Thomas C

EUROPEAN RAIL TIMETABLE

INDEPENDENT TRAVELLER'S EDITION

Summer 2009

Thomas Cook
Publishing

Published by
Thomas Cook Publishing,
Unit 9, Thomas Cook Business Park
Coningsby Road
Peterborough PE3 8SB
United Kingdom

ISBN 978-1-84848-132-9

Director of Publishing : Chris Young

Editor : Brendan Fox

Editorial team : John Potter, Reuben Turner, David Turpie, Chris Woodcock

Telephone (Sales) +44 (0)1733 416477 (Editorial) +44 (0)1733 416322
Fax +44 (0)1733 416688

e-mail (Sales): publishing-sales@thomascook.com
e-mail (Editorial): timetables@thomascook.com

Website and on-line bookshop : www.thomascookpublishing.com

Front cover photograph:

A Villach to Lienz train at Irschen, Austria (Table 971)
© Phil Wormald

Printed in the UK by CPI William Clowes, Beccles NR34 7TL

INTRODUCTION

This **Independent Traveller's Edition** is a specially enlarged version of the monthly **European Rail Timetable**, published by Thomas Cook for over 135 years and recognised throughout the world as the indispensable compendium of European rail schedules. The Independent Traveller's Edition appears twice yearly in Summer and Winter versions based on the June and December editions of the European Rail Timetable.

The much-loved **Thomas Cook European Rail Timetable** has for years been the travelling companion of the dedicated European rail-based tourist and business traveller. For travel further afield you need the **Thomas Cook Overseas Timetable** covering surface transport in North and South America, Asia, Africa and Australasia.

The intention of this special **Independent Traveller's Edition** is to make the timetable more widely available to the increasing numbers of holidaymakers who are touring Europe by train, whether using InterRail, Eurail or one of the other popular European rail passes, or simply travelling point to point. It includes additional information of use to rail travellers, especially those trying this kind of holiday for the first time.

Our feature on **Rail Passes** (pages v to xi) includes full details of the InterRail Global Pass and InterRail One Country Pass schemes (for European residents), as well as latest details of the various Eurail passes for those resident outside Europe. Many other passes are also featured, including a selection of citywide tickets and visitor cards for those visiting major European cities.

The **Country-by-Country** section (pages xii to xxxii) is packed with useful information about each country, and there is a chart of visa requirements on page xxxii. In the main body of the timetable, **Newslines** on page 3 has information about the latest changes and about the particular contents of this edition. Pages 10 to 11 help you make vital preparations for your journey, whilst a little time spent reading the notes on pages 4 to 9, explaining how to read the timetable, will be amply repaid when you get down to the task of planning your travels.

Whether you intend to travel only in one or two countries, or are attempting a spectacular grand tour of Europe, the timetables in this book will cover most of the routes you will need and will enable you to pre-plan your journey, which is often half the fun. Rail timetables are, however, always liable to change and you are recommended to consult the latest monthly edition of the European Rail Timetable or local information before travelling.

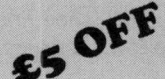

TRAVEL TIPS

ACCOMMODATION

Hotels:

Europe offers an excellent choice, from five-star hotels to room only. Your main problem may lie in finding something to suit your budget. Rooms in private houses are often a good, inexpensive and friendly option (local tourist offices often have lists), but you may be expected to stay for more than one night. The quality of cheaper hotels in Eastern Europe may still be less than inspiring and you may do better with a private room. Local tourist offices are almost always your best starting point if you haven't pre-booked. If they don't handle bookings themselves (there's usually a small charge), they will re-direct you to someone who does and/or supply you with the information to do it yourself – tell them your price horizons.

Hostels:

For those on a tight budget, the best bet is to join **HI** (Hostelling International); there's no age limit. Membership of a national association will entitle you to use over 5000 HI hostels in 60 different countries and, apart from camping, they often provide the cheapest accommodation. The norm is dormitory-style, but many hostels also have single and family rooms.

Many offer excellent-value dining and many have self-catering and/or laundry facilities. Some hostels are open 24 hours, but most have lock-out times and reception's hours are usually limited; advise them if you are arriving out of hours. Reservation is advisable – many hostels fill well in advance and even those with space are likely to limit your stay to three nights if you just turn up without booking. In winter (except around Christmas) you may be able to get special price deals.

Buy the HI's directory Europe, which lists hostel addresses, contact numbers, locations and facilities; the HI website is *www.iyhf.org.*

Camping:

This is obviously the cheapest accommodation if you're prepared to carry the equipment. There are campsites right across Europe, from basic (just toilets and showers) to luxury family-oriented sites with dining-rooms, swimming pools and complexes of permanent tents. The drawback is that sites are often miles from the city centres. There's no really good pan-European guide to campsites, but most tourist offices can provide a directory for their country.

WHAT TO TAKE WITH YOU

Luggage:

Backpack (not more than 50 litres for women or 60 litres for men) plus day sack; sort your luggage into see-through polythene bags (makes fishing out your socks from the backpack much easier), plus take plastic bags for dirty clothes etc, and elastic bands for sealing them.

Clothing:

Lightweight clothing, preferably of a type that doesn't need ironing; smart casual clothes for evening wear, swimsuit, sun hat, long-sleeved garment to cover shoulders (essential in some churches/temples; women may need head-scarves); non-slip foot-wear – and don't forget underwear! All-purpose hiking boots (useful for big walks around cities) or rubber sandals with chunky soles are good when it's hot; flip flops for the shower etc.

First Aid/Medical:

Insect repellent and antihistamine cream, sun-screen cream, after-sun lotion, water-sterilising tablets, something for headaches and tummy troubles, antiseptic spray or cream, medicated wet-wipes, plasters for blisters, bandage, contra-ceptives and tampons (especially if visiting Eastern Europe, where they can be sometimes difficult to get – or try the luxury shop in the city's biggest hotel). Spare spectacles/contact lenses and a copy of your prescription.

Overnight Equipment:

Lightweight sleeping-bag (optional), sheet liner (for hostelling), inflatable travel pillow, earplugs, and eyemask.

Documents:

Passport, tickets, photocopies of passport/visas (helps if you lose the passport itself) and travel insurance, travellers' cheques counterfoil, passport photos, student card, numbers of credit cards and where to phone if you lose them.

Other items:

A couple of lightweight towels, small bar of soap, water-bottle, pocket knife, torch (flashlight), sewing kit, padlock and chain (for anchoring your lug-gage), safety matches, mug and basic cutlery, toothbrush, travel wash, string (for a washing-line), travel adapter, universal bath plug (often missing from wash-basins), sunglasses, alarm clock, note-pad and pen, pocket calculator (to convert money), a money-belt and a good book/game (for long journeys).

EUROPEAN RAIL PASSES

Rail passes represent excellent value for train travellers who are touring around Europe (or parts of it) or making a number of journeys within a short period. They can offer substantial savings over point-to-point tickets, as well as greater flexibility. Passes may cover most of Europe (e.g. InterRail or Eurail), a specific group of countries, single countries, or just a certain area. InterRail passes are only available to European residents, whereas Eurail passes are only for non-European residents. Most passes cannot be used in your country of residence.

Passes either cover a specified number of consecutive days, or are of the *flexi* type where you get so many 'travel days' within a specified period (there are boxes on the pass where you write each date). Free travel requires the use of a travel day, whereas discounted travel does not.

With InterRail and Eurail *flexi* passes, direct night trains or ferries leaving after 1900 hrs can count as the next travel day (as long as it's not the first day of validity). Free overnight ferries count as either the day of departure or the next day. Passes generally cover the ordinary services of the national rail companies, but supplements often have to be paid for travel on high-speed services, night trains, and 'global price' trains. 'Private' railways may not accept passes but may give discounts to passholders. Extra charges always apply for travel in sleeping cars or couchettes.

Passes can be purchased from appointed agents and their websites, and some may be available from principal railway stations. Your passport may be required for identification, also one or two passport-size photos. In this feature USD = US dollars, € = euros, £ = pounds sterling.

InterRail

InterRail Global Pass

Area of validity

The *InterRail Global Pass* is valid for unlimited travel on the national railways of 30 European countries, namely Austria, Belgium, Bosnia-Herzegovina, Bulgaria, Croatia, Czech Republic, Denmark, Finland, France, Germany, Great Britain, Greece, Hungary, Republic of Ireland, Italy, Luxembourg, FYR Macedonia, Montenegro, the Netherlands, Norway, Poland, Portugal, Romania, Serbia, Slovakia, Slovenia, Spain, Sweden, Switzerland and Turkey. However, passes are **not** valid in the passholder's country of residence. Note that passes are no longer valid in Morocco or Northern Ireland.

Who can buy the pass?

Any national of a European country (including Russia) with a valid passport, or anyone who has lived in Europe for at least six months. Passes can be purchased up to three months before travel begins.

Periods of validity and prices

- Any 5 days within 10 days (flexi): adult 1st class €329/£305, adult 2nd class €249/£229, youth 2nd class €159/£145.
- Any 10 days within 22 days (flexi): adult 1st class €489/£449, adult 2nd class €359/£329, youth 2nd class €239/£219.
- 22 days (continuous): adult 1st class €629/£579, adult 2nd class €469/£429, youth 2nd class €309/£285.
- 1 month (continuous): adult 1st class €809/£745, adult 2nd class €599/£549, youth 2nd class €399/£369.

Youth prices are available to those aged 25 or under on the first day for which the pass is valid. Child fares for ages 4 to 11 are approximately half the price of the adult pass. Children under four travel free.

Day trains - supplements and reservation fees

Supplements or reservation fees are compulsory for certain types of high-speed or 'global price' train. The official website www.interrailnet.com gives full details. International examples (sample fees are 2nd class and subject to change): *Artesia* (France - Italy) €10; *Berlin - Warszawa Express* from €4; *Cisalpino* €5 - 15; *Eurostar* passholder fare from €75; *TGV* and *ICE* from / to France €3 - 5; *Thalys* passholder fare from €26; Talgo (France - Spain) €6.50; *X2000* Stockholm - København €7. Others include *EC* Milano - Nice €5; *EC* Venezia - Wien €7; EC72-75 Wien - Praha €7; *IC* Stockholm - Oslo €3. On other routes reservation is recommended, especially in July and August.

Domestic examples of compulsory reservation fees include: **Croatia** *IC* €1 - 5. **Czech Republic** *SC* €7. **Finland** *Pendolino* €3 - 5. **France** *TGV* €3 (peak €10), *Téoz* €3. **Germany** free on *ICE* (€11 on *ICE Sprinter*). **Greece** *ICity* €6 - 20, *IcityE* €9 - 33. **Hungary** *IC* €2.50. **Italy** *ES* and *ES City* €15, *AV* €20, *TBiz* €25. **Norway** long-distance trains €6.30. **Poland** *IC/EC* €5.30, *Ex* €3. **Portugal** *AP* €8, *IC* €4. **Romania** *IC* €3 - 18. **Slovakia** *IC/EC* €3, *SC* €7. **Spain** *AVE, Avant, Talgo 200* €10, most other long-distance trains €6.50. **Sweden** *X2000* €7.

The number of seats allocated to InterRail Pass holders may be limited (e.g. on *TGV* and *Thalys* trains). If sold out, you may have to buy an ordinary ticket. The fold-out Travel Report inside the ticket cover must be filled in for all journeys taken and ticket inspectors may ask to see it.

Night trains - supplements

Many night trains are globally priced and fares for passholders vary widely. *Elipsos* night trains France / Italy - Spain give discounted fares. Passes do not include sleeping accommodation, which is typically €15 to €69 for a couchette, and €30 to €197 for a berth in a sleeping car.

Discount in country of residence

Although the pass is not valid in the country of residence, passholders can obtain a reduction for one return ticket to the border or nearest airport. This is usually 50% (Bosnia 30%, Germany 25%, Spain 35%) but there is no discount in Great Britain, Czech Republic, Poland or Romania.

Validity on private railways

InterRail passes are valid on the national railway companies in each country, plus many of the privately run railways (some give discounts). For full details see the official InterRail website www.interrailnet.com. Selected details are as follows: **Berlin Night Express**: reduced fare if pass valid in Sweden. **Denmark**: free travel on Arriva and DSB-First, 50% discount on Hjørring - Hirtshals and Frederikshavn - Skagen. **France**: SNCF bus services free, 50% discount on CP (Nice - Digne), 50% on railways in Corsica. **Germany**: free on most regional services (not Züssow - Świnoujście). **Hungary**: GySEV services are included. **Netherlands**: Noordnet, Synthus, Veolia included. **Norway**: the Myrdal - Flåm line is treated as a private line and gives 30% discount. **Spain**: FEVE and FGC railways give 50% discount. **Sweden**: included are Arlanda Express, Arriva, DSB First, Inlandsbanan, MerResor, Skånetrafiken, Tågkompaniet, Västtrafik, Veolia. **Switzerland**: free travel on BLS, FART/SSIF, MOB, RhB, SOB, THURBO and ZB. Many others offer 50% discount, including AB, ASM, CJ, FB, Gornergratbahn, LEB, MBC, MVR, NStCM, Pilatusbahn, RA, Rigibahnen, RBS, SZU, TMR, TPC, TPF, TRN, WB, WSB. The MGB (Disentis - Brig - Zermatt and Göschenen - Andermatt) offer 50% to under-26s only. No discounts are available on the BRB or the narrow gauge railways in the Jungfrau area (BOB, JB, WAB). Discounted fare on William Tell Express (rail and boat tour).

Ferry services

The pass includes free deck passage between Italy and Greece on SuperFast Ferries and Blue Star Ferries (you pay port taxes €7, fuel surcharge, also high-season surcharge €10 June / Sept, €20 July / Aug. Free dormitories for 1st class pass holders). Also free on Scandlines.

Many other ferry companies offer discounts (not on cabins), for example: Balearia 50%, Color Line 50%, DFDS 25%, Endeavor Lines (Patras - Brindisi) 30% - 50%, Fjord1 Fylkesbaatane 50%, Grimaldi 20%, Irish Ferries 30%, Minoan Lines special fares, Sea France 50%, Stena Line 20% (30% on UK routes), Tallink Silja 30% - 50%, Viking Line 50%. There is no discount on SNCM ferries to Corsica.

Other services and discounts: passes are valid on Austrian lake services operated by ÖBB. Most Swiss lakes give 50% discount. DDSG offer 20% on Melk - Krems river cruises. Certain bus services in Scandinavia offer a 50% discount. Some railway museums offer free or discounted entry and a limited number of tourist attractions, hotels, hostels and cycle hire outlets offer discounts.

InterRail One Country Pass

Area of validity

The *InterRail One Country Pass* is valid for travel in any **one** of the participating countries above, with the exception of Bosnia-Herzegovina or Montenegro. It is **not** available for travel in the passholder's country of residence. Note that Benelux (Belgium, Luxembourg and the Netherlands) counts as one country. There are two passes for Greece - the *Greece Plus* variant includes ferry services between Italy and Greece operated by Attica (i.e. SuperFast Ferries and Blue Star Ferries). Eligibility / supplements / discounts are as for the *InterRail Global Pass*.

Periods of validity and prices

All passes are flexi passes, valid for 3, 4, 6 or 8 days within 1 month. Prices shown are for adult 1st class / adult 2nd class / youth (under 26) respectively, and are in euros. Further details: www.interrailnet.com.

- France, Germany, Great Britain, Norway, Sweden: 3 days €255/189/125, 4 days €285/209/139, 6 days €363/269/175, 8 days €404/299/194.
- Austria, Benelux, Finland, Greece 'Plus', Republic of Ireland, Italy, Spain, Switzerland: 3 days €147/109/71, 4 days €188/139/90, 6 days €255/189/123, 8 days €309/229/149.
- Croatia, Denmark, Greece, Hungary, Poland, Portugal, Romania: 3 days €93/69/45, 4 days €120/89/58, 6 days €161/119/77, 8 days €188/139/90.
- Bulgaria, Czech Republic, FYR Macedonia, Serbia, Slovakia, Slovenia, Turkey: 3 days €66/49/32, 4 days €93/69/45, 6 days €134/99/64, 8 days €161/119/77.

Eurail

Eurail Global Pass

Area of validity

The *Eurail Global Pass* is valid for unlimited travel on the national railways of 21 European countries, namely Austria, Belgium, Croatia, Czech Republic, Denmark, Finland, France, Germany, Greece, Hungary, the Republic of Ireland, Italy, Luxembourg, the Netherlands, Norway, Portugal, Romania, Slovenia, Spain, Sweden and Switzerland (the Czech Republic is new for 2009). Additional countries participate in the *Eurail Select Pass, Eurail Regional Pass* and *Eurail National Pass* (see below).

Who can buy the pass?

The pass can be purchased by anyone resident outside Europe (but excluding residents of the former USSR or Turkey). Passes are sold through official Eurail Sales Agents and can also be bought directly from Eurail through www.Eurail.com.

The option exists to buy the passes after arrival in Europe but it is much cheaper to buy them beforehand, and since you can buy them up to six months in advance, there is no point in waiting until the last minute. Pass validity cannot be changed once in Europe, and passes must be validated before first use.

Periods of validity and prices

Adult *Eurail Global Passes* are valid for first class travel (naturally you can also travel in second class), wheras the under-26 Youth version is for 2nd class travel only. Prices from eurail.com:

- 15 days: adult 689 USD, youth 449 USD.
- 21 days: adult 895 USD, youth 579 USD.
- 1 month: adult 1,109 USD, youth 719 USD.
- 2 months: adult 1,569 USD, youth 1,019 USD.
- 3 months: adult 1,935 USD, youth 1,259 USD.
- 10 days within 2 months: adult 815 USD, youth 529 USD.
- 15 days within 2 months: adult 1,069 USD, youth 695 USD.

Children aged 4 - 11 pay half fare, and children under 4 travel free (except if a reservation for a separate seat or bed is required).

Two or more people travelling together are eligible for the *Saver* rate, giving a reduction of 15% on the adult fare (there is no youth *Saver*, children aged 4 - 11 in the group pay half the *Saver* rate).

Supplements payable

Supplements are generally not required for *EC, IC, ICE* trains. *Thalys* charge a special passholder rate, as do other 'global price' trains (see the InterRail page for further details). French *TGV* and *Téoz* require the reservation fee only. In Spain most long-distance trains have a supplement / reservation fee (sample 2nd class rates: regional trains €4, long-distance €6.50, *AVE* Turista class €10; where meal provided in 1st / Preferente class €23.50). Supplements are also payable on *ICE Sprinter, Cisalpino* (€5 - 15), *Eurostar Italia* (€15 on *ES, ESc*, €20 on *AV*), *X2000* (€7-17) and *IcityE* in Greece (€9 - 33). As with all passes, sleeper / couchette supplements and seat reservations are extra.

Validity on other railways

Eurail passes are valid on the principal railway companies in each country, but may not be valid on 'private' or locally run railways (some give discounts). Selected details are as follows (some require reservations): **Denmark**: 50% discount on Hjørring - Hirtshals and Frederikshavn - Skagen. **France**: valid on RER in Paris (obtain a voucher), 50% discount on CP (Nice - Digne), 50% on railways in Corsica. **Hungary**: GySEV services are included, 50% discount on 'nostalgia' steam trips and the train to the railway museum. **Norway**: the Myrdal - Flåm line is treated as a 'private' line and gives 30% discount. **Spain**: FEVE and FGC railways give 50% discount. **Sweden**: most trains included (see under InterRail for a full list). **Switzerland**: free travel on many railways including BLS, CJ, FART/SSIF, MOB, RhB, SOB, SZU, THURBO, TMR, TPC, ZB. There is 50% discount on Vitznau - Rigi, the Pilatus line (and cable car) offers 30%, and there is a 25% discount on railways in the Jungfrau region (BOB, JB, WAB), the MGB (Disentis - Brig - Zermatt), and the Gornergratbahn. There are reductions on some cable cars as well. A list of bonuses is included in the Traveler's Guide issued with your pass. Note that *Eurostar* also offer special prices.

Ferry services

Free passage or fare reductions are available on various ferry services; the main ones are shown below. Ferry discounts usually exclude cabin accommodation, and other restrictions (such as compulsory reservation) may apply:

Balearia 20%; Color Line day sailings 50%; DFDS 25%; Grimaldi 20%, HML (Endeavor Lines) 30-50%; Irish Ferries 30%; Minoan Lines 20% (free deck passage on Italy-Greece routes if pass valid in both countries, summer surcharges €16 - 26); Sea France 50%; Scanlines free; Stena Line 20-30%; Superfast / Blue Star free passage on Italy-Greece routes if pass valid in both countries (summer surcharge €10-20, port tax €7, also fuel surcharge); Tallink-Silja 30-50%, Viking Line 50%.

Most boat services on the Swiss lakes are included in the pass, as are Austrian lake services operated by ÖBB. Bodensee ferries operated by BSB, SBS, ÖBB give 50% discount. There are also reductions on some river cruises (e.g. certain DDSG sailings); KD Line give free travel on their scheduled Rhine and Mosel boats.

Other discounts

The Europabus services in our Table **927** give 60% reduction, and certain bus services in Norway offer a 50% discount. Some railway museums offer free or discounted entry and a limited number of tourist attractions, hotels and hostels offer discounts. If in doubt, ask!

Note regarding flexi passes: free travel requires the use of a 'travel day', wheras discounted travel does not, provided it is within the overall validity of the pass. For free overnight travel by ferry you can enter either the day of departure or day of arrival. A direct overnight train leaving after 1900 hrs requires only the following day to be used as a 'travel day'.

International journeys using *Select, Regional* or *National Eurail* passes (below): the pass must be valid in both the country of departure and arrival to obtain free travel, but in only one of these for discounted travel.

Eurail Select Pass

A *Eurail Select Pass* allows unlimited travel in 3, 4 or 5 adjoining countries from the following (some are grouped together and count as one):

- Austria • Bulgaria / Montenegro / Serbia
- Benelux (Belgium / Netherlands / Luxembourg) • Croatia / Slovenia
- Denmark • Finland • France • Germany • Greece • Hungary
- Republic of Ireland • Italy • Norway • Portugal • Romania
- Spain • Sweden • Switzerland. • *NEW 2009* Czech Republic

'Adjoining' means linked by a direct train (not through another country) or shipping line included in the Eurail scheme; for example Italy's links include Spain and Greece, and France can be linked with Ireland.

The Select Pass is available for 5, 6, 8 or 10 travel days within a two-month period (the 5-country pass is also available for 15 days). The 5-day adult pass costs 439 / 489 / 539 USD for 3 / 4 / 5 countries respectively; 6 days costs 479 / 535 / 585 USD, 8 days 569 / 625 / 675 USD, 10 days 665 / 715 / 759 USD, and the 5-country 15-day pass costs 965 USD. The *Saver* pass for 2 or more people travelling together gives 15% reduction.

The Youth (under 26) pass is priced at 65% of the adult price and children aged 4 to 11 travel at half the adult fare. As with the *Eurail Global Pass*, the adult version gives 1st class travel, the youth version 2nd class. Eligibility, supplements, discounts etc are as for the *Global Pass* above.

Eurail Regional Pass

A *Eurail Regional Pass* allows unlimited travel in two European countries (or country combinations) as listed below. Conditions vary but all are available for 5, 6, 8 or 10 days within 2 months, and some also for 4, 7 or 9 days (Portugal - Spain also for 3 days). All are available in adult and saver 1st class versions (most also in 2nd class), and there is a youth 2nd class version for all except Portugal - Spain. Passes must be obtained before travelling to Europe, but those shown with the symbol § are also for sale in the countries where the pass is valid (but not to European residents). For current prices and further information see www.eurail.com. Eligibility, supplements, discounts etc are generally as for the *Global Pass* above.

- Austria - Croatia / Slovenia § • Austria - Czech Republic
- Austria - Germany • Austria - Hungary § • Austria - Switzerland
- Benelux - France • Benelux - Germany • Croatia / Slovenia - Hungary §
- Czech Republic - Germany • Denmark - Germany • France - Germany
- France - Italy • France - Spain • France - Switzerland
- Germany - Poland • Germany - Switzerland • Greece - Italy §
- Hungary - Romania § • Italy - Spain • Portugal - Spain
- Finland - Sweden • Denmark - Sweden • Norway - Sweden

Sample prices: France - Spain 4 days 1st / 2nd 349 / 309 USD, 10 days 559 / 519 USD. Hungary - Romania 1st class 5 / 10 days 259 / 379 USD.

Eurail One Country Passes

A *Eurail One Country Pass* allows unlimited travel in a single European country (or country combination) as listed below. Each pass has its own characteristics regarding class of travel, number of travel days, and availability of saver, youth and child versions. A few also have discounts for seniors. For prices and further information see www.eurail.com.

- Austria • Benelux • Croatia § • Czech Rep • Denmark • Finland
- Greece § • Hungary § • Ireland § • Italy § • Norway • Poland
- Portugal § • Romania § • Slovenia • Spain • Sweden.
- Scandinavia (Denmark, Finland, Norway, Sweden. 2nd class only. Youth 25% off). *NEW 2009:* • Bulgaria. (§ - for sale in Europe)

Sample prices: Benelux 5 days in 1 month adult 345 / 219 USD 1st / 2nd. Spain 3-10 days 259-529 USD 1st class, 209-425 USD 2nd class.

BritRail

Britrail is a pass for overseas visitors to Great Britain, allowing unlimited travel on the national rail network in England, Scotland and Wales. It is not available to residents of Great Britain, Northern Ireland, the Isle of Man or the Channel Islands. It is best to buy the pass before arriving in Britain. Prices shown are the US prices for 2009. Further information: www.britrail.com.

BritRail Consecutive Pass
Allows travel for a certain number of consecutive days, in either first or standard class. Children (5-15) travel at half the adult fare.

(USD prices)	Adult 1st class	Adult Standard	Senior (60+) 1st class	Youth (16-25) Standard §
3 days	305	199	259	159
4 days	379	249	319	199
8 days	535	359	455	285
15 days	799	535	679	425
22 days	1015	675	859	539
1 month	1195	795	1015	635

BritRail FlexiPass
The FlexiPass version gives 3, 4, 8 or 15 days travel within a two-month period.

(USD prices)	Adult 1st class	Adult Standard	Senior (60+) 1st class	Youth (16-25) Standard §
3 days in 2 months	375	255	319	205
4 days in 2 months	465	315	399	249
8 days in 2 months	679	459	579	365
15 days in 2 months	1025	689	869	555

§ – First-class youth passes are also available (at 80% of the adult 1st rates).

Britrail England Pass
Excludes Wales and Scotland. Prices are 20% cheaper than those shown above. Available in both the Consecutive and Flexi versions.

Discounts
Reductions are available on adult passes as follows, but only one type of discount can be used (this includes youth and senior discounts):

Eurail Passholder Discount: Those aged 16 to 25 with valid Eurail passes pay about 50% of the normal adult fare.

Party Discount: for 3 to 9 adults travelling in a group. Passengers 3 to 9 receive a 50% discount on the cost of their passes. The passes must be of the same type and duration and the party must travel together.

Family Discount: if you purchase any adult or senior pass, one accompanying child (aged 5–15) receives a free pass of the same type and duration. Any further children travelling receive a 50% discount. All children under 5 travel free.

Guest Pass Discount: a friend or relative who is a UK resident may accompany the pass holder. Both get 25% off the adult fare and must travel together at all times. The guest must carry proof of UK residence.

Two additional passes are available covering larger or smaller areas:

BritRail + Ireland
Adds Northern Ireland and the Republic of Ireland, plus a return ferry crossing (Stena Line / Irish Ferries). 5 days within one month costs 699 USD first class, 469 USD standard. 10 days within one month: 1245 / 839 USD first / standard. Not available to residents of the Republic of Ireland.

BritRail London Plus Pass
This 'flexi' pass allows unlimited rail travel in London and the surrounding area. You can visit such places as Canterbury, Salisbury, Bristol, Oxford, Cambridge, Kings Lynn, the whole coast from Colchester to Weymouth, and even get as far as Worcester. Children aged 5–15 pay 50% of the adult fare. No youth or senior discount available.

(USD prices)	Adult 1st class	Adult Standard
2 days within 8 days	209	139
4 days within 8 days	289	225
7 days within 15 days	369	269

Other International Passes

BALKAN FLEXIPASS

Unlimited 1st class travel in Bulgaria, Greece, Macedonia, Montenegro, Romania, Serbia and Turkey for any 5 / 10 / 15 days in one month. Available in the countries above (but not for residents of those countries), also in the USA. Typical US prices : adults 256 / 447 / 539 USD, youth (12-25) 153 / 268 / 324 USD, senior (60+) 206 / 359 / 433 USD. Children half adult fare. Supplements for *IC* trains. Gives 30% discount on Attica Group ferries (Superfast / Bluestar). A 2nd class version is also available if purchased within the countries where it is valid (e.g. unconfirmed prices in Greece: €82 / 144 / 172 adult, €49 / 82 / 98 youth, €66 / 115 / 138 senior).

BENELUX TOURRAIL

A flexi pass for travel in Belgium, Netherlands and Luxembourg for 5 days within one month. Prices €219 1st class, €139 2nd class. Under 26 version (2nd class only) €99. Special pass price available on Thalys. Available from principal stations, also from International Rail in the UK, who call it the Benelux Pass.

EUREGIO - BODENSEE TAGESKARTE

One day's unlimited travel in border region Austria / Germany / Switzerland surrounding Lake Constance. Includes buses and ferries. In Germany valid only on DB local trains. Adult 37 CHF / €28, family 74 CHF / €56. Zonal versions also available for smaller areas.

EUREGIO MAAS-RHEIN

One days unlimited travel in border region Belgium / Netherlands / Germany by rail and bus (covers Liège, Hasselt, Maastricht, Heerlen, Aachen, Düren). In Germany covers only local trains and buses. Price €15. At weekends / public holidays valid as a family ticket (2 adults plus 3 children under 12). Further information: www.euregio-ticket.com

EUROPEAN EAST PASS

Available to non-European residents; offers unlimited rail travel throughout Austria, Czech Republic, Hungary, Poland and Slovakia for any 5 days within a month. 1st class 299 USD, 2nd class 209 USD (up to 5 extra days 36 / 28 USD per day 1st / 2nd class). Children aged 4 - 11 half price. Discounts available on river cruises, steam trips in Hungary, Children's Railway etc.

ÖRESUND RUNDT

Two days unlimited travel on trains in the København, Malmö and Helsingborg area, 199 SEK / 179 DKK. A larger area extending further into Sweden (Ystad, Kristianstad) is also available for 249 SEK / 229 DKK. Children 7-15 half price. The Öresund can only be crossed by rail in one direction; ferry (included) must be used in the other direction. Although some sources have quoted that this ticket is no longer available in Denmark, København Tourist Office have told us that they still sell it.

SAAR-LOR-LUX TICKET

One day's unlimited 2nd class travel on Saturday or Sunday throughout Saarland (i.e. Saarbrücken area of Germany, local trains only), Lorraine (i.e. Metz, Nancy, Épinal area of France) and all of Luxembourg. Price €20. For groups of 2 - 5 people add €10 per extra person.

Railplus

Railplus cards are valid for one year and offer a discount of 25% on cross-border rail travel (excluding supplements) between the participating countries, which are Austria, Belgium, Bulgaria, Croatia, Czech Republic, Denmark, Finland, France, Germany, Great Britain, Greece, Hungary, Italy, Latvia, Lithuania, Luxembourg, Macedonia, Montenegro, Netherlands, Norway, Poland, Portugal, Romania, Serbia, Slovakia, Slovenia, Spain, Sweden, Switzerland and Ukraine.

France, Norway, Spain and Sweden only grant discounts to youth (12-25) and seniors (60+), and Ireland only to seniors. Cards are not available for sale in all participating countries, and you may be required to hold a national railcard for the country where you buy the pass, in addition to the Railplus card. Note that Rail Europe in the UK, who used to sell the Railplus Senior Card, no longer do so, although they do sell the SNCF Carte Senior, giving 25% off cross-border journeys.

Passes for Domestic Travel

Every effort has been made to show latest prices, but some may have changed. Most cities offer day tickets valid on public transport (some include local trains), and larger cities often have Visitor Cards, available from airports and tourist information offices (often also hotels and online).

AUSTRIA

European residents: see InterRail Global Pass and One Country Pass. Non-European residents: see Eurail Global Pass, Eurail Select/Regional/One Country Passes, European East Pass. See also Euregio-Bodensee Tageskarte.

Austria Pass: for non-Europeans, must be purchased outside Europe. 3 to 8 days within one month, 199/139 USD 1st/2nd class for 3 days plus 30/20 USD per extra day. Children aged 6-11 half price. Also valid on the private railway company Raab-Oedenburg Ebenfurter Eisenbahn. Discounts on selected river trips by DDSG, Wurm & Köck.

Einfach-Raus-Ticket: one day's 2nd class travel on regional trains for groups of 2 to 5 people, €28. On Mons to Fris not valid before 0900 hrs.

Discounts on ÖBB point to point tickets: **1-PLUS-Freizeitticket** discount of 25-40% for the 2nd to 5th people in a group travelling together, and bicycles may be taken free. **Gruppenticket** for groups of 6 or more, discounts of 30% up to 100km and 40% over 100km. **Vorteilscard** annual cards giving 50% discount; the *Classic* version is available to all but there are cheaper cards for families, seniors and those under 26.

Wien-Karte: unlimited travel on local transport in Vienna plus discounted museum entry, 72 hours €18.50. One child up to age 15 free.

Wien metro/tram/bus: 24 hours €5.70; 72 hours €13.60; 8 days €27.20; buy additional zone (€1.70) to include airport. Off-peak (after 0900 Mon-Fri) weekly ticket also available €14.00.

Other visitor cards giving local travel plus museum/sights discounts for 24/48/72 hours: **Salzburg Card** €24/32/37 (reduced by €2 outside May to Oct period); **Innsbruck Card** €25/30/35. Children half price.

BELARUS

There are no rail passes that we are aware of that are valid in Belarus.

Minsk: 10-day public transport passes are available from metro stations.

BELGIUM

European residents: see InterRail Global Pass and One Country Pass. Non-European residents: see Eurail Global Pass, Eurail Select/Regional/One Country Passes. See also Benelux Tourrail, Euregio.

Discounts on SNCB point to point tickets: **Rail Pass** (age 26+) allows 10 single journeys between two specified stations for €73 2nd class, €112 1st class, valid 1 year. **Go Pass** is under 26 version, €50 (2nd class). Various discounts are available for return journeys at weekends.

Carte Jump d'un Jour valid on all public transport in greater Brussels (including SNCB rail services), 1 day €4.50. **Carte 3 Jours** gives 3 days on local transport (STIB only) for €9.50. Cards for 5 or 10 journeys also available. **Brussels Card** gives public transport (STIB) plus museums, 24 hrs €19, 48 hrs €27, 72 hrs, €32.

BOSNIA-HERZEGOVINA

European residents: see InterRail Global Pass.

BULGARIA

European residents: see InterRail Global Pass and One Country Pass. Non-European residents: see Eurail Select/One Country Passes. See also Balkan Flexipass.

Sofiya: all SKGT local transport, 1 day 3 BGN, 5 days 12 BGN.

CROATIA

European residents: see InterRail Global Pass and One Country Pass. Non-European residents: see Eurail Select/Regional/One Country Passes.

Zagreb: day ticket (dnevne karte) for all trams/buses (zone 1): 25 HRK.

CZECH REPUBLIC

European residents: see InterRail Global Pass and One Country Pass. Non-European residents: see Eurail Global Pass (from 2009), Eurail Regional/One Country Pass, European East.

Kilometrická banka 2000 (KMB): a prepaid card giving 2000 km of 2nd class travel within 6 months, 2000 CZK. The conductor deducts the appropriate distance (minimum 100 km) for each trip.

SONE+: one day's travel on Sat or Sun for up to 5 people (max 2 adults), 2nd class, 150 CZK local trains, 450 CZK all trains except *SC*. SONE+PKP variant includes local trains in border area of Poland (add 100 CZK). Smaller regional areas also available,

Network tickets: ČD Net ticket valid one day, 2nd class 450 CZK (900 CZK for group of 2-5 people); extra charge for *SC* travel (200 CZK each). Regional variants (Regionet) also available.

Praha: all public transport including ČD trains, extending up to 50 km from the centre: 24 hrs 100 CZK, 3 days 330 CZK, 5 days 500 CZK.

Prague Card: 4-day admission card with 3-day transport add-on as above costs 1120 CZK (children and students 860 CZK).

DENMARK

European residents: see InterRail Global Pass and One Country Pass. Non-European residents: see Eurail Global Pass, Eurail Select/Regional/One Country Passes. See also Öresund Rundt.

Fares based on national zonal system. **Pendlerkort**: 30 day all-zone 2nd class ticket max fare 3,050 DKK, photocard required. 10-journey tickets also available. **DSB WildCard**: discount card for 16-25 year olds, giving up to 50% off tickets, 180 DKK.

København: **24-Hour Ticket** valid on bus, metro and DSB trains in greater København, 120 DKK. **Flexcard 7-Days** is a 7 day zonal card, from 205 DKK for 2 zones to 570 DKK for all 9 zones in København.

Copenhagen Card (CPH Card) gives public transport plus free entry to 60 attractions, 24 hrs 225 DKK (child 115), 72 hrs 450 DKK (child 225).

ESTONIA

There are no rail passes that we are aware of that are valid in Estonia.

Tallinn Card: free city transport, sightseeing tours, many museums etc; 6 hrs €12, 24 hrs €24, 48 hrs €28, 72 hrs €32. Under 14s half price.

FINLAND

European residents: see InterRail Global Pass and One Country Pass. Non-European residents: see Eurail Global Pass, Eurail Select/Regional/One Country Passes.

Finnrailpass: unlimited rail travel for 3/5/10 days in any 1 month; 1st class €195/260/353, 2nd class €131/175/237. Ages 6-16 half price. Seat reservation fees required for Pendolino trains. Available to non-Finnish residents. Can be purchased at main stations in Finland.

Helsinki Tourist Ticket: bus/tram/metro/local trains 1/3/5 days for €6/12/18 (children 7-16 half price); regional area also available.
Helsinki Card: public transport plus free entry to over 50 attractions, €33/45/55 for 24/48/72 hours (children 7-16: €13/16/19).

FRANCE

European residents: see InterRail Global Pass and One Country Pass. Non-European residents: see Eurail Global Pass, Eurail Select/Regional/One Country Passes.

France Railpass: only available to non-European residents, valid for 3 to 9 days within one month. Adult 3 days 293/250 USD 1st/2nd class plus 45/37 USD per extra day; Youth (12-25) 217/186 USD plus 33/28 USD per day; Senior (60+, 1st class only) 268 USD for 3 days plus 40 USD per day. Saver version for 2-5 people (must include at least 2 adults) gives around 15% discount. Children pay 50% of the adult (or Saver) fare. Special Passholder fare payable on *Eurostar*, *Thalys*, *Artesia*, night trains etc. Reservation fee payable on *TGV* and *Téoz*. 50% discount on CP, Corsica trains, Sea France. Further information: www.francerailpass.com

Discounts on point to point tickets: **Découverte Séjour**: 25% discount (15%-35% on *TGV* and *Corail Téoz*), blue periods only, min 200 km return trip, Sat night away. ***iDTGV*** are low-cost advance purchase tickets; book online for best deals.

Carte 12-25 and **Carte Sénior**: young person's railcard for those aged 12 - 25 (€49) and senior railcard for those over 60 (€56). Valid 1 year. Both give at least 25% discount (up to 50% for journeys purchased in advance). **Carte Escapades**: railcard for ages 26 - 59 giving at least 25% discount (min 200 km return, must spend Sat night away), €85.

Regional Tickets: several regions offer day tickets or discounted fares on TER (local) trains at weekends and holidays. Conditions vary and some only valid in Summer. Details generally available on TER website www.ter-sncf.com.

Paris Visite: public transport within greater Paris, plus free or discounted entry to 20 attractions: zones 1–3: €8.80/14.40/19.60/28.30 for 1/2/3/5 days. Zones 1–6 (includes airports): €18.50/28.30/39.70/48.40. Children 4-11 half price. **Mobilis**: Paris one-day ticket (not available on airport services), €5.80 (zones 1–2) to €16.40 (zones 1–6).

Lyon day ticket €4.50, covers all TCL tram/bus/metro/funicular.
Lille day ticket €3.50; similar tickets in most cities.

GERMANY

European residents: see InterRail Global Pass and One Country Pass. Non-European residents: see Eurail Global Pass, Eurail Select/Regional Passes. See also Euregio-Bodensee, Euregio Ticket, Sar-Lor-Lux Ticket.

German Rail Pass: for people resident outside Europe; 4 to 10 days unlimited travel within 1 month. 4 days €236/180 1st/2nd class; add €32/22 per extra day. Also **Youth Pass** for those under 26 (2nd class only) - 4 days €150, add €12 for each extra day. **Twin Pass** also available giving up to 50% for second adult. Available from Deutsche Bahn London and certain German stations, but not available to European residents. No supplements on *ICE*, *IC*, *EC*. 20% discount on Romantische Strasse and Burgenstrasse buses.

Passes for Domestic Travel

Schönes-Wochenende-Ticket: one day's unlimited travel on Saturday or Sunday (to 0300 following day) on local trains (IRE/RE/RB/S-Bahn), 2nd class. Price € 37 from machines, € 39 from ticket offices, € 40.70 on train. Valid for up to 5 people, buy on the day. Also valid on trams / buses in certain areas, and on certain rail lines across the border into Poland.

Quer-Durchs-Land-Ticket from August 2009, local trains throughout Germany after 0900, from € 34 (1 person) to € 54 (5 people).

Regional tickets (Länder-Tickets): one day's unlimited travel for up to 5 people on DB local trains (not before 0900 on Mon-Fri, valid to 0300 next day). **Baden-Württemberg** € 19 for one person, € 28 for 2-5 people. **Bayern** € 20 for one person, € 28 for 2-5 people. **Brandenburg-Berlin** € 26. **Hessen** (includes most buses) € 30. **Mecklenburg-Vorpommern** € 18 for one person, € 25 for 2-5 people. **Niedersachsen** € 20 for one person, € 28 for 2-5 people. **Nordrhein-Westfalen** (SchönerTagTicket) one person € 25, 2-5 people € 34. **Rheinland-Pfalz** and **Saarland** € 19 for one person, € 27 for 2-5 people. **Sachsen**, **Sachsen-Anhalt** and **Thüringen** € 19 for one person, € 28 for 2-5 people. **Schleswig-Holstein** € 30 (includes travel in Mecklenburg-Vorpommern and all public transport in Hamburg). Buy on the day from ticket machines (most cost € 2 more if purchased from travel centres).

Bahncard 25 / 50: valid for 1 year, giving discounts of 25% or 50% on all national DB trains for € 57 or € 225, 2nd class, passport photo required (1st class € 114 / 450). With Bahncard 50, travel companions get 50% and children under 15 travel free. Both cards entitle the holder to a 25% discount for international journeys between Germany and 29 European countries (discount not available where global fares are charged). Bahncards available at discounted prices to young people, families, seniors, disabled persons. **Mobility Bahncard 100** gives unlimited travel for 1 year, € 3,650 (1st class € 6,150). Bahncards also available from DB London.

Sparpreis 25 / 50: advance purchase tickets giving 25% or 50% discount, also 50% off for up to 4 travel companions. Weekend restrictions apply to 50% version. Group versions (6 +) available giving 50% to 70% off.

Harz: HSB narrow gauge railway 3 / 5 days € 42 / 47, child 6-11 50%.

Tageskarte (day ticket): most urban areas offer 24 / 48 / 72 hour tickets valid on most public transport; generally a zonal system operates.

Welcome Tickets: most public transport in selected cities, also includes free or reduced entry to many museums and visitor attractions. Buy from Tourist Information, main stations, some airports and hotels. Examples:

Berlin Welcome Card: one adult and up to 3 children under 14; 48 hours € 18.50, 72 hours € 25, 5 days € 34.50. Covers zones A, B and C and includes DB trains.

Dresden City Card: 48 hours € 21, includes some Elbe river trips.

Frankfurt Card: 1 day € 8.70, 2 days € 12.50; group ticket (up to 5) € 15 (1 day)/ € 24 (2 days). Includes travel from / to the airport.

Hamburg Card: Day Ticket (valid from 1800 hrs previous day) € 8.50. Also 3 days € 18.90, 5 days € 33.90. Group versions (up to 5) € 12.50 / 31.50 / 54.90.

Hannover Card: 1 day € 9.50, 3 days € 16, group ticket (up to 5) € 18 / 31.

Köln Welcome Card: 24 / 48 / 72 hours € 9 / 14 / 19, family (2 adults plus 3 children up to 14) € 18 / 28 / 38, group (up to 3 adults) € 18 / 28 / 38.

Leipzig Card: 1 day € 8.90, 3 days € 18.50, 3 day group (2 adults and up to 3 children under 14) € 34.

Nürnberg Card: 2 days € 19, children up to age 12 free.

GREAT BRITAIN

European residents: see InterRail Global Pass and One Country Pass. See also Britrail.

All-Line Rail Rover: covers whole National Rail network, 1st / standard class £650 / £430 (7 days), £990 / £650 (14 days). 34% discount for children aged 5-15 and holders of Senior and Disabled Persons railcards, and (standard class only) Young Persons railcard. Not valid on Eurostar, Heathrow Express, London Underground, private railways.

Freedom of Scotland Travelpass: all rail services in Scotland (includes Carlisle and Berwick) plus Caledonian MacBrayne ferry services and some buses. Standard class only. Valid 4 out of 8 days (£111) or 8 out of 15 days (£148); not before 0915 Mon to Fri (except on Glasgow - Oban / Mallaig services and north of Inverness). 34% discount with Young Persons / Senior / Disabled railcard; 50% discount for children (5-15). 20% discount on Northlink Ferries to Orkney and Shetland; 10% off sleeper fares to / from Scotland. Smaller areas also available: **Highland Rover**, 4 days out of 8 £72; **Central Scotland Rover** 3 days out of 7 £32.

Freedom of Wales Flexi Pass: gives 8 consecutive days travel on most buses in Wales, plus standard-class rail travel on any 4 days out of the 8 (not before 0915 Mon to Fri), price £74, children half price, railcard holders 34% discount. Includes Ffestiniog and Welsh Highland Railways, with discounts on other tourist railways and attractions. Tickets available online and at most staffed stations. Smaller areas also available: South Wales (£50), North and Mid Wales (£50).

A range of **Rover** tickets is available covering various areas, typically for 7 days, 3 in 7 days, 4 in 8 days, or 8 in 15 days. Most are not valid until after the morning peak on Monday to Friday. Examples: Anglia Plus, Coast and Peaks, Devon and Cornwall, East Midlands, Heart of England, Kent, North Country, North East, North West, Settle & Carlisle, Severn & Solent, Shakespeare Explorer, South West, Thames. **Ranger** day tickets also available, for example Cambrian Coast, Cheshire, Cornwall, Cumbrian Coast, Derbyshire, Devon, East Midlands, Lakes, Lancashire, Lincolnshire, North Downs, Oxfordshire, Settle & Carlisle line, South Pennines, Tyne & Tees, Valley Lines, West Midlands, West Yorkshire, Yorkshire Coast. Details: nationalrail.co.uk.

Railcards: annual cards giving 34% discount on most rail fares; 16-25 Railcard, Family, Senior, all £24. Disabled Persons £18, HM Forces £15. Network Railcard gives off-peak discount in South East England, £20.

London: Day Travelcards covers almost all transport (Underground / bus / rail) in the London area; peak version from £7.20 (central London, zones 1–2) to £14.80 (zones 1–6), off-peak version (not before 0930 Mon-Fri) from £5.60 to £7.50. 3-day Travelcards cost £18.40 (zones 1–2) or £42.40 (zones 1–6); off-peak all-zones version costs £21.20. 7 day tickets from £25.80 (central zones) to £47.60 (zones 1-6), no off-peak version. Children under 11 travel free with an Oyster photocard. Travelcard holders may take up to four children aged 11-15 for £1 each off-peak (otherwise half fare). Stored-value Oyster cards give best value; Visitor Oyster card preloaded with £10 credit costs £12 (also available online from www.visitlondon.com); can be topped up at numerous outlets.

All-day tickets (some off-peak) covering rail and bus are also available in Glasgow, Greater Manchester, Derbyshire, Merseyside, South Yorkshire, West Yorkshire, Tyneside and West Midlands. Most large bus companies have day and weekly tickets. 'Plus Bus' add-on tickets are available with many rail fares, giving bus travel in the specified city.

GREECE

European residents: see InterRail Global Pass and One Country Pass. Non-European residents: see Eurail Global Pass, Eurail Regional / One Country Passes. See also Balkan Flexipass.

Multiple journey card: unlimited journeys for 10 (€48.10), 20 (€72.20) or 30 (€96.30) days in 2nd class. Discounts available for up to 5 persons travelling together. Supplements not included. *Prices and availability are unconfirmed.*

Athens: 24-hour ticket valid on metro (including ISAP), trams and buses € 3, but excludes airport (weekly ticket € 10). A return to airport is € 10.

HUNGARY

European residents: see InterRail Global Pass and One Country Pass. Non-European residents: see Eurail Global Pass, Eurail Select / Regional / One Country Passes, European East.

Turista Bérlet: MÁV 7 and 10 day tickets are available for HUF 22,000 and 28,000 (in 1st class HUF 27,500 and 35,000). GySEV tickets also available for HUF 12,000 and 16,000 (in 1st class 15,000 / 20,000). A day ticket for the Balaton area is available for HUF 3,000 (1st class 3,760).

Budapest: BKV tram / metro / bus, 1 day HUF 1,500, 3 days HUF 3,700, 7 day travelcard HUF 4,400, 14 days HUF 5,950. Weekend family ticket HUF 2,100. **Budapest Card** also includes museums and discounts: 48 hours HUF 6,300, 72 hours HUF 7,500; 1 child up to 14 years old goes free. The **BKSZ bérlet** includes local rail services and is aimed at commuters.

IRELAND

REPUBLIC OF IRELAND ONLY:

European residents: see InterRail Global Pass and One Country Pass. Non-European residents: see Eurail Global / Select / National Passes. See also Britrail + Ireland.

Irish Explorer: any 5 days in 15 on IÉ rail services, € 160 (child € 80), standard class only.

Irish Explorer Rail and Bus: IÉ rail plus Bus Éireann services, any 8 days in 15, € 245 (child € 122).

Open Road passes; flexi passes giving 3 to 15 days travel on Bus Éireann services, € 54 to € 234.

Note that the Emerald Card and Irish Rover Rail Only (which covered the whole of Ireland) are no longer available. There is, however, an **Irish Rover Bus Only** pass.

Dublin area: bus and suburban rail 'short hop' (excludes Airlink): 1 day € 10.20, family (2 adults + 4 under 16s) € 15.60, 3 days € 20, 7 days € 34.50. Medium / long / giant hop cover Dublin hinterland for 7 days, € 52 to € 80 (photo-card required). Rambler (bus only, includes Airlink): 1 day € 6, family € 10. Freedom ticket gives bus plus city tour, 3 days € 25.

NORTHERN IRELAND ONLY:

Freedom of Northern Ireland: valid for 1 day (£15), 3 out of 8 days (£36) or 7 consecutive days (£53) on all Translink services (Northern Ireland Railways, Ulsterbus, Belfast Citybus). Children: 50% reduction. The one day ticket is now available from bus drivers and train conductors.

Passes for Domestic Travel

ITALY

European residents: see InterRail Global Pass and One Country Pass. Non-European residents: see Eurail Global Pass, Eurail Select/Regional/One Country Passes.

Roma: Roma Pass is a 3-day transport pass (€23) with museum discounts; first two visited are free. Vatican and Rome card (1 day €19, 3 days €25) gives transport plus 'Open' bus tour operated by Roma Cristiana. Biglietto Integrato Giornaliero (BIG) covers rail/metro/bus in urban area for one day, €4 (excludes Fiumicino airport, restrictions on rail/metro). Biglietto Turistico Integrato (BTI) valid 3 days €11, weekly ticket (CIS) €16. Roma & Lazio day ticket (BIRG) covers wider area in 7 zones (max €10.50), also 3 day ticket (BTR) max €28.50.

Milano: 24 hour ticket (abbonamento) on ATM city services (including local rail) €3.00, 48 hrs €5.50.

Napoli: 'Campania > artecard' is a museum/transport visitors card, with two types of 3 day ticket. The standard card allows free entry to any two museums with 50% off all others. The higher priced card allows free entry to all museums. Various areas available, prices from €16.

Venice Card: *Transport* version - public transport (including waterbuses) with other discounts €48/68 for 3/7 days. *Transport & Culture* version adds museums €73/96. *Junior* discounts for those under 29; add-on available for Alilaguna boats. ACTV bus/boats: 12/24/48 hrs €16/18/28.

Day tickets available in other major cities.

LATVIA

There are no rail passes that we are aware of that are valid in Latvia.

Riga Card: unlimited travel on public transport, also free/discounted museum entry. 10/14/18 LVL for 24/48/72 hours.

LITHUANIA

There are no rail passes that we are aware of that are valid in Lithuania.

Vilnius: 24 hr ticket on local buses 6 LTL, 72 hrs 14 LTL, 10 days 27 LTL.

LUXEMBOURG

European residents: see InterRail Global Pass and One Country Pass. Non-European residents: see Eurail Global Pass, Eurail Select/Regional Passes. See also Benelux Tourrail, Sar-Lor-Lux Ticket.

Billet longue durée: day ticket €4.00, unlimited 2nd-class travel on all public transport throughout the country; not valid to border points; valid to 0800 hrs following morning. Carnet of 5 day tickets €16.00. Oeko Pass: valid one month €45 2nd class, €67.50 1st class; from CFL offices.

Luxembourg Card: unlimited travel on trains and buses throughout the country, plus free entry to 56 attractions. 1 day €10; any 2 days €17, any 3 days €24 (the 2/3 day tickets must be used within two weeks). Family pass for 2-5 people (max. 3 adults) at twice one person rate.

MACEDONIA

European residents: see InterRail Global Pass and One Country Pass. See also Balkan Flexipass.

MONTENEGRO

European residents: see InterRail Global Pass. Non-European residents: see Eurail Select Pass. See also Balkan Flexipass.

NETHERLANDS

European residents: see InterRail Global Pass and One Country Pass. Non-European residents: see Eurail Global Pass, Eurail Select/Regional Passes. See also Benelux Tourrail, Euregio Ticket.

NS Day Card (Dagkaart) allows unlimited travel on Netherlands Railways for one day: €72.80 1st class, €42.90 2nd class, available at stations. **OV Dagkaart** costs €5.50 extra and includes buses, trams and metro throughout the country. Five NS Day Cards can be purchased in one transaction as a 5-Dagkaart (price is five times the above). Monthly and yearly versions also available, with or without OV add-on. Available from booking offices and ticket automats.

Railrunner: Up to 3 children (aged 4–11) may accompany an adult (aged 19+) for a flat rate of €2 per day. Excludes *Thalys*.

Zomertoer: 2 days' unlimited travel within any 7 day period between July 1 and Sept. 6. 2nd class only, €65 for 2 people, €85 for 3 people. **Zomertoer Plus** includes bus / tram / metro: €75 for 2, €99 for 3.

Amsterdam: GVB tram/bus/metro tickets. 24 hrs €7, 48 hrs €11.50, 72 hrs €15, 96 hrs €18. **I amsterdam Card**: tram/bus/metro/canal boat tour, plus free museum admission and discounts at various tourist attractions, 24/48/72 hrs: €33/43/53.

NORWAY

European residents: see InterRail Global Pass and One Country Pass. Non-European residents: see Eurail Global Pass, Eurail Select/Regional/One Country Passes.

Eurail Norway Pass: for non-Europeans: 3 to 8 days 2nd class travel within one month, 259 USD for 3 days, 395 USD for 8 days. Youth (under 26) get 25% reduction. 30% discount on Flåm Railway, various ferry discounts; not valid on Oslo Airport Express.

Oslo: 24 hour ticket for all public transport (Dagskort) 65 NOK, 7 days (Ukeskort) 200 NOK, children 4-16 half price. **Oslo Pass**: unlimited travel on buses, trams, underground and NSB local trains (up to Zone 4), free entry to attractions, discounts on sightseeing buses/boats: 24/48/72 hours 220/320/410 NOK (children 95/115/150 NOK).

Bergen Card: local bus travel plus free or discounted entry to various attractions, 24/48 hrs: 190/250 NOK (children aged 3-15, 75/100 NOK).

POLAND

European residents: see InterRail Global Pass and One Country Pass. Non-European residents: see Eurail Select/Regional/One Country Passes, European East.

Bilet Weekendowy (weekend ticket): unlimited travel on *Ex/IC/TLK* trains (except Berlin-Warszawa-Express) 1800 Fri to 2400 Sun and on public holidays, 149 PLZ 1st class, 99 PLZ 2nd class. Available from over 660 stations.

Bilet Turystyczny (tourist ticket): unlimited travel on PKP local trains 1800 Friday to 0600 Monday, 60 PLZ 2nd class, 80 PLZ 1st class. **Bilet Turystyczny + CD** adds border area of Czech Republic.

Tam, gdzie chcesz is a 2-day rover ticket valid 1000-2400 on Mon-Tues, Tues-Wed or Wed-Thurs, valid only on *IC, Ex, TLK* trains. Reservations compulsory (at 20% discount). Prices 157 PLN 2nd class, 217 PLN 1st.

Warsaw Tourist card: public transport within the city limits plus free or discounted entry to various attractions. 24/72 hours for 35/65 PLN.

PORTUGAL

European residents: see InterRail Global Pass and One Country Pass. Non-European residents: see Eurail Global Pass, Eurail Select/Regional/One Country Passes.

Intra-Rail: zonal (4 zones) pass for ages 12-30, 3 days (Fri-Sun) €55 (€49 with Youth Card), 10 days (starting Mon-Thurs) €185/159. Includes nights at youth hostels. Not valid on Alfa. Buy at major stations.

Lisboa: Carris tram/bus and metro - one-day ticket (bilhete 1 dia) €3.70. **Lisboa Card** (includes tourist attractions): 24/48/72 hrs for €16/27/33.50 (children 5-11 €9.50/14/17).

Train and Bus Tourist Ticket: day ticket valid on the CP Sintra and Cascais lines (also suburban trains Alcântara to Oriente), also on Scotturb bus network, €12. Buy from main stations in the area.

Coimbra: day ticket on local buses €3.20.

Porto: metro + STCP bus + local rail, all zones, 1 day €5, 3 days €11. **Porto Card** also includes free/discounted entry to tourist attractions, 1 day €7.50, 2 days €11.50, 3 days € 15.50.

ROMANIA

European residents: see InterRail Global Pass and One Country Pass. Non-European residents: see Eurail Global Pass, Eurail Select/Regional/One Country Passes. See also Balkan Flexipass.

Bucureşti: day ticket for urban tram/bus network 8 RON, 7 days 17 RON, 15 days 25 RON.

RUSSIA

Moskva: bus/tram tickets available from kiosks in strips of 10/20. Separate 10-trip tickets available for metro. Monthly *yediniy bilyet* covers bus/tram/metro. No tourist tickets. **St Peterburg**: bus/tram tickets available in packs of 10; multi-journey cards can be bought for the metro.

SERBIA

European residents: see InterRail Global Pass and One Country Pass. Non-European residents: see Eurail Select Pass. See Balkan Flexipass.

Beograd: urban transport seems to use single tickets; no day tickets.

SLOVAKIA

European residents: see InterRail Global Pass and One Country Pass. Non-European residents: see European East.

Bratislava: urban tram/bus network, 24 hrs €3.50, 48 hrs €6.50, 3 days €8, 7 days €12. **Bratislava City Card** includes walking tour and many discounts, 1 day €6, 2 days €10, 3 days €12, available from tourist offices.

SLOVENIA

European residents: see InterRail Global Pass and One Country Pass. Non-European residents: see Eurail Global Pass, Eurail Select/Regional/One Country Passes.

Ljubljana Card: city buses, museums and discounts, 72 hrs €12.50.

Passes for Domestic Travel

SPAIN

European residents: see InterRail Global Pass and One Country Pass. Non-European residents: see Eurail Global Pass, Eurail Select/Regional/One Country Passes.

Eurail Spain Pass: this pass for people resident outside Europe gives unlimited travel on RENFE main-line services for 3 to 10 days within a period of 2 months. 3 days: 259 USD 1st class, 209 USD 2nd class. Each extra day 36-39 USD 1st class, 30 USD 2nd class. Children aged 4-11 half fare. No youth or group discounts. Reservation compulsory on all long distance trains.

Barcelona T-Dia ticket: valid 1 day on all public transport (TMB, FGC, tram, local rail), from €5.80 (1 zone) to €16.50 (all 6 zones). Zone 1 travelcards available for 2/3/4/5 days €10.70/15.20/19.50/23.10. **Barcelona Card**: various discounts 2/3/4/5 days €26/31.50/36/42.

Madrid: Abono Turístico gives all public transport in Zone A, 1/2/3 days €5.20/8.80/11.60, also 5/7 days €17.60/23.60, children 50%. Also available for wider area (zone T) at double the price. **Madrid Card** adds free or reduced entry to various attractions, 24/48/72 hrs €45/58/72.

Sevilla Card: public transport plus free entry to most museums, 24 hrs €50, 48 hrs €60, 72 hrs €65. Tourist cards also available for Burgos, Córdoba and Zaragoza.

SWEDEN

European residents: see InterRail Global Pass and One Country Pass. Non-European residents: see Eurail Global Pass, Eurail Select/Regional/One Country Passes. See also Öresund Rundt.

SJ Sommarkort: a pass giving 5 days 2nd class travel out of 30 days during the period mid-June to mid-August, 1750 SEK. Also valid to Oslo and København. Available from main stations. *Subject to confirmation.*

Stockholm: all SL public transport in Greater Stockholm, 24 hours 100 SEK, 72 hours 200 SEK, (72-timmarskort Plus adds various museums, summer only, 250 SEK). Also 7 days 260 SEK, 30 days 690 SEK; reductions of about 40% for under 20s and over 65s. Annual cards also available. **Stockholm Card** includes free entry to museums, 375/495/595 SEK for 24/48/72 hours (children aged 7-17 180/210/230 SEK).

SWITZERLAND

European residents: see InterRail Global Pass and One Country Pass. Non-European residents: see Eurail Global Pass, Eurail Select/Regional Passes. See also Euregio-Bodensee.

Swiss Pass: available to all non-Swiss residents. Consecutive days on Swiss Railways, boats and most alpine postbuses and city buses. Valid for 4, 8, 15, 22 days or 1 month. 1st class £229/332/402 for 4/8/15 days, £464/510 for 22 days/1 month. 2nd class £153/221/268 for 4/8/15 days, £309/340 for 22 days/1 month. Youth Pass gives 25% reduction for under 26s. All versions give 50% reduction on many funicular and mountain railways. Also acts as a Museum Pass - free entrance to 400 sites. Children aged 6-15 travel free with a Family Card (issued free by Switzerland Tourism, London) if accompanied by a parent (not other relatives), otherwise half fare.

Swiss Flexi Pass: as above but valid for 3, 4, 5 or 6 days within 1 month. Prices 1st/2nd class £220/146 (3 days), £266/178 (4 days), £308/205 (5 days), £351/234 (6 days). No Youth discount.

Saver Program: applies to the Swiss Pass or Flexi Pass (not Youth Pass) - 15% reduction per person for 2-5 adults travelling together.

Swiss Transfer Ticket: return ticket from any airport/border station to any other Swiss station; use within 1 month. Each journey must be completed on day of validation and on the most direct route. 1st class £113, 2nd class £75. Family Card valid, see above. Cannot be obtained in Switzerland.

Swiss Card: as Swiss Transfer Ticket but also offers unlimited half-fare tickets for 1 month and 50% reduction on many private railways. 1st class £150, 2nd class £107. Family card valid, see above under Swiss Pass.

Swiss Half Fare Card: 50% off most public transport, price £58, valid one month. Annual cards also available.

Note that the above passes are available from Switzerland Tourism, London, tel. 02074 204900, also online. Also available (except Swiss Transfer ticket) at major Swiss stations; Swiss Card only at border/airport stations. None of the above passes are available to Swiss residents.

Regional Passes: several areas available, e.g. Bernese Oberland for 7 days (3 days unlimited 2nd class travel plus 4 at 50% discount) 230 CHF, or 15 days (5 plus 10), 277 CHF, available May to October. Other passes include Adventure Card Wallis, and Graubünden Summer Holiday Pass. Not available from the UK, obtain locally in Switzerland.

Bern: day ticket, all transport in city (zones 10/11) 20/12 CHF 1st/2nd class, all zones in region 64/38 CHF.

Genève: Day ticket (Carte 24 Heures) includes buses, trams, trains and boats: 10 CHF (valid for 2 people at weekends). A version valid 0900 hrs until midnight costs 7 CHF.

Zürich: Tageskarte gives 24 hours on all transport including SBB trains, 13.20/8 CHF 1st/2nd class (central zone only); all zones in Canton 51.20/30.80 CHF. Off-peak version is 9-UhrPass, all zones, not before 0900 Mon-Fri, 38/23 CHF (also available for use on 6 different days 204/124 CHF; monthly version also available). **Zürich Card** includes visitor attractions: 24 hours 19 CHF, 72 hours 38 CHF (children 13/26 CHF), includes airport. **Zürich Card Plus** covers the whole Canton of Zürich with additional discounts: 24 hours 36 CHF (children 24 CHF).

TURKEY

European residents: see InterRail Global Pass and One Country Pass.

UKRAINE

There are no rail passes that we are aware of that are valid in Ukraine.

Kyïv: a monthly travelcard is available but there are no tourist tickets.

Where to Buy your Pass

Sources of rail passes include the following. Many can also provide point to point tickets and further information about rail travel.

IN THE UNITED KINGDOM

Rail Pass Direct
Chase House, Gilbert Street, Ropley, Hampshire SO24 0BY
✆ 08700 84 14 13 fax 0870 751 5005 www.railpassdirect.co.uk

Deutsche Bahn UK (German Railways)
UK Booking Centre, PO Box 687a, Surbiton KT6 6UB
✆ 08718 80 80 66 (8p per minute) fax 08718 80 80 65
www.deutsche-bahn.co.uk

European Rail Ltd
Unit 25, Tileyard Studios, Tileyard Road, London N7 9AH
✆ 020 7619 1083 fax 020 7700 2164 www.europeanrail.com

Ffestiniog Travel
Unit 6, Snowdonia Business Park, Minffordd, Gwynedd LL48 6LD
✆ 01766 772 050 fax 01766 772 056 www.festtravel.co.uk

Rail Canterbury
39 Palace Street, Canterbury, Kent CT1 2DZ
✆ 01227 450 088 fax 01227 470 072 www.rail-canterbury.co.uk

RailChoice - International Rail
Chase House, Gilbert Street, Ropley, Hampshire SO24 0BY
✆ 0870 165 7300 fax 0208 659 7466 www.railchoice.co.uk

Rail Europe
Britain Visitor Centre, 1 Regent Street, London SW1Y 4LR
✆ 08705 848 848 www.raileurope.co.uk

Stephen Walker Travel
Assembly Rooms, Market Place, Boston, Lincs PE21 6LY
✆ 08707 466 400 fax 01205 35 23 23.

Trainseurope
4 Station Approach, March, Cambs PE15 8SJ
Also at St Pancras International (from June) and Cambridge Station
✆ 08717 00 77 22 fax 01354 660 444 www.trainseurope.co.uk

Ultima Travel
424 Chester Road, Little Sutton, South Wirral CH66 3RB
✆ 0151 339 6171 fax 0151 339 9199.

IN THE USA

Rail Europe Inc.
Toll-free ✆ 1-800-4EURAIL, 1-888-BRITRAIL or 1-800-EUROSTAR
www.raileurope.com

See also **Rick Steve's** comprehensive website: www.ricksteves.com

In other European countries passes are often available from the travel centres at major stations.

AUSTRIA

CAPITAL
Vienna (Wien).

CLIMATE
Moderate Continental climate. Warm summer; high snowfall in winter.

CURRENCY
Euro (EUR / €). 1 euro = 100 cent. For exchange rates see page 11.

EMBASSIES IN VIENNA
Australia: Mattiellistraße 2, ✆ 01 506 740. **Canada**: Laurenzerberg 2, ✆ 01 383 000. **New Zealand** (Consulate): Salesianergasse 15/3, ✆ 01 318 8505. **UK**: Jaurèsgasse 12, ✆ 01 716 130. **USA**: Boltzmanngasse 16, ✆ 01 313 390.

EMBASSIES OVERSEAS
Australia: 12 Talbot St, Forrest, Canberra, ACT 2603, ✆ 2 6295 1533. **Canada**: 445 Wilbrod St, Ottawa ON, KIN 6M7, ✆ 613 789 1444. **UK**: 18 Belgrave Mews West, London SW1X 8HU, ✆ 020 7344 3250. **USA**: 3524 International Court NW, Washington DC 20008, ✆ 202 895 6700.

LANGUAGE
German; English is widely spoken in tourist areas.

OPENING HOURS
Banks: mostly Mon, Tues, Wed, Fri 0800–1230 and 1330–1500, Thur 0800–1230 and 1330–1730. **Shops**: Mon–Fri 0800–1830 (some closing for a 1- or 2-hour lunch), Sat 0800–1200/1300 (in larger towns often until 1700). **Museums**: check locally.

POST OFFICES
Indicated by golden horn symbol; all handle poste restante (*postlagernde Briefe*). Open mostly Mon–Fri 0800–1200 and 1400–1800. Main and station post offices in larger cities open 24 hrs. Stamps (*Briefmarke*) also sold at Tabak/Trafik shops.

PUBLIC HOLIDAYS
Jan 1, Jan 6 (Epiphany), Easter Mon, May 1, Ascension Day, Whit Mon, Corpus Christi, Aug 15 (Assumption), Oct 26 (National Day), Nov 1 (All Saints), Dec 8 (Immaculate Conception), Dec 25, 26. For dates of movable holidays see page 2.

PUBLIC TRANSPORT
Most long-distance travel is by rail (see below). Inter-urban buses operated by ÖBB-Postbus (www.postbus.at); usually based by rail stations or post offices. City transport is efficient with integrated ticketing; buy tickets from machines or Tabak/Trafik booths. Wien has an extensive metro and tram system; for day tickets see Passes section. Other cities with tram networks include Graz, Innsbruck and Linz. Taxis are metered; extra charges for luggage (fixed charges in smaller towns).

RAIL TRAVEL
See Tables **950 - 999**. Operated by Österreichische Bundesbahnen (ÖBB) (www.oebb.at). Mostly electrified; fast and reliable; ÖIC or IC trains every 1–2 hrs with connecting regional trains. Other fast trains, with stops only in larger cities: ICE, ÖEC, EC and the new Railjet (RJ) services; D (ordinary express trains); REX (semi-fast/local trains). Most overnight trains convey sleeping-cars (up to three berths), couchettes (four/six berths) and 2nd-class seats. Seat reservations available on long-distance services. Most stations have left luggage facilities.

TELEPHONES
Dial in: ✆ +43 then number (omit initial 0). Outgoing: ✆ 00. Phonecards are sold at post offices and tobacconists (Tabak Trafiken). Operator assistance / enquiries: ✆ 1611 (national); ✆ 1613 (rest of Europe); ✆ 1614 (rest of world). Emergency: ✆ 112. Police: ✆ 133. Fire: ✆ 122. Ambulance: ✆ 144.

TIPPING
Hotels, restaurants, cafés and bars: service charge of 10–15% but tip of around 10% still expected. Taxis 10%.

TOURIST INFORMATION
Austrian National Tourist Office (www.austria.info). Staff invariably speak some English. Tourist office opening times vary widely, particularly restricted at weekends in smaller places. Usually called *Fremdenverkehrsbüro*; look for green ‘i’ sign. Main tourist office in Vienna: Albertinaplatz / Maysedergasse, ✆ 01 24 555.

TOURIST OFFICES OVERSEAS
Australia: 36 Carrington St, 1st floor, Sydney NSW 2000, ✆ 02 9299 3621, info@antosyd.org.au. **Canada**: 2 Bloor St West, Suite 400, Toronto ON, M4W 3E2, ✆ 416 967 3381, anto-tor@sympatico.ca. **UK**: 9-11 Richmond Buildings, off Dean St., London W1D 3HF, ✆ 020 7318 1651, info@anto.co.uk. **USA**: 120 West 45th St, 9th floor, New York NY 10036, ✆ 212 944 6885, travel@austria.info.

VISAS
See page xxxii for visa requirements.

BELGIUM

CAPITAL
Brussels (Bruxelles/Brussel).

CLIMATE
Rain prevalent at any time; warm summers, cold winters (often with snow).

CURRENCY
Euro (EUR / €). 1 euro = 100 cent. For exchange rates see page 11.

EMBASSIES IN BRUSSELS
Australia: rue Guimard 6-8, ✆ 02 286 0500. **Canada**: Avenue de Tervueren 2, ✆ 02 741 0611. **New Zealand**: square de Meeûs 1, ✆ 02 512 1040. **UK**: rue d'Arlon 85, ✆ 02 287 6211. **USA**: Regentlaan 27 Boulevard du Régent, ✆ 02 508 2111.

EMBASSIES OVERSEAS
Australia: 19 Arkana St, Yarralumla, Canberra, ACT 2600, ✆ 2 6273 2501. **Canada**: 360 Albert St, Suite 820, Ottawa ON, K1R 7X7, ✆ 613 236 7267. **UK**: 17 Grosvenor Crescent, London SW1X 7EE, ✆ 020 7470 3700. **USA**: 3330 Garfield St NW, Washington DC 20008, ✆ 202 333 6900.

LANGUAGE
Dutch (north), French (south) and German (east). Many speak both French and Dutch, plus often English and/or German.

OPENING HOURS
Many establishments close 1200–1400. **Banks**: Mon–Fri 0900–1600. **Shops**: Mon–Sat 0900/1000–1800/1900 (often later Fri). **Museums**: vary, but most open six days a week: 1000–1700 (usually Tues–Sun, Wed–Mon or Thur–Tues).

POST OFFICES
Postes / Posterijen / De Post open Mon–Fri 0900–1700 (very few open Sat morning). Stamps are also sold at newsagents.

PUBLIC HOLIDAYS
Jan 1, Easter Mon, May 1, Ascension Day, Whit Mon, July 21 (National Day), Aug 15 (Assumption), Nov 1 (All Saints), Nov 11 (Armistice), Dec 25. For dates of movable holidays see page 2. Transport and places that open usually keep Sunday times on public holidays.

PUBLIC TRANSPORT
National bus companies: De Lijn (Flanders), TEC (Wallonia, i.e. the French-speaking areas); few long-distance buses. Brussels has

extensive metro / tram / bus system operated by STIB with integrated ticketing; tickets can be purchased from tram / bus driver but it's cheaper to buy in advance from machines at metro stations or special kiosks (also offices labelled *Bootik*). For day tickets see Passes section. Some tram and bus stops are request stops – raise your hand. Taxis seldom stop in the street, so find a rank or phone; double rates outside city limits.

RAIL TRAVEL
See Tables **400 - 439**. Operated by NMBS (in Dutch) / SNCB (in French) (www.b-rail.be). Rail information offices: 'B' in an oval logo. Seat reservations available for international journeys only. Refreshments are not always available. Some platforms serve more than one train at a time; check carefully. Left luggage and cycle hire at many stations. Timetables usually in two sets: Mondays to Fridays and weekends/holidays.

TELEPHONES
Dial in: ✆ +32 then number (omit initial 0). Outgoing: ✆ 00. Phonecards are sold at post offices, newsagents and supermarkets. Some public phones accept credit cards. Emergency: ✆ 112. Police: ✆ 101. Fire, ambulance: ✆ 100.

TIPPING
Tipping in cafés, bars, restaurants and taxis is not the norm, as service is supposed to be included in the price, but is starting to be expected in places where staff are used to serving people from the international community (who often leave generous tips): 10 to 15%. Tip hairwashers in salons, delivery men, cloakroom / toilet attendants.

TOURIST INFORMATION
Toerisme Vlaanderen (www.toervl.be / www.visitflanders.co.uk). Office de Promotion du Tourisme de Wallonie et de Bruxelles (www.belgium-tourism.net). Dutch: *Dienst voor Toerisme*. French: *Office de Tourisme*. Brussels tourist office: Hôtel de Ville, Grand Place, ✆ 025 138 940. Most tourist offices have English-speaking staff and free English-language literature, but charge for walking itineraries and good street maps. Opening hours, especially in small places and off-season, are flexible.

TOURIST OFFICES OVERSEAS
UK: Tourism Flanders - Brussels, 1a Cavendish Square, London W1G 0LD. ✆ 020 7307 7738, info@visitflanders.co.uk; Belgian Tourist Office Brussels-Wallonia 217 Marsh Wall, London E14 9FJ. ✆ 020 7531 0390, ✆ 0800 954 5245 (to order brochures), info@belgiumtheplaceto.be. **USA / Canada**: 220 East 42nd St, Suite 3402, New York NY 10017, ✆ 212 758 8130, info@visitbelgium.com

VISAS
See page xxxii for visa requirements.

BULGARIA

CAPITAL
Sofia (Sofiya).

CLIMATE
Hot summers; wet spring and autumn; snow in winter (skiing popular).

CURRENCY
Lev (BGN or Lv.); 1 lev = 100 stotinki (st). Tied to euro. For exchange rates, see page 11. Credit cards are increasingly accepted.

EMBASSIES IN SOFIA
Australia (Consulate): ulitsa Trakia 37, ✆ 02 946 1334. **Canada**: (Consulate) ulitsa Moskovska 9, ✆ 02 969 9710. **New Zealand**: *refer to NZ Embassy in Belgium*. **UK**: ul. Moskovska 9, ✆ 02 933 9222. **USA**: ulitsa Kozyak 16, ✆ 02 937 5100.

EMBASSIES OVERSEAS
Australia: 33 Culgoa Circuit, O'Malley, Canberra, ACT 2606, ✆ 2 6286 9711. **Canada**: 325 Steward St, Ottawa ON, K1N 6K5, ✆ 613 789 3215. **UK**: 186–186 Queen's Gate, London SW7 5HL, ✆ 020 7584 9400. **USA**: 1621 22nd St NW, Washington DC 20008, ✆ 202 387 0174.

LANGUAGE
Bulgarian (written in the Cyrillic alphabet); English, German, Russian and French in tourist areas. Nodding the head indicates 'no' (*ne*); shaking it means 'yes' (*da*).

OPENING HOURS
Banks: Mon–Fri 0900–1500. Some exchange offices open longer hours and weekends. **Shops**: Mon–Fri 0800–2000, closed 1200–1400 outside major towns, Sat open 1000–1200. **Museums**: vary widely, but often 0800–1200, 1400–1830. Many close Mon or Tues.

POST OFFICES
Stamps (*marki*) are sold only at post offices (*poshta*), usually open Mon–Sat 0800–1730. Some close 1200–1400.

PUBLIC HOLIDAYS
Jan 1, Mar. 3 (National Day), Orthodox Easter Mon, May 1, May 24 (Education), Sept 6 (Union), Sept 22 (Independence), Nov. 1 (Spiritual Leaders), Dec 24, 25, 26. For dates of movable holidays see page 2.

PUBLIC TRANSPORT
There is an extensive bus network but quality is variable. They are slightly more expensive than trains but both are very cheap for hard-currency travellers. In Sofia buses and trams use the same ticket; punch it at the machine after boarding, get a new ticket if you change. For day tickets see Passes section.

RAIL TRAVEL
See Tables **1500 - 1560**. Bulgarian State Railways (BDZ), (www.bdz.bg) run express, fast and stopping trains. Often crowded; reservations are recommended (obligatory for express trains). Most long-distance trains provide a limited buffet service; certain services also convey a restaurant car. Overnight trains convey 1st- and 2nd-class sleeping cars and seats (also 2nd-class couchettes on certain trains between Sofia and Black Sea resorts). One platform may serve two tracks, platforms and tracks are both numbered. Signs at stations are in Cyrillic.

TELEPHONES
Dial in: ✆ +359 then number (omit initial 0). Outgoing: ✆ 00. Tokens (for local calls) and phonecards are sold at post offices and tobacconists. Police: ✆ 166. Fire: ✆ 160. Ambulance: ✆ 150.

TIPPING
Waiters and taxi drivers expect a tip of about 10%.

TOURIST INFORMATION
Bulgarian Tourism Authority (www.bulgariatravel.org). Main tourist office: 1 Sveta Nedelia Sq., 1040 Sofia, ✆ 029 335 845. There are tourist offices in all main cities and resorts.

TOURIST OFFICES OVERSEAS
UK and **USA**: Tourist information available at the Bulgarian Embassies listed above.

VISAS
See page xxxii for visa requirements. Passports must have 3 months validity remaining. Visitors staying with friends or family (i.e. not in paid accommodation) need to register on arrival.

CROATIA

CAPITAL
Zagreb.

CLIMATE
Continental on the Adriatic coast, with very warm summers.

CURRENCY

Kuna (HRK or kn); 1 kuna = 100 lipa. For exchange rates, see page 11. Credit cards are widely accepted.

EMBASSIES IN ZAGREB

Australia: Centar Kaptol, 3rd Floor, Nova Ves 11, ✆ 014 891 200. **Canada**: Prilaz Gjure Dezelica 4, ✆ 014 881 200. **New Zealand** (Consulate): Vlaska ulica 50A, ✆ 014 612 060. **UK**: Ivana Lučića 4, ✆ 016 009 100. **USA**: Ulica Thomasa Jeffersona 2, ✆ 016 612 200.

EMBASSIES OVERSEAS

Australia: 14 Jindalee Crescent, O'Malley, Canberra, ACT 2606, ✆ 2 6286 6988. **Canada**: 229 Chapel St, Ottawa ON, K1N 7Y6, ✆ 613 562 7820. **New Zealand** (consulate): 291 Lincoln Rd, Henderson, PO Box 83-200, Edmonton, Auckland, ✆ 9 836 5581. **UK**: 21 Conway St, London, W1T 6BN, ✆ 020 7387 2022. **USA**: 2343 Massachusetts Ave. NW, Washington DC 20008-2803, ✆ 202 588 5899.

LANGUAGE

Croatian. English, German and Italian spoken in tourist areas.

OPENING HOURS

Banks: Mon–Fri 0700–1900, Sat 0700–1300, but may vary, some banks may open Sun in larger cities. Most **shops**: Mon–Fri 0800–2000, Sat 0800–1400/1500; many shops also open Sun, especially in summer. Some shops close 1200–1600. Most open-air **markets** daily, mornings only. **Museums**: vary.

POST OFFICES

Usual hours: Mon–Fri 0700–1900 (some post offices in larger cities open until 2200), Sat 0700–1300. Stamps (*markice*) are sold at newsstands and tobacconists (*trafika*), Post boxes are yellow.

PUBLIC HOLIDAYS

Jan 1, Jan 6 (Epiphany), Easter Mon, May 1, Corpus Christi, June 22 (Antifascist Struggle), Aug. 5 (Nat. Thanksgiving), Aug. 15 (Assumption), Oct 8 (Independence), Nov 1 (All Saints), Dec. 25, 26. For dates of movable holidays see page 2. Many local Saints' holidays.

PUBLIC TRANSPORT

Buses and trams are cheap, regular and efficient. Zagreb and Osijek have tram networks. Jadrolinija maintains most domestic ferry lines; main office in Rijeka, ✆ +385 51 666 111.

RAIL TRAVEL

See Tables **1300 - 1359**. National railway company: Hrvatske željeznice (HŽ) (www.hznet.hr). Zagreb is a major hub for international trains. Efficient services but there is a limited network and services can be infrequent. Daytime trains on the Zagreb - Split line are operated by modern tilting diesel trains. Station amenities: generally left luggage, a bar, newsstand and WCs.

TELEPHONES

Dial in: ✆ +385 then number (omit initial 0). Outgoing: ✆ 00. Public phones accept phonecards only (sold at post offices, newsstands and tobacconists). Police: ✆ 92. Fire: ✆ 93. Ambulance: ✆ 94.

TIPPING

Leave 10% for good service in a restaurant. It's not necessary to tip in bars.

TOURIST INFORMATION

Croatian National Tourist Board (www.croatia.hr). Main office: Iblerov trg 10/IV, 10000 Zagreb, ✆ 014 699 333, info@htz.hr.

TOURIST OFFICES OVERSEAS

UK: Lanchesters, 162-164 Fulham Palace Rd, London, W6 9ER, ✆ 020 8563 7979, info@croatia-london.co.uk **USA**: 350 Fifth Ave., Suite 4003, New York NY 10118, ✆ 212 279 8672, cntony@earthlink.net

VISAS

See page xxxii for visa requirements.

CZECH REPUBLIC

CAPITAL

Prague (Praha).

CLIMATE

Mild summers and very cold winters.

CURRENCY

Czech crown or koruna (CZK or Kč); 1 koruna = 100 haléřu. For exchange rates, see page 11. Credit cards are widely accepted.

EMBASSIES IN PRAGUE

Australia (Consulate): 6th Floor, Solitaire Building, ulica Klimentska 10, ✆ 296 578 350. **Canada**: Muchova 6, ✆ 272 101 800. **New Zealand** (Consulate): Dykova 19, ✆ 222 514 672. **UK**: Thunovská 14, ✆ 257 402 111. **USA**: Tržíště 15, ✆ 257 022 000.

EMBASSIES OVERSEAS

Australia: 8 Culgoa Circuit, O'Malley, Canberra, ACT 2606, ✆ 2 6290 1386. **Canada**: 251 Cooper St., Ottawa ON, K2P 0G2, ✆ 613 562 3875. **UK**: 26–30 Kensington Palace Gardens, London W8 4QY, ✆ 020 7243 1115. **USA**: 3900 Spring of Freedom St NW, Washington DC 20008, ✆ 202 274 9100.

LANGUAGE

Czech. Czech and Slovak are closely related Slavic tongues. English, German and Russian are widely understood, but Russian is less popular.

OPENING HOURS

Banks: Mon–Fri 0800–1800. **Shops**: Mon–Fri 0900–1800, Sat 0900–1200 (often longer in Prague Sat–Sun). **Food shops**: usually open earlier plus on Sun. **Museums**: (usually) Tues–Sun 1000–1800. Most castles close Nov–Mar.

POST OFFICES

Usual opening hours are 0800–1900. Stamps also available from newsagents and tobacconists. Post boxes: orange and blue.

PUBLIC HOLIDAYS

Jan 1, Easter Mon, May 1, May 8 (Liberation), July 5 (Cyril & Methodius), July 6 (Jan Hus), Sept 28 (Statehood), Oct 28 (Founding), Nov. 17 (Freedom & Democracy), Dec 24, 25, 26. For dates of movable holidays see page 2.

PUBLIC TRANSPORT

Extensive long-distance bus network competing with the railways, run by ČSAD or increasingly by private companies. In Prague the long-distance bus station is close to Florenc metro station. If boarding at a bus station with a ticket window, buy your ticket in advance, otherwise pay the driver. Good urban networks with integrated ticketing. Prague (Praha) has metro and tram system - see Passes feature for day tickets. Other cities with trams include Brno, Ostrava, Plzeň, Olomouc, Liberec.

RAIL TRAVEL

See Tables **1100 - 1169**. National rail company is České Dráhy (ČD) (www.cd.cz). An extensive network with many branch lines and cheap fares, but sometimes crowded trains. The best mainline trains are classified *IC*, *EC* or *Ex*. The fastest Praha - Ostrava trains are classified *SC* meaning *SuperCity* and are operated by Pendolino tilting trains - a compulsory reservation fee of CZK 200 or €7.00 applies on these. Other fast (*R* for rychlík) trains are shown in our tables with just the train number. Semi-fast trains are *Sp* or spešný, local trains (very slow) are *Os* or osobný. Some branch lines are now operated by private companies. Many long-distance trains have dining or buffet cars. Seats for express trains may be reserved at least one hour before departure at the counter marked R at stations.

TELEPHONES

Dial in: ✆ +420 then number. Outgoing: ✆ 00. Payphones accept coins or phonecards (sold at post offices, tobacconists, newsstands, hotels and money exchange offices). Police: ✆ 158. Fire: ✆ 150. Ambulance: ✆ 155.

TIPPING

You should tip at pubs and restaurants, in hotels and taxis and hairdressers. In general, round up the nearest CZK 10 unless you are somewhere upmarket, when you should tip 10%.

TOURIST INFORMATION

Czech Tourism (www.czechtourism.com). Main office: Vinohradská 46, 120 41 Praha 2, Vinohrady, ✆ 221 580 111. Prague Information Service (www.pis.cz), Information centre, Old Town Hall, Staromestská námesti 1, Praha 1.

TOURIST OFFICES OVERSEAS

Canada: 2 Bloor Street West, Suite 1500, Toronto ON, M4W 3E2, ✆ 416 363 9928, info-ca@czechtourism.com **UK**: 13 Harley Street, London W1G 9QG, ✆ 020 7631 0427, info-uk@czechtourism.com **USA**: 1109 Madison Ave., New York NY 10028, ✆ 212 288 0830, info-usa@czechtourism.com

VISAS

See page xxxii for visa requirements.

DENMARK

CAPITAL

Copenhagen (København).

CLIMATE

Maritime climate. July–Aug is warmest, May–June often very pleasant, but rainier; Oct–Mar is wettest, with periods of frost.

CURRENCY

Danish crown or krone, DKK or kr; 1 krone = 100 øre. For exchange rates, see page 11.

EMBASSIES IN COPENHAGEN

Australia: Dampfaergevej 26, ✆ 70 26 36 76. **Canada**: Kristen Bernikowsgade 1, ✆ 33 48 32 00. **New Zealand** (Consulate): Store Strandstraede 21, ✆ 33 37 77 02. **UK**: Kastelsvej 36-40, ✆ 35 44 52 00. **USA**: Dag Hammarskjölds Allé 24, ✆ 33 41 71 00.

EMBASSIES OVERSEAS

Australia: 15 Hunter St, Yarralumla, Canberra, ACT 2600, ✆ 2 6270 5333. **Canada**: 47 Clarence St, Suite 450, Ottawa ON, K1N 9K1, ✆ 613 562 1811. **New Zealand** (Consulate): 273 Bleakhouse Rd, Howick, PO Box 619, Auckland 1015, ✆ 9 537 3099. **UK**: 55 Sloane St, London SW1X 9SR, ✆ 020 7333 0200. **USA**: 3200 Whitehaven St NW, Washington DC 20008-3683, ✆ 202 234 4300.

LANGUAGE

Danish. English is almost universally spoken.

OPENING HOURS

Banks (Copenhagen): Mon–Fri 0930–1600 (some until 1700; most until 1800 on Thur). Vary elsewhere. **Shops**: (mostly) Mon–Thur 0930–1730, Fri 0930–1900/2000, Sat 0900–1300/1400, though many in Copenhagen open until 1700 and may also open Sun. **Museums**: (mostly) daily 1000/1100–1600/1700. In winter, hours shorter and museums usually close Mon.

POST OFFICES

Mostly Mon–Fri 0900/1000–1700/1800, Sat 0900–1200 (but opening times vary greatly). Stamps also sold at newsagents.

PUBLIC HOLIDAYS

Jan 1, Maundy Thurs, Good Fri, Easter Sun/Mon, Common Prayer Day (4th Fri after Easter), Ascension, Whit Monday, June 5 (Constitution Day), Dec. 25, 26. For dates of movable holidays see page 2.

PUBLIC TRANSPORT

Long-distance travel is easiest by train (see below). Excellent regional and city bus services, many connecting with trains. Modern and efficient metro (www.m.dk) and suburban rail network in and around the capital; see Passes feature for day tickets. No trams in København; bus network can be tricky to fathom. Bridges or ferries link all the big islands. Taxis: green *Fri* sign when available; metered, and most accept major credit cards. Many cycle paths and bike hire shops; free use of City Bikes in Copenhagen central area (returnable coin required).

RAIL TRAVEL

See Tables **700 - 728**. Operator: Danske Statsbaner (DSB); (www.dsb.dk). Some independent lines, and certain former DSB services are now operated by private company ArrivaTog. *IC* trains reach up to 200 km/h. *Re* (regionaltog) trains are frequent, but slower. Refreshment trolley or vending machine available on most *IC* trains. Reservations are recommended (not compulsory) on *IC* and *Lyn* trains - DKK 20 in standard class; reservation included in business class. Reservations close 15 minutes before a train leaves its originating station. Nationwide reservations ✆ 70 13 14 15. Baggage lockers at most stations, usually DKK 20 per 24 hrs. Usually free trolleys, but you may need a (returnable) coin.

TELEPHONES

Dial in: ✆ +45 then number. Outgoing: ✆ 00. Most operators speak English. Phonecards are available from DSB kiosks, post offices and newsstands. Directory enquiries: ✆ 118. International operator/directory: ✆ 14. Emergency services: ✆ 112.

TIPPING

At least DKK 20 in restaurants. Elsewhere (taxis, cafés, bars, hotels etc) tipping is not expected.

TOURIST INFORMATION

Danish Tourist Board (www.visitdenmark.com). Nearly every decent-sized town in Denmark has a tourist office (*turistbureau*), normally found in the town hall or central square; they distribute maps, information and advice. Some will also book accommodation for a small fee, and change money.

TOURIST OFFICES OVERSEAS

UK: 55 Sloane St, London SW1X 9SY, ✆ 020 7259 5958, london@visitdenmark.com **USA / Canada**: P.O.Box 4649, Grand Central Station New York NY 10163-4649, ✆ 212 885 9700, info@goscandinavia.com

VISAS

See page xxxii for visa requirements.

ESTONIA

CAPITAL

Tallinn.

CLIMATE

Warm summers, cold, snowy winters; rain all year, heaviest in August.

CURRENCY

Estonian crown or kroon (EEK or kr); 1 kroon = 100 senti. For exchange rates, see page 11. Currency exchange facilities are limited, though cash machines (ATMs) are plentiful, especially in Tallinn.

EMBASSIES IN TALLINN

Australia (Consulate): c/- Standard Ltd Marja 9, ✆ 6 509 308.
Canada (Consulate): Toom Kooli 13, ✆ 6 273 308.
New Zealand: *refer to NZ Embassy in Poland.*
UK: Wismari 6, ✆ 6 674 700.

USA: Kentmanni 20, ✆ 6 688 100.

EMBASSIES OVERSEAS

Australia (Consulate): 40 Nicholson St. Balmain East, Sydney, NSW 2041, ✆ 2 8014 8999. **Canada**: 260 Dalhousie St, Suite 210, Ottawa ON, K1N 7E4, ✆ 613 789 4222. **UK**: 16 Hyde Park Gate, London SW7 5DG, ✆ 020 7589 3428. **USA**: 2131 Massachusetts Ave. NW, Washington DC 20008, ✆ 202 588 0101.

LANGUAGE

Estonian. Some Finnish is useful, plus Russian in Tallinn and the north-east.

OPENING HOURS

Banks: Mon–Fri 0900–1600. **Shops**: Mon–Fri 0900/1000–1800/1900, Sat 0900/1000–1500/1700; many also open Sun. **Museums**: days vary (usually closed Mon and/or Tues); hours commonly 1100–1600.

POST OFFICES

Post offices *(Eesti Post)* are generally open 0900–1800 Mon–Fri, 0930–1500 Sat. The central post office in Tallinn is located at Narva 1. Stamps are also sold at large hotels, newsstands, and tourist offices.

PUBLIC HOLIDAYS

Jan 1, Feb 24 (Independence), Good Friday, Easter Mon (unofficial), May 1, June 23 (Victory), June 24 (Midsummer), Aug 20 (Restoration of Independence), Dec 25, 26. For dates of movable holidays see page 2.

PUBLIC TRANSPORT

Long-distance bus services are often quicker, cleaner, and more efficient than rail, but getting pricier. The main operator is Eurolines (www.eurolines.ee). Book international journeys in advance at bus stations; pay the driver on rural and local services. Tallinn has a tram network.

RAIL TRAVEL

See Tables **1800 - 1890**. Local rail services are operated by Edelaraudtee (www.edel.ee), international services by GoRail (www.gorail.ee). Comfortable overnight train to Moskva; best to take berth in 2nd-class coupé (4-berth compartments); 1st-class *luxe* compartments (2-berth) also available. Reservations are compulsory for all sleepers; entry visa to Russia may need to be shown when booking. Very little English spoken at stations.

TELEPHONES

Dial in: ✆ +372 then number. Outgoing: ✆ 00. Pay phones take phonecards (from hotels, tourist offices, post offices, newsstands). Police: ✆ 110. Fire, ambulance: ✆ 112.

TIPPING

Not necessary to tip at the bar or counter, but tip 10% if served at your table. Round up taxi fares to a maximum of 10%.

TOURIST INFORMATION

Welcome to Estonia (www.visitestonia.com). Tallinn Tourist Information: Niguliste 2 / Kullassepa 4, 10146 Tallinn, ✆ 6457 777, turismiinfo@tallinnlv.ee. Ekspress Hotline (www.1182.ee), is an English-speaking information service covering all Estonian towns: ✆ 1182 (available only within Estonia).

TOURIST OFFICES OVERSEAS

UK: Tourism brochures available from the Estonian Embassy (see above) mon-fri 0900 - 1700. **Germany**: Baltikum Tourismus Zentrale, Katharinenstraße 19-20, 10711 Berlin, ✆ 030 89 00 90 91, info@baltikuminfo.de.

VISAS

See page xxxii for visa requirements.

FINLAND

CAPITAL

Helsinki (Helsingfors).

CLIMATE

Extremely long summer days; spring and autumn curtailed further north; continuous daylight for 70 days north of 70th parallel. Late June to mid-August best for far north, mid-May to September for south. Ski season: mid-January to mid-April.

CURRENCY

Euro (EUR / €). 1 euro = 100 cent. For exchange rates see page 11.

EMBASSIES IN HELSINKI

Australia (Consulate): c/- Tradimex Oy, museokatu 25B, ✆ 09 4777 6640. **Canada**: Pohjoisesplanadi 25B, ✆ 09 228 530.
New Zealand (Consulate): Johannesbrinken 2, ✆ 024 701 818.
UK: Itäinen Puistotie 17, ✆ 09 2286 5100.
USA: Itäinen Puistotie 14B, ✆ 09 616 250.

EMBASSIES OVERSEAS

Australia: 12 Darwin Ave., Yarralumla, Canberra, ACT 2600, ✆ 2 6273 3800. **Canada**: 55 Metcalfe St, Suite 850, Ottawa ON, K1P 6L5, ✆ 613 288 2233. **UK**: 38 Chesham Place, London SW1X 8HW, ✆ 020 7838 6200. **USA**: 3301 Massachusetts Ave. NW, Washington DC 20008, ✆ 202 298 5800.

LANGUAGE

Finnish, and, in the north, Lapp/Sami. Swedish, the second language, often appears on signs after the Finnish. English is widely spoken, especially in Helsinki. German is reasonably widespread.

OPENING HOURS

Banks: Mon–Fri 0915–1615, with regional variations. **Shops**: Mon–Fri 0900–2000, Sat 0900–1500, though many shops open Mon–Fri 0700–2100, Sat 0900–1800; many shops also open Sun, June–Aug. **Stores/food shops**: Mon–Sat 0900–1800/2000. **Museums**: usually close Mon, hours vary. Many close in winter.

POST OFFICES

Most *posti* open at least Mon–Fri 0900–1700. Stamps also sold at shops, hotels and bus and train stations. Yellow postboxes.

PUBLIC HOLIDAYS

Jan 1, Jan 6 (Epiphany), Good Friday, Easter Mon, May 1, Ascension, Midsummer (Sat falling June 20–26), All Saints (Sat falling Oct 31 - Nov 6), Dec 6 (Independence), Dec 24, 25, 26. For dates of movable holidays see page 2.

PUBLIC TRANSPORT

The national timetable book *Aikataulut / Tidtabeller* (in Finnish and Swedish, from bookshops) covers trains, buses, and boats in detail. Bus stations (*Linja-autoasema*) have restaurants and shops. There are more than 300 bus services daily from Helsinki to all parts of the country. The main long-distance bus operators are Matkahuolto (www.matkahuolto.fi) and the Expressbus consortium (www.expressbus.com). It is usually cheaper to buy tickets in advance. Bus stop signs show a black bus on a yellow background (local services) or a white bus on a blue background (long distance). Helsinki has metro / tram / bus network with integrated ticketing. Taxis can be hailed in the street: they are for hire when the yellow *taksi* sign is lit.

RAIL TRAVEL

See Tables **790 - 799**. National rail company: VR (www.vr.fi); tilting Pendolinos (up to 220 km/h) run on certain lines. Fares depend upon train type - those for *S220* (Pendolino), *IC* (InterCity) and *P* (express) trains include a seat reservation. Sleeping-cars: two or three berths per compartment (2nd class), single compartment (1st class). In winter sleeping accommodation generally costs less on Mondays to Thursdays. Rail station: *Rautatieasema* or *Järnvägsstation*; virtually all have baggage lockers.

TELEPHONES

Dial in: ✆ +358 then number (omit initial 0). Outgoing: ✆ 00. Phonecards are sold by *R-kiosk* newsstands, tourist offices, *Tele* offices, and some post offices. There are no public telephone booths in Helsinki. Directory enquiries: ✆ 020202. Emergency services: ✆ 112.

TIPPING

Service charge included in hotel and restaurant bills but leave coins for good service. Hotel and restaurant porters and sauna attendants expect a euro or two. Taxi drivers and hairdressers do not expect a tip.

TOURIST INFORMATION

Finnish Tourist Board (www.visitfinland.com). PO Box 625, Töölönkatu 11, 00101 Helsinki, ✆ 010 60 58 000, mek@visitfinland.com. Every Finnish town has a tourist office *(Matkailutoimistot)* where staff speak English. English literature, mostly free.

TOURIST OFFICES OVERSEAS

Australia: P.O. Box 1427, North Sydney NSW 2059 ✆ 02 9929 6044. **UK**: P.O. Box 33213, London W6 8JX ✆ 020 7365 2512, finlandinfo.lon@mek.fi. **USA**: 297 York Street, Jersey City, NJ 07302 ✆ 917 863 5484.

VISAS

See page xxxii for visa requirements.

FRANCE

CAPITAL

Paris, divided into *arrondissements* 1 to 20 (1er, 2^e^ etc).

CLIMATE

Cool–cold winters, mild–hot summers; south coast best Oct–Mar, Alps and Pyrenees, June and early July. Paris best spring and autumn.

CURRENCY

Euro (EUR/€). 1 euro = 100 cent. For exchange rates see page 11.

EMBASSIES IN PARIS

Australia: 4 rue Jean Rey, ✆ 01 40 59 33 00. **Canada**: 35 avenue Montaigne, ✆ 01 44 43 29 02. **New Zealand**: 7 ter rue Léonard de Vinci, ✆ 01 45 01 43 43. **UK**: 35 rue du Faubourg St Honoré, ✆ 01 44 51 31 00. **USA**: 2 avenue Gabriel, ✆ 01 43 12 22 22.

EMBASSIES OVERSEAS

Australia: 6 Perth Ave. Yarralumla, Canberra, ACT 2600, ✆ 2 6216 0100. **Canada**: 42 Sussex Drive, Ottawa ON, K1M 2C9, ✆ 613 789 1795. **New Zealand**: 34-42 Manners St, Wellington, ✆ 4 384 2555. **UK**: 58 Knightsbridge, London SW1X 7JT, ✆ 020 7258 6600. **USA**: 4101 Reservoir Rd, NW, Washington DC 20007, ✆ 202 944 6000.

LANGUAGE

French; many people can speak a little English, particularly in Paris.

OPENING HOURS

Paris and major towns: shops, banks and post offices are generally open 0900/1000–1700/1900 Mon-Fri, plus often Sat am/all day. Small shops can be open Sun am but closed Mon. **Provinces**: weekly closing is mostly Sun pm/all day and Mon; both shops and services generally close 1200–1400; services may have restricted opening times. Most **super/hypermarkets** open unti; 2100/2200. **Museums**: (mostly) 0900–1700, closing Mon and/or Tues; longer hours in summer; often free or discount rate on Sun. **Restaurants** serve 1200–1400 and 1900–2100 at least. Public holidays: services closed, food shops open am in general; check times with individual museums and tourist sights.

POST OFFICES

Called *La Poste*. Letter boxes are small, wall or pedestal-mounted, and yellow. Basic rate postage stamps (*timbres*) can also be bought from tobacconists (*Tabacs* or *Café-Tabacs*).

PUBLIC HOLIDAYS

Jan 1, Easter Mon, Whit Mon, May 1, May 8 (Victory), Ascension Day, July 14 (National Day), Aug 15 (Assumption), Nov 1 (All Saints), Nov 11 (Armistice), Dec 25. For dates of movable holidays see page 2. If a holiday falls on a Tuesday or Thursday, many businesses close additionally on the Monday or Friday.

PUBLIC TRANSPORT

In Paris, use the Métro where possible: clean, fast, cheap and easy. For urban and suburban transport, *carnets* (sets of 10 tickets) are cheaper than individual tickets; for day tickets see Passes feature. Bus and train timetable leaflets (free) are available from tourist offices, bus and rail stations. Many cities have modern tram/light rail networks; Lyon, Marseille and Toulouse also have metro systems. Bus services are infrequent after 2030 and on Sundays. Sparse public transport in rural areas, and few long-distance bus services. Licensed taxis (avoid others) are metered; white roof-lights when free; surcharges for luggage, extra passengers, and journeys beyond the centre.

RAIL TRAVEL

See Tables **250 - 399**. Société Nationale des Chemins de fer Français (SNCF) (www.sncf.com), ✆ 3635 (premium rate, in French), followed by 1 for traffic status, 2 for timetables, 3 for reservations and tickets, 4 for other services. Excellent network from Paris to major cities with *TGV* trains using dedicated high-speed lines (up to 320 km/h on the *Est Européen* line to eastern France) as well as conventional track. However, some cross-country journeys can be slow and infrequent. Trains can get very full at peak times, so to avoid having to spend the journey standing, book a seat. Prior reservation is compulsory on *TGV* high-speed trains and the charge is included in the ticket price; rail pass holders will have to pay at least the reservation fee. Tickets can cost more at busy times (known as 'white' periods). Long distance trains on several non-TGV routes are branded *Corail Téoz* using refurbished rolling stock - reservation is compulsory. Reservation is also compulsory on all overnight trains: most convey couchettes and reclining seats only (sleeping cars are only conveyed on international trains). A certain number of couchette compartments are reserved for women only or those with small children; otherwise, couchette accommodation is mixed. There is a minimal bar/trolley service on most long-distance trains. Larger stations have 24-hour coin-operated left-luggage lockers, and sometimes pay-showers.

TELEPHONES

Dial in: ✆ +33 then number (omit initial 0). Outgoing: ✆ 00. Most payphones have English instructions. Few accept coins; some take credit cards. Phonecards (*télécartes*) are sold by post offices, some tobacconists and certain tourist offices. Emergency: ✆ 112. Police: ✆ 17. Fire: ✆ 18. Ambulance: ✆ 15.

TIPPING

Not necessary to tip in bars or cafés although it is common practise to round up the price. In restaurants there is no obligation to tip, but if you wish to do so, leave €1–2.

TOURIST INFORMATION

Maison de la France (www.franceguide.com). 23 Place de Catalogne, 75685 Paris, ✆ 0 142 967 000. Local tourist offices: look for *Syndicat d'Initiative* or *Office de Tourisme*. Staff generally speak English. Many sell passes for local tourist sights or services and can organise accommodation (for a fee). Opening times are seasonal.

TOURIST OFFICES OVERSEAS

Australia: Level 13, 25 Bligh St, Sydney NSW 2000, ✆ 02 9231 5244, info.au@franceguide.com. **Canada**: 1800 avenue McGill College, Suite 1010, Montréal QC, H3A 3J6, ✆ 514 288 2026, canada@franceguide.com. **UK**: Lincoln House, 300 High Holborn, London WC1V 7JH, ✆ 0906 824 4123 (premium rate), info.uk@franceguide.com. **USA**: 825 Third Avenue, 29th floor, New York NY 10022, ✆ 514 288 1904, info.us@franceguide.com. Also in Los Angeles (✆ 310 271 6665) and Chicago (✆ 312 327 0290).

VISAS
See page xxxii for visa requirements.

GERMANY

CAPITAL
Berlin.

CURRENCY
Euro (EUR / €). 1 euro = 100 cent. For exchange rates see page 11.

EMBASSIES IN BERLIN
Australia: Wallstraße 76-79, ✆ 030 88 00 880.
Canada: Leipziger Platz 17, ✆ 030 203 120.
New Zealand: Friedrichstraße 60, ✆ 030 206 210.
UK: Wilhelmstraße 70, ✆ 030 204 570.
USA: Pariser Platz 2, ✆ 030 830 50.

EMBASSIES OVERSEAS
Australia: 119 Empire Circuit, Yarralumla, Canberra, ACT 2600, ✆ 2 6270 1911. **Canada**: 1 Waverley St, Ottawa ON, K2P 0T8, ✆ 613 232 1101. **New Zealand**: 90-92 Hobson St, Thorndon, Wellington, ✆ 4 473 6063. **UK**: Embassy, 23 Belgrave Sq., London SW1X 8PZ, ✆ 020 7824 1300. **USA**: 4645 Reservoir Rd NW, Washington DC, 20007-1998, ✆ 202 298 4000.

LANGUAGE
German; English and French widely spoken in the west, especially by young people, less so in the east.

OPENING HOURS
Vary; rule of thumb: **Banks**: Mon–Fri 0830–1300 and 1430–1600 (until 1730 Thur). **Shops**: Mon–Fri 0900–1830 (large department stores may open 0830/0900–2000) and Sat 0900–1600.
Museums: Tues–Sun 0900–1700 (until 2100 Thur).

POST OFFICES
Mon–Fri 0800–1800, Sat 0800–1200. Main post offices have poste restante (*Postlagernd*).

PUBLIC HOLIDAYS
Jan 1, Jan 6*, Good Fri, Easter Mon, May 1, Ascension Day, Whit Mon, Corpus Christi*, Aug 15*, Oct 3 (German Unity), Nov 1* (All Saints), Dec 24 (afternoon); Dec 25, Dec 26. For dates of movable holidays see page 2.
* Catholic feastdays, celebrated only in the south (see p. 363).

PUBLIC TRANSPORT
Most large cities have U-Bahn (U) underground railway and S-Bahn (S) urban rail service, many have trams. City travel passes cover these and other public transport, including local ferries in some cities (e.g. Hamburg). International passes usually cover S-Bahn. Single fares are expensive; a day card (*Tagesnetzkarte*) or multi-ride ticket (*Mehrfahrkarte*) pays for itself if you take more than three rides (see Passes feature for selected day tickets). Long-distance buses are not common.

RAIL TRAVEL
See Tables **800 - 949**. Deutsche Bahn (DB) (www.bahn.de).
✆ 01805 99 66 33 (14ct/min) for timetable and fares information, ticket purchase and reservations. Timetable freephone (automated): ✆ 0800 1507090. UK booking centre ✆ 08718 80 80 66 (8p per minute). Discounts of 25% or 50% are available on long-distance tickets if purchased at least 3 days in advance - 50% tickets have restrictions. Long-distance trains: *ICE* (modern high-speed trains; up to 300km/h; higher fares but no extra charge for InterRail holders), *IC, EC, EN, CNL, D*. Regional trains: *IRE, RE, RB* (modern, comfortable, link with long-distance network). Frequent local S-Bahn services operate in major cities. Some local services now operated by private railways. Overnight services convey sleeping-cars (up to three berths) and/or couchettes (up to six berths), also reclining seats - reservation is generally compulsory. Most long-distance trains convey a bistro or restaurant car. Seat reservations possible on long-distance trains. Stations are well staffed, often with left luggage and bicycle hire. *Hbf.* (Hauptbahnhof) means main (central) station; *Bf.* (Bahnhof) means station.

TELEPHONES
Dial in: ✆ + 49 then number (omit initial 0). Outgoing: ✆ 00. *Kartentelefon* boxes take phonecards only (available from newsagents, tobacconists and some kiosks). National directory enquiries: ✆ 11833 (11837 in English). International directory enquiries: ✆ 11834. Police: ✆ 110. Fire: ✆ 112. Ambulance: ✆ 112.

TIPPING
Not a must but customary for good service. Small sums are rounded up, while for larger sums you could add a tip of EUR 1, or up to 10% of the bill.

TOURIST INFORMATION
German National Tourist Office (www.germany-tourism.de). Main office: Beethovenstraße 69, 60325 Frankfurt am Main, ✆ 069 974 640, info@d-z-t.com Tourist offices are usually near rail stations. English is widely spoken; English-language maps and leaflets available. Most offer a room-finding service.

TOURIST OFFICES OVERSEAS
Australia: c/o Ink Publicity, Suite 502, Level 5, 5 Hunter St, Sydney NSW 2000, ✆ 02 9236 8982, germanytourism@smink.com.au. **Canada**: 480 University Avenue, Suite 1500, Toronto ON, M5G 1V2, ✆ 416 968 1685, info@-gnto.ca. **UK**: PO Box 2695, London W1A 3TN, ✆ 020 7317 0908, gntolon@d-z-t.com. **USA**: 122 East 42nd Street, Suite 2000, New York NY 10168-0072, ✆ 212 661 7200, GermanyInfo@d-z-t.com. Also in Chicago (✆ 773 539 6303) and Los Angeles (✆ 310 545 1350).

VISAS
See page xxxii for visa requirements.

GREECE

CAPITAL
Athens (Athina).

CLIMATE
Uncomfortably hot in June–Aug; often better to travel in spring or autumn.

CURRENCY
Euro (EUR / €). 1 euro = 100 cent. For exchange rates see page 11.

EMBASSIES IN ATHENS
Australia: Level 6, Thon Building, Kifisias / Alexandras, Ambelokipi, ✆ 210 870 4000. **Canada**: Ioannou Ghennadiou 4, ✆ 210 727 3400. **New Zealand** (Consulate): Kifissias 76, Ambelokipi, ✆ 210 692 4136. **UK**: Ploutarchou 1, ✆ 210 727 2600. **USA**: Vassilissis Sophias 91, ✆ 210 721 2951.

EMBASSIES OVERSEAS
Australia: 9 Turrana St, Yarralumla, Canberra, ACT 2600, ✆ 2 6273 3011. **Canada**: 76-80 MacLaren St, Ottawa ON, K2P 0K6, ✆ 613 238 6271. **UK**: 1A Holland Park, London W11 3TP, ✆ 020 7221 6467. **USA**: 2217 Massachusetts Ave. NW, Washington DC 20008, ✆ 202 939 1300.

LANGUAGE
Greek; English widely spoken in Athens and tourist areas (some German, French or Italian), less so in remote mainland areas.

OPENING HOURS
Banks: (usually) Mon–Thur 0800–1400, Fri 0830–1330, longer hours in peak holiday season. **Shops**: vary; in summer most close midday and reopen in the evening (Tue, Thu, Fri) 1700–2000. **Sites and museums**: mostly 0830–1500; Athens sites and other major archaeological sites open until 1900 or open until sunset in summer.

POST OFFICES

Normally Mon–Fri 0800–1300, Sat 0800–1200; money exchange, travellers cheques, Eurocheques. Stamps sold from vending machines outside post offices, street kiosks.

PUBLIC HOLIDAYS

Jan 1, Jan 6 (Epiphany), Shrove Monday (48 days before Easter*), Mar 25 (Independence), Good Friday*, Easter Monday*, May 1, Whit Monday*, Aug 15 (Assumption), Oct 28 (National Day), Dec 25, 26. Everything closes for Easter. Holidays related to Easter are according to the Orthodox calendar – dates usually differ from those of Western Easter (see page 2).

PUBLIC TRANSPORT

KTEL buses: fast, punctual, fairly comfortable long-distance services; well-organised stations in most towns (tickets available from bus terminals), website: www.ktel.org. Islands connected by ferries and hydrofoils; see Thomas Cook guide *Greek Island Hopping* (order form at the back of this edition). City transport: bus or (in Athens) trolleybus, tram and metro; services may be crowded. Outside Athens, taxis are plentiful and good value.

RAIL TRAVEL

See Tables **1400 - 1499**. Operator: Hellenic Railways (Organismós Sidiródromon Éllados; OSE) (www.ose.gr). Call centre for reservations and information (24-hour, english spoken): ✆ 1110. Limited rail network, especially north of Athens. Reservations are essential on most express trains. *ICity* and *ICityE* trains are fast and fairly punctual, but supplements can be expensive (€6 to 20 on *ICity* and €9 to 33 on *ICityE*). Stations: often no left luggage or English-speaking staff, but many have bars.

TELEPHONES

Dial in: ✆ +30 then number. Outgoing: ✆ 00. Payphones take phonecards only (on sale at most shops and street kiosks). Bars, restaurants, and kiosks often have privately owned metered phones: pay after making the call. Emergency: ✆ 112. Police: ✆ 100. Fire: ✆ 199. Ambulance: ✆ 166. Tourist police (24 hrs, English-speaking): ✆ 171.

TIPPING

Not necessary for restaurants or taxis.

TOURIST INFORMATION

Greek National Tourist Organisation (www.gnto.gr). Main office: Tsoha 7, 11521 Athens, ✆ 2 108 707 000. Athens information desk: Amalias 26, ✆ 2 103 310 392. Tourist offices provide sightseeing information, fact sheets, local and regional transport schedules.

TOURIST OFFICES OVERSEAS

Australia: 37-49 Pitt St, Sydney NSW 2000, ✆ 02 9241 1663, hto@tpg.com.au. **Canada**: 1500 Don Mills Road, Suite 102, Toronto ON, M3B 3K4, ✆ 416 968 2220, grnto.tor@on.aibn.com. **UK**: 4 Conduit St, London W1S 2DJ, ✆ 020 7495 9300, info@gnto.co.uk. **USA**: Olympic Tower, 645 Fifth Ave., Suite 903, New York NY 10022, ✆ 212 421 5777, info@greektourism.com.

VISAS

See page xxxii for visa requirements.

HUNGARY

CAPITAL

Budapest.

CURRENCY

Forint (HUF or Ft). For exchange rates see page 11. You can buy your currency at banks and official bureaux. Credit cards and small denomination travellers cheques are widely accepted. Euros are more useful than dollars or sterling.

EMBASSIES IN BUDAPEST

Australia: Királyhágó tér 8–9, ✆ 0 614 579 777. **Canada**: Ganz utca 12–14, ✆ 0 613 923 360. **New Zealand** (Consulate): Nagymazõ utca 50, ✆ 013 022 484. **UK**: Harmincad utca 6, ✆ 012 662 888. **USA**: Szabadság tér 12, ✆ 01 475 4400.

EMBASSIES OVERSEAS

Australia: 17 Beale Crescent, Deakin, Canberra, ACT 2600, ✆ 2 6282 3226. **Canada**: 299 Waverley St, Ottawa ON, K2P 0V9, ✆ 613 230 2717. **UK**: 35 Eaton Place, London SW1X 8BY, ✆ 020 7201 3440. **USA**: 3910 Shoemaker St NW, Washington DC 20008, ✆ 202 362 6730.

LANGUAGE

Hungarian. English and German are both widely understood.

OPENING HOURS

Food/tourist shops, markets, malls open Sun. **Banks**: commercial banks Mon–Thur 0800–1500, Fri 0800–1300. **Food shops**: Mon–Fri 0700–1900, others: 1000–1800 (Thur until 1900); shops close for lunch and half-day on Sat (1300). **Museums**: usually Tues–Sun 1000–1800, free one day a week, closed public holidays.

POST OFFICES

Mostly 0800–1800 Mon–Fri, 0800–1200 Sat. Stamps also sold at tobacconists. Major post offices cash Eurocheques and change western currency; all give cash for Visa Eurocard/Mastercard, Visa Electron and Maestro cards.

PUBLIC HOLIDAYS

Jan 1, Mar 15 (Revolution), Easter Sun/Mon, May 1, Whit Monday, Aug 20 (Constitution), Oct 23 (Republic), Dec 25, 26. For dates of movable holidays see page 2.

PUBLIC TRANSPORT

Long-distance buses: *Volánbusz* (www.volanbusz.hu), ✆ +36 1 382 0888. Extensive metro / tram / bus system in Budapest with integrated tickets; for day tickets see Passes section. Debrecen, Miskolc and Szeged also have trams. Ferry and hydrofoil services operate on the Danube.

RAIL TRAVEL

See Tables **1200 - 1299**. A comprehensive network operated by Hungarian State Railways (MÁV) (www.mav.hu) connects most towns and cities. Express services link Budapest to major centres and Lake Balaton: *IC* trains require compulsory reservation and supplement. InterPici (*IP*) trains are fast railcars connecting with *IC* trains, also with compulsory reservation. Most *EC* trains require a supplement but not reservation (for exceptions see page 485). Other trains include *gyorsvonat* (fast trains) and *sebesvonat* (semi-fast). Local trains (*személyvonat*) are very slow. Book sleepers well in advance.

TELEPHONES

Dial in: ✆ +36 then number (omit initial 06). Outgoing: ✆ 00. Payphones take HUF 10, 20, 50 and 100 coins or phonecards (sold at hotels, newsstands, tobacconists and post offices). Directory enquiries: ✆ 198 (International ✆ 199). Emergency: ✆ 112. Police: ✆ 107. Fire: ✆ 105. Ambulance: ✆ 104.

TIPPING

Round up by 5–15% for restaurants and taxis. People do not generally leave coins on the table; instead the usual practise is to make it clear that you are rounding up the sum. Service is included in some upmarket restaurants.

TOURIST INFORMATION

Hungarian National Tourist Office (www.hungarytourism.hu). Tourinform ✆ 06 80 630 800, info@hungarytourism.hu *Tourinform* branches throughout Hungary. English-speaking staff. The *Hungarian Tourist Card* (www.hungarycard.hu), giving various discounts, costs HUF 7140.

TOURIST OFFICES OVERSEAS

UK: 46 Eaton Place, London SW1X 8AL, ✆ 020 7823 1032, htlondon@hungarytourism.hu **USA**: 350 Fifth Avenue, Suite 7107, New York NY 10118, ✆ 212 695 1221, info@gotohungary.com

VISAS

See page xxxii for visa requirements.

IRELAND

CAPITAL

Dublin. For Northern Ireland see under United Kingdom.

CLIMATE

Cool, wet winters, mild spring and autumn. Intermittent rain is a common feature of the Irish weather.

CURRENCY

Euro (EUR / €). 1 euro = 100 cent. For exchange rates see page 11.

EMBASSIES IN DUBLIN

Australia: Fitzwilton House, Wilton Terrace, ✆ 01 664 5300. **Canada**: 7–8 Wilton Terrace, ✆ 01 234 4000. **New Zealand** (Consulate): P.O. Box 9999, ✆ 01 660 4233. **UK**: 29 Merrion Road, Ballsbridge, ✆ 01 205 3700. **USA**: 42 Elgin Road, ✆ 01 668 8777.

EMBASSIES OVERSEAS

Australia: 20 Arkana St, Yarralumla, Canberra, ACT 2600 ✆ 2 6273 3022. **Canada**: Suite 1105, 130 Albert St, Ottawa ON, K1P 5G4, ✆ 613 233 6281. **UK**: 17 Grosvenor Place, London SW1X 7HR, ✆ 020 7235 2171. **USA**: 2234 Massachusetts Ave. NW, Washington DC 20008, ✆ 202 462 3939.

LANGUAGE

Most people speak English. The Irish language (Gaeilge) is spoken in several areas (known as the Gaeltacht) scattered over seven counties and four provinces, mostly along the western seaboard. Official documents use both languages.

OPENING HOURS

Shops generally open Mon - Sat 0900 - 1730; most shopping centres stay open until 2000 on Thurs and Fri. Some shops open on Sunday, 1200 - 1800.

POST OFFICES

Postal service: *An Post*, www.anpost.ie. Most communities have a post office, usually open Mon-Fri 0900 - 1730 or 1800, Sat 0900 - 1300; often closed one hour at lunchtime (except main offices). Sub post offices often close at 1300 one day per week.

PUBLIC HOLIDAYS

January 1 (New Year's Day), March 17 (St Patrick's Day), Good Friday (bank holiday only), Easter Monday, first Monday in May, first Monday in June, first Monday in August, last Monday in October, December 25 (Christmas Day), December 26 (St Stephen's Day). Holidays falling at the weekend are transferred to the next following weekday.

PUBLIC TRANSPORT

A modern tramway system in Dublin called *Luas* (www.luas.ie) has two unconnected lines; the red line is the most useful for visitors as it connects Connolly and Heuston stations. Dublin Bus operates an extensive network throughout the capital, but journeys can be very slow in rush-hour traffic. Almost all bus services outside Dublin are operated by Bus Éireann (www.buseireann.ie), ✆ 01 836 6111 (daily 0830–1900). Long distance services leave from the Dublin bus station (*Busáras*) in Store St, near Connolly rail station.

RAIL TRAVEL

See Tables **230 - 249**. Rail services are operated by Iarnród Éireann (IÉ) (www.irishrail.ie). Timetable and fares enquiries: ✆ 01 850 366 222 (0900–1800 Mon-Sat, 1000–1800 Sun). The *Enterprise* express service Dublin - Belfast is operated jointly with Northern Ireland Railways. Local IÉ north-south electric line in Dublin is called DART.

TELEPHONES

Dial in: ✆ +353 then number (omit initial 0). Outgoing: ✆ 00 (048 for Northern Ireland). Pay phones take coins, phonecards or credit cards. Directory enquiries: ✆ 11811 / 11850 (International ✆ 11818). Operator assistance: ✆ 10 (International ✆ 114). Emergency services: ✆ 112 or 999.

TIPPING

A tip of 12 - 15% is expected in restaurants. Taxis 10%.

TOURIST INFORMATION

Fáilte Ireland (www.discoverireland.ie). Main office: 5th Floor, Bishop's Square, Redmond's Hill, Dublin 2, ✆ 014 763 400. Tourist offices offer a wide range of information, also accommodation bookings.

TOURIST OFFICES OVERSEAS

Australia: Level 5, 36 Carrington St, Sydney NSW 2000, ✆ 02 9299 6177. **Canada**: 2 Bloor St West, Suite 3403, Toronto ON, M4W 3E2, ✆ 416 925 6368. **UK**: 103 Wigmore St, London W1U 1QS, ✆ 020 7518 0800. **USA**: 345 Park Avenue, 17th floor, New York NY 10154, ✆ 212 418 0800.

VISAS

See page xxxii for visa requirements.

ITALY

CAPITAL

Rome (Roma).

CLIMATE

Very hot in July and Aug. May, June, and Sept are best for sightseeing. Holiday season ends mid Sept or Oct. Rome is crowded at Easter.

CURRENCY

Euro (EUR / €). 1 euro = 100 cent. For exchange rates see page 11.

EMBASSIES IN ROME

Australia: Via Antonio Bosio 5, ✆ 06 852 721. **Canada**: Via Zara 30, ✆ 06 854 441. **New Zealand**: Via Clitunno 44, ✆ 06 853 7501. **UK**: Via XX Settembre 80a, ✆ 06 4220 0001. **USA**: Via Vittorio Veneto 121, ✆ 06 46 741.

EMBASSIES OVERSEAS

Australia: 12 Grey St, Deakin, Canberra ACT 2600, ✆ 2 6273 3333. **Canada**: 275 Slater St, Ottawa ON, K1P 5H9, ✆ 613 232 2401. **New Zealand**: 34-38 Grant Rd, Thorndon, Wellington, ✆ 4 473 5339. **UK**: 14 Three Kings Yard, London W1K 4EH, ✆ 020 7312 2200. **USA**: 3000 Whitehaven St NW, Washington DC 20008, ✆ 202 612 4400.

LANGUAGE

Italian; standard Italian is spoken across the country though there are marked regional pronunciation differences. Some dialects in more remote areas. Many speak English in cities and tourist areas. In the south and Sicily, French is often more useful than English.

OPENING HOURS

Banks: Mon–Fri 0830–1330, 1430–1630. **Shops**: (usually) Mon–Sat 0830/0900–1230, 1530/1600–1900/1930; closed Mon am/Sat pm July/Aug. **Museums/sites**: usually Tues–Sun 0930–1900; last Sun of month free; most refuse entry within an hour of closing. Churches often close at lunchtime.

POST OFFICES

Mostly Mon–Fri 0830–1330/1350, Sat 0830–1150. Some counters (registered mail and telegrams) may differ; in main cities some open in the afternoon. Send anything urgent via express. *Posta prioritaria* stamps also guarantee a faster delivery. Stamps (*francobolli*) are available from tobacconists (*tabacchi*). Poste restante (*Fermo posta*) at most post offices.

PUBLIC HOLIDAYS

All over the country: Jan 1, Jan 6 (Epiphany), Easter Mon, Apr 25 (Liberation), May 1, June 2 (Republic), Aug 15 (Assumption, virtually nothing opens), Nov 1 (All Saints), Dec 8 (Immaculate Conception), Dec 25, Dec 26. For dates of movable holidays see page 2. Regional Saints' days: Apr 25 in Venice, June 24 in Florence, Genoa and Turin, June 29 in Rome, July 11 in Palermo, Sept 19 in Naples, Oct 4 in Bologna, Dec 6 in Bari, Dec 7 in Milan.

PUBLIC TRANSPORT

Buses are often crowded, but regular, and serve many areas inaccessible by rail. Services may be drastically reduced at weekends; this is not always made clear in timetables. Roma, Milano and Napoli have metro systems; most major cities have trams. Taxis (metered) can be expensive; steer clear of unofficial ones.

RAIL TRAVEL

See Tables **580 - 648**. The national operator is Trenitalia, a division of Ferrovie dello Stato (FS) (website www.trenitalia.com). National rail information ✆ 89 20 21 (+39 06 68 47 54 75 from abroad). High-speed express services operate between major cities; the latest stretch of high-speed line (Milano to Bologna) opened in December 2008, whilst Bologna - Firenze is due to open in December 2009, completing the core high-speed trunk route. 'Alta Velocità' (*AV*) are premium fare services using high-speed lines. 'Eurostar Italia' (*ES*) and 'Eurostar City' (*ESc*) trains also require payment of a higher fare. InterCity Plus (*ICp*) uses refurbished *IC* stock. Reservation is compulsory on *AV*, *ES*, *ESc* and *ICp* trains. Reservation is also possible on *IC*, *EC* and *ICN* (InterCityNight) trains. Other services are classified *Espresso* (long-distance domestic train, stopping only at main stations) and *Regionale* (stops at most stations). Services are reasonably punctual. Some long-distance trains do not carry passengers short distances. Sleepers: single or double berths in 1st class, three (occasionally doubles) in 2nd. Couchettes: four berths in 1st class, six in 2nd. Refreshments on most long-distance trains. There are often long queues at stations; buy tickets and make reservations at travel agencies (look for FS symbol).

TELEPHONES

Dial in: ✆+39 then number. Outgoing: ✆ 00. Public phones take phonecards *(carta telefonica)* available from any newsstand, tobacconist or coffee shop. Some take coins or credit cards (mostly in tourist areas). Metered phones (*scatti*) are common in bars and restaurants; pay the attendant after use. Phone directory assistance: ✆ 12. International enquiries: ✆ 176. Carabinieri: ✆ 112. Police: ✆ 113. Fire: ✆ 115. Ambulance: ✆ 118.

TIPPING

In restaurants you need to look at the menu to see if service charge is included. If not, a tip of 10% is fine depending on how generous you feel like being. The same percentage applies to taxi drivers. A helpful porter can expect up to €2.50.

TOURIST INFORMATION

Italian State Tourist Board (www.enit.it). Main office: Via Marghera 2/6, 00185 Roma, ✆ 0 649 711, sedecentrale@enit.it. Most towns and resorts have an *Azienda Autonoma di Soggiorno e Turismo* (AAST), many with their own websites, or *Pro Loco* (local tourist board).

TOURIST OFFICES OVERSEAS

Australia: Level 4, 46 Market St, Sydney NSW 2000, ✆ 02 9262 1666, italia@italiantourism.com.au. **Canada**: 175 Bloor Street East, Suite 907, South Tower, Toronto ON, M4W 3R8, ✆ 416 925 4882, enitto@italiantourism.com. **UK**: 1 Princes St, London W1B 2AY, ✆ 020 7399 3562, italy@italiantouristboard.co.uk. **USA**: 630 Fifth Avenue, Suite 1565, New York NY 10111, ✆ 212 245 5618, enitny@italiantourism.com. Also in Chicago (✆ 312 644 0996) and Los Angeles (✆ 310 820 1898).

VISAS

See page xxxii for visa requirements.

LATVIA

CAPITAL

Riga.

CLIMATE

Warm summers, cold, snowy winters; rain all year, heaviest in August.

CURRENCY

Lats (LVL or Ls) 1 lats = 100 santimu. For exchange rates, see page 11.

EMBASSIES IN RIGA

Australia (Consulate): Tomsona iela 33–1, ✆ 6722 4251. **Canada**: Baznicas iela 20/22, ✆ 6781 3945. **New Zealand**: *refer to NZ Embassy in Poland.* **UK**: Alunana iela 5, ✆ 6777 4700. **USA**: Raiņa bulvaris 7, ✆ 6703 6200.

EMBASSIES OVERSEAS

Australia (Consulate): 2 Mackennel Street, Melbourne, VIC 3079, ✆ 3 9499 6920. **Canada**: 350 Sparks St, Suite 1200, Ottawa ON, K1R 7S8, ✆ 613 238 6014. **UK**: 45 Nottingham Place, London W1U 5LY, ✆ 020 7312 0040. **USA**: 2306 Massachusetts Ave. NW, Washington DC 20008, ✆ 202 328 2840.

LANGUAGE

Latvian is the majority language. Russian is the first language of around 30% and is widely understood. English and German can often be of use, especially in the larger towns.

OPENING HOURS

Banks: mainly Mon–Fri 0900–1700, some Sat 0900–1300. **Shops**: Mon–Fri 0900/1000–1800/1900 and Sat 0900/1000–1700. Many close on Mon. **Museums**: days vary, but usually open Tues/Wed–Sun 1100–1700.

POST OFFICES

Mon–Fri 0900–1800, Sat 0900–1300. The main post office in Riga, at Brivibas bulvaris 19, is open 24 hrs. Postboxes are yellow.

PUBLIC HOLIDAYS

Jan 1, Good Friday, Easter Mon, May 1, June 23 (Ligo Day), June 24 (Saint John), Nov 18 (Republic), Dec 25, 26, 31. For dates of movable holidays see page 2.

PUBLIC TRANSPORT

Very cheap for Westerners. Taxis generally affordable (agree fare first if not metered). Beware of pickpockets on crowded buses and trams. Long-distance bus network preferred to slow domestic train service.

RAIL TRAVEL

See Table **1800 - 1899**. Comfortable overnight trains to Moscow and St Peterburg; best to take berth in 2nd-class coupé (4-berth compartment); 1st-class *luxe* compartments (2-berth) are also available. Reservation is compulsory for all sleepers; Russian-bound ones may require proof of entry visa when booking. Very little English spoken at stations.

TELEPHONES

Dial in: ✆ +371 then number. Outgoing: ✆ 00. Public phones take coins, phonecards or credit cards. Phonecards (LVL 2, 5, or 10) sold by shops, kiosks, hotels and post offices; look for the *Lattelekom* sign. Emergency: ✆ 112. Police: ✆ 02. Fire: ✆ 01. Ambulance: ✆ 03.

TIPPING

Not necessary to tip at the bar or counter, but tip 10% if served at your table. Round up taxi fares to a maximum of 10%.

TOURIST INFORMATION

Latvian Tourism Development Agency (www.latviatourism.lv). Pils Laukums 4, Riga 1050, ✆ 67 229 945, info@latviatourism.lv.

TOURIST OFFICES OVERSEAS

Germany: Baltikum Tourismus Zentrale, Katharinenstraße 19-20, 10711 Berlin, ✆ 030 89 00 90 91, info@baltikuminfo.de.
UK: Latvian Tourism Bureau, 72 Queensborough Terrace, London W2 3SH, ✆ 020 7229 8271, london@latviatourism.lv.

VISAS

See page xxxii for visa requirements. Applications may take up to 30 days; confirmed hotel reservations are required. Visas may also be valid for Estonia and Lithuania. Passports must be valid for at least 3 months following the stay. Visas issued on arrival at the airport (not train border crossings) are valid 10 days.

LITHUANIA

CAPITAL

Vilnius.

CLIMATE

Warm summers, cold, snowy winters; rain all year, heaviest in August.

CURRENCY

Litas (LTL or Lt); 1 litas = 100 centu (ct), singular centas. Travellers cheques and credit cards are widely accepted. For exchange rates see page 11.

EMBASSIES IN VILNIUS

Australia (Consulate): 23 Vilniaus St. ✆ 05 212 3369. **Canada** (Consulate): Jogailos St. 4, ✆ 05 249 0950. **New Zealand**: *refer to NZ Embassy in Poland.* **UK**: Antakalnio Str. 2, ✆ 05 246 2900. **USA**: Akmenu gatve 6, ✆ 05 266 5500.

EMBASSIES OVERSEAS

Australia (Consulate): 56 Somers St. Melbourne, VIC 3125, ✆ 3 9808 8300. **Canada**: 150 Metcalfe St. Suite 1600, Ottawa ON, K2P 1P1, ✆ 613 567 5458. **UK**: 84 Gloucester Pl., London W1U 6AU, ✆ 020 7486 6401. **USA**: 4590 MacArthur Blvd. NW, Suite 200, Washington DC 20007, ✆ 202 234 5860.

LANGUAGE

Lithuanian. Russian is the first language of around 10% of the population. English and German can often be of use, especially in the larger towns.

OPENING HOURS

Banks: mostly Mon–Thur 0900–1600, Fri 0900–1500. **Shops**: (large shops) Mon–Fri 1000/1100–1900; many also open Sat until 1600. Some close for lunch 1400–1500 and also on Sun and Mon. **Museums**: days vary, most close Mon and sometimes Tues and open at least Wed and Fri; often free on Wed; hours usually at least 1100–1700, check locally.

POST OFFICES

All towns have post offices *(Lietuvos Paštas)* with an international telephone service. Offices are generally open 0800–1830 Mon–Fri and 0800–1400 Sat. Smaller offices often close for an hour at midday.

PUBLIC HOLIDAYS

Jan 1, Feb 16 (Independence Day), Mar 11 (Restoration of Statehood), Easter Mon, May 1 (not banks), July 6 (King Mindaugas), Aug. 15 (Assumption), Nov 1 (All Saints), Dec 25, 26. For dates of movable holidays see page 2.

PUBLIC TRANSPORT

Similar to Latvia (see above).

RAIL TRAVEL

See Tables **1800 - 1899**. Major routes are to St Petersburg, Moscow, Kaliningrad, Warsaw, and Minsk. Warsaw trains have standard European couchettes and sleepers. Other overnight trains have 54-bunk open coaches (P), 4-bed compartments (K) and (on Moscow trains only) 2-bed compartments (M-2).

TELEPHONES

Dial in: ✆ +370 then number (omit initial 8). Outgoing: ✆ 00. Phonecards (*telefono kortelė*) are sold at newsstands and supermarkets. Emergency: ✆ 112. Police: ✆ 02. Fire: ✆ 01. Ambulance: ✆ 03.

TIPPING

Not necessary to tip at the bar or counter, but tip 10% if served at your table. Round up taxi fares to a maximum of 10%.

TOURIST INFORMATION

Lithuania State Department of Tourism (www.tourism.lt and www.travel.lt). Main tourist office in Vilnius: Vilniaus g. 22, LT-01119, Vilnius, ✆ 526 296 60, tic@vilnius.lt. There are tourist offices in most towns.

TOURIST OFFICES OVERSEAS

Germany: Baltikum Tourismus Zentrale, Katharinenstraße 19-20, 10711 Berlin, ✆ 030 89 00 90 91, info@baltikuminfo.de.

VISAS

See page xxxii for visa requirements.

LUXEMBOURG

CAPITAL

Luxembourg City (Ville de Luxembourg).

CLIMATE

Rain prevalent at any time; warm summers, cold winters (often with snow).

CURRENCY

Euro (EUR/€). 1 euro = 100 cent. For exchange rates see page 11.

EMBASSIES IN LUXEMBOURG

Australia: *refer to Australian Embassy in Belgium.* **Canada** (Consulate): 15, rue Guillaume Schneider, ✆ 27 05 70. **New Zealand**: *refer to NZ Embassy in Belgium.* **UK**: 5 Boulevard Joseph II, ✆ 22 98 64. **USA**: 22 Boulevard Emmanuel Servais, ✆ 46 01 23.

EMBASSIES OVERSEAS

Australia (Consulate): 6 Damour Ave, Sydney, NSW 2070, ✆ 2 9880 8002. **UK**: 27 Wilton Crescent, London SW1X 8SD, ✆ 020 7235 6961. **USA/Canada**: 2200 Massachusetts Ave. NW, Washington DC 20008, ✆ 202 265 4171.

LANGUAGE

Luxembourgish is the national tongue, but almost everybody also speaks fluent French and/or German, plus often at least some English.

OPENING HOURS

Many establishments take long lunch breaks. **Banks**: usually Mon–Fri 0830–1200 and 1400–1630 or later. **Shops**: Mon 1300/1400–1800; Tues–Sat 0800/0900–1800. **Museums**: most open six days a week (usually Tues–Sun).

POST OFFICES

Usually open Mon–Fri 0800–1200 and 1400–1700.

PUBLIC HOLIDAYS

Jan 1, Carnival (Monday before Shrove Tuesday), Easter Mon, May

1, Ascension, Whit Mon, Corpus Christi, June 23 (National Day), Aug 15 (Assumption), Nov 1 (All Saints), Dec 25, 26. For dates of movable holidays see page 2. When a holiday falls on a Sunday, the next working day becomes a substitute holiday.

PUBLIC TRANSPORT

Good bus network between most towns. Taxis not allowed to pick up passengers in the street; most stations have ranks.

RAIL TRAVEL

See Table **445** for local services. Operator: Société Nationale des Chemins de fer Luxembourgeois (CFL) (www.cfl.lu), ✆ +352 2489 2489. Frequent rail services converge on Luxembourg City. Inexpensive multi-ride passes (good for one hour or up to 24 hours) are valid on trains and local buses. Most rail stations are small with few facilities.

TELEPHONES

Dial in: ✆ +352 then number. Outgoing: ✆ 00. Phonecards (*Telekaarten*) are available from post offices and stations. Police: ✆ 113. Fire and ambulance: ✆ 112.

TIPPING

In restaurants, cafés and bars service charge is usually included (round up bill to the next euro). Taxi drivers EUR 2–5; porters EUR 1–2; hairdressers EUR 2; cloakroom attendants EUR 0.50; toilet attendants EUR 0.25.

TOURIST INFORMATION

Office National du Tourisme (www.ont.lu). Gare Centrale, P.O. Box 1001, L-1010 Luxembourg, ✆ 4 282 8220, info@visitluxembourg.lu. Information and hotel bookings: Luxembourg City Tourist Office, 30 Place Guillaume II, L-1648 Luxembourg, ✆ 222 809, touristinfo@lcto.lu (www.lcto.lu),

TOURIST OFFICES OVERSEAS

UK: Sicilian House, Sicilian Avenue, London WC1A 2QR, ✆ 020 7434 2800, tourism@luxembourg.co.uk. **USA**: 17 Beekman Place, New York NY 10022, ✆ 212 935 8888, info@visitluxembourg.com.

VISAS

See page xxxii for visa requirements.

NETHERLANDS

CAPITAL

Amsterdam is the capital city. The Hague (Den Haag) is the seat of government.

CLIMATE

Can be cold in winter; rain prevalent all year. Many attractions close Oct–Easter, while Apr–May is tulip time and the country is crowded; June–Sept can be pleasantly warm and is busy with tourists.

CURRENCY

Euro (EUR / €). 1 euro = 100 cent. For exchange rates see page 11.

EMBASSIES IN THE HAGUE

Australia: Carnegielaan 4, ✆ 0 70 31 08 200. **Canada**: Sophialaan 7, ✆ 0 70 31 11 600. **New Zealand**: Eisenhowerlaan 77, ✆ 0 70 34 69 324. **UK**: Lange Voorhout 10, ✆ 0 70 42 70 427. **USA**: Lange Voorhout 102, ✆ 0 70 31 02 209.

EMBASSIES OVERSEAS

Australia: 120 Empire Circuit, Yarralumla, Canberra, ACT 2600, ✆ 2 6220 9400. **Canada**: Constitution Square Building, 350 Albert St, Suite 2020, Ottawa ON, K1R 1A4, ✆ 613 237 5030. **New Zealand**: Investment House, cnr Ballance & Featherston Streets, Wellington, ✆ 4 471 6390. **UK**: 38 Hyde Park Gate, London SW7 5DP, ✆ 020 7590 3200. **USA**: 4200 Linnean Ave. NW, Washington DC 20008, ✆ 877 388 2443.

LANGUAGE

Dutch; English is very widely spoken.

OPENING HOURS

Banks: Mon–Fri 0900–1600/1700 (later Thur or Fri). **Shops**: Mon–Fri 0900/0930–1730/1800 (until 2100 Thur or Fri), Sat 0900/0930–1600/1700. Many close Mon morning. **Museums**: vary, but usually Mon–Sat 1000–1700, Sun 1100–1700 (some close Mon). In winter many have shorter hours.

POST OFFICES

Post offices *(TPG Post)* are generally open Mon–Fri 0830–1700; some also open on Sat 0830–1200. Many shops selling postcards also sell stamps. Post international mail in the left slot, marked *overige* (other), of the red *TPG* mailboxes.

PUBLIC HOLIDAYS

Jan 1, Good Fri, Easter Mon, Apr 30 (Queen's Birthday), May 5 (Liberation Day), Ascension Day, Whit Mon, Dec 25, Dec 26. For dates of movable holidays see page 2.

PUBLIC TRANSPORT

Premium rate number for all rail and bus enquiries (computerised, fast and accurate): ✆ 09 009 292 (www.9292ov.nl). Taxis are best boarded at ranks or ordered by phone as they seldom stop in the street. In many cities (not Amsterdam), shared *Treintaxis* have ranks at stations and yellow roof signs (€4.20 for anywhere within city limits; tickets from rail ticket offices). *Strippenkaarten* (from stations, city transport offices, post offices and sometimes VVV) are strip tickets, valid nation-wide on metros, buses, trams and some trains (2nd class) within city limits; zones apply; validate on boarding; valid one hour; change of transport allowed.

RAIL TRAVEL

See Tables **450 - 499**. National rail company Nederlandse Spoorwegen (NS) (www.ns.nl) provides most services, though private operators run local train services in some parts of the north and east. Through tickets can be purchased between all stations in the Netherlands, regardless of operator. Credit cards are not accepted, though larger stations usually have ATM machines from which cash can be obtained. Cycle hire and cycle and baggage storage are usually available at larger stations. Smaller stations are usually unstaffed, but all stations have ticket vending machines. Undated tickets must be validated before travel in one of the ticket stamping machines located at platform entrances. Travellers found to have boarded a train without a valid ticket must pay a fine of €35 plus the cost of their fare. Seat reservations are not available except for international journeys. The fastest domestic trains, calling at principal stations only, are classified *Intercity*. *Stoptreinen* call at all stations. Between these two categories are *sneltreinen* (fast trains) which miss out the less important stations.

TELEPHONES

Dial in: ✆ +31 then number (omit initial 0). Outgoing: ✆ 00. Green booths take only phonecards (*telefoonkaarten*), available from post offices, tourist offices (VVV), rail stations (NS), telecom shops (Primafoon) and major department stores (some booths also take credit cards). Orange / grey booths take coins, credit cards and *Telfort* phonecards, available from Holland Welcome Service (GWK), Wizzl shops and NS rail stations. Most information-line numbers are prefixed 0900 and are at premium rates. Operator: ✆ 0800 0410. International enquiries: ✆ 09 008 418. National enquiries: ✆ 09 008 008. Emergency services: ✆ 112.

TIPPING

Although service charges are included, it is customary in restaurants, bars and cafés to leave a tip of 5–10% if you are satisfied. Taxi drivers expect a 10% tip.

TOURIST INFORMATION

Netherlands Board of Tourism (www.holland.com), Vlietweg 15, 2260 MG Leidschendam, ✆ 070 370 5705, info@holland.com. Vereniging voor Vreemdelingenverkeer (VVV: signs show a triangle with three Vs). Tourist bureaux are all open at least Mon–Fri 0900–1700, Sat 1000–1200. The *Museumkaart* (EUR 35, under 25s EUR 17.50) obtainable from VVV and participating museums, is valid for one year and gives free entry to over 400 museums nationwide.

TOURIST OFFICES OVERSEAS

UK: PO Box 30783, London WC2B 6DH, ✆ 020 7539 7950, info-uk@holland.com. **USA / Canada**: 355 Lexington Ave., 19th floor, New York NY 10017, ✆ 212 370 7360, information@holland.com.

VISAS

See page xxxii for visa requirements.

NORWAY

CAPITAL

Oslo.

CLIMATE

Surprisingly mild considering it's so far north; can be very warm in summer, particularly inland; the coast is appreciably cooler. May and June are driest months, but quite cool; summer gets warmer and wetter as it progresses, and the western fjords have high rainfall year-round. Days are very long in summer: the sun never sets in high summer in the far north. July and Aug is the busiest period; Sept can be delightful. Winter is the time to see the Northern Lights (*Aurora Borealis*). Excellent snow for skiing Dec–Apr.

CURRENCY

Norwegian crown or krone (NOK or kr); 1 krone = 100 øre. For exchange rates see page 11. On slot machines, *femkrone* means a NOK 5 coin and *tikrone* a NOK 10 coin.

EMBASSIES IN OSLO

Australia (Consulate): Wilh. Wilhelmsen ASA, Strandveien 20, Lysaker, ✆ 67 58 48 48. **Canada**: Wergelandsveien 7, ✆ 22 99 53 00. **New Zealand** (Consulate): c/o Halfdan Ditlev-Simonsen & Co AS, Strandveien 50, Lysaker. ✆ 67 11 00 33. **UK**: Thomas Heftyesgate 8, ✆ 23 13 27 00. **USA**: Henrik Ibsens gate 48, ✆ 21 30 85 40.

EMBASSIES OVERSEAS

Australia: 17 Hunter St, Yarralumla, Canberra, ACT 2600, ✆ 2 6273 3444. **Canada**: 150 Metcalfe St. Suite 1300, Ottawa ON, K2P 1P1, ✆ 613 238 6571. **UK**: 25 Belgrave Sq., London, SW1X 8QD, ✆ 020 7591 5500. **USA**: 2720 34th St NW, Washington D.C. 20008, ✆ 202 333 6000.

LANGUAGE

Norwegian, which has two official versions: *Nynorsk* and *Bokmål*. Norwegian has three additional vowels: æ, ø, å, which (in that order) follow z. Almost everyone speaks English; if not, try German.

OPENING HOURS

Banks: Mon–Wed and Fri 0815–1500 (1530 in winter), Thur 0815–1700. In Oslo, some open later, in the country some close earlier. Many have minibank machines that accept Visa, MasterCard (Eurocard) and Cirrus. **Shops**: Mon–Fri 0900–1600/1700 (Thur 0900–1800/2000), Sat 0900–1300/1500, many open later, especially in Oslo. **Museums**: usually Tues–Sun 1000–1500/1600. Some open Mon, longer in summer and/or close completely in winter.

POST OFFICES

Usually Mon–Fri 0800/0830–1700, Sat 0830–1300. Yellow postboxes with red crown-and-posthorn symbol are for local mail; red boxes with yellow symbol for all other destinations.

PUBLIC HOLIDAYS

Jan 1, Maundy Thur, Good Fri, Easter Mon, May 1, Ascension Day, May 17 (Constitution Day), Whit Mon, Dec 25, 26. For dates of movable holidays see page 2.

PUBLIC TRANSPORT

Train, boat and bus schedules are linked to provide good connections. It is often worth using buses or boats to connect two dead-end rail lines (e.g. Bergen and Stavanger), rather than retracing your route. Rail passes sometimes offer good discounts, even free travel, on linking services. NorWay Bussekspress (www.nor-way.no), Karl Johans gate 2, N-0154 Oslo, ✆ 82 021 300 (premium rate) has the largest bus network with routes going as far north as Kirkenes. Long-distance buses are comfortable, with reclining seats, ample leg room. Tickets: buy on board or reserve, ✆ 81 544 444 (premium-rate). Taxis: metered, can be picked up at ranks or by phoning; treat independent taxis with caution.

RAIL TRAVEL

See Tables **770 - 789**. Operated by: Norges Statsbaner (NSB) (www.nsb.no). All trains convey 2nd-class seating. Most medium- and long-distance trains also convey *NSB Komfort* accommodation, a dedicated area with complimentary tea/coffee and newspapers (supplement payable). Sleeping cars have one-, two and three-berth compartments (passengers may reserve a berth in any category with a 2nd-class ticket). Long-distance trains convey refreshments. Reservation possible on all long-distance trains, ✆ (within Norway) 81 500 888, then dial 4 for an english speaking operator. Reserved seats not marked, but your confirmation specifies carriage and seat/berth numbers. Carriage numbers shown by the doors, berth numbers outside compartments, seat numbers on seat-backs or luggage racks. Stations: most have baggage lockers, larger stations have baggage trolleys. Narvesen chain (at most stations; open long hours) sells English-language publications and a good range of snacks.

TELEPHONES

Dial in: ✆ +47 then number. Outgoing: ✆ 00. *Telekort* (phonecards) are available from Narvesen newsstands and post offices. Card phones are green; some accept credit cards. Coin and card phones are usually grouped together. Directory enquiries: ✆ 180 (Nordic countries), ✆ 181 (other countries). Local operator: ✆ 117. International operator: ✆ 115. Operators speak English. These are all premium-rate. Police: ✆ 112. Fire: ✆ 110. Ambulance: ✆ 113.

TIPPING

Tip 10% in restaurants (but not bars/cafés) if you are satisfied with the food, service etc. Not necessary for taxis.

TOURIST INFORMATION

Innovation Norway (www.visitnorway.com). Main office: P.O. Box 448, Sentrum 0158 Oslo, ✆ 2200 2500. Tourist offices (*Turistkontorer*) and bureaux (*Reiselivslag / Turistinformasjon*) exist in almost all towns and provide free maps, brochures, etc.

TOURIST OFFICES OVERSEAS

UK: Charles House, 5 Regent St, London SW1Y 4LR, ✆ 020 7389 8800, london@innovationnorway.no. **USA**: 655 Third Avenue, 18th floor, New York NY 10017, ✆ 212 885 9700, usa@innovationnorway.no.

VISAS

See page xxxii for visa requirements.

POLAND

CAPITAL

Warsaw (Warszawa).

CLIMATE

Temperate, with warm summers and cold winters; rain falls throughout year.

CURRENCY

Złoty (PLN or zł), divided into 100 groszy. For exchange rates see page 11. British pounds, American dollars and (especially) euros are useful. *Kantor* exchange offices sometimes give better rates than banks and opening hours are longer. Credit cards are increasingly accepted but not universal.

EMBASSIES IN WARSAW

Australia: Ulica Nowogrodzka 11, ✆ 0 22 521 3444. **Canada**: Ulica Jana Matejki 1/5, ✆ 0 22 584 3100. **New Zealand**: Dom Dochodawy, Level 5, Aleje Ujazdowskie 51, ✆ 0 22 521 0500. **UK**: Aleje Róz 1,

✆ 0 22 311 0000. **USA**: Aleje Ujazdowskie 29/31, ✆ 0 22 504 2000.

EMBASSIES OVERSEAS

Australia: 7 Turrana St, Yarralumla, Canberra, ACT 2600, ✆ 2 6272 1000. **Canada**: 443 Daly Ave., Ottawa ON, K1N 6H3, ✆ 613 789 0468. **New Zealand**: 17 Upland Rd, Kelburn, Wellington, ✆ 4 475 9453. **UK**: 47 Portland Place, London W1B 1JH, ✆ 0870 774 2700. **USA**: 2640 16th St NW, Washington DC 20009, ✆ 202 234 3800.

LANGUAGE

Polish. Many older Poles speak German; younger Poles, particularly students, are likely to understand English. Russian is widely understood, but unpopular.

OPENING HOURS

Banks: Mon–Fri 0800–1600/1800, Sat 0800–1300. **Shops**: Mon–Fri 0800/1100–1900, Sat 0900–1300. **Food shops**: Mon–Fri 0600–1900, Sat 0600–1600. **Museums**: usually Tues–Sun 1000–1600; often closed public holidays and following day.

POST OFFICES

Known as *Poczta*; Mon–Fri 0700/0800–1800/2000, Sat 0800–1400 (main offices). City post offices are numbered (main office is always 1); number should be included in the post restante address. Post boxes: green (local mail), red (long-distance).

PUBLIC HOLIDAYS

Jan 1, Easter Mon, May 1, May 3 (Constitution), Corpus Christi, Aug 15 (Assumption), Nov 1 (All Saints), Nov 11 (Independence), Dec 25, 26. For dates of movable holidays see page 2.

PUBLIC TRANSPORT

PKS buses: cheap and sometimes more practical than trains. Main long-distance bus station in Warszawa is adjacent to the Zachodnia (western) station. Tickets normally include seat reservations (seat number is on back), bookable from bus station. In rural areas, bus drivers will often halt between official stops if you flag them down. Extensive tram networks in Warszawa and most other cities; Warszawa also has a modern north-south metro line.

RAIL TRAVEL

See Tables **1000 - 1099**. Cheap and punctual, run by Polskie Koleje Państwowe (PKP), www.pkp.pl. At stations, departures (*odjazdy*) are shown on yellow paper, arrivals (*przyjazdy*) on white. Intercity (IC), express (*ekspres* or Ex) and semi-express trains (*pospieszny*) are printed in red (all bookable). *Osobowy* trains are the slowest. Fares are about 50% higher for 1st class, but still cheap by western standards and probably worth it. Overnight trains usually have 1st/2nd-class sleepers, plus 2nd-class couchettes and seats. *TLK* are low cost, long distance trains on day and night services. Most long-distance trains have refreshments. Left luggage and refreshments in major stations. Few ticket clerks speak English.

TELEPHONES

Dial in: ✆ +48 then number (omit initial 0). Outgoing: ✆ 0*0 *(wait for tone after first 0)*. Older public phones take tokens (*żetony* – from post offices, hotels and Ruch kiosks). Newer phones accept phonecards. English-speaking operator: ✆ 903. Police: ✆ 997. Fire: ✆ 998. Ambulance: ✆ 999. Emergency (from mobile): ✆ 112.

TIPPING

An older system of rounding up has now been largely superseded by a flat rate 10% for table service in bars and restaurants, also for hairdressers, taxis and guides.

TOURIST INFORMATION

Polish National Tourist Office (www.poland.travel/). IT tourist information office can usually help with accommodation. Also Orbis offices, for tourist information, excursions and accommodation.

TOURIST OFFICES OVERSEAS

UK: Level 3, Westgate House, West Gate, London W5 1YY, ✆ 0870 067 5010, london@pot.gov.pl. **USA**: 5 Marine View Plaza, Hoboken NJ 07030-5722, ✆ 201 420 9910, info.na@poland.travel.

VISAS

See page xxxii for visa requirements.
For travellers in Germany, visas are obtainable from the Polish consulate in Berlin (www.berlin.polemb.net).

PORTUGAL

CAPITAL

Lisbon (Lisboa).

CLIMATE

Hotter and drier as you go south; southern inland parts very hot in summer; spring and autumn milder, but wetter. Mountains are very cold in winter.

CURRENCY

Euro (EUR/€). 1 euro = 100 cent. For exchange rates see page 11.

EMBASSIES IN LISBON

Australia: Avenida da Liberdade 200, ✆ 21 310 1500.
Canada: Avenida da Liberdade 196–200, ✆ 21 316 4600.
New Zealand: (Consulate) Rua do Periquito. Lote A-13, ✆ 21 370 5779. **UK**: Rua de São Bernado 33, ✆ 21 392 4000.
USA: Avenida das Forças Armadas, ✆ 21 727 3300.

EMBASSIES OVERSEAS

Australia: 23 Culgoa Circuit, O'Malley, Canberra, ACT 2606, ✆ 2 6290 1733. **Canada**: 645 Island Park Dr., Ottawa ON, K1Y OB8, ✆ 613 729 0883. **New Zealand**: (Consulate) 41/47 Dixon Street, Wellington, ✆ 4 382 7655. **UK**: 11 Belgrave Sq., London SW1X 8PP, ✆ 020 7235 5331. **USA**: 2125 Kalorama Rd. NW, Washington DC 20036, ✆ 202 328 8610.

LANGUAGE

Portuguese. Older people often speak French as second language, young people Spanish and/or English. English, French, and German in some tourist areas.

OPENING HOURS

Banks: Mon–Fri 0830–1445/1500. **Shops**: Mon–Fri 0900/1000–1300 and 1500–1900, Sat 0900–1300. City shopping centres often daily 1000–2300 or later. **Museums**: Tues–Sun 1000–1700/1800; some close for lunch and some are free on Sun. Palaces and castles usually close on Wed.

POST OFFICES

Post offices (*Correios*) are open Mon–Fri 0900–1800. The main offices in larger towns and at airports also open on Sat 0900–1300. Stamps (*selos*) can also be bought wherever you see the *Correios* symbol: a red-and-white horseback rider.

PUBLIC HOLIDAYS

Jan 1, Shrove Tues (47 days before Easter), Good Fri, Apr 25 (Freedom), May 1, Corpus Christi, June 10 (National Day), Aug 15 (Assumption), Oct 5 (Republic), Nov 1 (All Saints), Dec 1 (Independence), Dec 8 (Immaculate Conception), Dec 25. Many local saints' holidays. For dates of movable holidays see page 2.

PUBLIC TRANSPORT

Usually buy long-distance bus tickets before boarding. Bus stops: *paragem;* extend your arm to stop a bus. Taxis: black with green roofs or beige; illuminated signs; cheap, metered in cities, elsewhere fares negotiable; drivers may ask you to pay for their return journey; surcharges for luggage over 30 kg and night travel; 10% tip. City transport: single tickets can be bought as you board, but books of tickets or passes are cheaper; on boarding, insert 1–3 tickets (according to length of journey) in the machine behind the driver.

RAIL TRAVEL

See Tables **690 - 699**. Operator: Comboios de Portugal (CP) (www.cp.pt). Cheap and generally punctual; 1st/2nd class on long-distance. Fastest trains are *IC* and *AP* (Alfa Pendular), modern, fast; supplement payable; seat reservations compulsory, buffet cars. CP information line, ✆ 808 208 208. Left-luggage lockers in most stations.

TELEPHONES

Dial in: ✆ +351 then number. Outgoing: ✆ 00. Payphones take coins or phonecards (from Portugal Telecom shops, post offices, newsstands and hotels), and occasionally credit cards. International calls are best made at post offices; pay after the call. Operator: ✆ 118. Emergency services: ✆ 112.

TIPPING

Not necessary in hotels; customary to round up taxi fares and bills in cafeś/bars, though not essential. Tip 10% in restaurants.

TOURIST INFORMATION

Portuguese National Tourist Office (www.portugal.org). Portuguese Tourism Institute (www.visitportugal.com). info@visitportugal.com, ✆ 211 205 050

TOURIST OFFICES OVERSEAS

Canada: 60 Bloor St West, Suite 1005, Toronto ON, M4W 3B8, ✆ 416 921 7376. **UK**: 11 Belgrave Square, London SW1X 8PP, ✆ 0845 355 1212, tourism@portugaloffice.org.uk. **USA**: 590 Fifth Avenue, 4th floor, New York NY 10036-4704, ✆ 212 354 4403, tourism@portugal.org.

VISAS

See page xxxii for visa requirements.

ROMANIA

CAPITAL

Bucharest (Bucureşti).

CLIMATE

Hot inland in summer, coast cooled by breezes; milder in winter, snow inland, especially in the mountains.

CURRENCY

Leu (plural: lei). 1 leu = 100 bani. For exchange rates see page 11. Carry pounds, euros or, ideally, dollars, in small denominations, plus traveller's cheques; change cash (commission-free) at exchange kiosks or banks; as rates can vary it's wise to check a few places first. Keep hold of your exchange vouchers; avoid black market exchange (risk of theft). Credit cards are needed for car rental, and are accepted in better hotels and restaurants. *Bancomats* (automatic cash dispensers; accept most cards at good rates) in most cities.

EMBASSIES IN BUCHAREST

Australia (Consulate): Str. Buzesti 14–18, ✆ 021 316 7558. **Canada**: 1-3 Tuberozelor St, ✆ 021 307 5000. **New Zealand**: *refer to NZ Embassy in Belgium.* **UK**: Jules Michelet 24, ✆ 021 201 7200. **USA**: Tudor Arghezi 7–9, ✆ 021 200 3300.

EMBASSIES OVERSEAS

Australia: 4 Dalman Crescent, O'Malley, Canberra ACT 2606, ✆ 2 6286 2343. **Canada**: 655 Rideau St, Ottawa ON, K1N 6A3, ✆ 613 789 3709. **UK**: Arundel House, 4 Palace Green, London W8 4QD, ✆ 020 7937 9666. **USA**: 1607 23rd St NW, Washington DC, 20008, ✆ 202 332 4846.

LANGUAGE

Romanian. English is understood by younger people, plus some German, and Hungarian throughout Transylvania.

OPENING HOURS

Banks: Mon–Fri 0900–1200/1300; private exchange counters open longer. **Shops**: usually 0800/0900–1800/2000, plus Sat morning or all day; often close 1300–1500. Local food shops often 0600–late. Few except in Bucharest open Sun. **Museums**: usually 0900/1000–1700/1800; open weekends, closed Mon (and maybe Tues).

POST OFFICES

There are post offices *(Posta Romana)* in all towns, open 0700-1900 Mon–Fri and until 1300 Sat. Postboxes are red. Mail usually takes five days to reach western Europe and up to two weeks to reach the US.

PUBLIC HOLIDAYS

Jan 1, Jan 2, Easter Mon (Orthodox), May 1, Dec 1 (National Unity Day), Dec 25, 26. For dates of movable holidays see page 2.

PUBLIC TRANSPORT

Buy bus/tram/metro tickets in advance from kiosks (as a rule) and cancel on entry. Taxis are inexpensive; if the meter not in use agree a price first and always pay in lei, not foreign currency. Trains are best for long-distance travel, although bus routes are expanding and connect important towns and cities.

RAIL TRAVEL

See Tables **1600 - 1699**. Societatea Naţională de Transport Feroviar de Călători (CFR) operates an extensive network linking all major towns (www.cfr.ro/călători). Most main lines are electrified and quite fast, but branch lines services are very slow. Trains are fairly punctual and very cheap. Except for local trains, reserve and pay a speed supplement in advance (tickets issued abroad include the supplement): cheapest are *tren de persoane* (very slow), then *accelerat* (still cheap), *rapid*, and finally *IC* trains (prices approaching Western levels). Food is normally available only on *IC* trains and some *rapids*; drinks are sold on some other trains. Couchette (*cuşeta*) or sleeper (*vagon de dormit*) accommodation is inexpensive. A number of local services are now operated by private operators, such as Regiotrans.

TELEPHONES

Dial in: ✆ +40 then number (omit initial 0). Outgoing: ✆ 00. Operator-connected calls from hotels and post offices: pay after making the call. Blue public phones accept coins only, Oranges' phones take phonecards available from post offices and newsstands. Emergency: ✆ 112. Police: ✆ 955. Fire: ✆ 981. Ambulance: ✆ 961.

TIPPING

Small tips are appreciated for good service at restaurants, hotels and in taxis. Only tip 10% at top-notch restaurants.

TOURIST INFORMATION

Romanian National Tourist Office (www.romaniatourism.com). Main office in Bucharest: ✆ 0 213 149 957. Regional tourist information offices in all major centres.

TOURIST OFFICES OVERSEAS

UK: 22 New Cavendish St, London W1G 8TT, ✆ 020 7224 3692, romaniatravel@btconnect.com. **USA**: 355 Lexington Ave., 19th floor, New York NY 10017, ✆ 212 545 8484, info@romaniatourism.com.

VISAS

See page xxxii for visa requirements. Make sure you keep your visa papers when you enter – you'll pay a large fine if you don't have them when you leave Romania.

SLOVAKIA

CAPITAL

Bratislava.

CLIMATE

Mild summers and very cold winters.

CURRENCY

Euro (EUR / €). 1 euro = 100 cent. For exchange rates see page 11. Slovakia joined the Euro zone from January 1, 2009.

EMBASSIES IN BRATISLAVA

Australia: *refer to Australian Embassy in Austria.* **Canada**: Carlton Court Yard & Savoy Buildings, Mostova 2, ✆ 02 5920 4031. **New Zealand**: *refer to NZ Embassy in Germany.* **UK**: Panská 16, ✆ 02

5998 2000. **USA**: Hviezdoslavovo námestie 4, ✆ 02 5443 3338.

EMBASSIES OVERSEAS

Australia / New Zealand: 47 Culgoa Circuit, O'Malley, Canberra, ACT 2606, ✆ 2 6290 1516. **Canada**: 50 Rideau Terrace, Ottawa ON, K1M 2A1, ✆ 613 749 4442. **UK**: 25 Kensington Palace Gardens, London W8 4QY, ✆ 020 7243 0803. **USA**: 3523 International Court NW, Washington DC 20008, ✆ 202 237 1054.

LANGUAGE

Slovak, a Slavic tongue closely related to Czech. Some Russian (unpopular), German, Hungarian (especially in the south), plus a little English and French.

OPENING HOURS

Banks: Mon–Fri 0800–1800. **Shops**: Mon–Fri 0900–1800, Sat 0800–1200. **Food shops** usually open 0800 and Sun.
Museums: (usually) Tues–Sun 1000–1700. Most **castles** close on national holidays and Nov–Mar.

POST OFFICES

Usual post office hours: 0800–1900. Stamps are also available from newsagents and tobacconists. Post boxes are orange.

PUBLIC HOLIDAYS

Jan 1, Jan 6 (Epiphany), Good Fri, Easter Mon, May 1, July 5 (Cyril & Methodius), Aug 29 (National Day), Sept 1 (Constitution), Sept 15 (Virgin Mary), Nov 1 (All Saints), Nov 17 (Freedom and Democracy), Dec 24, 25, 26. For dates of movable holidays, see page 2.

PUBLIC TRANSPORT

There is a comprehensive long-distance bus network, often more direct than rail in upland areas. Buy tickets from the driver; priority is given to those with bookings.

RAIL TRAVEL

See Tables **1170 - 1199**. The national rail operator is Železničná spoločnosť (ŽSSK), running on the network of ŽSR. Trains are cheap, but often crowded. Apart from a small number of *EC* and *IC* trains (for which higher fares apply), the fastest trains are *expresný* (*Ex*) and *Rýchlik* (*R*). Cheaper are *zrýchlený* (semi-fast) and *osobný* (very slow). At stations, departures (*odjezdy*) are shown on yellow posters, arrivals (*prijezdy*) on white. Sleeping cars/couchettes (reserve at all main stations, well in advance in summer) are provided on most overnight trains. Seat reservations (at station counters marked R) are recommended for express trains. Reservation agency: MTA, Páričkova 29, Bratislava, ✆ 0 255 969 343.

TELEPHONES

Dial in: ✆ +421 then number (omit initial 0). Outgoing: ✆ 00. Public phones take coins or phonecards, available from post offices and selected newsstands. Information: ✆ 120 (national), ✆ 0149 (international). Emergency: ✆ 112. Police: ✆ 158. Fire: ✆ 150. Ambulance: ✆ 155.

TIPPING

Tipping is expected at hotels, hairdressers, in eateries and taxis. In general, round up to the next SKK 10, unless you are somewhere very upmarket, where you should tip 10%.

TOURIST INFORMATION

Slovak Tourist Board (www.slovakia.travel/). Main office: Námestie L'. Štúra 1, P.O. Box 35, 974 05 Banská Bystrica, ✆ 0 484 136 146, sacr@sacr.sk. Bratislava Information Service (www.bratislava.sk), Klobučnicka 2, 815 15 Bratislava, ✆ 0 254 433 715, info@bkis.sk. Staff speak English and can arrange accommodation.

TOURIST OFFICES OVERSEAS

Germany: Slowakische Zentrale für Tourismus, Zimmerstr. 27, D-10969, Berlin, ✆ +49 (0) 30 2594 2640, tourismus@botschaft-slowakei.de

VISAS

See page xxxii for visa requirements.

SLOVENIA

CAPITAL

Ljubljana.

CLIMATE

Warm summers, cold winters; Mediterranean climate along coast; snow in the mountains in winter.

CURRENCY

Euro (EUR / €). 1 euro = 100 cent. For exchange rates see page 11.

EMBASSIES IN LJUBLJANA

Australia (Consulate): Dunajska cesta 50, ✆ 01 425 4252. **Canada**: Trg Republike 3, ✆ 01 252 4444. **New Zealand**: (Consulate) Lek d.d., Verovskova 57, ✆ 01 580 2011. **UK**: Trg Republike 3, ✆ 01 200 3910. **USA**: Prešernova 31, ✆ 01 200 5500.

EMBASSIES OVERSEAS

Australia: 60 Marcus Clarke St, Canberra, ACT 2601, ✆ 2 6243 4830. **Canada**: 150 Metcalfe St. Suite 2101, Ottawa, ON, K2P 1P1, ✆ 613 565 5781. **UK**: 10 Little College St, London SW1P 3SH, ✆ 020 7222 5700. **USA**: 1525 New Hampshire Ave. NW, Washington DC 20036, ✆ 202 667 5363.

LANGUAGE

Slovenian. English, German and Italian are often spoken in tourist areas.

OPENING HOURS

Banks: vary, but mostly Mon–Fri 0830–1230 and 1400–1630, Sat 0830–1200. **Shops**: mostly Mon–Fri 0800–1900, Sat 0830–1200.
Museums: larger ones 1000–1800, many smaller ones 1000–1400; some close Mon.

POST OFFICES

Mon–Fri 0800–1800, Sat 0800–1200. Main post offices in larger centres may open evenings and on Sun. Ljubljana's main post office in Trg Osvobodilne Fronte 5, by the railway station, is open 24 hrs.

PUBLIC HOLIDAYS

Jan 1, 2, Feb 8 (Culture), Easter Sun/Mon, Apr 27 (Resistance), May 1, 2, June 25 (Statehood), Aug 15 (Assumption), Oct 31 (Reformation), Nov 1 (All Saints), Dec 25, 26. For dates of movable holidays, see page 2.

PUBLIC TRANSPORT

Long-distance bus services are frequent and inexpensive; normally, buy your ticket on boarding. Information: Trg Osvobodilne Fronte 5, next to Ljubljana station, ✆ 012 344 606. On city buses pay by dropping the exact flat fare or a cheaper token (available from newsstands and post offices) into the farebox next to the driver. Daily and weekly passes are available in the main cities.

RAIL TRAVEL

See Tables **1300 - 1359**. Operator: Slovenske železnice (SŽ) (www.slo-zeleznice.si). Information: ✆ 012 913 332 (+386 1 29 13 332 from abroad). Efficient network, but fewer services on Saturdays. Reserve for *ICS* trains; supplements are payable on other express services.

TELEPHONES

Dial in: ✆ +386 then number (omit initial 0). Outgoing: ✆ 00. Public phones take phonecards, available from post offices, newspaper kiosks and tobacconists. Police: ✆ 113. Fire and ambulance: ✆ 112.

TIPPING

No need to tip bar staff or taxi drivers, although you can round sums up as you wish. In restaurants add 10%.

TOURIST INFORMATION

Slovenian Tourist Board (www.slovenia.info). Main office: Krekov trg 10, SI-1000 Ljubljana, ✆ 01 306 45 75, stic@visitljubljana.si

TOURIST OFFICES OVERSEAS

UK: South Marlands, Itchingfield, Horsham, West Sussex RH13 0NN ✆ 0870 225 5305, info@slovenia.info
USA: 2929 East Commercial Boulevard, Suite 201, Fort Lauderdale, FL 33308, ✆ 954 491 0112, info@slovenia.info

VISAS

See page xxxii for visa requirements.

SPAIN

CAPITAL

Madrid.

CURRENCY

Euro (EUR / €). 1 euro = 100 cent. For exchange rates see page 11.

EMBASSIES IN MADRID

Australia: Paseo de la Castellana, 259D, Planta 24, ✆ 913 536 600. **Canada:** Núñez de Balboa 35, ✆ 914 233 250. **New Zealand**: Pinar 7, ✆ 915 230 226. **UK**: Fernando el Santo 16, ✆ 917 008 200. **USA**: Serrano 75, ✆ 915 872 200.

EMBASSIES OVERSEAS

Australia: 15 Arkana St, Yarralumla, Canberra, ACT 2600, ✆ 2 6273 3555. **Canada**: 74 Stanley Avenue, Ottawa ON, K1M 1P4, ✆ 613 747 2252. **UK**: 39 Chesham Place, London SW1X 8SB, ✆ 020 7235 5555. **USA**: 2375 Pennsylvania Ave. NW, Washington DC 20037, ✆ 202 452 0100.

LANGUAGE

Castilian Spanish is the most widely spoken language. There are three other official languages: Catalan in the east; Galician (*Galego*) in the north-west, and Basque (*Euskera*) in the Basque country and parts of Navarre. English is fairly widely spoken in tourist areas. Note that in Spanish listings *Ch* often comes after the *C*'s, *Ll* after the *L*'s, and *Ñ* after the *N*'s.

OPENING HOURS

Banks: Mon–Thur 0930–1630; Fri 0830–1400; Sat 0830–1300 (winter); Mon–Fri 0830–1400 (summer). **Shops**: Mon–Sat 0930/1000–1400 and 1700–2000/2030; major stores do not close for lunch, food shops often open Sun. **Museums**: vary, mostly open 0900/1000, close any time from 1400 to 2030. Few open Mon and some also close (or open half day) Sun. Expect to find most places closed 1300–1500/1600, especially in the south.

POST OFFICES

Most *Oficinas de Correos* are open 0830–1430 Mon–Fri, 0930–1300 Sat, although the main offices in large cities often stay open until around 2100 on Mon–Fri. Main offices offer poste restante *(lista de correos)*. Stamps *(sellos)* are also sold at tobacconists (estancos). Post overseas mail in the slot marked *Extranjero*.

PUBLIC HOLIDAYS

Jan 1, Jan 6 (Epiphany), several days at Easter, May 1, July 25, Aug 15 (Assumption), Oct 12 (National Day); Nov 1 (All Saints), Dec 6 (Constitution), Dec 8 (Immaculate Conception) and several days at Christmas. Not all of these are official holidays, but many places close anyway. Each region has at least four more public holidays, usually local saints' days (e.g. Andalucia Feb 28, Galacia July 25, Catalonia Sept 11). For the dates of movable holidays, see page 2.

PUBLIC TRANSPORT

Numerous regional bus companies provide a fairly comprehensive and cheap (if sometimes confusing) service. The largest bus operating groups are ALSA (www.alsa.es) and Avanzabus (www.avanzabus.com). City buses are efficient and there are metro systems in Madrid, Barcelona, València and Bilbao.

RAIL TRAVEL

See Tables **650 - 689**. National rail company: Red Nacional de los Ferrocarriles Españoles (RENFE) (www.renfe.es). FEVE and a number of regionally-controlled railways operate lines in coastal regions. General information: RENFE ✆ 902 240 202; FEVE ✆ 902 100 818; AVE (high-speed): ✆ 915 066 329; Grandes Líneas (other long-distance): ✆ 902 105 205; international: ✆ 934 901 122. Spain's high-speed network has expanded considerably over the last few years and the Barcelona - Madrid service has some of the fastest trains in Europe. As well as *AVE* high-speed trains, other long-distance categories include *Altaria, Alaris, Euromed, Talgo* (light articulated trains) and IC expresses (see page 321 for further train categories). *Diurno*: ordinary long-distance day train. *Estrella*: night train (including sleeper and/or couchette cars). A pricier alternative for night travel is the *Trenhotel* (hotel train), offering sleeping compartments with their own shower and WC. All convey 1st- and 2nd-class accommodation (*Preferente* and *Turista*; AVE also have a 'super-first' class: *Club*) and require advance reservation. *Regionales*: local stopping service; *Cercanías*: suburban trains. In remoter parts of country, services may be very infrequent. Reservation is compulsory on all services for which a train category (*Talgo, IC* etc) is shown in the timing column of this timetable. RENFE offer money back if their AVE trains on the Sevilla line arrive more than 5 minutes late!

TELEPHONES

Dial in: ✆ +34 then number. Outgoing: ✆ 00. Public phones usually have English instructions and accept coins or phonecard (*Teletarjeta*; sold in tobacconists, post offices and some shops). Payphones in bars are usually more expensive. Emergency (police / fire / ambulance): ✆ 112.

TIPPING

Not necessary to tip in bars and taxis; tipping is more common in restaurants but by no means obligatory. If you want to tip for good service, add around 5%.

TOURIST INFORMATION

Spanish Tourist Office / Turespaña (USA: www.okspain.org, www.spain.info, UK: www.tourspain.co.uk). Local *Oficinas de Turismo* can provide maps and information on accommodation and sightseeing, and generally have English-speaking staff. Regional offices stock information for the whole region, municipal offices cover only that city; larger towns have both types of office.

TOURIST OFFICES OVERSEAS

Canada: 2 Bloor Street West, Suite 3402, Toronto ON M4W 3E2, ✆ 416 961 3131, toronto@tourspain.es. **UK**: PO Box 4009, London W1A 6NB, ✆ 020 7486 8077, londres@tourspain.es. **USA**: 666 Fifth Avenue, 35th Floor, New York NY 10103, ✆ 212 265 8822, nuevayork@tourspain.es. Also in Chicago ✆ 312 642 1992, Los Angeles ✆ 323 658 7195, and Miami ✆ 305 358 8223.

VISAS

See page xxxii for visa requirements.

SWEDEN

CAPITAL

Stockholm.

CLIMATE

Often warm (especially in summer; continuous daylight in far north). Huge range between north and south; it can be mild in Skåne (far south) in Feb, but spring comes late May in the north. Winter generally very cold everywhere.

CURRENCY

Swedish crown or krona (SEK, kr, or Skr); 1 krona = 100 öre. For exchange rates see page 11. *Växlare* machines give change. The best exchange rate is obtained from Forex, which has branches at many stations. Keep receipts so that you can reconvert at no extra cost.

EMBASSIES IN STOCKHOLM

Australia: Sergels Torg 12, ✆ 08 613 2900. **Canada**: Tegelbacken 4, ✆ 08 453 3000. **New Zealand**: Stureplan 4C, ✆ 08 463 3116. **UK**: Skarpögatan 6–8, ✆ 08 671 3000. **USA**: Dag Hammarskjölds Väg 31, ✆ 08 783 5300.

EMBASSIES OVERSEAS

Australia: 5 Turrana St, Yarralumla, Canberra, ACT 2600, ✆ 2 6270 2700. **Canada**: 377 Dalhousie St, Ottawa ON, K1N 9N8, ✆ 613 244 8200. **New Zealand** (Consulate): Molesworth House, 101 Molesworth Street, Wellington, ✆ 4 499 9895.
UK: 11 Montagu Pl., London W1H 2AL, ✆ 020 7917 6400.
USA: 901 30th. Street NW, Washington DC 20007, ✆ 202 467 2600.

LANGUAGE

Swedish. English is widely spoken. Useful rail / bus / ferry words include *daglig* (daily), *vardagar* (Mon–Sat), and *helgdagar* (Sundays and holidays).

OPENING HOURS

Banks: Mon–Fri 0930–1500 (Thur, and Mon–Fri in some cities, until 1730). Some, especially at transport terminals, have longer hours. **Shops**: mostly Mon–Fri 0900/0930–1700/1800, Sat 0900/0930–1300/1600. In larger towns department stores open until 2000/2200; also some on Sun 1200–1600. **Museums**: vary widely. In winter, many attractions close Mon and some close altogether.

POST OFFICES

Generally Mon–Fri 0900–1800, Sat 1000–1300, but there are local variations. Stamps are also sold at newsagents and tobacconists. Post boxes: yellow (overseas), blue (local).

PUBLIC HOLIDAYS

Jan 1, Jan 6 (Epiphany), Good Friday, Easter Mon, May 1, Ascension Day, Whit Sun/Mon, June 6 (National Day), Midsummer Day (Sat falling June 20–26) plus Midsummer Eve (previous day), All Saints Day (Sat falling Oct 31 - Nov 6), Dec 24, 25, 26. Many places close early the previous day, or Fri if it's a long weekend. For dates of movable holidays, see page 2.

PUBLIC TRANSPORT

The transport system is highly efficient; ferries are covered (in whole or part) by rail passes and city transport cards. Swebus (www.swebus.se), ✆ 08 410 653 00 is the biggest operator of long-distance buses. Advance booking is required on some routes and always advisable in summer; bus terminals usually adjoin rail stations.

RAIL TRAVEL

See Tables **730 - 769**. National rail company: Statens Järnvägar (SJ) (www.sj.se). Some local lines are run by regional authorities or private companies such as Veolia Transport (www.veolia.se), who also operate a service to the far north. SJ information and sales line, ✆ (0) 771 757575, Veolia ✆ (0) 771 260 000. Supplements are required on *X2000* trains (up to 200 km/h). Sleeping-cars: one or two berths in 2nd class; couchettes: six berths; female-only compartment available. 1st-class sleeping-cars (en-suite shower and WC) on many overnight services; 2nd-class have wash-basins, shower and WC are at the end of the carriage. Long-distance trains have a refreshment service. Many trains have a family coach with a playroom, and facilities for the disabled. Seat reservations are compulsory on *X2000* and night trains. *X2000* services operate between Sweden and Copenhagen via the Öresund bridge and tunnel but it is better to use the frequent local trains for short journeys. 'C' (for Central) in timetables etc. means the town's main station. Large, detailed timetables are displayed for long-distance trains: yellow for departures, white for arrivals. *Biljetter* indicates the station ticket office. *Pressbyrån* kiosks (at most stations) sell snacks and English-language publications.

TELEPHONES

Dial in: ✆ +46 then number (omit initial 0). Outgoing: ✆ 00. Coin-operated phones take krona or euro. Most card phones accept credit / debit cards and *Telia* phonecards (*telefonkor-ten*), available from most newsagents, tobacconists, and *Pressbyrån* kiosks). Emergency services (police / fire / ambulance): ✆ 112.

TIPPING

Restaurants include a service charge but a tip of 10–15% is appreciated. Taxis 10%. Tip hotel staff, porters, cloakroom attendants etc. at your discretion.

TOURIST INFORMATION

Swedish Travel & Tourism Council (www.visitsweden.com). Tourist offices, of which there are 400 throughout the country, are called *Turistbyråer*. Stockholm City Tourist Centre: Sverigehuset, Hamngatan 27, 10327 Stockholm, ✆ 085 0828508, info@svb.stockholm.se.

TOURIST OFFICES OVERSEAS

UK: 5 Upper Montagu St, London W1H 2AG, ✆ 020 7108 6168, uk@visitsweden.com. **USA**: P.O. Box 4649, Grand Central Station, New York NY 10163-4649, ✆ 212 885 9700, usa@visitsweden.com.

VISAS

See page xxxii for visa requirements.

SWITZERLAND

CAPITAL

Berne (Bern).

CLIMATE

Rainfall spread throughout the year. May–Sept are best in the mountains. June or early July best for the wild flowers. Snow at high altitudes even in midsummer. Season in the lakes: Apr–Oct. July and Aug get very busy.

CURRENCY

Swiss franc (CHF or Sfr.); 1 franc = 100 centimes. For exchange rates, see page 11.

EMBASSIES IN BERNE

Australia (Consulate in Geneva): 2 Chemin des Fins, Geneva, ✆ 0 22 799 9100. **Canada**: Kirchenfeldstrasse 88, ✆ 0 31 357 3200. **New Zealand** (Consulate in Geneva): 2 Chemin des Fins, Geneva, ✆ 0 22 929 0350. **UK**: Thunstrasse 50, ✆ 0 31 359 7700. **USA**: Sulgeneckstrasse 19, ✆ 0 31 357 7011.

EMBASSIES OVERSEAS

Australia: 7 Melbourne Avenue, Forrest, Canberra, ACT 2603, ✆ 2 6162 8400. **Canada**: 5 Marlborough Avenue, Ottawa ON, K1N 8E6, ✆ 613 235 1837. **UK**: 16-18 Montagu Place, London W1H 2BQ, ✆ 020 7616 6000. **USA**: 2900 Cathedral Ave. NW, Washington DC 20008, ✆ 202 745 7900.

LANGUAGE

German, French, Italian, and Romansch are all official languages. Most Swiss people are at least bilingual. English is widespread.

OPENING HOURS

Banks: Mon–Fri 0800–1200 and 1400–1700. Money change desks in most rail stations, open longer hours. **Shops**: Mon–Fri 0800–1200 and 1330–1830, Sat 0800–1200 and 1330–1600. Many close Mon morning. In stations, shops open longer hours and on Sun. **Museums**: usually close Mon. Hours vary.

POST OFFICES

Usually Mon–Fri 0730–1200 and 1345–1830, Sat 0730–1100; longer in cities. Poste restante (*Postlagernd*) facilities are available at most post offices.

PUBLIC HOLIDAYS

Jan 1, Jan. 2, Good Fri, Easter Mon, Ascension Day, Whit Mon, Aug 1 (National Day), Dec 25, 26. Also May 1 and Corpus Christi in some areas. For dates of movable holidays see page 2.

PUBLIC TRANSPORT

Swiss buses are famously punctual. Yellow postbuses call at rail stations; free timetables from post offices. Swiss Pass valid (see Passes feature), surcharge for some scenic routes. The best way to get around centres is often on foot. Most cities have efficient tram and bus networks with integrated ticketing.

RAIL TRAVEL

See Tables **500 - 579**. The principal rail carrier is Swiss Federal Railways (SBB / CFF / FFS) (www.sbb.ch). Information: ✆ 0 900 300 300 (English-speaking operator). There are also many local lines with independent operators. Services are fast and punctual, trains spotlessly clean. Some international trains have sleepers (3 berths) and/or couchettes (up to 6 people). Sleepers can be booked up to 3 months in advance, couchettes/seats up to 2 months ahead. Reservations are required on some sightseeing trains (e.g. Glacier Express, Bernina-Express). All main stations have information offices (and usually tourist offices), shopping and eating facilities. Bicycle hire at most stations.

TELEPHONES

Dial in: ✆ +41 then number (omit initial 0). Outgoing: ✆ 00. Phonecards (*taxcard*) are available from Swisscom offices, post offices, newsagents and most rail stations in denominations of CHF 5, 10, 20, and 50. Some payphones accept Euros. National enquiries: ✆ 111. International operator: ✆ 1141. All operators speak English. Emergency: ✆ 112. Police: ✆ 117. Fire: ✆ 118. Ambulance: ✆ 114.

TIPPING

Not necessary or expected in restaurants or taxis.

TOURIST INFORMATION

Switzerland Tourism (www.myswitzerland.com). Main office: Tödistrasse 7, CH-8027 Zürich. International toll-free ✆ 00800 100 200 30 (information, reservations, etc.). There are Tourist Offices in almost every town and village. The standard of information is excellent.

TOURIST OFFICES OVERSEAS

Canada: 926 The East Mall, Toronto ON, M9B 6K1, ✆ 800 794 7795 (toll-free), info.caen@myswitzerland.com.
UK: 30 Bedford Street, London WC2E 9ED, ✆ 00800 100 200 30 (free-phone), info.uk@myswitzerland.com.
USA: 608 Fifth Ave., New York NY 10020, ✆ 011800 100 200 30 (toll-free), info.usa@myswitzerland.com.

VISAS

See page xxxii for visa requirements.

TURKEY

CAPITAL

Ankara.

CLIMATE

Very hot summers, more manageable in spring or autumn. Cool Nov–Mar.

CURRENCY

New Turkish lira (TRY or YTL). 1 lira = 100 kuruş. For exchange rates, see page 11. Credit cards are widely accepted.

CONSULATES IN ISTANBUL

Australia: Ritz carlton residences, Askerocaği Caddesi No 15, Elmadağ 34367, ✆ 0 212 243 1333. **Canada**: Istiklal Caddesi No 189/5, Beyoglu, ✆ 0 212 251 9838. **New Zealand**: (Embassy in Ankara) Iran Caddesi 13, Kavaklidere, Ankara, ✆ 0 312 467 9054.
UK: Mesrutiyet Caddesi No 34, Tepebasi Beyoglu, ✆ 0 212 334 6400. **USA**: İstinye Mahallesi, Kaplıcalar Mekvii No 2, İstinye 34460, ✆ 0 212 335 9000.

EMBASSIES OVERSEAS

Australia: 6 Moonah Place, Yarralumla, Canberra, ACT 2600, ✆ 2 6234 0000. **Canada**: 197 Wurtemburg St., Ottawa ON, K1N 8L9, ✆ 613 789 4044. **UK**: 43 Belgrave Sq., London SW1X 8PA, ✆ 020 7393 0202. **USA**: 2525 Massachusetts Ave, NW, Washington, DC 20008, ✆ 202 612 6700.

LANGUAGE

Turkish, which is written using the Latin alphabet. English and German are often understood.

OPENING HOURS

Banks: 0830–1200, 1300–1700, Mon–Fri (some private banks are open at lunchtime). Shops 0930–1900; until around 2400 in tourist areas. **Government offices**: 0830–1230, 1300–1700 (closed Sat and Sun). In Aegean and Mediterranean regions, many establishments stay open very late in summer. **Museums**: many close on Mon.

POST OFFICES

Post offices have PTT signs. Major offices: Airport, Beyoglu and Sirkeci open 24 hrs all week (limited services at night). Small offices: 0830–1700 (some close 1230–1300).

PUBLIC HOLIDAYS

Jan 1, Apr 23, May 1, 19, Aug 30, Oct 29. Religious festivals have movable dates and can affect travel arrangements and business opening times over an extended period. The main festival periods are *Kurban Bayrami* (Nov. 27 - 30 in 2009, Nov. 16 - 19 in 2010) and *Seker Bayrami* (Sept. 20 - 22 in 2009, Sept. 9 - 11 in 2010).

PUBLIC TRANSPORT

An excellent long-distance bus system, run by competing companies (amongst the best are Varan and Ulusoy), generally provides quicker journeys than rail. *Dolmuş* minibuses that pick up passengers like a taxi, but at much cheaper rates and operating along set routes, can be used for shorter journeys. Istanbul has a modern metro line, as well as a light-rail and tram route. TML (Turkish Maritime Lines) operates passenger ferries.

RAIL TRAVEL

See Table **1550** – for journeys in Asian Turkey beyond Istanbul, consult the *Thomas Cook Overseas Timetable*. Operator: TCDD (Turkish State Railways) (www.tcdd.gov.tr). Routes are tortuous and journeys slow, but a new high-speed route is now partially open between Istanbul and Ankara.

TELEPHONES

Dial in: ✆ +90 then number (omit initial 0). Outgoing: ✆ 00. Payphones take *Türk Telekom* phonecards (*Telekart*) available in 30, 60, and 100 units from post offices, shops, kiosks and some hotels. Hotels often charge very high rates. Directory enquiries: ✆ 118. International operator: ✆ 115. Emergency: ✆ 112. Police: ✆ 155. Fire: ✆ 110. Ambulance: ✆ 112.

TIPPING

A 10% tip is usual in restaurants, unless service is included. Do not tip barmen directly. 10–20% is customary at hair salons. Do not tip taxi drivers.

TOURIST INFORMATION

Turkish National Tourist Office (UK: www.goturkey.com, USA: www.tourismturkey.org). Ministry of Culture and Tourism: Atatürk Bulvarı 29, 06050 Opera, Ankara, ✆ 0312 309 0850.

TOURIST OFFICES OVERSEAS

UK: 4th Floor, 29-30 St James's Street, London SW1A 1HB, ✆ 020 7839 7778, info@gototurkey.co.uk. **USA**: 821 United Nations Plaza, New York NY 10017, ✆ 212 687 2194, info.ny@tourismturkey.org.

VISAS

See page xxxii for visa requirements.

UNITED KINGDOM

CAPITAL

London.

CLIMATE

Cool, wet winters, mild spring and autumn, winter can be more extreme. Wetter in the west. Aug and Bank Holiday weekends busiest in tourist areas.

CURRENCY

Pounds Sterling (GBP or £). £1 = 100 pence (p). For exchange rates, see page 11.

EMBASSIES IN LONDON

Australia (High Commission): Australia House, The Strand, ✆ 020 7379 4334. **Canada** (High Commission) Canada House, Trafalgar Square, ✆ 020 7258 6600. **New Zealand** (High Commission): New Zealand House, 80 Haymarket, ✆ 020 7930 8422. **USA**: 24 Grosvenor Square, ✆ 020 7499 9000.

EMBASSIES OVERSEAS

Australia (High Commission): Commonwealth Ave, Yarralumla, Canberra, ACT 2600, ✆ 2 6270 6666. **Canada** (High Commission): 80 Elgin St, Ottawa ON, K1P 5K7, ✆ 613 237 1530. **New Zealand** (High Commission): 44 Hill St, Wellington, ✆ 4 924 2888. **USA**: 3100 Massachusetts Ave. NW, Washington DC 20008, ✆ 202 588 6500.

LANGUAGE

English, plus Welsh in Wales and Gaelic in parts of Scotland.

OPENING HOURS

Banks: Mon–Fri 0930–1530 (or later); some open Sat morning. **Shops**: Mon–Sat 0900–1730. Many supermarkets and some small shops open longer, plus Sunday 1000–1600. **Museums**: usually Mon–Sat 0900/1000–1730/1800, half-day Sun.

POST OFFICES

Usually Mon–Fri 0930–1730, Sat 0930–1300; stamps sold in newsagents etc.

PUBLIC HOLIDAYS

Jan 1, Good Fri, Easter Mon *(not Scotland)*, Early May Bank Holiday (first Mon in May), Spring Bank Holiday (last Mon in May), Summer Bank Holiday (last Mon in August) *(not Scotland)*, Dec 25, 26. Scotland: *also* Jan 2, Summer Bank Holiday (first Monday in August). Northern Ireland: *also* Mar 17 (St Patrick), July 12 (Orangemen). Holidays falling at the weekend are transferred to the following weekday. For the dates of movable holidays, see page 2.

PUBLIC TRANSPORT

Intercity express bus services (coaches) are generally cheaper, but slower, than trains, and mostly require prebooking. The main long-distance coach operator in England and Wales is National Express (www.nationalexpress.com), or Citylink (www.citylink.co.uk) in Scotland. Comprehensive local bus network; most companies belong to large groups such as Stagecoach, First or Arriva. Bus stations are rarely adjacent to railway stations. Traveline (www.traveline.org.uk) is an on-line and telephone service for all UK timetables:
✆ 0871 200 22 23 (10p per minute). Extensive 'Underground' railway network in London operated by Transport for London (www.tfl.gov.uk) who also control the bus service using private companies.
In Northern Ireland, Ulsterbus (part of Translink) is the principal bus operator. (www.translink.co.uk)

RAIL TRAVEL

See Tables **100 - 234**. Passenger services in Great Britain are provided by a number of train operating companies, working together as National Rail (www.nationalrail.co.uk). Through tickets are available to all stations in the country. If asked, booking-office staff will quote the cheapest fare regardless of operator (time period restrictions apply to the very cheapest fares). National Rail enquiries: ✆ 08457 48 49 50. Fast trains, comfortable and frequent, have first and standard class. Other long- and medium-distance regional services are often standard-class only. Refreshments are often available on board. Sleepers: cabins are two-berth or (higher charge) single. Advance reservation (essential for sleepers) is available for most long-distance services - a fee may be charged. Travel between Saturday evening and Sunday afternoon is sometimes interrupted by engineering works and buses may replace trains.
In Northern Ireland, trains are operated by Northern Ireland Railways (NIR), part of Translink. NIR enquiries: ✆ 028 90 666 630.

TELEPHONES

Dial in: ✆ +44 then number (omit initial 0). Outgoing: ✆ 00. Payphones take coins, phonecards (sold at newsagents) or credit cards. Emergency services: ✆ 999 or 112.

TIPPING

Tip 10% in restaurants, except where service is included (becoming increasingly common), but not in pubs, self-service restaurants or bars. Tip taxis (10%) hailed in the street.

TOURIST INFORMATION

VisitBritain (www.visitbritain.com). Britain and London Visitor Centre: 1 Regent Street, London SW1Y 4XT, ✆ 0870 156 6366. There are local tourist offices in most towns and cities.

TOURIST OFFICES OVERSEAS

Australia: australia@visitbritain.org. **Canada**: 160 Bloor Street East, Suite 905, Toronto, ON, M4W 1B9 (not open to the public), britinfo@visitbritain.org. **New Zealand**: newzealand@visitbritain.org. **USA**: travelinfo@visitbritain.org, ✆ 1800 462 2748.

VISAS

See below for visa requirements.

VISA REQUIREMENTS

The table below shows whether nationals from selected countries (shown in columns) need visas to visit countries in Europe (shown in rows) - the symbol ▲ indicates that a visa **is** required. This information applies to tourist trips for up to 30 days - different requirements may apply for longer trips or for visits for other purposes, also if you are resident in a country other than your own. To enter certain countries you may need up to three months remaining validity on your passport.

The first row and column, labeled **Schengen area**, apply to the 25 European countries which have signed the Schengen Agreement whereby border controls between the member countries have been abolished. It is possible to obtain a single Schengen visa to cover all these countries, which are:

Austria, Belgium, Czech Republic, Denmark, Estonia, Finland, France, Germany, Greece, Hungary, Iceland, Italy, Latvia, Lithuania, Luxembourg, Malta, the Netherlands, Norway, Poland, Portugal, Slovakia, Slovenia, Spain, Sweden, Switzerland

Note that the Schengen area and the European Union (EU) differ in the following respects: Iceland, Norway and Switzerland are not in the EU but have implemented the Schengen agreement, whereas the United Kingdom and the Republic of Ireland are in the EU but have not implemented Schengen. Andorra is not included in the Schengen area.

Visas should generally be applied for in advance from an Embassy or Consulate of the country you are visiting, although sometimes they are available on arrival. Transit visas may be available for those travelling through a country in order to reach another, but these may also need to be purchased in advance. The information show below is given as a guide only - entry requirements may be subject to change.

NATIONALS OF →

▲ VISA REQUIRED

TRAVELLING TO ↓	Schengen area	Albania	Belarus	Bosnia-Herzegovina	Bulgaria	Croatia	Cyprus	Macedonia	Moldova	Montenegro	Romania	Russia	Serbia	Switzerland	Turkey	UK / Ireland	Ukraine	Australia	Canada	Japan	New Zealand	USA
Schengen area	–	▲	▲	▲	:	:	:	▲	▲	▲	:	▲	▲	:	▲	:	▲	:	:	:	:	:
Albania ◇	:	–	▲	▲	:	:	:	:	▲	:	:	▲	▲	:	:	:	▲	:	:	:	:	:
Belarus	▲	▲	–	▲	▲	▲	▲	:	:	:	▲	:	:	▲	▲	▲	:	▲	▲	▲	▲	▲
Bosnia-Herzegovina	:	▲	▲	–	:	:	:	:	▲	:	:	:	:	:	:	:	▲	:	:	:	:	:
Bulgaria	:	▲	▲	▲	–	:	:	▲	▲	▲	:	▲	▲	:	▲	:	▲	:	:	:	:	:
Croatia	:	▲	▲	:	:	–	:	:	▲	:	:	▲	:	:	:	:	▲	:	:	:	:	:
Cyprus	:	▲	▲	▲	:	:	–	▲	▲	▲	:	▲	▲	:	▲	:	▲	:	:	:	:	:
Macedonia	:	:	▲	:	:	:	:	–	▲	:	:	▲	:	:	:	:	▲[1]	:	:	:	:	:
Moldova	:	▲	:	▲	:	▲	:	▲	–	▲	:	:	▲	:	▲	:	:	▲	:	:	▲	:
Montenegro	:	:	:	:	:	:	:	:	▲	–	▲	:	:	:	▲	:	:	:	:	:	:	:
Romania	:	▲	▲	▲	:	:	:	▲	▲	▲	–	▲	▲	:	▲	:	▲	:	:	:	:	:
Russia	▲	▲	:	▲	▲	▲	▲	▲	:	▲	▲	–	▲	▲	▲	▲	:	▲	▲	▲	▲	▲
Serbia	:	▲	:	:	:	:	:	:	▲	:	:	:	–	:	▲	:	▲	:	:	:	:	:
Switzerland	:	▲	▲	▲	:	:	:	▲	▲	▲	:	▲	▲	–	▲	:	▲	:	:	:	:	:
Turkey	●[2]	●	●	:	:	:	●	:	●	:	●	●	●	:	–	●	●	●	●	:	:	●
UK / Ireland	:	▲	▲	▲	:	:	:	▲	▲	▲	:	▲	▲	:	▲	–	▲	:	:	:	:	:
Ukraine	:	▲	:	▲	▲	▲	:	▲	:	▲	▲	:	▲	:	▲	:	–	▲	:	:	▲	:

NOTES

▲ – Visa required (see also general notes above table).

▲[1] – Visa required except for organized tourist visits.

● – Sticker-type tourist visas must be purchased on entering the country (prices vary according to nationality, e.g. UK citizens pay GBP 10 per person, payable in £10 notes only).

●[2] – ● applies to nationals of Austria, Belgium, Hungary, Lithuania, Malta, Netherlands, Norway, Poland, Portugal, Slovakia, Slovenia and Spain.

◇ – Tax of 10 euro is payable on entry to Albania.

ISSN 0952-620X
Published Monthly

June 2009

Thomas Cook

EUROPEAN RAIL TIMETABLE

CONTENTS

TABLE DES MATIÈRES *INDICE DELLE MATERIE* *INHALTSVERZEICHNIS* *ÍNDICE DE MATERIAS*

INFORMATION

Thomas Cook Publishing		*Director of Publishing: Chris Young*
Editor	Brendan Fox	+44 (0)1733 416322
Editorial Team	John Potter	+44 (0)1733 417354
	Reuben Turner	+44 (0)1733 417478
	David Turpie	+44 (0)1733 417155
	Chris Woodcock	+44 (0)1733 416408
Commercial Manager	Lisa Bass	+44 (0)1733 402003
Subscriptions	Gemma Slater	+44 (0)1733 402002
Sales enquiries		+44 (0)1733 416477
Advertising		+44 (0)1733 416322
Fax		+44 (0)1733 416688
Rail Pass Direct		08700 841 413
e-mail (Sales)		publishing-sales@thomascook.com
e-mail (Editorial)		timetables@thomascook.com
Publishing homepage:		www.thomascookpublishing.com
Thomas Cook homepage:		www.thomascook.com

Thomas Cook Publishing, Unit 9
Coningsby Road, Peterborough PE3 8SB, UK

A division of Thomas Cook Tour Operations Ltd
Company Registration No. 3772199 England

Cover picture: A Matterhorn Gotthard Bahn (MGB) train on the steep descent into Göschenen (Table 576) © Phil Wormald

Printed in the UK by CPI William Clowes, Beccles NR34 7TL

RAIL – INTERNATIONAL

Selected winter timings from December 13 will appear from the September edition

RAIL – COUNTRY BY COUNTRY

SHIPPING

SPECIAL FEATURES

will appear in alternate editions as follows:

January **Sample Fares**, *March* **Cruise Trains and Rail Holidays**, *May* **Rail Passes**, *July* **Tourist Railways**, *September* **High-Speed Trains**, *November* **Night Trains**

CALENDAR

CALENDRIER CALENDARIO KALENDER CALENDARIO

2009

JANUARY

M	T	W	T	F	S	S
①	②	③	④	⑤	⑥	⑦
–	–	–	1	2	3	4
5	6	7	8	9	10	11
12	13	14	15	16	17	18
19	20	21	22	23	24	25
26	27	28	29	30	31	–

FEBRUARY

M	T	W	T	F	S	S
①	②	③	④	⑤	⑥	⑦
–	–	–	–	–	–	1
2	3	4	5	6	7	8
9	10	11	12	13	14	15
16	17	18	19	20	21	22
23	24	25	26	27	28	–

MARCH

M	T	W	T	F	S	S
①	②	③	④	⑤	⑥	⑦
30	31	–	–	–	–	1
2	3	4	5	6	7	8
9	10	11	12	13	14	15
16	17	18	19	20	21	22
23	24	25	26	27	28	29

APRIL

M	T	W	T	F	S	S
①	②	③	④	⑤	⑥	⑦
–	–	1	2	3	4	5
6	7	8	9	10	11	12
13	14	15	16	17	18	19
20	21	22	23	24	25	26
27	28	29	30	–	–	–

MAY

M	T	W	T	F	S	S
①	②	③	④	⑤	⑥	⑦
–	–	–	–	1	2	3
4	5	6	7	8	9	10
11	12	13	14	15	16	17
18	19	20	21	22	23	24
25	26	27	28	29	30	31

JUNE

M	T	W	T	F	S	S
①	②	③	④	⑤	⑥	⑦
1	2	3	4	5	6	7
8	9	10	11	12	13	14
15	16	17	18	19	20	21
22	23	24	25	26	27	28
29	30	–	–	–	–	–

JULY

M	T	W	T	F	S	S
①	②	③	④	⑤	⑥	⑦
–	–	1	2	3	4	5
6	7	8	9	10	11	12
13	14	15	16	17	18	19
20	21	22	23	24	25	26
27	28	29	30	31	–	–

AUGUST

M	T	W	T	F	S	S
①	②	③	④	⑤	⑥	⑦
31	–	–	–	–	1	2
3	4	5	6	7	8	9
10	11	12	13	14	15	16
17	18	19	20	21	22	23
24	25	26	27	28	29	30

SEPTEMBER

M	T	W	T	F	S	S
①	②	③	④	⑤	⑥	⑦
–	1	2	3	4	5	6
7	8	9	10	11	12	13
14	15	16	17	18	19	20
21	22	23	24	25	26	27
28	29	30	–	–	–	–

OCTOBER

M	T	W	T	F	S	S
①	②	③	④	⑤	⑥	⑦
–	–	–	1	2	3	4
5	6	7	8	9	10	11
12	13	14	15	16	17	18
19	20	21	22	23	24	25
26	27	28	29	30	31	–

NOVEMBER

M	T	W	T	F	S	S
①	②	③	④	⑤	⑥	⑦
30	–	–	–	–	–	1
2	3	4	5	6	7	8
9	10	11	12	13	14	15
16	17	18	19	20	21	22
23	24	25	26	27	28	29

DECEMBER

M	T	W	T	F	S	S
①	②	③	④	⑤	⑥	⑦
–	1	2	3	4	5	6
7	8	9	10	11	12	13
14	15	16	17	18	19	20
21	22	23	24	25	26	27
28	29	30	31	–	–	–

2010

JANUARY

M	T	W	T	F	S	S
①	②	③	④	⑤	⑥	⑦
–	–	–	–	1	2	3
4	5	6	7	8	9	10
11	12	13	14	15	16	17
18	19	20	21	22	23	24
25	26	27	28	29	30	31

FEBRUARY

M	T	W	T	F	S	S
①	②	③	④	⑤	⑥	⑦
1	2	3	4	5	6	7
8	9	10	11	12	13	14
15	16	17	18	19	20	21
22	23	24	25	26	27	28
–	–	–	–	–	–	–

MARCH

M	T	W	T	F	S	S
①	②	③	④	⑤	⑥	⑦
1	2	3	4	5	6	7
8	9	10	11	12	13	14
15	16	17	18	19	20	21
22	23	24	25	26	27	28
29	30	31	–	–	–	–

APRIL

M	T	W	T	F	S	S
①	②	③	④	⑤	⑥	⑦
–	–	–	1	2	3	4
5	6	7	8	9	10	11
12	13	14	15	16	17	18
19	20	21	22	23	24	25
26	27	28	29	30	–	–

MAY

M	T	W	T	F	S	S
①	②	③	④	⑤	⑥	⑦
31	–	–	–	–	1	2
3	4	5	6	7	8	9
10	11	12	13	14	15	16
17	18	19	20	21	22	23
24	25	26	27	28	29	30

JUNE

M	T	W	T	F	S	S
①	②	③	④	⑤	⑥	⑦
–	1	2	3	4	5	6
7	8	9	10	11	12	13
14	15	16	17	18	19	20
21	22	23	24	25	26	27
28	29	30	–	–	–	–

PUBLIC HOLIDAYS 2009

JOURS FÉRIÉS GIORNI FESTIVI FEIERTAGE DÍAS FESTIVOS

The dates given below are those of national public holidays (those falling on a Sunday may not be shown). They do not include regional or half-day holidays. Passengers intending to travel on public holidays, or on days immediately preceding or following them, are strongly recommended to reserve seats and to confirm timings locally. Further information regarding special transport conditions applying on holiday dates may be found in the introduction to each country.

Austria : Jan. 1, 6, Apr. 13, May 1, 21, June 1, 11, Aug. 15, Oct. 26, Nov. 1, Dec. 8, 25, 26.

Belarus : Jan. 1, 7, Mar. 8, 15, Apr. 17, 20, May 1, 9, July 3, Nov. 2, Dec. 25.

Belgium : Jan. 1, Apr. 13, May 1, 21, June 1, July 21, Aug. 15, Nov. 1, 11, Dec. 25.

Bosnia-Herzegovina : Jan. 1, 6, 7, 14, 15, 27, Mar. 1, Apr. 10, 13, May 1, Aug. 15, Nov. 1, 25, 26.

Bulgaria : Jan. 1, Mar. 3, Apr. 10, 13, May 1, 6, 24, Sept. 6, 22, Nov. 1, Dec. 24, 25, 26, 31.

Croatia : Jan. 1, 6, Apr. 13, May 1, June 11, 22, 25, Aug. 5, 15, Oct. 8, Nov. 1, Dec. 25, 26.

Czech Republic : Jan. 1, Apr. 13, May 1, 8, July 5, 6, Sept. 28, Oct. 28, Nov. 17, Dec. 24, 25, 26.

Denmark : Jan. 1, Apr. 9, 10, 13, May 8, 21, June 1, 5, Dec. 24, 25, 26.

Estonia : Jan. 1, Feb. 24, Apr. 10, May 1, June 23, 24, Aug. 20, Dec. 25, 26.

Finland : Jan. 1, 6, Apr. 10, 13, May 1, 21, June 20, Oct. 31, Dec. 6, 25, 26.

France : Jan. 1, Apr. 13, May 1, 8, 21, June 1, July 14, Aug. 15, Nov. 1, 11, Dec. 25.

Germany : Jan. 1, Apr. 10, 13, May 1, 21, June 1, Oct. 3, Dec. 25, 26. *Regional holidays: see page 363.*

Great Britain : *England & Wales*: Jan. 1, Apr. 10, 13, May 4, 25, Aug. 31, Dec. 25, 26, 28; *Scotland*: Jan. 1, 2, Apr. 10, May 4, 25, Aug. 3, Nov. 30, Dec. 25, 26, 28.

Greece : Jan. 1, 6, Mar. 2, 25, Apr. 17, 20, May 1, June 8, Aug. 15, Oct. 28, Dec. 25, 26.

Hungary : Jan. 1, Mar. 15, Apr. 13, May 1, June 1, Aug. 20, Oct. 23, Nov. 1, Dec. 25, 26.

Ireland (Northern) : Jan. 1, Mar. 17, Apr. 10, 13, May 4, 25, July 13, Aug. 31, Dec. 25, 26, 28.

Ireland (Republic) : Jan. 1, Mar. 17, Apr. 13, May 4, June 1, Aug. 3, Oct. 26, Dec. 25, 26.

Italy : Jan. 1, 6, Apr. 13, 25, May 1, June 2, Aug. 15, Nov. 1, Dec. 8, 25, 26.

Latvia : Jan. 1, Apr. 10, 13, May 1, 4, June 23, 24, Nov. 18, Dec. 25, 26, 31.

Lithuania : Jan. 1, Feb. 16, Mar. 11, Apr. 10, 13, May 1, 3, June 24, July 6, Aug. 15, Nov. 1, Dec. 25, 26.

Luxembourg : Jan. 1, Apr. 13, May 1, 21, June 1, 23, Aug. 15, Nov. 1, Dec. 25, 26.

Macedonia : Jan. 1, 6, 7, Mar. 8, Apr. 20, May 1, Aug. 2, Sept. 8.

Moldova : Jan. 1, 7, 8, Mar. 8, Apr. 20, May 1, 9, Aug. 27, 31.

Netherlands : Jan. 1, Apr. 10, 13, 30, May 21, June 1, Dec. 25, 26.

Norway : Jan. 1, Apr. 5, 9, 10, 13, May 1, 17, 21, June 1, Dec. 25, 26.

Poland : Jan. 1, Apr. 13, May 1, 3, June 11, Aug. 15, Nov. 1, 11, Dec. 25, 26.

Portugal : Jan. 1, Apr. 10, 25, May 1, June 10, 11, Aug. 15, Oct. 5, Nov. 1, Dec. 1, 8, 25.

Romania : Jan. 1, 2, Apr. 20, May 1, Dec. 1, 25, 26.

Russia : Jan. 1, 7, Feb. 23, Mar. 9, May 1, 9, 11, June 12, Nov. 4.

Serbia : Jan. 1, 7, Apr. 17, 20, 27, May 1, 9.

Slovakia : Jan. 1, 6, Apr. 10, 13, May 1, 8, July 5, Aug. 29, Sept. 1, 15, Nov. 1, 17, Dec. 24, 25, 26.

Slovenia : Jan. 1, 2, Feb. 8, Apr. 13, 27, May 1, 2, June 25, Aug. 15, Oct. 31, Nov. 1, Dec. 25, 26.

Spain : Jan. 1, 6, Mar. 19, Apr. 9, 10, May 1, Aug. 15, Oct. 12, Nov. 1, Dec. 6, 8, 25. *Some are regional.*

Sweden : Jan. 1, 6, Apr. 10, 13, May 1, 21, June 6, 20, Oct. 31, Dec. 25, 26.

Switzerland : Jan. 1, 2, Mar. 19, Apr. 10, 13, May 1, 21, June 1, 11, Aug. 1, 15, Sept. 20, Nov. 1, Dec. 8, 25, 26. *Some are regional holidays.*

Ukraine : Jan. 1, 7, Mar. 8, Apr. 17, 20, May 1, 2, 9, June 8, 28, Aug. 24.

MOVABLE HOLIDAYS

Fêtes mobiles – Feste mobile
Bewegliche Feste – Fiestas movibles

	2009	2010
Good Friday	Apr. 10*	Apr. 2
Easter Monday	Apr. 13*	Apr. 5
Ascension Day	May 21*	May 13
Whit Monday (Pentecost)	June 1*	May 24
Corpus Christi	June 11	June 3

* *1 week later in the Orthodox calendar*

TIME COMPARISON

COMPARAISON DES HEURES COMPARAZIONE DELLE ORE ZEITVERGLEICH COMPARACIÓN DE LAS HORAS

West European Time	*WINTER: GMT* *SUMMER: GMT +1*	Canaries, Faroes, Ireland, Portugal, United Kingdom, Iceland *(GMT all year)*
Central European Time	*WINTER: GMT +1* *SUMMER: GMT +2*	Albania, Austria, Belgium, Bosnia, Croatia, Czech Rep., Denmark, France, Germany, Hungary, Italy, Luxembourg, Macedonia, Malta, Montenegro, Netherlands, Norway, Poland, Serbia, Slovakia, Slovenia, Spain, Sweden, Switzerland
East European Time	*WINTER: GMT +2* *SUMMER: GMT +3*	Belarus, Bulgaria, Cyprus, Estonia, Finland, Greece, Kaliningrad, Latvia, Lithuania, Moldova, Romania, Turkey, Ukraine
Moskva Time	*WINTER: GMT +3* *SUMMER: GMT +4*	Western Russia *(except Kaliningrad)*

In 2009 clocks are advanced by one hour in all countries (except Iceland) between 0100 GMT on Mar. 29 and 0100 GMT on Oct. 25 *(GMT = Greenwich Mean Time = UTC)*

What's new this month

This edition shows where possible the new Summer 2009 schedules, which for the most part are valid from June 14. The new timetable in Great Britain, however, commenced on May 17 (and was shown in our May edition). Timings shown for Finland, Russia, Ukraine, Belarus and the Baltic States start on May 31.

CAR-CARRYING TRAINS

SNCF has withdrawn two routes from its summer schedules: Paris - Tarbes and Mulhouse - Narbonne.

INTERNATIONAL

A summary of the principal changes to international trains taking place from June 14 appears on page 46.

The situation with Cisalpino remains fluid with no date announced yet for the introduction of its new ETR 610 trains. At the moment three return trips between Zürich and Milano, *CIS* **17, 21, 25, 12, 16, 20**, require a change of trains at Lugano, and one return trip between Basel and Milano, *CIS* **51/56**, requires a change of trains at Domodossola. Trains *CIS* **35/40** Genève - Milano and *CIS* **37/42** Genève - Milano - Venezia will run 20–30 minutes later enroute due to being formed of conventional InterCity rolling stock instead of ETR 470 tilting trains.

GREAT BRITAIN

The summer timetable in Great Britain runs from May 17 to December 12. Services on Saturdays and Sundays are generally valid for shorter periods due to engineering work variations, and these are updated in our tables as necessary.

IRELAND

Iarnród Éireann (**IÉ**) has extended its current timetable from May 30 until mid September. This includes the Dublin Area Rapid Transit (**DART**) services. Bus Éireann has also confirmed that its timetable has been extended beyond May 11 until further notice.

Similarly, Northern Ireland Railways has extended its timetable until December 12. As reported last month, engineering work between Ballymena and Coleraine (Table **231**) from March 30 until June 28 has necessitated the closure of the route and a replacement bus service is in operation. Additionally, a bus service will run between Antrim and Coleraine on several dates in June. The service from June 29 is shown on page 40.

Ulsterbus issued a new timetable valid from May 5, 2009 and the Belfast to Armagh service (Table **232**) has been recast.

FRANCE

The French section shows timings from June 1, and as usual there are many services which change for the high-summer period, July 5 to August 30. In the case of Tables **280** to **285**, special versions showing this period will be found at the back of this edition on pages 539 to 542.

A number of new *TGV* services will be introduced from July 5. The first runs from Cherbourg and Caen to Dijon and Besançon (Table **275**), calling at Charles de Gaulle Airport and Marne la Vallée (for Disneyland Paris). This will take the northern part of the 'Grande Ceinture' line around Paris, reversing at Bobigny depot, as will a new Le Havre - Rouen - Strasbourg service (Table **391**). The latter train will also serve Charles de Gaulle airport, as well as all three of the intermediate stations on the *TGV Est Européen* line.

An additional pair of Toulouse - Lyon *TGV* trains numbered **5307** and **5385** will also be introduced from July 5, as shown in Tables **321** and **355**. A further innovation will be two local trains each way between St Malo and Granville, running July 5 - August 30 (Table **272**). Lastly there will be a new early-morning Troyes - Dijon train on Mondays to Fridays from July 6 (Table **380**), returning from Dijon via Troyes to Paris. Table **359** has been expanded to show the SNCF buses from Digne to Aix en Provence TGV station.

Many lines continue to be affected by engineering work entailing cancellations, diversions and bus substitution. Whilst we try to show these in individual tables where possible, many of the changes are arranged at short notice and are not notified to us in time to be shown in the tables. Additional details affecting the September to December period will be added in later editions.

BELGIUM

Minor changes to schedules are possible from June 14, but details were not received in time for this edition.

ITALY

A new timetable is due to be issued from June 14 but no details had been received as we went to press. We do not anticipate major changes, although some local services could be revised and timings should be checked locally before travel.

SPAIN

Trains **3271** 0720 Madrid to Barcelona and **3270** 0720 Barcelona to Madrid now run on Mondays to Thursdays instead of Mondays, Wednesdays and Thursdays.

Day trains **410/413** Salamanca - Bilbao, **530/533** Salamanca - Barcelona and overnight **930/933** Salamanca - Barcelona (Table **689**) are all planned to be withdrawn sometime in mid-June. Other changes expected are the conversion of the Madrid to Cadiz and Huelva services (Table **671**) from *Altaria* to *Alvia*; the conversion of some Barcelona to Alacant services (Table **672**) from *Euromed* to *Alvia*, and the upgrading of **930/933** Gijón to Barcelona sleeper service from *Estrella* to *Trenhotel*.

The *Alaris* trains between Madrid and València (Table **668**) which used to depart from Madrid Puerta de Atocha station will now depart from Madrid Chamartín and call at Madrid Atocha Cercanías (suburban station). A daily morning service to Gandia has been added.

DENMARK

Engineering work between Roskilde and Næstved will affect schedules until August 9 and many services, including the *EC* trains to Germany, will be diverted via Køge. Journey times will be increased by approximately 20 minutes (Table **720**). The new times for Table **721** are more complex as the work will be executed in two phases; March 28 - July 6 will be found in this issue and July 7 - August 9 will be shown in the July edition.

SWEDEN

The new summer schedules shown in this edition are valid from June 14 to August 15. Our August edition will show the services from August 16 onwards.

As is normal practice during the summer period, much engineering work is taking place throughout the country, affecting Tables **705**, **737**, **751**, **755** and **757**. Unfortunately, the complexity of the alternative services provided means we are unable to show the finer details and readers are invited to contact the editorial team for further information if intending to travel during this period.

FINLAND

The new schedules in Finland are valid from May 31 to September 6.

GERMANY

ICE services have returned to normal following the technical problems which have affected various routes since late last year.

Engineering work will affect a number of routes during this timetable period and a summary of known alterations can be found on page 363. The most significant work will involve the complete closure of the route between Bamberg and Forchheim (Tables **851** / **875**) for six weeks from August 1 to September 14. This is to allow upgrade work to take place in preparation for the extension of S-Bahn services from Nürnberg. During this period all trains are replaced by bus between Bamberg and Forchheim, with a limited train service operating between Forchheim and Nürnberg. *ICE* services from / to Berlin will operate every two hours to / from Bamberg with replacement express bus services operating between Bamberg and Nürnberg. Direct *ICE* trains will run every two hours between Berlin and Nürnberg / München via Erfurt and Würzburg. Full details of the amended long-distance service can be found in a special version of Table **851** on page 41.

CONTINUED ON PAGE 46

EXPLANATION OF STANDARD SYMBOLS

	EXPLANATION OF SYMBOLS	*EXPLICATION DES SIGNES*	*DELUCIDAZIONE DEI SEGNI*	*ZEICHENERKLÄRUNG*	*EXPLICACIÓN DE LOS SIGNOS*
	SERVICES	**SERVICES**	**SERVIZI**	**DIENSTE**	**SERVICIOS**
🚃12	Through service (1st and 2nd class seats)	Relation directe (places assises 1re et 2e classe)	Relazione diretta (con posti di 1a e 2a classe)	Direkte Verbindung (Sitzplätze 1. und 2. Klasse)	Relación directa (con asientos de 1a y 2a clase)
🛏	Sleeping car	Voiture-lits	Carrozza letti	Schlafwagen	Coche-camas
━	Couchette car	Voiture-couchettes	Carrozza cuccette	Liegewagen	Coche-literas
✕	Restaurant car	Voiture-restaurant	Carrozza ristorante	Speisewagen	Coche-restaurante
🍸	Snacks and drinks available *(see page 10)*	Voiture-bar ou vente ambulante *(voir page 10)*	Carrozza bar o servizio di buffet *(vedere pagina 10)*	Imbiss und Getränke im Zug *(siehe Seite 10)*	Servicio de cafetería o bar móvil *(véase pág. 10)*
2	Second class only	Uniquement deuxième classe	Sola seconda classe	Nur zweite Klasse	Sólo segunda clase
🚌	Bus or coach service	Service routier	Servizio automobilistico	Buslinie	Servicio de autobuses
🚢	Shipping service	Service maritime	Servizio marittimo	Schifffahrtslinie	Servicio marítimo
	DAYS OF RUNNING	**JOURS DE CIRCULATION**	**GIORNI DI EFFETTUAZIONE**	**VERKEHRSTAGE**	**DÍAS DE CIRCULACIÓN**
⚒	Mondays to Saturdays except holidays*	Du lundi au samedi, sauf les fêtes*	Dal lunedì al sabato, salvo i giorni festivi*	Montag bis Samstag außer Feiertage*	De lunes a sábado, excepto festivos*
Ⓐ	Mondays to Fridays except holidays*	Du lundi au vendredi, sauf les fêtes*	Dal lunedì al venerdì, salvo i giorni festivi*	Montag bis Freitag außer Feiertage*	De lunes a viernes, excepto festivos*
Ⓑ	Daily except Saturdays	Tous les jours sauf les samedis	Giornalmente, salvo il sabato	Täglich außer Samstag	Diario excepto sábados
Ⓒ	Saturdays, Sundays and holidays*	Les samedis, dimanches et fêtes*	Sabato, domenica e giorni festivi*	Samstage, Sonn- und Feiertage*	Sábados, domingos y festivos*
†	Sundays and holidays*	Les dimanches et fêtes*	Domenica e giorni festivi*	Sonn- und Feiertage*	Domingos y festivos*
①②	Mondays, Tuesdays	Les lundis, mardis	Lunedì, martedì	Montag, Dienstag	Lunes, martes
③④	Wednesdays, Thurdays	Les mercredis, jeudis	Mercoledì, giovedì	Mittwoch, Donnerstag	Miércoles, jueves
⑤⑥	Fridays, Saturdays	Les vendredis, samedis	Venerdì, sabato	Freitag, Samstag	Viernes, sábados
⑦	Sundays	Les dimanches	Domenica	Sonntag	Domingos
①–④	Mondays to Thursdays	Des lundis aux jeudis	Dal lunedì al giovedì	Montag bis Donnerstag	De lunes a jueves
	OTHER SYMBOLS	**AUTRES SIGNES**	**ALTRI SIMBOLI**	**SONSTIGE SYMBOLE**	**OTROS SÍMBOLOS**
IC **29**	Train number (**bold figures** above train times)	Numéro du train (en **caractères gras** au-dessus de l'horaire du train)	Numero del treno (in **neretto** sopra gli orari del treno)	Zugnummer (über den Fahrplanzeiten in **fetter Schrift** gesetzt)	Número del tren (figura en **negrita** encima del horario del tren)
◆	See footnotes (listed by train number)	Renvoi aux notes données en bas de page (dans l'ordre numérique des trains)	Vedi in calce alla pagina l'annotazione corrispondente al numero del treno	Siehe die nach Zugnummern geordneten Fußnoten	Véase al pie de la página la nota correspondiente al número del tren
🅁	Reservation compulsory	Réservation obligatoire	Prenotazione obbligatoria	Reservierung erforderlich	Reserva obligatoria
🏛	Frontier station	Gare frontalière	Stazione di frontiera	Grenzbahnhof	Estación fronteriza
✈	Airport	Aéroport	Aeroporto	Flughafen	Aeropuerto
|	Train does not stop	Sans arrêt	Il treno non ferma qui	Zug hält nicht	El tren no para aquí
━━	Separates two trains in the same column between which no connection is possible	Sépare deux trains de la même colonne qui ne sont pas en correspondance	Separa due treni della stessa colonna che non sono in coincidenza	Trennt zwei in derselben Spalte angegebene Züge, zwischen denen kein Anschluß besteht	Separa dos trenes de la misma columna entre los cuales no hay enlace
→	Continued in later column	Suite dans une colonne à droite	Continuazione più avanti a destra	Fortsetzung weiter rechts	Continuación a la derecha
←	Continued from earlier column	Suite d'une colonne à gauche	Seguito di una colonna a sinistra	Fortsetzung von links	Continuación desde la izquierda
v.v.	Vice versa	Vice versa	Viceversa	Umgekehrt	A la inversa
	** Public holiday dates for each country are given on page 2.* *Other, special symbols are explained in table footnotes or in the introduction to each country.*	** Les dates des fêtes légales nationales sont données en page 2.* *D'autres signes particuliers sont expliqués dans les notes ou bien dans l'avant-propos relatif à chaque pays.*	** Per le date dei giorni festivi civili nei diversi paesi vedere pagina 2.* *Altri segni particolari vengono spiegati nelle note in calce ai quadri o nella introduzione attinente a ogni paese.*	** Gesetzlichen Feiertage der jeweiligen Länder finden Sie auf Seite 2.* *Besondere Symbole sind in den Fußnoten bzw. in der Einleitung zu den einzelnen Ländern erklärt.*	** Las fechas de los días festivos en cada país figuran en la página 2.* *La explicación de otros signos particulares se da en las notas o en el preámbulo correspondiente a cada país.*

What is the European Rail Timetable?

The Thomas Cook European Rail Timetable is a concise guide to rail and ferry schedules throughout Europe. Needless to say, it cannot be comprehensive (it would run into thousands of pages), but through our knowledge and experience, together with valuable feedback from our readers, we can select those services which we believe will satisfy the needs of most travellers.

When do the services change?

There is a major annual timetable change in mid-December affecting almost all European countries, with a second change in mid-June affecting most, although the British summer timetable now starts in late May once again. The winter timetable in Denmark comes into effect in January rather than December, and Sweden has a further change in August. Russia and the other CIS countries have their main change at the end of May. Many holiday areas also have separate timetables for the high-summer period. In fact, changes can happen at any time of year, and railways issue amendments either on set dates or as and when necessary. Engineering work also causes frequent changes. Shipping schedules can change at any time, although many companies issue their timetables on a calendar year or seasonal basis.

Why do I need a subscription?

Apart from getting the latest available schedules, you will also be benefitting from advance information for the following season in relevant editions (see below) and also special features in alternate editions, covering the following topics: *January* **Sample Fares**, *March* **Cruise Trains and Rail Holidays**, *May* **Rail Passes**, *July* **Tourist Railways**, *September* **High-Speed Trains**, and *November* **Night Trains**. You may wish to keep a year's worth of timetables on your bookshelf so that you can refer to these features. Note that the Rail Passes feature also appears in the quarterly *Independent Travellers Edition*.

What about forthcoming schedule changes?

A major benefit of a full subscription is obtaining the latest available details of forthcoming changes to International services. Advance summer timings start in our February edition with an 18-page Summer Supplement, which is expanded to 34 pages in March and the full 50 pages in April and May. These summer versions of our international tables are corrected and updated as the information comes in. Winter Supplements appear in our September, October and November editions, leading up to the new schedules from mid-December.

How are the trains selected for inclusion?

People travel for many reasons, whether for leisure, business, sightseeing, visiting friends or relations, or just for the fun of it, and there are no hard and fast rules for selecting the services that we show. Naturally, major towns and inter-city services are shown as a matter of course, but the level of smaller places and local trains shown will depend on the country and even the area. It's surprising just how many minor lines we manage to squeeze in! Generally we will show a greater number of local trains in areas which are popular tourist destinations or where other services are sparse.

It is not possible to show suburban trains within cities or conurbations, or most outer-suburban routes to places close to large cities. However, where there are places of particular interest or importance in this category we do try to show brief details of frequency and journey time.

When should I use the International section?

The rail tables are divided into two sections - International (Tables **10** to **99**) and Country by Country (Tables **100** to **1999**). The International section contains most international routes, but for some services between adjacent countries (for example Stockholm - Oslo or Hamburg - Århus) it is necessary to use the relevant Country tables - the index or maps will guide you. Local trains which cross international frontiers will usually only be found in the Country sections.

Most international trains also carry passengers internally within each country and will therefore be found in the Country tables as well as the International section. Some services are primarily for international travel and will therefore only be found in the International section - this includes *Eurostar* trains (London - Paris / Brussels) and *Thalys* services between Paris and Brussels, as well as certain long-distance night trains.

What about places outside Europe?

No problem. Our sister publication in the blue cover, the **Thomas Cook Overseas Timetable**, is packed with rail, bus and ferry schedules for everywhere you can think of outside Europe, and plenty of other places you have probably never heard of! It is published six times per year and further details can be found on the order form at the back of this timetable.

Our on-line bookstore at www.thomascookpublishing.com has all of our publications, and there is a 10% discount for timetable orders.

New readers start here . . .

Table number and route

Other table showing trains between these places

Train numbers

Origin and destination of trains starting / finishing on other tables

Connecting trains *(in italics)*

References to footnotes. Standard symbols (*eg* R) are explained on page 4.

1078 KRAKÓW - KRYNICA and KOŠICE

km			387	43201	13209	385	381		383	33105	Ex 1315	311
			R ⚡ B		🍷 W	X	R ⚡ K 🍷		2		R ✕	R ⚡ C ✕
	Warszawa Cent. **1065**	d.	...	...	2105	...	0625	...	...	...	1700	...
	Katowice **1075**	d.	...	2245	|	...	|	...	...	...	|	...
0	**Kraków** Główny **1075**	d.	0019	0012	0147	...	0915	0925	*1402*	1645	1943	2150
5	Kraków Płaszów **1075**	d.	0026	0031	0213	...	0922	0934	*1410*	1651	1951	2157
78	Tarnów **1075**	d.	0129	0145	0320	0536	1018	1114	1512	1749	2051	2256
167	**Nowy Sacz**	d.	0317	0331	0505	0732	1156	1326	1658	1918	2220	0035
217	Muszyna	d.	0437	0453	0627	0841	1252	1502	1805	*2115*	...	0132
228	**Krynica**	a.	|	0510	0644	|	|	1525	|	*2140*	...	|
231	Plaveč	a.	0455	...	...	0903	1310	...	1825	...	...	0150
231	Plaveč 🏛	d.	0530	...	...	*0933*	1342	...	1902	...	...	0220
285	Prešov	d.	0643	...	...	*1055*	1512	...	2006	...	...	0346
318	**Košice**	a.	0716	...	...	*1220*z	1545	...	*2052*	...	...	0420
	Budapest Keleti **1290**	a.	...	...	...	...	...	...	...	...	...	0842

B – 1, 2 cl., 2 cl. and (12) Kraków - Bucureşti (- Constanţa in summer). See Table **95b**.

C – CRACOVIA – (12) Kraków - Pécs; 1, 2 cl. (also 2 cl. in summer) and ✕ Kraków - Budapest.

K – KARPATY – (12) Warszawa - Miskolc - Bucureşti; ✕ Warszawa - Plaveč and v.v.

W – 1, 2 cl., 2 cl. and (12) Warszawa - Krynica.

X – Not Sept. 30 - Dec. 7.

z – Change at Prešov.

⚡ – Supplement payable in Slovakia.

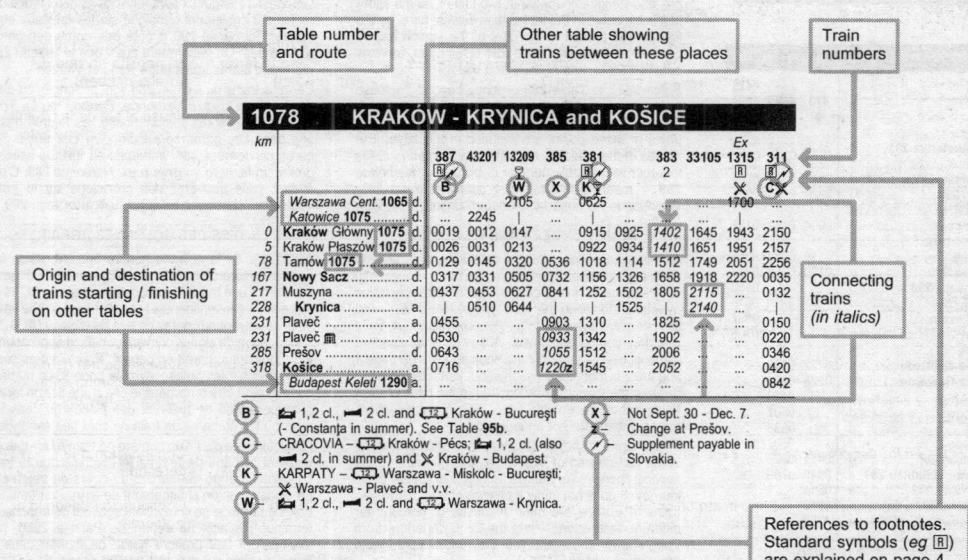

- *use the maps and index to find the tables you need*
- *trains run daily unless shown otherwise by a symbol or footnote*
- *always read the footnotes!*
- *for more detailed advice on how to use the timetable, see pages 6 to 9*

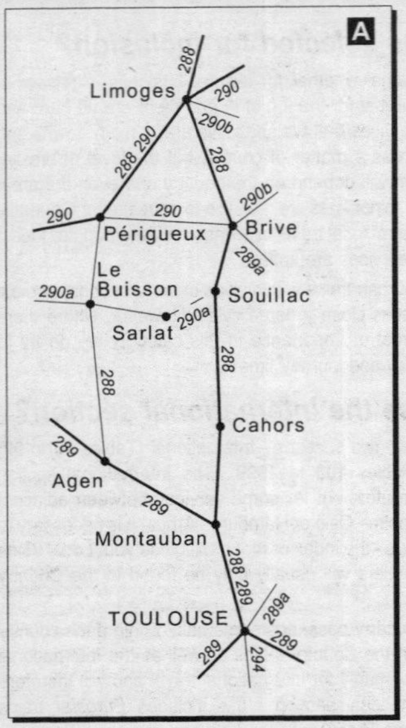

B

Agen, 288, 289
Brive la Gaillarde, 48, 288b, 289a, 290, 290b
Cahors, 288
Le Buisson, 288, 290a
Limoges, 288, 290, 290b
Montauban, 288, 289
Périgueux, 288, 290
Sarlat, 290a
Souillac, 288, 290a
TOULOUSE
▶ Aurillac, 289a
▶ Avignon, 313
▶ Bordeaux, 289
etc.

288

km	C		473 ♦	4425 ♦	4425 4423 Q
0	**Paris Austerlitz 291**	d.	2139	2256	2256
	Orléans	d.	*2237*	*2350*	*2350*
119	Les Aubrais-Orléans **291**	d.	2246	0004	0004
200	Vierzon **291**	d.	2329	0055	0055
236	Issoudun	d.	|	|	|
263	Châteauroux	d.	0004	0132	0132
341	La Souterraine	d.	|	|	|
400	**Limoges**	a.	0116	0254	0254
400	**Limoges 290**	d.	0120	0259	0312
499	Périgueux **290**	d.	|	|	0450
539	Les Eyzies	d.	|	|	0519
556	Le Buisson	d.	|	|	0537
651	**Agen**	a.	|	|	0705
459	Uzerche	d.	|	|	...
499	**Brive la Gaillarde**	a.	0222	0408	...
499	**Brive la Gaillarde**	d.	0225	0421	...
536	Souillac	d.	|	0449	...
559	Gourdon	d.	|	0507	...
600	Cahors	d.	|	0538	...
639	Caussade	d.	|	0607	...
662	Montauban **289**	d.	0411	0628	...
713	**Toulouse Matabiau 289**	a.	0440	0700	...
	Narbonne **289**	a.	0644	...	...
	Portbou **289**	a.	0842	...	...
	La Tour de Carol **294**	a.	0758	...	...

♦ – **NOTES** (LISTED BY TRAIN NUMBER):

473 – PARIS - CÔTE VERMEILLE – 1,2 cl. (T2), 1,2 cl. and 2 Paris - Portbou. Conveys, except when train **4415** runs, 2 and 1,2 cl. Paris - La Tour de Carol.

4425 – ⑤⑦ (also Dec. 25, Jan. 1, Apr. 8, May 15; not Dec. 24, 31, Apr. 7, May 17): 12 and 2 cl. Paris - Toulouse (also 1,2 cl. on ⑤**f**).

Q – ⑤ (also May 15; not May 17): 1,2 cl. and 2 Paris - Agen.

f – Also May 15; not May 17.

FINDING YOUR TRAIN

USING THE MAPS

The maps included in the timetable (see extract **A**, left) provide a diagrammatic index to services. Showing major places, line termini and junctions, they are the quickest way – if you already know the geographical location of the start and end points of your journey – of finding the table numbers you require, as indicated by the figures appearing beside each route.

The maps will also help you to work out routes and changing-points for journeys between places not connected by through services. For example, for a journey from Périgueux to Toulouse you will need to consult either Tables **290** and **288** (via Brive) or Tables **288** and **289** (via Agen).

Where services along a section of line appear in more than one table, then more than one number is shown alongside that section. An example in **A** is Limoges - Périgueux: trains (not necessarily the same ones) running on this section appear in Tables **288** and **290**.

A broken line (e.g. Sarlat - Souillac in **A**) indicates a bus link.

USING THE ALPHABETICAL INDEX

If you cannot find the start and end points of your journey on the maps (and many places are, of course, too small to feature), the alphabetical index on pages 13–28 lists all the places included in the timetable and the numbers of the tables in which those places appear. Extract **B** shows the list of places appearing in map **A**. In the case of major centres (see the entry for Toulouse) there are separate sub-entries for principal destinations reachable from that place.

Look up the two places between which you are travelling. If they have no table number in common, use the numbers given, together with the maps, to work out your route, and where you may need to change trains. It can often be helpful to start your search from the *smaller* of the two locations.

READING THE TABLES

THE STATION COLUMN

Services from Paris to Toulouse via Limoges appear in Table **288**, and an extract from that table is shown in **C**, left. As will be seen from the map, the stations shown between Périgueux and Agen inclusive lie on a branch from the main route of the table. This is indicated in the table by the fact that these station names are indented.

Just as the map showed that services between Limoges and Périgueux appear in two tables, so the same fact is indicated in the tables themselves: here, by the figures **290** printed to the right of the station names concerned. Similarly, Table **291** gives other services between Paris, Les Aubrais and Vierzon.

Some trains in Table **288** continue beyond Toulouse to Narbonne and Portbou and/or La Tour de Carol. For your convenience, the times of arrival of through trains at these points are included in the table. The names of the stations concerned are printed *in italics* together with a table number in **bold**, e.g. *Narbonne* **289** – meaning that for fuller details of trains from Toulouse to Narbonne you should consult Table **289**.

TRAIN NUMBERS AND HEADNOTES

At the head of the columns containing train timings there appear, when appropriate, the train number (e.g. **473**) – preceded in the case of special-category trains by letters indicating the train type (e.g. *EC* **69**) – and any standard symbols (⚒, 🍸 ...) or letters (**A**, **B** ...) referring you to footnotes. A key to the standard symbols used throughout the book appears on page 4 and there is more information about footnotes on page 8. Train numbers may be omitted in the case of local trains without reservable seats or in countries where train numbers are not announced.

When a train is shown with more than one number, as in the last column of extract **C**, this means that the service changes its number during the course of its journey. It does not imply a change of train. However, trains in Europe are often made up of portions for different destinations – see the 2256 departure from Paris shown here – and you should take care to join the correct portion.

DAYS OF RUNNING

Unless otherwise shown, days and dates of running given are those that apply at the station (referred to in a footnote if not shown in the table itself) where the train *starts* its journey. Thus the last train in extract **C** leaves Paris on *Friday* evening (⑤ in the footnotes) and, having travelled through the night, arrives at Agen on *Saturday* morning.

Continued on page 8 ▶

COMMENT TROUVER VOTRE TRAIN

EN UTILISANT LES CARTES

Les cartes (voir l'extrait **A** à gauche) donnent un répertoire schématique des relations reprises dans l'indicateur. Leur consultation – si vous savez déjà la location géographique de vos points de départ et d'arrivée – est le moyen le plus rapide de repérer les numéros des tableaux relatifs à votre parcours. Les chiffres à côté du tracé de chaque ligne renvoient aux tableaux correspondants. Les cartes vous aiderez aussi a établir votre itinéraire et, là où il n'y a pas de service direct, vos gares de changement. Pour un voyage entre Périgueux et Toulouse, par exemple, il faut consulter ou les tableaux **290** et **288** (en passant par Brive) ou bien le **288** et le **289** (par Agen).

Parfois l'ensemble des trains desservant une section sera reparti entre deux ou plusieurs tableaux. On notera dans l'extrait **A** l'exemple de la ligne Limoges - Périgueux: il circule entre ces deux villes des trains (pas forcément les mêmes) repris dans les deux tableaux **288** et **290**. Les traits pointillés (Sarlac - Souillac sur la carte **A**) indiquent des liaisons routières.

EN UTILISANT LE RÉPERTOIRE DES VILLES

Si vous ne savez pas localiser les points de départ et d'arrivée de votre itinéraire sur les cartes, ou s'ils sont trop petits pour y figurer, le répertoire des villes (pages 13 à 28) donne pour chaque localité mentionnée dans l'indicateur les numéros des tableaux qui s'y rapportent. Dans l'extrait **B** vous verrez la liste de toutes les villes de la carte **A**. Pour quelques grands nœuds ferroviaires (p.ex. Toulouse) les numéros des tableaux sont présentés selon les destinations.

Cherchez les deux bouts du parcours désiré sur la liste des villes. S'il n'y a aucun numéro de tableau en commun, recourez aux cartes pour établir votre itinéraire et les éventuels points de correspondance en se servant des numéros indiqués. Commencer par la ville de moindre importance peut faciliter la tâche.

COMMENT LIRE LES TABLEAUX

LA COLONNE DES GARES

Les trains de Paris à Toulouse par Limoges figurent sur le tableau **288**, dont un extrait apparaît sous la lettre **C** à gauche. En examinant la carte on verra que les gares comprises entre Périgueux et Agen sont situées sur une ligne d'embranchement. La mise en retrait sur le tableau des noms de ces gares indique la même circonstance.

Tout comme la carte a montré que les trains entre Limoges et Périgueux sont repris dans deux tableaux, ce fait est également témoigné sur les tableaux eux-mêmes: ici par le **290** à côté des noms des gares concernées. On remarquera aussi que le tableau **291** reprend d'autres trains entre Paris et Vierzon.

Certains trains du tableau **288** sont prolongés au-delà de Toulouse jusqu'à Narbonne, Portbou, ou La Tour de Carol. Par souci de commodité, les heures d'arrivée dans ces gares sont indiquées. Les noms des gares concernées sont imprimés en *italique* avec, à droite, un numéro en **gras** p.ex. *Narbonne* **289**. C'est à dire: vous trouverez des précisions sur le trajet Toulouse - Narbonne en consultant le tableau **289**.

L'EN-TÊTE DES COLONNES HORAIRES

À l'en-tête de la colonne horaire figurent, selon les cas, le numéro du train (p.ex. **473**) – précédé éventuellement d'une indication de catégorie (p.ex. *EC* **69**) – des signes conventionnels (⚒, 🍸 ...) et/ou une lettre vous renvoyant aux notes en bas du tableau (**A**, **B** ...). L'explication de signes conventionnels, d'application à tout l'indicateur, paraît en page 4. Pour d'autres commentaires sur les notes, voyez la page 8. Le numéro du train peut être omis dans le cas d'une liaison locale sans possibilité de réserver des places ou dans les pays où les numéros de train ne sont pas annoncés.

L'indication de plus d'un numéro de train à l'en-tête (la dernière colonne de l'extrait **C**) signifie que le train concerné change de numéro au cours du trajet: elle ne signale pas un changement de train. Pourtant, les trains en Europe se composant souvent de tranches à terminus distincts (le départ de Paris à 2256, par exemple), il faut prendre garde de monter dans la partie du train qui convient à votre destination.

JOURS DE CIRCULATION

Sauf indication contraire, les jours et les dates de circulation mentionnés sont ceux applicables à la *gare d'origine* du train (mentionnée si elle ne figure pas sur le tableau même dans les notes). Ainsi le dernier train de l'extrait **C** part de Paris les *vendredis* (⑤ dans les notes), arrive pourtant à Agen le *samedi*, le parcours s'achevant après minuit.

Suite à la page 8 ▶

COME TROVARE IL VOSTRO TRENO

USANDO LE CARTINE

Le cartine incluse nell'orario (vedi l'esempio A, a sinistra) forniscono un indice diagrammatico dei servizi. Sono il modo più rapido per trovare i numeri quadri-orario di cui avete bisogno - come indicato dai numeri che compaiono a fianco di ogni linea - se conoscete già la collocazione geografica dei punti di inizio e conclusione del vostro viaggio, perché indicano i luoghi principali, le stazioni terminali delle linee e i nodi ferroviari. Le cartine vi aiuteranno anche a studiare i percorsi e le stazioni dove cambiare per viaggi tra località non collegate da servizi diretti. Per esempio, per un viaggio da Périgueux a Toulouse dovrete consultare anche le tavole **290** e **288** (via Brive) oppure le tavole **288** e **289** (via Agen).

Nel caso in cui i servizi lungo la sezione di una linea appaiano in più di un quadro, allora a lato di quella sezione vengono indicati più numeri. Un caso nell'esempio A è Limoges - Périgueux: i treni (non necessariamente gli stessi) che percorrono questa linea compaiono nei quadri **288** e **290**. Una linea interrotta (per es. in A Sarlat - Souillac) indica un collegamento con autobus.

USANDO L'INDICE ALFABETICO

Se non riuscite a trovare sulle cartine i punti di partenza e di arrivo (e molte destinazioni sono naturalmente troppo piccole per essere indicate) l'indice alfabetico delle pagine 13–28 elenca le località incluse nell'orario e i numeri dei quadri in cui compaiono tali località. L'esempio B mostra la lista dei luoghi che compaiono nella cartina A, nel caso di centri maggiori (per esempio la voce Toulouse) ci sono delle voci separate per le principali destinazioni raggiungibili da quella località.

Se le due località tra le quali avete intenzione di viaggiare non hanno numeri di quadri in comune, usate i numeri dati, insieme alle cartine, per elaborare il vostro percorso, considerando che potreste dover cambiare treno. Spesso può essere di aiuto iniziare la ricerca dalle località più piccole.

COME LEGGERE I QUADRI ORARIO

LA COLONNA DEI STAZIONI

I servizi da Paris a Toulouse via Limoges compaiono nella tavola **288** e trovate un estratto del quadro C, a sinistra. Come si può vedere dalla cartina le stazioni tra Périgueux e Agen inclusa si trovano su una diramazione del percorso principale della tavola. Ciò è indicato nella tavola dal fatto che i nomi di queste stazioni sono rientrati.

Esattamente come la cartina mostra che i servizi tra Limoges e Périgueux appaiono in due quadri così lo stesso fatto è anche indicato nei quadri-orario. In questo caso accanto al numero **290** stampato sulla destra dei nomi delle stazioni interessate. In modo simile il quadro **291** riferisce altri servizi tra Paris, Les Aubrais e Vierzon.

Alcuni treni del quadro **288** proseguono oltre Toulouse verso Narbonne e Portbou e/o La Tour de Carol. Per vostra comodità gli orari di arrivo dei treni diretti con queste destinazioni sono inclusi nel quadro. I nomi delle stazioni interessate sono stampati *in corsivo* insieme con un numero di quadro in **grassetto**, per es. *Narbonne* **289**, il che significa che per ulteriori dettagli sui treni da Toulouse a Narbonne bisogna consultare il quadro **289**.

NUMERI DEI TRENI E NOTE DI TESTATA

In cima alla colonna che riporta l'orario del treno compare, dove necessario, il numero del treno (per es. **473**) – preceduto in caso di treni di categoria speciale dalle lettere indicanti il tipo di treno (per es. *EC* **69**) – e ogni altro simbolo standard (⚒, 🍸 ...) o lettera (**A**, **B**...) che si riferiscono alle note a piè di pagina. Una legenda dei simboli standard usati in tutto il volume compare a pagina 4 e trovate ulteriori informazioni sulle note a piè di pagina a pagina 9. I numeri dei treni possono essere omessi nel caso di treni locali senza possibilità di posti riservati o di paesi dove i numeri dei treni non vengono indicati.

Quando un treno è contrassegnato da più di un numero, come nell'ultima colonna dell'esempio C, significa che il servizio cambia numero nel corso del viaggio. Questo non implica comunque un cambio di treno. In Europa spesso i treni sono costituiti da sezioni con destinazioni diverse - come il treno in partenza da Paris alle 2256 qui mostrato - e bisogna fare attenzione a salire sui vagoni giusti.

GIORNI DI CIRCOLAZIONE

Salvo casi in cui sia diversamente indicato, i giorni e le date di circolazione si riferiscono alla stazione dove il treno inizia il suo viaggio (come viene riportato in una nota a piè di pagina se non nel quadro stesso). Così l'ultimo treno nell'esempio C lascia Paris il *venerdì* sera (⑤ nella nota a piè di pagina) e, viaggiando tutta la notte, arriva a Agen il *sabato* mattina.

Continua a pagina 9 ►

WIE FINDE ICH MEINEN ZUG?

MIT HILFE DER ÜBERSICHTSKARTEN

Kennen Sie die geographische Lage der Ausgangs- und Bestimmungsorte Ihrer Reise, dann empfehlen wir einen Blick in die im Kursbuch eingeschlossene Übersichtskarte (siehe den Auszug A links). Sie zeigen nicht nur die wichtigsten Orte, Endstationen und Knotenpunkte an, sondern neben den Strecken die Nummern der entsprechenden Fahrplantabellen. Die Karten helfen auch beim Aussuchen Ihres Reisewegs und der zweckmäßigen Anschlussstationen wenn Sie eine Reise ohne Direktverbindungen machen wollen. Möchten Sie, zum Beispiel, von Périgueux nach Toulouse, schlagen Sie entweder in den Tabellen **290** und **288** (Reiseweg über Brive) oder in den Tabellen **288** und **289** (über Agen) nach.

Manchmal ist der Gesamtverkehr einer bestimmten Strecke in keiner einzigen Tabelle zu finden. In solchen Fällen sind zwei oder mehrere Nummern angegeben. Ein Beispiel aus A ist Limoges - Périgueux: über diese Strecke verkehren Züge (nicht unbedingt dieselben), die in den Tabellen **280** und **290** dargestellt sind.

MIT HILFE DES ORTSVERZEICHNISSES

Können Sie Ihre Ausgangs- und Bestimmmungsorte auf den Karten nicht ermitteln (und natürlich sind viele kleine Orte ausgelassen), dann schlagen Sie in dem alphabetischen Ortsverzeichnis nach. Hier finden Sie alle die im Kursbuch erwähnten Orte mit den entsprechenden Fahrplannummern. Im Auszug B sehen Sie die Liste der in A dargestellten Orte. Für größere Knotenpunkte (z.B. Toulouse) sind die Tabellnummern nach den daraus erreichbaren Hauptbestimmungen getrennt. Suchen Sie Ihre Start- und Endbahnhöfe im Ortsverzeichnis nach. Haben diese keine gemeinsame Nummer, so ziehen Sie die Karten heran und wenden Sie die angegebenen Nummern an, um Ihre Reiseroute, sowie eventuell notwendige Umsteigeorte, herauszuarbeiten. Dazu empfehlen wir, Ihre Suche aus der Richtung des *kleineren* Ortes aufzunehmen.

WIE LESE ICH DIE FAHRPLÄNE?

DIE BAHNHOFSSPALTE

In der Tabelle **288** stehen Züge von Paris nach Toulouse über Limoges. Einen Auszug aus dieser Tabelle sehen Sie links (Abbildung C). Die Bahnhöfe zwischen Périgueux und Agen liegen – das sieht man in der Übersichtskarte – auf einer Nebenstrecke. Der gleiche Umstand ist in der Tabelle wegen des eingezogenen Drucks der betreffenden Bahnhofsnamen auch erkennbar.

In der Karte sehen wir, wie der Gesamtverkehr zwischen Limoges und Périgueux in zwei Tabellen steht. Dasselbe ist in der Tabelle angezeigt: hier durch die Nummer **290** neben den betreffenden Bahnhofsnamen. Gleicherweise ist das Vorhandsein anderer in der Tabelle **291** stehenden Züge zwischen Paris und Vierzon angezeigt. Einige Züge der Tabelle **288** fahren jenseits Toulouse fort, nach Narbonne, Portbou oder La Tour de Carol. Aus Übersichtlichkeitsgründe schließen wir die Ankunftzeiten dieser Züge auf ihren Endbahnhöfe in der Tabelle ein. Die betreffende Bahnhofsnamen sind *kursiv* gedruckt zusammen mit einer **fett** gedruckten Fahrplannummer (z.B. *Narbonne* **289**). Das bedeutet: Näheres über den Zugdienst Toulouse - Narbonne finden Sie in der Tabelle **289**.

ZUGNUMMERN UND KOPFNOTEN

Im Kopf der Zugspalte stehen, nach Bedarf: die Zugnummer (z.B. **473**), gelegentlich mit einem vorangehenden Hinweis auf die Zuggattung (z.B. *EC* **69**); Standard-Symbole (⚒, 🍸 ...); und möglicherweise ein buchstablicher Hinweis auf die Fußnoten (**A**, **B**...). Eine Erklärung der überall in dem Kursbuch verwendeten konventionellen Zeichen finden Sie auf Seite 4, sowie auf Seite 9 Näheres zum Thema Fußnoten. In einigen Fällen – Nahverkehrzüge ohne Reservierungsmöglichkeiten, Länder wo die Nummern nicht bekanntgemacht sind – können die Zugnummern ausgelassen werden.

Die Angabe von zwei Zugnummern, z.B. in der letzten Spalte des Auszugs C, bedeutet, dass die Nummer im Laufe der Reise wechselt, besagt aber keinen Umsteigebedarf. Merken Sie, jedoch, dass Züge in Europa oft aus Teilen mit verschiedenen Bestimmungen bestehen – siehe zum Beispiel die Abfahrt von Paris um 2256. Bemühen Sie sich darum, in den richtigen Teil des Zuges einzusteigen.

VERKEHRSTAGE

Die erwähnten Tage und Zeitabschnitte für Züge, die nicht täglich verkehren, gelten für den Ausgangsbahnhof des Zuges (wenn dieser nicht in der Tabelle steht, ist er in einer Fußnote erwähnt). Demgemäß fährt der letzte Zug des Auszugs C an *Freitag* ab (⑤ in den Noten), kommt aber an *Samstag* in Agen an, weil der Zug die Nacht über fährt.

Fortsetzung auf Seite 9 ►

COMO BUSCAR SU TREN

SIRVIÉNDOSE DE LOS MAPAS

Los mapas (véase el ejemplo A a la izquierda) ofrecen un índice esquemático de las relaciones presentadas en esta guía. Indican los centros principales, los puntos terminales y de empalme de cada línea, y señalan al lado de los trayectos los números de los cuadros horarios correspondientes. Por eso constituyen – si ya sabe localizar en ellos los puntos de inicio y conclusión de su viaje – el modo más rápido de encontrar los números de los cuadros que debe consultar. Los mapas le ayudarán también a estudiar su itinerario y, caso de que no haya servicio directo, sus puntos de enlace óptimos. La figura A demuestra, por ejemplo, que si propone viajar entre Périgueux y Toulouse debe consultar o los cuadros **290** y **288** (viaje por Brive) o bien el **288** y el **289** (por Agen).

A veces no se recoge en un solo cuadro todos los trenes recorriendo un determinado tramo de línea. Un ejemplo en el mapa A es la línea Limoges - Périgueux, recorrida por trenes (normalmente distintos) incluidos en los dos cuadros **288** y **290**. Se indica con una línea interrumpida (p.ej. Sarlat - Souillac) un servicio de autobuses.

SIRVIÉNDOSE DEL ÍNDICE ALFABÉTICO

Si no consigue localizar en los mapas los puntos de inicio y conclusión de su viaje (y muchos destinos, naturalmente, son demasiado pequeños para constar), acuda al índice alfabético en las páginas 13–28 donde encontrará el elenco de todos los lugares incluidos en la guía con los números de los cuadros horarios correspondientes. El ejemplo B da la lista de las localidades que constan en el mapa A. Verá que para los nodos mayores, como Toulouse, se señalan aparte los destinos principales. Si las dos localidades entre las cuales desea viajar carecen de número de cuadro en común, utilice los números facilitados, conjuntamente con los mapas, para establecer su itinerario y los puntos de éste en que pueda ser necesario que cambie de tren. Le puede resultar más fácil iniciar su búsqueda empezando con el lugar de *menor* importancia.

COMO LEER LOS CUADROS

LA COLUMNA DE LAS ESTACIONES

Los trenes de Paris a Toulouse por Limoges aparecen el el cuadro **288** y en la figura C a la izquierda se presenta un trozo de este cuadro. Como ya vimos en el mapa las estaciones entre Périgueux y Agen están situadas en un ramal de la línea principal, hecho representado en el cuadro por la impresión sangrada de los nombres de estas estaciones.

El mapa señala que los servicios entre Limoges y Périgueux figuran en dos cuadros horarios. Esto se evidencia también en el cuadro mismo: por la impresión del número **290** a la derecha de los nombres de las estaciones interesadas. De modo igual, se indica que en el cuadro **291** constan otros trenes entre Paris, Les Aubrais y Vierzon. Algunos trenes del cuadro **288** prosiguen más allá de Toulouse, hasta Narbonne o La Tour de Carol, y sus horas de llegada en estas localidades están incluidas en el cuadro. Se imprimen *en cursiva* los nombres de tales estaciones con, a la derecha, un número en **negrita** (p. ej. *Narbonne* **289**) – lo cual quiere decir que en el cuadro **289** encontrará detalles más amplios sobre el servicio de trenes entre Toulouse y Narbonne.

LAS NOTAS DEL ENCABEZAMIENTO

En el encabezamiento de cada columna horaria se dan, según los casos: el número del tren (p.ej. **473**), precedido eventualmente de letras indicando su tipo (p.ej. *EC* **69**), los signos convencionales (⚒, 🍸 ...) y/o letras (**A**, **B**...) le remitiendo a las notas al pie del cuadro. Encontrará en la página 4 una explicación de los signos convencionales de uso corriente en la guía, y se informa más ampliamente sobre las notas en la página 9. En algunos casos – trenes locales sin posibilidad de reservar plazas, o en países donde no se los comunican – se omiten los números de los trenes.

La indicación de más de un número de tren (véase la última columna del ejemplo C) quiere decir que el servicio cambia de número en el curso de su recorrido: no supone ningún cambio de tren. Sin embargo los trenes europeos se componen a menudo de secciones a destinos distintos – véase en el ejemplo el tren con salida de Paris a las 2256 – y conviene asegurarse de que suba en el coche justo.

DÍAS DE CIRCULACÍON

Salvo indicación contraria los días y las fechas de circulación son aquéllos aplicables en la estación de *origen* del tren (mencionada, si no figura en el cuadro mismo, en una nota). Así el último tren del ejemplo C, aunque sale de Paris por la noche del *viernes* (símbolo ⑤ en las notas), como acaba su viaje después de medianoche, llega a Agen por la mañana del *sábado*.

Sigue en la página 9 ►

289

D

	TGV 8503 ⚒k 🍷		162 163 ♦ 🍴
Paris Montparnasse **286** ....d.	0705	...	...
Paris Austerlitz **286 288** ....d.	|	...	...
Nantes **284** ....d.	|	...	...
Bordeaux St Jean ....d.	1005	1015	1115
Marmande ....d.	|	1059	|
Agen ....d.	1106	1129	|
Montauban **288** ....d.	1142	▬	|
Hendaye 287 ....d.	|	...	|
St Jean de Luz **287** ....d.	|	...	|
Biarritz **287** ....d.	|	...	|
Bayonne **287** ....d.	|	...	|
Puyoô ....d.	|	...	|
Pau **287** ....d.	|	...	|
Lourdes **287** ....d.	|	...	|
Tarbes 287 ....d.	|	...	|
Lannemezan ....d.	|	...	|
Montréjeau ....d.	|	...	|
Boussens ....d.	|	...	|
Toulouse Matabiau 288 ....a.	1209	⚒	1312
Toulouse Matabiau ....d.	...	1220	1316
Castelnaudary ....d.	...	1255	|
Carcassonne ....d.	...	1317	|
Lézignan ....d.	...	...	|
Narbonne ....a.	...	...	|
Marseille **313** ....a.	...	...	1642**z**
Nice **314** ....a.	...	...	1910**z**
Lyon Part Dieu **301** ....a.	...	...	...
Genève **309** ....a.	...	...	...
Perpignan **313** ....a.	...	...	...
Port Bou **313** ....a.	...	...	...

♦ – **NOTES** (LISTED BY TRAIN NUMBER):

162/3 – LE GRAND SUD – [12] and 🍴 Bordeaux - Nice.

k – Also Nov. 1, 11, May 16.

z – Arrives 10–12 minutes earlier from Mar. 10.

290

E

	6390 V		P	6380
Bordeaux St Jean ....d.	0747	0747	...	1051
Libourne ....d.	0809	0809	...	1112
Coutras ....d.	0821	0821	...	|
Périgueux ....a.	0910	0910	...	1206
Périgueux **288** ....d.	0912	0912	0933	1211
Brive la Gaillarde ....a.	1005	1005	|	|
Clermont Ferrand **290b** ..a.	1344	...	|	|
Limoges 288 ....a.	|	...	1041	1311
Limoges ....d.	|	...	...	1313
Guéret ....d.	|	...	...	1410
Montluçon ....d.	|	...	...	1505
Gannat ....d.	|	...	...	1608
St Germain des Fossés......d.	1447	...	...	1627
Roanne ....d.	1530	...	...	1708
Lyon Part Dieu ....a.	1650	...	...	1824
Lyon Perrache ....a.	1700	...	...	1834

P – ①-⑥ (not Dec. 25, Jan. 1, Apr. 8).

V – LE VENTADOUR – ⑤ (also Oct. 26 - Nov. 5, Dec. 19 - Jan. 7, ⑥⑦ Feb. 17 - Mar. 17, Apr. 6, 8, 13, 14, 20, 21, 27, 28, May 1, 3, 8, 10, 15, 19, 24; not May 17, 31).

The timetable extracts shown here are for purposes of illustration only.

Consult the full tables in this book for the latest information on the services mentioned.

Train services in Europe, and with them the tables in this book, are constantly evolving – which is why the Thomas Cook European Rail Timetable is published monthly.

▶ **Continued from page 6**

TRAIN TIMINGS

Timings are given in the 24-hour system – from 0000 hours (midnight departure) to 2400 hours (midnight arrival) – and are always expressed in local time at the place concerned (for time zones, see page 2). The station list indicates for each timing whether it is a departure (d.) or an arrival time (a.). Note, however, that the timing given for the *first* appearance of a train in a table is always a *departure* time, that for its *last* appearance is always an *arrival* time.

THROUGH TRAINS AND CONNECTIONS

Timings in normal (roman) type indicate a through service. Thus, in extract **D**, train **8503**, originating in Paris, runs from Bordeaux to Toulouse, calling at Agen and Montauban en route. The train does not stop at Marmande or, of course, at any of the stations on the branch from Hendaye: this is shown by the symbol | in the centre of the column against the names of the stations concerned.

As just seen, train **8503** does not call at Marmande; passengers travelling from Paris by this service can, however, reach Marmande by changing at Bordeaux to the train, shown in the following column, which leaves there at 1015.

Similarly, while train **8503** completes its journey at Toulouse, passengers wishing to continue to Castelnaudary or Carcassonne have a connecting train at 1220 on ⚒.

Note that, although shown in the same column, the services leaving Bordeaux at 1015 and Toulouse at 1220 are two different trains which do not connect with each other: this is confirmed by the symbol ▬ separating them.

Where timings are *in italics* they refer to a *connecting service* involving a change of trains. Thus, in extract **C** on page 6, train **473** from Paris does not call at Orléans, which is situated – as the indentation shows – on a branch from the main line. However, passengers from Orléans can take a connecting service at *2237* to the main-line station at Les Aubrais-Orléans and change there to train **473**. *Italic* timings always imply a *change of train*.

Warning! While the connections shown in the timetable are believed, on the basis of experience and operators' advice, to be feasible, it cannot be guaranteed that they will always be maintained in such cases as late running. Bear in mind, too, that at large city stations transfer between trains can involve a long walk with change of levels. You should judge for yourself how much time you wish to allow for making a connection 'comfortably'.

FOOTNOTES

When more information about a train needs to be given than can be expressed in standard symbols at the head of the timing column, you will be referred to a footnote.

The symbol ♦ in the headnotes means: refer to the footnote with the corresponding train number. A letter (**A**, **B** ...) means: refer to the footnote with that letter. As will be seen from the timetable extracts, footnotes give much important information about such things as days of running, train composition and through carriages, and you should always consult them when planning your journey.

A letter (**b**, **c** ...) beside a particular timing refers only to that timing. In extract **D**, for example, the **z** beside the last two timings for train **162/163** refers you to a note explaining that arrival times will be earlier from March 10 (but only at Marseille and Nice).

Note that where no days or dates are given, the train runs *daily*. Thus, in extract **E**, a train bearing the name *Le Ventadour* leaves Bordeaux at 0747 and runs via Brive to Lyon – but only on the dates shown in note **V**. Nevertheless, there is a service from Bordeaux to Brive at 0747 *daily* (shown in the following column). In other words, even when the Bordeaux - Lyon train does not run there is still a Bordeaux - Brive train at 0747.

If no other indication is given, trains convey both 1st and 2nd classes of accommodation. Trains conveying 2nd-class accommodation only are distinguished by '2' in the headnotes, by [2], ━ 2 cl., etc. in the footnotes, or by '2nd class' in the table heading .

WHERE ELSE TO LOOK IN THE TIMETABLE

Page 10 gives general information about travelling by train in Europe. You are also strongly advised to consult the introduction to each national section. Here you will find important information concerning each country's transport services, such as train categories, catering, the payability or otherwise of supplements, reservation requirements, etc.

▶ **Suite de la page 6**

LES HORAIRES DES TRAINS

Toutes les indications horaires sont donnés en heures locales (voir tableau de comparaison des heures à la page 2). Le départ à minuit est indiqué par 0000, l'arrivée à minuit par 2400. Il est précisé dans la colonne des gares s'il s'agit d'une heure de départ (d.) ou d'arrivée (a.). À noter, pourtant, que pour chaque train la *première* mention est toujours une heure de *départ*, la *dernière* toujours une heure d'*arrivée*.

TRAINS DIRECTS ET CORRESPONDANCES

Les heures en caractère droit indiquent des relations directes. Prenons l'exemple, dans l'extrait **D**, du train **8503** qui (ayant pour origine Paris) circule sur le parcours Bordeaux - Toulouse en effectuant des arrêts à Agen et à Montauban. Ce train ne dessert pas Marmande ni, bien sûr, aucune des gares de l'embranchement Hendaye - Toulouse: c'est le sens du symbole | placé au milieu de la colonne en face des noms de ces gares.

On notera que malgré la non desserte de Marmande par le train **8503**, cette ville est toujours accessible aux voyageurs venant de Paris: moyennant un changement vers le train, mentionné dans la colonne suivante, qui quitte Bordeaux à 1015.

Les voyageurs à destination de Castelnaudary et de Carcassonne ont également la possibilité de prendre à Toulouse les jours ouvrables (⚒) le train en correspondance qui part à 1220.

À noter pourtant le fait – comme en témoigne le symbole ▬ placé entre les deux trains de la deuxième colonne horaire – qu'il n'y a aucune correspondance *entre ces deux trains-là*.

Les heures en *italique* indiquent une *correspondance* et supposent dans tous les cas un changement de train. Ainsi, dans l'extrait **C** (page 6), on verra que le train **473** de Paris ne dessert pas Orléans, situé – comme l'indique la mise en retrait du son nom – sur une ligne d'embranchement. Les passagers en provenance d'Orléans ont pourtant la possibilité d'y prendre à *2237* un train en correspondance qui leur permettra de rejoindre le train **473** aux Aubrais-Orléans.

Attention! Nous nous sommes efforcés de ne mentionner dans l'indicateur que les correspondances réellement faisables, tenant compte surtout des conseils des compagnies exploitantes. Aucune correspondance n'est garantie pourtant. N'oubliez pas non plus que dans les grandes gares les changements peuvent entrainer une longue marche et l'emprunt d'escaliers. À vous de juger combien de temps vous voulez vous permettre pour effectuer un changement 'en tout confort'.

LES NOTES EN BAS DU TABLEAU

Parfois les signes conventionnels placés à l'en-tête de la colonne horaire ne suffisent pas à donner tous les renseignements nécessaires. Dans ces cas-là, il y a un renvoi aux notes en bas du tableau.

Le symbole ♦ à l'en-tête d'une colonne signifie qu'il faut consulter le note portant le numéro du train concerné. Les lettres (**A**, **B** ...) sont également expliquées en bas du tableau. Vu l'importance des précisions données dans les notes – jours de circulation, composition des trains, voitures directes, etc. – il faut toujours les consulter en préparant votre itinéraire.

Une lettre (**b**, **c** ...) placée après une heure de départ ou d'arrivée n'a rapport qu'à l'heure concernée. Ainsi, dans l'extrait **D**, le **z** des indications 1642**z** et 1910**z** du train **162/163** signifie qu'à partir du 10 mars les heures d'arrivée du train (à Marseille et à Nice exclusivement) seront avancées.

À noter que dans l'absence d'une mention particulière les trains circulent tous les jours. Dans l'extrait **E**, par exemple, *Le Ventadour* (départ de Bordeaux à 0747 pour Lyon par Brive) ne circule que les jours précisés dans la note **V**. La relation Bordeaux - Brive à 0747 est néanmoins *quotidienne*. Comme l'indique la deuxième colonne, il y a un train de Bordeaux à Brive à 0747 même les jours où *le Ventadour* ne circule pas.

Sauf indication contraire, les trains ont des places de 1re et de 2e classe. Les trains n'ayant que des places de 2e classe sont distingués par les mentions '2' à l'en-tête de la colonne, [2], ━ 2 cl., etc. dans les notes, ou '2nd class' à l'en-tête du tableau.

AUTRES PAGES À CONSULTER

Vous trouverez à la page 10 des renseignements d'application générale au sujet des voyages par train en Europe. Il vous est fortement recommandé de consulter aussi l'introduction à chaque section nationale: vous y trouverez des précisions concernant la classification des trains, les prestations offertes à bord des trains, les suppléments, la réservation des places, etc.

COME SI CONSULTA L'ORARIO – II

▶ Seguito della pagina 7

GLI ORARI DEI TRENI

Gli orari vengono forniti in base al sistema delle 24 ore - dalle 0000 (partenza di mezzanotte) alle 2400 (arrivo di mezzanotte) - e sono sempre espressi in ora locale (per i fusi orari vedere pagina 2). La lista delle stazioni indica per ogni orario se si tratta di un orario di partenza (d.) o di arrivo (a.). Notate, comunque, che l'orario che compare per *primo* in una tavola è sempre un orario di *partenza*, mentre quello che compare per *ultimo* è sempre un orario di *arrivo*.

TRENI DIRETTI E COINCIDENZE

L'orario in caratteri normali indica un servizio diretto. Così nell'esempio **D** il treno **8503**, che ha origine a Paris va da Bordeaux a Toulouse fermando lungo il percorso a Agen e Montauban. Il treno non ferma invece a Marmande né, naturalmente, in nessuna delle stazioni sulla diramazione di Hendaye: il che è indicato dal simbolo | nel centro della colonna accanto ai nomi delle stazioni interessate.

Come si è appena visto, il treno **8503** non passa da Marmande; i passeggeri che viaggiano da Paris con questo servizio possono comunque raggiungere Marmande cambiando a Bordeaux con il treno, mostrato nella colonna successiva, che parte alle 1015.

Allo stesso modo, dal momento che il treno **8503** termina il suo viaggio a Toulouse, i passeggeri che desiderano proseguire per Castelnaudary o Carcassonne hanno nei giorni feriali (⚒) un treno in coincidenza alle ore 1220.

Notate che, sebbene siano segnati nella stessa colonna, i servizi che lasciano Bordeaux alle 1015 e Toulouse alle 1220 sono due treni differenti che non hanno coincidenze: il che è indicato dal simbolo ▬ che li separa.

Dove gli orari sono *in corsivo* si riferiscono a un servizio *in coincidenza* che implica un cambio di treno. Perciò nell'essempio **C** a pagina 6 il treno **473** da Paris non ferma ad Orléans, che è situata - come mostra il rientro di riga - su una diramazione della linea principale. Comunque, i passeggeri provenienti da Orléans possono prendere un treno in coincidenza alle *2237* per la stazione principale della linea a Les Aubrais-Orléans e prendere lì il treno **473**. L'orario scritto *in corsivo* implica sempre un *cambio di treno*.

Attenzione! Mentre le coincidenze indicate nell'orario sono quelle ritenute realmente fattibili sulla base dell'esperienza e delle indicazioni delle amministrazioni ferroviarie, non può essere garantito che siano mantenute in caso di ritardi. Ricordate anche che nelle stazioni delle grandi città il trasferimento tra due treni può significare un lungo tratto da percorrere a piedi e con l'uso di scale. Dovrete giudicare da voi quanto tempo vi occorre per cambiare comodamente treno.

NOTE A PIÈ DI PAGINA

Quando sarà necessario dare maggiori informazioni su di un treno di quante possano essere interamente espresse in simboli standard, in cima alla colonna degli orari ci sarà un rimando a una nota a piè di pagina.

Il simbolo ♦ nelle note di testa significa: fate riferimento a una nota a piè di pagina con il numero corrispondente. Una lettera (**A**, **B**...) significa: fate riferimento alla nota con quella lettera. Come si vede dall'esempio **E** le note danno molte informazioni importanti come giorni di percorrenza, composizione dei treni e carrozze dirette, e occorre sempre consultarle quando programmate il vostro viaggio.

Una lettera (**b**, **c**...) accanto ad un particolare orario si riferisce soltanto a quell'orario. Nell'esempio **D** la lettera **z** accanto agli ultimi due orari per i treni **162/163** vi rimanda ad una nota che spiega che l'orario di arrivo sarà anticipato dal 10 di marzo (ma soltanto a Marseille e Nice).

Notate che quando non ci sono giorni e date il treno viaggia *ogni giorno*. Perciò nell'esempio **E** il treno chiamato *Le Ventadour* lascia Bordeaux alle 0747 e va via Brive a Lyon - ma solo nei giorni indicati nella nota **V**. Tuttavia c'è un servizio quotidiano da Bordeaux a Brive alle 0747 (indicato nella colonna successiva), in altre parole anche quando il treno Bordeaux-Lyon non fa servizio c'è comunque il treno Bordeaux-Brive alle 0747.

Se non ci sono altre indicazioni i treni hanno sia la prima sia la seconda classe. I treni con sole carrozze di seconda classe sono identificabili dal '2' nelle note di testata, nei simboli delle carrozze, nelle note a piè di pagina o dall'indicazione '2nd class' nell'intestazione del quadro.

ALTRE PAGINE DA CONSULTARE

A pagina 10 trovate delle informazioni generali sui viaggi in treno in Europa. Vi consigliamo vivamente di consultare anche l'introduzione a ciascuna sezione dedicata ad una nazione. Vi troverete importanti informazioni riguardanti i servizi di trasporto di ciascun paese, così come le categorie dei treni, la ristorazione, il pagamento di supplementi, le necessità di prenotazione, ecc.

BENUTZUNGSHINWEISE – II

▶ Fortsetzung der Seite 7

FAHRZEITANGABEN

Die Abfahrtzeit um Mitternacht ist 0000, die Ankunftzeit um Mitternacht ist 2400. Fahrzeiten sind immer in der jeweiligen Landeszeit angegeben (eine Zeitvergleichstabelle finden Sie auf Seite 2). Die Buchstaben d. (ab) und a. (an) nach den Ortsnamen in der Bahnhofsspalte kennzeichnen Abfahrt- bzw. Ankunftzeiten. Bermerken Sie jedoch, dass es sich stets bei der ersten für einen Zug angegebenen Zeit um eine Abfahrtzeit, bei der letzten um eine Ankunftzeit, handelt.

DIREKTE ZÜGE UND ANSCHLÜSSE

Normal (in gerader Schrift) gedruckte Zeitangaben verweisen auf direkte Verbindungen. Eine solche sieht man in dem Auszug **D**. Der Zug **8503** aus Paris verkehrt von Bordeaux nach Toulouse, hält auf den Bahnhöfen Agen und Montauban, fährt aber bei Marmande durch. Die auf die Seitenstrecken von Hendaye liegende Bahnhöfe bedient er natürlich auch nicht. Dies wird von dem in der Mitte der Zugspalte stehenden Symbol | gekennzeichnet.

Wie soeben erläutert: der Zug **8503** hält in Marmande nicht. Reisende aus Paris können Marmande trotzdem erreichen, mittels Umsteigen in Bordeaux in den in der nächsten Spalte angegebenen Zug (Abfahrt von Bordeaux um 1015).

Gleicherweise, obwohl der Zug **8503** nicht weiter als Toulouse fährt, haben die Passagiere, die ihre Reise bis Castelnaudary oder Carcassonne verlängern wollen, an Werktagen (⚒) einen Anschlusszug dennoch um 1220.

Merken Sie sich, dass die Züge mit den Abfahrtzeiten Bordeaux 1015 bzw. Toulouse 1220 verschiedene Züge und keine Anschlusszüge sind. Das Zeichen ▬ zwischen den beiden Zügen deutet dies an.

Kursiv gedruckte Zeitangaben weisen auf *Anschlussverbindungen* hin und bedeuten Umsteigen. Der Zug **473** in der Abbildung **C** (Seite 6), zum Beispiel, bedient Orléans nicht, weil diese Stadt auf einer Nebenstrecke liegt. Reisende aus Orléans haben jedoch die Möglichkeit, um *2237* einen Anschlusszug zu benutzen, also auf dem Hauptstreckenbahnhof Les Aubrais-Orléans in dem Zug **473** umzusteigen. *Kursiv* gedruckte Zeitangaben weisen immer auf das Umsteigen hin.

Achtung! Alle die im Kursbuch angezeigten Anschlussmöglichkeiten sind nach unserem besten Wissen und den Meldungen der Verkehrsbetriebe erreichbar. Anschlussversäumnisse durch Verspätung oder Ausfall von Zügen sind aber immer möglich. Merken Sie sich auch, dass man auf Großstadtbahnhöfe oft einen langen Umweg zu Fuß machen und Treppe benutzen muss. Beurteilen Sie bitte selbst, wieviel Zeit zum Umsteigen Sie benötigen.

FUSSNOTEN

Manchmal ist es nötig, Ergänzungsinformationen zu vermitteln, für welche die Standard-Symbole nicht genügen. In diesen Fällen wird es auf eine unter der Fahrplantabelle stehenden Fußnote hingewiesen.

Das Zeichen ♦ im Kopf der Zugspalte bedeutet: schlagen Sie die Note mit der Nummer des betreffenden Zuges nach. Ein Buchstabe (**A**, **B**...) weist auf die mit demselben Buchstaben bezeichneten Note hin. Die Fußnoten enthalten – so sieht man das in den Auszügen – viele wichtige Auskünfte: über Verkehrstage, Zugbildung, Kurswagen und so weiter. Lesen Sie immer die Fußnote bei der Planung Ihrer Reise

Ein Buchstabe (**b**, **c**...) neben einer bestimmten Zeitangabe gilt nur für diese Angabe. Das **z** hinter die zwei letzten Zeitangaben des Zuges **162/163** (im Auszug **D**), zum Beispiel, deutet auf das vom 10. Mai frühere Einlaufen dieses Zuges in Marseille und in Nice hin (aber *nur* dorthin).

Sofern nicht anders angemeldet, verkehren die Züge *täglich*. In dem Auszug **E**, fährt der Zug *Le Ventadour* von Bordeaux um 0747 ab und verkehrt nach Lyon über Brive – aber nur in dem in der Note **V** angegebenen Zeitabschnitt. Es ist jedoch in der nächsten Spalte ein Zug auch mit Abfahrt von Bordeaux um 0747 angegeben, diesmal aber ohne Hinweis auf eine bestimmte Verkehrsperiode. Das heißt, dass man *täglich* um 0747 von Bordeaux nach Brive fahren kann, auch wenn *Le Ventadour* nicht verkehrt.

Im Allgemeinen führen die Züge die 1. und 2. Wagenklasse. Abweichungen (das heißt, Züge mit nur 2. Klasse) sind durch die Erwähnungen '2' im Kopf der Zugspalte, (2), ━ 2 cl., usw. in der Noten, bzw. '2nd class' in der Tabellenüberschrift, erkennbar.

AUCH ZUM LESEN

Auf Seite 10 erscheinen allgemeine Auskünfte über das Thema Reisen mit der Bahn in Europa. Es ist auch sehr zu empfehlen, die Einleitungen zu jedem einzelnen Land zu lesen. Darin werden Sie wichtige Informationen über die Besonderheiten jedes Landes finden: Zugcharakterisierung, Services an Bord der Züge, Zuschlagpflicht, Reservierungsbedingungen usw.

MODO DE EMPLEO – II

▶ Continuación de la página 7

LAS INDICACIONES HORARIAS

Éstas se exprimen siempre en la hora del país interesado (véase el cuadro de comparación horaria en la página 2). Por 0000 se entiende una salida de medianoche, por 2400 una llegada a la misma hora. En la lista de las estaciones se aclara para todo horario si se trata de una salida (d.) o de una llegada (a.). Nótese sin embargo que en todos los casos el *primer* horario indicado para un tren determinado en las columnas es un horario de *salida*, el *último* un horario de *llegada*.

TRENES DIRECTOS Y ENLACES

Los horarios en caracteres normales representan servicios directos. Así, en el ejemplo **D**, el tren **8503**, naciendo en Paris, circula de Bordeaux a Toulouse, haciendo escala en Agen y Montauban. No para en Marmande ni, claro, en ninguna de las estaciones del ramal de Hendaye, lo cual está indicado por la presencia del símbolo | en el centro de la columna enfrente de los nombres de estas estaciones.

Como acabamos de ver, el tren **8503** no hace escala en Marmande. Sin embargo los pasajeros que vienen de Paris pueden llegar a esta localidad mediante un cambio de tren en Bordeaux, de donde pueden tomar el tren, indicado en la columna siguiente, que sale de Bordeaux a las 1015. Del mismo modo, los pasajeros del tren **8503** – si bien que acaba su recorrido en Toulouse – deseosos de llegar a Castelnaudary o a Carcassonne tienen a su disposición los días laborables (⚒) un tren de enlace a las 1220. Nótese que los trenes saliendo respectivamente de Bordeaux a las 1015 y de Toulouse a las 1220, si bien que están señalados en la misma columna, son dos trenes distintos entre los cuales no hay enlace, lo cual está indicado por el símbolo ▬ que los separa.

Se refiere, en el caso de horarios imprimidos en *cursivo*, a correspondencias, es decir servicios de enlace que suponen un *cambio de tren*. Así, en el ejemplo **C** de la página 6, el tren **473** de Paris no hace escala en Orléans, estación situada, como lo indica la impresión sangrada de su nombre, en un ramal. Sin embargo existe para los pasajeros deseando iniciar su viaje en Orléans un tren, saliendo de allí a las *2237*, que enlaza en la estación de la línea principal de Les Aubrais-Orléans con el tren **473**.

¡Ojo! Bien que creemos, apoyándonos en las indicaciones suministradas por las administraciones, que todos los enlaces indicados en la guía son factibles, no podemos garantizar que las correspondencias serán respectadas en la práctica, sobre todo en el caso de retrasos. Hay que ser consciente también que el transbordo en las estaciones de las grandes ciudades puede suponer un desplazamiento bastante largo a pie y el uso de escaleras. A usted de decidir cuánto tiempo le conviene para efectuar cómodamente los cambios de tren.

LAS NOTAS AL PIE DEL CUADRO

Cuando los signos convencionales no bastan para expresar toda la información que hay que comunicar acerca de un tren, entonces se remite el lector a una nota al pie del cuadro.

El símbolo ♦ en el encabezamiento de la columna quiere decir: consulte la nota que lleva el número del tren interesado. Una letra (**A**, **B**...) significa que hay que consultar la nota que lleva esta letra. Come se ve en los ejemplos, las notas comunican datos muy importantes como días de circulación, composición de los trenes, coches directos, y es imprescindible consultarlas cuando prepara su viaje. Una minúscula (**b**, **c**...) al lado de un horario determinado se refiere únicamente a ese horario. Por ejemplo, en **D**, la **z** al lado de los dos últimos horarios del tren **162/163** le remite a una nota que le explica que las llegadas serán anticipadas a partir del día 10 de marzo (pero *solo* en Marseille y Nice).

Nótese que en los casos donde no se comunica ningún día ni fecha la circulación del tren es *diaria*. Así, en el ejemplo **E**, el tren *Le Ventadour* sale de Bordeaux a las 0747 para Lyon por vía de Brive – pero sólo en los días indicados en la nota **V**. En la columna siguiente, sin embargo, se indica un servicio diario de Bordeaux a Brive. Es decir que hay una salida de Bordeaux para Brive a las 0747 aun cuando no circula *Le Ventadour*.

Salvo indicación contraria los trenes llevan coches de primera y de segunda clase. Los trenes que llevan exclusivamente coches de segunda clase están distinguidos o por la cifra '2' el la parte superior de la columna, por (2), ━ 2 cl., etc. en las notas, o por la mención '2nd class' en el encabezamiento general del cuadro.

OTRAS PÁGINAS QUE CONSULTAR

En la página 10 encontrará otras informaciones generales sobre el tema de los viajes por tren en Europa. Se le recomienda vivamente que consulte también los preámbulos al comienzo de cada sección nacional: le proporcionarán datos importantes sobre las particularidades de cada país: tipos de trenes, restauración, pago de suplementos, necesidades de reservación anticipada, etc.

The following is designed to be a concise guide to travelling in Europe by train. For more details of accommodation available, catering, supplements etc., see the introduction to each country.

BUYING YOUR TICKET

Train tickets must be purchased before travelling, either from travel agents or at the station ticket office (or machine). Where a station has neither a ticket office nor a ticket machine, the ticket may usually be purchased on the train.

Tickets which are not dated when purchased (for example in France, Italy and the Netherlands) must be validated before travel in one of the machines at the entrance to the platform.

In certain Eastern European countries foreign nationals may have to buy international rail tickets at the office of the state tourist board concerned and not at the railway station. The tickets can sometimes only be purchased in Western currency and buying tickets can take a long time.

All countries in Europe (except Albania) offer two classes of rail accommodation, usually 1st and 2nd class. 1st class is more comfortable and therefore more expensive than 2nd class. Local trains are often 2nd class only. In Southern and Eastern Europe, 1st class travel is advisable for visitors as fares are reasonable and 2nd class can be very overcrowded.

RESERVATIONS

Many express trains in Europe are restricted to passengers holding advance seat reservations, particularly in France, Sweden and Spain. This is shown by the symbol 🅁 in the tables, or by notes in the introduction to each country. All *TGV, Eurostar* and *Pendolino* trains require a reservation, as do all long-distance trains in Spain.

Reservations can usually be made up to two months in advance. A small fee is charged, but where a supplement is payable the reservation fee is often included. Reservations can often be made on other long-distance services and this is recommended at busy times.

SUPPLEMENTS

Many countries have faster or more luxurious train services for which an extra charge is made. This supplement is payable when the ticket is purchased and often includes the price of a seat reservation. The supplement can sometimes be paid on the train, but usually at extra cost. The introduction to each country gives further information. On certain high-speed services, the first class fare includes the provision of a meal.

RAIL PASSES

Tickets are available which give unlimited travel on all trains in a given area. These rail passes range from Eurail and InterRail passes which cover the whole of Western Europe for up to one month, to local passes which cover limited areas for 1 day. Passports may need to be shown when purchasing such tickets. A special feature on rail passes appears each year in our May edition and also in the quarterly Independent Travellers Edition.

FINDING YOUR TRAIN

At most stations departures are listed on large paper sheets (often yellow), and/or on electronic departure indicators. These list trains by departure, giving principal stops, and indicate from which platform they leave.

On each platform of principal European stations, a display board can be found giving details of the main trains calling at that platform. This includes the location of individual coaches, together with their destinations and the type of accommodation provided.

A sign may be carried on the side of the carriage indicating the train name, principal stops and destination and a label or sign near the door will indicate the number allocated to the carriage, which is shown on reservation tickets. 1st class accommodation is usually indicated by a yellow band above the windows and doors and/or a figure 1 near the door or on the windows

A sign above the compartment door will indicate seat numbers and which seats are reserved. In non-compartment trains, reserved seats have labels on their headrests. In some countries, notably Sweden and Yugoslavia, reserved seats are not marked and occupants will be asked to move when the passenger who has reserved the seat boards the train.

✕ CATERING 🍸

Many higher quality and long-distance trains in Europe have restaurant cars serving full meals, usually with waiter service, or serve meals at the passenger's seat. Such trains are identified with the symbol ✕ in the tables. Full meals may only be available at set times, sometimes with separate sittings, and may only be available to passengers holding first class tickets. However, the restaurant car is often supplemented by a counter or trolley service offering light snacks and drinks.

Other types of catering are shown with the symbol 🍸. This varies from a self-service buffet car serving light meals (sometimes called bistro or café) to a trolley which is wheeled through the train, serving only drinks and sandwiches. Where possible, the introduction to each country gives further information on the level of catering to be expected on particular types of train.

The catering shown may not be available throughout the journey and may be suspended or altered at weekends or on holidays.

SLEEPING CARS 🛏

Sleeping cars are shown as 🛏 in the timetables. Standard sleeping car types have bedroom style compartments with limited washing facilities and full bedding. Toilets are located at one or both ends of the coach. An attendant travels with each car or pair of cars and will serve drinks and continental breakfast at an extra charge. 1st class sleeping compartments have one or two berths (in Britain and Norway, and in older Swedish sleeping cars, two berth compartments require only 2nd class tickets) and 2nd class compartments have three berths. Some trains convey special T2 cabins, shown as 🛏 (T2) in the tables, with one berth in 1st class and two berths in 2nd class.

Compartments are allocated for occupation exclusively by men or by women except when married couples or families occupy all berths. Children travelling alone, or who cannot be accommodated in the same compartment as their family, are placed in women's compartments. In Russia and other countries of the former USSR, however, berths are allocated in strict order of booking and men and women often share the same compartments.

Some trains have communicating doors between sleeping compartments which can be opened to create a larger room if both compartments are occupied by the same family group. Berths can be reserved up to 2 months (3 months on certain trains) before the date of travel and early reservation is recommended as space is limited, especially on French ski trains and in Eastern Europe. Berths must be claimed within 15 minutes of boarding the train or they may be resold.

HOTEL TRAINS

A new generation of overnight trains known collectively as Hotel trains are now running on a selection of national and international routes. The facilities are of a higher standard than those offered in conventional sleeping cars, and special fares are payable. The trains fall into the following categories:

City Night Line: Most night trains radiating from Germany, as well as domestic overnight trains within Germany, now come under the *City Night Line* banner. They operate on around 30 routes serving nine countries, and are shown as *CNL* in our tables. *De Luxe* class consists of one or two berth cabins, with one or two moveable armchairs, a table and an en suite washroom containing toilet, washbasin and shower. *Comfort* compartments have two berths, the upper of which folds away against the cabin wall, and the lower becomes a seat for day use. There are also four berth family compartments as well as couchettes and reclining seats (sleeperettes). A first class ticket is required for *De Luxe* compartments (but no longer for single occupancy of a *Comfort* compartment). A new rule on *CNL* trains is that only entire compartments can be booked, so people travelling alone must book a single compartment rather than sharing with others.

Trenhotel (Spain). These trains, of the *Talgo* type, run on the international routes from Madrid to Paris and Lisboa, and from Barcelona to Paris, Zürich and Milano. They also run on internal routes within Spain, from Barcelona to A Coruña, Vigo, Málaga and Sevilla and v.v., and Madrid to A Coruña and Vigo and v.v. The highest class of accommodation is known as *Gran Clase*, which has shower and toilet facilities in each compartment and can be used for single or double occupancy.

Compartments with showers can also now be found on a number of services in Sweden, Norway and Italy, and other international routes include Wien to Zürich and Roma, the Amsterdam - Warszawa *Jan Kiepura* and the *Berlin Night Express* running between Berlin and Malmö. Further details of sleeper services are shown in our Night Trains feature in the November edition.

COUCHETTES ▬

Couchettes (▬) are a more basic form of overnight accommodation consisting of simple bunk beds with a sheet, blanket and pillow. The couchettes are converted from ordinary seating cars for the night, and there are usually 4 berths per compartment in 1st class, 6 berths in 2nd class. On certain trains (e.g. in Austria and Italy), 4 berth compartments are available to 2nd class passengers, at a higher supplement. Washing and toilet facilities are provided at the ends of each coach. Men and women are booked into the same compartments and are expected to sleep in daytime clothes. A small number of trains in Germany, however, have women-only couchette compartments.

WHEELCHAIR ACCESS ♿

High-quality main line and international trains are now often equipped to accommodate passengers in wheelchairs. Access ramps are available at many stations and some trains are fitted with special lifts. The following trains have at least one wheelchair space, often with accessible toilets:

International: all Eurostar trains, many EC and other trains. CityNightLine trains have a special compartment. *Austria:* many IC/EC trains. *Denmark:* IC and Lyn trains. *France:* all TGV trains and many other long distance services. *Germany:* all EC, ICE, IC and IR trains. *Italy:* all Pendolino and many EC or IC trains. *Netherlands:* most trains. *Sweden:* X2000 and most IC and IR trains, some sleeping cars. *Switzerland:* All IC, most EC and some regional trains. *Austria, Great Britain, Ireland, Poland:* certain trains only.

Most of these railways publish guides to accessibility, and some countries, for example France, provide special staff to help disabled travellers. Wheelchair users normally need to reserve in advance, stating their requirements. The Editor would welcome information for countries not listed.

CAR-SLEEPERS

Trains which convey motor cars operate throughout much of Europe and are shown in Table **1** for international services and Table **2** for other services. The motor cars are conveyed in special wagons while passengers travel in sleeping cars or couchettes, usually (but not always) in the same train.

LUGGAGE & BICYCLES

Luggage may be registered at many larger stations and sent separately by rail to your destination. In some countries, bicycles may also be registered in advance and certain local and some express trains will convey bicycles (there may be a charge). The relevant railways will advise exact details on request.

HEALTH REQUIREMENTS

It is not mandatory for visitors to Europe to be vaccinated against infectious diseases unless they are travelling from areas where these are endemic. For travellers' peace of mind, however, protection against the following diseases should be considered:

AIDS	Cholera
Hepatitis A	Hepatitis B
Polio	Rabies
Tetanus	Typhoid

Full information is available from the manual published by the World Health Organisation, and travellers should seek advice from their Travel Agent.

DRINKING WATER

Tap water is usually safe to drink in most parts of Europe. The water in washrooms or toilets on trains is, however, not suitable for drinking. Those who doubt the purity of the tap water are recommended to boil it, to use sterilisation tablets, or to drink bottled water.

CLIMATE

Most of Europe lies within the temperate zone but there can be considerable differences between North and South, East and West, as illustrated in the table below. Local temperatures are also affected by altitude and the difference between summer and winter temperatures tends to be less marked in coastal regions than in areas far removed from the sea.

	București	Dublin	Madrid	Moskva
JANUARY				
Highest	2°	8°	10°	− 6°
Lowest	− 6°	3°	3°	− 12°
Rain days	6	13	9	11
APRIL				
Highest	18°	11°	18°	10°
Lowest	6°	4°	7°	2°
Rain days	7	10	11	9
JULY				
Highest	29°	19°	31°	23°
Lowest	16°	11°	18°	14°
Rain days	7	9	3	12
OCTOBER				
Highest	18°	14°	19°	8°
Lowest	6°	8°	10°	2°
Rain days	5	11	9	10

Highest = Average highest daily temperature in °C
Lowest = Average lowest daily temperature in °C
Rain days = Average number of days with recorded precipitation

Source : World Weather Information Service

METRIC CONVERSION TABLES

The Celsius system of temperature measurement, the metric system of distance measurement and the twenty-four hour clock are used throughout this book. The tables below give Fahrenheit, mile and twelve-hour clock equivalents.

TEMPERATURE

°C	°F
−20	−4
−15	5
−10	14
−5	23
0	32
5	41
10	50
15	59
20	68
25	77
30	86
35	95
40	104

Conversion formulae :
°C = (°F – 32) x 5 / 9
°F = (°C x 9 / 5) + 32

DISTANCE

km	miles	km	miles	km	miles
1	0.62	45	27.96	300	186.41
2	1.24	50	31.07	400	248.55
3	1.86	55	34.18	500	310.69
4	2.49	60	37.28	600	372.82
5	3.11	65	40.39	700	434.96
6	3.73	70	43.50	800	497.10
7	4.35	75	46.60	900	559.23
8	4.97	80	49.71	1000	621.37
9	5.59	85	52.82	1100	683.51
10	6.21	90	55.92	1200	745.65
15	9.32	95	59.03	1300	807.78
20	12.43	100	62.14	1400	869.92
25	15.53	125	77.67	1500	932.06
30	18.64	150	93.21	2000	1242.74
35	21.75	175	108.74	3000	1864.11
40	24.85	200	124.27	4000	2485.48

TIME

Midnight departure	=	0000
1 am	=	0100
5 am	=	0500
5.30 am	=	0530
11 am	=	1100
12 noon	=	1200
1 pm	=	1300
3.45 pm	=	1545
Midnight arrival	=	2400

CURRENCY CONVERSION

The information shown below is intended to be indicative only. Rates fluctuate from day to day and commercial exchange rates normally include a commission element.

Country	unit	1 GBP=	1 USD=	1 EUR=	100 JPY=
Euro zone (‡)	**euro**	**1.12**	**0.74**	**1.00**	**0.77**
Albania	lek	148.34	97.22	132.17	101.98
Belarus	rubl	4224.94	2769.00	3764.46	2904.49
Bosnia	marka	2.20	1.44	1.96	1.51
Bulgaria	lev	2.20	1.44	1.96	1.51
Croatia	kuna	8.28	5.43	7.38	5.69
Czech Republic	koruna	30.19	19.79	26.90	20.76
Denmark	krone	8.36	5.48	7.45	5.74
Estonia	kroon	17.56	11.51	15.65	12.07
Hungary	forint	321.41	210.65	286.38	220.96
Iceland	krona	191.51	125.52	170.64	131.66
Latvia	lats	0.80	0.52	0.71	0.55
Lithuania	litas	3.88	2.54	3.45	2.66
Macedonia	denar	69.21	45.36	61.67	47.58
Moldova	leu	17.21	11.28	15.34	11.83
Norway	krone	9.89	6.48	8.82	6.80
Poland	złoty	5.00	3.28	4.46	3.44
Romania	leu nou	4.69	3.08	4.18	3.23
Russia	rubl	48.91	32.06	43.58	33.63
Serbia	dinar	105.92	69.42	94.38	72.82
Sweden	krona	11.90	7.80	10.61	8.18
Switzerland	franc	1.69	1.10	1.50	1.16
Turkey	yeni lira	2.38	1.56	2.12	1.64
Ukraine	hryvnya	11.65	7.63	10.38	8.01
United Kingdom	pound	1.00	0.66	0.89	0.69

‡ – Austria, Belgium, Cyprus, Finland, France, Germany, Greece, Ireland, Italy, Luxembourg, Malta, the Netherlands, Portugal, Slovakia, Slovenia, and Spain.

The euro is also legal tender in Andorra, Kosovo, Monaco, Montenegro, San Marino, and the Vatican City.

PASSPORTS AND VISAS

Nationals of one country intending to travel to or pass through another country normally require a valid passport and will also require a visa unless a special visa-abolition agreement has been made between the countries concerned. The limit of stay permitted in each country is usually 3 months.

Applications for visas should be made well in advance of the date of travel to the local consulate of the country concerned. Consuls usually make a charge for issuing a visa. Before issuing a transit visa, a consul normally requires to see the visa of the country of destination.

The possession of a valid passport or visa does not necessarily grant the holder automatic access to all areas of the country to be visited. Certain countries have zones which are restricted or prohibited to foreign nationals.

All border controls have been abolished, however, between those countries which have signed the **Schengen Agreement** (see list below), and a visa allowing entry to any of these countries is valid in all of them.

LIST OF SCHENGEN AREA COUNTRIES

Austria, Belgium, Czech Republic, Denmark, Estonia, Finland, France, Germany, Greece, Hungary, Iceland, Italy, Latvia, Lithuania, Luxembourg, Malta, Netherlands, Norway, Poland, Portugal, Slovakia, Slovenia, Spain, Sweden. Switzerland has also started to apply Schengen area rules.

GLOSSARY

	FRANÇAIS	ITALIANO	DEUTSCH	ESPAÑOL
additional trains	d'autres trains	ulteriori treni	weitere Züge	otros trenes
also	[circule] aussi	[si effettua] anche	[verkehrt] auch	[circula] también
alteration	modification	variazione	Änderung	modificación
approximately	environ	circa	ungefähr	aproximadamente
arrival, arrives (a.)	arrivée, arrive	arrivo, arriva	Ankunft, kommt an	llegada, llega
and at the same minutes past each hour until	puis toutes les heures aux mêmes minutes jusqu'à	poi ai stessi minuti di ogni ora fino a	und so weiter im Takt bis	luego a los mismos minutos de cada hora hasta
calls at	s'arrête à	ferma a	hält in	efectúa parada en
certain	déterminé	certo	bestimmt	determinado
change at	changer à	cambiare a	umsteigen in	cambiar en
composition	composition	composizione	Zugbildung	composición
confirmation	confirmation	conferma	Bestätigung	confirmación
connection	correspondance, relation	coincidenza, relazione	Anschluss, Verbindung	correspondencia, enlace
conveys	comporte, achemine	ha in composizione	befördert, führt	lleva
daily	tous les jours	giornalmente	täglich	diariamente
delay	retard	ritardo	Verspätung	retraso
departure, departs (d.)	départ, part	partenza, parte	Abfahrt, fährt ab	salida, sale
earlier	plus tôt	più presto	früher	más temprano
engineering work	travaux de voie	lavori sul binario	Bauarbeiten	obras de vía
even / uneven dates	jours pairs / impairs	giorni pari / dispari	gerade / ungerade Daten	fechas pares / impares
every 30 minutes	toutes les 30 minutes	ogni 30 minuti	alle 30 Minuten	cada 30 minutos
except	sauf	escluso	außer	excepto
fast(er)	(plus) rapide	(più) rapido	schnell(er)	(más) rápido
for	pour	per	für	para
from Rennes	(en provenance) de Rennes	(proviene) da Rennes	von Rennes	(procede) de Rennes
from Jan. 15	à partir du 15 janvier	dal 15 di gennaio	vom 15. Januar (an)	desde el 15 de enero
hourly	toutes les heures	ogni ora	stündlich	cada hora
hours (hrs)	heures	ore	Stunden	horas
journey	voyage, trajet	viaggio, percorso	Reise	viaje, trayecto
journey time	temps de parcours	tempo di tragitto	Reisezeit	duración del recorrido
later	plus tard	più tardi	später	más tarde
may	peut, peuvent	può, possono	kann, können	puede(n)
minutes (mins)	minutes	minuti	Minuten	minutos
not	ne [circule] pas	non [si effettua]	[verkehrt] nicht	no [circula]
not available	pas disponible	non disponibile	nicht erhältlich	no disponible
on the dates shown in Table **81**	les jours indiqués dans le tableau **81**	nei giorni indicati nel quadro **81**	an den in der Tabelle **81** angegebene Daten	los días indicados en el cuadro **81**
only	seulement	esclusivamente	nur	sólo
operator	entreprise de transports	azienda di trasporto	Verkehrsunternehmen	empresa de transportes
other	autre	altro	andere	otros
runs	circule	circola, si effettua	verkehrt	circula
sailing	traversée	traversata	Überfahrt	travesía
ship	bateau, navire	nave, battello	Schiff	barco
stopping trains	trains omnibus	treni regionali	Nahverkehrszüge	trenes regionales
stops	s'arrête	ferma	hält	efectúa parada
subject to	sous réserve de	soggetto a	vorbehaltlich	sujeto a
summer	été	estate	Sommer	verano
supplement payable	avec supplément	con pagamento di supplemento	zuschlagpflichtig	con pago de suplemento
then	puis	poi	dann	luego
through train	train direct	treno diretto	durchgehender Zug	tren directo
timings	horaires	orari	Zeitangaben	horarios
to York	vers, à destination de York	(diretto) a York	nach York	(continúa) a York
to / until July 23	jusqu'au 23 juillet	fino al 23 di luglio	bis zum 23. Juli	hasta el día 23 de julio
to pick up	pour laisser monter	per viaggiatori in partenza	zum Zusteigen	para recoger viajeros
to set down	pour laisser descendre	per viaggiatori in arrivo	zum Aussteigen	para dejar viajeros
unless otherwise shown	sauf indication contraire	salvo indicazione contraria	sofern nicht anders angezeigt	salvo indicación contraria
valid	valable	valido	gültig	válido
when train **44** runs	lors de la circulation du train **44**	quando circola il treno **44**	beim Verkehren des Zuges **44**	cuando circula el tren **44**
winter	hiver	inverno	Winter	invierno

PICTOGRAMS

Information
Information
Renseignements
Información

Ticket office
Fahrkartenschalter
Guichet
Despacho de billetes

Luggage office
Gepäckaufbewahrung
Consigne
Consigna

Luggage lockers
Gepäckschließfächer
Consigne automatique
Taquillas de equipaje

Ladies
Damen
Dames
Señoras

Gentlemen
Herren
Hommes
Caballeros

Lost property
Fundbüro
Objets trouvés
Objetos perdidos

Bureau de change
Geldwechsel
Bureau de change
Cambio

Post office
Postamt
Poste
Correos

Telephone
Telefon
Téléphone
Teléfono

Restaurant
Restaurant
Restaurant
Restaurante

Buffet
Buffet
Buffet
Comedor

Meeting point
Treffpunkt
Point de rencontre
Lugar de reunión

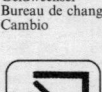

Entrance
Eingang
Entrée
Entrada

Exit
Ausgang
Sortie
Salida

Bus
Bus
Autobus
Autobús

Boat
Schiff
Bateau
Barco

Tram
Straßenbahn
Tramway
Tranvía

INDEX OF PLACES

by table number

🚆 Connection by train from the nearest station shown in this timetable.
⛴ Connection by boat from the nearest station shown in this timetable.
🚌 Connection by bus from the nearest station shown in this timetable.
10/355 Consult both indicated tables to find the best connecting services.

H

HAMBURG

HANNOVER

HEIDELBERG

HELSINKI

I

INNSBRUCK

İSTANBUL

PARIS ✈ CHARLES DE GAULLE

POZNAŃ

PRAHA

Q

R

ROMA

ROTTERDAM

St / Ste

ST PETERBURG

S

SALZBURG

SHEFFIELD

CRUISE TRAINS

The services shown in the European Rail Timetable are the regular scheduled services of the railway companies concerned. However, a number of specialised operators also run luxurious cruise trains taking several days to complete their journey. Overnight accommodation is provided either on the train or in hotels. Cruise trains are bookable only through the operating company or its appointed agents and normal rail tickets are not valid on these trains. A selection of operators is shown below.

The Royal Scotsman: luxury tours of Scotland starting from Edinburgh. Operator: Orient-Express Hotels, Trains & Cruises, 20 Upper Ground, London SE1 9PF, UK; ✆ 0845 077 2222 or +44 (0) 20 7960 0500, fax +44 (0) 207 921 4708. Website: www.royalscotsman.com

El Transcantábrico: 1000-km 8-day rail cruise along Spain's northern coast. Operator: El Transcantábrico, Plaza de los Ferroviarios, s/n. 33012 Oviedo, Spain. ✆ +34 985 981 711, fax +34 985 981 710. Website: www.transcantabrico.feve.es

Trans-Siberian Express: Tours by private hotel train along the Trans-Siberian Railway. Operator: GW Travel Ltd, Denzell House, Denzell Gardens, Dunham Road, Altrincham WA14 4QF, UK. ✆ +44 (0)161 928 9410, fax +44 (0)161 941 6101. Website: www.gwtravel.co.uk. USA agent: MIR Corporation, 85 South Washington Street, Suite 210, Seattle, Washington 98104, USA; ✆ +1 (206) 624 7289, fax +1 (206) 624 7360. Website: www.mircorp.com

Venice Simplon-Orient-Express: This well-known luxury train runs once or twice weekly from late March to early November, mostly on its established London - Paris - Venezia route. Operator: Orient-Express Hotels, Trains & Cruises, 20 Upper Ground, London SE1 9PF, UK; ✆ 0845 077 2222 or +44 (0) 20 7960 0500, fax +44 (0) 207 921 4708. Website: www.orient-express.com

For further details of these and other operators, see our annual Cruise Trains and Rail Holidays feature in the March edition

LIST OF ADVERTISERS

CITY STATION LOCATION PLANS

Passenger railway	Main station
Metro	Local station
Bus / tram line	Bus station
Ferry	Airport

Only those metro, bus, and tram lines which provide inter-station links or connect outlying main stations to the city centre are shown.

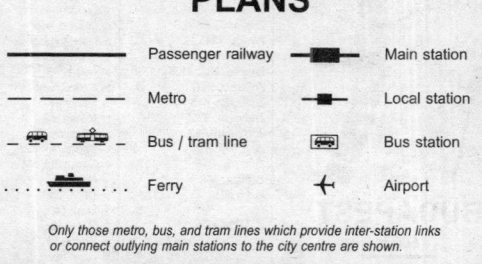

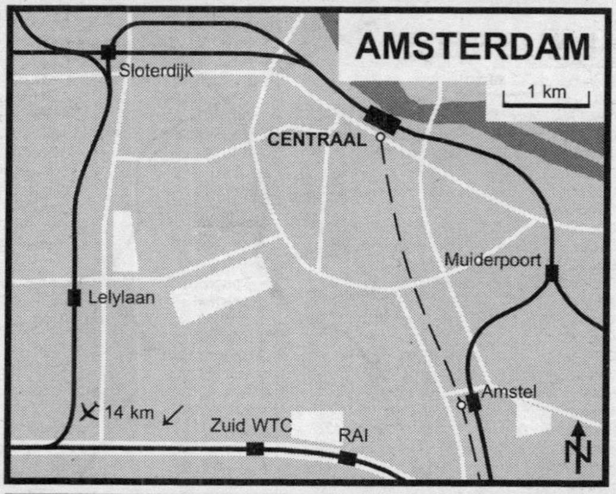

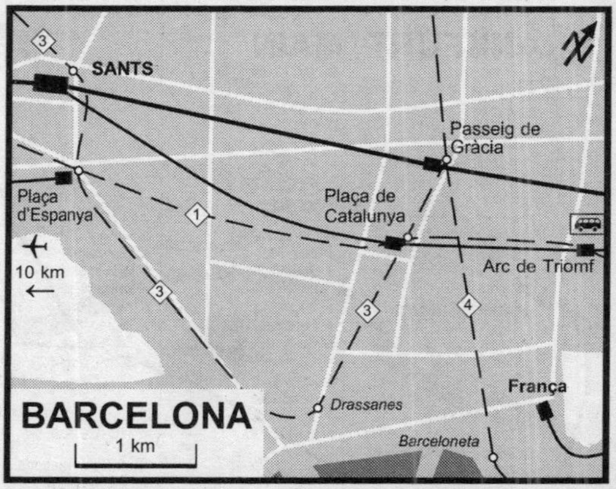

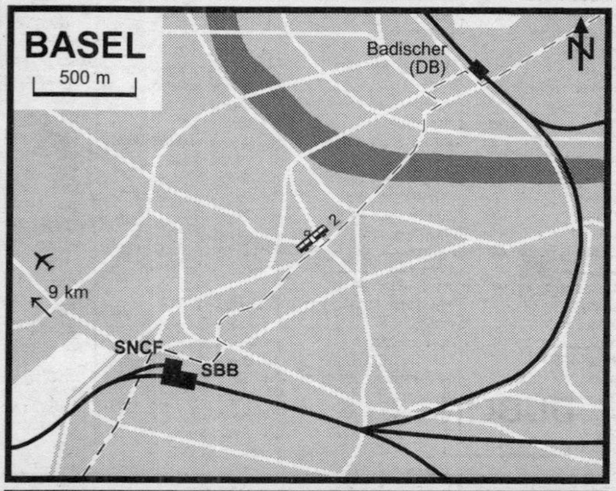

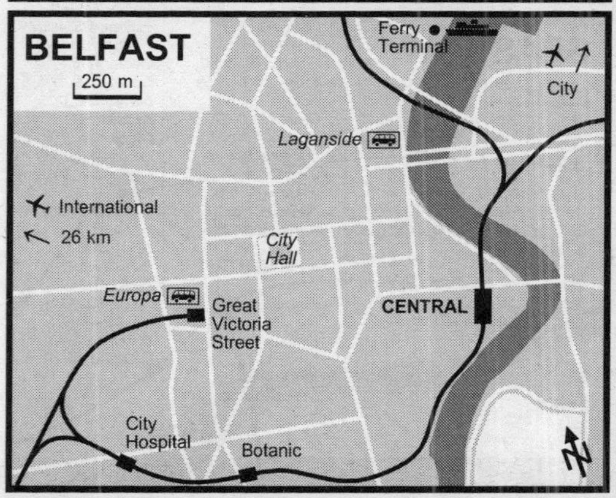

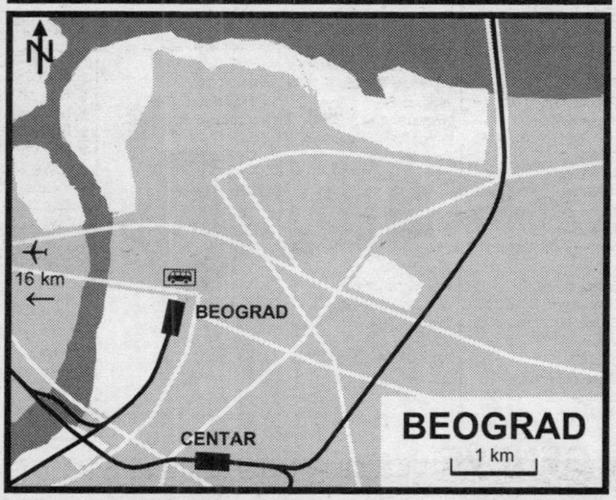

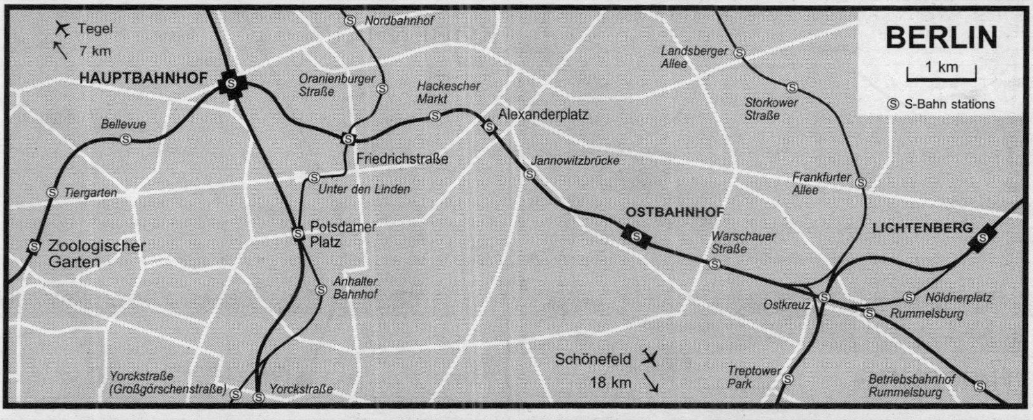

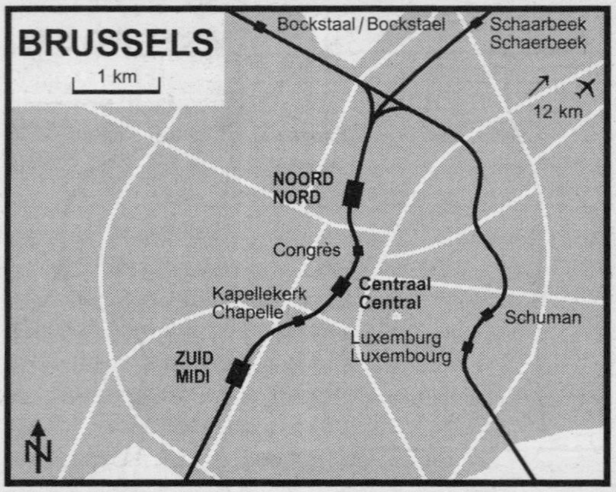
BRUSSELS
1 km
Bockstaal / Bockstael
Schaarbeek
Schaerbeek
12 km
NOORD
NORD
Congrès
Kapellekerk
Chapelle
Centraal
Central
Schuman
Luxemburg
Luxembourg
ZUID
MIDI

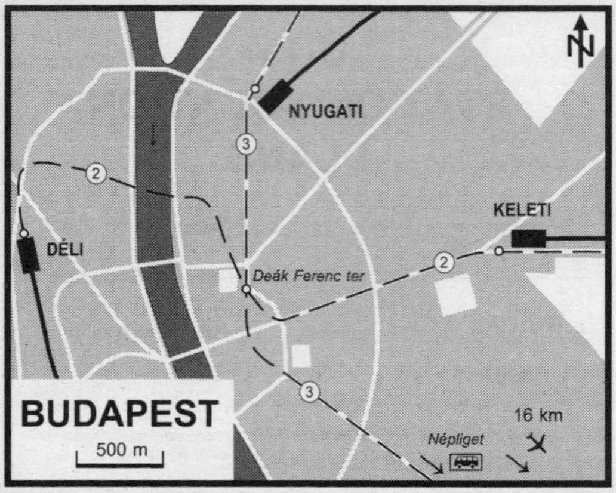
NYUGATI
3
2
DÉLI
KELETI
Deák Ferenc tér
2
3
BUDAPEST
500 m
16 km
Népliget

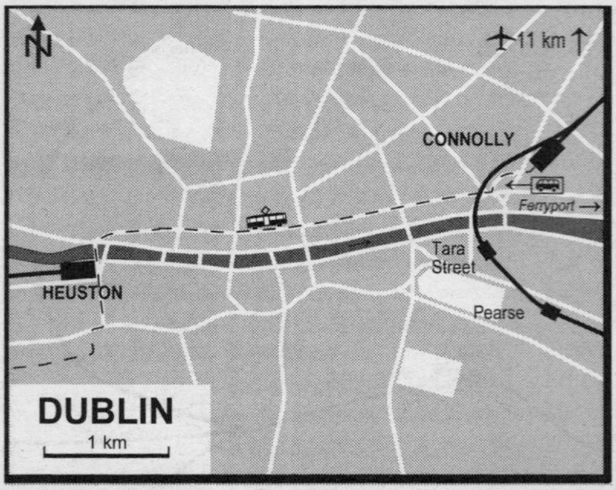
11 km
CONNOLLY
Ferryport
Tara
Street
HEUSTON
Pearse
DUBLIN
1 km

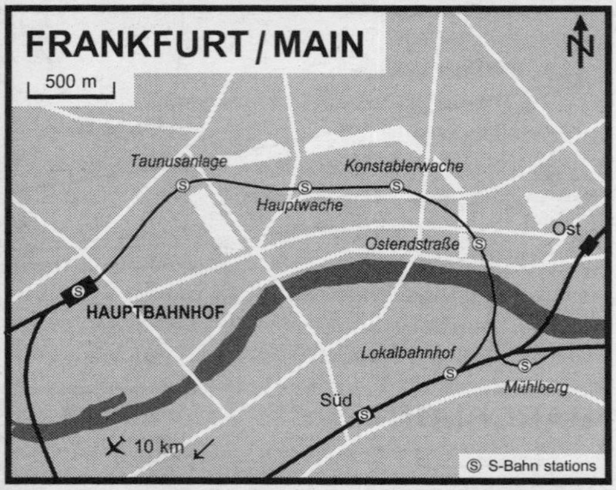
FRANKFURT / MAIN
500 m
Taunusanlage
Konstablerwache
Hauptwache
Ostendstraße
Ost
HAUPTBAHNHOF
Lokalbahnhof
Mühlberg
Süd
10 km
S S-Bahn stations

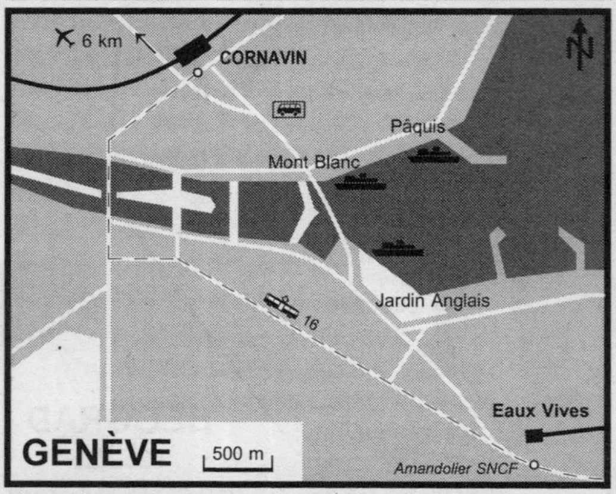
6 km
CORNAVIN
Pâquis
Mont Blanc
Jardin Anglais
16
Eaux Vives
GENÈVE
500 m
Amandolier SNCF

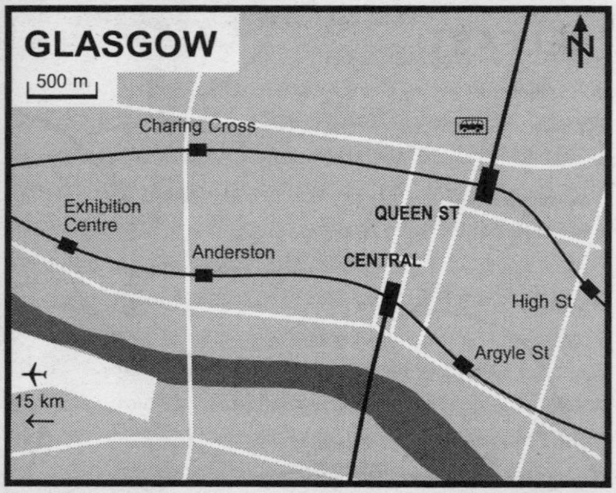
GLASGOW
500 m
Charing Cross
Exhibition
Centre
QUEEN ST
Anderston
CENTRAL
High St
Argyle St
15 km

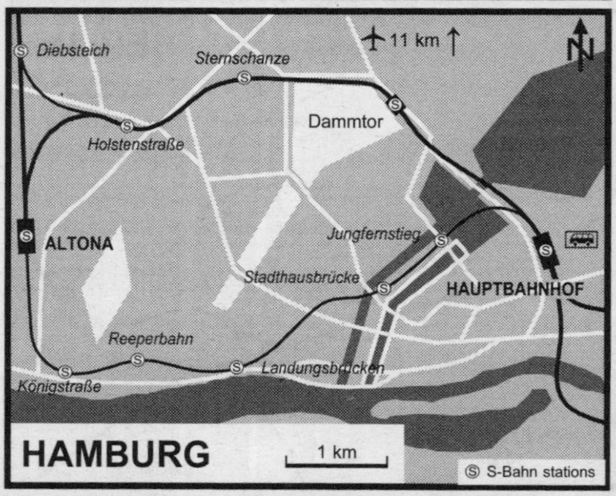
Diebsteich
Sternschanze
11 km
Dammtor
Holstenstraße
ALTONA
Jungfernstieg
Stadthausbrücke
HAUPTBAHNHOF
Reeperbahn
Landungsbrücken
Königstraße
HAMBURG
1 km
S S-Bahn stations

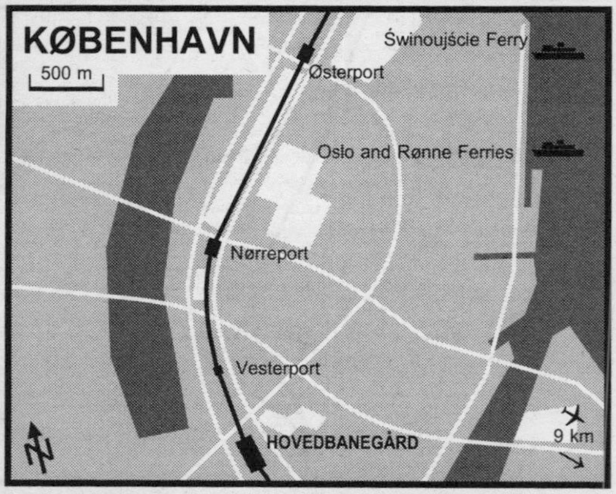
KØBENHAVN
500 m
Świnoujście Ferry
Østerport
Oslo and Rønne Ferries
Nørreport
Vesterport
HOVEDBANEGÅRD
9 km

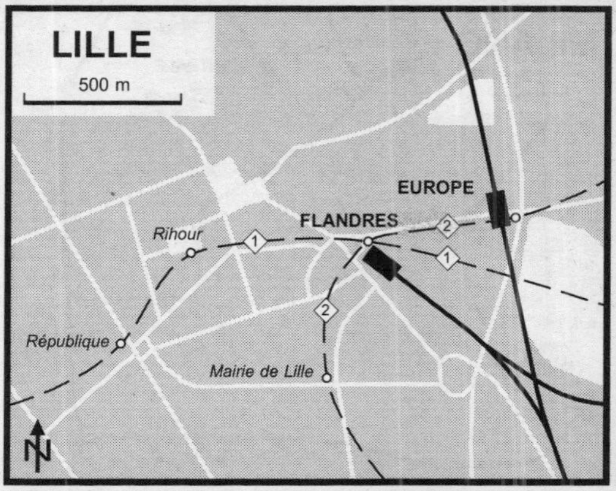
LILLE
500 m
EUROPE
FLANDRES
Rihour
République
Mairie de Lille
1
2

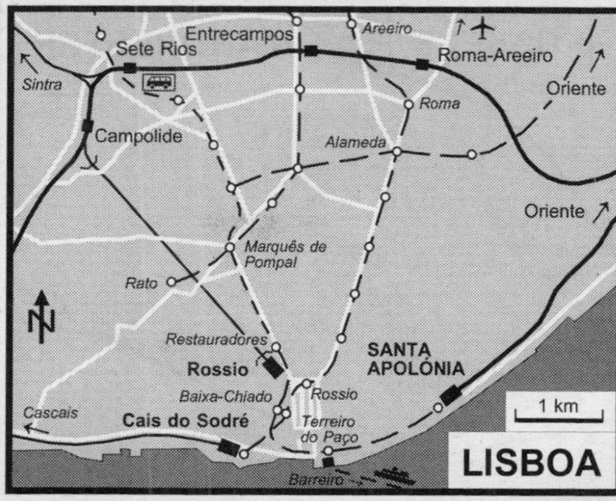
Entrecampos
Areeiro
Sete Rios
Roma-Areeiro
Sintra
Oriente
Roma
Campolide
Alameda
Oriente
Marquês de Pompal
Rato
Restauradores
Rossio
SANTA APOLÓNIA
Baixa-Chiado
Rossio
Cascais
Cais do Sodré
Terreiro do Paço
1 km
Barreiro
LISBOA

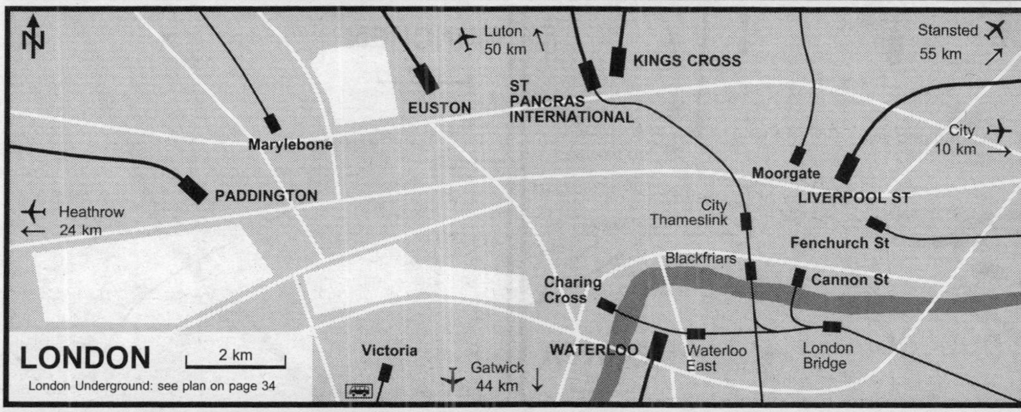
Luton
50 km
Stansted
55 km
KINGS CROSS
ST PANCRAS INTERNATIONAL
EUSTON
Marylebone
City
10 km
Moorgate
LIVERPOOL ST
PADDINGTON
Heathrow
24 km
City Thameslink
Fenchurch St
Blackfriars
Cannon St
Charing Cross
WATERLOO
Waterloo East
London Bridge
Victoria
Gatwick
44 km
LONDON
2 km
London Underground: see plan on page 34

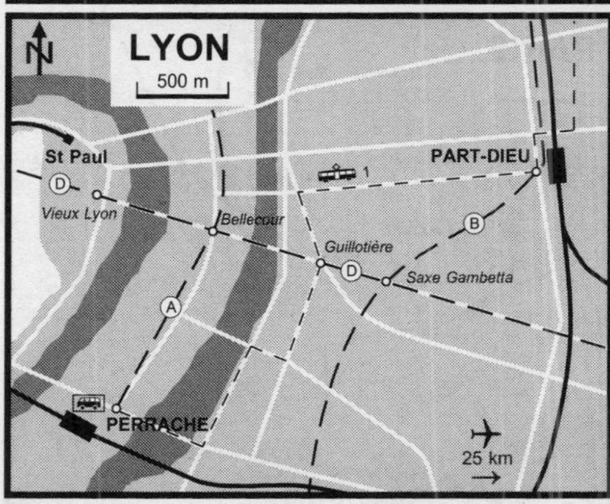
LYON
500 m
St Paul
PART-DIEU
1
D
Vieux Lyon
Bellecour
B
Guillotière
D
Saxe Gambetta
A
PERRACHE
25 km

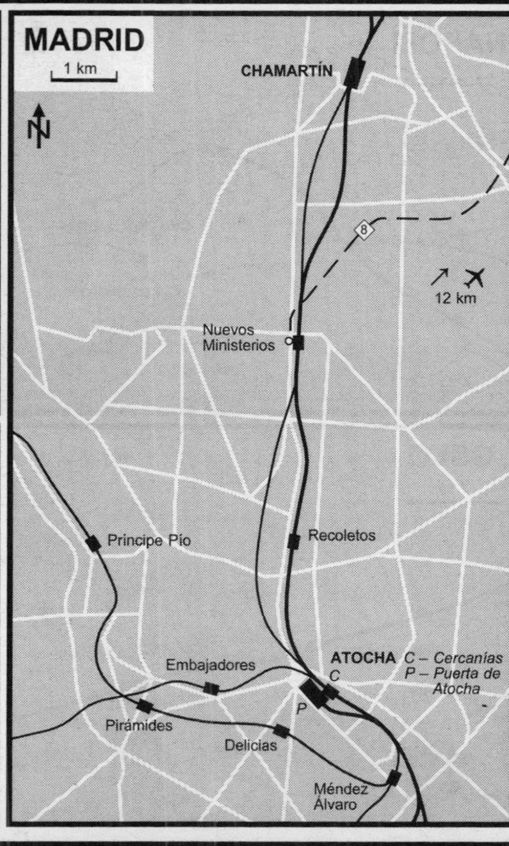
MADRID
1 km
CHAMARTÍN
8
12 km
Nuevos Ministerios
Príncipe Pío
Recoletos
Embajadores
ATOCHA
C
C – Cercanías
P – Puerta de Atocha
P
Pirámides
Delicias
Méndez Álvaro

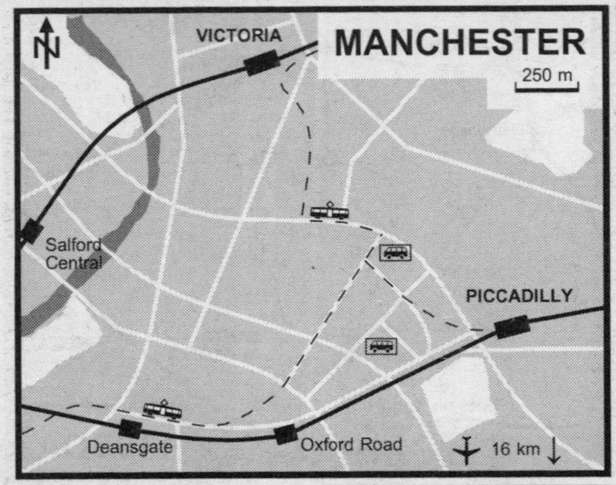
MANCHESTER
250 m
VICTORIA
Salford Central
PICCADILLY
Deansgate
Oxford Road
16 km

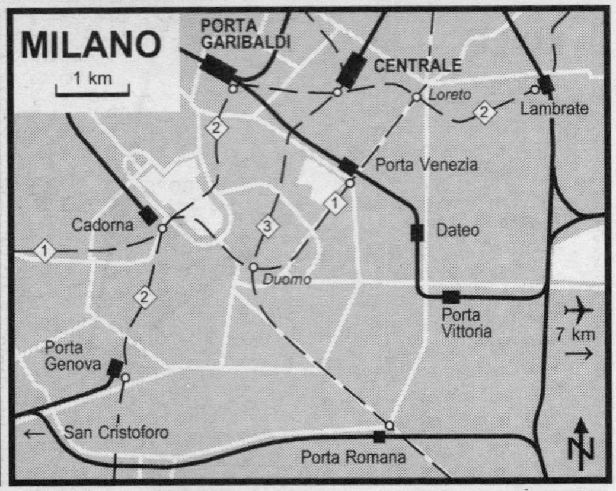
MILANO
1 km
PORTA GARIBALDI
CENTRALE
Loreto
Lambrate
Porta Venezia
Cadorna
Dateo
Duomo
Porta Vittoria
7 km
Porta Genova
San Cristoforo
Porta Romana

27 km
Savyolovsky
Rizhskaya
Yaroslavskaya
BELORUSSKAYA
(Smolenskaya)
OKTYABRSKAYA
(Leningradski vokzal)
Komsomolskaya
Kazanskaya
Kurskaya
KIYEVSKAYA
Paveletskaya
MOSKVA
1 km

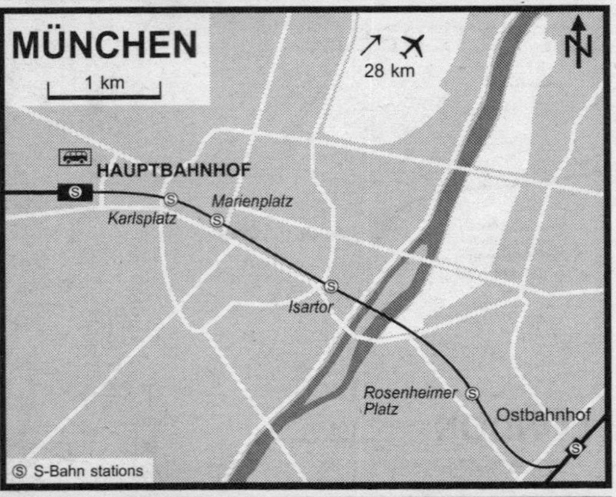
MÜNCHEN
1 km
28 km
HAUPTBAHNHOF
Karlsplatz
Marienplatz
Isartor
Rosenheimer Platz
Ostbahnhof
Ⓢ S-Bahn stations

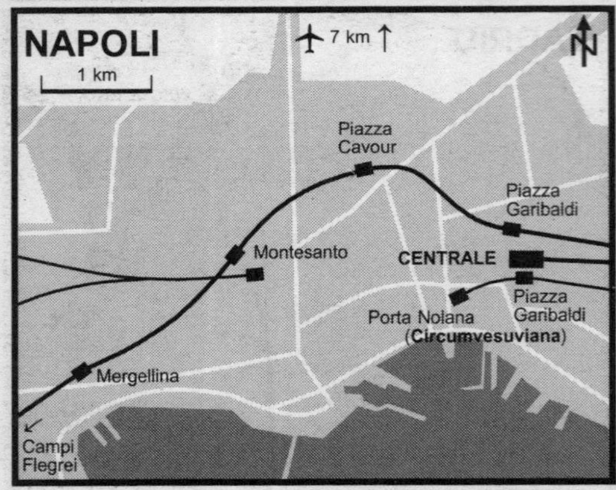
NAPOLI
1 km
7 km
Piazza Cavour
Piazza Garibaldi
Montesanto
CENTRALE
Piazza Garibaldi
Porta Nolana
(Circumvesuviana)
Mergellina
Campi Flegrei

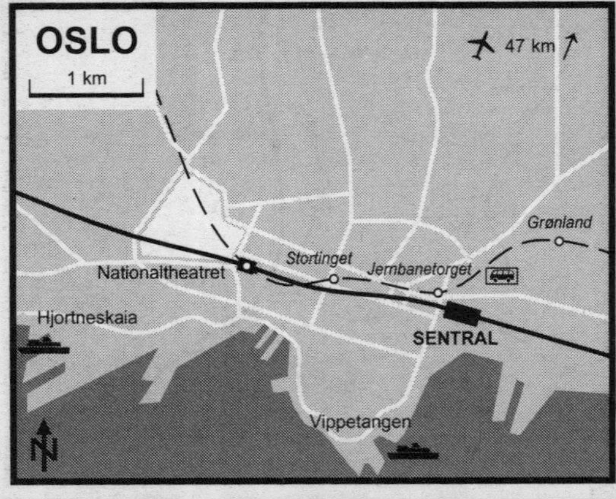
OSLO
1 km
47 km
Grønland
Nationaltheatret
Stortinget
Jernbanetorget
Hjortneskaia
SENTRAL
Vippetangen

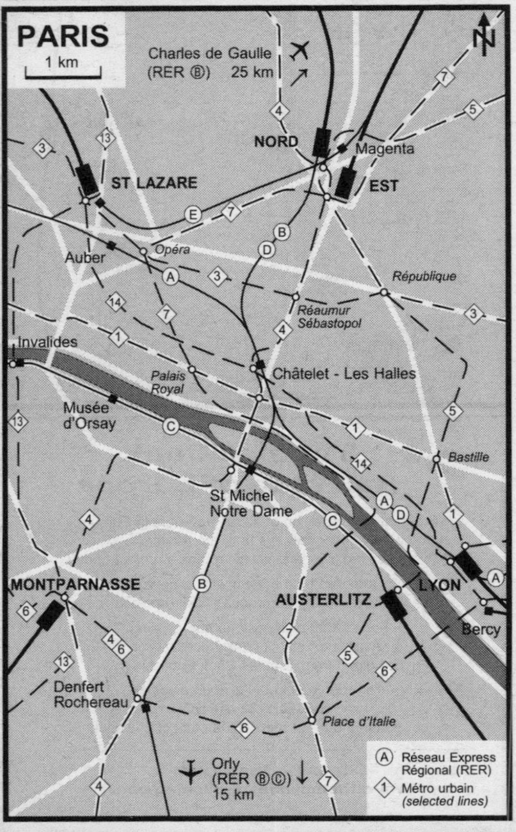
PARIS
1 km
Charles de Gaulle
(RER Ⓑ) 25 km
NORD
Magenta
ST LAZARE
EST
Opéra
Auber
République
Réaumur Sébastopol
Invalides
Châtelet - Les Halles
Palais Royal
Musée d'Orsay
Bastille
St Michel Notre Dame
LYON
MONTPARNASSE
AUSTERLITZ
Bercy
Denfert Rochereau
Place d'Italie
Orly
(RER ⒷⒸ)
15 km
Ⓐ Réseau Express Régional (RER)
◇ Métro urbain (selected lines)

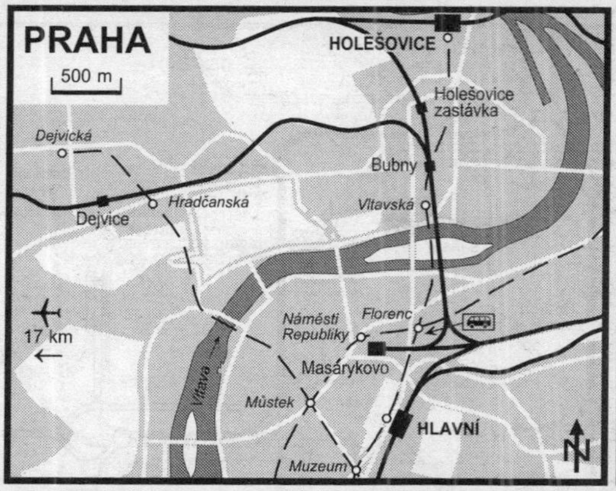
PRAHA
500 m
HOLEŠOVICE
Holešovice zastávka
Dejvická
Bubny
Dejvice
Hradčanská
Vltavská
17 km
Náměstí Republiky
Florenc
Masarykovo
Vltava
Můstek
HLAVNÍ
Muzeum
N

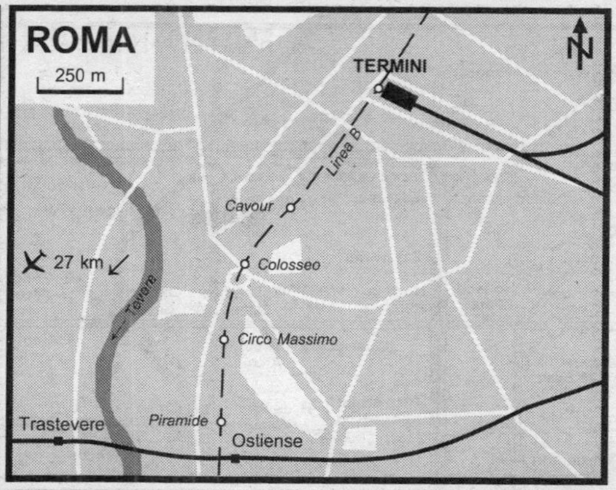
ROMA
250 m
TERMINI
N
Linea B
Cavour
27 km
Colosseo
Tevere
Circo Massimo
Trastevere
Piramide
Ostiense

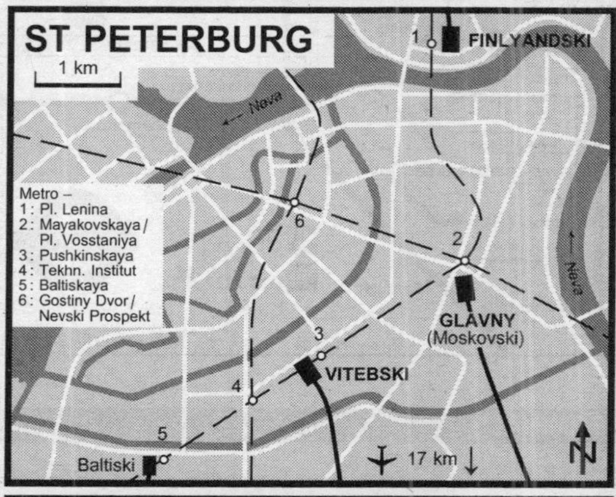
ST PETERBURG
1 km
1
FINLYANDSKI
Neva
Metro –
1: Pl. Lenina
2: Mayakovskaya / Pl. Vosstaniya
3: Pushkinskaya
4: Tekhn. Institut
5: Baltiskaya
6: Gostiny Dvor / Nevski Prospekt
6
2
Neva
GLAVNY (Moskovski)
3
VITEBSKI
4
5
Baltiski
17 km
N

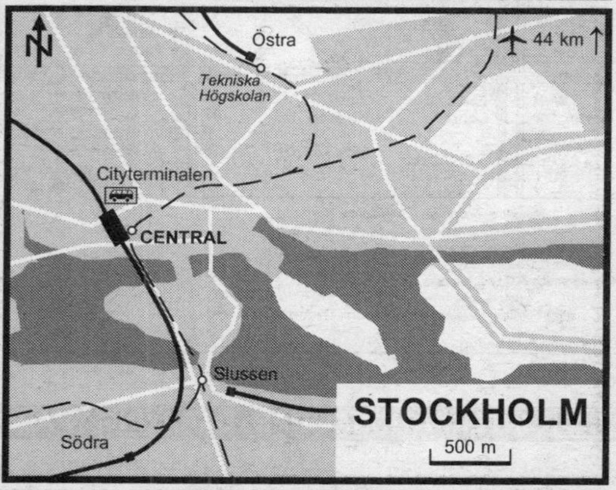
N
Östra
44 km
Tekniska Högskolan
Cityterminalen
CENTRAL
Slussen
STOCKHOLM
Södra
500 m

Mestre 9 km
13 km
VENEZIA
250 m
SANTA LUCIA
Piazzale Roma
Piazza S. Marco
N

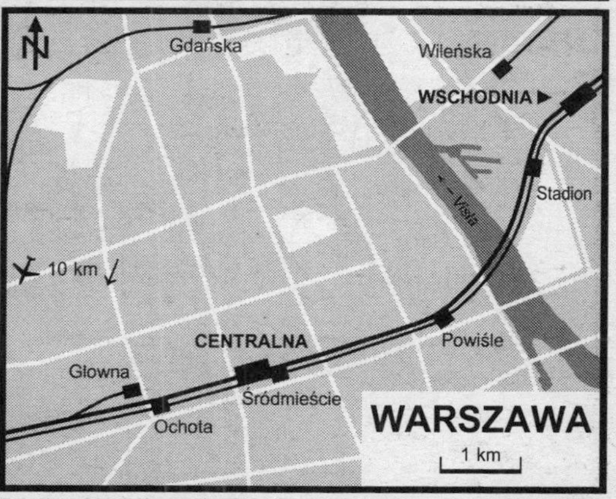
N
Gdańska
Wileńska
WSCHODNIA
Stadion
Wisła
10 km
CENTRALNA
Powiśle
Glowna
Śródmieście
Ochota
WARSZAWA
1 km

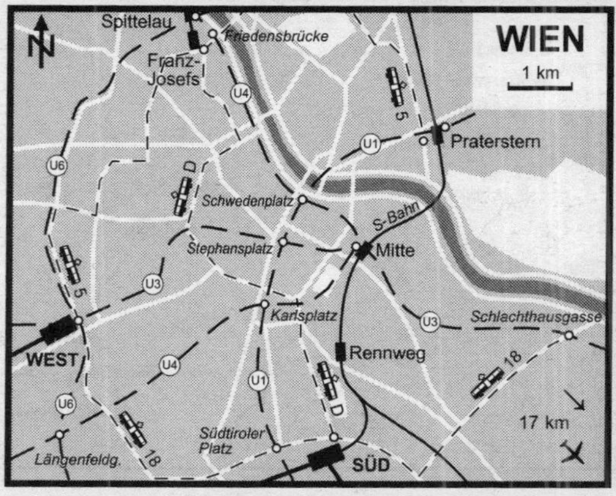
N
Spittelau
Friedensbrücke
Franz-Josefs
U4
WIEN
1 km
5
U1
Praterstern
U6
D
Schwedenplatz
S-Bahn
Stephansplatz
Mitte
5
U3
Karlsplatz
U3
Schlachthausgasse
WEST
U4
Rennweg
18
U1
D
U6
17 km
Südtiroler Platz
Längenfeldg.
18
SÜD

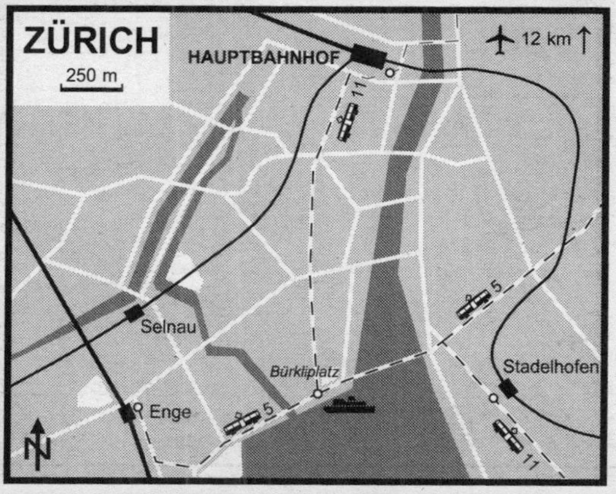
ZÜRICH
250 m
HAUPTBAHNHOF
12 km
11
5
Selnau
Stadelhofen
Bürkliplatz
Enge
5
N
11

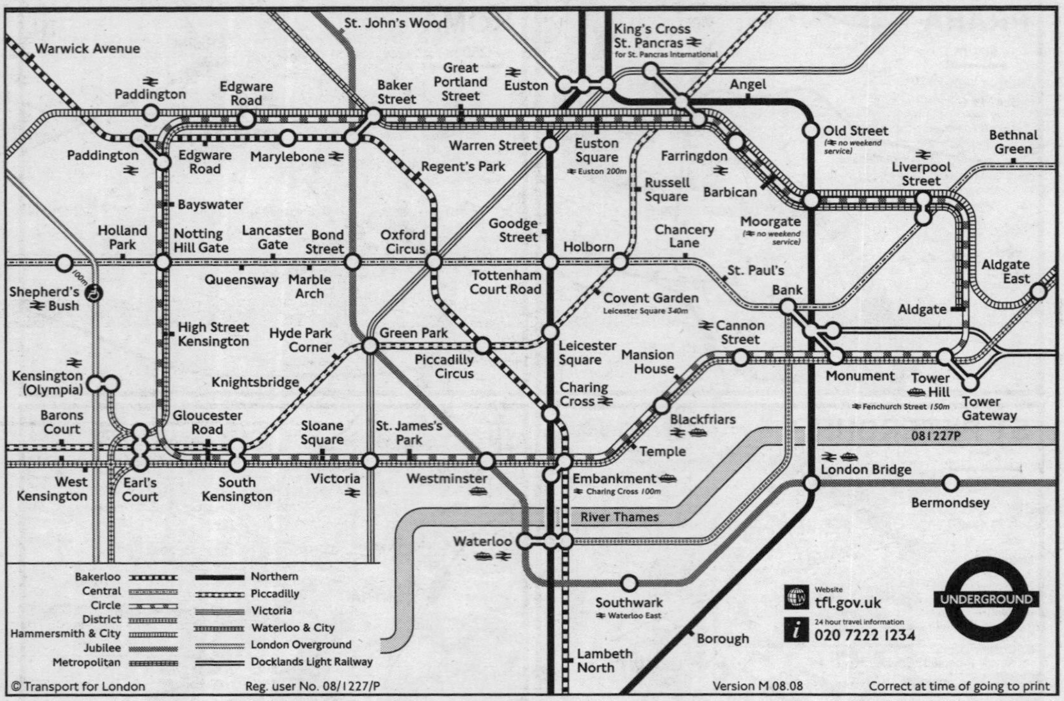
St. John's Wood
Warwick Avenue
King's Cross St. Pancras
for St. Pancras International
Paddington
Edgware Road
Baker Street
Great Portland Street
Euston
Angel
Paddington
Edgware Road
Marylebone
Warren Street
Euston Square
Euston 200m
Farringdon
Old Street
(no weekend service)
Bethnal Green
Liverpool Street
Regent's Park
Russell Square
Barbican
Bayswater
Goodge Street
Chancery Lane
Moorgate
(no weekend service)
Holland Park
Notting Hill Gate
Lancaster Gate
Bond Street
Oxford Circus
Holborn
St. Paul's
Aldgate East
Shepherd's Bush
100m
Queensway
Marble Arch
Tottenham Court Road
Covent Garden
Leicester Square 340m
Bank
Aldgate
High Street Kensington
Hyde Park Corner
Green Park
Cannon Street
Leicester Square
Mansion House
Kensington (Olympia)
Piccadilly Circus
Knightsbridge
Monument
Tower Hill
Charing Cross
Tower Gateway
Fenchurch Street 150m
Barons Court
Gloucester Road
Blackfriars
081227P
Sloane Square
St. James's Park
Temple
West Kensington
Earl's Court
South Kensington
Victoria
Westminster
Embankment
Charing Cross 100m
London Bridge
Bermondsey
River Thames
Waterloo
Southwark
Waterloo East
Borough
Lambeth North
Bakerloo
Central
Circle
District
Hammersmith & City
Jubilee
Metropolitan
Northern
Piccadilly
Victoria
Waterloo & City
London Overground
Docklands Light Railway
Website
tfl.gov.uk
24 hour travel information
020 7222 1234
UNDERGROUND
© Transport for London
Reg. user No. 08/1227/P
Version M 08.08
Correct at time of going to print

INTERNATIONAL CAR-CARRYING TRAIN TERMINALS

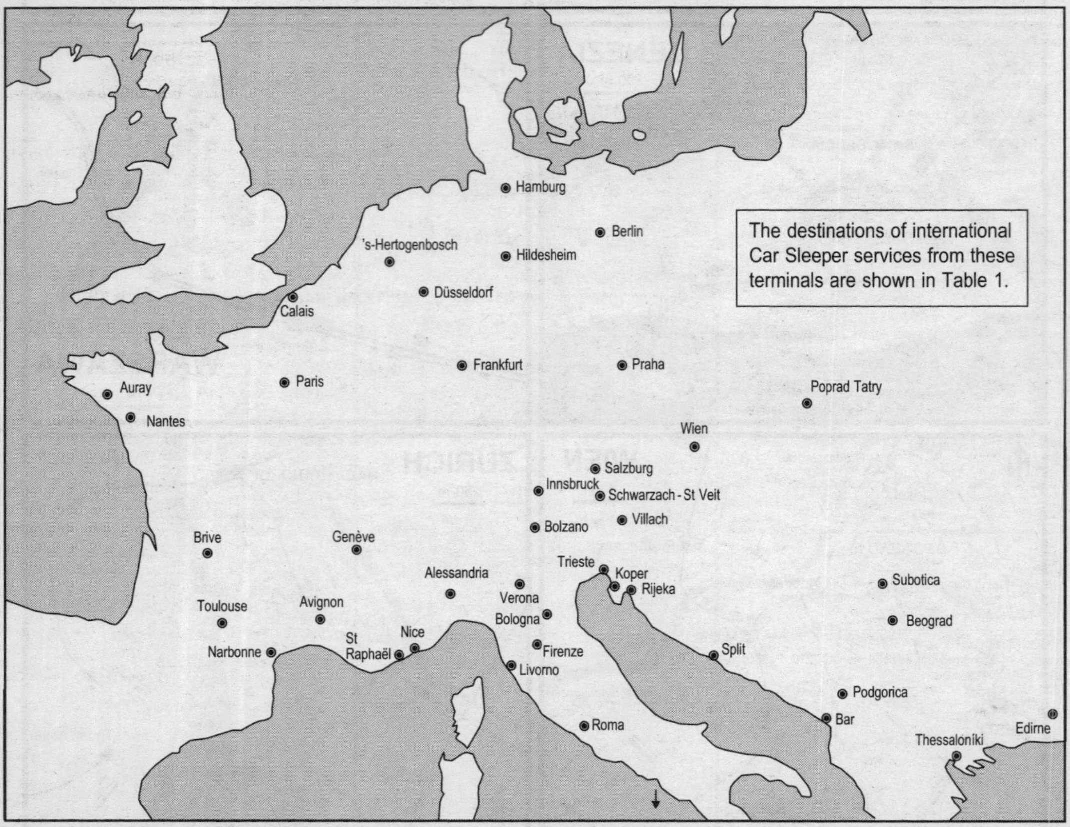
Hamburg
Berlin
's-Hertogenbosch
Hildesheim
Düsseldorf
Calais
Frankfurt
Praha
Auray
Paris
Nantes
Poprad Tatry
Wien
Salzburg
Innsbruck
Schwarzach - St Veit
Villach
Bolzano
Brive
Genève
Trieste
Koper
Rijeka
Alessandria
Verona
Subotica
Toulouse
Avignon
Bologna
Beograd
Narbonne
St Raphaël
Nice
Firenze
Livorno
Split
Podgorica
Bar
Roma
Edirne
Thessaloníki

The destinations of international Car Sleeper services from these terminals are shown in Table 1.

AUTO-TRAIN, AUTOREISEZÜGE, MOTORAIL

Car-carrying trains are composed of special wagons or vans for the conveyance of motorcars usually with sleeping cars and couchettes enabling the driver and passengers to travel overnight in comfort in the same train. Some services (particularly in France) convey vehicles separately allowing passengers a choice of trains for their own journey. Some shorter distance services run by day and convey seating coaches.

Cars are often loaded on the trains at separate stations from the passenger station and may be loaded some time before the passenger train departs. International car-carrying trains (including services from Calais) are shown in Table **1**, Domestic car-carrying trains (including services from Genève) in Table **2**. Some services also carry passengers without cars.

Details of Channel Tunnel shuttle services may be found on page 46. Austrian and Swiss alpine tunnel car-carrying trains are shown in the relevant country section - see pages 453 and 260 respectively for details.

Readers should be careful to check that dates refer to current schedules, as old dates may be left in the table until such time as current information is received. Loading and train times may vary on some dates, but will be confirmed by the agent when booking.

Full details of days and dates of running are shown only in the February, April, June, August, October and December editions of the European Rail Timetable. A summary of services is shown in other editions.

Some services shown in Table **1** are operated by organisations other than national railway companies. Contact details for these are:
Services from Germany: DB AutoZug, (UK booking centre); ✆ 08718 80 80 66.
Services from Netherlands: Euro-Express-Traincharter, Singelstraat 1a, 2613 EM Delft; ✆ +31 (0)15 213 36 36.
Services from Calais: French Motorail (Rail Europe), 1 Regent St, London SW1Y 4XT; ✆ 0844 848 4050.
Certain Eastern European services (see table for details):
Optima Tours, Karlstrasse 56, 80333 D-München; ✆ +49 89 54880 - 111, fax +49 89 54880 - 155.

SEE MAP PAGE 34

INTERNATIONAL CAR-CARRYING TRAINS 1

ALESSANDRIA to

DÜSSELDORF: ① Apr. 6 - Oct. 26, 2009.
Alessandria load 1530 - 1700, depart 1828, Düsseldorf Hbf arrive 0956.
Train **13372**: 🛏 1,2 cl., ▬ 2 cl. and ✕.

FRANKFURT: ①⑥ Apr. 4 - Oct. 31, 2009.
Alessandria load 1530 - 1700, depart 1828, Frankfurt Neu Isenburg arrive 0603.
Train **13370/2**: 🛏 1,2 cl., ▬ 2 cl. and ✕.

HAMBURG: ⑥ Apr. 4 - Oct. 31, 2009.
Alessandria load 1530 - 1700, depart 1828, Hamburg Altona arrive 1158.
Train **13370**: 🛏 1,2 cl., ▬ 2 cl. and ✕.

HILDESHEIM: ⑥ Apr. 4 - Oct. 31, 2009.
Alessandria load 1530 - 1700, depart 1828, Hildesheim arrive 0949.
Train **13370**: 🛏 1,2 cl., ▬ 2 cl. and ✕.

AVIGNON to

Loading at Avignon Sud (🚌 connection to Centre).

BERLIN: ① Apr. 6 - Oct. 26, 2009.
Avignon load 1745 - 1845, depart 2001, Berlin Wannsee arrive 1502.
Train **1362**: 🛏 1,2 cl., ▬ 2 cl. and ✕.

CALAIS: ⑥ May 16 - Sept. 12, 2009.
Avignon load 1730 - 2000, depart 2227, Calais arrive 0948.
▬ and 🍸.
Operator: French Motorail (see table heading).

HAMBURG: ④ Apr. 2 - Oct. 29, 2009 (also May 23).
Avignon load 1745 - 1845, depart 2000, Hamburg Altona arrive 1433.
Train **1372/6**: 🛏 1,2 cl., ▬ 2 cl. and ✕.

's-HERTOGENBOSCH: ⑥ June 6 - Sept. 5, 2009.
Timings not advised.
🛏 1,2 cl., ▬ 2 cl. and ✕.
Operator: Euro-Express-Traincharter (see table heading).

HILDESHEIM: ⑥ Apr. 4 - Oct. 31, 2009.
Avignon load 1745 - 1845, depart 2000, Hildesheim Hbf arrive 1152.
Train **1372**: 🛏 1,2 cl., ▬ 2 cl. and ✕.

BAR to

BEOGRAD: daily.
Bar loading times not advised, depart 2100, Beograd arrive 0632.
Train **434**: 🛏 1,2 cl. and ▬ 2 cl.

NOVI SAD: June 20 - Sept. 1, 2009.
Bar loading times not advised, depart 2010, Novi Sad arrive 0727.
Train **1138**: 🛏 1,2 cl., ▬ 2 cl., [2] and 🍸.

SUBOTICA: June 20 - Sept. 1, 2009.
Bar loading times not advised, depart 1800, Subotica arrive 0716.
Train **436**: 🛏 1,2 cl., ▬ 2 cl., [2] and 🍸.

BEOGRAD to

BAR: daily.
Beograd loading times not advised, depart 2210, Bar arrive 0800.
Train **435**: 🛏 1,2 cl. and ▬ 2 cl.

PODGORICA: daily.
Beograd loading times not advised, depart 2210, Podgorica arrive 0642.
Train **435**: 🛏 1,2 cl. and ▬ 2 cl.

BERLIN to

AVIGNON: ⑦ Apr. 5 - Oct. 25, 2009.
Berlin Wannsee load 1150 - 1220, depart 1311, Avignon arrive 0818.
Train **1360**: 🛏 1,2 cl., ▬ 2 cl. and ✕.

BOLZANO: ⑤ Dec. 19, 2008 - Oct. 30, 2009.
Berlin Wannsee load 1640 - 1720, depart 1803 (1603 Aug. 7 - Sept. 11), Bolzano arrive 0645.
Train **13301/5**: 🛏 1,2 cl., ▬ 2 cl. and ✕.

INNSBRUCK: ⑤ Dec. 19, 2008 - Mar. 27, 2009.
Timings not advised.
Train **13305**: 🛏 1,2 cl., ▬ 2 cl. and ✕.

NARBONNE: ⑦ Apr. 5 - Oct. 25, 2009.
Berlin Wannsee load 1120 - 1200, depart 1311, Narbonne arrive 1035.
Train **1360**: 🛏 1,2 cl., ▬ 2 cl. and ✕.

SCHWARZACH-ST VEIT: ⑤ Dec. 19, 2008 - Mar. 27, 2009.
Timings not advised.
Train **13395**: 🛏 1,2 cl., ▬ 2 cl. and ✕.

TRIESTE: ③ Apr. 1 - Oct. 28, 2009.
Berlin Wannsee load 1510 - 1540 (1410 - 1440 Aug. 5 - Sept. 9), depart 1703 (1603 Aug. 5 - Sept. 9), Trieste arrive 1014.
Train **13307**: 🛏 1,2 cl., ▬ 2 cl. and ✕.

VERONA: ⑤ Apr. 3 - Oct. 30, 2009.
Berlin Wannsee load 1600 - 1630 (1400 - 1430 Aug. 7 - Sept. 11), depart 1803 (1603 Aug. 7 - Sept. 11), Verona arrive 0903.
Train **13301**: 🛏 1,2 cl., ▬ 2 cl. and ✕.

VILLACH: ③ Apr. 1 - Oct. 28, 2009.
Berlin Wannsee load 1530 - 1610 (1430 - 1510 Aug. 5 - Sept. 9), depart 1703 (1603 Aug. 5 - Sept. 9), Villach Ost arrive 0643.
Train **13307**: 🛏 1,2 cl., ▬ 2 cl. and ✕.

WIEN: daily until Dec. 12, 2009.
Berlin Wannsee load 1620 - 1700, depart 1733, Wien Westbf arrive 0630.
Train **477/203**: 🛏 1,2 cl. and ▬ 2 cl.

BOLOGNA to

's-HERTOGENBOSCH: ⑥ June 6 - Sept. 5, 2009.
Timings not advised.
🛏 1,2 cl., ▬ 2 cl. and ✕.
Operator: Euro-Express-Traincharter (see table heading).

BOLZANO to

German services may be bookable only in Germany.

BERLIN: ⑥ Dec. 20, 2008 - Oct. 31, 2009.
Bolzano load 1830 - 1900, depart 2024, Berlin Wannsee arrive 0754 (0951 Aug. 2 - Sept. 13).
Train **13300/4**: 🛏 1,2 cl., ▬ 2 cl. and ✕.

DÜSSELDORF: ⑥ Dec. 20, 2008 - Apr. 25; ④⑥ Apr. 30 - Oct. 17, 2009 (also Oct. 24, 31).
Bolzano load 1830 - 1945, depart 2024 (2109⑥), Düsseldorf Hbf arrive 0840 (1025⑦).
Train **13316/20/24**: 🛏 1,2 cl., ▬ 2 cl. and ✕.

HAMBURG: ⑥ Dec. 20, 2008 - Apr. 25; ④⑥ Apr. 30 - May 30; ①④⑥ June 1 - Oct. 3; ⑥ Oct. 10 - 31, 2009 (also Oct. 1, 8, 15).
Bolzano load 1630 - 1900, depart 1825 - 2024, Hamburg Altona arrive 0935 (1034②, 1305⑤).
Train **13316/80/82**: 🛏 1,2 cl., ▬ 2 cl. and ✕.

HILDESHEIM: ⑥ Apr. 4 - May 30; ①⑥ June 1 - Sept. 28; ⑥ Oct. 3 - 31, 2009.
Bolzano load 1630 - 1710, depart 1825 (1851⑥), Bolzano arrive 0803 (0629⑦).
Train **13380/2**: 🛏 1,2 cl., ▬ 2 cl. and ✕.

BRIVE to

CALAIS: ⑥ May 16 - Sept. 12, 2009.
Brive load 1700 - 2100, depart 2246, Calais arrive 0735.
▬ and 🍸.
Operator: French Motorail (see table heading).

CALAIS to

Operator: French Motorail (see table heading).

AVIGNON: ⑤ May 15 - Sept. 11, 2009.
Calais load 1540 - 1740, depart 1805, Avignon arrive 0542.
▬ and 🍸.

BRIVE: ⑤ May 15 - Sept. 11, 2009.
Calais load 1815 - 2010, depart 2040, Brive arrive 0620.
▬ and 🍸.

NARBONNE: ⑤ May 15 - Sept. 11, 2009.
Calais load 1815 - 2010, depart 2040, Narbonne arrive 1011.
▬ and 🍸.

NICE: ⑤ May 15 - Sept. 11, 2009.
Calais load 1540 - 1740, depart 1805, Nice arrive 0957.
▬ and 🍸.

ST. RAPHAËL: ⑤ May 15 - Sept. 11, 2009.
Calais load 1540 - 1740, depart 1805, St. Raphaël arrive 0909.
▬ and 🍸.

TOULOUSE: ⑤ May 15 - Sept. 11, 2009.
Calais load 1815 - 2010, depart 2040, Toulouse arrive 0833.
▬ and 🍸.

DÜSSELDORF to

ALESSANDRIA: ⑦ Apr. 5 - Oct. 25, 2009.
Düsseldorf Hbf load 1440 - 1510, depart 1554, Alessandria 0725.
Train **13373**: 🛏 1,2 cl., ▬ 2 cl. and ✕.

BOLZANO: ⑤ Dec. 19, 2008 - Apr. 24; ③⑤ Apr. 29 - Oct. 16, 2009 (also Oct. 23, 30).
Düsseldorf Hbf load 1645 - 1800, depart 1735 (1854③), Bolzano arrive 0742 (0910④).
Train **13317/21/25**: 🛏 1,2 cl., ▬ 2 cl. and ✕.

INNSBRUCK: ⑤ Dec. 19, 2008 - Jan. 9; ②⑤ Jan. 13 - Mar. 27; ③ Apr. 1 - Oct. 28, 2009 (also Dec. 21, Jan. 4).
Düsseldorf load 2030 - 2050, depart 2155, Innsbruck arrive 0850.
Train **13325/7/9**: 🛏 1,2 cl., ▬ 2 cl. and ✕.

NARBONNE: ⑦ Mar. 1 - 29; ③ Apr. 1 - Oct. 28, 2009 (also Dec. 14, 28, Jan. 11, 25, Feb. 8, 22).
Düsseldorf Hbf load 1440 - 1510, depart 1554, Narbonne arrive 1004.
Train **1354**: 🛏 1,2 cl., ▬ 2 cl. and ✕.

SALZBURG: ⑤ Dec. 19, 2008 - Mar. 27; ⑦ Apr. 5 - Oct. 25, 2009 (also Dec. 21, 28, Jan. 4).
Düsseldorf Hbf load 2050 - 2110, depart 2155, Salzburg Hbf arrive 0804.
Train **13315/23**: 🛏 1,2 cl., ▬ 2 cl. and ✕.

TRIESTE: ⑤ Apr. 3 - Oct. 30, 2009.
Düsseldorf Hbf load 1330 - 1350, depart 1501, Trieste arrive 1014.
Train **13311**: 🛏 1,2 cl., ▬ 2 cl. and ✕.

VERONA: ⑤ Apr. 3 - Oct. 30, 2009.
Düsseldorf Hbf load 1615 - 1645, depart 1735, Verona arrive 0955.
Train **13321**: 🛏 1,2 cl., ▬ 2 cl. and ✕.

VILLACH: ⑤ Apr. 3 - Oct. 30, 2009.
Düsseldorf Hbf load 1345 - 1410, depart 1501, Villach Ost arrive 0643.
Train **13311**: 🛏 1,2 cl., ▬ 2 cl. and ✕.

EDIRNE to

VILLACH: ④ May 14 - June 18; ④⑦ June 21 - July 12; ①③④⑦ July 19 - Aug. 6; ①④⑤ Aug. 10 - 21; ①②③④⑤⑥ Aug. 22 - Sept. 11; ①④ Sept. 14 - Nov. 9, 2009 (also June 23, 29, Aug. 18).
Timings vary. ▬ 2 cl. (also 🛏 1, 2 cl. on some services).
Contact operator for further details.
Operator: Optima Tours (see table heading).

FIRENZE to

WIEN: ⑥ Apr. 4 - Sept. 26, 2009.
Firenze Campo di Marte load 1845 - 1930, depart 2055, Wien Süd arrive 0838.
Train **1236**: 🛏 1, 2 cl., ▬ 2 cl. and [12].

FRANKFURT (NEU ISENBURG) to

ALESSANDRIA: ⑤⑦ Apr. 3 - Oct. 30, 2009.
Frankfurt Neu Isenburg load 1800 - 1900, depart 1943, Alessandria arrive 0725.
Train **13371/3**: 🛏 1, 2 cl., ▬ 2 cl. and ✕.

NARBONNE: ⑦ Mar. 1 - 29; ③⑦ Apr. 1 - Oct. 28, 2009 (also Dec. 14, 28, Jan. 11, 25, Feb. 8, 22).
Frankfurt Neu Isenburg load 1830 - 1930 (1910 - 2000⑦), depart 1953 (2020⑦), Narbonne arrive 1004 (1035①).
Train **1354/60**: 🛏 1, 2 cl., ▬ 2 cl. and ✕.

TRIESTE: ⑤ Apr. 3 - Oct. 30, 2009.
Frankfurt Neu Isenburg load 1830 - 1900, depart 1921, Trieste arrive 1014.
Train **13311**: 🛏 1, 2 cl., ▬ 2 cl. and ✕.

VILLACH: ⑤ Apr. 3 - Oct. 30, 2009.
Frankfurt Neu Isenburg load 1800 - 1830, depart 1921, Villach Ost arrive 0643.
Train **13311**: 🛏 1, 2 cl., ▬ 2 cl. and ✕.

FRÉJUS ST. RAPHAEL – see St. Raphael

GENÈVE – see Table 2

HAMBURG to

ALESSANDRIA: ⑤ Apr. 3 - Oct. 30, 2009.
Hamburg Altona load 1110 - 1250, depart 1320, Alessandria arrive 0727 or 0745.
Train **13371**: 🛏 1, 2 cl., ▬ 2 cl. and ✕.

AVIGNON: ③ Apr. 1 - Oct. 28, 2009 (also May 22).
Hamburg Altona load 1210 - 1240, depart 1314, Avignon arrive 0820.
Train **1371/5**: 🛏 1, 2 cl., ▬ 2 cl. and ✕.

BOLZANO: ⑤ Dec. 19, 2008 - Apr. 24; ③⑤ Apr. 29 - May 22; ③⑤⑦ May 27 - Oct. 2; ⑤ Oct. 9 - 30, 2009 (also Oct. 7, 14).
Hamburg Altona load 1300 - 1735, depart 1343③ (1734⑦, 1759⑤), Bolzano arrive 0910 (0949⑥).
Train **13317/81/83**: 🛏 1, 2 cl., ▬ 2 cl. and ✕.

INNSBRUCK: ⑤ Dec. 19, 2008 - Jan. 9; ②⑤ Jan. 13 - Mar. 27, 2009 (also Dec. 21).
Timings not advised.
Train **13329/35/85**: 🛏 1, 2 cl., ▬ 2 cl. and ✕.

NARBONNE: ⑦ Mar. 1 - 29; ③⑤ Apr. 1 - Oct. 30, 2009 (also Dec. 14, 28, Jan. 11, 25, Feb. 8, 22).
Hamburg Altona load 1200 - 1230, depart 1314, Narbonne arrive 1035.
Train **1371/5**: 🛏 1, 2 cl., ▬ 2 cl. and ✕.

SCHWARZACH - ST VEIT: ⑤ Dec. 19, 2008 - Mar. 27, 2009.
Timings not advised.
Train **13395**: 🛏 1, 2 cl., ▬ 2 cl. and ✕.

TRIESTE: ⑦ Apr. 5 - May 17; ②⑦ May 19 - Sept. 29; ⑦ Oct. 4 - 25, 2009.
Hamburg Altona load 1235 - 1305 (1350 - 1420⑦), depart 1341 (1454⑦), Trieste arrive 1014.
Train **13393/97**: 🛏 1, 2 cl., ▬ 2 cl. and ✕.

VERONA: ⑤ Apr. 5 - 24; ③⑤ Apr. 29 - May 22; ③⑤⑦ May 27 - Oct. 2; ⑤ Oct. 9 - 30, 2009 (also Oct. 7, 14).
Hamburg Altona load 1240 - 1805, depart 1343 (1734⑦, 1759⑤), Verona arrive 1138 (1105①④).
Train **13317/81/3**: 🛏 1, 2 cl., ▬ 2 cl. and ✕.

VILLACH: ⑦ Apr. 5 - May 17; ②⑦ May 19 - Sept. 29; ⑦ Oct. 4 - 25, 2009.
Hamburg Altona load 1250 - 1320 (1400 - 1435⑦), depart 1341 (1454⑦), Villach Ost arrive 0643.
Train **13393/7**: 🛏 1, 2 cl., ▬ 2 cl. and ✕.

WIEN: daily until Dec. 12, 2009.
Hamburg Altona load 1915 - 1950, depart 2018, Wien Westbf arrive 0904.
Train **491**: 🛏 1, 2 cl. and ▬ 2 cl.

's-HERTOGENBOSCH to

AVIGNON: ⑤ June 5 - Sept. 4, 2009.
Timings not advised.
🛏 1, 2 cl., ▬ 2 cl. and ✕.
Operator: Euro-Express-Traincharter (see table heading).

BOLOGNA: ⑤ June 5 - Sept. 4, 2009.
Timings not advised.
🛏 1, 2 cl., ▬ 2 cl. and ✕.
Operator: Euro-Express-Traincharter (see table heading).

LIVORNO: ⑤ June 26 - Aug. 28, 2009.
Timings not advised.
🛏 1, 2 cl., ▬ 2 cl. and ✕.
Operator: Euro-Express-Traincharter (see table heading).

HILDESHEIM to

ALESSANDRIA: ⑤ Apr. 3 - Oct. 30, 2009.
Hildesheim load 1450 - 1530, depart 1643, Alessandria arrive 0727.
Train **13371**: 🛏 1, 2 cl., ▬ 2 cl. and ✕.

AVIGNON: ⑤ Apr. 3 - Oct. 30, 2009.
Hildesheim load 1320 - 1350, depart 1500, Avignon arrive 0736.
Train **1371**: 🛏 1, 2 cl., ▬ 2 cl. and ✕.

BOLZANO: ⑤ Apr. 3 - May 22; ⑤⑦ May 29 - Sept. 27; ⑤ Oct. 2 - 30, 2009.
Hildesheim load 1840 - 2010, depart 2134 (2005⑦), Bolzano arrive 0949 (0910①).
Train **13381/3**: 🛏 1, 2 cl., ▬ 2 cl. and ✕.

INNSBRUCK: ⑤ Dec. 19, 2008 - Mar. 27, 2009 (also Dec. 21).
Timings not advised.
Train **13335/85**: 🛏 1, 2 cl., ▬ 2 cl. and ✕.

NARBONNE: ⑦ Mar. 1 - 29; ③⑤ Apr. 1 - Oct. 30, 2009 (also Dec. 14, 28, Jan. 11, 25, Feb. 8, 22).
Hildesheim load 1410 - 1450, depart 1500 (1600⑤), Narbonne arrive 1035 (0945⑥).
Train **1371/5**: 🛏 1, 2 cl., ▬ 2 cl. and ✕.

VILLACH: ⑦ Apr. 5 - May 17; ②⑦ May 19 - Sept. 29; ⑦ Oct. 4 - 25, 2009.
Hildesheim load 1530 - 1610 (1700 - 1745⑦), depart 1658 (1827⑦), Villach Ost arrive 0643.
Train **13393/7**: 🛏 1, 2 cl., ▬ 2 cl. and ✕.

INNSBRUCK to

BERLIN: ⑥ Dec. 20, 2008 - Mar. 28, 2009.
Timings not advised.
Train **13304**: 🛏 1, 2 cl., ▬ 2 cl. and ✕.

DÜSSELDORF: ⑥ Dec. 20, 2008 - Jan. 10; ③⑥ Jan. 14 - Mar. 28; ④ Apr. 2 - Oct. 29, 2009 (also Dec. 22, Jan. 5).
Innsbruck load 1825 - 1855, depart 1938, Düsseldorf arrive 0625.
Train **13324/6/8**: 🛏 1, 2 cl., ▬ 2 cl. and ✕.

HAMBURG: ⑥ Dec. 20, 2008 - Jan. 10; ③⑥ Jan. 14 - Mar. 28, 2009 (also Dec. 22).
Innsbruck load 1900 - 1930, depart 2030, Hamburg Altona arrival time not advised.
Train **13328/84**: 🛏 1, 2 cl., ▬ 2 cl. and ✕.

HILDESHEIM: ⑥ Dec. 20, 2008 - Mar. 28, 2009 (also Dec. 22).
Timings not advised.
Train **13384**: 🛏 1, 2 cl., ▬ 2 cl. and ✕.

KOPER to

WIEN: ⑥ June 6 - Aug. 29, 2009.
Koper load 1945 - 2130, depart 2215, Wien Sud arrive 0717.
Train **1458**: ▬ 2 cl. and [2].

KOŠICE

PRAHA: daily except Dec. 24, 31.
Košice depart 2100, Praha Hlavni arrive 0709.
Train **424**: 🛏 1, 2 cl., ▬ 2 cl. and [2].

LIVORNO to

German services may be bookable only in Germany.

's-HERTOGENBOSCH: ⑥ June 27 - Aug. 29, 2009.
Timings not advised.
🛏 1, 2 cl., ▬ 2 cl. and ✕.
Operator: Euro-Express-Traincharter (see table heading).

NARBONNE to

Loading at Gare auto/train (🚌 connection)

BERLIN: ① Apr. 6 - Oct. 26, 2009.
Narbonne load 1500 - 1600, depart 1737, Berlin Wannsee arrive 1502.
Train **1362**: 🛏 1, 2 cl., ▬ 2 cl. and ✕.

CALAIS: ⑥ May 16 - Sept. 12, 2009.
Narbonne load 1400 - 1700, depart 1820, Calais arrive 0735.
▬ and 🍸.
Operator: French Motorail (see table heading).

DÜSSELDORF: ① Mar. 2 - 30; ④ Apr. 2 - Oct. 29, 2009 (also Dec. 1, 15, 29, Jan. 12, 26, Feb. 9, 23).
Narbonne load 1400 - 1500, depart 1645, Düsseldorf Hbf arrive 0956.
Train **1356**: 🛏 1, 2 cl., ▬ 2 cl. and ✕.

FRANKFURT: ① Mar. 2 - 30; ①④ Apr. 2 - Oct. 29, 2009 (also Dec. 1, 15, 29, Jan. 12, 26, Feb. 9, 23).
Narbonne load 1500 - 1600 (1400 - 1500④), depart 1737 (1645④), Frankfurt Neu Isenburg arrive 0753 (0603⑤).
Train **1356/62**: 🛏 1, 2 cl., ▬ 2 cl. and ✕.

HAMBURG: ① Mar. 2 - 30; ④⑥ Apr. 2 - Oct. 31, 2009 (also Dec. 1, 15, 29, Jan. 12, 26, Feb. 9, 23).
Narbonne load 1500 - 1600, depart 1737, Hamburg Altona arrive 1433 or 1442.
Train **1372/6**: 🛏 1, 2 cl., ▬ 2 cl. and ✕.

HILDESHEIM: ① Mar. 2 - 30; ④⑥ Apr. 2 - Oct. 31, 2009 (also Dec. 1, 15, 29, Jan. 12, 26, Feb. 9, 23).
Narbonne load 1500 - 1600, depart 1737, Hildesheim Hbf arrive 1152 or 1210.
Train **1372/6**: 🛏 1, 2 cl., ▬ 2 cl. and ✕.

NICE to

CALAIS: ⑥ May 16 - Sept. 12, 2009.
Nice load 1400 - 1630, depart 1806, Calais arrive 0948.
▬ and 🍸.
Operator: French Motorail (see table heading).

NOVI SAD to

BAR: June 19 - Aug. 31, 2009.
Novi Sad loading times not advised, depart 1940, Bar arrive 0705.
Train **1139**: 🛏 1, 2 cl., ▬ 2 cl., [2] and 🍸.

PODGORICA to

BEOGRAD: daily.
Podgorica loading times not advised, depart 2210, Beograd arrive 0632.
Train **434**: 🛏 1, 2 cl. and ▬ 2 cl.

POPRAD TATRY to

PRAHA: daily except Dec. 24, 31.
Poprad Tatry depart 2249, Praha Hlavni arrive 0709.
Train **424**: 🛏 1, 2 cl., ▬ 2 cl. and [2].

PRAHA to

KOŠICE: daily except Dec. 24, 31.
Praha Hlavní depart 2204, Košice arrive 0732.
Train **425**: 🛏 1, 2 cl., ▬ 2 cl. and [2].

POPRAD TATRY: daily except Dec. 24, 31.
Praha Hlavni depart 2204, Poprad Tatry arrive 0537
Train **425**: 🛏 1, 2 cl., ▬ 2 cl. and [2].

SPLIT: June 19 - Sept. 4, 2009.
Praha Hlavni depart 0918, Split arrive 0548.
Train **1475/1823**: 🛏 1, 2 cl. and ▬ 2 cl.

RIJEKA to

WIEN: ⑥ June 6 - Aug. 29, 2009.
Rijeka load 1900 - 2000, depart 2045, Wien Süd arrive 0717.
Train **480/1458**: ▬ 2 cl. and [2].

ROMA to

WIEN: ⑥ Apr. 4 - Sept. 26, 2009 (also Apr. 5, 13, May 1, 22, June 1, 11).
Roma Termini load 1430 - 1545, depart 1650 or 1720, Wien Süd arrive 0838 or 0857.
Train **1236/8**: 🛏 1, 2 cl., ▬ 2 cl. and [12].

ST RAPHAËL to

CALAIS: ⑥ May 16 - Sept. 12, 2009.
St Raphaël load 1600 - 1745, depart 1915, Calais arrive 0948.
▬ and 🍸.
Operator: French Motorail (see table heading).

SALZBURG to

DÜSSELDORF: ⑥ Dec. 20, 2008 - Mar. 28; ① Apr. 6 - Oct. 26, 2009 (also Dec. 22, 29, Jan. 5).
Loading time 1800 - 1850, Salzburg Hbf depart 1850, Düsseldorf Hbf arrive 0625.
Train **13314/22**: 🛏 1, 2 cl., ▬ 2 cl. and ✕.

SCHWARZACH - ST VEIT to

BERLIN: ⑥ Dec. 20, 2008 - Mar. 28, 2009.
Timings not advised.
Train **13394**: 🛏 1, 2 cl., ▬ 2 cl. and ✕.

HAMBURG: ⑥ Dec. 20, 2008 - Mar. 28, 2009.
Timings not advised.
Train **13394**: 🛏 1, 2 cl., ▬ 2 cl. and ✕.

SPLIT to

PRAHA: June 20 - Sept. 5, 2009.
Split depart 2050, Praha arrive 1840.
Train **1822/783/1474**: 🛏 1, 2 cl. and ▬ 2 cl.

WIEN: ⑥ June 6 - Aug. 29, 2009.
Split load 2015 - 2045, depart 2221, Wien Süd arrive 1405.
Train **824/158**: ▬ 2 cl.

SUBOTICA to

BAR: June 19 - Aug. 31, 2009.
Subotica loading times not advised, depart 1840, Bar arrive 0849.
Train **437**: 🛏 1, 2 cl., ▬ 2 cl., [2] and 🍸.

THESSALONÍKI to

VILLACH: ⑤ Aug. 15 - Sept. 5, 2008 (also July 27, Aug. 3).
Timings vary. ▬ 2 cl.
Contact operator for further details.
Operator: Optima Tours (see table heading).

TOULOUSE to

CALAIS: ⑥ May 16 - Sept. 12, 2009.
Toulouse load 1500 - 1830, depart 2019, Calais arrive 0735.
▬ and 🍸.
Operator: French Motorail (see table heading).

TRIESTE to

BERLIN: ④ Apr. 2 - Oct. 29, 2009.
Trieste load 1400 - 1445, depart 1552, Berlin Wannsee arrive 0903 (1006 Aug. 7 - Sept. 11).
Train **13306**: 🛏 1, 2 cl., ▬ 2 cl. and ✕.

DÜSSELDORF: ⑥ Apr. 4 - Oct. 31, 2009.
Trieste load 1400 - 1445, depart 1552, Düsseldorf Hbf arrive 0956.
Train **13310**: 🛏 1, 2 cl., ▬ 2 cl. and ✕.

FRANKFURT: ⑥ Apr. 4 - Oct. 31, 2009.
Trieste load 1400 - 1445, depart 1552, Frankfurt Neu Isenburg arrive 0600.
Train **13310**: 🛏 1, 2 cl., ▬ 2 cl. and ✕.

HAMBURG: ① Apr. 6 - May 11; ①③ May 18 - Sept. 30; ① Oct. 5 - 26, 2009.
Trieste load 1400 - 1445, depart 1552, Düsseldorf Hbf arrive 1133 (1112④).
Train **13392/96**: 🛏 1, 2 cl., ▬ 2 cl. and ✕.

VERONA to

German services may be bookable only in Germany.

BERLIN: ⑥ Apr. 4 - Oct. 31, 2009.
Verona load 1600 - 1645, depart 1755, Berlin Wannsee arrive 0754 (0951 Aug. 2 - Sept. 13).
Train **13300**: 🛏 1, 2 cl., ▬ 2 cl. and ✕.

DÜSSELDORF: ⑥ Apr. 4 - Oct. 31, 2009.
Verona load 1700 - 1745, depart 1855, Düsseldorf Hbf arrive 1025.
Train **13320**: 🛏 1, 2 cl., ▬ 2 cl. and ✕.

HAMBURG: ⑥ Apr. 4 - 25; ④⑥ Apr. 30 - May 30; ①④⑥ June 1 - Oct. 3; ⑥ Oct. 10 - 31, 2009 (also Oct. 1, 8, 15).
Verona load 1400 - 1515 (1600 - 1645④), depart 1553 (1755④, 1638⑥), Hamburg Altona arrive 0934 (1034②, 1305⑤).
Train **13316/80/2**: 🛏 1, 2 cl., ▬ 2 cl. and ✕.

VILLACH to

BERLIN: ④ Apr. 2 - Oct. 29, 2009.
Villach Ost load 1835 - 1920, depart 2009, Berlin Wannsee arrive 0903 (1006 Aug. 7 - Sept. 11).
Train **13306**: 🛏 1, 2 cl., ▬ 2 cl. and ✕.

DÜSSELDORF: ⑥ Apr. 4 - Oct. 31, 2009.
Villach Ost load 1835 - 1920, depart 2009, Düsseldorf Hbf arrive 0956.
Train **13310**: 🛏 1, 2 cl., ▬ 2 cl. and ✕.

EDIRNE: ②⑥ May 9 - June 30; ②③⑥ July 1 - 15; ①②③⑤⑥ July 17 - Aug. 8; ⑥ Aug. 15 - Oct. 10, 2009 (also Apr. 24, 27, 30, May 4, June 17, 25, 28, Oct. 24, Nov. 7).
Timings vary. ▬ 2 cl. (also 🛏 1, 2 cl. on some services).
Contact operator for further details.
Operator: Optima Tours (see table heading).

FRANKFURT: ⑥ Apr. 4 - Oct. 31, 2009.
Villach Ost load 1835 - 1920, depart 2009, Frankfurt Neu Isenburg arrive 0600.
Train **13310**: 🛏 1, 2 cl., ▬ 2 cl. and ✕.

HAMBURG: ① Apr. 6 - May 11; ①③ May 18 - Sept. 30; ① Oct. 5 - 26, 2009.
Villach Ost load 1835 - 1920, depart 2009, Hamburg Altona arrive 1112 (1133②).
Train **13392/6**: 🛏 1, 2 cl., ▬ 2 cl. and ✕.

HILDESHEIM: ① Apr. 6 - May 11; ①③ May 18 - Sept. 30; ① Oct. 5 - 26, 2009.
Villach Ost load 1835 - 1920, depart 2009, Hildesheim Hbf arrive 0830 (0915②).
Train **13392/6**: 🛏 1, 2 cl., ▬ 2 cl. and ✕.

THESSALONÍKI: ⑥ July 12 - Aug. 2, 2008 (also Aug. 14, 20).
Timings vary. ▬ 2 cl.
Contact operator for further details.
Operator: Optima Tours (see table heading).

WIEN to

BERLIN: daily until Dec. 12, 2009.
Wien Westbf load 2115 - 2150, depart 2212, Berlin Wannsee arrive 0943.
Train **202/476**: 🛏 1, 2 cl. and ▬ 2 cl.

FIRENZE: ⑤ Apr. 3 - Sept. 25, 2009.
Wien Süd load 1845 - 1905, depart 2023, Firenze Campo di Marte arrive 0705.
Train **1237**: 🛏 1, 2 cl., ▬ 2 cl. and [12].

HAMBURG: daily until Dec. 12, 2009.
Wien Westbf load 1925 - 1940, depart 1954, Hamburg Altona arrive 0804.
Train **490**: 🛏 1, 2 cl. and ▬ 2 cl.

KOPER: ⑤ June 5 - Aug. 28, 2009.
Wien Süd load 2130 - 2150, depart 2156, Koper arrive 0642.
Train **1459**: ▬ 2 cl. and [2].

RIJEKA: ⑤ June 5 - Aug. 28, 2009.
Wien Süd load 2110 - 2130, depart 2156, Rijeka arrive 0850.
Train **1459/481**: ▬ 2 cl. and [2].

ROMA: ⑤ Apr. 3 - Sept. 25, 2009 (also Apr. 4, 12, 30, May 20, 31, June 10).
Wien Süd load 1910 - 1930, depart 2023, Roma Termini arrive 1045.
Train **1237/9**: 🛏 1, 2 cl., ▬ 2 cl. and [12].

SPLIT: ⑤ June 5 - Aug. 28, 2009.
Wien Süd load 1500 - 1530, depart 1556, Split arrive 0655.
Train **159/825**: ▬ 2 cl.

AUSTRIA

to 12/12/09

Feldkirch - Graz: daily (day and overnight trains).
Feldkirch - Wien: daily (day and overnight trains).
Feldkirch - Villach: daily.
Graz - Feldkirch: daily (day and overnight trains).

Innsbruck - Wien: daily (day train).
Lienz - Wien: ⑥ until Apr. 11; ⑥ May 30 - Sept. 19 (also Apr. 13, 14, June 1, 2) (day train).
Villach - Feldkirch: daily.
Villach - Wien: daily (2 day trains).

Wien - Feldkirch: daily (day and overnight trains).
Wien - Innsbruck: daily (day train).
Wien - Lienz: ⑥ until Apr. 11; ⑥ May 30 - Sept. 19 (also Apr. 13, 14, June 1, 2) (day train).
Wien - Villach: daily (2 day trains).

CROATIA

to 12/12/09

Split - Zagreb: daily. Also additional train in summer.

Zagreb - Split: daily. Also additional train in summer.

FINLAND

to 12/12/09

Subject to alteration on and around holiday dates.

Helsinki - Kemijärvi: ⑤ May 29 - Dec. 11.
Helsinki - Kolari: ③⑤⑥ (also June 18; not June 19, 20).
Helsinki - Oulu: daily (not June 19).
Helsinki - Rovaniemi: daily.
Kemijärvi - Helsinki: ⑥ May 30 - Dec. 12.

Kolari - Helsinki: ④⑥⑦ (not June 20).
Kolari - Tampere: ④⑥⑦ (not June 20).
Kolari - Turku: *winter only.*
Oulu - Helsinki: daily (not June 20).
Rovaniemi - Helsinki: daily.
Rovaniemi - Tampere: daily (not June 19).
Rovaniemi - Turku: daily (not June 20).

Tampere - Kolari: ③⑤⑥ (also June 18; not June 19, 20).
Tampere - Rovaniemi: daily (not June 20).
Turku - Kolari: *winter only.*
Turku - Rovaniemi: daily (not June 19).

FRANCE

to 12/12/09

For services from Calais, see Table **1**.

Auray - Genève: daily June 19 - Sept. 5 (not Aug. 14, 15).
Auray - Lyon: daily June 19 - Sept. 5.
Auray - Metz: ⑥ June 20 - Sept. 19.
Auray - Strasbourg: ⑥ June 20 - Sept. 19.
Avignon - Metz: ⑥ June 20 - Sept. 19.
Avignon - Paris▲: daily Apr. 25 - Oct. 3; ②④⑥ Oct. 6 - Dec. 12 (not Aug. 10, Sept. 20).
Avignon - Seclin (Lille)▲: ⑥ June 20 - Sept. 19.
Avignon - Strasbourg: ⑥ June 20 - Sept. 19.
Biarritz - Genève: ⑥ June 27 - Sept. 5 (not Aug. 15).
Biarritz - Metz: ⑥ June 20 - Sept. 19.
Biarritz - Paris: ②④⑥ May 21 - June 25; daily June 25 - Sept. 5; ②④⑥ Sept. 8 - Oct. 1.
Biarritz - Strasbourg: ⑥ June 20 - Sept. 19.
Bordeaux - Marseille: ⑤⑥⑦ June 12 - Sept. 13 (not June 13, Sept. 12).
Bordeaux - Metz: ⑥ June 20 - Sept. 19.
Bordeaux - Paris▲: ②④⑥ May 21 - June 25; daily June 26 - Sept. 5; ②④⑦ Sept. 8 - Oct. 1; ②⑥ Oct. 3 - Dec. 12.
Bordeaux - St. Raphaël▲: ⑤⑥⑦ June 12 - Sept. 13 (not June 13, Sept. 12).
Bordeaux - Strasbourg: ⑥ June 20 - Sept. 19.
Briançon - Paris: ②④⑥ June 16 - Sept. 19 (also June 21; not June 20, Aug. 11).
Brive - Paris▲: ②④⑥ May 21 - June 25; daily June 26 - Sept. 5; ②④⑥ Sept. 8 - Oct. 1 (not June 23).
Fréjus-St. Raphaël – see St. Raphaël.
Genève - Auray: daily June 20 - Sept. 6 (not Aug. 15, 16).
Genève - Biarritz: ⑤ June 26 - Sept. 4 (not Aug. 14).
Genève - Nantes: daily June 20 - Sept. 6 (not Aug. 15, 16).
Genève - Paris▲: ②④⑥ June 20 - Sept. 5 (not Aug. 11, 15).
Lille – see Seclin (Lille).
Lyon - Auray: daily June 20 - Sept. 6.
Lyon - Nantes: daily June 20 - Sept. 6.
Lyon - Paris▲: ②④⑥ Apr. 25 - Oct. 3; ⑥ Oct. 10 - Dec. 12 (not Aug. 11, Sept. 12, 19).
Marseille - Bordeaux▲: ⑤⑥⑦ June 12 - Sept. 13 (not June 13, Sept. 12).
Marseille - Paris▲: daily Apr. 25 - Oct. 3; ②④⑥ Oct. 6 - Dec. 12 (not Aug. 10, Sept. 20).
Metz - Auray: ⑤ June 19 - Sept. 18.
Metz - Avignon: ⑤ June 19 - Sept. 18.
Metz - Biarritz: ⑤ June 19 - Sept. 18.
Metz - Bordeaux: ⑤ June 19 - Sept. 18.
Metz - Nantes: ⑤ June 19 - Sept. 18.
Metz - Narbonne: ⑤ June 19 - Sept. 18.
Metz - St. Raphaël: ⑤ June 19 - Sept. 18.
Nantes - Genève: daily June 19 - Sept. 5 (not Aug. 14, 15).
Nantes - Lyon: daily June 19 - Sept. 5.
Nantes - Metz: ⑥ June 20 - Sept. 19.
Nantes - St. Raphaël: daily June 19 - Sept. 6 (also June 12, 14, Sept. 11, 13).
Nantes - Strasbourg: ⑥ June 20 - Sept. 19.
Narbonne - Metz: ⑥ June 20 - Sept. 19.
Narbonne - Paris: ②④⑥ May 21 - June 25; daily June 26 - Sept. 5; ②④⑥ Sept. 8 - Oct. 1; ②⑥ Oct. 3 - Dec. 12.
Narbonne - Seclin (Lille)▲: ⑥ June 20 - Sept. 19.
Narbonne - Strasbourg: ⑥ June 20 - Sept. 19.
Nice - Paris: daily Apr. 25 - Oct. 3; ②④⑥ Oct. 6 - Dec. 12 (not Aug. 10, Sept. 20).
Paris - Avignon▲: daily Apr. 25 - Oct. 2; ①③⑤ Oct. 5 - Dec. 11 (not Aug. 10, Sept. 20).
Paris - Biarritz: ①③⑤ May 20 - June 24; daily June 25 - Sept. 4; ①③⑤ Sept. 7 - 30.
Paris - Bordeaux▲: ①③⑤ May 20 - June 24; daily June 25 - Sept. 4; ①③⑤ Sept. 7 - 30; ①⑤ Oct. 2 - Dec. 11.
Paris - Briançon: ①③⑤ June 15 - Sept. 18 (not Aug. 10).
Paris - Brive▲: ①③⑤ May 20 - June 24; daily June 25 - Sept. 4; ①③⑤ Sept. 7 - 30 (not June 22).
Paris - Genève▲: ①③⑤ June 19 - Sept. 4 (not Aug. 10, 14).
Paris - Lyon▲: ①③⑤ Apr. 27 - Oct. 2; ⑤ Oct. 9 - Dec. 11 (not Aug. 10, Sept. 11, 18).
Paris - Marseille▲: daily Apr. 25 - Oct. 2; ①③⑤ Oct. 5 - Dec. 11 (not Aug. 8, Sept. 20).
Paris - Narbonne: ①③⑤ May 20 - June 24; daily June 25 - Sept. 4; ①③⑤ Sept. 7 - 30; ①⑤ Oct. 2 - Dec. 11.
Paris - Nice: daily Apr. 25 - Oct. 2; ①③⑤ Oct. 5 - Dec. 11 (not Aug. 10, Sept. 20).
Paris - St. Raphaël: daily Apr. 25 - Oct. 2; ①③⑤ Oct. 5 - Dec. 11 (not Aug. 10, Sept. 20).
Paris - Toulon: daily Apr. 25 - Sept. 30 (not Aug. 10, Sept. 20).
Paris - Toulouse: ①③⑤ May 20 - June 24; daily June 25 - Sept. 4; ①③⑤ Sept. 7 - 30; ①⑤ Oct. 2 - Dec. 11.
St. Raphaël - Bordeaux▲: ⑤⑥⑦ June 12 - Sept. 13 (not June 13, Sept. 12).
St. Raphaël - Metz: ⑥ June 20 - Sept. 19.
St. Raphaël - Nantes: daily June 19 - Sept. 6 (also June 12, 14, Sept. 11, 13).
St. Raphaël - Paris: daily Apr. 25 - Oct. 3; ②④⑥ Oct. 6 - Dec. 12 (not Aug. 10, Sept. 20).
St. Raphaël - Seclin (Lille)▲: ⑥ June 20 - Sept. 19.
St. Raphaël - Strasbourg: ⑥ June 20 - Sept. 19.
Seclin (Lille) - Avignon▲: ⑤ June 19 - Sept. 18.
Seclin (Lille) - Narbonne▲: ⑤ June 19 - Sept. 18.
Seclin (Lille) - St. Raphaël▲: ⑤ June 19 - Sept. 18.
Strasbourg - Auray: ⑤ June 19 - Sept. 18.
Strasbourg - Avignon: ⑤ June 19 - Sept. 18.
Strasbourg - Biarritz: ⑤ June 19 - Sept. 18.
Strasbourg - Bordeaux: ⑤ June 19 - Sept. 18.
Strasbourg - Nantes: ⑤ June 19 - Sept. 18.
Strasbourg - Narbonne: ⑤ June 19 - Sept. 18.
Strasbourg - St. Raphaël: ⑤ June 19 - Sept. 18.
Toulon - Paris: daily Apr. 25 - Oct. 1 (not Aug. 10, Sept. 20).
Toulouse - Paris: ②④⑥ May 21 - June 25; daily June 26 - Sept. 5; ②④⑥ Sept. 8 - Oct. 1; ②⑥ Oct. 3 - Dec. 12.

▲ – These services offer the passenger a choice of departure times, usually including day and night trains.

GERMANY

to 31/10/09

Basel (Lörrach) - Hamburg Altona: ⑥ Nov. 1 - Jan. 31; ①⑥ Feb. 2 - 14; ①④⑥ Feb. 16 - May 2; ①④⑥⑦ May 4 - 17; ①③④⑤⑥⑦ May 18 - 31; daily June 1 - Sept. 13; ①②④⑤⑥⑦ Sept. 14 - Oct. 18; ①⑤⑥⑦ Oct. 19 - 31.

Basel (Lörrach) - Hildesheim: ⑥ Nov. 1 - Jan. 31; ①⑥ Feb. 2 - 14; ①④⑥ Feb. 16 - May 2; ①④⑥⑦ May 4 - 17; ①③④⑤⑥⑦ May 18 - 31; daily June 1 - Sept. 13; ①②④⑤⑥⑦ Sept. 14 - Oct. 18; ①⑤⑥⑦ Oct. 19 - 31.

Berlin Wannsee - München Ost: daily. [***CNL*** train].

Düsseldorf - München Ost: ⑤ Nov. 7 - Mar. 27; ③⑦ Apr. 1 - Oct. 28.

Hamburg Altona - Basel (Lörrach): ⑤ Nov. 7 - Jan. 30; ⑤⑦ Feb. 1 - 15; ③⑤⑦ Feb. 18 - May 3; ③⑤⑥⑦ May 6 - 17; ②③④⑤⑥⑦ May 19 - 31; daily June 1 - Sept. 13; ①③④⑤⑥⑦ Sept. 14 - Oct. 4; ③④⑤⑥⑦ Oct. 7 - 18; ④⑤⑥⑦ Oct. 22 - 30.

Hamburg Altona - München Ost: ③⑤ Jan. 2 - Mar. 27; ③⑤⑦ Apr. 1 - May 31; ①③⑤⑦ June 1 - Oct. 4; ③⑤⑦ Oct. 7 - 18; ⑤⑦ Oct. 23 - 30 (also Mar. 8, 15, 22, 29). Also daily ***CNL*** train.

Hildesheim - Basel (Lörrach): ⑤ Nov. 7 - Jan. 30; ⑤⑦ Feb. 1 - 15; ③⑤⑦ Feb. 18 - May 3; ③⑤⑥⑦ May 6 - 17; ②③④⑤⑥⑦ May 19 - 31; daily June 1 - Sept. 13; ①③④⑤⑥⑦ Sept. 14 - Oct. 4; ③④⑤⑥⑦ Oct. 7 - 18; ④⑤⑥⑦ Oct. 22 - 30.

Hildesheim - München Ost: ③⑤ Jan. 2 - Mar. 27; ③⑤⑦ Apr. 1 - May 31; ①③⑤⑦ June 1 - Oct. 4; ③⑤⑦ Oct. 7 - 18; ⑤⑦ Oct. 23 - 30 (also Mar. 8, 15, 22, 29).

München Ost - Berlin Wannsee: daily. [***CNL*** train].

München Ost - Düsseldorf: ⑥ Nov. 1 - Mar. 28; ①④ Apr. 2 - Oct. 29.

München Ost - Hamburg Altona: ④⑥ Jan. 1 - Mar. 28; ①④⑥ Apr. 2 - May 30; ①②④⑥ June 1 - Oct. 3; ①④⑥ Oct. 5 - 17; ①⑥ Oct. 19 - 31 (also Mar. 9, 16, 23, 30). Also daily ***CNL*** train.

München Ost - Hildesheim: ④⑥ Jan. 1 - Mar. 28; ①④⑥ Apr. 2 - May 30; ①②④⑥ June 1 - Oct. 3; ①④⑥ Oct. 5 - 17; ①⑥ Oct. 19 - 31 (also Mar. 9, 16, 23, 30).

Niebüll - Westerland: Daily shuttle service; 18 - 28 per day in summer, 12 - 14 per day in winter.

Westerland - Niebüll: Daily shuttle service; 18 - 28 per day in summer, 12 - 14 per day in winter.

CNL – *DB City Night Line* (see page **10** for description).

GREECE

to 12/12/09

Athína - Thessaloníki: daily (day and night trains).

Thessaloníki - Athína: daily (day and night trains).

ITALY

to 13/06/09

Bari - Bolzano: ⑤ until Mar. 20 and from June 5.
Bari - Milano: Apr. 9, 13, June 12.
Bari - Torino: ⑦ Jan. 11 - Apr. 5 (also Apr. 13, June 2; not Apr. 12, May 31).
Bologna - Catania: daily.
Bologna - Lamezia: ⑤ from June 12.
Bologna - Villa San Giovanni: daily.
Bolzano - Bari: ⑥ until Mar. 21 and from June 6.
Bolzano - Lamezia: ⑥ until Mar. 21.
Bolzano - Roma: ⑥ Jan. 10 - Feb. 7; ⑥⑦ Feb. 14 - Mar. 22.
Bolzano - Villa San Giovanni: ⑥ until Mar. 21.
Calalzo - Roma: ⑥ Jan. 10 - Mar. 21.
Catania - Bologna: daily.
Catania - Milano: *summer only.*
Catania - Roma: ⑤ Dec. 19 - June 12.
Catania - Torino: *summer only.*
Foggia - Torino: *summer only.*
Genova - Lamezia: ⑤⑥ Apr. 10 - May 2, and from June 12.
Genova - Villa San Giovanni: ⑤⑥ Apr. 10 - May 2, and from June 12.
Lamezia - Bologna: ⑥ from June 13.
Lamezia - Bolzano: ⑤ until Mar. 20.
Lamezia - Genova: ④⑤ Apr. 9 - May 1, and from June 11.
Lamezia - Milano: ⑤ Apr. 10 - May 1, and from June 12.
Lamezia - Roma: *summer only.*
Lamezia - Torino: ④ Apr. 9 - 30 (also June 11).
Milano - Bari: Apr. 14, June 13.
Milano - Catania: *summer only.*
Milano - Lamezia: ⑥ Apr. 11 - May 2, and from June 13.
Milano - Milazzo: *summer only.*
Milano - Palermo: *summer only.*
Milano - Villa San Giovanni: ⑥ Apr. 11 - May 2, and from June 13.
Milazzo - Milano: *summer only.*
Milazzo - Torino: *summer only.*
Napoli - Torino: ⑦ Jan. 11 - June 13 (also Apr. 13, June 2; not Apr. 12, May 31).
Palermo - Milano: *summer only.*
Palermo - Roma: *summer only.*
Palermo - Torino: *summer only.*
Roma - Bolzano: ⑤ Jan. 9 - Feb. 6; ⑤⑥ Feb. 13 - Mar. 21.
Roma - Calalzo: ⑤ Jan. 9 - Mar. 20.
Roma - Catania: ⑦ Dec. 14 - June 7.
Roma - Lamezia: *summer only.*
Roma - Palermo: *summer only.*
Roma - Torino: ⑦ Jan. 11 - June 13 (also Apr. 13, June 2; not Apr. 12, May 31).
Roma - Villa San Giovanni: ④⑥ Dec. 18 - June 13.
Torino - Bari: ⑤ Jan. 9 - June 12 (also Apr. 30; not May 1).
Torino - Catania: *summer only.*
Torino - Foggia: *summer only.*
Torino - Lamezia: ⑤ Apr. 10 - May 1 (also June 12).
Torino - Milazzo: *summer only.*
Torino - Napoli: ⑤ Jan. 9 - June 12 (not May 1).
Torino - Palermo: *summer only.*
Torino - Roma: ⑤ Jan. 9 - June 12 (not May 1).
Torino - Villa San Giovanni: ⑤ Dec. 19 - June 12.
also additional train: ⑤ Apr. 10 - May 1, June 12.
Venezia - Villa San Giovanni: June 12.
Villa San Giovanni - Bologna: daily.
Villa San Giovanni - Bolzano: ⑤ until Mar. 20.
Villa San Giovanni - Genova: ④⑤ Apr. 9 - May 1, and from June 11.
Villa San Giovanni - Milano: ⑤ Apr. 10 - May 1, and from June 12.
Villa San Giovanni - Roma: ⑤⑦ Dec. 14 - June 12.
Villa San Giovanni - Torino: ⑦ Dec. 14 - June 7
also additional train: ④ Apr. 9 - 30, June 11.
Villa San Giovanni - Venezia: June 13.

231 BELFAST - LONDONDERRY and PORTRUSH — NIR

Service valid June 29 - Dec. 12. **For service March 30 - June 28 see page 167**

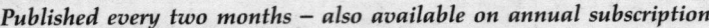

km		⚒	⑥	Ⓐ	Ⓐ	⚒	Ⓐ	⑥	⚒	Ⓐ	⑥	Ⓐ	Ⓐ	Ⓐ	⑥	Ⓐ	Ⓐ	⑥	Ⓐ	⑥		⑦	⑦	⑦	⑦	⑦
	Belfast GVSt. ★ .. d.	...	0840	0844	0916	1040	1218	1220	1415e	1520	1557	1600	1647	1715	1755	1756	1935	1950	2115	2120	...	0950	1250	1550	1850	2120
0	**Belfast Central** .... d.	0655	0850	0854	0925	1050	1228	1229	1425e	1530	1607	1610	1657	1725	1805	1805	1945	2000	2125	2130	...	1000	1300	1600	1900	2130
33	Antrim .... d.	0717	0913	0919	0952	1113	1251	1252	1451	1557	1630	1634	1722	1753	1827	1829	2009	2023	2149	2153	...	1024	1324	1624	1924	2154
52	Ballymena .... d.	0731	0930	0934	1005	1126	1310	1312	1505	1611	1650	1653	1736	1807	1841	1841	2030	2036	2203	2207	...	1038	1338	1638	1938	2208
97	**Coleraine** .... ▲ d.	0820	1015	1018	...	1210	1355	1357x	1550	...	1735	1735	1825	1857	1925	1930x	2112	2120	2247	2250	...	1122	1422	1722	2022	2250
107	Portrush .... ▲ a.	|	|	|	...	|	|	|	|	...	|	|	1835	1907	|	|	|	|	|	|	...	|	|	|	|	|
151	**Londonderry** .... a.	0910	1105	1105	...	1300	1445	1447	1640	...	1825	1825	...	...	2015	2018	2203	2210	2335	2340	...	1210	1510	1810	2110	2340

	Ⓐ	Ⓐ	⑥	Ⓐ	Ⓐ	⚒	Ⓐ	⚒	Ⓐ	⑥	⚒	Ⓐ	⚒	⑥	Ⓐ	⑥	Ⓐ	Ⓐ	⑥		⑦	⑦	⑦	⑦	⑦	⑦
Londonderry .... d.	...	...	0605	...	0635	0735	...	0930	1125	1125	1309	...	1505	1650	1705	1840	1838	2028	2035	...	1035	1335	...	1635	1935	2125
Portrush .... ▲ d.	...	0605	|	0635	|	|	...	|	|	|	|	...	|	|	|	|	|	|	|	...	|	|	1537	|	|	|
Coleraine .... ▲ d.	...	0617	0650	0648	0722	0820	...	1015	1212	1212	1355	...	1550	1736	1756	1925	1928	2113	2120	...	1122	1422	1550	1722	2022	2210
Ballymena .... d.	0631	0700	0735	0737	0805	0905	1022	1100	1257	1257	1438	1617	1635	1821	1841	2010	2015	2204	2207	...	1207	1507	1637	1807	2107	...
Antrim .... d.	0645	0715	0750	0752	0820	0918	1036	1113	1311	1310	1452	1631	1648	1842	1855	2023	2029	2218	2220	...	1220	1520	1650	1820	2120	...
Belfast Central ..... a.	0715	0746	0813	0821	0843	0943	1103	1137	1333	1334	1520	1655	1713	1908	1919	2047	2051	2240	2244	...	1243	1543	1714	1843	2143	...
Belfast GVSt. ★ ... a.	0722	...	0825	0833	0855	0955	1113	1150	1343	1345	1530	1705	1725	1918	1930	2100	2101	2250	2255	...	1255	1555	1725	1855	2155	...

km		Ⓐ	⑥	⚒	⑥	Ⓐ	⚒	⚒	⚒	⚒e	⚒	⚒e	⚒	⚒	⚒e	Ⓐy	⑥	Ⓐy	Ⓐ	⑥	Ⓐ	⑥	Ⓐ	⑥	Ⓐ	⑥	Ⓐ	⑥	
0	Coleraine .... d.	0725	0700	0830	0930	0935	1023	1130	1220	1315	1405	1510	1600	1700	1740	1825	1850	1857	1931	1935	2040	2045	2120	2130	2215	2220	2250	2255	...
10	Portrush .... a.	0737	0710	0842	0940	0947	1035	1142	1232	1327	1417	1522	1612	1712	1752	1835	1900	1907	1941	1945	2050	2055	2130	2140	2225	2230	2300	2305	...

	Ⓐy	Ⓐy	⑥	Ⓐ	⚒	⚒v	⚒	⚒	⚒	⚒v	⚒	⚒v	⚒	⑥	Ⓐ	⑥	Ⓐ	⚒	Ⓐ	⑥	Ⓐ	⚒	Ⓐ	⑥	Ⓐ	⑥	Ⓐ	⑥	
Portrush.......... d.	0605	0635	0635	0705	0758	0845	0953	1040	1150	1235	1333	1420	1530	1615	1620	1715	1718	1800	1843	1905	1915	1950	2055	2100	2140	2145	2230	2235	...
Coleraine .... a.	0615	0645	0645	0717	0810	0855	1005	1052	1202	1245	1345	1430	1542	1625	1632	1725	1730	1812	1853	1915	1925	2000	2105	2110	2150	2155	2240	2245	...

	⑦	⑦	⑦	⑦		⑦	⑦		⑦	⑦	⑦	⑦		
Coleraine .... d.	1040	1130	1340	1430	...	1640	1730	...	1940	2030	2215	2255	...	...
Portrush.......... a.	1050	1140	1350	1440	...	1650	1740	...	1950	2040	2225	2305	...	...

		⑦	⑦		⑦	⑦y	⑦	⑦		⑦	⑦	⑦	
Portrush...... d.	...	1100	1200	...	1400	1537	1700	1800	...	2000	2100	2235	...
Coleraine .... a.	...	1110	1210	...	1410	1547	1710	1810	...	2010	2110	2245	...

e – 5 mins. later on ⑥.
v – 5 mins. later on Ⓐ.
y – Through train to / from Belfast Great Victoria St.
▲ – **COLERAINE - PORTRUSH** (for all trains see panel).
★ – Belfast GVSt. (Belfast Great Victoria St.) is the nearest station to Belfast City Centre and the Europa Buscentre is adjacent.

BERLIN - LEIPZIG - SAALFELD - NÜRNBERG 851

Aug. 1 - Sept. 14 (see page 398 for service to July 31 and from Sept. 15)

km		RB 16843	ICE 1663 ①–⑤	ICE 1644 ①–⑥	ICE 1563 ①–⑥	RE 3481	ICE 1654 ①–⑥	ICE 1665 ①–⑥	IC 2154 ①–⑥	ICE 1565	RE 3483	ICE 1667 ①	ICE 1697 ②–⑦	X 80002	IC 2152 ①–⑥	IC 2152	ICE 1567 ①–⑤	ICE 1587 ⑥	ICE 1567 ⑦	RE 3485	ICE 1729 Ⓑ	ICE 1669 ⑥	IC 2150 2250	ICE 1569 ①–⑥	ICE 1589 ⑦
			✕	⊖	✕	◧	✕⊖	D✕	⊖	✕	◧	✕	G✕	△	⊖	⊖	✕	✕	✕	◧	R✕	✕	⊖	K✕	✕
	Hamburg Hbf **840** d.	...	...	...	...	...	...	...	...	...	...	0600	...	...	...	...	0708	...	...	...	...	0806	...	0908	...
0	**Berlin** Hbf **850** d.	...	...	...	...	...	0548	...	0639	0652	...	0752	0752	0757	0839	...	0858	0858	...	...	0952	0952	1039	1058	1058
98	Lutherstadt Wittenberg **850** d.	...	...	...	...	...	0633	...	0721	0736	...	0835	0835	|	0921	...	|	|	...	...	1035	1035	1121	|	|
135	Bitterfeld **850** d.	...	...	...	...	...	0649	...	0738	|	...	|	|	|	0938	...	|	|	...	...	|	|	1138	|	|
168	**Leipzig** Hbf a.	...	...	...	...	...	0705	...	|	0805	...	0905	0905	0916	|	...	1005	1005	...	...	1105	1105	|	1205	1205
168	**Leipzig** Hbf **850** d.	...	0501	0601	...	...	...	0711	|	0816	...	0911	0911	...	|	...	1016	1016	1016	...	1111	1111	|	1216	1216
	Halle (Saale) Hbf **850** d.	...	|	|	0602	...	...	|	0800	|	...	|	|	...	1000	1000	|	|	|	...	|	|	1200	|	|
222	Naumburg (Saale) Hbf **850** d.	...	|	0638	0645	...	...	|	0833	0851	...	|	|	...	1033	1033	1051	1051	1051	...	|	|	1233	1251	1251
261	**Jena** Paradies d.	...	|	...	0711	...	...	|	...	0917	...	|	|	...	...	...	1117	1117	1117	...	|	|	...	1317	1317
308	**Saalfeld** (Saale) d.	0525	✣	...	0741	0752	...	✣	...	0946	0952	✣	✣	...	...	...	1146	1146	1146	1152	✣	✣	...	1346	1346
372	Kronach d.	0628	|	...	|	0841	...	|	...	|	1041	|	|	...	...	...	|	|	|	1241	|	|	...	|	|
395	Lichtenfels **875** d.	0650	|	...	0832	0853	...	|	...	1038	1053	|	|	...	...	...	1238	1238	1238	1253	|	|	...	1438	1438
427	**Bamberg** **875** a.	*0722*	|	...	0848	*0922*	...	|	...	1055	*1122*	|	|	...	...	...	1255	1255	1255	*1322*	|	|	...	1455	1455
465	Erlangen **875** a.	*0827**	|	...	*1004**	|	...	|	...	*1204**	*1237**	|	|	...	...	...	*1404**	*1404**	*1404**	|	|	|	...	*1604**	*1604**
489	**Nürnberg** Hbf **875** a.	*0837**	0925	...	*1003**	*1037**	...	1125	...	*1215**	*1237**	1325	1325	...	...	...	*1415**	*1415**	*1415**	*1437**	1525	1525	...	*1613**	*1613**
	Augsburg Hbf **904** a.	...	1032	...	...	...	...	|	...	...	...	|	|	...	...	...	...	...	...	...	|	|	...	...	...
	München Hbf **904** a.	...	1110	...	...	...	...	1240	...	...	...	1439	1439	...	...	...	...	...	...	...	1640	1640	...	...	...

	RE 3487	ICE 309	IC 2356	ICE 1571	RE 3489	ICE 1673	IC 2354	ICE 1573	RE 3491	ICE 1675	IC 2352	ICE 1575	RE 3493	X 80004	ICE 1677	IC 2350 Ⓑ	ICE 1577 Ⓑ	ICE 1579 ⑥	RE 3495	ICE 905 ⑦	ICE 1619 ①–⑥	ICE 1519 Ⓑ	ICE 909 ⑤	CNL 1211 [R]	ICE 1521 ⑦
	◧	C✕	⊖	✕	◧	✕	⊖	✕	◧	✕	⊖	✕		R△	✕	⊖	✕	✕		✕	✕	✕	✕	B✕	✕
Hamburg Hbf **840** d.	...	...	...	1051	...	...	...	1308	...	...	...	1453	...	...	...	...	1708	...	...	1804	...	1908	2006	...	2121
Berlin Hbf **850** d.	...	1152	1239	1258	...	1352	1440	1458	...	1552	1639	1658	...	1706	1752	1839	1858	1858	...	1952	1952	2058	2152	2212	2312
Lutherstadt Wittenberg **850** d.	...	1235	1321	|	...	1435	1521	|	...	1635	1721	|	...	|	1835	1921	|	|	...	2035	2035	2140	2238	|	2354
Bitterfeld **850** d.	...	|	1338	|	...	|	1538	|	...	|	1738	|	...	|	|	1938	|	1958	...	|	|	|	|	|	|
Leipzig Hbf a.	...	1305	|	1405	...	1505	|	1605	...	1705	|	1805	...	1832	1905	|	2005	2015	...	2105	2105	2210	2307	|	0029
Leipzig Hbf **850** d.	...	1311	|	1416	...	1511	|	1616	...	1711	|	1816	...	...	1911	|	2011	2019	...	...	...	...	...	|	...
Halle (Saale) Hbf **850** d.	...	|	1400	|	...	|	1600	|	...	|	1800	|	...	...	|	2002	|	|	...	...	...	...	...	0045**u**	...
Naumburg (Saale) Hbf **850** d.	...	|	1433	1451	...	|	1633	1651	...	|	1833	1851	...	...	|	2033	2052	2052	...	...	...	...	...	|	...
Jena Paradies d.	...	|	...	1517	...	|	...	1717	...	|	...	1917	...	...	|	...	2117	2117	...	...	...	...	...	|	...
Saalfeld (Saale) d.	1352	✣	...	1546	1552	✣	...	1746	1752	✣	...	1946	1952	...	✣	...	2146	2146	2152	...	...	...	...	|	...
Kronach d.	1441	|	...	|	1641	|	...	|	1841	|	...	|	2041	...	|	...	|	|	2247	...	...	...	...	|	...
Lichtenfels d.	1453	|	...	1638	1653	|	...	1838	1853	|	...	2037	2053	...	|	...	2236	2236	2310	...	...	...	...	|	...
Bamberg a.	*1522*	|	...	1655	*1722*	|	...	1855	*1922*	|	...	2057	*2127*	...	|	...	2251	2251	*2342*	...	...	...	...	|	...
Erlangen a.	*1637**	|	...	*1804**	*1837**	|	...	*1945**	*2037**	|	...	*2150**	*2247**	...	|	...	*2345**	*2345**	*0054**	...	...	...	...	|	...
Nürnberg Hbf a.	*1637**	1725	...	*1813**	*1837**	1925	...	*2013**	*2037**	2125	...	*2225**	*2241**	...	2320	...	*0020**	*0020**	*0146**	...	...	...	...	|	...
Augsburg Hbf **904** a.	...	|	...	...	...	|	...	...	...	|	...	...	...	...	|	...	...	...	...	...	...	...	...	0646	...
München Hbf **904** a.	...	1838	...	...	...	2040	...	...	...	2240	...	...	...	...	0049	...	...	...	...	...	...	...	...	0731**o**	...

	ICE 1578 ①	ICE 1578 ①–⑥	ICE 1616 ①–⑤	CNL 1210 [R]	RB 16902 ①–⑤	ICE 1576 ①	ICE 1576	RB 16842 ①–⑥	ICE 1753 ②–⑤	ICE 1674 ①–⑥	X 80003	RE 3480	ICE 1574	IC 2353	ICE 1672 ①–⑤	ICE 1692 ⑥	RE 3482	ICE 1572	IC 2355	ICE 1670	RE 3484	ICE 1570	IC 2357	ICE 308	RE 3486
		§✕	✕	A✕		✕	✕		D✕	✕	R△		✕	⊖	✕	✕	◧	¶✕	⊖	✕	◧	✕	⊖	N✕	◧
München Hbf **904** d.	...	...	...	2304	...	0128	...	...	...	...	...	...	...	...	0431	0516	...	...	...	0720	...	...	...	0921	...
Augsburg Hbf **904** d.	...	...	...	2345	...	0208	...	...	...	...	...	...	...	...	0513	|	...	...	...	|	...	...	...	|	...
Nürnberg Hbf d.	...	...	...	|	...	0336	...	...	0413	*0440**	...	*0523**	*0550***v**	...	0635	0635	*0723**	*0750**	...	0835	*0923**	*0950**	...	1035	*1123**
Erlangen d.	...	...	...	|	...	|	...	...	|	*0512**	...	*0539**	|	...	|	|	*0725**	*0747***z**	...	|	*0945**	*0952**	...	|	*1122**
Bamberg d.	0302	...	...	|	...	|	...	...	|	0604	...	*0642*	0707	...	|	|	*0838*	0904	...	|	*1038*	1105	...	|	*1238*
Lichtenfels d.	0320	...	...	|	...	✣	...	0543	✣	0621	...	0704	0724	...	|	|	0904	0922	...	|	1104	1122	...	|	1304
Kronach d.	|	...	...	|	...	|	...	0607	|	|	...	0717	|	...	|	|	0917	|	...	|	1117	|	...	|	1317
Saalfeld (Saale) d.	0416	...	...	|	0508	|	...	0709	|	0717	...	0808	0815	...	✣	✣	1008	1015	...	✣	1208	1215	...	✣	1408
Jena Paradies d.	0442	...	...	|	0549	|	...	...	|	0744	...	...	0844	...	|	|	...	1044	...	|	...	1244	...	|	...
Naumburg (Saale) Hbf **850** d.	0505	...	...	|	0625	0715	0715	...	0814	|	...	...	0908	0925	|	|	...	1108	1125	|	...	1308	1325	|	...
Halle (Saale) Hbf **850** a.	|	...	...	0648**s**	0707	|	|	...	|	|	...	...	|	0956	|	|	...	|	1156	|	...	|	1356	|	...
Leipzig Hbf **850** a.	0542	...	...	|	...	0747	0747	...	0846	0841	...	...	0941	|	1046	1046	...	1141	|	1246	...	1341	|	1446	...
Leipzig Hbf d.	0548	0548	0651	|	...	0751	0751	...	...	0851	0926	...	0951	|	1051	1051	...	1151	|	1251	...	1351	|	1451	...
Bitterfeld **850** d.	|	|	0709	|	...	|	|	...	...	|	|	...	|	1020	|	|	...	|	1220	|	...	|	1420	|	...
Lutherstadt Wittenberg **850** d.	|	|	0725	|	...	|	|	...	...	0922	|	...	|	1036	1122	1122	...	|	1236	1322	...	|	1436	1522	...
Berlin Hbf **850** a.	0700	0700	0811	0959	...	0900	0900	...	...	1005	1050	...	1100	1116	1205	1205	...	1300	1316	1405	...	1500	1516	1605	...
Hamburg Hbf **840** a.	0852	0852	0956	...	...	...	...	...	...	1156	...	...	1301	...	...	...	...	1452**b**	...	...	...	1649**b**	...	...	...

	ICE 1568 Ⓑ	ICE 1588 ⑥	IC 2157 2257	ICE 1666 ⑥	ICE 1726 Ⓑ	RE 3488	ICE 1586 ⑤⑦	ICE 1566 T	IC 2259 2359	ICE 1684	X 80005	RE 3490	ICE 1564 ⑤–⑦	ICE 1584 ①–④	IC 2151	ICE 1662	ICE 1655 Ⓑ	RE 3492	ICE 1562 ①–⑥	ICE 1582 ⑦	IC 2153 Ⓑ	ICE 1660 ⑤⑦	RE 3494	ICE 1560	ICE 1647 1747
	K✕	✕	⊖	H✕	R✕	◧	✕	✕	Ⓑ⊖	‡✕	△	◧	✕	✕	⊖	D✕	✕⊖	◧	✕	✕	⊖	✕		✕	
München Hbf **904** d.	...	...	...	1120	1120	...	...	...	...	1320	...	...	...	...	...	1520	...	...	...	...	...	1720	...	1745	...
Augsburg Hbf **904** d.	...	...	...	|	|	...	...	...	...	|	...	...	...	...	...	|	...	...	...	...	...	|	...	1822	...
Nürnberg Hbf d.	*1150**	*1150**	...	1237	1237	*1323**	*1350**	*1350**	...	1436	...	*1523**	*1550**	*1550**	...	1635	...	*1723**	*1750**	*1750**	...	1835	*1923**	1937	...
Erlangen d.	*1153**	*1153**	...	|	|	*1345**	*1353**	*1353**	...	|	...	*1545**	*1552**	*1552**	...	|	...	*1745**	*1810**	*1810**	...	|	*1945**	|	...
Bamberg d.	1305	1305	...	|	|	*1438*	1505	1505	...	|	...	*1638*	1705	1705	...	|	...	*1838*	1905	1905	...	|	*2038*	|	...
Lichtenfels d.	1322	1322	...	|	|	1504	1522	1522	...	|	...	1704	1722	1722	...	|	...	1904	1922	1922	...	✣	2103	✣	...
Kronach d.	|	|	...	|	|	1517	|	|	...	|	...	1717	|	|	...	|	...	1917	|	|	...	|	2118	|	...
Saalfeld (Saale) d.	1415	1415	...	✣	✣	1608	1615	1615	...	✣	...	1808	1815	1815	...	✣	...	2008	2015	2015	...	|	2208	|	...
Jena Paradies d.	1444	1444	...	|	|	...	1644	1644	...	|	...	...	1844	1844	...	|	...	...	2044	2044	...	|	...	|	...
Naumburg (Saale) Hbf **850** d.	1508	1508	1525	|	|	...	1708	1708	1725	|	...	...	1908	1908	1925	|	...	...	2108	2108	2128	2219	...	2315	2322
Halle (Saale) Hbf **850** a.	|	|	1556	|	|	...	|	|	1756	|	...	...	|	|	1956	|	...	...	|	|	2200	|	...	|	2350
Leipzig Hbf **850** a.	1541	1541	|	1646	1646	...	1741	1741	|	1846	...	...	1941	1941	|	2046	...	...	2141	2141	...	2251	...	2345	...
Leipzig Hbf d.	1551	1551	|	1651	1651	...	1751	1751	|	1851	1855	...	1951	1951	|	...	2051	...	2151	2151	...	2301	...	...	...
Bitterfeld **850** d.	|	|	1620	|	|	...	|	|	1820	|	|	...	|	|	2020	...	|	...	|	|	...	|	...	...	...
Lutherstadt Wittenberg **850** d.	|	|	1636	1722	1722	...	|	|	1836	1922	|	...	|	|	2036	...	2122	...	|	|	...	2332	...	...	...
Berlin Hbf **850** a.	1659	1700	1716	1804	1805	...	1900	1900	1916	2005	2015	...	2100	2100	2116	...	2204	...	2300	2300	...	0014	...	...	...
Hamburg Hbf **840** a.	1852	...	...	1956	...	...	2052	...	...	2157**b**	...	...	2305	...	...	...	...	...	0043	...	...	...	...	...	...

A – Aug. 1 - Sept. 13. CAPELLA – 1 cl., 2 cl. and (reclining) München - Potsdam Hbf (a. 0902) - Berlin Wannsee (a. 0913) - Berlin Zoo (a. 0952) - Berlin Ostbahnhof (a. 1007).
B – Aug. 1 - Sept. 13. CAPELLA – 1 cl., 2 cl. and (reclining) Berlin Ostbahnhof (d. 2203) - Berlin Zoo (d. 2220) - Berlin Wannsee (d. 2254) - Potsdam Hbf (d. 2304) - München Ost.
C – and ✕ (Warnemünde - Rostock ⑥ -) Berlin - München - Innsbruck.
D – To / from Dresden (Table **842**).
G – To Garmisch on ⑥ (a. 1622).
H – From Garmisch (d. 0925).
K – From / to Kiel (Table **820**).
N – From Innsbruck (Table **951**)
R – To / from Rostock and Warnemünde (see Table **835**).
T – ①②③④⑥ only.

b – Ⓑ only.
o – München **Ost**.
s – Stops to set down only.
u – Stops to pick up only.
v – ①–⑥ only. By 🚌 Nürnberg - Bamberg.
z – *0808* on ⑥. By 🚌 Erlangen - Bamberg.

* – By 🚌 Bamberg - Erlangen or Nürnberg and v.v.
◧ – Saalfeld - Lichtenfels - Bayreuth / Hof and v.v.
△ – *InterConnex*. Operated by Veolia Verkehr GmbH. **DB tickets are not valid**.
✣ – Via Erfurt and Würzburg.
§ – Train number **908** on ⑥.
¶ – Train number **1592** on ⑥.
‡ – Train number **1664** on ⑥.

5 AIRPORT → CITY CENTRE LINKS

City Plans are on pages 29–33

Airport code and name	City	Distance	Journey	Transport ‡	City terminal	Table
AAR Aarhus	Århus	37 km	40 mins	🚌 flybus, connects with flights	Central train station	
ABZ Aberdeen, Dyce	Aberdeen	11 km	40 mins	🚌 **27**, ①–⑥ every 30–40 mins, ⑦ 70 - 125 mins	Guild Street. Also taxis to Dyce rail station	
ALC Alacant	Alacant	12 km	30 mins	🚌 **C6**, every 40 mins	Plaça del Mar	
AMS Amsterdam, Schiphol	Amsterdam	17 km	20 mins	Train, every 10 mins (every hour 2400 - 0600)	Centraal rail station	**451, 454**
	Rotterdam	65 km	45 mins	Train, every 30 mins (every hour 2400 - 0600)	Centraal rail station	**450, 454**
	Den Haag	43 km	35 mins	Train, every 30 mins (every hour 2400 - 0600)	Centraal rail station	**450, 454**
AOI Ancona, Falconara	Ancona	16 km	30 mins	1) 🚌 **9**, 2) Train hourly at peak times: 17 mins	Main rail station	
ATH Athína, Eleftherios Venizélos	Athína	27 km	41 mins	Metro (line **3**), every 30 mins	Syntagma	
	Pireás	41 km	90 mins	🚌 **X96**, every 15–20 mins	Platia Karaiskáki	
SOB Balaton, Sármellék	Keszthely	12 km	20 mins	🚌, connects with Ryanair flights	Rail station. Also 🚌 to Budapest Déli (190 mins), Siófok and Székesfehérvár	
BCN Barcelona, Aeroport del Prat	Barcelona	14 km	22 mins	Train, every 30 mins: 0608 - 2338	Sants. Also calls at Passeig de Gràcia rail station.	**659**
BSL Basel - Mulhouse - Freiburg	Basel	9 km	20 mins	🚌 **50**, ①–⑤ 8 per hour; ⑥⑦ 6 per hour	SBB rail station / Kannenfeldplatz	
	Freiburg	60 km	55 mins	🚌 ①–⑤ every 75–90 mins; ⑥⑦ every 2 hours	Rail station	
BHD Belfast, City, George Best	Belfast	2 km	15 mins	🚌 *Airlink* **600**, ①–⑥ every 20 mins; ⑦ every 40 mins	Europa Buscentre. Also train from Sydenham rail station.	
BFS Belfast, International	Belfast	26 km	40 mins	🚌 *Airbus* **300**, Ⓐ every 10 mins; ⑥ every 20; ⑦ every 30	Europa Buscentre (adjacent to Great Victoria St rail station)	
BEG Beograd, Nikola Tesla	Beograd	16 km	30 mins	🚌 **72**, every 32 minutes	Rail station	
SXF Berlin, Schönefeld	Berlin	24 km	27 mins	Train *AirportExpress* **RE7 / RB14** 2 per hour 0631 - 2331	Ost, Alexanderplatz, Hbf and Zoo rail stations	**847**
TXL Berlin, Tegel	Berlin	7 km	40 mins	🚌 *JetExpressBus TXL*, Ⓐ every 10 mins, Ⓒ every 20 mins	Hauptbahnhof rail station	
BIQ Biarritz - Anglet - Bayonne	Biarritz	3 km	22 mins	🚌 *STAB* **6**, every hour approx.	Town centre	
	Bayonne	7 km	28 mins	🚌 *STAB* **6**, every hour approx.	Rail station	
BIO Bilbao, Sondika	Bilbao	10 km	45 mins	🚌 Bizkaibus **A-3247**, every 30 mins 0615 - 0000	Plaza Moyúa (Metro station Moyúa)	
BHX Birmingham, International	Birmingham	12 km	11 mins	Train, ①–⑥ ± 7 per hour, ⑦ 5 per hour	New Street rail station from International	**129, 142, 143**
FRL Bologna, Forli	Bologna	66 km	85 mins	🚌, connects with Ryanair flights	Centrale rail station, also 🚌 to Forli rail station every 20 minutes	
BLQ Bologna, Guglielmo Marconi	Bologna	8 km	20 mins	🚌 *Aerobus* BLQ, every 15 mins 0600 - 2315	Centrale rail station	
BOD Bordeaux, Mérignac	Bordeaux	12 km	45 mins	🚌 Jet'Bus, every 45 mins 0745 - 2245	St Jean rail station	
BOH Bournemouth	Bournemouth	10 km	15 mins	🚌 **A 1** *Airport Shuttle*, hourly 0730 - 1830	Rail station, Bus station (Travel Interchange)	
BTS Bratislava, Milan Rastislav Štefánika	Bratislava	10 km	20 mins	🚌 **61**, 3 per hour	Main rail station (Hlavná stanica)	
BRE Bremen	Bremen	3 km	20 mins	Tram **6**, ①–⑥ every 10 mins, ⑦ every 20 mins	Main rail station	
VBS Brescia, Montichiari, Verona	Verona	50 km	45 mins	🚌, connects with Ryanair flights	Main rail station	
	Brescia	18 km	20 mins	🚌, connects with Ryanair flights	Main rail station	
BRS Bristol, International	Bristol	13 km	30 mins	🚌 *International Flyer*, ①–⑥ 2–4 per hour; ⑦ 2–4 per hour	Temple Meads rail station, also bus station	
BRU Brussels, National / Zaventem	Brussels	12 km	25 mins	Train, every 20 mins	Midi / Zuid rail station (also calls at Central and Nord)	**402**
OTP Bucureşti, Henri Coanda, Otopeni	Bucureşti	16 km	40 mins	🚌 **783**, ①–⑤ every 15 mins; ⑥⑦ every 30 mins	Piaţa Victoriei (800m from Nord station or 1 stop on subway)	
	Bucureşti	16 km	68 mins	🚌 to P.O. Aeroport H, then train; hourly from 0556	Nord station	
BUD Budapest, Ferihegy	Budapest	16 km	40 mins	🚌 **200**, every 10 - 20 mins	Kőbánya-Kispest metro station (metro connection to city centre)	
Terminal 1	Budapest	18 km	25 mins	Train, 2 - 6 per hour	Nyugati rail station. Ferihegy station is 200m from Terminal 1	
BZG Bydgoszcz	Bydgoszcz	4 km	20 mins	🚌 **80**	Main rail station	
CCF Carcassonne, Salvaza	Carcassonne	5 km	10 mins	🚌, connects with Ryanair flights	Place Davilla and Carcassonne rail station	
CWL Cardiff	Cardiff	19 km	40 mins	🚌 *Airbus Xpress* **X91**, ①–⑥ hourly, ⑦ every 2 hours	Central rail station, city centre	
	Cardiff	19 km	50 mins	🚌 to Rhoose then Train: ①–⑥ hourly, ⑦ every 2 hours	Central rail station	
CRL Charleroi, Brussels	Brussels	55 km	60 mins	🚌, connects with Ryanair flights	Brussels Midi (corner of Rue de France / Rue de l'Instruction)	
	Charleroi		9 mins	🚌 *Line A*, ①–⑤ 2 per hour, ⑥⑦ hourly	Main rail station	
ORK Cork	Cork	8 km	25 mins	🚌 **226**, hourly. Also SkyLink every 30 mins	Parnell Place Bus Station, then 🚌 **5** to rail station	
LDY Derry (Londonderry)	Londonderry	11 km	30 mins	🚌 connects with flights	Foyle Street Bus Station	
DNR Dinard - Pleurtuit - St-Malo	St Malo	14 km	20 mins	Taxis only. Dinard 6 km 10 mins		
DSA Doncaster - Sheffield	Doncaster	10 km	25 mins	🚌 **91, 707, X19**, ①–⑥ 4 per hour; ⑦ 2 per hour	Rail station	
DTM Dortmund, Wickede	Dortmund	10 km	25 mins	🚌 every hour, AirportExpress	Main rail station (Hbf). Also 🚌 to Holzwickede rail station.	
DRS Dresden	Dresden	15 km	23 mins	Train (S-Bahn **S2**) every 30 mins	Main rail stations (Hauptbahnhof and Neustadt)	**857a**
DUB Dublin	Dublin	11 km	35 mins	🚌 *Airlink* **747**, every 10 mins (15 - 20 mins on ⑦)	Bus station (Busaras), O'Connell Street	
	Dublin	11 km	45 mins	🚌 *Airlink* **748**, every 30 mins	Heuston rail station, Bus station (Busaras), Connolly rail station	
	Belfast	157 km	130 mins	🚌 **001 / 200**, hourly 24 hour service	Europa Buscentre (adjacent to Great Victoria St rail station)	
DBV Dubrovnik, Čilipi	Dubrovnik	24 km	30 mins	🚌 *Atlas Bus*, connects with flights	Bus station	
DUS Düsseldorf, International	Düsseldorf	7 km	12 mins	Train (S - Bahn **S7**) Ⓐ every 20 mins, Ⓒ every 30 mins	Main rail station (Hauptbahnhof)	**800, 802**
EMA East Midlands, Nottingham - - Leicester - Derby	East Midlands	10 km	15 mins	🚌 every 30 min. 0700 - 2330	East Midlands Parkway rail station	
	Nottingham	21 km	45 mins	🚌 *Skylink*, every 30 min. 0405 - 2305; (60 mins 2305 - 0405)	Rail station, Market Square	
	Derby	19 km	40 mins	🚌 *Skylink* every 30 min. 0720 - 1820; (60 mins 2045 - 0645)	Bus station (also departures at 0615,1920)	
	Loughborough	8 km	30 mins	🚌 *Skylink* every 30 min. 0745 - 2045; (60 mins 2155 - 0645)	Rail station	
	Leicester	23 km	60 mins	🚌 *Skylink* hourly 0740, 0842 - 1545, 1650 - 1950, 2055 - 0655	St Margaret's Bus station	
EDI Edinburgh, Turnhouse	Edinburgh	11 km	25 mins	🚌 *Airlink* **100**, every 10 mins. **N22** 2400-0600 every 30mins.	Haymarket rail station; Waverley Bridge (next to Waverley station)	
ERF Erfurt	Erfurt	6 km	22 mins	Tram, Line 4, Ⓐ every 10 mins, Ⓒ every 30 mins	Main rail station (Hauptbahnhof)	
EBJ Esbjerg	Esbjerg	12 km	21 mins	🚌 **8**, hourly	*Bybusterminal*	
FAO Faro	Faro	6 km	20 mins	🚌 *EVA*, **14, 16**, hourly	Bus station	
FLR Firenze, Amerigo Vespucci	Firenze	7 km	20 mins	🚌 Ataf *Vola in bus* **62**, every 30 mins	Santa Maria Novella rail station	
HHN Frankfurt, Hahn	Frankfurt	120 km	105 mins	🚌, connects with Ryanair flights	Mannheimer Straße, adjacent to main rail station (Hauptbahnhof)	
				Also 🚌 to Bingen, 60 mins; Heidelberg hbf, 140 mins; Koblenz, 70 mins; Köln hbf, 135 mins; Luxembourg, 105 mins; Mainz, 70 mins; Saarbrücken, 125 mins; Traben-Trarbach, 25 mins.		
FRA Frankfurt	Frankfurt	10 km	15 mins	Train (S-Bahn **S8** or **S9**), 4–6 times hourly	Main rail station (Hauptbahnhof)	**917a**
FDH Friedrichshafen	Friedrichshafen	4 km	7 mins	1–2 trains per hour	Main rail station (Stadt) or Harbour (Hafen)	**931**
GDN Gdańsk, Lech Walesa	Gdańsk	10 km	26 mins	🚌 **110**, 1–2 per hour	Wrzeszcz rail station, then 3 stops (every 15 mins) to Główny	
GVA Genève	Genève	6 km	6 mins	Train, 5 times hourly	Cornavin rail station	**500, 570**
GOA Genova, Cristoforo Colombo	Genova	7 km	20 mins	🚌 *Volabus* **100**, hourly	Principe rail station	
GRO Girona	Girona	12 km	25 mins	🚌, hourly	Rail / Bus station (Estación autobuses)	
	Barcelona	102 km	70 mins	🚌, connects with Ryanair flights	Estacio del Nord, corner of carrer Ali Bei 80 / Sicilia	
GLA Glasgow, International	Glasgow	15 km	25 mins	🚌 *GlasgowFlyer*, ①–⑥ every 10 mins, ⑦ every 15 mins.	Buchanan bus station	
PIK Glasgow, Prestwick	Glasgow	61 km	50 mins	Train, ①–⑥ every 30 mins, ⑦ every 60 minutes	Central station	**216**
GSE Göteborg, City	Göteborg	12 km	30 mins	🚌, connects with Ryanair, Air Berlin and WizzAir flights	Nils Ericson Terminalen (bus station) / Central rail station	
GOT Göteborg, Landvetter	Göteborg	25 km	30 mins	🚌, ①–⑤ 3 per hour, ⑥⑦ 2–3 per hour	Nils Ericson Terminalen (bus station) / Central rail station	
GRZ Graz	Graz	9 km	9 mins	Train ①–⑥ hourly, ⑦ every 2 hours	Main rail station (Hauptbahnhof)	
HAM Hamburg, Fuhlsbüttel	Hamburg	11 km	24 mins	Train (S-Bahn **S1**), every 10 mins	Main rail station (Hauptbahnhof)	
HAJ Hannover, Langenhagen	Hannover	15 km	17 mins	Train (S-Bahn **S5**), every 30 mins	Main rail station (Hauptbahnhof)	**809**
HEL Helsinki, Vantaa	Helsinki	19 km	35 mins	🚌 **615**, ①–⑤ every 15 mins, ⑥⑦ every 20–30 mins	Rail station (stop 10)	
	Tikkurila	7 km	22 mins	🚌 **61**, ①–⑤ every 10 mins, ⑥ 10–15 mins, ⑦ 15–20 mins	Rail station for trains to Helsinki (20 mins; 16 km)	
IOM Isle of Man, Ronaldsway	Douglas	16 km	30 mins	🚌 **1**, hourly (every 30 mins in peak periods)	Lord street	
IST İstanbul, Atatürk	İstanbul	24 km	40 mins	🚌, *Havaş Airport Shuttle* hourly 0400 - 2400	Taksim	
	İstanbul	24 km	60 mins	Metro to Zeytinburnu, then over bridge for Tram **T1**	Sirkeci rail station	
SAW İstanbul, Sabiha Gökçen	İstanbul	32 km	60 mins	🚌, 1–2 per hour, 0540–2040	Bus station. Also Pendik rail station is 4km from airport.	
FKB Karlsruhe - Baden-Baden	Baden-Baden	8 km	15 mins	🚌 **205**, connects with Ryanair flights	Rail station; also 🚌 **140** to Karlsruhe Hbf, 25min	
KTW Katowice, Pyrzowice	Katowice	34 km	50 mins	🚌 hourly	Main rail station	
KUN Kaunas	Kaunas	13 km	40 mins	🚌 **120, 29**	City centre	
	Vilnius	102 km	90 mins	🚌 connects with Ryanair flights	Hotel Panorama, close to bus and railway stations	
KLU Klagenfurt	Klagenfurt	5 km	25 mins	🚌 **45**, to Annabichl rail station, then train or 🚌 **40**	Main rail station and bus station	
KOC Knock	Charlestown	8 km	15 mins	🚌 **449A**, ①–⑥ 6 per day, ⑦ 5 per day	Rooney's public house.	
CPH København, Kastrup	København	12 km	15 mins	Train, every 10 mins	Main rail station (Hovedbanegård)	**703**
	Malmö	36 km	22 mins	Train, every 20 mins	Central rail station	**703**
CGN Köln / Bonn, Konrad Adenauer	Bonn	25 km	32 mins	🚌 **670**, ①–⑤ every 20–30 mins; ⑥⑦ every 30–60 mins	Main rail station (Hauptbahnhof)	
	Köln	15 km	16 mins	Train **S13**, ①–⑤ every 20 mins, ⑥⑦ every 30 mins	Main rail station (Hbf). Also to Mönchengladbach, Koblenz	**802**
KRK Kraków, Balice	Kraków	12 km	15 mins	Train, 2 per hour	Kraków Główny. Balice rail station is 200m from air terminal	
KBP Kyïv, Boryspil	Kyïv	34 km	60 mins	🚌 **322** *Polit*, 2–3 per hour	Main rail station	
LBA Leeds - Bradford	Leeds	16 km	40 mins	🚌 **757**, ①–⑥ every 30 mins, ⑦ every 60 mins	Main rail station and bus station	
	Bradford	11 km	40 mins	🚌 **747**, ①–⑥ every 30 mins, ⑦ every 60 mins	Interchange rail station	
LEJ Leipzig - Halle	Leipzig	20 km	14 mins	Train, every 30 mins	Main rail station (Hauptbahnhof)	**810**
	Halle	18 km	12 mins	Train, every 30 mins	Main rail station (Hauptbahnhof)	**810**
AOC Leipzig, Altenburg-Nobitz	Leipzig	75 km	70 mins	🚌 **250** *ThüSac*, connects with Ryanair flights	Main rail station. Also stops at Altenburg rail station after 15 mins.	

‡ – The frequencies shown apply during daytime on weekdays and are from the airport to the city centre. There may be fewer journeys in the evenings, at weekends and during the winter months. Extended 🚌 journey times could apply during peak hours.

¶ – Graz Airport - Feldkirchen rail station is located about 300 metres away from the airport.

City Plans are on pages 29–33

AIRPORT → CITY CENTRE LINKS 5

Airport code and name	City	Distance	Journey	Transport ‡	City terminal	Table
LNZ Linz, Blue Danube	Linz	12 km	19 mins	🚌, connects with Ryanair flights	Main rail station. Also free 🚌 to Hörsching rail station, 3 mins.	
LIS Lisboa, Portela	Lisboa	7 km	45 mins	🚌 *Aero-Bus* **91**, every 20 mins 0740–2040	Cais do Sodré, Rossio and Entrecampos rail stations	
LPL Liverpool, John Lennon	Liverpool	11 km	35 mins	🚌 **500**, every 30 mins 0645–2345	Lime Street rail stn, Paradise St. Interchange; also 🚌 **700** to Manchester	
LJU Ljubljana, Jože Pučnik, Brnik	Ljubljana	26 km	45 mins	🚌, Ⓐ hourly 0510–2010; © 0700, every 2 hours 1000–2000	Bus station (Avtobusna postaja)	
LCJ Łódź, Lublinek	Łódź	6 km	20 mins	🚌 **65**	Kaliska rail station	
LCY London, City	London	12 km	23 mins	Train (Docklands Light Railway), every 8–10 mins	Bank underground (tube) station	**140**
LGW London, Gatwick	London	44 km	30 mins	Train *Gatwick Express*, every 15 minutes	Victoria	**103, 140**
LHR London, Heathrow	London	24 km	15 mins	Train *Heathrow Express*, every 15 minutes	Paddington	**140**
	London	24 km	58 mins	Underground train (tube), every 4–10 mins	King's Cross St Pancras	**140**
LTN London, Luton	London	50 km	35 mins	6–7 per hour (🚌 between ✈ and Parkway rail station)	St Pancras International	**170, 140**
STN London, Stansted	London	55 km	46 mins	Train *Stansted Express*, every 15 minutes	Liverpool Street rail station	**140**
LBC Lübeck, Blankensee	Lübeck	8 km	30 mins	🚌 **6**, every 20 mins	Bus station (bus stop 5). Also train from Flughafen 300m walk	
	Hamburg	59 km	75 mins	🚌 *VHHAG*, connects with Ryanair flights	Corner Adenauerallee / Brockesstrasse (ZOB) near main rail station	
LUX Luxembourg, Findel	Luxembourg	7 km	25 mins	🚌 **16**, every 15 mins ①–⑤, every 20 mins ⑥	Central rail station	
LWO Lviv, Sknilov	Lvov	10 km		🚌, Taxi-bus *Marshrutka*	City Centre	
LYS Lyon, St Exupéry	Grenoble	91 km	65 mins	🚌 Satobus, hourly 0730 - 2330	Bus station (gare routière), Place de la Résistance	
	Lyon	25 km	50 mins	🚌 *Navette Aéroport*, every 20 mins 0600 - 2340	Part Dieu (journey 35 mins) and Perrache (50 mins) rail stations	
	Chambéry	87 km	60 mins	🚌, 4–5 times daily	Bus station (gare routière)	
MAD Madrid, Barajas	Madrid	12 km	45 mins	Metro (Line **8**) every 5 - 6 mins	Nuevos Ministerios rail / metro station (see city plans p31)	
AGP Málaga	Málaga	8 km	12 mins	Train, every 30 mins	Centro-Alameda and RENFE rail stations	**662**
MMX Malmö, Sturup	Malmö	30 km	45 mins	🚌 *flygbussarna*, connects with Sterling flights	Central rail station	
MAN Manchester	Manchester	16 km	14 mins	Train, up to 8 per hour (houry through the night)	Piccadilly rail station	
MBX Maribor, Orehova vas	Maribor	9 km	15 mins	🚌, connects with Ryanair flights	Bus station, stand 6	
MRS Marseille, Provence	Marseille	28 km	25 mins	🚌, every 20 mins	St Charles rail station; also 🚌 to Aix TGV rail stn. every 30 mins.	
FMM Memmingen	Memmingen	5 km	10 mins	🚌 **2, 810, 811**	Bus station. Train station is nearby; also 🚌 to München, 100 min.	
LIN Milano, Linate	Milano	9 km	20 mins	1) 🚌 **73** every 10 mins; 2) 🚌 *Starfly*, every 30 mins	1) Piazza S. Babila, Metro line 1; 2) Centrale rail station	
MXP Milano, Malpensa	Milano	45 km	40 mins	*Malpensa Express* train, every 30 mins	Cadorna and Bovisa rail stations	**583**
			50 mins	🚌 *Bus Express*, 2 per hour / *Shuttle Air* 3 per hour	Centrale rail station	
BGY Milano, Orio al Serio, Bergamo	Milano	45 km	60 mins	🚌, every 30 - 60 mins	Centrale rail station (Air Terminal)	
	Bergamo	4 km	15 mins	🚌, 2 per hour	Rail station	
DME Moskva, Domodedovo	Moskva	35 km	40 mins	Train, *Aeroekspress*, 1–2 per hour	Paveletskaya rail station	
SVO Moskva, Sheremetyevo	Moskva	29 km	30 mins	Train, *Aeroekspress*, every hour, approx	Savyolovsky rail station	
VKO Moskva, Vnukovo	Moskva	28 km	35 mins	Train, *Aeroekspress*, every hour, approx	Kiyevskaya rail station	
MUC München, International	München	37 km	40 mins	Train (S-Bahn **S1** for Hbf; **S8** for Ost), every 10 mins	Main rail stations (Hauptbahnhof, Ostbahnhof)	**892**
	Freising	6 km	24 mins	🚌 *MVV635*, every 20 mins	Rail station for connections to Regensburg, Passau	**878, 944**
NTE Nantes, Atlantique	Nantes	9 km	30 mins	🚌 *Tan Air*, ± hourly	Main rail station	
NAP Napoli, Capodichino	Napoli	7 km	20 mins	🚌 *ANM* **3S** line, every 30 mins	Piazza Garibaldi (Centrale rail station)	
NCL Newcastle, International	Newcastle	9 km	23 mins	Metro train, every 7 - 12 mins	Main rail station	
NCE Nice, Côte d'Azur	Nice	7 km	20 mins	🚌 **98**, ①–⑥ every 20 mins, ⑦ every 20–30 mins	SNCF rail station	
		8 km	6 mins	Train, from Nice St Augustin, 500m from Terminal 1	SNCF rail station	
NRN Niederrhein	Düsseldorf	70 km	75 mins	🚌, connects with Ryanair flights	Main rail station (Hauptbahnhof) Worringer Street	
	Düsseldorf	74 km	82 mins	🚌 **SW1**, to Weeze rail station, then train, Table **802**	Main rail station (Hauptbahnhof)	
FNI Nîmes - Arles - Camargue	Nîmes	12 km	20 mins	🚌, connects with Ryanair flights	Rail station	
NWI Norwich, International	Norwich	6 km	38 mins	🚌 **27**, ①–⑥ every 20 mins, ⑦ every 60 mins	City centre	
NUE Nürnberg	Nürnberg	6 km	12 mins	Train, U-bahn **U2**, 4–6 per hour	Main rail station (Hauptbahnhof)	
OSL Oslo, Gardermoen	Oslo	49 km	19 mins	Train, 2–4 per hour	Central rail station	
TRF Oslo, Sandefjord Torp	Oslo	140 km	110 mins	🚌 Torp Express, connects with Ryanair and WizzAir flights	Bus terminal. Also 🚌 to Sandefjord for train to Oslo	
PMO Palermo, Falcone-Borsellino	Palermo	24 km	45 mins	Train *Trinacria express*, ①–⑥ 2 per hour, ⑦ hourly	Centrale rail station	
PMI Palma, Mallorca	Palma	11 km	30 mins	🚌 **1**, every 15 mins	Paseo de Mallorca, Plaça d'Espanya (for rail stations), the Port	
BVA Paris, Beauvais	Paris	80 km	75 mins	🚌, connects with Ryanair and WizzAir flights	Porte Maillot, Metro (Line 1) for Châtelet Les Halles, Gare de Lyon	
CDG Paris, Charles de Gaulle	Paris	25 km	35 mins	RER train, (Line B), every 7–15 mins	Nord, Châtelet Les Halles, and St Michel stations	**398**
	Disneyland	23 km	45 mins	🚌 **VEA** Navette / Shuttle, every 20 minutes	Disneyland Resort, Disneyland hotels	
ORY Paris, Orly	Paris	15 km	35 mins	RER train, (Line C), every 15 mins	Austerlitz, St Michel, Musée d'Orsay, and Invalides stations	**398**
PGF Perpignan, Rivesaltes	Perpignan	5 km	15 mins	🚌, connects with Ryanair, Bmibaby flights	Rail station, Bus station (gare routière)	
PSA Pisa, Galileo Galilei	Pisa	2 km	5 mins	1) Train, 2 per hour 2) 🚌 *RedLAM*, every 10 mins	Central rail station (some trains continue to Firenze)	**614**
OPO Porto	Porto	17 km	35 mins	Metro Train, 2 per hour	Campanhã rail station	
POZ Poznań, Ławica	Poznań	6 km	20 mins	🚌 **L** *MPK*, every hour	Rail station	
PRG Praha, Ruzyně	Praha	17 km	60 mins	🚌 **119**, every 10 mins	Dejvická metro station, then Metro line A to muzeum (see City Plans)	
	Praha	16 km	30 mins	🚌 **AE** *Airport Express*, every 30 mins	Holešovice rail station	
PUY Pula	Pula	6 km	15 mins	🚌, connects with Ryanair flights	Town centre	
REU Reus	Reus	6 km	20 mins	🚌 **50**, *Hispano Igualadina* connects with Ryanair flights	Rail station	**652**
	Barcelona	90 km	80 mins	🚌 *Hispano Igualadina* connects with Ryanair flights	Sants rail station	
RZE Rzeszów, Jasionka	Rzeszów	10 km	15 mins	🚌 **L**, departs 1150, 1505 Ⓑ, 2120 Ⓑ	Main rail station and bus station	
KEF Reykjavík, Keflavík	Reykjavík	48 km	55 mins	🚌, connects with flights	Hótel Loftleidir	
RIX Riga	Riga	13 km	30 mins	🚌 **22**, every 10–30 mins	Abrenes iela (street) next to rail station	
RJK Rijeka	Rijeka	30 km	45 mins	🚌 Autotrolej, connects with flights	Bus station, Jelačić Square	
CIA Roma, Ciampino	Roma	15 km	40 mins	🚌 *Terravision*	Termini rail station	**622**
FCO Roma, Fiumicino	Roma	26 km	42 mins	Train, up to 4 per hour	Ostiense and Tiburtina rail stations	**622**
(also known as Leonardo da Vinci)		26 km	31 mins	*Leonardo Express* rail service, every 30 mins	Roma Termini	**622**
RTM Rotterdam	Rotterdam	5 km	20 mins	*Airport Shuttle* **33**, ①–⑤ every 10 mins, ⑥⑦ every 15 mins	Groot Handelsgebouw (adjacent to Centraal rail station)	
LED St Peterburg, Pulkovo II	St Peterburg	17 km	60 mins	🚌 **T-13**	Moskovskaya Metro station, Line 2 for Nevski Pr. (see City Plans)	
SZG Salzburg, W. A. Mozart	Salzburg	5 km	22 mins	🚌 **2**, ①–⑥ every 10 mins, ⑦ every 20 mins	Main rail station	
SOF Sofiya, International	Sofiya	10 km	25 mins	🚌 **84**, every 10–20 mins	University	
SOU Southampton	Southampton	8 km	8 mins	Train, 50 metres from terminal	Main rail station	**108, 126**
SPU Split, Kaštela	Split	16 km	50 mins	🚌 **37**, ①–⑤ every 20 mins, ⑥⑦ every 30 mins	Bus station. Departs 200m from Airport terminal.	
SVG Stavanger, Sola	Stavanger	14 km	30 mins	🚌, ①–⑤ every 20 mins, ⑥ 2 per hour, ⑦ hourly	Atlantic Hotel / Fiskepiren	
ARN Stockholm, Arlanda	Stockholm	44 km	20 mins	*Arlanda Express* train, every 15 mins	Central rail station	**747**
NYO Stockholm, Skavsta	Stockholm	103 km	80 mins	🚌, connects with Ryanair flights	Cityterminal (bus station), also 🚌 to Nyköping train station	
VST Stockholm, Västerås	Stockholm	107 km	75 mins	🚌, connects with Ryanair flights	Cityterminal (bus station), also 🚌 **941** to Västerås train station	
SXB Strasbourg, Entzheim	Strasbourg	12 km	20 mins	🚌, every 20–30 mins to Baggersee, then tram line **A**	Étoile / Homme de Fer / Gare Centrale (Central rail station)	
			12 mins	Train from Entzheim (5 mins walk) infrequent service	Strasbourg	
STR Stuttgart, Echterdingen	Stuttgart	14 km	27 mins	Train (S-Bahn **S2**, **S3**), 2–4 times hourly 0508 - 0008	Main rail station (Hauptbahnhof)	**932**
SZZ Szczecin, Goleniów	Szczecin	38 km	60 mins	🚌, connects with Ryanair flights	Szczecin Główny. Also 🚌, 7km, to Goleniów train station.	
TMP Tampere, Pirkkala	Tampere	18 km	25 mins	🚌, connects with Ryanair flights	City Centre (Rautatieasema)	
TRN Torino, Caselle	Torino	16 km	20 mins	*SATTI* train every 30 mins	Torino Dora rail station, Piazza Baldissera	
	Torino	16 km	40 mins	🚌, every 30–45 minutes	Torino Porta Nuova and Porta Susa	
TLS Toulouse, Blagnac	Toulouse	8 km	20 mins	🚌, every 20 minutes	Place Jeanne d'Arc / Matabiau rail / Bus station (gare routière)	
TRS Trieste, Ronchi dei Legionari	Trieste	33 km	50 mins	🚌 **51**, 2 per hour	Bus station, next to rail station	
	Monfalcone	4 km	17 mins	🚌 **10**, ①–⑥ 2–3 per hour; ⑦ hourly	Rail station	
TRD Trondheim, Værnes	Trondheim	33 km	37 mins	Train, ①–⑤ hourly, ⑥⑦ every two hours	Rail station. Værnes rail station is 220m from Airport terminal	**787**
VLC València	València	9 km	22 mins	Train, Lines **3**, **5**, Ⓐ every 6–9 mins; ⑥⑦ every 8–12 mins	Xátiva for Nord rail station	
VCE Venezia, Marco Polo	Venezia	12 km	21 mins	🚌 **5**, ①–⑥ every 30 mins; ⑦ every 60 mins	Santa Lucia rail station	
	Venezia		60 mins	Waterbus ± every 60 mins	Lido / Piazza S. Marco	
TSF Venezia, Treviso	Venezia	30 km	70 mins	🚌, connects with Ryanair flights	Mestre rail station, Piazzale Roma	
VRN Verona, Villafranca	Verona	12 km	20 mins	🚌, every 20 mins 0635 - 2335	Rail station	
VNO Vilnius	Vilnius	5 km	7 mins	Train, every 40 minutes	Rail station	
WAW Warszawa, Frederic Chopin, Okęcie	Warszawa	10 km	30 mins	🚌 **175** *Airport-City*, ①–⑤ every 20 mins, ⑥⑦ every 30 mins	Centralna rail station	
VIE Wien, Schwechat	Wien	21 km	16 mins	*CAT*, every 30 mins	Mitte rail station	**979**
	Wien	21 km	25 mins	S-bahn, every 30 mins	Mitte rail station	**979**
	Bratislava	45 km	70 mins	🚌 ÖBB-Bahn Bus / SAD Bratislava, hourly	AS Mlynské nivy (bus station)	**979**
WRO Wrocław, Copernicus	Wrocław	10 km	30 mins	🚌 **406**, ①–⑥ 2–3 per hour; ⑦ every 40 mins	Rail station, bus station	
ZAG Zagreb	Zagreb	17 km	25 mins	🚌, 1–2 per hour	Bus station (Autobusni kolodvor), Avenija Marina Drzica	
ZRH Zürich	Zürich	10 km	13 mins	Train, 7–8 per hour	Main rail station (**HB**)	**529**
ZQW Zweibrücken	Zweibrucken	4 km	10 mins	Taxi	Rail station. Also 🚌 to Saarbrücken.	

‡ – The frequencies shown apply during daytime on weekdays and are from the airport to the city centre. There may be fewer journeys in the evenings, at weekends and during the winter months. Extended 🚌 journey times could apply during peak hours.

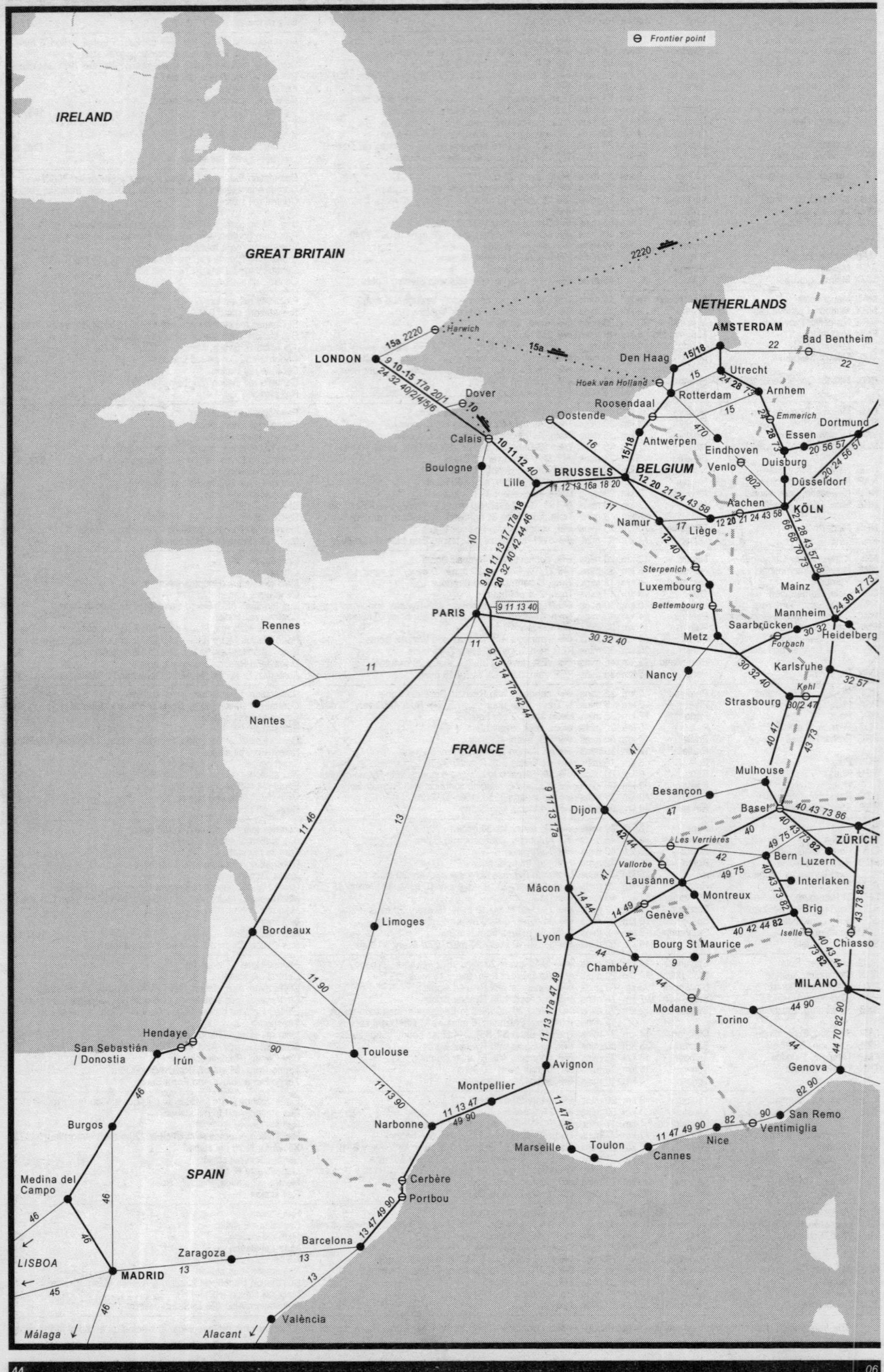
Frontier point
IRELAND
GREAT BRITAIN
NETHERLANDS
BELGIUM
FRANCE
SPAIN
LONDON
Harwich
Dover
Calais
Boulogne
Lille
Hoek van Holland
Den Haag
AMSTERDAM
Utrecht
Rotterdam
Roosendaal
Antwerpen
Oostende
BRUSSELS
Eindhoven
Venlo
Arnhem
Emmerich
Essen
Dortmund
Duisburg
Düsseldorf
KÖLN
Aachen
Liège
Namur
Bad Bentheim
Sterpenich
Luxembourg
Bettembourg
Metz
Mainz
Mannheim
Heidelberg
Saarbrücken
Forbach
Karlsruhe
Kehl
Strasbourg
Nancy
PARIS
Rennes
Nantes
Mulhouse
Besançon
Basel
ZÜRICH
Dijon
Les Verrières
Vallorbe
Bern
Luzern
Lausanne
Interlaken
Montreux
Mâcon
Genève
Brig
Iselle
Chiasso
Lyon
Bourg St Maurice
Chambéry
Modane
MILANO
Torino
Genova
Limoges
Bordeaux
Hendaye
San Sebastián / Donostia
Irún
Toulouse
Avignon
Montpellier
Narbonne
Marseille
Toulon
Cannes
Nice
Ventimiglia
San Remo
Burgos
Medina del Campo
Cerbère
Portbou
Barcelona
Zaragoza
MADRID
València
LISBOA
Málaga
Alacant

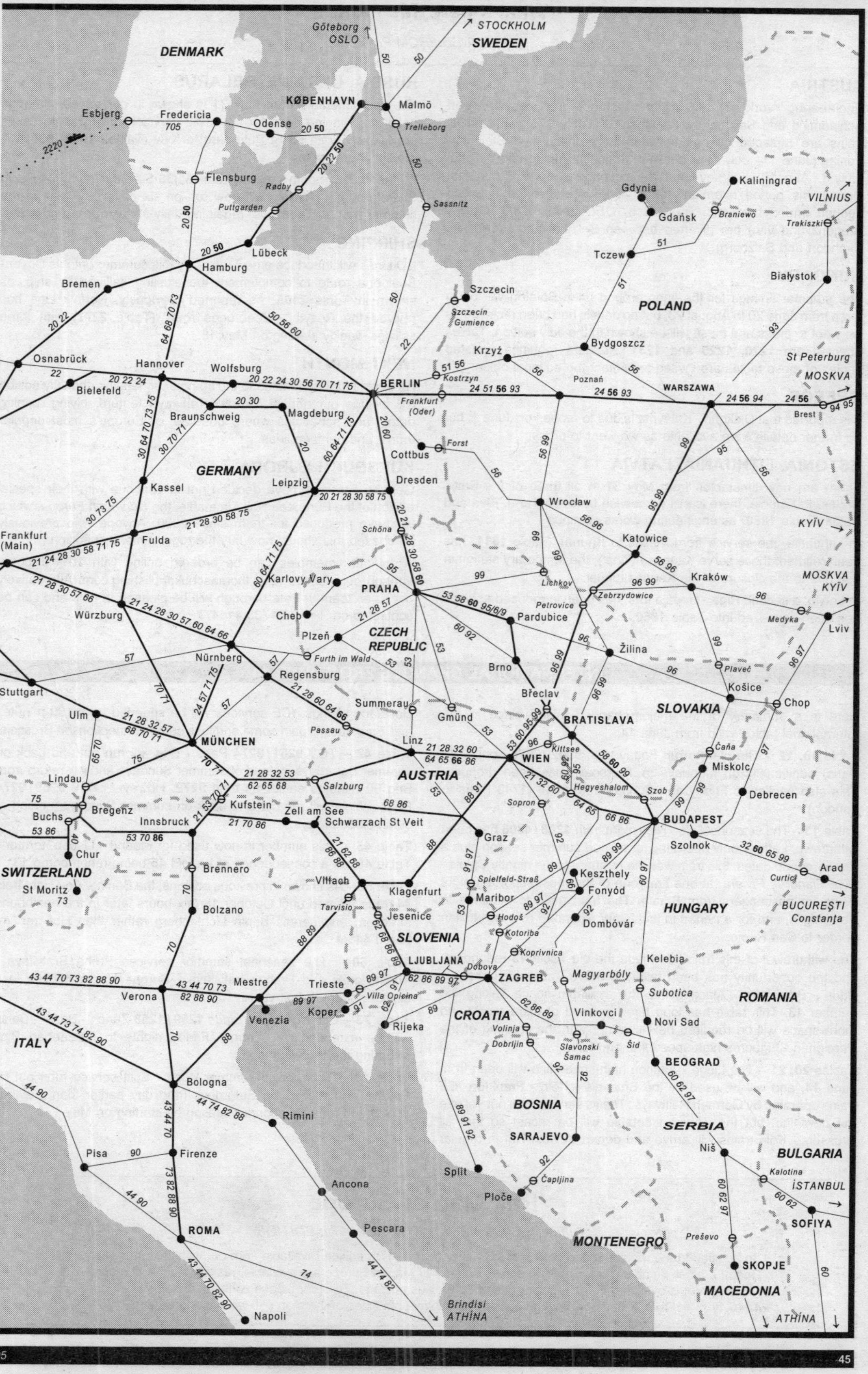

DENMARK
SWEDEN
POLAND
GERMANY
CZECH REPUBLIC
SLOVAKIA
AUSTRIA
SWITZERLAND
SLOVENIA
HUNGARY
CROATIA
BOSNIA
SERBIA
ROMANIA
BULGARIA
MONTENEGRO
MACEDONIA
ITALY
Göteborg
OSLO
STOCKHOLM
KØBENHAVN
Malmö
Trelleborg
Esbjerg
Fredericia
Odense
Flensburg
Rødby
Puttgarden
Sassnitz
Lübeck
Hamburg
Bremen
Osnabrück
Hannover
Bielefeld
Wolfsburg
Braunschweig
Magdeburg
BERLIN
Kostrzyn
Frankfurt (Oder)
Szczecin
Szczecin Gumience
Krzyż
Bydgoszcz
Poznań
Gdynia
Gdańsk
Tczew
Kaliningrad
Braniewo
Trakiszki
VILNIUS
Białystok
St Peterburg
MOSKVA
WARSZAWA
Brest
KYÏV
Cottbus
Forst
Dresden
Leipzig
Kassel
Fulda
Frankfurt (Main)
Würzburg
Nürnberg
Stuttgart
Ulm
Regensburg
Passau
Schöna
Karlovy Vary
Cheb
Plzeň
Furth im Wald
PRAHA
Pardubice
Brno
Wrocław
Katowice
Kraków
Lichkov
Petrovice
Zebrzydowice
Žilina
Medyka
Lviv
Plaveč
Košice
Chop
Čaňa
Miskolc
Debrecen
Summerau
Gmünd
Linz
Břeclav
BRATISLAVA
Kittsee
WIEN
Hegyeshalom
Sopron
Szob
BUDAPEST
Szolnok
Curtici
Arad
BUCUREŞTI
Constanţa
MÜNCHEN
Lindau
Bregenz
Buchs
Chur
St Moritz
Kufstein
Salzburg
Innsbruck
Zell am See
Schwarzach St Veit
Graz
Brennero
Bolzano
Villach
Tarvisio
Klagenfurt
Jesenice
Spielfeld-Straß
Maribor
Hodoš
Kotoriba
Koprivnica
Keszthely
Fonyód
Dombóvár
Magyarbóly
LJUBLJANA
Dobova
ZAGREB
Trieste
Villa Opicina
Koper
Rijeka
Volinja
Dobrljin
Vinkovci
Slavonski Šamac
Šid
Kelebia
Subotica
Novi Sad
BEOGRAD
SARAJEVO
Čapljina
Split
Ploče
Niš
Kalotina
SOFIYA
İSTANBUL
Preševo
SKOPJE
ATHÍNA
Verona
Mestre
Venezia
Bologna
Rimini
Pisa
Firenze
Ancona
Pescara
ROMA
Napoli
Brindisi
ATHÍNA

What's new this month

CONTINUED FROM PAGE 3

AUSTRIA

Engineering work will affect long-distance services between Schladming and Selzthal until August 10 (Table **975**); *EC* and *IC* trains are replaced by bus between Schladming and Stainach-Irdning (June 11 - July 7) or between Stainach-Irdning and Selzthal (July 8 - Aug. 10). Journey times are extended by up to 15 minutes. During this period overnight trains **464/5** are diverted between Leoben and Schwarzach via Villach. *ÖEC* trains **668/9** (Graz - Bregenz and v.v.) are diverted between Selzthal and Wörgl (via Kirchdorf and Salzburg).

HUNGARY

The summer timings for the lines around Lake Balaton will be in force from June 20 to August 23, but no details had been received as we went to press and these will be shown in the July edition. Tables affected are **1220**, **1225** and **1231**. Readers requiring updated copies of these tables are invited to contact the editorial office.

GREECE

It is reported that Diakoftó - Kalávrita is due to reopen on June 1, but no further details were available as we went to press.

ESTONIA, LITHUANIA, LATVIA

There are new timetables from May 31 in all three of the Baltic States. In Estonia, there is still no service between Tartu, Elva and Valga (Table **1880**) as engineering works continue.

In Lithuania, the service from Vilnius to Kaunas (Table **1811**) has been retimed; these serve Kaunas **I** ('one'), the temporary station in use due to the closure of the Kaunas tunnel.

In Latvia, a second Riga - Liepaja train has been introduced and this has been squeezed into Table **1860**.

RUSSIA, UKRAINE, BELARUS

The new timetable from May 31 is shown in our tables, although details of running days for domestic services are in some cases provisional. Train **53** St Peterburg to Kyïv (Tables **1920/1930**) will run six hours earlier.

Further to last month's report, trains **35/36** *Sibelius* and **33/34** *Repin* St Peterburg - Helsinki will now run on six days per week in the summer (not on Tuesdays) regaining daily status from August 31.

SHIPPING

L D Lines will introduce a new fast ferry this summer onto its Dover - Boulogne route to complement the existing sailings by ship, as shown in Table **2105**. As reported previously, Norfolk Line has revived the Rosyth - Zeebrugge route (Table **2277**) with three sailings weekly starting on May 18.

NEXT MONTH

As well as further updates to the summer schedules, the July edition will include our annual **Tourist Railways** feature, giving running dates, and schedules where possible, of Europe's most popular tourist and heritage lines.

KURSBUCH EUROPA

German Railways have decided not to continue with their special edition of the European Rail Timetable, the *Kursbuch Europa*, which we have produced for them since 2000. Anyone who previously purchased this should now buy the regular monthly edition.

All of our timetables can be ordered online with 10% discount through our website www.thomascookpublishing.com. Alternatively our sales team in Peterborough will be pleased to help and can be contacted on +44 (0)1733 416477.

INTERNATIONAL CHANGES FROM JUNE 14

Here is a summary of the major changes taking place in the International tables valid from June 14.

Table **10**, **12** – The plan to run Friday train **9002** (0626 London to Paris) additionally on Mondays to Thursdays has been dropped. This also applies to Friday and Sunday train **9049** (1743 Paris to London).

Table **13** – The seasonal Lille - Nice night train **4208 / 4308** has been withdrawn. Latterly only operating for a short summer season plus a few other odd dates, this train was the remnant of the nightly Calais - Nice *Flandres Riviera*, at one time one of the most important night trains for passengers from Britain. The train used to continue to Ventimiglia, and for a period in its history extended over the Italian border to San Remo.

The withdrawal of this train has made the old Table **13** redundant, and the opportunity has been taken to move Table **45**, London - Paris - Barcelona - Alacant, into the available space, taking the number **13**. This table has long been in need of extra room, and more space will be required next summer with the opening of the Perpignan - Figueres high-speed line and tunnel.

Tables **20**, **21** – The Liège - Aachen high-speed line will open from June 14, and will be used by the Brussels - Köln - Frankfurt *ICE* trains operated by German Railways. *Thalys* services will not yet use the new line, but the *Thalys* timetable will be recast so that all Brussels - Köln trains will arrive and depart at Köln Hbf in regular clockface timings. *ICE* services will be speeded up by 30 minutes and Eurostar will gain some and lose some connections at Brussels.

Table **42** – *TGV* **9261 / 9274** Paris - Brig will run out and back on summer Saturdays instead of summer Sundays and will return from Brig 90 minutes earlier as train **9272**. However, *TGV* **9269 / 9274** Paris - Aigle will run out and back on summer Sundays instead of summer Saturdays.

Table **45** – This number is now used for Madrid - Lisboa, formerly Table **48**, as a consequence of the old **45** being renumbered **13**.

Table **56** – As shown in previous editions, the Berlin - Kiev night train **441/0** is retimed until October 18 (six hours later in the eastbound direction) and serves Berlin Lichtenberg rather than Hbf, renumbered **445/4**.

Table **60** – The seasonal summer services Praha / Bratislava - Thessaloníki and Praha / Bratislava - Burgas / Varna will run in a similar pattern to last year.

Table **73** – *City Night Line Sirius* **1259 / 1258** Zürich - Basel - Berlin will be extended on summer Friday nights to Ostseebad Binz returning the following night.

Table **91** – The weekly summer Wien - Split service runs out on Fridays and returns on Saturdays (one day earlier than previous years) and runs for a longer season by starting on May 1.

INTERNATIONAL SERVICES

Services All trains convey first and second classes of seating accommodation unless otherwise noted. For information on types of sleeping car (🛏) and couchette car (▬) see page 10. Restaurant (✕) and buffet (🍷) cars vary considerably from country to country in standard of service offered. The catering car may not be carried or open for the whole journey.

Timings **Valid June 14, 2009 - December 12, 2009**. Services can change at short notice and passengers are advised to consult the latest Thomas Cook European Rail Timetable before travelling. International trains are not normally affected by public holidays, but may alter at Christmas and Easter - these changes (where known) are shown in the tables.

Tickets **Seat reservations** are available for most international trains and are advisable as some trains can get very crowded. **Supplements** are payable on **EuroCity** (*EC*) trains in most countries and on most InterCity trains – consult the introduction at the start of each country to see which supplements apply.

Listed below is a selection of the different types of trains found in the International Section.

DAY SERVICES:

AP	**Alfa Pendular**	Portuguese high-quality tilting express train.
Alvia	**Alvia**	The newest Spanish high-speed trains.
Alta	**Altaria**	Spanish quality express using light, articulated stock.
Arco	**Arco**	Spanish quality express train.
AV	**Alta Velocità**	Italian premium fare **ETR 500** services using high-speed lines.
AVE	***Alta Velocidad Española***	Spanish high-speed train.
CIS	***Cisalpino***	Italian **ETR 470** or **610** international high-speed (200 km/h) tilting train.
EC	**EuroCity**	Quality international express. Supplement may be payable.
Em	***Euromed***	Spanish 200 km/h trains.
☆	**Eurostar**	High speed (300 km/h) service between London - Paris and Brussels. Special fares payable. Three classes of service: (Business Premier, Leisure Select and Standard). Minimum check-in time 30 minutes. Non–smoking.
ES	**Eurostar Italia**	Italian high speed **ETR 450 / 460 / 500** (250 - 300 km/h) service.
ESc	**Eurostar City**	High speed loco-hauled services, premium fares payable.
Ex	**Express**	Express between Czech Republic and Slovakia.
IC	**InterCity**	Express train. Supplement may be payable.
ICE	**InterCity Express**	German high speed (230 - 320 km/h) service.
ICp	**InterCity** Plus	Italian express formed of new coaches, supplement payable.
IR	**InterRegio**	Inter-regional express usually with refurbished coaches.
RJ	**Railjet**	Austrian quality international express with Premium Class.
RX	**RegioExpress**	Swiss semi-fast regional train.
RB	**Regional Bahn**	German stopping train.
RE	**Regional Express**	German semi-fast train.
SC	**Super City**	Czech Pendolino **680** tilting train, supplement payable.
Talgo	**Talgo**	Spanish quality express using light, articulated stock.
⇄	***Thalys***	High-speed (300 km/h) international train Paris - Brussels - Amsterdam/Köln. Special fares apply. Non–smoking.
TGV	**Train à Grande Vitesse**	French high-speed (270 - 320 km/h) train.
X2000	**X2000**	Swedish high speed (210 km/h) tilting trains.

NIGHT SERVICES:

CNL	**City Night Line**	German brand name covering *CityNightLine*, DB NachtZug and UrlaubsExpress services. Facilities range from *Deluxe* sleeping cars (1 and 2 berth) with en-suite shower and WC, to modernised sleeper and couchette cars. Most trains convey shower facilities and 🍷 (also ✕ on certain services). Special fares apply and reservation is compulsory on most services.
D	**Durchgangszug** or **Schnellzug**	Overnight or international express. Some may only convey passengers to international destinations and are likely to be compulsory reservation, marked R.
EN	**EuroNight**	Quality international overnight express.
Estr	**Estrella**	Spanish night train.
Hotel	**Trenhotel**	Spanish international quality overnight train. Conveys Gran Clase / Grande Classe sleeping accommodation comprising *de luxe* (1 and 2 berth) compartments with en-suite shower and WC. Also conveys 1, 2 and 4 berth sleeping cars.
ICN	**InterCityNight**	Italian overnight train, supplement payable.

EUROTUNNEL

The frequent car-carrying service between Folkestone and Calais through the **Channel Tunnel** is operated by Eurotunnel. The service operates up to four times hourly (less frequently at night) and takes about 35 minutes. Passengers stay with their cars during the journey. Separate less-frequent trains operate for lorries, coaches, motorcycles, and cars with caravans. Reservations are advisable but passengers can buy tickets at the toll booths when they arrive at the terminal and board the next available shuttle.

Freephone customer information service: ✆ 080 00 96 99 92. Reservations: ✆ 08705 35 35 35.

INTERNATIONAL SERVICES FROM LONDON

INTERNATIONAL SERVICES FROM PARIS

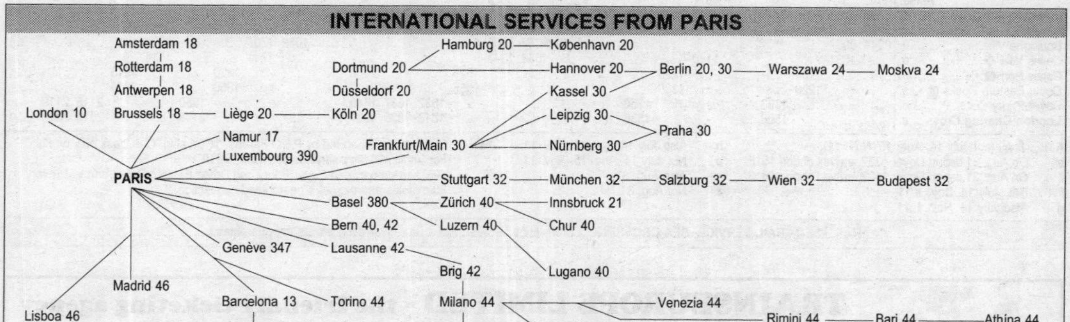

9 LONDON, BRUSSELS and LILLE - ST GERVAIS, BOURG ST MAURICE and BRIANÇON

Table 9 appears in winter editions only

10 LONDON - LILLE - PARIS and BRUSSELS *by Eurostar*

Minimum check-in time is 30 minutes. Not available for London - Ebbsfleet - Ashford or v.v. Special fares payable that include three classes of service.

All times shown are local times (France is one hour ahead of Great Britain). All Eurostar services are 🄡, non-smoking and convey ✕.

Service June 14 - Aug. 30.

km	km	*train number*	9078	9106	9002	9002	9004	9110	9006	9008	9114	9010	9120	9120	9116	9012	9014	9074	9016	9018	9126	9020	9022	9082	9024	9024
		notes		①-⑤	⑥	⑤	①-⑥	①-⑥	①-⑥	⑦	⑥	①-⑥	①-⑤		⑥				⑥				⑤	⑦	①-⑤	⑥⑦
		notes	**By**		**D**	**E**								**P**		**F**		**Z**				**C**	**G**			
0	0	**London St Pancras** .... d.	0525	0557	0622	0626	0655	0659	0727	0752	0757	0832	0834	0827	0859	0901	0926	0953	1000	1025	1057	1101	1132	1202	1229	1229
35	35	Ebbsfleet International....... d.	0542	|	0639	0642	|	0715	0745	0809	|	|	|	0845	0915	|	0942	|	|	|	1115	|	|	|	1245	1245
90	90	Ashford International .... d.	|	0627	|	|	0725	|	|	|	0828	|	|	|	|	|	|	1028	|	1055	|	|	|	|	|	|
166	166	Calais Fréthun .... a.	|	|	|	|	|	|	0929	|	|	|	|	|	|	|	|	|	|	|	|	|	|	|	|	1429
267	267	Lille Europe...................... a.	|	|	|	|	|	0924	|	|	|	|	|	1054	1124	1121	|	1224	|	|	1324	|	|	|	|	|
	373	**Brussels Midi / Zuid**...... a.	|	0856	|	|	|	1003	|	|	1056	|	1129	1133	1203	|	|	...	|	|	1403	|	|	|	|	|
492		**Paris Nord** .... a.	0850	...	0947	0947	1017	...	1056	1117	...	1147	...	...	...	1223	1247	...	1317	1347	...	1417	1447	1517	1550	1556

train number	9132	9026	9028	9030	9138	9034	9036	9144	9144	9144	9040	9148	9150	9044	9044	9046	9154	9048	9154	9050	9050	9052	9158	9054	9054	9056
notes		⑦	①-⑥					⑤	⑦	①-④		⑥⑦	①-⑤	①-⑤	⑥⑦	Ⓑ	⑦	①-⑤		⑥	Ⓑ	⑤		⑥⑦	①-⑤	⑦
notes						**H**												**J**	**S**			**K**				
London St Pancras..........d.	1257	1300	1332	1404	1434	1456	1529	1604	1604	1604	1625	1657	1727	1730	1731	1756	1821	1832	1834	1856	1902	1932	1934	2005	2005	2032
Ebbsfleet International ....d.	1315	|	|	|	|	1512	1545	|	|	|	|	1715	1745	|	|	1812	|	|	|	1912	|	|	|	|	|	|
Ashford International..........d.	|	|	|	|	|	|	|	|	|	|	1655	|	|	|	|	|	1855	|	|	|	|	|	|	|	|	|
Calais Fréthun ....a.	|	|	|	|	|	|	1729	|	1759	|	|	|	|	|	1926	|	|	|	|	|	|	|	|	|	2159	|
Lille Europe ....a.	1524	|	|	1624	1654	|	|	|	|	1824	|	1924	1954	|	|	|	2051	|	|	|	|	|	2154	|	|	|
Brussels Midi / Zuid ......a.	1603	|	|	|	1733	|	|	1859	1903	1903	|	2003	2033	|	|	|	2133	|	2133	|	|	|	2233	|	|	|
Paris Nord.....................a.	...	1617	1647	1726	...	1817	1856	...	...	...	1947	...	...	2047	2053	2117	...	2147	...	2217	2217	2247	...	2320	2326	2347

train number	9109	9005	9007	9113	9113	9113	9009	9011	9119	9015	9019	9181	9023	9025	9027	9133	9031	9033	9139	9035	9141	9037	9039	9039	9145	
notes	①-⑥	①-⑤	①-⑥	⑥	⑦		①-⑤		①-⑥					⑦		⑥⑦		⑦	⑥⑦	⑤⑥⑦	①-⑤		⑥⑦	①-⑤	①-⑤	
notes		**y**				**T**	**J**							**L**								**N**				
Paris Nord......................d.	...	0643	0713	...	...	...	0743	0807	...	0913	1013	...	1113	1143	1213	...	1301	1343	...	1413	...	1443	1507	1513	...	...
Brussels Midi / Zuid ......d.	0659	|	|	0759	0759	0805	|	|	0929	|	|	1129	|	|	|	1259	|	|	1429	|	1459	|	|	|	1559	...
Lille Europe ....d.	0735	|	|	|	0835	|	|	|	1005	|	|	1205	|	|	|	1335	1404	|	1505	|	1535	|	|	|	1635	...
Calais Fréthun ....d.	|	|	|	0902	|	|	|	0934	|	|	|	|	|	|	|	|	1434	|	|	|	|	|	1634	|	|	...
Ashford International.........a.	|	|	|	|	|	|	|	|	|	1006	|	|	|	|	|	|	|	|	|	|	|	|	1606	1606	|	...
Ebbsfleet International ....a.	|	|	|	|	|	|	|	0918	1015	|	|	|	|	|	|	1345	1418	|	|	|	|	|	|	|	1645	...
London St Pancras..........a.	0755	0758	0828	0856	0857	0856	0859	0934	1031	1036	1128	1226	1229	1259	1328	1403	1434	1459	1526	1529	1556	1559	1636	1636	1703	...

train number	9043	9045	9149	9149	9047	9049	9153	9051	9157	9053	9055	9055	9057	9059	9163	9059	9061	9063								
notes			⑦	①-⑤		⑤⑦			Ⓑ	①-⑤	⑦	①-⑤		①-⑤	Ⓑ	⑥⑦	⑦									
notes		**P**									**R**		**Z**		**U**											
Paris Nord......................d.	1613	1643	...	...	1713	1743	...	1813	...	1843	1913	1913	...	2013	...	2013	2043	2113	...	...	...	...	...	...	...	...
Brussels Midi / Zuid ....d.	|	|	1659	1659	|	|	1759	|	1859	|	|	|	...	|	2029	|	|	|	...	...	...	...	...	...	...	...
Lille Europe ....d.	|	|	1735	1735	|	|	1835	|	1935	|	|	|	2038	|	2105	|	|	|	...	...	...	...	...	...	...	...
Calais Fréthun ....d.	|	|	|	|	|	|	|	|	|	|	|	|	|	|	|	|	|	|	...	...	...	...	...	...	...	...
Ashford International..........a.	|	|	1733	1737	|	|	|	|	|	1936	|	|	2037	|	|	2106	|	|	...	...	...	...	...	...	...	...
Ebbsfleet International ....a.	1718	|	|	|	1818	|	1845	1918	|	|	|	2018	|	|	2115	2124	|	2218	...	...	...	...	...	...	...	...
London St Pancras..........a.	1734	1759	1803	1807	1834	1859	1903	1934	1956	2006	2029	2034	2112	2129	2133	2141	2159	2234	...	...	...	...	...	...	...	...

B – ①-⑤ (①-⑥ July 5 - Aug. 30).
C – ⑥⑦ (daily July 5 - Aug. 30).
D – ⑥ (not July 5 - Aug. 30).
E – ⑤ (⑤⑥ July 5 - Aug. 30).
F – ①-⑤ (Ⓑ July 5 - Aug. 30).
G – ⑤ (⑤⑥ July 5 - Aug. 30).
H – ⑥ July 5 - Aug. 30.
J – Not July 5 - Aug. 30.
K – ⑤ (⑤⑦ July 5 - Aug. 30).
L – ⑦ (⑤⑥⑦ July 5 - Aug. 30).
N – ①-⑥ July 5 - Aug. 30.
P – ⑦ July 5 - Aug. 30.
R – ⑦ (⑥⑦ July 5 - Aug. 30).
S – ①-⑤ (⑤ July 5 - Aug. 30).
T – ①-⑤ (① July 5 - Aug. 30).
U – Ⓑ (daily July 5 - Aug. 30).
Z – To / from Marne la Vallée - Chessy: (station for Disneyland). Table **17a**.
y – Not July 14.

10 LONDON – PARIS *by rail – sea – rail*

Other services are available by taking normal service trains between London and Dover (Tables **100**, **101**), sailings between Dover and Calais (Table **2110**) and normal service trains between Calais and Paris, by changing at Boulogne (Tables **260** and **261**), passengers making their own way between stations and docks at Dover and Calais, allowing at least 1 hour for connections.

French train number		⛴	2			⛴	2	**2032**			⛴	2	**2038**			⛴	2	2	**2042**			⛴	2	**2044**		
sea crossing (see below)	⑥	⑥	⑥		①-⑤	①-⑤	①-⑤			⑦	⑦	⑦	⑦		①-⑥	①-⑥	①-⑤	⑥			⑦	⑦	⑦	⑦		
notes			**g**		**z**		**f**			**x**		**g**	**h**		**z**		**f**	**g**			**x**		**g**	**h**		
London Charing Cross ....d.	0600	...	...	...	0700	...	...	...	...	0900	...	...	...	...	1023	...	...	...	...	...	1200	...	...	...	...	...
Dover Priory ✣...................a.	0759	...	...	...	0859	...	...	...	...	1049	...	...	...	...	1210	...	...	...	...	...	1349	...	...	...	...	...
Dover Eastern Docks 🏛 ✣d.	...	0925	...	...	...	1005	...	...	...	...	1215	...	...	...	...	1300	...	...	...	...	...	1425	...	...	...	...
Calais Port 🏛 ✣.................a.	...	1155	...	...	...	1235	...	...	...	...	1445	...	...	...	...	1530	...	...	...	...	...	1655	...	...	...	...
Calais Ville ✣.....................d.	...	...	1306	...	...	...	1349	...	...	...	...	1552	...	...	...	...	1644	1652	...	...	...	...	1746	...	...	...
Boulogne Ville.....................d.	...	...	1338	...	...	...	1423	1437	...	...	...	1626	1630	...	...	...	1721	1726	1742	...	...	...	1818	1832	...	...
Amiens ....a.	...	...	...	...	...	...	...	1602	...	...	...	...	1758	...	...	...	...	...	1858	...	...	...	...	2000	...	...
Paris Nord ....a.	...	...	...	...	...	...	...	1720	...	...	...	...	1920	...	...	...	...	...	2020	...	...	...	...	2123	...	...

French train number	**2003**	2	⛴			*TGV* **7229**	⛴			**2015**	2	2	⛴					**2025**	2	⛴		2	⛴			
sea crossing (see below)	①-⑥	①-⑥	①-⑥	①-⑥				①-⑥			⑦	①-⑥		⑦	⑥	①-⑤			①-⑤	①-⑤	①-⑤	⑥⑦	⑥⑦	⑥	⑦	
notes	**p**	**f**		**b**		🄡 **A**		**e**			**g**	**f**		**x**		**z**			**f**		**z**	**g**			**x**	
Paris Nord ....d.	0707	...	...	...	...	0958	...	...	...	1004	...	...	...	...	...	...	...	1419	...	...	...	...	...	...	...	...
Amiens ....d.	0828	...	...	...	...	|	...	...	...	1123	...	...	...	...	...	...	...	1535	...	...	...	...	...	...	...	...
Boulogne Ville.....................d.	0944	0957	...	...	...	|	...	...	...	1249	1258	1303	...	...	...	...	...	1659	1707	...	...	1739	...	...	...	...
Calais Ville ✣.....................a.	...	1031	...	...	...	1140	...	...	...	...	1333	1343	...	...	...	...	...	...	1741	...	...	1816	...	...	...	...
Calais Port 🏛 ✣..................d.	...	...	1150	...	...	...	1235	...	...	...	...	...	1525	...	...	...	...	...	...	1820	...	...	1945	...	...	...
Dover Eastern Docks 🏛 ✣a.	...	...	1220	...	...	...	1305	...	...	...	...	...	1555	...	...	...	...	...	...	1850	...	...	2015	...	...	...
Dover Priory ✣....................d.	...	...	...	1333	...	...	...	1350	...	...	...	...	...	1632	1637	1640	...	...	...	...	1950	...	...	2115	2119	...
London Charing Cross....a.	...	...	...	1506	...	...	...	1536	...	...	...	...	...	1818	1836	1837	...	...	...	...	2148	...	...	2318	2319	...

A – ①-⑥ (not July 14, Aug. 15, Nov. 11).
b – On Aug. 31 depart Dover 1332, arrive London 1518.
e – On Aug. 31 depart Dover 1432, arrive London 1618.
f – Not July 14, Nov. 1, 11.
g – Also July 14, Nov. 1, 11.
h – Also July 14, Aug. 15, Nov. 11.
p – Not July 14, Aug. 15, Nov. 11.
x – Also Aug. 31.
z – Not Aug. 31.
⛴ – Ship service, operated by P & O Ferries. ✕ on ship. One class only on ship. For additional ferry services see Table **2110**.
✣ – 🚐 service between Dover Priory and Dover Eastern Docks and v.v. (every 20 minutes approx, not a guaranteed connection).

RAIL – SEA – RAIL SERVICE SEA CROSSING: Connections between Rail - Sea - Rail services are not guaranteed.

LONDON / BRUSSELS - LILLE - CHARLES DE GAULLE ✈ - WESTERN / SOUTHERN FRANCE 11

Supplements are payable on *TGV* trains. Connections at Lille are not guaranteed. Other connections available via Paris.

km	*train type*	*TGV*	*TGV*	*TGV*	*TGV*	*TGV*	*TGV*	*TGV*	*TGV*	⇌	*TGV*	*TGV*	*TGV*	☆	☆	*TGV*	*TGV*	☆	☆	☆	*TGV*	*TGV*	*TGV*	*TGV*	*TGV*
	train number	**5102**	**9804**	**5104**	**5200**	**5110**	**9802**	**5212**	**8515**	**9928**	**5112**	**5214**	**5214**	**9110**	**9084**	**9826**	**5164**	**9120**	**9116**	**9012**	**9832**	**5114**	**6818**	**5224**	**5227**
	train number	**5103**	**9805**	**5105**	**5201**	**5111**	**9803**	[R]	[R]	**9929**	**5113**	**5213**	**5215**	[R]	[R]	**9827**	[R]	[R]	[R]	[R]	**9833**	**5115**	**6819**	**5225**	[R]
	notes	[R] 🍸	[R] 🍸	[R] 🍸	[R] 🍸	[R] 🍸	[R] 🍸	🍸	🍸	[R] 🍸	[R] 🍸	[R] 🍸	[R] 🍸	✕	✕	[R] 🍸	🍸	✕	✕	✕	[R]	[R] 🍸	[R] 🍸	[R] 🍸	🍸
			A	**B**	**r**					**G**				①–⑥	**P**			**H**	⑥	**J**	🍸				
	London St Pancras 12 d.	...	...	...	...	...	...	...	...	...	...	...	...	0659	0719	...	...	0827	0859	0901	...	...	...	...	...
	Ebbsfleet International **12** d.	...	...	...	...	...	...	...	...	...	...	...	...	0715	│	...	...	0845	0915	│	...	...	...	...	...
	Ashford International **12** d.	...	...	...	...	...	...	...	...	...	...	...	...	│	0755	...	...	│	│	│	...	...	...	...	...
	Brussels Midi / Zuid 12 d.	...	0540	...	...	...	0731	...	...	0819	...	...	...	│	│	1021	...	│	│	│	1110	...	...	...	...
	Lille Europe 12 a.	...	0615	...	...	...	│	...	...	│	...	...	...	0924	0952s	│	...	1054	1124	1121	1146	...	...	...	...
0	**Lille Europe** d.	0559	0625	0625	0558t	0643c	│	0759	...	│	0828	0846t	0846t	...	│	│	1030	...	...	...	1156	1156	...	1210	1210
	Douai d.	│	│	│	0628t	0709	│	│	...	│	│	0908t	0908t	...	│	│	│	...	...	...	│	│	...	│	│
	Arras d.	│	│	│	0647t	0727	│	│	...	│	│	0927t	0927t	...	│	│	│	...	...	...	│	│	...	│	│
128	TGV Haute Picardie d.	│	0653	0653	0707	0746	│	│	...	│	│	0952	0952	...	│	│	1103	...	...	...	│	│	...	1244	1244
241	Paris Charles de Gaulle ✈ a.	0649	0720	0720	0735	0816	0846	0851	...	│	0921	1022	1022	...	│	1136	1132	...	...	...	1247	1247	...	1312	1312
	Paris Charles de Gaulle ✈ d.	0654	0725	0725	0739	0821	0858	0858	...	│	0925	1027	1027	...	│	1142	1142	...	...	...	1258	1258	...	1316	1316
264	Marne la Vallée § d.	0710	0740	0740	0756	0835	0912	0912	...	│	0940	1042	1042	...	│	1156	1156	...	...	...	1311	1311	...	1329	1329
326	Massy TGV d.	│	│	│	0831	│	0946	0946	...	│	│	1117	1117	...	│	│	│	...	...	...	│	│	...	1401	1401
	Le Mans a.	│	│	│	│	│	│	│	...	│	│	1205	1205	...	│	│	│	...	...	...	│	│	...	1450	1450
	Rennes a.	│	│	│	│	│	│	│	...	│	│	│	1327	...	│	│	│	...	...	...	│	│	...	1607	│
	Angers St Laud a.	│	│	│	│	│	│	│	...	│	│	1250	...	...	│	│	│	...	...	...	│	│	...	...	1539
	Nantes a.	│	│	│	│	│	│	│	...	│	│	1333	...	...	│	│	│	...	...	...	│	│	...	...	1617
	St Pierre des Corps a.	│	│	│	0921	│	1035	1035	...	│	│	▬	...	...	│	│	│	...	...	...	│	│	...	...	...
	Poitiers a.	│	│	│	1011	│	1117	1117	...	│	│	...	...	...	│	│	│	...	...	...	│	│	...	...	...
	Angoulême a.	│	│	│	1058	│	1203	1203	...	│	│	...	...	...	│	│	│	...	...	...	│	│	...	...	...
	Bordeaux a.	│	│	│	1200	│	1305	1305	1315	│	│	...	...	...	│	│	│	...	...	...	│	│	...	...	...
	Irún a.	│	│	│	1428g	│	▬	...	1545	│	│	...	...	...	│	│	│	...	...	...	│	│	...	...	...
558	Le Creusot TGV a.	│	│	│	...	│	...	...	...	│	│	...	...	...	│	│	│	...	...	...	│	│	...	...	...
682	**Lyon Part Dieu** a.	0901	0931	0931	...	1031	...	...	...	│	1131	...	...	...	│	│	│	...	...	...	1501	1501	1537	...	...
	Lyon Perrache a.	│	│	│	...	│	...	...	...	│	│	*Talgo*	...	...	│	│	│	...	...	...	│	│	│	...	...
	Grenoble a.	│	│	│	...	│	...	...	...	│	│	**71**	...	...	│	│	│	...	...	...	│	│	│	...	...
	Valence TGV a.	│	1011	1011	...	1111	...	...	...	1150	1213	**70**	...	...	│	1404	1404	...	...	...	1541	│	│	...	...
	Avignon TGV a.	1009	│	│	...	1145	...	...	...	1227	│	[R] ✕	...	...	1408p	1439	1439	...	...	...	│	│	1643	...	...
	Nîmes a.	│	1057	1057	...	│	...	...	...	│	1258	**N** ⁄	...	...	...	│	│	...	...	...	1629	│	│	...	...
	Montpellier a.	│	1128	1128	...	│	...	...	...	│	1326	1509	...	...	...	│	│	...	...	...	1657	│	│	...	...
	Béziers a.	│	1213	1213	...	│	...	...	...	│	...	1553	...	...	...	│	│	...	...	...	1751	│	│	...	...
	Narbonne a.	│	1235	1235	...	│	...	...	...	│	...	1609	...	...	...	│	│	...	...	...	1807	│	│	...	...
	Toulouse Matabiau a.	│	1355	1355	...	│	...	...	...	│	...	│	...	...	...	│	│	...	...	...	│	│	│	...	...
	Perpignan a.	│	...	...	...	│	*TGV*	...	...	│	...	1652	...	...	...	│	│	...	...	...	1844	│	│	...	...
	Portbou 🏛 a.	│	...	...	...	│	**5148**	...	...	│	...	1748	...	...	...	│	│	...	...	...	...	│	│	...	...
	Barcelona França a.	│	...	...	...	│	**5149**	...	...	│	...	1959	...	...	...	│	│	...	...	...	...	│	│	...	...
	Aix en Provence TGV a.	1033	...	...	...	1210	[R] 🍸	...	...	1251	...	...	...	...	...	1502	1502	...	...	...	...	1633	│	...	...
	Marseille St Charles a.	1047	...	...	...	1225	1259	...	...	1308	...	...	...	...	...	1516	1516	...	...	...	...	1647	1717	...	...
	Toulon a.	1138	...	...	...	...	1339	...	...	...	...	...	...	...	...	1608	1608	...	...	...	...	...	1808	...	...
	St Raphaël - Valescure a.	1231	...	...	...	...	1432	...	...	...	...	...	...	...	...	1702	1702	...	...	...	...	...	1901	...	...
	Cannes a.	1255	...	...	...	...	1457	...	...	...	...	...	...	...	...	1726	1726	...	...	...	...	...	1926	...	...
	Nice a.	1325	...	...	...	...	1528	...	...	...	...	...	...	...	...	1755	1755	...	...	...	...	...	1955	...	...

train type	☆	☆	☆	*TGV*	*TGV*	☆	*TGV*	*TGV*		☆	*TGV*	*TGV*	*TGV*	*TGV*	*TGV*	*TGV*	☆	*TGV*	*TGV*	☆	*TGV*	☆	*TGV*	*TGV*	
train number	**9120**	**9116**	**9012**	**5218**	**5221**	**9074**	**9828**	**5117**		**9126**	**5232**	**5216**	**5216**	**5232**	**5118**	**5222/3**	**9132**	**9834**	**6181**	**9030**	**9836**	**9138**	**5236**	**5231**	
train number	[R]	[R]	[R]	**5219**	[R] 🍸	[R]	**9829**	**5116**		[R]	**5233**	**5229**	**5217**	**5205**	**5119**	[R] 🍸	[R]	**9835**	[R]	[R]	**9837**	[R]	**5238**	[R]	
notes	✕	✕	✕	[R] 🍸	⑦	✕	[R] 🍸	🍸		✕	[R] 🍸	[R] 🍸	[R] 🍸	[R] 🍸	[R] 🍸	⑤⑥	✕	[R] 🍸	🍸	✕	[R] 🍸	✕	[R] 🍸	🍸	
	H	⑥	**J**	**z**	**z**						**C**	⑦**k**	⑦**k**	**D**		**y**							**E**	**E**	
London St Pancras 12 d.	0827	0859	0901	...	...	0953	...	...	...	1057	...	...	...	...	...	...	1257	...	...	1404	...	1434	...	...	...
Ebbsfleet International **12** d.	0845	0915	│	...	...	│	...	...	...	1115	...	...	...	...	...	...	1315	...	...	│	...	│	...	...	...
Ashford International **12** d.	│	│	│	...	...	1028	...	...	...	│	...	...	...	...	...	...	│	...	...	│	...	│	...	...	...
Brussels Midi / Zuid 12 d.	│	│	│	...	...	│	1209	...	...	│	...	...	...	...	...	...	│	1509	...	│	1609	│	...	...	...
Lille Europe 12 a.	1054	1124	1121	...	...	1224s	1244	...	...	1324	...	...	...	...	...	...	1524	1546	...	1624	1644	1654	...	...	...
Lille Europe d.	...	...	...	1238x	1238x	│	1254	...	...	...	1447	1447	1447	1447	1458v	1540	...	1557	...	...	1654	...	1729	1729	...
Douai d.	...	...	...	│	│	│	│	...	...	...	│	│	│	│	│	│	...	│	...	...	│	...	│	│	...
Arras d.	...	...	...	│	│	│	│	...	...	...	│	│	│	│	│	│	...	│	...	...	│	...	│	│	...
TGV Haute Picardie d.	...	...	...	│	│	│	│	...	...	...	│	│	│	│	│	│	...	│	...	...	│	...	│	│	...
Paris Charles de Gaulle ✈ a.	...	...	...	1332	1332	│	1346	...	...	...	1538	1538	1538	1538	1548	1632	...	1647	...	...	1746	...	1820	1820	...
Paris Charles de Gaulle ✈ d.	...	...	...	1337	1337	│	1352	...	...	...	1542	1542	1542	1542	1553	1637	...	1652	...	...	1751	...	1824	1824	...
Marne la Vallée § d.	...	...	...	1351	1351	1331	1407	...	...	...	1557	1557	1557	1557	1610	1652	...	1710	...	...	1810	...	1840	1840	...
Massy TGV d.	...	...	...	1431	1431	...	│	...	...	...	1631	1631	1631	1636	│	1730	...	│	...	...	│	...	1917	1921	...
Le Mans a.	...	...	...	│	│	...	│	...	...	...	1719	│	│	│	│	│	...	│	...	...	│	...	2005	│	...
Rennes a.	...	...	...	│	│	...	│	...	...	...	1836	│	│	│	│	│	...	│	...	...	│	...	2125	│	...
Angers St Laud a.	...	...	...	│	│	...	│	...	...	...	...	│	1812	│	│	│	...	│	...	...	│	...	...	2105	...
Nantes a.	...	...	...	│	│	...	│	...	...	...	...	│	1854	│	│	│	...	│	...	...	│	...	...	2147	...
St Pierre des Corps a.	...	...	...	1521	1521	...	│	...	...	...	...	1721	1721f	1727	│	1821	...	│	...	...	│	...	...	2011f	...
Poitiers a.	...	...	...	1610	1610	...	│	...	...	...	...	1807	...	1809	│	1903	...	│	...	...	│	...	...	...	...
Angoulême a.	...	...	...	1655	1655	...	│	...	...	...	...	...	...	1859	│	1949	...	│	...	...	│	...	...	...	...
Bordeaux a.	...	...	...	1802	1802	...	│	...	...	...	...	...	...	2002	│	2051	...	│	...	...	│	...	...	...	...
Irún a.	...	...	...	│	2040	...	│	...	...	...	...	...	...	...	│	...	...	│	...	...	│	...	...	...	...
Le Creusot TGV a.	...	...	...	│	...	...	│	...	...	...	...	...	...	...	│	...	...	│	...	...	│	...	...	...	...
Lyon Part Dieu a.	...	...	...	│	...	...	1601	1707	...	...	...	...	...	...	1801	...	...	1901	...	...	2001	...	...	...	...
Lyon Perrache a.	...	...	...	│	...	...	│	│	...	...	...	...	...	...	│	...	...	│	...	...	│	...	...	...	...
Grenoble a.	...	...	...	│	...	...	│	│	...	...	...	...	...	...	│	...	...	│	...	...	│	...	...	...	...
Valence TGV a.	...	...	...	│	...	...	│	1742	...	...	...	...	...	...	│	...	...	│	...	...	2042	...	...	...	...
Avignon TGV a.	...	...	...	│	...	...	1709	│	...	...	...	...	...	...	│	...	...	2010	...	...	│	...	...	...	...
Nîmes a.	...	...	...	│	...	...	│	1830	...	...	...	...	...	...	1927	...	...	│	...	...	2127	...	...	...	...
Montpellier a.	...	...	...	│	...	...	│	1857	...	...	...	...	...	...	1955	...	...	│	...	...	2155	...	...	...	...
Béziers a.	...	...	...	│	...	...	│	1940	...	...	...	...	...	...	2044	...	...	│	...	...	2241j	...	...	...	...
Narbonne a.	...	...	...	│	...	...	│	1955	...	...	...	...	...	...	2101	...	...	│	...	...	2257j	...	...	...	...
Toulouse Matabiau a.	...	...	...	2011	...	...	│	2112	...	...	...	...	...	...	│	...	...	│	...	...	│	...	...	...	...
Perpignan a.	...	...	...	...	...	...	│	...	...	...	...	...	...	...	2135	...	...	│	...	...	2332j	...	...	...	...
Portbou 🏛 a.	...	...	...	...	...	...	│	...	...	...	...	...	...	...	...	...	...	│	...	...	...	...	...	...	...
Barcelona França a.	...	...	...	...	...	...	│	...	...	...	...	...	...	...	...	...	...	│	...	...	...	...	...	...	...
Aix en Provence TGV a.	...	...	...	...	...	...	1733	...	...	...	...	...	...	...	...	...	...	2033	2045	...	...	...	...	...	...
Marseille St Charles a.	...	...	...	...	...	...	1747	...	...	...	...	...	...	...	...	...	...	2047	│	...	...	...	...	...	...
Toulon a.	...	...	...	...	...	...	...	...	...	...	...	...	...	...	...	...	...	2140j	2133	...	...	...	...	...	...
St Raphaël - Valescure a.	...	...	...	...	...	...	...	...	...	...	...	...	...	...	...	...	...	...	2222	...	...	...	...	...	...
Cannes a.	...	...	...	...	...	...	...	...	...	...	...	...	...	...	...	...	...	...	2246	...	...	...	...	...	...
Nice a.	...	...	...	...	...	...	...	...	...	...	...	...	...	...	...	...	...	...	2314	...	...	...	...	...	...

A – ①–⑤ (not July 14).
B – ⑥⑦ (also July 14).
C – ①–⑥ (not July 14).
D – ①–④ (not July 14).
E – ⑧ (daily July 5 - Aug. 29).
G – THALYS SOLEIL – ⑥ June 27 - Aug. 22: 1,2 and 🍸 Amsterdam (depart 0532 see Table **18**) - Brussels - Marseille. ⑥ June 27 - Aug. 29: 1,2 and 🍸 Brussels - Marseille.
H – ⑦ July 5 - Aug. 30.
J – ①–⑤ (⑥ July 5 - Aug. 30).
N – CATALÁN TALGO – 1,2 and ✕ Montpellier - Barcelona. Special fares payable.
P – ⑥ July 11 - Sept. 5.
c – Lille **Flandres**, see note **x**. Departs 0647 on ⑥.
f – Runs Massy TGV - St Pierre des Corps - Angers St Laud - Nantes.
g – ⑥ only.
j – ⑤⑦ (also July 14).
k – Also July 14.
p – Avignon **Centre**.
r – Calls at Futuroscope 1004.
s – Stops to set down only.
t – On Sept. 20 departs Lille 35–39 minutes later and does not call Douai and Arras.
v – 1454 on ⑥⑦ (also Aug. 31).
x – Lille **Flandres**, 500 metres from Lille Europe; see City Plan on page 31.
y – To Hendaye, arrive 2313.
z – Calls at Futuroscope 1603.
☆ – Eurostar train. Special fares payable. Minimum check-in time 30 minutes. Valid June 14 - Aug. 30.
§ – Marne la Vallée - Chessy (station for Disneyland).
⁄ – Supplement payable.

11 LONDON / BRUSSELS - LILLE - CHARLES DE GAULLE ✈ - WESTERN / SOUTHERN FRANCE

Supplements payable on all *TGV* services. Connections at Lille are not guaranteed. Other connections available via Paris.

train type	☆	*TGV*	*TGV*	*TGV*	*TGV*	*TGV*	*TGV*	*TGV*	*TGV*	*TGV*	☆	*TGV*	*TGV*	*TGV*	*TGV*	*TGV*	☆	*TGV*	☆	*TGV*	*TGV*	*TGV*
train number	**9138**	**5123**	**5126**	**5124**	**5240**	**5130**	**5132**	**5242**	**5142**	**5142**	**9144**	**5136**	**5136**	**5248**	**5248**	**5234**	**9148**	**5138**	**9150**	**5210**	**5210**	**9846**
train number	🅁	🅁 🍷	**5127**	**5125**	**5241**	**5131**	**5133**	**5243**	**5135**	**5143**	🅁	**5137**	**5137**	**5249**	**5245**	**5235**	🅁	**5139**	🅁	**5211**	**5247**	🅁
notes	✕	①–⑥	🅁 🍷	🅁 🍷	🅁 🍷	🅁 🍷	🅁 🍷	🅁 🍷	🅁 🍷	🅁 🍷	✕	①–④	🅁 🍷	🅁 🍷	🅁 🍷	🅁 🍷	✕	🅁 🍷	✕	🅁 🍷	🅁 🍷	🍷
		k	⑦p	B	⑧	m	⑦p	C	D	D	①–④	k	⑤⑥	E	E	F	⑥⑦	⑦p	①–⑤	⑤⑦p	⑦p	
London St Pancras 12 d.	1434	...	...	...	...	...	...	...	...	...	1604	...	...	...	...	...	1657	...	1727	...	...	...
Ebbsfleet International **12** d.	│	...	...	...	...	...	...	...	...	...	│	...	...	...	...	...	1715	...	1745	...	...	...
Ashford International **12** d.	│	...	...	...	...	...	...	...	...	...	│	...	...	...	...	...	│	...	│	...	...	...
Brussels Midi / Zuid 12 d.	│	...	...	...	...	...	...	...	...	...	│	...	...	...	...	...	│	...	│	...	...	2036
Lille Europe 12 a.	1654	...	...	...	...	...	...	...	...	...	1824	...	...	...	...	...	1924	...	1954	...	...	│
Lille Europe d.	...	1752	1752	1752	1809	1842e	1842e	1829c	1931	1931	...	1915	1915	1939	1939	1939	...	2021e	...	2014	2014	│
Douai d.	...	│	│	│	│	│	│	│	│	│	...	1936	1936	│	│	│	...	2043	...	│	│	│
Arras d.	...	│	│	│	│	│	│	│	│	│	...	1952	1952	│	│	│	...	2059	...	│	│	│
TGV Haute Picardie d.	...	1823	1823	1823	1837	│	│	│	│	│	...	2015	2015	│	│	│	...	2119	...	│	│	│
Paris Charles de Gaulle ✈ a.	...	1850	1850	1850	1907	1936	1936	1921	2021	2021	...	2043	2043	2030	2030	2030	...	2146	...	2105	2105	2150
Paris Charles de Gaulle ✈ d.	...	1854	1854	1854	1911	1941	1941	1925	2026	2026	...	2048	2048	2034	2034	2034	...	2150	...	2109	2109	2155
Marne la Vallée § d.	...	1908	1908	1908	1927	1953	2008	1942	2040	2040	...	2103	2103	2050	2050	2050	...	2204	...	2125	2125	2207
Massy TGV d.	...	│	│	│	2000	...	│	2018	│	│	...	│	│	2131	2131	2131	...	│	...	2201	2201	...
Le Mans a.	...	│	│	│	│	...	│	│	│	│	...	│	│	2223	2223	2222	...	│	...	2250	2250	...
Rennes a.	...	│	│	│	│	...	│	│	│	│	...	│	│	2340	│	│	...	│	...	│	0010	...
Angers St Laud a.	...	│	│	│	│	...	│	│	│	│	...	│	│	...	2303	2301	...	│	...	2328	...	...
Nantes a.	...	│	│	│	│	...	│	│	│	│	...	│	│	...	2340	2338	...	│	...	0007	...	...
St Pierre des Corps a.	...	│	│	│	│	...	│	2110	│	│	...	│	│	...	...	...	...	│	...	...	...	...
Poitiers a.	...	│	│	│	2122	...	│	2158	│	│	...	│	│	...	...	...	...	│	...	...	...	...
Angoulême a.	...	│	│	│	2211	...	│	2247	│	│	...	│	│	...	...	...	...	│	...	...	...	...
Bordeaux a.	...	│	│	│	2313	...	│	2352	│	│	...	│	│	...	...	...	...	│	...	...	...	...
Irún a.	...	│	│	│	...	...	│	...	│	│	...	│	│	...	...	...	...	│	...	...	...	...
Le Creusot TGV a.	...	│	│	│	...	...	│	...	│	│	...	2220	2220	...	...	...	...	2319	...	...	...	...
Lyon Part Dieu a.	...	2101	│	2101	...	...	2201	...	2231	2231	...	2259	2259	...	...	...	...	2359	...	...	...	...
Lyon Perrache a.	...	│	│	│	...	...	│	...	│	│	...	...	│	...	...	...	...	0014	...	...	...	...
Grenoble a.	...	2225	│	│	...	...	2317	...	│	│	...	...	│	...	...	...	...	...	...	...	...	...
Valence TGV a.	...	...	2114	│	...	...	...	...	2315	│	...	...	2341	...	...	...	...	...	...	...	...	...
Avignon TGV a.	...	...	2148	2208	...	...	...	...	│	2343	...	...	0018	...	...	...	...	...	...	...	...	...
Nîmes a.	...	...	│	│	...	...	...	...	2400	│	...	...	│	...	...	...	...	...	...	...	...	...
Montpellier a.	...	...	│	│	...	...	...	...	0030	│	...	...	│	...	...	...	...	...	...	...	...	...
Béziers a.	...	...	│	│	...	...	...	...	...	│	...	...	│	...	...	...	...	...	...	...	...	...
Narbonne a.	...	...	│	│	...	...	...	...	...	│	...	...	│	...	...	...	...	...	...	...	...	...
Toulouse Matabiau a.	...	...	│	│	...	...	...	...	...	│	...	...	│	...	...	...	...	...	...	...	...	...
Perpignan a.	...	...	│	│	...	...	...	...	...	│	...	...	│	...	...	...	...	...	...	...	...	...
Aix en Provence TGV a.	...	...	│	2231	...	...	...	...	...	0006	...	...	0041	...	...	...	...	...	...	...	...	...
Marseille St Charles a.	...	...	2221	2246	...	...	...	...	...	0020	...	...	0055	...	...	...	...	...	...	...	...	...
Toulon a.	...	...	...	...	...	...	...	...	...	...	...	...	...	...	...	...	...	...	...	...	...	...
St Raphaël - Valescure a.	...	...	...	...	...	...	...	...	...	...	...	...	...	...	...	...	...	...	...	...	...	...
Cannes a.	...	...	...	...	...	...	...	...	...	...	...	...	...	...	...	...	...	...	...	...	...	...
Nice a.	...	...	...	...	...	...	...	...	...	...	...	...	...	...	...	...	...	...	...	...	...	...

train type or number		*TGV*	*TGV*	*TGV*	*TGV*	☆		*TGV*	*TGV*	*TGV*	*TGV*		*TGV*	*TGV*	*TGV*	*TGV*	*TGV*	☆				
train number		**9811**	**9807**	**5152**	**5154**	**9119**		**5158**	**5160**	**5254**	**5252**		**9854**	**5156**	**5260**	**9856**	**5260**	**9181**				
train number		🅁	🅁	**5153**	**5155**	🅁		**5159**	**5161**	**5255**	🅁		**9855**	**5157**	**5261**	**9857**	**5261**	🅁				
notes		🍷	🍷	🅁 🍷	🅁 🍷	✕		🅁 🍷	🅁 🍷	🅁 🍷	🍷		🅁 🍷	🅁 🍷	🅁 🍷	🅁 🍷	🅁 🍷	✕				
		G		G w	B	①–⑥		E	⑦p	B	B		G	A x	B	A	⑦p					
Nice d.	...	...	...	...	...	...	...	...	...	...	...	...	...	...	...	...	...	...	...	...	...	...
Cannes d.	...	...	...	...	...	...	...	...	...	...	...	...	...	...	...	...	...	...	...	...	...	...
St Raphaël - Valescure d.	...	...	...	...	...	...	...	...	...	...	...	...	...	...	...	...	...	...	...	...	...	...
Toulon d.	...	...	...	...	...	...	...	...	...	...	...	...	...	...	...	0519q	...	...	...	...	...	...
Marseille St Charles d.	...	...	...	...	...	...	...	0539	...	...	...	...	0539	...	...	0610	...	...	...	...	...	...
Aix en Provence TGV d.	...	...	...	...	...	...	...	0554	...	...	...	...	│	...	...	0624	...	...	...	...	...	...
Perpignan d.	...	...	...	...	...	...	...	│	...	...	...	...	│	...	...	│	...	...	...	...	...	...
Toulouse Matabiau d.	...	...	...	...	...	...	...	│	...	...	...	...	│	...	...	│	...	...	...	...	...	...
Narbonne d.	...	...	...	...	...	...	...	│	...	...	...	...	│	...	...	│	...	...	...	...	...	...
Béziers d.	...	...	...	...	...	...	...	│	...	...	...	...	│	...	...	│	...	...	...	...	...	...
Montpellier d.	...	...	...	...	...	...	...	│	...	...	...	...	│	...	...	│	...	...	...	...	...	...
Nîmes d.	...	...	...	...	...	...	...	│	...	...	...	...	│	...	...	│	...	...	...	...	...	...
Avignon TGV d.	...	...	...	...	...	...	...	0616	...	...	...	...	0611	...	...	0646	...	...	...	...	...	...
Valence TGV d.	...	...	...	...	...	...	...	0650	...	...	...	...	0645	...	...	│	...	...	...	...	...	...
Grenoble d.	...	...	...	...	0451	...	...	│	0540	...	...	...	│	...	...	│	...	...	...	...	...	...
Lyon Perrache d.	...	...	...	...	│	...	...	│	│	...	...	...	│	...	...	│	...	...	...	...	...	...
Lyon Part Dieu d.	...	...	...	...	0613	...	...	│	0659	...	...	...	0726	...	...	0756	...	...	...	...	...	...
Le Creusot TGV d.	...	...	...	...	0653	...	...	│	0741	...	...	...	│	...	...	│	...	...	...	...	...	...
Hendaye d.	...	...	...	...	│	...	...	│	│	...	...	...	│	...	...	│	...	...	...	...	...	...
Bordeaux d.	...	...	...	...	│	...	...	│	│	...	...	...	│	...	0535	│	0614	...	...	...	...	...
Angoulême d.	...	...	...	...	│	...	...	│	│	...	...	...	│	...	0637	│	0714	...	...	...	...	...
Poitiers d.	...	...	...	...	│	...	...	│	│	...	...	...	│	...	0724	│	0801	...	...	...	...	...
St Pierre des Corps d.	...	...	...	...	│	...	...	│	│	...	...	...	│	...	0803	│	0841	...	...	...	...	...
Nantes d.	...	...	...	...	│	...	...	│	│	...	0604	...	│	...	│	│	│	...	...	...	...	...
Angers St Laud d.	...	...	...	...	│	...	...	│	│	...	0643	...	│	...	│	│	│	...	...	...	...	...
Rennes d.	...	...	...	...	│	...	...	│	│	0610	│	...	│	...	│	│	│	...	...	...	...	...
Le Mans d.	...	...	...	...	│	...	...	│	│	0731	0731	...	│	...	│	│	│	...	...	...	...	...
Massy TGV d.	...	...	...	...	│	...	...	│	│	0821	0821	...	│	...	│	│	│	...	...	...	...	...
Marne la Vallée § d.	...	...	0727	0810	0817	...	...	0908	0859	0904	0904	...	0920	0922	0932	0949	1011	...	...	...	...	...
Paris Charles de Gaulle ✈ a.	...	...	0738	0820	0829	...	...	0918	0909	0914	0914	...	0930	0933	0942	1000	1021	...	...	...	...	...
Paris Charles de Gaulle ✈ d.	...	...	0745	0825	0837	...	...	...	0913	0918	0918	...	0940	0937	0947	1010	1026	...	...	...	...	...
TGV Haute Picardie d.	...	...	│	│	0909	...	...	...	0943	│	│	...	│	│	1019	│	1101	...	...	...	...	...
Arras a.	...	...	│	│	│	...	...	...	│	│	│	...	│	│	│	│	│	...	...	...	...	...
Douai a.	...	...	│	│	│	...	...	...	│	│	│	...	│	│	│	│	│	...	...	...	...	...
Lille Europe a.	...	...	│	0915	0937	...	...	...	1008	1008	1008	...	1028	1027	1046	1103	1128	...	...	...	...	...
Lille Europe 12 d.	...	0729	│	...	...	1005	...	...	...	...	...	...	1041	...	...	1115	...	1205	...	...	...	...
Brussels Midi / Zuid 12 a.	...	0803	0859	...	...	│	...	...	...	...	...	...	1115	...	...	1150	...	│	...	...	...	...
Ashford International **12** a.	...	...	...	...	...	│	...	...	...	...	...	...	...	...	...	...	...	│	...	...	...	...
Ebbsfleet International **12** a.	...	...	...	...	...	1015	...	...	...	...	...	...	...	...	...	...	...	│	...	...	...	...
London St Pancras 12 a.	...	...	...	...	...	1031	...	...	...	...	...	...	...	...	...	...	...	1226	...	...	...	...

A – ⑥⑦ (also July 14).
B – ①–⑥ (not July 14).
C – ⑤⑥⑦ (also July 14).
D – ⑦ (not July 5 - Aug. 30).
E – ⑥ (not July 11 - Aug. 29).
F – ①–④ (not July 14).
G – ①–⑤ (not July 14).

c – On July 14 depart from Lille **Flandres** at 1824.
e – Lille **Flandres**, 500 metres from Lille Europe; see City Plan on page 31.
k – Not July 14.
m – To Dijon (arrive 2139), and Besançon (2232) (Table **370**).
p – Also July 14.
q – ⑥ only.
w – From Besançon (depart 0540), and Dijon (0632) (Table **370**).

x – From Besançon (depart 0652, and Dijon (0744).
y – Also July 14.

§ – Marne la Vallée - Chessy. Station for Disneyland Paris.
☆ – Eurostar train. Special fares payable. Minimum check-in time 30 minutes. Valid June 14 - Aug. 30.

SOUTHERN / WESTERN FRANCE - CHARLES DE GAULLE ✈ - LILLE - BRUSSELS / LONDON 11

Supplements payable on all *TGV* services. Connections at Lille are not guaranteed. Other connections available via Paris.

train type or number	*TGV*	*TGV*	*TGV*	*TGV*	☆		*TGV*	*TGV*	☆	*TGV*	*TGV*	☆	☆	*TGV*	*TGV*	*TGV*	*TGV*	☆	☆	*TGV*	☆		
train number	**5144**	**5162**	**5264**	**5268**	**9133**		**9860**	**5166**	**9031**	**5270**	**5272**	**9139**	**9141**	**5276**	**5368**	**5198**	**9862**	**9149**	**9149**	**9864**	**9153**		
train number	R	**5163**	**5265**	R	R		R	R 🍷	R	**5271**	R	R	R	**5277**	R	R	**9863**	R	R	**9865**	R		
notes	🍷	R 🍷	R 🍷 x	🍷 Wx	🍴 ⑥⑦		🍷		🍴	R 🍷	🍷	🍴 ⑥⑦	🍴 ①–⑤	R 🍷	🍷 E	🍷	R 🍷	🍴 ⑦	🍴 ①–⑤	R 🍷	🍴		
Nice d.	...	...	...	...	...	...	...	...	...	...	...	...	...	...	...	0932	...	...	...	1032	...	...	...
Cannes d.	...	...	...	...	...	...	...	...	...	...	...	...	...	...	...	0950	...	...	...	1101	...	...	...
St Raphaël - Valescure d.	...	...	...	...	...	...	...	...	...	...	...	...	...	...	...	1026	...	...	...	1125	...	...	...
Toulon d.	...	...	...	...	...	...	0747j	...	...	...	...	...	...	...	...	1117	...	...	...	1218	...	...	...
Marseille St Charles d.	0710	...	...	...	...	...	0841	...	...	...	...	...	...	...	1133	1210	...	...	...	1310	...	...	...
Aix en Provence TGV d.	0725	...	...	...	...	...	0855	...	...	...	...	...	...	...	1147	|	...	...	...	|	...	...	...
Barcelona França d.	|	...	...	...	...	...	|	...	...	...	...	...	...	...	|	|	...	...	...	|	...	...	...
Cerbère 🏛 d.	|	...	...	...	...	...	|	...	...	...	...	...	...	...	|	|	...	...	...	|	...	...	...
Perpignan d.	|	0505f	...	...	...	...	|	0642	...	...	...	...	...	...	|	|	...	...	...	|	...	...	...
Toulouse Matabiau d.	|	|	0527	...	...	...	|	|	...	...	...	...	...	...	|	|	...	...	...	|	...	...	...
Narbonne d.	|	0544f	|	...	...	...	|	0721	...	...	...	...	...	...	|	|	...	...	...	|	...	...	...
Béziers d.	|	0601f	|	...	...	...	|	0737	...	...	...	...	...	...	|	|	...	...	...	|	...	...	...
Montpellier d.	|	0652	|	...	...	...	|	0826	...	...	...	...	...	...	|	|	1200	...	...	|	...	...	...
Nîmes d.	|	0718	|	...	...	...	|	0853	...	...	...	...	...	...	|	|	1227	...	...	|	...	...	...
Avignon TGV d.	0747	|	|	...	...	...	0918	|	...	...	...	...	...	...	1209	1245	|	...	...	1340	...	...	...
Valence TGV d.	|	0810	|	...	...	...	|	0938	...	...	...	...	...	...	1243	|	|	...	...	1414	...	...	...
Grenoble d.	|	|	|	...	...	...	|	|	...	...	...	...	...	...	|	|	|	...	...	|	...	...	...
Lyon Perrache d.	|	|	|	...	...	...	|	|	...	...	...	...	...	...	|	|	|	...	...	|	...	...	...
Lyon Part Dieu d.	0856	0856	|	...	...	...	1026	1026	...	...	...	...	...	...	1320	1350	1356	...	...	|	...	...	...
Le Creusot TGV d.	|	|	|	...	...	...	|	|	...	...	...	...	...	...	...	...	|	...	...	|	...	...	...
Hendaye d.	|	|	|	0524	...	...	|	|	...	...	...	...	...	0833e	...	...	|	...	...	|	...	...	...
Bordeaux d.	|	|	0750	0750	...	...	|	|	...	...	...	...	...	1057	...	...	|	...	...	|	...	...	...
Angoulême d.	|	|	0850	0850	...	...	|	|	...	...	...	...	...	1201	...	...	|	...	...	|	...	...	...
Poitiers d.	|	|	0936	0936	...	...	|	|	...	...	...	...	...	1250	...	...	|	...	...	|	...	...	...
St Pierre des Corps d.	|	|	1023	1023	...	...	|	|	...	...	...	...	...	1332	...	...	|	...	...	|	...	...	...
Nantes d.	|	|	|	|	...	...	|	|	...	0910	...	...	...	|	...	...	|	...	...	|	...	...	...
Angers St Laud d.	|	|	|	|	...	...	|	|	...	0948	...	...	...	|	...	...	|	...	...	|	...	...	...
Rennes d.	|	|	|	|	...	...	|	|	...	|	0915	...	...	|	...	...	|	...	...	|	...	...	...
Le Mans d.	|	|	|	|	...	...	|	|	...	1041	1041	...	...	|	...	...	|	...	...	|	...	...	...
Massy TGV d.	|	|	1116	1116	...	...	|	|	...	1141	1141	...	...	1427	...	...	|	...	...	|	...	...	...
Marne la Vallée § d.	1049	1049	1159	1159	...	...	1220	1220	...	1227	1227	...	...	1511	...	...	1550	...	...	1623	...	...	...
Paris Charles de Gaulle ✈ a.	1059	1059	1209	1209	...	...	1229	1229	...	1237	1237	...	...	1521	...	...	1600	...	...	1633	...	...	...
Paris Charles de Gaulle ✈ d.	1109	1109	1214	1214	...	...	1235	1235	...	1242	1242	...	...	1525	...	...	1610	...	...	1639	...	...	...
TGV Haute Picardie d.	|	|	|	|	...	...	|	|	...	1313	1313	...	...	|	...	...	1639	...	...	1710	...	...	...
Arras a.	1151	1151	|	|	...	...	|	|	...	|	|	...	...	|	...	...	|	...	...	|	...	...	...
Douai a.	1207	1207	|	|	...	...	|	|	...	|	|	...	...	|	...	...	|	...	...	|	...	...	...
Lille Europe a.	1233c	1233c	1306	1306	...	...	1326	1326	...	1341	1341	...	...	1615	...	...	1707	...	...	1736	...	...	...
Lille Europe 12 d.	...	...	...	...	1335	...	1336	...	1404	...	...	1505	1535	...	...	...	1721	1735	1735	1747	1835	...	...
Brussels Midi / Zuid 12 a.	...	...	...	...	|	...	1412	...	|	...	...	|	|	...	...	...	1756	|	|	1822	|	...	...
Ashford International **12** a.	...	...	...	...	|	...	...	...	|	...	...	|	|	...	...	...	...	1733	1737	...	|	...	...
Ebbsfleet International **12** a.	...	...	...	...	1345	...	...	...	1418	...	...	|	|	...	...	...	...	|	|	...	1845	...	...
London St Pancras 12 a.	...	...	...	...	1403	...	...	...	1434	...	...	1526	1556	...	...	...	...	1803	1807	...	1903	...	...

train type or number	*TGV*	*TGV*	*TGV*	☆	⇌		*Talgo*	*TGV*	*TGV*	*TGV*	☆	☆	*TGV*	*TGV*	*TGV*	*TGV*	*TGV*	*TGV*	*TGV*	*TGV*	*TGV*	*TGV*	
train number	**9866**	**5280**	**5278**	**9157**	**9954**		**73/72**	**9868**	**9816**	**9816**	**9087**	**9057**	**9868**	**5180**	**5180**	**5284**	**5290**	**5288**	**5184**	**5187**	**5292/3**	**5294**	
train number	**9867**	**5281**	R	R	**9955**		R 🍴	**9869**	**9817**	**5279**	R	R	**9869**	**5181**	**5181**	**5285**	R	**5289**	**5185**	**9887**	R	**5295**	
notes	R 🍷	R 🍷	🍷	🍴 ⑧	R 🍷 T		↗ N	R 🍷 C	R 🍷	R 🍷	🍴 X	🍴	R 🍷 A	R 🍷 P	R 🍷 Q	R 🍷 ⑧z	🍷	R 🍷	R 🍷	R 🍷 k	🍷 ①–⑥	R 🍷 ⑦h	
Nice d.	...	...	...	...	...	...	...	...	...	...	...	...	...	...	...	...	...	...	1531	...	...	...	...
Cannes d.	...	...	...	...	...	...	...	...	...	...	...	...	...	...	...	...	...	...	1601	...	...	...	...
St Raphaël - Valescure d.	...	...	...	...	...	...	...	...	...	...	...	...	...	...	...	...	...	...	1626	...	...	...	...
Toulon d.	...	...	...	...	...	...	...	...	...	...	...	...	...	...	...	...	...	...	1718	...	...	...	...
Marseille St Charles d.	1339	...	...	...	1409	...	...	...	...	...	...	...	...	1709	1709	...	...	...	1810	...	...	...	...
Aix en Provence TGV d.	1353	...	...	...	1424	...	...	...	...	...	...	...	...	1723	1723	...	...	...	1824	...	...	...	...
Barcelona França d.	|	...	...	...	|	...	0845	...	...	...	...	...	...	|	|	...	...	...	|	...	...	...	...
Cerbère 🏛 d.	|	...	...	...	|	...	1114	...	...	...	...	...	...	|	|	...	...	...	|	...	...	...	...
Perpignan d.	|	...	...	...	|	...	1145	1234	...	...	...	...	1410	|	|	...	...	...	|	...	...	...	...
Toulouse Matabiau d.	|	...	...	...	|	...	|	|	...	...	...	...	|	|	|	...	...	...	|	1610	...	...	...
Narbonne d.	|	...	...	...	|	...	1222	1314	...	...	...	...	1449	|	|	...	...	...	|	1728	...	...	...
Béziers d.	|	...	...	...	|	...	1239	1331	...	...	...	...	1507	|	|	...	...	...	|	1745	...	...	...
Montpellier d.	|	...	...	...	|	...	1322	1430	...	...	...	...	1600	|	|	...	...	...	|	1830	...	...	...
Nîmes d.	|	...	...	...	|	...	...	1457	...	...	...	...	1627	|	|	...	...	...	|	1857	...	...	...
Avignon TGV d.	1416	...	...	...	1446	...	...	|	...	...	1624g	...	|	|	|	...	...	...	1846	|	...	...	...
Valence TGV d.	|	...	...	...	1520	...	...	1544	...	...	|	...	|	1815	1815	...	...	...	|	1945	...	...	...
Grenoble d.	|	...	...	...	|	...	...	|	...	...	|	...	|	|	|	...	...	...	|	|	...	...	...
Lyon Perrache d.	|	...	...	...	|	...	...	|	...	...	|	...	|	|	|	...	...	...	|	|	...	...	...
Lyon Part Dieu d.	1526	...	...	...	|	...	...	1626	...	...	|	...	1756	1856	1856	...	...	...	1956	2026	...	...	...
Le Creusot TGV d.	|	...	...	...	|	...	...	|	...	...	|	...	|	|	|	...	...	...	|	|	...	...	...
Hendaye d.	|	...	...	...	|	...	...	|	...	...	|	...	|	|	|	...	...	...	|	|	1620j	...	...
Bordeaux d.	|	...	...	...	|	...	...	|	1422	1422	|	...	|	|	|	1643	...	...	|	|	1841	...	...
Angoulême d.	|	...	...	...	|	...	...	|	1526	1526	|	...	|	|	|	1745	...	...	|	|	1946	...	...
Poitiers d.	|	...	...	...	|	...	...	|	1614	1614	|	...	|	|	|	1833	...	...	|	|	2039	...	...
St Pierre des Corps d.	|	...	...	...	|	...	...	|	1656	1656	|	...	|	|	|	1928	...	...	|	|	2122	...	...
Nantes d.	|	...	1435	...	|	...	...	|	|	|	|	...	|	|	|	|	...	1835	|	|	|	...	...
Angers St Laud d.	|	...	1513	...	|	...	...	|	|	|	|	...	|	|	|	|	...	1912	|	|	|	...	...
Rennes d.	|	1435	|	...	|	...	...	|	|	|	|	...	|	|	|	|	1839	|	|	|	|	2020	...
Le Mans d.	|	1558	1558	...	|	...	...	|	|	|	|	...	|	|	|	|	2000	2000	|	|	|	2138	...
Massy TGV d.	|	1651	1651	...	|	...	...	|	1749	1749	|	...	|	|	|	2021	2050	2050	|	|	2217	2230	...
Marne la Vallée § d.	|	1732	1732	...	|	...	...	1820	1830	1830	|	1937	1950	2049	2049	2102	2134	2134	2150	2219	2256	2306	...
Paris Charles de Gaulle ✈ a.	1720	1741	1741	...	|	...	...	1830	1841	1841	|	|	2000	2103	2103	2112	2146	2146	2159	2228	2306	2316	...
Paris Charles de Gaulle ✈ d.	1724	1745	1745	...	|	...	...	1840	1848	1845	|	|	2010	2108	2108	2116	2150	2150	2209	2232	2310	2320	...
TGV Haute Picardie d.	|	|	|	...	|	...	...	|	|	|	|	|	|	2140	2140	2150	2220	2220	|	2302	2341	|	...
Arras a.	|	|	|	...	|	...	...	|	|	1924	|	|	|	|	2159	|	2238	2238	|	|	|	|	...
Douai a.	|	|	|	...	|	...	...	|	|	1942	|	|	|	|	2214	|	2254	2254	|	|	|	|	...
Lille Europe a.	1814	1838c	1838c	...	|	...	...	1936	|	2005c	|	|	2105	2206	2238	2219	2318	2318	2301	2328	0007	0010	...
Lille Europe 12 d.	1835	...	...	1935	|	...	...	1946	|	...	2032u	2038u	2115	...	...	...	...	...	...	2338	...	...	...
Brussels Midi / Zuid 12 a.	1910	...	...	|	1847	...	...	2022	2003	...	|	|	2152	...	...	...	...	...	...	0013k	...	...	...
Ashford International **12** a.	...	...	...	|	...	...	...	...	...	...	2033	2037	...	...	...	...	...	...	...	...	...	...	...
Ebbsfleet International **12** a.	...	...	...	|	...	...	...	...	...	...	|	|	...	...	...	...	...	...	...	...	...	...	...
London St Pancras 12 a.	...	...	...	1956	...	...	...	...	...	...	2109	2112	...	...	...	...	...	...	...	...	...	...	...

A – ①–⑤ (not July 14).
C – ⑥⑦ (also July 14).
E – ①–⑥ (not July 14).
N – CATALÁN TALGO – [12] and 🍴 Barcelona - Montpellier. Special fares payable.
P – ①–⑤ until July 3 and from Aug. 31.
Q – ⑥⑦ (daily July 4 - Aug. 30).
T – THALYS SOLEIL – ⑥ July 4 - Aug. 29: [12] and 🍷 Marseille - Brussels - Amsterdam (arrive 2136; Table **18**). ⑥ June 27 - Aug. 29: [12] and 🍷 Marseille - Brussels.

W – ①⑥ (not July 13).
X – ⑥ July 18 - Sept. 12.
c – Lille **Flandres**, 500 metres from Lille Europe; see City Plan on page 31.
e – ⑦ (not July 5 - Aug. 30).
f – ①⑥ (also July 15; not July 13).
g – Avignon **Centre**.
h – ⑦ (also July 14).
j – ⑥ only.

k – Runs to Brussels on ⑥ July - Aug. 29 (arrive next day).
u – Stops to pick up only.
x – Calls at Futuroscope 0947.
z – Calls at Futuroscope 1850.
↗ – Supplement payable.
§ – Marne la Vallée - Chessy, Station for Disneyland Paris.
☆ – Eurostar train. Special fares payable. Minimum check-in time 30 minutes. Valid June 14 – Aug. 30.

12 LONDON - LILLE - BRUSSELS *by Eurostar*

All times shown are local times (France and Belgium are one hour ahead of Great Britain).

For the complete service London - Lille see Table 10. For other services Lille - Brussels (by TGV) see Table 16a.

All Eurostar services are Ⓡ, non-smoking and convey ✕

Service June 14 - Aug. 30.

km	train type	☆			☆			☆		☆	☆		☆				☆				☆			EC J
	train number	9106			9110			9114		9120	9120		9116				9126				9132	⑥⑦		295
	notes	①–⑤			①–⑥			⑥		①–⑤	A		⑥											①–⑤
0	**London St Pancras** d.	0557	...	...	0659	...	...	0757	...	0834	0827	...	0859	...	...	...	1057	...	...	...	1257	...	...	...
35	Ebbsfleet International d.	|	...	...	0715	...	...	|	...	|	0845	...	0915	...	...	...	1115	...	...	...	1315	...	...	...
90	Ashford International d.	0627	...	...	|	...	...	0828	...	|	|	...	|	...	...	...	|	...	...	...	|	...	...	...
267	Lille Europe a.	|	...	...	0924	...	...	|	...	|	1054	...	1124	...	...	...	1324	...	...	...	1524	...	...	...
	Lille Europe d.	|	...	...	0928	...	...	|	...	|	1058	...	1128	...	...	...	1328	...	...	...	1528	...	...	...
373	**Brussels Midi / Zuid** a.	0856	0933	0957	1003	1033	1057	1056	1133	1129	1133	1157	1203	1233	1257	...	1403	1433	1457	...	1603	1633	1657	1727
	Brugge a.	*1027*	|	|	*1127*	|	|	*1227*	|	*1302*	*1302*	|	*1327*	|	|	...	*1527*	|	|	...	*1727*	|	|	|
	Leuven a.	...	|	1023	...	|	1123	...	|	...	...	1223	...	|	1323	...	...	|	1523	...	...	|	1723	|
	Liège Guillemins a.	...	|	1100	...	|	1200	...	|	...	...	1300	...	|	1400	...	...	|	1600	...	...	|	1800	|
	Namur a.	...	1039	...	...	1139	...	...	1239	...	...	...	...	1339	...	...	...	1539	...	...	...	1739	...	1832
	Luxembourg a.	...	1240	...	...	1337	...	...	1445	...	...	...	...	1542	...	...	...	1742	...	...	...	1947	...	2016

train type	☆					☆	☆	☆			☆		☆			☆	☆			☆				
train number	9138		①–⑤			9144	9144	9144			9148		9150			9154	9154			9158		⑥⑦		
notes			t			⑤	①–④	⑦w			⑥⑦		①–⑤			⑦	B					f		
London St Pancras d.	1434	...	...	...	...	1604	1604	1604	...	...	1657	...	1727	...	...	1821	1834	...	...	1934	...	...	...	...
Ebbsfleet International d.	|	...	...	...	...	|	|	|	...	...	1715	...	1745	...	...	|	|	...	...	|	...	...	...	...
Ashford International d.	|	...	...	...	...	|	|	|	...	...	|	...	|	...	...	1855	|	...	...	|	...	...	...	...
Lille Europe a.	1654	...	...	...	...	|	1824	|	...	...	1924	...	1954	...	...	2051	|	...	...	2154	...	...	...	...
Lille Europe d.	1658	...	...	...	...	|	1828	|	...	...	1928	...	1958	...	...	2058	|	...	...	2158	...	...	...	...
Brussels Midi / Zuid a.	1733	1757	1809	1833	...	1859	1903	1903	1933	1957	2003	2033	2033	2057	2133	2133	2133	2157	2203	2233	2257	2333	...	...
Brugge a.	*1902*	|	|	|	...	*2027*	*2027*	*2027*	|	|	*2127*	|	*2202*	|	|	*2302*	*2302*	|	|	*2358*	|	|	...	...
Leuven a.	...	1823	|	|	...	...	...	...	|	2023	...	|	...	2123	|	...	...	2223	|	...	2323	|	...	...
Liège Guillemins a.	...	1900	|	|	...	...	...	...	|	2100	...	|	...	2200	|	...	...	2300	|	...	0019	|	...	...
Namur a.	...	...	1912	1939	...	...	...	...	2039	...	...	2139	...	...	2239	...	...	...	2309	...	...	0046	...	...
Luxembourg a.	...	...	2103	2137	...	...	...	...	2237	...	...	2342	...	...	0040	...	...	...	...	...	...	...	...	...

train type				☆			☆	☆		☆				☆				☆				☆		
train number	⑥⑦		①–⑤	9109			9113	9113	①–⑤	9113	①–⑤			9119				9181				9133		
notes	f		t	①–⑥			⑥m	⑦	t	C	t			①–⑥								⑥⑦		
Luxembourg d.	...	...	...	...	...	...	...	...	...	...	0520	...	...	...	...	0719	...	...	...	...	0920	...	...	...
Namur d.	0436	...	0521	...	...	0620	...	...	...	...	0720	0751	...	...	...	0921	...	...	...	...	1121	...	...	...
Liège Guillemins d.	|	0443	|	...	0556	|	...	...	0639	...	|	|	0800	...	...	|	1000	...	...	1100	|	...	...	...
Leuven d.	|	0537	|	...	0637	|	...	...	|	...	|	|	0837	...	...	|	1035	...	...	1135	|	...	...	...
Brugge d.	|	|	|	*0524*	|	|	*0631*	*0631*	|	*0631*	|	|	|	*0758*	...	|	|	*0958*	...	|	|	*1131*	...	...
Brussels Midi / Zuid d.	0546	0603	0627	0659	0703	0727	0759	0759	0736	0805	0827	0857	0903	0929	...	1027	1103	1129	...	1203	1227	1259	...	...
Lille Europe a.	...	...	...	0732	...	...	|	0832	...	|	...	...	...	1002	...	...	...	1202	...	...	...	1332	...	...
Lille Europe d.	...	...	...	0735	...	...	|	0835	...	|	...	...	...	1005	...	...	...	1205	...	...	...	1335	...	...
Ashford International a.	...	...	...	|	...	...	|	|	...	|	...	...	...	|	...	...	...	|	...	...	...	|	...	...
Ebbsfleet International a.	...	...	...	|	...	...	|	|	...	|	...	...	...	1015	...	...	...	|	...	...	...	1345	...	...
London St Pancras a.	...	...	...	0755	...	...	0856	0857	...	0856	...	...	...	1031	...	...	...	1226	...	...	...	1403	...	...

train type	EC		☆		☆			☆			☆	☆			☆			☆		EC		☆		
train number	296		9139		9141			9145			9149	9149			9153			9157		90		9163		
notes	J		⑥⑦		①–⑤			①–⑤			⑦	①–⑤						⑧		V		D		
Luxembourg d.	1024	...	...	1124	...	...	1224	...	...	1324	...	...	...	1420	...	...	1520	...	...	1702	...	...	...	...
Namur d.	1221	...	...	1321	...	...	1421	...	...	1521	...	...	...	1621	...	...	1721	...	...	1848	...	...	...	...
Liège Guillemins d.	|	1300	...	|	...	1400	|	...	1500	|	...	...	1600	|	...	1700	|	...	...	|	1900	...	...	...
Leuven d.	|	1337	...	|	...	1437	|	...	1537	|	...	...	1635	|	...	1737	|	...	...	|	1937	...	...	...
Brugge d.	|	|	*1258*	|	*1331*	|	|	*1431*	|	|	*1531*	*1531*	|	|	*1631*	|	|	*1731*	...	|	|	*1858*	...	...
Brussels Midi / Zuid d.	1327	1403	1429	1427	1459	1503	1527	1559	1603	1627	1659	1659	1703	1727	1759	1803	1827	1859	...	1951	2003	2029	...	...
Lille Europe a.	...	...	1502	...	1532	...	...	1632	...	...	1732	1732	...	...	1832	...	...	1932	...	...	...	2102	...	...
Lille Europe d.	...	...	1505	...	1535	...	...	1635	...	...	1735	1735	...	...	1835	...	...	1935	...	...	...	2105	...	...
Ashford International a.	...	...	|	...	|	...	...	|	...	...	1733	1737	...	...	|	...	...	|	...	...	...	|	...	...
Ebbsfleet International a.	...	...	|	...	|	...	...	1645	...	...	|	|	...	...	1845	...	...	|	...	...	...	2115	...	...
London St Pancras a.	...	...	1526	...	1556	...	...	1703	...	...	1803	1807	...	...	1903	...	...	1956	...	...	...	2133	...	...

A – ⑦ July 5 - Aug. 30.
B – ①–⑤ (⑤ July 5 - Aug. 30).
C – ①–⑤ (① July 5 - Aug. 30).
D – ⑧ (daily July 5 - Aug. 30).
f – Also July 14, Nov. 11.
m – Calls at Calais Fréthun 0902.
t – Not July 14, Nov. 11.
w – Calls at Calais Fréthun 1759.
J – JEAN MONNET – 12 Brussels - Luxembourg - Basel and v.v.
V – VAUBAN – 12 Zürich - Basel - Brussels.
☆ – Eurostar train. Special fares payable. Minimum check-in time 30 minutes. Not available for London - Ebbsfleet - Ashford or v.v. journeys. Valid June 14 – Aug. 30.

INTERNATIONAL SERVICES FROM BRUSSELS

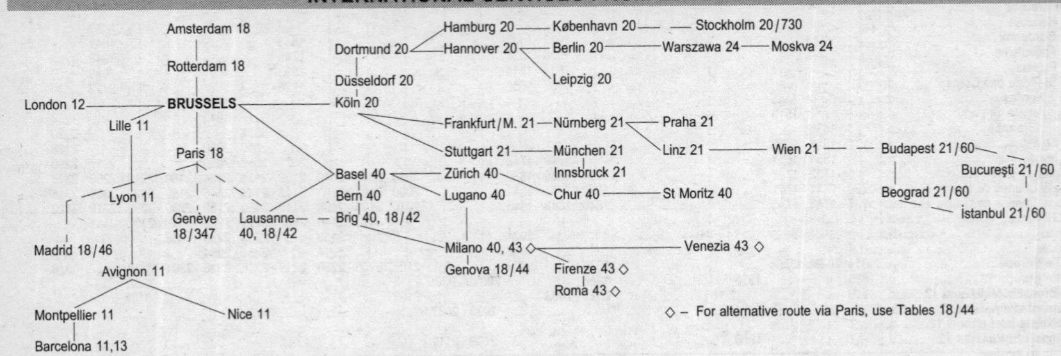

For explanation of standard symbols see page 4

LONDON / BRUSSELS - LILLE - PARIS - BARCELONA - ALACANT 13

train type	TGV				TGV	☆	TGV	Talgo	AVE	TGV			☆	Hotel		AVE	AVE	Em	☆			Talgo	AVE		
train number	9804				5112	9004	6209	70	3212	9832			9036	477		3090	3102	1101	9040	3731	3733	463	3122		
notes	9805		⑥⑦	⑧	5113	①–⑥		71		9833				476		⑧				®		462			
notes		2	2	2				K 🍷			2	2		J ❖						G	A	C 🍷		2	
London St Pancras 10 .. d.	...	...	...	...	...	0655	...	...	...	...	...	...	1529	...	...	...	...	...	1625	...	...	...	...	...	...
Brussels Midi/Zuid 12 d.	0540x	...	...	...	...	|	...	...	...	1110	...	...	|	...	...	...	...	...	|	...	...	...	...	...	...
Lille Europe 12 d.	0625	...	...	...	0828	|	...	...	...	1156	...	...	|	...	...	...	...	...	|	...	...	...	...	...	...
Paris Nord 10 a.	|	...	...	...	|	1017	...	...	...	|	...	...	1856	...	...	...	...	...	1947	...	...	...	...	...	...
Paris Austerlitz d.	|	...	...	...	|	...	...	...	...	|	...	...	...	2032	...	...	...	...	...	2156	2202	...	...	...	...
Paris Gare de Lyon d.	|	...	...	...	|	...	1120	...	...	|	...	...	...	|	...	...	...	...	...	|	|	...	...	...	...
Les Aubrais-Orléans d.	|	...	...	...	|	...	|	...	...	|	...	...	...	2133	...	...	...	...	...	2256	2302	...	...	...	...
Limoges d.	|	...	...	...	|	...	|	...	...	|	...	...	...	2355	...	...	...	...	...	|	0127	...	...	...	...
Lyon Part Dieu d.	0931	...	...	...	1131	...	|	...	...	1507	...	...	...	|	...	...	...	...	...	|	|	...	...	...	...
Montpellier d.	1128	1155	...	...	1326	...	1442	1509	...	1706	...	...	...	|	...	...	...	...	...	|	|	...	...	...	...
Narbonne d.	...	1256	...	...	...	...	...	1611	...	1827	...	...	...	|	...	...	...	...	...	0637	0658	0821	...	...	...
Perpignan d.	...	1340	...	...	...	...	...	1654	...	1844	1916	...	...	|	...	...	...	...	...	0722	0746	0857	...	...	...
Cerbère 🏛 a.	...	1420	...	...	...	...	...	1729	...	...	2001	...	...	|	...	...	...	...	...	0817	0850	0931	...	...	...
Portbou 🏛 a.	...	1428	1526	1559	...	...	...	1746	...	...	2009	2030e	...	|	...	...	...	...	...	0821	0854	0948	...	1029	...
Figueres a.	...	...	1546	1623	...	...	...	1811	...	...	...	2057	...	0624	...	...	...	...	...	...	...	1012	...	1054	...
Girona a.	...	...	1615	1701	...	...	...	1837	...	...	...	2127	...	0654	...	...	...	...	...	...	...	1040	...	1132	...
Barcelona França a.	...	...	|	|	...	...	...	1959	...	...	...	|	...	0824	0842	...	...	...	...	...	...	|	...	|	...
Barcelona Sants a.	...	...	1739	1839	...	...	...	...	2100	...	...	2256	...	...	0854	0930	1000	1000	...	...	...	1146	1200	1309	...
Zaragoza Delicias a.	...	...	...	...	...	...	...	...	2251	...	...	...	...	...	...	|	1151	|	...	...	...	|	1351	...	...
Madrid Puerta de Atocha .. a.	...	...	...	...	...	...	...	...	0017	...	...	...	...	...	...	1213	1323	|	...	...	...	|	1523	...	...
València Nord a.	...	...	...	...	...	...	...	...	...	...	...	...	...	...	...	...	...	1300	...	...	...	1515	...	...	...
Alacant Términal a.	...	...	...	...	...	...	...	...	...	...	...	...	...	...	...	...	...	1500	...	...	...	1724	...	...	...

train type			Talgo	TGV	☆	☆	TGV				TGV	AVE	Talgo	AVE				☆	AVE	Em	AVE	AVE	Hotel	☆	
train number			73	6212	9059	9059	9868				9868	3123	460	3133		3730	3732	9015	3163	1162	3171	3181	475	9023	
notes	①–⑤	⑥⑦	72		①–⑤	⑥⑦	9869		①–⑤		9869		461			G ®	B			⑧	⑧ p	⑧ q	474		
notes	2	2	T 🍷				P		2	2	Q		D 🍷		2								J		
Alacant Términal d.	...	...	...	...	...	...	...	...	...	...	...	...	1109	...	...	...	...	...	...	1420	...	...	...	...	...
València Nord d.	...	...	...	...	...	...	...	...	...	...	...	...	1308	...	...	...	...	...	...	1605	...	...	...	...	...
Madrid Puerta de Atocha .. d.	...	...	...	...	...	...	...	...	...	...	...	1230	|	1330	...	...	...	...	1630	|	1700	1800	...	...	...
Zaragoza Delicias d.	...	...	...	...	...	...	...	...	...	...	...	1349	|	1455	...	...	...	...	1749	|	|	|	...	...	...
Barcelona Sants d.	0716	0746	...	...	...	...	...	...	0916	...	...	1527	1642	1654	1716	...	...	...	1927	1910	1938	2043	...	...	...
Barcelona França d.	|	|	0845	...	...	...	...	...	|	...	...	...	|	...	|	...	...	...	...	...	...	...	2105	...	...
Girona d.	0902	0911	0955	...	...	...	...	...	1052	...	...	...	1748	...	1852	...	...	...	...	...	...	...	2217	...	...
Figueres d.	0940	0940	1025	...	...	...	...	...	1130	...	...	...	1815	...	1930	...	...	...	...	...	...	...	2247	...	...
Portbou 🏛 d.	1005	1000	1053	...	...	...	...	...	1155	...	...	...	1844	...	1956	...	...	...	...	...	...	...	|	...	...
Cerbère 🏛 d.	1010	...	1114	...	...	...	...	...	1200	1240	...	...	1902	...	2000	2121	2135	...	...	...	...	...	|	...	...
Perpignan d.	...	...	1145	...	...	...	1234	...	...	1320	1410	...	...	...	...	2210	2226	...	...	...	...	...	|	...	...
Narbonne d.	...	...	1222	...	...	...	1314	...	...	...	1449	...	...	...	...	2304	2330	...	...	...	...	...	|	...	...
Montpellier a.	...	...	1322	1423	...	...	1430	...	...	...	1600	...	...	...	...	|	|	...	...	...	...	...	|	...	...
Lyon Part Dieu a.	...	...	...	|	...	...	1626	...	...	...	1756	...	...	...	...	|	|	...	...	...	...	...	|	...	...
Limoges a.	...	...	...	|	...	...	|	...	...	...	|	...	...	...	...	|	0408	...	...	...	...	...	0504z	...	...
Les Aubrais-Orléans a.	...	...	...	|	...	...	|	...	...	...	|	...	...	...	...	0620	0634	...	...	...	...	...	0740z	...	...
Paris Gare de Lyon a.	...	...	...	1749	...	...	|	...	...	...	|	...	...	...	...	|	|	...	...	...	...	...	|	...	...
Paris Austerlitz a.	...	...	...	...	...	...	|	...	...	...	|	...	...	...	...	0730	0743	...	...	...	...	...	0900	...	...
Paris Nord 10 d.	...	...	...	...	2013	2013	|	...	...	...	|	...	...	...	...	...	...	0913	...	...	...	...	...	1113	...
Lille Europe 12 a.	...	...	...	...	|	|	1936	...	...	...	2105	...	...	...	...	...	...	|	...	...	...	...	...	|	...
Brussels Midi/Zuid 12 a.	...	...	...	...	|	|	2022	...	...	...	2152	...	...	...	...	...	...	|	...	...	...	...	...	|	...
London St Pancras 10 ... a.	...	...	...	...	2129	2141	...	...	...	...	...	...	...	...	...	...	...	1036	...	...	...	...	...	1229	...

A – ⑤⑥ June 26 - Sept. 5 (also July 13, Oct. 23): 🛏 1, 2 cl., and [2] (reclining) Paris - Portbou.
B – ⑥⑦ June 27 - Sept. 6 (also July 14, Nov. 1): 🛏 1, 2 cl. and [2] (reclining) Cerbère - Paris.
C – MARE NOSTRUM – [12] and 🍷 Montpellier - Portbou - Barcelona - Alacant - Cartagena (arrive 1952), ® ⁄ Special fares payable.
D – MARE NOSTRUM – [12] and 🍷 Lorca (depart 0820) - Alacant - Barcelona - Portbou - Montpellier, ® ⁄ Special fares payable.
G – *CORAIL LUNÉA* – 🛏 1, 2 cl., [2] (reclining) and 🍷 Paris - Portbou and Cerbère - Paris.
J – JOÁN MIRÓ *Trainhotel Elipsos* – 🛏 1, 2 cl., 🛏 1, 2 cl. (T4) [1] (reclining) and ✕ Paris - Barcelona and v.v. ® Special fares apply.
K – CATALÁN TALGO – [12] and ✕ Montpellier - Portbou - Barcelona and v.v. ® ⁄ Special fares payable.

P – ⑥⑦ (also July 14).
Q – ①–⑤ (not July 14).

c – Madrid **Chamartín**.
e – 2036 on ①–⑤.
p – Not Aug. 2–28.
q – Not June 24, Aug. 2–28.
t – 9–10 minutes earlier on ⑥.
x – ①–⑤ (not July 14).
z – Not June 21, 22, 23.

⁄ – Supplement payable.
Em – *Euromed* train, ® 🍷 ⁄.

TGV – *Train à Grande Vitesse* ® 🍷 ⁄.
AVE – Alta Velocidad Española ® 🍷 ⁄.
Talgo – *Talgo* ® ⁄ 🍷.
❖ – On June 22, 23 does not stop at Limoges and Les Aubrais-Orléans. On morning of July 1 arrive Figueres 0712, Girona 0744 and Barcelona 0929.
☆ – Eurostar train. Special fares payable. Minimum check-in time 30 minutes. Additional services are shown on Table **10**. Valid June 14 - Aug. 30.

LONDON - GENÈVE 14

For the full service Paris - Genève, see Table **341**. 90 minutes (including Eurostar check-in time of 30 minutes) has been allowed from Paris **Lyon** and Paris **Austerlitz** to Paris Nord; additional Eurostar services are available, see Table **10**.

train type	☆	☆	☆	TGV	☆	TGV	☆	TGV	☆	☆	TGV	☆	TGV	☆	TGV	☆	☆		
train number	9078	9002	9002	6569	9010	6573	9018	6577	9026	9028	6581	9030	6585	9036	6589	9044	9046	5595 5594	
notes	® ✕	® ✕	® ✕	♥	®	♥	®	♥	®	®	♥	®	♥	®	♥	®	®	🍷	
notes	①–⑤	⑥ D	⑤ E		✕ ①–⑥	⑧	✕		✕ ⑦	✕ ①–⑥		✕		✕	⑤	✕ ⑥⑦	✕ ⑧	A	
London St Pancras 10 d.	0525	0622	0626	...	0832	...	1025	...	1300	1332	...	1404	...	1529	...	1731	1756	...	...
Paris Nord 10 a.	0850	0947	0947	...	1147	...	1347	...	1617	1647	...	1726	...	1856	...	2053	2117	...	...
Paris Gare de Lyon d.	...	...	...	1110	...	1310	...	1504	...	...	1810	...	1908	...	2010	...	...	...	...
Paris Austerlitz d.	...	...	...	|	...	|	...	|	...	...	|	...	|	...	|	...	...	2246	...
Mâcon Loché TGV a.	...	...	...	|	...	|	...	1640	...	...	|	...	2044	...	|	...	...	|	...
La Roche sur Foron a.	...	...	...	|	...	|	...	|	...	...	|	...	|	...	|	...	...	0813	0918
Genève Cornavin a.	...	...	...	1435	...	1635	...	1835	...	...	2132	...	2245	...	2335	...	...	...	|
Genève Eaux Vives a.	...	...	...	...	...	...	...	...	...	...	...	...	...	...	...	...	...	...	0958

train type	TGV	☆	TGV	☆	TGV	☆	☆	☆		TGV	☆	☆	☆				☆		
train number	6560	9023	6564	9031	6568	9037	9039	9039		6572	9053	9055	9059			5596 5597	9011		
notes	♥	®	♥	®	♥	®	®	®		♥	®	®	®		①–⑤	🍷	®		
notes	①–⑤ k	✕		✕		✕ N	✕ ⑥⑦	✕ ①–⑤			✕ ①–⑤	✕ ⑦	✕ ⑥⑦		k	B	✕		
Genève Eaux Vives d.	...	...	...	...	...	...	...	...	...	...	...	...	...	...	1702	...	...	...	...
Genève Cornavin d.	0535	...	0717	...	0917	...	...	...	...	1317	...	...	...	...	|	...	...	...	...
La Roche sur Foron a.	|	...	|	...	|	...	...	...	...	|	...	...	...	...	1736	2158	...	...	...
Mâcon Loché TGV d.	|	...	|	...	|	...	...	...	...	|	...	...	...	...	...	|	...	...	...
Paris Austerlitz a.	|	...	|	...	|	...	...	...	...	|	...	...	...	...	...	0636	...	...	...
Paris Gare de Lyon a.	0903	...	1051	...	1249	...	...	...	...	1649	...	...	...	...	...	...	...	...	...
Paris Nord 10 d.	...	1113	...	1301	...	1443	1507	1513	...	...	1843	1913	2013	...	...	...	0807	...	...
London St Pancras 10 a.	...	1229	...	1434	...	1559	1636	1636	...	...	2006	2029	2141	...	...	...	0934	...	...

A – *CORAIL LUNÉA* – ⑤⑥⑦ (daily June 26 - Aug. 30): ® 🛏 1, 2 cl. and [2] (reclining) Paris - La Roche sur Foron - St Gervais.
B – *CORAIL LUNÉA* – ⑤⑥⑦ (daily June 26 - Aug. 30): ® 🛏 1, 2 cl. and [2] (reclining) St Gervais - La Roche sur Foron - Paris.
D – ⑥ (not July 5 - Aug. 30).
E – ⑤ (⑤⑥ July 5 - Aug. 30).

N – ①–⑥ July 5 - Aug. 30.
k – Not July 14.
☆ – Eurostar train. Minimum check-in time 30 minutes. Special fares payable. Connections across Paris between *TGV* and Eurostar services are not guaranteed. See Table **10**. Valid June 14 - Aug. 30.
♥ – *TGV Lyria* service. ® special fares payable. At-seat meal service in first class.

TRAIN NAMES: **6577** EUROCITY VERSAILLES **6569/6572** EUROCITY VOLTAIRE **6581/6568** EUROCITY HENRY DUNANT **6585/6564** EUROCITY J J ROUSSEAU

15 LONDON - ROTTERDAM - AMSTERDAM *by Eurostar*

Due to engineering works Aug. 15 – 22, *Thalys* services will not call at Schiphol, Den Haag HS, Rotterdam. Earlier departures and later arrivals will occur at Amsterdam.

train type	☆				☆	⇌	☆				☆	☆	⇌				☆	♀			☆				
train number	9106				9110	9319	9114				9120	9120	9323				9116				9126	9233			
notes	①-⑤	①-⑤			①-⑥	⑤⑦h	⑥	♀			①-⑤	A		♀			⑥	⑥				♀			
London St Pancras 12 d.	0557	...	...	...	0659	...	0757	...	...	...	0834	0827	...	...	...	...	0859	...	...	...	1057	...	...	...	...
Ebbsfleet International 12 d.	|	...	...	...	0715	...	|	...	...	...	|	0845	...	...	...	...	0915	...	...	...	1115	...	...	...	...
Ashford International d.	0627	...	...	...	|	...	0828	...	...	...	|	|	...	...	...	...	|	...	...	...	|	...	...	...	...
Lille Europe 12 d.	|	...	...	...	0928	...	|	...	...	...	|	1058	...	...	...	...	1128	...	...	...	1328	...	...	...	...
Brussels Midi / Zuid 12 a.	0856	...	...	...	1003	...	1056	...	...	...	1129	1133	...	...	...	...	1203	...	...	...	1403	...	...	...	...
Brussels Midi / Zuid d.	...	0918	...	...	...	1052	...	1115x	...	...	...	...	1152	1215x	...	...	...	1315	...	...	...	1515x	...	...	...
Mechelen a.	...	0940	...	...	...	|	...	1140	...	...	...	...	|	1240	...	...	...	1340	...	...	...	1540	...	...	...
Antwerpen Berchem a.	...	|	...	...	...	|	...	|	...	...	...	...	|	|	...	...	...	|	...	...	...	|	...	...	...
Antwerpen Centraal a.	...	0957	...	...	...	1132	...	1157	...	...	...	...	1232	1257	...	...	...	1357	...	...	...	1557	...	...	...
Roosendaal 🛃 a.	...	1028	...	1051	...	|	...	1228	...	1251	...	...	|	1328	...	1351	...	1428	...	1451	...	1628	...	1651	...
Breda a.	...	|	...	1108	...	|	...	|	...	1308	...	...	|	|	...	1408	...	|	...	1508	...	|	...	1708	...
Tilburg a.	...	|	...	1124	...	|	...	|	...	1324	...	...	|	|	...	1424	...	|	...	1524	...	|	...	1724	...
's-Hertogenbosch a.	...	|	...	1142	...	|	...	|	...	1342	...	...	|	|	...	1442	...	|	...	1542	...	|	...	1742	...
Nijmegen a.	...	|	...	1213	...	|	...	|	...	1413	...	...	|	|	...	1513	...	|	...	1613	...	|	...	1813	...
Arnhem a.	...	|	...	1235	...	|	...	|	...	1435	...	...	|	|	...	1535	...	|	...	1635	...	|	...	1835	...
Dordrecht a.	...	1053	...	...	...	|	...	1253	...	...	...	...	|	1353	...	...	...	1453	...	...	...	1653	...	...	...
Rotterdam Centraal a.	...	1106	1117	...	...	1236	...	1306	1317	...	...	...	1336	1406	1417	...	...	1506	1517	...	...	1706	1717	...	...
Utrecht Centraal a.	...	|	1156	...	...	|	...	|	1356	...	...	...	|	|	1456	...	...	|	1556	...	...	|	1756	...	...
Den Haag HS a.	...	1125	...	...	...	1256	...	1325	...	...	...	...	1356	1425	...	...	...	1525	...	...	...	1725	...	...	...
Schiphol ✈ a.	...	1149	...	...	...	1319	...	1349	...	...	...	...	1419	1449	...	...	...	1549	...	...	...	1749	...	...	...
Amsterdam Centraal a.	...	1206	...	...	...	1336	...	1406	...	...	...	...	1436	1506	...	...	...	1606	...	...	...	1806	...	...	...

train type	☆	⇌			☆	⇌			☆		☆	☆	⇌			☆	☆	⇌		☆	☆		☆		
train number	9132	9343	9245		9138	9347	9249		9144	♀	9144	9144	9355	9257		9148	9150	9359	9257	9154	9154	9265	9158	⑥⑦	①-⑤
notes		①-⑥	♀			⑦	♀		⑤	⑤	①-④	⑦		♀		⑥⑦	①-⑤	Ⓑ	♀	⑦	C			h	q
London St Pancras 12 d.	1257	p	...	...	1434	h	...	...	1604	...	1604	1604	...	...	...	1657	1727	...	...	1821	1834	...	1934	...	...
Ebbsfleet International 12 d.	1315	...	...	...	|	...	...	...	|	...	|	|	...	...	...	1715	1745	...	...	|	|	...	|	...	...
Ashford International d.	|	...	...	...	|	...	...	...	|	...	|	|	...	...	...	|	|	...	...	1855	|	...	|	...	...
Lille Europe 12 d.	1528	...	...	...	1658	...	...	...	|	...	1828	|	...	...	...	1928	1958	...	...	2058	|	...	2158	...	...
Brussels Midi / Zuid 12 a.	1603	...	...	...	1733	...	...	...	1859	...	1903	1903	...	...	...	2003	2033	...	...	2133	2133	...	2233	...	...
Brussels Midi / Zuid d.	...	1652	1715x	...	...	1752	1815x	...	...	1918	...	...	1952	2015x	...	...	...	2052	2115x	...	...	2215x	...	2305	2331
Mechelen a.	...	|	1740	...	...	|	1840	...	...	1940	...	...	|	2040	...	...	...	|	2140	...	...	2240	...	2345	0006
Antwerpen Berchem a.	...	|	|	...	...	|	|	...	...	|	...	...	|	|	...	...	...	|	|	...	...	|	...	2400	0033
Antwerpen Centraal a.	...	1732	1757	...	...	1832	1857	...	...	1957	...	...	2032	2057	...	...	...	2132	2157	...	...	2257	...	0006	0039
Roosendaal 🛃 a.	...	|	1828	1851	...	|	1928	1951	...	2029	...	...	|	2129	2151	...	...	|	2229	...	...	2329	...	...	...
Breda a.	...	|	|	1908	...	|	|	2008	...	|	...	...	|	|	2208	...	...	|	|	...	...	|	...	...	...
Tilburg a.	...	|	|	1924	...	|	|	2023	...	|	...	...	|	|	2224	...	...	|	|	...	...	|	...	...	...
's-Hertogenbosch a.	...	|	|	1942	...	|	|	2042	...	|	...	...	|	|	2242	...	...	|	|	...	...	|	...	...	...
Nijmegen a.	...	|	|	2013	...	|	|	2113	...	|	...	...	|	|	2313	...	...	|	|	...	...	|	...	...	...
Arnhem a.	...	|	|	2035	...	|	|	2135	...	|	...	...	|	|	2335	...	...	|	|	...	...	|	...	...	...
Dordrecht a.	...	|	1853	▬	...	|	1953	▬	...	2053	...	...	|	2153	▬	...	...	|	2253	...	...	2353	...	...	...
Rotterdam Centraal a.	...	1836	1906	1917	...	1936	2006	2017	...	2106	...	...	2136	2206	2232	...	...	2236c	2306	...	...	0006	...	...	...
Utrecht Centraal a.	...	|	|	1956	...	|	|	2056	...	|	...	...	|	|	2311	...	...	|	|	...	...	...	...	...	...
Den Haag HS a.	...	1856	1925	...	...	1956	2025	...	...	2125	...	...	2156	2225	...	...	...	2256c	2325	...	...	...	...	...	...
Schiphol ✈ a.	...	1919	1949	...	...	2019	2049	...	...	2149	...	...	2219	2249	...	...	...	2319c	2349	...	...	...	...	...	...
Amsterdam Centraal a.	...	1936	2006	...	...	2036	2106	...	...	2206	...	...	2236	2306	...	...	...	2336c	0006	...	...	...	...	...	...

train type	4527	4526	☆		☆	☆	4528	☆				☆					☆			⇌	☆			☆	☆
train number	①-⑤	⑥⑦	9109	⑥⑦	9113	9113	①-⑤	9113	①-⑤	①-⑤	9212	9119	⑦	①-⑥		9220	9181		♀	9326	9133		9232	9139	9141
notes	q	h	①-⑥	h	⑥	⑦	q	B	q	q	①-⑥	①-⑥	h	q		♀			⑥⑦	F	⑥⑦		♀	⑥⑦	①-⑤
Amsterdam Centraal d.	...	...	...	...	...	...	...	...	...	...	0556q	...	...	...	...	0756	...	...	0856	0926	...	...	1056	...	...
Schiphol ✈ △ d.	...	...	...	...	...	...	...	...	...	...	0612q	...	...	...	...	0812	...	...	0912	0942	...	...	1112	...	...
Den Haag HS d.	...	...	...	...	...	...	...	...	...	...	0636q	...	...	...	...	0836	...	...	0936	1006	...	...	1136	...	...
Utrecht Centraal d.	...	...	...	...	...	...	...	...	0603	...	|	...	0747	0803	...	|	...	...	|	|	...	...	|	...	...
Rotterdam Centraal d.	...	...	...	...	...	...	...	...	0642	...	0655	...	0839	0842	...	0855	...	...	0955	1026	...	...	1155	...	...
Dordrecht d.	...	...	...	...	...	...	...	...	...	...	0709	...	...	...	...	0909	...	...	1009	|	...	...	1209	...	...
Arnhem d.	...	...	...	...	...	...	...	...	...	...	|	...	...	...	0726f	|	...	0826	|	|	...	1026	|	...	...
Nijmegen d.	...	...	...	...	...	...	...	...	...	...	|	...	...	...	0748f	|	...	0848	|	|	...	1048	|	...	...
's-Hertogenbosch d.	...	...	...	...	...	...	...	...	...	0620	|	...	...	...	0819	|	...	0919	|	|	...	1119	|	...	...
Tilburg d.	...	...	...	...	...	...	...	...	...	0637	|	...	...	...	0837	|	...	0937	|	|	...	1137	|	...	...
Breda d.	...	...	...	...	...	...	...	...	...	0652	|	...	...	...	0852	|	...	0952	|	|	...	1152	|	...	...
Roosendaal 🛃 d.	...	...	...	...	...	...	...	...	...	0711	0734	...	...	...	0911	0934	...	1011	1034	|	...	1211	1234	...	...
Antwerpen Centraal d.	0520	0538	...	0638	...	...	0650	...	...	...	0803	...	...	...	...	1003	...	...	1103	1128	...	...	1303	...	...
Antwerpen Berchem d.	0526	0544	...	0644	...	...	0656	...	...	...	|	...	...	...	...	|	...	...	|	|	...	...	|	...	...
Mechelen d.	0540	0557	...	0657	...	...	0710	...	...	...	0820	...	...	...	...	1020	...	...	1120	|	...	...	1320	...	...
Brussels Midi / Zuid a.	0607	0626	...	0726	...	...	0735	...	...	...	0845v	...	...	...	...	1045v	...	...	1145	1208	...	...	1345v	...	...
Brussels Midi / Zuid 12 d.	...	...	0659	...	0759	0759	...	0805	...	...	...	0929	...	...	...	...	1129	...	...	...	1259	...	...	1429	1459
Lille Europe 12 a.	...	...	0732	...	|	0832	...	|	...	...	...	1002	...	...	...	...	1202	...	...	...	1332	...	...	1502	1535
Ashford International a.	...	...	|	...	|	|	...	|	...	...	...	|	...	...	...	...	|	...	...	...	|	...	...	|	|
Ebbsfleet International 12 a.	...	...	|	...	|	|	...	|	...	...	...	1015	...	...	...	...	|	...	...	...	1345	...	...	|	|
London St Pancras 12 a.	...	...	0755	...	0856	0857	...	0856	...	...	...	1031	...	...	...	...	1226	...	...	...	1403	...	...	1526	1556

train type			⇌				⇌		☆	☆			⇌		☆				⇌		☆				☆
train number		♀	9338			9240	9342		9149	9149		9244	9346		9153			9248	9350		9157			9256	9163
notes		①-⑤	Ⓑ			♀	⑥	Q	⑦	①-⑤		♀	Ⓑ	Q				♀	⑤⑦h	Q	Ⓑ			♀	D
Amsterdam Centraal d.	...	1156	1226	...	...	1256	1326	...	...	...	...	1356	1426	...	...	...	...	1456	1526	...	...	...	...	1656	...
Schiphol ✈ △ d.	...	1212	1242	...	...	1312	1342	...	...	...	...	1412	1442	...	...	...	...	1512	1542	...	...	...	...	1712	...
Den Haag HS d.	...	1236	1306	...	...	1336	1406	...	...	...	...	1436	1506	...	...	...	...	1536	1606	...	...	...	...	1736	...
Utrecht Centraal d.	...	|	|	1303	...	|	|	...	...	...	1403	|	|	...	...	1503	...	|	|	...	...	1703	...	|	...
Rotterdam Centraal d.	...	1255	1326	1342	...	1355	1426	...	...	...	1442	1455	1526	...	...	1542	...	1555	1626	...	...	1742	...	1755	...
Dordrecht d.	...	1309	|	▬	...	1409	|	...	...	...	▬	1509	|	...	...	...	...	1609	|	...	...	...	...	1809	...
Arnhem d.	1126	|	|	...	1226	|	|	...	...	...	1326	|	|	...	...	...	1426	|	|	...	...	...	1626	|	...
Nijmegen d.	1148	|	|	...	1248	|	|	...	...	...	1348	|	|	...	...	...	1448	|	|	...	...	...	1648	|	...
's-Hertogenbosch d.	1219	|	|	...	1319	|	|	...	...	...	1419	|	|	...	...	...	1519	|	|	...	...	...	1719	|	...
Tilburg d.	1237	|	|	...	1337	|	|	...	...	...	1437	|	|	...	...	...	1537	|	|	...	...	...	1737	|	...
Breda d.	1252	|	|	...	1352	|	|	...	...	...	1452	|	|	...	...	...	1552	|	|	...	...	...	1752	|	...
Roosendaal 🛃 d.	1311	1334	|	...	1411	1434	|	...	...	...	1511	1534	|	...	...	...	1611	1634	|	...	...	...	1811	1834	...
Antwerpen Centraal d.	...	1403	1428	...	...	1503	1528	1538	...	...	...	1603	1628	1638	...	...	...	1703	1728	1738	...	...	...	1903	...
Antwerpen Berchem d.	...	|	|	☆	...	|	|	1544	...	...	...	|	|	1644	...	...	...	|	|	1744	...	...	...	|	...
Mechelen d.	...	1420	|	9145	...	1520	|	1557	...	...	...	1620	|	1657	...	...	...	1720	|	1757	...	...	...	1920	...
Brussels Midi / Zuid a.	...	1442	1508	①-⑤	...	1545v	1608	1626	...	...	...	1645v	1708	1726	...	...	...	1745v	1808	1826	...	...	...	1945v	...
Brussels Midi / Zuid 12 d.	...	...	...	1559	...	...	...	...	1659	1659	...	...	...	...	1759	...	...	...	...	...	1859	...	...	...	2029
Lille Europe 12 a.	...	...	...	1632	...	...	...	...	1732	1732	...	...	...	...	1832	...	...	...	...	...	1932	...	...	...	2102
Ashford International a.	...	...	...	|	...	...	...	...	1733	1737	...	...	...	...	|	...	...	...	...	...	|	...	...	...	|
Ebbsfleet International 12 a.	...	...	...	1645	...	...	...	...	|	|	...	...	...	...	1845	...	...	...	...	...	|	...	...	...	2115
London St Pancras 12 a.	...	...	...	1703	...	...	...	...	1803	1807	...	...	...	...	1903	...	...	...	...	...	1956	...	...	...	2133

A – ⑦ July 5 - Aug. 30.
B – ①-⑤ (① July 5 - Aug. 30).
C – ①-⑤ (⑤ July 5 - Aug. 30).
D – Ⓑ (daily July 5 - Aug. 30).
F – ①⑤⑥⑦ (also Nov. 11).
Q – On ①-⑤ (not July 14, Nov. 11) runs 9–13 minutes later.

c – ⑤⑦ (also Nov. 2, 11).
f – ①-⑥.
h – Also Nov. 2, 11.
p – Not Nov. 2, 11.
q – Not July 14, Nov. 11.

v – On ①-⑤ (not July 14, Nov. 11) arrive Brussels Midi / Zuid 3 minutes earlier.
x – On ①-⑤ (not July 14, Nov. 11) depart Brussels Midi / Zuid 3 minutes later.

⇌ – *Thalys* high-speed train. Ⓡ ♀ Special fares payable.
△ – Trains stop to pick up only.
☆ – Eurostar train. Special fares payable. Minimum check-in time 30 minutes. Not available for London - Ebbsfleet - Ashford or v.v. journeys. Valid June 14 - Aug. 30.

LONDON - AMSTERDAM *by rail–sea–rail via Harwich - Hoek van Holland* 15a

notes	①-⑥	⑥	⑥	①-⑤	①-⑤	①-⑤	⑦	⑦	🚢					⑦	⑦	⑦	⑦	①-⑥	①-⑥	①-⑥	①-⑥	①-⑥	🚢	①-⑤				
London Liverpool Street .. d.	...	...	0618	...	0625	...	...	...	...	...	...	...	...	...	...	...	2000	...	...	...	...	2038	...	...	...	...	...	...
Peterborough d.	...	...	|	...	|	...	...	...	...	...	...	...	...	1746	...	...	|	...	1818	...	1945	|	...	...	...	...	...	...
Cambridge d.	...	...	|	...	|	...	...	...	...	...	...	...	...	|	1912	...	|	...	1908	1943	|	|	...	...	...	...	...	...
Norwich d.	...	0630	|	0625	|	...	0700	...	...	...	...	...	...	|	|	2000	|	2000	...	|	|	|	...	...	...	...	...	...
Ipswich d.	0700	0708	|	0708	|	...	0740	0745	...	...	...	...	...	1927	2035	2042	|	2040	...	2104	2127	|	...	...	...	...	...	...
Manningtree d.	|	0718	0726	0718	0732	0735	...	|	...	...	...	...	...	...	|	2052	2104	...	...	|	2137	2146	...	...	...	...	...	...
Harwich International ⛴ d.	0725	...	0744	...	...	0751	...	0810	0900	...	...	...	...	...	2102	...	2122	...	...	2128	...	2202	2345	...	...	...	...	...
Hoek van Holland Haven ⛴ a.	...	...	...	...	...	...	...	...	1615	1707	...	...	...	...	...	...	...	...	...	...	...	...	0745	0822	...	0837	...	...
Schiedam Centrum a.	...	...	...	...	...	...	...	...	...	1733	1746	...	...	...	...	...	...	...	...	...	...	...	...	0848	...	0903	0916	...
Rotterdam Centraal a.	...	...	...	...	...	...	...	...	...	1738	|	1758	...	...	...	...	...	...	...	...	...	...	...	0853	0858	0908	|	...
Den Haag HS a.	...	...	...	...	...	...	...	...	...	...	1802	1817	...	...	...	...	...	...	...	...	...	...	...	...	0917	...	0932	...
Schiphol ✈ a.	...	...	...	...	...	...	...	...	...	...	|	1845	...	...	...	...	...	...	...	...	...	...	...	...	0945	...	|	...
Amsterdam Centraal a.	...	...	...	...	...	...	...	...	...	...	1852	1903	...	...	...	...	...	...	...	...	...	...	...	...	1003	...	1022	...

notes			🚢	⑦	⑦	①-⑤	⑥	①-⑥	⑦	⑦	①-⑥	①-⑤	⑥				🚢	①-⑤	①-⑤	⑥	①-⑥	⑦	①-⑥	①-⑥	①-⑥	⑦	⑦	⑦
Amsterdam Centraal d.	1156	...	...	...	...	...	...	...	...	...	...	...	...	1859	1910	...	...	...	...	...	...	...	...	...	...	...	...	...
Schiphol ✈ d.	1212	...	...	...	...	...	...	...	...	...	...	...	...	1913	|	...	...	...	...	...	...	...	...	...	...	...	...	...
Den Haag HS d.	1234	...	...	...	...	...	...	...	...	...	...	...	...	1944	2000	...	...	...	...	...	...	...	...	...	...	...	...	...
Rotterdam Centraal d.	1253	1313	...	...	...	...	...	...	...	...	...	...	...	2002	2020	2043	...	...	...	...	...	...	...	...	...	...	...	...
Schiedam Centrum d.	...	1318	...	...	...	...	...	...	...	...	...	...	...	...	...	2048	...	...	...	...	...	...	...	...	...	...	...	...
Hoek van Holland Haven ⛴ d.	...	1342	1430	...	...	...	...	...	...	...	...	...	...	...	...	2112	2200	...	...	...	...	...	...	...	...	...	...	...
Harwich International ⛴ a.	...	...	2000	2058	...	2106	2106	...	2110	...	2134	...	...	...	...	...	0630	0710	...	0715	...	0725	0747	...	...	0830	...	...
Manningtree a.	...	...	...	2114	2118	2122	2122	2132	|	...	|	...	...	...	...	...	...	0722	0732	0728	0746c	0738	|	...	...	|	...	...
Ipswich a.	...	...	...	...	|	|	|	2142	2137	2144	2200	2243	2246	...	...	...	...	|	0741	|	0759	|	0815	...	0842	0855	0944	0955
Norwich a.	...	...	...	...	|	|	|	2228	...	2229	...	2329	2332	...	...	...	...	|	0827	|	|	|	|	...	0927	|	1029	|
Cambridge a.	...	...	...	...	|	|	|	...	...	...	...	...	...	...	...	...	...	|	...	|	|	|	0939	1000	...	1024	...	|
Peterborough a.	...	...	...	...	|	|	|	...	...	...	...	...	...	...	...	...	...	|	...	|	0938	|	...	1050	...	...	...	1136
London Liverpool Street .. a.	...	...	...	...	2242	2236	2238	...	...	...	...	...	...	...	...	...	...	0848	...	0839	...	0859	...	...	...	...	...	...

c – 0750 on ①-⑤.

SEA CROSSING (for rail / sea / rail journeys): 🚢 – Ship service, operated by Stena Line. [R] One class only on ship. ✕ on ship. A cabin berth is necessary on night sailings.

PARIS - BRUSSELS - OOSTENDE 16

For additional services change at Brussels Midi. Table **18** Paris - Brussels. Table **400 / 401** Brussels - Gent - Brugge. Table **400** Brussels - Oostende.

	⇌ 9313 ⑥	⇌ 9329 ⑦ g	⇌ 9455 ①-⑤ h	⇌ 9363 ⑦ g
Paris Nord 18 d.	0755	1155	1825	2025
Brussels Midi / Zuid 18 a.	0917	1317	1947	2147
Brussels Midi / Zuid d.	0926	1326	1959	2159
Gent Sint-Pieters a.	0959	1359	2030	2230
Brugge a.	1025	1425	2056	2256
Oostende a.	1040	1440	2111	2311

	⇌ 9308 ⑥	⇌ 9308 ①-⑤ h		⇌ 9454 ⑥⑦ g
Oostende d.	0610	0611	...	1750
Brugge d.	0625	0626	...	1805
Gent Sint-Pieters d.	0651	0653	...	1830
Brussels Midi / Zuid a.	0722	0725	...	1901
Brussels Midi / Zuid 18 d.	0743	0743	...	1913
Paris Nord 18 a.	0905	0905	...	2035

g – Also Nov. 2, 11.
h – Not Nov. 2, 11.

⇌ – *Thalys* high-speed train [R] 🍷 special fares payable.

LILLE - BRUSSELS (Summary Table) 16a

train type	*TGV*		☆	*TGV*	*TGV*	☆	☆	☆	*TGV*		☆	☆	*TGV*	*TGV*	☆	*TGV*	☆	*TGV*	☆	☆	*TGV*	☆	
train number	**9811**		**9110**	**9854**	**9856**	**9120**	**9116**	**9126**	**9860**		**9132**	**9138**	**9862**	**9864**	**9144**	**9866**	**9148**	**9868**	**9150**	**9154**	**9854**	**9158**	
train number				**9855**	**9857**				**9861**				**9863**	**9865**		**9867**		**9869**			**9855**		
notes	[R] 🍷			[R] 🍷	[R] 🍷				[R] 🍷				[R] 🍷	[R] 🍷		[R] 🍷		[R] 🍷			[R] 🍷		
notes	**A**		①-⑥	**A**	**B**	**C**	⑥								①-④		⑥⑦	**B**	①-⑤	⑦	**A**		
Lille Europe d.	0729	...	0928	1041	1115	1058	1128	1328	1336	...	1528	1658	1721	1747	1828	1835	1928	1946	1958	2058	2115	2158	...
Brussels Midi / Zuid a.	0803	...	1003	1115	1150	1133	1203	1403	1412	...	1603	1733	1756	1822	1903	1910	2003	2022	2033	2133	2152	2233	...

train type	*TGV*	☆		☆	☆		*TGV*	☆	*TGV*	☆		☆	☆	*TGV*	☆	*TGV*	☆	☆	☆		☆		
train number	**9804**	**9109**		**9113**	**9119**		**9832**	**9181**	**9828**	**9133**		**9139**	**9141**	**9834**	**9145**	**9836**	**9149**	**9153**	**9157**		**9163**		
train number	**9805**						**9833**		**9829**					**9835**		**9837**							
notes	[R] 🍷						[R] 🍷		[R] 🍷					[R] 🍷		[R] 🍷							
notes	**A**	①-⑥		⑦	①-⑥					⑥⑦		⑥⑦	①-⑤		①-⑤		⑧		⑧		**D**		
Brussels Midi / Zuid d.	0540	0659	...	0759	0929	...	1110	1129	1209	1259	...	1429	1459	1509	1559	1609	1659	1759	1859	...	2029	...	...
Lille Europe a.	0615	0732	...	0832	1002	...	1146	1202	1244	1332	...	1502	1532	1546	1632	1644	1732	1832	1932	...	2102	...	...

A – ①-⑤ (not July 14).
B – ⑥⑦ (also July 14).
C – ⑦ July 5 - Aug. 30.
D – ⑧ (daily July 5 - Aug. 30).

☆ – Eurostar train. Special fares payable. Minimum check-in time 30 minutes departing from Brussels. Valid June 14 - Aug. 30.

PARIS - CHARLEROI - NAMUR - LIÈGE 17

km	*train type*	⇌	⇌
	train number	**9499**	**9499**
	notes	①-⑤	⑥⑦
	notes	**p**	**q**
0	**Paris Nord** ▲ d.	1943	2016
282	Mons a.	2101	2133
323	Charleroi Sud a.	2133	2201
359	**Namur** a.	2206	2234
419	**Liège Guillemins** ▲ a.	2245	2314

train type	⇌	⇌
train number	**9496**	**9496**
notes	①-⑤	⑥⑦
notes	**p**	**q**
Liège Guillemins .. ▲ d.	0640	0647
Namur d.	0720	0726
Charleroi Sud d.	0756	0759
Mons d.	0825	0826
Paris Nord ▲ a.	0944	0944

LONDON - ASHFORD - AVIGNON / MARNE LA VALLÉE 17a

train type	☆	☆	
train number	**9084**	**9074**	
train number	**9085**		
notes	**P**		
London St Pancras d.	0719	0953	...
Ashford International d.	0755	1028	...
Lille Europe a.	0952**s**	1224**s**	...
Marne la Vallée § a.	|	1331	...
Avignon Centre a.	1408	...	...

train type	☆	☆	
train number	**9087**	**9057**	
train number	**9086**		
notes	**Q**		
Avignon Centre d.	1624	...	...
Marne la Vallée § d.	|	1937	...
Lille Europe d.	2032**u**	2038	...
Ashford International . a.	2033	2037	...
London St Pancras . a.	2109	2112	...

NOTES FOR TABLES 17 AND 17a

P – ⑥ July 11 - Sept. 5.
Q – ⑥ July 18 - Sept. 12.
p – Not July 21, Nov. 11.
q – Also July 21, Nov. 11.
s – Stops to set down only.
u – Stops to pick up only.
▲ – For other trains Paris - Liège see Table **20**.
§ – Marne la Vallée - Chessy (station for Disneyland).
⇌ – *Thalys* high-speed train. [R] 🍷. Special fares payable.
☆ – Eurostar train. Special fares payable. Minimum check-in time 30 minutes. Not available for London - Ashford or v.v. journeys.

18 AMSTERDAM - BRUSSELS - PARIS

Brussels - Disneyland: see Table 11

Due to engineering works Aug. 15 – 22, *Thalys* services will not call at Schiphol, Den Haag HS, Rotterdam. Earlier departures and later arrivals will occur at Amsterdam.

km	km	train number	9304	4527	9306	9308	4528	9208	9310	9310	9920/1	9412	9212	9314	9416	9216	9318	9418	9220	9322	9224	9326	9326	9328	
		train type	⇌		⇌	⇌			⇌	⇌	⇌	⇌		⇌	⇌		⇌	⇌		⇌		⇌	⇌	⇌	
		notes	①–④		①–⑤	①–⑥		①–⑥	⑥	①–⑥	A		①–⑥	①–⑥	①–⑤	🍷	⑥		🍷		🍷	F		⑤	
			b	K	f	f	K	🍷		b	⊕		🍷	f	b										
0	0	**Amsterdam Centraal** d.	...	...	...	...	...	...	...	...	0526	...	0556	0626	...	0656	0726	...	0756	0826	0856	0926	...	...	...
17	17	Schiphol ✈ ⊕ d.	...	...	...	...	...	...	...	...	0542	...	0612	0642	...	0712	0742	...	0812	0842	0912	0942	...	...	...
60	60	Den Haag HS d.	...	...	...	...	...	...	...	...	0606	...	0636	0706	...	0736	0806	...	0836	0906	0936	1006	...	...	...
82	82	**Rotterdam Centraal** d.	...	...	...	...	...	0555	...	...	0626	...	0655	0726	...	0755	0826	...	0855	0926	0955	1026	...	...	...
102	102	Dordrecht d.	...	...	...	...	...	0609	...	...	|	...	0709	|	...	0809	|	...	0909	|	1009	|	...	...	...
140	140	Roosendaal 🛃 d.	...	...	...	...	...	0634	...	...	|	...	0734	|	...	0834	|	...	0934	|	1034	|	...	...	...
184		**Antwerpen Centraal** d.	...	0550	0628	...	0650	0703	0725	...	0728	...	0803	0828	...	0903	0928	...	1003	1028	1103	1128	...	...	...
187	182	Antwerpen Berchem d.	...	0556	|	...	0656	|	|	...	|	...	|	|	...	|	|	...	|	|	|	|	...	...	...
208	203	Mechelen d.	...	0610	|	...	0710	0720	|	...	|	...	0820	|	...	0920	|	...	1020	|	1120	|	...	...	...
229	224	Brussels Nord / Noord a.	...	0626	|	...	0726	0736v	|	...	|	...	0836v	|	...	0936v	|	...	1036v	|	1136v	|	...	...	...
235	227	**Brussels Midi / Zuid** a.	...	0635	0708	...	0735	0745v	0805	...	|	...	0845v	0908	...	0945v	1008	...	1045v	1108	1145v	1208	...	...	...
235	227	**Brussels Midi / Zuid** d.	0643	...	0713	0743	...	...	0813	0813	0819	0843	...	0913	0943	...	1013	1013	...	1113	...	1213	1213	1243	...
547	540	**Paris Nord** a.	0805	...	0835	0905	...	...	0935	0935	...	1005	...	1035	1105	...	1135	1135	...	1235	...	1335	1335	1405	...

train number	9228	9430	9232		9436	9236	9338	9338	9240	9342	9342	9344	9244	9346	9348	9248	9450	9350	9352	9252	9354	9456	9256	9458	
train type		⇌			⇌		⇌	⇌		⇌	⇌	⇌		⇌	⇌		⇌	⇌	⇌		⇌	⇌		⇌	
notes	🍷		🍷			🍷		⑧	🍷	⑥		⑤⑦	🍷	⑧	⑧	🍷		⑤⑦	⑧	🍷		⑦	🍷		
												t						p	t			h			
Amsterdam Centraal d.	0956	...	1056	...	...	1156	...	1226	1256	1326	...	...	1356	1426	...	1456	...	1526	...	1556	1626	...	1656	...	...
Schiphol ✈ ⊕ d.	1012	...	1112	...	...	1212	...	1242	1312	1342	...	...	1412	1442	...	1512	...	1542	...	1612	1642	...	1712	...	...
Den Haag HS d.	1036	...	1136	...	...	1236	...	1306	1336	1406	...	...	1436	1506	...	1536	...	1606	...	1636	1706	...	1736	...	...
Rotterdam Centraal d.	1055	...	1155	...	...	1255	...	1326	1355	1426	...	...	1455	1526	...	1555	...	1626	...	1655	1726	...	1755	...	...
Dordrecht d.	1109	...	1209	...	...	1309	...	|	1409	|	...	...	1509	|	...	1609	...	|	...	1709	|	...	1809	...	...
Roosendaal 🛃 d.	1134	...	1234	...	...	1334	...	|	1434	|	...	...	1534	|	...	1634	...	|	...	1734	|	...	1834	...	...
Antwerpen Centraal d.	1203	...	1303	...	...	1403	...	1428	1503	1528	...	...	1603	1628	...	1703	...	1728	...	1803	1828	...	1903	...	...
Antwerpen Berchem d.	|	...	|	...	...	|	...	|	|	|	...	...	|	|	...	|	...	|	...	|	|	...	|	...	...
Mechelen d.	1220	...	1320	...	...	1420	...	|	1520	|	...	...	1620	|	...	1720	...	|	...	1820	|	...	1920	...	...
Brussels Nord / Noord a.	1236v	...	1336v	...	...	1436v	...	|	1536v	|	...	...	1636v	|	...	1736v	...	|	...	1836v	|	...	1936v	...	...
Brussels Midi / Zuid a.	1245v	...	1345v	...	...	1445v	...	1508	1545v	1608	...	...	1645v	1708	...	1745v	...	1808	...	1845v	1908	...	1945v	...	...
Brussels Midi / Zuid d.	...	1313	...	...	1443	...	1513	1513	...	1613	1613	1643	...	1713	1743	...	1813	1813	1843	...	1913	1943	...	2013	...
Paris Nord a.	...	1435	...	...	1605	...	1635	1635	...	1735	1735	1805	...	1835	1905	...	1935	1935	2005	...	2035	2105	...	2135	...

train number	9260	9462	9362	9264	9366	9268	9272	9276
train type		⇌	⇌		⇌			
notes	🍷		⑧	🍷	⑤⑦	🍷	🍷	⑥
					p			
Amsterdam Centraal d.	1756	...	1826	1856	...	1956	2056	2156
Schiphol ✈ ⊕ d.	1812	...	1842	1912	...	2012	2112	2212
Den Haag HS d.	1836	...	1906	1936	...	2036	2136	2236
Rotterdam Centraal d.	1855	...	1926	1955	...	2055	2155	2255
Dordrecht d.	1909	...	|	2009	...	2109	2209	2309
Roosendaal 🛃 d.	1934	...	|	2034	...	2134	2234	2334
Antwerpen Centraal d.	2003	...	2028	2103	...	2203	2303	0003
Antwerpen Berchem d.	|	...	|	|	...	|	|	|
Mechelen d.	2020	...	|	2120	...	2220	2320	0020
Brussels Nord / Noord a.	2036v	...	|	2136v	...	2236v	2336v	0036
Brussels Midi / Zuid a.	2045v	...	2108	2145v	...	2245v	2345v	0045
Brussels Midi / Zuid d.	...	2113	2113	...	2213	...	...	...
Paris Nord a.	...	2235	2235	...	2335	...	...	...

train number	9201	9205	9407	9307	9209	9309	9311	9311	9213	9313	
train type			⇌	⇌		⇌	⇌	⇌		⇌	
notes	①–⑥	🍷		①–⑤	🍷	①–⑤	①–⑥	⑥	🍷	①–⑥	
	🍷 g			f		b	f			f	
Paris Nord d.	...	...	0625	0625	...	0655	0725	0725	...	0755	...
Brussels Midi / Zuid a.	...	...	0747	0747	...	0817	0847	0847	...	0917	...
Brussels Midi / Zuid d.	0615x	0715x	...	0752	0815	...	...	0852	0915x	...	...
Brussels Nord / Noord d.	0624x	0724x	...	|	0824y	...	...	|	0924x	...	...
Mechelen a.	0640	0740	...	|	0840	...	...	|	0940	...	...
Antwerpen Berchem a.	|	|	...	|	|	...	...	|	|	...	...
Antwerpen Centraal a.	0657	0757	...	0832	0857	...	...	0932	0957	...	...
Roosendaal 🛃 a.	0728	0828	...	|	0928	...	...	|	1028	...	...
Dordrecht a.	0753	0853	...	|	0953	...	...	|	1053	...	...
Rotterdam Centraal a.	0806	0906	...	0936	1006	...	...	1036	1106	...	...
Den Haag HS a.	0825	0925	...	0956	1025	...	...	1056	1125	...	...
Schiphol ✈ a.	0849	0949	...	1019	1049	...	...	1119	1149	...	...
Amsterdam Centraal a.	0906	1006	...	1036	1106	...	...	1136	1206	...	...

train number	9315	9315	9217	9417	9319	9319	9221	9323	9225	9325	9229	9427	9329	9331	9233	9333	9237	9339	9339	9241	9341	9343	9343	9245	
train type	⇌	⇌		⇌	⇌	⇌		⇌		⇌		⇌	⇌	⇌		⇌		⇌	⇌		⇌	⇌	⇌		
notes		①–⑥	🍷	①–⑥		⑤⑦	🍷		🍷	①⑤⑥	🍷		⑤⑦		🍷		🍷		⑦	🍷	⑤		①–⑥	🍷	
		f		f	b	p				t			h						p		t		f		
Paris Nord d.	0825	0825	...	0855	0925	0925	...	1025	...	1055	...	1125	1155	1225	...	1255	...	1425	1425	...	1455	1525	1525	...	...
Brussels Midi / Zuid a.	0947	0947	...	1017	1047	1047	...	1147	...	1217	...	1247	1317	1347	...	1417	...	1547	1547	...	1617	1647	1647	...	...
Brussels Midi / Zuid d.	...	0952	1015x	...	...	1052	1115x	1152	1215x	...	1315x	...	...	1352	1415x	...	1515x	...	1552	1615x	...	...	1652	1715x	...
Brussels Nord / Noord d.	...	|	1024x	...	...	|	1124x	|	1224x	...	1324x	...	...	|	1424x	...	1524x	...	|	1624x	...	...	|	1724x	...
Mechelen a.	...	|	1040	...	...	|	1140	|	1240	...	1340	...	...	|	1440	...	1540	...	|	1640	...	...	|	1740	...
Antwerpen Berchem a.	...	|	|	...	...	|	|	|	|	...	|	...	...	|	|	...	|	...	|	|	...	...	|	|	...
Antwerpen Centraal a.	...	1032	1057	...	...	1132	1157	1232	1257	...	1357	...	...	1432	1457	...	1557	...	1632	1657	...	...	1732	1757	...
Roosendaal 🛃 a.	...	|	1128	...	...	|	1228	|	1328	...	1428	...	...	|	1528	...	1628	...	|	1728	...	...	|	1828	...
Dordrecht a.	...	|	1153	...	...	|	1253	|	1353	...	1453	...	...	|	1553	...	1653	...	|	1753	...	...	|	1853	...
Rotterdam Centraal a.	...	1136	1206	...	...	1236	1306	1336	1406	...	1506	...	...	1536	1606	...	1706	...	1736	1806	...	...	1836	1906	...
Den Haag HS a.	...	1156	1225	...	...	1256	1325	1356	1425	...	1525	...	...	1556	1625	...	1725	...	1756	1825	...	...	1856	1925	...
Schiphol ✈ a.	...	1219	1249	...	...	1319	1349	1419	1449	...	1549	...	...	1619	1649	...	1749	...	1819	1849	...	...	1919	1949	...
Amsterdam Centraal a.	...	1236	1306	...	...	1336	1406	1436	1506	...	1606	...	...	1636	1706	...	1806	...	1836	1906	...	...	1936	2006	...

train number	9345	9345	9347	9347	9249	9349	9954/5	9451	9253	9353	9355	9257	9457	9359	9359	9359	9261	9361	9363	9265	9365	9367	9369	9371	
train type	⇌	⇌	⇌	⇌		⇌	⇌	⇌		⇌	⇌		⇌	⇌	⇌	⇌		⇌	⇌		⇌	⇌	⇌	⇌	
notes	⑤⑥	①–⑤	⑧	⑦	🍷		B		🍷			🍷			⑧	⑤⑦	🍷	⑤⑦			⑤	⑦	①–⑥	⑦	
	g	D	t	p			⊗			C						p		p	E			p	f	p	
Paris Nord d.	1555	1555	1625	1625	...	1655	...	1725	...	1755	1825	...	1855	1925	1925	1925	...	1955	2025	...	2055	2125	2155	2231	...
Brussels Midi / Zuid a.	1717	1717	1747	1747	...	1817	1844	1847	...	1917	1947	...	2017	2047	2047	2047	...	2117	2147	...	2217	2247	2317	2353	...
Brussels Midi / Zuid d.	...	...	...	1752	1815x	...	|	...	1915x	...	1952	2015x	...	...	2052	2052	2115x	...	...	2215x	...	...	...	...	...
Brussels Nord / Noord d.	...	...	...	|	1824x	...	|	...	1924x	...	|	2024x	...	...	|	|	2124x	...	...	2224x	...	...	...	...	...
Mechelen a.	...	...	...	|	1840	...	|	...	1940	...	|	2040	...	...	|	|	2140	...	...	2240	...	...	...	...	...
Antwerpen Berchem a.	...	...	...	|	|	...	|	...	|	...	|	|	...	...	|	|	|	...	...	|	...	...	...	...	...
Antwerpen Centraal a.	...	...	...	1832	1857	...	1932	...	1957	...	2032	2057	...	...	2132	2132	2157	...	...	2257	...	...	...	...	...
Roosendaal 🛃 a.	...	...	...	|	1928	...	|	...	2028	...	|	2128	...	...	...	|	2228	...	...	2328	...	...	...	...	...
Dordrecht a.	...	...	...	|	1953	...	|	...	2053	...	|	2153	...	...	...	|	2253	...	...	2353	...	...	...	...	...
Rotterdam Centraal a.	...	...	...	1936	2006	...	2036	...	2106	...	2136	2206	...	...	...	2236	2306	...	...	0006	...	...	...	...	...
Den Haag HS a.	...	...	...	1956	2025	...	2056	...	2125	...	2156	2225	...	...	...	2256	2325	...	...	0025	...	...	...	...	...
Schiphol ✈ a.	...	...	...	2019	2049	...	2119	...	2149	...	2219	2249	...	...	...	2319	2349	...	...	0049	...	...	...	...	...
Amsterdam Centraal a.	...	...	...	2036	2106	...	2136	...	2206	...	2236	2306	...	...	...	2336	0006	...	...	0106	...	...	...	...	...

A – ⑥ June 27 - Aug. 22: *THALYS* SOLEIL – [12] and 🍷 Amsterdam - Brussels - Valence *TGV* - Marseille; (Table **11**).

B – ⑥ July 4 - Aug. 29: *THALYS* SOLEIL – [12] and 🍷 Marseille - Valence *TGV* - Brussels - Amsterdam; (Table **11**).

C – ②③④⑤ (not July 19 - Aug. 22).

D – ①–⑤ July 19 - Aug. 22.

E – Not ⑤.

F – ①⑤⑥⑦ (also Nov. 11).

K – ①–⑤ (not July 14 , Nov. 11).

b – Not July 19 - Aug. 22, Nov. 2, 11.

f – Not Nov. 2, 11.

g – Not Aug. 15.

h – Also Nov. 2, 11; not July 19 - Aug. 22.

p – Also Nov. 2, 11.

t – Not July 19 - Aug. 22.

v – On ①–⑤ (not July 14, Nov. 11) not call at Brussels Nord / Noord and arrive Brussels Midi / Zuid 3 minutes earlier.

x – On ①–⑤ (not July 14, Nov. 11) depart Brussels Midi / Zuid 3 minutes later and not call at Brussels Nord / Noord.

y – Not ①–⑤ (not Aug. 15).

⇌ – *Thalys* high-speed train. 🅁 🍷. Special fares payable.

⊗ – Calls to set down only.

⊕ – Calls to pick up only.

LONDON, PARIS and BRUSSELS - KÖLN, HAMBURG and BERLIN — 20

For the full service London - Brussels and v.v. see Table 12. For Paris - Brussels and v.v. see Table 18. Connections at Brussels are not guaranteed.

train type	ICE	RE	IC	ICE	IC	ICE	EC	RE	ICE		⇌	RE	ICE	IC	IC	IC	ICE	EC	☆	⇌	RE	ICE	IC	ICE	IC	ICE
train number	11	11010	231	857	2141	1549	379	10115	1028		9407	11012	557	2039	2116	2049	1641	179	9106	9415	11016	559	2114	37	2047	1643
notes	🍷		331 🍷	🍷	🍷	🍴	🍴		🍷				🍷	🍷	🍷	🍷	🍴	🍴	Ⓡ🍴 ①–⑤			🍷	🍷	D	🍷 Ⓑ	🍴
London St Pancras .. d.	...	...	...	...	...	...	...	...	...	...	...	...	...	...	...	...	...	...	0557	...	...	...	...	...	...	...
Ebbsfleet International d.	...	...	...	...	...	...	...	...	...	...	...	...	...	...	...	...	...	...	|	...	...	...	...	...	...	...
Ashford International .. d.	...	...	...	...	...	...	...	...	...	...	...	...	...	...	...	...	...	...	0627	...	...	...	...	...	...	...
Lille Europe .... d.	...	...	...	...	...	...	...	...	...	...	...	...	...	...	...	...	...	...	|	...	...	...	...	...	...	...
Paris Nord .... d.	...	...	...	...	...	...	...	...	...	...	0625	...	...	...	...	...	...	...	|	0825	...	...	...	...	...	...
Brussels Midi/Zuid ... a.	...	...	...	...	...	...	...	...	...	...	0747	...	...	...	...	...	...	...	0856	0947	...	...	...	...	...	...
Brussels Midi/Zuid ... d.	0718	...	...	...	...	...	...	...	...	...	0755	...	...	...	...	...	...	...	...	0959	...	...	...	...	...	...
Liège Guillemins .... a.	0811	...	...	...	...	...	...	...	...	...	0843	...	...	...	...	...	...	...	...	1043	...	...	...	...	...	...
Liège Guillemins .... d.	0814	...	...	...	...	...	...	...	...	...	0845	...	...	...	...	...	...	...	...	1045	...	...	...	...	...	...
Aachen 🏛 .... a.	0836	...	...	...	...	...	...	...	...	...	0936	...	...	...	...	...	...	...	...	1136	...	...	...	...	...	...
Köln Hbf .... a.	0915	...	...	...	...	...	...	...	...	...	1015	...	...	...	...	...	...	...	...	1215	...	...	...	...	...	...
Köln Hbf .... d.	...	0931	0948	0949	...	...	...	0951	1011	...	...	1031	1049	...	1111	1113	...	...	...	...	1231	1249	1311	...	1313	...
Wuppertal Hbf .... a.	...	|	|	1015	...	...	...	|	1041	...	...	|	1115	...	|	1141	...	...	...	...	|	1315	|	...	1341	...
Hagen Hbf .... a.	...	|	|	1033	...	...	...	|	1059	...	...	|	1133	...	|	1159	...	...	...	...	|	1333	|	...	1359	...
Düsseldorf Hbf .... a.	...	1000	1009	|	...	...	...	1021	|	...	...	1100	|	...	1132	|	...	...	...	...	1300	|	1332	...	|	...
Duisburg Hbf .... a.	...	1018	1023	|	...	...	...	1037	|	...	...	1118	|	...	1145	|	...	...	...	...	1318	|	1345	...	|	...
Oberhausen .... a.	...	1026	1031	|	...	...	...	|	|	...	...	1126	|	...	|	|	...	...	...	...	1326	|	|	...	|	...
Essen Hbf .... a.	...	...	|	|	...	...	...	1051	|	...	...	...	|	...	1158	|	...	...	...	...	...	|	1358	...	|	...
Bochum Hbf .... a.	...	...	|	|	...	...	...	1103	|	...	...	...	|	...	1209	|	...	...	...	...	...	|	1409	...	|	...
Dortmund Hbf .... a.	...	...	|	|	...	...	...	1115	1120	...	...	...	|	...	1221	1220	...	...	...	...	...	|	1421	...	1420	...
Hamm Hbf .... a.	...	...	|	1102	...	...	...	1145	|	...	...	...	1202	...	|	1243	...	...	...	...	...	1402	|	...	1443	...
Bielefeld Hbf .... a.	...	...	|	1135	...	...	...	...	|	...	...	...	1236	...	|	1313	...	...	...	...	...	1436	|	...	1513	...
Münster .... a.	...	...	1127	|	...	...	...	...	1155	...	...	...	|	...	1254	|	...	...	...	...	...	|	1454	...	|	...
Osnabrück Hbf ...... a.	...	...	...	|	...	...	...	...	1221	...	...	...	|	...	1321	|	...	...	...	...	...	|	1521	...	|	...
Bremen Hbf .... a.	...	...	...	|	...	...	...	...	1314	...	...	...	|	...	1414	|	...	...	...	...	...	|	1614	...	|	...
Hannover Hbf .... a.	...	...	...	1228	1236	...	...	...	|	...	...	...	1328	1336	|	1418	...	...	...	...	...	1528	|	...	1618	...
Hamburg Hbf .... a.	...	...	...	|	|	...	...	...	1412	...	...	...	|	|	1511	|	...	...	...	...	...	|	1712	1728	|	...
København H ⊙ a.	...	...	...	|	|	...	...	...	...	...	...	...	|	|	...	|	...	...	...	...	...	|	...	2211	|	...
Wolfsburg .... a.	...	...	...	1303	|	...	...	...	...	...	...	...	|	|	...	|	...	...	...	...	...	|	...	...	|	...
Braunschweig Hbf ...... a.	...	...	...	|	1309	...	...	...	...	...	...	...	|	1408	...	1509	...	...	...	...	...	|	...	...	1709	...
Magdeburg Hbf .... a.	...	...	...	|	1355	...	...	...	...	...	...	...	|	1457	...	1555	...	...	...	...	...	|	...	...	1755	...
Halle Hbf .... a.	...	...	...	|	1453	...	...	...	...	...	...	...	|	1550	...	1653	...	...	...	...	...	|	...	...	1853	...
Leipzig Hbf .... a.	...	...	...	|	1519	1551	...	...	...	...	...	...	|	1617	...	1719	1751	...	...	...	...	|	...	...	1919	1951
Berlin Hbf .... a.	...	...	...	1411	...	|	1435	...	...	...	...	...	1508	...	...	...	|	1635	...	...	...	1710	...	...	...	|
Berlin Ostbahnhof ... a.	...	...	...	1422	...	|	|	...	...	...	...	...	1519	...	...	...	|	|	...	...	...	1721	...	...	...	|
Dresden Hbf .... a.	...	...	...	...	...	1702	1710d	...	...	...	...	...	...	...	...	...	1902	1910d	...	...	...	...	...	...	...	2102
Bad Schandau 🏛 ... a.	...	...	...	...	...	...	1736	...	...	...	...	...	...	...	...	...	...	1936	...	...	...	...	...	...	...	...
Děčín .... a.	...	...	...	...	...	...	1753	...	...	...	...	...	...	...	...	...	...	1953	...	...	...	...	...	...	...	...
Praha Holešovice . a.	...	...	...	...	...	...	1918	...	...	...	...	...	...	...	...	...	...	2118	...	...	...	...	...	...	...	...
Praha hlavní .... a.	...	...	...	...	...	...	...	...	...	...	...	...	...	...	...	...	...	...	...	...	...	...	...	...	...	...

train type	☆	☆	☆	⇌	ICE	RE	ICE	RE	IC	☆	⇌	RE	ICE	IC	ICE	ICE	⇌	RE	ICE	IC	EC	☆	⇌	RE	ICE	ICE
train number	9114	9120	9120	9323	15	11020	651	10125	2112	9116	9427	11022	953	2045	1024	518	9431	11024	653	2135	100	9132	9443	11030	957	514
notes	Ⓡ🍴 ⑥	Ⓡ🍴 ①–⑤	Ⓡ🍴 A	Ⓡ🍷	🍷		🍷		🍷	Ⓡ🍴 ⑥			🍷 Ⓑ	🍷 Ⓑ	🍷	🍷			🍷	🍷	102 B	Ⓡ 🍴			🍷 Ⓑ	🍷
London St Pancras .. d.	0757	0834	0827	...	...	...	...	...	...	0859	...	...	...	...	...	...	...	...	...	...	...	1257	...	...	...	...
Ebbsfleet International d.	|	|	0845	...	...	...	...	...	...	0915	...	...	...	...	...	...	...	...	...	...	...	1315	...	...	...	...
Ashford International .. d.	0828	|	|	...	...	...	...	...	...	|	...	...	...	...	...	...	...	...	...	...	...	|	...	...	...	...
Lille Europe .... d.	|	|	1058	...	...	...	...	...	...	1128	...	...	...	...	...	...	...	...	...	...	...	1528	...	...	...	...
Paris Nord .... d.	|	|	|	1025	...	...	...	...	...	|	1125	...	...	...	...	...	1225	...	...	...	...	|	1525	...	...	...
Brussels Midi/Zuid ... a.	1056	1129	1133	1147	...	...	...	...	...	1203	1247	...	...	...	...	...	1347	...	...	...	...	1603	1647	...	...	...
Brussels Midi/Zuid ... d.	...	...	...	...	1218	...	...	...	...	▬	1259	...	...	...	...	...	1359	...	...	...	...	▬	1655	...	...	...
Liège Guillemins .... a.	...	...	...	...	1311	...	...	...	...	...	1343	...	...	...	...	...	1443	...	...	...	...	...	1743	...	...	...
Liège Guillemins .... d.	...	...	...	...	1314	...	...	...	...	...	1345	...	...	...	...	...	1445	...	...	...	...	...	1745	...	...	...
Aachen 🏛 .... a.	...	...	...	...	1336	...	...	...	...	...	1436	...	...	...	...	...	1536	...	...	...	...	...	1836	...	...	...
Köln Hbf .... a.	...	...	...	...	1415	...	...	...	...	...	1515	...	...	...	...	...	1615	...	...	...	...	...	1915	...	...	...
Köln Hbf .... d.	...	...	...	...	...	1431	1449	1451	1511	...	...	1531	1549	...	1611	1611	...	1631	1649	...	1711	...	...	1931	1949	2011
Wuppertal Hbf .... a.	...	...	...	...	...	|	1515	|	|	...	...	|	1615	...	1641	|	...	|	1715	...	|	...	...	|	2015	|
Hagen .... a.	...	...	...	...	...	|	1533	|	|	...	...	|	1633	...	1659	|	...	|	1733	...	|	...	...	|	2033	|
Düsseldorf Hbf .... a.	...	...	...	...	...	1500	|	1521	1532	...	...	1600	|	...	|	1632	...	1700	|	...	1732	...	...	2000	|	2032
Duisburg Hbf .... a.	...	...	...	...	...	1518	|	1537	1545	...	...	1618	|	...	|	1645	...	1718	|	...	1745	...	...	2018	|	2045
Oberhausen .... a.	...	...	...	...	...	1526	|	|	|	...	...	1626	|	...	|	|	...	1726	|	...	|	ICE	...	2026	|	|
Essen Hbf .... a.	...	...	...	...	...	...	|	1551	1558	...	...	...	|	...	|	1657	...	...	|	...	1758	945	...	...	|	2057
Bochum Hbf .... a.	...	...	...	...	...	...	|	1603	1609	...	...	...	|	...	|	1709	...	...	|	...	1809	🍷	...	...	|	2109
Dortmund Hbf .... a.	...	...	...	...	...	...	|	1615	1621	...	...	...	|	...	1720	1721	...	...	|	...	1821	1848	...	...	|	2121
Hamm .... a.	...	...	...	...	...	...	1602	1640	|	...	...	...	1702	...	|	...	...	...	1802	...	|	1906	...	...	2102	|
Bielefeld .... a.	...	...	...	...	...	...	1636	▬	|	...	...	...	1735	...	|	...	...	...	1835	...	|	1935	...	...	2135	|
Münster .... a.	...	...	...	...	...	...	|	IC	1654	...	...	...	|	...	1755	...	...	...	|	...	1854	|	...	...	|	2157
Osnabrück .... a.	...	...	...	...	...	...	|	**2133**	1721	...	...	...	|	...	1821	...	...	...	|	...	1921	|	...	...	|	2225
Bremen Hbf .... a.	...	...	...	...	...	...	|	🍷	1814	...	...	...	|	...	1914	...	...	...	|	...	2014	|	...	...	|	2320
Hannover Hbf .... a.	...	...	...	...	...	...	1728	1736	|	...	...	...	1828	1836	|	...	...	...	1928	1936	|	2028	...	...	2228	|
Hamburg Hbf .... a.	...	...	...	...	...	...	|	|	1912	...	...	...	|	|	2012	...	...	...	|	|	2112	|	...	...	|	0020
København H ⊙ a.	...	...	...	...	...	...	|	|	...	ICE	...	...	|	|	...	...	...	...	|	|	...	|	...	...	|	...
Wolfsburg .... a.	...	...	...	...	...	...	|	|	...	**1602**	...	...	|	|	...	...	...	...	|	|	...	2103	...	...	|	...
Braunschweig Hbf ..... a.	...	...	...	...	...	...	|	1808	...	**1662**	...	...	|	1909	...	...	...	...	|	2008	...	|	...	...	|	...
Magdeburg Hbf .... a.	...	...	...	...	...	...	|	1857	...	🍴	...	...	|	1955	...	...	...	...	|	2057	...	|	...	...	|	...
Halle .... a.	...	...	...	...	...	...	|	1950	...	Ⓑ	...	...	|	2053	...	...	...	...	|	2153	...	|	...	...	|	...
Leipzig Hbf .... a.	...	...	...	...	...	...	|	2017	...	2051	...	...	|	2119	...	...	...	...	|	2219	...	|	...	...	|	...
Berlin Hbf .... a.	...	...	...	...	...	...	1908	...	...	|	...	...	2011	...	...	...	...	...	2108	...	...	2221	...	...	0019	...
Berlin Ostbahnhof ... a.	...	...	...	...	...	...	1919	...	...	|	...	...	2022	...	...	...	...	...	2119	...	...	2232	...	...	0030	...
Dresden Hbf .... a.	...	...	...	...	...	...	...	...	...	2202	...	...	...	...	...	...	...	...	...	...	...	...	...	...	...	...
Bad Schandau 🏛 ... a.	...	...	...	...	...	...	...	...	...	...	...	...	...	...	...	...	...	...	...	...	...	...	...	...	...	...
Děčín .... a.	...	...	...	...	...	...	...	...	...	...	...	...	...	...	...	...	...	...	...	...	...	...	...	...	...	...
Praha Holešovice . a.	...	...	...	...	...	...	...	...	...	...	...	...	...	...	...	...	...	...	...	...	...	...	...	...	...	...
Praha hlavní .... a.	...	...	...	...	...	...	...	...	...	...	...	...	...	...	...	...	...	...	...	...	...	...	...	...	...	...

A – ⑦ July 5 - Aug. 30.

B – [1] (panorama car), [12] and 🍴 Chur - Basel - Köln - Dortmund - Hamburg (- Kiel ⑦).

D – [12] and 🍷 ✓ Hamburg - København and v.v. (Table **50**).

d – Departure time.

n – Departs 8 minutes later.

☆ – Eurostar train. Special fares payable. Minimum check-in time 30 minutes. Not available for London - Ebbsfleet - Ashford or v.v. journeys. Valid June 14 – Aug. 30.

⊙ – 🏛 between Hamburg and København is Rødby, see Table **720**.

⇌ – *Thalys* high-speed train. Ⓡ 🍷. Special fares payable.

✓ – Supplement payable.

For London - Esbjerg/København by rail and sea via Harwich, see DFDS Seaways Table 2220

20 LONDON, PARIS and BRUSSELS - KÖLN, HAMBURG and BERLIN

For the full service London - Brussels and v.v. see Table **12**. For Paris - Brussels and v.v. see Table **18**. Connections at Brussels are not guaranteed.

train type	☆	⇌	*ICE*	*RE*	*IC*	*ICE*	*ICE*	*IC*	⇌	*RE*	*RE*	*ICE*	*ICE*	*CNL*	*CNL*	*IC*	*IC*	☆	☆	☆	⇌	☆	*CNL*	*ICE*	*ICE*	
train number	**9138**	**9347**	**17**	**11032**	**2339**	**657**	**502**	**2318**	**9451**	**11034**	**10139**	**24**	**512**	**457**	**447**	**2020**	**2241**	**9144**	**9144**	**9148**	**9457**	**9036**	**451**	**988**	**672**	
notes	[R] ✕	Ⓑ	🍷	**11042**	Ⓑ	🍷 ⑦	**1002** 🍷	🍷 Ⓑ				🍷	🍷	[R] **C**	**482** [R] **E**	🍷	🍷 ①–⑥	[R] ✕ ⑤	[R] ✕ ①–④	[R] ✕ ⑥⑦	Ⓑ **p**	[R] ✕	[R] **A**	①–⑥		
London St Pancras .. d.	1434	...	...	...	...	...	...	...	...	...	...	...	...	...	...	...	...	1604	1604	1657	...	1529	...	...	...	...
Ebbsfleet International d.	|	...	...	...	...	...	...	...	...	...	...	...	...	...	...	...	...	|	|	1715	...	1545	...	...	...	...
Ashford International .. d.	|	...	...	...	...	...	...	...	...	...	...	...	...	...	...	...	...	|	|	|	...	|	...	...	...	...
Lille Europe .... d.	1658	...	...	...	...	...	...	...	...	...	...	...	...	...	...	...	...	|	1828	1928	...	|	...	...	...	...
Paris Nord .... d.	|	1625	...	...	...	...	...	...	1725	...	...	...	...	...	...	...	...	|	|	|	1855	1856	2020¶	...	...	...
Brussels Midi/Zuid ... a.	1733	1747	...	...	...	...	...	...	1847	...	...	...	...	...	...	...	...	1859	1903	2003	2017	...	|	...	...	...
Brussels Midi/Zuid ... d.	...	...	1818	...	...	...	...	...	1859	...	...	...	...	...	...	...	...			...	2025	...	|	...	...	...
Liège Guillemins .... a.	...	...	1911	...	...	...	...	...	1943	...	...	...	...	...	...	...	...	...	...	...	2111	...	|	...	...	...
Liège Guillemins .... d.	...	...	1914	...	...	...	...	...	1945	...	...	...	...	...	...	...	...	...	...	...	...	...	|	...	...	...
Aachen 🏛 .... a.	...	...	1936	...	...	...	...	...	2036	...	...	...	...	...	...	...	...	...	...	...	...	...	|	...	...	...
Köln Hbf .... a.	...	...	2015	...	...	...	...	...	2115	...	...	...	...	...	...	...	...	...	...	...	...	...	|	...	...	...
Köln Hbf .... d.	...	...	...	2031	2045	2049	2111	2111	...	2131	2151	2211	2211	2228	2228	0210	...	...	...	...	...	...	|	...	...	...
Wuppertal Hbf .... a.	...	...	...	|	|	2115	2141	|	...	|	|	2241	|	2315u	2315u	|	...	...	...	...	...	...	|	...	...	...
Hagen Hbf .... a.	...	...	...	|	|	2133	2159	|	...	|	|	2259	|	2334u	2334u	|	...	...	...	...	...	...	|	...	...	...
Düsseldorf Hbf .... a.	...	...	...	2100	2106	|	|	2132	...	2200	2221	|	2232	|	|	0232	...	...	...	...	...	...	|	...	...	...
Duisburg Hbf .... a.	...	...	...	2118	2128	|	|	2145	...	2218	2237	|	2245	|	|	0250	...	...	...	...	...	...	|	...	...	...
Oberhausen .... a.	...	...	...	2126	|	|	|	|	...	2226	|	|	|	|	|	|	...	...	...	...	...	...	|	...	...	...
Essen Hbf .... a.	...	...	...	...	2143	|	|	2158	...	...	2251	|	2257	|	|	0306	...	...	...	...	...	...	|	...	...	...
Bochum Hbf .... a.	...	...	...	...	2154	|	|	2209	...	...	2303	|	2309	|	|	0316	...	...	...	...	...	...	|	...	...	...
Dortmund Hbf .... a.	...	...	...	...	2207	|	2220	2221	...	...	2315	2322	2321	2356u	2356u	0329	...	...	...	...	...	...	|	...	...	...
Hamm .... a.	...	...	...	...	...	2202	2248	|	...	...	2345	...	|	0014u	0014u	|	...	...	...	...	...	...	|	...	...	...
Bielefeld Hbf .... a.	...	...	...	...	...	2236	2318	|	...	...	...	...	|	0043u	0043u	|	...	...	...	...	...	...	|	...	...	...
Münster .... a.	...	...	...	...	...	|	|	2254j	...	...	...	...	2357	|	|	0415	0538	...	...	...	...	...	|	...	...	...
Osnabrück Hbf ...... a.	...	...	...	...	...	|	|	...	...	...	...	...	...	|	|	0446	0601	*EC*	*ICE*	...	...	...	|	...	...	...
Bremen Hbf .... a.	...	...	...	...	...	|	|	...	...	...	...	...	...	|	|	0552	|	**31**	**33**	...	...	...	|	...	...	...
Hannover Hbf .... a.	...	...	...	...	...	2328	0026	...	...	...	...	...	...	|	|	|	0718	**T F**	**F**	...	...	...	0702s	0736	0820	...
Hamburg Hbf .... a.	...	...	...	...	...	|	...	...	...	...	...	...	...	|	**b**	0651	|	0725	0928	...	...	...	|	0856	0934	...
København H ⊙ a.	...	...	...	...	...	|	...	...	...	...	...	...	...	|	0959	...	|	1211	1411	...	...	...	|	...	...	...
Wolfsburg .... a.	...	...	...	...	...	|	...	...	...	...	...	...	...	|	...	...	0753	...	...	...	...	...	|	...	...	...
Braunschweig Hbf ...... a.	...	...	...	...	...	|	...	...	...	...	...	...	...	|	...	...	|	...	...	...	...	...	|	...	...	...
Magdeburg Hbf .... a.	...	...	...	...	...	|	...	...	...	...	...	...	...	|	...	...	|	...	...	...	...	...	|	...	...	...
Halle Hbf .... a.	...	...	...	...	...	|	...	...	...	...	...	...	...	|	...	...	|	...	...	...	...	...	|	...	...	...
Leipzig Hbf .... a.	...	...	...	...	...	|	...	...	...	...	...	...	...	|	...	...	|	...	...	...	...	...	|	...	...	...
Berlin Hbf .... a.	...	...	...	...	...	0112	...	...	...	...	...	...	...	|	...	...	0920	...	...	...	...	...	0902	...	...	...
Berlin Ostbahnhof ... a.	...	...	...	...	...	0122	...	...	...	...	...	...	...	|	...	...	0931	...	...	...	...	...	...	...	...	...
Dresden Hbf .... a.	...	...	...	...	...	...	...	...	...	...	...	...	...	0707	...	...	...	...	...	...	...	...	...	...	...	...
Bad Schandau 🏛 ... a.	...	...	...	...	...	...	...	...	...	...	...	...	...	0736	...	...	...	...	...	...	...	...	...	...	...	...
Děčín .... a.	...	...	...	...	...	...	...	...	...	...	...	...	...	0753	...	...	...	...	...	...	...	...	...	...	...	...
Praha Holešovice . a.	...	...	...	...	...	...	...	...	...	...	...	...	...	0918	...	...	...	...	...	...	...	...	...	...	...	...
Praha hlavní .... a.	...	...	...	...	...	...	...	...	...	...	...	...	...	0956	...	...	...	...	...	...	...	...	...	...	...	...

train type		⇌	☆		*ICE*	*CNL*	☆		*ICE*	*EC*	*IC*	*CNL*	*EN*	*ICE*	*IC*	*RE*	*RE*	⇌	☆							
train number		**9412**	**9119**		**887**	**450**	**9023**		**32**	**30**	**2021**	**483**	**456**	**501**	**2319**	**10104**	**11105**	**9418**	**9181**							
notes		①–⑥ **p**	[R] ✕ ①–⑥		**1087**	[R] **D**	[R] ✕		**F**	**S F**	🍷	**446** [R] **E**	[R] **C**	🍷	🍷 **P**		**P**		[R] ✕							
Praha hlavní .... d.	...	...	...	...	...	...	...	...	...	...	...	...	1829	...	...	...	...	...	...	...	...	...	...	...	...	...
Praha Holešovice . d.	...	...	...	...	...	...	...	...	...	...	...	...	1840	...	...	...	...	...	...	...	...	...	...	...	...	...
Děčín .... d.	...	...	...	...	...	...	...	...	...	...	...	...	2002	...	...	...	...	...	...	...	...	...	...	...	...	...
Bad Schandau 🏛 ... d.	...	...	...	...	...	...	...	...	...	...	...	...	2019	...	...	...	...	...	...	...	...	...	...	...	...	...
Dresden Hbf .... d.	...	...	...	...	...	...	...	...	...	...	...	...	2051	...	...	...	...	...	...	...	...	...	...	...	...	...
Berlin Ostbahnhof ... d.	...	...	...	...	...	...	...	...	...	...	...	...	|	...	...	...	...	...	...	...	...	...	...	...	...	...
Berlin Hbf .... d.	...	...	...	...	...	1958	...	...	...	...	...	...	|	...	...	...	...	...	...	...	...	...	...	...	...	...
Leipzig Hbf .... d.	...	...	...	...	...	|	...	...	...	...	...	...	|	...	...	...	...	...	...	...	...	...	...	...	...	...
Halle Hbf .... d.	...	...	...	...	...	|	...	...	...	...	...	...	|	...	...	...	...	...	...	...	...	...	...	...	...	...
Magdeburg Hbf .... d.	...	...	...	...	...	|	...	...	...	...	...	...	|	...	...	...	...	...	...	...	...	...	...	...	...	...
Braunschweig Hbf ..... d.	...	...	...	...	...	|	...	...	...	...	...	...	|	...	...	...	...	...	...	...	...	...	...	...	...	...
Wolfsburg .... d.	...	...	...	...	...	|	...	...	...	...	...	...	|	...	...	...	...	...	...	...	...	...	...	...	...	...
København H ⊙ d.	...	...	...	...	...	|	...	...	1542	1742	...	1853	|	...	...	...	...	...	...	...	...	...	...	...	...	...
Hamburg Hbf .... d.	...	...	...	...	2001	|	...	...	2016	2216	2246	**k**	|	...	...	...	...	...	...	...	...	...	...	...	...	...
Hannover Hbf .... d.	...	...	...	...	2121	2218	...	...	...	...	|	|	|	...	...	...	...	...	...	...	...	...	...	...	...	...
Bremen Hbf .... d.	...	...	...	...	...	|	...	...	...	...	2347	|	|	...	...	...	...	...	...	...	...	...	...	...	...	...
Osnabrück Hbf ...... d.	...	...	...	...	...	|	...	...	...	...	0045	|	|	...	...	...	...	...	...	...	...	...	...	...	...	...
Münster .... d.	...	...	...	...	...	|	...	...	...	...	0115	|	|	...	0504c	...	...	...	...	...	...	...	...	...	...	...
Bielefeld Hbf .... d.	...	...	...	...	...	|	...	...	...	...	|	0356s	0356s	...	|	...	...	...	...	...	...	...	...	...	...	...
Hamm .... d.	...	...	...	...	...	|	...	...	...	...	0137	0429s	0429s	...	|	0516	...	...	...	...	...	...	...	...	...	...
Dortmund Hbf .... d.	...	...	...	...	...	|	...	...	...	...	0203	0450s	0450s	0537	0538	0545	...	...	...	...	...	...	...	...	...	...
Bochum Hbf .... d.	...	...	...	...	...	|	...	...	...	...	0215	|	|	|	0549	0556	...	...	...	...	...	...	...	...	...	...
Essen Hbf .... d.	...	...	...	...	...	|	...	...	...	...	0228	|	|	|	0600	0609	...	...	...	...	...	...	...	...	...	...
Oberhausen .... d.	...	...	...	...	...	|	...	...	...	...	|	|	|	|	|	|	0634	...	...	...	...	...	...	...	...	...
Duisburg Hbf .... d.	...	...	...	...	...	|	...	...	...	...	0241	|	|	|	0613	0624	0642	...	...	...	...	...	...	...	...	...
Düsseldorf Hbf .... d.	...	...	...	...	...	|	...	...	...	...	0302	|	|	|	0627	0640	0658	...	...	...	...	...	...	...	...	...
Hagen Hbf .... d.	...	...	...	...	...	|	...	...	...	...	|	0521s	0521s	0557	|	|	|	...	...	...	...	...	...	...	...	...
Wuppertal Hbf .... d.	...	...	...	...	...	|	...	...	...	...	|	0539s	0539s	0614	|	|	|	...	...	...	...	...	...	...	...	...
Köln Hbf .... a.	...	...	...	...	...	|	...	...	...	...	0336	0614	0614	0646	0649	0711	0729	...	...	...	...	...	...	...	...	...
Köln Hbf .... d.	...	...	...	...	...	|	...	...	...	...	...	...	...	...	...	...	...	0745	...	...	...	...	...	...	...	...
Aachen 🏛 .... d.	...	...	...	...	...	|	...	...	...	...	...	...	...	...	...	...	...	0824	...	...	...	...	...	...	...	...
Liège Guillemins .... a.	...	...	...	...	...	|	...	...	...	...	...	...	...	...	...	...	...	0915	...	...	...	...	...	...	...	...
Liège Guillemins .... d.	...	0749	...	...	...	|	...	...	...	...	...	...	...	...	...	...	...	0917	...	...	...	...	...	...	...	...
Brussels Midi/Zuid ... a.	...	0835	...	...	...	|	...	...	...	...	...	...	...	...	...	...	...	1001	...	...	...	...	...	...	...	...
Brussels Midi/Zuid ... d.	...	0843	0929	...	...	|	...	...	...	...	...	...	...	...	...	...	...	1013	1129	...	...	...	...	...	...	...
Paris Nord .... a.	...	1005	|	...	...	0930h	1113	...	...	...	...	...	...	...	...	...	...	1135	|	...	...	...	...	...	...	...
Lille Europe .... a.	...	...	1002	...	...	...	|	...	...	...	...	...	...	...	...	...	...	...	1202	...	...	...	...	...	...	...
Ashford International . a.	...	...	|	...	...	...	|	...	...	...	...	...	...	...	...	...	...	...	|	...	...	...	...	...	...	...
Ebbsfleet International a.	...	...	1015	...	...	...	|	...	...	...	...	...	...	...	...	...	...	...	|	...	...	...	...	...	...	...
London St Pancras .. a.	...	...	1031	...	...	...	1229	...	...	...	...	...	...	...	...	...	...	...	1226	...	...	...	...	...	...	...

NOTES for pages 58 and 59

A – *City Night Line* PERSEUS ①⑤⑥⑦ (daily until Nov. 2) – 🛏 1, 2 cl., 🛏 2 cl. (including ladies only berths), (2) (reclining) and ✕ Paris - Metz (depart 2353; also 2247, 2301, 0003 on certain dates) - Forbach 🏛 - Saarbrücken (0059) - Göttingen (arrive 0611) - Hannover (0702) - Berlin Spandau (arrive 0850) - Berlin Hbf - Berlin Südkreuz (0911). [R] Special fares apply.

B – *ICE SPRINTER* – ①–④, supplement payable.

C – *City Night Line* KOPERNIKUS / PHOENIX – 🛏 1, 2 cl., 🛏 2 cl., (2) (reclining) and 🍷 Amsterdam - Köln - Berlin - Dresden - Praha and v.v. [R] Special fares apply.

D – *City Night Line* PERSEUS ④⑤⑥⑦ (daily until Nov. 1) – 🛏 1, 2 cl., 🛏 2 cl. (including ladies only berths), (2) (reclining) and ✕ Berlin Südkreuz (depart 1949; 1919 on ⑦) - Berlin Hbf (1958; 1936 on ⑦) - Berlin Spandau (2008; 1945 on ⑦) - Hannover (2218) - Göttingen (2331) - Saarbrücken (arrive 0459) - Forbach 🏛 - Metz (0615) - Paris. [R] Special fares apply.

E – *City Night Line* BOREALIS – 🛏 1, 2 cl., 🛏 2 cl., (2) (reclining) and 🍷 Amsterdam - Köln - København and v.v. ✕ Hannover - København and v.v. [R] Special fares apply.

F – (12) and 🍷 ⚡ Hamburg - København and v.v. (Table **50**).

G – Ⓑ (daily July 5 - Aug. 30).

P – ①–⑥ (not Oct. 3).

S – Apr. 4 - Oct. 25.

T – Apr. 4 - Oct. 26.

NOTES CONTINUED ON NEXT PAGE →

For København / Esbjerg - London by rail and sea via Harwich, see DFDS Seaways Table 2220

BERLIN, HAMBURG and KÖLN - BRUSSELS, PARIS and LONDON — 20

For the full service Brussels - London and v.v. see Table **12**. For Brussels - Paris and v.v. see Table **18**. Connections at Brussels are not guaranteed.

train type	ICE	RE	EC	ICE	⇌	RE	ICE	ICE	ICE	⇌	ICE	IC	IC	IC	ICE	RE	⇌	ICE	ICE	IC	ICE	IC	ICE	⇌	☆	☆
train number	25	10106	115	16	9322	29713	515	1094	27	9430	654	2013	2023	2044	954	11015	9438	1023	1642	2046	952	334	14	9346	9149	9149
notes	✕		🍷	🍷			✕	[R] 🍷 B	✕		✕	🍷	🍷	🍷 ①–⑥	✕ ①–⑥			🍷	①–⑥	🍷 ①–⑥	✕	🍷	🍷	Ⓑ	[R] ✕ ⑦	[R] ✕ ①–⑤
Praha hlavní d.	...	...	...	...	...	...	...	...	...	...	...	...	...	...	...	...	...	...	...	...	...	...	...	...	...	...
Praha Holešovice d.	...	...	...	...	...	...	...	...	...	...	...	...	...	...	...	...	...	...	...	...	...	...	...	...	...	...
Děčín d.	...	...	...	...	...	...	...	...	...	...	...	...	...	...	...	...	...	...	...	...	...	...	...	...	...	...
Bad Schandau 🏛 d.	...	...	...	...	...	...	...	...	...	...	...	...	...	...	...	...	...	...	...	...	...	...	...	...	...	...
Dresden Hbf d.	...	...	...	...	...	...	...	...	...	...	...	...	...	...	...	...	...	...	0654	...	...	...	...	...	...	...
Berlin Ostbahnhof d.	...	...	...	...	...	...	...	...	...	...	0640	...	...	...	0738	...	...	...	|	...	0938	...	...	...	...	...
Berlin Hauptbahnhof d.	...	...	...	...	...	...	...	...	...	...	0650	...	...	...	0748	...	...	...	|	...	0948	...	...	...	...	...
Leipzig Hbf d.	...	...	...	...	...	...	...	...	...	...	|	0436**c**	...	0640	|	...	...	...	0807	0840	|	...	...	...	...	...
Halle Hbf d.	...	...	...	...	...	...	...	...	...	...	|	0503**c**	...	0707	|	...	...	...	▬	0907	|	...	...	...	...	...
Magdeburg Hbf d.	...	...	...	...	...	...	...	...	...	...	|	0600**y**	...	0800	|	...	...	...	...	1000	|	...	...	...	...	...
Braunschweig Hbf d.	...	...	...	...	...	...	...	...	...	...	|	0651**y**	...	0851	|	...	...	...	...	1051	|	...	...	...	...	...
Wolfsburg d.	...	...	...	...	...	...	...	...	...	...	|	|	...	|	0855	...	...	...	...	|	1055	...	...	...	...	...
København H ⊙ d.	...	...	...	...	...	...	...	...	...	...	|	|	...	|	|	...	...	...	...	|	|	...	...	...	...	...
Hamburg Hbf d.	...	...	...	...	...	...	0537	0612	...	...	|	|	0746	|	|	...	...	0946	...	|	|	...	...	...	...	...
Hannover Hbf d.	...	...	...	...	...	...	|	|	...	...	0831	0740	|	0923	0931	...	...	|	...	1123	1131	...	...	...	...	...
Bremen Hbf d.	...	...	...	...	...	...	0637	|	...	...	|	|	0844	▬	|	...	...	1044	...	...	|	...	...	...	...	...
Osnabrück Hbf d.	...	...	...	...	...	...	0732	|	...	...	|	|	0937	...	|	...	...	1137	...	...	|	...	...	...	...	...
Münster d.	...	...	0631	...	...	0734	0801	|	...	...	|	|	1004	*ICE*	|	...	...	1203	*ICE*	...	|	1232	...	...	...	...
Bielefeld Hbf d.	...	...	|	...	...	|	|	|	...	...	0922	0842	|	**517**	1022	...	...	|	**519**	...	1222	|	...	...	...	...
Hamm d.	...	0616	|	...	...	0801	|	|	...	...	0954	0914	|	✕	1054	...	...	|	🍷	...	1254	|	...	...	...	...
Dortmund Hbf d.	0636	0645	|	...	...	|	0837	|	0838	...	|	0952	1036	1038	|	...	...	1236	1238	...	|	|	...	...	...	...
Bochum Hbf d.	|	0656	|	...	...	|	|	|	0849	...	|	1003	|	1049	|	...	...	|	1249	...	|	|	...	...	...	...
Essen Hbf d.	|	0709	|	...	...	|	|	0853**s**	0900	...	|	1014	|	1100	|	...	...	|	1300	...	|	|	...	...	...	...
Oberhausen d.	|	|	0727	...	...	|	|	|	|	...	|	|	|	|	|	1134	...	|	|	...	|	1327	...	...	...	...
Duisburg Hbf d.	|	0724	0735	...	...	|	|	|	0913	...	|	1032	|	1113	|	1142	...	|	1313	...	|	1334	...	...	...	...
Düsseldorf Hbf d.	|	0740	0752	...	...	|	|	0916**s**	0927	...	|	1050	|	1127	|	1158	...	|	1327	...	|	1348	...	...	...	...
Hagen Hbf d.	0657	|	|	...	...	0839	0857	|	|	...	1024	|	1057	|	1124	|	...	1257	|	...	1324	|	...	...	...	...
Wuppertal Hbf d.	0714	|	|	...	...	0904	0914	|	|	...	1041	|	1114	|	1141	|	...	1314	|	...	1341	|	...	...	...	...
Köln Hbf a.	0746	0811	0815	...	...	0938	0946	0941	0949	...	1109	1112	1146	1149	1209	1229	...	1346	1349	...	1409	1412	...	...	...	...
Köln Hbf d.	...	...	...	0844	...	▬	...	...	...	1045	▬	▬	...	...	...	...	1244	▬	...	...	...	...	1444	...	...	...
Aachen 🏛 d.	...	...	...	0921	...	☆	...	...	...	1124	☆	☆	...	...	...	...	1324	☆	...	...	...	...	1521	...	...	...
Liège Guillemins a.	...	...	...	0942	...	**9181**	...	...	...	1215	**9139**	**9141**	...	...	...	...	1415	**9145**	...	...	...	...	1542	...	...	...
Liège Guillemins d.	...	...	...	0944	...	[R]	...	...	...	1217	[R] ✕	[R] ✕	...	...	...	...	1417	[R] ✕	...	...	...	...	1544	...	...	...
Brussels Midi/Zuid a.	...	...	...	1035	...	✕	...	...	...	1301	⑥⑦	①–⑤	...	...	...	...	1501	①–⑤	...	...	...	...	1635	...	...	...
Brussels Midi/Zuid d.	...	...	...	...	1113	1129	...	...	...	1313	1429	1459	...	...	...	...	1513	1559	...	...	...	...	...	1713	1659	1659
Paris Nord a.	...	...	...	...	1235	|	...	...	...	1435	|	|	...	...	...	...	1635	|	...	...	...	...	...	1835	|	|
Lille Europe a.	...	...	...	...	...	1202	...	...	...	...	1502	1532	...	...	...	...	...	1632	...	...	...	...	...	...	1732	1732
Ashford International a.	...	...	...	...	...	|	...	...	...	...	|	|	...	...	...	...	...	|	...	...	...	...	...	...	1733	1737
Ebbsfleet International a.	...	...	...	...	...	|	...	...	...	...	|	|	...	...	...	...	...	1645	...	...	...	...	...	...	|	|
London St Pancras a.	...	...	...	...	...	1226	...	...	...	...	1526	1556	...	...	...	...	...	1703	...	...	...	...	...	...	1803	1807

train type	IC	IC	ICE	RE	EC	ICE	ICE	IC	IC	ICE	RE	⇌	☆	ICE	EC	ICE	IC	ICE	⇌	IC	RE	ICE	IC	ICE	RE	ICE
train number	2115	2130	650	11021	178	1640	38	2311	2038	558	11025	9458	9163	1025 1125	176	1548	2140	858	9462	2213	10130	1558	2036	556	11029	10
notes	🍷	🍷	✕		✕	🍷	F	🍷	🍷	✕			[R] ✕ G	🍷	✕	✕	🍷	✕	🍷	🍷		🍷	🍷	✕		🍷
Praha hlavní d.	...	...	...	...	0629	...	...	...	...	...	...	...	...	...	...	...	...	...	...	...	...	...	...	...	...	...
Praha Holešovice d.	...	...	...	...	0640	...	...	...	...	...	...	...	...	...	0840	...	...	...	...	...	...	...	...	...	...	...
Děčín d.	...	...	...	...	0802	...	...	...	...	...	...	...	...	...	1002	...	...	...	...	...	...	...	...	...	...	...
Bad Schandau 🏛 d.	...	...	...	...	0819	...	...	...	...	...	...	...	...	...	1019	...	...	...	...	...	...	...	...	...	...	...
Dresden Hbf d.	...	...	...	...	0846	0854	...	...	...	...	...	...	...	...	1046	1054	...	...	...	...	...	1154	...	...	...	...
Berlin Ostbahnhof d.	...	...	1040	...	▬	|	...	...	...	1240	...	...	...	...	▬	|	...	1338	...	...	...	|	...	1440	...	...
Berlin Hauptbahnhof d.	...	...	1050	...	...	|	...	...	...	1250	...	...	...	...	...	|	...	1348	...	...	...	|	...	1450	...	...
Leipzig Hbf d.	...	0942	|	...	...	1007	...	...	1142	|	...	...	...	...	...	1207	1240	|	...	...	...	1307	1342	|	...	...
Halle Hbf d.	...	1009	|	...	...	▬	...	...	1209	|	...	...	...	...	...	▬	1307	|	...	...	...	...	1409	|	...	...
Magdeburg Hbf d.	...	1100	|	...	...	...	...	...	1300	|	...	...	...	...	...	...	1400	|	...	...	...	...	1500	|	...	...
Braunschweig Hbf d.	...	1151	|	...	...	...	...	...	1351	|	...	...	...	...	...	...	1451	|	...	...	...	...	1551	|	...	...
Wolfsburg d.	...	|	|	...	...	...	...	...	|	|	...	...	...	...	...	...	|	1455	...	...	...	...	|	|	...	...
København H ⊙ d.	...	|	|	...	...	...	0742	...	|	|	...	...	...	...	...	...	|	|	...	...	...	...	|	|	...	...
Hamburg Hbf d.	1046	|	|	...	...	...	1216	1246	|	|	...	...	...	1346	...	...	|	|	...	1446	...	...	|	|	...	...
Hannover Hbf d.	|	1223	1231	...	...	...	...	|	1423	1431	...	...	...	|	...	...	1523	1531	...	|	...	...	1623	1631	...	...
Bremen Hbf d.	1144	...	|	...	...	...	...	1344	...	|	...	...	...	1444	...	...	...	|	...	1544	...	...	...	|	...	...
Osnabrück Hbf d.	1237	...	|	...	...	...	...	1437	...	|	...	...	...	1537	...	...	...	|	...	1637	...	...	...	|	...	...
Münster d.	1304	...	|	...	...	...	...	1504	...	|	...	...	...	1603	*ICE*	...	...	|	...	1704	...	...	...	|	...	...
Bielefeld Hbf d.	|	...	1322	...	...	...	...	|	...	1522	...	...	...	|	**613**	...	...	1622	...	|	...	...	...	1722	...	...
Hamm d.	|	...	1354	...	...	...	...	|	...	1554	...	...	...	|	🍷	...	...	1654	...	|	1720	...	...	1754	...	...
Dortmund Hbf d.	1338	...	|	...	...	...	...	1538	...	|	...	...	...	1636	1638	...	...	|	...	1738	1745	...	...	|	...	...
Bochum Hbf d.	1349	...	|	...	...	...	...	1549	...	|	...	...	...	|	1649	*RE*	...	|	...	1749	1756	...	...	|	...	...
Essen Hbf d.	1400	...	|	...	...	...	...	1600	...	|	...	...	...	|	1700	**11027**	...	|	...	1800	1809	...	...	|	...	...
Oberhausen d.	|	...	|	1434	...	...	...	|	...	|	1634	...	...	|	|	1734	...	|	...	|	|	...	...	|	1834	...
Duisburg Hbf d.	1413	...	|	1442	...	...	...	1613	...	|	1642	...	...	|	1713	1742	...	|	...	1813	1824	...	...	|	1842	...
Düsseldorf Hbf d.	1427	...	|	1458	...	...	...	1627	...	|	1658	...	...	|	1727	1758	...	|	...	1827	1840	...	...	|	1858	...
Hagen Hbf d.	|	...	1424	|	⇌	...	...	|	...	1624	|	...	...	1657	|	|	...	1724	...	|	|	...	...	1824	|	...
Wuppertal Hbf d.	|	...	1441	|	**9450**	...	...	|	...	1641	|	...	...	1714	|	|	...	1741	...	|	|	...	...	1841	|	...
Köln Hbf a.	1450	...	1509	1529	🍷	...	...	1649	...	1709	1729	...	...	1746	1749	1829	...	1809	...	1849	1911	...	...	1909	1929	...
Köln Hbf d.	...	...	...	...	1545	☆	...	...	...	...	...	1745	...	...	...	...	...	...	1845	...	...	...	...	...	...	1944
Aachen 🏛 d.	...	...	...	...	1624	**9157**	...	...	...	...	...	1824	...	...	...	...	...	...	1924	...	...	...	...	...	...	2021
Liège Guillemins a.	...	...	...	...	1715	[R]	...	...	...	...	...	1915	...	...	...	...	...	...	2015	...	...	...	...	...	...	2042
Liège Guillemins d.	...	...	...	...	1717	✕	...	...	...	...	...	1917	...	...	...	...	...	...	2017	...	...	...	...	...	...	2044
Brussels Midi/Zuid a.	...	...	...	...	1801	Ⓑ	...	...	...	...	...	2001	...	...	...	...	...	...	2101	...	...	...	...	...	...	2135
Brussels Midi/Zuid d.	...	...	...	...	1813	1859	...	...	...	...	...	2013	2029	...	...	...	...	...	2113	...	...	...	...	...	...	...
Paris Nord a.	...	...	...	...	1935	|	...	...	...	...	...	2135	|	...	...	...	...	...	2235	...	...	...	...	...	...	...
Lille Europe a.	...	...	...	...	...	1932	...	...	...	...	...	...	2102	...	...	...	...	...	...	...	...	...	...	...	...	...
Ashford International a.	...	...	...	...	...	|	...	...	...	...	...	...	|	...	...	...	...	...	...	...	...	...	...	...	...	...
Ebbsfleet International a.	...	...	...	...	...	|	...	...	...	...	...	...	2115	...	...	...	...	...	...	...	...	...	...	...	...	...
London St Pancras a.	...	...	...	...	...	1956	...	...	...	...	...	...	2133	...	...	...	...	...	...	...	...	...	...	...	...	...

← NOTES CONTINUED FROM PREVIOUS PAGE

- **b** – Via Flensburg (0547**s**), Padborg (0600**s**) and Odense (0818**s**).
- **c** – ① only.
- **h** – Paris **Est**. Arrive 1051 on Oct. 25, Nov. 8, 15.
- **j** – ⑦ only.
- **k** – Via Odense (2023**u**), Padborg (2218**u**) and Flensburg (2233**u**).
- **p** – Not Nov. 2, 11.
- **s** – Stops to set down only.
- **t** – Arrive 10 minutes earlier.
- **u** – Stops to pick up only.
- **y** – ①–⑥.
- ☆ – Eurostar train. Special fares payable. Minimum check-in time 30 minutes. Not available for London - Ebbsfleet - Ashford or v.v. journeys. Valid June 14 - Aug. 30. See Table **12**.
- ⇌ – *Thalys* high-speed train. [R] 🍷. Special fares payable.
- ⊙ – 🏛 between Hamburg and København is Rødby (Table **720**).
- ⫽ – Supplement payable.
- ¶ – Paris **Est**. Depart 1947 Sept. 28, 29, 30, Oct. 1, 2, 24, Nov. 6, 7, 9, 13, 14.

For København / Esbjerg - London by rail and sea via Harwich, see DFDS Seaways Table 2220

21 LONDON and BRUSSELS - FRANKFURT, WIEN and MÜNCHEN

train type	*ICE*	*ICE*	*ICE*	*RE*	*ICE*	*RE*	*IC*	*ICE*	⇌	*ICE*	*ICE*	*D*	*EC*	*EC*	*ICE*	*EC*	☆	⇌	*ICE*	*IC*	*ICE*	*ICE*	*IC*	*ICE*	*ICE*	*RE*
train number	**11**	**11**	**621**	**353**	**515**	**30021 30051**	**83**	**27**	**9407**	**105**	**595**	**1281**	**319**	**189**	**27**	**101**	**9106**	**9415**	**507**	**2023**	**597**	**109**	**2113**	**123**	**629**	**4259**
notes	🍷 ①–⑥	🍷 ⑦	🍷		🍷		♣	🍷 R		🍷	🍷	G	🍷 g	✕ ♣	🍷 R	🍷	🅁 ✕ ①–⑤		🍷		🍷	🍷	🍷	🍷	🍷 Ⓑ	
London St Pancras .. d.	...	...	...	...	...	...	...	...	...	...	...	...	...	...	...	...	0557	...	...	...	...	...	...	...	...	...
Ebbsfleet International d.	...	...	...	...	...	...	...	...	...	...	...	...	...	...	...	...	|	...	...	...	...	...	...	...	...	...
Ashford International .. d.	...	...	...	...	...	...	...	...	...	...	...	...	...	...	...	...	0627	...	...	...	...	...	...	...	...	...
Lille Europe .... d.	...	...	...	...	...	...	...	...	...	...	...	...	...	...	...	...	|	...	...	...	...	...	...	...	...	...
Paris Nord .... d.	...	...	...	...	...	...	...	...	0625	...	...	...	...	...	...	...	|	0825	...	...	...	...	...	...	...	...
Brussels Midi / Zuid .. a.	...	...	...	...	...	...	...	...	0747	...	...	...	...	...	...	...	0856	0947	...	...	...	...	...	...	...	...
Brussels Midi / Zuid .. d.	0718	0718	...	...	...	...	...	...	0755	...	...	...	...	...	...	...	...	0959	...	...	...	...	...	...	...	...
Liège Guillemins .... a.	0811	0811	...	...	...	...	...	...	0843	...	...	...	...	...	...	...	...	1043	...	...	...	...	...	...	...	...
Liège Guillemins .... d.	0814	0814	...	...	...	...	...	...	0845	...	...	...	...	...	...	...	...	1045	...	...	...	...	...	...	...	...
Aachen Hbf 🏛 .... a.	0836	0836	...	...	...	...	...	...	0936	...	...	...	...	...	...	...	...	1136	...	...	...	...	...	...	...	...
Köln Hbf .... a.	0915	0915	...	...	...	...	...	...	1015	...	...	...	...	...	...	...	...	1215	...	...	...	...	...	...	...	...
Köln Hbf .... d.	0920	0920	...	...	0954	...	...	0953	...	1054	...	...	...	...	...	1053	...	...	1254	...	...	...	1253	1320	...	...
Bonn Hbf .... a.	|	|	...	...	|	...	...	1012	...	|	...	...	...	...	...	1112	...	...	|	...	...	...	1312	|	...	...
Koblenz Hbf .... a.	⊖	⊖	...	...	⊖	...	...	1046	...	⊖	...	...	...	...	←	1146	...	...	⊖	...	...	...	1346	⊖	...	...
Mainz Hbf .... a.	|	|	...	...	|	...	...	1138	...	|	...	...	...	...	1140	1237	...	...	|	...	...	...	1437	|	...	...
Frankfurt Flughafen ✈ a.	1014	1026	...	...	1051	...	...	→	...	1151	...	...	...	...	1159	|	...	...	1351	1401	...	...	|	1414	...	...
Frankfurt (Main) Hbf. a.	1030	1040	1054	...	|	...	...	...	...	|	...	...	...	...	1213	|	...	...	|	1413	...	...	|	1430	1454	...
Würzburg Hbf .... a.	...	...	1203	...	|	...	...	...	...	|	...	...	...	...	1331	|	...	...	|	...	...	...	|	...	1603	...
Nürnberg Hbf .... a.	...	...	1259	1339	|	...	...	...	...	|	...	...	...	...	1428	|	...	...	|	...	...	...	|	...	1659	1736
Regensburg Hbf ..... a.	...	...	|	|	|	...	...	...	...	|	...	...	...	...	1522	|	...	...	|	...	...	...	|	...	...	1839
Praha hlavní **57** .. a.	...	...	|	1850	|	...	...	...	...	|	...	...	...	...	|	|	...	...	|	...	...	...	|	...	...	...
Mannheim Hbf .... a.	...	...	|	...	1124	...	...	...	...	1224	1231	...	...	...	|	1321	...	...	1424	...	1431	...	1521	...	...	...
Stuttgart Hbf .... a.	...	...	|	...	1208	...	...	...	...	...	1308	...	1358	...	|		...	...	...	...	1508	...	1622	...	...	...
Ulm Hbf .... a.	...	...	|	...	1306	...	...	...	...	...	1406	...	1453	...	|	...	...	...	...	...	1606	...	...	...	...	...
Augsburg Hbf .... a.	...	...	|	...	1350	...	...	...	...	...	1450	...	1539	...	|	...	...	...	...	...	1650	...	...	...	...	...
München Hbf .... a.	...	...	1404	...	1430	1446	1530	...	...	...	1530	1600	1616	1731	|	...	...	...	...	...	1730	1843	...	...	...	...
Salzburg .... a.	...	...	...	...	...	1647	|	...	...	...	...	|	1804	|	|	...	...	...	...	...	...	|	...	...	...	...
Kufstein 🏛 .... a.	...	...	...	...	...	...	1632	...	...	...	...	1711	...	1832	|	...	...	...	...	...	...	1939	...	...	...	...
Wörgl .... a.	...	...	...	...	...	...	1644	...	...	...	...	1724	...	1844	|	...	...	...	...	...	...	1949	...	...	...	...
Kitzbühel .... a.	...	...	...	...	...	...	|	...	...	...	...	1817	...	|	|	...	...	...	...	...	...	|	...	...	...	...
Zell am See .... a.	...	...	...	...	...	...	|	...	...	...	...	1911	...	|	|	...	...	...	...	...	...	|	...	...	...	...
Innsbruck .... a.	...	...	...	...	...	...	1721	...	...	...	...	...	...	1921	|	...	...	...	...	...	...	2026	...	...	...	...
Bad Gastein .... a.	...	...	...	...	...	...	...	...	...	...	...	...	...	...	|	...	...	...	...	...	...	...	...	...	...	...
Villach .... a.	...	...	...	...	...	...	...	...	...	...	...	...	...	...	|	...	...	...	...	...	...	...	...	...	...	...
Klagenfurt .... a.	...	...	...	...	...	...	...	...	...	...	...	...	...	...	|	*EC*	...	...	...	...	...	...	...	...	...	...
Passau 🏛 .... a.	...	...	...	...	...	...	...	...	...	...	...	...	...	...	1626	**969**	...	...	...	...	...	...	...	...	...	...
Linz .... a.	...	...	...	...	...	...	...	...	...	...	...	...	...	...	1743	✕	...	...	...	...	...	...	...	...	...	...
Wien Westbahnhof. a.	...	...	...	...	...	...	...	...	...	...	...	...	...	...	1922	1950	...	...	...	...	...	...	...	...	...	...
Budapest Keleti ▲.. a.	...	...	...	...	...	...	...	...	...	...	...	...	...	...	...	2249	...	...	...	...	...	...	...	...	...	...

train type / number	☆	☆	☆	⇌	*ICE*	*ICE*	*ICE*	*ICE*	*ICE*	*EC*	*IC*	☆	⇌	*ICE*	*ICE*	*IC*	*ICE*	*ICE*	⇌	*ICE*	*ICE*	*EN*	*IC*	*IC*	*ICE*	*EN*
train number	**9114**	**9120**	**9120**	**9323**	**15**	**721**	**509**	**599**	**229**	**391**	**2115**	**9116**	**9427**	**611**	**1655**	**2027 2327**	**817**	**725**	**9431**	**601**	**691**	**463**	**2027 2327**	**2311**	**127**	**409 469**
notes	🅁 ✕ ⑥	🅁 ✕ ①–⑤	🅁 ✕ S		🍷	🍷	🍷	🍷	🍷	🍷	🍷	🅁 ✕ ⑥		🍷	🍷	🍷	🍷	🍷		🍷	🍷	B	🍷	🍷	🍷	C
London St Pancras .. d.	0757	0834	0827	...	...	...	...	...	...	...	...	0859	...	...	...	...	...	...	...	...	...	...	...	...	...	...
Ebbsfleet International d.	|	|	0845	...	...	...	...	...	...	...	...	0915	...	...	...	...	...	...	...	...	...	...	...	...	...	...
Ashford International .. d.	0828	|	|	...	...	...	...	...	...	...	...	|	...	...	...	...	...	...	...	...	...	...	...	...	...	...
Lille Europe .... d.	|	|	1058	...	...	...	...	...	...	...	...	1128	...	...	...	...	...	...	...	...	...	...	...	...	...	...
Paris Nord .... d.	|	|	|	1025	...	...	...	...	...	...	...	|	1125	...	...	...	...	...	1225	...	...	...	...	...	...	...
Brussels Midi / Zuid .. a.	1056	1129	1133	1147	...	...	...	...	...	...	...	1203	1247	...	...	...	...	...	1347	...	...	...	...	...	...	...
Brussels Midi / Zuid .. d.	...	...	...	...	1218	...	...	...	...	...	...	...	1259	...	...	...	...	...	1359	...	...	...	...	...	...	...
Liège Guillemins .... a.	...	...	...	...	1311	...	...	...	...	...	...	...	1343	...	...	...	...	...	1443	...	...	...	...	...	...	...
Liège Guillemins .... d.	...	...	...	...	1314	...	...	...	...	...	...	...	1345	...	...	...	...	...	1445	...	...	...	...	...	...	...
Aachen Hbf 🏛 .... a.	...	...	...	...	1336	...	...	...	...	...	...	...	1436	...	...	...	...	...	1536	...	...	...	...	...	...	...
Köln Hbf .... a.	...	...	...	...	1415	...	...	...	...	...	...	...	1515	...	...	...	...	...	1615	...	...	...	...	...	...	...
Köln Hbf .... d.	...	...	...	...	1420	1428	1454	...	...	...	1453	...	...	1554	...	1553	1620	...	...	1654	...	...	...	1653	1720	...
Bonn Hbf .... a.	...	...	...	...	|	|	|	...	...	...	1512	...	...	|	...	1612	|	...	...	|	...	...	...	1712	|	...
Koblenz Hbf .... a.	...	...	...	...	⊖	⊖	⊖	...	...	...	1546	...	...	⊖	...	1646	⊖	...	...	⊖	...	...	←	1746	⊖	...
Mainz Hbf .... a.	...	...	...	...	|	|	|	...	...	...	1637	...	...	|	...	1738	|	...	...	|	...	...	1740	1837	|	...
Frankfurt Flughafen ✈ a.	...	...	...	...	1522	1534	1551	...	...	...	|	...	...	1651	1703	→	1727	1737	...	1751	...	..	1759	|	1814	...
Frankfurt (Main) Hbf. a.	...	...	...	...	1540	1548	|	...	1621	1620	|	...	...	|	1715	...	1741	1748	...	|	...	...	1813	|	1830	2000
Würzburg Hbf .... a.	...	...	...	...	...	1703	|	...	1731	|	|	...	...	|		...	...	1903	...	|	...	...	1931	|	...	|
Nürnberg Hbf .... a.	...	...	...	...	...	1759	|	...	1828	|	|	...	...	|	...	...	...	1959	...	|	...	...	2028	|	...	|
Regensburg Hbf ..... a.	...	...	...	...	...	|	|	...	1922	|	|	...	...	|	...	...	...	...	...	|	...	...	2131	|	...	|
Praha hlavní **57** .. a.	...	...	...	...	...	|	|	...	|	|	|	...	...	|	...	...	...	...	...	|	...	...	|	|	...	|
Mannheim Hbf .... a.	...	...	...	...	...	|	1624	1631	|	|	1721	...	...	1724	*CNL*	...	...	...	...	1824	1831	...	|	1921	...	2057**d**
Stuttgart Hbf .... a.	...	...	...	...	...	|	...	1708	|	1753	1822	...	...	1808	**485**	...	...	...	...	...	1908	...	|	2022	...	2307**d**
Ulm Hbf .... a.	...	...	...	...	...	|	...	1806	|	1853	...	...	...	1906	**363**	...	...	...	...	...	2006	...	|	...	...	0011**d**
Augsburg Hbf .... a.	...	...	...	...	...	|	...	1850	|	1939	...	...	...	1950	**D**	...	...	...	...	...	2050	...	|	...	...	|
München Hbf .... a.	...	...	...	...	...	1904	...	1930	|	2016	...	...	...	2030	2103	...	...	...	...	...	2133	2340	|	...	...	|
Salzburg .... a.	...	...	...	...	...	...	...	...	|	2209	...	...	...	...	|	...	...	...	...	...	...	0117	|	...	...	0313
Kufstein 🏛 .... a.	...	...	...	...	...	...	...	...	|	...	...	...	...	...	2207	...	...	...	...	...	...	|	|	...	...	|
Wörgl .... a.	...	...	...	...	...	...	...	...	|	...	...	...	...	...	2218	...	...	...	...	...	...	|	|	...	...	|
Kitzbühel .... a.	...						...	...	|	...	...	...	...	...	|	...	...	...	...	...	...	|	|	...	...	|
Zell am See .... a.	...						...	...	|	...	...	...	...	...	|	...	...	...	...	...	...	|	|	...	...	|
Innsbruck .... a.	...						...	...	|	...	...	...	...	...	2256	...	...	...	...	...	...	|	|	...	...	|
Bad Gastein .... a.	...						...	...	|	...	...	...	...	...	...	...	...	...	...	...	...	|	|	...	...	|
Villach .... a.	...						...	...	|	...	...	...	...	...	...	...	...	...	...	...	...	|	|	...	...	|
Klagenfurt .... a.	...						...	...	|	...	...	...	...	...	...	...	...	...	...	...	...	|	|	...	...	|
Passau 🏛 .... a.	...						...	...	2026	...	...	...	...	...	...	...	...	...	...	...	...	|	2242	...	...	|
Linz .... a.	...	...	...	...	...	...	...	...	2143	...	...	...	...	...	...	...	...	...	...	...	...	0340	...	...	...	0433
Wien Westbahnhof. a.	...	...	...	...	...	...	...	...	2322	...	...	...	...	...	...	...	...	...	...	...	...	0545**h**	...	...	...	0640
Budapest Keleti ▲.. a.	...	...	...	...	...	...	...	...	...	...	...	...	...	...	...	...	...	...	...	...	...	0854	...	...	...	1019

OTHER TRAIN NAMES:

IC **83** GARDA
R **353** KAREL ČAPEK
R **357** FRANZ KAFKA

B – KÁLMÁN IMRE – 🛏 1,2 cl., 🛌 2 cl. and (2) München - Wien - Budapest. Conveys 🛏 1, 2 cl. and 🛌 1, 2 cl. München - Wien - Budapest (**375**) - Bucureşti.
C – DANUBIUS – 🛏 1,2 cl., 🛌 2 cl., (2) and ✕ Frankfurt (**409**) - Karlruhe (**469**) - Salzburg 🏛 - Wien (**461**) - Budapest.
D – *CNL* LUPUS – 🛏 1,2 cl., 🛌 2 cl., (2) (reclining) and ✕ München - Innsbruck - Roma / Venezia. 🅁 Special fares apply. Table **70**.
G – GROSSGLOCKNER – ⑥ June 20 - Aug. 22: (12) München - Kufstein 🏛 - Wörgl - Zell am See.
R – (12) and ✕ Dortmund - Köln - Nürnberg - Wien.

S – ⑦ July 5 - Aug. 30.
d – Departure time.
g – To Graz (Table **68**).
h – Wien **Hütteldorf**.
⇌ – *Thalys* high-speed train. 🅁 🍷. Special fares payable.
▲ – 🏛 is at Hegyeshalom.

♣ – Special 'global' fares payable.
☆ – Eurostar train. Special fares payable. Minimum check-in time 30 minutes. Not available for London - Ebbsfleet - Ashford or v.v. journeys. Valid June 14 - Aug. 30.
⊖ – Via Köln - Frankfurt high speed line.

LONDON and BRUSSELS - FRANKFURT, WIEN and MÜNCHEN

train type	☆	⇌	ICE	ICE	ICE	ICE	CNL	☆	ICE	ICE	CNL	CNL	IC		⇌	ICE	IC	IC	CNL	EC	EC	☆	⇌		
train number	**9132**	**9443**	**911**	**615**	**1659**	**1029**	**421**	**9138**	**17**	**1029**	**421**	**459**	**2315**		**9451**	**617**	**2315**	**2321**	**419**	**81**	**111**	**9148**	**9457**		
notes	🅁		**821**	🍷	🍷	🍷	🅁	🅁	🍷	🍷	🅁	🅁	🍷			🍷	🍷	**2121**	🅁	✕♣		🅁	⑧		
	✕		🍷				**B**	✕			**B**	**A**						🍷	**H**	**K**		⑥⑦	**p**		
London St Pancras ....d.	1257	...	...	...	...	...	...	1434	...	...	...	...	...	...	...	...	...	...	...	...	...	1657	...	...	...
Ebbsfleet International ..d.	1315	...	...	...	...	...	...	|	...	...	...	...	...	...	...	...	...	...	...	...	...	1715	...	...	...
Ashford International ....d.	|	...	...	...	...	...	...	|	...	...	...	...	...	...	...	...	...	...	...	...	...	|	...	...	...
Lille Europe ....d.	1528	...	...	...	...	...	...	1658	...	...	...	...	...	...	...	...	...	...	...	...	...	1928	...	...	...
Paris Nord................d.	|	1525	...	...	...	...	...	|	...	...	...	...	...	...	1725	...	...	...	...	...	...	|	1855	...	...
Brussels Midi / Zuid....a.	1603	1647	...	...	...	...	...	1733	...	...	...	...	...	...	1847	...	...	...	...	...	...	2003	2017	...	...
Brussels Midi / Zuid....d.	...	1655	...	...	...	...	...	...	1818	...	...	...	...	...	1859	...	...	...	...	...	...	...	2025	...	...
Liège Guillemins ....a.	...	1743	...	...	...	...	...	...	1911	...	...	...	...	...	1943	...	...	...	...	...	...	...	2111	...	...
Liège Guillemins ....d.	...	1745	...	...	...	...	...	...	1914	...	...	...	...	...	1945	...	...	...	...	...	...	...	...	...	...
Aachen Hbf 🛃...............a.	...	1836	...	...	...	...	...	...	1936	...	...	...	...	...	2036	...	...	...	...	...	...	...	...	...	...
Köln Hbf ....a.	...	1915	...	...	...	...	...	...	2015	...	...	...	...	...	2115	...	...	...	...	...	...	...	...	...	...
Köln Hbf ....d.	...	...	1928	1958	...	1953	2006	...	2020	...	...	...	2053	...	...	2154	...	2153	2346	...	...	...	...	...	...
Bonn Hbf ....a.	...	...	|	|	...	2012	2034	...	|	...	...	...	2112	...	...	|	...	2212	0007**u**	...	...	...	...	...	...
Koblenz Hbf..................a.	...	...	⊖	⊖	...	2046	2115	...	⊖	...	...	...	2146	...	...	⊖	...	2246	0044**u**	...	...	...	...	...	...
Mainz Hbf.....................a.	...	...	|	|	...	2140	2212	...	|	...	...	...	2238	...	...	|	...	2338	|	...	...	...	...	...	...
Frankfurt Flughafen ✈ .a.	...	...	2035	2055	2100	2159	|	...	2114	...	←	...	...	...	...	2256	2300	2359	|	...	...	...	...	...	...
Frankfurt (Main) Hbf...a.	...	...	2049	|	2114	2213	2239	...	2130	2218	2305	0055**j**	...	...	...	|	2310	0013	|	...	...	...	...	...	...
Würzburg Hbf...........a.	...	...	2203**e**	|	...	2341	→	...	...	2341	|	|	...	...	...	|	...	...	|	...	...	...	...	...	...
Nürnberg Hbf..........a.	...	...	2259**e**	|	...	0038	...	...	...	0038	0136	|	...	...	...	|	...	...	|	...	...	...	...	...	...
Regensburg Hbf.......a.	...	...	|	|	...	...	...	...	...	...	0427	|	...	...	...	|	...	...	|	...	...	...	...	...	...
Praha hlavní **57** ....a.	...	...	|	|	...	...	...	...	...	...	|	1052	...	...	...	|	...	...	|	...	...	...	...	...	...
Mannheim Hbf ....a.	...	...	|	2131	...	...	...	...	...	...	|	▬	...	...	...	2337	...	...	|	...	...	...	...	...	...
Stuttgart Hbf ....a.	...	...	|	2208	...	...	...	...	...	...	|	...	...	...	...	0052	...	...	0419	...	...	...	...	...	...
Ulm Hbf.......................a.	...	...	|	2306	...	...	...	...	...	...	|	...	...	...	...	...	...	...	0542	...	...	...	...	...	...
Augsburg Hbf...............a.	...	...	|	2352	...	...	...	...	...	...	|	...	...	...	...	...	...	...	0633	...	...	...	...	...	...
München Hbf..............a.	...	...	0005**e**	0034	...	...	...	...	...	...	|	...	...	...	...	...	...	...	0716	0730	0827	...	...	...	...
Salzburg.....................a.	...	...	...	...	...	...	...	...	...	...	|	...	...	...	...	...	...	...	...	|	1006	...	...	...	...
Kufstein 🛃..................a.	...	...	...	...	...	...	...	...	...	...	|	...	...	...	...	...	...	...	...	0832	|	...	...	...	...
Wörgl..........................a.	...	...	...	...	...	...	...	...	...	...	|	...	...	...	...	...	...	...	...	0844	|	...	...	...	...
Kitzbühel.....................a.	...	...	...	...	...	...	...	...	...	...	|	...	...	...	...	...	...	...	...	|	|	...	...	...	...
Zell am See.................a.	...	...	...	...	...	...	...	...	...	...	|	...	...	...	...	...	...	...	...	|	|	...	...	...	...
Innsbruck.................a.	...	...	...	...	...	...	...	...	...	...	|	...	...	...	...	...	...	...	...	0921	|	...	...	...	...
Bad Gastein.................a.	...	...	...	...	...	...	...	...	...	...	|	...	...	...	...	...	...	...	...	...	1140	...	...	...	...
Villach.........................a.	...	...	...	...	...	...	...	...	...	...	|	...	...	...	...	...	...	...	...	...	1243	...	...	...	...
Klagenfurt ....a.	...	...	...	...	...	...	...	...	...	...	|	*EC*	...	...	...	...	...	...	...	...	1315	...	...	...	...
Passau 🛃 ....a.	...	...	...	...	...	...	...	...	...	...	0532	**943**	...	...	...	...	...	...	...	...	...	...	...	...	...
Linz.............................a.	...	...	...	...	...	...	...	...	...	...	0646	✕	...	...	...	...	...	...	...	...	...	...	...	...	...
Wien Westbahnhof...a.	...	...	...	...	...	...	...	...	...	...	0904	0950	...	...	...	...	...	...	...	...	...	...	...	...	...
Budapest Keleti ▲....a.	...	...	...	...	...	...	...	...	...	...	...	1249	...	...	...	...	...	...	...	...	...	...	...	...	...

train type	⇌	☆	EC	EC	CNL	CNL	EC	CNL	ICE	IC	ICE	⇌	IC	ICE	ICE	⇌	☆	CNL	ICE	ICE	ICE	ICE	⇌	☆	
train number	**9412**	**9119**	**110**	**80**	**418**	**458**	**968**	**420**	**828**	**2212**	**826**	**9418**	**2120**	**616**	**16**	**9322**	**9181**	**490**	**1028**	**822**	**818**	**614**	**9430**	**9137**	
notes	①–⑥	🅁✕	✕	✕	🅁	🅁	✕	🅁	①–⑤		🍷		**2320**	⊖	🍷		🅁	**420**	🍷	①–⑥	①–⑥	🍷		🅁✕	
notes	**p**	①–⑥			**H**	**A**		**C**					🍷	❖			✕	**400** **C** 🅁						⑥⑦	
Budapest Keleti ▲....d.	...	...	...	...	...	...	1510	...	...	...	...	...	...	...	...	...	...	...	...	...	...	...	...	...	...
Wien Westbahnhof ..d.	...	...	...	...	...	...	1808	1954	...	...	...	...	...	...	...	...	...	...	...	...	...	...	...	...	...
Linz.............................d.	...	...	...	...	...	...	...	2157	...	...	...	...	...	...	...	...	...	...	...	...	...	...	...	...	...
Passau 🛃 ....d.	...	...	...	...	...	...	...	|	...	...	...	...	...	...	...	...	...	...	...	...	...	...	...	...	...
Klagenfurt ....d.	...	...	1616	...	...	...	...	|	...	...	...	...	...	...	...	...	...	...	...	...	...	...	...	...	...
Villach.........................d.	...	...	1716	...	...	...	...	|	...	...	...	...	...	...	...	...	...	...	...	...	...	...	...	...	...
Bad Gastein.................d.	...	...	1820	...	...	...	...	|	...	...	...	...	...	...	...	...	...	...	...	...	...	...	...	...	...
Innsbruck.................d.	...	...	|	2036	1938	...	...	|	...	...	...	...	...	...	...	...	...	...	...	...	...	...	...	...	...
Zell am See.................d.	...	...	|	|	|	...	...	|	...	...	...	...	...	...	...	...	...	...	...	...	...	...	...	...	...
Kitzbühel.....................d.	...	...	|	|	|	...	...	|	...	...	...	...	...	...	...	...	...	...	...	...	...	...	...	...	...
Wörgl..........................d.	...	...	|	2113	2031	...	...	|	...	...	...	...	...	...	...	...	...	...	...	...	...	...	...	...	...
Kufstein 🛃..................d.	...	...	|	2124	2043	...	...	|	...	...	...	...	...	...	...	...	...	...	...	...	...	...	...	...	...
Salzburg.....................d.	...	...	1952	|	|	...	...	|	...	...	...	...	...	...	...	...	...	...	...	...	...	...	...	...	...
München Hbf..............d.	...	...	2135	2226	2244	...	...	|	...	...	0032**c**	...	...	0317	...	...	...	...	...	...	...	0523	...	...	...
Augsburg Hbf...............d.	...	...	...	...	2320	...	...	|	...	...	0112**c**	...	...	0357	...	...	...	...	...	...	...	0604	...	...	...
Ulm Hbf.......................d.	...	...	...	...	0010	...	...	|	...	...	0202**c**	...	...	0440	...	...	...	...	...	...	...	0651	...	...	...
Stuttgart Hbf ....d.	...	...	...	...	0126	...	...	|	...	...	0305	...	...	0551	...	...	...	...	...	...	...	0751	...	...	...
Mannheim Hbf ....d.	...	...	...	...	|	...	...	|	...	...	0440	...	...	0635	...	...	...	...	...	...	...	0835	...	...	...
Praha hlavní **57** ....d.	...	...	...	...	|	1829	...	|	...	...	|	...	...	|	...	...	...	...	...	...	...	|	...	...	...
Regensburg Hbf.......d.	...	...	...	...	|	|	...	|	...	...	|	...	...	|	...	...	...	...	...	...	...	|	...	...	...
Nürnberg Hbf..........d.	...	...	...	...	|	|	...	0240	...	...	|	...	...	|	...	...	...	...	0530	0600	...	|	...	...	...
Würzburg Hbf...........d.	...	...	...	...	|	|	...	|	...	...	|	...	...	|	...	...	...	←	0626	0656	...	|	...	...	...
Frankfurt (Main) Hbf..d.	...	...	...	...	|	0400**j**	...	0456	0505	...	0544	...	0542	|	0729	...	...	0615	0742	0810	0816	|	...	...	...
Frankfurt Flughafen ✈..d.	...	...	...	...	|	...	...	→	0524	...	0607	...	0558	0709	0743	...	...	|	0758	0824	0831	0909	...	...	...
Mainz Hbf.....................d.	...	...	...	...	|	...	...	...	|	...	|	...	0618	|	|	...	...	0646**s**	0820	|	|	|	...	...	...
Koblenz Hbf..................d.	...	...	...	...	0445**s**	...	...	...	⊖	0606	⊖	...	0712	⊖	⊖	...	...	0744**s**	0912	⊖	⊖	⊖	...	...	...
Bonn Hbf ....d.	...	...	...	...	0521**s**	...	...	...	|	0644	|	...	0744	|	|	...	...	0817**s**	0944	|	|	|	...	...	...
Köln Hbf....................a.	...	...	...	...	0545	...	...	...	0640	0705	0714**x**	...	0805	0805	0840	...	...	0842	1005	0914**x**	0940	1005	...	...	...
Köln Hbf....................d.	...	...	...	...	...	...	...	...	...	...	...	0745	...	...	0844	...	...	...	...	...	...	...	1045	...	...
Aachen Hbf 🛃...............d.	...	...	...	...	...	...	...	...	...	...	...	0824	...	...	0921	...	...	...	...	...	...	...	1124	...	...
Liège Guillemins ....a.	...	...	...	...	...	...	...	...	...	...	...	0915	...	...	0942	...	...	...	...	...	...	...	1215	...	...
Liège Guillemins ....d.	0749	...	...	...	...	...	...	...	...	...	...	0917	...	...	0944	...	...	...	...	...	...	...	1217	...	...
Brussels Midi / Zuid....a.	0835	...	...	...	...	...	...	...	...	...	...	1001	...	...	1035	...	...	...	...	...	...	...	1301	...	...
Brussels Midi / Zuid....d.	0843	0929	...	...	...	...	...	...	...	...	...	1013	...	...	...	1113	1129	...	...	...	...	...	1313	1429	...
Paris Nord................d.	1005	|	...	...	...	...	...	...	...	...	...	1135	...	...	...	1235	|	...	...	...	...	...	1435	|	...
Lille Europe ....a.	...	1002	...	...	...	...	...	...	...	...	...	...	...	...	...	...	1202	...	...	...	...	...	...	1502	...
Ashford International ....a.	...	|	...	...	...	...	...	...	...	...	...	...	...	...	...	...	|	...	...	...	...	...	...	|	...
Ebbsfleet International .a.	...	1015	...	...	...	...	...	...	...	...	...	...	...	...	...	...	|	...	...	...	...	...	...	|	...
London St Pancras ....a.	...	1031	...	...	...	...	...	...	...	...	...	...	...	...	...	...	1226	...	...	...	...	...	...	1526	...

A – *City Night Line* CANOPUS – 🛏 1,2 cl., ▬ 2 cl., [2] (reclining) and 🍷 Zürich - Basel - Frankfurt (Main) **Süd** - Děčín 🛃 - Praha and v.v. 🅁 Special fares apply.

B – *City Night Line* ERIDANUS – 🛏 1, 2 cl., ▬ 2 cl. (4, 6 berth), [2] (reclining) and 🍷: Amsterdam/ Dortmund - Köln - Frankfurt (**421**) - Nürnberg (**491**) - Passau 🛃 - Wien. ✕ Amsterdam / Dortmund - Köln - Frankfurt. 🅁 Special fares apply. For international journeys only.

C – *City Night Line* ERIDANUS – 🛏 1, 2 cl., ▬ 2 cl. (4, 6 berth), [2] (reclining) and 🍷: Wien (**490**) - Passau 🛃 - Nürnberg (**420**) - Frankfurt (**400**) - Köln - Amsterdam / Dortmund. ✕ Frankfurt - Köln - Amsterdam / Dortmund. 🅁 Special fares apply. For international journeys only.

H – ①⑤⑥⑦ (daily until Nov. 2) City Night Line POLLUX – 🛏 1,2 cl., 🛏 1, 2 cl. (T4), ▬ 2 cl. (4, 6 berth), [2] (reclining) and ✕ Amsterdam - Köln - München and v.v. 🅁 Special fares apply.

K – VAL GARDENA / GRÖDNERTAL – [12] and ✕ München - Innsbruck - Bolzano / Bozen.

c – ① only.
e – ⑤⑦.
j – Frankfurt (Main) **Süd**.
p – Not Nov. 2, 21.
s – Stops to set down only.
u – Stops to pick up only.
x – Köln **Messe/Deutz.**

☆ – Eurostar train. Special fares payable. Minimum check-in time 30 minutes. Not available for London - Ebbsfleet - Ashford or v.v. journeys. See Table **12**. Valid June 14 - Aug. 30.

⇌ – *Thalys* high-speed train. 🅁 🍷. Special fares payable.
⊖ – Via Köln - Frankfurt high speed line.
♣ – Special fares payable.
▲ – 🛃 is at Hegyeshalom.
❖ – Subject to alteration on certain dates.

21 MÜNCHEN, WIEN and FRANKFURT - BRUSSELS and LONDON

train type	EN	ICE	ICE	EN	EN	ICE	⇌	☆	☆	IC	ICE	ICE	R/RE	EC	ICE	ICE	☆	☆	☆	IC	ICE	ICE	ICE	⇌	☆
train number	460	728	1126	462	484	612	9438	9145	9149	2024	108	610	350	390	722	14	9149	9149	9153	2112	598	1024	508	9450	9157
notes	408	⊖	1026		358	🍷		🅁✗	🅁✗	🍷	✗	🍷		🍷	🍷	🍷	🅁✗	🅁✗	🅁	🍷	✗	🍷	🍷		🅁✗
notes	E			K	♣C			①–⑤	⑦					①–⑥			⑦	①–⑤	✗						⑧
Budapest Keleti ▲ d.	1905	...	...	2105	...	...	...	...	...	...	...	...	...	...	...	...	...	...	...	...	...	...	...	...	...
Wien Westbahnhof d.	2240	...	...	0009h	...	...	...	...	...	...	...	...	...	...	...	...	...	...	...	...	...	...	...	...	...
Linz d.	0038	...	...	0201	...	...	...	...	...	...	...	...	...	...	...	...	...	...	...	...	...	...	...	...	...
Passau ▦ d.	|	...	...	|	...	...	...	...	...	0719	...	...	...	...	...	...	...	...	...	...	...	...	...	...	...
Klagenfurt d.	|	...	...	|	...	...	...	...	...	|	...	...	...	...	...	...	...	...	...	...	...	...	...	...	...
Villach d.	|	...	...	|	...	...	...	...	...	|	...	...	...	...	...	...	...	...	...	...	...	...	...	...	...
Bad Gastein d.	|	...	...	|	...	...	...	...	...	|	...	...	...	...	...	...	...	...	...	...	...	...	...	...	...
Innsbruck d.	|	...	...	|	0434	...	...	...	...	|	0735	...	...	...	...	...	...	...	...	...	...	...	...	...	...
Zell am See d.	|	...	...	|	|	...	...	...	...	|	|	...	...	...	...	...	...	...	...	...	...	...	...	...	...
Kitzbühel d.	|	...	...	|	|	...	...	...	...	|	|	...	...	...	...	...	...	...	...	...	...	...	...	...	...
Wörgl d.	|	...	...	|	0514	...	...	...	...	|	0810	...	...	...	...	...	...	...	...	...	...	...	...	...	...
Kufstein ▦ d.	|	...	...	|	0530	...	...	...	...	|	0821	...	...	...	...	...	...	...	...	...	...	...	...	...	...
Salzburg d.	0210	...	...	0428	|	...	...	...	...	|	|	...	...	0753	...	...	...	...	...	...	...	...	...	...	...
München Hbf d.	|	...	...	0615	0630	0723	...	...	...	|	0916	0923	...	0935	0955	...	...	...	...	...	1023	...	...	...	...
Augsburg Hbf d.	|	...	...	...	...	0803	...	...	...	|	...	1003	...	...	|	...	...	...	...	...	1103	...	...	...	...
Ulm Hbf d.	0517s	...	...	...	...	0851	...	...	...	|	...	1051	...	...	|	...	...	...	...	...	1151	...	...	...	...
Stuttgart Hbf d.	0633s	...	...	...	...	0951	...	...	...	|	...	1151	...	...	|	...	...	...	...	1137	1251	...	...	...	...
Mannheim Hbf d.	0848s	...	...	...	...	1035	...	...	...	|	...	1235	...	...	|	...	...	...	...	1239	1328	...	1335	...	...
Praha hlavni **57** d.	|	...	...	...	...	|	...	...	...	|	...	|	0511	...	|	...	...	...	...	|	...	...	|	...	...
Regensburg Hbf d.	|	...	...	...	...	|	...	...	...	0827	...	|	|	...	|	...	...	...	...	|	...	...	|	...	...
Nürnberg Hbf d.	|	0800	...	...	...	|	...	...	...	0928	...	|	1009	...	1100	...	...	...	...	|	...	...	|	...	...
Würzburg Hbf d.	|	0856	...	...	...	|	...	...	...	1025	...	|	...	...	1156	...	...	...	...	|	...	...	|	...	...
Frankfurt (Main) Hbf d.	0957	1010	...	...	...	|	...	...	...	1144	...	|	...	...	1305	1329	...	...	...	|	...	1344	|	...	...
Frankfurt Flughafen ✈ d.	...	1024	...	...	...	1109	...	...	...	1158	...	1306	...	...	...	1343	...	...	...	|	...	1355	1409	...	...
Mainz Hbf d.	...	|	1020	...	...	|	...	...	...	1220	...	...	...	...	...	|	...	...	...	1320	...	...	|	...	...
Koblenz Hbf d.	...	⊖	1112	...	...	⊖	...	...	...	1312	...	...	...	...	...	⊖	...	...	...	1412	...	...	⊖	...	...
Bonn Hbf d.	...	|	1144	...	...	|	...	...	...	1344	...	...	...	...	...	|	...	...	...	1444	...	...	|	...	...
Köln Hbf a.	...	1140	1205	...	...	1205	...	...	...	1405	...	...	...	...	...	1440	...	...	...	1505	...	...	1505	...	...
Köln Hbf d.	...	...	...	...	...	...	1244	...	...	...	...	...	...	...	...	1444	...	...	...	...	...	...	...	1545	...
Aachen Hbf ▦ d.	...	...	...	...	...	...	1324	...	...	...	...	...	...	...	...	1521	...	...	...	...	...	...	...	1624	...
Liège Guillemins a.	...	...	...	...	...	...	1415	...	...	...	...	...	...	...	...	1542	...	...	...	...	...	...	...	1715	...
Liège Guillemins d.	...	...	...	...	...	...	1417	...	...	...	...	...	...	...	...	1544	...	...	...	...	...	...	...	1717	...
Brussels Midi / Zuid a.	...	...	...	...	...	...	1501	...	...	...	...	...	...	...	...	1635	...	...	...	...	...	...	...	1801	...
Brussels Midi / Zuid d.	...	...	...	...	...	...	1513	1559	1659	...	...	...	...	...	...	...	1659	1659	1759	...	...	...	...	1813	1859
Paris Nord a.	...	...	...	...	...	...	1635	|	|	...	...	...	...	...	...	...	|	|	|	...	...	...	...	1935	|
Lille Europe a.	...	...	...	...	...	...	...	1632	1732	...	...	...	...	...	...	...	1732	1732	1832	...	...	...	...	...	1932
Ashford International a.	...	...	...	...	...	...	...	|	1733	...	...	...	...	...	...	...	1733	1737	|	...	...	...	...	...	|
Ebbsfleet International a.	...	...	...	...	...	...	...	1645	|	...	...	...	...	...	...	...	|	|	1845	...	...	...	...	...	|
London St Pancras a.	...	...	...	...	...	...	...	1703	1803	...	...	...	...	...	...	...	1803	1807	1903	...	...	...	...	...	1956

train type	EC	D	ICE	ICE	ICE	EC	ICE	⇌	☆	ICE	IC	ICE	ICE	⇌	RJ	R/ALX	ICE	IC	EC	ICE	IC	ICE	ICE	ICE
train number	100	1280	596	506	28	318	626	9458	9163	122	188	1558	516	9462	60	354	26	118	6	1090	88	622	572	10
notes	102		✗	🍷	✗	🍷	🍷		🅁✗	🍷	D	🍷	🍷		✗		✗	🍷	🍷	594	♣	🍷	✗	🍷
notes		G				g			P		♣				H		R			✗				
Budapest Keleti ▲ d.	...	...	...	...	...	...	...	...	...	...	...	...	...	...	0710	...	...	...	...	...	...	...	...	...
Wien Westbahnhof d.	...	...	...	...	0840	...	...	...	...	...	...	...	...	...	1008	...	1040	...	...	...	...	...	...	...
Linz d.	...	...	...	...	1016	...	...	...	...	...	...	...	...	...	...	...	1216	...	...	...	...	...	...	...
Passau ▦ d.	...	...	...	...	1130	...	...	...	...	...	...	...	...	...	...	...	1330	...	...	...	...	...	...	...
Klagenfurt d.	...	...	...	...	|	...	...	...	...	...	...	...	...	...	...	...	|	...	...	...	...	...	...	...
Villach d.	...	...	...	...	|	...	...	...	...	...	...	...	...	...	...	...	|	...	...	...	...	...	...	...
Bad Gastein d.	...	...	...	...	|	...	...	...	...	...	...	...	...	...	...	...	|	...	...	...	...	...	...	...
Innsbruck d.	...	...	...	...	|	...	...	...	...	...	1036	...	...	...	...	...	|	0904	...	...	1236	...	...	...
Zell am See d.	...	0853	...	...	|	...	...	...	...	...	|	...	...	...	...	...	|	|	...	...	|	...	...	...
Kitzbühel d.	...	0944	...	...	|	...	...	...	...	...	|	...	...	...	...	...	|	|	...	...	|	...	...	...
Wörgl d.	...	1035	...	...	|	...	...	...	...	...	1113	...	...	...	...	...	|	|	...	...	1313	...	...	...
Kufstein ▦ d.	...	1046	...	...	|	...	...	...	...	...	1124	...	...	...	...	...	|	◐	...	...	1324	...	...	...
Salzburg d.	...	|	...	...	|	0957	...	...	...	...	|	...	...	...	...	...	|	|	...	...	|	...	...	...
München Hbf d.	...	1153	1223	...	|	1143	1255	...	...	...	1225	...	1323	...	...	...	|	|	...	1423	1427	1455	...	...
Augsburg Hbf d.	...	...	1303	...	|	1218	|	...	...	...	...	...	1403	...	...	...	|	|	...	1503	...	|	...	...
Ulm Hbf d.	...	...	1351	...	|	1305	|	...	...	...	...	...	1451	...	...	...	|	1356	...	1551	...	|	...	...
Stuttgart Hbf d.	...	...	1451	...	|	1405	|	...	...	...	...	...	1551	...	...	...	|	1512	...	1651	...	|	1727	...
Mannheim Hbf d.	1439	...	1528	1535	|	|	|	...	...	...	...	...	1635	...	...	...	|	1608	...	1731	...	|	1806	...
Praha hlavní **57** d.	|	...	...	|	|	|	|	...	...	...	...	...	|	...	...	0911	|	|	...	|	...	|	|	...
Regensburg Hbf d.	|	...	...	|	1232	|	|	...	...	...	...	...	|	...	...	1337	1433	|	...	|	...	|	|	...
Nürnberg Hbf d.	|	...	...	|	1328	|	1400	...	...	...	...	...	|	...	...	...	1527	|	...	|	...	1600	|	...
Würzburg Hbf d.	|	...	...	|	1427	|	1456	...	...	...	...	...	|	...	...	...	1627	|	...	|	...	1656	|	...
Frankfurt (Main) Hbf d.	|	...	...	|	1536	1540	1610	...	...	1629	...	1642	|	...	...	...	1736	|	...	1808	...	1805	|	1829
Frankfurt Flughafen ✈ d.	|	...	...	1609	...	...	1623	...	...	1643	...	1655	1709	...	...	...	...	|	...	...	...	...	1838	1843
Mainz Hbf d.	1520	...	...	|	...	...	|	...	...	|	...	...	|	...	...	...	...	1648	1720	...	...	...	...	|
Koblenz Hbf d.	1612	...	...	⊖	...	...	⊖	...	...	⊖	...	...	⊖	...	...	...	...	1743	1812	...	...	...	...	⊖
Bonn Hbf d.	1644	...	...	|	...	...	|	...	...	|	...	...	|	...	...	...	...	1822	1844	...	...	...	...	|
Köln Hbf a.	1705	...	...	1705	...	...	1732	...	...	1740	...	...	1805	...	...	...	...	1842	1905	...	...	...	...	1940
Köln Hbf d.	...	...	...	...	...	...	...	1745	...	...	...	...	...	1845	...	...	...	...	...	...	...	...	...	1944
Aachen Hbf ▦ d.	...	...	...	...	...	...	...	1824	...	...	...	...	...	1924	...	...	...	...	...	...	...	...	...	2021
Liège Guillemins a.	...	...	...	...	...	...	...	1915	...	...	...	...	...	2015	...	...	...	...	...	...	...	...	...	2042
Liège Guillemins d.	...	...	...	...	...	...	...	1917	...	...	...	...	...	2017	...	...	...	...	...	...	...	...	...	2044
Brussels Midi / Zuid a.	...	...	...	...	...	...	...	2001	...	...	...	...	...	2101	...	...	...	...	...	...	...	...	...	2135
Brussels Midi / Zuid d.	...	...	...	...	...	...	...	2013	2029	...	...	...	...	2113	...	...	...	...	...	...	...	...	...	...
Paris Nord d.	...	...	...	...	...	...	...	2135	|	...	...	...	...	2235	...	...	...	...	...	...	...	...	...	...
Lille Europe a.	...	...	...	...	...	...	...	...	2102	...	...	...	...	...	...	...	...	...	...	...	...	...	...	...
Ashford International a.	...	...	...	...	...	...	...	...	|	...	...	...	...	...	...	...	...	...	...	...	...	...	...	...
Ebbsfleet International a.	...	...	...	...	...	...	...	...	2115	...	...	...	...	...	...	...	...	...	...	...	...	...	...	...
London St Pancras a.	...	...	...	...	...	...	...	...	2133	...	...	...	...	...	...	...	...	...	...	...	...	...	...	...

C – *CNL* LUPUS – 🛏 1, 2 cl., ▬ 2 cl., [2] (reclining) and ✗ Roma / Venezia - Innsbruck - München. 🅁 Special fares apply. Table **70**.

D – GARDA – [12] Verona - Innsbruck - München.

E – DANUBIUS – 🛏 1, 2 cl., ▬ 2 cl., [2] and ✗ Budapest (**460**) - Wien (**468**) - Salzburg ▦ - Karlruhe (**408**) - Frankfurt.

G – GROSSGLOCKNER – ⑥ June 20 - Aug. 22: [12] Zell am See - Wörgl - Kufstein ▦ - München.

H – [1] (premium class), [1] (first class), [2] (economy class) and ✗ Budapest - Wien - München. ÖBB *Railjet* service.

K – KÁLMÁN IMRE – 🛏 1, 2 cl., ▬ 2 cl. and [2] Budapest - Wien - München. Conveys 🛏 1, 2 cl. București - Budapest - Wien - München.

P – ⑧ (daily July 5 - Aug. 30).

R – [12] and ✗ Wien - Nürnberg - Frankfurt - Köln - Dortmund.

c – ①–⑥.

g – From Graz (Table **68**).

h – Wien **Hütteldorf**.

☆ – Eurostar train. Special fares payable. Minimum check-in time 30 minutes. Not available for London - Ebbsfleet - Ashford or v.v. journeys. Valid June 14 – Aug. 30. See Table **12**.

▲ – ▦ is at Hegyeshalom.

◐ – ▦ is at Lindau and Bregenz.

♣ – Special 'global' fares payable.

⇌ – *Thalys* high-speed train. 🅁 🍷. Special fares payable.

⊖ – Via Köln - Frankfurt high speed line.

OTHER TRAIN NAMES:

IC **88** LEONARDO DA VINCI
R **350** KAREL ČAPEK
R **354** FRANZ KAFKA

AMSTERDAM - HAMBURG and BERLIN 22

train type		IC	IC		IC	IC		IC	IC	ICE		IC	IC		IC	ICE		IC	IC	IC	IC			IC
train number		141	2320		143	1028		245	145	1126 1026		147	2024		149	1024		241	241	2022	241			243
notes	①–⑥	🍷			🍷			⑥ 🍷	⑧ 🍷 A			🍷			🍷			⑤⑦ 🍷	①–④ 🍷		⑥ 🍷	⑥		🍷
Schiphol ✈ a.	...	0649	...	...	0849	...	...	1049	1049	...	...	1249	...	...	1449	...	...	1649	1649	...	1649	...	...	1849
Amsterdam Centraal d.	0657	|	...	0857	|	...	1057	|	|	...	1257	|	...	1457	|	...	1657	|	|	...	|	...	1857	|
Amsterdam Zuid WTC d.	|	0658	...	|	0858	...	|	1058	1058	...	|	1258	...	|	1458	...	|	1658	1658	...	1658	...	|	1858
Duivendrecht d.	|	0704	...	|	0904	...	|	1104	1104	...	|	1304	...	|	1504	...	|	1704	1704	...	1704	...	|	1904
Amersfoort d.	0732	0741	...	0932	0941	...	1132	1141	1141	...	1332	1341	...	1532	1541	...	1732	1741	1741	...	1741	...	1932	1941
Deventer d.	...	0820	...	...	1020	...	...	1220	1220	...	...	1420	...	...	1620	...	...	1820	1820	...	1820	...	▬	2020
Hengelo d.	...	0858	...	...	1058	...	...	1258	1258	...	...	1458	...	...	1658	...	...	1858	1858	...	1858	...	*RE*	2058
Bad Bentheim 🏛 a.	...	0918	...	...	1118	...	...	1318	1318	...	...	1518	...	...	1718	...	...	1918	1918	...	1918	1957	**14019**	2118
Rheine a.	...	0940	...	...	1140	...	...	1340	1340	...	...	1540	...	...	1740	...	...	1940	1940	...	...	2012	⑥	...
Osnabrück a.	...	1006	1023	...	1206	1223	...	1406	1406	1423	...	1606	1623	...	1806	1823	...	2006	2006	2023	...	2046	2116	...
Bremen Hbf a.	...	|	1114	...	|	1314	...	|	|	1514	...	|	1714	...	|	1914	...	|	|	2114	...	...	|	...
Hamburg Hbf a.	...	|	1211	...	|	1412	...	|	|	1612	...	|	1812	...	|	2012	...	|	|	2212	...	...	|	...
Minden a.	...	1047	...	...	1247	...	...	1447	1447	...	...	1647	...	...	1847	...	...	2047	2047	...	...	...	2206	...
Hannover Hbf a.	...	1118	...	...	1318	...	...	1518	1518	...	...	1718	...	...	1918	...	...	2118	2118	...	...	...	2250	...
Wolfsburg a.	...	1153	...	...	1353	...	...	1553	1553	...	...	1753	...	...	1953	...	...	2153	...	...	...	...	...	...
Stendal a.	...	1224	...	...	1424	...	...	1624	1624	...	...	1824	...	...	2024	...	...	2224	...	...	...	...	...	...
Berlin Hauptbahnhof a.	...	1320	...	...	1520	...	...	1720	1715	...	...	1915	...	...	2120	...	...	2320	...	...	...	...	...	...
Berlin Ostbahnhof a.	...	1332	...	...	1531	...	...	1731	|	...	...	1931	...	...	2131	...	...	2330	...	...	...	...	...	...
Szczecin Gł. a.	...	...	...	...	...	...	...	...	1934	...	...	...	...	...	...	...	...	...	...	...	...	...	...	...

train type	IC	ICE	IC		IC	IC	IC		ICE	IC	IC		IC	IC		ICE	IC		ICE	IC		IC	IC	
train number	242	515	242		240	2023	240		1023	148	248		2027 2327	146		1125 1025	144		929	142		2321 2121	140	
notes	⑦ 🍷		①–⑥ 🍷				①–⑥ 🍷			①–⑥ A 🍷	⑦ 🍷			🍷			🍷			🍷			🍷	
Szczecin Gł. d.	...	...	...	...	...	...	...	...	...	0610	...	...	...	...	...	...	...	...	...	...	...	...	...	...
Berlin Ostbahnhof d.	...	...	...	...	...	...	0626	...	...	|	0826	...	...	1026	...	...	1226	...	...	1426	...	...	1626	...
Berlin Hauptbahnhof d.	...	...	...	...	...	...	0637	...	...	0837	0837	...	...	1037	...	...	1236	...	...	1437	...	...	1637	...
Stendal d.	...	...	...	...	...	...	0734	...	...	0935	0935	...	...	1135	...	...	1335	...	...	1535	...	...	1735	...
Wolfsburg d.	...	...	...	...	...	...	0805	...	...	1005	1005	...	...	1205	...	...	1405	...	...	1605	...	...	1805	...
Hannover Hbf d.	...	...	0640	...	...	...	0840	...	...	1040	1040	...	...	1240	...	...	1440	...	...	1640	...	...	1840	...
Minden d.	...	...	0712	...	...	...	0912	...	...	1112	1112	...	...	1312	...	...	1512	...	...	1712	...	...	1912	...
Hamburg Hbf d.	...	0537	|	...	...	0746	|	...	0946	|	|	...	1146	|	...	1346	|	...	1546	|	...	1746	|	...
Bremen Hbf d.	...	0637	|	...	...	0844	|	...	1044	|	|	...	1244	|	...	1444	|	...	1644	|	...	1844	|	...
Osnabrück d.	...	0730	0753	...	...	0935	0953	...	1135	1153	1153	...	1335	1353	...	1535	1553	...	1735	1753	...	1935	1953	...
Rheine d.	...	...	0821	...	...	...	1021	...	...	1221	1221	...	...	1421	...	...	1621	...	...	1821	...	...	2021	...
Bad Bentheim 🏛 d.	0844	...	0844	...	1044	...	1044	...	...	1244	1244	...	...	1444	...	...	1644	...	...	1844	...	...	2044	...
Hengelo a.	0904	...	0904	...	1104	...	1104	...	...	1304	1304	...	...	1504	...	...	1704	...	...	1904	...	...	2104	...
Deventer a.	0942	...	0942	...	1142	...	1142	...	...	1342	1342	...	...	1542	...	...	1742	...	...	1942	...	...	2142	...
Amersfoort a.	1023	...	1023	1028	1223	...	1223	1228	...	1423	1423	1428	...	1623	1628	...	1821	1828	...	2023	2028	...	2223	2228
Duivendrecht a.	1057	...	1057	|	1257	...	1257	|	...	1457	1457	|	...	1657	|	...	1857	|	...	2057	|	...	2257	|
Amsterdam Zuid WTC a.	1102	...	1102	|	1302	...	1302	|	...	1502	1502	|	...	1702	|	...	1902	|	...	2102	|	...	2302	|
Amsterdam Centraal a.	|	...	|	1101	|	...	|	1301	...	|	|	1501	...	|	1701	...	|	1901	...	|	2101	...	|	2301
Schiphol ✈ a.	1109	...	1109	...	1309	...	1309	...	...	1509	1509	...	...	1709	...	...	1909	...	...	2109	...	...	2309	...

A – [12] and 🍷 Schiphol - Hannover - Berlin - 🏛 Tantow [ticket point] - 🏛 Szczecin Gumience - Szczecin and v.v.-

LONDON, PARIS and BRUSSELS - WARSZAWA and MOSKVA 24

train type	☆	⇌	EN	EN	EN		☆	451	
train number	9138	9451	447	472	482		9036	443	
notes	[R] ✕		A	C	E		[R]	①⑥	
notes			[R]	[R]	[R]		✕	P	
London St Pancras d.	1434	...	...	...	...	...	1529	...	...
Ebbsfleet International d.	|	...	...	...	...	...	1545	...	...
Lille Europe **12** d.	1658	...	...	...	...	...	|	...	...
Paris Nord d.	|	1725	...	...	...	...	1856	2020h	...
Brussels Midi / Zuid d.	1733	1859	...	...	...	...	...	|	...
Liège Guillemins d.	...	1945	...	...	...	...	...	|	...
Aachen 🏛 d.	...	2040	...	...	...	...	...	|	...
Amsterdam Centraal d.	...	|	1901	...	...	...	...	|	...
Köln Hbf d.	...	2115	2228	...	...	...	...	|	...
Dortmund Hbf d.	...	...	2356	...	...	...	...	|	...
Basel SBB d.	...	...	|	1804	...	...	...	|	...
Frankfurt (Main) Süd d.	...	...	|	2218	...	...	...	|	...
München Hbf d.	...	...	|	|	1900	...	...	|	...
Hannover d.	...	...	|	|	|	...	...	0713	...
Berlin Hbf a.	...	...	|	|	|	...	...	0902	...
Berlin Hbf d.	...	...	0423	0423	0423	...	...	1515	...
Berlin Ostbahnhof d.	...	...	0447	0447	0447	...	...	1532	...
Frankfurt (Oder) 🏛 d.	...	...	|	|	|	...	...	1711	...
Rzepin a.	...	...	0602	0602	0602	...	...	1740	...
Poznań Gł. a.	...	...	0733	0733	0733	...	...	1951	...
Warszawa Centralna a.	...	...	1035	1035	1035	...	...	2310	...
Warszawa Wschodnia a.	...	...	1052	1052	1052	...	...	2320	...
Warszawa Wschodnia d.	...	...	1250	1250	1250	...	...	2342	...
Terespol a.	...	...	1525	1525	1525	...	...	0245	...
Terespol d.	...	...	1555	1555	1555	...	...	0330	...
Brest 🏛 a.	...	...	1741	1741	1741	...	...	0516	...
Brest 🏛 d.	...	...	1942	1942	1942	...	...	0720	...
Baranavichy a.	...	...	2153	2153	2153	...	...	|	...
Minsk a.	...	...	2336	2336	2336	...	...	1046	...
Orsha Tsentralnaya § a.	...	...	0227	0227	0227	...	...	1332	...
Smolensk Tsentralny 🏛 § a.	...	...	0456	0456	0456	...	...	1601	...
Vyazma a.	...	...	0700	0700	0700	...	...	1745	...
Moskva Belorusskaya a.	...	...	1059	1059	1059	...	...	2035	...

train type	442	☆		EN	EN	EN	⇌	☆	
train number	450	9023		446	446	446	9418	9181	
notes	④⑥	[R] ✕		F	D	B	[R] ✕	[R]	
notes	Q			[R]	[R]	[R]		✕	
Moskva Belorusskaya d.	0800	...	...	2109	2109	2109	...	...	...
Vyazma d.	1032	...	...	0035	0035	0035	...	...	...
Smolensk Tsentralny 🏛 § d.	1212	...	...	0231	0231	0231	...	...	...
Orsha Tsentralnaya § d.	1250	...	...	0311	0311	0311	...	...	...
Minsk d.	1529	...	...	0625	0625	0625	...	...	...
Baranavichy d.	|	...	...	0826	0826	0826	...	...	...
Brest 🏛 a.	1855	...	...	1035	1035	1035	...	...	...
Brest 🏛 d.	2115	...	...	1250	1250	1250	...	...	...
Terespol a.	2033	...	...	1208	1208	1208	...	...	...
Terespol d.	2113	...	...	1248	1248	1248	...	...	...
Warszawa Wschodnia a.	2351	...	...	1529	1529	1529	...	...	...
Warszawa Wschodnia d.	0059	...	...	1742	1742	1742	...	...	...
Warszawa Centralna d.	0110	...	...	1755	1755	1755	...	...	...
Poznań Gł. d.	0429	...	...	2101	2101	2101	...	...	...
Rzepin d.	0617	...	...	2242	2242	2242	...	...	...
Frankfurt (Oder) 🏛 d.	0658	...	...	2310	2310	2310	...	...	...
Berlin Ostbahnhof d.	0823	...	...	0022	0022	0022	...	...	...
Berlin Hbf a.	0900	...	...	0032	0032	0032	...	...	...
Berlin Hbf d.	1936	...	...	|	|	|	...	...	...
Hannover d.	2218	...	...	|	|	|	...	...	...
München Hbf a.	|	...	...	0857	|	|	...	...	...
Frankfurt (Main) Süd a.	|	...	...	...	0654	|	...	...	...
Basel SBB a.	|	...	...	...	1037	|	...	...	...
Dortmund Hbf a.	|	...	...	...	...	0450	...	...	...
Köln Hbf a.	|	...	...	...	...	0614	0745	...	...
Amsterdam Centraal d.	|	...	...	...	...	1029	|	...	...
Aachen 🏛 a.	|	...	...	...	...	...	0820	...	...
Liège Guillemins a.	|	...	...	...	...	...	0915	...	...
Brussels Midi / Zuid a.	|	...	...	...	...	...	1001	1129	...
Paris Nord a.	0938h	1113	...	...	...	...	1135	|	...
Lille Europe **12** a.	...	|	...	...	...	...	...	1202	...
Ebbsfleet International a.	...	|	...	...	...	...	...	|	...
London St Pancras a.	...	1229	...	...	...	...	...	1226	...

A – JAN KIEPURA – 🛏 1, 2 cl. Amsterdam (**447**) - Köln - Warszawa (**11013**) - Brest (**12**) - Moskva (journey 2 nights). 🛏 1, 2 cl., ▬ 2 cl. and [2] Amsterdam - Warszawa. ✕ Rzepin - Warszawa and Brest - Moskva.

B – JAN KIEPURA – 🛏 1, 2 cl. Moskva (**11**) - Brest (**11014**) - Warszawa (**446**) - Köln - Amsterdam (journey 2 nights). 🛏 1, 2 cl., ▬ 2 cl. and [2] Warszawa - Amsterdam. ✕ Moskva - Brest and Warszawa - Rzepin.

C – JAN KIEPURA – 🛏 1, 2 cl. Basel (**472**) - Frankfurt - Fulda (**457**) - Hannover (**447**) - Warszawa - Moskva (journey 2 nights). 🛏 1, 2 cl. and ▬ 2 cl. Basel - Warszawa. ✕ Basel - Fulda and Rzepin - Warszawa.

D – JAN KIEPURA – 🛏 1, 2 cl. Moskva (**11**) - Warszawa (**446**) - Hannover (**483**) - Fulda (**473**) - Frankfurt - Basel (journey 2 nights). 🛏 1, 2 cl. and ▬ 2 cl. Warszawa - Basel. ✕ Warszawa - Rzepin and Fulda - Basel.

E – 🛏 1, 2 cl. München (**482**) - Nürnberg - Fulda - Hannover (**447**) - Warszawa - Moskva (journey 2 nights). 🛏 1, 2 cl. and ▬ 2 cl. München - Warszawa. ✕ München - Fulda and Rzepin - Warszawa.

F – 🛏 1, 2 cl. Moskva (**11**) - Warszawa (**446**) - Hannover (**483**) - Fulda - Nürnberg - München (journey 2 nights). 🛏 1, 2 cl. and ▬ 2 cl. ✕ Warszawa - Rzepin and Fulda - München.

P – ①⑥ (①④⑥ June 4 - Oct. 19) 🛏 1, 2 cl. Paris (**451**) - Berlin (**443**) - Moskva (journey 2 nights with a 6 hour stay in Berlin).

Q – ④⑥ (②④⑥ June 2 - Oct.17) 🛏 1, 2 cl. Moskva (**442**) - Berlin (**450**) - Paris (journey 2 nights with a 10 hour stay in Berlin).

h – Paris **Est**.

n – Depart 8 minutes later.

§ – 🏛: Osinovka (BY) / Krasnoye (RU).

⇌ – *Thalys* high-speed train. [R] 🍷. Special fares payable. For additional services see Tables **20, 21**.

☆ – Eurostar train. Special fares payable. Minimum check-in time 30 minutes. Not available for London - Ebbsfleet - Ashford or v.v. journeys. Valid June 14 - Aug. 30.

28 AMSTERDAM - FRANKFURT, WIEN and MÜNCHEN

train type		*ICE*	*ICE*		*ICE*	*ICE*	*ICE*	*ALX/R*		*ICE*	*ICE*	*ICE*	*ICE*		*ICE*	*ICE*	*ICE*		*ICE*	*ICE*	*ICE*	*EN*		*ICE*	*ICE*	
train number		**121**	**515**		**105**	**595**	**27**	**357**		**123**	**629**	**519**	**229**		**125**	**723**	**611**		**127**	**727**	**613**	**409 469**		**129**	**615**	
notes	①–⑥	①–⑥	🍷		🍷 Q	🍷	🍴			🍷	🍷 Ⓑ	🍷	🍴		🍷	🍷 Ⓑ	🍷		🍷 T	🍷 Ⓑ	🍷	R		🍷	🍷	
Amsterdam Centraal d.	...	0704	...	...	0804	...	...	...	...	1034	...	...	...	...	1234	...	...	...	1434	...	...	...	...	1634	...	...
Rotterdam Centraal d.	0632	|	...	0732	|	...	...	...	1002	|	...	...	...	1202	|	...	...	1402	|	...	...	...	1602	|	...	...
Utrecht Centraal d.	0711	0729	...	0811	0829	...	...	...	1041	1059	...	...	...	1241	1259	...	...	1441	1459	...	...	...	1641	1659	...	...
Arnhem ◐ d.	...	0808	...	...	0907	...	...	...	...	1137	...	...	...	...	1337	...	...	...	1537	...	...	...	...	1737	...	...
Oberhausen ◐ a.	...	0858	...	...	0958	...	...	...	...	1224	...	...	...	...	1424	...	...	...	1624	...	...	...	...	1824	...	...
Duisburg a.	...	0906	...	...	1006	...	...	...	...	1232	...	...	...	...	1432	...	...	...	1632	...	...	...	...	1832	...	...
Düsseldorf Hbf a.	...	0920	...	...	1020	...	...	...	...	1246	...	...	...	...	1446	...	...	...	1646	...	...	...	...	1846	...	...
Köln Hbf a.	...	0943t	...	...	1045	...	...	...	...	1312	...	...	...	...	1512	...	...	...	1712	...	...	...	...	1912	...	...
Köln Hbf d.	...	0951t	...	...	1054	...	...	...	...	1320	...	...	...	...	1520	...	...	...	1720	...	...	...	...	1920	...	...
Bonn Hbf a.	...	|	...	...	|	...	...	...	...	|	...	...	...	...	|	...	...	...	|	...	...	...	...	|	...	...
Koblenz a.	...	⊖	...	...	⊖	...	...	...	...	⊖	...	...	...	...	⊖	...	...	...	⊖	...	...	...	...	⊖	...	...
Mainz a.	...	|	...	...	|	...	...	...	...	|	...	...	...	...	|	...	...	...	|	...	...	...	...	|	...	...
Frankfurt Flughafen ✈ a.	...	1043	1054	...	1151	...	1201	...	...	1414	...	1454	...	...	1614	...	1654	...	1814	...	1854	...	...	2014	2054	...
Frankfurt (Main) Hbf a.	...	1102	|	...	|	...	1213	...	...	1430	1454	|	1621	...	1630	1654	|	...	1830	1854	|	2000	...	2030	|	...
Würzburg a.	...	...	|	...	|	...	1331	...	...	...	1603	|	1731	...	...	1803	|	...	...	2003	|	|	...	...	|	...
Nürnberg a.	...	...	|	...	|	...	1428	...	...	...	1659	|	1828	...	...	1859	|	...	...	2059	|	|	...	...	|	...
Regensburg a.	...	...	|	...	|	...	1522	1819	...	...	|	|	1922	...	...	|	|	...	...	|	|	|	...	...	|	...
Praha hlavní 58 a.	...	...	|	...	|	...	|	2250	...	...	|	|	|	...	...	|	|	...	...	|	|	|	...	...	|	...
Mannheim a.	...	...	1124	...	1224	1231	|	...	...	...	|	1524	|	...	...	|	1724	...	...	|	1924	2057d	...	...	2124	...
Stuttgart a.	...	...	1208	...	...	1308	|	...	...	...	|	1608	|	...	...	|	1808	...	...	|	2008	|	...	...	2208	...
Ulm a.	...	...	1306	...	...	1406	|	...	...	...	|	1706	|	...	...	|	*1906*	...	...	|	2106	|	...	...	2306	...
Augsburg a.	...	...	1350	...	...	1450	|	...	...	...	|	1750	|	...	...	|	*1950*	...	...	|	2150	|	...	...	2352	...
München Hbf a.	...	...	1430	...	...	1530	|	...	...	...	1804	1830	|	...	...	2004	*2030*	...	...	2204	2232	|	...	...	0034	...
Passau ▦ a.	...	...	...	...	...	...	1626	...	...	...	...	...	2026	...	...	...	...	...	...	...	...	|	...	...	...	...
Linz a.	...	...	...	...	...	...	1743	...	...	...	...	...	2143	...	...	...	...	...	...	...	...	0433	...	...	...	...
Wien Westbahnhof a.	...	...	...	...	...	...	1922	...	...	...	...	...	2322	...	...	...	...	...	...	...	...	0640	...	...	...	...

train type	*CNL*	*CNL*		*ICE*	*CNL*		*CNL*		*CNL*	
train number	**40401**	**421**		**227**	**459**		**457**		**419**	
notes	A	B		🍷	P		Ⓡ K		Ⓡ 🍷 F	
Amsterdam Centraal d.	1701	...	...	1834	...	...	1901	...	2031	...
Rotterdam Centraal d.	*1632*	...	1802	|	...	1832	|	2002	|	...
Utrecht Centraal d.	1729	...	1841	1859	...	1911	1929	2041	2101	...
Arnhem ◐ d.	1808	...	...	1937	...	...	2008	...	2138	...
Oberhausen ◐ a.	1914d	...	...	2024	...	...	2139d	...	2248d	...
Duisburg a.	|	...	...	2032	...	...	2147d	...	2256d	...
Düsseldorf Hbf a.	1935d	1935	...	2046	...	...	2202d	...	2312d	...
Köln Hbf a.	|	|	...	2112	...	...	|	...	|	...
Köln Hbf d.	2006	2006	...	2120	...	...	2228	...	2346	...
Bonn Hbf a.	2034d	2034d	...	|	...	...	|	...	0007d	...
Koblenz a.	2115d	2115d	...	⊖	...	...	|	...	0044d	...
Mainz a.	2212d	2212d	...	|	...	...	|	...	|	...
Frankfurt Flughafen ✈ a.	|	|	...	2218	...	...	|	...	|	...
Frankfurt (Main) Hbf a.	2239	2239	...	2234	0055k	...	|	...	|	...
Würzburg a.	|	|	...	...	|	...	|	...	|	...
Nürnberg a.	0136	0136	...	...	|	...	|	...	|	...
Regensburg a.	0427	0427	...	...	|	...	|	...	|	...
Praha hlavní 58 a.	|	|	...	...	1052	...	0956	...	|	...
Mannheim a.	|	|	...	...	...	...	...	...	|	...
Stuttgart a.	|	|	...	...	...	...	...	...	0419	...
Ulm a.	|	|	...	...	...	...	...	...	0542	...
Augsburg a.	|	|	...	...	...	...	...	...	0633	...
München Hbf a.	|	|	...	...	...	...	...	...	0716	...
Passau ▦ a.	0532	0532	...	...	...	...	...	...	...	...
Linz a.	0646	0646	...	...	...	...	...	...	...	...
Wien Westbahnhof a.	0904	0904	...	...	...	...	...	...	...	...

train type	*CNL*	*ICE*	*ICE*	*ICE*	*ICE*	*ICE*	*RE*	*EN*	*ICE*	*ICE*	*ICE*
train number	**458**	**616**	**226**	**614**	**820**	**128**	**4242**	**460 408**	**612**	**726**	**126**
notes	P	🍷 ✣	🍷	🍷	①–⑤	🍷		R	🍷	①–⑥	🍷 T
Wien Westbahnhof d.	...	...	...	...	...	...	...	2240	...	...	...
Linz d.	...	...	...	...	...	...	...	0038	...	...	...
Passau ▦ d.	...	...	...	...	...	...	0549	|	...	...	...
München Hbf d.	...	0317	...	0523	0551	...	|	|	0723	0755	...
Augsburg d.	...	0357	...	0604	|	...	|	|	0803	|	...
Ulm d.	...	0440	...	0651	|	...	|	|	0851	|	...
Stuttgart d.	...	0551	...	0751	|	...	|	|	0951	|	...
Mannheim d.	...	0635	...	0835	|	...	|	0848a	1035	|	...
Praha hlavní 57 d.	1829	|	...	|	|	...	|	|	|	|	...
Regensburg d.	|	|	...	|	*0541*	...	0720	|	|	|	...
Nürnberg d.	|	|	...	|	0700	...	0825	|	|	0900	...
Würzburg d.	|	|	...	|	0756	...	▬	|	|	0956	...
Frankfurt (Main) Hbf d.	0400k	|	0729	|	0905	0928	...	0957	|	1105	1128
Frankfurt Flughafen ✈ d.	...	0709	0743	0906	▬	0943	...	...	1106	...	1143
Mainz d.	...	|	|	▬	...	|	...	...	...	...	|
Koblenz d.	...	⊖	⊖	...	...	⊖	...	...	...	...	⊖
Bonn Hbf d.	...	|	|	...	...	|	...	...	...	...	|
Köln Hbf a.	...	0805	0840	...	...	1040	...	...	...	...	1240
Köln Hbf d.	...	...	0848	...	...	1048	...	...	...	...	1248
Düsseldorf Hbf d.	...	...	0915	...	...	1113	...	...	...	...	1314
Duisburg d.	...	...	0927	...	...	1126	...	...	...	...	1328
Oberhausen ◐ d.	...	...	0935	①–⑥	...	1135	...	...	...	...	1335
Arnhem ◐ a.	...	...	1023		...	1223	...	...	...	...	1423
Utrecht Centraal a.	...	...	1058	1103	1118	1258	1303	...	...	...	1458
Rotterdam Centraal a.	...	...	|	1142	1157	|	1342	...	...	...	*1542*
Amsterdam Centraal a.	...	...	1125	...	...	1325	...	...	...	...	1525

train type	*IC*	*ICE*	*R/RE*	*ICE*	*ICE*	*EC*	*ICE*	*ICE*	*ICE*	*ICE*	*R/ALX*	*ICE*	*ICE*	*ICE*	*ICE*	*ICE*	*ICE*		*CNL*	*CNL*		*ICE*	*ICE*		*CNL*	*CNL*
train number	**2024**	**610**	**350**	**722**	**124**	**100 102**	**28**	**596**	**626**	**122**	**354**	**26**	**1090 594**	**104**	**514**	**620 926 928**	**120**		**418**	**456**		**616**	**226**		**40420**	**420**
notes	🍷	🍷		🍷	🍷	🍷	🍷	🍷	🍷	🍷		🍷	🍷	🍷 Q	🍷		Ⓑ p		🍷 G	Ⓡ K		🍷 ✣	🍷		C	D
Wien Westbahnhof d.	...	...	...	...	...	...	0840	...	...	...	...	1040	...	...	...	...	...	...	...	...	...	...	...	...	1954	1954
Linz d.	...	...	...	...	...	...	1016	...	...	...	...	1216	...	...	...	...	...	...	...	...	...	...	...	...	2157	2157
Passau ▦ d.	0719	...	...	...	...	...	1130	...	...	...	...	1330	...	...	...	...	...	...	...	...	...	...	...	...	2306	2306
München Hbf d.	|	*0923*	...	0955	...	...	|	1223	1255	...	...	|	1423	...	1523	1555	...	...	2244	...	...	0317	...	...	|	|
Augsburg d.	|	*1003*	...	|	...	...	|	1303	|	...	...	|	1503	...	1603	|	...	...	2320	...	...	0357	...	...	|	|
Ulm d.	|	*1051*	...	|	...	...	|	1351	|	...	...	|	1551	...	1651	|	...	...	0010	...	...	0440	...	...	|	|
Stuttgart d.	|	1151	...	|	...	...	|	1451	|	...	...	|	1651	...	1751	|	...	...	0126	...	...	0551	...	...	|	|
Mannheim d.	|	1235	...	|	...	1439	|	1531	|	...	...	|	1728	1735	1835	|	...	...	|	...	...	0635	...	...	|	|
Praha hlavní 58 d.	|	|	0511	|	...	|	|	|	|	...	0911	|	...	|	|	|	...	...	|	1829	...	|	...	...	|	|
Regensburg d.	0827	|	|	*0919*	...	|	1232	|	|	...	1337	1433	...	|	|	|	...	...	|	|	...	|	...	...	0014	0014
Nürnberg d.	0928	|	1009	1100	...	|	1328	|	1400	...	▬	1527	...	|	|	1700	...	...	|	|	...	|	...	...	0240	0240
Würzburg d.	1025	|	...	1156	...	|	1427	|	1456	...	...	1627	...	|	|	1756	...	...	|	|	...	|	...	...	|	|
Frankfurt (Main) Hbf d.	1144	|	...	1305	1329	|	1536	1608	1605	1629	...	1742	...	|	|	1905	1928	...	|	|	...	|	0729	...	0456a	0456a
Frankfurt Flughafen ✈ d.	1158	1306	...	...	1343	|	...	...	...	1643	...	1755	...	1809	1906	...	1943	...	|	|	...	0709	0743	...	|	|
Mainz d.	1220	...	...	...	|	1520	...	...	...	|	...	...	...	|	▬	...	|	...	|	|	...	|	|	...	0646a	0646a
Koblenz d.	1312	...	...	...	⊖	1612	...	...	...	⊖	...	...	...	⊖	...	...	⊖	...	0445a	|	...	⊖	⊖	...	0744a	0744a
Bonn Hbf d.	1344	...	...	...	|	1644	...	...	...	|	...	...	...	|	...	...	|	...	0521a	|	...	|	|	...	0817a	0817a
Köln Hbf a.	1405	...	...	...	1440	1705	...	...	...	1740	...	...	...	1905	...	...	2040	...	0545a	0614a	...	0805	0840	...	0842	0842
Köln Hbf d.	...	...	...	...	1448	▬	...	...	...	1748	...	...	...	1917	...	...	2048	...	|	|	...	...	0848	...	|	|
Düsseldorf Hbf d.	...	...	...	...	1514	...	...	...	...	1813	...	...	...	1940	...	...	2113	...	0613a	0654a	...	...	0915	...	0909a	0909
Duisburg d.	...	...	...	...	1528	...	...	...	...	1826	...	...	...	1953	...	...	2126	...	0628a	0715a	...	...	0927	...	|	...
Oberhausen ◐ d.	...	...	...	...	1535	...	...	...	...	1835	...	...	...	2000	...	...	2135	...	0637a	0737a	...	...	0935	...	|	...
Arnhem ◐ a.	...	...	...	...	1623	...	...	...	...	1923	...	...	...	2053	...	...	2223	...	0753	0922	...	...	1023	...	1122	...
Utrecht Centraal a.	...	...	...	...	1658	1703	...	...	...	1958	2003	...	...	2128	2133	...	2258	2318	0828	0958	1018	...	1058	1118	1156	...
Rotterdam Centraal a.	...	...	...	...	|	1742	...	...	...	|	2042	...	...	|	2212	...	|	2357	|	|	1057	...	|	1157	|	...
Amsterdam Centraal a.	...	...	...	...	1725	...	...	...	...	2025	...	...	...	2155	...	...	2325	...	0859	1029	...	...	1125	...	1229	...

A – *City Night Line* ERIDANUS – ⑤⑥⑦: 🛏 1, 2 cl., ▬ 2 cl. (4, 6 berth), [2] (reclining) and 🍷: Amsterdam - Köln - Frankfurt - Passau ▦ - Wien. 🍴 Amsterdam - Frankfurt. Ⓡ Special fares apply. For international journeys only.

B – *City Night Line* ERIDANUS – ①②③④: 🛏 1, 2 cl., ▬ 2 cl. (4, 6 berth), [2] (reclining) and 🍷: Dortmund (depart 1826) - Köln - Frankfurt - Passau ▦ - Wien. 🍴 Dortmund - Frankfurt. Ⓡ Special fares apply. For international journeys only.

C – *City Night Line* ERIDANUS – ④⑤⑥: 🛏 1, 2 cl., ▬ 2 cl. (4, 6 berth), [2] (reclining) and 🍷: Wien - Passau ▦ - Frankfurt - Köln - Amsterdam. 🍴 Frankfurt - Amsterdam. Ⓡ Special fares apply. For international journeys only.

D – *City Night Line* ERIDANUS – ①②③⑦: 🛏 1, 2 cl., ▬ 2 cl. (4, 6 berth), [2] (reclining) and 🍷: Wien - Passau ▦ - Frankfurt - Köln - Dortmund (arrive 1006). 🍴 Frankfurt - Dortmund. Ⓡ Special fares apply. For international journeys only.

F – *City Night Line* POLLUX – ①⑤⑥⑦ (daily until Nov. 2): 🛏 1,2 cl., 🛏 1, 2 cl. (T4), ▬ 2 cl. (6 berth), [2] (reclining) and 🍷 Amsterdam - München. Ⓡ Special fares apply.

G – *City Night Line* POLLUX – ④⑤⑥⑦ (daily until Nov. 1): 🛏 1,2 cl., 🛏 1, 2 cl. (T4), ▬ 2 cl. (6 berth), [2] (reclining) and 🍷 München - Amsterdam. Ⓡ Special fares apply.

K – *City Night Line* KOPERNIKUS / PHOENIX – 🛏 1, 2 cl., ▬ 2 cl., [2] (reclining) and 🍷 Amsterdam - Köln - Berlin - Dresden - Praha and v.v. Ⓡ Special fares apply.

P – *City Night Line* CANOPUS – 🛏 1, 2 cl., ▬ 2 cl., [2] (reclining) and 🍷: Zürich - Basel - Frankfurt (Main) **Süd** - Děčín ▦ - Praha and v.v. 🍴 Basel - Frankfurt and v.v. Ⓡ Special fares apply.

Q – [12] and 🍷 Amsterdam - Köln - Mannheim - Basel and v.v.

R – DANUBIUS – 🛏 1, 2 cl., ▬ 2 cl., [2] and 🍴 Frankfurt - Salzburg ▦ - Wien - Budapest and v.v.

T – Apr. 3 - Oct. 25.

a – Arrival time.

d – Departure time.

k – Frankfurt (Main) **Süd**.

t – Köln **Messe / Deutz**.

◐ – ▦ between Arnhem and Oberhausen is Emmerich.

⊖ – Via Köln - Frankfurt high speed line.

✣ – Subject to alteration on certain dates.

For explanation of standard symbols see page 4

PARIS - FRANKFURT - BERLIN, LEIPZIG, DRESDEN and PRAHA 30

Alternative services Paris - Frankfurt are available via Brussels (Table **21**). Alternative services Paris - Berlin are available via Brussels (Table **20**).

train type	*ICE*	*ICE*	*ICE*	*EC*	*ICE*	*TGV*	*TGV*	*ICE*	*ICE*	*EC*	*ICE*	*ICE*	*ICE*	*ICE*	*ICE*	*ICE*	*ICE*	*ICE*		*ICE*	*CNL*		*CNL*	
train number	**9551**	**278**	**1559**	**379**	**623**	**9553**	**9553**	**276**	**1651**	**179**	**627**	**9555**	**370**	**1655**	**725**	**9557**	**1659**	**1029**		**9559**	**459**		**451**	
notes	♣	🍷	🍷	🍴	🍷	♣	♣	🍷	🍷	🍴	🍷	♣	🍷		🍷	♣	Ⓑ **k**	🍷		♣			[R]	
notes	①–⑥	**L**		**K**		⑦	①–⑥	**L**		**D**			**L**	Ⓑ 🍷		Ⓑ	🍷				**B**		**A**	
Paris Est d.	0658	...	...	...	...	0901	0909	...	...	...	...	1309	...	...	...	1709	...	...	...	1905	...	...	2020¶	...
Metz d.	│	...	...	...	...	│	│	...	...	...	...	│	...	...	...	│	...	...	...	│	...	...	2353x	...
Forbach 🏛 d.	0849	...	...	...	...	1049	│	...	...	...	...	│	...	...	...	│	...	...	...	2049	...	...	│	...
Saarbrücken a.	0857	...	...	...	...	1057	1057	...	...	...	...	1457	...	...	...	1857	...	...	...	2057	...	...	0059u	...
Kaiserlautern a.	0936	...	...	...	...	1136	1136	...	...	...	...	1536	...	...	...	1936	...	...	...	2136	...	...	│	...
Karlsruhe Hbf a.	│	...	...	...	...	│	│	...	...	...	...	│	...	...	...	│	...	...	...	│	...	...	│	...
Mannheim a.	1016	...	...	...	...	1216	1216	...	...	...	...	1616	...	...	...	2016	...	...	...	2216	...	...	│	...
Frankfurt (Main) Hbf a.	1058	...	...	...	...	1258	1258	...	...	...	...	1658	...	...	...	2058	...	...	...	2258	...	...	│	...
Frankfurt (Main) Hbf d.	...	1113	1119	...	1154	...	...	1313	1319	...	1354	...	1713	1720	1754	...	2119	2218	...	...	0055q	...	│	...
Würzburg a.	...	│	│	...	1303	...	...	│	│	...	1503	...	│	│	1903	...	│	2341	...	...	│	...	│	...
Nürnberg a.	...	│	│	...	1359	...	...	│	│	...	1559	...	│	│	1959	...	│	0038	...	...	│	...	│	...
Fulda a.	...	1209	1211	...	...	...	...	1409	1411	...	...	...	1809	1811	...	...	2211	...	...	...	│	...	│	...
Erfurt a.	...	│	1332	...	...	...	...	│	1533	...	...	...	│	1933	...	...	2331	...	...	...	0520	...	│	...
Leipzig Hbf a.	...	│	1441	...	...	...	...	│	1641	...	...	...	│	2041	...	...	0044r	...	...	...	0641	...	│	...
Dresden Hbf a.	...	│	1602	1710	...	...	...	│	1802	1910	...	...	│	...	...	...	...	...	...	...	0807	...	│	...
Děčín (🏛 = Schöna) a.	...	│	...	1753	...	...	...	│	...	1953	...	...	│	...	...	...	...	...	...	...	0912	...	│	...
Praha Holešovice a.	...	│	...	1918	...	...	...	│	...	2118	...	...	│	...	...	...	...	...	...	...	1040	...	│	...
Praha hlavní a.	...	│	...	...	...	...	...	│	...	...	...	...	│	...	...	...	...	...	...	...	1052	...	│	...
Kassel Wilhelmshöhe a.	...	1242	...	...	...	...	...	1442	...	...	...	...	1842	...	...	...	...	...	...	...	...	...	│	...
Gottingen a.	...	1301	...	...	...	...	...	1501	...	...	...	...	1901	...	...	...	...	...	...	...	...	...	0611	...
Hannover Hbf a.	...	│	...	...	...	...	...	│	...	...	...	...	│	...	...	...	...	...	...	...	...	...	0702	...
Braunschweig a.	...	1358	...	...	...	...	...	1558	...	...	...	...	1958	...	...	...	...	...	...	...	...	...	│	...
Wolfsburg a.	...	1416	...	...	...	...	...	1616	...	...	...	...	2016	...	...	...	...	...	...	...	...	...	│	...
Berlin Hauptbahnhof a.	...	1525	...	...	...	...	...	1725	...	...	...	...	2128	...	...	...	...	...	...	...	...	...	0902	...
Berlin Ostbahnhof a.	...	1537	...	...	...	...	...	1737	...	...	...	...	2138	...	...	...	...	...	...	...	...	...	...	...

train type	*CNL*	*ICE*	*ICE*	*ICE*	*ICE*	*ICE*	*ICE*	*ICE*	*ICE*	*ICE*	*ICE*	*ICE*	*ICE*	*EC*	*ICE*	*TGV*	*ICE*	*EC*	*ICE*	*ICE*	*ICE*		*CNL*	
train number	**458**	**9558**	**822**	**1656**	**373**	**9556**	**9556**	**724**	**1652**	**871**	**9554**	**626**	**279**	**176**	**1558**	**9552**	**622**	**378**	**1556**	**873**	**9550**		**450**	
notes		♣	🍷		🍷	♣	♣	🍷	🍷	🍷	♣	🍷	🍷	🍴	🍷	♣	🍷	🍴	🍷	🍷	♣		[R]	
notes	**B**	①–⑥	①–⑥	①–⑥	①–⑤	①–⑥	⑦						**L**	**G**				**E**			Ⓑ		**H**	
Berlin Ostbahnhof d.	...	...	...	...	0421	...	...	...	...	0821	...	...	1221	...	...	...	...	...	...	1421	...	...	...	...
Berlin Hauptbahnhof d.	...	...	...	...	0432	...	...	...	...	0832	...	...	1232	...	...	...	...	...	...	1432	...	...	1958c	...
Wolfsburg d.	...	...	...	...	0540	...	...	...	...	0940	...	...	1340	...	...	...	...	...	...	1540	...	...	│	...
Braunschweig d.	...	...	...	...	0558	...	...	...	...	0958	...	...	1358	...	...	...	...	...	...	1558	...	...	│	...
Hannover Hbf d.	...	...	...	...	│	...	...	...	...	│	...	...	│	...	...	...	...	...	...	│	...	...	2218	...
Gottingen d.	...	...	...	...	0650	...	...	...	...	1050	...	...	1450	...	...	...	...	...	...	1650	...	...	2331	...
Kassel Wilhelmshöhe d.	...	...	...	...	0710	...	...	...	...	1110	...	...	1510	...	...	...	...	...	...	1710	...	...	│	...
Praha hlavní d.	1829	...	...	...	│	...	...	...	...	│	...	...	│	...	...	...	...	...	..	│	...	...	│	...
Praha Holešovice d.	1840	...	...	...	│	...	...	...	...	│	...	...	│	0840	...	...	...	1040	...	│	...	...	│	...
Děčín (🏛 = Schöna) d.	2002	...	...	...	│	...	...	...	...	│	...	...	│	1002	...	...	...	1202	...	│	...	...	│	...
Dresden Hbf d.	2103	...	...	...	│	...	...	...	0754	│	...	...	│	1046	1154	...	...	1246	1354	│	...	...	│	...
Leipzig Hbf d.	2253	...	...	0501	│	...	...	...	0915	│	...	...	│	...	1315	...	...	...	1515	│	...	...	│	...
Erfurt d.	0117	...	...	0618	│	...	...	...	1022	│	...	...	│	...	1422	...	...	...	1622	│	...	...	│	...
Fulda d.	│	...	...	0744	0748	...	...	...	1144	1148	...	...	1548	...	1544	...	...	...	1744	1748	...	...	│	...
Nürnberg d.	│	...	0600	│	│	...	...	1000	│	│	...	1400	│	...	│	...	1600	...	│	│	...	...	│	...
Würzburg d.	│	...	0656	│	│	...	...	1056	│	│	...	1456	│	...	│	...	1656	...	│	│	...	...	│	...
Frankfurt (Main) Hbf a.	0359**q**	...	0805	0836	0844	...	...	1205	1236	1244	...	1605	1644	...	1636	...	1805	...	1836	1844	...	...	│	...
Frankfurt (Main) Hbf d.	...	0600	...	...	...	0901	0901	...	...	...	1301	...	...	...	...	1658	...	...	...	...	1901	...	│	...
Mannheim d.	...	0640	...	...	...	0941	0941	...	...	...	1341	...	...	...	...	1741	...	...	...	...	1941	...	│	...
Karlsruhe Hbf d.	...	│	...	...	...	│	│	...	...	...	│	...	...	...	...	│	...	...	...	...	│	...	│	...
Kaiserlautern d.	...	0722	...	...	...	1022	1022	...	...	...	1422	...	...	...	...	1822	...	...	...	...	2022	...	│	...
Saarbrücken d.	...	0800	...	...	...	1101	1101	...	...	...	1501	...	...	...	...	1901	...	...	...	...	2101	...	0520**s**	...
Forbach 🏛 a.	...	0808	...	...	...	│	1109	...	...	...	│	...	...	...	...	1909	...	...	...	...	│	...	│	...
Metz a.	...	│	...	...	...	│	│	...	...	...	│	...	...	...	...	│	...	...	...	...	│	...	0615**s**	...
Paris Est a.	...	0950	...	...	...	1249	1253	...	...	...	1650	...	...	...	...	2053**t**	...	...	...	...	2253	...	0930**e**	...

A – *City Night Line* PERSEUS ①⑤⑥⑦ (daily until Nov. 2): 🛏 1, 2 cl., couchette 2 cl. (including ladies only berths), [2] (reclining) and 🍴 Paris - Forbach 🏛 - Hannover - Berlin Spandau (arrive 0850) - Berlin Hbf - Berlin Südkreuz (0911). [R] Special fares apply. (Table **20**).

B – *City Night Line* CANOPUS – 🛏 1,2 cl., couchette 2 cl., [2] (reclining) and 🍷 Zürich - Basel - Frankfurt (Main) **Süd** - Děčín 🏛 - Praha and v.v. [R] Special fares apply.

D – ALOIS NEGRELLI – [12] and 🍴 Berlin - Dresden - Praha - Brno.

E – CARL MARIA VON WEBER – [12] and 🍴 Wien - Praha - Dresden - Berlin - Stralsund. To Ostseebad Binz on dates in Table **60**.

F – JAN JESENIUS – [12] and 🍴 Hamburg - Berlin - Dresden - Praha - Budapest.

G – ALOIS NEGRELLI – [12] and 🍴 Brno - Praha - Dresden - Berlin - Hamburg.

H – *City Night Line* PERSEUS ④⑤⑥⑦ (daily until Nov. 1): 🛏 1, 2 cl., couchette 2 cl. (including ladies only berths), [2] (reclining) and 🍴 Berlin Südkreuz (depart 1949; 1919 on ⑦) - Berlin Hbf - Berlin Spandau (2008; 1945 on ⑦) - Hannover - Forbach 🏛 - Paris. [R] Special fares apply. (Table **20**).

J – VINDOBONA – [12] and 🍴 Wien - Praha - Dresden - Berlin - Hamburg.

K – CARL MARIA VON WEBER – [12] and 🍴 Strlsund - Berlin - Dresden - Praha - Brno. From Ostseebad Binz on dates in Table **60**.

L – [12] and 🍷 Interlaken Ost - Basel - Mannheim - Berlin and v.v.

c – 1936 on ⑦.

e – Arrive 1051 on Oct. 25, Nov. 8, 15.

q – Frankfurt (Main) **Süd**.

r – ①⑥.

s – Stops to set down only.

t – 2057 on ⑥.

u – Stops to pick up only.

x – Stops to pick up only. Also departs 2247, 2301, 0003 on certain dates.

♣ – [R] (Paris - Saarbrücken and v.v.); supplement payable, 🍷.

¶ – 1947 on Sept. 28, 29, 30, Oct. 1, 2, 24, Nov. 6, 7, 9, 13, 14.

32 LONDON - PARIS - MÜNCHEN - WIEN - BUDAPEST - BUCUREŞTI

Alternative services London - München and London - Wien - Budapest are available via Brussels (Table **21**)

train type	EC	RJ	RJ	D		TGV	ICE	EC	RJ		☆	TGV	ICE	EC		☆	☆	TGV		☆	☆	TGV	ICE	EN	
train number	**361**	**65**	**67**	**347**		**9571**	**1091**	**115**	**69**		**9004**	**9573**	**597**	**117**		**9018**	**9020**	**9575**		**9024**	**9026**	**9577**	**693**	**463**	
train number/notes	✕	🍷	✕	✕			**593**	🍷	✕		①–⑥		🍷	🍷			⑥⑦				⑦	⑧	🍷		
notes				**M**			🍷										**U**							**J**	
London St Pancras 10 d.	...	...	...	...	...	...	...	...	...	...	0655	...	...	...	...	1025	1101	...	...	1229	1300	...	...	...	...
Paris Nord 10 a.	...	...	...	...	...	...	...	...	...	...	1017	...	...	...	...	1347	1417	...	...	1556	1617	...	...	...	...
Paris Est d.	...	...	...	...	...	0724	...	...	...	...	...	1124	...	...	...	...	...	1524	...	...	...	1724	...	...	...
Strasbourg d.	0653	...	...	...	...	0945	...	...	...	...	...	1345	...	...	...	...	...	1745	...	...	...	1946	...	...	...
Kehl 🛃 d.	0705	...	...	...	...	|	...	...	...	...	...	|	...	...	...	...	...	|	...	...	...	|	...	...	...
Baden Baden d.	0732	...	...	...	...	|	...	...	...	...	...	|	...	...	...	...	...	|	...	...	...	|	...	...	...
Karlsruhe Hbf d.	0806	...	...	...	...	1028	...	...	...	...	...	1428	...	...	...	...	...	1828	...	...	...	2030	...	...	...
Stuttgart Hbf d.	0853	...	...	...	...	1103	1112	1158	...	...	...	1503	1512	1558	...	...	...	1919	...	...	...	2105	2112	...	...
Ulm Hbf d.	0955	...	...	...	...	...	1208	1255	...	...	...	...	1608	1655	...	...	...	2017	...	...	...	...	2208	...	...
Augsburg Hbf d.	1038	...	...	...	...	...	1252	1341	...	...	...	...	1652	1741	...	...	...	2102	...	...	...	...	2252	...	...
München Pasing a.	1107s	...	...	...	...	...	1320s	|	...	...	...	...	1720s	|	...	...	...	|	...	...	...	...	2320s	...	...
München Hbf a.	1116	...	...	...	...	...	1330	1416	...	...	...	...	1730	1815	...	...	...	2138	...	...	...	...	2330	...	...
München Hbf d.	...	1126	1326	...	...	...	...	1421	1526	...	...	...	...	1820	...	...	...	...	...	...	...	...	...	2340	...
Salzburg Hbf 🛃 a.	...	1254	1454	...	...	...	...	1604	1654	...	...	...	...	2004	...	...	...	...	...	...	...	...	...	0117	...
Linz Hbf a.	...	1404	1604	...	...	...	...	...	1804	...	...	...	...	...	...	...	...	...	...	...	...	...	...	0340	...
St Pölten Hbf a.	...	1457	1657	...	...	...	...	...	1857	...	...	...	...	...	...	...	...	...	...	...	...	...	...	0458	...
Wien Westbahnhof a.	...	1540	1740	...	...	...	...	...	1940	...	...	...	...	...	...	...	...	...	...	...	...	...	...	0545h	...
Wien Westbahnhof d.	...	...	1750	1850	...	...	...	...	...	...	...	...	...	...	...	...	...	...	...	...	...	...	...	0600q	...
Hegyeshalom 🛃 a.	...	...	1854	1951	...	...	...	...	...	...	...	...	...	...	...	...	...	...	...	...	...	...	...	0653	...
Györ a.	...	...	1919	2027	...	...	...	...	...	...	...	...	...	...	...	...	...	...	...	...	...	...	...	0722	...
Budapest Keleti a.	...	...	2049	2219	...	...	...	...	...	...	...	...	...	...	...	...	...	...	...	...	...	...	...	0854	...
Bucureşti Nord a.	...	...	...	1359	...	...	...	...	...	...	...	...	...	...	...	...	...	...	...	...	...	...	...	2355	...

train type	☆	TGV	EN	EN	EN	☆	CNL	RJ	EN
train number	**9028**	**9217**	**469**	**409**	**409**	**9036**	**40451**	**63**	**371**
train number/notes	①–⑥		🍷	**469**	**469**		Ⓡ	✕	✕
notes			**A**	**B**	**461**		**G**		**R**
					C				
London St Pancras 10 d.	1332	...	...	...	...	1529	...	...	...
Paris Nord 10 a.	1647	...	...	...	...	1856	...	...	...
Paris Est d.	...	1754	...	...	...		2020¶	...	...
Strasbourg d.	...	2011	2037	...	...	...	|	...	...
Kehl 🛃 d.	...	...	2050	...	...	...	|	...	...
Baden Baden d.	...	...	2118	...	...	...	|	...	...
Karlsruhe Hbf d.	...	...	2156	2156	2156	...	|	...	...
Stuttgart Hbf d.	...	...	2307	2307	2307	...	0419	...	...
Ulm Hbf d.	...	...	0011	0011	0011	...	0542	...	...
Augsburg Hbf d.	...	...	|	|	|	...	0633	...	...
München Pasing a.	...	...	|	|	|	...	|	...	...
München Hbf a.	...	...	|	|	|	...	0716	...	...
München Hbf d.	...	...	|	|	|	...	...	0927	...
Salzburg Hbf 🛃 a.	...	...	0313	0313	0313	...	...	1054	...
Linz Hbf a.	...	...	0433	0433	0433	...	...	1204	...
St Pölten Hbf a.	...	...	0545	0545	0545	...	...	1257	...
Wien Westbahnhof a.	...	...	0640	0640	0640	...	...	1340	...
Wien Westbahnhof d.	...	...	...	...	0705	**355**	...	1350	...
Hegyeshalom 🛃 a.	...	...	...	...	0817	**1822**	...	1454	...
Györ a.	...	...	...	...	0846	**T**	...	1519	...
Budapest Keleti a.	...	...	...	...	1019	1313	...	1649	1913
Bucureşti Nord a.	...	...	...	...	...	0619	...	...	1028

train type	TGV	☆	EN	TGV	☆	☆	EC	ICE	TGV	☆	☆
train number	**9578**	**9027**	**462**	**9576**	**9035**	**9037**	**390**	**598**	**9574**	**9049**	**9051**
train number/notes	①–⑥				⑤⑥⑦		🍷	🍷		⑤⑦	
notes			**K**			**W**					
Bucureşti Nord d.	...	...	0550	...	...	...	...	...	...	...	...
Budapest Keleti d.	...	...	2105	...	...	...	...	...	...	...	...
Györ d.	...	...	2232	...	...	...	...	...	...	...	...
Hegyeshalom 🛃 d.	...	...	2301	...	...	...	...	...	...	...	...
Wien Westbahnhof a.	...	...	2353q	...	...	...	...	...	...	...	...
Wien Westbahnhof d.	...	...	0009h	...	...	...	...	...	...	...	...
St Pölten Hbf d.	...	...	0052	...	...	...	...	...	...	...	...
Linz Hbf d.	...	...	0201	...	...	...	0626c	...	...	...	...
Salzburg Hbf 🛃 d.	...	...	0428	...	...	...	0753c	...	...	...	...
München Hbf a.	...	...	0615	...	...	...	0935c	...	...	...	...
München Hbf d.	...	...	...	0621	...	...	0940	1023	...	...	...
München Pasing d.	...	...	...	|	...	...	|	1031u	...	...	...
Augsburg Hbf d.	...	...	...	0658	...	...	1017	1103	...	...	...
Ulm Hbf d.	...	...	...	0743	...	...	1105	1151	...	...	...
Stuttgart Hbf d.	0655	...	...	0855	...	...	1200	1247	1255	...	...
Karlsruhe Hbf d.	0732	...	...	0932	...	...		...	1332	...	...
Baden Baden d.	|	...	...	|	...	...	...	...	|	...	...
Kehl 🛃 d.	|	...	...	|	...	...	☆	...	|	...	...
Strasbourg a.	0813	...	...	1013	...	...	**9039**	...	1413z	...	...
Paris Est a.	1034	...	...	1234	...	...	①–⑤	...	1634z	...	...
Paris Nord 10 d.	...	1213	...	...	1413	1443	1513	...	...	1743	1813
London St Pancras 10 a.	...	1328	...	...	1529	1559	1636	...	...	1859	1934

train type	RJ	EC	ICE	TGV		D	RJ	EC	ICE	TGV	EC		EN	RJ	CNL	☆			EN	EN	EN	TGV	☆		
train number	**262**	**114**	**1090**	**9572**		**346**	**60**	**112**	**592**	**9570**	**360**		**370**	**66**	**40418**	**9023**		**1821**	**460**	**468**	**468**	**9210**	**9031**		
train number/notes	✕	🍷	**594**	⑥⑦		✕	✕	🍷	🍷	①–⑤	✕		✕	✕	Ⓡ			**354**	**468**	**408**	🍷	**9212**			
notes			🍷			**M**							**R**		**H**			**T**	**408**	**D**	**A**				
																			E						
Bucureşti Nord d.	...	...	...	...	...	1645	...	...	...	...	...	...	1950	...	...	...	...	2345	...	...	...	...	...	...	...
Budapest Keleti d.	...	...	...	...	...	0555	0710	...	...	...	...	...	0847	1310	...	...	...	1447	1905	...	...	...	...	...	...
Györ d.	...	...	...	...	...	0725	0837	...	...	...	...	...	...	1437	...	...	...	...	2033	...	...	...	...	...	...
Hegyeshalom 🛃 d.	...	...	...	...	...	0755	0906	...	...	...	...	...	...	1506	...	...	...	...	2106	...	...	...	...	...	...
Wien Westbahnhof a.	...	...	...	...	...	0859	1008	...	...	...	...	...	...	1608	...	...	...	...	2211	...	...	...	...	...	...
Wien Westbahnhof d.	0820	...	...	...	...	...	1020	...	...	...	...	...	...	1620	...	...	...	...	2240	2240	2240	...	...	...	...
St Pölten Hbf d.	0902	...	...	...	...	...	1102	...	...	...	...	...	...	|	...	...	...	...	2325	2325	2325	...	...	...	...
Linz Hbf d.	0953	...	...	...	...	...	1153	...	...	...	...	...	...	1753	...	...	...	...	0038	0038	0038	...	...	...	...
Salzburg Hbf 🛃 d.	1103	1152	...	...	...	...	1303	1352	...	...	...	...	...	1903	...	...	...	...	0210	0210	0210	...	...	...	...
München Hbf a.	1231	1335	...	...	...	...	1431	1535	...	...	...	...	...	2034	...	...	...	...	|	|	|	...	...	...	...
München Hbf d.	...	1340	1423	...	...	...	...	1541	1623	...	1643	...	...	...	2244	...	...	...	|	|	|	...	...	...	...
München Pasing d.	...	|	1431u	...	...	...	...	|	1631u	...	1651u	...	...	...	|	...	...	...	|	|	|	...	...	...	...
Augsburg Hbf d.	...	1417	1503	...	...	...	...	1617	1703	...	1722	...	...	...	2320u	...	...	...	|	|	|	...	...	...	...
Ulm Hbf d.	...	1505	1551	...	...	...	...	1705	1751	...	1805	...	...	...	0010u	...	...	...	0519	0519	0519	...	...	...	...
Stuttgart Hbf d.	...	1559	1647	1655	...	...	...	1800	1847	1855	1911	...	...	...	0126u	...	...	...	0643	0643	0643	...	...	...	...
Karlsruhe Hbf d.	...	...	...	1732	...	...	...	...	...	1932	2006	...	...	...	|	...	...	...	0754	0754	0754	...	...	...	...
Baden Baden d.	...	...	...	|	...	...	...	...	...	|	2024	...	...	...	|	...	...	...	...	...	0819	...	...	...	...
Kehl 🛃 d.	...	...	...	|	...	...	...	...	...	|	2051	...	...	...	|	...	...	...	...	...	0846	...	...	...	...
Strasbourg a.	...	...	...	1815	...	...	...	...	...	2015	2101	...	...	...	|	...	...	...	...	...	0859	0915	...	...	...
Paris Est a.	...	...	...	2037	...	...	...	...	...	2237	...	...	...	...	0930e	...	...	...	...	...	...	1134	...	...	...
Paris Nord 10 d.	...	...	...	...	...	...	...	...	...	...	...	...	...	...	...	1113	...	...	...	...	...	...	1301	...	...
London St Pancras 10 a.	...	...	...	...	...	...	...	...	...	...	...	...	...	...	...	1229	...	...	...	...	...	...	1434	...	...

A – ORIENT EXPRESS – 🛏 1,2 cl., ▬ 2 cl. and (2) Strasbourg - Wien and v.v.
B – DANUBIUS – 🛏 1, 2 cl., ▬ 2 cl. and (2) Frankfurt (**409**) - Karlruhe (**469**) - Salzburg 🛃 - Wien.
C – DANUBIUS – 🛏 1, 2 cl., ▬ 2 cl., (2) and ✕ Frankfurt (**409**) - Karlruhe (**469**) - Salzburg 🛃 - Wien (**461**) - Budapest.
D – DANUBIUS – 🛏 1, 2 cl., ▬ 2 cl. and (2) Wien (**468**) - Salzburg 🛃 - Karlruhe (**408**) - Frankfurt.
E – DANUBIUS – 🛏 1, 2 cl., ▬ 2 cl., (2) and ✕ Budapest (**460**) - Wien (**468**) - Salzburg 🛃 - Karlruhe (**408**) - Frankfurt.
G – *City Night Line* CASSIOPEIA ①⑤⑥⑦ (daily until Nov. 2) – 🛏 1, 2 cl., ▬ 2 cl. (including ladies only compartment), (2) and ✕ Paris - Metz (depart 2353) - Forbach 🛃 - Saarbrücken (0059) - München. Ⓡ Special fares apply.
H – *City Night Line* CASSIOPEIA ④⑤⑥⑦ (daily until Nov. 1) – 🛏 1, 2 cl., ▬ 2 cl. (including ladies only compartment), (2) and ✕ München - Saarbrücken (arrive 0459) - Forbach 🛃 - Metz (0615) - Paris. Ⓡ Special fares apply.
J – KÁLMÁN IMRE – 🛏 1,2 cl., ▬ 2 cl. and (2) München - Wien - Budapest. 🛏 1, 2 cl. and ▬ 1, 2 cl. München - Wien - Budapest (**375**) - Bucureşti. (12) and ✕ Budapest - Bucureşti.
K – KÁLMÁN IMRE – 🛏 1,2 cl., ▬ 2 cl. and (2) Budapest - Wien - München. 🛏 1, 2 cl. and ▬ 1, 2 cl. Bucureşti (**374**) - Budapest (**462**) - Wien - München. (12) and ✕ Bucureşti - Budapest.
M – DACIA – 🛏 1, 2 cl., ▬ 2 cl., (2) and ✕ Wien - Budapest - Bucureşti and v.v. (1) Wien - Budapest - Lökösháza and v.v.
R – *EuroNight* ISTER – 🛏 1, 2 cl., ▬ 1, 2 cl., (2) and ✕ Budapest - Bucureşti and v.v. 🛏 1, 2 cl. Budapest - Bucureşti - Sofiya - Thessaloníki and v.v.
T – 🛏 1, 2 cl. and (2) Venezia - Budapest - Bucureşti and v.v.
U – ⑥⑦ (daily July 5 - Aug. 30).
W – ①–⑥ July 5 - Aug. 30.

c – ①–⑥.
e – Arrive 1051 on Oct. 25, Nov. 8, 15.
h – Wien **Hütteldorf**.
q – Wien **Meidling**.
s – Calls to set down only.
u – Stops to pick up only.
z – On ⑤⑥⑦ arrive Strasbourg 1415, Paris 1637.

☆ – Eurostar train. Ⓡ, ✕. Special fares payable. Minimum check-in time 30 minutes. Valid June 14 - Aug. 30. Additional Eurostar services are available, see Table **10**.
¶ – 1947 on ①–⑤ Sept. 28 - Oct. 30, also Oct. 24, Nov. 2, 6, 7, 9, 13, 14.
TGV – Ⓡ, supplement payable, 🍷.
RJ – ÖBB *Railjet* service. (1) (premium class), (1) (first class), (2) (economy class) and ✕.

LONDON, PARIS and BRUSSELS - BASEL - ZÜRICH, INTERLAKEN, BRIG and MILANO 40

For Brussels - Köln - Basel - Milano services see Table **43**.

train type/number	TGV	IC	IC	IR	ICE	IC	TGV	IR	IC	IC	ICN	ICN	ICN	TGV	IR	ICE	ICN	IR	CIS	CIS	EC	IC	IC	ICN	ICN	ICN
train number	**9201**	**967**	**818**	**2169**	**271**	**569**	**9203**	**1571**	**969**	**820**	**620**	**1520**	**675**	**9211**	**1573**	**375**	**1622**	**2173**	**19**	**57**	**91**	**977**	**828**	**628**	**1528**	**683**
notes	♥ h	✕	✕	🍷	🍷	🍷	♥		✕	✕	✕	✕	🍷	**9213**	🍷	🍷	✕		Ⓡ ⊕	Ⓡ ⊕		🍷	🍷	✕	✕	🍷
	①–⑤						⑥							♥					✕	✕	**V**					
London St Pancras d.	...	...	...	...	...	...	...	...	...	...	...	...	...	...	...	...	...	...	...	...	...	...	...	...	...	...
Paris Nord a.	...	...	...	...	...	...	...	...	...	...	...	...	...	...	...	...	...	...	...	...	...	...	...	...	...	...
Paris Est d.	0624	...	...	...	...	...	0654	...	...	...	...	...	...	0824	...	...	...	...	...	...	...	...	...	...	...	...
Brussels Midi / Zuid § d.	│	...	...	...	...	...	│	...	...	...	...	...	...	│	...	...	...	...	...	...	0733	...	...	...	...	...
Namur § d.	│	...	...	...	...	...	│	...	...	...	...	...	...	│	...	...	...	...	...	...	0841	...	...	...	...	...
Luxembourg 🏛 § d.	│	...	...	...	...	...	│	...	...	...	...	...	...	│	...	...	...	...	...	...	1046	...	...	...	...	...
Thionville d.	│	...	...	...	...	...	│	...	...	...	...	...	...	│	...	...	...	...	...	...	1111	...	...	...	...	...
Metz d.	│	...	...	...	...	...	│	...	...	...	...	...	...	│	...	...	...	...	...	...	1132	...	...	...	...	...
Strasbourg d.	0847	...	...	...	...	...	0917	...	...	...	...	...	...	1047	...	...	...	...	...	...	1253	...	...	...	...	...
Mulhouse d.	0937	...	...	...	...	...	1006	...	...	...	...	...	...	1132	...	...	...	...	...	...	1355	...	...	...	...	...
Basel SNCF 🏛 ▷ a.	0956	...	...	...	...	...	1026	...	...	...	...	...	...	1152	...	...	...	...	...	...	1420	...	...	...	...	...
Basel SBB ▷ d.	...	1001	...	1003	1007	1033	━	1047	1101	...	1103	...	1103	1207	...	1201	1203	1203	...	1228	1447	1501	...	1503	...	1503
Zürich HB a.	...	│	...	│	1100	1126	...	1152	│	...	│	...	│	1300	1312	│	│	│	...	│	1552	│	...	│	...	│
Sargans a.	...	│	...	│	...	1232	...	1319	│	...	│	...	│	...	1419	│	│	│	...	│	1719	│	...	│	...	│
Landquart a.	...	│	...	│	...	1241	...	1332	│	...	│	...	│	...	1432	│	│	│	...	│	1732	│	...	│	...	│
Davos Platz a.	...	│	...	│	...	*1355*	...	*1455*	│	...	│	...	│	...	*1555*	│	│	│	...	│	*1855*	│	...	│	...	│
Chur a.	...	│	...	│	...	1252	...	1343	│	...	│	...	│	...	1443	│	│	│	...	│	1743	│	...	│	...	│
St Moritz a.	...	│	...	│	...	*1458*	...	*1558*	│	...	│	...	│	...	*1658*	│	│	│	...	│	*1958*	│	...	│	...	│
Luzern a.	...	│	...	1105	...	...	...	...	│	...	│	...	1205	...	...	│	│	1305	...	│	...	│	...	│	...	1605
Arth Goldau a.	...	│	...	1145	...	...	...	...	│	...	│	...	1245	...	...	│	│	1345	1350	│	...	│	...	│	...	1645
Bellinzona a.	...	│	...	1353	...	...	...	...	│	...	│	...	1423	...	...	│	│	1553	1523	│	...	│	...	│	...	1823
Locarno a.	...	│	...	1413	...	...	...	...	│	...	│	...	*1457*	...	...	│	│	1613	│	│	...	│	...	│	...	*1857*
Lugano a.	...	│	...	...	...	...	...	...	│	...	│	...	1446	...	...	│	│	━	1546	│	...	│	...	│	...	1846
Chiasso 🏛 a.	...	│	...	...	...	...	...	...	│	...	│	...	━	...	...	│	│	...	│	│	...	│	...	│	...	1908
Bern a.	...	1056	1107	...	...	...	...	...	1156	1207	│	...	...	...	...	1256	│	...	│	1327	...	1556	1607	│	...	...
Thun a.	...	1121	1124	...	...	...	...	...	1221	1224	│	...	...	...	...	1321	│	...	│	1352	...	1621	1624	│	...	...
Spiez a.	...	1131	1134	...	...	...	1205	...	1231	1234	│	...	...	...	...	1331	│	*ICN*	│	1402	...	1631	1634	│	...	...
Interlaken West a.	...	1151	│	...	...	...	1224	...	1251	│	│	...	...	...	...	1351	│	**522**	│	│	...	1651	│	│	...	...
Interlaken Ost a.	...	1157	│	...	...	...	1229	...	1257	│	│	...	...	...	...	1357	│	✕	│	│	...	1657	│	│	...	...
Biel/Bienne a.	...	...	│	...	...	...	...	...	...	│	1210	1216	*CIS*	...	...	...	1310	1319	│	│	...	...	│	1610	1616	...
Neuchâtel a.	...	...	│	...	...	...	...	...	...	│	1235	1232	**125**	...	...	...	1332	1335	│	│	...	...	│	1635	1632	...
Lausanne a.	...	...	│	...	...	...	...	...	...	│	│	1315	Ⓡ ¶	...	...	...	1415	│	│	│	...	...	│	│	1715	...
Genève a.	...	...	│	...	...	...	...	...	...	│	1346	...	🍷	...	...	...	...	1446	│	│	...	...	│	1746	...	...
Brig a.	...	...	1211	...	...	...	...	...	...	1311	...	...	1320	...	...	...	...	...	│	1440	...	...	1711	...	...	...
Como San Giovanni a.	...	...	...	...	...	...	...	...	...	...	...	...	◧	...	...	...	...	...	1614	◧	...	...	...	...	...	...
Milano a.	...	...	...	...	...	...	...	...	...	...	...	...	1535	...	...	...	...	...	1650	1640	...	...	...	...	...	...

train type/number	☆	☆	TGV	IC	IC	ICN	IR	CIS	EC	☆	☆	EC*	ICE	ICN	IR	ICN	☆	☆	TGV	IC	IC	IC	IR	IR	☆	EC
train number	**9006**	**9008**	**9215**	**979**	**830**	**1630**	**2181**	**23**	**101**	**9120**	**9116**	**97**	**279**	**1640**	**2191**	**693**	**9026**	**9028**	**9217**	**1093**	**1095**	**993**	**1597**	**2195**	**9132**	**295**
notes	①–⑥	⑦	♥	🍷	✕	✕		Ⓡ ⊕	✕	①–⑤	⑥		✕	✕			⑦	①–⑥	♥		**1097**					⑧
								✕				**A**														**J**
London St Pancras d.	0727	0752	...	...	...	...	...	...	...	0834	0859	...	...	...	...	...	1300	1332	...	...	...	...	...	...	1257	...
Paris Nord a.	1056	1117	...	...	...	...	...	...	...	│	│	...	...	...	...	...	1617	1647	...	...	...	...	...	...	│	...
Paris Est d.	...	...	1224	...	...	...	...	...	...	│	│	...	...	...	...	...	━	━	1754	...	...	...	...	...	│	...
Brussels Midi / Zuid § d.	...	...	│	...	...	...	...	...	...	1129	1203	1309	...	...	...	...	...	...	│	...	...	...	...	...	1603	1727
Namur § d.	...	...	│	...	...	...	...	...	...	━	...	1414	...	...	...	...	...	...	│	...	...	...	...	...	━	1834
Luxembourg 🏛 § d.	...	...	│	...	...	...	...	...	...	...	...	1610	...	...	...	...	...	...	│	...	...	...	...	...	...	2026
Thionville d.	...	...	│	...	...	...	...	...	...	...	...	1632	...	...	...	...	...	...	│	...	...	...	...	...	...	2051
Metz d.	...	...	│	...	...	...	...	...	...	...	...	1653	...	...	...	...	...	...	│	...	...	...	...	...	...	2115
Strasbourg d.	...	...	1447	...	...	...	...	...	...	*IC*	...	1823	...	...	...	...	...	*IC*	2015	...	...	...	...	...	...	2253
Mulhouse d.	...	...	1532	...	...	...	...	...	...	**1081**	...	1924	...	...	...	...	*IR*	**1091**	2057	...	...	...	...	...	*ICN*	2349
Basel SNCF 🏛 ▷ a.	...	...	1551	...	...	...	...	...	...	🍷	...	1948	...	...	...	...	**1593**	**1087**	2115	...	...	...	...	...	**1644**	0013
Basel SBB ▷ d.	...	...	1607	1601	...	1603	1603	...	...	1628	...	2014	2001	2003	2003	...	2047	2028	2133	2128	...	2201	...	2203	2203	━
Zürich HB a.	...	...	1700	│	...	│	│	...	1712	│	...	2124	│	│	│	...	2152	│	2226	│	...	│	2312	│	│	...
Sargans a.	...	...	...	│	...	│	│	...	1819	│	...	...	│	│	│	...	2319	│	...	│	...	│	0024	│	│	...
Landquart a.	...	...	...	│	...	│	│	...	1832	│	...	...	│	│	│	...	2334	│	...	│	...	│	0039	│	│	...
Davos Platz a.	...	...	...	│	...	│	│	...	*1955*	│	...	...	│	│	│	...	│	│	...	│	...	│	│	│	│	...
Chur a.	...	...	...	│	...	│	│	...	1833	│	...	...	│	│	│	...	2345	│	...	│	...	│	0049	│	│	...
St Moritz a.	...	...	...	│	...	│	│	...	*2058*	│	...	...	│	│	│	...	...	│	...	│	...	│	...	│	│	...
Luzern a.	...	...	...	│	...	│	1705	...	...	│	...	...	│	│	2105	...	...	│	...	│	...	│	...	2305	│	...
Arth Goldau a.	...	...	...	│	...	│	1745	1750	...	│	...	...	│	│	2145	2150	...	│	...	│	...	│	...	...	│	...
Bellinzona a.	...	...	...	│	...	│	1953	1923	...	│	...	...	│	│	━	2323	...	│	...	│	...	│	...	...	│	...
Locarno a.	...	...	...	│	...	│	2013	│	...	│	...	...	│	│	...	*2357*	...	│	...	│	...	│	...	...	│	...
Lugano a.	...	...	...	│	...	│	━	1946	...	│	...	...	│	│	...	2346	...	│	...	│	...	│	...	...	│	...
Chiasso 🏛 a.	...	...	...	│	...	│	...	│	...	│	...	...	│	│	...	0010	...	│	...	│	...	│	...	...	│	...
Bern a.	...	...	...	1656	1707	│	...	│	...	1727	...	...	2056	│	...	...	...	2127	...	2227	2235	2256	...	...	│	...
Thun a.	...	...	...	1721	1724	│	...	│	...	1752	...	...	2124	│	...	...	...	2152	...	...	2252	2325	...	...	│	...
Spiez a.	...	...	...	1731	1734	│	*ICN*	│	...	1802	...	...	2134	│	...	...	...	2202	...	...	2302	2335	...	...	│	...
Interlaken West a.	...	...	...	1751	│	│	**530**	│	...	│	...	...	2151	│	...	...	...	│	...	...	│	2353	...	...	│	*ICN*
Interlaken Ost a.	...	...	...	1757	│	│	✕	│	...	│	...	...	2157	│	*ICN*	...	...	│	...	...	│	2359	...	...	│	**1544**
Biel/Bienne a.	...	...	...	...	│	1710	1719	│	...	│	...	...	...	2110	**2540**	...	...	│	...	...	│	...	...	...	2310	2316
Neuchâtel a.	...	...	...	...	│	1732	1735	│	...	│	...	...	...	2132	✕	...	...	│	...	...	│	...	...	...	...	2332
Lausanne a.	...	...	...	...	│	1815	│	│	...	│	...	...	...	2215	2220	...	...	│	...	...	│	...	...	...	...	0015
Genève a.	...	...	...	...	│	...	1846	│	...	│	...	...	...	...	2304	...	...	│	...	...	│	...	...	...	...	...
Brig a.	...	...	...	...	1811	...	...	│	...	1840	...	...	...	...	...	...	...	2240v	...	...	2343	...	...	...	...	...
Como San Giovanni a.	...	...	...	...	...	...	...	2014	...	...	...	...	...	...	...	...	...	...	...	...	...	...	...	...	...	...
Milano a.	...	...	...	...	...	...	...	2050	...	...	...	...	...	...	...	...	...	...	...	...	...	...	...	...	...	...

LONDON - LILLE - STRASBOURG - BASEL

			TGV	TGV			☆	TGV					☆	☆	TGV	EC				
			5400	**9211**			**9110**	**5402**	①–⑥	⑦			**9138**	**9144**	**5416**	**295**				
			D	**9213**			①–⑥							①–④		⑧ **J**				
London St Pancras d.	...	...	...	...	...	...	0659	...	...	...	...	...	1434	1604	...	...	...	...	...	...
Lille Europe d.	...	...	0652	...	...	...	0924	1121c	...	...	...	...	1654	1824	1858	...	...	...	...	...
Strasbourg d.	...	...	1010	1047	...	...	...	1517	1553	1553	...	...	...	...	2217	2253	...	...	...	...
Basel SNCF a.	...	...	...	1150	...	...	...	...	1709	1716	...	...	...	...	...	0013	...	...	...	...

A – IRIS – (12) Brussels - Basel - Zürich.
D – ①–⑥ (not July 14).
J – JEAN MONNET – (12) Brussels - Basel.
V – VAUBAN – (12) Brussels - Basel - Zürich - Chur.

c – 1138 Sept. 20.
h – Not July 14.
v – 2301 on ⑦.

♥ – *TGV Lyria* service. Ⓡ 🍷 special fares payable.
* – *IR* in Switzerland.

⊕ – **ETR 470** *Cisalpino*. Ⓡ and supplement payable for international journeys. Ⓡ and *IC* supplement payable for internal journeys within Italy.
☆ – Eurostar train. Ⓡ ✕ Special fares payable. Minimum check-in time 30 minutes. Valid June 14 - Aug. 30.
▷ – Trains arrive at SNCF (French) platforms and depart from SBB (Swiss) platforms. Minimum connection time 10 minutes. Connections at Basel are not guaranteed.
◧ – 🏛 between Brig and Milano is Domodossola. Ticket point is **Iselle**.
§ – Additional services run Brussels - Namur - Luxembourg. (Table **430**).
¶ – Supplement payable in Italy (except with international tickets). *IC* in Italy.

OTHER TRAIN NAMES: *EC* **125** – CISALPINO LEMANO

40 LONDON, PARIS and BRUSSELS - BASEL - ZÜRICH, INTERLAKEN, BRIG and MILANO

For Milano - Basel - Köln - Brussels services see Table **43**.

train type	*IR*	*EC*	*IC*	*ICN*	*ICN*	*IR*	*TGV*	☆	*ICN*	*IR*	*ICN*	*ICN*	*IC*	*IC*	*IC*	*TGV*	☆	*CIS*	*IC*	*IC*		*ICN*	*ICN*	*ICN*	*EC**	☆
train number	**1556**	**296**	**1058**	**1511**	**611**	**1560**	**9212** **9210**	**9031**	**654**	**2166**	**1517**	**617**	**817**	**1066**	**566**	**9204**	**9043**	**50**	**1070**	**570**		**662**	**523**	**1623**	**90**	**9163**
notes		**B** ⑧		✕	✕		♥		🍷		✕	✕		✕	🍷	♥		Ⓡ ⊕ ✕		🍷	2		✕	✕	**V**	⑧ **U**
Milano d.	...	...	...	...	...	...	...	...	...	...	...	...	...	...	...	...	...	0725	...	...	...	...	...	...	...	...
Como San Giovanni d.	...	...	...	...	...	...	...	...	...	...	...	...	...	...	...	...	...	◧	...	...	...	...	...	...	...	...
Brig d.	...	...	...	...	...	...	...	...	...	...	...	...	0749	...	...	...	...	0920	...	...	...	...	...	...	...	...
Genève d.	...	...	...	...	...	...	...	...	...	...	...	0714	|	...	...	...	...	|	...	...	...	...	1014	...	...	...
Lausanne d.	...	...	...	0539	...	...	...	...	...	...	0745	|	|	...	...	...	...	|	...	...	...	...	|	1045	...	...
Neuchâtel d.	...	...	...	0624	...	...	...	...	...	...	0827	0824	|	...	...	...	...	|	...	...	...	...	1124	1127	...	...
Biel/Bienne d.	...	...	...	0640	0650	...	...	...	...	...	0842	0850	|	...	...	...	...	|	...	...	...	...	1140	1150	...	...
Interlaken Ost d.	...	...	0521	▬	|	...	...	...	...	...	...	|	|	0831	...	...	...	|	1031	...	...	...	...	|	...	...
Interlaken West d.	...	...	0526	...	|	...	...	...	...	...	...	|	|	0836	...	...	...	|	1034	...	...	...	...	|	...	...
Spiez d.	...	...	0550	...	|	...	...	...	...	...	...	|	0825	0854	...	...	...	0954	1054	...	...	...	...	|	...	...
Thun d.	...	...	0601	...	|	...	...	...	...	...	...	|	0837	0905	...	...	...	1005	1105	...	...	...	...	|	...	...
Bern d.	...	...	0634	...	|	...	...	...	...	...	...	|	0854	0934	...	...	...	1034	1134	...	...	...	...	|	...	...
Chiasso 🏛 d.	...	...	|	...	|	...	...	...	0544	...	...	|	...	|	...	...	...	|	|	...	...	0852	...	|	...	...
Lugano d.	...	...	|	...	|	...	...	...	0612	...	...	|	...	|	...	...	...	|	|	...	...	0912	...	|	...	...
Locarno d.	...	...	|	...	|	...	...	...	*0603*	...	...	|	...	|	...	...	...	|	|	...	0903	|	...	|	...	...
Bellinzona d.	...	...	|	*IR*	|	...	...	...	0636	...	...	|	...	|	...	...	...	|	|	...	0927	0936	...	|	...	...
Arth Goldau d.	...	...	|	**2454**	|	...	...	...	0809	0814	...	|	...	|	...	...	...	|	|	...	...	1114	...	|	...	...
Luzern d.	...	...	|	0630	|	...	...	...	...	0855	...	|	...	|	...	...	...	|	|	...	...	1155	...	|	...	...
St Moritz d.	...	...	|	|	|	...	...	...	...	|	...	|	...	|	...	...	...	|	|	*0804*	...	|	...	|	...	...
Chur d.	...	...	|	|	|	0513	...	...	...	|	...	|	...	|	0809	...	...	|	|	1009	...	|	...	|	...	...
Davos Platz d.	...	...	|	|	|	|	...	...	...	|	...	|	...	|	*0702*	...	...	|	|	*0902*	...	|	...	|	...	...
Landquart d.	...	...	|	|	|	0523	...	...	...	|	...	|	...	|	0819	...	...	|	|	1019	...	|	...	|	...	...
Sargans d.	...	...	|	|	|	0539	...	...	...	|	...	|	...	|	0828	...	...	|	|	1028	...	|	...	|	...	...
Zürich HB d.	0508	...	|	|	|	0647	0702	...	...	|	...	|	...	|	0934	...	...	|	|	1134	...	|	...	|	1136	...
Basel SBB ◁ a.	0612	...	0732	0744	0753	...	0757	...	...	0953	...	0953	...	1032	1027	...	...	1132	1232	1227	...	1253	...	1253	1247	...
Basel SNCF 🏛 ◁ d.	...	0646	▬	▬	...	...	0802	...	...	...	...	...	...	...	...	1102	...	...	...	...	...	...	...	...	1304	...
Mulhouse a.	...	0711	...	...	...	...	0825	...	...	...	...	...	...	...	...	1120	...	...	...	...	...	...	...	...	1332	...
Strasbourg a.	...	0803	...	...	...	...	0910	...	...	...	...	...	...	...	...	1210	...	...	...	...	...	...	...	...	1433	...
Metz a.	...	0927	...	...	...	...	|	...	...	...	...	...	...	...	...	|	...	...	...	...	...	...	...	...	1554	...
Thionville a.	...	0950	☆	☆	...	...	|	...	...	...	...	...	...	...	...	|	...	...	...	...	...	...	...	...	1615	...
Luxembourg 🏛 § a.	...	1014	**9139**	**9141**	...	...	|	...	...	...	...	...	...	...	...	|	...	...	...	...	...	...	...	...	1645	...
Namur § a.	...	1218	⑥⑦	①–⑤	...	...	|	...	...	...	...	...	...	...	...	|	...	...	...	...	...	...	...	...	1846	...
Brussels Midi / Zuid § a.	...	1327	1429	1459	...	...	|	...	...	...	...	...	...	...	...	|	...	...	...	...	...	...	...	...	1951	2029
Paris Est a.	...	...	|	|	...	...	1134	...	...	...	...	...	...	...	...	1434	...	...	...	...	...	...	...	...	...	|
Paris Nord d.	...	...	|	|	...	...	...	1301	...	...	...	...	...	...	...	...	1613	...	...	...	...	...	...	...	...	|
London St Pancras a.	...	...	1526	1556	...	...	...	1434	...	...	...	...	...	...	...	...	1734	...	...	...	...	...	...	...	...	2133

train type	*CIS*	*IR*	*IC*	*IC*	*ICN*	*ICN*	*IC*	*TGV*	☆	*CIS*	*CIS*	*ICN*	*IR*	*ICN*	*ICN*	*IC*	*IC*	*EC**	*CIS*	*IR*	*ICN*	*ICN*	*IC*	*IC*	*IC*	*TGV*
train number	**14**	**2174**	**827**	**974**	**1525**	**625**	**574**	**9216**	**9059**	**52**	**16**	**10016**	**2178**	**1529**	**629**	**978**	**576**	**96**	**18**	**2182**	**537**	**1637**	**837**	**986**	**582**	**9218** **9220**
notes	Ⓡ ⊕ ✕			🍷	🍷	✕	🍷	♥		Ⓡ ⊕ ✕	Ⓡ ⊕ ✕	🍷		✕	✕	🍷		**A**	Ⓡ ⊕ ✕		✕	✕		🍷		♥
Milano d.	0910	...	...	...	...	...	...	...	...	1120	1110	...	...	...	...	...	...	...	1310	...	...	...	...	...	...	...
Como San Giovanni d.	0945	...	...	...	...	...	...	...	...	◧	1145	...	...	...	...	...	...	...	1345	...	...	...	...	...	...	...
Brig d.	|	...	1249	...	...	...	...	...	...	1320	|	...	...	...	...	...	...	...	|	...	...	...	1649	...	...	...
Genève d.	|	...	|	...	...	1114	...	...	...	|	|	...	...	...	1314	...	...	...	|	...	1614	...	|	...	...	...
Lausanne d.	|	...	|	...	1145	|	...	...	...	|	|	...	...	1345	|	...	...	...	|	...	|	1645	|	...	...	...
Neuchâtel d.	|	...	|	...	1227	1224	...	...	...	|	|	...	...	1427	1424	...	...	...	|	...	1724	1727	|	...	...	...
Biel/Bienne d.	|	...	|	...	1242	1250	...	...	...	|	|	...	...	1442	1450	...	...	...	|	...	1740	1750	|	...	...	...
Interlaken Ost d.	|	...	|	1301	...	|	...	...	...	|	|	...	...	...	|	1401	...	...	|	...	...	|	|	1701	...	...
Interlaken West d.	|	...	|	1306	...	|	...	...	...	|	|	...	...	...	|	1406	...	...	|	...	...	|	|	1706	...	...
Spiez d.	|	...	1325	1323	...	|	...	...	...	1354	|	...	...	...	|	1423	...	...	|	...	...	|	1725	1723	...	...
Thun d.	|	...	1336	1333	...	|	...	...	...	1404	|	...	...	...	|	1434	...	...	|	...	...	|	1736	1733	...	...
Bern d.	|	...	1354	1404	...	|	...	...	...	1434	|	...	...	...	|	1504	...	...	|	...	...	|	1754	1804	...	...
Chiasso 🏛 d.	|	...	...	|	...	|	...	...	...	|	|	...	...	...	|	|	...	...	|	...	...	|	...	|	...	...
Lugano d.	1012	...	...	|	...	|	...	...	...	|	1210	1212	...	...	|	|	...	...	1412	...	...	|	...	|	...	...
Locarno d.	*1003*	...	...	|	...	|	...	...	...	|	...	|	1146	...	|	|	...	...	|	1346	...	|	...	|	...	...
Bellinzona d.	1036	...	...	|	...	|	...	...	...	|	...	1236	1206	...	|	|	...	...	1436	1406	...	|	...	|	...	...
Arth Goldau d.	1209	1214	...	|	...	|	...	...	...	|	...	1409	1414	...	|	|	...	...	1609	1614	...	|	...	|	...	...
Luzern d.	...	1255	...	|	...	|	...	...	...	|	...	...	1455	...	|	|	...	...	...	1655	...	|	...	|	...	...
St Moritz d.	...	|	...	|	...	|	*1002*	...	...	|	...	...	|	...	|	|	*1104*	...	...	|	...	|	...	|	*1402*	...
Chur d.	...	|	...	|	...	|	1209	...	...	|	...	...	|	...	|	|	1309	...	...	|	...	|	...	|	1609	...
Davos Platz d.	...	|	...	|	...	|	*1102*	...	...	|	...	...	|	...	|	|	*1202*	...	...	|	...	|	...	|	*1502*	...
Landquart d.	...	|	...	|	...	|	1219	...	...	|	...	...	|	...	|	|	1319	...	...	|	...	|	...	|	1619	...
Sargans d.	...	|	...	|	...	|	1228	...	...	|	...	...	|	...	|	|	1328	...	...	|	...	|	...	|	1628	...
Zürich HB d.	...	|	...	|	...	|	1323	1402	...	|	...	...	|	...	|	|	1423	1436	...	|	...	|	...	|	1723	1802
Basel SBB ◁ a.	...	1353	...	1455	...	1353	...	1457	...	1532	...	...	1553	...	1553	1555	...	1547	...	1753	...	1853	...	1855	...	1857
Basel SNCF 🏛 ◁ d.	...	...	...	...	...	...	...	1502	...	...	...	...	...	...	...	...	...	1604	...	...	...	...	...	...	...	1902
Mulhouse a.	...	...	...	...	...	...	...	1526	...	...	...	...	...	...	...	...	...	1632	...	...	...	...	...	...	...	1921
Strasbourg a.	...	...	...	...	...	...	...	1610	...	...	...	...	...	...	...	...	...	1732	...	...	...	...	...	...	...	2010
Metz a.	...	...	...	...	...	...	...	|	...	...	...	...	...	...	...	...	...	1854	...	...	...	...	...	...	...	|
Thionville a.	...	...	...	...	...	...	...	|	...	...	...	...	...	...	...	...	...	1915	...	...	...	...	...	...	...	|
Luxembourg 🏛 § a.	...	...	...	...	...	...	...	|	...	...	...	...	...	...	...	...	...	1936	...	...	...	...	...	...	...	|
Namur § a.	...	...	...	...	...	...	...	|	...	...	...	...	...	...	...	...	...	2139	...	...	...	...	...	...	...	|
Brussels Midi / Zuid § a.	...	...	...	...	...	...	...	|	...	...	...	...	...	...	...	...	...	2245	...	...	...	...	...	...	...	|
Paris Est a.	...	...	...	...	...	...	...	1834	...	...	...	...	...	...	...	...	...	...	...	...	...	...	...	...	...	2237
Paris Nord d.	...	...	...	...	...	...	...	...	2013	...	...	...	...	...	...	...	...	...	...	...	...	...	...	...	...	...
London St Pancras a.	...	...	...	...	...	...	...	...	2129**z**	...	...	...	...	...	...	...	...	...	...	...	...	...	...	...	...	...

BASEL - STRASBOURG - LILLE - LONDON

		TGV	*TGV*	☆					*TGV*	☆	☆	☆					*TGV*			
		5420	**5420**	**9181**			⑦	①–⑥	**5422**	**9145**	**9149**	**9153**			①–⑤	⑥⑦	**5426**			
		D	**E**							①–⑤	⑦						⑧			
Basel SNCF d.	...	...	...	...	...	...	1004	1018	...	...	...	...	...	...	1718	1718	...	...	...	...
Strasbourg d.	...	0611	0620	...	...	...	1134	1135	1206	...	...	...	...	...	1833	1842	1900	...	...	...
Lille Europe d.	...	0946	0946	1205	...	...	...	...	1559	1635	1735	1835	...	...	...	...	2223	...	...	...
London St Pancras a.	...	...	...	1226	...	...	...	...	...	1703	1803	1903	...	...	...	...	...	...	...	...

A – IRIS – (12) Zürich - Basel - Brussels.
B – JEAN MONNET – (12) Basel - Brussels.
D – ①–⑥ (not July 14).
E – ⑦ (also July 14).
U – ⑧ (daily July 5 - Aug. 30).
V – VAUBAN – (12) Zürich - Basel - Brussels.
z – 2141 on ⑥⑦.
♥ – *TGV Lyria* service. Ⓡ 🍷 special fares payable.

* – *IR* in Switzerland.
◧ – 🏛 between Brig and Milano is Domodossola. Ticket point is **Iselle**.
§ – Additional services run Luxembourg - Namur - Brussels. (Table **430**).
¶ – Supplement payable in Italy (except with international tickets).
☆ – Eurostar train. Ⓡ ✕ Special fares payable. Minimum check-in time 30 minutes. Valid June 14 - Aug. 30.
⊕ – **ETR 470** *Cisalpino*. Ⓡ and supplement payable for international journeys. Ⓡ and *IC* supplement payable for internal journeys within Italy.
◁ – Trains arrive at SBB (Swiss) platforms and depart from SNCF (French) platforms. Minimum connection time 10 minutes. Connections at Basel are not guaranteed.

LONDON and PARIS - BERN, LAUSANNE and BRIG — 42

train type	TGV	TGV	IR	IR	TGV	☆	☆	TGV	TGV	IR	☆	TGV	IR	☆	TGV	TGV	IR	IR	TGV	ICE	☆	TGV	IC	☆	TGV	EN
train number	**9261**	**9261**	**1725**	**1427**	**9281**	**9008**	**9010**	**9269**	**9269**	**1737**	**9014**	**9271**	**1739**	**9018**	**9273**	**9273**	**1743**	**1445**	**9285**	**279**	**9024**	**9287**	**989**	**9028**	**9277**	**311**
notes	♥ 🍷	♥ 🍷 B			♥ 🍷 ⑧	[R] 🍴 ⑦	[R] 🍴 ①–⑥	♥ 🍷	**9267** L ♥		[R] 🍴	♥ 🍷 ⑦		[R] 🍴	♥ 🍷	♥ 🍷 C			♥ 🍷 ⑤	🍷	[R] 🍴	♥ 🍷 H		[R] 🍴 ①–⑥	♥ 🍷	
London St Pancras 10 d.	...	...	...	...	...	0752	0832	...	...	...	0926	...	...	1025	...	...	...	...	...	...	1229	...	...	1332	...	...
Paris Nord 10 a.	...	...	...	...	...	1117	1147	...	...	...	1247	...	...	1347	...	...	...	...	...	...	1556	...	...	1647	...	...
Paris Gare de Lyon d.	0758	0758	...	...	0758	▬	...	1258	1258	...	▬	1410	...	▬	1558	1558	...	...	1558	...	...	1658	...	...	1758	...
Dijon d.	0938	0938	...	...	0938	...	...	1440	1440	...	...	1550	...	...	1738	1738	...	...	1738	...	...	1846	...	...	1938	...
Frasne a.	1056	1056	...	...	1056	*ICE*	...	1558	1558	...	...	1704	...	...	1857	1857	...	...	1857	...	...	2008	...	...	2056	...
Pontarlier 🏛 a.	|	|	...	...	1110	**373**	...	|	|	...	...	|	...	...	|	|	...	...	1911	...	...	2021	...	...	|	...
Neuchâtel a.	|	|	...	...	1156	🍷	...	|	|	...	...	|	...	...	|	|	...	...	1956	...	...	2107	...	...	|	...
Bern a.	|	|	...	...	1236	1304	...	|	|	...	...	|	...	...	|	|	...	...	2036	2107	...	2140	2207	...	|	...
Thun a.	|	|	...	...	...	1321	...	|	|	...	...	|	...	...	|	|	...	...	▬	2124	...	...	2224	...	|	...
Spiez a.	|	|	...	...	...	1331	...	|	|	...	...	|	...	...	|	|	...	...	...	2134	...	...	2234	...	|	...
Interlaken West a.	|	|	...	...	...	1351	...	|	|	...	...	|	...	...	|	|	...	...	...	2151	...	...	2251	...	|	...
Interlaken Ost a.	|	|	...	...	...	1357	...	|	|	...	*IR*	|	...	*IR*	|	|	...	...	...	2157	...	...	2257	...	|	...
Vallorbe 🏛 a.	1117	1117	...	...	...	...	...	1616	1616	...	**1439**	1722	...	**1441**	1916	1916	...	...	...	▬	...	...	...	...	2114	...
Lausanne a.	1152	1152	...	...	...	...	...	1652	1652	...		1758	...		1952	1952	...	...	...	...	...	...	...	...	2152	...
Lausanne d.	...	1157	1220	1245	...	...	...	...	1657	1720	1745	...	1820	1850	...	1957	2020	2045	...	...	...	...	...	...	...	2220
Montreux a.	...	1214	1239	1304	...	...	...	...	1714	1739	1804	...	1839	1909	...	2014	2039	2104	...	...	...	...	...	...	...	2239
Aigle a.	...	1226	1250	1315	...	...	...	...	1727	1750	1815	...	1850	1920	...	2025	2050	2115	...	...	...	...	...	...	...	2250
Bex a.	...	|	|	1323	...	...	...	...	...	|	1823	...	|	1927	...	|	2058	2123	...	...	...	...	...	...	...	2258
St Maurice a.	...	|	|	1327	...	...	...	...	...	|	1827	...	|	1931	...	|	2102	2127	...	...	...	...	...	...	...	2302
Martigny a.	...	1246	1307	▬	...	...	...	...	...	1807	▬	...	1907	▬	...	2043	2112	2137	...	...	...	...	...	...	...	2313
Sion a.	...	1302	1322	...	...	...	...	...	...	1822	...	...	1922	...	...	2100	2127	2152	...	...	...	...	...	...	...	2327
Sierre a.	...	1315	1333	...	...	...	...	...	...	1833	...	...	1933	...	...	2113	...	2203	①–⑥	⑦	...	...	...	...	...	2338
Visp a.	...	1336	1352	1357	...	...	...	...	...	1852	1910	...	1952	2010	...	2136	...	2222	2240	2322	...	...	...	...	...	2357
Zermatt a.	...	|	|	1454	...	...	...	...	...	|	2014	...	|	2114	...	|	...	|	2344	0025	...	...	...	...	...	|
Brig a.	...	1345	1402	...	...	...	...	...	...	1902	...	...	2002	...	...	2147	...	2230	...	...	...	...	...	...	...	0005

train type	IR	IR	TGV	☆		EN	TGV	IC	TGV	☆		IR	TGV	TGV	☆	☆		IR	TGV	TGV	IC	TGV		IR	TGV	TGV
train number	**1404**	**1706**	**9260**	**9031**		**316**	**9264**	**956**	**9284**	**9039**		**1720**	**9268**	**9268**	**9053**	**9055**		**1730**	**9272**	**9272**	**982**	**9288**		**1432**	**9274**	**9274**
notes			♥ 🍷	[R] 🍴			♥ 🍷	🍷	♥ 🍷	[R] 🍴			♥ 🍷	♥ 🍷 B	[R] 🍴 ①–⑤	[R] 🍴 ⑦			♥ 🍷	♥ 🍷 B	🍷	♥ 🍷 ⑧			♥ 🍷 G	♥ 🍷 L
Brig d.	0428	...	...	...	...	0657	...	...	...	...	...	1057	...	1101	...	...	...	1557	...	1541	...	...	...	1728	...	...
Zermatt d.	|	...	...	...	0539	|	...	...	...	...	0939	|	...	|	...	...	1439	|	...	|	...	...	1613	|	...	...
Visp d.	0436	...	...	...	0647	0707	...	...	...	...	1047	1107	...	1111	...	...	1547	1607	...	1549	...	...	1722	1736	...	...
Sierre d.	0455	...	...	...	▬	0726	...	...	...	...	▬	1126	...	1132	...	...	▬	1626	...	1611	...	...	...	1755	...	...
Sion d.	0506	0532	...	...	...	0737	...	...	...	...	...	1137	...	1143	...	...	...	1637	...	1626	...	...	...	1806	...	...
Martigny d.	0520	0545	...	...	...	0751	...	...	...	...	...	1151	...	1157	...	...	...	1651	...	1642	...	...	...	1820	...	...
St Maurice d.	0531	0556	...	...	0731	|	...	...	...	...	1126	|	...	|	...	...	1631	|	...	|	...	...	...	1831	...	...
Bex d.	0536	0601	...	...	0736	|	...	...	...	...	1131	|	...	|	...	...	1636	|	...	|	...	...	...	1836	...	...
Aigle d.	0543	0608	...	...	0743	0808	...	...	...	...	1138	1208	...	1215	...	...	1643	1708	...	1714	...	...	...	1843	...	1835
Montreux d.	0554	0619	...	...	0754	0819	...	...	...	...	1149	1219	...	1227	...	...	1654	1719	...	1727	...	...	...	1854	...	1849
Lausanne a.	0615	0640	...	...	0815	0840	...	...	...	...	1210	1240	...	1245	...	...	1715	1740	...	1745	...	...	...	1915	...	1908
Lausanne d.	...	...	0703	...	...	...	0903	...	...	...	...	...	1303	1303	...	...	...	...	1803	1803	...	...	...	...	1922	1922
Vallorbe 🏛 d.	...	...	0745	...	...	...	0940	...	...	...	...	...	1342	1342	...	...	...	...	1840	1840	...	...	...	...	2005	2005
Interlaken Ost d.	...	...	|	...	...	...	|	0701	...	...	...	...	|	|	...	...	...	...	|	|	1601	...	...	...	|	|
Interlaken West d.	...	...	|	...	...	...	|	0706	...	...	...	...	|	|	...	...	...	...	|	|	1606	...	...	...	|	|
Spiez d.	...	...	|	...	...	...	|	0723	...	...	...	...	|	|	...	...	...	...	|	|	1623	...	...	...	|	|
Thun d.	...	...	|	...	...	...	|	0734	...	...	...	...	|	|	...	...	...	...	|	|	1634	...	...	...	|	|
Bern d.	...	...	|	...	...	...	|	0752	0829	...	...	...	|	|	...	...	...	...	|	|	1652	1723	...	...	|	|
Neuchâtel d.	...	...	|	...	...	...	|	...	0902	...	...	...	|	|	...	...	...	...	|	|	...	1802	...	...	|	|
Pontarlier 🏛 d.	...	...	|	...	...	...	|	...	0945	...	...	...	|	|	...	...	...	...	|	|	...	1845	...	...	|	|
Frasne d.	...	...	0806	...	...	...	1007	...	1007	...	...	...	1403	1403	...	...	...	...	1906	1906	...	1906	...	...	2025	2025
Dijon d.	...	...	0924	...	...	...	1125	...	1125	...	...	...	1515	1515	...	...	...	...	2020	2020	...	2020	...	...	2143	2143
Paris Gare de Lyon a.	...	...	1103	...	...	...	1303	...	1303	...	...	...	1655	1655	...	...	...	...	2159	2159	...	2159	...	...	2324	2324
Paris Nord 10 d.	...	...	...	1301	...	...	...	...	...	1507	...	...	...	...	1843	1913	...	...	...	...	...	...	...	...	...	...
London St Pancras 10 a.	...	...	...	1434	...	...	...	...	...	1636	...	...	...	...	2006	2029	...	...	...	...	...	...	...	...	...	...

B – ⑥ July 11 - Aug. 29.
C – ⑤ July 10 - Aug. 28.
G – ⑤⑦ (also July 14).

H – ①②③④⑥⑦.
L – ⑦ July 5 - Aug. 30.

♥ – *TGV Lyria* service. [R]. Special fares payable. Supplement payable.
☆ – Eurostar train. Special fares payable. Minimum check-in time 30 minutes. Valid June 14 - Aug. 30. Additional Eurostar services are available, see Table **10**.
§ – Supplement payable in Italy (except with international tickets). *IC* in Italy.

BRUSSELS - KÖLN - MILANO, VENEZIA and ROMA — 43

For Eurostar and rail/sea connections from London see Table **12**.

train type	ICE	CIS	AV	⇌	EC	CIS	⇌	CNL	ESc	AV
train number	**373**	**57**	**9447**	**9407**	**101**	**23**	**9443**	**401**	**9707**	**9429**
notes	🍷	🍷 ⊕	[R] 🍴 ⁄		🍷	🍷 ⊕		**40421** A [R]	[R] 🍴 ⁄	[R] 🍴 ⁄
Brussels Midi / Zuid d.	...	...	...	0755	...	...	1655	...	...	...
Aachen 🏛 d.	...	...	...	0940	...	...	1840	...	...	...
Köln Hbf a.	...	...	...	1015	...	...	1915	...	...	...
Köln Hbf d.	...	...	...	▬	1053	...	▬	2006	...	...
Frankfurt Flughafen ✈ d.	...	...	...	...	|	...	...	|	...	...
Frankfurt (Main) Hbf d.	0850	...	...	*ES*	|	...	...	2249	...	...
Basel SNCF/SBB 🏛 d.	1147	1228	...	**9403**	1537	...	*E*	◐	...	...
Zürich HB d.	...	|	...	[R] 🍴	1652	1701**b**	**1911**	|	...	...
Chiasso 🏛 a.	...	|	...	⁄	...	|	**C**	0631	...	...
Milano Centrale a.	...	1640	1730	1735	...	2050	2320	0750	0805	0830
Verona a.	...	...	|	|	...	...	|	...	0927	|
Padova a.	...	...	|	1926	...	...	|	...	1010	|
Venezia Santa Lucia a.	...	...	|	1955	...	...	|	...	1040	|
Bologna a.	...	...	1835	...	...	...	|	...	...	0935
Firenze SMN a.	...	...	1939	...	...	...	|	...	...	1039
Roma Termini a.	...	...	2129	...	...	...	0723**t**	...	...	1229
Napoli Centrale a.	...	...	2305	...	...	...	1012	...	...	1405

train number	AV	ESc	AV	CNL	ICE	CNL	CIS	EC	ESc	AV	CIS	ICE
train number	**9444**	**9402**	**9446**	**400**	**16**	**400**	**50**	**100**	**9708**	**9426**	**52**	**870**
notes	[R] 🍴 ⁄	[R] ⁄ 🍷	[R] 🍴 ⁄	**40400** A [R]	⊖	[R] A	🍷 ⊕	🍷	[R] 🍴 ⁄	[R] 🍴 ⁄	🍷 ⊕ B	🍷
Napoli Centrale d.	1354	...	...	...	...	...	...	...	...	...	...	...
Roma Termini d.	1530	...	1630	...	...	...	...	...	...	0630	...	...
Firenze SMN d.	1719	...	1819	...	...	...	...	...	...	0819	...	...
Bologna d.	1824	...	1924	...	...	...	...	...	...	0924	...	...
Venezia Santa Lucia d.	|	1805	|	...	...	...	...	...	0750	|	0832**q**	...
Padova d.	|	1834	|	...	...	...	...	...	0819	|	0849	...
Verona d.	|	|	|	...	...	...	...	...	0902	|	0932	...
Milano Centrale d.	1929	2025	2029	2110e	...	...	0725	...	1025	1029	1120	...
Chiasso 🏛 d.	...	...	...	2221	...	...	|	...	▬	...	|	...
Zürich HB d.	...	...	...	|	...	...	|	...	...	...	|	...
Basel SBB/SNCF 🏛 a.	...	...	...	◐	...	←	1132	1218	...	...	1532	1612
Frankfurt (Main) Hbf a.	...	...	...	0545	0729	0615	...	|	...	...	...	1908
Frankfurt Flughafen ✈ a.	...	...	...	→	0740	|	...	|	⇌	...	...	...
Köln Hbf a.	...	...	...	...	0840	0842	...	1705	**9458**	...	...	...
Köln Hbf d.	...	...	...	...	0844	...	...	...	1745	...	...	...
Aachen 🏛 a.	...	...	...	...	0916	...	...	...	1820	...	...	...
Brussels Midi / Zuid a.	...	...	...	...	1035	...	...	...	2001	...	...	...

A – *City Night Line* APUS – 🛏 1, 2 cl., ▬ 2 cl. (4, 6 berth) and [2] (reclining) (Amsterdam ⑤⑥⑦ / Dortmund ①②③④ - Köln -) Frankfurt - Milano and v.v. 🍴 Amsterdam - Frankfurt - Karlsruhe and v.v. [R] Special fares apply.
B – [12] and 🍷 Trieste (depart 0635) - Venezia Mestre - Milano - Basel.
C – 🛏 1, 2 cl. (Excelsior), 🛏 1, 2 cl. (T2), 🛏 1, 2 cl., ▬ 2 cl. (4, 6 berth) and [12] Milano - Napoli.

b – 1709 on ⑥⑦ (also Dec. 8).

e – 2100 on ⑦ as *CNL* **1300**.
q – Venezia **Mestre**.
t – Roma **Tiburtina**.

⁄ – Supplement payable.
◐ – Frontier / ticketing point.

⊖ – Via Köln - Frankfurt high speed line.
⇌ – *Thalys* high-speed train. [R] 🍷. Special fares payable.
§ – Supplement payable in Italy (except with international tickets).
⊕ – **ETR 470** *Cisalpino*. Supplement payable for international journeys. *IC* supplement payable for internal journeys within Italy.

44 LONDON - PARIS - TORINO - MILANO - VENEZIA and ROMA

train type		TGV	EC	ICp	AV	ICp	ESc	ESc		☆		TGV			E	ICN		☆		TGV	E	E		
train number	17983	9241	159	533	9443	605	9781	9733		9014	17941	9247	2199	2117	901	785		9018	17943	9249	809	1911	10601	
notes	①–⑥	R ✕	R 🍷	🍷	R ✕	R 🍷	R ✕	R ✕				R ✕			O	⚡				R ✕				
	h	♣	⚡	⚡	⚡	⚡	⚡	⚡				♣				C				♣x	Q	H		
London St Pancras 10 12 d.	...	...	...	...	...	...	...	...	...	0926	...	...	...	...	...	...	...	1025	...	...	...	...	...	...
Lille Europe 11 d.	...	...	...	...	...	...	...	...	...	|	...	...	...	...	...	...	...	|	...	...	...	...	...	...
Paris Nord 10 a.	...	...	...	...	...	...	...	...	...	1247	...	...	...	...	...	...	...	1347	...	...	...	...	...	...
Paris Gare de Lyon d.	...	0742	...	...	...	...	...	...	...	...	...	1350	...	...	...	...	...	...	...	1524	...	...	...	...
Paris Gare de Bercy ✣ d.	...	|	...	...	...	...	...	...	...	...	...	|	...	...	...	...	...	...	...	|	...	...	...	...
Dijon d.	...	|	...	...	...	...	...	...	...	...	...	|	...	...	...	...	...	...	...	|	...	...	...	...
Lyon Perrache d.	...	|	...	...	...	...	...	...	...	...	...	|	...	...	...	...	...	...	...	|	...	...	...	...
Lyon Part Dieu d.	0841	|	...	...	...	...	...	...	...	...	1541	|	...	...	...	...	...	...	1641	|	...	...	...	...
Aix les Bains d.	|	|	...	...	...	...	...	...	...	...	|	|	...	...	...	...	...	...	|	|	...	...	...	...
Chambéry d.	0955	1045	...	...	...	...	...	...	...	...	1658	1711	...	...	...	...	...	...	1755	1826	...	...	...	...
Modane 🛃 d.	...	1155	...	...	...	...	...	...	...	...	...	1820	...	...	...	...	...	...	...	1930	...	...	...	...
Oulx ▲ a.	...	1228	...	...	...	...	...	...	...	...	...	1855	...	...	...	...	...	...	...	2005	...	...	...	...
Torino Porta Nuova § a.	...	|	...	1505	...	...	...	...	...	...	...	|	...	...	2105	...	...	...	...	|	2155	...	...	...
Torino Porta Susa § a.	...	1317	...	|	...	...	...	...	...	...	...	1945	...	...	|	...	...	...	...	2055	|	...	...	...
Novara a.	...	|	...	|	...	...	...	...	...	...	...	2041	...	...	|	...	...	...	...	|	|	...	...	...
Milano Centrale a.	...	1455	1510	|	1530	1600	1600	1605	...	...	...	2120	2225	2230	|	2300	...	...	...	2225	|	2320	0015	...
Alessandria a.	...	...	|	1600	|	|	|	|	...	...	...	...	|	|	2204	|	...	...	...	...	2257	|	|	...
Genova Piazza Principe a.	...	...	1642	1649	|	1742	|	|	...	...	...	...	0020	|	|	|	...	...	...	...	2350	|	|	...
La Spezia a.	...	...	...	1804	|	1917	|	|	...	...	...	...	...	|	|	|	...	...	...	...	0124	|	|	...
Viareggio a.	...	..	...	1838	|	1955	|	|	...	...	...	...	...	|	|	|	...	...	...	...	|	|	|	...
Pisa Centrale a.	...	...	...	1857	|	2012	|	|	...	...	...	...	...	|	|	|	...	...	...	...	0214	|	|	...
Livorno a.	...	...	...	1914	|	2030	|	|	...	...	...	...	...	|	|	|	...	...	...	...	0235	|	|	...
Grosseto a.	...	...	...	2032	|	...	|	|	...	...	...	...	...	|	|	|	...	...	...	...	0356	|	|	...
Brescia a.	...	...	...	|	|	...	|	1651	...	...	...	...	...	2333	|	|	...	...	...	...	|	|	0134	...
Verona Porta Nuova a.	...	...	...	|	|	...	|	1727	...	...	...	...	...	0020	|	|	...	...	...	...	|	|	0223	...
Vicenza a.	...	...	...	|	|	...	|	1754	...	...	...	...	...	...	|	|	...	...	...	...	|	|	...	...
Padova a.	...	...	...	|	|	...	|	1810	...	...	...	...	...	...	|	|	...	...	...	...	|	|	...	...
Venezia Mestre a.	...	...	...	|	|	...	|	1828	...	...	...	...	...	...	|	|	...	...	...	...	|	|	...	...
Venezia Santa Lucia a.	...	...	...	|	|	...	|	1840	...	...	...	...	...	...	|	|	...	...	...	...	|	|	...	...
Piacenza a.	...	...	...	|	|	...	1643	...	...	...	...	...	...	...	2312	2343	...	...	...	...	|	0008	...	...
Parma a.	...	...	...	|	|	...	1711	...	...	...	...	...	...	...	2349	0016	...	...	...	...	|	0059	...	...
Reggio Emilia a.	...	...	...	|	|	...	1728	...	...	...	...	...	...	...	0010	0038	...	...	...	...	|	|	...	...
Modena a.	...	...	...	|	|	...	1743	...	...	...	...	...	...	...	0025	0053	...	...	...	...	|	|	...	...
Bologna Centrale a.	...	...	...	|	1635	...	1811	...	...	...	...	...	...	...	0054	0124	...	...	...	...	|	|	...	...
Rimini a.	...	...	...	|	|	...	1934	...	...	...	...	...	...	...	0200	0235	...	...	...	...	|	|	...	...
Ancona a.	...	...	...	|	|	...	2047	...	...	...	...	...	...	...	0257	0333	...	...	...	...	|	|	...	...
Pescara Centrale a.	...	...	...	|	|	...	2225	...	...	...	...	...	...	...	0422	0459	...	...	...	...	|	|	...	...
Bari Centrale a.	...	...	...	|	|	...	...	...	...	...	...	...	...	...	0749	0826	...	...	...	...	|	|	...	...
Athína ⊖ a.	...	...	...	|	|	...	...	...	...	...	...	...	...	...	⊖	⊖	...	...	...	...	|	|	...	...
Brindisi a.	...	...	...	|	|	...	...	...	...	...	...	...	...	...	0924	...	...	...	...	...	|	|	...	...
Firenze SMN a.	...	...	...	|	1739	...	...	...	...	...	...	...	...	...	...	...	...	...	...	...	|	|	...	...
Roma Termini a.	...	...	...	2228	1929c	...	...	...	...	...	...	...	...	...	...	...	...	...	...	...	0551	0723t	...	...
Napoli Centrale a.	...	...	...	...	2105	...	...	...	...	...	...	...	...	...	...	...	...	...	...	...	0911	1012	...	...

train type			☆	EN		ICp ⚡	AV ⚡	ICp			☆	EN			AV	ESc	IC	ICp						
train number			9030	227	2121	501	9425	727			9036	221	2004	2179 1713	9425	9761	585	553						
notes				🛏		R 🍷	R ✕	R 🍷				🛏 ▬			R ✕	R ✕	🍷	R 🍷						
				A		①–⑥	①–⑥	⚡				B m			①–⑥ ⚡	⚡	⚡	⚡						
London St Pancras 10 12 d.	...	...	1404	...	...	...	...	...	...	...	1529	...	...	...		...	...	...	...	...	...	...	...	...
Lille Europe 11 d.	...	...	|	...	...	...	...	...	...	...	|	...	...	...	...	...	...	...	...	...	...	...	...	...
Paris Nord 10 a.	...	...	1726	...	...	...	...	...	...	...	1856	...	...	...	...	...	...	...	...	...	...	...	...	...
Paris Gare de Bercy ✣ d.	...	...	...	1852	...	...	...	...	...	...	...	2033	...	...	...	...	...	...	...	...	...	...	...	...
Dijon d.	...	...	...	2137	...	...	...	...	...	...	...	2321	...	...	...	...	...	...	...	...	...	...	...	...
Modane 🛃 d.	...	...	...	⊙	...	...	...	...	...	...	...	⊙	...	...	...	...	...	...	...	...	...	...	...	...
Milano Centrale a.	...	...	...	|	...	...	...	...	...	...	...	0538	0600	0625	0630	0700	0705	0915	...	...	...	...	...	...
Novara a.	...	...	...	|	...	...	...	...	...	...	...	|	0643	|	|	|	|	|	...	...	...	...	...	...
Torino Porta Nuova a.	...	...	...	|	...	...	...	...	...	...	...	|	0800	|	|	|	|	|	...	...	...	...	...	...
Genova Piazza Principe a.	...	...	...	|	...	...	...	...	...	...	...	|	...	0836	|	|	|	|	...	...	...	...	...	...
La Spezia a.	...	...	...	|	...	...	...	...	...	...	...	|	...	...	|	|	|	|	...	...	...	...	...	...
Viareggio a.	...	...	...	|	...	...	...	...	...	...	...	|	...	...	|	|	|	|	...	...	...	...	...	...
Pisa Centrale a.	...	...	...	|	...	...	...	...	...	...	...	|	...	...	|	|	|	|	...	...	...	...	...	...
Livorno a.	...	...	...	|	...	...	...	...	...	...	...	|	...	...	|	|	|	|	...	...	...	...	...	...
Grosseto a.	...	...	...	|	...	...	...	...	...	...	...	|	...	...	|	|	|	|	...	...	...	...	...	...
Brescia a.	...	...	...	|	...	...	...	...	...	...	...	0643	...	...	|	|	|	|	...	...	...	...	...	...
Verona Porta Nuova a.	...	...	...	|	...	...	...	...	...	...	...	0727	...	...	|	|	|	|	...	...	...	...	...	...
Vicenza a.	...	...	...	|	...	...	...	...	...	...	...	0813	...	...	|	|	|	|	...	...	...	...	...	...
Padova a.	...	...	...	|	...	...	...	...	...	...	...	0851	...	...	|	|	|	|	...	...	...	...	...	...
Venezia Mestre a.	...	...	...	|	...	...	...	...	...	...	...	0921	...	...	|	|	|	|	...	...	...	...	...	...
Venezia Santa Lucia a.	...	...	...	|	...	...	...	...	...	...	...	0934	...	...	|	|	|	|	...	...	...	...	...	...
Piacenza a.	...	...	...	0444	...	...	...	...	...	...	...	...	...	...	|	0738	0748	0954	...	...	...	...	...	...
Parma a.	...	...	...	0512	...	...	...	...	...	...	...	...	...	...	|	|	0812	1021	...	...	...	...	...	...
Reggio Emilia a.	...	...	...	|	...	...	...	...	...	...	...	...	...	...	|	|	0829	1038	...	...	...	...	...	...
Modena a.	...	...	...	|	...	...	...	...	...	...	...	...	...	...	|	|	0840	1051	...	...	...	...	...	...
Bologna Centrale a.	...	...	...	0558	0638	...	...	...	...	...	...	...	...	...	0735	0852	0904	1114	...	...	...	...	...	...
Rimini a.	...	...	...	|	0805	...	...	...	...	...	...	...	...	...	|	0951	|	1234	...	...	...	...	...	...
Ancona a.	...	...	...	|	0924	...	...	...	...	...	...	...	...	...	|	1051	|	1334	...	...	...	...	...	...
Pescara Centrale a.	...	...	...	|	...	...	...	...	...	...	...	...	...	...	|	1205	|	1509	...	...	...	...	...	...
Bari Centrale a.	...	...	...	|	...	...	...	...	...	...	...	...	...	...	|	1451	|	1841	...	...	...	...	...	...
Athína ⊖ a.	...	...	...	|	...	...	...	...	...	...	...	...	...	...	|	⊖	|	⊖	...	...	...	...	...	...
Brindisi a.	...	...	...	|	...	...	...	...	...	...	...	...	...	...	|	1555	|	...	...	...	...	...	...	...
Firenze SMN a.	...	...	...	0713	...	...	...	...	...	...	...	...	...	...	0839	...	1024j	...	...	...	...	...	...	...
Roma Termini a.	...	...	...	1013	...	1027	1044	1128	...	...	...	...	...	...	1029	...	1316	...	...	...	...	...	...	...
Napoli Centrale a.	...	...	...	...	...	1236	1205	1330	...	...	...	...	...	...	1205	...	1550	...	...	...	...	...	...	...

NOTES for pages 70 and 71

A – PALATINO *Trainhotel Artesia* – 🛏 1, 2 cl., ▬ 2 cl. (6 berth, 4 berth and ladies only 4 berth) and ✕: Paris - Bologna - Firenze - Roma and v.v.

B – STENDHAL *Trainhotel Artesia* – 🛏 1, 2 cl., ▬ 2 cl. (6 berth, 4 berth and ladies only 4 berth) and ✕: Paris - Milano - Venezia and v.v.

C – FRECCIA DEL LEVANTE – 🛏 1, 2 cl., 🛏 1, 2 cl. (T2), ▬ 2 cl. and (12) Milano - Bari - Taranto.

H – 🛏 1, 2 cl. (Excelsior), 🛏 1, 2 cl. (T2), 🛏 1, 2 cl., ▬ 2 cl. (4, 6 berth) and (12) Milano - Napoli and v.v.

K – FRECCIA SALENTINA – 🛏 1, 2 cl. (Excelsior), 🛏 1, 2 cl., ▬ 2 cl. (4 berth) and (12) Lecce - Brindisi - Milano.

O – FRECCIA ADRIATICA – 🛏 1, 2 cl. (T2), ▬ 2 cl. and (2) Torino - Brindisi - Lecce.

Q – 🛏 1, 2 cl. (Excelsior), 🛏 1, 2 cl., ▬ 2 cl. (4 berth) and (2) Torino - Roma - Napoli and v.v. 🛏 1, 2 cl. and ▬ 2 cl. (2) Torino - Roma and v.v.

c – Departs 15 minutes later.

h – Not July 14, Aug. 15, Nov. 11.

j – Firenze **Rifredi**.

k – Calls at Lyon St Exupéry TGV ✈, arrive 2124.

m – Calls at Dole, depart 2346.

p – Not July 14.

q – Also July 14.

t – Roma **Tiburtina**.

w – Calls at Dole, arrive 0509.

x – Calls at Lyon St Exupéry TGV ✈, depart 1720.

z – Arrive 2305.

NOTES CONTINUED ON NEXT PAGE →

OTHER TRAIN NAMES: **9241** – ALESSANDRO MANZONI **9247** – ALEXANDRE DUMAS **9249** – CARAVAGGIO

ROMA and VENEZIA - MILANO - TORINO - PARIS - LONDON 44

train type		TGV		☆	ICN	E	E			ICp	TGV				☆		ESc	IC	ESc	AV	ICp	ICp	TGV		
train number		9240	17910	9043	780	1910	806	2718	2710	500	9242	17912	17536	17914	9047		9760	582	9722	9436	606	516	9248	17928	
notes		[R] ✕		[R]	↯					[R]	[R] ✕	①–⑥			[R]		[R] ✕	🍷	[R] ✕	[R] ✕	[R] 🍷	[R] 🍷	[R] ✕		
		♣		✕	K	H	Q			↯	♣	p			✕		↯	↯	↯	↯	↯	↯	♣k	Ⓑ	
Napoli Centrale d.	...	...	...	...	...	2030	2108	...	...	...	...	...	...	...	...	...	...	...	...	0954	...	0730	...	...	...
Roma Termini d.	...	...	...	...	...	2306	2350	...	...	...	...	...	...	...	...	...	...	0841	...	1130	...	0946	...	...	...
Firenze SMN d.	...	...	...	...	...	|	|	...	...	...	...	...	...	...	...	...	...	1136j	...	1319	...	|	...	...	...
Brindisi d.	...	...	...	...	1932	|	|	...	...	...	...	...	...	...	...	...	...	|	...	|	...	|	...	...	...
Athína ⊖ d.	...	...	...	...	⊖	|	|	...	...	...	...	...	...	...	...	...	⊖	|	...	|	...	|	...	...	...
Bari Centrale d.	...	...	...	...	2100	|	|	...	...	...	...	...	...	...	...	...	0649	|	...	|	...	|	...	...	...
Pescara Centrale d.	...	...	...	...	0029	|	|	...	...	...	...	...	...	...	...	...	0953	|	...	|	...	|	...	...	...
Ancona d.	...	...	...	...	0158	|	|	...	...	...	...	...	...	...	...	...	1115	|	...	|	...	|	...	...	...
Rimini d.	...	...	...	...	0256	|	|	...	...	...	...	...	...	...	...	...	1209	|	...	|	...	|	...	...	...
Bologna Centrale d.	...	...	...	...	0412	|	|	...	...	...	...	...	...	...	...	...	1308	1256	...	1424	...	|	...	...	...
Modena d.	...	...	...	...	0435	|	|	...	...	...	...	...	...	...	...	...	|	1314	...	|	...	|	...	...	...
Reggio Emilia d.	...	...	...	...	0453	|	|	...	...	...	...	...	...	...	...	...	|	1328	...	|	...	|	...	...	...
Parma d.	...	...	...	...	0512	0521	|	...	...	...	...	...	...	...	...	...	|	1343	...	|	...	|	...	...	...
Piacenza d.	...	...	...	...	0554	0602	|	...	...	...	...	...	...	...	...	...	|	1418	..	|	...	|	...	...	...
Venezia Santa Lucia d.	...	...	...	...	|	|	|	...	...	...	...	...	...	...	...	...	|	|	1250	|	...	|	...	...	...
Venezia Mestre d.	...	...	...	...	|	|	|	...	...	...	...	...	...	...	...	...	|	|	1302	|	...	|	...	...	...
Padova d.	...	...	...	...	|	|	|	...	...	...	...	...	...	...	...	...	|	|	1319	|	...	|	...	...	...
Vicenza d.	...	...	...	...	|	|	|	...	...	...	...	...	...	...	...	...	|	|	1335	|	...	|	...	...	...
Verona Porta Nuova d.	...	...	...	...	|	|	|	...	0540	...	...	...	...	...	...	...	|	|	1402	|	...	|	...	...	...
Brescia d.	...	...	...	...	|	|	|	...	0627	...	...	...	...	...	...	...	|	|	1439	|	...	|	...	...	...
Grosseto d.	...	...	...	...	|	|	0154	...	|	...	...	...	...	...	...	...	|	|	|	|	...	1130	...	...	...
Livorno d.	...	...	...	...	|	|	0311	...	|	...	...	...	...	...	...	...	|	|	|	|	1126	1242	...	...	...
Pisa Centrale d.	...	...	...	...	|	|	0328	...	|	...	...	...	...	...	...	...	|	|	|	|	1144	1300	...	...	...
Viareggio d.	...	...	...	...	|	|	|	...	|	...	...	...	...	...	...	...	|	|	|	|	1202	|	...	...	...
La Spezia d.	...	...	...	...	|	|	0416	...	|	...	...	...	...	...	...	...	|	|	|	|	1240	1353	...	...	...
Genova Piazza Principe d.	...	...	...	...	|	|	0604	0545	|	0708	...	...	...	...	...	...	|	|	|	|	1419	1512	...	...	...
Alessandria d.	...	...	...	...	|	|	0705	|	|	0757	...	...	...	...	...	...	|	|	|	|	|	1557	...	...	...
Milano Centrale d.	...	0640	...	...	0705	0725	|	0740	0735	|	0810	...	...	...	...	...	1455	1500	1525	1529	1555	|	1610	...	...
Novara d.	...	0714	...	...	...	...	|	...	...	|	0844	...	...	...	...	...	...	...	...	...	...	|	|	...	...
Torino Porta Susa § d.	...	0811	...	...	...	...	|	...	...	|	0940	...	...	...	...	...	...	...	...	...	...	|	1735	...	...
Torino Porta Nuova § d.	...	|	...	...	...	...	0820	...	...	0855	|	...	...	...	...	...	...	...	...	...	...	1655	|	...	...
Oulx ▲ d.	...	0900	...	...	...	...	...	...	...	...	1030	...	...	...	...	...	...	...	...	...	...	...	1825	...	...
Modane 🏛 a.	...	0938	1029	...	...	...	...	...	...	...	1105	...	...	...	...	...	...	...	...	...	...	...	1905	...	...
Chambéry a.	...	1052	1151	...	...	...	...	...	...	...	1220	1301	1313	1401	...	...	...	...	...	...	...	...	2022	2101	...
Aix les Bains a.	...	|	|	...	...	...	...	...	...	...	|	|	1324	|	...	...	...	...	...	...	...	...	|	|	...
Lyon Part Dieu a.	...	|	1316	...	...	...	...	...	...	...	|	1416	...	1416	...	...	...	...	...	...	...	...	|	2221	...
Lyon Perrache a.	...	|	...	...	...	...	...	...	...	...	|	...	...	...	...	...	...	...	...	...	...	...	|	...	...
Dijon a.	...	|	...	...	...	...	...	...	...	...	|	...	...	...	...	...	...	...	...	...	...	...	|	...	...
Paris Gare de Bercy ✣ a.	...	|	...	...	...	...	...	...	...	...	|	...	...	...	...	...	...	...	...	...	...	...	|	...	...
Paris Gare de Lyon a.	...	1355	...	...	...	...	...	...	...	...	1515	...	...	...	...	...	...	...	...	...	...	...	2319	...	...
Paris Nord 10 d.	...	...	...	1613	...	...	...	...	...	...	...	...	...	...	1713	...	...	...	...	...	...	...	...	...	...
Lille Europe 11 d.	...	...	...	|	...	...	...	...	...	...	...	...	...	...	|	...	...	...	...	...	...	...	...	...	...
London St Pancras 10 12 a.	...	...	...	1734	...	...	...	...	...	...	...	...	...	...	1834	...	...	...	...	...	...	...	...	...	...

train type		ICp	AV		ICp	EC	ESc	IC	EN	TGV	☆	☆			EN	TGV	☆	☆							
train number		568	9450	2029	538	147	9768	592	220	5152	9119	9019			226	5156	9181	9023							
notes		[R] ✕	[R] ✕		[R]	148	[R] ✕	🍷	⊠ ◧	[R] 🍷					⊠ ◧	[R] 🍷									
		↯	Ⓑ ↯		↯	[R] 🍷 ↯	↯	↯	B w	①–⑤ p	①–⑥				A	⑥⑦ q									
Napoli Centrale d.	...	...	1654	...	1324		...	1424	...		...	...	...	...	...		...	...	...	...	...	...	...	...	...
Roma Termini d.	...	...	1830	...	1546	...	...	1644	...	...	...	...	...	...	1840	...	...	...	...	...	...	...	...	...	...
Firenze SMN d.	...	...	2019	...	|	...	...	1936j	...	...	...	...	...	...	2109	...	...	...	...	...	...	...	...	...	...
Brindisi d.	...	...	|	...	|	...	1402	|	...	...	...	...	...	...	|	...	...	...	...	...	...	...	...	...	...
Athína ⊖ d.	...	⊖	|	...	|	...	⊖	|	...	...	...	...	...	...	|	...	...	...	...	...	...	...	...	...	...
Bari Centrale d.	...	1113	|	...	|	...	1507	|	...	...	...	...	...	...	|	...	...	...	...	...	...	...	...	...	...
Pescara Centrale d.	...	1435	|	...	|	...	1750	|	...	...	...	...	...	...	|	...	...	...	...	...	...	...	...	...	...
Ancona d.	...	1620	|	...	|	...	1913	|	...	...	...	...	...	...	|	...	...	...	...	...	...	...	...	...	...
Rimini d.	...	1726	|	...	|	...	2007	|	...	...	...	...	...	...	|	...	...	...	...	...	...	...	...	...	...
Bologna Centrale d.	...	1856	2124	...	|	...	2103	2056	...	...	...	...	...	...	2231	...	...	...	...	...	...	...	...	...	...
Modena d.	...	1915	|	...	|	...	|	2115	...	...	...	...	...	...	|	...	...	...	...	...	...	...	...	...	...
Reggio Emilia d.	...	1929	|	...	|	...	|	2130	...	...	...	...	...	...	|	...	...	...	...	...	...	...	...	...	...
Parma d.	...	1945	|	...	|	...	|	2145	...	...	...	...	...	...	2314	...	...	...	...	...	...	...	...	...	...
Piacenza d.	...	2020	|	...	|	...	|	2220	...	...	...	...	...	...	2345	...	...	...	...	...	...	...	...	...	...
Venezia Santa Lucia d.	...	|	|	...	|	...	|	|	1957	...	...	...	...	...	|	...	...	...	...	...	...	...	...	...	...
Venezia Mestre d.	...	|	|	...	|	...	|	|	2009	...	...	...	...	...	|	...	...	...	...	...	...	...	...	...	...
Padova d.	...	|	|	...	|	...	|	|	2032	...	...	...	...	...	|	...	...	...	...	...	...	...	...	...	...
Vicenza d.	...	|	|	...	|	...	|	|	2052	...	...	...	...	...	|	...	...	...	...	...	...	...	...	...	...
Verona Porta Nuova d.	...	|	|	...	|	...	|	|	2124	...	...	...	...	...	|	...	...	...	...	...	...	...	...	...	...
Brescia d.	...	|	|	...	|	...	|	|	2206	...	...	...	...	...	|	...	...	...	...	...	...	...	...	...	...
Grosseto d.	...	|	|	...	1729	...	|	|	|	...	...	...	...	...	|	...	...	...	...	...	...	...	...	...	...
Livorno d.	...	|	|	...	1842	...	|	|	|	...	...	...	...	...	|	...	...	...	...	...	...	...	...	...	...
Pisa Centrale d.	...	|	|	...	1900	...	|	|	|	...	...	...	...	...	|	...	...	...	...	...	...	...	...	...	...
Viareggio d.	...	|	|	...	1917	...	|	|	|	...	...	...	...	...	|	...	...	...	...	...	...	...	...	...	...
La Spezia d.	...	|	|	...	1953	...	|	|	|	...	...	...	...	...	|	...	...	...	...	...	...	...	...	...	...
Genova Piazza Principe d.	...	|	|	...	2108	2119	|	|	|	...	...	...	...	...	|	...	...	...	...	...	...	...	...	...	...
Torino Porta Nuova d.	...	|	|	2050	...	|	|	|	|	...	...	...	...	...	|	...	...	...	...	...	...	...	...	...	...
Novara d.	...	|	|	2203	...	|	|	|	|	...	...	...	...	...	|	...	...	...	...	...	...	...	...	...	...
Milano Centrale d.	...	2105	2229	2245	...	2250	2255	2300	2335z	...	...	...	...	...	|	...	...	...	...	...	...	...	...	...	...
Modane 🏛 a.	...	...	...	...	...	...	...	...	⊙	...	...	...	...	...	⊙	...	...	...	...	...	...	...	...	...	...
Dijon a.	...	...	...	...	...	...	...	...	0536	0632	...	...	...	...	0633	0744	...	...	...	...	...	...	...	...	...
Paris Gare de Bercy ✣ a.	...	...	...	...	...	...	...	...	0819	|	...	...	...	...	0916	|	...	...	...	...	...	...	...	...	...
Paris Nord 10 d.	...	...	...	...	...	...	...	...	...	|	...	1013	...	...	...	|	...	1113	...	...	...	...	...	...	...
Lille Europe 11 d.	...	...	...	...	...	...	...	...	...	0915	1005	|	...	...	...	1027	1205	|	...	...	...	...	...	...	...
London St Pancras 10 12 a.	...	...	...	...	...	...	...	...	...	...	1031	1128	...	...	...	...	1226	1229	...	...	...	...	...	...	...

→ **NOTES CONTINUED FROM PREVIOUS PAGE**

♣ – *TGV Artesia* service. Special fares payable.

▲ – Station for the resorts of Cesana, Claviere and Sestriere.

✣ – Paris **Gare de Bercy**, 1km from **Gare de Lyon**; see City Plan of Paris page 32.

⊠ – For use by passengers making international journeys only. Special fares payable.

⊖ – For connections to Athína (by ⛴ Ancona / Bari - Pátra), see Tables **74, 2715, 2755**.

☆ – Eurostar train. Special fares payable. Minimum check-in time 30 minutes. Valid June 14 - Aug. 30. Additional Eurostar services are available, see Table **10**.

⊙ – Frontier / ticketing points 🏛 are Vallorbe and Domodossola (via Switzerland, non–EU nationals may require transit visas). Ticket point for Domodossola is **Iselle**.

§ – Local train services (Tables **585 / 586**) and metro services run between Torino **Porta Susa** and Torino **Porta Nuova**.

◧ – *Artesia* overnight services will be disrupted due to engineering work on the following dates. On June 6 and 20, train **221** will depart Paris Bercy at 1902 instead of 2033, Dijon at 2146 instead of 2321 and will not call at Dole. On June 7 and 21, train **221** will depart Paris Bercy at 1828 instead of 2033, Dijon at 2100 instead of 2321 and will not call at Dole. On the morning of June 7 and 21, train **226** will arrive Dijon 0916 instead of 0633 and Paris Bercy at 1157 instead of 0916. On the morning of June 8 and 22, train **226** will arrive Dijon 0845 instead of 0633 and Paris Bercy at 1122 instead of 0916. On the morning of June 7, 8, 21, 22, train **220** will arrive Dijon 0803 instead of 0536, Paris Bercy at 1033 instead of 0819 and will not call at Dole.
On Aug. 10, Sept. 21 Trains **220, 221, 226, 227** are cancelled.

OTHER TRAIN NAMES:	9240 – CARAVAGGIO	9242 – ALEXANDRE DUMAS	9248 – ALESSANDRO MANZONI

45 MADRID - LISBOA

train number / notes			Hotel 332 R ✕ A		
Madrid Chamartín d.	...	...	2225	...	...
Talavera de La Reina d.	...	...	0008	...	...
Navalmoral de La Mata d.	...	...	0038	...	...
Cáceres d.	...	...	0153	...	...
San Vicente de Alcántara d.	...	...	0307	...	...
Valencia de Alcántara 🏛 ES d.	...	...	0445	...	...
Marvão Beirã 🏛 PT d.	...	...	0404	...	...
Abrantes a.	...	...	0531	...	...
Entroncamento a.	...	...	0554	...	...
Lisboa Oriente a.	...	...	0730	...	...
Lisboa Santa Apolónia a.	...	...	0741	...	...

train number / notes			Hotel 335 R ✕ A		
Lisboa Santa Apolónia d.	...	...	2230	...	...
Lisboa Oriente d.	...	...	2239	...	...
Entroncamento d.	...	...	2354	...	...
Abrantes d.	...	...	0020	...	...
Marvão Beirãa 🏛 PT d.	...	...	0142	...	...
Valencia de Alcántara 🏛 ES d.	...	...	0340	...	...
San Vicente de Alcántara d.	...	...	0355	...	...
Cáceres a.	...	...	0505	...	...
Navalmoral de La Mata a.	...	...	0636	...	...
Talavera de La Reina a.	...	...	0713	...	...
Madrid Chamartín a.	...	...	0858	...	...

A – LUSITANIA *Hotel Train* – 🛏 *Gran Clase* (1, 2 berths), 🛏 *Preferente* (1, 2 berths), 🛏 1, 2 cl. (T4), [12] and ✕ Madrid - Lisboa and v.v. Special fares apply. From Lisboa, passengers can board from 2130; ✕ from 2200.

ES – Spain (Central European Time).
PT – Portugal (West European Time).

46 LONDON - PARIS - LISBOA, PORTO and MADRID

train type / number	TGV		TGV	Alvia		☆	TGV	313	IC	IC	Hotel	AVE		☆	Hotel		AVE	AVE	☆	☆		Alvia	AVE		Arco
train number	8505	413	8515	4166		9018	8543	312	521	523	752	2092		9030	409/8	18300	2102	2112	9044	9048	4053	4086	2162	18308	283
notes	R ⚡ 🍷	🍷 2	R ⚡ 🍷			R ✕	R ⚡ 🍷	R ✕ A	①–⑥ R 🍷	R 🍷	R ⚡ C			R ✕	R ✕ H	2 ①–⑤	①–⑥		R ✕ ⑥⑦	R ✕ ①–⑤	R F			2	E
London St Pancras 10 d.	...	...	...	...	...	1025	...	...	...	...	...	...	...	1404	...	...	...	...	1731	1832	...	...	...	...	...
Paris Nord 10 a.	...	...	...	...	...	1347	...	...	...	...	...	...	...	1726	...	...	...	...	2053	2147	...	...	...	...	...
Paris Montparnasse d.	0715	...	1010	...	...	...	1550	...	...	...	...	...	...	...	...	...	...	...	...	...	...	...	...	...	...
Paris Austerlitz d.	|	...	|	...	...	...	|	...	...	...	...	...	...	...	1945	...	...	...	...	...	2310	...	...	...	...
Blois d.	|	...	|	...	...	...	|	...	...	...	...	...	...	...	2108	...	...	...	...	...	|	...	...	...	...
Poitiers d.	|	...	|	...	...	...	|	...	...	...	...	...	...	...	2209	...	...	...	...	...	|	...	...	...	...
Bordeaux St Jean d.	1025	...	1315	...	...	...	1856	...	...	...	...	...	...	...	|	...	...	...	...	...	|	...	...	...	...
Hendaye d.	1245	...	1535	...	...	...	2119	...	...	...	...	...	...	...	|	...	...	...	...	...	0726	...	...	...	...
Irún 🏛 d.	1255	1320	1545	1620	...	...	2128	2200	...	...	...	...	...	...	|	...	...	...	...	...	0736	0815	...	...	0845
San Sebastián / Donostia a.	...	1335	...	1637	...	...	...	2218	...	...	...	...	...	...	|	...	...	...	...	...	...	0830	...	...	0901
Vitoria / Gasteiz a.	...	1514	...	1815	...	...	...	0014	...	...	...	...	...	...	0405	...	...	...	...	...	...	1007	...	...	1039
Burgos Rosa de Lima a.	...	1703	...	1938	...	...	...	0157	...	...	...	...	...	...	0520	...	...	...	...	...	...	1125	...	...	1212
Valladolid Campo Grande a.	...	1811	...	2046	...	...	...	0318	...	...	0500	...	...	...	0622	0726	...	...	...	...	...	1235	...	1348	...
Medina del Campo a.	...	1843	...	|	...	...	...	0352	...	...	0526	...	...	...	|	0800	...	...	...	...	...	|	...	1416	...
Salamanca a.	...	1937	...	|	...	...	...	0448	...	...	|	...	...	...	|	0859	...	...	...	...	...	|	...	1515	...
Coimbra-B ⊙ a.	...	...	...	|	...	...	...	0849	0931	1134	|	...	...	...	|	...	...	...	...	...	...	|	...	...	...
Lisboa Santa Apolónia a.	...	...	...	|	...	...	...	1103	|	|	|	...	...	...	|	...	...	...	...	...	...	|	...	...	...
Porto Campanhã a.	...	...	...	|	...	...	...	...	1039	1239	|	...	...	...	|	...	...	...	...	...	...	|	...	...	...
Madrid Chamartín a.	...	...	...	2208	...	...	...	...	...	...	0805	...	...	...	0910	...	...	...	...	...	...	1357	...	...	...
Madrid Puerta de Atocha a.	...	...	...	...	...	...	...	...	...	...	...	0935	...	...	...	...	1035	1130	...	...	...	...	1635	...	...
Málaga María Zambrano a.	...	...	...	...	...	...	...	...	...	...	...	1223	...	...	...	...	1315	1410	...	...	...	...	1915	...	...

train type / number	Alvia	TGV		TGV		Arco	AVE		Alvia		☆		AVE		Hotel	☆		AVE	Hotel	IC	310	TGV	☆		
train number	4087	8558	410	8584		280	2123	18306	4167	4052	9015		2153	18316	407/6	9019		2183	751	528	311	8524	9043		
notes		R ⚡ 🍷	🍷 2	R ⚡		E		2		R F	R ✕			2 ⑦	R ✕ H	R ✕			R ⚡ D	R 🍷	R ✕ B	R ⚡ 🍷	R ✕		
Málaga María Zambrano d.	...	...	...	...	...	...	1200	...	...	...	...	...	1500	...	...	...	...	1805	...	...	...	...	...	...	...
Madrid Puerta de Atocha d.	...	...	...	...	...	...	1440	...	...	...	...	...	1740	...	...	...	...	2040	...	...	...	...	...	...	...
Madrid Chamartín d.	0800	...	...	...	...	...	...	...	1610	...	...	...	...	...	1900	...	...	...	2230	...	...	...	...	...	...
Porto Campanhã d.	|	...	...	...	...	...	...	...	|	...	...	...	...	...	|	...	...	...	|	1652	...	...	...	...	...
Lisboa Santa Apolónia d.	|	...	...	...	...	...	...	...	|	...	...	...	...	...	|	...	...	...	|	|	1606	...	...	...	...
Coimbra-B ⊙ d.	|	...	...	...	...	...	...	...	|	...	...	...	...	...	|	...	...	...	|	1757	1824	...	...	...	...
Salamanca d.	|	...	1030	...	...	...	...	1350	|	...	...	...	...	1705	|	...	...	...	|	...	0005	...	...	...	...
Medina del Campo d.	|	...	1120	...	...	...	...	1448	|	...	...	...	...	1758	|	...	...	...	0051	...	0057	...	...	...	...
Valladolid Campo Grande d.	0919	...	1151	...	...	...	...	1514	1734	...	...	...	...	1837	2120	...	...	...	0120	...	0130	...	...	...	...
Burgos Rosa de Lima d.	1022	...	1304	...	...	1644	...	...	1837	...	...	...	...	...	2221	...	...	...	...	...	0258	...	...	...	...
Vitoria / Gasteiz d.	1140	...	1503	...	...	1813	...	...	1956	...	...	...	...	...	2339	...	...	...	...	...	0424	...	...	...	...
San Sebastián / Donostia d.	1324	...	1644	...	...	2005	...	...	2135	...	...	...	...	...	|	...	...	...	...	...	0634	...	...	...	...
Irún d.	1348s	...	1706	...	...	2027s	...	...	2157s	...	...	...	...	...	|	...	...	...	...	...	0659	...	...	...	...
Hendaye 🏛 a.	1354	1402	1713	1722	...	2035	...	...	2203	2219	...	...	...	...	|	...	...	...	...	...	0710	0753	...	...	...
Bordeaux St Jean a.	...	1627	...	1947	...	...	...	...	...	|	...	...	...	...	|	...	...	...	...	...	...	1021	...	...	...
Poitiers a.	...	|	...	2137	...	...	...	...	...	|	...	...	...	...	0555c	...	...	...	...	...	...	1211	...	...	...
Blois a.	...	|	...	|	...	...	...	...	...	|	...	...	...	...	0656c	...	...	...	...	...	...	|	...	...	...
Paris Austerlitz a.	...	|	...	|	...	...	...	...	...	0710	...	...	...	...	0827c	...	...	...	...	...	...	|	...	...	...
Paris Montparnasse a.	...	1945	...	2320	...	...	...	...	...	...	...	...	...	...	...	...	...	...	...	...	...	1345	...	...	...
Paris Nord 10 d.	...	...	...	...	...	...	...	...	...	...	0913	...	...	...	...	1013	...	...	...	...	...	...	1613	...	...
London St Pancras 10 a.	...	...	...	...	...	...	...	...	...	...	1036	...	...	...	...	1128	...	...	...	...	...	...	1734	...	...

A – SUREX / SUD EXPRESSO – 🛏 1, 2 cl., ▬ 2 cl., [2] and ✕ Irún - Vilar Formoso (**312**) - Lisboa.
B – SUD EXPRESSO / SUREX – 🛏 1, 2 cl., ▬ 2 cl., [2] and ✕ Lisboa - Vilar Formoso (**310**) - Hendaye.
C – ATLÁNTICO *Hotel Train* – Ⓑ (①–⑥ from Valladolid): 🛏, ▬ and [1] Ferrol - Valladolid - Madrid.
D – ATLÁNTICO *Hotel Train* – Ⓑ: 🛏, ▬ and [1] Madrid - Valladolid - Ferrol.
E – CAMINO DE SANTIAGO – [12] and 🍷 Irún - Burgos - A Coruña and A Coruña - Burgos - Hendaye.
F – *CORAIL LUNÉA* – ▬ 1, 2 cl. and [2] (reclining) Paris - Irún and Hendaye - Paris.
H – FRANCISCO DE GOYA *Trainhotel Elipsos* – From Paris: daily June 14 - Oct. 7; ①④⑤⑥⑦ Oct. 8 - Dec. 12; From Madrid: daily June 14 - Oct. 6; ③④⑤⑥⑦ Oct. 7 - Dec. 12: 🛏 1, 2 cl., 🛏 1, 2 cl. (T4), [1] (reclining) and ✕ Paris - Madrid and v.v. R Special fares apply.

c – On June 28 arrive Poitiers 0745, Blois 0846, Paris 1005.
s – Stops to set down only.

☆ – Eurostar train. Special fares payable. Minimum check-in time 30 minutes. Valid June 14 - Aug. 31. Additional services are shown on Table **10**.

Alvia – *Alvia* R 🍷 ⚡.
Arco – *Arco* R ⚡ 🍷.
Estr – *Estrella*. R 🍷 ⚡.
◐ – Via Pamplona.
⚡ – Supplement payable.
AVE – *Alta Velocidad Española* R 🍷 ⚡.
⊙ – 🏛 at Fuentes de Oñoro.

KÖLN and FRANKFURT - BARCELONA and NICE 47

train type / number	IC	4239	4248	ICE	ICE	87454	4293	ICE	ICE	TGV	87460	4297
train number	332	4238	4249	611	279	31964	4248	691	601	9570	31966	4296
notes	🍸 Ⓑ	[R] C	[R] J	🍸	🍸	2	[R] A	🍸	🍸	①–⑤	2	[R] D
Köln Hbf d.	1618	...	...	1554	...	...	...	...	1654	...	...	...
Luxembourg 🏛 d.	1934	1946	...	|	...	...	...	...	|	...	...	...
Metz d.	...	2041	2106	|	...	...	...	...	|	...	...	...
Nancy d.	...	2134	2219	|	...	...	...	...	|	...	...	...
Frankfurt (Main) Hbf d.	...	|	|	|	1650	...	...	1750	|	...	...	...
Mannheim d.	...	|	|	1724	1736	...	...	1828	1836	...	...	...
Karlsruhe d.	...	|	|	...	1800	...	...	▬	1900	1931	...	...
Offenburg d.	...	|	|	...	1827	1834	...	...	1927	|	2004	...
Kehl 🏛 d.	...	|	|	...	...	1852	...	...	▬	|	2022	...
Strasbourg d.	...	|	|	...	...	1904	2020	...	...	2015	2034	2100
Mulhouse d.	...	|	|	...	...	...	2134	...	...	...	...	2210
Besançon d.	...	|	|	...	...	...	2322	...	...	...	...	0001
Dijon d.	...	|	|	...	...	...	|	...	...	...	...	|
Lyon Part Dieu a.	...	|	|	...	...	...	|	*Talgo*	...	...	...	|
Avignon Centre a.	...	0412	|	...	...	...	|	**463**	...	...	...	0438
Arles a.	...	|	|	...	...	...	|	**462**	...	...	...	0506
Nîmes a.	...	|	0552	...	...	...	0552	M 🍸	...	...	...	|
Montpellier a.	...	|	0628	...	...	...	0628	0726	...	...	...	|
Béziers a.	...	|	0720	...	...	...	0720	0804	...	...	...	|
Narbonne a.	...	|	0739	...	...	...	0739	0819	...	...	...	|
Perpignan a.	...	|	0826	...	...	...	0826	0855	...	...	...	|
Cerbère a.	...	|	0916	...	...	...	0916	0921	2	...	...	|
Portbou 🏛 a.	...	|	0927	...	...	...	0927	0948	1029	...	...	|
Figueres a.	...	|	...	...	...	...	...	1012	1054	...	...	|
Girona a.	...	|	...	...	...	...	...	1040	1132	...	...	|
Barcelona Sants a.	...	|	...	...	...	...	...	1146	1309	...	...	|
Marseille St Charles a.	...	0532	...	...	...	...	...	...	...	...	...	0556
Toulon a.	...	0639	...	...	...	...	...	...	...	...	...	0707
Les Arcs - Draguignan a.	...	0717	...	...	...	...	...	...	...	...	...	0745
St Raphaël - Valescure a.	...	0734	...	...	...	...	...	...	...	...	...	0802
Cannes a.	...	0758	...	...	...	...	...	...	...	...	...	0827
Antibes a.	...	0810	...	...	...	...	...	...	...	...	...	0840
Nice a.	...	0828	...	...	...	...	...	...	...	...	...	0900

train type / number	4394	4330		4348	4348	87417	TGV	ICE	ICE
train number	4395	4331		4349	4393	31955	9571	76	600
notes	[R] D	[R] C y	2	[R] K	[R] B	2			🍸
Nice d.	2007	2034	...	...	...	...	...	...	...
Antibes d.	2023	2052	...	...	...	...	...	...	...
Cannes d.	2035	2105	...	...	...	...	...	...	...
St Raphaël - Valescure d.	2100	2131	...	...	...	...	...	...	...
Les Arcs - Draguignan d.	2117	2147	...	...	...	...	...	...	...
Toulon d.	2156	2226	...	...	...	...	...	...	...
Marseille St Charles d.	2253	2321	...	...	...	...	...	...	...
Barcelona Sants d.	|	|	1716	...	...	...	...	...	...
Girona d.	|	|	1852	...	...	...	...	...	...
Figueres d.	|	|	1930	...	...	...	...	...	...
Portbou d.	|	|	1956	...	...	...	...	...	...
Cerbère 🏛 d.	|	|	2000	2042	2042	...	...	...	...
Perpignan d.	|	|	▬	2133	2133	...	...	...	...
Narbonne d.	|	|	...	2215	2215	...	...	...	...
Béziers d.	|	|	...	2232	2232	...	...	...	...
Montpellier d.	|	|	...	2319	2319	...	...	...	...
Nîmes d.	|	|	...	2357	2357	...	...	...	...
Arles d.	2342	|	...	|	|	...	...	...	...
Avignon Centre d.	0014	0021	...	|	|	...	...	...	...
Lyon Part Dieu a.	|	|	...	|	|	...	...	...	...
Dijon a.	|	|	...	|	|	...	...	...	...
Besançon a.	0448	|	...	|	0530	...	...	...	...
Mulhouse a.	0637	|	...	|	0720	...	...	...	...
Strasbourg a.	0759	|	...	|	0834	0923	0945	...	...
Kehl 🏛 a.	...	|	...	|	...	0933	|	...	...
Offenburg a.	...	|	...	|	...	0952	|	...	...
Karlsruhe a.	...	|	...	|	...	...	1025	1051	1100
Mannheim a.	...	|	...	|	...	...	...	1114	1123
Frankfurt (Main) Hbf a.	...	|	*IC*	|	...	...	...	1153	|
Nancy a.	...	0654	**335**	0729	...	...	...	...	|
Metz a.	...	0745	🍸	0817	...	...	...	...	|
Luxembourg 🏛 a.	...	0845	1024	...	...	...	...	...	|
Köln Hbf a.	...	...	1342	....	...	...	...	...	1305

A – *CORAIL LUNÉA* – ⑤⑥⑦ Feb. 1 - June 21; daily June 26 - Sept. 5; ⑤⑦ Sept. 6 - Dec. 12 (also Sept. 12, 19, 26, Oct. 24, 31, Nov. 2, 3, 4): 🛏 1, 2 cl. and [2] (reclining) Strasbourg - Portbou.

B – *CORAIL LUNÉA* – ⑤⑥⑦ Feb. 1 - June 21; daily June 26 - Sept. 5; ⑤⑦ Sept. 6 - Dec. 12 (also Sept. 12, 19, 26, Oct. 24, 31, Nov. 2, 3, 4): 🛏 1, 2 cl. and [2] (reclining) Cerbère - Strasbourg.

C – *CORAIL LUNÉA* – ⑤⑥⑦ Feb. 1 - June 21; daily June 26 - Sept. 5; ⑤⑦ Sept. 6 - Dec. 12 (also Oct. 24, 31, Nov. 2, 3, 4, 5): 🛏 1, 2 cl. and [2] (reclining) Luxembourg - Nice and v.v.

D – *CORAIL LUNÉA* – ⑤⑥⑦ Feb. 1 - June 21; daily June 26 - Sept. 5; ⑤⑦ Sept. 6 - Dec. 12 (also Oct. 24, 31, Nov. 2, 3, 4, 5): 🛏 1, 2 cl. and [2] (reclining) Strasbourg - Nice and v.v.

J – *CORAIL LUNÉA* – ⑤⑥⑦ Feb. 1 - June 21; daily June 26 - Sept. 5; ⑤⑦ Sept. 6 - Dec. 12 (also Sept. 12, 19, 26, Oct. 24, 31, Nov. 2, 3, 4): 🛏 1, 2 cl. and [2] (reclining) Metz - Portbou.

K – *CORAIL LUNÉA* – ⑤⑥⑦ Feb. 1 - June 21; daily June 26 - Sept. 5; ⑤⑦ Sept. 6 - Dec. 12 (also Sept. 12, 19, 26, Oct. 24, 31, Nov. 2, 3, 4): 🛏 1, 2 cl. and [2] (reclining) Cerbère - Metz.

M – MARE NOSTRUM – [12] and 🍸 Montpellier - Barcelona - Alacant - Cartagena (arrive 1952), [R] ↗ Special fares payable.

y – Aug. 31 - Sept. 3 depart Nice 2011, runs up to 23 minutes earlier, depart Marseille 2313 and does not stop at Avignon.

BARCELONA - MARSEILLE, NICE, LYON, GENÈVE and ZÜRICH 49

train type / number	Talgo	TGV	IC	4657		Talgo		Hotel	
train number	73/2	6866/7	739	4656		460/1		EN 🍴 273/2	
notes	[R] ↗ W 🍸	[R] ↗ 🍸	🍸	★		[R] ↗ P 🍸		[R] B	
Barcelona Sants d.	...	...	...	...	...	1642	...	...	...
Barcelona França d.	0845	...	...	...	...	|	...	1938	...
Girona d.	0955	...	...	...	...	1748	...	2057	...
Figueres d.	1025	...	...	...	...	1815	...	2125	...
Portbou d.	1053	...	...	...	...	1844	...	|	...
Cerbère 🏛 d.	1114	...	...	...	...	1906	...	|	...
Perpignan a.	1143	...	...	...	...	1936	...	2244d	...
Narbonne a.	1220	...	...	...	...	2013	...	|	...
Béziers a.	1237	...	...	...	...	2027	...	|	...
Montpellier a.	1322	1356	...	1416	...	2109	...	|	...
Nîmes a.	...	1421	...	|	...	...	...	|	...
Marseille St Charles a.	...	|	...	1542	...	...	...	|	...
Nice a.	...	|	...	1825	...	...	...	|	...
Valence Ville a.	...	1510v	...	...	...	...	...	|	...
Lyon Part Dieu a.	...	1550	...	...	...	...	...	|	...
Genève 🏛 a.	...	1735	1745	...	...	...	...	0545	...
Lausanne a.	...	...	1818	...	...	...	...	0654	...
Fribourg a.	...	...	1903	...	...	...	...	0746	...
Bern a.	...	...	1926	...	...	...	...	0849	...
Zürich HB a.	...	...	2028	...	...	...	...	1007	...

train type / number	Talgo		4758	IC	TGV	Talgo		Hotel	
train number	463/2		4759	710	6816/7	70/71		EN 🍴 274/5	
notes	[R] ↗ M 🍸		★	🍸	[R] ↗ 🍸	[R] ↗ W 🍸		[R] C	
Zürich HB d.	...	...	...	0732	...	...	...	1927	...
Bern d.	...	...	...	0834	...	...	...	2108	...
Fribourg d.	...	...	...	0855	...	...	...	2145	...
Lausanne d.	...	...	...	0942	...	...	...	2238	...
Genève 🏛 d.	...	...	...	1015	1117	...	...	2335	...
Lyon Part Dieu d.	...	...	...	...	1307	...	...	|	...
Valence Ville d.	...	...	...	...	1346v	...	...	|	...
Nice d.	...	...	1001	...	|	...	...	|	...
Marseille St Charles d.	...	...	1242	...	|	...	...	|	...
Nîmes d.	...	...	|	...	1432	...	...	|	...
Montpellier d.	0726	...	1409	...	1457	1509	...	|	...
Béziers d.	0806	...	...	...	...	1555	...	|	...
Narbonne d.	0821	...	...	...	...	1611	...	|	...
Perpignan d.	0857	...	...	...	...	1654	...	0614a	...
Cerbère d.	0931	...	...	...	...	1729	...	|	...
Portbou 🏛 a.	0948	...	...	...	...	1748	...	|	...
Figueres a.	1012	...	...	...	...	1811	...	0744	...
Girona a.	1040	...	...	...	...	1837	...	0818	...
Barcelona França a.	|	...	...	...	...	1959	...	0943	...
Barcelona Sants a.	1146	...	...	...	...	...	...	...	...

B – PAU CASALS *Trainhotel Elipsos* – ②④⑦: 🛏 1, 2 cl., 🛏 1, 2 cl. (T4), [1] (reclining) and 🍴 Barcelona - Zürich.

C – PAU CASALS *Trainhotel Elipsos* – ①③⑤: 🛏 1, 2 cl., 🛏 1, 2 cl. (T4), [1] (reclining) and 🍴 Zürich - Barcelona.

M – MARE NOSTRUM – [12] and 🍸 Montpellier - Barcelona - Alacant - Cartagena (arrive 1952). Special fares payable.

P – MARE NOSTRUM – [12] and 🍸 Lorca (depart 0820) - Alacant - Barcelona - Montpellier. Special fares payable.

W – CATALÁN TALGO – [12] and 🍴 Barcelona - Montpellier and v.v. Special fares payable.

a – Arrival time.

d – Departure time.

v – Valence **TGV**.

↗ – Supplement payable.

★ – CORAIL TÉOZ, [R], 🍸.

50 OSLO, STOCKHOLM and KØBENHAVN - HAMBURG - BERLIN

Day Trains (for night trains see below)

⊠ Services are disrupted July 6 - Aug. 9 Oslo - Göteborg; A replacement 🚌 service will operate and journey times are extended ⊠.

✣ Services are disrupted July 6 - August 9 Göteborg - Malmo; A replacement 🚌 service will operate and journey times are extended ✣.

train type / number	[R]	[R]	[R]	[R]		*ICE*	*ICE*		*EC*	*EC*	*ICE*	*IC*	*EC*	*X2000*	*EC*	*IC*	*X2000*			*IC*	*EC*	*EC*	*ICE*	*IC*	
train number	**10003**	**5**	**3**	**1**		**38**	**38**		**238**	**238**	**1515**	**601**	**36**	**521**	**36**	**2071**	**523**		**1051**	**609**	**34**	**34**	**1519**	**2075**	
notes	G	J	F	K		🍷	🍷		🍷	🍷	1575	①–⑤	🍷	①–⑥	🍷	🍷	①–⑤		①–⑤	10609	🍷	🍷	Ⓑ	⑥	
notes	Ⓑ	Ⓑ	Ⓑ	Ⓑ		X c	R c		X c	Z c	🍷	P✣	X c		R c				L	Q	Y c	V c	🍷	🍷	
Oslo Sentral d.	1939	...	2132	...	...	...	...	...	...	...	...	...	...	...	...	...	...	...	...	...	...	...	...	...	...
Stockholm Central d.	|	2155	|	2306	...	...	...	...	...	...	...	...	...	0621	...	...	0721	...	...	...	...	...	...	...	...
Göteborg d.	0230	0230	0230	|	...	...	...	...	...	...	...	0727	...	|	...	...	|	...	0842	0927	...	...	...	...	...
Malmö d.	0620	0620	0620	0620	0642	...	...	0842	...	...	...	1019s	...	1046s	...	...	1146	1202	1202	1219s	...	...	...	...	...
København H. d.	...	...	...	...	0717	0726	0742	0917	0926	0942	...	1100	1126	1132	1142	...	...	1237	1237	1304	1326	1342	...	...	...
Rødby Ferry ⛴ d.	...	...	...	...	...	0934	0934	...	1134	1134	...	...	1334	...	1334	...	...	...	...	...	1534	1534	...	...	...
Puttgarden ⛴ a.	...	...	...	...	...	1035	1035	...	1235	1235	...	...	1435	...	1435	...	...	...	...	...	1635	1635	...	...	...
Lübeck Hbf a.	...	...	...	...	...	1136	1136	...	1336	1336	...	...	1536	...	1536	...	...	...	...	...	1736	1736	...	...	...
Hamburg Hbf a.	...	...	...	...	...	1216	1216	...	1416	1416	1453	...	1616	...	1616	1631	...	...	...	...	1816	1816	1908	1921	...
Berlin Hauptbahnhof a.	...	...	...	...	...	1427	1427	...	...	...	1631	...	...	...	...	1832	...	...	...	...	...	...	2048	2121	...

train type	*X2000*	*X2000*		**391**	*X2000*	*ICE*	*ICE*	*ICE*	*ICE*		*X2000*		*X2000*		**393**	*IC*	*IC*		*EC*	*EC*					
train number	**525**	**527**		①–⑤	**485**	**32**	**32**	**1521**	**1005**		**529**	**1069**	**531**		⑥	**603**	**10603**		**30**	**30**					
notes				⊠		🍷	🍷	⑦	**1015**						⊠	①–⑤	⑥⑦		🍷	🍷					
notes		O		🍷		X c	R c		①–⑥			P✣			🍷	P✣	P✣		N c	S c					
Oslo Sentral d.	...	...	...	0700	...	...	...	...	...	...	...	...	...	...	0900	...	...	...	...	...	...	...	...	...	...
Stockholm Central d.	0821	0921	...	|	...	...	...	...	...	...	1021	...	1121	...	|	...	...	...	...	...					
Göteborg d.	|	|	...	1052	1132	...	...	...	...	...	|	1142	|	...	1253	1327	1327	...	...	...					
Malmö d.	1246	1346	1402	...	1415s	...	...	...	...	...	1446	1502	1546	1602	...	1623s	1617	1642	...	...					
København H. d.	1342	...	1437	...	1502	1526	1542	...	...	...	1531	1537	...	1637	...	1701	...	1717	1726	1742					
Rødby Ferry ⛴ d.	...	...	...	...	...	1735	1735	...	...	...	...	...	...	...	...	...	...	...	1935	1935					
Puttgarden ⛴ a.	...	...	...	...	...	1835	1835	...	...	...	...	...	...	...	...	...	...	...	2035	2035					
Lübeck Hbf a.	...	...	...	...	...	1936	1936	...	...	...	...	...	...	...	...	...	...	...	2136	2136					
Hamburg Hbf a.	...	...	...	...	...	2016	2016	2121	2121	...	...	...	...	...	...	...	...	...	2216	2216	...	...	...	...	...
Berlin Hauptbahnhof a.	...	...	...	...	...	...	...	2309	2313	...	...	...	...	...	...	...	...	...	...	...	...	...	...	...	...

Services are subject to alteration around holidays, please refer to relevant countries for details.

train type	*ICE*	*EC*		*X2000*	*EC*		*X2000*	**396**	**398**	*X2000*	*X2000*		*ICE*	*ICE*		*X2000*	*ICE*		*IC*	*IC*	*X2000*	*X2000*			
train number	**1006**	**31**	**1050**	**538**	**31**		**492**	⑥	Ⓑ	**540**	**542**		**1518**	**33**	**1062**	**542**	**33**		**10604**	**604**	**544**	**546**			
notes	**1016**	🍷			🍷			⊠	⊠	Ⓑ			**908**	🍷			🍷		⑥⑦	①–⑤					
notes	🍷	T c	P		W c			🍷	🍷					R c	P		X c		P	P	Ⓑ				
Berlin Hauptbahnhof d.	0517	...	...	...	...	...	...	...	...	...	...	...	0713	...	...	...	...	...	...	...	...	...	...	...	...
Hamburg Hbf d.	0706	0725	...	...	0725	...	...	...	...	...	...	...	0852	0928	...	...	0928	...	...	...	...	...	...	...	...
Lübeck Hbf d.	...	0806	...	...	0806	...	...	...	...	...	...	...	...	1006	...	...	1006	...	...	...	...	...	...	...	...
Puttgarden ⛴ d.	...	0910	...	...	0910	...	...	...	...	...	...	...	...	1110	...	...	1110	...	...	...	...	...	...	...	...
Rødby Ferry ⛴ a.	...	1000	...	...	1000	...	...	...	...	...	...	...	...	1200	...	...	1200	...	...	...	...	...	...	...	...
København H. d.	...	1211	1223	...	1231	1243	1257	...	...	...	1419	...	...	1411	1423	...	1431	1443	...	1459	...	1619	...	...	...
Malmö a.	...	...	1258	1314	...	1318	1345u	...	...	1414	1514u	...	...	...	1458	1514	...	1518	1542	1537u	1614	1714u	...	...	...
Göteborg a.	...	...	1617	|	...	...	1632	1639	1746	|	|	...	...	...	1817	|	...	...	1830	1830	|	|	...	...	...
Stockholm Central a.	...	...	...	1739	...	...	...	|	|	1839	1939	...	...	...	...	1939	...	...	...	...	2039	2139	...	...	...
Oslo Sentral a.	...	...	...	...	...	...	...	2045	2145	...	...	...	...	...	...	...	...	...	...	...	...	...	...	...	...

train type	*ICE*	*EC*		*X2000*	*EC*		*IC*	*ICE*	*ICE*	*EC*		*EC*		[R]	[R]	[R]	[R]	*ICE*		*ICE*		*ICE*	*EC*	*EC*	
train number	**1514**	**35**	**1086**	**550**	**35**		**610**	**808**	**1512**	**237**		**237**		**4**	**6**	**202**	**10004**	**37**		**37**		**1508**	**39**	**39**	
notes	**1714**	🍷		Ⓑ	🍷					🍷		🍷		F	J	K	G	🍷		🍷			🍷	🍷	
notes		R c	P		X c		P h		Ⓑ	Z c		X c		Ⓑ	Ⓑ	Ⓑ	Ⓑ	R c		X c		Ⓑ	V c	Y c	
Berlin Hauptbahnhof d.	1125	...	...	...	...	...	...	1217	1316	...	...	...	...	...	...	...	...	1526	...	1526	...	1716	...	...	...
Hamburg Hbf d.	1301	1328	...	...	1328	...	...	1356	1452	1528	...	1528	...	...	...	...	...	1728	...	1728	...	1852	1928	1928	...
Lübeck Hbf d.	...	1406	...	...	1406	...	...	...	...	1606	...	1606	...	...	...	...	...	1806	...	1806	...	...	2006	2006	...
Puttgarden ⛴ d.	...	1510	...	...	1510	...	...	...	...	1710	...	1710	...	...	...	...	...	1910	...	1910	...	...	2110	2110	...
Rødby Ferry ⛴ a.	...	1600	...	...	1600	...	...	...	...	1800	...	1800	...	...	...	...	...	2000	...	2000	...	...	2200	2200	...
København H. d.	...	1811	1823	...	1827	1843	1859	...	...	2011	2023	2027	2043	...	...	...	...	2211	2223	2227	2243	...	0011	0024	0103
Malmö a.	...	...	1858	1914	...	1918	1942u	...	...	...	2058	...	2118	2308	2308	2308	2308	...	2258	...	2318	...	...	...	0138
Göteborg a.	...	...	2217	|	...	...	2232	...	...	...	...	...	...	0227	0227	|	0227	...	...	...	...	...	...	...	...
Stockholm Central a.	...	...	...	2339	...	...	...	...	...	...	...	...	...	|	0705	0554	|	...	...	...	...	...	...	...	...
Oslo Sentral a.	...	...	...	...	...	...	...	...	...	...	...	...	...	0700	...	...	0800	...	...	...	...	...	...	...	...

50 KØBENHAVN - KÖLN, AMSTERDAM, MÜNCHEN, BASEL and BERLIN

Night Trains (for day trains see above)

train type	**391**	**393**	*X2000*			*CNL*	*CNL*	*CNL*	*X2000*	**395**		*EN*
train number	①–⑤	⑥	**533**	**1081**		**483**	**483**	**483**	**541**	Ⓑ	**1105**	**211**
notes	⊠	⊠				**446**	**13483**	**473**		⊠		[R]
notes	🍷	🍷				**A**	**H**	**B**		🍷		**D b**
Oslo Sentral d.	0700	0900	...	...	...	...	...	...	...	1300	...	...
Stockholm Central d.	|	|	1221	...	...	...	...	...	1615	|	...	...
Göteborg d.	1052	1253	|	1342	...	...	...	...	|	1654	1742	...
Malmö d.	...	...	1646	1702	1742	...	...	...	|	...	|	...
København H. d.	...	...	1730	1737	1817	1853	1853	1853	|	...	|	*2043*
Malmö d.	...	...	...	...	...	|	|	|	2049	...	2052	2131
Odense d.	...	...	...	...	...	2023	2023	2023	...	...	...	|
Padborg ⛴ d.	...	...	...	...	...	2218	2218	2218	...	...	...	|
Flensburg ⛴ d.	...	...	...	...	...	2233	2233	2233	...	...	...	|
Köln 20 800 a.	...	...	...	...	...	0614	|	|	...	...	...	|
Amsterdam 22 a.	...	...	...	...	...	1029	|	|	...	...	...	|
München Hbf 900 a.	...	...	...	...	...	...	0857	|	...	...	...	|
Kufstein ⛴ a.	...	...	...	...	...	...	...	|	...	...	...	|
Wörgl a.	...	...	...	...	...	...	...	1037	...	...	...	|
Jenbach a.	...	...	...	...	...	...	...	...	...	...	...	|
Innsbruck a.	...	...	...	...	...	...	...	...	...	...	...	|
Basel SBB 912 a.	...	...	...	...	...	...	...	...	...	...	...	|
Berlin Hbf d.	...	...	...	...	...	...	...	...	...	...	...	0605

train type	*EN*			**394**	*X2000*	*CNL*	*CNL*	*CNL*		*X2000*	**396**	**398**
train number	**210**		**1026**	Ⓑ	**530**	**472**	**482**	**447**	**1038**	**534**	⑥	Ⓑ
notes	[R]					**482**	**13482**	**482**		**504**		
notes	**C b**			🍷		**B**	**H**	**A**			🍷	🍷
Berlin Hbf d.	2303	...	...	...	...	...	...	...	...	...	...	...
Basel SBB 912 d.	|	...	...	...	...	1804	...	...	...	...	...	...
Innsbruck d.	|	...	...	...	...	|	...	...	...	...	...	...
Jenbach d.	|	...	...	...	...	|	...	...	...	...	...	...
Wörgl d.	|	...	...	...	...	|	...	...	...	...	...	...
Kufstein ⛴ d.	|	...	...	...	...	|	...	...	...	...	...	...
München Hbf 900 d.	|	...	...	...	...	|	1900e	...	...	...	...	...
Amsterdam 22 d.	|	...	...	...	...	|	|	1901	...	...	...	...
Köln 20 800 d.	|	...	...	...	...	|	|	2228	...	...	...	...
Flensburg ⛴ a.	|	...	...	...	...	0547	0547	0547	...	...	...	...
Padborg ⛴ a.	|	...	...	...	...	0600	0600	0600	...	...	...	...
Odense a.	|	...	...	...	...	0818	0818	0818	...	...	...	...
Malmö a.	0808	0822	0908	...	0914	|	|	|	...	...	...	...
København H. d.	...	0857	|	...	|	0959	0959	0959	1023	...	...	...
Malmö a.	...	...	|	...	|	...	...	...	1058	1114	...	...
Göteborg a.	...	...	1217	1245	|	...	...	...	1417	|	1639	1746
Stockholm Central a.	...	...	...	|	1339	...	...	...	...	1540	|	|
Oslo Sentral a.	...	...	...	1645	...	...	...	...	...	...	2045	2145

A – *City Night Line* BOREALIS – 🛏 1, 2 cl., ▬ 2 cl., [2] (reclining) and 🍷 København - Köln - Amsterdam and v.v. [R] Special fares apply.

B – *City Night Line* AURORA – 🛏 1, 2 cl., ▬ 2 cl. (4, 6 berth), [2] (reclining) and ✕ København - Frankfurt - Basel and v.v. [R] Special fares apply.

C – BERLIN NIGHT EXPRESS – Daily May 2 - Aug. 23; ①④⑤⑥⑦ Aug. 24 - Sept. 27; ②④⑥ Sept. 28 - Oct. 10 (also Oct. 27, 31): 🛏 1, 2 cl. and ▬ 2 cl. Berlin - Malmö. [R] Special fares apply.

D – BERLIN NIGHT EXPRESS – Daily May 2 - Aug. 23; ③④⑤⑥⑦ Aug. 24 - Sept. 27; ③⑤⑦ Sept. 28 - Oct. 10 (also Oct. 23, 28): 🛏 1, 2 cl. and ▬ 2 cl. Malmö - Berlin. [R] Special fares apply.

F – Ⓑ June 14 - July 4; Aug. 10–30: 🛏 1, 2 cl., and ▬ 2 cl. Oslo - Göteborg - Malmö and v.v. [R].

G – Ⓑ July 5 - Aug. 9: 🛏 1, 2 cl., and ▬ 2 cl. Oslo - Göteborg - Malmö and v.v. [R].

H – *City Night Line* HANS CHRISTIAN ANDERSEN – 🛏 1, 2 cl., ▬ 2 cl., [2] (reclining) and ✕ København - München and v.v. [R] Special fares apply.

J – Ⓑ June 14 - Aug. 30: 🛏 1, 2 cl., ▬ 2 cl. and [2] Stockholm - Göteborg - Malmö and v.v. [R].

K – Ⓑ Aug. 31 - Dec. 12: 🛏 1, 2 cl., ▬ 2 cl. and [2] Stockholm - Malmö and v.v. [R].

L – ①–⑤ Aug. 10 - Dec. 12.

N – Apr. 3 - Aug. 9.

O – ⑤ (①–⑥ June 29 - Aug. 15).

P – June 14 - July 5; Aug. 10 - Dec. 12, for July 6 - Aug. 9 see note ✣.

Q – ⑥ (daily July 6 - Aug. 9).

R – Aug. 10 - Dec. 12.

S – Aug. 10 - Oct. 25.

T – Aug. 10 - Oct. 26.

V – Aug. 10 – 23.

W – Apr. 4 - Aug. 9.

X – June 14 - Aug. 9.

Y – June 19 - Aug. 9.

Z – Aug. 10 – 23, 28 – 30.

b – Train is conveyed by train-ferry Trelleborg ⛴ - Sassnitz Fährhafen ⛴ (Mukran) and v.v.

c – Passengers to / from Rødby or Puttgarden may be required to leave / board the train on board the ferry.

e – 1915 on ⑥⑦.

h – Not June 19.

s – Stops to set down only.

u – Calls to pick up only.

✣ – Services are disrupted enroute Göteborg - Malmo July 6 - Aug. 9; A replacement 🚌 service will operate and journey times are extended.

⊠ – Services are disrupted enroute Oslo - Göteborg July 6 - Aug. 9; A replacement 🚌 service will operate and journey times are extended.

X2000 – High speed train. [R] ✕.

BERLIN - GDAŃSK and KALININGRAD 51

train type			D	D				
train number			449	40449				
notes			A 🅁	C 🅁				
Berlin Lichtenberg d.	...	...	2104	2104	...	...	...	...
Kostrzyn ▦ d.	...	...	2244	|	...	...	...	...
Tczew a.	...	...	0748	|	...	...	...	...
Tczew d.	...	...	0758	|	...	...	...	...
Gdańsk Gł. a.	...	...	0824	|	...	...	...	...
Gdynia Gł. a.	...	...	0855	|	...	...	...	...
Malbork a.	...	...	...	0925	...	...	...	...
Malbork d.	...	...	...	0935	...	...	...	...
Elbląg a.	...	...	...	0959	...	...	...	...
Braniewo ▦ a.	...	...	...	1048	...	...	...	...
Kaliningrad § a.	...	...	...	1535	...	...	...	...

train type			D	D				
train number			448	40448				
notes			B 🅁	D 🅁				
Kaliningrad § d.	...	...	...	1823	...	...	...	...
Braniewo ▦ d.	...	...	...	1950	...	...	...	...
Elbląg d.	...	...	...	2040	...	...	...	...
Malbork a.	...	...	...	2107	...	...	...	...
Malbork d.	...	...	...	2117	...	...	...	...
Gdynia Gł. d.	...	...	2134	|	...	...	...	...
Gdańsk Gł. d.	...	...	2204	|	...	...	...	...
Tczew a.	...	...	2230	|	...	...	...	...
Tczew d.	...	...	2242	|	...	...	...	...
Kostrzyn ▦ a.	...	...	0617	|	...	...	...	...
Berlin Hbf a.	...	...	0806	0806	...	...	...	...

A – 🛏 1, 2 cl. Berlin (**449**) - Kostrzyn ▦ - Bydgoszcz (**65201**) - Tczew - Gdynia.

B – 🛏 1, 2 cl. Gdynia (**56200**) - Tczew - Bydgoszcz (**448**) - Kostrzyn ▦ - Berlin.

C – 🛏 1, 2 cl. Berlin (**40449**) - Kostrzyn ▦ - Bydgoszcz (**65200**) - Tczew (**55000**) - Braniewo ▦ (**7**) - Kaliningrad. (Table **1038**).

D – 🛏 1, 2 cl. Kaliningrad (**8**) - Braniewo ▦ (**55002**) - Tczew (**56200**) - Bydgoszcz (**40448**) - Kostrzyn ▦ - Berlin. (Table **1038**).

◐ – ▦ is at Kostrzyn (see Table **1000**).

§ – Moskva time (2 hours ahead of Polish time, 1 hour ahead of Kaliningrad time).

PRAHA - BŘECLAV - WIEN 53

train type	EC	EC*					EC		EC					EC	EC	EC	EC*		EC	EC	EC	EC			
train number	71	15		669	8605	2111	101		73		665	635	1931	566	275	103	17		75	173	277	105			
notes	✕	⊙				2	✕ A		🍸					✕	🍸	🍸	⊙		✕	✕ V		🍸			
Cheb d.	...	...	...	...	...	...	...	...	...	...	...	...	...	...	...	...	...	...	...	...	...	...	...	...	...
Plzeň hlavní d.	...	...	...	0803	...	...	...	...	...	...	1003	...	...	...	...	...	...	...	...	...	...	...	...	...	...
Praha Holešovice d.	...	...	...	|	...	...	...	...	0830	...	|	...	...	...	0930	...	...	...	1230	1330	1430	...	...	...	...
Praha hlavní d.	...	0557	...	|	...	...	0714	...	|	...	|	0914	...	...	|	...	1057	...	|	|	|	...	...	...	...
Tábor d.	...	|	...	|	...	...	0855	...	|	...	|	1055	...	...	|	...	|	...	|	|	|	...	...	...	...
Veselí nad Lužnicí d.	...	|	...	|	...	...	0921	...	|	...	|	1121	...	...	|	...	|	...	|	|	|	...	...	...	...
České Budějovice d.	...	|	...	0956	1001	...	1007	...	|	...	1156	1156	1212	...	|	...	|	...	|	|	|	...	...	...	...
Brno Hlavní d.	0716	0827	...	...	|	...	|	...	1116	...	...	...	|	...	1216	...	1327	...	1516	1616	1716	...	...	...	...
Břeclav ▦ d.	0802	0902	...	...	|	...	|	...	1202	...	...	...	|	...	1251	1302	1402	...	1602	1702	1751	1802	...	...	...
Summerau ▦ d.	|	|	...	...	|	...	1113	...	|	...	...	...	1336	...	...	|	|	...	|	|	...	|	...	...	...
Linz Hbf a.	|	|	...	...	|	...	1218	...	|	...	...	...	1443	1516	...	|	|	...	|	|	...	|	...	...	...
Salzburg a.	|	|	...	...	|	...	1347	...	|	...	...	...	...	1627	...	|	|	...	|	|	...	|	...	...	...
Zürich HB a.	|	|	...	...	|	...	...	...	|	...	...	...	...	...	...	|	|	...	|	|	...	|	...	...	...
Gmünd NÖ ▦ a.	|	|	...	...	1110	1129	...	...	|	...	...	...	...	...	...	|	|	...	|	|	...	|	...	...	...
Wien Franz-Josefs-Bf a.	|	|	...	...	...	1348	...	...	|	...	...	...	...	...	...	|	|	...	|	|	...	|	...	...	...
Wien Südbahnhof a.	0902	1002	...	...	...	...	...	...	1302	...	...	...	...	...	...	1402	1502	...	1702	1802	...	1902	...	...	...

train type					EC	EC	EC		CNL	
train number	645	925	361	1933	764	77	177	207	458	471
notes			2129 2119		✕	✕	✕ G	466 B	✕ C	203 P
Cheb d.	...	...	...	...	...	...	...	...	...	...
Plzeň hlavní d.	...	1603	...	...	...	...	...	...	...	...
Praha Holešovice d.	...	|	...	...	...	1630	1730	...	1840v	...
Praha hlavní d.	1514	|	...	...	...	|	|	1714	1829v	2140
Tábor d.	1655	|	...	...	...	|	|	1855	|	|
Veselí nad Lužnicí d.	1721	|	...	...	...	|	|	1921	|	|
České Budějovice d.	1756	1756	1819	1815	...	|	|	2034	|	|
Brno Hlavní d.	...	...	|	|	...	1916	2016	|	|	|
Břeclav ▦ d.	...	...	|	|	...	2002	2102	|	◧	0502
Summerau ▦ d.	...	...	|	1933	...	|	|	2147	|	|
Linz Hbf a.	...	...	|	2045	2053	|	|	2244	|	|
Salzburg a.	...	...	|	...	2158	|	|	0014	|	|
Zürich HB a.	...	...	|	...	...	|	|	0620	0917	|
Gmünd NÖ ▦ a.	...	...	1919	...	...	|	|	...	...	|
Wien Franz-Josefs-Bf a.	...	...	2158	...	...	|	|	...	...	|
Wien Südbahnhof a.	...	...	...	...	...	2102	2202	...	...	0630z

train type	EC				EC	EC	EC	EC		EC*	
train number	378	2100	924	640	76	104	276	172		14	
notes	✕ E	360 2			✕	🍸	🍸	✕ V		⊙	
Wien Südbahnhof d.	0558	...	...	...	0658	0858	...	0958	...	1058	...
Wien Franz-Josefs-Bf d.	|	0622	...	...	|	|	...	|	...	|	...
Gmünd NÖ ▦ d.	|	0847	...	...	|	|	...	|	...	|	...
Zürich HB d.	|	|	...	...	|	|	...	|	...	|	...
Salzburg d.	|	|	...	...	|	|	...	|	...	|	...
Linz Hbf d.	|	|	...	...	|	|	...	|	...	|	...
Summerau ▦ a.	|	|	...	...	|	|	...	|	...	|	...
Břeclav ▦ d.	0704	|	...	...	0804	0955	1004	1104	...	1157	...
Brno Hlavní d.	0741	|	...	...	0841	...	1041	1141	...	1232	...
České Budějovice a.	|	0946	1002	1001	|	...	|	|	...	|	...
Veselí nad Lužnicí a.	|	...	|	1032	|	...	|	|	...	|	...
Tábor a.	|	...	|	1057	|	...	|	|	...	|	...
Praha hlavní a.	|	...	|	1241	|	...	|	|	...	1501	...
Praha Holešovice a.	1029	...	|	...	1129	...	1329	1429	...	...	...
Plzeň hlavní a.	...	...	1158	...	...	...	...	...	...	...	...
Cheb a.	...	...	...	...	...	...	...	...	...	...	...

train type					EC		EC*		EC			EC		EC									CNL			
train number	1930	650	664		74		16		100	666		72		70		2114	1936	1934	1932		202		459	467		
notes					✕		⊙		✕ A			✕		✕		1760 2	1932 Z	1932 Y			470 Q		✕ C	206 B		
Wien Südbahnhof d.	...	...	...	...	1258	...	1558	...	...	...	...	1658	...	1858	...	...	...	...	...	...	2212z	...	...	...	...	...
Wien Franz-Josefs-Bf d.	...	...	...	...	|	...	|	...	...	...	...	|	...	|	...	1659	...	...	...	...	|	...	...	...	...	...
Gmünd NÖ ▦ d.	...	...	...	...	|	...	|	...	...	...	...	|	...	|	...	1928	...	...	...	...	|	...	...	...	...	...
Zürich HB d.	...	...	...	...	|	...	|	...	...	...	...	|	...	|	...	|	...	...	...	...	|	...	1944	2240	...	...
Salzburg d.	...	...	...	...	|	...	|	...	1422	...	...	|	...	|	...	|	...	...	...	...	|	...	|	0441	...	...
Linz Hbf d.	1308	...	...	...	|	...	|	...	1535	...	...	|	...	|	...	|	1808	1830	...	...	|	...	|	0614	...	...
Summerau ▦ a.	1414	...	...	...	|	...	|	...	1633	...	...	|	...	|	...	|	1926	1932	...	...	|	...	◧	0714	...	...
Břeclav ▦ d.	|	...	...	...	1404	...	1657	...	|	...	...	1804	...	2004	...	|	|	|	...	...	0127	...	|	|	...	...
Brno Hlavní d.	|	...	...	...	1441	...	1732	...	|	...	...	1841	...	2041	...	|	|	|	...	...	|	...	|	|	...	...
České Budějovice a.	1543	1601	1602	...	|	...	|	...	1748	1802	...	|	...	|	...	2029	2053	2053	2110	...	|	...	|	0820	...	...
Veselí nad Lužnicí a.	...	1632	|	...	|	...	|	...	1832	|	...	|	...	|	...	...	...	...	2151	...	|	...	|	0932	...	...
Tábor a.	...	1657	|	...	|	...	|	...	1857	|	...	|	...	|	...	...	...	...	2221	...	|	...	|	0957	...	...
Praha hlavní a.	...	1841	|	...	|	...	2001	...	2041	|	...	2131	...	2331	...	...	...	...	0005	...	0622	...	1052x	1141	...	...
Praha Holešovice a.	...	...	|	...	1729	...	...	...	...	|	...	...	...	...	...	...	...	...	...	...	...	...	1040x	...	...	...
Plzeň hlavní a.	...	...	1758	...	...	...	...	...	...	1958	...	...	...	...	...	...	...	...	...	...	...	...	...	...	...	...
Cheb a.	...	...	...	...	...	...	...	...	...	...	...	...	...	...	...	...	...	...	...	...	...	...	...	...	...	...

A – JÓŽE PLEČNIK – (12) and ✕ Praha - Linz - Salzburg and v.v.

B – MATTHIAS BRAUN – 🛏 1, 2 cl. and ▬ 2 cl. Praha - Summerau ▦ - Linz - Buchs ▦ - Zürich and v.v. (Table **86**). (12) Praha - Linz - Salzburg and v.v.

C – *City Night Line* CANOPUS – 🛏 1, 2 cl., ▬ 2 cl., (2) (reclining) and ✕ Zürich - Basel Bad Bf ▦ - Frankfurt (Main) Süd - Leipzig - Dresden - Bad Schandau ▦ - Praha Holešovice - Praha hlavní and v.v. 🅁 Special fares apply.

E – CARL MARIA VON WEBER – (12) and ✕ Wien - Praha - Berlin - Stralsund. To Ostseebad Binz on dates in Table **844**.

G – JOHANNES BRAHMS – (12) and ✕ Berlin - Dresden - Praha - Wien.

P – 🛏 1, 2 cl. Praha (**471**) - Přerov - Břeclav (**203**) - Wien.

Q – 🛏 1, 2 cl. Wien (**202**) - Břeclav (**470**) - Přerov - Praha.

V – VINDOBONA – (12) and ✕ Hamburg - Berlin - Praha - Wien and v.v.

Y – ①-⑤ (not Oct. 26, Dec. 8).

Z – ⑥⑦ (also Oct. 26, Dec. 8).

v – Train stops at Praha **hlavní** before Praha **Holešovice**.

x – Train stops at Praha **Holešovice** before Praha **hlavní**.

z – Wien **Westbahnhof**.

* – *SC* in Czech Republic.

⊙ – ČD 680 Pendolino (Czech Railways tilting train) 🅁 🍸 supplement payable.

◧ – ▦ at Basel Bad Bf and Bad Schandau.

OTHER TRAIN NAMES:			
	*EC** **14 / 15** – SMETANA	*EC* **70 / 71** – GUSTAV MAHLER	*EC* **74 / 75** – ZDENĚK FIBICH
	*EC** **16 / 17** – ANTONÍN DVOŘÁK	*EC* **72 / 73** – FRANZ SCHUBERT	*EC* **76 / 77** – GUSTAV KLIMT

56 KÖLN - BERLIN - WARSZAWA - MOSKVA

train type/number	EC				ICE	EC	ICE	EC	11011	11011	ICE	441	441	441					ICE	EC	ICE			
train number	41	12	10	12001	541	341	855	45	104	104	857	443	443	1249	445	445	445	445	859	47	651	449	449	447
notes	✕	11013	11001	68	🍷	[R] [·]	🍷	✕		132	🍷	14	20	64	30	668	84	282	🍷	✕	🍷	83704		[R]
	T	Z	P	C	①–⑥	W	A	T	V	EE	A	M	L	D	K	AA	G	S	A	T	A	DD	CC	J
Köln Hbf d.	...	...	...	...	0429	...	0749	...	...	...	0949	...	...	...	...	...	...	...	1149	...	1449	...	...	2228
Düsseldorf Hbf d.	...	...	...	...	0453	...	0753z	...	...	...	0953z	...	...	...	...	...	...	...	1153z	...	1453z	...	...	2202
Dortmund Hbf d.	...	...	...	...	0548	...	0848z	...	...	...	1048z	...	...	...	...	...	...	...	1248z	...	1548z	...	...	2356
Bielefeld Hbf d.	...	...	...	...	0638	...	0937	...	...	...	1137	...	...	...	...	...	...	...	1337	...	1638	...	...	0043
Hannover Hbf d.	...	...	...	...	0731	...	1031	...	...	...	1231	...	...	...	...	...	...	...	1431	...	1731	...	...	│
Hamburg Hbf d.	...	...	...	...	│	0705y	│	...	...	...	│	...	...	...	...	...	...	...	│	...	│	...	...	│
Berlin Zoo d.	...	...	...	...	│	│	│	...	...	...	│	1507	1507	1507	...	...	...	...	│	...	│	...	...	│
Berlin Hauptbahnhof d.	0629	...	...	...	0909s	0941	1211s	1229	...	...	1411s	1515	1515	1515	...	...	...	...	1611s	1629	1908s	...	...	0423
Berlin Ostbahnhof d.	0640u	...	...	...	0919	0951	1222	1240u	...	...	1422	1532	1532	1532	...	...	...	...	1622	1640u	1922	...	...	0447
Berlin Lichtenberg d.	│	...	...	...	...	│	...	│	...	...	...	│	│	│	2139	2139	2139	2139	...	│	...	2104	2104	│
Frankfurt (Oder) 🛃 d.	0733	...	...	...	...	│	...	1333	...	...	...	1711u	1711u	1711u	│	│	│	│	...	1733	...	│	│	│
Rzepin a.	0755	...	...	...	...	│	...	1355	...	...	...	1752u	1752u	1752u	2354u	2354u	2354u	2354u	...	1755	...	│	│	0602
Poznań Gł. a.	0927	...	...	...	...	│	...	1527	...	...	...	1956u	1956u	1956u	0138u	0138u	0138u	0138u	...	1927	...	0157	│	0733
Wrocław Gł. a.	│	...	...	...	...	1537	...	│	...	...	...	│	│	│	│	│	│	│	...	│	...	0432	│	│
Katowice a.	│	...	...	...	...	1820	...	│	...	...	...	│	│	│	│	│	│	│	...	│	...	0725	│	│
Kraków Gł. a.	│	...	...	...	...	1956	...	│	...	...	...	│	│	│	│	│	│	│	...	│	...	0918	│	│
Warszawa Centralna a.	1220	...	1530	1645	...	...	...	1820	2050	2050	...	2315u	2315u	2315u	0449u	0449u	0449u	0449u	...	2220	...	...	0810	1035
Warszawa Wschodnia a.	1232	1250	1540d	1654d	...	...	...	1837	2100d	2100d	...	2342u	2342u	2342u	0501u	0501u	0501u	0501u	...	2232	...	...	0827	1052
Terespol a.	...	1525	1842	│	...	...	...	...	0003	0003	...	0330u	0330u	0330u	│	│	│	│	...	...	...	...	...	1525
Brest 🛃 a.	...	1741	2058	│	...	...	...	...	0222	0222	...	0516r	0516r	0516r	│	│	│	│	...	...	...	...	...	1741
Yahodyn 🛃 a.	...	│	│	2300	...	...	...	...	│	│	...	│	│	│	1048	1048	1048	1048	...	...	...	...	...	│
Lviv a.	...	│	│	│	...	...	...	...	│	│	...	│	│	│	│	2255	│	│	...	...	...	...	...	│
Kyïv a.	...	│	│	1027	...	...	...	...	│	│	...	│	│	│	2112	...	│	2112	...	...	...	...	...	│
Odesa a.	...	│	│	...	...	...	...	...	│	│	...	│	│	│	...	...	0957	│	...	...	...	...	...	│
Simferopol a.	...	│	│	...	...	...	...	...	│	│	...	│	│	│	...	...	...	1330	...	...	...	...	...	│
Minsk a.	...	2336	0158	...	...	...	...	...	0804	0837	...	1046	1046	1114	...	...	...	...	...	...	...	...	...	2336
Orsha Tsentralnaya § a.	...	0227	0424	...	...	...	...	...	...	1136	...	1332	1330n	1408c	...	...	...	...	...	...	...	...	...	0227
St Peterburg Vitebski a.	...	│	│	...	...	...	...	...	...	│	...	│	0615	│	...	...	...	...	...	...	...	...	...	│
Smolensk Tsentralny 🛃 § a.	...	0456	0643	...	...	...	...	...	...	1408	...	1601	...	1652	...	...	...	...	...	...	...	...	...	0456
Moskva Belorusskaya ‡ a.	...	1059	1145	...	...	...	...	...	...	1954	...	2035	...	...	...	...	...	...	...	...	...	...	...	1059

train type/number	25			EC	ICE		EC	EC	ICE		EC	ICE				69	19	13			83	134	ICE
train number	103	103	67	46	858	9	44	340	844	11	40	1502	446	448	448	1248	442	442	40	29	84	84	652
notes	11008	11008	21000	✕	🍷	11002	✕	[R] [·]	🍷	11014	✕	700	[R]		38700	440	440	440	444	444	444	444	🍷
	EE	V	C	T	A	P	T	W		Z	T	🍷	E	CC	DD	B	Q	F	O	R	H	BB	A
Moskva Belorusskaya ‡ d.	1027	...	...	...	...	1650	...	...	...	2109	...	...	2109	...	...	...	...	0800	...	...	...	...	...
Smolensk Tsentralny 🛃 § d.	1620	...	...	...	...	2132	...	...	...	0231	...	...	0231	...	...	1117	...	1220	...	...	...	...	...
St Peterburg Vitebski d.	│	...	...	...	...	│	...	...	...	│	...	...	│	...	...	│	2355	│	...	...	...	...	...
Orsha Tsentralnaya § d.	1707	...	...	...	...	2153	...	...	...	0311	...	...	0311	...	...	1213	1250j	1250	...	...	...	...	...
Minsk d.	2040	2040	...	...	...	0019	...	...	...	0619	...	...	0619	...	...	1503	1529	1529	...	...	...	...	...
Simferopol d.	│	│	...	...	...	│	...	...	...	│	...	...	│	...	...	│	│	│	1537	...	...	...	...
Odesa d.	│	│	...	...	...	│	...	...	...	│	...	...	│	...	...	│	│	│	│	...	1822	...	...
Kyïv d.	│	│	1531	...	...	│	...	...	...	│	...	...	│	...	...	│	│	│	0924	0924	│	...	...
Lviv d.	│	│	│	...	...	│	...	...	...	│	...	...	│	...	...	│	│	│	│	│	│	0108	...
Yahodyn 🛃 d.	│	│	0317	...	...	│	...	...	...	│	...	...	│	...	...	│	│	│	1932	1932	1932	1932	...
Brest 🛃 d.	0240	0240	│	...	...	0532	...	...	...	1250	...	...	1250	...	...	2115f	2115	2115	│	│	│	│	...
Terespol d.	0238	0238	│	...	...	0530	...	...	...	1248	...	...	1248	...	...	2113	2113	2113	│	│	│	│	...
Warszawa Wschodnia d.	0549a	0549a	0811a	0723	...	0830a	1123	...	...	1529	1623	...	1742e	2118	...	2351s	2351s	2351s	2339s	2339s	2339s	2339s	...
Warszawa Centralna d.	0600	0600	0820	0735	...	0840	1135	...	...	...	1635	...	1755	2130	...	0107s	0107s	0107s	2352s	2352s	2352s	2352s	...
Kraków Gł. d.	...	...	...	│	...	...	│	0723	...	...	│	...	│	│	1945	│	│	│	│	│	│	│	...
Katowice d.	...	...	...	│	...	...	│	0854	...	...	│	...	│	│	2134	│	│	│	│	│	│	│	...
Wrocław Gł. d.	...	...	...	│	...	...	│	1132	...	...	│	...	│	│	0024	│	│	│	│	│	│	│	...
Poznań Gł. d.	...	...	...	1027	...	...	1427	│	...	...	1927	...	2101	│	0305	0429s	0429s	0429s	0310s	0310s	0310s	0310s	...
Rzepin d.	...	...	...	1200	...	...	1600	│	...	...	2100	...	2242	│	│	0617s	0617s	0617s	0500s	0500s	0500s	0500s	...
Frankfurt (Oder) 🛃 a.	...	...	...	1222	...	...	1622	│	...	...	2120	...	2308	│	│	0658s	0658s	0658s	│	│	│	│	...
Berlin Lichtenberg a.	...	...	...	│	...	...	│	│	...	...	│	...	│	0806	0806	│	│	│	0715	0715	0715	0715	...
Berlin Ostbahnhof a.	...	...	...	1315	1338	...	1715	1719	1738	...	2215	...	0002	...	...	0823	0823	0823	...	...	...	...	0840
Berlin Hauptbahnhof a.	...	...	...	1327	1348d	...	1727	1730	1748d	...	2227	2305	0029	...	...	0900	0900	0900	...	...	...	...	0850d
Berlin Zoo a.	...	...	...	...	│	...	...	│	│	...	...	│	│	...	...	0909	0909	0909	...	...	...	...	│
Hamburg Hbf a.	...	...	...	...	│	...	...	2024x	│	...	...	0043	│	...	...	...	...	...	...	...	...	...	│
Hannover Hbf a.	...	...	...	...	1528	...	...	...	1928	...	...	...	│	...	...	...	...	...	...	...	...	...	1028
Bielefeld Hbf a.	...	...	...	...	1620	...	...	...	2020	...	...	...	0356	...	...	...	...	...	...	...	...	...	1120
Dortmund Hbf a.	...	...	...	...	1709z	...	...	...	2110	...	...	...	0450	...	...	...	...	...	...	...	...	...	1209z
Düsseldorf Hbf a.	...	...	...	...	1805z	...	...	...	2147	...	...	...	0654	...	...	...	...	...	...	...	...	...	1305z
Köln Hbf a.	...	...	...	...	1809	...	...	...	2231	...	...	...	0614	...	...	...	...	...	...	...	...	...	1309

A – (12) and ✕ Köln - Wuppertal - Hamm - Berlin and Düsseldorf - Hamm - Berlin and v.v. Table **810**.

B – SARATOV EXPRESS – ④ (④⑥ June 4 - Oct. 10): 🛏 1, 2 cl. (1, 2, 4 berth) Saratov (**69**) (depart 1129) - Smolensk (depart ⑤) - Orscha - Terespol (**1248**) - Warszawa (**440**) - Berlin (arrive ⑥). ②: 🛏 2 cl. (3, 4 berth) Novosibirsk (**113**), also Rostov-na-Donu (**104**) (depart ④), Omsk ③ - Perm II ③ - Gorkii ④ - Orscha (**13**) (⑤) - Minsk - Terespol (**442**) - Berlin (arrive ⑥). (Table **1980**).

C – KYÏV EKSPRES / KIEV EXPRESS – 🛏 1, 2 cl. Warszawa - Kyïv and v.v.

D – SARATOV EXPRESS – ⑥ (①⑥ June 6 - Oct. 17): 🛏 1, 2 cl. (1, 2, 4 berth) Berlin (**441**) - Warszawa (**1249**) - Brest 🛃 (**70**) (arrive ⑦) - Orsha (**64**) - Smolensk - Saratov ① (arrive 1516). ⑥: 🛏 2 cl. (3, 4 berth) Berlin (**443**) - Brest 🛃 (**14**) - Orscha (**64**) - Gorkii (arrive ①) - Perm II ② - Omsk ③ - Novosibirsk ③, also Rostov-na-Donu ② (Table **1980**).

E – JAN KIEPURA – 🛏 1, 2 cl. Moskva (**11**) - Brest (**11014**) - Warszawa (**446**) - Köln - Amsterdam (journey 2 nights). 🛏 1, 2 cl., ▬ 2 cl., (2) and ✕ Warszawa (*EN* **446**) - Köln - Amsterdam. Table **24**.

F – MOSKVA EXPRESS – ②④⑥ Dec. 12 - May 30; ①②③④⑥ June 1 - Oct. 17; ②④⑥ Oct. 21 - Dec. 12: 🛏 1 cl. *Lux* and 🛏 1, 2 cl. Moskva (**13**) - Terespol (**442**) - Warszawa - Berlin. ✕ Moskva - Brest.

G – June 3 - Oct. 15 ①③④⑤⑥: 🛏 2 cl. Berlin (**445**) - Kovel (**84**) - Odesa (journey 2 nights).

H – May 30 - Oct. 14 ①②③④⑥: 🛏 2 cl. Odesa (**83**) - Kovel (**444**) - Berlin (journey 2 nights).

J – JAN KIEPURA – 🛏 1, 2 cl. Amsterdam (**447**) - Köln - Warszawa (**11013**) - Brest (**12**) - Moskva (journey 2 nights). 🛏 1, 2 cl., ▬ 2 cl., (2) and ✕ Amsterdam (*EN* **447**) - Köln - Warszawa. Table **24**.

K – June 1 - Oct. 18: 🛏 2 cl. Berlin (**445**) - Dorohusk (**30**) - Kyïv. ✕ Warszawa - Kyïv. Conveys on ④⑦ June 4 - Oct. 15: 🛏 2 cl. Berlin - Kyïv (**116**) - Kharkiv (journey 2 nights).

L – ⑤⑦ Dec. 14 - May 21: 🛏 2 cl. Berlin (**441**) - Warszawa (**443**) - Brest 🛃 (**14**) - Orsha (**20**) - St Peterburg (journey 2 nights).

M – MOSKVA EXPRESS – ③⑤⑦ Dec. 12 - May 31; ②③④⑤⑦ June 2 - Oct. 18; ③⑤⑦ Oct. 21 - Dec. 12: 🛏 1 cl. *Lux* and 🛏 1, 2 cl. Berlin (**443**) - Warszawa - Brest 🛃 (**14**) - Moskva. ✕ Brest - Moskva.

O – May 31 - Oct. 14 ③⑦: 🛏 2 cl. Simferopol (**40 / 39**) - Kyïv (**29**) - Dorohusk (**444**) - Berlin (journey 2 nights).

P – POLONEZ – 🛏 1, 2 cl., 🛏 1, 2 cl. (Lux) and 🍷 Warszawa - Moskva and v.v. ✕ Brest - Moskva and v.v.

Q – ③⑤ Dec. 12 - May 22: 🛏 2 cl. St Peterburg (**19**) - Orsha (**13**) - Terespol (**442**) - Warszawa (**440**) - Berlin (journey 2 nights).

R – May 31 - Oct. 17: 🛏 2 cl. Kyïv (**29**) - Dorohusk (**444**) - Berlin. ✕ Kyïv - Warszawa. Conveys on ②⑤ 🛏 2 cl. Kharkiv (**343**) - Kyïv (**29**) - Berlin (journey 2 nights).

S – June 2 - Oct. 13 ②⑤: 🛏 2 cl. Berlin (**445**) - Kyïv (**282**) - Simferopol (journey 2 nights).

T – BERLIN WARSZAWA EXPRESS – (12) and ✕ Berlin - Poznań - Warszawa and v.v. [R] Special fares apply. Supplement payable in Poland.

V – 🛏 1, 2 cl. Warszawa - Minsk and v.v.

W – WAWEL – (12) and 🍷 (Hamburg ①–⑥ -) Berlin - Cottbus - Forst 🛃 - Legnica - Wrocław - Kraków and Kraków - Wrocław - Legnica - Forst 🛃 - Cottbus - Berlin (- Hamburg ⑧).

Z – OST WEST – 🛏 1, 2 cl. Warszawa - Moskva and v.v.

AA – June 6 - Oct. 17 ⑥: 🛏 2 cl. Berlin (**445**) - Dorohusk (**30**) - Kovel (**668**) - Lutsk - Lviv.

BB – June 5 - Oct. 16 ⑤: 🛏 2 cl. Lviv (**134**) - Zdolbunov (**84**) - Kovel (**444**) - Dorohusk - Berlin (journey 2 nights).

CC – 🛏 1, 2 cl., ▬ 2 cl. and (2) (reclining) Berlin - Kostrzyn 🛃 - Warszawa and v.v. Conveys 🛏 1, 2 cl. Berlin - Kostrzyn 🛃 - Gdynia / Kaliningrad and v.v.

DD – 🛏 1, 2 cl., ▬ 2 cl. and (2) (reclining) Berlin - Kostrzyn 🛃 - Poznań - Kraków and v.v.

EE – 🛏 1, 2 cl. Warszawa - Moskva and v.v.

a – Arrival time.
c – Depart 1426.
d – Departure time.
e – Arrive 1529.
f – Arrive 1856.
j – Arrive 1047.
n – Depart 1637.
r – Depart 0720.
s – Stops to set down only.
u – Stops to pick up only.
x – ⑧.
y – ①–⑥.
z – For train number, days of running and possible earlier timings of Düsseldorf portion see Table **800**.
[·] – Supplement payable in Poland.
‡ – Also known as Moskva **Smolenskaya** station.
§ – 🛃: Osinovka (BY) / Krasnoye (RU).

Summary of Berlin - Lviv, Kyïv, Odesa, Simferopol service from Oct. 18.

train number	441	441	441	441
Berlin Hbf d.	1515	1515	1515	1515
Warszawa C. d.	2315	2315	2315	2315
Warszawa W. d.	2359	2359	2359	2359
Yahodyn 🛃 a.	0608	0608	0608	0608
Lviv a.	│	2300	│	│
Kyïv a.	1648	...	1650	1650
Odesa a.	...	...	0533	│
Simferopol a.	...	...	...	0845

train number	440	440	440	440
Simferopol d.	1534	...	...	...
Odesa d.	│	...	2300	...
Kyïv d.	0924	0924	│	...
Lviv d.	│	│	│	0102
Yahodyn 🛃 d.	1932	1932	1932	1932
Warszawa W a.	2339	2339	2339	2339
Warszawa C. a.	0107	0107	0107	0107
Berlin Hbf a.	0900	0900	0900	0900

DORTMUND - FRANKFURT - NÜRNBERG - PRAHA 57

train type	RE	RE¶	ICE	ICE	RE	RE	ALX¶		IC	ICE	ICE	ALX	RE¶		IC	IC	ICE	RE	RE	ALX¶		ICE	IC	CNL	
train number	3690	351	21	523*	19905	3583	355		2065	25	621	37978	353		2069	2023	629	19919	3599	357		17	2215	459	
notes			🍷	①–⑥					🍷	🍷	🍷	🍷			🍷	🍷	Ⓑ	19921				🍷	🍷	A	
Dortmund Hbf d.	...	...	...	0401	...	...	...	...	...	0636	...	...	...	...	...	1036	...	...	...	...	...	...	1938	...	...
Köln Hbf d.	...	...	...	0518t	...	...	...	...	...	0753	0944t	...	...	...	...	1153	1344t	...	...	...	...	2020	2053	...	...
Bonn Hbf d.	...	...	...	|	...	...	...	...	...	0814	|	...	...	...	...	1214	|	...	...	...	...	|	2114	...	...
Koblenz d.	...	...	...	⊖	...	...	...	...	...	0848	⊖	...	...	...	...	1248	⊖	...	...	...	...	⊖	2148	...	...
Mainz d.	...	...	...	|	...	...	...	...	...	0940	|	...	...	...	...	1340	|	...	...	...	...	|	2240	...	...
Frankfurt Flughafen ✈ d.	...	...	...	0637	...	...	...	...	...	1001	1037	...	...	...	...	1401	1437	...	...	...	...	2117	2300	...	...
Frankfurt (Main) Hbf d.	...	...	0622	0654	...	...	...	...	...	1021	1054	...	...	...	...	1413	1454	...	...	...	...	2130	2310	0055k	...
Würzburg Hbf d.	...	...	0734	0805	...	...	...	...	...	1134	1205	...	...	...	...	...	1605	...	...	...	...	...	...	|	...
Karlsruhe Hbf d.	...	...	|	|	...	...	...	...	0906	|	|	...	...	...	1306	...	|	...	...	...	...	...	...	|	...
Stuttgart Hbf d.	...	...	|	|	0640	...	...	...	1007	|	|	...	...	...	1407	...	|	1440	...	...	...	...	...	|	...
München Hbf d.	...	...	|	|	|	...	0844	...	|	|	|	1244	...	...	|	...	|	|	...	1643	...	...	...	|	...
Nürnberg Hbf d.	...	0540	0831	0859	0925	0936	|	...	1216	1228	1259	|	1339	...	1616	...	1659	1725	1736	|	...	...	...	|	...
Regensburg d.	0623	|	0922	...	...	|	1022	...	...	...	...	1419	|	...	...	...	...	...	|	1819	...	...	...	|	...
Schwandorf d.	0650	0655	...	...	...	1044	1056	...	...	...	...	1446	1456	...	...	...	...	...	1843	1856	...	...	...	|	...
Furth im Wald 🏛 d.	...	0749	...	...	...	...	1149	...	...	...	...	...	1549	...	...	...	...	...	...	1949	...	...	...	◧	...
Plzeň hlavní a.	...	0857	...	...	...	...	1257	...	...	...	...	...	1657	...	...	...	...	...	...	2057	...	...	...	|	...
Praha hlavní a.	...	1050	...	...	...	...	1450	...	...	...	...	...	1850	...	...	...	...	...	...	2250	...	...	...	1052	...

train type	RE¶	ALX	RE	ICE	ICE	IC	ALX¶	RE	RE	ICE	ICE	IC		RE¶	ALX	RE	ICE	ICE	ALX¶	RE		CNL	IC	ICE	
train number	350	37977	19906	722	1024	2068	354	3558	19914	624	26	2064		352	37985	19922	526	22	356	3574		458	2320	16	
notes		🍷	🍷	🍷	🍷	🍷			🍷	🍷	🍷	🍷			🍷		Ⓑ	🍷				A	🍷	🍷	
Praha hlavní d.	0511	...	...	...	...	...	0911	...	...	...	...	...	...	1311	...	...	...	...	1711	...	...	1829	...	...	...
Plzeň hlavní d.	0700	...	...	...	...	...	1100	...	...	...	...	...	...	1500	...	...	...	...	1900	...	...	|	...	...	...
Furth im Wald 🏛 a.	0811	...	...	...	...	...	1211	...	...	...	...	...	...	1611	...	...	...	...	2011	...	...	◧	...	...	...
Schwandorf a.	0903	0908	...	...	...	...	1303	1309	...	...	...	...	...	1703	1708	...	...	...	2105	2113	...	|	...	...	...
Regensburg a.	|	0937	...	...	...	...	1337	|	...	...	1433	...	...	|	1736	...	...	...	2148	|	...	|	...	...	...
Nürnberg Hbf a.	1009	|	1035	1100	...	1141	|	1421	1435	1500	1527	1541	...	1809	|	1835	1900	1927	|	2223	2335	|	...	...	...
München Hbf a.	...	1115	|	|	...	|	1515	...	|	|	|	|	...	...	1915	|	|	|	2324	...	|	|	...	...	...
Stuttgart Hbf a.	...	...	1318	|	...	1353	...	...	1718	|	|	1753	...	...	...	2118	|	|	...	...	|	|	...	...	...
Karlsruhe a.	...	...	...	|	...	1453	...	...	...	|	|	1853	...	...	...	...	|	|	...	...	|	|	...	...	...
Würzburg Hbf a.	...	...	...	1154	...	...	...	...	...	1554	1625	...	...	...	...	...	1954	2024	...	...	0056	|	...	...	...
Frankfurt (Main) Hbf a.	...	...	...	1305	1344	...	...	...	...	1705	1736	...	...	...	...	...	2105	2136	...	...	...	0400k	0532	0729	...
Frankfurt Flughafen ✈ a.	...	...	...	1321	1355	...	...	...	...	1721	1755	...	...	...	...	...	2121	2157	...	...	...	...	0555	0740	...
Mainz a.	...	...	...	|	1418	...	...	...	...	|	1818	...	...	...	...	...	|	2218	...	...	...	...	0616	|	...
Koblenz a.	...	...	...	⊖	1510	...	...	...	...	⊖	1910	...	...	...	...	...	⊖	2310	...	...	...	...	0710	⊖	...
Bonn Hbf a.	...	...	...	|	1542	...	...	...	...	|	1943	...	...	...	...	...	|	2342	...	...	...	...	0742	|	...
Köln Hbf a.	...	...	...	1414t	1605	...	...	...	...	1814t	2005	...	...	...	...	...	2219t	0005	...	...	...	...	0805	0840	...
Dortmund Hbf a.	...	...	...	...	1720	...	...	...	...	1929	2122	...	...	...	...	...	2338	0122	...	...	...	...	0920	...	...

A – *City Night Line* CANOPUS – 🛏 1,2 cl., ▬ 2 cl., (2) (reclining) and 🍷 Zürich - Basel - Frankfurt (Main) **Süd** - Děčín 🏛 - Praha and v.v. Ⓡ Special fares apply.

k – Frankfurt (Main) **Süd**.

t – Köln **Messe / Deutz**.

* – Train **1123** on ⑥.

¶ – *R* in the Czech Republic.

⊖ – Via Köln - Frankfurt high speed line.

◧ – 🏛 is Děčín; Ticketing point is Schöna.

ALX – Arriva Länderbahn Express.

TRAIN NAMES *RE* **351 / 352** JAN HUS *RE* **353 / 350** KAREL ČAPEK *ALX* **355 / 356** ALBERT EINSTEIN *ALX* **357 / 354** FRANZ KAFKA

BRUSSELS - KÖLN - FRANKFURT - LEIPZIG - DRESDEN - PRAHA 58

train type	CNL	D		ICE	ICE	EC	ICE	ICE	EC	ICE	EC	⇌	ICE	ICE	EC	⇌	ICE	ICE	EC	ICE	ICE	EN	
train number	459	61459		1543	1543	173	1745	1545	175	1547	177	9407	105	1549	379	9415	507	1641	179	15	1643	477	
notes	A			🍷 ①–⑥		🍴 C	🍷 ⑦f	🍷j ①–⑥	🍴 H	🍷	🍴 S	🍷	🍷	🍷	🍴 D	🍷	🍷	🍷	🍴 Q	🍷	🍷		
Brussels Midi / Zuid d.	...	...	...	...	...	...	...	...	...	...	...	0755	...	...	...	0959	...	...	...	1218	...	...	...
Köln Hbf d.	...	...	...	...	...	...	...	...	...	...	...	1015	1054	...	...	1215	1254	...	...	1420	...	...	...
Frankfurt Flughafen ✈ d.	...	...	...	...	...	...	...	0811	...	1011	...	...	1151	1211	...	...	1351	1411	...	1522	1611	...	...
Frankfurt (Main) Hbf d.	...	...	...	0618	...	...	0822	|	...	|	...	...	...	|	...	...	...	|	...	...	|	...	...
Frankfurt (Main) Süd d.	0055	...	...	|	...	...	|	0822	...	1022	...	...	...	1222	...	...	...	1422	...	...	1622	...	...
Fulda d.	|	0341	...	0715	...	...	0915	0915	...	1115	...	...	...	1315	...	...	...	1515	...	...	1715	...	...
Erfurt Hbf d.	0520s	0525	...	0838	...	...	1038	1038	...	1238	...	...	...	1438	...	...	...	1638	...	...	1838	...	...
Weimar d.	0540s	0542	...	0852	...	...	1052	1052	...	1252	...	...	...	1452	...	...	...	1652	...	...	1852	...	...
Leipzig d.	0641s	0651	...	0951	0951	...	1151	1151	...	1351	...	...	...	1551	...	...	...	1751	...	...	1951	...	...
Dresden Hbf d.	0807s	0816	...	1105	1102	1110	1305	1305	1310	1505	1510	...	...	1705	1710	...	...	1905	1910	...	2105	2210	...
Bad Schandau 🏛 ◧ d.	0850s	0853	...	...	...	1138	...	...	1338	...	1538	...	...	...	1738	...	...	...	1938	...	...	|	...
Děčín 🏛 ◧ d.	0912s	0915	...	...	...	1155	...	...	1355	...	1555	...	...	...	1755	...	...	...	1955	...	...	2255	...
Praha Holešovice a.	1040s	1040	...	...	...	1318	...	...	1518	...	1718	...	...	...	1918	...	...	...	2118	...	...	0018	...
Praha hlavní a.	1052	1052	...	...	...	|	...	...	|	...	|	...	...	...	...	...	...	...	...	...	...	0030	...
Wien Südbahnhof a.	...	...	...	...	...	1802	...	...	|	...	2202	...	...	...	...	...	...	...	...	...	...	...	...
Bratislava Hlavná a.	...	...	...	...	...	...	...	...	1947	...	...	...	...	...	...	...	...	...	...	...	...	...	...
Budapest Keleti a.	...	...	...	...	...	...	...	...	2232	...	...	...	...	...	...	...	...	...	...	...	...	...	...

train type	EC	ICE	ICE	⇌	EC	ICE	ICE	⇌	EC	ICE	ICE	EC	ICE	ICE	EC	ICE	ICE	EC	ICE	RE	RE	D	CNL
train number	178	1640	508	9450	176	1548	506	9458	378	1546	10	174	1744	1744	172	1742	1542	170	1740	17470	17472	61458	458
notes	🍴 T	🍷	🍷	🍷	🍴 P	🍷	🍷	🍷	🍴 F	🍷	🍷	🍴 H	🍷 ⑦	🍷 ①–⑤	🍴 C	🍷 ⑦	🍷 ①–⑤	🍴 L	Q	Ⓑ			A
Budapest Keleti d.	...	...	...	...	...	...	...	...	...	...	...	0528	...	...	...	...	...	0928	...	...	...	...	...
Bratislava Hlavná d.	...	...	...	...	...	...	...	...	...	...	...	0801	...	...	...	...	...	1201	...	...	...	...	...
Wien Südbahnhof d.	...	...	...	...	...	...	...	...	0558	...	...	|	...	...	0958	...	...	|	...	...	...	...	...
Praha hlavní d.	0629	...	...	...	...	...	...	...	|	...	...	|	...	...	|	...	...	|	...	...	...	1829	1829
Praha Holešovice d.	0640	...	...	...	0840	...	...	...	1040	...	...	1240	...	...	1440	...	...	1640	...	...	...	1840	1840u
Děčín 🏛 ◧ d.	0802	...	...	...	1002	...	...	...	1202	...	...	1402	...	...	1602	...	...	1802	...	...	...	2002	2002u
Bad Schandau 🏛 ◧ a.	0817	...	...	...	1017	...	...	...	1217	...	...	1417	...	...	1617	...	...	1817	...	...	...	2017	2019u
Dresden Hbf a.	0846	0854	...	...	1046	1054	...	...	1246	1254	...	1446	1454	1454	1646	1654	1654	1846	1854	1920	2020	2047	2115u
Leipzig a.	...	1007	...	...	...	1207	...	...	...	1407	...	...	1607	1607	...	1807	1807	...	2005	2101	2201	2242	2253u
Weimar a.	...	1105	...	...	...	1305	...	...	...	1505	...	...	1705	1705	...	1905	1905	...	...	...	...	0003	0005u
Erfurt Hbf a.	...	1118	...	...	...	1318	...	...	...	1518	...	...	1718	1718	...	1918	1918	...	...	...	...	0020	0117u
Fulda a.	...	1242	...	...	...	1442	...	...	...	1642	...	...	1842	1842	...	2042	2042	...	...	...	...	...	|
Frankfurt (Main) Süd a.	...	1335	...	...	...	1535	...	...	...	1735	...	...	1935	|	...	2138	2138	...	...	...	...	...	0359
Frankfurt (Main) Hbf a.	...	|	...	...	...	|	...	...	...	|	...	...	|	1940	...	|	2146	...	...	...	...	...	...
Frankfurt Flughafen ✈ a.	...	1348	1409	...	...	1548	1609	...	...	1748	1843	...	1948	...	...	2149	...	...	...	...	...	...	...
Köln Hbf a.	...	...	1505	1544	...	...	1705	1744	...	...	1940	...	...	...	...	...	...	...	...	...	...	...	...
Brussels Midi / Zuid a.	...	...	...	1801	...	...	...	2001	...	...	2135	...	...	...	...	...	...	...	...	...	...	...	...

A – *City Night Line* CANOPUS – 🛏 1,2 cl., ▬ 2 cl., (2) (reclining) and 🍷: Zürich - Basel - Frankfurt (Main) **Süd** - Děčín 🏛 - Praha and v.v. Ⓡ Special fares apply.
C – VINDOBONA – (12) and 🍴 Hamburg - Berlin - Dresden - Praha - Wien and v.v.
D – (12) and 🍴 Stralsund - Berlin - Dresden - Praha - Brno. From Ostseebad Binz on dates in Table **844**.
F – (12) and 🍴 Wien - Praha - Dresden - Berlin - Stralsund. To Ostseebad Binz on dates in Table **844**.
H – JAN JESENIUS – (12) and 🍴 Hamburg - Berlin - Dresden - Praha - Budapest and v.v.
L – HUNGARIA – (12) and 🍴 Berlin - Dresden - Praha - Budapest and v.v.
P – (12) and 🍴 Brno - Praha - Dresden - Berlin - Hamburg.
Q – (12) and 🍴 Berlin - Dresden - Praha - Brno.
S – JOHANNES BRAHMS – (12) and 🍴 Berlin - Dresden - Praha - Wien.
T – JOHANNES BRAHMS – (12) and 🍴 Praha - Dresden - Berlin.

Q – ①②③④⑦.
f – Also Oct. 3.
j – Not Oct. 3.
s – Stops to set down only.
u – Stops to pick up only.
◧ – Ticketing point is Schöna.

60 HAMBURG - BERLIN - PRAHA / WIEN - BUDAPEST - BUCUREŞTI and İSTANBUL

train type	EC	345	345	IC			355¶	EC	EC	EC	EN	371	463	463	EC	EC	EC	347¶	491				383	EC	EC	
train number	345	335	335	55	293	335	1822	273	275	171	371	463	[R]	491	173	277	175	341	81031	337	391	347¶	4663	77	133	
notes	✕			✕				✕	475	✕	✕	[R]		81031			✕	491						✕		
	J	FF	HH	⚡	W	K	C	P			R	F	AA	[R]	V			G	T	Y		E	LL			
Hamburg Hbf d.	...	...	...	...	...	...	...	...	...	...	...	...	...	KK	0628z	...	0833z	...	...	...	...	...	...	...	...	...
Berlin Hbf d.	...	...	...	...	...	...	...	...	...	0635	...	...	...	...	0835	...	1035	...	...	...	...	...	...	...	...	...
Dresden Hbf d.	...	...	...	...	...	...	...	...	...	0910	...	...	...	...	1110	...	1310	...	...	...	...	...	...	...	...	...
Bad Schandau 🛃 d.	...	...	...	...	...	...	...	...	...	0938	...	...	...	...	1138	...	1338	...	...	...	...	...	...	...	...	...
Děčín d.	...	...	...	...	...	...	...	...	...	0955	...	...	...	...	1155	...	1355	...	...	...	...	...	...	...	...	...
Praha Holešovice d.	...	...	...	...	...	...	...	0730	0930	1130	...	...	...	...	1330	1430	1530	...	...	...	...	...	...	1630	...	...
Praha hlavní d.	0528	0528	...	...	...	...	...	|	|	|	...	...	...	...	|	|	|	...	...	...	...	...	...	|	...	...
Pardubice d.	0636	0636	...	...	...	...	...	0836	1036	1236	...	...	...	...	1436	1536	1636	...	...	...	...	...	...	1736	...	...
Brno Hlavní d.	0816	0816	...	...	...	...	...	1016	1216	1416	...	...	...	...	1616	1716	1816	...	...	...	...	...	...	1916	...	...
Břeclav d.	0855	0855	...	...	...	...	...	1055	1255	1455	...	...	...	...	1702	1755	1855	...	...	...	...	...	...	1951	1955	...
Wien Südbahnhof a.	|	|	...	...	...	...	...	|	|	|	...	...	...	...	1802	|	|	...	...	...	...	...	...	2102	|	...
Wien Westbahnhof d.	|	|	...	...	...	...	...	|	|	|	...	...	...	...	...	|	|	1850	...	...	...	1850	...	...	|	...
Kúty 🛃 d.	0910	0910	...	...	...	...	...	1110	1310	1510	...	...	...	...	...	1810	1910	|	...	...	...	|	...	...	2010	...
Bratislava Hlavná d.	0950	0950	0950	...	...	...	...	1150	1347	1550	...	...	...	...	...	1850	1950	|	...	...	...	|	...	...	2050	...
Rajka 🛃 a.	|	|	|	...	...	...	...	|	...	|	...	...	...	...	...	...	|	|	...	...	...	|	...	...	...	...
Štúrovo 🛃 d.	1112	1112	1112	...	...	...	...	1312	...	1712	...	...	...	...	...	...	2112	|	...	...	...	|	...	...	...	...
Hegyeshalom 🛃 a.	|	|	|	...	...	...	...	|	...	|	...	...	...	...	...	...	|	1951	...	...	...	1951	...	...	...	...
Györ a.	|	|	|	...	...	...	...	|	...	|	...	...	...	...	...	...	|	2027	...	...	...	2027	...	...	...	...
Budapest Nyugati a.	|	|	|	...	...	...	...	|	...	|	...	...	...	...	...	...	|	|	...	...	...	|	...	...	...	...
Budapest Keleti a.	1232	1232	1232	...	...	...	...	1432	...	1832	...	...	...	...	...	...	2232	2219	...	...	...	2219	...	...	...	...
Budapest Keleti d.	1305	1305	1305	...	...	...	1313	...	...	...	1913	1913	...	...	...	...	...	2300	...	...	...	2313	...	...	...	...
Lökösháza a.	|	|	|	...	...	...	1610	...	...	...	2205	2205	...	...	...	...	...	|	...	...	...	0205	...	...	...	...
Curtici 🛃 a.	|	|	|	...	...	...	1742	...	...	...	2342	2342	...	...	...	...	...	|	...	...	...	0342	...	...	...	...
Arad a.	|	|	|	...	...	...	1814	...	...	...	0015	0015	...	...	...	...	...	|	...	...	...	0414	...	...	...	...
Timişoara a.	|	|	|	...	...	...	|	...	...	...	|	|	...	...	...	...	...	|	...	...	...	|	...	...	...	...
Craiova a.	|	|	|	...	...	...	0315	...	...	...	|	|	...	...	...	...	...	|	...	...	...	|	...	...	...	...
Braşov a.	|	|	|	...	...	...	|	...	...	...	0702	0702	...	...	...	...	...	|	...	...	...	1053	...	...	...	...
Bucureşti Nord a.	|	|	|	...	...	...	0619	...	...	...	1028	1028	...	...	...	...	...	|	...	...	...	1359	...	...	...	...
Bucureşti Nord d.	|	|	|	...	...	...	...	...	...	...	...	1216	1216	1216	...	...	...	|	...	...	...	...	2004	...	...	...
Ruse 🛃 a.	|	|	|	...	...	...	...	...	...	...	...	1445	1445	1445	...	...	...	|	...	...	...	...	2230	...	...	...
Varna a.	|	|	|	...	...	...	...	...	...	...	...	|	|	|	...	...	...	|	...	...	...	...	|	...	...	...
Burgas a.	|	|	|	...	...	...	...	...	...	...	...	|	|	|	...	...	...	|	...	...	...	...	|	...	...	...
Subotica 🛃 a.	1626	1626	1626	...	...	...	...	...	...	...	...	|	|	|	...	...	...	0206	...	...	...	...	|	...	...	...
Novi Sad a.	1858	1858	1858	...	...	...	...	...	...	...	...	|	|	|	...	...	...	0437	...	...	...	...	|	...	...	...
Beograd a.	2031	2031	2031	...	2115	2200	...	...	...	...	...	|	|	|	...	...	...	0613	0750	0750	1405	...	|	...	...	...
Niš a.	...	0152	0152	...	0110	0152	...	...	...	...	...	|	|	|	...	...	...	1137	1137	1137	1745	...	|	...	...	...
Tabanovci 🛃 a.	...	0545	0545	...	|	0545	...	...	...	...	...	|	|	|	...	...	...	|	|	1555	2138	...	|	...	...	...
Skopje a.	...	0650	0650	...	|	0650	...	...	...	...	...	|	|	|	...	...	...	|	|	1700	2250	...	|	...	...	...
Idoméni 🛃 a.	...	1105	1105	...	|	1105	...	...	...	...	...	|	|	|	...	...	...	|	|	2100	...	...	|	...	...	...
Dimitrovgrad 🛃 a.	...	|	|	...	0432	|	...	...	...	...	...	|	|	|	...	...	...	1457	1457	|	...	...	|	...	...	...
Kalotina Zapad 🛃 a.	...	|	|	...	0545	|	...	...	...	...	...	|	|	|	...	...	...	1604	1604	|	...	...	|	...	...	...
Sofiya a.	...	|	|	...	0715	|	...	...	...	...	...	2133	2133	|	...	...	...	1740	1740	|	...	...	0600	...	...	...
Svilengrad a.	...	|	|	...	...	|	...	...	...	...	...	|	|	0033	...	...	...	...	0033	|	...	...	...	...	...	...
Kapikule 🛃 a.	...	|	|	...	...	|	...	...	...	...	...	|	|	0130	...	...	...	...	0130	|	...	...	...	...	...	...
İstanbul Sirkeci a.	...	|	|	...	...	|	...	...	...	...	...	|	|	0825	...	...	...	...	0825	|	...	...	...	...	...	...
Kulata 🛃 a.	...	|	|	...	...	|	...	...	...	...	...	0230	0230	...	...	...	...	...	...	|	...	...	...	...	...	...
Thessaloníki a.	...	1231	1231	1454	...	1231	...	...	...	...	...	0524	0524	...	...	...	...	...	...	2233	...	...	...	...	...	...
Athína Lárisa a.	...	...	...	1949	...	...	...	...	...	...	...	...	...	...	...	...	...	...	...	...	...	...	...	...	...	...

train type	EC	SC		EC	EC	471	471	EN		463¶	EN
train number	177	19		379	179	477	477	477	375	375	477
notes	✕	⊙		✕	✕	375	375			[R]	203
		N		H		CC	SS	A	B	L	M
Hamburg Hbf d.	...	...	...	...	...	...	...	...	...	...	...
Berlin Hbf d.	1235	...	...	1435	1635	...	...	1900	...	...	1900
Dresden Hbf d.	1510	...	...	1710	1910	...	...	2210	...	...	2210
Bad Schandau 🛃 d.	1538	...	...	1738	1938	...	...	|	...	...	|
Děčín d.	1555	...	...	1755	1955	...	...	2255	...	...	2255
Praha Holešovice d.	1730	...	...	1930	2130	...	...	0020	...	...	0020
Praha hlavní d.	|	1823	...	|	|	2140	2140	0042	...	...	0042
Pardubice d.	1836	1925	...	2036	2236	2308	2308	|	...	...	|
Brno Hlavní d.	2016	2053	...	2214	0015	|	|	0327	...	...	0327
Břeclav d.	2102	2130	...	...	...	0335	0335	0446	...	...	0502
Wien Südbahnhof a.	2202	|	...	...	...	|	|	|	...	...	|
Wien Westbahnhof d.	...	|	...	...	...	|	|	|	...	0600q	0630
Kúty 🛃 d.	...	|	...	...	...	0350	0350	0501	...	|	...
Bratislava Hlavná d.	...	2220	...	...	...	0553	0553	0553	...	|	...
Rajka 🛃 a.	...	...	...	...	...	|	|	|	...	|	...
Štúrovo 🛃 d.	...	...	...	...	...	0718	0718	0718	...	|	...
Hegyeshalom 🛃 a.	...	...	...	...	...	|	|	|	...	0653	...
Györ a.	...	...	...	...	...	|	|	|	...	0722	...
Budapest Nyugati a.	...	...	...	...	...	|	|	|	...	|	...
Budapest Keleti a.	...	...	...	...	...	0832	0832	0832	...	0854	...
Budapest Keleti d.	...	...	...	...	...	0913	0913	...	0913	0913	...
Lökösháza a.	...	...	...	...	...	1205	1205	...	1205	1205	...
Curtici 🛃 a.	...	...	...	...	...	1342	1342	...	1342	1342	...
Arad a.	...	...	...	...	...	1414	1414	...	1414	1414	...
Timişoara a.	...	...	...	...	...	|	|	...	|	|	...
Craiova a.	...	...	...	...	...	|	|	...	|	|	...
Braşov a.	...	...	...	...	...	2049	2049	...	2049	2049	...
Bucureşti Nord a.	...	...	...	...	...	2355	2355	...	2355	2355	...
Bucureşti Nord d.	...	...	...	...	...	...	0130	...	...	...	...
Ruse 🛃 a.	...	...	...	...	...	...	0430	...	...	...	...
Varna a.	...	...	...	...	...	...	0655	...	...	...	...
Burgas a.	...	...	...	...	...	...	0923	...	...	...	...
Subotica 🛃 a.	...	...	...	...	...	...	...	...	...	...	...
Novi Sad a.	...	...	...	...	...	...	...	...	...	...	...
Beograd a.	...	...	...	...	...	...	...	...	...	...	...
Niš a.	...	...	...	...	...	...	...	...	...	...	...
Tabanovci 🛃 a.	...	...	...	...	...	...	...	...	...	...	...
Skopje a.	...	...	...	...	...	...	...	...	...	...	...
Idoméni 🛃 a.	...	...	...	...	...	...	...	...	...	...	...
Dimitrovgrad 🛃 a.	...	...	...	...	...	...	...	...	...	...	...
Kalotina Zapad 🛃 a.	...	...	...	...	...	...	...	...	...	...	...
Sofiya a.	...	...	...	...	...	...	...	...	...	...	...
Svilengrad a.	...	...	...	...	...	...	...	...	...	...	...
Kapikule 🛃 a.	...	...	...	...	...	...	...	...	...	...	...
İstanbul Sirkeci a.	...	...	...	...	...	...	...	...	...	...	...
Kulata 🛃 a.	...	...	...	...	...	...	...	...	...	...	...
Thessaloníki a.	...	...	...	...	...	...	...	...	...	...	...
Athína Lárisa a.	...	...	...	...	...	...	...	...	...	...	...

train type/number	EC	EC	SC	EC	EC	EC		81032	490	EC	
train number	178	176	18	378	132	76	390	490	340	174	
notes	✕	✕	⊙	✕		✕			346	✕	
			N	Q				T	G [R]		
Athína Lárisa d.	...	...	...	...	...	...	...	...	...	...	...
Thessaloníki d.	...	...	...	...	...	...	...	...	...	...	...
Kulata 🛃 d.	...	...	...	...	...	...	...	...	...	...	...
İstanbul Sirkeci d.	...	...	...	...	...	...	...	2200	...	...	...
Kapikule 🛃 d.	...	...	...	...	...	...	...	0405	...	...	...
Svilengrad d.	...	...	...	...	...	...	...	0505	...	...	...
Sofiya d.	...	...	...	...	...	...	...	1155	1155	...	...
Kalotina Zapad 🛃 d.	...	...	...	...	...	...	...	1303	1303	...	...
Dimitrovgrad 🛃 d.	...	...	...	...	...	...	...	1230	1230	...	...
Idomeni 🛃 d.	...	...	...	...	...	...	...	|	|	...	...
Skopje d.	...	...	...	...	...	...	0740	|	|	...	...
Tabanovci 🛃 d.	...	...	...	...	...	...	0844	|	|	...	...
Niš d.	...	...	...	...	...	...	1235	1520	1520	...	...
Beograd d.	...	...	...	...	...	...	1633	1918	2120	...	...
Novi Sad d.	...	...	...	...	...	...	...	...	2252	...	...
Subotica 🛃 d.	...	...	...	...	...	...	...	...	0125	...	...
Burgas d.	...	...	...	...	...	...	...	...	|	...	...
Varna d.	...	...	...	...	...	...	...	...	|	...	...
Ruse 🛃 d.	...	...	...	...	...	...	...	...	|	...	...
Bucureşti Nord a.	...	...	...	...	...	...	...	...	|	...	...
Bucureşti Nord d.	...	...	...	...	...	...	...	...	|	...	...
Braşov d.	...	...	...	...	...	...	...	...	|	...	...
Craiova d.	...	...	...	...	...	...	...	...	|	...	...
Timişoara d.	...	...	...	...	...	...	...	...	|	...	...
Arad d.	...	...	...	...	...	...	...	...	|	...	...
Curtici 🛃 d.	...	...	...	...	...	...	...	...	|	...	...
Lököshaza d.	...	...	...	...	...	...	...	...	|	...	...
Budapest Keleti a.	...	...	...	...	...	...	...	...	0504	...	...
Budapest Keleti d.	...	...	...	...	...	...	...	...	0555	0528	...
Budapest Nyugati d.	...	...	...	...	...	...	...	...	|	|	...
Györ d.	...	...	...	...	...	...	...	...	0725	|	...
Hegyeshalom 🛃 d.	...	...	...	...	...	...	...	...	0758	|	...
Štúrovo 🛃 d.	...	...	...	...	...	...	...	...	|	0641	...
Rajka 🛃 d.	...	...	...	...	...	...	...	...	|	|	...
Bratislava Hlavná d.	...	...	0539	...	0655	...	...	...	|	0801	...
Kúty 🛃 d.	...	...	|	...	0735	...	...	...	|	0841	...
Wien Westbahnhof a.	...	...	|	...	|	...	...	...	0859	|	...
Wien Südbahnhof d.	...	...	|	0558	|	0658	...	...	...	|	...
Břeclav d.	...	...	0631	0704	0748	0804	...	...	...	0904	...
Brno Hlavní d.	...	0541	0706	0741	...	0841	...	...	...	0941	...
Pardubice d.	...	0720	0833	0920	...	1020	...	...	...	1120	...
Praha hlavní d.	0629	|	0935	|	...	|	...	...	...	|	...
Praha Holešovice d.	0640	0840	...	1040	...	1129	...	...	...	1240	...
Děčín d.	0802	1002	...	1202	...	...	...	...	...	1402	...
Bad Schandau 🛃 a.	0817	1017	...	1217	...	...	...	...	...	1417	...
Dresden Hbf a.	0846	1046	...	1246	...	...	...	...	...	1446	...
Berlin Hbf a.	1119	1320	...	1518	...	...	...	...	...	1720	...
Hamburg Hbf a.	...	1526f	...	...	...	...	...	...	...	1927f	...

CONTINUED ON NEXT PAGE

İSTANBUL - BUCUREŞTI - BUDAPEST - WIEN / PRAHA - BERLIN - HAMBURG 60

train type/number train number notes	4662 382 Ⓡ LL	EC 276	346¶ E	EC 172 V	336 Y	81032 490 462 Ⓡ KK	462 Ⓡ AA	462 370 Ⓡ F	EN 370 ✕ R	EC 170 ✕	EC 274 474	EC 272 ✕ P	292 W	IC 52 Ⓡ⁄ ✕	334 K	1821 354¶ D	EC 344 ✕ J	344 GG	344 JJ	EN 202 476 X	374 B	EN 476 U	374 476 470 DD	374 476 470 TT	374 462 Ⓡ L
Athína Lárisa d.	...	...	...	...	...	...	...	...	...	...	...	...	...	1051	...	...	...	...	...	...	...	...	...	...	...
Thessaloníki d.	...	...	...	...	0945	...	2345	2345	...	...	...	...	...	1550	1705	...	...	1705	1705	...	...	...	...	...	...
Kulata 🛃 d.	...	...	...	...	│	...	0240	0240	...	...	...	...	...	...	│	...	...	│	│	...	...	...	...	...	...
İstanbul Sirkeci d.	...	...	...	...	│	2200	│	│	...	...	...	...	...	...	│	...	...	│	│	...	...	...	...	...	...
Kapikule 🛃 d.	...	...	...	...	│	0405	│	│	...	...	...	...	...	...	│	...	...	│	│	...	...	...	...	...	...
Svilengrad d.	...	...	...	...	│	0505	│	│	...	...	...	...	...	...	│	...	...	│	│	...	...	...	...	...	...
Sofiya d.	1930	...	...	...	│	│	0745	0745	...	...	...	...	2120	...	│	...	...	│	│	...	...	...	...	...	...
Kalotina Zapad 🛃 d.	│	...	...	...	│	│	│	│	...	...	...	...	2231	...	│	...	...	│	│	...	...	...	...	...	...
Dimitrovgrad 🛃 d.	│	...	...	...	│	│	│	│	...	...	...	...	2200	...	│	...	...	│	│	...	...	...	...	...	...
Idoméni 🛃 d.	│	...	...	...	1107	│	│	│	...	...	...	...	│	...	1830	...	...	1830	1830	...	...	...	...	...	...
Skopje d.	│	...	...	...	1305	│	│	│	...	...	...	...	│	...	2044	...	...	2044	2044	...	...	...	...	...	...
Tabanovci 🛃 d.	│	...	...	...	1415	│	│	│	...	...	...	...	│	...	2155	...	...	2155	2155	...	...	...	...	...	...
Niš d.	│	...	...	...	1835	│	│	│	...	...	...	...	0050	...	0148	...	...	0148	0148	...	...	...	...	...	...
Beograd d.	│	...	...	...	2233	│	│	│	...	...	...	...	0448	...	0544	...	0730	0730	0730	...	...	...	...	...	...
Novi Sad d.	│	...	...	...	...	│	│	│	...	...	...	...		...	...	...	0904	0904	0904	...	...	...	...	...	...
Subotica 🛃 d.	│	...	...	...	...	│	│	│	...	...	...	...	...	...	...	...	1136	1136	1136	...	...	...	...	...	...
Burgas d.	│	...	...	...	...	│	│	│	...	...	...	...	...	...	...	...	│	│	│	...	...	...	...	1925	...
Varna d.	│	...	...	...	...	│	│	│	...	...	...	...	...	...	...	...	│	│	│	...	...	...	...	2200	...
Ruse 🛃 d.	0315	...	...	...	...	1405	1405	1405	...	...	...	...	...	...	...	...	│	│	│	...	...	...	...	0215	...
Bucureşti Nord a.	0544	...	...	...	...	1719	1719	1719	...	...	...	...	...	...	...	...	│	│	│	...	...	...	...	0430	...
Bucureşti Nord d.	...	...	1645	...	...	...	...	1950	1950	...	...	...	...	...	...	2345	│	│	│	...	0550	...	0550	0550	0550
Braşov d.	...	...	1947	...	...	...	...	2248	2248	...	...	...	...	...	...	│	│	│	│	...	0904	...	0904	0904	0904
Craiova d.	...	...	│	...	...	...	...	│	│	...	...	...	...	...	...	0252	│	│	│	...	│	...	│	│	│
Timişoara d.	...	...	│	...	...	...	...	│	│	...	...	...	...	...	...	│	│	│	│	...	│	...	│	│	│
Arad d.	...	...	0226	...	...	...	...	0545	0545	...	...	...	...	...	...	1145	│	│	│	...	1552	...	1552	1552	1552
Curtici 🛃 d.	...	...	0253	...	...	...	...	0618	0618	...	...	...	...	...	...	1218	│	│	│	...	1618	...	1618	1618	1618
Lököshaza d.	...	...	0230	...	...	...	...	0555	0555	...	...	...	...	...	...	1144	│	│	│	...	1550	...	1550	1550	1550
Budapest Keleti a.	...	...	0517	...	...	...	...	0847	0847	...	...	...	...	...	...	1447	1453	1453	1453	...	1847	...	1847	1847	1847
Budapest Keleti d.	...	...	0555	...	...	...	...	...	...	0928	...	1328	...	...	...	...	1528	1528	1528	...	...	1958	1958	1958	2105
Budapest Nyugati d.	...	...	│	...	...	...	...	...	...	│	...	│	...	...	...	...	│	│	│	...	...	│	│	│	│
Győr d.	...	...	0725	...	...	...	...	...	...	│	...	│	...	...	...	...	│	│	│	...	...	│	│	│	2232
Hegyeshalom 🛃 d.	...	...	0758	...	...	...	...	...	...	│	...	│	...	...	...	...	│	│	│	...	...	│	│	│	2301
Štúrovo 🛃 d.	...	...	│	...	...	...	...	...	...	1041	...	1441	EC	...	...	...	1641	1641	1641	...	...	2120	2120	2120	│
Rajka 🛃 d.	...	...	│	...	...	...	...	...	...	│	...	│	**130**	...	...	...	│	│	│	...	...	│	│	│	│
Bratislava Hlavná d.	...	0907	│	...	...	...	...	...	...	1201	1401	1601	1655	EC	...	...	1801	1801	1801	...	...	2255	2255	2255	│
Kúty 🛃 d.	...	0948	│	...	...	...	...	...	...	1241	1441	1641	1735	**72**	...	...	1841	1841	...	...	...	2335	0041	0041	│
Wien Westbahnhof a.	...	│	0859	...	...	...	...	...	...	│	│	│	│	✕	...	...	│	│	...	2212	...	│	│	│	2353q
Wien Südbahnhof d.	...	│	...	0958	...	...	...	...	...	│	│	│	│	1658	...	...	│	│	...	│	...	│	│	│	...
Břeclav d.	...	1004	...	1104	...	...	...	...	...	1304	1504	1704	1750	1804	...	...	1904	1904	...	0015	...	0015	0127	0127	...
Brno Hlavní d.	...	1041	...	1141	...	...	...	...	...	1341	1541	1741	...	1841	...	...	1941	1941	...	0052	...	0052	│	│	...
Pardubice d.	...	1220	...	1320	...	...	...	...	...	1520	1720	1920	...	2020	...	...	2120	2120	...	│	...	│	0448	0448	...
Praha hlavní d.	...	│	...	│	...	...	...	...	...	│	1840	2031	...	2131	...	...	2231	2231	...	│	...	│	0622	0622	...
Praha Holešovice d.	...	1329	...	1440	...	...	...	...	...	1640	...	...	...	...	...	...	...	...	...	0340	...	0340	...	...	...
Děčín d.	...	...	...	1602	...	...	...	...	...	1802	...	...	...	...	...	...	...	...	...	0502	...	0502	...	...	...
Bad Schandau 🛃 a.	...	...	...	1617	...	...	...	...	...	1817	...	...	...	...	...	...	...	...	...	│	...	│	...	...	...
Dresden Hbf a.	...	...	...	1646	...	...	...	...	...	1846	...	...	...	...	...	...	...	...	...	0547	...	0547	...	...	...
Berlin Hbf a.	...	...	...	1920	...	...	...	...	...	2120	...	...	...	...	...	...	...	...	...	0914	...	0914	...	...	...
Hamburg Hbf a.	...	...	...	2132f	...	...	...	...	...	...	...	...	...	...	...	...	...	...	...	...	...	...	...	...	...

A – METROPOL – 🛏 1, 2 cl., ▬ 2 cl. and (2) Berlin **Wannsee** (depart 1733) - Berlin **Hbf** - Berlin **Ost** (1805) - Praha - Budapest.
B – PANNONIA – (12) and ✕ Ⓡ Budapest - Bucureşti and v.v.
C – MAROS / MUREŞ – (12) Budapest (**355**) - Arad - Targu Mureş. Conveys 🛏 1, 2 cl. and (2) Venezia (**241**) - Budapest (**355**) - Arad (**1822**) - Bucureşti (journey 2 nights) and conveys on May 31 - Sept. 20: ▬ 1, 2 cl. Venezia - Budapest - Bucureşti.
D – MUREŞ / MAROS – (12) Targu Mureş - Arad (**354**) - Budapest. Conveys 🛏 1, 2 cl. and (2) Bucureşti (**1822**) - Arad (**354**) - Budapest (**240**) - Venezia (journey 2 nights) and conveys on May 29 - Sept. 19: ▬ 1, 2 cl. Bucureşti - Budapest - Venezia.
E – DACIA – 🛏 1, 2 cl., ▬ 2 cl., (2) and ✕ Wien - Budapest - Bucureşti and v.v. (1) Wien - Budapest - Lökösháza and v.v. (12) Curtici - Bucureşti and v.v.
F – 🛏 1, 2 cl. Budapest (**371**) - Bucureşti (**463**) - Sofiya - Thessaloníki and Thessaloníki (**462**) - Sofiya - Bucureşti (**370**) - Budapest (journey 2 nights).
G – BEOGRAD – 🛏 1, 2 cl. and ▬ 2 cl. Wien - Budapest - Beograd and v.v. 🛏 1, 2 cl. Wien - Beograd - Sofiya and v.v. (2) Budapest - Beograd and v.v. (12) Beograd - Sofiya and v.v.
H – (12) and ✕ Stralsund (depart 1139) - Berlin - Praha - Brno (from Ostseebad Binz on dates shown in Table **844**).
J – AVALA – (12) and ✕ Praha - Budapest - Beograd and v.v. Conveys 🛏 2 cl. Moskva - Budapest - Beograd and v.v. (journey 2 nights, Table **97**). Conveys ②③⑥⑦ June 9 - Sept. 16: ▬ 2 cl. Praha - Budapest - Subotica - Bar (arrive 0849). Conveys ①③④⑦ June 10 - Sept. 17: ▬ 2 cl. Bar (depart 1800) - Subotica - Budapest - Praha.
K – HELLAS EXPRESS – 🛏 1, 2 cl., ▬ 2 cl. and (12) Beograd - Thessaloníki and v.v. 🛏 1, 2 cl., ▬ 2 cl. and (2) Beograd - Skopje and v.v.
L – KÁLMÁN IMRE – 🛏 1, 2 cl., ▬ 2 cl. and (2) München - Wien - Budapest and v.v. 🛏 1, 2 cl. and ▬ 1, 2 cl. München - Wien - Budapest (**375 / 374**) - Lökösháza - Bucureşti and v.v.
M – METROPOL – 🛏 1, 2 cl., ▬ 2 cl. and (2) Berlin **Wannsee** (depart 1733) - Berlin **Hbf** - Berlin **Ost** (1805) - Praha - Wien.
N – SLOVENSKÁ STRELA – (12) and ✕ Praha - Bratislava and v.v.
P – JAROSLAV HAŠEK – (12) and ✕ Praha - Budapest and v.v.
Q – CARL MARIA VON WEBER – (12) and ✕ Wien - Praha - Berlin - Stralsund (arrive 1822). To Ostseebad Binz on dates shown in Table **844**.
R – *EuroNight* ISTER – 🛏 1, 2 cl., ▬ 1, 2 cl., (2) and ✕ Budapest - Bucureşti and v.v. (12) Budapest - Lökösháza and v.v.
T – BALKAN EXPRESS – (12) Beograd - Sofiya and v.v. 🛏 1, 2 cl. Beograd - Sofia - İstanbul and v.v. Conveys June 1 - Oct. 30 from Sofia, June 2 - Oct. 31 from İstanbul: ▬ 2 cl. Sofia - İstanbul and v.v.
U – METROPOL – 🛏 1, 2 cl., ▬ 2 cl. and (2) Budapest - Praha - Berlin **Ost** (arrive 0907) - Berlin **Hbf** - Berlin **Wannsee** (0941).
V – VINDOBONA – (12) and ✕ Hamburg Altona - Hamburg Hbf - Berlin - Praha - Wien and v.v.
W – 🛏 1, 2 cl., ▬ 2 cl. and (12) Beograd - Sofiya and v.v.
X – METROPOL – 🛏 1, 2 cl., ▬ 2 cl. and (2) Wien - Praha - Berlin **Ost** (arrive 0907) - Berlin **Hbf** - Berlin **Wannsee** (0941).
Y – OLYMPUS – (12) Beograd - Skopje - Thessaloníki and v.v.
AA – ROMANIA – 🛏 1, 2 cl., ▬ 1, 2 cl. and 🍷 Bucureşti - Sofiya - Thessaloníki and v.v. (2) Bucureşti - Sofiya and v.v.
CC – AMICUS – 🛏 1, 2 cl. and (2) Praha (**471**) - Břeclav (**477**) - Budapest. June 12 - Sept. 30: 🛏 1, 2 cl. Praha (**471**) - Břeclav (**477**) - Budapest (**375**) - Bucureşti.
DD – AMICUS – 🛏 1, 2 cl. and (2) Budapest (**476**) - Břeclav (**470**) - Praha. June 12 - Sept. 29: 🛏 1, 2 cl. Bucureşti (**374**) - Budapest (**476**) - Břeclav (**470**) - Praha.
FF – ⑤ June 12 - Sept. 18: ▬ 2 cl. Praha - Thessaloniki.
GG – ⑥ June 13 - Sept. 19: ▬ 2 cl. Thessaloníki - Praha.
HH – ① June 15 - Sept. 14: ▬ 2 cl. Bratislava - Thessaloníki.
JJ – ② June 16 - Sept. 15: ▬ 2 cl. Thessaloníki - Bratislava.
KK – BOSPHOR – 🛏 1, 2 cl. and ▬ 2 cl. Bucureşti - İstanbul and v.v.
LL – BULGARIA EXPRESS – 🛏 1, 2 cl. and (12) Bucureşti - Sofiya and v.v. Conveys 🛏 2 cl. Moskva, Lviv, Kyïv and Minsk - Sofiya and v.v. on dates shown in Table **98**.
SS – ⑤ June 12 - Sept. 4: 🛏 2 cl. and ▬ 2 cl. Praha - Ruse 🛃 (**1183**) - Kaspichan (**1181**) - Varna. ②④⑥ June 11 - Sept. 5: 🛏 2 cl. and ▬ 2 cl. Praha - Ruse 🛃 (**1183**) - Kaspichan - Burgas. ⑥ June 13 - Sept. 5: ▬ 2 cl. Bratislava - Varna. ③⑤⑦ June 12 - Sept. 6: ▬ 2 cl. Bratislava - Burgas. (All journeys two nights).
TT – ⑦ June 14 - Sept. 6: 🛏 2 cl. and ▬ 2 cl. Varna (**1180**) - Kaspichan (**1182**) - Ruse 🛃 - Praha. ①④⑥ June 13 - Sept. 7: 🛏 2 cl. and ▬ 2 cl. Burgas (**1182**) - Praha. ⑦ June 14 - Sept. 6: ▬ 2 cl. Varna - Bratislava. ①④⑥ June 15 - Sept. 7: ▬ 2 cl. Burgas - Bratislava. (All journeys two nights).

a – Arrival time.
f – Arrive Hamburg **Altona** 14–16 minutes later.
n – Arrive 0804.
q – Wien **Meidling**.
r – Depart 2020.
x – Depart 2300.
z – Depart Hamburg **Altona** 14 minutes earlier.
⊙ – ČD 680 Pendolino (Czech Railways tilting train). Ⓡ supplement payable.
* – *SC* in Czech Republic.
⁄ – Supplement payable.
¶ – Train number for international bookings.
§ – It is reported that ▬ 2 cl. could replace the 🛏 1, 2 cl. on certain days.

OTHER TRAIN NAMES:

EC 70 / 71 –	ANTONÍN DVOŘÁK
EC 72 / 73 –	JOHANN GREGOR MENDEL
EC 74 / 75 –	SMETANA
EC 77 –	GUSTAV KLIMT
EC 174 / 175 –	JAN JESENIUS
EC 274 / 275 –	SLOVAN
EC 276 / 277 –	FRANTIŠEK KŘIŽÍK
391 –	BORA STANKOVIC
390 –	KOCO RACIN

62 MÜNCHEN - LJUBLJANA - ZAGREB - BEOGRAD - THESSALONÍKI

train type/number	IC	IC	EC111		IC	IC	EC113	EC	D			241	D			499		499				IC	
train number	592	313	EC211	483	690	311	EC213	115	315	491	337	413	413	391		741	481	481	415	293	335	55	
notes			🍷◧				🍷◧	✕					✕			419						✕	
			G	A			M	W	Y	D	K	R				L		C	F	H	E	⚡	
München Hbf d.	...	...	0827	...	...	...	1221	1421	...	...	...	...	...	...	...	2340	...	2340	...	...	...	...	...
Salzburg Hbf ▣ d.	0812	...	1012	...	1212	...	1412	1612	...	...	...	...	...	...	...	0134	...	0134	...	...	...	...	...
Bischofshofen d.	0855	...	1055	...	1255	...	1455	1655	...	...	...	...	...	...	...	|	...	|	...	...	...	...	...
Schwarzach St Veit d.	0911	...	1111	...	1311	...	1511	1711	...	...	...	...	...	...	...	0226	...	0226	0430	...	...	...	...
Bad Gastein d.	0941	...	1141	...	1341	...	1541	1741	...	...	...	...	...	...	...	|	...	|	0503	...	...	...	...
Villach Hbf d.	1043	1052	1254	...	1443	1452	1654	1843	1927	...	...	...	...	...	...	0407	...	0407	0626	...	...	...	...
Jesenice ▣ a.	...	1130	1330	...	...	1530	1730	...	2005	...	...	...	...	...	...	0444	...	0444	0706	...	...	...	...
Ljubljana a.	...	1232	1430	1453	...	1629	1830	...	2108	...	...	0200	...	...	...	0605	0620	0605	0810	...	...	...	...
Rijeka a.	...	...	|	1725	...	|	|	...	|	...	...	|	...	...	...	|	0851	0851	|	...	...	...	...
Dobova ▣ a.	...	...	1610	...	...	1811	2008	...	2250	...	...	0334	...	...	...	0750	...	...	0948	...	...	...	...
Zagreb a.	...	...	1657	...	...	1856	2055	...	2334	...	...	0418	...	...	...	0834	...	...	1034	...	...	...	...
Zagreb d.	...	...	1710	...	...	...	...	...	2355	...	...	0603	0603	...	...	0900	...	...	1100	...	...	...	...
Vinkovci a.	...	...	2020	...	...	...	...	...	0305	...	...	0914	0914	...	...	1206	...	...	1410	...	...	...	...
Šid ▣ a.	...	...	2120	...	...	...	...	...	0411	...	...	1019	1019	...	...	1336	...	...	1508	...	...	...	...
Beograd a.	...	...	2321	...	...	...	...	...	0621	0750	0750	1225	1225	1405	...	1538	...	...	1718	2115	2200	...	...
Niš a.	...	...	...	...	...	...	...	...	...	1137	1137	...	...	1745	...	...	...	...	...	0110	0152	...	...
Dimitrovgrad ▣ a.	...	...	...	...	...	...	...	...	...	1457	|	...	...	|	...	...	...	...	...	0432	|	...	...
Kalotina Zapad ▣ a.	...	...	...	...	...	...	...	...	...	1604	|	...	...	|	...	...	...	...	...	0545	|	...	...
Sofiya a.	...	...	...	...	...	...	...	...	...	1740	|	...	...	|	...	...	...	...	...	0715	|	...	...
Tabanovci ▣ a.	...	...	...	...	...	...	...	...	...	...	1555	...	...	2138	...	...	...	...	...	...	0545	...	...
Skopje a.	...	...	...	...	...	...	...	...	...	...	1700	...	...	2250	...	...	...	...	...	...	0650	...	...
Idoméni ▣ a.	...	...	...	...	...	...	...	...	...	...	2100	...	...	...	...	...	...	...	...	...	1105	...	...
Thessaloníki a.	...	...	...	...	...	...	...	...	...	...	2233	...	...	...	...	...	...	...	...	...	1231	1454	...
Athína Lárisa a.	...	...	...	...	...	...	...	...	...	...	...	...	...	...	...	...	...	...	...	...	...	1949	...

train type	IC				418	480	D	412		D	EC		EC212	IC	IC	EC§				EC210	IC	IC	
train number	52	334	414	480	748	498	412	240	390	314	114	490	EC112	310	691	64	336	292	482	EC110	312	593	
notes	Ⓡ⚡				498		✕				✕		🍷◧			🍷				🍷◧			
	✕	E	F		L	B		R		Y	W	D	M				K	H	A	G			
Athína Lárisa d.	1051	...	...	...	...	...	...	...	...	...	...	...	...	...	...	...	...	...	...	...	...	...	...
Thessaloníki d.	1550	1705	...	...	...	...	...	...	...	...	...	...	...	...	...	...	0945	...	...	...	...	...	...
Idoméni ▣ d.	...	1830	...	...	...	...	...	...	...	...	...	...	...	...	...	...	1107	...	...	...	...	...	...
Skopje d.	...	2044	...	...	...	...	...	...	0740	...	...	...	...	...	...	...	1305	...	...	...	...	...	...
Tabanovci ▣ d.	...	2155	...	...	...	...	...	...	0844	...	...	...	...	...	...	...	1415	...	...	...	...	...	...
Sofiya d.	...	|	...	...	...	...	...	...	|	...	...	1155	...	...	...	...	|	2120	...	...	...	...	...
Kalotina Zapad ▣ d.	...	|	...	...	...	...	...	...	|	...	...	1303	...	...	...	...	|	2231	...	...	...	...	...
Dimitrovgrad ▣ d.	...	|	...	...	...	...	...	...	|	...	...	1230	...	...	...	...	|	2200	...	...	...	...	...
Niš d.	...	0148	...	...	...	...	...	...	1235	...	...	1520	...	...	...	...	1835	0050	...	...	...	...	...
Beograd d.	...	0544	1035	...	1300	...	1535	1535	1633	2150	...	1918	...	...	...	...	2233	0448	...	0550	...	...	...
Šid ▣ d.	...	...	1332	...	1553	...	1828	1828	...	0054	...	...	...	...	...	...	...	...	...	0848	...	...	...
Vinkovci d.	...	...	1449	...	1725	...	1943	1943	...	0147	...	...	...	...	...	...	...	...	...	0949	...	...	...
Zagreb a.	...	...	1752	...	2050	...	2245	2245	...	0453	...	...	...	...	...	...	...	...	...	1256	...	...	...
Zagreb d.	...	...	1814	...	2110	...	...	2335	...	0500	...	...	0700	0900	...	...	...	...	...	1300	...	...	...
Dobova ▣ d.	...	...	1908	...	2154	....	...	0040	...	0545	...	...	0746	0946	...	...	...	...	...	1345	...	...	...
Rijeka d.	...	...	|	2045	|	2045	...	|	...	|	...	...	|	|	...	...	...	...	1257	|	...	...	...
Ljubljana d.	...	...	2048	2322	2350	2350	...	0212	...	0726	...	...	0927	1128	...	...	...	...	1525	1525	1652	...	...
Jesenice ▣ d.	...	...	2156	...	0054	0054	...	...	...	0829	...	...	1029	1229	...	...	...	...	...	1629	1757	...	...
Villach Hbf a.	...	...	2232	...	0130	0130	...	...	...	0906	0916	...	1104	1306	1316	...	...	...	...	1704	1832	1916	...
Bad Gastein a.	...	...	0015	...	|	|	...	...	...	...	1020	...	1220	...	1420	...	...	...	...	1820	...	2020	...
Schwarzach St Veit a.	...	...	0042	...	0318	0318	...	...	...	...	1049	...	1249	...	1449	...	...	...	...	1849	...	2049	...
Bischofshofen a.	...	...	...	...	|	|	...	...	...	...	1106	...	1306	...	1506	...	...	...	...	1906	...	2106	...
Salzburg Hbf ▣ a.	...	...	...	...	0409	0409	...	...	...	...	1148	...	1348	...	1548	1702	...	...	...	1948	...	2148	...
München Hbf a.	...	...	...	...	0615	0615	...	...	...	...	1335	...	1535	...	...	1833	...	...	...	2135	...	...	...

A – LJUBLJANA – [12] Ljubljana - Rijeka and v.v. Conveys [2] Wien - Ljubljana - Rijeka and v.v. Table **89a**.
B – Mar. 27 - Sept. 18 ▬ 2 cl. (also Apr. 29 - Sept. 18 🛏 1, 2 cl.) Rijeka - München.
C – Mar. 28 - Sept. 19 ▬ 2 cl. (also Apr. 30 - Sept. 19 🛏 1, 2 cl.) München - Rijeka.
D – BALKAN – 🛏 1, 2 cl. Beograd - Sofiya - Svilengrad - İstanbul and v.v. [12] Beograd - Sofiya and v.v.
E – HELLAS EXPRESS – 🛏 1, 2 cl., ▬ 2 cl. and [12] Beograd - Thessaloníki and v.v.
F – [2] Zürich (**465**) - Schwarzach St Veit (**415**) - Zagreb - Beograd and Beograd (**414**) - Zagreb - Schwarzach St Veit (**464**) - Zürich. [12] and ✕ Villach - Beograd and v.v. Table **86**.
G – [12] München - Villach - Jesenice ▣ - Beograd and v.v. [2] and ✕ Jesenice ▣ - Beograd and v.v.
H – 🛏 1, 2 cl., ▬ 2 cl. and [12] Beograd - Sofiya and v.v.
J – 🛏 1, 2 cl., ▬ 2 cl. and [2] Ljubljana - Zagreb - Beograd and v.v.
K – OLYMPUS – [12] Beograd - Thessaloníki and v.v.
L – LISINSKI – 🛏 1, 2 cl., ▬ 2 cl. and [2] München - Zagreb and v.v. [2] München - Beograd and v.v. 🛏 1, 2 cl. Praha - Zagreb and v.v.

M – [12] Frankfurt - Zagreb and v.v. ✕ München - Villach and v.v.
R – ▬ 2 cl. Venezia - Ljubljana - Beograd and v.v.
W – WÖRTHERSEE – [12] and ✕ Münster - Klagenfurt and Klagenfurt - Dortmund.
Y – 🛏 1, 2 cl., ▬ 2 cl. and [12] Villach - Beograd and v.v.

RJ – ÖBB *Railjet* service. [1] (premium class), [1] (first class), [2] (economy class) and ✕.
◧ – Supplement payable: Jesenice ▣ - Ljubljana - Zagreb - Beograd and v.v.
§ – Classified as *RJ* from Sept. 6.
⚡ – Supplement payable.

64 HAMBURG and BERLIN - WIEN - BUDAPEST

train type	ICE	RJ	ICE	ICE	ICE	ICE	EC	ICE	ICE	ICE	RJ	ICE	ICE	ICE	EC	ICE	ICE	ICE	ICE	ICE	ICE		EN	EC	
train number	21	63	1605	783	783	23	965	1727	785	25	67	1609	787	27	969	1711	789	29	1613	881	229		491	943	
notes	🍷	✕	①–⑥	⑥	①–⑥	🍷	✕	1607	🍷	🍷	✕	1709	🍷	🍷	✕	🍷	🍷	🍷	🍷	🍷	🍷			✕	
		B	✤					✤🍷			B	✤🍷				✤			✤				A		
Hamburg Hbf d.	...	...	...	0605x	...	...	...	...	0803x	...	...	...	1001x	...	...	...	1201x	...	...	1401x	...	...	2033	...	...
Hannover Hbf d.	...	...	...	0726	0726	...	...	...	0926	...	...	...	1126	...	...	...	1326	...	...	1526	...	...	2226	...	...
Berlin Hbf d.	...	...	...	|	|	...	...	0752	|	...	...	0952	|	...	...	1152	|	...	1352	|	...	...	|	...	...
Leipzig Hbf d.	...	...	0711	|	|	...	...	0911	|	...	...	1111	|	...	...	1311	|	...	1511	|	...	...	|	...	...
Nürnberg d.	0831	...	1020	1024	1024	1031	...	1220	1224	1231	...	1420	1424	1431	...	1620	1624	1631	1820	1824	1831	...	0324	...	...
Passau ▣ d.	1033	...	...	...	...	1233	...	...	...	1433	...	...	...	1633	...	...	...	1833	...	...	2033	...	0532a	...	...
Linz Hbf a.	1143	1207	...	...	...	1343	...	...	...	1543	1607	...	...	1743	...	...	...	1943	...	...	2143	...	0646	...	...
Wien Westbahnhof a.	1322	1340	...	...	...	1522	1550	...	...	1722	1740	...	...	1922	1950	...	...	2122	...	...	2322	...	0904	0950	...
Budapest Keleti § a.	...	1649	...	...	...	...	1849	...	...	...	2049	...	...	...	2249	...	...	...	...	...	...	...	...	1249	...

train type	ICE	ICE	ICE	ICE	ICE	ICE	RJ	ICE	ICE	ICE	EC	ICE	ICE	ICE	ICE	ICE	EC	ICE	ICE	ICE	RJ	ICE	EC	EN	
train number	228	880	1608	28	788	1706	60	26	786	1604	962	24	784	1602	1655	1502	964	22	782	1600	66	20	968	490	
notes	🍷	🍷	🍷	🍷	🍷	1606	✕	🍷	🍷	1704	✕	🍷	🍷	✤🍷	🍷	1722	✕	🍷	🍷	⑤⑦	✕	🍷	✕		
			✤			✤	B			✤🍷				⑧	⑧	✤🍷				✤	B			A	
Budapest Keleti § d.	...	...	...	...	...	...	0710	...	...	...	0910	...	...	...	...	...	1110	...	...	...	1310	...	1510	...	...
Wien Westbahnhof d.	0640	...	...	0840	...	...	1020	1040	...	...	1208	1240	...	...	...	...	1408	1440	...	...	1620	1640	1808	1954	...
Linz Hbf d.	0816	...	...	1016	...	...	1150	1216	...	...	...	1416	...	...	...	...	...	1616	...	...	1750	1816	...	2157	...
Passau ▣ a.	0922	...	...	1122	...	...	...	1322	...	...	...	1522	...	...	...	...	...	1722	...	...	...	1922	...	2306d	...
Nürnberg a.	1124	1133	1137	1325	1333	1337	...	1524	1533	1537	...	1724	1733	1737	...	1836	...	1924	1933	1937	...	2124	...	0113	...
Leipzig Hbf a.	...	|	1446	...	|	1646	...	...	|	1846	...	...	|	2046	2051	2141	...	...	|	2251	...	...	...	|	...
Berlin Hbf a.	...	|	1605	...	|	1805	...	...	|	2005	...	...	|	...	2204	2300	...	...	|	0014	...	...	...	|	...
Hannover Hbf a.	...	1432	...	...	1632	...	...	...	1832	...	...	...	2032	...	...	...	...	...	2240	...	...	...	...	0613	...
Hamburg Hbf a.	...	1555z	...	...	1754z	...	...	...	1954z	...	...	...	2154z	...	...	...	...	...	0003z	...	...	...	...	0750z	...

A – HANS ALBERS – 🛏 1, 2 cl., ▬ 2 cl., [2] and 🍷 Hamburg - Passau ▣ - Wien and v.v.
B – [1] (premium class), [1] (first class), [2] (economy class) and ✕ München - Wien - Budapest and v.v. ÖBB *Railjet* service.

a – Arrival time.
d – Departure time.

x – June 14 - July 19 depart 23–27 minutes earlier.
z – June 14 - July 19 arrive 25–26 minutes later.

§ – ▣ is at Hegyeshalom.
✤ – Due to engineering work between Leipzig and Nürnberg from Aug. 1 until Sept. 14, services are subject to alteration. See Table **851**.

MÜNCHEN - WIEN - BUDAPEST - BUCUREŞTI 65

train type	RJ	EN	EN		EC	EC §	EC	RJ		RJ	EC	EN	RJ	D	RJ	EC	D	ICE		IC	ICE	EC	EN	
train number	41	461	467	355	943	61	961	63		65	965	371	67	347	69	969	347	261		2265	661	391	463	
notes	✗	✗ G	✗ W	1822 C	✗	🍷	✗	✗		🍷	✗	✗ R	✗	✗ D	✗	✗	✗ D	🍷		Ⓑ	🍷	🍷	A	
München Hbf d.	...	...	...	...	...	0726	...	0927	...	1126	...	...	1326	...	1526	...	...	1723	...	1921	...	2024	2340	...
Salzburg Hbf 🏛 d.	...	0316	...	...	...	0900	...	1100	...	1300	...	...	1500	...	1700	...	...	1900	...	2107	2132	2215e	0218	...
Linz Hbf d.	...	0436	...	...	...	1007	...	1207	...	1407	...	...	1607	...	1807	...	...	2007	...	...	2243	2342e	0342	...
St Pölten Hbf d.	...	0547	...	...	...	1059	...	1259	...	1459	...	...	1659	...	1859	...	...	2059	...	...	2335	...	0500	...
Wien Westbahnhof a.	...	0640	...	...	...	1140	...	1340	...	1540	...	...	1740	...	1940	...	...	2140	...	...	0015	...	0545**h**	...
Wien Westbahnhof d.	0650	0705	0825	...	0950	...	1150	1350	...	...	1550	...	1750	1850	...	1950	...	...	...	...	...	...	0600**q**	...
Hegyeshalom 🏛 a.	0754	0817	0927	...	1054	...	1254	1454	...	...	1654	...	1854	1954	...	2054	...	...	...	...	...	...	0653	...
Győr a.	0819	0846	0957	...	1119	...	1319	1519	...	...	1719	...	1919	2027	...	2119	←	...	...	...	...	...	0722	...
Budapest Keleti a.	0949	1019	1134	1313	1249	...	1449	1649	...	...	1849	1913	2049	2219	...	2249	2313	...	...	...	...	...	0854	...
Bucureşti Nord a.	...	...	...	0619	...	...	...	...	...	...	...	1028	...	→	...	...	1359	...	...	...	...	...	2355	...

train type	EC	ICE	RJ	D	RJ		EN	EC	IC		EC	EC §		RJ		EC	RJ		EC	EN	EN	RJ	EN	
train number	390	260	262	346	60		370	962	746		964	64		66		968	68	1821	942	466	460	40	462	
notes	①–⑥	🍷	✗	✗ D	✗ S		✗ R	✗	🍷		✗	🍷		✗		✗	🍷	354 C	✗	✗ W	✗ H	✗	✗ B	
Bucureşti Nord d.	...	...	...	1645	...	...	1950	...	...	...	...	...	...	...	...	...	...	2345	...	...	...	...	0545	...
Budapest Keleti d.	...	...	...	0555	0710	...	0847	0910	...	...	1110	...	...	1310	...	1510	...	1447	1710	1805	1905	2010	2105	...
Győr d.	...	...	...	0725	0837	...	...	1037	...	...	1237	...	...	1437	...	1637	...	...	1837	1933	2033	2137	2232	...
Hegyeshalom 🏛 d.	...	...	...	0758	0906	...	...	1106	...	...	1306	...	...	1506	...	1706	...	...	1906	2004	2106	2206	2301	...
Wien Westbahnhof a.	...	...	...	0859	1008	...	...	1208	...	...	1408	...	...	1608	...	1808	...	...	2008	2105	2211	2308	2353**q**	...
Wien Westbahnhof d.	...	0614	0820	...	1020	...	...	...	1244	...	...	1420	...	1620	...	...	1820	...	...	...	2240	...	0009**h**	...
St Pölten Hbf d.	...	0655	0902	...	1102	...	...	...	1328	...	...	|	...	|	...	...	|	...	...	...	2325	...	0051	...
Linz Hbf d.	0626	0747	0953	...	1153	...	...	...	1432	...	...	1553	...	1753	...	...	1953	...	...	...	0038	...	0201	...
Salzburg Hbf 🏛 d.	0753	0902	1103	...	1303	...	...	...	1550	...	...	1702	...	1903	...	...	2102	...	...	...	0155	...	0428	...
München Hbf a.	0935	1031	1231	...	1431	...	...	...	...	...	...	1833	...	2034	...	...	2230	...	...	...	...	...	0615	...

A – KÁLMÁN IMRE – 🛏 1, 2 cl., ▬ 2 cl. and [2] München - Wien - Budapest. 🛏 1, 2 cl. and ▬ 1, 2 cl. München - Wien - Budapest (**375**) - Lökösháza - Bucureşti. [12] and ✗ Budapest - Bucureşti.
B – KÁLMÁN IMRE – 🛏 1, 2 cl., ▬ 2 cl. and [2] Budapest - Wien - München. 🛏 1, 2 cl. and ▬ 1, 2 cl. Bucureşti (**374**) - Budapest (**462**) - München. [12] and ✗ Bucureşti - Wien.
C – 🛏 1, 2 cl. and [2] Venezia - Budapest - Bucureşti and v.v.
D – DACIA – 🛏 1, 2 cl., ▬ 2 cl., [2] and ✗ Wien - Budapest - Bucureşti and v.v. [1] Wien - Budapest - Lökösháza and v.v.
G – DANUBIUS – 🛏 1, 2 cl., ▬ 2 cl., [2] and ✗ Frankfurt (**409**) - Karlruhe (**469**) - Salzburg 🏛 - Wien (**461**) - Budapest. [12] Wien - Budapest.
E – DANUBIUS – 🛏 1, 2 cl., ▬ 2 cl., [2] and ✗ Budapest (**460**) - Wien (**468**) - Salzburg 🏛 - Karlruhe (**408**) - Frankfurt. [12] Budapest and Wien.
R – *EuroNight* ISTER – 🛏 1, 2 cl., ▬ 1, 2 cl., [2] and ✗ Budapest - Bucureşti and v.v.

W – WIENER WALZER – [12] and ✗ Wien - Budapest and v.v.

e – Ⓑ only.
h – Wien **Hütteldorf**.
q – Wien **Meidling**.

RJ – ÖBB *Railjet* service. [1] (premium class), [1] (first class), [2] (economy class) and ✗.
§ – Classified as *RJ* from Sept. 6.

DORTMUND - KÖLN - FRANKFURT - WIEN - BUDAPEST 66

train type	ICE	RJ	ICE	EC	ICE	RJ	ICE	EC	ICE	ICE	EN	CNL
train number	21	63	23	965	25	67	27	969	29	229	461	421
notes	🍷	B	🍷	✗	🍷	B	🍷	✗	🍷	🍷	C	A
Dortmund Hbf d.	...	...	0433	...	0636	...	0838	...	...	...	...	...
Bochum Hbf d.	...	...	0445	...	|	...	0849	...	...	...	...	...
Essen Hbf d.	...	...	0456	...	⊙	...	0900	...	...	...	...	...
Duisburg Hbf d.	...	...	0508	...	|	...	0913	...	...	...	...	...
Düsseldorf Hbf d.	...	...	0523	...	|	...	0927	...	...	...	...	...
Köln Hbf d.	...	...	0553	...	0753	...	0953	...	...	...	...	...
Bonn Hbf d.	...	...	0614	...	0814	...	1014	...	...	...	...	...
Koblenz d.	...	...	0648	...	0848	...	1048	...	...	...	...	...
Mainz d.	...	...	0740	...	0940	...	1140	...	...	...	...	...
Frankfurt Flug. ✈ d.	...	...	0801	...	1001	...	1201	...	...	...	...	...
Frankfurt (M) Hbf d.	0622	...	0818	...	1021	...	1221	...	1416	1621	2000	2305
Würzburg d.	0734	...	0934	...	1134	...	1334	...	1534	1734	|	|
Nürnberg d.	0831	...	1031	...	1231	...	1431	...	1631	1831	△	0324
Regensburg d.	0924	...	1124	...	1324	...	1524	...	1724	1924	|	0430
Passau 🏛 d.	1033	...	1233	...	1433	...	1633	...	1833	2033	|	0535
Salzburg 🏛 a.	|	...	|	...	|	...	|	...	|	|	|	|
Linz a.	1143	...	1343	...	1543	...	1743	...	1943	2143	0433	0646
Wien Westbf a.	1322	1350	1522	1550	1722	1750	1922	1950	2122	2322	0640	0904
Hegyeshalom 🏛 a.	...	1454	...	1654	...	1854	...	2054	...	...	0817	...
Budapest Keleti a.	...	1649	...	1849	...	2049	...	2249	...	...	1019	...

train type	ICE	ICE	RJ	ICE	EC	ICE	EC	ICE	RJ	ICE	CNL	EC	EN
train number	228	28	60	26	962	24	964	22	66	20	490	942	460
notes	🍷	🍷	B	🍷	✗	🍷	✗	🍷	B	🍷	A	✗	C
Budapest Keleti d.	...	...	0710	...	0910	...	1110	...	1310	...	...	1710	1905
Hegyeshalom 🏛 d.	...	...	0906	...	1106	...	1306	...	1506	...	...	1906	2106
Wien Westbf d.	0640	0840	1008	1040	1208	1240	1408	1440	1608	1640	1954	2008	2240
Linz d.	0816	1016	...	1216	...	1416	...	1616	...	1816	2157	...	0038
Salzburg 🏛 d.	|	|	...	|	...	|	...	|	...	|	|	...	|
Passau 🏛 a.	0922	1122	...	1322	...	1522	...	1722	...	1922	2304	...	|
Regensburg a.	1031	1230	...	1431	...	1631	...	1831	...	2031	0012	...	|
Nürnberg a.	1124	1325	...	1524	...	1724	...	1924	...	2124	0113	...	△
Würzburg a.	1225	1425	...	1625	...	1825	...	2024	...	2227	|	...	|
Frankfurt (M) Hbf a.	1340	1536	...	1736	...	1936	...	2136	...	2339	0436	...	0957
Frankfurt Flug. ✈ a.	...	...	...	1755	...	1955	...	2157	...	...	...	...	...
Mainz a.	...	...	...	1818	...	2018	...	2218	...	...	...	...	...
Koblenz a.	...	...	...	1910	...	2110	...	2310	...	...	...	...	...
Bonn Hbf a.	...	...	...	1943	...	2142	...	2342	...	...	...	...	...
Köln Hbf a.	...	...	...	2005	...	2205	...	0005	...	...	...	...	...
Düsseldorf Hbf a.	...	...	...	|	...	|	...	0034	...	...	...	...	...
Duisburg Hbf a.	...	...	...	|	...	|	...	0047	...	...	...	...	...
Essen Hbf a.	...	...	...	⊙	...	⊙	...	0059	...	...	...	...	...
Bochum Hbf a.	...	...	...	|	...	|	...	0109	...	...	...	...	...
Dortmund Hbf a.	...	...	...	2122	...	2322	...	0122	...	...	...	...	...

A – *City Night Line* ERIDANUS – 🛏 1, 2 cl., ▬ 2 cl. (4, 6 berth), [2] (reclining) and 🍷: Amsterdam / Dortmund - Köln - Frankfurt - Passau 🏛 - Wien and v.v. Ⓡ Special fares apply. For international journeys only. (See Table **28** for dates of running).
B – [1] (premium class), [1] (first class), [2] (economy class) and ✗ München - Wien - Budapest and v.v. ÖBB *RailJet* service.
C – DANUBIUS – 🛏 1, 2 cl., ▬ 2 cl., [2] and ✗ Frankfurt - Salzburg 🏛 - Wien - Budapest and v.v. (Table **32**).

△ – Via Mannheim (Table **28**).
⊙ – Via Hagen, Wuppertal (Table **800**).

DORTMUND - KÖLN - MÜNCHEN - GRAZ and KLAGENFURT 68

train type / number	EC	EC	EC	EC	EC	EC	EC	EC	ICE	
train number	111	111 211	317	113	113 213	115	319	117	613	499
notes	🍷	H🍷	🍷 G	🍷	Z	✗ W	🍷	🍷 Ⓑ	🍷	L
Hamburg Hbf d.	...	...	...	...	...	...	...	...	...	...
Dortmund Hbf d.	...	...	...	...	...	...	...	...	1638	...
Bochum Hbf d.	...	...	...	...	...	...	...	...	1649	...
Essen Hbf d.	...	...	...	...	...	...	...	...	1700	...
Duisburg Hbf d.	...	...	...	...	...	0735	...	...	1713	...
Düsseldorf Hbf d.	...	...	...	...	...	0752	...	...	1727	...
Köln Hbf d.	...	...	...	...	...	0818	...	...	1754	...
Bonn Hbf d.	...	...	...	...	...	0837	...	...	|	...
Koblenz Hbf d.	...	...	...	...	...	0917	...	...	|	...
Mainz Hbf d.	...	...	...	...	...	1015	...	...	|	...
Frankfurt (Main) Hbf d.	...	...	...	0820	0820	|	1220	1420	|	...
Mannheim d.	...	...	0712	|	|	1103	|	|	1933	...
Heidelberg d.	...	...	|	0914	0914	|	1314	1514	|	...
Stuttgart Hbf d.	...	...	0758	0958	0958	1143	1358	1558	2012	...
Ulm d.	...	...	0855	1055	1055	1255	1455	1655	2108	...
Augsburg d.	...	...	0941	1141	1141	1341	1541	1741	2152	...
München Hbf d.	0827	0827	1021	1221	1221	1421	1622	1820	2232	2340
Salzburg 🏛 a.	1006	1006	1204	1404	1404	1604	1804	2004	...	0117
Bischofshofen a.	1053	1053	1302	1453	1453	1653	1902	2053	...	|
Selzthal a.	|	|	1440	|	|	|	2040	|	...	|
Graz a.	|	|	1622	|	|	|	2222	|	...	|
Schwarzach St Veit a.	1109	1109	...	1509	1509	1709	...	2109	...	0223
Villach Hbf a.	1243	1243	...	1643	1643	1843	...	2245	...	0352
Klagenfurt a.	1315	|	...	1715	|	1915	...	2317	...	|
Ljubljana a.	...	1430	...	...	1830	...	...	...	...	0605

train type / number	EC	EC	EC	EC	EC	EC	EC		ICE	
train number	318	114	112	212 112	316	110	210 110	498	612	
notes	🍷	✗ W	🍷	Z	🍷 G	🍷	H🍷	L	🍷	
Ljubljana d.	...	...	...	0927	...	...	1525	2350	...	...
Klagenfurt d.	...	0843	1033	|	...	1631	|	|	...	...
Villach Hbf d.	...	0916	1116	1116	...	1716	1716	0145	...	...
Schwarzach St Veit d.	...	1051	1251	1251	...	1851	1851	0320	...	...
Graz d.	0545	|	|	|	1138	|	|	|	...	...
Selzthal d.	0719	|	|	|	1319	|	|	|	...	...
Bischofshofen d.	0857	1108	1308	1308	1457	1908	1908	|	...	...
Salzburg 🏛 d.	0957	1152	1352	1352	1552	1952	1952	0428	...	...
München Hbf a.	1137	1335	1535	1535	1735	2135	2135	0615	0723	...
Augsburg a.	1216	1414	1615	1615	1815	...	...	...	0801	...
Ulm a.	1303	1503	1703	1703	1903	...	...	...	0849	...
Stuttgart Hbf a.	1400	1559	1800	1800	2000	...	...	...	0947	...
Heidelberg a.	1445	|	1845	1845	|	...	...	...	|	...
Mannheim a.	|	1656	|	|	2048	...	...	...	1026	...
Frankfurt (Main) Hbf a.	1540	|	1940	1940	...	...	...	...	|	...
Mainz Hbf a.	...	1740	...	...	...	...	...	...	|	...
Koblenz Hbf a.	...	1841	...	...	...	...	...	...	|	...
Bonn Hbf a.	...	1920	...	...	...	...	...	...	|	...
Köln Hbf a.	...	1942	...	...	...	...	...	...	1205	...
Düsseldorf Hbf a.	...	2009	...	...	...	...	...	...	1232	...
Duisburg Hbf a.	...	2023	...	...	...	...	...	...	1245	...
Essen Hbf a.	...	2039	...	...	...	...	...	...	1257	...
Bochum Hbf a.	...	2049	...	...	...	...	...	...	1309	...
Dortmund Hbf a.	...	2116	...	...	...	...	...	...	1321	...
Hamburg Hbf a.	...	...	...	...	...	...	...	...	...	...

G – [12] and 🍷 Saarbrücken - Mannheim - Graz and v.v.
H – [12] and 🍷 München - Villach - Ljubljana - Zagreb - Beograd and v.v.
L – LISINSKI – 🛏 1, 2 cl., ▬ 2 cl. and [2] München - Ljubljana - Zagreb and v.v.

W – WÖRTHERSEE – [12] and ✗ Münster - Klagenfurt and Klagenfurt - Dortmund.
Z – [12] and 🍷 Frankfurt - München - Villach - Ljubljana - Zagreb and v.v.

70 DORTMUND - MÜNCHEN - INNSBRUCK - VENEZIA and MILANO

train type	CNL	CNL	CNL	EC	IC	ICE	ICE	IC		IC	ICE	EC	IC	EC	ES	ICE	IC 89	IC	EC	ICE	IC	IC		D	IC
train type	1201	1289	419	81	515	699	521	85	1509	2021	525	361	87	669	9313	529	EC 92‡	649	115	623	2261	83	1515	1281	119
train number	[R]	[R]	[R]	♣✕	🍷	🍷	🍷	35085			925	✕	♣✕	🍷	[R]⚡	🍷	♣	🍷	✕	🍷	🍷	♣	2	H	🍷
notes	P	A	L	D				♣✕			🍷		V		✕		G		Q			T			K
Hamburg Hbf d.	...	2202	...	...	...	...	...	R	...	2246	...	...	...	...	...	...	...	...	...	...	...	...	...	...	...
Berlin Hbf d.	2212	|	...	...	...	...	...	...	...	|	...	...	...	...	...	...	...	...	...	...	...	...	...	...	...
Dortmund Hbf d.	|	|	...	...	...	...	...	...	...	0203	0523j	...	...	...	...	0723p	...	...	...	...	...	...	...	...	...
Bochum Hbf d.	|	|	...	...	...	...	...	...	...	0215	0535j	...	...	...	...	0735p	...	...	...	...	...	...	...	...	...
Essen Hbf d.	|	|	...	...	...	...	...	...	...	0228	0553j	...	...	...	...	0753	...	...	...	...	...	...	...	...	0823
Duisburg Hbf d.	|	|	2256	...	...	...	...	...	...	0241	0608j	...	...	...	...	0808	...	...	0735	...	...	...	...	...	0838
Dusseldorf Hbf d.	|	|	2312u	...	...	...	...	...	...	0302	0622j	...	...	...	...	0822	...	...	0752	...	...	...	...	...	0852
Köln Hbf d.	|	|	2346u	...	...	...	0420	...	...	0352	0644x	...	...	...	...	0844k	...	...	0818	1020	...	...	...	...	0918
Bonn Hbf d.	|	|	0007u	...	...	...	|	...	...	|	|	...	...	...	...	|	...	...	0837	|	...	...	...	...	0937
Koblenz Hbf d.	|	|	0044u	...	...	...	⊖	...	...	0530	⊖	...	...	...	...	⊖	...	...	0917	⊖	...	...	...	...	1017
Mainz Hbf d.	|	|	|	...	...	...	|	...	...	0629	|	...	...	...	...	|	...	...	1015	|	...	...	...	...	1113
Frankfurt Flughafen ✈ d.	|	|	|	...	...	...	0535	...	...	0648	0737	...	...	...	...	0937	...	...	|	1130	...	...	...	...	|
Frankfurt (Main) Hbf d.	|	|	|	...	...	...	0551	...	...	0702	0754	...	...	...	...	0954	...	...	|	1154	...	...	...	...	|
Mannheim Hbf d.	|	|	|	...	...	...	|	...	...	▬	|	...	...	...	...	|	...	...	1103	|	...	...	...	...	1154
Heidelberg Hbf d.	|	|	|	...	...	...	|	...	...	...	|	...	...	...	...	|	...	...	|	|	...	...	...	...	1206
Stuttgart Hbf d.	|	|	0419	...	...	0656	|	...	...	...	|	0853	...	...	...	|	...	...	1143f	|	1253	...	...	...	1257
Ulm Hbf d.	|	|	0544	...	...	0755	|	...	...	...	|	0955	...	...	...	|	...	...	1255	|	1355	...	...	...	1411
Lindau 🏛 a.	|	|	|	...	...	|	|	...	...	...	|	|	...	...	...	|	...	...	|	|	|	...	...	...	1554
Bregenz a.	|	|	|	...	...	|	|	...	...	...	|	|	...	...	...	|	...	...	|	|	|	...	...	...	1614
Bludenz a.	|	|	|	...	...	|	|	...	...	...	|	|	...	...	...	|	...	...	|	|	|	...	...	...	1702
Langen am Arlberg a.	|	|	|	...	...	|	|	...	...	...	|	|	...	...	...	|	...	...	|	|	|	...	...	...	1737
St Anton am Arlberg a.	|	|	|	...	...	|	|	...	...	...	|	|	...	...	...	|	...	...	|	|	|	...	...	...	1747
Landeck - Zams a.	|	|	|	...	...	|	|	...	...	...	|	|	...	...	...	|	...	...	|	|	|	...	...	...	1810
Augsburg Hbf d.	0554s	0622s	0636	...	...	0839	|	...	...	...	|	1038	...	...	...	|	...	...	1341	|	1438	...	...	...	|
München Hbf d.	0639	0705	0716	0730	...	0917	0904	0931	...	...	1104	1116	1130	...	...	1304	1330	...	1416	1504	1516	1530	...	1600	|
München Ost ▲ d.	...	...	...	0740	...	...	...	0940	...	...	▬	...	1140	...	...	▬	1340	...	...	...	...	1540	...	|	|
Kufstein 🏛 d.	...	...	...	0835	...	...	...	1035	...	...	...	...	1235	...	...	...	1435	...	...	...	...	1635	...	1714	|
Wörgl d.	...	...	...	0846	0900	...	...	1046	1058	...	...	...	1246	1300	...	...	1444a	1449	...	...	...	1646	1658	1736	|
Kitzbühel a.	...	...	...	|	0929	...	...	|	1127	...	...	...	|	1329	...	...	|	1518	...	...	...	|	1727	1817	|
St Johann in Tirol a.	...	...	...	|	0937	...	...	|	1135	...	...	...	|	1337	...	...	|	1526	...	...	...	|	1735	1826	|
Saalfelden a.	...	...	...	|	1007	...	...	|	1205	...	...	...	|	1407	...	...	|	1558	...	...	...	|	1805	1901	|
Zell am See a.	...	...	...	|	1019	...	...	|	1216	...	...	...	|	1416	...	...	|	1610	...	...	...	|	1816	1911	|
Jenbach a.	...	...	...	0859	...	...	...	1059	▬	...	...	...	1259	▬	...	...	1459	▬	...	...	...	1659	▬	...	|
Innsbruck Hbf a.	...	...	...	0921	...	...	...	1121	...	...	...	...	1321	...	...	...	1521	...	...	...	...	1721	...	...	1857
Innsbruck Hbf d.	...	...	...	0927	...	...	...	1127	...	*ESc*	*ESc*	...	1327	*CIS*	...	...	1527	...	...	...	...	1727	*ESc*	...	...
Brennero / Brenner 🏛 a.	...	...	...	|	...	...	...	|	...	**9727**	**9728**	...	|	**42**	...	...	|	...	...	...	...	|	**9749**	...	...
Bolzano / Bozen a.	...	...	...	1128	...	...	...	1329	...	[R]	🍷⚡	...	1529	[R]⚡	1606	...	1729	**2107**	...	...	...	1929	[R]	...	...
Trento a.	...	...	...	...	...	...	...	1401	...	✕⚡	[R]	...	1601	🍷⊕	1647	...	1801	...	...	...	...	2001	🍷⚡	...	...
Verona a.	...	...	...	...	...	...	...	1457	*AV*	1559	1532	...	1657	1732	1747	*ESc*	1901	1918	...	...	...	2101	2129	...	...
Venezia Santa Lucia a.	...	...	...	...	...	...	...	|	**9643**	1710	|	...	1810	|	|	**9783**	|	2051	...	...	...	...	2240	...	...
Milano Centrale a.	...	...	...	...	...	...	...	|	[R]⚡	...	1655	...	...	1900	|	🍷⚡	2035	...	...	...	...	...	...	...	...
Genova Piazza Principe a.	...	...	...	...	...	...	...	|	✕	...	*1945*	...	...	*2148*	|	[R]	...	...	...	...	...	...	...	...	...
Bologna Centrale a.	...	...	...	...	...	...	...	1611	1625	...	...	...	...	...	1902	1920	...	...	...	...	...	...	...	...	...
Firenze SMN a.	...	...	...	...	...	...	...	|	1723	...	...	...	...	...	2009	|	...	...	...	...	...	...	...	...	...
Roma Termini a.	...	...	...	...	...	...	...	|	1910	...	...	...	...	...	2159	|	...	...	...	...	...	...	...	...	...
Napoli Centrale a.	...	...	...	...	...	...	...	|	2046	...	...	...	...	...	...	|	...	...	...	...	...	...	...	...	...
Rimini a.	...	...	...	...	...	...	...	1743	...	...	...	...	...	...	...	2034	...	...	...	...	...	...	...	...	...

train type / number	EC	ICE	ICE	EC	ICE	ICE	ICE	ICE	CNL	CNL
train number	101	517	627	189	519	109	723	611	485	40485
notes	🍷	🍷	🍷	✕ S	🍷	🍷	🍷 Ⓑ	🍷	B	C
Hamburg Hbf d.	...	...	...	...	...	...	...	...	...	...
Berlin Hbf d.	...	...	...	...	...	...	...	...	...	...
Dortmund Hbf d.	...	1038	...	...	1238	...	...	1438	...	...
Bochum Hbf d.	...	1049	...	...	1249	...	...	1449	...	...
Essen Hbf d.	...	1100	...	...	1300	...	1453	1500	...	...
Duisburg Hbf d.	...	1113	...	...	1313	...	|	1513	...	...
Dusseldorf Hbf d.	...	1127	...	...	1327	...	1522	1527	...	...
Köln Hbf d.	...	1154	1220	...	1354	...	1544k	1554	...	...
Bonn Hbf d.	1114	|	|	...	|	...	|	|	...	...
Koblenz Hbf d.	1148	⊖	⊖	...	⊖	...	⊖	⊖	...	...
Mainz Hbf d.	1239	|	|	...	|	...	|	|	...	...
Frankfurt Flughafen ✈ d.	|	1254	1330	...	1454	...	1637	1654	...	...
Frankfurt (Main) Hbf d.	|	|	1354	...	|	...	1654	|	...	...
Mannheim Hbf d.	1321	1333	|	...	1533	...	|	1733	...	...
Heidelberg Hbf d.	...	|	|	...	|	...	|	|	...	...
Stuttgart Hbf d.	...	*1412*	|	...	1612	...	|	*1812*	...	...
Ulm Hbf d.	...	*1508*	|	...	1708	...	|	*1908*	...	...
Lindau 🏛 a.	...	|	|	...	|	...	|	|	...	...
Bregenz a.	...	|	|	...	|	...	|	|	...	...
Bludenz a.	...	|	|	...	|	...	|	|	...	...
Langen am Arlberg a.	...	|	|	...	|	...	|	|	...	...
St Anton am Arlberg a.	...	|	|	...	|	...	|	|	...	...
Landeck - Zams a.	...	|	|	...	|	...	|	|	...	...
Augsburg Hbf d.	...	*1552*	|	...	1752	...	|	*1952*	...	...
München Hbf d.	...	*1631*	1704	1731	1830	1843	2004	*2030*	2103	2103
München Ost ▲ d.	...	...	...	1741	▬	|	▬	...	|	|
Kufstein 🏛 d.	...	...	...	1835	**1517**	1940	2	...	2209	2209
Wörgl d.	...	...	...	1846	1858	1951	2058	...	2220	2220
Kitzbühel a.	...	...	...	|	1927	|	2127	...	|	|
St Johann in Tirol a.	...	...	...	|	1935	|	2135	...	|	|
Saalfelden a.	...	...	...	|	2005	|	2205	...	|	|
Zell am See a.	...	...	...	|	2016	|	2216	...	|	|
Jenbach a.	...	...	...	1859	...	2004	...	...	2235	2235
Innsbruck Hbf a.	...	...	...	1921	...	2026	...	...	2256	2256
Innsbruck Hbf d.	...	...	...	...	...	...	...	...	2305	2305
Brennero / Brenner 🏛 a.	...	...	...	...	...	...	...	...	2342	2342
Bolzano / Bozen a.	...	...	...	...	...	...	...	...	|	|
Trento a.	...	...	...	...	...	...	...	...	|	|
Verona a.	...	...	...	...	...	...	...	...	0237	0237
Venezia Santa Lucia a.	...	...	...	...	...	...	...	...	|	0638
Milano Centrale a.	...	...	...	...	...	...	...	...	|	...
Genova Piazza Principe a.	...	...	...	...	...	...	...	...	|	...
Bologna Centrale a.	...	...	...	...	...	...	...	...	0435	...
Firenze SMN a.	...	...	...	...	...	...	...	...	0618	...
Roma Termini a.	...	...	...	...	...	...	...	...	0905	...
Napoli Centrale a.	...	...	...	...	...	...	...	...	...	...
Rimini a.	...	...	...	...	...	...	...	...	...	...

train type		ICE	EC	D	ICE	IC		IC	ESc	IC 93‡	ICE
train number	1500	108	390	1280	596	118	1710	188	9704	IC 88	514
notes	2	🍷	🍷	J	🍷	🍷 K	2	♣ T	🍷⚡ [R]	♣ G	🍷
Rimini d.	...	...	...	...	...	...	...	...	...	...	...
Napoli Centrale d.	...	...	...	...	...	...	...	...	...	...	...
Roma Termini d.	...	...	...	...	...	...	...	...	...	...	...
Firenze SMN d.	...	...	...	...	...	...	...	...	...	...	...
Bologna Centrale d.	...	...	...	...	...	...	...	...	...	...	...
Genova Piazza Principe d.	...	...	...	...	...	...	...	...	...	...	...
Milano Centrale d.	...	...	...	...	...	...	...	...	...	0705	...
Venezia Santa Lucia d.	...	...	...	...	...	...	0514	...	0620	|	...
Verona d.	...	...	...	...	...	...	0643	0659	0730	0859	...
Trento d.	...	...	...	...	...	...	▬	0758	▬	0958	...
Bolzano / Bozen d.	...	...	...	...	...	...	...	0832	...	1032	...
Brennero / Brenner 🏛 d.	...	*0605*	...	...	...	...	...	|	...	|	...
Innsbruck Hbf a.	...	*0643*	...	...	...	...	...	1034	...	1232	...
Innsbruck Hbf d.	...	0735	...	...	...	0904	**1504**	1036	...	1236	...
Jenbach d.	...	0756	...	...	...	|	2	1057	...	1257	...
Zell am See d.	0612	|	...	0853	...	|	0946	|	...	|	...
Saalfelden d.	0625	|	...	0902	...	|	0955	|	...	|	...
St Johann in Tirol d.	0658	|	...	0935	...	|	1025	|	...	|	...
Kitzbühel d.	0706	|	...	0944	...	|	1033	|	...	|	...
Wörgl d.	0742	0810	...	1035	...	|	1102	1113	*ICE*	1313	...
Kufstein 🏛 a.	...	0820	...	1044	...	|	...	1122	**516**	1322	...
München Ost ▲ a.	...	|	...	|	...	|	...	1214	🍷	1414	...
München Hbf a.	...	0916	0940	1153	1223	|	...	1225	*1323*	1427	1523
Augsburg Hbf a.	...	...	1015	...	1301	|	...	...	*1401*	...	1601
Landeck - Zams d.	...	...	|	...	|	0952	...	...	|	...	|
St Anton am Arlberg d.	...	...	|	...	|	1015	...	...	|	...	|
Langen am Arlberg d.	...	...	|	...	|	1026	...	...	|	...	|
Bludenz d.	...	...	|	...	|	1057	...	...	|	...	|
Bregenz d.	...	...	|	...	|	1142	...	...	|	...	|
Lindau 🏛 d.	...	...	|	...	|	1202	...	...	|	...	|
Ulm Hbf a.	...	...	1103	...	1349	1345	...	...	*1449*	...	1649
Stuttgart Hbf a.	...	...	1200	...	1447	1458	...	...	*1547*	...	1747
Heidelberg Hbf a.	...	...	1245	...	|	1553	...	...	|	...	|
Mannheim Hbf a.	...	...	|	...	1528	1606	...	...	1626	...	1826
Frankfurt (Main) Hbf a.	...	...	1340	...	1608	|	...	...	|	...	|
Frankfurt Flughafen ✈ a.	...	...	...	...	...	|	...	...	1706	...	1906
Mainz Hbf a.	...	...	...	...	...	1646	...	...	|	...	|
Koblenz Hbf a.	...	...	...	...	...	1741	...	...	⊖	...	⊖
Bonn Hbf a.	...	...	...	...	...	1820	...	...	|	...	|
Köln Hbf a.	...	...	...	...	...	1842	...	...	1805	...	2005
Dusseldorf Hbf a.	...	...	...	...	...	1909	...	...	|	...	2032
Duisburg Hbf a.	...	...	...	...	...	1924	...	...	|	...	2045
Essen Hbf a.	...	...	...	...	...	1936	...	...	|	...	2057
Bochum Hbf a.	...	...	...	...	...	...	...	...	|	...	2109
Dortmund Hbf a.	...	...	...	...	...	...	...	...	1920	...	2121
Berlin Hbf a.	...	...	...	...	...	...	...	...	...	...	...
Hamburg Hbf a.	...	...	...	...	...	...	...	...	...	...	...

FOR NOTES SEE NEXT PAGE

MILANO and VENEZIA - INNSBRUCK - MÜNCHEN - DORTMUND 70

train type / number	EC	EC	ICE	EC	ESc	ESc	AV	IC	IC	ICE	ICE	IC	ES	ESc	IC	ICE		EC	CNL	CNL	CNL	CNL	CNL	ICE	
train number	**668**	**82**	**528**	**360**	**9713**	**9714**	**9428**	**84**	**2092**	**524**	**510**	**578**	**9310**	**9719**	**86**	**990**	**1514**	**80**	**318**	**1288**	**1200**	**484**	**40484**	**612**	
notes	🍷	♣✖	**924**	✖	🍷⌿	🍷⌿	[R]⌿	♣✖	Ⓑ	🍷	**1010**	🍷	[R]⌿	[R]⌿	♣✖	✖	2	✖	[R]	[R]	[R]	**B**	**C**	🍷	
		D	🍷		[R]	[R]	✖	**R**	🍷				✖	**W**	**V**			**S**	**L**	**A**	**P**				
Rimini d.	...	...	...	...	...	...	...	0953**h**	...	...	...	...	...	...	...	...	...	...	...	...	...	...	...	...	...
Napoli Centrale d.	...	...	...	...	...	...	...	|	...	...	...	0614	...	...	...	...	...	...	...	...	...	...	...	...	...
Roma Termini d.	...	...	...	...	...	...	0730	|	...	...	...	0833	0900	...	...	...	...	...	...	...	...	1910	...	...	...
Firenze SMN d.	...	...	...	...	...	...	0919	|	...	...	...	▬	1049	...	...	...	...	...	...	...	...	2153	...	...	...
Bologna Centrale d.	...	...	...	...	...	...	1020	1117	...	...	...	...	1154	...	...	...	...	...	...	...	...	2305	...	...	...
Genova Piazza Principe d.	...	...	...	...	...	...	▬	|	...	...	...	...	|	...	...	...	...	...	...	...	...	|	...	...	...
Milano Centrale d.	...	...	...	...	0935	...	...	|	...	...	...	...	|	1235	...	...	...	...	...	...	...	|	...	...	...
Venezia Santa Lucia d.	...	...	...	...	|	1050	...	|	...	...	...	...	|	|	1320	...	...	...	...	...	...	|	2251	...	...
Verona d.	...	...	...	...	1057	1200	...	1259	...	...	...	...	1259	1357	1459	...	...	...	...	...	...	0101	0101	...	...
Trento d.	...	...	...	...	▬	...	...	1358	...	...	...	...	...	▬	1558	...	...	...	...	...	...	|	|	...	...
Bolzano / Bozen d.	...	1232	...	...	...	...	...	1432	...	...	...	...	...	...	1632	...	...	...	...	...	...	|	|	...	...
Brennero / Brenner 🏛 d.	...	|	...	...	...	...	...	|	...	...	...	...	...	...	|	...	...	...	...	...	...	0356	0356	...	...
Innsbruck Hbf a.	...	1432	...	...	...	...	...	1632	...	...	...	...	...	...	1832	...	...	...	...	...	...	0430	0430	...	...
Innsbruck Hbf d.	...	1436	...	...	...	...	**1510**	1636	...	...	...	...	...	*IC*	1836	...	...	2036	...	...	...	0434	0434	...	...
Jenbach d.	...	1457	...	...	...	...	2	1657	...	...	...	...	...	**518**	1857	...	...	2057	...	...	...	0456	0456	...	...
Zell am See d.	1343	|	...	...	...	...	1540	|	...	...	...	...	...	1743	|	...	1946	|	...	...	...	|	|	...	...
Saalfelden d.	1353	|	...	...	...	...	1555	|	...	...	...	...	...	1753	|	...	1955	|	...	...	...	|	|	...	...
St Johann in Tirol d.	1421	|	...	...	...	...	1625	|	...	...	...	...	...	1821	|	...	2025	|	...	...	...	|	|	...	...
Kitzbühel d.	1429	|	...	...	...	...	1633	|	...	...	...	...	...	1829	|	...	2033	|	...	...	...	|	|	...	...
Wörgl d.	1458	1513	...	...	...	...	1702	1713	...	...	...	...	...	1858	1913	...	2102	2113	...	...	...	0514	0514	...	...
Kufstein 🏛 a.	...	1522	...	...	...	...	...	1722	...	...	...	...	...	...	1922	...	...	2122	...	...	...	0525	0525	...	...
München Ost ▲ a.	...	1614	...	...	...	...	...	1814	...	...	...	...	...	...	2014	...	...	2214	...	...	...	|	|	...	...
München Hbf a.	...	1626	1650	1643	...	...	...	1827	1844	1855	1923	...	...	...	2027	2040	...	2226	2244**d**	2252	2304	0630	0630	0723	...
Augsburg Hbf a.	...	...	|	1720	...	...	...	...	1917	|	2001	...	...	...	...	2114	...	...	2320**d**	2339**u**	2345**u**	...	...	0801	...
Landeck - Zams d.	...	...	|	|	...	...	...	...	|	|	|	...	...	...	...	|	...	...	|	|	|	...	...	|	...
St Anton am Arlberg d.	...	...	|	|	...	...	...	...	|	|	|	...	...	...	...	|	...	...	|	|	|	...	...	|	...
Langen am Arlberg d.	...	...	|	|	...	...	...	...	|	|	|	...	...	...	...	|	...	...	|	|	|	...	...	|	...
Bludenz d.	...	...	|	|	*IC*	...	...	...	|	|	|	...	...	...	...	|	...	...	|	|	|	...	...	|	...
Bregenz d.	...	...	|	|	**2110**	...	...	...	|	|	|	...	...	...	...	|	...	...	|	|	|	...	...	|	...
Lindau 🏛 a.	...	...	|	|	🍷	...	...	...	|	|	|	...	...	...	...	|	...	...	|	|	|	...	...	|	...
Ulm Hbf a.	...	...	|	1803	Ⓑ	...	...	...	2003	|	2049	...	...	...	...	2202	...	...	0010**d**	|	|	...	...	0849	...
Stuttgart Hbf a.	...	...	|	1907	1937	...	...	...	2107	|	2147	...	...	...	...	2300	...	...	0126**d**	|	|	...	...	0947	...
Heidelberg Hbf a.	...	...	|	...	2023	...	...	...	...	|	|	*IC*	...	...	...	|	...	...	|	|	|	...	...	|	...
Mannheim Hbf a.	...	...	|	...	2037	...	...	...	...	|	2228	**2020**	...	...	...	2342	...	...	|	|	|	...	...	1026	...
Frankfurt (Main) Hbf a.	...	...	2005	...	|	...	...	...	...	2205	2325**t**		...	...	...	0042**r**	...	...	|	|	|	...	...	|	...
Frankfurt Flughafen ✈ a.	...	...	2021	...	|	...	...	...	...	2221	2303	2328	...	...	...	0023**r**	...	...	|	|	|	...	...	1106	...
Mainz Hbf a.	...	...	|	...	2118	...	...	...	...	|	...	2345	...	...	...	...	...	...	|	|	|	...	...	|	...
Koblenz Hbf a.	...	...	⊖	...	2210	...	...	...	...	⊖	...	0045	...	...	...	...	...	...	0445**s**	|	|	...	...	⊖	...
Bonn Hbf a.	...	...	|	...	2242	...	...	...	...	|	...	0123	...	...	...	...	...	...	0521**s**	|	|	...	...	|	...
Köln Hbf a.	...	...	2113**k**	...	...	...	...	...	...	2341**k**	...	...	...	...	...	...	...	...	0545**s**	|	|	...	...	1205	...
Dusseldorf Hbf a.	...	...	2137	...	...	...	...	...	...	0005	...	...	...	...	...	...	...	...	0613**s**	|	|	...	...	1232	...
Duisburg Hbf a.	...	...	2149	...	...	...	...	...	...	0018	...	...	...	...	...	...	...	...	0628	|	|	...	...	1245	...
Essen Hbf a.	...	...	2202	...	...	...	...	...	...	0030	...	...	...	...	...	...	...	...	...	|	|	...	...	1257	...
Bochum Hbf a.	...	...	2214	...	...	...	...	...	...	0041	...	...	...	...	...	...	...	...	...	|	|	...	...	1309	...
Dortmund Hbf a.	...	...	2228	...	...	...	...	...	...	0053	...	...	...	...	...	...	...	...	...	|	|	...	...	1321	...
Berlin Hbf a.	...	...	...	...	...	...	...	...	...	...	...	...	...	...	...	...	...	...	...	|	0741	...	...	...	...
Hamburg Hbf a.	...	...	...	...	...	...	...	...	...	...	...	...	...	...	...	...	...	...	...	0754	...	...	...	...	...

A – *CNL* PYXIS – 🛏 1, 2 cl., ▬ 2 cl., [2] (reclining) and ✖ Hamburg - München and v.v. Special fares payable. Talgo stock.

B – *CNL* LUPUS – 🛏 1, 2 cl., ▬ 2 cl., [2] and ✖ München - Innsbruck - Roma and v.v. Special fares apply. [R] for journeys to / from Italy.

C – *CNL* PICTOR – 🛏 1, 2 cl., ▬ 2 cl. and [2] München - Venezia and v.v. ✖ München - Innsbruck and v.v.

D – VAL GARDENA / GRÖDNERTAL – [12] and ✖ München - Bolzano / Bozen and v.v.

G – LEONARDO DA VINCI – [12] München - Milano and v.v. 🍷 Brennero / Brenner - Milano and v.v.

H – ⑥ June 20 - Aug. 22: GROSSGLOCKNER – [12] München - Kufstein 🏛 - Wörgl - Zell am See.

J – ⑥ June 27 - Aug. 29: GROSSGLOCKNER – [12] Zell am See - Wörgl - Kufstein 🏛 - München.

K – [12] and 🍷 Munster - Köln - Stuttgart - Lindau 🏛 - Innsbruck and v.v.

L – ①⑤⑥⑦ (daily Mar. 27 - Nov. 2) City Night Line POLLUX – 🛏 1, 2 cl., 🛏 1, 2 cl. (T4), ▬ 2 cl. (4, 6 berth), [2] (reclining) and ✖ Amsterdam - Köln - München and v.v. [R] Special fares apply.

P – *CNL* CAPELLA – 🛏 1, 2 cl., ▬ 2 cl., [2] (reclining) and ✖ Berlin - München and v.v. Special fares payable. Talgo stock.

Q – WÖRTHERSEE – [12] and ✖ Münster - Klagenfurt and Klagenfurt - Dortmund.

R – MICHELANGELO – [12] and ✖ München - Rimini and v.v.

S – [12] and ✖ München - Innsbruck and v.v.

T – GARDA – [12] München - Verona and v.v.

V – TIEPOLO – [12] and ✖ München - Venezia and v.v.

W – ①–⑤ (not Dec. 8).

a – Arrival time.

d – Departure time.

f – Vaihingen (Enz). 29 km from Stuttgart.

h – 1003 on ⑥⑦ (also Dec. 8); Train **1284**.

j – Depart 9–16 minutes earlier on ⑥⑦ (also Dec. 8).

k – Köln **Messe / Deutz.**

p – ⑥⑦ only.

r – Train stops at Frankfurt Flughafen before Frankfurt (Main) Hbf.

s – Stops to set down only.

t – ①–⑥; train stops at Frankfurt Flughafen before Frankfurt (Main) Hbf.

u – Stops to pick up only.

x – Köln **Messe / Deutz**. Depart 0619 on ⑥⑦.

‡ – Train number Milano - Verona and v.v.

♣ – Special fares payable. Reservation compulsory for journeys to/from Italy.

⊖ – Via Köln - Frankfurt high speed line.

⌿ – Supplement payable.

▲ – Change here for München Airport (Table **892**).

⊕ – **ETR 470** *Cisalpino*. Supplement payable for international journeys. *IC* supplement payable for internal journeys within Italy.

BERLIN - INNSBRUCK 71

For other services from Berlin to Innsbruck, change at München (Tables **850** and **70**); for Dresden - München connections see Table **880**.

train type	CNL	ICE	ICE	ICE	ICE	ICE	ICE	ICE
train number	**1201**	**1603**	**781**	**1505**	**1507**	**1719**	**109**	**1513**
notes	[R]	①–⑥					**A**	
	B	❖		❖	❖	❖	❖	❖
Berlin Hbf d.	2212	...	...	0652	0858	1058	1258	1458
Leipzig Hbf d.	|	0501	...	0816	1016	1216	1416	1616
Nürnberg Hbf d.	|	0820	0827	1128	1328	1528	1728	1928
München Hbf a.	0639	...	0942	1240	1439	1640	1838	2040
	EC		*IC*	*IC*	*IC*	*EC*	|	*CNL*
	81		**87**	**89**	**83**	**189**	|	**485**
	E		**E**	**E**	**E**	**E**	|	**E**
München Hbf d.	0730	...	1130	1330	1530	1731	1841**x**	2103
Kufstein 🏛 a.	0832	...	1232	1432	1632	1832	1939**x**	2207
Innsbruck a.	0921	...	1321	1521	1721	1921	2026**x**	2256

train type	CNL	ICE	IC	IC	EC	IC		EC
train number	**484**	**108**	**188**	**88**	**82**	**84**		**80**
notes	**E**	**A**	**E**	**E**	**E**	**E**		**E**
		❖						
Innsbruck d.	0434	0735**z**	1036	1236	1436	1636	...	2036
Kufstein 🏛 d.	0530	0821**z**	1124	1324	1524	1724	...	2124
München Hbf a.	0630	0916**z**	1225	1427	1626	1827	...	2226
		|		*ICE*				*CNL*
	ICE	|	*ICE*	**1724**	*ICE*	*ICE*		**1200**
	1712	|	**1716**	**1104**	**1502**	**1500**		[R]
	❖	|	❖	❖	❖	❖		**C**
München Hbf d.	0720	0921	1320	1520	1720	1920	...	2304
Nürnberg Hbf a.	0831	1031	1431	1631	1831	2031	...	|
Leipzig Hbf a.	1141	1341	1741	1941	2141	2349	...	|
Berlin Hbf a.	1302	1500	1900	2100	2300	...	...	0741

A – [12] and ✖ Berlin - München - Kufstein 🏛 - Innsbruck and v.v.

B – *City Night Line* CAPELLA – 🛏 1, 2 cl., ▬ 2 cl., [2] (reclining) and ✖ Berlin Lichtenberg (depart 2149) - Berlin Ostbahnhof (2203) - Berlin Hbf - Berlin Zoo (2220) - Berlin Wannsee (2254) - München. Special fares payable. Talgo stock.

C – *City Night Line* CAPELLA – 🛏 1, 2 cl., ▬ 2 cl., [2] (reclining) and ✖ München - Berlin Wannsee (arrive 0709) - Berlin Zoo (0730) - Berlin Hbf - Berlin Ostbahnhof (0752) - Berlin Lichtenberg (0811). Special fares payable. Talgo stock.

E – See notes in Table **70** for details of this train.

x – ⑤⑥ only.

z – ⑥⑦ only.

❖ – Due to engineering work between Leipzig and Nürnberg from Aug. 1 until Sept. 14, services are subject to alteration. See Table **851**.

73 AMSTERDAM, BERLIN, DORTMUND and KÖLN - BASEL - ZÜRICH, MILANO and ROMA

For other connections Basel - Luzern - Chiasso see Table **550**, for Basel - Bern - Interlaken and Brig see Table **560**.

train type	*ICE*	*ICE*	*IC*	*ICE*	*ICE*	*ICN*	*CNL*	*ICE*	*IC*	*ICE*	*ICE*	*IR*	*CIS*	*ICE*	*ICE*	*IC*	*EC*	*ICE*	*ICE*	*ICE*	*ICE*	*ICE*	*EC*	*IC*	*ICN*
train number	**521**	**5**	**2021**	**511**	**271**	**10017**	**473**	**501**	**2319**	**513**	**373**	**2173**	**57**	**503**	**71**	**575**	**7**	**121**	**515**	**375**	**105**	**73**	**91**	**977**	**683**
notes	🍷	🍷 **M**		🍷	🍷	🍷	**C**	🍷	①–⑥	🍷	🍷	¶	🍴	🍷	🍷	🍷	🍴 **B**	①–⑥	🍷	🍷	🍷	🍷	🍷	🍷	🍷
København H. d.	...	...	...	...	...	...	1853	...	...	...	...	...	...	...	...	...	...	...	...	...	...	...	...	...	...
Hamburg Hbf d.	...	0025e	2246	...	...	...	0031	...	...	...	...	...	...	...	0618z	...	0442v	...	0537	...	...	0824z	...	...	...
Bremen Hbf d.	...	│	2347	...	...	...	│	...	...	...	...	...	...	...	│	...	0540v	...	0637	...	...	│	...	...	...
Berlin Hauptbahnhof d.	...	│	│	...	...	...	│	...	...	...	0432p	...	...	...	│	...	│	...	│	0632	...	│	...	...	...
Hannover Hbf d.	...	0150e	│	...	...	...	│	...	...	...	│	...	...	0540	0741	...	│	...	│	│	...	0941	...	...	...
Dortmund Hbf d.	...	│	0203	...	...	...	│	0537	...	0638	│	...	...	0737	│	...	0738	...	0837	│	...	│	...	...	...
Essen Hbf d.	...	│	0228	...	...	...	│	│	...	0700	│	...	...	│	│	...	0800	...	│	│	...	│	...	...	...
Amsterdam Centraal d.	...	│	│	...	...	...	│	│	...	│	│	...	...	│	│	...	│	0704	│	│	0804	│	...	...	...
Utrecht Centraal d.	...	│	│	...	...	...	│	│	...	│	│	...	...	│	│	...	│	0729	│	│	0829	│	...	...	...
Arnhem ⊙ d.	...	│	│	...	...	...	│	│	...	│	│	...	...	│	│	...	│	0808	│	│	0907	│	...	...	...
Duisburg Hbf d.	...	│	0241	...	...	...	│	**h**	...	0713	│	...	...	**h**	│	...	0813	0908	**h**	│	1008	│	...	...	...
Düsseldorf Hbf d.	...	│	0302	...	...	...	│	│	...	0727	│	...	...	│	│	...	0827	0923	│	│	1022	│	...	...	...
Köln Hbf d.	0420	│	0352	0554	...	...	│	0654	...	0754	│	...	...	0854	│	...	0853	0951x	0954	│	1054	│	...	...	...
Bonn Hbf d.	│	│	│	│	...	...	│	│	0714	│	│	...	...	│	│	...	0914	│	│	│	│	│	...	...	...
Koblenz Hbf d.	⊖	│	0530	⊖	...	...	│	⊖	0748	⊖	│	...	...	⊖	│	...	0948	⊖	⊖	│	⊖	│	...	...	...
Mainz Hbf d.	│	│	0629	│	...	...	│	│	0839	│	│	...	...	│	│	...	1039	│	│	│	│	│	...	...	...
Frankfurt Flughafen ✈ d.	0533	0555r	0646	0654	...	...	│	0754	│	0854	│	...	...	0954	│	...	│	1043	1054	│	1154	│	...	...	...
Frankfurt (Main) Hbf d.	...	0538r	▬	│	0650	...	0659j	│	│	│	0850	...	...	│	1005	...	│	▬	│	1050	│	1205	...	...	...
Mannheim Hbf d.	...	0627	...	0724	0736	...	0750s	0836	0921	0924	0936	...	...	1036	1044	...	1123	...	1124	1136	1236	1244	...	...	...
Karlsruhe Hbf d.	...	0656	...	▬	0800	...	0818s	0900	▬	▬	1000	...	...	1051	1108	...	1149	...	▬	1200	1300	1308	...	...	...
Freiburg (Brsg) Hbf d.	...	0802	...	...	0901	...	0939s	1002	...	...	1101	...	...	*1201*	1211	...	1255	...	...	1301	1401	1411	...	...	...
Basel Bad Bf 🏛 a.	...	0837	...	...	0936	...	1027s	1037	...	...	1136	...	...	*1236*	1247	...	1329	...	...	1336	1436	1447	...	...	...
Basel SBB a.	...	0847	...	...	0947	...	1037	1047	...	...	1147	...	...	*1247*	1255	...	1337	...	...	1347y	1447	1455	...	...	...
		│	*IC* **567** 🍷	*ICN* **671** 🍷	│		▬ *IC* **967**	*IC* **969**	*ICN* **675** 🍷	*IC* **571** 🍷	│			▬ *IC* **573**	▬		│	*IR* **2177** 🍷		│	▬	│			
Basel SBB ★ d.	...	0901	0933	0903	1007	...	1001	1101	1103	1133	1201	1203	1228	1233	...	1333	1407	1403	...	1401	...	1507	...	1501	1503
Bern a.	...	0956	│	│	│	...	1056	1156	│	│	1256	│	1327	│	...	│	│	│	...	1456	...	│	...	1556	│
Spiez a.	...	1031	│	│	│	...	1131	1231	│	│	1331	│	1402	│	...	│	│	│	*ICN*	1531	...	│	...	1631	│
Interlaken Ost a.	...	1057	│	│	│	...	1157	1257	│	│	1357	│	│	│	...	│	│	│	**10021**	1557	...	│	...	1657	│
Brig a.	...	*1111*f	│	│	│	...	*1211*f	*1311*f	│	│	*1411*f	│	1440	│	...	│	│	│	⊡	*1611*f	...	│	...	*1711*f	│
Domodossola 🏛 § a.	...	...	│	│	│	...	▬	▬	│	│	▬	│	1512	│	...	│	│	│	🍷	▬	...	│	...	...	│
Zürich HB a.	...	...	1026	│	1100	1109	...	...	│	1226	...	│	│	1326	...	1426	1500	│	1509	...	...	1600	1612	...	│
Landquart a.	...	...	1141	│	*1232*	│	...	...	│	1341	...	│	│	1441	...	1541	1632	│	│	...	...	▬	1732	...	│
Davos Platz a.	...	...	*1255*	│	│	│	...	...	│	*1455*	*CIS*	│	│	*1555*	...	*1655*	*1755*	│	│	...	...	...	*1855*	...	│
Chur a.	...	...	1152	│	*1243*	│	...	...	│	1352	**19**	│	│	1452	...	1552	1643	│	│	...	...	...	1743	...	│
St Moritz a.	...	...	*1358*	│	...	│	*CIS*	...	│	*1558*	Ⓡ	│	│	*1658*	...	*1758*	*1858*	│	│	*CIS*	...	...	*1958*	...	│
Luzern a.	...	...	...	1005	...	│	**17**	...	1205	▬	🍷	1305	│	▬	...	...	...	1505	│	**21**	...	...	...	...	1605
Arth-Goldau a.	...	...	...	1045	...	1146	Ⓡ	...	1245	...	1350	1345y	│	...	...	...	...	1545	1546	Ⓡ	*ESc*	...	...	...	1645
Bellinzona a.	...	...	...	1223	...	1323	🍷	*Esc*	1423	*AV*	1523	1553	│	*AV*	*Esc*	...	...	...	1723	🍷	**9745**	*AV*	...	...	1823
Lugano a.	...	...	...	1246	...	1346	1348	**9729**	1446	**9443**	1546	...	│	**9447**	**9403**	...	...	...	1746	1748	**9793**	**9451**	...	...	1846
Chiasso 🏛 a.	...	...	...	...	...	...	│	Ⓡ🍴	...	Ⓡ🍴	│	...	│	Ⓡ🍴	Ⓡ🍴	...	...	...	...	│	Ⓡ🍷	Ⓡ🍴	...	...	1908
Como San Giovanni a.	...	...	...	...	...	...	1414	⚡	...	⚡	│	...	│	⚡	⚡	...	...	...	...	1818	⚡	⚡	...	...	...
Milano Centrale a.	...	...	...	...	...	...	1450	1505	...	1530	1650	...	1640	1730	1735	...	...	...	...	1850	1905	1930	...	...	...
Venezia Santa Lucia a.	...	...	...	...	...	...	...	1740	...	│	...	...	1928k	│	1955	...	...	...	...	...	2150	│	...	...	...
Bologna Centrale a.	...	...	...	...	...	...	...	...	...	1635	...	...	...	1835	...	...	...	...	...	...	...	2035	...	...	...
Firenze SMN a.	...	...	...	...	...	...	...	...	...	1739	...	...	...	1939	...	...	...	...	...	...	...	2139	...	...	...
Roma Termini a.	...	...	...	...	...	...	...	...	...	1929	...	...	...	2129	...	...	...	...	...	...	...	2329	...	...	...

train type	*EC*	*ICE*	*ICE*	*IR*	*ICE*	*ICE*	*IR*	*IC*	*ICE*	*ICE*	*ICE*	*IR*	*ICE*	*ICE*	*ICE*	*ICN*	*ICE*	*IC*	*ICE*	*ICE*	*ICE*	*ICE*	*ICE*	*IC*	*EN*
train number	**101**	**517**	**871**	**2181**	**507**	**75**	**1585**	**2113**	**123**	**519**	**277**	**2187**	**599**	**509**	**77**	**691**	**125**	**2115**	**611**	**279**	**691**	**601**	**79**	**1093**	**313**
notes	🍴 **D**	🍷	🍷	¶	🍷	🍷		🍷	🍷	🍷	🍷		🍷	🍷	🍷	🍷	🍷	🍷	🍷	🍷	🍷	🍷	🍷		⚡ **N**
København H. d.	...	...	...	...	...	...	...	...	...	...	...	...	...	...	...	...	...	...	...	...	...	...	...	...	...
Hamburg Hbf d.	0646	...	...	...	...	1024z	...	...	...	...	...	...	...	...	1224z	...	...	...	...	...	...	...	1424z	...	...
Bremen Hbf d.	0744	...	...	...	...	│	...	...	...	...	...	...	...	...	│	...	...	...	...	...	...	...	│	...	...
Berlin Hauptbahnhof d.	│	...	0832	...	...	│	...	...	...	...	1031	...	1137	...	│	...	...	...	...	1232	1337	...	│	...	...
Hannover Hbf d.	│	...	│	...	...	1141	...	...	...	...	│	...	│	...	1341	...	...	...	...	│	│	...	1541	...	...
Dortmund Hbf d.	0938	1038	│	...	...	│	...	...	...	1238	│	...	│	...	│	...	...	...	1438	│	│	...	│	...	...
Essen Hbf d.	1000	1100	│	...	...	│	...	...	...	1300	│	...	│	...	│	...	...	...	1500	│	│	...	│	...	...
Amsterdam Centraal d.	│	│	│	...	...	│	...	...	1034	│	│	...	│	...	│	...	1234	...	│	│	│	...	│	...	...
Utrecht Centraal d.	│	│	│	...	...	│	...	...	1059	│	│	...	│	...	│	...	1259	...	│	│	│	...	│	...	...
Arnhem ⊙ d.	│	│	│	...	...	│	...	...	1137	│	│	...	│	...	│	...	1337	...	│	│	│	...	│	...	...
Duisburg Hbf d.	1013	1113	│	...	...	│	...	...	1234	1313	│	...	│	...	│	...	1434	...	1513	│	│	...	│	...	...
Düsseldorf Hbf d.	1027	1127	│	...	...	│	...	...	1248	1327	│	...	│	...	│	...	1448	...	1527	│	│	...	│	...	...
Köln Hbf d.	1053	1154	│	...	1254	│	...	...	1320	1354	│	...	│	1454	│	...	1520	...	1554	│	│	1654	│	...	...
Bonn Hbf d.	1114	│	│	...	│	│	...	1314	│	│	│	...	│	│	│	...	│	1514	│	│	│	│	│	...	...
Koblenz Hbf d.	1148	⊖	│	...	⊖	│	...	1348	⊖	⊖	│	...	│	⊖	│	...	⊖	1548	⊖	│	│	⊖	│	...	...
Mainz Hbf d.	1239	│	│	...	│	│	...	1439	│	│	│	...	│	│	│	...	│	1639	│	│	│	│	│	...	...
Frankfurt Flughafen ✈ d.	│	1254	│	...	1354	│	...	│	1417	1454	│	...	│	1554	│	...	1617	│	1654	│	│	1754	│	...	...
Frankfurt (Main) Hbf d.	│	│	1250	...	│	1405	...	│	1430	│	1450	...	1550	│	1605	...	1630	│	│	1650	1750	│	1805	...	...
Mannheim Hbf d.	1323	1324	1336	...	1426	1444	...	1521	▬	1524	1536	...	1628	1636	1644	...	▬	1721	1724	1736	1828	1826	1844	...	...
Karlsruhe Hbf d.	1349	...	1400	...	1451	1508	...	▬	...	▬	1600	...	▬	1700	1708	...	...	▬	...	1800	▬	1900	1908	...	...
Freiburg (Brsg) Hbf d.	1455	...	1501	...	*1559*	1611	...	...	...	...	1701	...	...	1801	1811	...	...	...	...	1901	...	2001	2011	...	...
Basel Bad Bf 🏛 a.	1529	...	1536	...	*1636*	1647	...	...	...	...	1736	...	...	1836	1847	...	...	...	...	1936	...	2036	2047	...	...
Basel SBB a.	1537	...	1547	...	*1647*	1655	...	...	...	...	1747	...	...	1847	1855	...	...	...	...	1947	...	2047	2055	...	...
	│		*IC* **979**		*IC* **581**	│		*IC* **981** 🍷	*ICN* **685** 🍷	*CIS* **59** 🍴	│		*IC* **587**	▬	│			*ICE* **987** 🍷		│	*IR* **2191**	▬	│		
Basel SBB ★ d.	1547	...	1601	1603	1633	1707	...	1701	1703	1728	1801	1803	1833	...	1907	1903	...	1901	...	2001	2003	...	2107	2128	...
Bern a.	│	...	1656	│	│	│	...	1756	│	1827	1856	│	│	...	│	│	...	1956	...	2056	│	...	│	2227	2304
Spiez a.	│	*CIS*	1731	│	│	│	...	1831	│	1902	1931	│	│	...	│	│	...	2031	...	2134	│	...	│	*2302*	2335u
Interlaken Ost a.	│	**23**	1757	│	│	│	...	1857	│	│	1957	│	│	...	│	│	*IR*	2054	...	2157	│	...	│	│	│
Brig a.	│	Ⓡ	*1811*f	│	│	│	...	*1911*f	│	1940	*2011*f	│	│	...	│	│	**1589**	*2111*f	...	*2239*‡	│	...	│	*0008*	0100d
Domodossola 🏛 § a.	│	🍷	...	│	│	│	...	...	│	2012	...	│	│	...	│	│	...	...	...	...	│	...	│	...	◐
Zürich HB a.	1652	1701b	...	│	1726	1800	1812	...	│	│	...	│	1926	...	2000	│	2012	...	...	...	│	...	2200	...	│
Landquart a.	1832	│	...	│	1841	▬	1932	...	│	│	...	│	2041	...	▬	│	2134	...	...	...	│	...	...	...	│
Davos Platz a.	*1955*	│	...	│	*1955*	*CIS*	*2057*	...	│	│	...	│	*2157*	*ICN*	...	│	*2257*	...	...	...	│	...	...	...	│
Chur a.	1843	│	...	│	1852	**23**	1943	...	│	│	...	│	2052	**10025**	...	│	2145	...	...	...	│	*ICN*	...	...	│
St Moritz a.	*2058*	│	...	│	*2058*	Ⓡ	*2159*	...	│	│	...	│	*2259*	Ⓡ	*CIS*	│	⊗	...	...	...	│	**693**	...	...	│
Luzern a.	...	│	...	1705	...	🍷	▬	...	1805	│	...	1905	...	🍷	**25**	2005	▬	...	...	...	2105	🍷	...	...	│
Arth-Goldau a.	...	1750	...	1745	...	1750	...	...	1845	│	...	1945	...	1950	Ⓡ	2045	...	...	...	...	2145	2150	...	...	│
Bellinzona a.	...	1923	...	1953	...	1923	*ESc*	...	2023	│	...	2153	...	2123	🍷	2223	...	...	...	...	...	2323	...	...	│
Lugano a.	...	1946	...	...	...	1946	**9753**	...	2046	│	...	2226	...	2146	2148	2246	*E*	...	...	...	...	2346	...	...	│
Chiasso 🏛 a.	...	│	...	...	...	│	Ⓡ🍷	...	2108	│	...	2257	...	...	│	2308	**1911**	...	...	...	...	0010	...	...	│
Como San Giovanni a.	...	2015	...	...	...	2015	⚡	...	...	│	...	...	...	...	2214	...	**E**	...	...	...	...	...	...	...	│
Milano Centrale a.	...	2050	...	...	...	2050	2105	...	...	2135	...	...	...	...	2250	...	2320	...	...	...	...	...	...	...	│
Venezia Santa Lucia a.	...	...	...	...	...	...	2356k	...	...	...	...	...	...	...	...	...	│	...	...	...	...	...	...	...	│
Bologna Centrale a.	...	...	...	...	...	...	...	...	...	...	...	...	...	...	...	...	│	...	...	...	...	...	...	...	0519
Firenze SMN a.	...	...	...	...	...	...	...	...	...	...	...	...	...	...	...	...	│	...	...	...	...	...	...	...	0641q
Roma Termini a.	...	...	...	...	...	...	...	...	...	...	...	...	...	...	...	...	0723t	...	...	...	...	...	...	...	0912

CONTINUED ON NEXT PAGE

AMSTERDAM, BERLIN, DORTMUND and KÖLN - ZÜRICH, MILANO and ROMA 73

train type	*IC*	*ICE*	*ICE*	*ICE*	*IR*	*IC*	*ICE*	*ICE*	*CNL*	*CNL*	*ICE*	*IC*	*IC*	*ICE*	*CNL*	*CNL*	*IC*	*CIS*	*IC*	*IC*	*CNL*	*IC*	*IR*	*CIS*	*AV*
train number	**2311**	**127**	**613**	**873**	**1567**	**993**	**227**	**673**	**401**	**40421**	**609**	**955**	**559**	**542**	**40419**	**479**	**561**	**15**	**959**	**458**	**1258**	**565**	**2165**	**15**	**9439**
notes	🍷	🍷	🍷	🍷			🍷	🍷			🍷	🍷	🍷	🍷		[R]	🍷	[R]	🍷		[R] ✖	🍷	¶	[R]	[R] ✖
notes		**T**							**P**	**Q**					**A**	**K**		🍷			**G**			🍷	⚡
København H .... d.	...	...	...	...	...	...	...	...	...	...	...	...	...	...	...	...	...	...	...	...	...	...	...	...	...
Hamburg Hbf .... d.	...	...	...	...	...	...	...	1824z	...	...	1946	...	...	...	...	1918	...	...	...	...	...	...	...	...	...
Bremen Hbf .... d.	...	...	...	...	...	...	...	|	...	...	2044	...	...	...	...	|	...	...	...	...	...	...	...	...	...
Berlin Hauptbahnhof .... d.	...	...	...	1432	...	...	...	|	...	...	|	...	...	1850	...	|	...	...	...	...	2222	...	...	...	...
Hannover Hbf .... d.	...	...	...	|	...	...	...	1941	...	...	|	...	...	2031	...	2218	...	...	...	...	|	...	...	...	...
Dortmund Hbf .... d.	...	...	1638	|	...	...	...	|	...	1826	2238	...	...	2212	...	|	...	...	...	...	|	...	...	...	...
Essen Hbf .... d.	...	...	1700	|	...	...	...	|	...	1904	2300	...	...	2236	...	|	...	...	...	...	|	...	...	...	...
Amsterdam Centraal .... d.	...	1434	|	|	...	...	1834	|	1701	|	|	...	...	|	2031	|	...	...	...	...	|	...	...	...	...
Utrecht Centraal .... d.	...	1459	|	|	...	...	1859	|	1729	|	|	...	...	|	2101u	|	...	...	...	...	|	...	...	...	...
Arnhem ⊙ .... d.	...	1537	|	|	...	...	1937	|	1808	|	|	...	...	|	2138u	|	...	...	...	...	|	...	...	...	...
Duisburg Hbf .... d.	...	1634	1713	|	...	...	2034	|	|	|	2313	...	...	2249	2256u	|	...	...	...	...	|	...	...	...	...
Düsseldorf Hbf .... d.	...	1648	1727	|	...	...	2048	|	1935	1935	2327	...	...	2308	2312u	|	...	...	...	...	|	...	...	...	...
Köln Hbf .... d.	...	1720	1754	|	...	...	2120	|	2006	2006	2353	...	...	2330	2346u	|	...	...	...	...	|	...	...	...	...
Bonn Hbf .... d.	1714	|	|	|	...	...	|	|	2034	2034	0014	...	...	▬	0007u	|	...	...	...	...	|	...	...	...	...
Koblenz Hbf .... d.	1748	⊖	⊖	|	...	...	⊖	|	2115	2115	0048	...	...	...	0044u	|	...	...	...	...	|	...	...	...	...
Mainz Hbf .... d.	1839	|	|	|	...	...	|	|	2212	2212	0143	...	...	...	|	|	...	...	...	...	|	...	...	...	...
Frankfurt Flughafen ✈ .... d.	|	1817	1854	|	...	...	2221	|	|	|	0205	...	...	...	|	|	...	...	...	...	|	...	...	...	...
Frankfurt (Main) Hbf .... d.	|	1830	|	1850	...	...	2234	2200	2249	2249	0222	...	...	...	|	|	...	...	...	0402j	0400j	...	...	...	...
Mannheim Hbf .... d.	1921	...	1924	1936	...	...	▬	▬	2332	2332	0302	...	...	...	|	0310s	...	...	...	0445	0443s	...	...	...	...
Karlsruhe Hbf .... d.	...	...	...	2000	...	...	...	...	2359	2359	0337	...	...	...	0437s	0437s	...	...	...	0542	0540s	...	...	...	...
Freiburg (Brsg) Hbf .... d.	...	...	...	2101	...	...	...	...	|	|	0452	...	...	...	0556s	0556s	...	...	...	0655	0653s	...	...	...	...
Basel Bad Bf 🏛 .... a.	...	...	...	2136	...	...	...	...	◐	◐	0537	...	...	...	0644s	0644s	...	...	...	0749	0746s	...	...	...	...
Basel SBB .... a.	...	...	...	2147	...	...	...	...	|	|	0547	...	...	...	0654s	0654s	...	...	...	0755	0755	...	...	...	...
									|	|	▬			*CIS*	|	|				▬	|				
				IC				*IR*	|	|				**51**	|	|				*IC*	|				
				795				**2195**	|	|				🍷	|	|				**810**	|				
Basel SBB ★ .... d.	...	...	...	2207	...	2201	...	2203	|	|	...	0601	0633	0628	|	|	...	...	0701	🍷	|	...	0803	...	...
Bern .... a.	...	...	...	|	...	2256	...	|	|	|	...	0656	|	0727	|	|	...	...	0756	0807	|	...	|	...	...
Spiez .... a.	...	...	...	|	...	2335	0012	|	|	|	...	0731	|	0802	|	|	...	...	0831	0834	|	...	|	...	...
Interlaken Ost .... a.	...	...	...	|	...	2359	|	|	|	|	...	0757	|	|	|	|	...	...	0857	|	|	...	|	...	...
Brig .... a.	...	...	...	|	...	...	0120	|	|	|	...	*0811*f	|	0840	|	|	...	...	▬	0911	|	...	|	...	...
Domodossola 🏛 § .... a.	...	...	...	|	...	...	...	|	|	|	...	▬	|	0912	|	|	...	...	...	...	|	...	|	...	...
Zürich HB .... a.	...	...	...	2259	2312	...	...	|	|	|	...	...	0726	|	0820	0820	0837	0901	...	...	0917	0937	|	...	...
Landquart .... a.	...	...	...	...	0039	...	...	|	|	|	...	...	0841	|	▬	▬	0941	|	...	...	...	1041	|	...	...
Davos Platz .... a.	...	...	...	...	|	...	...	|	|	|	...	...	*0955*	|	...	...	*1055*	|	...	...	...	*1155*	|	...	...
Chur .... a.	...	...	...	...	0049	...	...	|	|	|	...	...	0852	|	...	...	0952	|	...	...	...	1052	|	...	...
St Moritz .... a.	...	...	...	...	...	...	...	|	|	|	...	...	*1058*	|	...	...	*1158*	|	...	...	...	*1258*	|	...	...
Luzern .... a.	...	...	...	...	...	...	...	2305	|	|	...	...	...	|	...	...	...	|	...	...	...	...	0905	...	...
Arth-Goldau .... a.	...	...	...	...	...	...	...	*2351*	|	|	...	...	...	|	...	...	...	0945	...	...	...	...	0945	0950	...
Bellinzona .... a.	...	...	...	...	...	...	...	...	0540	0540	*ESc*	*AV*	...	|	*AV*	*ESc*	...	1121	*ESc*	...	...	...	1153	1121	...
Lugano .... a.	...	...	...	...	...	...	...	...	0608	0608	**9707**	**9429**	...	|	**9435**	**9715**	...	1144	**9723**	...	...	...	...	1144	...
Chiasso 🏛 .... a.	...	...	...	...	...	...	...	...	0631	0631	[R] 🍷	[R] ✖	...	|	[R] ✖	🍷	...	|	🍷	...	...	...	...	|	...
Como San Giovanni .... a.	...	...	...	...	...	...	...	...	0656	0656	⚡	⚡	...	|	⚡	⚡	...	1214	⚡	...	...	...	...	1214	...
Milano Centrale .... a.	...	...	...	...	...	...	...	...	0750	0750	0805	0830	...	1035	1130	1135	...	1250	1335	...	...	...	...	1250	1330
Venezia Santa Lucia .... a.	...	...	...	...	...	...	...	...	...	...	1040	|	...	...	|	1410	...	...	1610	...	...	...	...	*1610*	|
Bologna Centrale .... a.	...	...	...	...	...	...	...	...	...	...	...	0935	...	...	1235	...	...	...	...	...	...	...	...	...	1435
Firenze SMN .... a.	...	...	...	...	...	...	...	...	...	...	...	1039	...	...	1339	...	...	...	...	...	...	...	...	...	1539
Roma Termini .... a.	...	...	...	...	...	...	...	...	...	...	...	1229	...	...	1529	...	...	...	...	...	...	...	...	...	1729

A – *City Night Line* PEGASUS – ①⑤⑥⑦ (daily until Nov. 2): 🛏 1, 2 cl., 🛏 1, 2 cl. (T4), ▬ 2 cl. (4, 6 berth), 2 (reclining) and 🍷 Amsterdam - Mannheim - Basel - Zürich. [R] Special fares apply.

B – 12 and ✖ (Hamburg ①–⑥ v -) Dortmund - Köln - Basel - Zürich - Chur.

C – *City Night Line* AURORA – 🛏 1, 2 cl., ▬ 2 cl. (4, 6 berth), 2 and ✖ København - Basel. [R] Special fares apply.

D – 12 and ✖ Hamburg - Dortmund - Köln - Basel - Zürich - Chur.

E – 🛏 1, 2 cl., 🛏 1, 2 cl. (Excelsior), 🛏 1, 2 cl. (T2), ▬ 2 cl. and 2 Milano - Roma - Napoli.

G – *City Night Line* BERLINER – 🛏 1, 2 cl., 🛏 1, 2 cl. (T4), ▬ 2 cl. (4, 6 berth), 2 (reclining) and ✖ (Ostseebad Binz, depart 1820, ⑥ July 4 - Aug. 22) Berlin - Basel - Zürich. [R] Special fares apply. Conveys *City Night Line* **458** CANOPUS Praha - Dresden - Zürich (Table **75**).

K – *City Night Line* KOMET – ④⑤⑥⑦ (daily until Nov. 1): 🛏 1, 2 cl., 🛏 1, 2 cl. (T4), ▬ 2 cl. (4, 6 berth), 2 (reclining) and ✖ Hamburg - Hannover - Mannheim - Basel - Zürich. [R] Special fares apply.

M – 12 and 🍷 (Hamburg ① e) - Frankfurt - Basel - Interlaken Ost.

N – ROMA – 🛏 1, 2 cl. and ▬ 2 cl. (6 berth) Zürich - Bern - Roma.

P – *City Night Line* APUS – 🛏 1, 2 cl., ▬ 2 cl. (6 berth), 2 (reclining) and ✖: ⑤⑥⑦ Amsterdam - Frankfurt - Milano. [R] Special fares apply.

Q – *City Night Line* APUS – 🛏 1, 2 cl., ▬ 2 cl. (6 berth), 2 (reclining) and ✖: ①②③④ Dortmund - Frankfurt - Milano. [R] Special fares apply.

T – Apr. 3 - Oct. 25.

b – 1709 on ⑥⑦.

d – Departure time.

e – ① only.

f – Change at Bern.

h – Via Hagen and Wuppertal.

j – Frankfurt (Main) **Süd**.

k – Venezia **Mestre**.

p – ①–⑤.

q – Firenze **Campo di Marte**.

r – Train stops at Frankfurt (Main) Hbf before Frankfurt Flughafen.

s – Stops to set down only.

t – Roma **Tiburtina**.

u – Stops to pick up only.

v – ①–⑥.

x – Köln **Messe / Deutz**.

y – Connects with train in previous column.

z – June 14 - July 19 depart 22 minutes earlier.

¶ – To Locarno.

⊙ – 🏛 is at Emmerich.

§ – Ticket point is **Iselle**.

◐ – Ticket point / frontier.

⚡ – Supplement payable.

★ – Connections at Basel are not guaranteed.

⊖ – Via Köln - Frankfurt high speed line.

‡ – Change at Bern. 2301 on ⑦.

⊡ – Supplement payable in Italy (except with international tickets).

CIS – **ETR 470** *Cisalpino*. [R], Supplement payable for international journeys. *IC* supplement payable for internal journeys within Italy.

⊠ – Change at Landquart for St Moritz. Landquart depart 2147, Klosters arrive 2228, change trains, depart 2230, St Moritz arrive 2346.

OTHER TRAIN NAMES:

EC **109** – CISALPINO TICINO
EC **111** – CISALPINO SAN MARCO
EC **115** – CISALPINO MEDIOLANUM
EC **117** – CISALPINO VERDI
EC **119** – CISALPINO TIZIANO
EC **177** – CISALPINO MONTE CENERI
EC **179** – CISALPINO INSUBRIA

MILANO and ROMA - PATRAS - ATHÍNAI 74

train type	*ES*	*ESc*				*ESc*				
train number	**9353**	**9761**			**2320**	**9761**				
notes	[R] ✖ ⚡	[R] ✖ ⚡	⛴ *SF*			[R] ✖ ⚡	⛴ *SF*			
Milano Centrale .... d.	...	0700	...	...	...	0700	...	...	...	...
Bologna .... d.	...	0856	...	...	...	0856	...	...	...	...
Roma Termini .... d.	1400	|	...	...	0550	|	...	...	...	...
Foligno .... d.	|	|	...	...	0740	|	...	...	...	...
Ancona .... d.	|	1054	...	...	0955	1051	...	...	...	...
Ancona Marittima .... d.	|	|	...	...	...	...	1330	...	...	...
Pescara Centrale .... d.	|	1208	...	...	...	....	|	...	...	...
Caserta .... d.	1518	|	...	...	...	...	|	...	...	...
Foggia .... d.	1714	1350	...	...	...	...	|	...	...	...
Bari Centrale .... a.	1815	1451	...	...	...	...	|	...	...	...
Bari Marittima .... d.	...	...	2000	...	...	...	|	...	...	...
Patras .... a.	...	...	1230	...	...	...	1130	...	...	...
Athína Lárisa .... a.	...	...	❖	...	...	...	❖	...	...	...

train type		*ESc*	*ICp*	*ES*				*ES*	*ESc*	
train number		**9764**	**568**	**9354**			**2327**	**9331**	**9762**	
notes	⛴ *SF*	[R] ✖ ⚡	[R] ✖ ⚡	[R] ✖ ⚡		⛴ *SF*		[R] ✖ ⚡	[R] ✖ ⚡	
Athína Lárisa .... d.	❖	...	...	...	...	❖	...	...	...	...
Patras .... d.	1800	...	...	...	...	1430	...	...	...	...
Bari Marittima .... a.	0830	...	...	...	...	|	...	...	...	...
Bari Centrale .... d.	...	1105	1113	1344	...	|	...	...	...	...
Foggia .... a.	...	1207	1224	1445	...	|	...	...	...	...
Caserta .... a.	...	|	|	1637	...	|	...	...	...	...
Pescara Centrale .... a.	...	1347	1432	|	...	|	...	...	...	...
Ancona Marittma .... a.	...	|	|	|	...	1030	...	...	...	...
Ancona .... a.	...	1512	1617	|	...	...	1408	1523	1240	...
Foligno .... a.	...	|	|	|	...	...	1610	1658	|	...
Roma Termini .... a.	...	|	|	1800	...	...	1803	1824	|	...
Bologna .... a.	...	1706	1846	...	...	...	...	...	1504	...
Milano Centrale .... a.	...	1900	2105	...	...	...	...	...	1700	...

❖ – For shipping operators' bus connections see Table **2770**; for rail service see Table **1450**.

⚡ – Supplement payable.

SF – **Superfast Ferries**, for days of running see Tables **2715**, **2755**.

73 ROMA, MILANO and ZÜRICH - KÖLN, DORTMUND, BERLIN and AMSTERDAM

For other connections Basel - Luzern - Chiasso see Table **550**, for Basel - Bern - Interlaken and Brig see Table **560**.

train type	*ICE*	*IR*	*EN*	*TGV*	*ICN*	*IR*	*IC*	*IR*	*ICE*	*IC*	*IR*	*ICE*	*IC*	*ICN*	*IC*	*CIS*	*ICN*	*IR*	*EC*	*CIS*	*ICE*	*IR*	*ICN*	*ICE*	*IC*	*ICE*
train number	**78**	**1560**	**314**	**9210**	**650**	**2164**	**956**	**1562**	**76**	**562**	**2166**	**276**	**962**	**658**	**566**	**12**	**10012**	**2170**	**100**	**50**	**374**	**1572**	**662**	**72**	**968**	**122**
notes	🍷		⚡	**9212**					🍷			🍷		🍷		🅁	🍷		**102**	✕	🍷	🍷	🍷	🍷		🍷
			N	🍷⚡												🍷			**G**✕							
Roma Termini d.	...	...	1956	...	...	...	...	...	...	...	...	...	...	...	...	...	...	...	...	...	...	...	...	...	...	...
Firenze SMN d.	...	...	2157**q**	...	...	...	...	...	...	...	...	...	...	...	...	...	...	...	...	...	...	...	...	...	...	...
Bologna Centrale d.	...	...	2318	...	...	...	...	...	...	...	...	...	...	...	...	...	...	...	...	...	...	...	...	...	...	...
Venezia Santa Lucia d.	...	...	|	...	...	...	...	...	...	...	...	...	...	...	...	...	...	...	...	...	...	...	...	...	...	...
Milano Centrale d.	...	...	|	...	...	...	...	...	...	...	...	...	...	...	...	0710	...	...	...	0725	...	...	...	...	...	...
Como San Giovanni d.	...	...	|	...	...	...	...	...	...	...	...	...	...	...	...	0745	...	...	...	|	...	...	...	...	...	...
Chiasso 🏛 d.	...	...	|	...	0448	...	...	...	...	...	...	...	...	0644	...	|	...	0711	...	|	...	...	0852	...	...	...
Lugano d.	...	...	|	...	0512	...	...	...	...	...	...	...	...	0712	...	0810	0812	0737	...	|	...	...	0912	...	...	...
Bellinzona d.	...	...	|	...	0536	...	...	...	...	...	0606	...	...	0736	...	▬	0836	0806	...	|	...	...	0936	...	...	...
Arth-Goldau d.	...	...	|	...	0709	0714	...	...	...	...	0814	...	...	0914	...	...	1013	1014	...	|	...	...	1114	...	...	...
Luzern d.	...	...	|	...	▬	0755	...	...	...	...	0855	...	...	0955	...	...	|	1055	...	|	...	...	1155	...	...	...
St Moritz d.	...	...	|	...	...	|	...	...	...	...	|	...	...	|	*0540***k**	...	|	|	*0704*	|	...	*0804*	|	...	...	...
Chur d.	...	0513	|	...	...	|	...	0613	...	0709	|	...	...	|	0809	*ICE*	|	|	0916	|	...	1016	|	...	...	...
Davos Platz d.	...	|	|	...	...	|	...	|	...	*0550*	|	...	...	|	*0702*	**74**	|	|	*0802*	|	...	*0902*	|	...	...	...
Landquart d.	...	0523	|	...	*ICE*	|	...	0623	...	0719	|	...	...	|	0819	🍷	|	|	0926	|	...	1026	|	...	...	...
Zürich HB d.	0602	0647	|	0702	**278**	|	...	0747	0802	0834	|	...	...	|	0934	1002	1051	|	1102	|	...	1147	|	1202	...	...
Domodossola 🏛 § d.	|	▬	◐	|	🍷	|	...	▬	|	|	|	...	...	|	|	|	▬	|	|	0848	...	▬	|	|	...	...
Brig d.	|	...	0439**a**	|	*0547***f**	|	*0649***f**	...	|	|	|	*0749***f**	*0849***f**	|	|	|	...	|	|	0920	*0949***f**	*EC*	|	|	*1049***f**	...
Interlaken Ost d.	|	...	|	|	0601	|	0701	...	|	|	|	0801	0901	|	|	|	...	|	|	|	1001	**100/2**	|	|	1101	...
Spiez d.	|	...	0544**s**	|	0623	|	0723	...	|	|	|	0823	0923	|	|	|	...	|	|	0954	1023	**G**✕	|	|	1123	...
Bern d.	|	...	0620	|	0704	|	0804	...	|	|	|	0904	1004	|	|	|	...	|	|	1034	1104	←	|	|	1204	...
Basel SBB ★ a.	0657	...	...	0757	0755	0853	0855	...	0857	0927	0953	0955	1055	1053	1027	1057	...	1153	1157	1132	1155	1157	1253	1257	1255	...
	|	*ICE*			|	▬	▬		|	▬		|	▬	▬	▬	|	*ICE*	▬	|		|	|		|	*ICE*	
	|	**602**			|				|	*ICE*		|				|	**508**		|		|	|		|	**506**	
	|	🍷			|				|	**600**		|				|	🍷		|		|	|		|	🍷	
Basel SBB d.	0704	0712	...	...	0812	...	...	...	0904	*0912*	...	1012	...	...	...	1104	1112	...	1218	...	1212	1218	...	1304	*1312*	...
Basel Bad Bf 🏛 d.	0713	0721	...	...	0822	*ICE*	*ICE*	*IC*	0913	*0922*	...	1022	*ICE*	...	*IC*	1113	1122	IC	→	...	1222	1227	...	1313	*1322*	...
Freiburg (Brsg) Hbf d.	0749	0756	...	...	0857	**612**	**126**	**2114**	0949	*0957*	...	1057	**610**	*ICE*	**2112**	1149	1157	**2012**	...	...	1257	1304	...	1349	*1357*	...
Karlsruhe Hbf d.	0851	0901	...	...	1000	🍷	🍷	🍷	1051	1107	...	1200	🍷	**124**	🍷	1251	1300	🍷	...	...	1400	1412	...	1451	1507	...
Mannheim Hbf a.	0914	0924	...	...	1022	1035	**T**	1039	1114	1133	...	1222	1235	🍷	1239	1314	1323	1408	...	...	1422	1437	...	1514	1532	...
Frankfurt (Main) Hbf a.	0953	|	...	...	1108	|	1128	|	1153	|	...	1308	|	1328	|	1353	|	|	...	...	1508	|	...	1553	|	1629
Frankfurt Flughafen ✈ a.	|	1006	...	...	|	1106	1140	|	|	1206	...	|	1306	1340	|	|	1406	|	...	...	|	|	...	|	1606	1641
Mainz Hbf a.	|	|	...	...	|	|	|	1118	|	|	...	|	|	|	1318	|	|	1446	...	...	|	1518	...	|	|	|
Koblenz Hbf a.	|	⊖	...	...	|	⊖	⊖	1210	|	⊖	...	|	⊖	⊖	1410	|	⊖	1541	...	...	|	1610	...	|	⊖	⊖
Bonn Hbf a.	|	|	...	...	|	|	|	1242	|	|	...	|	|	|	1442	|	|	1620	...	...	|	1642	...	|	|	|
Köln Hbf a.	|	1105	...	...	|	1205	1240	1305	|	1305	...	|	1405	1440	1505	|	1505	1642	...	...	|	1705	...	|	1705	1740
Düsseldorf Hbf a.	|	...	...	...	|	1232	1311	1332	|	|	...	|	1432	1511	1532	|	|	1712	...	...	|	1732	...	|	|	1811
Duisburg Hbf a.	|	...	...	...	|	1245	1326	1345	|	**h**	...	|	1445	1526	1545	|	**h**	1725	...	...	|	1745	...	|	**h**	1824
Arnhem ⊙ a.	|	...	...	...	|	|	1423	|	|	|	...	|	|	1623	|	|	|	|	...	...	|	|	...	|	|	1923
Utrecht Centraal a.	|	...	...	...	|	|	1458	|	|	|	...	|	|	1658	|	|	|	|	...	...	|	|	...	|	|	1958
Amsterdam Centraal a.	|	...	...	...	|	|	1525	|	|	|	...	|	|	1725	|	|	|	|	...	...	|	|	...	|	|	2025
Essen Hbf a.	|	...	...	...	|	1257	...	1358	|	|	...	|	1457	...	1558	|	|	1740	...	...	|	1758	...	|	|	...
Dortmund Hbf a.	|	...	...	...	|	1321	...	1421	|	1420	...	|	1521	...	1621	|	1620	1805	...	...	|	1821	...	|	1820	...
Hannover Hbf a.	1217	...	...	...	|	...	...	|	1417	...	...	|	...	...	|	1617	...	2018	...	...	|	|	...	1817	...	...
Berlin Hauptbahnhof a.	|	...	...	...	1525	...	...	|	|	...	...	1725	...	...	|	|	...	...	...	...	1925	|	...	|	...	...
Bremen Hbf a.	|	...	...	...	...	...	...	1614	|	...	...	...	...	...	1814	|	...	...	...	...	...	2014	...	|	...	...
Hamburg Hbf a.	1334**z**	...	...	...	...	...	...	1712	1534**z**	...	...	...	...	...	1912	1734**z**	...	...	...	...	...	2112	...	1934**z**	...	...
København H. a.	...	...	...	...	...	...	...	...	...	...	...	...	...	...	...	...	...	...	...	...	...	...	...	...	...	...

train type	*CIS*	*IR*	*EC*	*ICE*	*ICE*	*EC*	*IC*	*IC*	*ESc*	*AV*	*IC*	*CIS*	*IR*	*IC*	*ICE*	*ICE*	*ES*	*ES*	*EC*	*ICE*	*ICE*	*ESc*	*ES*	*IR*	*CIS*	*ICE*
train number	**14**	**2174**	**6**	**370**	**516**	**6**	**574**	**974**	**9708**	**9426**	**576**	**52**	**2178**	**978**	**514**	**120**	**9712**	**9428**	**122**	**376**	**502**	**9792**	**9430**	**2182**	**18**	**272**
notes	✕	¶	✕	🍷	🍷	✕	🍷	🍷	🅁✕	🅁✕	🍷	✕	¶	🍷	🍷	Ⓑ	🅁✕	🅁✕	🍷	🍷	**1002**	🅁✕	🅁✕	¶	🅁	**372**
			G			**G**			**W**	⚡						🍷	⚡	⚡	⊡			**X**	⚡		🍷	
Roma Termini d.	...	...	...	...	...	...	...	...	...	0630	...	...	...	...	...	...	...	0730	...	...	...	...	0830	...	...	...
Firenze SMN d.	...	...	...	...	...	...	...	...	...	0819	...	...	...	...	...	...	...	0919	...	...	...	...	1019	...	...	...
Bologna Centrale d.	...	...	...	...	...	...	...	...	...	0924	...	...	...	...	...	...	...	1024	...	...	...	...	1124	...	...	...
Venezia Santa Lucia d.	*0514*	...	...	...	...	...	...	...	0750	|	...	0832**t**	...	...	...	...	0850	|	...	...	...	0950	|	...	...	...
Milano Centrale d.	0910	...	...	...	...	...	...	...	1025	1029	...	1120	...	...	...	...	1125	1129	1225	...	...	1225	1229	...	1310	...
Como San Giovanni d.	0945	...	...	...	...	...	...	...	▬	...	...	|	...	...	...	...	▬	▬	|	...	...	▬	▬	...	1344	...
Chiasso 🏛 d.	|	...	...	...	...	...	...	...	...	...	...	|	...	...	...	...	...	...	|	...	...	...	...	...	|	...
Lugano d.	1012	...	...	...	...	...	...	...	...	...	...	|	...	...	...	...	...	...	|	...	...	...	...	...	1412	...
Bellinzona d.	1036	1006	...	...	...	...	...	...	...	...	...	|	1206	...	...	...	...	*IC*	|	...	...	*IC*	...	1406	1436	...
Arth-Goldau d.	1213	1214	...	...	...	...	...	...	...	...	...	|	1414	...	...	...	...	**578**	|	...	...	**580**	...	1614	1609	...
Luzern d.	|	1255	...	...	...	...	...	...	...	...	...	|	1455	...	...	...	...	🍷	|	...	...	🍷	...	1655	|	...
St Moritz d.	|	|	*0904*	...	...	...	*1004*	...	...	...	*1104*	|	|	...	...	...	...	*1204*	|	...	...	*1304*	...	|	|	...
Chur d.	|	|	1116	...	...	...	1209	...	...	...	1309	|	|	...	...	...	...	1409	|	...	...	1509	...	|	|	...
Davos Platz d.	|	|	*1002*	...	...	...	*1102*	...	...	...	*1202*	|	|	...	...	...	...	*1302*	|	...	...	*1402*	...	|	|	...
Landquart d.	|	|	1126	...	...	...	1219	...	...	...	1319	|	|	...	...	...	...	1419	|	...	...	1519	*IC*	|	|	...
Zürich HB d.	1251	|	1302	...	...	...	1334	...	...	...	1434	|	|	...	...	...	...	1534	|	...	...	1634	**1080**	|	1651	1702
Domodossola 🏛 § d.	▬	|	|	...	...	...	|	...	...	...	|	1248	|	...	...	...	...	|	1410	...	...	|	🍷	|	...	|
Brig d.	1120	|	|	*1149***f**	...	...	|	*1249***f**	...	...	|	1320	|	*1349***f**	...	...	...	|	1440	*1449***f**	...	|	1520	|	...	|
Interlaken Ost d.	|	|	|	1201	...	...	|	1301	...	...	|	|	|	1401	...	...	...	|	...	1501	...	|	*1529*	|	...	|
Spiez d.	1154	|	|	1223	...	...	|	1323	...	...	|	1354	|	1423	...	...	...	|	...	1523	...	|	1554	|	...	|
Bern d.	1234	|	|	1304	...	←	|	1404	...		|	1434	|	1504	...	...	...	|	...	1604	...	|	1634	|	...	|
Basel SBB ★ a.	1332	1353	1357	1355	...	1357	1427	1455		...	1527	1532	1553	1555	...	...	...	1627	...	1655	...	1727	1732	1753	...	1757
			|	|		|		*ICE*	*ICE*					*ICE*						|		▬		*CNL*		|
			|	|		|		**70**	**104**					**870**						|				**472/82**		|
			|	|		|		🍷	🍷					🍷						|				**J**		|
Basel SBB d.	...	...	1418	1412	...	1418	...	1504	1512	...	...	...	...	1612	...	...	...	...	...	1704	*1712*	...	...	1804	...	1812
Basel Bad Bf 🏛 d.	...	...	→	1422	...	1427	...	1513	1522	...	...	...	...	1621	...	...	*IC*	...	...	1713	*1721*	*ICE*	...	1817**u**	...	1822
Freiburg (Brsg) Hbf d.	...	...	...	1457	...	1504	...	1549	1557	...	...	...	...	1656	...	...	**2318**	...	...	1749	*1756*	**592**	...	1904**u**	...	1857
Karlsruhe Hbf d.	...	...	...	1600	...	1612	...	1651	1700	...	...	...	...	1801	...	...	🍷	...	...	1851	1907	✕	...	2018**u**	...	2000
Mannheim Hbf a.	...	...	...	1622	1635	1637	...	1714	1723	...	...	...	...	1823	1835	...	1839	...	...	1914	1933	1931	...	2116**u**	...	2022
Frankfurt (Main) Hbf a.	...	...	...	1708	|	|	...	1753	|	...	...	...	...	1908	|	1928	|	...	...	1953	|	2008	...	2218**b**	...	2108
Frankfurt Flughafen ✈ a.	...	...	...	|	1706	|	...	|	1806	...	...	...	...	|	1906	1940	|	...	...	|	2006	|	...	|	...	...
Mainz Hbf a.	...	...	...	|	|	1718	...	|	|	...	...	...	...	|	|	|	1918	...	...	|	|	|	...	|	...	...
Koblenz Hbf a.	...	...	...	|	⊖	1810	...	|	⊖	...	...	...	...	|	⊖	⊖	2010	...	...	|	⊖	|	...	|	...	...
Bonn Hbf a.	...	...	...	|	|	1842	...	|	|	...	...	...	...	|	|	|	2042	...	...	|	|	|	...	|	...	...
Köln Hbf a.	...	...	...	|	1805	1905	...	|	1905	...	...	...	...	|	2005	2040	2105	...	...	|	2105	|	...	|	...	...
Düsseldorf Hbf a.	...	...	...	|	|	1932	...	|	1938	...	...	...	...	|	2032	2111	...	...	...	|	|	|	...	|	...	...
Duisburg Hbf a.	...	...	...	|	**h**	1945	...	|	1950	...	...	...	...	|	2045	2124	...	...	...	|	**h**	|	...	|	...	...
Arnhem ⊙ a.	...	...	...	|	|	|	...	|	2053	...	...	...	...	|	|	2223	...	...	...	|	|	|	...	|	...	...
Utrecht Centraal a.	...	...	...	|	|	|	...	|	2128	...	...	...	...	|	|	2258	...	...	...	|	|	|	...	|	...	...
Amsterdam Centraal a.	...	...	...	|	|	|	...	|	2155	...	...	...	...	|	|	2325	...	...	...	|	|	|	...	|	...	...
Essen Hbf a.	...	...	...	|	|	1958	...	|	...	...	...	...	...	|	2057	...	...	...	...	|	|	|	...	|	...	...
Dortmund Hbf a.	...	...	...	|	1920	2021	...	|	...	...	...	...	...	|	2121	...	...	...	...	|	2220	|	...	|	...	...
Hannover Hbf a.	...	...	...	|	...	|	...	2017	...	...	...	...	...	|	|	...	...	...	...	2217**j**	...	|	...	|	...	...
Berlin Hauptbahnhof a.	...	...	...	2128	...	|	...	|	...	...	...	...	...	2325	|	...	...	...	...	|	...	0027	...	|	...	...
Bremen Hbf a.	...	...	...	...	...	2218**e**	...	|	...	...	...	...	...	...	2320	...	...	...	...	|	...	...	...	|	...	...
Hamburg Hbf a.	...	...	...	...	...	2314**e**	...	2137**z**	...	...	...	...	...	...	0020	...	...	...	...	2344**j**	...	...	...	|	...	...
København H. a.	...	...	...	...	...	...	...	...	...	...	...	...	...	...	...	...	...	...	...	...	...	...	...	0959	...	...

CONTINUED ON NEXT PAGE

ROMA, MILANO and ZÜRICH - KÖLN, DORTMUND, BERLIN and AMSTERDAM 73

train type	IC	ESc	ICN	AV	CIS	ICN	IR	ICE	IC	IC	AV	ESc	CIS	IR	IC	CNL	ESc	AV	IC	CIS	ES	AV	CNL	CNL	CNL
train number	582	9718	674	9434	20	10020	1586	270	588	990	9438	9728	22	2192	590	478	9732	9440	794	56	9402	9446	1300	40400	400
notes	🍷	Ⓡ✕	🍷	Ⓡ✕	Ⓡ	🍷	🍷	🍷	🍷		Ⓡ✕	Ⓡ🍷	Ⓡ	¶		✕	Ⓡ✕	Ⓡ✕	🍷	✕	Ⓡ✕	Ⓡ✕	P	Q	R
		↯		↯	🍷						↯	↯	🍷			K	↯	↯			↯	↯	⑦	①②③	④⑤⑥
Roma Termini d.	...	...	...	1030	...	...	...	...	...	...	1230	...	...	...	...	...	...	1330	...	...	...	1630	...	...	...
Firenze SMN d.	...	...	...	1219	...	...	...	...	...	...	1419	...	...	...	...	...	...	1519	...	...	...	1819	...	...	...
Bologna Centrale d.	...	...	...	1324	...	...	...	...	...	...	1524	...	...	...	...	...	...	1624	...	...	...	1924	...	...	...
Venezia Santa Lucia d.	...	1150	...	|	...	...	...	...	...	...	|	1420	...	...	...	...	1520	|	...	...	1805	|	...	...	...
Milano Centrale d.	...	1425	...	1429	1510	...	...	...	...	...	1629	1655	1710	...	...	...	1755	1729	...	1825	2025	2029	2100	2110	2110
Como San Giovanni d.	...	▬	...	...	1544	...	...	...	...	...	▬	▬	1744	...	...	...	▬	...	...	|	▬	▬	|	2156	2156
Chiasso 🛂 d.	...	...	...	...	|	...	...	...	...	...	...	...	|	...	...	...	...	...	...	|	...	...	|	2221	2221
Lugano d.	...	...	1512	...	1610	1612	...	...	...	...	...	...	1812	1746	...	...	...	...	...	|	...	...	|	2244	2244
Bellinzona d.	...	...	1536	...	▬	1636	...	...	...	...	...	...	1836	1806	...	...	...	...	...	|	...	...	|	2312	2312
Arth-Goldau d.	...	...	1714	...	...	1813	...	...	...	...	...	...	2009	2014	...	...	...	...	...	|	...	...	|	0059	0059
Luzern d.	...	...	1755	...	...	|	...	...	...	...	...	...	▬	2055	...	...	...	...	...	|	...	...	|	|	|
St Moritz d.	*1404*	...	|	...	...	|	*1504*	...	*1604*	...	*CNL*	...	...	|	*1704*	...	*CNL*	...	*1804*	|	...	...	|	|	|
Chur d.	1609	...	|	...	...	|	1716	...	1809	...	**1259**	...	...	|	1909	...	**40478**	...	2013	|	...	...	|	|	|
Davos Platz d.	*1502*	...	|	...	...	|	*1602*	...	*1702*	...	✕	...	...	|	*1802*	...	✕	...	*1902*	|	...	...	|	|	|
Landquart d.	1619	*IC*	|	...	*IC*	|	1726		1819	...	**C**	...	...	|	1919	...	**A**	...	2023	|	...	...	|	|	|
Zürich HB d.	1734	**986**	|	...	**988**	1851	1847	1902	1934	...	1944	...	*IC*	|	2023	2042	2042	...	2202	|	...	...	|	|	|
Domodossola 🛂 § d.	|	🍷	|	...	🍷	...	...	|	|	...	|	...	**992**	|	...	|	|	...	|	1948	*ICE*	...	|	|	|
Brig d.	|	*1649*f	|	...	*1749*f	...	...	|	|	*1849*f	|	...	*1949*f	|	...	|	|	...	|	2020	**994**	...	2353	|	|
Interlaken Ost d.	|	1701	|	...	1801	...	...	|	|	1901	|	...	2001	|	...	|	|	...	|	|	2101	...	|	|	|
Spiez d.	|	1723	|	...	1823	...	...	|	|	1923	|	...	2023	|	...	|	|	...	|	2054	2123	...	|	|	|
Bern d.	|	1804	|	...	1904	...	...	|	|	2004	|	...	2104	|	...	|	|	...	|	2134	2204	...	|	|	|
Basel SBB ★ a.	1827	1855	1853	...	1955	...	...	1957	2027	2054	|	...	2155	2153	...	|	|	...	2257	2232	2255	...	|	|	|
			ICE **500** 🍷					|			|	*IC* **60459**	▬			|	|					*ICE* **608** 🍷	|	|	|
Basel SBB d.	...	...	1912	...	...	...	...	2012	...	...	2107u	2107	*ICE*	...	...	2207u	2207u	...	...	...	...	2326	|	|	|
Basel Bad Bf 🛂 d.	...	...	1921	...	...	...	...	2022	...	...	2121u	2121	**990**	...	...	2219u	2219u	...	...	...	...	2334	◐	◐	◐
Freiburg (Brsg) Hbf d.	...	...	1956	...	...	...	...	2057	...	...	2158u	2158	🍷	...	...	2257u	2257u	...	...	...	...	0014	|	|	|
Karlsruhe Hbf d.	...	...	2101	...	...	...	...	2200	...	...	2305u	2305	**d**	...	...	0011u	0011u	...	...	...	...	0129	0426s	0426s	0426s
Mannheim Hbf a.	...	...	2124	...	...	...	...	2222	...	...	0005u	2346	2351	...	...	|	|	...	...	...	...	0222	0454s	0454s	0454s
Frankfurt (Main) Hbf a.	...	...	|	...	...	...	...	2315	...	...	0055b	...	0042	...	...	|	|	...	...	...	...	0308	0600s	0545s	0545s
Frankfurt Flughafen ✈ a.	...	...	2206	...	...	...	...	...	...	...	|	...	0023	...	...	|	|	...	...	...	...	0330	|	|	|
Mainz Hbf a.	...	...	|								|	...	...	...	...	|	|	...	...	...	...	0406	0646s	0646s	0646s
Koblenz Hbf a.	...	...	⊖								|	...	...	...	...	|	0445s	...	...	...	...	0501	0744s	0744s	0744s
Bonn Hbf a.	...	...	|								|	...	...	...	...	|	0521s	...	...	...	...	0534	0817s	0817s	0817s
Köln Hbf a.	...	...	2312								|	...	...	...	...	|	0545s	...	...	...	...	0605	0842s	0842s	0842s
Düsseldorf Hbf a.	...	...	2338								|	...	...	...	...	|	0613s	...	...	...	...	0631	0909s	0909s	0909s
Duisburg Hbf a.	...	...	2355								|	...	...	...	...	|	0628s	...	...	...	...	0644	0931	0931	|
Arnhem ⊙ a.	...	...	|								|	...	...	...	...	|	0753s	...	...	...	...	|	|	|	1122
Utrecht Centraal a.	...	...	|								|	...	...	...	...	|	0828s	...	...	...	...	|	|	|	1156
Amsterdam Centraal a.	...	...	|								|	...	...	...	...	|	0859	...	...	...	...	|	|	|	1229
Essen Hbf a.	...	...	0007								|	...	...	...	...	|	...	...	...	...	...	0658	0944	0944	...
Dortmund Hbf a.	...	...	0030								|	...	...	...	...	|	...	...	...	...	...	0721	1006	1006	...
Hannover Hbf a.	...	...	...								|	...	...	...	...	0702s	...	...	...	...	...	|	...	...	...
Berlin Hauptbahnhof a.	...	...	...								0718	...	...	...	...	|	...	...	...	...	...	|	...	...	...
Bremen Hbf a.	...	...	...								...	...	...	...	...	|	...	...	...	...	...	0914	...	...	...
Hamburg Hbf a.	...	...	...	...	...	...	...	...	...	...	...	...	...	...	...	0906	...	...	...	...	...	1012	...	...	...
København H. a.	...	...	...	...	...	...	...	...	...	...	...	...	...	...	...	...	...	...	...	...	...	...	...	...	...

OTHER TRAIN NAMES:

EC **106** – CISALPINO TIZIANO
EC **108** – CISALPINO VERDI
EC **110** – CISALPINO TICINO
EC **114** – CISALPINO SAN MARCO
EC **120** – CISALPINO VALLESE
EC **122** – CISALPINO MONTE ROSA
EC **170** – CISALPINO MONTE CENERI
EC **172** – CISALPINO INSUBRIA
EC **174** – CISALPINO CANALETTO
EC **176** – CISALPINO CINQUE TERRE

A – *City Night Line* PEGASUS – ④⑤⑥⑦ (daily until Nov. 1): 1, 2 cl., 1, 2 cl. (T4), 2 cl. (4, 6 berth), (2) (reclining) and ✕ Zürich - Basel - Mannheim - Amsterdam. Ⓡ Special fares apply.
C – *City Night Line* SIRIUS – 1, 2 cl., 1, 2 cl. (T4), 2 cl. (4, 6 berth), (2) (reclining) and ✕ Zürich - Basel - Berlin (- Ostseebad Binz, arrive 1117, ⑥ July 4 - Aug. 22). Ⓡ Special fares apply. Conveys *City Night Line* **459** CANOPUS Zürich - Dresden - Praha, see Table **75**.
G – (12) and ✕ Chur - Basel - Köln - Dortmund (- Hamburg ⑧).
J – *City Night Line* AURORA – 1, 2 cl., 2 cl. (4, 6 berth), (2) (reclining) and ✕ Basel (**472**) - Fulda (**482**) - København. Ⓡ Special fares apply.
K – *City Night Line* KOMET – ④⑤⑥⑦ (daily until Nov. 1): 1, 2 cl., 1, 2 cl. (T4), 2 cl. (4, 6 berth), (2) (reclining) and ✕ Zürich - Basel - Mannheim - Hannover - Hamburg. Ⓡ Special fares apply.
N – ROMA – 1, 2 cl. and 2 cl. (6 berth) Roma - Bern - Zürich.
P – *City Night Line* APUS – 1, 2 cl., 2 cl. (6 berth), (2) (reclining) and ✕: ⑦ Milano - Brig - Frankfurt - Dortmund. Ⓡ Special fares apply.
Q – *City Night Line* APUS – 1, 2 cl., 2 cl. (6 berth), (2) (reclining) and ✕: ①②③ Milano - Chiasso - Frankfurt - Dortmund. Ⓡ Special fares apply.
R – *City Night Line* APUS – 1, 2 cl., 2 cl. (6 berth), (2) (reclining) and ✕: ④⑤⑥ Milano - Chiasso - Frankfurt - Amsterdam. Ⓡ Special fares apply.

T – Apr. 3 - Oct. 25.
W – ①–⑤ (not Nov. 8).
X – ⑥⑦ (also Nov. 8).

a – Arrival time.
b – Frankfurt (Main) **Süd**.
d – Train calls Mannheim - Frankfurt Flughafen ✈ - Frankfurt (Main) Hbf.
e – ⑧ only.
f – Change trains at Bern.
h – Via Wuppertal, Hagen.
j – ⑤⑦ only.
k – Depart 0542 on ⑦ (also Aug. 1).
q – Firenze **Campo di Marte**.
s – Stops to set down only.
t – Venezia **Mestre**.
u – Stops to pick up only.
y – Connects with train in previous column.

z – June 14 - July 19 arrive 16 minutes later.

★ – Connections at Basel are not guaranteed.
CIS – **ETR 470** *Cisalpino*. Supplement payable for international journeys. *IC* supplement payable for internal journeys within Italy.
⊖ – Via Köln - Frankfurt high speed line.
⊡ – Supplement payable in Italy.
§ – Ticket point is **Iselle**.
◐ – Ticket point / frontier.
↯ – Supplement payable.
⊙ – 🛂 is at Emmerich.
¶ – From Locarno.

For Table 74 see page 85

BERLIN - MÜNCHEN - ZÜRICH - BERN - GENÈVE 75

train type	CNL	CNL	CNL	EC	ICE	EC	ICE	EC	IR	ICE	EC
train number	1258	458	1201	196	1605	194	1709	192	2542	1711	190
notes	✕ A	✕ B	✕ D	✕ Z	①–⑥ ❖	✕ Z	**1609** ❖	✕ Z		🍷 ❖	✕ Z
Berlin Hbf d.	2222	...	2212	...	...	...	0952	...	...	1152	...
Dresden Hbf d.	|	2115	|	...	0554	...	|	...	...	|	...
Leipzig Hbf d.	|	2253	|	...	0711	...	1111	...	...	1311	...
Nürnberg Hbf d.	|	|	|	...	1023	...	1423	...	...	1629	...
München Hbf d.	|	|	0639	0712	1137	1234	1539	1634	...	1811	1834
Lindau 🛂 d.	|	|	▬	0955	▬	1456	...	1855	...	...	2056
Bregenz 🛂 d.	|	|	...	1006	...	1507	...	1906	...	...	2107
St Margrethen 🛂 a.	|	|	*ICN*	1018	...	1519	...	1918	...	...	2119
St Gallen a.	|	|	**1612**	1041	...	1541	...	1941	...	...	2141
Winterthur a.	|	|	🍷	1117	...	1617	...	2017	...	...	2217
Basel SBB (🛂 = Bad) a.	0755	0755	0803	|	...	|	...	|	...	...	|
Zürich Flughafen ✈ a.	|	|	|	1132	...	1632	...	2032	...	...	2232
Zürich HB a.	0917	0917	|	1144	...	1644	...	2044	...	...	2244
		IC **716** ✕	|	*IC* **822** 🍷	*IC* **722** ✕	*IC* **832** 🍷	*IC* **732** 🍷	*IC* **842**			*IC* **846**
Zürich HB d.	...	0932	|	1200	1232	1700	1732	2100	...	...	2300
Bern a.	...	1029	|	1257	1329	1757	1829	2157	2204	...	0002
Lausanne a.	...	1140	1015	...	1440	...	1940	...	2315	...	...
Genève a.	...	1215	...	...	1515	...	2015	...	0004	...	...
Genève Aéroport ✈ a.	...	1224	...	...	1524	...	2024	...	...	...	...

train type	IC	IR	IC	IR	IC	IC	IC	IC	ICN	CNL	CNL
train number	809	2515	815	2523	823	731	835	737	1641	1259	459
notes	🍷		✕		✕	🍷	🍷	✕	🍷	✕ A	✕ B
Genève Aéroport ✈ d.	...	...	...	1001	...	1436	...	1636	...	...	...
Genève d.	...	0610	...	1010	...	1445	...	1645	...	...	...
Lausanne d.	...	0645	...	1045	...	1520	...	1720	1845	...	...
Bern d.	0602	0756	0802	1156	1202	1632	1702	1832	|	...	...
Zürich HB a.	0702	▬	0858	▬	1258	1728	1758	1928	|	...	...
	EC **191** ✕Z		*EC* **193** ✕Z		*EC* **195** ✕Z	▬	*EC* **197** ✕Z	▬	|		
Zürich HB d.	0716	...	0916	...	1316	...	1816	...	|	1944	1944
Zürich Flughafen ✈ d.	0728	...	0928	...	1328	...	1828	...	|	|	|
Basel SBB (🛂 = Bad) d.	|	...	|	...	|	...	|	...	2053	2107	2107
Winterthur d.	0742	*ICE*	0942	*ICE*	1342	...	1842	...	...	|	|
St Gallen d.	0819	**1506**	1019	**1604**	1419	*ICE*	1919	*CNL*	...	|	|
St Margrethen 🛂 d.	0842	**1716**	1042	**1704**	1442	**1500**	1942	**1200**	...	|	|
Bregenz 🛂 d.	0855	🍷	1055	🍷	1455	🍷	1955	✕	...	|	|
Lindau 🛂 a.	0905	❖	1105	❖	1505	❖	2005	**D**	...	|	|
München Hbf a.	1128	1320	1328	1341	1728	1920	2245	2301	...	|	|
Nürnberg Hbf a.	...	1431	...	1523	...	2031	...	|	...	|	|
Leipzig Hbf a.	...	1741	...	1846	...	2349	...	|	...	|	0641
Dresden Hbf a.	...	|	...	|	...	...	...	|	...	|	0807
Berlin Hbf a.	...	1900	...	2005	...	...	...	0741	...	0718	...

A – *City Night Line* SIRIUS – 1, 2 cl., 1, 2 cl. (T4), 2 cl. (4, 6 berth), (2) (reclining) and ✕ Berlin - Frankfurt - Basel - Zürich and v.v. Ⓡ Special fares apply.
B – *City Night Line* CANOPUS – 1, 2 cl., 2 cl., (2) (reclining) and ✕ Praha - Dresden - Zürich and v.v. Ⓡ Special fares apply.
D – *City Night Line* CAPELLA – 1, 2 cl., 2 cl., (2) (reclining) and ✕ Berlin - München and v.v. Ⓡ Special fares apply. Talgo stock.
Z – (12) and ✕ München - Zürich and v.v.

❖ – Due to engineering work between Leipzig and Nürnberg Aug. 1 – Sept. 14, services are subject to alteration. See Table **851**.

82 GENÈVE, BASEL, ZÜRICH and LUZERN - MILANO - VENEZIA and ROMA

train type	*CIS*	*AV*	*ESc*	*IR*	*CIS*	*IR*	*CIS*	*ESc*	*EC⚡*	*ESc*	*AV*	*IC*	*CIS*	*ESc*	*AV*		*IR*	*IC*	*IR*	*IR*	*CIS*	*ESc*	*AV*	*ESc*	
train number	**35**	**9433**	**9791**	**1415**	**51**	**2159**	**13**	**9765**	**143 144**	**9715**	**9435**	**810**	**37**	**9777**	**9437**		**1419**	**1063**	**2715**	**2165**	**15**	**9767**	**9439**	**9723**	
notes	[R] 🍷 §	✕⚡ [R]	[R] 🍷 A		[R] 🍷 § ✤		[R] 🍷 ⊕	[R] ✕ ⚡	[R] 🍷	[R] ✕ ⚡	✕⚡ [R]	🍷	[R] 🍷 §	[R] ✕ ⚡	[R] ✕ ⚡			[R] 🍷			[R] 🍷 ⊕	[R] ✕ ⚡	[R] ✕ ⚡	[R] 🍷 ⚡	
Genève Aéroport ✈ d.	...	...	...	0547	...	...	...	...	...	...	...	...	0733	...	...	...	0747	...	...	...	...	...	...	...	...
Genève d.	0545	...	...	0556	...	...	...	...	...	...	...	...	0742	...	...	...	0756	...	...	...	...	...	...	...	...
Lausanne d.	0620	...	...	0645	...	...	...	...	...	...	...	...	0820	...	...	...	0845	...	...	...	...	...	...	...	...
Sion d.	0714	...	...	0754	...	...	...	...	...	...	...	...	0914	...	...	...	0954	...	...	...	...	...	...	...	...
Zürich HB d.	│	...	...	│	...	...	0701	...	...	...	...	...	│	...	...	...	│	...	...	...	0901	...	...	...	...
Basel SBB d.	│	...	...	│	0628	...	│	...	...	...	...	...	│	...	...	...	│	0828	...	0803	│	...	...	...	...
Olten d.	│	...	...	│	0700	...	│	...	...	...	...	...	│	...	...	...	│	0900	...	0830	│	...	...	...	...
Bern d.	│	...	...	│	0735	...	│	...	...	...	...	0807	│	...	...	...	│	0935	...	│	│	...	...	...	...
Spiez d.	│	...	...	│	0805	...	│	...	...	...	...	0836	│	...	...	...	│	1005	...	│	│	...	...	...	...
Luzern d.	│	...	...	│	│	0718	│	...	...	...	...	│	│	...	...	...	│	│	...	0918	│	...	...	...	...
Arth-Goldau d.	│	...	...	│	│	0745	0750	...	...	...	...	│	│	...	...	...	│	│	...	0945	0950	...	...	...	...
Bellinzona d.	│	...	...	│	│	...	0923	...	...	...	...	│	│	...	...	...	│	│	...	...	1123	...	...	...	...
Lugano d.	│	...	...	│	│	...	0948	...	...	...	...	│	│	...	...	...	│	│	...	...	1148	...	...	...	...
Chiasso 🏛 d.	│	...	...	│	│	...	│	...	...	...	...	│	│	...	...	...	│	│	...	...	│	...	...	...	...
Como San Giovanni a.	│	...	...	│	│	...	1014	...	...	...	...	│	│	...	...	...	│	│	...	...	1214	...	...	...	...
Visp d.	│	...	...	0824	0832	...	│	...	...	...	...	0903	│	...	...	...	1024	1032	...	...	│	...	...	...	...
Brig d.	0744	...	...	0830	0844	...	│	...	...	...	...	0911	0944	...	...	...	1030	1040	1044	...	│	...	...	...	...
Domodossola 🏛 ¶ a.	0812	...	...	...	0912	...	│	...	...	...	...	...	1012	...	...	...		...	1114	...	│	...	...	...	...
Stresa a.	0838	...	...	...	│	...	│	...	...	...	...	...	│	...	...	...	...	...	...	...	│	...	...	...	...
Arona a.	│	...	...	...	│	...	│	...	...	...	...	...	│	...	...	...	...	...	...	...	│	...	...	...	...
Milano Centrale a.	0935	...	...	...	1035	...	1050	...	...	...	...	...	1135	...	...	...	...	...	...	...	1250	...	...	...	...
Milano Centrale d.	...	1030	1035	...	...	...	1115	1105	1110	1135	1130	...	1205	1200	1230	...	...	...	...	...	...	1305	1330	1335	...
Genova PP ▲ a.	...	│	│	...	...	...	│	│	1242	│	│	...	│	│	│	...	...	...	...	...	...	│	│	│	...
Ventimiglia 🏛 a.	...	│	│	...	...	...	│	│	1507	│	│	...	│	│	│	...	...	...	...	...	...	│	│	│	...
Nice Ville a.	...	│	│	...	...	...	│	│	1559	│	│	...	│	│	│	...	...	...	...	...	...	│	│	│	...
Verona Porta Nuova a.	...	│	1157	...	...	...	│	│	...	1257	│	...	1327	│	│	...	...	...	...	...	...	│	│	1457	...
Venezia Santa Lucia a.	...	│	1310	...	...	...	│	│	...	1410	│	...	1440	│	│	...	...	...	...	...	...	│	│	1610	...
Bologna Centrale a.	...	1135	...	...	...	...	1258	1252	...	...	1235	...	...	1411	1335	...	...	...	...	...	...	1452	1435	...	...
Rimini a.	...	│	...	...	...	...	│	1351	...	...	│	...	...	1534	│	...	...	...	...	...	...	1551	│	...	...
Ancona a.	...	│	...	...	...	...	│	1441	...	...	│	...	...	1700	│	...	...	...	...	...	...	1641	│	...	...
Pescara Centrale a.	...	│	...	...	...	...	│	1605	...	...	│	...	...	...	│	...	...	...	...	...	...	1805	│	...	...
Bari Centrale a.	...	│	...	...	...	...	│	1853	...	...	│	...	...	...	│	...	...	...	...	...	...	2055	│	...	...
Brindisi a.	...	│	...	...	...	...	│	1957	...	...	│	...	...	...	│	...	...	...	...	...	...	...	│	...	...
Lecce a.	...	│	...	...	...	...	│	2023	...	...	│	...	...	...	│	...	...	...	...	...	...	...	│	...	...
Firenze SMN a.	...	1239	...	...	...	...	1415	...	...	...	1339	...	...	...	1439	...	...	...	...	...	...	...	1539	...	...
Roma Termini a.	...	1429	...	...	...	...	...	...	...	...	1529	...	...	...	1629	...	...	...	...	...	...	...	1729	...	...
Napoli Centrale a.	...	1605	...	...	...	...	...	...	...	...	...	...	...	...	1805	...	...	...	...	...	...	...	1905	...	...

train type	*IR*	*ICN*	*CIS*	*ES*	*ESc*	*EC⚡*	*IC*	*CIS*	*ESc*	*AV*	*ESc*	*IR*	*CIS*	*ICp*	*IR*	*CIS*	*CIS*	*AV*	*ES*	*IR*	*ICN*	*CIS*	*ICp*	*ESc*	*AV*
train number	**2169**	**10017**	**17**	**9769**	**9729**	**159 160**	**1069**	**125**	**9781**	**9445**	**9733**	**1427**	**57**	**659**	**2173**	**19**	**57**	**9447**	**9403**	**2177**	**10021**	**21**	**663**	**9745 9793**	**9451**
notes		[R] 🍷	[R] 🍷 ⊕	[R] ✕ ⚡	[R] ✕ ⚡	[R] 🍷	🍷	🍷 §	[R] ✕ ⚡	[R] ✕ ⚡	[R] 🍷 ⚡		[R] 🍷 C ⊕	[R] 🍷 ⚡		[R] 🍷 ⊕	[R] 🍷 C ⊕	[R] ✕ ⚡	[R] 🍷 ⚡		[R] 🍷	[R] 🍷 ⊕	[R] 🍷 ⚡	[R] 🍷	[R] ✕ ⚡
Genève Aéroport ✈ d.	...	...	...	...	...	...	...	...	...	...	...	1147	...	...	...	...	...	...	...	...	...	...	...	...	...
Genève d.	...	...	...	...	...	...	...	1107	...	...	...	1156	...	...	...	...	...	...	...	...	...	...	...	...	...
Lausanne d.	...	...	...	...	...	...	...	1146	...	...	...	1245	...	...	...	...	...	...	...	...	...	...	...	...	...
Sion d.	...	...	...	...	...	...	...	1243	...	...	...	1354	...	...	...	...	...	...	...	...	...	...	...	...	...
Zürich HB d.	...	1109	...	...	...	...	...	│	...	...	...	│	...	...	...	1309	...	...	...	...	1509	...	...	...	...
Basel SBB d.	1003	│	...	...	...	...	1028	│	...	...	...	│	1228	...	1203	│	...	...	...	1403	│	...	...	...	...
Oltern d.	1031	│	...	...	...	...	1100	│	...	...	...	│	1300	...	1231	│	...	...	...	1431	│	...	...	...	...
Bern d.	│	│	...	..	...	...	1135	│	...	...	...	│	1335	...	│	│	...	...	...	│	│	...	...	...	...
Spiez d.	│	│	...	...	...	...	1205	│	...	...	...	│	1405	...	│	│	...	...	...	│	│	...	...	...	...
Luzern d.	1118	│	...	...	...	...	│	│	...	...	...	│	│	...	1318	│	...	...	...	1518	│	...	...	...	...
Arth-Goldau d.	1145	1150	...	...	...	...	│	│	...	...	...	│	│	...	1345	1350	...	...	...	1545	1550	...	...	...	...
Bellinzona d.	...	1325	...	...	...	...	│	│	...	...	...	│	│	...	━	1525	...	...	...	━	1725	...	...	...	...
Lugano d.	...	1346	1348	...	...	...	│	│	...	...	...	│	│	...	...	1548	...	...	...	...	1746	1748	...	...	...
Chiasso 🏛 d.	...	...	│	...	...	...	│	│	...	...	...	│	│	...	...	│	...	...	...	...	...	│	...	...	...
Como San Giovanni a.	...	...	1414	...	...	...	│	│	...	...	...	│	│	...	...	1614	...	...	...	...	...	1814	...	...	...
Visp d.	...	...	│	...	...	...	1232	│	...	...	...	1424	1432	...	...	│	...	...	...	...	...	│	...	...	...
Brig d.	...	...	│	...	...	...	1240	1320	...	...	...	1430	1444	...	...	│	...	...	...	...	...	│	...	...	...
Domodossola 🏛 ¶ a.	...	...	│	...	...	...	━	1350	...	...	...	...	1512	...	...	│	...	...	...	...	...	│	...	...	...
Stresa a.	...	...	│	...	...	...	...	1430	...	...	...	...	│	...	...	│	...	...	...	...	...	│	...	...	...
Arona a.	...	...	│	...	...	...	...	1444	...	...	...	...	│	...	...	│	←	...	...	...	...	│	...	...	...
Milano Centrale a.	...	...	1450	...	...	...	...	1535	...	...	...	...	1640	...	...	1650	1640	...	...	...	...	1850	...	...	...
train type							*AV*								*ESc*						*ICp*				
train number							**9443**								**9783**						**661**				
notes							[R] ✕ ⚡								[R] ✕ ⚡						[R] 🍷 ⚡				
Milano Centrale d.	...	...	...	1505	1505	1510	1530	...	1600	1630	1605	...	1705	1700	1700	...	1705	1730	1735	1805	...	...	1905	1905	1930
Genova PP ▲ a.	...	...	...	│	│	1642	│	...	│	│	│	...	→	1842	│	...	│	│	│	1945	...	...	2042	│	│
Ventimiglia 🏛 a.	...	...	...	│	│	1907	│	...	│	│	│	...	...	2107	│	...	│	│	│	*2316*	...	...	*2316*	│	│
Nice Ville a.	...	...	...	│	│	2012	│	...	│	│	│	...	...	*0021*	│	...	│	│	│	...	...	...	...	│	│
Verona Porta Nuova a.	...	...	...	│	1627	...	│	...	│	│	1727	...	...	...	│	...	1827	│	│	...	...	...	...	2027	│
Venezia Santa Lucia a.	...	...	...	│	1740	...	│	...	│	│	1840	...	...	...	│	...	1928**q**	│	1955	...	...	...	...	2150	│
Bologna Centrale a.	...	...	...	1652	...	...	1635	...	1811	1735	...	...	...	...	1911	...	...	1835	...	...	...	...	...	...	2035
Rimini a.	...	...	...	1751	...	...	│	...	1934	│	...	...	...	...	2034	...	...	│	...	...	...	...	...	...	│
Ancona a.	...	...	...	1842	...	...	│	...	2047	│	...	...	...	...	2141	...	...	│	...	...	...	...	...	...	│
Pescara Centrale a.	...	...	...	1957	...	...	│	...	2225	│	...	...	...	...	2315	...	...	│	...	...	...	...	...	...	│
Bari Centrale a.	...	...	...	2304	...	...	│	...	...	│	...	...	...	...	...	...	...	│	...	...	...	...	...	...	│
Brindisi a.	...	...	...	...	...	...	│	...	...	│	...	...	...	...	...	...	...	│	...	...	...	...	...	...	│
Lecce a.	...	...	...	...	...	...	│	...	...	│	...	...	...	...	...	...	...	│	...	...	...	...	...	...	│
Firenze SMN a.	...	...	...	...	...	...	1739	...	...	1839	...	...	...	...	...	...	...	1939	...	...	...	...	...	...	2139
Roma Termini a.	...	...	...	...	...	...	1929	...	...	2029	...	...	...	...	...	...	...	2129	...	...	...	...	...	...	2329
Napoli Centrale a.	...	...	...	...	...	...	2105	...	...	2205	...	...	...	...	...	...	...	2305	...	...	...	...	...	...	...

A – ⑥⑦ (also Dec. 8).

C – 🛏12 and 🍷 Zürich - Milano - Venezia Mestre - Trieste (arrive 2118).

Q – CISALPINO – 🛏12 and ✕ Basel - Milano - Genova - La Spezia (arrive 1518).

g – Change at Genova and Ventimiglia.

q – Venezia **Mestre**.

r – Firenze **Rifredi**

✤ – Change trains at Domodossola.

⚡ – Supplement payable.

¶ – Ticket point is **Iselle**.

▲ – Genova **Piazza Principe**.

§ – Supplement payable in Italy (except with international tickets). *IC* in Italy.

⊕ – **ETR 470** *Cisalpino*. Supplement payable for international journeys. *IC* supplement payable for internal journeys within Italy.

GENÈVE, BASEL, STUTTGART, ZÜRICH and LUZERN - MILANO - VENEZIA and ROMA 82

train type	IC	CIS	ICp	ESc	AV	E	IR	CIS	ICp	IR	CIS		IC	CIS	ICN	IR	ICN	CIS	E	EN	IC	EN	AV	
train number	1077	127	665	9749	9453	923	2181	23	667	1439	59	2199	836	129	785	2187	10025	25	1911	311	993	313	9423	
notes	🍷	🍷	Ⓡ	Ⓡ✕	Ⓡ✕			Ⓡ🍷	Ⓡ⁄		Ⓡ🍷		🍷	🍷	Ⓡ⁄		Ⓡ	Ⓡ🍷	K	Ⓡ⁄		Ⓡ⁄	Ⓡ✕	
		§	⁄	⁄	⁄	T		⊕	Ⓑ		⊕			§	J		🍷	⊕		R	w	S	⁄	
Genève Aéroport ✈ d.	...	...	...	...	...	...	...	...	...	1647	...	...	...	...	...	...	...	...	...	2127	...	...	...	...
Genève d.	...	1510	...	...	...	...	...	...	...	1656	...	...	...	1807	...	...	...	...	...	2136	...	...	...	...
Lausanne d.	...	1546	...	...	...	...	...	...	...	1745	...	...	...	1846	...	...	...	...	...	2220	...	...	...	...
Sion d.	...	1643	...	...	...	...	...	...	...	1854	...	...	...	1943	...	...	...	...	...	2329	...	...	...	...
Zürich HB d.	...	|	...	...	...	...	...	1701p	...	|	...	...	...	|	...	...	1909	...	...	|	...	2123	...	...
Basel SBB d.	1428	|	...	...	...	...	1603	|	...	|	1728	...	...	|	...	1803	|	...	...	|	2201	|	...	...
Olten d.	1500	|	...	...	...	...	1631	|	...	|	1800	...	...	|	...	1836	|	...	...	|	2229	2159	...	...
Bern d.	1535	|	...	...	...	...	|	|	...	|	1835	...	1907	|	...	|	|	...	...	|	2256	2304	...	...
Spiez d.	1605	|	...	...	...	...	|	|	...	|	1905	...	1936	|	...	|	|	...	...	|	...	2335	...	...
Luzern d.	|	|	...	...	...	...	1718	|	...	|	|	...	|	|	...	1918	|	...	...	|	...	|	...	...
Arth-Goldau d.	|	|	...	...	...	...	1745	1750	...	|	|	...	|	|	...	1945	1950	...	...	|	...	|	...	...
Bellinzona d.	|	|	...	...	...	...	...	1923	...	|	|	...	|	|	...	...	2125	...	...	|	...	|	...	...
Lugano d.	|	|	...	...	...	...	...	1948	...	|	|	...	|	|	...	...	2146	2148	...	|	...	|	...	...
Chiasso 🏛 d.	|	|	...	...	...	...	...	|	...	|	|	...	|	|	...	...	...	|	...	|	...	|	...	...
Como San Giovanni a.	|	|	...	...	...	...	...	2014	...	|	|	...	|	|	...	...	...	2214	...	|	...	|	...	...
Visp d.	1632	|	...	...	...	...	...	|	...	1924	1932	...	2003	|	...	...	...	|	...	2359	...	|	...	...
Brig d.	1640	1720	...	...	...	...	...	|	...	1930	1944	...	2011	2020	...	...	...	|	...	|	...	0100	...	...
Domodossola 🏛 ¶ a.	...	1750	...	...	...	...	...	|	...	...	2012	...	▬	2050	...	...	...	|	...	|	...	|	...	...
Stresa a.	...	1830	...	...	...	...	...	|	...	...	|	...	...	2130	...	...	...	|	...	|	...	|	...	...
Arona a.	...	1844	...	...	...	...	...	|	...	...	|	...	...	2144	...	...	...	|	...	|	...	|	...	...
Milano Centrale a.	...	1935	...	...	...	...	...	2050	...	...	2135	...	...	2235	...	...	...	2250	...	|	...	|	...	...
								ESc 9753 Ⓡ✕ ⁄												|		|		
Milano Centrale d.	...	...	2005	2005	2030	2040	...	2105	2105	...	...	2225	2230	...	2300	...	...	...	2320	|	...	|	...	...
Genova PP ▲ a.	...	...	2148	|	|	|	...	|	2242	...	...	0020	|	...	|	...	...	...	|	|	...	|	...	...
Ventimiglia 🏛 a.	...	...	*0104*	|	|	|	...	|	0107	...	...	...	|	...	|	...	...	...	|	|	...	|	...	...
Nice Ville a.	...	...	...	|	|	|	...	|	...	...	...	...	|	...	|	...	...	...	|	|	...	|	...	...
Verona Porta Nuova a.	...	...	...	2127	|	|	...	2244	...	...	...	...	0020	...	|	...	...	...	|	|	...	|	...	...
Venezia Santa Lucia a.	...	...	...	2240	|	|	...	2356q	...	...	...	...	...	...	|	...	...	...	|	|	...	|	...	...
Bologna Centrale a.	...	...	...	...	2135	2314	...	...	...	...	...	...	...	...	0124	...	...	...	|	0519	...	0519	...	...
Rimini a.	...	...	...	...	|	0027	...	...	...	...	...	...	...	...	0235	...	...	...	|	|	...	|	...	...
Ancona a.	...	...	...	...	|	0137	...	...	...	...	...	...	...	...	0333	...	...	...	|	|	...	|	...	...
Pescara Centrale a.	...	...	...	...	|	0257	...	...	...	...	...	...	...	...	0459	...	...	...	|	|	...	|	...	...
Bari Centrale a.	...	...	...	...	|	0618	...	...	...	...	...	...	...	...	0826	...	...	...	|	|	...	|	...	...
Brindisi a.	...	...	...	...	|	0738	...	...	...	...	...	...	...	...	*1104*	...	...	...	|	|	...	|	...	...
Lecce a.	...	...	...	...	|	0810	...	...	...	...	...	...	...	...	*1205*	...	...	...	|	|	...	|	...	...
Firenze SMN a.	...	...	...	...	2242	...	...	...	...	...	...	...	...	...	...	...	...	...	|	0641b	...	0641b	...	...
Roma Termini a.	...	...	...	...	...	...	...	...	...	...	...	...	...	...	...	...	...	...	0723t	0912	...	0912	0944	...
Napoli Centrale a.	...	...	...	...	...	...	...	...	...	...	...	...	...	...	...	...	...	...	1012	...	...	...	1105	...

train type	CIS	ICN	IR	CIS	IR	ICN	E			IC	ICN	ICp	ESc	CIS	IR	E	AV	ICp	CIS	CIS	ICN	ESc	CIS	IR
train number	12	10012	2170	50	1414	780	1910	2710	2178	1072	784	651	9704	14	2174	926	9426	656	52	16	10016	9778	52	1424
notes	Ⓡ🍷	Ⓡ		Ⓡ🍷		Ⓡ⁄	K			🍷	Ⓡ⁄	Ⓡ⁄	Ⓡ✕	Ⓡ🍷			Ⓡ✕	Ⓡ	Ⓡ🍷	Ⓡ🍷	Ⓡ	Ⓡ🍷	Ⓡ🍷	
	⊕	🍷		⊕		E					J	⚒	⁄	⊕		T	⁄	🍷⁄	U⊕	⊕	🍷	⁄	U⊕	
Napoli Centrale d.	...	...	...	...	...	...	2030	...	...	...	...	...	...	...	...	...	...	...	...	...	...	...	...	...
Roma Termini d.	...	...	...	...	...	...	2259t	...	...	...	...	...	...	...	...	...	0630	...	...	...	...	...	...	...
Firenze SMN d.	...	...	...	...	...	...	|	...	...	...	...	...	...	...	...	...	0819	...	...	...	...	...	...	...
Lecce d.	...	...	...	...	...	1907	|	...	...	...	...	...	...	...	...	2205	|	...	...	...	...	...	...	...
Brindisi d.	...	...	...	...	...	1932	|	...	...	...	...	...	...	...	...	2236	|	...	...	...	...	...	...	...
Bari Centrale d.	...	...	...	...	...	2100	|	...	...	...	2259	...	...	...	...	2359	|	...	...	...	...	...	...	...
Pescara Centrale d.	...	...	...	...	...	0029	|	...	...	...	0204	...	...	...	...	0321	|	...	...	...	...	...	...	...
Ancona d.	...	...	...	...	...	0158	|	...	...	...	0330	...	...	...	...	0445	|	...	...	...	...	0620	...	...
Rimini d.	...	...	...	...	...	0256	|	...	...	...	0427	...	...	...	...	0541	|	...	...	...	...	0722	...	...
Bologna Centrale d.	...	...	...	...	...	0412	|	...	...	...	0548	...	...	...	...	0702	0924	...	...	...	...	0856	...	...
Venezia Santa Lucia d.	...	...	...	...	...	|	|	...	...	...	|	...	0620	...	...	|	|	...	0832q	...	...	|	...	...
Verona Porta Nuova d.	...	...	...	...	...	|	|	0540	...	...	|	...	0732	...	...	|	|	...	0932	...	...	|	...	...
Nice Ville d.	...	...	...	...	...	|	|	|	...	...	|	...	|	...	...	|	|	*0525j*	|	...	...	|	...	...
Ventimiglia 🏛 d.	...	...	...	...	...	|	|	|	...	...	|	0445	|	...	...	|	|	*0633*	|	...	...	|	...	...
Genova PP ▲ d.	...	...	...	...	...	|	|	|	0545	...	|	0719	|	...	...	|	|	0910	|	...	...	|	←	...
Milano Centrale a.	...	...	...	...	...	0705	0725	0735	0740	...	0820	0855	0855	...	...	0920	1029	1055	1055	...	...	1100	1055	...
									CIS 120 🍷 §										|				|	
Milano Centrale d.	0710	...	...	0725	...	...	...	...	0825	...	...	...	...	0910	...	...	...	...	1120	1110	...	...	1120	...
Arona d.	|	...	...	|	...	...	...	...	0916	...	...	...	...	|	...	...	...	...	→	|	...	...	|	...
Stresa d.	|	...	...	|	...	...	...	...	0929	...	...	...	...	|	...	...	...	...	...	|	...	...	|	...
Domodossola 🏛 ¶ d.	|	...	...	0848	...	...	...	...	1010	...	...	...	...	|	...	...	...	...	...	|	...	...	1248	...
Brig a.	|	...	...	0916	0928	...	...	...	1040	1120	...	...	...	|	...	...	...	...	...	|	...	...	1316	1328
Visp a.	|	...	...	0926	0936	...	...	...	|	1126	...	...	...	|	...	...	...	...	...	|	...	...	1326	1334
Como San Giovanni d.	0745	...	...	|	|	...	...	...	|	|	...	...	...	0945	...	...	...	...	...	1145	...	...	|	|
Chiasso 🏛 a.	|	...	...	|	|	...	...	...	|	|	...	...	...	|	...	...	...	...	...	|	...	...	|	|
Lugano a.	0810	0812	...	|	|	...	...	...	|	|	...	...	...	1010	...	...	...	...	...	1210	1212	...	|	|
Bellinzona a.	...	0834	...	|	|	...	...	...	|	|	...	...	...	1034	...	...	...	...	...	...	1234	...	|	|
Arth-Goldau a.	...	1009	1014	|	|	...	...	...	|	|	...	...	...	1209	1214	...	...	...	...	...	1409	...	|	|
Luzern a.	...	|	1041	|	|	...	...	...	|	|	...	...	...	|	1241	...	...	...	...	...	|	...	|	|
Spiez a.	...	|	...	0953	|	...	...	...	|	1153	...	...	...	|	|	...	...	...	...	...	|	...	1353	|
Bern a.	...	|	...	1023	|	...	...	...	|	1223	...	...	...	|	|	...	...	...	...	...	|	...	1423	|
Olten a.	...	|	...	1100	|	...	...	...	|	1300	...	...	...	|	1328	...	...	...	...	...	|	...	1500	|
Basel SBB a.	...	|	...	1132	|	...	...	...	|	1332	...	...	...	|	1353	...	...	...	...	...	|	...	1532	|
Zürich HB a.	...	1051	...	...	|	...	...	...	|	...	...	...	...	1251	...	...	...	...	...	...	1451	...	...	|
Sion a.	...	...	...	...	1004	...	...	...	1115	...	...	...	...	...	...	...	...	...	...	...	...	...	...	1404
Lausanne a.	...	...	...	...	1115	...	...	...	1214	...	...	...	...	...	...	...	...	...	...	...	...	...	...	1515
Genève a.	...	...	...	...	1204	...	...	...	1250	...	...	...	...	...	...	...	...	...	...	...	...	...	...	1604
Genève Aéroport ✈ a.	...	...	...	...	1213	...	...	...	...	...	...	...	...	...	...	...	...	...	...	...	...	...	...	1613

E – FRECCIA SALENTINA – 🛏 1, 2 cl., 🛏 1, 2 cl. (T2), ▬ 2 cl. (4, 6 berth) and (12) Milano - Lecce.

J – FRECCIA DEL LEVANTE – 🛏 1, 2 cl., 🛏 1, 2 cl. (T2), ▬ 2 cl. and (12) Milano - Bari.

K – 🛏 1, 2 cl. (Excelsior), 🛏 1, 2 cl. (T2), 🛏 1, 2 cl., ▬ 2 cl. (4, 6 berth) and (12) Milano - Napoli.

R – LUNA – 🛏 1, 2 cl. and ▬ 2 cl. Genève - Roma.

S – LUNA – 🛏 1, 2 cl. and ▬ 2 cl. Zürich - Roma.

T – 🛏 1, 2 cl. (T2), ▬ 2 cl. (4, 6 berth) and (2) Milano - Lecce.

U – (12) and 🍷 Trieste (depart 0635) - Venezia Mestre - Milano - Basel.

b – Firenze **Campo di Marte**.

j – ①–⑤ (not July 14, Nov. 11). Change at Ventimiglia and Genova.

p – 1709 on ⑥⑦.

q – Venezia **Mestre**.

t – Roma **Tiburtina**.

w – For Train **313** change trains at Bern.

⁄ – Supplement payable.

¶ – Ticket point is **Iselle**.

▲ – Genova **Piazza Principe**.

§ – Supplement payable in Italy (except with international tickets). *IC* in Italy.

⊕ – **ETR 470** *Cisalpino*. Supplement payable for international journeys. *IC* supplement payable for internal journeys within Italy.

82 ROMA, VENEZIA - MILANO - LUZERN, ZÜRICH, BASEL and GENÈVE

train type	ESc	AV	CIS	ESc	AV	ICp	IR	ESc	AV	ICp	CIS	ESc	AV	EC⚡	ESc	ICN	IR	ESc	AV	CIS	AV	ESc	CIS	IR
train number	**9712**	**9428**	**122**	**9792**	**9430**	**657/8**	**2182**	**9714**	**9432**	**662**	**124**	**9718**	**9434**	**139**	**9760**	**10020**	**2188**	**9722**	**9436**	**40**	**9438**	**9728**	**22**	**2192**
notes	[R]✕	[R]✕	🍸	[R]✕	[R]✕	[R]		[R]✕	[R]✕	[R]	🍸	[R]✕	[R]✕	**140**	[R]✕	[R]		[R]🍸	[R]✕	[R]🍸	[R]✕	[R]✕	[R]🍸	
	⚡	⚡	§	⑥⑦ **b**	⚡	⚡🍸		⚡	⚡	🍸⚡	§	⚡	⚡	🍸[R]	⚡	🍸		⚡	⚡	§	⚡	⚡	⊕	
Napoli Centrale d.	...	...	...	...	0654	...	...	...	0754	...	...	...	0854	...	...	...	...	...	0954	...	...	...	...	...
Roma Termini d.	...	0730	...	...	0830	...	...	...	0930	...	...	...	1030	...	...	...	...	...	1130	...	1230	...	...	...
Firenze SMN d.	...	0919	...	...	1019	...	...	...	1119	...	...	...	1219	...	...	...	...	...	1319	...	1419	...	...	...
Lecce d.	...	|	...	...	|	...	...	...	|	...	...	...	|	...	...	...	...	...	|	...	|	...	...	...
Brindisi d.	...	|	...	...	|	...	...	...	|	...	...	...	|	...	*0406*	...	...	...	|	...	|	...	...	...
Bari Centrale d.	...	|	...	...	|	...	...	...	|	...	...	...	|	...	0649	...	...	...	|	...	|	...	...	...
Pescara Centrale d.	...	|	...	...	|	...	...	...	|	...	...	...	|	...	0953	...	...	...	|	...	|	...	...	...
Ancona d.	...	|	...	...	|	...	...	...	|	...	...	...	|	...	1115	...	...	...	|	...	|	...	...	...
Rimini d.	...	|	...	...	|	...	...	...	|	...	...	...	|	...	1209	...	...	...	|	...	|	...	...	...
Bologna Centrale d.	...	1024	...	...	1124	...	...	...	1224	...	...	...	1324	...	1308	...	...	...	1424	...	1524	...	...	...
Venezia Santa Lucia d.	0850	|	...	0950	|	...	...	1050	|	...	...	1150	|	...	|	...	...	1250	|	...	|	1420	...	...
Verona Porta Nuova d.	1002	|	...	1102	|	...	...	1202	|	...	...	1302	|	...	|	...	...	1402	|	...	|	1532	...	...
Nice Ville d.	|	|	...	|	|	*0751***j**	...	|	|	...	...	|	|	1002	|	...	...	|	|	...	|	|	...	...
Ventimiglia 🏛 d.	|	|	...	|	|	0858	...	|	|	...	...	|	|	1058	|	...	...	|	|	...	|	|	...	...
Genova PP ▲ d.	|	|	...	|	|	1119	...	|	|	1219	...	|	|	1319	|	...	...	|	|	...	|	|	...	...
Milano Centrale a.	1125	1129	...	1225	1229	1255	...	1325	1329	1355	...	1425	1429	1450	1455	...	...	1525	1529	...	1629	1655	...	...
				▬		*CIS* **18** [R]🍸 ⊕						▬			*CIS* **20** [R]🍸 ⊕						▬			
Milano Centrale d.	...	...	1225	...	...	1310	...	...	...	...	1425	...	...	...	1510	...	...	...	...	1625	...	...	1710	...
Arona d.	...	...	1316	*IC*	...	|	...	...	...	...	1516	*IC*	...	...	|	...	...	...	...	|	...	...	|	...
Stresa d.	...	...	1329	**1080**	...	|	...	...	...	...	1529	**1086**	...	...	|	...	...	...	...	1721	*IC*	...	|	...
Domodossola 🏛 ¶ d.	...	...	1410	🍸	...	|	...	...	...	...	1610	🍸	...	...	|	...	...	...	...	1748	**1092**	...	|	...
Brig a.	...	...	1440	1520	...	|	...	...	...	...	1640	1720	...	...	|	...	...	...	...	1816	1920	...	|	...
Visp a.	...	...	|	1526	...	|	...	...	...	...	|	1726	...	...	|	...	...	...	...	|	1926	...	|	...
Como San Giovanni d.	...	...	|	|	...	1345	...	...	...	...	|	|	...	...	1545	...	...	...	...	|	|	...	1745	...
Chiasso 🏛 a.	...	...	|	|	...	|	...	...	...	...	|	|	...	...	|	...	...	...	...	|	|	...	|	...
Lugano a.	...	...	|	|	...	1410	...	...	...	...	|	|	...	...	1610	1612	...	...	...	|	|	...	1810	...
Bellinzona a.	...	...	|	|	...	1434	...	...	...	...	|	|	...	...	...	1634	...	...	...	|	|	...	1834	...
Arth-Goldau a.	...	...	|	|	...	1609	1614	...	...	...	|	|	...	...	...	1809	1814	...	...	|	|	...	2009	2014
Luzern a.	...	...	|	|	...	|	1641	...	...	...	|	|	...	...	...	|	1841	...	...	|	|	...	|	2041
Spiez a.	...	...	|	1553	...	|	|	...	...	...	|	1753	...	...	...	|	|	...	...	|	1953	...	|	|
Bern a.	...	...	|	1623	...	|	|	...	...	...	|	1823	...	...	...	|	|	...	...	|	2023	...	|	|
Olten a.	...	...	|	1700	...	|	1728	...	...	...	|	1900	...	...	...	|	1928	...	...	|	2100	...	|	2128
Basel SBB a.	...	...	|	1732	...	|	1753	...	...	...	|	1932	...	...	...	|	1953	...	...	|	2132	...	|	2153
Zürich HB a.	...	...	|	...	...	1651	...	...	...	...	|	...	...	...	...	1851	...	...	...	|	...	...	2051	...
Sion a.	...	...	1515	...	...	...	...	...	...	...	1715	...	...	...	...	...	...	...	...	1845	...	...	...	...
Lausanne a.	...	...	1614	...	...	...	...	...	...	...	1814	...	...	...	...	...	...	...	...	1940	...	...	...	...
Genève a.	...	...	1653	...	...	...	...	...	...	...	1853	...	...	...	...	...	...	...	...	2018	...	...	...	...
Genève Aéroport ✈ a.	...	...	...	...	...	...	...	...	...	...	...	...	...	...	...	...	...	...	...	...	...	...	...	...

train type/number	ESc	EC/IR	CIS	AV	ESc	ICp	ESc	CIS	IR	AV	ICp	CIS	IR	ESc	ICp	CIS	AV	ESc	CIS	CIS	IR	EN	IC	EN
train number	**9762**	**174**	**10156**	**9440**	**9732**	**664**	**9784**	**56**	**1440**	**9442**	**693**	**24**	**2196**	**9764**	**586**	**42**	**9444**	**9740**	**158**	**10158**	**2298**	**314**	**1058**	**314**
notes	[R]✕	[R]🍸	[R]	[R]✕	[R]✕	[R]	[R]✕	[R]✕		[R]✕	**694**	[R]🍸		[R]✕	[R]✕	[R]🍸	[R]✕	[R]✕	[R]🍸	[R]		[R]⚡	🍸	[R]⚡
	⚡		🍸	⚡	⚡	🍸⚡	⚡	§ ❖		⚡	[R]⚡	⊕		⚡	⚡	§	⚡	⚡	⊕	🍸		**S w**		**T**
Napoli Centrale d.	...	...	...	1154	...	...	...	...	...	1254	...	...	...	...	1024	...	1354	...	...	...	...	...	...	...
Roma Termini d.	...	...	...	1330	...	...	...	...	...	1430	...	...	...	...	1244**t**	...	1530	...	...	...	...	1956	...	1956
Firenze SMN d.	...	...	...	1519	...	...	...	...	...	1619	...	1554	...	...	1536**g**	...	1719	...	...	...	...	2157**f**	...	2157**f**
Lecce d.	0704	...	...	|	...	...	...	...	...	|	...	|	...	...	|	...	|	...	...	...	...	|	...	|
Brindisi d.	0728	...	...	|	...	...	...	...	...	|	...	|	...	...	|	...	|	...	...	...	...	|	...	|
Bari Centrale d.	0834	...	...	|	...	...	...	...	...	|	...	|	...	1105	|	...	|	...	...	...	...	|	...	|
Pescara Centrale d.	1119	...	...	|	...	...	...	...	...	|	...	|	...	1350	|	...	|	...	...	...	...	|	...	|
Ancona d.	1240	...	...	|	...	...	1310	...	...	|	...	|	...	1515	|	...	|	...	...	...	...	|	...	|
Rimini d.	1339	...	...	|	...	...	1426	...	...	|	...	|	...	1609	|	...	|	...	...	...	...	|	...	|
Bologna Centrale d.	1508	...	...	1624	...	...	1556	...	...	1724	...	1654	...	1710	1703	...	1824	...	...	...	...	2318	...	2318
Venezia Santa Lucia d.	|	...	...	|	1520	...	|	...	...	|	...	|	...	|	|	1620	|	1720	...	...	...	|	...	|
Verona Porta Nuova d.	|	...	...	|	1632	...	|	...	...	|	...	|	...	|	|	1732	|	1832	...	...	...	|	...	|
Nice Ville d.	|	...	...	|	|	...	|	...	...	|	*1335***j**	|	...	|	|	|	|	|	...	...	...	|	...	|
Ventimiglia 🏛 d.	|	...	...	|	|	...	|	...	...	|	1458	|	...	|	|	|	|	|	...	...	...	|	...	|
Genova PP ▲ d.	|	...	...	|	|	1619	|	...	...	|	1719	|	...	|	|	|	|	|	...	...	...	|	...	|
Milano Centrale a.	1700	...	...	1729	1755	1755	1800	...	...	1829	1850	1855	...	1900	1905	1900	1929	1955	...	...	...	|	...	|
				▬								|				|	▬					|		|
Milano Centrale d.	...	1735	...	...	...	...	...	1825	...	...	...	1910	...	...	...	1920	...	...	2010	...	...	|	...	|
Arona d.	...	|	...	...	...	...	...	|	...	...	...	|	...	...	...	|	...	...	|	...	...	|	...	|
Stresa d.	...	|	...	...	...	...	...	1921	...	...	...	|	...	...	...	|	*IC*	...	|	...	...	|	...	|
Domodossola 🏛 ¶ d.	...	|	...	...	...	...	...	1948	...	...	...	|	...	...	...	2048	**1096**	...	|	...	...	|	...	|
Brig a.	...	|	...	...	...	...	...	2016	2028	...	...	|	...	...	...	2116	2120	...	|	...	...	0439	...	|
Visp a.	...	|	...	...	...	...	...	2026	2034	...	...	|	...	...	...	|	2123	...	|	...	...	|	...	0703
Como San Giovanni d.	...	1820	...	...	...	...	...	|	|	...	...	1945	...	...	...	|	|	...	2045	...	...	|	...	|
Chiasso 🏛 a.	...	1840	...	...	...	...	...	|	|	...	...	|	...	...	...	|	|	...	|	...	...	|	...	|
Lugano a.	...	1904	1912	*IR*	...	...	...	|	|	...	...	2010	...	...	...	|	|	...	2110	2112	...	|	...	|
Bellinzona a.	...	...	1934	**2294**	...	...	...	|	|	...	...	2034	...	...	...	|	|	...	...	2134	...	|	...	|
Arth-Goldau a.	...	...	2109	2113	...	...	...	|	|	...	...	2209	2214	...	...	|	|	...	...	2309	2313	|	...	|
Luzern a.	...	...	2141	|	...	...	...	|	|	...	...	|	2241	...	...	|	|	...	...	2341	|	|	...	|
Spiez a.	...	...	|	|	...	...	...	2053	|	...	...	|	|	...	...	|	2153	...	...	|	|	0544	...	|
Bern a.	...	...	|	|	...	...	...	2123	|	...	...	|	|	...	...	|	2223	...	...	|	|	0620	0634	|
Olten a.	...	...	2227	|	...	...	...	2200	|	...	...	|	2328	...	...	|	...	...	...	0027	|	0745	0700	|
Basel SBB a.	...	...	2253	|	...	...	...	2232	|	...	...	|	2353	...	...	|	...	...	...	0056	|	|	0732	|
Zürich HB a.	...	...	...	2151	...	...	...	...	|	...	...	2251	...	...	...	|	...	...	...	...	2351	0842	...	|
Sion a.	...	...	...	...	...	...	...	...	2104	...	...	...	...	...	...	2149	...	...	...	...	...	...	...	0735
Lausanne a.	...	...	...	...	...	...	...	...	2215	...	...	...	...	...	...	2240	...	...	...	...	...	...	...	0840
Genève a.	...	...	...	...	...	...	...	...	*2304*	...	...	...	...	...	...	2315	...	...	...	...	...	...	...	0924
Genève Aéroport ✈ a.	...	...	...	...	...	...	...	...	*2313*	...	...	...	...	...	...	2324	...	...	...	...	...	...	...	0933

E – CISALPINO – (12) and 🍸 La Spezia (depart 1640) - Genova - Milano - Basel.
S – LUNA – 🛏 1,2 cl. and 🛌 2 cl. Roma - Zürich.
T – LUNA – 🛏 1,2 cl. and 🛌 2 cl. Roma - Genève.

b – Also Dec. 8.
f – Firenze **Campo di Marte**.
g – Firenze **Rifredi**.

j – ①–⑥ (not July 14, Nov. 11).
t – Roma **Tiburtina**.
w – For Basel on Train **1058**, change trains at Bern.

⚡ – Supplement payable.
¶ – Ticket point is **Iselle**.
▲ – Genova **Piazza Principe**.

❖ – Change trains at Domodossola.
§ – Supplement payable in Italy (except with international tickets). *IC* in Italy.
⊕ – **ETR 470** *Cisalpino*. Supplement payable for international journeys. *IC* supplement payable for internal journeys within Italy.

OTHER TRAIN NAMES FOR TABLE 82:

EC **106 / 119** –	CISALPINO TIZIANO	*EC* **121 / 128** –	CISALPINO MONTERVERDI	*EC* **170 / 177** –	CISALPINO MONTE CENERI
EC **108 / 117** –	CISALPINO VERDI	*EC* **123 / 124** –	CISALPINO BORROMEO	*EC* **171 / 178** –	CISALPINO TEODOLINDA
EC **109 / 110** –	CISALPINO TICINO	*EC* **125 / 126** –	CISALPINO LEMANO	*EC* **173 / 174** –	CISALPINO CANALETTO
EC **111 / 114** –	CISALPINO SAN MARCO	*EC* **127 / 120** –	CISALPINO VALLESE	*EC* **179 / 172** –	CISALPINO INSUBRIA
EC **115 / 116** –	CISALPINO MEDIOLANUM	*EC* **129 / 122** –	CISALPINO MONTE ROSA		

BASEL - ZÜRICH - INNSBRUCK - WIEN, ZAGREB and BUDAPEST 86

train type/number	EC	IC	EC	IC	IC	EC	EC	EC	EC	EC	EC	D	IC	IC	IC	EC	EC		IC	EC	IC	EN	EN	EN	IR	EN
train number	**561**	**515**	**111**	**559**	**169**	**565**	**669**	**669**	**113**	**113**	**163**	**347**	**649**	**611**	**573**	**315**	**161**	**1517**	**581**	**165**	**591**	**465**	**465**	**15465**	**1993**	**467**
notes	✕	🍸 ❖	**211**	🍸		✕	🍸 **W**	🍸 **V**	**213** 🍸	✕	✕ **B**	✕ **D**	🍸	❖	🍸	**E**	✕ **M**	2		✕ **P**	🍸	**H**	**415** **KT**	**415** **KS**		🍸 **A**
Basel SBB d.	...	...	...	0633	...	...	...	...	...	...	0814	...	...	...	1233	...	...	...	1633	...	2033	...	...	...	2114	...
Zürich HB d.	...	...	...	0726	0740	...	...	...	...	...	0940	...	...	...	1326	...	1340	...	1726	1740	2126	2140	2140	2140	2224	2240
Sargans d.	...	...	...	▬	0837	...	...	...	...	...	1037	...	...	...	▬	...	1437	...	▬	1837	▬	2237	2237	2237	▬	2337
Buchs 🛃 d.	...	...	...	...	0856	...	...	...	...	...	1102	...	...	...	...	...	1502	...	...	1902	...	2259	2259	2259	...	0005
Bregenz d.	0500	...	...	...	|	0844	0942	0942	...	...	|	...	...	...	...	...	|	...	...	|	...	|	|	|	...	|
Feldkirch a.	0522	...	...	...	0912	0920**d**	1017	1017	...	...	1118	...	...	...	...	...	1518	...	...	1918	...	2314	2314	2314	...	0020
Bludenz a.	0536	...	...	...	...	0932	1029	1029	...	...	1132	...	...	...	...	...	1532	...	...	1932	...	2345	2345	2359	...	0035
Langen am Arlberg a.	|	...	...	...	...	1000	1055	1055	...	...	1202	...	...	...	...	...	1600	...	...	2000	...	0020	0020	0035	...	|
St Anton am Arlberg a.	0611	...	...	...	...	1010	1106	1106	...	...	1212	...	...	...	...	...	1610	...	...	2010	...	0029	0029	0045	...	|
Landeck-Zams a.	0634	...	...	...	...	1033	1129	1129	...	...	1238	...	...	...	...	...	1633	...	...	2033	...	0053	0053	0108	...	|
Ötztal a.	0659	...	...	...	...	1057	1153	1153	...	...	1302	...	...	...	...	...	1657	...	...	2057	**1547**	|	|	|	...	|
Innsbruck Hbf a.	0726	0825	...	...	...	1121	1217	1217	...	...	1326	...	1412	...	...	...	1721	1819	...	2121	2	0140	0140	0154	...	0224
Jenbach a.	0749	0844	...	...	...	1149	1244	1244	...	...	1349	...	1432	...	...	...	1749	1842	...	2149		|	|	|	...	|
Wörgl a.	0803	0859	...	...	...	1203	1259	1259	...	...	1403	...	1448	...	...	...	1803	1857	...	2203	2208	0216	0216	0233	...	|
Kitzbühel a.	|	0929	...	...	...	|	1329	|	...	...	|	...	1518	...	...	...	|	1927	*EC*	|	2243	|	|	|	...	|
St Johann in Tirol a.	|	0937	...	...	...	|	1337	|	...	...	|	...	1526	...	*EC*	...	|	1935	**117**	|	2251	|	|	|	...	|
Saalfelden a.	|	1007	...	*EC*	...	|	1407	|	...	...	|	...	1558	...	**115**	...	|	2005	🍸	|	2322	|	|	|	...	|
Zell am See a.	|	1019	...	**111**	...	|	1419	◧	...	...	|	...	1610	...	✕	...	|	2016	Ⓑ	|	...	|	|	|	...	|
Schwarzach St Veit a.	|	1048	1111	1111	...	|	1448	|	1511	1511	|	...	1639	...	1711	...	|	2048	2111	|	...	0355	0355	0414	...	|
Bischofshofen a.	|	1110	|	|	...	|	1510	|	|	|	|	...	1655	1713	|	...	|	2111	|	|	...	0412	|	|	...	|
Selzthal a.	|	1240	|	|	...	|	1640	1640	|	|	|	...	...	1840	|	...	|	...	|	|	...	0539	|	|	**4270**	|
Graz Hbf a.	|	1422	|	|	...	|	1822	1822	|	|	|	...	...	2022	|	...	|	...	|	|	...	0737	|	|	2	|
Villach Hbf a.	|	▬	1243	1243	...	|	▬	...	1643	1643	|	...	...	...	1843	1927	|	...	2245	|	...	...	0609	0609	0620	|
Klagenfurt a.	|	...	|	1315	...	|	...	...	|	1715	|	...	...	...	1915	|	|	...	2317	|	...	...	|	|	0656	|
Jesenice 🛃 a.	|	...	1330	...	...	|	...	...	1730	...	|	...	...	...	...	2005	|	...	...	|	...	...	0706	0706	...	|
Ljubljana ⊙ a.	|	...	1430	...	...	|	...	...	1830	...	|	...	...	...	...	2108	|	...	...	|	...	...	0810	0810	...	|
Zagreb ⊙ a.	|	...	1657	...	...	|	...	...	2055	...	|	...	...	...	...	2334	|	...	...	|	...	...	1034	1034	...	|
Vinkovci ⊕ a.	|	...	2020	...	...	|	...	...	...	...	|	...	...	...	...	0305	|	...	...	|	...	...	1410	1410	...	|
Beograd ⊕ a.	|	*RJ*	2321	...	...	|	*RJ*	...	...	...	|	...	...	...	...	0621	|	...	...	|	...	...	1718	1718	...	|
Salzburg Hbf a.	0929	**63**	...	...	...	1329	**67**	...	...	...	1529	...	...	...	...	...	1929	...	...	2329	...	...	...	...	...	0424
Linz Hbf a.	1043	✕	...	...	...	1443	✕	...	...	...	1643	...	...	...	...	...	2043	...	...	...	...	...	...	...	...	0554
St Pölten a.	1137	**C**	...	...	...	1537	**C**	...	...	...	1737	...	...	...	...	...	2132	...	...	...	...	...	...	...	...	0708
Wien Westbahnhof a.	1224	1350	...	...	...	1624	1750	...	...	...	1824	1850	...	...	...	...	2218	...	...	...	...	...	...	...	...	0803
Hegyeshalom 🛃 a.	...	1454	...	...	...	...	1854	...	...	...	...	1953	...	...	...	...	...	...	...	...	...	...	...	...	...	0927
Győr a.	...	1519	...	...	...	...	1919	...	...	...	...	2027	...	...	...	...	...	...	...	...	...	...	...	...	...	0957
Budapest Keleti a.	...	1649	...	...	...	...	2049	...	...	...	...	2219	...	...	...	...	...	...	...	...	...	...	...	...	...	1134

train type/number	EC	IC		EC	EC	EC	D	EC	EC	RJ	EC	EC	EC	IC	IC	EC	EC	EC	EC	RJ	EC	EN	EC	EN	EN	EN
train number	**164**	**693**	**1504**	**160**	**314**	**114**	**346**	**162**	**212**	**60**	**668**	**668**	**564**	**310**	**691**	**962**	**566**	**210**	**110**	**66**	**660**	**466**	**539**	**414**	**414**	**464**
notes	✕ **P**	🍸	2	✕ **M**	**E**	✕	✕ **D**	✕ **B**	**112** ✕	✕ **C**	🍸 **V**	🍸 **W**	✕			✕	✕	**110**		✕ **C**	✕	🍸 **A**		**15464** **KS**	**464** **KT**	**H**
Budapest Keleti d.	...	...	...	...	...	...	0555	...	...	0710	...	...	...	...	...	0910	...	...	...	1310	...	1805	...	...	...	...
Győr d.	...	...	...	...	...	...	0725	...	...	0838	...	...	...	...	...	1037	...	...	...	1437	...	1933	...	...	...	...
Hegyeshalom 🛃 d.	...	...	...	...	...	...	0758	...	...	0906	...	...	...	...	...	1106	...	...	...	1506	...	2004	...	...	...	...
Wien Westbahnhof d.	...	...	...	0740	...	...	0859	0940	...	1008	...	...	1140	...	...	1208	1340	...	...	1608	1740	2125	...	...	...	...
St Pölten d.	...	...	...	0822	...	...	▬	1022	...	▬	...	...	1222	...	...	▬	1422	...	...	▬	1822	2209	...	...	...	...
Linz Hbf d.	...	...	...	0916	...	...	...	1116	...	...	...	...	1316	...	...	...	1516	...	...	...	1916	2314	...	...	...	...
Salzburg Hbf d.	0622	...	...	1031	...	...	...	1231	...	...	...	...	1431	...	...	...	1631	...	...	...	2030	0044	...	...	...	...
Beograd ⊕ d.	|	...	...	|	2150	...	...	|	...	...	...	...	|	...	...	...	|	0550	...	...	|	|	...	1035	1035	...
Vinkovci ⊕ d.	|	...	...	|	0147	...	...	|	...	...	...	...	|	...	...	...	|	0949	...	...	|	|	...	1449	1449	...
Zagreb ⊙ d.	|	...	...	|	0500	...	...	|	0700	*EC*	...	...	|	...	...	...	|	1300	...	...	|	|	...	1814	1814	...
Ljubljana ⊙ d.	|	...	...	|	0726	...	...	|	0927	**112**	...	...	|	1128	...	...	|	1525	...	...	|	|	...	2048	2048	...
Jesenice 🛃 d.	|	...	...	|	0829	...	...	|	1029	✕	...	...	|	1229	...	...	|	1629	...	...	|	|	...	2156	2156	...
Klagenfurt d.	|	0646	...	|	|	0843	...	|	|	1033	...	...	|	|	1246	...	|	|	1631	...	|	|	2215	|	|	...
Villach Hbf d.	|	0716	...	|	0906	0916	...	|	1116	1116	...	...	|	1306	1316	...	|	1716	1716	...	|	|	2236	2300	2300	...
Graz Hbf d.	|	|	...	|	▬	|	*EC*	|	|	|	0938	0938	|	▬	|	**1510**	|	|	|	**1514**	|	|	▬	|	|	2138
Selzthal d.	|	|	...	|	...	|	**542**	|	|	|	1119	1119	|	...	|	2	|	|	|	2	|	|	...	|	|	2339
Bischofshofen d.	|	|	*0855*	|	...	|	🍸	|	|	|	|	1249	|	...	|		|	|	|		|	|	...	|	|	0108
Schwarzach St Veit d.	|	0849	0912	|	...	1049	1121	|	1249	1249	|	1312	|	...	1449	1512	|	1849	1849	1912	|	|	...	0101	0145	0145
Zell am See d.	|	▬	0946	|	...	...	1152	|	...	...	◧	1343	|	...	▬	1546	|	...	...	1946	|	|	...	|	|	|
Saalfelden d.	|	...	0955	|	...	...	1201	|	...	...	|	1353	|	...	...	1555	|	...	...	1955	|	|	...	|	|	|
St Johann in Tirol d.	|	...	1025	|	...	...	1233	|	...	...	|	1421	|	...	...	1625	|	...	...	2025	|	|	...	|	|	|
Kitzbühel d.	|	...	1033	|	...	...	1241	|	...	...	|	1429	|	...	...	1633	|	...	...	2033	|	|	...	|	|	|
Wörgl d.	0749	...	1103	1156	...	...	1312	1356	...	...	1459	1459	1556	...	...	1703	1756	...	...	2103	2156	|	...	0255	|	|
Jenbach d.	0806	...	1119	1210	...	...	1326	1410	...	...	1513	1513	1610	...	...	1719	1810	...	...	2119	2210	|	...	|	|	|
Innsbruck Hbf d.	0839	...	1140	1239	...	...	1348	1439	...	...	1539	1539	1639	...	...	1740	1839	...	...	2140	2233	0241	...	0345	0402	0402
Ötztal d.	0903	...	...	1303	...	...	...	1503	...	...	1607	1607	1703	...	...	...	1903	...	...	...	2300	|	...	|	|	|
Landeck-Zams d.	0926	...	...	1326	...	...	...	1526	...	...	1634	1634	1726	...	...	...	1926	...	...	...	2322	|	...	0437	0456	0456
St Anton am Arlberg d.	0950	...	...	1350	...	...	...	1550	...	...	1657	1657	1750	*IC*	...	...	1950	...	...	...	2345	|	...	0503	0521	0521
Langen am Arlberg d.	1001	...	...	1401	...	...	...	1601	...	...	1708	1708	1801	**168**	...	...	2001	...	...	...	2356	|	...	0513	0531	0531
Bludenz d.	1028	...	...	1428	...	...	...	1628	...	...	1734	1734	1828		...	...	2028	...	...	...	0021	0427	...	0555	0615	0615
Feldkirch d.	1042	...	...	1442	...	...	...	1642	...	...	1750	1750	1844	1846	...	...	2042	...	...	...	0033	0446	...	0646	0646	0646
Bregenz a.	|	*IC*	...	|	*IC*	...	...	|	...	...	1822	1822	1915	|	*IC*	...	2105	...	...	...	0056	|	*IC*	|	|	|
Buchs 🛃 a.	1058	**572**	...	1458	**580**	...	...	1658	...	...	...	...	...	1902	**590**	...	...	...	...	...	...	0502	**558**	0702	0702	0702
Sargans a.	1122	🍸	...	1522	🍸	...	...	1722	...	...	...	...	...	1922		...	...	...	...	...	...	0522	🍸	0722	0722	0722
Zürich HB a.	1220	1234	...	1620	1634	...	...	1820	...	...	...	...	...	2020	2034	...	...	...	...	...	...	0620	0634	0820	0820	0820
Basel SBB a.	...	1327	...	...	1727	...	...	1947	...	...	...	...	...	...	2127	...	...	...	...	...	...	...	0727	*0927*	*0927*	*0927*

A – WIENER WALZER – 🛏 1, 2 cl., ▬ 2 cl., and [2] Zürich - Wien and v.v. Special fares payable. ▬ 2 cl. and [2] Zürich - Wien - Budapest and v.v. [12] and ✕ Wien - Budapest and v.v. 🛏 1, 2 cl. and ▬ 2 cl. Zürich - Linz - Praha and v.v. (see Table **53**).

B – TRANSALPIN – [1] (panorama car), [12] and ✕ Basel - Wien and v.v.

C – [1] (premium class), [1] (first class), [2] (economy class) and ✕ München - Wien - Budapest and v.v. ÖBB *Railjet* service.

D – DACIA – 🛏 1, 2 cl., ▬ 2 cl., [2] and ✕ Wien - Budapest - Bucureşti and v.v. [1] Wien - Budapest - Lökösháza and v.v.

E – 🛏 1, 2 cl., ▬ 2 cl. and [12] Villach - Beograd and v.v. Table **62**.

H – ZÜRICHSEE – 🛏 1,2 cl., ▬ 2 cl. and [2] Zürich - Graz and v.v. May 13 - Aug. 9 *EN***465** will arrive Graz 0910, and will not call at Bischofshofen and Selzthal. May 13 - Aug. 9 *EN***466** will depart Graz 1953, and will not call at Bischofshofen and Selzthal.

K – 🛏 1, 2 cl. and ▬ 2 cl. Zürich - Zagreb and v.v. [2] Zürich - Beograd and v.v. [12] and ✕ Villach - Beograd and v.v.

M – VORARLBERG – [12] and ✕ Zürich - Wien and v.v.

P – KAISERIN ELISABETH – [12] and ✕ Zürich - Salzburg and v.v.

S – ⑤⑥⑦ June 14–25; daily July 3 - Sept. 6; ⑤⑥⑦ Sept. 11 - Oct. 25 (also Oct. 31, Nov. 1).

T – Daily except on dates in note **S**.

V – May 14 - Aug. 10.

W – Aug. 11 - Dec. 12.

d – Departure time, arrive 0910.

⊙ – 🛃 between Ljubljana and Zagreb is Dobova.

⊕ – 🛃 between Vinkovci and Beograd is Šid.

◧ – Via Salzburg Hbf. (due to engineering work).

❖ – Due to engineering work between Bischofshofen and Selzthal, from May 14 until Aug. 10, services may be replaced by 🚌.

OTHER TRAIN NAMES: *EC* **960** – LISZT FERENC / FRANZ LISZT *EC* **962** – SEMMELWEIS IGNAC / IGNAZ SEMMELWEIS *EC* **967** – CSÁRDÁS

88 WIEN - VENEZIA, MILANO, ROMA and ANCONA

train type / number	🚌	AV	ESc	ESc	EC	IC	EC	ESc	AV	ESc	IC	IC	🚌	ESc	ES	IC	IC	EN	EN	EN	EN		EN	ES	ESc
train number	833	9641 9469	9765	9714	390	592	31	9728	9643	9769	715	533	835	9744	9485	648	596	235	235 9702	1237	1239	2121	237	9467	9712
notes	[R]	[R]✕	[R]✕ ⁄	[R]🍷 ⁄	①–⑥	🍷	A	[R]🍷 ⁄	[R]✕ ⁄	[R]✕ ⁄	🍷 ⁄	🍷	[R]	[R]🍷 ⁄	[R]✕ ⁄	🍷	🍷	R ⁄	V⁄	P ⁄	C ⁄		G ⁄	[R]✕ ⁄	[R]🍷 ⁄
Wien Südbahnhof d.	...	⁄	...	...	...	...	0623	...	...	...	...	1023	...	...	...	...	...	1923	1923	2023	2023	...	2040r	...	...
Bruck an der Mur d.	...	...	...	...	...	...	0815	...	...	...	...	1215	...	...	...	...	...	2125	2125	2222	2222	...	|	...	...
Klagenfurt Hbf d.	0605	...	...	...	...	...	1023	...	...	...	...	1423	1410	...	...	...	...	2338	2338	0021	0021	...	|	...	...
Linz Hbf d.	|	...	...	...	0626	...	|	...	...	...	...	|	|	...	...	1932	...	|	|	|	|	...	2232	...	...
Salzburg Hbf d.	|	...	...	...	0750	0812	|	...	...	...	...	|	|	...	...	2050	2110	|	|	|	|	...	0134	...	...
Villach Hbf d.	0650	...	...	...	...	1043	1047	...	...	...	...	1446	1456	...	...	▬	2343	0003	0003	0045	0045	...	0445	...	...
Tarvisio 🏛 a.	|	...	...	...	...	...	1109	...	...	...	...	...	|	...	...	...	...	0026	0026	0108	0108	...	0508	...	...
Udine a.	0825	...	...	...	...	...	1214	...	...	...	...	...	1630	...	...	...	...	|	|	0217	0217	...	0633	...	...
Venezia Mestre a.	1000	1054	...	1102	...	...	1409	1432	1454	...	1534	...	1805	1832	1847	...	...	0252	0252h	0332	0332	...	0821	0854	0902
Venezia Santa Lucia a.	1020x	|	...	|	...	...	1421	|	|	...	|	...	1825x	|	|	...	...	|	|	|	|	...	0834	|	|
Padova a.	...	1109	...	1117	...	...	...	1447	1509	...	1555	...	...	1847	1901	...	...	|	0552	0418	0418	...	...	0909	0917
Verona Porta Nuova a.	...	|	...	1200	...	...	...	1530	|	...	|	...	...	1930	|	**2075**	...	|	0643	|	|	...	...	|	1000
Milano Centrale a.	...	|	...	1325	...	...	...	1655	|	...	|	...	...	2055	|		...	|	0825	|	|	...	...	|	1125
Bologna Centrale a.	...	1221	1256	...	...	...	...	...	1621	1656	1712	...	...	...	2021	2038	...	0448	...	0541	0541	0638	...	1021	...
Firenze SMN a.	...	1323	|	...	...	...	...	...	1723	|	|	...	...	...	2123	|	...	0618	...	0705e	0705e	|	...	1123	...
Roma Termini a.	...	1510	|	...	...	...	...	...	1910	|	|	...	...	...	2310	|	...	0905	...	0957	1045	|	...	1310	...
Ravenna a.	...	...	|	...	...	...	...	...	...	|	|	...	...	...	...	|	...	...	...	...	...	|	...	...	...
Rimini a.	...	...	1351	...	...	...	...	...	...	1751	1834	...	...	...	...	2205	...	...	...	...	...	0805	...	...	...
Ancona a.	...	...	1441	...	...	...	...	...	...	1842	1947	...	...	...	...	2324	...	...	...	...	...	0924	...	...	...

train type / number	ES	ESc	🚌	IC	ESc	ESc	ES	EC	IC	EC	ESc	ES	🚌	ESc	ES	ESc	ICp	EN	ESc	EN	EN	EN	EN	IC	IC
train number	9462	9711	832	630	9719	9760	9470	30	593	391	9735	9478	834	9764	9478	9743	706	236	9768	1236	1238	234	9753 34	597	547
notes	[R]✕ ⁄	[R]✕ ⁄	[R]	🍷	[R]⁄ T	[R]✕ ⁄	[R]✕ ⁄	A	🍷	🍷 ⑧	[R]✕ ⁄	[R]✕ ⁄	[R]	[R]✕ ⁄	[R]✕ ⁄	[R] ⁄	[R] 🍷⁄	H ⁄	[R]✕ ⁄	Q ⁄	D ⁄	R ⁄	W⁄	🍷	🍷
Ancona d.	...	...	...	...	...	1115	...	...	...	...	...	...	...	1515	...	...	...	...	1913	...	...	...	...	...	...
Rimini d.	...	...	...	...	...	1209	...	...	...	...	...	...	...	1609	...	...	...	...	2007	...	...	...	...	...	...
Ravenna d.	...	...	...	...	...	|	...	...	...	...	...	...	...	|	...	...	...	...	|	...	...	...	...	...	...
Roma Termini d.	0650	...	...	...	...	|	1050	...	...	...	...	1450	...	|	1450	...	1445	...	|	1650	1720	1910	...	...	...
Firenze SMN d.	0837	...	...	...	...	|	1237	...	...	...	...	1637	...	|	1637	...	1733j	...	|	2055e	2055e	2153	...	...	...
Bologna Centrale d.	0938	...	...	...	...	1304	1338	...	...	...	...	1738	...	1706	1738	...	1828	...	2059	2220	2220	2320	...	...	...
Milano Centrale d.	|	0905	...	...	1235	...	|	...	...	...	1635	|	...	...	|	1835	|	...	...	|	|	|	2105	...	...
Verona Porta Nuova d.	|	1029	...	...	1359	...	|	...	...	...	1759	|	...	...	|	1959	|	...	...	|	|	|	2247	...	...
Padova d.	1051	1112	...	...	1442	...	1451	...	...	...	1842	1851	...	...	1851	2042	2014	...	...	2349	2349	0041	2338	...	...
Venezia Santa Lucia d.	|	|	1120x	...	|	...	|	1548	...	...	|	|	1920x	...	1917	|	|	2105	...	|	|	|	|	...	...
Venezia Mestre d.	1106	1128	1140	...	1458	...	1506	1600	...	...	1858	1906	1940	...	...	2058	2045	2118	...	0036	0036	0130	0130g	...	...
Udine d.	...	...	1315	...	...	...	...	1737	...	...	...	...	2115	...	...	...	...	2306	...	0157	0157	|	|	...	...
Tarvisio 🏛 d.	...	...	|	...	...	...	...	1852	...	...	...	...	|	...	...	...	...	0020	...	0319	0319	0352	0352	...	...
Villach Hbf a.	...	...	1450	1514	...	...	...	1913	1916	...	...	...	2250	...	...	...	...	0042	...	0341	0341	0415	0415	0616	...
Salzburg Hbf a.	...	...	|	|	...	...	...	|	2148	2215	...	...	|	...	...	...	...	0409	...	|	|	|	|	0848	0908
Linz Hbf a.	...	...	|	|	...	...	...	|	...	2342	...	...	|	...	...	...	...	0627	...	|	|	|	|	...	1027
Klagenfurt Hbf a.	...	...	1535	1537	...	...	...	1937	...	...	...	...	2335	...	...	...	...	|	...	0413	0413	0438	0438	...	...
Bruck an der Mur a.	...	...	...	1744	...	...	...	2144	...	...	...	...	...	...	...	...	...	|	...	0622	0622	0639	0639	...	...
Wien Südbahnhof a.	...	...	...	1935	...	...	...	2335	...	...	...	...	...	...	...	...	...	0827r	...	0838	0857	0842	0842	...	...

A – ALLEGRO JOHANN STRAUSS – [12] and ✕ [R] ♣ ⁄ Wien - Venezia and v.v.
C – Oct. 23, Dec. 4: 🛏 1, 2 cl. (T2), ━ 2 cl. and [2] [R] Wien - Firenze - Roma.
D – Oct. 25, Dec. 7: 🛏 1, 2 cl. (T2), ━ 2 cl. and [2] [R] Roma - Firenze - Wien.
G – ALLEGRO DON GIOVANNI – 🛏 1, 2 cl., ━ 2 cl. and [2] Wien (**744**) - Salzburg (**499**) - Villach (**237**) - Udine - Venezia.
H – ALLEGRO DON GIOVANNI – 🛏 1, 2 cl., ━ 2 cl. and [2] Venezia (**236**) - Udine - Villach (**498**) - Salzburg (**745**) - Wien.
P – ALLEGRO ROSSINI ⑤ June 19 - Sept. 25: 🛏 1, 2 cl. (T2), ━ 2 cl. and [2] Wien - Firenze - Roma.
Q – ALLEGRO ROSSINI ⑥ June 20 - Sept. 26: 🛏 1, 2 cl. (T2), ━ 2 cl. and [2] Roma - Firenze - Wien.
R – ALLEGRO TOSCA – 🛏 1, 2 cl., 🛏 1, 2 cl. (Excelsior), ━ 2 cl. and [2] Wien - Roma and v.v.
T – ①–⑤ (not Dec. 8).
V – 🛏 1, 2 cl. and ━ 2 cl. (4 berth) Wien (**235**) - Venezia Mestre (**9702**) - Milano.
W – 🛏 1, 2 cl. and ━ 2 cl. (4 berth) Milano (**9753**) - Venezia Mestre (**234**) - Wien.

e – Firenze **Campo di Marte**.

g – Arrive 2356.
h – Depart 0532.
j – Firenze **Rifredi**.
r – Wien **Westbahnhof**.
x – Venezia Piazzale Roma, see City Plans page **33**.

🚌 – ÖBB *IC Bus*. [R] Rail tickets valid. 1st and 2nd class. 🍷 in first class.
⁄ – Supplement payable.
♣ – Special "global fares" payable.

89 VENEZIA - LJUBLJANA - ZAGREB - BUDAPEST and BEOGRAD

train type		703			IC	IC	IC	EC	D	EN	EN
train number	703	205	247	520	501	284	201	30	315	241	241
notes	🍷			[R]	[R]🍷	✕				[R]	413
notes		MR	C	🍷		D	P	E	G	A♣	B♣
Venezia Santa Lucia d.	...	...	...	...	...	...	...	1548	...	2120	2120
Venezia Mestre d.	...	...	...	...	...	...	...	1600	...	2132	2132
Villach Hbf d.	...	...	...	...	...	...	...	1913	1927	|	|
Monfalcone d.	...	...	...	...	...	...	...	...	|	2259	2259
Villa Opicina 🏛 d.	...	...	...	...	...	...	...	...	|	2348	2348
Ljubljana d.	...	...	0840	...	...	...	...	...	2108	0200	0200
Dobova 🏛 d.	...	...	|	...	...	...	...	...	2250	0349	0349
Split d.	...	...	|	0738	...	...	...	...	|	|	|
Rijeka d.	0545	...	|	|	1145	...	...	...	|	|	|
Zagreb a.	0937	...	|	1310	1502	...	...	...	2334	0418	0418
Zagreb d.	...	0958	|	...	...	1545	1545	...	2355	0456	0603
Vinkovci a.	...	|	|	...	...	|	|	...	0305	|	0914
Šid 🏛 a.	...	|	|	...	...	|	|	...	0411	|	1019
Beograd a.	...	|	|	...	...	|	|	...	0621	|	1225
Koprivnica 🏛 d.	...	1123	|	...	...	1656	1656	...	...	0611	...
Kotoriba 🏛 d.	...	|	|	...	...	|	|	...	...	|	...
Hodoš 🏛 d.	...	|	1250	...	...	|	|	...	...	|	...
Zalaegerszeg a.	...	|	1334	...	...	|	|	...	...	|	...
Gyékényes a.	...	1137	|	...	...	1710	1710	...	...	0625	...
Nagykanizsa a.	...	1220	|	...	...	1745	1745	...	...	0717	...
Fonyód a.	...	1317	|	...	...	...	1907	...	...	0812	...
Siófok a.	...	1402	|	...	...	...	1952	...	...	0859	...
Székesfehérvár a.	...	1441	1641	...	...	...	2037	...	...	0941	...
Budapest Keleti a.	...	1609	1747x	...	...	...	2159	...	...	1059	...

train type	D	EC	IC		IC					EN	EN
train number	314	31	200	700	285	525	702	246	204	412	240
notes					✕	[R]	🍷			240	[R]
notes	G	E	P		D	🍷		C	MR	B♣	A♣
Budapest Keleti d.	...	...	0605	...	...	...	...	1203x	1405	...	1635
Székesfehérvár d.	...	...	0722	...	...	...	...	1317	1523	...	1749
Siófok d.	...	...	0808	...	...	...	...	|	1605	...	1830
Fonyód d.	...	...	0857	...	...	...	...	|	1650	...	1927
Nagykanizsa d.	...	...	0959	...	1116	...	...	|	1751	...	2032
Gyékényes d.	...	...	1032	...	1203	...	...	|	1830	...	2134
Zalaegerszeg d.	...	...	|	...	|	...	...	1618	|	...	|
Hodoš 🏛 a.	...	...	|	...	|	...	...	1725	|	...	|
Kotoriba 🏛 a.	...	...	|	...	|	...	...	|	|	...	|
Koprivnica 🏛 a.	...	...	1046	...	1217	...	...	|	1844	...	2144
Beograd d.	2150	...	|	...	|	...	...	|	|	1535	|
Šid 🏛 d.	0054	...	|	...	|	...	...	|	|	1828	|
Vinkovci d.	0147	...	|	...	|	...	...	|	|	1943	|
Zagreb a.	0453	...	1159	...	1333	...	...	|	2000	2245	2307
Zagreb d.	0500	...	...	1235	...	1522	1650	|	...	2335	2335
Rijeka a.	|	...	...	1628	...	|	2034	|	...	|	|
Split a.	|	...	...	...	...	2055	...	|	...	|	|
Dobova 🏛 a.	0529	...	...	...	...	...	...	|	...	0004	0004
Ljubljana a.	0722	...	...	...	...	...	...	2130	...	0212	0212
Villa Opicina 🏛 a.	|	...	...	...	...	...	...	...	...	0428	0428
Monfalcone a.	|	...	...	...	...	...	...	...	...	0542	0542
Villach Hbf a.	0906	1047	...	...	...	...	...	...	...	|	|
Venezia Mestre a.	...	1409	...	...	...	...	...	...	...	0704	0704
Venezia Santa Lucia a.	...	1420	...	...	...	...	...	...	...	0716	0716

A – VENEZIA – 🛏 1, 2 cl., ━ 2 cl., [2] and ✕ Venezia - Budapest and v.v. 🛏 1, 2 cl. and [2] Venezia - Budapest - Bucureşti and v.v. May 31 - Aug. 20: ━ 1, 2 cl. Venezia - Budapest - Bucureşti. May 29 - Aug. 18: ━ 1, 2 cl. Bucureşti - Budapest - Venezia.
B – ♣ [R] ━ 2 cl. Venezia - Zagreb - Beograd and v.v. ✕ Venezia - Zagreb and v.v. [12] and ✕ Zagreb - Beograd and v.v.
C – CITADELLA – [12] [R] Budapest - Hodoš - Murska Sobota - Ljubljana and v.v.
D – ZAGREB – [12] and ✕ Wien - Sopron 🏛 - Szombathely - Nagykanizsa - Gyékényes 🏛 - Zagreb and v.v. Table **92**.
E – ALLEGRO JOHANN STRAUSS – [12] and ✕ [R] ♣ ⁄ Venezia - Tarvisio 🏛 - Villach - Wien and v.v.
G – 🛏 1, 2 cl., ━ 2 cl. and [12] Villach - Tarvisio 🏛 - Ljubljana - Beograd and v.v.
M – Conveys on dates shown in Tables **95**/**97**: 🛏 1, 2 cl. Zagreb - Budapest - Kyïv / Moskva / St Peterburg and v.v.

P – KVARNER – [12] [R] Budapest - Zagreb and v.v.
R – MAESTRAL – [12] [R] Budapest - Zagreb and v.v.

x – Budapest **Déli.**

♣ – Special fares payable for journeys to or from Italy.
⁄ – Supplement payable.

BARCELONA, MARSEILLE and NICE - MILANO, ROMA and VENEZIA — 90

train type/number train number notes	4621 4620 [R] G	4620 4621 [R] C	EC 139 140 D	ESc 9729 [R]🍷 ↯	AV 9443 [R]🍴 ↯	ESc 9799 [R]🍴 ↯	TGV 5301 [R]🍷	TGV 5103 [R]🍷	◇	ICp 693 694 [R]↯	ESc 9745 793 🍷↯	AV 9451 [R]🍴 ↯	ICp 605 [R]🍴 ↯	ICp 539 [R] 🍷↯	4652 4653 [R] 🍷	EC 147 148 D	10601	ICN 761 [R] ↯		Hotel EN 272 371 11273 A	AV 9433 [R]🍴 ↯	ESc 9791 [R]🍴 ⑥⑦	ESc 9715 [R]🍴 ⑥⑦
Hendaye d.	...	1907	...	...	...	...	...	...	...	...	...	...	...	...	...	...	...	...	...		...	...	...
Bordeaux St Jean d.	2157	2157	...	...	...	...	...	...	...	...	...	...	...	...	0610	...	...	...	...		...	...	...
Toulouse d.	0013	0013	...	...	...	...	0654	...	...	...	...	...	...	...	0817	...	...	...	...	...	...	...	...
Barcelona França d.	|	|	...	...	...	...	|	...	...	...	...	...	...	...	|	...	...	...	...	1938	...	...	...
Girona d.	|	|	...	...	...	...	|	...	...	...	...	...	...	...	|	...	...	...	...	2057	...	...	...
Figueres d.	|	|	...	...	...	...	|	...	...	...	...	...	...	...	|	...	...	...	...	2125	...	...	...
Perpignan d.	|	|	...	...	...	...	|	...	...	...	...	...	...	...	|	...	...	...	...	2244	...	...	...
Montpellier d.	|	|	...	...	...	...	0915	...	...	...	...	...	...	...	1016	...	...	...	...	|	...	...	...
Marseille St Charles d.	0524	0524	...	...	...	...	1041	1059	...	...	...	...	...	...	1159	...	...	...	...	|	...	...	...
Toulon d.	0609	0609	...	...	...	...	...	1141	...	...	...	...	...	...	1241	...	...	...	...	|	...	...	...
Cannes d.	0730	0730	...	...	...	...	...	1258	...	...	...	...	...	...	1359	...	...	...	...	|	...	...	...
Nice d.	0758	0758	1002	...	...	...	...	1325	1356	...	...	...	...	...	1425	1759	...	...	...	|	...	...	...
Monaco-Monte Carlo d.	...	...	1018	...	...	...	...	...	1419	...	...	...	...	...	...	1817	...	...	...	|	...	...	...
Ventimiglia 🏛 d.	...	...	1058	...	...	...	...	...	1443	1458	...	...	...	...	...	1858	...	...	...	|	...	...	...
San Remo a.	...	...	1113	...	...	...	...	...	...	1513	...	...	...	...	...	1913	...	...	...	|	...	...	...
Genova Piazza Principe a.	...	...	1306	...	...	1452	...	...	...	1706	...	...	1748	1852	...	2106	...	2240	...	|	...	...	...
Torino Porta Susa a.	...	...	|	...	...	|	...	...	...	|	...	...	|	|	...	|	...	|	...	0812	...	...	...
Novara a.	...	...	|	...	...	|	...	...	...	|	...	...	|	|	...	|	...	|	...	0912	...	...	...
Milano Centrale a.	...	...	1450	1505	1530	|	...	...	...	1850	1905	1930	|	|	...	2250	0015	|	...	0959	1030	1035	1135
Verona a.	...	...	...	1627	|	|	...	...	...	...	2027	|	|	|	...	...	0223	|	...	...	|	1157	1257
Venezia Santa Lucia a.	...	...	...	1740	|	|	...	...	...	...	2150h	|	|	|	...	...	...	|	...	...	|	1310	1410
La Spezia a.	...	...	...	...	|	1604	...	...	...	...	...	|	1917	2004	...	...	...	2355	...	...	|	...	...
Pisa Centrale a.	...	...	...	...	|	1657	...	...	...	...	...	|	2012	2053	...	...	...	0047	...	...	|	...	...
Firenze **Rifredi** a.	...	...	...	...	1739v	|	...	...	...	...	...	2139v	...	2200v	...	...	...	|	...	...	1239v	...	...
Roma Termini a.	...	...	...	...	1929	2014	...	...	...	...	...	2329	...	...	...	...	...	|	...	...	1429	...	...
Napoli Centrale a.	...	...	...	...	2105	2236	...	...	...	...	...	...	...	...	...	...	...	0558y	...	...	1605	...	...

train type/number train number notes	E 806 F	ICp 654 [R] 🍷↯	ICp 691 692 [R]↯	◇	4764 4765 [R] 🍷		ICp 506 [R] 🍷↯	ESc 9708 [R]🍴 ①–⑤	CIS 52 [R]🍴 ↯	EC 143 144 D	TGV 6876 [R] 🍷		ICp 516 [R]🍴 ↯	ESc 9718 [R]🍴 ↯	AV 9434 [R]🍴 ↯	EC 159 160 D	4730 4731 [R] G	4730 4731 [R] C		AV 9442 [R]↯ 🍴	ESc 9738 [R]🍴 ↯	Hotel EN 372 274 11274 A	
Napoli Centrale d.	2108	...	...	...	...	...	...	...	...	...	...	...	0730	...	0854	...	...	...	...	1254	...		...
Roma Termini d.	0010o	...	...	...	...	...	...	...	...	...	...	...	0946	...	1030	...	...	...	...	1430	...		...
Firenze **Rifredi** d.	|	...	...	...	...	...	0751v	...	...	...	...	...	|	...	1219v	...	...	...	...	1619	...	...	...
Pisa Centrale d.	0328	0544	...	...	...	...	0902	...	...	...	...	...	1300	...	|	...	...	...	...	|	...	...	...
La Spezia d.	0416	0640	...	...	...	...	0953	...	...	...	...	...	1353	...	|	...	...	...	...	|	...	...	...
Venezia Santa Lucia d.	|	|	...	...	...	...	|	0750	0832q	...	...	...	|	1150	|	...	...	...	...	|	1650	...	...
Verona d.	|	|	...	...	...	...	|	0902	0932	...	...	...	|	1302	|	...	...	...	...	|	1802	...	...
Milano Centrale d.	|	|	0700	...	...	...	|	1025	1055	1110	...	...	|	1425	1429	1510	...	...	...	1829	1925	1940	...
Novara a.	|	|	|	...	...	...	|	...	...	|	...	...	|	...	...	|	...	...	...	...	...	2018	...
Torino Porta Susa d.	|	|	|	...	...	...	|	...	...	|	...	...	|	...	...	|	...	...	...	...	...	2118	...
Genova Piazza Principe d.	0601	0816	0855	...	...	...	1108	...	...	1255	...	...	1508	...	...	1655	...	...	...	...	...	|	...
San Remo d.	...	...	1050	...	...	...	...	...	...	1450	...	...	...	...	...	1850	...	...	...	...	...	|	...
Ventimiglia 🏛 a.	...	...	1107	1155	...	...	...	...	...	1507	...	...	...	...	...	1907	...	...	...	...	...	|	...
Monaco-Monte Carlo a.	...	...	...	1220	...	...	...	...	...	1542	...	...	...	...	...	1952	...	...	...	...	...	|	...
Nice a.	...	...	...	1242	1336	...	...	...	...	1559	1725	...	...	...	...	2012	2057z	2057z	...	...	...	|	...
Cannes a.	...	...	...	1322	1401	...	...	...	...	...	1754	...	...	...	...	...	2126z	2126z	...	...	...	|	...
Toulon a.	...	...	...	...	1519	...	...	...	...	...	1914	...	...	...	...	...	2246z	2246z	...	...	...	|	...
Marseille St Charles a.	...	...	...	...	1601	...	...	...	...	...	1958	...	...	...	...	...	2329z	2329z	...	...	...	|	...
Montpellier a.	...	...	...	...	1741	...	...	...	...	...	...	...	...	...	...	...	|	|	...	...	...	|	...
Perpignan a.	...	...	...	...	|	...	...	...	...	...	...	...	...	...	...	...	|	|	...	...	...	0614	...
Figueres a.	...	...	...	...	|	...	...	...	...	...	...	...	...	...	...	...	|	|	...	...	...	0744	...
Girona a.	...	...	...	...	|	...	...	...	...	...	...	...	...	...	...	...	|	|	...	...	...	0818	...
Barcelona França a.	...	...	...	...	|	...	...	...	...	...	...	...	...	...	...	...	|	|	...	...	...	0943	...
Toulouse a.	...	...	...	...	1945	...	...	...	...	...	...	...	...	...	...	...	0514	0514	...	...	...	...	...
Bordeaux St Jean a.	...	...	...	...	2150	...	...	...	...	...	...	...	...	...	...	...	0810	0810	...	...	...	...	...
Irún a.	...	...	...	...	...	...	...	...	...	...	...	...	...	...	...	...	...	1057	...	...	...	...	...

A – SALVADOR DALÍ *Train-hotel Elipsos* ②④⑦ from Barcelona; ①③⑤ from Milano: 🛏 1, 2 cl., 🛏 1, 2 cl. (T4), [1] (reclining) and 🍴 Barcelona - Milano and v.v. [R] special fares apply.
C – ⑤⑦ (daily June 19 - Sept. 6 and Oct. 23 - Nov. 4): *CORAIL LUNÉA* – couchette 1, 2 cl. and [2] (reclining) Hendaye - Nice and Nice - Irún.
D – [12] and 🍷 [R] ↯ Nice - Milano and v.v.
F – 🛏 1, 2 cl., 🛏 1, 2 cl. (Excelsior), couchette 2 cl. (4 berth) and [2] Napoli - Genova - Torino.
G – *CORAIL LUNÉA* – couchette 1, 2 cl. and [2] (reclining) Bordeaux - Nice and v.v.
h – 2140 on ⑥⑦.
o – Roma **Ostiense**.
q – Venezia **Mestre**.
t – Roma **Tiburtina**.
v – Firenze **SMN**.
y – Napoli **Campi Flegrei**.
z – On June 8–11, 15–18, 22–25, Sept. 28 - Oct. 1, Nov. 23–26, Nov. 30 - Dec. 3 departs Nice 2011 and runs 50 minutes earlier.
↯ – Supplement payable.
◇ – Stopping train.

WIEN - LJUBLJANA and ZAGREB — 91

train type train number notes	IC 251 🍷	ICS 13 [R]	EC 253 🍴	2803	2260	IC 285 🍴 B	EC 151 483 A		EC 255 🍴	3403	2268	IC 257 🍷	ICS 19 [R]	IC 311	IC 509	IC 259 🍷	IC 1615 ①–⑥ m	EC 159 🍴 C↯	EC 159 825 S↯	ICS 23 [R]	1459 K	1459 481 M	
Wien Süd ♣ d.	...	...	0556	...	...	0726	0756	...	0956	...	...	1156	...	...	...	1356	...	1556	1556	...	2156	2156	...
Graz Hbf d.	0634	...	0836	...	...	|	1036	...	1236	...	...	1436	...	...	...	1636	...	1836	1836	...	0036	0036	...
Spielfeld-Straß 🏛 d.	0721	...	0921	...	...	|	1121	...	1321	...	...	1521	...	...	...	1721	...	1921	1921	...	0123	0123	...
Maribor a.	0738	0817	0938	1015	...	|	1138	...	1338	1350	...	1538	1545	...	...	1738	1800	1938	1938	1945	0142	0142	...
Pragersko a.	...	0830	...	1034	...	|	1201	...	...	1417	...	...	1558	...	...	...	1816	2010	2010	1958	|	|	...
Zidani Most a.	...	0924	...	1147	1155	|	1306	...	...	1539	1600	...	1653	1731	...	...	1925	|	|	2053	|	|	...
Dobova 🏛 a.	...	|	...	1242	|	|	|	...	...	...	|	...	|	1811	...	...	|	2151	2151	|	|	|	...
Zagreb a.	...	|	...	...	|	1333	|	...	...	...	|	...	|	1856	...	...	|	2234	2234	|	|	|	...
Ljubljana a.	...	1009	...	...	1303	...	1406	...	...	...	1703	...	1738	...	1810	...	2025	...	|	2138	0351	0351	...
Koper a.	...	...	...	...	...	...	|	...	...	...	...	...	...	...	2032	...	...	...	|	...	0632	|	...
Rijeka a.	...	...	...	...	...	...	1725	...	...	...	...	...	...	...	...	...	...	...	|	...	...	0851	...
Split a.	...	...	...	...	...	...	...	...	...	...	...	...	...	...	...	...	...	...	0655	...	...	...	...

train type/number train number notes	IC 250 🍷	ICS 12 [R]	IC 252 🍷	IC 508	ICS 14 [R]	EC 158 🍴 C↯	EC 824 158 T↯	2259 ①–⑤ m	2912 ①–⑤ m	EC 254 🍴	ICS 18 [R]	EC 256 🍴		IC 506	5000	IC 258 🍷	IC 284 🍴 B	482 EC 150 A	IC 502	IC 350	1458 L	480 1458 N	
Split d.	...	...	...	...	...	...	2210	...	...	...	...	...	...	...	...	...	...	...	...	...	...	...	...
Rijeka d.	...	...	...	...	...	...	|	...	...	...	...	...	...	...	...	...	...	1257	...	...	...	2045	...
Koper d.	...	...	...	0525	...	...	|	...	...	...	...	...	...	...	...	...	...	|	1445	...	2215	|	...
Ljubljana d.	...	0545	...	0747	0805	...	|	0845	...	...	1213	...	...	1245	...	...	...	1600	1725	...	0050	0050	...
Zagreb d.	...	|	...	...	|	0725	0725	|	...	...	|	...	...	|	...	...	1545	|	|	...	|	|	...
Dobova 🏛 d.	...	|	...	...	|	0813	0813	|	...	...	|	...	...	|	...	...	|	|	|	...	|	|	...
Zidani Most d.	...	0630	...	...	0850	|	|	0952	1000	...	1259	...	...	1341	1400	...	|	1654	1824	...	|	|	...
Pragersko d.	...	0722	...	...	0941	0959	0959	...	1112	...	1354	...	...	...	1513	...	|	1803	1935	...	|	|	...
Maribor d.	0620	0736	0822	...	0953	1022	1022	...	1133	1222	1406	1422	...	...	1534	1622	|	1821	1952	2022	0305	0305	...
Spielfeld-Straß 🏛 a.	0637	...	0839	...	...	1039	1039	...	...	1239	...	1439	...	...	...	1639	|	1839	...	2039	0339	0339	...
Graz Hbf a.	0723	...	0923	...	...	1123	1123	...	...	1323	...	1523	...	...	...	1723	|	1923	...	2123	0423	0423	...
Wien Süd ♣ a.	1005	...	1205	...	...	1405	1405	...	...	1605	...	1805	...	...	...	2005	2132	2205	...	0005	0717	0717	...

A – EMONA – [12] and 🍴 Wien - Ljubljana and v.v. [2] Wien - Ljubljana - Rijeka and v.v. [12] Ljubljana - Rijeka and v.v.
B – ZAGREB – [12] and 🍴 Wien - Sopron 🏛 - Szombathely - Nagykanizsa - Gyékényes 🏛 - Zagreb and v.v. Table **92**.
C – CROATIA – [12] and 🍴 Wien - Zagreb and v.v.
K – ISTRIA – ⑤ June 5 - Aug. 28: couchette 2 cl. and [2] Wien - Koper.
L – ISTRIA – ⑥ June 6 - Aug. 29: couchette 2 cl. and [2] Koper - Wien.
M – ISTRIA – ⑤ June 5 - Aug. 28: couchette 2 cl. and [2] Wien - Rijeka.
N – ISTRIA – ⑥ June 6 - Aug. 29: couchette 2 cl. and [2] Rijeka - Wien.
S – ⑤ May 1 - Sept. 25: couchette 2 cl. Wien - Split.
T – ⑥ May 2 - Sept. 26: couchette 2 cl. Split - Wien.
m – Does not run on Slovenian Holidays.
↯ – Supplement payable.
♣ – Full name is Wien Südbahnhof.

92 BUDAPEST / ZAGREB - SARAJEVO

train number	397	IC 259		399	391
notes	G	A		H	
Zagreb d.	0855	...	...	2125	...
Sunja d.	1016	...	...	2246	...
Volinja 🏛 d.	1102	...	...	2332	...
Dobrljin 🏛 d.	1119	...	...	2355	...
Novi Grad § d.	1144	...	...	0011	...
Banja Luka d.	1315	...	...	0143	...
Budapest Keleti d.	|	0945	...	|	...
Dombóvár d.	|	1151	...	|	...
Pécs d.	|	1300	...	|	...
Magyarbóly 🏛 d.	|	1402	...	|	...
Beli Manastir 🏛 d.	|	1430	...	|	...
Osijek d.	|	1500	...	|	...
Slavonski Šamac 🏛 d.	|	1622	...	|	...
Šamac 🏛 d.	|	1648	...	|	...
Doboj d.	1512	1814	...	0345	...
Zenica d.	1647	1951	...	0512	...
Sarajevo a.	1805	2109	...	0639	...
Sarajevo d.	1818	...	...	...	0655
Mostar d.	2043	...	...	...	0906
Ploče d.	2216	...	...	...	1051

train number	IC 258	396	390	398	
notes	A	G		H	
Ploče d.	...	0605	1700	...	...
Mostar d.	...	0738	1840	...	...
Sarajevo a.	...	1002	2050	...	...
Sarajevo d.	0700	1027	...	2120	...
Zenica d.	0820	1147	...	2240	...
Doboj d.	1005	1329	...	0029	...
Šamac 🏛 d.	1131	|	...	|	...
Slavonski Šamac 🏛 d.	1157	|	...	|	...
Osijek d.	1304	|	...	|	...
Beli Manastir 🏛 d.	1347	|	...	|	...
Magyarbóly 🏛 a.	1400	|	...	|	...
Pécs a.	1502	|	...	|	...
Dombóvár a.	1611	|	...	|	...
Budapest Keleti a.	1814	|	...	|	...
Banja Luka d.	...	1529	...	0221	...
Novi Grad § d.	...	1657	...	0348	...
Dobrljin 🏛 d.	...	1728	...	0420	...
Volinja 🏛 d.	...	1758	...	0452	...
Sunja d.	...	1825	...	0522	...
Zagreb a.	...	1945	...	0642	...

PRAHA / WIEN - ZAGREB - SPLIT

train number	475 / 1475	IC 285
notes	C	E
Praha hlavní d.	0918	...
Pardubice d.	1036	...
Brno Hlavní d.	1216	...
Břeclav d.	1255	...
Kúty 🏛 d.	1310	...
Bratislava Hlavná d.	1447	...
Rajka 🏛 a.	1528	...
Győr a.	|	...
Wien Südbahnhof d.	|	0726
Sopron 🏛 d.	|	0835
Szombathely a.	1719	0933
Nagykanizsa a.	1900	1114
Gyékényes 🏛 a.	1926	1143
Koprivnica 🏛 a.	1954	1217
Zagreb a.	2123	1333
Split a.	0554	...

train number	474 / 1474	IC 284
notes	D	E
Split d.	2100	...
Zagreb d.	0640	1545
Koprivnica 🏛 d.	0812	1656
Gyékényes 🏛 d.	0851	1722
Nagykanizsa d.	0922	1756
Szombathely d.	1056	1935
Sopron 🏛 a.	|	2031
Wien Südbahnhof a.	|	2132
Győr d.	|	...
Rajka 🏛 d.	1301	...
Bratislava Hlavná a.	1341	...
Kúty 🏛 a.	1438	...
Břeclav a.	1454	...
Brno Hlavní a.	1539	...
Pardubice a.	1719	...
Praha hlavní a.	1840	...

A – DRAVA – (12) Budapest - Pécs - Magyarbóly - Sarajevo and v.v. (12) and ✕ Budapest - Pécs and v.v.
C – JADRAN June 19 - Sept. 4: 🛏 2 cl. ▬ 2 cl. and (2) Praha - Split.
D – JADRAN June 20 - Sept. 5: 🛏 2 cl., ▬ 2 cl. and (2) Split - Praha.
E – ZAGREB – (12) and ✕ Wien - Zagreb and v.v.
G – (12) Zagreb - Sarajevo - Ploče and v.v.
H – ▬ 2 cl. and (2) Zagreb - Sarajevo and v.v.
§ – Formerly Bosanski Novi.

93 BERLIN - WARSZAWA - VILNIUS

train number	🚌 99928		449	81200 / 81201	91001 / 910	194
notes	D R		A	B		2
Berlin Lichtenberg d.	...	...	2104	...	...	...
Warszawa Centralna a.	...	...	0028k	0056k	...	...
Warszawa Centralna d.	2300	...	...	0605	0725	...
Warszawa Wschodnia d.	|	...	...	0617	0734	...
Białystok d.	0200	...	...	...	1010	...
Suwałki d.	|	...	...	...	1244	...
Šeštokai 🏛 § a.	|	...	...	...	1448	1503
Kaunas a.	0720	...	...	...	...	*1709*x
Vilnius a.	0900	...	...	...	...	1756

train number	193 / 2	91002 / 910	448		🚌 99927	
notes			A		E R	
Vilnius d.	1140	...	...	...	2200	...
Kaunas d.	*1235*z	...	...	...	2330	...
Šeštokai 🏛 § d.	1443	1508	...	...	|	...
Suwałki a.	...	1514	...	...	|	...
Białystok a.	...	1745	...	...	0220	...
Warszawa Wschodnia a.	...	2021	2118	...	|	...
Warszawa Centralna a.	...	2030	|	...	0500	...
Warszawa Centralna d.	...	...	2130	...	...	...
Berlin Lichtenberg a.	...	...	0806	...	...	...

A – 🛏 1, 2 cl., ▬ 2 cl. and (2) (reclining) Berlin - Kostrzyn 🏛 - Krzyż - Warszawa.
B – (12) Szczecin - Krzyż - Poznań - Warszawa - Terespol.
D – ①③⑤ (daily June 13 - Sept. 12) 🚌 run by PKP InterCity. R.
E – ②④⑥ (daily June 14 - Sept. 13) 🚌 run by PKP InterCity. R.
k – Krzyż. Change trains.
x – Change at Marijampole (arrive 1539; depart 1558).
z – Change at Marijampole (arrive 1345; depart 1404).
§ – 🏛 at Trakiszki / Mockava.

94 MOSKVA / St PETERBURG - WARSZAWA

train number	19 / 442	13 / 442	19/13 / 103	25 / 103	103 / 11008	9 / 11002		11 / 446	11 / 11014
notes	G	N	A	S	T	R		P	Q
Moskva Belorusskaya d.	...	0800	...	1027	...	1650	...	2109	2109
Smolensk Tsentralny 🏛 § d.	...	1220	...	1620	...	2132	...	0231	0231
St Peterburg Vitebski d.	2355	|	2355	|	...	|	...	|	|
Orsha Tsentralnaya § d.	1250j	1250	1250j	1707	...	2153	...	0311	0311
Minsk d.	1529	1529	1529	2040	2040	0019	...	0619	0619
Brest 🏛 d.	2115	2115	0240	0240	0240	0532	...	1250	1250
Terespol a.	2033	2033	0158	0158	0158	0450	...	1208	1208
Warszawa Wschodnia a.	2351	2351	0549	0549	0549	0830	...	1529	1529
Warszawa Centralna a.	0107	0107	0600	0600	0600	0840	...	1750	...

train number	447 / 12	12 / 11013	10 / 11001		11011 / 104	104 / 132	104 / 14 / 20	443 / 14	443 / 20
notes	P	Q	R		T	S	B	M	H
Warszawa Centralna d.	1045	...	1530	...	2050	2050	2050	2315	2315
Warszawa Wschodnia d.	1250	1250	1540	...	2100	2100	2100	2342	2342
Terespol d.	1555	1555	1922	...	0036	0036	0036	0330	0330
Brest 🏛 a.	1741	1741	2058	...	0222	0222	0222	0516	0516
Minsk a.	2336	2336	0158	...	0804	0837	1046	1046	1046
Orsha Tsentralnaya § a.	0227	0227	0424	...	...	1136	1332c	1332	1332c
St Peterburg Vitebski a.	|	|	|	...	...	|	0615	|	0615
Smolensk Tsentralny 🏛 § a.	0456	0456	0648	...	...	1408	...	1601	...
Moskva Belorusskaya a.	1059	1059	1145	...	...	1954	...	2035	...

A – ①③⑤ Dec. 12 - May 29; ①②③⑤⑦ May 31 - Oct. 16; ①③⑤ Oct. 19 - Dec. 12: 🛏 2 cl. St Peterburg (**19**) - Orsha (**13**) - Brest (**103**) - Warszawa (journey 2 nights).
B – ③⑤⑦ Dec. 12 - May 31; ②③④⑤⑦ June 2 - Oct. 18; ③⑤⑦ Oct. 21 - Dec. 12: 🛏 2 cl. Warszawa (**104**) - Brest (**14**) - Orsha (**20**) - St Peterburg (journey 2 nights).
G – ①③⑤ Dec. 12 - May 29; ①②③⑤⑦ May 31 - Oct. 16; ①③⑤ Oct. 19 - Dec. 12: 🛏 2 cl. St Peterburg (**19**) - Orsha (**13**) - Terespol (**442**) - Warszawa - Berlin (journey 2 nights).
H – ③⑤⑦ Dec. 12 - May 31; ②③④⑤⑦ June 2 - Oct. 18; ③⑤⑦ Oct. 21 - Dec. 12: 🛏 2 cl. Berlin (**443**) - Warszawa - Brest 🏛 (**14**) - Orsha (**20**) - St Peterburg (journey 2 nights).
M – MOSKVA EXPRESS – ③⑤⑦ Dec. 12 - May 31; ②③④⑤⑦ June 2 - Oct. 18; ③⑤⑦ Oct. 21 - Dec. 12: 🛏 1 cl. *Lux* and 🛏 1, 2 cl. Berlin (**443**) - Warszawa - Brest 🏛 (**14**) - Moskva.
N – MOSKVA EXPRESS – ②④⑥ Dec. 12 - May 30; ①②③④⑥ June 1 - Oct. 17; ②④⑥ Oct. 21 - Dec. 12: 🛏 1 cl. *Lux* and 🛏 1, 2 cl. Moskva (**13**) - Terespol (**442**) - Warszawa - Berlin.
P – JAN KIEPURA – 🛏 1, 2 cl. Moskva - Warszawa - Köln - Amsterdam and v.v. (journey 2 nights; for timings of Basel, Amsterdam and München cars see Table **24**).
Q – OST–WEST – 🛏 1, 2 cl. Warszawa - Moskva and v.v.
R – POLONEZ – 🛏 1, 2 cl., 🛏 1, 2 cl. (Lux) and 🍸 Warszawa - Moskva and v.v. ✕ Brest - Moskva and v.v.
S – 🛏 1, 2 cl. Warszawa - Moskva and v.v.
T – 🛏 1, 2 cl. Minsk - Warszawa and v.v.
c – Depart 1637.
j – Arrive 1047.
§ – 🏛: Osinovka (BY) / Krasnoye (RU).

95 MOSKVA / St PETERBURG - WIEN, BRATISLAVA, BUDAPEST and PRAHA

train number	208	208	208	208	208	208	
notes	B	V	J	C	F	P	
Moskva Belorusskaya d.	...	2344	2344	2344	2344	...	...
Smolensk Tsentralny 🏛 § d.	...	0505	0505	0505	0505	...	...
St Peterburg Vitebski d.	1500	|	|	|	|	1500	...
Orsha Tsentralnaya § d.	0127	0542	0542	0542	0542	0127	...
Minsk d.	0408	0825	0825	0825	0825	0408	...
Brest 🏛 d.	1440x	1440z	1440z	1440z	1440z	1440x	...
Terespol a.	1358	1358	1358	1358	1358	1358	...
Łuków a.	1606	1606	1606	1606	1606	1606	...
Katowice a.	2225	2225	2225	2205	2205	2205	...
Bohumín 🏛 a.	0017	0017	0017	0017	0017	0017	...
Ostrava Hlavní a.	0051	0051	0051	0224	0224	0224	...
Břeclav a.	|	|	|	0412	0412	0412	...
Wien Westbahnhof a.	|	|	|	0630	|	|	...
Bratislava Hlavná a.	|	|	|	...	0540	0540	...
Budapest Keleti a.	|	|	|	...	0832	0832	...
Zagreb a.	|	|	|	...	...	2000	...
Olomouc a.	0200	0200	0200	...	...	...	...
Pardubice a.	0334	0334	0334	...	...	...	...
Praha hlavní a.	0507	0507	0507e	...	...	...	...
Karlovy Vary a.	...	...	1047	...	...	...	...
Cheb a.	...	...	1142	...	...	...	...

train number	209	209	209	209	209	209	
notes	Q	G	H	K	W	D	
Cheb d.	...	...	...	1614	...	...	...
Karlovy Vary d.	...	...	...	1706	...	...	...
Praha hlavní d.	...	...	...	2300f	2300	2300	...
Pardubice d.	...	...	...	0019	0019	0019	...
Olomouc d.	...	...	...	0153	0153	0153	...
Zagreb d.	0958	...	...	|	|	|	...
Budapest Keleti d.	1958	1958	...	|	|	|	...
Bratislava Hlavná d.	2255	2255	...	|	|	|	...
Wien Westbahnhof d.	|	|	2212	|	|	|	...
Břeclav d.	0018	0018	0018	|	|	|	...
Ostrava Hlavní d.	0208	0208	0208	0301	0301	0301	...
Bohumín 🏛 d.	0328	0328	0328	0328	0328	0328	...
Katowice d.	0520	0520	0520	0520	0520	0520	...
Łuków d.	1100	1100	1100	1100	1100	1100	...
Terespol d.	1318	1318	1318	1318	1318	1318	...
Brest 🏛 a.	1504c	1504c	1504c	1504c	1504c	1504c	...
Minsk a.	2102	2102	2102	2102	2102	2102	...
Orsha Tsentralnaya § a.	2344	2344	2344	2344	2344	2344	...
St Peterburg Vitebski a.	1243	|	|	|	|	1243	...
Smolensk Tsentralny 🏛 § a.	...	0214	0214	0214	0214	...	...
Moskva Belorusskaya a.	...	0805	0805	0805	0805	...	...

B – ③④ Dec. 12 - June 4; ①③④⑤⑥⑦ June 6 - Sept. 21; ③④ Sept. 23 - Dec. 12: 🛏 1, 2 cl. St Peterburg (**49**) - Brest (**208**) - Praha (journey 2 nights).
C – 🛏 1, 2 cl. Moskva (**21**) - Terespol (**208**) - Katowice - Bohumín (**203**) - Wien (journey 2 nights).
D – ⑤⑥ Dec. 12 - June 6; ①②③⑤⑥⑦ June 8 - Sept. 23; ⑤⑥ Sept. 25 - Dec. 12: 🛏 1, 2 cl. Praha (**209**) - Orsha (**61/62**) - St Peterburg (journey 2 nights).
F – 🛏 1, 2 cl. Moskva (**21**) - Terespol (**208**) - Katowice - Bohumín (**203**) - Břeclav (**477**) - Bratislava - Budapest (journey 2 nights).
G – 🛏 1, 2 cl. Budapest (**476**) - Bratislava - Břeclav (**202**) - Bohumín (**209**) - Katowice - Brest (**22**) - Moskva (journey 2 nights).
H – 🛏 1, 2 cl. Wien (**202**) - Bohumín (**209**) - Katowice - Brest (**22**) - Moskva (journey 2 nights).
J – 🛏 1, 2 cl. Moskva (**21**) - Terespol (**14012**) - Katowice - Bohumín (**208**) - Praha (**606**) - Cheb (journey 2 nights). ✕ Moskva - Brest.
K – 🛏 1, 2 cl. Cheb (**607**) - Praha (**209**) - Bohumín (**41012**) - Katowice - Brest (**22**) - Moskva (journey 2 nights). ✕ Brest - Moskva.
V – VLTAVA – 🛏 1, 2 cl. Moskva (**21**) - Terespol (**14012**) - Katowice - Bohumín (**208**) - Praha (journey 2 nights). ✕ Moskva - Brest.
W – VLTAVA – 🛏 1, 2 cl. Praha (**209**) - Bohumín (**41012**) - Katowice - Brest (**22**) - Moskva (journey 2 nights). ✕ Brest - Moskva.
P – ⑦ 🛏 1, 2 cl. St Peterburg (**49**) - Brest (**208**) - Katowice - Bohumín (**203**) - Břeclav (**477**) - Bratislava - Budapest (**204**) - Zagreb (journey 2 nights).
Q – ③ 🛏 1, 2 cl. Zagreb (**205**) - Budapest (**476**) - Bratislava - Břeclav (**202**) - Bohumín (**209**) - Katowice - Orsha (**61/62**) - St Peterburg (journey 2 nights).

c – Depart 1707.
e – Depart 0729.
f – Arrive 2030.
x – Arrive 0824.
z – Arrive 1226.
§ – 🏛: Osinovka (BY) / Krasnoye (RU).

PRAHA, WIEN and WROCŁAW - KYÏV — 96

train number	EC	609	609			201	7310	33011
train number	121	16	16	16	201	107	52	35
notes	✕	A	X		C	T	P	J❖
Praha hlavní d.	1109	...	...	...	2109	2109	...	...
Pardubice d.	1223	...	...	...	2225	2225	...	...
Česká Třebová d.	1306	...	...	...	2305	2305	...	...
Olomouc d.	1354	...	...	...	0003	0003	...	...
Wien Südbahnhof d.	|	1228	1228	...	|	|	...	...
Bratislava Hlavná d.	|	1410	1410	...	|	|	...	...
Žilina d.	1631	1705	1705	...	|	|	...	...
Košice a.	1921	2017	2017	...	|	|	...	...
Košice d.	...	2032	2032	...	|	|	...	...
Čierna nad Tisou 🏛 a.	...	2215	2215	...	|	|	...	...
Chop 🏛 a.	...	0012	0012	...	|	|	...	...
Bohumín 🏛 d.	...	|	|	...	0307	0307	...	...
Zebrzydowice 🏛 d.	...	|	|	...	0329	0329	...	...
Wrocław Główny d.	...	|	|	...	|	|	0835	...
Katowice d.	...	|	|	...	|	|	1130	...
Kraków Główny d.	...	|	|	...	1340e	1340e	1340	2115
Przemyśl a.	...	|	|	...	1736	1736	1736	0050
Przemysl d.	...	|	|	...	1924	1924	1924	0120
Mostiska II ◐ d.	...	|	|	...	2222	2222	2222	0327
Lviv a.	...	1031	1031	1057	2346	2346	2346	0447
Ternopil a.	...	1305	...	1305	0221	|	0221	0725
Kozyatyn a.	...	1759	...	1759	0805	|	0805	1218
Kyïv a.	...	2001	...	2000	1018	|	1018	1438
Odesa a.	...	...	...	...	...	1331	...	...

train number	51		108	7		7		33012
train number	3710	200	200	422	7	422	442	36
notes	P	D	U	B		Y	E	K❖
Odesa d.	...	...	1813	...	...	...	...	...
Kyïv d.	2042	2042	|	2358	2358	...	...	2241
Kozyatyn d.	2308	2308	|	0221	0221	...	...	0050
Ternopil d.	0434	0434	|	0744	0744	...	...	0723
Lviv d.	0718	0718	0718	1026	0959	1026	...	0835
Mostiska II ◐ d.	0937	0937	0937	|	...	|	...	1028
Przemyśl a.	0926	0926	0926	|	...	|	...	1008
Przemyśl d.	1130	1130	1130	|	...	|	...	1034
Kraków Główny a.	1538	1538c	1538c	|	...	|	...	1410
Katowice a.	1729	|	|	|	...	|	...	...
Wrocław Główny a.	2025	|	|	|	...	|	...	...
Zebrzydowice 🏛 a.	...	0047	0047	|	...	|	...	...
Bohumín 🏛 a.	...	0109	0109	|	...	|	...	...
Chop 🏛 d.	...	|	|	1825	...	1825	...	...
Čierna nad Tisou 🏛 d.	...	|	|	1952	...	1952	...	...
Košice a.	...	|	|	2130	...	2130	...	...
Košice d.	...	|	|	2202	...	2202	2202	...
Žilina a.	...	|	|	0119	...	0119	0119	...
Bratislava Hlavná a.	...	|	|	0508	...	0508	|	...
Wien Südbahnhof a.	...	|	|	0658	...	0658	|	...
Olomouc a.	...	0354	0354	...	...	...	0534	...
Česká Třebová a.	...	0447	0447	...	...	...	0628	...
Pardubice a.	...	0531	0531	...	...	...	0708	...
Praha hlavní a.	...	0654	0654	...	...	...	0830	...

A – ①②④⑤⑦: 🛏 1, 2 cl. Wien (**2522**) - Bratislava (**609**) - Košice (**8815**) - Čierna nad Tisou (**8860**) - Chop (**16**) - Kyïv.
B – ②③⑤⑥⑦: 🛏 1, 2 cl. Kyïv (**7**) - Chop (**8865**) - Čierna nad Tisou (**8814**) - Košice (**422**) - Žilina (**706**) - Bratislava (**2507**) - Wien (journey 2 nights).
C – 🛏 1, 2 cl. Praha (**201**) - Kraków (**7311**) - Przemyśl (**52**) - Kyïv (journey 2 nights). 🛏 1, 2 cl., ▬ 2 cl. and [12] Praha - Kraków.
D – 🛏 1, 2 cl. Kyïv (**51**) - Przemyśl (**3710**) - Kraków (**200**) - Praha (journey 2 nights). 🛏 1, 2 cl., ▬ 2 cl. and [12] Kraków - Praha.
E – ŠÍRAVA – 🛏 1, 2 cl., ▬ 2 cl. and [12] Humenné - Košice - Praha.
J – ❖ ③⑤⑦ GEORGIJ KIRPA: 🛏 2 cl. Kraków - Kyïv.
K – ❖ ②④⑥ GEORGIJ KIRPA: 🛏 2 cl. Kyïv - Kraków.
P – *TLK* 🛏 2 cl. Wrocław - Kraków - Przemyśl - Lviv - Kyïv and v.v.
T – ②④⑤⑦: 🛏 1, 2 cl. Praha - Odesa (journey 2 nights).
U – ②③⑤⑦: 🛏 1, 2 cl. Odesa - Praha (journey 2 nights).
X – ③⑥: 🛏 1, 2 cl. Wien - Lviv.
Y – ②⑤: 🛏 1, 2 cl. Lviv - Wien.

c – Depart 2215.
e – Arrive 0633.

❖ – Subject to confirmation.
◐ – 🏛 at Medyka / Mostiska **II** (Table **1056**).

MOSKVA - BUDAPEST, VENEZIA, BEOGRAD and ATHÍNAI — 97

train type/number	15	204	*EN* 240	335	*IC*	15	15	15	
notes		Ⓡ	Ⓡ ⁄		55				
notes	A		C	M	✕ ⁄	K	Y	Q	
Moskva Kiyevskaya d.	2213	...	...	...	...	2213	...	2213	...
Minsk d.	|	...	...	...	...	|	...	|	...
Kyïv d.	1110	...	...	...	...	1110	1110	1110	...
Lviv d.	2120	...	...	...	...	2120	2120	2120	...
Chop 🏛 d.	0500	...	...	...	...	0500	0500	0500	...
Debrecen a.	0825	...	...	...	...	0825	0825	0825	...
Szolnok a.	0954	...	...	...	...	0954	0954	0954	...
Budapest Keleti a.	1117	...	...	...	...	1117	1117	1117	...
Budapest Keleti d.	1305	1405	1635	...	...	1405	1405	1635	...
Siófok a.	|	1602	1828	...	...	1602	1602	1828	...
Zagreb a.	|	2000	2307	...	...	2000	2000	2307	...
Ljubljana a.	|	...	0212	...	...	...	...	0212	...
Trieste Centrale a.	|	...	|	...	...	...	...	|	...
Venezia Santa Lucia a.	|	...	0716	...	...	...	...	0716	...
Subotica 🏛 a.	1626	...	...	...	...	...	...	...	...
Novi Sad a.	1859	...	...	...	...	...	...	...	...
Beograd a.	2030	...	...	2200	...	...	...	...	...
Niš a.	...	...	...	0152	...	...	...	...	...
Skopje ⊖ a.	...	...	...	0650	...	...	...	...	...
Thessaloníki ⊡ a.	...	...	...	1231	1454	...	...	...	...
Athína Lárisa a.	...	...	...	...	1949	...	...	...	...

train type/number	*IC*	334	*EN* 241	703	16		16	16	16
notes	52		Ⓡ ⁄	205					
notes	✕ ⁄	M	C	Ⓡ	B		R	L	Z
Athína Lárisa d.	1051	...	...	...	...	...	...	...	...
Thessaloníki ⊡ d.	1550	1705	...	...	...	...	...	...	...
Skopje ⊖ d.	...	2040	...	...	...	...	...	...	...
Niš d.	...	0148	...	...	...	...	...	...	...
Beograd d.	...	0544	...	...	0730	...	...	...	...
Novi Sad d.	...	...	...	...	0904	...	...	...	...
Subotica 🏛 d.	...	...	...	...	1136	...	...	...	...
Venezia Santa Lucia d.	...	...	2120	...	|	...	2120	...	...
Trieste Centrale d.	...	...	|	...	|	...	|	...	...
Ljubljana d.	...	...	0200	...	|	...	0200	...	...
Zagreb d.	...	...	0456	0958	|	...	0456	0958	0958
Siófok d.	...	...	0901	1403	|	...	0901	1403	1403
Budapest Keleti a.	...	...	1059	1609	1453	...	1059	1609	1609
Budapest Keleti d.	...	...	...	...	1843	...	1843	1843	1843
Szolnok d.	...	...	...	...	2003	...	2003	2003	2003
Debrecen d.	...	...	...	...	2129	...	2129	2129	2129
Chop 🏛 a.	...	...	...	...	0113	...	0113	0113	0113
Lviv a.	...	...	...	...	1031	...	1031	1031	1031
Kyïv a.	...	...	...	...	2001	...	2001	2001	2001
Minsk a.	...	...	...	...	|	...	|	|	...
Moskva Kiyevskaya a.	...	...	...	...	0956	...	0956	0956	...

A – TISZA – 🛏 2 cl. Moskva (**15**) - Budapest (**345**) - Beograd (journey 2 nights).
B – TISZA – 🛏 2 cl. Beograd (**344**) - Budapest (**16**) - Moskva (journey 2 nights).
C – VENZIA – 🛏 1, 2 cl., ▬ 2 cl., [2] and ✕ Budapest - Ljubljana - Venezia and v.v.
K – ②④⑥: 🛏 1, 2 cl. Moskva (**15**) - Kyïv - Budapest (**204**) - Zagreb (journey 2 nights).
L – ②⑤⑦: 🛏 1, 2 cl. Zagreb (**205**) - Budapest (**16**) - Kyïv - Moskva (journey 2 nights).
M – HELLAS EXPRESS – 🛏 1, 2 cl., ▬ 2 cl. and [12] Beograd - Thessaloníki and v.v. 🛏 1, 2 cl., ▬ 2 cl. and [2] Beograd - Skopje and v.v.
Q – ⑦: 🛏 1, 2 cl. Moskva (**15**) - Budapest (**240**) - Venezia (journey 3 nights).
R – ③: 🛏 1, 2 cl. Venezia (**241**) - Budapest (**16**) - Moskva (journey 3 nights).
Y – ④: 🛏 1, 2 cl. Kyïv - Zagreb.
Z – ⑥: 🛏 1, 2 cl. Zagreb - Kyïv.

⊖ – 🏛 at Preševo / Tabanovci.
⊡ – 🏛 at Gevgelija / Idomeni.
⁄ – Ⓡ with supplement payable.

MOSKVA - BUCUREŞTI, SOFIYA and İSTANBUL — 98

train number			668	668	86			59	59	
train number	491		59	1183	383	383	383	1181	1183	
notes	M		F	W	N	B	A	V	K	
Moskva Kiyevskaya d.	...	...	...	...	...	2139	0025	0025	0025	...
St Peterburg Vit d.	...	...	...	...	...	|	|	|	|	...
Minsk d.	...	...	...	...	2050	|	|	|	|	...
Kyïv d.	...	...	...	...	1402	1540	1402	1402	1402	...
Lviv d.	...	...	2335	2335	|	|	|	|	|	...
Chernivtsi d.	...	...	0703	0703	0703	0703	0703	0703	0703	...
Vadul Siret 🏛 d.	...	...	1020	1020	1020	1020	1020	1020	1020	...
Bucureşti Nord a.	1216	...	1931	1931	1931	1931	1931	1931	1931	...
Constanţa a.	|	...	|	|	|	|	|	|	|	...
Ruse 🏛 a.	1445	...	2230	2230	2230	2230	2230	2230	2230	...
Varna a.	|	...	|	|	|	|	|	0655	|	...
Burgas a.	|	...	|	0923	|	|	|	...	0923	...
Sofiya a.	|	...	0600	...	0600	0600	0600	...	...	...
Kapikule 🏛 a.	0130	...	...	...	...	...	...	...	...	...
İstanbul Sirkeci a.	0819	...	...	...	...	...	...	...	...	...

train number	1180	1182			382	382	1182			
train number	382	382	382	382	85	604	382		490	
notes	Q	S	C	D	P	T	U		G	
İstanbul Sirkeci d.	...	...	...	...	...	...	...	...	2200	...
Kapikule 🏛 d.	...	...	...	...	...	...	...	...	0405	...
Sofiya d.	...	...	1930	1930	1930	1930	...	...	|	...
Burgas d.	...	1925	|	|	|	|	1925	...	|	...
Varna d.	2200	|	|	|	|	|	|	...	|	...
Ruse 🏛 d.	0315	0315	0315	0315	0315	0315	0315	...	1448	...
Constanţa d.	|	|	|	|	|	|	|	...	|	...
Bucureşti Nord d.	0626	0626	0626	0626	0626	0626	0626	...	1719	...
Vadul Siret 🏛 a.	1510	1510	1510	1510	1510	1510	1510	...	...	...
Chernivtsi a.	1816	1816	1816	1816	1816	1816	1816	...	...	...
Lviv a.	|	|	|	|	|	0805	0805	...	...	...
Kyïv a.	0929	0929	0929	0929x	0929z	...	...	...	...	...
Minsk a.	|	|	|	|	0601	...	...	...	...	...
St Peterburg Vit a.	|	|	|	|	...	...	...	...	...	...
Moskva Kiyevskaya a.	2236	2236	2236	0452	...	...	...	...	...	...

A – BULGARIA EXPRESS – June 14 - Sept 4: 🛏 1, 2 cl. Moskva (**59**) - Vadul Siret (**383**) - Bucureşti - Sofiya.
B – BULGARIA EXPRESS – Dec. 14 - June 12, Sept. 4 - Dec. 9: 🛏 1, 2 cl. Moskva (**3**) - Kyïv (**59**) - Vadul Siret (**383**) - Bucureşti - Ruse - Sofiya.
C – BULGARIA EXPRESS – June 14 - Sept. 3: 🛏 1, 2 cl. Sofiya (**382**) - Bucureşti - Vadul Siret (**60**) - Moskva.
D – BULGARIA EXPRESS – Dec. 14 - June 13, Sept. 4 - Dec. 9: 🛏 1, 2 cl. Sofiya (**382**) - Ruse - Bucureşti - Vadul Siret (**60**) - Kyïv (**142**) - Moskva.
F – ①④⑥ Dec. 13 - June 16; Sept. 5 - Dec. 10: 🛏 2 cl. Lviv (**76**) - Chernivtsi (**59**) - Vadul Siret (**383**) - Bucureşti - Ruse 🏛 (**4665**) - Sofiya.
G – 🛏 1, 2 cl. and ▬ 2 cl. İstanbul (**81032**) - Kapikule 🏛 (**490**) - Ruse 🏛 (**462**) - Bucureşti.
K – ④⑥ June 18 - Sept. 3: 🛏 2 cl. Moskva (**59**) - Vadul Siret (**383**) - Bucureşti - Ruse 🏛 (**1183**) - Burgas.
M – 🛏 1, 2 cl. and ▬ 2 cl. Bucureşti (**463**) - Ruse 🏛 (**491**) - Kapikule 🏛 (**81031**) - İstanbul.
N – ⑥ (also ② June 16 - Sept. 1): 🛏 2 cl. Minsk (**86**) - Kyïv (**59**) - Sofiya.
P – ② (also ⑤ June 19 - Sept. 4): 🛏 2 cl. Sofiya (**382**) - Kyïv (**86**) - Minsk.
Q – ②③④⑤⑦ June 16 - Sept. 6: 🛏 2 cl. Varna (**1180**) - Ruse 🏛 (**382**) - Bucureşti - Vadul Siret (**60**) - Moskva.
S – ①⑥ June 20 - Sept. 5: 🛏 2 cl. Burgas (**1182**) - Ruse 🏛 (**382**) - Bucureşti - Vadul Siret (**60**) - Moskva.
T – ①③⑥ Dec. 15 - June 18; Sept. 7 - Dec. 12: 🛏 2 cl. Sofiya (**60**) - Ruse 🏛 (**382**) - Bucureşti - Vadul Siret (**60**) - Chernivtsi (**604**) - Lviv.
U – ①⑥ June 20 - Sept. 5: 🛏 2 cl. Burgas - Lviv.
V – ①②③⑤⑦ June 14 - Sept. 4: 🛏 2 cl. Moskva (**59**) - Vadul Siret (**383**) - Bucureşti - Ruse 🏛 (**1181**) - Varna.
W – ④⑥ June 18 - Sept. 3: 🛏 2 cl. Lviv - Burgas.

x – Depart 1350 (Train **142**).
z – Depart 1818 (Train **86/85**).

99 WARSZAWA, WROCŁAW, KRAKÓW - PRAHA, WIEN, BUDAPEST and BUCUREŞTI

train type/number	EC	EC	EC				EC		EC	EC	EC	EC										1381	
train number	118	118	103	234	275	38108	114	38100	105	142	277	175		200	200	200	203	203	203	1381	1381	1375	1381
notes	[R]	103	[R]	🍷	475	38109	[R]	38101	[R]	✕		✕		203	203		477		200	537	375	1183	1375
notes	⊡	[R]⊡	✕⊡				✕⊡	🍷	✕⊡					477			[R]	[R]	[R]	1864		1181	1183
notes	V	W	R				X		Y					A	E	S	B	C	Q	G	J	L	N
Warszawa Wschodnia d.	...	...	0613	...	...	...	0913	...	1113	...	...	...	...	...	...	...	2047	2047	2047	...	...	...	...
Warszawa Centralna d.	...	...	0625	...	...	...	0925	...	1125	...	...	...	...	...	...	...	2100	2100	2100	...	...	...	...
Wrocław Główny d.	...	...	|	...	...	...	|	...	|	...	...	...	...	...	...	...	|	|	|	...	...	...	...
Lichkov d.	...	...	|	...	...	...	|	...	|	...	...	...	...	...	...	...	|	|	|	...	...	...	...
Kraków Gł. d.	0653	0653	|	...	...	0947	|	1147	|	...	...	...	...	2215	2215	2215	|	|	|	2245	2245	2245	2245
Tarnów d.	|	|	|	...	...	|	|	|	|	...	...	...	...	|	|	|	|	|	|	2350	2350	2350	2350
Katowice d.	|	|	0909	...	...	1129	1209	1329	1409	...	...	...	...	|	|	|	2353	2353	2353	|	|	|	|
Zebrzydowice d.	0916	0916	1016	...	...	...	1316	...	1516	...	...	...	...	0050	0050	0050	0105	0105	0105	|	|	|	|
Bohumín a.	0935	0935	1030	...	...	...	1329	...	1529	...	...	...	...	0109	0109	0109	0125	0125	0125	|	|	|	|
Bohumín d.	0950	1046	1046	...	...	...	1350	...	1546	...	...	...	...	0215	0215	0207	0215	0215	0207	|	|	|	|
Ostrava Hlavní a.	0959	1054	1054	1142	...	...	1359	...	1554	1601	...	...	...	0224	0224	0216	0224	0224	0216	|	|	|	|
Přerov a.	|	1144	1144	|	...	...	|	...	1644	|	...	...	...	|	|	0314	|	|	0314	|	|	|	|
Olomouc a.	1105	|	|	1305	...	...	1505	...	|	1705	...	...	...	|	|	0354	|	|	0354	|	|	|	|
Pardubice a.	1234	|	|	1434	...	...	1634	...	|	1834	...	...	...	|	|	0531	|	|	0531	|	|	|	|
Praha hlavní a.	1354	|	|	1554	...	...	1754	...	|	1954	...	...	...	|	|	0654	|	|	0654	|	|	|	|
Břeclav a.	...	1246	1246	...	1255	...	...	...	1746	...	1755	1855	...	0412	0412	...	0412	0412	...	|	|	|	|
Wien Südbahnhof a.	...	1402	1402	...	|	...	...	...	1902	...	|	|	...	|	0630z	...	|	0630z	...	|	|	|	|
Kúty a.	...	...	...	...	1308	...	...	...	...	...	1808	1908	...	0459	...	...	0459	...	...	|	|	|	|
Bratislava Hlavná a.	...	...	...	...	1347	...	...	...	...	...	1850	1947	...	0540	...	...	0540	...	...	|	|	|	|
Štúrovo a.	...	...	...	...	...	...	...	...	...	...	...	2108	...	0715	...	...	0715	...	...	|	|	|	|
Plaveč a.	...	...	...	...	...	...	...	...	...	...	...	|	...	|	...	...	|	...	...	0325	0325	0325	0325
Košice a.	...	...	...	...	...	...	...	...	...	...	...	|	...	|	...	...	|	...	...	0500	0500	0500	0500
Hidasnémeti a.	...	...	...	...	...	...	...	...	...	...	...	|	...	|	...	...	|	...	...	0633	0537	0537	0537
Miskolc a.	...	...	...	...	...	...	...	...	...	...	...	|	...	|	...	...	|	...	...	0726	0655	0655	0655
Budapest Keleti a.	...	...	...	...	...	...	...	...	...	...	...	2232	...	0832	...	...	0832	...	...	0927	|	|	|
Budapest Nyugati a.	...	...	...	...	...	...	...	...	...	...	...	...	...	...	...	...	...	...	...	|	|	|	|
Székesfehérvár a.	...	...	...	...	...	...	...	...	...	...	...	...	...	...	...	...	...	...	...	1120	|	|	|
Siófok a.	...	...	...	...	...	...	...	...	...	...	...	...	...	...	...	...	...	...	...	1159	|	|	|
Keszthely a.	...	...	...	...	...	...	...	...	...	...	...	...	...	...	...	...	...	...	...	1332	|	|	|
Szolnok a.	...	...	...	...	...	...	...	...	...	...	...	...	...	...	...	...	...	...	...	...	0953	0953	0953
Lőkösháza a.	...	...	...	...	...	...	...	...	...	...	...	...	...	...	...	...	...	...	...	...	1143	1143	1143
Curtici a.	...	...	...	...	...	...	...	...	...	...	...	...	...	...	...	...	...	...	...	...	1342	1412	1412
Arad a.	...	...	...	...	...	...	...	...	...	...	...	...	...	...	...	...	...	...	...	...	1414	1447	1447
Bucureşti Nord a.	...	...	...	...	...	...	...	...	...	...	...	...	...	...	...	...	...	...	...	...	2355	|	|
Varna a.	...	...	...	...	...	...	...	...	...	...	...	...	...	...	...	...	...	...	...	...	...	0655	|
Burgas a.	...	...	...	...	...	...	...	...	...	...	...	...	...	...	...	...	...	...	...	...	...	...	0923

train type/number	EC	EC	EC			EC		EC		EC	EC										1180		
train number	174	143	104	83100		115	83108	119	274	102	102		201	201	202	202	476	476	1863		1182	1182	
notes	✕	✕	[R]	83101		[R]	83109	[R]	474	[R]	119		202			201	202	202	536	374	1374	1374	
notes		⚡	✕⊡	🍷		✕⊡		⊡		✕⊡	[R]⊡		[R]		[R]		[R]	201	1380	1380	1380	1380	
notes			Y			X		V		R	W		Q	S	C	E	B	F	H	K	M	P	
Burgas d.	...	...	...	...	...	...	...	...	...	...	...	...	...	...	...	...	...	...	...	...	...	1925	...
Varna d.	...	...	...	...	...	...	...	...	...	...	...	...	...	...	...	...	...	...	...	...	2200	|	...
Bucureşti Nord d.	...	...	...	...	...	...	...	...	...	...	...	...	...	...	...	...	...	...	...	0550	|	|	...
Arad d.	...	...	...	...	...	...	...	...	...	...	...	...	...	...	...	...	...	...	...	1552	1423	1423	...
Curtici d.	...	...	...	...	...	...	...	...	...	...	...	...	...	...	...	...	...	...	...	1618	1543	1543	...
Lőkösháza d.	...	...	...	...	...	...	...	...	...	...	...	...	...	...	...	...	...	...	...	1610	1610	1610	...
Szolnok d.	...	...	...	...	...	...	...	...	...	...	...	...	...	...	...	...	...	...	...	1806	1806	1806	...
Keszthely d.	...	...	...	...	...	...	...	...	...	...	...	...	...	...	...	...	...	...	1435	|	|	|	...
Siófok d.	...	...	...	...	...	...	...	...	...	...	...	...	...	...	...	...	...	...	1603	|	|	|	...
Székesfehérvár d.	...	...	...	...	...	...	...	...	...	...	...	...	...	...	...	...	...	...	1653	|	|	|	...
Budapest Nyugati d.	...	...	...	...	...	...	...	...	...	...	...	...	...	...	...	...	...	...	|	|	|	|	...
Budapest Keleti d.	0528	...	...	...	...	...	...	...	...	...	...	...	...	...	...	...	1958	1958	1833	|	|	|	...
Miskolc d.	|	...	...	...	...	...	...	...	...	...	...	...	...	...	...	...	|	|	2034	2106	2106	2106	...
Hidasnémeti d.	|	...	...	...	...	...	...	...	...	...	...	...	...	...	...	...	|	|	2129	2223	2223	2223	...
Košice d.	|	...	...	...	...	...	...	...	...	...	...	...	...	...	...	...	|	|	2304	2304	2304	2304	...
Plaveč d.	|	...	...	...	...	...	...	...	...	...	...	...	...	...	...	...	|	|	0104	0104	0104	0104	...
Štúrovo d.	0641	...	...	...	...	...	...	...	...	...	...	...	...	...	...	...	2120	2120	|	|	|	|	...
Bratislava Hlavná d.	0801	...	...	...	...	...	...	...	1401	...	...	...	...	...	...	...	2255	2255	|	|	|	|	...
Kúty d.	0841	...	...	...	...	...	...	...	1441	...	...	...	...	...	...	...	2335	2335	|	|	|	|	...
Wien Südbahnhof d.	|	...	0858	...	...	...	...	...	|	1458	1458	...	...	...	2212z	2212z	|	|	|	|	|	|	...
Břeclav d.	0854	...	1008	...	...	...	...	...	1454	1608	1608	...	...	...	0018	0018	0018	0018	|	|	|	|	...
Praha hlavní d.	...	0809	|	...	...	1009	...	1409	...	|	|	...	2109	2109	|	|	|	|	|	|	|	|	...
Pardubice d.	...	0924	|	...	...	1124	...	1524	...	|	|	...	2225	2225	|	|	|	|	|	|	|	|	...
Olomouc d.	...	1054	|	...	...	1254	...	1654	...	|	|	...	0003	0003	|	|	|	|	|	|	|	|	...
Přerov d.	...	|	1112	...	...	|	...	|	...	1712	1712	...	0038	0038	|	|	|	|	|	|	|	|	...
Ostrava Hlavní d.	...	1200	1206	...	...	1402	...	1800	...	1806	1806	...	0138	0138	0208	0208	0208	0208	|	|	|	|	...
Bohumín a.	...	1208	1215	...	...	1410	...	1808	...	1815	1815	...	0147	0147	0217	0217	0217	0217	|	|	|	|	...
Bohumín d.	...	...	1234	...	...	1431	...	1838	...	1834	1838	...	0250	0307	0250	0307	0250	0307	|	|	|	|	...
Zebrzydowice d.	...	...	1250	...	...	1450	...	1858	...	1850	1858	...	0313	0329	0313	0329	0313	0329	|	|	|	|	...
Katowice a.	...	...	1357	1430	...	1557	1630	|	...	1957	|	...	0425	|	0425	|	0425	|	|	|	|	|	...
Tarnów a.	...	...	|	|	...	|	|	|	...	|	|	...	|	|	|	|	|	|	0421	0421	0421	0421	...
Kraków Gł. a.	...	...	|	1619	...	|	1819	2146	...	|	2146	...	|	0633	|	0633	|	0633	0529	0529	0529	0529	...
Lichkov a.	...	...	|	...	...	|	...	...	...	|	...	...	|	...	|	...	|	...	...	...	...	...	...
Wrocław Główny a.	...	...	|	...	...	|	...	...	...	|	...	...	|	...	|	...	|	...	...	...	...	...	...
Warszawa Centralna a.	...	...	1645	...	...	1845	...	...	...	2245	...	...	0720	...	0720	...	0720	...	...	...	...	...	...
Warszawa Wschodnia a.	...	...	1657	...	...	1857	...	...	...	2257	...	...	0737	...	0737	...	0737	...	...	...	...	...	...

A – 🛏 1, 2 cl. and ▬ 2 cl. Kraków (**200**) - Bohumín (**203**) - Břeclav (**477**) - Budapest.

B – 🛏 1, 2 cl., ▬ 2 cl. and [2] Warszawa - Bratislava - Budapest and v.v. Conveys 🛏 1, 2 cl. Moskva / Minsk - Budapest and v.v.

C – CHOPIN – 🛏 1, 2 cl., ▬ 2 cl. and [2] Warszawa - Wien and v.v. Conveys 🛏 1, 2 cl. Moskva - Wien and v.v.

E – 🛏 1, 2 cl. (also ▬ 2 cl. Apr. 29 - Sept. 26 from Kraków; Apr. 30 - Sept. 27 from Wien) Kraków - Wien and v.v.

F – 🛏 1, 2 cl. and ▬ 2 cl. Budapest (**476**) - Břeclav (**202**) - Bohumín (**201**) - Kraków.

G – CRACOVIA – June 18 - Aug. 30: ▬ 2 cl. and [2] Kraków (**381**) - Košice (**537**) - Budapest - Balatonszentgyörgy - Keszthely. ✕ Košice - Budapest - Keszthely.

H – CRACOVIA – June 19 - Aug. 31: ▬ 2 cl. and [2] Keszthely (**536**) - Balatonszentgyörgy - Budapest - Košice (**380**) - Kraków. ✕ Keszthely - Budapest - Košice.

J – CRACOVIA – June 18 - Aug. 30: [2] Kraków - Košice - Lőkösháza; June 20 - Aug. 30: ▬ 2 cl. and [2] Kraków - Bucureşti.

K – CRACOVIA – June 19 - Aug. 31: [2] Lőkösháza - Košice - Kraków; June 19 - Aug. 29: ▬ 2 cl. and [2] Bucureşti - Kraków.

L – ⑤ June 19 - Aug. 28: 🛏 1, 2 cl. Kraków (**381**) - Hidasnémeti (**1577**) - Lőkösháza (**1373**) - Curtici - Ruse (**1183 / 1181**) - Varna (journey 2 nights).

M – ⑦ June 21 - Aug. 30: 🛏 1, 2 cl. Varna (**1180 / 1182**) - Ruse (**1372**) - Curtici - Lőkösháza (**1578**) - Hidasnémeti (**380**) - Kraków (journey 2 nights).

N – ②④ June 18 - Aug. 27: 🛏 1, 2 cl. Kraków (**1381**) - Hidasnémeti - Lőkösháza (**1375**) - Curtici - Ruse (**1183**) - Burgas (journey 2 nights).

P – ④⑥ June 20 - Aug. 29: 🛏 1, 2 cl. Burgas (**1182**) - Ruse (**1372**) - Curtici - Lőkösháza (**1578**) - Hidasnémeti (**380**) - Kraków (journey 2 nights).

Q – 🛏 1, 2 cl., ▬ 2 cl. and [2] Warszawa - Praha and v.v.

R – POLONIA – [12] and ✕ Warszawa - Wien and v.v.

S – SILESIA – 🛏 1, 2 cl., ▬ 2 cl. and [12] Kraków - Praha and v.v.

V – COMENIUS – [12] and ✕ Kraków - Praha and v.v.

W – [2] Kraków - Wien and v.v. ✕ Kraków - Bohumín - Praha and v.v. ✕ Warszawa - Bohumín - Wien and v.v.

X – PRAHA – [12] and ✕ Warszawa - Praha and v.v.

Y – SOBIESKI – [12] and ✕ Warszawa - Wien and v.v.

z – Wien **Westbahnhof**.

⊡ – Supplement payable in Poland.

GREAT BRITAIN

SEE MAP PAGES 98–99

Operators: Passenger services are provided by a number of private passenger train companies operating the **National Rail** network on lines owned by the British national railway infrastructure company **Network Rail**. The following Network Rail codes are used in the table headings to indicate the operators of trains in each table:

AW	Arriva Trains Wales	GW	First Great Western	ME	Merseyrail	SW	South West Trains
CH	Chiltern Railways	HT	Hull Trains	NT	Northern Rail	TP	TransPennine Express
EM	East Midlands Trains	IL	Island Line	SE	Southeastern	VT	Virgin Trains
FC	First Capital Connect	LE	National Express East Anglia	SN	Southern	WS	Wrexham & Shropshire
GC	Grand Central Railway	LM	London Midland	SR	First ScotRail	XC	Arriva Cross Country
GR	National Express East Coast						

Timings: Except where indicated otherwise, timings are valid from **May 17, 2009** to **December 12, 2009**.
As service patterns at weekends (especially on ⑦) usually differ greatly from those applying on Mondays to Fridays, the timings in most tables are grouped by days of operation: Ⓐ = Mondays to Fridays; ⚒ = Mondays to Saturdays; ⑥ = Saturdays; ⑦ = Sundays. Track engineering work, affecting journey times, frequently takes place at weekends, so it is advisable to confirm your journey details locally if planning to travel in the period between the late evening of ⑥ and the late afternoon of ⑦. Confirm timings, too, if you intend travelling on public holidays (see page **2**) as there may be alterations to services at these times. Suburban and commuter services are the most likely to be affected; the majority of long-distance and cross-country trains marked Ⓐ and ⚒ run as normal on these dates. No trains (except limited Gatwick and Heathrow Express services) run on **December 25**, with only a limited service on certain routes on **December 26**. In Scotland only trains between Edinburgh / Glasgow and England run on **January 1**.

Services: Unless indicated otherwise (by '2' in the train column or '2nd class' in the table heading), trains convey both **first** (1st) and **standard** (2nd) classes of seated accommodation. Light refreshments (snacks, hot and cold drinks) are available from a **buffet car** or a **mobile trolley service** on board those trains marked 🍸 and ✕: the latter also convey a **restaurant car** or serve meals to passengers at their seats (this service is in some cases available to first-class ticket holders only). Note that catering facilities may not be available for the whole of a train's journey. **Sleeping-cars** (🛏) have one berth per compartment in first class and two in standard class.

Reservations: Seats on most long-distance trains and berths in sleeping-cars can be reserved in advance when purchasing travel tickets at rail stations or directly from train operating companies (quote the departure time of the train and your destination). Seat reservation is normally free of charge.

SE — LONDON - CHATHAM - DOVER and RAMSGATE — 100

For London to Canterbury and Dover via Ashford, see Table **101**

km		Ⓐ	Ⓐ	Ⓐ	Ⓐ	Ⓐ	Ⓐ	Ⓐ	Ⓐ	Ⓐ	Ⓐ	Ⓐ	Ⓐ	Ⓐ	Ⓐ	Ⓐ	Ⓐ	Ⓐ	Ⓐ	Ⓐ		Ⓐ	Ⓐ	Ⓐ	Ⓐ
0	**London** Victoria d.		...	...	0532	...	0616	...	0639	...	0707	0733	0803	0803	0833	0833	0903	0903	0933	0933	and at the same minutes past each hour until	1403	1403	1433	1433
55	**Chatham** d.		0536	...	0629	...	0717	...	0742	...	0808	0819	0848	0848	0918	0918	0947	0947	1017	1017		1447	1447	1517	1517
72	Sittingbourne d.		0554	...	0648	...	0735	...	0804	...	0827	0837	0904	0904	0934	0934	1002	1002	1033	1033		1502	1502	1532	1532
84	Faversham d.		0605	0613	0701	0704	0746	0751	0817	0819	0849	0847	0916	0918	0946	0948	1014	1016	1044	1047		1514	1516	1544	1546
99	Canterbury East d.		0619	|	|	0718	|	0808	0832	|	0904	|	|	0932	|	1008	|	1028	|	1101		|	1528	|	1600
124	**Dover** a.		0648	|	|	0745	|	0836	0900	|	0932	|	|	0952	|	1035	|	1045	|	1127		|	1544	|	1627
119	Margate d.		...	0645	0733	...	0818	...	...	0852	...	0920	0943	...	1019	...	1041	...	1115	...		1541	...	1615	...
128	**Ramsgate** a.		...	0656	0743	...	0829	...	...	0903	...	0930	0952	...	1030	...	1051	...	1127	...		1551	...	1626	...

	Ⓐ	Ⓐ	Ⓐ	Ⓐ	Ⓐ	Ⓐ	Ⓐ	Ⓐ	Ⓐ	Ⓐ	Ⓐ	Ⓐ	Ⓐ	Ⓐ	Ⓐ	Ⓐ	Ⓐ	Ⓐ	Ⓐ	Ⓐ	Ⓐ	Ⓐ	Ⓐ	Ⓐ	Ⓐ	Ⓐ
London Victoria d.	1503	1503	1533	1533	1603	1603	1623	1623	1642	1709	1709	1727	1748	1749	1804	1804	1833	1833	1903	1903	1933	1934	2003	2003	2033	2033
Chatham d.	1547	1547	1616	1616	1647	1647	1708	1708	1728	1756	1756	1810	1835	1834	1855	1855	1917	1917	1947	1947	2019	2019	2047	2047	2116	2116
Sittingbourne d.	1603	1603	1632	1632	1703	1703	1727	1727	1745	1815	1815	1827	1853	1852	1912	1912	1935	1935	2005	2005	2036	2036	2102	2102	2133	2133
Faversham d.	1615	1617	1644	1647	1715	1718	1741	1745	1803	1829	1834	1840	1905	1911	1924	1932	1947	1949	2019	2021	2048	2052	2116	2118	2145	2147
Canterbury East d.	|	1632	|	1701	|	1733	|	1800	1818	|	1849	|	|	1926	|	1947	|	2006	|	2036	|	2106	|	2132	|	2200
Dover a.	|	1659	|	1728	|	1803	|	1830	1848	|	1917	|	|	1955	|	2015	|	2033	|	2103	|	2133	|	2159	|	...
Margate d.	1647	...	1716	...	1745	...	1813	...	...	1903	...	1912	1934	...	1957	...	2020	...	2047	...	2119	...	2143	...	2216	...
Ramsgate a.	1658	...	1727	...	1756	...	1826	...	...	1917	...	1925	*1954*	...	*2018*	...	2032	...	2059	...	2130	...	2153	...	2227	...

	Ⓐ	Ⓐ	Ⓐ	Ⓐ	Ⓐ			⑥	⑥	⑥	⑥	⑥	⑥	⑥	⑥	⑥	⑥	⑥		⑥	⑥	⑥	⑥	⑥	⑥
London Victoria d.	2103	2103	2139	2203	2303	...	...		...	...	0539	...	0639	0639	0733	0733	0803	0803	and at the same minutes past each hour until	1803	1803	1833	1833	1903	1903
Chatham d.	2150	2150	2238	2246	2346	...	...		0546	...	0638	...	0738	0738	0817	0817	0847	0847		1847	1847	1917	1917	1949	1949
Sittingbourne d.	2205	2205	2255	2301	0001	...	...		0603	...	0655	...	0755	0755	0832	0832	0902	0902		1902	1902	1932	1932	2005	2005
Faversham d.	2217	2220	2313	2311	0012	...	...		0615	0617	0714	0716	0814	0816	0844	0846	0914	0916		1914	1916	1944	1946	2016	2018
Canterbury East d.	|	2234	2327	|	|	...	...		0629	|	|	0730	0830	|	|	0900	|	0931		|	1931	|	2000	|	2033
Dover a.	|	2301	2347	|	|	...	...		0656	|	|	0757	0857	|	|	0928	|	0946		|	1946	|	2028	|	2101
Margate d.	2248	...	...	2342	0043	...	...		...	0649	0746	...	...	0848	0915	...	0941	...		1941	...	2015	...	2047	...
Ramsgate a.	2259	...	...	2353	0054	...	...		...	0659	0758	...	...	0859	0926	...	0951	...		1951	...	2026	...	2057	...

	⑥	⑥	⑥	⑥	⑥	⑥	⑥			⑦	⑦	⑦	⑦		⑦	⑦	⑦	⑦	⑦						
London Victoria d.	2003	2003	2103	2103	2203	2203	2303	...	...		0735	0803	0803	and at the same minutes past each hour until	2103	2103	2203	2203	2303	...	...	...	...	...	...
Chatham d.	2049	2049	2149	2149	2249	2249	2349	...	...		0835	0846	0846		2146	2146	2246	2246	2346	...	...	...	...	...	...
Sittingbourne d.	2105	2105	2205	2205	2305	2305	0005	...	...		0849	0902	0902		2202	2202	2302	2302	0002	...	...	...	...	...	...
Faversham d.	2116	2118	2216	2218	2316	2318	0016	...	...		0900	0914	0916		2214	2216	2314	2316	0014	...	...	...	...	...	...
Canterbury East d.	|	2133	|	2233	|	2332	|	...	...		...	|	0930		|	2230	|	2330	|	...	...	...	...	...	...
Dover a.	|	2201	|	2303	|	2347	|	...	...		...	|	0958		|	2258	|	2346	|	...	...	...	...	...	...
Margate d.	2147	...	2247	...	2347	...	0047	...	...		...	0945	...		2245	...	2345	...	0045	...	...	...	...	...	...
Ramsgate a.	2157	...	2257	...	2357	...	0058	...	...		...	0956	...		2256	...	2356	...	0056	...	...	...	...	...	...

		Ⓐ	Ⓐ	Ⓐ	Ⓐ	Ⓐ	Ⓐ	Ⓐ	Ⓐ	Ⓐ	Ⓐ	Ⓐ	Ⓐ	Ⓐ	Ⓐ	Ⓐ	Ⓐ	Ⓐ	Ⓐ	Ⓐ	Ⓐ	Ⓐ	Ⓐ		Ⓐ
Ramsgate d.	Ⓐ	0438	...	0504	0528	...	0611	...	0630	...	0650	0722	...	0752	...	...	0817	...	0850	...	0922	...	0959	and at the same minutes past each hour until	...
Margate d.		0448	...	0514	0538	...	0622	...	0640	...	0700	0732	...	0802	...	...	0828	...	0902	...	0934	...	1008		...
Dover d.		|	0450	|	|	0549	|	0624	|	0645	|	|	0709	|	0750	0817	|	0904	|	0922	|	1004	|		1304
Canterbury East d.		|	0517	|	|	0616	|	0651	|	0713	|	|	0737	|	0818	0844	|	0921	|	0949	|	1021	|		1321
Faversham d.		0519	0531	0543	0610	0631	0653	0706	0713	0728	0732	0804	0807	0834	0838	0903	0903	0938	0938	1008	1008	1038	1038		1338
Sittingbourne d.		0528	0541	0554	0618	0641	0702	...	0724	...	0743	0812	0818	0843	0849	0913	0913	0947	0947	1017	1017	1047	1047		1347
Chatham d.		0546	0601	0613	0636	0702	0720	...	0743	...	0802	0829	0837	0900	0907	0930	0930	1003	1003	1033	1033	1103	1103		1403
London Victoria a.		0630	0659	0712	0724	0752	0811	...	0833	...	0853	0927	0937	0950	1007	1017	1017	1047	1047	1117	1117	1147	1147		1447

	Ⓐ	Ⓐ	Ⓐ	Ⓐ	Ⓐ	Ⓐ	Ⓐ	Ⓐ	Ⓐ	Ⓐ	Ⓐ	Ⓐ	Ⓐ	Ⓐ	Ⓐ	Ⓐ	Ⓐ	Ⓐ	Ⓐ	Ⓐ	Ⓐ	Ⓐ	Ⓐ	Ⓐ	Ⓐ	Ⓐ
Ramsgate d.	1259	...	1322	...	1359	...	1421	...	1457	...	1521	...	1552	...	1620	...	1648	...	1722	...	1750	...	1821	1848	...	1950
Margate d.	1308	...	1334	...	1408	...	1433	...	1506	...	1533	...	1604	...	1632	...	1659	...	1734	...	1801	...	1832	1859	...	2000
Dover d.	|	1322	|	1404	|	1420	|	1502	|	1520	|	1552	|	1620	|	1648	|	1722	|	1750	|	1821	|	|	1854	|
Canterbury East d.	|	1349	|	1421	|	1447	|	1519	|	1547	|	1619	|	1647	|	1716	|	1749	|	1818	|	1849	|	|	1922	|
Faversham d.	1338	1408	1408	1438	1438	1506	1506	1536	1536	1606	1606	1638	1638	1706	1706	1735	1735	1809	1809	1837	1837	1908	1908	1939	1939	2037
Sittingbourne d.	1347	1417	1417	1447	1447	1515	1515	1545	1545	1615	1615	1647	1647	1715	1715	1743	1743	1817	1817	1845	1845	1917	1917	1947	1947	2045
Chatham d.	1403	1433	1433	1503	1503	1531	1531	1601	1601	1631	1631	1703	1703	1731	1731	1800	1800	1835	1835	1902	1902	1933	1933	2004	2004	2102
London Victoria a.	1447	1517	1517	1547	1547	1617	1617	1651	1651	1717	1717	1757	1757	1817	1817	1848	1848	1917	1917	1949	1949	2019	2019	2049	2049	2147

	Ⓐ	Ⓐ	Ⓐ	Ⓐ	Ⓐ	Ⓐ	Ⓐ	Ⓐ	Ⓐ					⑥		⑥	⑥	⑥	⑥		⑥	⑥	⑥	⑥	⑥	⑥
Ramsgate d.	...	2050	...	...	2155	2210	...	2253	...	...	...	...	⑥	0438	...	...	0522	...	0559	and at the same minutes past each hour until	...	1822	...	1852	...	1952
Margate d.	...	2101	...	...	2206	2220	...	2304	...	...	...	...		0446	...	...	0534	...	0608		...	1834	...	1904	...	2004
Dover d.	1952	|	2052	2155	|	|	2301	|	...	...	...	...		|	...	0522	|	0604	|		1822	|	1852	|	1952	|
Canterbury East d.	2019	|	2120	2222	|	|	2318	|	...	...	...	...		|	...	0549	|	0621	|		1849	|	1919	|	2019	|
Faversham d.	2037	2138	2138	2235	2238	2248	2330	2336	2342	...	...	...		0512	...	0608	0608	0638	0638		1908	1908	1938	1938	2038	2038
Sittingbourne d.	2045	2147	2147	...	2247	2258	...	...	2352	...	...	...		0520	...	0617	0617	0647	0647		1917	1917	1947	1947	2047	2047
Chatham d.	2102	2203	2203	...	2303	2317	...	...	0011	...	...	...		0537	...	0633	0633	0703	0703		1933	1933	2003	2003	2103	2103
London Victoria a.	2147	2248	2248	...	2347	0018	...	...	0113	...	...	...		0632	...	0717	0717	0747	0747		2017	2017	2047	2047	2147	2147

	⑥	⑥		⑥	⑥	⑥	⑥	⑥				⑦	⑦		⑦	⑦		⑦	⑦		⑦	⑦			
Ramsgate d.	...	2052	...	...	2152	...	2255	...	...	...	⑦	...	0622	...	...	0722	and at the same minutes past each hour until	...	2122	...	...	2152	...	...	...
Margate d.	...	2104	...	...	2204	...	2306	...	...	...		...	0634	...	...	0734		...	2134	...	...	2204	...	...	...
Dover d.	2052	|	...	2152	|	2304	|	...	...	...		...	|	...	0722	|		2122	|	...	2152	|	...	...	...
Canterbury East d.	2119	|	...	2219	|	2322	|	...	...	...		...	|	...	0749	|		2149	|	...	2219	|	...	...	...
Faversham d.	2138	2138	...	2238	2238	2334	2338	2342	...	...		0632	0708	...	0808	0808		2208	2208	...	2232	2235	...	...	...
Sittingbourne d.	2147	2147	...	2247	2247	...	...	2352	...	...		0642	0717	...	0817	0817		2217	2217	...	...	2245	...	...	...
Chatham d.	2203	2203	...	2303	2303	...	...	0009	...	...		0701	0733	...	0833	0833		2233	2233	...	...	2303	...	...	...
London Victoria a.	2247	2247	...	2347	2347	...	...	0111	...	...		0801	0816	...	0916	0916		2316	2316	...	...	2359	...	...	...

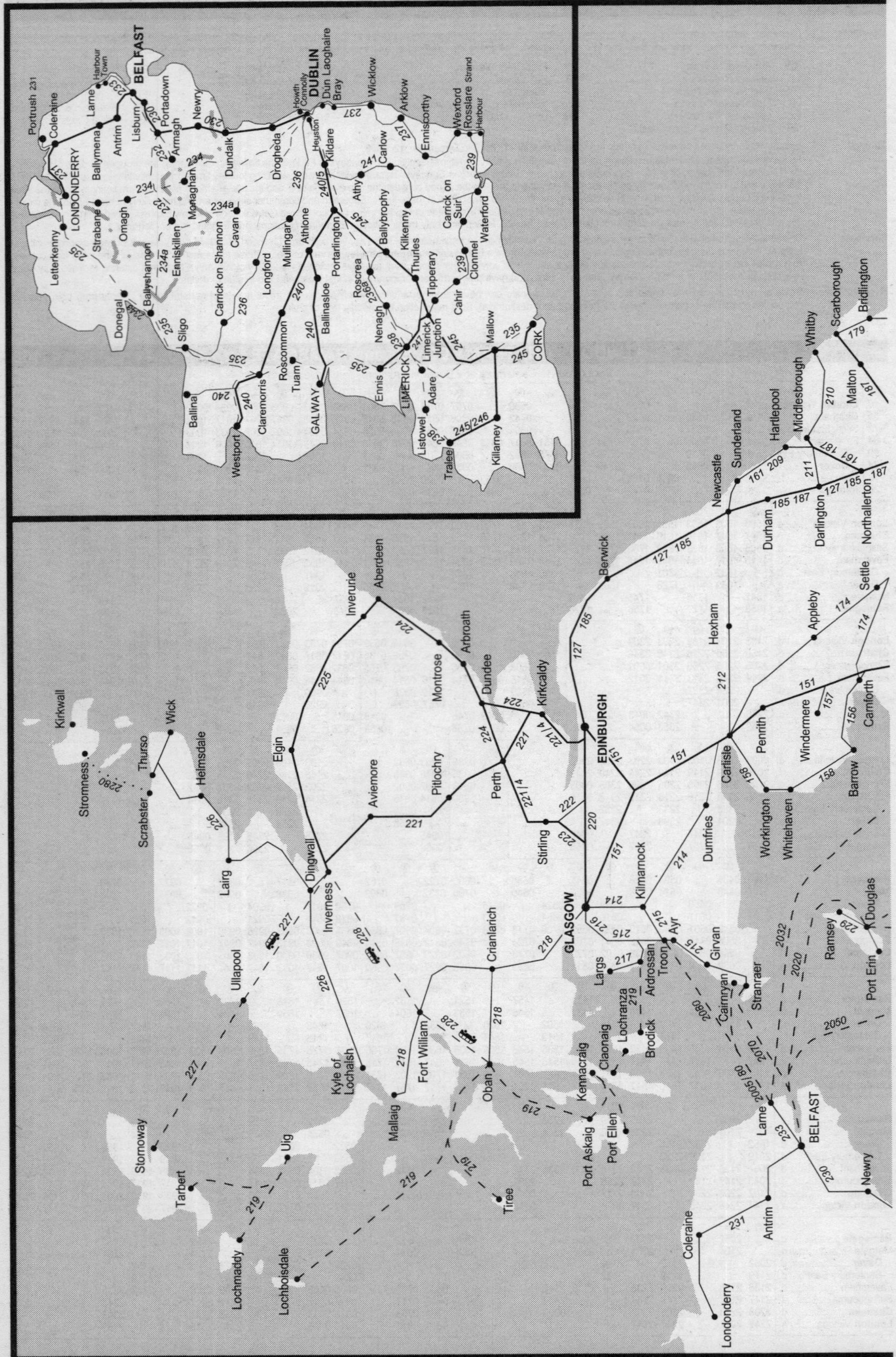

Kirkwall
Stromness
2280
Thurso
Wick
Scrabster
Helmsdale
226
Lairg
Dingwall
Inverness
Elgin
225
Inverurie
Aberdeen
224
Montrose
Arbroath
Dundee
Aviemore
221
Pitlochry
Perth
Kirkcaldy
221/4
EDINBURGH
Stirling
222
223
220
GLASGOW
Ullapool
227
Stornoway
Tarbert
Uig
219
Lochmaddy
Lochboisdale
Kyle of Lochalsh
228
Fort William
218
Mallaig
Crianlarich
Oban
Tiree
Kennacraig
Port Askaig
Port Ellen
Claonaig
Lochranza
Brodick
Largs
217
Ardrossan
Troon
Ayr
215
216
214
Kilmarnock
Girvan
Cairnryan
Stranraer
2060
2070
2005/80
Larne
233
BELFAST
230
Newry
Antrim
231
Coleraine
Londonderry
2032
2020
2050
Ramsey
229
Douglas
Port Erin
151
Dumfries
Carlisle
158
Workington
Whitehaven
Barrow
156
Carnforth
157
Windermere
Penrith
Appleby
174
Settle
212
Hexham
127
185
Berwick
Newcastle
Sunderland
161
209
Durham
187
Hartlepool
Middlesbrough
211
Darlington
Northallerton
210
Whitby
Scarborough
179
Malton
Bridlington
Portrush
Coleraine
Larne
Harbour
Town
BELFAST
Ballymena
Antrim
Lisburn
Portadown
Armagh
Newry
LONDONDERRY
Letterkenny
Strabane
Omagh
Enniskillen
Monaghan
Dundalk
Drogheda
Howth
Connolly
DUBLIN
Dún Laoghaire
Bray
Heuston
Kildare
Wicklow
Arklow
Enniscorthy
Wexford
Rosslare Strand
Rosslare Harbour
Carlow
Athy
Kilkenny
Carrick on Suir
Waterford
Ballybrophy
Portarlington
Athlone
Mullingar
Longford
Cavan
234a
Carrick on Shannon
Ballyshannon
Donegal
Sligo
Ballina
Westport
Claremorris
Roscommon
Tuam
Ballinasloe
GALWAY
Roscrea
Thurles
Tipperary
Cahir
Clonmel
Nenagh
Limerick Junction
LIMERICK
Ennis
Adare
Listowel
Tralee
Killarney
245/246
Mallow
CORK
235
236
237
238
239
240
240/5
241
245
247

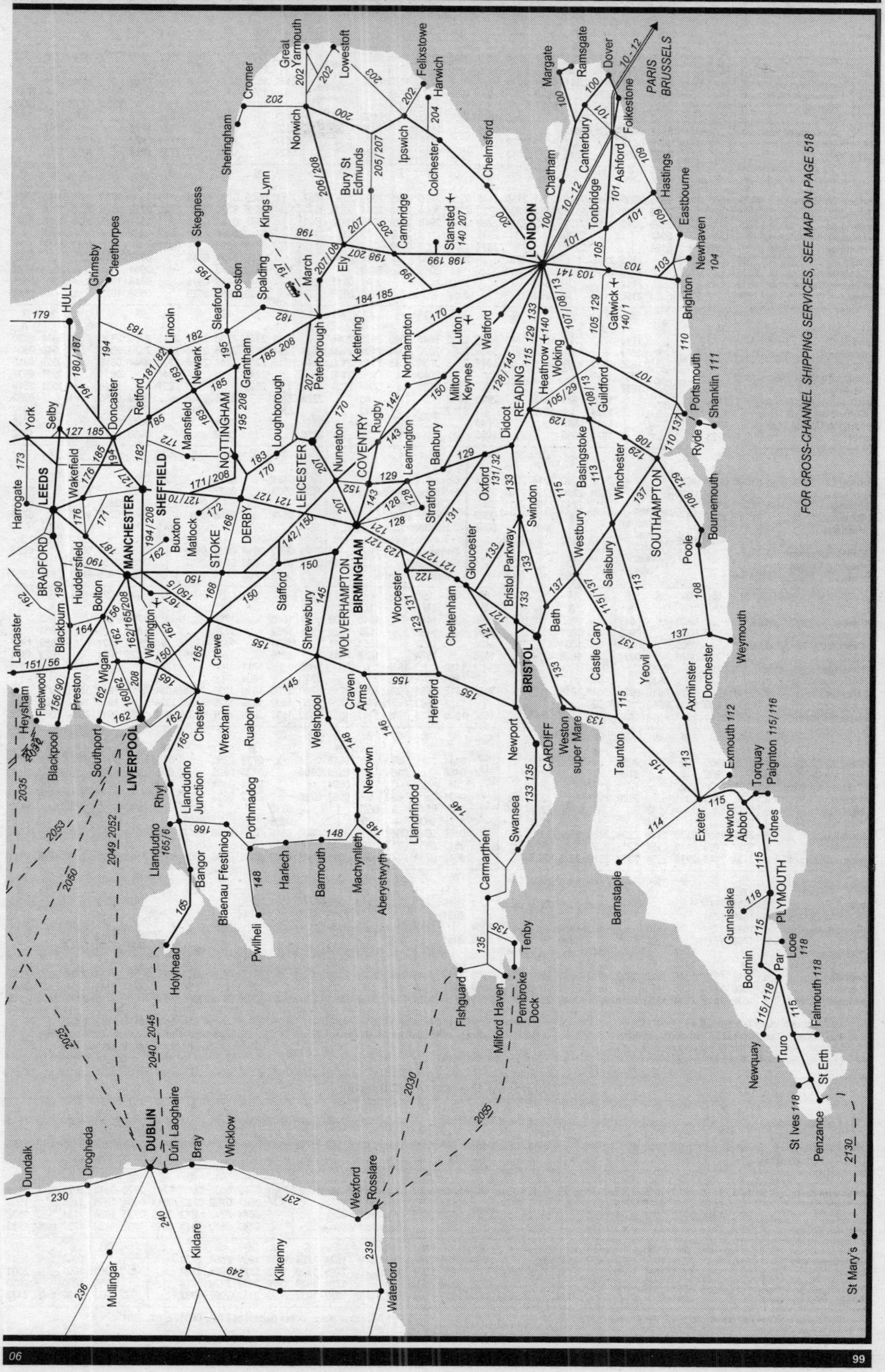
LONDON
BIRMINGHAM
MANCHESTER
LIVERPOOL
LEEDS
BRADFORD
SHEFFIELD
NOTTINGHAM
DERBY
LEICESTER
COVENTRY
WOLVERHAMPTON
STOKE
BRISTOL
CARDIFF
SOUTHAMPTON
PLYMOUTH
READING
HULL
DUBLIN
Dún Laoghaire
Bray
Wicklow
Drogheda
Dundalk
Mullingar
Kildare
Kilkenny
Waterford
Wexford
Rosslare
Lancaster
Heysham
Fleetwood
Blackpool
Preston
Southport
Wigan
Blackburn
Bolton
Huddersfield
Harrogate
York
Selby
Wakefield
Doncaster
Grimsby
Cleethorpes
Skegness
Lincoln
Retford
Newark
Mansfield
Sleaford
Boston
Spalding
Grantham
Kings Lynn
Sheringham
Cromer
Norwich
Great Yarmouth
Lowestoft
Ely
March
Peterborough
Bury St Edmunds
Ipswich
Felixstowe
Harwich
Colchester
Cambridge
Stansted 140 207
Chelmsford
Margate
Ramsgate
Canterbury
Dover
Folkestone
Chatham
Ashford
Tonbridge
Hastings
Eastbourne
Newhaven 104
Brighton
Gatwick 140/1
Guildford
Woking
Heathrow 140
Watford
Luton
Milton Keynes
Northampton
Kettering
Loughborough
Rugby
Nuneaton
Leamington
Stratford
Banbury
Oxford
Didcot
Swindon
Basingstoke
Winchester
Portsmouth
Ryde
Shanklin 111
Bournemouth
Poole
Weymouth
Dorchester
Salisbury
Westbury
Bath
Bristol Parkway
Gloucester
Cheltenham
Worcester
Hereford
Stafford
Shrewsbury
Crewe
Warrington
Chester
Wrexham
Ruabon
Welshpool
Craven Arms
Newtown
Llandrindod
Machynlleth
Aberystwyth
Barmouth
Harlech
Porthmadog
Pwllheli
Blaenau Ffestiniog
Llandudno
Llandudno Junction
Rhyl
Bangor
Holyhead
Buxton
Matlock
Newport
Swansea
Carmarthen
Tenby
Fishguard
Milford Haven
Pembroke Dock
Weston super Mare
Castle Cary
Taunton
Yeovil
Axminster
Exeter
Exmouth 112
Barnstaple
Newton Abbot
Torquay
Paignton 115/116
Totnes
Gunnislake
Looe 118
Par
Bodmin
Newquay
Truro
Falmouth 118
St Erth
St Ives 118
Penzance
St Mary's
PARIS
BRUSSELS
FOR CROSS-CHANNEL SHIPPING SERVICES, SEE MAP ON PAGE 518

101 LONDON - TONBRIDGE - HASTINGS and DOVER SE

For London to Canterbury and Dover via Chatham, see Table **100**

km		Ⓐ	Ⓐ	Ⓐ	Ⓐ	Ⓐ	Ⓐ	Ⓐ	Ⓐ	Ⓐ	Ⓐ	Ⓐ	Ⓐ		Ⓐ	Ⓐ	Ⓐ	Ⓐ	Ⓐ	Ⓐ	Ⓐ	Ⓐ	Ⓐ	Ⓐ
						A					A		A		A		A		A	A			A	
0	**London** Ch. Cross ⊕ d.	0530	0625	0700	0728	0752	0814	0854	0858	0945	0953	1045	1053	and at the same minutes past each hour until	1353	1445	1453	1545	1553	1646	1716	1734	1756	1800
36	Sevenoaks d.	0611	0700	0736	0805	0830	0847	|	0936	1016	|	1116	|		|	1516	|	1620	|	|	|	|	|	|
48	**Tonbridge** d.	0622	0711	0749	0819	0841	0857	0935	0947	1025	1031	1125	1131		1431	1525	1531	1629	1633	1725	|	1815	1835	|
55	Tunbridge Wells a.	*0654*	*0741*	|	0829	|	0909	|	|	1036	|	1135	|		|	1535	|	1639	|	|	1803	|	|	1847
100	**Hastings** a.	*0745*	*0829*	|	0907	|	0957	|	|	1117	|	1217	|		|	1619	|	1727	|	|	1851	|	|	1939
90	Ashford a.	0659	0752	0827	...	0918	...	1005	1025	...	1053	...	1153		1453	...	1553	...	1657	1757	...	1851	1914	...
113	**Canterbury** West a.	*0730*	*0817*	*0855*	...	0944	...	|	1046	...	1124	...	1220		1520	...	1621	...	1724	1829	...	|	1942	...
113	Folkestone Central a.	0723	0815	0848	...	0937	...	1029	...	...	1118	...	1212		1512	...	1621	...	1723	1822	...	1916	1938	...
124	**Dover** a.	0735	0827	0859	...	0948	...	1040	...	...	1130	...	1224		1524	...	1634	...	1735	1834	...	1929	1950	...

	Ⓐ	Ⓐ	Ⓐ	Ⓐ	Ⓐ	Ⓐ	Ⓐ	Ⓐ	Ⓐ	Ⓐ	Ⓐ	Ⓐ	Ⓐ	Ⓐ	Ⓐ	Ⓐ		⑥	⑥	⑥	⑥	⑥	⑥	⑥	⑥	⑥
	A		A																			A				
London Ch. Cross ⊕ d.	1830c	1850	1924	1945	2000	2030	2045	2100	2130	2145	2200	2230	2245	2300	2330	2337	⑥	0600	0700	0730	0745	0800	0830	0845	0945	0953
Sevenoaks d.	1858	1920	|	2020	2032	2104	2120	2134	2204	2220	2234	2304	2320	2334	0006	0010		0636	0736	0806	0820	0836	0906	0916	1016	|
Tonbridge d.	1907	1931	2003	2029	2043	2115	2129	2145	2215	2229	2245	2315	2329	2345	0017	0021		0647	0747	0815	0831	0847	0915	0926	1026	1031
Tunbridge Wells a.	|	1941	|	2042	|	|	2139	|	|	2239	|	|	2339	|	|	0031		*0710*	*0810*	|	0842	|	|	0937	1037	|
Hastings a.	|	2030	|	2121	|	|	2227	|	|	2327	|	|	0027	|	|	0119		*0758*	*0858*	|	0937	|	|	1017	1117	|
Ashford a.	1945	...	2038	...	2121	2152	...	2217	2252	...	2317	2352	...	0017	0054	...		0726	0824	0848	...	0926	0949	...	...	1052
Canterbury West a.	2015	...	2107	...	|	2216	...	|	2316	...	|	0015	...	*0118*	|	...		*0813*	*0913*	|	...	0954	|	...	...	1122
Folkestone Central a.	2012	...	2102	...	2144	...	...	2241	...	...	2341	...	...	0041	0118	...		0748	0845	0918	...	0946	1017	...	...	1121
Dover a.	2026	...	2114	...	2156	...	...	2252	...	...	2352	...	...	0052	0130	...		0759	0856	0929	...	0958	1028	...	...	1132

	⑥	⑥		⑥	⑥	⑥	⑥	⑥	⑥	⑥	⑥	⑥	⑥	⑥	⑥	⑥	⑥	⑥	⑥	⑥	⑥	⑥		⑦	⑦
		A			A																				A
London Ch. Cross ⊕ d.	1045	1053	and at the same minutes past each hour until	1745	1753	1823	1830	1845	1900	1930	1945	2000	2030	2045	2100	2130	2145	2200	2230	2245	2300	2330	⑦	0814	0830
Sevenoaks d.	1116	|		1816	|	|	1904	1917	1934	2004	2020	2034	2104	2120	2134	2204	2220	2236	2304	2320	2336	0004		0848	0904
Tonbridge d.	1126	1131		1826	1831	1903	1915	1926	1945	2015	2030	2045	2115	2130	2145	2215	2230	2247	2315	2330	2347	0018		0857	0915
Tunbridge Wells a.	1137	|		1837	|	|	|	1937	|	|	2040	|	|	2140	|	|	2240	|	|	2340	|	*0031*		0907	*0937*
Hastings a.	1217	|		1917	|	|	|	2017	|	|	2129	|	|	2227	|	|	2327	|	|	0027	|	*0118*		1001	*1019*
Ashford a.	...	1152		...	1852	1924	1948	...	2023	2048	...	2123	2148	...	2223	2248	...	2326	2348	...	0024	0055		...	0952
Canterbury West a.	...	1220		...	1924	|	2012	...	|	2112	...	|	2212	...	|	2312	...	|	0013	...	*0119*	|		...	1019
Folkestone Central a.	...	1211		...	1911	1947	...	...	2043	...	...	2143	...	...	2244	...	...	2348	...	...	0047	0116		...	1018
Dover a.	...	1223		...	1923	1958	...	...	2055	...	...	2155	...	...	2255	...	...	2359	...	...	0059	0127		...	1030

	⑦	⑦	⑦		⑦	⑦	⑦	⑦	⑦
		D					E		
London Ch. Cross ⊕ d.	0900	0914	0930	and at the same minutes past each hour until	2130	2200	2214	2230	2314
Sevenoaks d.	0934	0948	1004		2204	2234	2250	2304	2350
Tonbridge d.	0943	0957	1015		2215	2243	2259	2315	2359
Tunbridge Wells a.	|	1007	|		|	|	2309	|	0009
Hastings a.	|	1051	|		|	|	0001	|	0056
Ashford a.	1012	...	1052		2252	2312	...	2352	...
Canterbury West a.	|	...	1116		2316	|	...	|	...
Folkestone Central a.	1037	...	...		...	2338	...	0013	...
Dover a.	1049	...	...		...	2350	...	0025	...

		Ⓐ	Ⓐ	Ⓐ	Ⓐ	Ⓐ	Ⓐ	Ⓐ	Ⓐ	Ⓐ	Ⓐ
Dover d.	Ⓐ	0451	...	0525	...	...	0615	...	0656	...	...
Folkestone Central d.		0503	...	0537	...	...	0627	...	0709	...	...
Canterbury West d.		|	...	|	0542	...	|	0636	|	...	0716
Ashford d.		0524	...	0558	0607	...	0650	0702	0730	...	0745
Hastings d.		|	0516	|	|	0626	|	|	|	0702	|
Tunbridge Wells d.		|	0606	|	|	0716	|	|	|	0756	|
Tonbridge d.		0602	0618	0630	0645	|	0725	0742	0802	|	0825
Sevenoaks a.		0612	0630	0639	0657	|	0735	0752	0812	|	|
London Ch. Cross ⊡ a.		0646	0705	0714	0732	0805	0809	0826	0847	0851	0907

	Ⓐ	Ⓐ	Ⓐ	Ⓐ	Ⓐ	Ⓐ	Ⓐ		Ⓐ	Ⓐ	Ⓐ	Ⓐ	Ⓐ	Ⓐ	Ⓐ	Ⓐ	Ⓐ	Ⓐ	Ⓐ	Ⓐ	Ⓐ	Ⓐ	Ⓐ	Ⓐ	Ⓐ
					B		B		B		B		B	B		B		B						B	
Dover d.	0735	...	0810	...	0848	...	0950	and at the same minutes past each hour until	1350	...	1446	...	1540	1608	...	1640	...	1708	...	...	1752	...	...	1852	...
Folkestone Central d.	0747	...	0821	...	0900	...	1001		1402	...	1458	...	1552	1620	...	1652	...	1720	...	...	1804	...	...	1904	...
Canterbury West d.	*0747*	...	*0806*	...	0853	...	1006		1406	...	1502	...	1551	1611	...	1651	...	1711	1751	...	|	1827	...	1859	1927
Ashford d.	0810	...	0846	...	0921	...	1028		1428	...	1524	...	1619	1641	...	1719	...	1741	1816	...	1825	1851	...	1929	1951
Hastings d.	|	0750	|	0842	|	0930	|		|	1430	|	1535	|	|	1635	|	1711	|	|	1747	|	|	1847	|	|
Tunbridge Wells d.	|	0842	|	0936	|	1008	|		|	1508	|	1616	|	|	1730	|	1804	|	|	1843	|	|	1938	|	|
Tonbridge d.	0846	0900	0924	0946	0958	1018	1058		1458	1518	1554	1628	1651	1718	1740	1750	1816	1820	1846	1854	1911	1930	1948	2000	2031
Sevenoaks a.	0856	0909	0934	0955	|	1027	|		|	1527	1603	1637	1703	1730	1750	1802	1825	1829	1858	1904	|	1939	1957	2009	2040
London Ch. Cross ⊡ a.	0928c	0944	1007	1033	1036	1103	1136		1536	1603	1638	1719	1741	1807	1830	1837	1900	1907	1935	1942	1950	2018	2034	2048	2118

	Ⓐ	Ⓐ	Ⓐ	Ⓐ	Ⓐ	Ⓐ	Ⓐ	Ⓐ			⑥	⑥	⑥	⑥	⑥	⑥	⑥	⑥	⑥	⑥	⑥	⑥		⑥	⑥
															B			B	B		B			B	
Dover d.	...	1950	...	...	2056	...	...	2200	...	⑥	0444	...	0543	...	0618	0654	...	0723	0750	...	0850	...	and at the same minutes past each hour until	1550	...
Folkestone Central d.	...	2002	...	...	2108	...	...	2212	...		0456	...	0555	...	0629	0706	...	0735	0802	...	0902	...		1602	...
Canterbury West d.	...	|	2027	...	|	2127	...	|	...		|	...	|	...	0624	|	...	0724	0801	...	0906	...		1606	...
Ashford d.	...	2029	2051	...	2129	2151	...	2233	...		0521	...	0620	...	0652	0726	...	0752	0828	...	0928	...		1628	...
Hastings d.	1947	|	|	2047	|	|	2135	*2205*	...		|	0547	|	0616	|	|	0718	|	|	0818	|	0930		|	1647
Tunbridge Wells d.	2036	|	|	2136	|	|	2226	*2256*	...		|	0636	|	0706	|	|	0806	|	|	0905	|	1008		|	1736
Tonbridge d.	2048	2100	2130	2148	2200	2230	2242	2310	...		0600	0646	0659	0716	0731	0800	0816	0831	0858	0917	0958	1018		1658	1746
Sevenoaks a.	2057	2109	2139	2157	2209	2239	2251	2322	...		0612	0656	0711	0726	0743	0809	0826	0843	|	0927	|	1028		|	1755
London Ch. Cross ⊡ a.	2134	2148	2218	2234	2248	2318	2328	0001	...		0648	0734	0748	0805	0818	0848	0903	0918	0936	1003	1036	1103		1736	1833

	⑥	⑥	⑥	⑥	⑥	⑥	⑥	⑥	⑥	⑥	⑥	⑥	⑥	⑥	⑥			⑦	⑦	⑦		⑦	⑦	⑦	⑦
	B													B						G				H	B
Dover d.	1637	1719	...	...	1819	...	...	1919	...	...	2019	...	...	2115	2205	⑦	...	0732	...	...	and at the same minutes past each hour until	2032	...	...	2119
Folkestone Central d.	1649	1731	...	...	1831	...	...	1931	...	...	2031	...	...	2127	2216		...	0744	...	...		2044	...	...	2131
Canterbury West d.	1648	*1724*	...	1804	|	...	1904	|	...	2004	|	...	2104	2123	*2159*		...	|	0800	...		|	2100	...	2124
Ashford d.	1709	1751	...	1828	1851	...	1928	1951	...	2028	2051	...	2128	2152	2236		...	0804	0824	...		2104	2124	...	2154
Hastings d.	|	|	1747	|	|	1847	|	|	1947	|	|	2047	|	|	*2207*		...	*0718*	|	0854		|	|	2112	|
Tunbridge Wells d.	|	|	1836	|	|	1936	|	|	2036	|	|	2136	|	|	*2255*		...	*0808*	|	0939		|	|	2208	|
Tonbridge d.	1748	1830	1846	1900	1930	1946	2000	2030	2046	2100	2130	2146	2200	2230	2313		...	0833	0901	0949		2133	2202	2219	2231
Sevenoaks a.	1800	1842	1856	1909	1942	1956	2009	2042	2056	2109	2142	2156	2209	2242	2325		...	0843	0913	0958		2143	2214	2228	2243
London Ch. Cross ⊡ a.	1836	1919	1934	1949	2019	2034	2049	2119	2134	2149	2219	2234	2249	2318	0001		...	0918	0948	1035		2218	2248	2305	2319

A – (12) London - Canterbury; (12) London - Dover.
B – (12) Dover - London; (12) Canterbury - London.
D – London - Hastings in this pattern hourly until 1914.
E – London - Hastings in this pattern hourly from 2014.

G – Hastings - London in this pattern hourly until 1754.
H – Hastings - London in this pattern hourly from 1812.

c – London Cannon Street.

⊕ – London Charing Cross; trains also call (3 minutes later) at London Waterloo (East).
⊡ – London Charing Cross; trains also call (3–5 minutes earlier) at London Waterloo (East).

London – Maidstone – Canterbury

km			Ⓐ	Ⓐ	Ⓐ	Ⓐ		Ⓐ	Ⓐ	Ⓐ	Ⓐ	Ⓐ	Ⓐ	Ⓐ	Ⓐ	Ⓐ	Ⓐ	Ⓐ		⑥	⑥	⑥	⑥		⑥	⑥
0	**London** Victoria d.	Ⓐ	...	0610	0719	0818	and	1318	*1418*	*1518*	*1548*		*1848*	*1918*	*1948*	*2109*	*2209*	2309	⑥	...	0618	0718	0818	and	1518	*1618*
76	Maidstone East d.		0633	0723	0821	0917	hourly	1413	*1521*	*1619*	*1644*	*1754*	*2008*	*2020*	*2044*	*2213*	*2313*	0013		0619	0719	0819	0913	hourly	1613	*1713*
95	Ashford a.		0702	0752	0853	0946		1443	1553	1657	1735	1829	2038	2106	2152	2252	2352	0042		0648	0748	0848	0943		1643	1752
118	**Canterbury** West a.		0730	0817	0924	1012	until	1507	1621	1724	1805	1855	2107	2130	2216	2316	0015	0118		0714	0813	0913	1007	until	1707	1817

	⑥	⑥	⑥	⑥	⑥	⑥		⑦	⑦		⑦	⑦K
London Victoria d.	*1718*	*1818*	*1918*	*2018*	*2118*	2318	⑦	0742	0842	and	1742	1842
Maidstone East d.	*1813*	*1913*	*2019*	*2119*	*2219*	0019		0843	0943	hourly	1843	1943
Ashford a.	1852	1948	2148	2248	2348	0048		0912	1012		1912	2012
Canterbury West a.	1924	2012	2212	2312	0013	0119		0932	1033	until	1932	...

		Ⓐ	Ⓐ	Ⓐ	Ⓐ	Ⓐ	Ⓐ	Ⓐ		Ⓐ
Canterbury West d.	Ⓐ	0542	0636	0656	0747	0820	0943	1024	and	1424
Ashford d.		0607	0702	0722	0814	0904	1005	1105	hourly	1503
Maidstone East d.		*0644*	*0742*	*0812*	0843	0933	1034	1134		1532
London Victoria a.		*0749*	*0852*	*0919*	0949	1032	1132	1232	until	1633

	Ⓐ	Ⓐ	Ⓐ	Ⓐ	Ⓐ	Ⓐ	Ⓐ		⑥	⑥	⑥	⑥	⑥		⑥	⑥	⑥	⑥	⑥	⑥			⑦L	⑦		⑦
Canterbury West d.	1532	1611	1711	1827	1934	2027	2127	⑥		0624	0724	0835	0924	and	1624	1724	1804	1904	2004	2123	...	⑦	...	0944	and	1944
Ashford d.	1559	1641	1741	1851	1958	2051	2151		0600	0652	0752	0904	1005	hourly	1705	1805	1828	1928	2028	2152	...		0901	1001	hourly	2001
Maidstone East d.	1628	*1727*	*1829*	*1929*	2027	*2127*	*2237*		0630	*0729*	*0834*	*0934*	1034		1734	1829	*1929*	*2029*	*2129*	*2229*	...		0930	1030		2030
London Victoria a.	1733	*1832*	*1931*	*2031*	2129	*2232*	*2344*		0732	*0832*	*0932*	*1032*	1132	until	1832	1932	*2032*	*2132*	*2232*	*2332*	...		1032	1132	until	2132

K – Additional trains in this pattern at 1942, 2042, 2142, 2242.

L – Additional trains in this pattern at 0701, 0801, 2101, 2201.

FC, SN — LONDON - GATWICK ✈ - BRIGHTON and EASTBOURNE — 103

For details of the direct *Gatwick Express* service between London Victoria and Gatwick Airport, see Table **140**.

Services on ⑦ valid until September 6.

km		Ⓐ	Ⓐ	Ⓐ	Ⓐ	Ⓐ	Ⓐ	Ⓐ	Ⓐ	Ⓐ	Ⓐ	Ⓐ	Ⓐ	Ⓐ	Ⓐ	Ⓐ	Ⓐ		Ⓐ	Ⓐ	Ⓐ	Ⓐ	Ⓐ	Ⓐ
0	**London** Victoria ..... d.	Ⓐ	0532	0621	0632	0647	0733b	0747	0753b	0817	0821	0836	0847	0906	0917	0936	0947	and at the same minutes past each hour until	1606	1617	1636	1647	1706	1730
17	East Croydon ..... d.		0549	0638	0649	0703	0749	0803	0806	0833	0839	0853	0903	0922	0933	0952	1003		1622	1633	1652	1703	1722	|
43	**Gatwick** Airport ✈ ..... d.		0620	0704	0720	0719	0805	0819	0829	0849	0856	|	0919	|	0949	|	1019		|	1649	|	1720	|	1800
61	Haywards Heath ..... d.		0634	0721	0740	0733	0819	0832	0843	0913	0910	|	0934	|	1007	|	1034		|	1710	1723	1736	1746	1812
82	**Brighton** ..... a.		|	0742	0802	|	0836	|	0904	|	0926	0930	|	0958	|	1027	|		1700	|	1739	|	1810	1834
81	Lewes ..... a.		0649	...	...	0752	...	0851	...	0928	...	...	0952	...	1022	...	1051		...	1721	...	1756	...	...
106	**Eastbourne** ..... a.		0716	...	...	0814	...	0913	...	0950	...	...	1013	...	1044	...	1113		...	1748	...	1818	...	...

	Ⓐ	Ⓐ	Ⓐ	Ⓐ	Ⓐ	Ⓐ	Ⓐ	Ⓐ		Ⓐ	Ⓐ	Ⓐ	Ⓐ	Ⓐ	Ⓐ			⑥	⑥	⑥	⑥	⑥	⑥	⑥
London Victoria ..... d.	1736	1800	1806	1830	1847	1906	1917	1936	and at the same minutes past each hour until	2147	2206	2236	2247	2306	2332	...	⑥	0706	0721	0747	0806	0817	0821	0847
East Croydon ..... d.	1752	|	1822	|	1903	1922	1933	1952		2203	2222	2252	2303	2322	2352	...		0722	0737	0803	0822	0833	0837	0903
Gatwick Airport ✈ ..... d.	1807	1835	1838	1905	1920	|	1949	|		2219	|	|	2319	|	0015	...		|	0758	0819	|	0849	0855	0919
Haywards Heath ..... d.	1818	1847	1850	1917	1934	1945	2007	2017		2234	2245	2315	2334	2345	0031	...		|	0817	0834	|	0907	0917	0934
Brighton ..... a.	|	1910	|	1939	|	2002	|	2033		|	2300	2230	|	2359	0052	...		0758	0840	|	0858	|	0940	|
Lewes ..... a.	1838	...	1909	...	1953	...	2022	...		2251	...	...	2351	...	...	...		...	...	0848	...	0922	...	0951
Eastbourne ..... a.	1901	...	1941	...	2014	...	2048	...		2314	...	...	0016	...	...	...		...	...	0913	...	0944	...	1013

		⑥	⑥	⑥	⑥	⑥	⑥	⑥	⑥	⑥	⑥	⑥	⑥	⑥	⑥	⑥	⑥	⑥			⑦	⑦	⑦	⑦
London Victoria ..... d.	and at the same minutes past each hour until	1906	1917	1921	1947	2006	2017	2021	2047	2106	2117	2136	2147	2206	2236	2247	2302	2332	...	⑦	0632	0721	0821	0847
East Croydon ..... d.		1922	1933	1937	2003	2022	2033	2037	2103	2122	2133	2152	2203	2222	2252	2303	2318	2352	...		0652	0738	0838	0903
Gatwick Airport ✈ ..... d.		|	1949	1958	2019	|	2049	2055	2119	|	2149	|	2219	|	|	2319	2339	0014	...		0719	0758	0858	0919
Haywards Heath ..... d.		|	2007	2017	2034	|	2107	2117	2134	2145	2208	2215	2234	2245	2315	2334	2353	0034	...		0736	0821	0921	0930
Brighton ..... a.		1958	|	2040	|	2058	|	2140	|	2200	|	2230	|	2300	2330	|	0015	0055	...		0758	0841	0941	|
Lewes ..... a.		...	2022	...	2051	...	2122	...	2151	...	2223	...	2251	...	...	2351	...	...	...		...	...	...	0948
Eastbourne ..... a.		...	2048	...	2113	...	2148	...	2215	...	2248	...	2314	...	...	0016	...	...	...		...	...	...	1008

	⑦	⑦	⑦		⑦	⑦	⑦	⑦	⑦	⑦
London Victoria ..... d.	0906	0921	0947	and at the same minutes past each hour until	2106	2121	2147	2221	2247	2332
East Croydon ..... d.	0922	0938	1003		2122	2138	2203	2238	2303	2353
Gatwick Airport ✈ ..... d.	0938	0958	1019		2138	2158	2219	2258	2319	0015
Haywards Heath ..... d.	|	1021	1030		|	2215	2230	2315	2330	0031
Brighton ..... a.	1000	1041	|		2200	2235	|	2335	|	0052
Lewes ..... a.	...	...	1048		...	...	2248	...	2348	...
Eastbourne ..... a.	...	...	1108		...	...	2319	...	0020	...

		Ⓐ	Ⓐ	Ⓐ	Ⓐ	Ⓐ	Ⓐ	Ⓐ	Ⓐ
Eastbourne ..... d.	Ⓐ	0508	0542	...	...	0624	...	...	0657
Lewes ..... d.		0529	0605	...	...	0650	...	...	0723
Brighton ..... d.		|	|	0617	0640	|	0656	0715	|
Haywards Heath ..... d.		0546	0622	0635	0702	0713	0720	0735	0743
Gatwick Airport ✈ ..... d.		0558	0641	0653	0720	0729	0735	0750	|
East Croydon ..... d.		0614	0658	0715	|	0747	|	|	0814
London Victoria ..... a.		0632	0714b	0733	0750	0804b	0806	0820	0832

	Ⓐ	Ⓐ	Ⓐ	Ⓐ	Ⓐ	Ⓐ	Ⓐ	Ⓐ	Ⓐ	Ⓐ	Ⓐ	Ⓐ	Ⓐ	Ⓐ	Ⓐ		Ⓐ	Ⓐ	Ⓐ	Ⓐ	Ⓐ	Ⓐ	Ⓐ	Ⓐ
Eastbourne ..... d.	...	0715	...	0732	0757	...	0818	...	0856	...	0929	...	0956	...	1028	and at the same minutes past each hour until	...	1858	...	1931	...	...	2031	...
Lewes ..... d.	...	0743	...	0754	0823	...	0847	...	0917	...	0949	...	1020	...	1049		...	1921	...	1950	...	...	2050	...
Brighton ..... d.	0730	|	0744	|	|	0845	|	0919	|	0949	|	1019	|	1049	|		1919	|	1949	|	2019	2049	|	2119
Haywards Heath ..... d.	0751	0802	0806	0814	0844	0858	0904	|	0937	|	1009	|	1040	|	1105		|	1940	|	2010	|	|	2109	|
Gatwick Airport ✈ ..... d.	0805	|	0820	|	0855	0911	0922	|	0954	|	1024	|	1054	|	1124		|	1955	|	2025	|	|	2124	|
East Croydon ..... d.	|	0831	|	0846	0914	0926	0939	0955	1010	1024	1040	1056	1110	1124	1140		1954	2011	2024	2041	2054	2125	2140	2153
London Victoria ..... a.	0835	0850b	0852	0905	0932	0944	0958	1011	1027	1040	1057	1112	1127	1140	1157		2010	2028	2043	2058	2110	2141	2157	2210

	Ⓐ	Ⓐ	Ⓐ	Ⓐ	Ⓐ			⑥	⑥	⑥	⑥	⑥	⑥	⑥	⑥	⑥	⑥	⑥	⑥		⑥	⑥	⑥	⑥
Eastbourne ..... d.	...	2131	...	2215	...	...	⑥	...	...	...	...	0624	...	...	0658	...	0731	...	0758	and at the same minutes past each hour until	...	1858	...	1932
Lewes ..... d.	...	2150	...	2240	...	...		...	...	...	...	0650	...	...	0720	...	0750	...	0820		...	1920	...	1951
Brighton ..... d.	2149	|	2200	|	2302	...		0521	0550	0610	0649	|	0655	0719	|	0749	|	0819	|		1919	|	1949	|
Haywards Heath ..... d.	|	2206	2222	2258	2324	...		0537	0611	0640	|	0705	0716	|	0740	|	0805	|	0840		|	1940	|	2007
Gatwick Airport ✈ ..... d.	|	2224	2238	2312	2353	...		0553	0625	0655	|	0724	0738	|	0754	|	0824	|	0854		|	1954	|	2024
East Croydon ..... d.	2224	2240	2300	2330	0017	...		0611	0641	0711	0724	0740	0753	0756	0810	0824	0840	0856	0910		1956	2010	2024	2040
London Victoria ..... a.	2240	2257	2320	2352	0037	...		0630	0657	0727	0740	0757	0809	0812	0827	0840	0857	0912	0927		2012	2027	2040	2057

	⑥	⑥	⑥	⑥	⑥	⑥	⑥	⑥	⑥	⑥		⑦	⑦	⑦	⑦	⑦		⑦	⑦	⑦		⑦		⑦
Eastbourne ..... d.	...	...	2031	...	...	2131	...	2218	...	...	⑦	...	0658	...	0755	...	and at the same minutes past each hour until	...	...	2059	...	...	...	...
Lewes ..... d.	...	...	2050	...	...	2150	...	2240	...	...		...	0722	...	0822	...		...	...	2122	...	...	...	...
Brighton ..... d.	2019	2049	|	2119	2149	|	2200	|	2302	...		0704	|	0800	|	0840		2040	2104	|	...	2204	...	2302
Haywards Heath ..... d.	|	|	2106	|	|	2206	2222	2258	2324	...		0725	0740	0825	0840	|		|	2125	2140	...	2225	...	2324
Gatwick Airport ✈ ..... d.	|	|	2124	|	|	2223	2238	2312	2353	...		0742	0752	0842	0852	0902		2102	2142	2152	...	2242	...	2347
East Croydon ..... d.	2054	2124	2140	2154	2224	2240	2300	2330	0017	...		0800	0809	0900	0909	0917		2117	2200	2209	...	2300	...	0017
London Victoria ..... a.	2110	2140	2157	2210	2240	2258	2317	2352	0036	...		0817	0825	0917	0925	0933		2133	2217	2225	...	2317	...	0037

BEDFORD - LONDON ST. PANCRAS - BRIGHTON

Due to engineering work there are no through services between Bedford and Brighton on ©. On these days services between London and Brighton will start / terminate at **London Bridge**. For more information please contact First Capital Connect (✆ 0845 026 4700 www.firstcapitalconnect.co.uk) or National Rail Enquiries (✆ 08457 484 950 www.nationalrail.co.uk).

	Ⓐ	Ⓐ	Ⓐ	Ⓐ	Ⓐ	Ⓐ	Ⓐ	Ⓐ	Ⓐ		Ⓐ	Ⓐ	Ⓐ	Ⓐ	Ⓐ	Ⓐ	Ⓐ	Ⓐ	Ⓐ	Ⓐ	Ⓐ	Ⓐ	Ⓐ	Ⓐ
Bedford ..... 170 d.	0540	0600	0620	0700	0748	0820	0840	0854	0910	and at the same minutes past each hour until	1454	1510	1524	1610	1632	1710	1734	1810	1842	1854	1920	1950	2020	2050
Luton ..... 170 d.	0604	0624	0644	0724	0812	0844	0904	0918	0934		1518	1534	1548	1634	1656	1734	1758	1834	1906	1918	1944	2014	2044	2114
Luton Airport ✈ .. 170 d.	0606	0626	0646	0726	0814	0846	0906	0920	0936		1520	1536	1550	1636	1658	1736	1800	1836	1908	1920	1946	2016	2046	2116
St Albans City ..... d.	0618	0638	0658	0738	0826	0900	0918	0934	0948		1534	1548	1604	1648	1710	1748	1812	1848	1920	1933	1958	2028	2058	2128
London St Pancras 170 d.	0640	0700	0720	0800	0848	0920	0939	0954	1009		1554	1609	1624	1710	1734	1808	1838	1908	1942	1952	2022	2052	2122	2152
East Croydon ..... d.	0716	0732	0756	0836	0924	0954	1010	1024	1039		1624	1640	1700	1800	1809	1840	1910	1939	2014	2024	2054	2124	2154	2224
Gatwick Airport ✈ ..... d.	0732	0750	0812	0852	0941	1011	1026	1041	1056		1641	1656	1716	1812	1825	1856	1927	1956	2031	2041	2111	2141	2211	2241
Haywards Heath ..... d.	0748	0806	0828	0907	0957	1027	1040	1055	1108		1655	1710	1733	1830	1836	1912	1941	2010	2042	2057	2126	2158	2226	2258
Brighton ..... a.	0807	0827	0849	0923	1019	1049	1054	1117	1124		1717	1727	1757	1854	1904	1934	2000	2030	2058	2118	2148	2220	2248	2320

	Ⓐ	Ⓐ	Ⓐ	Ⓐ	Ⓐ	Ⓐ	Ⓐ	Ⓐ	Ⓐ	Ⓐ	Ⓐ		Ⓐ	Ⓐ	Ⓐ	Ⓐ	Ⓐ	Ⓐ	Ⓐ	Ⓐ	Ⓐ	Ⓐ	Ⓐ	Ⓐ
Brighton ..... d.	0509	0539	0609	0623	0700	0724	0802	0836	0907	0934	0937	and at the same minutes past each hour until	1607	1630	1704	1737	1807	1837	1907	1934	1937	2007	2034	2037
Haywards Heath ..... d.	0530	0600	0630	0644	0722	0746	0823	0900	0932	0948	0958		1626	1650	1718	1756	1832	1902	1932	1948	2002	2032	2048	2102
Gatwick Airport ✈ ..... d.	0546	0616	0646	0700	0737	0801	0838	0916	0946	1001	1016		1641	1707	1731	1816	1846	1916	1946	2001	2016	2046	2101	2116
East Croydon ..... d.	0602	0632	0702	0724	0754	0828	0854	0932	1002	1017	1032		1657	1728	1747	1832	1902	1932	2002	2017	2032	2102	2117	2132
London St Pancras. 170 d.	0633	0703	0732	0803	0831	0903	0931	1003	1033	1047	1103		1735	1805	1831	1905	1933	2003	2033	2047	2103	2133	2147	2203
St Albans City ..... d.	0655	0725	0753	0824	0851	0925	0951	1024	1054	1110	1124		1756	1826	1851	1926	1955	2025	2055	2109	2125	2155	2209	2225
Luton Airport ..... 170 d.	0707	0737	0805	0837	0900	0937	1000	1037	1106	1121	1137		1809	1839	|	1939	2007	2037	2107	2121	2137	2207	2221	2237
Luton ..... 170 d.	0710	0740	0808	0840	0904	0940	1004	1040	1109	1124	1140		1812	1842	1904	1942	2010	2040	2110	2124	2140	2210	2224	2240
Bedford ..... 170 a.	0736	0806	0834	0906	0926	1008	1026	1106	1136	1150	1206		1838	1908	1928	2008	2036	2106	2136	2150	2206	2236	2250	2306

b – London Bridge.

SN — BRIGHTON - NEWHAVEN - SEAFORD — 104

From Brighton: (Lewes *13 km* 15 mins, Newhaven *23 km* 29 mins, Seaford *27 km* 37 mins)

Ⓐ: 0545, 0600 **L**, 0639, 0652, 0710, 0740, 0813, 0845, 0910, 0940 and every 30 minutes until 1740; then 1808, 1817, 1838, 1908, 1940, 2010, 2040, 2104, 2140, 2204, 2234, 2334.

⑥: 0552, 0610, 0640 and every 30 minutes until until 2040; then 2104, 2140, 2204, 2234, 2334.

⑦: 0715, 0749, 0809, 0849, 0909, 0929 the at 09 and 29 minutes past each hour until 2209; then 2239.

L – Change at Lewes.

From Seaford (and **Newhaven Town** ▲ 7 minutes later):

Ⓐ: 0509, 0545, 0630, 0716, 0733, 0758, 0857, 0925, 0958 and at 25 and 58 minutes past each hour until 1825; then 1844, 1902, 1919, 1937, 1958, 2028, 2058, 2128, 2158, 2220, 2258, 2325.

⑥: 0505, 0628, 0658, 0728, 0758, 0825, 0858 and at 25 and 58 minutes past each hour until 1958; then 2028, 2058, 2128, 2158, 2220, 2258, 2325.

⑦: 0657, 0757, 0827, 0857 and at 27 and 57 minutes past each hour until 2127; then 2153, 2227, 2253.

▲ – ± 500m from **Newhaven Harbour**; most trains also call at the Harbour station.

105 GATWICK ✈ - TONBRIDGE and READING — GW, SE

km			Ⓐ	Ⓐ	Ⓐ	Ⓐ	Ⓐ	Ⓐ	Ⓐ	Ⓐ	Ⓐ		Ⓐ	Ⓐ		Ⓐ	Ⓐ	Ⓐ		Ⓐ	Ⓐ	Ⓐ	Ⓐ	Ⓐ
0	Gatwick Airport ✈ d.	Ⓐ	0531	...	0556	...	0700	...	0758	...	0907	...	1003	...	and at	1503	...	1603	...	...	1703	...	1803	...
10	Redhill d.		0544	0556	0614	0642	0711	0729	0809	0823	0924	...	1014	1022	the same	1514	1522	1614	...	1622	1714	1739	1814	1832
42	**Tonbridge** a.		|	0626	|	0715	|	0802	|	0853	|	...	|	1052	minutes	|	1552	|	...	1652	|	1811	|	1902
43	Guildford d.		0612	...	0642	...	0742	...	0837	...	0954	...	1043	...	past each	1543	...	1643	...	...	1744	...	1849	...
84	**Reading** a.		0658	...	0729	...	0828	...	0916	...	1023	...	1119	...	hour until	1623	...	1719	...	...	1824	...	1925	...

	Ⓐ	Ⓐ		Ⓐ	Ⓐ		Ⓐ	Ⓐ	Ⓐ		Ⓐ		Ⓐ	Ⓐ	Ⓐ				⑥	⑥	⑥		⑥	⑥
Gatwick Airport ✈ d.	...	1916	...	...	2003	...	...	2103	...	...	2222	...	...	2318	...	...	...	⑥	0531	0603	...	and at	...	2003
Redhill d.	1901	1927	...	1951	2014	...	2051	2114	2155	...	2233	...	2255	2329	2355	...	...		0542	0614	0622	the same	1922	2014
Tonbridge a.	1934	|	...	2021	|	...	2121	|	2225	...	|	...	2325	|	0015	...	...		|	|	0652	minutes	1952	|
Guildford d.	...	1955	...	...	2043	...	...	2143	...	...	2314	...	...	0001	...	...	...		0612	0644	...	past each	...	2044
Reading a.	...	2032	...	...	2119	...	...	2219	...	...	0001	...	...	0039	...	...	...		0703	0719	...	hour until	...	2119

	⑥	⑥	⑥	⑥	⑥	⑥	⑥				⑦	⑦	⑦	⑦	⑦		⑦	⑦		⑦	⑦	⑦		⑦
Gatwick Airport ✈ d.	...	2103	...	2222	...	2318	...	...	...	⑦	0606	0708	...	0808	...	and at	2108	...	...	2207	...	...	...	2307
Redhill d.	2051	2114	2151	2233	2255	2329	2355	...	...		0619	0719	0740	0819	0840	the same	2120	2140	...	2220	2240	2309	...	2320
Tonbridge a.	2121	|	2221	|	2325	|	0015	...	...		|	|	0810	|	0910	minutes	|	2210	...	|	2310	2339	...	|
Guildford d.	...	2144	...	2314	...	0001	...	...	...		0649	0750	...	0858	...	past each	2151	...	...	2259	...	...	...	2351
Reading a.	...	2219	...	2359	...	0037	...	...	...		0724	0834	...	0934	...	hour until	2237	...	...	2337	...	...	...	0037

		Ⓐ	Ⓐ	Ⓐ	Ⓐ	Ⓐ	Ⓐ	Ⓐ	Ⓐ	Ⓐ	Ⓐ	Ⓐ	Ⓐ		Ⓐ	Ⓐ	Ⓐ	Ⓐ	Ⓐ	Ⓐ	Ⓐ	Ⓐ	Ⓐ	Ⓐ
Reading d.	Ⓐ	...	0434	0534	...	0634	...	...	0734	...	0834	...	0934	and at	1434	...	1528	...	...	1634	...	1734	...	1834
Guildford d.		...	0510	0610	...	0710	...	...	0818	...	0913	...	1010	the same	1510	...	1610	...	...	1710	...	1818	...	1910
Tonbridge d.		0500	|	|	0647	|	0725	0759	|	0837	|	0919	|	minutes	|	1519	|	1619	1703	|	1749	|	1850	|
Redhill a.		0531	0539	0638	0718	0738	0756	0830	0846	0908	0942	0950	1038	past each	1538	1550	1645	1650	1725	1738	1821	1847	1921	1938
Gatwick Airport ✈ a.		...	0552	0656	...	0750	...	...	0901	...	0958	...	1050	hour until	1550	...	1658	...	...	1754	...	1900	...	1953

	Ⓐ	Ⓐ	Ⓐ	Ⓐ	Ⓐ	Ⓐ	Ⓐ	Ⓐ	Ⓐ			⑥	⑥	⑥	⑥	⑥	⑥	⑥	⑥		⑥	⑥	⑥	⑥
Reading d.	...	1934	...	2034	...	2134	...	2234	2334	...	⑥	0434	...	0534	...	0634	...	0734	...	and at	1734	...	1834	...
Guildford d.	...	2010	...	2110	...	2218	...	2318	0021	...		0510	...	0610	...	0710	...	0810	...	the same	1810	...	1910	...
Tonbridge d.	1910	|	2110	|	2210	|	2317	|	|	...		|	0524	|	0619	|	0719	|	0819	minutes	|	1819	|	1910
Redhill a.	1941	2038	2142	2149	2242	2248	2349	2358	0049	...		0538	0555	0638	0650	0738	0750	0838	0850	past each	1838	1850	1938	1945
Gatwick Airport ✈ a.	...	2050	...	2204	...	2304	...	0010	0102	...		0558	...	0650	...	0750	...	0850	...	hour until	1850	...	1950	...

	⑥	⑥	⑥	⑥	⑥	⑥	⑥	⑥	⑥			⑦	⑦	⑦	⑦	⑦		⑦	⑦	⑦	⑦	⑦	⑦	⑦
Reading d.	1934	...	...	2034	...	2134	...	2234	2334	...	⑦	0603	...	0703	...	0803	and at	...	2003	...	2103	...	2203	2315
Guildford d.	2010	...	...	2110	...	2218	...	2318	0021	...		0640	...	0747	...	0839	the same	...	2039	...	2147	...	2239	2359
Tonbridge d.	|	2010	2141	|	2210	|	2317	|	|	...		|	0741	|	0841	|	minutes	2041	|	2141	|	2224	|	|
Redhill a.	2038	2045	2141	2144	2242	2252	2349	2358	0049	...		0709	0812	0817	0912	0918	past each	2112	2118	2212	2218	2255	2318	0030
Gatwick Airport ✈ a.	2050	...	...	2159	...	2303	...	0010	0102	...		0727	...	0830	...	0932	hour until	...	2132	...	2231	...	2333	0041

107 LONDON - GUILDFORD - PORTSMOUTH — SW

km			Ⓐ		Ⓐ	Ⓐ		Ⓐ	Ⓐ		Ⓐ	Ⓐ	Ⓐ	Ⓐ		Ⓐ	Ⓐ	Ⓐ	Ⓐ	Ⓐ	Ⓐ	Ⓐ	Ⓐ
0	**London** Waterloo d.	Ⓐ	...	...	0500	0520	...	0615	0645	...	0730	0800	0830	0900	and at	1500	1530	1600	1630	1700	1730	1800	1830
39	Woking d.		...	...	0551	0611	...	0643	0713	...	0755	0825	0855	0925	the same	1525	1555	1625	1655	1725	1756	|	1858
49	**Guildford** d.		0515	...	0600	0625	...	0655	0725	...	0804	0839	0904	0934	minutes	1534	1604	1634	1704	1737	1808	1833	1908
69	Haslemere d.		0530	...	0625	0655	...	0720	0755	...	0825	0855	0921	0950	past	1550	1624	1651	1724	1752	1826	1852	1926
107	Havant d.		0602	...	0658	0728	...	0752	0827	...	0850	0920	0950	1016	each	1616	1650	1716	1750	1819	1851	1917	1951
118	Portsmouth & Southsea a.		0618	...	0716	0746	...	0807	0843	...	0902	0932	1002	1028	hour	1628	1702	1728	1802	1832	1903	1929	2003
120	**Portsmouth** Harbour a.		0622	...	0720	...	...	0812	0848	...	0907	0937	1007	1033	until	1633	1707	1735	1809	1839	1910	1936	2010

	Ⓐ	Ⓐ	Ⓐ	Ⓐ	Ⓐ	Ⓐ	Ⓐ	Ⓐ	Ⓐ	Ⓐ	Ⓐ			⑥	⑥		⑥	⑥	⑥		⑥	⑥	⑥
London Waterloo d.	1900	1930	2000	2030	2100	2130	2200	2230	2245	2315	2345	...	⑥	...	0520	...	0645	0730	0800	and at	1930	2000	2030
Woking d.	1925	1955	2025	2055	2125	2155	2225	2255	2313	2343	0017	...		...	0613	...	0713	0755	0825	the same	1955	2025	2055
Guildford d.	1937	2004	2034	2104	2134	2204	2234	2304	2325	2352	0030	...		0515	0625	...	0725	0804	0834	minutes	2004	2034	2104
Haslemere d.	1953	2022	2055	2122	2155	2225	2255	2325	2350	0013	0054	...		0529	0645	...	0745	0821	0850	past	2021	2050	2121
Havant d.	2018	2049	2119	2146	2219	2249	2319	2349	0022	0037	0126	...		0601	0720	...	0817	0850	0916	each	2050	2116	2146
Portsmouth & Southsea a.	2032	2101	2132	2158	2232	2304	2332	0002	0038	0050	0142	...		0617	0735	...	0832	0902	0928	hour	2102	2128	2158
Portsmouth Harbour a.	2037	2106	2137	2202	2237	2308	2337	0007	...	0055	...	...		0622	0740	...	0837	0907	0933	until	2107	2133	2203

	⑥	⑥	⑥	⑥	⑥	⑥	⑥			⑦	⑦	⑦	⑦	⑦	⑦	⑦		⑦	⑦	⑦	⑦	⑦	⑦
London Waterloo d.	2100	2130	2200	2230	2245	2315	2345	...	⑦	...	0800	0830	0900	0930	1000	1030	and at	2100	2130	2200	2230	2300	2330
Woking d.	2125	2155	2225	2255	2313	2343	0017	...		0732	0835	0904	0935	1004	1032	1102	the same	2132	2202	2232	2302	2332	0002
Guildford d.	2134	2204	2234	2304	2325	2352	0029	...		0742	0845	0914	0945	1014	1042	1112	minutes	2142	2212	2242	2312	2342	0012
Haslemere d.	2155	2225	2255	2325	2350	0013	0054	...		0807	0912	0929	1012	1029	1107	1127	past	2207	2227	2307	2327	0007	0027
Havant d.	2219	2249	2319	2349	0022	0037	0126	...		0839	0945	0952	1045	1053	1139	1151	each	2239	2251	2339	2351	0039	0051
Portsmouth & Southsea a.	2232	2302	2332	0002	0038	0050	0142	...		0853	0959	1006	1059	1105	1153	1204	hour	2253	2304	2353	0004	0053	0104
Portsmouth Harbour a.	2236	2308	2337	0007	...	0055	...	...		0857	1004	1011	1104	1111	1158	1211	until	2258	2309	2358	0009	0058	0109

		Ⓐ		Ⓐ	Ⓐ	Ⓐ	Ⓐ		Ⓐ	Ⓐ	Ⓐ	Ⓐ	Ⓐ	Ⓐ		Ⓐ	Ⓐ	Ⓐ	Ⓐ	Ⓐ	Ⓐ	Ⓐ	Ⓐ
Portsmouth Harbour d.	Ⓐ	0425	...	0514	0550	0615	0642	...	0713	0745	0815	0845	0915	0945	and at	1445	1515	1545	1615	1645	1715	1745	1815
Portsmouth & Southsea d.		0430	...	0519	0555	0620	0647	...	0718	0750	0820	0850	0920	0950	the same	1450	1520	1550	1620	1650	1720	1750	1820
Havant d.		0446	...	0536	0611	0634	0700	...	0732	0804	0834	0904	0934	1004	minutes	1504	1534	1604	1634	1704	1734	1804	1834
Haslemere d.		0521	...	0611	0647	0702	0735	...	0800	0832	0902	0932	1002	1032	past	1532	1602	1637	1702	1737	1802	1832	1902
Guildford d.		0550	...	0631	0707	0717	0754	...	0815	0854	0917	0947	1017	1047	each	1547	1617	1700	1717	1800	1817	1855	1921
Woking a.		0600	...	0639	0715	0725	|	...	0826	|	0927	0959	1025	1057	hour	1557	1625	1711	1725	1811	|	1903	1928
London Waterloo a.		0629	...	0712	0745	0754	0832	...	0855	0931	0955	1027	1051	1124	until	1624	1651	1743	1754	1843	1859	1929	1959

	Ⓐ	Ⓐ	Ⓐ	Ⓐ	Ⓐ	Ⓐ	Ⓐ	Ⓐ			⑥	⑥		⑥	⑥	⑥		⑥	⑥	⑥	⑥	⑥	⑥
Portsmouth Harbour d.	1845	1915	1945	2015	2045	2118	2218	2318	...	⑥	0438	0514	...	0619	0645	0715	and at	1615	1645	1717	1745	1815	1845
Portsmouth & Southsea d.	1850	1920	1950	2020	2050	2124	2224	2324	...		0443	0519	...	0624	0650	0720	the same	1620	1650	1724	1750	1820	1850
Havant d.	1904	1934	2004	2034	2104	2140	2240	2340	...		0459	0535	...	0640	0704	0734	minutes	1634	1704	1740	1804	1834	1904
Haslemere d.	1932	2002	2032	2102	2132	2215	2315	0015	...		0534	0610	...	0715	0732	0802	past	1702	1732	1815	1832	1902	1932
Guildford d.	1947	2017	2047	2117	2147	2239	2339	0037	...		0602	0632	...	0732	0747	0817	each	1717	1747	1832	1847	1917	1947
Woking a.	1957	2025	2057	2125	2157	2249	2349	...	...		0611	0644	...	0744	0757	0826	hour	1725	1757	1844	1857	1925	1957
London Waterloo a.	2023	2050	2127	2150	2227	2319	0030	...	...		0640	0713	...	0813	0823	0851	until	1751	1823	1913	1923	1951	2023

	⑥	⑥	⑥	⑥	⑥	⑥	⑥			⑦		⑦	⑦	⑦	⑦	⑦	⑦	⑦	⑦		⑦		⑦
Portsmouth Harbour d.	1915	1945	2015	2045	2118	2218	2318	...	⑦	0643	...	0729	0748	0829	0848	0932	0948	1032	1048	and at	2232	...	2248
Portsmouth & Southsea d.	1920	1950	2020	2050	2124	2224	2324	...		0648	...	0734	0753	0834	0853	0937	0953	1037	1053	the same	2237	...	2253
Havant d.	1934	2004	2034	2104	2140	2240	2340	...		0702	...	0747	0807	0847	0907	0950	1007	1050	1107	minutes	2250	...	2307
Haslemere d.	2002	2032	2102	2132	2215	2315	0015	...		0737	...	0814	0842	0914	0942	1017	1042	1117	1142	past	2317	...	2342
Guildford d.	2017	2047	2117	2149	2239	2339	0037	...		0805	...	0835	0905	0935	1005	1035	1105	1135	1205	each	2335	...	0005
Woking a.	2025	2057	2125	2157	2249	2349	...	...		0813	...	0842	0915	0942	1015	1042	1113	1142	1213	hour	2342	...	0013
London Waterloo a.	2050	2127	2150	2224	2318	0032	...	...		0849	...	0919	0949	1021	1049	1119	1149	1219	1249	until	0014	...	...

☛ 🍸 conveyed by trains from London at 0730 and 0830–2100 on Ⓐ; at 0900–1930 on ⑥; and hourly 1130–2030 on ⑦.

☛ 🍸 conveyed by trains from Portsmouth at 0514 and 0615–1845 on Ⓐ; at 0645–1645 and 1745 on ⑥; and hourly 0932–1832 on ⑦.

SW LONDON - SOUTHAMPTON - WEYMOUTH 108

For other trains Basingstoke - Bournemouth and v.v., see Table **129**

km		⚒	②–⑥	⚒	⚒	⚒	⑥	Ⓐ	Ⓐ	⑥	Ⓐ	⑥	⚒	⑥	Ⓐ	⚒	⑥	Ⓐ 🍷	⚒ 🍷	⚒ 🍷		⚒ 🍷	⚒ 🍷	⚒ 🍷
0	**London** Waterloo d.		0005	0105	...	...	...	...	0530	0530	...	...	0630	...	0612	0735	0805	0805	0835	0905	and	1435	1505	1535
39	Woking d.		0036	0142	...	...	...	...	0601	0601	...	...	0657	...	0650	0800	|	|	0900	|	at	1500	|	1600
77	Basingstoke d.		0057	0212**s**	...	...	...	0540	0621	0621	...	...	0718	...	0730	0820	0850	0850	|	0950	the	|	1550	|
107	Winchester d.		0113	0229**s**	...	...	...	0559	0638	0641	...	...	0734	...	0750	0837	0906	0906	0933	1006	same	1533	1606	1633
120	Southampton Airport d.		0127	0243**s**	...	...	...	0613	0653	0656	...	...	0748	...	0806	0851	0915	0915	0942	1015	minutes	1542	1615	1642
128	**Southampton** Central d.		0137	0253	...	...	0625	0625	0701	0705	0718	0725	0800	0822	0819	0900	0924	0924	0951	1024	past	1551	1624	1651
149	Brockenhurst d.		0153**s**	...	...	0616	0644	0644	0718	0722	0744	0744	0817	0844	0844	0916	0938	0938	1005	1038	each	1605	1638	1705
174	**Bournemouth** d.		0216	...	0611	0644	0711	0711	0746	0749	0811	0811	0844	0911	0911	0943	1004	1004	1024	1104	hour	1624	1704	1724
183	Poole d.		...	...	0624	0657	0724	0724	0758	0802	0824	0824	0857	0924	0924	0956	1014	1014	1037	1114	until	1637	1714	1737
219	Dorchester South d.		...	...	0658	0731	0758	0758	0833	0834	0858	0858	0929	0958	0958	1027	1049	1056	1105	1149		1705	1749	1805
230	**Weymouth** a.		...	...	0714	0742	0809	0814	0844	0845	0909	0909	0940	1009	1009	1035	1100	1107	1113	1200		1713	1802	1815

	⑥ 🍷	Ⓐ 🍷	⚒ 🍷	Ⓐ 🍷	⑥ 🍷	Ⓐ 🍷	⑥ 🍷	Ⓐ	Ⓐ 🍷	⑥ 🍷	Ⓐ 🍷	⑥ 🍷	⚒ 🍷	⑥ 🍷	Ⓐ 🍷	⚒	⚒ 🍷	⚒ 🍷	⚒	⚒ 🍷	⚒ 🍷	⚒	⚒ 🍷	⚒ 🍷	⚒
London Waterloo d.	1605	1605	1635	1705	1705	1735	1735	1748	1805	1805	1835	1835	1905	1935	1935	1939	2005	2035	2039	2105	2135	2139	2205	2235	2239
Woking d.	|	|	1700**b**	|	|	|	1800	1813	|	|	|	1900	|	2000	2000	|	|	2100	|	2132	2200	|	2232	2300	|
Basingstoke d.	1650	1650	|	|	1750	|	|	1833	|	1850	|	|	1950	|	|	2036	2050	|	2136	2153	|	2236	2253	|	2334
Winchester d.	1706	1706	1733	1801	1806	1831	1833	1850	1901	1906	1931	1933	2006	2033	2033	2052	2106	2133	2155	2209	2233	2255	2309	2333	2351
Southampton Airport d.	1715	1715	1742	1810	1815	1840	1842	1903	1910	1915	1940	1942	2015	2042	2042	2108	2115	2142	2211	2223	2242	2311	2323	2342	0006
Southampton Central d.	1724	1724	1751	1822	1824	1852	1851	1918	1919	1924	1952	1951	2024	2051	2051	2117	2122	2151	2218	2231	2251	2318	2331	2351	0015
Brockenhurst d.	1738	1738	1805	|	1838	|	1905	...	1936	1938	|	2005	2038	2105	2108	...	2143	2205	...	2250	2305	...	2350	0005	...
Bournemouth d.	1804	1809	1824	1850	1904	1921	1924	...	2007	2004	2021	2024	2104	2124	2127	...	2210	2224	...	2318	2329	...	0018	0024	...
Poole d.	1814	1819	1837	1903	1914	1934	1937	...	2019	2014	2034	2037	2114	2137	2139	...	2223	2237	...	2330	2342	...	0030	0036	...
Dorchester South d.	1849	1853	1905	1938	1949	2002	2005	...	2054	2049	2102	2105	2147	2210	2212	...	...	2309	...	...	0015	...	...	...	...
Weymouth a.	1900	1906	1917	1951	2001	2015	2013	...	2107	2100	2113	2113	2159	2221	2223	...	...	2320	...	...	0026	...	...	...	...

	⚒	⚒		⑦	⑦		⑦	⑦		⑦		⑦	⑦	⑦	⑦	⑦	⑦	⑦ 🍷		⑦	⑦ 🍷	⑦		⑦ 🍷
London Waterloo d.	2305	2339	...		0005	...	0105	...	...	...	...	...	0754	0835	0854	0935	0954	1035	and	2054	2135	2154	...	2254
Woking d.	2332	0008	...		0036	...	0142	...	...	...	...	...	0828	0909	0928	1009	1028	1107	at	2128	2207	2228	...	2328
Basingstoke d.	2353	0036	...		0057	...	0212**s**	...	...	0748	...	...	0848	0930	0948	1030	1048	1128	the	2148	2228	2248	...	2348
Winchester d.	0012	0053	...		0113	...	0229**s**	...	...	0808	...	...	0908	0946	1008	1046	1108	1144	same	2208	2244	2308	...	0008
Southampton Airport d.	0026	0106	...		0127	...	0243**s**	...	...	0827	...	...	0927	0955	1027	1055	1127	1153	minutes	2227	2253	2327	...	0027
Southampton Central d.	0036	0115	...		0137	...	0253	...	...	0835	...	0904	0935	1004	1035	1104	1135	1203	past	2235	2303	2335	...	0037
Brockenhurst d.	0052**s**	...	...		0153**s**	...	...	...	...	0857	...	0918	0957	1018	1057	1118	1157	1217	each	2257	2317	2354	...	0053**s**
Bournemouth d.	0116	...	...		0216	...	...	0840	...	0925	...	0940	1025	1040	1125	1140	1225	1240	hour	2325	2340	0022	...	0118
Poole d.	0130	...	...		...	...	...	0852	...	0934	...	0952	1034	1052	1134	1152	1234	1252	until	2334	2352	0035	...	0130
Dorchester South d.	...	...	...		...	...	...	0925	...	...	...	1025	...	1125	...	1225	...	1325		...	0025	...	...	...
Weymouth a.	...	...	...		...	...	...	0936	...	...	...	1036	...	1136	...	1236	...	1336		...	0036	...	...	...

	⚒	Ⓐ	⑥	Ⓐ 🍷	⑥	⑥ 🍷	Ⓐ 🍷	Ⓐ	Ⓐ 🍷	Ⓐ	⑥	⑥ 🍷	Ⓐ 🍷	Ⓐ	⑥ 🍷	Ⓐ 🍷	⑥ 🍷	Ⓐ 🍷	Ⓐ 🍷	⑥ 🍷	Ⓐ	Ⓐ 🍷	⑥ 🍷	Ⓐ 🍷	⑥ 🍷
Weymouth d.		...	...	...	...	...	...	...	...	...	...	...	0550	...	...	0620	0650	0650	...	0717	0725	0755	0758	0820	0820
Dorchester South d.		...	...	...	...	...	...	...	...	...	...	...	0602	...	...	0632	0702	0702	...	0733	0737	0807	0808	0833	0833
Poole d.		...	...	0457	...	0528	0542	...	0608	...	...	0628	0636	...	0707	0706	0741	0736	0755	0807	0811	0841	0835	0907	0906
Bournemouth d.		...	...	0512	...	0542	0554	...	0625	...	...	0642	0656	...	0722	0726	0759	0759	0810	0822	0826	0859	0859	0918	0922
Brockenhurst d.		...	...	0538	...	0610	0614	...	|	...	...	0710	|	...	0745	|	0815	0815	0841	0845	0853	0915	0915	0941	0945
Southampton Central d.		0455	0512	0555	0600	0630	0630	...	0700	0643	0700	0730	0730	0738	0800	0800	0830	0830	0900	0900	...	0930	0930	1000	1000
Southampton Airport d.		0502	0520	0603	0608	0638	0638	0650	0708	0654	0708	0738	0738	0749	0808	0808	0838	0838	0908	0908	...	0938	0938	1008	1008
Winchester d.		0518	0534	0618	0623	0652	0648	0705	0718	0711	0724	0748	0748	0806	0818	0818	0848	0848	0918	0918	...	0948	0948	1018	1018
Basingstoke d.		0539	0554	0635	0640	0709	|	|	|	0736	0742	|	|	0824	0836	0835	|	|	0936	0936	...	|	|	1036	1036
Woking a.		0605	0628	0653	0658	0727	|	0738	|	0808	0808	0821	|	0858	|	0853	0919	0922	0954	|	...	1020	1019	|	|
London Waterloo a.		0634	0709	0724	0731	0753	0747	0808	0816	0839	0838	0849	0850	0929	0920	0925	0949	0953	1023	1020	...	1049	1049	1120	1120

	Ⓐ 🍷	⑥ 🍷	⚒ 🍷	⚒ 🍷		⚒ 🍷	⚒ 🍷	⚒ 🍷	⑥ 🍷	Ⓐ 🍷	⚒ 🍷	⚒ 🍷	⚒ 🍷	⚒ 🍷	Ⓐ	⑥	⚒	⚒	⚒	⚒		⚒		⚒
Weymouth d.	0903	0903	0920	1003		1520	1603	1620	1703	1703	1720	1803	1820	1903	1920	1920	...	2010	...	2110	...	2210	...	2310
Dorchester South d.	0913	0913	0933	1013	and	1533	1613	1633	1713	1713	1733	1813	1833	1913	1938	1933	...	2022	...	2122	...	2222	...	2322
Poole d.	0940	0940	1007	1040	at	1607	1640	1707	1740	1740	1807	1840	1907	1940	2009	2007	...	2053	...	2154	...	2254	...	2354
Bournemouth d.	0955	0959	1022	1059	the	1622	1659	1722	1759	1759	1822	1859	1922	1959	2026	2022	...	2112	...	2212	...	2312	...	0003
Brockenhurst d.	1011	1015	1045	1115	same	1645	1715	1745	1815	1815	1845	1915	1945	2015	2045	2045	...	2140	...	2240	...	2340	...	...
Southampton Central d.	1030	1030	1100	1130	minutes	1700	1730	1800	1830	1830	1900	1930	2000	2030	2100	2100	2130	2200	2230	2300	...	2359	...	...
Southampton Airport d.	1038	1038	1108	1138	past	1708	1738	1808	1838	1838	1908	1938	2008	2038	2108	2108	2138	2208	2238	2308	...	0010	...	...
Winchester d.	1048	1048	1118	1148	each	1718	1748	1818	1848	1848	1918	1948	2018	2048	2118	2118	2148	2218	2254	2324	...	...	...	...
Basingstoke d.	|	|	1136	|	hour	1736	|	1836	|	|	1936	|	2036	|	2136	2136	|	2236	2313	2344	...	...	...	...
Woking a.	1119	1119	|	1219	until	|	1819	|	1919	1924	|	2019	|	2119	|	|	2219	2354	2333	0018	...	...	...	...
London Waterloo a.	1149	1149	1220	1249		1823	1849	1920	1949	1951	2020	2049	2124	2149	2222	2222	2249	2323	0010	0102	...	...	...	...

	⑦	⑦		⑦ 🍷		⑦	⑦ 🍷	⑦	⑦ 🍷	⑦	⑦ 🍷	⑦	⑦ 🍷	⑦	⑦ 🍷		⑦ 🍷	⑦		⑦		⑦	⑦	⑦
Weymouth d.		...	...	...	...	...	0743	...	0843	...	0948	...	1048	...	1148		1848	...	...	1958	...	2058	2158	2258
Dorchester South d.		...	...	...	...	...	0755	...	0855	...	1000	...	1100	...	1200	and	1900	...	...	2010	...	2110	2210	2310
Poole d.		...	...	0650	...	0750	0827	0855	0927	0955	1032	1055	1132	1155	1232	at	1932	1955	...	2050	...	2150	2250	2350
Bournemouth d.		...	...	0706	...	0806	0850	0906	0950	1006	1050	1106	1150	1206	1250	the	1950	2006	...	2106	...	2206	2306	0003
Brockenhurst d.		...	...	0734	...	0834	0909	0934	1009	1034	1109	1134	1209	1234	1309	same	2009	2034	...	2134	...	2234	2334	...
Southampton Central d.		0655	...	0755	...	0855	0925	0955	1025	1055	1125	1155	1225	1255	1325	minutes	2025	2055	...	2155	...	2255	2353	...
Southampton Airport d.		0703	...	0803	...	0903	0933	1003	1033	1103	1133	1203	1233	1303	1333	past	2033	2103	...	2203	...	2303	...	...
Winchester d.		0723	...	0823	...	0923	0942	1023	1042	1123	1142	1223	1242	1323	1342	each	2042	2123	...	2223	...	2323	...	...
Basingstoke d.		0744	...	0844	...	0944	1000	1044	1100	1144	1200	1244	1300	1344	1400	hour	2100	2144	...	2244	...	2344	...	...
Woking a.		0802	...	0902	...	1002	1019	1102	1118	1202	1218	1302	1318	1402	1418	until	2118	2202	...	2302	...	0002	...	...
London Waterloo a.		0842	...	0942	...	1042	1054	1140	1152	1240	1252	1340	1349	1437	1449		2149	2237	...	2337	...	0033	...	...

b – Stops to pick up only on Ⓐ.

s – Stops to set down only.

SN ASHFORD - HASTINGS - BRIGHTON 109

Services on ⑦ valid until September 6.

km		⚒	⚒		⚒		⚒		⚒		⚒		⚒		⑦	⑦		⑦		⑦		⑦		⑦	
0	**Ashford** d.		0623	...	0730	...	0830	and	2030	...	2130	...	2224	...		...	...	0816	...	0921	and	2121	...	2220	...
25	Rye d.		0648	...	0754	...	0854	hourly	2054	...	2157	...	2247	...		...	...	0841	...	0946	hourly	2146	...	2243	...
42	**Hastings** d.		0711	...	0812	...	0912	until	2112	...	2216	...	2309	...		0818	...	0904	...	1004	until	2204	...	2305	...
50	Bexhill d.		0722	...	0822	...	0922		2122	...	2225	...	*2322*	...		0828	...	0914	...	1014		2214	...	*2328*	...
67	Eastbourne a.		0737	...	0840	...	0937		2137	...	2241	...	*2343*	...		0849	...	0929	...	1029		2229	...	*2348*	...
93	Lewes a.		0807	...	0907	...	1007		2207	...	2307	...	*0008*	...		0918	...	0959	...	1059		2259	...	...	...
106	**Brighton** a.		0820	...	0920	...	1020		2220	...	2320	...	*0024*	...		*1000*	...	1012	...	1112		2312	...	...	...

	⚒	Ⓐ		⚒		⚒		⚒		⚒	⚒	Ⓐ	⑥		⑦	⑦		⑦		⑦		⑦		⑦	
Brighton d.		...	...	*0530*	...	0632	and	1932	...	2030	2130	2228	2228	...		...	...	*0709*	...	0820	and	2020	...	2120	...
Lewes d.		...	...	*0541*	...	0644	hourly	1944	...	2044	2144	2239	2239	...		...	...	*0725*	...	0832	hourly	2032	...	2132	...
Eastbourne d.		*0454*	...	0604	...	0708	until	2008	...	2108	2208	2303	2310	...		...	...	0758	...	0902	until	2102	...	2202	...
Bexhill d.		*0508*	...	0619	...	0723		2023	...	2123	2223	...	2324	...		...	...	0811	...	0916		2116	...	2216	...
Hastings d.		0530	...	0630	...	0734		2034	...	2134	2233	...	2334	...		0722	...	0822	...	0927		2127	...	2226	...
Rye d.		0553	...	0649	...	0754		2054	...	2157	...	...	...	...		0743	...	0841	...	0946		2146	...	...	...
Ashford a.		0615	...	0711	...	0816		2116	...	2219	...	...	...	...		0806	...	0903	...	1008		2208	...	...	...

☛ Additional trains operate Hastings - Eastbourne - Brighton and v.v.

110 BRIGHTON - PORTSMOUTH and SOUTHAMPTON — SN

Services on ⑦ valid until September 6.

km		⚒	⑥	Ⓐ	Ⓐ	⑥	Ⓐ	⑥	Ⓐ	⑥	Ⓐ	Ⓐ	Ⓐ	⑥	⚒	⑥	Ⓐ	⚒	⚒		⑥	Ⓐ	⑥
0	**Brighton** d.		0527	0530	0553	0601	0627	0633	0635	0703	0706	0715	0730	0733	0803	0833	0839	0903	0933	and at	1503	1503	1533
2	Hove d.		0531	0534	0557	0605	0631	0637	0639	0707	0710	0719	0734	0737	0807	0837	0843	0907	0937	the	1507	1507	1537
17	Worthing d.		0553	0555	0609	0623	0643	0655	0656	0725	0723	0736	0752	0755	0820	0855	0856	0925	0955	same	1525	1525	1555
36	Barnham d.		0615	0618	0624	0645	0705	0717	0718	0741	0744	0753	0814	0817	0841	0917	0916	0945	1017	minutes	1542	1547	1617
46	**Chichester** d.		0623	0626	0632	0653	0713	0725	0728	0749	0752	0801	0822	0825	0849	0925	0924	0953	1025	past each	1550	1555	1625
60	Havant d.		0637	0640	0653	0704	0731	0737	0741	0804	0803	0822	0837	0837	0901	0937	0938	1007	1037	hour	1605	1609	1637
71	Portsmouth & Southsea a.		|	|	0708	0716	|	|	0753	0816	|	0837	|	|	0917	|	|	1019	|	until	1617	1621	|
73	**Portsmouth** Harbour a.		|	|	0712	0720	|	|	0758	0820	|	0841	|	|	0921	|	|	1023	|	★	1621	1625	|
76	Fareham a.		0653	0659	...	...	0746	0753	...	...	0818	...	0854	0853	...	0953	0953	...	1053		...	...	1653
100	**Southampton** Central a.		0718	0724	...	...	0813	0817	...	...	0852	...	0919	0919	...	1017	1019	...	1119		...	...	1719

	Ⓐ	⑥	Ⓐ	⚒	⑥	Ⓐ	⚒	Ⓐ	⑥	Ⓐ	⑥	Ⓐ	⑥	⚒	⑥	Ⓐ	⚒	⚒	⚒	⚒		⑦	⑦	⑦
Brighton d.	1533	1603	1603	1633	1703	1703	1733	1800	1803	1828	1833	1900	1903	1929	1956	2003	2030	2103	2133	2203	...		0712	0718
Hove d.	1537	1607	1607	1637	1707	1707	1737	1804	1807	1832	1837	1904	1907	1933	2000	2007	2034	2107	2137	2207	...		0716	0722
Worthing d.	1555	1625	1625	1655	1725	1725	1755	1827	1825	1854	1855	1926	1929	1955	2022	2029	2056	2129	2159	2229	...		0728	0743
Barnham d.	1617	1642	1647	1717	1744	1747	1817	1849	1842	1912	1917	1948	1951	2017	2044	2051	2118	2151	2221	2251	...		0746	0806
Chichester d.	1625	1650	1655	1725	1752	1755	1825	1857	1850	1920	1925	1956	1959	2025	2052	2059	2126	2159	2229	2259	...		0754	0814
Havant d.	1637	1705	1709	1737	1806	1813	1837	1908	1905	1936	1937	2007	2010	2037	2110	2110	2137	2210	2243	2310	...		0809	0835
Portsmouth & Southsea a.	|	1717	1722	|	1818	1825	|	1921	1917	|	|	2020	2022	|	2122	2123	|	2222	2255	2323	...		0821	0848
Portsmouth Harbour a.	|	1721	...	|	1822	1831	|	1925	1921	|	|	...	2026	|	2126	2127	|	2226	2259	2327	...		0825	0852
Fareham a.	1653	...	...	1753	...	...	1853	...	...	1952	1953	...	...	2053	...	...	2154	...	...	...	...		...	...
Southampton Central a.	1728	...	...	1819	...	...	1920	...	...	2018	2019	...	...	2119	...	...	2220	...	...	...	...		...	...

	⑦	⑦	⑦		⑦	⑦		
Brighton d.	0812	0818	0912		2112	*2210*	...	...
Hove d.	0816	0822	0922	and at	2122	2219	...	...
Worthing d.	0828	0843	0943	the	2143	2235	...	...
Barnham d.	0846	0906	1006	same	2206	2256	...	...
Chichester d.	0854	0914	1014	minutes	2214	2304	...	...
Havant d.	0909	0935	1035	past each	2235	2322	...	...
Portsmouth & Southsea a.	0921	0948	1050	hour	2248	2334	...	...
Portsmouth Harbour a.	0925	0952	1054	until	2252	2338	...	...
Fareham a.	...	...	...	★	...	...	...	...
Southampton Central a.	...	...	...		...	...	...	...

	⚒	Ⓐ	Ⓐ	⑥	Ⓐ	⑥	Ⓐ	⑥	⑥
Southampton Central d.		...	...	...	0610	0633	...	...	0733
Fareham d.		...	...	...	0634	0656	...	...	0756
Portsmouth Harbour d.		0534	0604	0629	|	|	0720	0729	|
Portsmouth & Southsea d.		0538	0608	0633	|	|	0724	0733	|
Havant d.		0554	0620	0646	0653	0711	0736	0746	0811
Chichester d.		0615	0635	0700	0708	0725	0747	0800	0825
Barnham d.		0623	0643	0708	0716	0733	0755	0808	0833
Worthing d.		0645	0708	0726	0738	0756	0816	0826	0856
Hove d.		0706	0726	0744	0756	0814	0834	0844	0914
Brighton a.		0710	0730	0748	0800	0818	0838	0848	0918

	Ⓐ	⚒	⚒	⚒		⚒	⚒	⚒	⚒	⚒	⚒	Ⓐ	⚒	⑥	Ⓐ	⚒	Ⓐ	⑥	Ⓐ	⑥	⑥	Ⓐ	⚒
Southampton Central d.	0733	...	0833	...		1333	...	1427	...	1533	...	...	1633	...	...	1733	...	...	1833	1833	...	...	1933
Fareham d.	0758	...	0856	...	and at	1356	...	1500	...	1556	...	...	1656	...	...	1756	...	...	1856	1856	...	...	1956
Portsmouth Harbour d.	|	0829	|	0929	the	|	1429	|	1529	|	1629	1640	|	1729	1729	|	1828	1829	|	|	1929	1932	|
Portsmouth & Southsea d.	|	0833	|	0933	same	|	1433	|	1533	|	1633	1646	|	1733	1733	|	1832	1833	|	|	1933	1936	|
Havant d.	0813	0846	0911	0946	minutes	1411	1446	1514	1546	1611	1646	1700	1711	1746	1746	1811	1844	1846	1911	1911	1946	1944	2011
Chichester d.	0828	0900	0925	1000	past each	1425	1500	1525	1600	1625	1700	1721	1725	1800	1800	1825	1859	1900	1922	1925	1959	1959	2025
Barnham d.	0836	0908	0933	1008	hour	1433	1508	1533	1608	1633	1708	1729	1733	1808	1808	1833	1907	1908	1930	1933	2007	2007	2033
Worthing d.	0856	0926	0956	1026	until	1456	1526	1556	1626	1656	1726	1743	1756	1826	1825	1852	1924	1926	1952	1953	2023	2023	2052
Hove d.	0914	0944	1014	1044	★	1514	1544	1614	1644	1714	1744	1805	1814	1844	1847	1914	1945	1944	2014	2015	2045	2045	2114
Brighton a.	0918	0948	1018	1048		1518	1548	1618	1648	1718	1748	1809	1818	1848	1852	1918	1949	1948	2018	2019	2049	2049	2118

	⑥	Ⓐ	⚒	⑥	Ⓐ		⚒	⚒	Ⓐ	⑥	⚒		⑦	⑦	⑦		⑦		⑦		⑦		⑦
Southampton Central d.	...	...	2033	...	...	...	2113	...	2213	2213	...	...		...	...		...	...	...	...	...	...	...
Fareham d.	...	...	2056	...	...	...	2140	...	2237	2239	...	...		...	...	and at	...	...	...	...	...	...	...
Portsmouth Harbour d.	2028	...	|	2111	...	...	|	2215	|	|	2244	...		0705	0805	the	1905	...	2005	...	2105	...	2143
Portsmouth & Southsea d.	2032	2032	|	2115	2115	...	|	2219	|	|	2248	...		0709	0809	same	1909	...	2009	...	2109	...	2147
Havant d.	2044	2044	2111	2131	2131	...	2156	2235	2257	2255	2305	...		0727	0827	minutes	1927	...	2027	...	2127	...	2200
Chichester d.	2059	2059	2125	2152	2152	...	2207	2252	2311	2309	2317	...		0748	0848	past each	1948	...	2048	...	2148	...	2214
Barnham d.	2107	2107	2133	2200	2200	...	2215	2300	2319	2317	2325	...		0802	0902	hour	2002	...	2102	...	2202	...	2222
Worthing d.	2123	2123	2155	2222	2223	...	2252	2322	...	...	2359	...		0824	0924	until	2024	...	2124	...	2224	...	2302
Hove d.	2145	2145	2216	2244	2244	...	2314	2344	...	...	0021	...		0845	0945	★	2045	...	2145	...	2245	...	2325
Brighton a.	2149	2149	2221	2248	2248	...	2318	2348	...	...	0025	...		0849	0949		2049	...	2149	...	2249	...	2329

ADDITIONAL SERVICES OPERATED BY *GW*.

	Ⓐ 2	⑥ 2	⑦ 2	⑦ 2	Ⓐ 2	⑥ 2C	⑦ 2	⑦	
Brighton d.	0900	0900	1108	1545	1700	1700	1745	2143	...
Hove d.	0904	0904	1112	1549	1704	1704	1749	2147	...
Worthing d.	0922	0922	1127	1606	1722	1722	1806	2200	...
Barnham d.	0938	0941	1143	1623	1739	1738	1823	2215	...
Chichester d.	0947	0949	1155	1634	1747	1746	1834	2223	...
Havant d.	0959	1000	1210	1648	1758	1800	1848	2242	...
Portsmouth & Southsea a.	|	|	|	|	|	|	|	2257	...
Portsmouth Harbour a.	|	|	|	|	|	|	|	2301	...
Fareham a.	1014	1015	1231	1702	1812	1814	1902	...	...
Southampton Central a.	1041	1040	1253	1724	1841	1843	1924	...	...
Bristol Temple Meads **137** a.	1229	1229	1442	1922	2029	2035	2134	...	...
Worcester Shrub Hill **122** a.	1414	1415	|	...	2212	...	...	...	...
Cardiff Central **137** a.	...	...	1538	...	...	...	...	...	...

	⑥ 2	Ⓐ 2	⑦ 2	⑦ 2	⚒ 2	⑦ 2	⑦ 2		
Cardiff Central **137** d.	...	...	...	1015	...	1215	1640	...	...
Worcester Shrub Hill **122** d.	...	...	...	|	1106	|	|	...	...
Bristol Temple Meads **137** d.	...	...	...	1110	1239	1310	1740	...	...
Southampton Central d.	...	...	0831	1308	1434	1522	1927	...	...
Fareham d.	...	...	0852	1334	1455	1551	1949	...	...
Portsmouth Harbour d.	0648	0701	|	|	|	|	|	...	...
Portsmouth & Southsea d.	0654	0705	|	|	|	|	|	...	...
Havant d.	0708	0720	0911	1404	1510	1611	2011	...	...
Chichester d.	0720	0732	0922	1419	1521	1622	2022	...	...
Barnham d.	0728	0740	0930	1427	1529	1630	2030	...	...
Worthing d.	0750	0800	0945	1445	1548	1645	2051	...	...
Hove d.	0808	0814	0959	1458	1608	1659	2105	...	...
Brighton a.	0815	0820	1005	1504	1614	1705	2110	...	...

C – To Cheltenham Spa.

★ – Timings may vary by up to 5 minutes.

111 PORTSMOUTH - RYDE - SHANKLIN — 2nd class IL

PORTSMOUTH Harbour – **RYDE** Pierhead *Valid until September 20.* ⛴ (*Wightlink*)

0015, 0145⑥, 0415⚒, 0515⚒, 0545Ⓐ**a**, 0615, 0645Ⓐ**a**, 0715, 0745Ⓐ**a**, 0815, 0845⚒, 0915⑥⑦, 0945⚒, 1015, 1045⑥, 1115, 1145⑥, 1215Ⓑ, 1245⑥⑦, 1315⚒, 1345⑦, 1415⚒, 1445, 1515⑥⑦, 1545, 1615, 1645, 1715, 1745⚒, 1815, 1845Ⓐ, 1915, 2015, 2115, 2215, 2315.

RYDE Pierhead – **PORTSMOUTH** Harbour Journey time: ± 18 minutes

0045, 0215⑥, 0445⚒, 0545⚒, 0615Ⓐ**a**, 0645, 0715Ⓐ**a**, 0745, 0815Ⓐ**a**, 0845, 0915⚒, 0945⑥⑦, 1015⚒, 1045, 1115⑥, 1145, 1215⑥, 1245Ⓑ, 1315⑥⑦, 1345⚒, 1415⑦, 1445⚒, 1515, 1545⑥⑦, 1615, 1645, 1715, 1745, 1815⚒, 1845, 1915Ⓐ, 1945, 2045, 2145, 2245, 2345.

RYDE Pierhead – **SHANKLIN** *14 km*

0549⚒, 0608⚒, 0649, 0708⚒ and then at 49 and 08⚒ minutes past each hour until 1849, 1908, 1949, 2008⚒, 2049⑦, 2108⚒, 2149⑦, 2208⚒.

SHANKLIN – **RYDE** Pierhead Journey time: ± 24 minutes

0617⚒, 0636⚒, 0717, 0736 then at 17 and 36⚒ minutes past each hour until 2928, 1836, 1917, 1936, 2017Ⓑ, 2036⚒, 2117⑦, 2136⚒, 2217⑦, 2236⚒.

☛ Through fares including ferry travel are available. Allow at least 10 minutes for connections between trains and ferries. Ferry operator: Wightlink. ✆ 0871 376 4342. www.wightlink.co.uk

a – Not May 4, 25; Aug. 31.

112 EXETER - EXMOUTH — 2nd class GW

EXETER St Davids – Exeter Central – **EXMOUTH** *18 km*

Ⓐ: 0544, 0609, 0629, 0711, 0748, 0818 and every 30 minutes until 1548; then 1620, 1650, 1720, 1750, 1820, 1850, 1929, 2029, 2130, 2239, 2330.

⑥: 0544, 0629, 0711, 0748, 0818 and every 30 minutes until 1548; then 1620, 1650, 1720, 1750, 1820, 1850, 1926, 2026, 2127, 2236, 2310.

⑦: 0825, 0926, 1030, 1125, 1232, 1330, 1430, 1530, 1628, 1730, 1835, 1935, 2040, 2135, 2230, 2326.

EXMOUTH – Exeter Central – **EXETER** St Davids Journey time: ± 28 minutes

Ⓐ: 0615, 0646, 0715, 0753, 0823 and every 30 minutes until 1553; then 1625, 1655, 1725, 1755, 1828, 1855, 1933, 2001, 2101, 2204, 2310.

⑥: 0615, 0715, 0753, 0823 and every 30 minutes until 1553; then 1625, 1655, 1725, 1755, 1827, 1855, 1933, 2001, 2101, 2201, 2313, 2343.

⑦: 0908, 1000, 1105, 1205, 130 and hourly until 2010; then 2117, 2210, 2307, 2359.

SW LONDON - SALISBURY - EXETER 113

km		⚒	⚒	Ⓐ	⑥	⚒	⑥	Ⓐ	Ⓐ	⑥	⚒	⚒	Ⓐ	⑥	⚒	⚒	⑥	Ⓐ	⚒	⑥	Ⓐ	Ⓐ	⑥	Ⓐ	Ⓐ	⑥
							🍷	🍷	🍷	🍷	🍷B	🍷	🍷	🍷	🍷B	🍷	🍷P	🍷	🍷	🍷	🍷	🍷	🍷	🍷	🍷	🍷
0	**London** Waterloo ..... d.		...	...	...	...	0710	0710	0820	0820	0920	1020	1120	1120	1220	1320	1420	1420	1520	1620	1620	1650	1720	1720	1750	1820
39	Woking ..... d.		...	...	...	...	0736	0736	0846	0846	0946	1046	1146	1146	1246	1346	1446	1446	1546	1646	1646	1716u	1746	1746u	|	1846
77	Basingstoke ..... d.		...	...	...	...	0759	0757	0907	0907	1007	1107	1207	1207	1307	1407	1507	1507	1607	1707	1707	1737	1807	1807	1838	1907
107	Andover ..... d.		...	...	...	...	0821	0819	0924	0924	1024	1124	1224	1224	1324	1424	1524	1524	1624	1724	1729	1759	1824	1829	1900	1924
134	**Salisbury** ..... a.		...	...	...	...	0842	0839	0943	0942	1042	1142	1242	1242	1343	1442	1542	1542	1642	1742	1748	1818	1843	1848	1920	1945
134	**Salisbury** ..... d.		...	0608	0615	0712	0845	0845	0948	0948	1048	1148	1248	1248	1348	1448	1548	1548	1648	1748	1753	1823	1853	1853	1923	1953
169	Gillingham ..... d.		...	0642	0642	0743	0907	0907	1013	1013	1113	1213	1313	1310	1413	1513	1613	1613	1713	1813	1817	1848	1918	1918	1948	2018
190	Sherborne ..... d.		...	0657	0657	0758	0922	0922	1028	1028	1128	1228	1328	|	1428	1528	1628	1628	1728	1828	1833	1903	1933	1933	2003	2033
197	**Yeovil** Junction ..... a.		...	0703	0703	0804	0927	0927	1033	1033	1133	1233	1334	1327	1433	1534	1633	1633	1734	1833	1838	1911	1939	1938	2012	2038
197	**Yeovil** Junction ..... d.		0615	0708	0708	...	0929	0929	1035	1035	1135	1235	...	1328	1435	...	1635	1637	...	1835	1840	...	...	1940	...	2040
211	Crewkerne ..... d.		0624	0717	0717	...	0938	0938	1044	1044	|	1244	...	|	1444	...	1644	1646	...	1844	1849	...	...	1949	...	2049
233	Axminster ..... d.		0655	0737	0737	...	0952	0952	1104	1105	1155	1304	...	|	1504	...	1704	1706	...	1904	1905	...	...	2003	...	2111
249	Honiton ..... d.		0710	0749	0749	...	1004	1004	1116	1130	1207	1316	...	1400	1516	...	1716	1718	...	1930	1930	...	...	2015	...	2123
276	**Exeter** Central ..... a.		0731	0812	0824	...	1025	1028	1138	1155	1225	1338	...	1422	1538	...	1732	1733	...	1951	1952	...	...	2031	...	2148
277	**Exeter** St Davids ..... a.		0736	0815	0831	...	1029	1032	1142	1201	1230	1342	...	1426	1542	...	1736	1738	...	1957	1957	...	...	2036	...	2153
	Paignton **116** ..... a.		...	...	0923	...	1122	1129	...	...	|	...	...	1519	|	...	|	1840	...	...	...	...	...	...	...	...
	Plymouth **115** ..... a.		...	...	...	...	...	...	...	...	1357	...	...	...	1658	...	1903	...	...	...	...	...	...	...	...	...

	Ⓐ	Ⓐ	⑥	⑥	Ⓐ	⑥	Ⓐ			⑦	⑦	⑦	⑦	⑦	⑦	⑦	⑦	⑦	⑦	⑦	⑦	⑦	⑦	⑦	⑦	⑦	⑦
	🍷	🍷B	🍷	🍷	🍷	🍷	🍷						🍷	🍷	🍷	🍷	🍷B	🍷	🍷	🍷	🍷	🍷	🍷B	🍷	🍷	🍷
London Waterloo ..... d.	1820	1920	1920	2020	2020	2120	2120	...	...		...	...	0815	0915	1015	1115	1215	1315	1415	1515	1615	1715	1815	1915	2015	2115
Woking ..... d.	1846	1946	1946	2046	2046	2149	2149	...	...		...	...	0847	0947	1046	1146	1246	1346	1446	1546	1646	1746	1846	1946	2046	2146
Basingstoke ..... d.	1907	2007	2007	2107	2107	2212	2210	...	...		...	0808	0908	1008	1107	1207	1307	1407	1507	1607	1707	1807	1907	2007	2107	2207
Andover ..... d.	1929	2029	2024	2129	2129	2234	2232	...	...		...	0830	0930	1025	1129	1224	1329	1424	1529	1624	1729	1824	1929	2024	2129	2224
Salisbury ..... a.	1948	2049	2042	2148	2148	2253	2255	...	...		...	0849	0950	1041	1148	1240	1348	1440	1548	1640	1748	1840	1948	2040	2148	2244
Salisbury ..... d.	1953	2053	2053	2200	2204	2304	2304	...	...		0710	0854	0954	1050	1154	1250	1354	1450	1554	1654	1754	1850	1954	2054	2154	2248
Gillingham ..... d.	2018	2118	2118	2226	2229	2329s	2330s	...	...		0735	0919	1019	1115	1219	1315	1419	1515	1619	1719	1819	1915	2019	2119	2219	2315
Sherborne ..... d.	2033	2133	2133	2241	2244	2344s	2345s	...	...		0750	0934	1034	1130	1234	1330	1434	1530	1634	1734	1834	1930	2034	2134	2234	2330
Yeovil Junction ..... a.	2038	2138	2138	2247	2249	2351	2352	...	...		0755	0939	1039	1135	1240	1335	1440	1535	1640	1739	1840	1935	2040	2140	2240	2335
Yeovil Junction ..... d.	2040	2140	2140	...	2251	...	...	...	...		0757	0941	1041	1140	...	1340	...	1540	...	1740	...	1940	...	2140	...	2337
Crewkerne ..... d.	2049	2149	2149	...	2300	...	...	...	...		0806	0950	|	1149	...	1349	...	1549	...	1749	...	1949	...	2149	...	2346
Axminster ..... d.	2111	2203	2203	...	2314v	...	...	...	...		0820	1011	1101	1211	...	1411	...	1611	...	1811	...	2013	...	2211	...	2358
Honiton ..... d.	2123	2214	2215	...	2328v	...	...	...	...		0835	1023	1113	1223	...	1423	...	1623	...	1823	...	2025	...	2223	...	0010
Exeter Central ..... a.	2148	2236f	2238	...	2349v	...	...	...	...		0854	1044	1129	1244	...	1442	...	1645	...	1842	...	2044	...	2245	...	|
Exeter St Davids ..... a.	2154	2241f	2242	...	2354v	...	...	...	...		0859	1049	1133	1249	...	1446	...	1649	...	1846	...	2049	...	2249	...	0030
Paignton **116** ..... a.	...	...	...	...	...	...	...	...	...		...	1140	|	1347	...	1534	...	1743	...	...	...	2139	...	...	...	...
Plymouth **115** ..... a.	...	...	...	...	...	...	...	...	...		...	...	1244	...	...	...	...	...	...	...	...	...	...	...	...	...

	⚒	Ⓐ	Ⓐ	⑥	⚒	Ⓐ	⚒	⚒	⚒	⚒	⚒	Ⓐ	⑥	⚒	⚒	⚒	Ⓐ	⑥	Ⓐ	⑥	Ⓐ	⑥	Ⓐ	⑥	Ⓐ	⑥
									🍷B	🍷	🍷	🍷	🍷	🍷	🍷B	🍷	🍷	🍷	🍷B	🍷B	🍷	🍷	🍷	🍷	🍷	🍷
Plymouth **115** ..... d.		...	...	...	...	...	...	...	...	...	...	...	...	...	...	...	...	...	...	...	1447	1448	...	...	...	1742
Paignton **116** ..... d.		...	...	...	...	...	...	...	...	...	...	...	1014	...	...	1234	...	...	...	...	|	|	...	...	...	|
Exeter St Davids ..... d.		...	0510	0510	...	...	0641	...	0825	...	1010	...	1108	1210	...	1335	1410	1410	...	...	1610	1610	...	1810	1810	1910
Exeter Central ..... d.		...	0514	0514	...	...	0645	...	0830	...	1014	...	1112	1214	...	1339	1414	1414	...	...	1614	1614	...	1814	1814	1914
Honiton ..... d.		...	0538	0538	0620	...	0712	...	0846	...	1040	...	1128	1238	...	1357	1438	1438	...	...	1638	1638	...	1838	1839	1930
Axminster ..... d.		...	0549	0549	0631	...	0723	...	0857	...	1051	...	1139	1249	...	1408	1449	1449	...	...	1649	1649	...	1849	1850	1941
Crewkerne ..... d.		...	0602	0602	0644	...	0736	...	0910	...	1104	...	1200	1303	...	|	1503	1503	...	...	1705	1703	...	1903	1910	1954
Yeovil Junction ..... a.		...	0611	0611	0652	...	0745	...	0919	...	1113	...	1209	1312	...	1427	1512	1512	...	...	1714	1712	...	1912	1918	2003
Yeovil Junction ..... d.		0550	0620	0620	0654	0720	0750	0820	0920	1020	1120	1220	1220	1320	1350a	1428	1520	1520	1620	1620	1724	1720	1820	1920	1920	2020
Sherborne ..... d.		0556	0626	0626	0700	0726	0756	0826	0926	1026	1126	1226	1226	1326	1356a	|	1526	1526	1626	1626	1731	1726	1826	1926	1926	2026
Gillingham ..... d.		0612	0642	0642	0716	0744	0812	0842	0942	1042	1142	1242	1242	1342	1413a	1445	1545	1542	1642	1642	1748	1742	1848	1942	1948	2042
Salisbury ..... a.		0639	0707	0710	0740	0809	0837	0915	1015	1115	1215	1315	1315	1415	1435a	1515	1615	1615	1715	1715	1820	1815	1923	2020	2020	2120
Salisbury ..... d.		0645	0715	0720	0745	0815	0845	0920	1020	1120	1220	1320	1320	1420	1445	1520	1620	1620	1720	1720	1825	1820	1925	2025	2025	2125
Andover ..... d.		0705	0735	0737	0804	0835	0904	0937	1037	1137	1237	1337	1337	1437	1504	1537	1639	1637	1737	1737	1842	1837	1944	2044	2044	2144
Basingstoke ..... a.		0728	0758	0754	0828	0858	0927	0954	1055	1154	1254	1354	1354	1454	1527	1554	1655	1654	1754	1754	1859	1854	2008	2106	2108	2206
Woking ..... a.		|	0818	0817	0849	0918	0949	1015	1115	1215	1315	1415	1415	1515	1549	1615	1715	1715	1815	1815	1919	1915	2029	2129	2129	2228
London Waterloo ..... a.		0814	0846	0849	0919	0951	1019	1049	1149	1249	1349	1449	1449	1549	1619	1649	1744	1749	1845	1849	1949	1949	2100	2204	2204	2257

	Ⓐ	Ⓐ	⑥	⚒	①–④	⑤	⑥		⑦	⑦	⑦	⑦	⑦	⑦	⑦	⑦	⑦	⑦	⑦	⑦	⑦	⑦	⑦	⑦	⑦	⑦
	🍷	🍷	🍷							🍷	🍷	🍷	🍷	🍷	🍷	🍷	🍷	🍷B	🍷	🍷	🍷P	🍷	🍷			
Plymouth **115** ..... d.	1752	...	...	...	...	...	...	...		...	...	...	...	...	...	...	...	1406	...	...	1602	...	...	...	...	...
Paignton **116** ..... d.	|	1912	1914	...	...	...	...	...		...	...	...	...	...	...	1225	...	|	1530	1610	|	...	1824	...	...	2210
Exeter St Davids ..... d.	1910	2015	2015	2100	2230	2257	2257	...		...	...	0920	...	1120	...	1318	...	1520	1633	1718	1718	...	1920	...	2120	2310
Exeter Central ..... d.	1914	2019	2019	2104	2234	2301	2301	...		...	...	0924	...	1124	...	1322	...	1524	1637	1723	1723	...	1924	...	2124	2314
Honiton ..... d.	1931	2046	2046	2123	2258	2327	2328	...		...	0846	0946	...	1146	...	1346	...	1546	1655	1746	1746	...	1948	...	2146	2329s
Axminster ..... d.	1942	2057	2057	2145	2309	2338	2339	...		...	0857	0957	...	1157	...	1357	...	1557	1706	1757	1757	...	1959	...	2157	2340s
Crewkerne ..... d.	2008	2110	2110	2208	2322	2351	2352	...		...	0910	1010	...	1210	...	1410	...	1610	1719	1810	1810	...	2012	...	2210	0004s
Yeovil Junction ..... a.	2016	2119	2119	2217	2331	2359	0001	...		...	0918	1018	...	1218	...	1418	...	1618	1728	1818	1818	...	2021	...	2218	0013s
Yeovil Junction ..... d.	2020	2120	2120	2224	2234	0001	0002	...		0732	0925	1025	1125	1225	1325	1425	1525	1625	1729	1825	1825	1925	2025	2125	2225	|
Sherborne ..... d.	2026	2126	2126	2230	|	|	|	...		0738	0931	1031	1131	1231	1331	1431	1531	1631	1736	1831	1831	1931	2031	2131	2231	|
Gillingham ..... d.	2042	2142	2142	2246	|	|	|	...		0755	0947	1047	1147	1247	1347	1447	1547	1647	1751	1847	1847	1947	2047	2147	2247	|
Salisbury ..... a.	2120	2209	2207	2313	0028	0035	0036	...		0820	1021	1117	1221	1317	1421	1518	1621	1721	1822	1917	1917	2021	2121	2221	2317	0050
Salisbury ..... d.	2125	2225	2225	...	...	...	...	...		0826	1026	1126	1226	1326	1426	1526	1626	1726	1826	1926	1926	2026	2126	2226	...	...
Andover ..... d.	2144	2244	2244	...	...	...	...	...		0846	1046	1143	1246	1343	1446	1543	1646	1743	1846	1943	1943	2046	2143	2246	...	...
Basingstoke ..... a.	2208	2307	2307	...	...	...	...	...		0908	1108	1200	1308	1400	1508	1600	1708	1800	1908	2000	2000	2108	2200	2308	...	...
Woking ..... a.	2228	*2333*	*2332*	...	...	...	...	...		0930	1130	1223	1330	1423	1530	1623	1730	1823	1930	2023	2023	2130	2223	*2350*	...	...
London Waterloo ..... a.	2257	*0006*	*0010*	...	...	...	...	...		1008	1203	1303	1404	1458	1604	1658	1804	1858	2004	2058	2058	2204	2258	*0033*	...	...

London - Salisbury also at Ⓐ: 0750 and hourly until 1550; then 1850, 1950, 2220, 2335. ⑥: 0750 and hourly until 1950; then 2220, 2335. ⑦: 2215, 2335

Salisbury - London also at Ⓐ: 0512, 0540, 0945 and hourly until 1845. ⑥: 0512, 0542, 0617, 0645, 0820, 0945 and hourly until 1845. ⑦: 0642, 0723, 0926.

B – Conveys (12) London - Salisbury - Bristol and v.v.
P – To / from Penzance.
a – Ⓐ only.
f – ⑤ only.
s – Stops to set down only.
u – Stops to pick up only.
v – 7 minutes later on ⑤.

GW 2nd class BARNSTAPLE - EXETER 114

km		⚒	⚒	⚒	⚒		⚒	⚒	⚒	Ⓐ	Ⓐ	⚒	Ⓐ	⑥		⑦	⑦	⑦	⑦	⑦	⑦	⑦			
0	**Barnstaple** ..... d.		0709	0843	0943		1543	1709	1813	1916	1916	2023	2218	2218	...		1110	1317	1514	1720	1917	2130	...	...	...
28	Eggesford ..... d.		0739	0907	1007	and	1607	1738	1840	1942	1942	2048	2247	2247	...		1141	1342	1544	1750	1948	2155	...	...	...
51	Crediton ..... d.		0805	0937	1037	hourly	1637	1811	1911	2005	2005	2114	2313	2313	...		1208	1408	1614	1818	2016	2218	...	...	...
63	**Exeter** St Davids ..... a.		0818	0948	1048	until	1648	1824	1925	2018	2020	2131	2326	2326	...		1223	1423	1628	1833	2030	2230	...	...	...
64	**Exeter** Central ..... a.		0822	0951	1051		1653	1832	1929	2025	2040	2140	2330	...	...		1235	1433	1632	1838	2043	2234	...	...	...

	⚒	⚒		⚒	⚒	⚒	⚒		⚒	⚒	⚒	⚒		⚒		⑦	⑦	⑦	⑦	⑦	⑦	⑦			
Exeter Central ..... d.		...	...	0641	0819	0919	1017		1517	1653	1751	1849	...	2055	...		...	1135	1336	1539	1737	1936	...	...	...
Exeter St Davids ..... d.		0556	...	0650	0827	0927	1027	and	1527	1657	1757	1857	...	2100	...		0940	1158	1354	1601	1800	1958	...	...	...
Crediton ..... d.		0607	...	0701	0838	0938	1038	hourly	1538	1708	1811	1911	...	2114	...		1000	1210	1410	1623	1816	2015	...	...	...
Eggesford ..... d.		0632	...	0740	0908	1008	1108	until	1608	1738	1841	1943	...	2143	...		1028	1237	1438	1642	1845	2043	...	...	...
Barnstaple ..... a.		0658	...	0809	0937	1035	1135		1635	1807	1913	2010	...	2213	...		1058	1303	1508	1714	1912	2114	...	...	...

115 LONDON and BRISTOL - EXETER - PLYMOUTH - PENZANCE

GW, SW, XC

Services on Ⓐ valid until June 26, services on ⑥ valid until September 5, services on ⑦ valid until July 12.

For additional Exeter - Paignton *GW* and *SW* trains see Table **116**.

km	Operator		XC	GW	XC	GW	GW	GW	XC	GW	XC	GW	XC	GW	XC	GW	GW	GW	XC	GW	XC	GW	XC	GW	SW	GW
			①	②–⑤	②–⑤	①	Ⓐ	②–⑤	Ⓐ	Ⓐ	Ⓐ	Ⓐ	Ⓐ	Ⓐ	Ⓐ	Ⓐ	Ⓐ	Ⓐ	Ⓐ	Ⓐ	Ⓐ	Ⓐ	Ⓐ	Ⓐ	Ⓐ	Ⓐ
			🍷	🍷Z	🍷	🍷Z		2	🍷	2	🍷	2	🍷	🍷	🍷	🍷	🍷	2	🍷	🍷	🍷	🍷	🍷	2	🍷W	🍷
0	**London** Pad ☆ . 133 d.	Ⓐ	...	2345b	...	2350d	...	...	...	...	...	...	...	0730	...	0818	0906	...	...	1006	...	1000	...	...	...	1106
58	Reading ....132 133 d.		...	0037u	...	0037u	...	...	...	...	...	...	...	0757	...	0848	0932	...	...	1032e	...	1027	...	...	...	1132e
85	Newbury .... d.		...	|	...	|	...	...	...	...	...	...	...	|	...	0912	|	...	...	|	...	|	...	...	...	|
154	Westbury .... d.		...	|	...	|	...	...	...	...	...	...	...	Y	...	0959	|	...	...	|	...	Y	...	...	...	1222
186	Castle Cary .... d.		...	|	...	|	...	...	...	...	...	...	...	|	...	1016	|	...	...	|	...	|	...	...	...	1239
	B'ham New St **127**. d.		...	|	...	|	...	...	...	...	0642	...	0712	|	0812	|	|	...	0912	|	0942	|	1012	...	...	|
	Bristol T Meads .... d.		...	|	...	|	...	0529	0634	0626	0811	...	0844	0913	0944	|	|	...	1044	|	1115	1147	1144	...	...	|
230	Taunton .... d.		...	0322	...	|	...	0623	0708	0729	0843	...	0917	0946	1018	1038	1048	...	1118	|	1202	1229	1217	...	...	1302
253	Tiverton Parkway ...... d.		...	|	...	|	...	0639	0720	0744	|	...	0929	|	1030	1051	1101	...	1130	|	1214	|	1229	...	...	1315
279	**Exeter** St Davids .... a.		...	0414	...	0405	...	0657	0734	0803	0907	...	0943	1012	1046	1112	1118	...	1146	1209	1230	1255	1243	...	...	1332
279	**Exeter** St Davids **116** d.		...	0417	...	0435	...	0659	0736	0804	0908	0934	0945	1013	1048	...	1119	...	1148	1210	1232	1257	1245	...	1238	1334
299	Dawlish .... **116** d.		...	|	...	|	...	0720	|	0820	|	|	|	|	|	...	|	...	|	|	1244	1310	|	...	1301	|
303	Teignmouth .... **116** d.		...	|	...	|	...	0725	|	0825	|	|	|	|	|	...	|	...	|	|	1249	1316	|	...	1306	|
311	**Newton Abbot** .. **116** d.		...	0439	...	0456	...	0732	0757	0832	|	0955	1004	1034	1110	...	1139	...	1209	1231	1257	1324	1304	...	1313	1354
321	Torquay .... **116** d.		...	|	...	|	...	|	|	|	0937	|	|	|	|	...	|	...	|	|	1309	1335	|	...	|	|
324	**Paignton** .... **116** a.		...	|	...	|	...	|	|	|	0948	|	|	|	|	...	|	...	|	|	1320	1348	|	...	|	|
325	Totnes .... d.		...	|	...	|	...	0746	0809	0846	...	1008	1017	1047	1123	...	1153	...	1223	|	...	...	1317	...	1326	1407
363	**Plymouth** .... **118** a.		...	0518	...	0535	...	0816	0839	0916	...	1039	1048	1115	1156	...	1225	...	1256	1309	...	...	1348	...	1356	1439
363	**Plymouth** .... d.		0550	0550	0628	0640	0702	0820	...	0919	...	1040	...	1118	...	...	...	1239	...	1311	...	...	...	1354	...	...
370	Saltash .... d.		|	|	|	|	0715	0830	...	0930	...	1050	...	|	...	...	...	1254	...	|	...	...	...	1402	...	...
392	Liskeard .... **118** d.		0615	0615	0651	0709	0734	0851	...	0949	...	1109	...	1141	...	...	...	1306	...	1334	...	...	...	1421	...	...
406	Bodmin Parkway .... d.		0629	0629	0703	0723	0746	0903	...	1001	...	1121	...	1153	...	...	...	1318	...	1347	...	...	...	1433	...	...
419	Par .... **118** d.		0642	0642	0715	0737	0759	0915	...	1014	...	1133	...	1204	...	...	...	1330	...	1358	...	...	...	1445	...	...
452	**Newquay** .... **118** a.		|	|	|	|	|	|	...	|	...	|	...	|	...	...	...	|	...	|	...	...	...	|	...	...
426	St Austell .... d.		0650	0650	0722	0745	0807	0923	...	1022	...	1141	...	1212	...	...	...	1338	...	1406	...	...	...	1453	...	...
449	**Truro** .... **118** d.		0709	0709	0739	0805	0826	0941	...	1041	...	1158	...	1230	...	...	...	1356	...	1423	...	...	...	1511	...	...
464	Redruth .... d.		0723	0723	0750	0819	0838	0954	...	1054	...	1211	...	1242	...	...	...	1409	...	1436	...	...	...	1524	...	...
470	Camborne .... d.		0730	0730	0757	0826	0845	1000	...	1100	...	1217	...	1250	...	...	...	1415	...	1444	...	...	...	1530	...	...
482	St Erth .... **118** d.		0744	0744	0812	0843	0858	1011	...	1112	...	1228	...	1300	...	...	...	1426	...	1458	...	...	...	1542	...	...
491	**Penzance** .... a.		0800	0800	0824	0859	0911	1024	...	1127	...	1240	...	1318	...	...	...	1439	...	1511	...	...	...	1554	...	...

Operator	XC	GW	XC	GW	GW	XC	SW	XC	GW	XC	GW	GW	XC	XC	GW	XC	GW	GW	GW	XC	GW	GW	XC	GW	GW	GW
	Ⓐ	Ⓐ	Ⓐ	Ⓐ	Ⓐ	Ⓐ	Ⓐ	⑤	Ⓐ	Ⓐ	Ⓐ	Ⓐ	Ⓐ	Ⓐ	Ⓐ	Ⓐ	①–④	⑤	Ⓐ	Ⓐ	Ⓐ	Ⓐ	Ⓐ	①–④	⑤	Ⓐ
	🍷	✕	🍷	🍷	🍷	🍷	🍷W	🍷	🍷	🍷	2	🍷	🍷	🍷	🍷	🍷	🍷	🍷	🍷	🍷	🍷	✕	🍷	🍷	🍷	✕
London Pad ☆..**133** d.	...	1206	...	1218	1306	...	...	...	1406	...	...	1506	...	...	1606	...	1633	1633	1703	...	1733	1803	...	1836	1836	1903
Reading.......**132 133** d.	...	1232e	...	1248	1332e	...	...	...	1432e	...	...	1532e	...	...	1632e	...	1704	1704	1731e	...	1801	1831e	...	1903	1903	1932
Newbury .... d.	...	|	...	1312	|	...	...	...	|	...	...	|	...	...	|	...	1720	1720	1748	...	1817	|	...	1919	1919	1948
Westbury .... d.	...	|	...	1359	|	...	...	...	|	...	...	1622	...	...	|	...	1805	1805	|	...	1901	|	...	2005	2005	|
Castle Cary................ d.	...	|	...	1423	|	...	...	...	|	...	...	1641	...	...	|	...	1823	1823	|	...	1919	|	...	2022	2022	|
B'ham New St **127** d.	1112	|	1212	|	|	1312	...	1342	|	1412	...	|	1512	1542	|	1612	|	|	|	1712	|	|	1812	|	|	|
Bristol T Meads.... d.	1244	|	1344	|	|	1444	...	1513	|	1544	...	|	1644	1714	|	1744	|	|	|	1844	|	|	1944	|	|	|
Taunton .... d.	1318	|	1417	1446	1451	1518	...	1546	1550	1617	...	1705	1717	1746	1750	1817	1845	1845	1852	1917	1941	1948	2017	2045	2045	2053
Tiverton Parkway ...... d.	1330	|	1429	▬	1504	1530	...	1558	1603	1629	...	1718	1729	1758	1803	1829	1858	1858	1905	1929	1954	|	2029	2058	2058	|
Exeter St Davids .... a.	1346	1409	1443	...	1521	1546	...	1618	1619	1643	...	1734	1743	1813	1820	1843	1917	1917	1921	1943	2010	2013	2043	2116	2116	2121
Exeter St Davids **116** d.	1348	1411	1445	...	1524	1548	1552	▬	1622	1645	...	1736	1745	1814	1821	1845	...	1917	1923	1945	2019	2016	2045	...	2116	2122
Dawlish..............**116** d.	|	|	|	...	|	|	1606	...	|	|	...	|	|	1826	|	|	...	|	|	|	2041	|	|	...	|	|
Teignmouth...........**116** d.	|	|	|	...	|	|	1611	...	|	|	...	|	|	1831	|	|	...	|	|	|	2047	|	|	...	|	|
Newton Abbot...**116** d.	1409	1431	1504	...	1544	1609	1618	...	1642	1704	...	1757	1812	1840	1843	1904	...	1937	1943	2004	2054	2036	2104	...	2137	2143
Torquay.............**116** d.	|	|	|	GW	|	|	|	GW	|	|	...	|	|	1851	|	|	...	|	|	|	2107	|	|	...	|	|
Paignton ....**116** a.	|	|	|	Ⓐ	|	|	|	Ⓐ	|	|	...	|	|	1901	|	|	...	|	|	|	2120	|	|	...	|	|
Totnes .... d.	1423	|	1517	2	1558	1623	1631	2	1655	1717	...	1810	1824	...	1856	1917	...	|	1957	2017	...	2049	2117	...	|	2157
Plymouth...........**118** a.	1456	1509	1548	...	1629	1656	1701	...	1723	1748	...	1838	1856	...	1927	1948	...	2017	2025	2048	...	2117	2148	...	2215	2225
Plymouth.................. d.	...	1511	...	1557	...	...	...	1706	1726	...	1755	1844	1900	...	1931	1950	...	...	2028	2050	...	2119	...	...	...	2227
Saltash .... d.	...	|	...	1611	...	...	...	1720	1735	...	|	|	|	...	1940	|	...	...	2038	|	...	|	...	...	...	2236
Liskeard..............**118** d.	...	1534	...	1632	...	...	...	1742	1754	...	1819	1907	1923	...	1956	2013	...	...	2056	2113	...	2143	...	...	...	2255
Bodmin Parkway....... d.	...	1547	...	1644	...	...	...	...	1806	...	1831	1919	1935	...	2008	2026	...	...	2108	2126	...	2157	...	...	...	2310
Par ....**118** d.	...	1558	...	1656	...	...	...	...	1819	...	1843	1930	1945	...	2019	2036	...	...	2119	2138	...	2208	...	...	...	2320
Newquay ....**118** a.	...	|	...	|	...	...	...	...	|	...	|	|	|	...	|	|	...	...	|	|	...	|	...	...	...	|
St Austell .... d.	...	1606	...	1705	...	...	...	...	1827	...	1851	1938	1952	...	2027	2043	...	...	2127	2145	...	2216	...	...	...	2328
Truro..................**118** d.	...	1623	...	1724	...	...	...	...	1846	...	1908	1956	2010	...	2045	2100	...	...	2144	2203	...	2234	...	...	...	2346
Redruth .... d.	...	1636	...	1737	...	...	...	...	1857	...	1921	2008	2025	...	2057	2115	...	...	2157	2214	...	2246	...	...	...	2359
Camborne................... d.	...	1644	...	1743	...	...	...	...	1907	...	1927	2017	2033	...	2106	2122	...	...	2209	2223	...	|	...	...	...	0007
St Erth...............**118** d.	...	1655	...	1754	...	...	...	...	1920	...	1940	2027	2044	...	2116	2132	...	...	2217	2235	...	|	...	...	...	0018
Penzance.................... a	...	1711	...	1808	...	...	...	...	1936	...	1953	2044	2059	...	2133	2147	...	...	2231	2250	...	2315	...	...	...	0034

Operator	XC	XC	GW	XC	GW	GW	GW		GW	XC	GW	XC	GW	GW	GW	GW	XC	GW	XC	GW	GW	XC	GW	GW	XC	XC
	Ⓐ	Ⓐ	Ⓐ	Ⓐ	Ⓐ	Ⓐ	Ⓐ		⑥	⑥	⑥	⑥	⑥	⑥	⑥	⑥	⑥	⑥	⑥	⑥	⑥	⑥	⑥	⑥	⑥	⑥
			🍷		🍷	2C			🍷Z		2🍷	🍷	🍷	2		2🍷	🍷	2🍷	🍷	🍷	🍷	🍷	🍷	🍷	🍷	🍷
London Pad ☆..**133** d.	...	...	1945	...	2035	...	2145	⑥	2345c	...	...	...	...	...	...	...	...	...	...	0736	0730	...	0835	0906	...	...
Reading.......**132 133** d.	...	...	2011	...	2101	...	2211		0037	...	...	...	...	...	...	...	...	...	...	0806u	0757	...	0904u	0933u	...	...
Newbury .... d.	...	...	2027	...	2118	...	|		|	...	...	...	...	...	...	...	...	...	...	|	|	...	0921	|	...	...
Westbury .... d.	...	...	2105	...	2157	...	Y		|	...	...	...	...	...	...	...	...	...	...	|	Y	...	0958	|	...	...
Castle Cary................ d.	...	...	2127	...	2215	...	|		|	...	...	...	...	...	...	...	...	...	...	|	|	...	1016	|	...	...
B'ham New St **127** d.	1912	1942	|	2012	|	...	|		|	...	...	...	...	...	...	...	0642	...	0712	|	|	0812	|	|	0842	0912
Bristol T Meads.... d.	2044	2113	|	2144	|	2308	2335		|	...	0529	0608	...	0636	...	...	0811	...	0844	|	0917	0944	|	|	1020	1044
Taunton .... d.	2117	2146	2149	2217	2237	0019s	0037s		0322	...	0623	0717	...	0724	...	...	0843	...	0917	|	0951	1017	1037	1050	1102	1117
Tiverton Parkway ...... d.	2129	2158	2209	2229	2251	0034s	0050s		|	...	0639	0729	...	0741	...	...	|	...	0929	|	|	1029	|	1103	1114	1129
Exeter St Davids .... a.	2143	2232	2239	2255	2320	0108	0121		0414	...	0657	0743	...	0759	...	...	0907	...	0943	0952	1018	1046	1104	1121	1130	1143
Exeter St Davids **116** d.	2145	2233	2243	2256	2321	...	...		0417	...	0659	0745	...	0805	...	...	0908	0928	0945	0953	1019	1049	1106	1123	1133	1145
Dawlish..............**116** d.	|	|	|	|	|	...	...		|	...	0719	|	...	|	...	...	|	|	|	|	|	|	1125	|	|	|
Teignmouth...........**116** d.	|	|	|	|	|	...	...		|	...	0724	|	...	|	...	...	|	|	|	|	|	|	1131	|	|	|
Newton Abbot...**116** d.	2204	2253	2307	2322	2342	...	...		0439	...	0732	0804	...	0827	...	...	|	0949	1004	|	1040	1110	1140	1144	1154	1204
Torquay.............**116** d.	|	|	|	|	|	...	...		|	...	|	|	...	|	...	...	0937	|	|	|	|	|	1152	|	|	|
Paignton ....**116** a.	|	|	|	|	|	...	...		|	...	|	|	...	|	...	...	0949	|	|	|	|	|	1200	|	|	|
Totnes .... d.	2217	2304	2220	2334	2354	...	...		|	...	0745	0817	...	0839	...	...	...	1002	1017	|	1054	1123	...	1157	|	1217
Plymouth...........**118** a.	2248	2338	2355	0006	0025	...	...		0518	...	0815	0848	...	0909	...	...	...	1032	1048	1051	1122	1156	...	1226	1232	1248
Plymouth.................. d.	...	...	...	...	...	...	...		0550	0630	0818	...	0858	...	0926	0958	...	1033	...	1051	1124	...	...	1228	1239	...
Saltash .... d.	...	...	...	...	...	...	...		|	|	0829	...	|	...	|	1008	...	1043	...	|	|	...	...	|	|	...
Liskeard..............**118** d.	...	...	...	...	...	...	...		0615	0653	0850	...	0922	...	0949	1029	...	1102	...	|	1147	...	...	1251	1304	...
Bodmin Parkway....... d.	...	...	...	...	...	...	...		0629	0706	0902	...	0934	...	1001	1041	...	1114	...	|	1201	...	...	1304	1317	...
Par ....**118** d.	...	...	...	...	...	...	...		0642	0721	0914	...	0947	...	1015	1053	...	1126	...	1135	|	...	...	|	|	...
Newquay ....**118** a.	...	...	...	...	...	...	...		|	0825	|	...	1105	...	|	...	...	|	...	1245	|	...	...	|	1442	...
St Austell .... d.	...	...	...	...	...	...	...		0650	...	0921	...	...	...	1022	...	...	1137	...	...	1217	...	...	1321	...	...
Truro..................**118** d.	...	...	...	...	...	...	...		0709	...	0940	...	...	...	1040	...	...	1155	...	...	1234	...	...	1339	...	...
Redruth .... d.	...	...	...	...	...	...	...		0723	...	0953	...	...	...	1052	...	...	1208	...	...	1247	...	...	1351	...	...
Camborne................... d.	...	...	...	...	...	...	...		0730	...	0959	...	...	...	1100	...	...	1214	...	...	1254	...	...	1359	...	...
St Erth...............**118** d.	...	...	...	...	...	...	...		0744	...	1010	...	...	...	1117	...	...	1224	...	...	1306	...	...	1414	...	...
Penzance.................... a	...	...	...	...	...	...	...		0800	...	1023	...	...	...	1128	...	...	1237	...	...	1319	...	...	1427	...	...

A – From / to Aberdeen.
B – From / to Birmingham.
C – From / to Cardiff.
D – From / to Derby.
E – From / to Edinburgh.
G – From / to Glasgow.
K – From / to York.
L – From / to Leeds.
M – From / to Manchester.
N – From / to Newcastle.
U – From / to Dundee.
W – From / to London Waterloo.
Y – Via Swindon, Table **133**.
Z – Also conveys 🛏 1, 2 cl.
b – From London on ①–④.
c – From London on ⑤.
d – From London on ⑦.
e – Stops to pick up only until September 4.
s – Stops to set down only.
u – Stops to pick up only.
☆ – London Paddington.

LONDON and BRISTOL - EXETER - PLYMOUTH - PENZANCE

Services on Ⓐ valid until June 26, services on ⑥ valid until September 5, services on ⑦ valid until July 12:

For additional Exeter - Paignton *GW* and *SW* trains see Table **116**.

Operator	*GW*	*XC*	*SW*	*XC*	*GW*	*GW*	*XC*	*GW*	*GW*	*XC*	*GW*	*GW*	*GW*	*XC*	*SW*	*XC*	*GW*	*XC*	*GW*	*GW*	*XC*	*SW*	*GW*	*XC*	*GW*	*GW*
	⑥	⑥	⑥	⑥	⑥	⑥	⑥	⑥	⑥	⑥	⑥	⑥	⑥	⑥	⑥	⑥	⑥	⑥	⑥	⑥	⑥	⑥	⑥	⑥	⑥	⑥
	🍷	🍷	🍷**W**	🍷	🍷	🍷	🍷	🍷	🍷	🍷	2🍷	🍷	🍷	🍷	🍷**W**	🍷	🍷	🍷	2🍷	🍷	🍷	🍷**W**	🍷	🍷	🍷	🍷
London Pad ☆..**133** d.	1006	...	...	...	1035	1106	...	1135	1206	...	...	1235	1306	...	...	...	1406	...	...	1506	...	...	1606	...	1706	1630
Reading....... **132 133** d.	1033**u**	...	...	...	1104	1133**u**	...	1206**u**	1232**u**	...	...	1304	1332**u**	...	...	...	1433**u**	...	...	1533**u**	...	...	1632**u**	...	1732**u**	1657
Newbury.................. d.	|	...	...	...	|	|	...	|	|	...	...	1321	|	...	...	...	|	...	...	|	...	...	|	...	|	|
Westbury.................. d.	|	...	...	...	1155	|	...	|	|	...	...	1400	|	...	...	...	|	...	...	1623	...	...	|	...	1822	|
Castle Cary............... d.	|	...	...	...	1213	|	...	|	|	...	...	1418	|	...	...	...	|	...	...	1641	...	...	|	...	1841	**Y**
B'ham New St **127** d.	|	0942	...	1012	|	|	1112	|	|	1212	...	|	|	1312	...	1342	|	1412	...	|	1512	...	|	1612	|	|
Bristol T Meads.... d.	|	1113	...	1144	|	|	1244	|	|	1344	...	|	|	1444	...	1513	|	1544	...	|	1644	...	|	1744	|	1800
Taunton.................... d.	|	1203	...	1217	1236	1252	1317	|	|	1417	...	1441	1449	1517	...	1545	1549	1617	...	1703	1719	...	1748	1817	1902	1906
Tiverton Parkway...... d.	|	1215	...	|	1249	|	1329	|	|	1429	...	|	1502	|	...	1557	1602	1629	...	1716	1731	...	1801	1829	1915	1921
Exeter St Davids...... a.	1213	1231	...	1242	1306	1319	1343	|	1412	1443	...	1506	1520	1543	...	1612	1620	1643	...	1733	1747	...	1819	1843	1932	1937
Exeter St Davids **116** d.	1216	1234	1239	1245	1309	1321	1345	1356**u**	1414	1445	...	1509	1521	1545	1549	1613	1622	1645	...	1735	1749	1753	1821	1845	1934	1938
Dawlish...............**116** d.	|	1247	1302	|	1323	|	|	|	|	|	...	1527	|	|	1603	|	|	|	...	|	|	1808	|	|	|	|
Teignmouth.........**116** d.	|	1254	1307	|	1329	|	|	|	|	|	...	1533	|	|	1608	|	|	|	...	|	|	1813	|	|	|	|
Newton Abbot...**116** d.	1237	1302	1314	1304	1338	1342	1404	|	1435	1504	...	1541	1544	1604	1615	1340	1643	1704	...	1757	1811	1821	1843	1904	1954	1959
Torquay...........**116** d.	|	1314	|	|	1351	|	|	|	|	|	...	1555	|	|	|	1652	|	|	...	|	|	|	|	|	|	2012
Paignton ....**116** a.	|	1327	|	|	1400	|	|	|	|	|	...	1603	|	|	|	1704	|	|	...	|	|	|	|	|	|	2024
Totnes...................... d.	|	...	1328	1320	...	1355	1417	|	|	1517	...	...	1558	1620	1628	...	1655	1717	...	1810	1824	1834	1857	1917	2007	...
Plymouth...........**118** a.	1314	...	1357	1348	...	1423	1448	|	1511	1548	...	...	1625	1647	1658	...	1723	1748	...	1838	1842	1903	1928	1948	2036	...
Plymouth................. d.	1319	...	...	1348	...	1426	...	1456**u**	1512	...	1603	...	1627	1653	...	...	...	...	1752	1842	1901	1911	1929	1948	...	...
Saltash..................... d.	|	...	...	|	...	|	...	|	|	...	1611	...	|	|	...	...	...	...	1806	|	|	1919	|	|	...	...
Liskeard.............**118** d.	1344	...	...	1412	...	1449	...	|	1536	...	1632	...	1650	1716	...	...	...	...	1826	1906	1924	1938	1953	2011	...	...
Bodmin Parkway....... d.	1357	...	...	1425	...	1502	...	|	1549	...	1644	...	1703	1729	...	...	...	...	1838	1919	1937	1950	2006	2024	...	...
Par.......................**118** d.	1407	...	...	1435	...	|	...	1553	1559	...	1656	...	|	|	...	...	...	...	1851	1930	1947	2003	2016	2036	...	...
Newquay........**118** a.	|	...	...	|	...	|	...	1652	|	...	...	...	|	1849	...	...	...	...	|	|	|	|	|	|	...	...
St Austell.................. d.	1415	...	...	1443	...	1517	...	...	1607	...	...	...	1718	...	...	...	...	...	1858	1938	1955	2011	2024	2043	...	...
Truro..................**118** d.	1433	...	...	1501	...	1535	...	...	1624	...	...	...	1736	...	...	...	...	...	1916	1958	2013	2029	2042	2100	...	...
Redruth..................... d.	1445	...	...	1513	...	1547	...	...	1637	...	...	...	1748	...	...	...	...	...	1929	2008	2025	2041	2054	2112	...	...
Camborne.................. d.	1453	...	...	1521	...	1554	...	...	1645	...	...	...	1756	...	...	...	...	...	1935	2016	2032	2047	2103	2118	...	...
St Erth................**118** d.	1508	...	...	1531	...	1609	...	...	1656	...	...	...	1811	...	...	...	...	...	1946	2026	2043	|	2114	2130	...	...
Penzance................. a	1521	...	...	1550	...	1624	...	...	1713	...	...	...	1824	...	...	...	...	...	1957	2043	2059	2105	2130	2146	...	...

Operator	*GW*	*XC*	*GW*	*XC*	*XC*	*GW*	*XC*	*GW*	*XC*	*GW*	*GW*		*XC*	*GW*	*GW*	*GW*	*XC*	*GW*	*GW*	*SW*	*XC*	*GW*	*XC*	*GW*	*XC*	*GW*
	⑥	⑥	⑥	⑥	⑥	⑥	⑥	⑥	⑥	⑥	⑥		⑦	⑦	⑦	⑦	⑦	⑦	⑦	⑦	⑦	⑦	⑦	⑦	⑦	⑦
	2🍷	🍷	🍷	🍷	🍷	🍷	🍷	🍷	🍷	2**C**	🍷			2🍷	2	2	🍷	🍷	🍷	🍷**W**	🍷	🍷	🍷	🍷	🍷	2🍷
London Pad ☆..**133** d.	...	...	1806	...	...	1906	...	2006	...	...	2030	⑦	...	...	...	...	...	0800	0857	...	...	0957	...	1057	...	...
Reading....... **132 133** d.	...	...	1832**u**	...	...	1932	...	2031	...	...	2057		...	...	...	...	...	0838	0932	...	...	1032	...	1132	...	...
Newbury.................. d.	...	...	|	...	...	1949	...	2046	...	...	|		...	...	...	...	...	|	0948	...	...	|	...	|	...	...
Westbury.................. d.	...	...	|	...	...	2028	...	2124	...	...	**Y**		...	...	...	...	...	**Y**	1023	...	...	|	...	|	...	...
Castle Cary............... d.	...	...	|	...	...	2045	...	2143	...	...	|		...	...	...	...	...	|	|	...	...	1134	...	|	...	...
B'ham New St **127** d.	...	1712	|	1742	1812	|	1912	|	2012	...	|		...	...	...	...	...	|	|	...	0852	|	1012	|	1112	...
Bristol T Meads.... d.	...	1844	|	1937	1944	|	2044	|	2144	2155	2217		...	...	0745	0828	0944	1000	|	...	1044	|	1144	|	1244	...
Taunton.................... d.	...	1917	1947	2009	2017	2108	2117	2205	2217	2302	2219		...	...	0839	0930	1021	1033	1059	...	1121	1156	1217	1247	1317	...
Tiverton Parkway...... d.	...	1929	|	2021	2029	2121	2129	2218	2229	2317	2332		...	...	0854	0945	1033	1047	1112	...	1134	|	1229	|	1330	...
Exeter St Davids...... a.	...	1943	2014	2036	2043	2139	2145	2236	2244	2336	2353		...	...	0912	1004	1047	1104	1129	...	1148	1226	1247	1314	1347	...
Exeter St Davids **116** d.	...	1945	2015	2037	2045	2139	2145	2238	2245	...	...		...	...	0914	1005	1049	1106	1130	1140	1150	1228	1249	1315	1349	...
Dawlish...............**116** d.	...	|	|	2049	|	|	|	2250	|	...	...		...	...	0930	1018	|	1119	|	|	|	|	|	|	|	...
Teignmouth.........**116** d.	...	|	|	2054	|	|	|	2256	|	...	...		...	...	0935	1023	|	1125	|	|	|	|	|	|	|	...
Newton Abbot...**116** d.	...	2004	2037	2103	2104	2200	2209	2304	2313	...	...		...	...	0943	1031	1109	1132	1152	1201	1209	1249	1310	1337	1410	...
Torquay...........**116** d.	...	|	|	2115	|	|	|	|	|	...	...		...	...	|	|	|	|	|	|	|	|	|	|	|	...
Paignton ....**116** a.	...	|	|	2127	|	|	|	|	|	...	...		...	...	|	|	|	|	|	|	|	|	|	|	|	...
Totnes...................... d.	...	2017	2051	...	2117	2214	2223	2317	2328	...	...		...	...	0956	1044	1121	1145	1204	1214	1224	1302	1323	|	1423	...
Plymouth...........**118** a.	...	2048	2119	...	2148	2242	2255	2347	2359	...	...		...	...	1026	1112	1153	1213	1232	1244	1255	1333	1356	1414	1453	...
Plymouth................. d.	2042	2058	2120	...	...	...	...	...	...	...	...		0905	0917	1030	1114	...	1215	1235	...	1255	1333	...	1415	...	1458
Saltash..................... d.	2050	|	|	...	...	...	...	...	...	...	...		|	0930	1044	1122	...	|	|	...	|	|	...	|	...	1506
Liskeard.............**118** d.	2109	2125	2144	...	...	...	...	...	...	...	...		0930	0949	1108	1144	...	1239	1257	...	1318	1358	...	1443	...	1525
Bodmin Parkway....... d.	2121	2138	2159	...	...	...	...	...	...	...	...		0943	1001	1122	1156	...	1255	1310	...	1330	1410	...	1455	...	1537
Par.......................**118** d.	2133	2148	2209	...	...	...	...	...	...	...	...		|	1014	1134	1208	...	1307	1321	...	1340	1424	...	|	...	1550
Newquay........**118** a.	|	|	|	...	...	...	...	...	...	...	...		1115	|	|	|	...	|	|	...	|	1530	...	|	...	|
St Austell.................. d.	2144	2155	2217	...	...	...	...	...	...	...	...		...	1021	1142	1215	...	1314	1328	...	1347	...	...	1512	...	1557
Truro..................**118** d.	2202	2219	2235	...	...	...	...	...	...	...	...		...	1040	1200	1233	...	1331	1347	...	1404	...	...	1528	...	1616
Redruth..................... d.	2215	2230	2247	...	...	...	...	...	...	...	...		...	1053	1214	1247	...	1344	1359	...	1416	...	...	1540	...	1629
Camborne.................. d.	2221	2236	2256	...	...	...	...	...	...	...	...		...	1059	1220	1253	...	1351	1407	...	1423	...	...	1547	...	1635
St Erth................**118** d.	2231	2246	2309	...	...	...	...	...	...	...	...		...	1110	1231	1304	...	1404	1419	...	1433	...	...	1558	...	1646
Penzance................. a	2243	2302	2324	...	...	...	...	...	...	...	...		...	1124	1245	1316	...	1418	1435	...	1448	...	...	1611	...	1700

Operator	*GW*	*GW*	*XC*	*GW*	*GW*	*XC*	*GW*	*GW*	*XC*	*XC*	*GW*	*XC*	*GW*	*GW*	*XC*	*GW*	*XC*	*GW*	*XC*	*GW*	*XC*	*XC*	*GW*	*GW*	*XC*	*GW*
	⑦	⑦	⑦	⑦	⑦	⑦	⑦	⑦	⑦	⑦	⑦	⑦	⑦	⑦	⑦	⑦	⑦	⑦	⑦	⑦	⑦	⑦	⑦	⑦	⑦	⑦
	🍷	🍷	🍷	🍷	🍷	🍷	2	🍷	🍷	🍷	🍷	🍷	🍷	2	🍷	🍷	🍷	🍷	🍷	🍷	🍷	🍷	🍷	🍷	🍷	🍷
London Pad ☆..**133** d.	1127	1157	...	1200	1257	...	...	1357	...	...	1457	...	1557	...	...	1657	...	1757	...	1857	...	...	1900	1957	...	2057
Reading....... **132 133** d.	1202	1232	...	1237	1332	...	...	1432	...	...	1532	...	1632	...	...	1732	...	1832	...	1932	...	...	1937	2032	...	2132
Newbury.................. d.	|	1248	...	|	|	...	...	1448	...	...	|	...	1648	...	...	|	...	1848	...	|	...	...	|	2049	...	|
Westbury.................. d.	1303	|	...	**Y**	1419	...	...	|	...	...	|	...	1724	...	...	|	...	1928	...	|	...	...	**Y**	2128	...	|
Castle Cary............... d.	1319	|	...	|	|	...	...	1535	...	...	|	...	1741	...	...	|	...	|	...	2029	...	...	|	2146	...	|
B'ham New St **127** d.	|	|	1212	|	|	1312	...	|	1412	1442	|	1512	|	...	1612	|	1712	|	1812	|	1842	1912	|	|	2012	|
Bristol T Meads.... d.	|	|	1344	1356	|	1444	...	|	1544	1614	|	1644	|	...	1744	|	1844	|	1944	|	2019	2044	2057	|	2144	|
Taunton.................... d.	1342	1350	1417	1430	1455	1517	...	1555	1617	1646	1652	1717	1803	...	1821	1849	1917	2002	2017	2051	2059	2117	2152	2206	2217	2249**s**
Tiverton Parkway...... d.	1355	1405	1429	|	1508	1529	...	|	1629	1658	1705	1729	1817	...	1833	1901	1929	2016	2029	2104	2112	2129	2205	2219	2229	2303**s**
Exeter St Davids...... a.	1412	1423	1444	1457	1524	1544	...	1622	1647	1713	1721	1744	1837	...	1848	1918	1948	2033	2047	2121	2126	2144	2222	2237	2244	2320
Exeter St Davids **116** d.	1413	1424	1445	1457	1525	1545	1605	1623	1649	1714	1723	1745	1838	...	1849	1920	1949	2033	2048	2122	2130	2145	...	2237	2245	...
Dawlish...............**116** d.	1430	|	|	|	|	|	1620	|	|	1726	|	|	|	...	|	|	|	|	|	2136	2143	|	...	|	|	...
Teignmouth.........**116** d.	1436	|	|	|	|	|	1625	|	|	1731	|	|	|	...	|	|	|	|	|	2142	2148	|	...	|	|	...
Newton Abbot...**116** d.	1444	1448	1504	1518	1546	1604	1631	1642	1710	1739	1743	1805	1900	...	1909	1940	2009	2055	2108	2149	2156	2204	...	2258	2306	...
Torquay...........**116** d.	1455	|	|	|	|	|	|	|	|	1750	|	|	|	...	|	|	|	|	|	|	2207	|	...	|	|	...
Paignton ....**116** a.	1504	|	|	|	|	|	|	|	|	1802	|	|	|	...	|	|	|	|	|	|	2219	|	...	|	|	...
Totnes...................... d.	...	1501	1517	|	1600	1617	1647	1658	1723	...	1757	1817	|	...	1921	1953	2021	2110	2120	2203	...	2217	...	2311	2321	...
Plymouth...........**118** a.	...	1529	1548	1600	1629	1648	1717	1729	1756	...	1824	1848	1938	...	1953	2021	2048	2137	2152	2231	...	2248	...	2344	2354	...
Plymouth................. d.	...	1531	...	...	1635	...	1735	...	...	...	1826	1855	...	1943	...	2023	2050	2140	...	...	...	...	...	...	...	...
Saltash..................... d.	...	|	...	...	|	...	1744	...	...	...	|	|	...	1951	...	|	|	|	...	...	...	...	...	...	...	...
Liskeard.............**118** d.	...	1555	...	...	1657	...	1806	...	...	...	1850	1918	...	2010	...	2047	2113	2203	...	...	...	...	...	...	...	...
Bodmin Parkway....... d.	...	1607	...	...	1709	...	1818	...	...	...	1902	1930	...	2022	...	2100	2125	2214	...	...	...	...	...	...	...	...
Par.......................**118** d.	...	1618	...	...	1722	...	1830	...	...	...	1914	1940	...	2035	...	2111	2135	2227	...	...	...	...	...	...	...	...
Newquay........**118** a.	...	|	...	...	|	...	|	...	...	...	|	|	...	|	...	|	|	|	...	...	...	...	...	...	...	...
St Austell.................. d.	...	1626	...	...	1728	...	1837	...	...	...	1921	1951	...	2042	...	2118	2142	2235	...	...	...	...	...	...	...	...
Truro..................**118** d.	...	1643	...	...	1747	...	1855	...	...	...	1938	2008	...	2109	...	2136	2159	2251	...	...	...	...	...	...	...	...
Redruth..................... d.	...	1656	...	...	1759	...	1908	...	...	...	1951	2019	...	2122	...	2148	2210	2305	...	...	...	...	...	...	...	...
Camborne.................. d.	...	1703	...	...	1806	...	1914	...	...	...	1958	2027	...	2128	...	2156	2221	2311	...	...	...	...	...	...	...	...
St Erth................**118** d.	...	1716	...	...	1819	...	1925	...	...	...	2011	2037	...	2139	...	2208	2231	2323	...	...	...	...	...	...	...	...
Penzance................. a	...	1733	...	...	1835	...	1938	...	...	...	2023	2052	...	2151	...	2221	2246	2338	...	...	...	...	...	...	...	...

A – From / to Aberdeen.
B – From / to Birmingham.
C – From / to Cardiff.
D – From / to Derby.
E – From / to Edinburgh.
G – From / to Glasgow.

K – From / to York.
L – From / to Leeds.
M – From / to Manchester.
N – From / to Newcastle.
U – From / to Dundee.
W – From / to London Waterloo.

Y – Via Swindon, Table **133**.
Z – Also conveys 🛏 1, 2 cl.
b – From London on ①–④.
c – From London on ⑤.
d – From London on ⑦.

s – Stops to set down only.
u – Stops to pick up only.

☆ – London Paddington.

115 PENZANCE - PLYMOUTH - EXETER - BRISTOL and LONDON

GW, SW, XC

Services on Ⓐ valid until June 26, services on ⑥ valid until September 5, services on ⑦ valid until July 12.

For additional Paignton - Exeter *GW* and *SW* trains see Table **116**.

Operator		*GW*	*GW*	*XC*	*GW*	*GW*	*GW*	*GW*	*XC*	*XC*	*GW*	*GW*	*GW*	*GW*	*GW*	*XC*	*GW*	*XC*	*XC*	*GW*	*XC*	*GW*	*GW*	*XC*	*XC*	*GW*
		Ⓐ	Ⓐ	Ⓐ	Ⓐ	Ⓐ	Ⓐ	Ⓐ	Ⓐ	Ⓐ	Ⓐ	Ⓐ	Ⓐ	Ⓐ	Ⓐ	Ⓐ	Ⓐ	Ⓐ	Ⓐ	Ⓐ	Ⓐ	Ⓐ	Ⓐ	Ⓐ	Ⓐ	Ⓐ
		🍷	2	🍷	🍷	🍷	🍷	🍷	🍷	🍷	🍴	2	🍷	🍷	2	🍷	🍷	🍷	🍷	🍷	🍷	🍷	🍷	🍷	🍷	🍴
Penzance d.	Ⓐ	...	...	...	...	...	...	...	...	...	0505	0521	...	0541	0600	0628	0648	...	...	0737	0828	0844	...	...	0940	1000
St Erth 118 d.		...	...	...	...	...	...	...	...	...	|	|	...	|	0608	0636	0659	...	...	0747	0836	0855	...	...	0948	1011
Camborne d.		...	...	...	...	...	...	...	...	...	|	0540	...	0600	0622	0646	0710	...	...	0801	0846	0907	...	...	1001	1022
Redruth d.		...	...	...	...	...	...	...	...	...	0526	|	...	0607	0628	0652	0717	...	...	0808	0852	0914	...	...	1008	1029
Truro 118 d.		...	...	...	...	...	...	...	...	...	0539	0555	...	0619	0640	0704	0729	...	...	0821	0904	0926	...	...	1019	1041
St Austell d.		...	...	...	...	...	...	...	...	...	0556	—	...	0637	0657	0720	0747	...	...	0838	0920	0944	...	...	1035	1059
Newquay 118 d.		...	...	...	...	...	...	...	...	...	|	...	...	|	|	|	|	...	...	|	|	|	...	...	|	|
Par 118 d.		...	...	...	...	...	...	...	...	...	|	...	...	0644	0704	0728	0755	...	...	0846	0928	0951	...	...	1043	1107
Bodmin Parkway d.		...	...	...	...	...	...	...	...	...	0612	*XC*	...	0658	0717	0739	0808	...	...	0900	0939	1003	...	...	1057	1118
Liskeard 118 d.		...	...	...	...	...	...	...	...	...	0624	Ⓐ	...	0711	0730	0751	0821	...	...	0913	0951	1016	...	...	1109	1131
Saltash d.		...	...	...	...	...	...	...	...	...	|	🍷E	...	0731	0749	|	0839	...	...	0931	|	|	...	...	|	|
Plymouth a.		...	...	...	...	...	...	...	...	...	0649		...	0742	0805	0820	0851	...	...	0942	1015	1040	...	...	1137	1156
Plymouth 118 d.		...	...	0520	...	0530	0541	0600	0625	...	0655	0725	...	0747	0807	0825	0855	0925	...	0945	1025	1044	...	1125	1150	1200
Totnes d.		...	...	0545	...	0557	0608	|	0650	...	|	0750	...	0814	0836	0850	0922	0950	...	1014	1050	|	...	1150	1215	1229
Paignton 116 d.		...	...	|	...	|	|	|	|	0700	|	|	0738	|	|	|	|	|	1005	|	|	|	...	|	|	|
Torquay 116 d.		...	...	|	...	|	|	|	|	0706	|	|	0744	|	|	|	|	|	1011	|	|	|	...	|	|	|
Newton Abbot 116 d.		...	...	0602	...	0610	0622	0635	0703	0717	0730	0803	0806	0827	0850	0903	0935	1003	1022	1027	1103	|	...	1203	1228	1242
Teignmouth 116 d.		...	...	|	...	0617	|	|	|	0724	|	|	0813	|	0857	|	|	|	1029	1035	|	|	...	|	|	|
Dawlish 116 d.		...	...	|	...	0623	|	|	|	0729	|	|	0819	|	0902	|	|	|	1034	1041	|	|	...	|	|	|
Exeter St Davids 116 a.		...	...	0621	...	0636	0643	0654	0721	0741	0750	0821	0839	0847	0921	0921	0955	1021	1046	1054	1121	1137	...	1221	1246	1302
Exeter St Davids d.		0546	0600	0623	0630	0638	0645	0655	0723	0743	0752	0823	0840	0849	...	0923	0957	1023	1048	1056	1123	1139	1155	1223	1248	1304
Tiverton Parkway d.		0602	0618	0637	|	0653	0700	|	0737	0756	|	0837	|	0904	...	0937	1012	1037	1102	1111	1137	|	1209	1237	1302	1319
Taunton d.		0617	0635	0651	0654	0708	0715	0719	0751	0811	0817	0851	0905	0919	...	0951	1027	1051	1116	1126	1151	|	1224	1251	1316	1334
Bristol T Meads a.		|	0743	0726	0758	|	0825	|	0827	0855	|	0927	0956	|	...	1026	|	1124	1153	1159	1224	|	|	1324	1356	|
B'ham New St 127 a.		|	...	0856	|	|	|	|	0956	1026	|	1056	|	|	...	1156	|	1256	1326	|	1356	|	|	1456	1526	|
Castle Cary d.		0638	...	...	|	0730	|	|	...	...	|	...	|	0940	...	...	|	...	...	|	...	|	1245	...	...	|
Westbury d.		0705	...	...	Y	0751	Y	|	...	...	|	...	Y	0959	...	...	1103	...	...	Y	...	|	1305	...	...	|
Newbury d.		0746	...	...	|	0830	|	|	...	...	|	...	|	|	...	...	|	...	...	|	...	|	1349	...	...	|
Reading 132 133 a.		0807	...	...	0914	0851	0944	0833	...	...	0933	...	1111	1051	...	...	1151	...	...	1311	...	1317	1417	...	...	1451
London Pad ☆ 133 a.		0838	...	...	0944	0921	1014	0900	...	...	1002	...	1140	1123	...	...	1225	...	...	1340	...	1344	1444	...	...	1523

Operator	*XC*	*GW*	*GW*	*XC*	*XC*	*GW*	*GW*	*XC*	*SW*	*GW*	*GW*	*XC*	*XC*	*GW*	*XC*	*GW*	*GW*	*XC*	*SW*	*GW*	*XC*	*GW*	*GW*	*GW*	*GW*	*GW*
	Ⓐ	Ⓐ	Ⓐ	Ⓐ	Ⓐ	Ⓐ	Ⓐ	Ⓐ	Ⓐ	Ⓐ	Ⓐ	Ⓐ	⑤	Ⓐ	Ⓐ	Ⓐ	Ⓐ	Ⓐ	Ⓐ	Ⓐ	Ⓐ	①–④	⑤	①–④	⑤	Ⓐ
	🍷	2	🍴	🍷	🍷	2	🍷	🍷	🍷W	2	🍷	🍷	🍷	🍷	🍷	2	🍷	🍷	W	🍷	🍷	2	2	🍷	🍷	🍷
Penzance d.	...	1046	...	...	...	1145	...	...	...	1254	...	...	...	1400	...	1449	...	...	...	1600	...	1644	1644	...	...	1738
St Erth 118 d.	...	1054	...	...	...	1153	...	...	...	1302	...	...	...	1411	...	1457	...	...	...	1611	...	1652	1652	...	...	1748
Camborne d.	...	1107	...	...	...	1206	...	...	...	1315	...	...	...	1422	...	1510	...	...	...	1623	...	1705	1705	...	...	1803
Redruth d.	...	1113	...	...	...	1212	...	...	...	1321	...	...	...	1429	...	1516	...	...	...	1630	...	1711	1711	...	...	1810
Truro 118 d.	...	1125	...	...	...	1224	...	...	...	1333	...	...	...	1441	...	1527	...	...	...	1642	...	1724	1724	...	...	1823
St Austell d.	...	1142	...	...	...	1241	...	...	...	1350	...	...	...	1459	...	1544	...	...	...	1700	...	1741	1741	...	...	1840
Newquay 118 d.	...	|	...	...	...	|	...	...	...	|	...	...	...	|	...	|	...	...	...	|	...	|	|	...	...	|
Par 118 d.	...	1150	...	...	...	1249	...	...	...	1357	...	...	...	1506	...	1552	...	...	...	1708	...	1748	1748	...	...	1848
Bodmin Parkway d.	...	1202	...	...	...	1255	...	...	...	1410	...	...	...	1518	...	1604	...	...	...	1722	...	1801	1801	...	...	1859
Liskeard 118 d.	...	1215	...	...	...	1314	...	...	...	1423	...	...	...	1532	...	1617	...	...	...	1736	*1749*	1814	1814	...	...	1912
Saltash d.	...	1234	...	...	...	1334	...	...	...	1441	...	...	...	|	...	1637	...	...	...	|	*1807*	1832	1832	...	...	|
Plymouth a.	...	1246	...	...	...	1344	...	...	...	1451	...	...	...	1557	...	1652	...	...	...	1759	*1818*	1842	1842	...	...	1937
Plymouth 118 d.	1221	...	1255	1321	...	1346	...	1425	1447	...	1500	1521	...	1600	1625	...	1657	1721	1752	1800	1825	1843	1843	...	...	1940
Totnes d.	1248	...	1322	1348	...	1415	...	1450	1516	...	1527	1548	...	1627	1650	...	1727	1748	1821	1830	1850	1913	1913	...	...	2007
Paignton 116 d.	|	...	|	|	1401	|	1415	|	|	...	|	|	...	|	|	...	|	|	|	|	|	|	|	...	...	|
Torquay 116 d.	|	...	|	|	1407	|	1421	|	|	...	|	|	...	|	|	...	|	|	|	|	|	|	|	...	...	|
Newton Abbot 116 d.	1301	...	1335	1401	1418	1428	1433	1503	1529	...	1540	1601	...	1640	1703	...	1740	1801	1833	1843	1903	1925	1925	...	...	2020
Teignmouth 116 d.	|	...	|	|	1425	—	1440	|	1536	...	|	|	...	|	|	...	|	|	1840	|	|	|	|	...	...	|
Dawlish 116 d.	|	...	|	|	1430	*GW*	1446	|	1541	...	|	|	...	|	|	...	|	|	1845	|	|	|	|	...	...	|
Exeter St Davids 116 a.	1321	...	1355	1421	1442	Ⓐ	1459	1521	1556	...	1600	1621	...	1700	1721	...	1800	1821	1859	1903	1921	1948	1948	...	...	2040
Exeter St Davids d.	1323	...	1357	1423	1444	🍷	1500	1523	...	...	1600	1623	1653	1700	1723	...	1800	1823	...	1905	1923	...	1948	1954	...	2042
Tiverton Parkway d.	1338	...	|	1438	1457		1516	1537	...	...	1616	1637	1707	1716	1737	...	1816	1838	...	1920	1937	...	2005	2009	...	2057
Taunton d.	1353	...	1423	1453	1512	1519	1530	1551	...	...	1630	1653	1721	1730	1751	...	1830	1853	...	1935	1951	...	2021	2024	2026	2112
Bristol T Meads a.	1427	...	|	1527	1557	|	|	1627	...	...	|	1727	1754	|	1824	...	|	1827	...	|	2024	...	...	|	|	2145
B'ham New St 127 a.	1556	...	|	1656	1726	|	|	1756	...	...	|	1856	1926	|	1956	...	|	2056	...	|	2206	...	...	|	|	|
Castle Cary d.	...	...	1444	...	...	1541	|	...	...	...	|	...	...	|	...	...	1853	...	...	|	...	...	...	2045	2045	|
Westbury d.	...	...	1503	...	...	1609	|	...	...	...	|	...	...	|	...	...	1911	...	...	|	...	...	...	2104	2104	Y
Newbury d.	...	...	|	...	...	1649	|	...	...	...	|	...	...	|	...	...	1945	...	...	|	...	...	...	2142	2142	|
Reading 132 133 a.	...	...	1551	...	...	1717	1651	...	...	...	1751	...	...	1851	...	...	2007	...	...	2051	...	...	...	2200	2200	2303
London Pad ☆ 133 a.	...	...	1621	...	...	1754	1724	...	...	...	1821	...	...	1924	...	...	2039	...	...	2121	...	...	...	2230	2232	2342

Operator	*XC*	*GW*	*GW*	*GW*	*GW*	*GW*	*XC*		*XC*	*GW*	*XC*	*XC*	*GW*	*GW*	*XC*	*GW*	*GW*	*XC*	*XC*	*GW*	*GW*	*XC*	*GW*	*XC*	*XC*	*GW*
	Ⓐ	Ⓐ	Ⓐ	Ⓐ	⑤	①–④	Ⓐ		⑥	⑥	⑥	⑥	⑥	⑥	⑥	⑥	⑥	⑥	⑥	⑥	⑥	⑥	⑥	⑥	⑥	⑥
	🍷	2	2	🍷	🍷Z	🍷Z	🍷		🍷	2	🍷	🍷	🍷	🍷	🍷	🍷	2	🍷	🍷	🍷	🍷	🍷	🍷	🍷	🍷	🍷
Penzance d.	...	1913	...	2014	2145	2145	2208	⑥	...	0522	...	...	...	...	...	...	0601	0630	...	0650	...	...	0722	...	0825	0842
St Erth 118 d.	...	1921	...	2025	2155	2155	2216		...	|	...	...	...	...	...	...	0608	0638	...	0701	...	...	0734	...	0833	0854
Camborne d.	...	1934	...	2040	2207	2207	2230		...	0539	...	...	...	...	...	...	0621	0651	...	0712	...	...	0748	...	0843	0905
Redruth d.	...	1940	...	2047	2214	2214	2236		...	0545	...	...	...	...	...	...	0627	0657	...	0719	...	...	0755	...	0849	0912
Truro 118 d.	...	1952	...	2100	2227	2227	2248		...	0556	...	...	...	...	...	...	0639	0709	...	0731	...	...	0809	...	0902	0926
St Austell d.	...	2009	...	2117	2245	2245	2304		...	—	...	...	...	...	...	...	0656	0725	...	0749	...	...	0826	...	0918	0943
Newquay 118 d.	...	|	...	|	|	|	|		...	...	...	...	...	...	...	...	|	|	...	|	...	...	|	...	|	|
Par 118 d.	...	2016	...	|	2253	2253	2312		...	...	...	...	...	...	...	...	0703	0732	...	0756	...	...	0834	...	0926	0951
Bodmin Parkway d.	...	2029	...	2137	2305	2305	2326		...	*GW*	...	...	...	...	...	...	0716	0746	...	0810	...	...	0847	...	0937	1002
Liskeard 118 d.	...	2043	...	2150	2320	2320	2339		...	⑥	...	...	...	...	...	...	0730	0758	...	0823	...	...	0900	...	0949	1015
Saltash d.	...	2103	...	|	|	|	|		...	🍷	...	...	...	...	...	...	0749	|	...	|	...	...	0920	...	|	|
Plymouth a.	...	2118	...	2217	2347	2347	0008		...		...	...	...	...	...	...	0805	0822	...	0848	...	...	0930	...	1018	1039
Plymouth 118 d.	...	—	2123	—	2351	2351	...		0525	0540	0625	...	...	0655	0725	0747	0806	0825	0840	0852	...	0925	0934	...	1025	1043
Totnes d.	...	...	2152	...	0019	0019	...		0550	0607	0650	...	...	|	0750	0814	0835	0850	0905	0919	...	0950	1001	...	1050	|
Paignton 116 d.	2010	...	|	...	|	|	...		|	|	|	0700	...	|	|	|	|	|	|	|	0920	|	|	1005	|	|
Torquay 116 d.	2016	...	|	...	|	|	...		|	|	|	0706	...	|	|	|	|	|	|	|	0927	|	|	1012	|	|
Newton Abbot 116 d.	2027	...	2204	*GW*	0032	0032	...		0603	0620	0703	0718	...	0731	0803	0827	0848	0903	0918	0932	0939	1003	1014	1023	1103	|
Teignmouth 116 d.	|	...	2211	Ⓐ	|	|	...		|	|	|	0725	...	|	|	|	0855	|	|	|	0948	|	|	1032	|	|
Dawlish 116 d.	|	*GW*	2216	2	|	|	...		|	|	|	0730	...	|	|	|	0900	|	|	|	0955	|	|	1038	|	|
Exeter St Davids 116 a.	2046	Ⓐ	2238		0054	0054	...		0621	0640	0721	0746	...	0751	0821	0847	0916	0921	0936	0952	1013	1021	1034	1050	1121	1136
Exeter St Davids d.	2048	🍷	...	2111	0114	0114	...		0623	0641	0723	0748	0728	0753	0823	0849	...	0923	0939	0954	1015	1023	1037	1052	1123	1139
Tiverton Parkway d.	2101		...	2128	|	|	...		0637	0656	0737	|	0743	|	0837	0904	...	0937	0952	1009	1030	1037	|	1106	1137	|
Taunton d.	2116	2129	...	2147	0233	0233	...		0651	0711	0751	0812	0758	0819	0851	0919	...	0951	1007	1024	1045	1051	1102	1120	1151	|
Bristol T Meads a.	2151	2230	...	2234	|	|	...		0725	|	0824	0845	0857	|	0925	|	...	1026	1051	|	1119	1126	|	1157	1225	|
B'ham New St 127 a.	2344	|	...	...	|	|	...		0856	|	0956	1026	|	|	1056	|	...	1156	1226	|	|	1256	|	1326	1356	|
Castle Cary d.	...	|	...	...	|	|	...		...	0733	...	...	Y	|	...	0940	...	...	...	|	Y	...	1123	...	...	|
Westbury d.	...	Y	...	...	|	|	...		...	0756	...	...	|	|	...	0959	...	...	...	1102	|	...	1143	...	...	|
Newbury d.	...	|	...	...	|	|	...		...	0833	...	...	|	|	...	|	...	...	...	|	|	...	|	...	...	|
Reading 132 133 a.	...	2355	...	...	0417s	0427s	...		...	0852	...	...	1009	0935	...	1051	...	...	...	1151	1248	...	1241	...	...	1317
London Pad ☆ 133 a.	...	0033	...	...	0543	0543	...		...	0921	...	...	1038	1008	...	1124	...	...	...	1223	1322	...	1314	...	...	1354

A – From / to Aberdeen.
B – From / to Birmingham.
C – From / to Cardiff.
D – From / to Derby.
E – From / to Edinburgh.
G – From / to Glasgow.
K – From / to York.
L – From / to Leeds.
M – From / to Manchester.
N – From / to Newcastle.
U – From / to Dundee.
W – From / to London Waterloo.
Y – Via Swindon, Table **133**.
Z – Also conveys 🛏 1, 2 cl.
b – From London on ①–④.
c – From London on ⑤.
d – From London on ⑦.
s – Stops to set down only.
u – Stops to pick up only.

GW, SW, XC

PENZANCE - PLYMOUTH - EXETER - BRISTOL and LONDON 115

Services on Ⓐ valid until June 26, services on ⑥ valid until September 5, services on ⑦ valid until July 12.

For additional Paignton - Exeter *GW* and *SW* trains see Table **116**.

Operator	*XC*	*GW*	*XC*	*GW*	*GW*	*GW*	*GW*	*XC*	*XC*	*GW*	*GW*	*XC*	*SW*	*GW*	*GW*	*XC*	*GW*	*XC*	*GW*	*GW*	*XC*	*XC*	*SW*	*GW*	*XC*	*XC*
	⑥	⑥	⑥	⑥	⑥	⑥	⑥	⑥	⑥	⑥	⑥	⑥	⑥	⑥	⑥	⑥	⑥	⑥	⑥	⑥	⑥	⑥	⑥	⑥	⑥	⑥
	🍷	🍷	🍷	2 🍷	🍷	🍷	🍷	🍷	🍷	🍷	🍷	🍷	🍷 W	🍷	2 🍷	🍷	🍷	🍷	2 🍷	🍷	🍷	🍷	W	🍷	🍷	🍷
Penzance d.	...	0955	...	...	1100	...	...	...	...	1158	...	...	...	...	1300	...	1400	...	1449	...	...	...	...	1553	1625	...
St Erth **118** d.	...	1007	...	...	1112	...	...	...	...	1210	...	...	...	...	1311	...	1411	...	1457	...	...	...	...	1604	1638	...
Camborne d.	...	1021	...	...	1126	...	...	...	...	1224	...	...	...	...	1323	...	1422	...	1510	...	...	...	...	1615	1647	...
Redruth d.	...	1028	...	...	1133	...	...	...	...	1231	...	...	...	...	1329	...	1429	...	1516	...	...	...	...	1622	1654	...
Truro **118** d.	...	1042	...	...	1147	...	...	...	...	1245	...	...	...	...	1341	...	1441	...	1528	...	...	...	...	1634	1706	...
St Austell d.	...	1059	...	...	1204	...	...	...	...	1302	...	...	...	...	1357	...	1459	...	1545	...	...	...	...	1652	1724	...
Newquay **118** d.	0930	|	...	...	|	1122	...	...	...	|	...	...	...	1314	|	...	|	...	|	...	1520	...	...	|	|	...
Par **118** d.	|	1107	...	1132	|	1227	...	...	...	|	...	...	...	1416	1424	...	1506	...	1553	...	|	...	...	1659	|	...
Bodmin Parkway d.	|	1119	...	1145	1221	|	...	...	...	1319	...	...	...	|	1438	...	1518	...	1606	...	1636	...	...	1713	1740	...
Liskeard **118** d.	|	1133	...	1158	1234	|	...	...	...	1332	...	...	...	|	1451	...	1534	...	1619	...	1650	...	...	1726	1753	...
Saltash d.	|	|	...	1220	|	|	...	...	...	|	...	...	...	|	1509	...	|	...	1638	...	|	...	...	|	|	...
Plymouth a.	1118	1159	...	1229	1259	1311s	...	...	...	1357	...	...	...	1503	1521	...	1557	...	1648	...	1715	...	...	1751	1818	...
Plymouth **118** d.	1121	1159	1221	1229	1301	|	...	1325	...	1359	...	1425	1448	1505	...	1525	1600	1625	...	...	1721	...	1742	1754	1821	1832
Totnes d.	1148	1229	1248	1259	1329	|	...	1350	...	|	...	1450	1517	|	...	1550	1627	1650	...	...	1748	...	1811	1821	1848	1857
Paignton **116** d.	|	|	|	|	|	|	1307	|	1347	|	1430	|	|	|	...	|	|	|	...	1703	|	1803	|	|	|	|
Torquay **116** d.	|	|	|	|	|	|	1314	|	1354	|	1436	|	|	|	...	|	|	|	...	1710	|	1810	|	|	|	|
Newton Abbot **116** d.	1201	1242	1301	1311	1342	|	1326	1403	1406	1436	1450	1503	1530	1544	...	1603	1640	1703	...	1722	1801	1822	1825	1834	1901	1910
Teignmouth **116** d.	|	|	|	|	|	|	1335	|	1415	|	1458	|	1537	|	...	|	|	|	...	1730	|	|	1832	|	|	1917
Dawlish **116** d.	|	|	|	|	|	|	1343	|	1423	|	1504	|	1542	|	...	|	|	|	...	1737	|	|	1836	|	|	1922
Exeter St Davids **116** a.	1221	1302	1321	1333	1402	1415s	1408	1421	1436	1455	1528	1521	1600	1605	...	1621	1700	1721	...	1754	1821	1847	1900	1854	1921	1932
Exeter St Davids d.	1223	1304	1323	...	1405	|	1411	1423	1438	1459	1532	1523	...	1607	...	1623	1701	1723	...	1802	1823	1852	...	1856	1923	1945
Tiverton Parkway d.	1239	1319	1339	...	|	|	|	1437	|	1514	|	1537	...	|	...	1637	1717	1737	...	1817	1837	1905	...	1911	|	1958
Taunton d.	1254	1334	1354	...	1430	|	1444	1451	1504	1529	1557	1551	...	1632	...	1651	1731	1751	...	1832	1851	1920	...	1926	1949	2014
Bristol T Meads a.	1327	|	1427	...	|	|	|	1527	1548	|	|	1624	...	|	...	1725	|	1825	...	|	1926	1955	...	|	2024	2056
B'ham New St **127** a.	1456	|	1556	...	|	|	|	1656	1726	|	|	1756	...	|	...	1856	|	1956	...	|	2056	2141	...	|	2156	2227
Castle Cary d.	...	|	...	...	|	|	1508	...	...	|	1618	...	...	|	...	...	|	...	...	1853	...	...	...	1947	...	...
Westbury d.	...	|	...	...	|	|	1528	...	...	|	1638	...	...	|	...	...	|	...	...	1912	...	...	...	2006	...	...
Newbury d.	...	|	...	...	|	|	1605	...	...	|	|	...	...	|	...	...	|	...	...	1948	...	...	...	|	...	...
Reading **132 133** a.	...	1451	...	...	1549	1559	1628	...	...	1649	1735	...	...	1751	...	...	1849	...	...	2006	...	...	...	2058	...	...
London Pad ☆ **133** a.	...	1523	...	...	1621	1629	1659	...	...	1721	1808	...	...	1821	...	...	1922	...	...	2045	...	...	...	2132	...	...

Operator	*GW*	*GW*	*GW*	*GW*	*GW*	*GW*	*XC*	*GW*	*XC*		*GW*	*GW*	*GW*	*XC*	*GW*	*XC*	*GW*	*GW*	*XC*	*GW*	*XC*	*XC*	*XC*	*GW*	*XC*	*GW*
	⑥	⑥	⑥	⑥	⑥	⑥	⑥	⑥	⑥	⑦	⑦	⑦	⑦	⑦	⑦	⑦	⑦	⑦	⑦	⑦	⑦	⑦	⑦	⑦	⑦	⑦
	2 🍷	🍷	🍷	🍷	2	2 🍷		2	🍷		2 C	🍷	🍷	🍷	🍷	🍷	🍷	🍷	🍷	🍷	🍷	🍷	🍷	🍷	🍷	🍷
Penzance d.	...	1645	...	1737	...	1906	...	...	2132		...	...	...	...	...	...	0837	...	0930	0950	...	...	...	1100	...	1142
St Erth **118** d.	...	1654	...	1748	...	1914	...	...	2140		...	...	...	...	...	...	0847	...	0938	1002	...	...	...	1110	...	1153
Camborne d.	...	1708	...	1802	...	1927	...	...	2151		...	...	...	...	...	...	0902	...	0948	1013	...	...	...	1122	...	1204
Redruth d.	...	1715	...	1809	...	1933	...	...	2158		...	...	...	...	...	...	0908	...	0954	1019	...	...	...	1128	...	1211
Truro **118** d.	...	1727	...	1822	...	1945	...	...	2209		...	...	...	...	...	...	0921	...	1006	1031	...	...	...	1142	...	1224
St Austell d.	...	1745	...	1839	...	2002	...	...	2226		...	...	...	...	...	...	0938	...	1024	1049	...	...	...	1158	...	1241
Newquay **118** d.	...	|	1718	|	...	|	1958	2120	|		...	...	...	...	...	...	|	...	|	|	...	...	...	|	1130	|
Par **118** d.	...	1751	1821	1847	1859	2009	|	2206	2333		...	...	...	...	...	...	0946	...	1031	1056	...	...	...	1206	|	1249
Bodmin Parkway d.	...	1804	1833	1858	1912	2022	2108	2221	2244		...	...	...	...	...	...	0958	...	1042	1109	...	...	...	1218	1241	1300
Liskeard **118** d.	...	1817	1846	1911	1925	2035	2121	2234	2257		...	...	...	...	...	...	1011	...	1054	1122	...	...	...	1232	1254	1315
Saltash d.	...	1839	|	|	1945	2056	|	2253	|		...	...	...	...	...	...	1031	...	|	|	...	...	...	|	|	|
Plymouth a.	...	1851	1911	1936	1954	2110	2151	2309	2326		...	...	...	...	...	...	1040	...	1117	1145	...	...	...	1257	1317	1340
Plymouth **118** d.	1842	...	1912	1939	—	2115	...	...	...		...	...	0840	0855	0945	0955	1040	1054	1125	1145	1200	1225	...	1300	1321	1344
Totnes d.	1913	...	|	2006	...	2144	...	...	...		...	...	0908	0920	1013	1020	1110	|	1150	1216	|	1250	...	1327	1348	1411
Paignton **116** d.	|	...	|	|	...	|	...	...	...		...	...	|	|	|	|	|	|	|	|	|	|	1308	|	|	|
Torquay **116** d.	|	...	|	|	...	|	...	...	...		...	...	|	|	|	|	|	|	|	|	|	|	1314	|	|	|
Newton Abbot **116** d.	1926	...	1950	2019	...	2156	...	...	...		...	...	0921	0933	1026	1033	1125	1132	1203	1230	1236	1303	1326	1340	1401	1425
Teignmouth **116** d.	1933	...	|	|	...	2203	...	...	...		...	...	0928	|	|	|	|	|	|	|	|	|	1333	|	|	|
Dawlish **116** d.	1939	...	|	|	*GW*	2208	...	...	...		...	...	0934	|	|	|	|	|	|	|	|	|	1338	|	|	|
Exeter St Davids **116** a.	1952	...	2009	2038	⑥	2230	...	...	...		...	...	0948	0953	1046	1053	1145	1152	1221	1250	1255	1321	1349	1400	1421	1445
Exeter St Davids d.	...	...	2011	2040	🍷	...	...	...	...		0810	0838	0949	0955	1048	1055	1147	1154	1223	1251	1257	1323	1351	1402	1423	1446
Tiverton Parkway d.	...	...	|	2057		...	...	...	...		0827	0853	|	1009	1102	1109	|	1209	1237	|	1310	1337	1405	1416	1437	|
Taunton d.	...	...	2038	2111	2130	...	...	...	...		0843	0908	1015	1023	1117	1123	1213	1223	1251	1317	1325	1351	1419	1431	1453	1511
Bristol T Meads a.	...	...	|	2144	2230	...	...	...	...		0945	|	|	1056	1152	1156	|	1257	1324	|	1357	1424	1456	|	1527	|
B'ham New St **127** a.	...	...	|	|	|	...	...	...	...		...	|	|	1250	|	1350	|	|	1450	|	1526	1550	1626	|	1650	|
Castle Cary d.	...	...	|	Y	Y	...	...	...	...		...	0929	|	...	Y	...	1234	Y	...	|	...	...	...	|	...	1553
Westbury d.	...	...	|	|	|	...	...	...	...		...	0949	1053	...	|	...	1253	|	...	1357	...	...	...	|	...	1551
Newbury d.	...	...	|	|	|	...	...	...	...		...	1026	1126	...	|	...	1330	|	...	|	...	...	...	|	...	1629
Reading **132 133** a.	...	...	2158	2301	2352	...	...	...	...		...	1044	1147	...	1313	...	1348	1413	...	1443	...	...	...	1548	...	1647
London Pad ☆ **133** a.	...	...	2226	2338	0033	...	...	...	...		...	1122	1232	...	1355	...	1424	1455	...	1525	...	...	...	1624	...	1728

Operator	*SW*	*GW*	*XC*	*XC*	*GW*	*GW*	*XC*	*GW*	*GW*	*SW*	*GW*	*XC*	*GW*	*GW*	*XC*	*GW*	*XC*	*GW*	*XC*	*GW*	*GW*	*GW*	*XC*	*GW*	*GW*	*GW*
	⑦	⑦	⑦	⑦	⑦	⑦	⑦	⑦	⑦	⑦	⑦	⑦	⑦	⑦	⑦	⑦	⑦	⑦	⑦	⑦	⑦	⑦	⑦	⑦	⑦	⑦
	🍷	2	🍷	🍷	🍷	🍷	🍷	🍷	🍷	🍷	🍷	🍷	🍷	2 🍷	🍷	🍷	🍷	🍷	🍷	🍷	🍷	🍷	🍷	2	2 🍷	🍷 Z
Penzance d.	...	1215	...	1230	1255	...	...	...	...	1350	...	...	1445	1506	1530	1545	...	...	...	1720	1750	...	...	1900	2000	2115
St Erth **118** d.	...	1222	...	1240	1306	...	...	...	...	1400	...	...	1456	1515	1538	1557	...	...	...	1730	1759	...	...	1908	2009	2125
Camborne d.	...	1234	...	1255	1317	...	...	...	...	1413	...	...	1507	1528	1548	1608	...	...	...	1742	1811	...	...	1919	2021	2137
Redruth d.	...	1240	...	1301	1323	...	...	...	...	1419	...	...	1514	1534	1554	1615	...	...	...	1749	1817	...	...	1925	2027	2144
Truro **118** d.	...	1252	...	1313	1335	...	...	...	...	1432	...	...	1526	1546	1606	1628	...	...	...	1800	1829	...	...	1937	2040	2159
St Austell d.	...	1310	...	1330	1354	...	...	...	...	1448	...	...	1544	1603	1622	1645	...	...	...	1819	1846	...	...	1954	2057	2217
Newquay **118** d.	...	|	...	|	|	...	...	...	...	|	...	...	|	|	|	|	...	1615	...	|	|	...	...	|	|	|
Par **118** d.	...	1318	...	1337	1400	...	...	...	...	1456	...	...	1551	1610	1630	1652	...	1715	...	1826	1854	...	...	2002	2104	|
Bodmin Parkway d.	...	1332	...	1351	1413	...	...	...	...	1508	...	...	1603	1623	1641	1704	...	1730	...	1838	1906	...	...	2014	2116	2234
Liskeard **118** d.	...	1346	...	1403	1427	...	...	...	...	1522	...	...	1616	1636	1653	1717	...	1743	...	1851	1922	...	...	2027	2130	2249
Saltash d.	...	1406	...	|	|	...	...	...	...	1545	...	...	|	1656	|	|	...	|	...	|	|	...	...	2047	|	|
Plymouth a.	...	1415	...	1427	1452	...	...	...	...	1553	...	...	1641	1704	1717	1742	...	1809	...	1915	1946	...	...	2058	2159	2315
Plymouth **118** d.	1406	...	1421	1435	1455	1505	1521	1545	...	1602	1610	1625	1645	1708	1725	1745	...	1810	1821	1915	...	1955	2025	2115	...	2320
Totnes d.	1435	...	1448	1500	1522	1534	1548	1611	...	1631	1642	1650	1712	1738	1750	1812	...	1839	1848	1946	...	|	2050	2142	...	2348
Paignton **116** d.	|	...	|	|	|	|	|	|	1545	|	|	|	|	|	|	|	1817	|	|	|	...	|	|	|	...	|
Torquay **116** d.	|	...	|	|	|	|	|	|	1551	|	|	|	|	|	|	|	1823	|	|	|	...	|	|	|	...	|
Newton Abbot **116** d.	1447	...	1501	1512	1535	1547	1601	1624	1605	1643	1655	1703	1725	1751	1803	1825	1836	1851	1901	1959	...	2032	2103	2155	...	0001
Teignmouth **116** d.	1454	...	|	|	|	|	|	|	1613	|	|	|	|	1759	|	|	|	|	|	|	...	|	|	2202	...	|
Dawlish **116** d.	1459	...	|	|	|	|	|	|	1618	|	|	|	|	1804	|	|	|	|	|	|	...	|	|	2207	...	|
Exeter St Davids **116** a.	1515	...	1521	1531	1555	1607	1621	1644	1636	1705	1715	1721	1745	1818	1821	1845	1854	1912	1921	2019	...	2053	2121	2221	...	0036
Exeter St Davids d.	...	...	1523	1533	1558	1609	1623	1645	1638	...	1717	1723	1747	...	1823	1847	1856	1914	1923	2020	...	2055	2123	...	...	0127
Tiverton Parkway d.	...	...	1538	1546	1613	1624	1638	1701	1703	...	1732	1738	1802	...	1837	|	1910	1929	1953	2036	...	2110	2137	...	...	|
Taunton d.	...	...	1553	1601	1628	1639	1653	1715	|	...	1746	1751	1817	...	1851	1911	1924	1943	2027	2049	...	2123	2151	...	...	|
Bristol T Meads a.	...	...	1627	1653	|	1722	1727	|	1753	...	1823	1827	|	...	1927	|	1957	|	2156	|	...	2158	2306	...	...	|
B'ham New St **127** a.	...	...	1750	1827	|	|	1856	|	|	...	|	1950	|	...	2050	|	2131	|	...	|	...	|	...	...	...	|
Castle Cary d.	...	...	...	...	|	Y	...	1737	Y	...	Y	...	|	...	...	|	...	2005	...	2112	...	Y	...	...	...	|
Westbury d.	...	...	...	...	|	|	...	1757	|	...	|	...	1858	...	...	|	...	2025	...	2130	...	|	...	...	...	|
Newbury d.	...	...	...	...	|	|	...	1834	|	...	|	...	|	...	...	2015	...	|	...	2208	...	|	...	...	...	|
Reading **132 133** a.	...	...	...	...	1748	1844	...	1853	1915	...	1943	...	1943	...	...	2034	...	2112	...	2228	...	2326	...	...	...	0417s
London Pad ☆ **133** a.	...	...	...	...	1826	1928	...	1942	1955	...	2025	...	2023	...	...	2113	...	2156	...	2317	...	0006	...	...	...	0505

A – From / to Aberdeen.
B – From / to Birmingham.
C – From / to Cardiff.
D – From / to Derby.
E – From / to Edinburgh.
G – From / to Glasgow.
K – From / to York.
L – From / to Leeds.
M – From / to Manchester.
N – From / to Newcastle.
U – From / to Dundee.
W – From / to London Waterloo.
Y – Via Swindon, Table **133**.
Z – Also conveys 🛏 1, 2 cl.
b – From London on ①–④.
c – From London on ⑤.
d – From London on ⑦.
s – Stops to set down only.
u – Stops to pick up only.

116 Local Trains EXETER - PAIGNTON

2nd class GW, SW

For details of long distance *GW* and *XC* services to / from Paignton see Table **115**. Services on ⑥ valid until September 5, services on ⑦ valid until July 12.

km		Ⓐ																				
		GW	GW	GW	GW	GW	SW	GW	GW	GW	GW	GW	GW	GW	GW	GW	SW	GW	GW	GW	GW	
		Ⓐ	Ⓐ	Ⓐ	Ⓐ	Ⓐ	Ⓐ	Ⓐ	Ⓐ	Ⓐ	Ⓐ	Ⓐ	Ⓐ	Ⓐ	Ⓐ	Ⓐ	Ⓐ	Ⓐ	Ⓐ	Ⓐ	Ⓐ	
							◇W										◇W					
0	**Exeter** St Davids **113** d.	0611	0720	0750	0856	0956	1037	1056	1156	1301	1356	1456	1558	1626	1656	1726	1749	1826	1928	2134	2237	...
20	Dawlish d.	0631	0740	0810	0925	1016	1053	1116	1228	1322	1428	1516	1618	1646	1716	1753	1808	1846	1948	2203	2257	...
24	Teignmouth d.	0636	0745	0815	0930	1021	1058	1121	1233	1327	1433	1521	1623	1651	1721	1758	1813	1851	1953	2208	2302	...
32	**Newton Abbot** d.	0645	0754	0824	0939	1041	1113	1130	1241	1336	1441	1530	1632	1700	1730	1809	1821	1909	2009	2216	2310	...
42	Torquay d.	0656	0805	0835	0950	1052	1123	1141	1253	1347	1452	1541	1644	1711	1741	1820	1834	1920	2020	2227	2321	...
45	**Paignton** 🚂 a.	0706	0814	0844	0957	1059	1129	1151	1300	1356	1500	1549	1653	1720	1751	1828	1840	1928	2028	2235	2329	...

⑥																					
	GW	GW	SW	GW	GW	GW	SW	GW	GW	GW	GW	SW	GW	GW	GW	GW	SW	GW	GW	GW	GW	
	⑥	⑥	⑥	⑥	⑥	⑥	⑥	⑥	⑥	⑥	⑥	⑥	⑥	⑥	⑥	⑥	⑥	⑥	⑥	⑥	⑥	
			◇S				◇W					◇W					◇					
Exeter St Davids **113** d.	0611	0750	0837	0856	0958	1025	1036	1056	1156	1256	1402	1432	1456	1557	1656	1726	1805	1826	1917	2006	2056	...
Dawlish d.	0631	0810	0850	0924	1019	|	1051	1116	1217	1316	1430	1447	1516	1616	1716	1753	1820	1846	1937	2036	2116	...
Teignmouth d.	0636	0815	0855	0930	1024	|	1056	1121	1223	1321	1435	1452	1521	1621	1721	1758	1825	1851	1942	2041	2121	...
Newton Abbot d.	0645	0824	0906	0938	1034	1047	1104	1130	1232	1330	1448	1500	1530	1631	1730	1809	1833	1901	1951	2049	2130	...
Torquay d.	0656	0835	0917	0950	1045	1058	1115	1141	1244	1341	1459	1513	1541	1642	1741	1820	1844	1912	2002	2100	2141	...
Paignton 🚂 a.	0705	0842	0923	0957	1051	1106	1122	1149	1251	1349	1506	1519	1549	1651	1751	1828	1852	1921	2010	2108	2148	...

⑦															
	GW	GW	SW	GW	SW	GW	SW	GW	SW	GW	GW	GW	SW	GW	
	⑦	⑦	⑦	⑦	⑦	⑦	⑦	⑦	⑦	⑦	⑦	⑦	⑦	⑦	
			◇B		◇W		◇W		◇W				◇W		
Exeter St Davids **113** d.	0905	1008	1054	1236	1301	1354	1452	1517	1657	1750	1852	2004	2056	2149	...
Dawlish d.	0925	1028	1109	1306	1314	1414	|	1544	1710	1810	1912	2024	2109	2210	...
Teignmouth d.	0930	1033	1114	1311	1319	1419	|	1549	1715	1815	1917	2029	2114	2215	...
Newton Abbot d.	0939	1042	1123	1320	1328	1429	1517	1557	1726	1824	1926	2038	2122	2224	...
Torquay d.	0950	1053	1134	1331	1339	1440	1528	1609	1737	1835	1937	2049	2133	2235	...
Paignton 🚂 a.	0957	1101	1140	1338	1347	1447	1634	1617	1743	1842	1944	2056	2139	2242	...

Ⓐ																						
	GW	GW	GW	GW	GW	GW	GW	GW	SW	GW	GW	GW	GW	GW	GW	GW	GW	SW	GW	GW	GW	GW	
	Ⓐ	Ⓐ	Ⓐ	Ⓐ	Ⓐ	Ⓐ	Ⓐ	Ⓐ	Ⓐ	Ⓐ	Ⓐ	Ⓐ	Ⓐ	Ⓐ	Ⓐ	Ⓐ	Ⓐ	Ⓐ	Ⓐ	Ⓐ	Ⓐ	Ⓐ	
									◇W									◇B					
Paignton 🚂 d.	0607	0634	0707	0823	0913	1023	1123	1213	1235	1313	1422	1519	1612	1655	1725	1752	1835	1912	1931	2032	2240	2340	...
Torquay d.	0612	0639	0714	0828	0918	1028	1128	1218	1241	1318	1427	1524	1617	1700	1730	1757	1840	1918	1936	2037	2245	2345	...
Newton Abbot d.	0625	0652	0734	0841	0939	1041	1141	1232	1253	1341	1440	1543	1630	1713	1743	1810	1853	1931	1949	2050	2258	2358	...
Teignmouth d.	0632	0658	0741	0848	0946	1048	1148	1239	1300	1348	1447	1551	1637	1720	1750	1817	1900	1938	1956	2057	2305	0005	...
Dawlish d.	0637	0703	0746	0853	0951	1053	1153	1244	1305	1353	1452	1556	1642	1725	1755	1822	1905	1943	2002	2102	2310	0009	...
Exeter St Davids **113** a.	0706	0733	0810	0915	1017	1117	1216	1313	1326	1416	1515	1618	1711	1748	1818	1846	1935	1959	2024	2127	2334	0034	...

⑥																						
	GW	GW	GW	GW	SW	GW	GW	GW	SW	GW	GW	GW	SW	GW	GW	GW	GW	SW	GW	GW	GW	GW	
	⑥	⑥	⑥	⑥	⑥	⑥	⑥	⑥	⑥	⑥	⑥	⑥	⑥	⑥	⑥	⑥	⑥	⑥	⑥	⑥	⑥	⑥	
					◇W				◇W				◇					◇B					
Paignton 🚂 d.	0613	0651	0811	0904	1014	1055	1123	1213	1234	1258	1422	1513	1552	1612	1723	1752	1853	1914	1923	2013	2113	2153	...
Torquay d.	0618	0656	0816	0909	1020	1100	1128	1218	1240	1303	1427	1518	1558	1617	1728	1757	1858	1920	1928	2018	2118	2158	...
Newton Abbot d.	0631	0709	0837	0922	1033	1123	1141	1232	1252	1321	1440	1534	1610	1630	1741	1810	1914	1932	1941	2031	2131	2211	...
Teignmouth d.	0638	0716	0844	0929	1040	1130	1148	1239	1259	1328	1447	1542	1617	1638	1749	1817	1922	1939	1948	2038	2138	2218	...
Dawlish d.	0643	0721	0849	0934	1045	1135	1153	1244	1304	1333	1452	1547	1622	1643	1754	1822	1927	1944	1953	2043	2143	2223	...
Exeter St Davids **113** a.	0705	0744	0912	1008	1100	1157	1216	1313	1325	1400	1515	1617	1635	1712	1817	1843	1948	2003	2022	2105	2205	2245	...

⑦														
	GW	SW	GW	GW	GW	SW	SW	GW	SW	GW	GW	GW	SW	GW
	⑦	⑦	⑦	⑦	⑦	⑦	⑦	⑦	⑦	⑦	⑦	⑦	⑦	⑦
		◇W				◇W	◇W		◇W				◇S	
Paignton 🚂 d.	1005	1225	1252	1404	1500	1530	1610	1720	1824	1855	1955	2100	2210	2300
Torquay d.	1010	1231	1257	1409	1505	1536	1616	1725	1830	1900	2000	2105	2216	2305
Newton Abbot d.	1039	1244	1310	1435	1518	1551	1630	1738	1842	1913	2013	2118	2230	2318
Teignmouth d.	1046	1251	1318	1442	1525	1558	|	1745	1849	1920	2020	2125	2237	2325
Dawlish d.	1051	1256	1323	1447	1530	1603	|	1750	1854	1925	2025	2130	2242	2330
Exeter St Davids **113** a.	1114	1309	1345	1510	1552	1618	1653	1813	1909	1950	2047	2152	2257	2352

B – To / from Basingstoke.
S – To / from Salisbury.
W – To / from London Waterloo.
◇ – Also conveys 1.

🚂 – **PAIGNTON - KINGSWEAR** (for ⛴ to Dartmouth, inclusive tickets available). Services operate on ②④⑥⑦ Apr. 1 - Oct. 31 (daily Jun. - Sept.).
Operator: Paignton & Dartmouth Steam Railway. ✆ (0)1803 555872.

118 CORNISH BRANCH LINES and BUS CONNECTIONS

2nd class GW

Rail tickets are generally **not** valid on 🚌 services shown in this table.

PLYMOUTH – GUNNISLAKE *Service on ⑦ valid until September 20.* 24 km

⚒: 0512Ⓐ, 0644, 0850⑥, 0857Ⓐ, 1045, 1255, 1447⑥, 1455Ⓐ, 1639, 1821, 2130.
⑦: 0912, 1117, 1313, 1517, 1741.

GUNNISLAKE – PLYMOUTH Journey time: ± 45 minutes

⚒: 0556Ⓐ, 0732, 0945, 1135, 1345, 1545, 1729, 1916, 2219.
⑦: 1018, 1207, 1402, 1607, 1837.

LISKEARD – LOOE *Services on ⑥⑦ valid until September 6.* 14 km

Ⓐ: 0604, 0710, 0841, 0955, 1115, 1212, 1319, 1428, 1539, 1640, 1802, 1915.
⑥: 0604, 0710, 0841, 0954, 1115, 1221, 1324, 1425, 1542, 1656, 1800, 1929, 2040.
⑦: 1015, 1126, 1245, 1404, 1507, 1624, 1811, 2015.

LOOE – LISKEARD Journey time: ± 29 minutes

Ⓐ: 0637, 0747, 0915, 1031, 1144, 1244, 1351, 1458, 1611, 1715, 1834, 1949.
⑥: 0637, 0744, 0916, 1041, 1154, 1253, 1358, 1454, 1616, 1729, 1834, 2001, 2112.
⑦: 1047, 158, 1324, 1436, 1539, 1705, 1843, 2051.

PAR – NEWQUAY *Services on ⑥⑦ valid until September 6.* 33 km

Ⓐ: 0601, 0919, 1210, 1402, 1610, 1829, 2028.
⑥: 0721 **P**, 0947 **P**, 1135 **L**, 1543 **L**, 2021.
⑦: 0900, 1152, 1424 **P**, 1636, 1845.
L – From London Paddington, Table **115**. **P** – From Plymouth, Table **115**.

NEWQUAY – PAR Journey time: ± 55 minutes

Ⓐ: 0657, 1013, 1303, 1458, 1722, 1925, 2126.
⑥: 1122 **L**, 1314 **L**, 1718 **L**, 2120 **P**.
⑦: 0954, 1300, 1615 **L**, 1732, 1940.
L – From London Paddington, Table **115**. **P** – From Plymouth, Table **115**.

TRURO – FALMOUTH Docks 20 km

Ⓐ: 0610, 0637, 0716, 0748, 0820, 0850 and every 30 minutes until 1650; then 1727, 1758, 1829, 1900, 2001, 2103, 2206.
⑥: 0610, 0637, 0716, 0748, 0820, 0850 and every 30 minutes until 1650; then 1727, 1758, 1829, 1900, 2001, 2103, 2206.
⑦: 1045, 1215, 1337, 1431, 1535, 1700, 1810, 2003, 2104, 2203.

FALMOUTH Docks – TRURO Journey time: ± 23 minutes

Ⓐ: 0637, 0717, 0748, 0820, 0850, and every 30 minutes until 1650; then 1727, 1758, 1829, 1900, 1927, 2029, 2130, 2233.
⑥: 0637, 0717, 0748, 0820, 0850, and every 30 minutes until 1650; then 1727, 1758, 1829, 1900, 1927, 2029, 2130, 2233.
⑦: 1112, 1244, 1403, 1457, 1600, 1730, 1843, 2030, 2130, 2235.

ST ERTH – ST IVES *Service on ⑦ valid until September 6.* 7 km

Ⓐ: 0645 **p**, 0714, 0805, 0905 **p**, 0938, 1011 and every 30 minutes until 2041; then 2138.
⑥: 0645 **p**, 0714, 0801, 0905 **p**, 0938, 1011 and every 30 minutes until 1641; then 1712, 1759, 1858 **p**, 1950, 2046, 2146.
⑦: 0859 **p**, 0930, 1000, 1030, 1111 and every 30 minutes until 1641; then 1724, 1824, 1930.
p – 2 Penzance - St Ives (departs Penzance 8 minutes earlier).

ST IVES – ST ERTH Journey time: ± 14 minutes

Ⓐ: 0659, 0728, 0819 **q**, 0922, 0953, 1025 and every 30 minutes until 2055; then 2154 **q**.
⑥: 0700, 0728, 0815 **q**, 0922, 0952, 1025 and every 30 minutes until 1625; then 1657, 1727, 1817, 1928, 2010, 2112, 2202 **q**.
⑦: 0915, 0945, 1015, 1050, 1125, 1156 and at 25 and 56 minutes past the hour until 1656; then 1740, 1840, 1940 **q**.
q – 2 St Ives - Penzance (journey time St Ives - Penzance: ± 25 minutes).

BODMIN PARKWAY – PADSTOW Western Greyhound 🚌 service **555**

Buses call at **Wadebridge** 30 minutes after Bodmin Parkway.
⚒: 0725, 0830 and hourly until 1530; then 1630Ⓐ, 1730, 1830, 1930, 2200.
⑦: 0930, 1130, 1330, 1530, 1730, 1930.

PADSTOW – BODMIN PARKWAY Journey time: ± 62 minutes

Buses call at **Wadebridge** 25 minutes after Padstow.
⚒: 0630 and hourly until 1830; then 2030.
⑦: 0830, 1030, 1230, 1430, 1630, 1830.

ST AUSTELL Railway Station **– THE EDEN PROJECT** First Truronian 🚌 service **T9**

Ⓐ: 0835, 0850, 0930, 0935, 1030, 035, 1055, 1135, 1140, 1235, 1240, 1310, 1335, 1350, 1435, 1515, 1535, 1550, 1635, 1650, 1730.
⑥: 0850, 0930, 1030, 1140, 1240, 1250, 1350, 1535, 1550, 1635, 1650, 1720, 1730.
⑦: 0850, 1000, 1040, 1135, 1230, 1335, 1500, 1520, 1540, 1630, 1635, 1720, 1735.

THE EDEN PROJECT – ST AUSTELL Railway Station Journey time: ± 20 minutes

Ⓐ: 0900, 0910, 0950, 1000, 1100, 1200, 1210, 1300, 1310, 1400, 1500, 1505, 1600, 1630, 1700, 1710, 1800.
⑥: 0910, 0950, 1100, 1210, 1310, 1420, 1505, 1630, 1700, 1710, 1800.
⑦: 1010, 1020, 1100, 1155, 1250, 1440, 1520, 1615, 1635, 1700, 1710, 1750, 1800.

AW, XC — CARDIFF - GLOUCESTER - BIRMINGHAM - NOTTINGHAM — 121

Services on ⑥ valid until September 5, services on ⑦ valid until July 12. For faster *XC* services Birmingham - Derby and v.v. see Table **127**.

km	Operator		XC	XC	XC	XC	XC	XC	AW	XC	XC	XC	AW	XC	XC	XC	AW	XC	XC	AW	XC	XC	XC	XC	AW
		⚒	⚒	⚒	⚒	⚒	⑥	Ⓐ	⚒2	⚒	⚒	⚒A	⚒2	⚒	⚒	⚒	⚒2	⚒	⚒	⚒2	⚒	⚒	⚒	⚒	⚒2
0	**Cardiff** Central d.		...	...	...	...	...	...	0612	0640	...	0700	0712	0745	...	0845	0912	...	0945	1012	...	1045	...	1145	1212
19	Newport d.		...	...	...	...	...	...	0628	0655	...	0714	0727	0800	...	0900	0927	...	1000	1027	...	1100	...	1200	1227
47	Chepstow d.		...	...	...	...	...	...	0649	0716	...	|	0749	|	...	|	0949	...	|	1049	...	|	...	|	1249
91	**Gloucester** ... 122 133 d.		...	...	...	...	0706	0710	0721	0746	...	|	0821	0846	...	0944	1021	...	1046	1121	...	1146	...	1246	1322
101	Cheltenham .. 122 133 d.		...	...	...	...	0718	0721	0734	0756	...	0842	0834	0856	...	0956	1034	...	1056	1134	...	1156	...	1256	1335
174	**Birmingham** New St a.		...	...	...	...	0808	0816	...	0845	...	0926	...	0945	...	1045	...	...	1145	...	...	1245	...	1345	...
174	**Birmingham** New St d.		0619	0649	0719	0749	0819	0819	...	0849	0919	...	...	0949	1019	1049	...	1119	1149	...	1219	1249	1319	1349	...
202	Tamworth d.		0639	0707	0738	0807	0837	0837	...	0907	0939	...	...	1007	1037	1107	...	1139	1207	...	1237	1307	1339	1407	...
222	Burton on Trent d.		0651	0719	0750	0819	0849	0849	...	0919	0951	...	...	1019	1049	1119	...	1151	1219	...	1249	1319	1351	1419	...
241	Derby a.		0705	0735	0805	0835	0905	0904	...	0935	1005	...	...	1035	1105	1135	...	1205	1235	...	1305	1335	1405	1435	...
267	**Nottingham** a.		0741	0810	0836	0905	0936	0937	...	1005	1036	...	...	1105	1136	1205	...	1236	1305	...	1336	1405	1436	1505	...

Operator	XC	XC	AW	XC	XC	XC	XC	AW	XC	XC	AW	AW	XC	XC	AW	XC	XC	AW	XC	XC	XC	XC	XC	AW	XC
	⚒	⚒	⚒2	⚒	⚒	⚒	⚒	⚒2	⚒	⚒	Ⓐ2F	⑥2	⚒	⚒	⚒2	⚒	⚒	⚒2	Ⓐ	⑥	Ⓐ	Ⓐ	⑥	⚒2	⑥
Cardiff Central d.	...	1245	1312	...	1345	...	1445	1512	...	1545	1605	1612	...	1645	1712	...	1745	1812	1845	1845	2000	...	2000	2015	2050
Newport d.	...	1300	1327	...	1400	...	1500	1527	...	1600	1621	1627	...	1700	1727	...	1800	1827	1900	1900	2015	...	2015	2030	2105
Chepstow d.	...	|	1349	...	|	...	|	1549	...	|	1644	1649	...	|	1749	...	|	1849	|	|	|	...	2036	2052	|
Gloucester .... 122 133 d.	...	1346	1421	...	1446	...	1546	1621	...	1646	1722	1721	...	1746	1822	...	1846	1921	1946	1947	2057	...	2106	2123	2149
Cheltenham .... 122 133 d.	...	1356	1434	...	1456	...	1556	1634	...	1656	1734	1734	...	1756	1834	...	1856	1934	1957	1958	2108	...	2118	2134	2200
Birmingham New St a.	...	1445	...	...	1545	...	1645	...	...	1745	...	...	...	1845	...	...	1945	...	2045	2040	2157	...	2207	...	2242
Birmingham New St d.	1419	1449	...	1519	1549	1619	1649	...	1719	1749	...	...	1819	1849	...	1919	1949	...	2049	2049	...	2210	2210	...	...
Tamworth d.	1437	1507	...	1539	1607	1637	1707	...	1739	1807	...	...	1837	1907	...	1939	2007	...	2109	2108	...	2228	2227	...	...
Burton on Trent d.	1449	1519	...	1551	1619	1649	1719	...	1751	1819	...	...	1849	1919	...	1951	2019	...	2123	2120	...	2240	2239	...	...
Derby a.	1505	1535	...	1605	1635	1705	1735	...	1805	1835	...	...	1905	1935	...	2005	2035	...	2140	2135	...	2254	2255	...	...
Nottingham a.	1536	1605	...	1636	1705	1736	1805	...	1836	1905	...	...	1936	2005	...	2036	2110	...	2210	2210	...	2330	2333	...	...

Operator	XC	XC	XC	AW	XC	AW		XC	XC	AW	XC	XC	AW	XC	AW	XC	XC	AW	XC	XC	AW	XC	AW	XC	AW
	⑥	Ⓐ	Ⓐ	Ⓐ2	Ⓐ	Ⓐ2	⑦	⑦	⑦	⑦	⑦	⑦	⑦	⑦	⑦	⑦	⑦	⑦	⑦	⑦	⑦	⑦	⑦	⑦	⑦
Cardiff Central d.	...	...	2100	2114	2150	2319		...	1020	1030	1120	1220	1230	1350	1430	1450	1550	1630	1650	1750	1830	1950	2030	2050	2230
Newport d.	...	...	2115	2129	2205	2337		...	1034	1045	1134	1234	1245	1404	1445	1504	1604	1645	1704	1804	1845	2004	2045	2104	2249
Chepstow d.	...	...	|	2152	|	0009		...	|	1107	|	|	1307	|	1507	|	|	1707	|	|	1907	|	2107	|	2317
Gloucester .... 122 133 d.	...	...	2206	2223	2247	0039		...	1118	1145	1218	1318	1344	1447	1538	1547	1647	1738	1747	1847	1942	2047	2140	2147	2350
Cheltenham .... 122 133 d.	...	...	2217	2236	2258	0053		...	1129	1157	1229	1329	1357	1458	1551	1558	1658	1751	1758	1858	1952	2058	...	2158	...
Birmingham New St a.	...	...	2335	...	0004			...	1228	...	1334	1428	...	1540	...	1640	1740	...	1840	1940	...	2145	...	2240	...
Birmingham New St d.	2249	2309	...	...	...	...		1149	1249	...	1349	1449	...	1549	...	1649	1749	...	1849	1949	...	2149	...	2249	...
Tamworth d.	2308	2328	...	...	...	...		1207	1307	...	1407	1509	...	1607	...	1707	1807	...	1909	2007	...	2209	...	2307	...
Burton on Trent d.	2320	2340	...	...	...	...		1219	1319	...	1419	1521	...	1619	...	1719	1819	...	1921	2019	...	2221	...	2319	...
Derby a.	2338	2359	...	...	...	...		1234	1331	...	1434	1534	...	1634	...	1734	1834	...	1934	2036	...	2234	...	2334	...
Nottingham a.	...	0020	...	...	...	...		1308	1408	...	1508	1608	...	1709	...	1808	1902	...	1959	2108	...	2308	...	2359	...

Operator		XC	AW	XC	XC	AW	XC	XC	XC	XC	AW	XC	XC	XC	AW	XC	XC	XC	XC	XC	XC	AW	XC	XC	XC
	⚒	⚒	⚒2	⚒	⚒B	⚒2	⚒	⚒	⚒	⚒	⚒2	⚒	⑥	Ⓐ	⚒2	⚒	⑥	Ⓐ	⚒	⑥	Ⓐ	⚒2	⚒	⑥	Ⓐ
Nottingham d.		...	...	0557	0637	...	0656	0735	0808	0836	...	0908	0920	0937	...	1008	1020	1037	1108	1120	1137	...	1208	1220	1237
Derby d.		...	...	0636	0706	...	0735	0806	0836	0906	...	0936	0957	1006	...	1036	1057	1106	1136	1157	1206	...	1236	1257	1306
Burton on Trent d.		...	...	0648	0718	...	0749	0818	0848	0918	...	0948	1018	1018	...	1048	1118	1118	1148	1218	1218	...	1248	1318	1320
Tamworth d.		...	...	0700	0730	...	0801	0830	0900	0930	...	1000	1030	1030	...	1100	1130	1130	1200	1230	1230	...	1300	1330	1333
Birmingham New St a.		...	...	0724	0755a	...	0824	0856	0924	0956	...	1024	1056	1056	...	1124	1156	1156	1224	1256	1256	...	1324	1356	1356
Birmingham New St d.		0542	...	0730	...	...	0830	...	0930	...	...	1030	...	...	...	1130	...	...	1230	...	...	...	1330	...	...
Cheltenham .... 122 133 d.		0643	0745	0816a	...	0845	0911	...	1011	...	1045	1111	...	...	1145	1211	...	...	1311	...	...	1345	1411	...	...
Gloucester .... 122 133 a.		0654	0756	0826a	...	0856	0921	...	1021	...	1056	1121	...	...	1156	1221	...	...	1321	...	...	1356	1421	...	...
Chepstow a.		0729	0827	|	...	0927	|	...	|	...	1127	|	...	...	1227	|	...	...	|	...	...	1427	|	...	...
Newport a.		0752	0850	0911a	...	0950	1011a	...	1111a	...	1150	1211a	...	...	1250	1311a	...	...	1411a	...	...	1451	1511a	...	...
Cardiff Central a.		0813	0910	0931a	...	1010	1031a	...	1131a	...	1210	1231a	...	...	1310	1331a	...	...	1431a	...	...	1510	1531a	...	...

Operator	AW	XC	XC	XC	XC	XC	XC	AW	XC	XC	XC	AW	XC	XC	XC	AW	XC	XC	XC	XC	AW	XC	XC	XC	XC
	⚒2	⚒	⑥	Ⓐ	⚒	⑥	Ⓐ	⚒2	⚒	⑥	Ⓐ	⚒2	⚒	⑥	Ⓐ	⚒2	⚒	ⒶA	⑥	Ⓐ	⚒2	⚒	⑥	Ⓐ	⚒
Nottingham d.	...	1308	1320	1337	1408	1420	1437	...	1508	1520	1537	...	1608	1620	1637	...	1708	...	1720	1737	...	1808	1820	1837	1908
Derby d.	...	1336	1357	1406	1436	1457	1506	...	1536	1557	1606	...	1636	1657	1706	...	1736	...	1757	1806	...	1836	1857	1906	1936
Burton on Trent d.	...	1348	1418	1418	1448	1518	1518	...	1548	1618	1618	...	1648	1718	1718	...	1748	...	1818	1820	...	1848	1918	1918	1948
Tamworth d.	...	1400	1430	1430	1500	1530	1530	...	1600	1630	1630	...	1700	1730	1730	...	1800	...	1830	1833	...	1900	1930	1930	2000
Birmingham New St a.	...	1424	1456	1456	1524	1556	1556	...	1624	1656	1656	...	1724	1756	1756	...	1824	...	1900	1856	...	1924	1956	1956	2024
Birmingham New St d.	...	1430	...	...	1530	...	...	...	1630	...	...	...	1730	...	...	...	1830	1842	...	...	...	1930	...	...	2030
Cheltenham ... 122 133 d.	1445	1511	...	...	1611	...	...	1645	1715a	...	...	1745	1818	...	...	1845	1915a	1925	...	...	1945	2011	...	...	2111
Gloucester .... 122 133 a.	1456	1521	...	...	1621	...	...	1656	1725a	...	...	1756	1828	...	...	1856	1925a	|	...	...	1956	2021	...	...	2121
Chepstow a.	1527	|	...	...	|	...	...	1727	|	...	...	1827	|	...	...	1927	|	|	...	...	2027	|	...	...	|
Newport a.	1550	1611a	...	...	1711a	...	...	1750	1811a	...	...	1850	1914a	...	...	1950	2011a	2047	...	...	2051	2111	...	...	2214
Cardiff Central a.	1610	1631a	...	...	1731a	...	...	1810	1831a	...	...	1910	1935a	...	...	2012	2031a	2107	...	...	2110	2132	...	...	2239

Operator	XC	XC	AW	XC	XC	XC		XC	XC	AW	XC	XC	AW	XC	XC	AW	XC	XC	AW	XC	XC	AW	XC	XC	XC
	⑥	Ⓐ	⚒2	Ⓐ	⑥	⚒	⑦	⑦	⑦	⑦	⑦	⑦	⑦	⑦	⑦	⑦	⑦	⑦	⑦	⑦	⑦	⑦	⑦	⑦	⑦
Nottingham d.	1920	1937	...	2037	2020	2137		...	...	...	1109	1205	...	1305	1405	...	1505	1605	...	1700	1805	...	1910	2010	2105
Derby d.	1957	2006	...	2106	2057	2210		...	...	...	1136	1236	...	1335	1436	...	1536	1635	...	1735	1835	...	1935	2035	2136
Burton on Trent d.	2018	2018	...	2120	2118	2221		...	...	...	1148	1248	...	1349	1448	...	1548	1648	...	1748	1848	...	1948	2047	2148
Tamworth d.	2030	2030	...	2133	2130	2233		...	...	...	1200	1300	...	1401	1500	...	1600	1700	...	1800	1900	...	2000	2102	2200
Birmingham New St a.	2056	2056	...	2157	2200	2305		...	...	...	1223	1321	...	1421	1521	...	1623	1721	...	1821	1921	...	2025	2120	2227
Birmingham New St d.	...	...	...	...	...	...		0952	1130	...	1230	1330	...	1430	1530	...	1630	1730	...	1830	1930	...	...	...	...
Cheltenham ... 122 133 d.	...	...	2145	...	...	...		1052	1211	1218	1311	1411	1418	1511	1611	1618	1711	1811	1818	1914	2011	2018	...	...	...
Gloucester .... 122 133 a.	...	...	2158	...	...	...		1102	1221	1226	1321	1421	1429	1521	1621	1627	1721	1821	1829	1924	2021	2031	...	...	...
Chepstow a.	...	...	2227	...	...	...		|	|	1302	|	|	1502	|	|	1702	|	|	1902	|	|	2102	...	...	...
Newport a.	...	...	2259	...	...	...		1145	1304	1325	1404	1504	1525	1604	1704	1731	1804	1904	1925	2009	2104	2125	...	...	...
Cardiff Central a.	...	...	2321	...	...	...		1206	1325	1345	1425	1525	1545	1625	1725	1751	1825	1925	1947	2030	2125	2143	...	...	...

A – Via Bristol Temple Meads (Table **127**). B – To Bournemouth (Table **129**). F – To / from Fishguard Harbour. a – 4–6 minutes earlier on ⑥.

GW, LM 2nd class — BRISTOL - GLOUCESTER - WORCESTER — 122

km			Ⓐ	Ⓐ	Ⓐ	Ⓐ	ⒶT	ⒶS	ⒶW	ⒶR	ⒶW	ⒶS	ⒶW	Ⓐ	ⒶW	Ⓐ	ⒶT	ⒶR	Ⓐ				⑥	⑥	⑥
0	**Bristol** TM d.	Ⓐ	...	0734	...	0841	0941	1041	1141	1241	1341	1441	1541	1641	1741	1841	1941	2041	2211	...	...	⑥★	...	0741	...
9	Bristol Parkway d.		...	0748	...	0852	0952	1052	1152	1252	1352	1452	1552	1652	1752	1852	1952	2052	2222	...	...		...	0752	...
62	**Gloucester** a.		...	0829	...	0933	1032	1134	1231	1331	1430	1532	1632	1732	1832	1930	2032	2130	2302	...	...		...	0832	...
						|	Ⓐ◇	|	Ⓐ◇	|	Ⓐ◇	|	Ⓐ◇	|	Ⓐ◇	|	|	|							
62	**Gloucester** ... 121 133 d.		0601	...	0715	0938	1113	1136	1316	1338	1513	1537	1710	1738	1910	1938	2036	2134	...	...	...		0550	...	0715
72	Cheltenham .. 121 133 d.		0612	...	0725	0948	1123	1148	1327	1348	1525	1548	1724	1748	1922	1948	2048	2146	...	...	...		0600	...	0725
84	Ashchurch § d.		0621	...	0734	0955	1131	1155	1334	1355	1532	1555	1731	1755	1929	1955	...	2154	...	...	...		0609	...	0734
108	**Worcester** Shrub Hill .. a.		0642	...	0754	1014	1148	1214	1354	1414	1552	1622	1755	1819	1952	2015	...	2212	...	...	...		0633	...	0752

	⑥◇	⑥	⑥W	⑥S	⑥W	⑥R	⑥W	⑥S	⑥W	⑥	⑥	⑥W	⑥	⑥R	⑥			⑦	⑦	⑦	⑦	⑦	⑦		
Bristol TM d.	...	0841	0938	1041	1141	1241	1341	1441	1541	1641	1741	1841	1941	2041	2206	...	⑦★	0944	1244	1444	1643	1840	2043	...	...
Bristol Parkway d.	...	0852	0949	1052	1152	1252	1352	1452	1552	1652	1752	1852	1952	2052	2218	...		0955	1255	1456	1655	1851	2055	...	...
Gloucester a.	...	0933	1029	1132	1231	1334	1432	1532	1632	1733	1834	1933	2033	2134	2301	...		1034	1334	1541	1734	1931	2135	...	...
		|	⑥◇	|	⑥◇	|	⑥◇	|	⑥◇	|	⑥◇	|	|	|				|	|	|	|	|	|		
Gloucester .... 121 133 d.	0807	0938	1101	1138	1301	1338	1505	1538	1705	1738	1905	1938	2038	2140	...	...		1038	1338	1552	1751	1938	2141	...	...
Cheltenham ... 121 133 d.	0818	0948	1118	1149	1318	1349	1518	1548	1718	1748	1918	1948	2046	2149	...	...		1049	1350	1603	1803	1948	2149	...	...
Ashchurch § d.	0825	0957	1125	1157	1325	1357	1525	1557	1725	1757	1925	1955	...	...	...	...		...	1359	1611	1811	1957	...	...	...
Worcester Shrub Hill ... a.	0851	1014	1142	1215	1352	1415	1557	1614	1749	1815	1948	2015	...	...	...	...		...	1424	1634	1831	2018	...	...	...

For footnotes and return service see next page.

122 BRISTOL - GLOUCESTER - WORCESTER

2nd class GW, LM

		Ⓐ	Ⓐ	ⒶW	ⒶW	ⒶT	Ⓐ◇	ⒶR	Ⓐ◇	ⒶW	Ⓐ◇	ⒶW	ⒶW	Ⓐ◇	ⒶS	Ⓐ◇	ⒶW	Ⓐ	Ⓐ	⑤B			⑥	⑥	⑥W
Worcester Shrub Hill...d.	Ⓐ	...	...	0709	...	0900	0956	1106	1215	1306	1413	1506	...	1601	1706	1814	1906	2131	2232	2345	...	⑥	...	...	0648
Ashchurch §...d.		...	...	0725	...	0921	1010	1121	1230	1321	1427	1521	...	1623	1721	1829	1921	2152	2251	2359	...		...	...	0704
Cheltenham ... **121 133** d.		...	0657	0735	...	0931	1019	1132	1240	1331	1436	1531	...	1636	1740	1838	1931	2205	2305	0008	...	★	...	0648	0714
Gloucester.... **121 133** a.		...	0707	0744	...	0941	1029	1142	1253	1341	1453	1541	...	1653	1750	...	1939	2221	2318	0018	...		...	0658	0725
			|	|		|	ⒶW	|	— ⒶT	|	— ⒶT	|		ⒶT		— Ⓐ	|	— Ⓐ	— Ⓐ					|	|
Gloucester...d.		0620	0711	0750	0842	0942	1042	1142	1242	1342	1442	1542	1642	1742	...	1842	1942	2115	2249	...	...		0621	0702	0740
Bristol Parkway...a.		0658	0748	0825	0919	1018	1119	1219	1319	1418	1519	1618	1719	1819	...	1919	2018	2152	2316	...	...		0700	0739	0818
Bristol TM...a.		0715	0802	0837	0935	1038	1135	1235	1336	1440	1537	1638	1737	1837	...	1936	2038	2210	2337	...	...		0713	0754	0834

	⑥◇	⑥T	⑥◇	⑥R	⑥◇	⑥W	⑥◇	⑥W	⑥◇	⑥T	⑥◇	⑥W	⑥	⑥			⑦	⑦	⑦	⑦	⑦	⑦			
Worcester Shrub Hill...d.	0715	0908	1014	1108	1211	1254	1410	1508	1611	1708	1810	1908	...	2131	...	⑦	...	...	1436	1640	1840	2036	...	...	...
Ashchurch §...d.	0730	0925	1029	1124	1225	1310	1425	1524	1626	1724	1825	1924	...	2151	...		...	...	1451	1658	1855	2053	...	...	...
Cheltenham ... **121 133** d.	0739	0935	1040	1134	1236	1320	1434	1534	1635	1734	1834	1934	2102	2201	...	★	1005	1200	1501	1708	1906	2103	...	...	...
Gloucester.... **121 133** a.	0750	0944	1052	1144	1251	1332	1451	1542	1651	1744	1852	19424	2112	2210	...		1015	1210	1510	1716	1915	2113	...	...	...
	⑥W	|	— ⑥W	|	— ⑥T	|	— ⑥T	|	— ⑥W	|	— ⑥	|	|				|	|	|	|	|	|			
Gloucester...d.	0842	0946	1042	1146	1242	1342	1442	1546	1642	1746	1842	1946	2116	...	...		1019	1214	1513	1720	1918	2115	...	...	...
Bristol Parkway...a.	0919	1024	1119	1124	1319	1421	1518	1624	1719	1824	1921	2023	2153	...	...		1055	1251	1549	1757	1955	2153	...	...	...
Bristol TM...a.	0935	1039	1135	1239	1335	1437	1534	1639	1735	1839	1938	2039	2204	...	...		1108	1309	1609	1810	2008	2207	...	...	...

B – From Birmingham New St (dep. 2300).
R – To / from Brighton.
S – From / to Southampton.
T – From / to Westbury.
W – From / to Weymouth.
§ – Ashchurch for Tewkesbury.
◇ – Operated by *LM*.
★ – Services on ⑥ valid until September 5, services on ⑦ valid until July 12.

123 BIRMINGHAM - WORCESTER - HEREFORD

2nd class LM

Services on ⑦ valid until November 1. For additional services Worcester Shrub Hill - Hereford and v.v., see Table **131**.

km			Ⓐ	Ⓐ	Ⓐ	Ⓐ	Ⓐ	Ⓐ	Ⓐ	Ⓐ	Ⓐ	Ⓐ	Ⓐ	Ⓐ	Ⓐ	Ⓐ	Ⓐ	Ⓐ	Ⓐ	Ⓐ	Ⓐ	Ⓐ			⑥	⑥
0	**Birmingham** New St..d.	Ⓐ	...	0659	0759	0849	0949	1049	1149	1249	1349	1449	1549	1649	1719	1749	1819	1919	1949	2059	2200	2300	...	⑥	...	0649
21	Bromsgrove...d.		...	0723	0821	0911	1011	1111	1211	1311	1413	1511	1611	1711	1745	|	1846	1940	2009	2123	2223	2320	...		...	0711
32	Droitwich...d.		...	0733	0831	0921	1023	1121	1221	1322	1423	1521	1621	1722	1755	1819	1856	1950	2025	2133	2234	2330	...		...	0721
41	Worcester Shrub Hill a.		0600	|	|	|	|	|	|	|	|	|	|	1729	1804	1828	1911	2001	2034	|	2248	2339	...		0630	|
41	Worcester Foregate St a.		0602	0741	0839	0929	1031	1131	1230	1330	1431	1531	1631	1735	1811	1834	*1948*	2014	*2045*	2141	*2307*	...	...		0632	0729
54	Great Malvern...a.		0615	0754	0852	0942	1045	1144	1242	1343	1445	1544	1644	1747	1824	1847	*2002*	2026	*2058*	2154	*2319*	...	...		0644	0741
65	Ledbury...a.		0627	0813	0906	0956	1058	1158	1256	1357	1457	1558	1658	1801	1836	1901	*2016*	2039	*2112*	2210	...	...	...		0657	0755
87	**Hereford**...a.		0650	0834	0930	1019	1120	1222	1318	1422	1519	1622	1720	1823	1857	1926	*2037*	2100	*2136*	2232	...	...	...		0714	0821

	⑥	⑥	⑥	⑥	⑥	⑥	⑥	⑥	⑥	⑥	⑥	⑥	⑥	⑥			⑦	⑦	⑦	⑦	⑦	⑦	⑦	⑦	⑦	⑦
Birmingham New St. d.	0749	0849	0949	1049	1149	1249	1349	1449	1549	1649	1749	1849	1919	2059	...	⑦	1018‡	1118‡	1218‡	1320	1418‡	1518‡	1600	1800	1900	2100
Bromsgrove...d.	0811	0911	1011	1111	1211	1311	1411	1511	1611	1711	1811	1911	1942	2121	...		|	|	|	1343	|	|	1621	1821	1921	2121
Droitwich...d.	0821	0921	1021	1121	1221	1321	1421	1521	1621	1721	1819	1921	1957	2131	...		1104	1206	1306	1354	1506	1604	1630	1830	1931	2131
Worcester Shrub Hill a.	|	|	|	|	|	|	|	|	|	|	1827	1928	|	|	...		1111	1214	1313	1401	1514	|	1641	1838	1941	2138
Worcester Foregate St a.	0829	0929	1029	1129	1229	1329	1429	1529	1629	1729	1833	1935	2005	2139	...		1127	*1315*	1331	1423	...	1612	1646	1844	*2015*	2144
Great Malvern...a.	0842	0942	1042	1142	1242	1342	1442	1542	1642	1741	1846	1950	2018	2154	...		1139	*1329*	1343	1435	...	...	1701	1856	*2029*	2157
Ledbury...a.	0856	0956	1056	1156	1256	1356	1456	1556	1656	1755	1859	...	2038	2213	...		*1235*	*1343*	...	1448	...	...	*1742*	1910	...	2209
Hereford...a.	0920	1021	1120	1221	1320	1421	1518	1619	1720	1821	1920	...	2059	2234	...		*1255*	*1405*	...	1510	...	...	*1801*	1931	...	2230

		Ⓐ	Ⓐ	Ⓐ	Ⓐ	Ⓐ	Ⓐ	Ⓐ	Ⓐ	Ⓐ	Ⓐ	Ⓐ	Ⓐ	Ⓐ	Ⓐ	Ⓐ	Ⓐ	Ⓐ	Ⓐ	Ⓐ			⑥	⑥	⑥	⑥
Hereford...d.	Ⓐ	...	...	...	0708	0734	...	0849	0940	1040	1140	1239	1341	1440	1540	1640	1740	1848	1950	2130	...	⑥	...	...	0740	0840
Ledbury...d.		...	...	...	0724	0751	...	0908	0958	1059	1157	1300	1359	1459	1600	1659	1801	1904	2018	2147	...		...	...	0758	0858
Great Malvern...d.		0550	0648	0705	0739	0803	0838	0919	1010	1110	1211	1311	1411	1510	1611	1710	1813	1915	2029	2158	...		0620	...	0810	0910
Worcester Foregate St d.		0602	0659	0717	0751	0819	0851	0931	1023	1123	1223	1323	1423	1523	1623	1724	1825	1927	2042	2210	...		0631	...	0822	0922
Worcester Shrub Hill d.		|	0706	0724	0757	|	|	0937	|	|	|	|	|	|	|	|	|	|	|	|	...		|	0733	|	|
Droitwich...d.		0612	0714	0732	0805	0830	0900	0945	1033	1133	1233	1332	1432	1533	1633	1733	1834	1936	2049	2217	...		0640	0740	0831	0931
Bromsgrove...d.		0621	0725	|	|	0841	0909	0954	1042	1142	1242	1342	1442	1542	1642	1743	1842	1946	2059	2227	...		0650	0750	0840	0940
Birmingham New St. a.		0645	0745	0809	0837	0907	0942	1024	1113	1213	1313	1413	1513	1613	1713	1813	1912	2020	2123	2257	...		0716	0816	0911	1011

	⑥	⑥	⑥	⑥	⑥	⑥	⑥	⑥	⑥	⑥	⑥	⑥	⑥			⑦	⑦	⑦	⑦	⑦	⑦	⑦	⑦	⑦	⑦	
Hereford...d.	0936	1040	1140	1240	1340	1440	1540	1640	1740	1911	2000	2133	2243	...	⑦	...	...	...	...	...	...	1530	*1630*	*1830*	2005	...
Ledbury...d.	0958	1058	1158	1258	1358	1457	1558	1658	1758	1928	2016	2149	2302	...		...	...	...	...	...	...	1551	*1647*	*1848*	2021	...
Great Malvern...d.	1010	1110	1210	1310	1410	1510	1610	1710	1810	1940	2028	2200	2314	...		*0900*	1002	1056	1204	...	1435	1603	1716	*1908*	2032	...
Worcester Foregate St d.	1022	1122	1222	1322	1422	1522	1622	1722	1824	1951	2042	2218	2325	...		*0912*	1016	1120	1216	1320	1445	1615	1728	*1824*	2044	...
Worcester Shrub Hill d.	|	|	|	|	|	|	|	|	|	...	|	2220	2331	...		0921	1022	|	1221	|	1451	1633	1734	1953	2050	...
Droitwich...d.	1033	1133	1233	1333	1433	1533	1633	1734	1835	...	2049	...	...	...		0932	1030	1129	1229	1329	1459	1641	1742	2001	2058	...
Bromsgrove...d.	1042	1142	1242	1342	1442	1542	1642	1743	1844	...	2059	...	...	...		|	|	|	|	|	1509	1651	1752	2010	2108	...
Birmingham New St. a.	1111	1211	1311	1411	1511	1611	1711	1811	1911	...	2122	...	...	...		1020‡	1117‡	1217‡	1317‡	1417‡	1537	1717	1813	2036	2142	...

BIRMINGHAM SNOW HILL - KIDDERMINSTER - WORCESTER

Most trains call at Birmingham Moor Street 4 minutes before / after Snow Hill

km			Ⓐ	⑥	Ⓐ	⑥	Ⓐ	⑥	Ⓐ	Ⓐ	⑥	⚒	⚒	⚒	⚒	⑥	Ⓐ	⚒	Ⓐ	⑥	⚒	⑥	Ⓐ	⑥	Ⓐ	⑥
0	**Birmingham** Snow Hill d.	⚒	0620	0635	0653	0705	0723	0753	0753	0843	0853	0913	1013	1113	1213	1313	1313	1413	1513	1513	1613	1713	1713	1745	1753	1823
30	Kidderminster...d.		0700	0716	0735	0746	0803	0829	0831	0920	0929	0949	1049	1149	1249	1349	1351	1449	1549	1549	1649	1749	1754	1822	1832	1859
45	Droitwich...d.		0712	0729	0747	0758	0817	0840	0844	0932	0940	1001	1101	1201	1301	1401	1403	1501	1601	1601	1701	1803	1806	1835	1846	1913
54	**Worcester** Shrub Hill a.		|	0739	|	0806	0824	|	|	0942	0949	|	|	|	|	|	1411	|	1610	|	|	1814	1818	|	1858	1921
54	**Worcester** Foregate St a.		0722	...	0757	0812	0830	0849	0859	...	...	1009	1110	1211	1310	1409	...	1509	...	1609	1712	...	...	1843	...	...

	Ⓐ	⑥	⚒	⑥	Ⓐ	⚒	⑥	Ⓐ	⑥	Ⓐ			⑦	⑦	⑦	⑦	⑦	⑦	⑦	⑦	⑦	⑦	⑦	⑦	⑦	⑦
Birmingham Snow Hill d.	1843	1857	1927	1955	1957	2055	2155	2157	2256	2300	...	⑦	0930	1018	1118	1218	1320	1418	1518	1618	1720	1818	1918	2018	2145	2255
Kidderminster...d.	1920	1937	2007	2035	2037	2136	2235	2238	2337	2340	...		1004	1052	1155	1254	1355	1454	1552	1652	1754	1855	1952	2053	2218	2329
Droitwich...d.	1932	1949	2019	2047	2050	2147	2246	2249	2348	2352	...		1015	1104	1206	1306	1407	1506	1604	1704	1806	1906	2008	2105	2230	2340
Worcester Shrub Hill a.	|	1957	2029	2054	2100	2158	2255	2257	2356	0001	...		1023	1111	1214	1313	|	|	|	|	1813	1914	2015	2125	2237	2348
Worcester Foregate St a.	1941	...	...	2100	...	2204a	2300	2307	...	...	...		1029	1127	...	1331	1420	1514	1612	1712	...	...	...	2131	2243	...

		Ⓐ	⑥	Ⓐ	⑥	Ⓐ	⑥	Ⓐ	⑥	⚒	⚒	⑥	Ⓐ		⚒	Ⓐ	⑥	⚒	Ⓐ	⑥	Ⓐ	⑥	⑥	Ⓐ	Ⓐ	⑥
Worcester Foregate St d.	⚒	0647	...	...	0743	0804	...	0835	0856	...	...	1147	1150	...	1246	...	1347	...	1540	1546	1647	...	1748	1755	1847	1849
Worcester Shrub Hill d.		|	0658	0715	|	|	0814	0841	|	0947	1047	|	|	...	|	1347	|	1443	1547	|	|	1647	|	|	|	|
Droitwich...d.		0655	0706	0723	0752	0811	0822	0849	0905	0955	1055	1156	1158	...	1255	1355	1356	1455	1555	1555	1656	1655	1757	1804	1856	1858
Kidderminster...d.		0709	0722	0737	0806	0822	0836	0906	0916	1006	1106	1206	1210	...	1306	1406	1406	1506	1606	1606	1706	1706	1807	1817	1910	1911
Birmingham Snow Hill a.		0749	0805	0816	0845	0905	0916	0945	0955	1045	1145	1245	1245	...	1345	1445	1445	1545	1645	1645	1745	1745	1845	1855	1953	1955

	Ⓐ	⑥	⑥	Ⓐ	Ⓐ	⑥	Ⓐ	⑥				⑦	⑦	⑦	⑦	⑦	⑦	⑦	⑦	⑦	⑦	⑦	⑦	⑦	⑦	⑦
Worcester Foregate St d.	1945	1952	...	...	...	2142	2217	...	...	...	⑦	...	1016	1120	1216	1320	1420	1520	...	1620	1720	1820	...	...	...	2217
Worcester Shrub Hill d.	|	|	2052	2053	2152	2152	2227	2248	...	...		0921	1022	|	1221	|	|	|	1546	|	|	|	1938	2034	2122	2226
Droitwich...d.	1954	2001	2100	2101	2200	2200	2235	2256	...	...		0932	1030	1129	1229	1329	1429	1529	1554	1629	1729	1829	1946	2042	2130	2234
Kidderminster...d.	2010	2011	2111	2111	2210	2210	2245	2306	...	...		0942	1040	1139	1239	1339	1439	1539	1604	1639	1739	1839	1956	2052	2141	2244
Birmingham Snow Hill a.	2053	2054	2153	2153	2253	2253	2324	2337	...	...		1020	1117	1217	1322	1417	1517	1617	1635	1717	1817	1919	2033	2128	2218	2321

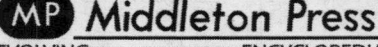

a – Ⓐ only.
‡ – Birmingham Snow Hill.

Services on ⑥ valid until September 5. Services on ⑦ valid until July 12.

km	Operator		XC	XC	XC	XC	XC	XC	XC	XC	XC	XC	XC	XC	XC	XC	XC	XC	XC	XC	XC	XC	XC	XC	XC
			Ⓐ	Ⓐ	Ⓐ	Ⓐ	Ⓐ	Ⓐ**R**	Ⓐ	Ⓐ	Ⓐ**R**	Ⓐ**C**	Ⓐ	Ⓐ**R**	Ⓐ**T**	Ⓐ	Ⓐ**R**	Ⓐ	Ⓐ**P**	Ⓐ**R**	Ⓐ	Ⓐ**A**	Ⓐ**R**	Ⓐ**T**	Ⓐ**P**
	Plymouth **115** d.	Ⓐ	...	...	...	...	...	...	...	0520	...	...	0625	...	...	0725	...	...	0825	...	...	0925	...	...	1025
	Exeter **115** d.		...	...	...	...	...	...	...	0637	...	...	0723	...	0743	0823	...	...	0923	...	...	1023	...	1048	1123
0	**Bristol** Temple Meads d.		...	...	...	...	0615	...	0700	0730	...	0800	0830	...	0900	0930	...	1000	1030	...	1100	1130	...	1200	1230
10	**Bristol** Parkway d.		...	...	...	...	0625	...	0710	0740	...	0810	0840	...	0910	0940	...	1010	1040	...	1110	1140	...	1210	1240
72	Cheltenham d.		...	...	...	...	0712	...	0742	0812	...	0842	0912	...	0942	1012	...	1042	1112	...	1142	1212	...	1242	1312
145	**Birmingham** New St a.		...	...	...	...	0756	...	0826	0856	...	0926	0956	...	1026	1056	...	1126	1156	...	1226	1256	...	1326	1356
145	**Birmingham** New St d.		0600	0630	0703	0730	0803	0830	0831	0903	0930	0931	1003	1030	1031	1103	1130	1131	1203	1230	1231	1303	1330	1331	1403
	Manchester Piccadilly **150** a.		|	|	|	|	|	|	1000	|	|	1100	|	|	1200	|	|	1300	|	|	1400	|	|	1500	|
173	Tamworth d.		0615	0646	0719	0746	0819	|	...	|	|	...	1019	|	...	|	|	...	1219	|	...	|	|	...	1419
193	Burton on Trent d.		|	0656	0729	0757	0829	|	...	0926	|	...	|	|	...	1126	|	...	|	|	...	1326	|	...	|
212	**Derby** 170 a.		0635	0711	0742	0811	0842	0911	...	0939	1011	...	1039	1111	...	1139	1211	...	1239	1311	...	1339	1411	...	1439
250	Chesterfield 170 a.		|	0731	0802	0832	0902	|	...	1002	|	...	1102	|	...	1202	|	...	1302	|	...	1402	|	...	1502
270	**Sheffield** 170 194 a.		0706	0748	0817	0851	0917	0946	...	1017	1046	...	1117	1146	...	1218	1246	...	1317	1346	...	1417	1446	...	1517
299	Doncaster 185 194 a.		|	0824	|	0920	|	1015	...	|	1115	...	|	1215	...	|	1320	...	|	1417	...	|	1516	...	|
316	Wakefield Westgate 185 a.		0736	|	0846	|	0946	|	...	1046	|	...	1146	|	...	1246	|	...	1346	|	...	1446	|	...	1546
332	**Leeds** 185 a.		0752	|	0902	|	1002	|	...	1102	|	...	1202	|	...	1302	|	...	1402	|	...	1502	|	...	1602
344	**York** 185 187 a.		0823	0847	0933	0948	1029	1040	...	1129	1145	...	1229	1245	...	1329	1346	...	1429	1443	...	1529	1540	...	1629
415	Darlington 185 187 a.		0855	0920	1004	1017	1059	1112	...	1158	1220	...	1300	1313	...	1400	1416	...	1458	1516	...	1606	1611	...	1657
450	Durham 185 187 a.		0913	0937	1021	1034	1117	1129	...	1222	1238	...	1318	1330	...	1418	1434	...	1515	1534	...	1624	1629	...	1714
473	**Newcastle** 185 187 a.		0926	1000	1036	1057	1132	1154	...	1236	1305	...	1333	1351	...	1436	1456	...	1531	1558	...	1637	1651	...	1734
529	Alnmouth 185 a.		0955	...	|	...	1200	...	...	|	...	...	1400	...	...	|	...	...	1601	...	...	|	...	...	1801
581	Berwick upon Tweed 185 a.		|	...	1120	...	|	...	...	1321	...	...	|	...	...	1521	...	...	|	...	...	1725	...	...	|
673	**Edinburgh** 185 a.		1102	...	1213	...	1310	...	...	1414	...	...	1510	...	...	1616	...	...	1709	...	...	1813	...	...	1903
766	**Glasgow** Central 185 a.		...	...	...	...	...	...	...	...	...	...	...	...	...	...	...	...	...	...	...	...	...	...	2025

Operator	XC	XC	XC	XC	XC	XC	XC	XC	XC	XC	XC	XC	XC	XC	XC	XC	EM	XC	XC	XC	XC	EM	EM	XC	XC
	Ⓐ**R**	Ⓐ	Ⓐ**D**	Ⓐ**R**	Ⓐ**P**	Ⓐ	Ⓐ**R**	Ⓐ	Ⓐ	Ⓐ**R**	Ⓐ**T**	Ⓐ	Ⓐ**R**	Ⓐ	Ⓐ	Ⓐ**R**	Ⓐ**L**	①–④	⑤	Ⓐ	Ⓐ**R**	Ⓐ**L**	Ⓐ**L**	Ⓐ	Ⓐ
Plymouth **115** d.	...	...	1125	...	1150	1221	...	...	1321	...	...	1425	...	...	1521	...	...	...	...	1625	...	...	...	...	1721
Exeter **115** d.	...	...	1223	...	1248	1323	...	...	1423	...	1444	1523	...	...	1623	...	...	...	1653	1723	...	...	...	...	1823
Bristol Temple Meads d.	...	1300	1330	...	1400	1430	...	1500	1530	...	1600	1630	...	1700	1730	...	...	1800	1800	1830	...	...	...	1900	1930
Bristol Parkway d.	...	1310	1340	...	1410	1440	...	1510	1540	...	1610	1640	...	1710	1740	...	...	1810	1810	1840	...	...	...	1910	1940
Cheltenham d.	...	1342	1412	...	1442	1512	...	1542	1612	...	1642	1712	...	1742	1812	...	...	1842	1842	1912	...	...	...	1942	2012
Birmingham New St a.	...	1426	1456	...	1526	1556	...	1626	1656	...	1726	1756	...	1826	1856	...	...	1926	1926	1956	...	...	...	2028	2056
Birmingham New St d.	1430	1431	1503	1530	1531	1603	1630	1631	1703	1730	1731	1803	1830	1831	1903	1930	...	1931	1931	2003	2030	...	...	2031	2103
Manchester Piccadilly **150** a.	|	1600	|	|	1700	|	|	1800	|	|	1900	|	|	2000	|	|	...	2100	2100	|	|	...	...	2200	|
Tamworth d.	|	...	|	|	...	1621	|	...	|	|	...	1819	|	...	|	|	...	...	...	2019	|	...	...	...	2121
Burton on Trent d.	|	...	1526	|	...	|	|	...	1728	|	...	|	|	...	1928	|	...	...	...	|	|	...	...	...	2133
Derby 170 a.	1511	...	1539	1611	...	1639	1711	...	1739	1811	...	1839	1911	...	1941	2011	...	...	...	2039	2111	2134	...	...	2146
Chesterfield 170 a.	|	...	1602	|	...	1703	|	...	1802	|	...	1902	1929	...	2002	|	2053	...	...	2102	2134	2153	2220	...	2207
Sheffield 170 194 a.	1546	...	1617	1646	...	1719	1745	...	1818	1849	...	1920	1947	...	2018	2049	2113	...	...	2116	2148	2216	2237	...	2226
Doncaster 185 194 a.	1615	...	|	1715	...	|	|	...	|	1917	...	|	2020	...	|	2120	|	...	...	|	2229	|	|	...	|
Wakefield Westgate 185 a.	|	...	1646	|	...	1746	1812	...	1846	|	...	1949	|	...	2053	|	2154	...	...	2148	|	2246	2317	...	2311
Leeds 185 a.	|	...	1702	|	...	1804	1831	...	1902	|	...	2006	|	...	2109	|	2212	...	...	2208	|	2305	2336	...	2330
York 185 187 a.	1640	...	1730	1740	...	1831	1858	...	1930	1944	...	2031	2046	...	2139	2145	...	...	...	...	2259	...	...	...	...
Darlington 185 187 a.	1708	...	1759	1815	...	1900	1938	...	2004	2012	...	2107	2120	...	...	2213	...	...	...	...	...	...	...	...	...
Durham 185 187 a.	1731	...	1817	1833	...	1918	1955	...	2022	2030	...	2125	2138	...	...	2230	...	...	...	...	...	...	...	...	...
Newcastle 185 187 a.	1754	...	1836	1855	...	1934	2018	...	2038	2048	...	2139	2200	...	...	2256	...	...	...	...	...	...	...	...	...
Alnmouth 185 a.	...	...	|	...	...	2004	...	...	|	2127	...	2211	...	...	...	...	...	...	...	...	...	...	...	...	...
Berwick upon Tweed 185 a.	...	...	1924	...	...	|	...	...	2127	2147	...	2232	...	...	...	...	...	...	...	...	...	...	...	...	...
Edinburgh 185 a.	...	...	2015	...	...	2112	...	...	2222	2235	...	2323	...	...	...	...	...	...	...	...	...	...	...	...	...
Glasgow Central 185 a.	...	...	...	...	...	2235	...	...	...	...	...	...	...	...	...	...	...	...	...	...	...	...	...	...	...

Operator	XC	XC	XC			XC	XC	XC	XC	EM	XC	XC	XC	XC	XC	XC	XC	XC	XC	XC	XC	XC	XC	XC	XC
	Ⓐ	Ⓐ	Ⓐ**T**			⑥	⑥	⑥	⑥	⑥**LK**	⑥	⑥**R**	⑥	⑥	⑥**C**	⑥**B**	⑥	⑥**R**	⑥**T**	⑥	⑥**R**	⑥	⑥**P**	⑥**R**	⑥
Plymouth **115** d.	...	1825	...	...	⑥	...	...	...	...	...	...	...	...	0525	...	...	0625	...	...	0725	...	...	0825	...	0840
Exeter **115** d.	...	1923	2048	...		...	...	...	...	...	...	...	...	0623	...	...	0723	...	0748	0823	...	...	0923	...	0939
Bristol Temple Meads d.	2000	2030	2200	...		...	...	...	...	...	0615	...	0700	0730	0800	...	0830	...	0900	0930	...	1000	1030	...	1100
Bristol Parkway d.	2010	2040	2210	...		...	...	...	...	...	0625	...	0710	0740	0810	...	0840	...	0910	0940	...	1010	1040	...	1110
Cheltenham d.	2042	2116	2242	...		...	...	...	...	...	0712	...	0742	0812	0842	...	0912	...	0942	1012	...	1042	1112	...	1142
Birmingham New St a.	2143	2206	2344	...		...	...	...	...	...	0756	...	0826	0856	0926	...	0956	...	1026	1056	...	1126	1156	...	1226
Birmingham New St d.	...	...	...	...		0555	0630	0703	0730	...	0803	0830	0831	0903	0931	0930	1003	1030	1031	1103	1130	1131	1203	1230	1231
Manchester Piccadilly **150** a.	...	...	...	...		|	|	|	|	...	|	|	1000	|	1100	|	|	|	1200	|	|	1300	|	|	1400
Tamworth d.	...	...	...	...		0612	0646	0719	0747	...	0819	|	...	|	...	|	1019	|	...	|	|	...	1219	|	...
Burton on Trent d.	...	...	...	...		0622	0656	0729	0758	...	0829	|	...	0926	...	|	|	|	...	1126	|	...	|	|	...
Derby 170 a.	...	...	...	...		0635	0709	0743	0809	0828	0842	0909	...	0942	...	1009	1042	1109	...	1142	1209	...	1242	1309	...
Chesterfield 170 a.	...	...	...	...		0655	0729	0802	0829	0846	0902	|	...	1002	...	|	1102	|	...	1202	|	...	1302	|	...
Sheffield 170 194 a.	...	...	...	...		0709	0748	0817	0846	0907	0917	0946	...	1017	...	1046	1117	1146	...	1217	1246	...	1317	1346	...
Doncaster 185 194 a.	...	...	...	...		|	0823	|	0921	0953	|	1018	...	|	...	1116	|	1216	...	|	1319	...	|	1416	...
Wakefield Westgate 185 a.	...	...	...	...		0736	|	0846	|	|	0946	|	...	1046	...	|	1146	|	...	1246	|	...	1346	|	...
Leeds 185 a.	...	...	...	...		0752	|	0902	|	|	1002	|	...	1102	...	|	1202	|	...	1302	|	...	1402	|	...
York 185 187 a.	...	...	...	...		0825	0849	0930	0945	1016	1030	1044	...	1132	...	1144	1230	1244	...	1332	1344	...	1430	1444	...
Darlington 185 187 a.	...	...	...	...		0854	0918	0959	1013	...	1059	1116	...	1159	...	1214	1301	1312	...	1359	1416	...	1459	1515	...
Durham 185 187 a.	...	...	...	...		0911	0935	1016	1030	...	1116	1133	...	1216	...	1234	1318	1329	...	1416	1434	...	1516	1532	...
Newcastle 185 187 a.	...	...	...	...		0926	0959	|	1051	...	1132	1154	...	1233	...	1255	1333	1350	...	1432	1455	...	1532	1551	...
Alnmouth 185 a.	...	...	...	...		0955	...	1033	...	...	1159	...	...	|	...	...	1359	...	...	|	...	...	1602	...	...
Berwick upon Tweed 185 a.	...	...	...	...		|	...	1117	...	...	|	...	...	1317	...	...	|	...	...	1517	...	...	|	...	...
Edinburgh 185 a.	...	...	...	...		1102	...	1212	...	...	1306	...	...	1412	...	...	1509	...	...	1610	...	...	1714	...	...
Glasgow Central 185 a.	...	...	...	...		...	...	...	...	...	...	...	...	...	...	...	...	...	...	...	...	...	...	...	...

Operator	XC	XC	XC	XC	XC	XC	XC	XC	XC	XC	XC	XC	XC	XC	XC	XC	XC	XC	XC	XC	EM	XC	XC	XC	EM
	⑥**A**	⑥**R**	⑥**T**	⑥**P**	⑥**R**	⑥	⑥**ND**	⑥**R**	⑥	⑥	⑥**R**	⑥	⑥	⑥**R**	⑥**T**	⑥	⑥**R**	⑥	⑥	⑥**R**	⑥**L**	⑥	⑥	⑥**R**	⑥**L**
Plymouth **115** d.	0925	...	...	1025	...	...	1121	...	...	1221	...	...	1325	...	...	1425	...	...	1525	...	...	...	1625	...	...
Exeter **115** d.	1023	...	1048	1123	...	...	1223	...	...	1323	...	...	1423	...	1438	1523	...	...	1623	...	...	...	1723	...	...
Bristol Temple Meads d.	1130	...	1200	1230	...	1300	1330	...	1400	1430	...	1500	1530	...	1600	1630	...	1700	1730	...	...	1800	1830	...	...
Bristol Parkway d.	1140	...	1210	1240	...	1310	1340	...	1410	1440	...	1510	1540	...	1610	1640	...	1710	1740	...	...	1810	1840	...	...
Cheltenham d.	1212	...	1242	1312	...	1342	1412	...	1442	1512	...	1542	1612	...	1642	1712	...	1742	1812	...	...	1842	1912	...	...
Birmingham New St a.	1256	...	1326	1356	...	1426	1456	...	1526	1556	...	1626	1656	...	1726	1756	...	1826	1856	...	...	1926	1956	...	...
Birmingham New St d.	1303	1330	1331	1403	1430	1431	1503	1530	1531	1603	1630	1631	1703	1730	1731	1803	1830	1831	1903	1930	...	1931	2003	2030	...
Manchester Piccadilly **150** a.	|	|	1500	|	|	1600	|	|	1700	|	|	1800	|	|	1900	|	|	2000	|	|	...	2100	|	|	...
Tamworth d.	|	|	...	1419	|	...	|	|	...	1619	|	...	|	|	...	1819	|	...	|	|	...	...	2019	2046	...
Burton on Trent d.	1326	|	...	|	|	...	1526	|	...	|	|	...	1726	|	...	|	|	...	1926	|	...	...	|	2056	...
Derby 170 a.	1342	1409	...	1442	1509	...	1542	1609	...	1642	1709	...	1742	1809	...	1842	1909	...	1942	2009	...	...	2042	2109	2143
Chesterfield 170 a.	1402	|	...	1502	|	...	1602	|	...	1702	|	...	1802	|	...	1902	1929	...	2002	2029	2052	...	2102	2129	2212
Sheffield 170 194 a.	1417	1446	...	1517	1546	...	1618	1646	...	1719	1744	...	1818	1847	...	1918	1951	...	2018	2049	2114	...	2118	2144	2234
Doncaster 185 194 a.	|	1516	...	|	1616	...	|	1719	...	|	|	...	|	1918	...	|	2016	...	|	2125	|	...	|	2219	|
Wakefield Westgate 185 a.	1446	|	...	1546	|	...	1646	|	...	1747	1814	...	1846	|	...	1946	|	...	2046	|	2152	...	2146	|	2305
Leeds 185 a.	1502	|	...	1602	|	...	1702	|	...	1802	1832	...	1902	|	...	2002	|	...	2105	|	2210	...	2207	|	2323
York 185 187 a.	1532	1544	...	1630	1644	...	1731	1744	...	1831	1859	...	1931	1944	...	2031	2040	...	2203	2148	...	...	...	2248	...
Darlington 185 187 a.	1559	1613	...	1659	1712	...	1800	1812	...	1901	1937	...	2003	2012	...	2104	2114	...	...	2221	...	...	...	...	...
Durham 185 187 a.	1616	1632	...	1716	1729	...	1818	1829	...	1919	1954	...	2021	2029	...	2121	2132	...	...	2241	...	...	...	...	...
Newcastle 185 187 a.	1632	1651	...	1732	1753	...	1837	1850	...	1935	2018	...	2033	2045	...	2133	2155	...	...	2310	...	...	...	...	...
Alnmouth 185 a.	|	...	...	1801	...	...	|	...	...	2003	...	...	|	2116	...	2159	...	...	...	...	...	...	...	...	...
Berwick upon Tweed 185 a.	1717	...	...	|	...	...	1925	...	...	|	...	...	2119	2137	...	2220	...	...	...	...	...	...	...	...	...
Edinburgh 185 a.	1805	...	...	1907	...	...	2015	...	...	2110	...	...	2215	2228	...	2309	...	...	...	...	...	...	...	...	...
Glasgow Central 185 a.	...	...	...	2029	...	...	...	...	...	2223	...	...	...	...	...	...	...	...	...	...	...	...	...	...	...

FOR NOTES SEE PAGE 115 →

127 EDINBURGH - YORK - SHEFFIELD - BIRMINGHAM - BRISTOL

All services 🍷 EM, XC

Services on ⑥ valid until September 5. Services on ⑦ valid until July 12.

Operator	XC ⑥	XC ⑥B	XC ⑥N	XC ⑥T	XC ⑥P	XC ⑥			XC ⑦	EM ⑦E	XC ⑦	XC ⑦	XC ⑦	XC ⑦	XC ⑦A	XC ⑦	XC ⑦		XC ⑦R		XC ⑦	XC ⑦R	XC ⑦	XC ⑦	EM ⑦L
Plymouth **115** d.	...	...	1721	...	1821	1832	...	⑦	...	...	...	...	...	...	0855	...	0955	...	...	...	1125	...	1200	1225	...
Exeter **115** d.	...	...	1823	1852	1923	1945	...		...	...	...	...	...	...	0955	...	1055	...	...	...	1223	...	1257	1323	...
Bristol Temple Meads d.	1900	...	1930	2000	2030	2100	...		...	...	...	0900	1010	...	1100	...	1200	...	...	...	1330	...	1400	1430	...
Bristol Parkway d.	1910	...	1940	2010	2040	2110	...		...	...	...	0910	1023	...	1110	...	1210	...	...	...	1340	...	1410	1440	...
Cheltenham d.	1942	...	2012	2042	2112	2142	...		...	...	...	0957	1056	...	1142	...	1242	...	...	...	1412	...	1442	1512	...
Birmingham New St a.	2026	...	2056	2141	2156	2227	...		...	...	...	1056	1156	...	1250	...	1350	...	...	...	1450	...	1526	1550	...
Birmingham New St d.	2031	2103	2057	...	2157	...	...		0903	...	1003	1103	1203	1230	1303	1330	1403	...	1430	...	1503	1530	1531	1603	...
Manchester Piccadilly **150** a.	2205	|	2248	...	|	...	...		|	...	|	|	|	|	|	|	|	...	|	...	|	|	1700	|	...
Tamworth d.	...	2119	...	...	|	...	...		0919	...	1019	|	1219	|	|	|	1419	...	|	...	|	|	...	1619	...
Burton on Trent d.	...	2129	...	...	|	...	...		0929	...	1029	1126	|	|	1326	|	|	...	|	...	1526	|	...	|	...
Derby 170 a.	...	2142	...	...	2231	...	...		0942	1044	1042	1141	1242	1309	1342	1409	1442	...	1505	...	1542	1605	...	1642	1655
Chesterfield 170 a.	...	2207	...	...	2252	...	...		1002	1108	1102	1204	1302	1329	1402	1429	1502	...	|	...	1602	|	...	1702	1716
Sheffield 170 194 a.	...	2223	...	...	2308	...	...		1018	1128	1116	1218	1317	1345	1417	1447	1517	...	1547	...	1618	1648	...	1718	1732
Doncaster 185 194 a.	...	2247	...	...	|	...	...		|	1152	|	|	|	1413	|	1513	|	...	1615	...	|	1713	...	|	|
Wakefield Westgate 185 a.	...	2309	...	...	|	...	...		1044	|	1144	1244	1344	|	1444	|	1544	...	|	...	1644	|	...	1745	1806
Leeds 185 a.	...	2329	...	...	2356	...	...		1102	|	1202	1302	1402	|	1502	|	1602	...	|	...	1702	|	...	1802	1824
York 185 187 a.	...	...	...	...	...	...	...		1134	1215	1232	1332	1432	1443	1532	1543	1632	...	1640	...	1732	1742	...	1832	...
Darlington 185 187 a.	...	...	...	...	...	...	...		1203	...	1301	1401	1507	1515	1601	1612	1701	...	1714	...	1801	1810	...	1901	...
Durham 185 187 a.	...	...	...	...	...	...	...		1220	...	1318	1418	1524	1532	1618	1630	1718	...	1732	...	1818	1827	...	1918	...
Newcastle 185 187 a.	...	...	...	...	...	...	...		1235	...	1334	1434	1538	1551	1634	1650	1734	...	1753	...	1834	1847	...	1934	...
Alnmouth 185 a.	...	...	...	...	...	...	...		|	...	1400	|	1607	...	|	...	1801	...	...	...	|	...	...	2004	...
Berwick upon Tweed 185 a.	...	...	...	...	...	...	...		1320	...	|	1519	|	...	1719	...	|	...	...	...	1919	...	...	|	...
Edinburgh 185 a.	...	...	...	...	...	...	...		1415	...	1507	1612	1714	...	1807	...	1908	...	...	...	2007	...	...	2111	...
Glasgow Central 185 a.	...	...	...	...	...	...	...		...	...	...	...	...	...	...	...	...	...	...	...	2117	...	...	2219	...

Operator	XC ⑦R	XC ⑦T		XC ⑦N	XC ⑦	XC ⑦R	XC ⑦		XC ⑦R	XC ⑦P		XC ⑦	XC ⑦R	XC ⑦		XC ⑦	EM ⑦L	XC ⑦	XC ⑦P	EM ⑦L		XC ⑦T	XC ⑦		XC ⑦
Plymouth **115** d.	...	...	...	1321	...	...	1421	...	...	1435	...	1521	...	...	...	1625	...	...	1725	...	...	...	1821	...	...
Exeter **115** d.	...	1351	...	1423	...	...	1523	...	...	1533	...	1623	...	...	...	1723	...	...	1823	...	...	1856	1923	...	...
Bristol Temple Meads d.	...	1500	...	1530	1600	...	1630	...	...	1700	...	1730	...	1800	...	1830	...	1900	1930	...	...	2000	2030	...	2210
Bristol Parkway d.	...	1510	...	1540	1610	...	1640	...	...	1710	...	1740	...	1810	...	1840	...	1910	1940	...	...	2010	2040	...	2220
Cheltenham d.	...	1542	...	1612	1642	...	1712	...	...	1742	...	1812	...	1842	...	1912	...	1942	2012	...	...	2042	2112	...	2252
Birmingham New St a.	...	1626	...	1650	1726	...	1750	...	...	1827	...	1856	...	1926	...	1950	...	2026	2050	...	...	2131	2156	...	2344
Birmingham New St d.	1630	1631	...	1703	1731	1730	1803	...	1830	1831	...	1903	1930	1931	...	2003	...	2031	2103	...	...	...	2203	...	...
Manchester Piccadilly **150** a.	|	1800	...	|	1900	|	|	...	|	2000	...	|	|	2100	...	|	...	2200	|	...	...	...	|	...	...
Tamworth d.	|	...	...	|	...	|	1821	...	|	...	...	|	|	...	...	2019	...	...	|	...	...	...	2222	...	...
Burton on Trent d.	|	...	...	1726	...	|	|	...	|	...	...	1928	|	...	...	|	...	...	2126	...	...	...	2235	...	...
Derby 170 a.	1705	...	...	1742	...	1805	1842	...	1905	...	...	1942	2005	...	...	2042	2048	...	2144	2243	...	...	2249	...	...
Chesterfield 170 a.	|	...	...	1802	...	|	1904	...	|	...	...	2002	|	...	...	2102	2109	...	2202	2307	...	...	2313	...	...
Sheffield 170 194 a.	1748	...	...	1819	...	1846	1920	...	1939	...	...	2018	2038	...	...	2116	2125	...	2218	2327	...	...	2334	...	...
Doncaster 185 194 a.	1813	...	...	|	...	1913	|	...	2016	...	...	|	2119	...	...	|	|	...	|	|	...	...	|	...	...
Wakefield Westgate 185 a.	1833	...	...	1847	...	|	1948	...	|	...	...	2046	|	...	...	2144	2205	...	2245	2354	...	...	|	...	...
Leeds 185 a.	1853	...	...	1904	...	|	2005	...	|	...	...	2103	|	...	...	2208	2226	...	2308	0031	...	...	0049	...	...
York 185 187 a.	1921	...	...	1932	...	1942	2032	...	2044	...	...	2137	2142	...	...	...	...	...	...	...	...	...	...	...	...
Darlington 185 187 a.	1951	...	...	2003	...	2010	2103	...	2118	...	...	...	2210	...	...	...	...	...	...	...	...	...	...	...	...
Durham 185 187 a.	2008	...	...	2021	...	2027	2121	...	2136	...	...	...	2227	...	...	...	...	...	...	...	...	...	...	...	...
Newcastle 185 187 a.	2030	...	...	2037	...	2043	2137	...	2159	...	...	...	2248	...	...	...	...	...	...	...	...	...	...	...	...
Alnmouth 185 a.	...	...	...	|	...	2115	2205	...	...	...	...	...	...	...	...	...	...	...	...	...	...	...	...	...	...
Berwick upon Tweed 185 a.	...	...	...	2123	...	2136	2228	...	...	...	...	...	...	...	...	...	...	...	...	...	...	...	...	...	...
Edinburgh 185 a.	...	...	...	2220	...	2225	2319	...	...	...	...	...	...	...	...	...	...	...	...	...	...	...	...	...	...
Glasgow Central 185 a.	...	...	...	...	...	...	...	...	...	...	...	...	...	...	...	...	...	...	...	...	...	...	...	...	...

Operator		XC ⒶT	XC Ⓐ	XC ⒶR	EM ⒶL	XC Ⓐ	XC ⒶB	XC Ⓐ	XC ⒶR	EM ⒶL	XC Ⓐ	XC Ⓐ	XC ⒶR	XC ⒶT	XC Ⓐ	XC ⒶR	XC Ⓐ	XC Ⓐ	XC ⒶR	XC Ⓐ	XC Ⓐ	XC ⒶR	XC Ⓐ	XC ⒶD	XC ⒶR
Glasgow 185 d.	Ⓐ	...	...	...	...	...	...	...	...	...	...	...	...	...	...	...	...	...	...	...	0600	...	...	...	...
Edinburgh 185 d.		...	...	...	...	...	...	...	...	...	...	...	...	...	...	...	...	0608	0644	...	0708	...	...	0810	...
Berwick upon Tweed 185 d.		...	...	...	...	...	...	...	...	...	...	...	...	...	...	...	...	0649	0723	...	0751	...	...	0852	...
Alnmouth 185 d.		...	...	...	...	...	...	...	...	...	...	...	...	...	...	...	...	0710	0747	...	|	...	...	|	...
Newcastle 185 187 d.		...	...	...	...	...	...	...	...	...	...	...	0621	...	0644	0723	...	0744	0824	...	0840	0933	...	0943	1025
Durham 185 187 d.		...	...	...	...	...	...	...	...	...	...	...	0639	...	0655	0737	...	|	0840	...	0852	0948	...	0955	1041
Darlington 185 187 d.		...	...	...	...	...	...	...	...	...	...	...	0656	...	0712	0755	...	0812	0857	...	0912	1005	...	1012	1058
York 185 187 d.		...	...	...	...	...	...	...	...	...	...	0632	0727	...	0744	0827	...	0844	0927	...	0944	1034	...	1044	1127
Leeds 185 d.		...	...	...	0525	...	...	0600	0615	0634	...	0705	|	...	0811	|	...	0911	|	...	1011	|	...	1111	|
Wakefield Westgate 185 d.		...	...	...	0537	...	...	0612	0627	0646	...	0718	|	...	0823	|	...	0923	|	...	1023	|	...	1123	|
Doncaster 185 194 d.		...	...	...	0557	...	...	|	0645	|	...	|	0752	...	|	0851	...	|	0956	...	|	1058	...	|	1154
Sheffield 170 194 d.		...	...	0601	0627	...	...	0650	0718	0732	...	0753	0820	...	0854	0823	...	0954	1023	...	1054	1123	...	1154	1223
Chesterfield 170 d.		...	...	0626	0639	...	...	0704	0730	0745	...	0806	0832	...	0906	|	...	1006	|	...	1106	|	...	1206	|
Derby 170 d.		...	0610	0647	0703	...	0706	0726	0750	...	...	0828	0853	...	0928	0953	...	1028	1053	...	1128	1153	...	1228	1253
Burton on Trent d.		...	0620	0657	...	...	0718	0737	0800	...	...	0838	|	...	0938	|	...	|	|	...	|	|	...	|	|
Tamworth d.		...	0631	0708	...	...	0730	0749	0811	...	...	0849	|	...	|	|	...	1048	|	...	|	|	...	1248	|
Manchester Piccadilly **150** d.		...	|	|	...	0600	|	|	|	...	0706	|	|	0807	|	|	0907	|	|	1007	|	|	1107	|	|
Birmingham New St a.		...	0652	0727	...	0731	0756	0809	0829	...	0831	0909	0927	0931	1007	1027	1031	1109	1127	1131	1204	1227	1231	1309	1327
Birmingham New St d.		0642	0712	...	...	0742	...	0812	...	...	0842	0912	...	0942	1012	...	1042	1112	...	1142	1212	...	1242	1312	...
Cheltenham a.		0723	0751	...	...	0823	...	0851	...	...	0923	0951	...	1023	1051	...	1123	1151	...	1223	1251	...	1323	1351	...
Bristol Parkway a.		0756	0827	...	...	0856	...	0925	...	...	0956	1026	...	1056	1126	...	1156	1226	...	1256	1324	...	1356	1427	...
Bristol Temple Meads a.		0808	0841	...	...	0913	...	0941	...	...	1013	1041	...	1113	1138	...	1213	1241	...	1313	1339	...	1413	1441	...
Exeter **115** a.		0907	0943	...	...	...	...	1046	...	...	...	1146	...	1230	1243	...	...	1346	...	...	1443	...	...	1546	...
Plymouth **115** a.		...	1048	...	...	...	...	1156	...	...	...	1256	...	...	1348	...	...	1456	...	...	1548	...	...	1656	...

Operator	XC ⑤	XC ①–④	XC ⒶD	XC ⒶR	XC Ⓐ	XC ⒶP	XC ⒶR	XC ⒶT	XC ⒶAP	XC ⒶR	XC Ⓐ	XC ⒶP	XC ⒶR	XC Ⓐ	XC Ⓐ	XC ⒶR	XC ⒶC	XC Ⓐ	XC ⒶR	XC Ⓐ	XC Ⓐ	XC ⒶR	XC Ⓐ	XC Ⓐ	XC Ⓐ
Glasgow 185 d.	...	...	...	...	...	0900	...	...	...	...	...	...	...	...	...	...	...	...	...	...	...	...	...	...	...
Edinburgh 185 d.	...	...	0907	...	...	1008	...	...	1108	...	...	1205	...	...	1306	...	...	1408	...	...	1508	...	...	1607	...
Berwick upon Tweed 185 d.	...	...	0951	...	...	|	...	...	1151	...	...	|	...	...	1351	...	...	|	...	...	1551	...	...	|	...
Alnmouth 185 d.	...	...	|	...	...	1105	...	...	|	...	...	1306	...	...	|	...	...	1505	...	...	|	...	...	1709	...
Newcastle 185 187 d.	...	...	1043	1127	...	1140	1219	...	1243	1334	...	1344	1427	...	1440	1522	...	1540	1632	...	1640	1717	...	1743	1820
Durham 185 187 d.	...	...	1055	1139	...	1152	1235	...	1255	1346	...	1352	1440	...	1452	1534	...	1552	1648	...	1652	1733	...	1755	1836
Darlington 185 187 d.	...	...	1112	1156	...	1211	1253	...	1312	1403	...	1412	1457	...	1512	1551	...	1612	1705	...	1712	1750	...	1812	1856
York 185 187 d.	...	...	1144	1227	...	1244	1326	...	1344	1432	...	1444	1529	...	1544	1625	...	1644	1734	...	1744	1824	...	1844	1929
Leeds 185 d.	...	...	1211	|	...	1311	|	...	1411	|	...	1511	|	...	1611	|	...	1711	|	...	1811	|	...	1911	|
Wakefield Westgate 185 d.	...	...	1223	|	...	1323	|	...	1423	|	...	1523	|	...	1623	|	...	1723	|	...	1823	|	...	1923	|
Doncaster 185 194 d.	...	...	|	1255	...	|	1355	...	|	1457	...	|	1555	...	|	1653	...	|	1758	...	|	1852	...	|	1957
Sheffield 170 194 d.	...	...	1254	1323	...	1354	1423	...	1454	1523	...	1554	1623	...	1654	1723	...	1754	1823	...	1854	1923	...	1954	2023
Chesterfield 170 d.	...	...	1306	|	...	1406	|	...	1506	|	...	1606	|	...	1706	|	...	1806	|	...	1906	|	...	2006	|
Derby 170 d.	...	...	1328	1353	...	1428	1453	...	1528	1553	...	1628	1653	...	1728	1753	...	1828	1853	...	1928	1953	...	2028	2053
Burton on Trent d.	...	...	1338	|	...	|	|	...	1538	|	...	|	|	...	1738	|	...	|	|	...	1938	|	...	|	|
Tamworth d.	...	...	|	|	...	1448	|	...	|	|	...	1648	|	...	|	|	...	1848	|	...	|	|	...	2048	|
Manchester Piccadilly **150** d.	1207	1207	|	|	1307	|	|	1407	|	|	1507	|	|	1607	|	|	1706	|	|	1805	|	|	1907	|	|
Birmingham New St a.	1331	1331	1407	1427	1431	1507	1527	1531	1608	1627	1631	1707	1727	1731	1807	1827	1831	1908	1927	1931	2009	2027	2031	2107	2140
Birmingham New St d.	1342	1342	1412	...	1442	1512	...	1542	1612	...	1642	1712	...	1742	1812	...	1842	1912	...	1942	2012	...	2042	2112	...
Cheltenham a.	1423	1423	1451	...	1523	1551	...	1623	1651	...	1723	1751	...	1823	1851	...	1923	1951	...	2023	2051	...	2123	2151	...
Bristol Parkway a.	1456	1456	1524	...	1556	1626	...	1656	1724	...	1756	1824	...	1908	1927	...	1956	2027	...	2056	2125	...	2200	2223	...
Bristol Temple Meads a.	1513	1513	1541	...	1613	1641	...	1713	1741	...	1813	1841	...	1925	1939	...	2013	2041	...	2113	2138	...	2219	2241	...
Exeter **115** a.	1618	...	1643	...	...	1743	...	1813	1843	...	...	1943	...	...	2043	...	...	2143	...	2232	2255	...	...	...	...
Plymouth **115** a.	...	...	1748	...	...	1856	...	...	1948	...	...	2048	...	...	2148	...	...	2248	...	2338	0006	...	...	...	...

FOR NOTES SEE NEXT PAGE →

EM, XC All services

EDINBURGH - YORK - SHEFFIELD - BIRMINGHAM - BRISTOL 127

Services on ⑥ valid until September 5. Services on ⑦ valid until July 12.

Operator	XC Ⓐ	XC Ⓐ	XC Ⓐ		⑥	XC ⑥T	XC ⑥	XC ⑥R	XC ⑥	XC ⑥B	XC ⑥	XC ⑥R	EM ⑥L	XC ⑥N	XC ⑥	XC ⑥R	EM ⑥L	XC ⑥T	XC ⑥P	XC ⑥R	XC ⑥	XC ⑥	XC ⑥R	XC ⑥	XC ⑥
Glasgow 185 d.	...	...	...	...		...	...	...	...	...	...	...	...	...	...	...	...	...	...	...	...	...	...	...	...
Edinburgh 185 d.	1708	...	1805	...		...	...	...	...	...	...	...	...	...	...	...	...	...	...	...	...	0612	0655	...	0705
Berwick upon Tweed 185 d.	1751	...	1848	...		...	...	...	...	...	...	...	...	...	...	...	...	...	...	...	...	0651	0735	...	0748
Alnmouth 185 d.	|	...	1908	...		...	...	...	...	...	...	...	...	...	...	...	...	...	...	...	...	0711	0755	...	|
Newcastle 185 187 d.	1840	1925	1943	...		...	...	...	...	...	...	...	...	...	...	0620	...	...	0642	0725	...	0744	0830	...	0840
Durham 185 187 d.	1852	1944	1955	...		...	...	...	...	...	...	...	...	...	...	0639	...	...	0656	0738	...	0756	0842	...	0856
Darlington 185 187 d.	1912	2004	2012	...		...	...	...	...	...	...	...	...	...	...	0656	...	...	0713	0755	...	0813	0859	...	0913
York 185 187 d.	1944	2032	2044	...		...	...	...	...	...	...	...	...	...	0609	0725	...	...	0744	0827	...	0844	0928	...	0944
Leeds 185 d.	2011	|	2111	...		...	...	...	...	...	0600	0615	0634	...	0705	|	0734	...	0811	|	...	0911	|	...	1011
Wakefield Westgate 185 d.	2023	|	2123	...		...	...	...	...	...	0612	0629	0646	...	0718	|	0746	...	0823	|	...	0923	|	...	1023
Doncaster 185 194 d.	|	2057	|	...		...	...	...	...	...	|	0647	|	...	|	0752	|	...	|	0853	...	|	0953	...	|
Sheffield 170 194 d.	2054	2126	2200	...		...	...	0601	...	...	0650	0718	0732	...	0754	0820	0832	...	0854	0923	...	0954	1023	...	1054
Chesterfield 170 d.	2106	|	2224	...		...	...	0626	...	...	0703	0730	0745	...	0806	0832	0845	...	0906	|	...	1006	|	...	1106
Derby 170 d.	2128	2200	2245	...		...	0610	0647	...	0706	0725	0750	...	...	0828	0853	...	...	0928	0953	...	1028	1053	...	1128
Burton on Trent d.	2138	|	2256	...		...	0620	0657	...	0718	0736	0800	...	...	0838	|	...	...	0938	|	...	|	|	...	1138
Tamworth d.	2149	|	2306	...		...	0631	0708	...	0730	0748	0811	...	...	0848	|	...	...	|	|	...	1048	|	...	|
Manchester Piccadilly 150 d.	|	|	|	...		...	|	|	0600	|	|	|	...	0700	|	|	...	0800	|	|	0907	|	|	1007	|
Birmingham New St a.	2207	2254	2334	...		...	0650	0727	0731	0750	0808	0829	...	0837	0907	0927	...	0938	1006	1027	1031	1107	1127	1131	1207
Birmingham New St d.	2216	...	...	...		0642	0712	...	0742	...	0812	...	...	0842	0912	...	...	0942	1012	...	1042	1112	...	1142	1212
Cheltenham a.	2331	...	...	...		0723	0751	...	0823	...	0851	...	...	0924	0951	...	...	1024	1051	...	1123	1151	...	1223	1251
Bristol Parkway a.	0004	...	...	...		0756	0824	...	0856	...	0925	...	...	0957	1026	...	...	1057	1125	...	1156	1229	...	1256	1324
Bristol Temple Meads a.	0018	...	...	...		0811	0838	...	0913	...	0938	...	...	1013	1041	...	...	1113	1138	...	1213	1241	...	1313	1338
Exeter 115 a.	...	...	...	...		0907	0943	...	...	...	1046	...	...	1130	1143	...	...	1231	1242	...	...	1343	...	...	1443
Plymouth 115 a.	...	...	...	...		...	1048	...	...	...	1156	...	...	1232	1248	...	...	...	1348	...	...	1448	...	...	1548

Operator	XC ⑥R	XC ⑥	XC ⑥N	XC ⑥R	XC ⑥T	XC ⑥D	XC ⑥R	XC ⑥	XC ⑥P	XC ⑥R	XC ⑥	XC ⑥AP	XC ⑥R	XC ⑥	XC ⑥P	XC ⑥R	XC ⑥T	XC ⑥	XC ⑥R	XC ⑥C	XC ⑥	XC ⑥R	XC ⑥	XC ⑥	EM ⑥KL
Glasgow 185 d.	...	...	0700	...	...	...	...	...	0900	...	...	...	...	...	...	...	...	...	...	...	...	...	...	...	...
Edinburgh 185 d.	...	...	0805	...	...	0905	...	...	1005	...	...	1105	...	...	1205	...	...	1305	...	...	1405	...	...	1505	...
Berwick upon Tweed 185 d.	...	...	0847	...	...	0948	...	...	|	...	...	1148	...	...	|	...	...	1348	...	...	|	...	...	1548	...
Alnmouth 185 d.	...	...	0909	...	...	|	...	...	1104	...	...	|	...	...	1305	...	...	|	...	...	1505	...	...	|	...
Newcastle 185 187 d.	0925	...	0940	1025	...	1044	1120	...	1140	1222	...	1244	1327	...	1344	1422	...	1444	1525	...	1544	1622	...	1644	...
Durham 185 187 d.	0937	...	0955	1038	...	1056	1134	...	1155	1238	...	1256	1339	...	1356	1434	...	1456	1538	...	1556	1638	...	1656	...
Darlington 185 187 d.	0956	...	1012	1056	...	1113	1156	...	1212	1255	...	1313	1358	...	1413	1452	...	1513	1556	...	1613	1656	...	1713	...
York 185 187 d.	1025	...	1044	1127	...	1144	1225	...	1244	1327	...	1344	1427	...	1444	1526	...	1544	1625	...	1644	1725	...	1744	1749
Leeds 185 d.	|	...	1111	|	...	1211	|	...	1311	|	...	1411	|	...	1511	|	...	1611	|	...	1711	|	...	1811	|
Wakefield Westgate 185 d.	|	...	1123	|	...	1223	|	...	1323	|	...	1423	|	...	1523	|	...	1623	|	...	1723	|	...	1823	|
Doncaster 185 194 d.	1053	...	|	1155	...	|	1252	...	|	1354	...	|	1456	...	|	1555	...	|	1653	...	|	1755	...	|	1818
Sheffield 170 194 d.	1123	...	1154	1223	...	1254	1323	...	1354	1423	...	1454	1523	...	1554	1623	...	1654	1723	...	1754	1823	...	1854	1847
Chesterfield 170 d.	|	...	1206	|	...	1306	|	...	1406	|	...	1506	|	...	1606	|	...	1706	|	...	1806	|	...	1906	|
Derby 170 d.	1153	...	1228	1253	...	1328	1353	...	1428	1453	...	1528	1553	...	1628	1653	...	1728	1753	...	1828	1853	...	1928	1919
Burton on Trent d.	|	...	|	|	...	1338	|	...	|	|	...	1538	|	...	|	|	...	1738	|	...	|	|	...	1938	...
Tamworth d.	|	...	1248	|	...	|	|	...	1448	|	...	|	|	...	1648	|	...	|	|	...	1848	|	...	|	...
Manchester Piccadilly 150 d.	|	1107	|	|	1207	|	|	1307	|	|	1407	|	|	1507	|	|	1607	|	|	1706	|	|	1805	|	...
Birmingham New St a.	1227	1231	1309	1327	1331	1407	1427	1431	1508	1527	1531	1607	1627	1631	1707	1727	1731	1807	1827	1831	1907	1927	1931	2007	...
Birmingham New St d.	...	1242	1312	...	1342	1412	...	1442	1512	...	1542	1612	...	1642	1712	...	1742	1812	...	1842	1912	...	1942	2012	...
Cheltenham a.	...	1325	1351	...	1423	1451	...	1523	1551	...	1623	1651	...	1723	1751	...	1823	1851	...	1923	1951	...	2023	2051	...
Bristol Parkway a.	...	1358	1426	...	1456	1524	...	1556	1626	...	1656	1724	...	1756	1826	...	1908	1926	...	1956	2026	...	2056	2123	...
Bristol Temple Meads a.	...	1413	1441	...	1513	1541	...	1613	1641	...	1713	1738	...	1813	1841	...	1927	1941	...	2013	2041	...	2113	2135	...
Exeter 115 a.	...	...	1543	...	1612	1643	...	...	1747	...	...	1843	...	...	1943	...	2036	2043	...	...	2145	...	...	2244	...
Plymouth 115 a.	...	...	1647	...	...	1748	...	...	1852	...	...	1848	...	...	2048	...	...	2148	...	...	2255	...	...	2359	...

Operator	XC ⑥R	XC ⑥	XC ⑥	XC ⑥	XC ⑥	XC ⑥	XC ⑥		⑦	XC ⑦P	XC ⑦	XC ⑦	EM ⑦L	XC ⑦	EM ⑦L	XC ⑦	XC ⑦	XC ⑦T	XC ⑦P	XC ⑦R	XC ⑦	XC ⑦	EM ⑦L	XC ⑦R	XC ⑦
Glasgow 185 d.	...	...	...	...	...	...	...	...		...	...	...	...	...	...	...	...	...	...	...	...	...	...	...	...
Edinburgh 185 d.	...	...	1605	...	1708	...	1805	...		...	...	...	...	...	...	...	0850	...	0950	...	...	1050	...	...	...
Berwick upon Tweed 185 d.	...	...	|	...	1748	...	1848	...		...	...	...	...	...	...	...	0933	...	|	...	...	1133	...	...	...
Alnmouth 185 d.	...	...	1705	...	|	...	1908	...		...	...	...	...	...	...	...	|	...	1047	...	...	|	...	...	...
Newcastle 185 187 d.	1722	...	1744	1822	1844	1925	1943	...		...	...	...	...	...	...	0925	1025	...	1125	...	...	1225	...	1315	...
Durham 185 187 d.	1738	...	1756	1838	1856	1937	1956	...		...	...	...	...	...	...	0938	1037	...	1137	...	...	1237	...	1330	...
Darlington 185 187 d.	1755	...	1813	1856	1913	1954	2013	...		...	...	...	...	...	...	0955	1054	...	1154	...	...	1254	...	1347	...
York 185 187 d.	1825	...	1844	1925	1944	2023	2044	...		...	...	...	...	0928	...	1028	1128	...	1228	...	...	1328	...	1419	...
Leeds 185 d.	|	...	1911	|	2011	|	2111	...		...	0809	0900	0944	1000	1020	1100	1200	...	1300	...	...	1400	1405	|	...
Wakefield Westgate 185 d.	|	...	1923	|	2023	|	2123	...		...	0822	0912	0958	1012	1032	1112	1212	...	1312	...	...	1412	1418	|	...
Doncaster 185 194 d.	1851	...	|	1953	|	|	|	...		...	|	0932	|	1030	|	1130	1230	...	1330	...	...	|	|	1450	...
Sheffield 170 194 d.	1923	...	1954	2023	2054	2123	2154	...		...	0855	0957	1028	1057	1106	1157	1257	...	1357	1420	...	1450	1502	1520	...
Chesterfield 170 d.	|	...	2006	|	2106	2135	2206	...		...	0907	1009	1041	1109	1125	1209	1309	...	1409	1432	...	1502	1515	|	...
Derby 170 d.	1953	...	2028	2053	2128	2157	2226	...		...	0930	1033	...	1130	1147	1230	1332	...	1430	1453	...	1523	...	1551	...
Burton on Trent d.	|	...	|	|	2138	2207	2237	...		...	|	1044	...	1141	...	|	1341	...	|	|	...	1535	...	|	...
Tamworth d.	|	...	2048	|	|	2218	2247	...		...	0949	|	...	|	...	1248	|	...	1448	|	...	|	...	|	...
Manchester Piccadilly 150 d.	|	1907	|	|	|	|	|	...		...	|	|	...	|	...	|	|	1307	|	|	1407	|	...	|	1507
Birmingham New St a.	2027	2031	2107	2131	2212	2248	2311	...		...	1010	1112	...	1207	...	1307	1410	1431	1507	1527	1531	1600	...	1627	1631
Birmingham New St d.	...	2042	2112	...	...	...	...	...		0852	1014	1112	...	1212	...	1312	1412	1442	1512	...	1542	1612	...	...	1642
Cheltenham a.	...	2123	2151	...	...	...	...	...		0950	1055	1150	...	1250	...	1350	1450	1524	1550	...	1624	1650	...	...	1724
Bristol Parkway a.	...	2157	2223	...	...	...	...	...		1023	1128	1226	...	1323	...	1423	1525	1600	1623	...	1657	1723	...	...	1802
Bristol Temple Meads a.	...	2213	2241	...	...	...	...	...		1035	1141	1239	...	1335	...	1435	1538	1613	1635	...	1713	1735	...	...	1814
Exeter 115 a.	...	...	...	...	...	...	...	...		1148	1247	1347	...	1444	...	1544	1647	1713	1744	...	...	1848	...	...	...
Plymouth 115 a.	...	...	...	...	...	...	...	...		1255	1356	1408	...	1548	...	1648	1756	...	1848	...	...	1953	...	...	...

Operator	XC ⑦P	XC ⑦R	XC ⑦	XC ⑦	XC ⑦R	XC ⑦T	XC ⑦A	XC ⑦R	XC ⑦	XC ⑦	EM ⑦L	XC ⑦S	XC ⑦	XC ⑦	XC ⑦	XC ⑦	XC ⑦	XC ⑦		
Glasgow 185 d.	...	...	...	1137	...	...	...	...	...	1345	...	...	...	...	...	...	...	...	...	...
Edinburgh 185 d.	1150	...	...	1250	1333	...	1350	...	...	1450	...	...	...	1550	...	...	1650	1750	...	...
Berwick upon Tweed 185 d.	|	...	...	1333	1418	...	|	...	...	1533	...	...	...	|	...	...	1733	|	...	...
Alnmouth 185 d.	1247	...	...	|	1438	...	1447	...	...	|	...	...	...	1647	...	...	|	1851	...	...
Newcastle 185 187 d.	1325	1418	...	1425	1518	...	1525	1618	...	1625	...	1718	...	1725	1818	...	1825	1925	...	...
Durham 185 187 d.	1337	1430	...	1437	1530	...	1537	1630	...	1637	...	1733	...	1737	1833	...	1837	1937	...	...
Darlington 185 187 d.	1354	1447	...	1454	1547	...	1554	1647	...	1654	...	1750	...	1754	1850	...	1854	1954	...	...
York 185 187 d.	1428	1520	...	1528	1620	...	1628	1720	...	1728	1740	1820	...	1828	1920	...	1928	2028	...	...
Leeds 185 d.	1500	|	...	1600	|	...	1700	|	...	1800	|	|	...	1900	|	...	2000	2100	...	...
Wakefield Westgate 185 d.	1512	|	...	1612	|	...	1712	|	...	1812	|	|	...	1912	|	...	2012	2112	...	...
Doncaster 185 194 d.	|	1550	...	|	1650	...	|	1720	...	|	1806	1850	...	|	1950	...	|	|	...	...
Sheffield 170 194 d.	1550	1620	...	1650	1720	...	1750	1820	...	1850	1832	1920	...	1950	2020	...	2050	2150	...	...
Chesterfield 170 d.	1602	|	...	1702	|	...	1802	|	...	1902	1844	|	...	2002	|	...	2102	2202	...	...
Derby 170 d.	1623	1651	...	1723	1751	...	1823	1851	...	1923	1908	1951	...	2023	2100	...	2123	2223	...	...
Burton on Trent d.	|	|	...	1735	|	...	|	|	...	1935	...	|	...	|	|	...	2135	2235	...	...
Tamworth d.	1643	|	...	|	|	...	1843	|	...	|	...	|	...	2043	|	...	2146	2246	...	...
Manchester Piccadilly 150 d.	|	|	1607	|	|	1707	|	|	1807	|	...	|	1907	|	|	2007	|	|	...	...
Birmingham New St a.	1702	1727	1731	1800	1827	1831	1902	1927	1931	2000	...	2027	2031	2101	2137	2139	2200	2309	...	...
Birmingham New St d.	1712	...	1742	1812	...	1842	1912	...	1942	2012	...	...	2042	2112	...	2142	2212	...	...	...
Cheltenham a.	1750	...	1824	1850	...	1924	1950	...	2024	2050	...	...	2124	2150	...	2224	2250	...	...	...
Bristol Parkway a.	1823	...	1908	1923	...	2000	2023	...	2057	2123	...	...	2159	2224	...	2257	2324	...	...	...
Bristol Temple Meads a.	1837	...	1925	1935	...	2014	2035	...	2114	2135	...	...	2214	2241	...	2314	2341	...	...	...
Exeter 115 a.	1948	...	...	2047	...	2126	2144	...	...	2244	...	...	...	...	...	...	...	...	...	...
Plymouth 115 a.	2048	...	...	2152	...	...	2248	...	...	2354	...	...	...	...	...	...	...	...	...	...

A – To / from Aberdeen.
B – To / from Bournemouth.
C – To / from Cardiff.
D – To / from Dundee.
E – To / from Leicester.
K – To / from Scarborough.
L – To / from London St Pancras.
N – To / from Newquay.
P – To / from Penzance.
R – To / from Reading.
S – To / from Southampton.
T – To / from Paignton.

128 LONDON - LEAMINGTON - STRATFORD and BIRMINGHAM

2nd class CH

km		Ⓐ	Ⓐ	Ⓐ	Ⓐ	Ⓐ	Ⓐ	Ⓐ	Ⓐ	Ⓐ	Ⓐ	Ⓐ	Ⓐ	Ⓐ	Ⓐ	Ⓐ		Ⓐ	Ⓐ	Ⓐ	Ⓐ	Ⓐ	Ⓐ	Ⓐ
0	**London** Marylebone ‡d.		...	...	0600	0650	0720	0723	0750	0820	0850	0854	0920	0950	1020	1050	...	1054	1120	1150	1220	1250	1254	1320
45	High Wycombe ‡d.		...	0607	0642	0720	0750	0800	0820	0850	0920	0925	0950	1020	1050	|	...	1128	1150	|	1250	|	1328	1350
111	Banbury 129 ‡d.		...	0702	0738	0805	0835	0845	0857	0935	0957	1014	1035	1057	1135	1157	...	1217	1235	1257	1335	1357	1417	1435
143	**Leamington Spa** 129 d.		0655	0722	...	0824	0853	0903	0915	0954	1015	1034	1054	1115	1154	1215	...	1238	1254	1315	1354	1415	1438	1454
146	Warwick d.		0658	0726	...	0828	0857	0908	0919	0958	1019	1038	1059	1119	1159	1219	...	1242	1259	1319	1359	1419	1442	1459
167	**Stratford upon Avon** a.		0730	|	...	|	|	0940	|	|	|	1109	|	|	|	|	...	1311	|	|	|	|	1509	|
169	Solihull d.		...	0750	...	0848	0920	...	0938	1022	1038	...	1118	1138	1222	1238	...	...	1318	1338	1422	1439	...	1518
180	**Birmingham** Snow Hill a.		...	0814	...	0907	0941	...	1001	1041	1101	...	1141	1201	1242	1302	...	...	1341	1401	1442	1502	...	1541

	Ⓐ	Ⓐ	Ⓐ	Ⓐ	Ⓐ	Ⓐ	Ⓐ		Ⓐ	Ⓐ	Ⓐ	Ⓐ	Ⓐ	Ⓐ	Ⓐ	Ⓐ	Ⓐ	Ⓐ	Ⓐ	Ⓐ	Ⓐ	Ⓐ	⑤	
London Marylebone ‡d.	1350	1420	1450	1454	1520	1600	1630	...	1636	1700	1730	1741	1800	1830	1900	1930	1933	2000	2030	2100	2133	2220	2310	...
High Wycombe ‡d.	|	1450	|	1528	1550	|	|	...	1705	|	|	1815	|	|	|	|	2004	|	2100	|	|	|	2345	...
Banbury 129 ‡d.	1457	1535	1557	1617	1635	1703	1733	...	1749	1803	1839	1858	1903	1936	2003	2038	2049	2106	2147	2210	2242	2330	0033	...
Leamington Spa 129 d.	1515	1554	1615	1638	1654	1722	1750	...	1807	1823	1858	1916	1922	1954	2023	2056	2107	2125	2205	2230	2300	2348	0052	...
Warwick d.	1519	1559	1619	1642	1659	1727	1756	...	1814p	1829p	1903	1920	1928p	1959	2029p	2100	2112	2131p	2210	2235p	2305	2353	0056	...
Stratford upon Avon a.	|	|	|	1712	|	|	|	...	1841	|	|	1951	|	|	|	|	2143	|	|	|	|	|	...	...
Solihull d.	1538	1622	1638	...	1720	1748	1817	...	...	1845	1927	...	1944	2022	2045	2124	...	2147	2235	2251	2323	0012	...	...
Birmingham Snow Hill a.	1601	1642	1701	...	1741	1812	1841	...	...	1901	1947	...	2001	2044	2103	2147	...	2204	2258	2305	2345	0032	...	...

	⑥	⑥	⑥	⑥	⑥	⑥	⑥	⑥	⑥	⑥	⑥	⑥	⑥	⑥		⑥	⑥	⑥	⑥	⑥	⑥	⑥	⑥	⑥
London Marylebone ‡d.		...	0627	...	0724	0818	0845	0854	0918	0945	1018	1050	1053	1120	...	1150	1220	1250	1253	1320	1350	1420	1450	1453
High Wycombe ‡d.		0610	0713	...	0810	0851	0914	0928	0951	1015	1048	|	1127	1149	...	|	1250	|	1327	1350	|	1450	|	1527
Banbury 129 ‡d.		0702	0801	0840	0858	0939	0958	1019	1039	1058	1135	1158	1219	1234	...	1258	1335	1358	1419	1435	1458	1535	1558	1619
Leamington Spa 129 d.		0721	0820	0900	0917	0958	1017	1038	1058	1117	1154	1217	1238	1253	...	1317	1354	1417	1438	1454	1517	1554	1617	1638
Warwick d.		0725	0824	0904	0921	1002	1021	1042	1102	1121	1159	1221	1242	1259	...	1321	1359	1421	1442	1459	1521	1559	1621	1642
Stratford upon Avon a.		|	|	0936	|	|	|	1113	|	|	|	|	1311	|	...	|	|	|	1510	|	|	|	|	1711
Solihull d.		0745	0850	...	0941	1022	1045	...	1122	1142	1222	1241	...	1319	...	1342	1422	1441	...	1519	1541	1622	1642	...
Birmingham Snow Hill a.		0808	0911	...	1002	1041	1104	...	1141	1201	1242	1301	...	1341	...	1401	1442	1501	...	1541	1601	1641	1702	...

	⑥	⑥	⑥	⑥	⑥	⑥	⑥	⑥	⑥	⑥	⑥	⑥	⑥	⑥	⑥		⑦	⑦	⑦	⑦	⑦	⑦	⑦	⑦
London Marylebone ‡d.	1520	1550	1620	1650	1653	1720	1750	1820	1850	1853	1920	2000	2050	2200	2245	...		0810	0915	0933	1017	1050	1120	1133
High Wycombe ‡d.	1549	|	1650	|	1727	1750	|	1850	|	1927	1950	2030	2121	|	2320	...		0840	0949	1008	1051	|	1154	1208
Banbury 129 ‡d.	1634	1658	1735	1758	1819	1835	1903	1935	2003	2019	2035	2119	2207	2306	0014	...		0927	1036	1101	1138	1202	1241	1301
Leamington Spa 129 d.	1653	1717	1754	1817	1838	1854	1923	1953	2023	2038	2054	2138	2227	2324	...	...		0946	1058	1121	1158	1222	1301	1321
Warwick d.	1659	1721	1759	1821	1842	1859	1927	1959	2027	2042	2059	2142	2231	2328	...	...		0951	1102	1125	1202	1227p	1305	1325
Stratford upon Avon a.	|	|	|	|	1913	|	|	|	|	2110	|	|	|	|	...	...		|	|	1159	|	|	|	1354
Solihull d.	1722	1742	1822	1841	...	1922	1948	2022	2047	...	2122	2203	2251	2349	...	...		1014	1123	...	1225	1244	1325	...
Birmingham Snow Hill a.	1741	1802	1841	1904	...	1941	2006	2042	2106	...	2141	2226	2310	0010	...	...		1039	1145	...	1244	1303	1346	...

	⑦	⑦	⑦	⑦	⑦	⑦	⑦	⑦	⑦	⑦	⑦	⑦	⑦	⑦	⑦	⑦	⑦	⑦	⑦	⑦	⑦	⑦	⑦	
London Marylebone ‡d.	1150	1220	1250	1320	1333	1350	1420	1450	1520	1533	1550	1620	1657	1720	1735	1757	1820	1857	1922	1957	2020	2050	2200	...
High Wycombe ‡d.	|	1254	|	1354	1408	|	1454	|	1554	1608	|	1654	|	1754	1810	|	1854	|	1956	|	2054	2124	|	...
Banbury 129 ‡d.	1305	1341	1402	1441	1501	1505	1540	1602	1641	1701	1705	1741	1809	1841	1901	1909	1941	2009	2044	2109	2141	2211	2306	...
Leamington Spa 129 d.	1326	1401	1422	1501	1521	1525	1559	1622	1701	1721	1725	1801	1829	1901	1921	1929	2003	2029	2103	2129	2201	2231	2324	...
Warwick d.	1331p	1405	1427p	1505	1525	1531p	1603	1627p	1705	1725	1731p	1805	1834p	1905	1925	1934p	2008	2034p	2108	2134p	2205	2235	2328	...
Stratford upon Avon a.	|	|	|	|	1554	|	|	|	|	1754	|	|	|	|	1954	|	|	|	|	|	|	|	|	...
Solihull d.	1347	1426	1444	1525	...	1548	1626	1644	1725	...	1747	1829	1851	1927	...	1951	2030	2051	2129	2151	2225	2259	2347	...
Birmingham Snow Hill a.	1408	1445	1503	1549	...	1606	1649	1703	1746	...	1807	1849	1910	1946	...	2010	2053	2110	2148	2210	2245	2318	0008	...

	Ⓐ	Ⓐ	Ⓐ	Ⓐ	Ⓐ	Ⓐ	Ⓐ	Ⓐ	Ⓐ	Ⓐ	Ⓐ	Ⓐ	Ⓐ	Ⓐ	Ⓐ		Ⓐ	Ⓐ	Ⓐ	Ⓐ	Ⓐ	Ⓐ	Ⓐ	Ⓐ
Birmingham Snow Hill d.		...	0543	...	0614	...	0650	0714	...	0745	0812	0852	0912	...	0952	...	1012	1052	1112	...	1152	1212	1252	1312
Solihull d.		...	0556	...	0627	...	0703	0728	...	0758	0825	0905	0925	...	1005	...	1025	1105	1125	...	1205	1225	1305	1325
Stratford upon Avon d.		...	|	0610	|	0646	|	|	0736	|	|	|	|	0942	|	...	|	|	|	1140	|	|	|	|
Warwick d.		0540	0615	0638	0644p	0713	0719p	0748	0805	0823	0844	0924	0949	1010	1024	...	1049	1124	1145	1203	1224	1249	1324	1345
Leamington Spa 129 d.		0545	0620	0645	0649	0718	0724	0752	0809	0827	0849	0929	0954	1014	1029	...	1054	1129	1152	1208	1229	1254	1329	1352
Banbury 129 ‡d.		0603	0638	...	0707	0736	0742	0810	0828	0845	0909	0947	1012	1032	1047	...	1112	1147	1209	1227	1247	1312	1347	1409
High Wycombe ‡d.		|	|	...	|	|	|	|	0916	|	0948	|	1057	1117	...	...	1157	|	1253	1317	|	1357	|	1453
London Marylebone ‡a.		0718	0753	...	0816	0851	0854	0925	0955	1001	1025	1058	1130	1157	1202	...	1230	1259	1329	1356	1359	1430	1459	1528

	Ⓐ	Ⓐ	Ⓐ	Ⓐ	Ⓐ	Ⓐ		Ⓐ	Ⓐ	Ⓐ	Ⓐ		Ⓐ	Ⓐ	Ⓐ	Ⓐ	Ⓐ	Ⓐ		Ⓐ	Ⓐ		Ⓐ	
Birmingham Snow Hill d.	...	1352	1412	1452	1512	...	...	1552	1612	1652	1710	...	...	1752	1812	1912	...	...	...	2012	2115	...	...	...
Solihull d.	...	1405	1425	1505	1525	...	...	1605	1625	1705	1723	...	...	1805	1825	1925	...	...	...	2025	2127	...	...	...
Stratford upon Avon d.	1340	|	|	|	|	1540	...	|	|	|	|	...	1740	|	|	|	1943	2000	...	|	|	...	2300	...
Warwick d.	1403	1424	1449	1524	1544	1603	...	1624	1649	1723	1749	...	1808	1826	1849	1950	2009	2023	...	2050	2151	...	2321	...
Leamington Spa 129 d.	1408	1429	1454	1529	1549	1608	...	1629	1654	1728	1754	...	1812	1830	1854	1954	2014	2033	...	2054	2155	...	2325	...
Banbury 129 ‡d.	1427	1447	1512	1547	1607	1627	...	1647	1712	1746	1812	...	1832	1848	1912	2012	2032	...	...	2112	2214	...	2343	...
High Wycombe ‡d.	1516	|	1557	|	1653	1719	...	1726	1756	1830	1857	...	1920	1928	1959	2056	2120	...	...	2156	2259	...	...	...
London Marylebone ‡a.	1553	1600	1631	1701	1731	1756	...	1805	1833	1908	1933	...	1958	2006	2035	2132	2157	...	...	2232	2333	...	...	...

	⑥	⑥	⑥	⑥	⑥	⑥	⑥	⑥	⑥	⑥	⑥	⑥	⑥	⑥	⑥		⑥	⑥	⑥	⑥	⑥	⑥	⑥	⑥
Birmingham Snow Hill d.		0612	0637	0712	...	0752	0812	0852	0912	...	0952	1012	1052	1112	...	...	1152	1212	1252	1312	...	1352	1412	1452
Solihull d.		0625	0650	0725	...	0805	0825	0905	0925	...	1005	1025	1105	1125	...	...	1205	1225	1305	1325	...	1405	1425	1505
Stratford upon Avon d.		|	|	|	0735	|	|	|	|	0938	|	|	|	|	1138	...	|	|	|	|	1340	|	|	|
Warwick d.		0645	0709	0748	0804	0825	0849	0925	0947	1004	1025	1048	1125	1145	1204	...	1225	1248	1325	1345	1404	1425	1448	1525
Leamington Spa 129 d.		0649	0714	0753	0809	0830	0853	0930	0952	1009	1030	1053	1130	1149	1209	...	1230	1253	1330	1349	1409	1430	1453	1530
Banbury 129 ‡d.		0707	0737	0813	0829	0849	0913	0949	1013	1029	1049	1113	1149	1207	1229	...	1249	1313	1349	1407	1429	1449	1513	1549
High Wycombe ‡d.		0753	|	0857	0918	|	0957	|	1057	1118	|	1157	|	1253	1318	...	|	1357	|	1453	1518	|	1557	|
London Marylebone ‡a.		0829	0847	0930	0955	1001	1034	1102	1132	1156	1159	1230	1301	1326	1358	...	1401	1432	1501	1530	1558	1601	1637	1659

	⑥	⑥	⑥	⑥	⑥	⑥	⑥	⑥	⑥	⑥	⑥	⑥	⑥			⑦	⑦	⑦	⑦	⑦	⑦	⑦	⑦	⑦
Birmingham Snow Hill d.	1512	...	1552	1612	1652	1712	...	1752	1812	1910	...	2010	2111	...	...		0840	0910	0940	...	1010	1040	1110	1140
Solihull d.	1525	...	1605	1625	1705	1725	...	1805	1825	1923	...	2023	2123	...	...		0852	0922	0952	...	1022	1052	1122	1152
Stratford upon Avon d.	|	1539	|	|	|	|	1736	|	|	|	1953	|	|	...	...		|	|	|	1000	|	|	|	|
Warwick d.	1545	1604	1625	1648	1725	1748	1804	1825	1849	1947	2019	2047	2147	...	...		0912	0941	1009p	1025	1041	1112p	1141	1209p
Leamington Spa 129 d.	1549	1609	1630	1653	1730	1753	1809	1830	1853	1952	2023	2052	2152	...	...		0917	0947	1016	1029	1047	1118	1147	1216
Banbury 129 ‡d.	1607	1629	1649	1713	1749	1813	1829	1849	1913	2013	2042	2115	2215	...	...		0936	1006	1035	1048	1106	1137	1206	1235
High Wycombe ‡d.	1653	1718	|	1757	1828	1857	1918	1928	2000	2100	2133	2202	2304	...	...		|	|	1122	1136	|	1225	|	1322
London Marylebone ‡a.	1729	1758	1801	1832	1902	1930	1956	2002	2037	2137	2221	2240	2340	...	...		1051	1123	1158	1217	1222	1301	1322	1358

	⑦	⑦	⑦	⑦	⑦	⑦	⑦	⑦		⑦	⑦	⑦	⑦	⑦	⑦	⑦	⑦	⑦	⑦		⑦	⑦	⑦	⑦
Birmingham Snow Hill d.	...	1210	1240	1310	1340	...	1410	1440	...	1510	1540	...	1610	1640	1710	1740	...	1810	1840	...	1910	...	2015	2115
Solihull d.	...	1222	1252	1322	1352	...	1422	1452	...	1522	1552	...	1622	1652	1722	1752	...	1822	1852	...	1921	...	2028	2128
Stratford upon Avon d.	1200	|	|	|	|	1400	|	|	...	|	|	1600	|	|	|	|	1800	|	|	...	|	1957	|	|
Warwick d.	1225	1241	1309p	1341	1412p	1425	1442	1509p	...	1541	1612p	1625	1641	1709p	1741	1812p	1825	1841	1909p	...	1946	2022	2049	2149
Leamington Spa 129 d.	1229	1247	1316	1347	1418	1429	1447	1516	...	1547	1618	1629	1647	1716	1747	1818	1829	1847	1916	...	1954	2026	2054	2154
Banbury 129 ‡d.	1248	1306	1335	1406	1437	1448	1506	1535	...	1606	1637	1648	1706	1735	1806	1837	1848	1906	1935	...	2013	2048	2113	2215
High Wycombe ‡d.	1336	|	1422	|	1525	1536	|	1622	...	|	1725	1736	|	1822	|	1925	1936	|	2022	...	2103	2136	2203	2307
London Marylebone ‡a.	1416	1422	1500	1523	1601	1616	1622	1658	...	1723	1802	1816	1821	1858	1922	2002	2016	2021	2058	...	2152	2216	2252	2353

p – Warwick Parkway.

‡ – Additional trains run London - Banbury and v.v.

Stratford upon Avon – Birmingham Snow Hill

2nd class LM

⚒: 0631 Ⓐ, 0654 Ⓐ, 0700 ⑥, 0723 Ⓐ, 0745, 0827 and hourly until 1527; then 1623, 1727, 1758, 1819 ⑥, 1826 Ⓐ, 1846 ⑥, 1850 Ⓐ, 1927, 2027.

⑦: *Valid until November 1.* 0928, 1028 and hourly until 1928.

☛ Trains also call at Birmingham Moor St. All trains and buses call at **Henley in Arden** (*13 km*, ± 13 mins by train, 21 mins by bus, from Stratford).

Birmingham Snow Hill – Stratford upon Avon

40 km Journey: ± 55 mins

⚒: 0558 Ⓐ, 0629 Ⓐ, 0643 Ⓐ, 0720 ⑥, 0725 Ⓐ, 0747⑥, 0827, 0927 and hourly until 1525; then 1627, 1702 Ⓐ, 1727, 1747, 1827, 1927, 2027.

⑦: *Valid until November 1.* 0919, 1022, 1119, 1219 and hourly until 1819.

☛ Trains also call (3 mins later) at Birmingham Moor St. All trains and buses (except the 0558 Ⓐ) call at **Henley in Arden** (*27 km*, ± 38 mins by train, 99 mins by bus, from Birmingham).

XC All services 🍷 BOURNEMOUTH - READING - BIRMINGHAM 129

Services on ⑥ valid until September 5. Services on ⑦ valid until July 12.

km			Ⓐ	Ⓐ	Ⓐ	Ⓐ	Ⓐ	Ⓐ	Ⓐ	Ⓐ	Ⓐ	Ⓐ	Ⓐ	Ⓐ	Ⓐ	Ⓐ	Ⓐ	Ⓐ	Ⓐ	Ⓐ	Ⓐ	Ⓐ E	Ⓐ	Ⓐ
0	**Bournemouth** ... 108 d.	Ⓐ	...	...	...	...	0630	...	0730	...	0845	...	0945	...	1045	...	1145	...	1245	...	1345	...	1445	...
25	Brockenhurst ... 108 d.		...	...	...	...	0649	...	0749	...	0900	...	1000	...	1100	...	1200	...	1300	...	1400	...	1500	...
46	**Southampton** Central ... 108 d.		0515	...	0615	...	0715	...	0815	...	0915	...	1015	...	1115	...	1215	...	1315	...	1415	...	1515	...
54	**Southampton** Airport ✈ . 108 d.		0522	...	0622	...	0722	...	0822	...	0922	...	1022	...	1122	...	1222	...	1322	...	1422	...	1522	...
67	Winchester ... 108 d.		0531	...	0631	...	0731	...	0831	...	0931	...	1031	...	1131	...	1231	...	1331	...	1431	...	1531	...
97	Basingstoke ... 108 d.		0547	...	0647	...	0747	...	0847	...	0947	...	1047	...	1147	...	1247	...	1347	...	1447	...	1547	...
122	**Reading** ... 105 132 d.		0610	0640	0710	0740	0810	0840	0910	0940	1010	1040	1110	1140	1210	1240	1310	1340	1410	1440	1510	1540	1610	1640
166	Oxford ... 132 d.		0635	0705	0735	0805	0835	0905	0935	1005	1035	1105	1135	1205	1235	1305	1335	1405	1435	1505	1535	1605	1635	1705
203	Banbury ... 128 d.		0654	0725	0754	0825	0854	0925	0954	1025	1054	1125	1154	1225	1254	1325	1354	1425	1454	1525	1554	1625	1654	1725
235	**Leamington Spa** ... 128 d.		0712	0743	0812	0843	0912	0943	1012	1043	1112	1143	1212	1243	1312	1343	1412	1443	1512	1543	1612	1643	1712	1743
250	Coventry ... 142 143 d.		0727	|	0827	|	0927	|	1027	|	1127	|	1227	|	1327	|	1427	|	1527	|	1627	|	1727	|
267	Birmingham Intl. ✈ . 142 143 d.		0738	|	0838	|	0938	|	1038	|	1138	|	1238	|	1338	|	1438	|	1538	|	1638	|	1738	|
280	**Birmingham** New St. 142 143 a.		0749	0817	0849	0917	0949	1017	1049	1117	1149	1217	1249	1317	1349	1417	1449	1517	1549	1617	1649	1717	1749	1817
	Manchester Piccadilly 150 .. a.		0940	|	1040	|	1140	|	1240	|	1340	|	1440	|	1540	|	1640	|	1740	|	1840	|	1940	|
	York 127 ... a.		...	1040	...	1145	...	1245	...	1346	...	1443	...	1540	...	1640	...	1740	...	1858	...	1944	...	2046
	Newcastle 127 ... a.		...	1154	...	1305	...	1351	...	1456	...	1558	...	1651	...	1754	...	1855	...	2018	...	2048	...	2200

	Ⓐ	Ⓐ	Ⓐ	Ⓐ	Ⓐ	Ⓐ	Ⓐ	Ⓐ	Ⓐ	Ⓐ			⑥	⑥	⑥	⑥	⑥	⑥	⑥	⑥	⑥	⑥	⑥	⑥
Bournemouth ... 108 d.	1545	...	1645	...	1745	...	1845	...	1945	...	...	⑥	...	...	...	0625	0637	...	0745	...	0845	...	0945	...
Brockenhurst ... 108 d.	1600	...	1700	...	1800	...	1900	...	2000	...	...		...	...	...	0639	0655	...	0800	...	0900	...	1000	...
Southampton Central ... 108 d.	1615	...	1715	...	1815	...	1915	...	2015	...	...		0509	...	0615	0653	0715	...	0815	...	0915	...	1015	...
Southampton Airport ✈ 108 d.	1622	...	1722	...	1822	...	1922	...	2022	...	...		0516	...	0622	0701	0722	...	0822	...	0922	...	1022	...
Winchester ... 108 d.	1631	...	1731	...	1831	...	1931	...	2031	...	...		0525	...	0631	0709	0731	...	0831	...	0931	...	1031	...
Basingstoke ... 108 d.	1647	...	1747	...	1847	...	1947	...	2047	...	...		0541	...	0647	0725	0747	...	0847	...	0947	...	1047	...
Reading ... 105 132 d.	1710	1740	1810	1840	1910	1940	2010	2040	2110	2145	...		0610	0646	0710	0745	0810	0840	0910	0940	1010	1040	1110	1140
Oxford ... 132 d.	1735	1805	1835	1905	1935	2005	2035	2122	2135	2230	...		0636	0712	0736	0815	0836	0907	0936	1007	1036	1107	1136	1207
Banbury ... 128 d.	1754	1825	1854	1925	1954	2025	2054	2141	2154	2253	...		0653	0731	0753	0835	0853	0925	0953	1025	1053	1125	1153	1225
Leamington Spa ... 128 d.	1812	1843	1912	1943	2012	2043	2112	2200	2212	2312	...		0711	0749	0811	0853	0911	0943	1011	1043	1111	1143	1211	1243
Coventry ... 142 143 d.	1827	|	1927	|	2027	|	2127	|	2224	|	...		0727	|	0827	|	0927	|	1027	|	1127	|	1227	|
Birmingham Intl. ✈ 142 143 d.	1838	|	1938	|	2038	|	2138	|	2234	|	...		0738	|	0838	|	0938	|	1038	|	1138	|	1238	|
Birmingham New St 142 143 a.	1849	1917	1949	2017	2049	2122	2149	2235	2250	2355	...		0749	0817	0849	0917	0949	1017	1049	1117	1149	1217	1249	1317
Manchester Piccadilly 150 . a.	2040	|	2140	|	2240	...	2340	...	...	...	...		0940	|	1040	|	1140	|	1240	|	1340	|	1440	|
York 127 ... a.	...	2145	...	2259	...	...	...	...	...	...	...		...	1044	...	1144	...	1244	...	1344	...	1444	...	1544
Newcastle 127 ... a.	...	2256	...	...	...	...	...	...	...	...	...		...	1154	...	1255	...	1350	...	1455	...	1551	...	1651

	⑥	⑥	⑥	⑥	⑥		⑥	⑥	⑥ E	⑥	⑥		⑥	⑥	⑥	⑥	⑥ L		⑥	⑥	⑥	⑥		⑥
Bournemouth ... 108 d.	1045	...	1145	...	1245	...	...	1345	...	1445	...	...	1545	...	1645	...	1745	...	...	1845	...	1945	...	...
Brockenhurst ... 108 d.	1100	...	1200	...	1300	...	...	1400	...	1500	...	...	1600	...	1700	...	1800	...	...	1900	...	2000	...	...
Southampton Central ... 108 d.	1115	...	1215	...	1315	...	...	1415	...	1515	...	...	1615	...	1715	...	1815	...	...	1915	...	2015	...	...
Southampton Airport ✈ 108 d.	1122	...	1222	...	1322	...	...	1422	...	1522	...	...	1622	...	1722	...	1822	...	...	1922	...	2022	...	...
Winchester ... 108 d.	1131	...	1231	...	1331	...	...	1431	...	1531	...	...	1631	...	1731	...	1831	...	...	1931	...	2031	...	...
Basingstoke ... 108 d.	1147	...	1247	...	1347	...	...	1447	...	1547	...	...	1647	...	1747	...	1847	...	...	1947	...	2047	...	...
Reading ... 105 132 d.	1210	1240	1310	1340	1410	...	1440	1510	1540	1610	1640	...	1710	1740	1810	1840	1910	...	1940	2010	2040	2110	...	2140
Oxford ... 132 d.	1236	1307	1336	1407	1436	...	1507	1536	1607	1636	1707	...	1736	1807	1836	1907	1936	...	2007	2036	2107	2136	...	2207
Banbury ... 128 d.	1253	1325	1353	1425	1453	...	1525	1553	1625	1653	1725	...	1753	1825	1853	1925	1953	...	2025	2053	2125	2153	...	2225
Leamington Spa ... 128 d.	1311	1343	1411	1443	1511	...	1543	1611	1643	1711	1743	...	1811	1843	1911	1943	2011	...	2043	2111	2143	2211	...	2243
Coventry ... 142 143 d.	1327	|	1427	|	1527	...	|	1627	|	1727	|	...	1827	|	1927	|	2027	...	|	2127	2156	2227	...	|
Birmingham Intl. ✈ 142 143 d.	1338	|	1438	|	1538	...	|	1638	|	1738	|	...	1838	|	1938	|	2038	...	|	2138	2213	2238	...	|
Birmingham New St 142 143 a.	1349	1417	1449	1517	1549	...	1617	1649	1717	1749	1817	...	1849	1917	1949	2017	2049	...	2117	2149	2225	2254	...	2317
Manchester Piccadilly 150 . a.	1540	|	1640	|	1740	...	|	1840	|	1940	|	...	2040	|	2140	|	...	...	...	2335	...	...	...	...
York 127 ... a.	...	1644	...	1744	...	...	1859	...	1944	...	2040	...	...	2148	...	2248	...	...	...	...	...	...	...	...
Newcastle 127 ... a.	...	1753	...	1850	...	...	2018	...	2137	...	2155	...	...	2310	...	...	...	...	...	...	...	...	...	...

		⑦	⑦	⑦	⑦	⑦	⑦	⑦	⑦	⑦	⑦	⑦ E	⑦	⑦	⑦	⑦	⑦	⑦	⑦	⑦	⑦	⑦	⑦	⑦
Bournemouth ... 108 d.	⑦	...	...	0940	1040	...	1140	...	1240	...	1340	...	1440	...	1540	...	1640	...	1740	...	1840	...	1940	...
Brockenhurst ... 108 d.		...	...	0957	1057	...	1157	...	1257	...	1357	...	1457	...	1557	...	1657	...	1757	...	1857	...	1957	...
Southampton Central ... 108 d.		...	0915	1015	1115	...	1215	...	1315	...	1415	...	1515	...	1615	...	1715	...	1815	...	1915	...	2015	...
Southampton Airport ✈ 108 d.		...	0922	1022	1122	...	1222	...	1322	...	1422	...	1522	...	1622	...	1722	...	1822	...	1922	...	2022	...
Winchester ... 108 d.		...	0931	1031	1131	...	1231	...	1331	...	1431	...	1531	...	1631	...	1731	...	1831	...	1931	...	2031	...
Basingstoke ... 108 d.		...	0947	1047	1147	...	1247	...	1347	...	1447	...	1547	...	1647	...	1747	...	1847	...	1947	...	2047	...
Reading ... 105 132 d.		0911	1011	1111	1211	1254	1311	1340	1411	1440	1511	1540	1611	1640	1711	1740	1811	1840	1911	1940	2011	2040	2111	2140
Oxford ... 132 d.		0937	1037	1137	1237	1317	1337	1406	1437	1506	1537	1606	1637	1706	1737	1806	1837	1906	1937	2006	2037	2106	2137	2206
Banbury ... 128 d.		0953	1053	1153	1253	1335	1353	1425	1453	1525	1553	1625	1653	1725	1753	1825	1853	1925	1953	2025	2053	2125	2153	2225
Leamington Spa ... 128 d.		1011	1111	1211	1311	1353	1411	1443	1511	1543	1611	1643	1711	1743	1811	1843	1911	1943	2011	2043	2111	2143	2211	2243
Coventry ... 142 143 d.		1028	1128	1228	1326	|	1426	|	1526	|	1626	|	1726	|	1826	|	1926	1954	2026	2054	2126	2154	2223	2254
Birmingham Intl. ✈ 142 143 d.		1040	1140	1240	1338	|	1438	|	1538	|	1638	|	1738	|	1838	|	1938	2004	2038	2104	2138	2204	2233	2304
Birmingham New St 142 143 a.		1051	1151	1251	1349	1418	1449	1509	1549	1609	1649	1709	1749	1809	1849	1909	1949	2015	2049	2120	2149	2220	2306	2335
Manchester Piccadilly 150 . a.		1240	1340	1440	1540	|	1640	|	1740	|	1840	|	1940	|	2040	|	2140	|	2240	...	2345	...	...	...
York 127 ... a.		...	...	...	...	1640	...	1742	...	1921	...	1942	...	2044	...	2142	...	2253	...	...	...	...	...	...
Newcastle 127 ... a.		...	...	...	...	1753	...	1847	...	2030	...	2043	...	2159	...	2248	...	...	...	...	...	...	...	...

E – To / from Edinburgh.

L – To / from Leeds.

129 BIRMINGHAM - READING - BOURNEMOUTH

All services 🍷 XC

Services on ⑥ valid until September 5. Services on ⑦ valid until July 12.

		Ⓐ	Ⓐ	Ⓐ	Ⓐ	Ⓐ	Ⓐ	Ⓐ	Ⓐ	Ⓐ	Ⓐ	Ⓐ	Ⓐ	Ⓐ	Ⓐ	Ⓐ	Ⓐ	Ⓐ	Ⓐ	Ⓐ	Ⓐ	Ⓐ	Ⓐ
					S	D	L						E										
Newcastle **127** d.	Ⓐ	...	...	...	...	...	...	...	0621	...	0723	...	0824	...	0933	...	1025	...	1127	...	1219	...	1334
York **127** d.		...	...	...	...	...	...	...	0727	...	0827	...	0927	...	1034	...	1127	...	1227	...	1326	...	1432
Manchester Piccadilly **150** d.		...	...	0500	...	...	...	0726	|	0827	|	0927	|	1027	|	1127	|	1227	|	1327	|	1427	|
Birmingham New St **142 143** d.		0604	0633	0704	0733	0804	0833	0904	0933	1004	1033	1104	1133	1204	1233	1304	1333	1404	1433	1504	1533	1604	1633
Birmingham Intl. ✈ **142 143** d.		0614	|	0714	|	0814	|	0914	|	1014	|	1114	|	1214	|	1314	|	1414	|	1514	|	1614	|
Coventry **142 143** d.		0625	|	0725	|	0825	|	0925	|	1025	|	1125	|	1225	|	1325	|	1425	|	1525	|	1625	|
Leamington Spa **128** d.		0638	0700	0738	0800	0838	0900	0938	1000	1038	1100	1138	1200	1238	1300	1338	1400	1438	1500	1538	1600	1638	1700
Banbury **128** a.		0654	0718	0754	0818	0854	0918	0954	1018	1054	1118	1154	1218	1254	1318	1354	1418	1454	1518	1554	1618	1654	1718
Oxford **132** a.		0714	0741	0814	0841	0914	0941	1014	1041	1114	1141	1214	1241	1314	1341	1414	1441	1514	1541	1614	1641	1714	1741
Reading **105 132** a.		0740	0813	0840	0913	0940	1013	1040	1113	1140	1213	1240	1313	1340	1413	1440	1513	1540	1613	1640	1713	1740	1813
Basingstoke **108** a.		0808	...	0908	...	1008	...	1108	...	1208	...	1308	...	1408	...	1507	...	1608	...	1708	...	1808	...
Winchester **108** a.		0824	...	0924	...	1024	...	1124	...	1224	...	1324	...	1424	...	1524	...	1624	...	1724	...	1824	...
Southampton Airport ✈ **108** a.		0832	...	0932	...	1032	...	1132	...	1232	...	1332	...	1432	...	1532	...	1632	...	1732	...	1833	...
Southampton Central **108** a.		0841	...	0943	...	1043	...	1143	...	1241	...	1341	...	1440	...	1541	...	1641	...	1741	...	1841	...
Brockenhurst **108** a.		0850	...	0957	...	1057	...	1157	...	1256	...	1356	...	1456	...	1556	...	1656	...	1756	...	1856	...
Bournemouth **108** a.		0915	...	1015	...	1115	...	1215	...	1315	...	1415	...	1515	...	1615	...	1715	...	1815	...	1915	...

	Ⓐ	Ⓐ	Ⓐ	Ⓐ	Ⓐ	Ⓐ	Ⓐ	Ⓐ	Ⓐ	Ⓐ			⑥	⑥	⑥	⑥	⑥	⑥	⑥	⑥	⑥	⑥	⑥
																S	D	L					
Newcastle **127** d.	...	1427	...	1522	...	1632	...	1717	...	...	...	⑥	...	...	...	...	...	...	...	0620	...	0725	...
York **127** d.	...	1529	...	1625	...	1734	...	1824	...	...	...		...	...	...	...	...	...	...	0725	...	0827	...
Manchester Piccadilly **150** d.	1527	|	1627	|	1727	|	1827	|	1927	...	...		...	...	0511	...	...	...	0727	|	0827	|	0927
Birmingham New St **142 143** d.	1704	1733	1804	1833	1904	1933	2004	2033	2104	2204	...		0604	0633	0704	0733	0804	0833	0904	0933	1004	1033	1104
Birmingham Intl. ✈ **142 143** d.	1714	|	1814	|	1914	|	2014	|	2114	2214	...		0614	|	0714	|	0814	|	0914	|	1014	|	1114
Coventry **142 143** d.	1725	|	1825	|	1925	|	2025	|	2125	2225	...		0625	|	0725	|	0825	|	0925	|	1025	|	1125
Leamington Spa **128** d.	1738	1800	1838	1900	1938	2000	2038	2100	2138	2238	...		0638	0700	0738	0800	0838	0900	0938	1000	1038	1100	1138
Banbury **128** a.	1754	1818	1854	1918	1954	2018	2054	2118	2154	2254	...		0654	0717	0754	0817	0854	0917	0954	1017	1054	1117	1154
Oxford **132** a.	1814	1841	1914	1941	2014	2041	2114	2141	2214	2314	...		0714	0740	0814	0840	0914	0940	1014	1040	1114	1140	1214
Reading **105 132** a.	1840	1913	1940	2013	2040	2113	2140	2219	2240	2357	...		0740	0813	0840	0913	0940	1013	1040	1113	1140	1213	1240
Basingstoke **108** a.	1908	...	2009	...	2108	...	2208	...	2212	...	...		0808	...	0908	...	1008	...	1108	...	1208	...	1308
Winchester **108** a.	1924	...	2024	...	2124	...	2224	...	2228	...	...		0824	...	0924	...	1024	...	1124	...	1224	...	1324
Southampton Airport ✈ **108** a.	1933	...	2033	...	2133	...	2232	...	2337	...	...		0832	...	0932	...	1032	...	1132	...	1232	...	1332
Southampton Central **108** a.	1941	...	2041	...	2141	...	2241	...	0052	...	...		0841	...	0940	...	1040	...	1141	...	1241	...	1341
Brockenhurst **108** a.	1956	...	2056	...	2156	...	2356	...	...	...	...		0856	...	0957	...	1057	...	1157	...	1257	...	1357
Bournemouth **108** a.	2015	...	2115	...	2221	...	2321	...	...	...	...		0915	...	1015	...	1115	...	1215	...	1315	...	1415

	⑥	⑥	⑥	⑥	⑥	⑥	⑥	⑥	⑥	⑥	⑥	⑥	⑥	⑥	⑥	⑥	⑥	⑥	⑥	⑥			⑦
	E																						
Newcastle **127** d.	0830	...	0925	...	1025	...	1120	...	1222	...	1327	...	1422	...	1525	...	1622	...	1722	...	...	⑦	...
York **127** d.	0928	...	1025	...	1127	...	1225	...	1327	...	1427	...	1526	...	1625	...	1725	...	1825	...	...		...
Manchester Piccadilly **150** d.	|	1027	|	1127	|	1227	|	1327	|	1427	|	1527	|	1627	|	1727	|	1827	|	1927	...		...
Birmingham New St **142 143** d.	1133	1204	1233	1304	1333	1404	1433	1504	1533	1604	1633	1704	1733	1804	1833	1904	1933	2004	2033	2104	...		0904
Birmingham Intl. ✈ **142 143** d.	|	1214	|	1314	|	1414	|	1514	|	1614	|	1714	|	1814	|	1914	|	2014	|	2114	...		0914
Coventry **142 143** d.	|	1225	|	1325	|	1425	|	1525	|	1625	|	1725	|	1825	|	1925	|	2025	|	2125	...		0925
Leamington Spa **128** d.	1200	1238	1300	1338	1400	1438	1500	1538	1600	1638	1700	1738	1800	1838	1900	1938	2000	2038	2100	2138	...		0938
Banbury **128** a.	1217	1254	1317	1354	1417	1454	1517	1554	1617	1654	1717	1754	1817	1854	1917	1954	2017	2054	2117	2154	...		0954
Oxford **132** a.	1240	1314	1340	1414	1440	1514	1540	1514	1640	1714	1740	1814	1840	1914	1940	2014	2040	2114	2140	2214	...		1014
Reading **105 132** a.	1313	1340	1413	1440	1513	1540	1613	1640	1713	1740	1813	1840	1913	1940	2013	2040	2113	2140	2213	2240	...		1042
Basingstoke **108** a.	...	1408	...	1508	...	1608	...	1708	...	1808	...	1908	...	2008	...	2108	...	2208	...	2311	...		1109
Winchester **108** a.	...	1424	...	1524	...	1624	...	1724	...	1824	...	1924	...	2024	...	2124	...	2224	...	2327	...		1124
Southampton Airport ✈ **108** a.	...	1433	...	1532	...	1632	...	1732	...	1832	...	1932	...	2032	...	2132	...	2232	...	2335	...		1133
Southampton Central **108** a.	...	1441	...	1541	...	1641	...	1741	...	1840	...	1941	...	2041	...	2141	...	2241	...	2348	...		1142
Brockenhurst **108** a.	...	1457	...	1557	...	1657	...	1757	...	1857	...	1957	...	2057	...	2157	...	2257	...	...	...		1201
Bournemouth **108** a.	...	1515	...	1615	...	1715	...	1815	...	1915	...	2015	...	2115	...	2215	...	2321	...	...	...		1227

	⑦	⑦	⑦	⑦	⑦	⑦	⑦	⑦	⑦	⑦	⑦	⑦	⑦	⑦	⑦	⑦	⑦	⑦	⑦	⑦	⑦		⑦
									D		S						E						
Newcastle **127** d.	...	...	...	...	...	...	...	...	...	...	...	...	1315	...	1418	...	1518	...	1618	...	1718	...	...
York **127** d.	...	...	...	...	...	...	...	...	...	...	...	...	1419	...	1520	...	1620	...	1720	...	1820	...	...
Manchester Piccadilly **150** d.	0827	0927	...	1026	...	1126	...	1226	...	1327	...	1427	|	1527	|	1627	|	1727	|	1827	|	...	1927
Birmingham New St **142 143** d.	1004	1104	1133	1204	1233	1304	1333	1404	1433	1504	1533	1604	1633	1704	1729	1804	1833	1904	1933	2004	2033	...	2104
Birmingham Intl. ✈ **142 143** d.	1014	1114	|	1214	|	1314	|	1414	|	1514	|	1614	|	1714	|	1814	|	1914	|	2014	|	...	2114
Coventry **142 143** d.	1025	1125	|	1225	|	1325	|	1425	|	1525	|	1625	|	1725	|	1825	|	1925	|	2025	|	...	2124
Leamington Spa **128** d.	1038	1138	1200	1238	1300	1338	1400	1438	1500	1538	1600	1638	1700	1738	1800	1838	1900	1938	2000	2038	2100	...	2135
Banbury **128** a.	1054	1154	1218	1254	1318	1354	1418	1454	1518	1554	1618	1654	1718	1754	1818	1854	1918	1954	2018	2054	2118	...	|
Oxford **132** a.	1114	1214	1247	1314	1341	1414	1445	1514	1541	1614	1641	1714	1741	1814	1845	1914	1941	2014	2041	2114	2138	...	2208
Reading **105 132** a.	1142	1242	1315	1342	1413	1442	1515	1542	1613	1642	1715	1742	1813	1842	1915	1942	2013	2042	2113	2142	2212	...	2242
Basingstoke **108** a.	1209	1309	...	1409	...	1509	...	1609	...	1709	...	1809	...	1909	...	2009	...	2109	...	2211	2230	...	...
Winchester **108** a.	1224	1324	...	1424	...	1524	...	1624	...	1724	...	1824	...	1924	...	2024	...	2124	...	2226	|	...	...
Southampton Airport ✈ **108** a.	1233	1333	...	1433	...	1533	...	1633	...	1733	...	1833	...	1933	...	2033	...	2133	...	2235	2335	...	...
Southampton Central **108** a.	1242	1342	...	1442	...	1542	...	1642	...	1740	...	1842	...	1940	...	2042	...	2142	...	2247	2347	...	...
Brockenhurst **108** a.	1301	1401	...	1501	...	1601	...	1701	...	1801	...	1901	...	2001	...	2101	...	2201	...	...	...	...	...
Bournemouth **108** a.	1327	1427	...	1527	...	1627	...	1727	...	1827	...	1927	...	2027	...	2127	...	2227	...	...	...	...	...

A – To / from Aberdeen.
D – To / from Derby.
E – To / from Edinburgh.
G – To / from Glasgow.
L – To / from Leeds.
S – To / from Sheffield.

GW LONDON - WORCESTER - HEREFORD 131

Services on ⑦ valid until September 6.

km			Ⓐ	Ⓐ	Ⓐ 🍷	Ⓐ 🍷	Ⓐ 🍷	Ⓐ 🍷	Ⓐ 🍷	Ⓐ	Ⓐ	Ⓐ 🍷	Ⓐ	Ⓐ 🍷	Ⓐ 🍷	Ⓐ 🍷	Ⓐ 🍷	Ⓐ 🍷 A	Ⓐ 🍷 A			⑥	⑥	⑥	⑥ 🍷
0	**London** Paddington ..... 132 d.	Ⓐ	...	0542	0648	0822	0921	1022	1122	1321	1421	1551	...	1722	1751	1821	1922	2020	2148	...	⑥	0521	0621	0721	0821
58	Reading ..... 132 d.		...	0621	0721	0853	0953	1053	1153	1353	1453	1622	...	1750	1821	1851	1937	2051	2223	...		0554	0653	0753	0854
103	**Oxford** ..... 132 d.		...	0654	0804	0921	1026	1119	1219	1419	1519	1647	1731	1816	1854	1919	2022	2117	2252	...		0624	0718	0820	0920
148	Moreton in Marsh ..... d.		0537	0731	0834	0959	1101	1157	1257	1457	1558	1726	1815	1855	1935	1959	2100	2155	2334	...		0702	0800	0900	1000
172	Evesham ..... a.		0551	0751	0853	1019	1116	1217	1317	1517	...	1746	1833	1915	1952	2019	2120	2215	2354	...		0721	0822	0922	1019
172	Evesham ..... d.		0606	0756	0854	1029	1118	1229	1319	1519	...	1747	1841	1921	1957	2020	2125	2216	2355	...		0723	0824	0924	1024
194	**Worcester** Shrub Hill ..... 123 a.		0630	0817	0916	1051	1135	1250	1339	1539	...	1808	1911	1944	2023	2041	2145	2236	0016	...		0742	0844	0943	1044
195	**Worcester** Foregate St. 123 a.		0636	0821	0919	1055	1142	1254	1343	1547	...	...	1917	1948	...	2045	2152	2247	...	...		0746	0848	0948	1048
208	Great Malvern ..... 123 a.		...	0837	0934	1109	...	1307	1400	1604	...	...	...	2002	...	2058	2209	2303	...	...		0804	0907	1005	1101
219	Ledbury ..... 123 a.		...	...	...	1123	...	1323	...	...	...	...	...	2016	...	2112	2235	...	...	...		...	...	...	1121
241	**Hereford** ..... 123 a.		...	...	...	1147	...	1348	...	...	...	...	...	2037	...	2136	2257	...	...	...		...	...	...	1140

	⑥ 🍷	⑥ 🍷	⑥ 🍷	⑥ 🍷	⑥ 🍷	⑥ 🍷	⑥ 🍷	⑥ 🍷	⑥ 🍷	⑥			⑦	⑦ 🍷	⑦ 🍷	⑦ 🍷		⑦ 🍷	⑦ 🍷	⑦ 🍷	⑦ 🍷		⑦ 🍷	⑦	⑦ 🍷
London Paddington ..... 132 d.	1021	1121	1321	1421	1521	1621	1721	1821	1950	2150	...	⑦	0803	0935	1042	1242	...	1442	1542	1642	1742	...	1842	1942	2127
Reading ..... 132 d.	1054	1154	1354	1454	1554	1654	1754	1854	2023	2222	...		0844	1012	1120	1320	...	1520	1621	1721	1821	...	1920	2020	2210
Oxford ..... 132 d.	1120	1224	1420	1520	1620	1720	1820	1920	2049	2250	...		0915	1043	1150	1350	...	1550	1650	1750	1853	...	1950	2050	2240
Moreton in Marsh ..... d.	1200	1303	1503	1600	1700	1803	1900	2000	2128	2329	...		0957	1123	1230	1431	...	1629	1724	1829	1929	...	2030	2127	2322
Evesham ..... a.	1219	1322	1522	1619	1722	1822	1919	2019	2146	2347	...		1015	1142	1249	1447	...	1648	1740	1848	1948	...	2049	2144	2340
Evesham ..... d.	1221	1328	1528	1625	1724	1825	1922	2027	2149	2349	...		1017	1144	1252	1449	...	1650	1748	1851	1951	...	2055	2148	2343
Worcester Shrub Hill ..... 123 a.	1241	1348	1548	1644	1744	1844	1941	2046	2208	0011	...		1036	1203	1311	1509	...	1710	1808	1911	2008	...	2114	2207	0004
Worcester Foregate St. 123 a.	1248	1352	1552	1648	1748	1854	1945	2050	2211	...	...		1038	1207	1315	1513	...	1714	...	1915	2015	...	2118	2224	...
Great Malvern ..... 123 a.	1301	1409	1609	1706	1805	1907	...	2104	2227	...	...		1054	1221	1329	1526	...	1727	...	1929	2029	...	2132	2240	...
Ledbury ..... 123 a.	1321	...	...	...	...	1921	...	2118	...	...	...		...	1235	1343	1541	...	1742	...	...	...	...	2146	...	...
Hereford ..... 123 a.	1340	...	...	...	...	1945	...	2137	...	...	...		...	1258	1405	1606	...	1801	...	...	...	...	2205	...	...

		Ⓐ 🍷	Ⓐ 🍷	Ⓐ	Ⓐ	Ⓐ	Ⓐ	Ⓐ 🍷	Ⓐ 🍷	Ⓐ 🍷	Ⓐ 🍷	Ⓐ	Ⓐ 🍷	Ⓐ	Ⓐ 🍷	Ⓐ	⑤ A	①–④ B	⑤	①–④ B			⑥ 🍷	⑥ 🍷	⑥ 🍷
Hereford ..... 123 d.	Ⓐ	...	...	0535	...	0643	...	...	...	1311	...	...	1511	...	...	...	...	...	2153	2153	...	⑥	...	...	0710
Ledbury ..... 123 d.		...	...	0552	...	0659	...	...	...	1328	...	...	1527	...	...	...	...	...	2211	2211	...		...	...	0730
Great Malvern ..... 123 d.		...	0517	0605	...	0714	0858	0954	...	1347	1434	...	1540	1700	...	...	...	...	2224	2224	...		0539	0635	0743
Worcester Foregate St. 123 d.		...	0531	0620	0650	0730	0909	1005	1206	1402	1452	...	1601	1720	1847	1927	2059	2059	2239	2239	...		0554	0650	0758
Worcester Shrub Hill ..... 123 d.		0502	0535	0626	0652	0735	0912	1008	1208	1406	1456	...	1606	1724	1850	1929	2103	2103	2243	2243	...		0558	0654	0803
Evesham ..... a.		0516	0553	0644	0709	0753	0929	1026	1226	1424	1514	...	1624	1743	1917	1954	2122	2122	2301	2301	...		0615	0711	0820
Evesham ..... d.		0518	0555	0645	0710	0754	0930	1027	1227	1426	1522	...	1630	1749	1919	2022	2127	2127	2306	2306	...		0625	0725	0827
Moreton in Marsh ..... d.		0548	0616	0706	0726	0815	0949	1048	1248	1447	1543	1614	1651	1810	1936	2043	2148	2148	2326	2326	...		0646	0745	0848
Oxford ..... 132 a.		0625	0653	0746	0812	0849	1025	1127	1324	1524	1627	1649	1737	1901	2023	2120	2227	2227	2359	2359	...		0726	0826	0926
Reading ..... 132 a.		0657	0726	0822	...	0915	1055	1155	1355	1555	1655	...	1802	1926	2055	...	2322	2258	0038	0038	...		0754	0856	0955
London Paddington ..... 132 a.		0729	0759	0853	...	0947	1130	1229	1429	1627	1727	...	1830	2000	2129	...	2338	2337	0111	0117	...		0829	0929	1029

	⑥ 🍷	⑥ 🍷	⑥ 🍷	⑥ 🍷	⑥ 🍷	⑥ 🍷	⑥ 🍷	⑥ 🍷	⑥ 🍷	⑥	⑥	⑥			⑦ 🍷	⑦	⑦	⑦ 🍷	⑦ 🍷	⑦ 🍷	⑦ 🍷	⑦ 🍷	⑦ 🍷	⑦	⑦
Hereford ..... 123 d.	...	...	...	1213	...	1510	...	...	...	...	2020	...	...	⑦	...	...	...	1328	1430	...	1630	...	1830	...	...
Ledbury ..... 123 d.	...	...	...	1232	...	1529	...	...	...	...	2040	...	...		...	...	...	1346	1455	...	1647	...	1848	...	...
Great Malvern ..... 123 d.	0843	0943	1032	1245	1432	1543	1632	1743	1829	...	2053	2240	...		0900	1107	1310	1359	1508	...	1700	...	1908	2008	2055
Worcester Foregate St. 123 d.	0856	0958	1058	1300	1457	1559	1658	1758	1844	2002	2110	2251	...		0912	1119	1323	1414	1524	...	1722	...	1925	2025	2110
Worcester Shrub Hill ..... 123 d.	0903	1003	1102	1305	1501	1606	1702	1803	1900	2006	2125	2255	...		0916	1123	1327	1419	1526	1627	1727	1825	1929	2028	2118
Evesham ..... a.	0920	1021	1119	1324	1518	1623	1719	1820	1917	2023	2142	2313	...		0933	1140	1344	1436	1544	1645	1745	1845	1945	2046	2136
Evesham ..... d.	0927	1027	1127	1326	1524	1628	1727	1827	1927	2037	2154	...	...		0934	1146	1347	1451	1551	1652	1750	1853	1953	2053	2153
Moreton in Marsh ..... d.	0948	1048	1148	1348	1545	1648	1748	1848	1948	2058	2215	...	...		0955	1207	1407	1509	1612	1712	1807	1913	2013	2113	2213
Oxford ..... 132 a.	1028	1126	1226	1426	1626	1726	1826	1926	2027	2136	2256	...	...		1034	1242	1442	1548	1650	1750	1840	1949	2049	2149	2248
Reading ..... 132 a.	1055	1155	1254	1455	1655	1755	1855	1955	2052	2204	2330	...	...		1107	1309	1509	1619	1721	1821	1909	2022	2119	2222	...
London Paddington ..... 132 a.	1129	1229	1329	1529	1729	1829	1929	2029	2129	2239	0010	...	...		1154	1353	1553	1706	1810	1908	1953	2106	2207	2315	...

A – Until September 4.
B – Until September 3.

GW LONDON - OXFORD 132

Services on ⑥ valid until September 5, services on ⑦ valid until July 12.

Frequent additional but slower services operate London Paddington - Reading - Oxford and v.v.

km			Ⓐ	Ⓐ	Ⓐ	Ⓐ	Ⓐ	Ⓐ	Ⓐ	Ⓐ	Ⓐ	Ⓐ	Ⓐ	Ⓐ	Ⓐ	Ⓐ	Ⓐ	Ⓐ	Ⓐ	Ⓐ	Ⓐ	Ⓐ	Ⓐ	Ⓐ
0	**London** Paddington. 115 133 d.	Ⓐ	0558	0633	0722	0752	0822	0851	0921	0950	1022	1051	1122	1150	1222	1250	1321	1351	1421	1450	1522	1551	1622	1651
58	Reading ..... 115 133 d.		0630	0705	0753	0822	0853	0922	0953	1022	1053	1122	1153	1222	1253	1322	1353	1422	1453	1521	1553	1622	1658	1717
102	**Oxford** ..... 131 a.		0659	0739	0819	0848	0920	0952	1018	1048	1118	1152	1218	1248	1319	1351	1418	1448	1518	1550	1619	1647	1723	1748

	Ⓐ	Ⓐ	Ⓐ	Ⓐ	Ⓐ	Ⓐ	Ⓐ	Ⓐ	Ⓐ	Ⓐ	⑤	①–④	⑤	①–④	⑤	①–④			⑥	⑥	⑥	⑥	⑥	⑥
London Paddington 115 133 d.	1722	1751	1821	1851	1922	1950	2020	2051	2121	2148	2221	2221	2248	2248	2320	2320	...	⑥	0550	0621	0650	0721	0750	0821
Reading ..... 115 133 d.	1750	1821	1851	1922	1953	2022	2051	2123	2154	2223	2253	2306	2321	2334	2354	0004	...		0623	0653	0722	0753	0823	0853
Oxford ..... 131 a.	1815	1848	1918	1950	2021	2049	2116	2153	2224	2251	2326	2339	2349	0013	0029	0034	...		0652	0718	0748	0819	0848	0918

	⑥	⑥	⑥	⑥	⑥	⑥	⑥	⑥	⑥	⑥	⑥	⑥	⑥	⑥	⑥	⑥	⑥	⑥	⑥	⑥	⑥	⑥	⑥	⑥
London Paddington 115 133 d.	0850	0921	0950	1021	1050	1121	1150	1221	1250	1321	1350	1421	1450	1521	1550	1621	1650	1721	1750	1821	1850	1921	1950	2021
Reading ..... 115 133 d.	0923	0954	1023	1054	1123	1154	1220	1254	1323	1354	1423	1454	1523	1554	1623	1654	1723	1754	1823	1854	1923	1954	2023	2053
Oxford ..... 131 a.	0948	1020	1048	1119	1148	1218	1248	1320	1348	1418	1448	1518	1548	1618	1648	1718	1748	1818	1848	1918	1948	2020	2047	2120

	⑥	⑥	⑥	⑥	⑥	⑥			⑦	⑦	⑦	⑦	⑦	⑦	⑦	⑦	⑦	⑦	⑦	⑦	⑦	⑦	⑦	⑦
London Paddington 115 133 d.	2050	2121	2150	2232	2300	2333	...	⑦	0803	0842	0935	1042	1142	1242	1342	1442	1542	1642	1742	1842	1942	2042	2127	2242
Reading ..... 115 133 d.	2124	2152	2222	2307	2334	0008	...		0844	0926	1012	1120	1222	1320	1421	1520	1621	1721	1821	1920	2020	2122	2210	2320
Oxford ..... 131 a.	2153	2221	2249	2342	0004	0038	...		0915	0954	1042	1150	1250	1350	1450	1550	1649	1750	1850	1950	2048	2151	2239	*0010**

		Ⓐ	Ⓐ	Ⓐ	Ⓐ	Ⓐ	Ⓐ	Ⓐ	Ⓐ	Ⓐ	Ⓐ	Ⓐ	Ⓐ	Ⓐ	Ⓐ	Ⓐ	Ⓐ	Ⓐ	Ⓐ	Ⓐ	Ⓐ	Ⓐ	Ⓐ	Ⓐ
Oxford ..... 131 d.	Ⓐ	0602	0628	0656	0710	0731	0751	0806	0850	0901	0931	1001	1031	1101	1131	1201	1231	1301	1331	1401	1431	1501	1531	1601
Reading ..... 115 133 a.		0630	0657	0726	|	0756	0822	0836	0915	0932	0955	1025	1055	1125	1152	1225	1255	1325	1355	1425	1455	1526	1555	1625
London Paddington 115 133 a.		0709	0729	0759	0824	0829	0853	0910	0947	1010	1028	1059	1130	1158	1225	1300	1328	1359	1429	1501	1528	1600	1628	1658

	Ⓐ	Ⓐ	Ⓐ	Ⓐ	Ⓐ	Ⓐ	Ⓐ	Ⓐ	Ⓐ	Ⓐ	⑤	①–④	⑤	①–④	Ⓐ			⑥	⑥	⑥	⑥	⑥	⑥	⑥
Oxford ..... 131 d.	1631	1701	1737	1801	1831	1901	1931	2001	2031	2101	2131	2131	2233	2233	2305	...	⑥	0631	0701	0731	0801	0831	0901	0931
Reading ..... 115 133 a.	1655	1725	1802	1825	1855	1926	1955	2025	2055	2125	2206	2206	2258	2258	2334	...		0700	0727	0754	0824	0856	0925	0955
London Paddington 115 133 a.	1728	1759	1830	1859	1929	2000	2029	2057	2129	2158	2240	2252	2330	2337	0021	...		0737	0759	0829	0859	0929	0959	1029

	⑥	⑥	⑥	⑥	⑥	⑥	⑥	⑥	⑥	⑥	⑥	⑥	⑥	⑥	⑥	⑥	⑥	⑥	⑥	⑥	⑥	⑥	⑥	⑥
Oxford ..... 131 d.	1001	1031	1101	1131	1201	1231	1301	1331	1401	1431	1501	1531	1601	1631	1701	1731	1801	1831	1901	1931	2001	2031	2101	2137
Reading ..... 115 133 a.	1025	1055	1124	1155	1224	1254	1325	1355	1425	1455	1525	1555	1624	1655	1725	1755	1825	1855	1925	1955	2025	2052	2125	2204
London Paddington 115 133 a.	1059	1129	1159	1229	1259	1329	1359	1429	1459	1529	1559	1626	1656	1729	1759	1829	1859	1929	1959	2029	2059	2129	2159	2239

	⑥	⑥	⑥			⑦	⑦	⑦	⑦	⑦	⑦	⑦	⑦	⑦	⑦	⑦	⑦	⑦	⑦	⑦	⑦	⑦		
Oxford ..... 131 d.	2208	2231	2301	...	⑦	0805	0838	0938	1038	1138	1242	1338	1442	1550	1650	1750	1840	1950	2050	2150	2221	*2300**	...	...
Reading ..... 115 133 a.	2234	2255	2330	...		0847	0906	1006	1107	1210	1309	1410	1509	1619	1721	1821	1913	2022	2119	2222	2300	2352	...	...
London Paddington 115 133 a.	2308	2336	0010	...		0943	0946	1053	1154	1251	1353	1452	1535	1706	1810	1908	1953	2106	2207	2315	2354	0035	...	...

* – By 🚌, change at Didcot Parkway.

133 LONDON - BRISTOL - CARDIFF - SWANSEA - CARMARTHEN

Most services 🍸 GW

Services on ⑦ valid until July 12. For other services Cardiff - Swansea - South West Wales see Table **135**.

km			Ⓐ	Ⓐ	Ⓐ	Ⓐ	Ⓐ	Ⓐ	Ⓐ	Ⓐ	Ⓐ	Ⓐ	Ⓐ	Ⓐ	Ⓐ	Ⓐ	Ⓐ	Ⓐ	Ⓐ	Ⓐ	Ⓐ	Ⓐ	Ⓐ	Ⓐ	Ⓐ
							2W			**Z**							**2**						**T**		
0	**London** Paddington 115 d.	Ⓐ	0527	0530	0630	0645	...	0700	0715	0730	0745	0748	0800	0815	0830	0845	...	0900	0915	0930	0945	0948	1000	1015	1030
58	Reading 115 d.		0557	0607	0657	0711	...	0727	0741	0757	0811	0816	0827	0841	0857	0911	...	0927	0941	0957	1011	1016	1027	1041	1057
85	Didcot d.		|	0622	0712	|	...	0742	0756	|	|	0833	0842	0856	0912	|	...	|	0956	1012	|	1033	|	1056	1112
124	**Swindon** d.		0625	0650	0730	0740	0754	0800	0815	0825	0840	0854	0900	0915	0930	0940	0954	0955	1015	1030	1040	1054	1055	1115	1130
164	Stroud d.		|	0725	|	|	0822	|	|	|	|	0922	|	|	|	|	1022	|	|	|	|	1122	|	|	|
183	Gloucester 121 122 d.		|	0749	|	|	0850	|	|	|	|	0944	|	|	|	|	1050	|	|	|	|	1144	|	|	|
194	**Cheltenham** 121 122 a.		|	0804	|	|	0903	|	|	|	|	1003	|	|	|	|	1103	|	|	|	|	1203	|	|	|
151	Chippenham d.		0640	...	0745	|	...	0815	|	0840	|	...	0915	|	0945	|	...	1010	|	1045	|	...	1110	|	1145
172	Bath a.		0653	...	0800	|	...	0830	|	0855	|	...	0928	|	1000	|	...	1025	|	1100	|	...	1125	|	1200
180	**Bristol** Parkway d.		|	...	|	0807	...	|	0842	|	0907	...	|	0942	|	1007	...	|	1042	|	1107	...	|	1142	|
190	**Bristol** T. Meads **115** a.		0708	...	0817	|	...	0844	|	0910	|	...	0944	|	1015	|	...	1039	|	1115	|	...	1142	|	1215
221	Weston super Mare a.		|	...	...	|	...	...	|	|	|	...	...	|	...	|	...	...	|	...	|	...	1206	|	...
	Taunton 115 a.		|	...	...	|	...	...	|	0945	|	...	...	|	...	|	...	...	|	...	|	...	1229	|	...
215	Newport 135 a.		0744	...	...	0830	...	...	0905	...	0929	...	...	1004	...	1029	...	...	1105	...	1131	...	...	1204	...
234	**Cardiff** Central 135 a.		0801	...	...	0848	...	...	0922	...	0948	...	...	1021	...	1047	...	...	1123	...	1148	...	...	1221	...
266	Bridgend 135 a.		0822	...	...	0909	...	...	...	...	1009	...	...	...	...	1109	...	...	...	...	1209	...	...	...	...
286	Port Talbot Parkway 135 a.		0835	...	...	0923	...	...	...	...	1023	...	...	...	...	1123	...	...	...	...	1223	...	...	...	...
295	Neath 135 a.		0844	...	...	0930	...	...	...	...	1030	...	...	...	...	1130	...	...	...	...	1230	...	...	...	...
307	**Swansea** 135 a.		0857	...	...	0946	...	...	...	...	1044	...	...	...	...	1143	...	...	...	...	1245	...	...	...	...
325	Llanelli 135 a.		...	...	...	...	...	...	...	...	...	...	...	...	...	...	...	...	...	...	...	...	...	...	...
358	**Carmarthen** 135 a.		...	...	...	...	...	...	...	...	...	...	...	...	...	...	...	...	...	...	...	...	...	...	...

	Ⓐ	Ⓐ	Ⓐ	Ⓐ	Ⓐ	Ⓐ	Ⓐ	Ⓐ	Ⓐ	Ⓐ	Ⓐ	Ⓐ	Ⓐ	Ⓐ	Ⓐ	Ⓐ	Ⓐ	Ⓐ	Ⓐ	Ⓐ	Ⓐ	Ⓐ	Ⓐ	Ⓐ	Ⓐ
		2										2										2			
London Paddington 115 d.	1045	...	1100	1115	1130	1145	1148	1200	1215	1230	1245	...	1300	1315	1330	1345	1348	1400	1415	1430	1445	...	1500	1515	1530
Reading 115 d.	1111	...	1127	1141	1157	1211	1216	1227	1241	1257	1311	...	1327	1341	1357	1411	1416	1427	1441	1457	1511	...	1527	1541	1557
Didcot d.	|	...	|	1156	1212	|	1233	|	1256	1312	|	...	|	1356	1412	|	1433	|	1456	1512	|	...	|	1556	1612
Swindon d.	1140	1154	1155	1215	1230	1240	1254	1255	1315	1330	1340	1354	1355	1415	1430	1440	1454	1455	1515	1530	1540	1554	1555	1615	1630
Stroud d.	|	1222	|	|	|	|	1322	|	|	|	|	1422	|	|	|	|	1522	|	|	|	|	1622	|	|	|
Gloucester 121 122 d.	|	1250	|	|	|	|	1344	|	|	|	|	1450	|	|	|	|	1544	|	|	|	|	1650	|	|	|
Cheltenham 121 122 a.	|	1303	|	|	|	|	1403	|	|	|	|	1503	|	|	|	|	1603	|	|	|	|	1703	|	|	|
Chippenham d.	|	...	1210	|	1245	|	...	1310	|	1345	|	...	1410	|	1445	|	...	1510	|	1545	|	...	1610	|	1645
Bath a.	|	...	1225	|	1300	|	...	1325	|	1400	|	...	1425	|	1500	|	...	1525	|	1600	|	...	1625	|	1700
Bristol Parkway d.	1207	...	|	1242	|	1307	...	|	1342	|	1407	...	|	1442	|	1507	...	|	1542	|	1607	...	|	1642	|
Bristol T. Meads **115** a.	|	...	1239	|	1315	|	...	1341	|	1415	|	...	1439	|	1515	|	...	1540	|	1615	|	...	1639	|	1715
Weston super Mare a.	|	...	...	|	...	|	...	...	|	...	|	...	...	|	...	|	...	...	|	1652	|	...	...	|	1752
Taunton 115 a.	|	...	...	|	...	|	...	...	|	...	|	...	...	|	...	|	...	...	|	...	|	...	...	|	...
Newport 135 a.	1229	...	...	1304	...	1329	...	...	1404	...	1429	...	...	1505	...	1529	...	...	1604	...	1629	...	...	1705	...
Cardiff Central 135 a.	1248	...	...	1322	...	1348	...	...	1421	...	1448	...	...	1523	...	1548	...	...	1621	...	1648	...	...	1722	...
Bridgend 135 a.	1309	...	...	...	...	1409	...	...	...	...	1509	...	...	...	...	1609	...	...	...	...	1709	...	...	...	...
Port Talbot Parkway 135 a.	1323	...	...	...	...	1423	...	...	...	...	1523	...	...	...	...	1623	...	...	...	...	1723	...	...	...	...
Neath 135 a.	1330	...	...	...	...	1430	...	...	...	...	1530	...	...	...	...	1630	...	...	...	...	1730	...	...	...	...
Swansea 135 a.	1344	...	...	...	...	1444	...	...	...	...	1544	...	...	...	...	1645	...	...	...	...	1744	...	...	...	...
Llanelli 135 a.	...	...	...	...	...	...	...	...	...	...	...	...	...	...	...	...	...	...	...	...	...	...	...	...	...
Carmarthen 135 a.	...	...	...	...	...	...	...	...	...	...	...	...	...	...	...	...	...	...	...	...	...	...	...	...	...

	Ⓐ	Ⓐ	Ⓐ	Ⓐ	Ⓐ	Ⓐ	Ⓐ	Ⓐ	Ⓐ	Ⓐ	Ⓐ	Ⓐ	Ⓐ	Ⓐ	Ⓐ	Ⓐ	Ⓐ	Ⓐ	Ⓐ	Ⓐ	Ⓐ	Ⓐ	Ⓐ	Ⓐ	Ⓐ
							2													**2W**					
London Paddington 115 d.	1545	1548	1600	1615	1630	1645	...	1700	1715	1730	1745	1748	1800	1815	1830	1845	1848	1900	1915	...	1930	1948	2000	2015	2045
Reading 115 d.	1611	1616	1627	1641	1657	1711	...	1727	1741	1757	1811	1816	1827	1841	1857	1911	1916	1927	1941	...	1957	2016	2027	2041	2111
Didcot d.	1640	1633	|	1656	1712	1726	...	1742	1756	1812	|	1833	1842	1856	1912	|	1933	1942	1956	...	2012	2033	2042	2056	2126
Swindon d.	|	1654	1655	1715	1730	1745	1754	1800	1815	1830	1840	1854	1900	1915	1930	1940	1954	2000	2015	2023	2030	2054	2100	2115	2145
Stroud d.	|	1722	|	|	|	|	1822	|	|	|	|	1922	|	|	|	|	2022	|	|	2052	|	2126	|	|	|
Gloucester 121 122 d.	|	1746	|	|	|	|	1850	|	|	|	|	1945	|	|	|	|	2044	|	|	2113	|	2147	|	|	|
Cheltenham 121 122 a.	|	1803	|	|	|	|	1903	|	|	|	|	2003	|	|	|	|	2103	|	|	2129	|	2203	|	|	|
Chippenham d.	|	...	1710	|	1745	|	...	1815	|	1845	|	...	1915	|	1945	|	...	2015	|	...	2045	...	2115	|	2200
Bath a.	|	...	1725	|	1800	|	...	1828	|	1900	|	...	1928	|	2000	|	...	2028	|	...	2100	...	2128	|	2211
Bristol Parkway d.	1707	...	|	1742	|	1812	...	|	1842	|	1910	...	|	1942	|	2007	...	|	2042	...	|	...	|	2142	|
Bristol T. Meads **115** a.	|	...	1741	|	1815	|	...	1844	|	1915	|	...	1943	|	2015	|	...	2044	|	...	2115	...	2144	|	2230
Weston super Mare a.	|	...	...	|	1852	|	...	...	|	1949	|	...	...	|	2055	|	...	...	|	...	2150	...	...	|	...
Taunton 115 a.	|	...	...	|	1930	|	...	...	|	2023	|	...	...	|	...	|	...	...	|	...	...	...	...	|	...
Newport 135 a.	1729	...	...	1805	...	1836	...	...	1910	...	1937	...	...	2006	...	2029	...	...	2104	...	...	...	...	2204	...
Cardiff Central 135 a.	1748	...	...	1822	...	1853	...	...	1927	...	1953	...	...	2027	...	2048	...	...	2121	...	...	...	...	2225	...
Bridgend 135 a.	1809	...	...	1844	...	1915	...	...	1949	...	2015	...	...	2048	...	2109	...	...	2144	...	...	...	...	2257	...
Port Talbot Parkway 135 a.	1823	...	...	1857	...	1928	...	...	2002	...	2028	...	...	2101	...	2123	...	...	2157	...	...	...	...	2310	...
Neath 135 a.	1830	...	...	1904	...	1936	...	...	2010	...	2036	...	...	2109	...	2130	...	...	2205	...	...	...	...	2317	...
Swansea 135 a.	1848	...	...	1919	...	1949	...	...	2024	...	2049	...	...	2125	...	2146	...	...	2218	...	...	...	...	2332	...
Llanelli 135 a.	...	...	...	...	...	...	...	...	...	...	2116	...	...	...	...	...	...	...	...	...	...	...	...	...	...
Carmarthen 135 a.	...	...	...	...	...	...	...	...	...	...	2148	...	...	...	...	...	...	...	...	...	...	...	...	...	...

	Ⓐ	Ⓐ	Ⓐ	⑤	①–④	Ⓐ	⑤	①–④	⑤	①–④			⑥		⑥	⑥	⑥	⑥	⑥	⑥	⑥		⑥	⑥	⑥
	2		**E c**			2										**Z**					**P b**		**b**		
London Paddington 115 d.	...	2115	2145	2215	2215	...	2245	2245	2330	2330	...	⑥	0630	...	0700	0730	0745	0800	0815	0830	0845	...	0900	0930	0945
Reading 115 d.	...	2141	2211	2241	2250	...	2311	2321	0002	0008	...		0657	...	0727	0757	0811	0827	0841	0857	0911	...	0927	0957	1011
Didcot d.	...	2200	2230	2301	2309	...	2330	2339	0025	0026	...		0712	...	|	0812	|	|	0856	0912	|	...	|	1012	|
Swindon d.	2154	2220	2250	2321	2326	2333	2350	2358	0043	0046	...		0730	...	0755	0830	0840	0855	0915	0930	0945	...	0955	1030	1040
Stroud d.	2222	|	|	|	|	0002	|	|	|	|	...		|	...	|	|	|	|	0945	|	|	...	|	|	|
Gloucester 121 122 d.	2245	|	|	|	|	0024	|	|	|	|	...		|	...	|	|	|	|	1006	|	|	...	|	|	|
Cheltenham 121 122 a.	2303	|	|	|	|	...	|	|	|	|	...		|	...	|	|	|	|	1023	|	|	...	|	|	|
Chippenham d.	...	|	2305	2335	2341	...	|	|	0058	0100	...		0745	...	0810	0845	|	0910	...	0945	|	...	1010	1045	|
Bath a.	...	|	2319	2349	2356	...	|	|	0113	0115	...		0800	...	0824	0900	|	0924	...	1000	|	...	1025	1100	|
Bristol Parkway d.	...	2246	|	|	|	...	0017	0025	|	|	...		|	...	|	|	0907	|	...	|	1007	...	|	|	1107
Bristol T. Meads **115** a.	...	|	2333	0003	0010	...	|	|	0127	0129	...		0815	...	0839	0915	|	0939	...	1015	|	...	1039	1115	|
Weston super Mare a.	...	|	0006s	...	...	...	|	|	|	|	...		...	...	...	|	|	...	...	...	|	...	1107	...	|
Taunton 115 a.	...	|	0037s	...	...	...	|	|	|	|	...		...	...	...	0950	|	...	...	...	|	...	...	...	|
Newport 135 a.	...	2315	...	...	...	...	0039	0054	0203s	0210s	...		...	...	...	...	0931	...	...	...	1031	...	...	...	1131
Cardiff Central 135 a.	...	2339	...	...	...	...	0055	0114	0222	0233	...		...	...	...	...	0948	...	...	...	1048	...	...	...	1148
Bridgend 135 a.	...	2359	...	...	...	...	0120	0139	...	...	...		...	...	...	...	1009	...	...	...	1109	...	...	...	1209
Port Talbot Parkway 135 a.	...	0011	...	...	...	...	0133	0152	...	...	...		...	...	...	...	1023	...	...	...	1122	...	...	...	1223
Neath 135 a.	...	0019	...	...	...	...	0141	0159	...	...	...		...	...	...	...	1030	...	...	...	1130	...	...	...	1230
Swansea 135 a.	...	0034	...	...	...	...	0154	0215	...	...	...		...	...	...	...	1044	...	...	...	1143	...	...	...	1244
Llanelli 135 a.	...	...	...	...	...	...	...	...	...	...	...		...	...	...	...	...	...	...	...	...	...	...	...	...
Carmarthen 135 a.	...	...	...	...	...	...	...	...	...	...	...		...	...	...	...	...	...	...	...	...	...	...	...	...

E – To / from Exeter.
M – To / from Plymouth.
P – To / from Pembroke Dock.
R – To / from Worcester.
S – To / from Southampton.
T – To / from Paignton.
W – To / from Westbury.
Z – To / from Penzance.
b – Until September 5.
c – Until September 4.
s – Stops to set down only.
u – Stops to pick up only.

GW Most services 🍸 LONDON - BRISTOL - CARDIFF - SWANSEA - CARMARTHEN 133

Services on ⑦ valid until July 12. For other services Cardiff - Swansea - South West Wales see Table **135**.

	⑥	⑥	⑥	⑥	⑥	⑥	⑥	⑥	⑥	⑥	⑥	⑥	⑥	⑥	⑥	⑥	⑥	⑥	⑥	⑥	⑥	⑥	⑥	⑥	⑥
						2					**b**			2					**b**			2	**b**		
London Paddington..... **115** d.	1000	1015	1030	1045	1100	...	1130	1145	1200	1215	1230	1245	1300	...	1330	1345	1400	1415	1430	1445	1500	...	1530	1545	1600
Reading..... **115** d.	1027	1041	1057	1111	1127	...	1157	1211	1227	1241	1257	1311	1327	...	1357	1411	1427	1441	1457	1511	1527	...	1557	1611	1627
Didcot..... d.	|	1056	1112	|	|	...	1212	|	|	1256	1312	|	|	...	1412	|	|	1456	1512	|	|	...	1612	|	|
Swindon..... d.	1055	1115	1130	1140	1155	1214	1230	1240	1255	1315	1330	1340	1355	1414	1430	1440	1455	1515	1530	1540	1555	1614	1630	1640	1655
Stroud..... d.	|	1145	|	|	|	1243	|	|	|	1345	|	|	|	1443	|	|	|	1545	|	|	|	1643	|	|	|
Gloucester..... **121 122** d.	|	1207	|	|	|	1248	|	|	|	1406	|	|	|	1508	|	|	|	1606	|	|	|	1708	|	|	|
Cheltenham..... **121 122** a.	|	1323	|	|	|	1322	|	|	|	1423	|	|	|	1525	|	|	|	1623	|	|	|	1725	|	|	|
Chippenham..... d.	1110	...	1145	|	1210	...	1245	|	1310	...	1345	|	1410	...	1445	|	1510	...	1545	|	1610	...	1645	|	1710
Bath..... a.	1125	...	1200	|	1225	...	1300	|	1325	...	1400	|	1425	...	1500	|	1525	...	1600	|	1625	...	1700	|	1725
Bristol Parkway..... d.	|	...	|	1207	|	...	|	1307	|	...	|	1407	|	...	|	1507	|	...	|	1607	|	...	|	1707	|
Bristol T. Meads **115**..... a.	1139	...	1215	|	1240	...	1315	|	1340	...	1415	|	1439	...	1515	|	1539	...	1615	|	1639	...	1715	|	1739
Weston super Mare..... a.	...	...	1236	|	...	...	...	|	...	...	1436	|	...	...	...	|	...	...	1636	|	...	...	1736	|	...
Taunton 115..... a.	...	...	...	|	...	...	...	|	...	...	...	|	...	...	...	|	...	...	...	|	...	...	...	|	...
Newport..... **135** a.	...	...	...	1231	...	...	...	1331	...	...	...	1431	...	...	...	1531	...	...	...	1631	...	...	...	1731	...
Cardiff Central..... **135** a.	...	...	...	1248	...	...	...	1348	...	...	...	1448	...	...	...	1548	...	...	...	1648	...	...	...	1748	...
Bridgend..... **135** a.	...	...	...	1309	...	...	...	1410	...	...	...	1509	...	...	...	1609	...	...	...	1709	...	...	...	1809	...
Port Talbot Parkway..... **135** a.	...	...	...	1323	...	...	...	1423	...	...	...	1523	...	...	...	1623	...	...	...	1723	...	...	...	1823	...
Neath..... **135** a.	...	...	...	1330	...	...	...	1430	...	...	...	1530	...	...	...	1630	...	...	...	1730	...	...	...	1830	...
Swansea..... **135** a.	...	...	...	1344	...	...	...	1444	...	...	...	1544	...	...	...	1644	...	...	...	1744	...	...	...	1847	...
Llanelli..... **135** a.	...	...	...	...	...	...	...	...	...	...	...	...	...	...	...	...	...	...	...	...	...	...	...	...	...
Carmarthen..... **135** a.	...	...	...	...	...	...	...	...	...	...	...	...	...	...	...	...	...	...	...	...	...	...	...	...	...

	⑥	⑥	⑥	⑥	⑥	⑥	⑥		⑥	⑥	⑥	⑥	⑥	⑥	⑥	⑥	⑥	⑥	⑥	⑥	⑥	⑥	⑥	⑥	⑥
		T			2									2					**E**		**b**	2		**d**	**d**
London Paddington..... **115** d.	1615	1630	1645	1700	...	1730	1745	...	1800	1815	1830	1845	1900	...	1930	1945	2000	2015	2030	2045	2130	...	2200	2230	2330
Reading..... **115** d.	1641	1657	1711	1727	...	1757	1811	...	1827	1841	1857	1911	1927	...	1957	2011	2027	2041	2057	2111	2157	...	2227	2300	2359
Didcot..... d.	1656	1712	|	|	...	1812	|	...	|	1856	1912	|	|	...	2012	|	2042	2056	2112	|	2212	...	2242	2322	0018
Swindon..... d.	1715	1730	1740	1755	1814	1830	1840	...	1855	1915	1930	1940	1955	2000	2030	2040	2100	2115	2130	2146	2230	2235	2300	2341	0037
Stroud..... d.	1745	|	1816	|	1843	|	|	...	|	1945	|	|	|	2030	|	|	|	2145	|	|	|	2304	|	|	|
Gloucester..... **121 122** d.	1806	|	1846	|	1908	|	|	...	|	2006	|	|	|	2051	|	|	|	2205	|	|	|	2325	|	|	|
Cheltenham..... **121 122** a.	1823	|	|	|	1925	|	|	...	|	2023	|	|	|	2105	|	|	|	2223	|	|	|	...	|	|	|
Chippenham..... d.	...	1745	|	1810	...	1845	|	...	1911	...	1946	|	2010	...	2045	|	2115	...	2145	|	2245	...	|	2356	0052
Bath..... a.	...	1800	|	1825	...	1900	|	...	1925	...	2000	|	2025	...	2100	|	2130	...	2200	|	2300	...	|	0010	0107
Bristol Parkway..... d.	...	|	1807	|	...	|	1913	...	|	...	|	2007	|	...	|	2107	|	...	|	2211	|	...	2329	|	|
Bristol T. Meads **115**..... a.	...	1815	|	1839	...	1915	|	...	1940	...	2015	|	2042	...	2115	|	2145	...	2215	|	2315	...	|	0025	0123
Weston super Mare..... a.	...	1836	|	...	...	1952	|	...	...	...	2036	|	2126	...	...	|	...	...	2248**s**	|	...	...	|	...	...
Taunton 115..... a.	...	1906	|	...	...	...	|	...	...	...	2106	|	2200	...	...	|	...	...	2318	|	...	...	|	...	...
Newport..... **135** a.	...	...	1831	...	...	...	1936	...	...	...	...	2031	...	...	...	2131	...	...	...	2246	...	...	2358	...	...
Cardiff Central..... **135** a.	...	...	1848	...	...	...	1953	...	...	...	...	2048	...	...	...	2148	...	...	...	2306	...	...	0019	...	...
Bridgend..... **135** a.	...	...	1909	...	...	...	2014	...	...	...	...	2109	...	...	...	2209	...	...	...	2328	...	...	...	...	...
Port Talbot Parkway..... **135** a.	...	...	1923	...	...	...	2027	...	...	...	...	2123	...	...	...	2222	...	...	...	2341	...	...	...	...	...
Neath..... **135** a.	...	...	1930	...	...	...	2036	...	...	...	...	2130	...	...	...	2230	...	...	...	2349	...	...	...	...	...
Swansea..... **135** a.	...	...	1944	...	...	...	2049	...	...	...	...	2145	...	...	...	2244	...	...	...	0002	...	...	...	...	...
Llanelli..... **135** a.	...	...	...	...	...	...	2125	...	...	...	...	...	...	...	...	...	...	...	...	...	...	...	...	...	...
Carmarthen..... **135** a.	...	...	...	...	...	...	2155	...	...	...	...	...	...	...	...	...	...	...	...	...	...	...	...	...	...

		⑦	⑦	⑦	⑦	⑦	⑦	⑦	⑦	⑦	⑦	⑦	⑦	⑦	⑦	⑦	⑦	⑦	⑦	⑦	⑦	⑦	⑦	⑦	⑦
		Z					2						**M**				2								
London Paddington..... **115** d.	⑦	0800	0830	0835	0900	0930	...	1000	1027	1037	1100	1137	1200	1227	1237	1300	...	1337	1400	1427	1437	1500	1537	1600	1627
Reading..... **115** d.		0838	0916	0920	0937	1005	...	1037	1105	1114	1137	1214	1237	1305	1314	1337	...	1414	1437	1505	1514	1537	1616	1637	1705
Didcot..... d.		0853	0931	|	0953	1021	...	1053	|	1130	1153	1230	1253	|	1330	1353	...	1430	1453	|	1530	1553	1632	1653	|
Swindon..... d.		0912	0950	0955	1010	1040	1045	1110	1135	1147	1210	1247	1311	1340	1347	1411	1421	1447	1511	1535	1547	1611	1651	1711	1739
Stroud..... d.		|	|	1023	|	|	1114	|	1205	|	|	|	|	1409	|	|	1451	|	|	1604	|	|	|	|	1807
Gloucester..... **121 122** d.		|	|	1044	|	|	1135	|	1226	|	|	|	|	1432	|	|	1519	|	|	1625	|	|	|	|	1828
Cheltenham..... **121 122** a.		|	|	1102	|	|	1148	|	1246	|	|	|	|	1448	|	|	1533	|	|	1646	|	|	|	|	1848
Chippenham..... d.		0929	|	...	1026	|	...	1126	...	|	1226	|	1326	...	|	1426	...	|	1526	...	|	1626	|	1726	...
Bath..... a.		0945	|	...	1041	|	...	1141	...	|	1240	|	1340	...	|	1440	...	|	1540	...	|	1640	|	1742	...
Bristol Parkway..... d.		|	1017	...	|	1107	...	|	...	1216	|	1316	|	...	1416	|	...	1516	|	...	1616	|	1718	|	...
Bristol T. Meads **115**..... a.		0959	|	...	1056	|	...	1157	...	|	1254	|	1356	...	|	1455	...	|	1555	...	|	1655	|	1757	...
Weston super Mare..... a.		|	|	...	...	|	...	1231	...	|	1352	|	|	...	|	...	...	|	...	...	|	1736	|	...	...
Taunton 115..... a.		1033	|	...	...	|	...	...	...	|	...	|	1430	...	|	...	...	|	...	...	|	1801	|	...	...
Newport..... **135** a.		...	1038	...	...	1130	...	...	...	1237	...	1339	...	...	1439	...	...	1537	...	...	1639	...	1739	...	...
Cardiff Central..... **135** a.		...	1055	...	...	1147	...	...	...	1254	...	1356	...	...	1456	...	...	1554	...	...	1656	...	1756	...	...
Bridgend..... **135** a.		...	1117	...	...	1209	...	...	...	1316	...	1419	...	...	1518	...	...	1616	...	...	1718	...	1818	...	...
Port Talbot Parkway..... **135** a.		...	1130	...	...	1222	...	...	...	1329	...	1431	...	...	1531	...	...	1629	...	...	1731	...	1831	...	...
Neath..... **135** a.		...	1137	...	...	1229	...	...	...	1336	...	1438	...	...	1538	...	...	1636	...	...	1738	...	1839	...	...
Swansea..... **135** a.		...	1152	...	...	1244	...	...	...	1350	...	1458	...	...	1552	...	...	1650	...	...	1752	...	1855	...	...
Llanelli..... **135** a.		...	...	...	...	...	...	...	...	1422	...	...	...	...	1621	...	...	...	...	...	1820	...	...	...	...
Carmarthen..... **135** a.		...	...	...	...	...	...	...	...	1453	...	...	...	...	1651	...	...	...	...	...	1852	...	...	...	...

	⑦	⑦	⑦		⑦	⑦	⑦	⑦		⑦	⑦	⑦	⑦	⑦	⑦	⑦	⑦		⑦	⑦	⑦	⑦		⑦	⑦
			2								**E**	2**W**									2				
London Paddington..... **115** d.	1637	1700	...	...	1730	1737	1800	1827	...	1837	1900	...	1930	1937	2000	2029	2037	...	2100	2137	...	2203	...	2303	2337
Reading..... **115** d.	1716	1737	...	...	1804	1816	1837	1905	...	1916	1937	...	2005	2016	2037	2105	2116	...	2137	2215	...	2250	...	2346	2355
Didcot..... d.	1732	1753	...	...	|	1832	1853	|	...	1932	1953	...	|	2032	2053	|	2132	...	2153	2232	...	2306	...	|	0015
Swindon..... d.	1751	1811	1822	...	1833	1851	1911	1936	...	1951	2011	2024	2034	2051	2111	2136	2152	...	2214	2251	2257	2326	...	0022**s**	0052**s**
Stroud..... d.	|	|	1850	...	|	|	|	2004	...	|	|	2053	|	|	|	2204	|	...	|	|	2326	|	...	|	|
Gloucester..... **121 122** d.	|	|	1918	...	|	|	|	2025	...	|	|	2116	|	|	|	2225	|	...	|	|	2347	|	...	|	|
Cheltenham..... **121 122** a.	|	|	*1947*	...	|	|	|	2046	...	|	|	2128	|	|	|	2246	|	...	|	|	0004	|	...	|	|
Chippenham..... d.	|	1826	...	...	1852	|	1926	...	...	|	2026	...	2049	|	2126	...	|	...	2228	|	...	2341	...	0037**s**	0108**s**
Bath..... a.	|	1840	...	...	1912	|	1940	...	...	|	2040	...	2105	|	2140	...	|	...	2245	|	...	2355	...	0052**s**	0122**s**
Bristol Parkway..... d.	1818	|	...	...	|	1918	|	...	...	2018	|	...	|	2118	|	...	2219	...	|	2318	...	|	...	|	|
Bristol T. Meads **115**..... a.	|	1855	...	...	1928	|	1955	...	...	|	2055	...	2122	|	2155	...	|	...	2258	|	...	0010	...	0106	0138
Weston super Mare..... a.	|	...	...	...	2002	|	...	...	...	|	2127	...	...	|	...	...	|	...	2332	|	...	...	...	...	...
Taunton 115..... a.	|	...	...	...	...	|	...	...	...	|	2150	...	...	|	...	...	|	...	...	|	...	...	...	...	...
Newport..... **135** a.	1841	...	...	...	...	1939	...	...	...	2039	...	...	...	2144	...	...	2246	...	...	2346	...	...	...	...	...
Cardiff Central..... **135** a.	1858	...	...	...	...	1956	...	...	...	2056	...	...	...	2204	...	...	2307	...	...	0006	...	...	...	...	...
Bridgend..... **135** a.	1919	...	...	...	...	2018	...	...	...	2118	...	...	...	2226	...	...	2329	...	...	0028	...	...	...	...	...
Port Talbot Parkway..... **135** a.	1932	...	...	...	...	2031	...	...	...	2131	...	...	...	2239	...	...	2342	...	...	0041	...	...	...	...	...
Neath..... **135** a.	1940	...	...	...	...	2039	...	...	...	2138	...	...	...	2247	...	...	2349	...	...	0049	...	...	...	...	...
Swansea..... **135** a.	1954	...	...	...	...	2055	...	...	...	2152	...	...	...	2300	...	...	0003	...	...	0102	...	...	...	...	...
Llanelli..... **135** a.	...	...	...	...	...	...	...	...	...	...	...	...	...	...	...	...	...	...	...	...	...	...	...	...	...
Carmarthen..... **135** a.	...	...	...	...	...	...	...	...	...	...	...	...	...	...	...	...	...	...	...	...	...	...	...	...	...

E – To / from Exeter.
M – To / from Plymouth.
P – To / from Pembroke Dock.
R – To / from Worcester.
S – To / from Southampton.
T – To / from Paignton.
W – To / from Westbury.
Z – To / from Penzance.
b – Until September 5.
d – Until July 11 and from September 12.
s – Stops to set down only.
u – Stops to pick up only.

133 CARMARTHEN - SWANSEA - CARDIFF - BRISTOL - LONDON

Most services 🍷 GW

Services on ⑦ valid until July 12. For other services Cardiff - Swansea - South West Wales see Table **135**.

Ⓐ	Ⓐ	Ⓐ	Ⓐ	Ⓐ	Ⓐ	Ⓐ	Ⓐ	Ⓐ	Ⓐ	Ⓐ	Ⓐ	Ⓐ	Ⓐ	Ⓐ	Ⓐ	Ⓐ	Ⓐ	Ⓐ	Ⓐ	Ⓐ	Ⓐ	Ⓐ	Ⓐ	Ⓐ
		2S							a								E		M					
Carmarthen 135 d.	...	...	...	...	...	...	...	...	...	...	...	...	...	...	...	...	...	...	...	...	...	...	...	...
Llanelli 135 d.	...	...	...	...	...	...	...	...	...	...	...	...	...	...	...	...	...	...	...	...	...	...	...	...
Swansea 135 d.	...	...	...	0359	...	0458	...	...	...	0527	...	...	0559	...	0629	...	...	0659	...	0729	...	...	0759	...
Neath 135 d.	...	...	...	0410	...	0510	...	...	...	0539	...	...	0610	...	0640	...	...	0710	...	0740	...	...	0810	...
Port Talbot Parkway 135 d.	...	...	...	0418	...	0518	...	...	...	0546	...	...	0618	...	0648	...	...	0718	...	0748	...	...	0818	...
Bridgend 135 d.	...	...	...	0430	...	0529	...	...	...	0558	...	...	0630	...	0700	...	...	0730	...	0800	...	...	0830	...
Cardiff Central 135 d.	...	...	...	0515	...	0554	...	...	...	0623	...	...	0655	...	0725	...	...	0755	...	0825	...	...	0855	...
Newport 135 d.	...	...	...	0533	...	0608	...	...	...	0637	...	...	0709	...	0739	...	...	0809	...	0839	...	...	0909	...
Taunton 115 d.	...	...	...	|	...	|	...	...	...	|	...	...	|	...	|	...	0654	|	0715	|	...	...	|	...
Weston super Mare d.	...	...	...	|	...	|	...	...	...	|	...	0620	|	0649	|	...	0724	|	0749	|	...	...	|	...
Bristol T. Meads **115** d.	0447	...	0530	|	0600	|	...	0630	0640	|	...	0700	|	0730	|	...	0800	|	0830	|	...	0900	|	0930
Bristol Parkway d.	0457u	...	|	0601	|	0631	...	|	|	0700	...	|	0732	|	0802	...	|	0832	|	0902	...	|	0932	|
Bath d.	|	...	0543	|	0613	|	...	0643	0652	|	...	0713	|	0743	|	...	0813	|	0843	|	...	0913	|	0943
Chippenham d.	|	...	0555	|	0625	|	...	0655	0705	|	...	0725	|	0755	|	...	0825	|	0855	|	...	0925	|	0955
Cheltenham 121 122 d.	|	...	|	|	|	|	0555	|	|	|	0630	|	|	|	|	0730	|	|	|	|	0831	|	|	|
Gloucester 121 122 d.	|	0519	|	|	|	|	0612	|	|	|	0647	|	|	|	|	0745	|	|	|	|	0846	|	|	|
Stroud d.	|	0537	|	|	|	|	0631	|	|	|	0706	|	|	|	|	0804	|	|	|	|	0904	|	|	|
Swindon d.	0523	0606	0611	0628	0641	0658	0702	0711	0721	0727	0736	0741	0759	0811	0829	0833	0841	0859	0911	0929	0935	0941	0959	1011
Didcot a.	0541	...	0628	0645	0658	|	0719	0728	|	0743	0754	0800	0816	0828	0846	0852	0858	|	0928	|	0952	|	1016	1028
Reading 115 a.	0557	...	0643	0702	0714	0729	0736	0744	|	0801	0813	0816	0833	0844	0902	0908	0914	0927	0944	1001	1007	1009	1032	1044
London Paddington 115 a.	0624	...	0716	0732	0744	0802	0807	0814	0817	0832	0840	0844	0906	0914	0929	0939	0944	0959	1014	1030	1037	1049	1102	1114

	Ⓐ	Ⓐ	Ⓐ	Ⓐ	Ⓐ	Ⓐ	Ⓐ	Ⓐ	Ⓐ	Ⓐ	Ⓐ	Ⓐ	Ⓐ	Ⓐ	Ⓐ	Ⓐ	Ⓐ	Ⓐ	Ⓐ	Ⓐ	Ⓐ	Ⓐ	Ⓐ	Ⓐ	Ⓐ
		T	2									Z	2										2		
Carmarthen 135 d.	0730	...	...	...	...	...	...	...	...	...	...	...	...	...	...	...	...	...	...	...	...	...	...	...	...
Llanelli 135 d.	0804	...	...	...	...	...	...	...	...	...	...	...	...	...	...	...	...	...	...	...	...	...	...	...	...
Swansea 135 d.	0829	...	...	...	...	0929	...	...	...	...	1029	...	...	...	...	1129	...	...	...	...	1229	...	...	...	...
Neath 135 d.	0840	...	...	...	...	0940	...	...	...	...	1040	...	...	...	...	1140	...	...	...	...	1240	...	...	...	...
Port Talbot Parkway 135 d.	0848	...	...	...	...	0948	...	...	...	...	1048	...	...	...	...	1148	...	...	...	...	1248	...	...	...	...
Bridgend 135 d.	0900	...	...	...	...	1000	...	...	...	...	1100	...	...	...	...	1200	...	...	...	...	1300	...	...	...	...
Cardiff Central 135 d.	0925	...	...	0955	...	1025	...	...	1055	...	1125	...	...	1155	...	1225	...	...	1255	...	1325	...	...	1355	...
Newport 135 d.	0939	...	...	1009	...	1039	...	...	1109	...	1139	...	...	1209	...	1239	...	...	1309	...	1339	...	...	1409	...
Taunton 115 d.	|	0905	...	|	...	|	...	...	|	...	|	1126	...	|	...	|	...	...	|	...	|	...	...	|	...
Weston super Mare d.	|	0928	...	|	...	|	...	...	|	...	|	|	...	|	...	|	...	...	|	...	|	...	...	|	...
Bristol T. Meads **115** d.	|	1000	...	|	1030	|	...	1100	|	1130	|	1200	...	|	1230	|	...	1300	|	1330	|	1400	...	|	1430
Bristol Parkway d.	1002	|	...	1032	|	1102	...	|	1132	|	1202	|	...	1232	|	1302	...	|	1332	|	1402	|	...	1432	|
Bath d.	|	1013	...	|	1043	|	...	1113	|	1143	|	1213	...	|	1243	|	...	1313	|	1343	|	1413	...	|	1443
Chippenham d.	|	1025	...	|	1055	|	...	1125	|	1155	|	1225	...	|	1255	|	...	1325	|	1355	|	1425	...	|	1455
Cheltenham 121 122 d.	|	|	0940	|	|	|	1031	|	|	|	|	|	1140	|	|	|	1231	|	|	|	|	|	1340	|	|
Gloucester 121 122 d.	|	|	0954	|	|	|	1046	|	|	|	|	|	1154	|	|	|	1246	|	|	|	|	|	1354	|	|
Stroud d.	|	|	1011	|	|	|	1104	|	|	|	|	|	1211	|	|	|	1304	|	|	|	|	|	1411	|	|
Swindon d.	1029	1041	1042	1059	1111	1129	1135	1141	1159	1211	1229	1241	1242	1259	1311	1329	1335	1341	1359	1411	1429	1441	1442	1459	1511
Didcot a.	1046	|	...	1116	1128	|	1152	|	1216	1228	1246	|	...	1316	1328	|	1352	|	1416	1428	1446	|	...	1516	1528
Reading 115 a.	1101	1111	...	1132	1144	1200	1207	1209	1232	1244	1301	1311	...	1332	1344	1400	1407	1409	1432	1444	1501	1509	...	1532	1544
London Paddington 115 a.	1132	1140	...	1200	1214	1232	1239	1242	1308	1314	1330	1340	...	1406	1414	1432	1437	1440	1507	1514	1530	1539	...	1609	1614

	Ⓐ	Ⓐ	Ⓐ	Ⓐ	Ⓐ	Ⓐ	Ⓐ	Ⓐ	Ⓐ	Ⓐ	Ⓐ	Ⓐ	Ⓐ	Ⓐ	Ⓐ	Ⓐ	Ⓐ	Ⓐ	Ⓐ	Ⓐ	Ⓐ	Ⓐ	Ⓐ	Ⓐ	Ⓐ
								2										2RS							2
Carmarthen 135 d.	...	...	...	...	...	...	...	...	...	...	...	...	...	...	...	...	...	...	...	...	...	...	...	...	...
Llanelli 135 d.	...	...	...	...	...	...	...	...	...	...	...	...	...	...	...	...	...	...	...	...	...	...	...	...	...
Swansea 135 d.	1329	...	...	...	...	1429	...	...	...	...	1529	...	...	...	...	1629	...	...	...	...	1729	...	...	1829	...
Neath 135 d.	1340	...	...	...	...	1440	...	...	...	...	1540	...	...	...	...	1640	...	...	...	...	1740	...	...	1840	...
Port Talbot Parkway 135 d.	1348	...	...	...	...	1448	...	...	...	...	1548	...	...	...	...	1648	...	...	...	...	1748	...	...	1848	...
Bridgend 135 d.	1400	...	...	...	...	1500	...	...	...	...	1600	...	...	...	...	1700	...	...	...	...	1800	...	...	1900	...
Cardiff Central 135 d.	1425	...	...	1455	...	1425	...	...	1555	...	1625	...	...	1655	...	1725	...	...	1755	...	1825	...	...	1925	...
Newport 135 d.	1439	...	...	1509	...	1539	...	...	1609	...	1639	...	...	1709	...	1739	...	...	1809	...	1839	...	...	1939	...
Taunton 115 d.	|	...	...	|	...	|	...	...	|	...	|	...	...	|	...	|	...	...	|	...	|	...	...	|	...
Weston super Mare d.	|	...	...	|	...	|	...	...	|	...	|	...	...	|	1710	|	...	...	|	1810	|	...	...	|	...
Bristol T. Meads **115** d.	|	...	1500	|	1530	|	1600	...	|	1630	|	...	1700	|	1730	|	1800	...	|	1830	|	...	1930	|	...
Bristol Parkway d.	1502	...	|	1532	|	1602	|	...	1632	|	1702	...	|	1732	|	1802	|	...	1832	|	1902	...	|	2002	...
Bath d.	|	...	1513	|	1543	|	1613	...	|	1643	|	...	1713	|	1743	|	1813	...	|	1843	|	...	1943	|	...
Chippenham d.	|	...	1525	|	1555	|	1625	...	|	1655	|	...	1725	|	1755	|	1825	...	|	1855	|	...	1955	|	...
Cheltenham 121 122 d.	|	1431	|	|	|	|	|	1540	|	|	|	1631	|	|	|	|	|	1740	|	|	|	1831	|	|	2000
Gloucester 121 122 d.	|	1446	|	|	|	|	|	1554	|	|	|	1646	|	|	|	|	|	1754	|	|	|	1852	|	|	2013
Stroud d.	|	1504	|	|	|	|	|	1611	|	|	|	1704	|	|	|	|	|	1811	|	|	|	1910	|	|	2030
Swindon d.	1529	1535	1541	1559	1611	1629	1641	1642	1659	1711	1729	1735	1741	1759	1811	1829	1841	1841	1859	1911	1929	1941	2011	2029	2102
Didcot a.	|	1552	|	1616	1628	1646	|	...	1716	1728	|	1752	|	1816	1828	1846	|	...	1916	1928	|	1958	2028	2046	...
Reading 115 a.	1601	1607	1611	1632	1644	1701	1709	...	1732	1744	1757	1807	1813	1832	1847	1901	1909	...	1932	1945	2000	2014	2044	2101	...
London Paddington 115 a.	1630	1639	1644	1701	1714	1730	1739	...	1802	1814	1824	1839	1844	1902	1914	1932	1938	...	2007	2014	2032	2046	2114	2132	...

	Ⓐ	⑥	①–④	Ⓐ	Ⓐ	⑤	Ⓐ	Ⓐ	Ⓐ	
				2	Z			2		
Carmarthen 135 d.	...	...	...	...	...	...	...	...	...	...
Llanelli 135 d.	...	...	...	...	...	...	...	...	...	...
Swansea 135 d.	...	1929	1929	...	...	2029	2029	...	...	...
Neath 135 d.	...	1940	1940	...	...	2040	2040	...	...	...
Port Talbot Parkway 135 d.	...	1948	1948	...	...	2048	2048	...	...	...
Bridgend 135 d.	...	2000	2000	...	...	2100	2100	...	...	...
Cardiff Central 135 d.	...	2025	2025	...	...	2125	2125	...	...	...
Newport 135 d.	...	2039	2039	...	...	2139	2139	...	...	...
Taunton 115 d.	...	|	|	...	2112	|	|	...	2129	...
Weston super Mare d.	...	|	|	...	|	|	|	...	2158	...
Bristol T. Meads **115** d.	2030	|	|	...	2147	|	|	...	2233	...
Bristol Parkway d.	|	2102	2102	...	|	2202	2202	...	|	...
Bath d.	2043	|	|	...	2200	|	|	...	2246	...
Chippenham d.	2055	|	|	...	2212	|	|	...	2258	...
Cheltenham 121 122 d.	|	|	|	2048	|	|	|	2200	|	...
Gloucester 121 122 d.	|	|	|	2105	|	|	|	2213	|	...
Stroud d.	|	|	|	2123	|	|	|	2230	|	...
Swindon d.	2111	2129	2129	2153	2233	2233	2233	2302	2315	...
Didcot a.	2127	2150	2150	...	2246	|	|	...	2333	...
Reading 115 a.	2143	2211	2211	...	2303	2307	2307	...	2355	...
London Paddington 115 a.	2214	2244	2255	...	2340	2341	2351	...	0033	...

⑥	⑥	⑥	⑥	⑥	⑥	⑥	⑥	⑥	⑥	⑥	⑥	⑥	⑥	⑥
		2												
Carmarthen 135 d.	...	...	...	...	...	...	...	...	...	...	...	...	...	...
Llanelli 135 d.	...	...	...	...	...	...	...	...	...	...	...	...	...	...
Swansea 135 d.	...	...	0359	0459	...	0529	...	0559	...	0629	...	...	0659	...
Neath 135 d.	...	...	0410	0510	...	0540	...	0610	...	0640	...	...	0710	...
Port Talbot Parkway 135 d.	...	...	0418	0518	...	0548	...	0618	...	0648	...	...	0718	...
Bridgend 135 d.	...	...	0430	0530	...	0600	...	0630	...	0700	...	...	0730	...
Cardiff Central 135 d.	...	...	0455	0555	...	0625	...	0655	...	0725	...	...	0755	...
Newport 135 d.	...	...	0509	0609	...	0639	...	0709	...	0739	...	...	0809	...
Taunton 115 d.	...	...	|	|	...	|	...	|	...	|	...	0655	|	...
Weston super Mare d.	...	...	|	|	...	|	0624	|	...	|	...	0725	|	...
Bristol T. Meads **115** d.	0530	...	0600	|	0630	|	0700	|	0730	|	...	0800	|	0830
Bristol Parkway d.	|	...	0542	0632	|	0702	|	0732	|	0802	...	|	0832	|
Bath d.	0543	...	0613	|	0643	|	0713	|	0743	|	...	0813	|	0843
Chippenham d.	0555	...	0625	|	0655	|	0725	|	0755	|	...	0825	|	0855
Cheltenham 121 122 d.	|	0530	|	|	|	|	|	|	|	|	0729	|	|	|
Gloucester 121 122 d.	|	0544	|	|	|	|	|	|	|	|	0745	|	|	|
Stroud d.	|	0601	|	|	|	|	|	|	|	|	0803	|	|	|
Swindon d.	0611	0632	0641	0659	0711	0729	0741	0759	0811	0829	0835	0841	0859	0911
Didcot a.	0628	...	0658	0716	0728	0746	0759	0816	0828	0846	0851	0858	0916	0928
Reading 115 a.	0643	...	0714	0732	0744	0801	0814	0832	0844	0902	0907	0914	0933	0944
London Paddington 115 a.	0714	...	0744	0808	0814	0832	0844	0902	0914	0932	0937	0944	1002	1014

E – To / from Exeter.
M – To / from Plymouth.
P – To / from Pembroke Dock.
R – To / from Worcester.
S – To / from Southampton.
T – To / from Paignton.
W – To / from Westbury.
Z – To / from Penzance.
a – Until June 27 and from September 7.
s – Stops to set down only.
u – Stops to pick up only.

GW Most services 🍸 **CARMARTHEN - SWANSEA - CARDIFF - BRISTOL - LONDON** **133**

Services on ⑦ valid until July 12. For other services Cardiff - Swansea - South West Wales see Table **135**.

	⑥	⑥ E	⑥	⑥ b	⑥	⑥	⑥ 2	⑥	⑥	⑥	⑥	⑥ Tb	⑥	⑥ b	⑥ 2	⑥	⑥	⑥	⑥	⑥ b	⑥ Pb	⑥	⑥ 2	⑥	⑥
Carmarthen 135 d.	...	...	...	...	...	...	...	...	...	...	...	...	0935	...	...	...	...	...	...	...	1136	...	...	...	...
Llanelli 135 d.	...	...	...	...	...	...	...	...	...	...	...	...	1003	...	...	...	...	...	...	...	1203	...	...	...	...
Swansea 135 d.	0729	...	...	...	0829	...	...	...	0929	...	...	...	1029	...	...	...	1129	...	...	...	1229	...	...	...	1329
Neath 135 d.	0740	...	...	...	0840	...	...	...	0940	...	...	...	1040	...	...	...	1140	...	...	...	1240	...	...	...	1340
Port Talbot Parkway 135 d.	0748	...	...	...	0848	...	...	...	0948	...	...	...	1048	...	...	...	1148	...	...	...	1248	...	...	...	1348
Bridgend 135 d.	0800	...	...	...	0900	...	...	...	1000	...	...	...	1100	...	...	...	1200	...	...	...	1300	...	...	...	1400
Cardiff Central 135 d.	0825	...	...	...	0925	...	...	...	1025	...	...	...	1125	...	...	...	1225	...	...	...	1325	...	...	...	1425
Newport 135 d.	0839	...	...	...	0939	...	...	...	1039	...	...	...	1139	...	...	...	1239	...	...	...	1339	...	...	...	1439
Taunton 115 d.	|	0758	...	...	|	...	...	...	|	...	...	...	|	...	...	...	|	...	...	...	|	...	...	...	|
Weston super Mare d.	|	0829	...	...	|	...	...	...	|	...	...	1045	|	1133	...	...	|	...	...	1301	|	...	...	...	|
Bristol T. Meads **115** d.	|	0900	...	0930	|	1000	...	1030	|	1100	...	1130	|	1200	...	1230	|	1300	...	1330	|	1400	...	1430	|
Bristol Parkway d.	0902	|	...	|	1002	|	...	|	1102	|	...	|	1202	|	...	|	1302	|	...	|	1402	|	...	|	1502
Bath d.	|	0913	...	0943	|	1013	...	1043	|	1113	...	1143	|	1213	...	1243	|	1313	...	1343	|	1413	...	1443	|
Chippenham d.	|	0925	...	0955	|	1025	...	1055	|	1125	...	1155	|	1225	...	1255	|	1325	...	1355	|	1425	...	1455	|
Cheltenham 121 122 d.	|	|	0900	|	|	|	1001	|	|	|	1100	|	|	|	1201	|	|	|	1300	|	|	|	1401	|	|
Gloucester 121 122 d.	|	|	0916	|	|	|	1015	|	|	|	1116	|	|	|	1215	|	|	|	1316	|	|	|	1415	|	|
Stroud d.	|	|	0934	|	|	|	1032	|	|	|	1134	|	|	|	1232	|	|	|	1334	|	|	|	1432	|	|
Swindon d.	0927	0941	1004	1011	1029	1041	1102	1111	1129	1141	1204	1211	1229	1241	1302	1311	1329	1341	1404	1411	1429	1441	1502	1511	1529
Didcot a.	0946	|	1021	1028	1046	|	...	1128	1146	|	1221	1228	1246	|	...	1328	1346	|	1421	1429	|	|	...	1528	1546
Reading 115 a.	1001	1009	1035	1045	1101	1112	...	1144	1202	1209	1236	1248	1301	1309	...	1344	1402	1409	1436	1444	1501	1509	...	1544	1602
London Paddington 115 a.	1032	1038	1108	1114	1132	1140	...	1214	1232	1239	1310	1322	1332	1339	...	1414	1432	1439	1509	1514	1532	1539	...	1614	1632

	⑥	⑥	⑥ b	⑥	⑥	⑥ 2	⑥	⑥	⑥	⑥	⑥ b	⑥	⑥	⑥ 2	⑥ b	⑥ Pb	⑥	⑥	⑥	⑥ 2W	⑥	⑥		⑥ Zb	⑥
Carmarthen 135 d.	...	...	...	...	...	...	...	...	...	...	...	...	...	...	...	1607	...	...	...	...	...	...	...	...	...
Llanelli 135 d.	...	...	...	...	...	...	...	...	...	...	...	...	...	...	...	1704	...	...	...	...	...	...	...	...	...
Swansea 135 d.	...	...	...	1429	...	...	...	1529	...	...	...	1629	...	...	...	1729	...	...	1829	...	...	1929	...	...	...
Neath 135 d.	...	...	...	1440	...	...	...	1540	...	...	...	1640	...	...	...	1740	...	...	1840	...	...	1940	...	...	...
Port Talbot Parkway 135 d.	...	...	...	1448	...	...	...	1548	...	...	...	1648	...	...	...	1748	...	...	1848	...	...	1948	...	...	...
Bridgend 135 d.	...	...	...	1500	...	...	...	1600	...	...	...	1700	...	...	...	1800	...	...	1900	...	...	2000	...	...	...
Cardiff Central 135 d.	...	...	...	1525	...	...	...	1625	...	...	...	1725	...	...	...	1825	...	...	1925	...	...	2025	...	...	...
Newport 135 d.	...	...	...	1539	...	...	...	1639	...	...	...	1739	...	...	...	1839	...	...	1939	...	...	2039	...	...	...
Taunton 115 d.	...	...	...	|	...	...	...	|	...	...	...	|	...	...	...	|	...	...	|	...	...	|	...	2111	2130
Weston super Mare d.	...	...	1501	|	...	...	...	|	...	...	1701	|	...	...	1801	|	...	...	|	...	2010	|	...	|	2159
Bristol T. Meads **115** d.	1500	...	1530	|	1600	...	1630	|	1700	...	1730	|	1800	...	1830	|	...	1930	|	...	2033	|	...	2144	2233
Bristol Parkway d.	|	...	|	1602	|	...	|	1702	|	...	|	1802	|	...	|	1902	...	|	2002	...	|	2102	...	|	|
Bath d.	1513	...	1543	|	1613	...	1643	|	1713	...	1743	|	1813	...	1843	|	...	1943	|	...	2046	|	...	2200	2246
Chippenham d.	1525	...	1555	|	1625	...	1655	|	1725	...	1755	|	1825	...	1855	|	...	1955	|	...	2058	|	...	2212	2258
Cheltenham 121 122 d.	|	1500	|	|	|	1601	|	|	|	1700	|	|	|	1801	|	|	1900	|	|	2001	|	|	...	|	|
Gloucester 121 122 d.	|	1516	|	|	|	1615	|	|	|	1716	|	|	|	1815	|	|	1916	|	|	2015	|	|	...	|	|
Stroud d.	|	1534	|	|	|	1632	|	|	|	1734	|	|	|	1832	|	|	1934	|	|	2032	|	|	...	|	|
Swindon d.	1541	1604	1611	1629	1641	1702	1711	1729	1741	1804	1811	1829	1841	1902	1911	1929	2004	2011	2029	2103	2114	2129	...	2228	2314
Didcot a.	|	1621	1628	1646	|	...	1728	1746	|	1821	1828	1846	|	...	1928	|	2021	2028	2046	...	2131	2146	...	2245	2331
Reading 115 a.	1609	1636	1644	1701	1709	...	1744	1801	1809	1836	1843	1901	1909	...	1943	2000	2036	2044	2107	...	2148	2158	...	2301	2352
London Paddington 115 a.	1642	1706	1714	1732	1738	...	1814	1832	1838	1908	1914	1932	1939	...	2014	2032	2107	2114	2136	...	2216	2232	...	2338	0033

		⑦	⑦	⑦	⑦	⑦	⑦ 2	⑦	⑦	⑦	⑦	⑦	⑦ M	⑦	⑦	⑦ 2	⑦ M	⑦	⑦	⑦	⑦	⑦	⑦	⑦	⑦
Carmarthen 135 d.	⑦	...	...	...	...	...	...	...	...	...	...	...	...	...	...	...	...	...	...	...	...	...	...	...	...
Llanelli 135 d.		...	...	...	...	...	...	...	...	...	...	...	...	...	...	...	...	...	...	...	...	...	...	...	...
Swansea 135 d.		...	...	...	...	0759	...	...	0859	...	...	0959	...	...	1059	...	...	1159	...	...	1259	...	1359	...	...
Neath 135 d.		...	...	...	...	0811	...	...	0911	...	...	1011	...	...	1111	...	...	1211	...	...	1311	...	1411	...	...
Port Talbot Parkway 135 d.		...	...	...	...	0818	...	...	0918	...	...	1018	...	...	1118	...	...	1218	...	...	1318	...	1418	...	...
Bridgend 135 d.		...	...	...	...	0830	...	...	0930	...	...	1030	...	...	1130	...	...	1230	...	...	1330	...	1430	...	...
Cardiff Central 135 d.		...	...	0745	...	0855	...	...	0955	...	...	1055	...	...	1155	...	...	1255	...	...	1355	...	1455	...	...
Newport 135 d.		...	...	0803	...	0909	...	...	1009	...	...	1109	...	...	1209	...	...	1309	...	...	1409	...	1509	...	...
Taunton 115 d.		...	...	|	...	|	...	...	|	...	...	|	1117	...	|	...	1223	|	...	...	|	...	|	...	...
Weston super Mare d.		...	...	|	0826	|	...	...	|	...	1021	|	|	...	|	...	|	|	1321	...	|	1421	|	...	...
Bristol T. Meads **115** d.		0740	0810	|	0900	|	...	1000	|	1030	1100	|	1200	...	|	...	1300	|	1400	...	|	1500	|	1600	...
Bristol Parkway d.		|	|	0834	|	0932	...	|	1032	|	|	1132	|	...	1232	...	|	1332	|	...	1432	|	1532	|	...
Bath d.		0753	0823	|	0913	|	...	1013	|	1043	1113	|	1213	...	|	...	1313	|	1413	...	|	1513	|	1613	...
Chippenham d.		0805	0835	|	0925	|	...	1025	|	1055	1125	|	1225	...	|	...	1325	|	1425	...	|	1525	|	1625	...
Cheltenham 121 122 d.		|	|	|	|	|	0935	|	|	|	|	|	|	1146	|	1235	|	|	|	1346	|	|	|	|	1546
Gloucester 121 122 d.		|	|	|	|	|	0949	|	|	|	|	|	|	1204	|	1249	|	|	|	1404	|	|	|	|	1604
Stroud d.		|	|	|	|	|	1006	|	|	|	|	|	|	1223	|	1306	|	|	|	1422	|	|	|	|	1622
Swindon d.		0820	0850	0900	0941	0959	1035	1041	1059	1111	1141	1159	1241	1253	1259	1336	1341	1359	1441	1451	1459	1541	1559	1641	1651
Didcot a.		0839	0909	|	0958	1016	...	1058	1116	|	1158	1216	1258	|	1316	...	1358	1416	1458	|	1516	1558	1616	1658	|
Reading 115 a.		0855	0926	0929	1012	1031	...	1113	1131	1142	1213	1231	1313	1322	1331	...	1413	1431	1514	1519	1531	1614	1631	1714	1719
London Paddington 115 a.		0934	1006	1010	1055	1110	...	1155	1209	1228	1255	1310	1355	1408	1409	...	1455	1509	1555	1608	1610	1653	1710	1753	1808

	⑦	⑦	⑦ 2	⑦		⑦	⑦ M	⑦ T	⑦	⑦		⑦ M	⑦	⑦	⑦	⑦ 2	⑦	⑦		⑦	⑦	⑦	⑦ 2		⑦ M
Carmarthen 135 d.	...	...	...	...	...	...	...	...	...	1609	...	...	...	...	...	...	...	...	...	1805	...	1909	...	...	...
Llanelli 135 d.	...	...	...	...	...	...	...	...	...	1636	...	...	...	...	...	...	...	...	...	1832	...	1936	...	...	...
Swansea 135 d.	1459	...	...	...	...	1559	...	...	...	1659	...	...	...	1759	...	...	...	...	...	1859	...	1959	...	...	...
Neath 135 d.	1511	...	...	...	...	1511	...	...	...	1711	...	...	...	1811	...	...	...	...	...	1911	...	2011	...	...	...
Port Talbot Parkway 135 d.	1518	...	...	...	...	1618	...	...	...	1718	...	...	...	1818	...	...	...	...	...	1918	...	2018	...	...	...
Bridgend 135 d.	1530	...	...	...	...	1630	...	...	...	1730	...	...	...	1830	...	...	...	...	...	1930	...	2030	...	...	...
Cardiff Central 135 d.	1555	...	...	...	...	1655	...	...	...	1755	...	...	...	1855	...	...	...	...	...	1955	...	2055	...	...	...
Newport 135 d.	1609	...	...	...	...	1709	...	...	...	1809	...	...	...	1909	...	...	...	...	...	2009	...	2109	...	...	...
Taunton 115 d.	|	...	...	...	...	|	1639	1703	...	|	...	1746	...	|	1823	...	...	...	...	|	...	|	...	...	2123
Weston super Mare d.	|	...	...	...	...	|	1701	1724	...	|	...	|	...	|	1853	...	...	...	...	|	2038	|	...	...	|
Bristol T. Meads **115** d.	|	1630	...	1700	...	|	1730	1800	...	|	...	1830	1900	|	1930	...	2000	...	...	|	2100	|	...	...	2205
Bristol Parkway d.	1632	|	...	|	...	1732	|	|	...	1832	...	|	|	1932	|	...	|	...	...	2032	|	2132	...	...	|
Bath d.	|	1643	...	1713	...	|	1743	1813	...	|	...	1843	1913	|	1943	...	2013	...	...	|	2113	|	...	...	2219
Chippenham d.	|	1655	...	1725	...	|	1755	1825	...	|	...	1855	1925	|	1955	...	2025	...	...	|	2125	|	...	...	2231
Cheltenham 121 122 d.	|	|	1633	|	...	|	|	|	1746	|	...	|	|	|	|	*1914*	|	1946	...	|	|	|	2146	...	|
Gloucester 121 122 d.	|	|	1647	|	...	|	|	|	1805	|	...	|	|	|	|	1934	|	2005	...	|	|	|	2159	...	|
Stroud d.	|	|	1704	|	...	|	|	|	1823	|	...	|	|	|	|	1953	|	2023	...	|	|	|	2217	...	|
Swindon d.	1659	1711	1734	1741	...	1759	1811	1841	1853	1859	...	1911	1941	1959	2011	2023	2041	2054	...	2059	2141	2159	2247	...	2252
Didcot a.	1716	|	...	1758	...	1816	|	1859	|	1916	...	|	1958	2016	|	...	2059	|	...	2116	2200	|	...	...	2310
Reading 115 a.	1731	1742	...	1814	...	1831	1844	1915	1923	1931	...	1943	2014	2031	2042	...	2116	2125	...	2131	2217	2235	...	...	2326
London Paddington 115 a.	1815	1823	...	1853	...	1910	1928	1955	2007	2012	...	2025	2053	2111	2121	...	2156	2207	...	2216	2308	2322	...	...	0006

E – To/ from Exeter.
M – To/ from Plymouth.
P – To/ from Pembroke Dock.
R – To/ from Worcester.
S – To/ from Southampton.
T – To/ from Paignton.
W – To/ from Westbury.
Z – To/ from Penzance.
b – Until September 5.
s – Stops to set down only.
u – Stops to pick up only.

135 CARDIFF - SWANSEA - SOUTH WEST WALES

Most services ⚲ 2nd class AW

Services on ⑦ valid until September 6. For *GW* services London - Bristol - Cardiff - Swansea see Table **133**.

km		⚒	⚒	⚒	⚒	⑥ c	⚒	Ⓐ R	⑥ R	⚒ S	⑥	Ⓐ R	⑥ R	Ⓐ	⚒	⚒	⑥ Gc	Ⓐ	⑥ c	Ⓐ	⚒	⑥ c	⚒	Ⓐ
	Manchester Piccadilly **155** d.	...	...	...	...	...	...	...	...	...	...	...	...	...	0630	...	...	0730	0730	...	0830	...	0930	...
0	**Cardiff** Central **133** d.	...	...	...	0540	...	0652	0758	0804	0809	...	0904	0904	...	1004	1054	1048	1104	1104	...	1204	...	1304	...
32	Bridgend **133** d.	...	...	...	0608	...	0712	0817	0823	0829	...	0923	0923	...	1023	|	1109	1123	1123	...	1223	...	1323	...
52	Port Talbot **133** d.	...	...	...	0624	...	0728	0830	0836	0845	...	0936	0936	...	1036	|	1123	1136	1136	...	1236	...	1336	...
61	Neath **133** d.	...	...	...	0635	...	0739	0837	0843	0856	...	0943	0943	...	1043	|	1130	1143	1143	...	1243	...	1343	...
73	**Swansea** **133** a.	...	...	...	0652	...	0755	0849	0855	0913	...	0955	0956	...	1055	|	1143	1155	1155	...	1255	...	1355	...
73	**Swansea** d.	...	...	0550	0654	0724	0805	0900	0900	0915	0950	1000	1005	1005	1100	|	1151	1200	1205	1205	1300	1335	1400	1405
91	Llanelli **133** d.	...	...	0608	0711	0745	0823	0919	0919	0932	1008	1016	1024	1024	1117	1158	1208	1216	1221	1224	1316	1353	1416	1424
124	**Carmarthen** **133** a.	...	...	0640	0742	0813	0853	0951	0951	...	1040	1041	1051	1056	1145	|	1240	1241	1251	1256	1341	1427	1441	1456
124	**Carmarthen** d.	0545	0605	0643	0744	0820	0856a	0955	0955	...	1056	...	...	1059	1145	|	1246	...	...	1259	1344	1447	...	1459
147	Whitland d.	0559	0620	0658	0800	0839	0910a	1014	1014	...	1110	...	...	1113	1200	1234	1305	...	...	1313	1359	1501	...	1513
172	Tenby d.	0630	|	0742	|	0912	0943a	|	|	...	1141	...	...	1143	|	|	1341	...	...	1343	|	1533	...	1543
191	**Pembroke Dock** a.	0704	|	0817	|	0949	1017a	|	|	...	1217	...	...	1217	|	|	1414	...	...	1417	|	1607	...	1617
174	Haverfordwest d.	...	0641	...	0822	...	...	1035	1035	...	...	...	...	...	1221	|	...	...	...	...	1420	...	...	...
188	**Milford Haven** a.	...	0704	...	0844	...	...	1058	1058	...	...	...	...	...	1247	|	...	...	...	...	1444	...	...	...
191	Fishguard a.	...	...	...	...	...	...	...	...	...	...	...	...	...	...	1315	...	...	...	...	...	...	...	...
	Rosslare ⛴ **2030** a.	...	...	...	...	...	...	...	...	...	...	...	...	...	...	*1800*	...	...	...	...	...	...	...	...

	⚒	⚒	Ⓐ	⑥ c	⚒	⚒	⚒	⑥	Ⓐ	⚒	⚒	Ⓐ	⑥	Ⓐ	⑥	⚒	⑥	Ⓐ	⑦	⑦	⑦	⑦	⑦	⑦ H
Manchester Piccadilly **155** d.	1030	1130	...	...	1230	...	1330	1430	1430	1530	1630	1730	1730	1830	1830	...	...	...	...	...	...	...	...	...
Cardiff Central **133** d.	1404	1504	...	...	1604	...	1704	1804	1804	1904	2000	2106	2106	2213	2216	...	2243	2315	...	...	0830	...	0955	1120
Bridgend **133** d.	1423	1523	...	...	1623	...	1725	1823	1824	1923	2022	2128	2128	2233	2236	...	2310	2345	...	...	0858	...	1015	1140
Port Talbot **133** d.	1436	1536	...	...	1636	...	1739	1836	1842	1938	2035	2143	2143	2247	2250	...	2327	0001	...	...	0914	...	1029	1154
Neath **133** d.	1443	1543	...	...	1643	...	1749	1843	1849	1948	|	2150	2150	2255	2258	...	2338	0012	...	...	0925	...	1037	1202
Swansea **133** a.	1455	1555	...	...	1655	...	1805	1856	1901	2005	|	2203	2203	2307	2310	...	2353	0028	...	...	0940	...	1049	1214
Swansea d.	1500	1600	1605	1605	1705	1751	1809	1905	1905	2010	|	2227	2227	2310	2313	2345	0008	0045	...	...	0945	...	1054	1217
Llanelli **133** d.	1519	1616	1624	1624	1723	1809	1826	1925	1925	2026	2105	2244	2244	2328	2331	0001	0025s	0102s	...	...	1006	...	1112	1235
Carmarthen **133** a.	1544	1646	1656	1656	1752	1841	1900	1950	1950	2055	2130	2313	2313	0004	0007	0027	0101	0137	...	...	1037	...	1143	1305
Carmarthen d.	1547	...	1659	1705	1755	1905	...	1955	1955	2100	2204	2317	2317	...	...	0030	...	...	0820	0935	1039	1046	1150	1308
Whitland d.	1602	...	1713	1732	1814	1919	...	2010	2010	2114	2221	2332	2332	...	...	0045	...	...	0835	0948	1055	1101	1205	1324
Tenby d.	|	...	1743	1801	|	1952	...	|	|	2145	|	|	|	...	...	|	...	...	|	1016	|	1132	1239	|
Pembroke Dock a.	|	...	1817	1835	|	2022	...	|	|	2220	|	|	|	...	...	|	...	...	|	1049	|	1203	...	|
Haverfordwest d.	1623	...	...	...	1835	...	...	2031	2031	...	2242	2354	2353	...	...	|	...	...	0856	...	1118	...	...	|
Milford Haven a.	1646	...	...	...	1858	...	...	2054	2054	...	2305	0011	...	...	...	|	...	...	0915	...	1137	...	...	|
Fishguard a.	...	...	...	...	...	...	...	...	...	...	...	...	...	...	...	0126	...	...	...	...	...	...	...	1400
Rosslare ⛴ **2030** a.	...	...	...	...	...	...	...	...	...	...	...	...	...	...	...	*0615*	...	...	...	...	...	...	...	*1800*

	⑦	⑦	⑦	⑦	⑦	⑦	⑦	⑦	⑦	⑦
Manchester Piccadilly **155** d.	...	...	1030	...	1230	1430	1430	...	...	...
Cardiff Central **133** d.	...	...	1406	...	1620	1807	1807	2022	2132	2235
Bridgend **133** d.	...	...	1425	...	1647	1827	1827	2042	2159	2254
Port Talbot **133** d.	...	...	1438	...	1700	1839	1839	2054	2214	2307
Neath **133** d.	...	...	1446	...	1707	1846	1846	2101	2225	2314
Swansea **133** a.	...	...	1501	...	1719	1859	1859	2115	2241	2326
Swansea d.	...	...	1506	...	1724	1920	1920	2119	2310	2332
Llanelli **133** d.	...	...	1525	...	1741	1939	1939	2136	2329	2349
Carmarthen **133** a.	...	...	1550	...	1813	2004	2004	2206	2357	0019
Carmarthen d.	1405	1420	1605	1700	1816	2009	2009	2211	...	0021
Whitland d.	1421	1434	1620	1719	1832	2028	2035	2227	...	0036
Tenby d.	|	1521	|	1750	|	2100	|	|	...	|
Pembroke Dock a.	|	1555	|	1825	|	2135	|	|	...	|
Haverfordwest d.	1444	...	1641	...	1854	...	2057	2248	...	|
Milford Haven a.	1505	...	1704	...	1917	...	2120	2311	...	|
Fishguard a.	...	...	...	...	...	...	...	...	...	0117
Rosslare ⛴ **2030** a.	...	...	...	...	...	...	...	...	...	*0615*

	⚒	⚒	⚒	⚒	⚒	⚒	⚒ S	Ⓐ
Rosslare ⛴ **2030** d.	*2115p*	...	...	...	...	...	...	...
Fishguard d.	0150	...	...	...	...	...	...	...
Milford Haven d.	|	...	...	...	0605	0705	...	...
Haverfordwest d.	|	...	...	...	0620	0720	...	...
Pembroke Dock d.	|	...	...	...	|	|	...	0705
Tenby d.	|	...	...	...	|	|	...	0736
Whitland d.	0222	...	...	...	0640	0740	...	0806
Carmarthen a.	0239	...	...	...	0656	0756	...	0824
Carmarthen **133** d.	0244	0504	0550	0618	0700	0759	...	0830
Llanelli **133** d.	0306	0528	0618	0645	0724	0827	0845	0909
Swansea a.	0325	|	0637	0709	0743	0846	0908	0922
Swansea **133** d.	*0359*	|	0640	0716	0745	0855	0910	0955
Neath **133** d.	*0410*	|	0651	0724	0756	0906	0925	1006
Port Talbot **133** d.	*0418*	0601	0658	0735	0803	0913	0936	1013
Bridgend **133** d.	*0430*	0615	0717	0750	0817	0925	0952	1025
Cardiff Central **133** a.	*0456*	0643	0740	0834	0844	0947	1017	1048
Manchester Piccadilly **155** a.	...	1015	1115	...	1215	1315	...	1415

	⑥	⑥ c	⚒	⑥ c	Ⓐ	⚒	⑥ Gc	⚒	⚒	⚒	⚒	⚒ E	⚒	⚒	⚒	⑥ Gc	Ⓐ	⚒	⑥	⚒	Ⓐ	⚒ C	Ⓐ	⑥	⑥
Rosslare ⛴ **2030** d.	...	...	...	...	...	...	...	...	...	...	...	*0900*	...	...	...	...	...	...	...	...	...	...	...	...	...
Fishguard d.	...	...	...	...	...	...	...	...	...	...	...	1327	...	...	...	...	...	...	...	...	...	...	...	...	...
Milford Haven d.	...	...	0910	...	...	...	...	1110	...	...	1310	|	...	...	1510	...	...	...	...	1710	...	...	1910	1910	...
Haverfordwest d.	...	...	0925	...	...	...	...	1125	...	...	1325	|	...	...	1525	...	...	...	...	1725	...	...	1925	1925	...
Pembroke Dock d.	0705	0835	|	...	0905	...	1002	|	1105a	...	|	|	1305	...	|	1455	1505	...	1635	|	1705	...	|	|	1916
Tenby d.	0736	0908	|	...	0940	...	1038	|	1141	...	|	|	1341	...	|	1535	1542	...	1703	|	1743	...	|	|	1947
Whitland d.	0806	0939	0945	1008	1009	...	1109	1145	1209	...	1345	1359	1410	...	1545	1609	1611	...	1731	1745	1810	...	1945	1945	2014
Carmarthen a.	0825	...	1001	1026	1026	...	1127	1201	1227	...	1401	1416	1427	...	1601	1626	1628	...	1748	1802	1827	...	2002	2002	2033
Carmarthen **133** d.	0900	...	1005	1030	1030	1100	1136	1205	1230	1300	1405	1419	1430	1505	1605	1633	1631	1701	1830	1806	1830	1908	2005	2005	2035
Llanelli **133** d.	0927	...	1028	1055	1055	1128	1203	1229	1255	1328	1429	1443	1500	1529	1629	1704	1701	1729	1900	1834	1859	1932	2029	2029	2106
Swansea a.	0946	...	1045	1116	1122	1146	1222	1246	1322	1348	1448	|	1522	1546	1648	1721	1722	1746	1922	1853	1922	1949	2050	2050	2124
Swansea **133** d.	0955	...	1055	...	...	1155	1229	1250	...	1355	1455	|	...	1555	1655	1729	...	1755	...	1910	...	2000	2055	2055	2135
Neath **133** d.	1006	...	1106	...	...	1206	1240	1306	...	1406	1506	|	...	1606	1706	1740	...	1806	...	1925	...	2011	2106	2106	2150
Port Talbot **133** d.	1013	...	1113	...	...	1213	1248	1313	...	1413	1513	|	...	1613	1713	1748	...	1813	...	1936	...	2018	2113	2113	2201
Bridgend **133** d.	1025	...	1125	...	...	1225	1300	1325	...	1425	1525	|	...	1625	1725	1800	...	1826	...	1951	...	2030	2125	2125	2216
Cardiff Central **133** a.	1047	...	1147	...	...	1247	1322	1347	...	1447	1548	1604	...	1647	1747	1822	...	1847	...	2018	...	2051	2147	2149	2239
Manchester Piccadilly **155** a.	1415	...	1515	...	...	1615	...	1715	...	1815	1915	...	...	2015	2115	...	...	2215	...	...	...	...	...	...	...

	Ⓐ	⚒	⑥	⚒	Ⓐ	⚒	⚒	⑦	⑦	⑦	⑦	⑦	⑦	⑦	⑦	⑦	⑦	⑦ R	⑦ S	⑦ H	⑦	⑦	⑦	⑦
Rosslare ⛴ **2030** d.	...	...	...	...	...	...	...	*2115p*	...	...	...	...	...	*0900*	...	...	...	...	...	...	...	...	...	...
Fishguard d.	...	...	...	...	...	...	...	0150	...	...	...	...	...	1430	...	...	...	...	...	...	...	...	...	...
Milford Haven d.	...	2120	...	...	...	...	2315	|	0925	...	...	1335	...	|	1535	...	1735	...	...	...	1935	2135	...	2315
Haverfordwest d.	...	2135	...	...	...	...	2330	|	0940	...	...	1350	...	|	1550	...	1750	...	...	...	1950	2150	...	2330
Pembroke Dock d.	1916	|	...	2111	...	2224	|	|	|	1100	1240	|	...	|	|	1605	|	...	...	1905	|	|	2205	|
Tenby d.	1947	|	...	2144	...	2251	|	|	|	1134	1308	|	1358	|	|	1633	|	...	...	1933	|	|	2233	|
Whitland d.	2016	2155	...	2215	...	2320	2357	0222	1000	1201	1339	1412	1429	1502	1610	1704	1810	...	...	2004	2012	2213	2304	2351
Carmarthen a.	2033	2216	...	2232	...	2340	0018	0238	1016	1217	1357	1428	1446	1520	1626	1725	1827	...	...	2021	2030	2230	2325	0007
Carmarthen **133** d.	2036	...	...	2335	...	...	...	0241	1020	1235	1400	1442	...	...	1631	...	...	1835	...	2035	...	2235	...	...
Llanelli **133** d.	2110	...	...	2305	...	...	...	0304	1048	1304	1430	1505	...	...	1659	...	...	1903	1952	2105	...	2305	...	...
Swansea a.	2133	...	...	2329	...	...	...	0321	1110	1321	1451	1523	...	...	1718	...	...	1926	2013	2126	...	2327	...	...
Swansea **133** d.	2135	...	2220	...	2232	...	...	0335	1122	1346	...	1530	...	...	1735	...	...	1936	2035	2135	...	2337	...	...
Neath **133** d.	2150	...	2235	...	2247	...	...	0346	1137	1357	...	1541	...	...	1747	...	...	1947	2046	2150	...	2348	...	...
Port Talbot **133** d.	2201	...	2246	...	2258	...	...	0353	1148	1404	...	1548	...	...	1754	...	...	1954	2054	2201	...	2356	...	...
Bridgend **133** d.	2216	...	2301	...	2313	...	...	0405	1202	1416	...	1600	...	...	1806	...	...	2006	2107	2216	...	0009	...	...
Cardiff Central **133** a.	2239	...	2326	...	2338	...	...	0430	1230	1437	...	1629	...	...	1827	...	...	2027	2130	2244	...	0050	...	...
Manchester Piccadilly **155** a.	...	...	...	...	...	...	...	...	1615	1815	...	2015	...	...	2215	...	...	...	...	...	...	...	...	...

C – To / from Chester.
E – To Cheltenham on Ⓐ.
G – 12 London Paddington - Pembroke Dock and v.v. Operated By *GW*.
H – To / from Hereford.
R – To / from Crewe.
S – To / from Shrewsbury.

a – Ⓐ only.
c – Until September 5.
p – Previous day.
s – Stops to set down only.

Services on ⑥⑦ valid until September 6.

km	Ⓐ	Ⓐ	Ⓐ	Ⓐ 🍷	Ⓐ	Ⓐ	Ⓐ 🍷	Ⓐ	Ⓐ 🍷	Ⓐ TW	Ⓐ ◇	Ⓐ	Ⓐ 🍷	Ⓐ GW	Ⓐ 🍷	Ⓐ	Ⓐ	Ⓐ 🍷	Ⓐ GW	Ⓐ 🍷	Ⓐ B	Ⓐ ◇	Ⓐ 🍷
0	**Cardiff** Central .... 133 135 d.	...	...	...	...	...	0628	...	0730	...	...	...	0830	...	0930	...	...	1030	...	1130	...	...	1230
19	Newport.................. 133 135 d.	...	...	...	...	...	0642	...	0744	...	...	...	0844	...	0944	...	...	1044	...	1144	...	...	1244
	Bristol Parkway .... 133 d.	...	...	...	...	...	|	0725	|	0825	...	...	|	0919	|	...	1019	|	1119	|	1219	...	|
61	**Bristol** Temple Meads... 133 d.	...	...	0544	...	0644	0722	0749	0822	0841	0850	0905	0922	0949	1022	...	1049	1122	1149	1222	1239	1310	1322
80	Bath .... 133 d.	...	...	0601	...	0702	0736	0807	0837	0858	0907	0921	0936	1007	1036	...	1107	1136	1207	1236	1257	1322	1336
95	Bradford on Avon.................d.	...	...	0618	...	0718	0747	0822	0847	0914	0920	0933	|	1022	1047	...	1122	1147	1222	1247	1312	1335	1347
100	Trowbridge ....d.	...	...	0625	0650	0724	0753	0828	0853	0920	0927	0939	0951	1028	1053	...	1128	1153	1228	1253	1318	1342	1353
107	**Westbury**...........................d.	0524	0549	0637	0658	0733	0801	0836	0901	0927	0939	0948	0958	1036	1101	1107	1136	1201	1236	1301	1327	1353	1402
114	Warminster.........................d.	0532	0556	0643	0710	...	0808	...	0908	...	0946	...	1006	...	1108	1116	...	1208	...	1308	1336	1400	1408
146	**Salisbury** .... 113 d.	0553	0620	0711	0736	...	0832	...	0932	...	1020	...	1030	...	1132	1139	...	1232	...	1332	1359	1445	1432
	London Waterloo........ 113 a.	...	|	|	|	...	|	...	|	...	1149	...	|	...	|	|	...	|	...	|	|	1619	|
173	Romsey...............................d.	...	0638	0730	0756	...	0850	...	0950	...	...	...	1048	...	1150	1200	...	1250	...	1350	1420	...	1450
184	**Southampton** Central ....a.	...	0649	0741	0809	...	0904	...	1004	...	...	...	1104	...	1204	1219	...	1304	...	1404	1432	...	1504
208	Fareham..............................a.	...	0714	0805	...	...	0927	...	1027	...	...	...	1127	...	1227	...	...	1327	...	1427	1455	...	1527
225	Portsmouth & Southsea ....a.	...	0738	0824	...	...	0945	...	1045	...	...	...	1145	...	1245	...	...	1345	...	1445	...	...	1545
226	**Portsmouth** Harbour.............a.	...	0745	0830	...	...	0954	...	1054	...	...	...	1154	...	1254	...	...	1354	...	1454	...	...	1554

	Ⓐ G	Ⓐ 🍷	Ⓐ W	Ⓐ 🍷	Ⓐ G	Ⓐ ◇	Ⓐ 🍷	Ⓐ W	Ⓐ	Ⓐ 🍷	Ⓐ GW	Ⓐ	Ⓐ 🍷	Ⓐ C	Ⓐ T	Ⓐ 🍷	Ⓐ G	Ⓐ 🍷	Ⓐ W	Ⓐ 🍷	Ⓐ	Ⓐ ◇		Ⓐ
Cardiff Central .... 133 135 d.	...	1330	...	1430	...	...	1530	...	...	1630	...	...	1730	...	...	1830	...	1930	...	2030	...	...	...	...
Newport.................. 133 135 d.	...	1344	...	1444	...	...	1544	...	...	1644	...	...	1744	...	...	1844	...	1944	...	2044	...	...	...	...
Bristol Parkway .... 133 d.	1319	|	1419	|	1519	...	|	1619	1646	|	1719	1746	|	1819	...	|	1919	|	2019	|	...	...	...	...
Bristol Temple Meads... 133 d.	1349	1422	1449	1522	1543	1552	1622	1649	1707	1722	1749	1807	1822	1849	...	1922	1949	2022	2049	2122	2200	2225	...	2316
Bath .... 133 d.	1407	1436	1507	1536	1601	1607	1636	1707	1725	1736	1807	1825	1836	1907	...	1937	2007	2037	2107	2137	2218	2238	...	2335
Bradford on Avon.................d.	1422	1447	1522	1547	1615	1622	1647	1722	1740	1747	1822	1840	1847	1922	...	1947	2022	2047	2122	2147	2234	2251	...	2351
Trowbridge ....d.	1428	1453	1528	1553	1621	1628	1653	1728	1746	1753	1828	1846	1853	1928	1920	1953	2028	2053	2128	2153	2240	2257	...	2357
Westbury...........................d.	1436	1501	1536	1601	1628	1639	1701	1736	1756	1801	1836	1856	1901	1936	1940	2001	2036	2101	2135	2201	2247	2304	...	0004
Warminster.........................d.	...	1508	...	1608	...	1647	1708	...	...	1808	...	...	1908	...	1949	2008	...	2108	...	2208	...	2311	...	...
Salisbury .... 113 d.	...	1532	...	1632	...	1720	1732	...	...	1832	...	...	1932	...	2013	2032	...	2132	...	2232	...	2334	...	...
London Waterloo........ 113 a.	...	|	...	|	...	1845	|	...	...	|	...	...	|	...	|	|	...	|	...	|	...	...	...	...
Romsey...............................d.	...	1550	...	1650	...	...	1750	...	...	1850	...	...	1950	...	2035	2050	...	2150	...	2250	...	...	...	...
Southampton Central ....a.	...	1604	...	1704	...	...	1804	...	...	1904	...	...	2004	...	2048	2104	...	2202	...	2303	...	...	...	...
Fareham..............................a.	...	1627	...	1727	...	...	1827	...	...	1927	...	...	2027	...	...	2127	...	2242	...	2325	...	...	...	...
Portsmouth & Southsea ....a.	...	1645	...	1745	...	...	1852	...	...	1945	...	...	2045	...	...	2145	...	2259	...	2344	...	...	...	...
Portsmouth Harbour.............a.	...	1654	...	1754	...	...	1858	...	...	1954	...	...	2054	...	...	2152	...	2304	...	2353	...	...	...	...

⑥	⑥	⑥	⑥	⑥	⑥	⑥	⑥ 🍷	⑥ TW	⑥ ◇	⑥ 🍷	⑥ GW	⑥ 🍷	⑥	⑥ T	⑥ 🍷	⑥ GW	⑥ 🍷	⑥ B	⑥ ◇	⑥ 🍷	⑥ G	⑥ 🍷	⑥ TW
Cardiff Central .... 133 135 d.	...	...	...	...	0630	...	0730	...	...	0830	...	0930	...	...	1030	...	1130	...	...	1230	...	1330	...
Newport.................. 133 135 d.	...	...	...	...	0644	...	0744	...	...	0844	...	0944	...	...	1044	...	1144	...	...	1244	...	1344	...
Bristol Parkway .... 133 d.	...	...	...	...	|	...	|	0820	...	|	0919	|	...	1025	|	1119	|	1225	...	|	1319	|	1421
Bristol Temple Meads... 133 d.	...	0549	...	0649	0722	0749	0822	0841	0850	0922	0949	1022	...	1049	1122	1149	1222	1243	1315	1322	1349	1422	1449
Bath .... 133 d.	...	0607	...	0707	0736	0807	0836	0858	0907	0936	1007	1036	...	1107	1136	1207	1236	1300	1327	1336	1407	1436	1507
Bradford on Avon.................d.	...	0622	...	0722	0747	0822	0847	0914	0920	0947	1022	1047	...	1122	1147	1222	1247	1313	1340	1347	1422	1447	1522
Trowbridge ....d.	...	0628	...	0728	0753	0828	0853	0920	0927	0953	1028	1053	...	1128	1153	1228	1253	1319	1347	1353	1428	1453	1528
Westbury...........................d.	0526	0639	0706	0735	0801	0835	0901	0927	0939	1003	1034	1101	1107	1135	1201	1235	1301	1327	1354	1401	1435	1501	1535
Warminster.........................d.	0534	0646	0715	...	0808	...	0908	...	0946	1008	...	1108	1116	...	1208	...	1308	1336	1402	1408	...	1508	...
Salisbury .... 113 d.	0558	0724	0737	...	0833	...	0933	...	1020	1032	...	1133	1139	...	1233	...	1333	1359	1445	1433	...	1533	...
London Waterloo........ 113 a.	...	|	|	...	|	...	|	...	1149	|	...	|	|	...	|	...	|	|	1619	|	...	|	...
Romsey...............................d.	...	0744	0756	...	0851	...	0951	...	...	1050	...	1151	1200	...	1251	...	1351	1419	...	1451	...	1551	...
Southampton Central ....a.	...	0802	0807	...	0902	...	1002	...	...	1102	...	1202	1220	...	1302	...	1402	1432	...	1502	...	1602	...
Fareham..............................a.	...	0827	...	...	0927	...	1027	...	...	1127	...	1227	...	...	1327	...	1427	1454	...	1527	...	1627	...
Portsmouth & Southsea ....a.	...	0846	...	...	0946	...	1046	...	...	1146	...	1246	...	...	1346	...	1446	...	...	1546	...	1646	...
Portsmouth Harbour.............a.	...	0852	...	...	0952	...	1053	...	...	1152	...	1252	...	...	1352	...	1452	...	...	1552	...	1652	...

	⑥ 🍷	⑥	⑥ ◇	⑥ 🍷	⑥ W	⑥ 🍷	⑥ GW	⑥ 🍷	⑥	⑥	⑥ 🍷	⑥ G	⑥ 🍷	⑥ W	⑥ 🍷	⑥	⑥ ◇	⑥		⑦ 🍷	⑦ W		⑦ 🍷
Cardiff Central .... 133 135 d.	1430	...	...	1530	...	1630	...	1730	...	...	1730	...	1930	...	2030	...	...	...	...	0805	...	...	0915
Newport.................. 133 135 d.	1444	...	...	1544	...	1644	...	1744	...	...	1844	...	1944	...	2044	...	...	...	...	0823	...	...	0929
Bristol Parkway .... 133 d.	|	1518	...	|	1624	|	1719	|	...	1825	|	1921	|	2023	|	...	...	...	...	|	...	...	|
Bristol Temple Meads... 133 d.	1522	1538	1552	1622	1649	1722	1749	1822	...	1849	1922	1949	2022	2049	2122	2151	2223	2310	...	0910	0915	...	1010
Bath .... 133 d.	1536	1556	1607	1636	1707	1736	1807	1836	...	1907	1936	2007	2036	2107	2137	2207	2236	2327	...	0927	0933	...	1022
Bradford on Avon.................d.	1547	1612	1624	1647	1722	1747	1822	1847	...	1922	1947	2022	2047	2122	2147	2222	2247	2342	...	0939	0949	...	1038
Trowbridge ....d.	1553	1618	1630	1653	1728	1753	1828	1853	...	1928	1953	2028	2053	2128	2153	2228	2253	2348	...	0945	0955	...	1044
Westbury...........................d.	1601	1628	1639	1701	1735	1801	1835	1901	1909	1935	2001	2035	2101	2136	2201	2237	2304	2355	...	0955	1002	...	1100
Warminster.........................d.	1608	...	1647	1708	...	1808	...	1908	1918	...	2008	...	2108	...	2208	...	2311	...	...	1004	...	...	1107
Salisbury .... 113 d.	1633	...	1720	1733	...	1833	...	1933	1941	...	2033	...	2133	...	2232	...	2334	...	...	1031	...	...	1131
London Waterloo........ 113 a.	|	...	1849	|	...	|	...	|	|	...	|	...	|	...	|	...	...	...	...	|	...	...	|
Romsey...............................d.	1651	...	...	1751	...	1851	...	1951	2002	...	2051	...	2151	...	2252	...	...	...	...	1050	...	...	1149
Southampton Central ....a.	1702	...	...	1802	...	1902	...	2002	2018	...	2102	...	2202	...	2302	...	...	...	...	1100	...	...	1204
Fareham..............................a.	1727	...	...	1827	...	1927	...	2027	...	...	2127	...	2226	...	2328	...	...	...	...	1125	...	...	1228
Portsmouth & Southsea ....a.	1746	...	...	1847	...	1946	...	2045	...	...	2146	...	2244	...	2345	...	...	...	...	1144	...	...	1247
Portsmouth Harbour.............a.	1752	...	...	1852	...	1952	...	2051	...	...	2152	...	2252	...	2349	...	...	...	...	1153	...	...	1253

	⑦ 🍷 B	⑦ 🍷	⑦ 🍷 B		⑦ 🍷	⑦ 🍷	⑦ ◇	⑦ 🍷		⑦ 🍷	⑦ 🍷 B	⑦ W		⑦ 🍷	⑦ 🍷	⑦ 🍷	⑦ 🍷		⑦ W	⑦ 🍷	⑦ ◇		⑦	⑦ 🍷
Cardiff Central .... 133 135 d.	1015	1115	1215	...	1315	1415	...	1515	...	1615	1640	...	...	1715	1745	1815	1915	...	...	2015	...	...	...	2205
Newport.................. 133 135 d.	1029	1129	1229	...	1329	1429	...	1529	...	1629	1654	...	...	1729	1759	1829	1929	...	...	2029	...	...	...	2224
Bristol Parkway .... 133 d.	|	|	|	...	|	|	...	|	...	|	|	...	...	|	|	|	|	...	...	|	...	...	...	|
Bristol Temple Meads... 133 d.	1110	1210	1310	...	1410	1510	1604	1610	...	1710	1740	1744	...	1810	1850	1910	2010	...	2050	2110	2135	...	2215	2310
Bath .... 133 d.	1127	1222	1327	...	1424	1527	1620	1624	...	1727	1752	1801	...	1827	1902	1927	2022	...	2107	2123	2149	...	2232	2322
Bradford on Avon.................d.	1139	1238	1339	...	1439	1539	1631	1641	...	1739	1804	1817	...	1839	1914	1939	2038	...	2124	2134	2200	...	2249	2334
Trowbridge ....d.	1146	1244	1346	...	1445	1545	1637	1647	...	1745	1811	1823	...	1845	1920	1945	2044	...	2130	2140	2206	...	2255	2340
Westbury...........................d.	1203	1257	1403	...	1500	1558	1646	1658	...	1800	1819	1830	...	1858	1929	1953	2055	...	2137	2155	2215	...	2302	2350
Warminster.........................d.	1212	1304	1412	...	1507	1607	1653	1707	...	1807	1828	...	...	1905	1937	2002	2102	...	...	2202	2222	...	...	2359
Salisbury .... 113 d.	1236	1329	1448	...	1531	1631	1726	1731	...	1831	1857	...	...	1929	2000	2030	2129	...	...	2229	2246	...	...	...
London Waterloo........ 113 a.	|	|	|	...	|	|	1858	|	...	|	|	...	...	|	|	|	|	...	...	|	...	...	...	...
Romsey...............................d.	1256	1347	1510	...	1551	1649	...	1749	...	1849	1915	...	...	1948	2019	2048	2147	...	...	2248	...	...	...	...
Southampton Central ....a.	1306	1358	1520	...	1605	1704	...	1804	...	1904	1926	...	...	1958	2029	2059	2158	...	...	2259	...	...	...	...
Fareham..............................a.	1333	1422	1550	...	1628	1728	...	1828	...	1928	1948	...	...	2024	2054	2122	2222	...	...	2321	...	...	...	...
Portsmouth & Southsea ....a.	...	1441	...	...	1647	1747	...	1847	...	1947	...	...	...	2043	2115	2139	2239	...	...	2340	...	...	...	...
Portsmouth Harbour.............a.	...	1448	...	...	1653	1753	...	1851	...	1953	...	...	...	2049	2126	2148	2246	...	...	2348	...	...	...	...

(BRISTOL -) WESTBURY - WEYMOUTH

km		Ⓐ	Ⓐ T	Ⓐ G	Ⓐ G	Ⓐ	Ⓐ	Ⓐ G	Ⓐ	⑥	⑥ T	⑥ G	⑥ G	⑥ T	⑥	⑥ G	⑥	⑦	⑦	⑦	⑦	⑦
	Bristol T Meads........d.	*0544*	0841	0949	1149	1449	1649	1749	2049	*0549*	0841	0949	1149	1449	1649	1749	2049	...	0915	*1310*	1744	2050
0	**Westbury**....................d.	0644	0930	1036	1237	1536	1738	1839	2135	0647	0930	1035	1236	1536	1738	1836	2139	0900	1003	1415	1830	2138
9	Frome..........................d.	0654	0939	1046	1247	1546	1747	1849	2149	0656	0939	1045	1248	1546	1747	1846	2149	0909	1012	1428	1839	2148
32	Castle Cary ....d.	0710	0956	1103	1304	1610	1805	1906	2206	0715	0956	1102	1305	1603	1805	1905	2206	0926	1029	1446	1900	2205
51	Yeovil Pen Mill..............d.	0734	1009	1116	1317	1623	1824	1919	2220	0739	1010	1116	1318	1616	1819	1919	2219	0940	1043	1500	1914	2218
84	Dorchester West..........d.	0808	1042	1151	1354	1657	1858	1955	2253	0814	1040	1156	1355	1656	1854	1954	2253	1013	1116	1533	1948	2252
95	**Weymouth**...................a.	0821	1056	1208	1409	1710	1912	2008	2307	0826	1055	1208	1408	1707	1908	2008	2305	1025	1127	1545	2001	2303

B – To Brighton.
C – From Cheltenham.
G – From Gloucester.
T – From Worcester.
W – To Weymouth.
◇ – Operated by *SW*. Conveys 🚃.
* – By 🚌.

137 PORTSMOUTH and WEYMOUTH - SALISBURY - BRISTOL - CARDIFF

2nd class GW

Services on ⑥⑦ valid until September 6.

Ⓐ	Ⓐ		Ⓐ G	Ⓐ	Ⓐ ◇	Ⓐ W	Ⓐ	Ⓐ 🍷	Ⓐ W	Ⓐ G	Ⓐ 🍷	Ⓐ	Ⓐ 🍷	Ⓐ GW	Ⓐ 🍷	Ⓐ ◇	Ⓐ B	Ⓐ 🍷	Ⓐ GW	Ⓐ 🍷	Ⓐ	Ⓐ T	Ⓐ 🍷
Portsmouth Harbour d.	...	...	...	...	...	...	...	0600	...	...	0651	...	0822	...	0922	...	...	1022	...	1122	...	...	1222
Portsmouth & Southsea d.	...	...	...	...	...	...	...	0604	...	...	0655	...	0827	...	0927	...	...	1027	...	1127	...	...	1227
Fareham d.	...	...	...	...	...	...	...	0624	...	...	0718	...	0847	...	0947	...	1014	1047	...	1147	...	...	1247
Southampton Central d.	...	...	...	...	...	...	...	0646	...	...	0747	0823	0910	...	1010	...	1042	1110	...	1210	...	1226	1310
Romsey d.	...	...	...	...	...	...	...	0700	...	...	0800	0835	0921	...	1021	...	1054	1121	...	1221	...	1239	1321
London Waterloo 113 d.	...	...	...	...	...	...	...	|	...	...	|	|	|	...	|	0920	|	|	...	|	...	|	|
Salisbury 113 d.	...	...	0604	...	0640	...	...	0719	...	...	0821	0903	0941	...	1041	1052	1114	1141	...	1241	...	1306	1341
Warminster d.	...	...	0625	...	0700	...	0723	0739	...	...	0841	0923	1001	...	1101	1112	1133	1201	...	1301	...	1331	1401
Westbury d.	0558	...	0634	0655	0707	0718	0738	0754	0817	0845	0854	0938	1008	1038	1108	1119	1138	1208	1249	1308	1338	1342	1408
Trowbridge d.	0604	...	0640	0701	0713	0724	0744	0800	0823	0851	0900	0944	1014	1044	1114	1125	1144	1214	1255	1314	1344	1351	1414
Bradford on Avon d.	0615	...	0646	0707	0720	0730	0750	0806	0829	0857	0908	0950	1020	1050	1120	1131	1150	1220	1301	1320	1350	1357	1420
Bath 133 a.	0626	...	0702	0724	0732	0747	0806	0821	0845	0913	0920	1006	1033	1106	1133	1145	1206	1233	1317	1333	1406	1413	1433
Bristol Temple Meads 133 a.	0645	...	0721	0745	0752	0806	0829	0839	0904	0935	0939	1029	1047	1129	1147	1205	1229	1247	1336	1347	|	1435	1447
Bristol Parkway 133 a.	|	...	0748	|	...	0829	0852	|	0928	0952	|	1052	|	1152	|	...	1252	|	1352	|	1437	1451	|
Newport 133 135 a.	0727	...	...	0826	...	...	...	0925	...	...	1023	...	1126	...	1224	...	...	1325	...	1424	...	...	1525
Cardiff Central 133 135 a.	0745	...	...	0846	...	...	...	0943	...	...	1042	...	1144	...	1242	...	...	1344	...	1445	...	...	1543

	Ⓐ ◇	Ⓐ GW	Ⓐ 🍷	Ⓐ	Ⓐ 🍷	Ⓐ GW	Ⓐ 🍷	Ⓐ	Ⓐ 🍷		Ⓐ C	①–④ 🍷	⑤ 🍷	Ⓐ W	Ⓐ B	Ⓐ 🍷	Ⓐ	Ⓐ 🍷	Ⓐ ◇	Ⓐ W	Ⓐ 🍷	Ⓐ	Ⓐ	Ⓐ
Portsmouth Harbour d.	...	...	1322	...	1422	...	1522	...	1622	...	...	1722	1722	...	...	1822	...	1922	...	...	2022	...	...	2122
Portsmouth & Southsea d.	...	...	1327	...	1427	...	1527	...	1627	...	...	1727	1727	...	...	1827	...	1927	...	...	2027	...	...	2127
Fareham d.	...	...	1347	...	1447	...	1547	...	1647	...	...	1747	1747	...	1813	1847	...	1947	...	...	2047	...	...	2147
Southampton Central d.	...	...	1410	...	1510	...	1610	...	1710	...	...	1810	1810	...	1842	1910	...	2010	...	...	2110	2120	...	2222
Romsey d.	...	...	1421	...	1521	...	1621	...	1721	...	...	1821	1821	...	1854	1921	...	2021	...	...	2121	2131	...	2233
London Waterloo 113 d.	1220	...	|	...	|	...	|	...	|	...	...	|	|	...	|	|	...	|	1920	...	|	|	...	|
Salisbury 113 d.	1352	...	1441	...	1541	...	1641	...	1741	...	...	1841	1841	...	1913	1941	...	2041	2057	...	2141	2153	...	2300
Warminster d.	1412	...	1501	1528	1601	...	1701	1728	1801	...	...	1901	1901	...	1932	2001	...	2101	2117	...	2201	2215	...	2320
Westbury d.	1419	1445	1508	1538	1608	1638	1708	1738	1808	...	1838	1908	1908	1917	1941	2008	2038	2108	2124	2155	2208	2225	2232	2330
Trowbridge d.	1425	1451	1514	1544	1614	1644	1714	1744	1814	...	1844	1914	1914	1923	1947	2014	2044	2114	2130	2201	2214	...	2238	...
Bradford on Avon d.	1431	1457	1520	1550	1620	1650	1720	1750	1820	...	1850	1920	1920	1929	1953	2020	2050	2120	2136	2207	2220	...	2244	...
Bath 133 a.	1445	1513	1533	1605	1633	1706	1733	1806	1835	...	1906	1935	1935	1946	2010	2035	2106	2135	2151	2224	2233	...	2300	...
Bristol Temple Meads 133 a.	1505	1534	1547	1629	1647	1729	1747	1828	1850	...	1929	1949	1949	2005	2029	2050	2129	2150	2206	2245	2247	...	2321	...
Bristol Parkway 133 a.	...	1552	|	1652	|	1752	|	1852	|	...	1952	...	|	...	2052	|	...	|	...	...	|	...	...	...
Newport 133 135 a.	...	...	1624	...	1727	...	1827	...	1927	...	...	...	2028	...	...	2127	...	2237	...	...	2335	...	...	...
Cardiff Central 133 135 a.	...	...	1643	...	1745	...	1845	...	1945	...	...	...	2046	...	...	2145	...	2259	...	...	2358	...	...	...

⑥	⑥ G	⑥	⑥ ◇	⑥	⑥	⑥ GW	⑥	⑥ T		⑥	⑥ GW	⑥	⑥ ◇	⑥ GB	⑥		⑥ GW	⑥	⑥	⑥	⑥ ◇	⑥ GW	⑥
Portsmouth Harbour d.	...	...	...	...	0600	...	0705	...	...	0822	...	0922	...	...	1022	...	...	1122	...	1222	...	...	1322
Portsmouth & Southsea d.	...	...	...	...	0604	...	0709	...	...	0827	...	0927	...	...	1027	...	...	1127	...	1227	...	...	1327
Fareham d.	...	...	...	...	0628	...	0730	...	...	0847	...	0947	...	1016	1047	...	...	1147	...	1247	...	...	1347
Southampton Central d.	...	...	...	...	0652	...	0754	0827	...	0910	...	1010	...	1042	1110	...	...	1210	1227	1310	...	...	1410
Romsey d.	...	...	...	...	0711	...	0812	0838	...	0921	...	1021	...	1053	1121	...	...	1221	1238	1321	...	...	1421
London Waterloo 113 d.	...	...	...	...	|	...	|	|	...	|	...	|	0920	|	|	...	...	|	|	|	1220	...	|
Salisbury 113 d.	0603	...	0640	...	0730	...	0834	0904	...	0941	...	1041	1052	1113	1141	...	...	1241	1304	1341	1352	...	1441
Warminster d.	0623	...	0700	0723	0750	...	0854	0925	...	1001	...	1101	1112	1134	1201	...	...	1301	1325	1401	1412	...	1501
Westbury d.	0638	0651	0707	0738	0802	0817	0908	0938	...	1008	1038	1108	1119	1138	1208	...	1252	1308	1338	1408	1419	1448	1508
Trowbridge d.	0644	0657	0713	0744	0808	0823	0914	0944	...	1014	1044	1114	1125	1144	1214	...	1258	1314	1344	1414	1425	1454	1514
Bradford on Avon d.	0649	0703	0719	0750	0814	0829	0920	0950	...	1020	1050	1120	1131	1150	1220	...	1304	1320	1350	1420	1431	1500	1520
Bath 133 a.	0706	0720	0732	0807	0831	0845	0933	1007	...	1034	1108	1133	1145	1208	1233	...	1316	1333	1408	1433	1445	1517	1534
Bristol Temple Meads 133 a.	0729	0739	0752	0830	0845	0905	0947	1029	...	1048	1129	1147	1200	1229	1247	...	1336	1347	1429	1447	1505	1535	1548
Bristol Parkway 133 a.	0752	|	...	0852	|	0949	|	1052	...	|	1152	|	...	1252	|	...	1352	|	1452	|	...	1552	|
Newport 133 135 a.	...	0826	...	...	0924	...	1023	...	...	1124	...	1223	...	...	1325	...	...	1423	...	1524	...	...	1623
Cardiff Central 133 135 a.	...	0845	...	...	0942	...	1042	...	...	1143	...	1241	...	...	1342	...	...	1443	...	1542	...	...	1641

	⑥	⑥	⑥ GW	⑥	⑥	⑥		⑥	⑥ W	⑥ BC	⑥	⑥	⑥	⑥ ◇	⑥ W	⑥	⑥		⑦	⑦		⑦ 🍷		⑦ 🍷
Portsmouth Harbour d.	...	1422	...	1522	...	1622	...	1722	...	...	1822	...	1922	...	...	2022	...	...		...	...	0908	...	1108
Portsmouth & Southsea d.	...	1427	...	1527	...	1627	...	1727	...	...	1827	...	1927	...	...	2027	...	...		...	...	0912	...	1112
Fareham d.	...	1447	...	1547	...	1647	...	1747	...	1815	1847	...	1947	...	...	2048	...	...		...	...	0932	...	1132
Southampton Central d.	...	1510	...	1610	...	1710	...	1810	...	1845	1910	...	2010	...	...	2112	2127	...		...	...	0954	...	1154
Romsey d.	...	1521	...	1621	...	1721	...	1821	...	1856	1921	...	2021	...	...	2123	2138	...		...	...	1005	...	1206
London Waterloo 113 d.	...	|	...	|	...	|	...	|	...	|	|	...	|	1920	...	|	|	...		...	...	|	...	|
Salisbury 113 d.	...	1541	...	1641	...	1741	...	1841	...	1916	1941	...	2041	2057	...	2143	2204	...		...	...	1030	...	1228
Warminster d.	1528	1601	1628	1701	...	1801	...	1901	...	1937	2001	...	2101	2117	...	2203	2225	...		...	...	1050	...	1248
Westbury d.	1538	1608	1638	1708	1744	1808	...	1908	1917	1948	2008	2038	2108	2124	2155	2208	2238	...		0956	...	1058	...	1255
Trowbridge d.	1544	1614	1644	1714	1750	1814	...	1914	1923	1954	2014	2044	2114	2130	2201	2214	2244	...		1002	...	1104	...	1301
Bradford on Avon d.	1550	1620	1650	1720	1756	1820	...	1920	1929	2000	2020	2050	2120	2136	2207	2220	2250	...		1007	...	1110	...	1307
Bath 133 a.	1607	1633	1707	1733	1811	1833	...	1933	1945	2016	2033	2107	2137	2150	2224	2235	2308	...		1024	...	1125	...	1325
Bristol Temple Meads 133 a.	1630	1647	1729	1747	1835	1847	...	1947	2004	2035	2047	2126	2151	2206	2245	2250	2328	...		1043	...	1143	...	1343
Bristol Parkway 133 a.	1652	|	1752	|	1852	|	...	|	...	2055	|	...	|	...	...	|	...	...		...	...	|	...	|
Newport 133 135 a.	...	1726	...	1825	...	1923	...	2023	...	...	2123	...	2236	...	...	2334	...	...		...	...	1224	...	1421
Cardiff Central 133 135 a.	...	1745	...	1843	...	1942	...	2041	...	...	2141	...	2256	...	...	2354	...	...		...	...	1239	...	1437

	⑦ B	⑦ ◇	⑦ 🍷		⑦ W	⑦ 🍷		⑦ 🍷			⑦ 🍷		⑦ B	⑦ 🍷	⑦ W	⑦ 🍷	⑦ ◇	⑦ B	⑦ 🍷		⑦ W	⑦ 🍷		⑦ 🍷
Portsmouth Harbour d.	...	...	1308	...	...	1408	...	1508	...	...	1608	...	...	1708	...	1808	...	...	1908	...	...	2008	...	2203
Portsmouth & Southsea d.	...	...	1312	...	...	1412	...	1512	...	...	1612	...	...	1712	...	1812	...	...	1912	...	...	2012	...	2212
Fareham d.	1232	...	1332	...	...	1432	...	1532	...	...	1632	...	1703	1732	...	1832	...	1903	1932	...	...	2032	...	2232
Southampton Central d.	1254	...	1354	...	...	1454	...	1554	...	...	1654	...	1726	1754	...	1854	...	1930	1954	...	...	2054	...	|
Romsey d.	1306	...	1406	...	...	1506	...	1606	...	...	1706	...	1739	1806	...	1906	...	1942	2006	...	...	2106	...	2309
London Waterloo 113 d.	|	1215	|	...	...	|	...	|	...	...	|	...	|	|	...	|	1815	|	|	...	...	|	...	|
Salisbury 113 d.	1328	1358	1428	...	...	1528	...	1628	...	...	1728	...	1802	1828	...	1928	1958	2003	2028	...	...	2128	...	2328
Warminster d.	1347	1418	1448	...	...	1548	...	1648	...	...	1748	...	1822	1848	...	1948	2018	2028	2048	...	...	2148	...	2353
Westbury d.	1355	1425	1501	...	1541	1558	...	1659	...	...	1801	...	1834	1901	1930	2001	2031	2039	2101	...	2146	2201	...	0002
Trowbridge d.	1401	1432	1507	...	1547	1604	...	1705	...	...	1807	...	1840	1907	1936	2007	2037	2045	2107	...	2152	2207	...	...
Bradford on Avon d.	1407	1438	1513	...	1552	1610	...	1711	...	...	|	...	1846	1913	1942	2013	2043	2052	2113	...	2158	2213	...	...
Bath 133 a.	1423	1454	1527	...	1608	1628	...	1725	...	...	1825	...	1903	1927	2001	2027	2059	2115	2127	...	2215	2228	...	...
Bristol Temple Meads 133 a.	1442	1508	1540	...	1628	1641	...	1743	...	...	1838	...	1922	1940	2020	2040	2116	2134	2140	...	2234	2241	...	...
Bristol Parkway 133 a.	|	...	|	...	...	|	...	|	...	...	|	...	...	|	...	|	...	...	|	...	...	|	...	...
Newport 133 135 a.	1521	...	1621	...	...	1724	...	1821	...	...	1921	...	...	2024	...	2121	...	...	2233	...	...	2328	...	...
Cardiff Central 133 135 a.	1538	...	1639	...	...	1740	...	1839	...	...	1938	...	...	2040	...	2138	...	...	2258	...	...	2349	...	...

WEYMOUTH - WESTBURY (- BRISTOL)

Ⓐ	Ⓐ	Ⓐ	Ⓐ G	Ⓐ G	Ⓐ G	Ⓐ G	Ⓐ	Ⓐ		⑥	⑥ G	⑥ G	⑥ G	⑥ G	⑥	⑥	⑥		⑦	⑦	⑦	⑦	⑦	⑦
Weymouth d.	0535	0640	0850	1110	1310	1510	1730	2024	...		0640	0852	1110	1310	1610	1730	2024	...		1111	1410	1613	1800	2009
Dorchester West d.	0549	0653	0904	1124	1325	1525	1745	2037	...		0653	0905	1126	1324	1626	1744	2037	...		1124	1423	1626	1813	2022
Yeovil Pen Mill d.	0621	0731	0936	1203	1404	1557	1819	2110	...		0730	0938	1202	1405	1703	1824	2110	...		1157	1459	1659	1846	2055
Castle Cary d.	0646	0743	0951	1222	1416	1610	1836	2122	...		0743	0957	1222	1418	1715	1842	2122	...		1211	1512	1711	1859	2116
Frome d.	0705	0802	1015	1239	1435	1629	1905	2141	...		0802	1017	1240	1437	1734	1906	2141	...		1229	1531	1730	1918	2135
Westbury a.	0714	0815	1025	1248	1444	1638	1917	2151	...		0812	1027	1249	1447	1743	1916	2151	...		1239	1540	1739	1927	2144
Bristol Temple Meads a.	0806	0904	1129	1336	1534	1729	2005	2245	...		0905	1129	1336	1535	1835	2004	2245	...		*1343*	1628	1828	2020	2234

B – To Brighton.
C – To Cheltenham.
G – To Gloucester.
T – To Worcester.
W – From Weymouth.
◇ – Operated by *SW*. Conveys 🚃.
* – By 🚌.

LONDON AIRPORT LINKS 140

Gatwick ✈

GATWICK EXPRESS daily non-stop rail service from / to **London Victoria**. Journey time: 30 minutes (35 minutes on ⑦). ✆ +44 (0) 845 850 1530.

From Victoria:
0001, 0030, 0330, 0430; then every 15 minutes 0500–2345.

From Gatwick:
0005, 0020, 0035, 0050, 0135, 0435 ⚒, 0450 ⑦, 0520 ⚒, 0525 ⑦; then every 15 minutes 0550–2350.

Other rail services:
Table **103** – London Victoria - Gatwick - Brighton; and Bedford (***A***) - Luton (***A***) - London St Pancras (***AB***) - Gatwick - Brighton.
Table **105** – Reading (***C***) - Gatwick.

A – Connections from / to Leicester, Nottingham, Derby and Sheffield (Table **170**).
B – Connections from / to Paris and Brussels (Table **10**).
C – Connections from / to Exeter and the South West (Table **115**), Birmingham (Table **129**), Worcester (Table **131**), Bristol and South Wales (Table **133**).

Heathrow ✈

HEATHROW EXPRESS daily non-stop rail service from / to **London Paddington**. Journey times: 15 mins to Heathrow Central ★ (Terminals 1 / 2 / 3), 21 mins to Heathrow Terminal 5.
From Paddington: Every 15 minutes 0510–2325.
From Heathrow Terminal 5: Every 15 minutes 0503–2342 (6 minutes later from Heathrow Central).
★ – Free rail transfer services operate every 15 minutes Heathrow Central to Heathrow Terminal 4 and v.v.

PICCADILLY LINE (London Underground) service.
Frequent trains (every 4–10 mins) 0530 – 2300 on ①–⑥, 0730 – 2330 on ⑦, between King's Cross St Pancras and all Heathrow terminals via Central London. Journey time: 50–58 minutes.

RAILAIR LINK 🚌 service from / to **Reading** rail station.

From Reading:
Ⓐ: 0400, 0500, 0530, 0555, 0608, 0620, 0640 and every 20 minutes until 0840; then 0905, 0925 and every 20 minutes until 1805; then 1835, 1905, 1935, 2005, 2035, 2105, 2205, 2305.
Ⓒ: 0400, 0500, 0545, 0615 and every 30 minutes until 1945; then 2025, 2055, 2205, 2305.

From Heathrow Central Bus Station (8–10 minutes later from Terminal 5):
Ⓐ: 0005, 0500, 0600, 0630, 0657, 0720, 0740 and every 20 minutes until 1000; then 1015, 1035 and every 20 minutes until 1915; then 1940, 2010, 2040, 2110, 2140, 2215, 2305.
Ⓒ: 0005, 0500, 0600, 0700, 0730 and every 30 minutes until 1900; then 1920, 1950, 2020, 2050, 2130, 2200, 2305.

Approximate journey times in minutes from Reading: 39 to Terminal 5, 48 to Terminal 1, 51 to Terminal 2, 54 to Terminal 3. Approximate journey time Heathrow Central to Reading: 49 minutes.

RAILAIR LINK 🚌 from / to **Woking** rail station.

From Woking: Journey time to Heathrow Central Bus Station: 50–70 minutes △
0530 Ⓐ, 0600 Ⓐ, 0630, 0700 and every 30 minutes until 2100; then 2200.
△ – 30–50 minutes to Terminal 4.

From Heathrow Central Bus Station ▽: Journey time to Woking: 50–70 minutes
0545 Ⓐ, 0615 Ⓐ, 0645, 0715 and every 30 minutes until 2015, then 2100, 2200, 2300.
▽ – 15 minutes later from Terminal 4.

Luton ✈

Frequent *First Capital Connect* trains from / to **London Kings Cross Thameslink**, **London Blackfriars**, **Gatwick** and **Brighton** serve Luton Airport Parkway station ★.
East Midlands Trains express services (Table **170**) from / to **London St Pancras**, **Leicester**, **Nottingham**, **Derby** and **Sheffield** serve both Luton main rail station and Airport station ★.
★ – A frequent shuttle 🚌 service operates between each of the rail stations and the airport terminal.

🚌 service **Milton Keynes - Luton** ✈ (journey time 55 minutes) for train connections from / to **Birmingham** (Table **143**), **Liverpool** and **Manchester** (Table **150**).

From Milton Keynes rail station:
⚒: 0640, 0740, 0840, 0955, 1055 and hourly until 2055, then 2155 Ⓐ.
⑦: 0920, 1120, 1220 and hourly until 2120.

From Luton ✈:
⚒: 0550, 0650, 0750, 0905, 1005 and hourly until 2005; then 2105 Ⓐ.
⑦: 0820, 1020, 1220, 1320 and hourly until 2020.

Stansted ✈

STANSTED EXPRESS rail link service from / to **London Liverpool St**. Journey time: ± 45 minutes. Operating company: *one* ✆ +44 (0) 845 600 7245.

From London Liverpool St:
⚒: 0410 ⑥, 0440, 0510, 0525 and every 15 minutes until 2255; then 2325.
⑦: 0410, 0440, 0510, 0540, 0610, 0625 and every 15 minutes until 2255; then 2325.

From Stansted ✈:
⚒: 0030, 0100 ⑥, 0130 ⑥, 0530 ⑥, 0600, 0615 and every 15 minutes until 2345; then 2359.
⑦: 0030, 0530, 0600, 0630, 0700, 0715 and every 15 minutes until 2345; then 2359.

Trains call at **Tottenham Hale** for London Underground (Victoria Line) connections to / from Kings Cross, Euston, and Victoria stations.
For *Arriva Cross Country* services to / from **Cambridge**, **Peterborough** and **Birmingham**, see Table **207**.

City ✈

DOCKLANDS LIGHT RAILWAY from / to **Bank** (interchange with London Underground: Central, Circle, District, Northern, and Waterloo & City Lines).
Trains run every 7–10 minutes 0530–0030 on ⚒, 0700–2330 on ⑦. Journey time: ± 22 minutes.

Inter - Airport 🚌 links

From **Gatwick** to **Heathrow** *Journey 70 minutes*
0050, 0250, 0420, 0520, 0605, 0635, 0705, 0750, 0820 and every 30 minutes until 2350.

From **Gatwick** to **Luton** *Journey 150 minutes*
0250, 0450, 0635, 0850, 1050 and every 2 hours until 1850, then 2150.

From **Gatwick** to **Stansted** *Journey 165 minutes*
0420, 0520, 0605, 0705, 0820, 0920 and hourly until 1920, then 2120, 2220.

From **Heathrow** to **Gatwick** *Journey 70 minutes*
0005, 0205, 0435, 0505 and every 30 minutes until 2205, then 2305.

From **Heathrow** to **Luton** *Journey 70 minutes*
0410, 0520 and at 10 mins past even hours, 20 mins past uneven hours until 2010, 2120, then 2310.

From **Heathrow** to **Stansted** *Journey 85 minutes*
0540, 0640 and hourly until 2040, then 2240, 2340.

From **Luton** to **Gatwick** *Journey 145 minutes*
0050, 0450, 0630 Ⓐ, 0650 Ⓒ, 0850, 1050 and every 2 hours until 2250.

From **Luton** to **Heathrow** *Journey 65 minutes*
0050, 0450, 0535, 0630 Ⓐ, 0650 Ⓒ, 0735, 0850 and at 35 mins past uneven hours, 50 mins past even hours until 2135, 2250.

From **Stansted** to **Heathrow** *(80 mins)* and **Gatwick** *(160 mins)*
0305, 0405, 0605, 0650 Ⓐ, 0705 Ⓒ, 0805, 0905 and hourly until 2005.

SN EAST CROYDON - MILTON KEYNES 141

km																									
		⚒	⑥	Ⓐ	⑥	Ⓐ	⑥	Ⓐ	⑥	Ⓐ	⑥	Ⓐ	⑥	⚒		Ⓐ	⑥	Ⓐ	⑥	⑥	Ⓐ	Ⓐ	⑥	⑥	Ⓐ
0	**East Croydon** d.		...	...	...	...	0610	...	0710	...	0810	...	0910	1010	and	1808	1810	1907	1907	...	...	...	...	...	...
12	Clapham Junction d.		0538	0555	0608	0638	0638	0738	0738	0838	0838	0938	0938	1038	hourly	1838	1838	1938	1938	2025	2038	2138	2138	2238	2238
18	Kensington Olympia d.		0549	0607	0622	0649	0650	0750	0750	0850	0850	0950	0950	1050	until	1850	1850	1950	1950	2036	2050	2150	2157	2250	2250
40	Watford Junction d.		0619	0635	0650	0719	0719	0820	0819	0920	0919	1020	1019	1119	★	1921	1921	2019	2015	2106	2119	2223	2227	2319	2323
88	**Milton Keynes** a.		0700	...	...	0803	0800	0901	0900	1001	1000	1101	1100	1201		2006	...	2101	...	...	2204	...	...	...	...

	⑦	⑦	⑦	⑦	⑦	⑦		⑦	⑦	
East Croydon d.		...	...	...	...	...	and	...	...	...
Clapham Junction d.		0815	0915	1015	1115	1205	hourly	2115	2215	...
Kensington Olympia d.		0826	0926	1026	1126	1216	until	2126	2226	...
Watford Junction d.		0858	0958	1058	1158	1246		2158	2258	...
Milton Keynes a.		...	...	...	...	...		...	...	...

	⚒	Ⓐ	⑥	Ⓐ	⑥	Ⓐ	⑥	⚒		⚒
Milton Keynes d.		...	...	...	...	0701	0713	0813	and	1713
Watford Junction d.		0554	0551	0653	0655	0738	0752	0851	hourly	1751
Kensington Olympia d.		0621	0622	0721	0722	0806	0822	0922	until	1821
Clapham Junction a.		0632	0633	0732	0733	0817	0833	0935	★	1833
East Croydon a.		...	0657	...	0757	...	0857	0957		1902

	Ⓐ	⑥	Ⓐ	⑥	⑥	Ⓐ	⑥	Ⓐ	Ⓐ	⑥	Ⓐ	⑥	Ⓐ		⑦	⑦	⑦	⑦	⑦		⑦	⑦	⑦		⑦
Milton Keynes d.	1813	1813	1913	1913	...	2013	...	2113	...	...	2211	...	...	...		...	...	...	...	and	...	...	...	...	...
Watford Junction d.	1851	1851	1953	1951	2043	2051	2143	2151	2227	2248	2253	2325	2329	...		0917	1017	1117	1222	hourly	2022	2117	2217	...	2317
Kensington Olympia d.	1920	1922	2023	2022	2108	2125	2210	2225	2251	2315	2323	2351	2356	...		0947	1047	1147	1247	until	2047	2147	2247	...	2347
Clapham Junction a.	1930	1933	2032	2033	2121	2134	2221	2234	2301	2326	2333	0002	0007	...		0958	1058	1158	1258		2058	2158	2258	...	2358
East Croydon a.	...	1957	...	2057	...	...	...	...	...	...	...	...	...	...		...	...	...	...		...	...	...	...	0022

★ – Timings may vary by up to 5 minutes.

142 LONDON - NORTHAMPTON - BIRMINGHAM and CREWE

LM

Services on ⑦ valid until July 12. For faster trains London Euston - Birmingham and v.v. see Table **143**.

km	Ⓐ	Ⓐ	Ⓐ	Ⓐ	Ⓐ	Ⓐ	Ⓐ	Ⓐ	Ⓐ		Ⓐ	Ⓐ	Ⓐ	Ⓐ	Ⓐ	Ⓐ	Ⓐ	Ⓐ	Ⓐ	Ⓐ	Ⓐ	Ⓐ
0	**London** Euston ... 150 151 ▼ d.	...	...	...	0530	0624	0653	0746	0754	and at the same minutes past each hour until	1546	1554	1648	1724	1754	1824	1849	1954	2046	2113	...	2154
27	Watford Junction ▼ d.	...	...	...	0549	0641	0710	0801	0811		1601	1611	|	1743	1811	1844	|	2011	|	|	...	2211
78	Milton Keynes ... 150 151 ▼ d.	0521	...	...	0637	0723	0749	0825	0849		1625	1649	1731	1820	1847	1919	1934	2049	2131	2158	...	2257
104	**Northampton** ▼ a.	0537	...	...	0654	0740	0806	0840	0906		1640	1706	1749	1836	1907	1936	1953	2106	2149	2215	...	2316
104	**Northampton** d.	0542	0617	0638	0656	0745	0817	0845	0917		1645	1717	Ⓐ 1756	1841	1917	1942	1956	2117	2156	2217	2256	...
134	Rugby ... 150 ▶ d.	0602	0637	0658	0716	0803	0837	0903	0937		1703	1737	1816	1903	1937	2003	2016	2137	2216	2237	2316	...
152	Coventry ▶ d.	|	0649	|	0729	|	0849	|	0949		|	1749	1828	...	1949	|	2029	2149	2229	2249	2329	...
170	**Birmingham** Int'l ▶ d.	|	0704	|	0745	|	0904	|	1004		|	1804	1845	...	2004	|	2045	2204	2245	2304	2347	...
183	**Birmingham** New St ▶ a.	|	0716	|	0803	|	0916	|	1016		|	1816	1901	...	2016	|	2101	2216	2303	2316	0004	...
158	Nuneaton d.	0615	...	0711	...	0816	...	0916	...		1716	...	...	...	...	2016	...	...	...	...	...	...
192	Stafford ... 150 151 d.	0659	...	0754	...	0854	...	0954	...		1820	...	...	...	...	|	...	...	...	...	...	...
216	Stoke on Trent ... 150 d.	0726	...	0813	...	0913	...	1013	...		1841	...	...	...	...	2105	...	...	...	...	...	...
250	**Crewe** ... 150 151 a.	0748	...	0838	...	0938	...	1038	...		1905	...	...	...	...	2127	...	...	...	...	...	...

⑥	⑥	⑥	⑥	⑥	⑥	⑥	⑥	⑥	⑥	⑥	⑥	⑥	⑥	⑥		⑥	⑥	⑥	⑥	⑥	⑥	⑥
London Euston .. 150 151 ▼ d.	...	...	...	...	0534	0624	...	0704	0746	...	0846	0846	0946	0946	and at the same minutes past each hour until ★	1746	1754	1846	1854	1944	2034	2128
Watford Junction ▼ d.	...	...	...	...	0553	0641	...	0723	0801	...	|	|	1001	1001		1801	1811	1901	1911	2001	2051	2145
Milton Keynes ..... 150 151 ▼ d.	0521	...	...	...	0640	0723	...	0809	0825	...	0923	0923	1024	1024		1825	1849	1925	1948	2044	2133	2225
Northampton ▼ a.	0537	...	...	...	0657	0740	...	0829	0841	...	0939	0939	1040	1040		1840	1909	1941	2006	2103	2159	2247
Northampton d.	0542	0617	0638	0656	⑥ 0717	0745	0756	...	0845	0856	0945	0956	1045	1056		⑥ 1845	⑥ 1917	⑥ 1945	⑥ 2017	⑥ 2117	⑥ 2217	⑥ 2256
Rugby ... 150 ▶ d.	0600	0637	0656	0716	0737	0804	0816	...	0903	0916	1003	1016	1103	1116		1903	1937	2003	2043	2137	2237	2316
Coventry ▶ d.	|	0649	|	0729	0749	|	0829	...	|	0929	|	1029	|	1129		|	1949	|	2054	2149	2249	2329
Birmingham Int'l ▶ d.	|	0704	|	0745	0804	|	0845	...	|	0945	|	1045	|	1145		|	2004	|	2112	2204	2304	2347
Birmingham New St ▶ a.	|	0716	|	0801	0816	|	0901	...	|	1001	|	1101	|	1201		|	2016	|	2125	2216	2316	0004
Nuneaton d.	0616	...	0710	...	...	0817	...	...	0916	...	1016	...	1116	...		1916	...	2016	...	...	...	...
Stafford ... 150 151 d.	0654	...	0754	...	...	0854	...	...	0954	...	1054	...	1154	...		1953	...	2055	...	...	...	...
Stoke on Trent ... 150 d.	0713	...	0813	...	...	0913	...	...	1013	...	1113	...	1213	...		2013	...	2116	...	...	...	...
Crewe ... 150 151 a.	0738	...	0837	...	...	0937	...	...	1037	...	1137	...	1237	...		2035	...	2138	...	...	...	...

⑦	⑦	⑦	⑦	⑦	⑦	⑦	⑦	⑦	⑦	⑦	⑦A	⑦	⑦A		⑦	⑦	⑦	⑦	⑦	⑦	⑦	⑦
London Euston .. 150 151 ▼ d.	0723	0750	0823	0853	0923	0953	1023	1053	1123	1234	1250	1334	1350	then each train runs every two hours until	1834	1850	1934	1950	2034	2128	2158	2334
Watford Junction ▼ d.	0742	0809	0842	0912	0943	1012	1042	1112	1142	1251	1307	1351	1406		1851	1906	1951	2006	2051	2147	2217	2353
Milton Keynes ..... 150 151 ▼ d.	0832	0850	0927	0958	1028	1058	1127	1158	1227	1329	1336	1429	1442		1928	1942	2029	2041	2129	2232	2303	0042
Northampton ▼ a.	0850	0908	0945	1016	1046	1116	1145	1216	1245	1346	|	1446	|		1946	|	2046	|	2146	2250	2321	0100
Northampton d.	...	⑦ 0850*	⑦ 0915*	...	⑦ 1015*	⑦ 1055*	⑦ 1115*	...	⑦ 1215*	⑦ 1315*	|	⑦ 1415*	|		⑦ 1915*	|	⑦ 2015*	|	⑦ 2115*	⑦ 2215*	⑦ 2332*	...
Rugby ... 150 ▶ d.	...	0950	1020	...	1121	1156	1221	...	1315	1415	1416	1515	1508		2015	2016	2115	2106	2215	2315	0024*	...
Coventry ▶ d.	...	1004	1034	...	1134	|	1234	...	1329	1429	|	1528	...		2029	|	2129	...	2229	2329	0104*	...
Birmingham Int'l ▶ d.	...	1013	1051	...	1151	|	1252	...	1347	1447	|	1547	...		2047	|	2147	...	2247	2347	...	...
Birmingham New St ▶ a.	...	1030	1103	...	1203	|	1303	...	1358	1458	|	1558	...		2058	|	2158	...	2258	2358	...	...
Nuneaton d.	...	...	...	...	...	1210	...	...	...	...	1430	...	...		...	2030	...	...	...	...	...	...
Stafford ... 150 151 d.	...	...	...	...	...	1300	...	...	...	...	1516	...	...		...	2116	...	...	...	...	...	...
Stoke on Trent ... 150 d.	...	...	...	...	...	|	...	...	...	...	1541	...	...		...	2143	...	...	...	...	...	...
Crewe ... 150 151 a.	...	...	...	...	...	1334	...	...	...	...	1607	...	...		...	2211	...	...	...	...	...	...

Ⓐ	Ⓐ	Ⓐ	Ⓐ	Ⓐ	Ⓐ	Ⓐ	Ⓐ	Ⓐ	Ⓐ	Ⓐ		Ⓐ	Ⓐ	Ⓐ	Ⓐ	Ⓐ	Ⓐ	Ⓐ	Ⓐ	Ⓐ	①–④	Ⓐ
Crewe ... 150 151 d.	...	...	...	...	...	...	0635	...	0733	...	and at the same minutes past each hour until	1633	...	1733	...	1833	...	...	...	...	...	...
Stoke on Trent ... 150 d.	...	...	...	...	...	...	0658	...	0754	...		1654	...	1754	...	1854	...	...	...	...	...	...
Stafford ... 150 151 d.	...	...	...	...	...	...	0722	...	0821	...		1721	...	1821	...	1921	...	...	...	...	...	...
Nuneaton d.	...	...	0630	...	...	...	0802	...	0903	...		1802	...	1902	...	2002	...	...	...	...	...	...
Birmingham New St ▷ d.	...	...	|	0553	...	0653	|	0753	|	0853		|	1753	|	1853	|	1953	2053	2133	2153	...	2253
Birmingham Int'l ▷ d.	...	...	|	0605	...	0705	|	0805	|	0905		|	1805	|	1905	|	2005	2105	2145	2205	...	2305
Coventry ▷ d.	...	...	|	0621	...	0721	|	0821	|	0921		|	1821	|	1921	|	2021	2121	2201	2221	...	2321
Rugby ... 150 ▷ d.	0520	0608	|	0633	0704	0733	0818	0833	0920	0933		1819	1833	1921	1933	2019	2033	2133	2213	2233	...	2333
Northampton ▷ d.	0541	0633	0647	0654	0726	0754	0841	0855	0942	0954		1842	1854	1944	1954	2044	2054	2154	2234	2255	...	2354
Northampton ▽ d.	0545	0637	...	0703	0732	0805	0847	0905	0950	1005		1850	1905	1950	2005	...	2105	2205	2252	① 2330	2346	...
Milton Keynes ... 150 151 ▽ d.	0602	0655	...	0719	0747	0821	0900	0921	1005	1021		1904	1921	2004	2021	...	2121	2222	2310	2348	0004	...
Watford Junction ▽ d.	0633	|	...	|	0825	|	0928	0957	1030	1057		1929	1958	2029	2057	...	2157	2302	2356	0030	0046	...
London Euston ... 150 151 ▽ a.	0650	0743	...	0806	0845	0911	0944	1020	1049	1118		1949	2020	2049	2118	...	2220	2325	0018	0052	0108	...

⑥	⑥	⑥	⑥	⑥	⑥	⑥	⑥	⑥	⑥		⑥	⑥	⑥	⑥	⑥	⑥	⑥	⑥	⑥	⑥		⑥
Crewe ... 150 151 d.	...	...	...	...	0638	...	0733	...	0833	and at the same minutes past each hour until	...	1633	...	1733	...	1833	...	...	...	...	...	...
Stoke on Trent ... 150 d.	...	...	...	...	0700	...	0754	...	0854		...	1654	...	1754	...	1854	...	...	...	...	...	...
Stafford ... 150 151 d.	...	...	...	...	0726	...	0823	...	0921		...	1721	...	1821	...	1821	...	...	...	...	...	...
Nuneaton d.	...	...	...	...	0804	...	0904	...	1002		...	1802	...	1902	...	2002	...	...	...	...	...	...
Birmingham New St ▷ d.	...	...	0653	0733	|	0833	|	0933	|		1733	|	1753	|	1853	|	1953	2053	2133	2153	...	2253
Birmingham Int'l ▷ d.	...	...	0705	0745	|	0845	|	0945	|		1745	|	1805	|	1905	|	2005	2105	2145	2205	...	2305
Coventry ▷ d.	...	...	0721	0801	|	0901	|	1001	|		1801	|	1821	|	1921	|	2021	2121	2201	2221	...	2321
Rugby ... 150 ▷ d.	...	...	0733	0813	0820	0913	0920	1013	1018		1813	1818	1833	1918	1933	2018	2033	2133	2213	2233	...	2333
Northampton ▷ d.	...	...	0754	0834	0840	0934	0941	1034	1038		1834	1838	1854	1938	1954	2038	2054	2154	2234	2254	...	2354
Northampton ▽ d.	0605	0705	⑥ 0805	0850	0850	0950	0950	1050	1050		1850	1850	⑥ 1905	...	⑥ 1959	...	⑥ 2100	⑥ 2200	⑥ 2255	⑥ 2330	...	...
Milton Keynes ... 150 151 ▽ d.	0621	0721	0821	0903	0903	1004	1004	1104	1104		1904	1904	1921	...	2016	...	2116	2218	2311	2346	...	...
Watford Junction ▽ d.	0700	0757	0857	0934	0934	1029	1029	1129	1129		1929	1929	1959	...	2049	...	2150	2304	2357	0018	...	...
London Euston ... 150 151 ▽ a.	0720	0819	0918	0951	0951	1048	1048	1148	1148		1948	1948	2019	...	2108	...	2211	2327	0017	0042	...	...

⑦	⑦	⑦	⑦	⑦	⑦	⑦	⑦	⑦A	⑦	⑦A		⑦	⑦A	⑦	⑦A	⑦	⑦A	⑦	⑦A	⑦	⑦	⑦
Crewe ... 150 151 d.	...	...	...	...	...	...	...	...	...	1138	then each train runs every two hours until	...	...	...	1738	...	...	...	1936	...	...	...
Stoke on Trent ... 150 d.	...	...	...	...	...	...	...	...	...	|		...	...	...	1759	...	...	...	1957	...	...	...
Stafford ... 150 151 d.	...	...	...	...	...	...	...	...	...	1210		...	...	...	1818	...	...	...	2016	...	...	...
Nuneaton d.	...	...	...	...	...	...	...	...	...	1258		...	...	...	1858	...	...	...	2058	...	...	...
Birmingham New St ▷ d.	...	...	...	0834	0914	1014	1114	...	1214	|		1714	...	1814	|	1914	...	2014	|	2114	...	2214
Birmingham Int'l ▷ d.	...	...	...	0945	0925	1025	1125	...	1225	|		1725	...	1825	|	1925	...	2025	|	2125	...	2225
Coventry ▷ d.	...	...	...	0900	0944	1044	1144	...	1244	|		1744	...	1844	|	1944	...	2044	|	2144	...	2244
Rugby ... 150 ▷ d.	...	...	...	—	1001	1100	1200	1229	1300	1327		1800	1829	1900	1930	2000	2040	2100	2121	2157	...	2257
Northampton ▷ d.	...	...	...	...	1101*	1201*	1301*	|	1401*	|		1901*	|	2001*	|	2101*	|	2201*	|	2301*	...	0001*
Northampton ▽ d.	0823	0853	0930	⑦ 1007	⑦ 1037	⑦ 1125	⑦ 1225	|	⑦ 1325	|		⑦ 1825	|	⑦ 1925	|	⑦ 2025	|	⑦ 2125	|	⑦ 2225	2255	...
Milton Keynes ... 150 151 ▽ d.	0841	0911	0948	1024	1055	1142	1241	1305	1341	1405		1841	1905	1941	2006	2041	2107	2144	2211	2244	2315	...
Watford Junction ▽ d.	0923	0953	1030	1105	1137	1218	1317	1333	1417	1433		1917	1933	2017	2033	2128	2136	2227	2253	2324	2357	...
London Euston ... 150 151 ▽ a.	0943	1013	1050	1126	1157	1237	1337	1354	1437	1454		1937	1953	2037	2052	2148	2157	2247	2313	2346	0017	...

▼ – Additional trains **London Euston - Northampton**:
Ⓐ: 0713**n** and hourly until 1613**n**; then 1648**n**, 1713**n**, 1746**n**, 1813**n**, 1913**n**, 1946**n**, 2013**n**, 2054, 2146**n**, 2224, 2254, 2324.
⑥: 0754, 0854, 0913**n**, 0954 and then at 13 (note **n** applies) and 54 minutes past the hour until 1713**n**; then 1813**n**, 1913**n**, 2107, 2154, 2234, 2304, 2348.
⑦: 1153, 2102, 2228, 2258.

▶ – Additional trains **Northampton - Birmingham New Street**:
Ⓐ: 0517, 0556, 0717, 0756 and hourly until 1756; then 1817, 1856, 2017, 2056.
⑥: 0556, 0817, 0917 and hourly until 1717; then 1856, 1956, 2056, 2156.

A – Until July 12.
n – Does not call at Watford Junction.

▽ – Additional trains **Northampton - London Euston**:
Ⓐ: 0617, 0713**n**, 0738**n**, 0825**n**, 0925**n** and hourly until 2025**n**; then 2132.
⑥: 0733, 0825**n**, 0905, 0925**n** and at 05 and 25 (note **n** applies) until 1805; then 1831, 1931, 2021, 2112.
⑦: 1107.

▷ – Additional trains **Birmingham New Street - Northampton**:
Ⓐ: 0633, 0733 and hourly until 1633; then 1713, 1733, 1833, 1933, 2033.
⑥: 0633, 0753 and hourly until 1653; then 1833, 1933, 2033.

★ – The 1546 from London Euston calls Stafford 1820, Stoke 1841 and arrives Crewe 1905.
* – By 🚌.

VT LONDON - BIRMINGHAM - WOLVERHAMPTON 143

For slower services London - Northampton - Birmingham see Table **142**.

km			Ⓐ	⚒	Ⓐ		⚒	⚒	⚒			Ⓐ	⑥	⚒		⚒	Ⓐ	⑥		Ⓐ	⑥A	Ⓐ
0	**London** Euston 150 d.	⚒	0603	0623	0643	...	0703	0723	0743	and at	...	1803	1803	1823	...	1843	1903	1902	...	1923	1930	1943
28	Watford Junction △ 150 d.		|	0637	|	...	|	0737	|	the same	...	|	|	1837	...	|	|	|	...	1937	|	|
80	Milton Keynes 150 d.		|	|	0713	...	|	|	0813	minutes	...	|	|	|	...	1913u	|	|	...	|	2006	2013
133	Rugby 150 d.		0651	|	|	...	0751	|	|	past each	...	1851	1851	|	...	|	1951	1951	...	|	|	|
151	**Coventry** a.		0701	0722	0742	...	0801	0822	0842	hour until	...	1901	1901	1922	...	1942	2001	2003	...	2022	2049	2042
168	Birmingham Int'l ✈ a.		0712	0733	0753	...	0812	0833	0853		...	1912	1912	1933	...	1953	2012	2014	...	2033	2100	2053
182	**Birmingham** New St a.		0727	0745	0808	...	0827	0845	0908		...	1927	1925	1945	...	2008	2027	2030	...	2045	2113	2106
190	Sandwell & Dudley a.		...	0757	...	...	...	0857	...	▲	...	...	1953	1958	...	...	...	2053	...	2058	|	2123
202	**Wolverhampton** a.		...	0811	...	...	...	0911	...		...	...	2008	2012	...	...	...	2108	...	2112	2149	2138

	Ⓐ	⑥A	Ⓐ		⑥A	Ⓐ	Ⓐ		⑥A		Ⓐ		Ⓐ	①–④	⑤			⑦B	⑦B			⑦B	⑦
London Euston 150 d.	2003	2007	2023	...	2029	2043	2103	...	2124	...	2143	...	2243	2343	2343	...	⑦	0850	0950	...	...	1050	1145
Watford Junction △ 150 d.	|	2023	2037	...	2045	|	|	...	2140	...	2158	...	2257	|	|	...		0905	1004	...	...	1105	1201
Milton Keynes 150 d.	|	|	|	...	2127	2113	2134	...	2218	...	2224	...	2324	0026	0026	...		0939	1039	...	...	1139	1227
Rugby 150 d.	2051	|	|	...	2211	|	2156	...	2252	...	|	...	0005s	0100s	0105s	...		1002	1102	...	...	1202	1247
Coventry a.	2101	2135	2122	...	2222	2142	2206	...	2302	...	2311	...	0017s	0113s	0118s	...		1023	1122	...	...	1223	1256
Birmingham Int'l ✈ a.	2112	2153	2133	...	2233	2153	2217	...	2313	...	2322	...	0028s	0123s	0129s	...		1034	1133	...	...	1234	1307
Birmingham New St a.	2125	2205	2146	...	2245	2206	2229	...	2325	...	2335	...	0040s	0135s	0141s	...		1047	1145	...	...	1247	1322
Sandwell & Dudley a.	|	2224	2158	...	2256	2223	2240	...	2337	...	2346	...	|	|	|	...		1059	1158	...	...	1259	...
Wolverhampton a.	2155	2238	2212	...	2310	2238	2255	...	2351	...	2359	...	0110	0205	0217	...		1113	1217	...	...	1313	...

		⑦	⑦	⑦			⑦	⑦	⑦		⑦	⑦	⑦		⑦	⑦	⑦		⑦B	⑦B		⑦B
London Euston 150 d.	...	1218	1238	1258		...	1818	1838	1858	...	1918	1938	1958	...	2018	2038	2054	...	2154	2224	...	2324
Watford Junction △ 150 d.	...	1232	|	|	and at	...	1832	|	|	...	1932	|	|	...	2032	|	2111	...	2208	2238	...	2339
Milton Keynes 150 d.	...	|	1311	|	the same	...	|	1911	|	...	|	2011	|	...	|	2116	2145	...	2244	2311	...	0011
Rugby 150 d.	...	|	|	1349	minutes	...	|	|	1949	...	|	|	2049	...	|	|	2206	...	2320	2343	...	0047s
Coventry a.	...	1320	1340	1400	past each	...	1920	1940	2000	...	2020	2040	2100	...	2120	2146	2215	...	2333	2354	...	0057s
Birmingham Int'l ✈ a.	...	1331	1351	1411	hour until	...	1931	1951	2011	...	2031	2051	2111	...	2131	2157	2226	...	2351	0008	...	0108s
Birmingham New St a.	...	1344	1406	1425		...	1944	2006	2023	...	2044	2104	2124	...	2144	2209	2239	...	0004	0022	...	0121s
Sandwell & Dudley a.	...	1356	...	...		...	1956	...	2046	...	2056	2115	2136	...	2156	2224	2252	...	|	|	...	|
Wolverhampton a.	...	1410	...	...		...	2010	...	2057	...	2110	2131	2151	...	2210	2239	2306	...	0028	0055	...	0153

		Ⓐ	⑥	Ⓐ	Ⓐ	⑥	⚒		Ⓐ	⑥	Ⓐ		⑥	Ⓐ	Ⓐ	⑥		⚒	⚒		Ⓐ		⑥
Wolverhampton d.	⚒	0500	...	0520	0545	0545	0604	...	0627	0627	0645	...	0645	0704	...	0704	...	...	0744	...	...	...	0806
Sandwell & Dudley d.		|	...	0530	0556	0556	0615	...	0637	0637	0656	...	0656	0715	...	0715	...	...	0756	...	...	...	|
Birmingham New St d.		0529	0550	0550	0610	0610	0630	...	0650	0650	0710	...	0710	0730	...	0730	...	0750	0810	...	0830	...	0830
Birmingham Int'l ✈ d.		0539	0600	0600	0620	0620	0639	...	0700	0700	0720	...	0720	|	0741	0740	...	0800	0820	...	0839	...	0839
Coventry d.		0550	0610	0611	0631	0631	0651	...	0711	0711	0731	...	0731	|	0752	0752	...	0811	0831	...	0851	...	0851
Rugby 150 d.		0603	0624	|	|	|	|	...	|	0723	|	...	|	|	|	|	...	0823	|	...	|	...	|
Milton Keynes 150 a.		0623	|	0638	0700	0659	|	...	0740s	|	|	...	|	|	|	0819	...	|	|	...	0919	...	0919
Watford Junction ▽ 150 a.		0643	|	|	|	0719	0738	...	|	|	|	...	0815	|	|	|	...	|	0917	...	|	...	|
London Euston 150 a.		0702	0716	0715	0736	0738	0756	...	0817	0814	0834	...	0834	0842	0849	0854	...	0914	0935	...	0954	...	0955

	⚒	⚒	⚒		⚒		Ⓐ	⑥		Ⓐ	Ⓐ		Ⓐ	⑥A		Ⓐ	⑥A	Ⓐ	⑥A	Ⓐ		Ⓐ
Wolverhampton d.	...	0845	...		...	...	1845	1845	...	...	...	...	1945	1945	...	...	2045	2047	2145	2145	...	2245
Sandwell & Dudley d.	...	0856	...	and at	...	...	1856	1856	...	...	...	...	1956	1956	...	...	2056	2057	2157	2156	...	2255
Birmingham New St d.	0850	0910	0930	the same	1850	...	1910	1910	...	1930	1950	...	2010	2010	...	2050	2110	2110	2210	2210	...	2310
Birmingham Int'l ✈ d.	0900	0920	0939	minutes	1900	...	1920	1920	...	1939	2000	...	2020	2020	...	2100	2120	2120	2220	2220	...	2320
Coventry d.	0911	0931	0951	past each	1911	...	1931	1931	...	1951	2011	...	2031	2031	...	2111	2131	2131	2231	2231	...	2331
Rugby 150 d.	0923	|	|	hour until	1923	...	|	1944	...	|	2023	...	|	2043	...	2123	2143	|	2243	2243	...	2344
Milton Keynes 150 a.	|	|	1019		|	...	|	2007	...	2019	|	...	2059	2122	...	|	2219	2159	2316s	2303s	...	0022s
Watford Junction ▽ 150 a.	|	1015	|		|	...	2015	2034	...	|	|	...	2119	2155	...	|	2244	2220	0001	2324	...	0052
London Euston 150 a.	1014	1034	1054		2017	...	2034	2056	...	2054	2114	...	2138	2216	...	2233	2306	2258	0022	0003	...	0113

		⑦		⑦		⑦		⑦	⑦	⑦	⑦		⑦		⑦	⑦	⑦		⑦	⑦B	⑦B	⑦B
Wolverhampton d.	⑦	0805	...	0905	...	1005	...	1105	...	1145	...		...	...	1845	...	1945	...	...	2105	2205	2237
Sandwell & Dudley d.		0815	...	0916	...	1015	...	1115	...	1157	...	and at	...	...	1856	...	1956	...	...	2115	2215	2247
Birmingham New St d.		0830	...	0930	...	1030	...	1130	1150	1210	1230	the same	1850	...	1910	1930	2010	...	2030	2130	2230	2300
Birmingham Int'l ✈ d.		0840	...	0940	...	1040	...	1140	1200	1220	1239	minutes	1901	...	1920	1939	2020	...	2040	2140	2240	2310
Coventry d.		0851	...	0951	...	1051	...	1151	1211	1231	1251	past each	1911	...	1931	1951	2031	...	2051	2151	2251	2321
Rugby 150 d.		0904	...	1004	...	1104	...	1205	1225	|	|	hour until	1926	...	|	|	|	...	2105	2205	2305	2335
Milton Keynes 150 a.		0939	...	1039	...	1137	...	1226	|	|	1319		|	...	|	2019	|	...	2128	2229	2329	2357s
Watford Junction ▽ 150 a.		1007	...	1110	...	1207	...	|	|	1318	|		|	...	2016	|	2132	...	2203	2258	0001	0035
London Euston 150 a.		1028	...	1131	...	1227	...	1304	1319	1339	1359		2020	...	2036	2102	2154	...	2224	2318	0022	0102

A – Until September 5.
B – Until July 12.
s – Stops to set down only.
u – Stops to pick up only.
△ – Trains stop here to pick up only.
▽ – Trains stop here to set down only.
▲ – The 1643 and 1743 services from London call at Milton Keynes to pick up only.

145 LONDON and BIRMINGHAM - SHREWSBURY - CHESTER

2nd class AW, LM, WS

Services on ⑦ valid until July 12.

km	⚒		Ⓐ	ⒶV	⚒A	Ⓐ	⑥	⚒	⚒		⚒A	ⒶW	⑥	Ⓐ	⑥W	⚒B	⚒	⚒		⚒B	⚒		⚒	⑥W
	London Marylebone	d.	...	...	...	...	...	...	...	...	...	0643	...	...	0720	...	...	...	...	...	...	...	...	1124
	Banbury	d.	...	...	...	...	...	...	...	...	...	0800u	...	...	0831u	...	...	...	...	...	...	...	...	1238u
	Tame Bridge Parkway	d.	...	...	...	...	...	...	...	...	...	|	...	...	0940	...	...	...	...	...	...	...	...	1340
0	**Birmingham** International	d.	...	...	...	...	...	0709	...	...	0809	|	0909	0909	|	1009	...	1109	...	1209	...	...	1309	|
13	**Birmingham** New St ◇	d.	...	...	0624	...	...	0722	...	...	0824	|	0924	0924	|	1024	...	1124	...	1224	...	...	1323	|
34	Wolverhampton ◇	d.	...	...	0642	...	...	0741	...	...	0843	|	0943	0943	0959u	1043	...	1143	...	1243	...	...	1343	1359u
59	Telford Central ◇	d.	...	...	0659	...	...	0758	...	...	0859	0941	0959	1003	1019	1059	...	1159	...	1259	...	...	1359	1419
65	Wellington ◇	d.	...	...	0705	...	...	0804	...	...	0906	|	1006	1010	1025	1106	...	1206	...	1306	...	...	1406	1425
	Cardiff Central **155**	d.	...	...	|	0510	0521	|	0720	...	|	|	|	|	|	|	0920	|	...	|	1120	...	|	|
81	**Shrewsbury** ◇	d.	0610	...	0718	0724	0724	0824	0924	...	0919	1003	1022	1026	1042	1119	1124	1222	...	1319	1324	...	1422	1442
110	Gobowen	d.	0630	...	...	0743	0743	0843	0943	...	...	1024	1042	1046	1103	...	1143	1242	...	...	1343	...	1442	1503
122	Ruabon	d.	0642	...	...	0754	0754	0855	0954	...	...	1036	1054	1057	1115	...	1154	1254	...	...	1354	...	1454	1515
129	Wrexham General	d.	0649	0700	...	0801	0801	0901	1001	...	...	1044	1100	1104	1124	...	1202	1300	...	...	1402	...	1500	1524
149	**Chester**	a.	0707	0719	...	0820	0819	0919	1020	...	...	...	1120	1121	...	...	1219	1319	...	...	1420	...	1521	...
	Holyhead **165**	a.	...	...	...	1005	1005	1119	1213	...	...	...	1319	1319	...	...	1414	1511	...	...	1614	...	1711	...

		⚒B	⚒	ⒶW	⚒	⚒		⚒A	Ⓐf	⚒	⑥W	⚒A	⚒	ⒶW		⚒	⚒A		⑥L	Ⓐ	⑥W	⚒	ⒶW	⑥	Ⓐ
London Marylebone	d.	...	...	1217	...	...	...	...	...	...	1524	...	...	1633	...	...	...	...	...	...	1824	...	2003	...	...
Banbury	d.	...	...	1330u	...	...	...	...	...	...	1638u	...	...	|	...	...	...	...	...	...	1938u	...	2116u	...	...
Tame Bridge Parkway	d.	...	...	1438	...	...	...	...	...	...	1742	...	...	1840	...	...	...	...	...	...	2040	...	2214	...	...
Birmingham International	d.	1409	...	|	1509	...	...	1609	...	1709	|	1809	...	|	...	1909	2009	...	...	...	|	2109	|	...	...
Birmingham New St ◇	d.	1424	...	|	1524	...	...	1624	...	1724	|	1824	...	|	...	1924	2024	...	...	...	|	2124	|	...	...
Wolverhampton ◇	d.	1443	...	1453u	1543	...	...	1643	...	1743	1759u	1843	...	1858u	...	1943	2043	...	...	...	2055u	2142	2230u	...	...
Telford Central ◇	d.	1459	...	1513	1559	...	...	1659	...	1759	1819	1859	...	1915	...	1959	2059	...	...	...	2115	2159	2250	...	...
Wellington ◇	d.	1506	...	1519	1606	...	...	1706	...	1806	1825	1906	...	1921	...	2006	2106	...	...	...	2121	2205	2257	...	...
Cardiff Central **155**	d.	|	1320	|	|	1520	...	|	1615	|	|	|	1720	|	...	|	|	...	1934	1934	|	|	|	...	...
Shrewsbury ◇	d.	1519	1524	1532	1622	1724	...	1719	1809	1824	1842	1920	1924	1939	...	2024	2119	...	2137	2139	2147	2223	2315	2333	2337
Gobowen	d.	...	1542	...	1642	1743	...	...	|	1843	1903	...	1943	2003	...	2043	...	...	2156	2158	2214	2242	2336	2352	2356
Ruabon	d.	...	1554	...	1654	1754	...	...	b	1855	1915	...	1954	2015	...	2055	...	...	2207	2209	2226	2254	2348	0004	0008
Wrexham General	d.	...	1602	...	1702	1801	...	...	|	1902	1924	...	2002	2023	...	2101	...	...	2213	2215	2235	2301	2357	0014	0014
Chester	a.	...	1621	...	1722	1821	...	...	1909	1920	...	...	2020	...	...	2119	...	...	2231	2234	...	2318	...	0031	0034
Holyhead **165**	a.	...	1819	...	1916	2016	...	...	2049	2121	...	...	2219	...	...	...	...	...	...	0055	...	...	...	...	...

⑦		⑦	⑦	⑦W	⑦A			⑦	⑦A	⑦	⑦B			⑦	⑦	⑦A	⑦			⑦W	⑦	⑦A	⑦W	⑦
London Marylebone	d.	...	...	0930	...	...	...	...	...	...	...	...	...	...	...	...	...	...	...	1615	...	...	1832	...
Banbury	d.	...	...	1042u	...	...	...	...	...	...	...	...	...	...	...	...	...	...	...	1729u	...	...	1946u	...
Tame Bridge Parkway	d.	...	...	1146	...	...	...	...	...	...	...	...	...	...	...	...	...	...	...	1830	...	...	2047	...
Birmingham International	d.	...	1048	|	1208	...	...	1305	1407	1507	1607	...	...	...	1707	1807	...	...	...	|	1907	2008	|	...
Birmingham New St ◇	d.	...	1105	|	1224	...	...	1324	1424	1524	1624	...	...	...	1724	1824	...	...	...	|	1924	2024	|	...
Wolverhampton ◇	d.	...	1127	1203u	1241	...	...	1342	1443	1543	1643	...	...	...	1743	1843	...	...	...	1854u	1943	2043	2101u	...
Telford Central ◇	d.	...	1154	1223	1257	...	...	1409	1459	1609	1659	...	...	...	1809	1859	...	...	...	1917	2009	2059	2121	...
Wellington ◇	d.	...	1201	1229	1304	...	...	1415	1506	1617	1706	...	...	...	1816	1906	...	...	...	1923	2017	2106	2127	...
Cardiff Central **155**	d.	...	|	|	|	...	...	|	|	|	|	...	...	1520	|	|	1720	...	...	|	|	|	|	...
Shrewsbury ◇	d.	1016	1216	1247	1317	...	...	1430	1519	1632	1719	...	...	1730	1830	1920	1932	...	...	1950	2034	2119	2143	...
Gobowen	d.	1035	1236	1308	...	...	...	1450	...	1651	...	...	...	1749	1850	...	1951	...	...	2011	2053	...	2204	...
Ruabon	d.	1046	1248	1320	...	...	...	1502	...	1703	...	...	...	1801	1902	...	2003	...	...	2023	2105	...	2216	...
Wrexham General	d.	1053	1255	1330	...	...	...	1508	...	1710	...	...	...	1808	1908	...	2010	...	...	2031	2112	...	2226	2235
Chester	a.	1111	1319	...	...	...	...	1529	...	1728	...	...	...	1825	1926	...	2031	...	...	...	2130	...	...	2253
Holyhead **165**	a.	...	...	...	...	...	...	...	...	1925	...	...	...	2020	2130	...	2238	...	...	...	...	...	...	...

⚒		ⒶW	Ⓐ	⑥W	⑥	Ⓐ	⚒A	ⒶW	Ⓐf	Ⓐ	⑥	Ⓐ	⑥	⚒C	⑥W	Ⓐ	⑥	Ⓐ	⑥	⚒B	ⒶW	⚒	⑥W	⚒
Holyhead **165**	d.	...	...	...	0425	0425	...	...	0532	0511	0522	0627	0633	...	...	0715	0715	0805	0820	...	...	0923	...	1033
Chester	d.	...	0515	*0537*	0612	0622	...	...	0708	0722	0722	0822	0822	...	...	0930	0930	1022	1022	...	...	1122	...	1222
Wrexham General	d.	0512	0531	0618	0638	0639	...	0723	|	0744	0744	0838	0838	...	0926	0946	0946	1038	1038	...	1123	1144	1220	1238
Ruabon	d.	|	0538	0626	0645	0646	...	0731	c	0751	0751	0845	0845	...	0934	0953	0953	1045	1045	...	1131	1151	1228	1245
Gobowen	d.	0527	0550	0637	0651	0658	...	0743	|	0803	0803	0857	0857	...	0944	1005	1005	1057	1057	...	1143	1203	1237	1257
Shrewsbury □	d.	0552	0610	0705	0717	0718	0731	0807	0809	0831	0831	0917	0917	0931	1008	1035	1031	1117	1117	1131	1207	1231	1303	1317
Cardiff Central **155**	a.	|	0817	|	0923	0922	|	|	0958	|	|	1119	1120	|	|	|	|	1320	1320	|	|	|	|	1521
Wellington □	d.	|	...	0718	...	...	0745	0821	...	0845	0845	...	...	0945	1021	1049	1045	...	...	1145	1221	1245	1316	...
Telford Central □	d.	0609	...	0724	...	...	0751	0827	...	0851	0851	...	...	0951	1027	1055	1051	...	...	1151	1227	1251	1322	...
Wolverhampton □	a.	|	...	0747s	...	...	0809	|	...	0908	0908	...	...	1008	1047s	1112	1108	...	...	1208	1247s	1308	1347s	...
Birmingham New St □	a.	|	...	|	...	...	0828	|	...	0926	0926	...	...	1026	|	1130	1126	...	...	1226	|	1326	|	...
Birmingham International	a.	|	...	|	...	...	0850	|	...	0950	0950	...	...	1050	|	1150	1150	...	...	1250	|	1350	|	...
Tame Bridge Parkway	a.	0641	...	0801	...	...	...	0902	...	...	...	...	...	...	1101	...	...	...	...	...	1302	...	1401	...
Banbury	d.	0746s	...	0906s	...	...	...	1006s	...	...	...	...	...	...	1212s	...	...	...	...	...	1406s	...	1507s	...
London Marylebone	a.	0857	...	1024	...	...	...	1123	...	...	...	...	...	...	1327	...	...	...	...	...	1523	...	1623	...

		⚒B	⚒	⚒	⚒B	ⒶW	⚒	Ⓐ	⑥	⚒B	⚒	⑥W	Ⓐ	⑥	⚒A	Ⓐ	⑥	ⒶV	⑥	Ⓐ	ⒶA	⑥A	Ⓐ	⑥	⚒
Holyhead **165**	d.	...	1123	1238	...	...	1323	1432	1423	...	1523	...	1636	1638	...	1721	1721	...	...	...	...	...	1921	1921	...
Chester	d.	...	1322	1422	...	...	1522	1622	1622	...	1722	...	1820	1822	...	1927	1927	2027	2027	...	...	...	2121	2122	2228
Wrexham General	d.	...	1344	1438	...	...	1544	1638	1638	...	1744	1818	1836	1838	...	1943	1943	2044	2043	2049	...	...	2137	2139	2244
Ruabon	d.	...	1351	1445	...	...	1551	1645	1645	...	1751	1826	1843	1845	...	1950	1950	...	2051	2057	...	...	2144	2147	2251
Gobowen	d.	...	1403	1457	...	...	1603	1657	1657	...	1803	1837	1855	1857	...	2002	2002	...	2102	2108	...	...	2156	2201	2303
Shrewsbury □	d.	1331	1431	1517	1531	1607	1631	1717	1717	1731	1831	1905	1915	1918	1932	2022	2023	...	2122	2128	2133	2131	2218	2231	2326
Cardiff Central **155**	a.	|	|	1718	|	|	|	1920	1926	|	|	|	2119	2120	|	2304	...	...	...	...	|	|	|	|	|
Wellington □	d.	1345	1445	...	1545	|	1645	...	...	1745	1845	1918	...	...	1946	...	...	...	...	...	2147	2145	2232	2245	2340
Telford Central □	d.	1351	1451	...	1551	1624	1651	...	...	1751	1851	1924	...	...	1952	...	...	...	...	...	2153	2151	2238	2251	2347
Wolverhampton □	a.	1408	1508	...	1608	1647s	1708	...	...	1808	1908	1949s	...	...	2009	...	...	...	...	...	2210	2208	2255	2308	0017
Birmingham New St □	a.	1426	1526	...	1626	|	1726	...	...	1826	1926	|	...	...	2027	...	...	...	...	...	2230	2226	2326	2324	...
Birmingham International	a.	1450	1550	...	1650	|	1750	...	...	1850	1950	|	...	...	2050	...	...	...	...	...	...	...	...	...	...
Tame Bridge Parkway	a.	...	...	...	...	1702	...	...	...	...	...	2002	...	...	...	...	...	...	...	...	...	...	...	...	...
Banbury	d.	...	...	...	...	1803s	...	...	...	...	...	2108s	...	...	...	...	...	...	...	...	...	...	...	...	...
London Marylebone	a.	...	...	...	...	1922	...	...	...	...	...	2222	...	...	...	...	...	...	...	...	...	...	...	...	...

⑦		⑦	⑦	⑦W	⑦A	⑦	⑦	⑦A	⑦W	⑦	⑦B	⑦	⑦B	⑦W	⑦	⑦			⑦A	⑦	⑦A	⑦		⑦
Holyhead **165**	d.	...	...	...	...	...	1020	...	...	...	...	...	...	...	...	1625	...	...	...	...	...	...	...	...
Chester	d.	0808	0912	...	...	1122	1222	...	...	1322	...	1531	...	...	1722	1824	...	...	...	1925	...	2124	...	2204
Wrexham General	d.	0826	0930	1047	...	1139	1238	...	1311	1339	...	1548	...	1703	1739	1840	...	...	...	1942	...	2143	...	2222
Ruabon	d.	...	0936	1055	...	1146	1245	...	1319	1346	...	1555	...	1711	1746	1847	...	...	...	1949	...	2150	...	...
Gobowen	d.	...	0948	1107	...	1158	1257	...	1331	1358	...	1607	...	1723	1758	1859	...	...	...	2001	...	2201	...	...
Shrewsbury □	d.	...	1010	1131	1140	1220	1317	1331	1356	1420	1533	1629	1733	1756	1820	1919	...	...	1931	2023	2131	2223	...	...
Cardiff Central **155**	a.	...	|	|	|	|	1530	|	|	|	|	|	|	|	|	2130	...	...	|	|	|	|	...	...
Wellington □	d.	...	1023	1144	1154	1234	...	1345	1409	1434	1547	1643	1747	1809	1834	...	...	...	1945	2037	2145	2237	...	...
Telford Central □	d.	...	1031	1150	1200	1241	...	1351	1415	1441	1553	1650	1753	1815	1841	...	...	...	1951	2044	2151	2245	...	...
Wolverhampton □	a.	...	1057	1210s	1217	1308	...	1408	1436s	1508	1610	1717	1810	1835s	1908	...	...	...	2008	2111	2208	2316	...	...
Birmingham New St □	a.	...	1114	|	1234	1324	...	1424	|	1524	1626	1735	1828	|	1924	...	...	...	2024	2128	2228	...	...	...
Birmingham International	a.	...	1132	|	1256	1356	...	1456	|	1556	1656	1756	1856	|	1956	...	...	...	2056	2156	2255	...	...	...
Tame Bridge Parkway	a.	...	...	1226	...	...	...	...	1451	...	...	...	...	1850	...	...	...	...	...	...	...	...	...	...
Banbury	d.	...	...	1334s	...	...	...	...	1605s	...	...	...	...	1958s	...	...	...	...	...	...	...	...	...	...
London Marylebone	a.	...	...	1448	...	...	...	...	1718	...	...	...	...	2113	...	...	...	...	...	...	...	...	...	...

A – To / from Aberystwyth.
B – To / from Aberystwyth and Pwllheli.
C – To / from Aberystwyth and Barmouth.
L – To / from Llandudno Junction.
W – Operated by *WS*. Conveys [12] and 🍷 (✕ in 1st class).
V – Operated by *VT*. To / from London Euston, Table **150**. Conveys [12].

X – From January 26.
a – ⑥ only.
b – Via Crewe (arrives 1845).
c – Via Crewe (departs 0735).
f – Also conveys [1].
s – Stops to set down only.
u – Stops to pick up only.

◇ – Additional trains **Birmingham New St - Shrewsbury** (±70 minutes. Operator *LM*): 0551Ⓐ, 0705⑥, 0727Ⓐ, 0805⚒ and hourly until 2105⚒; then 2205⑥, 2221Ⓐ.

□ – Additional trains **Shrewsbury - Birmingham New St** (±70 minutes. Operator *LM*): 0528Ⓐ, 0558Ⓐ, 0647⑥, 0655Ⓐ, 0714Ⓐ, 0747⚒ and hourly until 2147⚒.

AW 2nd class — SHREWSBURY - LLANDRINDOD - SWANSEA — 146

km		⚒	⚒ C	⚒		⚒	⚒		⑦	⑦	⑦
0	**Shrewsbury** .... **162** d.		0519	0905	...	1405	1805	...		1207	1625
20	Church Stretton .. **162** d.		0536	0922	...	1423	1823	...		1224	1642
32	Craven Arms ...... **162** d.		0550	0935	...	1436	1835	...		1236	1654
52	Knighton .... d.		0612	0957	...	1458	1857	...		1258	1717
84	**Llandrindod** .... a.		0648	1033	...	1534	1933	...		1333	1753
84	**Llandrindod** .... d.		0653	1033	...	1536	1933	...		1336	1755
110	Llanwrtyd .... d.		0722	1107	...	1605	2011	...		1408	1824
128	**Llandovery** .... d.		0746	1131	...	1630	2035	...		1432	1849
146	Llandeilo .... d.		0807	1152	...	1650	2056	...		1505	1909
159	Pantyffynnon .... d.		0823	1208	...	1707	2112	...		1521	1926
178	**Llanelli** .... **136** a.		0841	1228	...	1726a	2140	...		1540	1947
196	**Swansea** .... **136** a.		0908	1301	...	1806	2213	...		1613	2013

	⚒	⚒	⚒ C	⚒	⚒			⑦	⑦	⑦
Swansea .... **136** d.		0436	0915	1316	1821	...	...		1104	1516
Llanelli .... **136** d.		0453	0935	1335	1839	...	...		1127	1535
Pantyffynnon .... d.		0513	0955	1354	1858	...	...		1147	1555
Llandeilo .... d.		0532	1014	1414	1918	...	...		1207	1614
Llandovery .... d.		0554	1036	1436	1940	...	...		1229	1636
Llanwrtyd .... d.		0619	1105	1500	2006	...	...		1253	1701
Llandrindod .... a.		0647	1134	1529	2035	...	...		1322	1729
Llandrindod .... d.		0655	1138	1539	2039	...	...		1345	1758
Knighton .... d.		0731	1215	1615	2116	...	...		1421	1834
Craven Arms .... **162** d.		0752	1236	1636	2137	...	...		1442	1858
Church Stretton ... **162** d.		0805	1249	1649	2150	...	...		1455	1911
Shrewsbury .... **162** a.		0821	1307	1710	2207	...	...		1513	1929

C – From / to Cardiff.

a – 1732 on ⑥.

AW 2nd class — SHREWSBURY - ABERYSTWYTH and PWLLHELI — 148

Services on ⑦ valid until July 12.

km		⚒	⚒	⚒		⚒	⚒		Ⓐ	⚒ 🍷	⚒		②④ 🚂 A	①③⑤ 🚂 A		⚒ 🍷	⚒	⚒ 🍷	⚒	⚒ 🍷	⚒		⚒ 🍷	⚒
	Birmingham New St **145** ..... d.		...	...	...	...	...	...	...	0624	...	...	...	...	...	0824	...	1024	1024	1224	1224	...	1424	1424
0	**Shrewsbury 145** .... d.		...	...	...	...	...	...	...	0727	...	...	...	...	...	0927	...	1127	1127	1327	1327	...	1527	1527
32	Welshpool .... d.		...	...	...	...	...	...	...	0749	...	...	...	...	...	0949	...	1149	1149	1349	1349	...	1549	1549
54	Newtown .... d.		...	...	...	...	...	...	...	0805	...	...	...	...	...	1005	...	1205	1205	1405	1405	...	1605	1605
63	Caersws .... d.		...	...	...	...	...	...	...	0814	...	...	...	...	...	1014	...	1214	1214	1414	1414	...	1614	1614
98	**Machynlleth** .... d.		0435	0515	...	0630	0649	...	0807	0849	0905	...	1005	1005	...	1049	1100	1249	1256	1449	1456	...	1649	1700
104	Dovey Junction .... d.		0442	0522	...	0637	0656	...	0814	0856	0912	...	1010	1010	...	1056	1107	1256	1303	1456	1503	...	1656	1707
118	Borth .... d.		0453	|	...	0648	|	...	0825	0907	|	...	|	|	...	1107	|	1307	|	1507	|	...	1707	|
131	**Aberystwyth** .... a.		0512	|	...	0707	|	...	0844	0926	|	...	|	|	...	1126	|	1326	|	1526	|	...	1726	|
114	Aberdovey .... d.		...	0534	...	...	0707	...	...	...	0923	...	|	|	...	...	1119	...	1314	...	1514	...	...	1718
120	Tywyn .... d.		...	0540	...	...	0715	...	...	...	0930	...	1033	1033	...	...	1126	...	1322	...	1522	...	...	1726
135	Fairbourne .... d.		...	0557	...	...	0733	...	...	...	0948	...	|	|	...	...	1144	...	1340	...	1540	...	...	1744
139	**Barmouth** .... d.		...	0609	...	...	0750	...	...	...	0957	...	1102	1102	...	...	1156	...	1352	...	1552	...	...	1756
156	Harlech .... d.		...	0629	...	...	0832t	...	...	...	1021	...	1123	1123	...	...	1225f	...	1431t	...	1621f	...	...	1826f
165	Penrhyndeudraeth .... d.		...	|	...	...	0843	...	...	...	1032	...	|	|	...	...	1236	...	1442	...	1632	...	...	1837
167	Minffordd **166** .... d.		...	|	...	...	0846	...	...	...	1036	...	1142	1142	...	...	1240	...	1445	...	1635	...	...	1840
170	Porthmadog .... d.		...	0645	...	...	0852	...	...	...	1042	...	1149	1219a	...	...	1247	...	1453	...	1642	...	...	1846
178	Criccieth .... d.		...	|	...	...	0859	...	...	...	1050	...	...	|	...	...	1255	...	1501	...	1650	...	...	1854
191	**Pwllheli** .... a.		...	0705	...	...	0913	...	...	...	1109	...	...	1240	...	...	1314	...	1518	...	1709	...	...	1913

	⚒ 🍷	⑤		⚒ 🍷	⚒		⚒		⑦	⑦	⑦	⑦		⑦	⑦	⑦ 🍷	⑦		⑦ 🍷	⑦ 🍷	⑦		⑦ 🍷	⑦
Birmingham New St **145** ..... d.	1624	...	...	1824	...	...	2024	...		...	...	...	...	...	...	1224	...	...	1424	1624	1624	...	1824	2024
Shrewsbury 145 .... d.	1727	...	...	1927	...	...	2142	...		...	0833	...	...	...	...	1325	...	...	1526	1726	1726	...	1927	2126
Welshpool .... d.	1749	...	...	1949	...	...	2204	...		...	0856	...	...	...	...	1347	...	...	1549	1748	1748	...	1949	2148
Newtown .... d.	1805	...	...	2005	...	...	2220	...		...	0912	...	...	...	...	1403	...	...	1605	1804	1804	...	2005	2204
Caersws .... d.	1814	...	...	2014	...	...	2229	...		...	0921	...	...	...	...	1412	...	...	1614	1813	1813	...	2014	2213
Machynlleth .... d.	1849	1900	...	2049	2117	...	2305	...		0830	0955	0956	...	1050	1235	1449	1500	...	1649	1849	1855	...	2049	2246
Dovey Junction .... d.	1856	1907	...	2056	2124	...	2312	...		0837	1002	1003	...	1057	1242	1456	1507	...	1656	1856	1902	...	2056	2253
Borth .... d.	1907	|	...	2107	|	...	2323	...		0848	1012	|	...	1108	1253	1507	|	...	1707	1907	|	...	2107	2304
Aberystwyth .... a.	1926	|	...	2126	|	...	2342	...		0905	1029	|	...	1125	1310	1526	|	...	1726	1926	|	...	2126	2323
Aberdovey .... d.	...	1919	...	...	2135	...	...	...		...	...	1014	...	...	...	...	1519	...	...	...	1914	...	...	...
Tywyn .... d.	...	1925	...	...	2142	...	...	...		...	...	1021	...	...	...	...	1530	...	...	...	1920	...	...	...
Fairbourne .... d.	...	1944	...	...	2159	...	...	...		...	...	1039	...	...	...	...	1548	...	...	...	1938	...	...	...
Barmouth .... d.	...	1955	...	...	2208	...	...	...		...	...	1047	...	...	...	...	1557	...	...	...	1947	...	...	...
Harlech .... d.	...	...	...	...	2229	...	...	...		...	...	1110	...	...	...	...	1621	...	...	...	2011	...	...	...
Penrhyndeudraeth .... d.	...	...	...	...	2240	...	...	...		...	...	1122	...	...	...	...	1633	...	...	...	2023	...	...	...
Minffordd **166** .... d.	...	...	...	...	2244	...	...	...		...	...	1124	...	...	...	...	1636	...	...	...	2026	...	...	...
Porthmadog .... d.	...	...	...	...	2248	...	...	...		...	...	1130	...	...	...	...	1641	...	...	...	2031	...	...	...
Criccieth .... d.	...	...	...	...	2256	...	...	...		...	...	1137	...	...	...	...	1648	...	...	...	2038	...	...	...
Pwllheli .... a.	...	...	...	...	2313	...	...	...		...	...	1154	...	...	...	...	1706	...	...	...	2056	...	...	...

	⚒	Ⓐ 🍷	⑥ 🍷	⚒	⚒ 🍷		⚒	⚒	⚒ 🍷	⚒	⚒ 🍷		⚒	⚒ 🍷	⚒	⚒ 🍷		①③⑤ 🚂 A	②④ 🚂 A		⚒	⚒ 🍷	⚒	⚒
Pwllheli .... d.		...	...	...	...	...	0621	0728	...	0936	...	...	1138	...	1342	...	...	1415	...	...	1532	...	1738	...
Criccieth .... d.		...	...	...	...	...	0635	0742	...	0949	...	...	1151	...	1355	...	...	|	...	...	1545	...	1751	...
Porthmadog .... d.		...	...	...	...	...	0647f	0751	...	0958	...	...	1202	...	1406	...	...	1455	1455	...	1556	...	1802	...
Minffordd **166** .... d.		...	...	...	...	...	0651	0755	...	1002	...	...	1206	...	1410	...	...	1500	1500	...	1600	...	1806	...
Penrhyndeudraeth .... d.		...	...	...	...	...	0654	0758	...	1005	...	...	1209	...	1413	...	...	|	|	...	1603	...	1809	...
Harlech .... d.		...	...	...	...	...	0720t	0833t	...	1022f	...	...	1225f	...	1430f	...	...	1523	1523	...	1620f	...	1825f	...
Barmouth .... d.		...	...	0646	...	...	0748	0859	...	1049	...	...	1249	...	1452	...	...	1550	1550	...	1650	...	1849	...
Fairbourne .... d.		...	...	0653	...	...	0756	0906	...	1056	...	...	1256	...	1459	...	...	|	|	...	1657	...	1856	...
Tywyn .... d.		...	...	0716f	...	...	0816	0931f	...	1127t	...	...	1323f	...	1523f	...	...	1622	1622	...	1727f	...	1926f	...
Aberdovey .... d.		...	...	0722	...	...	0822	0937	...	1133	...	...	1329	...	1529	...	...	|	|	...	1733	...	1932	...
Aberystwyth .... d.		0530	0530	|	0730	...	|	|	0930	|	1130	...	|	1330	|	1530	...	|	|	...	|	1730	|	1930
Borth .... d.		0543	0543	|	0743	...	|	|	0943	|	1143	...	|	1343	|	1543	...	|	|	...	|	1743	|	1943
Dovey Junction .... d.		0554	0554	0735	0754	...	0835	0950	0954	1146	1154	...	1341	1354	1541	1554	...	1653	1653	...	1746	1754	1946	1954
Machynlleth .... d.		0607	0607	0807	0807	...	0844	1007	1007	1207	1207	...	1407	1407	1607	1607	...	1659	1659	...	1802	1807	1958	2007
Caersws .... d.		0637	0637	0837	0837	...	...	1037	1037	1237	1237	...	1437	1437	1637	1637	...	...	...	...	...	1837	...	2037
Newtown .... d.		0646	0646	0846	0846	...	...	1046	1046	1246	1246	...	1446	1446	1646	1646	...	...	...	...	...	1846	...	2046
Welshpool .... d.		0701	0701	0901	0901	...	...	1101	1101	1301	1301	...	1501	1501	1701	1701	...	...	...	...	...	1901	...	2101
Shrewsbury 145 .... a.		0725	0728	0925	0925	...	...	1125	1125	1325	1325	...	1525	1525	1725	1725	...	...	...	...	...	1928	...	2127
Birmingham New St **145** ..... a.		0827	0828	1026	1026	...	...	1226	1226	1426	1426	...	1626	1626	1826	1826	...	...	...	...	...	2027	...	2230

	⚒		⚒	⑤		⑥	Ⓐ		⑦	⑦ 🍷		⑦ 🍷		⑦	⑦ 🍷		⑦	⑦ 🍷		⑦ 🍷	⑦	⑦	⑦	⑦
Pwllheli .... d.	...	...	2000	...	...	...	...	...		...	...	...	...	1155	...	...	1355	...	...	...	1745	...	...	...
Criccieth .... d.	...	...	2013	...	...	...	...	...		...	...	...	...	1208	...	...	1408	...	...	...	1759	...	...	...
Porthmadog .... d.	...	...	2023	...	...	...	...	...		...	...	...	...	1218	...	...	1420	...	...	...	1808	...	...	...
Minffordd **166** .... d.	...	...	2027	...	...	...	...	...		...	...	...	...	1223	...	...	1424	...	...	...	1813	...	...	...
Penrhyndeudraeth .... d.	...	...	2030	...	...	...	...	...		...	...	...	...	1226	...	...	1427	...	...	...	1816	...	...	...
Harlech .... d.	...	...	2046f	...	...	...	...	...		...	...	...	...	1238	...	...	1439	...	...	...	1828	...	...	...
Barmouth .... d.	...	...	2114	2212	...	...	...	...		...	...	...	...	1302	...	...	1502	...	...	...	1852	...	...	...
Fairbourne .... d.	...	...	2121	2219	...	...	...	...		...	...	...	...	1309	...	...	1509	...	...	...	1859	...	...	...
Tywyn .... d.	...	...	2146f	2238	...	...	...	...		...	...	...	...	1328	...	...	1527	...	...	...	1922	...	...	...
Aberdovey .... d.	...	...	2152	2244	...	...	...	...		...	...	...	...	1334	...	...	1533	...	...	...	1928	...	...	...
Aberystwyth .... d.	2136	...	|	|	...	2346	2353	...		0910	...	1130	...	|	1330	...	|	1530	...	1730	|	1930	2130	2330
Borth .... d.	2149	...	|	|	...	2359	0006	...		0923	...	1143	...	|	1343	...	|	1543	...	1743	|	1943	2143	2343
Dovey Junction .... d.	2200	...	2206	2257	...	0010	0017	...		0934	...	1154	...	1347	1354	...	1546	1554	...	1754	1941	1954	2154	2354
Machynlleth .... d.	2207	...	2216	2303	...	0117	0024	...		1005	...	1205	...	1407	1407	...	1607	1607	...	1807	1954	2007	2204	0004
Caersws .... d.	...	...	...	...	...	...	...	...		1035	...	1235	...	1437	1437	...	1637	1637	...	1837	...	2037	...	...
Newtown .... d.	...	...	...	...	...	...	...	...		1044	...	1244	...	1446	1446	...	1646	1646	...	1846	...	2046	...	...
Welshpool .... d.	...	...	...	...	...	...	...	...		1102	...	1259	...	1501	1501	...	1701	1701	...	1901	...	2101	...	...
Shrewsbury 145 .... a.	...	...	...	...	...	...	...	...		1125	...	1323	...	1525	1525	...	1727	1727	...	1925	...	2125	...	...
Birmingham New St **145** ..... a.	...	...	...	...	...	...	...	...		1234	...	1424	...	1626	1626	...	1828	1828	...	2024	...	2228	...	...

A – Ⓐ July 27 - August 28. Ⓡ. Operated by West Coast Railways. National Rail tickets not valid. To book ✆ 01524 732100. www.westcoastrailways.co.uk.

a – Arrives 1149.

f – Arrives 5 - 10 minutes earlier.

t – Arrives 15 - 20 minutes earlier.

🚂 – Steam train.

150 LONDON and BIRMINGHAM - CHESTER, MANCHESTER and LIVERPOOL

AW, LM, VT, XC

Services on ⑥ valid until October 31, services on ⑦ valid until July 12. For services to Scotland see Table **151**. For slower services London - Crewe see Table **142**.

km	Operator		VT	XC	LM	XC	XC	VT	LM	VT	VT	VT	XC		LM	VT	XC	LM	VT	VT	VT	VT	VT	XC	LM	VT
			⚒H	⚒	⚒	Ⓐ	⑥	Ⓐv	⚒	ⒶGv	⑥Gv	Ⓐ	⚒		⚒	⚒v	⚒	⚒	⚒	Ⓐ	⑥	Ⓐ	⚒	⚒S	⚒	⚒
0	**London** Euston d.	⚒	...	...	...	...	...	0535	...	0547	0605	0617	...	...	...	0636	...	...	0655	0707	0707	0710	0720	...	...	0735
80	Milton Keynes d.		...	...	...	...	...	0610	...	0622	0641	0647	...	...	...	|	...	...	0727	|	|	0740u	0750	...	...	0806
131	Rugby d.		...	...	...	...	...	|	...	0644	0703	|	...	...	...	|	...	...	|	|	|	|	|	...	...	|
155	Nuneaton d.		...	...	...	...	...	0639	...	|	|	|	...	...	...	|	...	...	|	|	|	|	|	...	...	|
	Birmingham New St d.		0530	0557	0601	0620	0631	|	0636	|	|	|	0657	...	0701	|	0731	0736	|	|	|	|	|	0757	0801	|
	Wolverhampton d.		0548	0614	0618	0640	0649	|	0651	|	|	|	0714	...	0718	|	0749	0753	|	|	|	|	|	0814	0819	|
215	**Stafford** d.		0601	0629	0636	0654	0701	0703	0705	|	0734	|	0729	...	0736	|	|	0809	|	0823	0823	|	|	0829	0836	|
235	Stoke on Trent d.		|	0650	|	0712	0718	|	|	|	|	0745	|	...	|	|	0818	|	0824	|	|	|	0848	0854	|	|
267	Macclesfield d.		|	0711	|	0730	0736	|	|	|	|	0801	|	...	|	|	0835	|	0841	|	|	|	|	0911	|	|
254	**Crewe** 165 d.		0623	|	0657	|	|	0724	0731	0732	0755	|	0752	...	0758	0811	|	0831	|	|	0843	0849	|	|	0858	0911
288	**Chester** 165 a.		0644	|	|	|	|	|	|	...	...	|	|	...	|	|	|	|	|	|	|	0912	|	|	|	|
	Stockport d.		...	0727	|	0745	0749	|	|	...	...	0816	0820	...	|	0837	0849j	|	0855	|	|	...	0916	0927	|	0936
296	**Manchester** P'dilly a.		...	0740	|	0801	0800	|	|	...	...	0828	0840	...	|	0849	0900	|	0907	|	|	...	0928	0940	|	0949
290	Runcorn a.		...	...	0722	...	...	0740	0801	...	...	...	...	...	0824	...	...	0848	...	0854	0859	...	...	...	0922	...
312	**Liverpool** Lime St a.		...	...	0741	...	...	0802	0822	...	...	...	...	...	0845	...	...	0909	...	0915	0921	...	...	...	0942	...

Operator	XC	LM	VT	VT	VT	VT	XC		LM	VT	XC	LM	VT	VT	VT	VT	VT	XC	LM	VT	XC	LM	VT	VT	VT	VT
	⚒B	⚒	⚒	⚒	⚒A	⚒	⚒S		⚒	⚒	⚒C	⚒	⑥Hv	⚒	⚒	ⒶH	⚒	⚒U	⚒	⚒	⚒T	⚒	⚒	⚒	⚒	⚒
London Euston d.	...	...	0800	0807	0810	0820	...	...	...	0840	...	...	0850	0900	0907	0910	0920	...	...	0940	...	...	1000	1007	1010	1020
Milton Keynes d.	...	...	|	|	0840u	0850	...	...	...	|	...	...	0925	|	|	0940u	0950	...	...	|	...	...	|	|	1040u	1050
Rugby d.	...	...	|	|	|	|	...	...	...	|	...	...	|	|	|	|	|	...	...	|	...	...	|	|	|	|
Nuneaton d.	...	...	|	|	|	|	...	...	...	|	...	...	|	|	|	|	|	...	...	|	...	...	|	|	|	|
Birmingham New St d.	0831	0836	|	|	|	|	0857	...	0901	|	0931	0936	|	|	|	|	|	0957	1001	|	1031	1036	|	|	|	|
Wolverhampton d.	0849	0853	|	|	|	|	0914	...	0919	|	0949	0953	|	|	|	|	|	1014	1019	|	1049	1053	|	|	|	|
Stafford d.	|	0909	|	0923	|	|	0929	...	0935	|	|	1009	|	|	1023	|	|	1029	1035	|	|	1109	|	1123	|	|
Stoke on Trent d.	0918	|	0924	|	|	0948	0954	...	|	|	1018	|	|	1024	|	|	1048	1054	|	|	1118	|	1124	|	|	1148
Macclesfield d.	|	|	0941	|	|	|	1011	...	|	|	|	|	|	1041	|	|	|	1111	|	|	|	|	1141	|	|	|
Crewe 165 d.	|	0931	|	|	0949	|	|	...	0957	1011	|	1031	1045	|	|	1049	|	|	1057	1111	|	1131	|	|	1149	|
Chester 165 a.	|	|	|	|	1012	|	|	...	|	|	|	|	1112	|	|	1109	|	|	|	|	|	|	|	|	1212	|
Stockport d.	|	|	0955	|	...	1016	1027	...	|	1036	|	|	...	1055	|	...	1116	1127	|	1136	|	|	1155	|	...	1216
Manchester P'dilly a.	1000	|	1007	|	...	1028	1040	...	|	1049	1100	|	...	1107	|	...	1128	1140	|	1149	1200	|	1207	|	...	1228
Runcorn a.	...	0948	...	0954	...	...	...	...	1021	...	...	1048	...	...	1054	...	...	...	1121	...	...	1148	...	1154	...	...
Liverpool Lime St a.	...	1009	...	1015	...	...	...	...	1043	...	...	1109	...	...	1115	...	...	...	1142	...	...	1209	...	1215	...	...

Operator	XC	LM	VT	XC	LM	VT	VT	VT	VT	XC	LM	VT	XC	LM		VT	VT	VT	VT	XC	LM	VT	XC	LM	VT	VT
	⚒U	⚒	⚒	⚒B	⚒	⚒	⚒	⚒	⚒	⚒U	⚒	⚒	⚒C	⚒		⚒	⚒	⚒	⚒	⚒U	⚒	⚒	⚒T	⚒	⚒	⚒
London Euston d.	...	...	1040	...	...	1100	1107	1110	1120	...	...	1140	...	...	...	1200	1207	1210	1220	...	...	1240	...	...	1300	1307
Milton Keynes d.	...	...	|	...	...	|	|	1140u	1150	...	...	|	...	...	...	|	|	1240u	1250	...	...	|	...	...	|	|
Rugby d.	...	...	|	...	...	|	|	|	|	...	...	|	...	...	...	|	|	|	|	...	...	|	...	...	|	|
Nuneaton d.	...	...	|	...	...	|	|	|	|	...	...	|	...	...	...	|	|	|	|	...	...	|	...	...	|	|
Birmingham New St d.	1057	1101	|	1131	1136	|	|	|	|	1157	1201	|	1231	1236	...	|	|	|	|	1257	1301	|	1331	1336	|	|
Wolverhampton d.	1114	1119	|	1149	1153	|	|	|	|	1214	1219	|	1249	1253	...	|	|	|	|	1314	1319	|	1349	1353	|	|
Stafford d.	1129	1135	|	|	1209	|	1223	|	|	1229	1235	|	|	1309	...	|	1323	|	|	1329	1335	|	|	1409	|	1423
Stoke on Trent d.	1154	|	|	1218	|	1224	|	|	1248	1254	|	|	1318	|	...	1324	|	|	1348	1354	|	|	1418	|	1424	|
Macclesfield d.	1211	|	|	|	|	1241	|	|	|	1311	|	|	|	|	...	1341	|	|	|	1411	|	|	|	|	1441	|
Crewe 165 d.	|	1157	1211	|	1231	|	|	1249	|	|	1257	1311	|	1331	...	|	|	1349	|	|	1357	1411	|	1431	|	|
Chester 165 a.	|	|	|	|	|	|	|	1312	|	|	|	|	|	|	...	|	|	1412	|	|	|	|	|	|	|	|
Stockport d.	1227	|	1236	|	|	1255	|	...	1316	1327	|	1336	|	|	...	1355	|	...	1416	1427	|	1436	|	|	1455	|
Manchester P'dilly a.	1240	|	1249	1300	|	1307	|	...	1328	1340	|	1349	1400	|	...	1407	|	...	1428	1440	|	1449	1500	|	1507	|
Runcorn a.	...	1221	...	...	1248	...	1254	...	...	...	1321	...	...	1348	...	...	1354	...	...	...	1421	...	...	1448	...	1454
Liverpool Lime St a.	...	1243	...	...	1309	...	1315	...	...	...	1342	...	...	1409	...	...	1415	...	...	...	1442	...	...	1509	...	1515

Operator	VT	VT	XC	LM	VT	XC	LM	VT	VT	VT	VT	XC	LM	VT	XC	LM	VT	VT	VT	VT	XC		LM	VT	XC	LM
	⚒	⚒	⚒U	⚒	⚒	⚒B	⚒	⚒	⚒	⚒h	⚒	⚒U	⚒	⚒	⚒D	⚒	⚒	⚒	⚒	⚒	⚒U		⚒	⚒	⚒B	⚒
London Euston d.	1310	1320	...	...	1340	...	...	1400	1407	1410	1420	...	...	1440	...	...	1500	1507	1510	1520	...	...	...	1540	...	...
Milton Keynes d.	1340u	1350	...	...	|	...	...	|	|	1440u	1450	...	...	|	...	...	|	|	1540u	1550	...	...	...	|	...	...
Rugby d.	|	|	...	...	|	...	...	|	|	|	|	...	...	|	...	...	|	|	|	|	...	...	...	|	...	...
Nuneaton d.	|	|	...	...	|	...	...	|	|	|	|	...	...	|	...	...	|	|	|	|	...	...	...	|	...	...
Birmingham New St d.	|	|	1357	1401	|	1431	1436	|	|	|	|	1457	1501	|	1531	1536	|	|	|	|	1557	...	1601	|	1631	1636
Wolverhampton d.	|	|	1414	1419	|	1449	1453	|	|	|	|	1514	1519	|	1549	1553	|	|	|	|	1614	...	1619	|	1649	1653
Stafford d.	|	|	1429	1435	|	|	1509	|	1523	|	|	1529	1535	|	|	1609	|	1623	|	|	1629	...	1635	|	|	1709
Stoke on Trent d.	|	1448	1454	|	|	1518	|	1524	|	|	1548	1554	|	|	1618	|	1624	|	|	1648	1654	...	|	|	1718	|
Macclesfield d.	|	|	1511	|	|	|	|	1541	|	|	|	1611	|	|	|	|	1641	|	|	|	1711	...	|	|	|	|
Crewe 165 d.	1450	|	|	1457	1511	|	1531	|	|	1549	|	|	1557	1612	|	1631	|	|	1649	|	|	...	1657	1711	|	1731
Chester 165 a.	1512	|	|	|	|	|	|	|	|	1612	|	|	|	|	|	|	|	|	1712	|	|	...	|	|	|	|
Stockport d.	...	1516	1527	|	1536	|	|	1555	|	...	1616	1627	|	1636	|	|	1654	|	...	1716	1727	...	|	1736	|	|
Manchester P'dilly a.	...	1528	1540	|	1549	1600	|	1607	|	...	1628	1640	|	1649	1700	|	1707	|	...	1728	1740	...	|	1749	1800	|
Runcorn a.	...	...	...	1521	...	...	1548	...	1554	...	...	...	1624	...	...	1648	...	1654	...	...	...	...	1721	...	...	1748
Liverpool Lime St a.	...	...	...	1542	...	...	1609	...	1615	...	...	...	1643	...	...	1709	...	1715	...	...	...	...	1742	...	...	1809

Operator	VT	VT	VT	VT	XC	LM	VT	VT		VT	XC	LM	VT	VT	VT	VT	VT	VT	XC	LM	LM	VT	VT	XC	LM	LM
	⚒	⚒	⚒X	⚒	⚒U	⚒	ⒶP	⑥		⚒	⚒T	⚒	⚒	⑥	Ⓐ	⑥H	ⒶH	⚒	⚒U	⑥	Ⓐ	Ⓐ	⚒	⚒B	Ⓐ	⑥
London Euston d.	1600	1607	1610	1620	...	...	1633	1633	...	1640	...	...	1700	1707	1707	1710	1710	1720	...	...	...	1733	1740	...	...	...
Milton Keynes d.	|	|	1640u	1650t	...	...	|	|	...	|	...	...	|	|	|	1740u	1740u	1750t	...	...	...	|	|	...	...	...
Rugby d.	|	|	|	|	...	...	1722	|	...	|	...	...	|	|	|	|	|	|	...	...	...	1822	|	...	...	...
Nuneaton d.	|	|	|	|	...	...	|	|	...	|	...	...	|	1803	|	|	1812	|	...	...	...	|	|	...	...	...
Birmingham New St d.	|	|	|	|	1657	1701	|	|	...	|	1731	1736	|	|	|	|	|	|	1757	1801	1801	|	|	1831	1836	1836
Wolverhampton d.	|	|	|	|	1714	1719	|	|	...	|	1749	1753	|	|	|	|	|	|	1814	1819	1819	|	|	1849	1853	1853
Stafford d.	|	1723	|	|	1729	1736	1756	1758	...	|	|	1809	|	1827	1825	|	|	|	1829	1835	1835	1856	|	|	1909	1909
Stoke on Trent d.	1724	|	|	1748	1754	|	|	|	...	|	1818	|	1824	|	|	|	|	1848	1854	|	|	|	|	1918	|	|
Macclesfield d.	1741	|	|	|	1811	|	|	|	...	|	|	|	1841	|	|	|	|	|	1911	|	|	|	|	|	|	|
Crewe d.	|	|	1749	|	|	1800	1818	|	...	1811	|	1831	|	|	1845	1850	1856	|	|	1859	1902	1918	1911	|	1931	1937
Chester a.	|	|	1809	|	|	|	...	|	...	|	|	|	|	|	|	1910	1916	|	|	...	|	|	|	|	|	|
Stockport d.	1755	|	...	1816	1827	|	...	|	...	1836	|	|	1855	|	|	...	...	1916	1927	...	|	|	1936	|	|	|
Manchester P'dilly a.	1807	|	...	1828	1840	|	...	|	...	1849	1900	|	1907	|	|	...	...	1928	1940	...	|	|	1949	2000	|	|
Runcorn a.	...	1754	...	...	...	1823	...	1831	...	...	...	1857	...	1858	1902	...	...	...	...	...	1922	1934	...	...	1955	2005
Liverpool Lime St a.	...	1815	...	...	...	1843	...	1854	...	...	...	1917	...	1919	1923	...	...	...	...	...	1942	1955	...	...	2023	2026

Operator	VT	VT	VT	VT	VT	VT	XC	LM	VT	VT	VT	XC		LM	VT	VT	VT	VT	VT	VT	VT	XC	VT	VT	VT	XC
	⚒	⑥	Ⓐ	ⒶW	⑥	⚒	⚒U	⚒	Ⓐ	⑥	⚒	⚒B		⚒	⑥	⑥★	Ⓐ	⑥★	Ⓐ	ⒶH	Ⓐ	⚒U	Ⓐ	⚒	⑥	⚒B
London Euston d.	1800	1807	1807	1810	1810	1820	...	...	1833	1833	1840	...	...	...	1854a	1857	1900	1905	1907	1910	1920	...	1940	...	1925b	...
Milton Keynes d.	|	|	|	1840u	1840u	1850t	...	...	|	|	|	...	...	...	|	|	|	1936	|	1940u	1950	...	|	...	|	...
Rugby d.	|	|	|	|	|	|	...	...	1922	|	|	...	...	...	|	|	|	|	|	|	|	...	|	...	|	...
Nuneaton d.	|	|	|	1913	|	|	...	...	|	|	|	...	...	...	|	1956	|	|	2003	|	|	...	|	...	|	...
Birmingham New St d.	|	|	|	|	|	|	1857	1901	|	|	|	1931	...	1936	|	|	|	|	|	|	|	1957	|	2020	|	2031
Wolverhampton d.	|	|	|	|	|	|	1914	1919	|	|	|	1949	...	1953	|	|	|	|	|	|	|	2014	|	2037	|	2049
Stafford d.	|	1923	1925	|	|	|	1929	1936	1956	1959	|	|	...	2009	|	2024	|	|	2027	|	|	2029	2104	2050	|	|
Stoke on Trent d.	1924	|	|	|	|	1948	1954	|	|	|	|	2019	...	|	2024	|	2024	2037	|	|	2048	2054	|	|	|	2118
Macclesfield d.	1941	|	|	|	|	|	2011	|	|	|	|	|	...	|	2041	|	2041	|	|	|	|	2111	|	|	|	2138j
Crewe 165 d.	|	|	1945	1956	1950	|	|	2001	2018	|	2011	|	...	2031	|	2048	|	|	|	2050	|	|	|	2114	2119	|
Chester 165 a.	|	|	|	2016	2012	|	|	...	|	|	|	|	...	|	|	|	|	|	|	2110	|	|	|	...	|	|
Stockport d.	1955	|	|	...	...	2016	2027	...	|	|	2036	|	...	|	2055	|	2055	2116	|	...	2116	2127	|	...	2144	2153j
Manchester P'dilly a.	2007	|	|	...	...	2028	2040	...	|	|	2049	2100	...	|	2107	|	2107	2128	|	...	2128	2140	2155	...	2156	2205
Runcorn a.	...	1954	2001	...	...	...	...	...	2034	2032	...	...	...	2055	...	2105	...	...	2100	...	...	...	...	...	...	...
Liverpool Lime St a.	...	2015	2022	...	...	...	...	...	2055	2053	...	...	...	2115	...	2126	...	...	2121	...	...	...	...	...	...	...

FOR NOTES SEE NEXT PAGE ► ► ►

AW, LM, VT, XC — LONDON and BIRMINGHAM - CHESTER, MANCHESTER and LIVERPOOL — 150

Services on ⑥ valid until October 31, services on ⑦ valid until July 12. For services to Scotland see Table **151**. For slower services London - Crewe see Table **142**.

Operator	LM	LM	VT	VT	XC	XC	VT	VT	VT	VT		VT	VT	LM	LM	VT	XC	XC	VT	VT	VT	XC	XC	LM	VT	AW
	Ⓐ	⑥	Ⓐ	Ⓐ	Ⓐ**U**	⑥**EK**	Ⓐ	⑥★	Ⓐ**K**	Ⓐ**Qv**		Ⓐ	Ⓐ**Q**	Ⓐ	⑥	Ⓐ	Ⓐ**U**	⑥**KU**	Ⓐ	Ⓐ**Pv**	⑥★	Ⓐ	⑥	Ⓐ	Ⓐ	Ⓐ**2H**
London Euston d.	...	...	2000	2007	...	...	2010	1941	1947	2014	...	2040	...	...	...	2100	...	...	2107	2110	2026	...	...	...	2140	...
Milton Keynes d.	...	...	|	|	...	...	2040u	|	2051	|	...	|	...	...	...	2131	...	...	2138	|	2122	...	...	...	|	...
Rugby d.	...	...	|	|	...	...	|	2052	|	2135	...	|	...	...	...	|	...	...	|	2203	|	...	...	...	|	...
Nuneaton d.	...	...	|	2103	...	...	|	|	2133	|	...	|	...	...	...	|	...	...	2207	|	|	...	...	...	|	...
Birmingham New St d.	2036	2036	|	|	2057	2057	|	|	|	|	...	|	2120	2136	2136	|	2157	2157	|	|	|	2228	2231	2236	|	2255
Wolverhampton d.	2053	2053	|	|	2116	2114	|	|	|	|	...	|	2141	2153	2153	|	2216	2214	|	|	|	2246	2249	2257	|	2313
Stafford d.	2109	2109	|	2127	2129	2130	|	2137	2200	|	...	|	2155	2209	2209	|	2229	2229	|	2234	2236	2259	2303	2313	|	2330
Stoke on Trent d.	|	|	2123	|	2154	|	|	|	|	|	...	|	|	|	|	2228	2254	|	|	|	|	2320	|	|	2336s	|
Macclesfield d.	|	|	2140	|	2211	|	|	|	|	|	...	|	|	|	|	2244	2311	|	|	|	|	|	|	|	2352s	|
Crewe 165 d.	2131	2130	|	|	|	|	2150	2203	2227	2238	...	2213	2218	2231	2234	|	|	|	2248	2254	2301	|	2328	2343	|	2357
Chester 165 a.	|	...	|	|	|	|	2215	|	|	...	...	|	...	|	...	|	|	|	|	...	|	|	|	...	|	0018
Stockport d.	|	...	2155	|	2225	2235	...	|	2251	...	...	2238	...	|	...	2258	2325	2321	|	...	2326	|	2353s	...	0008s	...
Manchester P'dilly a.	|	...	2207	|	2240	2248	...	|	2304	...	...	2251	...	|	...	2311	2340	2335	|	...	2339	0015g	0009	...	0021	...
Runcorn d.	2153	...	...	2158	...	...	...	2220	...	...	...	...	...	2256	...	...	...	...	2307	...	...	...	...	...	...	...
Liverpool Lime St a.	2214	...	...	2220	...	...	...	2241	...	...	...	...	...	2321	...	...	...	...	2355	...	...	...	...	...	...	...

Operator	AW	LM	VT			VT	XC	VT	VT	VT	LM	VT	XC	VT	VT	LM		VT	XC	VT	VT	LM	VT	XC	VT	VT
	⑥2	Ⓐ	Ⓐ			⑦**P**	⑦	⑦	⑦	⑦	⑦	⑦**G**	⑦	⑦	⑦	⑦		⑦**G**	⑦**R**	⑦	⑦	⑦	⑦**G**	⑦**B**	⑦	⑦
London Euston d.	...	...	2200	...	⑦	...	...	0810	0815	0820	...	0845	...	0915	0920	...	...	0945	...	1015	1020	...	1045	...	1115	1120
Milton Keynes d.	...	...	2239	...		...	...	0855	|	0905	...	0933	...	|	1007	...	...	1033	...	|	1107	...	1132	...	1204	1209
Rugby d.	...	...	2319	...		...	...	|	|	|	...	0956	...	|	|	...	...	1057	...	|	|	...	1155	...	|	|
Nuneaton d.	...	...	2330	...	▲	...	...	|	0930	|	...	|	...	1038	|	...	...	|	...	1135	|	...	|	...	|	|
Birmingham New St d.	2255	2309	|	...		0845	0901	|	|	|	0941	|	1000	|	|	1042	...	|	1059	|	|	1142	|	1201	|	|
Wolverhampton d.	2313	2335	|	...		0904	0919	|	|	|	0957	|	1018	|	|	1029	...	|	1117	|	|	1159	|	1219	|	|
Stafford d.	|	2352	0002s	...		0919	0932	|	0958	1005	1014	|	1032	1105	1102	1117	...	|	1130	1201	1207	1216	|	1234	1255	|
Stoke on Trent d.	|	|	|	...		|	|	|	|	|	|	|	|	|	|	|	...	|	|	|	|	|	|	|	|	|
Macclesfield d.	|	|	|	...		|	|	|	|	|	|	|	|	|	|	|	...	|	|	|	|	|	|	|	|	|
Crewe 165 d.	0034	0016	0028s	...		0943	0959	1019	1031	|	1039	1052	|	1132	|	1138	...	1154	|	1221	|	1238	1249	|	1318	|
Chester 165 a.	...	...	|	...		...	|	|	|	|	|	...	|	|	|	|	...	...	|	|	|	|	...	|	|	|
Stockport d.	...	...	0059s	...		...	1024	1040	|	1052	|	...	1121	|	1155	|	...	...	1219	|	1252	|	...	1318	|	1345
Manchester P'dilly a.	...	...	0113	...		...	1040	1054	|	1104	|	...	1138	|	1209	|	...	...	1240	|	1304	|	...	1340	|	1359
Runcorn d.	...	...	...	...		...	...	...	1047	...	1101	...	...	1148	...	1200	...	...	...	1237	...	1300	...	...	1334	...
Liverpool Lime St a.	...	...	...	...		...	...	...	1108	...	1121	...	...	1209	...	1220	...	...	...	1303	...	1320	...	...	1356	...

Operator	LM	VT	VT	XC	VT	XC	LM	VT	VT	VT	XC	VT		XC	LM	VT	VT	VT	XC	VT	XC	LM	VT	VT	VT	VT
	⑦	⑦	⑦	⑦**U**	⑦	⑦	⑦	⑦	⑦	⑦	⑦**U**	⑦		⑦	⑦	⑦	⑦	⑦	⑦**U**	⑦	⑦**M**	⑦	⑦	⑦	⑦	⑦
London Euston d.	...	1202	1215	...	1235	...	...	1255	1302	1315	...	1335	...	...	...	1355	1402	1415	...	1435	...	...	1455	1502	1505	1515
Milton Keynes d.	...	|	1248	...	|	...	...	|	|	1348	...	|	...	...	...	|	|	1448	...	|	...	...	|	|	1538u	1548
Rugby d.	...	|	|	...	|	...	...	|	|	|	...	|	...	...	...	|	|	|	...	|	...	...	|	|	|	|
Nuneaton d.	...	|	|	...	|	...	...	|	|	|	...	|	...	...	...	|	|	|	...	|	...	...	|	|	|	|
Birmingham New St d.	1235	|	|	1301	|	1331	1335	|	|	|	1401	|	...	1431	1435	|	|	|	1501	|	1531	1535	|	|	|	|
Wolverhampton d.	1252	|	|	1319	|	1349	1352	|	|	|	1419	|	...	1449	1452	|	|	|	1519	|	1549	1552	|	|	|	|
Stafford d.	1310	1325	|	1334	|	|	1410	|	1422	|	1434	|	...	|	1510	|	1525	|	1534	|	|	1610	|	1621	|	|
Stoke on Trent d.	|	|	1350	|	|	1419	|	1426	|	1450	1456	|	...	1519	|	1525	|	1550	1556	|	1619	|	1624	|	|	1650
Macclesfield d.	|	|	|	|	|	|	|	1442	|	|	1514	|	...	|	|	1542	|	|	1614	|	|	|	1642	|	|	|
Crewe 165 d.	1331	1345	|	|	1413	|	1431	|	1445	|	|	1513	...	|	1531	|	1545	|	|	1613	|	1634	|	|	1657	|
Chester 165 a.	|	|	|	|	|	|	|	|	|	|	|	|	...	|	|	|	|	|	|	|	|	|	|	|	1719	|
Stockport d.	|	|	1418	1422	1438	|	|	1456	|	1518	1528	1538	...	|	|	1556	|	1618	1628	1638	|	|	1656	|	...	1718
Manchester P'dilly a.	|	|	1430	1440	1451	1500	|	1509	|	1530	1540	1551	...	1600	|	1609	|	1630	1640	1651	1700	|	1709	|	...	1730
Runcorn d.	1353	1401	...	...	...	...	1453	...	1501	...	...	...	...	...	1553	...	1601	...	...	...	...	1655	...	1658	...	...
Liverpool Lime St a.	1413	1423	...	...	...	...	1513	...	1523	...	...	...	...	...	1613	...	1622	...	...	...	...	1716	...	1722	...	...

Operator	XC	VT	XC	LM	VT	VT	VT	VT		XC	VT	XC	LM	VT	VT	VT	VT	XC	VT	XC	LM	VT	VT	VT	VT	XC
	⑦**A**	⑦	⑦**T**	⑦	⑦	⑦	⑦	⑦		⑦**U**	⑦	⑦**B**	⑦	⑦	⑦	⑦**H**	⑦	⑦**U**	⑦	⑦**Z**	⑦	⑦	⑦	⑦**H**	⑦	⑦**U**
London Euston d.	...	1535	...	...	1555	1602	1605	1615	...	...	1635	...	...	1655	1702	1705	1715	...	1735	...	...	1755	1802	1805	1815	...
Milton Keynes d.	...	|	...	...	|	|	1639u	1648	...	...	|	...	...	|	|	1738u	1748	...	|	...	...	|	|	1838u	1848	...
Rugby d.	...	|	...	...	|	|	|	|	...	...	|	...	...	|	|	|	|	...	|	...	...	|	|	|	|	...
Nuneaton d.	...	|	...	...	|	|	|	|	...	...	|	...	...	|	|	1810	|	...	|	...	...	|	|	|	|	...
Birmingham New St d.	1601	|	1631	1635	|	|	|	|	...	1701	|	1731	1735	|	|	|	|	1801	|	1831	1835	|	|	|	|	1901
Wolverhampton d.	1619	|	1649	1652	|	|	|	|	...	1719	|	1749	1752	|	|	|	|	1819	|	1849	1852	|	|	|	|	1919
Stafford d.	1636	|	|	1710	|	1725	|	|	...	1736	|	|	1810	|	1825	|	|	1839	|	|	1910	|	1925	|	|	1938
Stoke on Trent d.	1656	|	1719	|	1725	|	|	1750	...	1756	|	1819	|	1825	|	|	1850	1858	|	1919	|	1925	|	|	1950	1956
Macclesfield d.	1714	|	|	|	1742	|	|	|	...	1814	|	|	|	1842	|	|	|	1916	|	|	|	1942	|	|	|	2014
Crewe 165 d.	|	1713	|	1731	|	|	1757	|	...	|	1813	|	1831	|	|	1856	|	|	1913	|	1931	|	|	1957	|	|
Chester 165 a.	|	|	|	|	|	|	1819	|	...	|	|	|	|	|	|	1914	|	|	|	|	|	|	|	2016	|	|
Stockport d.	1730	1738	|	|	1756	|	...	1818	...	1828	1838	|	|	1856	|	...	1918	1928	1938	|	|	1956	|	...	2018	2028
Manchester P'dilly a.	1740	1751	1800	|	1809	|	...	1830	...	1840	1851	1900	|	1909	|	...	1930	1940	1951	2000	|	2009	|	...	2030	2040
Runcorn d.	...	...	...	1753	...	1756	...	...	...	...	...	...	1853	...	1856	...	...	...	...	...	1953	...	1957	...	...	...
Liverpool Lime St a.	...	...	...	1813	...	1819	...	...	...	...	...	...	1913	...	1919	...	...	...	...	...	2013	...	2019	...	...	...

Operator	VT	XC	LM	VT	VT	VT	VT	XC	VT	VT	XC	VT	VT	VT		VT	XC	VT	LM	VT	AW	XC	VT	VT	AW	VT
	⑦	⑦**B**	⑦	⑦	⑦	⑦**H**	⑦	⑦**U**	⑦	⑦	⑦**B**	⑦	⑦	⑦		⑦	⑦**U**	⑦	⑦	⑦**P**	⑦	⑦**U**	⑦	⑦	⑦**H**	⑦
London Euston d.	1835	...	...	1855	1902	1905	1915	...	...	1935	...	1955	2002	2005	...	2015	...	2035	...	2050	...	...	2120	2124	...	2150
Milton Keynes d.	|	...	...	|	|	1938u	1948	...	...	|	...	|	|	2038	...	2049	...	|	...	2139	...	...	|	2213	...	2238
Rugby d.	|	...	...	|	|	|	|	...	...	|	...	|	|	|	...	|	...	|	...	2200	...	...	|	|	...	2306
Nuneaton d.	|	...	...	|	2001	|	|	...	...	|	...	|	2101	|	...	|	...	|	...	|	...	...	2253	|	...	2326
Birmingham New St d.	|	1931	1935	|	|	|	|	2001	2020	|	2031	|	|	|	...	|	2101	|	2135	|	2124	2201	|	|	2255	|
Wolverhampton d.	|	1949	1952	|	|	|	|	2019	2038	|	2049	|	|	|	...	|	2119	|	2153	|	2143	2219	|	|	2315	|
Stafford d.	|	|	2010	|	2030	|	|	2038	2052	|	2119	|	|	2133	...	|	2156	2204	2214	|	|	2238	2319	|	2331	2353s
Stoke on Trent d.	|	2021	|	2025	|	|	2050	2057	|	|	|	2125	|	|	...	2150	2214	|	|	|	|	2255	|	2330	|	|
Macclesfield d.	|	|	|	2042	|	|	|	2115	|	|	|	2142	|	|	...	|	|	|	|	|	|	2313	|	2349	|	|
Crewe 165 d.	2013	|	2031	|	2050	2058	|	|	2110	2114	|	|	2146	2155	...	|	|	2223	2236	2249	2305	|	2347	|	0010	0016s
Chester 165 a.	|	|	|	|	|	2117	|	|	...	|	|	|	|	|	...	|	|	|	...	...	2326	|	|	|	0031	|
Stockport d.	2038	|	|	2056	|	...	2118	2128	...	2139	|	2156	|	|	...	2218	2228	2248	...	...	...	2327	|	0005	...	0045s
Manchester P'dilly a.	2051	2100	|	2109	|	...	2130	2140	...	2152	2200	2209	|	|	...	2230	2240	2300	...	...	...	2341	|	0017	...	0058
Runcorn d.	...	...	2053	...	2106	...	...	...	...	...	...	...	2202	2221	...	...	...	...	...	...	...	...	0007	...	...	...
Liverpool Lime St a.	...	...	2113	...	2127	...	...	...	...	...	...	...	2223	2232	...	...	...	...	...	...	...	...	0034	...	...	...

A – To Bangor on Ⓐ.
B – From Bristol.
C – From Bristol (from Plymouth on ⑥ May 16 - Sept. 5).
D – From Penzance on Ⓐ. From Bristol on ⑥ (from Penzance on ⑥ May 16 - Sept. 5).
E – From Newquay.
G – To Glasgow.
H – To Holyhead.
K – May 23 - Jul. 11.
L – To Llandudno Junction.
M – From Plymouth.
P – To Preston.
Q – To Preston. May 23 - Sept. 5.
R – From Reading.

S – From Southampton.
T – From Paignton.
U – From Bournemouth.
W – To Holyhead. Conveys (12) London Euston - Chester - Wrexham (arrive 2044).
X – To Bangor on Ⓐ, to Holyhead on ⑥.
Y – From Bristol on ①②③④⑥, from Exeter on ⑤.
Z – From Penzance.

a – From Sept. 12, departs 1900.
b – From Sept. 12, departs 1940.
g – Arrives 0037 on ②③.
h – To Holyhead on ⑥.
j – ⑥ only.

s – Stops to set down only.
t – Stops to pick up only on Ⓐ.
u – Stops to pick up only.
v – Also calls at Watford Junction 13–18 minutes after London Euston to pick up only.

★ – May 23 - Sept. 5.

▲ – Due to engineering work on ⑦ buses replace trains Stafford - Stoke on Trent - Macclesfield until around 1400.

150 LIVERPOOL, MANCHESTER and CHESTER - BIRMINGHAM and LONDON

AW, LM, VT, XC

Services on ⑥ valid until October 31, services on ⑦ valid until July 12. For services from Scotland see Table **151**. For slower services Crewe - London see Table **142**

Operator		AW	VT	VT	XC	VT	VT	VT	LM	VT	VT	VT	XC	XC	VT	VT	VT	LM	VT	VT	VT	VT	VT	LM	VT	VT
		⚒2	Ⓐ	⑥v	⚒U	Ⓐ	ⒶP	⑥v	⚒	Ⓐ	⑥	⑥L	ⒶB	⑥B	Ⓐ	Ⓐ	⑥	⚒	ⒶD	Ⓐv	⚒	Ⓐ	⑥	⚒	Ⓐ	Ⓐ
Liverpool Lime St ..... d.	⚒	...	...	...	...	0527	...	0547	...	...	...	...	...	...	...	0605	...	...	...	...	...	...	0645	0631	...	0700
Runcorn ..... d.		...	...	...	...	0543	...	0603	...	...	...	...	...	...	...	0621	...	...	...	...	...	...	0701	0649	...	0715u
Manchester P'dilly .. d.		...	0505	0525	0500k	|	...	|	...	0555	0555	...	0600	0600	0610	|	0610	...	...	0627	0635	0643	|	|	0700	|
Stockport ..... d.		...	0513	0534	|	|	...	|	...	0603	0603	...	0608	0608	0618	|	0618	...	...	0635	0643	0651	|	|	0707u	|
Chester ..... **165** d.		0423	|	|	|	|	...	|	...	|	|	...	|	|	|	|	|	...	0626	|	|	|	|	|	|	|
Crewe ..... **165** d.		0500	0536	0600	0547	0602	...	|	0620	0629	0629	...	0638	|	|	|	|	0647	0653	|	|	0717	0720	0716	|	|
Macclesfield ..... d.		|	|	|	|	|	...	|	|	|	|	...	|	0621	0631	|	0631	|	|	0648	0655	|	|	|	|	|
Stoke on Trent ..... d.		|	|	|	0607	|	...	|	|	|	|	...	|	0639	0648	|	0648	|	|	0706	0712	|	|	|	|	|
Stafford ..... d.		0524	0555	0619	0625	0621	...	0635	0641	|	|	...	0658	0658	|	0653	|	0712	|	0728	|	0735	0739	0741	|	|
Wolverhampton ..... a.		0538	|	|	0639	|	...	|	0657	|	|	...	0712	0712	|	|	|	0728	|	0743	|	|	|	0757	|	|
Birmingham New St a.		0555	|	|	0658	|	...	|	0718	|	|	...	0731	0731	|	|	|	0748	|	0805	|	|	|	0817	|	|
Nuneaton ..... d.		...	0617	|	...	|	...	0657	...	0706	|	...	...	...	|	|	|	...	0732	|	|	|	|	...	|	|
Rugby ..... a.		...	0630	0649	...	0652	0706	|	...	|	|	...	...	...	0728	|	|	...	|	|	0752	|	|	...	|	|
Milton Keynes ..... a.		...	0651	0711	...	0712	|	|	...	|	0731	0737	...	...	|	|	|	...	|	|	|	|	|	...	|	|
London Euston ..... a.		...	0728	0754	...	0750	0800	0805	...	0811	0810	0814	...	...	0822	0826	0827	...	0836	0934	0849	0855	0859	...	0858	0901

Operator	VT	XC	XC	VT	VT	LM	VT	VT	XC	VT	VT	VT	VT	LM	VT	XC	XC	LM	VT	VT	XC	VT	LM	VT	VT	VT
	⑥	ⒶB	⑥Q★	⚒	⑥	⚒	ⒶV	⑥	⚒U	⑥	Ⓐv	Ⓐ	⑥	⚒	⚒	ⒶT	⑥T★	⚒	⚒	⚒H	⚒U	⚒	⚒	⑥	Ⓐ	⚒
Liverpool Lime St ..... d.	...	...	...	...	...	0705	...	0719	...	...	...	0748	0748	0734	...	...	...	0804	...	...	...	...	0834	0848	0848	...
Runcorn ..... d.	...	...	...	...	...	0723	...	0736	...	...	...	0804	0804	0752	...	...	...	0825	...	...	...	...	0852	0904	0904	...
Manchester P'dilly .. d.	0655	0706	0700	0715	...	|	...	|	0726	0735	0735	|	|	|	0755	0807	0800	|	0815	...	0827	0835	|	|	|	0855
Stockport ..... d.	0704	|	0709	0723	...	|	...	|	0735	0743	0743	|	|	|	0804	|	0809	|	0823	...	0835	0842	|	|	|	0904
Chester ..... **165** d.	|	|	|	|	0717	|	0735	|	|	|	|	|	|	|	|	|	|	|	|	0835	|	|	|	|	|	|
Crewe ..... **165** d.	0729	|	|	|	0738	0749	0757	0755	|	|	|	|	|	0822	0829	|	|	0849	|	0856	|	|	0922	|	|	0929
Macclesfield ..... d.	|	|	0725	|	|	|	|	|	0749	0756	0756	|	|	|	|	|	0825	|	|	|	0849	0855	|	|	|	|
Stoke on Trent ..... d.	|	0744	0744	0750	|	|	|	|	0807	0812	0812	|	|	|	|	0844	0845	|	0850	|	0907	0912	|	|	|	|
Stafford ..... d.	|	|	|	|	|	0810	|	0816	0825	|	|	0836	0836	0843	|	|	|	0910	|	|	0925	|	0943	0936	0936	|
Wolverhampton ..... a.	|	0813	0816	|	|	0828	|	|	0839	|	|	|	|	0858	|	0913	0917	0927	|	|	0939	|	0956	|	|	|
Birmingham New St a.	|	0831	0837	|	|	0847	|	|	0858	|	|	|	|	0918	|	0931	0938	0947	|	|	0958	|	1017	|	|	|
Nuneaton ..... d.	|	...	...	|	|	...	|	|	...	|	0844	|	0858	...	|	...	...	...	|	|	...	|	...	0958	|	|
Rugby ..... a.	|	...	...	|	|	...	0845	|	...	|	|	|	|	...	|	...	...	...	|	|	...	|	...	|	|	|
Milton Keynes ..... a.	|	...	...	0846t	|	...	|	|	...	|	|	|	|	...	|	...	...	...	0946	1001s	...	|	...	|	|	|
London Euston ..... a.	0904	...	...	0923	0930	...	0938	0946	...	0942	0952	0956	1001	...	1004	...	...	...	1023	1038	...	1042	...	1101	1056	1104

Operator	XC	LM	VT	VT	XC	VT	VT	LM	VT	XC	LM	VT	VT	XC	VT	VT	LM	VT	XC	LM	VT	VT	XC	VT	VT	LM
	⚒B	⚒	⚒	⚒h	⚒U	⚒	⚒	⚒	⚒	⚒B	⚒	⚒	⚒H	⚒U	⚒	⚒	⚒	⚒	⚒B	⚒	⚒	⚒	⚒U	⚒	⚒	⚒
Liverpool Lime St ..... d.	...	0904	...	...	...	...	0948	0934	...	...	1004	...	...	...	...	1048	1034	...	...	1104	...	...	...	...	1148	1134
Runcorn ..... d.	...	0925	...	...	...	...	1004	0952	...	...	1025	...	...	...	...	1104	1052	...	...	1125	...	...	...	...	1204	1152
Manchester P'dilly .. d.	0907	|	0915	...	0927	0935	|	|	0955	1007	|	1015	...	1027	1035	|	|	1055	1107	|	1115	...	1127	1135	|	|
Stockport ..... d.	|	|	0923	...	0935	0942	|	|	1004	|	|	1023	...	1035	1042	|	|	1104	|	|	1123	...	1135	1142	|	|
Chester ..... **165** d.	|	|	|	0935	|	|	|	|	|	|	|	|	1035	|	|	|	|	|	|	|	|	1135	|	|	|	|
Crewe ..... **165** d.	|	0949	|	0956	|	|	|	1022	1029	|	1049	|	1056	|	|	|	1122	1129	|	1149	|	1156	|	|	|	1222
Macclesfield ..... d.	|	|	|	|	0949	0955	|	|	|	|	|	|	|	1049	1055	|	|	|	|	|	|	|	1149	1155	|	|
Stoke on Trent ..... d.	0944	|	0950	|	1007	1011	|	|	|	1044	|	1050	|	1107	1111	|	|	|	1144	|	1150	|	1207	1211	|	|
Stafford ..... d.	|	1010	|	|	1025	|	1036	1043	|	|	1110	|	|	1125	|	1136	1143	|	|	1210	|	|	1224	|	1236	1243
Wolverhampton ..... a.	1013	1027	|	|	1039	|	|	1056	|	1113	1127	|	|	1139	|	|	1156	|	1213	1227	|	|	1239	|	|	1256
Birmingham New St a.	1031	1047	|	|	1058	|	|	1118	|	1131	1147	|	|	1158	|	|	1217	|	1231	1247	|	|	1258	|	|	1317
Nuneaton ..... d.	...	...	|	|	...	|	|	...	|	...	...	|	|	...	|	|	...	|	...	...	|	|	...	|	|	...
Rugby ..... a.	...	...	|	|	...	|	|	...	|	...	...	|	|	...	|	|	...	|	...	...	|	|	...	|	|	...
Milton Keynes ..... a.	...	...	1046	1101s	...	|	|	...	|	...	...	1146	1201s	...	|	|	...	|	...	...	1246	1301s	...	|	|	...
London Euston ..... a.	...	...	1123	1138	...	1142	1156	...	1204	...	...	1223	1238	...	1242	1256	...	1304	...	...	1323	1338	...	1342	1356	...

Operator	VT	XC	LM	VT	XC	VT	VT	VT	LM	VT	XC	LM	VT	VT	XC	VT	VT	LM	VT	XC	LM	VT	VT	XC	VT	VT
	⚒	⚒A	⚒	⚒	⚒U	⚒	⚒	⚒	⚒	⚒	⚒B	⚒	⚒	⚒N	⚒U	⚒	⚒	⚒	⚒	⚒K	⚒	⚒	⚒	⚒U	⚒	⚒
Liverpool Lime St ..... d.	...	...	1204	...	...	...	...	1248	1234	...	...	1304	...	...	...	...	1348	1334	...	...	1404	...	...	...	...	1448
Runcorn ..... d.	...	...	1225	...	...	...	...	1304	1252	...	...	1325	...	...	...	...	1404	1352	...	...	1425	...	...	...	...	1504
Manchester P'dilly .. d.	1155	1207	|	1215	1227	...	1235	|	|	1255	1307	|	1315	...	1327	1335	|	|	1355	1407	|	1415	...	1427	1435	|
Stockport ..... d.	1204	|	|	1223	1235	...	1242	|	|	1304	|	|	1323	...	1335	1342	|	|	1404	|	|	1423	...	1435	1442	|
Chester ..... **165** d.	|	|	|	|	|	1235	|	|	|	|	|	|	|	1335	|	|	|	|	|	|	|	|	1435	|	|	|
Crewe ..... **165** d.	1229	|	1249	|	|	1256	|	|	1322	1329	|	1349	|	1356	|	|	|	1422	1429	|	1449	|	1456	|	|	|
Macclesfield ..... d.	|	|	|	|	1249	|	1255	|	|	|	|	|	|	|	1349	1355	|	|	|	|	|	|	|	1449	1455	|
Stoke on Trent ..... d.	|	1244	|	1250	1307	|	1311	|	|	|	1344	|	1350	|	1407	1411	|	|	|	1444	|	1450	|	1507	1511	|
Stafford ..... d.	|	|	1310	|	1325	|	|	1336	1343	|	|	1410	|	|	1425	|	1436	1446	|	|	1510	|	|	1525	|	1536
Wolverhampton ..... a.	|	1313	1327	|	1339	|	|	|	1356	|	1413	1427	|	|	1439	|	|	1459	|	1513	1527	|	|	1539	|	|
Birmingham New St a.	|	1331	1347	|	1358	|	|	|	1417	|	1431	1447	|	|	1458	|	|	1520	|	1531	1547	|	|	1558	|	|
Nuneaton ..... d.	|	...	...	|	...	|	|	|	...	|	...	...	|	|	...	|	|	...	|	...	...	|	|	...	|	|
Rugby ..... a.	|	...	...	|	...	|	|	|	...	|	...	...	|	|	...	|	|	...	|	...	...	|	|	...	|	|
Milton Keynes ..... a.	|	...	...	1346	...	1401s	|	|	...	|	...	...	1446	1501s	...	|	|	...	|	...	...	1546	1601s	...	|	|
London Euston ..... a.	1404	...	...	1424	...	1438	1442	1456	...	1504	...	...	1523	1538	...	1542	1556	...	1604	...	...	1623	1638	...	1642	1656

Operator	LM	VT	XC	LM	VT	VT	XC	VT	VT	LM	VT	VT	LM	VT	VT	VT	XC	VT	VT	VT	LM	VT	VT	XC	LM	VT
	⚒	⚒	⚒B	⚒	⚒	⚒X	⚒U	⚒	⚒	⚒	⚒	⚒J	⚒	⚒	⑥H	Ⓐ	⚒U	⚒	⑥	Ⓐ	⚒	⑥	Ⓐv	⚒C	⚒	⚒
Liverpool Lime St ..... d.	1434	...	...	1504	...	...	...	...	1548	1534	...	...	1604	...	...	...	...	...	1648	1648	1634	...	...	...	1704	...
Runcorn ..... d.	1452	...	...	1525	...	...	...	...	1604	1552	...	...	1625	...	...	...	...	...	1704	1704	1652	...	...	...	1725	...
Manchester P'dilly .. d.	|	1455	1507	|	1515	...	1527	1535	|	|	1555	1607	|	1615	...	...	1627	1635	|	|	|	1655	1655	1706	|	1715
Stockport ..... d.	|	1504	|	|	1523	...	1535	1542	|	|	1604	|	|	1623	...	...	1635	1642	|	|	|	1704	1704	|	|	1723
Chester ..... **165** d.	|	|	|	|	|	1535	|	|	|	|	|	|	|	|	1620	1635	|	|	|	|	|	|	|	|	|	|
Crewe ..... **165** d.	1522	1529	|	1549	|	1556	|	|	|	1622	1629	|	1649	|	1656	1656	|	|	|	|	1722	1729	1729	|	1749	|
Macclesfield ..... d.	|	|	|	|	|	|	1549	1555	|	|	|	|	|	|	|	|	1649	1656	|	|	|	|	|	1727	|	|
Stoke on Trent ..... d.	|	|	1544	|	1550	|	1607	1611	|	|	|	1644	|	1650	|	|	1707	1712	|	|	|	|	|	1744	|	1750
Stafford ..... d.	1543	|	|	1610	|	|	1625	|	1636	1646	|	|	1710	|	|	|	1725	|	1736	1736	1743	|	|	|	1810	|
Wolverhampton ..... a.	1556	|	1613	1626	|	|	1639	|	|	1659	|	1713	1727	|	|	|	1739	|	|	|	1756	|	|	1813	1827	|
Birmingham New St a.	1617	|	1631	1647	|	|	1658	|	|	1720	|	1731	1747	|	|	|	1758	|	|	|	1817	|	|	1831	1848	|
Nuneaton ..... d.	...	|	...	...	|	|	...	|	|	...	|	...	...	|	|	|	...	|	|	|	...	|	|	...	...	|
Rugby ..... a.	...	|	...	...	|	|	...	|	|	...	|	...	...	|	|	|	...	|	|	|	...	|	|	...	...	|
Milton Keynes ..... a.	...	|	...	...	1646	1701s	...	|	|	...	|	...	...	1746	1801	1801s	...	|	|	1823	...	|	|	...	...	1846
London Euston ..... a.	...	1704	...	...	1723	1738	...	1742	1757	...	1806	...	...	1823	1838	1838	...	1842	1856	1859	...	1904	1908	...	...	1923

Operator	VT	XC	XC	VT	VT	VT	LM	VT	VT	XC	LM	VT	XC	VT	VT	LM	VT	VT	VT	VT	XC	LM	LM	VT	VT	VT
	Ⓐ	ⒶU	⑥U	⚒	⑥	Ⓐv	⚒	⑥	Ⓐ	⚒F	⚒	⚒	⚒U	Ⓐ	⑥	⚒	Ⓐv	⑥	Ⓐ	⑥	⚒Bj	⑥	Ⓐ	ⒶG	Ⓐ	Ⓐ
Liverpool Lime St ..... d.	...	...	...	...	1748	1748	1734	...	...	...	1804	...	...	...	...	1834	1848	1848	...	...	...	1904	1911	...	...	...
Runcorn ..... d.	...	...	...	...	1804	1804	1752	...	...	...	1825	...	...	...	...	1844	1904	1904	...	...	...	1923	1929	...	...	...
Manchester P'dilly .. d.	...	1727	1727	1735	|	|	|	1755	1755	1805	|	1815	1827	1835	1835	|	|	|	1855	1855	1907	|	|	...	1915	...
Stockport ..... d.	...	1735	1735	1743	|	|	|	1804	1804	|	|	1823	1835	1842	1842	|	|	|	1904	1904	|	|	|	...	1923	...
Chester ..... **165** d.	1735	|	|	|	|	|	|	|	|	|	|	|	|	|	|	|	|	|	|	|	|	|	|	...	|	1935
Crewe ..... **165** d.	1756	|	|	|	|	|	1822	1829	1829	|	1849	|	|	|	|	1918	1923	|	1929	1929	|	1951	1955	...	|	1956
Macclesfield ..... d.	|	|	|	1755	|	|	|	|	|	1825	|	|	|	1855	1855	|	|	|	|	|	|	|	|	...	1936	|
Stoke on Trent ..... d.	|	|	1807	1812	|	|	|	|	|	1844	|	1850	1907	1912	1912	|	|	|	|	|	1944	|	|	...	1952	|
Stafford ..... d.	|	1825	1825	|	1836	1836	1843	|	|	|	1910	|	1925	|	|	1942	1943	1936	|	|	|	2012	2016	...	|	|
Wolverhampton ..... a.	|	1839	1839	|	|	|	1856	|	|	1913	1927	|	1939	|	|	1957	|	|	|	|	2013	2028	2029	...	|	|
Birmingham New St a.	|	1858	1858	|	|	|	1917	|	|	1931	1947	|	1958	|	|	2017	|	|	|	|	2031	2047	2047	...	|	|
Nuneaton ..... d.	|	...	...	|	|	|	...	|	|	...	...	|	...	|	|	...	|	|	|	|	...	...	...	...	|	|
Rugby ..... a.	|	...	...	|	|	|	...	|	|	...	...	|	...	|	|	...	|	|	|	|	...	...	...	...	|	|
Milton Keynes ..... a.	1901s	...	...	|	|	1942s	...	|	1931	...	...	1946	...	|	|	...	|	|	2032	|	...	...	...	2045	2048	2103s
London Euston ..... a.	1938	...	...	1942	1956	2002	...	2004	2008	...	...	2023f	...	2042	2116a	...	2106	2125b	2110	2158c	...	...	...	2124	2125	2142

FOR NOTES SEE NEXT PAGE ▶ ▶ ▶

AW, LM, VT, XC — LIVERPOOL, MANCHESTER and CHESTER - BIRMINGHAM and LONDON — 150

Services on ⑥ valid until October 31, services on ⑦ valid until July 12. For services from Scotland see Table **151**. For slower services Crewe - London see Table **142**.

Operator	VT	XC	VT	LM	VT	VT	VT	XC	VT	LM	VT	VT	VT	XC	VT		LM	XC	VT	VT	VT	VT	VT	VT	XC	XC
	⑥Cv	⚒S	⑥★	⚒	Ⓐv	Ⓐ	⑥	⚒j	ⒶP	Ⓐ	⑥C	ⒶG	Ⓐv	⚒	⑥v		⚒	⑥	ⒶGv	Ⓐv	Ⓐv	⑥G	ⒶN	⑥E	Ⓐ	⑥O
Liverpool Lime St ..... d.	...	...	...	1934	1948	...	1948	...	...	2004	...	...	...	...	...	...	2034	...	...	...	2048	...	...	...	...	...
Runcorn ..... d.	...	...	...	1952	2004	...	2004	...	...	2025	...	...	...	...	...	...	2052	...	...	...	2104	...	...	...	...	...
Manchester P'dilly .. d.	...	1927	1935	|	|	1955	|	2007	...	|	...	...	2015	2027	2035	...	|	2106	...	2115	|	...	...	...	2127	2127
Stockport ..... d.	...	1935	1942	|	|	2004	|	|	...	|	...	...	2023	2035	2043	...	|	|	...	2123	|	...	...	...	2135	2135
Chester ..... 165 d.	...	|	|	|	|	|	|	|	...	|	...	...	|	|	|	...	|	|	...	|	|	...	2135	...	|	|
Crewe ..... 165 d.	...	|	|	2018	2023	2029	|	|	2041	2047	2047	2054	|	|	|	...	2117	|	...	|	2124	2144	2156	2204	|	|
Macclesfield ..... d.	...	1949	1955	|	|	|	|	|	|	|	|	|	2036	2049	2056	...	|	|	...	2136	|	|	|	|	2149	|
Stoke on Trent ..... d.	...	2007	2012	|	|	|	|	2044	|	|	|	|	2053	2107	2113	...	|	2144	...	2153	|	|	|	|	2207	|
Stafford ..... d.	...	2025	|	2042	|	2048	2036	|	|	2110	|	2114	|	2125	|	...	2141	|	...	|	2144	2209	|	2229	2225	2233
Wolverhampton ..... a.	...	2039	|	2057	|	|	|	2113	|	2126	|	2130	|	2139	|	...	2157	2213	...	|	|	2223	2227	2242	2239	2250
Birmingham New St a.	...	2058	|	2118	|	|	|	2136	|	2147	|	2151	|	2203	|	...	2217	2237	...	|	|	2247	2250	2301	2303	2322
Nuneaton ..... d.	...	...	|	...	2102	|	|	...	|	...	|	...	|	...	|	...	...	...	...	|	2216	...	...	...	...	...
Rugby ..... a.	...	...	|	...	|	|	|	...	2127	...	|	...	|	...	|	...	...	...	...	|	2230	...	...	...	...	...
Milton Keynes ..... a.	2059	...	2126	...	|	2135	|	...	2147	...	2211	...	2150	...	2228	...	...	...	2237	2249	2254	...	...	...	...	...
London Euston ..... a.	2203	...	2221	...	2209	2212	2243d	...	2246	...	2303	...	2251	...	2336	...	...	...	2338	2350	2353	...	...	...	...	...

Operator	LM	LM	XC			VT	VT	VT	XC	VT	VT	VT	XC	VT	LM	VT	VT	XC	VT	VT	VT		VT	XC	VT	VT
	Ⓐ	⑥	Ⓐ		⑦	⑦v	⑦	⑦v	⑦U	⑦v	⑦Pv	⑦	⑦U	⑦	⑦	⑦P	⑦v	⑦U	⑦	⑦v	⑦		⑦	⑦U	⑦	⑦
Liverpool Lime St ..... d.	2134	2134	...	...		...	0815	...	...	0838	...	...	...	0936	...	...	...	...	...	1038	...	...	...	...	...	1148
Runcorn ..... d.	2152	2152	...	...		...	0834	...	...	0854	...	...	...	0952	...	...	...	...	...	1054	...	...	...	...	...	1204
Manchester P'dilly .. d.	|	|	2207	...		0805	|	0820	0827	|	...	0920	0927	|	...	...	1020	1026	1035	|	1109	...	...	1127	1135	|
Stockport ..... d.	|	|	|	...	▲	0814	|	0828	0836	|	...	0927	0936	|	...	...	1029	1035	1043	|	1117	...	...	1137	1143	|
Chester ..... 165 d.	|	|	|	...		|	|	|	|	|	...	|	|	|	...	...	|	|	|	|	|	...	1128	|	|	|
Crewe ..... 165 d.	2220	2220	|	...		0843	|	0857	0904	0913	0943	|	|	1012	1020	1043	1055	|	|	1114	|	...	1149	|	|	|
Macclesfield ..... d.	|	|	2229	...		|	|	|	|	|	|	|	|	|	|	|	|	|	|	|	|	...	|	|	|	|
Stoke on Trent ..... d.	|	|	2247	...		|	|	|	|	|	|	|	|	|	|	|	|	|	|	|	|	...	|	|	|	|
Stafford ..... d.	2241	2245	2307	...		0909	|	|	0929	0939	|	1017	1026	1040	1045	|	|	1125	1138	1142	1200	...	|	1227	1228	1236
Wolverhampton ..... a.	2257	2301	2319	...		|	|	|	0941	|	|	|	1040	|	1101	|	|	1137	|	|	|	...	|	1240	|	|
Birmingham New St a.	2318	2320	2340	...		|	|	|	0958	|	|	|	1059	|	1118	|	|	1157	|	|	|	...	|	1258	|	|
Nuneaton ..... d.	...	...	...	...		|	|	|	...	1001	|	|	...	1102	...	|	|	...	|	1204	|	...	1230	...	|	|
Rugby ..... a.	...	...	...	...		|	|	|	...	|	1038	|	...	|	...	1138	|	...	|	|	|	...	|	...	|	|
Milton Keynes ..... a.	...	...	...	...		|	1013	|	...	|	1104	1118	...	1148	...	1204	|	...	1229	|	1250	...	1303s	...	|	|
London Euston ..... a.	...	...	...	...		1058	1103	1108	...	1144	1204	1208	...	1238	...	1251	1258	...	1309	1315	1331	...	1344	...	1353	1403

Operator	VT	VT	VT	VT	XC	VT	VT		LM	VT	VT	VT	XC	VT	VT		LM	VT	XC	VT	VT	XC	VT	VT	LM	VT
	⑦	⑦	⑦	⑦H	⑦U	⑦	⑦		⑦	⑦	⑦	⑦H	⑦U	⑦	⑦		⑦	⑦	⑦B	⑦	⑦H	⑦U	⑦	⑦	⑦	⑦
Liverpool Lime St ..... d.	1134	...	...	...	...	...	1248	...	1234	...	...	...	...	...	1348	...	1334	...	...	...	...	...	...	1448	1434	...
Runcorn ..... d.	1152	...	...	...	...	...	1304	...	1252	...	...	...	...	...	1404	...	1352	...	...	...	...	...	...	1504	1452	...
Manchester P'dilly .. d.	|	1155	1215	...	1226	1235	|	...	|	1255	1315	...	1327	1335	|	...	|	1355	1407	1415	...	1427	1435	|	|	1455
Stockport ..... d.	|	1205	1223	...	1236	1244	|	...	|	1305	1322	...	1336	1342	|	...	|	1404	|	1422	...	1436	1442	|	|	1504
Chester ..... 165 d.	|	|	|	1233	|	|	|	...	|	|	|	1328	|	|	|	...	|	|	|	|	1433	|	|	|	|	|
Crewe ..... 165 d.	1222	1230	|	1254	|	|	|	...	1322	1330	|	1349	|	|	|	...	1422	1429	|	|	1454	|	|	|	1522	1529
Macclesfield ..... d.	|	|	|	|	|	|	|	...	|	|	|	|	1349	1355	|	...	|	|	|	|	|	1449	1455	|	|	|
Stoke on Trent ..... d.	|	|	|	|	|	|	|	...	|	|	1350	|	1407	1412	|	...	|	|	1443	1450	|	1507	1512	|	|	|
Stafford ..... d.	1242	|	1306	|	1327	1329	1336	...	1343	|	|	|	1425	|	1436	...	1443	|	|	|	|	1525	|	1536	1543	|
Wolverhampton ..... a.	1259	|	|	|	1340	|	|	...	1358	|	|	|	1440	|	|	...	1458	|	1513	|	|	1540	|	|	1558	|
Birmingham New St a.	1316	|	|	|	1358	|	|	...	1415	|	|	|	1458	|	|	...	1515	|	1531	|	|	1558	|	|	1615	|
Nuneaton ..... d.	...	|	|	|	...	|	|	...	...	|	|	1431	...	|	|	...	...	|	...	|	|	...	|	|	...	|
Rugby ..... a.	...	|	|	|	...	|	|	...	...	|	|	|	...	|	|	...	...	|	...	|	|	...	|	|	...	|
Milton Keynes ..... a.	...	|	1354	1402s	...	|	|	...	...	|	1449	1504s	...	|	|	...	...	|	...	1549	1604s	...	|	|	...	|
London Euston ..... a.	...	1412	1440	1443	...	1452	1503	...	...	1512	1530	1545	...	1548	1603	...	...	1611	...	1630	1644	...	1648	1703	...	1711

Operator	XC	VT	VT	XC		VT	VT	VT	VT	XC	VT	VT	XC	VT	VT	LM	VT	XC	VT	VT		XC	VT	VT	VT	VT
	⑦B	⑦	⑦H	⑦U		⑦	⑦	⑦	⑦	⑦B	⑦	⑦	⑦U	⑦	⑦	⑦	⑦	⑦T	⑦	⑦		⑦U	⑦	⑦	⑦	⑦
Liverpool Lime St ..... d.	...	...	...	...	...	...	1548	1534	...	...	...	1618	...	...	1648	1634	...	...	...	...	...	...	...	1748	1734	...
Runcorn ..... d.	...	...	...	...	...	...	1604	1552	...	...	...	1634	...	...	1704	1652	...	...	...	...	...	...	...	1804	1752	...
Manchester P'dilly .. d.	1507	1515	...	1527	...	1535	|	|	1555	1607	1615	|	1627	1635	|	|	1655	1707	1715	...	...	1727	1735	|	|	1755
Stockport ..... d.	|	1522	...	1536	...	1542	|	|	1604	|	1623	|	1636	1642	|	|	1704	|	1722	...	...	1736	1742	|	|	1804
Chester ..... 165 d.	|	|	1533	|	...	|	|	|	|	|	|	|	|	|	|	|	|	|	|	1735	...	|	|	|	|	|
Crewe ..... 165 d.	|	|	1554	|	...	|	|	1622	1629	|	|	1653	|	|	|	1722	1729	|	|	1755	...	|	|	|	1822	1829
Macclesfield ..... d.	|	|	|	1549	...	1555	|	|	|	|	|	|	1649	1655	|	|	|	|	|	|	...	1749	1755	|	|	|
Stoke on Trent ..... d.	1543	1550	|	1607	...	1612	|	|	|	1643	1650	|	1707	1712	|	|	|	1743	1750	|	...	1807	1812	|	|	|
Stafford ..... d.	|	|	|	1625	...	|	1637	1643	|	|	|	|	1725	|	1736	1743	|	|	|	|	...	1825	|	1836	1843	|
Wolverhampton ..... a.	1613	|	|	1640	...	|	|	1658	|	1713	|	|	1740	|	|	1758	|	1813	|	|	...	1840	|	|	1858	|
Birmingham New St a.	1631	|	|	1658	...	|	|	1715	|	1731	|	|	1758	|	|	1815	|	1831	|	|	...	1858	|	|	1915	|
Nuneaton ..... d.	...	|	|	...	...	|	|	...	|	...	|	|	...	|	|	...	|	...	|	|	...	...	|	|	...	|
Rugby ..... a.	...	|	|	...	...	|	|	...	|	...	|	|	...	|	|	...	|	...	|	|	...	...	|	|	...	|
Milton Keynes ..... a.	...	1649	1703s	...	...	|	|	...	|	...	1749	1803s	...	|	|	...	|	...	1849	1903s	...	...	|	|	...	|
London Euston ..... a.	...	1730	1744	...	...	1748	1804	...	1811	...	1830	1844	...	1848	1903	...	1911	...	1930	1944	...	...	1948	2003	...	20116

Operator	XC	VT	VT	XC	VT	VT	VT	VT		XC	VT	XC	VT	LM	VT	XC	VT	AW	VT	LM	VT	VT	XC		LM	XC
	⑦B	⑦	⑦	⑦S	⑦	⑦	⑦	⑦		⑦B	⑦	⑦R	⑦	⑦	⑦	⑦B	⑦Gv	⑦H	⑦	⑦	⑦v	⑦v	⑦		⑦	⑦
Liverpool Lime St ..... d.	...	...	...	...	...	1848	1834	...	...	...	...	...	...	1934	1948	...	...	...	...	2034	...	2048	...	...	2134	...
Runcorn ..... d.	...	...	...	...	...	1904	1852	...	...	...	...	...	...	1952	2004	...	...	...	...	2052	...	2104	...	...	2152	...
Manchester P'dilly .. d.	1807	1815	...	1827	1835	|	|	1855	...	1907	1915	1927	1935	|	|	2007	...	...	2020	|	2055	|	2107	...	|	2207
Stockport ..... d.	|	1822	...	1836	1842	|	|	1907	...	|	1922	1935	1942	|	|	2016	...	...	2027	|	2103	|	2116	...	|	2216
Chester ..... 165 d.	|	|	1835	|	|	|	|	|	...	|	|	|	|	|	|	|	...	2027	|	|	|	|	|	...	|	|
Crewe ..... 165 d.	|	|	1855	|	|	|	1922	1929	...	|	|	|	|	2018	2024	|	2047	2052	|	2117	|	2124	|	...	2222	|
Macclesfield ..... d.	|	|	|	1849	1855	|	|	|	...	|	|	1948	1955	|	|	2029	|	|	2040	|	2115	|	2129	...	|	2229
Stoke on Trent ..... d.	1843	1850	|	1907	1912	|	|	|	...	1943	1950	2007	2012	|	|	2047	|	|	2057	|	2133	|	2147	...	|	2247
Stafford ..... d.	|	|	|	1925	|	1936	1943	|	...	|	|	2025	|	2038	2044	2109	|	2116	|	2138	|	2144	2207	...	2244	2306
Wolverhampton ..... a.	1913	|	|	1940	|	|	1958	|	...	2013	|	2039	|	2055	|	2121	|	2134	|	2155	|	|	2220	...	2300	2318
Birmingham New St a.	1931	|	|	1958	|	|	2015	|	...	2031	|	2100	|	2115	|	2139	|	2152	|	2215	|	|	2245	...	2317	2341
Nuneaton ..... d.	...	|	|	...	|	|	...	|	...	...	|	...	|	...	|	...	|	...	|	...	|	2215	...	...	...	...
Rugby ..... a.	...	|	|	...	|	|	...	|	...	...	|	...	|	...	|	...	|	...	|	...	|	2229	...	...	...	...
Milton Keynes ..... a.	...	1949	2003s	...	|	|	...	|	...	...	2048	...	|	...	2138	...	2155	...	2203	...	2237	2253	...	...	...	...
London Euston ..... a.	...	2030	2044	...	2048	210	...	2114	...	...	2134	...	2204	...	2229	...	2253	...	2257	...	2332	2354	...	...	...	...

A – To Bristol on ①–④, to Exeter on ⑤, to Paignton on ⑥ (to Bristol on ⑥ Sept. 5 - Oct. 31).
B – To Bristol.
C – From Glasgow. May 23 - Sept. 5.
D – From Holyhead. Conveys 🛏12 Lancaster (depart 0535) - Crewe - London Euston.
E – From Edinburgh.
F – To Plymouth on Ⓐ, to Bristol on ⑥ (To Plymouth on ⑥ Sept. 12 - Oct. 31).
G – From Glasgow.
H – From Holyhead.
J – To Bristol on Ⓐ, to Paignton on ⑥ (To Bristol on ⑥ Sept. 12 - Oct. 31).
K – To Paignton on Ⓐ, to Bristol on ⑥ (To Paignton on ⑥ Sept. 12 - Oct. 31).
L – From Llandudno Junction.

M – To Plymouth.
N – From Bangor on Ⓐ.
O – May 23 - Jul. 11.
P – From Preston.
Q – To Newquay.
R – To Reading.
S – To Southampton.
T – To Paignton.
U – To Bournemouth.
V – From Holyhead. Conveys 🛏12 Wrexham (depart 0700) - Chester - London Euston.
X – From Holyhead on Ⓐ.

a – From September 12, arrives 2101.
b – From September 12, arrives 2115.
c – From September 12, arrives 2118.

d – From September 12, arrives 2217.
f – 5 minutes later on ⑥.
h – From Holyhead on ⑥.
j – Also calls at Stockport on ⑥.
k – Departs 0511 on ⑥.
s – Stops to set down only.
t – Stops to set down only on Ⓐ.
u – Stops to pick up only.
v – Also calls at Watford Junction 13–18 minutes before London Euston to set down only.

★ – May 23 - Sept. 5.

▲ – Due to engineering work on ⑦ buses replace trains Stafford - Stoke on Trent - Macclesfield until around 1400.

151 LONDON and BIRMINGHAM - PRESTON - EDINBURGH and GLASGOW

TP, VT

Services on ⑥ valid until October 31, services on ⑦ valid until July 12.

⚒

km	Operator	VT ⚒	TP Ⓐ	TP ⚒M	VT ⚒	VT ⒶA	VT ⑥A	TP ⒶM		VT Ⓐ	VT ⑥	VT ⚒	VT ⚒	TP ⑥M	VT ⚒	VT ⚒	TP ⒶM	TP ⑥M	VT Ⓐ	VT Ⓐ	VT Ⓐ	VT ⑥	VT ⚒
254	**London Euston 150** d.	...	...	...	...	0547	0605	...	...	...	...	0730	...	...	0830	...	...	...	0930	...	1030	1030	...
	Birmingham New St .. **150** d.	...	...	...	0617	│	│	...	...	0719	0720	│	0820	...	│	0920	...	...	│	1020	│	│	1120
	Wolverhampton d.	...	...	...	0634	│	│	...	...	0736	0737	│	0837	...	│	0937	...	...	│	1037	│	│	1137
0	**Crewe** d.	0557	...	...	0709	0732	0753	...	...	0809	0809	│	0909	...	│	1009	...	...	│	1109	│	│	1209
39	Warrington Bank Quay d.	0614	...	...	0727	0749	0812	...	...	0827	0828	0914	0927	...	1014	1027	...	...	1114	1127	1214	1214	1227
58	Wigan North Western ..... **160** d.	0625	...	...	0738	0800	0823	...	...	0838	0839	0925	0938	...	1025	1038	...	...	1125	1138	1225	1225	1238
82	*Manchester P'dilly* **156** d.	│	0603	0633	│	│	│	0745	...	│	│	│	│	0916	│	│	1016	1016	│	│	│	│	│
82	**Preston 156** d.	0640	0644	0716	0753	0815	0837	0824	...	0853	0854	0941	0953	0958	1041	1053	1058	1058	1141	1153	1241	1241	1253
116	Lancaster **156** d.	0654	0701	0732	0809	0830	0852	0840	...	0908	0909	0955	1008	1014	1055	1108	1114	1114	1155	1208	1300	1255	1308
147	Oxenholme **156** d.	0710	0715	│	0823	0843	0906	0854	...	│	│	│	1024	1028	1108	│	1128	1128	│	1224	...	2309	1324
199	Penrith d.	0735	│	0809	│	│	0932	0920	...	0945	0946	1031	│	1053	│	1145	1153	1153	1230	│	...	│	│
227	**Carlisle** d.	0751	0757	0826	0903	0922	0948	0937	...	1001	1004	1047	1103	1111	1147	1203	1211	1211	1247	1303	...	1347	1403
269	Lockerbie d.	0810	0816	│	│	│	│	0956	...	│	│	│	│	1131	│	│	1230	1230	│	│	...	│	│
392	**Edinburgh** a.	│	0922	│	1022	│	│	1110	...	│	│	│	1222	│	│	│	│	1340	│	1422	...	│	│
392	**Glasgow** Central a.	0914	...	0945	...	1036	1103	...	...	1116	1117	1201	...	1232	1301	1319	1331	...	1401	...	...	1501	1517

Operator	TP ⚒M	VT ⚒	VT ⚒	TP ⑥M	VT Ⓐ	VT ⑥	VT ⚒	TP ⒶM	TP ⑥M	VT Ⓐ	VT ⑥	VT ⚒	VT Ⓐ	VT ⑥		VT Ⓐ	VT ⑥	TP ⚒M	VT Ⓐ	VT Ⓐ	TP Ⓐ	VT Ⓐ	VT ⑥	VT Ⓐ
London Euston 150 d.	...	1130	...	...	1230	1230	...	...	...	1330	1330	...	1430	1430	...	...	...	...	1530	...	...	1630	1630	...
Birmingham New St .. **150** d.	...	│	1220	...	│	│	1320	...	...	│	│	1420	│	│	...	1520	1520	...	│	1620	...	│	│	1720
Wolverhampton d.	...	│	1237	...	│	│	1337	...	...	│	│	1437	│	│	...	1537	1537	...	│	1637	...	│	│	1737
Crewe d.	...	│	1309	...	│	│	1409	...	...	│	│	1509	│	│	...	1609	1609	...	│	1709	...	│	│	1809
Warrington Bank Quay d.	...	1314	1327	...	1414	1414	1427	...	...	1514	1514	1527	1617	1614	...	1627	1627	...	1714	1727	...	│	1814	1827
Wigan North Western...... **160** d.	...	1325	1338	...	1425	1425	1438	...	...	1525	1525	1538	1629	1625	...	1638	1638	...	1725	1738	...	│	1825	1838
Manchester P'dilly **156** d.	1216	│	│	1316	│	│	│	1416	1416	│	│	│	│	│	...	│	│	1616	│	│	1715	│	│	│
Preston 156 d.	1258	1341	1353	1358	1441	1441	1453	1458	1458	1541	1541	1553	1644	1641	...	1653	1653	1700	1741	1753	1758	1832	1841	1853
Lancaster **156** d.	1314	1355	1408	1414	1500	1455	1509	1514	1514	│	1546	1608	1700	1655	...	1710	1710	1716	1755	1808	1818	│	1855	1908
Oxenholme **156** d.	1328	1408	│	1428	...	│	1524	│	1528	1606	1609	│	...	│	...	1725	1725	1730	1808	1823	│	│	1909	1924
Penrith d.	1353	│	1445	1453	...	1530	│	1553	1553	1631	│	1645	...	1730	...	1751	│	│	│	1849	1853	│	1934	│
Carlisle d.	1411	1447	1502	1511	...	1547	1603	1610	1610	1647	1647	1702	...	1747	...	1807	1804	1811	1847	1904	1911	│	1951	2003
Lockerbie d.	1430	│	│	1533	...	│	│	1629	1629	│	│	│	...	│	...	│	│	1830	│	│	│	│	│	│
Edinburgh a.	1542	│	1622	│	...	│	│	1739	1739	│	│	1822	...	│	...	│	│	1939	│	2024	│	│	│	│
Glasgow Central a.	...	1601	...	1642	...	1701	1718	...	...	1801	1801	...	...	1901	...	1919	1917	...	2001	...	2030	2040	2101	2117

Operator	TP ⒶM	TP ⑥M	VT ⒶA	VT Ⓐ		VT Ⓐ	VT Ⓐ	VT Ⓐ	VT ⑥	VT Ⓐ	VT ⑥		VT Ⓐ	VT ⑥	VT ⑤	VT ⑥	VT Ⓐ	VT ⒶA	VT ⑥AB	VT Ⓐ	VT ⒶA	VT ⑥AC		VT ⒶA
London Euston 150 d.	...	...	1633	1657	...	1730	1730	...	...	1757	1830	...	...	...	1846	1919	1930	...	2014	2030	...	2030	...	2110
Birmingham New St .. **150** d.	...	...	│	│	...	│	│	1820	1820	│	│	...	1920	1920	│	│	│	2020	│	│	2120	│	...	│
Wolverhampton d.	...	...	│	│	...	│	│	1837	1837	│	│	...	1937	1937	│	│	│	2037	│	│	2141	│	...	│
Crewe d.	...	...	1818	│	...	│	│	1909	1909	│	│	...	2009	2009	│	2103	2103	2114	2240	│	2219	2240	...	2255
Warrington Bank Quay d.	...	...	1836	1850	...	1914	1914	1927	1927	1950	2014	...	2027	2027	2126s	2120	2120	...	2257	2223	2237	2257	...	2313
Wigan North Western...... **160** d.	...	...	1847	1901	...	1925	1925	1938	1938	2001	2025	...	2038	2038	2138s	2132	2131	...	2308	2234	2247	2308	...	2324
Manchester P'dilly **156** d.	1816	1816	│	│	...	│	│	│	│	│	│	...	│	│	│	│	│	...	│	│	│	│	...	│
Preston 156 d.	1900	1900	1902	1915	...	1941	1941	1953	1959	2015	2041	...	2053	2059	2155s	2149	2145	...	2322	2253	2305	2322	...	2343
Lancaster **156** d.	1916	1916	...	1930	...	1955	1955	2008	...	2030	2055	...	2108	...	...	...	2200	...	...	...	...	...	...	...
Oxenholme **156** d.	1932	1930	...	1945	...	2008	2008	│	...	│	2109	...	2124	...	...	...	2213	...	...	...	...	...	...	...
Penrith d.	1956	1955	...	2010	...	│	2034	2045	...	│	2134	...	│	...	...	...	2239	...	...	...	...	...	...	...
Carlisle d.	2013	2013	...	2025	...	2047	2050	2103	...	2118	215	...	2203	...	...	...	2256	...	...	...	...	...	...	...
Lockerbie d.	│	2032	...	2044	...	│	│	│	...	2137	│	...	│	...	...	...	│	...	...	...	...	...	...	...
Edinburgh a.	2139	2132	...	│	...	│	│	2222	...	│	│	...	│	...	...	...	│	...	...	...	...	...	...	...
Glasgow Central a.	...	...	...	2147	...	2201	2201	...	...	2239	2304	...	2317	...	...	...	0009	...	...	...	...	...	...	...

⑦

Operator	VT ⑦A	TP ⑦M		VT ⑦	VT ⑦		VT ⑦A	VT ⑦		VT ⑦A	VT ⑦		TP ⑦M	VT ⑦A		VT ⑦	TP ⑦M		VT ⑦	VT ⑦		TP ⑦M	VT ⑦
London Euston 150 d.	...	...	...	...	...	...	0845	...	...	0945	...	...	...	1045	...	...	...	...	1225	...	...	...	1325
Birmingham New St .. **150** d.	0845	...	...	0920	...	...	│	1015	...	│	1120	...	...	│	...	1220	...	...	│	1320	...	...	│
Wolverhampton d.	0904	...	...	0937	...	...	│	1032	...	│	1137	...	...	│	...	1236	...	...	│	1337	...	...	│
Crewe d.	0945	...	...	1014	1021	...	1054	1109	...	1156	1209	...	...	1251	...	1309	...	...	│	1411	...	...	│
Warrington Bank Quay d.	1002	...	...	1032	1037	...	1113	1127	...	1213	1227	...	...	1308	...	1327	...	...	1416	1429	...	...	1516
Wigan North Western...... **160** d.	1013	...	...	1043	1048	...	1124	1138	...	1224	1238	...	...	1319	...	1338	...	...	1427	1440	...	...	1527
Manchester P'dilly **156** d.	│	0946	...	│	│	...	│	│	...	│	│	...	1216	│	...	│	1316	...	│	│	...	1416	│
Preston 156 d.	1030	1039	...	1057	1106	...	1138	1153	...	1239	1253	...	1258	1337	...	1353	1401	...	1442	1455	...	1500	1542
Lancaster **156** d.	...	1055	...	...	1122	...	1153	1208	...	1254	1308	...	1314	1352	...	1408	1416	...	1458	1511	...	1516	1558
Oxenholme **156** d.	...	1109	...	...	...	...	1206	1224	...	1307	1324	...	1328	1405	...	│	1431	...	│	1525	...	1630	1611
Penrith d.	...	1135	...	...	...	...	1232	│	...	1333	│	...	1354	1431	...	1445	1456	...	1532	│	...	1554	│
Carlisle d.	...	1152	...	...	...	...	1247	1303	...	1352	1403	...	1411	1447	...	1503	1513	...	1548	1605	...	1613	1649
Lockerbie d.	...	1211	...	...	...	...	│	│	...	│	│	...	1430	│	...	│	│	...	│	│	...	1631	│
Edinburgh a.	...	│	...	...	...	...	│	1422	...	│	│	...	1535	│	...	1622	│	...	│	│	...	1737	│
Glasgow Central a.	...	1315	...	...	...	...	1359	...	...	1506	1523	...	...	1609	...	...	1635	...	1703	1717	...	...	1803

Operator	VT ⑦	VT ⑦		VT ⑦	TP ⑦M		VT ⑦	VT ⑦		TP ⑦M	VT ⑦		VT ⑦	TP ⑦M		VT ⑦	VT ⑦		VT ⑦	VT ⑦		VT ⑦	VT ⑦A	VT ⑦A
London Euston 150 d.	...	1425	...	...	...	...	1525	...	...	...	1625	...	...	...	...	1725	1825	...	...	1925	...	2025	...	2050
Birmingham New St .. **150** d.	1420	│	...	1520	...	...	│	1620	...	...	│	...	1720	...	...	│	│	...	1920	│	...	│	2120	│
Stafford d.	1437	│	...	1537	...	...	│	1637u	...	...	│	...	1737u	...	...	│	│	...	1937	│	...	│	2138	│
Crewe d.	1511	│	...	1611	...	...	│	1711	...	...	│	...	1811	...	...	│	│	...	2011	│	...	2213	2218	2251
Warrington Bank Quay d.	1529	1616	...	1629	...	...	1716	1729	...	...	1817	...	1829	...	...	1916	2016	...	2029	2116	...	2230	2236	2308
Wigan North Western...... **160** d.	1540	1627	...	1640	...	...	1727	1740	...	...	1828	...	1840	...	...	1927	2027	...	2040	2127	...	2241	2247	2319
Manchester P'dilly **156** d.	│	│	...	│	1616	...	│	│	...	1716	│	...	│	1816	...	│	│	...	│	│	...	│	│	│
Preston 156 d.	1555	1642	...	1655	1702	...	1742	1755	...	1802	1842	...	1855	1900	...	1942	2042	...	2055	2142	...	2258	2307	2339
Lancaster **156** d.	1610	1657	...	1710	1718	...	1757	1810	...	1818	1858	...	1910	1916	...	1957	2057	...	2110	2157	...	...	...	...
Oxenholme **156** d.	│	│	...	1725	1732	...	1810	1825	...	1832	1911	...	1926	1930	...	2010	2111	...	2126	2211	...	...	...	...
Penrith d.	1647	1732	...	│	1757	...	│	1851	...	1856	1936	...	│	1954	...	2036	2136	...	│	2236	...	...	...	...
Carlisle d.	1704	1748	...	1805	1815	...	1849	1906	...	1915	1953	...	2005	2013	...	2052	2152	...	2205	2252	...	...	...	...
Lockerbie d.	│	│	...	│	│	...	│	│	...	1933	│	...	│	2031	...	│	│	...	2223	│	...	...	...	...
Edinburgh a.	1822	│	...	│	1937	...	│	2024	...	│	│	...	│	2137	...	│	│	...	│	│	...	...	...	...
Glasgow Central a.	...	1900	...	1917	...	...	2003	...	...	2045	2108	...	2117	...	...	2207	2308	...	2335	0002	...	...	...	...

A – This service makes additional stops between London / Birmingham and Crewe. See Table **150** For details.
B – May 23 - Sept. 5.
C – Sept. 12 - Dec. 12.
M – From Manchester Airport.
s – Calls to set down only.
u – Calls to pick up only.

TP, VT — GLASGOW and EDINBURGH - PRESTON - BIRMINGHAM and LONDON — 151

Services on ⑥ valid until October 31, services on ⑦ valid until July 12.

Operator		VT	VT	VT		VT	VT	VT	VT	VT	TP	VT	VT		VT	VT	TP	VT	VT	VT		VT	VT		TP
		Ⓐ A	⑥ A	Ⓐ A		⚒	Ⓐ	⑥	⚒	⚒	Ⓐ M	Ⓐ	⑥		⚒	⚒	⚒ M	⚒	⚒	⚒		⚒	⚒		⑥ M
Glasgow Central d.	⚒	...	...	...	...	...	0425	0425	...	0540	...	0550	0550	...	0630	...	0710	0735	0800	0840	...	...	0940	...	...
Edinburgh d.		...	...	...	...	...	|	|	...	|	0536	|	|	...	|	0652	|	|	|	|	...	0852	|	...	0922
Lockerbie d.		...	...	...	...	...	|	|	...	|	|	|	|	...	0725	|	0806	|	|	|	...	|	|	...	1024
Carlisle d.		...	...	...	...	...	0543	0543	...	0649	|	0704	0703	...	0746	0807	0830	0849	0909	0949	...	1007	1049	...	1052
Penrith d.		...	...	...	...	...	0557	0558	...	|	|	0719	0718	...	0800	0822	0844	|	|	1003	...	|	|	...	1107
Oxenholme **156** d.		...	...	...	...	...	0620	0620	...	0724	|	0742	0742	...	0823	|	0911	0923	|	|	...	1042	1123	...	1131
Lancaster **156** d.		...	0540	0535	...	...	0635	0636	0658	0738	0747	0757	0757	...	0838	0857	0926	0938	0957	1038	...	1057	1138	...	1146
Preston 156 d.		0530	0558	0600	...	0616	0656	0658	0717	0758	0812	0817	0817	...	0858	0917	0947	0958	1017	1058	...	1117	1158	...	1210
Manchester P'dilly **156** a.		|	|	|	...	|	|	|	|	|	0856	|	|	...	|	|	1027	|	|	|	...	|	|	...	1256
Wigan North Western **160** d.		0545	0609	0611	...	0627	0708	0710	0728	0809	...	0828	0828	...	0909	0928	...	1009	1028	1109	...	1128	1209	...	...
Warrington Bank Quay d.		0556	0620	0622	...	0638	0718	0720	0739	0820	...	0839	0839	...	0920	0939	...	1020	1039	1120	...	1139	1220	...	...
Crewe d.		|	|	0653	...	0701	|	|	0801	|	...	0901	0901	...	|	1001	...	|	1101	|	...	1201	|	...	...
Wolverhampton a.		|	|	|	...	0732	|	|	0831	|	...	0931	0931	...	|	1031	...	|	1131	|	...	1231	|	...	...
Birmingham New St **150** a.		|	|	|	...	0755	|	|	0856	|	...	0956	0955	...	|	1055	...	|	1156	|	...	1255	|	...	...
London Euston **150** a.		0800	0814	0836	...	...	0909	0912	...	1012	...	...	...	...	1112	...	...	1212	...	1312	...	...	1412	...	...

Operator	VT	TP		TP	TP	VT		VT	VT	VT	VT		VT	TP	TP	VT	VT	TP		VT	VT	VT	VT	TP	TP
	⚒	Ⓐ M		Ⓐ M	⑥ M	⚒		⚒	Ⓐ	⑥	Ⓐ		⚒	Ⓐ M	⑥ M	⚒	⚒	⑥ M		Ⓐ	⑥	Ⓐ	⚒	Ⓐ M	⑥ M
Glasgow Central d.	1000	...	...	1010	1010	1040	...	...	1140	1140	...	...	1200	...	...	1240	...	1300	...	1340	1340	...	1400	1410	1410
Edinburgh d.	|	0955	...	|	|	|	...	1052	|	|	...	...	|	1208	1208	|	1252	|	...	|	|	...	|	|	|
Lockerbie d.	|	1100	...	|	|	|	...	|	|	|	...	...	|	1306	1306	|	|	1358	...	|	|	...	|	1506	|
Carlisle d.	1109	1133	...	1133	1128	1149	...	1207	1249	1249	...	...	1309	1330	1330	1349	1407	1430	...	1449	1449	...	1509	1530	1530
Penrith d.	1124	1147	...	1147	1142	|	...	|	1303	1303	...	...	|	|	|	|	1422	1445	...	|	|	...	|	1544	1544
Oxenholme **156** d.	|	1211	...	1211	1207	1223	...	1243	|	|	...	...	|	1410	1406	1424	|	1509	...	1524	1523	...	1544	1608	1608
Lancaster **156** d.	|	1226	...	1226	1223	1238	...	1257	|	1338	1339	...	1358	|	1422	1438	1457	1526	...	|	1538	1539	|	1623	1626
Preston 156 d.	1217	1247	...	1247	1247	1258	...	1317	1353	1358	1359	...	1417	1447	1447	1458	1517	1547	...	1553	1558	1559	1617	1647	1647
Manchester P'dilly **156** a.	|	1327	...	1327	1327	|	...	|	|	|	|	...	|	1527	1527	|	|	1627	...	|	|	|	|	1727	1727
Wigan North Western **160** d.	1228	...	...	...	...	1309	...	1328	|	1409	1410	...	1428	...	...	1509	1528	...	...	|	1609	1610	1628	...	...
Warrington Bank Quay d.	1239	...	...	...	...	1320	...	1339	|	1420	1421	...	1439	...	...	1520	1539	...	...	|	1620	1621	1639	...	...
Crewe d.	1301	...	...	...	...	|	...	1401	|	|	|	...	1501	...	...	|	1601	...	...	|	|	|	1701	...	...
Wolverhampton a.	1331	...	...	...	...	|	...	1431	|	|	|	...	1531	...	...	|	1631	...	...	|	|	|	1731	...	...
Birmingham New St **150** a.	1356	...	...	...	...	|	...	1455	|	|	|	...	1556	...	...	|	1655	...	...	|	|	|	1756	...	...
London Euston **150** a.	...	...	...	...	...	1512	...	...	1604	1612	1611	...	...	...	...	1712	...	...	...	1801	1812	1811	...	...	...

Operator	VT	VT	VT	VT		VT	TP	VT	VT		VT	TP	VT	VT	VT	TP		VT	VT	VT		VT	VT		TP
	⚒	⚒	Ⓐ	⑥		⚒	⚒ M	Ⓐ A	⑥ A B		⚒	⑥ M	Ⓐ A	⑥ A B	⑥	⑥ M		Ⓐ A	⑥ A	Ⓐ		⑥ A	Ⓐ		Ⓐ
Glasgow Central d.	1440	...	...	1540	...	1600	...	1640	1640	...	...	1707	1740	1740	1800	...	...	1840	1840	...	...	...	2010	...	...
Edinburgh d.	|	1452	...	|	...	|	1611	|	|	...	1652	|	|	|	|	1811	...	|	|	1852	...	1852	|	...	2011
Lockerbie d.	|	|	...	|	...	|	1710	|	|	...	|	1805	1832	1832	|	1910	...	|	|	|	...	|	2107	...	2112
Carlisle d.	1549	1607	...	1649	...	1709	1733	1751	1752	...	1807	1829	1854	1852	1909	1933	...	1949	1949	2008	...	2007	2126	...	2136
Penrith d.	|	1622	...	1703	...	|	1748	1805	|	...	|	1844	1909	1906	|	1948	...	|	2003	|	...	2022	2141	...	|
Oxenholme **156** d.	1624	|	...	|	...	1744	|	1829	1826	...	1842	1908	1932	1929	|	2012	...	2024	2026	2042	...	2045	2205	...	2212
Lancaster **156** d.	1638	1657	1736	1738	...	|	1826	1844	1841	...	1857	1926	1947	1944	1956	2026	...	2038	2041	2057	...	2100	2220	...	2226
Preston 156 d.	1658	1717	1756	1758	...	1817	1847	1904	1901	...	1917	1947	2008	2004	2017	2047	...	2058	2101	2117	...	2120	2240	...	2247
Manchester P'dilly **156** a.	|	|	|	|	...	|	1927	|	|	...	|	2027	|	|	|	2127	...	|	|	|	...	|	|	...	2344
Wigan North Western **160** d.	1709	1728	1808	1809	...	1828	...	1916	1912	...	1928	...	2019	2015	2028	...	...	2109	2112	2128	...	2131	2252	...	...
Warrington Bank Quay d.	1720	1739	1819	1820	...	1839	...	1927	1923	...	1939	...	2031	2026	2039	...	...	2120	2123	2139	...	2142	2303	...	...
Crewe d.	|	1801	|	|	...	1901	...	|	|	...	2001	...	2054	2047	2101	...	...	|	2144	2201	...	2204	2326	...	...
Wolverhampton a.	|	1831	|	|	...	1931	...	|	|	...	2033	...	2130	|	2131	...	...	|	2223	2232	...	2242	...	...	...
Birmingham New St **150** a.	|	1855	|	|	...	1956	...	|	|	...	2055	...	2151	|	2155	...	...	|	2247	2255	...	2301	...	...	...
London Euston **150** a.	1913	...	2013	2015	...	...	...	2124	2203	...	...	...	...	2303	...	...	...	2338	...	...	...	...	...	...	...

Operator		VT		VT		VT	VT		VT	VT		VT	VT		VT	TP			VT	VT		VT	VT		TP
		⑦ A		⑦ A		⑦	⑦		⑦	⑦		⑦	⑦		⑦	⑦ M			⑦	⑦		⑦	⑦		⑦ M
Glasgow Central d.	⑦	...	...	...	...	...	...	...	...	...	...	...	1032	...	...	...	...	...	1132	1151	...	1240	...	...	...
Edinburgh d.		...	...	...	...	...	...	...	...	...	...	...	|	...	1052	1110	...	...	|	|	...	|	1252	...	1309
Lockerbie d.		...	...	...	...	...	...	...	...	...	...	...	|	...	|	1208	...	...	|	|	...	|	|	...	1407
Carlisle d.		...	...	...	...	...	...	...	...	1046	...	...	1146	...	1207	1232	...	...	1249	1309	...	1354	1407	...	1431
Penrith d.		...	...	...	...	...	...	...	...	1100	...	...	1200	...	|	1246	...	...	|	|	...	|	1422	...	1446
Oxenholme **156** d.		...	...	...	...	...	...	...	...	1123	...	...	1224	...	1243	1310	...	...	1323	|	...	1428	|	...	1510
Lancaster **156** d.		...	...	...	...	...	...	...	...	1138	...	1200	1238	...	1257	1326	...	...	1338	1358	...	1443	1457	...	1525
Preston 156 d.		0900	...	1000	...	1017	1058	...	1117	1158	...	1217	1258	...	1317	1347	...	...	1358	1417	...	1503	1517	...	1547
Manchester P'dilly **156** a.		|	...	|	...	|	|	...	|	|	...	|	|	...	|	1427	...	...	|	|	...	|	|	...	1627
Wigan North Western **160** d.		0911	...	1011	...	1028	1109	...	1128	1209	...	1228	1309	...	1328	...	...	...	1409	1428	...	1514	1528	...	...
Warrington Bank Quay d.		0922	...	1022	...	1039	1120	...	1139	1220	...	1239	1320	...	1339	...	...	...	1420	1439	...	1525	1539	...	...
Crewe d.		0943	...	1043	...	1103	|	...	1201	|	...	1301	|	...	1401	...	...	...	|	1501	...	|	1601	...	...
Wolverhampton a.		|	...	|	...	1141	|	...	1234	|	...	1331	|	...	1433	...	...	...	|	1531	...	|	1634	...	...
Birmingham New St **150** a.		|	...	|	...	1205	|	...	1255	|	...	1355	|	...	1455	...	...	...	|	1555	...	|	1655	...	...
London Euston **150** a.		1204	...	1251	...	...	1323	...	...	1418	...	...	1518	...	...		...	...	1618	...	...	1723	...	...	...

Operator	VT		VT	VT		VT		TP	VT		VT		TP	VT		VT		TP	VT		TP	VT		TP	VT
	⑦		⑦	⑦		⑦		⑦ M	⑦		⑦		⑦ M	⑦		⑦		⑦ M	⑦ A		⑦ M	⑦ A		⑦ M	⑦
Glasgow Central d.	1335	...	1356	1436	...	...	...	1506	1535	...	1555	...	...	1636	...	...	...	1706	1736	...	...	1835	...	...	2006
Edinburgh d.	|	...	|	|	...	1452	...	|	|	...	|	...	1610	|	...	1652	...	|	|	...	1810	|	...	1957	|
Lockerbie d.	|	...	|	|	...	|	...	1607	|	...	|	...	1708	|	...	|	...	|	1832	...	1908	|	...	|	2102
Carlisle d.	1449	...	1509	1549	...	1607	...	1630	1649	...	1709	...	1732	1751	...	1807	...	1828	1852	...	1932	1944	...	2115	2124
Penrith d.	|	...	|	|	...	1622	...	1644	1703	...	|	...	1746	1805	...	|	...	1842	1906	...	1946	|	...	|	2139
Oxenholme **156** d.	1523	...	1544	1623	...	|	...	1708	|	...	1744	...	1810	1828	...	1842	...	1907	1929	...	2010	2019	...	|	2203
Lancaster **156** d.	1538	...	|	1638	...	1657	...	1723	1738	...	|	...	1826	1843	...	1857	...	1922	1944	...	2026	2034	...	2203	2218
Preston 156 d.	1558	...	1617	1658	...	1717	...	1747	1758	...	1817	...	1847	1903	...	1917	...	1947	2004	...	2047	2055	...	2229	2338
Manchester P'dilly **156** a.	|	...	|	|	...	|	...	1827	|	...	|	...	1927	|	...	|	...	2027	|	...	2127	|	...	2314	|
Wigan North Western **160** d.	1609	...	1628	1709	...	1728	...	...	1809	...	1828	...	...	1914	...	1928	...	...	2015	...	...	2107	...	...	2250
Warrington Bank Quay d.	1620	...	1639	1720	...	1739	...	...	1820	...	1839	...	...	1925	...	1939	...	...	2026	...	...	2118	...	...	2301
Crewe d.	|	...	1701	|	...	1801	...	...	|	...	1901	...	...	|	...	2001	...	...	2047	...	...	2140	...	...	2320
Stafford a.	|	...	1731	|	...	1832	...	...	|	...	1931	...	...	|	...	2034	...	...	|	...	...	2217	...	...	...
Birmingham New St **150** a.	|	...	1755	|	...	1855	...	...	|	...	1955	...	...	|	...	2057	...	...	|	...	...	2240	...	...	...
London Euston **150** a.	1818	...	...	1918	...	...	...	...	2018	...	...	...	...	2127	...	...	...	...	2253	...	...	...	...	...	...

A – This service makes additional stops between Crewe and Birmingham / London. See Table **150** For details.
B – May 23 - Sept. 5.
M – To / from Manchester Airport.
s – Calls to set down only.
u – Calls to pick up only.
***** – By 🚌.

LM — NUNEATON - COVENTRY — 152

From NUNEATON — *16 km*

Ⓐ: 0637, 0737, 0828, 0930, 1110 and hourly until 2110; then 2220.
⑥: 0647, 0814, 0915 and hourly until 1815; then 1946, 2115, 2215.
⑦: 1230, 1411, 1511, 1611, 1711, 1811, 2011, 2200.

From COVENTRY — *Journey time:* ± 18 minutes

Ⓐ: 0612, 0706, 0804, 0906, 1045 and houry until 2045; then 2144.
⑥: 0616, 0716, 0845 and hourly until 1845; then 2015, 2145.
⑦: 1155, 1346, 1446, 1546, 1646, 1746, 1946, 2135.

155 MANCHESTER - CREWE - HEREFORD - CARDIFF

Most services 🍷 2nd class AW

km			Ⓐ	⑥	⚒ M	Ⓐ	⑥		⚒ C	⚒	⚒ M	Ⓐ f	⚒ C	⚒	⚒ M		⚒ C	⚒	⚒ M	⚒ C	⚒	⚒ M	⚒ C	⚒	⚒ M	Ⓐ P
0	**Manchester** P'dilly d.	⚒	...	...	...	...	...	...	...	...	0630	...	0730	...	0830	...	0930	...	1030	1130	...	1230	1330	...	1430	1530
10	Stockport d.		...	...	...	...	...	...	...	...	0639	...	0739	...	0839	...	0939	...	1039	1139	...	1239	1339	...	1439	1539
	Holyhead **165** d.		...	...	...	...	...	...	...	0425	|	0532	|	0627r	|	...	|	0805t	|	|	1033	|	|	1238	|	|
	Chester **145 165** d.		...	...	...	0515	...	...	...	0612b	|	0708	|	0822	|	...	|	1022	|	|	1222	|	|	1422	|	|
50	**Crewe** ‡ d.		...	...	0454	|	...	...	0555	|	0709r	0735	0808	|	0912	...	1012	|	1112	1212	|	1312	1412	|	1512	1612
	Whitchurch ‡ d.		...	...	0512	|	...	...	0615	|	|	|	0827	|	|	...	|	|	|	|	|	|	|	|	|	1631
103	**Shrewsbury** ‡ a.		...	...	0533	0610	...	...	0641	0718	0742	0809	0848	0917	0941	...	1041	1117	1141	1241	1317	1341	1441	1517	1541	1652
103	**Shrewsbury** 146 d.		...	...	0540	0613	0613	...	0644	0719	0744	0810	0850	0921	0944	...	1044	1121	1144	1244	1321	1344	1444	1521	1544	1653
123	Church Stretton 146 d.		...	...	0555	0629	0629	...	0659	|	0759	|	|	|	0959	...	1059	|	1159	1259	|	1359	1459	|	1559	1709
135	Craven Arms 146 d.		...	...	0603	0637	0637	...	0707	|	0807	|	|	|	1007	...	1107	|	1207	1307	|	1407	1507	|	1607	1717
146	Ludlow d.		...	...	0611	0645	0645	...	0715	0747	0815	|	0917	0948	1015	...	1115	1148	1215	1315	1348	1415	1515	1548	1615	1725
164	Leominster d.		...	...	0622	0656	0656	...	0726	0758	0826	|	0928	|	1026	...	1126	|	1226	1326	|	1426	1526	|	1626	1735
184	**Hereford** d.		0523	0542	0642r	0713	0713	...	0744	0814	0842	|	0944	1012	1042	...	1142	1212	1242	1342	1412	1442	1542	1612	1642	1751
223	Abergavenny d.		0548	0607	0705r	0736	0736	...	0807	0837	0905	|	1007	1035	1105	...	1205	1235	1305	1405	1435	1505	1605	1635	1705	1814
238	Pontypool & New Inn d.		0559	0618	0715r	0746	0746	...	|	0847	|	|	1017	|	|	...	|	1245	|	|	1445	|	|	1645	|	|
243	Cwmbrân d.		0604	0623	0720r	0751	0751	...	0819	0852	0917	|	1022	1048	1118	...	1218	1250	1318	1418	1450	1518	1618	1650	1718	1827
254	Newport a.		0615	0634	0733r	0801	0801	...	0834	0901	0930	0940	1034	1057	1130	...	1229r	1259	1334	1434	1459	1530	1630	1659	1733	1841
273	**Cardiff** Central a.		0656	0654	0751r	0817	0819	...	0855	0923	0954	0958	1055	1115r	1155	...	1254	1320	1354	1454	1521	1554	1654	1718	1754	1859

	⑥ P	Ⓐ	⑥		⚒ M	Ⓐ M	⑥ W	Ⓐ	⑥	⚒ C	Ⓐ	⑥	Ⓐ	⑥ c	⑥ d	⑥	⑥ 🚌 c	Ⓐ	⚒			⑦ F	⑦	⑦ M	⑦	⑦ M
Manchester P'dilly d.	1530	...	...	...	1630	1730	1730	...	...	1830	1930	1930	2030	2030	2030	2130	...	2135	2235	...	⑦	...	0930	1030	1124e	1230
Stockport d.	1539	...	...	...	1639	1740	1740	...	...	1839	1939	1939	2039	2039	2039	2139	...	2144	2244	...		...	0939	1039	1140	1240
Holyhead **165** d.	|	1432	1423	...	|	|	|	1636	1638	|	|	|	|	|	|	|	...	|	|	...		...	|	|	|	|
Chester **145 165** d.	|	1622	1622	...	|	|	|	1820	1822	|	|	|	|	|	|	|	...	|	|	...		...	|	|	|	|
Crewe ‡ d.	1612	|	|	...	1712	1812	1812	|	|	1912	2012	2012	2112	2111	2111	2212	...	2212	2314	...		...	1011	1113	1213	1313
Whitchurch ‡ d.	1631	|	|	...	|	1831	1831	|	|	1933	|	|	2133	2130	2130	2233	...	2233	2334	...		...	1034	|	|	1333
Shrewsbury ‡ a.	1652	1717	1717	...	1741	1852	1852	1915	1918	1959	2045	2044	2159	2156	2156	2303	...	2259	0004	...		...	1100	1141	1241	1357
Shrewsbury 146 d.	1653	1721	1721	...	1744	1856	1853	1916	1919	2001	2051	2046	2201	2156	2156	—	...	2301	...	...		*0750**	1102	1144	1244	1400
Church Stretton 146 d.	1709	|	|	...	1759	1911	1909	|	|	2016	2106	2059	2216	2212	2212	...	...	2316	...	...		*0815**	1118	|	|	|
Craven Arms 146 d.	1717	|	|	...	1807	1919	1917	|	|	2024	2114	2107	2224	2220	2220	...	...	2324	...	...		*0835**	1126	|	|	|
Ludlow d.	1725	1748	1749	...	1815	1927	1925	1945	1948	2032	2122	2117	2232	2228	2228	⑥	...	2332	...	...		*0855**	1135	1211	1311	1427
Leominster d.	1735	|	|	...	1826	1938	1935	|	|	2043	2133	2128	2243	2238	2238	d	...	2343	...	...		*0920**	1146	1222	1322	1438
Hereford d.	1751	1812	1816	...	1842	1954	1950	2010	2012	2101	2154	2145	2259	2255	2255	2313	2302	2359	...	...		1011	1203	1242	1339	1455
Abergavenny d.	1814	1835	1839	...	1905	2017	2014	2033	2035	2124	2219	2208	2322	...	2317	2336	2342	0025	...	...		1034	1227	1305	1402	1518
Pontypool & New Inn d.	|	1845	1849	...	|	|	|	2043	2045	|	2229	2218	|	...	2327	|	2357	0034	...	...		1045	|	1315	|	|
Cwmbrân d.	1827	1850	1854	...	1918	2029	2027	2048	2050	2136	2234	2223	2335	...	2332	2348	0007	0039	...	...		1050	1240	1320	1414	1530
Newport a.	1837	1859	1904	...	1932	2042	2037	2057	2059	2148	2244	2241	2346	...	2343	0004	0022	0049	...	...		1100	1250	1339	1425	1542
Cardiff Central a.	1854	1920	1926	...	1949	2058	2054	2119	2120	2209	2304	2305	0011	...	0008	0024	0052	0110	...	...		1117	1312	1357	1446	1600

	⑦	⑦ MP	⑦	⑦	⑦	⑦	⑦	⑦	⑦	⑦	
Manchester P'dilly d.	1330	1430	1530	1630	1730	...	1830	1930	2030	...	...
Stockport d.	1339	1439	1539	1639	1739	...	1839	1939	2039	...	...
Holyhead **165** d.	|	|	|	|	|	1625	|	|	|	...	...
Chester **145 165** d.	|	|	|	|	|	1824	|	|	|	...	...
Crewe ‡ d.	1413	1513	1613	1713	1813	|	1913	2013	2113	2320	...
Whitchurch ‡ d.	|	|	|	1733	|	|	1932	|	2134	2343	...
Shrewsbury ‡ a.	1441	1541	1641	1800	1841	1919	1957	2041	2200	0011	...
Shrewsbury 146 d.	1444	1544	1644	1802	1844	1922	1959	2044	2202	...	...
Church Stretton 146 d.	1459	|	1659	|	|	1938	|	2059	2218	...	...
Craven Arms 146 d.	1507	|	1707	|	|	1946	|	2107	2227	...	...
Ludlow d.	1515	1611	1715	1830	1911	1954	2027	2115	2235	...	...
Leominster d.	1526	1622	1726	1840	|	2005	2037	2126	2247	...	...
Hereford d.	1543	1642	1743	1857	1935	2021	2053	2143	2304	...	...
Abergavenny d.	1606	1705	1806	1920	1958	2044	2116	2206	2327	...	...
Pontypool & New Inn d.	1616	|	1816	|	|	2054	|	2216	2338	...	...
Cwmbrân d.	1621	1717	1821	1933	2011	2059	2129	2221	2343	...	...
Newport a.	1634	1734	1834	1944	2028	2108	2140	2231	2353	...	...
Cardiff Central a.	1656	1749	1855	2005	2049	2130	2205	2257	0019	...	...

		⑥	②–⑤	Ⓐ	⑥	Ⓐ	⑥	⚒	⚒ C	Ⓐ
Cardiff Central d.	⚒	0030	0030	0435	0440	0510	0521	0540	0650	0720
Newport d.		0053	0059	0453	0457	0528	0535	0554	0704	0734
Cwmbrân d.		0104	0110	0504	0507	0538	0545	0604	0715	0745
Pontypool & New Inn d.		0110	0116	0509	0513	0544	0551	0610	|	0749
Abergavenny d.		0120	0127	0519	0522	0553	0600	0619	0728	0800
Hereford d.		0148	0155	0548	0548	0625	0626	0649	0755	0828
Leominster d.		0201	—	0602	0602	0638	0640	0702	0808	|
Ludlow d.		0213	...	0613	0613	0649	0651	0713	0819	0849
Craven Arms 146 d.		0222	...	0621	0621	0658	0659	0722	0828	|
Church Stretton 146 d.		0233	...	0630	0630	0707	0708	0731	0837	|
Shrewsbury 146 a.		...	...	0644	0644	0721	0722	0745	0851	0915
Shrewsbury ‡ d.		...	⑥	0646	0646	0724	0724	0746	0853	0924
Whitchurch ‡ d.		...		0706	|	|	|	0806	|	|
Crewe ‡ a.		...	0627	0725	0725	|	|	0826	0925	|
Chester **145 165** a.		...	|	|	|	0820	0819	|	|	1020
Holyhead **165** a.		...	|	|	|	1005	1005	|	|	1213
Stockport a.		...	0654	0754	0754	...	...	0858	0958	...
Manchester P'dilly a.		...	0709	0808	0808	...	...	0915	1015	...

	⑥	⚒ C	⚒ M	⚒	⚒ M	Ⓐ C	⑥ P	⚒	Ⓐ M	⑥ M	⚒ C	⚒	⚒ M	Ⓐ C	⑥	⚒	⚒ M	Ⓐ f	⑥	⚒ C	⚒	⚒ M	Ⓐ C	⑥ C	Ⓐ	⑥ L
Cardiff Central d.	0720	0750	0850	0920	0950	1050	1050	1120	1150	1150	1250	1320	1350	1450	1450	1520	1550	1615	1619	1650	1720	1750	1850	1850	1934	1934
Newport d.	0734	0805	0905	0934	1005	1105	1105	1134	1205	1205	1305	1334	1405	1505	1505	1534	1605	1629	1634	1705	1734	1805	1906	1905	1948	1948
Cwmbrân d.	0745	0815	0915	0945	1015	1115	1115	1145	1215	1215	1315	1345	1415	1515	1515	1544	1615	1639	1644	1715	1745	1815	1916	1915	1958	1958
Pontypool & New Inn d.	0749	|	|	0949	|	|	|	1150	|	|	|	1350	|	|	|	1549	1621	|	1650	|	1749	1821	|	|	2003	2003
Abergavenny d.	0800	0828	0928	1000	1028	1128	1128	1201	1228	1232	1328	1401	1428	1528	1528	1559	1630	1655	1703	1728	1800	1830	1932	1928	2012	2013
Hereford d.	0828	0855	0955	1028	1055	1155	1155	1228	1255	1258	1355	1428	1455	1555	1555	1628	1656	|	...	1755	1828	1857	1958	1955	2039	2039
Leominster d.	|	0908	1008	|	1108	1208	1208	|	1308	1311	1408	|	1508	1608	1608	|	1708	|	...	1808	1841	1908	2011	2008	2053	2052
Ludlow d.	0849	0919	1019	1049	1119	1219	1219	1249	1319	1322	1419	1449	1519	1619	1619	1649	1719	|	...	1819	1852	1919	2022	2019	2104	2103
Craven Arms 146 d.	|	0928	1028	|	1128	1228	1228	|	1328	1328	1428	|	1528	1628	|	|	1728	|	...	1828	|	1928	2028	2028	2112	2112
Church Stretton 146 d.	|	0937	1037	|	1137	1237	1237	|	1337	1347	1437	|	1537	|	|	|	1737	|	...	1837	|	1937	2037	2037	2121	2121
Shrewsbury 146 a.	0915	0951	1051	1115	1151	1251	1254	1315	1351	1354	1451	1515	1551	1650	1645	1715	1753	1808	...	1851	1918	1953	2054	2051	2137	2135
Shrewsbury ‡ d.	0924	0953	1053	1124	1153	1253	1255	1324	1353	1355	1453	1524	1553	1652	1648	1724	1754	1809	...	1853	1924	1955	2055	2053	2139	2137
Whitchurch ‡ d.	|	|	|	|	|	|	|	|	|	|	|	|	|	|	1709	|	|	|	...	|	|	|	|	|	|	|
Crewe ‡ a.	|	1026	1125	|	1225	1325	1326	|	1426	1426	1525	|	1626	1726	1725	|	1825	1845	...	1925	|	2026	2126	2127	|	|
Chester **145 165** a.	1019	|	|	1219	|	|	|	1420	|	|	|	1621	|	|	|	1821	|	1909	...	|	2020	|	|	|	2234	2231
Holyhead **165** a.	1211	|	|	1414	|	|	|	1614	|	|	|	1819	|	|	|	2016	|	2049	...	|	2219	|	|	|	0055	...
Stockport a.	...	1058	1158	...	1258	1358	1358	...	1458	1458	1558	...	1658	1758	1758	...	1858	...	...	1958	...	2058	2158	2158	...	...
Manchester P'dilly a.	...	1115	1215	...	1315	1415	1415	...	1515	1515	1615	...	1715	1815	1815	...	1915	...	...	2015	...	2115	2215	2215	...	...

	⚒	⚒ C	⑥ Ma	Ⓐ			⑦ A	⑦ B	⑦	⑦	⑦	⑦	⑦ D	⑦	⑦ E	⑦	⑦	⑦ M	⑦	⑦	⑦ M	⑦	⑦	⑦ C		⑦ P
Cardiff Central d.	2010	2053	2149	2155	...	⑦	...	...	0830	0935	1040	1145	1245	1345	1500	1520	1600	1645	1720	1740	1845	1945	...	2040	...	2250
Newport d.	2026	2110	2207	2213	...		...	...	0849	0950	1054	1159	1259	1359	1514	1534	1614	1659	1734	1754	1859	2000	...	2055	...	2310
Cwmbrân d.	2036	2121	2219	2223	...		...	...	0859	1000	1104	1209	1309	1409	1525	1544	1625	1709	1744	1804	1909	2010	...	2105	...	2319
Pontypool & New Inn d.	2042	|	2224	2229	...		...	...	0905	1006	1110	1215	|	1415	|	1549	|	1715	|	1810	|	2016	...	2111	...	2325
Abergavenny d.	2051	2134	2134	2239	...		...	...	0914	1016	1119	1224	1322	1424	1538	1600	1638	1724	1758	1820	1922	2026	...	2121	...	2335
Hereford d.	2117	2200	2258	2307	...		...	...	0943	1043	1152	1258	1355	1450	1604	1626	1704	1753	1824	1849	1949	2054	...	2149	...	0004
Leominster d.	2131	2214	...	2320	...		...	...	0957	1056	1205	1311	1408	1504	|	1639	|	1807	|	1903	2003	2108	...	2202	...	...
Ludlow d.	2142	2225	...	2332	...		...	...	1008	1107	1216	1322	1419	1515	1625	1650	1726	1818	1845	1914	2014	2119	...	2214	...	...
Craven Arms 146 d.	2150	2234	...	2341	...		...	...	1016	|	1225	|	1428	|	|	1700	|	1826	|	|	2022	2129	...	2223	...	...
Church Stretton 146 d.	2202	2242	...	2351	...		...	...	1025	|	1234	|	1437	|	|	1709	|	1835	|	|	2031	2138	...	2233	...	...
Shrewsbury 146 a.	2217	2256	...	0006	...		...	...	1039	1133	1250	1348	1451	1541	1651	1723	1752	1849	1911	1940	2045	2155	...	2248	...	...
Shrewsbury ‡ d.	2219	2301	...	0007	...		0955	0955	1041	1136	1252	1351	1453	1542	1653	1730	1754	1851	1932	1941	2048	...	2232	2254	...	...
Whitchurch ‡ d.	2243	2325	...	0032	...		|	|	1101	1202	|	|	|	1608	|	|	|	|	|	2006	|	...	|	2320	...	...
Crewe ‡ a.	2304	2353	...	0100	...		1026	1031	1121	1225	1326	1425	1525	1629	1725	|	1825	1922	|	2027	2121	...	2302	2347	...	...
Chester **145 165** a.	|	0027	...	...	...		|	|	|	|	|	|	|	|	|	1825	|	|	2031	|	|	...	2326	...	...	...
Holyhead **165** a.	|	...	...	...	...		|	|	|	|	|	|	|	|	|	2020	|	|	2238	|	|	...	...	...	...	...
Stockport a.	2332	...	...	...	...		1058	1100	1140	1258	1358	1458	1558	1658	1758	...	1858	1958	...	2057	2158	...	...	...	...	...
Manchester P'dilly a.	2348	...	...	...	...		1115	1115	1202	1315	1415	1615	1615	1715	1815	...	1915	2015	...	2114	2215	...	...	...	...	...

A – Jul. 19 - Sept. 13.
B – May 17 - Jul. 12.
C – To / from Carmarthen.
D – May 17 - Sept. 6 from Milford Haven; Sept. 13 - Dec. 12 from Carmarthen.
E – May 17 - Sept. 6 from Milford Haven; Sept. 13 - Dec. 12 from Carmarthen.
F – To Fishguard Harbour.
L – To / from Llandudno Junction.
M – To / from Milford Haven.
P – To / from Pembroke Dock.
W – To Haverfordwest.
a – Jul. 12 - Dec. 12.
b – 0622 on Ⓐ.
c – May 23 - Jul. 11.
d – Jul. 18 - Dec. 12.
f – Conveys [1].
e – Sept. 13 - Dec. 12., departs 1130.
r – 4–8 minutes later on ⑥.
t – 0820 on ⑥.
‡ – Additional services operate between these stations.
***** – By 🚌.

NT, TP MANCHESTER - PRESTON - BLACKPOOL and BARROW 156

Services on ⑦ valid until September 6. 1st class not available on *NT* services.

km		NT ⒶC	TP ⚒	TP ⒶE	TP ⚒Z	TP ⚒	TP ⚒E	NT ⚒C	TP ⑦	TP ⚒	NT Ⓐ	TP ⚒W	TP ⑦	TP Ⓐ	TP ⑥G	TP ⑦	TP ⚒	TP ⑥	TP ⚒	TP ⑦	TP ⑦G	TP ⚒B	NT ⑥C	NT Ⓐ	TP ⚒	TP ⑦
0	**Manchester** Airport d.	...	0529	*0537*	0618	0700	0728	...	0755	0800	...	0825	0830	0900	0900	0900	0900	...	0929	0930	0930	1000	...	...	1029	1029
16	**Manchester** P'dilly d.	...	0546	0603	0633	0715	0745	...	0811	0815	...	0846	0846	0916	0916	0916	0916	...	0946	0946	0946	1016	...	...	1046	1043
34	Bolton d.	...	0602	0619	0650	0731	0759	...	0830	0832	...	0907	0905	0933	0933	0933	0933	...	1007	1005	1005	1033	...	...	1107	1105
66	**Preston** d.	0522	0634	0644	0720	0759	0824	0838t	0857	0859	...	0945	0934	1000	0958	1000	1008	1004	1038	1034	1039	1058	...	...	1138	1134
94	**Blackpool** North a.	|	0703	|	|	0829	|	|	0925	0925	...	|	1000	|	|	|	1035	|	1105	1100	|	|	...	...	1205	1200
100	Lancaster d.	0542	...	0701	0736	...	0840	0858t	...	...	0939	1001	...	1016	1014	1016	...	1020	...	...	1055	1114	1128	1131	...	...
	Oxenholme a.	|	...	0715	|	...	0854	|	...	...	|	1017	...	|	1028	|	...	|	...	...	1109	1128	|	|	...	...
110	Carnforth d.	0552	...	...	0745	...	...	0908t	...	...	0949	...	...	1025	...	1024	...	1029	...	...	...	...	1137	1141	...	...
119	Arnside d.	0603	...	...	0755	...	...	0919t	...	...	1000	...	...	1034	...	1034	...	1037	...	...	...	...	1148	1152	...	...
124	Grange over Sands d.	0609	...	...	0800	...	...	0925t	...	...	1006	...	...	1039	...	1040	...	1043	...	...	...	...	1154	1158	...	...
140	Ulverston d.	0625	...	...	0816	...	...	0941t	...	...	1023	...	...	1052	...	1056	...	1055	...	...	...	...	1210	1215	...	...
156	**Barrow in Furness** a.	0647	...	...	0839	...	...	1003t	...	...	1047	...	...	1112	...	1119	...	1115	...	...	...	...	1232	1239	...	...

	TP ⚒	TP ⑦	TP ⚒	TP ⑦	TP E	NT ⚒D	TP ⚒	TP ⑦	TP Ⓐ	TP ⑦	TP ⑥G	TP ⑦G	NT ⑥C	TP ⚒	TP ⑥	TP ⑦	TP ⑥E	TP ⑦E	TP ⒶE	TP ⒶWa	NT ⒶC	TP ⚒	TP ⑦	TP ⚒	TP ⑦	NT ⚒M
Manchester Airport d.	1100	1100	1129	1130	1200	...	1229	1230	1300	1300	1300	1300	...	1329	1329	1330	1400	1400	1400	1400	...	1429	1430	1500	1500	...
Manchester P'dilly d.	1116	1116	1146	1146	1216	...	1246	1246	1316	1316	1316	1316	...	1346	1346	1346	1416	1416	1416	1416	...	1446	1446	1516	1516	...
Bolton d.	1133	1133	1207	1205	1233	...	1307	1305	1333	1333	1333	1333	...	1407	1407	1405	1433	1433	1433	1433	...	1507	1505	1533	1533	...
Preston d.	1158	1202	1238	1234	1258	...	1338	1334	1358	1405	1358	1401	...	1438	1445	1434	1458	1500	1458	1504	...	1538	1534	1558	1600	...
Blackpool North a.	|	|	1305	1300	|	...	1405	1400	|	|	|	|	...	1505	|	1500	|	|	|	|	...	1605	1600	|	|	...
Lancaster d.	1214	1218	...	...	1314	1332	...	...	1414	1421	1414	1416	1422	...	1501	...	1514	1516	1514	1520	1533	...	...	1614	1616	1654t
Oxenholme a.	|	|	...	...	1328	|	...	...	|	|	1428	1430	|	...	|	...	1528	1530	...	1537	|	...	...	|	|	|
Carnforth d.	1223	1226	...	...	...	1341	...	...	1423	1430	...	...	1432	...	1509	...	...	...	...	...	1543	...	...	1622	1624	1705t
Arnside d.	1231	1236	...	...	...	1352	...	...	1431	1440	...	...	1442	...	1518	...	...	...	...	...	1554	...	...	1632	1634	1716t
Grange over Sands d.	1237	1242	...	...	...	1358	...	...	1437	1445	...	...	1448	...	1523	...	...	...	...	...	1600	...	...	1638	1640	1722t
Ulverston d.	1249	1258	...	...	...	1414	...	...	1449	1501	...	...	1505	...	1536	...	...	...	...	...	1617	...	...	1654	1656	1739t
Barrow in Furness a.	1310	1321	...	...	...	1438	...	...	1510	1524	...	...	1526	...	1556	...	...	...	...	...	1639	...	...	1718	1719	1802t

	TP ⚒	TP ⑦	NT Ⓐ	TP ⚒WY	TP ⑦WY	NT ⑥	NT Ⓐ	TP ⚒	TP ⑦	TP ⑦G	TP ⑥	TP Ⓐ	TP ⑦	TP ⚒	TP ⑦	TP ⑥⑦F	TP ⒶY	TP ⑥	TP ⚒	TP ⑦	TP ⚒	TP ⑦	TP ⚒	TP ⑦	TP ⚒	TP ⚒
Manchester Airport d.	1529	1530	...	1600	1600	...	...	1629	1630	1700	1700	1700	1700	1727	1730	1800	1800	...	1829	1830	1900	1900	1929	1930	2000	2029
Manchester P'dilly d.	1546	1546	...	1616	1616	...	1627	1646	1646	1716	1715	1715	1716	1746	1746	1816	1816	...	1846	1846	1916	1916	1946	1946	2016	2046
Bolton d.	1607	1605	...	1633	1633	...	1649	1706	1705	1733	1732	1732	1733	1807	1805	1833	1833	...	1907	1905	1933	1933	2007	2005	2033	2107
Preston d.	1638	1634	...	1704	1706	...	1728	1732	1734	1802	1758	1758	1806	1840	1834	1900	1904	1904	1938	1934	1958	2000	2038	2034	2058	2138
Blackpool North a.	1707	1700	...	|	|	...	|	1802	1800	|	|	|	|	1909	1900	|	|	|	2005	2000	|	|	2106	2100	|	2206
Lancaster d.	...	...	1719	1721	1722	1732	1748	...	...	1818	1814	1825	1822	...	...	1916	1920	1920	...	...	2014t	2016	...	...	2114t	...
Oxenholme a.	...	...	|	1741	1738	|	|	...	...	1832	|	|	|	...	...	1930	|	|	...	...	|	|	...	...	|	...
Carnforth d.	...	...	1728	...	...	1743	1800	...	...	...	1824	1835	1831	...	...	...	1929	1929	...	...	2022t	2024	...	...	2122t	...
Arnside d.	...	...	1740	...	...	1753	1811	...	...	...	1834	1845	1841	...	...	...	1939	1939	...	...	2032t	2034	...	...	2132t	...
Grange over Sands d.	...	...	1746	...	...	1759	1819	...	...	...	1840	1851	1846	...	...	...	1944	1944	...	...	2038t	2040	...	...	2138t	...
Ulverston d.	...	...	1802	...	...	1816	1836	...	...	...	1856	1907	1902	...	...	...	2000	2000	...	...	2054t	2056	...	...	2154t	...
Barrow in Furness a.	...	...	1825	...	...	1838	1859	...	...	...	1919	1930	1926	...	...	...	2024	2024	...	...	2117t	2119	...	...	2217t	...

	TP ⑦	NT ⑦	NT Ⓐ	NT ⑥	TP ⚒	TP ⑦	NT ⑥	TP Ⓐ	TP ⚒	TP ⑦
Manchester Airport d.	2030	...	...	...	2129	2130	2200	2200	2229	2230
Manchester P'dilly d.	2046	...	...	...	2146	2146	2216	2216	2246	2246
Bolton d.	2105	...	...	...	2207	2205	2233	2233	2307	2305
Preston d.	2134	...	2151	2159	2235	2234	2255	2313	2335	2347
Blackpool North a.	2200	...	|	|	2301	2300	|	|	0001	0014
Lancaster d.	...	2205	2211	2219	...	...	2311	2329	...	...
Oxenholme a.	...	|	|	|	...	...	|	|	...	...
Carnforth d.	...	2215	2221	2229	...	...	2320	2337	...	...
Arnside d.	...	2226	2232	2240	...	...	2330	2347	...	...
Grange over Sands d.	...	2232	2238	2246	...	...	2335	2353	...	...
Ulverston d.	...	2248	2254	2302	...	...	2351	0009	...	...
Barrow in Furness a.	...	2310	2316	2324	...	...	0015	0032	...	...

	TP ⚒	TP ⚒	TP ⚒	TP ⚒	TP ⚒	TP Ⓐ	TP ⒶE	TP ⑦	TP ⚒	NT ⒶM	TP Ⓐ
Barrow in Furness d.	0435	...	0531	...	0619	...	...	...	...	0700	0728
Ulverston d.	0450	...	0546	...	0638	...	...	...	...	0719	0745
Grange over Sands d.	0503	...	0559	...	0654	...	...	...	...	0736	0800
Arnside d.	0510	...	0606	...	0700	...	...	...	...	0743	0806
Carnforth d.	0520	...	0616	...	0712	...	...	...	...	0754	0818
Oxenholme d.	0528	...	|	...	|	...	...	...	...	|	|
Lancaster d.	...	...	0626	...	0722	...	0747	0748	...	0804	0826
Blackpool North d.	...	0545	|	0634	|	0710	|	|	0736d	|	|
Preston d.	...	0610	0647	0703	0747	0747	0812	0814	0812	0829	0847
Bolton d.	...	0635	0708	0735	0808	0808	0835	0837	0835	...	0908
Manchester P'dilly a.	...	0656	0727	0756	0827	0827	0856	0859	0856	...	0927
Manchester Airport a.	...	0717	0747	0817	0847	0847	0919	0919	0919	...	0947

	TP ⑦	TP ⚒	NT Ⓐ	TP ⚒G	NT ⑥	TP	TP	TP	NT ⚒	TP ⚒W	TP ⑥E	TP ⑥	TP	TP ⑦	TP ⚒	TP ⑥G	TP ⒶA	TP ⑦	TP ⚒	NT ⚒C	TP ⚒W	TP ⑦E	TP	TP ⑦	TP ⚒a	TP ⚒b
Barrow in Furness d.	...	...	0800	...	0825	...	0923	...	1016	...	...	...	...	1115	1125	...	...	...	...	1211	...	...	...	1322	1325	1325
Ulverston d.	...	...	0819	...	0844	...	0942	...	1034	...	...	...	...	1134	1140	...	...	...	...	1229	...	...	...	1341	1340	1340
Grange over Sands d.	...	...	0936	...	0902	...	0958	...	1051	...	...	...	...	1150	1153	...	...	...	...	1245	...	...	...	1357	1353	1353
Arnside d.	...	...	0843	...	0908	...	1004	...	1057	...	...	...	...	1156	1200	...	...	...	...	1251	...	...	...	1403	1400	1400
Carnforth d.	...	...	0854	...	0920	...	1016	...	1108	...	...	...	...	1208	1209	...	...	...	...	1302	...	...	...	1415	1409	1409
Oxenholme d.	...	...	|	0911	|	...	|	...	|	1110	1131	...	...	|	|	1207	1211	...	...	|	1309	1310	...	|	|	|
Lancaster d.	...	...	0907	0926	0933	...	1026	...	1120	1126	1146	...	...	1219	1218	1223	1226	...	...	1315	1326	1326	...	1525	1418	1418
Blackpool North d.	0844	0845	...	|	...	0944	|	1044	...	|	|	1132	1144	|	|	|	|	1244	1245	...	|	|	1344	|	|	|
Preston d.	0910	0910	...	0947	...	1010	1047	1110	...	1147	1210	1210	1210	1247	1237	1247	1247	1310	1310	...	1347	1347	1410	1447	1447	1437
Bolton d.	0935	0935	...	1008	...	1035	1108	1135	...	1208	1235	1235	1235	1308	...	1308	1308	1335	1335	...	1408	1408	1435	1508	1508	...
Manchester P'dilly a.	0957	0956	...	1027	...	1056	1127	1157	...	1227	1256	1256	1257	1327	...	1327	1327	1357	1356	...	1427	1427	1457	1527	1527	...
Manchester Airport a.	1013	1017	...	1047	...	1117	1147	1217	...	1247	1317	1317	1317	1347	...	1347	1347	1417	1417	...	1447	1447	1517	1547	1547	...

	TP ⚒E	TP ⑦	TP ⚒	NT ⚒	TP ⒶW	TP ⑥G	TP ⑦E	TP ⑦	TP ⚒	NT ⑥C	TP ⑦	TP ⑥E	TP ⒶY	TP ⚒	TP ⑦	TP ⑥	TP ⑦	TP ⑦G	TP ⑥	TP Ⓐ	NT Ⓐ	TP ⑦W	TP ⑦	TP ⚒W	TP ⒶW	TP ⑥
Barrow in Furness d.	...	...	...	1416	...	...	...	...	...	1518	1522	...	1525	...	...	1622	1625	...	...	...	1620	...	...	...	1721	1721
Ulverston d.	...	...	...	1435	...	...	...	...	...	1536	1541	...	1540	...	...	1637	1640	...	...	...	1638	...	...	...	1738	1738
Grange over Sands d.	...	...	...	1451	...	...	...	...	...	1553	1557	...	1553	...	...	1650	1653	...	...	...	1650	...	...	...	1753	1753
Arnside d.	...	...	...	1457	...	...	...	...	...	1559	1603	...	1600	...	...	1657	1700	...	...	...	1654	...	...	...	1759	1759
Carnforth d.	...	...	...	1508	...	...	...	...	...	1610	1615	...	1609	...	...	1706	1709	...	...	...	1711	...	...	...	1809	1809
Oxenholme d.	1406c	...	...	|	1509	1509	1510	...	...	|	|	1608	|	...	...	|	|	1708	...	...	|	1716	...	1730	|	|
Lancaster d.	|	...	...	1521	1526	1526	1525	...	...	1623	1625	1626	1618	...	...	1715	1718	1723	...	...	1725	1733	...	1748	1820	1817
Blackpool North d.	|	1444	1445	...	|	|	|	1544	1545	...	|	|	|	1641	1644	|	|	|	1711	1720	...	|	1740	|	...	|
Preston d.	1447	1510	1510	...	1547	1547	1547	1610	1610	...	1647	1647	1647	1710	1710	1747	1747	1747	1747	1747	...	1810	1810	1808	...	1836
Bolton d.	1508	1535	1535	...	1608	1608	1608	1635	1635	...	1708	1708	1708	1735	1735	1808	1808	1808	1808	1808	...	1835	1835	1835	...	...
Manchester P'dilly a.	1527	1557	1556	...	1627	1627	1627	1657	1656	...	1727	1727	1727	1756	1757	1827	1827	1827	1827	1827	...	1857	1857	1856	...	...
Manchester Airport a.	1547	1617	1617	...	1647	1647	1647	1717	1717	...	1747	1748	1748	1817	1817	1847	1847	1847	1847	1847	...	1917	1917	1917	...	...

	TP ⑦E	TP ⚒E	NT Ⓐ	TP ⑦	TP ⚒	TP ⒶW	NT ⚒C	TP ⑦	TP ⑦G	TP ⑥G	TP ⑦	TP ⚒	TP ⑦E	TP ⚒E	TP ⑦	TP ⚒	TP ⑥	NT ⑦	TP Ⓐ	TP ⚒	TP ⑦	TP ⑦E	TP ⒶE	TP ⚒	NT ⚒	TP ⑦
Barrow in Furness d.	...	...	1743	...	...	...	1803	1815	...	...	...	...	...	...	...	...	1942	2002	2007	...	...	...	...	...	2143	...
Ulverston d.	...	...	1759	...	...	...	1821	1834	...	...	...	...	...	...	...	...	2001	2021	2026	...	...	...	...	...	2201	...
Grange over Sands d.	...	...	|	...	...	...	1837	1850	...	...	...	...	...	...	...	...	2017	2037	2042	...	...	...	...	...	2217	...
Arnside d.	...	...	|	...	...	...	1843	1856	...	...	...	...	...	...	...	...	2023	2043	2048	...	...	...	...	...	2223	...
Carnforth d.	...	...	1823	...	...	...	1854	1907	...	...	...	...	...	...	...	...	2037	2054	2101	...	...	...	...	...	2234	...
Oxenholme d.	1810	...	|	...	...	1833	|	|	1907	1908	...	...	2010	2012	...	...	|	|	|	...	...	...	2212	...	|	...
Lancaster d.	1826	1826	1838	...	...	1850	1905	1917	1922	1926	...	...	2026	2026	...	...	2045	2107	2111	...	...	2203	2226	...	2245	...
Blackpool North d.	|	|	...	1844	1845	|	|	|	|	|	1944	1945	|	|	2044	2045	|	...	|	2145	2156	|	|	2245	|	2300
Preston d.	1847	1847	...	1910	1910	1913	1930	1947	1947	1947	2010	2010	2047	2047	2110	2111	2115	...	2131	2210	2229	2229	2247	2310	2310	2328
Bolton d.	1908	1908	...	1935	1935	1940	...	2008	2008	2008	2035	2035	2108	2108	2135	2135	2139	...	|	2235	2251	2251	|	2335	...	2359
Manchester P'dilly a.	1927	1927	...	1957	1956	2002	...	2027	2027	2027	2057	2056	2127	2127	2157	2156	2202	...	2230	2256	2314	2314	2344	2353	...	0015
Manchester Airport a.	1947	1950	...	2017	2017	2024	...	2047	2047	2047	2117	2117	2147	2147	2217	2217	2257	...	2247	2317	2330	2330	...	0022	...	0030

A – From Edinburgh and Glasgow.
B – To Glasgow on Ⓐ, to Edinburgh on ⑥.
C – To Carlisle.
D – To Carlisle on ⑥.
E – To / from Edinburgh.
F – To Glasgow on ⑥, to Edinburgh on ⑦.
G – To / from Glasgow.
M – To / from Millom.
W – To / from Windermere.
Y – Conveys 12 Manchester Airport - Edinburgh and v.v.
Z – Conveys 12 Manchester Airport - Glasgow and v.v.
a – May 18 - Jun. 20 and Sept. 7 - Dec. 12.
b – Jun. 22 - Sept. 4.
c – 1410 on Ⓐ.
d – 0744 on ⑥.
t – 3–6 minutes later on ⑥.
u – Calls to pick up only.

157 PRESTON - OXENHOLME - WINDERMERE TP

km		⚒	⚒b	⚒	⚒	⚒	⚒	⚒	⚒	⚒	Ⓐ	⑥	⚒	⚒	⑥	Ⓐ	⑥	Ⓐ	⚒	⑥	Ⓐ	⚒	Ⓐ	⑦	⑦c	⑦d
	Manchester Airport **156** d.		...	...	...	...	0825	...	...	...	...	...	...	...	1600	1600	...	...	...	...	...	...	...		...	...
0	**Preston** d.		...	...	...	...	0945	1104	...	1304	...	...	1504a	...	1704	1705	...	...	...	...	...	...	...		1005	1045
34	Lancaster d.		0545	...	...	...	1001	1120	...	1320	...	...	1520a	...	1721	1725	...	1829	...	...	...	...	...		1021	1101
68	**Oxenholme** d.		0621	0721	0827	0914	1018	1137	1228	1337	1424	1433	1538	1628	1738	1742	1830	1846	1937	2023	2027	2115	2220		1038	1118
72	Kendal d.		0625	0725	0831	0918	1022	1141	1232	1341	1428	1437	1543	1632	1742	1747	1834	1850	1941	2027	2031	2119	2224		1042	1122
84	**Windermere** a.		0641	0740	0846	0933	1039	1156	1247	1356	1444	1452	1600	1648	1800	1804	1849	1908	1956	2042	2046	2134	2239		1100	1140

	⑦c	⑦	⑦		⑦	⑦c	⑦	⑦	⑦	⑦
Manchester Airport **156** d.	...	...	...	and	...	1600	...	...	...	...
Preston d.	...	...	...	hourly	...	1706	...	...	...	...
Lancaster d.	...	...	...	until	...	1722	...	...	...	...
Oxenholme d.	1133	1233	1333		1633	1739	1739	1837	1929	2033
Kendal d.	1137	1237	1337		1637	1744	1744	1841	1933	2037
Windermere a.	1152	1252	1352		1652	1802	1802	1856	1945	2052

	⚒	⚒	⚒	⚒	⚒	⚒	⚒	⚒	⚒	Ⓐ
Windermere d.		0650	0757	0850	0941	1049	1159	1251	1400	1448
Kendal d.		0704	0811	0901	0955	1103	1213	1302	1414	1502
Oxenholme a.		0709	0816	0906	1000	1108	1218	1307	1419	1507
Lancaster a.		...	...	...	1018	1125	...	1326	...	1526
Preston a.		...	...	...	1037	1145	...	1345	...	1545
Manchester Airport **156** a.		...	...	...	...	1247	...	1447	...	1647

	⑥	⚒	⚒	⑥	Ⓐ	⑥	Ⓐ	⚒	⑥	Ⓐ	Ⓐ	⑥	Ⓐ		⑦	⑦c	⑦	⑦		⑦c	⑦d	⑦	⑦	⑦	⑦
Windermere d.	1459	1602	1706	1802	1812	1900	1910	2000	2047	2050	2140	2140	2245	...		1102	1158	1258	and	1658	1658	1804	1900	1950	2100
Kendal d.	1513	1614	1720	1816	1826	1914	1921	2014	2058	2104	2154	2154	2259	...		1116	1212	1312	hourly	1709	1712	1818	1914	2001	2114
Oxenholme a.	1518	1619	1725	1821	1831	1919	1927	2019	2104	2109	2159	2159	2304	...		1121	1218	1317	until	1715	1717	1823	1919	2006	2119
Lancaster a.	...	...	1747	...	1849	...	...	...	...	...	...	2217	2323	...		...	...	...		1732	...	...	...	...	2137
Preston a.	...	...	1806	...	1910	...	...	...	...	...	...	2238	...	...		...	...	...		1751	...	...	...	...	2158
Manchester Airport **156** a.	...	...	1917	...	2024	...	...	...	...	...	...	...	...	...		...	...	...		1917	...	...	...	...	...

a – Ⓐ only.
b – Via Morcambe (depart 0558).
c – May 17 - Sept. 6.
d – Sept. 13 - Dec. 12.

158 BARROW - WHITEHAVEN - CARLISLE 2nd class NT

km		⚒	⑥	Ⓐ	Ⓐ P	⑥	⚒	Ⓐ	⑥	⑥	Ⓐ	⚒ P	Ⓐ	⑥	⑥	⑦	Ⓐ	Ⓐ	⑥	Ⓐ	⑥	⑥	Ⓐ	⑦	⑥	Ⓐ
	Lancaster **156** d.	...	...	...	0542	...	...	...	...	...	...	0858	...	...	...	...	...	...	1128	...	...	1332	...	...	1422	1533
0	**Barrow in Furness** d.	...	0600	0600	0650	0705	0801	...	...	0907	0910	1011	1119	1122	...	...	...	1231	1234	1331	1350	1450	1454	...	1533	1641
26	Millom d.	...	0626	0629	0719	0734	0829	...	...	0935	0938	1039	1147	1150	...	...	...	1259	1302	1358	1418	1518	1522	...	1601	1709
47	Ravenglass ‡ 🚂 d.	...	0642	0647	0737	0752	0844	...	...	0952	0955	1056	1204	1207	...	...	...	1315	1319	1415	1435	1535	1539	...	1618	1726
56	Sellafield d.	...	0655	0702	0751	0806	0858	...	...	1004	1010	1110	1215	1219	...	...	...	1328	1331	1427	1447	1551	1551	...	1630	1739
74	**Whitehaven** d.	0630	0717	0725	0811	0826	...	0902	0915	1024	1028	1129	1235	1239	1254	1257	1305	1347	1351	1448	1506	1611	1611	1628	1656	1758
85	Workington d.	0648	0736	0743	0829	0844	...	0920	0933	1042	1046	1147	1253	...	1312	1315	1322	1405	1409	1506	1524	1629	1629	1646	1714	1816
92	Maryport d.	0656	0744	0751	0837	0852	...	0928	0941	1050	1054	1155	1301	...	1320	1323	1330	1413	1417	1514	1532	1637	1637	1654	1722	1826
119	Wigton d.	0715	0803	0811	0857	0912	...	0947	1000	1109	1113	1214	1321	...	1339	1342	1350	1432	1436	1533	1552	1657	1657	1713	1742	1846
138	**Carlisle** a.	0738	0826	0834	0921	0936	...	1013	1024	1134	1137	1239	1345	...	1404	1407	1411	1457	1501	1558	1616	1721	1721	1737	1806	1908

	⑥	Ⓐ	Ⓐ	⚒	⑦	⑥	⚒	⑥	Ⓐ	⚒
Lancaster **156** d.	...	...	1654	...	...	1659	...	...	...	...
Barrow in Furness d.	1725	1728	1805	...	...	1810	...	1930	1935	2125
Millom d.	1753	1758	1835	...	...	1840	...	2000	2005	2155
Ravenglass ‡ 🚂 d.	1810	1815	...	...	...	...	...	...	...	—
Sellafield d.	1822	1827	...	...	...	...	...	...	...	Ⓐ
Whitehaven d.	1843	1855	...	1931	2028	...	2030	...	...	2150
Workington d.	1901	1912	...	1949	2046	...	2048	...	...	2210
Maryport d.	1909	1920	...	1957	2054	...	2056	...	...	...
Wigton d.	1928	1940	...	2016	2113	...	2115	...	...	...
Carlisle a.	1953	2004	...	2041	2138	...	2139	...	...	...

	Ⓐ P	⑥	Ⓐ		⑥	Ⓐ	⚒	⚒		⑥	Ⓐ
Carlisle d.	...	...	...	...	...	...	0744	...	...	0837	0844
Wigton d.	...	...	...	...	...	...	0801	...	...	0854	0901
Maryport d.	...	...	0600	...	0626	...	0821	...	...	0914	0921
Workington d.	...	...	0609	...	0637	...	0833	...	...	0926	0933
Whitehaven d.	...	...	0628	...	0657	0728	0854	...	...	0945	0952
Sellafield d.	...	...	0648	...	0722	0748	...	0907	...	1003	1011
Ravenglass ‡ 🚂 d.	...	...	0657	...	0732	0757	...	0916	...	1013	1020
Millom d.	0610	0610	0717	...	0751	0815	...	0936	...	1032	1040
Barrow in Furness a.	0642	0642	0749	...	0824	0849	...	1007	...	1107	1114
Lancaster **156** a.	0803	...	0907	...	0933	...	...	1120	...	...	...

	⚒	⚒		⑥	⑥		Ⓐ	Ⓐ	⑥	Ⓐ	⑥	⑦	Ⓐ P	⑥ P	⑥	Ⓐ		Ⓐ	⑥	⚒	⑥⑦	Ⓐ	⑥	Ⓐ	⑥	Ⓑ
Carlisle d.	0940	1043	...	1139	...	...	1149	1247	1248	1420	1421	1500	1512	1525	1630	1631	...	1727	1740	1811	1900	1915	2005	2033	2145	2150
Wigton d.	0957	1100	...	1156	...	...	1206	1304	1305	1437	1438	1517	1529	1542	1647	1648	...	1744	1757	1828	1917	1932	2022	2050	2202	2207
Maryport d.	1017	1120	...	1216	...	...	1226	1324	1325	1457	1458	1537	1549	1602	1707	1708	...	1804	1817	1848	1937	1952	2042	2110	2222	2227
Workington d.	1029	1132	...	1228	...	...	1238	1336	1337	1509	1510	1549	1601	1614	1719	1720	...	1816	1829	1900	1949	2004	2054	2122	2234	2239
Whitehaven d.	1048	1151	...	1249	1254	...	1259	1356	1357	1528	1530	1610	1620	1634	1739	1739	...	1835	1848	1923	2010	2025	2115	2143	2255	2300
Sellafield d.	1108	1210	...	...	1312	...	...	1414	1415	1554	1550	...	1642	1653	1759	1803	...	1854	1906	—	...	...	...	—	...	...
Ravenglass ‡ 🚂 d.	1118	1220	...	...	1321	...	...	1423	1424	1604	1559	...	1652	1703	1808	1814	...	1903	1916	⚒	...	...	...	⚒	...	...
Millom d.	1137	1239	...	...	1341	...	...	1443	1444	1625	1619	...	1713	1722	1828	1834	...	1923	1936	2010	...	...	...	2202	...	...
Barrow in Furness a.	1209	1314	...	...	1413	...	...	1517	1516	1659	1653	...	1747	1755	1902	1910	...	1957	2010	2044	...	...	...	2235	...	...
Lancaster **156** a.	1315	...	...	...	1521	...	...	...	1623	...	...	...	1904	1904	...	...	...	...	...	...	...	...	...	...	...	...

P – From / to Preston.
‡ – Ravenglass for Eskdale.
🚂 – **RAVENGLASS - DALEGARTH**. Narrow gauge (0.381m). Services operate daily Mar. 21 - Oct. 25. Operator: Ravenglass and Eskdale Railway. ✆ (0)1229 717171. www.ravenglass-railway.co.uk

159 Sleeper trains LONDON - SCOTLAND SR

km		⑦ B	⑦ A	Ⓐ	⑦ A	⑦ B	⑤	①–④		
0	**London** Euston **150** d.	2007	2055	2115	2327	2232	2350	2350	...	...
28	Watford Junction **150** d.	|	2117	2133	2347	|	0010	0010	...	...
254	Crewe **150 152** d.	|	2342	2354	|	|	|	|	...	...
336	Preston **152** d.	|	0030	0052	|	|	|	|	...	...
481	Carlisle **152** a.	|	|	|	0504	|	0518	0511	...	...
625	Motherwell **152** a.	|	|	|	0701	0739	0700	0701	...	...
646	**Glasgow** Central **152** ◧ a.	|	|	|	0718	0757	0621	0718	...	...
646	**Edinburgh 152** ◧ a.	|	|	|	0720	0625	0713	0720	...	...
	Perth **221** a.	0539	0539	0539	...	...	...	...	...	...
	Dundee **224** a.	0608	0608	0608	...	...	...	...	...	...
	Aberdeen **224** ◧ a.	0735	0735	0735	...	...	...	...	...	...
	Inverness **221** a.	0830	0830	0830	...	...	...	...	...	...
	Fort William **218** a.	0954	0954	0954	...	...	...	...	...	...

	①–④	⑤	⑦ A	⑦ A	⑦ A	⑦ B	①–④	⑤	
Fort William **218** d.	...	...	...	...	1900	1900	1950	1950	...
Inverness **221** d.	...	...	...	...	2025	2025	2038	2038	...
Aberdeen **224** d.	...	...	...	...	2142	2142	2140	2140	...
Dundee **224** d.	...	...	...	...	2306	2306	2306	2306	...
Perth **221** d.	...	...	...	...	2300	2300	2321	2321	...
Edinburgh 152 d.	2340	2340	2315	2315	|	|	|	|	...
Glasgow Central **152** d.	2340	2340	2315	2140	|	|	|	|	...
Motherwell **152** d.	2356	2356	2331	2201	|	|	|	|	...
Carlisle **152** d.	0140	0140	0108	|	|	|	|	|	...
Preston **152** a.	|	|	|	|	0433	|	0432	0432	...
Crewe **150 152** a.	|	|	|	|	0537	|	0532	0524	...
Watford Junction **150** a.	0614	0627	0623	|	|	|	|	|	...
London Euston **150** ◧ a.	0637	0650	0646	0705	0747	0747	0747	0748	...

☛ All trains in this table convey 🛏 1, 2 cl., 🚃2 (reservation compulsory) and 🍷.
A – May 17 and Jul 12. - Dec. 6.
B – May 24 - July 5.
◧ – Sleeping-car passengers may occupy their cabins until 0800 following arrival at these stations.

160 PRESTON - LIVERPOOL 2nd class NT

km		⚒	⚒	⚒		Ⓐ	⑥	⑦		⚒	⑦		⚒	⑦		⚒	⑦		⚒	⑦		⚒	⑦
	Blackpool North **156 190** d.	...	0702	...	...	*0829*	0838	0850	...	0937	0950	and at	1937	1950	...	2038	2050	...	...	2150	...	2214	2244
0	**Preston 151 156 190** d.	*0616*	0730	*0758*	...	0904	0904	0915	...	1004	1015	the same	2004	2015	...	2104	2115	...	*2117*a	2215	...	2243	2309
24	Wigan North Western **151** ‡ d.	0638	0750	0828	...	0924	0924	0936	...	1024	1036	minutes past	2024	2036	...	2123	2136	...	2225	2236	...	2303	2330
38	St Helens Central ‡ d.	0656	0806	0846	...	0939	0939	0953	...	1039	1053	each hour	2039	2053	...	2141	2153	...	2243	2254	...	2321	2347
57	**Liverpool** Lime St ‡ a.	0728	0835	0918	...	1002	1002	1022	...	1102	1122	until	2102	2122	...	2214	2222	...	2315	2323	...	2354	0016

	⚒	⚒		⑦	⚒		⑦	⚒	⚒	⑦	⚒	Ⓐ	⑥	⑦	⚒	⑦	⚒	⑦	⚒	⑦	⑦		⚒
Liverpool Lime St ‡ d.	0657	0757	...	0831	0857	and at	1631	1657	1727	1731	1744	1801	1801	1831	1923	1931	2025	2031	2142	2131	2231	...	2302
St Helens Central ‡ d.	0715	0815	...	0858	0915	the same	1658	1715	1750	1758	1811	1830	1830	1858	1941	1958	2043	2058	2211	2158	2258	...	2331
Wigan North Western **151** ‡ d.	0731	0831	...	0914	0931	minutes past	1714	1731	1805	1814	1831	1849	1849	1914	1955	2014	2057	2114	2228	2214	2314	...	2348
Preston 151 156 190 a.	0756	0855	...	0937	0954	each hour	1737	1754	1831	1837	1854	1915	1915	1937	2018	2037	2122	2137	2254	2237	2335	...	0016
Blackpool North **156 190** a.	0818s	0920s	...	1007	1020	until	1807	1820	*1909*	1907	1920	*2000*	...	2007	2044	2107	2153	2207	2321	2307	0004	...	...

a – 2120 on ⑥. May 17 - Oct. 31.
s – ⑥ only.
‡ – Additional services operate Wigan - Liverpool and v.v.

GC SUNDERLAND - YORK - LONDON 161

km	Station	Ⓐ ✕		Ⓐ ✕		Ⓐ ✕		
0	**Sunderland** 211 d.	0641	...	1230	...	1730	...	...
29	Hartlepool 211 d.	0708	...	1254	...	1756	...	...
53	Eaglescliffe d.	0728	...	1316	...	1815	...	...
76	Northallerton 186 187 d.	0745	...	1338	...	1836	...	...
89	Thirsk 187 d.	0756	...	1347	...	1845	...	...
124	**York** 186 187 a.	0817	...	1407	...	1904	...	...
124	**York** 185 d.	0821	...	1410	...	1906	...	...
428	**London** Kings Cross 185 a.	1031	...	1605	...	2109	...	...

km	Station	⑥ 🍷		⑥ 🍷		⑥ 🍷		
0	**Sunderland** 211 d.	0653	...	1230	...	1730	...	...
29	Hartlepool 211 d.	0717	...	1254	...	1756	...	...
53	Eaglescliffe d.	0745	...	1313	...	1828	...	...
76	Northallerton 186 187 d.	0806	...	1331	...	1845	...	...
89	Thirsk 187 d.	0815	...	1342	...	1854	...	...
124	**York** 186 187 a.	0844	...	1403	...	1913	...	...
124	**York** 185 d.	0847	...	1405	...	1916	...	...
428	**London** Kings Cross 185 a.	1048	...	1604	...	2116	...	...

km	Station	⑦ 🍷		⑦ 🍷		⑦ 🍷	
0	**Sunderland** 211 d.	0910	...	1342	...	1842	...
29	Hartlepool 211 d.	0934	...	1406	...	1906	...
53	Eaglescliffe d.	0955	...	1434	...	1925	...
76	Northallerton 186 187 d.	1012	...	1453	...	1948	...
89	Thirsk 187 d.	1026	...	1506	...	1957	...
124	**York** 186 187 a.	1045	...	1528	...	2013	...
124	**York** 185 d.	1047	...	1531	...	2015	...
428	**London** Kings Cross 185 a.	1251	...	1724	...	2217	...

Station	Ⓐ ✕		Ⓐ ✕		Ⓐ ✕		
London Kings Cross 185 d.	0804	...	1127	...	1650	...	...
York 185 a.	1002	...	1319	...	1844	...	...
York 186 187 d.	1014	...	1322	...	1847	...	...
Thirsk 187 d.	1030	...	1338	...	1905	...	...
Northallerton 186 187 d.	1039	...	1347	...	1916	...	...
Eaglescliffe a.	1057	...	1404	...	1933	...	...
Hartlepool 211 a.	1120	...	1423	...	2000	...	...
Sunderland 211 a.	1150	...	1450	...	2035	...	...

Station	⑥ 🍷		⑥ 🍷		⑥ 🍷		
London Kings Cross 185 d.	0757	...	1127	...	1650	...	...
York 185 a.	0957	...	1325	...	1846	...	...
York 186 187 d.	1000	...	1330	...	1848	...	...
Thirsk 187 d.	1021	...	1351	...	1920	...	...
Northallerton 186 187 d.	1032	...	1409	...	1929	...	...
Eaglescliffe a.	1048	...	1426	...	1948	...	...
Hartlepool 211 a.	1120	...	1445	...	2007	...	...
Sunderland 211 a.	1150	...	1515	...	2034	...	...

Station	⑦ 🍷		⑦ 🍷		⑦ 🍷		
London Kings Cross 185 d.	0907	...	1345	...	1820	...	...
York 185 a.	1114	...	1551	...	2023	...	...
York 186 187 d.	1118	...	1554	...	2025	...	...
Thirsk 187 d.	1135	...	1610	...	2042	...	...
Northallerton 186 187 d.	1144	...	1620	...	2050	...	...
Eaglescliffe a.	1202	...	1639	...	2112	...	...
Hartlepool 211 a.	1221	...	1658	...	2136	...	...
Sunderland 211 a.	1251	...	1736	...	2206	...	...

2nd class MANCHESTER and LIVERPOOL local services 162

Manchester – Blackburn – Clitheroe

NT

km	⚒	⚒	⚒	⚒	⚒	⚒	⚒	⚒	and at	⚒	⚒	⚒	⚒	⚒	⚒	⚒	⚒		⚒	⚒	⚒	Ⓐ	⑥
0	**Manchester** Victoria d.	...	0555	0654p	0723	0800	0829	0900	the same	1500	1540	1623	1700	1723	1800	1823	1900	...	2000	2100	2200	2300	2305
17	Bolton d.	...	0612	0719	0742	0820	0849	0920	minutes past	1520	1600	1643	1720	1743	1820	1843	1920	...	2020	2120	2220	2320	2324
39	Blackburn d.	0625	0652	0747	0820	0852	0920	0952	each hour	1552	1631	1719	1753	1814	1849	1921	1952	...	2052	2152	2251	2351	2354
57	**Clitheroe** a.	0650	0715	0812	...	0917	...	1017	until	1617	1656	1744	1818	...	1914	...	2017	...	2117	2217	2316	...	...

⑦	⑦A	⑦B		⑦A		⑦A	⑦B		⑦A		⑦A	⑦B		⑦A	⑦B	and at		⑦A	⑦B		⑦A		
Manchester Victoria d.	0801	0801	...	...	...	0900	0900	...	...	...	1000	1000	...	1100	1100	the same	...	2100	2100	...	2200	...	...
Bolton d.	0820	0821	...	...	...	0920	0920	...	...	...	1020	1020	...	1120	1120	minutes past	...	2120	2120	...	2220	...	...
Blackburn d.	0857	0849	...	0927	...	1002	0948	...	1022	...	1048	1048	...	1148	1148	each hour	...	2148	2148	...	2248	...	...
Clitheroe a.	0920	0936*	...	0950	...	1013	1036*	...	1044	...	1113	1136*	...	1213	1236*	until	...	2213	2236*	...	...	...	...

⚒	⚒		⚒	⚒	⚒	⚒	⚒	⚒	⚒	and at	⚒	⚒	⚒	⚒	⚒	⚒	⚒		⚒	⚒	⚒	Ⓐ	⑥
Clitheroe d.	...	...	...	0707	0740	...	0826	...	0940	the same	1440	1526	1640	1709	1809	1840	...	...	1940	2040	2140	2240	2246
Blackburn d.	0628	...	0700	0729	0803	0832	0903	0931	1003	minutes past	1503	1551	1703	1731	1831	1903	1931	...	2003	2103	2203	2303	2309
Bolton d.	0655	...	0730	0758	0830	0902	0930	1000	1030	each hour	1530	1617	1730	1801	1901	1931	2002	...	2030	2130	2230	2330	2336
Manchester Victoria a.	0726	...	0751	0825	0851	0926	0951	1023	1051	until	1553	1640	1754	1826	1922	1952	2023	...	2051	2151	2251	2350	2359

⑦	⑦	⑦B	⑦A	⑦B	⑦A	⑦B	⑦A	and at	⑦B	⑦A	⑦A	⑦B	⑦A	⑦B	⑦A	⑦A	⑦B	⑦A	⑦B	⑦A		⑦B	⑦A
Clitheroe d.	...	0919*	0940	1019*	1040	1119*	1140	the same	1719*	1740	1758	1819*	1840	1919*	1940	1955	2019*	2040	2119*	2140	...	2219*	2240
Blackburn d.	0903	1003	1003	1103	1103	1203	1203	minutes past	1803	1803	1823	1903	1903	2003	2003	2022	2103	2103	2203	2203	...	2303	2303
Bolton d.	0930	1030	1030	1130	1130	1230	1230	each hour	1830	1830	...	1930	1930	2030	2030	...	2130	2130	2230	2230	...	2330	2330
Manchester Victoria a.	0951	1051	1051	1151	1151	1251	1251	until	1851	1851	...	1951	1951	2051	2051	...	2151	2151	2251	2251	...	2351	2351

A – May 17 - Sept. 6. B – Sept. 13 - Dec. 13. p – Manchester Piccadilly. * – By 🚌.

Manchester – Buxton

Journey time: ± 56 minutes *41 km* NT

From Manchester Piccadilly:

Trains call at Stockport ± 11 minutes and at New Mills Newtown ± 31 minutes later.

Ⓐ: 0649, 0752, 0852, 0952, 1052, 1152, 1252, 1352, 1452, 1552, 1621, 1651, 1723, 1752, 1821, 1852, 1952, 2052, 2152, 2310.

⑥: 0649, 0752, 0852, 0952, 1052, 1152, 1252, 1352, 1452, 1552, 1652; then 1721, 1752, 1852, 1952, 2052, 2152, 2310.

⑦: 0855, 0951 and hourly until 2252.

From Buxton:

Trains call at New Mills Newtown ± 21 minutes and at Stockport ± 46 minutes later.

Ⓐ: 0559, 0623, 0650, 0724, 0748, 0827, 0927, 1030, 1127, 1230, 1325, 1430, 1547, 1630, 1659, 1727, 1759, 1827, 1927, 2027, 2127, 2256.

⑥: 0559, 0627, 0727, 0756, 0827, 0927, 1030, 1127, 1230, 1327, 1430, 1527, 1630, 1727, 1827, 1927, 2027, 2256.

⑦: 0823, 0919, 1023, 1126, 1227 and hourly until 2227.

Manchester – Northwich – Chester

Journey time: ± 87 minutes *73 km* NT

From Manchester Piccadilly:

Trains call at Stockport ± 9 mins, Altrincham ± 26 mins, and Northwich ± 53 mins later.

Ⓐ: 0617, 0717 and hourly until 1617; then 1709, 1817, 1917, 2017, 2117, 2217, 2317.

⑥: 0617, 0717 and hourly until 2317.

⑦: 0923, 1122, 1322, 1522, 1722, 1922, 2122.

From Chester:

Trains call at Northwich 28 mins, at Altrincham ± 55 mins, and at Stockport ± 73 mins later.

Ⓐ: 0605, 0635, 0703, 0735, 0807 and hourly until 2107; then 2248.

⑥: 0605, 0703, 0807 and hourly until 2007; then 2133, 2249.

⑦: 0859, 1103, 1308, 1508, 1708, 1908, 2108.

Manchester – St Helens – Liverpool

Journey time: ± 63 minutes *51 km* NT

From Manchester Victoria:

Trains call at St Helens Junction ± 29 minutes later.

⚒: 0539, 0609, 0709, 0739, 0809, 0839 and hourly until 1639; then 1709, 1737, 1839, 1939, 2039, 2139, 2239, 2309.

⑦: 0850**P a**, 0950**P** and hourly until 2250**P**.

From Liverpool Lime Street:

Trains call at St Helens Junction ± 28 minutes later.

⚒: 0546, 0646, 0716, 0746, 0844, 0946 and hourly until 1546; then 1616, 1646, 1710, 1735, 1748, 1846, 1912, 2012, 2112, 2212, 2316.

⑦: 0805**Q a**, 0901**Q** and hourly until 2301**Q**.

P – On ⑦ trains start from Manchester Piccadilly, not Victoria.
Q – On ⑦ trains terminate at Manchester Piccadilly, not Victoria.
a – May 17 - Sept. 6.

☛ Manchester - Warrington - Liverpool and v.v.: see Tables **187**, **208**.
St Helens Central - Liverpool and v.v.: see Table **160**.

Manchester – Wigan – Southport

Journey time: ± 71 minutes *62 km* NT

From Manchester Piccadilly:

Trains call at Bolton ± 20 minutes and at Wigan Wallgate ± 39 minutes later.

⚒: 0706Ⓐ**v**, 0710⑥**v**, 0811Ⓐ**v**, 0822 and hourly until 1822; then 1920, 2020, 2120, 2236.

⑦: 0835**b**, 0839**c v**, 0935, 1026**b**, 1035**c**, 1127**c**, 1135**b**, 1230**c**, 1235**b**, 1335 and hourly until 2035.

From Southport:

Trains call at Wigan Wallgate ± 30 minutes and at Bolton ± 48 minutes later.

⚒: 0623, 0722, 0824 and hourly until 1724; then 1817, 1923, 2023, 2123**v**, 2218.

⑦: 0909, 1005 and hourly until 2205.

v – Manchester Victoria.
b – May 17 - Sept. 6.
c – Sept. 13 - Dec. 13.
☛ Additional trains (not calling at Bolton) run Manchester Victoria - Southport and v.v. on ⚒.

Liverpool – Birkenhead – Chester

Journey time: 43 minutes *29 km* ME

From Liverpool Lime Street:

Trains call at Birkenhead Central 9 minutes later.

⚒: 0538, 0608, 0643 and every 30 minutes until 1613; then 1635Ⓐ, 1643⑥, 1650Ⓐ, 1705Ⓐ, 1713⑥, 1720Ⓐ, 1733Ⓐ, 1743⑥, 1750Ⓐ, 1813, 1843 and every 30 minutes until 2343.

⑦: 0813, 0843 and every 30 minutes until 2343.

From Chester:

Trains call at Birkenhead Central 34 minutes later.

⚒: 0600, 0630, 0700, 0722Ⓐ, 0730⑥, 0737Ⓐ, 0752Ⓐ, 0800⑥, 0807Ⓐ, 0830, 0900 and every 30 minutes until 2300.

⑦: 0800, 0830 and every 30 minutes until 2300.

Liverpool – Southport

Journey time: 44 minutes *30 km* ME

From Liverpool Central:

⚒: 0608, 0623 and every 15 minutes until 2308; then 2323, 2338 (also 1713 Ⓐ).

⑦: 0808, 0823, 0853 and every 30 minutes until 2253; then 2338.

From Southport:

⚒: 0543, 0558 and every 15 minutes until 2258, then 2316 (also 0748 Ⓐ, 0803 Ⓐ).

⑦: 0758, 0828 and every 30 minutes until 2258; then 2316.

165 HOLYHEAD - CREWE and MANCHESTER

Most services 🍸 2nd class AW, VT

Services on ⑦ valid until September 6. For ⛴ connections to / from **Dublin** see Table **2040**.

km		⚒	⚒	⚒	⚒ C	⚒	Ⓐ ◇	⚒	Ⓐ B	⚒	⑥ B	Ⓐ C□	Ⓐ ◇	⚒	Ⓐ C	⑥ C	⑥ ◇	Ⓐ ◇	⚒	⚒ B	⑥ D◇	⚒	Ⓐ C	⑥ C
0	**Holyhead** d.		...	...	0425	...	0450	...	0511	...	0522	0532	0553	...	0627	0633	0650	0655	...	0715	0755	...	0805	0820
40	Bangor d.		...	...	0457	...	0516	...	0540	...	0601	0602	0620	...	0708	0708	0717	0722	...	0802	0822	...	0902	0902
	Llandudno ‡ d.		...	...	|	...	|	...	|	...	|	|	|	0634	|	|	|	|	0745	|	|	0845	|	|
64	Llandudno Junction ‡ d.		0438	...	0515	...	0534	0546	0607	...	0624	0621	0638	0644	0725	0725	0735	0740	0754	0825	0840	0854	0925	0925
71	Colwyn Bay d.		0444	...	0521	...	0540	0552	0613	...	0630	|	0644	0650	0731	0731	0742	0747	0800	0831	0847	0900	0931	0931
81	Abergele & Pensarn d.		0451	...	|	...	|	0559	|	...	|	|	|	0657	|	|	|	|	0807	|	|	0907	|	|
88	Rhyl d.		0457	...	0531	...	0551	0605	0623	...	0640	0636	0655	0703	0742	0742	0753	0758	0813	0841	0858	0913	0941	0941
94	Prestatyn d.		0502	...	0537	...	|	0610	0629	...	0646	|	0700	0708	0747	0747	0759	0804	0819	0847	0904	0919	0947	0947
116	Flint d.		0516	...	0550	...	|	0624	0642	...	0659	0652	|	0721	0801	0801	0812	0817	0832	0900	0918	0932	1000	1000
136	**Chester 145 150** ▼ a.		0533	0538	0605	0613	0619	0641	0659	0712	0715	0707	0725	0738	0822	0815	0826	0831	0850	0915	0931	0950	1015	1015
170	**Crewe 150** ▼ a.		0558	|	...	|	0647	0703	...	|	...	0732	0754	|	...	...	0854	0854	|	...	0954	|	...	...
	London Euston 150 a.		...	|	...	|	0836	...	...	|	...	...	0938	|	...	...	1038	1038	|	...	1138	|	...	...
165	Warrington Bank Quay a.		...	0605	...	0639	...	...	...	0738	...	...	...	0806	...	...	...	...	0918	...	...	1018	...	...
201	**Manchester** Piccadilly a.		...	0646	...	0718	...	...	...	0818	...	...	...	0850	...	...	...	...	0957	...	...	1057	...	...

	Ⓐ ◇	⑥ ◇	⚒	⚒ B	⚒	⚒ C	⚒	⚒ B	Ⓐ ◇	⚒	⚒ C	⚒	⚒ B	Ⓐ ◇	⚒	Ⓐ	⑥ C	Ⓐ C	⑥ ◇	⑥	Ⓐ	Ⓐ B	⑥ B	⑥
Holyhead d.	0855	0855	...	0923	...	1033	...	1123	...	...	1238	...	1323	1358	...	...	1423	1432	1436	...	...	1523	1523	...
Bangor d.	0922	0922	...	1002	...	1106	...	1202	1224	...	1307	...	1402	1425	...	...	1454	1502	1506	...	...	1602	1602	...
Llandudno ‡ d.	|	|	0945	|	1044	|	1144	|	|	1244	|	1344	|	|	1440	1508	|	|	|	1544	1608	|	|	1644
Llandudno Junction ‡ d.	0940	0940	0954	1025	1053	1125	1153	1225	1242	1253	1325	1353	1425	1443	1449	1517	1517	1525	1525	1553	1617	1625	1625	1653
Colwyn Bay d.	0947	0947	1000	1031	1059	1131	1159	1231	1248	1259	1331	1359	1431	1450	1455	1523	1523	1531	1533	1559	1623	1631	1631	1659
Abergele & Pensarn d.	|	|	1007	|	1106	|	1206	|	1259	1306	|	1406	|	|	1502	|	|	1538	|	1606	|	1638	|	1706
Rhyl d.	0958	0958	1013	1041	1112	1141	1212	1241	1305	1312	1341	1412	1441	1500	1508	1534	1534	1544	1546	1612	1634	1644	1641	1712
Prestatyn d.	1004	1003	1019	1047	1118	1147	1218	1247	1318	1318	1347	1418	1447	|	1514	1539	1539	1549	|	1618	1639	1650	1647	1718
Flint d.	1017	|	1032	1100	1131	1200	1231	1300	|	1331	1400	1431	1500	|	1527	1553	1553	1603	|	1631	1653	1703	1700	1731
Chester 145 150 ▼ a.	1031	1028	1050	1115	1149	1215	1249	1315	1332	1349	1415	1449	1517	1527	1546	1610	1607	1616	1617	1649	1710	1717	1714	1749
Crewe 150 ▼ a.	1054	1054	|	...	|	...	|	...	1354	|	...	|	...	1554	|	|	...	...	1644	|	|	...	...	|
London Euston 150 a.	1238	1238	|	...	|	...	|	...	1538	|	...	|	...	1738	|	|	...	...	1838	|	|	...	...	|
Warrington Bank Quay a.	...	...	1118	...	1218	...	1318	...	...	1418	...	1518	...	...	1616	1651	...	...	...	1718	1749	...	...	1818
Manchester Piccadilly a.	...	...	1157	...	1257	...	1357	...	...	1457	...	1557	...	...	1657	1730	...	...	...	1757	1828	...	...	1857

	Ⓐ	Ⓐ C	⑥ C	⑥	Ⓐ	⚒	⚒	⚒	⚒	⚒ B	Ⓐ B◇	⚒	⚒	⚒	⚒	⚒		⑦	⑦	⑦	⑦	⑦	⑦	⑦
Holyhead d.	...	1636	1638	...	...	1721	...	1823	...	1921	...	...	...	2037	...	...	...		...	...	0750	0840	...	...
Bangor d.	...	1704	1707	...	...	1800	...	1902	...	2000	2020	...	...	2106	...	...	...		...	0743	0828	0908	...	...
Llandudno ‡ d.	1707	|	|	1744	...	|	1844	|	1942	|	|	2042	...	|	2145	...	...		...	|	|	|	...	...
Llandudno Junction ‡ d.	1716	1722	1725	1753	...	1823	1853	1925	1951	2023	2038	2051	...	2129	2155	...	...		...	0801	0851	0926	...	...
Colwyn Bay d.	1722	1728	1731	1759	...	1829	1859	1931	1957	2029	2044	2057	...	2135	2201	...	...		...	0807	0857	0932	...	...
Abergele & Pensarn d.	|	1735	|	1806	...	|	1906	|	2004	|	|	2104	...	2142	2209	...	...		...	0814	|	0939	...	...
Rhyl d.	1733	1741	1741	1812	...	1839	1912	1941	2010	2039	2055	2110	...	2148	2216	...	...		...	0820	0908	0945	...	...
Prestatyn d.	1738	1747	1747	1818	...	1845	1918	1947	2016	2045	2100	2116	...	2153	2222	...	...		...	0825	|	0950	...	...
Flint d.	1752	1802	1800	1831	...	1858	1931	2000	2029	2058	2114	2129	...	2207	2237	...	...		...	0839	|	1004	...	...
Chester 145 150 ▼ a.	1811	1816	1815	1849	1850	1915	1949	2015	2047	2115	2128	2147	2152	2223	2259	2322	...		0841	0856	0939	1021	1036	1136
Crewe 150 ▼ a.	|	...	...	|	|	...	|	2041	|	...	2154	...	|	2246	2326	|	...		|	0922	|	1052	|	|
London Euston 150 a.	|	...	...	|	|	...	|	...	|	...	...	...	|	...	...	|	...		|	...	|	...	|	|
Warrington Bank Quay a.	1845	...	...	1918	1918	...	2018	...	2116	...	...	...	2218	...	...	2349	...		0908	...	1007	...	1103	1203
Manchester Piccadilly a.	1929	...	...	1957	1957	...	2057	...	2157	...	...	...	2258	...	...	0028	...		0948	...	1050	...	1141	1241

	⑦ C	⑦ ◇	⑦	⑦ ◇	⑦	⑦ ◇	⑦	⑦ ◇	⑦	⑦		⑦		⑦ C	⑦	⑦	⑦	⑦ B	⑦	⑦ W	⑦	⑦	⑦	⑦
Holyhead d.	1020	1055	...	1148	...	1247	...	1355	...	1430	...	1540	...	1625	...	1730	...	1825	...	1915	...	...	2035	2140
Bangor d.	1059	1122	...	1215	...	1314	...	1422	...	1508	...	1608	...	1704	...	1759	...	1904	...	1954	...	...	2114	2211
Llandudno ‡ d.	|	|	...	|	...	|	...	|	...	|	...	|	...	|	...	|	...	|	...	|	...	...	|	|
Llandudno Junction ‡ d.	1122	1140	...	1233	...	1332	...	1440	...	1526	...	1635	...	1725	...	1824	...	1924	...	2017	...	...	2137	2229
Colwyn Bay d.	1128	1147	...	1240	...	1339	...	1446	...	1532	...	1641	...	1731	...	1830	...	1930	...	2023	...	...	2143	2235
Abergele & Pensarn d.	1135	|	...	|	...	|	...	|	...	1539	...	1648	...	1738	...	1837	...	1937	...	2030	...	...	2150	|
Rhyl d.	1141	1158	...	1251	...	1350	...	1457	...	1545	...	1654	...	1744	...	1843	...	1943	...	2036	...	...	2156	2245
Prestatyn d.	1146	1203	...	1257	...	1356	...	1503	...	1551	...	1659	...	1749	...	1848	...	1948	...	2041	...	...	2201	2251
Flint d.	1200	1217	...	|	...	1409	...	|	...	1604	...	1713	...	1803	...	1902	...	2002	...	2055	...	...	2215	2304
Chester 145 150 ▼ a.	1218	1230	1236	1321	1336	1423	1436	1531	1536	1621	...	1732	...	1820	1836	1919	1936	2019	2036	2113	2136	2209	2232	2318
Crewe 150 ▼ a.	...	1252	|	1347	|	1452	|	1552	|	|	...	|	...	...	|	1944	|	2083	|	...	|	|	2259	...
London Euston 150 a.	...	1443	|	1545	|	1644	|	1744	|	|	...	|	...	...	|	...	|	...	|	...	|	|	...	...
Warrington Bank Quay a.	...	...	1303	...	1403	...	1503	...	1603	1703	...	1803	...	...	1903	...	2003	...	2103	...	2203	2236	...	...
Manchester Piccadilly a.	...	...	1341	...	1440	...	1541	...	1641	1741	...	1841	...	...	1941	...	2041	...	2141	...	2241	2315	...	...

	⚒	⚒ B◇	⚒	Ⓐ	⑥	⚒	Ⓐ C	⑥ C	⚒	⚒ B	⚒	Ⓐ ◇	⑥ C	Ⓐ C	⚒	Ⓐ ◇	⑥ ◇	⚒ B	⚒	⚒ C	⚒	⚒ B	⚒	⚒ C
Manchester Piccadilly d.		...	0550	...	...	0650	...	...	0750	...	0850	...	...	...	0950	...	...	...	1050	...	1150	...	1250	...
Warrington Bank Quay d.		...	0626	...	...	0722	...	...	0824	...	0926	...	...	...	1026	...	...	...	1126	...	1226	...	1326	...
London Euston 150 d.		...	|	...	...	|	...	...	|	...	|	0810	...	...	|	0910	0850	...	|	...	|	...	|	...
Crewe 150 ▼ d.		0623	|	0654	0703	|	...	...	|	...	|	0949	...	...	|	1049	1045	...	|	...	|	...	|	...
Chester 145 150 ▼ d.		0644	0655	0726	0726	0755	0820	0826	0855	0926	0955	1016	1026	1026	1055	1116	1116	1126	1155	1226	1254	1326	1355	1426
Flint d.		0657	0710	0739	0739	0810	0839	0839	0910	0939	1010	1029	1039	1039	1110	|	|	1139	1210	1239	1310	1339	1410	1439
Prestatyn d.		0710	0723	0752	0752	0823	0852	0852	0923	0952	1023	1042	1052	1052	1123	|	|	1152	1223	1252	1323	1352	1423	1452
Rhyl d.		0716	0729	0758	0758	0829	0858	0858	0929	0958	1029	1048	1058	1058	1129	1143	1145	1158	1229	1258	1329	1358	1429	1458
Abergele & Pensarn d.		|	0735	|	|	0835	|	|	0935	|	1035	|	|	|	1135	|	|	|	1235	|	1335	|	1435	|
Colwyn Bay d.		0727	0743	0809	0809	0843	0909	0909	0943	1009	1043	1059	1109	1109	1143	1154	1158	1209	1243	1309	1343	1409	1443	1509
Llandudno Junction ‡ d.		0733	0750	0815	0815	0850	0915	0915	0950	1015	1050	1106	1115	1115	1150	1201	1205	1215	1250	1315	1350	1415	1450	1515
Llandudno ‡ a.		|	0806	|	|	0906	|	|	1006	|	1106	|	|	|	1206	|	|	|	1306	|	1406	|	1506	|
Bangor d.		0750	...	0838	0838	...	0932	0932	...	1038	...	1127	1138	1140	...	1217	1224	1238	...	1332	...	1438	...	1532
Holyhead a.		0823	...	0919	0919	...	1005	1005	...	1119	...	...	1211	1213	...	1250	1256	1319	...	1414	...	1511	...	1614

	⚒	⚒ B	⚒	⑥ D◇	⚒ C	⚒	⚒ B	⚒	Ⓐ ◇	⑥ D◇	Ⓐ	⚒ C	⚒	Ⓐ C□	⑥ ◇	Ⓐ ◇	⚒ B	⚒	Ⓐ ◇	⚒ C	⚒	Ⓐ ◇	⑥	Ⓐ
Manchester Piccadilly d.	1350	...	1450	...	...	1550	...	1650	...	...	1719	...	1750	...	...	...	...	1850	...	...	1950	...	...	...
Warrington Bank Quay d.	1426	...	1526	...	...	1626	...	1726	...	...	1753	...	1824	...	...	...	...	1926	...	...	2026	...	...	...
London Euston 150 d.	|	...	|	1410	...	|	...	|	1610	1610	|	...	|	...	1710	1710	...	|	1810	...	|	1910	...	...
Crewe 150 ▼ d.	|	...	|	1549	...	|	...	|	1749	1749	|	...	|	1846	1850	1856	...	|	1956	...	|	2050	2100	2100
Chester 145 150 ▼ d.	1455	1526	1555	1612	1626	1655	1726	1755	1811	1816	1822	1826	1855	1910	1917	1922	1931	1955	2022	2031	2057	2117	2126	2130
Flint d.	1510	1539	1610	1625	1639	1710	1741	1810	1824	1829	...	1839	1910	1924	1930	1935	1946	...	|	2044	...	2130	2141	2145
Prestatyn d.	1523	1552	1623	1638	1652	1723	1754	1823	1837	1842	...	1852	1923	|	1943	1948	1959	...	|	2058	...	2143	2154	2159
Rhyl d.	1529	1558	1629	1645	1658	1729	1800	1829	1843	1849	...	1858	1929	1942	1950	1955	2005	...	2049	2104	...	2150	2200	2205
Abergele & Pensarn d.	1535	|	1635	|	|	1735	1806	1835	|	|	...	|	1935	|	|	|	2011	...	|	|	...	|	2206	2211
Colwyn Bay d.	1543	1609	1643	1656	1709	1743	1814	1843	1854	1900	...	1909	1943	|	2001	2006	2019	...	2100	2115	...	2201	2214	2219
Llandudno Junction ‡ d.	1550	1615	1650	1702	1715	1750	1821	1850	1901	1906	...	1915	1950	1956	2007	2012	2026	...	2107	2121	...	2207	2221	2226
Llandudno ‡ a.	1606	|	1706	|	|	1806	|	1906	|	|	...	|	2006	|	|	|	|	...	|	|	...	|	|	|
Bangor d.	...	1638	...	1719	1738	...	1843	...	1922	1923	...	1932	...	2014	2024	2029	2048	...	2123	2138	...	2224	2243	2248
Holyhead a.	...	1711	...	1751	1819	...	1916	...	...	1955	...	2016	...	2049	2056	2102	2121	...	2156	2219	...	2256	2315	2321

‡ – All trains Llandudno Junction - Llandudno. Journey time ± 10 minutes.

⚒ : 0613, 0651, 0730, 0750, 0825, 0850, 0926, 0950, 1000, 1026, 1050, 1126, 1150, 1226, 1250, 1300, 1326, 1350, 1426, 1450, 1526⑥, 1550, 1600⑥, 1604Ⓐ, 1626⑥, 1650, 1726⑥, 1750, 1826, 1841, 1850, 1926, 1950, 2024, 2125.

⑦ : 1000, 1050, 1125, 1200, 1242, 1258, 1335, 1402, 1500, 1530, 1604, 1830.

‡ – All trains Llandudno - Llandudno Junction. Journey time ± 10 minutes.

⚒ : 0634, 0710, 0745, 0810, 0845, 0910, 0945, 1010, 1020, 1044, 1110, 1144, 1210, 1244, 1310, 1320, 1344, 1410, 1440, 1508, 1544⑥, 1608, 1620, 1644⑥, 1707, 1808, 1844, 1903, 1910, 1942, 2008, 2042, 2145.

⑦ : 1022, 1107, 1140, 1218, 1319, 1330, 1350, 1420, 1511, 1545, 1616, 1855.

FOR FOOTNOTES SEE NEXT PAGE.

MANCHESTER and CREWE - HOLYHEAD — 165

AW, VT 2nd class Most services 🍷

Services on ⑦ valid until September 6. For ⛴ connections to / from **Dublin** see Table **2040**.

	⚒	Ⓐ C	⑥ C	⚒	Ⓐ	⑥	⚒	Ⓐ B		⑦	⑦	⑦	⑦ 🚌	⑦	⑦	⑦ ◇	⑦	⑦	⑦	⑦	⑦	⑦	⑦	⑦
Manchester Piccadilly d.	2050	...	...	2150	2212	2226	2314	...	...	⑦	...	...	0744	...	0956	...	1055	...	1156	...	1256	...	1356	...
Warrington Bank Quay d.	2126	...	...	2224	2259	2259	2348	...	...		...	...	0842	...	1028	...	1130	...	1228	...	1329	...	1428	...
London Euston **150** d.	|	...	...	|	|	|	|	...	...		...	...	|	...	|	...	|	...	|	...	|	...	|	...
Crewe 150 ▼ d.	|	...	...	|	|	|	|	2357	...		...	0827	|	0927	|	1040	|	1127	|	1227	|	1327	|	1427
Chester 145 150 ▼ d.	2154	2256	2236	2251	2326	2326	0015	0040	...		0620	0902	0938	0948	1059	1108	1157	1203	1255	1302	1344	1402	1455	1502
Flint d.	...	2311	2251	...	...	...	...	0053	...		0633	0915	...	1003	...	|	...	1218	...	1317	...	1417	...	1517
Prestatyn d.	...	2324	2305	...	...	...	...	0106	...		0646	0928	...	1016	...	1131	...	1231	...	1330	...	1430	...	1530
Rhyl d.	...	2330	2311	...	...	...	...	0112	...		0652	0934	...	1022	...	1138	...	1237	...	1336	...	1436	...	1536
Abergele & Pensarn d.	...	2336	2317	...	...	...	...	|	...		|	|	...	1028	...	|	...	|	...	1342	...	1442	...	1542
Colwyn Bay d.	...	2344	2325	...	...	...	...	0123	...		0703	0945	...	1036	...	1149	...	1248	...	1350	...	1450	...	1550
Llandudno Junction ‡ d.	...	2351	2333	...	...	...	...	0129	...		0709	0954	...	1043	...	1155	...	1254	...	1357	...	1457	...	1557
Llandudno ‡ a.	...	|	|	...	...	...	...	|	...		|	|	...	|	...	|	...	|	...	|	...	|	...	|
Bangor d.	...	0013	*0038**	...	...	...	...	0145	...		0729	1011	...	1105	...	1212	...	1311	...	1419	...	1514	...	1619
Holyhead a.	...	0055	*0202**	...	...	...	...	0215	...		0800	1048	...	1148	...	1243	...	1345	...	1455	...	1555	...	1655

	⑦	⑦	⑦	⑦	⑦ B	⑦	⑦ C	⑦	⑦	⑦ ◇	⑦ B	⑦	⑦ ◇	⑦ C	⑦	⑦ ◇	⑦	⑦	⑦	⑦	⑦		⑦	⑦ B
Manchester Piccadilly d.	1456	...	1556	...	...	1656	...	...	1756	...	...	1856	...	...	1956	...	2056	...	2156	...	2256	...	2325	...
Warrington Bank Quay d.	1529	...	1628	...	...	1728	...	...	1828	...	...	1929	...	...	2030	...	2128	...	2228	...	2328	...	2356	...
London Euston **150** d.	|	...	|	...	...	|	...	...	|	1705	...	|	1805	...	|	1905	|	...	|	...	|	...	|	...
Crewe 150 ▼ d.	|	1527	|	1627	...	|	...	1827	|	1856	...	|	1957	...	|	2058	|	2127	|	2229	|	...	|	0010
Chester 145 150 ▼ d.	1556	1602	1655	1702	1732	1755	1830	1855	1855	1921	1938	1956	2022	2036	2057	2119	2155	2200	2255	2300	2355	...	0024	0035
Flint d.	...	1617	...	1717	1747	...	1845	1910	...	|	1953	...	2035	2051	...	2132	...	2215	...	2315	...	...	...	0048
Prestatyn d.	...	1630	...	1730	1800	...	1858	1923	...	1944	2006	...	2049	2104	...	2146	...	2228	...	2328	...	...	...	0101
Rhyl d.	...	1636	...	1736	1806	...	1904	1929	...	1951	2012	...	2055	2110	...	2152	...	2234	...	2334	...	...	...	0107
Abergele & Pensarn d.	...	1642	...	1742	1812	...	1910	1935	...	|	2018	...	|	2116	...	|	...	2240	...	|	...	...	...	|
Colwyn Bay d.	...	1650	...	1750	1820	...	1918	1943	...	2002	2026	...	2106	2124	...	2203	...	2248	...	2345	...	...	...	0118
Llandudno Junction ‡ d.	...	1657	...	1757	1827	...	1925	1950	...	2014	2033	...	2113	2131	...	2210	...	2255	...	2351	...	...	...	0125
Llandudno ‡ a.	...	|	...	|	|	...	|	|	...	|	|	...	|	|	...	|	...	|	...	|	...	...	...	|
Bangor d.	...	1714	...	1819	1844	...	1947	2012	...	2031	2055	...	2129	2154	...	2226	...	2312	...	0014	...	...	...	0141
Holyhead a.	...	1755	...	1855	1925	...	2020	2047	...	2102	2130	...	2202	2238	...	2259	...	2352	...	0049	...	...	...	0215

▼ – Additional trains Chester - Crewe. Journey time ± 24 minutes.
⚒: 0455, 0551, 0755 and hourly until 2055.
⑦: 0757, 0827, 0927, 0957 and hourly until 2057; then 2127, 2157, 2257

▼ – Additional trains Cewe - Chester. Journey time ± 24 minutes.
⚒: 0721, 0821 and hourly until 2121; then 2321, 2358⑥ **C**, 0002Ⓐ **C**.
⑦: 0957 and hourly until 1557; then 1657◇, 1757◇, 1927, 2027, 2157, 2305**B**, 2338.

B – To / from Birmingham, Table **145** or **150**.
C – To / from Cardiff, Table **131**.
D – Until October 31.
W – To Wolverhampton.
▼ – For additional trains Crewe - Chester and v.v. see above.

‡ – For full service Llandudno Junction - Llandudno and v.v. see previous page.
◇ – Operated by *VT*. Conveys 🛏12.
□ – Also conveys 🛏1.
* – by 🚌.

LLANDUDNO - BLAENAU FFESTINIOG - PORTHMADOG — 166

AW 2nd class

km		⚒	⚒		⚒	⑦ A	⑦ 🚌 B	F	Fa	⚒	⑦ 🚌 B	⑦ A	F	⑦ A	Ⓐ 🚌 B	⚒	Fa	⚒					
0	**Llandudno** 165 d.	...	*0710*	...	1020	1022	1015	...	...	1320	1315	1330	...	*1545*	1600	1620	...	1903	...	...	...	...	...
5	**Llandudno** Junction 165 d.	0535	0739	...	1033	1032	1035	...	...	1333	1335	1340	...	1615	1620	1633	...	1920	...	...	...	...	...
18	Llanrwst d.	0553	0802	...	1055	1054	1100	...	...	1355	1400	1402	...	1637	1645	1655	...	1942	...	...	...	...	...
24	Betws y Coed d.	0559	0808	...	1101	1100	1110	...	...	1401	1410	1408	...	1643	1655	1701	...	1948	...	...	...	...	...
44	**Blaenau Ffestiniog** d.	0626	0840	...	1133	1130	1145	1150	1340	1433	1445	1438	1510	1713	1730	1733	1735	2019	...	...	...	...	...
63	Minffordd 149 a.	...	...	...	...	...	...	1250	1440	...	...	...	1610	...	...	...	1830	...	...	...	...	...	...
66	**Porthmadog** Harbour a.	...	...	...	...	...	...	1305	1450	...	...	...	1620	...	...	...	1845	...	...	...	...	...	...

		⚒	⚒		F	⑦ A	⚒	⑦ 🚌 B	Fa	F	⚒	⑦ A	⑦ 🚌 B	Fa	⑦ A	⚒	⑦ 🚌 B	⚒					
Porthmadog Harbour d.	...	...	...	...	1015	...	...	...	1145	1335	...	...	...	1600	...	...	...	...	...	...	...	...	...
Minffordd 149 d.	...	...	...	...	1025	...	...	...	1155	1345	...	...	...	1610	...	...	...	...	...	...	...	...	...
Blaenau Ffestiniog d.	...	0630	0852	...	1125	1145	1152	1150	1300	1445	1452	1503	1500	1715	1730	1737	1750	2023	...	...	...	...	...
Betws y Coed d.	...	0656	0919	...	...	1211	1219	1220	...	...	1519	1529	1530	...	1757	1804	1820	2050	...	...	...	...	...
Llanrwst d.	...	0702	0925	...	...	1217	1225	1230	...	...	1525	1535	1540	...	1803	1810	1830	2056	...	...	...	...	...
Llandudno Junction 165 a.	...	0726	0951	...	...	1240	1251	1300	...	...	1551	1559	1610	...	1829	1835	1900	2123	...	...	...	...	...
Llandudno 165 a.	...	*0806*	1008	...	...	1251	1309	1320	...	...	1613	*1614*	1630	...	1840	1849	1920	2135	...	...	...	...	...

A – Until September 6.
B – From September 13.
F – Ffestiniog Railway (www.festrail.co.uk ✆ +44 (0) 1766 516 000). Service shown valid until August 31.

a – Not May 1, 8, 11, 15, 18, 22; June 1, 5, 8, 12.

CREWE - MANCHESTER AIRPORT ✈ — 167

NT 2nd class

From CREWE *37 km*

⚒: 0044 ②-⑥, 0633, 0730⑥, 0831, 0933 and hourly until 1833.
⑦: *No direct trains. Connections available by changing at* **Wilmslow**.
Valid until July 12: 0959, 1228, 1428, 1631, 1828, 2028, 2223.

From MANCHESTER AIRPORT ✈ Journey: ± 33 minutes (50 - 60 minutes on ⑦)

⚒: 0605, 0711, 0811, 0911 and hourly until 1811.
⑦: *No direct trains. Connections available by changing at* **Wilmslow**.
Valid until July 12: 0909, 1108, 1306, 1506, 1706, 1906, 2106.

CREWE - STOKE - DERBY — 168

EM 2nd class

Services on ⑦ valid until July 12.

km			⚒	Ⓐ	⑥	⚒		⚒	Ⓐ	⑥			⑦	⑦	⑦	⑦	⑦	⑦	⑦	⑦		
0	**Crewe** d.	⚒	0607	0658	0707	0807	and hourly until	1907	2045	2045	...	⑦	1404	1505	1610	1708	1809	1908	2010	2116	...	...
24	Stoke on Trent d.		0633	0724	0733	0833		1933	2118	2119	...		1429	1532	1635	1735	1836	1935	2039	2142	...	...
33	Blythe Bridge d.		0645	0736	0745	0845		1945	2129	2131	...		1441	1544	1647	1753	1852	1950	2051	2159	...	...
51	Uttoxeter d.		0658	0749	0758	0858		1958	2142	2144	...		1453	1556	1700	1805	1904	2003	2104	2212	...	...
82	**Derby** a.		0725	0816	0824	0924		2024	2210	2211	...		1521	1624	1727	1828	1928	2030	2134	2240	...	...

		⚒	⚒	⚒	Ⓐ	⑥		⑥	Ⓐ	⑥ A			⑦	⑦	⑦	⑦	⑦	⑦	⑦			
Derby d.	⚒	0640	0740	0842	0940	0942	and hourly until	1942	2040	2042	...	⑦	1444	1544	1644	1744	1844	1944	2044	...	...	...
Uttoxeter d.		0705	0807	0907	1007	1007		2007	2107	2107	...		1509	1609	1709	1811	1909	2010	2109	...	...	...
Blythe Bridge d.		0719	0821	0921	1021	1021		2021	2121	2121	...		1523	1623	1723	1825	1923	2024	2123	...	...	...
Stoke on Trent a.		0731	0833	0933	1033	1033		2033	2133	2133	...		1535	1635	1737	1838	1936	2037	2136	...	...	...
Crewe a.		0801	0859	0959	1059	1101		2104	2159	2201	...		1609	1703	1802	1906	2003	2110	2210	...	...	...

A – From July 18.

170 LONDON - LEICESTER - NOTTINGHAM, DERBY and SHEFFIELD

All services 🍷 EM

Services on ⑦ valid until July 12.

km		⚒	Ⓐ	⑥	Ⓐ	⑥	⚒	⚒	Ⓐ	⑥	⚒	⚒	⚒	⚒	⚒	⚒	⚒	⚒	⚒	⚒	⚒	⚒	⚒	⚒	⚒
						Z							Ca										Ca		
0	**London** St Pancras 103 d.		0610	0610	0637	0637	0655	0700	0725	...	0730	0755	0800	0815	0825	0830	0855	0900	0915	0925	0930	0955	1000	1015	1025
47	Luton ✈ Parkway 103 d.		|	|	|	|	0716	|	|	...	0751	|	|	|	|	0851	|	|	|	|	0951	|	|	|	|
49	Luton 103 d.		0633	0633	0659	0659	|	0723	|	...	|	|	0823	|	|	|	|	0923	|	|	|	|	1023	|	|
80	Bedford 103 d.		0648	0648	|	|	|	0738	|	...	0807	|	0838	|	|	0907	|	0938	|	|	1007	|	1038	|	|
105	Wellingborough d.		0701	0701	|	|	|	0751	|	...	0820	|	0851	|	|	0920	|	0951	|	|	1020	|	1051	|	|
116	Kettering d.		0708	0708	0728	0728	|	0801	|	...	0827	|	0900	|	|	0927	|	1000	|	|	1027	|	1100	|	|
133	Market Harborough d.		0718	0718	0738	0738	|	0812	0821	...	0837	|	...	0912	|	0937	|	...	1012	|	1037	|	...	1112	|
159	**Leicester** 191 d.		0736	0736	0757	0755	0806	0830	0838	0838	0854	0904	...	0930	0935	0954	1004	...	1030	1035	1054	1104	...	1130	1135
180	Loughborough 191 d.		0747	0747	0807	0805	0817	0841	0848	0849	0904	|	...	|	0945	1005	|	...	|	1045	1104	|	...	|	1145
	East Midlands Parkway 191 d.		0754	|	|	|	|	0850	0856	0856	|	|	...	0946	0953	|	|	...	1046	1053	|	|	...	1146	1153
204	**Nottingham** 191 a.		|	|	|	|	0842	0903	|	|	0926	|	...	0959	|	1026	|	...	1059	|	1126	|	...	1159	|
207	**Derby 127** a.		0811	0816	0824	0826	...	...	0915	0920	...	0926	...	...	1016	...	1026	...	...	1116	...	1126	...	...	1216
246	Chesterfield **127 208** d.		...	...	0847	0847	...	...	...	...	...	0947	...	...	...	...	1049	...	...	...	...	1147	...	...	...
265	**Sheffield 127 208** a.		...	...	0904	0907	...	...	...	...	...	1004	...	...	...	...	1104	...	...	...	...	1204	...	...	...

	⚒	⚒	⚒	⚒	⚒	⚒	⚒	⚒	⚒	⚒	⚒	⚒	⚒	⚒	⚒	⚒	⚒	⚒	⚒	⚒	⚒	⚒	⚒	⚒	⚒
			Ca					Ca					Ca					C					C		
London St Pancras 103 d.	1030	1055	1100	1115	1125	1130	1155	1200	1215	1225	1230	1255	1300	1315	1325	1330	1355	1400	1415	1425	1430	1455	1500	1515	1525
Luton ✈ Parkway 103 d.	1051	|	|	|	|	1151	|	|	|	|	1251	|	|	|	|	1351	|	|	|	|	1451	|	|	|	|
Luton 103 d.	|	|	1123	|	|	|	|	1223	|	|	|	|	1323	|	|	|	|	1423	|	|	|	|	1523	|	|
Bedford 103 d.	1107	|	1138	|	|	1207	|	1238	|	|	1307	|	1338	|	|	1407	|	1438	|	|	1507	|	1538	|	|
Wellingborough d.	1120	|	1151	|	|	1220	|	1251	|	|	1320	|	1350	|	|	1420	|	1451	|	|	1520	|	1551	|	|
Kettering d.	1127	|	1200	|	|	1227	|	1303	|	|	1327	|	1400	|	|	1427	|	1500	|	|	1527	|	1601	|	|
Market Harborough d.	1137	|	...	1212	|	1237	|	...	1312	|	1337	|	...	1412	|	1437	|	...	1512	|	1537	|	...	1612	|
Leicester 191 d.	1154	1204	...	1230	1235	1254	1304	...	1330	1335	1354	1404	...	1430	1435	1454	1504	...	1530	1535	1554	1604	...	1630	1635
Loughborough 191 d.	1204	|	...	|	1245	1304	|	...	|	1345	1404	|	...	|	1445	1504	|	...	|	1545	1604	|	...	|	1645
East Midlands Parkway 191 d.	|	|	...	1246	1253	|	|	...	1345	1353	|	|	...	1446	1453	|	|	...	1546	1553	|	|	...	1645	1652
Nottingham 191 a.	1226	|	...	1259	|	1327	|	...	1359	|	1426	|	...	1459	|	1526	|	...	1559	|	1626	|	...	1659	|
Derby 127 a.	...	1226	...	...	1316	...	1326	...	...	1416	...	1426	...	...	1516	...	1526	...	...	1616	...	1626	...	...	1716
Chesterfield **127 208** d.	...	1247	...	...	...	...	1347	...	...	...	...	1447	...	...	...	...	1547	...	...	...	...	1647	...	...	...
Sheffield 127 208 a.	...	1304	...	...	...	...	1404	...	...	...	...	1504	...	...	...	...	1604	...	...	...	...	1704	...	...	...

	⚒	⚒	⚒	⚒	⚒	⚒	⚒	Ⓐ	⑥	⑥	Ⓐ	⑥	Ⓐ	⑥	⚒	Ⓐ	Ⓐ	⑥	Ⓐ	⑥	⑥	Ⓐ	⑥	Ⓐ	⑥
			C					A	C					P			M	C	L	L				P	
London St Pancras 103 d.	1530	1555	1600	1615	1625	1630	1655	1700	1700	1715	1715	1725	1730	1730	1755	1745	1800	1800	1815	1815	1825	1825	1830	1830	1855
Luton ✈ Parkway 103 d.	1551	|	|	|	|	1651	|	|	|	|	|	|	|	1751	|	1810	|	|	|	|	|	|	1851	1854	|
Luton 103 d.	|	|	1623	|	|	|	|	|	1723	|	1742	|	|	|	|	|	1823	1823	|	|	|	1851	|	|	|
Bedford 103 d.	1607	|	1638	|	|	1707	|	1735	1738	|	|	|	|	1807	|	|	1838	1838	|	|	|	|	1907	1911	|
Wellingborough d.	1620	|	1651	|	|	1720	|	1748	1751	|	|	|	1818	1820	|	1845	1851	1851	1902	|	|	|	1920	1924	|
Kettering d.	1627	|	1701	|	|	1727	|	1804	1801	|	|	|	1826	1827	|	1856	1910	1901	1910	|	|	|	1927	1932	|
Market Harborough d.	1637	|	...	1712	|	1737	|	|	...	1812	1819	|	1836	1837	|	1907	...	...	|	1912	|	1928	1937	|	|
Leicester 191 d.	1654	1704	...	1730	1735	1754	1804	1829	...	1830	1837	1835	1855	1854	1904	1925	...	...	1936	1930	1935	1946	1954	1957	2004
Loughborough 191 d.	1704	|	...	|	1745	1804	|	1840	...	|	1853	1845	1905	1904	|	1936	...	...	1947	|	1945	1957	2004	|	|
East Midlands Parkway 191 d.	|	|	...	1746	1753	|	|	1847	...	1846	|	1853	1912	|	|	1944	...	...	1955	1946	1953	|	|	2012	|
Nottingham 191 a.	1726	|	...	1759	|	1830	|	|	...	1859	1910	|	1927	1926	|	1958	...	...	2008	1959	2016	|	2026	2028	|
Derby 127 a.	...	1726	...	...	1815	...	1826	1915	...	...	...	1916	...	...	1928	2035	...	...	|	|	...	2019	...	...	2026
Chesterfield **127 208** d.	...	1747	...	...	...	...	1847	...	...	...	...	...	...	...	1947	...	...	...	2053	2053	...	...	...	...	2047
Sheffield 127 208 a.	...	1804	...	...	...	...	1904	...	...	...	...	...	...	...	2006	...	...	...	2113	2114	...	...	...	...	2100

	Ⓐ	⚒	⑥	Ⓐ	⑥	Ⓐ	⑥	Ⓐ	⚒	⚒	Ⓐ	⑥	⚒	Ⓐ	⑥	⑥	Ⓐ	⑥	Ⓐ	Ⓐ	⑥	⑥	⑥	Ⓐ	⑥
		C						L	L	C					b	c		b	c		d	e	c		b
London St Pancras 103 d.	1855	1900	1915	1915	1925	1925	1930	1930	1955	2000	2015	2015	2025	2030	2030	2030	2055	2055	2055	2100	2100	2100	2100	2125	2125
Luton ✈ Parkway 103 d.	|	|	|	|	|	|	1951	1951	|	|	|	|	|	2051	2051	2051	|	|	|	|	|	|	|	|	|
Luton 103 d.	|	1923	|	|	|	|	|	|	|	2023	|	|	|	|	|	|	|	|	|	2123	2123	2123	2123	|	|
Bedford 103 d.	|	1938	|	|	|	|	2007	2007	|	2038	|	|	|	2107	2107	2107	|	|	|	2138	2138	2138	2138	|	|
Wellingborough d.	|	1951	|	|	|	|	2020	2020	|	2051	|	|	|	2120	2120	2120	|	|	|	2151	2151	2151	2151	|	|
Kettering d.	|	2001	|	|	|	2014	2027	|	|	2101	|	|	|	2127	2127	2127	|	|	|	2158	2201	2201	2201	|	|
Market Harborough d.	1954	...	2012	2012	|	2024	2037	2037	|	...	2110	2112	|	2137	2137	2137	|	|	|	2208	2212	2212	2212	2223	2220
Leicester 191 d.	2013	...	2030	2030	2035	2041	2054	2054	2106	...	2126	2130	2135	2154	2154	2154	2204	2204	2204	2228	2230	2230	2230	2241	2237
Loughborough 191 d.	2024	...	|	|	2045	2051	2104	2104	|	...	|	|	2145	2204	2204	2212	|	|	|	|	|	|	|	2252	2248
East Midlands Parkway 191 d.	2032	...	2046	2045	2053	2101	|	|	|	...	2143	2146	2153	2227	2227	2236	|	|	|	2246	|	2241	2249	2301	2225
Nottingham 191 a.	|	...	2059	2105	|	|	2126	2129	|	...	2158	2201	|	...	...	...	|	|	|	|	2246	|	|	2312	2306
Derby 127 a.	2046	...	...	...	2113	2115	...	|	2132	...	...	...	2212	...	...	...	2226	2226	2243	2259	2302	2302	2315	...	...
Chesterfield **127 208** d.	2109	...	...	...	...	...	...	2221	2156	...	...	...	...	...	...	...	2247	2247	2305	...	...	...	...	...	...
Sheffield 127 208 a.	2129	...	...	...	...	...	...	2237	2216	...	...	...	...	...	...	...	2304	2300	2318	...	...	...	...	...	...

	⑥	⑥	⑥	⑥	Ⓐ	Ⓐ	⑥	⑥	Ⓐ	⑥	Ⓐ	⑦	⑦	⑦	⑦	⑦	⑦	⑦	⑦	⑦	⑦	⑦	⑦	⑦	⑦
	c	e	d	c			d						Y												L
London St Pancras 103 d.	2125	2130	2130	2130	2130	2200	2200	2200	2225	2225	2315		...	0900	0930	1000	1030	1100	1130	1200	1230	1300	1330	1400	1430
Luton ✈ Parkway 103 d.	|	2151	2151	2151	2153	|	|	|	2248	2303	|		...	0927	|	1027	|	1129	1156	1227	1257	1329	1403	1429	|
Luton 103 d.	|	|	|	|	|	2224	2235	2235	|	|	2346		...	|	0959	|	1100	1132	1159	1230	1300	1333	1406	|	1501
Bedford 103 d.	|	2207	2207	2207	2209	2240	2258	2258	2304	2328	0010		...	0952	1021	1050	1125	1155	1225	1256	1326	1356	1421	1447	1517
Wellingborough d.	|	2220	2220	2220	2222	2253	2316	2316	2317	2341	0023		...	1006	1037	1104	1139	1209	1240	1310	1340	1410	1435	1500	1531
Kettering d.	|	2227	2227	2227	2231	2301	2324	2324	2336	2350	0040		...	1015	1044	1113	1146	1216	1247	1317	1349	1417	1443	1508	1539
Market Harborough d.	2220	2237	2237	2237	2242	2312	2335	2335	2347	0001	0050		...	1026	1054	1124	1156	1226	1258	1327	1400	1427	1454	1518	1550
Leicester 191 d.	2237	2254	2254	2254	2302	2330	2353	2353	0003	0019	0105		1010	1048	1116	1146	1219	1247	1319	1348	1422	1448	1518	1539	1619
Loughborough 191 d.	2257	2307	2304	2314	2313	2341	0004	0012	0014	0030	0115		1021	1059	1126	1157	1229	1257	1330	1358	1433	1458	1529	1549	1630
East Midlands Parkway 191 d.	2308	2314	2314	2325	2324	2350	0013	0023	0022	0038	0123		|	1107	1134	1205	1237	1305	1337	1406	1441	1506	1537	1557	1638
Nottingham 191 a.	2319	|	|	|	|	0014	0029	0040	|	|	0144		|	1122	|	1218	|	1319	|	1422	|	1520	|	1612	|
Derby 127 a.	...	2329	2337	0025	2350	...	...	...	0042	0053	0208		1040	...	1149	...	1251	...	1352	...	1500	...	1556	...	1655
Chesterfield **127 208** d.	...	...	...	...	...	...	...	...	0106	...	...		1109	...	1210	...	1312	...	1413	...	1522	...	1618	...	1717
Sheffield 127 208 a.	...	...	...	...	...	...	...	...	0121	...	...		1128	...	1229	...	1328	...	1428	...	1537	...	1633	...	1732

	⑦	⑦	⑦	⑦	⑦	⑦	⑦	⑦	⑦	⑦	⑦	⑦	⑦	⑦	⑦	⑦	⑦	⑦	⑦	⑦	⑦	⑦	⑦	⑦	⑦
												L													
London St Pancras 103 d.	1500	1530	1600	1625	1630	1655	1700	1725	1730	1755	1800	1825	1830	1855	1900	1925	1930	1955	2000	2025	2030	2100	2130	2230	2300
Luton ✈ Parkway 103 d.	1529	|	1629	|	|	|	1721	|	|	|	1821	|	|	|	1921	|	|	|	2023	|	|	2123	|	2253	2328
Luton 103 d.	|	1601	|	|	1652	|	|	|	1752	|	|	|	1852	|	|	|	1952	|	|	|	2054	|	2154	|	|
Bedford 103 d.	1547	1617	1647	|	1715	|	1745	|	1815	|	1845	|	1915	|	1945	|	2015	|	2048	|	2118	2147	2217	2317	2352
Wellingborough d.	1601	1631	1700	|	1728	|	1758	|	1828	|	1858	|	1928	|	1958	|	2028	|	2100	|	2131	2200	2230	2331	0006
Kettering d.	1609	1639	1708	|	1736	|	1806	|	1836	|	1906	|	1936	|	2006	|	2036	|	2108	|	2139	2208	2238	2338	0013
Market Harborough d.	1620	1650	1718	|	1746	|	1816	|	1846	|	1916	|	1946	|	2016	|	2046	|	2118	|	2150	2218	2248	2348	0023
Leicester 191 d.	1643	1712	1739	1749	1810	1822	1837	1846	1911	1921	1937	1949	2007	2020	2037	2049	2107	2119	2139	2149	2213	2239	2309	0009	0044
Loughborough 191 d.	1654	1724	1749	|	1820	|	1847	|	1921	|	1947	|	2017	|	2047	|	2117	2130	2149	2201	|	2249	2319	0019	0054
East Midlands Parkway 191 d.	1702	1732	1757	1805	1828	1836	1855	1900	1929	1935	1955	2008	2025	2034	2055	2105	2125	2139	2157	2209	2229	2257	2327	0027	0102
Nottingham 191 a.	1714	|	1814	|	|	1850	1907	|	|	1950	2008	|	|	2048	2112	|	|	2150	2211	|	|	2318	|	0048	|
Derby 127 a.	...	1751	...	1817	1848	...	...	1914	1949	...	...	2020	2048	...	...	2117	2144	...	...	2222	2241	...	2349	...	0121
Chesterfield **127 208** d.	...	|	...	1840	...	...	...	1935	...	...	...	2043	...	...	...	2140	...	...	...	...	2309	...	0010	...	...
Sheffield 127 208 a.	...	1829	...	1857	...	...	...	1949	...	...	...	2058	...	...	...	2155	...	...	...	...	2327	...	0024	...	...

KETTERING - CORBY. *Journey 9 minutes.*

From **Kettering**:

⚒: 0738⑥, 0832Ⓐ, 0928**S**, 1131**S**, 1231**S**, 1331**S**, 1415**S**, 1501**S**, 1601**S**, 1701**S**, 1801⑥**S**, 1808Ⓐ**S**, 1901⑥**S**, 1910Ⓐ**S**, 2001**S**, 2101**S**, 2205, 2259⑥, 2305Ⓐ.

⑦: 0955, 1055, 1155, 1255, 1355, 1455, 1545, 1645, 1750, 1850, 1945, 2046, 2155.

From **Corby**:

⚒: 0637Ⓐ**S**, 0708, 0803Ⓐ, 0815⑥**S**, 0915**S**, 1114**S**, 1215**S**, 1315**S**, 1405**S**, 1443**S**, 1543**S**, 1643**S**, 1743**S**, 1843**S**, 1943**S**, 2043**S**, 2143, 2243.

⑦: 0930, 1025, 1125, 1230, 1330, 1425, 1525, 1625, 1720, 1820, 1920, 2020, 2125.

FOR FOOTNOTES, SEE NEXT PAGE.

EM All services 🍷

SHEFFIELD, DERBY and NOTTINGHAM - LEICESTER - LONDON 170

Services on ⑦ valid until July 12.

	⚒	⚒	①	Ⓐ	Ⓐ	⑥	Ⓐ	Ⓐ	⑥	⑥	Ⓐ	Ⓐ	⑥	⑥	Ⓐ	Ⓐ	⑥	Ⓐ	⑥	Ⓐ	⑥	Ⓐ	⑥	⑥	Ⓐ
			f	g				N									L							C	
Sheffield 127 208 d.		...	...	...	...	...	...	...	0527	...	0527	...	...	...	0556	...	0625	0627	...	...	...	0647	...	...	...
Chesterfield **127 208** d.		...	...	...	...	...	...	...	0539	...	0539	...	...	...	0609	...	0637	0639	...	...	...	0659	...	...	...
Derby 127 d.		...	0455	0455	0517	0525	...	...	0601	...	0603	...	0618	...	0632	...	0701	0703	...	...	0718	0721	...	...	0724
Nottingham **191** d.		...	|	|	|	|	0535	...	|	0602	|	0628	|	0628	|	0648	|	|	0702	0710	|	|	0728	...	|
East Midlands Parkway **191** d.		...	0506	0506	|	0539	0546	...	|	|	0616	0640	0632	0639	|	0701	|	|	|	0725	0732	0734	0739	...	|
Loughborough **191** d.		...	0514	0514	|	0547	0554	...	|	0620	0624	|	0640	|	0652	|	|	0722	0720	|	0740	0742	|	...	0747
Leicester **191** d.		0440	0526	0526	0544	0559	0608	...	0625	0633	0638	0657	0653	0657	0706	0716	0725	0735	0733	0742	0753	0755	0757	...	0801
Market Harborough d.		|	0541	0541	0558	0614	0623	...	|	0647	0653	0712	|	0712	|	0731	|	|	0747	0758	|	|	0812	...	0816
Kettering d.		0501	0551	0551	0609	0626	0634	0647	|	0656	0705	0722	0726	|	0729	0741	|	0759	0756	0809	|	0817	|	0826	0828
Wellingborough d.		0509	0559	0559	0617	0634	0642	0656	|	0704	0713	0730	0734	|	0738	0749	|	0807	0804	|	|	0825	|	0834	0839
Bedford **103** d.		0532	|	|	0632	0649	|	0713	|	0719	|	|	0749	|	0755	|	|	|	0819	0829	|	|	|	0849	0902
Luton **103** d.		|	0624	0624	|	0705	|	0729	|	|	|	0756	0805	|	|	0815	|	|	|	|	|	|	|	0905	0919
Luton ✈ Parkway **103** d.		0555	|	|	|	|	0708	|	|	0735	0740	|	|	|	0812	|	|	|	0835	|	|	|	|	|	|
London St Pancras **103** a.		0621	0654	0654	0714	0731	0736	0755	0734	0800	0809	0826	0831	0812	0838	0844	0834	0857	0901	0908	0906	0913	0912	0929	0947

	Ⓐ	⚒	⚒	Ⓐ	⑥	⚒	⚒	⚒	⚒	⚒	⑥	Ⓐ	⚒	⚒	⚒	⚒	⚒	⚒	⚒	⚒	⚒	⚒	⚒	⚒	⚒
			P			L	C				L							C					C		
Sheffield 127 208 d.	...	0727	...	0741	...	0732	...	0827	...	...	0832	...	...	0927	...	...	...	...	1027	...	...	...	...	1127	...
Chesterfield **127 208** d.	...	0739	...	|	...	0745	...	0839	...	...	0845	...	...	0939	...	...	...	...	1039	...	...	...	...	1139	...
Derby 127 d.	...	0801	...	0816	0818	|	...	0901	...	0918	|	...	...	1001	...	1018	...	...	1101	...	1118	...	...	1201	...
Nottingham **191** d.	0750	|	0802	|	|	0828	...	|	0902	|	0928	0928	...	|	1002	|	1028	...	|	1102	|	1128	...	|	1202
East Midlands Parkway **191** d.	0801	|	|	0832	0832	0839	...	|	|	0932	0939	0939	...	|	|	1032	1039	...	|	|	1132	1139	...	|	|
Loughborough **191** d.	|	|	0820	0840	0840	|	...	|	0920	0940	|	|	...	|	1020	1040	|	...	|	1120	1140	|	...	|	1220
Leicester **191** d.	0818	0825	0833	0853	0853	0857	...	0925	0933	0953	0957	0957	...	1025	1033	1053	1057	...	1125	1133	1153	1157	...	1225	1233
Market Harborough d.	|	|	0847	|	|	0912	...	|	0947	|	1012	1012	...	|	1047	|	1112	...	|	1147	|	1212	...	|	1247
Kettering d.	|	|	0856	|	|	|	0926	|	0956	|	|	|	1024	|	1056	|	|	1125	|	1156	|	|	1226	|	1256
Wellingborough d.	|	|	0904	|	|	|	0934	|	1004	|	|	|	1032	|	1104	|	|	1133	|	1204	|	|	1234	|	1304
Bedford **103** d.	|	|	0918	|	|	|	0948	|	1018	|	|	|	1049	|	1118	|	|	1149	|	1219	|	|	1249	|	1318
Luton **103** d.	|	|	|	|	|	|	1004	|	|	|	|	|	1105	|	|	|	|	1205	|	|	|	|	1305	|	|
Luton ✈ Parkway **103** d.	|	|	0934	|	|	|	|	|	1034	|	|	|	|	|	1134	|	|	|	|	1235	|	|	|	|	1334
London St Pancras **103** a.	0930	0937	1000	1006	1006	1019	1030	1034	1101	1106	1112	1119	1129	1134	1203	1207	1212	1229	1234	1301	1307	1313	1329	1334	1402

	⚒	⚒	⚒	⚒	⚒	⚒	⚒	⚒	⚒	⚒	⚒	⚒	⚒	⚒	⚒	⚒	⚒	⚒	⚒	⚒	⑥	Ⓐ	⑥	Ⓐ	⚒
			C					C					Ca					Ca							Ca
Sheffield 127 208 d.	...	...	...	1227	...	...	...	...	1327	...	...	...	...	1427	...	...	...	...	1527	...	...	...	...	...	...
Chesterfield **127 208** d.	...	...	...	1239	...	...	...	...	1339	...	...	...	...	1439	...	...	...	...	1539	...	...	...	...	...	...
Derby 127 d.	1218	...	...	1301	...	1318	...	...	1401	...	1418	...	...	1501	...	1518	...	...	1601	...	1618	1618	...	...	...
Nottingham **191** d.	|	1228	...	|	1302	|	1328	...	|	1402	|	1428	...	|	1502	|	1528	...	|	1602	|	|	1628	1628	...
East Midlands Parkway **191** d.	1232	1239	...	|	|	1332	1339	...	|	|	1432	1439	...	|	|	1532	1539	...	|	|	1632	1632	1639	1639	...
Loughborough **191** d.	1240	|	...	|	1320	1340	|	...	|	1420	1440	|	...	|	1520	1540	|	...	|	1620	1640	1640	|	|	...
Leicester **191** d.	1253	1257	...	1325	1333	1353	1357	...	1425	1433	1453	1457	...	1525	1533	1553	1557	...	1625	1633	1653	1653	1657	1657	...
Market Harborough d.	|	1312	...	|	1347	|	1412	...	|	1447	|	1512	...	|	1547	|	1612	...	|	1647	|	|	1712	1712	...
Kettering d.	|	|	1326	|	1356	|	|	1426	|	1456	|	|	1526	|	1556	|	|	1626	|	1656	|	1715	|	|	1726
Wellingborough d.	|	|	1334	|	1404	|	|	1434	|	1504	|	|	1534	|	1604	|	|	1634	|	1704	|	|	|	|	1734
Bedford **103** d.	|	|	1349	|	1419	|	|	1449	|	1519	|	|	1549	|	1619	|	|	1649	|	1719	|	|	|	|	1749
Luton **103** d.	|	|	1405	|	|	|	|	1505	|	|	|	|	1605	|	|	|	|	1705	|	|	|	|	|	1750	1805
Luton ✈ Parkway **103** d.	|	|	|	|	1435	|	|	|	|	1535	|	|	|	|	1635	|	|	|	|	1734	|	|	|	|	|
London St Pancras **103** a.	1407	1414	1429	1439	1501	1507	1513	1529	1534	1601	1606	1613	1629	1634	1701	1707	1720	1729	1734	1806	1806	1813	1812	1819	1829

	⑥	Ⓐ	⚒	Ⓐ	⑥	⚒	⚒	⚒	⚒	⚒	⚒	⚒	⚒	⚒	⑥	Ⓐ	⚒	⚒	⚒	⚒	Ⓐ	⑥	⑥	Ⓐ	⑥
							Ca					Ca			Z			Ca			Ca	Ca			
Sheffield 127 208 d.	1627	1627	...	...	...	...	...	1727	...	...	...	...	1827	...	1847	...	...	...	1927	...	...	...	...	...	2027
Chesterfield **127 208** d.	1639	1639	...	...	...	...	...	1739	...	...	...	...	1839	...	|	...	...	...	1939	...	...	...	...	...	2039
Derby 127 d.	1701	1701	...	1718	1718	...	...	1801	...	1818	...	...	1901	...	1921	1918	...	...	2001	...	...	...	...	...	2101
Nottingham **191** d.	|	|	1702	|	|	1728	...	|	1802	|	1828	...	|	1902	|	|	1928	...	|	2002	...	...	2043	2102	|
East Midlands Parkway **191** d.	|	|	|	1733	1732	1739	...	|	|	1832	1839	...	|	|	1935	1932	1939	...	|	2016	...	...	2055	2115	2114
Loughborough **191** d.	|	|	1720	1741	1740	|	...	|	1820	1840	|	...	|	1920	1941	1940	|	...	|	2024	...	...	2103	2122	2123
Leicester **191** d.	1725	1725	1733	1753	1753	1757	...	1825	1833	1853	1857	...	1925	1933	1955	1953	1957	...	2025	2036	...	...	2115	2133	2139
Market Harborough d.	|	|	1747	|	|	1812	...	|	1847	|	1912	...	|	1947	|	|	2012	...	|	2050	...	...	2129	2147	...
Kettering d.	|	|	1756	1815	|	|	1826	|	1856	|	|	1926	|	1956	|	|	|	2026	|	2059	2117	2124	2138	2157	...
Wellingborough d.	|	|	1804	|	|	|	1834	|	1904	|	|	1934	|	2004	|	|	|	2034	|	2107	2126	2132	2147	2205	...
Bedford **103** d.	|	|	1819	|	|	|	1849	|	1919	|	|	1948	|	2018	|	|	|	2053	|	2121	2153	2145	2201	2219	...
Luton **103** d.	|	1815	|	|	|	|	1905	|	|	|	|	2008	|	|	|	|	|	2108	|	|	2209	2207	2218	2235	...
Luton ✈ Parkway **103** d.	|	|	1835	|	|	|	|	|	1934	|	|	|	|	2034	|	|	|	|	|	2137	|	|	2221	2239	...
London St Pancras **103** a.	1834	1839	1901	1908	1909	1919	1934	1938	2006	2009	2015	2035	2038	2106	2108	2110	2115	2134	2141	2206	2235	2240	2259	2304	...

	⑥	Ⓐ	Ⓐ		⑦	⑦	⑦		⑦	⑦	⑦		⑦	⑦	⑦		⑦	⑦	⑦	⑦	⑦	⑦	⑦	⑦	⑦
																		L	L						
Sheffield 127 208 d.	...	2039	...	...		...	...	...	...	...	...	...	...	0917	...	...	1017	1028	1106	...	1224	...	1320	...	1407
Chesterfield **127 208** d.	...	2053	...	...		...	...	...	...	...	...	...	...	0929	...	...	1029	1041	1125	...	1237	...	1333	...	1420
Derby 127 d.	...	2120	...	...		0650	...	...	0752	...	0847	...	...	0951	...	...	1052	|	1148	...	1302	...	1354	...	1448
Nottingham **191** d.	2114	|	2128	...		|	0728	...	|	0819	|	...	0915	|	1015	...	|	1119	|	1215	|	1314	|	1430	|
East Midlands Parkway **191** d.	|	2133	|	...		0702	0738	...	0803	0832	0902	...	0926	1005	1030	...	1106	1130	1201	1230	1316	1330	1409	1443	1508
Loughborough **191** d.	2132	2141	2147	...		|	|	...	0811	0839	0910	...	0934	1013	1038	...	1114	1138	1209	1238	1324	1338	1417	1451	1515
Leicester **191** d.	2145	2155	2200	...		0720	0754	...	0823	0852	0922	...	0949	1025	1053	...	1126	1153	1223	1253	1336	1353	1429	1504	1527
Market Harborough d.	2159	|	2214	...		0738	0811	...	0840	0909	0939	...	1007	1039	1108	...	1140	1208	1238	1308	1350	1408	1443	1518	|
Kettering d.	2215	|	2224	...		0749	0821	...	0850	0919	0949	...	1018	1049	1119	...	1149	1219	1249	1319	1400	1419	1453	1528	|
Wellingborough d.	2222	|	2232	...		0801	0832	...	0902	0930	1002	...	1026	1057	1127	...	1158	1227	1257	1327	1407	1429	1500	1535	|
Bedford **103** d.	2237	|	2246	...		0815	0845	...	0914	0945	1014	...	1045	1114	1145	...	1215	1246	1315	1346	1425	1452	1525	1555	|
Luton **103** d.	2300	|	2302	...		0834	|	...	0939	|	1039	...	|	1139	|	...	1240	|	1339	|	1449	|	1542	|	1625
Luton ✈ Parkway **103** d.	|	|	|	...		|	0907	...	|	1010	|	...	1110	|	1209	...	|	1310	|	1410	|	1511	|	1614	|
London St Pancras **103** a.	2335	2307	2333	...		0919	0949	...	1019	1049	1119	...	1149	1219	1250	...	1319	1351	1419	1444	1522	1545	1615	1645	1655

	⑦		⑦	⑦	⑦	⑦	⑦	⑦	⑦		⑦	⑦	⑦		⑦	⑦	⑦	⑦		⑦	⑦	⑦		⑦	⑦
				L														Y							
Sheffield 127 208 d.	...	...	...	1502	1532	...	...	...	1629	...	...	...	...	...	1729	...	...	1832	...	...	1931	2003	...	...	2213
Chesterfield **127 208** d.	...	...	...	1515	1544	...	...	...	1643	...	...	...	...	...	1743	...	...	1844	...	...	1944	2017	...	...	2227
Derby 127 d.	...	...	...	|	1614	...	...	1647	1709	...	...	...	1747	...	1807	...	...	1909	...	...	2006	2053	...	...	2304
Nottingham **191** d.	1510	...	1536	|	|	1618	1645	|	|	...	1720	1734	|	...	|	1810	1844	|	...	1946	|	|	...	2113	...
East Midlands Parkway **191** d.	1523	...	1546	1552	1625	1631	1655	1701	1721	...	1732	1749	1801	...	1820	1825	1854	1926	...	1958	2021	2105	...	2123	...
Loughborough **191** d.	1530	...	|	1601	|	1639	|	1709	|	...	1740	|	1809	...	|	1833	1902	1933	...	2006	2030	|	...	2131	...
Leicester **191** d.	1544	...	1603	1615	1641	1652	1713	1722	1740	...	1752	1808	1821	...	1840	1845	1915	1945	...	2018	2044	2124	...	2143	...
Market Harborough d.	1601	...	|	1630	|	1706	|	1736	|	...	1806	|	1835	...	|	1905	1931	2003	...	2032	2059	2139	...	2157	...
Kettering d.	1611	...	|	1641	|	1716	|	1746	|	...	1816	|	1845	...	|	1915	1941	2013	...	2042	2110	2150	...	2207	...
Wellingborough d.	1618	...	|	1649	|	1723	|	1753	|	...	1823	|	1852	...	|	1922	1948	2021	...	2049	2118	2158	...	2214	...
Bedford **103** d.	1635	...	|	1707	|	1740	|	1812	|	...	1840	|	1910	...	|	1940	2007	2040	...	2108	2137	2218	...	2232	...
Luton **103** d.	|	...	|	1725	|	|	|	1829	|	...	|	|	1929	...	|	|	2026	|	...	2123	2152	2237	...	2250	...
Luton ✈ Parkway **103** d.	1653	...	|	|	|	1759	|	|	|	...	1859	|	|	...	|	1959	|	2055	...	|	|	|	...	|	...
London St Pancras **103** a.	1727	...	1731	1759	1804	1829	1834	1859	1904	...	1929	1934	1959	...	2004	2029	2057	2127	...	2157	2227	2312	...	2328	...

A – Conveys (12) London St Pancras - Corby.
C – To / from Corby.
L – To / from Leeds, Table **127**.
M – To Corby, Oakham (arrive 1942) and Melton Mowbray (arrive 1955).
N – From Melton Mowbray (depart 0602) Oakham (depart 0614) and Corby.
P – To / from Lincoln, Table **191**.

S – To / from London St Pancras.
Y – To / from York, Table **127**.
Z – To / from Scarborough. May 23 - Sept. 5.

a – Waits at Kettering for up to 31 minutes before departing for Corby / London.
b – ⑥ May 23 - Jul. 11 and Sept. 12 - Dec. 12.
c – ⑥ 18 Jul. - 5 Sept.
d – ⑥ May 23 - Jul. 11.
e – ⑥ Sept. 12 - Dec. 12.
f – ① May 17 - Aug. 31.
g – Ⓐ Sept. 1 - Dec. 11.

FOR SERVICES KETTERING – CORBY AND V.V., SEE PREVIOUS PAGE.

171 NOTTINGHAM - SHEFFIELD - BARNSLEY - HUDDERSFIELD and LEEDS

2nd class EM, NT

Services on ⑦ valid until July 12. For services Sheffield - Leeds and v.v. via Doncaster and Wakefield Westgate see Table **127**.

km			NT	NT	EM	NT	NT	NT	NT	EM	NT	NT	NT	EM	NT	NT		EM	NT	EM	NT	NT	NT	EM	NT
			Ⓐ	⚒	⚒	⚒	Ⓐ	⑥	Ⓐ	⚒	⚒	⚒	⚒	⚒	⚒	⚒		⚒	⚒	⚒	⚒	⚒	⚒	⚒	⚒
					L					L				L				L		L				L	
0	**Nottingham** .. 170 208 d.	⚒	...	...	0518	...	...	...	0623	0640	...	0713	...	0745	0815a	...	and at the same minutes past each hour until ★	1545	1615	1645	...	1715	...	1745	1815
18	Langley Mill d.		...	...	|	...	...	...	0638	|	...	0730	...	|	0831	...		|	1632	|	...	1731	...	1802	1832
29	Alfreton d.		...	...	|	...	...	...	0646	0702	...	0738	...	0807	0839	...		1607	1640	1707	...	1739	...	1808	1840
45	Chesterfield ... 170 208 d.		...	...	0549	...	0626	...	0658	0713	...	0750	...	0818	0851	...		1618	1651	1718	...	1752	...	1818	1852
64	**Sheffield** ...... 170 208 a.		...	...	0615	...	0646	...	0718	0731	...	0808	...	0838	0915	...		1638	1717	1734	...	1815	...	1839	1915
64	**Sheffield** .... 127 d.		0536	0606	...	0636	0649	0706	0720	...	0736	0818	0836	...	0918	0936		...	1718	...	1736	1818	1836	...	1918
70	Meadowhall d.		0542	0612	...	0642	0655	0712	0726	...	0742	0824	0842	...	0924	0942		...	1724	...	1742	1824	1842	...	1924
90	Barnsley d.		0601	0633	...	0701	0712	0733	0742	...	0801	0842	0901	...	0942	1001		...	1742	...	1803	1842	1908r	...	1942
123	**Huddersfield** .... 187 a.		0649	|	...	0749	|	|	|	...	0849	|	0949	...	|	1049		...	|	...	1857r	|	1956r	...	|
107	Wakefield Kirkgate ..... d.		...	0650	...	...	0728	0750	0758	...	...	0858	...	...	0958	...		...	1758	...	...	1858	...	...	1958
130	**Leeds** .... 127 187 a.		...	0728	...	...	0751	0825	0821	...	...	0919	...	...	1018	...		...	1818	...	...	1923	...	...	2019

	NT	EM	NT	EM	NT	NT	NT	NT	EM	EM	NT	NT	NT	NT	NT	NT	NT	EM		NT	NT	NT	EM	NT	NT	EM
	⚒	⚒	⚒	⚒	⚒	Ⓐ	⑥	⑥	Ⓐ	⑥	⑥	⚒	Ⓐ	①–④	Ⓐ	⑥	⚒	Ⓐ		⑦	⑦	⑦	⑦	⑦	⑦	⑦
		L		L			C	D	A	A			B					A					L			L
Nottingham .. 170 208 d.	...	1845	1915	1940	...	...	...	...	2015	2015	2038	...	2045	...	2111	2115	...	2143	⑦	...	...	...	0931	1006	...	1040
Langley Mill d.	...	|	1932	|	...	...	...	...	2033	2033	2102	...	|	...	2131	2131	...	2201		...	...	...	|	1027	...	|
Alfreton d.	...	1907	1940	2001	...	...	...	...	2041	2041	2110	...	|	...	2139	2139	...	2209		...	...	...	0953	1035	...	1103
Chesterfield .. 170 208 d.	...	1918	1952	2011	...	...	...	...	2053	2053	2122	...	2128	...	2200	2150	...	2221		...	...	...	1008	1054	...	1114
Sheffield ...... 170 208 a.	...	1939	2015	2028	...	...	...	...	2113	2114	2140	...	2154	...	2219	2214	...	2237		...	...	...	1032	1115	...	1135
Sheffield .... 127 d.	1936	...	2018	...	2041	2109	2106	2106	2125	2124	...	2141	...	2206	...	...	2241	2248		0839	0917	0939	...	1117	1149	...
Meadowhall d.	1942	...	2024	...	2047	2115	2112	2112	|	|	...	2147	...	2212	...	...	2247	|		0845	0923	0945	...	1123	1155	...
Barnsley d.	2008	...	2042	...	2108	2136	2133	2133	|	|	...	2208	...	2233	...	...	2308	|		0910	0937	1006	...	1137	1216	...
Huddersfield .... 187 a.	2055	...	|	...	2156	|	|	|	|	|	...	2257	...	|	...	...	0001	|		|	|	1053	...	|	1303	...
Wakefield Kirkgate ..... d.	...	...	2058	...	...	2152	2150	2152	2155k	2153k	...	...	...	2250	...	...	...	2318k		0932	0955	...	...	1153	...	...
Leeds .... 127 187 a.	...	...	2122	...	...	2228	2214	2228	2212	2210	...	...	...	2328	...	...	...	2336		0952	1019	...	...	1218	...	...

	NT	NT	EM	NT	EM	NT	NT	EM	NT	EM	NT	NT	EM	NT	NT	NT	EM	NT	EM	NT	EM	NT	NT	EM	NT	NT
	⑦	⑦	⑦	⑦	⑦	⑦	⑦	⑦	⑦	⑦	⑦	⑦	⑦	⑦	⑦	⑦	⑦	⑦	⑦	⑦	⑦	⑦	⑦	⑦	⑦	⑦
			L		L			L		L			L				L		L		L			L		
Nottingham .. 170 208 d.	1115	...	1146	1219	1239	...	1311	1338	1419	1438	...	1512	1554	...	1614	...	1640	1714	1737	1814	1837	...	1919	1938	2013	2120
Langley Mill d.	1131	...	|	1235	1256	...	1327	1355	1435	1455	...	1534	|	...	1630	...	1700	1730	1754	1830	1854	...	1935	|	2029	2141
Alfreton d.	1139	...	1208	1243	1304	...	1335	1403	1443	1503	...	1542	1604	...	1638	...	1708	1738	1802	1838	1902	...	1943	2000	2037	2149
Chesterfield .. 170 208 d.	1151	...	1218	1254	1317	...	1351	1418	1454	1513	...	1553	1623	...	1650	...	1720	1749	1817	1849	1912	...	1954	2010	2048	2208
Sheffield ...... 170 208 a.	1215	...	1235	1315	1333	...	1415	1436	1515	1531	...	1615	1639	...	1715	...	1740	1815	1834	1915	1931	...	2015	2031	2114	2232
Sheffield .... 127 d.	1216	1235	...	1317	...	1339	1417	...	1517	...	1539	1617	...	1654	1717	1739	...	1817	...	1916	...	1939	2017	*2039*	...	*2239*
Meadowhall d.	1223	1241	...	1323	...	1345	1423	...	1523	...	1543	1623	...	1700	1723	1746	...	1823	...	1923	...	1945	2023	*2045*	...	*2245*
Barnsley d.	1237	1306	...	1337	...	1406	1437	...	1537	...	1604	1637	...	1715	1737	1810	...	1837	...	1937	...	2006	2037	*2110*	...	*2310*
Huddersfield .... 187 a.	|	1353	...	|	...	1453	|	...	|	...	1653	|	...	1805	|	1858	...	|	...	|	...	2053	|	|	...	|
Wakefield Kirkgate ..... d.	1253	...	...	1353	...	...	1453	...	1553	...	...	1653	...	...	1753	...	...	1853	...	1957	...	...	2053	*2130*	...	*2330*
Leeds .... 127 187 a.	1318	...	...	1418	...	...	1518	...	1618	...	...	1718	...	...	1818	...	...	1917	...	2027	...	...	2118	*2154*	...	*0008*

		NT	NT	NT	NT	NT	EM	NT	NT	EM	NT	EM	NT	NT	EM	NT	NT	EM		NT	NT	EM	NT	NT	EM
		Ⓐ	⑥	Ⓐ	⑥	Ⓐ	⚒	⚒	⚒	⑥	⚒	⚒	⚒	⚒	⚒	⚒	⚒	⚒		⚒	⚒	⚒	⚒	⚒	⑥
							A			A		L			L			L				L			L
Leeds .... 127 187 d.	⚒	...	...	...	...	0605	0634	...	0705	0734	...	...	0802	...	...	0905	...	...	and at the same minutes past each hour until	1605	...	...	1705	...	...
Wakefield Kirkgate ..... d.		...	...	...	...	0621	0646k	...	0723	0746k	...	...	0823	...	...	0923	...	...		1623	...	...	1723	...	...
Huddersfield .... 187 d.		...	...	...	...	|	|	0610	|	|	0710	...	|	0810	...	|	0913	...		|	1613	...	|	1713	...
Barnsley d.		...	...	...	0621	0638	|	0658	0740	|	0758	...	0840	0858	...	0940	1001	...		1640	1701	...	1740	1801	...
Meadowhall d.		...	...	...	0642	0649	|	0720	0753	|	0818	...	0852	0921	...	0952	1019	...		1652	1721	...	1751	1820	...
Sheffield .... 127 a.		...	...	...	0655	0700	0725	0729	0805	0821	0829	...	0902	0930	...	1002	1030	...		1702	1732	...	1802	1830	...
Sheffield ...... 170 208 d.		0505	0554	0600	0703	0703	0732	...	0805	0832	...	0838	0905	...	0938	1005	...	1038		1705	...	1744	1805	...	1838
Chesterfield .. 170 208 d.		0520	0619	0616	0720	0720	0745	...	0824	0845	...	0853	0922	...	0953	1022	...	1053		1722	...	1758	1822	...	1853
Alfreton d.		|	0630	0630	0733	0733	0756	...	0835	0856	...	0903	0933	...	1003	1033	...	1103		1733	...	1808	1833	...	1903
Langley Mill d.		|	0637	0637	0740	0740	0804	...	0842	|	...	|	0940	...	|	1040	...	|		1740	...	|	1840	...	|
Nottingham .. 170 208 a.		0612	0704	0708	0802	0802	0823	...	0902	0918	...	0930	1001	...	1030	1101	...	1130		1801	...	1833	1900	...	1933

	EM	NT	NT	NT	EM	NT	NT	NT	EM	NT	EM	NT	NT	NT	EM	NT	NT	EM		NT	NT	NT	NT	EM	NT	NT
	Ⓐ	⚒	Ⓐ	⑥	⚒	Ⓐ	⚒	⚒	⚒	⚒	⚒	⚒	⚒	⚒	⑥	⚒	⚒	Ⓐ		⑦	⑦	⑦	⑦	⑦	⑦	⑦
	L				L				L		L													L		
Leeds .... 127 187 d.	...	1805	...	...	...	1743	1905	...	...	1943	...	...	2037	...	...	2137	...	...	⑦	...	0837	0855	...	...	0954	...
Wakefield Kirkgate ..... d.	...	1823	...	...	...	|	1923	...	...	2000	...	...	2107	...	...	2207	...	...		...	0900	0914	...	...	1011	...
Huddersfield .... 187 d.	...	|	1756	1813	...	1822	|	1918	...	|	...	2018	|	2118	...	|	2218	...		...	|	|	0919	...	|	1015
Barnsley d.	...	1840	1855	1901	...	1910	1940	2006	...	2016	...	2111	2124	2206	...	2225	2306	...		...	0924	0941	1012	...	1038	1103
Meadowhall d.	...	1852	1916	1920	...	1930	1952	2024	...	2031	...	2128	2146	2225	...	2247	2326	...		...	0941	0955	1033	...	1051	1120
Sheffield .... 127 a.	...	1903	1927	1930	...	1940	2004	2036	...	2044	...	2140	2158	2236	...	2258	2336	...		...	0955	1004	1043	...	1100	1128
Sheffield ...... 170 208 d.	1845	1905	...	...	1938	...	2005	...	2041	...	2138	...	...	...	2235	...	...	2338		0900	...	1007	...	1049	1103	...
Chesterfield .. 170 208 d.	1901	1922	...	...	1953	...	2022	...	2058	...	2154	...	...	...	2251	...	...	0002		0917	...	1024	...	1104	1120	...
Alfreton d.	1911	1933	...	...	2004	...	2033	...	2109	...	2205	...	...	...	|	...	...	|		0928	...	1035	...	1114	1131	...
Langley Mill d.	|	1940	...	...	|	...	2040	...	|	...	2212	...	...	...	|	...	...	|		0935	...	1042	...	|	1138	...
Nottingham .. 170 208 a.	1938	2000	...	...	2031	...	2101	...	2138r	...	2238r	...	...	...	2333	...	...	0041		0955	...	1102	...	1138	1158	...

	NT	NT	NT	EM	NT	EM	NT	EM	NT	NT	EM	NT	EM	NT	NT	EM	NT	EM	NT	NT	EM	NT	EM	NT	EM	EM
	⑦	⑦	⑦	⑦	⑦	⑦	⑦	⑦	⑦	⑦	⑦	⑦	⑦	⑦	⑦	⑦	⑦	⑦	⑦	⑦	⑦	⑦	⑦	⑦	⑦	⑦
				L		L		L			L		L			L		L			L		L		L	
Leeds .... 127 187 d.	1051	1129	...	...	1229	...	...	...	1348	...	...	1505	...	...	1605	...	1654	...	...	1805	...	1904	...	...	...	...
Wakefield Kirkgate ..... d.	1113	1146	...	...	1246	...	...	...	1411	...	...	1522	...	...	1622	...	1711	...	...	1822	...	1920	...	...	...	...
Huddersfield .... 187 d.	|	|	1129	...	|	...	1319	...	|	1415	...	|	...	1519	|	...	|	...	1719	|	...	|	...	1919	...	...
Barnsley d.	1133	1206	1217	...	1306	...	1412	...	1441	1503	...	1542	...	1612	1642	...	1741	...	1812	1842	...	1940	...	2012	...	...
Meadowhall d.	1146	1217	1235	...	1318	...	1433	...	1454	1521	...	1556	...	1633	1656	...	1756	...	1833	1856	...	1954	...	2034	...	...
Sheffield .... 127 a.	1156	1229	1247	...	1329	...	1447	...	1506	1528	...	1605	...	1643	1705	...	1805	...	1844	1905	...	2004	...	2043	...	...
Sheffield ...... 170 208 d.	1200	1231	...	1249	1331	1349	...	1453	1507	...	1543	1607	1640	...	1707	1739	1807	1841	...	1907	1940	2006	2040	...	2140	2329
Chesterfield .. 170 208 d.	1218	1249	...	1303	1348	1403	...	1507	1525	...	1557	1625	1656	...	1724	1754	1825	1856	...	1925	1955	2022	2055	...	2154	2343
Alfreton d.	1229	1259	...	1314	1359	1414	...	1518	1536	...	1608	1636	1707	...	1735	1804	1836	1906	...	1936	2006	2033	2106	...	2205	2354
Langley Mill d.	1236	1307	...	|	1406	|	...	1525	1543	...	1615	1643	1714	...	1743	1812	1843	1914	...	1943	2014	2040	2114	...	2212	0001
Nottingham .. 170 208 a.	1256	1326	...	1339	1426	1440	...	1544	1603	...	1633	1703	1732	...	1803	1829	1903	1936	...	2003	2031	2101	2136	...	2235	0023

A – (12) London St Pancras - Leeds and v.v., Table **170**.
B – Via Derby (dep. 2106).
C – May 23 - Jul. 11.
D – Jul. 18 - Dec. 12.
L – (2) (Norwich -) Nottingham - Sheffield (- Liverpool) and v.v., see Table **208**.
a – 0811 on ⑥.
k – Wakefield Westgate.
r – 5–6 minutes earlier on ⑥.
★ – On ⑥ the 1115 Nottingham - Leeds does not call at Chesterfield.

172 NOTTINGHAM and DERBY local services

EM 2nd class

Nottingham – Mansfield – Worksop

Services valid until September 26.

Journey time: ± 65 minutes *51 km*

From Nottingham:
Trains call at Mansfield ± 35 minutes later.
⚒: 0540, 0605, 0659, 0825 and hourly until 1725; then 1755, 1855, 1955, 2055, 2205.
⑦: 0826 (until Sept. 6), 0926, 1426, 1726.

From Worksop:
Trains call at Mansfield ± 32 minutes later.
⚒: 0550, 0656, 0738 and hourly until 1642; then 1745, 1841, 1921, 2015, 2120, 2220.
⑦: 0938 (until Sept. 6), 1038, 1538, 1840.

Derby – Matlock

Services on ⚒ valid until September 5; on ⑦ valid until July 12.

Journey time: ± 31 minutes *28 km*

From Derby:
Ⓐ: 0538, 0650, 0750 and hourly until 1650; then 1754, 1854, 1950, 2056, 2216.
⑥: 0540, 0648, 0752, 0847 and hourly until 2047; then 2152.
⑦: 0958, 1157, 1400, 1529, 1757, 1926, 2156.

From Matlock:
Ⓐ: 0622, 0737, 0838 and hourly until 2038; then 2139, 2255.
⑥: 0621, 0744 and hourly until 1744; then 1841, 1941, 2043, 2141, 2255.
⑦: 1042, 1238, 1438, 1642, 1840, 2059, 2242.

NT 2nd class — LEEDS - HARROGATE - YORK — 173

km			⚒	Ⓐ	⑥	⚒	⑥	Ⓐ	⑥	Ⓐ	⚒	⚒	⚒	⚒	⚒	⚒		⚒	⚒	⚒	⚒	Ⓐ	⚒
0	**Leeds** 127 185 187 d.	⚒	0607	0629	0637	0713	0739	0743	0754	0759	0829	0859	0929	0959	1029	1059	and at	1629	1659	1713	1729	1744	1759
29	**Harrogate** d.		0645	0705	0714	0749	0816	0816	0829	0834	0905	0935	1005	1035	1105	1135	the same minutes	1708	1735	1749	1805	1816	1835
36	Knaresborough d.		0655	0719	0723	0759	0828	0828	0840	0845	0915	0945	1014	1045	1114	1145	past each	1721	1745	1800	1814	1826	1845
62	**York** 127 185 187 a.		0721	0748	0751	0827	0859	0858	...	...	0947	...	1046	...	1147	...	hour until	1748	...	...	...	1846	...

	⚒	Ⓐ	⚒	⚒	⑥	Ⓐ	⚒	⑥	Ⓐ			⑦	⑦		⑦	⑦	⑦	⑦	⑦	⑦	⑦	⑦	⑦	⑦
Leeds 127 185 187 d.	1829	1859	1929	2029	2120	2129	2229	2321	2329	...	⑦	0954	1054	...	1254	1454	1554	1654	1754	1854	1954	2116	2223	2322
Harrogate d.	1905	1935	2005	2105	2156	2205	2308	2358	0006	...		1031	1130	...	1330	1530	1630	1730	1830	1930	2030	2153	2300	2359
Knaresborough d.	1914	1945	2014	2114	2206	2215	...	...	...	...		...	1140	...	1340	1540	1645	1744	1844	1944	2045	2203	...	...
York 127 185 187 a.	1945	...	2045	2148	...	...	...	...	...	...		...	1207	...	1408	1608	1710	1810	1912	2012	2115	...	...	...

	⚒	Ⓐ	⑥	Ⓐ	Ⓐ A	⑥	Ⓐ	⑥ A	Ⓐ	⑥	Ⓐ	⚒	⑥	Ⓐ		⑥	Ⓐ	⚒	⚒	⚒		⚒	⑥
York 127 185 187 d.	...	...	...	...	...	0653	0652	...	...	...	...	0757	...	...	...	0845	0845	0910	...	1011	and at	...	1654
Knaresborough d.	...	...	0647	0700	...	0721	0724	...	0742	0751	0756	0821	0851	0856	...	0909	0910	0935	1005	1035	the same minutes	1705	1718
Harrogate d.	0606	0630	0656	0711	0728	0731	0740	0744	0751	0800	0806	0830	0900	0905	...	0918	0919	0944	1014	1044	past each	1714	1730
Leeds 127 185 187 a.	0644	0708	0734	0748	0757	0808	0817	0810	0829	0838	0840	0908	0937	0937	...	0955	0956	1022	1052	1122	hour until	1755	1807

	Ⓐ	⚒	⚒	⚒	Ⓐ	⚒	⚒	Ⓐ	⑥	Ⓐ		⑦	⑦	⑦		⑦	⑦	⑦	⑦	⑦	⑦	⑦	⑦	⑦
York 127 185 187 d.	1654	1717	...	1811	...	1911	2011	2111	2157	2211	⑦	...	...	...	...	1218	1420	1618	1717	1817	1917	2018	2126	...
Knaresborough d.	1718	1741	1805	1835	1905	1935	2035	2135	2221	2236		...	...	1142	...	1242	1444	1642	1742	1842	1942	2042	2150	...
Harrogate d.	1737	1750	1818	1844	1914	1944	2044	2145	2237	2247		0953	1053	1153	...	1253	1453	1653	1753	1853	1953	2053	2202	2305
Leeds 127 185 187 a.	1817	1828	1855	1922	1952	2022	2122	2223	2314	2324		1030	1130	1230	...	1330	1530	1730	1830	1930	2030	2130	2240	2343

A – (1,2) and 🍷 Harrogate - Leeds - London Kings Cross and v.v. Operated by *GR*. See Table **185**.

NT 2nd class — LEEDS - LANCASTER and CARLISLE — 174

Services on ⑦ valid until November 1

km		Ⓐ	Ⓐ	⑥	⑥	⚒	⑦ f	⚒	⑦	⚒	⚒ A	⚒	⑦ f	⚒	⑦	⚒	⚒	⑦	⑥ z	⑥	Ⓐ	⑦	⑦	⑥ y	Ⓐ	Ⓐ
0	**Leeds** 176 d.	...	...	0555	0619	0819	0840	0849	0900	0947	1019	1049	1051	1249	1315	1349	1449	1457	...	1639	1639	1721	1733	1750	1756	1919
17	Shipley d.	...	...	0608	0632	0832	0853	0902	0914	1002	1032	1102	1104	1302	1329	1403	1502	1510	...	1655	1655	1734	1746	1803	1808	1932
27	Keighley 176 d.	...	...	0621	0642	0843	0906	0912	0928	1012	1042	1112	1114	1312	1339	1414	1512	1520	...	1710	1710	1744	1756	1814	1824	1942
42	**Skipton** 176 d.	0540	...	0640	0656	0900	0926	0926	0946	1026	1100	1126	1129	1326	1354	1434	1526	1536	1645	1725	1724	1800	1811	1835	1841	2000
58	Hellifield d.	0555	...	0654	0708	0914	0940	0940	0957	|	1114	1137	1144	1340	1408	1448	1537	1550	1659	1740	1739	1814	1822	1849	1855	2015
66	Giggleswick d.	0608	...	0707	|	0925	0952	|	|	|	1125	|	1154	|	|	1459	|	1600	|	1750	1749	1825	|	|	|	|
103	Carnforth 157 a.	0643	...	0742	|	1000	1028	|	|	|	1200	|	1230	|	|	1534	|	1636	|	1826	1829	1900	|	|	|	|
113	**Lancaster** 157 a.	0653	...	0752	|	1012	1039	|	|	|	1211	|	1244	|	|	1547r	|	1646	|	1838	1842	1914	|	|	|	|
120	Morecambe a.	*0736*	...	*0846*	|	1040	1055	|	|	|	1239	|	1309	|	|	1609r	|	1701	|	1859	1901	1930	|	|	|	|
66	Settle d.	...	...	...	0715	...	...	0950	1006	1044	...	1146	...	1348	1417	...	1545	...	1707	...	...	...	1830	1857	1903	2024
76	Horton in Ribblesdale d.	...	...	...	0724	...	...	0958	1015	|	...	1154	...	1357	1426	...	1553	...	1716	...	...	...	1839	1906	1912	2032
84	Ribblehead d.	...	...	...	0732	...	...	1006	1023	|	...	1202	...	1405	1434	...	1601	...	1724	...	...	...	1847	1914	1920	2042
99	Garsdale d.	...	...	...	0747	...	...	1021	1039	|	...	1217	...	1420	1450	...	1616	...	1739	...	...	...	1902	1929	1935	...
115	Kirkby Stephen d.	...	0728	...	0759	...	...	1034	1052	1122	...	1230	...	1432	1503	...	1629	...	1751	...	...	...	1915	1941	1947	...
132	Appleby d.	...	0740	...	0812	...	...	1047	1105	1136	...	1243	...	1445	1515	...	1641	...	1804	...	...	...	1928	1954	2000	...
166	Armathwaite d.	...	0808	...	0839	...	...	1115	1133	|	...	1311	...	1512	1543	...	1709	...	1831	...	...	...	1956	2021	2027	...
182	**Carlisle** a.	...	0824	...	0858	...	...	1134	1149	1217	...	1329	...	1532	1600	...	1728	...	1851	...	...	...	2013	2041	2047	...

	⚒	Ⓐ	⑥	⑥	Ⓐ	⑥⑦	⚒	⚒	⑦ f	⚒ B	⑦	⑦ f	Ⓐ	⑥ y	Ⓐ	Ⓐ	⑥	⑥	⚒	⑦	⑦	⑥	Ⓐ	⚒	⑦	⚒
Carlisle d.	...	0620	...	0752	0853	0925	...	1151	...	...	1351	...	1400	1426	1503	...	1549	...	1618	1637	...	1800	1807	...	...	...
Armathwaite d.	...	0634	...	0806	0907	0939	...	1205	...	...	1405	...	1414	1440	|	...	|	...	1632	1651	...	1814	1821	...	...	...
Appleby d.	...	0702	...	0834	0935	1007	...	1233	...	...	1433	...	1443	1509	1540	...	1626	...	1701	1720	...	1842	1849	...	...	...
Kirkby Stephen d.	...	0717	...	0847	0948	1021	...	1246	...	...	1447	...	1456	1522	1553	...	1639	...	1714	1734	...	1856	1902	...	...	...
Garsdale d.	...	▬	...	0900	1002	1034	...	1259	...	...	1500	...	1509	1535	|	...	|	...	1727	1747	...	1909	1915	...	...	...
Ribblehead d.	0714	...	...	0915	1017	1049	...	1314	...	...	1515	...	1523	1549	|	...	|	...	1742	1802	...	1924	1930	...	...	2100
Horton in Ribblesdale d.	0721	...	...	0921	1024	1056	...	1320	...	...	1522	...	1530	1556	|	...	|	...	1748	1809	...	1931	1936	...	...	2106
Settle d.	0729	Ⓐ	...	0929	1032	1104	...	1328	...	...	1530	...	1539	1604	1635	...	1716	...	1757	1819	...	1939	1944	...	...	2114
Morecambe d.	|	*0619*	*0738*	|	|	|	1041	|	1220	1329	|	1446	|	|	|	1619	|	1619	|	|	1745	|	|	1908	2000	|
Lancaster 157 d.	|	0710	0824	|	|	|	1100	|	1248	1348	|	|	|	|	|	|	|	1640	|	|	1804	|	|	1924	2020	|
Carnforth 157 d.	|	0720	0834	|	|	|	1110	|	1258	1358	|	1500	|	|	|	1632	|	1650	|	|	1814	|	|	1934	2030	|
Giggleswick d.	|	0754	0908	|	|	|	1145	|	1332	1433	|	1535	|	|	|	1710	|	1725	|	|	1849	|	|	2009	2105	|
Hellifield d.	0737	0806	0920	0937	1039	1111	1157	1337	1344	1444	1539	1548	1548	1611	|	1722	|	1736	1806	1826	1900	1947	1952	2021	2116	2123
Skipton 176 d.	0756	0827	0942	0957	1059	1128	1214	1358	1402	1510	1557	1608	1612	1628	1658	1740	1741	1758	1828	1843	1918	2007	2007	2038	2133	2140
Keighley 176 d.	0809	0837	0952	1008	1109	1138	1224	1409	1412	1520	1607	1618	1622	1638	1708	1750	1751	1808	1838	1853	1928	2017	2017	2048	2143	*2201*
Shipley d.	0819	0847	1002	1019	1118	1149	1232	1418	1421	1530	1616	1629	1631	1649	1720	1758	1800	1819	1848	1903	1938	2028	2028	2057	2154	*2214*
Leeds 176 a.	0837	0904	1022	1034	1136	1206	1254	1437	1439	1547	1633	1647	1651	1707	1740	1815	1817	1839	1907	1920	1956	2044	2044	2117	2210	*2232*

A – To Heysham Port (a. 1257).
B – From Heysham Port (d. 1315).
f – Until Sept. 13.
r – 2–7 minutes earlier on ⑥.
y – Until Oct. 31.
z – From Nov. 7.

NT 2nd class — WEST YORKSHIRE local services — 176

LEEDS – BRADFORD Forster Square *22 km*

Ⓐ : 0649, 0739, 0810, 0840 and every 30 minutes until 1610; then 1635, 1710, 1736, 1810, 1840, 1910, 1959.

⑥ : 0710, 0810, 0840 and every 30 minutes until 1610; then 1635, 1710, 1740, 1810, 1840, 1910, 2043.

⑦ : 0834 and hourly until 1534 (see note **A**); then 1635, 1737, 1834, 1934, 2034, 2134, 2234.

BRADFORD Forster Square **– LEEDS** Journey : ± 21 minutes

Ⓐ : 0601, 0630, 0655, 0759, 0826, 0901, 0931 and every 30 minutes until 1801; then 1827, 1901, 1931.

⑥ : 0601, 0701, 0733, 0759, 0831, 0901 and every 30 minutes until 1931.

⑦ : 0902 and houry until 2302.

A – Nov. 8 - Dec. 6, no 1334 service from Leeds.

LEEDS – BRADFORD Interchange *Services on ⑦ valid until July 12.* *15 km*

Ⓐ : 0508, 0551, 0603, 0622, 0637, 0651, 0708, 0722, 0737, 0751 and at 08, 22, 37 and 51 minutes past each hour until 2008; then 2037, 2108, 2137, 2208, 2237, 2308.

⑥ : 0537, 0551, 0616, 0637, 0651, 0708, 0722, 0737, 0751 and at 08, 22, 37 and 51 minutes past each hour until 2008; then 2037, 2108, 2137, 2208, 2237, 2300.

⑦ : 0803, 0821, 0845, 0923, 0953, 1012, 1053 and at 12 and 54 minutes past each hour until 1812; then 1842, 1903, 1942, 2003, 2012, 2042, 2104, 2135, 2205, 2235, 2322.

BRADFORD Interchange **– LEEDS** Journey : ± 20 minutes

Ⓐ : 0618, 0648, 0703, 0719, 0734, 0750 and at 03, 19, 34 and 50 minutes past each hour until 2019; then 2037, 2104, 2137, 2204, 23219, 2237, 2304, 2330

⑥ : 0626, 0704, 0719, 0734, 0750, and at 03, 19, 34 and 50 minutes past each hour until 2019; then 2037, 2104, 2137, 2204, 2237, 2304.

⑦ : 0831, 0921, 1002, 1025, 1102, 1125, 1144, 1225, 1244 and at 25 and 44 minutes past each hour until 1944; then 2007, 2031, 2107, 2138, 2202, 2232, 2302, 2349.

BRADFORD Forster Square **– ILKLEY** *22 km*

⚒ : 0615, 0644Ⓐ, 0711Ⓐ, 0715⑥, 0746Ⓐ, 0816, 0846 and every 30 minutes until 1616; then 1644, 1716, 1746, 1816, 1846, 1941, 2038, 2138, 2238, 2320.

⑦ : 1038, 1238, 1438, 1638, 1838, 2038, 2238.

ILKLEY – BRADFORD Forster Square Journey : ± 31 minutes

⚒ : 0617, 0650Ⓐ, 0722, 0750Ⓐ, 0821, 0851, 0921, 0951 and every 30 minutes until 1921; then 2005, 2040, 2140, 2240.

⑦ : 0953, 1153, 1353, 1553, 1753, 1953, 2153.

TABLE CONTINUES ON NEXT PAGE ▶ ▶ ▶

176 WEST YORKSHIRE local services — 2nd class NT

BRADFORD Forster Square – **SKIPTON** *30 km*

Ⓐ: 0610, 0640, 0715, 0742, 0811 and every 30 minutes until 1611; then 1640, 1711, 1738, 1811, 1841, 1907, 1936, 2007, 2105, 2205, 2309.

⑥: 0610, 0711, 0811, 0841 and every 30 minutes until 1841; then 1907, 1936, 2007, 2105, 2205, 2305.

⑦: 1048, 1248, 1448, 1648, 1848, 2048, 2248.

SKIPTON – BRADFORD Forster Square — Journey: ± 38 minutes

Ⓐ: 0602, 0627, 0701, 0732, 0801, 0832, 0902 and every 30 minutes until 1602; then 1636, 1702, 1728, 1802, 1832, 1900, 1932, 1954, 2054, 2154.

⑥: 0602, 0701, 0732, 0801, 0832, 0902 and every 30 minutes until 1702; then 1730, 1802, 1832, 1900, 1932, 1954, 2054, 2154.

⑦: 0936, 1137, 1337, 1537, 1737, 1937, 2139.

HUDDERSFIELD – WAKEFIELD Westgate *No service on ⑦ 25 km*

⚒: 0532Ⓐ, 0641, 0732⑥, 0749Ⓐ, 0837, 0935 and hourly until 2135.

WAKEFIELD Westgate – **HUDDERSFIELD** — Journey: ± 33 minutes

⚒: 0630Ⓐ, 0729, 0829 and hourly (see note **B**) until 2129; then 2242.

B – 14xx service departs 1438 on ⑥.

LEEDS – DONCASTER stopping trains *48 km*

Ⓐ: 0619, 0727, 0819, 0919 and hourly until 1919; then 2021, 2128, 2239.

⑥: 0619, 0726, 0819, 0919 and hourly until 1819; then 1922, 2021, 2134, 2216.

⑦: 1009, 1209, 1409, 1609, 1809, 2020, 2109.

DONCASTER – LEEDS stopping trains — Journey: ± 48 minutes

Ⓐ: 0625, 0714, 0758, 0826, 0914, 1014, 1126, 1225, 1327, 1427, 1514, 1614, 1727, 1827, 1927, 2038, 2138, 2230.

⑥: 0625, 0714, 0826, 0914 and hourly until 1514; then 1627, 1727, 1827, 1927, 2045, 2128, 2252.

⑦: 0910, 1110, 1310, 1510, 1710, 1930, 2149.

LEEDS – ILKLEY *26 km*

⚒: 0602, 0627Ⓐ, 0702Ⓐ, 0729Ⓐ, 0735Ⓐ, 0802, 0832 and every 30 minutes until 1702; then 1715Ⓐ, 1732, 1802, 1832, 1902, 1932, 2002, 2106, 2206, 2315.

⑦: 0912 and hourly until 2212; then 2314.

ILKLEY – LEEDS — Journey: ± 30 minutes

⚒: 0609, 0640Ⓐ, 0710, 0740Ⓐ, 0805Ⓐ, 0810⑥, 0817Ⓐ, 0840, 0910 and every 30 minutes until 1640; then 1710⑥, 1714Ⓐ, 1740, 1804Ⓐ, 1810, 1840, 1910, 1940, 2021, 2121, 2221, 2321.

⑦: 0930, 1021 and hourly until 2321.

LEEDS – SKIPTON *See also Table **174** on previous page* *42 km*

Ⓐ: 0555, 0621, 0656, 0725, 0751, 0825, 0856, 0926 and every 30 minutes until 1626; then 1656, 1726, 1750, 1826, 1850, 1925, 1956, 2026, 2055, 2126, 2156, 2226, 2256, 2318.

⑥: 0555, 0619, 0656, 0756, 0825, 0849, 0856, 0926 and every 30 minutes until 1856; then 1925, 2006, 2026, 2055, 2126, 2156, 2226, 2256, 2318.

⑦: 0840, 0900, 1008, 1108 and hourly until 2208; then 2310.

SKIPTON – LEEDS — Journey: ± 45 minutes

Ⓐ: 0618, 0642, 0708, 0724, 0747, 0815, 0843, 0918, 0948 and every 30 minutes until 1618; then 1649, 1719, 1749, 1816, 1848, 1918, 1948, 2018, 2048, 2118, 2148, 2218.

⑥: 0647, 0747, 0756, 0818, 0848 and every 30 mins until 1618; then 1649, 1719, 1749, 1816, 1848, 1918, 1948, 2007, 2018, 2048, 2118, 2148, 2218.

⑦: 0835, 0915, 1015 and hourly until 1815; then 1924, 2015, 2115, 2215, 2315.

179 HULL - BRIDLINGTON - SCARBOROUGH — NT 2nd class

km		⚒	⚒A	⚒B	⑦C	⚒	⑦C	⚒	⑦C	⑦D	⚒	⑦C	⑦D	⚒	⚒	⑦C	⑦D	⚒A	ⒶB	⑥B	⑦C	⑦D	⚒A		⚒B
0	**Hull** 178 181 187 d.	0654	0814	0814	0925	0944	1025	1114	1200	1200	1314	1400	1400	1444	1600	1605	1657	1730	1730	1730	1800	1900	1914	...	1914
13	Beverley d.	0707	0827	0828	0938	0957	1038	1127	1213	1213	1327	1413	1413	1457	1613	1618	1710	1743	1745	1745	1813	1913	1927	...	1928
31	Driffield d.	0724	0841	0843	0955	1011	1052	1139	1227	1227	1339	1427	1427	1511	1630	1632	1724	1800	1802	1802	1825	1927	1941	...	1942
50	**Bridlington** a.	0739	0856	0900	1010	1028	1107	1154	1242	1244	1355	1442	1444	1528	1648	1647	1741	1815	1818	1820	1838	1944	1957	...	1959
50	**Bridlington** d.	0747	0900	0902	1012	1035	1110	1204	1245	...	1404	1445	...	1530	1654	1653	...	1818	1821	1822	1845	...	1959	...	2021
71	Filey d.	0809	0922	0924	1034	1057	1132	1226	1307	...	1426	1507	...	1552	1716	1715	...	1840	1843	1844	1907	...	2021	...	2023
87	**Scarborough** 187 a.	0829	0940	0941	1052	1117	1149	1243	1324	...	1445	1525	...	1610	1735	1733	...	1857	1904	1901	1924	...	2039	...	2042

	⚒		⚒	⚒B	⚒A	⑦C	⚒	⑦C	⑦D	⚒B	⚒A	⑦C	⑦D	⚒	⑦C	⚒B	⚒A	⑦D		⚒	⑦C	⑦C	⑦D	⚒A	⚒B
Scarborough 187 d.	0650	...	0900	0957	1000	1114	1128	1208	...	1322	1328	1408	...	1454	1608	1615	1618	...	...	1738	1808	1937	...	2000	2000
Filey d.	0704	...	0914	1011	1014	1128	1142	1222	...	1340	1342	1422	...	1508	1622	1629	1632	...	...	1752	1822	1951	...	2014	2014
Bridlington a.	0727	...	0937	1034	1036	1150	1204	1244	...	1404	1404	1444	...	1530	1644	1653	1653	...	...	1816	1844	2013	...	2036	2038
Bridlington d.	0731	...	0940	1039	1042	1153	1209	1253	1253	1409	1412	1453	1453	1537	1653	1703	1706	1750	...	1822	1853	2015	2015	2038	2040
Driffield d.	0746	...	0955	1054	1057	1208	1222	1306	1308	1422	1425	1506	1508	1552	1706	1717	1720	1805	...	1837	1908	2030	2030	2057	2055
Beverley d.	0806	...	1010	1109	1111	1222	1236	1318	1322	1436	1437	1518	1527	1607	1718	1732	1734	1819	...	1853	1924	2044	2044	2113	2111
Hull 178 181 187 a.	0823	...	1026	1126	1126	1237	1254	1334	1337	1453	1453	1534	1537	1624	1734	1749	1749	1834	...	1912	1940	2059	2059	2123	2128

☛ Additional trains **Hull - Bridlington** at 0624⚒, 0714⚒, 0752⚒, 0900⑦**C**, 0915⚒, 1014⚒**B**, 1044⚒, 1129⑦**C**, 1144⚒, 1214⚒, 1244⚒, 1300⑦**C**, 1344⚒, 1414⚒, 1505⑦**C**, 1520⚒, 1652⚒, 1657⑦**C**, 1720⑦**C**, 1800⚒, 1900⑦**C**, 2010Ⓐ, 2014⑥, 2148⚒.

Additional trains **Bridlington - Hull** at 0644⚒, 0712⚒, 0806⚒, 0903⚒, 0953⑦**C**, 1010⚒, 1109⚒, 1139⚒, 1239⚒, 1309⚒, 1339⚒, 1353⑦**C**, 1439⚒, 1509⚒, 1550⑦**C**, 1611⚒, 1721⑦**C**, 1744⚒, 1753⑦**C**, 1814⑦**C**, 1907⚒, 1957⑦**C**, 2132⚒, 2240⚒.

A – May 18 - Sept. 5.
B – Sept. 7 - Dec. 12.
C – May 17 - Sept. 20.
D – Sept. 27 - Dec. 6.

180 HULL - SELBY - YORK and DONCASTER — GR, HT, NT

Services valid until June 21. *NT* services convey 2nd class only.

km		HT Ⓐ	GR ⑥	NT ⑥	GR Ⓐ	NT Ⓐ	HT ⑥	HT Ⓐ	NT ⑦	NT ⚒	HT ⑥	HT Ⓐ	HT ⑦	NT ⚒	NT ⑦	HT ⑦	HT Ⓐ	HT ⑥	NT ⚒	HT ⑦	NT ⑦	NT ⑥	NT Ⓐ	HT ⑥	HT Ⓐ	NT ⑦	NT ⚒
0	**Hull** d.	0625	0650	0657	0700	0707	0802	0812	0854	0902	1006	1012	1012	1105	1154	1212	1245	1305	1312	1410	1428	1451	1506	1506	1518	1601	1610
50	Selby d.	0700	0723	0740	0732	0748	0837	0845	0925	0938	1041	1047	1047	1139	1225	1247	1320	1340	1354	1445	1504	1522	1538	1542	1557	1632	1647
84	**York** a.	|	|	0815	|	0821	|	|	0954	1010	|	|	|	1210	1250	|	|	|	1426	|	1530	1553	1606	|	|	1657	1713
	Doncaster 185 a.	0716	0740	...	0753	...	0900	0902	...	...	1101	1104	1103	...	...	1305	1337	1403	...	1505	...	...	...	1601	1615	...	...
	London KC ■ a.	0917	0926	...	0945	...	1052	1051	...	...	1247	1244	1248	...	...	1454	1520	1550	...	1650	...	...	...	1745	1812	...	...

	HT ⑦	HT Ⓐ	NT ⚒	NT ⑦	GR ⑦	HT ⑥	NT ⑥	HT ⑦	NT Ⓐ	HT Ⓐ	NT ⑦
Hull d.	1621	1706	1718	1723	1730	1812	1846	1848	1910	1918	2022
Selby d.	1656	1743	1806	1754	1805	1847	1922	1923	1947	1953	2053
York a.	|	|	1836	1823	|	|	1956	|	2016	|	2120
Doncaster 185 a.	1714	1801	...	...	1823	1904	...	1943	...	2010	...
London KC ■ a.	1906	1849	...	...	2023	2046	...	2134	...	2158	...

	NT ⚒	HT Ⓐ	NT ⚒	NT ⑦	HT ⑥	HT Ⓐ	NT ⑥	NT Ⓐ	NT ⑦	HT ⑦	NT ⑦	HT ⚒
London KC ■ d.	...	0720	...	...	0934	0948	...	...	...	1044	...	1148
Doncaster 185 d.	...	0906	...	...	1124	1136	...	...	...	1224	...	1327
York d.	0730	|	0952	1040	|	|	1149	1153	1205	|	1323	|
Selby d.	0750	0922	1012	1059	1140	1152	1209	1218	1224	1242	1342	1343
Hull a.	0846	1004	1056	1138	1220	1232	1254	1302	1303	1321	1421	1425

	NT ⑥	NT Ⓐ	NT ⑦	NT Ⓐ	NT ⑥	HT Ⓐ	HT ⑥	NT ⑦	HT ⑦	NT ⚒	NT ⑦	NT ⑥	HT ⑦	HT Ⓐ	NT ⚒	HT ⑥	GR Ⓐ	NT ⑦	HT ⑦	NT ⑥	GR ⑥	HT Ⓐ	HT ⑥	NT ⑦	HT ⑦	NT Ⓐ	HT Ⓐ
London KC ■ d.	...	...	...	...	...	1333	1348	...	1444	...	...	...	1544	1605	...	1705	1719	...	1744	...	1840	1850	1941	...	2010	...	2030
Doncaster 185 d.	...	...	...	...	...	1512	1527	...	1623	...	...	...	1735	1742	...	1848	1905	...	1924	...	2027	2031	2120	...	2155	...	2212
York d.	1338	1345	1442	1459	1505	|	|	1543	|	1612	1710	1718	|	|	1813	|	|	1910	|	2017	|	|	|	2141	|	2203	|
Selby d.	1404	1409	1501	1519	1524	1528	1543	1602	1642	1639	1731	1737	1750	1800	1842	1908	1921	1930	1940	2036	2044	2047	2136	2200	2209	2222	2230
Hull a.	1445	1448	1540	1558	1603	1610	1622	1641	1721	1727	1810	1821	1832	1840	1932	1947	2000	2009	2022	2122	2127	2128	2216	2239	2250	2308	2313

■ – London Kings Cross, Table **185**.

181 LINCOLN - SHEFFIELD — 2nd class NT

km		⚒	⚒	⚒	⚒		⚒	⚒	⚒	⚒	⚒	⚒	⑥	Ⓐ	⚒		⑦	⑦	⑦	⑦	⑦	⑦	⑦
0	**Lincoln** d.		...	0704	0827	and at	1627	1722	...	1824	1943	2027	2124	2127	...	...		...	1515	1735	1935	2115	...
26	Gainsborough Lea Road d.		...	0726	0849	the same	1649	1744	...	1846	2005	2049	2146	2149	...	...		...	1537	1757	1957	2137	...
40	Retford d.		0703	0740	0903	minutes	1703	1758	1814	1904	2019	2103	2200	2203	2245	...		1450	1551	1811	2011	2151	2224
52	Worksop d.		0716	0752	0915	past each	1715	1810	1825	1916	2031	2115	2212	2215	2258	...		1501	1603	1823	2023	2203	2235
78	**Sheffield** a.		0748	0826	0949	hour until	1749	1835	1857	1954	2105	2146	2246	2250	2333	...		1533	1636	1855	2056	2234	2307

	⚒	⚒	⚒	⚒	⚒	⚒		⚒	⚒	⚒	⚒	⚒	⚒	⚒	⚒		⑦	⑦	⑦	⑦	⑦	⑦	⑦
Sheffield d.		0539	0546	0643	0730	0844	and at	1644	1724	1744	1845	1948	2044	2144	2244	...		1342	1357	1602	1802	1926	2106
Worksop d.		0601	0623	0714	0759	0913	the same	1713	1752	1813	1914	2017	2123	2214	2322	...		1402	1426	1630	1830	1954	2134
Retford d.		0610	0638	0724	0809	0923	minutes	1723	1807	1823	1924	2027	...	2228	...	...		1414	1439	1639	1840	2004	2149
Gainsborough Lea Road d.		0625	...	0738	0824	0938	past each	1738	...	1838	1939	2042	...	...	...	...		1426	...	1654	1854	2018	...
Lincoln a.		0653	...	0806	0852	1006	hour until	1806	...	1907	2006	2110	...	...	...	...		1454	...	1721	1922	2045	...

EM 2nd class — PETERBOROUGH - LINCOLN - DONCASTER — 182

km		⚒	⚒	⚒	⚒	⑥	Ⓐ	⚒	⚒	⚒	Ⓐ	⚒	⚒	⚒	⑥	Ⓐ	⑥	⚒	⚒	⚒	⚒	⚒	⚒	⚒	⚒
0	**Peterborough** 185 d.	0630	...	...	0730	...	...	0833	0933	...	1038	1148	...	1241	...	1340	...	1510	1625	1730	...	...	1836	...	2027
27	Spalding d.	0656	...	...	0756	...	...	0857	0957	...	1101	1210	...	1303	...	1402	...	1532	1649	1758	...	...	1902	...	2054
57	Sleaford d.	...	0657	0742	...	...	0846	0925	1025	...	1130	1242	...	1332	...	1432	...	1614	1718	...	1754	1900	...	2007	...
91	**Lincoln** a.	...	0727	0812	...	0915	0916	0959	1059	1154	1204	1314	...	1405	1410	1505	1510	1648	1751	...	1827	1932	...	2041	...
117	Gainsborough Lea Rd d.	...	...	...	...	0937	0940	...	...	1217	...	1339a	...	...	1432	...	1532	...	...	...	1857a	1953	...	...	...
151	**Doncaster** 182 a.	...	...	...	...	1007	1008	...	...	1247	...	1415a	...	...	1501	...	1601	...	...	...	1925a	2023	...	...	...

	⚒	⚒	⚒	⚒	Ⓐ	⚒	⚒	⚒	Ⓐ	⚒	⚒	⚒	Ⓐ	Ⓐ	⚒	⚒	⑥	⚒	⚒	⚒	⚒	Ⓐ	⚒	⚒	⚒
Doncaster 182 d.	...	...	...	...	...	...	...	1022	...	...	1304	...	...	1427	*1507*x	...	1627	...	...	...	...	1934	...	...	2033
Gainsborough Lea Road d.	...	...	...	...	...	...	...	1052	...	...	1330	...	...	1454	*1533*x	...	1656	...	...	...	...	2000	...	...	2100
Lincoln d.	...	0705	...	0800	0910	1015	1110	1116	1208	1330	1354	1441	1512	1518	1603	1715	1720	...	1812	1910	...	2026	...	2048	2126
Sleaford d.	...	0736	...	0834	0942	1050	1142	...	1242	1402	...	1516	1543	...	1634	1747	...	...	1843	1941	...	...	...	2119	...
Spalding d.	0700	...	0800	0902	1007	1115	1207	...	1307	1427	...	1541	...	...	1659	...	...	1802	...	...	1953	...	2058	...	...
Peterborough 185 a.	0725	...	0825	0927	1031	1141	1234	...	1332	1453	...	1609	...	...	1724	...	...	1827	...	...	2021	...	2126	...	...

a – Ⓐ only. x – ⑥ only.

EM 2nd class — GRIMSBY - LINCOLN - NEWARK - NOTTINGHAM - LEICESTER — 183

km			⚒	Ⓐ	⚒ L	⚒	⚒	⚒	⚒	⚒	⚒	⚒	⚒	⚒	⚒	⚒	⚒	⚒	⚒	⚒	⚒	⚒	⚒	Ⓐ	⚒
	Cleethorpes 194 d.		...	0549	...	...	...	...	...	...	...	...	...	...	...	...	...	...	...	...	...	...	...	...	...
0	**Grimsby** Town 194 d.	⚒	...	0556	...	...	0703	...	...	...	0928	...	...	1128	...	...	...	...	1352	...	...	1603	...	...	...
47	Market Rasen d.		...	0632	...	...	0739	...	...	...	1003	...	...	1203	...	...	...	...	1427	...	...	1636	...	...	...
71	**Lincoln** d.		0526	0653	0708	0729	0759	0835	0911	0931	1023	1036	1142	1223	1230	1340	1405	1435	1448	1530	1635	1657	1728	1818	1835
97	Newark North Gate 185 a.		0556	0722	|	|	0825	|	0936	|	1052	|	|	1252	|	|	1433	|	1514	|	|	1725	|	1844	|
98	Newark Castle d.		0609	...	0733	0756	...	0904	...	0954	...	1103	1204	...	1257	1405	...	1501	...	1557	1703	...	1756	...	1902
126	**Nottingham** a.		0645	...	0757	0830	...	0930	...	1030	...	1129	1230	...	1330	1430	...	1530	...	1630	1730	...	1831	...	1929
126	**Nottingham** 170 d.		...	...	0802	0832	...	0932	...	1032	...	1132	1232	...	1332	1432	...	1532	...	1632	1732	...	1832	...	1932
	East Midlands Parkway 170 d.		...	...	|	0843	...	0943	...	1043	...	1143	1243	...	1343	1443	...	1543	...	1646	1746	...	1843	...	1946
150	Loughborough 170 d.		...	...	0820	0854	...	0954	...	1054	...	1154	1254	...	1354	1454	...	1554	...	1656	1756	...	1854	...	1956
170	**Leicester** 170 a.		...	...	0832	0921	...	1021	...	1122	...	1221	1321	...	1421	1521	...	1621	...	1723	1824	...	1921	...	2023

	⚒	⑥	⑥	⑥ D	⑥ E	⚒	Ⓐ	Ⓐ	Ⓐ		⑦	⑦	⑦ A	⑦ B	⑦ A	⑦ A	⑦ A	⑦	⑦	⑦ A	⑦	⑦ A	⑦ B	⑦ A	⑦
Cleethorpes 194 d.	...	...	...	...	...	...	...	2115	...	⑦	...	...	1356	...	...	...	...	...	...	1818	...	1954	...	...	...
Grimsby Town 194 d.	1828	...	1945	...	...	...	...	2122	...		...	...	1403	...	...	...	...	...	...	1825	...	2007	...	...	...
Market Rasen d.	1904	...	2018	...	...	...	...	2155	...		...	...	1437	...	...	...	...	...	...	1859	...	2041	...	...	...
Lincoln d.	1925	1935	2037	...	...	2045	2140	2218	2238		1105	1300	1500	1500	1550	1710	1725	1810	1910	1924	2010	2100	2100	2126	2210
Newark North Gate 185 a.	1954	|	▬	...	...	|	|	▬	|		1130	1325	1528	1528	1614	|	1749	|	|	1948	|	2127	2127	2150	|
Newark Castle d.	...	2003	...	...	...	2110	2205	...	2257		...	...	1542	1542	...	1738	...	1839	1940	...	2040	2140	2140	...	2239
Nottingham a.	...	2030	⑥	...	...	2139	2234	⑥	2333		...	...	1611	1611	...	1808	...	1917	2008	...	2108	2209	2209	...	2317
Nottingham 170 d.	...	...	2032	2132	2132	...	...	2310	...		...	...	...	...	...	...	...	...	...	...	...	...	...	...	...
East Midlands Parkway 170 d.	...	...	2046	2143	2143	...	...	2321	...		...	...	...	...	...	...	...	...	...	...	...	...	...	...	...
Loughborough 170 d.	...	...	2056	2154	2153	...	...	2329	...		...	...	...	...	...	...	...	...	...	...	...	...	...	...	...
Leicester 170 a.	...	...	2123	2220	...	...	...	2354	...		...	...	...	...	...	...	...	...	...	...	...	...	...	...	...

		⚒	⚒	⚒	⚒	⑥	Ⓐ	⚒	⚒	⚒	⚒	⚒	⚒	⚒	⚒	⚒	⚒	⚒	⚒	⚒	⚒	Ⓐ	⚒	⑥	Ⓐ
Leicester 170 d.	⚒	...	...	...	0633	...	...	0725	0825	...	0925	1025	...	1125	...	1225	...	1325	...	1425	1525	...	1625	...	...
Loughborough 170 d.		...	...	...	0657	...	...	0746	0847	...	0947	1047	...	1147	...	1247	...	1347	...	1447	1547	...	1647	...	...
East Midlands Parkway 170 d.		...	...	...	0708	...	...	0757	0857	...	0957	1057	...	1157	...	1257	...	1357	...	1457	1557	...	1657	...	...
Nottingham 170 a.		...	...	...	0728	...	...	0816	0913	...	1013	1114	...	1213	...	1314	...	1413	...	1513	1613	...	1713	...	...
Nottingham d.		...	0655	...	▬	0801	0805	...	0923	...	1029	1117	...	1227	...	1317	...	1429	...	1527	1614	...	1717	...	1750
Newark Castle d.		...	0729	...	⚒	0837	0841	...	0950	...	1058	1151	...	1253	...	1351	...	1455	...	1553	1648	...	1753	...	1814
Newark Northgate 185 d.		...	|	0745a	0831	|	|	...	|	0957	|	|	1204	|	1302	|	1436	|	1536	|	|	1734	|	1805	|
Lincoln d.		0557	0758	0817	0902	0908	0908	...	1017	1023	1130	1221	1237	1320	1330	1423	1501	1522	1603	1625	1714	1803	1826	1833	1848
Market Rasen d.		0613	...	0834	...	...	...	...	...	1040	...	...	1254	...	...	...	1517	...	...	...	*1737*	...	...	1849	...
Grimsby Town 194 a.		0656	...	0915	...	...	...	...	...	1121	...	...	1336	...	...	...	1557	...	...	...	*1817*	...	...	1929	...
Cleethorpes 194 a.		...	...	...	...	...	...	...	...	...	...	...	...	...	...	...	...	...	...	...	...	...	...	...	...

	⚒	Ⓐ	Ⓐ	⑥	⑥ L	⚒	⚒	Ⓐ L	⚒	⚒	Ⓐ		⑦ A	⑦	⑦ A	⑦ A	⑦	⑦ A	⑦	⑦	⑦ A	⑦	⑦	⑦ A	⑦
Leicester 170 d.	1725	...	...	1825	1854	...	1925	1957	2025	2125	...	⑦	...	...	...	...	...	...	...	...	...	...	...	...	...
Loughborough 170 d.	1747	...	...	1846	1904	...	1947	|	2047	2146	...		...	...	...	...	...	...	...	...	...	...	...	...	...
East Midlands Parkway 170 d.	1757	...	...	1857	|	...	1957	2012	2057	2157	...		...	...	...	...	...	...	...	...	...	...	...	...	...
Nottingham 170 a.	1813	...	...	1914	1926	...	2020	2028	2116	2216	...		...	...	...	...	...	...	...	...	...	...	...	...	...
Nottingham d.	1815	...	1925	...	1929	...	2029x	2029	2125x	...	2225		...	...	1529	...	1635	...	1730	1837	...	1937	2037	...	2226
Newark Castle d.	1850	...	1950	...	1959	...	2057x	2057	2157x	...	2256		...	...	1555	...	1700	...	1805	1902	...	2002	2102	...	2301
Newark Northgate 185 d.	|	1924	|	...	|	2030	|	|	2209x	...	2308		1135	1335	|	1637	|	1756	|	1917	1955	|	|	2200	2315
Lincoln d.	1922	1955	2017	...	2026	2056	2124x	2124	2240x	...	2340		1202	1402	1623	1708	1732	1822	1838	1948	2021	2034	2134	2227	2346
Market Rasen d.	...	2012	...	...	...	2115a	...	...	...	...	...		1218b	...	1639	...	...	1838	...	...	...	...	...	...	...
Grimsby Town 194 a.	...	2052	...	...	...	...	...	...	...	...	...		1253b	...	1714	...	...	1913	...	...	...	...	...	...	...
Cleethorpes 194 a.	...	2102	...	...	...	...	...	...	...	...	...		1316b	...	1723	...	...	1924	...	...	...	...	...	...	...

A – May 17 - Sept. 6.
B – Sept. 13 - Dec. 6.
D – May 23 - July 11 and Sept. 12 - Dec. 12.
E – July 18 - Sept. 5.
L – (12) Lincoln - London St Pancras and v.v.
a – Ⓐ only.
b – May 17 - Sept. 6.
x – ⑥ only.

FC — LONDON - PETERBOROUGH stopping trains — 184

km			②–⑤	①	②–⑤	①	Ⓐ		Ⓐ	Ⓐ	✤	Ⓐ	Ⓐ	Ⓐ	Ⓐ	Ⓐ	Ⓐ	Ⓐ	Ⓐ	Ⓐ	Ⓐ	Ⓐ	Ⓐ
0	**London** Kings Cross 185 d.	Ⓐ	0036	0036	0136	0136	0522	...	0622	0636	and at the same minutes past each hour until	1522	1536	1640	1710	1714	1744	1810	1814	1840	1910	1922	2007
44	Stevenage 185 d.		0112	0123	0218	0223	0558	...	0646	0712		1546	1612	|	|	1740	1809	|	1839	|	|	1947	|
95	Huntingdon a.		0155s	0204s	0259s	0301s	0635	...	0720	0747		1620	1647	1725	1757	1816	1845	1857	1915	1925	2000	2023	2049
123	**Peterborough** 185 a.		0217	0226	0321	0323	0654	...	0738	0809		1637	1704	1743	1822	1833	1903	1914	1932	1943	2024	2040	2105

	Ⓐ	Ⓐ	Ⓐ	Ⓐ	Ⓐ	Ⓐ			⑥	⑥		⑥		⑥	⑥	⑥	✤	⑥	⑥	⑥	⑥	⑥	⑥
London Kings Cross 185 d.	2022	2107	2122	2207	2222	2322	...	⑥	0001	0036	...	0136	...	0522	0622	0636	and at the same minutes past each hour until	2122	2136	2222	2252	2322	2352
Stevenage 185 d.	2047	|	2147	|	2246	2346	...		0020s	0112	...	0218	...	0558	0646	0712		2146	2212	2246	2320	2358	|
Huntingdon a.	2123	2151	2223	2251	2326	0026	...		0104s	0155s	...	0259s	...	0635	0720	0747		2220	2247	2320	2359	0034	0102s
Peterborough 185 a.	2140	2207	2240	2317	2342	0042	...		0124	0217	...	0321	...	0656	0736	0805		2236	2306	2343	0020	0054	0121

		⑦j	⑦j	⑦j	⑦	✤	⑦	⑦	⑦
London Kings Cross 185 d.	⑦	0036	0722	0822	0922	and hourly until	2122	2222	2325
Stevenage 185 d.		0116	0750	0846	0946		2146	2246	2349
Huntingdon a.		0307*	0829	0920	1020		2220	2327	0033
Peterborough 185 a.		0347*	0850	0939	1036		2236	2349	0058

		Ⓐ	Ⓐ	Ⓐ	Ⓐ	Ⓐ	Ⓐ	Ⓐ	Ⓐ
Peterborough 185 d.	Ⓐ	0330	0412	0512	0540	0600	0621	0632	0654
Huntingdon d.		0344	0426	0526	0555	0615	0636	0647	0709
Stevenage 185 d.		0418	0504	0603	0625	0652	|	0724	0736
London Kings Cross 185 a.		0504	0555	0630	0652	0725	0728	0750	0759

	Ⓐ	Ⓐ	Ⓐ	Ⓐ	Ⓐ	Ⓐ	Ⓐ	Ⓐ	Ⓐ	✤	Ⓐ	Ⓐ	Ⓐ	Ⓐ	Ⓐ	Ⓐ	Ⓐ	Ⓐ	Ⓐ	Ⓐ		⑥	⑥
Peterborough 185 d.	0714	0726	0733	0758	0816	0845	0915	0944	1015	and at the same minutes past each hour until	1720	1756	1820	1844	1915	1941	2016	2055	2128	2230	⑥	0330	0412
Huntingdon d.	0732	0740	0750	0812	0831	0900	0930	0959	1033		1741	1812	1841	1859	1933	1959	2033	2112	2142	2244		0344	0426
Stevenage 185 d.	0759	|	0827	0839	0905	0934	0956	1033	1109		1817	1848	1917	1933	2009	2033	2109	2147	2217	2322		0418	0504
London Kings Cross 185 a.	0822	0831	0856	0903	0932	1002	1022	1102	1149		1858	1915	1958	2003	2049	2100	2148	2214	2256	0004		0504	0555

	⑥	⑥	⑥	✤	⑥	⑥	⑥	⑥j	⑥			⑦j	⑦j	⑦	⑦	⑦	⑦	✤	⑦	⑦		⑦
Peterborough 185 d.	0514	0545	0618	and at the same minutes past each hour until	2045	2117	2145	2218	2242	...	⑦	0507*	0550	0745	0845	0945	1045	and hourly until	2045	2145	...	2251
Huntingdon d.	0528	0559	0633		2059	2133	2159	2233	2256	...		0547*	0604	0759	0859	0959	1059		2059	2159	...	2305
Stevenage 185 d.	0609	0633	0709		2133	2209	2233	2309	2330	...		0735	0641	0833	0933	1033	1133		2133	2233	...	2339
London Kings Cross 185 a.	0649	0702	0749		2202	2249	2316	2353	0011	...		0818	0717	0900	1000	1101	1200		2200	2309	...	0014

j – Until Sept. 6.
s – Stops to set down only.
* – By bus. Change at Letchworth.
✤ – Timings may vary by a few minutes on some journeys.

185 LONDON - HULL, LEEDS and YORK - NEWCASTLE - EDINBURGH GR (unless otherwise stated)

Services on ⑦ valid until September 6. All services convey 🍷.

km			Ⓐ	Ⓐ	Ⓐ	Ⓐ	Ⓐ	Ⓐ	Ⓐ	Ⓐ	Ⓐ	Ⓐ	Ⓐ	Ⓐ	Ⓐ	Ⓐ	Ⓐ	Ⓐ	Ⓐ	Ⓐ	Ⓐ	Ⓐ	Ⓐ	Ⓐ	Ⓐ
					A						H				G								H		
0	**London** Kings Cross **184** d.	Ⓐ	...	...	...	0600	0615	0635	0700	0710	0720	0730	0735	0800	0804	0810	0830	0840	0900	0910	0930	0935	0948	1000	1010
44	Stevenage **184** d.		...	...	...	0619	0634	|	0719	0729	0744**u**	0750	0756	|	|	|	0849	|	|	|	0949	0954	1009**u**	|	|
123	Peterborough **184 208** d.		...	...	...	0651	0706	0721	0751	0801	|	0821	|	0846	|	0859	0921	0928	0947	0957	1021	1027	|	1045	1056
170	Grantham **208** d.		...	...	...	0710	0725	0740	|	|	0829	0845	|	|	|	|	|	0949	|	|	|	1046	1055	|	1116
193	Newark North Gate d.		...	...	...	0722	0737	|	|	0828	|	|	|	|	|	|	0948	|	|	|	1048	|	|	|	1128
223	Retford d.		...	...	...	0737	0752	|	|	|	0850	|	|	|	|	|	|	1012	|	|	|	|	1117	|	1143
251	**Doncaster 178** d.		...	0615	...	0751	0808	0812	|	0858	0905	0917	|	|	|	|	|	1030	1035	|	1112	1119	1132	|	1159
330	**Hull 178** a.		...	|	...	|	|	|	|	|	1004	|	|	|	|	|	|	|	|	|	|	|	1232	|	|
283	Wakefield Westgate **127** a.		...	|	...	0810	|	0836	|	0916	...	|	0930	|	|	1001	|	1051	|	1057	|	1136	...	|	1216
299	**Leeds 127 187** a.		...	|	0710	0832	|	0852	|	0936	...	|	0946	|	|	1021	|	1109	|	1118	|	1155	...	|	1236
303	**York 127 187** d.		...	0637	0737	...	0833	...	0858	...	...	0942	...	0955	1014	...	1036	...	1103	...	1141	...	...	1154	...
351	Northallerton **187** d.		...	|	|	...	|	...	|	...	...	|	...	|	1039	...	|	...	|	...	1200	...	...	|	...
374	Darlington **127 187** d.		...	0706	0805	...	0903	...	0931	...	...	1012	...	1023	...	...	1106	...	1134	...	1214	...	...	1226	...
409	Durham **127 187** d.		...	0723	0823	...	0920	...	|	...	...	|	...	1040	...	...	1123	...	|	...	1232	...	...	|	...
432	**Newcastle 127 187** d.		0625	0741	0841	...	0938	...	1004	...	...	1044	...	1059	...	...	1142	...	1205	...	1250	...	...	1257	...
540	Berwick upon Tweed **127** d.		0714	0829	0930	...	1021	...	1047	...	...	...	...	1142	...	...	...	...	1253	...	...	...	...	|	...
632	**Edinburgh 127** a.		0805	0919	1020	...	1109	...	1132	...	...	...	...	1231	...	...	...	...	1338	...	...	...	...	1425	...
725	**Glasgow** Central **127** a.		0922	1029	...	...	...	...	1247	...	...	...	...	...	...	...	...	...	1447	...	...	...	...	...	...

	Ⓐ	Ⓐ	Ⓐ	Ⓐ	Ⓐ	Ⓐ	Ⓐ	Ⓐ	Ⓐ	Ⓐ	Ⓐ	Ⓐ	Ⓐ	Ⓐ	Ⓐ	Ⓐ	Ⓐ	Ⓐ	Ⓐ	Ⓐ	Ⓐ	Ⓐ	Ⓐ	Ⓐ	Ⓐ
	A				G			H	N							H		A							
London Kings Cross **184** d.	1030	1035	1100	1110	1127	1130	1135	1148	1200	1210	1230	1235	1300	1310	1330	1333	1335	1400	1410	1430	1435	1500	1510	1530	1535
Stevenage **184** d.	|	|	|	|	|	1150	1154	|	|	1229	|	1257	|	|	|	|	|	|	|	|	1454	|	|	|	1554
Peterborough **184 208** d.	1117	1123	1146	1156	|	1221	1227	|	1247	1301	1317	|	1346	1358	|	|	1425	|	1456	1516	|	|	1557	1617	1626
Grantham **208** d.	|	1142	|	1215	|	|	1246	1254	|	1320	|	1342	|	1417	|	1435	1444	|	1515	|	|	|	1618	|	1645
Newark North Gate d.	|	1155	|	1227	|	1250	1258	|	|	|	|	1355	|	1429	|	|	1501	|	1527	|	|	|	1629	|	|
Retford d.	|	|	|	|	|	|	|	1316	|	1342	|	|	|	|	1448	1456	|	|	|	|	|	|	1645	|	|
Doncaster 178 d.	|	1219	|	1258	|	1315	|	1329	|	1357	1407	1421	1434	1453	1503	1511	1529	1530	1555	|	1610	|	1701	1709	1719
Hull 178 a.	|	|	|	|	|	|	|	1425	|	|	|	|	|	|	|	1610	|	|	|	|	|	|	|	|	|
Wakefield Westgate **127** a.	|	1236	|	1317	|	|	1337	...	|	1414	|	1439	|	1514	|	...	1551	|	1615	|	1630	|	1718	|	1736
Leeds 127 187 a.	|	1254	|	1341	|	|	1355	...	|	1435	|	1501	|	1535	|	...	1609	|	1635	|	1648	|	1736	|	1756
York 127 187 d.	1229	...	1252	...	1322	1342	...	...	1402	...	1436	...	1500	...	1528	...	...	1555	...	1622	...	1646	...	1736	...
Northallerton **187** d.	|	...	|	...	1347	|	...	...	|	...	1458	...	|	...	|	...	...	|	...	|	...	|	...	1756	...
Darlington **127 187** d.	|	...	1320	...	...	1411	...	...	|	...	1511	...	1528	...	1601	...	...	1623	...	1651	...	|	...	1810	...
Durham **127 187** d.	|	...	|	...	...	1428	...	...	|	...	1529	...	|	...	|	...	...	|	...	1708	...	|	...	1827	...
Newcastle 127 187 d.	1324	...	1351	...	...	1447	...	...	1500	...	1547	...	1559	...	1632	...	...	1654	...	1726	...	1740	...	1846	...
Berwick upon Tweed **127** d.	|	...	1434	...	...	...	...	...	|	...	...	...	1642	...	|	...	...	1738	...	...	...	1827	...	|	...
Edinburgh 127 a.	1453	...	1519	...	...	...	...	...	1627	...	...	...	1733	...	1804	...	...	1826	...	...	...	1913	...	2026	...
Glasgow Central **127** a.	...	...	1627	...	...	...	...	...	...	...	...	...	1841	...	...	...	...	...	...	...	...	2018	...	...	...

	Ⓐ	Ⓐ	Ⓐ	Ⓐ	Ⓐ	Ⓐ	Ⓐ	Ⓐ	Ⓐ	Ⓐ	Ⓐ	Ⓐ	Ⓐ	Ⓐ	Ⓐ	Ⓐ	Ⓐ	Ⓐ	Ⓐ	Ⓐ	⑤	Ⓐ	Ⓐ	Ⓐ	Ⓐ
	A	H				G					B			J				H							H
London Kings Cross **184** d.	1600	1605	1610	1630	1635	1650	1700	1703	1719	1730	1733	1800	1749	1803	1819	1830	1835	1850	1900	1903	1930	1933	2000	2003	2030
Stevenage **184** d.	|	|	|	1649	|	|	|	|	|	|	1752	|	|	|	|	1850	|	|	|	|	|	|	|	|	|
Peterborough **184 208** d.	|	|	1656	|	1725	|	|	1751	1807	1817	|	|	1839	1854	1907	|	1925	|	1947	1953	|	2022	2046	2053	|
Grantham **208** d.	|	1707	1715	1734	|	|	|	1810	|	|	1840	|	1905	1915	|	1935	|	1956	2006	|	|	2041	|	2114	2132
Newark North Gate d.	|	|	1727	1746	|	|	|	|	1835	|	|	|	1917	|	1934	|	1954	|	|	2022	|	2053	|	2126	|
Retford d.	|	1728	|	|	1804	|	|	|	|	|	1902	|	|	|	|	1957	|	2018	|	|	|	|	2123	|	2153
Doncaster 178 d.	1730	1741	|	1810	1819	|	|	1843	1904	|	1917	1928	1942	1948	|	2015	2019	2030	2038	2050	|	2120	2139	2153	2211
Hull 178 a.	|	1840	|	|	|	|	|	|	2000	|	|	|	|	|	|	|	|	2128	|	|	|	|	|	|	2313
Wakefield Westgate **127** a.	|	...	1804	|	1836	|	|	1900	...	|	1934	|	2001	2007	|	|	2038	...	|	2115	|	2137	|	2213	...
Leeds 127 187 a.	|	...	1823	|	1855	|	|	1920	...	|	1952	|	2021	2024	|	|	2055	...	|	2135	|	2155	|	2233	...
York 127 187 d.	1756	...	...	1839	...	1847	1853	...	...	1925	...	1953	...	...	2023	2044	...	...	2103	...	2123	...	2203	...	...
Northallerton **187** d.	|	...	...	1900	...	1916	|	...	...	|	...	|	...	...	|	2103	...	...	|	...	|	...	2223	...	...
Darlington **127 187** d.	1827	...	...	1913	...	...	1921	...	...	1953	...	2023	...	...	2051	2116	...	...	2131	...	2154	...	2236	...	...
Durham **127 187** d.	|	...	...	1931	...	...	|	...	...	2010	...	|	...	...	2109	2134	...	...	2149	...	2213	...	2253	...	...
Newcastle 127 187 d.	1859	...	...	1949	...	...	1954	...	...	2029	...	2054	...	...	2127	2153	...	...	2208	...	2231	...	2316	...	...
Berwick upon Tweed **127** d.	1943	...	...	|	...	...	|	...	...	2122	...	2137	...	...	...	2237**f**	...	...	2300**f**	...	...	...	...	...	...
Edinburgh 127 a.	2029	...	...	2116**f**	...	...	2121	...	...	2214	...	2223	...	...	...	2330**f**	...	...	2354**f**	...	...	...	...	...	...
Glasgow Central **127** a.	...	...	...	...	...	...	...	...	...	...	...	2332	...	...	...	...	...	...	...	...	...	...	...	...	...

	Ⓐ	Ⓐ	Ⓐ	Ⓐ	Ⓐ		⑥	⑥	⑥	⑥	⑥	⑥	⑥	⑥	⑥	⑥	⑥	⑥	⑥	⑥	⑥	⑥	⑥	⑥	⑥
									A				G							H			A		
London Kings Cross **184** d.	2033	2100	2130	2200	2330	⑥	...	...	...	0615	0700	0710	0757	0800	0810	0830	0900	0905	0930	0934	1000	1010	1030	1040	1100
Stevenage **184** d.	|	2120	|	|	|		...	...	...	0634	|	|	|	0820	|	0849	|	0924	0949	|	|	|	|	|	|
Peterborough **184 208** d.	2120	2154	2217	2247	0023**s**		...	...	...	0706	0746	0756	|	0851	0857	0921	0946	|	1021	|	1046	1056	1118	1127	1146
Grantham **208** d.	2139	|	2238	2308	0044**s**		...	...	...	0725	0805	0815	|	|	0916	0940	|	|	1040	1044	|	1115	|	1148	|
Newark North Gate d.	2151	2223	2249	2319	0056**s**		...	...	...	0737	0817	0827	|	|	0928	|	|	1018	|	|	|	1127	|	|	|
Retford d.	|	|	2305	|	|		...	...	...	0752	|	0842	|	|	|	|	1024	|	|	1106	|	|	|	|	|
Doncaster 178 d.	2218	2248	2324	2349	0124**s**		...	0620	...	0808	0842	0858	|	0937	0957	1012	1040	1048	1114	1124	1132	1154	|	1220	1234
Hull 178 a.	|	|	|	|	|		...	|	...	|	|	|	|	|	|	|	|	|	|	1220	|	|	|	|	|
Wakefield Westgate **127** a.	2235	|	2342	|	|		...	|	...	|	|	0915	|	|	1014	|	|	1111	|	...	|	1213	|	|	|
Leeds 127 187 a.	2253	|	2359	|	0237		...	|	0710	|	|	0936	|	|	1035	|	|	1135	|	...	|	1235	|	|	|
York 127 187 d.	...	2314	...	0041	...		...	0642	0735	0833	0906	...	1000	1003	...	1042	1104	...	1141	...	1157	...	1229	1249	1258
Northallerton **187** d.	...	|	...	...	...		...	0701	|	|	|	...	1032	|	...	|	|	...	|	...	1220	...	|	|	|
Darlington **127 187** d.	...	2350	...	...	...		...	0715	0805	0901	0936	...	...	1031	...	1111	1133	...	1210	...	1233	...	|	1317	1326
Durham **127 187** d.	...	0007	...	...	...		...	0733	0822	0918	|	...	...	1048	...	|	|	...	1227	...	|	...	|	1335	|
Newcastle 127 187 d.	...	0041	...	...	...		0630	0752	0845	0936	1007	...	...	1108	...	1145	1203	...	1246	...	1304	...	1326	1353	1401
Berwick upon Tweed **127** d.	...	...	...	...	...		0719	0842	0929	1021	1050	...	...	|	...	1228	|	...	1329	...	|	...	|	...	1444
Edinburgh 127 a.	...	...	...	...	...		0809	0932	1021	1110	1137	...	...	1240	...	1316	1328	...	1416	...	1432	...	1453	...	1529
Glasgow Central **127** a.	...	...	...	...	...		0915	1048	...	...	1250	...	...	...	...	...	1447	...	...	...	...	...	...	...	1650

	⑥	⑥	⑥	⑥	⑥	⑥	⑥	⑥	⑥	⑥	⑥	⑥	⑥	⑥	⑥	⑥	⑥	⑥	⑥	⑥	⑥	⑥	⑥	⑥	⑥
		G		H	N						H	A						G		H	K				C
London Kings Cross **184** d.	1110	1127	1130	1148	1200	1210	1230	1300	1310	1330	1348	1400	1430	1500	1530	1600	1630	1650	1700	1705	1730	1740	1800	1803	1830
Stevenage **184** d.	|	|	1150	|	|	|	|	|	|	1349	|	|	|	|	1549	|	|	|	|	|	1750	|	|	|	|
Peterborough **184 208** d.	1156	|	1221	|	1247	1256	1316	1346	1356	1421	|	1447	1516	1546	1621	1646	1716	|	1746	|	1821	1827	1846	1852	|
Grantham **208** d.	1216	|	1242	1249	|	1315	1335	|	1416	1440	1447	|	1535	|	1640	|	1735	|	|	1810	1842	1848	|	|	1930
Newark North Gate d.	1228	|	|	|	|	1327	|	|	1428	1452	|	|	1547	|	1652	|	1747	|	|	|	1854	1900	|	1920	|
Retford d.	1243	|	|	1313	|	|	|	|	1442	|	1512	|	1602	|	|	|	1802	|	|	1831	|	|	|	|	|
Doncaster 178 d.	1259	|	1315	1326	|	1353	1407	1434	1458	|	1526	1536	1621	1632	1716	1735	1818	|	1834	1846	1918	1925	1934	|	2002
Hull 178 a.	|	|	|	1422	|	|	|	|	|	|	1622	|	|	|	|	|	|	|	|	1947	|	|	|	|	|
Wakefield Westgate **127** a.	1316	|	|	...	|	1413	|	|	1515	|	...	|	1638	|	1733	|	1835	|	|	...	1935	|	|	2000	2019
Leeds 127 187 a.	1335	|	|	...	|	1435	|	|	1535	|	...	|	1701	|	1753	|	1853	|	|	...	1951	|	|	2022	2035
York 127 187 d.	...	1330	1341	...	1357	...	1436	1500	...	1541	...	1601	...	1657	...	1803	...	1848	1858	...	...	1956	2002	...	...
Northallerton **187** d.	...	1409	|	...	|	...	1455	|	...	|	...	|	...	|	...	1822	...	1929	|	...	...	|	|	...	...
Darlington **127 187** d.	...	...	1409	...	|	...	1508	1528	...	1609	...	1629	...	1727	...	1835	...	...	1926	...	...	2024	2031	...	...
Durham **127 187** d.	...	...	1427	...	|	...	1526	1545	...	1626	...	|	...	1745	...	|	...	...	1943	...	...	2041	|	...	...
Newcastle 127 187 d.	...	...	1445	...	1458	...	1543	1603	...	1644	...	1701	...	1802	...	1906	...	...	2001	...	...	2100	2103	...	...
Berwick upon Tweed **127** d.	...	...	|	...	1542	...	|	1652	...	|	...	|	...	1845	...	1949	...	...	|	...	...	...	2157	...	...
Edinburgh 127 a.	...	...	1618	...	1630	...	1719	1738	...	1812	...	1828	...	1934	...	2037	...	...	2131	...	...	...	2244	...	...
Glasgow Central **127** a.	...	...	...	...	...	...	...	1850	...	...	...	...	...	2044	...	...	...	...	2246	...	...	...	...	...	...

A – To / from Aberdeen.
B – To Bradford Forster Square (a. 2022).
C – To Bradford Forster Square (a. 2106).
D – From Bradford Forster Square (d. 0630).
E – From Bradford Forster Square (d. 0733).
G – 12 London - Sunderland and v.v. Operated by *GC*.
H – 12 London - Hull and v.v. Operated by *HT*.
J – To Keighley (a. 2057**s**) and Skipton (a. 2113).
K – To Keighley (a. 2017**s**) and Skipton (a. 2031).
L – From Skipton (d. 0655) and Keighley (d. 0705**u**).
M – From Skipton (d. 0655) and Keighley (d. 0707**u**).
N – To / from Inverness.

NOTES CONTINUE ON NEXT PAGE →

GR (unless otherwise stated) **LONDON - HULL, LEEDS and YORK - NEWCASTLE - EDINBURGH** **185**

Services on ⑦ valid until September 6. All services convey 🍸.

	⑥	⑥	⑥	⑥	⑥	⑥	⑥	⑦	⑦	⑦	⑦	⑦	⑦	⑦	⑦	⑦	⑦	⑦	⑦	⑦	⑦	⑦	⑦	⑦	⑦
					H							G						H	A				N		
London Kings Cross 184 d.	1835	1840	1900	1930	1941	2000	2030		...	...	0900	0907	0910	0930	1000	1010	1030	1044	1100	1110	1200	1210	1230	1300	1310
Stevenage 184 d.	|	|	1919	|	|	|	|		...	...	0920	|	|	|	|	|	1049	|	|	|	|	1229	|	1319	|
Peterborough 184 208 d.	1921	1927	1951	2016	|	2046	2117		...	...	0949	|	0957	1014	1046	1059	1119	|	1145	1154	1244	1259	1315	1351	1357
Grantham 208 d.	|	|	|	2035	2043	2105	2138		...	...	1011	|	|	|	|	1121	|	1146	|	1216	|	1321	|	|	1419
Newark North Gate d.	|	1955	|	2047	|	2117	2149		...	...	|	|	1031	|	1116	|	|	|	|	1228	1314	|	|	|	1431
Retford d.	|	2011	|	|	2105	2132	|		...	...	|	|	1046	|	|	1143	|	1207	|	1243	|	1343	|	|	|
Doncaster 178 d.	2008	2027	2040	2112	2120	2148	2214		...	0943	1044	|	1103	1106	1141	1200	1210	1223	1239	1300	1342	1359	1409	1442	1457
Hull 178 a.	|	2127	|	|	2216	|	|		...	|	|	|	|	|	|	|	|	1321	|	|	|	|	|	|	|
Wakefield Westgate 127 a.	|	...	|	|	...	2205	|		...	|	|	|	1120	|	|	1218	|	...	|	1317	|	1416	|	|	1514
Leeds 127 187 a.	|	...	|	|	...	2224	|		...	|	|	|	1139	|	|	1236	|	...	|	1336	|	1436	|	|	1533
York 127 187 d.	2041	...	2106	2142	...	...	2239		0900	1006	1109	1118	...	1130	1206	...	1244	...	1307	...	1406	...	1435	1507	...
Northallerton 187 d.	|	...	2126	|	...	...	|		0920	|	|	1144	...	|	|	...	|	...	|	...	1425	...	|	|	...
Darlington 127 187 d.	2109	...	2141	2210	...	...	2308		0933	1034	1137	...	...	1158	1234	...	1312	...	1335	...	1438	...	1503	1535	...
Durham 127 187 d.	2127	...	2158	2227	...	...	2325		0950	1051	1154	...	...	|	1252	...	|	...	1353	...	1456	...	|	1554	...
Newcastle 127 187 d.	2145	...	2216	2245	...	...	2346		1010	1111	1215	...	...	1231	1309	...	1343	...	1413	...	1514	...	1534	1611	...
Berwick upon Tweed 127 d.	...	...	...	...	...	...	...		1103	1154	1258	...	...	|	|	...	1426	...	|	...	1557	...	|	|	...
Edinburgh 127 a.	...	...	...	...	...	...	...		1157	1238	1346	...	...	1402	1435	...	1510	...	1541	...	1646	...	1700	1737	...
Glasgow Central 127 a.	...	...	...	...	...	...	...		1305	1354	...	...	...	...	...	...	1614	...	...	...	...	...	...	1844	...

	⑦	⑦	⑦	⑦	⑦	⑦	⑦	⑦	⑦	⑦	⑦	⑦	⑦	⑦	⑦	⑦	⑦	⑦	⑦	⑦	⑦	⑦	⑦	⑦	⑦
		G	A			H				H								H			G				
London Kings Cross 184 d.	1330	1345	1400	1410	1430	1444	1500	1510	1530	1544	1600	1610	1630	1640	1700	1710	1730	1744	1800	1810	1820	1830	1840	1900	1910
Stevenage 184 d.	1349	|	|	|	|	|	1519	|	|	1604u	|	1629	1649	|	|	|	1749	|	|	|	|	1850	|	|	|
Peterborough 184 208 d.	1419	|	1445	1454	1514	|	1549	1555	1615	|	1645	1659	1719	1725	1746	1754	1819	|	1845	1855	|	1919	1925	1944	1956
Grantham 208 d.	|	|	|	1516	|	1547	|	1618	1639	1649	|	|	|	1747	|	1817	|	1846	1906	|	|	|	1947	|	2019
Newark North Gate d.	|	|	|	1528	|	|	|	1631	1650	|	|	|	|	|	1816	|	1849	|	|	1926	|	|	|	|	2030
Retford d.	|	|	|	1543	|	1608	|	|	|	1710	|	1739	|	|	|	|	|	1907	|	1942	|	|	|	|	|
Doncaster 178 d.	1510	|	1539	1600	1609	1622	|	1657	1720	1725	1740	1755	1811	|	1843	1850	1920	1923	1942	1959	|	2012	2020	2035	2056
Hull 178 a.	|	|	|	|	|	1721	|	|	|	1832	|	|	|	|	|	|	|	2022	|	|	|	|	|	|	2156
Wakefield Westgate 127 a.	|	|	|	1617	|	...	|	1714	|	...	|	1812	|	1838	|	1907	|	...	|	2016	|	|	2038	|	...
Leeds 127 187 a.	|	|	|	1636	|	...	|	1734	|	...	|	1832	|	1859	|	1927	|	...	|	2039	|	|	2059	|	...
York 127 187 d.	1538	1554	1606	...	1642	...	1705	...	1747	...	1807	...	1842	...	1907	...	1947	...	2008	...	2025	2040	...	2102	...
Northallerton 187 d.	|	1620	|	...	|	...	|	...	|	...	|	...	1901	...	|	...	2008	...	|	...	2050	2100	...	|	...
Darlington 127 187 d.	1608	...	1634	...	1710	...	1733	...	1816	...	1835	...	1915	...	1936	...	2021	...	2036	...	...	2113	...	2130	...
Durham 127 187 d.	1625	...	|	...	|	...	|	...	1833	...	|	...	1933	...	1953	...	2038	...	|	...	...	2131	...	|	...
Newcastle 127 187 d.	1644	...	1707	...	1741	...	1805	...	1852	...	1907	...	1951	...	2011	...	2056	...	2107	...	...	2153	...	2202	...
Berwick upon Tweed 127 d.	1737	...	|	...	1828	...	1848	...	...	...	|	...	...	...	2054	...	...	...	2157	...	...	2237	...	...	...
Edinburgh 127 a.	1825	...	1833	...	1914	...	1933	...	...	...	2035	...	...	...	2138	...	...	...	2244	...	...	2329	...	...	...
Glasgow Central 127 a.	...	...	...	...	...	...	2037	...	...	...	...	...	...	...	2245	...	...	...	...	...	...	...	...	...	...

	⑦	⑦	⑦	⑦	⑦	⑦	⑦	⑦	⑦	⑦
					H					
London Kings Cross 184 d.	1930	1935	2000	2003	2010	2030	2100	2130	2200	2210
Stevenage 184 d.	1949	1954	|	|	2030u	|	|	|	|	|
Peterborough 184 208 d.	2019	2025	2044	2050	|	2114	2146	2215	2245	2259s
Grantham 208 d.	|	|	|	|	2119	2136	|	2239	|	2331s
Newark North Gate d.	|	|	|	|	|	2148	|	2250	|	2342s
Retford d.	|	|	|	|	2140	2203	|	2306	|	|
Doncaster 178 d.	2110	2123	2136	|	2154	2220	2243	2327	2345	0012s
Hull 178 a.	|	|	|	|	2250	|	|	|	|	|
Wakefield Westgate 127 a.	2127	|	|	2157	...	2237	|	|	|	|
Leeds 127 187 a.	2146	|	|	2216	...	2300	|	0024	|	0118
York 127 187 d.	...	2148	2202	...	...	...	2311	...	0039	...
Northallerton 187 d.	...	|	|	...	...	...	2347	...	...	...
Darlington 127 187 d.	...	2227	2243	...	...	...	2359	...	...	...
Durham 127 187 d.	...	2244	2301	...	...	...	0017	...	...	...
Newcastle 127 187 d.	...	2314	2334	...	...	...	0050	...	...	...
Berwick upon Tweed 127 d.	...	...	...	...	...	...	...	...	...	...
Edinburgh 127 a.	...	...	...	...	...	...	...	...	...	...
Glasgow Central 127 a.	...	...	...	...	...	...	...	...	...	...

	Ⓐ	Ⓐ	Ⓐ	Ⓐ	①	②–⑤	Ⓐ	Ⓐ	Ⓐ	Ⓐ
Glasgow Central 127 d.		...	...	...	...	...	...	...	...	...
Edinburgh 127 d.		...	...	...	...	...	...	...	...	...
Berwick upon Tweed 127 d.		...	...	...	...	...	...	...	...	...
Newcastle 127 187 d.		...	...	...	0420	0430	...	0525	...	0600
Durham 127 187 d.		...	...	...	0434	0444	...	0538	...	0612
Darlington 127 187 d.		...	...	...	0452	0502	...	0556	...	0630
Northallerton 187 d.		...	...	...	0518	0528	...	0608	...	|
York 127 187 d.		...	...	...	0600	0600	...	0630	...	0700
Leeds 127 187 d.		...	0505	0530	|	|	0605	|	0640	|
Wakefield Westgate 127 d.		...	0517	0542	|	|	0618	|	0652	|
Hull 178 d.		...	|	|	|	|	|	|	|	|
Doncaster 127 178 d.		...	0535	0600	0623	0623	|	0654	|	|
Retford d.		...	0550	|	|	|	0648	|	|	|
Newark North Gate d.		...	0605	0624	0646	0646	0704	|	0729	|
Grantham 208 d.		...	0618	0637	0659	0659	0717	0725	|	|
Peterborough 184 208 a.		0610	0637	0658	0718	0718	0737	0745	|	0803
Stevenage 184 a.		|	|	|	|	|	|	|	|	|
London Kings Cross 184 a.		0700	0730	0753	0813	0813	0833	0843	0846	0859

	Ⓐ	Ⓐ	Ⓐ	Ⓐ	Ⓐ	Ⓐ	Ⓐ	Ⓐ	Ⓐ	Ⓐ	Ⓐ	Ⓐ	Ⓐ	Ⓐ	Ⓐ	Ⓐ	Ⓐ	Ⓐ	Ⓐ	Ⓐ	Ⓐ	Ⓐ	Ⓐ	Ⓐ	Ⓐ
	H	D				L			P	G		H									H				
Glasgow Central 127 d.	...	...	...	...	...	...	...	...	...	...	...	...	...	...	...	...	...	...	...	0650	...	...	...	0750	...
Edinburgh 127 d.	...	...	...	...	...	...	...	0550	...	...	0600	...	...	...	...	0700	...	...	...	0800	...	...	...	0900	...
Berwick upon Tweed 127 d.	...	...	...	...	...	...	...	0629	...	...	0643	...	...	...	...	0742	...	...	...	|	...	...	...	0939	...
Newcastle 127 187 d.	...	...	...	0630	...	...	0700	0720	...	...	0740	...	...	0752	...	0832	...	0900	...	0930	...	...	...	1034	...
Durham 127 187 d.	...	...	...	0644	...	...	0712	|	...	...	|	...	...	0804	...	0845	...	0912	...	|	...	...	...	1047	...
Darlington 127 187 d.	...	...	...	0702	...	...	0730	|	...	...	|	...	...	0822	...	0905	...	0931	...	0958	...	...	...	1106	...
Northallerton 187 d.	...	...	...	0713	...	...	|	|	...	0745	|	...	...	|	...	|	...	0943	...	|	...	...	...	|	...
York 127 187 d.	...	...	...	0736	...	...	0800	0811	...	0821	0836	...	...	0852	...	0935	...	1006	...	1029	...	...	...	1135	...
Leeds 127 187 d.	...	0700	0720	|	...	0740	|	|	0805	|	|	...	0840	|	0905	|	0940	|	1005	|	...	1040	1105	|	1140
Wakefield Westgate 127 d.	...	0712	0732	|	...	0752	|	|	0817	|	|	...	0852	|	0918	|	0952	|	1018	|	...	1052	1117	|	1154
Hull 178 d.	0625	|	|	|	0700	|	|	|	|	|	|	0812	|	|	|	|	|	|	|	|	1012	|	|	|	|
Doncaster 127 178 d.	0718	0730	|	|	0755	|	|	|	0837	|	|	0902	0912	0917	0936	1004	1015	1030	1035	1053	1105	1113	1137	1200	1212
Retford d.	0732	|	|	|	|	0819	|	|	|	|	|	0916	|	|	0951	|	|	|	|	1108	1120	|	|	|	|
Newark North Gate d.	|	|	|	|	|	0834	|	|	|	|	|	|	0937	0943	1006	|	1038	|	1059	|	|	1141	|	|	1237
Grantham 208 d.	0757	|	|	|	0829	|	|	0900	|	|	0928	0942	|	0955	|	1038	|	|	1111	|	1140	1154	1209	|	|
Peterborough 184 208 a.	|	|	0832	|	0850	|	|	|	0926	|	0947	|	1005	1015	1036	1057	1106	1116	1131	1148	|	1213	1228	1246	1305
Stevenage 184 a.	|	|	|	0906	|	|	|	|	0957	|	|	|	|	|	1106	|	|	1147	|	|	|	1243	|	1316	|
London Kings Cross 184 a.	0917	0907	0926	0935	0945	0951	0955	1010	1025	1031	1040	1051	1059	1114	1134	1151	1203	1217	1225	1242	1244	1310	1322	1343	1402

	Ⓐ	Ⓐ	Ⓐ	Ⓐ	Ⓐ	Ⓐ	Ⓐ	Ⓐ	Ⓐ	Ⓐ	Ⓐ	Ⓐ	Ⓐ	Ⓐ	Ⓐ	Ⓐ	Ⓐ	Ⓐ	Ⓐ	Ⓐ	Ⓐ	Ⓐ	Ⓐ	Ⓐ	Ⓐ
				A		H			N		G			A							H				
Glasgow Central 127 d.	...	...	...	...	...	...	...	0950	...	...	...	...	...	...	...	...	...	1150	...	...	...	...	...	...	...
Edinburgh 127 d.	0930	...	...	1030	...	...	...	1100	1130	...	...	...	1200	1230	...	...	...	1300	...	...	...	...	1400	...	...
Berwick upon Tweed 127 d.	1010	...	...	|	...	...	...	1139	|	...	...	...	1239	|	...	...	...	1341	...	...	...	...	1439	...	...
Newcastle 127 187 d.	1101	...	1130	1159	...	...	...	1235	1301	...	...	...	1329	1400	...	...	1405	1434	...	1455	...	...	1530	...	1555
Durham 127 187 d.	|	...	1144	|	...	...	...	1248	|	...	...	...	|	|	...	...	1417	|	...	1507	...	...	|	...	1608
Darlington 127 187 d.	1129	...	1202	|	...	...	...	1306	|	...	...	...	1356	|	...	...	1437	1504	...	1525	...	...	1602	...	1626
Northallerton 187 d.	|	...	|	|	...	...	...	|	|	...	1338	...	|	|	...	...	1449	|	...	|	...	...	|	...	|
York 127 187 d.	1159	...	1232	1253	...	...	...	1336	1354	...	1410	...	1426	1453	...	...	1511	1535	...	1554	...	...	1632	...	1656
Leeds 127 187 d.	|	1205	|	|	1240	...	1305	|	|	1340	|	1405	|	|	1440	1505	|	|	1540	|	...	1605	|	1640	|
Wakefield Westgate 127 d.	|	1217	|	|	1252	...	1318	|	|	1353	|	1418	|	|	1452	1517	|	|	1552	|	...	1617	|	1652	|
Hull 178 d.	|	|	|	|	|	1245	|	|	|	|	|	|	|	|	|	|	|	|	|	|	1518	|	|	|	|
Doncaster 127 178 d.	|	1236	1255	|	1314	1337	1338	1403	|	1415	|	|	1450	|	1515	|	1536	1600	|	|	1615	1636	|	1710	1720
Retford d.	|	1251	|	|	|	|	1355	|	|	|	|	|	|	|	|	|	1551	|	|	|	1634	|	|	|	|
Newark North Gate d.	|	|	|	|	1342	|	1410	|	|	|	|	|	1513	|	1541	|	1606	|	|	|	|	1700	|	1733	1744
Grantham 208 d.	|	1314	|	|	|	1409	1423	|	|	|	|	1503	1526	|	1554	|	1619	|	|	1644	1655	|	|	|	1757
Peterborough 184 208 a.	1311	|	1342	1402	1409	|	1442	1449	|	1505	|	1522	1545	1601	|	1618	|	1647	1651	1704	|	1727	|	1801	|
Stevenage 184 a.	|	|	1417	|	|	|	1512	|	|	|	|	1552	1617	|	|	1648	|	|	|	1734	1746s	|	|	|	1842
London Kings Cross 184 a.	1410	1420	1444	1457	1505	1520	1540	1544	1550	1558	1605	1622	1646	1657	1704	1715	1730	1741	1746	1804	1812	1824	1827	1854	1912

NOTES FOR TABLE 185 CONTINUED

P – From Harrogate (d. 0728).
Q – From Harrogate (d. 0744).

f – ⑤ only.
s – Stops to set down only.

u – Stops to pick up only.

185 EDINBURGH - NEWCASTLE - YORK, LEEDS and HULL - LONDON GR (unless otherwise stated)

Services on ⑦ valid until September 6. All services convey 🍸.

	Ⓐ	Ⓐ	Ⓐ	Ⓐ	Ⓐ	Ⓐ	Ⓐ	Ⓐ	Ⓐ	Ⓐ	Ⓐ	Ⓐ	Ⓐ	Ⓐ	Ⓐ	Ⓐ	Ⓐ	Ⓐ	Ⓐ	⑥	⑥	⑥	⑥	⑥	⑥
			H						G				H		A										
Glasgow Central .... **127** d.	1350	...	...	...	...	...	...	...	...	...	...	1550	...	...	...	...	...	1750	1950		...	...	...	...	...
Edinburgh .... **127** d.	1500	...	...	...	...	...	1600	...	...	...	...	1700	...	...	1730	1835	...	1900	2100		...	...	...	...	...
Berwick upon Tweed..... **127** d.	|	...	...	...	...	...	1643	...	...	...	...	|	...	...	1817	1920	...	1947	2143		...	...	...	...	...
Newcastle..............**127 187** d.	1628	...	...	...	1655	...	1732	...	...	1810	...	1835	...	...	1908	2020	...	2038	2245		...	0430	...	0600	...
Durham ....**127 187** d.	|	...	...	...	1707	...	|	...	...	1822	...	|	...	...	|	...	...	2051	2300		...	0445	...	0612	...
Darlington ....**127 187** d.	|	...	...	...	1725	...	1759	...	...	1840	...	1904	...	...	1938	...	...	2109	2318		...	0503	...	0630	...
Northallerton .... **187** d.	|	...	...	...	|	...	|	...	1836	1851	...	|	...	...	|	...	...	|	|		...	0530	...	|	...
York.......................**127 187** d.	1721	...	...	...	1755	...	1831	...	1906	1913	...	1935	...	...	2009	...	...	2140	0016		...	0600	...	0700	...
Leeds ....**127 187** d.	|	1705	...	1740	|	1805	|	1840	|	|	1905	|	...	1940	|	...	2040	|	...		0505	|	0610	|	0700
Wakefield Westgate **127**... d.	|	1717	...	1752	|	1817	|	1852	|	|	1917	|	...	1952	|	...	2055	|	...		0517	|	0622	|	0712
Hull 178 .... d.	|	|	1706	|	|	|	|	|	|	|	|	|	1918	|	|	...	|	|	...		|	|	|	|	|
Doncaster 127 178 .... d.	|	1737	1803	1811	1821	1835	1854	1911	|	1937	1935	2000	2010	2014	2032	...	2112	2203	...		0535	0623	0640	0723	0730
Retford .... d.	|	1757	1817	|	1836	|	|	|	|	|	|	|	|	|	|	...	2127	|	...		0550	|	0655	|	|
Newark North Gate .... d.	|	|	|	1834	1851	|	1917	1934	|	|	2005	|	|	2037	|	...	2142	2226	...		0605	|	0710	|	0753
Grantham **208**...................... d.	|	|	1837	1847	|	|	|	1949	|	|	2017	|	2041	2050	|	...	2155	2239	...		0617	|	0723	|	0806
Peterborough 184 208........ a.	1826	|	|	1906	1919	1925	1945	|	|	2027	2037	2046	|	2109	2120	...	2214	2258	...		0637	0709	0742	0809	0826
Stevenage **184** .... a.	|	1900	1924s	|	1950	|	2016	2035	|	|	|	2117	2130s	|	2152	...	2251s	2335s	...		|	|	|	|	|
London Kings Cross **184** .... a.	1919	1929	1949	1959	2018	2021	2044	2103	2109	2120	2133	2144	2158	2204	2220	...	2332	0015	...		0729	0804	0840	0903	0918

	⑥	⑥	⑥	⑥	⑥	⑥	⑥	⑥	⑥	⑥	⑥	⑥	⑥	⑥	⑥	⑥	⑥	⑥	⑥	⑥	⑥	⑥	⑥	⑥	⑥
			M		E	Q		G	H							H							A		
Glasgow Central .... **127** d.	...	...	...	...	...	...	...	...	...	...	...	...	...	...	0650	...	...	...	0750	...	...	0850	...	...	0950
Edinburgh .... **127** d.	...	...	...	...	...	...	...	...	...	0615	...	0700	0730	...	0800	...	0835	...	0900	0930	...	1000	1030	...	1100
Berwick upon Tweed..... **127** d.	...	...	...	...	...	...	...	...	...	0658	...	0740	0809	...	|	...	0914	...	0941	1010	...	|	|	...	1139
Newcastle..............**127 187** d.	...	0635	...	0700	...	...	0730	...	...	0754	...	0833	0900	...	0932	...	1003	...	1032	1100	...	1129	1200	...	1233
Durham ....**127 187** d.	...	0648	...	0712	...	...	0742	...	...	|	...	0846	0913	...	|	...	|	...	1045	|	...	1142	1213	...	1246
Darlington ....**127 187** d.	...	0706	...	0730	...	...	0800	...	...	0821	...	0904	0931	...	1001	...	1031	...	1103	1127	...	1201	1231	...	1304
Northallerton .... **187** d.	...	|	...	0741	...	...	|	0806	...	|	...	|	0942	...	|	...	|	...	|	|	...	|	|	...	|
York.......................**127 187** d.	...	0736	...	0803	...	...	0830	0847	...	0851	...	0935	1005	...	1031	...	1100	...	1133	1159	...	1231	1302	...	1334
Leeds ....**127 187** d.	...	|	0740	|	0805	0815	|	|	...	|	0905	|	|	1005	|	...	|	1105	|	|	1205	|	|	1305	|
Wakefield Westgate **127**... d.	...	|	0752	|	0818	|	|	|	...	|	0917	|	|	1018	|	...	|	1117	|	|	1217	|	|	1317	|
Hull 178 .... d.	0650	|	|	|	|	|	|	|	0802	|	|	|	|	|	|	1006	|	|	|	|	|	|	|	|	|
Doncaster 127 178 .... d.	0740	0800	|	|	|	0845	0855	|	0901	0915	0935	1003	1029	1036	1055	1102	1124	1139	1157	1221	1235	1257	|	1338	1358
Retford .... d.	|	|	0820	|	|	|	0910	|	0921	|	|	|	|	|	1110	1117	|	|	|	|	1250	|	|	|	|
Newark North Gate .... d.	|	0824	0834	|	0854	|	|	|	|	|	1000	|	|	1100	|	|	|	1201	|	|	1305	|	|	1401	|
Grantham **208**...................... d.	|	0837	0846	|	0906	|	|	|	0942	|	1012	|	|	1112	|	1138	1155	1214	1228	|	1317	|	|	|	1429
Peterborough 184 208........ a.	0832	0857	0906	0915	0926	0932	0951	|	|	1006	1032	1054	1120	1132	1149	|	1219	1233	1249	1307	|	1343	1413	1429	1449
Stevenage **184** .... a.	|	|	|	0945	|	|	|	|	|	|	1102	|	1150	|	|	|	|	1303	|	|	|	1416	|	|	|
London Kings Cross **184** .... a.	0926	0951	1000	1013	1020	1026	1044	1048	1052	1058	1133	1150	1217	1224	1242	1247	1311	1333	1344	1359	1427	1443	1510	1521	1542

	⑥	⑥	⑥	⑥	⑥	⑥	⑥	⑥	⑥	⑥	⑥	⑥	⑥	⑥	⑥	⑥	⑥	⑥	⑥	⑥	⑥	⑥	⑦	⑦	⑦
	H	N	G			A			H							H		G		A					
Glasgow Central .... **127** d.	...	...	...	...	...	...	...	1150	...	...	...	...	1350	...	...	...	...	...	1550	...	...	1750		...	...
Edinburgh .... **127** d.	...	1130	...	...	1200	1230	...	1300	...	1330	...	1400	1500	...	1600	...	...	...	1700	1730	...	1900		...	...
Berwick upon Tweed..... **127** d.	...	|	...	...	1239	|	...	|	...	1409	...	1439	|	...	1639	...	...	...	|	1813	...	1946		...	...
Newcastle..............**127 187** d.	...	1304	...	...	1331	1359	...	1429	...	1459	...	1528	1629	...	1729	...	...	...	1834	1906	...	2047		...	0800
Durham ....**127 187** d.	...	|	...	...	1344	1412	...	1442	...	1526	...	1542	1642	...	|	...	...	...	1847	|	...	2100		...	0812
Darlington ....**127 187** d.	...	|	...	...	1402	1430	...	1500	...	|	...	1604	1700	...	1759	...	...	...	1905	1934	...	2118		...	0830
Northallerton .... **187** d.	...	|	1331	...	1413	|	...	|	...	|	...	|	|	...	|	...	...	1845	|	|	...	2130		...	|
York.......................**127 187** d.	...	1357	1405	...	1437	1501	...	1530	...	1557	...	1634	1731	...	1829	...	...	1916	1936	2006	...	2152		...	0900
Leeds ....**127 187** d.	...	|	|	1405	|	|	1505	|	...	|	1605	|	|	1740	|	...	1840	|	|	|	2015	|		0825	|
Wakefield Westgate **127**... d.	...	|	|	1417	|	|	1517	|	...	|	1617	|	|	1752	|	...	1854	|	|	|	2031	|		0837	|
Hull 178 .... d.	1305	|	|	|	|	|	|	|	1506	|	|	|	|	|	|	1812	|	|	|	|	|	|		|	|
Doncaster 127 178 .... d.	1404	|	|	1435	1504	|	1535	1555	1602	1621	1638	1658	1755	1810	1852	1905	1914	|	2004	2030	2048	2217		0855	0925
Retford .... d.	1419	|	|	1450	|	|	|	|	1617	|	1653	|	|	1825	|	1920	1929	|	|	|	2103	...		|	0940
Newark North Gate .... d.	|	|	|	1505	|	|	1602	|	|	|	1708	|	1818	1840	|	|	1944	|	|	|	2118	...		0918	|
Grantham **208**...................... d.	1439	|	|	1518	|	|	1615	|	1637	1652	|	1729	|	1852	|	1940	1956	|	|	|	2131	...		0931	1002
Peterborough 184 208........ a.	|	1504	|	1538	1550	|	1634	1642	|	1711	1736	1748	1846	1912	1938	|	2018	|	2051	2121	2150	...		0953	1024
Stevenage **184** .... a.	|	|	|	|	1621	|	1706	1716	|	|	|	1819	|	1943	2007	|	2048	|	2120	2154	2220	...		|	1055
London Kings Cross **184** .... a.	1550	1603	1604	1634	1647	1658	1733	1743	1745	1810	1828	1846	1940	2012	2035	2046	2115	2116	2148	2220	2247	...		1048	1123

	⑦	⑦	⑦	⑦	⑦	⑦	⑦	⑦	⑦	⑦	⑦	⑦	⑦	⑦	⑦	⑦	⑦	⑦	⑦	⑦	⑦	⑦	⑦	⑦	⑦
				H	G						H									H	A		G		N
Glasgow Central .... **127** d.	...	...	...	...	...	...	...	...	...	...	...	...	...	...	...	...	...	...	1050	...	...	...	...	...	...
Edinburgh .... **127** d.	...	...	...	...	...	...	0900	...	0930	1000	...	1030	...	1100	...	1130	...	1200	...	1230	...	...	1300	...	1330
Berwick upon Tweed..... **127** d.	...	...	...	...	...	...	0939	...	|	1039	...	1109	...	|	...	|	...	1239	...	|	...	...	1339	...	1411
Newcastle..............**127 187** d.	...	0900	0930	...	...	...	1030	...	1057	1132	...	1200	...	1232	...	1301	1324	1332	...	1402	...	...	1432	...	1501
Durham ....**127 187** d.	...	0912	|	...	...	...	|	...	1110	|	...	|	...	1245	...	|	|	1345	...	|	...	...	|	...	1515
Darlington ....**127 187** d.	...	0930	0959	...	...	...	1059	...	|	|	...	1227	...	1303	...	1328	1351	1405	...	1430	...	...	1459	...	1533
Northallerton .... **187** d.	...	0943	|	...	1012	...	|	...	|	|	...	|	...	|	...	1339	|	|	...	|	...	1453	1510	...	|
York.......................**127 187** d.	...	1004	1028	...	1047	...	1129	...	1153	1229	...	1257	...	1337	...	1402	1422	1436	...	1502	...	1531	1534	...	1603
Leeds ....**127 187** d.	0940	|	|	...	|	1040	|	1140	|	|	...	|	1240	|	1340	|	|	|	...	|	1440	|	|	1540	|
Wakefield Westgate **127**... d.	0952	|	|	...	|	1052	|	1152	|	|	...	|	1252	|	1352	|	|	|	...	|	1452	|	|	1552	|
Hull 178 .... d.	|	|	|	1012	|	|	|	|	|	|	1212	|	|	|	|	|	|	|	1410	|	|	|	|	|	|
Doncaster 127 178 .... d.	1010	1028	1053	1104	|	1113	1153	1210	|	1254	1306	1321	1311	1401	1410	1426	1448	1500	1505	|	1510	|	1558	1610	1628
Retford .... d.	|	|	|	1119	|	1128	|	|	|	|	1321	|	1334	|	|	|	|	|	1520	|	1525	|	|	|	|
Newark North Gate .... d.	1032	1051	|	|	|	1142	|	|	1236	|	|	|	1348	|	1433	|	|	|	|	|	1539	|	1620	|	|
Grantham **208**...................... d.	|	1103	|	1139	|	1154	|	1241	|	1326	1340	|	1400	|	|	1456	|	|	1540	|	1552	|	|	1640	|
Peterborough 184 208........ a.	1102	1125	1143	|	|	1216	1240	|	1306	|	|	1410	1422	1448	|	|	1535	1547	|	|	1613	|	1651	1701	1718
Stevenage **184** .... a.	|	1155	|	|	|	|	|	|	1336	1416	1429s	|	|	|	1528	|	|	1618	|	|	1649	|	1721	|	|
London Kings Cross **184** .... a.	1155	1223	1240	1248	1251	1314	1339	1350	1404	1444	1454	1509	1516	1542	1555	1610	1629	1646	1650	1711	1718	1724	1749	1755	1815

	⑦	⑦	⑦	⑦	⑦	⑦	⑦	⑦	⑦	⑦	⑦	⑦	⑦	⑦	⑦	⑦	⑦	⑦	⑦	⑦	⑦	⑦	⑦		
			H		A									A	H			G							
Glasgow Central .... **127** d.	1250	...	...	...	...	...	...	...	...	...	...	1450	...	...	...	1550	...	...	...	...	1750	...	1950	...	...
Edinburgh .... **127** d.	1400	...	...	...	1430	...	1500	...	1530	...	...	1600	...	1630	...	1700	1730	...	...	1800	1900	2000	2100	...	...
Berwick upon Tweed..... **127** d.	|	...	...	...	|	...	1539	...	1609	...	...	|	...	1709	...	|	|	...	...	1839	|	2043	2144	...	...
Newcastle..............**127 187** d.	1530	...	...	1550	1601	...	1633	...	1704	...	1712	1730	...	1810	...	1829	1855	...	...	1935	2031	2140	2241	...	...
Durham ....**127 187** d.	|	...	...	|	1614	...	1646	...	|	...	1724	|	...	|	...	1843	1908	...	...	1948	|	2153	...	...	...
Darlington ....**127 187** d.	1559	...	...	1620	1632	...	1704	...	1731	...	1742	1759	...	|	...	1901	1926	...	...	2006	2058	2211	...	...	...
Northallerton .... **187** d.	|	...	...	1632	|	...	|	...	1742	...	|	|	...	|	...	|	1939	1948	...	|	|	2241	...	...	...
York.......................**127 187** d.	1629	...	...	1653	1703	...	1736	...	1805	...	1812	1829	...	1905	...	1931	2002	2015	...	2036	2128	2319	...	...	...
Leeds ....**127 187** d.	|	1640	...	|	|	1705	|	1740	|	...	|	|	1840	|	...	|	|	|	2015	|	|	...	...	...	...
Wakefield Westgate **127**... d.	|	1652	...	|	|	1718	|	1752	|	...	|	|	1852	|	...	|	|	|	2027	|	|	...	...	...	...
Hull 178 .... d.	|	|	1621	|	|	|	|	|	|	1730	|	|	|	|	1848	|	|	|	|	|	|	...	...	...	...
Doncaster 127 178 .... d.	1653	1710	1715	1719	1728	1736	1803	|	1831	1823	1837	1853	1910	1931	1943	1954	2026	|	2047	2100	2152	...	...	...	...
Retford .... d.	|	|	1730	|	|	1751	|	|	|	1844	|	|	|	|	1958	|	|	|	|	2115	|	...	...	...	...
Newark North Gate .... d.	|	|	|	1746	|	1805	|	|	|	|	1902	|	|	|	|	2016	|	|	|	2134	|	...	...	...	...
Grantham **208**...................... d.	|	1740	1749	|	|	|	|	1837	|	1906	|	|	1940	|	2018	|	2056	|	|	|	2222	...	...	...	...
Peterborough 184 208........ a.	1740	1802	|	|	1826	|	1850	1859	1918	1928	1933	1940	2001	2022	|	2046	2117	|	2135	2203	2243	...	...	...	...
Stevenage **184** .... a.	1816	|	|	1848	|	1902	1921	|	|	|	2007	2018	2032	2054	2109s	2120	2148	|	2209	2234	|	...	...	...	...
London Kings Cross **184** .... a.	1843	1855	1906	1916	1921	1933	1948	1952	2014	2023	2034	2043	2101	2125	2134	2147	2216	2217	2237	2314	2350	...	...	...	...

← **FOR NOTES SEE PAGES 150 AND 151**

TP NEWCASTLE and MIDDLESBROUGH - YORK - LEEDS - MANCHESTER and LIVERPOOL 187

Services on ⑦ valid until September 6. For Arriva Cross Country and National Express East Coast services Newcastle - York and v.v., see Tables **127** and **185**.

km			⚒	⚒	⚒	⚒	⚒	⚒	⚒	Ⓐ	⑥	⚒	Ⓐ	⑥	⚒	⚒	Ⓐ	⑥	Ⓐ	⑥	⚒	⚒	⚒	⚒	⚒	⚒
0	**Newcastle** 127 185 d.	⚒	...	...	...	...	...	...	...	...	...	0613	...	...	...	...	...	...	0726	0733	...	...	...	...	...	0912
23	Durham 127 185 d.		...	...	...	...	...	...	...	...	...	0629	...	...	...	...	...	...	0743	0749	...	...	...	...	...	0927
	Middlesbrough d.		...	...	...	...	...	0557	...	...	...	|	...	...	...	0721	...	...	|	|	...	...	...	0900	...	|
58	Darlington 127 185 d.		...	...	...	...	...	|	...	...	...	0646	...	...	...	|	...	...	0800	0806	...	...	...	|	...	0944
81	Northallerton 185 d.		...	...	...	...	...	0625	...	...	...	0658	...	...	...	0748	...	...	0812	0818	...	...	...	0927	...	0956
93	Thirsk d.		...	...	...	...	...	0633	...	...	...	0706	...	...	...	0756	...	...	0820	0826	...	...	...	0935	...	|
	Scarborough d.		...	...	...	...	...	|	...	0630	0634	|	0700	0704	...	|	0738	0747	|	|	...	...	0847	|	...	|
	Malton d.		...	...	...	...	...	|	...	0653	0657	|	0723	0727	...	|	0801	0810	|	|	...	...	0910	|	...	|
129	**York** 127 185 d.		0526	...	0557	0628	...	0654	...	0723	0728	0740	0754	0758	...	0824	0840	0840	0858	0858	...	0928	0940	0958	...	1028
	Hull d.		|	...	|	|	0600	|	0635	|	|	|	|	|	0733	|	|	|	|	|	0840	|	|	|	0940	|
	Selby d.		|	...	|	|	0635	|	0707	|	|	|	|	|	0807	|	|	|	|	|	0911	|	|	|	1011	|
170	**Leeds** 127 190 d.		0555	...	0625	0655	0708	0723	0738	0755	0755	0808	0825	0825	0840	0855	0908	0908	0925	0925	0940	0955	1008	1025	1040	1055
185	Dewsbury 190 d.		0606	...	0636	0706	|	0734	|	0806	0806	|	0836	0836	|	0906	|	|	0936	0936	|	1006	|	1036	|	1106
198	**Huddersfield** d.		0615	...	0645	0716	0726	0744	0757	0816	0816	0826	0845	0845	0859	0916	0926	0926	0946	0946	0959	1016	1026	1046	1059	1116
227	Stalybridge d.		0633	...	0704	0734	0744	0802	0817	|	|	0844	|	|	|	|	0944	0944	|	|	|	|	1044	|	|	|
239	**Manchester** P'dilly a.		0650	0707	0719	0751	0805	0819	0836	0851	0851	0905	0919	0919	0936	0949	1005	1005	1019	1019	1036	1049	1105	1119	1136	1149
255	M'chester Airport ✈ a.		0712	|	0742	0812	|	0842	...	0912	0912	|	0942	0942	...	1012	|	|	1042	1042	...	1112	|	1142	...	1212
265	Warrington Central a.		...	0729	...	...	0829	...	...	...	...	0929	...	...	...	...	1029	1029	...	...	...	...	1129	...	...	...
295	**Liverpool** Lime St a.		...	0757	...	...	0857	...	...	...	...	0957	...	...	...	...	1057	1057	...	...	...	...	1157	...	...	...

	⚒	⚒	⚒	⚒	⚒	⚒	⚒	⚒	⚒	⚒	⚒	⚒	⚒	⚒	⚒	⚒	⚒	Ⓐ	⑥	⚒	⚒	⚒	⚒	⚒	⚒	⚒
Newcastle 127 185 d.	...	...	...	1012	...	...	...	1115	...	...	...	1215	...	...	...	1315	...	...	...	...	1412	...	...	...	1509	...
Durham 127 185 d.	...	...	...	1027	...	...	...	1127	...	...	...	1227	...	...	...	1327	...	...	...	...	1424	...	...	...	1525	...
Middlesbrough d.	...	0959	...	|	...	1100	...	|	...	1200	...	|	...	1250	...	|	...	1350	1400	...	|	...	1450	...	|	...
Darlington 127 185 d.	...	|	...	1044	...	|	...	1144	...	|	...	1244	...	|	...	1344	...	|	|	...	1444	...	|	...	1542	...
Northallerton 185 d.	...	1027	...	1056	...	1127	...	1156	...	1227	...	1256	...	1317	...	1356	...	1417	1427	...	1456	...	1517	...	1553	...
Thirsk d.	...	1035	...	|	...	1135	...	|	...	1235	...	|	...	1325	...	|	...	1425	1435	...	|	...	1525	...	|	...
Scarborough d.	0947	|	...	|	1047	|	...	|	1147	|	...	|	1247	|	...	|	1347	|	|	...	|	1447	|	...	|	1547
Malton d.	1010	|	...	|	1110	|	...	|	1210	|	...	|	1310	|	...	|	1410	|	|	...	|	1510	|	...	|	1610
York 127 185 d.	1040	1058	...	1128	1140	1158	...	1228	1239	1258	...	1328	1340	1358	...	1428	1440	1458	1458	...	1528	1540	1558	...	1628	1640
Hull d.	|	|	1038	|	|	|	1138	|	|	|	1238	|	|	|	1338	|	|	|	|	1438	|	|	|	1540	|	|
Selby d.	|	|	1109	|	|	|	1209	|	|	|	1309	|	|	|	1409	|	|	|	|	1509	|	|	|	1611	|	|
Leeds 127 190 d.	1108	1125	1140	1155	1208	1225	1240	1255	1308	1325	1340	1355	1408	1425	1437	1455	1508	1525	1525	1540	1555	1608	1625	1640	1655	1708
Dewsbury 190 d.	|	1136	|	1206	|	1236	|	1306	|	1336	|	1406	|	1436	|	1506	|	1536	1536	|	1606	|	1636	|	1706	|
Huddersfield d.	1126	1146	1159	1216	1226	1246	1258	1316	1326	1346	1359	1416	1426	1446	1456	1516	1526	1546	1546	1559	1616	1626	1646	1659	1716	1726
Stalybridge d.	1144	|	|	|	1244	|	|	|	1344	|	|	|	1444	|	|	|	1544	|	|	|	|	1644	|	1718	|	1744
Manchester P'dilly a.	1205	1219	1236	1249	1305	1319	1336	1349	1405	1419	1436	1449	1505	1519	1536	1549	1605	1619	1619	1636	1649	1705	1721	1737	1749	1805
M'chester Airport ✈ a.	|	1242	...	1312	|	1342	...	1412	|	1442	...	1512	|	1542	...	1612	|	1642	1642	...	1712	|	...	...	1812	|
Warrington Central a.	1229	...	...	...	1329	...	...	...	1429	...	...	...	1529	...	...	...	1629	...	...	...	...	1729	...	...	...	1829
Liverpool Lime St a.	1257	...	...	...	1357	...	...	...	1457	...	...	...	1557	...	...	...	1657	...	...	...	...	1800	...	...	...	1859

	⚒	⚒	⚒	⚒	⚒	⑥E	Ⓐ	⑥	⚒d	Ⓐ	⑥A	⑥B	⑥A	⑥B	Ⓐ	Ⓐ	⑥	⚒	⚒	⚒	⑥	Ⓐ	⚒	⚒	Ⓐ	Ⓐ
Newcastle 127 185 d.	...	...	1606	...	...	....	...	...	1701	...	...	...	...	...	...	...	...	...	...	...	1852	1858	...	...	...	...
Durham 127 185 d.	...	...	1621	...	...	....	...	...	1713	...	...	...	...	...	...	...	...	...	...	...	1904	1910	...	...	...	...
Middlesbrough d.	1550	...	|	...	...	....	1650	1700	|	...	...	...	...	...	...	1750	1807	...	...	1900	|	|	...	...	2000	...
Darlington 127 185 d.	|	...	1639	...	...	....	|	|	1730	...	...	...	...	...	...	|	|	...	...	|	1922	1927	...	...	2031	...
Northallerton 185 d.	1617	...	1650	...	...	....	1717	1727	1742	...	...	...	...	...	...	1817	1835	...	...	1927	1936	1938	...	...	2042	...
Thirsk d.	1625	...	1658	...	...	....	1725	1735	|	...	...	...	...	...	...	1825	1843	...	...	1935	|	|	...	...	2050	...
Scarborough d.	|	...	|	...	1647	1703	|	|	|	...	1745	1745	...	...	1747	|	|	...	1847	|	|	|	...	1947	|	2037
Malton d.	|	...	|	...	1710	|	|	|	|	...	1808	1808	...	...	1810	|	|	...	1910	|	|	|	...	2010	|	2100
York 127 185 d.	1658	...	1728	...	1740	1746	1758	1758	1809	...	1838	1838	...	...	1840	1910	1910	...	1939	1958	2010	2010	...	2040	2110	2128
Hull d.	|	1640	|	1701	|	....	|	|	|	1758	|	|	1803	1803	|	|	|	1859	|	...	|	|	1956	|	|	...
Selby d.	|	1711	|	1732	|	....	|	|	|	1831	|	|	1834	1834	|	|	|	1930	|	...	|	|	2027	|	|	...
Leeds 127 190 d.	1726	1740	1755	1802	1808	....	1825	1825	1840	1855	1904	1908	1908	1858	1908	1940	1940	1956	2008	...	2040	2040	2056	2108	2140	...
Dewsbury 190 d.	1736	|	1806	1813a	|	....	1836	1836	|	1906	...	|	|	....	|	1951	1951	...	|	...	2051	2051	...	|	2151	...
Huddersfield d.	1746	1759	1816	1823a	1826	....	1846	1846	1858	1916	...	1926	1926	....	1926	2000	2000	...	2026	...	2100	2100	...	2126	2200	...
Stalybridge d.	|	1818	|	...	1844	....	|	|	|	|	...	1944	1944	....	1944	|	|	...	2044	...	|	|	...	2144	|	...
Manchester P'dilly a.	1819	|	1849	...	1905	....	1921	1921	1933	1957	...	2005	2005	....	2005	2033	2033	...	2105	...	2133	2133	...	2205	2233	...
M'chester Airport ✈ a.	1842	1837	1913	...	|	....	...	...	1959	...	...	|	|	....	|	2057	2057	...	|	...	2157	2157	...	|	2257	...
Warrington Central a.	...	...	...	...	1929	....	...	...	...	...	...	2029	2029	....	2029	...	...	...	2129	...	...	...	...	2229	...	...
Liverpool Lime St a.	...	...	...	...	1957	....	...	...	...	...	...	2059	2059	....	2059	...	...	...	2157	...	...	...	...	2258	...	...

	⚒	⚒	Ⓐ	⚒	⑥B	Ⓐ	⑥A	⑥B		⑦	⑦	⑦	⑦	⑦	⑦	⑦	⑦	⑦	⑦	⑦	⑦	⑦	⑦	⑦	⑦	⑦
Newcastle 127 185 d.	...	...	...	...	....	2147	...	...	⑦	...	...	...	...	0806	...	...	...	0933	...	...	...	1103	...	...	1205	...
Durham 127 185 d.	...	...	...	...	....	2200	...	...		...	...	...	...	0818	...	...	...	0948	...	...	...	1115	...	...	1217	...
Middlesbrough d.	2050	...	2140	...	....	|	2150	2150		...	...	...	...	|	...	...	...	|	1015	...	...	|	...	...	|	...
Darlington 127 185 d.	|	...	2208	...	....	2217	2219	2219		...	...	...	...	0835	...	...	...	1005	|	...	...	1132	...	...	1234	...
Northallerton 185 d.	2117	...	2219	...	....	2228	2230	2230		...	...	...	...	0847	...	...	...	1016	1042	...	...	1142	...	...	|	...
Thirsk d.	|	...	2227	...	....	|	2238	2238		...	...	...	...	|	...	...	...	|	1051	...	...	|	...	...	|	...
Scarborough d.	|	...	|	2207	....	|	|	|		...	...	...	...	|	...	...	0920	|	|	...	1050	|	...	1150	|	...
Malton d.	|	...	|	2230	....	|	|	|		...	...	...	...	|	...	...	0943	|	|	...	1115	|	...	1213	|	...
York 127 185 d.	2142	...	2252	2257	....	2307	2307	2307		0612	0712	0810	0840	0915	...	...	1015	1045	1115	...	1145	1215	...	1245	1315	...
Hull d.	|	2133	...	...	....	|	|	|		|	|	|	|	|	0900	...	|	|	|	1058	|	|	1200	|	|	1258
Selby d.	|	2207	...	...	....	|	|	|		|	|	|	|	|	0931	...	|	|	|	1129	|	|	1233	|	|	1329
Leeds 127 190 d.	2208	2240	...	...	....	2335	2335	2333		0640	0740	0840	0910	0940	1006	...	1040	1110	1140	1159	1210	1240	1259	1310	1340	1359
Dewsbury 190 d.	|	2251	...	...	....	2346	2346	*0010**		0651	0751	0851	|	0951	|	...	1051	|	1151	|	|	1251	|	|	1351	|
Huddersfield d.	2226	2300	...	...	2356	2356	2356	*0035**		0701	0801	0901	0928	1001	1026	...	1100	1128	1201	1217	1228	1301	1317	1328	1401	1417
Stalybridge d.	2244	|	...	...	|	|	|	....		0719	0819	0919	0946	|	1046	...	|	1146	|	|	1246	|	|	1346	|	|
Manchester P'dilly a.	2305	2337	...	...	0030	0054	0041	....		0734	0834	0934	1005	1034	1105	1107	1134	1205	1234	1254	1305	1334	1354	1405	1434	1454
M'chester Airport ✈ a.	...	...	...	...	0048	0110	0100	....		0755	0855	0955	|	1055	...	|	1155	|	1255	...	|	1355	...	|	1455	...
Warrington Central a.	...	...	...	...	....	...	...	...		...	...	...	1029	...	...	1129	...	1229	...	...	1329	...	...	1429	...	...
Liverpool Lime St a.	...	...	...	...	....	...	...	...		...	...	...	1057	...	...	1159	...	1257	...	...	1357	...	...	1457	...	...

	⑦	⑦	⑦	⑦	⑦	⑦	⑦	⑦	⑦	⑦	⑦	⑦	⑦	⑦	⑦	⑦	⑦	⑦	⑦	⑦	⑦	⑦	⑦	⑦	⑦	⑦
Newcastle 127 185 d.	...	1306	...	...	1408	...	...	1507	...	...	1608	...	...	1652	...	...	1757	...	...	1906	...	...	2007	...	...	...
Durham 127 185 d.	...	1318	...	...	1420	...	...	1522	...	...	1620	...	...	1708	...	...	1809	...	...	1917	...	...	2019	...	...	...
Middlesbrough d.	1245	|	...	...	|	...	1445	|	...	...	|	...	1645	|	...	...	|	...	1845	|	...	2007	|	...	...	2207
Darlington 127 185 d.	|	1335	...	...	1437	...	|	1540	...	...	1637	...	|	1726	...	...	1826	...	|	1935	...	|	2036	...	...	|
Northallerton 185 d.	1312	|	...	...	1448	...	1512	|	...	...	1648	...	1712	1738	...	...	|	...	1914	|	...	2034	2048	...	...	2234
Thirsk d.	1322	|	...	...	|	...	1521	|	...	...	|	...	1721	|	...	...	|	...	1923	|	...	2042	|	...	...	2242
Scarborough d.	|	|	...	1350	|	...	|	|	...	1550	|	...	|	|	...	1750	|	...	|	|	1950	|	|	...	2120	|
Malton d.	|	|	...	1413	|	...	|	|	...	1613	|	...	|	|	...	1813	|	...	|	|	2013	|	|	...	2143	|
York 127 185 d.	1345	1415	1433	1445	1515	...	1545	1615	1633	1645	1715	...	1745	1815	1833	1845	1915	...	1945	2015	2045	2102	2115	...	2212	2312
Hull d.	|	|	|	|	|	1458	|	|	|	|	|	1658	|	|	|	|	|	1858	|	|	|	...	|	2100	|	|
Selby d.	|	|	|	|	|	1529	|	|	|	|	|	1729	|	|	|	|	|	1929	|	|	|	...	|	2131	|	|
Leeds 127 190 d.	1410	1440	1459	1510	1540	1559	1610	1640	1659	1710	1740	1759	1810	1840	1859	1910	1940	1959	2010	2040	2110	...	2140	2159	2240	2340
Dewsbury 190 d.	|	1451	|	|	1551	|	|	1651	|	|	1751	|	|	1851	|	|	1951	|	|	2051	|	...	2151	...	|	2351
Huddersfield d.	1428	1501	1517	1528	1601	1617	1628	1701	1717	1728	1801	1817	1828	1901	1917	1928	2001	2017	2028	2101	2128	...	2201	...	2258	0001
Stalybridge d.	1446	|	|	1546	|	|	1646	|	|	1746	|	|	1846	|	|	1946	|	|	2046	2119	|	...	2219	...	2319	|
Manchester P'dilly a.	1505	1534	1554	1605	1634	1654	1705	1734	1754	1805	1834	1854	1905	1934	1954	2005	2034	2054	2105	2136	2205	...	2234	...	2336	0043
M'chester Airport ✈ a.	|	1555	...	|	1655	...	|	1755	...	|	1855	...	|	1955	...	|	2055	...	|	...	|	...	2255	...	...	0100
Warrington Central a.	1529	...	...	1629	...	...	1729	...	...	1829	...	...	1929	...	...	2029	...	...	2129	...	2229	...	...	...	...	...
Liverpool Lime St a.	1547	...	...	1657	...	...	1757	...	...	1857	...	...	1957	...	...	2057	...	...	2157	...	2257	...	...	...	...	...

A – May 23 - Sept. 5.
B – Sept. 12 - Dec. 12.
E – To London St. Pancras. May 23 - Sept. 5. Operated by *EM*.
a – Ⓐ only.
d – Also calls at Dewsbury on ⑥.

* – By 🚌.

☛ Additional trains **York - Leeds - Huddersfield - Manchester Piccadilly - Manchester Airport**: 0146②–⑤, 0152①⑥, 0244⑥⑦, 0252Ⓐ, 0352⑥, 0359⑦, 0400②–⑤, 0422①, 0512⑦.

187 LIVERPOOL and MANCHESTER - LEEDS - YORK - MIDDLESBROUGH and NEWCASTLE TP

Services on ⑥ valid until September 6. For Arriva Cross Country and National Express East Coast services Newcastle - York and v.v., see Tables **127** and **185.**

⚒	⚒	⑥	⑥	Ⓐ	⚒	⚒	⚒	⚒	Ⓐ	⑥	⚒	Ⓐ	⑥	Ⓐ	⚒	⚒	⚒	⚒	⚒	⑥E	⚒	⚒	⚒	⚒	⚒
Liverpool Lime St d.	...	...	...	...	...	...	...	...	...	...	0616	0616	...	...	...	...	0716	...	...	...	...	0822	...	...	...
Warrington Central d.	...	...	...	...	...	...	...	...	...	...	0638	0638	...	...	...	...	0740	...	...	...	...	0844	...	...	...
M'chester Airport ✈ d.	...	0400	...	0400	...	0537	...	...	0623	0623	|	|	0705	0705	...	0733	|	0805	...	...	0835	|	0905	...	0935
Manchester P'dilly d.	...	0415	...	0415	0539	0557	0621	...	0654	0654	0711	0711	0726	0726	0736	0755	0810	0826	0842	...	0855	0911	0926	0942	0957
Stalybridge d.	...	|	...	|	0552	|	|	...	0707	0707	0726	0726	|	|	0749	0809	0826	|	|	...	|	0926	|	|	|
Huddersfield d.	...	0457	...	0516	0611	0627	0656	...	0726	0726	0745	0745	0757	0757	0810	0830	0845	0857	0916	...	0927	0945	0957	1016	1027
Dewsbury **190** d.	...	|	...	|	|	0637	0706	...	|	|	0755	0755	0807	0807	0820	0839	|	0907	|	...	0937	|	1007	|	1037
Leeds **127 190** d.	...	0519	...	0540	0635	0655	0723	...	0750	0750	0812	0812	0827	0827	0838	0857	0912	0927	0938	...	0957	1012	1027	1038	1057
Selby d.	...	|	...	|	|	|	0743	...	|	|	|	|	|	|	0858	|	|	|	0957	...	|	|	|	1057	|
Hull a.	...	|	...	|	|	|	0820	...	|	|	|	|	|	|	0931	|	|	|	1034	...	|	|	|	1134	|
York **127 185** d.	0554	0602	0638	0638	0706	0725	...	0732	0823	0823	0838	0842	0857	0903	...	0926	0938	0956	...	1024	1026	1038	1054	...	1126
Malton d.	|	...	0702	0702	|	0749	...	|	|	|	0902	|	|	|	...	|	1002	|	...	|	|	1102	|	...	|
Scarborough a.	|	...	0730	0730	|	0815	...	|	|	|	0930	|	|	|	...	|	1032	|	...	1106	|	1130	|	...	|
Thirsk d.	0610	...	...	...	0722	...	...	0754	0839	0845	...	|	|	|	...	0945	...	|	...	...	1045	...	|	...	1142
Northallerton **185** d.	0618	...	...	...	0730	...	...	0801	0848	0856	...	0902	0917	0924	...	0954	...	1020	...	...	1055	...	1115	...	1155
Darlington **127 185** d.	0629	...	...	...	0741	...	...	|	|	|	...	0914	0929	0936	...	|	...	1032	...	...	|	...	1127	...	|
Middlesbrough a.	0701	...	...	...	|	...	...	0836	0921	0932	...	|	|	|	...	1030	...	|	...	...	1130	...	|	...	1230
Durham **127 185** a.	...	...	...	...	0758	...	...	...	...	...	...	0931	0946	0953	...	...	...	1053	...	...	...	...	1144	...	...
Newcastle **127 185** a.	...	...	...	...	0818	...	...	...	...	...	...	0949	1002	1010	...	...	...	1114	...	...	...	...	1200	...	...

	⚒	⑥	Ⓐ	⚒	⚒	⚒	⚒	⚒	⚒	⚒	⚒	⚒	⚒	⚒	⚒	⚒	⚒	⚒	⚒	⚒	⚒	⚒	⚒	⚒	Ⓐ	⑥
Liverpool Lime St d.	0922	...	...	...	...	1022	...	...	...	1122	...	...	...	1222	...	...	...	1322	...	...	...	1422	...	...	...	...
Warrington Central d.	0944	...	...	...	...	1044	...	...	...	1144	...	...	...	1244	...	...	...	1344	...	...	...	1444	...	...	...	...
M'chester Airport ✈ d.	|	1005	1005	...	1035	|	1105	...	1135	|	1205	...	1235	|	1305	...	1335	|	1405	...	1435	|	1505	...	1535	1535
Manchester P'dilly d.	1011	1027	1027	1042	1057	1111	1127	1142	1157	1211	1227	1242	1257	1311	1327	1342	1357	1411	1427	1442	1457	1511	1527	1542	1557	1557
Stalybridge d.	1026	|	|	|	|	1126	|	|	|	1226	|	|	|	1326	|	|	|	1426	|	|	|	1526	|	|	|	|
Huddersfield d.	1045	1057	1057	1116	1127	1145	1157	1216	1227	1245	1257	1316	1327	1345	1357	1416	1427	1445	1457	1516	1527	1545	1557	1616	1627	1627
Dewsbury **190** d.	|	1107	1107	|	1137	|	1207	|	1237	|	1307	|	1337	|	1407	|	1437	|	1507	|	1537	|	1607	|	1637	1637
Leeds **127 190** d.	1112	1127	1127	1138	1157	1212	1227	1238	1257	1312	1327	1338	1357	1412	1427	1438	1457	1512	1527	1538	1557	1612	1627	1638	1657	1657
Selby d.	|	|	|	1157	|	|	|	1257	|	|	|	1357	|	|	|	1457	|	|	|	1557	|	|	|	1700	|	|
Hull a.	|	|	|	1236	|	|	|	1334	|	|	|	1434	|	|	|	1534	|	|	|	1635	|	|	|	1737	|	|
York **127 185** d.	1138	1154	1201	...	1226	1238	1254	...	1326	1338	1354	...	1426	1438	1454	...	1526	1538	1554	...	1626	1638	1658	...	1726	1726
Malton d.	1202	|	|	...	|	1302	|	...	|	1402	|	...	|	1502	|	...	|	1602	...	...	|	1702	|	...	1750	|
Scarborough a.	1230	|	|	...	|	1330	|	...	|	1430	|	...	|	1530	|	...	|	1630	...	...	|	1730	|	...	1817	|
Thirsk d.	...	|	|	...	1246	...	|	...	1343	...	|	...	1442	...	|	...	1546	...	...	...	1644	...	1714	...	...	1740
Northallerton **185** d.	...	1215	1221	...	1255	...	1319	...	1355	...	1415	...	1453	...	1522	...	1555	...	...	...	1655	...	1722	...	...	1751
Darlington **127 185** d.	...	1227	1233	...	|	...	1331	...	|	...	1427	...	|	...	1534	...	|	...	...	...	|	...	1736	...	...	|
Middlesbrough a.	...	|	|	...	1330	...	|	...	1430	...	|	...	1535	...	|	...	1630	...	...	...	1733	...	|	...	...	1832
Durham **127 185** a.	...	1245	1250	...	...	...	1351	...	...	...	1450	...	...	...	1551	...	...	...	...	...	...	...	1756	...	...	...
Newcastle **127 185** a.	...	1300	1308	...	...	...	1412	...	...	...	1506	...	...	...	1612	...	...	...	...	...	...	...	1817	...	...	...

	Ⓐ	⑥	⚒	⚒	⚒	⚒	⚒	⚒	⚒	⚒	Ⓐ	⚒	⚒	⚒	⚒	⚒	⚒	⚒	⑥B	⑥B	Ⓐ	⑥A	⑥	Ⓐ	⚒	Ⓐ
Liverpool Lime St d.	1522	1522	...	...	...	1622	...	...	...	1722	...	...	...	1822	...	...	1922	...	2022	...	2022	2022	...	...	...	2230
Warrington Central d.	1544	1544	...	...	...	1644	...	...	...	1744	...	...	...	1844	...	...	1944	...	2044	...	2044	2044	...	...	...	2252
M'chester Airport ✈ d.	|	|	1605	...	1635	|	1705	...	1735	|	...	...	1835	|	1919	...	|	2020	|	...	|	|	2120	2120	2222	|
Manchester P'dilly d.	1611	1611	1627	1642	1656	1711	1726	1742	1756	1811	1825	1842	1857	1911	1942	...	2011	2042	2111	...	2111	2111	2142	2142	2242	2321
Stalybridge d.	1626	1626	|	|	1709	1726	1739	|	1809	1826	|	|	|	1926	|	...	2026	|	2126	...	2126	2126	2155	2155	2255	2334
Huddersfield d.	1645	1645	1657	1716	1728	1745	1757	1816	1827	1845	1857	1916	1927	1945	2016	...	2045	2116	2145	...	2145	2145	2215	2216	2316	2353
Dewsbury **190** d.	|	|	1707	|	1737	|	1807	|	1837	|	1907	|	1937	|	2026	...	|	2126	|	...	|	|	2226	2226	2326	|
Leeds **127 190** d.	1712	1712	1724	1738	1757	1812	1827	1838	1857	1912	1927	1938	1957	2012	2045	2105	2112	2142	2212	2222	2222	2222	2242	2242	2342	0034
Selby d.	|	|	|	1804	|	|	|	1900	|	|	|	2000	|	|	|	2127	|	|	|	2244	2244	2244	|	|	|	|
Hull a.	|	|	|	1846	|	|	|	1937	|	|	|	2039	|	|	|	2205	|	|	|	2321	2321	2321	|	|	|	|
York **127 185** d.	1743	1738	1800	...	1826	1838	1856	...	1926	1938	1955	...	2026	2038	2111	...	2141	2211	2235	...	...	...	2308	2320	0011	0114
Malton d.	|	1802	1824a	...	|	1902	|	...	|	2002	...	...	|	2102	|	...	...	2239	...	...	...	...	...	|	...	...
Scarborough a.	|	1829	1851a	...	|	1933	|	...	|	2030	...	...	|	2130	|	...	...	2306	...	...	...	...	...	|	...	...
Thirsk d.	1759	...	...	...	1844	...	|	...	1942	...	...	...	2043	...	2128	...	...	...	...	...	...	...	...	2335	...	...
Northallerton **185** d.	1809	...	...	...	1855	...	1920	...	1950	...	...	...	2051	...	2136	...	...	...	...	...	...	...	...	2355	...	...
Darlington **127 185** d.	|	...	...	...	|	...	1933	...	|	...	...	...	|	...	2147	...	...	...	...	...	...	...	...	0006	...	...
Middlesbrough a.	1842	...	...	...	1930	...	|	...	2030	...	...	...	2125	...	|	...	...	...	...	...	...	...	...	|	...	...
Durham **127 185** a.	...	...	...	...	...	...	1950	...	...	...	...	...	...	...	2207	...	...	...	...	...	...	...	...	0024	...	...
Newcastle **127 185** a.	...	...	...	...	...	...	2010	...	...	...	...	...	...	...	2223	...	...	...	...	...	...	...	...	0056	...	...

	⑥A	⑥B	⑤	①–④	⑥A	⑥B		⑦	⑦	⑦	⑦	⑦	⑦	⑦	⑦	⑦	⑦	⑦	⑦	⑦	⑦	⑦	⑦	⑦	⑦	⑦
Liverpool Lime St d.	2230	2230	...	...	...	...	...		...	...	...	...	...	...	0822	...	0922	...	1022	...	...	1122	...	...	1222	...
Warrington Central d.	2252	2252	...	...	...	...	...		...	...	...	...	...	...	0844	...	0944	...	1044	...	...	1144	...	...	1244	...
M'chester Airport ✈ d.	|	|	2318	2318	2324	2324*	...		0624	0724	...	0806	...	...	|	0920	|	1019	|	1117	...	|	1220	...	|	1320
Manchester P'dilly d.	2321	2321	2338	2338	2341	2349*	...		0642	0742	...	0832	...	...	0911	0942	1011	1042	1111	1142	1202	1211	1242	1302	1311	1342
Stalybridge d.	2334	2334	|	|	|	|	...		0655	0755	...	0845	...	...	0924	|	1024	|	1124	|	|	1224	|	|	1324	|
Huddersfield d.	2353	2352	0008	0026	0026	0049*	...		0712	0812	...	0904	...	...	0943	1012	1043	1112	1143	1212	1233	1243	1312	1333	1343	1412
Dewsbury **190** d.	|	*0019**	0017s	0035s	0035s	|	...		0722	0822	...	0912	...	...	|	1021	|	1121	|	1221	|	|	1321	|	|	1421
Leeds **127 190** d.	0016	*0044**	0035	0054	0054	0124*	...		0740	0840	0912	0940	1012	...	1020	1040	1112	1140	1212	1240	1300	1312	1340	1357	1412	1440
Selby d.	|	...	|	|	|	|	...		|	|	|	|	|	...	1043	|	|	|	|	|	1323	|	|	|	|	|
Hull a.	|	...	|	|	|	|	...		|	|	|	|	|	...	1118	|	|	|	|	|	1400	|	|	|	|	|
York **127 185** d.	0044	...	0118	0143	0122	0209*	...		0821	0909	0940	1013	1040	1045	...	1115	1143	1215	1240	1315	...	1340	1415	1424	1440	1515
Malton d.	...	...	...	...	...	...	...		|	|	1004	|	|	|	...	|	1208	|	|	|	...	1404	|	...	|	|
Scarborough a.	...	...	...	...	...	...	...		|	|	1032	|	1128	|	...	|	1232	|	|	|	...	1432	|	...	|	|
Thirsk d.	...	...	...	...	...	...	...		0837	|	...	|	...	1104	...	|	...	|	1302	|	...	...	|	...	1502	|
Northallerton **185** d.	...	...	...	...	...	...	...		0845	0930	...	1035	...	1112	...	1135	...	1235	1310	1335	...	...	1435	...	1510	1535
Darlington **127 185** d.	...	...	...	...	...	...	...		0857	0941	...	1046	...	|	...	1147	...	1246	|	1346	...	...	1446	...	|	1546
Middlesbrough a.	...	...	...	...	...	...	...		0926	|	...	|	...	1148	...	|	...	|	1344	|	...	...	|	...	1552	|
Durham **127 185** a.	...	...	...	...	...	...	...		...	0958	...	1108	...	...	...	1203	...	1303	...	1403	...	...	1503	...	...	1603
Newcastle **127 185** a.	...	...	...	...	...	...	...		...	1018	...	1123	...	...	...	1220	...	1320	...	1422	...	...	1520	...	...	1620

	⑦	⑦	⑦	⑦	⑦	⑦	⑦	⑦	⑦	⑦	⑦	⑦	⑦	⑦	⑦	⑦	⑦	⑦	⑦C	⑦D	⑦	⑦	⑦	⑦	⑦	⑦
Liverpool Lime St d.	...	1322	...	...	1422	...	...	1522	...	...	1622	...	...	1722	...	...	1822	...	...	...	1922	...	2022	...	...	2152
Warrington Central d.	...	1344	...	...	1444	...	...	1544	...	...	1644	...	...	1744	...	...	1844	...	...	...	1944	...	2044	...	...	2214
M'chester Airport ✈ d.	...	|	1420	...	|	1520	...	|	1620	...	|	1720	...	|	1820	...	|	1920	...	...	|	2020	|	...	2120	|
Manchester P'dilly d.	1402	1411	1442	1502	1511	1542	1602	1611	1642	1702	1711	1742	1802	1811	1842	1902	1911	1942	2006	2006	2011	2042	2111	...	2142	2242
Stalybridge d.	|	1424	|	|	1524	|	|	1624	|	|	1724	|	|	1824	|	|	1924	|	|	|	2024	|	2124	...	|	2255
Huddersfield d.	1433	1443	1512	1533	1543	1612	1633	1643	1712	1733	1743	1812	1833	1843	1912	1933	1943	2012	2037	2037	2043	2112	2143	...	2212	2314
Dewsbury **190** d.	|	|	1521	|	|	1621	|	|	1721	|	|	1821	|	|	1921	|	|	2021	|	|	|	2121	|	...	2221	2323
Leeds **127 190** d.	1500	1512	1540	1557	1612	1640	1700	1712	1740	1757	1812	1840	1900	1912	1940	1957	2012	2040	2104	2104	2112	2140	2212	2220	2240	2340
Selby d.	1523	|	|	|	|	|	1723	|	|	|	|	|	1923	|	|	2016	|	|	2123	2138	|	|	|	2242	|	|
Hull a.	1600	|	|	|	|	|	1800	|	|	|	|	|	2000	|	|	2053	|	|	2201	2213	|	|	|	2318	|	|
York **127 185** d.	...	1540	1615	1624	1640	1714	...	1740	1814	1824	1840	1914	...	1940	2013	...	2040	2108	...	...	2138	2210	2242	...	2311	0010
Malton d.	...	1604	|	...	|	|	...	1804	|	...	|	|	...	2004	|	...	2104	|	...	...	...	2234	|	...	...	...
Scarborough a.	...	1632	|	...	|	|	...	1832	|	...	|	|	...	2032	|	...	2132	|	...	...	...	2302	|	...	...	...
Thirsk d.	...	...	|	...	1702	|	...	...	|	...	1859	|	...	...	2030	...	...	2126	...	...	...	...	2306	...	...	...
Northallerton **185** d.	...	...	1635	...	1710	1735	...	...	1835	...	1907	1935	...	...	2038	...	...	2134	...	...	...	...	2316	...	...	...
Darlington **127 185** d.	...	...	1646	...	|	1746	...	...	1846	...	|	1946	...	...	|	...	...	2146	...	...	...	...	2332	...	...	...
Middlesbrough a.	...	...	|	...	1743	|	...	...	|	...	1940	|	...	...	2112	...	...	|	...	...	...	...	|	...	...	...
Durham **127 185** a.	...	...	1703	...	...	1803	...	...	1903	...	...	2003	...	...	...	...	...	2203	...	...	...	...	2349	...	...	...
Newcastle **127 185** a.	...	...	1720	...	...	1822	...	...	1920	...	...	2022	...	...	...	...	...	2220	...	...	...	...	0021	...	...	...

A – May 23 - Sept. 5.
B – Sept. 12 - Dec. 12.
C – May 17 - Jul. 12.
D – Jul. 19 - Sept. 6.
E – Fom London St. Pancras. May 23 - Sept. 5. Operated by *EM*.

a – Ⓐ only.
d – Also calls at Dewsbury on ⑥.
* – By 🚌.
☛ Additional trains **Manchester Airport - Manchester Piccadilly - Leeds - York:** 0100⚒, 0122⑦, 0443⑦.

Services on ⑥⑦ valid until July 12.

km			Ⓐ	⑥	Ⓐ	Ⓐ	⑥	Ⓐ	⑥	Ⓐ	⑥	Ⓐ	Ⓐ	⚒	Ⓐ	⑥	Ⓐ	⑥	Ⓐ	⚒	Ⓐ	⑥	Ⓐ	⑥
0	**Leeds** 127 187 d.	⚒	0508	...	0551	0603	0603	0613	...	0637	...	0651	0708	0713	0737	...	0751	0758	0808	0813	0837	...	0851	0858
15	Bradford Interchange d.		0532	*0520**	0614	0624	|	|	*0600**	0700	*0620**	0714	0731	|	0800	*0710**	0812	|	0832	|	0900	*0810**	0913	|
28	**Halifax** d.		0544	*0545**	0626	0636	|	|	*0625**	0712	*0645**	0726	0744	|	0812	*0735**	0824	|	0844	|	0912	*0835**	0925	|
	Dewsbury 187 d.		|	|	|	|	|	0629	|	|	|	|	|	0729	|	|	|	|	|	0831	|	|	|	|
42	Hebden Bridge d.		0600	0628	0638	0652	0638	0708	0708	0728	0732	0738	0756	0808	0828	0830	0836	0838	0856	0908	0928	0930	0936	0937
63	Burnley Manchester Rd d.		|	|	0657	|	0657	|	|	|	|	0757	|	|	|	|	0857	0857	|	|	|	|	0956	0956
72	Accrington d.		|	|	0706	|	0706	|	|	|	|	0806	|	|	|	|	0906	0906	|	|	|	|	1006	1006
81	Blackburn d.		|	|	0716	|	0716	|	|	|	|	0814	|	|	|	|	0914	0914	|	|	|	|	1014	1014
100	**Preston** 152 a.		|	|	0736	|	0736	|	|	|	|	0838	|	|	|	|	0932	0932	|	|	|	|	1032	1032
129	**Blackpool** North 152 a.		|	|	0805	|	0805	|	|	|	|	0905	|	|	|	|	1000	1000	|	|	|	|	1100	1100
49	Todmorden d.		0608	0635	...	0659	...	0715	0715	0736	0744	...	0804	0815	0836	0837	...	...	0904	0915	0936	0937	...	...
63	Rochdale d.		0624	0655	...	0715	...	0730	0730	0752	0800	...	0814	0830	0851	0851	...	...	0914	0930	0951	0951	...	...
81	**Manchester** Victoria a.		0648	0717	...	0737	...	0753	0753	0814	0822	...	0838	0853	0908	0908	...	...	0932	0953	1007	1007	...	...

		⑥	⑥	Ⓐ	Ⓐ	⑥	Ⓐ	⑥	Ⓐ	⑥	⑥	Ⓐ	Ⓐ	⑥			⑦	⑦		⑦	⑦		⑦
Leeds 127 187 d.	and at the same minutes (✣) past each hour until	...	1858	1908	1937	1943	1951	1955	2037	2043	2145	2137	2237	2247	...	⑦	0829	0902	...	0913	0945	...	0956
Bradford Interchange d.		*1810**	|	1932	2000	|	2013	|	2100	|	|	2200	2300	|	...		|	|	...	|	|	...	|
Halifax d.		*1835**	|	1944	2012	|	2025	|	2112	|	|	2212	2312	|	...		|	|	...	|	|	...	|
Dewsbury 187 d.		|	|	|	|	|	|	|	|	|	|	|	|	|	...		|	|	...	|	|	...	|
Hebden Bridge d.		1930	1938	1956	2028	2028	2037	2038	2128	2128	2228	2228	2328	2328	...		0917	0931	...	0953	1020	...	1045
Burnley Manchester Rd d.		|	1956	|	|	|	2056	2056	|	|	|	|	|	|	...		|	0950	...	|	1038	...	|
Accrington d.		|	2005	|	|	|	2105	2105	|	|	|	|	|	|	...		|	0959	...	|	1047	...	|
Blackburn d.		|	2014	|	|	|	2114	2114	|	|	|	|	|	|	...		|	1007	...	|	1056	...	|
Preston 152 a.		|	2032	|	|	|	2132	2132	|	|	|	|	|	|	...		|	1027	...	|	1113	...	|
Blackpool North 152 a.		|	2100	|	|	|	2200	2200	|	|	|	|	|	|	...		|	1053	...	|	1139	...	|
Todmorden d.		1937	...	2004	2036	2036	...	...	2136	2136	2236	2236	2336	2336	...		0924	...	...	1000	...	...	1052
Rochdale d.		1952	...	2014	2052	2052	...	...	2152	2152	2252	2352	2352	2352	...		0941	...	...	1017	...	...	1109
Manchester Victoria a.		2015	...	2032	2114	2114	...	...	2214	2214	2308	2314	0008	0008	...		1002	...	...	1038	...	...	1130

	⑦	⑦	⑦	⑦		⑦	⑦	⑦	⑦	⑦	⑦	⑦	⑦	⑦	⑦	⑦	⑦	⑦	⑦	⑦	⑦		⑦	⑦
Leeds 127 187 d.	1034	1053	1149	1153	...	1237	1305	1346	1353	1436	1503	1547	1603	1635	1703	1746	1803	1834	1916	1949	2020	...	2035	2147
Bradford Interchange d.	|	|	|	|	...	|	|	|	|	|	|	|	|	|	|	|	|	|	|	|	|	...	|	|
Halifax d.	|	|	|	|	...	|	|	|	|	|	|	|	|	|	|	|	|	|	|	|	|	...	|	|
Dewsbury 187 d.	|	|	|	|	...	|	|	|	|	|	|	|	|	|	|	|	|	|	|	|	|	...	|	|
Hebden Bridge d.	1119	1145	1219	1245	...	1319	1345	1419	1445	1519	1545	1619	1645	1719	1745	1819	1845	1919	1956	2019	2056	...	2119	2227
Burnley Manchester Rd d.	1138	|	1238	|	...	1338	|	1438	|	1538	|	1638	|	1738	|	1838	|	1938	|	2038	|	...	2138	|
Accrington d.	1147	|	1247	|	...	1347	|	1447	|	1547	|	1647	|	1747	|	1847	|	1947	|	2047	|	...	2147	|
Blackburn d.	1155	|	1255	|	...	1355	|	1455	|	1555	|	1655	|	1755	|	1855	|	1956	|	2055	|	...	2155	|
Preston 152 a.	1213	|	1313	|	...	1413	|	1513	|	1613	|	1713	|	1813	|	1913	|	2014	|	2113	|	...	2213	|
Blackpool North 152 a.	1238	|	1338	|	...	1438	|	1540	|	1638	|	1738	|	1838	|	1938	|	2039	|	2138	|	...	2238	|
Todmorden d.	...	1152	...	1252	...	...	1352	...	1452	...	1552	...	1652	...	1752	...	1852	...	2004	...	2104	...	...	2234
Rochdale d.	...	1209	...	1309	...	...	1409	...	1509	...	1609	...	1709	...	1809	...	1909	...	2020	...	2120	...	...	2251
Manchester Victoria a.	...	1230	...	1330	...	...	1430	...	1530	...	1630	...	1730	...	1830	...	1930	...	2041	...	2141	...	...	2312

		⑥	Ⓐ	Ⓐ	⑥	Ⓐ	⑥	⚒	Ⓐ	⑥	Ⓐ	⑥	Ⓐ	⚒	Ⓐ	⑥	Ⓐ	Ⓐ	⑥		⑥	⚒	Ⓐ
Manchester Victoria d.	Ⓐ	...	...	0617	0621	0643	0643	0658	...	...	0717	0747	0748	0800	...	...	0821	0848	0847	and at the same minutes (✣) past each hour until	1741	1800	...
Rochdale d.		...	...	0637	0635	0656	0656	0718	...	...	0737	0800	0801	0820	...	...	0835	0901	0900		1801	1818	...
Todmorden d.		...	...	0654	0652	0708	0708	0735	...	...	0754	0812	0813	0834	...	...	0852	0913	0912		1814	1935	...
Blackpool North 152 d.		0529	0529	|	|	|	|	|	0628	0628	|	|	|	|	0729	0729	|	|	|		|	|	1714
Preston 152 d.		0554	0554	|	|	|	|	|	0654	0654	|	|	|	|	0754	0754	|	|	|		|	|	1744
Blackburn d.		0610	0610	|	|	|	|	|	0710	0710	|	|	|	|	0810	0810	|	|	|		|	|	1811
Accrington d.		0617	0617	|	|	|	|	|	0717	0717	|	|	|	|	0817	0817	|	|	|		|	|	1819
Burnley Manchester Rd d.		0626	0626	|	|	|	|	|	0726	0726	|	|	|	|	0826	0826	|	|	|		|	|	1828
Hebden Bridge d.		0650	0650	0700	0658	0716	0714	0741	0750	0750	0800	0818	0821	0841	0850	0850	0900	0921	0918		1820	1842	1850
Dewsbury 187 d.		|	|	|	|	|	|	0811	|	|	|	|	|	0912	|	0916	|	|	|		|	1913	|
Halifax d.		|	0703	0716	*0725**	0733	*0810**	|	0803	|	0816	*0910**	0833	|	0903	|	0916	0933	*1010**		*1910**	|	1903
Bradford Interchange d.		|	0720	0734	*0755**	0750	*0840**	|	0820	|	0834	*0940**	0850	|	0920	|	0934	0950	*1040**		*1940**	|	1919
Leeds 127 187 a.		0732	0739	0757	...	0810	...	0833	0839	0841	0856	...	0912	0931	0939	0941	0958	1012	...		...	1933	1940

	⑥	Ⓐ	Ⓐ	⑥	⚒	Ⓐ	⑥	Ⓐ	⑥	⑥	Ⓐ	⑥	Ⓐ	⑥	Ⓐ	Ⓐ	⑥	Ⓐ			⑦	⑦	⑦	⑦
Manchester Victoria d.	...	1821	1848	1848	1900	...	...	1921	1920	2021	2021	...	...	2121	2121	2221	2254	2320	...	⑦	0908	...	1008	...
Rochdale d.	...	1836	1901	1901	1919	...	...	1941	1941	2041	2041	...	...	2141	2141	2241	2307	2341	...		0928	...	1028	...
Todmorden d.	...	1853	1913	1913	1934	...	...	1958	1959	2058	2058	...	...	2158	2158	2258	2321	2358	...		0945	...	1045	...
Blackpool North 152 d.	1718	|	|	|	|	1829	1829	|	|	|	|	2029	2029	|	|	|	|	|	...		|	0911	|	1011
Preston 152 d.	1744	|	|	|	|	1854	1854	|	|	|	|	2054	2054	|	|	|	|	|	...		|	0937	|	1037
Blackburn d.	1811	|	|	|	|	1910	1910	|	|	|	|	2110	2110	|	|	|	|	|	...		|	0954	|	1055
Accrington d.	1819	|	|	|	|	1917	1917	|	|	|	|	2117	2117	|	|	|	|	|	...		|	1001	|	1103
Burnley Manchester Rd d.	1828	|	|	|	|	1926	1926	|	|	|	|	2128	2128	|	|	|	|	|	...		|	1010	|	1112
Hebden Bridge d.	1850	1900	1920	1921	1941	1950	1950	2005	*2020**	2105	2105	2151	2151	2205	2205	2304	2331	0004	...		0952	1032	1052	1134
Dewsbury 187 d.	1917	|	|	|	2012	|	2017	|	|	|	|	|	|	|	|	|	|	|	...		|	|	|	|
Halifax d.	|	1916	1932	*2010**	|	2003	|	2021	*2100**	|	2121	|	2203	|	2221	2320	|	0020	...		|	|	|	|
Bradford Interchange d.	|	1934	1950	*2040**	|	2019	|	2037	*2130**	|	2137	|	2219	|	2237	2337	|	0037	...		|	|	|	|
Leeds 127 187 a.	1943	1958	2012	...	2032	2038	2036	2101	...	2146	2201	2227	2241	2247	2301	0001	0012	0055	...		1034	1109	1130	1211

	⑦	⑦	⑦	⑦	⑦	⑦	⑦	⑦	⑦	⑦	⑦	⑦	⑦	⑦	⑦	⑦	⑦	⑦	⑦	⑦	⑦	⑦		⑦
Manchester Victoria d.	1108	...	1208	...	1308	...	1408	...	1508	...	1608	...	1708	...	1808	...	1908	...	2008	...	2108	...	...	2208
Rochdale d.	1128	...	1228	...	1328	...	1428	...	1528	...	1628	...	1728	...	1828	...	1928	...	2028	...	2128	...	...	2228
Todmorden d.	1145	...	1245	...	1345	...	1445	...	1545	...	1645	...	1745	...	1845	...	1945	...	2045	...	2145	...	...	2245
Blackpool North 152 d.	|	1113	|	1211	|	1313	|	1411	|	1513	|	1611	|	1711	|	1811	|	1913	|	2011	|	2113	...	|
Preston 152 d.	|	1138	|	1237	|	1338	|	1437	|	1537	|	1637	|	1737	|	1837	|	1937	|	2037	|	2138	...	|
Blackburn d.	|	1154	|	1254	|	1354	|	1454	|	1554	|	1654	|	1754	|	1844	|	1954	|	2054	|	2154	...	|
Accrington d.	|	1201	|	1301	|	1401	|	1501	|	1301	|	1701	|	1801	|	1901	|	2001	|	2101	|	2201	...	|
Burnley Manchester Rd d.	|	1210	|	1310	|	1410	|	1510	|	1610	|	1710	|	1810	|	1910	|	2010	|	2110	|	2210	...	|
Hebden Bridge d.	1152	1232	1252	1332	1352	1432	1452	1532	1552	1632	1652	1732	1752	1832	1852	1932	1952	2032	2052	2132	2152	2232	...	2252
Dewsbury 187 d.	|	|	|	|	|	|	|	|	|	|	|	|	|	|	|	|	|	|	|	|	|	|	...	|
Halifax d.	|	|	|	|	|	|	|	|	|	|	|	|	|	|	|	|	|	|	|	|	|	|	...	|
Bradford Interchange d.	|	|	|	|	|	|	|	|	|	|	|	|	|	|	|	|	|	|	|	|	|	|	...	|
Leeds 127 187 a.	1244	1310	1330	1408	1444	1511	1530	1611	1644	1712	1730	1811	1844	1911	1930	2008	2042	2108	2130	2209	2244	2309	...	2330

* – By 🚌.

✣ – Timings may vary by up to 5 minutes on some journeys.

Rail Replacement Buses on ⑦.

Due to engineering work, buses replace trains Bradford Interchange - Hebden Bridge and v.v.

From **Bradford Interchange**: 0830 and hourly until 1930, 2020; then 2115, 2210.
From **Hebdon Bridge**: 1000 and hourly until 2300.

Journey time ± 50–60 minutes.

194 HULL and CLEETHORPES - DONCASTER - SHEFFIELD - MANCHESTER — NT, TP

Services valid until June 21. *NT* services convey 2nd class only.

For services Hull - Selby - Doncaster (- London Kings Cross), see Table **180**. For *TP* services Hull - Leeds - Manchester, see Table **187**.

km		⚒	*TP*	*NT*	*TP*	*NT*	*TP*	*TP*	*NT*	*TP*	*NT*	*NT*	*NT*	*NT*	*TP*	*NT*	*NT*		*TP*	*NT*	*NT*	*TP*	*NT*
			⚒	⚒	⚒	⚒	⑥	Ⓐ	⚒	⚒	⚒	Ⓐ	⑥	⚒	⚒	⚒	⚒		⚒	⚒	⚒	⚒	⚒
0	**Hull** d.		...	0520	...	0607	...	...	0640	...	0736	0804	0806	0828	...	0856	0925	and	...	1557	1627	...	1654
38	Goole d.		...	0547	...	0642	...	...	0715	...	0813	0830	0834	0901	...	0922	0958	at	...	1623	1704	...	1722
	Cleethorpes d.		...	|	0518	|	0618	0618	|	0718	|	|	|	|	0828	|	|	the	1528	|	|	1628	|
	Grimsby Town d.		...	|	0526	|	0626	0626	|	0726	|	|	|	|	0836	|	|	same	1536	|	|	1636	|
	Scunthorpe ‡ d.		...	|	0600	|	0700	0700	|	0800	|	|	|	|	0910	|	|	minutes	1610	|	|	1710	|
66	**Doncaster** ‡ a.		...	0616	0638	0714	0733	0733	0745	0830	0843	0855	0857	0931	0940	0946	1027	past	1640	1646	1734	1740	1747
66	**Doncaster** ‡ d.		0540	0625	0640	...	0735	0735	0746	0841	...	0856	0859	...	0942	0948	...	each	1642	1647	...	1742	1748
90	Meadowhall ‡ d.		0558	0652	0658	...	0753	0753	0822	0901	...	0915	0919	...	1001	1007	...	hour	1701	1706	...	1801	1806
96	**Sheffield** ‡ a.		0608	0707	0706	...	0800	0800	0832	0908	...	0926	0928	...	1008	1020	...	until	1708	1719	...	1808	1819
96	**Sheffield** 208 d.		0611	...	0709	...	0805	0805	...	0911	...	...	...	...	1011	...	...		1711	...	...	1810	...
156	Stockport 208 a.		0653	...	0753	...	0853	0853	...	0953	...	...	...	...	1053	...	...	▽	1753	...	...	1853	...
165	**Manchester** Piccadilly 208 a.		0702	...	0802	...	0902	0902	...	1002	...	...	...	...	1102	...	...		1802	...	...	1902	...
181	**Manchester** Airport a.		0726	...	0829	...	0926	0933	...	1026	...	...	...	...	1126	...	...		1826	...	...	1928	...

km		*TP*	*NT*	*NT*	*NT*	*TP*	*NT*	*NT*	*NT*	*TP*	*NT*	*TP*	*TP*	*NT*	*NT*	*NT*	*NT*		⑦	*NT*	*TP*	*TP*	*TP*	*TP*
		⚒	⚒	Ⓐ	⑥	⚒	⚒	⚒	⚒	⚒	⚒	Ⓐ	⑥	⑥	Ⓐ	Ⓐ	⑥			⑦	⑦	⑦	⑦	⑦
	Hull d.	...	1752	1742	1742	...	1822	1853	1924	...	2003	...	...	2051	2056	2220	2222	...		0842	0941	...	1041	...
	Goole d.	...	|	1819	1819	...	1855	1919	1958	...	2036	...	...	2117	2122	2251	2248	...		0915	1009	...	1109	...
0	**Cleethorpes** d.	1728	|	|	|	1828	|	|	|	1928	|	2028	2028	|	|	|	|	...		|	|	0928	|	1028
5	Grimsby Town d.	1736	|	|	|	1836	|	|	|	1936	|	2036	2036	|	|	|	|	...		|	|	0936	|	1036
47	Scunthorpe ‡ d.	1810	|	|	|	1910	|	|	|	2010	|	2110	2110	|	|	|	|	...		|	|	1010	|	1110
84	**Doncaster** ‡ a.	1840	1845	1851	1851	1940	1927	1946	2030	2040	2105	2140	2140	2146	2145	2321	2318	...		0938	1036	1040	1132	1140
84	**Doncaster** ‡ d.	1842	1847	1855	...	1942	...	1949	...	2042	2107	2142	2142	2148	2148	2322	2319	...		0939	...	1042	1133	1142
107	Meadowhall ‡ d.	1901	1906	1925	...	2001	...	2007	...	2107	2135	2158	2158	2209	2209	2354	2349	...		1000	...	1100	1152	1200
113	**Sheffield** ‡ a.	1908	1917	1935	...	2008	...	2018	...	2117	2146	2208	2210	2221	2221	0004	2359	...		1009	...	1107	1203	1207
113	**Sheffield** 208 d.	1911	...	...	...	2011	...	...	...	...	...	2211	...	...	...	...	...	...		...	...	1110	...	1210
173	Stockport 208 a.	1953	...	...	...	2053	...	...	...	...	...	2253	...	...	...	...	...	...		...	...	1152	...	1252
182	**Manchester** Piccadilly 208 a.	2002	...	...	...	2102	...	...	...	...	...	2302	...	...	...	...	...	...		...	...	1206	...	1306
198	**Manchester** Airport a.	2035	...	...	...	2135	...	...	...	...	...	2326	...	...	...	...	...	...		...	...	1229	...	1329

	TP	*TP*	*TP*	*TP*	*TP*	*TP*		*TP*	*TP*		*TP*	*TP*	*TP*	*TP*		*TP*	*TP*		*TP*	*TP*		*TP*	*TP*	*TP*
	⑦	⑦	⑦	⑦	⑦	⑦		⑦	⑦		⑦	⑦	⑦	⑦		⑦	⑦		⑦	⑦		⑦	⑦	⑦
Hull d.	1141	...	1241	1341	...	1441	...	...	1541	...	...	1641	...	1741	...	...	1838	...	...	...	...	2030	...	2115
Goole d.	1209	...	1309	1409	...	1509	...	...	1609	...	...	1709	...	1809	...	...	1906	...	...	...	...	2058	...	2148
Cleethorpes d.	|	1128	|	|	1328	|	...	1428	|	...	1528	|	1628	|	...	1728	|	...	1828	1928	...	|	2028	|
Grimsby Town d.	|	1136	|	|	1336	|	...	1436	|	...	1536	|	1636	|	...	1736	|	...	1836	1936	...	|	2036	|
Scunthorpe ‡ d.	|	1210	|	|	1410	|	...	1510	|	...	1610	|	1710	|	...	1810	|	...	1910	2010	...	|	2110	|
Doncaster ‡ a.	1232	1240	1332	1432	1440	1532	...	1540	1632	...	1640	1731	1740	1833	...	1840	1935	...	1940	2040	...	2121	2140	2217
Doncaster ‡ d.	...	1242	1334	1433	1442	1533	...	1542	1633	...	1642	1732	1742	1834	...	1842	1937	...	1942	2042	...	2123	2142	2220
Meadowhall ‡ d.	...	1300	1353	1453	1500	1552	...	1600	1653	...	1700	1753	1800	1853	...	1900	1957	...	2000	2100	...	2145	2204	2250
Sheffield ‡ a.	...	1307	1404	1503	1507	1601	...	1607	1703	...	1707	1801	1807	1903	...	1907	2006	...	2007	2107	...	2156	2215	2258
Sheffield 208 d.	...	1310	...	...	1511	...	...	1611	...	...	1711	...	1811	...	...	1911	...	...	2011	2111	...	...	...	...
Stockport 208 a.	...	1352	...	...	1553	...	...	1653	...	...	1753	...	1853	...	...	1953	...	...	2053	2153	...	...	...	...
Manchester Piccadilly 208 a.	...	1406	...	...	1606	...	...	1706	...	...	1806	...	1906	...	...	2006	...	...	2106	2206	...	...	...	...
Manchester Airport a.	...	1429	...	...	1629	...	...	1729	...	...	1829	...	1929	...	...	2029	...	...	2129	2229	...	...	...	...

	⚒	*NT*	*TP*	*NT*	*NT*	*TP*	*NT*	*NT*	*NT*	*TP*	*NT*	*NT*	*TP*	*NT*	*NT*		*TP*	*NT*	*NT*	*TP*	*NT*	*NT*	*NT*
		⚒	⚒	⚒	⚒	⚒	⑥	Ⓐ	⚒	⚒	⚒	⚒	⚒	⚒	⚒		⚒	⚒	⚒	⚒	⑥	Ⓐ	Ⓐ
Manchester Airport d.		...	0515	...	...	0655	...	...	...	0754	...	...	0855	...	...	and	1455	...	...	1555	...	...	...
Manchester Piccadilly 208 d.		...	0544	...	...	0720	...	...	...	0820	...	...	0920	...	...	at	1520	...	...	1620	...	...	...
Stockport 208 d.		...	0552	...	...	0728	...	...	...	0828	...	...	0928	...	...	the	1528	...	...	1628	...	...	...
Sheffield 208 a.		...	0649	...	...	0810	...	...	...	0908	...	...	1008	...	...	same	1608	...	...	1708	...	...	...
Sheffield ‡ d.		0529	0655	...	0741	0811	...	...	0841	0811	...	0941	1011	...	1041	minutes	1611	...	1641	1711	...	...	1741
Meadowhall ‡ d.		0535	0701	...	0747	0817	...	...	0847	0917	...	0945	1017	...	1047	past	1617	...	1647	1717	...	...	1747
Doncaster ‡ a.		0606	0722	...	0820	0840	...	...	0912	0940	...	1011	1040	...	1109	each	1640	...	1712	1740	...	...	1813
Doncaster ‡ d.		0614	0724	0728	0822	0842	0848	0856	0916	0942	0946	1016	1042	1046	1117	hour	1642	1646	1714	1742	1748	1756	1816
Scunthorpe ‡ d.		|	0750	|	|	0908	|	|	|	1008	|	|	1108	|	|	until	1708	|	|	1808	|	|	|
Grimsby Town a.		|	0826	|	|	0942	|	|	|	1044	|	|	1145	|	|		1743	|	|	1845	|	|	|
Cleethorpes a.		|	0846	|	|	0958	|	|	|	1059	|	|	1157	|	|	▼	1754	|	|	1859	|	|	|
Goole d.		0639	...	0753	0842	...	0914	0921	0939	...	1011	1035	...	1112	1137		...	1711	1735	...	1813	1821	1836
Hull a.		0722	...	0836	0913	...	0955	0959	1010	...	1053	1112	...	1153	1209		...	1753	1810	...	1857	1904	1909

	NT	*TP*	*NT*	*NT*	*TP*	*NT*	*NT*	*NT*	*TP*	*NT*	*NT*	*TP*	*NT*	*TP*	*TP*		⑦	*NT*	*NT*	*NT*	*TP*	*NT*	*NT*	*NT*
	⑥	Ⓐ	Ⓐ	⑥	Ⓐ	⑥	Ⓐ	⚒	⚒	Ⓐ	Ⓐ	⚒	⚒	⑥	Ⓐ			⑦	⑦	⑦	⑦	⑦	⑦	⑦
Manchester Airport d.	...	1655	...	...	1755	...	...	...	1855	...	...	1955	...	2047	2047	...		...	...	...	...	...	1044	...
Manchester Piccadilly 208 d.	...	1720	...	...	1820	...	...	...	1918	...	...	2020	...	2120	2120	...		...	...	...	...	...	1118	...
Stockport 208 d.	...	1728	...	...	1828	...	...	...	1926	...	...	2028	...	2128	2128	...		...	...	...	...	...	1127	...
Sheffield 208 a.	...	1815	...	...	1910	...	...	...	2008	...	...	2108	...	2208	2208	...		...	...	...	...	...	1208	...
Sheffield ‡ d.	1741	1824	1841	1841	1911	...	...	1944	2011	...	2015	2111	2114	2211	2211	...		0800	...	0845	0952	1026	1211	1228
Meadowhall ‡ d.	1747	1829	1847	1847	1917	...	...	1950	2017	...	2021	2117	2121	2217	2217	...		0806	...	0851	0957	1032	1216	1234
Doncaster ‡ a.	1812	1853	1911	1910	1940	...	...	2011	2040	...	2055	2140	2155	2236	2240	...		0838	...	0922	1026	1051	1239	1254
Doncaster ‡ d.	1824	1855	1914	1913	1942	1947	1951	2011	2042	2044	2056	2142	2156	2238	2242	...		...	0907	0926	1028	1053	1242	1255
Scunthorpe ‡ d.	|	1923	|	|	2008	|	|	|	2108	|	|	2208	|	2313	2318	...		...	|	|	1055	|	1310	|
Grimsby Town a.	|	1958	|	|	2042	|	|	|	2145	|	|	2246	|	2349	2357	...		...	|	|	1129	|	1345	|
Cleethorpes a.	|	2009	|	|	2055	|	|	|	2159	|	|	2259	|	0002	0009	...		...	|	|	1144	|	1357	|
Goole d.	1844	...	1934	1934	...	2012	2017	2033	...	|	2123	...	2222	...	...	...		...	0935	0947	...	1112	...	1315
Hull a.	1915	...	2007	2011	...	2052	2055	2106	...	2145	...	...	2258	...	...	...		...	...	1021	...	1146	...	1348

	TP	*NT*	*TP*	*NT*	*TP*	*NT*		*TP*	*NT*		*TP*	*NT*	*TP*	*NT*		*TP*	*NT*		*TP*	*TP*		*NT*	*TP*	*NT*
	⑦	⑦	⑦	⑦	⑦	⑦		⑦	⑦		⑦	⑦	⑦	⑦		⑦	⑦		⑦	⑦		⑦	⑦	⑦
Manchester Airport d.	*1133*	...	1255	...	1355	...	...	1455	...	...	1555	...	1655	...	...	1755	...	...	1855	1955	...	...	...	...
Manchester Piccadilly 208 d.	1218	...	1320	...	1420	...	...	1520	...	...	1620	...	1720	...	...	1820	...	...	1920	2018	...	...	...	...
Stockport 208 d.	1228	...	1328	...	1428	...	...	1528	...	...	1628	...	1728	...	...	1828	...	...	1928	2027	...	...	...	...
Sheffield 208 a.	1308	...	1408	...	1508	...	...	1608	...	...	1708	...	1808	...	...	1908	...	...	2008	2108	...	...	...	...
Sheffield ‡ d.	1311	1324	1411	1428	1511	1528	...	1611	1628	...	1711	1728	1811	1828	...	1911	2002	...	2011	2111	...	2124	2230	2226
Meadowhall ‡ d.	1316	1330	1416	1434	1516	1534	...	1616	1634	...	1716	1734	1816	1835	...	1916	2009	...	2061	2116	...	2130	2236	2232
Doncaster ‡ a.	1335	1402	1435	1456	1539	1555	...	1639	1654	...	1739	1757	1839	1854	...	1939	2030	...	2039	2139	...	2203	2256	2304
Doncaster ‡ d.	...	1404	1442	1459	1542	1556	...	1642	1656	...	1742	1803	1842	1855	...	1942	2030	...	2042	2142	...	2204	2258	2307
Scunthorpe ‡ d.	...	|	1510	|	1610	|	...	1710	|	...	1810	|	1910	|	...	2010	|	...	2110	2210	...	|	2324	|
Grimsby Town a.	...	|	1545	|	1645	|	...	1745	|	...	1845	|	1945	|	...	2045	|	...	2145	2245	...	|	2358	|
Cleethorpes a.	...	|	1558	|	1658	|	...	1757	|	...	1858	|	1957	|	...	2058	|	...	2158	2258	...	|	0010	|
Goole d.	...	1425	...	1519	...	1617	...	...	1715	...	...	1822	...	1921	...	...	2049	...	...	...	...	2223	...	2328
Hull a.	...	1459	...	1557	...	1650	...	...	1749	...	...	1857	...	1955	...	...	2123	...	...	...	...	2256	...	0002

▽ – Timings may vary by up to 5 minutes. Variations to this pattern:
1028⑥ Cleethorpes - Manchester Airport arrives 1333.
1428⚒ Cleethorpes - Manchester Airport arrives 1732.

▼ – Timings may vary by up to 5 minutes.

‡ – Additional services operate between these stations.

2nd class EM — SKEGNESS - NOTTINGHAM — 195

Services on ⑦ valid until September 6

km		⚒	⚒	⚒	Ⓐ	⑥	Ⓐ	⑥		⚒	⚒	⚒	S	⚒		⚒	⚒	⚒	⚒	Ⓐ	⑥		⚒	Ⓐ	⑥
0	**Skegness** d.	...	...	0708	0810	0815	0905	0915	...	1015	1115	1215	1315	1415	...	1509	1610	1730	1814	1914	1919	...	2015	2100	2109
38	Boston d.	...	0614	0745	0845	0850	0940	0950	...	1050	1150	1250	1350	1450	...	1544	1646	1805	1849	1949	1954	...	2050	2135	2144
66	Sleaford d.	...	0636	0811	0907	0912	1002	1014	...	1112	1212	1312	1413	1512	...	1610	1713	1827	1913	2012	2018	...	2112	2158	2205
89	Grantham a.	...	0706	0842	0935	0941	1031	1043	...	1141	1242	1342	1442	1542	...	1641	1742	|	1941	2041	2045	...	2143	|	|
89	Grantham **208** d.	0610	0710	0845	0940	0945	1034	1045	...	1145	1245	1345	1445	1545	...	1645	1745	|	1945	2045	2048	...	2147	|	|
126	**Nottingham** **208** a.	0654	0753	0922	1018	1022	1113	1124	...	1223	1322	1422	1522	1623	...	1722	1822	1922	2028	2122	2124	...	2224	2252	2257

⑦	⑦	⑦	⑦	⑦	⑦	⑦	⑦	⑦	⑦	⑦
Skegness d.	...	1014	1108	1227	1408	1504	1622	1807	1915	2043
Boston d.	0906	1049	1143	1302	1443	1542	1657	1842	1950	2118
Sleaford d.	0928	1111	1205	1324	1505	1604	1719	1904	2012	2141
Grantham a.	0957	1140	1234	|	1535	1633	|	1933	2041	2210
Grantham **208** d.	1001	1145	1239	|	1540	1637	|	1937	2045	2213
Nottingham **208** a.	1037	1227	1315	1419	1617	1713	1813	2014	2121	2249

⚒	⚒	⚒	⚒	⚒	⑥	Ⓐ	⑥	Ⓐ	S	V
Nottingham **208** d.	0510	...	0550	0645	0730	0735	0845	0845	0955	1045
Grantham **208** a.	0549	...	0627	0723	0807	0812	0927	0926	|	1122
Grantham d.	...	...	0631	0726	0816	0816	0930	0936	|	1126
Sleaford d.	...	...	0657	0752	0845	0845	0956	1004	1044	1152
Boston d.	...	0625	0724	0820	0912	0912	1022	1029	1111	1218
Skegness a.	...	0703	0806	0859	0951	0951	1101	1108	1150	1257

	T	V	T	Ⓐ	⑥	V	T	⚒	⚒	⚒	⚒	Ⓐ	⑥	⚒	
Nottingham **208** d.	1045	1145	1150	1245	1245	1345	1350	1445	1545	1645	1745	1845	1845	2051	...
Grantham **208** a.	1128	1219	1228	1323	1328	1421	1428	1523	1625	1728	1826	1921	1928	2132	...
Grantham d.	1131	1223	1231	1327	1329	1423	1431	1526	1629	1732	1829	1924	1931	2136	...
Sleaford d.	1157	1249	1257	1355	1355	1451	1457	1552	1655	1801	1855	1953	2000	2201	...
Boston d.	1224	1315	1324	1421	1421	1517	1523	1620	1721	1826	1921	2017	2024	2232	...
Skegness a.	1303	1354	1403	1500	1502	1556	1602	1700	1803	1905	2001	2055	2102	...	...

⑦	⑦	⑦	⑦	⑦	⑦	⑦	⑦	⑦	⑦	⑦
Nottingham **208** d.	...	0900	0940	1109	1155	1403	1456	1621	1817	1948
Grantham **208** a.	...	|	1014	1144	1229	1437	1531	1703	1851	2022
Grantham d.	...	|	1018	1149	1235	1441	1536	1707	1855	2026
Sleaford d.	...	0949	1044	1215	1301	1509	1604	1736	1921	2052
Boston d.	0931	1016	1110	1241	1327	1539	1631	1802	1950	2120
Skegness a.	1007	1055	1149	1320	1406	1618	1710	1841	2029	...

S – Ⓐ (also ⑥ from Sept. 12). T – ⑥ July 18 - Sept. 5. V – Ⓐ (also ⑥ until July 11 and from Sept. 12).

First *Excel* service X1 — PETERBOROUGH - KINGS LYNN — 197

⚒	Ⓐ	Ⓐ		⚒	⚒		⚒	⚒	⚒	⚒	⚒			⑦	⑦	⑦		⑦
Peterborough rail station d.	0643	0713	...	0748	0818	and every	1918	2018	2118	2218	2318	...	...	0818	0918	and every	2318
Wisbech bus station a.	0730	0800	...	0835	0905	30 minutes	2005	2105	2205	2305	0005	...	...	0905	1005	60 minutes	0005
Kings Lynn bus station a.	0807	0837	...	0907	0937	until	2037	2137	2237	2337	0037	...	...	0937	1037	until	0037

⚒	Ⓐ	Ⓐ	⚒	⚒	⚒	⚒		⚒	⚒	⚒	⚒	⚒		⑦	⑦	⑦		⑦
Kings Lynn bus station d.	0524	0554	0629	0659	0729	0759	and every	1759	1859	1959	2059	2159	...	0659	0759	and every	2159
Wisbech bus station d.	0556	0626	0701	0731	0801	0831	30 minutes	1831	1931	2031	2131	2231	...	0731	0831	60 minutes	2231
Peterborough rail station a.	0638	0708	0743	0813	0843	0813	until	1913	2013	2113	2213	2313	...	0813	0913	until	2313

Rail Link service – through rail tickets are available.

FC — LONDON - ELY - KINGS LYNN — 198

km	Ⓐ	Ⓐ	Ⓐ	Ⓐ	Ⓐ	Ⓐ	Ⓐ		Ⓐ	Ⓐ	Ⓐ	Ⓐ	Ⓐ	Ⓐ	Ⓐ	Ⓐ	Ⓐ	Ⓐ	Ⓐ	Ⓐ	Ⓐ	Ⓐ	Ⓐ
0	**London** Kings Cross ¶ d.	...	0545	0645	0715	0745	0845	and	1545	1558r	1644	1658r	1744	1814	1758r	1844	1858r	1945	2015	2045	2115	2215	2315
93	Cambridge ¶ **205** d.	0618	0658	0735	0804	0838	0935	hourly	1635	1722	1739	1814	1839	1905	1919	1939	2015	2040	2110	2135	2210	2310	0013
117	**Ely** **205** a.	0633	0713	0751	0819	0853	0950	until ★	1650	1738	1755	1830	1855	1918	1934	1955	2030	2055	2125	2154	2225	2325	0029
142	Downham Market a.	0652	0729	0807	0837	0910	1006		1706	...	1812	1847	1912	1938	1952	2012	2047	2111	2141	2209z	2241	2341	0045z
160	**Kings Lynn** a.	0710	0745	0823	0853	0925	1021		1721	...	1828	1905	1928	1956	2010	2028	2105	2126	2156	2224z	2256	2356	0100z

⑥	⑥	⑥	⑥	⑥		⑥	⑥	⑥	⑥	⑥	⑥	⑥		⑦	⑦y		⑦		⑦	⑦	⑦	
London Kings Cross ¶ d.	...	0645	0658r	0745	and	1645	1745	1845	1945	2045	2152	2312	...	0752	...	0915	and	2115	2215	2315	...
Cambridge ¶ **205** d.	0632	0733	0820	0833	hourly	1733	1840	1940	2040	2140	2255	0019	...	0907	...	1005	hourly	2204	2311	0019	...
Ely **205** a.	0647	0748	0836	0848	until ★	1748	1855	1955	2055	2155	2310	0034	...	0922	...	1019	until ★	2219	2326	0038	...
Downham Market a.	0703	0804	...	0904		1804	1912	2012	2112	2212	2326	0050	...	0938	...	1035		2235	2342	...	...
Kings Lynn a.	0720	0821	...	0921		1821	1926	2026	2126	2226	2340	0107	...	0952	...	1050		2250	2359	...	...

Ⓐ	Ⓐ	Ⓐ	Ⓐ	Ⓐ	Ⓐ	Ⓐ	Ⓐ	Ⓐ	Ⓐ	Ⓐ		Ⓐ		Ⓐ	Ⓐ	Ⓐ		Ⓐ	Ⓐ	Ⓐ	Ⓐ	Ⓐ	Ⓐ
Kings Lynn d.	...	0519	0552	0618	0652	0723	0755	0827	0859	0959	...	1056	and	1456	1556	1654	...	1736	1836	1939	2039	2136	2232
Downham Market d.	...	0533	0605	0632	0705	0736	0808	0840	0912	1012	...	1109	hourly	1509	1609	1707	...	1749	1849	1952	2052	2149	2245
Ely **205** d.	0526	0552	0622	0650	0722	0754	0825	0857	0929	1029	...	1126	until ★	1526	1626	1724	...	1806	1906	2009	2109	2206	2302
Cambridge ¶ **205** a.	0544	0610	0640	0708	0740	0814	0844	0916	0947	1047	...	1144		1544	1644	1743	...	1822	1922	2026	2127	2223	2319
London Kings Cross ¶ a.	0638	0734r	0739	0834r	0839	0912	0942	1013	1046	1139	...	1233		1633	1738	1838	...	1934	2033	2130	2230	2335	0042

⑥	⑥	⑥		⑥	⑥	⑥	⑥	⑥	⑥		⑦	⑦	⑦	⑦		⑦		⑦	⑦	⑦		
Kings Lynn d.	0556	0656	and	1756	1834	1934	2034	2134	2315	...	0828	0928	1028	and	1928	...	2028	2128	2228	...	...
Downham Market d.	0609	0709	hourly	1809	1847	1947	2047	2147	2328	...	0841	0941	1041	hourly	1941	...	2041	2141	2241	...	...
Ely **205** d.	0626	0726	until ★	1826	1905	2005	2105	2205	2344	...	0858	0958	1058	until ★	1958	...	2058	2158	2258	...	...
Cambridge ¶ **205** a.	0644	0744		1844	1921	2021	2121	2221	0002	...	0916	1016	1116		2016	...	2116	2216	2315	...	...
London Kings Cross ¶ a.	0734	0833		1933	2032	2132	2234	2347	...	...	1008	1108	1208		2108	...	2209	2319	0032	...	...

r – London Liverpool Street. y – Until Sept. 6. z – ⑤ only. ★ – Timings may vary by up to 4 minutes. ¶ – **London - Cambridge** and v.v., see Table **199**.

FC, LE — LONDON - CAMBRIDGE — 199

London Kings Cross – **Cambridge** ★ Operator: FC *93 km*

Ⓐ: 0007, 0545, 0645, 0715 and every 30 minutes until 1615, then 1644, 1714, 1744, 1814, 1844, 1915, 1945, 2015, 2045, 2115, 2152, 2215, 2252, 2315.

⑥: 0007, 0545, 0645, 0745, 0815 and every 30 minutes until 1945; then 1952, 2045, 2152, 2312.

⑦: 0004, 0652, 0752, 0852, 0915, 0952, and at 15 and 52 minutes past each hour until 2315.

Cambridge – **London** Kings Cross ★ Journey time: ± 55 minutes

Ⓐ: 0545, 0615 and every 30 minutes until 0845; then 0920, 0950, 1020, 1050, 1115, 1145 and every 30 minutes until 1945; then 2028, 2045, 2128, 2145, 2228, 2319.

⑥: 0545, 0628, 0645, 0728, 0745, 0815 and every 30 minutes until 1945; then 2028, 2045, 2128, 2145, 2228.

⑦: 0728, 0828, 0920, 0928 and at 20 and 28 minutes past each hour until 1328; then 1415, 1428, 1514, 1528, 1615, 1628, 1720, 1728, 1820, 1828, 1920, 1928, 2020, 2028, 2120, 2128, 2220, 2241, 2315.

London Liverpool St – **Cambridge** Operator: LE *90 km*

Ⓐ: 0528, 0558, 0628 and every 30 minutes until 2328, 2358⑤.
Also: 1643, 1713, 1743, 1813, 1843, 1913.

⑥: 0558, 0628 and every 30 minutes until 2358.

⑦: 0743, 0828, 0928 and hourly until 2228.

★ – Selected trains.

Cambridge – **London** Liverpool St Journey time: ± 80 minutes

Ⓐ: 0448, 0521, 0541, 0551, 0618, 0621, 0648, 0651, 0718, 0721, 0748, 0751, 0818, 0821, 0851, 0932, 0948, 1032, 1048, 1132, 1151, 1232, 1251, 1332, 1351, 1432, 1451, 1521, 1551 and every 30 minutes until 1951; then 2032, 2051, 2132, 2151, 2232, 2251.

⑥: 0425, 0521, 0551, 0632, 0651 and at 32 and 51 minutes past each hour until 2251.

⑦: 0732, 0832 and hourly until 2232.

200 LONDON - IPSWICH - NORWICH

LE

For London - Lowestoft trains see Table **203**. For London - Harwich trains see Table **204**.

km			Ⓐ P	Ⓐ	Ⓐ	Ⓐ	Ⓐ P	Ⓐ	Ⓐ 🍷	Ⓐ L	Ⓐ 🍷	Ⓐ	Ⓐ 🍷	Ⓐ	Ⓐ 🍷	Ⓐ 🍷	Ⓐ L	Ⓐ 🍷	Ⓐ 🍷	Ⓐ P	Ⓐ 🍷	Ⓐ 🍷	Ⓐ L	Ⓐ 🍷	Ⓐ 🍷
0	**London** Liverpool St. ‡ d.	Ⓐ	...	...	0600	0625	0638	0700	0730	0738	0800	0802	0830	0838	0900	0930	0938	1000	1030	1038	1100	1130	1138	1200	1230
48	Chelmsford ‡ d.		...	...	│	0657	0712	│	0804	0812	│	0835	0902	0912	│	1002	1012	│	1102	1112	│	1202	1212	│	1302
84	**Colchester** ‡ d.		0535	0622	0650	0722	0741	0750	0824	0838	0850	0904	0924	0938	0950	1024	1038	1050	1122	1138	1150	1222	1238	1250	1322
97	Manningtree d.		0544	0631	0659	0732	0750	0759	0834	│	0859	0912	0934	0946	0959	1034	│	1059	1131	│	1159	1231	│	1259	1331
111	**Ipswich** 205 207 d.		0601	0642	0709	0742	0802	0809	0844	0856	0909	0923	0944	0958	1009	1044	1056	1109	1142	1202	1209	1242	1256	1309	1342
130	Stowmarket 205 207 d.		0612	0653	0720	0753	0813	0820	0855	...	│	...	0955	...	│	1055	...	│	1153	1213	│	1253	...	│	1353
153	Diss d.		...	0705	0732	0805	...	0832	0907	...	0930	...	1007	...	1030	1107	...	1130	1205	...	1230	1305	...	1330	1405
185	**Norwich** a.		...	0727	0754	0827	...	0854	0927	...	0952	...	1027	...	1052	1127	...	1152	1227	...	1252	1327	...	1352	1427

	Ⓐ P	Ⓐ 🍷	Ⓐ 🍷	Ⓐ L	Ⓐ 🍷	Ⓐ 🍷	Ⓐ P	Ⓐ 🍷	Ⓐ 🍷	Ⓐ L	Ⓐ 🍷	Ⓐ 🍷	Ⓐ P	Ⓐ 🍷	Ⓐ	Ⓐ 🍷	Ⓐ 🍷	Ⓐ 🍷	Ⓐ 🍷	Ⓐ 🍷	Ⓐ 🍷	Ⓐ 🍷	Ⓐ L	Ⓐ 🍷	Ⓐ 🍷
London Liverpool St. ‡ d.	1238	1300	1330	1338	1400	1430	1438	1500	1530	1538	1600	1630	1632	1700	1720	1730	1750	1800	1820	1830	1900	1930	1932	2000	2030
Chelmsford ‡ d.	1312	│	1402	1412	│	1502	1512	│	1559	1612u	1631	│	│	│	1751	│	│	│	│	│	│	2000	│	│	2103
Colchester ‡ d.	1338	1350	1422	1438	1450	1522	1538	1550	1622	1641	1650	1718	1726	│	1811	│	1843	1853	1912	1923	1953	2021	2026	2050	2123
Manningtree d.	│	1359	1431	│	1459	1531	│	1559	1631	│	1659	│	1735	│	1819	1827	1852	1902	1921	│	2002	2030	│	2059	2132
Ipswich 205 207 d.	1402	1409	1442	1456	1509	1542	1602	1609	1642	1658	1709	1734	1749	1759	1833	1837	1903	1912	1932	1940	2012	2041	2044	2109	2143
Stowmarket 205 207 d.	1413	│	1453	...	│	1553	1613	│	1653	...	1720	1745	1803	│	...	1848	│	1923	│	1951	2023	2052	...	2120	2154
Diss d.	...	1430	1505	...	1530	1605	...	1630	1705	...	1732	1757	...	1820	...	1900	│	1935	│	2003	2035	2104	...	2132	2206
Norwich a.	...	1452	1527	...	1552	1627	...	1652	1727	...	1755	1820	...	1842	...	1923	1944	1958	2014	2026	2057	2126	...	2154	2228

	Ⓐ L	Ⓐ 🍷	Ⓐ	Ⓐ	Ⓐ 🍷	Ⓐ	Ⓐ 🍷		⑥ P	⑥	⑥	⑥	⑥ P	⑥	⑥ 🍷	⑥ L	⑥ 🍷	⑥ 🍷	⑥ P	⑥ 🍷	⑥ 🍷	⑥ L	⑥ 🍷 Yz	⑥ 🍷	⑥ P
London Liverpool St. ‡ d.	2100	2130	2138	2200	2230	2300	2330	⑥	...	0530	...	0630	0638	0700	0730	0738	0800	0830	0838	0900	0930	0938	1000	1030	1038
Chelmsford ‡ d.	│	2203	2212u	2231	2303	2333	0003		...	0607	...	0702	0712	│	0802	0812	│	0902	0912	│	1002	1012	│	1102	1112
Colchester ‡ d.	2150	2223	2238	2254	2323	2357	0023		0538	0637	...	0722	0738	0750	0822	0838	0850	0922	0938	0950	1022	1038	1050	1122	1138
Manningtree d.	2158	2232	│	2302	2332	0004	0032		0546	0645	...	0731	0746	0759	0831	│	0859	0931	0946	0959	1031	│	1059	1131	│
Ipswich 205 207 d.	2207	2243	2256	2314	2343	0020	0044		0600	0656	0709	0742	0802	0809	0842	0902	0909	0942	1002	1009	1042	1056	1109	1142	1202
Stowmarket 205 207 d.	...	2254	...	...	2354	...	0055		0611	...	0720	0753	0813	│	0853	...	│	0953	1013	│	1053	...	│	1153	1213
Diss d.	...	2307	...	...	0007	...	0108		...	...	0732	0805	...	0830	0905	...	0930	1005	...	1030	1105	...	1130	1205	...
Norwich a.	...	2329	...	...	0045	...	0145		...	...	0752	0827	...	0852	0927	...	0952	1027	...	1052	1127	...	1152	1227	...

	⑥ 🍷	⑥ 🍷	⑥ L	⑥ 🍷 Yz	⑥ 🍷	⑥ P	⑥ 🍷	⑥ 🍷	⑥ L	⑥ 🍷	⑥ 🍷	⑥ P	⑥ 🍷	⑥ 🍷	⑥ L	⑥ 🍷	⑥ 🍷	⑥ P	⑥ 🍷	⑥ 🍷	⑥ L	⑥ 🍷	⑥ 🍷	⑥ P	⑥ 🍷
London Liverpool St. ‡ d.	1100	1130	1138	1200	1230	1238	1300	1330	1338	1400	1430	1438	1500	1530	1538	1600	1630	1638	1700	1730	1746	1800	1830	1846	1900
Chelmsford ‡ d.	│	1202	1212	│	1302	1312	│	1402	1412	│	1502	1512	│	1602	1612	│	1702	1712	│	1802	1816u	│	1902	1916u	│
Colchester ‡ d.	1150	1222	1238	1250	1322	1338	1350	1422	1438	1450	1522	1538	1550	1622	1638	1650	1722	1738	1750	1822	1840	1850	1922	1940	1950
Manningtree d.	1159	1231	│	1259	1331	│	1359	1431	│	1459	1531	│	1559	1631	│	1659	1731	│	1759	1831	│	1859	1931	│	1959
Ipswich 205 207 d.	1209	1242	1256	1309	1342	1402	1409	1442	1456	1509	1542	1602	1609	1642	1656	1709	1742	1802	1809	1842	1856	1909	1942	2002	2009
Stowmarket 205 207 d.	│	1253	...	│	1353	1413	│	1453	...	│	1553	1613	│	1653	...	1720	1753	1813	│	1853	...	│	1953	2013	│
Diss d.	1230	1305	...	1330	1405	...	1430	1505	...	1530	1605	...	1630	1705	...	1732	1805	...	1830	1905	...	1930	2005	...	2030
Norwich a.	1252	1327	...	1352	1427	...	1452	1527	...	1552	1627	...	1652	1727	...	1752	1827	...	1852	1927	...	1952	2027	...	2052

	⑥ 🍷	⑥ L	⑥ 🍷	⑥ 🍷	⑥ L	⑥ 🍷	⑥	⑥	⑥ 🍷	⑥	⑥ 🍷		⑦	⑦	⑦	⑦	⑦	⑦ 🍷		⑦	⑦ 🍷		⑦	⑦
London Liverpool St. ‡ d.	1930	1938	2000	2030	2100	2130	2134	2200	2230	2300	2330	⑦	...	...	0802	0830	0902	0930		2202	2230	...	2302	2330
Chelmsford ‡ d.	2003	2012	│	2103	│	2204	2212	2237	2304	2337	0004		...	...	0842	│	0942	│	and at the same minutes past each hour until	2242	│	...	2342	│
Colchester ‡ d.	2023	2038	2050	2123	2150	2226	2238	2300	2326	0001	0029		0740	0812	0912	0924	1012	1024		2312	2324	...	0012	0028
Manningtree d.	2032	│	2059	2132	2158	2235	│	2308	2335	0008	0038		0748	0820	0920	0933	1020	1033		2320	2333	...	0020	0037
Ipswich 205 207 d.	2043	2056	2109	2143	2209	2246	2256	2320	2346	0024	0050		0800	0832	0932	0944	1032	1044		2332	2344	...	0036	0048
Stowmarket 205 207 d.	2054	...	│	2154	...	2257	...	...	2357	...	0101		...	...	...	0955	...	1055		...	2355	...	...	0059
Diss d.	2106	...	2130	2206	...	2310	...	...	0010	...	0114		...	...	...	1007	...	1107		...	0007	...	...	0111
Norwich a.	2128	...	2152	2228	...	2332	...	...	0032	...	0136		...	...	...	1029	...	1129		...	0039	...	...	0143

		Ⓐ 🍷	Ⓐ 🍷	Ⓐ 🍷	Ⓐ 🍷	Ⓐ 🍷	Ⓐ 🍷	Ⓐ 🍷	Ⓐ Y	Ⓐ 🍷	Ⓐ 🍷	Ⓐ 🍷	Ⓐ P	Ⓐ 🍷	Ⓐ 🍷	Ⓐ L	Ⓐ 🍷	Ⓐ 🍷	Ⓐ P	Ⓐ 🍷	Ⓐ 🍷	Ⓐ L	Ⓐ 🍷	Ⓐ 🍷	Ⓐ P
Norwich d.	Ⓐ	0510	0540	0610	0625	0640	0655	0710	0730	0740	0800	0830	...	0900	0930	...	1000	1030	...	1100	1130	...	1200	1230	...
Diss d.		0528	0558	0628	0643	0658	0713	0728	│	0758	0817	0847	...	0917	0947	...	1017	1047	...	1117	1147	...	1217	1247	...
Stowmarket 205 207 d.		0540	0610	0640	0655	0710	0725	0740	│	0810	0829	│	0912	0929	│	...	1029	│	1112	1129	│	...	1229	│	1312
Ipswich 205 207 d.		0553	0623	0653	0708	0723	0738	0753	0818	0823	0842	0908	0930	0942	1008	1030	1042	1108	1130	1142	1208	1230	1242	1308	1330
Manningtree d.		0603	0633	0703	0718	0733	0748	0803	│	0833	0852	0918	│	0952	1018	│	1052	1118	│	1152	1218	│	1252	1318	│
Colchester ‡ d.		0615	0645	0715	0730	0745	0800	0815	│	0845	0903	0929	0949	1003	1029	1049	1103	1129	1149	1203	1229	1249	1303	1329	1349
Chelmsford ‡ d.		│	│	│	│	│	│	│	│	0902	│	0947	1010s	│	1046	1111	│	1146	1211	│	1246	1311	│	1346	1411
London Liverpool St. ‡ a.		0710	0737	0809	0823	0839	0855	0910	0925	0940	0956	1024	1046	1054	1124	1145	1154	1224	1245	1254	1324	1345	1354	1424	1445

	Ⓐ 🍷	Ⓐ 🍷	Ⓐ L	Ⓐ 🍷	Ⓐ 🍷	Ⓐ P	Ⓐ	Ⓐ 🍷	Ⓐ 🍷	Ⓐ 🍷	Ⓐ 🍷	Ⓐ P	Ⓐ 🍷	Ⓐ 🍷	Ⓐ L	Ⓐ 🍷	Ⓐ 🍷	Ⓐ P	Ⓐ 🍷	Ⓐ	Ⓐ L	Ⓐ 🍷	Ⓐ	Ⓐ P	Ⓐ 🍷
Norwich d.	1300	1330	...	1400	1430	...	...	1500	1530	1600	1630	...	1700	1730	...	1800	1830	...	1900	...	...	2000	...	...	2100
Diss d.	1317	1347	...	1417	1447	...	...	1517	1547	1618	1648	...	1718	1748	...	1817	1847	...	1917	...	...	2017	...	...	2117
Stowmarket 205 207 d.	1329	│	...	1429	│	1512	...	1529	│	1630	│	1712	1730	1800	...	1829	│	1912	1929	...	...	2029	...	2108	2129
Ipswich 205 207 d.	1342	1408	1430	1442	1508	1526	...	1542	1608	1642	1708	1730	1742	1811	1830	1842	1908	1927	1942	2008	2030	2042	2108	2127	2142
Manningtree d.	1352	1418	│	1452	1518	│	...	1552	1618	1652	1718	│	1752	1821	│	1852	1918	1937	1952	2018	│	2052	2118	2137	2152
Colchester ‡ d.	1403	1429	1449	1503	1529	1543	1547	1603	1629	1703	1729	1749	1803	1832	1849	1903	1929	1948	2003	2029	2049	2103	2129	2149	2203
Chelmsford ‡ d.	│	1446	1511	│	1546	...	1614	│	1646	│	1746	1813	│	1849	1913	│	1946	2011	│	2046	2111	│	2146	2211	│
London Liverpool St. ‡ a.	1454	1524	1545	1554	1624	...	1649	1654	1724	1754	1824	1849	1854	1927	1947	1954	2024	2046	2054	2121	2146	2154	2223	2246	2254

	Ⓐ	Ⓐ	Ⓐ	Ⓐ P	Ⓐ			⑥ 🍷	⑥ 🍷	⑥	⑥ 🍷	⑥ 🍷	⑥ L	⑥ 🍷	⑥ 🍷	⑥ L	⑥ 🍷	⑥ 🍷	⑥ P	⑥ 🍷	⑥ 🍷	⑥ L	⑥ 🍷	⑥ 🍷	⑥ P
Norwich d.	...	2200	...	...	2305	...	⑥	0500	0530	...	0600	0630	...	0700	0730	...	0800	0830	...	0900	0930	...	1000	1030	...
Diss d.	...	2217	...	...	2322	...		0517	0547	...	0617	0647	...	0717	0747	...	0817	0847	...	0917	0947	...	1017	1047	...
Stowmarket 205 207 d.	...	2229	...	2324	2334	...		0529	│	...	0629	│	...	0729	│	...	0829	│	0912	0929	│	...	1029	│	1114
Ipswich 205 207 d.	2208	2242	2322	2338	2348	...		0542	0608	0630	0642	0708	0730	0742	0808	0830	0842	0908	0930	0942	1008	1030	1042	1108	1130
Manningtree d.	2218	2252	2331	2348	...	...		0552	0618	│	0652	0718	│	0752	0818	│	0852	0918	│	0952	1018	│	1052	1118	│
Colchester ‡ d.	2229	2303	2341	2358	...	...		0603	0629	0649	0703	0729	0749	0803	0829	0849	0903	0929	0949	1003	1029	1049	1103	1129	1149
Chelmsford ‡ d.	2256	2324	...	...	...	...		│	0646	0711	│	0746	0811	│	0846	0906s	│	0946	1006s	│	1046	1106s	│	1146	1211
London Liverpool St. ‡ a.	2334	0003	...	...	...	...		0654	0724	0745	0754	0824	0845	0854	0924	0938	0954	1024	1038	1054	1124	1142	1154	1224	1245

	⑥ 🍷 Yz	⑥ 🍷	⑥ L	⑥ 🍷	⑥ 🍷	⑥ P	⑥ 🍷	⑥ 🍷	⑥ L	⑥ 🍷 Yz	⑥ 🍷	⑥ P	⑥ 🍷	⑥ 🍷	⑥ L	⑥ 🍷	⑥ 🍷	⑥ P	⑥ 🍷	⑥ 🍷	⑥ L	⑥ 🍷	⑥ 🍷	⑥ P	⑥ 🍷
Norwich d.	1100	1130	...	1200	1230	...	1300	1330	...	1400	1430	...	1500	1530	...	1600	1630	...	1700	1730	...	1800	1830	...	1900
Diss d.	1117	1147	...	1217	1247	...	1317	1347	...	1417	1447	...	1517	1547	...	1617	1647	...	1717	1747	...	1817	1847	...	1917
Stowmarket 205 207 d.	1129	│	...	1229	│	1312	1329	│	...	1429	│	1512	1529	│	...	1629	│	1712	1729	1759	...	1829	│	1912	1929
Ipswich 205 207 d.	1142	1208	1230	1242	1308	1330	1342	1408	1430	1442	1508	1530	1542	1608	1630	1642	1708	1730	1742	1811	1830	1842	1908	1927	1942
Manningtree d.	1152	1218	│	1252	1318	│	1352	1418	│	1452	1518	│	1552	1618	│	1652	1718	│	1752	1821	│	1852	1918	1937	1952
Colchester ‡ d.	1203	1229	1249	1303	1329	1349	1403	1429	1449	1503	1529	1549	1603	1629	1649	1703	1729	1749	1803	1832	1849	1903	1929	1949	2003
Chelmsford ‡ d.	│	1246	1311	│	1346	1411	│	1446	1511	│	1546	1611	│	1646	1711	│	1746	1811	│	1849	1911	│	1946	2011	│
London Liverpool St. ‡ a.	1254	1324	1345	1354	1424	1445	1454	1524	1545	1554	1624	1645	1654	1724	1745	1754	1824	1845	1854	1926	1945	1954	2024	2045	2054

	⑥	⑥ L	⑥ 🍷	⑥	⑥ P	⑥ 🍷	⑥	⑥	⑥ P	⑥			⑦ 🍷	⑦	⑦ 🍷	⑦		⑦ 🍷	⑦		⑦	⑦	⑦	⑦
Norwich d.	...	...	2000	...	...	2100	...	2200	...	2305	...	⑦	0700	...	0800	...		2000	...	...	2100	...	2200	2305
Diss d.	...	...	2017	...	...	2117	...	2217	...	2322	...		0717	...	0817	...	and at the same minutes past each hour until	2017	...	...	2117	...	2217	2322
Stowmarket 205 207 d.	...	...	2029	...	2112	2129	...	2229	2317	2334	...		0729	...	0829	...		2029	...	...	2129	...	2229	2334
Ipswich 205 207 d.	2008	2030	2042	2108	2127	2142	2208	2242	2335	2350	...		0742	0808	0842	0908		2042	2108	...	2142	2208	2242	2348
Manningtree d.	2018	│	2052	2118	2137	2152	2218	2252	2345	...	...		0752	0818	0852	0918		2052	2118	...	2152	2218	2252	...
Colchester ‡ d.	2029	2049	2103	2129	2149	2203	2229	2303	2356	...	...		0803	0830	0903	0930		2103	2130	...	2203	2230	2303	...
Chelmsford ‡ d.	2046	2111	│	2146	2211	│	2256	2324	...	...	...		│	0857	│	0957		│	2157	...	│	2257	2324	...
London Liverpool St. ‡ a.	2119	2149	2158	2225	2249	2258	2338	0007	...	...	...		0903	0942	1001	1042		2201	2242	...	2301	2342	0007	...

L – To / from Lowestoft, Table **203**.
P – To / from Peterborough, Table **207**.
Y – To / from Great Yarmouth.
s – Stops to set down only.
u – Stops to pick up only.
z – Until Sept. 26.
‡ – Frequent additional services available London - Chelmsford - Colchester and v.v.

LE 2nd class — NORWICH and IPSWICH local services — 202

NORWICH – GREAT YARMOUTH *30 km (33 km via Reedham)*

Ⓐ: 0515, 0634, 0705, 0736 **r**, 0836, 0936, 1036 **r**, 1136, 1236, 1336, 1436, 1536, 1640, 1705, 1736, 1840, 1936, 2040, 2140, 2300.

⑥: 0536 **r**, 0636, 0705, 0736 **r**, 0836, 0936, 1000 ♣, 1036 **r**, 1136, 1200 ♣, 1236, 1336, 1436, 1536, 1640, 1705, 1736, 1840, 1936, 2040, 2140, 2300.

⑦: 0736 **r**, 0845, 0936 **r**, 1045, 1136 **r**, 1245, 1336 **r**, 1445, 1536 **r**, 1645, 1736 **r**, 1845, 1936 **r**, 2045, 2136 **r**, 2236.

GREAT YARMOUTH – NORWICH Journey time: ± 32 mins

Ⓐ: 0555, 0640 ✣, 0717, 0744, 0817, 0917, 1017, 1117, 1217, 1317, 1412 **r**, 1517, 1617, 1717, 1747 **r**, 1817, 1917, 2017, 2117, 2217, 2333 **r**.

⑥: 0617, 0717, 0744, 0817, 0917, 1008 ♣, 1017, 1117, 1217, 1310 ♣, 1317, 1412 **r**, 1517, 1617, 1717, 1747 **r**, 1817, 1917, 2017, 2117, 2217, 2333 **r**.

⑦: 0820 **r**, 0922, 1018 **r**, 1122, 1218 **r**, 1322, 1420 **r**, 1522, 1618 **r**, 1722, 1818 **r**, 1922, 2022 **r**, 2122, 2222 **r**, 2320 **r**.

NORWICH – LOWESTOFT *38 km*

⚒: 0545 Ⓐ **r**, 0549 ⑥ **r**, 0624 Ⓐ **r**, 0655 ⑥ **r**, 0657 Ⓐ **r**, 0754 **r**, 0857, 0957 **r**, 1057, 1157 **r**, 1257, 1357 **r**, 1457 **r**, 1557 **r**, 1657 **r**, 1757 **r**, 1857 **r**, 1957 **r**, 2057 **r**, 2157 **r**, 2240 **r**.

⑦: 0725, 0857 **r**, 1057 **r**, 1257 **r**, 1457 **r**, 1657 **r**, 1857 **r**, 2057 **r**.

LOWESTOFT – NORWICH Journey time: ± 38 mins

⚒: 0536 Ⓐ **r**, 0640 **r**, 0740 **r**, 0755 Ⓐ **r**, 0842 **r**, 0942 **r**, 1050, 1142 **r**, 1250, 1342 **r**, 1450, 1542 **r**, 1647 **r**, 1747 **r**, 1847 **r**, 1947 **r**, 2050, 2142 **r**, 2245 **r**, 2330 **r**.

⑦: 0950 **r**, 1150 **r**, 1350 **r**, 1550 **r**, 1750 **r**, 1950 **r**, 2150 **r**, 2335 **r**.

NORWICH – CROMER – SHERINGHAM *49 km*

⚒: 0520, 0545 ⑥, 0550 Ⓐ, 0715, 0823, 0945, 1045 and hourly until 1945; then 2115, 2245.

⑦: 0836, 0945 **A**, 1036, 1145 **A**, 1236, 1345 **A**, 1436, 1545 **A**, 1636, 1745 **A**, 1836, 1945 **A**, 2036.

SHERINGHAM – CROMER (△) – NORWICH Journey time: ± 57 mins

⚒: 0622 ⑥, 0632 Ⓐ, 0717, 0825, 0946, 1046 and hourly until 1546; then 1649, 1748, 1849, 1948, 2049, 2216, 2346.

⑦: 0943, 1043 **A**, 1143, 1243 **A**, 1343, 1443 **A**, 1543, 1643 **A**, 1743, 1843 **A**, 1943, 2043 **A**, 2143.

IPSWICH – FELIXSTOWE *25 km*

⚒: 0504 Ⓐ, 0604 Ⓐ, 0627 ⑥, 0713 Ⓐ, 0727 ⑥, 0827, 0927 and hourly until 2027; then 2227.

⑦: 1055 **A**, 1155 and hourly until 1955.

FELIXSTOWE – IPSWICH Journey time: ± 25 mins

⚒: 0534 Ⓐ, 0638 Ⓐ, 0656 ⑥, 0750 Ⓐ, 0756 ⑥, 0856, 0956 and hourly until 2056; then 2256.

⑦: 1125 **A**, 1225 and hourly until 2025.

A – Until Sept. 6.

r – Calls at **Reedham**: *20 km*, 18–21 minutes from Norwich; *14 km*, 12–14 minutes from Yarmouth; *18 km*, 18–21 minutes from Lowestoft.

✣ – (12) from / to London Liverpool St.

♣ – Until Sept. 26. (12) from / to London Liverpool St.

△ – Trains depart Cromer 11 minutes after leaving Sheringham. Additional journey Cromer - Norwich at 0603 on Ⓐ.

LE — (LONDON -) IPSWICH - LOWESTOFT — 203

km			Ⓐ	⑥	Ⓐ	⚒	⚒	⚒	⚒	⚒	Ⓐ	Ⓐ	⑥	Ⓐ	⑥	⚒			⑦	⑦	⑦	⑦	⑦	⑦	⑦
	London Liverpool St d.	⚒	...	...	*0600*	0738	0938	1138	1338	1538	*1700*	*1730*	1746	1932	1938	2100	...	⑦	*0830*	*1030*	*1230*	*1430*	*1630*	*1830*	*2030*
	Colchester d.		*0622*	*0538*	*0650*	0838	1038	1238	1438	1638	*1726*	*1811*	1840	2026	2038	2150	...		*0924*	*1124*	*1324*	*1524*	*1724*	*1924*	*2124*
0	**Ipswich** d.		0647	0650	0732	0902	1102	1302	1502	1702	1813	1855	1902	2052	2102	2215	...		1000	1200	1400	1600	1800	2000	2200
17	Woodbridge d.		0706	0709	0755	0921	1121	1321	1521	1721	1832	1914	1921	2111	2121	2234	...		1019	1219	1419	1619	1819	2019	2219
36	Saxmundham d.		0727	0730	0817	0942	1142	1342	1542	1742	1853	1935	1942	2132	2142	2255	...		1040	1240	1440	1640	1840	2040	2240
65	Beccles d.		0758	0801	...	1013	1213	1413	1613	1813	1931	2006	2013	2203	2213	2326	...		1111	1311	1511	1711	1911	2111	2311
79	**Lowestoft** a.		0817	0820	...	1032	1232	1432	1632	1833	1950	2025	2032	2222	2232	2345	...		1130	1330	1530	1730	1930	2130	2330

		Ⓐ	⑥	Ⓐ	⑥	Ⓐ	⚒	⚒	⚒	⑥	Ⓐ	⚒	Ⓐ	⑥		⚒			⑦	⑦	⑦	⑦	⑦	⑦	⑦
Lowestoft d.	⚒	0531	0558	0644	0658	...	0858	1058	1258	1458	1458	1658	1843	1858	...	2058	...	⑦	0805	1005	1205	1405	1605	1805	2005
Beccles d.		0547	0614	0700	0714	...	0914	1114	1314	1514	1514	1714	1859	1914	...	2114	...		0821	1021	1221	1421	1621	1821	2021
Saxmundham d.		0619	0646	0732	0746	0821	0946	1146	1346	1546	1546	1746	1936	1946	...	2146	...		0853	1053	1253	1453	1653	1853	2053
Woodbridge d.		0640	0707	0753	0807	0842	1007	1207	1407	1607	1607	1807	1957	2007	...	2207	...		0914	1114	1314	1514	1714	1914	2114
Ipswich a.		0659	0726	0812	0826	0901	1026	1226	1426	1626	1626	1826	2016	2026	...	2226	...		0933	1133	1333	1533	1733	1933	2133
Colchester a.		*0728*	0748	*0843*	0848	*0927*	1048	1248	1448	1648	*1648*	1848	2048	2048	...	*2301*	...		*1001*	*1201*	*1401*	*1601*	*1801*	*2001*	*2201*
London Liverpool St a.		*0823*	0845	0925	0938	*1024*	1145	1345	1545	1745	*1749*	1947	2146	2149	...	*0007*	...		*1103*	*1301*	*1501*	*1701*	*1901*	*2101*	*2301*

LE — HARWICH - MANNINGTREE (- LONDON) — 204

For boat trains Harwich International – London and v.v., see Table **15a**

km			Ⓐ	Ⓐ	Ⓐ	Ⓐ		Ⓐ	Ⓐ	Ⓐ	Ⓐ	Ⓐ	Ⓐ	Ⓐ	Ⓐ	Ⓐ	Ⓐ	Ⓐ	Ⓐ			⑥	⑥		⑥
0	**Harwich Town** d.	Ⓐ	0537	0622	0708	0800		1500	1605	1700	1753	1825	1853	1928	2000	2033	2100	2154	2305	...	⑥	0600	0700		2000
3	Harwich International d.		0542	0627	0713	0806	and	1506	1611	1706	1758	1830	1858	1933	2006	2038	2106	2159	2310	...		0606	0706	and	2006
18	**Manningtree** 200 a.		0558	0643	0729	0822	hourly	1522	1627	1722	1814	1846	1914	1949	2022	2056	2122	2215	2326	...		0622	0722	hourly	2022
	Colchester 200 a.		*0613*	0653	*0743*	0832	until	1532	1640	1732	*1830*	*1901*	*1927*	*2001*	2032	2106	2132	*2228*	*2341*	...		0632	0732	until	2032
	London Liverpool St 200 a.		*0710*	*0759*	*0839*	0933		1635	1749	1836	*1927*	*1954*	*2024*	*2054*	2133	*2219*	2236	*2334*	...	...		0733	0833		2138

	⑥	⑥	⑥			⑦	⑦		⑦	⑦
Harwich Town d.	2100	2154	2310	...	⑦	0853	0953		2153	2253
Harwich International d.	2106	2159	2315	...		0858	0958	and	2158	2258
Manningtree 200 a.	2122	2215	2331	...		0914	1014	hourly	2214	2314
Colchester 200 a.	2132	*2228*	*2345*	...		*0929*	*1029*	until	*2229*	2324
London Liverpool St 200 a.	2238	*2338*	...	...		*1042*	*1142*		*2342*	...

		Ⓐ	Ⓐ	Ⓐ	Ⓐ	Ⓐ	Ⓐ	Ⓐ		Ⓐ
London Liverpool St 200 d.	Ⓐ	...	...	*0625*	0718	*0808*	0918	1018		1615
Colchester 200 d.		0543	*0622*	*0722*	0821	0914	1021	1118	and	1713
Manningtree 200 d.		0551	0636	0735	0829	0922	1029	1126	hourly	1721
Harwich International d.		0609	0652	0751	0846	0939	1047	1144	until	1738
Harwich Town a.		0614	0657	0756	0851	0944	1052	1149		1745

	Ⓐ	Ⓐ	Ⓐ	Ⓐ	Ⓐ	Ⓐ	Ⓐ	Ⓐ	Ⓐ			⑥	⑥	⑥		⑥	⑥	⑥			⑦	⑦		⑦	
London Liverpool St 200 d.	1645	*1720*	*1750*	*1820*	*1900*	1918	2018	*2130*	*2230*	...	⑥	...	...	0618		2018	*2130*	*2230*	...	⑦	...	*0802*		*2102*	...
Colchester 200 d.	1747	*1811*	*1843*	*1912*	*1953*	2017	2117	*2223*	*2323*	...		0518	0618	0718	and	2118	*2226*	*2326*	...		0818	*0912*	and	*2212*	...
Manningtree 200 d.	1755	1823	1857	1927	2007	2025	2125	2238	2338	...		0526	0626	0726	hourly	2126	2238	2338	...		0826	0926	hourly	2226	...
Harwich International d.	1812	1839	1913	1943	2023	2042	2142	2254	2354	...		0544	0644	0744	until	2144	2254	2354	...		0842	0942	until	2242	...
Harwich Town a.	1819	1846	1918	1948	2028	2047	2147	2259	2359	...		0549	0649	0749		2149	2259	2359	...		0847	0947		2247	...

LE 2nd class — IPSWICH - CAMBRIDGE — 205

km			⚒	⚒	Ⓐ	⑥	⚒		⚒	⑥	Ⓐ	⚒				⑦	⑦	⑦	⑦	⑦	⑦	⑦	⑦	
0	**Ipswich** d.	⚒	0510	0613	0652	0716	0816		1916	2016	2116	2216	...	...	⑦	0845	0902	1102	1302	1502	1702	1902	2102	...
19	Stowmarket d.		0526	0629	0708	0732	0832	and	1932	2032	2132	2232	...	...		0859	0918	1118	1318	1518	1718	1918	2118	...
42	Bury St. Edmunds d.		0549	0651	0730	0755	0855	hourly	1955	2055	2155	2255	...	...		0917	0940	1140	1340	1540	1740	1940	2140	...
65	Newmarket d.		0610	0713	0751	0817	0915	until	2017	2115	2215	...	...	...		...	1000	1200	1400	1600	1800	2000	2200	...
88	**Cambridge** a.		0636	0739	0819	0839	0939		2039	2139	2239	...	...	...		...	1024	1224	1424	1624	1824	2024	2224	...

		Ⓐ	⚒		⚒	⚒		⚒		⑥		Ⓐ				⑦	⑦	⑦	⑦	⑦	⑦	⑦	⑦	
Cambridge d.	⚒	...	...	...	0641	0743		2043	...	2143	...	2243	...	...	⑦	...	1112	1312	1512	1712	1912	2112	2300	...
Newmarket d.		...	...	...	0701	0803	and	2103	...	2204	...	2304	...	...		...	1134	1334	1534	1734	1934	2134	2321	...
Bury St. Edmunds d.		0536	0622	...	0723	0823	hourly	2123	...	2225	...	2325	...	...		0955	1155	1355	1555	1755	1955	2155	2342	...
Stowmarket d.		0557	0644	...	0745	0845	until	2145	...	2246	...	2346	...	...		1017	1217	1417	1617	1817	2017	2217	0004	...
Ipswich a.		0615	0703	...	0803	0903		2203	...	2303	...	0003	...	...		1034	1234	1434	1634	1834	2034	2234	0021	...

LE 2nd class — CAMBRIDGE - NORWICH — 206

km			Ⓐ	Ⓐ	Ⓐ	Ⓐ		Ⓐ	Ⓐ	Ⓐ	Ⓐ	Ⓐ	Ⓐ			⑥	⑥	⑥		⑥	⑥			⑦
0	**Cambridge** 205 207 d.	Ⓐ	0605	0705	0812	0912	and	1712	1809	1925	2020	2113	2255	...	⑥	0608	0700	0812	and	2112	2230	...	⑦	1046
24	Ely 207 d.		0620	0720	0828	0927	hourly	1727	1824	1940	2036	2129	2310	...		0623	0715	0827	hourly	2127	2245	...		1102
63	Thetford d.		0645	0748	0853	0952	until	1752	1848	2004	2100	2154	2334	...		0648	0742	0852	until	2152	2309	...		1129
110	**Norwich** 200 208 a.		0730	0830	0930	1030		1830	1925	2042	2138	2231	0012	...		0729	0824	0930		2230	2345	...		1209

	⑦	⑦	⑦	⑦	⑦	⑦	⑦	⑦	⑦
Cambridge 205 207 d.	1246	1346	1446	1538	1642	1742	1842	1948	2148
Ely 207 d.	1302	1402	1502	1553	1657	1757	1857	2003	2203
Thetford d.	1329	1426	1526	1620	1721	1821	1921	2027	2227
Norwich 200 208 a.	1409	1509	1609	1658	1759	1859	1959	2109	2305

		Ⓐ	Ⓐ	Ⓐ	Ⓐ		Ⓐ	Ⓐ	Ⓐ
Norwich 200 208 d.	Ⓐ	0533	0633	0737	0840	and	1638	1735	1840
Thetford d.		0605	0705	0809	0912	hourly	1712	1812	1912
Ely 207 a.		0630	0730	0837	0938	until	1738	1838	1937
Cambridge 205 207 a.		0651	0751	0855	0958		1758	1858	1958

	Ⓐ	Ⓐ	Ⓐ			⑥	⑥		⑥	⑥	⑥	⑥	⑥	⑥	⑥	⑥			⑦	⑦		⑦	⑦	⑦
Norwich 200 208 d.	1945	2115	2240	...	⑥	0538	0640	and	1440	1535	1638	1735	1840	1940	2040	2240	...	⑦	0915	1115	and	1715	1815	2015
Thetford d.	2017	2147	2312	...		0610	0712	hourly	1512	1612	1712	1812	1912	2012	2112	2312	...		0947	1147	hourly	1747	1847	2047
Ely 207 a.	2044	2214	2338	...		0635	0737	until	1537	1637	1737	1837	1937	2037	2137	2337	...		1019	1219	until	1812	1912	2112
Cambridge 205 207 a.	2104	2233	0002	...		0655	0758		1558	1658	1758	1858	1958	2058	2158	2358	...		1036	1236		1832	1932	2132

207 IPSWICH, STANSTED AIRPORT and CAMBRIDGE - PETERBOROUGH - BIRMINGHAM *EM, LE, XC*

Subject to alteration on ⑥⑦ July 18 - September 6 owing to engineering work between Peterborough and Leicester

km		⚒	XC Ⓐ	XC ⑥	XC ⑥	XC Ⓐ		LE ⚒	XC Ⓐ	XC ⑥	XC ⚒		LE ⚒	XC ⚒	XC ⚒		LE ⚒	XC ⚒	XC ⚒		LE ⚒	XC ⚒	XC ⚒		LE ⚒	XC ⚒
	London Liverpool St **200** d.		...	...	...	...	...	...	...	...	...	...	0638	...	...	...	0838j	...	...	...	1038	...	...	...	1238	...
0	**Ipswich** 205 d.		...	...	...	...	...	0600	...	...	...	...	0802	...	...	...	1002	...	...	...	1202	...	...	...	1402	...
19	Stowmarket 205 d.		...	...	...	...	...	0611	...	...	...	...	0813	...	...	...	1013	...	...	...	1213	...	...	...	1413	...
42	Bury St. Edmunds 205 d.		...	...	...	...	...	0627	...	...	...	...	0829	...	...	...	1029	...	...	...	1229	...	...	...	1429	...
	Stansted Airport d.		...	...	0525	0521	...	|	0606	0625	0721y	...	|	0821y	0921y	...	|	1021y	1125	...	|	1225	1325	...	|	1425
	Cambridge 205 d.		0515	0515	0555	0555	...	|	0652	0656	0800	...	|	0900	1000	...	|	1100	1200	...	|	1300	1400	...	|	1500
82	Ely 208 d.		0530	0530	0610	0610	...	0657	0708	0711	0815	...	0858	0915	1015	...	1058	1115	1215	...	1258	1315	1415	...	1458	1515
108	March d.		0546	0546	0628	0628	...	0714	0726	0729	0831	...	0915	0931	1031	...	1115	1131	1231	...	1315	1331	1431	...	1515	1531
132	**Peterborough** 208 a.		0608	0608	0650	0650	...	0739	0749	0751	0850	...	0938	0950	1050	...	1137	1151	1250	...	1337	1351	1450	...	1537	1551
132	**Peterborough** d.		0610	0610	0652	0652	...	...	0750	0752	0852	...	...	0952	1052	...	...	1152	1252	...	...	1352	1452	...	...	1552
151	Stamford d.		0623	0623	0705	0705	...	...	0805	0805	0905	...	...	1005	1105	...	...	1205	1305	...	...	1405	1505	...	...	1605
173	Oakham d.		0639	0639	0721	0721	...	...	0821	0821	0921	...	...	1021	1121	...	...	1221	1321	...	...	1421	1521	...	...	1621
193	Melton Mowbray d.		0650	0650	0733	0733	...	...	0833	0833	0933	...	...	1033	1133	...	...	1233	1333	...	...	1433	1533	...	...	1633
216	**Leicester** ▼ d.		0710	0716	0749	0749	...	...	0849	0849	0949	...	...	1049	1149	...	...	1249	1349	...	...	1449	1549	...	...	1649
246	Nuneaton ▼ d.		0730	0736	0810	0817	...	...	0910	0910	1010	...	...	1110	1210	...	...	1310	1410	...	...	1510	1610	...	...	1710
278	**Birmingham** New St. ▼ a.		0803	0809	0843	0850	...	...	0943	0943	1043	...	...	1143	1243	...	...	1343	1443	...	...	1543	1643	...	...	1743

km		XC Ⓐ	XC ⑥			LE ⚒	XC ⚒	XC Ⓐ	XC ⑥	LE Ⓐ	LE ⑥	XC ⚒	XC ⚒		EM 2Ⓐ	LE ⑥	XC Ⓐ	LE Ⓐ	⑦	LE ⑦z	LE ⑦	XC ⑦	XC ⑦	LE ⑦	XC ⑦	XC ⑦
	London Liverpool St **200** d.	...	...	...	...	1438	...	...	...	1632	1638	...	...	...	...	1846	...	*1900*		...	...	...	...	...	...	...
	Ipswich 205 d.	...	...	...	...	1602	...	...	...	1749	1802	...	...	...	...	2002	...	2016		0755	0955	...	...	1155	...	...
	Stowmarket 205 d.	...	...	...	...	1613	...	...	...	1803	1813	...	...	...	...	2013	...	2030		0807	1007	...	...	1207	...	...
	Bury St. Edmunds 205 d.	...	...	...	...	1629	...	...	...	1823	1829	...	...	...	...	2029	...	2050		0823	1023	...	...	1223	...	...
0	**Stansted Airport** d.	1520	1525	...	...	|	1625	1718	1725	|	|	1821y	1921y	...	...	|	2021	|		|	|	1025	1125	|	1225	1325
40	**Cambridge** 205 d.	1600	1600	...	...	|	1700	1751	1800	|	|	1900	2000	...	...	|	2100	|		|	|	1056	1156	|	1256	1356
64	Ely 208 d.	1615	1615	...	...	1658	1715	1806	1815	1901	1858	1915	2015	...	...	2058	2115	2119		0852	1052	1111	1211	1252	1311	1411
89	March d.	1631	1631	...	...	1715	1731	1825	1833	1917	1915	1931	2031	...	...	2115	2131	2136		0909	1109	1127	1227	1309	1327	1427
113	**Peterborough** 208 a.	1649	1650	...	...	1737	1751	1850	1850	1942	1937	1951	2050	...	...	2137	2149	2158		0936	1136	1150	1250	1336	1350	1450
113	**Peterborough** d.	1652	1652	...	...	...	1752	1852	1852	...	...	1952	2052	...	2130	...	2152	...		...	...	1152	1252	...	1352	1452
131	Stamford d.	1705	1705	...	...	...	1805	1905	1905	...	...	2005	2105	...	2143	...	2205	...		...	...	1205	1305	...	1405	1505
154	Oakham d.	1721	1721	...	...	...	1821	1921	1921	...	...	2021	2121	...	2158	...	2221	...		...	...	1221	1321	...	1421	1521
174	Melton Mowbray d.	1733	1733	...	...	...	1833	1933	1933	...	...	2033	2133	...	2211	...	2233	...		...	...	1233	1333	...	1433	1533
197	**Leicester** ▼ d.	1749	1749	...	...	...	1849	1949	1949	...	...	2049	2149	...	...	...	2249	...		...	...	1249	1349	...	1449	1549
227	Nuneaton ▼ d.	1817	1810	...	...	...	1910	2010	2010	...	...	2110	2210	...	...	...	2310	...		...	...	1309	1409	...	1509	1609
259	**Birmingham** New St. ▼ a.	1850	1843	...	...	...	1943	2043	2043	...	...	2143	2243	...	...	...	2343	...		...	...	1342	1442	...	1542	1642

	LE ⑦	XC ⑦	XC ⑦	LE ⑦	XC ⑦	XC ⑦	LE ⑦	XC ⑦	XC ⑦
London Liverpool St **200** d.	...	...	...	...	...	...	...	...	...
Ipswich 205 d.	1355	...	...	1555	...	...	1755	...	...
Stowmarket 205 d.	1407	...	...	1607	...	...	1807	...	...
Bury St. Edmunds 205 d.	1423	...	...	1623	...	...	1823	...	...
Stansted Airport d.	|	1425	1525	|	1625	1725	|	1825	1925
Cambridge 205 d.	|	1456	1556	|	1656	1756	|	1856	1956
Ely 208 d.	1452	1511	1611	1652	1711	1811	1852	1911	2011
March d.	1509	1527	1627	1709	1727	1827	1909	1927	2027
Peterborough 208 a.	1536	1550	1650	1731	1750	1851	1932	1950	2050
Peterborough d.	...	1552	1652	...	1752	1852	...	1952	2052
Stamford d.	...	1605	1705	...	1805	1905	...	2005	2105
Oakham d.	...	1621	1721	...	1821	1921	...	2021	2121
Melton Mowbray d.	...	1632	1732	...	1833	1933	...	2033	2133
Leicester ▼ d.	...	1648	1748	...	1849	1949	...	2049	2149
Nuneaton ▼ d.	...	1709	1809	...	1909	2009	...	2109	2209
Birmingham New St. ▼ a.	...	1742	1842	...	1942	2042	...	2142	2242

	⚒	EM 2ⒶA	EM 2⑥A	XC Ⓐ	XC ⑥	EM 2⚒A		LE ⑥	LE Ⓐ	XC ⚒		XC Ⓐ
Birmingham New St. ▽ d.		...	...	0522	0522	...	...	...	...	0622	...	0722
Nuneaton ▽ d.		...	...	0550	0552	...	...	...	...	0652	...	0751
Leicester ▽ d.		...	...	0611	0613	...	...	...	...	0715	...	0817
Melton Mowbray d.		0529	0537	0627	0631	0652	...	...	...	0731	...	0833
Oakham d.		0541	0549	0640	0643	0704	...	...	...	0743	...	0845
Stamford d.		0602	0606	0654	0657	0718	...	...	...	0759	...	0901
Peterborough a.		0617	0619	0707	0711	0733	...	...	...	0816	...	0917
Peterborough 208 d.		0627	0627	0709	0713	0735	...	0745	0746	0818	...	0918
March a.		0642	0642	0729	0732	0750	...	0804	0805	0834	...	0934
Ely 208 a.		0701	0701	0752	0752	0811	...	0830	0830	0852	...	0952
Cambridge 205 a.		...	...	0807	0808	...	...	|	|	0908	...	1008
Stansted Airport a.		...	...	0845	0845	...	...	|	|	0945	...	1045
Bury St. Edmunds 205 d.		...	...	...	...	...	...	0856	0856	...	...	...
Stowmarket 205 d.		...	...	...	...	...	...	0912	0912	...	...	...
Ipswich 205 a.		...	...	...	...	...	...	0925	0926	...	...	...
London Liverpool St. **200** a.		...	...	...	...	...	...	1038	1046	...	...	...

	XC ⑥	LE Ⓐ	LE ⑥	XC ⚒		XC ⚒	LE ⚒	XC ⚒		XC ⚒	LE Ⓐ	LE ⑥	XC ⚒		XC ⚒	LE ⚒	XC ⚒		XC ⚒	LE ⚒	XC ⚒	XC Ⓐ		XC ⚒		LE Ⓐ
Birmingham New St. ▽ d.	0722	...	...	0822	...	0922	...	1022	...	1122	...	...	1222	...	1322	...	1422	...	1522	...	1622	1652	...	1722	...	...
Nuneaton ▽ d.	0752	...	...	0851	...	0952	...	1052	...	1152	...	...	1252	...	1352	...	1452	...	1552	...	1652	1722	...	1752	...	...
Leicester ▽ d.	0815	...	...	0915	...	1015	...	1115	...	1215	...	...	1315	...	1415	...	1515	...	1615	...	1715	1750	...	1815	...	...
Melton Mowbray d.	0831	...	...	0931	...	1031	...	1131	...	1231	...	...	1331	...	1431	...	1531	...	1631	...	1731	1807	...	1831	...	...
Oakham d.	0843	...	...	0943	...	1043	...	1143	...	1243	...	...	1343	...	1443	...	1543	...	1643	...	1743	1819	...	1843	...	...
Stamford d.	0859	...	...	0959	...	1059	...	1159	...	1259	...	...	1359	...	1459	...	1559	...	1659	...	1759	1840	...	1859	...	...
Peterborough a.	0922	...	...	1016	...	1115	...	1216	...	1315	...	...	1416	...	1515	...	1616	...	1717	...	1814	1857	...	1916	...	...
Peterborough 208 d.	0923	0945	0955	1018	...	1116	1145	1218	...	1316	1345	1345	1418	...	1516	1545	1618	...	1718	1745	1814	1859	...	1918	...	1946
March a.	0939	1004	1014	1034	...	1134	1204	1234	...	1334	1404	1404	1434	...	1534	1604	1634	...	1737	1804	1834	1915	...	1934	...	2005
Ely 208 a.	0958	1026	1032	1052	...	1152	1230	1252	...	1353	1430	1430	1452	...	1552	1630	1652	...	1759	1830	1852	1933	...	1952	...	2027
Cambridge 205 a.	1016	|	|	1108	...	1208	|	1308	...	1408	|	|	1508	...	1608	|	1708	...	1816	|	1908	1955	...	2008	...	|
Stansted Airport a.	1050	|	|	1145	...	1245	|	1345	...	1445	|	|	1545	...	1645	|	1745	...	1853	|	1945	...	...	2045	...	|
Bury St. Edmunds 205 d.	...	1056	1058	...	...	...	1256	...	...	...	1456	1456	...	...	...	1656	...	...	...	1856	...	...	...	...	...	2052
Stowmarket 205 d.	...	1112	1114	...	...	...	1312	...	...	...	1512	1512	...	...	...	1712	...	...	...	1912	...	...	...	...	...	2108
Ipswich 205 a.	...	1125	1127	...	...	...	1327	...	...	...	1525	1525	...	...	...	1727	...	...	...	1925	...	...	...	...	...	2125
London Liverpool St **200** a.	...	1245	1245	...	...	...	1445	...	...	...	*1648*	1645	...	...	...	1849	...	...	...	2046	...	...	...	...	...	2246

	LE ⑥	XC ⚒		XC ⚒	LE ⑥	LE Ⓐ	XC ⚒		⑦	LE ⑦z	LE ⑦	XC ⑦	LE ⑦	XC ⑦	XC ⑦	LE ⑦	XC ⑦	XC ⑦	LE ⑦	XC ⑦	XC ⑦	LE ⑦	XC ⑦	XC ⑦		XC ⑦
Birmingham New St. ▽ d.	...	1822	...	1922	...	...	2022	...		...	...	1122	...	1222	1322	...	1422	1522	...	1622	1722	...	1822	1922	...	2022
Nuneaton ▽ d.	...	1852	...	1952	...	...	2052	...		...	...	1152	...	1252	1352	...	1452	1552	...	1652	1752	...	1852	1952	...	2051
Leicester ▽ d.	...	1915	...	2015	...	...	2115	...		...	...	1215	...	1315	1415	...	1515	1615	...	1715	1815	...	1915	2015	...	2115
Melton Mowbray d.	...	1931	...	2031	...	...	2131	...		...	...	1233	...	1333	1433	...	1533	1631	...	1733	1831	...	1931	2031	...	2131
Oakham d.	...	1943	...	2043	...	...	2143	...		...	...	1245	...	1345	1445	...	1545	1643	...	1745	1843	...	1943	2043	...	2143
Stamford d.	...	1959	...	2059	...	...	2159	...		...	...	1301	...	1401	1501	...	1601	1659	...	1801	1859	...	1959	2059	...	2159
Peterborough a.	...	2016	...	2115	...	...	2216	...		...	...	1316	...	1416	1516	...	1616	1714	...	1816	1914	...	2014	2114	...	2214
Peterborough 208 d.	1945	2018	...	2116	2145	2205	2216	...		0946	1146	1318	1346	1418	1518	1546	1618	1718	1746	1818	1918	1944	2018	2118	...	2218
March a.	2004	2034	...	2134	2204	2224	2234	...		1005	1205	1334	1405	1434	1534	1605	1634	1734	1805	1834	1934	2003	2034	2134	...	2234
Ely 208 a.	2030	2052	...	2152	2230	2242	2255	...		1030	1230	1358	1430	1458	1558	1630	1652	1752	1830	1852	1952	2022	2052	2152	...	2252
Cambridge 205 a.	|	2108	...	2210	|	|	2315	...		|	|	1418	|	1517	1617	|	1707	1807	|	1907	2007	|	2107	2207	...	2312
Stansted Airport a.	|	2145	...	2245	|	|	...	...		|	|	1450	|	1550	1650	|	1745	1845	|	1945	2045	|	2145	2245	...	...
Bury St. Edmunds 205 d.	2056	...	...	...	2258	2308	...	...		1056	1256	...	1456	...	...	1656	...	...	1856	...	...	2047	...	...	...	...
Stowmarket 205 d.	2112	...	...	...	2317	2324	...	...		1112	1312	...	1512	...	...	1712	...	...	1912	...	...	2105	...	...	...	...
Ipswich 205 a.	2127	...	...	...	2332	2337	...	...		1125	1325	...	1527	...	...	1725	...	...	1927	...	...	2118	...	...	...	...
London Liverpool St. **200** a.	2249	...	...	...	...	...	...	...		...	...	...	...	...	...	...	...	...	...	...	...	...	...	...	...	...

▼ – Additional *XC* services **Leicester - Birmingham New Street**. *Journey 60 minutes.*
Ⓐ : 0616, 0643, 0724, 0816 and hourly until 2116.
⑥ : 0549, 0649, 0816 and hourly until 2216.
⑦ : 1119 and hourly until 1619; then 1716, 1816, 1919, 2008, 2119, 2219.
☛ Services call at **Hinckley** (± 18–20 minutes), **Nuneaton** (± 24–27 minutes) and **Coleshill Parkway** ★ (± 42–44 minutes) after Leicester.

▽ – Additional *XC* services **Birmingham New Street - Leicester**. *Journey 60 minutes.*
Ⓐ : 0552 and hourly until 1552; then 1609, 1709, 1752, 1852, 1952, 2052, 2219.
⑥ : 0552 and hourly until 2052; then 2222.
⑦ : 0952 and hourly until 2052; then 2222.
☛ Services call at **Coleshill Parkway** ★ (± 13–16 minutes), **Nuneaton** (± 30–33 minutes) and **Hinckley** (± 37–40 minutes) after Birmingham.

A – 2 Nottingham - Norwich (see Table **208**).
j – Connection on Ⓐ.
y – 4–5 minutes later on ⑥.
z – Until Sept. 6.

★ – 🚌 connections available to NEC and Birmingham International Airport.

EM 2nd class — NORWICH - NOTTINGHAM - SHEFFIELD - MANCHESTER - LIVERPOOL — 208

Services on ⑦ valid until September 6

km	⚒	⚒	⚒	⚒	⚒ m	⚒ m	Ⓐ m	⑥ m	⑥	Ⓐ	⚒	⚒	⚒	⚒	⚒	⚒	Ⓐ	⑥	⚒	⚒ m	⚒	Ⓐ A	
0	**Norwich** 206 d.	...	...	...	0550	0652	0757	0757	0857	0857	0957	1057	1157	1257	1357	1457	1552	1552	1657	1754	1857	...	...
49	Thetford 206 d.	...	...	...	0623	0720	0824	0824	0924	0924	1024	1124	1224	1324	1424	1524	1627	1623	1727	1827	1924	...	...
86	Ely 206 207 d.	...	...	...	0651	0744	0849	0854	0951	0952	1052	1152	1252	1352	1452	1552	1652	1652	1752	1852	1952	...	...
135	**Peterborough** 207 d.	...	...	...	0727	0830	0927	0930	1028	1030	1125	1225	1326	1426	1526	1627	1728	1727	1826	1931	2027	2130	...
181	Grantham d.	...	...	...	0758	0858	0958	0958	1058	1113	1156	1258	1358	1458	1558	1658	1759	1803	1858	2003	2058	|	...
218	**Nottingham** a.	...	...	...	0838	0936	1036	1036	1135	1143	1236	1336	1436	1536	1636	1736	1836	1836	1936	2037	2135	2250	...
218	**Nottingham** 170 172 d.	0518	0640	0745	0845	0945	1045	1045	1145	1145	1245	1345	1445	1545	1645	1745	1845	1845	1940	...	...	...	...
264	Chesterfield 170 172 d.	0549	0713	0818	0918	1018	1118	1118	1218	1218	1318	1418	1518	1618	1718	1818	1918	1918	2011	...	...	...	...
283	**Sheffield** 170 172 a.	0615	0731	0838	0938	1038	1138	1138	1238	1238	1338	1438	1538	1638	1734	1838	1939	1939	2028	...	...	...	...
283	**Sheffield** 187 d.	0620	0735	0842	0942	1042	1142	1142	1242	1242	1342	1442	1542	1642	1740	1842	1942	1942	2031	...	...	...	...
343	Stockport 187 a.	0722	0824	0925	1025	1125	1225	1225	1325	1325	1425	1525	1625	1725	1825	1925	2025	2025	2120	...	...	...	...
352	**Manchester** Piccadilly 187 a.	0734	0836	0936	1036	1136	1236	1236	1336	1336	1436	1536	1636	1737	1836	1936	2036	2037	2132	...	...	...	...
378	Warrington a.	0753	0857	0957	1057	1157	1257	1257	1357	1357	1457	1557	1657	1803	1857	1957	2057	...	...	...	...	...	...
389	Widnes a.	0801	0905	1005	1105	1205	1305	1305	1405	1405	1505	1605	1705	1811	1905	2005	2105	...	...	...	...	...	...
408	**Liverpool** Lime St. a.	0831	0931	1031	1131	1231	1331	1331	1431	1431	1531	1631	1731	1835	1935	2035	2135	...	...	...	...	...	...

⑦	⑦ z	⑦ y	⑦ z	⑦	⑦		⑦	⑦		⑦	⑦	⑦ z	⑦ y		⑦	⑦	⑦		⑦	⑦	⑦		
Norwich 206 d.	...	...	...	...	...	...	0933	1047	...	...	...	1349	1349	...	1447	1553	1657	...	1756	1857	2052	...	...
Thetford 206 d.	...	...	...	...	...	...	1000	1114	...	...	...	1416	1416	...	1514	1620	1724	...	1823	1924	2119	...	...
Ely 206 207 d.	...	...	...	...	...	...	1032	1139	...	...	...	1445	1445	...	1548	|	1748	...	1848	1949	2144	...	...
Peterborough 207 d.	...	...	...	...	...	...	1111	1218	...	...	...	1526	1526	...	1624	1714	1830	...	1926	2030	2222	...	...
Grantham d.	...	...	...	...	...	...	1156	1247	...	...	...	1602	1559	...	1656	1755	1901	...	1957	2103	2251	...	...
Nottingham a.	...	...	...	...	...	...	1233	1326	...	...	...	1631	1628	...	1725	1829	1930	...	2031	2135	2326	...	...
Nottingham 170 172 d.	0906	0931	0931	1040	1146	...	1239	1338	...	1438	1544	1634	1640	...	1737	1837	1938	...	...	...	...	...	...
Chesterfield 170 172 d.	0951	1008	1008	1114	1218	...	1317	1418	...	1513	1623	1720	1720	...	1817	1912	2010	...	...	...	...	...	...
Sheffield 170 172 a.	1016	1032	1030	1135	1235	...	1333	1436	...	1531	1639	1740	1740	...	1834	1931	2031	...	...	...	...	...	...
Sheffield 187 d.	1041	1041	1041	1138	1241	...	1338	1439	...	1537	1644	1744	1744	...	1837	1935	2035	...	...	...	...	...	...
Stockport 187 a.	1126	1126	1125	1225	1325	...	1425	1525	...	1625	1727	1825	1825	...	1925	2025	2124	...	...	...	...	...	...
Manchester Piccadilly 187 a.	1138	1138	1137	1237	1337	...	1437	1537	...	1637	1737	1837	1837	...	1937	2038	2136	...	...	...	...	...	...
Warrington a.	1158	1158	|	1258	1358	...	1458	1558	...	1658	1758	1858	1858	...	1958	...	...	...	...	...	...	...	...
Widnes a.	1206	1206	|	1306	1406	...	1506	1606	...	1706	1806	1906	1906	...	2006	...	...	...	...	...	...	...	...
Liverpool Lime St. a.	1230	1230	1230	1330	1430	...	1530	1630	...	1730	1830	1930	1930	...	2030	...	...	...	...	...	...	...	...

⚒	Ⓐ Am	⑥x Am	⑥ wm	⑥x Am	Ⓐ	⑥ wm	⑥ w	Ⓐ	Ⓐ	⑥	⚒	⚒	⚒	⚒	⚒	⚒	⚒	⑥	Ⓐ m	⑥ m	⚒	Ⓐ	⑥
Liverpool Lime St. d.	...	...	...	...	...	...	...	...	...	...	0647	0742	0852	0952	1052	1152	1252	1352	1452	1452	1552	1652	1652
Widnes d.	...	...	...	...	...	...	...	...	...	...	0707	0805	0911	1011	1111	1211	1311	1411	1511	1511	1611	1711	1711
Warrington d.	...	...	...	...	...	...	...	...	...	...	0715	0813	0919	1019	1119	1219	1319	1419	1519	1519	1619	1719	1719
Manchester Piccadilly 187 d.	...	...	...	...	...	...	...	...	...	...	0742	0843	0943	1043	1143	1243	1343	1443	1543	1543	1643	1743	1743
Stockport 187 d.	...	...	...	...	...	...	...	...	...	...	0754	0854	0954	1054	1154	1254	1354	1454	1554	1554	1654	1754	1754
Sheffield 187 a.	...	...	...	...	...	...	...	...	...	...	0834	0935	1035	1135	1235	1335	1435	1535	1635	1635	1737	1841	1834
Sheffield 170 172 d.	...	...	...	...	...	...	...	...	...	...	0838	0938	1038	1138	1238	1338	1438	1538	1638	1638	1744	1845	1838
Chesterfield 170 172 d.	...	...	...	...	...	...	...	...	...	...	0853	0953	1053	1153	1253	1353	1453	1553	1656	1653	1758	1901	1853
Nottingham 170 172 a.	...	...	...	...	...	...	...	...	...	...	0930	1030	1130	1230	1330	1431	1530	1633	1731	1729	1833	1938	1933
Nottingham d.	0451	0504	0510	0554	0556	0630	0745	0752	0834	0834	0934	1034	1134	1234	1334	1434	1534	...	1734	1734	1834	...	...
Grantham d.	|	|	0551	|	|	|	0816	0825	0911	0911	1008	1106	1207	1306	1407	1507	1607	...	1812	1815	1905	...	...
Peterborough 207 d.	0627f	0627f	0627	0735	0735	0735	0846	0859	0940	0946	1044	1138	1240	1338	1440	1535	1636r	...	1842	1842	1937	...	...
Ely 206 207 a.	0701	0701	0701	0811	0811	0813	0919	0941	1013	1019	1116	1211	1313	1411	1514	1609	1709r	...	1924	1920	2012	...	...
Thetford 206 a.	0728	0730	0730	0836	0836	0839	0944	1005	1038	1044	1141r	1235	1339	1435	1538	1634	1733r	...	1949	1944	2035	...	...
Norwich 206 a.	0813	0813	0813	0915	0913	0918	1019	1043	1113	1118	1213r	1313	1413	1513	1613	1713	1813r	...	2022	2018	2113	...	...

	⚒	⚒	⚒	⑥	Ⓐ		⑦	⑦ m	⑦	⑦	⑦	⑦		⑦	⑦		⑦	⑦	⑦	⑦	⑦	⑦		⑦
Liverpool Lime St. d.	1752	1852	1952	2052	2137	...		...	...	...	...	...	...	1252	1352	...	1452	1552	1652	1752	1852	1952	...	2122
Widnes d.	1811	1911	2011	2111	2155	...		...	...	...	...	...	...	1311	1411	...	1511	1611	1711	1811	1911	2011	...	2139
Warrington d.	1819	1919	2019	2119	2203	...		...	...	...	...	...	...	1319	1419	...	1519	1619	1719	1819	1919	2019	...	2147
Manchester Piccadilly d.	1843	1943	2043	2143	2228	...		...	...	...	...	1244	...	1344	1444	...	1544	1644	1744	1844	1944	2044	...	2211
Stockport d.	1854	1954	2054	2152	2237	...		...	...	...	...	1254	...	1354	1454	...	1554	1654	1754	1854	1954	2054	...	2228
Sheffield a.	1935	2036	2135	2231	2335	...		...	...	...	...	1342	...	1443	1533	...	1636	1736	1837	1934	2034	2136	...	2323
Sheffield d.	1938	2041	2138	2235	2338	...		...	1049	...	1249	1349	...	1453	1543	...	1640	1739	1841	1940	2040	2140	...	2329
Chesterfield d.	1953	2058	2154	2251	0002	...		...	1104	...	1303	1403	...	1507	1557	...	1656	1754	1856	1955	2055	2154	...	2342
Nottingham a.	2031	2138t	2238t	2333	0041	...		...	1138	...	1339	1440	...	1544	1633	...	1732	1829	1936	2036	2136	2235	...	0023
Nottingham d.	2034	...	...	...	...	...		0952	1145	1239	1341	1445	...	1547	1645	...	1736	1843	...	...	...	...	...	...
Grantham d.	2107	...	...	...	...	...		1030	1218	1314	1414	|	...	1620	1725f	...	1818	1916	...	...	...	...	...	...
Peterborough d.	2136	...	...	...	...	...		1109	1253	1343	1442	1605	...	1653	1753	...	1847	1958	...	...	...	...	...	...
Ely a.	2210r	...	...	...	...	...		1148	1332	1421	1521	1638	...	1731	1831	...	1920	2031	...	...	...	...	...	...
Thetford a.	2234r	...	...	...	...	...		1220	1357	1448	1548	1702	...	1756	1855	...	1948	2055	...	...	...	...	...	...
Norwich a.	2318r	...	...	...	...	...		1305	1435	1528	1635	1735	...	1829	1929	...	2028	2135	...	...	...	...	...	...

A – Via Melton Mowbray, Table **207**.
f – Arrives 8–10 minutes earlier.
m – Also calls at March (± 15 minutes from Peterborough and Ely).
r – 3–6 minutes later on ⑥.
t – 3–6 minutes earlier on ⑥.
w – July 18 - Sept. 5.
x – Until July 11 and from Sept. 12.
y – Until July 12.
z – July 19 - Sept. 6.

NT 2nd class — MIDDLESBROUGH - NEWCASTLE — 209

km	⚒	Ⓐ	⚒ S	⚒	⚒		⚒ S	⚒		⚒	⚒	⚒	⚒		⑦	⑦	⑦		⑦		⑦	⑦		⑦
0	**Middlesbrough** 211 d.	0545	0649	0656	0732	...	0742	0832	and at the same minutes past each hour until	1730	1830	1920	2030	...		0930	1130	...	1330	...	1530	1730	...	1930
25	Darlington 211 d.	0614	0720	|	|	...	0815	|		|	|	|	|	...		|	|	...	|	...	|	|	...	|
9	Stockton d.	|	|	0708	0743	...	|	0843		1741	1841	1931	2041	...		0941	1141	...	1341	...	1541	1741	...	1941
28	Hartlepool d.	|	|	0727	0802	...	|	0900		1802	1900	1949	2100	...		1000	1200	...	1400	...	1600	1800	...	2000
57	Sunderland d.	|	|	0755	0828	...	|	0928		1830	1927	2027	2127	...		1028	1228	...	1428	...	1628	1828	...	2028
77	**Newcastle** a.	0655	0802	0817	0852	...	0900	0954		1853	1948	2049	2148	...		1050	1248	...	1448	...	1649	1848	...	2049

⚒	⚒	⚒	⚒		⚒	⚒	⚒	⚒	⚒	Ⓐ	⑥	⑥	Ⓐ		⑦	⑦p	⑦q		⑦	⑦	⑦	⑦	⑦	⑦S
Newcastle d.	0600	0700	0730	and at the same minutes past each hour until	1630	1653	1729	1830	1928	2045	2100	2150	2200	...		0945	1000	...	1200	1359	1600	1800	2000	2106
Sunderland d.	0620	0720	0750		1650	1715	1750	1850	1950	2105	2120	|	|	...		1006	1020	...	1221	1421	1621	1821	2021	|
Hartlepool d.	0646	0745	0815		1715	1739	1815	1915	2015	2129	2145	|	|	...		1031	1045	...	1245	1445	1645	1845	2045	|
Stockton d.	...	0804	0833		1733	1757	1833	1933	2033	2147	2203	|	|	...		1049	1103	...	1304	1504	1704	1904	2104	|
Darlington 211 d.	...	|	|		|	|	|	|	|	|	|	2230	2242	...		|	|	...	|	|	|	|	|	2145
Middlesbrough 211 a.	...	0822	0849		1749	1816	1848	1948	2050	2202	2218	2257	2310	...		1103	1118	...	1320	1519	1725	1918	2120	2207

S – To/from Saltburn, Table **211**.
p – Until Sept. 13.
q – From Sept. 20.

NT 2nd class — MIDDLESBROUGH - WHITBY — 210

km		Ⓐ	Ⓐ	Ⓐ		Ⓐ	Ⓐ		⑥	⑥	⑥		⑥	⑥		⑦	⑦h	⑦h		⑦h	⑦h		⑦h	
0	**Middlesbrough** 209 211 d.		0708	1038	...	1416	1740	...		0706	1038	...	1412	1738	...		0847	0945	...	1106	1417	...	1529	...
46	Grosmont ◧ d.		0820	1144	...	1522	1846	...		0814	1144	...	1518	1844	...		0953	1057	...	1213	1523	...	1637	...
56	**Whitby** ◧ a.		0841	1205	...	1543	1907	...		0835	1205	...	1539	1905	...		1014	1118	...	1233	1544	...	1658	...

	Ⓐ	Ⓐ	Ⓐ		Ⓐ	Ⓐ		⑥	⑥	⑥		⑥	⑥		⑦	⑦h	⑦h		⑦h	⑦h		⑦h	
Whitby ◧ d.		0852	1241	...	1605	1915	...		0845	1241	...	1550	1915	...		1024	1243	...	1557	1709	...	1800	...
Grosmont ◧ d.		0909	1258	...	1622	1932	...		0902	1258	...	1607	1932	...		1041	1300	...	1614	1726	...	1817	...
Middlesbrough 209 211 a.		1018	1407	...	1735	2041	...		1011	1407	...	1716	2041	...		1202	1409	...	1725	1835	...	1928	...

h – Until Sept. 13.
◧ – The North Yorkshire Moors Railway operate steam services (Whitby -) Grosmont - Pickering and v.v. in summer. ✆ 01751 472508, fax 01751 476048.

211 BISHOP AUCKLAND - MIDDLESBROUGH - SALTBURN
2nd class NT

Services on ⑦ valid until September 13

km		Ⓐ	Ⓐ	Ⓐ	Ⓐ	Ⓐ	Ⓐ	Ⓐ	Ⓐ	Ⓐ	Ⓐ	Ⓐ	Ⓐ
0	**Bishop Auckland** d.	0721	...	0925	1003	1140	1340	1530	1630	1803	1903	2115	...
4	Shildon d.	0726	...	0930	1008	1145	1345	1535	1635	1808	1908	2120	...
	Newcastle 209 d.	|	|	|	|	|	|	|	|	|	|	|	2200
19	**Darlington** ▶ d.	0748	0810	0953	1030	1207	1408	1557	1659	1833	1931	2144	2242
43	**Middlesbrough** ▶ d.	0812	0839	1024	1055	1232	1433	1624	1724	1859	1956	2209	2310
55	Redcar Central ▶ d.	...	0851	1035	1105	1242	1443	1636	1735	1909	2006	2220	...
63	**Saltburn** ▶ a.	...	0907	1052	1122	1258	1459	1655	1752	1926	2023	2237	...

	⑥	⑥	⑥	⑥	⑥	⑥	⑥	⑥	⑥	⑥	⑥
Bishop Auckland d.	0735	0923	0953	1140	1326	1532	1700	1800	1859	2117	...
Shildon d.	0740	0928	0958	1145	1331	1537	1705	1805	1904	2122	...
Newcastle 209 d.	|	|	|	|	|	|	|	|	|	|	2150
Darlington ▶ d.	0809	0951	1020	1206	1353	1600	1727	1830	1927	2144	2230
Middlesbrough ▶ d.	0839	1020	1054	1233	1420	1623	1754	1901	1954	2209	2257
Redcar Central ▶ d.	0851	1030	1104	1243	1431	1635	1806	1901	2004	2220	...
Saltburn ▶ a.	0908	1047	1120	1259	1448	1652	1823	1928	2021	2237	...

	⑦	⑦	⑦	⑦	⑦	⑦	⑦	⑦	⑦	⑦
Bishop Auckland d.	0840	1029	1240	1449	1656	...	1849	...	1955	...
Shildon d.	0845	1034	1245	1454	1701	...	1854	...	2000	...
Newcastle 209 d.	|	|	|	|	|	...	|	...	|	2106
Darlington ▶ d.	0907	1104	1310	1516	1724	1831	1916	1932	2032	2145
Middlesbrough ▶ d.	0940	1130	1335	1542	1750	1854	...	1958	2058	2208
Redcar Central ▶ d.	...	1141	1346	1552	1801	1904	...	2008	2108	2218
Saltburn ▶ a.	...	1157	1402	1608	1817	1919	...	2023	2124	2234

	Ⓐ	Ⓐ	Ⓐ	Ⓐ	Ⓐ	Ⓐ	Ⓐ	Ⓐ	Ⓐ	Ⓐ	Ⓐ	Ⓐ	Ⓐ
Saltburn ▷ d.	...	...	0624	0717	0738	0830	1000	1200	1400	1503	1630	1730	1930
Redcar Central ▷ d.	...	...	0637	0730	0751	0843	1013	1213	1413	1516	1643	1743	1943
Middlesbrough ▷ d.	0545	...	0649	0742	0802	0855	1024	1224	1424	1527	1657	1755	1955
Darlington ▷ d.	0614	0647	0720	0815	0833	0926	1055	1255	1454	1557	1728	1832	2030
Newcastle 209 a.	0655	|	0802	0900	|	|	|	|	|	|	|	|	|
Shildon d.	...	0706	...	...	0852	0945	1114	1314	1513	1616	1747	1851	2049
Bishop Auckland a.	...	0718	...	...	0859	0952	1121	1321	1519	1624	1755	1858	2056

	⑥	⑥	⑥	⑥	⑥	⑥	⑥	⑥	⑥	⑥	⑥	⑥	⑥
Saltburn ▷ d.	...	...	0624	0717	0738	0830	1000	1156	1358	1530	1630	1728	1935
Redcar Central ▷ d.	...	...	0637	0730	0751	0843	1013	1209	1411	1543	1643	1741	1948
Middlesbrough ▷ d.	0550	...	0649	0742	0802	0855	1024	1220	1423	1555	1655	1756	1959
Darlington ▷ d.	0618	0648	0720	0815	0838	0924	1057	1250	1453	1625	1730	1826	2036
Newcastle 209 a.	...	|	0802	0900	|	|	|	|	|	|	|	|	|
Shildon d.	...	0707	...	...	0857	0943	1116	1309	1512	1644	1749	1845	2055
Bishop Auckland a.	...	0719	...	...	0904	0950	1123	1316	1520	1652	1758	1853	2102

	⑦	⑦	⑦	⑦	⑦	⑦	⑦
Saltburn ▷ d.	...	...	1100	1300	1520	*1648*	*1720*
Redcar Central ▷ d.	...	...	1113	1313	1533	*1701*	*1733*
Middlesbrough ▷ d.	...	0915	1124	1325	1550	1725	1837
Darlington ▷ d.	0805	0951	1154	1406	1622	1815	1923
Newcastle 209 a.	|	|	|	|	|	|	|
Shildon d.	0824	1010	1213	1425	1641	1834	1942
Bishop Auckland a.	0834	1020	1219	1431	1646	1839	1947

▶ – Additional trains Darlington - Middlesbrough - Redcar - Saltburn:
Ⓐ: 0640, 0705, 0724, 0900, 0936, 1100, 1135, 1230, 1256, 1330, 1432, 1500, 1530, 1630, 1734, 1803, 2030.
⑥: 0640, 0658, 0719, 0856, 0923, 1047, 1130, 1235, 1258, 1331, 1435, 1504, 1532, 1627, 1704, 1802, 2030.
⑦: 0841, 0920, 1003, 1202, 1410, 1542, 1619, 1831.

▷ – Additional trains Saltburn - Redcar - Middlesbrough - Darlington:
Ⓐ: 0800, 0921, 1030, 1100, 1130, 1230, 1300, 1330, 1430, 1530, 1555, 1700, 1800, 1830, 1900, 2030, 2130, 2240.
⑥: 0800, 0913, 1030, 1100, 1130, 1230, 1300, 1330, 1430, 1500, 1600, 1659, 1800, 1828, 1900, 2030, 2130, 2240.
⑦: 0936, 1028, 1201, 1414, 1625, 1648, 1827, 1923, 2031, 2130, 2238.

212 NEWCASTLE - CARLISLE
2nd class NT

Valid until September 6

km		Ⓐ	⑥ G	Ⓐ G	⚒	⚒	⚒	⚒	⚒	⚒	⚒ S	⑥	Ⓐ	⚒	⚒	⚒	⚒ W	⚒ S	⚒	⚒	⚒	Ⓐ	⑥	⚒	Ⓐ
0	**Newcastle** ‡ d.	0630	0635	0654	0756	0824	0853	0924	1024	1122	1239	1324	1326	1354	1424	1524	1624	1713	1754	1824	1910	2010	2014	2122	2230
36	Hexham ‡ d.	0710	0711	0720	0840	0859	0939	0955	1055	1156	1308	1356	1359	1436	1457	1556	1703	1745	1831	1903	1949	2051	2055	2201	2311
62	Haltwhistle d.	...	0733	0743	...	0921	...	1016	1114	1219	1326	1414	1418	...	1517	1618	1723	1808	1854	1921	2009	...	...	2223	...
99	**Carlisle** a.	...	0808	0817	...	0956	...	1047	1146	1254	1400	1445	1454	...	1549	1656	1758	1846	1929	1957	2042	...	...	2258	...

	⑦	⑦	⑦	⑦	⑦	⑦	⑦	⑦	⑦	⑦	⑦
Newcastle d.	0910	1010	1110	1210	1310	1410	1510	1610	1710	1810	2015
Hexham d.	0949	1049	1149	1249	1349	1449	1551	1649	1749	1849	2054
Haltwhistle d.	1011	1111	1208	1311	1408	1508	1611	1710	1808	1911	2116
Carlisle a.	1045	1145	1238	1345	1438	1540	1645	1740	1838	1945	2150

	⚒	⚒	⚒ D	⚒	⚒ R	⚒	⚒	⚒	⚒	⚒ S	⚒	⚒	⑥	Ⓐ	⚒	⚒	⚒ G	⚒	⚒	⚒	Ⓐ
Carlisle d.	...	0625	0713	0829	0933	...	1033	1134	1230	1336	1436	1526	1629	1637	...	1720	1818	1945	...	2120	...
Haltwhistle d.	...	0656	0745	0901	1001	...	1101	1202	1301	1405	1504	1556	1700	1708	...	1752	1846	2013	...	2152	...
Hexham ‡ d.	0613	0718	0807	0923	1019	1044	1121	1223	1323	1424	1522	1616	1722	1731	1844	1814	1904	2031	2114	2214	2314
Newcastle ‡ a.	0652	0804	0857	1001	1055	1125	1159	1257	1400	1459	1600	1650	1759	1808	1927	1856	1947	2114	2156	2259	2357

	⑦	⑦	⑦	⑦	⑦		⑦	⑦	⑦	⑦	⑦		⑦
Carlisle d.	0905	1005	1112	1205	1312	...	1412	1505	1612	1712	1805	...	2015
Haltwhistle d.	0936	1036	1140	1236	1340	...	1440	1536	1640	1740	1836	...	2043
Hexham ‡ d.	0959	1059	1159	1259	1359	...	1459	1559	1659	1759	1859	...	2059
Newcastle ‡ a.	1040	1140	1240	1340	1440	...	1540	1640	1740	1840	1940	...	2143

D – From Dumfries. R – From Girvan. W – To Whitehaven. ‡ – Additional local trains run Newcastle - Hexham and v.v. on ⚒.
G – To / from Glasgow. S – To / from Stranraer.

214 CARLISLE - DUMFRIES - GLASGOW
2nd class SR

km		⚒	⚒	⑥	Ⓐ	⑥	⚒	⑥	⑦	⚒	⑦	⚒	Ⓐ	⑥	⑥	⚒	⑥	⚒	⚒	⑦	⑥	Ⓐ	⑥	⑦	⑥	Ⓐ
	Newcastle 212 d.	...	...	0635	0654	...	...	...	...	...	...	1239	...	...	...	...	...	...	1713	...	...	...	...	...	...	...
0	**Carlisle** 154 d.	0540	0609	0819	0819	0952	1107	1218	1253	1309	1347	1422	1500	1502	1522	1614	1724	1758	1852	1935	2008	2108	2108	2112	2256	2307
28	Annan d.	0600	0631	0838	0838	1012	1126	1238	1312	1329	1407	1442	1520	1525	1543	1634	1744	1817	1913	1954	2028	2128	2128	2132	2316	2327
53	**Dumfries** d.	0618	0650	0855	0855	1029	1143	1255	1328	1347	1424	1458	1539	1541	1600	1653	1801	1834	1930	2011	2044	2144	2145	2149	2333	2344
124	Auchinleck d.	...	0738	0944	0943	...	1231	...	1416	1435	...	1548	1628	1629	...	...	...	1922	2018	2059	2132	2232	...	...	...	...
146	**Kilmarnock 215** d.	...	0758	1004	1004	...	1250	...	1435	1455	...	1609	1646	1647	...	...	...	1950	2038	2118	2150	2250	...	...	...	...
	Stranraer 215 a.	...	|	|	|	...	|	...	|	|	...	1755	...	...	...	...	...	|	2224	|	|	|	...	...	...	...
185	**Glasgow** Central 154 a.	...	0837	1041	1041	...	1329	...	1514	1533	...	...	1731	1731	...	...	...	2027	...	2155	2227	2328	...	...	...	...

	⚒	⚒	⚒ G	⑥	Ⓐ	⑥	⚒	⚒	⑦	⚒	⑥	⑦	⑥	Ⓐ	⑥	⑦	⚒	⚒	⑥	⚒	⑥	⑦	Ⓐ	⑥	⑦
Glasgow Central 154 d.	...	...	...	0828	0828	...	0953	...	...	1203	...	...	1303	1303	...	1448	...	1548	...	2003	...	...	2203	2203	2228
Stranraer 215 d.	...	...	...	|	|	...	|	1000	...	|	...	...	|	|	...	|	...	|	...	|	...	...	|	|	|
Kilmarnock 215 d.	...	...	0741	0909	0913	...	1039	1147	...	1241	...	...	1342	1342	...	1528	...	1627	...	2040	...	...	2243	2243	2305
Auchinleck d.	...	...	0757	0925	0929	...	1056	1204	...	1257	...	...	1359	1359	...	1545	...	1644	...	2057	...	...	2259	2259	2322
Dumfries d.	0628	0734	0849	1015	1017	1039	1147	1254	1300	1348	1426	1437	1447	1447	1615	1635	1701	1731	1820	2147	2210	2214	2349	2353	0012
Annan d.	0643	0749	0906	1030	1032	1054	1202	1309	1315	1403	1441	1452	1504	1504	1630	1650	1716	1747	1835	2202	2225	2229	0006	0008	0027
Carlisle 154 a.	0708	0811	0928	1054	1056	1114	1226	1332	1337	1426	1503	1516	1526	1533	1652	1718	1738	1816	1859	2224	2247	2251	0026	0034	0049
Newcastle 212 a.	0857	...	1055	...	...	...	...	1459	...	...	...	...	...	...	...	...	...	1947	...	...	...	...	...	...	...

G – From Girvan, Table **215**.

215 GLASGOW and KILMARNOCK - STRANRAER
2nd class SR

km		⚒	⚒		Ⓐ	⑥	⚒	⚒		⚒ N	⚒	⚒	⑥	Ⓐ	⚒	⚒ N	⚒		⑦ p	⑦ q	⑦	⑦
0	**Glasgow** Central 216 d.	...	0713	...	0903	0903	1142	...	...	...	...	...	...	...	...	...	...	...	1137	1143	1625	...
12	Paisley Gilmour St 216 d.	...	0724	...	|	|	1153	...	...	...	...	...	...	...	...	...	...	...	1148	1154	1639	...
43	Kilwinning 216 d.	...	0741	...	|	|	1210	...	...	...	...	...	...	...	...	...	...	...	1205	1211	1656	...
	Kilmarnock 214 d.	...	|	0910	0954	0955	|	1310	...	1609	1631	...	1811	1815	...	2038	2244	...	|	|	|	2244
56	Troon 216 d.	...	|	0924	1006	1007	|	1322	...	1621	1644	...	1824	1827	...	2051	2256	...	|	|	|	2256
61	Prestwick Airport ✈ 216 d.	...	|	0929	1011	1012	|	1327	...	|	1649	...	1829	1832	...	|	2301	...	|	|	|	2301
67	**Ayr** 216 d.	0600	0800	0943	1022	1022	1230	1338	...	1634	1700	1810	1838	1839	1931	2101	2311	...	1230	1230	1719	2311
101	Girvan d.	0627	0826	1009	1051	1051	1301	1405	...	1700	1727	1837	...	...	1957	2127	2337	...	1256	1256	1747	2337
121	Barrhill d.	...	0845	1035	...	...	1320	...	...	1719	...	...	...	...	2016	2146	0001	...	1314	1314	1806	0001
163	**Stranraer** a.	...	0921	1111	...	...	1356	...	...	1755	...	...	...	...	2052	2224	0037	...	1351	1351	1842	0037
	Belfast Port ⛴ 2070 a.	...	*1150*	...	...	...	*1640*	...	...	*2210*	...	...	...	...	...	...	...	...	*1640*	*1640*	*2210*	...

N – From Newcastle.
p – Not Nov. 29, Dec. 6.
q – Nov. 29, Dec. 6 only.

SR 2nd class STRANRAER - KILMARNOCK and GLASGOW 215

km		⚒	⚒ N	⚒	⚒ N	⚒	⚒		⚒	⚒	⚒	⚒	⚒	⚒		Ⓐ		⑦	⑦		⑦		⑦	
	Belfast Port ⛴ **2070** d.		...	...	*0725*	...	...	...	...	*1215*	...	...	*1705*	...	...	...	...		*0725*	...	*1215*	...	*1705*	...
0	**Stranraer** d.		...	0709	1000	...	1148	...	...	1437	...	...	1940	2110	...	2325	...		1040	...	1440	...	1940	...
42	Barrhill d.		...	0743	1034	...	1222	...	...	1511	...	...	2019	2150	...	2359	...		1114	...	1514	...	2015	...
61	Girvan d.		0640	0801	1052	1140	1240	...	1440	1529	1732	1842	2037	2208	...	0019	...		1132	...	1532	...	2033	...
96	**Ayr** 216 d.		0710	0836	1122	1209	1309	...	1517	1556	1803	1909	2106	2238	...	0047	...		1200	...	1559	...	2100	...
102	Prestwick Airport ✈ 216 d.		|	0843	|	1216	1316	...	1524	|	...	1916	|	|	...	...	...		|	...	|	...	|	...
106	Troon 216 d.		0718	0848	1130	1221	1321	...	1529	|	...	1921	|	|	...	...	...		|	...	|	...	|	...
120	**Kilmarnock 214** a.		0740	0903	1146	1237	1337	...	1542	|	...	1942	|	|	...	...	...		|	...	|	...	|	...
	Kilwinning 216 d.		...	|	...	...	|	...	|	1613	...	...	2121	2254	...	...	...		1215	...	1614	...	2115	...
	Paisley Gilmour St 216 a.		...	|	...	...	|	...	|	1633	...	...	2144	2314	...	...	...		1236	...	1637	...	2136	...
	Glasgow Central 216 a.		...	0950	...	...	1427	...	1632	1645	...	...	2155	2326	...	...	...		1251	...	1649	...	2148	...

N – To Newcastle.

SR 2nd class GLASGOW - AYR 216

Services on ⑦ valid until September 27

km		⚒	⚒	⚒	⚒	⚒	❖⊡	⚒	⚒			⑦	⑦	⑦		⑦	⑦	⑦		⑦		
0	**Glasgow** Central 215 d.		0600	0630	0700	0730	and at	2300	2330	...	...		0900	0930	and at	1800	1830	1900	and at	2300	...	...
12	Paisley Gilmour St 215 d.		0611	0641	0711	0741	the same	2311	2341	...	...		0911	0941	the same	1811	1841	1911	the same	2311	...	...
43	Kilwinning 215 d.		0629	0659	0729	0759	minutes	2329	2359	...	...		0929	0959	minutes	1829	1859	1929	minutes	2329	...	...
48	Irvine d.		0633	0703	0733	0803	past	2333	0003	...	...		0933	1003	past	1833	1903	1933	past	2333	...	...
56	Troon 215 d.		0639	0711	0739	0811	each	2339	0011	...	...		0941	1009	each	1841	1909	1941	each	2341	...	...
61	Prestwick Airport ✈ 215 d.		0643	0715	0743	0815	hour	2343	0015	...	...		0945	1013	hour	1845	1913	1945	hour	2345	...	...
67	**Ayr** 215 a.		0652	0724	0752	0825	until	2352	0025	...	...		0954	1022	until	1854	1922	1954	until	2354	...	...

	⚒	⚒	⚒	⚒	⚒	⚒	❖	⚒	⚒	⚒	⚒	⚒	⚒		⑦	⑦	⑦		⑦	⑦	⑦	⑦	⑦
Ayr 215 d.		0540	0613	0643	0713	0743	and at	1913	1943	2043	2143	2213	2300	...		0913	0943	and at	1913	1943	2043	2143	2300
Prestwick Airport ✈ 215 d.		0548	0621	0651	0721	0750	the same	1920	1950	2050	2150	2221	2308	...		0920	0950	the same	1920	1950	2050	2150	2307
Troon 215 d.		0552	0625	0655	0725	0754	minutes	1924	1954	2054	2154	2225	2312	...		0924	0954	minutes	1924	1954	2054	2154	2311
Irvine d.		0559	0632	0702	0732	0759	past	1929	2001	2101	2159	2232	2319	...		0929	1001	past	1929	2001	2101	2201	2318
Kilwinning 215 d.		0604	0637	0707	0737	0804	each	1934	2006	2106	2204	2237	2324	...		0934	1006	each	1934	2006	2106	2206	2323
Paisley Gilmour St 215 a.		0632	0655	0726	0757	0823	hour	1953	2024	2124	2225	2257	2346	...		0953	1020	hour	1953	2024	2124	2224	2341
Glasgow Central 215 a.		0643	0707	0738	0809	0834	until	2004	2036	2136	2236	2309	2358	...		1004	1036	until	2004	2036	2136	2236	2353

⊡ – The 1730 Ⓐ service from Glasgow stops at Paisley to pick up only and does not call at Kilwinning.

❖ – Timings may vary by up to 8 minutes.

SR 2nd class GLASGOW - ARDROSSAN - LARGS 217

Services on ⑦ valid until September 27

km		⚒	⚒	⚒	⚒	Ⓐ	⚒	⚒	⚒	⚒	❖	⚒	⚒	⚒	⚒	⚒	⚒	⚒	⚒	⚒	❖	⚒	⚒
0	**Glasgow** Central 215 d.		0615	0645	0715	0815	0833	0845	0915	0945	and at	1515	1545	1618	1650	1720	1735	1745	1815	1845	and at	2215	2245
12	Paisley Gilmour St 215 d.		0626	0656	0726	0826	0844	0856	0926	0956	the same	1526	1556	1629	1701	1732	1746	1756	1826	1856	the same	2226	2256
43	Kilwinning 215 d.		0654	0720	0752	0854	0910	0918	0954	1020	minutes	1554	1618	1657	1727	1754	1814	1820	1854	1918	minutes	2254	2318
50	**Ardrossan** Sth Beach d.		0702	0730	0802	0902	0918	0926	1002	1028	past	1602	1626	1711	1737	1803	1822	1828	1902	1926	past each	2302	2326
54	Fairlie d.		0713	...	0814	...	...	0937	...	1039	each hour	...	1637	1722	...	1814	...	1839	...	1937	hour until	...	2337
69	**Largs** a.		0720	...	0822	...	...	0944	...	1047	until	...	1644	1728	...	1820	...	1848	...	1944		...	2344

	⚒	Ⓐ		⑦	⑦		⑦			
Glasgow Central 215 d.	2315	2345	⑦	0840	0940		2240	...	...	...
Paisley Gilmour St 215 d.	2326	2356		0851	0951	and	2251	...	...	...
Kilwinning 215 d.	2354	0024		0915	1019	hourly	2318	...	...	...
Ardrossan Sth Beach d.	0002	0032		0923	1027	until	2326	...	...	...
Fairlie d.	0014j	0043f		...	1039		2338	...	...	...
Largs a.	0019j	0049f		...	1045		2344	...	...	...

		⚒	⚒	Ⓐ	⚒	Ⓐ	Ⓐ	Ⓐ	⑥	⚒
Largs d.	⚒	...	0641	0723	0742	...	0828	...	0851	...
Fairlie d.		...	0646	0728	0747	...	0833	...	0856	...
Ardrossan South Beach d.		0634	0657	0739	0758	0817	0844	0907	0907	0936
Kilwinning 215 d.		0643	0710	0749	0808	0825	0853	0916	0916	0945
Paisley Gilmour St 215 a.		0711	0734	0813	0834	0853	0917	0940	0940	1011
Glasgow Central 215 a.		0722	0747	0824	0846	0904	0930	0953	0953	1022

	⚒	⚒	❖	⚒	⚒	⚒	⚒	⚒	⚒	⚒	⚒	❖	⚒	⚒			⑦	⑦	⑦	❖	⑦	⑦	
Largs d.	0953	...	and at	1553	...	1650	...	1735	...	...	1853	and at	...	2253	...	⑦	0853	0958	1053		2153	2258	...
Fairlie d.	0958	...	the same	1558	...	1655	...	1740	...	...	1858	the same	...	2258	...		0858	1003	1058	and	2158	2303	...
Ardrossan Sth Beach d.	1009	1034	minutes	1609	1634	1706	1740	1751	1806	1834	1909	minutes	2234	2309	...		0909	1014	1109	hourly	2209	2314	...
Kilwinning 215 d.	1018	1043	past	1618	1643	1715	1748	1800	1816	1843	1918	past	2243	2318	...		0918	1023	1118	until	2218	2327	...
Paisley Gilmour St 215 a.	1040	1111	each hour	1640	1711	1741	1812	1823	1840	1911	1940	each hour	2311	2342	...		0947	1052	1147		2247	2355	...
Glasgow Central 215 a.	1052	1122	until	1652	1722	1755	1823	1836	1852	1922	1952	until	2322	2354	...		0958	1103	1158		2258	0005	...

f – ⑤ only.

j – ①②③④⑥ only.

❖ – Timings may vary by up to 5 minutes.

SR 2nd class Most services 🍷 GLASGOW - OBAN, FORT WILLIAM and MALLAIG 218

km		⚒	⚒ A	⚒	B	G	C	G	D	F	E		
	Edinburgh **220** d.	...	0450	*0715*	*0715*	...	*0800*	*0800*	*0930*	*1100*	*1100*	*1700*	*1700*
0	**Glasgow** Queen St. d.	...	*0530*a	0821	0821	...	0907	0955	1037	1220	1220	1820	1820
10	Westerton d.	...	0556	|	|	...	|	|	|	|	|	|	|
16	Dalmuir d.	...	0604	0839	0839	...	0926	1013	1050	1235	1235	1835	1835
26	Dumbarton Central d.	...	|	0848	0848	...	0934	1022	1104	1243	1243	1844	1844
40	Helensburgh Upper d.	...	0628	0906	0906	...	0952	1040	1123	1303	1303	1903	1903
51	Garelochhead d.	...	0641	0917	0917	...	1004	1051	1134	1314	1314	1914	1914
68	Arrochar & Tarbet d.	...	0707	0937	0937	...	1027	1111	1154	1334	1334	1934	1934
81	Ardlui d.	...	0721r	0953	0953	...	1039	1127	1208	1351	1353	1952	1952
95	**Crianlarich** a.	...	0742	1009	1009	...	1055	1143	1224	1411	1411	2008	2008
95	**Crianlarich** d.	...	0743	1015	1021	...	1058	1149	1227	1415	1421	2014	2017
123	Dalmally d.	...	|	1042	|	...	|	1216	1257	1442	|	2041	|
142	Taynuilt d.	...	|	1103	|	...	|	1237	1318	1503	|	2102	|
162	**Oban** a.	...	|	1127	|	...	|	1301	1342	1529	|	2126	|
115	Bridge of Orchy d.	...	0813	▬	1046	...	1123	...	...	...	1446	...	2042
140	Rannoch d.	...	0845	...	1108	...	1145	...	...	...	1508	...	2107
177	Roy Bridge d.	...	0929r	...	1146	...	1223	...	...	...	1546	...	2145
183	Spean Bridge d.	...	0937	...	1154	...	1230	...	...	...	1553	...	2152
197	**Fort William** a.	...	0954	S	1207	...	1243	...	...	...	1608	...	2205
197	**Fort William** d.	0830	...	1020	1212	1212	1248	...	...	...	1619	...	2210
223	Glenfinnan d.	0903	...	|	1246	1245	1321	...	...	...	1654	...	2243
251	Arisaig d.	0936	...	|	1318	1318	1354	...	...	...	1727	...	2316
259	Morar d.	0944	...	|	1326	1326	1401	...	...	...	1735	...	2324
264	**Mallaig** a.	0952	...	1225	1334	1334	1408	...	...	...	1743	...	2331

	Ⓐ	⚒	⚒	J	E	C	S			⑦ A	E	Ⓐ A
Mallaig d.	...	...	0603	...	1010	...	1410	1605	...	...	1815	...
Morar d.	...	...	0609	...	1016	...	|	1611	...	...	1821	...
Arisaig d.	...	...	0619	...	1026	...	|	1621	...	...	1831	...
Glenfinnan d.	...	...	0651	...	1057	...	|	1651	...	...	1903	...
Fort William a.	...	...	0725	...	1132	...	1602	1727	...	...	1937	...
Fort William d.	...	...	0742	...	1139	...	▬	1737	...	1900	...	1950
Spean Bridge d.	...	...	0755	...	1153	...	...	1750	...	1920	...	2010
Roy Bridge d.	...	...	0802	...	1200	...	...	1757	...	1927r	...	2017r
Rannoch d.	...	...	0843	...	1242	...	...	1836	...	2015	...	2106
Bridge of Orchy d.	...	...	0903	...	1302	...	H	1856	...	2047	...	2134
Oban d.	...	0811	|	1211	|	1256	1611	|	1811	|	...	|
Taynuilt d.	...	0835	|	1235	|	1320	1639	|	1835	|	...	|
Dalmally d.	...	0856	|	1256	|	1341	1700	|	1856	|	...	|
Crianlarich a.	...	0930	0930	1333	1333	1410	1728	1926	1928	2116	...	2204
Crianlarich d.	...	0936	0936	1336	1336	1412	1731	1933	1933	2118	...	2205
Ardlui d.	...	0952	0952	1352	1352	1428	1747	1953	1953	2139r	...	2226r
Arrochar & Tarbet d.	0708	1007	1007	1407	1407	1443	1802	2008	2008	2157	...	2244
Garelochhead d.	0730	1029	1029	1427	1427	1503	1822	2028	2028	2223	...	2310
Helensburgh Upper d.	0742	1041	1041	1439	1439	1515	1834	2040	2040	2237	...	2324
Dumbarton Central a.	0757	1058	1058	1456	1456	1528	1847	2053	2053	|	...	|
Dalmuir a.	|	1108	1108	1505	1505	1537	1856	2105	2105	2302	...	2349
Westerton a.	|	|	|	|	|	|	|	|	|	2311	...	2356
Glasgow Queen St. a.	0837	1130	1130	1531	1531	1558	1918	2129	2129	|	...	*0020*
Edinburgh **220** a.	*0948*	*1235*	*1235*	*1653*	*1653*	*1722*	*2021*	*2250*t	*2250*t	0015	...	0050

A – 🅁. 🛏(12) (limited accommodation), 🛏 1, 2 cl. and 🍷 London - Fort William and v.v. (Table **159**).
B – ⑥ (also Ⓐ from Sept. 28).
C – Ⓐ until Sept. 25.
D – ⑥ until Oct. 24.
E – ⚒ (also ⑦ until Sept. 27).
F – ⚒ (also ⑦ until Oct. 25).
G – ⑦ until Sept. 27.
H – ⑥⑦ until Sept. 27; ⑥ Oct. 3 - 24.

J – ⑥⑦ until Sept. 27; daily Sept. 28 - Oct. 25; ⚒ from Oct. 26.
S – 🚂 ①–⑤ May 18 - June 26; daily June 27 - Aug. 30; ①–⑤ Aug. 31 - Oct. 9. Operated by West Coast Railways. National Rail tickets not valid. To book ✆ 01524 732100. www.westcoastrailways.co.uk.

a – ①–⑤ only.
r – Stops on request.
t – *2324* on ⑦.

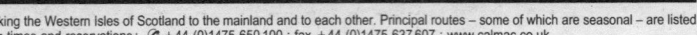

219 SCOTTISH ISLAND FERRIES

Caledonian MacBrayne Ltd operates numerous ferry services linking the Western Isles of Scotland to the mainland and to each other. Principal routes – some of which are seasonal – are listed below (see also the map on page **98**). Service frequencies, sailing-times and reservations: ✆ +44 (0)1475 650 100 ; fax +44 (0)1475 637 607 ; www.calmac.co.uk

Ardrossan – Brodick (Arran)
Claonaig – Lochranza (Arran)
Kennacraig – Port Askaig (Islay)
Kennacraig – Port Ellen (Islay)
Kilchoan – Tobermory (Mull)
Leverburgh (Harris) – Otternish (North Uist)
Mallaig – Armadale (Skye)
Mallaig – Eigg, Muck, Rum and Canna
Oban – Castlebay (Barra) and Lochboisdale (South Uist)
Oban – Coll and Tiree
Oban – Colonsay, Port Askaig (Islay) and Kennacraig
Oban – Craignure (Mull)
Uig (Skye) – Lochmaddy (North Uist)
Uig (Skye) – Tarbert (Harris)
Ullapool – Stornaway (Lewis)
Wemyss Bay – Rothesay (Bute)

220 EDINBURGH - GLASGOW SR

From EDINBURGH *76 km*

⚒: 0555, 0630, 0645Ⓐ, 0700 and every 15 minutes until 1930; then 2000 and every 30 minutes until 2330.

⑦: 0800, 0900, 1000, 1100, 1200, 1230 and every 30 minutes until 2100; then 2200, 2300, 2330.

☛ All services call at Falkirk High (*41 km* ± 27 mins from Edinburgh).

From GLASGOW Queen St Journey time: ± 51 minutes

⚒: 0600, 0630, 0645Ⓐ, 0700 and every 15 minutes until 1930; then 2000 and every 30 minutes until 2330.

⑦: 0750, 0830, 0930, 1030, 1130, 1230, 1300 and every 30 minutes until 2130; then 2230, 2330.

☛ All services call at Falkirk High (*35 km* ± 21 mins from Glasgow).

221 EDINBURGH and GLASGOW - INVERNESS

Most services 🍷 GR, SR

km		⚒ A	⚒ D	⚒	⚒	⚒	⚒	⚒	⚒	⚒	⚒	⚒	⚒	⚒ Ga	⚒	⚒	⚒	⚒
	London Kings Cross **185** d.	2116d	...	...	...	...	...	...	...	...	...	...	...	1200	...	...	...	...
0	**Edinburgh** **224** d.	|	0629	...	0833	0935	...	1034	1135	1335	1435	1535	...	1633	1741	1935	2037	2239
42	Kirkcaldy **224** d.	|	0703	...	0906	1009	...	1110	1208u	1407u	1509	1609	...	|	1816	2010	2117	2324
54	Markinch **224** d.	|	0712	...	0915	1018	...	1120	1217	1417	1518	1618	...	|	1825	2019	2126	2333
	Glasgow Queen St. **224** d.	|	|	0706	|	|	1011	|	|	|	|	|	1611	|	|	|	|	|
	Stirling **224** d.	0456	|	0733	|	|	1042	|	|	|	|	|	1637	1720	|	|	|	|
91	**Perth** **224** d.	0540	0747	0804	0950	1052	1119	1154	1253	1454	1553	1653	1718	1800	1859	2054	2200	0007
116	Dunkeld & Birnam d.	0601	—	0829	|	...	1138	...	1311	1511	...	...	1737	|	1917	2111	...	...
137	Pitlochry d.	0616	...	0842	1019	...	1151	...	1324	1524	...	...	1750	1833	1930	2124	...	...
148	Blair Atholl d.	0626	...	0852	|	...	1201	...	1333	1534	...	...	1759	|	|	2134	...	...
186	Dalwhinnie d.	0657	...	0916	|	...	1225	...	|	1601	...	...	|	|	|	2200	...	...
202	Newtonmore d.	0710	⚒	0927	|	...	|	...	1411	|	...	...	1832	|	|	2211	...	...
207	Kingussie d.	|		0932	1101	...	1238	...	1416	1614	...	...	1837	1917	2012	2221	...	...
226	Aviemore d.	0742	0757	0944	1114	...	1250	...	1428	1627	...	...	1848	1929	2025	2232	...	...
282	**Inverness** a.	0830	0843	1029	1154	...	1337	...	1506	1705	...	...	1934	2008	2103	2314	...	...

km	⑦	⑦	⑦	⑦ E	⑦ G	⑦ E	⑦
	London Kings Cross **185** d.	...	...	...	1230	...	...
0	**Edinburgh** **224** d.	0925	1350	...	1712	...	2236
42	Kirkcaldy **224** d.	1010	1428	...	|	...	|
54	Markinch **224** d.	|	|	...	|	...	|
	Glasgow Queen St. **224** d.	|	|	1440	|	1810	|
	Stirling **224** d.	|	|	1509	1752	1839	2327
91	**Perth** **224** d.	1052	1513	1546	1829	1916	0007
116	Dunkeld & Birnam d.	1109	1531	|	|	1934	...
137	Pitlochry d.	1122	1544	1616	1900	1947	...
148	Blair Atholl d.	1133	1554	|	|	1956	...
186	Dalwhinnie d.	1200	1619	|	|	2021	...
202	Newtonmore d.	1210	1629	|	|	2031	...
207	Kingussie d.	1216	1634	1659	1952	2036	...
226	Aviemore d.	1228	1648	1712	2004	2050	...
282	**Inverness** a.	1309	1738	1750	2044	2134	...

	⚒	⚒	⚒ Ge	⚒	⚒	⚒	⚒	⚒	⚒	⚒	⚒	⚒	⚒	⚒	⚒	⚒	Ⓐ B
Inverness d.	...	0646	0755	0918	...	1047	...	1254	1451	...	...	1656	...	1843	2015	...	2038
Aviemore d.	...	0722	0829	1001	...	1133	...	1331	1528	...	...	1735	...	1929	2100	...	2130
Kingussie d.	...	0733	0842	1014	...	1145	...	1344	1540	...	...	1748	...	1942	2112	...	2144
Newtonmore d.	...	|	|	1018	...	|	...	1348	|	...	...	1752	...	1946	2117	...	2152
Dalwhinnie d.	...	|	|	1030	...	|	...	|	1553	...	...	|	...	1958	2128	...	2206
Blair Atholl d.	0712	|	|	1051	...	|	...	1418	|	...	...	1822	...	2019	2150	...	2232
Pitlochry d.	0726	0816	0923	1101	...	1227	...	1428	1623	...	...	1834	...	2029	2202	...	2244
Dunkeld & Birnam d.	0739	0827	|	1116	...	1240	...	1440	1635	...	...	1846	...	2041	2215	...	2259
Perth **224** d.	0759	0847	0955	1137	1159	1301	1358	1500	1655	1700	1800	1909	1957	2102	2230	2238	2322
Stirling **224** a.	|	|	1030	1213	|	|	|	|	1729	|	|	|	|	|	2305	|	0008
Glasgow Queen St **224** a.	|	|	|	1246	|	|	|	|	1809	|	|	|	|	|	2338	|	|
Markinch **224** d.	0831	|	|	...	1229	1331	1429	1537	...	1739	1834	1944	2029	2132	...	2310	|
Kirkcaldy **224** d.	0841	0924	|	...	1239	1341	1439	1547	...	1748	1844	1954	2039	2142	...	|	|
Edinburgh **224** a.	0925	1001	1115	...	1319	1425	1519	1623	...	1825	1921	2029	2119	2219	...	0019	|
London Kings Cross **185** a.	...	...	1550p	...	...	...	...	...	...	...	...	...	...	...	...	...	0747c

	⑦	⑦ Gf	⑦	⑦	⑦	⑦	⑦ B
Inverness d.	...	0938	1230	1325	1615	1830	2025
Aviemore d.	...	1017	1317	1402	1655	1909	2110
Kingussie d.	...	1030	1330	1415	1714	1922	2124
Newtonmore d.	...	1035	1335	|	|	1926	2131
Dalwhinnie d.	...	|	1346	|	|	1939	2145
Blair Atholl d.	...	1107	1408	|	1747	2002	2211
Pitlochry d.	...	1123	1417	1454	1756	2011	2223
Dunkeld & Birnam d.	...	1136	1430	|	1809	2024	2238
Perth **224** d.	0927	1156	1450	1525	1827	2046	2301
Stirling **224** a.	1002	1233	1522	|	1902	|	2347
Glasgow Queen St **224** a.	|	|	1556	|	1936	|	|
Markinch **224** d.	|	|	...	|	...	|	|
Kirkcaldy **224** d.	|	|	...	1603	...	2125	|
Edinburgh **224** a.	1058	1318	...	1642	...	2205	|
London Kings Cross **185** a.	...	1815	...	...	...	...	0747c

A – [R]. [sleeper] 1, 2 class and [couchette 2]. Train stops to set down only.
B – [R]. [sleeper] 1, 2 class and [couchette 2]. Train stops to pick up only.
D – To / from Dundee.
E – To Elgin.
G – Operated by *GR*.

a – Via Falkirk Grahamston (d. 1704).
c – London Euston.
d – London Euston. Departs previous day. Departs 2057 on ⑦.
e – Via Falkirk Grahamston (d. 1045).
f – Via Falkirk Grahamston (d. 1249).

p – 1603 on ⑥.
u – Stops to pick up only.

222 EDINBURGH - STIRLING SR

From EDINBURGH *75 km*

Ⓐ: 0518, 0633, 0704, 0733, 0803 and every 30 minutes until 2034; then 2133, 2233, 2333.

⑥: 0518, 0633, 0704, 0733 and every 30 minutes until 2034; then 2133, 2233, 2333.

⑦: 0934 and hourly until 2134 (also 1712) then 2236.

From STIRLING Journey time: ± 50 minutes

Ⓐ: 0530, 0636, 0716, 0729, 0749, 0805 and every 30 minutes until 2106; then 2206, 2314.

⑥: 0530, 0636, 0716, 0805 and every 30 minutes until 2106; then 2206, 2314.

⑦: 0905, 1002, 1106 and hourly until 1806 (also 1233); then 1912, 2006, 2106, 2206.

☛ All trains (except the 1725 Ⓐ from Edinburgh and the 0729 Ⓐ from Stirling) call at **Falkirk Grahamston**: *41 km* (± 30 minutes) from Edinburgh; *34 km* (± 20 minutes) from Stirling.

Timings may vary by up to 4 minutes

223 GLASGOW - STIRLING SR

From GLASGOW Queen St *47 km*

Ⓐ: 0555, 0613, 0648, 0706, 0718, 0741, 0748 and at 18, 41 and 48 minutes past each hour until 2218 (also 1611; not 1641); then 2248, 2318.

⑥: 0555, 0613, 0648, 0706, 0718, 0741, 0748 and at 18, 41 and 48 minutes past each hour until 2218; then 2248, 2318.

⑦: 0938, 1015, 1115, 1145, 1215, 1315, 1345, 1415, 1440, 1515, 1545, 1615, 1715, 1745, 1810, 1815, 1915, 1945, 2015, 2115, 2145, 2215, 2335.

From STIRLING Journey time: ± 35 minutes

Ⓐ: 0553, 0621, 0652, 0722, 0738, 0753, 0806, 0821, 0844, 0851, 0921, 0944, 0951 and at 21, 43 and 51 minutes past each hour until 2251 (not 1851); then 2305.

⑥: 0553, 0621, 0652, 0722, 0740, 0753, 0806, 0821, 0844, 0851, 0913, 0921, 0944, 0951 and at 21, 43 and 51 minutes past each hour until 2251 (not 1851); then 2305.

⑦: 0928, 0938, 1028, 1125, 1138, 1225, 1325, 1338, 1425, 1522, 1526, 1538, 1625, 1725, 1738, 1828, 1902, 1924, 1954, 2025, 2125, 2138.

Timings may vary by up to 3 minutes

224 EDINBURGH and GLASGOW - ABERDEEN

Most services 🍷 GR, SR, XC

km		⚒ N	⚒ Y	⚒ V	⚒ x	⚒	⚒ x	⚒ D	⚒	⚒ V	⚒	⚒	⚒ V	⚒	⚒		Ⓐ	⑥	⑥	Ⓐ	⚒	⚒ Lg	⚒	⚒
	London Kings Cross **185** d.	...	2116q	...	...	...	...	...	...	...	...	...	...	...	...	...	...	...	...	...	...	...	...	...
0	**Edinburgh** **221** d.	...	|	...	...	0530	0533	...	0629	0730	...	0800	0829	...	0859	...	0930	0930	...	...	1000	1027	...	1100
42	Kirkcaldy **221** d.	...	0517	...	...	0602	|	...	0703	0802	...	0833	|	...	0933	...	|	|	...	...	1034	1104	...	1133
54	Markinch **221** d.	...	|	...	...	0611	0639	...	0712	0811	...	0842	|	...	0942	...	|	|	...	...	1043	|	...	1142
82	Leuchars d.	...	0546	...	...	0632	0658	...	|	0832	...	0906	0923	...	1003	...	|	1023	...	...	1104	1129	...	1203
	Glasgow Queen St **221** d.	...	|	...	...	|	|	0555	|	|	0741	|	|	0841	|	...	|	|	0941	0941	|	|	1041	|
	Stirling **221** d.	...	|	...	...	|	|	0624	|	|	0807	|	|	0907	|	...	|	|	1007	1007	|	|	1107	|
	Perth **221** d.	...	|	0601	...	|	|	0700	0747	|	0841	|	|	0936	|	...	|	|	1036	1036	|	|	1136	|
95	**Dundee** d.	...	0608	0623	0640	0651	0718	0723	0813	0845	0904	0921	0937	1000	1018	...	1033	1036	1100	1100	1120	1144	1200	1218
123	Arbroath d.	...	0631	0640	0656	0710	...	0739	...	0902	0923	...	0953	1017	...	...	1050	1053	1118	1118	...	1201	1217	...
145	Montrose d.	0625	0647	0656	0711	0723	...	0754	...	0916	0938	...	|	1031	...	...	1104	1107	1132	1134	...	1217	1232	...
184	Stonehaven d.	0649	0713	0722	0732	0748	...	0818	...	0938	|	...	1029	1053	...	...	1126	1129	|	1204	...	1242	|	...
210	**Aberdeen** a.	0713	0735	0744	0755	0813	...	0839	...	0957	1016	...	1053	1117	...	...	1145	1148	1214	1233	...	1307	1314	...

A – From Birmingham New Street (from Plymouth until Nov. 1).
B – Sept. 12 - Dec. 12. From Plymouth.
C – To Birmingham New Street (from Plymouth until Nov. 1).
D – To / from Dyce.
E – To / from Penzance.
L – To / from Leeds.
N – To / from Inverness.

P – To / from Plymouth.
V – To / from Inverurie.
W – May 17 - Sept. 5. From Newquay.
Y – [R]. [sleeper] 1, 2 class and [couchette 2]. Train stops to set down only.
Z – [R]. [sleeper] 1, 2 class and [couchette 2]. Train stops to pick up only.

a – 1510 on ⑥.
g – Operated by *GR*.
j – London Euston.
q – London Euston. Previous day. 2057 on ⑦.
x – Operated by *XC*.

SR **EDINBURGH and GLASGOW - ABERDEEN** **224**

	⚒	⚒	⚒	⚒ V	⚒	⚒	⚒ V	⚒	⚒	⚒	⚒	⚒ g	⚒	⚒ V	⚒	⚒	⚒ V	⑥	Ⓐ	Ⓐ 2	⚒ 2	⚒	⑥	Ⓐ	Ⓐ
London Kings Cross **185** .. d.	...	...	...	...	...	...	...	...	...	...	...	1030	...	...	...	...	...	...	...	...	...	...	...	...	...
Edinburgh **221** d.	1130	...	1200	1230	...	1300	1330	...	1400	1430	...	1500	1503	1530	...	1600	1629	...	...	...	1703	1735	...	...	1800
Kirkcaldy **221** d.	|	...	1235	|	...	1333	|	...	1433	|	...	1536	1542	|	...	1633	|	...	...	...	1739	|	...	...	1840
Markinch **221** d.	|	...	1242	|	...	1342	|	...	1442	|	...	|	1551	|	...	1642	|	...	...	...	1748	|	...	...	1851
Leuchars d.	1223	...	1303	1323	...	1403	1423	...	1503	1523	...	1600	1612	1623	...	1703	1724	...	...	...	1812	1835	...	...	1912
Glasgow Queen St ... **221** d.	|	1141	|	|	1241	|	|	1341	|	|	1441	|	|	|	1541	|	|	1641	1641	1712	|	|	1741	1740	|
Stirling **221** d.	|	1207	|	|	1307	|	|	1407	|	|	1507	|	|	|	1607	|	|	1707	|	1745	|	|	1807	1815	|
Perth **221** d.	|	1237	|	|	1336	|	|	1436	|	|	1536	|	|	|	1636	|	|	1736	1737	1823	|	|	1844	1853	|
Dundee d.	1237	1300	1318	1336	1400	1418	1436	1500	1518	1537	1600	1618	1628	1636	1700	1720	1739	1800	1800	...	1834	1848	1915	1916	1927
Arbroath d.	1253	1319	...	1353	1418	...	1453	1519	...	1554	1617	1636	...	1654	1720	...	1802	1820	1820	...	...	1904	1934	1935	...
Montrose d.	|	1333	...	1407	1432	...	|	1538	...	1608	1631	1652	...	1708	1733	...	1816	|	|	...	...	1922	1948	1949	...
Stonehaven d.	1327	|	...	1429	1454	...	1527	|	...	1630	|	1715	...	1733	1755	...	1841	1854	1853	...	...	1943	2010	2011	...
Aberdeen a.	1346	1412	...	1453	1513	...	1546	1619	...	1650	1711	1737	...	1752	1815	...	1900	1913	1913	...	...	2006	2029	2032	...

	⑥ Px	Ⓐ Px	2	⚒ g	⚒	⚒	⚒ N	⚒	2	Ⓐ Px	⑥ Bx	⑥ Wx	Ⓐ g	⚒ 2	⑥ 2	Ⓐ 2	Ⓐ	⑥	Ⓐ	⚒ 2	⚒ 2	⚒	⑦	⑦ x	⑦ g
London Kings Cross **185** .. d.	...	...	...	1400	...	...	...	...	...	...	...	...	1600	...	...	...	...	...	...	...	...	...		...	...
Edinburgh **221** d.	1808	1816	...	1830	...	1900	1930	...	2000	2015	2022	2022	2032	...	2100	2109	2140	...	...	2209	...	2309		0804	0910
Kirkcaldy **221** d.	1842	1900	...	1911	...	1933	|	...	2045	2051	2100	2101	2109	...	2145	2154	2212	...	...	2254	...	2354		0837	0949
Markinch **221** d.	1851	1909	...	|	...	1942	|	...	2054	2100	2110	2111	|	...	2154	2203	|	...	...	2303	...	0003		|	|
Leuchars d.	1912	1930	...	1938	...	2003	2028	...	2115	2122	2132	2136	2133	...	2215	2224	2234	...	...	2329	...	0024		|	1013
Glasgow Queen St ... **221** d.	|	|	1811	|	1841	|	|	1941	|	|	|	|	|	2041	|	|	|	2141	2141	|	2248	|		|	|
Stirling **221** d.	|	|	1841	|	1907	|	|	2007	|	|	|	|	|	2107	|	|	|	2207	2207	|	2333	|		|	|
Perth **221** d.	|	|	1919	|	1943	|	|	2036	|	|	|	|	|	2143	|	|	|	2235	2236	|	0013	|		|	|
Dundee d.	1925	1946	...	1953	2009	2020	2041	2100	2130	2145	2152	2157	2148	2208	2230	2239	2249	2258	2303	2344	...	0039		0914	1028
Arbroath d.	1942	2002	...	2010	2025	...	2058	2117	...	...	...	...	2205	2225	...	...	2305	2317	2322	...	...	...		0930	1045
Montrose d.	2002	2016	...	2026	2040	...	2112	|	...	...	...	...	2222	2239	...	...	2324	2333	2340	...	...	...		0944	1101
Stonehaven d.	2023	2036	...	2049	|	...	2134	2154	...	...	...	...	2245	2301	...	...	2345	2355	0005	...	...	...		1005	1124
Aberdeen a.	2046	2057	...	2112	2118	...	2153	2213	...	...	...	...	2307	2320	...	...	0008	0018	0025	...	...	...		1028	1147

	⑦ 2	⑦	⑦	⑦ 2	⑦	⑦	⑦ 2	⑦	⑦ 2	⑦	⑦ g		⑦	⑦ 2	⑦	⑦	⑦ Ax	⑦ g	⑦ 2	⑦	⑦	⑦	⑦ 2	⑦ 2	⑦
London Kings Cross **185** .. d.	...	...	...	...	...	...	...	...	...	...	1100	...	...	...	...	...	...	1400	...	...	...	...	...	...	...
Edinburgh 221 d.	0915	...	1055	1115	...	1240	1315	...	1515	...	1600	...	1705	1715	1745	...	1810	1842	1915	...	2100	...	2225	2236	...
Kirkcaldy **221** d.	1003	...	1131	1203	...	1316	1405	...	1603	...	1641	...	1738	1800	1812	...	1844	1919	2000	...	2134	...	2310	|	...
Markinch **221** d.	1012	...	|	1212	...	|	1414	...	1612	...	|	...	|	1809	|	...	1853	|	2009	...	2143	...	2319	|	...
Leuchars (for St Andrews) ... d.	1033	...	1155	1233	...	1340	1435	...	1633	...	1706	...	1802	1830	|	...	1914	1943	2030	...	2205	...	2340	|	...
Glasgow Queen St **221** ... d.	|	0938	|	|	1145	|	|	1345	|	1545	|	...	|	|	|	1745	|	|	|	1945	|	2145	|	|	2335
Stirling **221** d.	|	1012	|	|	1212	|	|	1412	|	1612	|	...	|	|	|	1812	|	|	|	2012	|	2211	|	2327	0014
Perth 221 d.	|	1047	|	|	1247	|	|	1448	|	1647	|	...	|	|	1845	1845	|	|	|	2047	|	2246	|	0007	0056
Dundee d.	1050	1111	1208	1248	1311	1353	1450	1511	1648	1711	1724	...	1815	1846	1909	1909	1930	1958	2045	2111	2218	2309	2356	...	...
Arbroath d.	...	1127	1225	...	1327	1410	...	1527	...	1727	1742	...	1832	...	1927	1927	1946	2015	...	2127	2235	2326	...	...	...
Montrose d.	...	1142	1237	...	1342	1424	...	1542	...	1742	1800	...	1846	...	1942	1942	2000	2031	...	2142	2249	2341	...	...	...
Stonehaven d.	...	1206	1259	...	1403	1446	...	1606	...	1803	1823	...	1908	...	2006	2006	2023	2054	...	2203	2311	0002	...	...	...
Aberdeen a.	...	1230	1323	...	1423	1505	...	1626	...	1823	1846	...	1930	...	2029	2029	2047	2117	...	2224	2333	0025	...	...	...

km		⚒	⚒	⚒ 2	⚒ 2	Ⓐ 2	⚒ Px	⚒		⚒ 2	⚒ 2	⚒ Px	⚒	⚒	⚒	⚒ N	⚒ V		⚒ g	⚒ Ex	⚒ 2	⚒	⚒	⚒ 2	
0	**Aberdeen** d.		...	...	...	...	...	0533	...	0556	...	...	0633	...	...	0713	0740	...	0752	0820	...	0842	0907	...	...
26	Stonehaven d.		...	...	...	...	...	0552	...	0612	...	...	0652	...	...	0729	0756	...	0809	0838	...	|	|	...	...
65	Montrose d.		...	...	...	...	...	0617	...	0634	...	...	0713	...	...	0754	0818	...	0832	0859	...	0918	0946	...	...
87	Arbroath d.		...	...	...	...	...	0631	...	0648	...	...	0727	...	...	0808	0832	...	0848	0915	...	0932	1000	...	...
115	**Dundee** d.		...	...	0605	...	0632	0652	...	0708	0720	0735	0752	0759	0818	0827	0853	...	0906	0933	0942	0952	1017	1034	...
149	**Perth** **221** d.		0510	0516	|	0609	|	0715	...	|	|	|	0812	|	0841	|	0915	...	|	|	|	1014	|	|	...
202	Stirling **221** d.		|	0553	|	0652	|	0753	...	|	|	|	0844	|	0913	|	|	...	|	|	|	1043	|	|	...
249	**Glasgow** Queen St ... **221** a.		|	0634	|	0734	|	0834	...	|	|	|	0915	|	0945	|	1014	...	|	|	|	1115	|	|	...
	Leuchars d.		|	...	0616	...	0646	...	...	0720	0732	0748	...	|	...	0839	...	...	0920	0947	0955	...	1029	1046	...
	Markinch **221** d.		0544	...	0639	...	0711	...	...	|	0756	0811	...	0831	...	|	...	...	|	1009	1017	...	|	1108	...
	Kirkcaldy **221** d.		0553	...	0649	...	0721	...	...	0748	0806	0820	...	0841	...	|	...	...	0944	1017	1027	...	|	1118	...
	Edinburgh **221** a.		0646	...	0742	...	0805	...	...	0826	0855	0858	...	0925	...	0940	...	...	1027	1101	1109	...	1129	1201	...
	London Kings Cross **186** ... a.		...	...	...	...	...	...	...	...	...	...	...	...	...	...	...	...	1457a	...	...	...	...	...	...

	⚒ D	⚒ g	⚒ 2	⚒	⚒ V	⚒	⚒		⚒ V	⚒	⚒	⚒	⚒ 2	⚒		⚒	⚒ 2	⚒	⚒ g		⚒	⚒ 2	⚒ V	⚒ 2	⚒
Aberdeen d.	0937	0952	...	1038	1105	...	1142	...	1207	...	1242	1306	...	1342	...	1407	...	1439	1449	...	1533	...	1601	...	1637
Stonehaven d.	0953	1009	...	|	1121	...	|	...	1226	...	1258	1322	...	|	...	1423	...	|	1506	...	1549	...	1618	...	1653
Montrose d.	1015	1032	...	1114	1146	...	1217	...	|	...	1317	1344	...	1417	...	|	...	1512	1529	...	1611	...	|	...	1713
Arbroath d.	1029	1049	...	1128	1200	...	1231	...	1300	...	1331	1358	...	1431	...	1500	...	1526	1545	...	1625	...	1655	...	1729
Dundee d.	1052	1106	1130	1149	1217	1234	1252	...	1317	1334	1350	1417	1434	1452	...	1517	1535	1549	1603	...	1646	1650	1717	1726	1751
Perth **221** d.	1114	|	|	1211	|	|	1314	...	|	|	1411	|	|	1514	...	|	|	1611	|	...	1711	|	|	|	1812
Stirling **221** d.	1143	|	|	1242	|	|	1343	...	|	|	1440	|	|	1543	...	|	|	1643	|	...	1742	|	|	|	1842
Glasgow Queen St ... **221** a.	1215	|	|	1314	|	|	1415	...	|	|	1515	|	|	1615	...	|	|	1717	|	...	1815	|	|	|	1914
Leuchars d.	...	1120	1145	...	1229	1246	...	...	1329	1346	...	1429	1446	...	...	1529	1547	...	1617	...	...	1702	1729	1739	...
Markinch **221** d.	...	|	1208	...	|	1308	...	...	|	1408	...	|	1508	...	...	|	1608	...	|	...	...	1723	|	1804	...
Kirkcaldy **221** d.	...	1144	1217	...	|	1318	...	...	|	1418	...	|	1518	...	...	|	1619	...	1645	...	...	1733	|	1813	...
Edinburgh **221** a.	...	1225	1255	...	1327	1357	...	...	1428	1455	...	1527	1555	...	...	1627	1656	...	1727	...	...	1822	1832	1850	...
London Kings Cross **185** .. a.	...	1658	...	...	...	...	...	...	...	...	...	...	...	...	...	...	...	...	2220	...	...	...	...	...	...

	⚒ V	⚒ 2	⚒	⑥		Ⓐ g	⚒	⚒ V	⚒ 2	⚒	⚒ 2V		⚒	⚒	⑥ x	Ⓐ x	Ⓐ Z	①–④	⑤		⑦	⑦ 2	⑦	⑦ 2	⑦
Aberdeen d.	1710	...	1736	1813	...	1816	1833	1910	...	1946	2005	...	2042	2106	2117	2132	2140	2230	2322	...		...	...	...	0927
Stonehaven d.	|	...	1752	1829	...	1833	|	1926	...	2005	2021	...	2058	2122	2135	2149	2201	2249	2341	...		...	...	...	0943
Montrose d.	1749	...	1817	1851	...	1856	1910	1951	...	2023	2043	...	2120	2144	2155	2210	2225	2313	0005	...		...	...	...	1008
Arbroath d.	1803	...	1831	1905	...	1912	1924	2005	...	2037	2057	...	2134	2158	2211	2226	2243	2328	0020	...		...	...	...	1022
Dundee d.	1819	1846	1852	1922	...	1930	1946	2021	2042	2056	2116	...	2152	2215	2229	2243	2306	2351	0043	...		0725	0845	0925	1043
Perth **221** d.	|	|	1914	|	...	|	2011	|	|	2117	|	...	2214	|	|	|	|	0015	0107	...		|	0903	|	1105
Stirling **221** d.	|	|	1943	|	...	|	2040	|	|	2145	|	...	2243	|	|	|	|	...	...	...		|	0938	|	1138
Glasgow Queen St ... **221** a.	|	|	2015	|	...	|	2114	|	|	2219	|	...	2315	|	|	|	|	...	...	...		|	1015	|	1211
Leuchars d.	1831	1856	...	1934	...	1944	...	2033	2054	...	2128	...	...	2227	2242	2256	2325	...	...	...		0737	...	0937	...
Markinch **221** d.	|	1919	...	|	...	|	...	|	2116	...	2151	...	...	2252	2303	2318	|	...	...	...		0759	...	0959	...
Kirkcaldy **221** d.	|	1928	...	2000	...	2008	...	|	2126	...	2159	...	...	2301	2312	2326	2354	...	...	...		0808	...	1008	...
Edinburgh **221** a.	1934	2013	...	2036	...	2048	...	2132	2216	...	2250	...	...	2352	0011	0010	|	...	...	...		0900	...	1106	...
London Kings Cross **185** .. a.	...	...	...	...	...	...	...	...	...	...	...	...	...	...	...	...	0747j	...	...	...		...	...	...	...

	⑦ g	⑦ 2	⑦ Cx	⑦	⑦ g	⑦ 2	⑦		⑦ g	⑦ 2	⑦	⑦	⑦ 2	⑦	⑦	⑦ 2	⑦	⑦		⑦	⑦ x		⑦ Z	⑦	
Aberdeen d.	0948	...	1112	1129	1147	...	1327	...	1350	...	1510	1530	...	1710	1747	...	1910	1935	...	2010	2128	...	2142	2229	...
Stonehaven d.	1005	...	1129	1145	1204	...	1342	...	1407	...	1526	1546	...	1726	1803	...	1926	1951	...	2026	2145	...	2202	2248	...
Montrose d.	1028	...	1150	1207	1227	...	1407	...	1430	...	1548	1608	...	1748	1828	...	1948	2013	...	2048	2206	...	2227	2311	...
Arbroath d.	1045	...	1206	1221	1243	...	1421	...	1446	...	1602	1622	...	1802	1842	...	2002	2027	...	2102	2222	...	2245	2325	...
Dundee d.	1102	1125	1225	1243	1301	1325	1443	...	1504	1525	1625	1643	1725	1819	1902	1927	2020	2043	...	2121	2239	...	2309	2347	...
Perth **221** d.	|	|	|	1305	|	|	1505	...	|	|	|	1705	|	|	1924	|	|	2105	...	|	|	...	|	0009	...
Stirling **221** d.	|	|	|	1338	|	|	1538	...	|	|	|	1738	|	|	1954	|	|	2138	...	|	|	...	|	...	...
Glasgow Queen St ... **221** a.	|	|	|	1411	|	|	1612	...	|	|	|	1812	|	|	2031	|	|	2215	...	|	|	...	|	...	...
Leuchars d.	1116	1137	1238	...	1315	1337	...	...	1518	1537	1637	...	1737	1831	...	1939	2032	...	...	2133	2252	...	2328	...	...
Markinch **221** d.	|	1159	|	...	|	1359	...	...	|	1559	|	...	1759	|	...	2001	|	...	...	2154	2314	...	|	...	...
Kirkcaldy **221** d.	1140	1208	1303	...	1339	1408	...	...	1542	1608	1702	...	1807	1856	...	2010	2059	...	...	2205	2322	...	2356	...	...
Edinburgh **221** a.	1224	1306	1342	...	1424	1506	...	...	1625	1659	1741	...	1900	1935	...	2101	2136	...	...	2243	0003	...	|	...	...
London Kings Cross **185** .. a.	1711	...	...	...	1921	...	...	...	2125	...	...	...	...	...	...	...	...	...	...	...	...	...	0747j	...	...

225 INVERNESS - ELGIN - ABERDEEN — SR

km		⚒ E	⚒	⚒ G	⚒	⚒	⚒	⚒	⚒	⚒	⚒	⚒	⚒ 🍷	⚒ 2	⚒	
0	**Inverness** d.	0457	0558	...	0710	0903	1058	1242	1427	...	1521	1711	1810	1957	2120	...
24	Nairn d.	0514	0615	...	0728	0921	1115	1259	1444	...	1540	1728	1827	2014	2137	...
40	Forres d.	0525	0626	...	0739	0937	1126	1310	1455	...	1551	1739	1838	2025	2148	...
59	**Elgin** d.	0540	0642	...	0800	0953	1142	1326	1511	...	1607	1758	1855	2041	2206	...
89	Keith d.	0602	0703	...	0821	1012	1203	1347	1532	...	1628	1819	1916	...	2227	...
109	Huntly d.	0616	0719	...	0845	1030	1217	1401	1546	...	1647	1840	1937	...	2247	...
130	Insch d.	0632	0735	...	0903	1049	1235	1419	1604	...	1704	1856	1953	...	2303	...
147	**Inverurie** d.	0645	0749	...	0915	1101	1247	1431	1618	...	1716	1909	2005	...	2316	...
164	Dyce ✈ d.	0658	0803	0908	0927	1115	1302	1443	1631	1705	1730	1921	2019	...	2328	...
174	**Aberdeen** a.	0710	0814	0919	0938	1126	1313	1454	1641	1716	1741	1932	2030	...	2339	...

⑦	⑦ 🍷	⑦ 🍷	⑦ 🍷	⑦ 🍷	⑦ G🍷	⑦ 🍷	⑦ G🍷
Inverness d.	0955	1230	1527	1712	1800	2100	2142
Nairn d.	1012	1247	1544	1730	1817	2117	2159
Forres d.	1023	1258	1555	1741	1828	2128	2210
Elgin d.	1038	1313	1610	1756	1844	2144	2226
Keith d.	1059	1335	1632	1818	...	2205	...
Huntly d.	1118	1352	1646	1837	...	2219	...
Insch d.	1134	1408	1702	1853	...	2235	...
Inverurie d.	1147	1420	1714	1905	...	2247	...
Dyce ✈ d.	1159	1432	1730	1917	...	2259	...
Aberdeen a.	1210	1443	1741	1928	...	2310	...

	⚒	⚒	⚒ M	⚒	⚒ G	⚒	⚒		⚒	⚒	⚒	⚒	⚒	⚒	⚒ E	
Aberdeen d.	...	0620	0714	0823	0850	1014	1159	...	1340	1525	1643	1718	1820	2007	2155	...
Dyce ✈ d.	...	0630	0731	0836	0901	1023	1208	...	1353	1538	1652	1729	1829	2020	2205	...
Inverurie d.	...	0646	0749	0848	...	1035	1220	...	1405	1550	...	1741	1841	2032	2217	...
Insch d.	...	0658	0801	0903	...	1047	1233	...	1417	1602	...	1753	1853	2044	2229	...
Huntly d.	...	0719	0817	0919	...	1103	1249	...	1433	1618	...	1809	1909	2100	2246	...
Keith d.	...	0733	0831	0933	...	1118	1303	...	1447	1634	...	1826	1924	2114	2300	...
Elgin d.	0700	0758	0853	0953	...	1142	1327	...	1511	1656	...	1854	1946	2136	2322	...
Forres d.	0714	0812	0907	1011	...	1156	1341	...	1525	1710	...	1908	2000	2155	2336	...
Nairn d.	0727	0823	0922	1022	...	1207	1352	...	1541	1729	...	1919	2015	2206	2347	...
Inverness a.	0748	0841	0940	1040	...	1225	1410	...	1559	1747	...	1938	2033	2224	0005	...

⑦	⑦ 🍷	⑦ 🍷		⑦ 🍷	⑦ 🍷		⑦ 🍷
Aberdeen d.	1000	1300	...	1525	1718	...	2100
Dyce ✈ d.	1009	1309	...	1534	1729	...	2109
Inverurie d.	1021	1321	...	1547	1741	...	2121
Insch d.	1033	1333	...	1559	1753	...	2133
Huntly d.	1049	1351	...	1615	1809	...	2149
Keith d.	1105	1404	...	1635	1824	...	2209
Elgin d.	1127	1426	...	1658	1846	...	2231
Forres d.	1141	1440	...	1712	1900	...	2245
Nairn d.	1152	1451	...	1732	1911	...	2256
Inverness a.	1210	1510	...	1750	1929	...	2314

Other trains on ⚒:
Inverurie – Aberdeen at 0714 **G**, 0822, 1038 **E**, 1135 **E**, 1338, 1524 **E**, 1638 **E**, 1843 **E**, 1940 **E**, 2124.
Aberdeen – Inverurie at 0750 **P**, 1000 **E**, 1104 **E**, 1250, 1456 **E**, 1555 **E**, 1756 **E**, 1907 **E**, 2056, 2250.

E – To / from Edinburgh.
G – To / from Glasgow.
M – From Montrose.
P – From Perth.

226 NORTH HIGHLAND BRANCHES — 2nd class SR

INVERNESS - THURSO and WICK

km		⚒	⚒ 🍷	⚒ 🍷	⚒	⑦p	⑦q 🍷
0	**Inverness** ‡ d.	0706	1038	1356	1752	1755	1804
16	Beauly ‡ d.	0720	1052	|	1806	1809	1818
21	Muir of Ord ‡ d.	0729	1058	1419	1812	1815	1824
30	Dingwall ‡ d.	0743	1107	1428	1829	1829	1835
51	Invergordon ‡ d.	0800	1126	1446	1847	1847	1853
71	Tain ‡ d.	0818	1145	1504	1905	1905	1910
93	Ardgay ‡ d.	0833	1200	1521	1924	1924	1924
108	Lairg d.	0852	1219	1544	1944	1944	1944
136	Golspie d.	0916	1243	1608	2008	2008	2007
146	Brora d.	0930	1254	1618	2018	2018	2018
163	Helmsdale d.	0946	1309	1633	2033	2033	2033
237	Georgemas Jcn a.	1049	1412	1733	2133	2133	2133
248	**Thurso** a.	1101	1424	1745	2145	2145	2145
248	**Thurso** d.	1104	1426	1747	2147	2147	2147
237	Georgemas Jcn d.	1114	1437	1758	2157	2157	2157
260	**Wick** a.	1132	1455	1815	2214	2214	2214

	⚒	⚒ 🍷	⚒ 🍷	† 🍷	⚒ 🍷	⚒ 🍷
Wick d.	...	0620	0812	1153	1236	1600
Georgemas Jcn d.	...	0637	0829	1210	1253	1617
Thurso a.	...	0646	0838	1219	1302	1626
Thurso d.	...	0648	0841	1222	1305	1629
Georgemas Jcn d.	...	0700	0853	1234	1317	1641
Helmsdale d.	...	0801	0947	1333	1418	1740
Brora d.	...	0816	1003	1348	1433	1755
Golspie d.	...	0826	1011	1358	1442	1804
Lairg d.	0634	0853	1038	1424	1508	1830
Ardgay ‡ d.	0651	0911	1051	1440	1525	1849
Tain ‡ d.	0706	0926	1107	1455	1541	1905
Invergordon ‡ d.	0724	0944	1126	1512	1558	1922
Dingwall ‡ d.	0742	1004	1145	1530	1619	1941
Muir of Ord ‡ d.	0752	1013	1155	1542	1630	1950
Beauly ‡ d.	0757	1019	|	1547	|	1956
Inverness ‡ a.	0812	1035	1213	1602	1647	2010

‡ – Additional trains operate Inverness - Invergordon (- Tain - Ardgay) and v.v.:
From Inverness: 1000† **T**, 1249† **T**, 1439⚒ **N**, 1521† **N**, 1715⚒ **A**, 2053 **T**, 2320⑤⑥ **T**.
From Invergordon: 0658⚒ **A**, 1126† **T**, 1416† **T**, 1619† **N**, 1539⚒ **N**, 1958⚒ **A**, 2220 **T**.

A – From / to Ardgay.
N – From / to Invergordon.
T – From / to Tain.
p – Until Sept. 27.
q – From Oct. 4.

INVERNESS - KYLE OF LOCHALSH

km		⚒	⚒	⑦	⚒ 🍷	⚒	⑦ p
0	**Inverness** d.	0900	1103	1111	1331	1752	1755
16	Beauly d.	0914	|	1125	1345	1806	1809
21	Muir of Ord d.	0920	1120	1131	1351	1812	1815
30	Dingwall d.	0931	1131	1144	1401	1826	1829
49	Garve d.	0953	1153	1205	1426	1849	1852
75	Achnasheen d.	1019	1218	1231	1452	1917	1918
104	Strathcarron d.	1046	1245	1258	1519	1946	1947
116	Stromeferry d.	1104	1303	1316	|	2004	2005
124	Plockton d.	1116	1315	1328	1547	2015	2016
133	**Kyle of Lochalsh** a.	1128	1328	1340	1600	2029	2029

	⚒	⑦ p	⚒	⚒ 🍷	⑦	⚒	
Kyle of Lochalsh d.	0621	1121	1203	1437	1522	1715	...
Plockton d.	0633	1133	1215	1449	1534	1727	...
Stromeferry d.	0644	1144	1226	|	1545	1738	...
Strathcarron d.	0702	1202	1247	1516	1603	1756	...
Achnasheen d.	0729	1229	1315	1547	1630	1823	...
Garve d.	0755	1257	1341	1612	1656	1849	...
Dingwall d.	0816	1320	1403	1637	1718	1913	...
Muir of Ord d.	0829	1334	1415	1646	1729	1925	...
Beauly d.	0835	1339	1420	1652	1734	1930	...
Inverness a.	0853	1354	1436	1709	1749	1949	...

227 🚌 / ⛴ INVERNESS - ULLAPOOL - STORNOWAY

	C	A	C	B	D	C				
Inverness 🚌 d.	0705	0810	1330	1500	1540	1950	...	...	...	...
Ullapool 🚌 a.	0825	0930	1450	1620	1700	2110	...	...	...	...
Ullapool ⛴ d.	0930	1025	1550	1735	1815	2200	...	...	...	...
Stornoway ⛴ a.	1215	1310	1835	2020	2100	0045	...	...	...	...

	C	A	C	B	D	C				
Stornoway ⛴ d.	0615	0700	1240	1350	1430	1900	...	...	...	...
Ullapool ⛴ a.	0900	0945	1525	1635	1715	2145	...	...	...	...
Ullapool 🚌 d.	0905	0950	1530	1640	1720	2150	...	...	...	...
Inverness 🚌 a.	1025	1110	1650	1800	1840	2310	...	...	...	...

A – ①②④⑥ Jun. 22 - Aug. 29; ⚒ Aug. 31 - Oct. 3.
B – ①②④ Jun. 22 - Aug. 27; Ⓐ Aug. 31 - Oct. 3.
C – ③⑤ Jun. 24 - Aug. 28.
D – ⑥ Jun. 22 - Oct. 3.

🚌 Operated by Scottish Citylink (service **961**) www.citylink.co.uk, ✆ +44 (0) 8705 50 50 50. Runs in conjunction with Ullapool - Stornoway ferry.

⛴ Operated by Caledonian MacBrayne Ltd. Latest passenger check-in: 30 minutes before departure.

228 🚌 INVERNESS - FORT WILLIAM - OBAN

Valid until October 4, 2009.

Service number	919 ⚒	918 ⚒	919	919	918 ⚒	919	919	918 ⚒	19 ⚒	919 ⚒	
Inverness d.	0845	...	1045	1245	...	1445	1645	...	1715	1845	...
Fort Augustus d.	0948	...	1148	1348	...	1548	1748	...	1818	1943	...
Fort William d.	1045	1100	1245	1445	1500	1645	1845	1900	1915	2045	...
Ballachulish d.	...	1127	...	...	1527	...	...	1927	...	...	...
Oban a.	...	1227	...	...	1627	...	...	2027	...	...	...

Service number	319 ⚒	919 ⚒	918 ⚒	919	919	918 ⚒	919	919	918 ⚒	919	
Oban d.	...	...	0840	...	...	1240	...	...	1640	...	...
Ballachulish d.	...	...	0939	...	...	1339	...	...	1739	...	...
Fort William d.	0730	0815	1008	1030	1215	1408	1415	1615	1808	1815	...
Fort Augustus d.	0822	0912	...	1127	1312	...	1512	1712	...	1907	...
Inverness a.	0920	1015	...	1230	1415	...	1615	1815	...	2005	...

☛ Operated by Highland Country Buses / Scottish Citylink: www.citylink.co.uk, ✆ +44 (0) 8705 50 50 50.

229 ISLE OF MAN RAILWAYS — ✆ +44 (0)1624 663366

km	*Manx Electric Railway*	A	C	B	D	B	A	C	B	B	D	C	C				
0	**Douglas** Derby Castle ‡ d.	0940	1010	1040	1110	1140	1240	1340	1410	1510	1540	1610	1640	...	...	...	...
4	Groudle d.	0952	1022	1052	1122	1152	1252	1352	1422	1522	1552	1622	1652	...	...	...	...
11	Laxey ▲ d.	1010	1040	1110	1140	1210	1310	1410	1440	1540	1610	1640	1710	...	...	...	...
29	**Ramsey** a.	1055	1125	1155	1225	1255	1355	1455	1525	1625	1655	...	1755	...	...	...	...

	B	A	C	B	D	B	A	C	B	C	C	D				
Ramsey d.	1010	1110	1140	1210	1240	1340	1440	1510	1540	...	1640	1710	...	...	...	...
Laxey ▲ d.	1055	1155	1225	1255	1325	1425	1525	1555	1625	1655	1725	1755	...	...	...	...
Groudle d.	1113	1213	1243	1313	1343	1443	1543	1613	1643	1713	1743	1813	...	...	...	...
Douglas Derby Castle ‡ a.	1125	1225	1255	1325	1355	1455	1555	1625	1655	1725	1755	1825	...	...	...	...

A – Daily Apr. 6 - Nov. 1.
B – Daily Apr. 6 - Sept. 27.
C – Daily May 25 - Sept. 6.
D – Daily Jun. 29 - Aug. 28.

‡ – 🚌 services **23, 24, 25, 26** connect Derby Castle and the Steam Railway Station.

▲ – **Snaefell Mountain Railway** operates daily until Nov. 1, subject to weather conditions. First departure from Laxey 1015, last departure 1545. Journey time to summit: 30 mins.

Service Apr. 6 - Nov. 1 (★ until Sept. 27)

km	*Isle of Man Steam Railway*			★				★		
0	**Douglas** Railway Station ‡ d.	1020	...	1220	...	1420	...	1620	...	...
9	Santon *(request stop)* d.	1041	...	1241	...	1441	...	1641	...	...
16	**Castletown** d.	1057	...	1257	...	1457	...	1657	...	...
25	Port Erin a.	1117	...	1317	...	1517	...	1717	...	...

Service Apr. 6 - Nov. 1 (★ until Sept. 27)

	★				★				
Port Erin d.	1020	...	1220	...	1420	...	1620	...	...
Castletown d.	1042	...	1242	...	1442	...	1642	...	...
Santon *(request stop)* d.	1058	...	1258	...	1458	...	1658	...	...
Douglas Railway Station ‡ a.	1117	...	1317	...	1517	...	1717	...	...

IRELAND

SEE MAP PAGE 98

Operators: Iarnród Éireann (**IÉ**) and Northern Ireland Railways (**NIR**), Bus Éireann, Ulsterbus and Dublin Area Rapid Transit (**DART**). Most cross-border services are jointly operated.

Timings: Rail: **NIR** services are valid until **December 12, 2009.**
IÉ and **DART** services are valid from **December 14, 2008** until **September 2009.**
Bus: **Ulsterbus** services are valid from **May 5, 2009** until further notice.
Bus Éireann services are valid from **May 11, 2009** until further notice.

Rail services: Except for *Enterprise* cross-border expresses (for details, see Table **230** below), **all trains** convey *Standard* (2nd) class seating. Most express trains in the Republic of Ireland, as noted in the tables, also have first class accommodation.
On public holiday dates in the **Republic of Ireland**, DART trains run as on Sundays; outer-suburban services to or from Drogheda and Dundalk do not run. Other services may be amended, though most main-line trains run normally. All services are subject to alteration during the Christmas, New Year and Easter holiday periods.

Bus services: **Bus Éireann** and **Ulsterbus**: services are shown in detail where there is no comparable rail service; only basic information is given for other routes. Buses do not always call at the rail station, but usually stop nearby. Where possible the stop details are given in the station bank or as a footnote. On longer routes, a change of bus may be required – please check with the driver. At holiday times bus travellers should consult detailed leaflets or seek further information from the operator. **Bus Éireann**: ✆ +353 1 836 6111 (Dublin) or + 353 21 450 8188 (Cork); **Ulsterbus**: ✆ + 028 9033 3000 (Translink, Belfast). **Dublin Busaras** (bus station) is a 5 minute walk from Dublin Connolly station.

The Dublin Tram service (Luas) connects Dublin Connolly and Heuston stations at frequent intervals. Journey time is 14 minutes, depending on traffic conditions. See Dublin City Plan on page 30.

NIR, IÉ BELFAST - DUNDALK - DUBLIN 230

Enterprise express trains (*E*) convey Standard (2nd) class and Premium (1st) class seating, 🍸 (Café Bar and trolley service) and ✕ (at-seat meal service in Premium)

km		Ⓐ	Ⓐ	⑥	Ⓐ	⚒	⚒ *E*	⑥	⚒	⚒ *E*	⚒	⚒	⚒	⚒ *E*	⚒	⚒	⚒ *E*	⚒	⚒ *E*	⚒	⑤	⚒	⚒ *E*	⚒	⚒	⑥	Ⓐ
0	**Belfast Central** § d.	...	...	...	...	...	0650	...	0750x	0800	...	...	1000	1035	...	1200	1235	1330	1410	...	...	1530	1610	...	...	1700	1710
13	Lisburn § d.	...	...	...	...	...	|	...	0801z	|	...	...	1032	|	...	1231	|	1401	|	...	...	1602	|	...	...	1732	1731
42	Portadown § d.	...	...	...	...	...	0721	...	0826z	0831	...	...	1057	1101	...	1257	1301	1428	1441	...	...	1630	1641	...	...	1800	1800
71	Newry d.	...	...	...	...	...	0742	...	▬	0852	...	...	▬	1122	...	▬	1322	▬	1502	...	...	▬	1702	...	...	1825	1825
95	**Dundalk** d.	0540	0635	0703	0703	...	0757	0810	Ⓐ	|	0955	1045	⚒	1138	...	⚒	1338	⚒	1520	...	1620	⚒	1717	...	...	...	...
131	Drogheda d.	0604	0659	0729	0727	0758	0820	0835	0832	|	1020	1109	1135	1200	1208	1303	1359	1415	1541	1555	1645	1655	1738	1748	1805	...	...
148	Balbriggan d.	0617	0713	0745	0742	0811	|	0850	0847	|	1033	1123	1150	|	1223	1318	|	1430	|	1610	|	1711	|	|	1819	...	...
154	Skerries d.	0623	0720	0751	0749	0817	|	0856	0853	|	1039	1130	1156	|	1229	1324	|	1436	|	1616	|	1717	|	|	1825	...	...
168	Malahide d.	|	|	0806	|	0832	|	0913	0909	|	|	1145	1211	|	1244	1339	|	1451	|	1631	|	1735	|	|	1840	...	...
183	**Dublin Connolly** a.	0654	0755	0824	0828	0859	0905	0929	0929	0955	1112	1202	1229	1240	1304	1357	1440	1510	1620	1657	1734	1756	1820	1830	1858	...	...

	Ⓐ	⚒ *E*	⚒	⚒ *E*	⚒	⑦	⑦ *E*	⑦ *E*	⑦ *E*	⑦ *E*	⑦ *E*
Belfast Central § d.	1750	1810	1900	2010	...	...	1000	1300	1500	1600	1900
Lisburn § d.	1811	|	1937	|	...	...	1016	*1301*	*1501*	*1601*	*1901*
Portadown § d.	1836	1841	2005	2041	...	...	1040	1332	1532	1632	1932
Newry d.	▬	1902	▬	2102	...	...	1102	1354	1554	1654	1954
Dundalk d.	⚒	1920	⚒	2120	...	0920	1119	1413	1613	1713	2013
Drogheda d.	1855	1941	2000	2141	2205	0945	1140	1434	1634	1734	2034
Balbriggan d.	1910	|	2014	|	2219	1000	|	|	|	|	|
Skerries d.	1916	|	2020	|	2226	1006	|	|	|	|	|
Malahide d.	1931	|	2035	|	2242	1021	|	|	|	|	|
Dublin Connolly a.	1953	2020	2054	2220	2300	1040	1213	1513	1715	1815	2105

	Ⓐ	⚒	Ⓐ	⚒ *E*	⚒	⚒ *E*	⚒	⚒	⚒ *E*	⚒	⚒	⚒ *E*
Dublin Connolly d.	...	...	0711	0735	0853	0935	1003e	1035	1100	1106	1237	1320
Malahide d.	...	...	0725	|	0912	|	1025	1053	|	1127	1255	|
Skerries d.	...	...	0739	|	0926	|	1039	1107	|	1141	1310	|
Balbriggan d.	...	...	0745	|	0932	|	1045	1113	|	1147	1315	|
Drogheda d.	...	...	0800	0805	0946	1006	1100	1127	1133	1204	1335	1350
Dundalk d.	...	...	...	0830	1010	1030	▬	▬	1155	▬	▬	1415
Newry d.	0650	0735	...	0848	...	1048	Ⓐ	⑥	1213	Ⓐ	⑥	1433
Portadown § d.	0720	0800	...	0909	...	1109	1115	1130	1234	1245	1300	1454
Lisburn § a.	0745	0825	...	*0940*p	...	|	1140	1155	|	1310	1325	|
Belfast Central § a.	0805	0848g	...	0945g	...	1145g	1210	1224	1315	1340	1354	1535h

	⚒	⚒ *E*	⚒	⚒	⚒ *E*	⚒ g	⑥	Ⓐ	Ⓐ	⑥	Ⓐ	⑥	⚒	⚒ *E*	⚒	Ⓐ	⚒ *E*	⚒	⚒	Ⓐ	⚒	⑦ *E*	⑦ *E*	⑦ *E*	⑦ *E*	⑦ *E*	⑦
Dublin Connolly d.	1322	1520	1549	1623	1650	1651	...	...	1721	1721	1758	1759	1840	1900	1921	2017	2050	...	2125	2229	2320	1000	1300	1600	1800	1900	2122
Malahide d.	1340	|	1609	1643	|	1710	...	...	|	1739	1820	1820	|	|	1942	2035	|	...	2143	2248	2335	|	|	|	|	|	2140
Skerries d.	1355	|	1623	1658	|	1725	...	...	1745	1754	1835	1834	1901	|	1956	2049	|	...	2157	2302	2350	|	|	|	|	|	2154
Balbriggan d.	1400	|	1629	1703	|	1731	...	...	1751	1759	1840	1840	1907	|	2002	2055	|	...	2203	2308	2355	|	|	|	|	|	2200
Drogheda d.	1418	1553f	1645	1720	|	1746	...	...	1807	1816	1857	1857	1922	1931	2018	2111	2115	...	2219	2324	0016	1030	1330	1630	1830	1930	2219
Dundalk d.	...	1615	▬	...	1743	▬	...	...	1832	1840	1922	...	1946	1955	▬	▬	2140	...	2243v	2348	0040	1052	1352	1652	1852	1952	2243
Newry d.	...	1633	⚒h	...	1801	⚒g	1835	1935	...	...	...	...	...	2013	Ⓐ	⑥	2158	...	...	...	...	1110	1410	1710	1910	2010	...
Portadown § d.	...	1654	1705	...	1822	1830	1900	2000	...	...	...	...	...	2034	2045	2100	2219	2230	...	...	...	1132	1432	1732	1932	2032	...
Lisburn § a.	...	|	1730	...	|	1855	1925	2025	...	...	...	...	...	|	2110	2125	|	2255	...	...	...	1201	*1525*	*1825*	*2025*	*2125*	...
Belfast Central § a.	...	1735h	1800	...	1858	1925	1954	2055	...	...	...	...	...	2110	2140	2154	2255	2325	...	...	...	1216	1507	1807	2010	2107	...

e – 1006 on ⑥.
f – Not ⑤.
g – 3–6 minutes later on ⑥.
h – 5 minutes earlier on ⑥.
p – *0955* on ⑥.
v – ⑤ only.
x – Belfast **Great Victoria Street**. On ⑥ depart Belfast **Central** 0730, arrive Portadown 0827.
z – On ⑥ depart Lisburn 0801, arrive Portadown 0827.
§ – Other local trains run Belfast - Lisburn - Portadown and v.v.

NIR BELFAST - LONDONDERRY and PORTRUSH 231

Service valid March 30 – June 28. For service June 29 - Dec. 12 see page 40

🚌 will run between Ballymena and Coleraine and v.v. 🚌 will run between Antrim - Coleraine June 13, 14, 20, 21, 27, 28.

km		⑥	Ⓐ	⑥	Ⓐ	⑥	Ⓐ	⑥	Ⓐ	⑥	Ⓐ	Ⓐ	⑥	Ⓐ	Ⓐ	Ⓐ	⑥	Ⓐ	⑥	Ⓐ	⑥	⑦	⑦	⑦	⑦	⑦
	Belfast GVSt. ★ d.	...	...	0810	0844	1010	1040	1210	1240	1410	1440	1600	1610	1647	1715	1756	1810	1935	2010	2115	2210	0950	1250	1550	1850	2120
0	**Belfast Central** d.	0620	0655	0820	0854	1017	1050	1220	1250	1420	1450	1610	1620	1657	1725	1805	1820	1945	2020	2125	2220	1000	1300	1600	1900	2130
33	Antrim d.	0645	0718	0844	0918	1044	1113	1244	1313	1444	1512	1635	1644	1722	1755	1829	1844	2009	2042	2149	2243	1024	1324	1624	1924	2154
52	Ballymena d.	*0705*	*0733*	*0905*	*0931*	*1105*	*1128*	*1305*	*1328*	*1505*	*1528*	*1648*	*1705*	*1738*	*1808*	*1842*	*1905*	*2022*	*2105*	*2205*	2258	*1040*	*1340*	*1640*	*1940*	2208
97	**Coleraine** ▲ d.	0807	0833	1007	1033	1207	1233	1407	1433	1607	1633	1757	1807	1847	1915	1945	2007	2133	2207	*2250*	...	1135	1435	1735	2035	...
107	Portrush ▲ a.	|	|	|	|	|	|	|	|	|	|	|	|	1859	1925	|	|	|	|	...	...	|	|	|	|	...
151	**Londonderry** a.	0855	0920	1055	1120	1255	1320	1455	1520	1655	1720	1845	1855	...	...	2033	2055	2220	2255	...	...	1223	1523	1823	2123	...

	Ⓐ	Ⓐ	⑥	Ⓐ	Ⓐ	⑥	Ⓐ	⑥	Ⓐ	Ⓐ	⑥	⑥	Ⓐ	⑥	Ⓐ	⑥	Ⓐ	Ⓐ	⑥	Ⓐ	⑥	⑦	⑦	⑦	⑦	⑦
Londonderry d.	...	...	...	...	0610	0720	0745	0920	0945	1145	1120	1320	1345	1520	1545	1720	1725	1855	1920	...	...	1015	1315	...	1615	1915
Portrush ▲ d.	...	0555	...	0625	|	|	|	|	|	|	|	|	|	|	|	|	|	|	|	...	...	|	|	1520	|	|
Coleraine ▲ d.	...	*0607*	...	*0637*	*0655*	*0805*	*0830*	*1005*	*1030*	*1230*	*1205*	*1405*	*1430*	*1605*	*1630*	*1805*	*1815*	*1940*	*2005*	...	...	*1105*	*1405*	*1540*	*1705*	*2005*
Ballymena d.	0631	0700	0705	0738	0807	0905	0936	1105	1135	1335	1305	1505	1540	1705	1741	1905	1918	2035	2105	2225	2305	1207	1507	1647	1807	2107
Antrim d.	0645	0715	0720	0753	0820	0920	0950	1120	1148	1350	1320	1520	1555	1718	1755	1918	1932	2049	2120	2239	2320	1220	1520	1700	1820	2120
Belfast Central a.	0715	0746	0742	0821	0843	0942	1012	1142	1212	1412	1342	1542	1621	1742	1825	1942	1954	2111	2142	2301	2342	1243	1543	1723	1843	2143
Belfast GVSt. ★ a.	0722	...	0755	0833	0855	0955	1025	1155	1225	1425	1355	1555	1631	1755	1836	1955	2005	2121	2155	2312	...	1255	1555	1735	1855	2155

km		Ⓐ	Ⓐ	Ⓐ	Ⓐ	Ⓐ	Ⓐ	Ⓐ	Ⓐ	Ⓐ	Ⓐ	Ⓐ	Ⓐ	Ⓐ	Ⓐ	Ⓐ	Ⓐ	Ⓐ	Ⓐ	Ⓐ	⑥	⑥	⑥	⑥	⑥	⑥		⑥
0	Coleraine d.	0730	0800	0835	0915	1000	1035	1135	1235	1335	1435	1535	1635	1720	1753	1822	1847	1915	1947	2100	0655	0810	0930	1010	1130	1210	and hourly until	2110
10	Portrush a.	0742	0810	0845	0927	1010	1045	1145	1245	1345	1445	1545	1645	1730	1805	1832	1859	1925	1657	2110	0705	0820	0940	1020	1140	1220		2120

	Ⓐ	Ⓐ	Ⓐ	Ⓐ	Ⓐ	Ⓐ	Ⓐ	Ⓐ	Ⓐ	Ⓐ	Ⓐ	Ⓐ	Ⓐ	Ⓐ	Ⓐ	Ⓐ	Ⓐ	Ⓐ	Ⓐ	Ⓐ	Ⓐ	⑥	⑥	⑥	⑥	⑥		⑥
Portrush d.	0555	0625	0746	0818	0850	0935	1018	1118	1218	1318	1418	1518	1618	1705	1740	1808	1825	1903	1930	2005	2118	0750	0830	0950	1030	1150	and hourly until	2150
Coleraine a.	0607	0637	0758	0828	0900	0947	1028	1128	1228	1328	1428	1528	1628	1715	1750	1820	1845	1913	1940	2015	2128	0800	0840	1000	1040	1200		2200

	⑦	⑦	⑦	⑦	⑦	⑦	⑦	⑦	⑦	⑦	⑦	⑦	
Coleraine d.	1030	1105	1140	1330	1405	1440	1630	1705	1740	1930	2005	2040	...
Portrush a.	1042	1115	1152	1342	1415	1452	1642	1715	1752	1942	2015	2052	...

		⑦	⑦	⑦	⑦	⑦	⑦	⑦	⑦	⑦	⑦	⑦	⑦
Portrush d.	...	1050	1120	1205	1350	1420	1520	1650	1720	1805	1950	2020	2105
Coleraine a.	...	1102	1130	1217	1402	1430	1532	1702	1730	1817	2002	2030	2117

▲ – **COLERAINE - PORTRUSH** (for all trains see panel).
★ – Belfast GVSt. (Belfast Great Victoria St.) is the nearest station to Belfast City Centre and the Europa Buscentre is adjacent.

Ulsterbus 212 express 🚌 service, Belfast - Londonderry. Journey time: 1 hour 40 minutes.
Ⓐ: 0645, 0800, 0830, 0900, 0930 and every 30 minutes until 1900, 1930 then 2030, 2130, 2300; also 1545, 1745.
⑥: 0645, 0930, 1030, 1130, 1230, 1330, 1400 and every 30 minutes to 1800, 1830 then 1930, 2030, 2130, 2300.
⑦: 0830, 1000, 1130, 1330, 1430, 1600, 1730, 1930, 2030, 2130, 2215.

Ulsterbus 212 express 🚌 service, Londonderry - Belfast. Journey time: 1 hour 40 minutes.
Ⓐ: 0530, 0545, 0600, 0630, 0700, 0730, 0745, 0800, 0830 and every 30 minutes until 1630, 1700 then 1800, 1930, 2100.
⑥: 0700, 0800, 0830, 0900, 0930, 1000, 1030, 1100, 1130, 1200, 1230, 1300, 1400, 1500, 1600, 1700, 1800, 1930, 2100.
⑦: 0800, 0900, 1030, 1200, 1330, 1500, 1600, 1700, 1800, 1900.

232 BELFAST - ENNISKILLEN and ARMAGH

Ulsterbus **251**, **261**

From Belfast ★ to Enniskillen (Bus Stn) (journey time 2 hours 15 mins)

Ⓐ: 0805, 0905 and hourly until 1905, 2005.
⑥: 0905, 1005, 1105, 1205, 1305, 1505, 1605, 1805, 2005.
⑦: 1605, 2005.

From Enniskillen (Bus Stn) to Belfast ★

Ⓐ: 0725, 0825, and hourly until 1625, 1725, 1825◧.
⑥: 0725, 0925, 1025, 1225, 1325, 1525, 1725.
⑦: 1225, 1525, 1725, 1825.

From Belfast ★ to Armagh (Bus Stn) (journey time 1 hour 25 mins)

Ⓐ: 0800, 0935, 1035, 1135, 1235, 1335, 1435, 1645, 1715, 1735, 1835, 1935, 2115.
⑥: 1035, 1235, 1435, 1735, 1835, 2005.
⑦: 1335, 1735, 2015, 2200.

From Armagh (Bus Stn) to Belfast ★

Ⓐ: 0630, 0715, 0800, 0900, 1000, 1100, 1200, 1300, 1500, 1600, 1700, 1800.
⑥: 0730, 0900, 1100, 1300, 1600, 1700.
⑦: 1210, 1410, 1610, 1830, 2015.

Buses call at **Portadown (Market Street)** 40–75 minutes from Belfast and **Portadown (Northern Bank)** 20–30 minutes from Armagh (Bus Stn).

◧ – Change at Dungannon; arrive Europa Buscentre 2140.

★ – Europa Buscentre / Great Victoria St. Rail Station.

233 BELFAST - LARNE

NIR

From Belfast Central – Ⓐ: 0553 **H**, 0648, 0732 **H**, 0842 **H**, and hourly until 1342 **H**, 1442, 1512 **H**, 1612, 1635, 1715 **H**, 1735, 1810, 1850, 1930 **H**, 2030 **H**, 2130 **H**, 2230 **H**, 2330 **H**.
⑥: 0612 **H**, 0712 **H**, and hourly until 2012 **H**, 2113 **H**, 2212, 2312 **H**.
⑦: 0833 **H**, 1003 **H**, 1133 **H**, 1303 **H**, 1433 **H**, 1603 **H**, 1733 **H**, 1903 **H**, 2033 **H**, 2203 **H**.

From Larne Town – Ⓐ: 0600, 0628 **S**, 0656 **S**, 0728 **S**, 0755, 0813 **S**, 0900 **S**, 1000 **S** and hourly until 1500 **S**, 1545, 1633 **S**, 1715, 1743, 1820, 1845, 1915, 1950, 2033 **S**, 2133 **S**, 2233 **S**.
⑥: 0550 **S**, 0630 **S**, 0730 **S**, 0830 **S** and hourly until 2030 **S**, 2130 **S**, 2230 **S**.
⑦: 0826 **S**, 0956 **S**, 1126 **S**, 1256**S**, 1426 **S**, 1556 **S**, 1726 **S**, 1856 **S**, 2026 **S**, 2156 **S**.

Trains call at: **Carrickfergus** 27–29 minutes from Belfast and 28–31 minutes from Larne and **Whitehead** 38–40 minutes from Belfast, 18–21 minutes from Larne.

Trains marked **H** arrive Larne **Harbour** 4 minutes after Larne **Town**. Trains marked **S** depart Larne **Harbour** 3 minutes before Larne **Town**. Journey time Belfast Central - Larne Harbour 57–65 mins.

234 DUBLIN - LONDONDERRY

Bus Éireann **33** / Ulsterbus **274**

Dublin ● d.	0400	0715	0915	1000	1145	1345	1545	1745	1945	2145	2300
Dublin Airport ✈ △ d.	0420	0735	0935	1020	1205	1405	1605	1805	2005	2205	2320
Monaghan a.	0545	0910	1110	1155	1340	1540	1740	1940	2140	2340	0055
Monaghan d.	0600	0925	1125	1210	1355	1555	1755	1955	2155	2340	0055
Omagh ▽ a.	0650	1010	1210	1255	1440	1640	1840	2040	2240	0025	0140
Strabane ▽ a.	0720	1045	1245	1330	1515	1715	1915	2115	2315	0100	0215
Londonderry a.	0745	1115	1315	1400	1545	1745	1945	2145	2345	0130	0245

Londonderry d.	0045	0415	0615	0815	1015	1115	1215	1415	1615	1815	2045
Strabane △ d.	0105	0445	0645	0845	1045	1145	1245	1445	1645	1845	2115
Omagh △ d.	0130	0520	0720	0920	1120	1220	1320	1520	1720	1920	2150
Monaghan a.	0210	0605	0805	1005	1205	1305	1405	1605	1805	2005	2235
Monaghan d.	0210	0605	0820	1020	1220	1320	1420	1620	1820	2020	2250
Dublin Airport ✈ ▽ a.	0350	0755	0955	1155	1350	1455	1555	1755	1955	2155	0025
Dublin ● a.	0410	0815	1015	1215	1410	1515	1615	1815	2015	2215	0045

△ – Buses stop here to pick up only. ▽ – Buses stop here to set down only. ● – Dublin **Busaras**. ☛ The calling point in each town is the bus station unless otherwise indicated.

234a DUBLIN - DONEGAL

Bus Éireann **30**

				⑤					⑦		
Dublin ● d.	0700	0930	1130	1300	1300	1500	1700	1900	2100	2200	2400
Dublin Airport ✈ △ d.	0720	0950	1150	|	1320	1520	1720	1920	|	2220	0020
Navan ◧ d.	0810	1040	1240	|	1410	1610	1810	2010	|	2250	0050
Cavan d.	0925c	1155c	1355c	1450	1525c	1725u	1925u	2125u	2250	0005c	0150
Enniskillen d.	1010	1240	1440	1555	1610	1810	2010	2210	2335	0055	0240
Ballyshannon d.	1055	1325	1525	|	1655	1855	2055	2255	|	0140	0325
Donegal ⊡ a.	1120	1350	1550	1700	1720	1920	2120	2320	0030	0205	0350

							⑦			
Donegal ⊡ d.	0200	0500	0700	0900	1100	1300	1500	1500	1645	1830
Ballyshannon d.	0225	0525	0725	0925	1125	1325	|	1525	1710	1855
Enniskillen d.	0305	0605	0810	1010	1210	1410	1600	1610	1755	1940
Cavan d.	0350	0650	0910c	1110c	1310c	1510c	1645u	1710c	1840s	2040c
Navan ◐ d.	0445	0745	1010	1210	1410	1610	|	1810	1955	2140
Dublin Airport ✈ ▽ a.	0535	0835	1100	1300	1500	1700	|	1900	2045	2230
Dublin ● a.	0555	0855	1120	1320	1520	1720	1840	1920	2105	2250

c – Arrive 15 minutes earlier.
s – Stops to set down only.
u – Stops to pick up only.
● – Dublin **Busaras**.
◐ – Navan **Bypass**.
◧ – Navan **Mercy Convent**.
⊡ – Donegal **Abbey Hotel**.
△ – Buses stop here to pick up only.
▽ – Buses stop here to set down only.

235 LONDONDERRY - GALWAY and GALWAY - CORK

Bus Éireann **51**, **64**

	⚒	⚒	⚒	⚒	⚒	⚒	⑦	⑦	⑦	⑦
Londonderry d.	...	0720	0830	1200	1600	1830	...	1130	1440	1715
Letterkenny d.	...	0755	0905	1235	1635	1905	...	1205	1515	1750
Donegal (Abbey Hotel) d.	...	0845	0955	1330	1730	1955	...	1255	1605	1840
Ballyshannon d.	...	0905	1015	1350	1750	2015	...	1315	1625	1900
Sligo d.	0815	1000	1115	1500	1900	2100	1115	1415	1720	2000
Knock d.	0925	1110	1225	1610	2010	...	1220	1525	1830	2110
Claremorris (Dalton St.) d.	|	1122	|	1622	|	...	1232	|	|	2122
Galway (Bus Station) ✣ a.	1045	1230	1345	1730	2130	...	1345	1645	1950	2230

	⚒	⚒	⚒	⚒	⚒	⚒	⑦	⑦	⑦	⑦
Cork d.	...	0825	1025	1225	1525	1825	0825	1025	1525	1825
Mallow (Town Park) d.	...	0900	1100	1300	1600	1900	0900	1100	1600	1900
Charleville d.	...	0930	1130	1330	1630	1930	0930	1130	1630	1930
Limerick (Rail Station) a.	...	1010	1210	1410	1710	2010	1010	1210	1710	2010
Limerick (Rail Station) d.	0825	1025	1225	1425	1725	2025	1025	1225	1725	2025
Shannon Airport ✈ d.	0855	1055	1255	1455	1755	2055	1055	1255	1755	2055
Ennis d.	0925	1125	1325	1525	1825	2125	1125	1325	1825	2125
Galway (Bus Station) ✣ a.	1045	1245	1445	1645	1945	2245	1245	1445	1945	2245

	⚒	⚒	⚒	⚒	⚒	⚒	⑦	⑦	⑦	⑦
Galway (Bus Station) ✣ d.	0705	1205	1405	1505	1705	1905	0705	1005	1505	1805
Ennis d.	0820	1320	1520	1620	1820	2020	0820	1120	1620	1920
Shannon Airport ✈ d.	0850	1350	1550	1650	1850	2050	0850	1150	1650	1950
Limerick (Rail Station) a.	0920	1420	1620	1720	1920	2120	0920	1220	1720	2020
Limerick (Rail Station) d.	0935	1435	1635	1735	1935	...	0935	1235	1735	2035
Charleville d.	1010	1510	1710	1810	2010	...	1010	1310	1810	2110
Mallow (Town Park) d.	1040	1540	1740	1840	2040	...	1040	1340	1840	2140
Cork a.	1125	1625	1825	1925	2125	...	1125	1425	1925	2225

	⚒	⚒	⚒	⚒	⚒	⑤	⑦	⑦	⑦	⑦
Galway (Bus Station) ✣ d.	0900	1200	1400	1600	1815	...	1000	1400	1600	2100
Claremorris (Dalton St.) d.	|	1308	|	|	1923	...	|	|	|	2208
Knock d.	1020	1320	1520	1720	1935	...	1120	1520	1720	2220
Sligo d.	1145	1445	1645	1845	2045	2050	1245	1645	1900	2330
Ballyshannon d.	1225	1525	1725	1925	...	2130	1325	1725	1940	...
Donegal (Abbey Hotel) d.	1250	1550	1750	1950	...	2155	1350	1750	2005	...
Letterkenny d.	1340	1640	1840	2040	...	2245	1440	1840	2055	...
Londonderry a.	1415	1715	1915	2115	...	2325	1515	1915	2130	...

✣ – Change buses at Galway. Minimum connection time 45 minutes.

☛ The calling point in each town is the bus station unless otherwise indicated.

236 DUBLIN - SLIGO

IÉ

km		Ⓐ 🍷	⚒ 🍷	⚒ 🍷	⚒ 🍷	⚒ 🍷	⚒ 🍷	⚒ 🍷	Ⓐ	Ⓐ	Ⓐ	⚒ 🍷	
0	**Dublin Connolly** d.	0705	0905	1105	1305	1505	1600	1705	1715	1805	1818	1905	...
26	Maynooth d.	0732	0934	1133	1332	1533	1627	1731e	1757	1832	1901	1937	...
83	Mullingar d.	0815	1014	1213	1413	1613	1712	1810	1843	1914	1950	2017	...
125	**Longford** d.	0844	1043	1242	1441	1642	1741	1840	1923	1946	2020	2046	...
143	Dromod d.	0858	1057	1256	1455	1656	1800	1855	...	...	...	2100	...
159	Carrick on Shannon d.	0914	1113	1311	1511	1711	1816	1911	...	...	...	2117	...
173	Boyle d.	0933	1145	1333	1533	1733	1827	1933	...	...	...	2130	...
219	**Sligo** a.	1010	1210	1410	1610	1810	1910	2010	...	...	...	2208	...

km			⑦ 🍷		⑦ 🍷	⑦ 🍷	⑦ 🍷	⑦ 🍷	⑦ 🍷		
0	**Dublin Connolly** d.	...	0905	...	1305	1505	1600	1705	1905	...	...
26	Maynooth d.	...	0932	...	1333	1533	1626	1730	1933	...	...
83	Mullingar d.	...	1012	...	1412	1612	1712	1810	2015	...	...
125	**Longford** d.	...	1041	...	1441	1641	1741	1841	2044	...	...
143	Dromod d.	...	1055	...	1455	1655	1800	1855	2058	...	...
159	Carrick on Shannon d.	...	1112	...	1511	1711	1816	1911	2115	...	...
173	Boyle d.	...	1133	...	1533	1733	1827	1933	2128	...	...
219	**Sligo** a.	...	1210	...	1610	1810	1910	2010	2205	...	...

	Ⓐ	Ⓐ 🍷	⚒ 🍷	⚒ 🍷	⚒ 🍷	⚒ 🍷	⚒ 🍷	⚒ 🍷	⚒ 🍷	Ⓐ	
Sligo d.	...	0545	0700	0900	1100	1300	1500	1700	1900	...	...
Boyle d.	...	0616	0732	0932	1132	1332	1532	1732	1932	...	...
Carrick on Shannon d.	...	0627	0744	0944	1144	1344	1544	1744	1944	...	...
Dromod d.	...	0642	0758	0958	1158	1358	1558	1758	1958	...	...
Longford d.	0615	0657	0814	1014	1214	1414	1614	1814	2022	2050	...
Mullingar d.	0648	0726	0853	1051	1250	1451	1650	1850	2056	2122	...
Maynooth d.	0730	0810	0933	1131	1330	1531	1730	1934	2136	2201	...
Dublin Connolly a.	0820	0847	1003	1158	1359	1559	1800	2006	2205	2230	...

		⑦ 🍷	⑦ 🍷	⑦ 🍷	⑦ 🍷	⑦ 🍷	⑦ 🍷					
Sligo d.	...	0900	1100	1300	1500	1700	1900	...	...	...	...	...
Boyle d.	...	0932	1132	1332	1532	1732	1932	...	...	...	...	...
Carrick on Shannon d.	...	0944	1144	1344	1544	1744	1944	...	...	...	...	...
Dromod d.	...	0958	1158	1358	1558	1758	1958	...	...	...	...	...
Longford d.	...	1014	1214	1414	1614	1816	2014	...	...	...	...	...
Mullingar d.	...	1051	1245	1451	1651	1851	2054	...	...	...	...	...
Maynooth d.	...	1130	1322	1528	1728	1928	2135	...	...	...	...	...
Dublin Connolly a.	...	1203	1354	1559	1805	2005	2210	...	...	...	...	...

e – ⑥ only.

236a BALLYBROPHY - ROSCREA - LIMERICK

IÉ

km		Ⓐ	⚒ ◇🍷	⚒		Ⓐ	⚒ ◇🍷	⚒		⑦ ◇🍷	⑦
0	Dublin Heuston d.	...	0900	...	...	...	1725	...	...	1825	...
107	Ballybrophy d.	...	1005	1010	...	...	1845	1855	...	1943	1950
123	Roscrea d.	...	...	1027	...	...	...	1912	...	...	2007
154	Nenagh d.	0755	...	1102	...	1845	...	1947	...	...	2042
199	**Limerick** a.	0845	...	1155	...	1935	...	2039	...	...	2135

	⚒	⚒ ◇🍷		⚒	⚒ 🍷	Ⓐ		⑦	⑦ ◇🍷	
Limerick d.	0640	...	...	1645	...	1747	...	1745	...	...
Nenagh d.	0735	...	...	1739	...	1840	...	1838	...	...
Roscrea d.	0810	...	...	1814	...	...	...	1913	...	...
Ballybrophy a.	0829	0835	...	1831	1844	...	...	1930	1939	...
Dublin Heuston a.	...	0955	...	...	2008	...	...	...	2105	...

◇ – Also conveys 1st class.

IÉ — DUBLIN - ROSSLARE — 237

km		Ⓐ	⚒	⚒	⚒🍷	Ⓐ	Ⓐ	Ⓐ	⚒🍷§	⑦	⑦🍷	⑦🍷§
0	**Dublin Connolly** ▲ d.	...	0726	1135	1305	1640	1725	...	1837	0949	1320	1830
11	Dún Laoghaire ▲ d.	...	0752	1157	1320	|	1749	...	1853	1009	1336	1845
21	Bray ▲ d.	...	0815	1216	1337	1723	1806	...	1910	1029	1353	1900
47	Wicklow d.	...	0838	1244	1400	1749	1835	...	1938	1053	1417	1925
80	Arklow d.	0544	0906	1313	1429	1818	1906	...	2011	1125	1446	1954
97	Gorey d.	0557	0920	1327	1447	1833	1920	...	2025	1139	1500	2008
126	Enniscorthy d.	0625	0940	...	1503	...	1939	1950	2049	1159	1525	2028
150	**Wexford** d.	0648	1004	...	1527	...	...	2013	2112	1223	1550	2052
160	Rosslare Strand d.	0712	1022	...	1544	...	...	2030	2129	1240	1608	2109
166	**Rosslare** Europort a.	0718	1028	...	1553	...	...	2037	2135	1248	1616	2117

	Ⓐ	Ⓐ	⑥	⚒🍷§	⚒🍷	⚒	⚒	Ⓐ	Ⓐ	Ⓐ	⑦🍷	⑦🍷	⑦
Rosslare Europort d.	...	0535	...	0740	1300	...	1740	...	1855	...	0855	1435	1750
Rosslare Strand d.	...	0541	...	0745	1306	...	1745	...	1901	...	0900	1440	1755
Wexford d.	...	0600	...	0804	1325	...	1805	...	1920	...	0920	1500	1815
Enniscorthy d.	...	0623	...	0827	1348	...	1828	...	1942	2005	0943	1523	1838
Gorey d.	0600	0645	0645	0850	1410	1448	1850	1923	...	2027	1005	1547	1900
Arklow d.	0613	0659	0659	0905	1431	1500	1904	1935	...	2040	1018	1600	1913
Wicklow d.	0644	0733	0733	0939	1501	1530	1938	2010	...	2109	1053	1630	1953
Bray ▲ d.	0713	0805	0805	1001	1523	1601	2001	2037	...	2133	1117	1653	2016
Dún Laoghaire ▲ d.	0731	0823	0823	1018	1538	1622	2017	2057	...	2150	1134	1713	2037
Dublin Connolly ▲ a.	0758	0851	0851	1036	1603	1641	2032	2118	...	2212	1152	1730	2054

▲ – Additional surburban trains (*DART*) run Howth - Dublin Connolly - Dún Laoghaire - Bray. Trains run every 10–15 minutes on ⚒, every 20–30 minutes on ⑦.

§ – Does not connect with Ferry: Rosslare - Fishguard and v.v.

Bus Éireann 12, 13 — 🚌 DUBLIN - LIMERICK - TRALEE — 238

									⑦			
Dublin Busaras d.	...	...	0730	0930	1130	1330	1530	1630	...	1730	1830	2000
Kildare (Boyle's) d.	...	...	0830	1030	1230	1430	1630	1730	...	1830	1930	2100
Portlaoise (JFL Ave.) d.	...	...	0900	1100	1300	1500	1700	1800	...	1900	2000	2130
Roscrea d.	...	...	0950	1150	1350	1550	1750	1850	...	1950	2050	2220
Nenagh d.	...	...	1025	1225	1425	1625	1825	1925	...	2025	2125	2255
Limerick (Bus Stn) ❖ a.	...	...	1110	1310	1510	1710	1910	2010	...	2110	2210	2340
Limerick (Bus Stn) ❖ d.	0835	0935	1135	1335	1535	1735	1935	2035	2035	2135	...	...
Adare d.	0855	0955	1155	1355	1555	1755	1955	2055	2055	2155	...	...
Newcastlewest d.	0920	1020	1220	1420	1620	1820	2020	2120	2120	2220	...	...
Abbeyfeale d.	0940	1040	1240	1440	1640	1840	2040	2140	2140	2240	...	...
Listowel (Square) d.	1000	1100	1300	1500	1700	1900	2100	...	2200	2300	...	...
Tralee (Station) a.	1040	1140	1340	1540	1740	1940	2140	...	2240	2340	...	...

		⚒										
Tralee (Station) d.	...	0615	...	0800	0900	1100	1300	1500	...	1700	1800	1900
Listowel (Square) d.	...	0645	...	0830	0930	1130	1330	1530	...	1730	1830	1930
Abbeyfeale d.	...	0710	...	0855	0955	1155	1355	1555	1655	1755	1855	1955
Newcastlewest d.	...	0730	...	0915	1015	1215	1415	1615	1715	1815	1915	2015
Adare d.	...	0755	...	0940	1040	1240	1440	1640	1740	1840	1940	2040
Limerick (Bus Stn) ❖ a.	...	0820	...	1005	1105	1305	1505	1705	1805	1905	2005	2105
Limerick (Bus Stn) ❖ d.	0730	...	0830	1030	1130	1330	1530	1730	1830	1930	...	...
Nenagh d.	0810	...	0910	1110	1210	1410	1610	1810	1910	2010	...	...
Roscrea d.	0840	...	0940	1140	1240	1440	1640	1840	1940	2040	...	...
Portlaoise (JFL Ave.) d.	0930	...	1030	1230	1330	1530	1730	1930	2030	2130	...	...
Kildare (Boyle's) d.	1000	...	1100	1300	1400	1600	1800	2000	2100	2200	...	...
Dublin Busaras a.	1110	...	1210	1410	1510	1710	1910	2110	2210	2310	...	...

Dublin - Limerick (service **12**) also: 0830, 1030, 1230, 1430.
Limerick - Dublin (service **12**) also: 0930, 1230, 1430, 1630.

❖ – A change of 🚌 is required at Limerick (Bus Station). Adjacent to Limerick railway station.

IÉ; Bus Éireann 40, 55, 372 — LIMERICK - WATERFORD - ROSSLARE — 239

km		⚒	⚒	⚒	⚒		🚌	🚌 ⚒	🚌	🚌 ⚒	🚌 x
0	**Limerick** d.	*0755*	*1055*	*1455*	*1755*	...	0825	1230	1615	1730	2030
35	**Limerick Jct.** d.	0850	1145	1546	1845	...	0855	1300	1645	1800	2100
40	Tipperary d.	0902	1156	1556	1856	...	0900	1305	1650	1805	2105
62	Cahir d.	0926	1220	1620	1920	...	0930	1335	1720	1835	2135
79	Clonmel d.	0944	1238	1638	1938	...	0950	1355	1740	1855	2155
101	Carrick on Suir d.	1008	1302	1707	2002	...	1010	1415	1800	1915	2215
124	**Waterford** a.	1032	1326	1732	2026	...	1055	1455	1840	1955	2255
	Waterford d.	...	...	1734	...	...	*1130c*	*1630*	*1930*	...	...
	Wexford d.	...	...	|	...	...	*1230c*	*1730*	*2030*	...	...
186	**Rosslare** Europort a.	...	...	1850	...	...	*1255c*	*1830e*	*2050*	...	...

	⚒	⚒	⚒	⚒	⚒	🚌	🚌	🚌	🚌	🚌
Rosslare Europort d.	...	0705	...	...	...	*0700x*	*0900c*	*1300*	*1440*	*1900*
Wexford d.	...	|	...	...	...	*0725x*	*0925c*	*1325*	*1505*	*1925*
Waterford a.	...	0823	...	...	...	*0845*	*1025*	*1425*	*1605*	*2020*
Waterford d.	0635	...	0935	1230	1638	0850	1050	1450	1650	2030
Carrick on Suir d.	0700	...	1009	1303	1704	0920	1120	1520	1720	2100
Clonmel d.	0723	...	1033	1326	1727	0945	1145	1545	1745	2125
Cahir d.	0742	...	1052	1345	1746	1010	1210	1610	1810	2150
Tipperary d.	0805	...	1115	1409	1809	1035	1235	1635	1835	2215
Limerick Jct. a.	0817	...	1125	1419	1819	1040	1240	1640	1840	2220
Limerick a.	*0915*	...	*1212*	*1508*	*1903*	1115	1315	1715	1915	2300

c – ⚒ only. e – Change additionally at Wexford. x – 10–15 minutes later on ⑦.

Additional journeys: – Limerick - Waterford 🚌 0930 ⚒, 1130, 1430, 1840 ⑦. Waterford - Limerick 🚌 0750 ⚒, 1250 ⚒, 1750 ⚒, 1830 ⑦. Waterford - Wexford 🚌 0700, 0900 ⚒. Wexford - Waterford 🚌: 1720 Ⓐ; 1745 ⑦; 1840 Ⓐ.

Buses call at rail stations **except**: Limerick (Bus Station), Limerick Junction (Bit and Bridle Pub), Tipperary (Abbey St), Cahir (Castle St), Carrick (Greenside), Waterford (Bus Station).

IÉ — ❖ DUBLIN - GALWAY, BALLINA and WESTPORT ❖ — 240

km		⚒	⚒h ◇🍴	⚒ 🍷	⚒ 🍷	⚒ 🍷	⚒ 🍷	⚒ ◇🍷	⑤ 🍷	⚒h ◇🍴	⚒	⚒ 🍷	⚒	⚒ 🍷	⚒ 🍷	⑦ 🍷	⑦	⑦ 🍷	⑦ 🍷	⑦	⑦ ◇🍷	⑦ 🍷	⑦ 🍷	⑦	⑦ ◇🍷	⑦
0	**Dublin Heuston 245** d.	...	0710	0820	0910	1110	1240	1435	1615	1650	1710	1745	...	1750	1915	0840	...	1210	1305	...	1345	1605	1805	...	1850	2040
48	Kildare **245** d.	...	|	|	0948	1144	1314	|	1653	|	1747	|	...	|	1951	0918	...	|	1342	...	|	|	1842	...	1924	|
67	Portarlington **245** d.	...	0754	|	1002	|	1329	1519	1708	|	1805	|	...	1839	2007	0932	...	|	1355	...	|	1650	1856	...	1938	2128
93	Tullamore d.	...	0812	0924	1021	1212	1347	1539	1727	|	1823	|	...	1858	2025	0951	...	|	1413	...	|	1708	1914	...	1959	2146
129	**Athlone** d.	0705	0845	0954	1048	1245	1414	1605	1753	1813	1853	1909	...	1932	2051	1026	1035	|	1445	...	1506	1739	1956	...	2031	2215
152	Ballinasloe d.	0721	0903	|	1105	1303	|	1623	|	1831	...	|	...	1950	2109	1045	|	|	|	...	1529	1757	|	...	2049	2233
187	Athenry d.	0800	0931	|	1137	1329	|	1650	|	1856	...	|	...	2012	2134	1116	|	|	|	...	1556	1831	|	...	2115	2256
208	**Galway** a.	0821	0955	|	1159	1351	|	1715	|	1916	...	|	...	2031	2155	1140	|	1438	|	...	1618	1847	|	...	2134	2315
160	Roscommon d.	...	...	1020	—	...	1442	—	1821	...	...	1937	...	...	...	...	1058	—	1520	...	...	...	2020	...	...	...
186	Castlerea d.	...	...	1040	...	...	1503	...	1841	...	...	1957	...	...	...	...	1119	...	1541	...	...	...	2040	...	...	...
204	Ballyhaunis d.	...	...	1055	...	...	1518	...	1856	...	...	2012	...	...	...	...	1134	...	1556	...	...	...	2055	...	...	...
222	Claremorris d.	...	...	1110	⚒	...	1532	⚒	1913	...	...	2027	...	...	...	...	1148	⑦	1610	...	...	...	2110	...	...	...
240	Manulla Junction § d.	...	...	1125	1128	...	1548	1551	|	...	...	2042	2045	...	...	...	1203	1207	1625	1629	...	...	2125	2128	...	...
273	**Ballina** a.	...	...	|	1157	...	|	1619	2002	...	...	|	2113	...	...	...	|	1236	|	1657	...	...	|	2156	...	...
246	Castlebar d.	...	...	1136	...	...	1558	...	...	...	...	2051	...	...	...	...	1213	...	1635	...	...	...	2135	...	...	...
264	**Westport** a.	...	...	1158	...	...	1621	...	...	...	...	2114	...	...	...	...	1231	...	1650	...	...	...	2151	...	...	...

	Ⓐ	Ⓐ 🍷	⚒h ◇🍴	⚒	⚒ 🍷	⚒ 🍷	⚒h ◇🍴	⚒ 🍷	⚒	⚒ 🍷	⚒ 🍷	⚒	⚒ 🍷	Ⓐ	⑦ 🍷	⑦	⑦ 🍷	⑦ 🍷	⑦ 🍷	⑦	⑦ 🍷	⑦ 🍷	⑦ 🍷	⑦ ◇🍷	⑦	⑦ 🍷
Westport d.	...	...	...	...	0700	...	...	...	...	1310	...	...	1805	...	...	...	0745	...	...	...	1425	...	1530	...	...	1755
Castlebar d.	...	...	...	...	0713	...	...	...	...	1323	...	...	1818	...	...	...	0758	...	...	...	1438	...	1543	...	...	1808
Ballina d.	...	...	...	0650	|	...	...	...	1300	|	...	1755	|	...	...	0735	|	...	...	1415	|	...	|	...	1745	|
Manulla Junction § d.	...	...	...	0718	0722	...	...	...	1328	1332	...	1823	1828	...	...	0803	0807	...	...	1443	1447	...	|	...	1813	1817
Claremorris d.	...	...	...	...	0737	...	...	...	...	1347	...	—	1843	...	...	...	0822	...	...	—	1502	...	1612	...	...	1836
Ballyhaunis d.	...	...	...	...	0753	...	...	...	...	1403	...	...	1859	...	...	...	0838	...	...	...	1518	...	1629	...	...	1852
Castlerea d.	...	...	...	...	0808	...	...	...	...	1417	...	⚒	1913	...	...	...	0853	...	...	⑦	1533	...	1645	...	...	1907
Roscommon d.	...	...	...	...	0829	...	...	...	...	1438	...	◇🍷	1935	...	...	...	0914	...	...	◇🍷	1602	...	1707	...	...	1928
Galway d.	...	0520	0715	...	|	0915	1050	1310	...	|	1505	1805	|	2145	0825	...	|	1130	1320	1455	|	1615	|	1815	...	|
Athenry d.	...	0533	0728	...	|	0928	1103	1328	...	|	1518	1818	|	2208	0838	...	|	|	1335	1508	|	1631	|	1828	...	|
Ballinasloe d.	...	0559	0751	...	|	0956	1130	1354	...	|	1545	1853	|	2237	0904	...	|	|	1405	1531	|	1657	|	1857	...	|
Athlone d.	0505	0617	0808	...	0855	1013	1147	1413	...	1508	1606	1910	2005	2255	0921	...	0941	|	1423	1548	1629	1718	1742	1914	...	1955
Tullamore d.	0531	0646	0837	...	0925	1043	1216	1443	...	1536	1635	1939	2046	...	0950	...	1015	|	1506	1617	1658	1748	1814	1940	...	2023
Portarlington **245** d.	0550	0706	|	...	0944	|	1238	1503	...	1601	1654	1958	2105	...	1012	...	1038	|	1531	1637	|	1811	1836	2004	...	2043
Kildare **245** d.	0604	0718	|	...	|	|	|	|	...	1614	|	|	|	...	1024	...	|	|	|	1649	|	1826	1851	2016	...	|
Dublin Heuston 245 a.	0700	0810	0945	...	1036	1158	1338	1603	...	1651	1748	2057	2157	...	1110	...	1131	1354	1628	1731	1829	1910	1934	2057	...	2137

h – 🍴 on Ⓐ, 🍷 on ⑥. ◇ – Also conveys [1]. § – Passenger transfer point only. ❖ – Services affected by engineering works on ⑥⑦.

IÉ — ❖ DUBLIN - KILKENNY - WATERFORD ❖ — 241

km		⚒ 🍷	⚒ 🍷	⚒h ◇🍴	⚒ 🍷	⚒ 🍷	⚒	⚒ ◇🍷	Ⓐ	⑦ 🍷	⑦ 🍷	⑦ ◇🍷	⑦ 🍷
0	**Dublin Heuston** △ d.	0730	0930	1130	1505	1625	1735	1825	2005	0930	1430	1735	1840
48	Kildare △ d.	0811	1011	1204	1545	1712	|	|	2043	1010	1512	1813	1914
72	Athy d.	0831	1031	1223	1604	1730	1829	1918	2106	1030	1533	1831	1926
90	Carlow d.	0854	1046	1238	1621	1745	1845	1933	2119	1048	1555	1845	1953
106	Muine Bheag d.	0906	1100	1253	1636	1759	...	1947	...	1102	1609	1859	2007
130	**Kilkenny** a.	0925	1119	1312	1654	1818	...	2006	...	1121	1628	1923	2026
	Kilkenny d.	0929	1123	1321	1701	1828	...	2015	...	1131	1632	1932	2035
147	Thomastown d.	0941	|	1333	1713	1840	...	2027	...	1142	1644	1944	2047
179	**Waterford** a.	1009	1202	1353	1740	1905	...	2050	...	1211	1713	2010	2109

	Ⓐ	⚒ 🍷	⚒h ◇🍴	⚒ 🍷	⚒ 🍷	⚒ ◇🍷	⚒ 🍷	Ⓐ	⑦ ◇🍷	⑦ 🍷	⑦ 🍷	⑦ 🍷
Waterford d.	...	0610	0735	1045	1315	1500	1825	...	0925	1300	1430	1800
Thomastown d.	...	0630	0755	1107	|	1521	1855	...	0949	1321	1450	1824
Kilkenny a.	...	0647	0812	1123	1358	1538	1912	...	1007	1337	1509	1842
Kilkenny d.	...	0656	0821	1127	1403	1548	1919	...	1016	1347	1518	1848
Muine Bheag d.	...	0711	0837	1143	1419	1603	1947	...	1032	1404	1535	1905
Carlow d.	0630	0724	0850	1201	1432	1621	2002	2125	1046	1417	1551	1919
Athy d.	0641	0737	0905	1222	1448	1633	2018	2137	1059	1430	1605	1934
Kildare △ d.	0659	0759	0925	1241	1508	1653	2040	2154	1118	1451	1625	1954
Dublin Heuston △ a.	0752	0845	1005	1326	1553	1734	2126	2240	1208	1534	1708	2042

h – 🍴 on Ⓐ, 🍷 on ⑥. ◇ – Also conveys [1]. △ – For additional trains Dublin - Kildare and v.v, see Tables **240**, **245**. ❖ – Services affected by engineering works on ⑥⑦.

245 ❖ DUBLIN - LIMERICK, TRALEE and CORK ❖ IÉ

km		⚒h ◇✕	⚒	⚒h ◇✕	⚒	⚒ ◇🍷	⚒ 🍷	⚒ ◇🍷	⚒	⚒ ◇🍷	⚒ 🍷	⚒h ◇✕	⚒	⚒h ◇✕	⚒ 🍷	⚒ ◇🍷	⚒	⚒h ◇✕	⚒ 🍷	⚒h ◇✕	⚒	⚒h ◇✕	Hh ◇✕	⑤ ◇✕	⚒ 🍷
0	**Dublin Heuston** .. **240** d.	0700	...	0800	...	0900	0925	1000	...	1100	1125	1200	...	1300	1325	1400	...	1500	1525	1600	...	1700	1705	1705	1725
48	Kildare .... **240** d.	|	...	|	...	|	1000	|	...	|	1158	|	...	|	1358	|	...	|	1558	|	...	|	|	|	1807
67	Portarlington ...... **240** d.	|	...	|	...	|	1013	|	...	|	1213	|	...	|	1412	|	...	|	1612	|	...	|	|	|	1819
82	Portlaoise .... d.	0753	...	|	...	|	1024	|	...	|	1224	|	...	|	1424	|	...	|	1624	|	...	|	|	|	1831
107	Ballybrophy .... d.	|	...	|	...	1005	|	|	...	|	|	|	...	|	1439	|	...	|	1639	|	...	|	|	|	1845
127	Templemore .... d.	|	...	|	...	|	1048	|	...	|	1248	|	...	|	1451	|	...	|	1651	|	...	|	1819	1819	1857
139	Thurles .... d.	0822	...	0919	...	|	1057	1119	...	1219	1257	1319	...	|	1500	1519	...	|	1700	1719	...	|	1828	1835	1907
172	**Limerick Junction** .. § d.	0844	0846	0941	0943	|	|	1141	1143	|	|	1341	1343	|	|	1541	1543	|	|	1741	1832	1838	|	|	|
208	**Limerick** .... § a.	|	0915	|	1012	|	1148	|	1212	|	1348	|	1412	|	1554	|	1612	|	1751	|	1903	|	1917	1917	1955
**	Ennis .... a.	|	*1000*	|	*1145*	|	*1325*	|	*1325*	|	*1500*	|	*1500*	|	*1700*	|	*1700*	|	*1840*	|	*2010*	|	*2010*	2010	...
208	Charleville .... d.	|	...	|	...	1058	...	|	...	1258	...	|	...	1455	...	|	...	1655	...	|	...	|	...	...	...
232	**Mallow** .... **246** d.	0918	...	1015	...	1115	...	1215	...	1315	...	1415	...	1512	...	1615	...	1712	...	1815	...	1912	...	...	...
	Tralee **246** .... a.	|	...	|	...	|	...	|	...	|	...	|	...	|	...	|	...	|	...	|	...	|	...	...	...
266	**Cork** .... **246** a.	0953	...	1050	...	1150	...	1250	...	1350	...	1450	...	1545	...	1650	...	1745	...	1850	...	1945	...	...	...

	⚒h ◇✕	⚒	⚒h ◇✕	⚒	⚒	⚒ ◇🍷	⚒ ◇🍷	⚒	⚒ ◇	⚒	⑦ 🍷	⑦	⑦	⑦ ◇🍷	⑦	⑦ ◇🍷	⑦ ◇🍷	⑦ ◇🍷	⑦ 🍷	⑦ ◇🍷	⑦ ◇🍷	⑦ 🍷	⑦ ◇🍷	⑦ ◇🍷	⑦ ◇🍷
Dublin Heuston ... **240** d.	1800	...	1830	...	1835	1900	2000	...	2100	...	0810	...	...	1000	...	1125	1200	1300	1325	1400	1500	1525	1600	1700	1800
Kildare .... **240** d.	|	...	|	...	1912	|	2034	...	|	...	|	...	...	|	...	1200	|	|	1400	|	|	1600	|	|	|
Portarlington ...... **240** d.	|	...	|	...	1925	|	|	...	2145	...	|	...	...	|	...	1213	|	|	1413	|	|	1613	|	|	|
Portlaoise .... d.	|	...	|	...	1936	1953	|	...	2156	...	0909	...	...	|	...	1224	|	|	1424	|	|	1624	|	|	|
Ballybrophy .... d.	|	...	|	...	1953	|	|	...	|	...	|	...	...	|	...	1239	|	|	1439	|	|	1639	|	|	|
Templemore .... d.	|	...	|	...	2006	|	|	...	|	...	|	...	...	|	...	1251	|	|	1451	|	|	1651	|	|	|
Thurles .... d.	1926	...	1954	...	2016	2024	2122	...	2225	...	0945	...	...	1119	...	1300	1319	1419	1500	1519	1619	1700	1719	1819	1919
Limerick Junction ... § d.	1948	1952	|	...	...	|	2144	2148	2249	2248	1008	1012	...	1141	1143	|	1341	|	|	1541	|	|	1741	|	1941
Limerick .... § a.	|	2029	|	...	...	|	|	2216	|	2316	|	1040	...	|	1211	1351	*1409*	|	1551	*1611*	|	1751	*1811*	|	|
Ennis .... a.	|	...	|	...	...	|	|	...	|	...	|	*1130*	...	|	*1310*	*1520*	*1520*	|	*1720*	*1720*	|	*1905*	*1905*	|	|
Charleville .... d.	|	...	2034	...	...	2103	|	...	|	...	1034	...	...	|	...	...	|	1458	...	|	|	...	|	|	|
Mallow .... **246** d.	2020	...	2055	2100	...	2118	2220	...	2321	...	1052	...	1100	1215	...	...	1415	1515	...	1615	1712	...	1815	1912	|
Tralee **246** .... a.	|	...	2235	|	...	|	|	...	|	...	1228	...	|	|	...	...	|	|	...	|	|	...	|	|	|
Cork .... **246** a.	2052	...	...	2126	...	2155	2255	...	2355	...	...	...	1128	1250	...	...	1450	1550	...	1650	1745	...	1850	1945	2045

	⑦ 🍷	⑦ ◇🍷	⑦ ◇🍷	⑦	⑦	⑦ ◇🍷	⑦ ◇	⑦ 🍷
Dublin Heuston .. **240** d.	1825	1900	1910	...	...	1925	2100	2135
Kildare .... **240** d.	1905	|	|	...	...	2005	|	2210
Portarlington ...... **240** d.	1917	|	1955	...	...	2017	2145	2223
Portlaoise .... d.	1929	|	|	...	...	2029	|	2234
Ballybrophy .... d.	1943	|	|	...	...	2043	|	|
Templemore .... d.	1955	|	|	...	...	2055	|	2301
Thurles .... d.	2005	2019	2032	...	...	2105	2222	2310
Limerick Junction .. § d.	|	|	2054	2028	...	|	2244	|
Limerick .... § a.	2052	|	|	2126	...	2150	|	2355
Ennis .... a.	*2135*	|	|	...	...	...	|	...
Charleville .... d.	...	|	2114	...	...	...	|	...
Mallow .... **246** d.	...	2112	2129	...	2135	...	2318	...
Tralee **246** .... a.	...	|	2315	...	|	...	|	...
Cork .... **246** a.	...	2145	...	...	2203	...	2355	...

	⚒ 🍷	⚒ ◇🍷	⚒ 🍷	⚒	⚒h ◇✕	⚒h ◇✕	⚒	⚒h ◇✕	⚒	⚒	⚒	⚒h ◇✕
Cork .... **246** d.	...	0505	...	...	0630	...	...	0730	0830	...	...	...
Tralee **246** .... d.	...	|	...	...	|	...	...	|	|	...	...	0715
Mallow .... **246** d.	...	0527	...	...	0652	...	...	0752	0855	...	...	0857
Charleville .... d.	...	0542	...	...	|	...	...	|	...	...	...	0910
Ennis .... d.	...	|	...	...	|	*0645*	...	|	...	0800	...	|
Limerick .... § d.	0535	|	0635	0655	|	0735	0755	|	...	0840	0855	|
Limerick Junction .... § d.	|	0604	|	0722	0726	|	0825	0829	...	...	0927	0932
Thurles .... d.	0618	0625	0718	...	|	0818	...	0849	...	...	...	0952
Templemore .... d.	0627	0634	0728	...	|	|	...	|	...	...	...	|
Ballybrophy .... d.	|	0647	|	...	|	0835	...	|	...	...	...	|
Portlaoise .... d.	0651	0710	0750	...	|	0850	...	|	...	...	...	|
Portarlington ...... **240** d.	|	0722	0804	...	|	|	...	|	...	...	...	|
Kildare .... **240** d.	0713	|	0814	...	|	|	...	|	...	...	...	|
Dublin Heuston ...... **240** a.	0757	0823	0905	...	0915	0955	...	1020	...	...	...	1115

	⚒	⚒ ◇🍷	⚒ ◇🍷	⚒	⚒ ◇🍷	⚒ 🍷	⚒h ◇✕	⚒	⚒h ◇✕	⚒ 🍷	⚒ ◇🍷	⚒	⚒	⚒ ◇🍷	⚒h ◇✕	⚒ 🍷	⚒	⚒h ◇✕	⚒ ◇🍷	⚒	⚒	⚒ ◇🍷	⚒	⚒ ◇🍷	
Cork .... **246** d.	...	0930	1030	...	1130	...	1230	...	1330	...	1430	...	...	1530	1630	...	...	1730	1830	...	...	1930	...	2030	...
Tralee **246** .... d.	...	|	|	...	|	...	|	...	|	...	|	...	...	|	|	...	...	|	|	...	...	|	...	|	...
Mallow .... **246** d.	...	0952	1052	...	1152	...	1252	...	1352	...	1452	...	...	1552	1652	...	...	1752	1852	...	...	1952	...	2052	...
Charleville .... d.	...	|	1107	...	|	...	|	...	|	...	1507	...	...	|	1707	...	...	|	1907	...	...	|	...	|	...
Ennis .... d.	...	|	|	*1005*	|	*1150*	|	...	|	*1330*	|	1505		|	|	...	*1705*	|	|	1845	...	|	...	|	...
Limerick .... § d.	0955	|	|	1155	|	1235	|	1355	|	1415	|	1545	1555	|	|	1735	1755	|	|	1925	1950	|	...	|	...
Limerick Junction ... § d.	1023	1026	|	1223	1226	|	|	1423	1426	|	|	...	1623	1626	|	|	1823	1826	|	...	2020	2026	...	|	...
Thurles .... d.	...	1046	|	...	1246	1317	|	...	1446	1459	1546	...	...	1646	|	1822	...	1846	|	...	...	2046	2100	2143	...
Templemore .... d.	...	|	1151	...	|	1327	|	...	|	1507	|	...	...	|	1751	1830	...	|	|	...	...	|	2109	|	...
Ballybrophy .... d.	...	|	|	...	|	1337	|	...	|	|	|	...	...	|	|	1844	...	|	|	...	...	|	2122	|	...
Portlaoise .... d.	...	1115	|	...	|	1352	1409	...	|	1531	|	...	...	|	|	1857	...	|	|	...	...	|	2139	2214	...
Portarlington ...... **240** d.	...	|	|	...	|	1403	|	...	|	1542	|	...	...	|	|	1909	...	|	|	...	...	|	2149	|	...
Kildare .... **240** d.	...	|	|	...	|	1415	|	...	|	1554	|	...	...	|	|	1921	...	|	|	...	...	|	2202	|	...
Dublin Heuston ... **240** a.	...	1225	1320	...	1420	1500	1515	...	1620	1635	1715	...	...	1820	1920	2008	...	2020	2115	...	...	2220	2247	2315	...

	⑦ ◇🍷	⑦ 🍷	⑦ ◇🍷	⑦ ◇🍷	⑦ 🍷	⑦ ◇🍷	⑦	⑦ ◇🍷	⑦ ◇🍷	⑦ ◇🍷	⑦	⑦🍷 ◇	⑦	⑦ ◇🍷	⑦ 🍷	⑦ ◇🍷	⑦	⑦ ◇🍷	⑦ 🍷	⑦ ◇🍷	⑦	⑦ 🍷	⑦	⑦	⑦ 🍷
Cork .... **246** d.	0830	...	...	1030	...	1230	...	1330	...	1430	1450	...	...	1530	...	1630	...	1730	...	1830	...	...	...	...	1930
Tralee **246** .... d.	|	...	...	|	...	|	...	|	...	|	|	1345	...	|	...	|	...	|	...	|	...	1745	...	...	|
Mallow .... **246** d.	0852	...	...	1052	...	1252	...	1352	...	1452	1515	1522	...	1552	...	1652	...	1752	...	1852	...	1927	...	...	1952
Charleville .... d.	0907	...	...	1107	...	1307	...	|	...	1507	...	1537	...	|	...	1707	...	|	...	1907	...	|	...	...	|
Ennis .... d.	|	*0750*	*0945*	|	*1145*	|	...	|	*1350*	|	...	|	...	|	*1545*	|	...	|	*1740*	|	...	|	1910	...	|
Limerick .... § d.	|	0835	1035	|	1235	|	1355	|	1435	|	...	|	1555	|	1635	|	1755	|	1835	|	1855	|	1950	1955	|
Limerick Junction ... § d.	0929	|	|	1129	|	|	1423	1426	|	|	...	|	1623	1626	|	|	1823	1826	|	|	1923	2006	...	2023	2026
Thurles .... d.	|	0918	1118	|	1318	1346	...	1446	1518	1546	...	1617	...	1646	1718	1746	...	1846	1918	1946	...	2029	...	...	2046
Templemore .... d.	|	0926	1126	|	1326	|	...	|	1526	|	...	|	...	|	1726	|	...	|	1928	|	...	|	...	...	|
Ballybrophy .... d.	|	0938	|	|	1338	|	...	|	1538	|	...	|	...	|	1738	|	...	|	1939	|	...	|	...	...	|
Portlaoise .... d.	|	0953	1150	|	1353	|	...	|	1553	|	...	|	...	|	1753	|	...	|	1958	|	...	|	...	...	|
Portarlington ...... **240** d.	|	|	1202	|	1405	|	...	|	1605	|	...	|	...	|	1805	|	...	|	2012	|	...	|	...	...	|
Kildare .... **240** d.	|	1013	1214	|	1417	|	...	|	1617	|	...	|	...	|	1817	|	...	|	2024	|	...	|	...	...	|
Dublin Heuston ... **240** a.	1120	1055	1257	1320	1500	1520	...	1620	1700	1720	...	1745	...	1820	1905	1920	...	2020	2105	2120	...	2206	...	...	2220

H – ①②③④⑥. h – ✕ on Ⓐ, 🍷 on ⑥. ◇ – Also conveys [1]. § – See also Table **247**. ** – Limerick - Ennis : *40 km*. ❖ – Services affected by engineering works on ⑥⑦.

246 (DUBLIN -) CORK - MALLOW - TRALEE IÉ

km		⚒	⚒	⚒	⚒	⚒	⚒	⚒	⚒h ◇✕	⚒			⑦	⑦	⑦ 🍷	⑦	⑦	⑦	⑦ ◇🍷		
	Dublin Heuston **245** d.	...	*0700*	*0900*	*1100*	*1300*	*1500*	*1700*	1830	*2000*	...	...	...	...	0810	*1000*	*1300*	*1500*	1910	...	...
0	**Cork** .... **245** d.	0615	0850	*1030*	*1230*	*1430*	*1655*	*1855*	*2030*	2220	...	...	...	*0830*	*1015*	1210	1450	*1630*	*2055*	...	...
34	**Mallow** .... **245** d.	0656	0925	1125	1325	1525	1725	1925	2055	2250	...	...	0755	0925	1052	1245	1528	1725	2129	...	...
66	Millstreet .... d.	0719	0948	1148	1348	1548	1748	1948	2123	2314	...	...	|	0948	1117	1308	1551	1748	2159	...	...
100	Killarney .... d.	0750	1029	1229	1429	1629	1829	2029	2156	2344	...	...	0849	1019	1151	1339	1629	1829	2232	...	...
134	**Tralee** .... **245** a.	0825	1103	1303	1503	1703	1903	2103	2235	0019	...	...	0923	1053	1228	1420	1705	1905	2315	...	...

	⚒	⚒h ◇✕	⚒	⚒	⚒	⚒	⚒	⚒	⚒			⑦	⑦	⑦ ◇🍷	⑦	⑦	⑦ 🍷	⑦			
Tralee .... **245** d.	0525	0715	0915	1115	1315	1515	1715	1915	2115	...	...	0715	1115	1345	1515	1715	1745	1915	...	...	...
Killarney .... d.	0600	0752	0950	1150	1350	1550	1750	1950	2149	...	...	0749	1150	1422	1550	1750	1829	1950	...	...	...
Millstreet .... d.	0624	0822	1017	1217	1417	1617	1817	2017	2222	...	...	0816	1217	1452	1617	1817	1859	2017	...	...	...
Mallow .... **245** d.	0700	0857	1044	1244	1444	1644	1844	2100	2247	...	...	0845	1256	1522	1641	1856	1927	2051	...	...	...
Cork .... **245** a.	0724	*0925*	*1111*	*1311*	*1511*	*1745*	*1945*	2126	2321	...	...	*0923*	1320	*1650*	*1711*	1925	|	2115	...	...	...
Dublin Heuston **245** ... a.	*0915*	1115	*1320*	*1515*	*1715*	*1920*	*2115*	*2315*	...	...	...	*1120*	1515	1745	*1920*	*2120*	2206	...	...	...	...

NOTES

h – ✕ on Ⓐ, 🍷 on ⑥.
◇ – Also conveys [1].

Will the times be the same in the next edition?

They may be, but many of the services in this timetable are likely to change frequently, and without advance notice.

For details of subscription rates, see the order form at the back of this book.

247 LIMERICK JUNCTION - LIMERICK IÉ

Shuttle service connecting with main-line trains. *35 km*. Journey time : 25–40 minutes. For through services to or from Dublin Heuston see Table **245** above. For notes see Table 246.

From Limerick Junction ⚒: 0800, 0846, 0943, 1032, 1143, 1232, 1343, 1440, 1543, 1632, 1832, 1952, 2032, 2148, 2248. ⑦: 1012, 1143, 1343, 1432, 1543, 1632, 1743, 1832, 1955, 2058.
From Limerick ⚒: 0655, 0755, 0855, 0955, 1055, 1155, 1255, 1355, 1455, 1555, 1755, 1900, 1950, 2105, 2200. ⑦: 0930, 1055, 1255, 1355, 1455, 1555, 1655, 1755, 1855, 1955.

FRANCE

SEE MAP PAGES 172/3

Operator: Société Nationale des Chemins de Fer Français (SNCF), unless otherwise shown.

Services: Most trains convey first and second classes of accommodation; some purely local services are second class only. *TGV* (*train à grande vitesse*) trains have a bar car in the centre of the train selling drinks and light refreshments. Selected *TGV* trains have an at-seat meal service in first class. On *Téoz* services refreshments are available from a trolley wheeled through the train. Certain other long-distance trains also have refreshments available (sometimes seasonal or on certain days of the week), but it is not possible to identify these in the tables as this information is no longer supplied. Regional and local trains (outside Paris) are classified *TER* (*Train Express Regional*). Domestic night trains are classified *Lunéa* - sleeping accommodation consists of modern four-berth couchettes (first class) or six-berth couchettes (second class). Women-only compartments are available on request. There are no sleeping cars on domestic trains in France. Note that all luggage placed on luggage racks must be labelled.

Timings: Valid **June 1 - December 12, 2009**. Amended services operate on and around public holidays and, whilst we try to show holiday variations, passengers are advised to confirm their train times locally before travelling during these periods. Public holidays in 2009 are Jan. 1, Easter Monday (Apr. 13), May 1, 8, Ascension Day (May 21), Whit Monday (June 1), July 14, Aug. 15, Nov. 1, 11, Dec. 25. **Engineering work** can often affect schedules; major changes are shown in the tables where possible but other changes may occur at short notice. Where a train is shown *subject to alteration* on certain dates this often means that part of the journey may be provided by bus, often with earlier departure or later arrival times.

Tickets: **Seat reservations** are compulsory for travel by all *TGV*, *Téoz* and *Lunéa* trains, and are also available for a small fee on most other long distance trains. Advance reservations are recommended for travel to ski resorts during the winter sports season. **Supplements** (which include the cost of seat reservation) are payable for travel in *TGV*, *Téoz* and *Lunéa* trains. Rail tickets must be date-stamped by the holder before boarding the train using the self-service validating machines (composteurs) at the platform entrances – this applies to all tickets except passes and hand-written tickets. Note that where two *TGV* units are coupled together, they will often carry different train numbers for reservation purposes.

Note: The *TGV* services **Lille Europe - Charles de Gaulle ✈ - Marne-la-Vallée - Lyon / Bordeaux / Rennes / Nantes** are shown in the International section (Table **11**).

PARIS - LILLE - TOURCOING — 250

TGV Nord high-speed trains

For slower trains via Douai see Table **256**. For **Charles de Gaulle ✈ - Lille** see Table **11**. Certain trains continue to Dunkerque, Calais or Boulogne - see Table **265**.

km		*TGV* 7001	*TGV* 7005	*TGV* 7207	*TGV* 7211	*TGV* 7015	*TGV* 7021	*TGV* 7229*	*TGV* 7033	*TGV* 7235	*TGV* 7043		*TGV* 7045	*TGV* 7049	*TGV* 7053	*TGV* 7059	*TGV* 7061	*TGV* 7065	*TGV* 7275	*TGV* 7277	*TGV* 7281	*TGV* 7079	*TGV* 7285	*TGV* 7087
		①	Ⓐ	Ⓐ		①–⑥							Ⓐ		Ⓐ		Ⓐ		Ⓐ		Ⓐ	⑤		Ⓐ
		Jg				Jn									J		J					J	‡	J
0	**Paris Nord** d.	0628	0658	0728	0758	0828	0858	0958	1058	1158	1258	...	1428	1458	1528	1558	1628	1658	1728	1758	1828	1849	1858	1928
227	**Lille Europe** a.	|	|	0827	|	|	|	1057	|	|	|	...	|	|	|	|	|	|	1827	|	1926	|	1956	|
227	**Lille Flandres** a.	0730	0800	...	0900	0930	1000	...	1200	1303	1400	...	1530	1600	1630	1700	1730	1800	...	1900	...	1951	...	2030
227	**Lille Flandres 405** d.	...	...	...	0912	...	...	...	...	1313	...	...	...	...	...	...	...	...	...	1910	...	...	...	...
237	Roubaix **405** a.	...	...	...	0926	...	...	...	...	1327	...	...	...	...	...	...	...	...	...	1924	...	...	...	...
240	**Tourcoing 405** a.	...	...	...	0932	...	...	...	...	1333	...	...	...	...	...	...	...	...	...	1930	...	...	...	...

	TGV 7091	*TGV* 7291	*TGV* 7093	*TGV* 7089	*TGV* 7293	*TGV* 7097	*TGV* 7099	*TGV* 7099	*TGV* 7095
	⑦	①–⑥	⑥	Ⓐ	⑦	⑤⑦		①–⑥	⑦
	e	n		⊡	e	e	J⊡	K⊡	K⊡
Paris Nord d.	1958	1958	2058	2058	2058	2158	2258	2258	2258
Lille Europe a.	|	|	|	|	|	|	|	|	|
Lille Flandres a.	2100	2100	2200	2219	2200	2300	0018	0018r	0029r
Lille Flandres 405 d.	...	2112	...	...	2212	...	...	...	...
Roubaix **405** a.	...	2126	...	...	2225	...	...	...	...
Tourcoing 405 a.	...	2132	...	...	2232	...	...	...	...

	TGV 7000	*TGV* 7002	*TGV* 7206	*TGV* 7214	*TGV* 7220	*TGV* 7222	*TGV* 7022	*TGV* 7022	*TGV* 7028
	Ⓐ	Ⓐ	①–⑥	Ⓐ	①–⑥	⑦	①–⑥		Ⓐ
	J		n		n	e	Jn	K	J
Tourcoing 405 d.	...	...	0630	...	...	0747	...	...	...
Roubaix **405** d.	...	...	0636	...	...	0753	...	...	...
Lille Flandres 405 a.	...	...	0650	...	...	0807	...	...	...
Lille Flandres d.	0600	0630	0700	...	...	0817	0817	0817	0830
Lille Europe d.	|	|	|	0732	0802	|	|	|	|
Paris Nord a.	0702	0732	0802	0832	0902	0920	0920	0920	0932

	TGV 7030	*TGV* 7036	*TGV* 7040	*TGV* 7246	*TGV* 7050	*TGV* 7254		*TGV* 7256	*TGV* 7058	*TGV* 7062	*TGV* 7066	*TGV* 7070	*TGV* 7072	*TGV* 7074	*TGV* 7082	*TGV* 7288	*TGV* 7088		*TGV* 7092	*TGV* 7292	*TGV* 7294	*TGV* 7098	*TGV* 7298	*TGV* 7096	
						①–⑥			Ⓐ		Ⓐ		Ⓐ		Ⓐ	Ⓑ	⑥		Ⓒ	Ⓐ	⑤⑦	⑥	⑦	Ⓐ	
						n			J		J		J		J						e		e	⊡	
Tourcoing 405 d.	...	...	...	1130	...	...	...	1430	...	...	...	...	...	...	...	...	...	...	...	...	2030	...	...	...	...
Roubaix **405** d.	...	...	...	1136	...	...	...	1436	...	...	...	...	...	...	...	...	...	...	...	...	2036	...	...	...	...
Lille Flandres 405 a.	...	...	...	1150	...	...	...	1450	...	...	...	...	...	...	...	...	...	...	...	...	2050	...	...	...	...
Lille Flandres d.	...	1000	1100	1200	1300	...	...	1500	1530	1600	1630	1700	1730	1800	1830	...	1900	...	...	...	2100	...	...	...	...
Lille Europe d.	0902	|	|	|	|	1324	...	|	|	|	|	|	|	|	|	1902	|	...	2002	2011	|	2202	2202	2209	...
Paris Nord a.	1002	1102	1202	1302	1402	1426	...	1602	1632	1702	1732	1802	1832	1902	1932	2002	2002	...	2102	2111	2202	2302	2302	2323	...

J – To July 4 / from Aug. 31.
K – July 5 - Aug. 30.
e – Also June 1, July 14.
g – Also June 2; not June 1.
n – Not June 1, July 14.
r – 0053 on July 15; 0032 on Sept. 20, 21.
TGV – Ⓡ, supplement payable.
⊡ – Via Arras (Table **256**).
‡ – Also runs as **7289** on ⑦.
* – Runs as **7029** on ⑦ (also June 1, July 14).

PARIS - LAON — 251

km		⚒	⚒	†	⑥t	Ⓐ			Ⓐ	†	⑥t	Ⓐ		Ⓐ	⑥t	Ⓐ	Ⓒ	Ⓐ	Ⓐ	Ⓒ	Ⓐ			Ⓐ	
0	**Paris Nord** d.	0558	0712	0806	0806	0831	0957	...	1202	1246	1326	1326	...	1448	1448	1530	1600	1631	1745	1752	1847	...	2005	2118	...
61	Crépy-en-Valois d.	0651	0744	0838	0856	0908	1038	...	1244	1322	1402	1403	...	1536	1534	1612	1634	1706	1831	1832	1927	...	2043	2153	...
105	Soissons d.	0730	0814	0912	0928	0938	1110	...	1316	1355	1431	1434	...	1614	1611	1645	1703	1735	1903	1901	1958	...	2113	2223	...
140	**Laon** a.	0755	0838	0939	0954	1004	1136	...	1340	1425	1456	1501	...	1652	1648	1709	1731	1804	1931	1926	2023	...	2139	2248	...

	Ⓐ	Ⓐ	Ⓐ	⑥t	†	⚒	†	⚒	Ⓐ	Ⓒ	⚒	†	Ⓐ	⑥t	†	Ⓐ	†	Ⓐ	⑥t	Ⓑh	Ⓐ	⚒	†	Ⓐ	†
Laon d.	0506	0532	0640	0640	0710	0753	0848	0933	1119	1125	1222	1231	1405	1554	1602	1621	1718	1718	1739	1803	1907	2013	2029	2114	2107
Soissons d.	0533	0600	0710	0708	0737	0822	0916	1001	1148	1151	1254	1258	1432	1625	1627	1649	1743	1749	1806	1831	1935	2041	2054	2143	2134
Crépy-en-Valois d.	0601	0630	0741	0740	0806	0852	0947	1031	1220	1220	1329	1330	1502	1657	1702	1724	1816	1821	1841	1900	2006	2112	2122	2215	2208
Paris Nord a.	0637	0706	0826	0818	0853	0927	1022	1110	1253	1253	1417	1420	1539	1749	1753	1802	1855	1902	1918	1937	2039	2158	2201	2305	2305

h – Also Aug. 15.
t – Not Aug. 15.

AMIENS - LAON - REIMS — 252

Some trains 2nd class only

km		⑥t	Ⓐ	Ⓐ	†	⚒	⚒	⑦e	⑥	Ⓐ	Ⓑh	⑥t	Ⓐ	Ⓐ	Ⓐ	Ⓒ	Ⓒ	Ⓐ	⑦e	Ⓒ	Ⓐ	⚒	Ⓐ		†
0	**Amiens** d.	0602	0611	0724	0800	0830	...	...	...	*1107**	1226z	1237	1453z	...	1611*	1612	...	...	...	1805	1806	1847	...	*1927*a	2125
	Cambrai **257** d.	|	|	|	|	|	0858	...	...	|	|	|	|	...	|	|	...	...	...	|	|	|	...	|	|
	St Quentin **255/7** d.	|	|	|	|	|	0941	...	...	|	|	|	|	1637	|	|	1716	1730	...	|	|	|	1940	|	|
80	Tergnier **255/7** a.	0710	0720	0831	0907	0932	0958	...	...	*1220**	1334	1345	1550	1656	1714*	1717	1735	1751	...	1908	1911	1955	2000	*2027*a	2228
80	Tergnier d.	0724	0733	0832	0912	...	1000	...	...	1233	1346	1348	1551	1658	1722	...	1749	1806	...	1922	1924	...	2002	2037	2230
108	Laon a.	0753	0802	0859	0935	...	1023	...	...	1300	1411	1415	1613	1720	1745	...	1814	1831	...	1948	1950	...	2028	2102	2252
108	Laon d.	...	0803	...	...	...	1027	1210	1256	1301	...	...	*1703*	*1732*	...	...	*1837*r	1833	1925	1949v	...	...	2030	...	...
160	**Reims** a.	...	0844	...	...	...	1107	1256	1343	1354	...	...	*1740*	*1807*	...	...	*1925*r	1925	2012	2026v	...	...	2105	...	...

	Ⓐ	⚒	Ⓐ	⚒	†	⚒y	Ⓐ	⑦e	Ⓐ	Ⓒ	Ⓐ	Ⓐ	⑥t	Ⓐ	⑥	Ⓐ	Ⓒ	Ⓐ	Ⓐ	†	Ⓐ	Ⓐ	⑦e	⚒	
Reims d.	...	...	...	0627	...	...	0735	1058	1118	...	1217	...	1225	1509	1509	...	...	...	1653	1705	1729	...	1830	1845	...
Laon a.	...	...	...	0709	...	...	0811	1145	1152	...	1304	...	1313	1543	1545	...	...	...	1737	1741	1820	...	1916	1933	...
Laon d.	0553	0628	0654	0711	0720	0742	0813	...	1156	1202	...	1313	1314	1544	...	1627	1706	*1722*	1739	1743	1826	...	...	*1945*a	2005
Tergnier a.	0615	0653	0720	0731	0745	0809	0836	...	1222	1225	...	1339	1337	1608	...	1651	1732	*1748*	1757	1805	1850	...	...	*2011*a	2031
Tergnier **255/7** d.	0624	0655	0722	0736	0747	0812	...	...	1233	1233	...	1341	...	1614	...	1652	1742	1807	1758	...	1852	1858	...	...	2038
St Quentin **255/7** a.	0643	|	|	0752	|	|	...	...	|	|	...	|	...	1630	...	|	|	|	1816	...	|	1916	...	...	|
Cambrai **257** a.	...	|	|	0839	|	|	...	...	|	|	...	|	...	...	...	|	|	|	...	...	|	...	...	...	|
Amiens a.	...	0801	0825	...	0843	0911	...	...	1337z	1339	...	1444z	...	...	...	1753	1848	1913	...	...	1956	...	...	...	2144

a – Ⓐ only.
e – Also July 14, Nov. 11.
h – Also Aug. 15.
r – ⑥ only.
t – Not Aug. 15.
v – On † June 28 - Aug. 30 Laon d. 2009, Reims a. 2043.
y – Subject to alteration Tergnier - Amiens Oct. 19 - 26.
z – By 🚌 Amiens - Chaulnes and v.v. on certain dates.
* – By 🚌 on certain dates.
Additional journey on ⚒: Laon d. 0636 - Reims a. 0725.

Seaside Special: ⑦ June 28 - Aug. 30 (also July 14, Aug. 15):
Reims *0720* → Laon a. *0756* d. 0820 → Tergnier 0842 → Abbeville 1009 → Le Tréport 1044.
Le Tréport 1740 → Abbeville 1815 → Tergnier 1935 → Laon a. 1957 / d. *2009* → Reims *2043*.

🚌 AMIENS - TGV HAUTE-PICARDIE — 253

SNCF 🚌 service

All *TGV* departures and arrivals at TGV Haute-Picardie (Table **11**) have 🚌 connections from / to Amiens and St Quentin. Departs 50 - 60 mins before the train; journey 40 minutes. Reservations for the 🚌 should be made at the same time as for the *TGV* service.

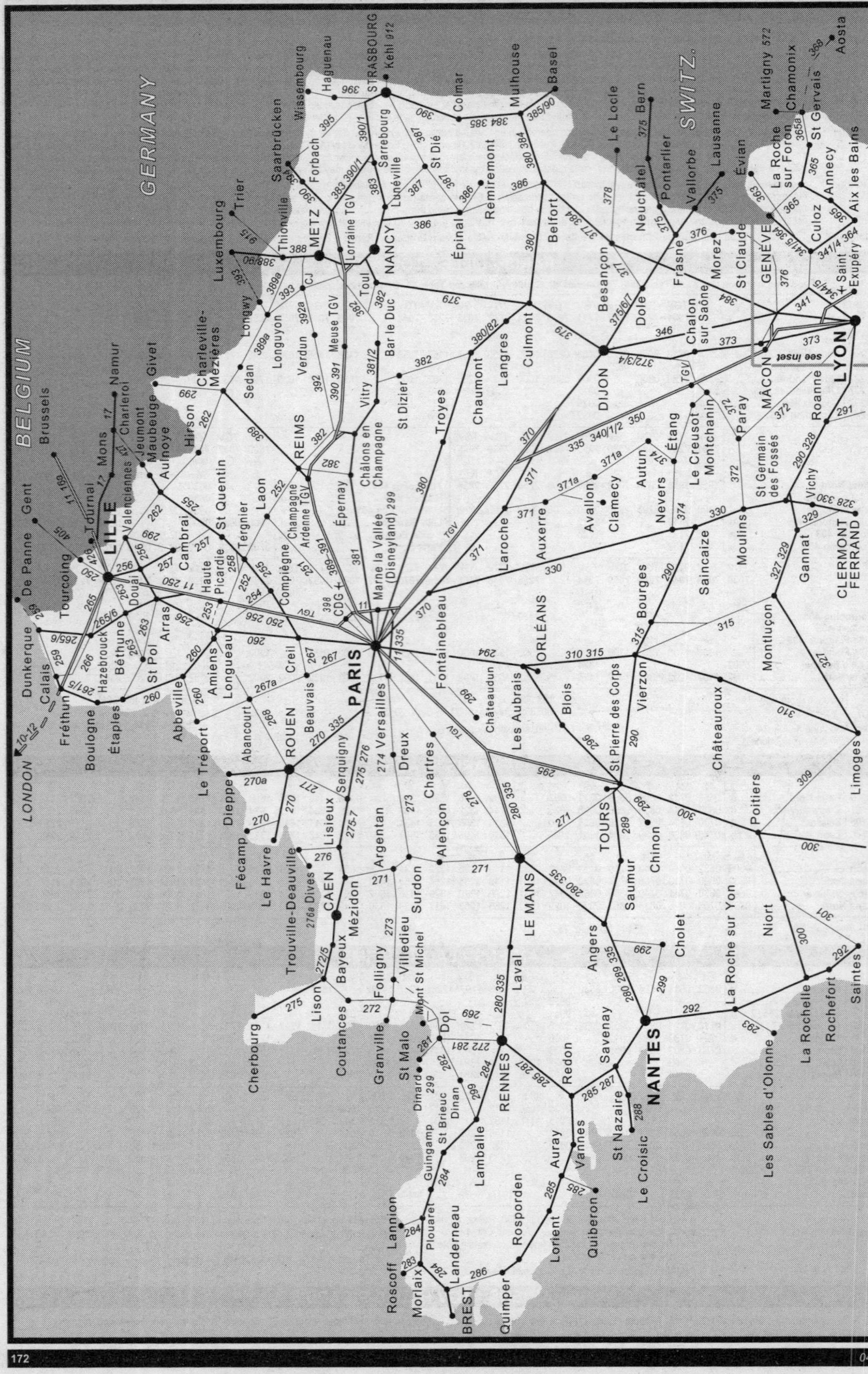
BELGIUM
GERMANY
SWITZ.
LONDON
Dunkerque
De Panne
Gent
Brussels
Namur
Mons
Charleroi
Tournai
Tourcoing
LILLE
Calais
Fréthun
Boulogne
Étaples
Hazebrouck
Béthune
Douai
Valenciennes
Jeumont
Maubeuge
Aulnoye
Givet
Hirson
Charleville-Mézières
Sedan
Longwy
Luxembourg
Trier
Thionville
METZ
Saarbrücken
Forbach
Wissembourg
Haguenau
STRASBOURG
Kehl
Sarrebourg
Lunéville
NANCY
Lorraine TGV
Toul
Bar le Duc
Verdun
Longuyon
Meuse TGV
St Dié
Épinal
Remiremont
Colmar
Mulhouse
Basel
Belfort
Besançon
Le Locle
Bern
Neuchâtel
Pontarlier
Frasne
Vallorbe
Lausanne
Morez
St Claude
Évian
GENÈVE
La Roche sur Foron
Martigny
Chamonix
St Gervais
Annecy
Aosta
Culoz
Aix les Bains
Saint Exupéry
LYON
see inset
Dole
DIJON
Chalon sur Saône
MÂCON
Paray
Montchanin
Le Creusot
Étang
Roanne
Vichy
St Germain des Fossés
CLERMONT FERRAND
Gannat
Moulins
Nevers
Saincaize
Autun
Avallon
Clamecy
Auxerre
Laroche
Culmont
Langres
Chaumont
Troyes
St Dizier
Vitry
Châlons en Champagne
Épernay
REIMS
Champagne Ardenne TGV
Laon
Tergnier
St Quentin
Cambrai
Arras
St Pol
Haute Picardie
Compiègne
Amiens
Longueau
Abbeville
Le Tréport
Abancourt
Beauvais
Creil
CDG
Marne la Vallée (Disneyland)
PARIS
Fontainebleau
Versailles
Dreux
Chartres
Châteaudun
ROUEN
Dieppe
Fécamp
Le Havre
Serquigny
Lisieux
Trouville-Deauville
Dives
CAEN
Mézidon
Argentan
Surdon
Alençon
Bayeux
Lison
Cherbourg
Coutances
Folligny
Villedieu
Granville
Mont St Michel
Dol
St Malo
Dinard
Dinan
St Brieuc
Guingamp
Lamballe
Lannion
Plouaret
Roscoff
Morlaix
Landerneau
BREST
Quimper
Rosporden
Lorient
Auray
Quiberon
Vannes
Redon
RENNES
Laval
LE MANS
Angers
Savenay
St Nazaire
Le Croisic
NANTES
Cholet
Saumur
TOURS
Chinon
St Pierre des Corps
Blois
Les Aubrais
ORLÉANS
Vierzon
Bourges
Châteauroux
Montluçon
Limoges
Poitiers
Niort
La Roche sur Yon
Les Sables d'Olonne
La Rochelle
Rochefort
Saintes
TGV

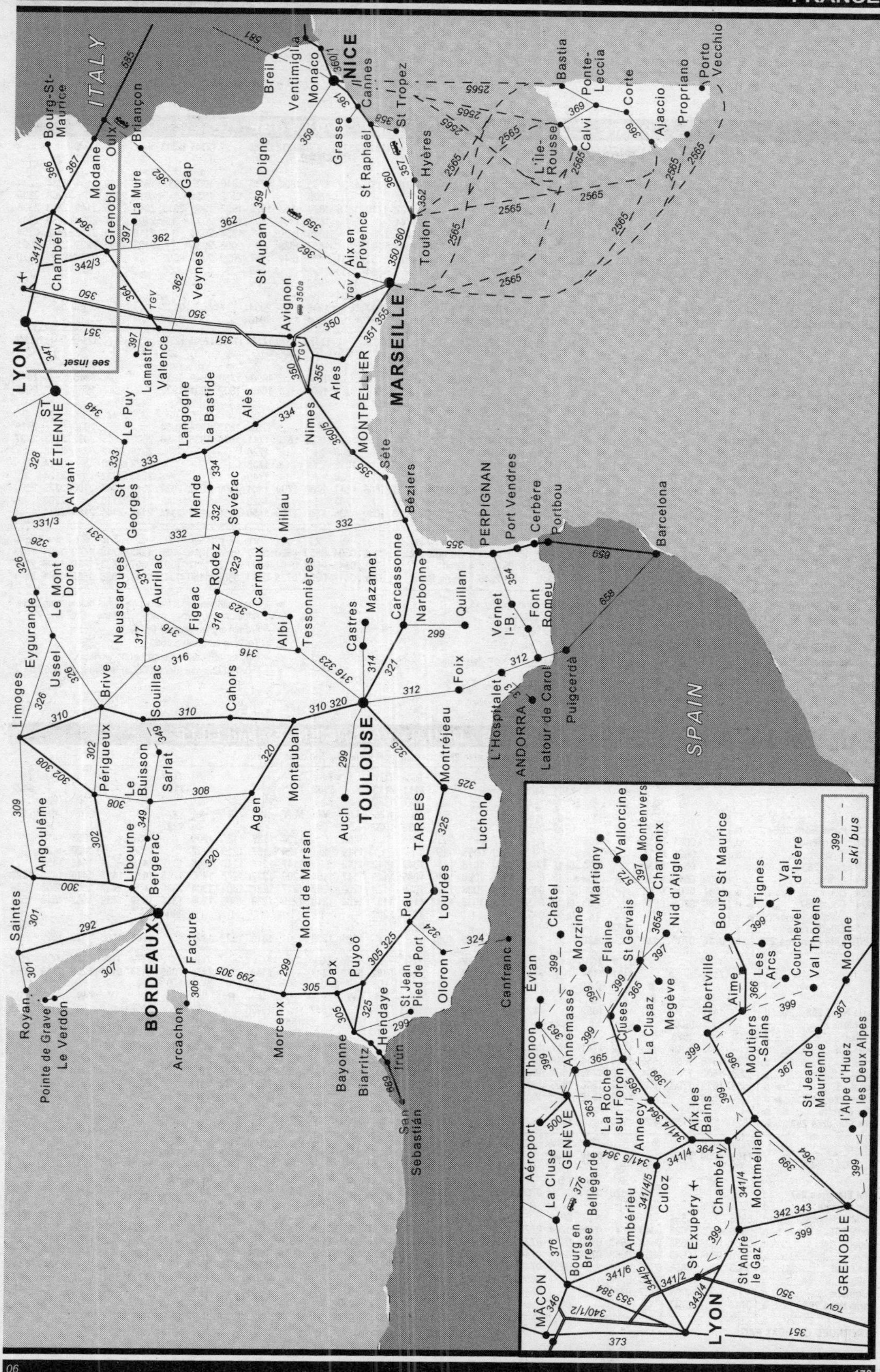
ITALY
SPAIN
LYON
ST ÉTIENNE
MARSEILLE
NICE
TOULOUSE
BORDEAUX
MONTPELLIER
PERPIGNAN
TARBES
see inset
Bourg-St-Maurice
Modane
Oulx
Briançon
Chambéry
Grenoble
La Mure
Gap
Digne
Breil
Ventimiglia
Monaco
Cannes
Grasse
St Raphaël
St Tropez
Hyères
Toulon
Aix en Provence
St Auban
Veynes
Valence
Lamastre
Avignon
Arles
Nîmes
Alès
La Bastide
Langogne
Le Puy
Mende
Sévérac
Millau
Sète
Béziers
Narbonne
Carcassonne
Quillan
Port Vendres
Cerbère
Portbou
Barcelona
Vernet I-B.
Font Romeu
Puigcerdà
Latour de Carol
ANDORRA
L'Hospitalet
Foix
Castres
Mazamet
Albi
Tessonnières
Carmaux
Rodez
Figeac
Aurillac
Neussargues
St Georges
Arvant
Le Mont Dore
Eygurande
Ussel
Limoges
Brive
Souillac
Cahors
Montauban
Agen
Sarlat
Le Buisson
Périgueux
Bergerac
Libourne
Angoulême
Saintes
Royan
Pointe de Grave
Le Verdon
Arcachon
Facture
Morcenx
Mont de Marsan
Dax
Puyoô
Pau
Lourdes
Montréjeau
Luchon
Auch
Bayonne
Biarritz
Hendaye
Irún
San Sebastián
St Jean Pied de Port
Oloron
Canfranc
Bastia
Ponte-Leccia
Corte
Calvi
L'Île-Rousse
Ajaccio
Propriano
Porto Vecchio
TGV
Mâcon
Bourg en Bresse
La Cluse
Ambérieu
Bellegarde
Aéroport
GENÈVE
Culoz
St Exupéry
St André le Gaz
Chambéry
Montmélian
Aix les Bains
Annecy
La Roche sur Foron
Annemasse
Thonon
Évian
Châtel
Morzine
Cluses
La Clusaz
Megève
St Gervais
Flaine
Martigny
Vallorcine
Montenvers
Chamonix
Nid d'Aigle
Albertville
Bourg St Maurice
Aime
Les Arcs
Tignes
Val d'Isère
Moutiers -Salins
Courchevel
Val Thorens
St Jean de Maurienne
Modane
l'Alpe d'Huez
les Deux Alpes
GRENOBLE
399 ski bus

254 AMIENS - COMPIÈGNE

km		Ⓐ	⑥t	⚒	†	Ⓐ		Ⓐ		⚒	†	⚒	†
0	**Amiens** d.	0553	0608	0805	0920	1049	1224	1439	1617	1733	1837	1857	2224
5	Longueau d.	0604	0614	0817	0927	1056	1230	1446	1624	1741	1845	1903	2231
76	**Compiègne** a.	0734	0738	0931	1034	1203	1351	1556	1758r	1856	2001	2021	2341

	⚒	⚒	†	①g	Ⓐ		Ⓐ		Ⓐ	†	⚒	†
Compiègne d.	0602	0700	0754	0811	1045	1229	1435	1623	1724	1840	1904	2020
Longueau a.	0720	0811	0903	0927	1158	1349	1548	1739	1855	1958	2013	2124
Amiens a.	0727	0822	0910	0934	1205	1356	1555	1746	1902	2005	2020	2131

g – Also June 2, July 15, Nov. 12; not June 1.
r – 1751 on Ⓒ.
t – Not Aug. 15.

255 PARIS - COMPIÈGNE - ST QUENTIN - MAUBEUGE

km		12301 Ⓐ c	12305 ①–⑥ b	Ⓐ	12309 Ⓑ J	12313 ⊖	12319 ①–⑥ b	12321 ⚒ J	†	12327 Ⓒ z	12325 Ⓐ c	Ⓒ	Ⓐ	12331	2335	Ⓐ	12337 Ⓐ c	12339 Ⓑ c	†	12341 ①–⑥ n	12343	Ⓒ s	Ⓐ	12349 Ⓑ c	⑥ t	Ⓑ h
0	**Paris Nord** ▶ d.	0640	0734	0749	0837	1037	1207	1237	1243	1437	1437	1616	1616	1637	1737	1740	1804	1837	1840	1907	1937	1943	2010	2104	2134	2234
51	Creil ▶ d.	0707	|	0823	|	|	1234	|	1316	|	|	1643	1642	|	|	1805	|	|	1912	1934	|	2019	2042	|	2208	2305
84	**Compiègne** ▶ d.	0726	0816	0847	0917	1118	1259	1319	1339	1518	1532	1705	1722	1719	1818	1824	1853	1925	1932	1959	2019	2048	2105	2145	2243	2328
108	Noyon d.	0741	|	0900	|	|	1314	|	1352	|	|	1719	1744	|	|	1836	1908	|	1944	2013	|	2107	2127	2200	2258	2342
124	Chauny d.	0754	|	0911	|	|	1326	|	1402	|	|	1730	1755	|	|	1845	1920	|	1954	2026	|	2116	2139	2213	2308	2354
131	Tergnier **257** d.	0802	|	0918	|	|	1334	|	1409	|	|	1743	1803	|	|	1852	1928	|	2006	2034	|	2122	2145	2221	2315	0001
154	**St Quentin 257** a.	0816	0848	...	0951	1153	1348	1352	1422	1551	1605	1802	1820	1752	1851	▬	1942	1957	2020	2049	2053	...	...	2234	2327	0020
154	**St Quentin 257** d.	...	0850	...	...	1153	...	1354	...	1553	1607	...	...	1754	1853	Ⓒ	...	1959	...	...	2055	...	...	2236v	...	...
181	Busigny **257** d.	...	|	...	...	|	...	|	...	|	|	...	...	|	1911	1920	...	|	...	...	|	...	...	|	...	...
207	*Cambrai Ville* **257** a.	...	|	...	...	|	...	|	...	|	|	...	...	|	1934	|	...	|	...	...	|	...	...	|	...	...
217	Aulnoye Aymeries **262** d.	...	0924	...	...	1228	...	1427	...	1626	1638	...	...	1827	...	1946	...	2034	...	...	2127	...	...	2315v	...	...
229	**Maubeuge 262** d.	...	0934	...	...	1242	...	1438	...	1636	1650	...	...	1837	...	2001	...	2045	...	...	2137	...	...	...	...	...

	12302 ①–⑥ n	12304 Ⓐ c	2306 Ⓐ c	†	⑥ t	Ⓐ	12308 s	12312 Ⓐ c	2312 Ⓒ u	12316 Ⓐ c	12318	12320 J⊖	⑦ y	12326 ⊖	Ⓐ	12330 Ⓐ J	12330 Ⓑ J	12334	12336 Ⓑ m	12338 Ⓒ u	12340 Ⓐ c	Ⓐ	†	12342 ⑦ e	†	12346 ⑦ J
Maubeuge 262 d.	...	0549	...	...	...	...	0647	...	...	...	1048	...	...	1450	...	1549	...	1628v	1750	1849	1913	...	...	1945	...	2042
Aulnoye Aymeries **262** d.	...	0601	...	...	...	...	0700	...	...	...	1100	...	...	1502	...	1601	...	1640v	1802	1901	1925	...	...	1957	...	2055
Cambrai Ville **257** d.	...	|	0614	...	...	...	|	...	0728	...	|	...	...	|	...	|	...	|	|	|	|	...	...	|	...	|
Busigny **257** d.	...	|	0642	0645	...	0700	|	...	0757	...	|	...	...	|	...	|	...	|	|	|	|	...	...	|	...	|
St Quentin 257 a.	...	0631	0656	0703	...	0717	0730	...	0811	...	1129	...	...	1531	...	1630	...	1709v	1832	1934	1954	...	...	2030	...	2125
St Quentin 257 d.	0600	0633	0658	0705	0710	0719	0732	0812	0813	1008	1131	1210	1441	1533	...	1632	1632	1711	1834	1936	1956	2000	...	2032	2053	2127
Tergnier **257** d.	0617	|	|	0720	0724	0732	|	0829	0828	1024	|	1230	1457	|	1608	|	|	1728	|	|	|	2015	2012	|	2108	|
Chauny d.	0625	|	|	0727	0730	0738	|	0837	0837	1032	|	1238	1503	|	1615	|	|	1736	|	|	|	2022	2020	|	2114	|
Noyon d.	0637	|	0724	0737	0740	0748	|	0850	0849	1043	|	1249	1513	|	1626	|	|	1749	|	|	|	2033	2032	|	2124	|
Compiègne ▶ d.	0652	0710	0739	0751	0752	0801	0808	0905	0904	1059	1208	1304	1531	1609	1641	1709	1709	1804	1909	2012	2032	2047	2048	2108	2139	2202
Creil ▶ d.	|	|	|	0814	0814	0822	|	0925	0925	1124	|	1324	1607	|	1703	|	|	1823	|	|	|	2110	2110	|	2208	|
Paris Nord ▶ a.	0741	0750	0820	0847	0847	0847	0853	0950	0950	1150	1250	1350	1638	1650	1738	1750	1750	1850	1950	2056	2114	2144	2144	2150	2241	2244

Also:	⑥t	†d	Ⓒ	Ⓐ	Ⓐ◧	Ⓐ	Ⓒ	Ⓐ	Ⓐ	Ⓑh
Paris Nord d.	0634	0640	0904	1040	1422	1707	1749	1819	1840	2134
Creil d.	0708	0714	0944	1114	1504	1741	1823	1853	1913	2208
Compiègne a.	0751	0752	1016	1149	1541	1810	1906	1919	1947	2246

Also:	Ⓐ	⚒§	⚒	⑦v◐	⑥t	Ⓒ	Ⓒ	Ⓐ	Ⓑh	⑥t	Ⓑh	⑥t
Compiègne d.	0504	0559	0620	0657	0657	1048	1226	1242	1719	1740	1824	2023
Creil d.	0543	0624	0704	0717	0735	1117	1307	1307	1803	1806	1906	2107
Paris Nord a.	0617	0650	0738	0741	0805	1150	1341	1341	1838	1838	1941	2141

J – To July 5/from Aug. 31.
b – Not June 1, July 14, Nov. 11.
c – Not July 13.
d – To Tergnier (a. 0833), St Quentin (a. 0901).
e – Also June 1, July 14; not July 12.
h – Also Aug. 15.
m – Not July 12, 13.
n – Not June 1, July 14.
s – Not July 14.
t – Not Aug. 15.
u – Also July 13.
v – ⑦ (also June 1, July 14).
y – Also Aug. 15.
z – Also July 13; not July 12.
▶ – For additional local trains see panel below main table. Additional suburban trains run Paris - Creil and v.v.
◐ – From Tergnier (depart 0618).
◧ – To Tergnier (arrive 1613).
⊖ – May be affected by engineering work.
§ – From St Quentin (depart 0508). Arrive Paris 0659 on ⑥.

256 PARIS and AMIENS - ARRAS - DOUAI - VALENCIENNES and LILLE

For fast trains Paris - Lille see Table **250**. Certain local trains are 2nd class only.

km ★		⚒	Ⓐ	Ⓐ	◇ Ⓐ	⑥ t	TGV 7101 ① Jg	TGV 7105 ①–⑥ n⊗	Ⓐ R	†	⑥ Rt	TGV 7111 ⑥⑦ e	TGV 7113 ①–⑤ n⊗	J⊖	TGV 5163 W	M⊖	† K	G	Ⓐ ⊖	TGV 7121 C	Ⓐ ⊖	†	⑥ t	Ⓐ ⊕	TGV 5422 S
0	**Paris Nord 265** d.	...	...	...	...	...	0722	0752	...	...	...	0952	1022	...	...	...	...	...	...	1222	...	...	...	...	...
131	**Amiens** d.	...	0601	0655	...	0705	|	|	0817	0932	0935	|	|	1050	...	1100	1137	1155	1208	|	1337	...	1359	1410	...
162	Albert d.	...	0625	0715	...	0728	|	|	0840	0955	0956	|	|	1119	...	1123	1157	1219	1227	|	1359	...	1420	1429	...
199	Arras **265** a.	...	0647	0734	...	0750	0812	0842	0900	1018	1014	1042	1112	1142	...	1147	1217	1246	1248	1312	1418	...	1444	1452	...
199	Arras d.	0609	0649	0736	0747	0752	0815	0845	0901	1020	1016	1045	1115	1147	1154	1200	1222	1248	1250	1315	1419	1417	1446	1454	1523
224	Douai a.	0637	0704	0752	|	0806	0830	0900	0914	1036	1030	1059	1129	1202	1207	1217	1237	1303	1304	1330	1437	1437	1500	1508	1538
224	Douai **257** ▶ d.	0639	0706	0804	|	0808	0838	0910	0915	1038	1032	1109	1137	1204	1210	1219	1239	1305	1306	1338	1439	1439	1502	1510	1541
260	Valenciennes ▶ a.	|	|	|	|	|	0904	0937	|	|	|	1135	1202	|	|	|	|	|	|	1404	|	|	|	|	|
257	**Lille Europe** a.	|	|	|	0807	|	...	...	|	|	|	...	...	|	|	|	|	|	|	...	|	|	|	|	1559
257	**Lille Flandres 257** a.	0716	0730	0826	...	0830	...	...	0937	1059	1052	...	...	1231	1233	1301	1316	1327	1327	...	1508	1508	1523	1529	...

		TGV 7131	Ⓐ ⊖	⑥ P	TGV 7137 E	TGV 7139 ①–④ J		TGV 7141 Ⓑ	†	TGV 7343 Ⓐ	Ⓐ	TGV 7145 F	TGV 5192 Ⓐ JW	TGV 5279 W	TGV 7347 Ⓑ	Ⓐ	TGV 7149 ①–④ J	R	TGV 7151 ⑤–⑦ e	TGV 7089 Ⓐ	TGV 7155 Ⓐ	TGV 5181 Y	TGV 5288 W	TGV 7159 ⑦ e	TGV 7099 ⊡
Paris Nord 265 d.	...	1452	...	...	1622	1652	...	1722	...	1752	...	1822	...	...	1852	...	1922	...	1952	2058	2058	...	...	2152	2258
Amiens d.	...	|	1600z	...	|	|	1658x	|	1751	|	1803	|	...	...	|	*1852*	|	1939	|	|	|	...	...	|	|
Albert d.	...	|	1623	...	|	|	1722	|	1814	|	1825	|	...	...	|	*1920*	|	2002	|	|	|	...	...	|	|
Arras **265** a.	...	1542	1648	...	1712	1741	1747	1812	1839	1842	1845	1912	...	...	1941	*1946*	2012	2021	2042	2149	2149	...	...	2242	2348
Arras d.	1539	1548	1650	1650	1715	1744	1749	1815	1841	...	1847	1915	1922	1928	...	1951	2015	2023	2048	2153	2156	2202	2240	2245	2354
Douai a.	1556	1602	1704	1704	1729	1758	1804	1829	1854	...	1910	1929	1937	1942	...	2007	2029	2037	2103	|	2211	2214	2254	2300	⊡
Douai **257** ▶ d.	1558	1612	1706	1706	1737	1806	1806	1837	1856	...	1912	1937	1939	1945	...	2009	2037	2039	2111	|	2219	2217	2257	2310	⊡
Valenciennes ▶ a.	|	1639	|	|	1802	1840	|	1903	|	...	|	2003	|	|	...	|	2104	|	2137	|	2246	|	|	2337	|
Lille Europe a.	|	...	|	|	...	...	|	...	|	...	|	...	2003	|	...	|	...	|	...	|	...	2238	2318	...	|
Lille Flandres 257 a.	1621	...	1733	1727	...	...	1832	...	1914	...	1941	...	...	2005	...	2031	...	2058	...	2219	...	...	...	...	0018

	TGV 7100 Ⓐ J	TGV 5200 W	TGV 7102 Ⓐ	⑥ t	Ⓐ R	TGV 5110 W	TGV 7104 B	⑥ t	Ⓐ	TGV 7108 ①–⑥ n	⑥ Rt	†	Ⓐ	TGV 7110 ⑦ e	TGV 5214 W	⚒ J		TGV 7118 L	Ⓐ R⊖	TGV 5402 S	⑥ t	Ⓐ ⊖	†	TGV 7124 ①–⑥ n	Ⓐ ⊖
Lille Flandres 257 d.	...	...	...	0620	0620	0643	...	0704	0705	...	0805	0805	0805	...	...	0910	1010	...	1037	...	1203	1202	1202	...	1256r
Lille Europe d.	...	0558	...	|	|	|	...	|	|	...	|	|	|	...	0846	|	|	...	|	1121	|	|	|	...	|
Valenciennes ▶ d.	0533	|	0554	|	|	|	0638	|	|	0733	|	|	|	0813	|	|	|	1006	|	|	|	|	|	1156	|
Douai **257** ▶ a.	0558	0625	0625	0640	0641	0706	0704	0727	0726	0759	0827	0824	0830	0841	0906	0934	1035	1032	1055	1139	1224	1224	1224	1222	1321
Douai d.	0606	0628	0633	0642	0643	0709	0712	0728	0727	0810	0829	0826	0832	0849	0908	0936	1037	1042	1057	1142	1226	1226	1226	1232	1323
Arras a.	0620	0644	0649	0655	0658	0724	0728	0744	0740	0825	0843	0839	0846	0903	0925	0954	1054	1059	1110	1155	1240	1241	1242	1246	1338
Arras **265** d.	0623	...	0656	0657	0701	...	0735	0746	0742	0835	0845	0841	0848	0906	...	...	1056c	1106	1119	...	1242	1243	...	1249	1340
Albert d.	|	...	|	0716	0720	...	|	0809	0805	|	0906	0904	0916	|	...	...	1122c	|	1137	...	1310	1311	...	|	1407
Amiens a.	|	...	|	0737	0741	...	|	0840	0829	|	0925	0923	0936	|	...	...	1145c	|	1158	...	...	1341	...	|	1428
Paris Nord 265 a.	0714	...	0747	...	...	...	0826	...	...	0926	...	...	...	0956	...	...	...	1156	...	...	...	...	...	1338	...

CONTINUED ON NEXT PAGE

LILLE and VALENCIENNES - DOUAI - ARRAS - AMIENS and PARIS 256

For fast trains Paris - Lille see Table **250**. Certain local trains are 2nd class only.

			TGV 7136			TGV 7342			TGV 7144		TGV 7148		
	Ⓒ	⑥ t	D		Ⓐ	N	Ⓐ	⑥ y	Ⓑ	Ⓐ R	Ⓑ	Ⓒ R	Ⓐ
Lille Flandres 257 d.	1301	1410	...	1540	1605	...	1634	1638	...	1705	...	1805	1804
Lille Europe d.	|	|	...	|	|	...	|	|	...	|	...	|	|
Valenciennes ▶ d.	|	|	1438	|	|	...	|	|	1641	|	1739	|	|
Douai **257** ▶ a.	1322	1439	1504	1607	1630	...	1656	1701	1707	1725	1805	1826	1829
Douai d.	1324	1441	1512	1609	1632	...	1658	1703	1717	1730	1813	1828	1831
Arras a.	1340	1500	1528	1629	1650	...	1713	1719	1733	1745	1829	1846	1851
Arras **265** d.	1342	...	1535	1632	...	1706	*1725*	...	1736	1747	1836	1848	1852
Albert d.	1408	...	|	1656	...	|	*1755*	...	|	1807	|	1910	1920
Amiens a.	1428	...	|	1719	...	|	*1817*	...	|	1826	|	1932	1944
Paris Nord 265 a.	...	...	1626	...	...	1756	...	...	1826	...	1926	...	...

	◇	TGV 7152		TGV 5136	TGV 7156	TGV 7154		TGV 7158	TGV 5138	TGV 7160		TGV 7096
	Ⓐ	⑤⑥	Ⓐ	①–⑥ W	⑦ e	①–④ n	Ⓐ	⑤	⑦ We	⑦ e		Ⓐ
Lille Flandres 257 d.	...	...	1909	...	...	...	2013	...	2021	...	2110	2209
Lille Europe d.	1839	...	|	1915	...	...	|	...	|	...	|	|
Valenciennes ▶ d.	|	1845	|	|	1938	1942	|	2008	|	2038	|	|
Douai **257** ▶ a.	|	1910	1928	1933	2004	2008	2037	2034	2040	2106	2136	|
Douai d.	|	1918	1930	1936	2012	2018	2039	2042	2043	2116	2138	|
Arras a.	1900	1933	1943	1949	2028	2032	2054	2058	2056	2132	2156	2229
Arras **265** d.	...	1940	1945	...	2035	2035	2055	2105	...	2135	...	2232
Albert d.	...	|	2007	...	|	|	2119	|	...	|	...	|
Amiens a.	...	|	2028	...	|	|	2141	|	...	|	...	|
Paris Nord 265 a.	...	2032	...	...	2126	2126	...	2156	...	2226	...	2323

Some trains are 2nd class only

LOCAL TRAINS DOUAI - VALENCIENNES

	⚒	⚒	Ⓐ	⚒	Ⓐ		⚒	†	Ⓐ		Ⓐ	⚒		⚒	b	Ⓐ		Ⓐ	Ⓐ	†	Ⓐ	⚒u	Ⓐ	⑥	Ⓐ	†
Douai d.	0600	0658	0725	0753	0814	0855	0953	1048	1155	1216	1248	1312	1351	1623	1650	1721	1754	1822	1854	1914	1921	1958	2046	2116	2143	2214
Valenciennes a.	0629	0727	0758	0834	0847	0933	1021	1116	1227	1251	1321	1347	1422	1659	1718	1754	1833	1852	1927	1949	1952	2032	2118	2147	2216	2246

	Ⓐ	⚒	Ⓐ	⚒	⚒	Ⓑh	Ⓐ	Ⓐ	Ⓒ	†	⑥t	Ⓐ	⚒		⚒	⚒		Ⓐ	⑥P	Ⓑh	⚒	Ⓑh	Ⓐ	⑥t	Ⓑh	Ⓐ
Valenciennes d.	0508	0545	0624	0654	0753	0803	0839	0934	0946	1120	1148	1201	1223	1300	1402	1455	1602	1650	1650	1719	1751	1820	1858	1856	1928	2142
Douai a.	0537	0616	0700	0727	0826	0837	0910	1004	1015	1151	1218	1230	1257	1336	1435	1524	1638	1725	1725	1754	1825	1852	1932	1935	1958	2212

B – ①–⑤ to July 6 (not June 1); ① July 20 - Aug. 24 (also July 15); ①–⑤ from Aug. 31.
C – ⑤⑥ to July 4; ⑥ July 11 - Aug. 29; ⑤⑥ from Sept. 4.
D – ⑥⑦ (also ⑤ to July 3 / from Sept. 4), also June 1, July 14.
E – ⑤ (also ⑥ July 11 - Aug. 29).
F – Daily to July 4; ①–⑤ July 6 - Aug. 28 (not July 14); daily from Aug. 31.
G – ⑥ (also ⑦ to June 28 / from Sept. 6), also June 1; not Aug. 15.
J – To July 5 / from Aug. 31.
K – July 5 - Aug. 30.
L – ①⑥⑦ (also June 1, 2, July 14, 15; not July 13).
M – ①–⑥ July 4 - Aug. 29 (not July 14, Aug. 15).
N – Daily to July 4; ⑦ July 5 - Aug. 23 (also July 14); daily from Aug. 30.
P – To June 27 / from Sept. 5.
R – To / from Rouen (Table **268**).
S – To / from Strasbourg (Table **391**).
W – For origin / destination see Table **11**.
Y – For origin / destination (also days of running) see Table **11**.
b – Will not run on ⑥ July 4 - Aug. 29.
c – Ⓒ only.
e – Also June 1, July 14.
g – Also June 2; not June 1.
h – Also Aug. 15.
n – Not June 1, July 14.
r – Depart 1249 July 6 - Aug. 28.
t – Not Aug. 15.
u – Runs 14 minutes later on ⑥ July 4 - Aug. 29.
x – 1700 on Ⓒ.
y – Not Aug. 15. On ⑥ July 4 - Aug. 29 Douai d. 1718, Arras a. 1733.
z – 1556 on ⑤.
TGV –Ⓡ, supplement payable.
◇ – TER à Grande Vitesse (via high-speed line). Supplement *Côte d'Opale* is payable (€3 per day).
★ – Paris - Arras via high-speed line is *179 km*.
▶ – For local trains see panel below main table.
⊖ – May be affected by engineering work Amiens - Arras and v.v.
⊕ – On Ⓐ Sept. 14 - Oct. 9 runs up to 30 minutes later.
⊗ – Subject to alteration Douai - Valenciennes on Ⓐ Aug. 31 - Sept. 11.
⊡ – Calls at Douai (0008, train **7095**) on night of ⑦ July 5 - Aug. 30, arrive Lille Flandres 0029.

LILLE - CAMBRAI - ST QUENTIN 257

For other journeys Paris - Cambrai change at Douai (see Table **256** for Paris - Douai). Certain trains are 2nd class only.

km		Ⓐ	Ⓐc	Ⓐ	Ⓒd	⚒	Ⓐ	Ⓐ	⚒	⚒		†	Ⓐ
0	**Lille Flandres 256** d.	...	...	0534	...	*0620*	...	*0647*	0733	...	0850	...	*0910*n
34	Douai **256** a.	...	...	0610	...	*0641*	...	*0723*	0800	...	0917	...	*0934*n
34	Douai d.	...	...	0612	...	0649	...	0728	0802	...	0919	...	0944
66	**Cambrai Ville** a.	...	...	0657	...	0723	...	0757	0830	...	0947	...	1014
66	**Cambrai Ville** d.	0520	0614	...	0728	...	0743	...	...	0858	...	1000	...
82	Caudry d.	0535	0629	...	0743	...	0757	...	...	0911	...	1013	...
92	Busigny **255** d.	0546	0642	...	0757	...	0807	...	...	0923	...	1022	...
119	**St Quentin 255** d.	0607	0658	...	0813	...	0827	...	...	0941	...	1044	...
142	Tergnier **255** a.	...	|	...	0826	...	...	...	...	0958	...	...	...
273	*Paris Nord* **255** a.	...	0820	...	0950	...	...	...	...	R	...	...	...

km		⚒	†	⚒	⚒J	⚒	⚒	†	⑥t	⑥P	Ⓑ	⑥t	Ⓐ
0	**Lille Flandres 256** d.	...	1108	...	1130	*1202*	...	*1301*	...	1505	*1540*	*1540*	...
34	Douai **256** a.	...	1131	...	1200	*1224*	...	*1322*	...	1529	*1607*	*1607*	...
34	Douai d.	...	1133	...	1202	1238	1342	1342	...	1531	1625	1627	...
66	**Cambrai Ville** a.	...	1201	...	1235	1315	1413	1414	...	1559	1658	1658	...
66	**Cambrai Ville** d.	1040	...	1216	...	1317	...	1416	1431	...	...	1700	1715
82	Caudry d.	1053	...	1234	...	1333	...	1429	1444	...	...	1714	1734
92	Busigny **255** d.	1103	...	1248	...	1344	...	1438	1452	...	...	1724	1747
119	**St Quentin 255** d.	1125	...	1309	...	...	...	...	1514	...	...	1746	1808
142	Tergnier **255** a.	...	...	...	...	...	...	...	...	...	...	...	...
273	*Paris Nord* **255** a.	...	...	...	...	...	...	...	...	...	...	...	...

	Ⓐ	Ⓒ	Ⓐ	Ⓐ	†	⚒	Ⓐ	⑥t	Ⓐ	Ⓐ
Lille Flandres 256 d.	*1634*	1705	*1705*	1738	1818	...	1838	1920	*1909*	*2013*
Douai **256** a.	*1656*	1729	*1725*	1802	1842	...	1903	1942	*1928*	*2037*
Douai d.	1705	1731	1734	1810	1844	1844	1909	1944	1950	2043
Cambrai Ville a.	1737	1801	1810	1840	1913	1913	1943	2014	2018	2113
Cambrai Ville d.	...	1805	1812	1842	1916	...	1945	2016	...	...
Caudry d.	...	1818	1828	1858	1928	...	1959	2029	...	...
Busigny **255** d.	...	1827	1840	1910	1939	...	2008	2037	...	...
St Quentin 255 d.	...	1846	1859	1930	2001	...	2028	...	...	...
Tergnier **255** a.	...	1906	1916	...	...	...	...	...	...	...
Paris Nord **255** a.	...	...	...	...	...	...	...	...	...	...

	Ⓐ	Ⓐ	Ⓐ	⚒	Ⓐ	Ⓐ	⑥t	Ⓐ	⚒ R
Paris Nord **255** d.	...	...	...	...	...	...	...	...	
Tergnier **255** d.	...	...	0524	...	...	...	...	...	0736
St Quentin 255 d.	...	0512	0538	0617	...	0650	0650	...	0755
Busigny **255** d.	...	0536	0556	0635	...	0712	0714	...	0819
Caudry d.	...	0544	0603	0643	...	0722	0724	...	0828
Cambrai Ville a.	...	0555	0614	0655	...	0736	0737	...	0839
Cambrai Ville d.	0513	0557	0623	0657	0716	0804	0805	0834	...
Douai a.	0543	0628	0652	0731	0755	0833	0833	0903	...
Douai **256** d.	*0557*	0630	*0706*	0733	*0804*	0835	0837	...	...
Lille Flandres 256 a.	*0636*	0659	*0730*	0759	*0826*	0902	0902	...	...

	⚒	†	⚒	⚒	†	⚒	⚒	Ⓑh	Ⓐ	⑥t	†	Ⓐ
Paris Nord **255** d.	...	...	...	...	...	...	...	...	...	...	...	...
Tergnier **255** d.	...	...	...	...	...	...	...	...	...	...	...	...
St Quentin 255 d.	...	...	0858	...	1120	...	1202	...	1402	1402	...	...
Busigny **255** d.	...	...	0923	...	1141	...	1225	...	1423	1423	1423	...
Caudry d.	...	...	0935	...	1151	...	1235	...	1432	1432	1433	...
Cambrai Ville a.	...	...	0949	...	1203	...	1247	...	1444	1444	1444	...
Cambrai Ville d.	0855	0852	...	1129	1205	1210	1249	1319	...	1446	1446	1632
Douai a.	0918	0919	...	1157	1234	1236	1320	1345	...	1515	1515	1704
Douai **256** d.	0920	0921	...	*1204*n	*1244*r	1237	...	1347	...	*1558*	*1558*	...
Lille Flandres 256 a.	0941	0947	...	*1231*n	*1322*r	1304	...	1410	...	*1621*	*1621*	...

	⑥t	Ⓐ	Ⓒ	Ⓐ	⑥t	†	Ⓐ	Ⓐ	†	⑥t		
Paris Nord **255** d.	...	...	...	...	...	...	...	...	...	...	1737	...
Tergnier **255** d.	...	...	...	...	...	...	...	...	1811	...	|	...
St Quentin 255 d.	1602	...	...	...	...	1724	1720	1830	1829	1832	1853	2103
Busigny **255** d.	1624	1638	...	...	...	1743	1745	1853	1854	1854	1911	2126
Caudry d.	1634	1648	...	...	...	1753	1756	1902	1903	1903	1922	2136
Cambrai Ville a.	1646	1701	...	...	...	1804	1808	1914	1914	1914	1934	2148
Cambrai Ville d.	...	1703	1703	1741	1809	1809	1814	1917	1917	1917	...	...
Douai a.	...	1731	1731	1816	1833	1833	1849	1946	1947	1947	...	...
Douai **256** d.	...	1733	1733	*1829*	1835	1835	*1912*	1949	1949	1949	...	...
Lille Flandres 256 a.	...	1801	1758	*1856*	1858	1858	*1941*	2015	2015	2014	...	...

J – To July 4 / from Aug. 31.
P – To June 27 / from Sept. 5.
R – To / from Reims (Table **252**).
c – Not July 13.
d – Also July 13.
h – Also Aug. 15.
n – To July 4 / from Aug. 31.
r – On ⑦ July 5 - Aug. 30 d. 1239, a. 1316.
t – Not Aug. 15.

AMIENS - ST QUENTIN 258

2nd class only

km		Ⓐ	⑥t	Ⓐ	⚒⊖	†	⚒§	Ⓐ§	Ⓐ	⚒	†z	Ⓐ
0	Amiens d.	0638	0650	0749	0830	1025	1212	1442	1718	1826	1851	2035
76	St Quentin a.	0734	0747	0844	1001	1121	1310	1539	1811	1926	1945	2133

	⑥t	Ⓐ	Ⓐ	†		⚒§	Ⓐ§	Ⓐ	Ⓐ	⑥t	†
St Quentin d.	0629	0637	0745	0755	...	1220	1324	1716	1841	1851	2017
Amiens a.	0724	0736	0840	0852	...	1317	1425	1813	1937	1951	2116

t – Not Aug. 15.
z – On † June 28 - Aug. 30 d. 1913, a. 2008.
⊖ – Via Tergnier (depart 0941).
§ – Liable to alteration due to engineeering work.

CALAIS - DUNKERQUE - DE PANNE 259

km			Ⓐ	Ⓐ	⑥P		ⒶJ	⑥P	Ⓐ	
0	**Calais Ville** d.	...	0534	0638	0638	...	1222	1222	1719	...
23	Gravelines d.	...	0553	0701	0701	...	1249	1249	1742	...
46	**Dunkerque** a.	...	0616	0731	0731	...	1316	1316	1810	...

	Ⓐ	⑥P	🚌 Ⓐ	⚒J	⑥P	Ⓐ		Ⓐ	Ⓐ
Dunkerque d.	0629	0629	0734	1217	1328	1542	...	1711	1827
Gravelines d.	0701	0701	0825	1247	1352	1609	...	1743	1855
Calais Ville a.	0724	0724	0855	1309	1412	1627	...	1806	1918

J – To July 4 / from Aug. 31.
P – To June 27 / from Sept. 5.

🚌 **BOULOGNE - CALAIS - DUNKERQUE** (serving the railway stations) is operated by Autocars BCD ✆ 03 21 83 51 51, approx. 4 journeys on Ⓐ, 2 journeys on ⑥ (no service on ⑦). Additional journeys run between Calais and Dunkerque (approx 8 journeys on Ⓐ, 1 on ⑥).

🚌 **DUNKERQUE GARE - ADINKERKE (DE PANNE STATION)** Operator DK'BUS Marine. Journey 40 - 50 minutes. Connects at De Panne station with coastal tram service (Table **404**).
From Dunkerque Gare: ⚒ (service 2): 0702 and approx hourly to 2006. † (service 3): 0755 and hourly to 1955.
From Adinkerke: ⚒ (service 2): 0704, 0807 and approx hourly to 2106. † (service 3): 0910 and hourly to 1910, 2014, 2105.

260 PARIS - AMIENS - BOULOGNE

For *TGV* service Paris - Boulogne / Calais (and connections via Hazebrouck) see Table **265**. Other services available by changing at Lille (Tables **250** and **266**).

km					12001		2003	🚌		2007	2007	🚌		12011		2015	🚌	12019		🚌		12023		2025	🚌
		Ⓐ	⚒	Ⓐ	Ⓐ	⑦	①–⑥	①–⑥	⑥		⑦	†	⚒	①–⑥	†			Ⓐ					Ⓐ		⚒
					J	K	n ⊖	n	t		e ⊖			B		▽		J						▽ a	
0	**Paris Nord** △ d.	...	...	...	0634	...	0707	...	0710	0804	0804	...	0819	0910	0919	1004	...	1104	...	...	1137	1231	...	1419	...
51	Creil △ d.	...	...	...	0701	...	0734	...	0744	0831	0831	...	0853	0940	0953	|	...	|	...	...	1211	1257	...	|	...
66	Clermont-de-l'Oise △ d.	...	...	...	|	...	|	...	0802	|	|	...	0903	0951	1010	|	...	|	...	...	1228	|	...	|	...
126	Longueau d.	...	...	...	0738	...	0812	...	0846	0909	0909	...	0950	1027	1054	1107	...	1204	...	...	1317	1338	...	1519	...
131	**Amiens** a.	...	...	...	0744	...	0817	...	0852	0914	0914	...	0955	1033	1059	1112	...	1210	...	...	1323	1344	...	1524	...
131	**Amiens** d.	...	...	0638	...	0834	0828	...	...	...	0925	...	...	...	...	1123	...	▬	1223	...	...	...	1428	1535	...
176	Abbeville d.	...	...	0715	...	0903	0853	0907	...	...	0950	1000	...	...	...	1148	1151	...	1312	1322	...	...	1514	1601	1606
213	Le Treport a.	...	...	|	...	0938	|	1015	...	...	|	1106	...	...	...	|	1259	⚒	...	1430	...	...	|	|	1713
216	Rang du Fliers ⊙ d.	0611	0656	0745	...	...	0917	...	...	...	1024	...	...	...	...	1221	...	1303	...	...	...	...	1543	1631	...
227	Étaples-Le Touquet § d.	0619	0704	0755	...	...	0927	...	...	...	1034	...	...	...	...	1231	...	1311	...	...	...	...	1552	1641	...
254	**Boulogne Ville** § a.	0642	0722	0823	...	...	0944	...	...	...	1051	...	...	...	...	1249	...	1333	...	...	...	...	1608	1659	...
	Calais Ville **261** a.	0718	0807	...	...	...	...	...	...	...	...	...	...	...	...	...	...	1416	...	...	...	...	...	...	...

					12031		2033				12035			12037	12039	2041	🚌				2045	2045	2049	2049	
	Ⓒ	Ⓐ	Ⓐ	Ⓒ	①–⑥	Ⓐ		Ⓐ	⑥	Ⓒ	Ⓐ	Ⓐ	Ⓐ		Ⓐ		⑤⑥	†	Ⓐ	⑥	①–⑤	⑤		⑦	
				▷	w		▽		t		h				h	▽	y			t	u		G	z ▽	
Paris Nord △ d.	...	...	...	...	1610	...	1704	...	...	1719	1734	...	1749	1807	1834	1904	...	1910	1910	1940	2004	2004	2107	2107	2149
Creil △ d.	...	...	...	...	|	...	|	...	...	1753	|	...	1823	|	|	|	...	1940	1949	2012	2032	2032	|	|	2219
Clermont-de-l'Oise △ d.	...	...	...	...	|	...	|	...	...	1810	|	...	1833	|	1908	|	...	1956	2006	2028	|	|	|	|	2234
Longueau d.	...	...	...	...	1710	...	1804	...	...	1859	1834	...	1927	1911	1945	2004	...	2037	2056	2108	2109	2109	2207	2207	2317
Amiens a.	...	...	...	...	1716	...	1809	...	...	1905	1839	...	1933	1917	1951	2008	...	2042	2102	2113	2114	2114	2212	2212	2323
Amiens d.	*1557*	...	*1650*	...	...	1724	1820	...	*1837*	...	...	1900	...	...	...	2019	...	...	...	...	...	2125	...	2223	...
Abbeville d.	1645	...	1742	...	...	1756	1846	1854	1921	...	...	1945	...	...	...	2046	2054	...	...	...	...	2150	...	2248	...
Le Treport a.	1734	...	1829	...	...	|	|	1941	2008	...	...	...	...	...	...	|	2202	...	...	...	...	|	...	|	...
Rang du Fliers ⊙ d.	...	...	...	1817	...	1825	1916	...	...	...	...	...	...	...	...	2119	...	...	...	...	...	2223	...	2321	...
Étaples-Le Touquet § d.	...	1729	...	1826	...	1834	1925	...	...	...	...	...	...	...	...	2129	...	...	...	...	...	2233	...	2331	...
Boulogne Ville § a.	...	1752	...	1843	...	1849	1942	...	...	...	...	...	...	...	...	2146	...	...	...	...	...	2250	...	2348	...
Calais Ville **261** a.	...	...	...	1921	...	1949	...	...	...	...	...	...	...	...	...	...	...	...	...	...	...	...	...	...	...

			2004	2004			12006	2008	12010			12012			2014			12018	12020	🚌	2022			12026	
	Ⓐ	⑥	①	①–⑥	†	⑥	Ⓐ	①–⑥	Ⓑ	⚒	Ⓐ	Ⓐ	⑥	⚒			Ⓐ	①–⑥	Ⓐ	Ⓒ		⚒	Ⓐ	①–⑥	⚒
		t	g	u		t		n ⊡	h			h	t	J	▽			n	J		♠ ▽			J	
Calais Ville **261** d.	...	...	...	...	...	...	...	...	...	...	0548	...	0601	...	...	...	...	...	...	...	...	...	...	...	...
Boulogne Ville § d.	...	...	0429	...	...	...	...	0538	...	...	0628	...	0636	...	0746	...	...	...	...	...	1046	1220	...	...	...
Étaples-Le Touquet § d.	...	...	0447	...	...	...	...	0556	...	...	0644	...	0653	...	0804	...	...	...	...	...	1104	1239	...	...	...
Rang du Fliers ⊙ d.	...	...	0457	...	...	...	...	0606	...	...	0654	...	0702	...	0815	...	...	...	...	...	1115	1247	...	...	...
Le Treport d.	...	...	|	...	...	...	...	|	...	0632	|	...	|	0732	|	...	*0755*r	...	...	1020	|	▬	...	...	*1202*r
Abbeville d.	...	...	0530	...	...	...	*0557*	0638	...	0719	0724	...	0732	0814	0838	...	0919	...	...	1128	1138	...	1229	...	1322
Amiens a.	...	...	0554	...	...	...	*0639*	0701	...	...	0759	...	0812	...	0902	...	1005	...	...	...	1202	...	1305	...	1407
Amiens d.	0520	0533	0605	0605	0612	0641	0646	0715	0747	...	...	0812	...	...	0913	0930	...	1012	1112	...	1213	1218	...	1311	...
Longueau d.	0526	0538	0613	0613	0618	0647	0654	0723	0755	...	...	0821	...	...	0921	0935	...	1020	1120	...	1221	1228	...	1319	...
Clermont-de-l'Oise △ d.	0616	0620	0650	0650	0706	0731	|	|	|	...	...	|	...	...	|	1019	...	|	|	...	|	1318	...	|	...
Creil △ a.	0632	0633	|	|	0721	0745	|	|	|	...	...	|	...	...	|	1036	...	|	|	...	|	1332	...	1356	...
Paris Nord △ a.	0708	0708	0723	0723	0759	0817	0753	0823	0856	...	...	0923	...	...	1020	1111	...	1120	1220	...	1320	1412	...	1423	...

				12030			🚌	2032		12036	🚌		2038	2038		🚌	2042			2044	2044			12046	2048
	Ⓐ	⑥	†	☆	Ⓒ	Ⓐ			Ⓐ	Ⓑ	Ⓑ	Ⓐ		⑦	Ⓐ			†	Ⓐ	Ⓑ	⑦	⑦	Ⓐ	Ⓑ	⑦
		t						▽		b				e ▽	J		▽			h	v ▽	K		L	e ▽
Calais Ville **261** d.	1227	1227	...	...	...	...	...	...	...	...	...	...	...	...	...	...	...	...	...	...	...	...	...	...	...
Boulogne Ville § d.	1314	1319	1324	...	...	...	...	1437	...	...	...	1619	...	1630	1648	...	1741	...	1824	...	1832	...	2015	...	2048
Étaples-Le Touquet § d.	1334	1337	1340	...	...	...	...	1455	...	...	...	1640	...	1649	1707	...	1800	...	1852	...	1850	...	2031	...	2106
Rang du Fliers ⊙ d.	1343	1347	1349	...	...	...	...	1505	...	...	...	1648	...	1659	▬	...	1809	...	1901	...	1901	...	2039	...	2117
Le Treport d.	|	|	*1301*r	...	...	...	1437c	|	...	...	1600	|	...	|	...	1720	|	...	|	...	|	1912	▬	...	|
Abbeville d.	1411	1419	1422	...	...	...	1523	1539	...	...	1708	1720	...	1733		1823	1834	...	1932	...	1935	1948		...	2140
Amiens a.	1445	1456	1501	...	...	...	...	1602	...	...	...	1756	...	1758	Ⓒ	...	1858	...	1959	...	2000	2018	†	...	2205
Amiens d.	...	...	...	1508	1524	1534	...	1613	1625	1708	...	...	1809	1809	1822	...	1909	1931	...	2011	2011	...	2025	2112	2216
Longueau d.	...	...	...	1516	1529	1540	...	1621	1631	1716	...	...	1817	1817	1828	...	1916	1937	...	2018	2018	...	2032	2120	2224
Clermont-de-l'Oise △ d.	...	...	...	|	1616	1619	...	|	1719	|	...	...	|	|	1919	...	|	2021	...	|	|	...	2115	2156	|
Creil △ a.	...	...	...	1552	1632	1632	...	|	1732	1752	...	...	1852	1852	1935	...	1955	2037	...	2053	2053	...	2131	|	|
Paris Nord △ a.	...	...	...	1620	1708	1708	...	1720	1808	1820	...	...	1920	1920	2011	...	2020	2111	...	2123	2123	...	2208	2229	2323

- **B** – ①–⑥ to July 10 (not June 1); ①–⑤ July 15 - Aug. 28; ①–⑥ from Aug. 31.
- **G** – Daily to July 10; ⑧ July 12 - Aug. 30 (not July 13); daily from Aug. 31.
- **J** – To July 4 / from Aug. 31.
- **K** – ⑦ June 28 - Aug. 30 (also July 14).
- **L** – Ⓑ to July 5 / from Aug. 31 (not Nov. 11).
- **a** – Depart Paris 1416 on Nov. 23, 25, 27.
- **b** – Not July 13, Nov. 11.
- **c** – 1413 on ⑥.
- **e** – Also June 1, July 14.
- **g** – Also June 2, July 15; not June 1, July 13.
- **h** – Not July 13.
- **n** – Not June 1, July 14.
- **r** – Connection by 🚌.
- **t** – Not Aug. 15.
- **u** – Not June 1, July 13, 14.
- **v** – Also July 14.
- **w** – Not June 1, July 14, Nov. 23 - 27.
- **y** – Also June 1, July 13, 14, Nov. 10; not Aug. 15.
- **z** – Also June 1; not Oct. 25, Nov. 1.
- ⊡ – By 🚌 Boulogne - Abbeville on Aug. 15.
- ⊖ – By 🚌 Amiens - Boulogne on June 28, Aug. 16, Dec. 5, 6.
- ⊙ – Rang du Fliers-Verton-Berck.
- ☆ – Will not call at Creil on ⑥.
- △ – Frequent local trains run Paris - Creil. Infrequent local trains run Paris or Creil - Clermont-de-l'Oise.
- ▽ – By 🚌 Boulogne - Abbeville and v.v. June 1, 28, Aug. 15, 16.
- ▷ – To Lille Flandres (Table **261**).
- ♠ – On Ⓐ to June 26 runs later: Boulogne 1108, Amiens a. 1243 / d. 1254, Paris a. 1420.
- § – See also Table **263**.

261 BOULOGNE - CALAIS

km		Ⓐ	Ⓐ	⚒	⚒		⚒	①–④	†	⑤	Ⓐ	⑥	⚒	†	⑥	Ⓐ	Ⓐ	⑥	†	Ⓒ	⑥	Ⓐ	Ⓒ	Ⓐ
								m				t	⊕		t			t	△		△t			
0	**Boulogne Ville** d.	0602	0644	0702	0724	0829	0957	1036	1057	1138	1157	1157	1224	1258	1303	1305	1335	1335	1346	1444	1517	1613	1644	1707
7	Wimille-Wimereux d.	0609	0651	0711	0733	0837	1006	1043	1104	1146	1205	1205	1232	1307	1311	1313	1343	1343	|	1451	1524	1621	1652	1715
17	Marquise-Rinxent d.	0617	0659	0718	0740	0845	1015	1051	1112	1153	1213	1212	1239	1315	1320	1321	1352	1351	1357	1459	1532	1628	1700	1723
34	Calais Fréthun **265** d.	0629	0711	0733	0756	0856	|	|	|	|	1224	1223	1250	|	1334	1335	1407	1405	1409	|	1544	1639	|	1735
42	**Calais Ville 265** a.	0637	0718	0741	0807	0903	1031	1108	1128	1210	1231	1230	1258	1333	1343	1343	1414	1416	1416	1517	1551	1649	1716	1741
	Lille Flandres **266** a.	0758	...	0858	...	1033*	...	1238*	1250	...	1403	1403	...	1508	1511	...	...	...	...	1643	...	...	1840	...

	Ⓐ	Ⓒ	Ⓐ	Ⓒ	Ⓐ	Ⓐ	Ⓒ	Ⓐ
					⊖	▷		
Boulogne Ville d.	1731	1739	1818	1845	1842	1909	1949	1952
Wimille-Wimereux d.	1740	1747	1827	1854	1850	1918	1959	1958
Marquise-Rinxent d.	1751	1755	1835	1903	1857	1926	2006	2005
Calais Fréthun **265** d.	1808	|	1852	|	1908	1940	2016	2016
Calais Ville 265 a.	1817	1816	1901	1921	1915	1949	2023	2023
Lille Flandres **266** a.	2002	1947	...	2059	...	...	...	2158

	Ⓐ	⑥	Ⓐ	⑥	Ⓐ	Ⓐ	⑥	Ⓐ	⑥	Ⓐ	†
	▷	t ▷		t			t	J	t		
Lille Flandres **266** d.	...	...	...	...	...	0627	...	0700	0727	0800	...
Calais Ville 265 d.	0548	0601	0642	0647	0739	0804	0804	0822	0904	0916	0951
Calais Fréthun **265** d.	|	|	0651	0656	|	0812	0811	0829	0911	0925	0958
Marquise-Rinxent d.	0611	0618	0711	0714	0755	0825	0822	0840	0922	0937	1011
Wimille-Wimereux d.	0619	0627	0719	0723	0803	0832	0830	0847	0929	0947	1020
Boulogne Ville a.	0626	0634	0727	0732	0809	0839	0837	0854	0936	0954	1027

	Ⓐ	Ⓒ	Ⓐ	⑥	Ⓒ	⑥	Ⓐ	Ⓐ	⑥	Ⓐ	⑥	Ⓐ	Ⓒ	Ⓐ	Ⓒ	Ⓐ	Ⓒ	Ⓐ	Ⓐ	Ⓐ	Ⓐ	Ⓒ	Ⓐ	Ⓒ
			▷	t ▷		J	J		t		t			▽	⊖									
Lille Flandres **266** d.	0815	0922	...	...	1124	...	...	...	...	...	1338	1403	1421	...	...	1600	1621	...	1700	...	1806	1821	1915	2020
Calais Ville 265 d.	0953	1046	1227	1227	1306	1327	1327	1349	1433	1433	1503	1529	1552	1644	1652	1727	1746	1754	1820	1910	1931	1950	2041	2154
Calais Fréthun **265** d.	1000	|	1236	1237	|	1334	|	1356	1442	1442	1510	|	|	1653	1659	1736	|	1805	1828	1918	1940	|	2049	|
Marquise-Rinxent d.	1012	1104	1255	1255	1323	1347	1348	1407	1452	1453	1523	1547	1610	1706	1711	1754	1803	1818	1841	1933	1952	2007	2101	2212
Wimille-Wimereux d.	1020	1112	1304	1303	1331	1355	1357	1415	1459	1502	1532	1557	1618	1714	1719	1802	1811	1827	1851	1941	2000	2015	2108	2220
Boulogne Ville a.	1027	1119	1312	1310	1338	1402	1404	1423	1505	1509	1540	1604	1626	1721	1726	1810	1818	1834	1858	1948	2007	2022	2115	2228

- **J** – To July 3 / from Aug. 31.
- **m** – Not June 1, July 14, Nov. 11.
- **t** – Not Aug. 15.
- △ – From Lille via Bethune and St Pol (Table **263**).
- ▽ – To Lille via St Pol and Bethune (Table **263**).
- ▷ – To / from Amiens (Table **260**).
- ⊖ – To / from Arras (Table **263**).
- ⊕ – Subject to alteration on Ⓐ Sept. 7 - 18.
- * – Subject to alteration on Ⓐ Sept. 21 - Oct. 9.

Certain trains 2nd class — LILLE - VALENCIENNES - MAUBEUGE and CHARLEVILLE MÉZIÈRES — 262

km		Ⓐ ⊖	⚒	Ⓐ	⚒	⚒	Ⓐ J	Ⓐ J	Ⓐ	⑥ t	⚒	Ⓐ		⑥ t	†	Ⓐ	†	†	⚒ J	Ⓐ	⑥ t	⚒			⚒ △	⚒
0	**Lille Flandres** d.	0554	*0554*	0655	0655	...	0750	...	0815	0817	...	0850	0917	...	...	...	1117	...	1200	1219	1219	...	1318	...	1415	...
48	Valenciennes d.	0635	*0635*	0736	0736	...	0832	...	0856	0856	...	0931	0955	...	...	...	1157	...	1233	1257	1257	...	1357	...	1453	...
82	Aulnoye Aymeries a.	0704	*0704*	0802	0802	...	0901	...	0925	0925	...	0957	1022	...	...	...	1227	...	1301	1324	1324	...	1423	...	1520	...
82	Aulnoye Aymeries d.	0706	0716	0810	0812	0835	0909	0909	0928	0928	0938	1005	1027	1039	1041	1044	1235	1235	1303	1333	1333	1332	1430	1437	1522	1540
94	**Maubeuge** a.	0718	|	0822	|	0848	|	0922	0941	0941	|	|	1038	|	|	|	|	1249	1315	|	|	1347	1443	|	1534	|
104	Jeumont a.	0727	|	0832	|	0901	|	0932	0951	0949	|	|	1046	|	|	|	|	1257	1324	|	|	1359	1451	|	1543	|
94	Avesnes d.	...	0732	...	0828	...	0921	...	...	...	0950	1016	...	1050	1058	1057	1246	...	...	1344	1344	...	...	1448	...	1552
123	Hirson a.	...	0758	...	0855	...	0946	...	...	...	1013	1039	...	1114	1124	1121	1310	...	...	1407	1406	...	...	1512	...	1622
184	**Charleville-Mézières** a.	...	...	...	0936	...	...	...	...	...	...	1120	...	...	1202	...	...	...	...	...	1450	...	...	...	...	...

	Ⓐ J	Ⓐ	Ⓐ	Ⓐ			Ⓐ	Ⓐ	Ⓐ	Ⓐ	Ⓐ	Ⓐ	Ⓐ	Ⓒ	Ⓐ	Ⓒ	Ⓐ	Ⓐ J	Ⓐ J	Ⓐ	Ⓐ	Ⓐ	Ⓒ		Ⓐ	Ⓐ J
Lille Flandres d.	1515	...	1550	1550	1616	...	1650	1716	1716	1727	...	1808	...	1813	1819	...	1846	1853	...	1928	...	2016	2018	...	2116	...
Valenciennes d.	1555	...	1628	1628	1658	...	1729	1752	1756	1808	...	1838	1842	1856	1859	...	1921	1932	...	2008	...	2056	2057	...	2153	...
Aulnoye Aymeries a.	1621	...	1654	1654	1728	...	1756	1813	|	1837	...	1900	|	1925	1928	...	|	1958	...	2036	...	2124	2125	...	2220	...
Aulnoye Aymeries d.	1623	1645	1703	1707	1730	1740	1802	1814	|	1839	1847	1902	|	1935	1933	1946	|	2005	2007	2038	2047	2131	2132	2136	2222	2235
Maubeuge a.	1634	|	1718	|	1742	|	1815	1823	|	1855	|	1911	|	|	1945	2001	|	|	2019	2049	|	2143	2144	|	2232	|
Jeumont a.	1641	|	1730	|	1751	|	1826	1832	|	1904	|	1920	|	|	1955	2012	|	|	2028	2058	|	2152	2155	|	2240	|
Avesnes d.	...	1658	...	1718	...	1756	...	...	1822	...	1903	...	1916	1946	...	...	1947	2016	...	...	2059	...	...	2150	...	2246
Hirson a.	...	1725	...	1741	...	1821	...	...	1841	...	1927	...	1938	2011	...	...	2009	2040	...	...	2124	...	...	2217	...	2310
Charleville-Mézières a.	...	...	...	...	...	1900v	...	...	1919	...	...	...	...	2052	...	...	2050	...	...	...	...	...	...	...	...	...

	Ⓐ	Ⓐ J	⚒	⚒	Ⓐ	Ⓐ	⚒	⚒	△	Ⓐ	Ⓐ J	⚒	▽	Ⓐ	Ⓒ		Ⓐ J	Ⓐ	Ⓐ	Ⓒ		Ⓐ J	⚒	⚒ ⊖	⚒	⑥ △
Charleville-Mézières d.	...	...	...	...	...	0600	...	...	...	...	...	...	...	...	...	...	...	...	0956	1013	...	...	...	...	...	1150
Hirson d.	...	0518	0545	...	...	0637	0614	0644	...	...	0720	0748	...	0825	0832	...	0936	...	1031	1055	...	1115	1149	...	...	1228
Avesnes d.	...	0542	0607	...	...	0658	0640	0709	...	...	0744	0814	...	0847	0856	...	1000	...	1053	1120	...	1143	1215	...	...	1255
Jeumont d.	0501	*0527*r	|	0611	0635	|	|	|	0707	0738	|	|	0815	|	|	0912	|	1003	|	|	1114	|	|	1215	1232	|
Maubeuge d.	0508	*0535*r	|	0619	0644	|	|	|	0716	0746	|	|	0823	|	|	0920	|	1011	|	|	1122	|	|	1223	1244	|
Aulnoye Aymeries a.	0519	0551	0623	0631	0652	|	0651	0723	0729	0757	0753	0828	0835	0857	0911	0932	1011	1021	|	1129	1134	1154	1229	1235	1302	1306
Aulnoye Aymeries d.	0521	0600	...	0633	0655	|	0706	...	0731	0759	0804	...	0837	...	...	0934	...	1023	|	...	1136	1204	...	1237	...	1316
Valenciennes d.	0552	0627	...	0704	0717	0724	0738	...	0800	0821	0831	...	0908	...	...	1003	...	1052	1121	...	1206	1232	...	1307	...	1344
Lille Flandres a.	0630	0700	...	0742	0746	0751	0817	...	0838	0850	0907	...	0944	...	...	1042	...	1132	1148	...	1245	1306	...	1346	...	1428

	Ⓐ	†	†	Ⓐ	Ⓐ	†	†	⑥ t	⚒ ⊖	Ⓐ J	Ⓐ	Ⓐ	Ⓐ △	Ⓐ J	Ⓐ J	†	†	⚒	⚒ ⊖	Ⓐ ⊕	†	Ⓐ	†	†	⚒	⚒
Charleville-Mézières d.	1153	1309	...	...	...	...	...	...	...	...	...	...	...	...	...	...	...	...	...	...	...	...	...	1921	...	2045
Hirson d.	1233	1347	...	1421	...	1534	...	1540	...	...	1616	1645	...	...	1719	1737	...	1749	...	...	1855	1951	...	2000	...	2127
Avesnes d.	1258	1410	...	1444	...	1601	...	1606	...	...	1639	1710	...	...	1741	1801	...	1815	...	...	1919	2015	...	2026	...	2150
Jeumont d.	|	|	1404	|	1500	|	1555	|	1610	1626	|	|	1706	1727	|	|	1803	|	1812	1856	*1901*r	|	2020	|	2123	|
Maubeuge d.	|	|	1413	|	1508	|	1604	|	1617	1638	|	|	1714	1736	|	|	1812	|	1820	1905	*1912*r	|	2028	|	2130	|
Aulnoye Aymeries a.	1308	1420	1425	1454	1521	1615	1616	1615	1627	1652	1649	1724	1725	1749	1752	1814	1824	1829	1831	1919	1929	2027	2038	2035	2141	2201
Aulnoye Aymeries d.	1319	...	1427	...	1523	...	1624	...	1629	...	1703	...	1735	...	1759	...	1826	...	1833	1921	1938	...	...	2047	...	2209
Valenciennes d.	1348	...	1500	...	1550	...	1655	...	1700	...	1730	...	1805	...	1824	...	1859	...	1902	1953	2006	...	...	2112	...	2235
Lille Flandres a.	1427	...	1542	...	1627	...	1737	...	1739	...	1805	...	1843	...	1903	...	1942	...	1943	2035	2044	...	...	2149	...	2312

LOCAL TRAINS LILLE - VALENCIENNES

	Ⓐ J	⚒	⚒	Ⓐ	Ⓐ	⑥ t	†	Ⓐ	†	⚒	Ⓐ J	⑥ J	Ⓐ	Ⓐ	Ⓐ	⑥ t	†	Ⓐ	Ⓐ	Ⓐ	†	⑥ z	Ⓐ	Ⓐ	Ⓒ	Ⓐ
Lille Flandres d.	0537	0634	0737	0832	0945	1011	1011	1137	1224	1235	1337	1342	1535	1637	1700	1721	1721	1733	1750	1832	1911	1921	1941	2037	2120	2229
Valenciennes a.	0620	0723	0824	0915	1031	1055	1059	1223	1308	1325	1425	1425	1622	1724	1742	1807	1805	1819	1827	1915	1958	2007	2027	2121	2205	2315

	⚒	Ⓐ	⚒	Ⓐ	Ⓐ	⑥ t	Ⓐ	†	Ⓐ	Ⓐ	⑥ J	Ⓐ	⑥ J	†	Ⓒ	Ⓐ	Ⓐ	†	⑥ J	⑥ K	Ⓐ	Ⓐ	⑥ t	Ⓐ J		
Valenciennes d.	0439	0537	0634	0650	0742	0750	0835	1123	1139	1235	1235	1334	1352	1354	1553	1634	1736	1814	1815	1821	1836	1936	2017	2035	...	...
Lille Flandres a.	0526	0623	0724	0734	0829	0832	0924	1213	1225	1323	1323	1423	1440	1440	1641	1722	1822	1903	1903	1905	1918	2023	2104	2123	...	...

J – To July 3/from Aug. 31.
K – ⑥ July 4 - Aug. 29 (not Aug. 15).
r – Change at Aulnoye Aymeries.
t – Also Aug. 15.
v – † only.
z – On ⑥ July 4 - Aug. 29 (not Aug. 15) d. 1933, a. 2020.
⊖ – Runs up to 10 minutes earlier July 4 - Aug. 29.
△ – Timings vary ± 4 minutes July 4 - Aug. 29.
▽ – On ⑥ July 4 - Aug. 29 (not Aug. 15) Jeumont 0830, Maubeuge 0838, Aulnoye 0854, Valenciennes 0922, Lille 1007.
⊕ – On Ⓐ July 6 - Aug. 28 Valenciennes 1952, Lille 2042.

Certain trains 2nd class — BOULOGNE - ST POL - ARRAS and LILLE — 263

km		Ⓐ	Ⓐ	⚒	Ⓐ	⑥ t	Ⓐ	Ⓐ	⚒	Ⓐ	⑥ t	Ⓐ	† J	†	†	Ⓐ	⑥ t	Ⓐ		Ⓐ	⚒	Ⓐ	†	Ⓐ	Ⓐ	†
	Calais Ville **260** d.	...	...	...	...	...	...	...	...	...	...	...	...	...	...	...	...	...	...	...	...	...	...	...	...	...
0	**Boulogne Ville** § d.	...	...	0519	...	...	...	...	0652	...	...	0850	0908	...	...	...	...	...	...	...	1229	...	1346	...	1527	1537
27	Étaples Le Touquet § d.	...	...	0553	...	...	...	...	0711	...	...	0940	0933	...	...	...	...	...	...	...	1300	...	1404	...	1546	1556
39	Montreuil sur Mer d.	...	...	0603	...	...	...	...	0721	...	...	0952	0944	...	...	...	...	...	...	...	1310	...	1415	...	1556	1606
88	St Pol sur Ternoise a.	...	...	0646	...	...	...	...	0802	...	...	1030	1021	...	...	...	...	...	...	...	1357	...	1453	...	1640	1645
88	St Pol sur Ternoise d.	0543	0618	0648	0658	0716	...	0727	0811z	0813	0816	...	1029	1029	1047	1116	1116	1216	...	1323	1404	...	1455	...	1648	1647
127	**Arras** a.	|	|	0725	|	|	...	0759	0845z	|	|	...	1101	1101	|	|	|	|	...	1359	1438	...	1522	...	1724	1717
120	Béthune a.	0614	0648	...	0729	0746	...	...	...	0845	0846	...	...	...	1117	1148	1146	1248	...	...	...	...	...	...	...	...
120	Béthune ▶ d.	0616	0650	...	0731	0748	0750	...	...	0847	0848	...	...	...	1119	1150	1148	1251	1319	...	...	1501	...	1719	...	...
162	**Lille Flandres** ▶ a.	0658	0725	...	0818	0824	0825	...	...	0925	0924	...	...	...	1158	1225r	1224	1325	1358	...	...	1546	...	1758	...	...

	Ⓐ	Ⓒ	Ⓒ	Ⓐ	Ⓐ	Ⓐ	Ⓒ	Ⓒ	Ⓐ	†
Calais Ville **260** d.	...	...	...	...	...	1644	1652	...	1754	...
Boulogne Ville § d.	...	1646	...	...	...	1723	1728	...	1842	...
Étaples Le Touquet § d.	...	1705	...	...	...	1803	1807	...	1909	...
Montreuil sur Mer d.	...	1716	...	...	...	1813	1817	...	1919	...
St Pol sur Ternoise a.	...	1759	...	...	...	1904	1855	...	2004	...
St Pol sur Ternoise d.	1737	1808	1810	...	1826	1906	1857	1921	...	...
Arras a.	1816	|	1841	...	1906	|	1924	|	...	...
Béthune a.	...	1838	...	...	...	1937	...	1947	...	...
Béthune ▶ d.	...	1847	...	1850	...	*1950*	...	1948	...	2019
Lille Flandres ▶ a.	...	1924	...	1925	...	*2025*	...	2024	...	2058

	⚒	⚒	Ⓐ	Ⓐ	Ⓐ	⑥ t	Ⓐ	Ⓐ	† J	†
Lille Flandres ▷ d.	...	...	...	0642	0735	0802	0835	...	0902	...
Béthune ▷ a.	...	...	...	0730	0811	0842	0908	...	0942	...
Béthune d.	...	...	...	0732	...	...	0910	...	0944	...
Arras d.	...	...	0640	|	...	...	|	0909	|	0942
St Pol sur Ternoise a.	...	...	0723	0802	...	...	0937	0943	1015	1017
St Pol sur Ternoise d.	0554	0712	...	...	...	...	...	0945	...	1026
Montreuil sur Mer d.	0647	0803	...	...	...	...	...	1031	...	1105
Étaples Le Touquet § d.	0712	0813	...	...	...	...	...	1040	...	1115
Boulogne Ville § a.	0737	0835	...	...	...	...	...	1100	...	1132
Calais Ville **260** a.	...	...	...	...	...	...	...	...	...	...

	⑥ J	⑥ t	†	†	Ⓐ	⑥ t	Ⓐ	⚒	Ⓐ	⑥ t	b	Ⓐ J	Ⓐ △	Ⓐ	Ⓐ	Ⓒ J	Ⓐ	Ⓐ	Ⓐ	Ⓐ	Ⓒ	Ⓒ J		Ⓐ	⑥ J	Ⓐ
Lille Flandres ▷ d.	0902	...	...	1133	...	...	1235r	...	...	1236	1402	...	1535	...	1635	...	...	1735	...	...	1802	...	...	*1902*	1902	1940
Béthune ▷ a.	0948	...	...	1209	...	...	1310	...	...	1312	1442	...	1610	...	1710	...	...	1810	...	...	1841	...	...	*1939*	1942	2020
Béthune d.	0950	...	...	1211	...	...	1312	...	...	1314	...	...	1622	...	1712	...	...	1812	...	...	1842	...	...	1947	1948	2022
Arras d.	|	0942	1143	|	1223	1223	|	1319	...	|	...	1608	|	1645	|	1736	1736	|	1822	1842	|	1849	1935	|	|	|
St Pol sur Ternoise a.	1020	1017	1215	1242	1259	1259	1343	1355	...	1348	...	1644	1652	1721	1743	1803	1813	1843	1859	1913	1912	1924	2006	2017	2018	2052
St Pol sur Ternoise d.	...	1028	...	1244	...	1301	...	...	1406	1406	...	...	...	1724	...	1808	1815	...	...	1914	...	1926	...	2019	2020	...
Montreuil sur Mer d.	...	1106	...	1319	...	1353	...	...	1448	1449	...	...	...	1816	...	1856	1857	...	...	2002	...	2004	...	2101	2100	...
Étaples Le Touquet § d.	...	1115	...	1328	...	1402	...	...	1456	1458	...	...	...	1826	...	1906	1908	...	...	2013	...	2016	...	2111	2110	...
Boulogne Ville § a.	...	1133	...	1344	...	1419	...	...	...	1516	...	...	...	1841	...	1921	1926	...	...	2029	...	2032	...	2127	2127	...
Calais Ville **260** a.	...	...	...	1416	...	...	...	...	...	1551	...	...	...	1915	...	...	...	...	...	...	...	...	...	...	...	...

J – To July 3/from Aug. 31.
b – On Ⓐ July 6-31 d. 1334, a. 1435.
r – Subject to alteration Lille - Don Sainghin and v.v. July 6-31.
t – Not Aug. 15.
u – Depart 1300 July 6-31.
z – On ⑥ July 4 - Aug. 29 (not Aug. 15) St Pol d. 0829, Arras a. 0908.

§ – See also Table **260**.

▶ – **Additional trains** Béthune - Lille (journey 35-52 minutes):
Ⓐ: 0531, 0600, 0631, 0700, 0719, 0819, 1231, 1300, 1550, 1631, 1700, 1731, 1750, 1819, 1833, 1900, 2031.
⑥t: 0646, 0726, 0819, 1019, 1226, 1419, 1626, 1719.
†: 0826, 0919, 1226, 1626, 1719, 1819, 1926.

▷ – **Additional trains** Lille - Béthune (journey 35-52 minutes):
Ⓐ: 0542, 0610, 0702, 1202, 1242**u**, 1602, 1642, 1702, 1742, 1802, 1835, 1910, 2042.
⑥t: 0642, 0902, 1002, 1202, 1242, 1602, 1742, 1902, 1942, 2102.
†: 0902, 1002, 1142, 1602, 1742, 1942, 2102.

△ – Subject to alteration July 6-31.

Ⓐ – Mondays to Fridays, except holidays Ⓑ – Daily except Saturdays Ⓒ – Saturdays, Sundays and holidays

For Eurostar services Paris - Calais Fréthun see Table 10

265 PARIS and LILLE - DUNKERQUE and CALAIS

Fast trains

For local trains Arras / Lille - Hazebrouck - Dunkerque / Calais see Table **266** (selected connections Hazebrouck - Calais are shown below). For Paris - Lille see Table **250**.

km		◇ Ⓐ	◇ Ⓐ		*TGV* 7207 Ⓐ	*TGV* 7301 Ⓐ	◇	🚌	*TGV* 7303 ⑥	*TGV* 7229 ①–⑥ n	◇ † s	*TGV* 7311 ⑥⑦ e	Ⓒ	◇ ⚒	⚒	◇ ⚒ u	*TGV* 7321 ①–⑥ n	⑥ t	◇ †	🚌 †	*TGV* 7331 E	Ⓒ	◇ Ⓐ	◇ Ⓐ	🚌 Ⓐ
0	**Paris Nord** .... **256** d.	...	...	...	0728	0722	...	...	0822	0958	...	0952	...	...	...	...	1222	...	...	...	1452	...	...	...	...
199	Arras .... **256** d.	...	...	...	|	0818	...	...	0915	|	...	1048	...	...	...	...	1318	...	...	...	1545	...	...	...	...
219	Lens ....d.	...	...	...	|	0832	...	...	0928	|	...	1102	...	...	...	...	1332	...	...	...	1600	...	...	...	...
238	Béthune ....d.	...	...	...	|	0845	...	...	0941	|	...	1115	...	...	...	...	1345	...	...	...	1618	...	...	...	...
	Lille Europe ....d.	0722	0822	...	0832	|	0912	...	|	1101	1119	|	...	1247	...	1303	|	...	1554	...	|	...	1715	1721	...
272	Hazebrouck ....d.	|	|	...	|	0908	|	...	1006	|	|	1137	1201	|	...	|	1407	1414	|	...	1641	1656	|	|	...
Δ 312	**Dunkerque** ....a.	0757	|	...	0905	0929	|	...	1028	|	1151	1158	|	|	...	1336	1429	|	|	...	1702	|	1749	|	...
293	St Omer ....d.	...	|	...	...	...	|	...	...	|	...	...	1216	|	...	...	...	1428	|	...	...	1709	...	|	...
	Calais Fréthun ....a.	...	0850	0856	...	...	0940	0950	...	1131	...	...	|	1315	1334	...	...	|	1622	1639	...	|	...	1749	1757
336	**Calais Ville** ....a.	...	|	0903	...	...	|	1007	...	1140	...	...	1248	|	1343	...	...	1453	|	1654	...	1738	...	|	1812
	Boulogne **260** ....a.	...	0925	...	...	...	1009	...	...	...	...	...	1338	1344	...	...	...	1540	1650	...	...	1818	...	1817	...

	◇ ⑥ t	🚌 ⑥ t	*TGV* 7337 ⑤–⑦ e	*TGV* 7339 ①–④ n	◇ ⑦ d	🚌 †	*TGV* 7275 ①–⑤ n	Ⓐ	◇ ⑥ k	*TGV* 7343 ①–⑤ n	*TGV* 7281 ①–⑤ n	*TGV* 7285	🚌	*TGV* 7289 ⑦ e	*TGV* 7347 Ⓑ	Ⓐ	Ⓒ	*TGV* 7351 ⑤–⑦ e	◇ †	🚌 †	*TGV* 7357 ⑤
Paris Nord .... **256** d.	...	...	1622	1652	...	...	1728	...	...	1752	1828	1858	...	1858	1852	...	...	1952	...	...	2131
Arras .... **256** d.	...	...	1718	1747	...	...	|	...	...	1845	|	|	...	|	1944	...	...	2045	...	...	2224
Lens ....d.	...	...	1733	1801	...	...	|	...	...	1858	|	|	...	|	1957	...	...	2059	...	...	2238
Béthune ....d.	...	...	1746	1818	...	...	|	...	...	1911	|	|	...	|	2009	...	...	2112	...	...	2251
Lille Europe ....d.	1731	...	|	|	1825	...	1830	...	1905	|	1930	2000	...	2003	|	...	...	|	2213	...	|
Hazebrouck ....d.	|	...	1809	1841	|	...	|	...	|	1933	|	|	...	|	2032	2049	2059	2135	|	...	2313
Dunkerque ....a.	|	...	1830*	1902	|	...	|	...	1937	|	2001	|	...	2035	2053	|	|	2156	|	...	2335
St Omer ....d.	|	...	...	...	|	...	|	...	...	1946	...	|	...	...	...	2102	2114	...	|	...	...
Calais Fréthun ....a.	1759	1807	...	...	1854	1910	1858	1908	...	...	...	2031	2039	...	...	|	|	...	2241	2249	...
Calais Ville ....a.	|	1822	...	...	|	1925	|	1915	...	...	...	|	2054	...	...	2132	2144	...	|	2304	...
Boulogne **260** ....a.	1829	...	...	...	1922	...	1927	...	...	...	...	2101	...	...	...	...	2228	...	2309	...	...

Alternative connections are available by using *TGV* trains between Paris and Lille Flandres (Table **250**) and local trains between Lille Flandres and Dunkerque / Calais (Table **266**)

	TGV 7302 B	Ⓐ J	*TGV* 7304 ①–⑤ n	◇ Ⓐ	*TGV* 7214 ①–⑤ n	🚌 Ⓐ	*TGV* 7220 ①–⑥ n	*TGV* 7308 ①⑥ v	🚌 ⚒	◇ ⚒	◇ Ⓐ		☆	*TGV* 7318 ⊕	Ⓐ	◇ Ⓐ	◇ † s	🚌 †	◇ †	🚌 Ⓐ	◇ Ⓐ	🚌 ⑥	◇ ⑥ t△	◇ ⑥ t	*TGV* 7254 ①–⑥ n
Boulogne **260** ....d.	...	...	...	...	...	...	0656	...	...	0744	...	...	0829	...	...	0940	...	...	1042	...	1133	...	1139	...	...
Calais Ville ....d.	...	0542	...	...	...	0706	|	...	0750	|	...	...	0913	...	0953	|	...	1048	|	1139	|	1145	|	...	1235
Calais Fréthun ....d.	...	|	...	...	...	0721	0729	...	0805	0813	...	...	|	...	1000	1011	...	1103	1111	1154	1202	1200	1208	...	1244
St Omer ....d.	...	0611	0623	...	...	...	|	...	...	|	...	...	0946	...	...	|	...	...	|	...	|	...	|	...	|
Dunkerque ....d.	0535	|	|	0642	0646	...	|	0717	...	|	0814	...	|	0944	...	|	1035	...	|	...	|	...	|	1227	|
Hazebrouck ....d.	0559	0624	0638	|	|	...	|	0740	...	|	|	...	0959	1008	...	|	|	...	|	...	|	...	|	|	|
Lille Europe ....a.	|	...	|	0712	0719	...	0758	|	...	0843	0847	...	...	|	...	1043	1107	...	1142	...	1232	...	1238	1300	1314
Béthune ....d.	0621	...	0700	...	|	...	|	0802	...	...	...	...	...	1030	...	...	...	...	...	...	...	...	...	...	|
Lens ....d.	0634	...	0712	...	|	...	|	0815	...	...	...	...	...	1043	...	...	...	...	...	...	...	...	...	...	|
Arras .... **256** d.	0656	...	0735	...	|	...	|	0835	...	...	...	...	...	1106	...	...	...	...	...	...	...	...	...	...	|
Paris Nord .... **256** a.	0747	...	0826	...	0832	...	0902	0926	...	...	...	...	...	1156	...	...	...	...	...	...	...	...	...	...	1426

	†	*TGV* 7336 ⊕	Ⓐ	Ⓒ	*TGV* 7342 D⊕	◇ Ⓐ	🚌 ⚒	◇ ⚒	*TGV* 7348 ⊕	🚌 †	◇ †	◇ Ⓐ	◇ ⑥ k	*TGV* 7288 Ⓑ	*TGV* 7352 ⑦ e⊕	Ⓒ	*TGV* 7356 ⑦ e⊕	Ⓐ	*TGV* 7292 ①–⑤ n	🚌 ⑥	◇ ⑥ t	*TGV* 7358 ⑤	🚌 †	◇ †	*TGV* 7298 ⑦ e
Boulogne **260** ....d.	1258	...	...	1444	...	...	...	1600	...	...	1714	...	...	...	...	1739	...	...	1904	...	1906	...	...	1946	...
Calais Ville ....d.	1343	...	1525	1527	...	...	1609	|	...	1721	|	...	...	...	...	1826	...	1910	|	1906	|	...	1953	|	...
Calais Fréthun ....d.	|	...	|	|	...	...	1624	1632	...	1736	1744	...	...	...	...	|	...	1918	1934	1921	1936	...	2008	2016	...
St Omer ....d.	1415	...	1556	1556	...	...	...	|	...	...	|	...	...	...	1832	1900	...	...	|	...	|	...	...	|	...
Dunkerque ....d.	|	1413	|	|	1552	1623	...	|	1711	...	|	1801	1816	1823	|	|	1912	...	|	...	|	1943	...	|	2115
Hazebrouck ....d.	1429	1437	1608	1608	1616	|	...	|	1737	...	|	|	|	|	1847	1913	1937	...	|	...	|	2007	...	|	|
Lille Europe ....a.	...	|	...	...	|	1658	...	1703	|	...	1815	1834	1847	1855	|	...	|	...	2003	...	2006	|	...	2045	2147
Béthune ....d.	...	1459	...	...	1639	...	...	...	1800	...	...	...	...	|	1909	...	2000	...	|	...	...	2029	...	...	|
Lens ....d.	...	1512	...	...	1651	...	...	...	1813	...	...	...	...	|	1921	...	2013	...	|	...	...	2042	...	...	|
Arras .... **256** d.	...	1535	...	...	1706	...	...	...	1836	...	...	...	...	|	1936	...	2035	...	|	...	...	2105	...	...	|
Paris Nord .... **256** a.	...	1626	...	...	1756	...	...	...	1926	...	...	...	...	2002	2026	...	2126	...	2111	...	...	2156	...	...	2302

FOR NOTES SEE BELOW TABLE 266 ON NEXT PAGE →

Subject to alteration Paris - Lens - Dunkerque and v.v. on October 18

266 ARRAS and LILLE - DUNKERQUE and CALAIS

Local trains

km	*See also Table 265*	⚒	Ⓐ	Ⓐ	⚒	Ⓐ J	⚒	Ⓐ	Ⓐ	⑥ t	Ⓐ	Ⓐ	Ⓒ	Ⓐ ▽	†	Ⓐ ⊖	⑥ t	Ⓐ	Ⓐ ⊗	Ⓐ	†	Ⓒ	†	Ⓐ ▷	⚒ ▷	Ⓐ ▽
0	**Arras** ....d.	...	...	0605	...	...	0634	...	...	...	0721	...	...	...	...	...	0805	0805	...	0845	0852	...	...	...	0920	...
20	Lens ....d.	...	...	0621	...	...	0650	...	...	...	0739	...	...	...	...	...	0822	0822	...	0901	0908	...	...	...	0937	...
39	Béthune ....d.	0603a	...	0638	...	...	0710	...	...	...	0800	...	...	...	...	...	0850	0853	...	0918	0926	...	...	...	0955	...
• 46	**Lille Flandres** ....d.	|	0627	|	0641	0700	|	0715	0731	0727	|	0800	0813	0815	...	0841	|	|	0900	|	|	0922	...	0931	|	0958
• 25	Armentières ....d.	|	0642	|	0655	0715	|	0730	|	0746	|	|	0828	0830	...	0857	|	|	0917	|	|	0939	...	0946	|	1012
73	Hazebrouck ....a.	0632a	0700	0706	0719	0729	0737	0754	0801	0803	0825	0831	0848	0854	...	0914	0917	0920	0938	0943	0952	0955	←	1004	1019	1028
73	Hazebrouck ....d.	0634	0702	0708	0721	0731	0738	0756	0803	0805	...	0833	0850	0856	0900	0916	0919	...	0940	...	→	0957	1009	1006	1021	1030
113	**Dunkerque** ....a.	|	|	0734	0753	|	0804	|	0829	|	...	|	0923	|	|	0943	0945	...	|	...	...	|	1041	1031	1044	|
94	St Omer ....d.	0653	0720	...	...	0745	...	0811	...	0821	...	0845	...	0910	0914	...	...	...	0953	...	...	1009	...	...	...	1043
137	**Calais Ville** ....a.	0729	0748	...	...	0812	...	0842	...	0848	...	0907	...	0943	0940	...	...	...	1018	...	...	1037	...	...	...	1113
	Boulogne **260** ....a.	...	0839	...	...	0854	...	...	...	0936	...	0954	...	1027	...	...	...	...	...	...	...	1119	...	...	...	...

	Ⓒ	Ⓒ	Ⓒ	Ⓐ	⚒ ▷	Ⓐ ▷	⑥ t	⚒ g	Ⓐ	⚒ ▷	†	⑥ t	Ⓐ	⑥ t	Ⓐ	Ⓐ	Ⓒ	†	Ⓐ	b	Ⓐ	Ⓐ	Ⓒ	Ⓒ	Ⓐ	Ⓐ
Arras ....d.	...	1052	...	...	...	1215	...	...	...	1220	...	...	...	1324	1324	...	...	1402	1442	...	...	1537	...	1548	...	...
Lens ....d.	...	1110	...	...	...	1230	...	...	...	1243	...	...	...	1341	1341	...	...	1419	1500	...	...	1603	...	1606	...	...
Béthune ....d.	...	1128	...	...	...	1247	...	...	...	1306	...	...	...	1357	1359	...	...	1436	1520	...	...	1625	...	1624	...	1648
Lille Flandres ....d.	1017	|	1124	1200	1232	|	...	1241	1300	|	1316	1338	1339	|	|	1403	1421	|	|	1532	1600	|	1621	|	1632	|
Armentières ....d.	1034	|	1139	1217	|	|	...	1302	|	|	1334	1353	1354	|	|	1418	1439	|	|	1549	|	|	1636	|	|	|
Hazebrouck ....a.	1053	1156	1159	1236	1306	1311	...	1318	1329	1336	1356	1412	1414	1420	1425	1436	1457	1500	1547	1607	1628	1650	1654	1650	1704	1718
Hazebrouck ....d.	1055	1209	1201	1238	1308	1313	1316	1320	1331	1338	1357	1414	1416	1422	1449	1438	1459	1502	...	1612	1630	1652	1656	1705	1706	1719
Dunkerque ....a.	1124	1245	*1245*	|	1333	|	|	1356	|	1406	1421	|	1440	1447	1523	*1523*	|	1528	...	1645	|	1717	|	1733	1733	|
St Omer ....d.	...	...	1216	1251	...	1329	1334	...	1345	...	...	1428	...	...	...	1451	1513	...	...	...	1645	...	1709	...	...	1735
Calais Ville ....a.	...	...	1248	1316	...	1358	1407	...	1410	...	...	1453	...	...	...	1520	1542	...	...	...	1711	...	1738	...	...	1802
Boulogne **260** ....a.	...	...	1338	...	...	...	1505	...	...	...	...	1540	...	...	...	1604	1626	...	...	...	1810	...	1818	...	...	...

	Ⓐ	Ⓐ	Ⓒ	Ⓐ		Ⓐ	Ⓐ	Ⓐ	Ⓒ	Ⓐ J	Ⓐ	Ⓐ	Ⓐ	Ⓐ	Ⓒ	Ⓐ	†	⑥ t	Ⓐ	Ⓒ	Ⓐ	Ⓒ	q	Ⓐ	y	†
Arras ....d.	...	1644	...	...	1722	...	...	1727	...	...	1806	...	...	1851	...	...	1926	1936	...	...	2020	2030	...	...	2151	...
Lens ....d.	...	1700	...	...	1738	...	...	1749	...	...	1824	...	...	1906	...	...	1942	1953	...	...	2039	2046	...	...	2206	...
Béthune ....d.	...	1720	...	...	1756	...	...	1824r	...	...	1844	...	...	1923	...	...	2000	2012	...	...	2059	2103	...	...	2225	...
Lille Flandres ....d.	1700	|	1718	1729	|	1745	1806	|	1821	1832	|	1841	1915	|	1921	1930	|	|	2015	2020	|	|	2108	2208	|	2223
Armentières ....d.	|	|	1736	|	|	1803	|	|	1838	|	|	1856	|	|	1938	1944	|	|	2030	2036	|	|	2126	2224	|	2238
Hazebrouck ....a.	1730	1749	1752	1759	1820	1822	1844	1851	1857	1901	1908	1914	1946	1951	1956	2001	2025	2036	2047	2057	2128	2126	2147	2245	2250	2257
Hazebrouck ....d.	1732	1751	1754	1801	1822a	1825	1846	1853	1859	1903	1910	1916	1948	...	1958	2003	...	2038	2049	2059	...	2128	2151	2247	...	2259
Dunkerque ....a.	|	1823	1826	|	1848a	1859	|	1915	|	1928	|	1949	|	...	2032	2037	...	2103	*2123*	|	...	2153	2223	2311	...	|
St Omer ....d.	1746	...	...	1819	...	...	1859	...	1911	...	1928	...	2000	...	...	...	...	...	2102	2114	...	...	...	...	...	2313
Calais Ville ....a.	1811	...	...	1848	...	...	1921	...	1940	...	1957	...	2028	...	...	...	...	...	2132	2144	...	...	...	...	...	2342
Boulogne **260** ....a.	1858	...	...	...	...	...	2007	...	2022	...	...	...	2115	...	...	...	...	...	...	2228	...	...	...	...	...	...

Table 266 is subject to alteration on Oct. 18

CALAIS and DUNKERQUE - LILLE and ARRAS — 266

Local trains (some 2nd class only)

	Ⓐ	⚒	Ⓐ J	⚒	Ⓐ	Ⓐ	⚒	†	Ⓐ	⑥ t	⑥ t	Ⓐ	Ⓐ	⑥ t	Ⓐ	⚒	Ⓐ	⚒	Ⓒ	Ⓐ ☆	Ⓐ		☆	Ⓐ ⊙	Ⓐ ⊡	Ⓐ
Boulogne **260** d.	...	...	...	...	...	...	...	...	0602	...	...	...	...	...	...	0702	...	...	...	...	...	...	0829	...	...	...
Calais Ville 260 d.	0503	...	0542	...	0558	...	...	...	0647	0643	...	...	0705	0705	...	0749	...	...	...	0838	...	...	0913	...	...	...
St Omer d.	0529	...	0611	...	0629	...	...	...	0712	0715	...	...	0739	0743	...	0815	...	...	...	0908	...	...	0946	...	...	...
Dunkerque d.	*0507*	0541a	|	0559	|	0620	0636	...	|	|	0655	0701	|	|	0737	*0748*	0821	...	0842	|	0910	0911c	|	1023	1044	...
Hazebrouck a.	0542	0607a	0624	0633	0642	0654	0704	...	0725	0733	0730	0736	0754	0756	0802	0830	0845	...	0910	0921	0935	0944c	0959	1047	1112	...
Hazebrouck d.	0544	0609	0626	0639	0644	0656	0706	0724	0727	0735	0737	0739	0756	0758	0804	0832	0847	0854	0912	0923	0937	0945	1001	1049	1114	...
Armentières d.	0601	|	|	0703	|	0716	|	|	|	|	0804	0805	|	0822	|	|	0903	|	0932	0947	1001	|	1017	1110	|	...
Lille Flandres a.	0617	|	0658	0721	|	0731	|	|	0758	0802	0819	0821	|	0842	0831	0858	0917	|	0947	1003	1019	|	1033	1125	|	←
Béthune d.	...	0637	...	...	0715	...	0743	0750	...	...	...	...	0824	...	...	...	...	0924	...	...	...	1012	...	...	1139	1220
Lens d.	...	0655	...	...	0734	...	0759	0807	...	...	...	...	0841	...	...	...	...	0942	...	...	...	1030	...	...	→	1239
Arras a.	...	0714	...	...	0746	...	0821	0820	...	...	...	...	0855	...	...	...	...	0959	...	...	...	1049	...	...	...	1259

	Ⓐ ☆	Ⓒ	Ⓐ ⊙	⑥ t	Ⓐ ☆	⑥ t	†	⚒ ⊙	⚒ ⊙	⚒ ⊡	Ⓐ	⑥ t	Ⓐ	Ⓒ	Ⓒ	†	⑥ t	Ⓐ	⑥ t	Ⓐ	Ⓐ	Ⓐ	Ⓐ	Ⓐ	Ⓒ	Ⓒ
Boulogne **260** d.	...	...	...	...	1036z	...	1057	...	...	...	...	1157	1157	...	...	1258	1303	...	...	...	...	...	...	...	1444	...
Calais Ville 260 d.	1038	...	...	...	1118	1120	1136	...	...	...	1231	1240	1246	...	...	1343	1353	...	...	1438	...	...	...	1525	1527	...
St Omer d.	1107	...	...	...	1148	1150	1202	...	...	...	1256	1310	1313	...	...	1415	1425	...	...	1506	...	...	...	1556	1556	...
Dunkerque d.	|	1057	1108	1118	|	|	|	1157	...	1212	|	|	|	1307	1343	|	|	...	1438	|	...	1512	1535	|	*1531*	1531
Hazebrouck a.	1120	1121	1143	1146	1205	1202	1213	1225	...	1244	1314	1321	1327	1335	1417	1429	1438	...	1506	1519	...	1545	1602	1608	1608	1603
Hazebrouck d.	1122	1123	1145	1148	1207	1204	1215	1227	1229	1246	1316	1328	1329	1337	1419	1431	1440	1454	1508	1521	1541	1547	1604	1610	1610	1626
Armentières d.	1142	1141	1204	|	1224	1225	1234	|	|	1309	|	1348	1348	1356	|	1452	1457	|	1528	1542	|	1607	|	1628	1627	|
Lille Flandres a.	1158	1157	1220	|	1238	1240	1250	1259	|	1330	1348	1403	1403	1411	|	1508	1511	|	1542	1558	|	1622	|	1645	1643	|
Béthune d.	...	...	...	1216	...	...	...	...	1302	...	...	...	...	...	1448	...	...	1522	...	...	1606	...	1644	...	...	1652
Lens d.	...	...	...	1234	...	...	...	...	1320	...	...	...	...	...	1506	...	...	1540	...	...	1626	...	1702	...	...	1710
Arras a.	...	...	...	1253	...	...	...	...	1335	...	...	...	...	...	1522	...	...	1555	...	...	1642	...	1717	...	...	1724

	Ⓐ	Ⓐ	Ⓒ	Ⓐ		Ⓐ J	Ⓐ	Ⓐ	Ⓐ	Ⓒ	Ⓐ	Ⓒ	Ⓐ	Ⓒ	Ⓐ	Ⓐ	Ⓒ	Ⓐ		Ⓒ	Ⓐ	Ⓐ	Ⓒ	Ⓐ	Ⓒ	Ⓐ
Boulogne **260** d.	...	...	...	...	...	...	...	...	...	1644	...	...	...	...	...	...	1739	1731	...	...	...	...	1845	...	...	1952
Calais Ville 260 d.	...	...	...	1617	...	...	...	1715	...	1726	...	...	1746	...	...	...	1826	1827	...	...	1914	...	1932	...	...	2036
St Omer d.	...	...	...	1647	...	...	...	1744	...	1755	...	...	1815	...	...	...	1900	1856	...	...	1942	...	2005	...	...	2108
Dunkerque d.	1614	...	1633	|	1639a	1715	1726	|	...	*1725*	...	...	|	1807	1810	1836	|	*1845*	1845	1917	|	1930	|	...	2050	|
Hazebrouck a.	1644	...	1659	1700	1715a	1740	1758	1801	...	1806	...	...	1828	1836	1843	1858	1913	1914	1917	1945	1956	1959	2018	...	2115	2120
Hazebrouck d.	1646	1649	1701	1702	1717	1742	1800	1803	1806	1808	1815	1824	1830	1838	1845	1900	1915	1923	1918	1947	...	2001	2020	2037	2117	2122
Armentières d.	1706	|	1721	1726	|	1806	|	|	1830	1825	|	|	|	1858	1909	|	1933	1946	|	2004	...	2022	2043	|	2135	2142
Lille Flandres a.	1721	|	1739	1744	|	1821	1831	|	1846	1840	|	|	1858	1915	1923	1930	1947	2002	|	2020	...	2038	2059	|	2150	2158
Béthune d.	...	1723	...	...	1746	...	...	1829	...	...	1845	1853	...	...	...	...	...	...	1943	...	...	...	...	2105	...	...
Lens d.	...	1742	...	...	1803	...	...	1851	...	...	1903	1912	...	...	...	...	...	...	2004	...	...	...	...	2123	...	...
Arras a.	...	1759	...	...	1822	...	...	1902	...	...	1918	1929	...	...	...	...	...	...	2020	...	...	...	...	2138	...	...

NOTES FOR TABLES 265 AND 266

- **B** – ①–⑤ to July 3; ① July 6 - Aug. 24 (also July 15; not July 13); ①–⑤ from Aug. 31.
- **D** – Daily to July 4; ⑦ July 5 - Aug. 23 (also July 14); daily from Aug. 30.
- **E** – Daily to July 5; ⑤⑥⑦ July 5 - Aug. 29 (also July 14); daily from Aug. 30.
- **J** – To July 3 / from Aug. 31.
- **a** – Ⓐ only.
- **b** – Runs 3 minutes later on Ⓒ (arrive Dunkerque 1638).
- **c** – Ⓒ only.
- **d** – Also June 1, July 14, Aug. 15.
- **e** – Also June 1, July 14.
- **g** – Depart Lille 1246 on Ⓐ.
- **k** – Not Aug. 15, Nov. 7.
- **n** – Not June 1, July 14.
- **q** – On Ⓒ depart Lille 2118.
- **r** – Arrive 1807.
- **s** – Not Nov. 8.
- **t** – Not Aug. 15.
- **u** – Not on ①–⑤ Sept. 28 - Oct. 9, Oct. 26 - Nov. 13.
- **v** – Also June 2, July 15; not June 1, July 13.
- **y** – Runs 6 - 12 minutes later on Ⓐ.
- **z** – ①–④ (not holidays).
- *TGV* – Ⓡ, supplement payable.
- ⊖ – Subject to alteration Hazebrouck - Dunkerque on Ⓐ Sept. 14 - Oct. 9.
- △ – Runs 4 minutes later on ⑥ July 4 - Aug. 29.
- ▷ – Subject to alteration on Ⓐ Sept. 14 - 25.
- ▽ – Subject to alteration Hazebrouck - Calais on Ⓐ Sept. 7 - 18.
- ◇ – TER à Grande Vitesse (TER GV) via high-speed line (1, 2 class), operated by *TGV* unit. Supplement *Côte d'Opale* payable (€3, valid all day). Reservation not necessary.
- ⊕ – Subject to alteration Dunkerque - Hazebrouck on Ⓐ July 6 - 31, Ⓐ Oct. 26 - Nov. 13. On Oct. 18 runs up to 30 mins earlier.
- ⊗ – Subject to alteration Hazebrouck - Calais on Ⓐ Sept. 7 - Oct. 9.
- ⊡ – Subject to alteration on Ⓐ Sept. 14 - Oct. 9.
- ⊙ – Subject to alteration on Ⓐ Sept. 28 - Oct. 9.
- ☆ – Subject to alteration on Ⓐ Sept. 21 - Oct. 9.
- Δ – *303 km* by *TGV* via Lille Europe.
- • – Distance from Hazebrouck.
- * – Subject to alteration on Nov. 7.
- 🚌 – Connecting SNCF bus service.

PARIS - BEAUVAIS — 267

km		June 1 - July 11 / Aug. 30 - Dec. 12 →	Ⓐ	⑥	Ⓐ	Ⓐ	⑥	†	†	Ⓐ	⑥	Ⓐ			⚒	Ⓐ	Ⓒ	Ⓐ	⑥	Ⓐ	Ⓐ	Ⓒ	Ⓐ
0	**Paris Nord** d.		0615	0632	0656	0741	0748	0801	0903	0929	0933	1018	1118	1218	1318	1418	1433	1618	1630	1649	1718	1733	1748
80	**Beauvais** a.		0730	0739	0807	0853	0902	0908	1011	1042	1050	1131	1235	1336	1439	1537	1549	1730	1740	1759	1833	1844	1906

	⑥	Ⓐ	Ⓐ	Ⓒ	Ⓐ	Ⓐ	⑥	Ⓑ	Ⓒ	July 12 - Aug. 29 →	Ⓐ	⑥	Ⓐ	⑥	†	Ⓐ	†	Ⓐ	⑥	Ⓐ			⚒	Ⓐ
Paris Nord d.	1801	1818	1836*	1901	1918	1949	1948	2048	2148		0615	0632	0648	0748	0801	0803	0903	0931	0933	1031	1131	1218	1331	1431
Beauvais a.	1913	1927	1959	2011	2030	2100	2105	2202	2300		0730	0739	0756	0905	0915	0916	1011	1039	1042	1134	1237	1340	1442	1537

	Ⓒ	Ⓐ	⑥	Ⓐ	Ⓐ	Ⓐ	Ⓒ	Ⓐ	⑥	Ⓐ	Ⓒ	Ⓐ	⑥	Ⓐ	Ⓑ	Ⓒ
Paris Nord d.	1431	1603	1618	1636	1706	1736	1748	1806	1818	1839*	1918	1936	1948	2003	2048	2148
Beauvais a.	1545	1713	1740	1756	1827	1901	1904	1919	1942	2009	2027	2058	2057	2123	2202	2301

	June 1 - July 11 / Aug. 30 - Dec. 12 →	Ⓐ	⑥
Beauvais d.		0508	0511
Paris Nord a.		0630	0624

	Ⓐ	⑥	†	Ⓐ	Ⓐ	⑥	†	Ⓐ	⑥	Ⓐ	†		⚒	⚒	†	⚒		Ⓐ	⑥	Ⓒ	Ⓐ	Ⓐ	†	⑥	Ⓐ	⑥
Beauvais d.	0612	0621	0633	0642	0713	0719	0742	0759	0845	0847	0922	1027	1144	1239	1253	1349	1428	1558	1613	1717	1740	1814	1824	1826	1908	1918
Paris Nord a.	0725	0731	0745	0757	0829	0831	0855	0914	1000	0958	1029	1145	1300	1400	1401	1500	1546	1716	1730	1831	1849	1933	1931	1932	2018	2032

	†	⑥	†	Ⓐ	†	July 12 - Aug. 29 →	⑥	Ⓐ	Ⓐ	⑥	†	Ⓐ	Ⓐ	†	⑥	Ⓐ	⑥	Ⓐ	†		⚒	†	⚒	⚒
Beauvais d.	1924	2004	2008	2010	2111		0507	0515	0614	0611	0625	0642	0716	0720	0722	0748	0846	0855	0922	1025	1148	1253	1256	1358
Paris Nord a.	2031	2108	2129	2117	2217		0618	0631	0731	0730	0732	0801	0831	0831	0845	0902	1002	1016	1029	1133	1304	1401	1404	1503

		⑥	Ⓐ	Ⓒ	Ⓐ	⑥	Ⓐ	†	Ⓐ	†	⑥	†	⑥	Ⓐ	†
Beauvais d.	1421	1550	1559	1655	1750	1802	1814	1824	1910	1911	1918	2008	2012	2010	2111
Paris Nord a.	1532	1659	1708	1815	1901	1915	1933	1931	2020	2023	2032	2129	2116	2117	2217

Most trains call at Persan-Beaumont (30 mins from Paris).
Trains also run Creil - Beauvais (11 on Ⓐ, 7 on ⑥, 4 on †).

* – From suburban platforms.

July 13 - ⑥ service runs; **Aug. 15** - ⑦ service runs.

BEAUVAIS - LE TRÉPORT — 267a

km		Ⓐ J	①⑥ R	† W	† S	⚒ M	⚒	⑤	⚒	Ⓐ	⑥ L	⑥ N	† W	† J	† K	⑥ t	⑤ L	⑤ M
	Paris Nord **267** d.	...	...	0801	0803	...	...	...	...	...	...	...	...	...	...	...	...	...
0	**Beauvais** d.	0734	0907	0910	0917	0921	1243	1453	1759	1844	1900	1909	1902	2027	2032	2032	2041	2058
49	Abancourt d.	0829	0952	0955	0957	1004	1335	1538	1849	1936	1945	1954	1956	2115	2115	2115	2125	2142
103	Eu d.	0913	1039	1041	|	1054	1420	1629	...	2021	2031	2040	2041	2159	2159	2201	2210	2227
106	**Le Tréport** a.	0917	1044	1046	1039	1059	1425	1633	...	2025	2035	2044	2046	2203	2203	2205	2215	2232

	Ⓐ	Ⓐ M	Ⓐ L	⑥ N	⑥ L	†	① P	① Q	⚒	† K	† J	⑤	†	⚒	† J	† K	† S	
Le Tréport d.	...	0610	0613	0645	0650	0740	0951	1007	1205	1241	1247	1545	1648	1720	1835	1835	2028	...
Eu d.	...	0614	0618	0650	0655	0745	0956	1012	1210	1246	1252	1550	1653	1724	1840	1840	2032	...
Abancourt d.	0618	0657	0706	0735	0740	0832	1047	1058	1259	1329	1335	1647	1738	1815	1924	1927	2116	...
Beauvais a.	0708	0743	0749	0821	0826	0916	1132	1143	1344	1416	1422	1731	1822	1903	2006	2007	2152	...
Paris Nord **267** a.	...	...	...	...	...	...	...	...	...	...	...	...	1931	...	2129	2118	2254	...

- **J** – To July 5 / from Aug. 30.
- **K** – July 12 - Aug. 23.
- **L** – To July 11 / from Aug. 31.
- **M** – July 13 - Aug. 29.
- **N** – ⑥ July 18 - Aug. 29 (not Aug. 15).
- **P** – ① to July 6 (also June 2; not June 1); ① from Aug. 31 (also Nov. 12).
- **Q** – ① July 13 - Aug. 24 (also July 15).
- **R** – ①⑥ to July 6 (also June 2, July 7 - 11; not June 1); ①⑥ from Aug. 31 (also Nov. 12).
- **S** – June 28 - Aug. 30.
- **W** – To June 21 / from Sept. 6.
- **t** – Not Aug. 15.

AMIENS - ROUEN — 268

TEMPORARILY RELOCATED TO PAGE 237

269 RENNES / ST MALO - LE MONT ST MICHEL

By Keolis Emeraude

68 km	⚒z		†	W	⑧S	⑥S
Rennes (Gare SNCF) .... d.	0930	1130	1230	1730	1830	1840
Le Mont St Michel .... a.	1050	1300	1400	1900	2000	2010

	b		
Le Mont St Michel .... d.	0930	1430	1715
Rennes (Gare SNCF) .... a.	1050	1550	1845

Service to July 4, 2009. Connections (not guaranteed) are available at Rennes with *TGV* services to/from Paris. Special fares are available in conjunction with rail tickets.

S – July 5 - Aug. 23.
W – Aug. 25 - July 4.

b – Not June 1.
z – 10 minutes later July 5 - Aug. 23 (subject to confirmation).

St Malo - Le Mont St Michel (change at Pontorson, journey approx 2 hours): ***To July 4, 2009***
From St Malo (Gare SNCF) 0940, 1630, change at Pontorson, arrive Le Mont St Michel 1135, 1811.
From Le Mont St Michel 0902⑥, 0927Ⓐ, 1550, change at Pontorson, arrive St Malo 1110⚒, 1740.

270 PARIS - ROUEN - LE HAVRE

km							3101			13101	3103	3103		13103	3105	3105	13105		3191	3107	3193			13107	3109
		Ⓐ	⑥	⑥	Ⓐ	⚒	Ⓐ	Ⓐ	⑥	Ⓐ	⑥	①–⑤	⑦		Ⓒ	Ⓐ	①–⑥	†	⑦	Ⓐ	⑥	⑥	⚒		①–⑥
			t	t			J	K	t	J		n	e				n		De		D	t			n
0	**Paris St Lazare** § .... d.	...	...	...	...	0611	0653	...	...	0720	0750	0753	...	0820	0850	0853	1020	...	1036	1050	1050	...	...	1220	1250
57	Mantes la Jolie § .... d.	...	...	...	0627	0644	|	...	0737	0752	|	|	...	0853	|	|	1052	...	1108	|	|	...	...	1252	|
79	Vernon (Eure) .... d.	...	...	...	0645	0707	|	...	0750	0806	|	|	...	0908	|	|	1108	...	1126	|	|	...	...	1306	|
111	Val de Reuil .... d.	...	...	...	0706	0729	|	...	0812	0828	|	|	...	0929	|	|	1129	...	1147	|	|	...	...	1328	|
126	Oissel .... d.	...	...	...	0717	0739	|	...	0824	0838	|	|	...	0939	|	|	1139	...	1158	|	|	...	...	1338	|
140	**Rouen** Rive-Droite ...... a.	...	...	...	0727	0750	0801	...	0838	0849	0901	0901	...	0950	1001	1001	1150	...	1207	1201	1201	...	...	1349	1401
140	**Rouen** Rive-Droite ...... d.	0632	0634	0700	...	...	0804	0804	...	...	0904	0904	0904	...	1004	1004	...	1201	...	1204	...	1210	1249	...	1404
178	Yvetot .... d.	0654	0656	0731	...	...	0825	0825	...	...	0925	0925	0925	...	1025	1025	...	1222	...	1225	...	1230	1320	...	1425
203	Bréauté-Beuzeville ▲ . d.	0707	0708	0750	...	...	0840	0840	...	...	0940	0940	0940	...	1040	1040	...	1237	...	1240	...	1243	1339	...	1440
228	**Le Havre** .... a.	0724	0723	0813	...	...	0855	0855	...	...	0955	0955	0955	...	1055	1055	...	1252	...	1255	...	1257	1402	...	1455

	3143	3111	3113	13109	3115	3117		3119	13111	3121			3123	13113	13115	3125		13117	13117	3127	3129	13119	3131		
		⑤	⑥				⑥	⑥		Ⓐ	†	Ⓐ		Ⓒ	Ⓐ		Ⓐ	⑥	†	①–④	⑤	Ⓐ	Ⓐ	Ⓒ	Ⓐ
	X	J				B	t		F				C						J	Ju	L				
Paris St Lazare § .... d.	1350	1350	1350	1420	1450	1550	...	1620	1620	1650	...	1653	1725	1720	1730	1750	1753	1820	1820	1825	1825	1830	1850	...	1853
Mantes la Jolie § .... d.	|	|	|	1452	|	|	...	1652	1652	|	...	1725	|	1752	|	|	1825	1852	1852	|	|	|	|	...	1925
Vernon (Eure) .... d.	|	|	|	1506	|	|	...	1707	1708	|	...	1747	|	1808	1811	|	1847	1908	1908	|	|	1911	|	...	1947
Val de Reuil .... d.	|	|	|	1528	|	|	...	1728	1729	|	...	1810	|	1829	1833	|	1910	1929	1929	|	|	1933	|	...	2009
Oissel .... d.	|	|	|	1538	|	|	...	1738	1739	|	...	1819	|	1839	1844	|	1919	1939	1939	|	|	1944	|	...	2019
Rouen Rive-Droite .... a.	1457	1501	1501	1549	1601	1701	...	1749	1750	1801	...	...	1836	1850	1855	1901	...	1950	1950	1936	1936	1955	2001	...	2031
Rouen Rive-Droite .... d.	1500	...	1504	...	1604	1704	1704	1752	...	1804	1804	...	1839	...	...	1904	...	...	...	...	1939	...	2004	2004	...
Yvetot .... d.	1522	...	1525	...	1625	1725	1725	1813	...	1825	1825	...	1900	...	...	1925	...	...	...	...	2000	...	2025	2027	...
Bréauté-Beuzeville ▲ .. d.	1537	...	1540	...	1640	1740	1740	1829	...	1840	1840	...	1915	...	...	1940	...	...	...	...	2015	...	2040	2040	...
Le Havre .... a.	1552	...	1555	...	1655	1755	1755	1843	...	1855	1855	...	1930	...	...	1955	...	...	...	...	2030	...	2056	2056	...

	13121	13123	3133	5376	5438	5348	13125	3135	3137	13127	3137	3139	13129	3141
	⑦	Ⓐ		*TGV*	*TGV*	*TGV*	Ⓐ	⑥	①–④	⑤	⑦	⑤		⑤⑦
	e		G	♥	P♠	Q♠	J						N	z
Paris St Lazare § .... d.	1920	1930	1950	...	...	...	2020	2020	2120	2120	2120	2150	2320	2350
Mantes la Jolie § .... d.	1952	|	|	2030	2104	2104	2052	2052	2152	2152	2152	|	2352	0022
Vernon (Eure) .... d.	2007	2011	|	|	|	|	2106	2107	2206	2208	2206	|	0006	0037
Val de Reuil .... d.	2028	2033	|	|	|	|	2128	2128	2228	2229	2228	|	0028	0058
Oissel .... d.	2038	2044	|	|	|	|	2138	2138	2238	2239	2238	|	0038	0108
Rouen Rive-Droite .... a.	2049	2055	2101	2114	2143	2155	2149	2147	2249	2250	2249	2301	0049	0119
Rouen Rive-Droite .... d.	...	...	2104	2118	2146	2158	...	2150	2252	...	2252	2304	...	0122
Yvetot .... d.	...	...	2125	|	|	|	...	2211	2313	...	2313	2325	...	0143
Bréauté-Beuzeville ▲ .. d.	...	...	2140	|	|	|	...	2226	2328	...	2328	2340	...	0158
Le Havre .... a.	...	...	2155	2200	2228	2240r	...	2241	2343	...	2343	2355	...	0213

		13100	13102	3100		13104
	Ⓐ	Ⓐ	⑥	Ⓐ	Ⓐ	Ⓐ
						J
Le Havre .... d.	...	...	...	0531	...	...
Bréauté-Beuzeville ▲ .... d.	...	...	...	0548	...	...
Yvetot .... d.	...	...	...	0603	...	...
Rouen Rive-Droite .... a.	...	...	...	0623	...	...
Rouen Rive-Droite .... d.	0526	0555	0609	0626	...	0649
Oissel .... d.	0538	0605	0619	|	0638	|
Val de Reuil .... d.	0548	0615	0630	|	0648	0706
Vernon (Eure) .... d.	0611	0638	0653	|	0711	0724
Mantes la Jolie § .... a.	0631	0656	0706	|	0731	|
Paris St Lazare § .... a.	0708	0735	0740	0738	0808	0815

	13106	3104	13108	3102			3106	5436	13110		5316	3108	13112		13114	3110	3112	13116	3114	13118	3116		3118	13120	3120
	Ⓐ	⑥	⑦	Ⓐ	Ⓐ	⑥	Ⓐ	*TGV*	①–⑥	Ⓐ	*TGV*		⚒	Ⓐ	Ⓑ	⑥	①–⑥	⑥	⑦		①–⑥	⑥	Ⓐ		
			e	L		t		R♠	n		♥						n	J	e		n	t	J		
Le Havre .... d.	...	0613	...	0631	...	0643	0702	0720	...	0725	0755	0803	...	0903	...	0913	1003	...	1103	...	1203	1245	1303	...	1403
Bréauté-Beuzeville ▲ .. d.	...	0628	...	0648	...	0707	0719	|	...	0741	|	0819	...	0919	...	0928	1019	...	1119	...	1219	1309	1319	...	1419
Yvetot .... d.	...	0643	...	0703	...	0725	0734	|	...	0756	|	0834	...	0934	...	0943	1034	...	1134	...	1234	1327	1334	...	1434
Rouen Rive-Droite .... a.	...	0705	...	0723	...	0756	0756	0801	...	0825	0840	0856	...	0956	...	1005	1056	...	1156	...	1256	1358	1356	...	1456
Rouen Rive-Droite .... d.	0659	0709	0709	0726	...	...	0759	0804	0809	...	0845	0859	0910	...	1009	1009	1059	1109	1159	1209	1259	...	1359	1409	1459
Oissel .... d.	0709	0719	0719	|	0738	...	|	|	0819	...	|	|	0921	...	1019	1019	|	1119	|	1219	|	...	|	1419	|
Val de Reuil .... d.	0719	0730	0730	|	0748	...	|	|	0830	...	|	|	0931	...	1030	1030	|	1130	|	1230	|	...	|	1430	|
Vernon (Eure) .... d.	0742	0753	0753	|	0811	...	|	|	0853	...	|	|	0953	...	1053	1053	|	1153	|	1253	|	...	|	1453	|
Mantes la Jolie § .... a.	0756	0806	0806	|	0831	...	|	0852	0906	...	0930	|	1006	...	1106	1106	|	1206	|	1306	|	...	|	1506	|
Paris St Lazare § .... a.	0835	0840	0840	0838	0908	...	0915	...	0940	...	...	1010	1040	...	1140	1140	1210	1240	1310	1340	1410	...	1510	1540	1610

	3122	3138		13122	3124	3190	3192	13124	3126		3128		13126		3130		13128	3194	3132		3134		13130		3136
	⑤		Ⓐ	⑦	Ⓐ	⑦	⑥	Ⓐ	⑦			Ⓐ	⑦	⑥		⑥	Ⓐ	⑦			Ⓑ	⑥	⑦		⑦
		Y		e		De	D		e				e	t	E	t		De				t	e		e
Le Havre .... d.	...	1504	...	...	1603	...	...	...	1613	...	1703	...	...	...	1803	1803	...	...	1913	...	2003	2003	...	...	2113
Bréauté-Beuzeville ▲ .. d.	...	1519	...	...	1619	...	...	...	1628	...	1719	...	...	...	1819	1820	...	...	1928	...	2019	2020	...	...	2128
Yvetot .... d.	...	1534	...	...	1634	...	...	...	1643	...	1734	...	...	...	1834	1835	...	...	1943	...	2034	2035	...	...	2143
Rouen Rive-Droite .... a.	...	1555	...	...	1656	...	...	...	1705	...	1756	...	...	...	1856	1856	...	...	2005	...	2056	2056	...	...	2205
Rouen Rive-Droite .... d.	1559	1559	1609	1609	1659	1659	1709	1709	1709	...	1759	1809	1809	1825	1859	...	1912	1959	2009	...	2059	...	2109	...	2209
Oissel .... d.	|	|	1619	1619	|	|	1719	1719	1719	...	|	1819	1819	1839	|	...	|	|	2019	...	|	...	2119	...	2219
Val de Reuil .... d.	|	|	1630	1630	|	|	1730	1730	1730	...	|	1830	1830	1851	|	...	1930	|	2030	...	|	...	2130	...	2230
Vernon (Eure) .... d.	|	|	1653	1653	|	|	1753	1753	1753	...	|	1852	1853	1912	|	...	1953	|	2053	...	|	...	2153	...	2253
Mantes la Jolie § .... a.	|	|	1706	1706	|	|	1806	1806	1806	...	|	1906	1906	1925	|	...	2006	|	2108	...	|	...	2206	...	2308
Paris St Lazare § .... a.	1710	1720	1740	1740	1810	1810	1840	1840	1840	...	1910	1940	1940	...	2010	...	2040	2110	2140	...	2210	...	2240	...	2340

B – Ⓐ to July 3; ⑤ July 10 - Aug. 21; Ⓐ from Aug. 24.
C – Ⓐ to July 10; ⑤ July 17 - Aug. 21; Ⓐ from Aug. 24.
D – (12) Paris - Rouen - Dieppe and v.v. (Table **270a**).
E – Ⓑ to July 5; ⑤⑦ July 10 - Aug. 21 (also July 14); Ⓑ from Aug. 23.
F – Ⓑ to June 28; Ⓐ June 29 - Aug. 21; Ⓑ from Aug. 24.
G – Daily to July 10; Ⓑ July 12 - Aug. 21; daily from Aug. 23.
J – To July 4/from Aug. 24.
K – July 6 - Aug. 21.
L – To July 10/from Aug. 24.

N – ①②③④⑥ (not June 1, July 14, Nov. 11).
P – ⑦ from July 5 (also July 14).
Q – ①–⑥ from July 6 (not July 14).
R – Daily from July 5.
X – July 10 only.
Y – June 1, July 14, Aug. 16, 23, Nov. 1 only.

e – Also June 1, July 14.
n – Not June 1, July 14.
r – 2245 on ⑥.

t – Not Aug. 15.
u – Not June 1, Nov. 10, 11.
z – Also June 1, July 14, Nov. 11.

TGV – Ⓡ, supplement payable, 🍷.

♥ – To/from Lyon and Marseille (Table **335**).
♠ – To/from Strasbourg via Charles de Gaulle ✈ (Table **391**).
▲ – Connecting trains run Bréauté-Beuzeville - Fécamp and v.v.
§ – Frequent suburban trains run Paris - Mantes-la-Jolie and v.v.

270a ROUEN - DIEPPE

km		⚒	Ⓐ	Ⓐ	†	⚒		Ⓐ	⑦	⑥	⑥		⑥	⑥	Ⓐ	Ⓐ	Ⓐ		Ⓐ	⑥	Ⓐ		Ⓐ	Ⓐ	Ⓒ
									e		t	G	t	t						St					
	Paris St Lazare **270**.d.	...	...	...	...	...	...	...	1036	1050	...	...	...	...	...	...	...	...	...	...	...	...	...	...	...
0	**Rouen** Rive-Droite ...... d.	0640	0714	0730	0841	0914	1014	1214	1224	1216	1241	1341	1414	1514	1614	1642	1714	1741	1814	1814	1844	1914	2014	2124	2124
63	**Dieppe** .... a.	0742	0758	0843	0942	0958	1059	1258	1306	1258	1341	1440	1459	1559	1658	1746	1800	1844	1858	1859	1941	1958	2058	2206	2210

	Ⓐ	⚒	Ⓐ	Ⓐ	Ⓒ	Ⓐ	⚒		⚒	⑥	†	Ⓐ	Ⓐ	⑦	Ⓐ	⑥	Ⓒ	Ⓐ	†	⚒	⑦	Ⓐ	⚒	†	†
										t				e			S				e				S
Dieppe .... d.	0534	0619	0701	0714	0751	0801	0814	1001	1201	1310	1310	1314	1401	1559	1601	1609	1701	1715	1801	1813	1900	1901	2001	2014	2101
Rouen Rive-Droite .... a.	0618	0718	0747	0820	0835	0846	0919	1046	1246	1419	1409	1419	1446	1644	1647	1654	1746	1819	1846	1919	1944	1947	2046	2113	2146
Paris St Lazare **270**..a.	...	...	...	...	...	...	...	...	...	...	...	...	...	1810	...	1840	...	...	...	...	2110	...	...	...	...

G – Ⓐ to June 12; Ⓑ June 14 - Sept. 13 (also Aug. 15); Ⓐ from Sept. 14.
S – June 13 - Sept. 13.
e – Also June 1, July 14.
t – Not Aug. 15.

CAEN - LE MANS - TOURS 271

Some trains 2nd class only

km		⚒	Ⓐ	Ⓐ	⚒	▷	⑥ t	⚒ c	Ⓑ h	⑥ t	⑤	P		⑥ t◇	†	①–④ m	⑤	⚒	⑥t 🚌	⑦ q	Ⓐ	⑦ s	Ⓐ	⑥ t	Ⓐ	⑦ e
0	**Caen** ... **275** d.	...	0527**z**	0600	0727	0832	...	1035	...	...	1300	1300	...	...	1617	1622	1622	...	...	...	1731	1748	1819	1830	1952	2135
23	Mézidon ... **275** d.	...	0544**z**	0616	0741	0852	...	1052	...	...	1317	1317	...	...	1634	1637	1637	...	...	...	1747	1806	1834	1844	2006	2150
67	Argentan ... **273** d.	...	0612	0647	0810	0918	...	1113	...	...	1347	1347	...	...	1704	1707	1707	...	...	...	1822	1834	1905	1910	2032	2212
82	Surdon ... **273** d.	...	|	0659	0820	|	...	1123	...	...	1357	1357	...	...	|	|	|	...	...	...	1832	1847	1916	1919	2041	|
91	Sées ... d.	...	0627	0707	0827	|	...	1130	...	...	1404	1404	...	...	1719	1722	1722	...	...	...	1840	1856	1923	1926	2049	2227
111	Alençon ... d.	...	0641	0722	0840	0944	...	1142	...	...	1419	1419	...	1644	1733	1736	1736	...	...	...	1853	1912	1937	1939	2100	2240
166	**Le Mans** ... a.	...	0731	0809	0909	1012	...	1218	...	...	1447	1447	...	1715	1808	1809	1809	...	...	...	...	1941	2008	2008	...	2308
166	**Le Mans** ... d.	0627	0732	...	...	1016	1212	...	1242	1309	1450	1450	1643	...	1811	*1820*	1824	1840	...	1911	...	2003	2019	...	...	...
215	Château du Loir ... d.	0656	0804	...	...	1047	1255	...	1312	1339	1518	1518	1719	...	1842	*1847*	1854	1922	1950	1950	...	2035	2053	...	...	...
262	St Pierre des Corps .. a.	|	|	...	...	1117	|	...	|	|	|	1545	|	...	|	|	1923	...	|	|	...	|	|	...	...	...
265	**Tours** ... a.	0735	0834	...	...	*1134*	1332	...	1340	1407	1548	1555	1747	...	1911	*1915*	1933	...	2035	2024	...	2105	2127	...	...	...

	Ⓐ	① g	⚒	① g	Ⓐ d	⚒	†	⚒ b	†	⚒	⚒ △	⑥ t	Ⓐ ▽	①–④ m	⑤	†	⚒	⑥ t	①–④ m	⑤	Ⓑ	⑤	†	①–④ m	†	⑤⑦ v
Tours ... d.	...	0545	...	0600	0644	0756	0900	0919	1040	...	1149	1225	1405	...	1523	1651	1701	...	...	...	1831	...	...	...	2005	2144
St Pierre des Corps ... d.	...	|	...	|	|	|	0911	0929	1050	...	|	|	|	...	|	|	|	...	...	...	|	...	...	...	2017	2153
Château du Loir ... d.	...	0614	...	0637	0719	0826	0940	1000	1119	...	1219	1305	1434	...	1555	1723	1734	...	...	...	1902	...	...	...	2049	2222
Le Mans ... a.	...	0650	...	0718	0804	0856	1009	1031	1149	...	1250	1348	1504	...	1622	1751	1801	...	...	...	1934	...	...	...	2118	2252
Le Mans ... d.	0628**z**	...	0705	...	*0849*	...	1030	1037	*1214*	1236	...	...	1513	...	1625	1805	1805	1858	1914	1914	...	1957	2004	2031	2120	...
Alençon ... d.	0700	...	0749	...	*0931*	...	1100	1107	*1250*	1325	...	...	1548	1722	1722	1837	1837	1927	1952	1957	...	2030	2039	2111	2152	...
Sées ... d.	0712	...	0801	...	...	...	1113	1120	...	1336	...	...	1601	1734	1736	1852	1853	1939	2004	2010	...	2043	2054	2124	2206	...
Surdon ... **273** d.	0718	...	0809	...	...	...	1120	1127	...	1343	...	...	|	1740	1744	1901	1901	1946	2011	2018	...	2051	2102	2132	|	...
Argentan ... **273** d.	0728	...	0819	...	...	...	1130	1139	...	1352	...	...	1614	1750	1756	1912	1914	1956	2020	2028	...	2101	2115	2142	2221	...
Mézidon ... **275** d.	0753	...	0846	...	...	...	1153	1203	...	1418	...	...	1638	1819	1829	1942	1949	2021	2046	2056	...	2129	2143	...	|	...
Caen ... **275** a.	0808	...	0901	...	...	...	1206	1217	...	1432	...	...	1652	1833	1844	1957	2005	2035	2100	2112	...	2145	2159	...	2259	...

P – Daily except ⑤ (not Dec. 12).
b – Not Le Mans - Caen Oct. 19-23, 26-30, Nov. 16-20, 30, Dec. 1-4.
c – Not Sept. 28 - Oct. 2, Nov. 23-27, Dec. 7-12.
d – Not Le Mans - Alençon on Nov. 16-20, 30, Dec. 1-4.
e – Also June 1, July 14; not July 12.
g – Also June 2, July 15, Nov. 12; not June 1.

h – Also Aug. 15.
m – Not June 1, July 14, Nov. 11.
q – Also June 1, July 14, Nov. 11.
s – Also June 1, July 14; not July 12.
t – Not Aug. 15.
v – Also June 1, July 14, Nov. 10.

z – ① (also June 2, July 15; not June 1, July 13).
△ – Runs 15 mins later on Ⓐ to Aug. 14 and Ⓐ Oct. 19-30.
▽ – Le Mans - Caen is subject to alteration Oct. 5-9.
▷ – Not Oct. 12-16, Nov. 23-27, Dec. 7-12.
◇ – Additional journey on ⑥**t**: Alençon 1841, Le Mans 1912.

CAEN - COUTANCES - RENNES 272

Some trains 2nd class only

km		① L	⚒	⑥	M	① L	Ⓐ	Ⓐ	⑥	⑦ Ku	Ⓐ K	K 🚌	Ⓒ K		Ⓐ		Ⓒ 🚌	Ⓐ	E	F		K	⚒	⑤ K	⑤ J
0	**Caen** ... **275** d.	0542	0625	0713	0713	0713	0833	0913	0913	0913	...	...	...	1113	1213	1233	...	1333	1413	1413	...	...	1605	1643	1643
30	Bayeux ... **275** d.	0558	0649	0731	0730	0730	0856	0930	0930	0930	...	...	...	1130	1231	1258	...	1356	1430	1430	...	...	1627	1700	1700
57	Lison ... **275** d.	0613	0709	0747	0747	0747	0914	0946	0946	0946	...	...	...	1146	1248	1318	...	1415	1446	1446	...	...	1646	1716	1716
75	St Lô ... **275** d.	0628	0722	0800	0801	0805	0926	1000	1001	1001	...	...	...	1201	1300	1333	1339	1429	1501	1500	...	...	1658	1730	1730
105	**Coutances** ... d.	0654	0741	0821	0822	0827	...	1021	1025	1025	...	1028	...	1221	1323	...	1411	...	1522	1521	...	...	...	1752	1801
	Granville ▲ ... a.	*0743***n**	*0817***a**	*0857*	*0908***x**	|	...	...	|	|	1047	1058	1108	*1300***c**	*1400*	...	1441	...	*1557*	*1557*	...	1723	...	*1827*	*1827*
132	Folligny ... d.	0719	...	...	0843	0849	...	...	1046	1046	1058	...	1119	...	...	...	...	...	1541	...	...	1734	...	1812	1822
151	Avranches ... d.	0736	...	...	0859	0907	...	...	1101	1101	1113	...	1138	...	...	...	...	...	1556	...	...	1749	...	1827	1839
173	Pontorson ⊡ ... d.	0757	...	...	0916	0926	...	...	1117	1117	1130	...	1155	...	...	...	...	...	1614	...	...	1805	...	1846	1857
194	Dol ... **281** d.	0818	...	...	0934	0946	...	...	1134	1134	1151	...	1216	...	...	...	...	...	1633	...	...	1827	...	1905	1917
	St Malo ... **281** a.	|	...	...	|	|	...	...	|	|	1205	...	1230	...	...	...	...	...	|	...	...	1841	...	|	|
252	**Rennes** ... **281** a.	0850	...	...	1007	1018	...	...	1205	1205	...	...	...	...	...	...	...	...	1705	...	...	...	...	1935	1952

	⑥ Kt	P	Ⓐ	⑤J 🚌	⚒	Ⓐ		⑤	†	
Caen ... **275** d.	1713	1713	1733	...	1805	1833	1905	1905	1905	...
Bayeux ... **275** d.	1730	1730	1756	...	1829	1858	1928	1928	1928	...
Lison ... **275** d.	1746	1746	1815	...	1849	1918	1946	1946	1946	...
St Lô ... **275** d.	1800	1800	1828	1834	1902	1933	2001	2001	2001	...
Coutances ... d.	1823	1831	...	1906	1925	...	2021	2023	2028	...
Granville ▲ ... a.	|	*1900*	...	1936	...	...	...	*2057*	*2057*	...
Folligny ... d.	1849	1852	...	...	...	...	...	2044	2049	...
Avranches ... d.	1904	1908	...	...	...	...	...	2100	2104	...
Pontorson ⊡ ... d.	1920	1925	...	...	...	...	...	2117	2120	...
Dol ... **281** d.	1937	1943	...	...	...	...	...	2135	2137	...
St Malo ... **281** a.	|	|	...	...	...	...	...	|	|	...
Rennes ... **281** a.	2006	2015	...	...	...	...	...	2208	2208	...

	⚒	⚒	① L	②–⑤ 🚌 §			⑥	⑦ Ku	Ⓐ	Ⓐ
Rennes ... **281** d.	...	...	0550	...	...	...	0838	0838	0906	...
St Malo ... **281** d.	...	...	|	...	...	...	|	|	|	...
Dol ... **281** d.	...	...	0625	...	...	...	0911	0911	0938	...
Pontorson ⊡ ... d.	...	...	0642	...	...	...	0928	0928	0956	...
Avranches ... d.	...	...	0703	...	...	...	0949	0949	1020	...
Folligny ... d.	...	...	0718	...	...	...	1003	1003	1035	...
Granville ▲ ... d.	...	*0615***r**	*0648***n**	0651	...	...	*0945*	*0945*	*1018*	...
Coutances ... d.	0603	*0646**	0742	0721	...	0830	1026	1026	1058	...
St Lô ... **275** d.	0627	0728	0803	0755	...	0853	1047	1047	1120	1229
Lison ... **275** d.	0643	0743	0816	0816	0827	0910	1101	1101	1136	1244
Bayeux ... **275** d.	0700	0800	0830	...	0841	0925	1116	1116	1151	1301
Caen ... **275** a.	0723	0822	0846	...	0856	0943	1132	1132	1207	1323

	⚒	Ⓐ K	Ⓒ K	Ⓐ	Ⓐ	⑦ Je	Ⓐ 🚌		⑤ J	①–⑥ Kv	⑦ Ku	H 🚌	Ⓐ	R	⑤ K	⑤ J	①–④ m	①–④ m	⑥⑦ Je	⑤	K	⑤	†	⑥ Kt	⑦ Je
Rennes ... **281** d.	...	...	...	...	...	1251	...	...	1451	1451	1451	...	...	...	1605	1615	...	1640	1645	...	...	1821	1842	1851	2045
St Malo ... **281** d.	...	1052	1123	...	...	|	...	...	|	|	|	...	...	...	|	|	...	|	|	...	1736	|	|	|	|
Dol ... **281** d.	...	1111	1143	...	...	1323	...	...	1522	1522	1522	...	...	...	1636	1647	...	1717	1717	...	1757	1900	1913	1922	2116
Pontorson ⊡ ... d.	...	1127	1159	...	...	1340	...	...	1539	1539	1538	...	...	...	1653	1704	...	1734	1734	...	1813	1917	1929	1939	2133
Avranches ... d.	...	1148	1221	...	...	1400	...	...	1602	1602	1558	...	...	...	1713	1725	...	1755	1755	...	1834	1939	1950	2000	2154
Folligny ... d.	...	1202	1235	...	...	1415	...	...	1618	1618	1613	...	...	...	1728	1739	...	1809	1809	...	1848	1954	2004	2015	2209
Granville ▲ ... d.	*1155*	1213	1245	*1255***z**	...	*1345***n**	...	...	*1557*	*1557*	*1557*	...	...	*1654***s**	*1713*	*1723*	*1720**	*1755*	*1755*	...	1858	*1942*	*1949*	*1957*	*2139***n**
Coutances ... d.	1236	...	...	1335	...	1437	1547	...	1639	1639	1636	1647	...	1734	1753	1803	*1750**	1837	1837	1837	...	2022	2029	2037	2231
St Lô ... **275** d.	1301	...	...	1358	1500	1500	1619	1629	1700	1700	1658	1719	1729	1759	1829	1829	1833	1901	1901	1901	...	2043	2050	2058	2252
Lison ... **275** d.	1314	...	...	1411	1513	1513	...	1642	1712	1712	1713	...	1742	1811	1841	1841	1845	1914	1914	1914	...	2056	2103	2113	2306
Bayeux ... **275** d.	1329	...	...	1427	1528	1528	...	1700	1728	1728	1728	...	1800	1827	1856	1856	1901	1929	1929	1929	...	2111	2118	2128	2321
Caen ... **275** a.	1347	...	...	1445	1543	1545	...	1722	1745	1745	1745	...	1822	1845	1913	1913	1922	1945	1945	1945	...	2128	2135	2145	2337

E – ①⑤⑥⑦ (daily July 3 - Aug. 27), also June 2, Nov. 11.
F – Daily except dates in note **E**.
G – ①⑤⑥⑦ to July 4 / from Aug. 31 (also June 2, Nov. 11).
H – ①–④ to July 2 / from Aug. 31 (not June 1, Nov. 11).
J – To July 4 / from Aug. 31.
K – July 5 - Aug. 30.
L – ① to June 29 / from Aug. 31 (also June 2; not June 1).
M – ②–⑤ (also ① July 6 - Aug. 24), not June 2, July 14, Nov. 11.
P – ①–④ (also ⑥⑦ to July 4 / from Aug. 31); not July 14.
R – Daily except ⑤.
S – ⑥⑦ Apr. 11 - Sept. 27 (daily July 1 - Aug. 31), also June 1.

T – ①–⑤ July 1 - Aug. 31 (not July 14). Depart 0706 July 1-3.
U – ⑥⑦ Apr. 11 - Sept. 27 (also June 1, July 14).
a – Ⓐ only.
c – Ⓒ (daily July 4 - Aug. 30).
e – Also June 1, Nov. 11.
m – Not June 1, July 14, Nov. 11.
n – 🚌 Folligny - Granville and v.v.
r – ⑥ only.
s – ①②③④⑦ (also ⑥ July 11 - Aug. 29).
t – Not Aug. 15.

u – Also July 14.
v – Not July 14.
x – Ⓐ July 6 - Aug. 28. 🚌 Folligny - Granville.
z – ⑤ to July 3; Ⓐ July 6 - Aug. 28; ⑤ from Sept. 4.
▲ – *Italic* times: connection by 🚌.
⊡ – 10 km from Mont St Michel.
§ – Not June 1, July 14, Nov. 11.
* – By 🚌.

GRANVILLE - FOLLIGNY - (RENNES)
🚌 connections Granville - Folligny
(see above for rail connections to Rennes)
🚌 journey 20 minutes
0648 ① **L**, 0813 **M**, 0819 ① **L**, 1511 **G**, 1742 ⑤ **K**, 1752 ⑤ **J**, 1822 Ⓒ **J**, 2014 ⑤, 2019 †.

(RENNES) - FOLLIGNY - GRANVILLE
🚌 connections Folligny - Granville
(see above for rail connections from Rennes)
🚌 journey 20 minutes
0723 ① **L**, 1040 Ⓐ, 1420 ⑦ **J**, 1623 ⑤ **J**, 1744 ⑤ **J**, 1814 **J** (not ⑤), 1959 ⑤ **J**, 2009 ⑦ **J**, 2214 ⑦ **J**.

PARIS - MONT ST MICHEL special rail / 🚌 service
By 🚌 Villedieu - Mont St Michel (see Table **273** for rail portion), 🅁

	T	U
Paris Montparnasse ... d.	0710	0837
Le Mont St Michel ... a.	1105	1230

	S
Le Mont St Michel ... d.	1810
Paris Montparnasse ... a.	2219

PARIS - DREUX - GRANVILLE 273

TEMPORARILY RELOCATED TO PAGE 224

274 PARIS - VERSAILLES

RER (express Métro) Line C: **Paris Austerlitz** - St Michel Notre Dame - **Versailles Rive Gauche** (for Château). Every 15 - 30 minutes. Journey 40 minutes.
Alternative service: RER Line C: Paris Austerlitz - St Michel Notre Dame - Versailles Chantiers. Journey 39 minutes.
SNCF suburban services: Paris St Lazare - Versailles Rive Droite (journey 28 - 35 minutes); Paris Montparnasse - Versailles Chantiers (journey 12 - 28 minutes). See also Table **278**.

275 PARIS - CAEN - CHERBOURG

For other trains Paris - Lisieux (- Trouville-Deauville) see Table **276**. Many fast trains have 🍸

km		3325 ① g	⚒	Ⓐ	Ⓐ J	⚒ u	⚒	3331 Ⓐ	3301 Ⓐ	Ⓐ		3333 ⑥	⑥ t	3327 X	Ⓐ	3335 Ⓐ	Ⓐ	3303 Ⓒ	3337 ⑥	3339 ⑦ e	Ⓒ	3305 Ⓐ	Ⓐ	3341 Ⓒ	Ⓒ	3307 Ⓐ
0	**Paris St Lazare** ▷ d.	0025	...	...	...	...	...	0645	0707	...	...	0745	...	0802	...	0846	...	0910	0945	0945	...	1010	...	1145	...	1210
57	Mantes la Jolie ▷ d.	|	...	...	...	...	...	|	|	...	...	|	...	|	...	|	...	|	|	|	...	|	...	|	...	|
108	Evreux ▷ d.	0132	...	...	0609	...	...	0740	|	...	...	0840	...	|	...	0940	...	|	1040	1040	...	|	...	1240	...	|
160	Bernay d.	0211	...	...	0646	...	...	0807	|	...	...	0907	...	|	...	1007	...	|	1107	1107	...	|	...	1307	...	|
191	Lisieux 277 d.	0240	...	*0609*	0701	...	0744	0826	|	...	0844	0926	...	|	0944	1026	...	|	1126	1126	...	|	...	1326	...	|
216	Mézidon 271 277 d.	|	...	*0624*	0715	...	0759	|	|	...	0859	|	...	|	0959	|	...	|	|	|	...	|	...	|	...	|
239	**Caen** 271 277 a.	0317	...	*0643*	0733	...	0818	0851	0855	...	0918	0951	...	1002	1018	1051	...	1057	1151	1151	...	1157	...	1351	...	1357
239	**Caen** 272 d.	0320	0559	0659	...	0759	...	...	0857	0913	...	...	0959	1004	...	...	1059	1059	1153	...	1159	1159	1259	...	1359	1359
269	Bayeux 272 d.	0349	0615	0715	...	0815	...	...	|	0930	...	...	1015	1023	...	...	1115	1116	1210	...	1216	1216	1315	...	1415	1416
296	Lison 272 d.	0411	0630	0730	...	0830	...	...	|	0946	...	...	1030	1039	...	...	1130	1130	1225	...	1230	1230	1330	...	1430	1430
314	St Lô 272 a.	|	|	|	...	|	...	...	|	0959	...	...	|	|	...	...	|	|	1240	...	|	|	|	...	|	|
314	Carentan d.	0424	0640	0740	...	0840	...	...	|	...	...	...	1040	1052	...	...	1140	1141	...	...	1241	1241	1340	...	1441	1441
343	Valognes d.	0444	0656	0756	...	0856	...	...	|	...	...	...	1056	1109	...	...	1156	1155	...	...	1256	1255	1356	...	1456	1455
371	**Cherbourg** a.	0500	0711	0811	...	0911	...	...	0953	...	...	...	1111	1124	...	...	1211	1209	...	...	1311	1309	1411	...	1511	1509

	3309 ⑥	Ⓐ	3343 Ⓐ	Ⓐ	3345 ⑤ s	3347 Ⓒ	3311 Ⓐ	Ⓐ	3313 Ⓒ	Ⓐ		3349 Ⓐ	3315 Ⓐ	Ⓐ	3351	3317 Ⓐ ▽	Ⓒ	3353 Ⓐ	3319 ⑤	3321 Ⓒ	3355 M	3361 L	TGV 5348 ♠ F	3323 Ⓑ	3357 ⑥	3359 B
Paris St Lazare ▷ d.	1310	...	1345	...	1410	1445	1510	...	1610	...	...	1645	1710	...	1745	1810	...	1845	1905	1910	1945	1959	...	2045	2045	2145
Mantes la Jolie ▷ d.	|	...	|	...	|	|	|	...	|	...	...	|	|	...	|	|	...	|	|	|	|	2038	2040	|	|	|
Evreux ▷ d.	|	...	1440	...	1505	1540	|	...	|	...	...	1740	|	...	1840	|	...	1940	|	|	2040	2106	2109	2140	2140	2240
Bernay d.	|	...	1507	...	1532	1607	|	...	|	...	...	1807	|	...	1907	|	...	2007	|	|	2107	2132	|	2207	2207	2306
Lisieux 277 d.	|	1444	1526	...	1551	1626	|	1644	|	1725	1744	1826	|	1844	1926	|	...	2026	|	|	2126	2151	2153	2224	2226	2325
Mézidon 271 277 d.	|	1459	|	...	|	|	|	1659	|	1740	1759	|	|	1859	|	|	...	|	|	|	|	|	|	|	|	|
Caen 271 277 a.	1457	1518	1551	...	1616	1651	1657	1718	1757	1759	1818	1851	1857	1918	1951	1957	...	2051	2057	2057	2151	2217	2221	2245	2251	2351
Caen 272 d.	1459	...	...	1559	...	...	1659	...	1759	1801	1821	...	1859	...	...	1959	1959	2054	2101	2059	...	...	2224	2247	...	...
Bayeux 272 d.	1516	...	...	1615	...	...	1716	...	1816	1816	1839	...	1916	...	...	2015	2015	2111	2118	2116	...	...	|	2302	...	...
Lison 272 d.	1530	...	...	1630	...	...	1730	...	1833	1830	1855	...	1930	...	...	2030	2030	2127	2133	2130	...	...	|	2317	...	...
St Lô 272 a.	|	...	...	|	...	...	|	...	|	|	|	...	|	...	...	|	|	2140	|	|	...	...	|	|	...	...
Carentan d.	1541	...	...	1640	...	...	1741	...	1844	1840	1905	...	1941	...	...	2040	2040	...	2143	2141	...	...	|	2327	...	...
Valognes d.	1555	...	...	1656	...	...	1755	...	1858	1856	1919	...	1955	...	...	2055	2056	...	2157	2155	...	...	|	2341	...	...
Cherbourg a.	1609	...	...	1711	...	...	1809	...	1911	1911	1934	...	2009	...	...	2110	2111	...	2212	2209	...	...	2328	2356	...	...

	3330 Ⓐ	3332 ①–⑥ n§	Ⓐ	3300 Ⓐ	TGV 5330 ♠ D	3334 Ⓐ	3336 Ⓒ	⚒	TGV 5330 ♠ E	Ⓐ	Ⓒ	3302		3338	⚒		3340 ⑤	3304 H	†	3306 ⑤	3342 Ⓒ	Ⓐ	⚒	3344 Ⓐ	3324 Y	3308
Cherbourg d.	...	...	...	0556	0620	...	...	0630	0655	0724	...	0746	...	...	0946	...	...	1046	1146	1200	...	...	1246	...	1315	1346
Valognes d.	...	...	...	0612	|	...	...	0645	|	0739	...	0802	...	...	1001	...	...	1102	1201	1217	...	...	1301	...	1333	1402
Carentan d.	...	...	...	0626	|	...	...	0701	|	0755	...	0816	...	...	1017	...	...	1116	1217	1232	...	...	1317	...	1349	1416
St Lô 272 d.	...	...	...	|	|	0651	...	|	|	|	...	|	0853	...	|	...	...	|	|	|	...	...	|	...	|	|
Lison 272 d.	...	...	...	0637	|	0705	...	0712	|	0806	...	0827	0910	...	1028	...	...	1127	1228	|	...	...	1328	...	1401	1427
Bayeux 272 d.	...	...	...	0651	|	0721	...	0729	|	0820	...	0841	0925	...	1042	...	...	1141	1242	|	...	...	1342	...	1416	1441
Caen 272 a.	...	...	...	0706	0728	0738	...	0750	0801	0836	...	0856	0943	...	1058	...	...	1156	1258	1306	...	...	1358	...	1433	1456
Caen 271 277 d.	0508	0608	0642	0708	0733	0742	0742	0752	0804	0842	0842	0858	...	1008	...	1112	1155	1158	...	1308	1308	1312	...	1408	1435	1458
Mézidon 271 277 d.	|	|	0701	|	|	|	|	0812	|	0901	0901	|	...	|	...	1131	|	|	...	|	|	1331	...	|	|	|
Lisieux 277 d.	0536	0636	0715	|	0801	0811	0810	0825	0834	0915	0915	|	...	1036	...	1145	|	|	...	1337	1336	1345	...	1436	1500	|
Bernay d.	0554	0654	...	|	|	0829	0829	...	|	...	...	|	...	1054	...	...	|	|	...	1354	1354	...	...	1454	1518	|
Evreux ▷ d.	0620	0720	...	|	0846	0855	0855	...	0920	...	...	|	...	1120	...	...	|	|	...	1420	1420	...	...	1520	1544	|
Mantes la Jolie ▷ a.	|	|	...	|	0911	0921	0921	...	0947	...	...	|	...	|	...	...	|	|	...	|	|	...	...	|	|	|
Paris St Lazare ▷ a.	0717	0818	...	0858	...	0957	0957	...	...	...	...	1046	...	1216	...	...	1346	1345	...	1516	1516	...	...	1616	1640	1646

	3326 Z	Ⓐ	† K	3346 Ⓒ	Ⓐ		3348	Ⓐ	⚒	3312 ⑦ e	3310 Ⓐ	Ⓐ J	3328 W	Ⓐ	†	3314 ①–⑤ b	3316 ⑥	3350 ⑦ e	Ⓐ	⑥ t	3318 ⑦ e	3352 ⑦ e	3320 Ⓐ	Ⓐ	3322 ⑦ e	
Cherbourg d.	1355	...	...	...	...	1546	...	...	1624	1646	1700	...	1715	...	1741	1746	1755	...	1824	1824	1846	...	1912	1946	2016	...
Valognes d.	1413	...	...	...	...	1601	...	...	1640	1702	|	...	1733	...	1756	1802	1811	...	1840	1839	1902	...	1928	2001	2032	...
Carentan d.	1430	...	...	...	...	1617	...	...	1655	1716	|	...	1748	...	1810	1816	1825	...	1855	1855	1916	...	1942	2017	2046	...
St Lô 272 d.	|	1500	1500	...	...	|	...	...	|	|	|	...	|	...	|	|	|	1819	|	|	|	...	|	|	|	...
Lison 272 d.	1442	1513	1513	...	...	1628	...	...	1706	1727	|	...	1801	...	1821	1827	1836	1832	1906	1906	1927	...	1953	2028	2057	...
Bayeux 272 d.	1459	1528	1528	...	...	1642	...	...	1720	1741	|	...	1816	...	1835	1841	1851	1848	1920	1920	1941	...	2007	2042	2111	...
Caen 272 a.	1516	1543	1545	...	...	1658	...	...	1736	1756	1756	...	1833	...	1851	1856	1905	1905	1936	1936	1956	...	2022	2058	2126	...
Caen 271 277 d.	1518	1545	...	1608	1642	...	1708	1722	1742	1758	1758	1824	1835	1842	...	1858	1908	1908	1938	...	1958	2008	2024	...	2128	...
Mézidon 271 277 d.	|	1559	...	|	1701	...	|	1742	1801	|	|	1843	|	1901	...	|	|	|	1957	...	|	|	|	...	|	...
Lisieux 277 d.	|	1612	...	1636	1715	...	1736	1756	1815	|	|	1855	|	1914	...	|	1936	1936	2011	...	|	2036	2049	...	|	...
Bernay d.	|	...	...	1654	...	...	1754	...	...	|	|	1911	|	...	...	|	1954	1954	...	...	|	2054	|	...	|	...
Evreux ▷ d.	|	...	...	1720	...	...	1820	...	...	|	|	1947	|	...	...	|	2020	2020	...	...	|	2120	|	...	|	...
Mantes la Jolie ▷ a.	|	...	...	|	...	...	|	...	...	|	|	...	|	...	...	|	|	|	...	...	|	|	|	...	|	...
Paris St Lazare ▷ a.	1715	...	...	1816	...	...	1916	...	...	1946	1946	...	2030	...	...	2046	2116	2116	...	...	2146	2216	2216	...	2316	...

LOCAL TRAINS PARIS - EVREUX △

	Ⓐ	Ⓐ	Ⓐ	Ⓐ	Ⓐ	Ⓐ	Ⓐ	Ⓐ	
Paris St Lazare d.	0907	1110	1310	1610	1713	1813	1913	2013	...
Mantes la Jolie d.	0941	1144	1344	1644	1747	1847	1947	2047	...
Evreux a.	1017	1220	1417	1715	1820	1920	2022	2120	...

	Ⓐ	Ⓐ	Ⓐ	Ⓐ d		Ⓐ	Ⓐ	Ⓐ
Evreux d.	0539	0639	0739	0841	...	1139	1339	1740
Mantes la Jolie a.	0616	0716	0816	0916	...	1213	1413	1813
Paris St Lazare a.	0652	0755	0855	0954	...	1248	1448	1849

TGV CHERBOURG - DIJON - BESANÇON *From July 5*

See above for other stations	*TGV* 5330 D	*TGV* 5330 E
Cherbourg d.	0620	0655
Caen d.	0733	0804
Charles de Gaulle ✈ a.	1108	1116
Marne la Vallée-Chessy a.	1052*	1131
Dijon a.	1318	1318
Besançon a.	1405	1405

	TGV 5348 F
Besançon d.	1621
Dijon d.	1709
Marne la Vallée-Chessy d.	1848
Charles de Gaulle ✈ d.	1904
Caen a.	2221
Cherbourg a.	2328

B – Ⓐ to July 2; ⑤ July 3 - Aug. 21; Ⓐ from Aug. 24.
D – ① from July 6 (also July 15).
E – ②–⑦ from July 5 (not July 15).
F – Daily from July 5.
H – ①②③④⑥ (not June 1, July 14, Aug. 15, Nov. 11).
J – To July 3/from Aug. 31.
K – July 5 - Aug. 30.
L – To July 4.
M – From July 5.
W – July 14, Aug. 16.

X – July 4, 11, Oct. 24, 31 only.
Y – June 1, July 14, Aug. 2, 9, 16, 23, 30, Nov. 1 only.
Z – June 1, Nov. 1 only.

b – Not July 14, Nov. 11.
d – On ① from July 6 (also July 15) depart Evreux 0826, arrive Mantes 0900, Paris 0935.
e – Also June 1, July 14, Nov. 11.
g – Also June 2; not June 1.
n – Not June 1, July 14, Nov. 11.
s – Also July 11, Oct. 24.

t – Not Aug. 15.
u – Runs 15 minutes later on ②–⑤ (not June 2).

♠ – To/from Dijon and Besançon (see panel below table).
▷ – For additional trains see panel below main table.
△ – Frequent suburban trains run Paris - Mantes-la-Jolie. Additional local trains run Mantes la Jolie - Evreux.
▽ – On ⑤ July 10 - Aug. 21 depart Paris 1805, Caen 1958.
§ – Depart Caen 0606 on Aug. 15.
* – Calls before Charles de Gaulle ✈.

PARIS - LISIEUX - TROUVILLE DEAUVILLE — 276

km		3371 Ⓐ	3373 Ⓒ	3375 ①–⑤ B	3377 ⑥⑦ S	3379 Ⓐ d	3381 ⑥ T	3383 ⑤	3385 ⑤ L	3389 ⑥⑦ Y	3393 Ⓐ
0	**Paris St Lazare** ▷ d.	0746	0845	0944	1010	1145	1345	1545	1633	1820	1910
108	Evreux ▷ d.	0840	0940	|	1107	1240	1441	1640	|	1915	2006
160	Bernay ▷ d.	0907	1007	|	1133	1307	1507	1707	|	1941	2031
191	Lisieux ▷ d.	0927	1026	|	1152	1326	1526	1726	1817	2000	2050
221	**Trouville-Deauville** a.	0948	1047	1131	1213	1347	1547	1746	1838	2028	2112

	3370 Ⓐ	3372 Ⓐ b	3374 ⑥⑦ X	3376 ①–⑤ B◇	3378 ⑦ e	3380 Ⓒ	3382 ⑦ W	3384 Ⓐ	3386 ⑦ M	3388 ⑦ W
Trouville-Deauville d.	0712	1107	1411	1425	1638	1812	1853	1911	2033	2058
Lisieux ▷ d.	0736	1136	1436	1448	1706	1836	|	1936	|	2121
Bernay ▷ d.	0754	1154	1455	1506	1724	1854	|	1955	|	2140
Evreux ▷ d.	0820	1220	1521	1532	1750	1920	|	2020	|	2207
Paris St Lazare ▷ a.	0918	1316	1616	1628	1847	2016	2046	2116	2226	2305

	⚒		Ⓑh		⑥t		Ⓐ		⚒		Ⓒ		Ⓐ		⚒	†		Ⓐ	⑥N		v				
Lisieux d.	0735	...	0835	...	0935	...	1034	...	1235	...	1335	...	1535	...	1635	1635	...	1835	1835	...	1935	...	...	...	...
Trouville-Deauville a.	0757	...	0857	...	0957	...	1056	...	1257	...	1357	...	1557	...	1657	1658	...	1857	1857	...	1955	...	...	...	...

	⚒	†		Ⓐ	⑥N		Ⓒ	Ⓐ		⑥t	Ⓐ		⑤	Ⓒ		Ⓐ				Ⓐv		†		Ⓐ	
Trouville-Deauville d.	0700	0738	...	0804	0804	...	1004	1004	...	1149	1204	...	1302	1304	...	1404	...	1604	1702	1804	...	2000z	...	2017	...
Lisieux a.	0722	0800	...	0826	0826	...	1024	1026	...	1219	1226	...	1324	1326	...	1426	...	1626	1726	1826	...	2026	...	2039	...

B – ①–⑤ July 6 - Aug. 21 (not July 14).
L – ⑤ July 10 - Aug. 21. Additional journey on same dates: Paris d. 1810, Lisieux d. 1951, Trouville a. 2013 (train **3387**).
M – ⑦ July 5 - Aug. 23 (also July 14).
N – ⑥ July 11 - Aug. 22 (not Aug. 15).
S – ⑥ May 16 - Oct. 31, also ⑦ July 5 - Aug. 23 (also July 14).
T – ⑥ May 30 - Sept. 26 (also Oct. 24, 31).
W – ⑦ June 7 - Sept. 27 (also July 14).

X – ⑥⑦ July 5 - Aug. 23 (also June 1, July 14, Nov. 1).
Y – ⑥⑦ July 5 - Aug. 23 (also July 14). Runs 20 - 25 minutes later on ⑥ July 11 - Aug. 8 and Aug. 22 (train **3391**).

b – Also runs on ⑥ July 11 - Aug. 22.
d – Additional journey runs July 11, Oct. 24, 31 (depart Paris 1212, non-stop to Trouville-Deauville, arrive 1408).
e – Also June 1, July 14.
h – Also Aug. 15.

t – Not Aug. 15.
v – Not on ⑤ July 10 - Aug. 21.
z – 2004 to June 28 / from Aug. 30.

▷ – For other trains see Table **275**.
◇ – Additional train on June 1 and Nov. 11: Trouville-Deauville d. 1550, non-stop to Paris, a. 1756.

TROUVILLE DEAUVILLE - DIVES CABOURG — 276a

24 km Journey 30 minutes

Service to July 4 and from Aug. 24:

From Trouville Deauville: 1102 Ⓒ, 1223 ⑥ **E**, 1416 Ⓒ, 1557 ⑥ **S**, 1645 ⑦, 2126 ④, 2126 ⑤.

From Dives Cabourg: 0620 ① **g**, 1138 ⑥ **E**, 1222 ⑥ **F**, 1222 ⑦, 1322 ⑥ **E**, 1511 ⑥ **S**, 1558 ⑦, 1731 Ⓒ.

Service July 5 - Aug. 23:

From Trouville Deauville: 0809 Ⓐ, 0955 Ⓐ, 1102 Ⓒ, 1141 Ⓐ, 1223 Ⓒ, 1557 ⑥, 1609 Ⓐ, 1645 ⑦, 1754 Ⓐ, 1917 ⑦ **c**, 2002 ⑥ **t**, 2008 **R**, 2023 ⑤, 2038 ⑦ **c**, 2107 ⑥ **t**, 2126 **R**, 2138 ⑤.

From Dives Cabourg: 0620 Ⓐ, 0913 Ⓐ, 1022 Ⓒ, 1031 Ⓐ, 1138 Ⓒ, 1322 Ⓐ, 1332 Ⓒ, 1511 ⑥, 1522 Ⓐ, 1558 ⑦, 1710 Ⓐ, 1731 Ⓒ, 1831 Ⓐ, 1953 ⑦ **c**, 2047 **R**, 2100 ⑤.

E – To Oct. 31.
F – From Nov. 7.
R – ①–④ (not July 14).

S – ⑥ May 30 - Sept. 26 (also Oct. 24, 31).
c – Also July 14, Aug. 15.
g – Also June 2; not June 1.

t – Not Aug. 15.

Additional journeys run on July 3.

ROUEN - LISIEUX - CAEN — 277

km		Ⓐ	⑥t	Ⓐ		Ⓐ	⑥t	†		①g	②–⑤w	†	⑥t		⑤	⑤	†		⚒				Ⓑh	
0	**Rouen Rive Droite** d.	0610	0704	0710	...	1004	1004	1004	...	1204	1202	1204	1304	...	1504	1604	1604	...	1704	...	1804	...	1904	...
23	Elbeuf-St Aubin d.	0625	0720	0725	...	1020	1020	1020	...	1220	1218	1220	1320	...	1520	1620	1620	...	1720	...	1820	...	1920	...
73	Serquigny d.	0654	|	|	...	|	1048	|	...	1248	1251	1248	1348	...	|	1648	1648	...	1745	...	1853	...	|	...
83	Bernay ▷ d.	0701	0751	0757	...	1052	1055	1052	...	1255	1259	1255	1355	...	1551	1655	1655	...	1752	...	1900	...	1952	...
114	Lisieux ▷ d.	0718	0807	0813	...	1108	1112	1107	...	1312	1319	1312	1412	...	1607	1712	1712	...	1809	...	1917	...	2008	...
139	Mézidon **271** ▷ d.	0733	0822	0828	...	1122	1126	1122	...	1326	1336	1326	1426	...	1622	1726	1726	...	1824	...	1932	...	2022	...
162	**Caen 271** ▷ a.	0748	0836	0842	...	1136	1140	1136	...	1340	1352	1340	1440	...	1636	1740	1740	...	1838	...	1946	...	2036	...

	Ⓐ		⑥t	Ⓐ				①–④m	⑤	Ⓒ		Ⓐ	Ⓒ		Ⓐ	Ⓒ		Ⓐ		⑤	⑥S	†		
Caen 271 ▷ d.	0555	...	0717	0720	...	1020	...	1205	1215	1215	...	1715	1722	...	1813	1817	...	1915	...	2003	2028	2028	...	...
Mézidon **271** ▷ d.	0609	...	0732	0735	...	1035	...	1221	1229	1230	...	1729	1736	...	1827	1832	...	1929	...	2017	2042	2042	...	...
Lisieux ▷ d.	0623	...	0746	0749	...	1049	...	1238	1243	1246	...	1743	1750	...	1841	1846	...	1943	...	2031	2056	2056	...	...
Bernay ▷ d.	0640	...	0803	0806	...	1107	...	1258	1300	1303	...	1800	1807	...	1857	1903	...	2000	...	2047	2113	2114	...	...
Serquigny d.	0648	...	0811	0814	...	|	...	1307	1307	1311	...	|	|	...	1905	1911	...	|	...	|	|	|	...	...
Elbeuf-St Aubin d.	0721	...	0839	0839	...	1139	...	1339	1339	1339	...	1832	1839	...	1933	1939	...	2032	...	2118	2145	2145	...	...
Rouen Rive Droite a.	0736	...	0855	0855	...	1155	...	1355	1355	1355	...	1848	1855	...	1948	1955	...	2048	...	2134	2200	2200	...	...

S – ⑥ Apr. 4 - Sept. 26 (not Aug. 15).
g – Also June 2, July 15; not June 1, July 13.
h – Also Aug. 15.

m – Not June 1, July 14, Nov. 11.
t – Not Aug. 15.
w – Also July 13; not June 2, July 14, 15, Nov. 11.

▷ – See also Table **275**.

PARIS - CHARTRES - LE MANS — 278

For TGV trains Paris - Le Mans see Table 280

km		Ⓐ	Ⓐ	⚒	⚒	⚒	Ⓐb	c		d	k			Ⓐ	⚒	†	Ⓐ					Ⓐ	Ⓐ		
0	**Paris Montparnasse 274** d.	...	0534	0619	0649	0719	0749	0819	...	0934	1034	...	1134	1204	1234	1234	1304	1334	...	1434	1534	1604	1625	1634	...
17	Versailles Chantiers **274** d.	...	0547	0632	0702	0732	0802	0832	...	0947	1047	...	1147	1217	1247	1247	1317	1347	...	1447	1547	1617	1639	1647	...
48	Rambouillet d.	...	|	0649	|	0754	|	0853	...	1004	1104	...	1204	|	1304	1304	|	1404	...	1504	1604	1634	|	1704	...
88	**Chartres** d.	0610	0644	0727	0741	0832	0857	0920	...	1042	1134	...	1244	1312	1334	1334	1414	1442	...	1534	1644	1712	1720	1744	...
149	Nogent le Rotrou d.	0657	0731	...	0816	...	...	0956	...	...	1208	...	1329	...	1411	1410	1459	...	...	1608	1730	...	1758	1830	...
211	**Le Mans** a.	0745	...	...	0849	...	...	1035	...	...	1246	...	...	...	1447	...	...	...	...	1650	1815	...	1839	1915	...

	Ⓐ	Ⓐ	Ⓒ	Ⓐ		Ⓐ		Ⓐ	Ⓐ	Ⓐ	Ⓐ	Ⓒ	Ⓐ	Ⓐ			Ⓐ			Ⓑ	▽		△		
Paris Montparnasse 274 d.	1704	1719	1719	1728	1734	1749	...	1804	1819	1825	1834	1834	1849	1904	...	1934	2004	2034	...	2134	2234	...	0034	...	...
Versailles Chantiers **274** d.	1717	1732	1732	1742	1747	1802	...	1817	1832	1839	1847	1847	1902	1917	...	1947	2017	2047	...	2147	2247	...	0047	...	...
Rambouillet d.	1734	1749	|	|	1804	1819	...	1834	1849	|	1904	1904	1919	1934	...	2004	2034	2104	...	2204	2304	...	0104	...	...
Chartres d.	1812	1819	1812	1824	1842	1849	...	1912	1919	1924	1944	1944	1949	2012	...	2034	2112	2142	...	2234	2342	...	0142	...	...
Nogent le Rotrou d.	...	...	1854	1904	...	1942	...	...	...	2003	2036	2037	...	...	...	2109	...	...	...	2311	...	...	...	...	...
Le Mans a.	...	...	1934	1945	...	...	...	...	...	2043	...	2120	...	...	...	2148z	...	...	...	2347	...	...	...	...	...

	Ⓐ	⑥t	Ⓐ	Ⓐ	⑥t	Ⓐ	Ⓒ	Ⓐ	Ⓐ	⑥t	Ⓐ	Ⓐ	Ⓐ	Ⓒ	Ⓐ	⑥t	Ⓐ	†	⚒		Ⓐ	Ⓒ			y
Le Mans d.	...	...	0400	...	...	...	...	...	0535	...	...	...	...	...	...	...	...	...	0656	...	0748	...	...	0920	...
Nogent le Rotrou d.	...	...	0436	...	...	...	...	0551	0614	...	...	...	0644	0649	0655	...	...	...	0756	...	0837	0837	...	0959	...
Chartres d.	0427	0457	0511	0534	0557	0604	0627	0630	0657	0657	0700	0727	0734	0739	0749	0757	0810	0835	0835	...	0927	0927	...	1035	1127
Rambouillet d.	|	0536	0536	0614	0636	0644	0706	0659	|	0736	0729	|	0759	0806	0829	0836	0839	0906	0906	...	1006	1006	...	1106	1206
Versailles Chantiers **274** d.	0523	0553	0553	0633	0653	0703	0723	0718	0736	0753	0748	0806	0818	0823	0848	0853	0903	0923	0923	...	1023	1023	...	1123	1223
Paris Montparnasse 274 a.	0534	0604	0604	0645	0704	0715	0734	0730	0750	0804	0800	0820	0830	0835	0900	0904	0915	0934	0936	...	1035	1035	...	1134	1234

	x	Ⓐy	y	†	⚒			Ⓐ		Ⓐ		Ⓐ	Ⓐ			Ⓐ	Ⓒ			Ⓑ		Ⓐ§	†		
Le Mans d.	1117	...	...	1259	1324	...	...	...	1524	...	...	...	1645	1730	...	1745	...	...	1930	...	...	...	2124	...	...
Nogent le Rotrou d.	1158	...	...	1346	1359	...	...	...	1559	...	1637	...	1737	1805	...	1837	1837	...	2005	...	...	...	2159	...	...
Chartres d.	1235	1257	1327	1435	1435	...	1527	1557	1635	1657	1727	1757	1827	1841	...	1927	1927	...	2041	2127	...	2235	2235	...	...
Rambouillet d.	1306	|	1406	1506	1506	...	1606	|	1706	|	1806	|	|	1906	...	2006	2006	...	2106	2206	...	2306	2306	...	...
Versailles Chantiers **274** d.	1323	1353	1423	1523	1523	...	1623	1653	1723	1753	1823	1853	1918	1923	...	2023	2023	...	2123	2223	...	2323	2323	...	...
Paris Montparnasse 274 a.	1334	1404	1434	1534	1534	...	1634	1704	1734	1804	1834	1904	1930	1934	...	2035	2034	...	2134	2234	...	2334	2334	...	...

b – Runs 10 - 15 minutes later Oct. 12 - 23.
c – Will not run Chartres - Le Mans on ①–⑤ Oct. 12 - 23.
d – On Oct. 12 - 23 runs 12 minutes earlier.
k – Will not run Nogent le Rotrou - Le Mans on Ⓐ Aug. 31 - Sept. 11 or Chartres - Le Mans on Ⓐ Oct. 12 - Nov. 6. On Ⓐ Oct. 12 - 23 depart Paris (for Chartres) at 1019.

t – Not Aug. 15.
x – Will not run Chartres - Nogent le Rotrou on Ⓐ Aug. 31 - Sept. 11. Subject to alteration on Ⓐ Oct. 26 - Nov. 6.
y – Subject to alteration on Ⓐ Oct. 26 - Nov. 6.
z – ⑤–⑦ and holidays.

△ – Runs up to 9 minutes earlier Sept. 22 - Nov. 7. Subject to alteration on ②–⑥ Sept. 29 - Oct. 10.
▽ – Subject to alteration on Sept. 7 - 10, 14 - 18.
§ – Subject to alteration on Sept. 7 - 10, 14 - 18, 28 - 30, Oct. 1, 2, 5 - 9.

280 PARIS - LE MANS - RENNES and NANTES

TGV Atlantique

Service to July 4 / from Aug. 31. *For service July 5 - Aug. 30 see page 539*

TGV trains convey 🍸. Many trains continue to destinations in Tables **281**, **284**, **285**, **288** and **293**. For other trains Massy - Nantes via St Pierre des Corps see Table **335**.

km				TGV 8801	TGV 8001	TGV 8903	TGV 8603*	TGV 8805		TGV 8081	TGV 8807	TGV 8009*	TGV 8909	TGV 8611	TGV 5486	TGV 8913	TGV 8715			TGV 8921*	TGV 8619	TGV 8617	TGV 5214	TGV 5213
		⚒	Ⓐ	Ⓐ	Ⓐ	Ⓐ	①–⑥	①–⑥ n	Ⓐ	Ⓐ	①–⑥ n				☆			†		①–⑥ n	Ⓒ	Ⓐ		
	Lille Europe **11** d.	...	...	...	...	...	...	...	...	...	...	...	...	...	...	...	...	...	...	...	...	...	0846	0846
	Charles de Gaulle ✈ d.	...	...	...	...	...	...	...	...	...	...	...	...	...	...	...	...	...	...	...	...	...	1027	1027
	Marne la Vallée - Chessy § d.	...	...	...	...	...	...	...	...	...	...	...	...	...	0900	...	...	...	...	...	...	...	1042	1042
0	**Paris Montparnasse** d.	...	...	0630	0635	0700	0705	0730	...	0735	0800	0805	0900	0905	|	1000	1005	...	...	1100	1105	1105	|	|
14	Massy TGV d.	...	...	|	|	|	|	0741	...	0747	|	|	|	|	0933	|	|	...	...	|	|	|	1117	1117
202	**Le Mans** d.	0625r	0650	0728	0733	|	|	0832	0840	|	|	0902	|	|	1023	1057	|	1104	1104	|	1202	1202	1209	1213
292	Laval d.	0728	|	|	0815	|	|	|	|	|	|	0943	|	|	|	|	|	1150	|	|	1244	1244	|	|
327	Vitré d.	0755	|	|	|	|	|	|	|	|	|	|	|	|	|	|	|	1214	|	|	|	1304	|	|
365	**Rennes** a.	0815	|	|	0852	|	0908	|	|	0949	|	1020	|	1108	|	|	1208	1245	|	|	1321	1323	1327	|
251	Sablé d.	...	0713	|	...	|	...	0852	0859	...	|	...	|	...	|	|	...	...	1124	|	...	...	...	|
299	Angers St Laud **289** d.	...	0738	0806	...	|	...	0916	0922	...	0933	...	1033	...	1102	1137	...	...	1145	|	...	...	...	1253
387	**Nantes 289** a.	...	0818	0842	...	0901	...	0952	1002	...	1008	...	1108	...	1140	1213	...	...	1231	1259	...	...	...	1333

	TGV 5350	TGV 5360	TGV 5365	TGV 8823	TGV 5470	TGV 8717	TGV 8929	TGV 8621	TGV 5224	TGV 5227	TGV 8933*	TGV 8623*	TGV 8625	TGV 8835		TGV 8837*	TGV 8729*	TGV 5375	TGV 5371	TGV 8843	TGV 8033*	TGV 8031		TGV 5232	TGV 5216
	Ⓑ ♠	⑥ ♣	⑥ ♣	▽	☆		⑤	⑤				Ⓐ	Ⓒ	⑤	⑤			⑦ ♠e	⑦ ♠e	Ⓑ	Ⓑ	⑥	⚒	①–⑥ n	⑦ e
Lille Europe **11** d.	...	...	...	...	...	...	...	...	1210	1210	...	...	...	...	...	...	...	...	...	...	...	...	...	1447	1447
Charles de Gaulle ✈ d.	...	...	...	...	...	...	...	...	1316	1316	...	...	...	...	...	...	...	...	...	...	...	...	...	1542	1542
Marne la Vallée - Chessy § d.	...	...	...	...	1122	...	...	...	1329	1329	...	...	...	...	...	...	...	...	...	...	...	...	...	1557	1557
Paris Montparnasse d.	...	...	...	1200	|	1205	1300	1305	|	|	1400	1405	1405	1430	...	1500	1505	...	...	1600	1605	1605	...	|	|
Massy TGV d.	1131	1131	1131	|	1200	|	|	|	1401	1401	|	|	|	|	...	|	|	1532	1532	|	|	|	...	1631	1631
Le Mans d.	1222	1222	1225	|	1252	1302	|	1402	1453	1502	1457	|	|	1524	1535	|	|	1622	1626	|	|	1702	1706	1722	|
Laval d.	|	|	|	|	1335	|	|	|	|	|	|	1539	1539	...	|	|	|	|	1709	|	|	1743	|	|	|
Vitré d.	|	|	|	|	|	|	|	|	|	|	|	|	1558	...	|	|	|	|	|	|	|	|	|	|	◐
Rennes a.	1340	1333	|	|	1410	1413	|	1515	1607	|	|	1615	1619	...	|	|	1708	|	1743	|	1808	1820	|	1836	|
Sablé d.	...	...	|	1315	...	...	|	...	...	|	|	...	...	...	1555	|	...	|	...	|	...	...	1726	...	|
Angers St Laud **289** d.	...	...	1305	1339	...	...	1435	...	...	1542	1538	...	...	...	1618	1632	...	1702	...	1733	...	...	1749	...	1815
Nantes 289 a.	...	...	1342	1414	...	...	1511	...	...	1617	1612	...	...	...	1657	1707	...	1736	...	1808	...	...	1830	...	1854

	TGV 8737*			TGV 8845	TGV 8847	TGV 8747*		TGV 8743	TGV 8953*	TGV 8645	TGV 8649*	TGV 8957	TGV 8955	TGV 8861	TGV 8655*	TGV 8659	TGV 8653	TGV 8095	TGV 8965	TGV 8873	TGV 8867	TGV 8869	TGV 8871	TGV 5373	TGV 5363
	Ⓐ	Ⓐ	†	Ⓐ	Ⓐ	①–⑥ n	Ⓐ	⑦ e		①–④ n	⑤	Ⓒ	Ⓐ	Ⓐ	Ⓐ	⑦ e	⑥	Ⓐ	①–⑥ n	Ⓒ	①–④ n	⑤	Ⓐ	①–⑥ ♠n	①–⑥ ♠n
Lille Europe **11** d.	...	...	...	...	...	...	...	...	...	...	...	...	...	...	...	...	...	...	...	...	...	...	...	...	...
Charles de Gaulle ✈ d.	...	...	...	...	...	...	...	...	...	...	...	...	...	...	...	...	...	...	...	...	...	...	...	...	...
Marne la Vallée - Chessy § d.	...	...	...	...	...	...	...	...	...	...	...	...	...	...	...	...	...	...	...	...	...	...	...	...	...
Paris Montparnasse d.	1635	...	...	1650	1700	1705	...	1705	1730	1735	1735	1750	1750	1800	1805	1805	1805	1835	1830	1845	1845	1845	1900	...	...
Massy TGV d.	|	...	...	|	|	|	...	|	|	|	|	|	|	|	|	|	|	|	|	|	|	|	|	1901	1901
Le Mans d.	1732	1738	1745	1747	|	|	1800	1801	|	|	1832	1847	1847	|	|	1902	1902	|	|	1942	1942	1942	|	1952	1957
Laval d.	1813	1823	|	|	|	|	|	1843	|	1909	1913	|	|	|	|	|	1943	2012	|	|	|	|	|	2034	|
Vitré d.	|	1842	|	|	|	|	|	|	|	|	|	|	|	|	|	|	2003	2031	|	|	|	|	|	|	|
Rennes a.	1850	1904	|	|	|	1908	|	1920	|	1945	1950	|	|	|	2008	2015	2024	2049	|	|	|	|	|	2110	|
Sablé d.	...	...	1805	|	|	...	1820	...	|	...	...	|	|	|	...	...	...	...	|	2002	2002	2002	|	...	|
Angers St Laud **289** d.	...	...	1828	1826	1832	...	1843	...	|	...	...	1927	1931	|	...	...	...	...	|	2025	2031	2031	|	...	2038
Nantes 289 a.	...	...	1908	1906	1910	...	1923	...	1930	...	...	2003	2008	2002	...	...	...	...	2033	2102	2108	2112	2102	...	2116

	TGV 8665	TGV 8669	TGV 5236*		TGV 5231	TGV 8761*	TGV 8879*	TGV 8071*	TGV 5387	TGV 8777	TGV 8887*	TGV 5488	TGV 8077	TGV 8679	TGV 8069	TGV 5234	TGV 5248	TGV 5245	TGV 5390	TGV 5210	TGV 5247	TGV 8893*	TGV 8041*	TGV 8045*	
	①–⑥	⑦ e	Ⓑ	Ⓑ	Ⓑ	①–⑥ n	Ⓑ		①–④ ♣n	⑤		☆	①–④ n	⑤	⑦ e	①–④ n	⑥	⑥	⑤⑦ ♣e	⑤⑦ e	⑦ e	Ⓑ d	⑤ △	⑦ e	
Lille Europe **11** d.	...	...	1729	...	1729	...	...	...	...	...	...	...	...	...	...	1939	1939	1939	...	2014	2014	...	...	...	...
Charles de Gaulle ✈ d.	...	...	1824	...	1824	...	...	...	...	...	...	...	...	...	...	2034	2034	2034	...	2109	2109	...	...	...	...
Marne la Vallée - Chessy § d.	...	...	1840	...	1840	...	...	...	...	...	...	2024	...	...	...	2050	2050	2050	...	2125	2125	...	...	...	...
Paris Montparnasse d.	1905	1905	|	...	|	1935	2000	2005	...	2035	2100	|	2105	2105	2105	|	|	|	...	|	|	2200	2205	2205	...
Massy TGV d.	|	|	1917	...	1921	|	|	|	2032	|	|	2101	|	|	|	2131	2131	2131	2137	2201	2201	|	|	|	...
Le Mans d.	2002	|	2008	2020	|	|	|	2102	2122	2132	|	2157	|	2202	2202	2222	2223	2226	2227	2253	2258	2257	|	|	...
Laval d.	|	2039	2048	|	|	|	|	2143	|	|	|	|	|	|	2244	|	2304	|	|	|	|	|	2340	2343	...
Vitré d.	|	2058	|	|	◐	|	|	|	|	|	|	|	|	2258	|	|	|	|	|	|	|	|	|	|	...
Rennes a.	2115	2119	2125	|	|	2138	|	2220	2234	2243	|	|	2308	2317	2323	|	2340	|	2339	|	0010	|	0016	0019	...
Sablé d.	...	...	...	2040	|	...	|	...	...	...	|	|	...	...	...	|	...	|	...	|	...	|	...	...	...
Angers St Laud **289** d.	...	...	...	2103	2108	...	2133	...	...	...	2231	2239	...	...	...	2304	...	2305	...	2331	...	2337	...	...	...
Nantes 289 a.	...	...	...	2143	2147	...	2208	...	...	...	2308	2314	...	...	...	2338	...	2340	...	0007	...	0016	...	...	...

	TGV 8800	TGV 8802	TGV 8002	TGV 8804	TGV 8690	TGV 5252	TGV 5254	TGV 8904*	TGV 8706*	TGV 8808	TGV 8806		TGV 8910	TGV 8608	TGV 8610		TGV 8820	TGV 8812	TGV 8712	TGV 5312		TGV 8814	TGV 8012	TGV 8014	TGV 8816
	① g	Ⓐ ⊕	Ⓐ	Ⓐ	Ⓐ	①–⑥ n	①–⑥ n	Ⓐ	Ⓐ	Ⓐ	⑥	Ⓐ	Ⓐ	⑥ u	Ⓐ	Ⓐ	Ⓐ	Ⓒ	Ⓐ	♠	Ⓐ	Ⓐ	Ⓐ	Ⓒ	Ⓐ
Nantes 289 d.	0500	0530	...	0600	...	0604	...	0630	...	...	0634	0634	0700	...	...	...	0730	0730	...	0735	0739	0800	...	...	0830
Angers St Laud **289** d.	0542	0608	...	0639	...	0643	...	|	...	0715	0715	0719	|	...	...	...	0809	0809	...	0813	0820	|	...	...	0907
Sablé d.	|	0630	...	|	...	|	...	|	...	|	|	0744	|	...	...	...	|	|	...	|	0841	|	...	...	|
Rennes d.	|	|	0535	|	0605	|	0610	|	0635	|	|	|	|	0705	0705	0710	|	|	0735	|	|	|	0805	0805	|
Vitré d.	|	|	0556	|	|	|	|	|	|	|	|	|	|	|	|	0728	|	|	|	|	|	|	|	|	|
Laval d.	|	|	0616	|	0639	|	|	|	|	|	|	|	|	|	|	0748	|	|	|	|	|	|	0841	0841	|
Le Mans d.	0623	0652	0703	|	|	0731	0731	|	|	0759	0759	0805	|	|	0819	0835	|	0849	0849	0854	0903	|	0925	0929	|
Massy TGV a.	|	|	|	|	|	0818	0818	|	|	|	|	...	|	|	|	...	|	|	|	0943	...	|	|	|	|
Paris Montparnasse a.	0720	0750	0800	0810	0820	|	|	0835	0840	0855	0855	...	0905	0910	0915	...	0940	0945	0945	...	...	1005	1020	1025	1040
Marne la Vallée - Chessy § a.	...	...	...	...	...	0900	0900	...	...	...	...	...	...	...	...	...	...	...	...	...	...	...	...	...	...
Charles de Gaulle ✈ a.	...	...	...	...	...	0914	0914	...	...	...	...	...	...	...	...	...	...	...	...	...	...	...	...	...	...
Lille Europe **11** a.	...	...	...	...	...	1008	1008	...	...	...	...	...	...	...	...	...	...	...	...	...	...	...	...	...	...

	TGV 5478	TGV 8618*	TGV 8016	TGV 8818	TGV 5318	TGV 5272	TGV 5270	TGV 8922	TGV 8620*	TGV 8028		TGV 8828	TGV 8022	TGV 8926	TGV 5324	TGV 5322	TGV 8932	TGV 8834	TGV 8084	TGV 8730*	TGV 8836	TGV 5326	TGV 5278	TGV 5280	TGV 8844
	☆	①–⑥ n	⑦ q		♠					① g		Ⓐ	Ⓐ	⑥	H ♣	♠	⑦ e	Ⓐ				⑤⑥ ♠			⑤
Nantes 289 d.	0834	...	...	0900	...	...	0910	1100	...	...	1144	1200	...	1200	...	1252	1300	1300	...	...	1400	...	1435	...	...
Angers St Laud **289** d.	0913	...	...	0937	...	...	0948	1138	...	...	1227	1237	...	1238	...	1337	|	|	...	...	1438	...	1513	...	...
Sablé d.	|	...	...	|	...	...	|	|	...	...	1248	|	...	|	...	|	|	|	...	...	|	...	|	...	...
Rennes d.	|	0905	0905	|	0910	0915	|	|	1105	1125	|	|	1205	|	1230	|	|	|	1305	1405	|	1414	|	1435	...
Vitré d.	|	|	|	|	|	|	|	|	|	|	|	|	|	|	|	◐	|	|	|	|	|	|	|	|	...
Laval d.	|	|	|	|	0946	0952	|	|	1142	|	|	|	|	|	|	|	|	|	1340	|	|	|	|	|	...
Le Mans d.	0956	|	|	1019	1029	1041	1041	|	1228	|	1309	|	1319	1319	1351	|	|	1413	|	|	1519	1529	1558	1558	1609
Massy TGV a.	1047	|	|	|	1118	1133	1133	|	|	|	...	|	|	|	1438	1518	|	|	|	|	|	1618	1647	1647	|
Paris Montparnasse a.	|	1110	1110	1115	...	|	|	1310	1325	1330	...	1410	1415	1415	...	...	1505	1510	1515	1610	1615	...	|	|	1705
Marne la Vallée - Chessy § a.	1123	...	...	...	...	1223	1223	...	...	...	...	...	...	...	...	...	...	...	...	...	...	...	1728	1728	...
Charles de Gaulle ✈ a.	...	...	...	...	...	1237	1237	...	...	...	...	...	...	...	...	...	...	...	...	...	...	...	1741	1741	...
Lille Europe **11** a.	...	...	...	...	...	1341	1341	...	...	...	...	...	...	...	...	...	...	...	...	...	...	...	1838z	1838z	...

D – ⑤ to June 26.
E – ⑦ to June 28.
H – ①②③④⑦ only.
d – Runs up to 30 minutes earlier on Ⓐ June 2 - 26, Aug. 31, Sept. 1 - 3, Oct. 5 - Dec. 4.

e – Also June 1.
g – Also June 2; not June 1.
n – Not June 1.
q – Also June 1, July 14; not July 12.
r – 0637 on ⑥.
u – Not June 20.

x – Arrive Paris up to 80 mins later ①–④ to June 25, also ①–④ Oct. 5 - Dec. 3.
y – 2310 to June 25; 2320 Oct. 5 - Dec. 3.
z – Lille **Flandres**.

TGV – Ⓡ, supplement payable, 🍸.

NOTES CONTINUED ON NEXT PAGE →

NANTES and RENNES - LE MANS - PARIS 280

Service to July 4/from Aug. 31. *For service July 5 - Aug. 30 see page 540*

	TGV 8942	TGV 8040 ⑤⑦	TGV 8042 ①–④ n	TGV 5346 ①–④ ♠n	TGV 5480 ☆	Ⓑ	⑥	TGV 8848 Ⓑ	TGV 8646	TGV 8752	TGV 8950	TGV 5334 ⑦ ♣e	TGV 5460 ☆	†	TGV 8956* Ⓐ	TGV 8090 ⑥	Ⓐ	TGV 8088 Ⓑ	TGV 8660 Ⓑ	TGV 8862 ①–④ n	TGV 8862 ⑤	TGV 8860 Ⓒ	TGV 8864* Ⓐ	TGV 8762	TGV 8864 ⑦ e
Nantes 289 d.	1500	...	...	...	1520	1527	1527	1600	...	...	1700	1708	...	1724	1730	...	1734	...	...	1800	1800	1800	1830	...	1830
Angers St Laud **289** d.	1537	...	...	...	1600	1609	1610	1637	...	...	1739	1744	...	1806	|	...	1816	...	...	1838	1838	1838	|	...	|
Sablé d.	|	...	...	...	|	1631	1633	|	...	...	|	|	...	1827	|	...	1838	...	...	1901	1901	1858	|	...	|
Rennes d.	|	1505	1505	1514	|	|	|	|	1605	1705	|	|	1710	|	|	1735	|	1735	1805	|	|	|	|	1835	|
Vitré d.	|	|	|	|	|	|	|	|	|	|	|	|	|	|	|	|	|	1757	|	|	|	|	|	|	|
Laval d.	|	|	|	|	|	|	|	|	1641	|	|	|	1746	|	|	1812	|	1819	|	|	|	|	|	|	|
Le Mans d.	|	|	1619	1630	1640	1652	1703	|	1725	|	1819	1825	1835	1848	|	1859	1859	1904	|	|	|	|	|	|	1948
Massy TGV a.	|	|	|	1717	1727	...	...	|	|	|	|	1912	1922	...	|	|	...	|	|	|	|	|	|	|	|
Paris Montparnasse a.	1710	1715	1715	...	|	...	...	1810	1820	1910	1915	...	|	...	1935	1955	...	2000	2010	2015	2020	2020	2035	2040	2045
Marne la Vallée - Chessy § a.	...	...	...	...	1803	...	...	...	...	...	...	...	2003	...	...	...	...	...	...	...	...	...	...	...	...
Charles de Gaulle ✈ a.	...	...	...	...	...	...	...	...	...	...	...	...	...	...	...	...	...	...	...	...	...	...	...	...	...
Lille Europe **11** a.	...	...	...	...	...	...	...	...	...	...	...	...	...	...	...	...	...	...	...	...	...	...	...	...	...

	TGV 5338 ⑦ ♣e	TGV 5290	TGV 5288	TGV 8668*	TGV 8866*	TGV 5344 ⑤ ♣	TGV 5342 ⑤ ♣	TGV 8986 ⑦ e	TGV 8774* ⑦ e	TGV 8980*	TGV 8780 ①–④ n	TGV 8782 ⑤	TGV 8096 Ⓒ	†	TGV 5294 ⑦ e	TGV 8688 ⑦ e	TGV 8894 ①–④ n	TGV 8682* Ⓑ	TGV 8890* ⑤	TGV 8896 ⑦ e	TGV 8076 ⑤ D‡	TGV 8996 ⑦ e	TGV 8686 ⑦ e	TGV 8898 ⑦ E	TGV 8078 ⑦ E
Nantes 289 d.	...	...	1835	...	1900	...	1904	1930	...	2000	...	...	...	1934	...	...	2045	...	2100	2100	...	2200	...	2230	...
Angers St Laud **289** d.	...	...	1912	...	1939	...	1944	|	...	2039	...	...	...	2048	...	...	2122	...	2139	2143	...	|	...	2308	...
Sablé d.	...	...	|	...	|	...	|	|	...	|	...	...	...	2111	...	...	|	...	|	|	...	|	...	|	...
Rennes d.	1827	1839	|	1905	|	1909	|	|	1935	|	2005	2005	2005	|	2020	2035	|	2105	|	|	2130	|	2205	|	2245
Vitré d.	|	|	|	|	|	|	|	|	|	|	|	|	2027	|	|	|	|	|	|	|	|	|	|	|	|
Laval d.	|	|	|	|	|	|	|	|	|	|	2041	2044	2047	|	|	|	|	|	|	|	2204	|	|	|	2319
Le Mans d.	1952	2000	2000	|	2019	2030	2030	|	|	|	|	2129	2132	2135	2138	|	|	|	2219	2225	|	|	|	|	|
Massy TGV a.	2042	2048	2048	|	|	2118	2118	|	|	|	|	|	|	...	2227	|	|	|	|	|	|	|	|	|	|
Paris Montparnasse a.	...	|	|	2110	2115	...	...	2135	2140	2210x	2215	2225	2230	...	|	2240	2255y	2310	2315	2325	0001	0005	0010	0040	0055
Marne la Vallée - Chessy § a.	...	2129	2129	...	...	...	...	...	...	...	...	...	...	...	2301	...	...	...	...	...	...	...	...	...	...
Charles de Gaulle ✈ a.	...	2146	2146	...	...	...	...	...	...	...	...	...	...	...	2316	...	...	...	...	...	...	...	...	...	...
Lille Europe **11** a.	...	2318	2318	...	...	...	...	...	...	...	...	...	...	...	0010	...	...	...	...	...	...	...	...	...	...

NOTES - CONTINUED FROM PREVIOUS PAGE

♣ – From/to Lyon (Table **335**).
♠ – From/to Lyon and Marseille (Table **335**).
◐ – Via St Pierre des Corps (Table **335**).
☆ – From/to Strasbourg (Table **391**).
△ – Runs 20 minutes earlier on ⑤ to June 21, also ⑤ Oct. 9 - Dec. 4.
▽ – Depart 5 minutes earlier on ① Oct. 12 - Nov. 2.
⊕ – Depart 0524 on Sept. 1 - 4.
§ – Station for Disneyland Paris.
‡ – On July 3 runs 20 minutes earlier.

Engineering work - June 13/14
Certain services are subject to alteration with earlier departures (on June 14 applies only until 0900 hrs).

* – **The train number shown is altered as below:**
5236 runs as 5238 on ⑤.
8009 runs as 8711 on Ⓒ.
8033 runs as 8633 on ⑤⑦.
8041 runs as 8073 from Sept. 4.
8045 runs as 8075 from Sept. 6.
8071 runs as 8773 on ⑦.
8603 also runs as 8705 on Ⓐ.
8618 also runs as 8718.
8620 runs as 8622 on Ⓒ. Also runs as 8722 ①–⑥, 8724 ⑦.
8623 runs as 8023 on ⑤.
8649 also runs as 8691.
8655 runs as 8657 on ⑤ (also runs as 8759 on ①–④).
8668 runs as 8670 on Ⓒ.
8682 runs as 8696/8794 on ⑦ (also as 8790 on ⑤).
8706 runs as 8704 on ①.
8729 runs as 8027 on ⑤.
8730 runs as 8734 on ⑦, also as 8634 on Ⓐ, 8636 on ⑦.
8737 runs as 8739 on ⑤.
8747 runs as 8741 on ⑥; also runs as 8643 on ①–④.
8761 runs as 8763 on ⑤.
8774 also runs as 8676.
8837 runs as 8937 on ⑥.
8864 runs as 8964 on ⑤.
8866 runs as 8966 on ⑦.
8879 runs as 8979 on ⑤.
8887 runs as 8987 on ⑤.
8890 runs as 8892 from Sept. 4.
8893 runs as 8895 on certain days.
8904 runs as 8902 on ①.
8921 runs as 8819 on ⑤, 8919 on ⑥ (arrive 1304 on ⑥).
8933 runs as 8833 on ⑤⑥.
8953 runs as 8951 on ⑤.
8956 runs as 8856 on ⑤.
8980 runs as 8880 on ⑤.

Certain trains change numbers June 27 - July 4 (this affects trains 8611, 8660, 8805, 8950)

Note - on Nov. 11 service is generally as on normal weekdays.

RENNES - ST MALO 281

Some trains 2nd class only

Service to July 4/from Aug. 31. *For service July 5 - Aug. 30 see page 540*

km	*TGV trains,* Ⓡ		TGV 8081 Ⓐ	TGV 8091 Ⓒ	TGV 8083		TGV 8089 ⑥	TGV 8095 Ⓐ	TGV 8099 ⑦ e	
	Paris Montparnasse **280** d.	...	0735	0805	1005	...	1505	1835	1905	...
0	**Rennes 272** d.	...	0952	1027	1215	...	1715	2058	2126	...
58	Dol **272** d.	...	1025	1058	|	...	|	2132	|	...
81	**St Malo** a.	...	1038	1113	1258	...	1758	2147	2210	...

TGV trains, Ⓡ	TGV 8080 Ⓐ		TGV 8084		TGV 8088 Ⓑ	TGV 8090 ⑥		TGV 8096 Ⓒ	
St Malo d.	0605	...	1213	...	1640	1640	...	1915	...
Dol **272** d.	0621	...	|	...	1656	1655	...	|	...
Rennes 272 a.	0655	...	1300	...	1730	1730	...	2000	...
Paris Montparnasse **280** a.	0915	...	1515	...	2000	1955	...	2230	...

	⚒	⚒	b	Ⓒ	Ⓐ	③⑥ h	⚒	†	⚒	⑤	Ⓒ	Ⓐ Q	Ⓐ P	Ⓐ Q	Ⓐ	†	Ⓐ	Ⓑ	⑥	Ⓐ	Ⓒ	①–④ m	⑤	†	⚒	⑤
Rennes 272 d.	0630	0730	0920	1130	1230	1300	1340	1350	1430	1530	1630	1630	1645	1700	1730	1730	1800	1830	1830	1900	1930	2000	2020	2030	2150	2253
Dol **272** d.	0709	0809	0956	1209	1310	1342	1414	1426	1506	1606	1706	1711	1729	1735	1806	1808	1844	1906	1912	1938	2006	2038	2058	2104	2228	2327
St Malo a.	0730	0825	1010	1222	1328	1400	1430	1440	1520	1620	1719	1727	1744	1750	1828	1822	1903	1922	1930	1952	2022	2051	2112	2117	2241	2341

	⚒	Ⓐ	⚒	Ⓐ	Ⓒ	Ⓐ	⚒	†	⑥	③ h	†	⚒		Ⓐ	†	⑤	Ⓒ	Ⓐ	Ⓑ	Ⓐ Q	⑥	†	Ⓐ P	Ⓐ Q		⑦
St Malo d.	0547	0620	0647	0717	0750	0750	0949	0950	1050	1220	1248	1250	1450	1547	1548	1650	1719	1720	1750	1820	1820	1830	1840	1850	1950	2048
Dol **272** d.	0601	0638	0701	0734	0805	0805	1002	1005	1108	1239	1302	1309	1504	1601	1602	1703	1732	1738	1809	1836	1838	1844	1857	1906	2003	2102
Rennes 272 a.	0641	0719	0744	0816	0841	0845	1039	1046	1148	1321	1341	1350	1538	1636	1642	1736	1808	1817	1850	1916	1918	1919	1936	1948	2038	2136

P – To July 4.
Q – From Aug. 31.
b – Runs 10 minutes later on Ⓒ.
e – Also June 1.
h – Not Nov. 11.
m – Not June 1, Nov. 11.

DOL - DINAN 282

2nd class

Service to July 4/from Aug. 31. *For service July 5 - Aug. 30 see page 540*

km		Ⓐ	⑥	Ⓐ ⊙	Ⓒ ⊙	⑥	Ⓐ	†	⑥	Ⓒ	Ⓐ	Ⓐ	†	①–④ n	⑤	†	⑤⑥
0	Dol d.	0702	0818	1032	1105	1350	1420	1433	1511	1725	1730	1814	1920	2045	2105	2110	2235
28	Dinan a.	0725	0841	1054	1128	1413	1443	1456	1542	1806	1801	1842	1943	2108	2128	2133	2258

	Ⓐ	⚒	⑥		Ⓒ	Ⓐ	⑥	⑤	①–④	⑥⑦	Ⓐ		† ⊙	⑤	①–④ n	⑥	†
Dinan d.	0630	0732	0927	...	1230	1232	1432	1617	1624	1624	1657	...	1816	1849	1910	1936	2034
Dol a.	0657	0800	0957	...	1255	1300	1455	1640	1647	1647	1720	...	1839	1912	1933	1959	2057

n – Not June 1.
⊙ – To/from St Brieuc (Table **299**).

No rail service June 9 - 19 (replacement 🚌 will operate).. Certain journeys replaced by 🚌 on Ⓐ Sept. 14 - 25.

MORLAIX - ROSCOFF 283

2nd class

Service to July 4/from Aug. 31. *For service July 5 - Aug. 30 see page 540*

km		🚌 Ⓐ	🚌 ⚒	Ⓐ △	⑥	†	⚒	†	🚌 ⑥	🚌 ①–④ b	🚌 ⑤	🚌 ①–④ n	🚌 Ⓒ	🚌 ⑤	🚌 †	🚌 ①–④ n	🚌 ⑤
0	**Morlaix** d.	0803	0929	1053	1100	1151	1305	1519	1515	1640	1705	1756	1806	1950	2010	2057	2122
28	**Roscoff** a.	0833	1004	1122	1128	1220	1334	1548	1545	1710	1735	1831	1841	2025	2040	2132	2157

	🚌 Ⓐ ⊖	🚌 ⑥	🚌 Ⓐ ⊖		⚒ ▽	🚌 †	🚌 ⚒	†	⑥	Ⓐ	🚌 ⑥	†	🚌 ①–④ n		🚌 Ⓐ	🚌 †	🚌 ⑤
Roscoff d.	0643	0830	0835	...	1133	1135	1330	1339	1437r	1528	1630	1634	1712	...	1839	1925	2030
Morlaix a.	0713	0905	0910	...	1201	1210	1405	1409	1508	1556	1705	1702	1742	...	1914	2000	2105

b – Schooldays only.
n – Not June 1, Nov. 11.
r – 1440 from Aug. 31.
△ – Runs 7 minutes later on Ⓐ to July 4. By 🚌 Aug. 31 - Sept. 11.
▽ – By 🚌 Aug. 31 - Sept. 25.
⊖ – Subject to confirmation from Aug. 31.

All services call at St Pol de Léon (*21 km*/15 mins from Morlaix). 🚌 call at Roscoff port on days of sailings.

284 RENNES - ST BRIEUC - MORLAIX - BREST

Service to July 4 / from Aug. 31. *For service July 5 - Aug. 30 see page 541*

km	TGV trains convey 🍸	Ⓐ	Ⓐ	Ⓐ	⑥ t	Ⓐ u	Ⓐ	⑥ x	55803 Ⓐ	Ⓐ	⑥	TGV 8603 ①-⑥ n	⚒	Ⓐ ▽	†	⑥	Ⓐ E	TGV 8613 C	TGV 8693 C	⚒ C	TGV 8611 B△	⚒ B§	Ⓑ B§	⑥ B	③ w
	Paris ⊡ **280** d.	...	...	...	...	...	...	...	...	...	...	0705	...	...	...	...	...	0905	0905	...	0905	...	...	...	...
0	**Rennes** d.	...	...	0605	...	...	0620	0640	0700	0720	0830	0911	...	...	1006	1035	1032	1111	1119	...	1111	...	...	...	...
80	Lamballe **299** d.	...	...	0647	...	0704	0724	0745	|	0809	0909	|	...	...	1043	1111	1112	|	1159	...	1152	...	...	...	...
101	**St Brieuc 299** d.	...	...	0701	0708	0723	0737	0759	0748	0823	0922	1000	...	...	1055	1124	1130	|	1212	...	1205	...	...	1215	1235
132	Guingamp d.	...	...	0719	0724	0746	...	...	|	...	0940	1017	1026	...	1113	1142	...	|	1230	...	1223	...	1230	1235	1302
158	Plouaret-Trégor d.	...	...	0734	0738	0802	...	...	|	...	0954	|	1043	...	1127	1156	...	|	1246	...	|	...	1246	1252	1322
175	Lannion a.	...	...	|	|	0818	...	...	|	...	|	|	1059	...	*1151*	*1230*	...	|	1302	...	|	...	1303	1309	1339
189	Morlaix d.	0616	0637	0759	0800	...	...	...	0831	...	1012	1046	...	1055	1145	1214	...	1235	...	1245	1252	1301	...	...	...
215	Landivisiau d.	0632	0700	0814	0815	...	...	...	|	...	1027	|	...	1111	1159	1229	...	|	...	1308	|	1324	...	...	...
230	Landerneau **286** d.	0643	0715	0830	0828	...	...	...	|	...	1036	|	...	1121	1209	1238	...	|	...	1321	|	1337	...	...	...
248	**Brest 286** a.	0657	0732	0842	0840	...	...	...	0902	...	1048	1120	...	1134	1220	1250	...	1308	...	1338	1325	1354	...	...	...

	⑥	TGV 8619 Ⓒ	TGV 8617 Ⓐ		TGV 8627 ①-④ n	⑤	⑥⑦	Ⓐ	①-④ m	TGV 8621 ⑤	⑤	①-④ m	⑦	⑤	TGV 8623 ①-④ n	TGV 8625 ⑥⑦		⑥	①-④ m	⑤	Ⓐ F	†	Ⓐ	Ⓐ	TGV 8633 ⑤⑦
Paris ⊡ **280** d.	...	1105	1105	...	1205	...	...	...	...	1305	...	...	...	...	1405	1405	...	...	...	...	...	...	...	...	1605
Rennes d.	1236	1324	1326	1333	1420	1426	1426	...	...	1518	...	...	...	1603	1618	1622	...	...	...	1650	1700	1723	1746	...	1812
Lamballe **299** d.	1312	|	|	1435	|	1501	1502	...	...	1559	...	...	...	1639	|	1703	...	...	1713	1729	1801	1759	1821	...	|
St Brieuc 299 d.	1325	1413	1417	1450	1511	1514	1514	...	...	1612	...	...	...	1652	1707	1716	...	1732	1735	1742	1815	1812	1834	...	1900
Guingamp d.	1344	1430	1434	...	1530	1532	1532	...	...	1629	...	...	...	1710	1724	1734	...	1800	1801	1800	...	1830	1852	...	1918
Plouaret-Trégor d.	1359	1446	1449	...	|	1546	1546	...	1637	|	...	...	1703	1724	|	|	...	1821	1820	1816	...	1844	1907	1931	|
Lannion a.	|	*1507*	*1511*	...	|	*1615*r	|	...	1654	|	...	...	1720	*1746*	|	|	...	1837	1837	*1842*	...	*1917*	|	1948	|
Morlaix d.	1418	1505	1507	...	1600	1604	1604	1630	...	1658	1705	1722	...	1742	1753	1803	1809	...	...	1836	...	1902	1924	...	1946
Landivisiau d.	1433	|	|	...	|	|	1619	1646	...	|	1727	1745	...	1757	|	|	1827	...	...	1855	...	1917	1939	...	|
Landerneau **286** d.	1442	1530	1533	...	|	1626	1628	1656	...	|	1739	1758	...	1806	|	|	1837	...	...	1906	...	1926	1949	...	2011
Brest 286 a.	1454	1542	1545	...	1630	1638	1640	1708	...	1732	1756	1815	...	1818	1827	1838	1853	...	...	1918	...	1938	2000	...	2023

	55845 ①-④ m	†	⑥	Ⓑ	TGV 8647 ⑤	⑤	TGV 8643 ①-④ m	①-④ m	🚌 ①-④ m	Ⓐ	†	TGV 8645 ①-④ n	TGV 8691 ⑤	TGV 8649 ⑤	TGV 8655 ①-④ n	TGV 8657 ⑤	TGV 8659 ⑦	⑦	TGV 8653 ⑥	TGV 8665 ①-⑥ n	TGV 8669 ⑦		TGV 5238 ⑤ ♥	TGV 8679 ⑤	TGV 8689 ⑦ q
Paris ⊡ **280** d.	...	...	...	...	1710	...	1705	...	...	...	...	1735	1735	1735	1805	1805	1805	...	1805	1905	1905	...	...	2105	2355
Rennes d.	1821	...	1846	1838	|	1920	1914	...	...	1925	1935	1948	2001	1953	2011	2011	2018	...	2027	2120	2122	...	2130	2320	|
Lamballe **299** d.	1858	...	1921	1936	|	2001	|	...	...	2017	2011	2029	2041	|	|	|	|	...	|	2202	2204	...	2212	|	|
St Brieuc 299 d.	1911	...	1934	1949	1959	2014	2003	...	...	2028	2024	2040	2054	|	2059	2103	2108	...	2118	2215	2217	...	2226	0013	0423
Guingamp d.	|	...	1951	...	|	2033	2020	2028	...	...	2042	...	2111	|	|	2123	2126	2134	2134	2232	2234	...	2245	0031	0440
Plouaret-Trégor d.	|	2005	2006	...	|	2049	|	2045	...	...	2057	...	|	|	|	|	|	2151	|	2247	2249	2252	|	|	|
Lannion a.	|	2022	*2028*	...	|	*2109*	|	2101	...	...	*2119*	...	2141	|	|	|	|	2207	|	|	|	2311	|	|	|
Morlaix d.	|	...	2023	...	|	2107	2049	...	2055	...	2113	...	...	2119	|	2151	2154	...	2202	2305	2307	...	2316	0101	0512
Landivisiau d.	|	...	2038	...	|	|	|	...	2113	...	2128	...	...	|	|	|	|	...	|	|	|	...	|	|	|
Landerneau **286** d.	|	...	2048	...	|	2131	|	...	2133	...	2138	...	...	|	|	|	|	...	|	2330	|	...	|	|	0537
Brest 286 a.	2023	...	2059	...	2109	2142	2122	...	...	...	2149	...	...	2153	2208	2222	2229	...	2236	2343	2341	...	2348	0132	0552

	TGV 8690 ①-⑤	TGV 8608 ⑥ v	① g	TGV 8610 ①-⑤	Ⓐ	⑥ x	Ⓐ	Ⓐ u	55802 Ⓐ	Ⓐ	† y	Ⓐ	⑥	TGV 8618 ①-⑥ n⊕	Ⓐ	Ⓐ	⑥	Ⓐ	⑥⑦	TGV 8622 ⑥⑦	TGV 8620 Ⓐ ⊗	⑥	†	†	Ⓐ z
Brest 286 d.	...	0448	...	0452	...	...	0528	...	0545	...	...	...	...	0648	0702	0749	0818	...	...	0844	0848	1022	...	1037	1132
Landerneau **286** d.	...	|	...	|	...	...	0541	...	|	...	...	...	...	0701	0720	0802	0833	...	...	|	|	1034	...	1049	1144
Landivisiau d.	...	|	...	|	...	...	0551	...	|	...	...	...	...	|	0732	0812	0845	...	...	|	|	|	...	1058	1154
Morlaix d.	...	0519	...	0523	...	...	0606	...	0615	...	...	...	...	0723	0755	0827	0908	...	...	0916	0921	1055	...	1113	1210
Lannion d.	...	|	0510	|	...	...	...	...	*0606*	...	...	0656	0656	|	...	—	—	0908	0910	|	|	|	1055	|	—
Plouaret-Trégor d.	...	|	0525	|	...	...	...	...	0631	...	...	0711	0711	|	...	...	...	0924	0927	0935	|	|	1112	1130	...
Guingamp d.	...	0548	0542	0552	...	...	...	0631	0645	0707	0720	0731	0734	0752	...	†	⚒ z	0940		0951	0951	1124	...	1144	Ⓐ c
St Brieuc 299 d.	0510	0607	...	0609	0617	0633	...	0651	0703	0730	0738	0751	0756	0811	...	0935	0934	...	...	1011	1011	1141	...	1201	1221
Lamballe **299** d.	0522	0619	...	|	0628	0645	...	0707	0717	0744	0751	...	...	|	...	0946	0946	...	...	|	|	1152	...	1212	1235
Rennes a.	0600	0700	...	0700	0725	0748	...	...	0755	0840	0850	...	...	0900	...	1040	1047	...	...	1056	1056	1230	...	1250	1345
Paris ⊡ **280** a.	0820	0910	...	0915	...	...	...	...	...	...	...	...	...	1110	...	...	...	...	...	1325	1325	...	...	...	...

	⑥	TGV 8634 ①-⑤	TGV 8636 ⑦	⑤	⚒		†	TGV 8646	①-④ m	⑥	⑤-⑦ d	①-④ m	Ⓑ B	TGV 8660 Ⓑ B	TGV 8658 C	TGV 8662 C	†	⑤	①-④ m	TGV 5290 ⑦ ♠	⑤	①-④ m	⑥	TGV 8670 ⑥⑦	TGV 8668 Ⓐ
Brest 286 d.	1142	1148	1151	1207	1229	...	1308	1345	1433	...	1437	1529	...	1544	...	1546	1602	...	...	1621	1621	...	...	1644	1700
Landerneau **286** d.	1154	|	|	1219	1247	...	1326	|	1445	...	1449	1542	...	|	...	|	1614	...	...	|	1634	...	...	|	|
Landivisiau d.	1203	|	|	1228	1300	...	1338	|	1455	...	1459	1552	...	|	...	|	1624	...	...	|	1644	...	...	|	|
Morlaix d.	1219	1220	1223	1244	1323	...	1401	1418	1512	...	1514	1607	...	1615	...	1618	1640	...	...	1654	1659	...	...	1716	|
Lannion d.	*1150*	*1211*	|	|	...	1403*	...	|	|	1512	|	...	1605	|	1603	|	*1633*	...	...	|	*1650*	1702	1700	|	|
Plouaret-Trégor d.	1235	1238	|	1301	...	1420	...	|	1529	1528	1531	...	1622	1633	1621	|	1657	...	...	|	1719	1717	1717	|	|
Guingamp d.	1250	1253	1253	1315	...	1436	...	1448	1544	...	1546	...	...	1647	1636	|	1712	...	...	1725	1737	1734	1731	1746	|
St Brieuc 299 d.	1306	1312	1312	1332	...	1455	...	1509	1601	...	1603	...	...	1710	1705	1705	1729	1729	1731	1744	1756	1755	...	1807	1812
Lamballe **299** d.	1318	|	|	1343	...	...	...	1521	1614	...	1614	...	...	1722	1718	1718	1741	1745	1744	1757	1810	...	...	1820	|
Rennes a.	1355	1400	1400	1421	...	...	...	1600	1653	...	1655	...	...	1800	1800	1800	1817	1839	1825	1834	1854	...	...	1900	1900
Paris ⊡ **280** a.	...	1610	1610	...	...	...	...	1820	...	...	...	...	...	2010	2010	2010	...	...	...	...	...	...	...	2110	2110

	⑥	①-④ m	⑤	⚒ s	TGV 8676 ⑦	Ⓐ	†	Ⓐ	⑦ d	TGV 8688 ⑦	⑦ d	Ⓐ	⑤	⑥	⑤⑥	①-④ m	TGV 8696 ⑦	TGV 8682 ①-⑤	†	①-④ m	⑤	TGV 8686 ⑦	⑤	⑦	⑦
Brest 286 d.	...	...	...	1705	1718	...	1725	1745	...	1811	...	1805	...	...	1834	...	...	1851	1902	1920	1935	1950	...	...	2058
Landerneau **286** d.	...	...	...	1721	|	...	1738	1757	...	|	...	1822	...	...	1847	...	...	|	1914	1937	1952	2002	...	...	2110
Landivisiau d.	...	...	...	1732	|	...	1748	|	...	|	...	1834	...	...	1857	...	...	|	1923	1949	2005	|	...	...	|
Morlaix d.	...	...	...	1749	1751	...	1806	1819	...	1842	...	1858	...	...	1912	...	...	1924	1939	2005	2020	2025	...	...	2131
Lannion d.	...	1735	1753	|	|	...	*1757*	|	1819	|	...	...	1851	1904	|	1911	1921	|	|	...	...	|	2020	2029	*2127*
Plouaret-Trégor d.	...	1752	1810	1815	|	...	1825	|	1836	|	...	...	1908	1921	1927	1927	|	|	1956	...	...	|	2037	2046	2149
Guingamp d.	...	1807	1825	...	1821	...	1841	1848	1856	1917	...	...	...	...	1944	1944	1950	1954	2010	...	...	|	...	...	2203
St Brieuc 299 d.	1825	1827	...	...	1839	1839	1900	1905	1915	1940	1947	...	...	...	2000	...	2009	2013	2027	...	...	2108	...	...	2220
Lamballe **299** d.	1839	...	...	...	|	1853	1913	1917	...	|	2001	...	...	...	2012	...	2022	|	2038	...	...	|	...	...	2232
Rennes a.	1944	...	...	...	1926	1945	1955	1955	...	2030	2055	...	...	...	2050	...	2100	2100	2115	...	...	2156	...	...	2310
Paris ⊡ **280** a.	...	...	...	...	2140	...	...	...	...	2240	...	...	...	...	...	...	2310	2310	...	...	...	0010	...	...	...

B – To June 26 / from Aug. 31.
C – June 27 - July 4.
E – To July 3 / from Sept. 14.
F – To July 3.
c – From Aug. 31 St Brieuc d. 1235, Lamballe d. 1247.
d – Also June 1, Nov. 11.
g – Also June 2, Nov. 12; not June 1.
m – Not June 1, Nov. 11.
n – Not June 1.
q – Not June 7, Nov. 15, 22.

r – By 🚌.
s – From Aug. 31 will not run on ⑤.
t – Not Sept. 26.
u – From / to Dinan, Table **299**.
v – Not Oct. 10.
w – Not Nov. 11.
x – Not Oct. 10.
y – Not Oct. 11.
z – Not Sept. 14 - 25.
TGV –Ⓡ, supplement payable, 🍸.

⊡ – Paris Montparnasse.
⊕ – On Sept. 26 subject to alteration Brest - Guingamp.
⊗ – Not Sept. 14 - 25 Brest - Rennes.
△ – Runs 15 minutes later Rennes - Brest on Aug. 31, Sept. 1 - 4, 7 - 11.
▽ – Not on Ⓐ Aug. 31 - Sept. 11.
♥ – From Lille Europe, depart 1729 (Table **11**).
♠ – To Lille Europe, arrive 2318 (Table **11**).
§ – Runs 13 - 15 minutes later on Ⓐ Aug. 31 - Sept. 11.
* – Subject to alteration Sept. 7 - 11.

RENNES and NANTES - QUIMPER 285

Service to July 4 / from Aug. 31. *For service July 5 - Aug. 30 see page 542*

km								4548 4549	4546 4547					TGV 8705							TGV 8711	TGV 26321	TGV 26341			
		Ⓐ	Ⓐ	⑥	Ⓐ	Ⓐ	⑥	[R]	[R]	Ⓐ	Ⓐ	Ⓐ	Ⓒ	Ⓐ	⑥	⑥	†	Ⓐ	†	⑥	⑥⑦	①–⑥		Ⓐ	Ⓐ	⑥
				⊕				X	X					⊖				C			B	C	D	B§	B§	
0	*Paris* ⊡ **280** .... d.	...	...	...	...	...	...	...	...	...	...	...	...	0705	...	...	...	...	...	...	0805	0830	0835	...	...	...
365	**Rennes 287** .... d.	...	...	...	0626	...	0625	...	...	0645	...	0723	0830	0914	0925	...	0930	1000	...	...	1023	|	1047	1030	...	1118
	Nantes .... ◧ d.	...	...	...	|	0612	|	0641	0641	|	0651	|	|	|	|	0910	|	|	1003	1008	|	|	|	|	1019	|
	Savenay .... ◧ d.	...	...	...	|	0636	|	|	|	|	0715	|	|	|	|	|	|	|	1026	1030	|	|	|	|	1041	|
437	Redon **287** .... ◧ d.	...	...	...	0712	0712	0711	0725	0726	0737	0744	0759	0908	|	1007	1007	1005	1039	1053	1056	1101	|	1125	1117	1117	1153
492	Vannes .... d.	...	0637	0642	0742	0742	...	0754	0754	0808	...	0825	...	1014	1033	1033	1030	1109	...	...	1128	1136	1152	1147	1147	1223
511	Auray .... d.	...	0652	0657	0754	0754	...	0808	0811	0819	...	|	...	1027	1044	1044	1043	1122	...	...	1141	1149	1205	1200	1200	1236
545	Lorient .... d.	0645	0725	0724	0815	0815	...	0829	0831	0843	...	0852	...	1047	1103	1103	1102	1144	...	...	1200	1209	1225	1221	1221	1258
565	Quimperlé .... d.	0657	0743	...	0827	0827	...	0844	0845	...	...	|	...	|	1115	1115	1114	1156	...	...	|	|	|	1233	1233	1310
612	**Quimper** .... a.	0728	0813	...	0853	0853	...	0915	0915	...	...	0926	...	1123	1142	1142	1142	1223	...	...	1235	1243	1259	1259	1259	1336

		TGV 8715				TGV 8717			13895	TGV 8723										TGV 8729						
	Ⓐ		⑥	⑥	Ⓐ					⑤	①–④	⑤	①–④	①–④	⑥	⑥	†	⑤	⑤		①–④	⑤	Ⓐ	†	Ⓑ	⑤
	C							◇			m		m	m						A	m					
Paris ⊡ **280** .... d.	...	1005	...	...	...	1205	...	...	...	1345	...	...	...	...	...	...	...	...	...	1505	...	...	...	...	...	...
Rennes 287 .... d.	...	1211	...	...	1341	1416	...	1426	...	|	...	1610	1639	...	1637	...	...	...	1654	1711	...	1727	...	...	1745	...
Nantes .... ◧ d.	1140	|	1227	1312	|	|	...	|	1450	|	...	|	|	1622	|	1622	1622	1622	|	|	...	|	1705u	1723	|	1809
Savenay .... ◧ d.	1203	|	1249	1336	|	|	...	|	|	|	...	|	|	1644	|	1643	1644	1645	|	|	...	|	1748	1748	|	|
Redon **287** .... ◧ d.	1229	1249	1316	1403	1417	|	...	1503	1535	|	...	1649	1723	1723	1723	1723	1712	1716	1733	|	1755	1804	1821	1813	1828	1853
Vannes .... d.	1257	1316	1345	...	1444	1517	...	...	1605	1647	1708	1719	1748	1748	1753	1753	...	...	1800	1812	1826	1830	...	...	1857	1922
Auray .... d.	1310	1329	1357	...	1457	1530	...	...	1618	1700	1721	1732	1801	1801	1805	1805	...	...	1813	1826	1840	...	...	...	1910	1935
Lorient .... d.	1329	1350	1419	...	1514	1551	1600	...	1640	1720	1754	1753	1820	1820	1826	1826	...	...	1834	1847	1905	...	...	...	1931	1957
Quimperlé .... d.	1341	1403	1431	...	...	|	1612	...	1652	|	1812	1804	|	|	1838	1838	...	...	1846	|	...	...	...	...	1943	2008
Quimper .... a.	1408	1431	1457	...	...	1626	1642	...	1719	1754	1845	1832	1854	1854	1904	1904	...	...	1913	1924	...	...	...	...	2009	2035

		3854 3855	TGV 5232		TGV 8737	TGV 8739	TGV 8747	TGV 8741	TGV 8743	TGV 8759	TGV 8757						TGV 5236	TGV 5236	3856	TGV 8763		TGV 8761	TGV 8773	TGV 8777		TGV 8799
	⑥	♠	⑤	⑦	①–④	⑤	Ⓐ	⑥	⑦	①–④	⑤	Ⓐ	①–④	†	⑥	†	①–④	⑦	⑤⑦	⑤			⑦	⑤		⑦
			♥		m					n			m				♥	♥	♠w		L	L				q
Paris ⊡ **280** .... d.	...	...	...	...	1635	1635	1705	1705	1705	1805	1810	...	...	...	...	...	...	...	...	1935	...	1935	2005	2035	...	2355
Rennes 287 .... d.	1815	...	1844	...	1853	1855	1911	1911	1923	2014	|	...	2020	2030	2034	...	2129	2129	...	2141	...	2141	2223	2246	...	|
Nantes .... ◧ d.	|	1818	|	...	|	|	|	|	|	|	|	1944	|	|	|	2043	|	|	2116	|	2126	|	|	|	...	|
Savenay .... ◧ d.	|	1841	|	...	|	|	|	|	|	|	|	2015	|	|	|	2104	|	|	2141	|	2147	|	|	|	...	|
Redon **287** .... ◧ d.	1855	1910	1928	1924	1931	1937	|	1949	|	|	|	2044	2108	2106	2111	2135	2206	2206	2207	2219	2212	2219	2300	2323	...	|
Vannes .... d.	...	1942	1955	1953	1959	2004	2016	2015	2025	2114	2115	...	2137	2132	...	...	2233	2233	...	2246	...	2246	2327	2350	...	0449
Auray .... d.	...	1957	2009	2008	...	2017	2029	2028	2039	|	2128	...	...	2145	...	...	2246	2246	...	2258	...	2258	2340	0003	...	0505
Lorient .... d.	...	2018	2028	2030	...	2036	2049	2048	2059	2142	2148	...	...	2204	...	...	2303	2305	...	2318	...	2318	2359	0023	...	0525
Quimperlé .... d.	...	|	2040	2041	...	|	2102	2102	|	|	|	...	...	2215	...	...	...	2319	...	|	...	2332	0012	0036	...	|
Quimper .... a.	...	2056	2107	2107	...	2116	2128	2130	2132	2216	2222	...	...	2242	...	...	...	2346	...	2355	...	2359	0041	0104	...	0600

	TGV 8704	TGV 8706	TGV 8712						TGV 8718	TGV 5272				3832 3833		TGV 8724	TGV 8722			13894	TGV 8730	TGV 8734				
	①	②–⑤	Ⓐ	Ⓐ	Ⓐ	Ⓒ	Ⓐ	Ⓐ	①–⑥	①–⑥		⑥	Ⓐ	♠	Ⓐ	⑦	①–⑥		Ⓒ		①–⑥	⑦	①–④	①–④	⑤	⑤
	g	j							n	♣n					⊖		n				n		m	m		
Quimper .... d.	0418	...	0523	...	0532	...	0613	0613	0635	0646r	...	0705	0725	0739	0800	0840	0842	...	1007	1112	1144	1147	1234	1234	1240	1325
Quimperlé .... d.	|	...	|	...	0559	...	|	|	0704	0715r	...	0734	0752	|	0827	0908	0910	...	1035	1139	|	|	1301	1301	1308	1353
Lorient .... d.	0452	0457	0601	...	0611	...	0647	0647	0717	0729	...	0748	0805	0819	0838	0922	0925	...	1049	1153	1219	1222	1314	1314	1321	1406
Auray .... d.	0511	|	|	...	0632	...	0704	0704	0737	0749	...	...	0826	0841	...	0941	0944	...	1107	1218	1239	1242	1333	1333	1341	1423
Vannes .... d.	0524	0524	0630	...	0645	...	0717	0717	0750	0802	...	...	0838	0856	...	0955	0958	...	1120	1233	1254	1255	1347	1347	1354	1436
Redon **287** .... d.	0553	0553	|	0650	0716	0736	0747	0750	0820	0829	...	...	0909	0928	...	1024	|	...	1147	1303	1321	|	1420	1423	1420	1508
Savenay .... ◧ d.	|	|	|	0734	|	|	|	0817	|	|	...	...	|	|	...	|	|	...	|	1327	|	|	|	1446	|	1530
Nantes .... ◧ a.	|	|	|	0810	|	|	|	0840	|	|	...	...	|	1012	...	|	|	...	|	1350	|	|	|	1507	|	1550
Rennes 287 .... ◧ a.	0630	0630	0730	...	0755	0814	0826	...	0856	0904	...	...	0945	...	...	1100	1100	...	1220	...	1357	1357	1455	...	1455	...
Paris ⊡ **280** .... a.	0840	0840	0945	...	...	...	...	...	1110	...	...	...	...	...	...	1325	1325	...	...	...	1610	1610	...	...	...	...

						TGV 8752											TGV 8762							TGV 8774		
	⑥	⑥	†	†	Ⓐ		Ⓐ	†	⑦	①–④	①–④	①–④	†	⑤	⑤	†		⚒	⑦	Ⓐ	⑥	①–④	†	⑦	⑥	①–④
										m	m	m										m▽				m
Quimper .... d.	1333	1333	1337	...	...	1437	1512	...	...	...	...	...	1547	1547	...	...	1617c	...	1633	...	...	1715	...	1717	...	...
Quimperlé .... d.	1400	1400	1404	...	...	1505	1539	...	...	...	...	...	1614	1614	...	...	|	...	1700	...	...	|	...	|	...	...
Lorient .... d.	1412	1412	1417	...	...	1523	1552	...	...	...	1630	...	1627	1632	...	...	1654	...	1712	1714	1740	1750	...	1753	...	1755
Auray .... d.	1434	1434	1439	...	...	1542	1614	...	...	...	1651	...	1649	1654	...	...	1715	...	1734	1739	1807	|	...	1811	...	1820
Vannes .... d.	1446	1446	1451	...	...	1556	1627	...	1645	...	1703	...	1703	1707	...	...	1730	...	1746	1755	1819	1821	...	1824	...	1834
Redon **287** .... d.	1520	1526	1522	1526	1538	1626	1658	1658	1716	1719	1730	1741	1736	1737	1745	1749	|	1809	1818	...	1847	1847	1851	1854	1901	1904
Savenay .... ◧ d.	|	1549	|	1549	|	|	1722	1730	|	|	...	1813	|	|	1816	1815	|	|	|	...	...	|	1919	|	1928	...
Nantes .... ◧ a.	|	1610	|	1610	|	|	1745	1750	|	|	...	1835	|	|	1840	1836	|	|	|	...	...	|	1941	|	1950	...
Rennes 287 .... ◧ a.	1555	...	1555	...	1616	1700	...	...	1750	1807	...	...	1811	1811	...	...	1829	1906	1855	...	...	1920	...	1930	...	...
Paris ⊡ **280** .... a.	...	...	...	...	...	1910	...	...	...	...	...	...	...	...	...	...	2040	...	...	...	...	...	...	2140	...	...

	4446 4447					TGV 8776	TGV 8780	TGV 8782					4448 4449		TGV 8794				TGV 8790			TGV 8798				
	[R]	①–④	⑤	Ⓐ	⑥	⑦	①–④	⑤	†	†	①–④	⑤	[R]		⑦	①–④	①–④	⑤	⑤	†	†	⑦	①–④	⑤	†	L
	X	m					n				m		X			m	m						m	△		
Quimper .... d.	1715	1728	1735	...	1740	1746	1748	1750	1757	...	...	1757	1820	...	1836	1838	1838	...	1846	1918	...	1950	2000	2003	2025	...
Quimperlé .... d.	1747	1800	1803	...	1808	|	|	|	1825	...	←	1830	1851	...	1905	1905	1905	...	|	1945	...	|	2027	2030	2053	...
Lorient .... d.	1803	1816	1815	...	1820	1822	1827	1827	1838	...	1835	1846	1906	...	1919	1918	1918	...	1922	1958	...	2025	2039	2042	2107	...
Auray .... d.	1856	→	1833	...	1839	1842	1847	1847	1857	...	1905	1917	1926	...	1939	1935	1935	...	1941	2021	...	2046	2100	2102	2127	...
Vannes .... d.	1911	...	1845	...	1851	1857	1901	1901	1910	...	1918	1929	1941	...	1953	1948	1948	...	1955	2034	...	2059	2111	2114	2140	...
Redon **287** .... d.	1940	...	1918	1921	1922	|	|	|	1937	1951	...	...	2010	...	2020	2021	2026	2026	|	2105	2130	|	2141	2144	2207	2227
Savenay .... ◧ d.	|	...	|	1949	|	|	|	|	|	2019	...	...	|	...	|	|	2052	2054	|	|	2155	|	...	2211	|	|
Nantes .... ◧ a.	2025	...	|	2012	|	|	|	|	|	2039	...	...	2053	...	|	|	2115	2116	|	|	2216	|	...	2233	|	|
Rennes 287 .... ◧ a.	...	...	1950	...	1955	|	2000	2000	2010	...	...	...	...	...	2056	2055	...	...	2056	2139	...	2200	...	...	2240	2305
Paris ⊡ **280** .... a.	...	...	...	...	...	2200	2215	2225	...	...	...	...	...	...	2310	...	...	...	2310	...	...	0010	...	...	...	...

A – Daily except ⑤.
B – To June 26 / from Aug. 31.
C – June 27 - July 3.
D – July 4 only.
L – ①②③④⑥ (not June 1).
X – For days of running and composition see Table **290** Night Trains panel.

c – 1613 on July 2-4.
g – Also June 2; not June 1.
j – Not June 2, Nov. 11.
m – Not June 1, Nov. 11.
n – Not June 1.
q – Not June 7, Nov. 15, 22.
r – ①⑥ (also June 2; not June 1).
u – Depart 1725 on ⑤ (arrive Redon 1817).
w – Also June 1, Nov. 11.

TGV – [R], supplement payable, 🍷.

⊡ – Paris Montparnasse.
◇ – On Ⓒ depart 1430, arrive 1507.
◧ – See also **287** Nantes - Redon, **287/8** Nantes - Savenay.
♥ – From Lille Europe (**5232** departs 1447, **5236** departs 1729, Table **11**).
♣ – To Lille Europe (arrive 1341, Table **11**).
♠ – To / from Bordeaux (Table **292**).
⊕ – Not Sept. 26, Oct. 17, 24, Nov. 14.
⊗ – Not Nov. 2-6, 9, 10, 12, 13.
⊖ – Not Oct. 10-30.
⊖ – Not Nov. 3-13.
△ – Not Oct. 16, 30, Nov. 13.
▽ – On June 22-25, 29, 30, July 1, 2, Aug. 31, Sept. 1-3 runs up to 9 mins earlier.

§ – Subject to alteration Sept. 14 - Oct. 2 Nantes - Redon and Sept. 14-18, Oct. 19-30 Redon - Quimper.

AURAY - QUIBERON

⑥⑦ June 13-21, ⑥⑦ Sept. 5-13:

From Auray: 1050, 1345, 1545, 1830.
From Quiberon: 1145, 1440, 1730, 1945.
Journey 45 minutes.

For daily service **June 27 - Aug. 30** see page 542.

🚌 operates 4-5 times daily all year.

286 BREST - QUIMPER

2nd class

km		→	Ⓐ	Ⓐ	⑥ t	⚒	†	△	⑤	Ⓒ	Ⓐ	†	①–④ n	⑤	⑥	⑤	⑦ e	→	Ⓐ ◇	Ⓐ	⑥	⊗	†
0	**Brest 284** d.	To	0553	0716	0719	0920	1019	1201	1535	1659	1713	1832	1841	1844	1920	2001	2006	July 5	0553	0716	0719	0920	1108
18	Landerneau **284** d.	July 4	0606	0728	0732	0931	1033	1215	1548	1712	1725	1845	1855	|	1935	2017	2021	to	0606	0728	0732	0931	1121
72	Châteaulin d.	and from	0644	0804	0812	1009	1109	1250	1624	1749	1803	1920	1927	1927	2013	2052	2059	Aug. 30	0644	0804	0812	1009	1157
102	**Quimper** a.	Aug. 31	0705	0825	0832	1029	1130	1311	1646	1810	1823	1940	1948	1949	2033	2113	2119		0705	0825	0832	1029	1218

	→	Ⓐ	⑥ t	⑤	Ⓒ	Ⓐ	Ⓐ	⑥ t	†	⑤	⑦ z
Brest 284 d.	July 5	1201	1210	1535	1710	1715	1856	1901	1908	2001	2017
Landerneau **284** d.	to	1215	1224	1548	1725	1730	|	1916	1920	2017	2033
Châteaulin d.	Aug. 30	1250	1259	1624	1803	1809	1941	1954	1956	2053	2109
Quimper a.		1311	1320	1646	1823	1829	2002	2014	2020	2113	2129

	→	Ⓐ	Ⓐ ⊗	⑥	†	⚒ ⊕		△
Quimper d.	To	0621	0741	0749	0925	0946	...	1443
Châteaulin d.	July 4	0646	0806	0814	0946	1011	...	1504
Landerneau **284** d.	and from	0725	0841	0852	1021	1047	...	1539
Brest 284 a.	Aug. 31	0737	0854	0904	1034	1100	...	1552

	→	⑤	Ⓒ	Ⓐ	†	①–④ n	⑤	⑤	⑦ e	→	Ⓐ	Ⓐ	⑥ t			⑤	Ⓒ	Ⓐ	①–④ m	†	⑤	⑤	⑦ z
Quimper d.	To	1601	1727	1740	1857	1905	1905	2029	2035	July 5	0621	0741	0749	0946	1449	1601	1740	1746	1918	1933	1918	2029	2045
Châteaulin d.	July 4	1626	1751	1805	1922	1929	1929	2054	2101	to	0646	0806	0814	1011	1510	1626	1805	1811	1943	1958	1943	2054	2111
Landerneau **284** d.	and from	1704	1830	1843	1957	|	2003	2135	2141	Aug. 30	0725	0841	0852	1047	1545	1704	1843	1850	|	2031	2018	2135	2149
Brest 284 a.	Aug. 31	1720	1843	1856	2010	2013	2016	2147	2153		0737	0854	0904	1100	1558	1720	1856	1902	2029	2045	2031	2147	2203

e – Also June 1, Nov. 11.
m – Not July 14.
n – Not Nov. 11.
t – Not Aug. 15.
z – Also July 14.

⊕ – Subject to alteration Landerneau - Brest on Ⓐ Aug. 31 - Sept. 11.
⊗ – Subject to alteration Landerneau - Brest and v.v. on Ⓐ Sept. 14 - 25.
△ – Subject to alteration on ①–④ Sept. 21 - Oct. 15.
◇ – To Lorient (arrive 0751).

Additional journeys by *CAT* 🚌, journey approx 90 minutes:
From Brest : 0700 Ⓐ, 1000 Ⓐ, 1415 †, 1440 ⚒, 1612 ⑤, 1800 Ⓐ.
From Quimper : 0713 Ⓐ, 1135 ⑤, 1247 †, 1255 ⚒, 1639 ⚒, 1720 ①–④, 1730 ⑤, 1740 †. *Timings subject to confirmation*

287 RENNES - REDON - NANTES

TEMPORARILY RELOCATED TO PAGE 237

288 NANTES - ST NAZAIRE - LE CROISIC

km	*TGV* trains convey 🍸	Ⓐ	⑥ J	B	Ⓐ	⑥ t	Ⓐ	† K	*TGV* 8903 Ⓐ	*TGV* 8905 C	Ⓐ J⊗	⑥ Ot	† O§	*TGV* 8909	⚒ K	Ⓐ ☉	▷	*TGV* 8919 ⑥ J	*TGV* 8921 ①–④ J	Ⓐ J	Ⓐ JO	*TGV* 8925 K	K	⑥ J	*TGV* 8929 ⑤ P
	Paris ⊡ **280** d.	...	...	...	...	...	...	...	0700	0730	...	...	...	0900	...	...	...	1100	1100	...	...	1200	...	...	1300
0	**Nantes 285/7** d.	0645	0656	0656	0753	0800	0800	0905	0905	0956	1005	1003	1007	1112	1150	1200	1223	1307	1303	1312	1355	1417	1424	1504	1515
39	Savenay **285/7** d.	0710	0722	0720	0821	0832	0834	0935	|	|	1026	1026	1040	|	1213	1233	1244	|	|	1334	1429	|	1445	1539	|
64	**St Nazaire** d.	0731	0741	0739	0835	0850	0858	0949	0939	1031	1041	1042	1055	1148	1226	1248	1258	1344	1344	1348	1445	1453	1500	1556	1550
79	Pornichet d.	...	...	0752	...	0901	0910	1000	...	1044	1051	1054	1105	|	1238	...	1309	1356	|	...	...	1504	1513	1608	|
83	La Baule Escoublac d.	...	...	0800	...	0908	0918	1006	...	1051	1058	1102	1113	1204	1245	...	1319	1403	1403	...	...	1511	1523	1615	1606
90	**Le Croisic** a.	...	...	0815	...	0918	0930	1017	...	1103	1111	1116	1126	1217	1258	...	1332	1416	1412	...	...	1526	1536	1627	1615

	TGV 8929 ⑤ Q	⑤ J	*TGV* 8933 L	Ⓐ	*TGV* 8937 ⑥	①–④ m	⑤	⑥ t	⑦ Tq	Ⓐ T	⚒	⚒ K	*TGV* 5216 ⑦ ♥e	⑤⑥ Ot	⑦ q	①–④ m	①–④ m	*TGV* 8953 D	*TGV* 8951 ⑤	①–④ m	⑥	⑤	⑦ q	*TGV* 8965 ①–⑥ n	①–④ Jd
Paris ⊡ **280** d.	1300	...	1400	...	1500	...	...	...	...	...	...	...	...	...	...	...	...	1730	1730	...	...	...	...	1830	...
Nantes 285/7 d.	1515	1605	1616	1643	1710	1721	1730	1735	1807	1802	1834	1834	1858	1900	1906	1907	1927	1935	1936	...	...	1927	2018	2037	2132
Savenay **285/7** d.	|	1640	|	1704	|	1745	1753	1801	1832	|	1910	1910	|	|	1928	1945	2001	|	|	←	...	2005	2045	|	2154
St Nazaire d.	1550	1659	1652	1728	1747	1803	1810	1818	1847	1843	1923	1924	1934	1934	1943	2006	2016	2009	2012	2021	2021	2025	2113	2112	2209
Pornichet d.	1601	1711	|	1739	|	1814	1823	1829	1858	1857	...	1935	1946	1945	1955	→	...	...	2024	2032	2032	2035	2124	|	2219
La Baule Escoublac d.	1608	1719	1709	1747	1802	1821	1831	1838	1907	1906	...	1942	1952	1952	2002	...	...	...	2031	2040	2040	2044	2131	2128	2224
Le Croisic a.	1621	1730	1717	1800	1811	1835	1844	1851	1922	1919	...	1956	2004	2006	2015	...	...	...	2043	2053	2053	2056	2144	2137	2235

	TGV 5231 F ♥	⑤ J	⑥ Kt	*TGV* 8979 ⑤	Y	①–④ Kn	*TGV* 8987 ⑤	⑦ q	⑤⑥ w	①–④ Jc	
Paris ⊡ **280** d.	...	...	...	2000	...	...	2100	...	...	...	...
Nantes 285/7 d.	2150	2157	2205	2212	2220	2220	2310	2322	2323	2325	...
Savenay **285/7** d.	|	2218	2228	|	2249	2249	|	2345	2354	2353	...
St Nazaire d.	2225	2233	2241	2248	2303	2305	2347	0001	0008	0006	...
Pornichet d.	2237	2246	...	2300	...	2317	|	0012	0018	...	...
La Baule Escoublac d.	2244	2253	...	2307	...	2324	0003	0021	0025	...	...
Le Croisic a.	2257	2306	...	2319	...	2337	0012	0035	0036	...	...

	① Jv	Ⓐ K	*TGV* 8902 ① g	*TGV* 8904 ②–⑤ Ju	*TGV* 8906 ②–⑤ Ka	Ⓐ J	⑥ t	*TGV* 8908 ① Kb	Ⓐ K
Le Croisic d.	0456	0512	...	...	...	...	0547	0554	...
La Baule Escoublac d.	0509	0523	...	...	...	...	0557	0605	...
Pornichet d.	0516	0530	...	...	...	...	0602	|	...
St Nazaire d.	0527	0544	0547	0551	0551	0559	0613	0621	0626
Savenay **285/7** d.	0541	...	0602	|	|	0624	0627	|	0646
Nantes 285/7 a.	0605	...	0625	0625	0625	0650	0648	0655	0720
Paris ⊡ **280** a.	...	...	0835	0835	0855	...	...	0905	...

	Ⓐ J	⚒	Ⓐ	Ⓐ	Ⓐ	Ⓒ O	*TGV* 5270 U ♥	† K	Ⓒ J	⑥ Kt	Ⓐ ▽	B	*TGV* 8922 ▽	Ⓐ J☆	*TGV* 8932 E	*TGV* 8930 Ⓐ K	Ⓐ	Ⓒ	Ⓐ	*TGV* 8942	Ⓐ	Ⓑ ◧	*TGV* 8952 ①–④ G	*TGV* 5334 ⑦ ♠Ks	Ⓐ
Le Croisic d.	0610	...	0634	...	0730	0730	0800	0848	0852	0852	0852	0939	0954	1141	1146	1146	...	1220	...	1351	...	1509	1546	1559	...
La Baule Escoublac d.	0624	...	0646	...	0744	0744	0813	0901	0906	0906	0905	0952	1005	1152	1202	1202	...	1232	...	1402	...	1522	1557	1611	...
Pornichet d.	0632	...	0653	...	0751	0751	0820	0906	0911	0911	0912	0959	|	1200	1210	1210	...	1239	...	|	...	1529	|	1618	...
St Nazaire d.	0644	0649	0705	0744	0803	0803	0833	0917	0922	0922	0924	1010	1021	1210	1222	1222	1237	1250	1402	1418	1453	1540	1614	1629	1632
Savenay **285/7** d.	0659	0709	0729	0758	0821	0822	|	0932	0936	0936	0944	1024	|	|	|	|	1258	1307	1418	|	1508	1558	|	|	1650
Nantes 285/7 a.	0720	0743	0750	0819	0847	0846	0906	0953	0957	0957	1005	1045	1055	1242	1255	1255	1333	1335	1450	1455	1540	1619	1648	1704	1714
Paris ⊡ **280** a.	...	...	...	...	...	...	...	...	...	...	...	...	1310	...	1505	1510	...	...	...	1710	...	...	1915	...	...

	TGV 8956 ①–④ Gc	*TGV* 8958 ①–⑥ R	*TGV* 8958 ⑦ K	⑥ t	Ⓐ O	†	Ⓐ	*TGV* 8964 ⑤	*TGV* 8966 ⑦ e	①–④ m	† Kr	Ⓐ z	⑥ Ot	*TGV* 8980 A	† O	Ⓐ	⑤ J	①–④ Jd	†	N	⑤ K	*TGV* 8996 ⑦ e	Ⓐ y	⑤	
Le Croisic d.	...	1605	1616	1641	...	1652	...	1717	1748	...	1759	1816	1823	1855	1902	...	1939	1943	2019	2026	2028	2040	...	...	...
La Baule Escoublac d.	...	1620	1630	1653	...	1707	...	1732	1802	...	1811	1830	1836	1906	1917	...	1951	1955	2031	2039	2043	2054	...	...	...
Pornichet d.	...	1627	1636	1659	...	1714	...	1739	1808	...	1819	1835	1843	|	1923	...	1956	2000	2037	2045	2051	2100	...	...	...
St Nazaire d.	1650	1641	1650	1710	1704	1727	1736	1751	1821	1823	1830	1847	1856	1921	1935	1939	2007	2011	2049	2056	2101	2115	2120	2214	...
Savenay **285/7** d.	|	|	|	1723	1727	1744	1754	|	|	1838	1844	1909	1912	|	|	1954	2022	2026	2108	2111	2116	|	2136	2232	...
Nantes 285/7 a.	1725	1718	1725	1750	1800	1816	1818	1825	1855	1910	1920	1940	1939	1955	2009	2020	2045	2049	2135	2133	2137	2155	2205	2252	...
Paris ⊡ **280** a.	1935	1935	1935	...	...	...	...	2035	2115	...	...	...	...	2210	...	...	...	...	...	...	...	0005	...	...	...

A – Daily except ⑤.
B – Ⓐ (⚒ July 6 - Aug. 29).
C – ①–⑥ June 27 - Aug. 29 (not July 14).
D – ①②③④⑥ (also ⑦ to June 28 / from Sept. 6), not July 14.
E – ⑦ (also ⑥ July 11 - Aug. 29), also July 14, Aug. 15.
F – ⑤ to July 3; ①–⑥ July 6 - Aug. 29 (not July 14); ⑤ from Sept. 4.
G – To June 26 / from Aug. 31.
J – To July 4 / from Aug. 31.
K – July 5 - Aug. 30.
L – ①②③④⑦.
N – ①②③④⑥ July 6 - Aug. 29 (not July 14).
O – To/from Orléans (Table **289**).
P – ⑤ to June 26 / from Sept. 4.
Q – ⑤ July 3 - Aug. 28.
R – ①–⑥ June 29 - Aug. 29 (not July 14). On July 4 runs up to 20 minutes earlier.

T – (12) Le Croisic - Nantes - Tours and v.v.
U – ①⑥ (daily July 4 - Aug. 30), also June 2; not June 1.
Y – ⑦ (also ①②③④ to July 2 / from Aug. 31), also July 14, Aug. 15. Will not run Oct. 6, 13 - 29, Nov. 3 - 5, 10.

a – Also July 13; not July 15.
b – Also July 15; not July 13.
c – Not June 1, Nov. 11.
d – Not Nov. 11.
e – Also June 1, July 14.
g – Also June 2, July 15; not June 1, July 13.
m – Not June 1, July 14, Nov. 11.
n – Not June 1, July 14.
q – Also June 1, July 14, Nov. 11.
r – On Aug. 15 departs up to 13 minutes earlier.
s – Also July 14.
t – Not Aug. 15.
u – Not June 2.
v – Also June 2; not June 1.
w – Not Aug. 15, Oct. 16, 30.
y – Not Oct. 12 - 15.
z – Not July 13.

TGV – Ⓡ, supplement payable, 🍸.

♥ – To/from Lille Europe (Table **11**).
♠ – To Lyon and Grenoble (Table **335**).
◧ – On Oct. 12 - 16 by 🚌 Le Croisic - St Nazaire.
⊡ – Paris Montparnasse.
☉ – Subject to alteration on Sept. 14 - 18, 28 - 30, Oct. 1, 2.
▽ – Subject to alteration Sept. 21 - 25.
▷ – Subject to alteration Sept. 15 - 18, Oct. 12 - 16, Nov. 10.
☆ – Subject to alteration Sept. 14 - Oct. 2, Oct. 26, Nov. 4, 13 - 20.
⊗ – Subject to alteration on Sept. 14 - 18.
§ – Not June 7.

NANTES - ANGERS - TOURS 289

For other *TGV* trains Nantes - Lyon (via Massy) see Table **335**. For night trains see panel below Table **290**

km		TGV 5302		TGV 5304	4402							TGV 5322	4406	TGV 5328												
		①-④ m	Ⓐ	⑥	⑥ t	Ⓐ ☆	Ⓐ d	Ⓒ	Ⓐ d	Ⓐ		♠	† c	Ⓐ b	⑤	Ⓐ	⑦ e	①-④ n	⑤	†	⑥ t	Ⓐ	⑦ e	⑥ t	†	⑦ ⊖e
	Le Croisic **288** d.	...	...	...	...	...	...	0730	...	...	...	...	...	...	...	...	...	...	...	...	...	...	...	1823	1902	...
0	**Nantes 280** d.	0455	...	0630	0658	0706	0837	0849	...	1123	...	1252	1505	1555	...	1630	1630	1636	1636	...	...	1818	1854	1945	2012	2218
88	Angers St Laud **280** d.	0536	0655	0708	0739	0743	0921	0931	1100	1201	1231	1337	1548	1633	1640	1710	1711	1750	1750	1749	1810	1859	1934	2030	2051	2301
132	Saumur d.	0559	0720	0730	0801	0805	0944	0954	1121	1222	1303	|	1610	1656	1710	1732	1732	1815	1815	1822	1842	1920	1958	2056	2112	2322
196	St Pierre des Corps a.	0629	|	0804	|	0837	1022	1032	|	1255	|	1426	|	1724	|	|	1802	|	1852	1858	1920	1952	|	2134	2141	2352
199	**Tours** a.	*0639*	0759	*0814*	0834	*0847*	1033	*1045*	1158	*1305*	1355	*1437*	1643	*1737*	1750	1804	1812	1854	1902	1911	1931	*2010*	2035	*2144*	*2151*	0002
202	St Pierre des Corps a.	|	...	|	0850	|	...	|	...	|	...	|	1710	|	...	1816	...	...	...	...	...	|	...	|	|	...
	Orléans **296** a.	|	...	|	|	0935	...	1128	...	1349	...	|	|	|	...	1912	...	...	...	...	...	2044	...	2226	2232	...
	Lyon Part Dieu **290** a.	0935	...	1103	1324	...	...	...	...	...	...	1731	2149	2031	...	...	...	...	...	...	...	...	...	...	...	...

						TGV 5352								TGV 5368							TGV 5378	TGV 5231	4506		TGV 5380
	Ⓐ	† K	Ⓐ	⑥ t	†	Ⓐ ♣	Ⓐ ⊕	Ⓐ ‡	⚒	Ⓐ	§	Ⓐ	⑥ t⊖	†	①-⑥ ♠n	⑤⑥ t	Ⓐ	①-④ f	⚒	⑤	†	⑦ ♠e	F ♥	⑤-⑦ x		k
Lyon Part Dieu **290** d.	...	...	...	...	...	...	0656	...	...	...	...	...	...	...	1326	...	...	...	...	...	...	1656	...	1526	...	1826
Orléans **296** d.	...	...	0641	0728	0728	...	|	1109	...	...	...	...	...	...	|	1630	...	1727	...	...	1759	|	...	|	...	|
St Pierre des Corps d.	...	...	|	|	|	...	|	|	...	...	...	...	...	...	|	|	...	|	...	...	|	|	...	2005	...	|
Tours d.	0639	0711	*0728*	*0809*	*0809*	0914	*0943*	*1151*	1228	1325	1432	1611	1611	1619	*1612*	*1709*	1732	*1803*	1837	1837	*1845*	*1939*	*2002*	2021	2042	*2112*
St Pierre des Corps d.	|	|	0738	0820	0820	|	0954	1201	|	1336	|	|	|	|	1626	1723	|	1819	|	|	1855	1955	2014	|	2053	2125
Saumur d.	0716	0749	0810	0856	0856	0955	|	1232	1317	1412	1505	1649	1648	1656	|	1755	1822	1851	1929	1930	1927	|	|	2053	2130	2158
Angers St Laud **280** d.	0744	0811	0833	0921	0921	1023	1049	1257	1349	...	1528	1714	1713	1720	1722	1817	1845	1914	...	1954	1950	2049	2108	2117	2206u	2219
Nantes 280 a.	0826	0854	0910	1001	1001	...	1125	1337	...	...	1608	1759	1759	1804	1803	1857	...	1956	...	...	2029	2127	2147	2158	...	2304
Le Croisic **288** a.	...	...	1116	1126	...	...	...	...	...	...	...	1919	...	1922	...	2006	...	...	...	...	...	...	2257y	...	...	...

FOR NOTES SEE BELOW **Additional trains**: Saumur - Tours 0635 ⚒, 0813 Ⓐ, 0836 Ⓒ, 1623 ⑤, 1626 ⑦ **q**, 1657 ⑥ **t**, 1702 ⑤, 1704 ①-④ **n**, 1710 †, 1850 †.
Tours - Saumur 0719 Ⓐ, 1202 †, 1450 ⑤, 1450 ⑥, 1933 Ⓑ, 2315 ⑦ **q**.

TOURS - BOURGES - LYON 290

For faster *TGV* trains Nantes / Tours - Massy - Lyon and v.v. see Table **335**. For night trains see panel below table

km				16831		4402	4402				16834			4406			4406							
		⚒	Ⓐ		⚒ ⊡	① p⊗	⑥ t△	⚒	†	⚒		⑤⑥ t		△ ⚒	⑤	†	† c	⚒	Ⓐ	Ⓑ ⊡			Ⓐ	⑦ w
	Nantes **289** d.	...	...	...	...	...	0658	...	...	...	...	...	...	...	...	...	1505	...	...	...	...	...	...	...
0	**Tours** d.	...	0617	...	0703	0845	0845	1008	1008	...	1213	1241	1331	1505	1608	1627	1705	1706	...	1817	1838	1928	2050	2050
3	St Pierre des Corps d.	...	0624	...	0710	0852	0852	1015	1015	...	1220	1248	1338	1512	1614	1633	1712	1713	...	1824	1845	1935	2057	2057
	Orléans **315** d.	...	|	0707	|	|	|	|	|	...	|	|	|	|	|	|	|	|	...	|	|	|	|	|
113	Vierzon **315** d.	...	0737	0748	0824	0951	0951	1128	1135	...	1328	1400	1457	1616	1726	1800	1814	1821	...	1937	2011	2103	2211	2213
145	**Bourges 315** ▷ d.	0741	0755	0806	0842	1010	1010	1144	1154	1217	1348	1420	1516	1636	1749	...	1835	1838	1845	1957	...	2128	...	2233
	Nevers d.	|	...	*0820*	|	|	|	▬	|	|	*1400*	...	|	*1652*v	|	...	*1847*	...	|	|	...	|	...	|
203	Saincaize d.	|	...	0836	|	1043	1043	...	|	|	1418	...	|	1709	|	...	1907	...	|	|	...	|	...	|
214	**Nevers 330** ▷ a.	0831	...	*0856*	0918	|	|	...	1229	1308	*1440*	...	1552	*1727*v	1828	...	*1928*	...	1935	2033	...	2210	...	*2338*
252	Moulins-sur-Allier **330** d.	...	...	0901	...	1111	1111	⚒	...	...	1444	...	...	1735	...	...	1936	...	...	...	...	...	...	...
293	St Germain des Fossés **328** d.	...	...	|	...	1135	1135	1135	...	...	|	...	...	1758	...	...	2000	...	...	...	...	...	...	...
360	Roanne **328** d.	...	...	⊙	...	1216	1216	1216	...	...	⊙	...	...	1839	...	...	2041	...	...	...	...	...	...	...
457	**Lyon Part Dieu 328** a.	...	...	1143	...	1324	1324	1324	...	...	|	...	...	1947	...	...	2149	...	...	...	...	...	...	...
461	**Lyon Perrache 328** a.	...	...	1158	...	1338	1338	1338	...	...	1727	...	...	2001	...	...	2205	...	...	...	...	...	...	...

								4504	4504				16842				4506						16846	
	⚒	⚒	Ⓐ	⚒	⚒		⊡ j	①-⑥ z▽	①⑥ s▽	Ⓐ	⑥ t	⑤				Ⓐ	▽		⚒	Ⓑ ⊡	Ⓐ	⑤⑦ w		†
Lyon Perrache 328 d.	...	...	...	...	...	...	...	0904	0904	...	...	...	1226	...	...	...	1511	...	...	...	...	...	1751	...
Lyon Part Dieu 328 d.	...	...	...	...	...	...	...	0918	0918	...	...	...	1239	...	...	...	1526	...	...	...	...	...	1804	...
Roanne **328** d.	...	...	...	...	...	...	...	1032	1032	...	...	...	⊙	...	...	...	1637	...	...	...	...	...	⊙	...
St Germain des Fossés **328** d.	...	...	...	...	...	...	...	1112	1114	...	...	...	|	...	...	...	1719	...	...	...	...	...	|	...
Moulins-sur-Allier **330** d.	...	...	...	...	...	...	...	▬	1138	...	...	...	1522	...	...	...	1742	...	...	...	...	...	2055	...
Nevers 330 ▷ d.	...	...	0549	0658	0741	...	0922	...	|	1233	1315	...	*1528*	1625	1643	1737	*1751*r	...	1830	1921	2002	...	*2104*	2120
Saincaize d.	...	...	|	|	|	...	|	...	1206	|	|	...	1548	|	|	|	1808	...	|	|	|	...	2120	|
Nevers a.	...	...	|	|	|	...	|	⚒	|	|	|	...	*1611*	|	|	|	*1825*r	...	|	|	|	...	*2138*	|
Bourges 315 ▷ d.	...	...	0636	0740	0831	0858	0958	1215	1238	1322	1405	1532	1620	1716	1724	1826	1840	1848	1920	2009	2051	2135	2151	2209
Vierzon **315** d.	0602	0633	0657	0801	...	0915	1017	1237	1300	...	...	1550	1640	...	1749	...	1902	1915	...	2029	...	2155	2211	...
Orléans **315** a.	|	|	|	|	...	|	|	|	|	...	...	|	|	...	|	...	|	|	...	|	...	|	2250	...
St Pierre des Corps a.	0724	0759	0807	0915	...	1028	1127	1348	1402	...	...	1658	1748	...	1901	...	2003	2031	...	2147	...	2254	...	...
Tours a.	0731	0806	0814	0922	...	1035	1134	1355	1409	...	...	1705	1755	...	1908	...	2010	2038	...	2154	...	2301	...	...
Nantes **289** a.	...	...	...	...	...	...	...	...	...	...	...	...	...	...	...	...	2158x	...	...	...	...	...	...	...

also:	⚒	⚒	Ⓐ	⚒	†	⚒		⚒	⚒
Bourges d.	0640	0911	1622	1725	1753	1933	Nevers d.	0633	0904
Nevers a.	0730	1001	1713	1815	1843	2024	Bourges a.	0723	0953

Night Trains	4548 4549 Ⓡ S◇	4546 4547 Ⓡ V◇
Genève d.	...	1944
Bellegarde d.	...	2014
Lyon Perrache d.	2207	|
Lyon Part Dieu d.	2221	2134
Lyon Perrache d.	|	2223
St Pierre des Corps a.	0456	0456
Saumur a.	0528	0528
Angers a.	0551	0549
Nantes a.	0637	0633
Quimper **285** a.	0915	0915

Night Trains	4446 4447 Ⓡ U◇	4448 4449 Ⓡ R◇
Quimper **285** d.	1715h	1820
Nantes d.	2105	2105
Angers d.	2152	2152
Saumur d.	2214	2214
St Pierre des Corps d.	2247	2247
Lyon Perrache a.	0637	|
Lyon Part Dieu a.	0729	0632
Lyon Perrache a.	|	0646
Bellegarde a.	0856	...
Genève a.	0932	...

NOTES FOR TABLES 289 AND 290

F – Ⓑ (daily July 5 - Aug. 30).
K – July 5 - Aug. 30.
R – ⑤ to June 12 (also June 1); ⑤⑦ from Sept. 6 (daily Oct. 23 - Nov. 4).
S – ⑤⑦ to June 19; ⑤⑦ from Sept. 11 (daily Oct. 23 - Nov. 4).
U – June 19 - Sept. 5.
V – June 20 - Sept. 6 (not June 21, 28, July 5 - 7).
b – To Grenoble on ⑤ (train **5332**), arrive 2153.
c – Not June 7 Nantes - Tours.
d – Not June 2 - 5, Sept. 28 - Oct. 9.
e – Also June 1, July 14.
f – Not June 1, July 14, Nov. 11.
h – 1656 on ⑦, 1650 on Aug. 15.
j – Arrives up to 13 mins later Sept. 14 - 25.
k – From Montpellier (Table **350**).
m – Not June 1, July 13, 14.
n – Not June 1, July 14.
p – Also June 2, July 15; not June 1, July 13.
q – Also June 1, July 14, Nov. 11; not July 12.
r – Daily except ⑥ (runs Aug. 15).
s – Also June 2, July 15; not June 1, July 13, Aug. 15.
t – Not Aug. 15.
u – ⑤⑦ (also June 1, July 14, Nov. 11).
v – Ⓐ only.
w – Also June 1, July 14, Nov. 11.
x – ⑤⑥⑦ (also June 1, July 14, Nov. 11; not June 6).
y – ⑤ (also ①-⑥ July 6 - Aug. 29, not July 14).
z – Not July 13, 14, Aug. 15, Nov. 11.

TGV – Ⓡ, supplement payable, 🍸.
⊙ – Via Paray le Monial (Table **372**).
⊡ – Tours - Nevers - Dijon and v.v. (Table **374**).
⊖ – To / from Rennes (Table **287**).
◇ – 🛏 1, 2 cl. and (2) (reclining).
⊕ – On Sept. 14 - 25 will not call at St Pierre des Corps (arrive Angers 1026, Nantes 1104).
⊗ – On Oct. 5 runs up to 20 minutes earlier.
♥ – From Lille (Table **11**).
♠ – To / from Marseille (Table **335**).
♣ – Not June 2, 3, Sept. 14 - 25.
▽ – On June 27 will not call at Lyon Part Dieu (departs Lyon Perrache 12 - 17 mins earlier).
△ – On June 27 will not call at Lyon Part Dieu (arrive Lyon Perrache 20 minutes later).
▷ – Bourges - Nevers: see also panel below.
☆ – Arrive Orléans 0951 Ⓐ Sept. 14 - Oct. 16.
§ – On June 7 depart Tours 1407.
‡ – On Ⓐ Nov. 9 - 27 depart Orléans 1058.

ROANNE - ST ÉTIENNE 291

km		Ⓐ	Ⓐ	⚒	Ⓐ	⚒		Ⓐ		Ⓐ§	§		△	Ⓐ△	Ⓐ△		Ⓑ§			Ⓐ				†
0	**Roanne** d.	0527	0547	0612	0641	0715	...	0818	0841	0941	1041	...	1237	1343	1445	...	1541	1641	...	1719	1818	1925	...	2047
80	**St Étienne** Châteaucreux a.	0647	0707	0732	0803	0838	...	0938	1003	1103	1204	...	1403	1503	1603	...	1703	1803	...	1843	1938	2044	...	2203

		Ⓐ	⚒	⚒			Ⓐ	△		Ⓐ△	△		§	Ⓐ§			Ⓐ	⚒			Ⓐ			
St Étienne Châteaucreux d.	...	0550	0621	0714	...	0815	0850	0950	...	1150	1233	...	1450	1550	1650	...	1715	1750	1822	...	1850	1950	2050	...
Roanne a.	...	0704	0743	0829	...	0929	1004	1104	...	1304	1341	...	1604	1704	1804	...	1823	1905	1936	...	2005	2104	2204	...

△ – Partly by 🚌 on Ⓐ to June 13 and Ⓐ Oct. 12 - Nov. 6 in altered timings.
§ – Partly by 🚌 on Ⓐ to June 13 in altered timings.

292 NANTES - LA ROCHELLE - BORDEAUX

km		Ⓐ	13899 ①–⑥ q	Ⓐ ◇	†	① Jg	⚒	3829 ① D	3829 ⑥ K	⚒	3832 3833	3831 ⑤ E	3831 ⑦ Kc	3835	⑤	①–④ n◇	Ⓐ	Ⓐ	⑤	A	3837	3839 ⑤⑦ e	①–④ Jn	4624 4625 🅁 N△
	Quimper **285** d.	...	...	...	...	...	...	...	...	...	0739	...	...	...	...	...	...	...	...	...	...	...	...	...
0	**Nantes 293** d.	...	...	...	...	...	...	0731	0805	...	1016	1209	1209	1409	...	...	...	...	...	...	1727	1900	1933	2034
77	La Roche sur Yon **293** d.	...	...	...	...	...	...	0821	0850	...	1101	1304	1254	1455	...	...	...	...	...	...	1812	1950	2031	2118
180	**La Rochelle** ▷ d.	...	0606	0642	0750	0751	0820	0933	0955	1122	1206	1424	1358	1558	1638	1649	...	1719	1753	1807	1917	2054	2134	2219
209	Rochefort ▷ d.	...	0632	0705	0815	0816	0848	0955	1016	1144	1226	1452	1418	1619	1701	1712	...	1747	1817	1836	1937	2114	...	2239
253	Saintes d.	0601	0702	0741	0845	0846	...	1024	1047	1218	1257	1552	1449	1648	1737	1747	1755	...	1858	1913	2007	2144	...	2310
376	**Bordeaux St Jean** a.	0750	0837	...	1016	1015	...	1151	1204	1351	1419	1719	1607	1814	...	...	1936	...	2046	...	2132	2304	...	0028
	Toulouse **320** a.	...	...	...	...	...	...	...	...	...	...	...	...	2054	...	...	...	...	...	...	...	...	...	|
	Marseille **355** a.	...	...	...	...	...	...	...	...	...	...	...	...	...	...	...	...	...	...	...	...	...	...	0644
	Nice **360** a.	...	...	...	...	...	...	...	...	...	...	...	...	...	...	...	...	...	...	...	...	...	...	0928

	②–⑤ M	4724 4725 🅁 N▽	Ⓐ	Ⓐ ◇	⑥ K	C	3848 ①⑥ B	3852	3850 ⑤ F§	3850 ⑦ Kc	⑥	Ⓐ	3854 3855	⚒	◇	3856 ⊖	Ⓐ	Ⓑ y	⑥ t	3858 ⑤	3858 ⑦ e	3888 ①–④ n	13898 ⑤⑦	⑤ J
Nice **360** d.	...	1832	...	...	...	...	...	...	...	...	...	...	...	...	...	...	...	...	...	...	...	...	...	...
Marseille **355** d.	...	2215	...	...	...	...	...	...	...	...	...	...	...	...	...	...	...	...	...	...	...	...	...	...
Toulouse **320** d.	...	|	...	...	...	...	...	0754r	...	...	...	...	...	...	...	...	...	...	...	...	...	...	...	...
Bordeaux St Jean d.	...	0457	...	...	0741	0819	0830	1034	1136	1151	1211	1220	1403	...	...	1703	1717	1757	1818	1851	1905	1905	2004	2140
Saintes d.	...	0618	0636	0736	0910	0946	0951	1155	1301	1313	1342	1349	1525	...	1742	1827	1905	1946	2009	2014	2028	2036	2144	2316
Rochefort ▷ d.	...	0647	0715	0814	0942	1018	1021	1223	1334	1343	1413	1418	1554	1714	1820	1859	...	...	...	2044	2058	2105	2215	2346
La Rochelle ▷ d.	0643	0727	0747	0836	1003	1040	1042	1244	1356	1405	1433	1438	1615	1745	1845	1922	...	...	...	2105	2119	2124	2240	0008
La Roche sur Yon **293** d.	0750	0830	...	...	...	...	1147	1351	1502	1511	...	...	1721	...	...	2028	...	...	...	2208	2220	...	...	...
Nantes 293 a.	0846	0916	...	...	...	...	1230	1438	1544	1552	...	...	1810	...	...	2113	...	...	...	2252	2304	...	...	...
Quimper **285** a.	...	...	...	...	...	...	...	...	...	...	...	...	2056	...	...	...	...	...	...	...	...	...	...	...

A – Daily except ⑤. Starts from Porte Dauphine (1759).
B – ①⑥ July 11 - Aug. 29 (not July 27). Also runs Bordeaux - La Rochelle on July 6.
C – ⑦ (also ⑥ to July 4 / from Sept. 5), not Aug. 15.
D – ① July 13 - Aug. 24 (not July 20).
E – ⑤ July 17 - Aug. 28 (not July 24).
F – ⑤ July 10 - Aug. 28 (not July 17, 31).
J – To July 4 and from Aug. 31.
K – July 5 - Aug. 30.
M – ②–⑤ to July 3 / from Sept. 1 (not Nov. 11).
N – ⑤⑦ (daily June 19 - Sept. 6, Oct. 23 - Nov. 4). 1,2 cl., (2) (reclining) Nantes - Nice and v.v.
c – Also July 14.
e – Also June 1, July 14.
g – Also June 2; not June 1.
n – Not June 1, July 14, Nov. 11.
q – Not June 1.
r – 0643 on Ⓐ Oct. 12 - Nov. 20.
t – Not Aug. 15.
y – On † depart 1756, arrive 1932.
◇ – To / from Angoulême (Table **301**).
△ – On June 5, 27, Sept. 5 runs up to 45 minutes earlier. On June 13 arrive Marseille 0737, Nice 1025.
▽ – On morning of June 28, Sept. 6 arrives up to 50 minutes later.
▷ – Additional local trains run La Rochelle Porte Dauphine - La Rochelle - Rochefort.
⊖ – Extended to Rennes on ⑤⑦ (also July 14, Nov. 11).
§ – Subject to alteration La Roche sur Yon - Nantes on July 24.

293 NANTES - LES SABLES D'OLONNE

For TGV trains see below — ***Local trains:*** **to July 4 and from Aug. 31** — *Subject to alteration Sept. 26 - Nov. 8*

km		Ⓐ	⚒	Ⓐ	⑥	†	†	Ⓐ	Ⓒ	⑤	Ⓐ	⑥		Ⓐ	Ⓐ	Ⓐ	Ⓒ	Ⓐ	⑤	⑥	Ⓑ	⑤⑦ d	†	⑤	⑤⑦ d
0	**Nantes 292** d.	...	0708	0857	0922	0926	1030	1233	1232	...	1424	1424	...	1635	1645	1735	1735	1815	1926	1926	2043	2043	2129	2132	2230
77	La Roche sur Yon **292** d.	0737	0830	0948	1010	1031	1119	1325	1338	1358	1511	1514	...	1722	1808	1843	1846	1906	2018	2020	2135	2137	2223	2223	2318
114	**Les Sables d'Olonne** a.	0808	0900	1015	1038	1058	1146	1353	1405	1427	1540	...	...	1751	1840	1914	1919	1933	...	2050	...	2205	2251	2251	...

	Ⓐ	⑥	Ⓐ	Ⓐ	Ⓒ	Ⓐ	Ⓐ			⑥	Ⓐ	Ⓐ	Ⓒ	Ⓐ	Ⓒ	Ⓐ	Ⓐ	⑦ d	Ⓐ	⑥	Ⓐ	†	Ⓐ	Ⓐ	†
Les Sables d'Olonne d.	0525	...	0634	0701	0724	0735	...	0917	...	1125	1130	1222	1219	1358	1415	1511	1637	1713	1719	1808	1810	1931	1950	...	...
La Roche sur Yon **292** d.	0553	0600	0700	0730	0752	0806	0852	0945	...	1152	1156	1250	1250	1426	1442	1540	1705	1741	1754	1836	1841	2000	2017	2028	2120
Nantes 292 a.	0644	0648	0748	0820	0850	...	0953	1038	...	1240	1242	1345	1345	1510	...	1628	1802	1843	1847	1938	1943	2050	...	2113	2208

For TGV trains see below — ***Local trains:*** **July 5 - Aug. 30**

km		Ⓐ	⚒		†	Ⓐ		⑤	Ⓐ B			Ⓐ		⚒	Ⓐ		Ⓐ	Ⓒ	Ⓐ	Ⓐ		⑤⑦ u	⑤⑦ u		
0	**Nantes 292** d.	...	0708	...	0902	0912	...	1118	1151	1233	...	1424	...	1635	1645	...	1735	1735	1815	1823	...	2132	2230	...	...
77	La Roche sur Yon **292** d.	0737	0830	...	1005	0959	...	1207	1239	1325	...	1511	...	1722	1808	...	1843	1846	1906	1937	...	2223	2318	...	...
114	**Les Sables d'Olonne** a.	0808	0900	...	1031	1025	...	1236	1307	1353	...	1540	...	1751	1840	...	1914	1919	1933	2007	...	2251	...	...	...

	⑥ t	⚒	Ⓐ	Ⓐ		Ⓐ	⚒			⑦ E	⑤	C	⑤⑦ q	①–④ m		⑦	Ⓐ	Ⓐ	†	⑥ t	Ⓐ	Ⓒ	Ⓐ	⑦	†
Les Sables d'Olonne d.	...	0600z	...	0701	0724	0735	0917	...	1206	1257	1326	1428	1458	1512	...	1620	1637	1722	1725	1808	1810	1938	*1938*	2024	...
La Roche sur Yon **292** d.	0600	0628	0653	0730	0752	0806	0945	...	1237	1326	1401	1455	1527	1540	...	1648	1705	1754	1752	1836	1841	2003	2028	2053	2115
Nantes 292 a.	0648	0720	0748	0820	0850	...	1038	...	1337	1409	1446	...	1614	1629	...	1745	1802	1847	1838	1938	1943	2049	2113	...	2208

TGV trains

TGV trains, 🅁	*TGV* 8913 J	*TGV* 8923 K	*TGV* 8955 Ⓐ	*TGV* 8957 Ⓒ
Paris M'parnasse **280** d.	1000	1100	1750	1750
Nantes d.	1224	1314	2020	2015
La Roche sur Yon d.	1307	1358	2103	2058
Les Sables d'Olonne a.	1332	1423	2128	2123

TGV trains, 🅁	*TGV* 8910 Ⓐ J	*TGV* 8936 Ⓑ K	*TGV* 8926 ⑥	*TGV* 8950 L	*TGV* 8962 M	*TGV* 8986 ⑦ e
Les Sables d'Olonne d.	0543	1043	1043	1547	1617	1810
La Roche sur Yon d.	0609	1110	1110	1613	1644	1836
Nantes a.	0652	1151	1152	1655	1725	1920
Paris M'parnasse **280** a.	0905	1410	1415	1915	1935	2135

B – Daily except ⑤ (will not run July 26, Aug. 2, 9, 16, 23).
C – Daily except ⑤ (will not run on Aug. 1).
E – ⑦ July 26 - Aug. 30.
J – To July 4 / from Aug. 31.
K – July 5 - Aug. 30.
L – To June 28 / from Aug. 31.
M – ①–⑥ June 29 - Aug. 29 (not July 14).

d – Also June 1, Nov. 11.
e – Also June 1, July 14.
m – Not July 14, 20 - 23.
q – Also July 14, Aug. 15; not July 24.
t – Not Aug. 15.
u – Also July 14.
z – ②–⑤ (not July 14, 15).
TGV – 🅁, supplement payable, 🍸.

294 PARIS - LES AUBRAIS - ORLÉANS

Selected trains

km		⚒	Ⓐ L	⚒	⚒		★	P		⚒	⚒			⚒	⚒		⑤		Ⓐ			Ⓑ	⚒	†	H
0	**Paris Austerlitz** § d.	0556	0624	0649	0703	0725	0754	0808	0921	1038	1048	1141	1218	1210	1241	1335	1456	1548	1632	1703	1721	1736	1805	1805	1818
56	Étampes § d.	0624	|	0719	|	|	|	|	|	|	|	|	|	1238	|	|	|	|	|	|	1750	|	|	|	|
119	Les Aubrais-Orléans a.	0717	0721	0816	0756	0821	0847	0905	1017	1153	1145	1234	1311	1330	1337	1431	1553	1646	1729	1803	1845	1830	1903	1903	1928
121	**Orléans** a.	0722	0727	0822	*0807*	*0833*	*0856*	0911	*1029*	1159	1151	1240	*1319*	1336	*1346*	1439	*1602*	*1655*	1735	1809	1849	*1840*	1909	*1913*	1933

	Ⓑ	⑤ J			G	⑤⑦	D		C	
Paris Austerlitz § d.	1836	1849	1903	1952	2048	2048	2152	2252	2344	...
Étampes § d.	|	|	|	|	|	|	|	|	|	...
Les Aubrais-Orléans a.	1933	1946	1955	2048	2145	2144	2251	2354	0045	...
Orléans a.	1939	1954	*2012*	2054	2151	*2156*	2257	*0005*	0050	...

	⚒	R	⚒	⚒	Ⓐ	⚒	⚒	† J	B	⚒	
Orléans d.	0504	0608	*0621*	0618	*0650*	0704	*0725*	0738	*0735*	0750	0841
Les Aubrais-Orléans d.	0509	0614	0629	0624	0658	0711	0736	0743	0745	0755	0846
Étampes § a.	|	|	|	0726	|	|	|	|	|	0841	|
Paris Austerlitz § a.	0611	0713	0727	0803	0800	0812	0830	0841	0841	0913	0944

	†	⚒ u	u		⚒ u	⚒ d	u	⚒	Ⓐ	Ⓒ	† J	u	⚒			⚒			Ⓑ	L	†	Ⓐ	⑦ e		
Orléans d.	0857	0941	1036	*1125*	1140	1227	1231	*1320*	*1356*	1434	1601	1633	1719	*1751*	1813	*1821*	1854	...	1924	*1956*	2043	2059	*2123*	2219	...
Les Aubrais-Orléans d.	0902	0946	1041	1134	1145	1232	1238	1328	1405	1439	1606	1638	1724	1801	1819	1832	1859	...	1930	2006	2049	2104	2131	2225	...
Étampes § a.	|	|	|	|	|	1328	|	|	|	|	|	1705	|	|	1921	|	|	...	|	|	2119	|	|	|	...
Paris Austerlitz § a.	1023	1044	1140	1228	1244	1356	1336	1423	1505	1538	1704	1735	1838	1859	1951	1926	1957	...	2052	2105	2150	2204	2223	2321r	...

B – ⚒ to June 27; Ⓐ June 29 - Aug. 28; ⚒ from Aug. 31.
C – Daily to July 4; ⑦ July 5 - Aug. 30 (also July 14); daily from Aug. 31.
D – ⑤⑦ (also June 1, July 14, Aug. 15, Nov. 11).
G – ①–④ (not June 1, July 13, 14, Nov. 11).
H – ①–④ (not June 1, July 14, Nov. 11).
J – To July 4 / from Aug. 31.
L – To June 26 / from Aug. 31.
P – Ⓐ (also ⑥ to July 4 / from Aug. 29).
R – ②–⑤ to July 3 / from Sept. 1 (not Nov. 11).
d – Runs up to 18 minutes earlier on Ⓐ Nov. 9 - 27.
e – Also June 1, July 14.
r – 2335 on ①–④ to June 25, Oct. 5 - Dec. 3.
u – Subject to alteration Sept. 12 - Oct. 16.
★ – CORAIL TÉOZ. 🅁, 🍸.
§ – Suburban trains run Paris Austerlitz - Étampes and v.v. approximately every 30 minutes (journey 55 minutes).

PARIS - TOURS — 295

TGV trains

km	*TGV* trains convey 🍸	*TGV* 8405	*TGV* 8315 ①-⑥ n	*TGV* 5200	*TGV* 8317	*TGV* 5212 9802 b	*TGV* 8417*		*TGV* 8323	*TGV* 8333 ‡	*TGV* 5218	*TGV* 8441 ‡	*TGV* 8343 ⑤	*TGV* 8345 ⑤	*TGV* 8349 ①-④ n	*TGV* 5216 ⑦ e	*TGV* 5205 ①-④ n	*TGV* 8347 ⑤ J	*TGV* 8353 ⑤	*TGV* 8451	*TGV* 5222 ⑤⑥	*TGV* 8363 ①-④ n	*TGV* 8357 ⑤	*TGV* 8365 D	*TGV* 8367 Ⓐ ¶
	Lille Europe **11** d.	...	...	0558	...	0759	...	...	...	...	1238v	...	...	...	...	1447	1447	...	...	...	1540	...	...	...	...
	Charles de Gaulle ✈ d.	...	...	0739	...	0858	...	...	...	...	1337	...	...	...	...	1542	1542	...	...	...	1637	...	...	...	...
	Marne la Vallée - Chessy d.	...	...	0756	...	0912	...	...	...	...	1351	...	...	...	...	1557	1557	...	...	...	1652	...	...	...	...
0	**Paris Montparnasse** d.	0650	0750	|	0910	|	1050	...	1225	1350	|	1515	1535	1610	1615	|	|	1645	1655	1715	|	1740	1755	1810	1840
14	Massy-TGV d.	0702	|	0831	|	0946	|	...	|	|	1431	|	|	|	|	1631	1636	|	|	|	1730	|	|	|	|
162	Vendôme-Villiers TGV d.	|	0835	|	|	|	|	...	1310	|	|	|	|	1654	|	|	|	|	|	|	|	|	1839	1855	1923
221	St Pierre des Corps a.	0752	0853	0921	1006	1035	1146	...	1327	1447	1521	1611	1631	1712	1712	1721	1727	1740	1751	1811	1821	1835	1858	1914	1942
221	St Pierre des Corps d.	*0757*	0855	*0926*	*1011*	*1040*	*1158*	...	1330	*1455*	*1526*	*1616*	1633	1714	1714	*1726*	*1732*	1743	*1756*	*1816*	*1829*	1837	1900	1916	1945
224	**Tours** a.	*0802*	0900	*0931*	*1016*	*1045*	*1203*	...	1335	*1500*	*1531*	*1621*	1639	1719	1719	*1731*	*1737*	1748	*1801*	*1821*	*1834*	1842	1905	1921	1950

TGV trains convey 🍸	*TGV* 8469	*TGV* 5231 F	*TGV* 8375 ①-⑥ n	*TGV* 8377 ⑦ e	*TGV* 5242 ⑤-⑦ e	*TGV* 8483 ①-④ J	*TGV* 8383 ⑤⑦ e	*TGV* 8489 ⑦ e	*TGV* 8391 ⑤ ▷	*TGV* 8497 ⑤
Lille Europe **11** d.	...	1729	...	...	1829r	...	...	...	...	...
Charles de Gaulle ✈ d.	...	1824	...	...	1925	...	...	...	...	...
Marne la Vallée - Chessy d.	...	1840	...	...	1942	...	...	...	...	...
Paris Montparnasse d.	1850	|	1930	1930	|	2020	2030	2110	2120	2135
Massy-TGV d.	|	1921	|	|	2018	|	|	|	|	|
Vendôme-Villiers TGV d.	|	|	2015	|	|	2105	2114	|	|	|
St Pierre des Corps a.	1946	2011	2033	2025	2110	2124	2132	2206	2216	2231
St Pierre des Corps d.	*1952*	*2017*	2036	*2030*	*2115*	*2134*	2134	*2211*	*2224*	*2236*
Tours a.	*1957*	*2022*	2041	*2035*	*2120*	*2139*	2139	*2216*	*2229*	*2241*

	TGV 8300 ①-④ n	*TGV* 8320 ⑤	*TGV* 8302 Ⓐ	*TGV* 8332 ⑥	*TGV* 8304 Ⓐ J	*TGV* 5260 ①-⑥ n	*TGV* 8310 ①-⑥ n	*TGV* 8312 ⑦ e	*TGV* 5260 ⑦ e	*TGV* 8414
Tours d.	0610	0624	0652	0727	0740	*0752*	0806	*0809*	*0829*	*0926*
St Pierre des Corps a.	0615	0629	0657	0732	0745	*0757*	0811	*0814*	*0834*	*0931*
St Pierre des Corps d.	0618	0632	0700	0735	0747	0803	0814	0823	0841	0938
Vendôme-Villiers TGV d.	0640	0653	0722	0757	|	|	0837	|	|	|
Massy-TGV a.	|	0728	|	|	|	|	|	|	|	|
Paris Montparnasse a.	0725	0740	0805	0840	0845	|	0920	0920	|	1035
Marne la Vallée - Chessy a.	...	...	...	...	...	0926	...	...	1006	...
Charles de Gaulle ✈ a.	...	...	...	...	...	0942	...	...	1021	...
Lille Europe **11** a.	...	...	...	...	...	1046	...	...	1128	...

	TGV 5264	*TGV* 8318 ①-④ J	*TGV* 8420 ◇	*TGV* 8322	*TGV* 8324	*TGV* 5276	*TGV* 8328 ⑤	*TGV* 8436	*TGV* 8540	*TGV* 9816 5279 b	*TGV* 8346 Ⓑ	*TGV* 8548	*TGV* 8350 ⑤	*TGV* 8358 ⑤ J	*TGV* 8364 ⑤-⑦ e	*TGV* 8362 ①-④ n	*TGV* 5284 Ⓑ	*TGV* 8466 ⑦ e	*TGV* 8472* ①-⑥ n⊙	*TGV* 8474* ⑦ e	*TGV* 8378 ⑦ e	*TGV* 5292 ①-⑥ n	*TGV* 8584	*TGV* 8386 ⑤	*TGV* 8390 ⑦ e§
Tours d.	*1012*	1020	*1024*	1209	*1252*	*1320*	1412	*1441*	*1612*	*1643*	1712	*1742*	1755	1829	*1855*	*1911*	*1917*	*1957*	*2020*	*2035*	2054	*2112*	*2208*	*2236*	*2307*
St Pierre des Corps a.	*1017*	1025	*1029*	1214	*1257*	*1325*	1417	*1446*	*1617*	*1648*	1717	*1747*	1800	1834	*1900*	*1916*	*1922*	*2002*	*2025*	*2040*	2059	*2117*	*2213*	*2241*	*2312*
St Pierre des Corps d.	1023	1038	1038	1217	1302	1332	1422	1452	1622	1656	1720	1753	1805	1836	1908	1923	1928	2007	2032	2048	2101	2122	2221	2252	2318
Vendôme-Villiers TGV d.	|	|	|	1237	|	|	|	|	|	|	1748	|	|	1857	|	|	|	|	|	|	2122	|	|	|	|
Massy-TGV a.	1113	|	|	|	|	1423	|	|	|	1747	|	|	|	|	|	|	2018	|	|	2138	|	2213	|	|	|
Paris Montparnasse a.	|	1135	1135	1320	1400	|	1520	1550	1720	|	1835	1850	1905	1940	2005	2020	|	2105	2130	2150	2205	|	2320	2350	0015
Marne la Vallée - Chessy a.	1154	...	...	...	...	1506	...	...	...	1826	...	...	...	...	...	...	2057	...	...	...	...	2251	...	...	...
Charles de Gaulle ✈ a.	1209	...	...	...	...	1521	...	...	...	1841	...	...	...	...	...	...	2112	...	...	...	...	2306	...	...	...
Lille Europe **11** a.	1306	...	...	...	...	1615	...	...	...	2005v	...	...	...	...	...	...	2219	...	...	...	...	0007	...	...	...

D – ①②③④⑦ (also ⑥ to July 4 / from Sept. 5).
F – Ⓑ (daily July 5 - Aug. 30).
J – To July 4 / from Aug. 31.
b – To / from Lille Europe and Brussels (Table **11**).
e – Also June 1, July 14.
n – Not June 1, July 14.
r – On July 14 depart Lille **Flandres** at 1824.

v – Lille **Flandres**.
TGV – Ⓡ, supplement payable, 🍸.
▷ – Train number **8393** on ⑤ Apr. 3 - Aug. 28.
◇ – Train number **8422** on ⑦ **e**.
⊙ – On ⑤ runs 5 minutes later St Pierre des Corps - Paris.

¶ – Train number **8371** on ⑤.
‡ – On ⑦ **e 8333** is numbered **8331**; **8441** is **8547**.
§ – Train number **8394** on ⑦ to June 28 (also June 1).
* – In July / Aug. train numbers are altered as follows: **8417** is **8521** on ⑥, **8472** is **8476**, **8474** is **8478**.

ORLÉANS - BLOIS - TOURS — 296

For fast *TGV* services Paris - Tours and v.v. see Table **295**

km		⚒	Ⓐ	Ⓐ	⚒	Ⓒ	Ⓐ	Ⓐ L	4003 N	⚒		†			Ⓐ	Ⓐ	⚒	⚒		⚒		⑤	⑤	
	Paris Austerlitz **294** d.	...	...	...	...	...	...	0624	0624	...	0725	...	...	0921	...	...	1048	...	1141	1241	1335	...	1456	...
0	**Orléans** d.	...	0641	0624	0702	0728	0728	0737	0737	0746	*0813*	0851	...	*1010*	1021	1109	1201	1221	1250	*1331*	1449	1540	*1546*	...
2	Les Aubrais-Orléans d.	...	|	|	|	|	|	0723x	0723x	|	0823	|	...	1019	1030	|	1147x	|	1236x	1339	1433x	|	1555	...
30	Beaugency d.	...	|	0643	0723	|	|	0759	0759	0815	0841	0918	...	1038	1055	|	1222	1246	1312	|	1510	1557	|	...
61	Blois d.	0637	0708	0713	0743	0755	0755	0823	0823	0840	0902	0943	...	1100	1113	1137	1244	1311	1334	1408	1531	1616	1625	...
93	Amboise d.	0704	|	0733	0801	|	|	0845	0845	...	0922	1008	...	1121	...	|	1305	1337	1354	|	1552	1634	|	...
115	St Pierre des Corps a.	0719	0735	0744	0814	0818	0818	0900	0858	...	0936	1023	...	1133	...	1200	1316	1351	1406	1434	1603	1647	1650	...
118	**Tours** a.	0725	*0745*	0751	0820	*0829*	0825	0907	*0910*	...	0943	1030	...	1140	...	*1209*	1323	1358	1413	1441	1610	1653	1659	...
	Nantes **289** a.	...	0910	...	...	1001	...	...	...	...	...	...	...	...	...	1337	...	...	...	...	...	...	...	...

	①-④ m	⑤	⑤⑥ t	①-④ m	Ⓐ		①-④ m	†	⚒	†	Ⓐ	⚒		⑥	Ⓑ	Ⓐ	†	⚒	Ⓑ	Ⓐ		Ⓑ		
Paris Austerlitz **294** d.	...	...	...	...	...	1548	...	...	...	...	1632	...	1706	1706	1736	...	1805	1805	1836	...	1952	...	...	2252
Orléans d.	1558	1607	1630	1607	...	*1641*	1727	1713	1735	1759	1745	...	1819	1819	*1822*	1850	*1858*	1919	1949	1954	2104	2141	...	*2344*
Les Aubrais-Orléans d.	|	|	|	|	...	1648	|	|	|	|	1731x	...	1805x	1805x	1832	|	1906	1905x	1935x	|	2050x	2153	...	2356
Beaugency d.	1616	1634	|	1634	...	1706	|	1739	1802	|	1808	...	1839	1839	|	1917	1924	1941	|	2021	2125	2212	...	|
Blois d.	1635	1651	1658	1701	1701	1728	1754	1805	1826	1826	1832	1842	1859	1901	1906	1942	1945	2003	2024	2039	2147	2232	...	0024
Amboise d.	1654	...	|	1728	1728	1749	|	1830	...	1840	1853	1908	...	1922	|	2007	2005	2024	...	...	2208	2251	...	|
St Pierre des Corps a.	1704	...	1721	1744	1744	1801	1817	1845	...	1853	1904	1923	...	1933	1929	2022	2017	2038	...	...	2220	2302	...	0050
Tours a.	1711	...	*1731*	1751	1751	1808	*1828*	1853	...	*1903*	1911	1930	...	1938	1936	2029	2024	2045	...	...	2226	2308	...	0055
Nantes **289** a.	...	...	1857	...	...	...	1956	...	...	2029	...	...	...	...	...	...	...	...	...	...	...	...	...	...

	⚒	⚒	Ⓐ	⚒	⚒	Ⓐ	⚒		⚒	Ⓐ	⚒	Ⓐ	Ⓐ		†	Ⓒ	⚒			⚒	⑥ t	Ⓐ	Ⓐ	Ⓒ
Nantes **289** d.	...	...	...	...	...	...	...	...	...	...	...	0706	...	...	...	0849	...	...	...	...	...	...	1123	...
Tours d.	...	0532	...	...	0631	...	0647	0708	...	0802	0813	*0829*	...	0904	0940	*1024*	1027	...	1101	...	1230	1229	*1247*	1304
St Pierre des Corps d.	...	0539	...	...	0638	...	0653	0715	...	0809	0820	0839	...	0911	0947	1034	1034	...	1108	...	1236	1236	1257	1310
Amboise d.	...	0551	...	...	0649	...	0710	0727	...	|	0832	|	...	0924	1005	1047	|	...	1120	...	1251	1253	|	1323
Blois d.	0549	0613	0628	0632	0707	0714	0735	0749	0753	0836	0852	0906	0924	0946	1030	1104	1101	...	1141	1227	1316	1325	1322	1344
Beaugency d.	0610	0634	|	0652	|	0732	...	0811	0819	|	0912	|	0943	1006	1055	|	|	...	1201	1253	...	1346	|	1404
Les Aubrais-Orléans a.	0627	0709v	0656	|	0732	|	...	0844v	|	|	0944v	|	|	1040v	|	|	1143v	...	1234v	1319	...	1403	|	1437v
Orléans a.	*0636*	0654	*0705*	0719	*0742*	0800	...	0831	0846	0905	0931	0935	1010	1039	1121	1128	1130	...	1221	1328	...	*1412*	1349	1424
Paris Austerlitz **294** a.	0727	0812	0800	...	0830	...	...	0944	...	...	1044	...	...	1140	...	...	1244	...	1336	...	...	1505	...	1538

		Ⓐ	Ⓐ		Ⓐ			Ⓐ		4004 N	L	⑦ M	Ⓐ	†	Ⓐ	Ⓐ	⑥ t			⑥ t	†		†	Ⓐ
Nantes **289** d.	...	...	...	...	...	...	...	1630	...	...	...	...	...	...	...	1818	...	...	...	1945	2012	...	...	...
Tours d.	1500	1550	1630	1656	...	1723	1735	1811	...	*1814*	1842	1851	1852	1911	1911	*1939*	1947	2047	...	*2126*	*2133*	...	2219	2223
St Pierre des Corps d.	1506	1557	1636	1703	...	1730	1740	1818	...	1827	1849	1858	1858	1918	1918	1954	1954	2053	...	2136	2143	...	2225	2230
Amboise d.	1520	1611	1652	|	...	1743	1756	|	...	1840	1901	1911	1914	1931	1930	|	2006	2106	...	|	|	...	2236	2242
Blois d.	1541	1631	1718	1730	1735	1804	1820	1843	...	1902	1924	1933	1938	1953	1954	2019	2025	2128	...	2200	2207	...	2256	2301
Beaugency d.	1601	1658	...	|	1801	1825	1839	|	...	1922	1945	1954	...	2013	2012	|	2043	2149	...	|	|	...	2314	2320
Les Aubrais-Orléans a.	1636v	|	...	1758	|	|	|	|	...	2004v	2004	2013	...	2047v	|	|	|	2223v	...	|	|	...	|	|
Orléans a.	1621	1725	...	*1806*	1828	1844	1905	1912	...	1944	*2013*	*2021*	...	2033	2029	2044	2101	2209	...	2226	2232	...	2331	2339
Paris Austerlitz **294** a.	1735	...	...	1859	...	1957	...	...	...	2105	2105	2113	...	2150	...	...	...	2321	...	...	...	...	...	...

L – To June 26 / from Aug. 31.
M – ⑦ June 28 - Aug. 30 (also July 14, Aug. 15).
N – June 27 - Aug. 30. To / from Royan (Table **301**).
m – Not June 1, July 14, Nov. 11.

t – Not Aug. 15.
v – Calls after Orléans.
x – Calls before Orléans.

299 OTHER LOCAL SERVICES

ANGERS - CHOLET: *60 km* Journey 50 - 65 minutes

Angers depart: 0646 Ⓐ, 0722 Ⓐ, 0754 ⚒ **J**, 0938 ⚒, 1148 Ⓐ, 1151 Ⓒ, 1303 Ⓐ, 1310 ⑥ **t**, 1556 **J**, 1556 Ⓐ **K**, 1638 ⑥, 1638 ⑦ **K**, 1725 Ⓐ **J**, 1741 Ⓐ, 1846 ⚒, 1934 Ⓑ, 2042 †, 2043 ⚒, 2138 ⑤, 2244 Ⓐ **J**, 2245 ⑦.

Cholet depart: 0611 Ⓐ, 0633 ⚒, 0655 Ⓐ, 0711 ⑥ **t**, 0744 Ⓐ, 0842 ⚒, 0844 †, 1046 ⚒, 1237 ⚒, 1352 †, 1357 ⚒, 1648 Ⓑ **J**, 1737, 1840 ⑦, 1843 Ⓐ, 1941 Ⓑ, 1944 ⑥, 2204 ⑦.

BAYONNE - ST JEAN PIED DE PORT *50 km*

	①	M	⚒				⚒		⑤⑦	
	g		J	K	J	K	H	K	J	
Bayonne ... d.	0745	0824	1158	1437	1506	1720	1812	1958	2106	...
St Jean Pied de Port ... a.	0858	0937	1311	1550	1619	1834	1935	2111	2218	...

	Ⓐ		⑥					†		
	J	K	J			K	H	J	K	
St Jean Pied de Port ... d.	0619	0643	0658	0945	1320	1556	1635	1839	1839	...
Bayonne ... a.	0737	0758	0816	1058	1433	1709	1748	1951	1951	...

BORDEAUX - MONT DE MARSAN *147 km*

	⚒	Ⓐ			⚒	†	⚒			Q	⑤
Bordeaux 305 ... d.	...	0636	0836	1036	1236	1336	1436	1726	...	2136	2156
Morcenx **305** ... d.	0658	0735	0935	1135	1335	1435	1535	1825	1935	2235	2255
Mont de Marsan .. a.	0727	0759	0955	1158	1358	1455	1555	1848	1959	2255	2315

	Ⓐ	⚒	⚒		⚒				Ⓑh	Ⓒ	
Mont de Marsan .. d.	0554	0624	0804	1004	1204	1404	1614	1754	1904	2004	...
Morcenx **305** ... d.	0616	0650	0826	1026	1226	1426	1634	1824	1926	2026	...
Bordeaux 305 ... a.	0716	...	0925	1125	1325	1525	1735	...	2025	...	...

CARCASSONNE - LIMOUX - QUILLAN

Rail journeys 1000 - 1500 hrs are replaced by 🚌 on Ⓐ May 25 - June 19

km											
		🚌	⚒	🚌†	⚒	⚒	🚌†	⚒	⚒	⚒	🚌†
0	Carcassonne ... d.	0610	0717	0915	1050	1237	1326	1611	1731	1845	1839
26	Limoux ... a.	0643	0747	0948	1120	1307	1359	1641	1801	1915	1912
54	Quillan ... a.	0723	...	1028	*1210*r	1343	1439	*1735*r	...	1951	1952

	⚒	⚒	🚌†	⚒	🚌†	⚒	⚒	🚌†	⚒	🚌⚒	🚌†
Quillan ... d.	0602	...	0736	*1035*r	1040	1354	*1555*r	1606	...	1750	2007
Limoux ... d.	0637	0755	0816	1127	1122	1429	1646	1650	1808	1833	2047
Carcassonne ... a.	0708	0826	0849	1157	1200	1500	1717	1727	1840	1910	2120

CHARLEVILLE MÉZIÈRES - GIVET: *64 km* Journey 65 - 75 minutes

Note: service is by 🚌 July 5 - Aug. 30.

Charleville Mézières depart: 0605 ⚒, 0650 ⚒, 0743 Ⓐ, 1010 ⚒, 1115, 1220 ⚒, 1258 ⑥, 1330, 1440, 1615, 1635 Ⓐ, 1730 ⚒, 1819 Ⓐ, 1837 Ⓐ, 1908 Ⓐ, 1915 ⑥, 1932 Ⓑ, 2040 **y**.

Givet depart: 0450 Ⓐ, 0511 ⑥, 0520 Ⓐ, 0553 Ⓐ, 0609 ⑥, 0645 Ⓐ, 0653 Ⓒ, 0738 ⑥, 0743 Ⓐ, 1010, 1209 ⑥, 1233 ⚒, 1349 Ⓐ, 1358 ⑥, 1451 Ⓑ, 1610 Ⓑ, 1713 ⚒, 1740 †, 1747 Ⓐ, 1753 ⑥, 1821 Ⓐ, 1905 Ⓑ.

DINARD - ST MALO

🚌 : 7 - 10 times per day (3 - 5 on †), journey 24 minutes. Operator: TIV. *11 km*

⛴ : *Le Bus de Mer* passenger ferry operates 10 - 15 times daily from April to October. Journey time 10 minutes.

LILLE - LENS: *39 km* Journey 31 - 48 minutes

Lille Flandres depart: 0548 Ⓐ, 0700 ⚒, 0724 Ⓐ, 0756 ⑥ **E**, 0759 Ⓐ **J**, 0825 Ⓐ, 0902 ⚒, 1003 †, 1142 ⑥ **t**, 1156 Ⓑ, 1242 ⚒, 1329, 1558, 1626 Ⓐ, 1658 **J**, 1658 Ⓒ **K**, 1723 Ⓐ, 1758, 1827 Ⓐ, 1858 Ⓐ, 1934 ⑥ **t**, 1942 Ⓑ, 2026.

Lens depart: 0524 ⚒, 0626 ⚒, 0652 ⚒ **E**, 0652 Ⓐ **F**, 0724 ⚒, 0756 ⚒, 0827 Ⓐ, 0851 **E**, 0851 † **F**, 0958 ⑥ **t**, 1054 Ⓒ, 1119 ⚒ **E**, 1119 Ⓐ **F**, 1230 ⚒, 1255 Ⓐ, 1258 †, 1342 ⑥ **t**, 1431 Ⓒ, 1556 Ⓐ **J**, 1556 ⑥ **t**, 1630 Ⓑ, 1658 ⚒, 1730 †, 1737 Ⓐ, 1758 ⚒, 1850 ⚒, 1900 †, 2002.

NANTES - CHOLET: *65 km* Journey 51 - 65 minutes

Nantes depart: 0634 ⚒, 0805 Ⓐ 🚌, 0915 ⑥ 🚌, 1237 ‡, 1635 ⚒ 🚌, 1709 Ⓐ, 1844 **A**.

Cholet depart: 0607 ⚒, 0635 Ⓐ 🚌, 0739 Ⓐ, 1219 ⑦ **J**, 1240 ⚒ 🚌, 1654 Ⓐ, 1825 Ⓐ, 2042 ⑦.

PARIS - CHÂTEAUDUN - VENDÔME

Subject to alteration June 29 - Aug. 7. Certain journeys continue to Tours

km										
			⚒		⑤	Ⓐ	⚒	⑦	⑤	⑦
0	Paris Austerlitz ... d.	0825	1152	1350	1618	1748	1854	1916	2211	2239
134	Châteaudun ... a.	0958	1319	1519	1749	1926	2026	2043	2339	0006
178	Vendôme ... a.	1038	...	1601	1829	...	2107	2122	...	...

	⚒	⚒		⑤	⚒		⑦	⑤	⑦	
Vendôme ... d.	0537	...	...	1437	...	1616	1742	...	2001	...
Châteaudun ... d.	0617	0721	1023	1525	1525	1656	1821	2033	2047	...
Paris Austerlitz ... a.	0756	0857	1153	1655	1655	1829	1954	2201	2215	...

PARIS - DISNEYLAND (Marne la Vallée - Chessy): *32 km* Journey 39 minutes

Trains run approximately every 15 minutes 0500 - 2400 on RER Line A:
Paris Châtelet les Halles - Paris Gare de Lyon - Marne la Vallée Chessy (for Disneyland).
Operator: RATP. For *TGV* services serving Marne la Vallée see Tables **11**, **391**.

ST BRIEUC - DINAN

km												
		Ⓐ	Ⓐ	⑥	†	⚒		⑥	Ⓐ	†	⚒	†
		J	K	t	J n	J	K	J	J	J ◇	K	K
0	St Brieuc **284** . d.	0651	0652	0717	1231	1320	1320	1713	1718	1714	1722	1730
21	Lamballe **284** . d.	0708	0709	0735	1248	1336	1336	1730	1736	1733	1739	1748
62	Dinan ... a.	0743	0745	0809	1323	1412	1412	1805	1810	1812	1814	1825

	Ⓐ	⑥	Ⓐ	Ⓐ	Ⓐ§	Ⓒ		⑥	Ⓐ	⚒	†
		t	△	◇ K	◇ J	◇ q		J	J	K	
Dinan ... d.	0627	0657	0749	1051	1057	1131	...	1820	1831	1831	1920
Lamballe **284** ... a.	0702	0730	0821	1123	1128	1206	...	1853	1905	1905	1954
St Brieuc **284** ... a.	0719	0747	0835	1141	1147	1221	...	1912	1923	1923	2012

TOULOUSE - AUCH: *88 km* Journey 90 - 100 minutes

Subject to alteration July 11, 12, 18, 19, Dec. 12. 🚌 serves Toulouse gare routière.

Toulouse Matabiau depart: 0627 Ⓐ, 0727 **b**, 1040 **a**, 1227, 1427 Ⓐ **b**, 1615 ⚒ 🚌, 1627 Ⓐ **b**, 1727 **b**, 1827, 2027, 2120 🚌.

Auch depart: 0607 Ⓐ, 0707, 0747 ⚒ 🚌, 0807 Ⓐ, 0907, 1107, 1407 Ⓐ **a**, 1407 Ⓒ, 1500 🚌, 1707, 1807, 1907.

TOURS - CHINON: *49 km* Journey 45 - 50 minutes (70 minutes by 🚌)

Note: service is by 🚌 July 14 - Aug. 30.

Tours depart: 0534 Ⓐ, 0640 ⚒ 🚌, 0735 Ⓐ, 0800 † 🚌, 0909 ⑥ **J**, 0915 Ⓐ 🚌, 1145 † 🚌, 1220 ⚒, 1410, 1633 ⚒, 1719 Ⓐ, 1750 Ⓐ 🚌, 1832, 1929 Ⓐ, 2058 ⑤⑦.

Chinon depart: 0635 Ⓐ, 0639 ⑥, 0714 Ⓐ, 0745 ⚒, 0837 Ⓐ, 0919 🚌, 1100 Ⓐ 🚌, 1116 ⑥, 1314 ⚒, 1335 † 🚌, 1516 ⑥, 1615 Ⓑ, 1728 ⚒ **J**, 1728 Ⓐ **K**, 1816 Ⓐ, 1915 ①–④ **m** 🚌, 1934 ⑤⑥, 1946 †, 2010 ⑤ 🚌.

VALENCIENNES - CAMBRAI: *40 km* Journey 36 - 44 minutes

Valenciennes depart: 0631 ⚒, 0726 ⚒, 0807 ⚒, 1013 Ⓐ, 1220 Ⓐ **J**, 1220 ⑥ **t**, 1309 ⚒ **J**, 1309 Ⓐ **K**, 1717, 1744 Ⓐ, 1837 Ⓐ, 1928 Ⓐ, 2010 †.

Cambrai depart: 0603 Ⓐ, 0644 ⚒, 0744 ⚒ **J**, 0744 Ⓐ **K**, 0752 ⑥ **K t**, 0759 Ⓐ **J**, 0957 ⑥ **t**, 1102 Ⓐ, 1209 Ⓐ, 1211 ⑥ **J**, 1314 Ⓐ **J**, 1352 ⑥ **t**, 1712 Ⓐ, 1812 Ⓒ, 1836 Ⓐ, 1921 †, 1942 Ⓐ.

A – Daily except ⑤ (runs daily July 4 - Aug. 30).
E – To June 28 / from Aug. 31.
F – June 29 - Aug. 30.
H – To July 4 / from Sept. 1.
J – To July 4 / from Aug. 31.
K – July 5 - Aug. 30.
M – ②–⑦ (daily June 30 - Aug. 31), also June 1, Oct. 26, Nov. 2; not June 2, Sept. 2, Nov. 5.
Q – ①②③④⑦ (also Aug. 15).

a – Depart / arrive Toulouse Arènes (connection by métro with main station).
b – From Toulouse Arènes (13 minutes later) on Ⓐ to Aug. 28.
g – ① to June 29 / from Sept. 7 (also June 2, Sept. 2, Nov. 5; not June 1, Oct. 26, Nov. 2).

h – Also Aug. 15.
m – Not holidays.
n – On June 14 runs 10 minutes later.
q – Not June 13, 14, Nov. 11.
r – By 🚌.
t – Not Aug. 15.
y – 2100 on ⑤.

◇ – To / from Dol (Table **282**).
△ – Subject to alteration Aug. 31 - Sept. 11.
§ – Subject to alteration June 8 - 19, Aug. 31 - Sept. 11.
‡ – Subject to alteration on ①–④ Oct. 5 - 29.

300 NOTES FOR TABLE 300 (for page 193 opposite) →

A – Daily except ⑤.
B – ①–⑥ (daily June 29 - Aug. 30).
D – Also runs on ⑥ July 11 - Aug. 29.
F – ⑦ (also ①–④ July 6 - Aug. 27).
J – To July 4 / from Aug. 31.
K – July 5 - Aug. 30.
M – ①②③④⑦ only.
N – ①②③④⑥ (not June 1, July 14).
P – ①②③④⑥ (not June 1, July 14, Aug. 15, Nov. 11).
R – Will not run on ⑥ July 11 - Aug. 29.
S – ⑥ July 11 - Aug. 29.

b – On June 13 runs up to 25 minutes earlier.
c – Ⓒ only.
e – Also June 1, July 14.
g – Also June 2, July 15, Nov. 12; not June 1.
n – Not June 1, July 14.
q – Not June 1, July 13, 14, Aug. 14, Nov. 10, 11.
r – Arrival time varies by up to 30 mins later on certain dates.

t – Not Aug. 15.
u – On ⑥ Poitiers d. 0723, Niort 0814, La Rochelle 0851.
w – Runs up to 20 minutes earlier on June 2 - 5, July 27 - 30.
y – Runs up to 50 minutes earlier on ⑤ to June 26 and ⑤ Oct. 9 - Dec. 4; up to 20 minutes earlier on ⑤ Sept. 4 - Oct. 2 (also July 3).
z – Lille **Flandres**.

TGV – Ⓡ, supplement payable, 🍷.

♥ – From Lyon (Table **335**).
♣ – (12) Brussels (d. 0731) - Bordeaux (Table **11**); (12) Lille Europe (train **5212**) - Charles de Gaulle ✈ - Bordeaux.
◧ – Runs 8 minutes earlier on ⑤.
☆ – From Strasbourg (Table **391**).
▷ – On July 14 depart Lille **Flandres** at 1824.
⊕ – Runs up to 25 mins earlier Aug. 24 - Sept. 4.
⊖ – Not for journeys to/from Poitiers or Châtellerault.
◇ – Runs up to 30 minutes earlier on certain dates - please enquire when reserving seats.
• – Train number **8393** July 3 - Aug. 28.

PARIS - POITIERS - LA ROCHELLE and BORDEAUX 300

km	*TGV* trains convey 🍷							*TGV* 8501		*TGV* 8405	*TGV* 8305		*TGV* 8505	*TGV* 8507		*TGV* 8411	*TGV* 8511	*TGV* 8513	*TGV* 5200	*TGV* 5200	*TGV* 5203	*TGV* 5356	*TGV* 8317	*TGV* 8415	*TGV* 9802
		Ⓐ	Ⓐ	⚒	⚒	①	②–⑤	Ⓐ	②–⑤		①–⑥	†		①–⑥	⑥	⑦	Ⓐ	Ⓒ		⑥	⑥	⑥		①–⑥	♣
			w	u		g	q		q		n			n◇	t	e	◇				K	♥		n⊕	
	Lille Europe **11** d.	...	...	...	...	...	...	...	...	...	...	...	...	...	...	...	...	...	0558	0558	0558	...	...	...	0759
	Charles de Gaulle ✈ d.	...	...	...	...	...	...	...	...	...	...	...	...	...	...	...	...	...	0739	0739	0739	...	...	...	0858
	Marne la Vallee - Chessy d.	...	...	...	...	...	...	...	...	...	...	...	...	...	...	...	...	...	0756	0756	0756	...	...	...	0912
0	**Paris Montparnasse 295** d.	...	...	...	...	...	...	0610	...	0650	0720	...	0715	0745	...	0755	0810	0810	|	|	|	...	0910	0915	|
14	Massy TGV **295** d.	...	...	...	...	...	...	|	...	0702	|	...	|	|	...	|	|	|	0831	0831	0831	0901	|	|	0946
	Tours d.	...	...	...	0601	0642	0649	|	...	*0745*	|	...	|	|	0825	|	|	|	*0913*	*0913*	*0913*	*0944*	*0956*	|	*1024*
221	St Pierre des Corps **295** d.	...	...	...	|	|	|	|	...	0755	|	...	|	|	0840	|	|	|	0925	0925	0925	0954	1009	|	1038
289	Châtellerault d.	...	...	...	0652	0715	0719	|	...	0823	|	...	|	|	0908	|	|	|	|	|	|	|	|	|	|
311	Futuroscope ⊖ d.	...	...	...	|	|	|	|	...	|	|	...	|	|	|	|	0936	0936	1004	1004	1004	1037	|	|	|
321	**Poitiers** a.	...	...	...	0726	0731	0734	0739	←	0838	0848	...	|	0914	0922	0922	|	|	1011	1011	1011	1044	1047	|	1117
321	**Poitiers** d.	0620	0624	0719	...	0733	→	0742	0754	0846	0851	0901	|	0917	0925	0925	|	|	1014	1014	1018	...	1050	|	1120
401	Niort d.	0724	|	0802	...	0826	...	|	0840	|	0937	0946	|	|	1016	|	|	|	|	|	1106	...	1136	|	|
468	**La Rochelle** a.	0804	|	0840	...	0907	...	|	0920	|	1016	1028	|	|	1055	|	|	|	|	|	1146	...	1216	|	|
434	Angoulême d.	...	0730	...	...	...	...	|	...	0935	...	...	|	1003	...	1013	|	|	1101	1101	...	...	...	|	1206
517	Coutras **302** d.	...	0817	...	...	...	...	|	...	|	...	...	|	|	...	|	|	|	|	|	...	...	...	|	|
533	Libourne **302** d.	...	0827	...	...	...	...	|	...	|	...	...	|	1047	...	1053	|	|	|	|	...	...	...	|	|
570	**Bordeaux St Jean 302** a.	...	0852	...	...	...	...	0920	...	1034c	...	...	1020	1111	...	1116	1119	1120	1200	1200	...	...	...	1218	1305
	Hendaye **305** a.	...	...	...	...	...	...	|	...	...	...	...	1246	|	...	...	|	|	...	1422	...	...	...	...	...
	Irún **305** a.	...	...	...	...	...	...	|	...	...	...	...	1255	|	...	...	|	|	...	1432	...	...	...	...	...
	Tarbes **305** a.	...	...	...	...	...	...	|	...	...	...	...	...	1353	...	...	|	|	...	...	...	...	...	...	...
	Toulouse **320** a.	...	...	...	...	...	...	1133r	...	...	...	...	...	...	...	...	1323	1329	...	...	...	...	...	...	...

	TGV 8515	*TGV* 8516		*TGV* 8319	*TGV* 8417	*TGV* 8521	*TGV* 5450		*TGV* 8519	*TGV* 8417		*TGV* 8525	*TGV* 8525	*TGV* 8429	*TGV* 8329	*TGV* 8333	*TGV* 8331	*TGV* 8535	*TGV* 8335		*TGV* 8539	*TGV* 5218	*TGV* 5221	*TGV* 8339	
					◇	⑥		⚒		⑥		Ⓐ	⑥	⑤	⑤	①–⑥	⑦		⑤	⑤					†
	◇	◇			R	S	☆		◇	S	◇	◇	◇	D	D	n	e						F	N	J
Lille Europe **11** d.	...	...	...	...	...	...	...	...	...	...	...	...	...	...	...	...	...	...	...	...	...	1238z	1238z	...	...
Charles de Gaulle ✈ d.	...	...	...	...	...	...	...	...	...	...	...	...	...	...	...	...	...	...	...	...	...	1337	1337	...	...
Marne la Vallee - Chessy d.	...	...	...	...	...	...	1023	...	...	...	...	...	...	...	...	...	...	...	...	...	...	1351	1351	...	...
Paris Montparnasse 295 d.	1010	1010	...	1045	1050	1050	|	...	1130	1135	...	1210	1210	1310	1310	1350	1350	1410	1420	...	1440	|	|	1445	...
Massy TGV **295** d.	|	|	...	|	|	|	1101	...	|	|	...	|	|	|	|	|	|	|	|	...	|	1431	1431	|	...
Tours d.	|	|	...	|	*1139*	*1139*	*1139*	...	|	|	1225	|	|	|	|	*1442*	*1442*	|	|	...	|	*1512*	*1512*	|	...
St Pierre des Corps **295** d.	|	|	...	|	1149	1149	1156	...	|	|	|	|	|	|	|	1457	1457	|	|	...	|	1525	1525	|	...
Châtellerault d.	|	|	...	|	|	|	|	...	|	|	1310	|	|	|	|	1532	1531	|	|	...	|	|	|	|	...
Futuroscope ⊖ d.	|	|	...	|	|	|	1233	...	|	|	|	|	|	|	|	|	|	|	|	...	|	1603	1603	|	...
Poitiers a.	|	|	...	1212	|	|	1240	...	|	|	1335	1339	1339	1437	1437	1547	1546	|	|	...	|	1610	1610	1616	...
Poitiers d.	|	|	...	1215	|	|	1243	1257	|	|	...	1341	1342	1440	1445	...	1549	|	|	1558	|	1612	1612	1619	1619
Niort d.	|	|	...	1258	|	|	|	1359	|	|	...	|	|	|	1527	...	1636	|	1634	1646	|	|	|	1702	1706
La Rochelle a.	|	|	...	1334	|	|	|	1448	|	|	...	|	|	|	1606	...	1716	|	1713	1729	|	|	|	1741	1746
Angoulême d.	|	|	1227	...	1313	1313	1329	...	|	|	...	1426	1429	1526	...	...	...	1618	...	...	|	1658	1658	...	...
Coutras **302** d.	|	|	1315	...	|	|	|	...	|	|	...	|	|	|	...	...	...	|	...	...	|	|	|	...	...
Libourne **302** d.	|	|	1327	...	1358	1358	|	...	|	|	...	|	|	|	...	...	...	|	...	...	|	1738	1738	...	...
Bordeaux St Jean 302 a.	1311	1311	1355	...	1423	1423	1428	...	1432	1436	...	1524	1528	1625	...	...	...	1714	...	...	1738	1802	1802	...	...
Hendaye **305** a.	1536	|	...	...	...	1645	...	...	|	...	...	1745	1749	...	...	...	...	|	...	...	|	|	2030	...	...
Irún **305** a.	1545	|	...	...	...	1653	...	...	|	...	...	...	...	...	...	...	...	|	...	...	|	|	2040	...	...
Tarbes **305** a.	...	1605	...	...	...	...	...	...	|	...	...	...	...	...	...	...	...	|	...	...	2039	|	...	...	...
Toulouse **320** a.	...	...	...	...	...	...	...	...	1642	...	...	...	...	...	...	...	...	1922	...	...	...	2011	...	...	...

	TGV 5452		*TGV* 8441	*TGV* 8547			*TGV* 8543	*TGV* 8551	*TGV* 8445	*TGV* 8545	*TGV* 5229	*TGV* 5205				*TGV* 8353		*TGV* 5452	*TGV* 5222	*TGV* 8451	*TGV* 8355	*TGV* 8549	*TGV* 8557	*TGV* 8361	
	⑤–⑦	⑤		⑦	Ⓒ	Ⓐ		①–④	①–④	⑤	⑦	①–④	⑤⑦	⑤	①–④	⑤		①–④	⑤⑥		⑦				⚒
	☆e		B	J				J	Kn		e	n	e		n		A	☆n			e			M	◧
Lille Europe **11** d.	...	...	...	...	...	...	...	...	...	...	1447	1447	...	...	...	...	...	...	1540	...	...	...	...	...	...
Charles de Gaulle ✈ d.	...	...	...	...	...	...	...	...	...	...	1542	1542	...	...	...	...	...	...	1637	...	...	...	...	...	...
Marne la Vallee - Chessy d.	1421	...	...	...	...	...	...	...	...	...	1557	1557	...	...	...	...	...	1657	1652	...	...	...	...	...	...
Paris Montparnasse 295 d.	|	...	1515	1515	...	...	1550	1610	1610	1620	|	|	...	...	...	1655	...	|	|	1715	1715	1720	1745	1755	...
Massy TGV **295** d.	1501	...	|	|	...	...	|	|	|	|	1631	1636	...	...	...	|	...	1731	1730	|	|	|	|	|	...
Tours d.	*1540*	...	*1600*	*1600*	...	...	|	|	|	|	*1715*	*1715*	...	1712	...	*1742*	1736	*1814*	*1814*	*1803*	*1803*	|	|	|	1848
St Pierre des Corps **295** d.	1555	...	1614	1614	...	...	|	|	|	|	1730	1730	...	|	...	1754	|	1824	1824	1814	1814	|	|	|	|
Châtellerault d.	|	...	|	|	...	...	|	|	|	|	|	|	...	1759	...	|	1824	|	|	1843	1843	|	|	|	1932
Futuroscope ⊖ d.	|	...	|	|	...	...	|	|	|	|	|	|	...	|	...	|	|	|	|	1901	1901	|	|	|	|
Poitiers a.	1633	...	1652	1652	...	...	|	1737	1738	|	1807	1809	...	1814	...	1833	1840	1902	1903	1908	1908	|	|	1922	1947
Poitiers d.	1636	1646	1655	1655	1708	1727	|	1740	1741	|	...	1812	...	*1822*	1831	1836	...	1905	1906	1915	1920	|	|	1927	...
Niort d.	|	1737	|	|	1754	1817	|	|	|	|	...	|	...	|	1922	1922	...	|	|	|	2002	|	|	2014	...
La Rochelle a.	|	1817	|	|	1834	1909	|	|	|	|	...	|	...	|	2005	2001	...	|	|	|	2041	|	|	2052	...
Angoulême d.	1721	...	1744	1744	...	...	|	|	|	|	...	1901	1900	*1940*	...	...	...	1950	1951	2008	...	|	1958	...	...
Coutras **302** d.	|	...	|	|	...	...	|	|	|	|	...	|	2000	...	...	...	...	|	|	|	...	|	|	...	...
Libourne **302** d.	|	...	1825	1825	...	...	|	|	|	|	...	|	2012	...	...	...	...	|	|	2049	...	|	|	...	...
Bordeaux St Jean 302 a.	1823	...	1848	1848	...	...	1852	1917	1920	1918	...	2002	2041	...	...	...	...	2051	2051	2111	...	2023	2056	...	...
Hendaye **305** a.	...	...	...	|	...	...	2118	|	...	|	...	...	...	...	...	...	...	...	2313	...	...	|	|	...	...
Irún **305** a.	...	...	...	|	...	...	2128	|	...	|	...	...	...	...	...	...	...	...	...	...	...	|	|	...	...
Tarbes **305** a.	...	...	...	2150	...	...	...	2215	...	2213	...	...	...	...	...	...	...	...	...	...	...	|	2347	...	...
Toulouse **320** a.	...	...	...	...	...	...	...	...	...	...	...	...	...	...	...	...	...	...	...	...	...	2236	...	...	...

	TGV 8359	*TGV* 8565	*TGV* 8469	*TGV* 8369		*TGV* 8477	*TGV* 8577	*TGV* 8579	*TGV* 8377	*TGV* 8479	*TGV* 5240	*TGV* 5454				*TGV* 8379	*TGV* 5242	*TGV* 8483	*TGV* 8495	*TGV* 8489	*TGV* 8491	*TGV* 8391*	*TGV* 8497		*TGV* 8589
	⑤	Ⓑ			⑤	①–④	⑤	⑤	⑦		Ⓑ			⑦	†	⑤	⑤–⑦	①–④	⑤	⑦	⑤	⑤	⑤		⑤⑦
				N		n			e			☆	P	e			e▷	J	J	e					y
Lille Europe **11** d.	...	...	...	...	...	...	...	...	...	...	1809	...	...	...	...	...	1829	...	...	...	...	...	...	...	...
Charles de Gaulle ✈ d.	...	...	...	...	...	...	...	...	...	...	1911	...	...	...	...	...	1925	...	...	...	...	...	...	...	...
Marne la Vallee - Chessy d.	...	...	...	...	...	...	...	...	...	...	1927	1912	...	...	...	...	1942	...	...	...	...	...	...	...	...
Paris Montparnasse 295 d.	1820	1825	1850	1850	...	1925	1925	1925	1930	1950	|	|	...	...	...	2020	|	2020	2110	2110	2115	2120	2135	...	2250
Massy TGV **295** d.	|	|	|	|	...	|	|	|	|	|	2000	1951	...	...	...	|	2018	|	|	|	|	|	|	...	|
Tours d.	|	|	*1939*	*1939*	...	|	|	|	*2019*	|	|	*2035*	...	2039	...	|	*2101*	*2112*	|	*2158*	|	*2208*	*2208*	...	*2337*
St Pierre des Corps **295** d.	|	|	1949	1949	...	|	|	|	2028	|	|	2047	...	2050	...	|	2113	2127	|	2209	|	2219	2233	...	2356
Châtellerault d.	|	|	2018	2018	...	|	|	|	|	|	|	|	...	2130	...	2138	|	2200	|	2238	2233	|	|	...	|
Futuroscope ⊖ d.	|	|	|	|	...	|	|	|	|	|	|	|	...	|	...	|	|	|	|	|	|	|	|	...	|
Poitiers a.	1947	|	2033	2033	...	|	|	|	2107	2118	2122	2127	...	2145	...	2153	2158	2215	|	2253	2248	|	2312	...	0048
Poitiers d.	1958	|	2036	2040	2041	|	|	|	2110	2120	2126	2130	2146	...	2155	2156	2201	2218	|	2256	2251	|	2315	...	0056
Niort d.	2046	|	|	2121	2125	|	|	|	2156	|	|	|	2233	...	2251	2241	|	|	|	|	|	2341	|	...	|
La Rochelle a.	2124	|	|	2156	2206	|	|	|	2236	|	|	|	2311	...	2327	2320	|	|	|	|	|	0024	|	...	|
Angoulême d.	...	|	2122	...	...	|	|	|	...	2208	2213	2219	...	...	...	...	2249	2304	|	2343	2343	...	0001	...	|
Coutras **302** d.	...	|	|	...	...	|	|	|	...	|	|	|	...	...	...	...	|	|	|	|	|	...	|	...	|
Libourne **302** d.	...	|	2202	...	...	|	|	|	...	|	|	|	...	...	...	...	|	|	|	0027	0024	...	|	...	|
Bordeaux St Jean 302 a.	...	2126	2225	...	...	2229	2229	2229	...	2308	2313	2318	...	...	...	...	2352	0003	0009	0050	0052	...	0102	...	|
Hendaye **305** a.	...	2346	...	...	...	...	0049	|	...	...	...	...	...	...	...	...	...	...	...	...	...	...	...	...	|
Irún **305** a.	...	...	...	...	...	...	...	|	...	...	...	...	...	...	...	...	...	...	...	...	...	...	...	...	|
Tarbes **305** a.	...	...	...	...	...	...	...	|	...	...	...	...	...	...	...	...	...	...	...	...	...	...	...	...	0703
Toulouse **320** a.	...	...	...	...	...	...	...	0043	...	...	...	...	...	...	...	...	...	...	...	...	...	...	...	...	...

← **FOR NOTES SEE FOOT OF PREVIOUS PAGE**

For overnight trains Paris - Irún / Tarbes see Table **305**

Engineering work – timings may vary by a few minutes (especially morning of June 13, 14); please enquire when making reservations.

300 BORDEAUX and LA ROCHELLE - POITIERS - PARIS

TGV trains convey 🍸	TGV 8308 ① g	TGV 8406 Ⓐ	⑥ t	Ⓐ	TGV 8408 Ⓐ	TGV 8306 ①–⑥ n	TGV 5260 ①–⑥ n	TGV 8312 ⑦ e	Ⓐ	TGV 8410 ①–⑥ n	TGV 8412 E	TGV 5260 ⑦ e	⑥ t	TGV 5440 ☆	Ⓐ	⑦ J	TGV 8414	TGV 8314 ① Jy	TGV 8416 E	TGV 8316 K	⚒ J	TGV 5264	TGV 5268 ①⑥ g	TGV 8518 ①–⑥ n
Toulouse **320** d.	...	...	...	...	...	...	...	...	...	...	...	...	...	...	...	...	...	...	...	...	...	0527	...	0608
Tarbes **305** d.	...	...	...	...	...	...	...	...	...	...	...	...	...	...	...	...	...	...	...	...	...	|	...	|
Hendaye **305** d.	...	...	...	...	...	...	...	...	...	...	...	...	...	...	...	...	...	...	...	...	...	|	0524	|
Bordeaux St Jean 302 d.	...	0440	...	...	0513	...	0535	...	...	0552	0627	0614	...	0633	...	...	0659	...	0728	...	...	0750	0750	0828
Libourne **302** d.	...	0506	...	...	|	...	|	...	...	0619	|	|	...	|	...	...	0724	...	|	...	...	|	|	|
Coutras **302** d.	...	|	...	...	|	...	|	...	...	|	|	|	...	|	...	...	|	...	|	...	...	|	|	|
Angoulême d.	...	0547	...	...	0611	...	0637	...	...	0700	|	0714	...	0733	...	...	0805	...	|	...	...	0850	0850	|
La Rochelle d.	...	|	...	...	|	0545	|	...	...	|	|	|	0640	|	0653	0715	|	0727	|	0746	0746	|	|	|
Niort d.	...	|	...	...	|	0626	|	...	...	|	|	|	0721	|	0738	0754	|	0804	|	0827	0828	|	|	|
Poitiers a.	...	0633	...	...	|	0714	0722	...	...	0746	|	0758	0805	0817	0823	0839	0851	0843	|	0912	0915	0933	0933	|
Poitiers d.	0506	0636	0641	0641	|	0717	0724	0733	0736	0749	|	0800	...	0820	...	...	0856	0856	|	0915	...	0936	0936	|
Futuroscope ⊖ d.	|	|	|	|	|	|	|	|	|	|	|	|	...	|	...	...	|	|	|	|	...	0947	0947	|
Châtellerault d.	|	0654	0659	0659	|	|	|	0751	0753	0806	|	|	...	|	...	...	|	|	|	|	...	|	|	|
St Pierre-des-Corps **295** a.	0546	|	|	|	|	|	0800	0818	|	|	|	0838	...	0859	...	...	0935	0935	|	|	...	1020	1020	|
Tours a.	*0556*	|	0747	0753	|	|	*0814*	*0830*	0830	|	|	*0847*	...	*0910*	...	...	*0947*	*0947*	|	|	...	*1030*	*1030*	|
Massy TGV **295** a.	0637	|	...	...	|	|	|	...	...	|	|	|	...	0952	...	...	|	|	|	|	...	1113	1113	|
Paris Austerlitz **296** a.	|	|	...	...	|	|	|	|	...	|	|	|	...	|	...	...	|	|	|	|	...	|	|	|
Paris Montparnasse 295 a.	0650	0815	...	...	0830	0850	|	0920	...	0925	0930	|	...	|	...	...	1035	1035	1030	1050	...	|	|	1130
Marne la Vallee - Chessy a.	...	...	...	...	...	...	0926	...	...	...	...	1006	...	1034	...	...	...	...	...	...	...	1154	1154	...
Charles de Gaulle ✈ a.	...	...	...	...	...	...	0942	...	...	...	...	1021	...	...	...	...	...	...	...	...	...	1209	1209	...
Lille Europe **11** a.	...	...	...	...	...	...	1046	...	...	...	...	1128	...	...	...	...	...	...	...	...	...	1306	1306	...

	TGV 8420 ①–⑥ n	TGV 8422 ⑦ e	TGV 5442 ☆ ©	TGV 8524 △	TGV 8527 △	TGV 8324	TGV 5442 ☆ Ⓐ		TGV 5276	TGV 8528 ▽	TGV 8530 S	TGV 8330 ⑤ J	Ⓐ	TGV 8436	TGV 8334	TGV 8534 ◇	TGV 8541	TGV 8542 Ⓐ J	TGV 8438 Ⓐ §	TGV 8442 ⑥ K	TGV 8338	TGV 9816 ♣	TGV 8444	TGV 8548
Toulouse **320** d.	...	...	...	...	...	...	...	...	...	0922	...	...	...	...	...	...	...	...	...	...	...	...	...	1313u
Tarbes **305** d.	...	...	...	...	0726	...	...	...	...	|	...	...	...	...	...	...	1052	...	...	...	...	...	...	|
Hendaye **305** d.	...	...	...	0753	|	...	...	...	0833x	|	0930	...	...	...	...	1021	|	1117	...	...	...	...	...	|
Bordeaux St Jean 302 d.	...	0755	1019	1026	1026	...	1030	...	1057	1124	1157	...	...	1201	...	1251	1355	1355	1416	1416	...	1422	1456	1525
Libourne **302** d.	...	|	|	|	|	...	|	...	|	|	|	...	...	1227	...	|	|	|	|	|	...	1446	|	|
Coutras **302** d.	...	|	|	|	|	...	|	...	|	|	|	...	...	|	...	|	|	|	|	|	...	|	|	|
Angoulême d.	0854	0857	1123	1128	1128	...	1135	...	1201	|	|	...	...	1311	...	|	1457	1457	|	|	...	1526	|	1625
La Rochelle d.	|	|	|	|	|	1056	|	...	|	|	|	...	1200	|	1228	|	|	|	|	|	1447	|	|	|
Niort d.	|	|	|	|	|	1138	|	...	|	|	|	...	1246	|	1309	|	|	|	|	|	1524	|	|	|
Poitiers a.	0945	0947	1207	1211	1211	1217	1222	...	1248	|	|	...	1346	1357	1353	|	|	|	1555	1555	1604	1611	|	1709
Poitiers d.	0948	0950	1210	1214	1214	1220	1225	1232	1250	|	|	1331	...	1403	1403	|	|	|	1557	1557	1607	1614	|	1712
Futuroscope ⊖ d.	|	|	|	|	|	|	|	|	|	|	|	|	...	|	|	|	|	|	|	|	|	|	|	|
Châtellerault d.	1004	1008	|	|	|	|	|	1315	|	|	|	|	...	1422	1422	|	|	|	|	|	|	|	|	|
St Pierre-des-Corps **295** a.	1030	1035	1248	|	|	1259	1304	|	1328	|	|	1422	...	1449	1449	|	1619	1619	|	|	|	1652	|	1750
Tours a.	*1045*	*1045*	*1259*	|	|	*1315*	*1315*	1406	*1339*	|	|	|	...	*1459*	*1459*	|	*1632*	*1632*	|	|	|	*1702*	|	*1801*
Massy TGV **295** a.	|	|	1342	|	|	|	1358	...	1423	|	|	|	...	|	|	|	|	|	|	|	|	1747	|	|
Paris Austerlitz **296** a.	|	|	|	|	|	|	|	...	|	|	|	|	...	|	|	|	|	|	|	|	|	|	|	|
Paris Montparnasse 295 a.	1135	1135	|	1345	1345	1400	|	...	|	1440	1505	1520	...	1550	1550	1555	1720	1720	1730	1730	1740	|	1800	1850
Marne la Vallee - Chessy a.	...	...	1421	...	...	...	1437	...	1506	...	...	...	...	...	...	...	...	...	...	...	...	1826	...	...
Charles de Gaulle ✈ a.	...	...	...	...	...	...	...	...	1521	...	...	...	...	...	...	...	...	...	...	...	...	1841	...	...
Lille Europe **11** a.	...	...	...	...	...	...	...	...	1615	...	...	...	...	...	...	...	...	...	...	...	...	2005c	...	...

	TGV 8348 ⑤	⚒	†	TGV 5444 ⑦ ☆e	TGV 8558	Ⓐ	TGV 8354 ①–④ n	TGV 8364 ⑤–⑦ e	TGV 5284 Ⓑ	TGV 8456 ⑤–⑦ e		TGV 8362 ①–④ n	TGV 5446 ①–⑥ ☆n	TGV 8563	Ⓑ	TGV 8466 ⑦ e	TGV 5336 ⑦ ♥e	TGV 8370 ⑤⑦ e	TGV 8370 ⑦ F	TGV 8472 ①–⑥ n‡	⑦ e	TGV 8474 ⑦ e‡	⑤	G
Toulouse **320** d.	...	...	...	...	...	...	...	...	...	...	...	...	...	...	...	...	...	...	...	...	...	...	...	...
Tarbes **305** d.	...	...	...	...	...	...	...	...	...	...	...	...	...	1437	...	...	...	...	...	...	...	...	...	...
Hendaye **305** d.	...	...	...	...	1402	...	...	...	...	...	...	...	...	|	...	...	...	...	...	...	...	...	...	...
Bordeaux St Jean 302 d.	...	...	...	1613	1632	...	...	...	1643	1647	...	...	1708	1725	...	1733	...	...	...	1751	...	1803	...	1754
Libourne **302** d.	...	...	...	|	|	...	...	...	|	|	...	...	|	|	...	|	...	...	...	1821	...	1829	...	1829
Coutras **302** d.	...	...	...	|	|	...	...	...	|	|	...	...	|	|	...	|	...	...	...	|	...	|	...	1857
Angoulême d.	...	...	...	1714	1734	...	...	...	1745	1750	...	...	1812	|	...	1835	...	...	...	1904	...	1910	...	1945
La Rochelle d.	1549	...	...	|	|	1625	...	1647	|	|	...	1707	|	|	1735	|	...	...	1750	|	1802	|	1812	...
Niort d.	1630	...	...	|	|	1707	...	1728	|	|	...	1748	|	|	1818	|	...	...	1832	|	1848	|	1903	...
Poitiers a.	1714	...	...	1802	|	1759	...	1813	1830	1838	...	1837	1856	|	1910	1922	...	...	1937	1948	1948	1957	1959	...
Poitiers d.	1717	1735	1735	1805	|	...	1821	1821	1833	1841	...	1840	1902	|	1912	1925	1932	1941	1941	1951	...	2006	...	...
Futuroscope ⊖ d.	|	|	|	1815	|	...	|	|	1850	|	...	|	1913	|	|	|	1943	1952	1952	|	...	|	...	...
Châtellerault d.	|	1809	1801	|	|	...	1840	1839	|	|	...	|	|	|	1929	|	|	|	|	|	...	|	...	...
St Pierre-des-Corps **295** a.	1755	|	|	1851	|	...	|	1905	1925	|	...	1920	1946	|	|	2004	2018	|	|	2029	...	2045	...	...
Tours a.	*1808*	1858	1848	*1903*	|	...	|	*1915*	*1938*	|	...	*1930*	*1957*	|	1959	*2015*	*2035*	|	|	*2045*	...	*2054*	...	...
Massy TGV **295** a.	|	...	...	1943	|	...	|	|	2018	|	...	|	2043	|	...	|	2118	|	|	|	...	2138	...	...
Paris Austerlitz **296** a.	|	...	...	|	|	...	|	|	|	|	...	|	|	|	...	|	|	|	|	|	...	|	...	...
Paris Montparnasse 295 a.	1905	...	...	|	1945	...	2005	2005	|	2015	...	2020	|	2035	...	2105	...	2120	2120	2130r	...	2150	...	...
Marne la Vallee - Chessy a.	...	...	...	2025	...	...	...	...	2057	...	...	...	2120	...	...	...	...	...	...	...	...	...	...	...
Charles de Gaulle ✈ a.	...	...	...	...	...	...	...	...	2112	...	...	...	...	...	...	...	...	...	...	...	...	...	...	...
Lille Europe **11** a.	...	...	...	...	...	...	...	...	2219	...	...	...	...	...	...	...	...	...	...	...	...	...	...	...

	⑥	TGV 8568 Ⓑ	TGV 8374 L	TGV 8570 ⑥	TGV 8382 ⑤	†	TGV 5286 ⑥ K	TGV 5292 ⑥	TGV 5292 Ⓐ	⑦ e	TGV 8384 ⑦ e	TGV 8488 ⑦ Kd	TGV 8580 Ⓑ	⚒	TGV 8584	TGV 8583	TGV 8494 ⑦ e	TGV 8496 ⑤	TGV 8586 ⑦ J	TGV 8590 ⑦ e	TGV 8386 ⑤ b	TGV 8390 ⑦ e	TGV 8392 ⑦ Kd	TGV 8498 ⑦ d
Toulouse **320** d.	...	1610	...	1631	...	...	...	...	...	...	...	...	1736	...	...	...	...	...	1826	...	...	...	...	...
Tarbes **305** d.	...	|	...	|	...	...	...	...	...	...	...	...	|	...	...	1650	...	...	|	...	...	...	...	...
Hendaye **305** d.	...	|	...	|	...	...	...	1620	...	...	...	...	|	...	1722	|	...	...	|	1816	...	...	...	...
Bordeaux St Jean 302 d.	1759	1823	...	1846	...	1831	...	1841	1841	...	...	1920	1947	...	1951	1951	2017	2030	2041	2041	...	...	...	2130
Libourne **302** d.	1833	|	...	|	...	1909	...	|	|	...	...	|	|	...	|	|	2042	|	|	|	...	...	...	|
Coutras **302** d.	1844	|	...	|	...	1918	...	|	|	...	...	|	|	...	|	|	|	|	|	|	...	...	...	|
Angoulême d.	1931	|	...	|	...	2004	...	1946	1951	...	...	|	|	...	2053	2053	2123	2130	|	|	...	...	...	2235
La Rochelle d.	...	|	1828	|	1855	...	1858	|	|	1906	1929	|	|	1945	|	|	|	|	|	|	2050	2112	2150	|
Niort d.	...	|	1909	|	1932	...	1941	|	|	1947	2006	|	|	2030	|	|	|	|	|	|	2131	2153	2227	|
Poitiers a.	...	|	1954	|	2012	...	2029	2033	2035	2038	2046	|	|	2130	2137	2137	2214	2214	|	|	|	2236	|	2318
Poitiers d.	...	|	2002	|	2017	...	2040	2040	2039	...	2049	|	|	...	2140	2140	2222	2218	|	|	|	2239	|	2321
Futuroscope ⊖ d.	...	|	2014	|	|	...	2050	2050	|	...	|	|	|	...	|	|	|	|	|	|	|	|	|	|
Châtellerault d.	...	|	|	|	|	...	|	|	|	...	|	|	|	...	|	|	2241	|	|	|	|	|	|	|
St Pierre-des-Corps **295** a.	...	|	|	|	|	...	2124	2124	2119	...	|	|	|	...	2218	2218	|	|	|	|	2249	2316	|	|
Tours a.	...	|	|	|	|	...	*2139*	*2139*	*2139*	...	|	|	|	...	*2229*	*2229*	|	|	|	|	*2308*	*2326*	|	|
Massy TGV **295** a.	...	|	|	|	|	...	2217	2217	2213	...	|	|	|	...	|	|	|	|	|	|	|	|	|	|
Paris Austerlitz **296** a.	...	|	|	|	|	...	|	|	|	...	|	|	|	...	|	|	|	|	|	|	|	|	|	|
Paris Montparnasse 295 a.	...	2130	2140	2150	2150	...	|	|	|	...	2220	2225	2250s	...	2320s	2320s	0000	2345	2345	2345	2350	0015	0035	0050
Marne la Vallee - Chessy a.	...	...	...	...	...	...	2251	2251	2251	...	...	...	...	...	...	...	...	...	...	...	...	...	...	...
Charles de Gaulle ✈ a.	...	...	...	...	...	...	2306	2306	2306	...	...	...	...	...	...	...	...	...	...	...	...	...	...	...
Lille Europe **11** a.	...	...	...	...	...	...	0007	0007	0000	...	...	...	...	...	...	...	...	...	...	...	...	...	...	...

Engineering work – timings may vary by a few minutes (especially on June 13); please enquire when making reservations.

E – Ⓐ to July 3; ① July 6 - Aug. 24 (also July 15; not July 13); ①–⑤ from Aug. 31.
F – ⑦ July 5 - Aug. 30 (also June 1, July 14, Nov. 11; not July 12).
G – ⑤ to June 26; Ⓐ June 29 - Aug. 28; ⑤ from Sept. 4.
J – To July 4 / from Aug. 31.
K – July 5 - Aug. 30.
L – ①②③④⑥ (not June 1, July 14).
S – June 27 - Sept. 20.

NOTES CONTINUED AT FOOT OF NEXT PAGE →

ANGOULÊME - SAINTES - ROYAN — 301

Some trains 2nd class

km		Ⓐ ◇	Ⓐ	Ⓒ K	Ⓐ	K	Ⓐ J△	M	4003 S	K	Ⓐ △	S	P△	⚒ P△	S	◇	⑤⑦ e	①–④ Jc	G	H	①–④ Kv	⑤	⚒	†	Ⓐ ▽	Ⓐ
	Paris Austerlitz ◐ ... d.	...	...	...	...	...	...	...	0624	...	...	...	...	...	...	...	...	...	...	...	...	...	...	...	...	...
0	**Angoulême** ... d.	0613	...	...	0721	...	0939	1017	1110	...	1236	...	...	1437	1437	1639	...	...	...	...	...	...	1750	...	...	1907
49	Cognac ... d.	0702	...	...	0804	...	1017	1100	1148	...	1315	...	...	1516	1529	1719	...	...	...	...	...	...	1831	...	...	1945
	Niort ... d.	|	0655	...	|	0941	|	|	|	1150	|	1315	1323	|	|	|	1652	...	1709	1720	...	1742	|	1825	1834	|
75	**Saintes** ... a.	0722	0758	...	0825	1035	1037	1119	1211	1246	1334	1408	1415	1535	1548	1739	1747	...	1803	1821	...	1840	1851	1939	1946	2004
75	**Saintes** ... d.	*0733*	0800	0801	...	1038	1044	1125	1233	1302	...	1410	1417	1543	1558	...	1749	1752	1806	1840	1840	...	1903z	...	...	2021
111	**Royan** ... a.	*0800*	0831	0832	...	1106	1111	1155	1304	1330	...	1440	1443	1614	1626	...	1816	1819	1834	1910	1911	...	1930z	...	...	2048

	⑥ t	L	H	†	①–④ Kv	⑥ Kt	⑤	⑤	Ⓑ J	Ⓑ K
Paris Austerlitz ◐ ... d.	...	...	...	...	...	...	...	...	...	...
Angoulême ... d.	1905	2016	2023	...	...	...	...	2126	2221	2221
Cognac ... d.	1943	2100	2101	...	...	...	...	2204	2307	2307
Niort ... d.	|	|	|	2029	2029	...	2054	|	|	|
Saintes ... a.	2002	2118	2120	2126	2126	...	2150	2223	2327	2327
Saintes ... d.	...	...	2127	2137	2137	2137	2154	2230	2332	2339
Royan ... a.	...	...	2154	2205	2205	2205	2220	2257	0002	0008

	Ⓐ	E	Ⓐ J	Ⓐ K	① b§	②–⑤ Kd	A	Ⓐ ◇	⑥ t	F	△	△
Royan ... d.	...	...	0605	...	0629	0629	0656	...	0710	0814	...	0958
Saintes ... a.	...	...	0631	...	0657	0657	0723	...	0736	0840	...	1024
Saintes ... d.	0542	0615	0640	0640	0711	0713	...	0743	0742	...	0957	1036
Niort ... a.	|	0729	|	|	0811	0822	...	|	|	...	|	1130
Cognac ... d.	0600	...	0701	0701	...	...	...	0803	0802	...	1017	...
Angoulême ... a.	0641	...	0746	0746	...	...	...	0843	0840	...	1055	...
Paris Austerlitz ◐ a.	...	...	...	...	...	...	...	...	...	...	...	...

	⚒ K	S	Ⓐ △	P△		Ⓐ J△	K	4004 S	①–④ Jc	①–④ Kv	⑥ t	⑤⑦ e	⑤⑦ e	☆	①–④ Kv	†	①–④ Jc	⑥ t	⑤	①–④ m	⑤	G	⑤⑦ e	⑤ K	†	†
Royan ... d.	1136	1205	...	1224	...	1340	1340	1420	...	1525	1547*	1547*	...	1708	1709	1821	...	...	*1821*	1852	...	1935	1935	2057	2107	...
Saintes ... a.	1204	1231	...	1250	...	1407	1407	1451	...	1555	1623	1623	...	1734	1736	1848	...	...	*1848*	1919	...	2002	2001	2124	2134	...
Saintes ... d.	1206	...	1233	...	1345	1418	1418	1507	1611	1612	1634	1624	1637	1747	1805	1853	1900	1900	1913	1925	1925	...	2013	...	2158	2200
Niort ... a.	1303	...	|	...	|	1510	1510	|	|	|	|	1722	|	|	1901	1959	2005	2005	2014	|	|	...	|	...	|	2257
Cognac ... d.	...	...	1251	...	1405	...	...	1527	1631	1631	1654	...	1655	1808	...	...	...	...	...	1946	1946	...	2034	...	2218	...
Angoulême ... a.	...	...	1335	...	1441	...	...	1605	1715	1716	1736	...	1736	1852	...	...	...	...	...	2023	2023	...	2116	...	2258	...
Paris Austerlitz ◐ ... a.	...	...	...	...	...	...	...	2105	...	...	...	...	...	...	...	...	...	...	...	...	...	...	...	...	...	...

A – ②–⑤ (also ① July 6 - Aug. 27), not June 2, July 14, 15, Nov. 11.
E – Ⓐ to June 26; ① June 29 - Aug. 17; Ⓐ from Aug. 24.
F – ⚒ (daily June 29 - Aug. 30).
G – ①②③④⑥ July 6 - Aug. 29 (not July 14, Aug. 15).
H – ①②③④⑥ to July 4 / from Aug. 31 (not June 1, Nov. 11).
J – To July 4 / from Aug. 31.
K – July 5 - Aug. 30.
L – Daily except dates in note **H**.
M – Ⓒ (daily July 4 - Aug. 28).

P – To June 26 / from Aug. 31.
S – June 27 - Aug. 30.
b – Also July 15; not July 13.
c – Not June 1, Nov. 11.
d – Also July 13; not July 15.
e – Also June 1, July 14, Nov. 11.
m – Not June 1, July 14, Nov. 11.
t – Not Aug. 15.
v – Not July 14.
z – ⑤⑥ (not Aug. 15).

◐ – See Table **300** for *TGV* connections at Niort or Angoulême.
◇ – To / from La Rochelle (Table **292**).
△ – Subject to alteration from Oct. 2.
▽ – On ⑤ depart 1844, arrive 1957. On ①–④ July 6 - Aug. 27 (not July 14) depart 1825, arrive 1939.
☆ – Change at Saintes ①–④ (not July 14, Aug. 14, Nov. 11).
§ – To Poitiers (arrive 0859).
* – 1555 to June 26 and from Sept. 4.

BORDEAUX - PÉRIGUEUX - BRIVE and LIMOGES — 302

km		Ⓐ	⚒	4490 ⑤ ◇v	R	⑥	Ⓐ ▽	4492 ⑥ ⊖	4480 q	⚒	⚒		①–④ m	⑤	† J	† K	Ⓐ	⑥ t	⑤⑥ t	Ⓑ h	Ⓑ ⊡	Ⓑ h	⚒	Ⓑ	⑤⑦ e	†
0	**Bordeaux 300** ... d.	0607	0641	0734	0734	...	0814	0908	1047	...	1226	1359	1559	1559	1621	1653	1659	1659	...	1738	1807	...	1856	2009	2009	2155
37	Libourne **300** ... d.	0633	0715	0800	0800	...	|	|	1113	...	1252	1425	|	1624	1646	1718	1727	1727	...	1809	1835	...	1929	2036	2036	2220
53	Coutras **300** ... d.	0645	0726	0812	0814	...	|	|	1123	...	1302	1436	|	1633	|	1729	1736	1737	...	1821	|	...	1943	2046	2046	2230
93	Mussidan ... d.	0711	0753	0840	0842	...	|	|	1144	...	1332	1504	|	1700	1714	1759	1805	1806	...	1850	1906	...	2011	2112	2112	2252
129	Périgueux ... a.	0735	0822	0902	0907	...	0920	1022	1202	...	1358	1528	1707	1720	1735	1820	1825	1826	...	1911	1925	...	2042	2133	2133	2314
129	Périgueux **308** ... d.	*0740*	...	0904	0909	0925	0925	1024	1208	1219	...	...	1715	...	1740	1840	1835	*1840*	1846	...	1932	1942	...	...	2138	...
203	**Brive la Gaillarde** ... a.	|	...	0958	1006	|	|	1109	|	1310	...	...	|	...	|	|	|	|	1951	...	|	2035	...	...	|	...
228	**Limoges 308** ... a.	*0839*	...	...	...	1024	1024	...	1306	...	...	...	1820	...	1855	1951	2000	*1951*	...	...	2048	...	...	...	2249	...
639	*Lyon Part Dieu* **327** .. a.	...	...	...	...	...	...	...	1816	...	...	...	...	...	...	...	...	...	...	...	...	...	...	...	...	...
643	*Lyon Perrache* **327** .. a.	...	...	...	...	...	...	...	1829	...	...	...	...	...	...	...	...	...	...	...	...	...	...	...	...	...

	⚒	Ⓐ	Ⓐ	⚒	Ⓐ	Ⓒ d		⚒	⑥	Ⓑ	⑤		Ⓑ h	①–④	§	⑤		Ⓐ	4590 ⑤ ◇v	4595 ⑦ ⊖	⑥ J	4580 q	Ⓐ	†	
Lyon Perrache **327** ... d.	...	...	...	...	...	...	...	...	...	...	...	...	...	...	...	...	...	...	...	...	...	1250	...	...	...
Lyon Part Dieu **327** ... d.	...	...	...	...	...	...	...	...	...	...	...	...	...	...	...	...	...	...	...	...	...	1304	...	...	...
Limoges 308 ... d.	...	...	0611	...	...	0718	...	1021r	*1110*x	*1110*x	...	1455	...	1705	1705	...	...	1735	...	...	...	1809	1835	...	2156
Brive la Gaillarde ... d.	...	...	|	...	...	|	0731	|	|	|	...	|	*1557*c	|	|	*1708*	...	|	1801	1801	1803	|	|	...	|
Périgueux **308** ... a.	...	...	0722	...	...	0825	0822	1119r	*1206*x	*1206*x	...	1559	*1647*c	1815	1815	*1807*	...	1852	1857	1856	1858	1906	2005	...	2257
Périgueux ... d.	0559	0652	0734	0734	0800	...	0834	1125	1215	1218	1439	1606	1658	1820	...	1820	1836	...	1900	1859	...	1916	...	2031	...
Mussidan ... d.	0625	0714	0755	0755	|	...	0855	1145	1240	1240	1459	1627	1723	|	...	1841	1905	...	|	|	...	1935	...	2053	...
Coutras **300** ... d.	0701	0742	0822	0822	|	...	0921	1210	1310	1310	1523	1654	1756	|	...	1905	1936	...	|	|	...	1956	...	2117	...
Libourne **300** ... d.	0713	0754	0832	0832	|	...	0931	1222	1320	1320	1534	1705	1808	|	...	1915	1946	...	1952	1951	...	2009	...	2128	...
Bordeaux St Jean 300 . a.	0741	0820	0858	0858	0913	...	0958z	1249	1346	1347	1558	1731	1836	1927	...	1939	2012	...	2018	2017	...	2036	...	2152	...

ADDITIONAL TRAINS PÉRIGUEUX - BRIVE / LIMOGES

	Ⓐ	Ⓐ J			K	u	†		⑤	Ⓑ ⊙	† J
Périgueux ... d.	0629	0735	0740	1319	1323	1428	1454	1602	1652	1658	1840
Brive la Gaillarde ... a.	0726	0833	|	|	1420	|	1545	|	|	1754	|
Limoges ... a.	...	...	0839	1429	...	1535	...	1709	1801	...	1951

	Ⓐ	Ⓐ	⑥		⚒ b	①–④ Jn	①–④ Jn	⑤	Ⓑ	†	Ⓑ
Limoges ... d.	...	...	...	1248	...	...	...	...	2035	...	2302
Brive la Gaillarde d.	0620	1045	1110	|	1349	1612	1822	2037	|	2115	|
Périgueux ... a.	0724	1135	1200	1355	1450	1714	1922	2127	2136	2205	2359

J – To July 4 / from Aug. 31.
K – July 5 - Aug. 30.
R – ①②③④⑥ to July 4 / from Aug. 31 (not June 1, Oct. 26 - - 29, Nov. 2 - 4, ① Nov. 9 - Dec. 7).

b – ⚒ (daily June 29 - Aug. 30). Not on Ⓐ from Nov. 30.
c – † (daily July 5 - Aug. 29), not Aug. 1.
d – Not June 7, 21.
e – Also June 1, July 14.
h – Also Aug. 15.
m – Not June 1, July 14, Nov. 11.

n – Not June 1, Nov. 11.
q – Not June 6. On June 27 will not call at Lyon Part Dieu (Perrache a. 1858 / d. 1231).
r – ⚒ June 13 - Oct. 17 (also June 6); ⑥ Oct. 24 - Nov. 28; ⚒ from Nov. 30.
t – Not Aug. 15.
u – Not June 25, 26.
v – Also Oct. 26 - 29, Nov. 2 - 4.
x – ⚒ to Oct. 17; ⑥ Oct. 24 - Nov. 28; ⚒ from Nov. 30.
z – 1013 on June 8 - 12, Nov. 23 - 27.

⊖ – To / from Clermont Ferrand (Table **326**).
◇ – To / from Ussel (Table **326**).
⊡ – On ⑤ **J** Bordeaux d. 1806 (Périgueux a. 1933 / d. 1946).
⊙ – On ①–④ **m** depart 1802, arrive 1907.
▽ – Subject to alteration from Oct. 19.
§ – Through train to Bordeaux on ⑤ (next column).

Certain trains are subject to alteration on June 6.

← NOTES FOR TABLE 300 (continued from page 194) — 300

b – Not July 3, ⑤ Sept. 4 - Oct. 2. Arrive Paris 0011 to June 27 (also Oct. 10 - Dec. 5).
c – Lille **Flandres**.
d – Also July 14.
e – Also June 1, July 14.
g – Also June 2, July 15; not June 1, July 13.
n – Not June 1, July 14.
r – 2135 on ⑤.
s – Arrive Paris 15 minutes later on ①–④ to June 26, ①–④ Oct. 5 - Dec. 3; arrive up to 50 minutes later on ⑤ to June 25; ⑤ Oct. 9 - Dec. 4.

t – Not Aug. 15.
u – Depart 1300 on Ⓐ June 3 - 26 (1236 on June 18, 19).
x – ⑦ (also ③–⑤ July 8 - Aug. 28), also June 1, July 13, 14.
y – Also June 2; not June 1.
TGV – Ⓡ, supplement payable, 🍷.
♥ – To Lyon (Table **335**).
♣ – (12) Bordeaux - Brussels (Table **11**); (12) Bordeaux - Charles de Gaulle ✈ (**5279**) - Lille Flandres.
☆ – To Strasbourg (Table **391**).
⊖ – Not for journeys to/from Poitiers or Châtellerault.

△ – Arrive Paris 1420 on Ⓐ Aug. 4 - Sept. 4.
▽ – Arrive Paris 1450 on Ⓐ June 15 - July 3.
◇ – Timings may vary by a few minutes.
§ – Train number **8442** on ⑤.
‡ – From Arcachon June 27 - Aug. 30 (**8476** ⚒, **8478** ⑦).

Certain journeys start from Arcachon – see Table **306**.

305 BORDEAUX - TARBES and IRÚN

All *TGV* convey 🍷

km		Ⓐ	Ⓐ	Ⓐ H	Ⓐ J	L	P		†	4730 ℝ U	4778 4779 ℝ ♥	J◇	Ⓒ K	Ⓐ K	*TGV* 8505 ⊕	Ⓐ d	† K	*TGV* 8507 ①–⑥ n◇	Ⓐ ◇	*TGV* 5200 ⑥	⑥ J	N	N	*TGV* 8515 ◇	*TGV* 8516 ◇
	Lille Europe 11 d.	...	...	...	...	...	...	...	...	...	...	...	...	...	...	...	...	...	...	0558	...	...	...	...	...
	Charles de Gaulle ✈ d.	...	...	...	...	...	...	...	...	...	...	...	...	...	...	...	...	...	...	0739	...	...	...	...	...
	Paris M'parnasse 300 d.	...	...	...	...	...	...	...	...	...	...	...	...	...	0715	...	...	0745	...	|	...	...	...	1010	1010
	Paris Austerlitz 300 d.	...	...	...	...	...	...	...	...	...	...	...	...	...	|	...	...	|	...	|	...	...	...	|	|
0	**Bordeaux St Jean** d.	...	...	0627	0627	0701	0727	...	...	0825	...	...	0947	0947	1025	...	...	1116	...	1205	...	1219	1219	1315	1315
109	Morcenx d.	...	...	0727	0725	0814	0821	...	...	|	...	...	1043	1118*	|	...	...	|	...	|	...	1312	1312	|	|
148	Dax a.	...	...	0745	0745	0841	0841	...	...	0939	...	...	1102	1140	1130	...	...	|	...	1310	...	1331	1331	1423	1423
148	Dax d.	0615	0650	0750	0755	0844	0844	0848	0848	0942	0952	1055	1105	1143	1133	1200	...	|	1245	1313	1325	1336	1340	1426	1430
179	Puyoô 325 d.	|	|	|	0813	|	|	0906	0906	|	|	|	|	|	|	1217	...	|	|	|	|	|	1358	|	|
193	Orthez 325 d.	|	|	|	0824	|	|	0917	0917	|	|	|	|	|	|	1228	...	|	|	|	|	|	1409	|	1459
233	Pau 325 d.	|	|	|	0850	|	|	0942	0944	|	|	|	|	|	|	1253	...	1312	|	|	|	|	1434	|	1524
272	Lourdes 325 d.	|	|	|	0918r	|	|	...	1012	|	|	|	|	|	|	...	...	1339	|	|	|	|	...	|	1550
293	**Tarbes 325** a.	|	|	|	0932r	|	|	...	1027	|	|	|	|	|	|	...	...	1353	|	|	|	|	...	|	1605
199	**Bayonne 325** d.	0704	0735	0820	...	0918	0918	...	...	1015	1024	1138	1138	1218	1204	...	1234	...	1331	1342	1410	1408	...	1455	...
209	Biarritz 325 d.	0715	0746	0832	...	0928	0929	...	...	1027	1036	1149	1148	1228	1217	...	1244	...	1342	1354	1421	1419	...	1509	...
222	St Jean de Luz 325 d.	0730	0801	0846	...	0940	0944	...	...	1041	1051	1204	1202	1240	1232	...	1258	...	1357	1408	1436	1433	...	1524	...
235	Hendaye 325 a.	0744	0815	0900	...	0952	0957	...	...	1054	1103	1218	1214	1257	1246	...	1310	...	1410	1422	1450	1448	...	1536	...
237	**Irún 325** a.	...	...	...	...	...	...	...	...	1104	1113	...	...	...	1255	...	...	...	...	1432	...	...	...	1545	...

	TGV 8521 ⑥ S	R	14013 ⑤	Ⓐ J	⑥ Kt	B	*TGV* 8525 ①–⑥ n◧	Ⓐ	† K	Ⓐ		⊡	⚒	*TGV* 8539	G	*TGV* 5221 F	14171 14170	*TGV* 8543	4678 4679 ℝ ♣	*TGV* 8547 ⑦ J	*TGV* 8551 ①–④ J	*TGV* 8545 ⑤	*TGV* 5222 ⑤⑥	*TGV* 8557	A
Lille Europe 11 d.	...	...	...	...	...	...	...	...	...	...	...	...	...	...	...	1238z	...	...	...	...	...	...	1540	...	...
Charles de Gaulle ✈ d.	...	...	...	...	...	...	...	...	...	...	...	...	...	...	...	1337	...	...	...	...	...	...	1637	...	...
Paris M'parnasse 300 d.	1050	...	...	...	...	...	1210	...	...	...	...	...	...	1440	...	|	...	1550	...	1515	1610	1620	|	1745	...
Paris Austerlitz 300 d.	|	...	...	...	...	...	|	...	...	...	...	...	...	|	...	|	...	|	...	|	|	|	|	|	...
Bordeaux St Jean d.	1428	1427	1429	...	...	...	1528	...	...	...	1637	...	...	1742	1747	1811	1828	1856	...	1900	1922	1922	2055	2100	...
Morcenx d.	|	1520	|	...	...	...	|	...	...	...	1730	...	...	|	1849	|	1922	|	...	|	|	|	|	|	...
Dax a.	1535	1540	1534	...	...	...	1630	...	...	...	1750	...	...	1853	1908	1917	1945	2002	...	2010	2035	2034	2200	2207	...
Dax d.	1538	1543	1536	1548	1553	1608	1633	1645	...	1706	1753	1758	1825	1856	1911	1920	1946	2005	2010	2013	2038	2037	2203	2210	2214
Puyoô 325 d.	|	|	|	1606	1611	1625	|	|	...	|	|	1816	|	|	|	|	2006	|	2029	|	|	|	|	|	|
Orthez 325 d.	|	|	|	1616	1623	1636	|	|	...	|	|	1826	|	|	|	|	2018	|	2041	2044	2109	2107	|	2241	|
Pau 325 d.	|	|	|	1641	1650	1702	|	|	...	|	|	1851	|	1950	|	|	2048	|	2107	2109	2133	2132	|	2306	|
Lourdes 325 d.	|	|	|	...	1717	1729	|	|	...	|	|	...	|	2024	|	|	2118	|	2138	2136	2200	2159	|	2332	|
Tarbes 325 a.	|	|	|	...	1733	1744	|	|	...	|	|	...	|	2039	|	|	2134	|	2152	2150	2215	2213	|	2347	|
Bayonne 325 d.	1609	1613	1604	...	...	...	1704	1730	1730	1751	1826	...	1910	...	1943	1950	...	2036	...	...	...	...	2233	...	2247
Biarritz 325 d.	1622	1625	1617	...	...	...	1718	1741	1741	1803	1839	...	1921	...	1954	2002	...	2049	...	...	...	...	2245	...	2258
St Jean de Luz 325 d.	1636	1640	1631	...	...	...	1732	1756	1756	1817	1852	...	1936	...	2009	2018	...	2104	...	...	...	...	2301	...	2312
Hendaye 325 a.	1645	1654	1643	...	...	...	1745	1810	1810	1832	1905	...	1950	...	2024	2030	...	2118	...	...	...	...	2313	...	2324
Irún 325 a.	1653	...	...	...	...	...	...	...	...	...	...	...	...	...	...	2040	...	2128	...	...	...	...	...	...	...

	TGV 8565 Ⓑ	*TGV* 8577 ⑤	⑤	14003 ⑥⑦ e‡	*TGV* 8589 ⑤⑦ y	*TGV* 7997 V	4053 ℝ Z◇	4054 ℝ Z◇	
Lille Europe 11 d.	...	...	...	...	...	...	...	...	...
Charles de Gaulle ✈ d.	...	...	...	...	...	...	...	...	...
Paris M'parnasse 300 d.	1825	1925	...	...	2250	2255	...	...	...
Paris Austerlitz 300 d.	|	|	...	...	|	|	2310	2310	...
Bordeaux St Jean d.	2130	2233	...	2231	|	|	|	|	...
Morcenx d.	|	|	...	|	|	|	0534	0534	...
Dax a.	|	2335	...	2338	0507	0538	0557	0557	...
Dax d.	|	2338	2349	2340	0510	0541	0607	0626	...
Puyoô 325 d.	|	|	0010	|	|	|	|	|	...
Orthez 325 d.	|	|	0021	|	0546	|	|	0655	...
Pau 325 d.	|	|	0050	|	0620	|	|	0722	...
Lourdes 325 d.	|	|	0117	|	0648	|	|	0749	...
Tarbes 325 a.	|	|	0133	|	0703	|	|	0806	...
Bayonne 325 d.	2306	0009	...	0007	...	0618	0636	...	...
Biarritz 325 d.	2318	0022	...	0019	...	0631	0650	...	...
St Jean de Luz 325 d.	2332	0036	...	0033	...	0645	0709	...	...
Hendaye 325 a.	2346	0049	...	0046	...	0656	0724	...	...
Irún 325 a.	...	...	...	...	...	...	0736	...	...

	Ⓐ K	Ⓐ J	14161 ①⑥ Ku	⑥ J	Ⓐ J	*TGV* 5268 ①⑥ g	14163 ②–⑤ Kv	*TGV* 8523 Ⓐ J	Ⓐ	N	N ⊙
Hendaye 325 d.	...	0507	...	...	...	0524	...	...	...	...	0629
St Jean de Luz 325 d.	...	0521	...	...	...	0536	...	...	...	...	0642
Biarritz 325 d.	...	0537	...	...	...	0552	...	...	...	...	0658
Bayonne 325 d.	0545	0551	...	...	...	0606	...	...	0634	...	0712
Tarbes 325 d.	|	|	0440	0447	0451a	|	...	0535	|	...	|
Lourdes 325 d.	|	|	0456	0503	0508a	|	...	0552	|	...	|
Pau 325 d.	|	|	0526	0533	0537	|	0545	0620	|	0647	|
Orthez 325 d.	|	|	0554	0600	0602	|	0612	0645	|	0712	|
Puyoô 325 d.	|	|	0605	0611	0612	|	0623	|	|	0722	|
Dax a.	0619	0624	0624	0629	0629	0634	0641	0711	0719	0739	0744
Dax d.	...	0640	0640	0640	...	0637	0643	0714	...	0749	0749
Morcenx d.	...	0701	0702	0702	...	|	0703	|	...	0808	0808
Bordeaux St Jean a.	...	0802	0805	0804	...	0743	0803	0823	...	0901	0901
Paris Austerlitz 300 a.	...	...	...	...	...	|	...	|	...	...	...
Paris Montparnasse a.	...	...	...	...	...	|	...	1130	...	...	...
Charles de Gaulle ✈ a.	...	...	...	...	...	1209	...	...	...	...	...
Lille Europe 11 a.	...	...	...	...	...	1306	...	...	...	...	...

	⚒	*TGV* 8527 △	*TGV* 8524 △	4778 4779 ℝ ♥	*TGV* 5276 C	Y◇	14167 J▷	K⊗	*TGV* 8530 M◇	Ⓐ J⊖	*TGV* 8534 ◇	Ⓐ K	*TGV* 8542 Ⓐ J	*TGV* 8541	◇	q	*TGV* 8558	Ⓐ b	⑤⑦	*TGV* 8563	†	①–④ m	Ⓑ	*TGV* 5292 ⑥	①–④ Qn	①–④ m
Hendaye 325 d.	0720	...	0753	...	0833	0905	...	...	0930	...	1021	1106	1117	...	1237	1307	1402	...	...	...	...	...	1600	1620	1635	...
St Jean de Luz 325 d.	0734	...	0807	...	0846	0918	...	...	0944	...	1035	1119	1130	...	1251	1321	1417	...	...	...	...	...	1613	1632	1648	...
Biarritz 325 d.	0750	...	0824	...	0902	0933	...	...	0957	...	1052	1133	1147	...	1307	1334	1434	...	...	...	...	...	1629	1648	1703	...
Bayonne 325 d.	0803	...	0838	...	0916	0947	...	...	1009	...	1105	1144	1201	...	1319	1346	1449	...	1526	...	...	...	1643	1701	1716	...
Tarbes 325 d.	|	0726	|	0745	|	|	0840	0902	|	...	|	|	|	1052	|	|	|	...	|	1437	1521	...	|	|	|	...
Lourdes 325 d.	|	0745	|	0804	|	|	0857	0917	|	...	|	|	|	1116	|	|	|	...	|	1455	1536	...	|	|	|	...
Pau 325 d.	|	0813	|	0835	|	|	0926	0945	|	1027	|	|	|	1143	|	|	|	1436	|	1523	1606	1606	|	|	|	1656
Orthez 325 d.	|	|	|	0903	|	|	0955	1011	|	1052	|	|	|	|	|	|	|	1501	|	|	1634	1631	|	|	|	1721
Puyoô 325 d.	|	|	|	|	|	|	1007	1021	|	1103	|	|	|	|	|	|	|	1512	|	|	1646	1643	|	|	|	1734
Dax a.	0837	0904	0909	0929	0944	1019	1025	1038	1037	1119	1134	1214	1229	1234	1405	1416	1516	1528	1600	1609	1705	1705	1715	1729	1800	1752
Dax d.	...	0914	0914	...	0947	...	1027	...	1042	1122	1137	1217	1239	1239	...	1419	1519	1531	...	1612	1707	1720	1720	1732	...	1754
Morcenx d.	...	|	|	...	|	...	1049	...	|	1141	|	1237	|	|	...	1439	|	1551	...	|	1729	1739	1739	|	...	1832
Bordeaux St Jean a.	...	1021	1021	...	1052	...	1145	...	1149	1236	1246	1333	1350	1350	...	1535	1627	1646	...	1720	1829	1833	1833	1837	...	1942
Paris Austerlitz 300 a.	...	|	|	...	|	...	...	...	|	...	|	...	|	|	...	...	|	...	...	|	...	...	...	|	...	...
Paris M'parnasse 300 a.	...	1345	1345	...	|	...	...	...	1500	...	1555	...	1720	1720	...	...	1945	...	...	2035	...	...	...	|	...	...
Charles de Gaulle ✈ a.	...	...	...	...	1521	...	...	...	...	...	...	...	...	...	...	...	...	...	...	...	...	...	...	2306	...	...
Lille Europe 11 a.	...	...	...	...	1615	...	...	...	...	...	...	...	...	...	...	...	...	...	...	...	...	...	...	0007	...	...

	14006 ⑦ e	⑤	14008 ⑤	*TGV* 8584	*TGV* 8583	⚒	*TGV* 8590 ⑦ e	4678 4679 ℝ ♣	Ⓐ	⚒	⑤⑥ k	⚒	4620 ℝ T	†	†	*TGV* 8595 ⑦ D	⚒ K	† K	◇ 4052 ℝ ⑦Zc	◇ 4051 ℝ ⑦Zc	◇ 4052 ℝ Zh	◇ 4051 ℝ Zh	*TGV* 8595 ⑤ E	*TGV* 7990 ⑤ f	*TGV* 7996 W	*TGV* 7996 ⑦ e
Hendaye 325 d.	1706	...	1703	1722	...	1732	1816	1826	1835	...	...	1900	1907	...	1857	...	1955	2055	2135	...	2219	...	...	2210	2210	2235
St Jean de Luz 325 d.	1717	...	1715	1735	...	1745	1828	1838	1848	...	...	1913	1920	...	1911	...	2009	2109	2152	...	2236	...	...	2228	2228	2253
Biarritz 325 d.	1733	...	1730	1751	...	1801	1844	1853	1904	...	...	1928	1935	...	1927	...	2022	2122	2212	...	2256	...	...	2246	2245	2310
Bayonne 325 d.	1747	...	1744	1804	...	1813	1858	1907	1916	...	...	1941	1949	...	1941	...	2032	2132	2227	...	2311	...	...	2302	2303	2326
Tarbes 325 d.	|	...	|	|	1650	|	|	|	|	...	1832	|	|	1830	|	2101	...	...	|	2117	|	2200	2243	|	|	|
Lourdes 325 d.	|	...	|	|	1710	|	|	|	|	...	1847	|	|	1845	|	2120	...	...	|	2137	|	2220	2302	|	|	|
Pau 325 d.	|	1700	|	|	1737	|	|	|	|	1916	1916	|	|	1915	|	2149	...	...	|	2206	|	2249	2330	|	|	|
Orthez 325 d.	|	1725	|	|	1803	|	|	|	|	1940	1940	|	|	1941	|	2215	...	...	|	2231	|	2314	2356	|	|	|
Puyoô 325 d.	|	1735	|	|	|	|	|	|	|	1951	1951	|	|	1951	|	|	...	...	|	|	|	|	|	|	|	|
Dax a.	1820	1800	1820	1834	1829	1857	|	1937	2000	2009	2009	2013	2022	2009	2013	2243	...	...	2256	2301	2340	2344	0022	|	|	|
Dax d.	1822	...	1824	1839	1839	...	|	...	...	2018	2018	2018	2024	...	2033	2246	...	...	2323	2323	0007	0007	0025	|	|	|
Morcenx d.	1844	...	1845	|	|	...	|	...	...	2036	2037	2036	|	...	2053	|	...	...	2348	2348	0032	0032	|	|	|	|
Bordeaux St Jean a.	1939	...	1939	1947	1947	...	2036	...	...	2135	2132	2135	2139	...	2156	|	...	...	|	|	|	|	|	0100	0100	0109
Paris Austerlitz 300 a.	...	...	...	|	|	...	|	...	...	...	...	...	...	...	...	|	...	...	0710	0710	0710	0710	|	|	|	|
Paris M'parnasse 300 a.	...	...	...	2320s	2320s	...	2345	...	...	...	...	...	...	...	...	0555	...	...	...	...	...	...	0645x	0745	0600	0600
Charles de Gaulle ✈ a.	...	...	...	...	...	...	...	...	...	...	...	...	...	...	...	...	...	...	...	...	...	...	...	...	...	...
Lille Europe 11 a.	...	...	...	...	...	...	...	...	...	...	...	...	...	...	...	...	...	...	...	...	...	...	...	...	...	...

BORDEAUX - TARBES and IRÚN 305

A – Ⓐ (also ⑦ to June 28 / from Sept. 6).
B – ⑦ July 5 - Aug. 30 (also Aug. 15, 17 - 20, 24 - 27). On July 5, Aug. 2 runs 7 minutes earlier.
C – ⑦ (also ③-⑤ July 8 - Aug. 28), also June 1, July 13, 14.
D – ⑦ to July 5 / from Aug. 30.
E – ⑤ (also ⑦ July 12 - Aug. 23), also July 14.
F – ⑦ (also ①-④ July 6 - Aug. 27).
G – Ⓐ to July 3; ⑤ July 10 - Aug. 28; Ⓐ from Aug. 31.
H – Ⓐ to July 3; Ⓐ Aug. 31 - Sept. 4.
J – To July 4 / from Aug. 31.
K – July 5 - Aug. 30.
L – June 27 - Sept. 6.
M – June 27 - Sept. 20.
N – Ⓐ (daily July 5 - Aug. 30).
P – Ⓒ to June 21; daily Sept. 7 - Nov. 22, Nov. 28 - Dec. 12.
Q – To Sept. 3.
R – ①②③④ (also ⑦ July 5 - Aug. 30), not June 1, Nov. 11.
S – ⑥ July 11 - Aug. 29.
T – ⑤⑦ (daily June 19 - Sept. 6, Oct. 23 - Nov. 4), also June 1. ▬ 2 cl. and ⊏2⊐ (reclining) Hendaye - Bordeaux - Nice.
U – Runs from Nice on ⑤⑦ (daily June 19 - Sept. 6, Oct. 23 - Nov. 4). ▬ 2 cl. and ⊏2⊐ (reclining) Nice - Bordeaux - Irún. Terminates at Bayonne on certain dates (from Nice on ⑦ from Sept. 7, also Oct. 24 - 29, Nov. 1 - 4).
V – ⑤⑦ (daily July 3 - Aug. 30), also June 20, Sept. 26, Oct. 3, 10, 24, Nov. 7, 14, Dec. 12. Depart Paris 2205 on ⑤ to June 26, ⑤ Oct. 9 - Dec. 4; dep 2235 on July 3, ⑤ Sept. 4 - Oct. 2.
W – ①②③④⑥ July 4 - Aug. 29 (also June 20, Sept. 26, Oct. 3, 10, 24, Nov. 7, 14, Dec. 12).

Y – June 8 - 12, June 29 - July 3, Aug. 31 - Sept. 4 (also runs from Bayonne on Ⓐ from Sept. 7).
Z – *CORAIL LUNÉA* – ▬ 1, 2 cl. and ⊏2⊐ (reclining).
a – ① to June 29 / from Aug. 31 (also June 2; not June 1).
b – Subject to alteration Pau - Dax on Ⓐ to June 26, Sept. 14 - 25, Oct. 12 - Nov. 6.
c – ⑦ to July 5 / from Aug. 30.
d – Ⓐ June 29 - July 6; ① July 13 - Aug. 10; Ⓐ Aug. 17 - Oct. 9; Ⓐ from Nov. 9.
e – Also June 1, July 14.
f – Not June 12.
g – Also June 2, July 15; not June 1, July 13.
h – Not dates in note **c**.
k – Not Aug. 15, Oct. 23, 30, Nov. 6.
m – Not June 1, July 14, Nov. 11.
n – Not June 1, July 14.
q – ⑥⑦ July 5 - 26 (also July 13, 14, Aug. 31 - Sept. 4).
r – ⑤ to July 3 / from Sept. 4.
s – Arrive Paris 15 minutes later on ①-④ to June 26, ①-④ Oct. 5 - Dec. 3; arrive up to 50 minutes later on ⑤ to June 25; ⑤ Oct. 9 - Dec. 4.
t – Not Aug. 15.
u – Also July 15.
v – Not July 14, 15.
x – Arrive 0555 on ① July 13 - Aug. 24 (also July 15).
y – Runs up to 50 minutes earlier on ⑤ to June 26 and ⑤ Oct. 9 - Dec. 4; up to 20 minutes earlier on ⑤ Sept. 4 - Oct. 2 (also July 3).
z – Lille Flandres.

TGV – 🅁, supplement payable, 🍸.
♥ – *CORAIL LUNÉA* – for days of running see Table **325**. ▬ 1, 2 cl. and ⊏2⊐ (reclining) Genève - Bayonne - Irún.
♣ – *CORAIL LUNÉA* – for days of running see Table **325**. ▬ 1, 2 cl. and ⊏2⊐ (reclining) Hendaye - Genève.
◧ – Depart Paris 1150 on Ⓐ Aug. 24 - Sept. 4 (train **8529**), also Aug. 3.
◇ – Timings may vary due to engineering work - please enquire before travel.
△ – Arrive Paris 1420 on Ⓐ Aug. 4 - Sept. 4.
▷ – On Sept. 1 runs 45 minutes later. Depart Tarbes 0825 on Ⓐ Oct. 5 - 21.
⊡ – Not Sept. 11.
⊙ – On July 5 starts from Dax.
⊖ – Runs 30 minutes later on Ⓐ to July 3, Sept. 14 - 29, Oct. 12 - Nov. 6 (not Sept. 15, 23).
⊕ – On Ⓐ to June 26 (also Nov. 23 - 27) runs later from Bordeaux and terminates at Hendaye (a. 1320).
⊗ – Not Aug. 5.
‡ – Runs earlier on Oct. 31 (depart Bordeaux 2151).
* – Arrive 1042.

Note: where a change of train is shown at Dax, certain trains may have a through car to / from Bordeaux. Check before boarding.

BORDEAUX - ARCACHON 306

Local services : to July 4 and from Aug. 31

	⚒	Ⓐ	⚒‡	Ⓐ‡	‡	‡		Ⓐ	Ⓒ	Ⓐ				Ⓐ		Ⓐu	Ⓐ		Ⓐ		Ⓐ			Ⓑ	⑤⑦	⑥
Bordeaux St Jean ... d.	0641	0711	0741	0811	0841	1041	1141	1241	1241	1319	1341	1441	1541	1611	1641	1707	1731	1751	1811	1841	1911	1941	2041	2141	2241	0001
Facture Biganos .... d.	0711	0741	0811	0841	0911	1111	1211	1315	1311	1353	1411	1511	1611	1641	1711	1741	1801	1824	1843	1911	1943	2011	2111	2211	2311	0032
Arcachon .... ⊖ a.	0733	0803	0833	0903	0933	1133	1233	1340	1333	1417	1433	1533	1633	1703	1733	1806	1823	1850	1904	1933	2004	2033	2133	2233	2333	0054

	Ⓐ	⚒	Ⓐ	Ⓐ	Ⓐ	⚒	Ⓐ	⚒				‡	Ⓐ‡	Ⓒ		Ⓐ		Ⓐ		Ⓐ		Ⓑ	⚒	†		
Arcachon .... ⊖ d.	0556	0612	0635	0646	0707	0726	0756	0826	0926	1026	1126	1226	1256	1426	1526	1603	1623	1654	1726	1756	1826	1926	2026	2126	...	...
Facture-Biganos .... d.	0618	0634	0659	0705	0731	0748	0818	0848	0948	1048	1148	1248	1318	1448	1548	1628	1645	1717	1748	1818	1848	1948	2048	2148	...	...
Bordeaux St Jean .... a.	0647	0707	0723	0735	0758	0817	0847	0917	1017	1117	1217	1317	1345	1517	1617	1700	1714	1749	1817	1847	1917	2017	2117	2217	...	...

Local services : July 5 - Aug. 30

		⚒				Ⓐ	Ⓒ					Ⓐu	Ⓐv	⑥	Ⓑ	Ⓐ						⑥t		
Bordeaux St Jean .... d.	0641	0741	0841	1041	1141	1241	1241	1341	1441	1541	1641	1707	1731	1751	1751	1815r	1841	1941	2041	2141	2241	0001	...	...
Facture Biganos.................... d.	0711	0811	0911	1111	1211	1315	1311	1411	1511	1611	1711	1741	1801	1824	1822	1843	1911	2011	2111	2211	2311	0032	...	...
Arcachon .... ⊖ a.	0733	0833	0933	1133	1233	1340	1333	1433	1533	1633	1733	1806	1823	1847	1850	1909	1933	2033	2133	2233	2333	0054	...	...

	Ⓐ	⚒	Ⓐ	Ⓐ	Ⓐ		⚒					Ⓐ	Ⓒ			Ⓐ			Ⓐ				†	
Arcachon .... ⊖ d.	0556	0612	0635	0646	0707	0726	0826	0926	0956	1126	1226	1256	1326	1426	1526	1603	1623	1726	1756	1826	1926	2026	2126	2226
Facture-Biganos..................... d.	0618	0634	0659	0705	0731	0748	0848	0948	1018	1148	1248	1318	1348	1448	1548	1628	1645	1748	1818	1848	1948	2048	2148	2248
Bordeaux St Jean .... a.	0647	0707	0723	0735	0758	0817	0917	1017	1047	1217	1317	1345	1417	1517	1617	1700	1714	1817	1847	1917	2017	2117	2217	2317

km	*TGV services,* 🅁	*TGV* **8411** ⑦ e	*TGV* **8415** ①-⑥ n△	*TGV* **8427** S§	*TGV* **8467** ⑤
	Paris M. ◐ **300** ... d.	0755*	0915	1210	1825
0	**Bordeaux St Jean** .. d.	1120	1225	1536	2135
40	Facture Biganos..... d.	1143	1250	1559	2158
56	La Teste .... a.	|	|	|	2208
59	**Arcachon** .... a.	1158	1305	1614	2215

TGV services, 🅁	*TGV* **8438** ①-④ n	*TGV* **8456** ⑤-⑦ e	*TGV* **8476** ①-⑥ Sc	*TGV* **8478** ⑦ Sx	*TGV* **8482** ⑦ e
Arcachon .... d.	1333	1557	1708	1719	1852
La Teste .... d.	|	|	|	|	1859
Facture-Biganos ...... d.	1349	1616	1724	1735	1913
Bordeaux St Jean . a.	1411	1642	1746	1758	1935
Paris M. ◐ **300** .... a.	1730	2015	2135	2150	2255

S – June 27 - Aug. 30.
c – Not July 14.
e – Also June 1, July 14.
n – Not June 1, July 14, Nov. 30, Dec. 1 - 3.
r – 1811 on ⑤.
t – Not Aug. 15.
u – Depart 1711 on ⑤.
v – Not July 6, 7, 23, Aug. 17, 18.
x – Also July 14.
TGV – 🅁, supplement, 🍸.
△ – Depart Paris 0910 on June 13; 0850 on Ⓐ Aug. 24 - Sept. 4.
‡ – Subject to alteration Nov. 21 - Dec. 4.
§ – Depart Paris 1205 on June 13, 1150 on Aug. 3.
* – 5 minutes earlier on June 14.

⊖ – Trains also call at La Teste, 5 minutes from Arcachon.
◐ – Paris Montparnasse.

BORDEAUX - LE VERDON - POINTE DE GRAVE 307

Some trains 2nd class

July 5 - August 30

km		Ⓐ					Ⓐ		†	Ⓐ	
0	**Bordeaux** St Jean ..... d.	0705	0905	1105	1305	1605	1700	1805	1935	1945	...
23	Blanquefort .... d.	0748	0948	1148	1348	1648	1748	1848	2014	2016	...
39	Margaux .... d.	0808	1008	1208	1408	1708	1808	1908	2038	2035	...
61	Pauillac...................... d.	0832	1032	1232	1432	1732	1832	1932	2102	2055	...
80	Lesparre .... d.	0847	1047	1247	1447	1747	1846	1947	2116	2110	...
106	Soulac sur Mer .... d.	0906	1106	1306	1506	1806	...	2006	...	2129	...
113	**Le Verdon**................. a.	0913	1113	1313	1513	1813	...	2013	...	2136	...
116	Pointe de Grave § ...... a.	0918	1118	1318	1518	1818	...	...	...	...	...

	⚒	Ⓐ								
Pointe de Grave § ..... d.	...	...	...	0936	1143	1343	...	1643	1843	...
Le Verdon................ d.	...	0648	0748	0941	1148	1348	...	1648	1848	...
Soulac sur Mer .... d.	...	0656	0756	0949	1156	1356	...	1656	1856	...
Lesparre .... d.	0615	0715	0815	1009	1215	1415	...	1715	1915	...
Pauillac.................... d.	0633	0733	0833	1033	1233	1433	...	1733	1933	...
Margaux .... d.	0654	0754	0854	1054	1254	1454	...	1754	1954	...
Blanquefort .... d.	0715	0815	0915	1115	1315	1515	...	1815	2015	...
Bordeaux St Jean .... a.	0754	0854	0954	1154	1354	1554	...	1854	2054	...

To July 4 / from August 31

km		Ⓐ	⚒ d	Ⓐ	Ⓒ	⚒ n	Ⓐ n	🚌 Ⓐ	Ⓐ	Ⓒ	🚌 ⑥		🚌 Ⓐ	Ⓐ		⑤⑦ w	①-④ m
0	**Bordeaux** St Jean......d.	0631	0705	0805	0905	1105	1205	...	1305	1305	...	1605	...	1700	1805	1935	1945
23	Blanquefort.................d.	0710	0748	0848	0948	1148	1248	...	1348	1348	...	1648	...	1748	1848	2014	2016
39	Margaux......................d.	0730	0808	0908	1008	1208	1308	...	1408	1408	...	1708	...	1808	1908	2038	2035
61	Pauillac.......................d.	0751	0832	0932	1032	1232	1332	...	1432	1432	...	1732	...	1832	1932	2102	2054
80	Lesparre......................d.	0805	0847	0946	1047	1246	1347	1415	1446	1447	1500	1746	1805	1847	1947	2116	...
106	Soulac sur Mer ....d.	...	0906	...	1106	...	1406	1453	...	1506	1538	...	1842	1906	2006	...	...
113	**Le Verdon**..................d.	...	0913	...	1113	...	1413	1505*	...	1513	1550*	...	1851*	1913	2013	...	...
116	Pointe de Grave §.......a.	...	...	...	...	...	...	1510	...	...	1555	...	1855	...	...	...	...

	Ⓐ	Ⓐ	⑥	Ⓐ	Ⓐ	Ⓒ	⑥	Ⓐ n	🚌 ⚒	b	Ⓐ		Ⓐ	🚌 †	Ⓐ	Ⓒ	
Pointe de Grave §........d.	...	...	...	...	...	...	...	...	1055	...	...	...	...	1655	...	...	...
Le Verdon...................d.	...	...	...	0626	...	0748	0948	...	1102*	1148	...	1548	...	1701*	...	1748	...
Soulac sur Mer ....d.	...	...	...	0633	...	0756	0956	...	1111	1156	...	1556	...	1712	...	1756	...
Lesparre ....d.	...	0554	0615	0652	0815	0815	1015	1115	1200	1215	1415	1615	1715	1800	1815	1815	...
Pauillac.........................d.	0531	0609	0633	0707	0833	0833	1033	1133	...	1233	1433	1633	1733	...	1833	1833	...
Margaux ....d.	0556	0628	0654	0729	0854	0854	1054	1154	...	1254	1454	1654	1754	...	1854	1854	...
Blanquefort ....d.	0615	0647	0715	0749	0915	0915	1115	1215	...	1315	1515	1715	1815	...	1915	1915	...
Bordeaux St Jean.......a.	0654	0729	0754	0827	0954	0954	1154	1254	...	1354	1554	1755	1854	...	1956	1954	...

b – Subject to alteration on Ⓐ to June 26 and Ⓐ Sept. 7 - Oct. 16.
d – Subject to alteration on Ⓐ to June 26.
m – Not June 1, Nov. 10, 11.
n – Subject to alteration on Ⓐ Sept. 7 - Oct. 16.
w – Also June 1, Nov. 11.

* – Serves village centre, not rail station.

§ – ⛴ Pointe de Grave - Royan:
Mar. 27 - June 25, Sept. 1 - 21:
From Pointe de Grave: 0715, 0855, 1025, 1155, 1325, 1510, 1640, 1825, 1955.
From Royan: 0750, 0930, 1100, 1230, 1400, 1545, 1715, 1900, 2030.
June 26 - Aug. 31: every 30 - 45 minutes. (0630 - 2030 from Pointe de Grave, 0715 - 2115 from Royan).
Sept. 22 - Mar. 25: 6 - 7 sailings per day.
✆ 05 56 73 37 73. www.gironde.fr

308 LIMOGES - PÉRIGUEUX - AGEN

2nd class

km		Ⓐ	F	⚒	†	Ⓐ	⚒	⚒	Ⓐ	⑤	†
0	**Limoges 302** d.	...	...	1110	...	...	...	...	1735	1735	...
99	Périgueux **302** a.	...	...	1206	...	...	...	...	1852	1852	...
99	Périgueux d.	0720	0951	1208	1405	1604	1722	1820	1914	1914	1914
139	Les Eyzies d.	0750	1021	1243	1436	1636	1759	1857	1947	1947	1947
156	Le Buisson a.	0805	1036	1258	1451	1651	1814	1912	2001	2002	2002
156	Le Buisson d.	0806	1037	1259	1452	1652	1815	...	...	2004	2004
251	**Agen** a.	0928	1218	1416	1615	1814	1942	...	...	2123	2123

	Ⓐ	†	d	E	†K	⑥t	†c	⑥	Ⓑ	⑤J
Agen d.	0641	...	1107	1502	1625	1625	...	1828	1828	2043
Le Buisson a.	0800	...	1223	1616	1739	1739	...	1951	1951	2200
Le Buisson d.	0815	0845	1224	1617	1740	1740	1813	1953	2003	2201
Les Eyzies d.	0830	0900	1244	1635	1756	1800	1830	2008	2019	2217
Périgueux a.	0905	0935	1314	1704	1826	1830	1909	2039	2049	2248
Périgueux **302** d.	...	...	1319	...	...	...	...	...	...	...
Limoges 302 a.	...	...	1429	...	...	...	...	...	...	...

E – Ⓐ (also ⑦ to June 28 / from Sept. 6).
F – Ⓒ (daily July 4 - Aug. 28).
J – To July 4 / from Aug. 31.
K – † July 5 - Aug. 30.
c – Runs 6-8 minutes later July 5 - Aug. 30.
d – From June 14.
t – Not Aug. 15.

309 LIMOGES - ANGOULÊME and POITIERS

km		①	⑥t	R	⑥	ⒶK				⑤	†	⑤
0	**Limoges** d.	0530	0530	0635	0821	0821	1226	...	1707	1836	1836	2042
122	**Angoulême** a.	0722	0722	0842	1006	1006	1420	...	1856	2029	2029	2235

	⚒	ⒶJ	⚒	†	⑤	G	H	F	⑤	†K
Angoulême d.	0550	0754	1223	1510	1632	1805	1835	1900	2011	2125
Limoges a.	0758	0941	1416	1653	1825	2010	2039	2100	2201	2257

Rail service Limoges - Poitiers to July 5. *Service is by 🚌 July 6 - Nov. 29 in revised timings.*

km		Ⓐ			⑤⑥	†	⑤			⑤	†	
0	**Limoges** d.	0527	0635	...	1342	1504	1610	...	1725	1834	1834	...
139	**Poitiers** a.	0731	0834	...	1549	1659	1809	...	1931	2053	2050	...

	Ⓐ	⑤–⑦	⑤–⑦			b		⑤	†	
Poitiers d.	0612	1055	1236	...	1817	1942	...	2150	2150	...
Limoges a.	0821	1253	1436	...	2026	2143	...	2350	2350	...

F – ⑤⑥⑦ (also June 1, July 13, 14, Nov. 11).
G – ①–④ July 6 - Aug. 27 (not July 14).
H – ①–④ to July 2 / from Aug. 31 (not June 1, Nov. 11).
J – To July 4 / from Aug. 31.
K – July 5 - Aug. 30.
R – ②–⑤ to July 3; Ⓐ from Aug. 31.
b – ⚒ to June 23; ⑤⑥ June 26 - July 4.
t – Not Aug. 15.

310 PARIS - LIMOGES - TOULOUSE

For faster TGV services Paris - Agen - Toulouse and v.v. see Table 320. Additional relief trains run on peak dates.

km								★ 3601			★ 3611		★ 3621		★ 3623			★ 3631				★ 3635		★ 3637
		⚒	Ⓐ		⑥	⚒	⚒	Ⓐ §	Ⓐ	Ⓐ	⊗	†	k	⚒	P	Ⓐ	Ⓒ	Y		⑥ t	Ⓐ	⑤⑦ q	⑤⑦ e	
	Lille Europe d.	...	...	...	...	...	...	...	...	...	...	...	...	...	...	...	...	...	...	...	...	...	...	...
0	**Paris Austerlitz 294 315** d.	...	...	...	...	...	...	0638	...	...	0754	...	0909	...	0924	...	...	1025	...	...	...	1250	...	1254
	Orléans 315 d.	...	...	...	...	...	0630	|	...	0800	*0841*	...	|	...	|	1016	1016	|	...	1214	1307	|	...	|
119	Les Aubrais-Orléans **294 315** d.	...	...	...	...	...	|	|	...	0808	0849	...	|	...	|	1026	1026	|	...	|	1315	|	...	|
200	Vierzon **315** d.	...	...	...	...	0636	0729	|	...	0904	|	...	1040	...	|	1115	1115	|	...	1314	1409	|	...	1422
236	Issoudun d.	...	...	...	...	0659	0750	0822	...	0921	|	...	|	...	|	1133	1133	|	...	1335	1429	|	...	1441
263	Châteauroux d.	...	...	...	...	0716	0805a	0837	...	0935	0950	...	1111	...	1126	1147	1146	|	...	1350	1442	1447	...	1458
294	Argenton sur Creuse d.	...	...	...	...	0734	0820a	|	...	0949	|	...	|	...	|	1203	...	|	...	1406	▬	|	...	1516
341	La Souterraine d.	...	...	...	...	0802	0846a	|	...	...	1026	...	1147	...	1203	1230	...	|	...	1435	...	|	...	1541
400	**Limoges** a.	...	...	...	...	0835	▬	0937	...	...	1054	...	1216	...	1233	1303	...	1314	...	1509	...	1552	...	1610
400	**Limoges** d.	...	...	0621	0734	▬	...	0939	...	...	1056	...	1218	1227	...	...	...	1317	...	...	...	1554	...	...
459	Uzerche d.	...	...	0657	0814	...	...	|	...	...	1132	...	1255	1313	...	...	...	|	...	...	...	1631	...	...
499	**Brive la Gaillarde** a.	...	...	0726	0843	...	...	1036	...	...	1157	...	1321	1341	...	...	...	1416	...	...	...	1656	...	...
499	**Brive la Gaillarde** d.	...	0603	0732	...	...	...	...	1112	...	1159	1204	...	...	...	...	...	1419	...	...	...	...	1713	...
536	Souillac d.	...	0628	0756	...	...	...	...	1135	...	|	1227	...	...	...	...	...	1445	...	...	...	...	1738	...
559	Gourdon d.	...	0643	0811	...	...	⚒	...	1149	...	|	1242	...	...	...	...	...	1500	...	...	Ⓑ	...	1753	...
600	Cahors d.	0622	0710	0838	...	...	1048	...	1215	...	1304	1308	...	...	...	...	...	1528	...	...	1823	...	1823	...
639	Caussade d.	0649	0735	0903	...	Ⓐ	1114	...	1239	...	|	1333	...	...	...	...	...	1554	...	...	1850	...	1850	...
662	Montauban **320** d.	0708	0752	0919	...	1045	1131	...	1254	...	1340	1348	...	...	...	...	...	1610	...	...	1907	...	1907	...
713	**Toulouse Matabiau 320** a.	0734	0828	0946	...	1121	1159	...	1320	...	1407	1413	...	...	...	...	...	1637	...	...	1947	...	1947	...
	Portbou **355** a.	...	...	...	...	...	...	...	...	...	...	...	...	...	...	...	...	...	...	...	...	...	...	...

	★ 3641	★ 3641					★ 3651				★ 3657	★ 3661			★ 3665	★ 3667		*TGV* 5298	★ 3673	★ 3681	*TGV* 5298		3731	3751
	①–⑤ n	⑥⑦ u	⚒	Ⓐ	Ⓐ	Ⓐ	Ⓐ	Ⓒ	⑦ e	Ⓐ	Ⓐ	Ⓑ	Ⓐ	†	⑤–⑦ e△		Ⓐ	⑦ ♠	⑤		①–⑥ ♣		♦ Ⓡ	♦ Ⓡ
Lille Europe d.	...	...	...	...	...	...	...	...	...	...	...	...	...	...	...	...	...	1740	...	...	1820	...	...	...
Paris Austerlitz 294 315 d.	1403	1403	...	...	...	...	1610	...	...	...	1702	1732	...	...	1821	1832	...	|	1919	1949	|	...	2156	2256
Orléans 315 d.	|	|	...	...	...	...	|	1647	1647	1709	|	|	...	...	|	|	1929	*2004*	|	|	*2046*	...	*2248*	*2344*
Les Aubrais-Orléans **294 315** d.	|	|	...	...	...	...	|	1656	1656	|	|	|	...	...	|	|	|	2012	|	|	2054	...	2256	2359
Vierzon **315** d.	|	|	...	...	1636	...	1737	1751	1751	1757	|	|	1903	...	1952	2001	2025	2053	|	2121	2129	...	2338	|
Issoudun d.	|	|	...	...	1656	...	|	1811	1811	1818	|	|	1925	...	|	2020	2043	|	|	|	|	...	|	|
Châteauroux d.	1554	1554	1605	1638	1713	...	1812	1827	1829	1836	1901	1927	1942	1942	2023	2036	2057	2124	|	2151	2202	...	|	|
Argenton sur Creuse d.	|	|	1622	1655	▬	...	|	...	1845	1851	|	|	1958	1958	|	2054	...	|	|	|	|	...	|	|
La Souterraine d.	|	|	▬	1724	...	...	1849	...	1915	1921	1938	|	2026	2026	|	2119	...	2203	|	|	2240	...	|	|
Limoges a.	1655	1655	Ⓐ	1800	†	...	1918	...	1948	1955	2006	2027	2057	2057	2124	2149	...	2232	2208	2252	2309	...	0108	|
Limoges d.	1659	1659	1730	...	1826	1830	1920	...	...	...	...	2029	...	...	2126	...	...	2235	...	2254	2312	...	0110	|
Uzerche d.	|	|	1816	...	1915	1918	|	...	...	...	...	2104	...	...	2203	...	...	|	...	|	|	...	|	|
Brive la Gaillarde a.	1759	1759	1845	...	1945	1945	2018	...	...	...	...	2128	...	...	2228	...	...	2333	...	2353	0012	...	|	|
Brive la Gaillarde d.	1802	1802	...	...	1949	...	...	...	...	...	...	2130	...	...	2238	...	...	...	...	...	...	...	|	|
Souillac d.	1827	|	...	...	2012	...	...	...	...	...	...	2156	...	...	2303	...	...	...	...	...	...	...	|	0441x
Gourdon d.	1843	|	...	...	2028	...	...	...	...	...	...	2212	...	...	2319	...	...	...	...	...	...	...	|	0457x
Cahors d.	1910	1902	...	...	2055	...	...	...	...	...	...	2239	...	...	2346	...	...	...	...	...	...	...	|	0525
Caussade d.	|	|	...	...	2120	...	...	...	...	...	...	...	...	...	|	...	...	...	...	...	...	...	|	0553x
Montauban **320** d.	|	|	...	...	2136	...	...	...	...	...	...	...	...	...	|	...	...	...	...	...	...	...	|	0610
Toulouse Matabiau 320 a.	2015	2006	...	...	2202	...	...	...	...	...	...	...	...	...	0048	...	...	...	...	...	...	...	|	0641
Portbou **355** a.	...	...	...	...	...	...	...	...	...	...	...	...	...	...	...	...	...	...	...	...	...	...	0821	...

		★ 3600	★ 3604		★ 3606		*TGV* 5296			★ 3610	★ 3612			★ 3620				★ 3624		★ 3626	★ 3630		★ 3640	
	⚒	Ⓐ §		⚒	Ⓐ	⚒	♥	Ⓐ	Ⓐ	①–⑥	⑦ b	① g	⚒	①–⑥ n	⚒	†	Ⓐ	▽	Ⓐ	⑦ e		⚒	⊡	⑥ t
Cerbère **355** d.	...	...	...	...	...	...	...	...	...	...	...	...	...	...	...	...	...	...	...	...	0750	...	...	...
Toulouse Matabiau 320 d.	...	...	...	...	...	...	...	...	...	...	...	0633	0657	0722	...	0726	0734	...	0949	...	1124	...	...	1223
Montauban **320** d.	...	...	...	...	...	...	...	...	...	...	...	0705	0732	0750	...	0757	0811	...	1025	...	1151	...	...	1303
Caussade d.	...	...	...	...	...	...	...	...	...	...	...	0720	0749	|	...	0813	▬	...	▬	...	1207	...	...	1319
Cahors d.	...	...	...	...	...	...	...	...	...	0633	...	0744	0819	0829	...	0840	...	...	...	...	1234	...	...	1345
Gourdon d.	...	...	...	...	...	...	...	...	...	0701	...	0810	0843	|	...	0905	...	...	...	...	1300	...	...	▬
Souillac d.	...	...	...	...	...	...	...	...	...	0718	...	0825	0858	|	...	0920	...	...	...	...	1317	...	...	...
Brive la Gaillarde a.	...	...	...	...	...	...	...	...	...	0742	...	0848	0921	0929	...	0942	...	...	Ⓒ	...	1341	...	...	...
Brive la Gaillarde d.	...	0450	...	...	...	0618	0640	0728	...	0745	0745	▬	▬	0931	...	▬	...	...	1240	1308	1345	...	1443	...
Uzerche d.	...	0515	...	...	...	0646	|	0755	...	|	|	...	...	|	...	...	⚒	...	1310	1334	|	...	1508	...
Limoges a.	...	0551	...	...	...	0730	0735	0833	...	0844	0844	...	Ⓐ	1029	...	...	...	...	1356	1412	1444	...	1545	...
Limoges d.	0524	0553	0603	0607	0700	0741a	0738	▬	...	0847	0847	...	1016	1032	...	...	1250	1350	...	1415	1448	...	1548	...
La Souterraine d.	0555	|	0634	0640	0731	0815a	0814	...	0903	|	|	Ⓐ	1051	1103	...	⚒	1334	1421	...	|	|	...	|	⑥
Argenton sur Creuse d.	0624	|	|	0707	|	...	|	...	0930	|	|	←	1119	|	←		1400	1445	...	|	|	1630	|	←
Châteauroux d.	0641	0654	0712	0732	0808	...	0852	0857	0945	0950	0950	0957	1134	1141	1146	1228	1419	1503	...	1518	|	1646	1652	1658
Issoudun d.	0656	|	0729	0750	|	...	|	0911	→	|	|	1011	→	|	1200	1244	...	1520	...	|	|	→	|	1715
Vierzon **315** d.	0724	|	0748	0812	|	...	0922	0933	...	|	|	1033	...	|	1222	1306	...	1540	...	|	|	...	|	1758•
Les Aubrais-Orléans **294 315** a.	|	|	|	|	|	...	0954	|	...	|	|	|	...	|	1313	1352	...	|	...	|	|	...	|	1853
Orléans 315 a.	0818	|	|	0859	|	...	*1002*	1021	...	|	|	1117	...	|	1323	1400	...	|	...	|	|	...	|	1900
Paris Austerlitz 294 315 a.	...	0844	0916	...	0958	...	|	...	...	1143	1143	...	...	1339	...	...	...	1707	...	1710	1738r	...	1844	...
Lille Europe a.	...	...	...	...	...	...	1226	...	...	...	...	...	...	...	...	...	...	...	...	...	...	...	...	...

TOULOUSE - LIMOGES - PARIS 310

	⚒	★ 3652 ⑦ e	★ 3654 ⑤	⚒	⚒ ⊕	★ 3660 ①–⑥ n	★ 3664 ⑦ e	Ⓐ	†	★ 3672 ⑦ e	†	★ 3680 Ⓑ ⊙	Ⓑ z	Ⓐ	⑥	★ 3690 E	★ 3690 F	⑤	①–④ m	⑤	①–④ m ‡	Ⓐ	Ⓒ	3750 ◆ 🄁	3730 ◆ 🄁
Cerbère **355** d.	...	...	...	...	...	...	...	...	...	...	...	...	...	...	...	...	...	...	...	...	...	...	...	...	2121
Toulouse Matabiau 320 d.	...	1346	...	...	1346	...	...	1353	...	1508	...	...	...	...	...	1653	1703	1713	1753	1801	...	1849	1936	2235	0056
Montauban **320** d.	...	|	...	...	1413	...	...	1427	...	|	...	...	...	...	1707	|	|	1755	1828	1828	...	1938	2003	2308	|
Caussade d.	...	|	...	...	1428	...	...	▬	...	|	...	...	...	...	1726	|	|	1813	1843	1842	...	1955	2019	2324c	|
Cahors d.	...	1452	...	...	1454	...	...	...	...	1613	1645	...	...	1730	1754	1757	1807	1840	1908	1908	...	2021	2046	2352	|
Gourdon d.	...	1519	...	...	1520	...	...	...	...	1640	1711	...	...	1759	1819	1825	|	1905	1934	1934	...	...	2113	0020c	|
Souillac d.	...	1537	...	...	1535	...	...	...	...	1656	1727	...	...	1814	1834	1842	|	1920	1950	1950	...	...	2129	0036c	|
Brive la Gaillarde a.	...	1601	...	...	1558	...	...	...	...	1720	1750	...	...	1840	1857	1906	1906	1943	2014	2014	...	...	2154	|	|
Brive la Gaillarde d.	...	1604	...	...	▬	1620	...	...	...	1723	▬	1758	1829	...	...	1908	1908	...	...	2016	2041	...	2156	|	|
Uzerche d.	...	|	...	...	...	|	...	...	...	|		1823	1859	...	...	|	|	...	...	2042	2106	...	2221	|	|
Limoges a.	...	1702	...	...	...	1717	...	Ⓐ	...	1823	⑤	1900	1942	...	...	2006	2006	...	...	2119	2144	...	2258	|	|
Limoges d.	1638	1705	1705	...	†	1720	1720	1740	1755	1826	1826	1903	...	...	...	2008	2008	...	...	...	...	...	...	|	|
La Souterraine d.	1717	|	|	...		1751	1751	1823	1836	|	1916	1934	...	...	...	|	|	...	...	...	...	...	...	|	|
Argenton sur Creuse d.	1743	|	|	←	1743	1814	1815	1852	1904	|	1947	|	...	...	...	|	|	...	...	...	...	...	...	|	|
Châteauroux d.	1801	1809	1809	1813	1813	1831	1834	1907	1919	1930	2020	2013	...	...	...	2112	2112	...	...	...	...	...	...	|	|
Issoudun d.	→	|	|	1830	1830	1846	1850	...	...	|	2038	|	...	...	...	|	|	...	...	...	...	...	...	|	|
Vierzon **315** d.	...	1840	1840	1909	1913	1905	1910	...	...	|	2059	2044	...	...	...	2143	2143	...	...	...	...	...	...	|	0538
Les Aubrais-Orléans **294 315** a.	...	|	|	1955	1959	|	|	...	...	|	...	|	...	...	...	2220	2220	...	...	...	...	...	...	0548	0620
Orléans 315 a.	...	|	|	2005	2007	|	|	...	...	|	...	|	...	...	...	*2229*	*2229*	...	...	...	...	...	...	*0602*	*0629*
Paris Austerlitz 294 315 a.	...	2008	2008	...	...	2034	2037	...	...	2121	...	2212	...	...	...	2318	2318	...	...	...	...	...	...	0652	0730
Lille Europe a.	...	...	...	...	...	...	...	...	...	...	...	...	...	...	...	...	...	...	...	...	...	...	...	...	...

◆ – **NOTES** (LISTED BY TRAIN NUMBER):

3730 – *CORAIL LUNÉA* – 🛏 1,2 cl. and [2] (reclining) Cerbère - Paris and Latour de Carol (**3970**) - Toulouse - Paris. Depart Cerbère 2030 June 26 - Sept. 6 (also Nov. 1); timings from Toulouse may vary.

3731 – *CORAIL LUNÉA* – 🛏 1,2 cl., [2] (reclining) Paris - Portbou; 🛏 1,2 cl. and [2] (reclining) Paris - Latour de Carol (train **3971**).

3750 – *CORAIL LUNÉA* – 🛏 1,2 cl., [2] (reclining) Toulouse - Paris. Train **3752** on dates in note **c**. Conveys (from Brive) portions from Rodez and Albi on dates in Table **316**.

3751 – *CORAIL LUNÉA* – 🛏 1,2 cl. and [2] (reclining) Paris - Toulouse. Train **3753** on dates in note **x**. Conveys (to Brive) portions for Rodez and Albi on dates in Table **316**.

E – ⑤ to June 12; ①⑤⑦ from June 14 (also July 15; not July 13).
F – Daily except dates in note **E**.
P – ⑤⑥ June 26 - Aug. 29 (also Oct. 24, 31; not June 27).
Y – To Cerbère (Table **355**). On Ⓐ June 15 - July 17 (not July 13) and Ⓐ Sept. 7 - 25 depart Montauban 1632, arrive Toulouse 1657. Additional relief train **3629** runs on July 4, 11, Aug. 1, 15, Oct. 24, 31, depart Paris 1017, arrive Toulouse 1633.

a – Ⓐ only.
b – Not June 1. On June 21 starts from Limoges.
c – Calls on night of ⑤⑥⑦ (also June 1, July 13, 14, Nov. 11).
e – Also June 1, July 14.
g – Also June 2; not June 1.
k – Runs 5 minutes later Limoges - Brive on ⑤ to June 26 / from Sept. 4. On Ⓐ Sept. 7 - 25 runs 30 - 45 minutes later La Souterraine - Brive.
m – Not June 1, July 14, Nov. 11.

n – Not June 1, July 14.
q – Not July 13, Aug. 15, Oct. 31, Nov. 10, 11. On June 26 runs only to Limoges.
r – 1749 Sept. 28 - Oct. 2.
t – Not Aug. 15.
u – Also June 1, July 14, Nov. 11. Arrive Toulouse 2015 on ⑦.
x – Calls on morning of ①⑥⑦ (also June 2, July 14, 15, Nov. 12).
z – Runs 15 minutes later on †.

TGV – 🄁, supplement payable, 🍷.

⊡ – Runs up to 30 minutes earlier on June 25, 26.
⊙ – On June 26 starts from Limoges.
⊕ – Runs up to 22 minutes earlier on Ⓐ June 15 - July 17.
⊗ – Arrives up to 50 minutes later Sept. 28 - Oct. 2.
◇ – 🛏 1,2 cl. and [2] (reclining).
△ – On ⑦ July 5 - Aug. 30 depart Brive 2230, Souillac 2255, Gourdon 2310, Cahors 2337, arrive Toulouse 0039.
▽ – On Ⓐ Oct. 12 - Nov. 6 runs up to 22 minutes earlier.
★ – CORAIL TÉOZ. 🄁. 🍷.
♥ – Also calls at Marne la Vallée (a. 1117), Charles de Gaulle ✈ (a. 1131). On June 21, 23 starts from Limoges.
♠ – Also June 1, July 14. Also calls at Charles de Gaulle ✈ (1835), Marne la Vallée (1853).
♣ – Also June 1, July 14. Also calls at Charles de Gaulle ✈ (1917), Marne la Vallée (1933).
• – Arrive 1735.
‡ – On June 22 runs 45 minutes earlier.
§ – On June 24 - 26 timings may vary by a few minutes.

TOULOUSE - LATOUR DE CAROL 312

Subject to alteration June 20, 21

Service to June 26

km		3971 ◇ 🄁									
	Paris Austerlitz **310** d.	2156	...	...	...	...	...	...	...	...	...
0	**Toulouse Matabiau** d.	|	0650	0750	0850	1050	1450	1650	1750	1850	1950
65	Pamiers d.	0545	0750	0850	0950	1150	1550	1750	1850	1950	2050
83	Foix a.	0555	0800	0905	1000	1200	1600	1800	1905	2000	2105
83	Foix d.	*0620**	0801	0906	1001	1201	1601	1801	1906	2001	*2115**
99	Tarascon sur Ariège a.	*0639**	0814	0920	1014	1214	1614	1814	1920	2014	|
99	Tarascon sur Ariège d.	*0639**	*0824**	*0930**	*1024**	*1224**	*1624**	*1824**	*1930**	*2024**	|
123	Ax les Thermes a.	*0719**	*0904**	*1005**	*1104**	*1304**	*1704**	*1904**	*2005**	*2104**	*2210**
144	L'Hospitalet ⊖ a.	*0745**	*0930**	...	*1130**	*1330**	*1730**	*1930**	...	*2130**	...
163	**Latour de Carol** a.	*0817**	*1002**	...	*1202**	*1402**	*1802**	*2002**	...	*2202**	...

	Ⓐ				Ⓐ				3970 ◇ 🄁
Latour de Carol d.	*0502**	*0702**	*0902**	*1302**	*1530**	...	*1702**	*1902**	*1902**
L'Hospitalet ⊖ d.	*0534**	*0734**	*0934**	*1334**	*1600**	...	*1734**	*1934**	*1934**
Ax les Thermes d.	*0600**	*0800**	*1000**	*1400**	*1625**	...	*1800**	*2000**	*2000**
Tarascon sur Ariège a.	*0640**	*0840**	*1040**	*1440**	*1655**	...	*1840**	*2040**	*2040**
Tarascon sur Ariège d.	0650	0850	1050	1450	*1655**	1743	1850	2050	*2040**
Foix a.	0704	0904	1104	1504	*1720**	1759	1904	2104	*2100**
Foix d.	0705	0907	1107	1507	1734	1802	1907	2107	2220
Pamiers d.	0721	0921	1121	1521	1751	1821	1921	2121	2237
Toulouse Matabiau a.	0816	1016	1216	1616	1846	1916	2016	2216	|
Paris Austerlitz **310** a.	...	...	...	...	...	...	...	...	0730

Service June 27 - Dec. 12

km		3971 ◇ 🄁									
	Paris Austerlitz **310** d.	2156	...	...	...	...	...	...	...	...	...
0	**Toulouse Matabiau** d.	|	0650	0750	0850	1050	1450	1650	1750	1850	1950
65	Pamiers d.	0545	0750	0850	0950	1150	1550	1750	1850	1950	2050
83	Foix a.	0555	0800	0905	1000	1200	1600	1800	1905	2000	2105
83	Foix d.	0558	0801	0906	1001	1201	1601	1801	1906	2001	2106
123	Ax les Thermes d.	0647	0849	0945	1049	1249	1649	1849	1945	2049	2145
144	L'Hospitalet ⊖ a.	0720	0920	...	1120	1320	1720	1920	...	2120	...
163	**Latour de Carol** a.	0751	0952	...	1152	1352	1752	1952	...	2152	...

	Ⓐ		Ⓒ	Ⓐ		Ⓐ				3970 ◇ 🄁
Latour de Carol d.	0521	0721	0921	*0913**	1321	*1530**	...	1721	1921	2021
L'Hospitalet ⊖ d.	0552	0752	0952	*0940**	1352	*1600**	...	1752	1952	2049
Ax les Thermes d.	0620	0820	1020	1020	1420	*1625**	1716	1820	2020	2120
Foix a.	0704	0904	1104	1104	1504	*1720**	1759	1904	2104	2210
Foix d.	0705	0907	1107	1107	1507	1734	1802	1907	2107	2220
Pamiers d.	0721	0921	1121	1121	1521	1751	1821	1921	2121	2237
Toulouse Matabiau a.	0816	1016	1216	1216	1616	1846	1916	2016	2216	|
Paris Austerlitz **310** a.	...	...	...	...	...	...	...	...	...	0730

◇ – 🛏 1,2 cl. and [2] (reclining).
⊖ – Full name: Andorre-L'Hospitalet. For 🚌 connections to / from Andorra see Table **313**.
* – By 🚌.

ANDORRA 🚌 313

Subject to cancellation when mountain passes are closed by snow

🚌		☆				⊖		
Andorre-L'Hospitalet (Gare) d.	0735	0935	1945	...	...	and	...	...
Pas de la Casa d.	0815	1001	2000	0815	0845	every	2045	2145
Soldeu ⊙ d.	0840	...	2025	0830	0855	30 mins	2055	2155
Andorra la Vella a.	0905	...	2105	0915	0940	until	2140	2240

🚌		☆				⊖		
Andorra la Vella d.	0545	...	1700	0715	0745	and	2015	2045
Soldeu ⊙ d.	0610	...	1735	0800	0825	every	2100	2125
Pas de la Casa d.	0640	1245	1815	0815	0840	30 mins	2115	2140
Andorre-L'Hospitalet (Gare) a.	0710	1310	1930	...	...	untill	...	...

⊙ – Also calls at Canillo, Encamp and Escaldes.
⊖ – Joint service with Cooperativa Interurbana.

☆ – Operated by SNCF. Terminates on French side of the border, 100 metre walk from central bus stop in Pas de la Casa.

Operator: La Hispano Andorrana, Av. Santa Coloma, entre 85 - 87, Andorra la Vella, ✆ + 376 821 372. www.andorrabus.com
Additional service: approx hourly (5 per day on ⑦) Escaldes - Andorra la Vella - Sant Julià de Lòria - Seu d'Urgell (Spain).

TOULOUSE - CASTRES - MAZAMET 314

Most trains 2nd class

From Oct. 5 service will be by 🚌 St Sulpice - Castres - Mazamet and v.v.

km		Ⓐ				Ⓐ	Ⓐ	Ⓐ			
0	**Toulouse Matabiau** d.	0645	0744	1145	1346	1546	1640	1724	1742	1846	2046
86	Castres a.	0753	0852	1255	1453	1653	1753	1834	1854	1953	2155
105	**Mazamet** a.	0820	0923	1320	1520	1720	1818	1903	1927	2020	2220

	Ⓐ	Ⓐ		Ⓐ	Ⓐ			Ⓐ		
Mazamet d.	0556	0631	0731	...	0931	1126	1431	1731	1822	1931
Castres d.	0625	0655	0756	0854	0956	1152	1456	1756	1857	1957
Toulouse Matabiau d.	0737	0804	0905	1004	1104	1304	1603	1903	2004	2104

315 PARIS - VIERZON - BOURGES - MONTLUÇON

Some trains 2nd class

Services to Montluçon are subject to alteration Sept. 29 - Nov. 6

km				3903	3905					3909						3913	3913				3917	3923	3925		3921
		⚒	♥	Ⓐ ⊖	⑥	⚒	†					Ⓐ	Ⓐ	⚒	Ⓐ	Ⓑ	⑤	N	⚒	†		⑦ G	⑦ F	⑦ e	⑤
0	**Paris Austerlitz** 310 d.	...	...	0703	0703	...	...	...	...	1218	...	...	...	...	...	1716	1716	...	...	...	1903	2048	2048	...	2048
	Orléans 310 d.	...	0707	*0747*	*0747*	...	...	0900	...	*1303*	1457	...	1629	...	1757	|	|	...	1828	...	*1947*	*2137*	*2137*	...	*2137*
119	Les Aubrais-Orléans 310 d.	...	|	0758	0758	...	...	0909	...	1313	|	...	|	...	|	|	|	...	1837	...	1957	2146	2147	...	2146
200	Vierzon 310 a.	...	0746	0831	0835	...	...	0957	...	1345	1544	...	1720	...	1842	1845	1845	...	1928	...	2035	2221	2222	...	2221
200	Vierzon ▷ d.	...	0748	0846	0838	0842	...	1002	1050	1347	1546	*1646*	1740	...	1843	1847	1847	1851	1929	...	2037	2231	2232	2235	2230
	Bourges ▷ a.	...	0804	0903	0855	|	...	1026	|	1403	1607	*1712*	1806	...	1859	1904	1904	|	1952	...	2053	2247	2250	|	2249
	Bourges d.	0530	...	...	...	|	1025	...	|	1413	...	1745	...	1822	...	...	1914	|	...	2004	2111	...	...	|	...
291	St Amand-Montrond-Orval d.	0653	...	...	...	0937	1111	...	1144	1456	...	1840	...	1916	...	...	2001	1942	...	2048	2159	...	...	2329	...
341	**Montluçon** a.	0734	...	...	...	1010	...	...	1218	1528	...	1916	...	...	...	...	2033	2022	...	2130	2236	...	...	0002	...

		3904		3906			3908		3914							3918	3920						3924	
	⚒	⚒	B	⚒	⑥ E	Ⓐ	Ⓐ		⚒	①–⑥ n	†	⚒	Ⓐ ⊗	Ⓑ	D		⚒	†	Ⓐ	†	Ⓐ	Ⓐ	Ⓐ	⑦ e	♥
Montluçon d.	...	0508	...	0615	...	...	...	0856	1108	...	...	...	...	...	...	...	1558	1630	1726	1755	...	...	1843	1902	...
St Amand-Montrond-Orval d.	...	0543	...	0650	...	...	...	0936	1146	...	1149	1310	...	...	...	...	1633	1705	1810	1838	...	...	1921	1943	...
Bourges a.	...	0630	...	|	...	...	...	1020	|	...	1231	1355	...	...	...	...	1723	1751	1907	1925	...	...	|	2026	...
Bourges ▷ d.	0608	...	0645	|	0733	0735	0804	1037	|	1232	...	...	1514	1603	...	1632	1735	1808	...	...	1934	...	|	2038	2151
Vierzon ▷ a.	0627	...	0703	0740	0750	0754	0831	1058	1242	1248	...	...	1534	1622	...	1655	1752	1824	...	...	1953	...	2021	2054	2209
Vierzon 310 d.	0632	...	0705	...	0752	0756	0836	1100	...	1253	...	...	1545	...	1632	1658	1754	1826	...	...	...	2010	...	2056	2211
Les Aubrais-Orléans 310 a.	0721	...	0743	...	0830	|	|	1132	...	1326	...	...	1631	...	1708	1748	1830	1905	...	...	...	2056	...	2129	|
Orléans 310 a.	0733	...	*0755*	...	*0840*	0828	0925	*1141*	...	*1333*	...	...	1640	...	*1719*	1756	*1840*	*1913*	...	...	...	2104	...	*2139*	2250
Paris Austerlitz 310 a.	...	...	0841	...	0928	...	...	1228	...	1423	...	...	...	...	1810	...	1926	2005	...	...	...	...	...	2223	...

ADDITIONAL TRAINS VIERZON - BOURGES (see also Table **290**)

	Ⓐ	⚒	Ⓐ	Ⓒ		⑥J	⚒	⚒	Ⓐ	
Vierzon d.	0625	0657	0759	0909	1046	1215	1351	1431	1646	1826
Bourges a.	0650	0723	0826	0933	1105	1241	1415	1450	1712	1851

	⚒	†	⚒		⚒	⚒		Ⓐ	Ⓐ	†	Ⓑ
Bourges d.	0702	0720	0840	0858	1215	1247	1741	1814	1934	1955	2009
Vierzon a.	0728	0740	0906	0914	1235	1313	1808	1833	1953	2021	2026

B – ⚒ to June 27; Ⓐ June 29 - Aug. 28; ⚒ from Aug. 31.
D – ⑥ to July 3; ⑦ July 5 - Aug. 30 (also July 14); Ⓑ from Aug. 31.
E – ⑥ July 4 - Aug. 29.
F – ⑦ July 5 - Aug. 30 (also July 14; not July 12).
G – ⑦ to June 28 / from Sept. 6 (also Apr. 13, June 1).
J – To July 4 / from Sept. 5.
N – ①②③④⑦ (not June 1, July 14, Nov. 11).
c – ⚒ only.
e – Also June 1, July 14.
n – Not June 1, July 14.
z – † only.
♥ – To / from Lyon (Table **290**).
▷ – See also panel below table (also Table **290**).
⊖ – Arrives 20 minutes later on Ⓐ Aug. 17 - 25.
⊗ – Departs up to 9 minutes earlier on Ⓐ Sept. 2 - 11.

316 BRIVE and AURILLAC - FIGEAC - TOULOUSE

Some trains 2nd class

km		3751/3 3755	3751/3 3755																					
		△ Ⓡ	△ E Ⓡ		Ⓐ			Ⓐ d	Ⓐ	⚒		Ⓐ	Ⓐ	🚌 Ⓐ				Ⓐ					⑤ J	
	Paris Austerlitz 310 d.	2256	2256	...	...	...	...	...	...	...	...	...	...	...	...	...	...	...	...	...	...	...	...	...
0	**Brive la Gaillarde 317** d.	|	|	...	...	0550	...	...	0830	...	...	1102	...	...	...	1330	...	1611	...	...	1827	...	...	2136
27	St Denis-près-Martel **317** d.	0422	0422	...	...	0613	...	...	0856	...	...	1123	...	...	...	1351	...	1632	...	...	1900	...	...	2212
45	Rocamadour-Padirac d.	0442	0442	...	...	0632	...	...	0915	...	...	1141	...	...	...	1410	...	1651	...	...	1919	...	...	2231
	Clermont Ferrand **331** d.	|	|	...	...	|	...	...	|	0636r	...	|	...	...	...	|	...	|	...	...	|	...	...	|
◧	**Aurillac** d.	|	|	...	...	|	0655v	...	|	0904	...	|	...	...	1305	|	...	|	1652	1830	|	...	2119	|
88	Figeac d.	0521	0521	...	0612	0705	0809	0906	0954	1015	1015	1214	1207	...	1416	1444	...	1725	1812	1949	1953	...	2231	2305
94	Capdenac a.	0528	0528	...	0619	0706	0815	0912	1000	1021	1021	1220	1213	...	1422	1450	...	1731	1819	...	1959	...	2238	2311
94	Capdenac d.	0529	0529	...	0621	0723	0822	0913	...	1023	1023	...	1221	1225	1424	1453	...	1733	1821	...	2000	...	...	2312z
161	**Rodez 323** a.	0641	0641	...	|	0828	|	1021	...	|	|	...	|	1340	|	1602	...	1841	|	...	2102	...	...	0019z
	Carmaux **323** a.	...	0804	...	|	...	|	...	...	|	|	...	|	...	|	...	...	...	|	...	...	...	...	...
	Albi 323 a.	...	0824	...	|	...	|	...	...	|	|	...	|	...	|	...	...	...	|	...	...	...	...	...
123	Villefranche de Rouergue d.	...	...	...	0650	...	0851	...	...	1052	1052	...	1251	...	1452	...	...	...	1851	...	...	...	...	...
140	Najac d.	...	...	...	0705	...	0905	...	...	1107	1107	...	1305	...	1507	...	...	...	1905	...	...	...	...	...
193	Gaillac **323** a.	...	...	...	0752	...	0951	...	...	1150	1150	...	1352	...	1552	...	...	...	1950	...	...	...	...	...
247	**Toulouse Matabiau 323** a.	...	...	...	0834	...	1033	...	...	1233	1233	...	1434	...	1633	...	...	...	2034	...	...	...	...	...

																							3754 3750/2	3754 3750/2
	⚒	⚒	†	Ⓐ ⊕	Ⓐ	Ⓐ d		Ⓐ	d	⊖	🚌				⑤	🚌 Ⓐ	Ⓐ	⑤			Ⓐ		△ Ⓡ	△ F Ⓡ
Toulouse Matabiau 323 d.	...	...	...	...	0634	...	0837	...	...	1237	...	...	...	1635	1635	...	...	...	1836	...	1945	...	...	...
Gaillac **323** d.	...	...	...	...	0717	...	0915	...	...	1318	...	...	...	1717	1717	...	...	...	1915	...	2030	...	...	...
Najac d.	...	...	...	...	0804	...	1005	...	...	1406	...	...	...	1803	1803	...	...	...	2004	...	2115	...	...	...
Villefranche de Rouergue d.	...	...	...	...	0819	...	1020	...	...	1421	...	...	...	1819	1819	...	...	...	2019	...	2130	...	...	...
Albi 323 d.	...	...	...	...	|	...	|	...	...	|	...	...	...	|	|	...	...	...	|	...	|	...	...	2038
Carmaux **323** d.	...	...	...	...	|	...	|	...	...	|	...	...	...	|	|	...	...	...	|	...	|	...	...	2058
Rodez 323 d.	...	0644	...	...	|	0838	|	...	1143	|	1400	...	1625	|	|	1730	...	...	|	2011	|	...	2230	2230
Capdenac a.	...	0752	...	...	0848	0945	1049	...	1250	1449	1516	...	1730	1849	1849	1849	...	...	2046	2115	2156	...	2343	2343
Capdenac d.	0555	0754	0754	...	0849	0946	1059	1110	1251	1451	...	1526	1732	1854	1854	1849	...	1912	2049	2117	2157	...	2344	2344
Figeac d.	0603	0801	0801	0838	0856	0953	1106	1117	1258	1459	...	1534	1739	1900	1906	1904	1920	1920	2057	2125	2204	...	2353	2353
Aurillac a.	0722	|	|	0958	...	...	1215v	|	|	1609	...	|	|	...	2018	...	|	|	2210	|	*2329*s	...	|	|
Clermont Ferrand **331** a.	...	|	|	...	...	...	...	|	|	1855	...	|	|	...	...	...	|	|	...	|	...	...	|	|
Rocamadour-Padirac d.	...	0834	0834	...	...	...	...	1156	1331	...	...	1613	1813	...	...	...	1956	1956	...	|	...	...	0033	0033
St Denis-près-Martel **317** d.	...	0853	0853	...	...	...	...	1214	1352	...	...	1634	1838	...	...	...	2014	2014	...	2212	...	...	0052	0052
Brive la Gaillarde 317 a.	...	0914	0914	...	...	...	...	1234	1417	...	...	1655	1903	...	...	...	2036	2036	...	2233	...	...	|	|
Paris Austerlitz **310** a.	...	...	...	...	...	...	...	...	...	...	...	...	...	...	...	...	...	...	...	...	...	...	0652	0652

E – From Paris on ⑤ to June 12 / from Oct. 16.
F – ⑦ to June 14 / from Oct. 18.
J – To July 3 / from Sept. 4.
d – Subject to alteration Oct. 12 - 16.
r – ⚒ to June 27 / from Aug. 29.
s – ⑤ only. Connection by 🚌.
v – ⚒ only.
z – Not ⑥.
◧ – Aurillac is *65* km from Figeac.
△ – 🛏 1,2 cl. and 💺2 (reclining).
⊖ – Subject to alteration Aurillac - Arvant June 29 - Sept. 10.
⊕ – Subject to alteration Nov. 24 - 26.

317 BRIVE - AURILLAC

km									
		K	Ⓐ ⊗		⑥ t	⊗		Ⓑ h	⑥
0	**Brive la Gaillarde 316** d.	0758	1050	...	1205	1431	...	1806	2143	2233
27	St Denis-près-Martel **316** d.	0822	1113	...	1228	1456	...	1832	2205	2257
102	**Aurillac** a.	0934	1231	...	1340	1622	...	1949	2316	0007

	⚒	⚒		⊕	†	F		◇	
Aurillac d.	0545	0737	...	1144	1415	1545	...	1718	...
St Denis-près-Martel **316** d.	0700	0858	...	1302	1532	1705	...	1832	...
Brive la Gaillarde 316 a.	0724	0921	...	1326	1553	1726	...	1855	...

F – ⑤ to July 3; ⚒ July 10 - Aug. 29; ⑤ from Sept. 4.
K – July 5 - Aug. 23.
h – Also Aug. 15.
t – Not Aug. 15.
◇ – From Neussargues on dates in Table **331**.
⊕ – Subject to alteration on Ⓐ Aug. 31 - Oct. 2 (also Sept. 5, 6).
⊗ – Subject to alteration on Ⓐ Aug. 31 - Oct. 2.

BORDEAUX - TOULOUSE 320

km		TGV 5171 ♦ d	4652 4653 ★	⚒	4654 4655 ★	TGV 8501 Ⓐ	†	4656 4657 ★ ⊖	TGV 8511 Ⓐ ◇	TGV 8513 Ⓒ	4660 4661 ★ ◇	TGV 8519 ◇		4662 4663 ★ ◇	4664 4665 ★	TGV 8535	R	TGV 5218 ♦	3835	14109 Ⓐ N	14111 ⑦ e	⑥ t	TGV 8549	4621 🅁 ♦	TGV 8579 ⑤	4624 4625 🅁 ♦
	Paris M'parnasse **300** d.	...	...	...	...	0610	...	...	0810	0810	...	1130	...	...	...	1410	...	...	...	...	...	...	1720	...	1925	...
	Nantes **292** d.	...	...	...	...	|	...	...	|	|	...	|	...	...	...	|	...	...	1409	...	...	...	|	...	|	2034
0	**Bordeaux St Jean** d.	0543	0610	0727	0827	0923	1016	1010	1123	1124	1238	1436	1441	1459	1638	1718	1722	1806	1837	1930	1930	1939	2028	2157	2237	0045
79	Marmande d.	|	|	0811	0907	|	1059	|	|	|	|	|	1539	|	|	|	1806	|	1919	2008	2019	2027	|	2236	|	|
136	Agen d.	0646	|	0849	0938	1027	1138	|	|	1227	1346	1539	1618	|	1742	1821	1849	1908	1949	2038	2100	2100	2132	2305	2340	|
206	Montauban d.	|	|	0934	1015	1104	1223	|	|	1303	|	1616	...	|	1820	1856	1936	1944	2026	2119	2146	...	2210	2342	0017	|
257	**Toulouse Matabiau** a.	0744	0812	0958	1041	1133	1247	1212	1323	1329	1446	1642	...	1700	1846	1922	2002	2011	2051	2145	2212	...	2236	0008	0043	|
	Narbonne **321** a.	0857	|	...	1202	...	...	|	...	...	1602	...	...	|	2004	...	...	...	...	...	...	...	...	|	...	|
	Marseille **355** a.	...	1142	...	1442	...	...	1542	...	...	1842	...	...	2042	2242	...	...	...	...	...	...	...	...	0509	...	0644
	Nice **360** a.	...	1425	...	...	...	...	1825	...	...	...	...	...	...	...	...	...	...	...	...	...	...	...	0758	...	0928

	⑥ t	Ⓐ g	TGV 5264 ♦	4730 🅁 ♦	TGV 8518 ①–⑥ n	14100 Ⓐ	†	3852		TGV 8528 ▽	4752 4753 ★ v	4754 4755 ★	4756 4757 ★ q	TGV 8548 u		TGV 8568 Ⓑ	4758 4759 ★	TGV 8570 ⑥		TGV 8580 Ⓑ	4762 4763 ★	TGV 8586 ⑦ J	4764 4765 ★	TGV 5116 ♦	4766 ★ ⑤⑦ w	4724 4725 🅁 ♦
Nice **360** d.	...	...	...	2057	...	...	...	...	...	...	...	...	...	...	...	...	1001	...	...	...	...	...	1336	...	...	1832
Marseille **355** d.	...	...	...	0010	...	...	...	...	...	...	0614	0714	0914	...	...	...	1242	...	...	...	1414	...	1615	...	1842	2215
Narbonne **321** d.	...	...	...	|	...	...	...	...	...	...	|	0952	1151	...	...	...	|	...	...	...	1652	...	|	1958	2124	|
Toulouse Matabiau d.	...	...	0527	0536	0608	0653r	...	0754	...	0922	0946	1115	1309	1313	...	1610	1621	1631	1658	1736	1810	1826	1950	2117	2252	|
Montauban d.	...	...	0554	0609	0636	0722	...	0822	...	|	|	1142	|	1342	...	1638	|	1701	1725	1803	1838	1853	|	|	2325	|
Agen d.	0525	0614	0631	0646	0714	0756	0833	0859	0950	|	|	1219	1411	1419	1439	1716	|	1740	1811	1840	1914	1931	|	2219	|	|
Marmande d.	0554	0647	|	0717	|	0826	0907	0929	1025	|	|	1249	|	|	1514	|	|	|	1850	|	1944	|	|	|	|	|
Bordeaux St Jean a.	0638	0730	0739	0810	0817	0903	0955	1007	1112	1119	1146	1326	1513	1520	1559	1818	1823	1841	1934	1942	2021	2032	2150	2320	0101	0437
Nantes **292** a.	...	...	...	...	|	...	...	1438	...	|	...	...	...	|	...	|	...	|	...	|	...	|	...	...	...	0916
Paris M'parnasse **300** a.	...	...	...	...	1130	...	...	...	...	1440	...	...	...	1850	...	2130	...	2150	...	2250s	...	2345	...	...	...	...

FOR NOTES SEE TABLE 321 BELOW

TOULOUSE - NARBONNE 321

Other night trains: Hendaye / Bordeaux - Marseille - Nice see Table **355**; Hendaye - Genève see Table **355**; Nantes - Marseille - Nice see Table **320** or **355**

km		3731 🅁 ♦	Ⓐ	TGV 5301 d		TGV 5171 ♦ d	S	4652 4653 ★	4654 4655 ★	a	TGV 5307 Ⓐ E△	4656 4657 ★ ⊖	TGV 5307 Ⓒ E	TGV 5315 Ⓑ	4660 4661 ★ ◇	⚒	TGV 5186 L§	4658 4659 ★ H	3631 ★	4662 4663 ★ ◇	Ⓐ	Q		4664 4665 ★	4666 4667 ★ ⑤⑦ y
	Paris Austerlitz **310** d.	2156	...	...	...	...	...	...	...	...	...	...	...	...	...	...	...	...	1025	...	...	...	...	...	
	Bordeaux **320** d.	|	...	...	...	0543	...	0610	0827	...	...	1010	...	...	1238	...	...	...	|	1459	...	...	...	1638	...
0	**Toulouse Matabiau** ▷ d.	|	...	0654	0705	0749	0804	0817	1045	1153	1210	1217	1340	1434	1451	...	1610	1614	1642	1704	...	1730	1844	1851	1951
55	Castelnaudary d.	0519	0615	|	0743	|	0834	|	1113	1224	|	|	|	|	|	1600	|	1643	1720	|	1733	1802	1909	|	|
91	Carcassonne ▷ d.	0540	0636	0742	0806	|	0903	|	1134	1246	1300	|	1423	1518	1534	1627	1656	1703	1739	|	1755	1822	1927	1936	2035
128	Lézignan d.	0602	0653	|	0825	|	|	|	|	1308	|	|	|	|	|	1646	|	|	|	|	1814	...	1945	|	|
150	**Narbonne** a.	0617	0707	0809	0838	0857	0932	|	1202	1321	1329	|	1450	1545	1602	1658	1724	1732	1807	|	1827	...	1957	2004	2104
	Marseille **355** a.	|	...	1041	...	|	|	1142	1442	...	|	1542	|	|	1842	...	|	2014	|	2042	...	...	|	2242	2342
	Nice **360** a.	|	...	...	...	|	|	1425	...	...	|	1825	|	|	...	...	|	2255	|	...	...	...	|	...	...
	Lyon Part Dieu **350/1** a.	|	...	...	...	1149	|	...	...	...	1620	...	1746	1846	...	...	2020	...	|	...	...	...	|	...	...
	Perpignan **355** a.	0718	...	...	...	...	1032	...	...	...	...	...	...	...	...	...	...	...	1907	...	...	...	2052	...	...
	Cerbère **355** a.	0812	...	...	...	...	1113	...	...	...	...	...	...	...	...	...	...	...	1956	...	...	...	...	...	...
	Portbou **355** a.	0821	...	...	...	...	...	...	...	...	...	...	...	...	...	...	...	...	...	...	...	...	...	...	...

	Ⓐ h	Ⓐ	⚒	Ⓐ b	4752 4753 ★ v	3630 ★	4754 4755 ★	TGV 5355 Ⓑ	4756 4757 ★ q		TGV 5104 L‡	4768 ★ F	4758 4759 ★	U b	4762 4763 ★	Ⓐ	Ⓐ	4764 4765 ★		S	TGV 5116 ♦	4766 ★ ⑤⑦ w	TGV 5385 E	TGV 5398	3730 🅁 ♦
Cerbère **355** d.	...	...	...	...	...	0750	...	...	...	1039	...	...	...	...	...	...	...	...	...	1730	...	...	...	...	2121
Perpignan **355** d.	...	...	...	...	...	0840	...	...	...	1119	...	...	...	...	...	...	...	...	...	1812	...	...	...	...	2210
Lyon Part Dieu **350/1** d.	...	...	...	...	...	|	...	0710	...	|	0937	...	...	...	...	...	...	...	...	|	1707	...	1911	...	|
Nice **360** d.	...	...	...	...	...	|	...	|	...	|	|	0832	1001	...	...	...	...	1336	...	|	|	...	|	...	|
Marseille **355** d.	...	...	...	...	0614	|	0714	|	0914	|	|	1114	1242	...	1414	...	...	1615	...	|	|	1842	|	1932	|
Narbonne d.	0649	0722	0744	0816	|	0938	0952	1002	|	1210	1238	1358	|	1533	1652	...	1824	|	1847	1912	1958	2124	2158	2204	2304
Lézignan d.	0703	0739	0801	0829	|	|	|	|	|	1223	|	|	|	1546	|	...	1838	|	1900	|	|	|	|	|	2319
Carcassonne ▷ d.	0725	0759	0821	0847	|	1011	1023	1034	|	1244	1310	1429	|	1608	1723	1729	1903	|	1919	1944	2028	2155	|	2236	2340
Castelnaudary d.	0746	0821	0841	0908	|	1032	1043	|	|	1306	|	1450	|	1629	|	1751	1925	|	1939	2007	|	|	|	|	0000
Toulouse Matabiau ▷ a.	0824	...	0912	...	0942	1101	1111	1121	1305	1342x	1355	1517	1612	1659	1806	1825	...	1945	...	2038	2112	2248	2309	2321	0036
Bordeaux **320** a.	...	...	...	...	1146	|	1326	...	1513	...	...	...	1823	...	2021	...	...	2150	...	...	2320	0101	...	...	|
Paris Austerlitz **310** a.	...	...	...	...	...	1738z	...	...	...	...	...	...	...	...	...	...	...	...	...	...	...	...	...	...	0730

♦ – **NOTES FOR TABLES 320/1** (LISTED BY TRAIN NUMBER):

3730 – *CORAIL LUNÉA* – 🛏 1,2 cl. and (2) (reclining) Cerbère - Paris. Depart Cerbère 2030 June 26 - Sept. 6 (also Nov. 1); other timings may vary.
3731 – *CORAIL LUNÉA* – 🛏 1,2 cl. and (2) (reclining) Paris - Portbou.
4621 – *CORAIL LUNÉA* – 🛏 1,2 cl. and (2) (reclining) Bordeaux - Nice. Starts from Hendaye on dates in Table **305**.
4624/5 – For days of running see Table **292**. 🛏 1,2 cl. and (2) (reclining) Nantes - Nice. Timings from Nantes vary – see Table **292**.
4724/5 – For days of running see Table **292**. 🛏 1,2 cl. and (2) (reclining) Nice - Nantes.
4730 – *CORAIL LUNÉA* – 🛏 1,2 cl. and (2) (reclining) Nice - Bordeaux. To Irún on dates in Table **305**.
5116 – (12) and 🍷 Dijon - Lyon - Bordeaux.
5171 – (12) and 🍷 Bordeaux - Toulouse - Lyon - Dijon.
5218 – (12) and 🍷 Lille Flandres - Charles de Gaulle ✈ - Bordeaux - Toulouse (Table **11**).
5264 – (12) and 🍷 Toulouse - Bordeaux - Charles de Gaulle ✈ - Lille Europe (Table **11**).

E – From July 5.
F – ⑤⑥⑦ June 26 - Aug. 30 (also June 1, July 14, Oct. 23, 24, 30, 31, Nov. 1, 2, 11).
H – ⑤⑥⑦ June 26 - Aug. 30 (also June 1, July 14, Oct. 23, 24, 30, 31, Nov. 1, 2).
J – To July 4 / from Aug. 31.
L – (12) Toulouse - Lyon - Charles de Gaulle ✈ - Lille Europe and v.v. (Table **11**).
N – Ⓐ to July 3; Ⓐ Aug. 31 - Oct. 9; Ⓐ from Nov. 23.
P – ⚒ to June 13; Ⓐ June 15 - Aug. 21; ⚒ from Aug. 24.
Q – Ⓑ to June 28; Ⓐ June 29 - Aug. 28; Ⓑ from Aug. 31.
R – Daily to Agen, Ⓑ to Toulouse.
S – ⑥⑦ June 20 - Aug. 23 (also July 14).
U – Daily to Carcassonne, Ⓑ to Toulouse.
Y – Daily to June 14; Ⓐ June 15 - Aug. 21; daily from Aug. 24.

a – To Montpellier (also Avignon Centre on Ⓐ). Depart Toulouse 1129 on Ⓐ Aug. 3 - 14, Sept. 21 - 25; depart 1123 Sept. 28 - Oct. 2.
b – To / from Montpellier and Avignon Centre.
d – Not June 30, July 1.
e – Also June 1, July 14.
g – On Ⓐ July 6 - Aug. 28 depart Agen 0601, Marmande 0638.
h – From Nimes, Table **355**. On ① (not Apr. 13, June 1) runs 8 - 12 minutes later Lézignan - Toulouse.
n – Not June 1, July 14.
q – Depart Marseille 0836 on June 29, 30, July 1.
r – 0612 June 15 - July 3.
s – Arrive Paris 15 minutes later on ①–④ to June 26, ①–④ Oct. 5 - Dec. 3; arrive up to 50 minutes later on ⑤ to June 25; ⑤ Oct. 9 - Dec. 4.
t – Not Aug. 15.
u – Runs earlier on Ⓐ June 3 - 26 (depart Toulouse 1300) and on June 18, 19 (depart 1236).
v – Subject to alteration on June 18, 19.
w – Also June 1, July 14, Oct. 24, 31, Nov. 2, 11.
x – 1430 on Ⓐ Aug. 17 - 28; 1419 on Sept. 28 - Oct. 2.
y – Also June 1, July 14, Nov. 2.
z – 1749 Sept. 28 - Oct. 2.

TGV – 🅁, supplement payable, 🍷.
★ – *CORAIL TÉOZ*, 🅁, 🍷.
◇ – Runs up to 40 minutes earlier on certain dates - please enquire when reserving seats.
△ – Depart Toulouse 1143 Aug. 31 - Sept. 18. Runs up to 20 minutes earlier Sept. 28 - Oct. 2.
▽ – Arrive Paris 1450 on Ⓐ June 15 - July 3.
⊖ – On June 18, 19 depart Bordeaux 0957, on Ⓐ Aug. 17 - 28 depart 0952. Runs later on June 15 - 17 (Bordeaux 1030, Marseille 1800, Nice 2056) and Ⓐ Aug. 3 - 14 (Bordeaux 1030, Marseille 1702, Nice 2017).
‡ – Train **9804** on Ⓐ (from Brussels).
§ – To Brussels on ⑥ July 11 - Aug. 29 (train **9887**).

▷ – Additional local trains Toulouse - Carcassonne (journey approx one hour):
From Toulouse: 0617 **P**, 0721 Ⓐ, 1618 Ⓐ, 1759 Ⓑ, 1936 ⚒.
From Carcassonne: 0610 ⚒, 0643 Ⓐ, , 0731 ⑥, 1544 Ⓐ, 1637 Ⓐ, 1833 **Y**.

323 TOULOUSE - ALBI - RODEZ - MILLAU

Most trains 2nd class

km		Ⓐ				Ⓐ		⑥🚌	Ⓐn				Ⓑ🚌		Ⓐ		⚒🚌	Ⓐ			Ⓐ		P[R]	Ⓐ	
0	**Toulouse Matabiau 316** d.	0619	...	0719	0900	1017	1120	...	...	1158	1300	1419	...	1558	1656	1710	...	1730	1800	...	1815	1858	...	1928	2120
54	Gaillac **316** d.	0701	...	0806	0953	1104	1205	...	...	1244	1353	1501	...	1652	1741	1756	...	1820	1854	...	1905	1939	...	2021	2214
58	Tessonnières **316** d.	|	...	|	1001	|	|	...	...	1249	1358	|	...	1657	1746	|	...	1824	|	...	1911	|	...	2027	2222
75	**Albi Ville** d.	0715	...	0826	1016	1117	1224	...	...	1305	1412	1515	...	1711	1804	1815	...	1841	1909	...	1925	2001	2038	2045	2237
92	Carmaux d.	0732	...	0845	1032	1132	1242	...	...	1322	1431	1532	...	1729	...	1831	...	1905	1925	...	...	2018	2058	2103	2255
158	**Rodez** d.	0830	0852	0947	...	1230	1345	1410	1427	...	...	1628	1636	...	...	1937	1942	...	2025	2106	...	2119	2207	...	...
202	Sévérac-le-Château **332** d.	...	0936	...	...	...	...	1454	1511	...	...	...	1717	...	...	...	2023	...	...	2147	...	...	...	...	...
232	**Millau 332** a.	...	1005	...	...	...	...	1530	1538	...	...	...	1751	...	...	...	2053	...	...	2214	...	...	...	...	...

	Ⓐ	Ⓐ			Ⓐ	P[R]				Ⓐ🚌			Ⓒ🚌	Ⓐ	Ⓐ	Ⓐ				Ⓐn	Ⓐ	†🚌		Ⓒ	
Millau 332 d.	...	...	...	...	...	...	0618	...	...	0900	...	...	1005	1027	...	...	...	...	...	1605	...	1650	...	1917	...
Sévérac-le-Château **332** d.	...	...	...	...	...	...	0648	...	...	0930	...	...	1040	1057	...	...	...	...	...	1636	...	1725	...	1951	...
Rodez d.	...	...	...	...	0633	0708	0729	0744	0833	1014	1024	...	1130	1138	1233	...	1433	...	1634	1716	1731	1808	1824	2033	2058
Carmaux d.	0508	0553	0622	0652	0733	0806	...	0846	0933	...	1133	1204	...	...	1330	1453	1533	1652	1731	...	1832	...	1926	...	2153
Albi Ville d.	0526	0614	0642	0716	0750	0824	...	0904	0949	...	1150	1223	...	...	1346	1516	1550	1720	1748	...	1849	...	1943	...	2209
Tessonnières **316** d.	0540	0630	0657	0732	|	...	...	|	|	...	|	1237	...	...	|	1532	|	1734	|	...	|	...	|	...	|
Gaillac **316** d.	0545	0635	0701	0737	0806	...	...	0925	1005	...	1205	1243	...	...	1405	1537	1604	1740	1806	...	1915	...	2002	...	2226
Toulouse Matabiau 316 a.	0638	0727	0752	0830	0845	...	...	1008	1043	...	1246	1329	...	...	1449	1625	1643	1833	1844	...	1953	...	2043	...	2304

P – 🛏 1, 2 cl. and 💺 (reclining) Paris - Rodez - Albi and v.v. For days of running see Table **316**.

n – Subject to alteration June 2-4, Oct. 6-8.

***Major engineering work**: all services are liable to alteration, with partial bus substitution. Please check before travel as timings are likely to be affected.*

324 PAU - OLORON - CANFRANC

km		Ⓐd	d	d		Ⓑh	⚒⊖	†	⚒		⑤
0	**Pau** d.	0730	0905	1208	1345	1532	1705	1749	1831	1957	2138
36	Oloron-Ste-Marie a.	0806	0943	1246	1423	1610	1743	1827	1909	2035	2216
36	Oloron-Ste-Marie 🚌 d.	*0816*	*0950*	...	*1440*	...	*1749*r	*1835*	*1914*	...	...
58	Bedous (Gare) 🚌 d.	*0841*	*1015*	...	*1505*	...	*1814*r	*1900*	*1939*	...	...
73	Urdos 🏛 🚌 d.	*0901*	*1035*	...	*1525*	...	*1834*r	*1920*	*1959*	...	...
90	**Canfranc** (Gare) 🚌 a.	*0937*	*1111*	...	*1601*	...	...	...	...	...	...

	Ⓐn	Ⓒ	Ⓐd	d	Ⓐd	Ⓒ	△	⚒⊖	†	⚒◇
Canfranc (Gare) 🚌 d.	...	...	...	...	*1120*	...	*1257*	*1612*	*1654*	...
Urdos 🏛 🚌 d.	...	...	...	...	*1152*	...	*1329*	*1644*	*1726*	...
Bedous (Gare) 🚌 d.	...	...	...	...	*1212*	...	*1349*	*1704*	*1746*	...
Oloron-Ste-Marie 🚌 a.	...	...	...	...	*1241*	...	*1418*	*1733*	*1815*	...
Oloron-Ste-Marie d.	0647	0719	0813	1052	1251	1251	1428	1748	1832	1914
Pau a.	0725	0757	0851	1130	1329	1329	1506	1826	1910	1952

d – Subject to alteration on Ⓐ June 2-26.
h – Also Aug. 15; not Sept. 1, Nov. 5.
n – On ① (also June 2, July 15; not June 1, July 13) d. 0630, a. 0708.
r – ⑤ only.

⊖ – Subject to alteration on Sept. 1.
△ – Subject to alteration on Nov. 5.
◇ – Additional journeys: 1615 Ⓐ ⊖, 1640 †, 2105 † (2201 on † July 12 - Aug. 23).

🚌 – By SNCF bus Oloron - Canfranc and v.v.

325 HENDAYE - BAYONNE - TARBES - TOULOUSE

Timings may vary by a few minutes due to engineering work

km						14140		14142 14144		14150						14132	14132				4678 4679	3990		
		Ⓐ		B	Ⓐ			▽	⚒ ☆			⑤⑥ ⊗	①–④ m	Ⓑ	† J	E	F	Ⓐ ⊡	†	Ⓐ	[R] G	[R] Y	† J	† K
0	**Hendaye 305** d.	...	...	...	...	0600	...	0831	...	...	...	...	...	...	...	...	...	...	...	...	1826	...	...	...
13	**St Jean de Luz 305** d.	...	...	...	...	0611	...	0843	...	...	...	...	...	...	...	...	...	...	...	...	1838	...	...	...
26	Biarritz **305** § d.	...	...	...	...	0627	...	0856	...	...	...	...	...	...	...	...	...	...	...	...	1853	...	...	...
36	**Bayonne 305** § a.	...	...	...	...	0639	...	0912	...	...	...	...	...	...	...	...	...	...	...	...	1905	...	...	...
36	**Bayonne 305** § d.	...	...	0544x	0610	0700	...	0936	...	1215	...	...	...	...	...	1622	1622	1717	1808	1819	1907	...	2008	2111
	Dax **305** d.	...	...	|	|	|	...	|	...	|	...	...	...	...	...	|	|	|	|	|	1957	...	|	|
87	Puyoô **305** d.	...	...	0619x	0658	0737	...	|	...	1255	...	...	...	...	...	1657	1657	1757	1843	1858	2018	...	2057	2145
101	Orthez **305** d.	...	...	0631x	0709	0748	...	|	...	1306	...	...	...	...	...	1709	1709	1807	1854	1908	2031	...	2110	2156
141	**Pau 305** d.	...	0559a	0701	0738	0812	...	1043	...	1336	...	1600	...	...	...	1736	1734	1833	1918	1935	2107	...	2139	2219
180	Lourdes **305** d.	0553	0630b	0731	0806	0841	...	1111	...	1405	...	1631	1631	...	1754	1806	1805	1908	1951	...	2138	...	2210	2247
201	**Tarbes 305** d.	0609	0648	0748	0820	0859	1048	1127	...	1422	1444	1647	1647	...	1810	1823	1824	1925	2007	...	2155	...	2225	2302
238	Lannemezan d.	0632	0715	0826	...	0924	1113	|	...	|	1508	1714	1714	...	1839	1851	1856	...	...	...	2219	...	...	...
◧	Luchon ▶ d.	|	|	|	...	|	|	|	1112	|	|	|	|	1723u	|	|	|	...	...	...	|	2136	...	...
255	Montréjeau d.	0644	0727	0839	...	0937	1124	|	1211	|	1520	1725	1725	1829	1852	1903	1908	...	...	...	|	2256	...	...
268	St Gaudens d.	0653	0737	0849	...	0947	1134	|	1223	|	1530	1735	1735	1839	1903	1914	1925	...	...	...	2239	2308	...	...
293	Boussens d.	0707	0751	0904	...	1002	1149	|	1237	|	1544	1749	1749	1859	1920	1929	1941	...	...	...	|	2322	...	...
359	**Toulouse Matabiau** a.	0756	0850	0956	...	1036	1222	1250	1325	1553	1621	1838	1838	1950	1958	2006	2020	...	...	...	2324	0003	...	...

			3991	4778 4779					14131		14143	14145				14147 14149								
	Ⓐ	⚒	[R] W	[R] H	Ⓐ	⚒	☆	☆	△	⚒ ⊕	Ⓐ	Ⓒ	⚒	Ⓐ	⑤ J			Ⓑ	⑤⑦ w	Ⓐ K	Ⓐ J		⊙	⑤⑦
Toulouse Matabiau d.	...	...	0541	0609	0614	0715	0731	0910	1011	1210	1400	1400	1437	...	1600	1632	1715	1715	1715	1745	1811	1940	2115	2341
Boussens d.	...	...	0623	|	0708	|	0823	0945	1051	1300	1438	1438	1527	...	1640	|	1757	1757	1757	1836	1902	2030	2202	0019
St Gaudens d.	...	...	0638	0656	0729	0815	0837	1000	1106	1314	1452	1452	1543	...	1655	|	1812	1812	1812	1855	1915	2045	2216	0033
Montréjeau d.	...	...	0707	|	0740	0826	0903	1011	1118	1324	1502	1502	1551	...	1704	|	1822	1822	1822	1905	1925	2056	2226	0047
Luchon ▶ a.	...	...	0802	|	|	|	0956	|	|	|	|	|	...	...	|	|	|	|	|	|	|	|	|	|
Lannemezan d.	...	...	...	0717	0755	0837	...	1022	1130	1336	1515	1515	...	...	1716	|	1833	1833	1833	1917	1936	2110	2237	|
Tarbes 305 d.	...	0623	...	0745	0823	0904	...	1044	1157	1403	1540	1540	...	1713	1740	1755	1856	1858	1858	1940	1959	2140	2305	0126
Lourdes **305** d.	...	0640	...	0804	...	0920p	...	...	1215	1417	1556	1556	...	1728	...	1811	...	1913	1913	...	...	2157	2320	0144
Pau 305 d.	0633	0712	...	0835	...	...	...	...	1245	1447z	1625	1625	...	1756	...	1837	...	1941	1943	...	...	2229	2348v	0209
Orthez **305** d.	0657	0736	...	0903	...	...	...	...	1309	...	1651	1651	...	1821	...	|	...	...	2005	...	...	2258c	...	...
Puyoô **305** d.	0709	0748	...	|	...	...	...	...	1322	...	1704	1704	...	1832	...	|	...	...	2020	...	...	2310c	...	...
Dax d.	|	|	...	0952	...	...	...	...	|	...	|	|	...	|	...	|	...	...	|	...	...	|	...	...
Bayonne 305 § a.	0749	0824	...	1021	...	...	...	...	1355	...	1745	1742	...	1910	...	1942	...	...	2056	...	...	2343c	...	...
Bayonne 305 § d.	...	...	...	1024	...	...	...	...	...	...	1805	1802	...	...	...	2002	...	...	2116r	...	...	...	...	...
Biarritz **305** § d.	...	...	...	1036	...	...	...	...	...	...	1817	1813	...	...	...	2013	...	...	2128r	...	...	...	...	...
St Jean de Luz **305** d.	...	...	...	1051	...	...	...	...	...	...	1834	1828	...	...	...	2028	...	...	2142r	...	...	...	...	...
Hendaye **305** a.	...	...	...	1103	...	...	...	...	...	...	1847	1843	...	...	...	2041	...	...	2154r	...	...	...	...	...
Irún 305 a.	...	...	...	1113	...	...	...	...	...	...	...	...	...	...	...	2050	...	...	...	...	...	...	...	...

B – ⚒ (daily July 5 - Aug. 30).
E – ⚒ (daily June 29 - Sept. 5).
F – † to June 28 / from Sept. 6.
G – *CORAIL LUNÉA* – ⑤⑦ (daily June 19 - Sept. 6, Oct. 23 - Nov. 4), also June 1, Nov. 11. 🛏 1, 2 cl., 💺 (reclining) Hendaye - Lyon - Genève. Timings vary (on ⑥ June 27 - Sept. 5 depart Hendaye 1813).
H – *CORAIL LUNÉA* – from Genève (next day from Toulouse) on ⑤⑦ (daily June 19 - Sept. 6, Oct. 23 - Nov. 4), also June 1, Nov. 11. 🛏 1, 2 cl. and 💺 (reclining) Genève - Lyon - Irún.
J – To July 4 / from Aug. 31.
K – July 5 - Aug. 30.
W – From Paris on ⑤ (daily June 26 - Aug. 29). 🛏 1, 2 cl. Paris Austerlitz (d. 2156) - Luchon.
Y – ⑦ (daily June 27 - Aug. 29). 🛏 1, 2 cl. Luchon - Paris Austerlitz (arrive 0730).

a – Ⓐ (daily July 5 - Aug. 30).
b – Ⓑ (daily July 5 - Aug. 30).
c – ⑤⑦ (daily July 5 - Aug. 29), also June 1, Nov. 11.
m – Not June 1, July 14, Nov. 11. Arrive Toulouse 1858 Oct. 22 - Nov. 11.
p – ①⑥ (also June 2; not June 1, Aug. 15, Oct. 5, 12, 19).
r – ⑤⑦ to June 26 / from Sept. 11.
u – † only.
v – ⑤⑥ only.
w – Also June 1, July 14, Aug. 15, Nov. 11.
x – ① June 8 - 29 (also June 2), ②③④⑤⑦ July 5 - Aug. 30 (also July 13, Aug. 15; not July 15); ① from Sept. 7.
z – ⑤⑥ (not Aug. 15, Oct. 9, 16).
◧ – Montréjeau - Luchon is 35 km.
▽ – Runs 3 minutes earlier Hendaye - Bayonne on † to June 21 / from Sept. 13.

△ – Runs up to 12 minutes earlier on Ⓐ July 13 - Aug. 7, Oct. 5 - 21. Arrives later (Bayonne 1424) on Ⓐ Aug. 31 - Sept. 11.
⊡ – Arrive Tarbes 1955 Oct. 22 - Nov. 6.
⊕ – Runs approx 20 minutes later Aug. 31 - Sept. 11.
⊗ – Runs up to 7 minutes earlier on Oct. 23, 30, Nov. 6.
⊙ – On July 11 arrives up to 40 minutes later.
☆ – Subject to alteration on Ⓐ Aug. 31 - Sept. 11.
§ – 🚌 services available to / from Biarritz town.
▶ – 🚌 connections Luchon - Montréjeau and v.v.: From Luchon 0620 ⚒, 0830, 1005 ⚒, 1358, 1616 ⚒, 1755 ⚒, 1945 †. From Montréjeau 0720 ⚒, 0805 ⚒, 1130, 1405 ⚒, 1527 †, 1557 ⚒, 1830, 2103. Journey 50 - 53 mins.

BRIVE / LIMOGES - USSEL - CLERMONT FERRAND 326

Brive - Ussel is service to July 5 / from Aug. 22 (service is by 🚌 July 6 - Aug. 21)

km		Ⓐ	⑥	4490 ⑤E	4492 ⑥F		⑤	⑤	⚒	†
	Bordeaux 302 d.	...	...	0734	0908	...	...	...	...	...
0	**Brive la Gaillarde** d.	0617	0617	1001	1111	1316	1540	1615	1734	1816
26	Tulle d.	0645	0645	1037	1146	1344	1606	1645	1809	1843
79	Meymac d.	0737	0737	1135	1244	1433	1705	1743	1857	1943
92	**Ussel** a.	0750	0750	1149	1258	1446	1718	1755	1910	1955
	Clermont Ferrand § a.	1012	...	...	1455	...	1924	1951	...	2202

	①g			4595 ⑦G	4591 ⑤E		⑤	†	⑦R	†
Clermont Ferrand § d.	...	...	1009	1409	...	...	1726	...	1845	2042
Ussel d.	0537	0847	1227	1612	1612	1612	1928	1928	2040	2242
Meymac d.	0550	0900	1245	1627	1627	1627	1942	1942	2053	2255
Tulle d.	0646	0954	1343	1734	1734	1734	2035	2035	2155	2349
Brive la Gaillarde a.	0710	1021	1409	1756	1756	1757	2057	2057	2218	0010
Bordeaux 302 a.	...	...	...	2017	2018	...	...	...	...	...

km		⚒	ⒶL	🚌 ⑥t	🚌		🚌 ⑤J	4492 ⑥F	Ⓐ	🚌 ⑥	🚌 ⑤y	🚌 ⑦s	🚌 ⚒	⚒	†	🚌 Ⓒ	🚌 ⑥t	†	🚌 H	⑤L	⑤L	🚌 ⑤	⑤	H	🚌 ⑦e	⑦L
	Brive la Gaillarde § d.	...	0617	...	...	...	...	1111	...	...	...	...	...	...	...	...	...	...	...	1540	1615	...	...	...	...	1816
	Limoges § d.	...	|	...	...	...	...	|	...	...	...	...	...	1321	1321	...	...	...	...	|	|	...	1700	1714	...	|
0	**Ussel** d.	...	0811	...	1032	...	1200	1302	...	...	...	...	...	1520	1529	1620	...	...	...	1721	1759	...	1930	1930	...	1958
18	Eygurande-Merlines d.	...	0828	...	1052	...	1222	1320	...	...	...	...	...	1538	1547	1636	...	...	...	1739	1818	...	1949	1948	...	2020
*13	**Le Mont Dore** d.	0558	*0822*c	0850	|	1103	*1218*	|	1426	1432	1446	1452	1534	|	*1546*c	|	1655	1653	1730	*1734*c	|	1943	|	|	2016	|
*8	La Bourboule d.	0605	*0830*c	0858	|	1111	*1226*	|	1433	1440	1454	1500	1540	|	*1552*c	|	1703	1700	1738	*1742*c	|	1951	|	|	2024	|
40	Laqueuille d.	0616	0853	0910	1112	1122	1244	1345	1444	1453	1507	1513	1553	1603	1612	1705	1715	1718	1750	1804	1846	2003	2014	2013	2036	2047
100	Royat-Chamalières d.	0725	1003	|	...	1224	|	1448	1548	1600	...	...	...	|	|	...	|	1827	|	|	|	...	2126	2114	...	2153
105	**Clermont Ferrand** a.	0735	1012	1010	...	1233	1335	1455	1558	1615	...	...	...	1714	1721	...	1815	1835	1855	1924	1955	...	2133	2121	...	2202

	⚒	🚌 ⚒	🚌 ①g	L	🚌 ⑤y	🚌 ⑥t	Ⓑh	🚌	4595 ⑦G	🚌 ⑤J	🚌 ⚒	🚌 †	S	🚌 ⑥t	🚌 ⑥t	⑤L	🚌 ⑦z	†	Ⓐ	🚌 H	⑦R	🚌 H	⑤	🚌 ⑤	†L	🚌 ⑤
Clermont Ferrand d.	0610	...	...	1009	...	1240	1248	...	1409	1417	...	...	1644	1737	...	1726	1750	1758	1758	...	1845	1935	2012	...	2042	*2135*
Royat-Chamalières d.	0618	...	...	1018	...	|	1256	...	1416	|	...	...	1652	|	...	1734	|	1807	1807	...	1854	|	2019	...	2050	|
Laqueuille d.	0726	0730	0903	1127	1249	1353	1403	1407	1520	1512	1607	1621	1759	1837	1842	1845	|	1915	1927	1931	1954	2035	2129	2134	2157	2236
La Bourboule a.	|	0743	0916	*1135*c	1300	1406	1413	|	*1541*c	*1530*	1620	1634	1809	1849	|	|	|	1926	1938	|	|	2047	2139	|	*2212*c	2248
Le Mont Dore a.	|	0751	0924	*1141*c	1309	1414	1420	|	*1549*c	*1536*	1628	1642	1817	1857	|	|	|	1933	1945	|	|	2055	2147	|	*2220*c	2256
Eygurande-Merlines d.	0752	...	...	1152	...	...	...	1427	1546	1534	...	...	...	...	1900	1911	|	...	...	1951	2021	...	...	2152	2222	...
Ussel a.	0808	...	...	1209	...	...	...	1447	1603	1554	...	...	...	...	1920	1927	1918	...	...	2011	2037	...	...	2212	2238	...
Limoges § a.	1010	...	...	|	...	...	...	...	|	...	...	...	...	...	...	|	...	...	...	...	|	...	...	...	|	...
Brive la Gaillarde § a.	...	...	...	1409	...	...	...	...	1756	...	...	...	...	...	...	2057	...	...	...	...	2218	...	...	...	0010	...

LIMOGES - USSEL

km		Ⓐ	Ⓐ	⑥		⑤	⑥	H	†	⑤	
0	**Limoges** d.	0537	1023	1119	1321	1700	1700	1714	1714	1835	2034
98	Meymac d.	0721	1205	1301	1502	1913	1913	1913	1902	2019	2216
111	**Ussel** a.	0733	1218	1313	1515	1925	1925	1925	1914	2032	2228

	⚒	⚒	⑥J	D	†	†	⑤	⑥J	†	Ⓐ	⑥K
Ussel d.	0617	0817	*1227*	1245	1518	1557	*1612*	*1612*	1801	1801	1801
Meymac d.	0630	0831	1258	1258	1531	1617	1636	1636	1814	1814	1814
Limoges a.	0816	1010	1442	1442	1710	1800	1822	1822	1958	2000	2000

D – Ⓑ (daily July 5 - Aug. 21).
E – ⑤ to July 3 / from Aug. 28 (also Oct. 26 - 29, Nov. 2 - 4).
F – ⑥ to July 4 / from Aug. 22 (not Sept. 26, Oct. 3, 10).
G – ⑦ to July 5 / from Aug. 23 (also June 1; not Sept. 27, Oct. 4, 11).
H – ①-④ (not June 1, July 14, Nov. 11).
J – To July 4 / from Aug. 31.
K – July 5 - Aug. 30.
L – To July 6 / from Aug. 28.
R – ⑦ to June 28 / from Aug. 23 (also June 1, Nov. 11).
S – June 7 - Sept. 19.
c – Connection by 🚌.
e – Also June 1, July 14, Nov. 11; not Nov. 1.
g – Also June 2, Nov. 12; not June 1.
h – Also Aug. 15.
s – Also June 1; not Nov. 1.
t – Not Aug. 15.
y – To July 3.
z – Also June 1, Nov. 11; not July 19 - Aug. 23.
§ – See other part of this table.
* – Distance from Laqueuille.

Brive - Ussel
Service is by 🚌 July 6 - Aug. 21
Ussel / Le Mont Dore - Clermont Ferrand
Subject to alteration Sept. 22 - Oct. 16

LIMOGES - MONTLUÇON - LYON 327

km		🚌 ⚒	①q	🚌 ⒶJ	D	4403 ⚒v	4480 u	🚌 Ⓐ		⑤
	Bordeaux 302 d.	...	...	...	...	...	1047	...	...	...
0	**Limoges** d.	...	0558	...	0805	...	1313	...	1553	1840
78	Guéret d.	...	0701	...	0908	...	1416	...	1705	1944
156	**Montluçon 329** d.	0730	0758	1000	1007	...	1515	1743	1804	2045
224	Gannat 329 d.	0850	—	|	1108	...	1619	1906	—	...
247	**St Germain des Fossés** d.	|	...	1124	1121	1135	|	|	Ⓐ	...
	Vichy 330 a.	0919	0929	...	...	|	|	1927	1937	...
314	Roanne 328 d.	...	1014	...	...	1216	1713	...	2021	...
411	**Lyon Part Dieu 328** a.	...	1117	...	...	1324	1816	...	2125	...
411	**Lyon Perrache 328** a.	...	1129	...	...	1338	1829	...	2137	...

	①g	⚒	4504 ⚒v	🚌 E	4580 u	N		🚌 Ⓑh		⑤⑦r
Lyon Perrache 328 d.	...	...	0904	...	1250	...	1621	...	1720	...
Lyon Part Dieu 328 d.	...	...	0918	...	1304	...	1634	...	1734	...
Roanne 328 d.	...	...	1032	...	1414	...	1744	...	1839	...
Vichy 330 d.	...	...	|	...	|	...	1828	1839	1921	...
St Germain des Fossés d.	...	...	1112	1135	|	...	—	|	|	...
Gannat 329 d.	...	...	...	|	1508	...	⑤⑦r	|	*1953*c	...
Montluçon 329 d.	0617	0800	...	1301	1605	1845	1912	2006	*2111*c	2146
Guéret d.	0738	0910	...	...	1704	1948	2012	...	...	2243
Limoges a.	0842	1015	...	...	1804	2052	2110	...	...	2343
Bordeaux 302 a.	...	...	...	...	2036	...	...	...	...	...

D – ⑥ (daily July 4 - Aug. 30).
E – Ⓐ (also ⑥ July 4 - Aug. 29)
J – To July 3 / from Aug. 31.
N – ①②③④⑥ July 6 - Aug. 29 (not July 14, Aug. 15).
c – Connection by 🚌.
g – Also June 2, July 15, Nov. 12; not June 1.
h – Also Aug. 15.
q – ① to June 29 / from Aug. 31 (also June 2, Nov. 12; not June 1).
r – Also June 1, July 14, Aug. 15, Nov. 11.
u – Not June 6.
v – Not July 13.

June 27
On June 27 trains do not call at Lyon Part Dieu. Departures from Lyon Perrache are approx 20 minutes earlier and arrivals approx 20 minutes later.

CLERMONT FERRAND - LYON 328

km		⚒		⚒ v		§		†	⚒	Ⓐ	†
0	**Clermont Ferrand** ▷ d.	0623	0858	*1040*	1213	1406	1504	1744	1756	1906	1958
14	Riom-Châtel-Guyon ▷ d.	0633	0907	*1052*	1223	1415	1513	1754	1805	1915	2007
55	Vichy 330 d.	0656	0929	|	1245	1436	1535	1818	1826	1937	2028
65	St Germain des Fossés d.	|	|	1135	|	|	|	|	|	|	|
132	Roanne 290 ▶ d.	0745	1014	1216	1332	1521	1620	1907	1914	2021	2114
229	**Lyon Part Dieu 290** ▶ a.	0856	1117	1324	1443	1625	1724	2017	2017	2125	2217
229	**Lyon Perrache 290** a.	0908	1129	1338	1455	1637	1736	2029	2029	2137	2229

	⚒	‡			B				
Lyon Perrache 290 d.	0620	1120	1420	1511	...	1621	1720	1820	2020
Lyon Part Dieu 290 ▶ d.	0634	1134	1434	1526	...	1634	1734	1834	2034
Roanne 290 ▶ d.	0739	1239	1539	1637	...	1744	1839	1949	2139
St Germain des Fossés d.	|	|	|	1717	1739	|	|	|	|
Vichy 330 d.	0823	1322	1624	...	1747	1829	1922	2036	2222
Riom-Châtel-Guyon ▷ d.	0847	1343	1648	...	1810	1853	1944	2101	2244
Clermont Ferrand ▷ a.	0856	1352	1656	...	1821	1902	1952	2111	2252

CLERMONT FERRAND - ST ÉTIENNE

km		⚒				
0	**Clermont Ferrand** d.	0749	0903	1116	1611	1823
112	Montbrison d.	0936	1048	1301	1801	2016
145	**St Étienne** C'creux a.	1008	1124	1336	1840	2050

	⚒	Ⓐ				
St Étienne C'creux d.	0608	0807	1228	1404	1729	1915
Montbrison d.	0653	0846	1259	1434	1803	1944
Clermont Ferrand a.	0849	...	1437	1610	1944	2124

June 27
On June 27 trains do not call at Lyon Part Dieu. Departures from Lyon Perrache are approx 20 mins earlier and arrivals approx 20 mins later.

B – Ⓐ (daily July 6 - Aug. 30).
v – Not July 13.
§ – Train **5528** on ⑤⑦ (daily July 5 - Aug. 22).
‡ – Train **5526** on ⑤⑦ (daily July 5 - Aug. 22).
▷ – See also Tables **329** and **330**.

▶ – Local trains Roanne - Lyon Part Dieu (journey 90 minutes):
From Roanne: 0522 Ⓐ, 0559, 0627, 0711 ⚒, 0722 ⑥, 0729 Ⓑ, 0829, 0929, 1123 ⚒,
From Lyon Part Dieu: 0808 ⚒, 1008, 1208, 1508, 1608, 1708, 1800, 1908 Ⓐ, 2008 Ⓑ, 2108.

2nd class MONTLUÇON - CLERMONT FERRAND 329

km		⚒	Ⓐ	†	Ⓐc		Ⓒ	Ⓑ		†
0	**Montluçon 327** d.	0600	0715	0840	0929	1228	*1515*	1710	1821	1925
68	Gannat 327 d.	0705	0817	0936	1032	1334	1641	1814	1929	2022
96	Riom-Châtel-Guyon d.	0730	0836	0952	1053	1355	1709	1831	1947	2040
110	**Clermont Ferrand** a.	0744	0845	1002	1103	1404	1721	1841	1956	2049

	Ⓐ	⚒	Ⓐ	†	⚒		Ⓐ	Ⓑh	⑥t	Ⓑh	⑤⑦z
Clermont Ferrand d.	0555	0654	0744	1037	1303	*1418*	1615	1733	1808	1820	2003
Riom-Châtel-Guyon d.	0609	0704	0758	1047	1314	*1431*	1624	1745	1821	1830	2013
Gannat 327 d.	0625	0723	0818	1107	1336	1508	1643	1811	1849	1849	2039
Montluçon 327 a.	0726	0828	0918	1208	1438	1605	1740	1906	1957	1953	2137

c – Subject to alteration Sept. 28 - Oct. 9.
h – Also Aug. 15.
t – Not Aug. 15.
z – Also June 1, July 13, 14, Nov. 10, 11.

330 PARIS - NEVERS - CLERMONT FERRAND

Some trains 2nd class

km					5951	5953	5955		5957		5959	5963		5967		5971		5975			5979	5981	5983	5985
					🅁★	🅁★	🅁★		🅁★		🅁★	🅁★		🅁★		🅁★		🅁★			🅁★	🅁★	🅁★	🅁★
		Ⓐ	⚒	Ⓑ	①–⑥			⚒		Ⓐ				⑤	Ⓐ		†	Ⓐ	⚒	†	Ⓑ	⑤		
					n	R			S				L					J					A	T
0	**Paris Gare de Lyon** ▶ d.	...	...	...	0701	0801	0901	...	1101	...	1301	1401	...	1501	...	1601	...	1701	...	...	1801	1901	1901	2101
254	**Nevers** ▶ d.	...	0640	...	0857	0957	1057	...	1257	...	1457	1557	...	1657	...	1757	...	|	...	...	1957	2057	2057	2257
	Dijon **372** d.	...	|	...	|	|	|	...	|	...	|	|	...	|	...	|	...	|	1716	*1716*	|	|	|	|
314	Moulins sur Allier d.	0650	0727	0810	0927	1027	1127	1231	1326	1431	1527	1627	1651	1727	1811	1827	1834	|	1956	1958	2027	2127	2127	2327
355	St Germain des Fossés d.	0721	0804	0834	|	|	|	1258	|	1454	|	|	1722	|	1836	|	1900	|	2021	2023	|	2147	|	|
365	Vichy ▷ d.	0730	0813	0842	0953	1053	1153	1306	1353	1502	1554	1653	1730	1753	1844	1853	1908	|	2030	2032	2053	2157	2154	2353
406	Riom-Châtel-Guyon ▷ d.	0752	0840	0904	1016	1116	1216	1329	1416	1523	1616	1716	1753	1816	1906	1916	1929	|	2052	2054	2116	2222	2217	0017
420	**Clermont Ferrand** ▷ a.	0802	0852	0912	1025	1125	1225	1342	1425	1532	1625	1725	1802	1825	1915	1925	1937	2000	2100	2102	2125	2230	2225	0025

	5948	5950	5954		5958		5962		5966			5968	5970	5974		5978		5982		5986		5990		
	🅁★	🅁★	🅁★		🅁★		🅁★		🅁★			🅁★	🅁★	🅁★		🅁★		🅁★		🅁★		🅁★		
	①	②–⑤	Ⓐ	Ⓐ	⑥	⚒		©	①–⑥	⚒	⑥			⑦	Ⓐ			Ⓑ	⚒	⑦	Ⓐ			⑦
	g	w	J				△		u		t	V		e						e				d
Clermont Ferrand ▷ d.	0523	0529	0601	0616	0629	0740	0829	0834	1029	1040	1130	1229	1329	1429	1530	1629	1659	1729	1800	1829	1830	1929	2030	2259
Riom-Châtel-Guyon ▷ d.	0534	0540	|	0626	0640	0749	0840	0844	1040	1052	1139	1240	1340	1440	1539	1640	1708	1740	1809	1840	1839	1940	2040	2309
Vichy ▷ d.	0556	0602	|	0649	0702	0810	0902	0907	1102	|	1202	1302	1402	1502	1603	1702	1730	1802	1833	1902	1902	2002	2104	2332
St Germain des Fossés d.	0606	|	|	0658	|	0818	|	0916	|	1132	1211	|	|	|	1611	|	1738	|	1841	|	1911	|	2113	2341
Moulins sur Allier d.	0627	0629	|	0734	0729	0841	0929	0942	1129	1200	1237	1329	1429	1529	1637	1729	1801	1829	1904	1929	1935	2029	2140	0009
Dijon **372** a.	|	|	|	1010	|	|	|	1220	|	...	...	|	|	|	...	|	...	|	...	|	...	|	...	...
Nevers ▶ d.	0657	0658	|	...	0758	0910	0958	...	1157	...	...	1358	1458	1558	...	1758	...	1858	...	1958	...	2058	...	...
Paris Gare de Lyon ▶ a.	0852	0852	0900	...	0952	...	1152	...	1352	...	...	1552	1652	1752	...	1952	...	2052	...	2152	...	2252	...	...

STOPPING TRAINS PARIS (BERCY) - NEVERS

km			5901	5905		5909		5911	5915	5917	5919	5921
		⚒	Ⓐ			⚒	Ⓑ	Ⓐ	Ⓐ	©	Ⓐ	†
0	**Paris Bercy** d.	...	0703	0903	...	1403	...	1635	1759	1803	1931	2003
119	Montargis d.	...	0804	1003	...	1503	...	1801	1903	1903	2050	2103
155	Gien d.	...	0826	1026	...	1524	...	1823	1924	1926	2112	2124
196	Cosne d.	0721	0850	1050	1243	1546	1743	1847	1946	1951	2137	2147
228	La Charité d.	0753	0909	1109	1313	1605	1813	1904	2005	2007	2156	2205
254	**Nevers** d.	0825	0929	1129	1346	1624	1843	1926	2024	2028	2216	2224

	5900	5904	5906	5908		5910	5912		5914	5916	
	Ⓐ	Ⓐ	⑥	Ⓐ	⚒		Ⓐ	⚒	†		Ⓐ
Nevers d.	0500	0600	0623	0728	0909	1028	1428	1524	1639	1823	2009
La Charité d.	0520	0620	0643	0747	0940	1047	1447	1554	1653	1843	2040
Cosne d.	0539	0639	0703	0806	1009	1106	1506	1623	1711	1903	2109
Gien d.	0602	0702	0726	0829	...	1128	1528	...	1734	1926	...
Montargis d.	0626	0726	0750	0850	...	1150	1550	...	1755	1950	...
Paris Bercy a.	0733	0833	0849	0949	...	1249	1649	...	1852	2049	...

A – Daily except ⑤.
J – To July 3 / from Aug. 31.
L – To July 10 / from Aug. 31.
R – July 4, 11, 12, Aug. 1, Oct. 24, 31 only.
S – July 3, 4, 11, Oct. 24, 31 only.
T – July 3, 10, 17, 31, Oct. 23, 30 only.
V – July 3, 4, 11, Oct. 24, 30, 31 only.

d – Also June 1, July 14, Nov. 11.
e – Also June 1, July 14, Aug. 15, Nov. 11.
g – Also June 2, July 15, Nov. 12; not June 1, July 13.
n – Not June 1, July 14, Aug. 15, Nov. 11.
t – Not Aug. 15.
u – Not June 1, July 14, Aug. 15, Oct. 12 - 23, Nov. 11.
w – Also July 13; not June 2, July 14, 15, Nov. 11, 12.

★ – *CORAIL TÉOZ* service, 🅁, 🍸.
▶ – For additional trains see below main table.
▷ – See also Tables **328** and **329**.
△ – Runs up to 25 minutes earlier on Sept. 15 - 18.

331 CLERMONT FERRAND - NEUSSARGUES - AURILLAC

km											
		⚒						Ⓑ	⚒	Ⓑ	⑤⑦
		⊡	⊙			E	⊙	⊙	⊙	h⊙	d
0	**Clermont Ferrand** ▷ d.	0636	1038	1242	...	...	1637	1738	1842	1942	2135
36	Issoire ▷ d.	0702	1104	1309	...	...	1705	1806	1909	2008	2201
61	Arvant ▷ d.	0728	1124	1330	...	...	1723	1823	1927	2025	2221
85	Massiac-Blesle d.	0749	1148	1352	...	...	1745	1846	1948	2045	2242
111	**Neussargues** a.	0809	1208	1415	...	...	1805	1907	2010	2107	2302
111	**Neussargues** d.	0810	1209	...	1443	1609	1806	1908	2012	2113	2303
120	Murat (Cantal) d.	0819	1218	...	1452	1618	1817	1918	2022	2122	2312
131	Le Lioran d.	0831	1229	...	1504	1629	1828	|	2036	2136	2323
168	**Aurillac** a.	0902	1259	...	1534	1702	1858	1958	2105	2204	2353
476	*Toulouse* **316** a.	1233	...	...	...	...	...	...	...	...	...

	⚒	Ⓐ					Ⓐ	Ⓑ	⑦	⑤
	⊙	z⊙	⊙			⊙	⊙	h⊙	d⊙	J
Toulouse **316** d.	...	...	...	...	...	1237	...	...	...	...
Aurillac ◇ d.	0553	0737	1034	1331	...	1632	1731	1828	2017	2036
Le Lioran ◇ d.	0625	|	1106	1403	...	1703	1803	1904	2049	2110
Murat (Cantal) d.	0637	0820	1118	1415	...	1715	1816	1917	2101	2124
Neussargues a.	0644	0829	1126	1423	...	1723	1824	1925	2108	2132
Neussargues d.	0645	0830	1127	...	1433	1724	1825	1926	2111	2133
Massiac-Blesle d.	0706	0850	1151	...	1456	1747	1848	1949	2132	2154
Arvant ▷ d.	0726	|	1212	...	1518	1811	1909	2009	2152	2215
Issoire ▷ d.	0745	0925	1231	...	1538	1830	1927	2028	2211	2234
Clermont Ferrand ▷ a.	0814	0954	1258	...	1603	1855	1952	2056	2239	2259

E – ⑤ to July 10 / from Sept. 4. To Brive (Table **317**).
J – To July 3 / from Sept. 4.
d – Also June 1, July 14, Nov. 11.
h – Also Aug. 15.
z – Also runs on ⑥ July 18 - Aug. 29.

▷ – See also Table **333**.
⊡ – Subject to alteration (with 🚌 substitution) June 29 - Aug. 28.
⊙ – By 🚌 Neussarges - Arvant and v.v. June 29 - Aug. 28 (in the same timings).

332 CLERMONT FERRAND - MILLAU - BÉZIERS

Some trains 2nd class

km						15941	15941			
		⚒	①	⚒		†	⚒	⑤	†	⑤
			g	b	h			◇		
0	**Clermont Ferrand** ▷ d.	...	...	...	...	1242	1242	...	...	...
85	Massiac-Blesle ▷ d.	...	...	...	...	1352	1352	...	...	...
111	**Neussargues** ▷ d.	...	...	...	...	1437	1437	...	1728	2140
130	St Flour d.	...	...	...	...	1459	1503	...	1750	2202
168	St Chély d'Apcher d.	...	...	1147	...	1539	1548	1645	1828	2240
201	Marvejols d.	...	...	1226	1242	1617	1629	1720	1903	2316
236	**Mende** a.	...	...	|	1329	|	|	|	|	|
243	Sévérac le Château d.	...	...	1310	...	1704	1716	1810	1947	2357
273	Millau ⊙ d.	0542	0848	1350	...	1733	1746	1843	2016	0024
352	Bédarieux ▶ d.	0658	1008	1508	...	1849	1902	2002	2132	...
394	**Béziers** ▶ a.	0730	1040	1540	...	1924	1936	2036	2205	...

		15940									
									🚌		
	⚒		†	⑤	①–④	Ⓐ	†	⚒		⑦	⑤
					m				E	q	u
Béziers ▶ d.	...	0910	...	1238	1300	...	1814	1826	...	1857	2055
Bédarieux ▶ d.	...	0943	...	1311	1337	...	1850	1901	...	1936	2128
Millau ⊙ d.	0853	1103	1415	1427	1500	1842	2007	2021	2033	2100	2245
Sévérac le Château d.	0920	1133	1443	1456	...	1910	...	...	2102	2128	...
Mende d.	|	*1125*r	|	|	...	|	...	...	|	|	...
Marvejols d.	1010	1223	1526	1538	...	1954	...	...	2212	2216	...
St Chély d'Apcher d.	1044	1301	1603	1612	...	2029	...	...	2242	2250	...
St Flour d.	...	1342	1641	...	...	2108c	...	...	...	...	...
Neussargues ▷ a.	...	1402	1700	...	...	2128c	...	...	...	...	...
Massiac-Blesle ▷ a.	...	1455	...	...	...	...	...	...	...	...	...
Clermont Ferrand ▷ a.	...	1603	...	...	...	...	...	...	...	...	...

SNCF 🚌 service	🚌	🚌	🚌	🚌	🚌	🚌	🚌	🚌	🚌	🚌
	⚒				⑦e	Ⓑ	Ⓐ	⑤	⑤	Ⓑ
Clermont Ferrand ▷ d.	...	...	1640	...	1737	...	...	1940	...	2145
Massiac-Blesle ▷ d.	0805	1155	|	1750	1830	1849	1952	|	2051	|
St Flour d.	0830	1219	|	1815	1852	1914	2017	|	2116	2303
St Chély d'Apcher d.	...	...	1815	...	...	...	...	2115	...	2324
Marvejols d.	...	...	1853	...	...	...	...	2151	...	2358
Mende a.	...	...	1930	...	...	...	...	2230	...	0037

SNCF 🚌 service	🚌	🚌	🚌	🚌	🚌	🚌	🚌	🚌	🚌	🚌
	⚒	Ⓐ			⑦e	⑦e	d	⑤	Ⓐ	⑦e
Mende d.	...	0700	...	1000	...	1507	...	1552	...	...
Marvejols d.	...	0740	...	1050	...	1549	...	1634	...	1815
St Chély d'Apcher d.	...	0816	...	1128	...	1625	...	1710	...	1854
St Flour d.	0631	0843	1116	|	1553	1653	1705	1738	1813	1918
Massiac-Blesle ▷ a.	0656	|	1140	|	1620	|	1729	|	1838	|
Clermont Ferrand ▷ a.	...	1000	...	1300	1719	1811	...	1856	...	2040

E – Ⓐ (also ⑦ July 5 - Aug. 30).
b – Arrive Millau 1338. On ①–④ Millau d. 1404, Bédarieux 1521, Béziers 1554. On ①–④ Sept. 14 - Oct. 29 by 🚌 Millau - Bédarieux (arrive Béziers 1554).
c – St Chély d'Apcher - Neussargues runs on ⑤ only.
d – On ⑤ runs to Arvant, arrive 1745 (not calling at Massiac-Blesle).
e – Also June 1, July 14, Nov. 11.
g – To June 29 / from Sept. 7 (also June 2, Nov. 5; not June 1, Oct. 26, Nov. 2).
h – Subject to alteration on June 8, 15, 22.

m – ①–④ to Sept. 10 / from Nov. 2 (not June 1, July 14, Nov. 11).
q – ⑦ to June 28 / from Sept. 6 (also June 1, Nov. 4; not Oct.25, Nov. 1). From Montpellier (d. 1802).
r – ⚒ only (subject to alteration June 8, 15, 22).
u – Also runs on ⑥ July 4 - Aug. 29 (not Aug. 15).

▷ – For connections see Table **331**.
◇ – To Montpellier (arrive 2139) on ⑤ to June 26 / from Sept. 4 (not Oct. 30).

▶ – Additional trains Bédarieux - Béziers and v.v.:
From Bédarieux: 0616 ⚒, 0658 †, 0750 ⚒, 1202, 1508 †, 1735.
From Béziers: 0702 ⚒, 0757, 1300 ©, 1652, 1741 Ⓐ.

⊙ – Additional SNCF 🚌 service Millau - Montpellier and v.v.:
From Millau 0700 ⚒, 0710 †, 1716. From Montpellier 0710, 1715 ⚒, 2115 ⑤, 2210. Journey 95 - 125 minutes.

CLERMONT FERRAND - LE PUY EN VELAY — 333

On Ⓐ May 11 - June 26 trains may be replaced by 🚌 between St Georges d'Aurac and Le Puy

km		Ⓐ	①–⑥ ▽	🚌 ⚒	Ⓐ		🚌 Ⓒ	⑥	Ⓐ ▽	Ⓒ ▽	🚌 Ⓒ	Ⓐ	🚌 Ⓐ	Ⓐ ▽	🚌 Ⓐ	Ⓐ ▽	Ⓒ ▽	🚌 G	Ⓑ	🚌 ⑤	Ⓐ	Ⓑ	🚌 ⑤	⑦ e
0	**Clermont Ferrand** 331 d.	0602	0648	...	0929	1038	...	1208	1208	1235	...	1242	...	1641	...	...	1710	...	1738	...	1900	1942	...	2106
36	Issoire 331 d.	0628	0714	...	0955	1104	...	1237	1239	1300	...	1309	...	1714	...	...	1740	...	1806	...	1930	2008	...	2130
61	Arvant 331 d.	0647	0735	...	1014	1123	1128	1257	1259	1319	...	1329	1335	1735	...	←	1800	...	1822	1830	1951	2024	2029	2149
71	Brioude d.	0656	0746	...	1022	...	1139	1306	1308	1328	1335	...	1348	1744	1750	1756	1813	1815	...	1843	2001	...	2040	2203
95	St Georges d'Aurac d.	0721	|	...	1044	...	|	1325	|	|	|	...	|	→	|	1819	|	|	...	1911	2022	...	|	2224
103	Langeac d.	|	0813	0820	|	...	1207	|	1335	1355	|	...	|	...	|	1827	1844	|	...	1920	|	...	2107	|
147	**Le Puy en Velay** a.	0810	...	0906	1133	...	1252	1415	...	...	1442	...	1455	...	1850	...	...	1915	...	2003	2111	...	2150	2312

	① g	②–⑤ w	⑥ L		🚌	▽	⚒		🚌 Ⓐ	Ⓐ ▽	🚌 Ⓒ	Ⓒ ▽		Ⓐ	†	🚌 ⑥ t	⑥		🚌 Ⓐ	🚌 ⑦ e	Ⓑ	Ⓑ ▽	⑦ e	
Le Puy en Velay d.	0545	0631	0801	...	1131	...	1158	...	1644	...	1702	...	...	1726	1743	1748	...	...	1842	1859	...	...	2020	...
Langeac d.	|	|	|	...	|	1215	|	...	|	1725	|	1744	...	|	|	1835	...	...	|	|	...	2130	|	...
St Georges d'Aurac d.	0633	0719	0847	...	|	|	1246	...	|	1734	|	1753	...	1820	1837	|	...	...	|	|	...	|	2110	...
Brioude d.	0701	0745	0907	...	1231	1241	1309	...	1744	1754	1802	1812	...	1838	1857	1912	1922	...	1940	1945	...	2155	2130	...
Arvant 331 d.	0710	0753	0917	...	...	|	1318	...	...	1803	...	1822	...	|	|	...	1930	...	1955	1958	2009	2205	2139	...
Issoire 331 d.	0733	0814	0938	...	...	1308	1338	...	...	1822	...	1842	...	1901	1919	...	1951	...	...	...	2028	2225	2200	...
Clermont Ferrand 331 a.	0802	0842	1006	...	...	1336	1408	...	...	1848	...	1908	...	1929	1950	...	2029	...	...	...	2056	2254	2228	...

G – ⑥ (also ⑦ to Aug. 30), also June 1, July 14.
L – To July 11/from Sept. 5.
e – Also June 1, July 14, Nov. 11.
g – Also June 2, Sept 2; not June 1, July 13 - Aug. 24.
t – Not Aug. 15.
w – Also ① July 13 - Aug. 24; not June 2, Sept. 2
▽ – Through train to Nimes or beyond (see Table **334**).

CLERMONT FERRAND and MENDE - NIMES - MONTPELLIER — 334

On Ⓐ Sept. 14 - Oct. 31 service may be by 🚌 between Langeac and Langogne. Timings will not be affected.

km		⚒ c	⑦ c	①–⑥	🚌 ⚒	①–⑥ c	15947 Ⓐ	15957 Ⓒ	◇	Ⓐ	Ⓒ
0	*Clermont Ferrand* 333 d.	...	...	0648	...	...	1208	1235	...	1641	1710
103	**Langeac** d.	...	...	0815	...	...	1336	1356	...	1828	1845
170	Langogne d.	...	...	1018	...	1230	1531	1549	...	2045	2045
*47	**Mende** d.	0510	0835	|	1130	|	*1350*x	*1350*x	1650	|	|
188	La Bastide-St Laurent d.	0628	0957	1038	1240	1249	1551	1610	1807	2107	2107
241	Grand Combe la Pise d.	0720	1051	1136	...	1342	1645	1704	1908	2200	2200
254	Alès ▶ d.	0740	1115	1203	...	1412	1702	1721	1927	2216	2216
303	**Nimes 355** ▶ a.	0818	1152	1245	...	1448	1740	1800	2007	2254	2254
	Marseille 355 a.	|	|	...	...	...	1914	1947	|	...	...
353	**Montpellier 355** a.	0847	1221	...	...	...	...	...	2036	...	...

	⚒ b c		⚒	Ⓐ	15942 Ⓐ	15952 Ⓒ	🚌	Ⓑ	◇
Montpellier 355 d.	0643	...	...	...	...	...	...	1624	1740
Marseille 355 d.	|	...	...	...	1128	1128	...	|	|
Nimes 355 ▶ d.	0713	0800	...	1245r	1312	1312	...	1714	1808
Alès ▶ d.	0806	0842	...	1327	1357	1357	...	1802	1851
Grand Combe la Pise d.	0820	0858	...	1343	1413	1413	...	1818	1909
La Bastide-St Laurent d.	0914	0956	1010	1440	1510	1521	1600	1916	2005
Mende a.	|	|	1123	1555	|	|	1710	|	2135v
Langogne d.	0936	1017	...	...	1532	1550	...	1935	...
Langeac a.	...	1214	...	...	1724	1743	...	2129	...
Clermont Ferrand 333 a.	...	1336	...	...	1848	1908	...	2254	...

b – From Béziers on Ⓐ (depart 0555).
c – Change at Alès.
r – 1233 on Ⓒ.
v – 2115 on ⑦ to June 28/from Sept. 6.
x – Connection by 🚌.
◇ – Change at Alès on certain dates.
* – Distance from La Bastide.
▶ – Additional services Alès - Nimes and v.v.:
From Alès 0600 ⚒, 0640 Ⓐ, 0704, 0810 Ⓐ, 0841, 0920 Ⓐ, 1113 Ⓐ, 1205 Ⓐ, 1254, 1513, 1615 🚌, 1805 Ⓑ, 1845 🚌.
From Nimes 0626 Ⓐ, 0655 Ⓐ, 0904 Ⓐ, 1022 Ⓐ, 1053, 1223 Ⓐ, 1520 🚌, 1635, 1714 ⑥, 1900 Ⓐ, 1945 🚌, 2055, 2145 🚌.

TGV services — LYON - MASSY - TOURS, RENNES and NANTES — 335

For slower services via Bourges see Table **290**. For Lille - Massy - Rennes/Nantes see Table **11**. For Strasbourg - Massy - Rennes/Nantes see Table **391**.

	TGV 5352 ① g	*TGV* 5352 Ⓐ	*TGV* 5356 ⑥		*TGV* 5350 Ⓑ	*TGV* 5360 ⑥	*TGV* 5364 ⑥ u	*TGV* 5365 ⑥		*TGV* 5374 ⑦ e	*TGV* 5371 ⑦ e	*TGV* 5368 ①–⑥ n	*TGV* 5233 ①–⑥ ♥n		*TGV* 5372 ①–⑥ n	*TGV* 5363 ①–⑥ n	*TGV* 5378 ⑦ e	*TGV* 5236 ⑦ ♥e		*TGV* 5380 ◇	*TGV* 5387 ①–④ ◇n		*TGV* 5390 ⑤⑦ e	
Bourg St Maurice d.	...	...	...	...	...	...	...	...	...	...	...	...	...	...	...	...	...	...	...	...	...	...	...	...
Chambéry d.	...	...	...	...	...	...	...	...	...	...	...	...	...	...	...	...	...	...	...	...	...	...	...	...
Grenoble 343 d.	0532	...	...	...	...	...	0811	...	...	...	...	...	...	...	...	...	...	...	...	...	...	...	...	...
Marseille 350 d.	|	...	...	...	0739	...	|	...	...	1133	1133	1133	...	...	1507	1507	1507	...	...	...	...	...	...	...
Avignon TGV 350 d.	|	...	...	...	|	...	|	...	...	1209	1209	1209	...	...	1546	1546	1546	...	...	...	...	...	...	...
Lyon Perrache d.	|	...	...	...	|	...	|	...	...	|	|	|	...	...	|	|	|	...	...	...	...	...	1907	...
Lyon Part Dieu d.	0656	0656	0656	...	0926	0926	0926	0926	...	1326	1326	1326	...	...	1656	1656	1656	...	...	1826	1826	...	1926	...
Massy TGV d.	0901	0901	0901	...	1131	1131	1131	1131	...	1532	1532	1534	1631	...	1901	1901	1901	1917	...	2032	2032	...	2137	...
St Pierre des Corps a.	0951	0951	0951	...	|	|	|	|	...	|	|	1622	|	...	|	|	1953	|	...	2129	|	...	|	...
Futuroscope 300 a.	|	|	1028	...	|	|	|	|	...	|	|	|	|	...	|	|	|	|	...	|	|	...	|	...
Poitiers 300 a.	|	|	1044	...	|	|	|	|	...	|	|	|	|	...	|	|	|	|	...	|	|	...	|	...
Le Mans 280 a.	|	|	...	...	1219	1217	1217	1217	...	1619	1619	|	1719	...	1949	1949	|	2005	...	|	2119	...	2224	...
Rennes 280 a.	|	|	...	...	1340	1333	1333	|	...	|	1743	|	1836	...	2110	|	|	2125	...	|	2234	...	2339	...
Angers St Laud 280 a.	1046	1046	...	...	...	...	...	1302	...	1659	...	1719	...	...	...	2035	2046	...	...	2223	...	...	...	...
Nantes 280 a.	1125	1125	...	...	...	...	...	1342	...	1736	...	1803	...	...	...	2116	2127	...	...	2304	...	...	...	...

	TGV 5302 ①–④ n	*TGV* 5304 ⑥	*TGV* 8712 Ⓐ J	*TGV* 5312	*TGV* 5311 △	*TGV* 8818	*TGV* 5318		*TGV* 5324 G	*TGV* 5322	*TGV* 8836	*TGV* 5326 ⑤⑥	*TGV* 5346 ①–④ n		*TGV* 5332 ⑤	*TGV* 5328 ①–④ n		*TGV* 5334 ⑦ e	*TGV* 5338 ⑦ v		*TGV* 5344 ⑤	*TGV* 5342 ⑤	*TGV* 5336 ⑦ e	*TGV* 5340 ⑦ e
Nantes 280 d.	0455	0630	...	0735	0735	0900	...	...	...	1252	1400	...	...	...	1555	1555	...	1708	...	...	...	1904	...	1849
Angers St Laud 280 d.	0536	0708	...	0813	0813	0937	...	...	...	1337	1438	...	...	...	1633	1633	...	1744	...	...	...	1944	...	1927
Rennes 280 d.	|	|	0735	|	|	|	0910	...	1230	|	|	1414	1514	...	|	|	...	|	1827	...	1909	|	...	|
Le Mans 280 d.	|	|	0846	0854	0854	1016	1029	...	1351	|	1516	1529	1630	...	|	|	...	1825	1952	...	2030	2030	...	|
Poitiers 300 d.	|	|	...	|	|	...	|	...	|	|	...	|	|	...	|	|	...	|	|	...	|	|	1932	|
Futuroscope 300 a.	|	|	...	|	|	...	|	...	|	|	...	|	|	...	|	|	...	|	|	...	|	|	1943	|
St Pierre des Corps d.	0632	0807	...	|	|	...	|	...	|	1430	...	|	|	...	1727	1727	...	|	|	...	|	|	2028	2028
Massy TGV d.	0723	0901	...	0949	0949	...	1121	...	1446	1521	...	1621	1720	...	1821	1821	...	1915	2045	...	2121	2121	2126	2126
Lyon Part Dieu a.	0935	1103	...	1201	1201	...	1331	...	1655	1731	...	1831	1931	...	2031	2031	...	2131	2255	...	2332	2332	2331	2331
Lyon Perrache a.	0950	1115	...	|	...	...	|	...	1710z	|	...	|	|	...	|	2046	...	|	|	...	2346	2346	2347	2347
Avignon TGV 350 a.	...	...	...	1309	...	...	1446	...	...	1846	...	1945	2046	...	|	...	...	|	0016	...	...	...	...	...
Marseille 350 a.	...	...	...	1346	...	...	1523	...	...	1918	...	2024	2117	...	|	...	...	|	0055	...	...	...	...	...
Grenoble 343 a.	...	...	...	...	...	...	...	...	...	...	...	...	...	...	2153	...	...	2253	...	...	...	...	...	...
Chambéry a.	...	...	...	...	...	...	...	...	...	...	...	...	...	...	...	...	...	...	...	...	...	...	...	...
Bourg St Maurice a.	...	...	...	...	...	...	...	...	...	...	...	...	...	...	...	...	...	...	...	...	...	...	...	...

LYON - ROUEN	*TGV* 5366 ⑥ y	*TGV* 5376
Marseille 350 d.	...	1539
Avignon TGV 350 d.	...	1610
Lyon Perrache d.	1216	|
Lyon Part Dieu d.	1231	1726
Massy-Palaiseau d.	1458	1938
Versailles Chantiers d.	1518	1956
Mantes la Jolie a.	|	2027
Rouen Rive Droite a.	1646	2123
Le Havre 270 a.	...	2212

ROUEN - LYON	*TGV* 5316	*TGV* 5320 ⑦ e
Le Havre 270 d.	0750	...
Rouen Rive Droite d.	0843	1243r
Mantes la Jolie d.	0933	|
Versailles Chantiers d.	1006	1359
Massy-Palaiseau d.	1022	1416
Lyon Part Dieu a.	1231	1621
Lyon Perrache a.	|	1641
Avignon TGV 350 a.	1347	...
Marseille 350 a.	1418	...

G – ①②③④⑦ (not June 1, July 14, Nov. 11).
J – To July 3/from Aug. 31.
e – Also June 1, July 14.
g – Also June 2, July 15; not June 1, July 13.
n – Not June 1, July 14.
r – 1233 July 5 - Sept. 13, 1236 on July 14.
u – Not June 20, 27, July 18, Sept. 5.
v – Also June 1, July 14; not Sept. 13 - Oct. 4.
y – To Sept. 5.
z – ⑦ (also June 1, July 14).

TGV – Ⓡ, supplement payable, 🍷.
♥ – To/from Lille (Table **11**).
◇ – From Montpellier (depart 1630, Table **350**).
△ – To Montpellier (arrive 1355, Table **350**).

340 PARIS - LYON *TGV Sud-Est*

For Charles de Gaulle ✈ - Marne la Vallée - Lyon see Table **11**. For Paris - Lyon St Exupéry ✈ see Table **342**. Trains not serving Lyon Perrache continue to/from other destinations.

km	*TGV* trains convey 🍷	*TGV* 6601 Ⓐ	*TGV* 6641 Ⓐ J	*TGV* 6681 ①–⑥ n	*TGV* 6603 ①–⑥ m		*TGV* 6643	*TGV* 6605		*TGV* 6645 ①–④ J	*TGV* 6607 ①–⑥ n		*TGV* 6609	*TGV* 6611		*TGV* 6613	*TGV* 6685	*TGV* 6615		*TGV* 6657 ⑤ J	*TGV* 6617		*TGV* 6619	*TGV* 6621
0	**Paris Gare de Lyon** ▷ d.	0554	0624	0654	0654	...	0724	0754	...	0824	0854	...	0954	1054	...	1154	1254	1254	...	1324	1354	...	1454	1554
303	Le Creusot TGV d.	0718	|	|	|	...	|	0918	...	|	|	...	1118	|	...	|	|	|	...	|	1518	...	|	1719
363	Mâcon Loché TGV ▷ a.	|	|	|	|	...	0901	|	...	|	|	...	|	|	...	|	|	|	...	|	|	...	|	|
427	**Lyon Part-Dieu** a.	0757	0821	0851	0851	...	0924	0957	...	1021	1051	...	1157	1251	...	1351	1451	1451	...	1521	1557	...	1651	1757
431	**Lyon Perrache** a.	0809	0833	...	0903	...	0936	1009	...	1033	1103	...	1209	1303	...	1403	...	1503	...	1533	1609	...	1703	1809

	TGV 6659 Ⓐ J	*TGV* 6687	*TGV* 6623 q		*TGV* 6663 ①–⑤ J	*TGV* 6663 ⑤ K	*TGV* 6627		*TGV* 6665 Ⓑ J	*TGV* 6665 ⑤ K	*TGV* 6689	*TGV* 6629 s		*TGV* 6669 ⑤	*TGV* 6631		*TGV* 6671 ⑦ p	*TGV* 6633 Ⓑ		*TGV* 6673 ⑤ J	*TGV* 6635 E		*TGV* 5139 ⑦ ⊡ e	*TGV* 6675 ⑦ e
Paris Gare de Lyon ▷ d.	1624	1654	1654	...	1724	1724	1754	...	1824	1824	1854	1854	...	1924	1954	...	2024	2054	...	2124	2154	...	...	2224
Le Creusot TGV d.	|	|	|	...	|	|	1918	...	|	|	|	|	...	|	2118	...	|	|	...	|	|	...	2321	|
Mâcon Loché TGV ▷ a.	|	|	|	...	|	|	|	...	|	|	|	|	...	|	|	...	|	|	...	|	|	...	|	|
Lyon Part-Dieu a.	1821	1853	1853	...	1921	1921	1957	...	2021	2021	2051	2051	...	2121	2157	...	2221	2251	...	2321	2351	...	2359	0021
Lyon Perrache a.	1833	...	1905	...	1933	1933	2009	...	2033	2033	...	2103	...	2133	2209	...	2233	2303	...	2333	0003	...	0014	0033

	TGV 6640 ① Jg	*TGV* 6602 Ⓐ	*TGV* 5154 ①–⑥ ⊙n		*TGV* 6642 Ⓐ J	*TGV* 6642 ① Kv	*TGV* 6604 ①–⑥ m	*TGV* 6690 ①–⑥ n		*TGV* 6648 J	*TGV* 6648 Ⓒ K	*TGV* 6644 ① Jg	*TGV* 6608 Ⓐ J	*TGV* 6608 Ⓒ J	*TGV* 6608 K		*TGV* 6610	*TGV* 6612	*TGV* 6692	*TGV* 6614		*TGV* 6616	*TGV* 6618	*TGV* 6694
Lyon Perrache d.	0516	0546	...	...	0616	0616	0641	...	...	0716	0716	0731	0746	0746	0746	...	0846	0946	...	1040	...	1146	1241	...
Lyon Part-Dieu d.	0530	0600	0613	...	0630	0630	0700	0700	...	0730	0730	0745	0800	0800	0800	...	0900	1000	1100	1100	...	1200	1300	1300
Mâcon Loché TGV ▷ d.	|	0626	|	...	|	|	|	|	...	|	|	|	|	0827	0827	...	|	|	|	|	...	|	|	|
Le Creusot TGV d.	|	0647	0651	...	|	|	|	|	...	|	|	|	0841	0848	0848	...	|	1041	|	|	...	|	1344	1344
Paris Gare de Lyon ▷ a.	0727	0807	...	...	0827	0827	0857	0857	...	0927	0927	0943	1003	1009	1009	...	1057	1203	1257	1257	...	1359	1505	1505

	TGV 6620 A	*TGV* 6620 ⑤		*TGV* 6622	*TGV* 6624		*TGV* 6664 ⑤	*TGV* 6626	*TGV* 6668 Ⓐ J	*TGV* 6668 ⑤ K	*TGV* 6628	*TGV* 6638 Ⓑ J		*TGV* 6696	*TGV* 6630 u	*TGV* 6632	*TGV* 6674 ⑦ e	*TGV* 6634 N	*TGV* 6636 ⑤		*TGV* 6588 ⑦ e△	*TGV* 6676 ⑤	*TGV* 6676 ⑦ p	*TGV* 6678 ⑦ e
Lyon Perrache d.	1346	1346	...	1446	1546	...	1616	1646	1716	1716	1746	1816	...	...	1841	1946	2016	2046	2046	...	...	2146	2146	2242
Lyon Part-Dieu d.	1400	1400	...	1500	1600	...	1630	1700	1730	1730	1800	1830	...	1900	1900	2000	2030	2100	2100	...	...	2200	2200	2300
Mâcon Loché TGV ▷ d.	|	|	...	|	|	...	|	|	|	|	|	|	...	|	|	|	|	|	|	...	...	|	2226	|
Le Creusot TGV d.	|	1440	...	|	1640	...	|	|	|	|	1841	|	...	|	|	2041	|	|	2140	...	2236	|	|	|
Paris Gare de Lyon ▷ a.	1559	1603	...	1659	1803	...	1827	1857	1927	1927	2003	2027	...	2057	2057	2203	2227	2257	2303	...	2359	2359	0003	0057

A – Daily except ⑤.
E – Ⓑ to July 3; ⑤⑦ July 5 - Aug. 30 (also July 14); Ⓑ from Aug. 31. Train number **6637** on ⑤.
J – To July 4 / from Aug. 31.
K – July 5 - Aug. 30.
N – ①②③④⑦ only.

e – Also June 1, July 14.
g – Also June 2; not June 1.

m – Not June 1, July 14, 24, 28 - 31, Aug. 4 - 7, 11 - 14, 21.
n – Not June 1, July 14.
p – Also June 1, July 14; not July 12.
q – Not Aug. 3 - 6, 10 - 13.
s – Not on July 12 or ①–④ July 27 - Aug. 20.
u – Not on July 12 or ①–⑤ July 20 - Aug. 21.
v – Also July 15; not July 13.

TGV –[R], supplement payable, 🍷.

▷ – For other trains Paris - Mâcon Loché TGV and v.v. see Table **341**.
△ – From Genève (Table **341**).
⊙ – Grenoble - Lyon - Lille Europe (Table **11**).
⊡ – Lille Flandres - Lyon (Table **11**).

341 PARIS - GENÈVE, CHAMBÉRY and ANNECY *TGV trains*

For the night trains Paris Austerlitz - Aix les Bains - Chambéry - Bourg St Maurice / Modane see Tables **368** and **369** (Paris - Annecy see Table **367**).

km	All trains convey 🍷	*TGV* 6931 B	*TGV* 6561	*TGV* 9241 M △	*TGV* 6935 ⑦ Kc	*TGV* 6565 Ⓐ	*TGV* 6937	*TGV* 6939	*TGV* 6569 F		*TGV* 6573 Ⓑ	*TGV* 9247 M △	*TGV* 6941		*TGV* 6577	*TGV* 9249 M △	*TGV* 6947	*TGV* 6949 Ⓑ	*TGV* 6581	*TGV* 6951	*TGV* 6585	*TGV* 6953 ⑤	*TGV* 6589 ⑤
0	**Paris Gare de Lyon** 340 d.	0650	0710	0742	0850	0910	0950	1050	1110	...	1310	1350	1350	...	1504	1524	1650	1750	1810	1850	1908	1950	2010
365	Mâcon Loché TGV 340 d.	|	|	|	|	|	1129	|	|	...	|	1528	1528	...	1643	|	|	1928	|	|	2046	2128	|
406	Bourg-en-Bresse d.	|	0903	|	|	|	|	|	1303	...	1504	|	|	...	1704	|	|	1950	|	|	2109	|	|
	Lyon St Exupéry TGV ✈ 342 d.	0846	|	|	1047	|	|	1247	|	...	|	|	|	...	|	1720	1846	|	|	2046	|	|	|
489	Culoz 345 d.	|	|	|	|	|	|	|	|	...	|	|	|	...	|	|	|	|	|	|	2156	|	|
522	Bellegarde ▲ 345 a.	|	1007	|	|	1203	|	|	1407	...	1607	|	|	...	1807	|	|	|	2103	|	2217	|	2306
555	**Genève** 345 a.	|	1035	|	|	1232	|	|	1435	...	1635	|	|	...	1835	|	|	|	2132	|	2245	|	2335
*532	Chambéry a.	0942	...	1041	1151	...	|	1343	...	...	...	1708	|	...	...	1821	1943	|	...	2143	...	2300	...
*532	Chambéry 344 364 d.	0951	...	...	1200	...	|	1352	...	...	...	...	|	...	...	...	1952	|	...	2152	...	|	...
*546	Aix les Bains 344 364 a.	1001	...	...	1210	...	1250	1401	...	...	...	...	1652	...	...	...	2002	2052	...	2201	...	2245z	...
*585	**Annecy** 344 364 a.	1032	...	...	1253	...	1330	1432	...	...	...	...	1730	...	...	...	2032	2129	...	2232	...	...	...

All trains convey 🍷	*TGV* 6560 Ⓐ	*TGV* 6960 ①–⑥ n	*TGV* 6962 Ⓐ J	*TGV* 6564		*TGV* 6964 D	*TGV* 6568 E	*TGV* 6968	*TGV* 9240 M △		*TGV* 9242 M △	*TGV* 6972	*TGV* 6572 ⊡	*TGV* 6976	*TGV* 6576 R	*TGV* 6576 S		*TGV* 6580 Ⓐ	*TGV* 6980 Ⓑ	*TGV* 6984 Ⓑ	*TGV* 6584	*TGV* 9248 M △	*TGV* 6588 ⑦ e⊖
Annecy 344 364 d.	...	0532	0632	...	...	0830	...	0935	...	...	...	1232	...	1535	...	...	...	...	1735	1832	...	...	...
Aix les Bains 344 364 d.	...	0601	0709	...	...	0907	...	1004	...	...	...	1309	...	1604	...	...	...	...	1804	1910	...	...	...
Chambéry 344 364 a.	...	0612	|	...	...	|	...	1014	...	...	...	|	...	1614	...	...	...	...	1815	|	...	...	...
Chambéry **348** d.	...	0622	|	...	...	|	...	1024	1058	...	1225	|	...	1624	...	...	...	...	1826	|	...	2027	...
Genève 345 d.	0535	|	|	0717	...	|	0917	|	|	...	|	|	1317	|	1614	1614	...	1717	|	|	1917	|	2017
Bellegarde ▲ 345 d.	0603	|	|	0749	...	|	0948	|	|	...	|	|	1348	|	1641	1641	...	1748	|	|	1948	|	2049
Culoz 345 d.	|	|	|	|	...	|	|	|	|	...	|	|	|	|	|	|	...	1810	|	|	|	|	|
Lyon St Exupéry TGV ✈ 342 a.	|	|	|	|	...	|	|	|	|	...	|	|	|	|	|	|	...	|	|	|	|	2124	|
Bourg-en-Bresse d.	0710	|	|	0856	...	|	1056	|	|	...	|	|	1454	|	|	1748	...	1856	|	|	2056	|	2158
Mâcon Loché TGV 340 d.	|	|	0829	|	...	1030	|	1146	|	...	|	1430	|	|	1807	1816	...	|	|	2029	|	|	|
Paris Gare de Lyon 340 a.	0903	0915	1007	1051	...	1207	1249	1323	1355	...	1515	1607	1649	1915	1943	1955	...	2049	2115	2207	2249	2319	2359

B – Daily to July 4; ①–⑤ July 6 - Aug. 28 (not July 14); ①–⑥ from Aug. 31.
D – ⑥⑦ to June 28; daily July 4 - Aug. 30; ⑥⑦ from Sept. 5.
E – ⑥⑦ to June 14; daily June 20 - Aug. 30; ⑥⑦ Sept. 5 - Oct. 11; daily from Oct. 17.
F – Daily to Sept. 13; ⑥⑦ Sept. 19 - Oct. 11; daily Oct. 17 - Nov. 22 (also Nov. 28, 29); daily from Dec. 5.
J – To July 4 / from Aug. 31.
K – July 5 - Aug. 30.
M – (12) Paris - Modane - Torino - Milano and v.v. (Table **44**).
R – ①–⑤ (also ⑥ June 27 - Aug. 29), not June 1, July 14.
S – ⑦ (also ⑥ to June 20 / from Sept. 5), also June 1, July 14.

c – Also July 14.

e – Also June 1, July 14.
n – Not June 1, July 14.
z – Calls before Chambéry.

TGV –[R], supplement payable, 🍷.

* – Via Lyon St Exupéry TGV (Paris - Aix les Bains via Bourg en Bresse = *511* km).
△ – Special 'global' fares payable.
▲ – Additional trains operate Paris - Bellegarde - (Évian les Bains) and v.v. at weekends – see Table **363**.
⊖ – Also calls at Le Creusot TGV (d. 2236).
⊡ – Arrive Paris 1710 on June 10 - 12.

PARIS - LYON ST EXUPÉRY ✈ - GRENOBLE 342

Shows complete service Paris - Lyon St Exupéry ✈ and v.v. Journeys not serving Grenoble continue to destinations in other tables

km	All trains convey 🍷	TGV 6901 Ⓐ	TGV 6931 F	TGV 6191 ①–⑥ n	TGV 6905 E	TGV 6911 ①–⑤ n	TGV 6193	TGV 6913 ⑥⑦ e‡	TGV 6939	TGV 6917 A‡	TGV 6917 ⑤		TGV 6919 ①–④ n	TGV 6919 ⑤–⑦ e‡	TGV 9249	TGV 6921 J⊗	TGV 6947	TGV 6195 ⊙	TGV 6923 ⑤⑦ e	TGV 6925 ①–⑤ n	TGV 6951	TGV 6927 ⑤	TGV 6197	TGV 6927 B	TGV 6929 ⑤⑦ e△
0	**Paris Gare de Lyon** d.	0638	0650	0750	0750	0938	0942	1038	1050	1138	1138	...	1338	1338	1524	1638	1650	1746	1746	1838	1850	1938	1946	1946	2038
441	Lyon St Exupéry ✈ a.	|	0843	0943	0943	|	1135	|	1244	|	1333	...	1531	|	1717	|	1843	1939	1939	|	2043	|	2139	2139	|
441	Lyon St Exupéry ✈ d.	|	...	...	0947	|	...	|	...	|	1345	...	1533	|	...	|	...	...	1947	|	...	|	...	2146	|
553	**Grenoble** a.	0933	...	...	1050	1233	...	1334	...	1433	1450	...	1634	1634	...	1933	...	...	2050	2133	...	2236	...	2248	2333

	TGV 6900 ①–④ Jv	TGV 6192 ①–⑤ n	TGV 6902 Ⓐ d		TGV 6904 ①–⑥ u	TGV 6194		TGV 6908 ⊕	TGV 6910 D§		TGV 6196	TGV 6916 §		TGV 6920 ⊗	TGV 6198		TGV 6922 Ⓐ J	TGV 6924 A⊗		TGV 6926 ⑤	TGV 6918 ⑦ e	TGV 9248		TGV 6928 ⑦ L	TGV 6928 ⑦ M
Grenoble d.	0521	...	0601	...	0725	...	...	1005	1205	...	...	1322	...	1605	...	...	1805	1921	...	2005	2005	...	...	2122	2158
Lyon St Exupéry ✈ a.	|	...	0710	...	0830	...	...	1109	1314	...	...	|	...	1710	...	...	1910	|	...	2110	2110	...	...	|	|
Lyon St Exupéry ✈ d.	|	0647	0713	...	0833	0933	...	1112	1317	...	1417	|	...	1713	1816	...	1913	|	...	2113	2113	2127	...	|	|
Paris Gare de Lyon a.	0819	0841	0907	...	1027	1127	...	1307	1511	...	1611	1619	...	1907	2015	...	2107	2219	...	2307	2307	2319	...	0021	0052

A – Daily except ⑤.
B – ①②③④⑥⑦ to June 14, June 29 - July 12, from Sept. 6 (also June 21, 28, and ⑥⑦ July 19 - Aug. 30).
D – Daily to Aug. 29; Ⓑ from Aug. 30.
E – ①–⑥ to July 3 (not June 1, 20, 27); ⑥ July 4 - Aug. 22 (not July 18); ①–⑥ from Aug. 29 (not Sept. 5).
F – Daily to July 4; ①–⑤ July 6 - Aug. 28 (not July 14); ①–⑥ from Aug. 31.
J – To July 4 / from Aug. 31.
L – ⑦ Sept. 6 - Dec. 6.
M – ⑦ Apr. 5 - Aug. 30 (also June 1).
d – Not July 17 Grenoble - St Exupéry.
e – Also June 1, July 14.
n – Not June 1, July 14.
u – Not June 1, July 14, Sept. 5. Will not run June 20, 27, July 17, 18 Grenoble - St Exupéry.
v – Not June 1, July 14, Nov. 11.
TGV – 🅁, supplement payable, 🍷.
⊙ – Train **6923** on ⑤⑦.
△ – Not June 26.
⊕ – Not June 20, 21, 27, 28, July 17 - 19, Sept. 5, 6 Grenoble - St Exupéry.
⊗ – Subject to alteration June 20, 27, Sept. 5.
§ – Not June 20, 27 Grenoble - St Exupéry.
‡ – Subject to alteration June 20, 27, July 18, Sept. 5.

LYON - GRENOBLE 343

Subject to alteration on June 20, 21, 27, 28, July 17 - 19, Sept. 5, 6

km		⚒		⚒		Ⓐ	◇		◇	Ⓐ	◇	Ⓐ	◇	Ⓐ	◇	Ⓐ	◇	Ⓐ	◇	◇		◇		◇	Ⓐ	◇
0	**Lyon Part-Dieu** . 344 d.	0557	0645	0703	0745	0815	0845	0945	1045	1115	1145	1215	1245	1315	1345	1415	1445	1515	1545	1603	...	1645	1715	1745	1811	1845
41	Bourgoin-Jallieu . 344 d.	0627	0715	0732	0813	|	0913	1013	1115	|	1214	|	1314	|	1413	|	1513	|	1613	1632	...	1713	1745	1815	1836	1912
56	La Tour du Pin... 344 d.	0638	0726	0742	0825	|	0924	1024	1126	|	1224	|	1325	|	1424	|	1525	|	1624	1643	...	1725	1755	1825	|	1924
104	Voiron d.	0711	0755	0815	0855	|	0954	1054	1155	|	1254	|	1354	|	1454	|	1555	|	1654	1714	...	1754	1825	1854	|	1954
129	**Grenoble** a.	0730	0814	0834	0914	0930	1014	1114	1214	1230	1314	1332	1413	1429	1514	1529	1614	1630	1714	1733	...	1814	1846	1914	1930	2014

	Ⓐ		TGV 5333 ⑤ Nf	d	TGV 5123 ①–⑥ Ls	TGV 5335 ⑦ N	d	TGV 5132 ⑦ L	⑤–⑦ P	🚌 Ⓐ
Lyon Part-Dieu .... 344 d.	1915	1945	2037	2045	2111	2137	2145	2207	2245	2310*
Bourgoin-Jallieu .... 344 d.	1943	2013	|	2116	|	|	2215	|	2314	2355
La Tour du Pin...... 344 d.	1954	2023	|	2126	|	|	2227	|	2325	|
Voiron d.	2028	2054	|	2154	|	|	2256	|	2355	|
Grenoble a.	2046	2114	2153	2214	2225	2253	2313	2317	0011	0055

	TGV 5154 ①–⑥ Lm	⚒ u	TGV 5352 ① Ng	TGV 5160 ⑦ Le	◇	Ⓐ	⚒ ◇	Ⓐ	◇	TGV 5364 ⑥ N
Grenoble d.	0451	0455	0532	0540	0544	0615	0642	0712	0742	0811
Voiron d.	|	0515	|	|	0603	0634	0700	|	0800	|
La Tour du Pin .... 344 d.	|	0545	|	|	|	0706	0731	0759	0832	|
Bourgoin-Jallieu .... 344 d.	|	0557	|	|	0642	0717	0743	0810	0844	|
Lyon Part-Dieu .... 344 a.	0604	0629	0650	0653	0712	0746	0812	0842	0912	0920

	Ⓐ	◇	Ⓐ	◇	Ⓐ	◇	Ⓐ	◇	Ⓐ	◇	Ⓐ	◇			Ⓐ		Ⓐ	◇	Ⓐ	◇	Ⓐ	◇	🚌 Ⓐ		b	
Grenoble d.	0826	0842	0926	0942	1026	1042	1126	1142	1226	1242	1326	1344	1442	1542	1625	1642	1723	1742	1823	1842	1926	1942	2015	2042	2142	...
Voiron d.	|	0900	|	1000	|	1100	|	1200	|	1300	|	1401	1500	1600	1642	1700	1742	1800	|	1900	|	2000	|	2100	2200	...
La Tour du Pin..... 344 d.	|	0930	|	1031	|	1132	|	1231	|	1331	|	1431	1531	1631	1713	1730	1814	1831	1910	1931	|	2031	|	2131	2231	...
Bourgoin-Jallieu ... 344 d.	|	0942	|	1043	|	1143	|	1243	|	1343	|	1443	1543	1643	1725	1741	1824	1843	1921	1943	|	2043	|	2142	2243	...
Lyon Part-Dieu ... 344 a.	0942	1012	1042	1112	1142	1212	1242	1312	1342	1412	1442	1512	1612	1712	1759	1812	1859	1912	1946	2012	2042	2112	2145*	2212	2312	...

L – 🚆12 Grenoble - Charles de Gaulle ✈ - Lille Europe and v.v. (Table **11**).
N – 🚆12 Grenoble - Massy - Nantes and v.v. (Table **335**).
P – ⑤–⑦ to June 21 / from Sept. 6 (not June 19).
b – Not June 15 - 20, 22 - 27, ①–④ July 20 - Sept. 3.
d – Not on ①–④ June 15 - 25, July 13 - Sept. 3.
e – Also June 1, July 14.
f – Not on ⑤ July 31 - Aug. 21.
g – Also June 2, July 15; not June 1, July 13.
m – Not June 16 - 20, 23 - 27, July 14, 17 - 25, ⑥ Aug. 1 - Sept. 5.
s – Not June 15 - 18, 20 - 25, July 13 - 16, 18, 20 - 23, July 27 - Sept. 3, Sept. 5.
u – Not June 15 - 27, ⑥ Aug. 1 - 29.
TGV – 🅁, supplement payable, 🍷.
◇ – To / from Dijon (Table **373**).
* – Bus station on eastern side of station (Rue de la Villette).

LYON - CHAMBÉRY - ANNECY 344

km		D△	🚌 ⚒			⚒	⚒		◇	🚌		⊕	⊕	🚌		⚒ d	§		△			△	⊖	
	Lyon Perrache d.	...	...	...	...	...	...	...	...	...	...	...	...	...	...	1316	...	...	...	...	...	...	...	...
0	**Lyon Part Dieu** 343 d.	0631	0638*	...	0738	0741	0841	...	0941	0938*	1038	1038	1138	1138*	1241	1338	1441	1445	1541	...	1638	1641	1738	...
41	Bourgoin-Jallieu 343 d.	0658	|	...	|	0807	0906	...	|	|	|	|	|	|	1305	|	1506	|	|	...	|	1706	|	...
56	La Tour du Pin 343 d.	0709	|	...	|	|	|	...	|	|	|	|	|	|	|	|	|	|	|	...	|	|	|	...
50	Ambérieu ▷ d.	|	|	...	0809	|	|	...	|	|	1109	1109	1212	|	|	|	|	1510	|	...	1709	|	1808	...
•106	**Chambéry** a.	0757	|	...	|	0901	0955	...	1059	|	|	1215r	1311r	|	1356	1450	1559	|	1658	...	|	1755	|	...
•106	**Chambéry** 341 364 d.	...	|	0814	|	...	...	1014	...	|	|	|	|	|	1405	1456	...	|	...	1714	|	...	|	...
•120	Aix les Bains 341 364 a.	...	|	0825	0855	...	...	1025	...	|	1159	1159	1256	|	1416	1507	...	1557	...	1725	1756	...	1854	...
•159	**Annecy** 341 364 a.	...	0830	0908	0933	...	...	1107	...	1130	1245	...	...	1330	1457	1556	...	1642	...	1814	1852	...	1929	...

	B§		§		⚒		🚌 ⑤	🚌 ⑦J
Lyon Perrache d.	...	...	...	...	...	...	...	...
Lyon Part Dieu 343 d.	1741	1841	1941	...	2041	2141	...	2235*
Bourgoin-Jallieu 343 d.	|	|	|	...	|	2209	...	|
La Tour du Pin 343 d.	|	1913	|	...	|	|	...	|
Ambérieu ▷ d.	|	|	|	...	|	|	...	|
Chambéry a.	1859	1956	2059	...	2156	2258	...	|
Chambéry 341 364 d.	...	2004	...	2114	2205	...	2305	|
Aix les Bains 341 364 a.	...	2015	...	2125	2216	...	|	|
Annecy 341 364 a.	...	2055	...	2204	2249	...	2357	0025

		⚒		D§	△				§		🚌 ⚒
Annecy 341 364 d.	...	0523	0609	...	...	0730	...	0800	...	...	0925
Aix les Bains 341 364 d.	...	0601	0644	...	...	0814	...	0835	0914	...	|
Chambéry 341 364 a.	...	|	0655	...	...	|	...	0846	|	...	|
Chambéry d.	0557	|	0701	0735	0801	|	...	...	0901r	...	|
Ambérieu ▷ d.	|	0654	|	|	|	0901	...	...	0959	...	|
La Tour du Pin 343 d.	|	|	|	0817	|	|	...	...	|	...	|
Bourgoin-Jallieu 343 d.	0651	|	0752	0828	0851	|	...	...	|	...	|
Lyon Part Dieu 343 a.	0716	0727	0816	0854	0916	0926	...	...	1026	...	1115*
Lyon Perrache a.	...-	...	...	...	...	...	...	...	...	...	...

	⊗	⊗	△		🚌 Ⓐ	⚒	🚌					▷		▽◇	◇		§	🚌		Ⓑ		△		Ⓑ
Annecy 341 364 d.	...	1039	...	...	1135	...	1235	...	1333	...	1435	...	1500	...	...	1629	...	1735	1815	...	1900	...	1931	...
Aix les Bains 341 364 d.	1116	1116	...	1216	|	...	|	...	1408	...	1516	1516	1535	...	...	1712	...	|	1849	...	1936	...	2013	...
Chambéry 341 364 a.	|	|	...	|	|	...	|	...	|	...	|	|	1546	...	...	|	...	|	|	...	1946	...	|	...
Chambéry d.	1101r	|	1159	1204r	|	1301	|	1401	|	...	|	1501r	...	1601	1701	|	1801	|	|	1901	...	2001	|	2101
Ambérieu ▷ d.	1201	1201	|	1300	|	|	|	|	1453	...	1601	1601	...	|	|	1800	|	|	1940	|	...	|	2101	|
La Tour du Pin 343 d.	|	|	|	|	|	|	|	|	|	...	|	|	...	|	|	|	|	|	|	|	...	2044	|	|
Bourgoin-Jallieu 343 d.	|	|	1251	|	|	|	|	1452	|	...	|	|	...	1652	|	|	1852	|	|	|	...	|	|	|
Lyon Part Dieu 343 a.	1226	1226	1316	1323	1330*	1416	1430*	1516	1517	...	1626	1626	...	1716	1816	1826	1916	1930*	2006	2016	...	2116	2126	2221
Lyon Perrache a.	1247	1247	...	...	...	...	...	...	...	...	...	...	...	...	...	...	...	...	...	...	...	...	...	...

B – Ⓑ (daily June 21 - Sept. 4).
D – ⚒ (daily June 22 - Sept. 6).
J – To June 21 / from Sept. 6 (not Oct. 25).
d – Subject to alteration on June 6.
r – Via Aix les Bains.
z – Subject to alteration on Ⓐ Oct. 12 - 23.
◇ – To / from Dijon (Table **373**).
△ – To / from Modane (Table **367**).
▽ – From Modane on dates in Table **367**.
▷ – Subject to alteration on Ⓐ June 22 - July 10.
⊖ – To Annemasse and Évian les Bains (Tables **365** / **363**).
⊕ – Subject to alteration on Ⓐ June 15 - July 6, Oct. 12 - 23.
⊗ – On Ⓐ June 10 - 19, July 7 - 10 will not call at Part Dieu.
§ – To / from Bourg St Maurice (Table **365**).
• – Distances via Ambérieu: Chambéry *138 km*, Aix les Bains *124 km*, Annecy *163 km*.
* – Eastern side of station (Rue de la Villette).

345 LYON - BELLEGARDE - GENÈVE

Certain trains convey through portions Lyon - Bellegarde - Annemasse - St Gervais (see Table **365**)

km														*TGV*	⊖	⊖				*TGV*			*TGV*	
				4678 4679										**6866**						**6886**			**6874**	
		①–⑤	①–⑤	®Z		①–⑤	⚒		d	①–⑤	b			M	Ⓐ	Ⓒ	Ⓒy	①–⑤		N			L	
0	**Lyon Part Dieu** 344 d.	...	...	0651	0704	...	0804	0904	1104	...	1304	...	1504	1556	1704	1704	...	...	...	1804	1904	2004	2056	...
50	Ambérieu 344 d.	...	...	|	0730	...	0829	0929	1130	...	1329	...	1530	|	1731	1730	...	...	...	|	1930	2032	|	...
102	Culoz d.	...	...	|	0804	...	0902	1002	1202	...	1402	...	1602	|	1805	1807	...	...	...	|	2003	2106	|	...
135	Bellegarde 341 364 d.	0618	0645	|	0830	0845	0929	1028	1228	1346	1428	1507	1628	1712	1830	1827	1830	1848	1905	1917	2028	2132	2207	...
168	**Genève** 341 364 a.	0654	0726	0837	0857	0926	0957	1057	1257	1426	1457	1532	1657	1735	1857v	...	1857	1926	1932	1942	2057	2157	2233	...

				TGV						*TGV*				*TGV*										**4778**
				6806						**6816**				**6818**										**4779**
	⚒		①–⑤	L	Ⓐ	Ⓒ	Ⓒ		h	M	Ⓐ	①–⑤		N					①–⑤	Ⓐ	①–⑤			®Y
Genève 341 364 d.	0558	0658	0735	0817	0858	0858	...	1017	1058	1117	1142	1205	1258	1344	1358	1417	1624	1658	1735	1817	1838	1858	1958	2044
Bellegarde 341 364 d.	0628	0729	0812	0848	0928	0923	0928	1047	1126	1145	1222	1251	1328	1411	1425	1446	1653	1728	1811	1846	1914	1932	2027	|
Culoz d.	0649	0752	...	|	0955	...	0956	...	1147	|	...	...	1351	|	1451	...	...	1750	...	...	...	1954	2051	|
Ambérieu 344 d.	0724	0823	...	|	1036	...	1036	...	1223	|	...	...	1423	|	1523	...	...	1823	...	...	...	2023	2123	|
Lyon Part Dieu 344 a.	0751	0847	...	1001	1102	...	1107	...	1247	1255	...	...	1447	1531	1553	...	...	1847	...	...	...	2047	2147	2245

L – (12) Genève - Lyon - Marseille and v.v. (Table **350**).
M – (12) Genève - Lyon - Montpellier and v.v. (Table **350**).
N – (12) Genève - Lyon - Marseille - Nice and v.v. (Table **350**).
Y – 1, 2 cl. and (2) (reclining) Genève - Lyon - Toulouse - Irún. For days of running see Table **355**.

Z – 1, 2 cl. and (2) (reclining) Hendaye - Toulouse - Lyon - Genève. For days of running see Table **355**.
b – Subject to alteration on ①–⑤ June 22 - July 10.
d – Not on ①–⑤ June 15 - July 10.
h – Subject to alteration on ①–⑤ June 8 - July 10 (also June 5).
v – Ⓐ to June 19 / from Sept. 7.

y – ⑥ (also ⑦ to June 14 / from Sept. 13), also June 14, Nov. 11.
TGV – ®, supplement payable, 🍷.
⊖ – From Lyon Perrache, depart 1650.

346 MÂCON - BOURG EN BRESSE - AMBÉRIEU - (LYON)

Mostly 2nd class

km																										
		②–⑤	🚌	Ⓐ	🚌	🚌 Ⓐ	Ⓐ	🚌 ⑥t	Ⓐ	🚌 ⚒	🚌	🚌	Ⓐ	🚌	🚌 ⑥t	Ⓐ	🚌	🚌	Ⓐ	🚌 ⑥t	🚌 Ⓐ	Ⓐ	🚌	🚌	🚌	🚌
0	**Mâcon Ville** d.	...	...	*0655*	0710	0725	...	...	0810	...	0925	...	1156c	...	1255	1310	1455	...	1648	1655	...	1755	...	1855	...	2055
37	Bourg en Bresse ▷ d.	0653	0712	0730	0815	0805	0827	0827	0841	0927	1025	1027	1224	1312	1350	1340	1555	1627	1724	1750	1825	1826	1827	1955	2027	2150
68	Ambérieu ▷ a.	0711	0750	0750	...	...	0850	0905	...	1005	...	1105	1248	1350	...	...	...	1705	1750	...	1855	...	1905	...	2105	...
118	**Lyon Part-Dieu** ▷ a.	0747	...	0826	...	...	...	...	...	...	...	...	...	...	...	...	...	...	...	...	...	...	...	...	...	...

	🚌 Ⓐ	h	🚌 ⑥t	Ⓐd	🚌	h	Ⓐ	🚌 ⑥t	Ⓐ	🚌 ⑥t	🚌	🚌	Ⓐz	🚌	🚌 ⑥t	Ⓐ	Ⓐ	🚌	🚌	Ⓐ	Ⓐ	H	🚌	🚌	🚌	⚒
Lyon Part-Dieu ▷ d.	...	...	...	...	...	...	...	...	...	...	...	...	...	...	...	...	...	...	...	...	...	1838	...	...	...	2112
Ambérieu ▷ d.	...	...	0700	0707	0800	...	0916	0917	...	...	1217	...	1317	1417	...	...	...	...	1717	...	1817	1908	...	1917	2117	2154
Bourg en Bresse ▷ d.	0640	0731	0740	0734	0842	0932	0940	0957	1231	1232	1257	1332	1341	1457	1532	1612	1713	1732	1757	1832	1840	1927	1932	1957	2157	2212
Mâcon Ville a.	0715	0804	...	...	...	1004	...	...	1303	1335	...	1435	...	...	1635	1644	1746	1835	...	1904	...	...	2030	...	...	...

H – ①–④ (not June 1, July 14).
a – Ⓐ only.
c – By 🚌 (depart 1114) on Ⓐ June 22 - July 3.
d – To Dijon (see panel to right).
e – Also June 1, July 14.
h – By 🚌 on Ⓒ (arrive Mâcon Ville 30 minutes later).
t – Not Aug. 15.
z – By 🚌 (arrive 1357) to June 19, also Oct. 12-23.

km		⚒		⚒	Ⓐ		
0	Dijon d.	0645	0941	1249	1728	1756	1924
86	Louhans d.	0758	1052	1404	1843	1856	2039
140	Bourg en Bresse a.	0830	1124	1436	1917	1930	2112
171	Ambérieu a.	...	...	...	1944	...	...

	Ⓐ		⚒		Ⓑ
Ambérieu d.	...	0707a	...	...	...
Bourg en Bresse d.	0534	0736	1136	1720	1839
Louhans d.	0608	0810	1215	1754	1913
Dijon a.	0716	0912	1335	1855	2009

▷ – Lyon - Ambérieu: see also Tables **344**/**345**. Lyon - Bourg en Bresse: see also Tables **353** and **384**.

347 LYON - ST ÉTIENNE

km	*TGV* trains convey 🍷												*TGV*													
			⚒	⚒	⚒	⚒		⚒	Ⓐ	Ⓐ		Ⓐ	**6681** P		Ⓐ		Ⓐ		Ⓐ			Ⓐ		⚒		Ⓐ
	Paris ▽ **340** d.	...	...	...	...	...	...	...	...	...	...	...	0654	...	...	...	...	...	...	...	...	...	...	...	...	...
0	**Lyon Part-Dieu** d.	0019	0619	...	0649	...	0719	...	0749	...	0819	0849	0858	0919	0949	1019	1049	1119	1149	1219	...	1249	1319	1349	1419	1449
	Lyon Perrache d.	|	|	0636	|	0706	|	0733	|	0806	|	|	|	|	|	|	|	|	|	|	1236	|	|	|	|	|
22	Givors Ville d.	0039	0638	0654	0708	0724	0739	0754	0808	0824	0838	0909	|	0938	1009	1038	1108	1138	1208	1238	1254	1308	1339	1409	1439	1508
47	St Chamond d.	0059	0658	0715	0728	0745	0759	0815	0828	0844	0858	0928	|	0958	1028	1057	1128	1158	1228	1258	1318	1328	1358	1428	1458	1528
59	**St Étienne** ⊙ a.	0108	0708	0724	0738	0754	0808	0824	0838	0854	0908	0938	0941	1008	1038	1108	1138	1208	1238	1310	1329	1338	1408	1438	1508	1538

	TGV															*TGV*							*TGV*			
	6685		Ⓐ	Ⓐ			Ⓑ	Ⓑ			Ⓐ	Ⓐ			Ⓐ	**6687**	Ⓐ			Ⓐ		Ⓑ	**6689**		Ⓑ	
Paris ▽ **340** d.	1254	...	...	...	...	...	...	...	...	...	...	...	...	...	...	1654	...	...	...	...	...	...	1854	...	...	...
Lyon Part-Dieu d.	1458	1519	1549	...	1619	...	1649	...	1719	...	1749	...	1819	...	1849	1900	...	1919	...	1949	2019	2049	2058	2119	2219	2319
Lyon Perrache d.	|	|	|	1606	|	1636	|	1706	|	1736	|	1806	|	1836	|	|	1906	|	1936	|	|	|	|	|	|	|
Givors Ville d.	|	1539	1609	1625	1639	1655	1708	1724	1739	1754	1808	1824	1839	1854	1908	|	1924	1939	1954	2008	2038	2108	|	2139	2238	2338
St Chamond d.	|	1559	1628	1649	1659	1719	1728	1745	1759	1815	1828	1845	1859	1915	1928	|	1945	1959	2015	2028	2058	2128	|	2158	2258	2358
St Étienne ⊙ a.	1541	1608	1638	1700	1708	1731	1738	1754	1808	1824	1838	1854	1908	1924	1938	1941	1954	2008	2024	2038	2108	2138	2141	2208	2308	0008

			TGV																*TGV*					*TGV*		
	⚒		**6691** P	⚒	Ⓐ		⚒	⚒	Ⓐ	⚒		⚒	Ⓐ	⚒		⚒	Ⓐ		**6693**	Ⓐ				**6695**	⚒	
St Étienne ⊙ d.	0518	0548	0615	0618	0631	0648	0701	0718	0731	0735	0748	0801	0818	0831	0848	0901	0918	0948	1014	1018	1048	1118	1148	1214	1218	1248
St Chamond d.	0528	0559	|	0629	0641	0658	0711	0729	0741	0746	0759	0810	0830	0840	0857	0910	0929	0959	|	1029	1057	1129	1158	|	1228	1259
Givors Ville d.	0550	0620	|	0650	0703	0719	0732	0750	0802	0807	0820	0832	0850	0902	0919	0932	0950	1020	|	1050	1119	1150	1220	|	1250	1320
Lyon Perrache a.	|	|	|	|	0723	|	0750	|	0820	|	|	0850	|	0920	|	0950	|	|	|	|	|	|	|	|	|	|
Lyon Part-Dieu a.	0608	0638	0654	0708	...	0738	...	0808	...	0826	0838	...	0908	...	0938	...	1008	1038	1054	1108	1138	1208	1238	1254	1308	1338
Paris ▽ **340** a.	...	...	0857	...	...	...	...	...	...	...	...	...	...	...	...	...	...	...	1257	...	...	...	...	1505	...	...

																TGV										
		Ⓐ	◇	Ⓐ		Ⓐ	Ⓐ	Ⓐ	Ⓐ				Ⓐ			**6697**	Ⓐ		Ⓑ		Ⓑ		Ⓑ			
St Étienne ⊙ d.	1301	1318	1348	1418	1448	1518	1613	1618	1631	1648	1701	1718	1731	1748	1801	1814	1818	1831	1848	1901	1918	1948	2018	2048	2118	2218
St Chamond d.	1311	1329	1359	1429	1459	1529	|	1629	1640	1659	1710	1729	1741	1759	1811	|	1829	1840	1859	1911	1929	1959	2029	2059	2129	2229
Givors Ville d.	1332	1349	1420	1450	1520	1550	|	1650	1702	1720	1732	1750	1802	1820	1832	|	1850	1902	1920	1932	1951	2020	2048	2120	2150	2250
Lyon Perrache a.	1350	|	|	|	|	|	|	|	1720	|	1750	|	1820	|	1850	|	|	1920	|	1950	|	|	|	|	|	|
Lyon Part-Dieu a.	...	1408	1438	1508	1538	1608	1654	1708	...	1738	...	1808	...	1838	...	1854	1908	...	1938	...	2008	2038	2108	2138	2208	2308
Paris ▽ **340** a.	...	...	...	...	...	...	...	...	...	...	...	...	...	...	...	2057	...	...	...	...	...	...	...	...	...	...

P – ①–⑥ (not June 1, July 14).
TGV – ®, supplement payable, 🍷.

◇ – From Le Puy en Velay (Table **348**).
▽ – Paris Gare de Lyon.
⊙ – St Étienne Châteaucreux.

Additional journeys: Lyon Perrache - St Étienne 0536 Ⓐ; St Étienne - Lyon Perrache 0531 ⚒, 0601 ⚒, 1548 Ⓐ.

348 ST ÉTIENNE - LE PUY

km		⚒		⚒					Ⓐ		
	Lyon Part Dieu **347** d.	...	...	...	...	...	...	...	...	...	...
0	**St Étienne** ⊙ d.	0612	0813	0953	1222	1553	1713	1818	1913	2019	2152
15	Firminy d.	0630	0831	1012	1240	1611	1735	1836	1935	2037	2214
88	**Le Puy en Velay** a.	0741	0938	1116	1354	1720	1836	1949	2039	2138	2315

	⚒	Ⓐ	†	⚒			⚒	Ⓑ		†
Le Puy en Velay d.	0603	0746	0806	0837	1039	1209	1617	1735	1841	1911
Firminy d.	0713	0852	0913	0943	1144	1321	1725	1856	1953	2016
St Étienne ⊙ a.	0738	0909	0931	1000	1201	1343	1743	1912	2010	2034
Lyon Part Dieu **347** a.	...	...	...	...	...	1438	...	...	...	2138

⊙ – St Étienne Châteaucreux.

Additional journeys: Le Puy - St Étienne 0445 Ⓐ, 0535 Ⓐ.

BORDEAUX - BERGERAC - SARLAT - SOUILLAC — 349

Some trains 2nd class

km		① Jy	Ⓐ	⑥ Kt	⚒ z		⚒	†	Ⓐ K	Ⓐ J▽	Ⓒ J	Ⓒ K	Ⓐ	Ⓐ ▽	⊗			Ⓐ ▷		Ⓐ w		⚒	⑤		Ⓑ
0	**Bordeaux St Jean 300/2** d.	...	0556	...	0706	...	0800	0833	...	...	1042	1041	1226	...	1334	...	1604	1651	...	1729	1811	1919	2036	...	2145
37	Libourne **300/2** d.	...	0625	...	0745	...	0829	0911	1107	1117	1117	1117	1251	1257	1403	...	1631	1723	...	1813	1845	1949	2108	...	2215
99	Bergerac d.	0550	0727	0727	0849	...	0915	1006	1208	1205	1205	1224	...	1356	1449	...	1724	1818	...	1919	1933	2040	2202	...	2300
135	Le Buisson a.	0630	0805	0806	0921	...	...	1040	1245	1240	1240	1302	...	...	1521	...	1803	...	...	...	2008	...	2236	...	...
135	Le Buisson d.	0631	0816	0807	0922	...	...	1048	1246	1241	1241	1303	...	...	1522	...	1805x	...	...	...	2013	...	2237	...	...
168	**Sarlat** a.	0715	0900	0851	1004	...	...	1130	1330	1323	1323	1346	...	...	1604	...	1848x	...	...	...	2055	...	2319	...	...

	① g	⚒		Ⓐ z	① b	②–⑤ d	⑥ t				†	Ⓐ ▽	Ⓒ J	Ⓐ J▽	Ⓐ	Ⓒ K	Ⓐ K	Ⓐ ▽	E▽	Ⓒ K		Ⓑ h			⑤⑦ u
Sarlat d.	...	...	...	...	0527	0601	...	...	0729	...	...	...	1015	1015	...	1010	1010	...	1205	1226	1607	...	...	1735	1941
Le Buisson a.	...	...	...	...	0611	0644	...	...	0810	...	...	...	1056	1056	...	1053	1053	...	1247	1308	1647	...	...	1818	2021
Le Buisson d.	...	...	...	...	0645	0645	...	...	0813	...	...	...	1057	1057	...	1054	1054	...	1252	1309	1648	...	...	1819	2022
Bergerac d.	0520	0601	...	0642	0726	0726	0725	...	0852	...	1013	1013	1131	1131	...	1136	1136	1215	1330	1347	1721	1819	...	1857	2055
Libourne **300/2** a.	0606	0653	...	0741	0816	0816	0816	...	0939	...	1102	1102	1217	1217	1222	1222	1222	1312	1418	1434	1811	1917	...	1947	2141
Bordeaux St Jean 300/2 a.	0632	0725	...	0810	0847	0847	0845	...	1009	...	1130	...	1245	...	1249	1255	...	1341	1450	1502	1840	1953	...	2032	2208

km	By 🚌 §	① s		③ s	†	H	⑥ v	Ⓐ s		†	
0	**Sarlat** d.	0802	1219	1310	1552	1638	1737	1815	...	1858	...
30	**Souillac** a.	0843	1300	1352	1633	1720	1818	1857	...	1939	...

By 🚌 §	Ⓐ s		⑥ t				⑤ s	⑦ s		⑦ K
Souillac d.	0645	...	0910	...	1501	...	1843	1843	...	2142
Sarlat a.	0726	...	0951	...	1539	...	1921	1921	...	2222

E – Ⓐ (daily to July 4 / from Aug. 31).
H – ①②④⑤ (school term only).
J – To July 4 / from Aug. 31.
K – July 5 - Aug. 30.
b – Also June 2; not June 1, July 6 - Aug. 24.
d – Also ① July 6 - Aug. 24; not June 1, 2, July 14, Nov. 11.
g – Also June 2; not June 1, July 6 - Aug. 24, Nov. 2 - Dec. 7.
h – Also Aug. 15.

s – School term only.
t – Not Aug. 15.
u – ⑤⑦ (daily July 5 - Aug. 29).
v – ⑥ (also ⚒ July 2 - Sept. 2).
w – Also runs on ⑥ July 11 - Aug. 29.
x – On ⑤ Le Buisson d. 1828, Sarlat a. 1910.
y – Also June 2; not June 1.
z – Subject to alteration on ① Nov. 2 - Dec. 7.

▽ – Subject to alteration Sept. 28 - Oct. 2.
▷ – Subject to alteration on ②–④ Nov. 2 - Dec. 10.
⊗ – By 🚌 Libourne - Bergerac Sept. 28 - Oct. 2.
§ – Rail tickets not valid. Most journeys continue beyond the SNCF stations to and from the town centres of Sarlat and Souillac.

PARIS and LYON - MONTPELLIER, MARSEILLE and NICE via high-speed line — 350

TGV Méditerranée

km	All *TGV* trains are 🅁	*TGV* 6831 ① g	*TGV* 6815 Ⓐ ⊕	*TGV* 5355 Ⓑ	*TGV* 6803 ⑥	*TGV* 6801 Ⓐ	*TGV* 6805 Ⓒ	*TGV* 6101 Ⓐ	*TGV* 6201 Ⓐ	*TGV* 6813	*TGV* 6133 Ⓐ	*TGV* 6811 Ⓒ	*TGV* 6103	*TGV* 5301 A	*TGV* 6203	*TGV* 5102	*TGV* 6171	*TGV* 9804 Ⓐ	*TGV* 5104 Ⓒ	*TGV* 6105	*TGV* 6205	*TGV* 6807	*TGV* 6809 Ⓐ ⊡u	*TGV* 6165 K
	Brussels Midi **11** d.	...	...	...	...	...	...	...	...	...	...	...	...	...	...	...	...	0540	...	...	...	...	...	...
	Lille Europe **11** d.	...	...	...	...	...	...	...	...	...	...	...	...	...	...	0559	...	0625	0625	...	...	...	...	...
	Charles de Gaulle ✈ d.	...	...	...	...	...	...	...	...	...	...	...	...	...	...	0654	...	0725	0725	...	...	...	...	...
	Marne la Vallée-Chessy § d.	...	...	...	...	...	...	...	...	...	...	...	...	...	...	0710	...	0740	0740	...	...	...	...	...
0	**Paris Gare de Lyon** d.	...	...	...	...	...	...	0616	0620	...	0642	...	0716	...	0720	|	0746	|	|	0816	0820	...	...	0846
	Genève **345** d.	...	...	...	...	...	...	|	|	...	|	...	|	...	|	|	|	|	|	|	|	0817	...	|
	Dijon **373** d.	...	...	...	...	0549	...	|	|	0616x	|	0645	|	...	|	|	|	|	|	|	|	|	...	|
△	**Lyon Part Dieu** d.	0050p	0635	0710	0711	0737	0737	|	|	0811	|	0837	|	...	|	0907	|	0937	0937	|	|	1007	1015	|
527	Valence TGV d.	|	|	|	|	0815	0816	|	0834	|	|	0915	|	...	|	|	|	1014	1014	|	1034	|	1052	|
657	**Avignon TGV** d.	|	0741	|	|	0851	|	0859	|	|	|	0951	0958	1005	|	1012	1027	|	|	|	|	1113	1127	1129
686	Nîmes **355** d.	|	|	0831	0831	|	|	|	0919	0930	|	|	|	|	1013	|	|	1100	1100	|	1120	|	|	|
736	**Montpellier 355** a.	|	|	0855	0855	|	|	|	0944	0959	|	|	|	|	1038	|	|	1128	1128	|	1145	|	|	|
	Sète **355** a.	|	|	|	|	|	|	|	...	...	|	|	|	|	1057	|	|	|	|	|	...	|	|	|
	Agde **355** a.	|	|	|	|	|	|	|	...	...	|	|	|	|	1112	|	|	|	|	|	...	|	|	|
	Béziers **355** a.	|	|	0941	0941	|	|	|	...	...	|	|	|	|	1125	|	|	1213	1213	|	...	|	|	|
	Narbonne **355** a.	|	|	0959	0959	|	|	|	...	...	|	|	|	|	1141	|	|	1235	1235	|	...	|	|	|
	Toulouse **321** a.	|	|	1121	|	|	|	|	...	...	|	|	|	|	|	|	|	1356	1355	|	...	|	|	|
	Perpignan 355 a.	|	|	...	1037	|	|	|	...	...	|	|	|	|	1216	|	|	...	...	|	...	|	|	|
731	Aix en Provence TGV d.	|	0805	...	...	|	|	0922	...	...	0943	|	1024	1029	...	1036	|	...	...	|	...	1136	|	|
750	**Marseille St Charles** a.	|	0817	...	...	0920	0917	0933	...	...	|	1021	1035	1041	...	1047	|	...	...	1118	...	1147	1156	|
750	**Marseille St Charles 360** d.	|	0829	...	...	...	0929	...	...	...	|	...	...	...	...	1059	|	...	...	1129	...	...	...	|
817	**Toulon 360** a.	0539	0908	...	...	...	1009	...	...	...	1036	...	...	...	...	1138	|	...	...	1210	...	...	...	1233
885	Les Arcs-Draguignan **360** a.	0614	|	...	...	...	|	...	...	...	...	...	...	...	...	1213	1205	...	...	...	...	...	...	|
911	St Raphaël-Valescure **360** a.	0632	1001	...	...	...	1102	...	...	...	...	...	...	...	...	1231	1222	...	...	...	...	...	...	1321
944	Cannes **360** a.	0656	1025	...	...	...	1127	...	...	...	...	...	...	...	...	1255	1247	...	...	...	...	...	...	1346
955	Antibes **360** a.	0709	1037	...	...	...	1139	...	...	...	...	...	...	...	...	1307	1258	...	...	...	...	...	...	1358
975	**Nice 360** a.	0730	1055	...	...	...	1155	...	...	...	...	...	...	...	...	1325	1317	...	...	...	...	...	...	1417

	TGV 5110	*TGV* 6107 ①–⑥ n	*TGV* 6207	*TGV* 6173	*TGV* 5148 M‡	*TGV* 9928 T	*TGV* 5112	*TGV* 6109 ◇	*TGV* 5312 N	*TGV* 5311 N	*TGV* 5316 H	*TGV* 6111	*TGV* 6209	*TGV* 6816	*TGV* 6175 w	*TGV* 5405 S	*TGV* 9826	*TGV* 5164	*TGV* 5318 R	*TGV* 6113	*TGV* 6211	*TGV* 9832	*TGV* 5115	*TGV* 6177
Brussels Midi **11** d.	...	...	...	...	...	0819	...	...	...	...	...	...	...	...	...	...	1021	...	...	...	...	1110	...	...
Lille Europe **11** d.	0643c	...	...	...	...	|	0828	...	...	...	...	...	...	...	...	...	|	1030	...	...	...	1156	1156	...
Charles de Gaulle ✈ d.	0821	...	...	...	...	|	0925	...	...	...	...	...	...	...	...	...	1143	1143	...	...	...	1258	1258	...
Marne la Vallée-Chessy § d.	0835	...	...	...	...	|	0940	...	...	...	...	...	...	...	...	...	1156	1156	...	...	...	1311	1311	...
Paris Gare de Lyon d.	|	0916	0920	0946	...	|	|	1016	...	...	...	1116	1120	...	1146	...	|	|	...	1316	1320	|	|	1346
Genève **345** d.	|	|	|	|	...	|	|	|	...	...	...	|	|	1117	|	...	|	|	...	|	|	|	|	|
Dijon **373** d.	|	|	|	|	0916	|	|	|	...	...	...	|	|	|	|	...	|	|	...	|	|	|	|	|
Lyon Part Dieu d.	1037	|	|	|	1107	|	1137	|	1207	1211	1237	|	|	1307	|	1323	|	|	1337	|	|	1507	1511	|
Valence TGV d.	1114	|	|	|	|	1200	1216	|	|	|	1315	|	1334	1346	|	|	1407	1407	1414	|	1534	1546	|	|
Avignon TGV d.	1148	1159	|	|	1216	1234	|	|	1312	|	1350	1359	|	|	|	1433	1442	1442	1449	1559	|	|	|	1630
Nîmes **355** d.	|	|	1220	|	|	|	1301	|	|	1330	|	|	1418	1432	|	|	|	|	|	|	1619	1632	|	|
Montpellier 355 a.	|	|	1247	|	|	|	1326	|	|	1355	|	|	1442	1457	|	|	|	|	|	|	1644	1657	|	|
Sète **355** a.	|	|	...	|	|	|	...	|	|	...	|	|	1501	...	|	|	|	|	|	|	1705s	1721	|	|
Agde **355** a.	|	|	...	|	|	|	...	|	|	...	|	|	1517	...	|	|	|	|	|	|	1720s	1737	|	|
Béziers **355** a.	|	|	...	|	|	|	...	|	|	...	|	|	1531	...	|	|	|	|	|	|	1735s	1751	|	|
Narbonne **355** a.	|	|	...	|	|	|	...	|	|	...	|	|	1547	...	|	|	|	|	|	|	1751s	1807	|	|
Toulouse **321** a.	|	|	...	|	|	|	...	|	|	...	|	|	|	...	|	|	|	|	|	|	|	|	|	|
Perpignan 355 a.	|	|	...	|	|	|	...	|	|	...	|	|	1625	...	|	|	|	|	|	|	1827s	1844	|	|
Aix en Provence TGV d.	1213	1222	...	1246	|	1258	...	|	1335	...	|	1422	...	...	1446	1457	1505	1505	1512	1622	...	...	1636	|
Marseille St Charles a.	1225	1235	...	|	1247	1315	...	1321	1346	...	1418	1435	...	...	|	1513	1516	1516	1523	1634	...	...	1647	|
Marseille St Charles 360 d.	...	...	...	|	1259	...	...	1333	...	...	...	...	...	...	|	...	1529	1529	...	...	...	...	...	|
Toulon 360 a.	...	...	...	|	1339	...	...	1412	...	...	...	...	...	...	1533	...	1608	1608	...	...	...	...	...	1733
Les Arcs-Draguignan **360** a.	...	...	...	1405	|	...	...	...	...	...	...	...	...	...	|	...	1646	1646	...	...	...	...	...	1809z
St Raphaël-Valescure **360** a.	...	...	...	1422	1432	...	...	...	...	...	...	...	...	...	1622	...	1702	1702	...	...	...	...	...	1823
Cannes **360** a.	...	...	...	1446	1457	...	...	...	...	...	...	...	...	...	1647	...	1726	1726	...	...	...	...	...	1848
Antibes **360** a.	...	...	...	1457	1509	...	...	...	...	...	...	...	...	...	1659	...	1737	1737	...	...	...	...	...	1859
Nice 360 a.	...	...	...	1515	1528	...	...	...	...	...	...	...	...	...	1717	...	1755	1755	...	...	...	...	...	1917

A – [12] Toulouse - Montpellier - Marseille (Table **355**).
H – [12] Le Havre - Rouen - Lyon - Marseille (Table **335**).
K – July 5 - Aug. 30.
M – From Metz d. 0611, Nancy d. 0651 (Table **379**).
N – From Nantes via Massy TGV (Table **335**).
R – From Rennes via Massy TGV (Table **335**).
S – From Strasbourg (Table **384**).
T – ⑥ June 27 - Aug. 29. *Thalys* train. Calls at Valence, Avignon and Aix to set down only.

c – Lille **Flandres**. Depart 0647 on certain ⑥.
g – Also June 2, July 15; not June 1, July 13.
n – Not June 1, July 14.
p – Lyon **Perrache**.
s – July 5 - Aug. 30.
u – On Ⓐ July 6 - Aug. 28 Valence a. 1052 / d. 1101, Avignon TGV d. 1143, Marseille a. 1215.
w – To Ventimiglia (Table **360**).
x – ①⑥ (also June 2, July 15; not June 1, July 13).

z – Calls Sept. 20 - Dec. 12 only.
TGV – 🅁, supplement payable, 🍸.
◇ – To Hyères (Table **352**).
⊡ – From Melun (Table **370**).
§ – Station for Disneyland Paris.
‡ – On July 8, 9, 28 - 30, Sept. 14 - 18 depart Dijon 0910.
△ – Distance Lyon Part Dieu - Valence TGV = *104 km*.
⊕ – Will not run Marseille - Nice on June 8 - 26, Nov. 9 - 13.

350 PARIS and LYON - MONTPELLIER, MARSEILLE and NICE via high-speed line *TGV Méditerranée*

All *TGV* trains are 🅁	*TGV* 6115	*TGV* 6818	*TGV* 9828	*TGV* 6821	*TGV* 6117	*TGV* 6213	*TGV* 5117	*TGV* 6179	*TGV* 5322	*TGV* 6119	*TGV* 6231	*TGV* 6829	*TGV* 5118	*TGV* 6121	*TGV* 5326	*TGV* 6123	*TGV* 6215	*TGV* 9834	*TGV* 5385	*TGV* 5398	*TGV* 6181	*TGV* 5346	*TGV* 6127	*TGV* 6187
											Ⓐ				⑤⑥							①–④		⑤
							B	L	N	△	J				R				Q	A		Rn	Z	
Brussels Midi **11** d.	...	...	1209	...	...	...	...	...	...	...	...	...	...	...	...	...	...	1509	...	...	...	...	...	...
Lille Europe **11** d.	...	...	1254	...	...	...	...	...	...	...	...	...	1454o	...	...	...	...	1557	...	...	...	...	...	...
Charles de Gaulle ✈ d.	...	...	1352	...	...	...	...	...	...	...	...	...	1553	...	...	...	...	1652	...	...	...	...	...	...
Marne la Vallée-Chessy § d.	...	...	1407	...	...	...	...	...	...	...	...	...	1610	...	...	...	...	1710	...	...	...	...	...	...
Paris Gare de Lyon d.	1416	...	|	...	1516	1520	...	1546	...	1616	1620	...	|	1646	...	1716	1720	|	...	...	1742	...	1816	1816
Genève **345** d.	|	1344	|	...	|	|	...	|	...	|	|	...	|	|	...	|	|	|	...	...	|	...	|	|
Dijon **373** d.	|	|	|	...	|	|	1516y	|	...	|	|	1611	|	|	...	|	|	|	...	...	|	...	|	|
Lyon Part Dieu d.	|	1537	1607	1637	|	|	1707	|	1737	|	|	1803	1807	|	1837	|	|	1907	1911	...	|	1937	|	|
Valence TGV d.	|	|	|	1716	|	1735	1745	|	1814	|	1834	1844	|	|	1914	|	1935	|	|	...	|	2014	|	|
Avignon TGV d.	|	1646	1712	|	1759	|	|	|	1849	|	|	|	|	1929	1948	1959	|	2013	|	2014	|	2049	|	|
Nîmes **355** d.	|	|	|	|	|	|	1833	|	|	|	1920	|	1930	|	|	|	2020	|	2030	2034	|	|	|	|
Montpellier 355 a.	|	|	|	|	|	1841	1857	|	|	|	1944	|	1959	|	|	|	2044	|	2057	2101	|	|	|	|
Sète **355** a.	|	|	|	|	|	1900	|	|	|	|	...	|	2013	|	|	|	2103	|	|	2119	|	|	|	|
Agde **355** a.	|	|	|	|	|	1915	|	|	|	|	...	|	2030	|	|	|	2118	|	|	|	|	|	|	|
Béziers **355** a.	|	|	|	|	|	1929	1940	|	|	|	...	|	2044	|	|	|	2131	|	2138	2144	|	|	|	|
Narbonne **355** a.	|	|	|	|	|	1944	1955	|	|	|	...	|	2101	|	|	|	2147	|	2155	2201	|	|	|	|
Toulouse **321** a.	|	|	|	|	|	|	2112	|	|	|	...	|	|	|	|	|	|	|	2309	2321	|	|	|	|
Perpignan 355 a.	|	|	|	|	|	2021	...	|	|	|	...	|	2135	|	|	|	2223	|	...	...	|	|	|	|
Aix en Provence TGV d.	|	|	1736	1811	1822	...	...	1845	|	|	...	|	...	|	2011	2022	...	2036	...	...	2045	|	|	|
Marseille St Charles a.	1721	1717	1747	1825	1834	...	...	|	1918	1922	...	1942	...	1958	2024	2034	...	2047	...	...	|	2117	2121	2121
Marseille St Charles 360 d.	...	1729	...	...	...	...	...	|	...	1933	...	1959	...	...	...	...	...	2059r	...	...	|	...	...	2133
Toulon 360 a.	...	1808	...	...	...	...	...	|	...	2012	...	2038	...	...	...	...	...	2140r	...	...	2133	...	...	2212
Les Arcs-Draguignan **360** a.	...	|	...	...	...	...	...	2007	...	...	...	|	...	...	...	...	...	...	...	...	|	...	...	|
St Raphaël-Valescure **360** a.	...	1901	...	...	...	...	...	2025	...	...	...	2131	...	...	...	...	...	...	...	...	2222	...	...	2300
Cannes **360** a.	...	1926	...	...	...	...	...	2049	...	...	...	2155	...	...	...	...	...	...	...	...	2246	...	...	2325
Antibes **360** a.	...	1937	...	...	...	...	...	2100	...	...	...	2207	...	...	...	...	...	...	...	...	2257	...	...	2336
Nice 360 a.	...	1955	...	...	...	...	...	2117	...	...	...	2225	...	...	...	...	...	...	...	...	2314	...	...	2353

	TGV 6217	*TGV* 6217	*TGV* 9836	*TGV* 9836	*TGV* 6183	*TGV* 6125	*TGV* 6135	*TGV* 5126	*TGV* 6129	*TGV* 5124	*TGV* 6219	*TGV* 6219	*TGV* 6219	*TGV* 6131	*TGV* 6221	*TGV* 5142	*TGV* 5135	*TGV* 6137	*TGV* 6225	*TGV* 5136	*TGV* 5136	*TGV* 5338	*TGV* 7989	*TGV* 7995
				⑤⑦			Ⓑ	⑦		①–⑥		①–④	⑤			⑦	⑦	⑤⑦	⑤⑦	①–⑥	⑤⑥	⑦	⑤–⑦	⑤–⑦
		J		r	W	Y		e		n		J				J	J	q	q	n⊖		Re	E‡	E
Brussels Midi **11** d.	...	...	1609	1609	...	...	...	...	...	...	...	...	...	...	...	...	...	...	...	...	...	...	...	...
Lille Europe **11** d.	...	...	1654	1654	...	...	...	1752	...	1752	...	...	...	...	...	1931	1931	...	...	1915	1915	...	...	...
Charles de Gaulle ✈ d.	...	...	1751	1751	...	...	...	1854	...	1854	...	...	...	...	...	2026	2026	...	...	2048	2048	...	...	...
Marne la Vallée-Chessy § d.	...	...	1810	1810	...	...	...	1908	...	1908	...	...	...	...	...	2040	2040	...	...	2103	2103	...	...	...
Paris Gare de Lyon d.	1820	1820	|	|	1842	1842	1846	|	1916	|	1920	1920	1920	2016	2020	|	|	2116	2120	|	|	...	2220	2220
Genève **345** d.	|	|	|	|	|	|	|	|	|	|	|	|	|	|	|	|	|	|	|	|	|	...	|	|
Dijon **373** d.	|	|	|	|	|	|	|	|	|	|	|	|	|	|	|	|	|	|	|	|	|	...	|	|
Lyon Part Dieu d.	|	|	2007	2007	|	|	|	|	|	2107	|	|	|	|	|	2237	2241	|	|	2259	2305	2305	|	|
Valence TGV d.	2034	2034	2045	2045	|	|	|	2117	|	|	|	|	|	|	2234	|	2318	|	2334	...	2344	2342	|	|
Avignon TGV d.	|	|	|	|	|	|	2129	2151	2159	2211	|	|	|	2258	|	2346	|	0000	|	...	0021	0019	|	|
Nîmes **355** d.	2119	2119	2130	2130	|	|	|	|	|	|	2213	2213	2213	|	2320	|	0005	|	0019	...	|	|	|	0510
Montpellier 355 a.	2144	2144	2155	2155	|	|	|	|	|	|	2238	2238	2238	|	2355	|	0030	|	0045	...	|	|	|	0536
Sète **355** a.	...	2205	...	2213	|	|	|	|	|	|	...	|	2259	|	...	|	...	|	...	...	|	|	|	|
Agde **355** a.	...	2222	...	2228	|	|	|	|	|	|	...	|	2314	|	...	|	...	|	...	...	|	|	|	|
Béziers **355** a.	...	2236	...	2241	|	|	|	|	|	|	...	2325	2329	|	...	|	...	|	...	...	|	|	|	0623
Narbonne **355** a.	...	...	...	2257	|	|	|	|	|	|	...	...	2345	|	...	|	...	|	...	...	|	|	|	0641
Toulouse **321** a.	...	...	...	|	|	|	|	|	|	|	...	...	|	|	...	|	...	|	...	...	|	|	|	|
Perpignan 355 a.	...	...	...	2332	|	|	|	|	|	|	...	...	0021	|	...	|	...	|	...	...	|	|	|	0733
Aix en Provence TGV d.	...	...	...	...	2151	2151	|	|	2222	2234	...	...	...	|	...	0009	...	0023	...	...	0044	0044	|	...
Marseille St Charles a.	...	...	...	...	|	|	2158	2221	2234	2246	...	...	...	2326	...	0020	...	0035	...	...	0055	0055	0514	...
Marseille St Charles 360 d.	...	...	...	...	|	|	...	...	2249	...	...	...	...	2338u	...	...	...	...	...	...	...	...	0528	...
Toulon 360 a.	...	...	...	...	2237	2237	...	...	2329	...	...	...	...	0019u	...	...	...	...	...	...	...	...	0615	...
Les Arcs-Draguignan **360** a.	...	...	...	...	|	...	...	...	...	...	...	...	...	...	...	...	...	...	...	...	...	...	|	...
St Raphaël-Valescure **360** a.	...	...	...	...	2325	...	...	...	...	...	...	...	...	...	...	...	...	...	...	...	...	...	0715	...
Cannes **360** a.	...	...	...	...	2349	...	...	...	...	...	...	...	...	...	...	...	...	...	...	...	...	...	0750	...
Antibes **360** a.	...	...	...	...	0000	...	...	...	...	...	...	...	...	...	...	...	...	...	...	...	...	...	0802	...
Nice 360 a.	...	...	...	...	0017	...	...	...	...	...	...	...	...	...	...	...	...	...	...	...	...	...	0823	...

	TGV 6102	*TGV* 9854	*TGV* 5158	*TGV* 6202	*TGV* 6104	*TGV* 9856	*TGV* 9856	*TGV* 6852	*TGV* 6136	*TGV* 6136	*TGV* 6230	*TGV* 6230	*TGV* 5162	*TGV* 5162	*TGV* 5144	*TGV* 6204	*TGV* 6106	*TGV* 5350	*TGV* 6850	*TGV* 6108	*TGV* 5166	*TGV* 9860	*TGV* 9860	*TGV* 6172
	Ⓐ	Ⓐ	⑥	Ⓐ	Ⓐ	⑥	⑦	Ⓐ		Ⓒ	Ⓐ	Ⓐ		①⑥				Ⓑ	Ⓒ	①–⑥			⑥	
			J	J			e					J		b				R		n				
Nice 360 d.	...	...	...	...	...	...	...	...	...	...	...	...	...	...	...	...	...	...	...	...	...	...	...	0639
Antibes **360** d.	...	...	...	...	...	...	...	...	...	...	...	...	...	...	...	...	...	...	...	...	...	...	...	0656
Cannes **360** d.	...	...	...	...	...	...	...	...	...	...	...	...	...	...	...	...	...	...	...	...	...	...	...	0707
St Raphaël-Valescure **360** d.	...	...	...	...	...	...	...	...	...	...	...	...	...	...	...	...	...	...	...	...	...	...	...	0731
Les Arcs-Draguignan **360** d.	...	...	...	...	...	...	...	...	...	...	...	...	...	...	...	...	...	...	...	...	...	...	...	|
Toulon 360 d.	...	...	...	...	0523	0519	...	...	...	0537	...	...	...	...	...	...	...	...	...	0723	...	...	0747	0820
Marseille St Charles 360 a.	...	...	...	...	|	0559	...	...	...	0616	...	...	...	...	...	...	...	...	...	0809	...	...	0829	|
Marseille St Charles d.	0528	0539	0539	...	|	0610	0610	0610	0628	0628	...	...	...	...	0710	...	0728	0739	0810	0828	...	0841	0841	|
Aix en Provence TGV d.	0542	|	0554	...	0617	0624	0624	0626	|	|	...	...	...	...	0725	...	0743	0754	0824	|	...	0855	0855	|
Perpignan 355 d.	|	|	|	...	|	|	|	|	|	|	...	...	...	0505	|	...	|	|	|	|	0642	|	|	|
Toulouse **321** d.	|	|	|	...	|	|	|	|	|	|	...	...	...	|	|	...	|	|	|	|	|	|	|	|
Narbonne **355** d.	|	|	|	...	|	|	|	|	|	|	...	...	...	0544	|	...	|	|	|	|	0721	|	|	|
Béziers **355** d.	|	|	|	0447	|	|	|	|	|	|	...	0534	...	0601	|	...	|	|	|	|	0737	|	|	|
Agde **355** d.	|	|	|	0501	|	|	|	|	|	|	...	0548	...	0615	|	...	|	|	|	|	0752	|	|	|
Sète **355** d.	|	|	|	0517	|	|	|	|	|	|	...	0604	...	0630	|	...	|	|	|	|	0808	|	|	|
Montpellier 355 d.	|	|	|	0539	|	|	|	|	|	|	0623	0623	0652	0652	|	0720	|	|	|	|	0826	|	|	|
Nîmes **355** d.	|	|	|	0605	|	|	|	|	|	|	0650	0650	0718	0718	|	0750	|	|	|	|	0853	|	|	|
Avignon TGV d.	0604	0611	0616	|	0640	0646	0646	|	|	|	|	|	|	|	0747	|	0805	|	|	|	|	0918	0918	0931
Valence TGV d.	|	0645	0650	0656	|	|	|	|	|	|	0736	0736	0810	0810	|	|	|	0846	|	|	0938	|	|	|
Lyon Part Dieu a.	|	0720	|	|	|	0750	0750	0750	|	|	|	|	0846	0846	0850	|	|	0920	0950	|	1016	1020	1020	|
Dijon **373** a.	|	|	|	|	|	|	|	0943	|	|	|	|	|	|	|	|	|	...	1143	|	|	|	|	|
Genève **345** a.	|	|	|	|	|	|	|	...	|	|	|	|	|	|	|	|	|	...	...	|	|	|	|	|
Paris Gare de Lyon a.	0845	|	|	0911	0919	|	|	...	0931	0931	0949	0949	|	|	|	1041	1045	...	...	1131	|	|	|	1211
Marne la Vallée-Chessy § a.	...	0915	0857	...	...	0945	0945	...	...	...	...	...	1045	1045	1045	...	...	...	...	...	1216	1216	1216	...
Charles de Gaulle ✈ a.	...	0930	0918	...	...	1000	1000	...	...	...	...	...	1059	1059	1059	...	...	...	...	...	1229	1229	1229	...
Lille Europe **11** a.	...	1028	...	...	...	1103	1103	...	...	...	...	...	1233v	1233v	1233v	...	...	...	...	...	1326	1326	1326	...
Brussels Midi **11** a.	...	1115	...	...	...	1150	1150	...	...	...	...	...	...	...	...	...	...	...	...	...	...	1412	1412	...

NOTES FOR PAGES 210/211

- **A** – 12 Toulouse - Montpellier - Marseille and v.v. (Table **355**).
- **B** – 12 Dijon - Lyon - Toulouse - Bordeaux and v.v.
- **D** – Daily to July 4; ⑤⑦ July 5 - Aug. 28 (also July 14); daily from Aug. 30.
- **E** – ⑤⑥⑦ (also June 1; not Sept. 20). Perpignan portion will not run on Oct. 25.
- **F** – ⑤⑥⑦ (also June 1, July 14).
- **G** – Daily to Sept. 18; ⑥⑦ Sept. 19 - Dec. 12.
- **H** – 12 Marseille - Lyon - Rouen - Le Havre.
- **J** – To July 4 / from Aug. 31.
- **K** – July 5 - Aug. 30.
- **L** – Daily to Sept. 17; ⑤⑥ Sept. 18 - Dec. 12.
- **M** – To Metz (Table **379**), arrive Nancy 1759, Metz 1848.
- **N** – To / from Nantes via Massy TGV (Table **335**).
- **Q** – From July 5.
- **R** – To / from Rennes via Massy TGV (Table **335**).
- **S** – To Strasbourg (Table **384**).
- **T** – ⑥ June 27 - Aug. 29. *Thalys* train. Calls at Aix, Avignon and Valence to pick up only.
- **U** – ⑤⑥⑦ (also June 1, July 13, 14, Nov. 10, 11).
- **V** – ⑦ to Aug. 2 / from Nov. 29 (also June 1, July 14).
- **W** – ⑤ (daily July 5 - Aug. 30).
- **X** – ⑦ to June 28 (also June 1); daily July 5 - Aug. 30; ⑦ from Sept. 6.
- **Y** – Daily except ⑤ to July 4 / from Aug. 31.
- **Z** – Daily except ⑤.

TGV Méditerranée NICE, MARSEILLE and MONTPELLIER - LYON and PARIS via high-speed line 350

All *TGV* trains are 🅁	*TGV* 6206	*TGV* 6112	*TGV* 5301	*TGV* 5170	*TGV* 6854	*TGV* 6114	*TGV* 6208	*TGV* 5368	*TGV* 5374	*TGV* 9862	*TGV* 5198	*TGV* 6174	*TGV* 6116	*TGV* 6232	*TGV* 5430	*TGV* 9864	*TGV* 6176	*TGV* 6210	*TGV* 6210	*TGV* 6118	*TGV* 6866	*TGV* 9866	*TGV* 9954	*TGV* 6120
								①–⑥	⑦e															
			A	B				Nn	NR		M	w	△		S			J	K				T	
Nice 360 d.	...	...	...	...	0732	...	...	...	...	...	0932	0941	...	...	...	1032	1041	...	...	...	...	...	...	...
Antibes **360** d.	...	...	...	...	0750	...	...	...	...	...	0950	0959	...	...	...	1049	1059	...	...	...	...	...	...	...
Cannes **360** d.	...	...	...	...	0801	...	...	...	...	...	1001	1010	...	...	...	1101	1110	...	...	...	...	...	...	...
St Raphaël-Valescure **360** d.	...	...	...	...	0825	...	...	...	...	...	1026	1035	...	...	...	1125	1135	...	...	...	...	...	...	...
Les Arcs-Draguignan **360** d.	...	...	...	...	|	...	...	...	...	...	|	1051	...	...	...	1142	1151	...	...	...	...	...	...	...
Toulon 360 d.	...	...	...	...	0919	...	...	...	...	...	1117	|	1138	...	...	1218	|	...	...	...	...	...	...	1320a
Marseille St Charles 360 a.	...	...	...	...	0959	...	...	...	...	...	1159	|	1217	...	...	1259	|	...	...	...	...	...	...	1410a
Marseille St Charles d.	...	0928	...	...	1010	1028	...	1133	1133	...	1210	|	1228	...	1246	1310	|	...	...	1328	...	1339	1410	1428
Aix en Provence TGV d.	...	0943	...	...	1025	1042	...	1147	1147	...	|	1213	|	...	1300	|	|	...	...	1343	...	1353	1424	1443
Perpignan 355 d.	0732	|	...	...	|	|	...	|	|	...	|	|	|	...	|	|	|	...	1135	|	...	|	|	|
Toulouse **321** d.	|	|	0654	0749	|	|	...	|	|	...	|	|	|	...	|	|	|	...	|	|	...	|	|	|
Narbonne **355** d.	0816	|	0812	0859	|	|	...	|	|	...	|	|	|	...	|	|	|	...	1210	|	...	|	|	|
Béziers **355** d.	0832	|	0827	0916	|	|	...	|	|	...	|	|	|	...	|	|	|	...	1226	|	...	|	|	|
Agde **355** d.	0846	|	|	|	|	|	...	|	|	...	|	|	|	...	|	|	|	...	1241	|	...	|	|	|
Sète **355** d.	0901	|	0855	|	|	|	...	|	|	...	|	|	|	...	|	|	|	...	1255	|	...	|	|	|
Montpellier 355 d.	0922	|	0915	0959	|	|	1021	|	|	1200	|	|	|	1223	|	|	|	1318	1318	|	1356	|	|	|
Nîmes **355** d.	0950	|	0943	1026	|	|	1050	|	|	1227	|	|	|	1250	|	|	|	1348	1348	|	1424	|	|	|
Avignon TGV d.	|	1005	1002	|	1049	|	|	1209	1209	|	1245	1238	|	|	1324	1340	1332	|	|	1405	|	1416	1446	|
Valence TGV d.	|	|	...	1112	|	|	1136	1243	1243	|	|	|	|	1336	|	1414	|	|	|	|	1513	|	1520	|
Lyon Part Dieu a.	|	|	...	1149	1155	|	|	1320	1320	1346	1350	|	|	|	1430	|	|	|	|	|	1550	1520	|	|
Dijon **373** a.	|	|	...	1354	...	|	|	...	...	|	1539	|	|	|	...	|	|	|	|	|	|	|	|	|
Genève **345** a.	|	|	...	...	...	|	|	...	...	|	...	|	|	|	...	|	|	|	|	|	1735	|	|	|
Paris Gare de Lyon a.	1241	1245	...	...	...	1337	1349	...	...	|	...	1519	1531	1549	...	|	1615	1641	1641	1645	...	|	|	1737
Marne la Vallée-Chessy § a.	...	...	...	...	...	...	...	...	...	1546	...	...	...	...	...	1619	...	...	...	...	...	|	|	...
Charles de Gaulle ✈ a.	...	...	...	...	...	...	...	...	...	1600	...	...	...	...	...	1633	...	...	...	...	...	1720	|	...
Lille Europe **11** a.	...	...	...	...	...	...	...	...	...	1707	...	...	...	...	...	1736	...	...	...	...	...	1814	|	...
Brussels Midi **11** a.	...	...	...	...	...	...	...	...	...	1756	...	...	...	...	...	1822	...	...	...	...	...	1910	1844	...

	TGV 6212	*TGV* 9868	*TGV* 5307	*TGV* 5372	*TGV* 5378	*TGV* 6122	*TGV* 6214	*TGV* 5376	*TGV* 6124	*TGV* 9868	*TGV* 5307	*TGV* 6886	*TGV* 6178	*TGV* 6126	*TGV* 6216	*TGV* 5380	*TGV* 6168	*TGV* 5314	*TGV* 6868	*TGV* 5180	*TGV* 6218	*TGV* 6218	*TGV* 6128	*TGV* 6870
		Ⓒ	Ⓐ	①–⑥	⑦					Ⓐ	Ⓒ			Ⓑ				Ⓑ	⑥					
			Q	Rn	Ne			H			Q		G			N	X				J	K	◇	⊡
Nice 360 d.	...	...	...	...	...	...	...	...	...	...	...	1329	1341	...	...	...	1442	...	...	...	...	...	...	...
Antibes **360** d.	...	...	...	...	...	...	...	...	...	...	...	1347	1400	...	...	...	1459	...	...	...	...	...	...	...
Cannes **360** d.	...	...	...	...	...	...	...	...	...	...	...	1358	1411	...	...	...	1510	...	...	...	...	...	...	...
St Raphaël-Valescure **360** d.	...	...	...	...	...	...	...	...	...	...	...	1422	1436	...	...	...	1535	...	...	...	...	...	...	...
Les Arcs-Draguignan **360** d.	...	...	...	...	...	...	...	...	...	...	...	|	1453	...	...	...	|	...	...	...	...	...	...	...
Toulon 360 d.	...	...	...	...	...	...	...	...	...	...	...	1515	|	...	...	...	1624	...	...	...	...	...	1630	...
Marseille St Charles 360 a.	...	...	...	...	...	...	...	...	...	...	...	1557	|	...	...	...	|	...	...	...	...	...	1709	...
Marseille St Charles d.	...	...	...	1507	1507	1528	...	1539	1558	...	...	1610	|	1628	...	...	|	...	...	1709	...	...	1727	1741
Aix en Provence TGV d.	...	...	...	1523	1523	|	...	|	|	...	...	|	1619	|	...	...	|	...	...	1723	...	...	1743	|
Perpignan 355 d.	...	1234	...	|	|	|	1336	|	|	1410	...	|	|	|	...	...	|	...	1510	|	1531	1531	|	|
Toulouse **321** d.	...	|	1210	|	|	|	|	|	|	|	1336	|	|	|	...	...	|	1434	|	|	|	|	|	|
Narbonne **355** d.	...	1314	1331	|	|	|	1417	|	|	1449	1450	|	|	|	...	...	|	1548	1548	|	1610	1610	|	|
Béziers **355** d.	...	1331	1346	|	|	|	1433	|	|	1507	1507	|	|	|	...	...	|	1604	1604	|	1627	1627	|	|
Agde **355** d.	...	1351	|	|	|	|	1447	|	|	1521	1522	|	|	|	...	...	|	|	|	|	|	1641	|	|
Sète **355** d.	...	1407	|	|	|	|	1503	|	|	1537	1538	|	|	|	...	...	|	|	|	|	|	1656	|	|
Montpellier 355 d.	1423	1430	1430	|	|	|	1526	|	|	1600	1600	|	|	|	1620	1630	|	1650	1650	|	1717	1717	|	|
Nîmes **355** d.	1450	1457	1457	|	|	|	1553	|	|	1627	1627	|	|	|	1650	1700	|	1720	1720	|	1744	1744	|	|
Avignon TGV d.	|	|	|	1546	1546	1600	|	1610	1630	|	|	1645	|	|	|	|	1728	|	|	|	|	|	1804	1813
Valence TGV d.	1537	1544	1544	|	|	|	|	1645	|	|	|	|	|	|	1736	1745	|	|	|	1815	1828	1828	|	1849
Lyon Part Dieu a.	|	1620	1620	1650	1650	|	|	1720	|	1746	1746	1750	|	|	|	1820	|	1846	1846	1850	|	|	|	1927
Dijon **373** a.	|	|	...	...	...	|	|	...	|	|	...	|	|	|	|	...	|	...	...	|	|	|	|	...
Genève **345** a.	|	|	...	...	...	|	|	...	|	|	...	1942	|	|	|	...	|	...	...	|	|	|	|	...
Paris Gare de Lyon a.	1749	|	...	...	...	1841	1845	...	1911	|	...	...	1919	1931	1949	...	2011	...	...	|	2041	2041	2045	...
Marne la Vallée-Chessy § a.	...	1816	...	...	...	...	...	...	...	1946	...	...	...	...	...	...	...	...	...	2045	...	...	...	...
Charles de Gaulle ✈ a.	...	1830	...	...	...	...	...	...	...	2000	...	...	...	...	...	...	...	...	...	2103	...	...	...	...
Lille Europe **11** a.	...	1936	...	...	...	...	...	...	...	2105	...	...	...	...	...	...	...	...	...	2206x	...	...	...	...
Brussels Midi **11** a.	...	2022	...	...	...	...	...	...	...	2152	...	...	...	...	...	...	...	...	...	...	...	...	...	...

	TGV 6130	*TGV* 6130	*TGV* 5184	*TGV* 6170	*TGV* 5186	*TGV* 6138	*TGV* 6220	*TGV* 6184	*TGV* 6874	*TGV* 6222	*TGV* 6880	*TGV* 6132	*TGV* 5398	*TGV* 6876	*TGV* 6180	*TGV* 6134	*TGV* 6226	*TGV* 6224	*TGV* 6140	*TGV* 6186	*TGV* 6228	*TGV* 6142	*TGV* 7994	*TGV* 7988
																	⑤	⑦	⑤	⑦	⑦	⑦	⑤–⑦	⑤–⑦
	J	K		K	s								A			D		e		V	e	e	F	U▽
Nice 360 d.	...	...	1531	1539	...	...	...	1641	...	...	...	...	...	1732	1741	...	...	...	...	1841	...	...	...	2038
Antibes **360** d.	...	...	1549	1559	...	...	...	1659	...	...	...	...	...	1750	1758	...	...	...	...	1900	...	...	...	2101
Cannes **360** d.	...	...	1601	1610	...	...	...	1710	...	...	...	...	...	1802	1810	...	...	...	...	1911	...	...	...	2116
St Raphaël-Valescure **360** d.	...	...	1626	1635	...	...	...	1734	...	...	...	...	...	1827	1835	...	...	...	...	1935	...	...	...	2143
Les Arcs-Draguignan **360** d.	...	...	1642	|	...	...	...	|	...	...	...	...	...	|	|	...	...	...	...	|	...	...	...	|
Toulon 360 d.	...	...	1718	1723	...	...	...	1825	...	...	...	...	...	1919	1923	...	...	...	...	2023	...	...	...	2239
Marseille St Charles 360 a.	...	...	1759	|	...	...	...	|	...	...	...	...	...	1959	|	...	...	...	...	|	...	...	...	2318
Marseille St Charles d.	1758	1758	1810	|	...	1828	...	|	1909	...	...	1928	1932	2010	|	2028	...	...	2058	|	...	2128	...	2333
Aix en Provence TGV d.	1812	|	1824	1818	...	|	...	1914	1924	...	...	1943	1951	|	2013	|	...	...	2112	2119	...	2143	...	|
Perpignan 355 d.	|	|	|	|	...	|	...	|	|	1737	...	|	|	|	|	|	...	1837	|	|	...	|	2200	|
Toulouse **321** d.	|	|	|	|	1610	|	...	|	|	|	...	|	|	|	|	|	...	|	|	|	...	|	|	|
Narbonne **355** d.	|	|	|	|	1728	|	...	|	|	1817	...	|	|	|	|	|	...	1914	|	|	...	|	2239	|
Béziers **355** d.	|	|	|	|	1745	|	...	|	|	1834	...	|	|	|	|	|	...	1931	|	|	...	|	2256	|
Agde **355** d.	|	|	|	|	|	|	...	|	|	1848	...	|	|	|	|	|	...	1945	|	|	...	|	|	|
Sète **355** d.	|	|	|	|	|	|	...	|	|	1903	...	|	|	|	|	|	...	2000	|	|	...	|	|	|
Montpellier 355 d.	|	|	|	|	1830	|	1823	|	|	1923	1927	|	|	|	|	|	2023	2023	|	|	2117	|	2347	|
Nîmes **355** d.	|	|	|	|	1857	|	1850	|	|	1950	1955	|	|	|	|	|	2050	2050	|	|	2144	|	0015	|
Avignon TGV d.	|	1830	1846	|	|	|	|	|	1946	|	|	2005	2011	|	|	2059	|	|	2135	|	|	2205	|	|
Valence TGV d.	|	|	|	|	1945	|	1936	|	|	|	2044	|	...	2111	|	|	2136	2136	|	|	2228	|	|	|
Lyon Part Dieu a.	|	|	1950	|	2020	|	|	|	2050	|	2120	|	...	2150	|	|	|	|	|	|	|	|	|	|
Dijon **373** a.	|	|	|	|	|	|	|	|	|	|	2305r	|	...	2343	|	|	|	|	|	|	|	|	|	|
Genève **345** a.	|	|	|	|	|	|	|	|	2233	|	...	|	...	...	|	|	|	|	|	|	|	|	|	|
Paris Gare de Lyon a.	2111	2111	|	2120	|	2131	2149	2211	...	2241	...	2245	...	...	2311	2336	2347	2347	0015	0011	0041	0045	0720	0720
Marne la Vallée-Chessy § a.	...	...	2146	...	2214	...	...	...	...	...	...	...	...	...	...	...	...	...	...	...	...	...	...	...
Charles de Gaulle ✈ a.	...	...	2159	...	2228	...	...	...	...	...	...	...	...	...	...	...	...	...	...	...	...	...	...	...
Lille Europe **11** a.	...	...	2301	...	2332	...	...	...	...	...	...	...	...	...	...	...	...	...	...	...	...	...	...	...
Brussels Midi **11** a.	...	...	...	...	0013s	...	...	...	...	...	...	...	...	...	...	...	...	...	...	...	...	...	...	...

NOTES FOR PAGES 210/211 – CONTINUED

a – Will not run on Ⓐ June 8-26, Sept. 28 - Oct. 2, Nov. 23 - Dec. 4.
b – Also June 2, July 15; not June 1, July 13.
e – Also June 1, July 14.
n – Not June 1, July 14.
o – 1458 on ①–⑤ (not June 1, Aug. 31).
q – Also June 1, July 14.
r – ⑤⑦ (also June 1, July 14).
s – Runs to Brussels on ⑥ July 11 - Aug. 29 (arrive next day), train number **9887**.
u – Not June 8-12, 15-19, 22-26, Nov. 9, 10, 12, 13.
v – Lille **Flandres**.
w – From Ventimiglia (Table **360**).
x – On Ⓒ (daily July 5 - Aug. 28) arrive 2238 or 2242.
y – 1506 on July 28-30.

TGV –🅁, supplement payable, 🍷.

⊡ – To Melun (Table **370**) on ①–④ (not June 1, July 14). On other dates train number is **6872**.
◇ – To/from Hyères (Table **352**).
△ – To/from Hyères on dates in Table **352**.
▽ – Runs earlier on June 12, 19, 26, Oct. 2, Nov. 27, Dec. 4 (Nice 1925, Cannes 2001).
⊖ – Also calls at Le Creusot TGV (a. 2220).
§ – Station for Disneyland Paris.
‡ – On June 20 Paris d. 2315. Departures from Paris on June 26, July 3, 10, 31 arrive up to 2 hours later. On ⑤ Sept. 18 - Nov. 6 Paris d. 2210.

← FOR OTHER NOTES SEE PREVIOUS PAGE

350a 🚌 AVIGNON CENTRE - AVIGNON TGV

City 🚌 service *Navette TGV* operated by TCRA ✆ 04 32 74 18 32. Journey time 13 minutes (10 minutes Gare TGV - Avignon Centre). Rail tickets not valid. *Valid to Dec. 12, 2009*

Avignon Centre (Poste) ▲ depart: 0544 Ⓐ, 0614 Ⓐ, 0623 Ⓒ, 0643, 0716, 0737, 0828, 0850, 0903, 0923, 0940, 0955, 1018, 1045, 1059, 1120, 1131, 1146, 1210, 1237, 1304, 1322, 1337, 1405, 1415, 1433, 1456, 1520, 1533, 1603, 1619, 1634, 1650, 1725, 1742, 1802, 1823, 1901, 1918, 1931, 1949, 2004, 2026, 2101, 2121, 2137, 2158, 2235.

Avignon TGV depart: 0618 Ⓐ, 0653, 0714, 0754, 0812, 0847, 0910, 0925, 0940, 1005, 1020, 1036, 1100, 1120, 1135, 1150, 1206, 1226, 1252, 1319, 1347, 1357, 1420, 1440, 1456, 1516, 1553, 1607, 1617, 1637, 1652, 1719, 1742, 1803, 1837, 1856, 1915, 1936, 1953, 2006, 2021, 2106, 2115, 2145, 2206, 2218, 2305.

▲ – Cross road in front of station, through city 'gate', turn first left, first bus stop. On ⑦ (until approx 1300) departs from Cité Administrative (cross road, through ramparts, first stop on the right).

351 LYON - VALENCE - AVIGNON - MARSEILLE

Via 'classic' line. For TGV trains via high-speed line see Table 350. Night trains Paris - Nice are shown in Table 360.

km	All *TGV* trains are 🅁	⚒	⚒		17705		*TGV* 6191 ①–⑥ n	17709	⚒	*TGV* 6193	17357 b	17713		17717	4240 4241 S	4251 4240 S		17721		⚒	17725		*TGV* 6295 ⑤⑦ q	
	Paris Gare de Lyon ▲ d.	...	...	...	...	...	0750	...	...	0942	...	...	...	...	...	...	...	...	...	...	...	...	1710	...
	Luxembourg **379** d.	...	...	...	...	...	|	...	...	|	...	...	...	...	...	...	...	...	...	...	...	...	|	...
	Metz **379** d.	...	...	...	...	...	|	...	...	|	...	...	...	...	0820r	...	...	...	...	...	...	...	|	...
	Strasbourg **384** d.	...	...	...	...	...	|	...	...	|	...	...	...	...	|	0816	...	...	...	...	...	...	|	...
	Dijon **373** d.	...	...	...	...	...	|	...	...	|	...	...	...	...	1216	1216	...	...	...	...	...	...	|	...
	Genève **345** d.	...	...	...	...	...	|	...	...	|	...	...	...	...	|	|	...	...	...	...	...	...	|	...
	Lyon St Exupéry TGV ✈ d.	...	...	...	...	...	0951	...	...	1142	...	...	...	...	|	|	...	...	...	...	...	...	|	...
0	**Lyon Perrache** ▶ d.	...	...	...	...	...	|	...	...	|	...	...	...	...	|	|	...	...	...	...	...	1738	|	...
0	**Lyon Part-Dieu** ▶ d.	...	...	...	0725	...	|	0925	1025	|	1111	1125	1225	1327	1405	1405	...	1525	...	1625	1725	|	|	1825
32	Vienne ▶ d.	...	...	...	0744	...	|	0944	1044	|	1131	1145	1244	1348	|	|	...	1544	...	1644	1745	1800	|	1844
87	Tain-Hermitage-Tournon ▶ d.	...	...	...	0819	...	|	1018	1124	|	|	1217	1324	1425	|	|	...	1617	...	1725	1817	1841	|	1924
105	**Valence Ville** ▶ a.	...	...	...	0829	...	1020	1029	1135	1212	1221	1228	1333	1436	1503	1503	...	1628	...	1736	1828	1851	1928	1935
105	**Valence Ville** d.	0555	0645	0715	0832	0945	1023	1032	1145	1215	...	1231	1335	1439	1506	1506	...	1631	1715	1745	1831	1913	1931	1939
150	Montélimar d.	0619	0713	0744	0857	1015	1046	1056	1214	1237	...	1257	1359	1500	|	|	...	1656	1744	1813	1856	1942	1956	2007
202	Orange d.	0651	0748	0820	0932	1049	|	1133	1249	1304	...	1332	1432	1534	|	|	...	1732	1820	1849	1932	2019	2031	2043
230	**Avignon Centre** a.	0714	0810	0843	0946	1113	1120	1146	1313	1317	...	1346	1447	1547	1603	1603	...	1746	1843	1913	1946	2043	2049	2105
230	**Avignon Centre** ▶ d.	0720	...	...	0949	...	...	1149	...	1321	...	1349	...	1550	1606	1606	...	1749	...	...	1949	...	2053	...
	Montpellier **355** a.	|	...	...	|	...	...	|	...	|	...	|	...	|	1707	1707	...	|	...	...	|	...	|	...
	Béziers **355** a.	|	...	...	|	...	...	|	...	|	...	|	...	|	1759	1759	...	|	...	...	|	...	|	...
	Perpignan **355** a.	|	...	...	|	...	...	|	...	|	...	|	...	|	1903	1903	...	|	...	...	|	...	|	...
	Portbou **355** a.	|	...	...	|	...	...	|	...	|	...	|	...	|	2009	2009	...	|	...	...	|	...	|	...
265	Arles § ▶ d.	0739	...	...	1008	...	...	1208	...	1340	...	1408	...	1610	...	...	...	1808	...	...	2009	...	2112	...
299	Miramas § ▶ d.	0800	...	...	1026	...	...	1226	...	1400	...	1426	...	1628	...	...	...	1826	...	...	2026	...	2130	...
351	**Marseille** St Charles § ▶ a.	0837	...	...	1054	...	...	1254	...	...	...	1454	...	1654	...	...	...	1854	...	...	2054	...	...	...
	Toulon **360** a.	...	...	...	...	...	...	...	...	...	...	...	...	...	...	...	...	...	...	...	...	...	...	...
	Nice **360** a.	...	...	...	...	...	...	...	...	...	...	...	...	...	...	...	...	...	...	...	...	...	...	...

	TGV 6195 N	17729	4264 4265 ⑤	*TGV* 6197	4778 4779 ♦ 🅁	4238 4239 ♦ 🅁	4296 4297 ♦ 🅁
Paris Gare de Lyon ▲ d.	1746	...	...	1946	...	...	...
Luxembourg **379** d.	|	...	...	|	...	1946	...
Metz **379** d.	|	...	1530	|	...	2041	...
Strasbourg **384** d.	|	...	|	|	...	|	2100
Dijon **373** d.	|	...	1907	|	...	|	|
Genève **345** d.	|	...	|	|	2044	|	|
Lyon St Exupéry TGV ✈ d.	1942	...	|	2142	|	|	|
Lyon Perrache ▶ d.	|	...	|	|	|	|	|
Lyon Part-Dieu ▶ d.	|	1925	2102	|	2250	|	|
Vienne ▶ d.	|	1945	2124	|	|	|	|
Tain-Hermitage-Tournon ▶ d.	|	2017	|	|	|	|	|
Valence Ville ▶ a.	2012	2028	2203	2212	2351	|	|
Valence Ville d.	2015	2031	2207	2215	2354	|	|
Montélimar d.	2037	2056	2230	2237	|	|	|
Orange d.	2103	2132	2308	|	|	|	|
Avignon Centre a.	2117	2146	2324	2312	|	0412	0438
Avignon Centre ▶ d.	2121	2149	2329	...	|	0423	0446
Montpellier **355** a.	|	|	0034	...	|	|	|
Béziers **355** a.	|	|	...	...	c	|	|
Perpignan **355** a.	|	|	...	...	...	|	|
Portbou **355** a.	|	|	...	...	...	|	|
Arles § ▶ d.	2139	2209	...	...	...	|	0508
Miramas § ▶ d.	2158	2227	...	...	...	|	|
Marseille St Charles § ▶ a.	...	2258	...	...	...	0532	0556
Toulon **360** a.	...	...	...	...	...	0639	0707
Nice **360** a.	...	...	...	...	...	0828	0900

	TGV 6192 Ⓐ	⚒	17702 ⚒	Ⓐ	Ⓒ	⚒		*TGV* 6194	17706	17704	4340 4341 T	4340 4351 T
Nice **360** d.	...	...	...	...	...	...	...	...	...	...	...	...
Toulon **360** d.	...	...	...	...	...	...	...	...	...	...	...	...
Marseille St Charles § ▶ d.	...	...	0503	...	...	...	...	...	0703	0903	...	...
Miramas § ▶ d.	...	...	0533	...	...	...	...	0715	0733	0933	...	...
Arles § ▶ d.	...	...	0552	...	...	...	...	0735	0751	0951	...	...
Cerbère **355** d.	...	...	|	...	...	...	...	|	|	|	0625	0625
Perpignan **355** d.	...	...	|	...	...	...	...	|	|	|	0716	0716
Béziers **355** d.	...	...	|	...	...	...	...	|	|	|	0818	0818
Montpellier **355** d.	...	...	|	...	...	...	...	|	|	|	0907	0907
Avignon Centre ▶ a.	...	...	0609	...	...	...	...	0752	0809	1009	1015	1015
Avignon Centre d.	0511	0524	0612	0616	0616	0646	0716	0755	0812	1012	1019	1019
Orange d.	|	0540	0628	0641	0641	0711	0741	0810	0828	1028	|	|
Montélimar d.	0550	0617	0704	0718	0718	0747	0817	0836	0903	1104	1111	1111
Valence Ville a.	0612	0644	0725	0744	0744	0814	0844	0858	0925	1125	1133	1133
Valence Ville ▶ d.	0615	0707	0728	0807	...	0822	...	0900	0928	1128	1137	1137
Tain-Hermitage-Tournon ▶ d.	|	0718	0740	0818	...	0833	...	|	0940	1139	|	|
Vienne ▶ d.	|	0758	0813	0901	...	0913	...	|	1012	1212	|	|
Lyon Part-Dieu ▶ a.	|	|	0834	|	...	0934	...	|	1034	1234	1246	1246
Lyon Perrache ▶ a.	|	0819	...	0919	...	...	...	|	...	...	|	|
Lyon St Exupéry TGV ✈ a.	0644	...	...	...	...	...	...	0930	...	...	|	|
Genève **345** a.	|	...	...	...	...	...	...	|	...	...	|	|
Dijon **373** a.	|	...	...	...	...	...	...	|	...	...	1439	1439
Strasbourg **384** a.	|	...	...	...	...	...	...	|	...	...	|	1827
Metz **379** a.	|	...	...	...	...	...	...	|	...	...	1807	...
Luxembourg **379** a.	|	...	...	...	...	...	...	|	...	...	...	...
Paris Gare de Lyon ▲ a.	0841	...	...	...	...	...	...	1127	...	...	...	...

		17352 b	17714	*TGV* 6196			17716	17718	*TGV* 6198 ①–⑥ J	*TGV* 6198 L		Ⓐ	Ⓐ	† s	17724			⚒	Ⓑ	4322 4323 ⑦ u		4394 4395 ♦ 🅁	4330 4331 ♦ 🅁	4678 4679 ♦ 🅁
Nice **360** d.	...	...	...	...	...	...	...	...	...	...	...	...	...	...	...	...	...	...	...	...	...	2007	2034	...
Toulon **360** d.	...	...	...	...	...	...	...	...	...	...	...	...	...	...	...	...	...	...	...	...	...	2156	2226	...
Marseille St Charles § ▶ d.	...	...	1103	...	...	...	1403	1503	...	...	...	...	...	...	1703	...	...	...	1903	...	...	2253	2321	...
Miramas § ▶ d.	...	...	1133	...	...	...	1433	1533	1558	1554	...	...	...	...	1733	...	...	...	1933	...	...	|	|	...
Arles § ▶ d.	...	...	1152	...	...	...	1452	1552	1618	1615	...	...	...	...	1752	...	...	...	1953	...	...	2342	|	...
Cerbère **355** d.	...	...	|	...	...	...	|	|	|	|	...	...	...	...	|	...	...	...	|	1650	...	|	|	...
Perpignan **355** d.	...	...	|	...	...	...	|	|	|	|	...	...	...	...	|	...	...	...	|	1742	...	|	|	...
Béziers **355** d.	...	...	|	...	...	...	|	|	|	|	...	...	...	...	|	...	...	...	|	1846	...	|	|	c
Montpellier **355** d.	...	...	|	...	...	...	|	|	|	|	...	...	...	...	|	...	...	...	|	1937	...	|	|	|
Avignon Centre ▶ a.	...	...	1209	...	...	...	1511	1609	1634	1630	...	...	...	...	1809	...	...	...	2013	2047	...	0001	0018	|
Avignon Centre d.	1146	...	1212	1239	1316	...	1514	1612	1637	1637	1646	1716	1746	1803	1812	1846	1935	1935	2016	2050	...	0014	0021	|
Orange d.	1211	...	1230	|	1339	...	1530	1628	1652	1653	1711	1742	1810	1822	1828	1910	2001	2001	2034	|	...	|	|	|
Montélimar d.	1247	...	1307	1320	1413	...	1605	1705	1719	1719	1748	1821	...	1857	1905	1947	2038	2038	2110	2130	...	|	|	|
Valence Ville a.	1314	...	1330	1341	1441	...	1625	1725	1741	1741	1816	1850	...	1921	1925	2014	2105	2105	2135	2151	...	|	|	0527
Valence Ville ▶ d.	...	1330	1338	1344	...	...	1628	1728	1744	1744	1818	...	...	...	1928	2025	...	2122	...	2155	...	|	|	0530
Tain-Hermitage-Tournon ▶ d.	...	|	1350	|	...	...	1639	1740	|	|	1830	...	...	...	1943	2036	...	2134	...	|	...	|	|	|
Vienne ▶ d.	...	|	1426	|	...	...	1714	1814	|	|	1911	...	...	...	2023	2114	...	2213	...	|	...	|	|	|
Lyon Part-Dieu ▶ a.	...	1434	1446	|	...	...	1734	1834	|	|	1931	...	...	...	2046	2134	...	2235	...	2251	...	|	|	0644
Lyon Perrache ▶ a.	...	...	...	|	...	...	...	...	|	|	...	...	...	...	...	...	...	...	...	|	...	|	|	|
Lyon St Exupéry TGV ✈ a.	...	...	...	1414	...	...	...	...	1813	1815	...	...	...	...	...	...	...	...	...	|	...	|	|	|
Genève **345** a.	...	...	...	|	...	...	...	...	|	|	...	...	...	...	...	...	...	...	...	|	...	|	|	0837
Dijon **373** a.	...	...	...	|	...	...	...	...	|	|	...	...	...	...	...	...	...	...	...	|	...	|	|	...
Strasbourg **384** a.	...	...	...	|	...	...	...	...	|	|	...	...	...	...	...	...	...	...	...	0520	...	0759	|	...
Metz **379** a.	...	...	...	|	...	...	...	...	|	|	...	...	...	...	...	...	...	...	...	...	...	...	0745	...
Luxembourg **379** a.	...	...	...	|	...	...	...	...	|	|	...	...	...	...	...	...	...	...	...	...	...	...	0845	...
Paris Gare de Lyon ▲ a.	...	...	...	1611	...	...	...	...	2011	2015	...	...	...	...	...	...	...	...	...	...	...	...	...	...

FOR ADDITIONAL LOCAL SERVICES SEE NEXT PAGE

LYON - VALENCE - AVIGNON - MARSEILLE 351

ADDITIONAL TRAINS LYON - VALENCE — Some trains 2nd class only

		⚒	⚒		Ⓐ	Ⓐ	Ⓐ		⚒			Ⓐ		Ⓐ		Ⓐ	Ⓑh	Ⓐ						
Lyon Perrache d.	...	0538	...	...	0638	0738	...	...	1338	...	...	1538	1638	1708	...	1810	1838	1908	1938	...	...	...	...	...
Lyon Part Dieu d.	...	|	0625	...	|	|	0825	...	|	1425	...	|	|	|	...	|	|	|	|	...	2025	...	2125	...
Vienne d.	...	0601	0645	...	0700	0757	0845	...	1359	1444	...	1600	1700	1731	...	1830	1900	1929	2000	...	2045	...	2144	...
Tain-Hermitage-Tournon d.	...	0640	0724	...	0741	0840	0924	...	1440	1525	...	1640	1740	1811	...	1910	1940	2010	2040	...	2124	...	2224	...
Valence Ville a.	...	0651	0734	...	0751	0851	0935	...	1451	1535	...	1651	1751	1821	...	1921	1951	2021	2051	...	2135	...	2235	...

		Ⓐ	Ⓐ	⚒	⚒		⚒		Ⓐ				⚒	Ⓑh		⚒	Ⓑh				Ⓑh	⑦e	†	
Valence Ville d.	...	0537	0607	0622	0637	...	0737	...	1022	...	1222	...	1422	1507	...	1607	1707	...	1807	...	1907	1924	2145	...
Tain-Hermitage-Tournon d.	...	0548	0618	0633	0649	...	0748	...	1033	...	1233	...	1433	1518	...	1618	1718	...	1818	...	1918	1936	2155	...
Vienne d.	...	0628	0657	0713	0728	...	0827	...	1113	...	1313	...	1513	1558	...	1658	1758	...	1857	...	1958	2011	2227	...
Lyon Part Dieu a.	...	|	|	0734	|	...	|	...	1134	...	1334	...	1534	|	...	|	|	...	|	...	|	2030	2247	...
Lyon Perrache a.	...	0649	0719	...	0749	...	0850	...	...	...	...	...	...	1619	...	1719	1819	...	1919	...	2019	...	...	...

ADDITIONAL TRAINS AVIGNON - MARSEILLE — Some trains 2nd class only

	Ⓐ	⚒	Ⓐ	Ⓐ		⚒	⚒	Ⓐ	Ⓐ		⚒	x	x	Ⓐ		Ⓐ		Ⓐ			Ⓐ		
Avignon Centre d.	0549	0551	0620	0621	0644	0720	0721	0751	0820	...	1220	1221	1357	1620	1621	1720	1721	1751	1820	1851	1920	1933	2110
Arles 355 d.	0609	|	0640	|	0704	0739	|	|	0840	...	1239	|	|	1640	|	1739	|	|	1840	|	1940	|	2130
Salon de Provence d.	|	0634	|	0719	|	|	0819	0841	|	...	...	1319	1449	|	1719	|	1819	1842	|	1943	|	2030	|
Miramas d.	0631	0645	0701	0730	0727	0800	0832	0850	0901	1245	...	1330	1500	1701	1730	1801	1830	1851	1901	1952	2003	2039	2151
Vitrolles Aéroport Marseille ‡ 355 d.	0650	0709	0720	0749	0809	0820	0851	...	0920	1309	...	1349	1518	1720	1754	1821	1848	...	1920	...	...	...	2210
Marseille St Charles 355 a.	0706	0733	0738	0806	0756	0837	0908	...	0938	1333	...	1408	1534	1738	1814	1838	1911	...	1938	...	...	...	2230

	⚒			⚒	⚒	Ⓐ			v	⚒	z		Ⓐ		Ⓐ	Ⓐ			Ⓐ	Ⓐ			
Marseille St Charles 355 d.	...	0618	0636	0718	...	0748	0818	...	...	...	1218	1318	1418	1546	1619	...	1646	...	1722	1746	1846	...	2045
Vitrolles Aéroport Marseille ‡ 355 d.	...	0635	0659	0736	...	0805	0837	...	...	...	1242	1335	1443	1603	1635	...	1701	...	1745	1803	1903	...	2102
Miramas d.	0625	0655	0725	0755	0802	0823	0857	...	1125	...	1307	1355	1506	1625	1659	1702	1725	...	1810	1825	1925	...	2123
Salon de Provence d.	0634	|	0734	|	0811	...	|	...	1134	...	1317	|	...	1634	|	1711	1734	...	|	1835	1934	...	|
Arles 355 d.	|	0717	|	0816	|	...	0918	...	|	1315	|	1416	...	|	1721	|	|	...	1831	|	|	...	2144
Avignon Centre a.	0730	0734	0830	0834	0900	...	0935	...	1231	1334	1411	1433	...	1730	1738	1800	1830	...	1849	1922	2030	...	2201

♦ – **NOTES** (LISTED BY TRAIN NUMBER)

4238/9 – *CORAIL LUNÉA* – 🛏 1,2 cl. and (2) (reclining) Luxembourg - Metz - Nice. For dates of running see Table **379**.

4296/7 – *CORAIL LUNÉA* – 🛏 1,2 cl. and (2) (reclining) Strasbourg - Nice. Train **4294/5** on certain dates. For dates of running see Table **384**.

4330/1 – *CORAIL LUNÉA* – 🛏 1,2 cl. and (2) (reclining) Nice - Metz - Luxembourg. For dates of running see Table **379**.

4394/5 – *CORAIL LUNÉA* – 🛏 1,2 cl. and (2) (reclining) Nice - Strasbourg. For dates of running see Table **384**. Train **4388/9** certain dates. Strasbourg 0834 certain dates.

4678/9 – *CORAIL LUNÉA* – for days of running and composition see Table **355**.

4778/9 – *CORAIL LUNÉA* – for days of running and composition see Table **355**.

J – ①–⑥ to July 4 / from Aug. 31.
L – ⑦ (daily July 7 - Aug. 29).
N – ①②③④⑥ (not June 1, July 14).
S – June 13 - Sept. 20 (not July 20).
T – June 14 - Sept. 21.

b – To / from Briançon (Table **362**).
c – To Irún / from Hendaye (Table **355**).
e – Also June 1, July 14, Nov. 11.
h – Also Aug. 15.
n – Not June 1, July 14.
q – Also June 1, July 14.
r – 0833 on ©.
s – To Chambéry (Table **364**).
u – Also June 1, July 14; not May 31, July 12.

v – Not Oct. 5 - 9, 12 - 16.
x – Not via Salon de Provence on Oct. 5 - 9, 12 - 16.
z – On Oct. 5 - 9, 12 - 16 arrive Avignon 1343 (not via Salon de Provence).

TGV – Ⓡ, supplement payable, 🍷.

▲ – For *TGV* services via high-speed line see Table **340** Paris - Lyon, Table **350** Paris - Marseille / Montpellier.
▶ – For additional trains Lyon - Valence Ville and Avignon - Marseille see separate panel.
§ – See also Table **355**.
‡ – Vitrolles Aéroport Marseille-Provence. A shuttle bus runs to the airport terminal (journey 5 mins).

TOULON - HYÈRES 352

Subject to alteration Toulon - Hyères and v.v. Oct. 27 - 30

km											
						TGV **6109**				*TGV* **6119** E	
			Ⓐ								
	Paris ◇ **350** d.	...	...	...	...	1016	...	...	...	1616	...
	Marseille **360** d.	...	...	...	...	1333	...	1703	1803	1933	...
0	**Toulon** d.	0631	0723	0846	1215	1416	1715	1802	1910	2016	...
20	**Hyères** a.	0651	0744	0907	1236	1431	1736	1823	1931	2031	...

					TGV **6116** F		*TGV* **6128**			
	⚒		Ⓐ							
Hyères d.	0617	0704	0804	1027	1112	1304	1610	1833	1954	...
Toulon a.	0638	0725	0825	1049	1128	1325	1626	1853	2016	...
Marseille **360** a.	0737	0825	0925	1155	1217	1426	1709	1955	...	...
Paris ◇ **350** a.	...	...	...	...	1531	...	2045	...	...	...

E – ⑤⑦ (daily July 3 - Aug. 29), also June 1.
F – ⑥⑦ (daily June 27 - Aug. 28), also June 1.

TGV – Ⓡ, supplement payable, 🍷.

◇ – Paris Gare de Lyon.

LYON - BOURG EN BRESSE 353

Most trains 2nd class only

For long-distance trains see Table **384**. For local trains via Ambérieu see Table **346**

km																								
		Ⓐ	⚒	Ⓐ			Ⓐ	Ⓑ	⚒			Ⓐ			Ⓐ	Ⓐ	Ⓐ			⚒		Ⓐ	⚒	
0	Lyon Perrache d.	0604	0703	0852	...	0952	...	1211	1256	...	1404	1518	1604	...	...	1704	...	1804	...	1852	2004	2027	...	...
5	Lyon Part Dieu d.	0626	0716	0904	...	1004	1056	1226	1308	...	1416	1530	1616	...	1704	1716	1811	1816	...	1904	2016	2044	2104	...
65	Bourg en Bresse a.	0734	0826	0957	...	1104	1204	1328	1358	...	1516	1634	1723	...	1753	1836	1901	1927	...	1957	2117	2147	2200	...

	⚒	Ⓐ	⚒	Ⓐ			Ⓐ		Ⓐ		Ⓐ			Ⓐ	Ⓒ				⚒		Ⓐ	Ⓒ	⚒	
Bourg en Bresse d.	0536	0611	0636	0709	...	0736	0804	...	0932	1036	1136	1236	...	1404	1429	...	1636	1729	1812	...	1904	1936	2004	...
Lyon Part Dieu a.	0639	0713	0739	0801	...	0839	0855	...	1039	1139	1239	1339	...	1456	1539	...	1739	1825	1906	...	1953	2039	2055	...
Lyon Perrache a.	0651	0725	0751	0813	...	0851	0912	...	...	1154	1251	1351	...	1508	1551	...	1751	1837	...	...	2005	2051	...	...

PERPIGNAN - VILLEFRANCHE - LATOUR DE CAROL 354

km	△									
		⚒				Ⓐ		Ⓑ		⑤K
0	**Perpignan** d.	0639	0747	0850	1226	1505	1711	1843	1958	2100
40	Prades-Molitg les Bains d.	0721	0829	0929	1308	1544	1753	1925	2040	2139
46	**Villefranche-Vernet les Bains** a.	0728	0836	0936	1315	1551	1800	1932	2047	2146

△								
	⚒				Ⓐ			Ⓑ
Villefranche-Vernet les Bains d.	0638	0746	1105	1225	1345	1710	1842	1958
Prades-Molitg les Bains d.	0645	0753	1112	1232	1352	1717	1849	2005
Perpignan a.	0723	0831	1150	1310	1430	1755	1927	2042

Villefranche - Latour de Carol is narrow gauge, 2nd class only ('Petit Train Jaune'). In summer most trains include open sightseeing carriages.

	June 1 - July 4 and Aug. 31 - Dec. 12 →	Pn	E	S	F	⑦R	H	u		July 5 - Aug. 30 →								
Villefranche-Vernet les Bains d.		0905	0905	1005	1330	1610	1725	1825	...		0710	0900	1000	1120	1345	1545	1730	1830
Mont Louis la Cabanasse d.		1018	1040	1133	1443	1746	1842	1936	...		0820	1027	1124	1254	1502	1702	1847	1936
Font Romeu-Odeillo-Via a.		1038	1059	1149	1503	1802	1858	1952	...		0836	1045	1140	1310	1518	1718	1906	1955
Font Romeu-Odeillo-Via d.		1041	1102	1154	...	1805	1901	1954	...		...	1048	1145	...	1523	...	1908	1956
Bourg Madame d.		1138	1159	1245	...	1852	1945	2039	...		...	1148	1235	...	1607	...	1959	2050
Latour de Carol a.		1152	1212	1300	...	1906	2001	2053	...		...	1201	1248	...	1620	...	2016	2103

		June 1 - July 4 and Aug. 31 - Dec. 12 →	①G	▽n	S	T	u	E		July 5 - Aug. 30 →								
0	**Latour de Carol** d.		0525	0810	0905	...	1527	1620	...		...	0900	1025	...	1335	1457	...	1730
7	Bourg Madame d.		0539	0827	0922	...	1542	1635	...		...	0917	1040	...	1352	1512	...	1744
28	Font Romeu-Odeillo-Via a.		0620	0912	1015	...	1635	1730	...		...	1003	1138	...	1439	1610	...	1825
28	Font Romeu-Odeillo-Via d.		0622	0917	1021	1520	1638	1734	...		0917	1008	1142	1340	1444	1637	1740	1828
35	Mont Louis la Cabanasse d.		0638	0935	1040	1540	1659	1756	...		0936	1030	1206	1404	1509	1702	1759	1851
63	**Villefranche-Vernet les Bains** a.		0737	1051	1155	1650	1809	1908	...		1047	1200	1315	1520	1627	1812	1913	2000

E – June 1, 6, 7, June 13 - July 4, Aug. 31 - Oct. 4.
F – June 1, 6, 7, June 13 - July 4, Sept. 7 - Oct. 4; ⑥⑦ Oct. 10 - 25, daily from Oct. 26.
G – June 2, 8, ① Sept. 7 - 28, ① Oct. 26 - Dec. 7.
H – June 1, 5 - 7, June 12 - July 4, Aug. 31 - Oct. 4.

K – ⑤ July 10 - Aug. 28.
P – June 2 - 5, 8 - 12, ⑥⑦ Oct. 10 - 25; daily from Oct. 26.
R – ⑦ Oct. 11 - Dec. 6.
S – June 1, 6, 7, June 13 - July 4, Aug. 31 - Sept. 27.
T – June 1, 6, 7, June 13 - July 4, Aug. 31 - Dec. 12.

n – Subject to alteration on Ⓐ to June 12.
u – Subject to alteration June 2 - 4, 8 - 11.

△ – On Oct. 25 service is by 🚌.
▽ – No rail service on ①–⑤ Oct. 5 - 23.

355 AVIGNON and MARSEILLE - NARBONNE - PORTBOU

km		Ⓐ	3731 ♦ [R]	Ⓐ	3733 ♦ [R]	Ⓐ	TGV 7995 ⑤–⑦ N	3741 ♦ [R]	Ⓐ	4248 4249 P [R]	4293 4248 Q [R]	Ⓐ	463 [R] ✕ ♦ ⁄	Ⓐ	4752 4753 ★	⚒	⚒	⚒		⚒	4754 4755 ★	TGV 6803 ⑥	TGV 5355 Ⓑ	Ⓐ d
	Paris Gare de Lyon **350** d.	...	...	...	...	...	2220	...	...	...	...	...	...	...	...	...	...	...	...	...	...	...	...	...
	Paris Austerlitz **310** d.	...	2156	...	2202	...	|	2218	...	...	...	...	...	...	...	...	...	...	...	...	...	...	...	...
	Brussels Midi **11** d.	...	|	...	|	...	|	|	...	...	...	...	...	...	...	...	...	...	...	...	...	...	...	...
	Lille Europe **11** d.	...	|	...	|	...	|	|	...	...	...	...	...	...	...	...	...	...	...	...	...	...	...	...
	Charles de Gaulle ✈ **350** d.	...	|	...	|	...	|	|	...	...	...	...	...	...	...	...	...	...	...	...	...	...	...	...
	Metz **379** d.	...	|	...	|	...	|	|	...	2106	...	...	...	...	...	...	...	...	...	...	...	...	...	...
	Strasbourg **384** d.	...	|	...	|	...	|	|	...	|	2020	...	...	...	...	...	...	...	...	...	...	...	...	...
	Dijon **373** d.	...	|	...	|	...	|	|	...	|	|	...	...	...	...	...	...	...	...	...	...	...	...	...
	Genève **345** d.	...	|	...	|	...	|	|	...	|	|	...	...	...	...	...	...	...	...	...	...	...	...	...
	Lyon Part Dieu **350** d.	...	|	...	|	...	|	|	...	|	|	...	...	...	...	...	...	...	...	...	...	0711	0710	...
	Nice **360** d.	...	|	...	|	...	|	|	...	|	|	...	...	...	...	...	...	...	...	...	...	|	|	...
▵	**Marseille St Charles** d.	...	|	...	|	...	|	|	...	|	|	...	...	...	0614	...	...	0624	...	...	0714	|	|	...
	Vitrolles Aéroport Marseille ‡ d.	...	|	...	|	...	|	|	...	|	|	...	...	...	|	...	...	0641	...	...	|	|	|	...
	Arles d.	...	|	...	|	...	|	|	...	|	|	...	...	...	|	...	...	0722	...	...	0759	|	|	...
0	**Avignon Centre** d.	...	|	...	|	...	|	|	...	|	|	0602	...	...	|	...	0638	|	0726	...	|	|	|	...
21	Tarascon-sur-Rhône d.	...	|	...	|	...	|	|	...	|	|	0615	...	...	|	...	0650	0732	0739	...	|	|	|	...
49	Nimes a.	...	|	...	|	...	0506	|	...	0552	0552	0630	...	...	|	...	0712	0746	0756	...	0823	0828	0828	...
49	Nimes d.	...	|	...	|	0515	0510	|	...	0555	0555	0632	...	0655	|	...	0719	...	0758	0820	0825	0831	0831	0841
99	**Montpellier** a.	...	|	...	|	0546	0536	|	...	0628	0628	0700	...	0727	0740	...	0754	...	0829	0847	0851	0855	0855	0911
99	**Montpellier** d.	...	|	...	|	0549	0540	|	0620	0632	0632	0703	0726	0730	0744	...	0758	...	0832	▬	0855	0859	0859	0914
126	Sète d.	...	|	...	|	0608	|	|	0644	0652	0652	0723	|	0747	|	...	0818	...	0851	...	0912	|	|	0934
149	Agde d.	...	|	...	|	0620	|	|	0700	0708	0708	0737	|	0802	|	...	0833	...	0906	...	|	|	|	0949
170	Béziers d.	...	|	...	|	0633	0627	|	0716	0722	0722	0752	0806	0816	|	...	0845	...	0921	...	0937	0943	0943	1004
196	**Narbonne** a.	...	0617	...	0638	0647	0641	0658	0734	0739	0739	0807	0819	0830	|	...	...	...	0937	E	0950	0959	0959	1020
196	**Narbonne** d.	...	0637	0642	0658	0649	0653	0718	0737	0748	0748	0816	0821	...	|	0846	...	...	0939	0948	0952	1002	1002	...
	Carcassonne **321** a.	...	|	|	|	0723r	|	|	|	|	|	0846	|	...	|	|	...	...	|	|	1021	|	1032	...
	Toulouse **321** a.	...	|	|	|	0824r	|	|	|	|	|	...	|	...	0942	|	...	...	|	|	1111	|	1121	...
	Irún **325** a.	...	|	|	|	...	|	|	|	|	|	...	|	...	|	|	...	...	|	|	|	|	▬	...
	Bordeaux **320** a.	...	|	|	|	...	|	|	|	|	|	...	|	...	1146*	|	...	...	|	|	1326	|	...	...
	Nantes **292** a.	...	|	|	|	...	|	|	|	|	|	...	|	...	...	|	...	...	|	|	...	|	...	...
259	**Perpignan** a.	...	0718	0728	0742	...	0733	0804	0821	0826	0826	...	0855	...	...	0933	...	...	1023	1032	...	1037	←	...
259	**Perpignan** d.	0620	0722	...	0746	...	...	0808	...	0830	0830	...	0857	...	...	0936	...	...	→	1034	...	...	1045	...
281	Argelès sur Mer d.	0639	0744	...	0809	...	...	0827	...	0850	0850	...	|	...	...	0954	...	...	...	1052	...	...	1104	...
286	Collioure d.	0645	0752	...	0818	...	...	0833	...	0857	0857	...	|	...	...	0959	...	...	...	1058	...	...	1110	...
289	Port Vendres d.	0649	0757	...	0823	...	...	0838	...	0902	0902	...	|	...	...	1003	...	...	...	1101	...	...	1114	...
294	Banyuls sur Mer d.	0654	0805	...	0831	...	...	0845	...	0909	0909	...	|	...	...	1009	...	...	...	1107	...	...	1119	...
301	Cerbère a.	0700	0812	...	0839	...	...	0851	...	0916	0916	...	0921	...	...	1015	...	...	...	1113	...	...	1126	...
303	**Portbou** a.	...	0821	...	0854	...	...	...	...	0927	0927	...	0948	...	...	...	...	...	...	...	...	...	...	...

	TGV 6201 Ⓐ		TGV 6813	⊡	TGV 6203		4756 4757 ★		TGV 5104 Ⓒ	TGV 9804 Ⓐ		TGV 6205		⑦	TGV 6207	4768 4769 ★ F	⚒	15942 15943 C	TGV 5112	TGV 5311 △	⚒	4758 4759 ★		TGV 6209
Paris Gare de Lyon **350** d.	0620	...	...	...	0720	...	...	...	...	...	...	0820	...	...	0920	...	...	...	...	...	...	...	...	1120
Paris Austerlitz **310** d.	|	...	...	...	|	...	...	...	...	...	...	|	...	...	|	...	...	...	...	...	...	...	...	|
Brussels Midi **11** d.	|	...	...	...	|	...	...	...	...	0540	...	|	...	...	|	...	...	...	...	...	...	...	...	|
Lille Europe **11** d.	|	...	...	...	|	...	...	...	0625	0625	...	|	...	...	|	...	...	...	0828	...	...	...	...	|
Charles de Gaulle ✈ **350** d.	|	...	...	...	|	...	...	...	0725	0725	...	|	...	...	|	...	...	...	0925	...	...	...	...	|
Metz **379** d.	|	...	...	...	|	...	...	...	|	|	...	|	...	...	|	...	...	...	|	...	...	...	...	|
Strasbourg **384** d.	|	...	...	...	|	...	...	...	|	|	...	|	...	...	|	...	...	...	|	...	...	...	...	|
Dijon **373** d.	|	...	0616x	...	|	...	...	...	|	|	...	|	...	...	|	...	...	...	|	...	...	...	...	|
Genève **345** d.	|	...	|	...	|	...	...	...	|	|	...	|	...	...	|	...	...	...	|	...	...	...	...	|
Lyon Part Dieu **350** d.	|	...	0811	...	|	...	...	...	0937	0937	...	|	...	...	|	...	...	...	1137	1211	...	...	...	|
Nice **360** d.	|	...	|	...	|	...	...	...	|	|	...	|	...	...	|	0832	...	...	|	|	...	1001	...	|
Marseille St Charles d.	|	0806	|	...	|	...	0914	...	|	|	...	|	...	...	|	1114	...	1128	|	|	...	1242	...	|
Vitrolles Aéroport Marseille ‡ d.	|	0821	|	...	|	...	|	...	|	|	...	|	...	...	|	|	...	|	|	|	...	|	...	|
Arles d.	|	0857	|	...	|	...	0959	...	|	|	...	|	...	...	|	1158	...	1226	|	|	...	|	...	|
Avignon Centre d.	|	|	|	0902	|	...	|	1021	|	|	...	|	...	...	|	|	1156	|	|	|	...	|	1327	|
Tarascon-sur-Rhône d.	|	0907	|	0915	|	...	|	1034	|	|	...	|	...	...	|	|	1209	1238	|	|	...	|	1339	|
Nimes a.	0916	0923	0927	0932	1010	...	1023	1048	1057	1057	...	1117	...	...	1217	1223	1232	1255	1258	1327	...	|	1353	1415
Nimes d.	0919	0925	0930	0934	1013	...	1025	1051	1100	1100	1113	1120	...	1155	1220	1225	1235	▬	1301	1330	1338	|	1356	1418
Montpellier a.	0944	0955	0959	1004	1038	...	1051	1122	1128	1128	1141	1145	←	1221	1247	1251	1305	...	1326	1355	1405	1409	1423	1442
Montpellier d.	...	...	...	1007	1043	...	1055	▬	1132	1132	→	...	1155	...	...	1255	1308	...	▬	...	1408	1413	1426	1447
Sète d.	...	...	...	1030	1059	...	|	...	|	|	...	...	1213	...	...	1313	1327	...	...	...	1432	|	1445	1504
Agde d.	...	...	...	1045	1114	...	|	...	|	|	...	...	1227	...	...	1328	1340	...	...	...	1447	|	1459	1520
Béziers d.	...	...	...	1059	1128	...	1133	...	1216	1216	...	...	1241	...	...	1342	1400	Ⓒ	⚒	...	1458	|	1512	1534
Narbonne a.	...	...	...	1114	1141	...	1149	...	1235	1235	...	...	1256	...	...	1356	1415	K	←	...	...	|	1526	1547
Narbonne d.	...	...	...	1116	1144	...	1151	1220	1238	1238	...	...	1258	...	...	1358	→	1426	1452	...	...	|	1533	1550
Carcassonne **321** a.	...	...	...	|	|	...	1220	|	1308	1309	...	...	|	...	...	1427	...	|	|	...	...	|	1608	|
Toulouse **321** a.	...	...	...	|	|	...	1305	|	1355	1356	...	...	|	...	...	1517	...	|	|	...	...	1612	1659z	|
Irún **325** a.	...	...	...	|	|	...	|	|	...	...	...	...	|	...	...	...	...	|	|	...	...	|	...	|
Bordeaux **320** a.	...	...	...	|	|	...	1513	|	...	...	...	...	|	...	...	...	...	|	|	...	...	1823*	...	|
Nantes **292** a.	...	...	...	|	|	...	...	|	...	...	...	...	|	...	...	...	...	|	|	...	...	...	...	|
Perpignan a.	...	...	...	1157	1216	←	...	1308	...	...	...	...	1336	...	...	...	...	1512	1532	...	...	...	...	1625
Perpignan d.	...	...	...	→	...	1226	...	...	...	...	...	...	1340	...	...	...	...	1514	1534	...	...	...	...	...
Argelès sur Mer d.	...	...	...	...	...	1244	...	...	...	...	...	...	1358	...	...	...	...	1531	1551	...	...	...	...	...
Collioure d.	...	...	...	...	...	1250	...	...	...	...	...	...	1404	...	...	...	...	1537	1556	...	...	...	...	...
Port Vendres d.	...	...	...	...	...	1254	...	...	...	...	...	...	1408	...	...	...	...	1540	1600	...	...	...	...	...
Banyuls sur Mer d.	...	...	...	...	...	1259	...	...	...	...	...	...	1413	...	...	...	...	1546	1605	...	...	...	...	...
Cerbère a.	...	...	...	...	...	1306	...	...	...	...	...	...	1420	...	...	...	...	1552	1611	...	...	...	...	...
Portbou a.	...	...	...	...	...	...	...	...	...	...	...	...	1428	...	...	...	...	...	...	...	...	...	...	...

♦ – **NOTES** (LISTED BY TRAIN NUMBER)

463 – MARE NOSTRUM – [12] and ✕ Montpellier - Barcelona - Alacant - Murcia - Cartagena. In France calls to pick up only.

3731 – *CORAIL LUNÉA* – couchette 1, 2 cl. and [2] (reclining) Paris - Toulouse - Narbonne - Portbou.

3733 – ⑤⑥ June 26 - Sept. 5 (also July 13, Oct. 23). couchette 1, 2 cl., [2] (reclining) Paris - Toulouse - Narbonne - Portbou.

3741 – ①②③④⑦ June 28 - Sept. 3 (not July 13). couchette 1, 2 cl. and [2] (reclining) Paris - Toulouse - Narbonne - Cerbère.

C – [12] Marseille - Clermont Ferrand (Table **334**).

E – ⑥⑦ June 20 - Aug. 23 (also July 14): [12] Toulouse (depart 0804) - Cerbère.

F – ⑤⑥⑦ June 26 - Aug. 30 (also June 1, July 14, Oct. 23, 24, 30, 31, Nov. 1, 2, 11).

K – July 5 - Aug. 30.

N – ⑤⑥⑦ (not Sept. 20, Oct. 24).

P – *CORAIL LUNÉA* – ⑤⑥⑦ to June 28 (also June 1); daily June 29 - Sept. 6; ⑤⑥⑦ Sept. 11 - 27; ⑤⑦ from Oct. 2 (also Oct. 24, 31, Nov. 2 - 4). couchette 1, 2 cl., [2] (reclining) Metz - Portbou.

Q – *CORAIL LUNÉA* – ⑤⑥⑦ to June 28 (also June 1); daily June 29 - Sept. 6; ⑤⑥⑦ Sept. 11 - 27; ⑤⑦ from Oct. 2 (also Oct. 24, 31, Nov. 2 - 4). couchette 1, 2 cl., [2] (reclining) Strasbourg - Dijon (**4293**) - Portbou.

d – Also runs on ⑥ Montpellier - Béziers.

r – On ① arrive Carcassonne 0735, Toulouse 0836.

x – ①⑥ (also June 2, July 15; not June 1, July 13).

z – Ⓐ (also ⑦ to June 28 / from Sept. 6). Subject to alteration on ①–④ Nov. 9 - Dec. 10.

TGV – [R], supplement payable, 🍷.

⁄ – Special 'global' fares payable.

△ – From Nantes (Table **335**).

⊡ – On Ⓐ June 2 - 19 and Ⓐ Nov. 2 - 13 Narbonne d. 1147, Perpignan a. 1224.

★ – *CORAIL TÉOZ*, [R], 🍷.

▵ – *135 km* from Nîmes via Avignon TGV, *128 km* via Arles.

‡ – Vitrolles Aéroport Marseille-Provence. A shuttle bus runs to the airport terminal (journey 5 mins).

* – Not on ①–④ Nov. 9 - Dec. 10.

AVIGNON and MARSEILLE - NARBONNE - PORTBOU 355

	TGV 6816	70 71 ◆ ⁄ R ✕		⚒	4762 4763 ★	Ⓐ	TGV 6211	TGV 6211 K	Ⓐ	TGV 9833	3631 ★	4240 4241 S	U	4764 4765 ★	Ⓐ		TGV 6213		⚒	TGV 5117	◇	Ⓑ	⚒	⚒	TGV 6231 Ⓐ J
Paris Gare de Lyon **350** d.	...	...	...	...	...	...	1320	1320	...	...	...	...	...	...	...	...	1520	...	...	...	...	...	...	...	1620
Paris Austerlitz **310** d.	...	...	...	...	...	...	|	|	...	...	1025	...	...	...	...	...	|	...	...	...	...	...	...	...	|
Brussels Midi **11** d.	...	...	...	...	...	...	|	|	...	1110	|	...	...	...	...	...	|	...	...	...	...	...	...	...	|
Lille Europe **11** d.	...	...	...	...	...	...	|	|	...	1156	|	...	...	...	...	...	|	...	...	...	...	...	...	...	|
Charles de Gaulle ✈ **350** d.	...	...	...	...	...	...	|	|	...	1258	|	...	...	...	...	...	|	...	...	...	...	...	...	...	|
Metz **379** d.	...	...	...	...	...	...	|	|	...	|	|	0820z	...	...	...	...	|	...	...	...	...	...	...	...	|
Strasbourg **384** d.	...	...	...	...	...	...	|	|	...	|	|	0816	...	...	...	...	|	...	...	...	...	...	...	...	|
Dijon **373** d.	...	...	...	...	...	...	|	|	...	|	|	1216	...	...	...	...	|	...	...	1516r	...	...	...	...	|
Genève **345** d.	1117	...	...	...	...	...	|	|	...	|	|	|	...	...	...	...	|	...	...	|	...	...	...	...	|
Lyon Part Dieu **350** d.	1307	...	...	...	...	...	|	|	...	1507	|	1405	...	...	...	...	|	...	...	1707	...	...	...	...	|
Nice **360** d.	|	...	...	...	...	...	|	|	...	|	|	|	...	1336	...	...	|	...	...	|	...	...	...	...	|
Marseille St Charles d.	|	...	...	...	1414	...	|	|	...	|	|	|	...	1615	...	...	|	...	...	|	...	1714	...	...	|
Vitrolles Aéroport Marseille ‡ d.	|	...	...	...	|	...	|	|	...	|	|	|	...	|	...	...	|	...	...	|	...	1732	...	...	|
Arles d.	|	...	...	...	1459	...	|	|	...	|	|	|	...	|	...	...	|	...	...	|	...	1815	...	...	|
Avignon Centre d.	|	...	...	...	|	1516s	|	|	...	|	|	1606	1606	|	...	1702	|	1732	1757	|	...	|	...	1832	|
Tarascon-sur-Rhône d.	|	...	...	...	|	|	|	|	...	|	|	|	1619	|	...	1715	|	1747	1810	|	...	1826	...	1844	|
Nimes a.	1429	...	...	...	1523	1552	1616	1616	...	1629	|	1634	1634	|	...	1730	|	1804	1826	1830	...	1840	←	1906	1917
Nimes d.	1432	...	...	1455	1525	1554	1619	1619	1623	1632	|	1637	1637	|	1655	1733	|	1807	→	1833	...	1843	1846	...	1920
Montpellier a.	1457	...	...	1525	1551	1623	1644	1644	1653	1657	|	1707	1707	1741	1737	1803	1841	1836	...	1857	...	1914	1929	...	1944
Montpellier d.	...	1509	...	1528	1555	1626	...	1650	1657	1706	|	1710	1710	1745	1750	1806	1846	1839	...	1901	...	1917	1931	...	...
Sète d.	...	|	...	1550	1612	1646	...	1707	1717	1723	|	1731	1731	|	1813	1831	1903	1908	...	|	...	1937	1951	...	...
Agde d.	...	|	...	1606	|	1701	...	1723	1731	1740	|	1747	1747	|	1829	1848	1918	1922	...	|	...	1950	2005	...	...
Béziers d.	...	1555	...	1621	1637	1714	...	1737	1744	1754	|	1801	1801	|	1843	1905	1931	1936	...	1943	...	2004	2017	...	...
Narbonne a.	...	1609	...	1639	1650	1734	...	1751	1757	1807	1807	1815	1815	|	1859	1921	1944	1949	...	1955	...	2017	...	...	...
Narbonne d.	...	1611	1616	▬	1652	1737	...	1752	...	1810	1827	1818	1818	|	...	...	1947	...	...	1958	2011	...	...	...	...
Carcassonne **321** a.	...	|	|	...	1721	|	...	|	...	|	|	|	|	|	...	...	|	...	...	2026	|	...	...	...	...
Toulouse **321** a.	...	|	|	...	1806	|	...	|	...	|	|	|	|	1945	...	...	|	...	...	2112	|	...	...	...	...
Irún **325** a.	...	|	|	...	|	|	...	|	...	|	|	|	|	|	...	...	|	...	...	|	|	...	...	...	...
Bordeaux **320** a.	...	|	|	...	2021	|	...	|	...	|	|	|	|	2150	...	...	|	...	...	2320	|	...	...	...	...
Nantes **292** a.	...	|	|	...	...	|	...	|	...	|	|	|	|	...	...	...	|	...	...	...	|	...	...	...	...
Perpignan a.	...	1652	1700	...	...	1821	...	1827	...	1844	1907	1903	1903	...	...	...	2021	...	...	...	2052	...	...	...	...
Perpignan d.	...	1654	1703	1726	...	1823	...	...	...	...	1911	1916	1916	...	...	...	...	...	...	...	...	...	...	...	...
Argelès sur Mer d.	...	|	1718	1743	...	1840	...	...	...	...	1930	1936	1936	...	...	...	...	...	...	...	...	...	...	...	...
Collioure d.	...	|	1724	1749	...	1845	...	...	...	...	1937	1942	1942	...	...	...	...	...	...	...	...	...	...	...	...
Port Vendres d.	...	|	1727	1753	...	1849	...	...	...	...	1942	1947	1947	...	...	...	...	...	...	...	...	...	...	...	...
Banyuls sur Mer d.	...	|	1732	1758	...	1854	...	...	...	...	1949	1954	1954	...	...	...	...	...	...	...	...	...	...	...	...
Cerbère a.	...	1719	1737	1804	...	1900	...	...	...	...	1956	2001	2001	...	...	...	...	...	...	...	...	...	...	...	...
Portbou a.	...	1746	...	1812	...	...	...	...	...	...	...	2009	2009	...	...	...	...	...	...	...	...	...	...	...	...

	TGV 5118				4766 ★ ⑤⑦ p		TGV 6215	TGV 5385 R	TGV 5398			TGV 6217	TGV 6217 J	TGV 9836	TGV 9836 ⑤⑦ e	TGV 6219	TGV 6219 ⑤	Q	TGV 6221	4724 4725 ◆ R	TGV 5135 ⑦ J e	4264 4265 ⑤	TGV 6225 ⑤⑦ e	4778 4779 ◆ R	4730 ◆ R
Paris Gare de Lyon **350** d.	...	...	...	...	...	...	1720	...	...	...	...	1820	1820	...	...	1920	1920	...	2020	...	...	...	2120	...	...
Paris Austerlitz **310** d.	...	...	...	...	...	...	|	...	...	...	...	|	|	...	...	|	|	...	|	...	...	...	|	...	...
Brussels Midi **11** d.	...	...	...	...	...	...	|	...	...	...	...	|	|	1609	1609	|	|	...	|	...	...	...	|	...	...
Lille Europe **11** d.	1454c	...	...	...	...	...	|	...	...	...	...	|	|	1654	1654	|	|	...	|	...	1931	...	|	...	...
Charles de Gaulle ✈ **350** d.	1553	...	...	...	...	...	|	...	...	...	...	|	|	1751	1751	|	|	...	|	...	2026	...	|	...	...
Metz **379** d.	|	...	...	...	...	...	|	...	...	...	...	|	|	|	|	|	|	...	|	...	|	1530	|	...	...
Strasbourg **384** d.	|	...	...	...	...	...	|	...	...	...	...	|	|	|	|	|	|	...	|	...	|	|	|	...	...
Dijon **373** d.	|	...	...	...	...	...	|	...	...	...	...	|	|	|	|	|	|	...	|	...	|	1907	|	...	...
Genève **345** d.	|	...	...	...	...	...	|	...	...	...	...	|	|	|	|	|	|	...	|	...	|	|	|	2044	...
Lyon Part Dieu **350** d.	1807	...	...	...	...	...	|	1911	...	...	...	|	|	2007	2007	|	|	...	|	...	2241	2102	|	2250	...
Nice **360** d.	|	...	...	...	...	...	|	|	...	...	...	|	|	|	|	|	|	...	|	1832	|	|	|	|	2057
Marseille St Charles d.	|	...	1818	...	1842	...	|	|	1932	...	1914	|	|	|	|	|	|	...	|	2215	|	|	|	|	0010
Vitrolles Aéroport Marseille ‡ d.	|	...	1836	...	|	...	|	|	|	...	1933	|	|	|	|	|	|	...	|	|	|	|	|	|	|
Arles d.	|	...	1917	...	1930	...	|	|	|	...	2014	|	|	|	|	|	|	...	|	|	|	|	|	|	|
Avignon Centre d.	|	1902	|	...	|	...	|	|	2014v	1958	|	|	|	|	|	|	|	...	|	|	|	2329	|	|	|
Tarascon-sur-Rhône d.	|	1916	1926	...	|	...	|	|	|	2019	2024	|	|	|	|	|	|	...	|	|	|	2342	|	|	|
Nimes a.	1927	1931	1940	...	1953	...	2017	2027	2031	2035	2039	2116	2116	2127	2127	2210	2210	...	2317	2330	0002	0001	0016	|	|
Nimes d.	1930	...	1942	...	1955	2009	2020	2030	2034	...	2042	2119	2119	2130	2130	2213	2213	...	2320	2333	0005	0003	0019	|	|
Montpellier a.	1955	...	2012	...	2022	2036	2044	2057	2101	...	2108	2144	2144	2155	2155	2238	2238	...	2355	0003	0030	0034	0045	|	|
Montpellier d.	1959	...	2015	...	2026	2039	2049	2101	2105	...	2111	...	2149	...	2159	2244x	2244	2248	...	0007	...	...	...	|	|
Sète d.	2016	...	2035	...	2043	2058	2105	|	2122	...	2129	...	2207	...	2215	|	2301	2307	...	|	...	...	...	|	|
Agde d.	2032	...	2049	...	|	2112	2120	|	|	...	2143	...	2224	...	2230	|	2317	2320	...	|	...	...	...	|	|
Béziers d.	2047	...	2103	...	2108	2123	2134	2140	2147	...	2156	...	2236	...	2244	2325x	2331	2332	...	|	...	...	...	|	|
Narbonne a.	2101	...	2117	...	2122	...	2147	2155	2201	...	2209	...	...	...	2257	...	2345	2345	...	|	...	...	...	|	|
Narbonne d.	2104	...	...	2120	2124	...	2150	2158	2204	...	*2219*	...	...	...	2300	...	2348	...	...	|	...	...	...	|	|
Carcassonne **321** a.	|	...	...	|	2153	...	|	|	2233	...	|	...	...	...	|	...	|	...	...	|	...	...	...	|	|
Toulouse **321** a.	|	...	...	|	2248	...	|	2309	2321	...	|	...	...	...	|	...	|	...	...	|	...	...	...	0510	0515
Irún **325** a.	|	...	...	|	|	...	|	...	...	...	|	...	...	...	|	...	|	...	...	|	...	...	...	1113	|
Bordeaux **320** a.	|	...	...	|	0101	...	|	...	...	...	|	...	...	...	|	...	|	...	...	0437	...	...	...	...	0810
Nantes **292** a.	|	...	...	|	...	...	|	...	...	...	|	...	...	...	|	...	|	...	...	0916y	...	...	...	...	...
Perpignan a.	2135	...	...	2158	...	...	2223	...	...	...	*2257*	...	...	...	2332	...	0021	...	...	...	...	...	...	...	...
Perpignan d.	...	...	...	2200	...	...	...	...	...	...	...	...	...	...	...	...	...	...	...	...	...	...	...	...	...
Argelès sur Mer d.	...	...	...	2216	...	...	...	...	...	...	...	...	...	...	...	...	...	...	...	...	...	...	...	...	...
Collioure d.	...	...	...	2222	...	...	...	...	...	...	...	...	...	...	...	...	...	...	...	...	...	...	...	...	...
Port Vendres d.	...	...	...	2225	...	...	...	...	...	...	...	...	...	...	...	...	...	...	...	...	...	...	...	...	...
Banyuls sur Mer d.	...	...	...	2231	...	...	...	...	...	...	...	...	...	...	...	...	...	...	...	...	...	...	...	...	...
Cerbère a.	...	...	...	2237	...	...	...	...	...	...	...	...	...	...	...	...	...	...	...	...	...	...	...	...	...
Portbou a.	...	...	...	...	...	...	...	...	...	...	...	...	...	...	...	...	...	...	...	...	...	...	...	...	...

◆ – **NOTES** (LISTED BY TRAIN NUMBER)

70/1 – CATALAN TALGO – [12] and ✕ Montpellier - Barcelona. In France calls to pick up only.

4730 – *CORAIL LUNÉA* – ▬ 1,2 cl. and [2] (reclining) Nice - Bordeaux. To Irún on dates in Table **305**. On ①–④ June 8-25, Sept. 28 - Oct. 1, Nov. 23 - Dec. 3 depart Nice 2011, Marseille 2325. Train number **14730** on certain dates.

4724/5 – ⑤⑦ (daily June 19 - Sept. 4, Oct. 23 - Nov. 4), also June 1; not June 5. ▬ 1,2 cl. and [2] (reclining) Nice - Nantes.

4778/9 – *CORAIL LUNÉA* – ⑤⑦ (daily June 19 - Sept. 6, Oct. 23 - Nov. 4), also June 1. ▬ 1,2 cl. and [2] (reclining) Genève - Lyon - Irún. Train number **14778** on certain dates.

J – To July 4 / from Aug. 31.
K – July 5 - Aug. 30.
Q – ⑦ to June 28; ①②③④⑥⑦ July 5 - Aug. 29 (not July 13); ⑦ from Aug. 30.
R – From July 5.
S – June 13 - Sept. 20 (not July 20): [12] Metz - Dijon - Portbou; [12] Strasbourg (**4251/0**) - Dijon - Portbou.
U – Dec. 14 - June 12, Sept. 21 - Dec. 12.

c – 1458 on ①–⑤ (not June 1, Aug. 31).
e – Also June 1, July 14.
p – Also June 1, July 14, Oct. 24, 31, Nov. 2, 11.
r – 1506 on July 28 - 30.
s – 1527 on Ⓐ Apr. 14 - June 12, Ⓐ July 13 - Oct. 9 (not July 27).
v – Avignon **TGV** station.
x – ①–④ to July 2 / from Aug. 31 (not June 1).
y – 1009 on June 28, Sept. 6; 1052 on June 6.
z – 0833 on ©.

TGV – R, supplement payable, 🍸.

⁄ – Special 'global' fares payable.
★ – *CORAIL TÉOZ*, R, 🍸.
◇ – From Toulouse.
‡ – Vitrolles Aéroport Marseille-Provence. A shuttle bus runs to the airport terminal (journey 5 mins).

355 CERBÈRE - NARBONNE - AVIGNON and MARSEILLE

		4624 4625		TGV 6202				TGV 6230		TGV 5162	TGV 5162		TGV 6204						TGV 5166		4340 4341		TGV 5301	TGV 6206	
	Ⓐ	♦ 🅁	Ⓐ	Ⓐ	Ⓐ	Ⓐ	⑥	Ⓐ	Ⓐ		①⑥ b			Ⓐ	Ⓐ	⚒	⚒	†			S	⚒			Ⓐ W
Cerbère d.	...	...	...	...	...	...	...	...	...	...	...	...	...	...	...	...	0540	0540	...	...	0625	0640	...	...	...
Banyuls sur Mer d.	...	...	...	...	...	...	...	...	...	...	...	...	...	...	...	...	0547	0547	...	...	0634	0647	...	...	...
Port Vendres d.	...	...	...	...	...	...	...	...	...	...	...	...	...	...	...	...	0552	0552	...	...	0641	0652	...	...	...
Collioure d.	...	...	...	...	...	...	...	...	...	...	...	...	...	...	...	...	0556	0556	...	...	0647	0656	...	...	...
Argelès sur Mer d.	...	...	...	...	...	...	...	...	...	...	...	...	...	...	...	...	0601	0601	...	...	0654	0702	...	...	...
Perpignan a.	...	...	...	...	...	...	...	...	...	...	...	...	...	...	...	...	0620	0620	...	...	0713	0719	...	...	...
Perpignan d.	...	...	...	...	...	...	...	...	...	...	0505	...	...	...	0552	...	0622	0622	0642	...	0716	0721	...	0732	...
Nantes 292 d.	...	2034	...	...	...	...	...	...	...	...	|	...	...	...	|	...	|	|	|	...	|	|	...	|	...
Bordeaux 320 d.	...	0045	...	...	...	...	...	...	...	...	|	...	...	...	|	...	|	|	|	...	|	|	...	|	...
Hendaye 325 d.	...	|	...	...	...	...	...	...	...	...	|	...	...	...	|	...	|	|	|	...	|	|	...	|	...
Toulouse 321 d.	...	|	...	...	...	...	...	...	...	...	|	...	...	...	|	...	|	|	|	...	|	|	0654	|	...
Carcassonne 321 d.	...	|	...	...	...	...	...	...	...	...	|	...	...	...	|	...	|	|	|	0714	|	|	0742	|	...
Narbonne a.	...	|	...	...	...	...	...	...	...	...	0541	...	...	...	0643	...	0710	0710	0718	0748	0800	0805	0809	0814	...
Narbonne d.	...	|	0428	...	...	...	...	...	...	...	0544	0557	...	...	0647	0653	0724	0724	0721	0758	0802	...	0812	0816	0822
Béziers d.	...	|	0443	0447r	...	0523	...	0534r	0555	...	0601	0612	...	...	0702	0708	0745	0745	0737	0813	0818	...	0827	0832	0838
Agde d.	...	|	0455	0501r	...	0536	...	0548r	0608	...	0615	0627	...	...	0716	0722	0758	0758	0752	0827	0832	...	|	0846	0852
Sète d.	...	|	0510	0517r	...	0552	...	0604r	0622	...	0630	0645	...	...	0731	0739	0813	0813	0808	0841	0848	...	0855	0901	0908
Montpellier a.	...	0504	0529	0534r	←	0610	...	0619r	0640	...	0645	0708	...	...	0748	0804	0830	0830	0822	0859	0903	...	0910	0916	0923
Montpellier d.	...	0508	→	0539	0602	0613	0613	0623	0643	0652	0652	0711	0720	...	0751	0807	0836	...	0826	0904	0907	...	0915	0922	0926
Nimes a.	...	0536	...	0602	0629	0705	0705	0647	0710	0715	0715	0740	0747	...	0823	0837	0906	...	0850	0933	0936	...	0941	0947	0953
Nimes d.	0530	0539	...	0605	0631	0707	0707	0650	...	0718	0718	0742	0750	0806	...	0843	...	...	0853	0935	0939	...	0943	0950	...
Tarascon-sur-Rhône d.	0549	|	...	|	0647	0730	0730	|	...	|	|	0758	|	0830	...	0900	...	...	|	0950	|	...	|	|	...
Avignon Centre a.	0600	|	...	|	|	0742	0742	|	...	|	|	|	|	0842	...	0912	...	...	|	1002	1015	...	1002v	|	...
Arles d.	...	|	...	|	0658	...	...	|	...	|	|	0810	|	...	...	...	...	...	|	...	|	...	|	|	...
Vitrolles Aéroport Marseille ‡ d.	...	|	...	|	|	...	...	|	...	|	|	|	|	...	...	...	...	...	|	...	|	...	|	|	...
Marseille St Charles a.	...	0644	...	|	0751	...	...	|	...	|	|	0856	|	...	...	...	...	...	|	...	|	...	1041	|	...
Nice 360 a.	...	0928	...	|	...	...	...	|	...	|	|	...	|	...	...	...	...	...	|	...	|	...	...	|	...
Lyon Part Dieu 350 a.	...	...	...	|	...	...	...	|	...	0846	0846	...	|	...	...	...	...	...	1016	...	1246	...	...	|	...
Genève 345 a.	...	...	...	|	...	...	...	|	...	|	|	...	|	...	...	...	...	...	|	...	|	...	...	|	...
Dijon 373 a.	...	...	...	|	...	...	...	|	...	|	|	...	|	...	...	...	...	...	|	...	1439	...	...	|	...
Strasbourg 384 a.	...	...	...	|	...	...	...	|	...	|	|	...	|	...	...	...	...	...	|	...	1827	...	...	|	...
Metz 392 a.	...	...	...	|	...	...	...	|	...	|	|	...	|	...	...	...	...	...	|	...	1807	...	...	|	...
Charles de Gaulle ✈ 350 a.	...	...	...	|	...	...	...	|	...	1059	1059	...	|	...	...	...	...	...	1229	...	...	...	...	|	...
Lille Europe 11 a.	...	...	...	|	...	...	...	|	...	1233x	1233x	...	|	...	...	...	...	...	1326	...	...	...	...	|	...
Brussels Midi 11 a.	...	...	...	|	...	...	...	|	...	...	...	...	|	...	...	...	...	...	...	...	...	...	...	|	...
Paris Austerlitz 310 a.	...	...	...	|	...	...	...	|	...	...	...	...	|	...	...	...	...	...	...	...	...	...	...	|	...
Paris Gare de Lyon 350 a.	...	...	...	0911	...	...	...	0949	...	...	...	...	1041	...	...	...	...	...	...	...	...	...	...	1241	...

		TGV 5170	4652 4653	TGV 6208	3630		TGV 9862			TGV 6232			4654 4655	TGV 6210	TGV 6210	72 73		TGV 6866			4656 4657	TGV 6212	TGV 9868	TGV 5307	
			★		★							⊡	★ ▽	J	K	♦⚡ 🅁✕			E	D	★		⑥⑦ e	Ⓐ R	Ⓐ
Cerbère d.	0718	...	...	...	0750	...	...	...	...	...	...	1039	...	...	...	1114	...	...	1125	...	...	...	...	...	...
Banyuls sur Mer d.	0725	...	...	...	0800	...	...	...	...	...	...	1045	...	...	...	|	...	...	1131	...	...	...	...	...	...
Port Vendres d.	0731	...	...	...	0806	...	...	...	...	...	...	1050	...	...	...	|	...	...	1136	...	...	...	...	...	...
Collioure d.	0735	...	...	...	0811	...	...	...	...	...	...	1054	...	...	...	|	...	...	1140	...	...	...	...	...	...
Argelès sur Mer d.	0741	...	...	...	0818	...	...	...	...	...	...	1059	...	...	...	|	...	...	1145	...	...	...	...	...	...
Perpignan a.	0800	...	...	...	0836	...	...	...	...	...	...	1117	...	...	...	1143	...	...	1201	...	...	...	...	...	...
Perpignan d.	0805	...	...	...	0840	...	...	...	1027	...	...	1119	...	...	1135	1145	...	...	1203	1203	...	...	1234	...	...
Nantes 292 d.	|	...	...	...	|	...	...	...	|	...	...	|	...	...	|	|	...	...	|	|	...	...	|	...	...
Bordeaux 320 d.	|	0543	0610	...	|	...	...	...	|	...	...	|	0827	...	|	|	...	...	|	|	1010	...	|	...	...
Hendaye 325 d.	|	|	|	...	|	...	...	...	|	...	...	|	|	...	|	|	...	...	|	|	|	...	|	...	...
Toulouse 321 d.	|	0749	0817	...	|	...	...	...	|	...	...	|	1045	...	|	|	...	...	|	|	1217	...	|	1210	1153
Carcassonne 321 d.	|	|	|	...	|	...	...	...	|	...	...	|	1134	...	|	|	1208	...	|	|	|	...	|	1300	1246
Narbonne a.	0845	0857	|	...	0916	...	...	...	1110	...	...	1158	1202	...	1207	1220	1238	...	1250	1250	|	...	1311	1329	1321
Narbonne d.	0848	0859	|	...	0938	...	...	1050	1112	...	...	...	1204	...	1210	1222	1245	...	...	...	|	...	1314	1331	1336
Béziers d.	0903	0916	|	...	|	...	...	1105	1127	...	...	...	1220	...	1226	1239	1300	...	...	...	|	...	1331	1346	1352
Agde d.	0915	|	|	...	|	...	...	1117	1140	...	...	...	|	...	1241	|	1313	...	...	...	|	...	1351	|	1404
Sète d.	0928	|	|	...	|	...	...	1132	1155	...	...	...	1245	...	1255	|	1327	...	...	...	|	...	1407	|	1419
Montpellier a.	0946	0952	1012	...	|	...	...	1150	1213	...	←	...	1300	...	1312	1322	1346	...	...	...	1412	...	1425	1423	1440
Montpellier d.	0948	0959	1016	1021	|	...	1200	1204	→	1223	1243	...	1304	1318	1318	...	1349	1356	...	...	1416	1423	1430	1430	1443
Nimes a.	1016	1023	|	1047	|	...	1224	1233	...	1247	1314	...	1329	1345	1345	...	1417	1422	...	...	|	1447	1454	1454	1511
Nimes d.	1018	1026	|	1050	|	1216	1227	...	...	1250	1317	...	1332	1348	1348	...	...	1425	...	...	|	1450	1457	1457	1516
Tarascon-sur-Rhône d.	1033	|	|	|	|	1231	|	...	...	|	1335	...	|	|	|	...	...	|	...	...	|	|	|	|	1531
Avignon Centre a.	|	|	|	|	|	1244	|	...	...	|	1347	...	|	|	|	...	...	|	...	...	|	|	|	|	1542
Arles d.	1044	|	|	|	|	...	|	...	...	|	...	...	1358	|	|	...	...	|	...	...	|	|	|	|	...
Vitrolles Aéroport Marseille ‡ d.	1121	|	|	|	|	...	|	...	...	|	...	...	|	|	|	...	...	|	...	...	|	|	|	|	...
Marseille St Charles a.	1138	|	1142	|	|	...	|	...	...	|	...	...	1442	|	|	...	...	|	...	...	1542	|	|	|	...
Nice 360 a.	...	|	1425	|	|	...	|	...	...	|	...	...	...	|	|	...	...	|	...	...	1825	|	|	|	...
Lyon Part Dieu 350 a.	...	1149	...	|	|	...	1346	...	...	|	...	...	...	|	|	...	...	1550	...	...	...	|	1620	1620	...
Genève 345 a.	...	|	...	|	|	...	|	...	...	|	...	...	...	|	|	...	...	1735	...	...	...	|	|	...	...
Dijon 373 a.	...	1354	...	|	|	...	|	...	...	|	...	...	...	|	|	...	...	...	...	...	...	|	|	...	...
Strasbourg 384 a.	...	...	...	|	|	...	|	...	...	|	...	...	...	|	|	...	...	...	...	...	...	|	|	...	...
Metz 392 a.	...	...	...	|	|	...	|	...	...	|	...	...	...	|	|	...	...	...	...	...	...	|	|	...	...
Charles de Gaulle ✈ 350 a.	...	...	...	|	|	...	1600	...	...	|	...	...	...	|	|	...	...	...	...	...	...	|	1830	...	...
Lille Europe 11 a.	...	...	...	|	|	...	1707	...	...	|	...	...	...	|	|	...	...	...	...	...	...	|	1936	...	...
Brussels Midi 11 a.	...	...	...	|	|	...	1756	...	...	|	...	...	...	|	|	...	...	...	...	...	...	|	2022	...	...
Paris Austerlitz 310 a.	...	...	...	|	1738	...	...	...	...	|	...	...	...	|	|	...	...	...	...	...	...	|	...	...	...
Paris Gare de Lyon 350 a.	...	...	...	1349	...	...	...	...	...	1549	...	...	...	1641	1641	...	...	...	...	...	...	1749	...	...	...

♦ – **NOTES FOR PAGES 216/217** (LISTED BY TRAIN NUMBER)

72/3 – *CATALAN TALGO* – [12] and ✕ Barcelona - Montpellier.

460 – *MARE NOSTRUM* – [12] and ✕ Lorca - Murcia - Alacant - Barcelona - Montpellier. After Cerbère calls to set down only.

3730 – *CORAIL LUNÉA* – 🛏 1,2 cl. and [2] (reclining) Cerbère - Paris.

3732 – ⑥⑦ June 27 - Sept. 6 (also July 14, Nov. 1). 🛏 1,2 cl. and [2] (reclining) Cerbère - Paris.

3740 – ①-⑤ June 29 - Sept. 4 (not July 14). 🛏 1,2 cl. and [2] (reclining) Cerbère - Paris.

4620/1 – *CORAIL LUNÉA* – 🛏 1,2 cl. and [2] (reclining) Bordeaux - Nice. From Hendaye on dates in Table **305**.

4624/5 – ⑤⑦ (daily June 19 - Sept. 6, Oct. 23 - Nov. 4), also June 1; not June 5 🛏 1,2 cl. and [2] (reclining) Nantes - Nice. Timings from Nantes vary – see Table **292**.

4678/9 – *CORAIL LUNÉA* – ⑤⑦ (daily June 19 - Sept. 6, Oct. 23 - Nov. 4), also June 1. 🛏 1,2 cl. and [2] (reclining) Hendaye - Lyon - Genève. Depart Hendaye 1813 on ⑥ June 27 - Sept. 5.

C – [12] Clermont Ferrand - Marseille (Table **334**).
D – ⚒ (daily July 5 - Aug. 30).
E – ①-⑥ June 2 - July 4; ⑦ July 5 - Aug. 30 (also July 14, Aug. 15); ①-⑥ Aug. 31 - Oct. 3.
F – Ⓑ to June 28; Ⓐ June 29 - Aug. 28; Ⓑ from Aug. 31.
G – ⑥⑦ June 20 - Aug. 23 (also July 14, Aug. 15).
H – ⑤⑥⑦ June 26 - Aug. 30 (also June 1, July 14, Oct. 23, 24, 30, 31, Nov. 1, 2).
J – To July 4 / from Aug. 31.
K – July 5 - Aug. 30.
N – ⑤⑥⑦ (daily July 3 - Aug. 30).

P – ⑤⑥⑦ to June 28 (also June 1); daily June 29 - Sept. 6; ⑤⑥⑦ Sept. 11 - 27; ⑤⑦ from Oct. 2 (also Oct. 24, 31, Nov. 2 - 4). 🛏 1,2 cl. and [2] (reclining) Cerbère - Metz.
Q – ⑤⑥⑦ to June 28 (also June 1); daily June 29 - Sept. 6; ⑤⑥⑦ Sept. 11 - 27; ⑤⑦ from Oct. 2 (also Oct. 24, 31, Nov. 2 - 4). 🛏 1,2 cl. and [2] (reclining) Cerbère - Dijon (**4392**) - Strasbourg.
R – From July 5.
S – June 14 - Sept. 21. [12] Cerbère - Dijon - Metz; [12] Cerbère - Dijon (**4351**) - Strasbourg.
W – Ⓐ Dec. 14 - June 12, Sept. 22 - Dec. 11 (also June 13).

b – Also June 2, July 15; not June 1, July 13.
c – Also July 14.
d – Also June 1, July 14; not July 12.
e – Also June 1, July 14.
n – Not June 1, July 14.
r – Ⓐ to July 3 / from Aug. 31.
s – Runs to Brussels on ⑥ July 11 - Aug. 29 (arrive next day), train number **9887**.
v – Avignon **TGV** station.
x – Lille **Flandres**.
y – Also June 1, July 14, Nov. 2.
z – ⑤⑦ (also June 1, July 14).

NOTES CONTINUED ON NEXT PAGE →

CERBÈRE - NARBONNE - AVIGNON and MARSEILLE 355

	Ⓒ		TGV 6214		TGV 5307 ⑥⑦ Rc	TGV 9868 ①–⑤ n		TGV 6216	TGV 5380 △	Ⓒ K	TGV 5314 Ⓑ	TGV 6868 ⑥	4660 4661 ★ ⊕		TGV 6218 J	TGV 6218 K	15947 C⊙	Ⓐ		Ⓐ		TGV 6220	TGV 5186 s	4658 4659 ★ H	
Cerbère d.	...	1240	...	...	...	...	...	...	...	1417	...	...	...	...	...	...	...	...	...	...	1545	...	...	...	...
Banyuls sur Mer d.	...	1248	...	...	...	...	...	...	...	1424	...	...	...	...	...	...	...	...	...	...	1553	...	...	...	...
Port Vendres d.	...	1253	...	...	...	...	...	...	...	1429	...	...	...	...	...	...	...	...	...	...	1559	...	...	...	...
Collioure d.	...	1256	...	...	...	...	...	...	...	1433	...	...	...	...	...	...	...	...	...	...	1604	...	...	...	...
Argelès sur Mer d.	...	1302	...	...	...	...	...	...	...	1438	...	...	...	...	...	...	...	...	...	...	1611	...	...	...	...
Perpignan a.	...	1320	...	...	...	...	...	...	...	1456	...	...	...	...	...	...	...	...	...	...	1628	...	...	...	...
Perpignan d.	...	1323	1336	...	...	1410	...	...	...	▬	...	1510	...	...	1531	1531	...	...	...	1549	1630	...	...	...	...
Nantes **292** d.	...	|	|	...	...	|	...	...	...	...	...	|	...	...	|	|	...	...	...	|	|	...	...	...	...
Bordeaux **320** d.	...	|	|	...	...	|	...	...	...	...	...	|	1238	...	|	|	...	...	...	|	|	...	...	...	...
Hendaye **325** d.	...	|	|	...	...	|	...	...	...	...	...	|	|	...	|	|	...	...	...	|	|	...	...	...	...
Toulouse **321** d.	1153	|	|	...	1336	|	...	...	...	...	1434	|	1451	...	|	|	...	...	...	|	|	...	1610	1614	...
Carcassonne **321** d.	1246	|	|	...	1419	|	...	...	...	...	1518	|	1534	...	|	|	...	...	...	|	|	...	1656	1703	...
Narbonne a.	1321	1409	1413	...	1447	1446	...	...	...	...	1545	1545	1602	...	1607	1607	...	...	...	1631	1706	...	1725	1732	...
Narbonne d.	1336	1411	1417	1425	1450	1449	...	...	...	...	1548	1548	1604	1555	1610	1610	...	1617	...	1633	1708	...	1728	1734	...
Béziers d.	1351	1426	1433	1443	1507	1507	1514	...	...	...	1604	1604	1620	1609	1627	1627	...	1633	1646	1653	1723	...	1745	1749	...
Agde d.	1403	1439	1447	1457	1522	1521	1527	...	...	...	|	|	|	1620	|	1641	...	1647	1659	1707	1736	...	|	1803	...
Sète d.	1417	1455	1503	1512	1538	1537	1543	...	...	...	|	|	1645	1634	|	1656	...	1701	1716	1721	1751	...	|	1819	...
Montpellier a.	1437	1514	1520	1527	1555	1554	1601	...	...	...	1643	1643	1700	1651	1711	1711	...	1719	1736	1741	1809	...	1825	1834	...
Montpellier d.	...	1517	1526	1530	1600	1600	1604	1620	1630	...	1650	1650	1704	1654	1717	1717	...	1722	1740	1744	1814	1823	1830	1838	1846
Nimes a.	...	1544	1550	1557	1624	1624	1630	1647	1657	...	1717	1717	1728	1734	1741	1741	...	1757	1805	1826	1843	1847	1854	1902	1913
Nimes d.	...	...	1553	1600	1627	1627	1639	1650	1700	1706	1720	1720	1730	1736	1744	1744	1800	1804	...	...	1846	1850	1857	1904	1916
Tarascon-sur-Rhône d.	...	...	|	|	|	|	1701	|	|	1730	|	|	|	1751	|	|	1816	1827	...	...	1903	|	|	|	1932
Avignon Centre a.	...	...	|	|	|	|	1712	|	|	1742	|	|	|	1803	|	|	|	1839	...	...	1915	|	|	|	|
Arles d.	...	...	|	1627	|	|	...	|	|	...	|	|	1758	...	|	|	1827	...	...	...	...	|	|	1930	1946
Vitrolles Aéroport Marseille ‡ d.	...	...	|	1711	|	|	...	|	|	...	|	|	|	...	|	|	|	...	...	...	...	|	|	|	2024
Marseille St Charles a.	...	...	|	1734	|	|	...	|	|	...	|	|	1842	...	|	|	1914	...	...	...	...	|	|	2014	2038
Nice **360** a.	...	...	|	...	|	|	...	|	|	...	|	|	...	...	|	|	...	...	...	...	...	|	|	2255	...
Lyon Part Dieu **350** a.	...	...	|	...	1746	1746	...	|	1820	...	1846	1846	...	...	|	|	...	...	...	...	...	|	2020	...	...
Genève **345** a.	...	...	|	...	...	|	...	|	...	...	...	...	...	...	|	|	...	...	...	...	...	|	|	...	...
Dijon **373** a.	...	...	|	...	...	|	...	|	...	...	...	...	...	...	|	|	...	...	...	...	...	|	|	...	...
Strasbourg **384** a.	...	...	|	...	...	|	...	|	...	...	...	...	...	...	|	|	...	...	...	...	...	|	|	...	...
Metz **392** a.	...	...	|	...	...	|	...	|	...	...	...	...	...	...	|	|	...	...	...	...	...	|	|	...	...
Charles de Gaulle ✈ **350** a.	...	...	|	...	...	2000	...	|	...	...	...	...	...	...	|	|	...	...	...	...	...	|	2228	...	...
Lille Europe **11** a.	...	...	|	...	...	2105	...	|	...	...	...	...	...	...	|	|	...	...	...	...	...	|	2328	...	...
Brussels Midi **11** a.	...	...	|	...	...	2152	...	|	...	...	...	...	...	...	|	|	...	...	...	...	...	|	0013s	...	...
Paris Austerlitz **310** a.	...	...	|	...	...	...	...	|	...	...	...	...	...	...	|	|	...	...	...	...	...	|	...	...	...
Paris Gare de Lyon **350** a.	...	...	1845	...	...	...	...	1949	...	...	...	...	...	...	2041	2041	...	...	...	...	...	2149	...	...	...

	4662 4663 ★ ⊗	TGV 6222	TGV 6880	⚒	4322 4323 ⑦ d	F	Ⓒ G	⑦ K§	TGV 6226 ⑤	TGV 6224 ⑦ e	Ⓐ		4664 4665 ★	TGV 6228 ⑦ e	460 [R]✕ ♦⚡	⑦	4666 4667 ⑤⑦ ★y	3740 ♦ [R]	4348 4349 P [R]	4348 4392 Q [R]	TGV 7994 ⑤–⑦ N	3730 ♦ [R]	3732 ♦ [R]	4620 4621 ♦ [R]	4678 4679 ♦ [R]
Cerbère d.	...	...	...	...	1650	1725	1730	...	...	...	...	1823	...	...	1906	...	...	2028	2042	2042	...	2121	2135	...	...
Banyuls sur Mer d.	...	...	...	...	1659	1732	1737	...	...	...	...	1830	...	...	|	...	...	2036	2051	2051	...	2129	2144	...	...
Port Vendres d.	...	...	...	...	1706	1737	1742	...	...	...	...	1835	...	...	|	...	...	2043	2058	2058	...	2136	2150	...	...
Collioure d.	...	...	...	...	1712	1741	1746	...	...	...	...	1839	...	...	|	...	...	2049	2103	2103	...	2141	2155	...	...
Argelès sur Mer d.	...	...	...	...	1719	1747	1752	...	...	...	...	1844	...	...	|	...	...	2056	2110	2110	...	2148	2202	...	...
Perpignan a.	...	...	...	...	1739	1806	1810	...	...	...	...	1901	...	...	1936	...	...	2114	2129	2129	...	2206	2222	...	...
Perpignan d.	...	1737	...	1743	1742	1808	1812	...	...	1837	...	1903	...	...	1939	1957	...	2118	2133	2133	2200	2210	2226	...	...
Nantes **292** d.	...	|	...	|	|	|	|	...	...	|	...	|	...	...	|	|	...	|	|	|	|	|	|	...	...
Bordeaux **320** d.	1459	|	...	|	|	|	|	...	...	|	...	|	1638	...	|	|	...	|	|	|	|	|	|	2157	...
Hendaye **325** d.	|	|	...	|	|	|	|	...	...	|	...	|	|	...	|	|	...	|	|	|	|	|	|	|	1826
Toulouse **321** d.	1704	|	...	|	|	|	|	...	...	|	...	|	1851	...	|	|	1951	|	|	|	|	|	|	0013	0019
Carcassonne **321** d.	|	|	...	|	|	|	|	...	...	|	...	|	1936	...	|	|	2035	|	|	|	|	|	|	|	|
Narbonne a.	|	1814	...	1829	1828	1853	1857	...	...	1911	...	1948	2004	...	2013	2032	2104	2204	2211	2211	2235	2244	2310	|	|
Narbonne d.	|	1817	...	1831	1830	1856	...	1905	...	1914	1930	...	2006	...	2015	2034	2106	2226	2215	2215	2239	2304	2330	|	|
Béziers d.	|	1834	...	1849	1846	1912	...	1920	...	1931	1947	...	2022	...	2029	2049	2121	|	2232	2232	2256	|	|	|	|
Agde d.	|	1848	...	1901	1900	1925	...	1933	...	1945	2000	...	|	...	|	2101	|	|	2246	2246	|	|	|	|	|
Sète d.	|	1903	...	1916	1916	1940	...	1947	...	2000	2016	...	|	...	|	2115	2146	|	2302	2302	|	|	|	|	|
Montpellier a.	1900	1917	...	1934	1933	1957	...	2006	...	2017	2031	...	2100	...	2109	2137	2201	|	2317	2317	2343	|	|	|	|
Montpellier d.	1904	1923	1927	1937	1937	2000	...	2008	2023	2023	2034	...	2104	2117	...	2140	2205	|	2319	2319	2347	|	|	|	|
Nimes a.	|	1947	1952	2006	2009	2029	...	2037	2047	2047	2106	...	2128	2141	...	2210	2229	|	2347	2347	0012	|	|	|	|
Nimes d.	|	1950	1955	...	2012	2032	...	2040	2050	2050	...	...	2130	2144	...	...	2231	|	2357	2357	0015	|	|	|	|
Tarascon-sur-Rhône d.	|	|	|	...	2030	2049	...	2055	|	|	...	...	|	|	...	...	|	|	|	|	|	|	|	|	|
Avignon Centre a.	|	|	|	...	2047	2102	...	2107	|	|	...	...	|	|	...	...	|	|	|	|	|	|	|	|	|
Arles d.	|	|	|	...	|	...	...	...	|	|	...	...	2156	|	...	...	2256	|	|	|	|	|	|	|	|
Vitrolles Aéroport Marseille ‡ d.	|	|	|	...	|	...	...	...	|	|	...	...	|	|	...	...	|	|	|	|	|	|	|	|	|
Marseille St Charles a.	2042	|	|	...	|	...	...	...	|	|	...	...	2242	|	...	...	2342	|	|	|	|	|	|	0509	|
Nice **360** a.	...	|	|	...	|	...	...	...	|	|	...	...	...	|	...	...	...	|	|	|	|	|	|	0758	|
Lyon Part Dieu **350** a.	...	|	2120	...	2251	...	...	...	|	|	...	...	...	|	...	...	...	|	|	|	|	|	|	...	0644
Genève **345** a.	...	|	|	...	|	...	...	...	|	|	...	...	...	|	...	...	...	|	|	|	|	|	|	...	0837
Dijon **373** a.	...	|	2305z	...	|	...	...	...	|	|	...	...	...	|	...	...	...	|	|	|	|	|	|	...	...
Strasbourg **384** a.	...	|	...	...	0520	...	...	...	|	|	...	...	...	|	...	...	...	|	|	0834	|	|	|	...	...
Metz **392** a.	...	|	...	...	...	...	...	...	|	|	...	...	...	|	...	...	...	|	0817	...	|	|	|	...	...
Charles de Gaulle ✈ **350** a.	...	|	...	...	...	...	...	...	|	|	...	...	...	|	...	...	...	|	...	...	|	|	|	...	...
Lille Europe **11** a.	...	|	...	...	...	...	...	...	|	|	...	...	...	|	...	...	...	|	...	...	|	|	|	...	...
Brussels Midi **11** a.	...	|	...	...	...	...	...	...	|	|	...	...	...	|	...	...	...	|	...	...	|	|	|	...	...
Paris Austerlitz **310** a.	...	|	...	...	...	...	...	...	|	|	...	...	...	|	...	...	...	0658	...	...	|	0730	0743	...	...
Paris Gare de Lyon **350** a.	...	2241	...	...	...	...	...	...	2347	2347	...	...	...	0041	...	...	...	...	...	...	0720	...	...	...	...

NOTES (CONTINUED FROM PREVIOUS PAGE)

TGV –[R], supplement payable.

⚡ – Special 'global' fares payable.

★ – *CORAIL TÉOZ* [R], 🍸.

⊡ – To Toulouse (Table **321**).

⊙ – On Ⓒ Nimes 1805, Tarascon 1822, Arles 1844, Marseille 1947.

▽ – Not on Ⓐ Nov. 9 - Dec. 11.

△ – To Nantes (Table **335**).

⊕ – On Ⓐ Oct. 12 - Nov. 20 depart Bordeaux 1149, Toulouse 1418.

⊗ – On Ⓐ Oct. 12 - Nov. 20 Bordeaux 1504, Toulouse 1711, Montpellier 1922 / 1930, Marseille 2129.

‡ – Vitrolles Aéroport Marseille-Provence. A shuttle bus runs to the airport terminal (journey 5 mins).

§ – Also July 14, Aug. 15.

SODETRAV 🚌 route 103 — 🚌 TOULON - ST TROPEZ 357

Daily July 6 - Aug. 30. ***See below table for service June 8 - July 5***

km		†	⚒	N	②⑥						
0	**Toulon** Gare SNCF d.	0615	0615	0800	0815	1035	1235	1340	1630	1835	1955
23	Hyères, Gare Routière d.	0643	0645	0827	0842	1110	1313	1420	1657	1915	2030
46	Le Lavandou d.	0714	0717	0857	0912	1145	1348	1455	1725	1950	2104
67	Cavalaire-sur-Mer d.	0744	0728	0933	0948	1217	1420	1527	1757	2020	2132
78	Gassin - La Foux a.	0806	0810	0955	1010	1239	1444	1550	1822	2040	2152
84	**St Tropez** a.	0815	*0850*	1015	*1045*	1257	1505	1610	1842	2053	2202

			⚒	†					
St Tropez d.	0530	0710	*0820*	0900	1100r	1250	1450	1720	1940
Gassin - La Foux d.	0540	0720	0900	0910	1115	1305	1505	1735	1955
Cavalaire-sur-Mer d.	0600	0740	0924	0937	1142	1332	1532	1752	2019
Le Lavandou d.	0628	0810	0959	1007	1214	1404	1604	1835	2047
Hyères, Gare Routière d.	0700	0844	1034	1037	|	1439	1641	1913	2120
Toulon Gare SNCF a.	0735	0919	1110	1110	1255	1514	1720	1952	2150

Service June 8 - July 5: From Toulon: 0615**z**, 0730⑦, 0800⚒**z**, 0920, 1120, 1310, 1430, 1600, 1830;
From St Tropez: 0535, 0820⚒**z**, 0900⑦, 1030⚒**z**, 1040⑦, 1220, 1350, 1555, 1745, 1930.

Operator: SODETRAV, BP 007, 83401 Hyères Les Palmiers. ✆ 04 94 12 55 12 www.sodetrav.fr *Service from Sept. 1 is likely to be similar to the service June 8 - July 5.*

N – ①③④⑤⑦ only. **r** – *1040* on ②⑥. **z** – Change at La Foux on ⚒.

358 🚌 ST RAPHAËL - ST TROPEZ

SODETRAV 🚌 route 104 / 100

Daily July 6 - Aug. 30. *See right-hand panel for service June 8 - July 5 and Sept. 1 - 28*

km																		
0	**St Raphaël** (Parking Kennedy) ▲ d.	...	0735	0855	0930	...	1015	1145	1310	1450	1600	...	1725	1845	1930	...	2100	2215
4	Fréjus (Av. Provence) d.	...	0740	0903	0938	...	1025	1155	1315	1455	1605	...	1735	1855	1935	...	2105	2220
9	St Aygulf d.	...	0755	0918	0948	...	1040	1210	1330	1510	1620	...	1750	1910	1950	...	2120	2235
	Les Arcs (Gare SNCF) d.	0725	|	|	|	1035	|	|	|	|	|	1715	|	|	|	2035	|	|
23	Ste Maxime (Office du Tourisme) d.	0757	0820	0943	1013	1107	1110	1240	1355	1535	1645	1750	1815	1940	2015	2107	2145	2300
28	Port Grimaud d.	0819	0838	1005	|	1132	1137	1305	1410	|	1702	1812	1837	|	|	2127	|	2315
29	Gassin - La Foux a.	0828	0845	1013	1119	1140	1145	1315	1415	1625	1710	1819	1845	2025	2100	2134	2225	2320
35	**St Tropez** (Gare Routière) a.	0840	0900	1028	1144	1200	1213	1333	1435	1645	1725	1835	1900	2040	2110	2145	2235	2330

St Tropez (Gare Routière) d.	0600	...	0710	0820	0910	0920	1000	1130	1220	1310	1410	1500	1535	1550	1705	1815	1850	1950
Gassin - La Foux d.	0605	...	0720	0830	0922	0932	1015	1145	1230	1320	1425	1515	1545	1602	1725	1835	1910	2005
Port Grimaud d.	0612	...	|	0835	0933	0940	1023	1153	1238	1325	1430	1520	1553	1610	1735	|	1919	|
Ste Maxime (Office du Tourisme) d.	0630	0635	0800	0852	1001	0954	1054	1220	1305	1348	1450	1545	1613	1637	1800	1925	1944	2055
Les Arcs (Gare SNCF) a.	|	0710	|	|	|	1025	|	|	|	|	|	|	1650	|	|	|	2015	|
St Aygulf d.	0647	...	0820	0925	1038	...	1125	1250	1330	1418	1520	1615	...	1707	1835	2000	...	2125
Fréjus (Av. Provence) d.	0657	...	0830	0935	1048	...	1135	1300	1340	1428	1530	1625	...	1717	1845	2010	...	2135
St Raphaël (Gare SNCF) △ a.	0705	...	0840	0945	1105	...	1150	1315	1355	1440	1540	1635	...	1732	1900	2025	...	2150

June 8 - July 5, Sept. 1 – 28

St Raphaël ▲ - St Tropez:
⚒: 0625, 0840*, 1000, 1230*, 1320, 1455, 1600, 1740*, 1910, 2115*.
†: 0730*, 0800, 1020*, 1225*, 1320, 1600, 1745*, 1900, 2100*.

Les Arcs - Port Grimaud - St Tropez:
1020 ⚒, 1430 †, 1840 †, 2035 ⚒ c.

June 8 - July 5, Sept. 1 – 28

St Tropez - St Raphaël:
⚒: 0620, 0750*, 0845, 1020*, 1225, 1410*, 1520*, 1630*, 1815, 1930.
†: 0625, 0845*, 1020, 1225, 1400, 1530*, 1635*, 1830, 1930.

St Tropez - Port Grimaud - Les Arcs:
0900 ⚒, 1310 †, 1720 †, 1900 ⚒.

Service by 🚌, operated by SODETRAV, BP 007, 83401 Hyères Les Palmiers. ✆ 04 94 12 55 12 www.sodetrav.fr c – Change at Ste Maxime. * – Via Port Grimaud.
▲ – Does not serve Gare SNCF in this direction due to road works. A free shuttle service runs from Gare SNCF to Parking Kennedy. △ – Continues to Parking Kennedy, arriving 10 mins later.

359 NICE - ANNOT - DIGNE - ST AUBAN and VEYNES

2nd class only

km	CP ▲	①								
0	**Nice** (Gare CP) d.	...	0625	...	0850	1255	...	1715	1813	...
65	Puget Théniers d.	...	0748	...	1015	1420	...	1839	1937	...
72	Entrevaux d.	...	0756	...	1023	1428	...	1848	1945	...
87	Annot d.	0541	0816	...	1042	1446	...	1908	2001	...
106	Thorame Haute d.	0605	0841	...	1106	1510	...	1932	...	...
118	St André les Alpes d.	0619	0854	...	1119	1524	...	1945	...	...
166	**Digne** a.	0715	0950	...	1216	1620	...	2041	...	...

CP ▲		⚒	†						
Digne d.	...	...	...	0729	1055	...	1425	1730	...
St. André les Alpes d.	...	...	...	0826	1153	...	1523	1828	...
Thorame Haute d.	...	...	...	0840	1206	...	1536	1841	...
Annot d.	...	0540	0639	0906	1231	...	1602	1910	...
Entrevaux d.	...	0558	0657	0923	1248	...	1620	1927	...
Puget Théniers d.	...	0606	0705	0931	1256	...	1628	1936	...
Nice (Gare CP) a.	...	0731	0830	1054	1421	...	1752	2057	...

SNCF 🚌	🚌 ⚒	🚌 ①v	🚌	🚌	🚌	🚌	🚌 ⑤	🚌 ⑦n	🚌 ⑧h	🚌 ⑥t
Digne (Gare) d.	0520	0600	0825	1140	1155	1710	1720	1750	1948	2015
Château Arnoux § **362** d.	|	0625*	|	|	1223*	|	1748*	1818*	2020	2041*
Sisteron **362** d.	|	0640	|	|	1240	|	1805	1835	...	2058
Veynes-Dévoluy 362 a.	|	0745	|	|	1340	|	1905	1935	...	2200
Manosque-Gréoux **362** a.	0608	...	0907	1222	...	1757	...	...	...	...
Aix en Provence TGV a.	0710	...	1010	1330	...	1900	...	...	...	...

SNCF 🚌	🚌	🚌 ⚒	🚌	🚌	🚌	🚌 ⑤	🚌 ⑤	🚌 ⑦n	🚌
Aix en Provence TGV d.	...	0930	1255	...	1520	...	...	...	2055
Manosque-Gréoux **362** d.	...	1030	1355	...	1610	...	...	...	2145
Veynes-Dévoluy 362 d.	0645	|	|	1445	|	1615	2020	2020	|
Sisteron **362** d.	0743	|	|	1543	|	1713	2113	2113	|
Château Arnoux § **362** d.	0800*	|	|	1556*	|	1730*	2130*	2130*	|
Digne (Gare) a.	0825	1115	1435	1622	1655	1755	2155	2155	2230

h – Also Aug. 15.
n – Not Nov. 1.
t – Not Aug. 15.
v – Also Sept. 2; not Oct. 26, Nov. 2.
§ – Château Arnoux - St Auban.
* – Town hall (Mairie), not rail station.
▲ – Narrow gauge railway, operated by Chemins de Fer de Provence (CP).

360 MARSEILLE - TOULON - NICE - VENTIMIGLIA

km	All *TGV* trains are [R]	*TGV* 6831 ① g	17471 Ⓐ	4620 4621 [R] B	*TGV* 7989 ⑤–⑦ E	4238 4239 [R] D	5771 [R] P	4296 4297 [R] S	4624 4625 [R] N		17475	*EC* 139 [R]§ M	*TGV* 6815 ①–⑤ n⊕	17479 Ⓐ ☆	*TGV* 6805 ⑥⑦ e	*TGV* 6171	*TGV* 5102	*TGV* 6165 K	4652 4653 ★		17483 Ⓐ	*TGV* 6173	*TGV* 5148 ⊗
	Paris Gare de Lyon **350** d.	...	...	...	2220	...	2225a	...	...	...	...	...	...	...	...	0746	...	0846	...	...	...	0946	...
	Lille Europe **11** d.	...	...	...	|	...	|	...	...	...	...	...	...	...	...	|	0559	|	...	...	...	|	...
	Metz **379** d.	...	...	...	|	2041	|	...	...	...	...	...	...	...	...	|	|	|	...	...	...	|	0611
	Strasbourg **384** d.	...	...	...	|	|	|	2100	...	...	...	...	...	...	...	|	|	|	...	...	...	|	|
	Dijon **373** d.	...	...	...	|	|	|	|	...	...	...	...	...	...	...	|	|	|	...	...	...	|	0916
	Genève **345** d.	...	...	...	|	|	|	|	...	...	...	...	...	...	...	|	|	|	...	...	...	|	|
	Lyon Part-Dieu **350** d.	0050p	...	...	|	|	|	|	...	...	...	...	0635	...	0737	|	0907	|	...	...	...	|	1107
	Nantes **292** d.	|	...	...	|	|	|	|	2034	...	...	...	|	...	|	|	|	|	...	...	...	|	|
	Bordeaux **320** d.	|	...	2157	|	|	|	|	0045	...	...	...	|	...	|	|	|	|	0610	...	...	|	|
	Toulouse **321** d.	|	...	0013	|	|	|	|	|	...	...	...	|	...	|	|	|	|	0817	...	...	|	|
	Montpellier **355** d.	|	...	|	|	|	|	|	0508	...	...	...	|	...	|	|	|	|	1016	...	...	|	|
0	**Marseille St Charles** 350 ▶ d.	|	0518	0524	0528	0559	|	0627	0659	...	0726	...	0829	0925	0929	|	1059	|	1159	...	1219	|	1259
67	**Toulon** 350 ▶ a.	0539	0557	0606	0615	0639	0634	0707	0739	...	0805	...	0908	1006	1009	|	1138	1233	1239	...	1303	|	1339
67	**Toulon** d.	0542	0559	0609	0619	0642	0637	0710	0742	...	0807	...	0911	1008	1012	|	1141	1236	1241	1245	1306	|	1342
100	Carnoules d.	|	0618	|	|	|	|	|	|	...	0827	...	|	1026	|	|	|	|	|	1315	|	|	|
135	Les Arcs-Draguignan ▷ d.	0617	0638	0646	|	0719	0714	0747	0819	...	0847	...	|	1046	|	1207	1216	|	1318	1343	1349	1407	|
158	Fréjus ▷ d.	|	0653	|	|	|	|	|	|	...	0901	...	|	1101	|	|	|	|	|	...	1404	|	|
162	St Raphaël-Valescure ▷ d.	0635	0658	0705	0719	0737	0742	0805	0837	...	0906	...	1005	1106	1106	1225	1234	1324	1335	...	1409	1426	1436
195	**Cannes** ▷ d.	0659	0725	0730	0754	0801	0812	0830	0901	...	0929	...	1029	1128	1130	1250	1258	1349	1359	...	1432	1450	1501
206	Antibes ▷ d.	0712	0736	0742	0806	0812	0826	0842	0912	...	0940	...	1040	1140	1142	1301	1310	1401	1409	...	1443	1500	1512
229	**Nice Ville** ▷ a.	0730	0754	0758	0823	0828	0847	0900	0928	...	0955	...	1055	1155	1155	1317	1325	1417	1425	...	1457	1515	1528
229	**Nice Ville** ▷ d.	...	...	...	...	...	0852	...	...	...	...	1002	...	...	...	...	...	...	...	...	...	...	...
245	Monaco-Monte Carlo ▷ d.	...	...	...	...	...	0917	...	...	...	...	1018	...	...	...	...	...	...	...	...	...	...	...
252	Menton ▷ d.	...	...	...	...	...	0928	...	...	...	...	1028	...	...	...	...	...	...	...	...	...	...	...
262	**Ventimiglia** ▷ a.	...	...	...	...	...	0939	...	...	...	...	1039	...	...	...	...	...	...	...	...	...	...	...

	17487	*TGV* 6175		*EC* 147 [R]§ M	*TGV* 9826 C	4656 4657 ★ y	Ⓐ	17491 Ⓐ ⊡	*TGV* 6177 T	*TGV* 6177 U		*TGV* 6818	17495		*TGV* 6179 R	Ⓑ	*TGV* 6829	4658 4659 ★ H	*TGV* 6181	17499 Q	*TGV* 6187 ⑤	17499 ⑤⑦ q	*TGV* 6183 ⑤ W
Paris Gare de Lyon **350** d.	...	1146	...	...	...	...	...	...	1346	1346	...	...	...	...	1546	...	...	...	1742	...	1816	...	1842
Lille Europe **11** d.	...	|	...	...	1030	...	...	...	|	|	...	...	...	...	|	...	...	...	|	...	|	...	|
Metz **379** d.	...	|	...	...	|	...	...	...	|	|	...	...	...	...	|	...	...	...	|	...	|	...	|
Strasbourg **384** d.	...	|	...	...	|	...	...	...	|	|	...	...	...	...	|	...	...	...	|	...	|	...	|
Dijon **373** d.	...	|	...	...	|	...	...	...	|	|	...	...	...	...	|	...	1611	...	|	...	|	...	|
Genève **345** d.	...	|	...	...	|	...	...	...	|	|	...	1344	...	...	|	...	|	...	|	...	|	...	|
Lyon Part-Dieu **350** d.	...	|	...	...	|	...	...	...	|	|	...	1537	...	...	|	...	1803	...	|	...	|	...	|
Nantes **292** d.	...	|	...	...	|	...	...	...	|	|	...	|	...	...	|	...	|	...	|	...	|	...	|
Bordeaux **320** d.	...	|	...	...	|	1010	...	...	|	|	...	|	...	...	|	...	|	...	|	...	|	...	|
Toulouse **321** d.	...	|	...	...	|	1217	...	...	|	|	...	|	...	...	|	...	|	1614	|	...	|	...	|
Montpellier **355** d.	...	|	...	...	|	1416	...	...	|	|	...	|	...	...	|	...	|	1838	|	...	|	...	|
Marseille St Charles 350 ▶ d.	1429	|	...	...	1529	1557	...	1622	|	|	...	1729	1759	...	|	...	1959	2029	|	2059	2133	2129	|
Toulon 350 ▶ a.	1508	1533	...	...	1608	1638	...	1708	1733	1733	...	1808	1838	...	|	...	2038	2109	2133	2138	2212	2208	2237
Toulon d.	1511	1536	1544	...	1611	1640	1644	1710	1736	1736	1744	1811	1840	1844	|	1944	2041	2111	2136	2141	2215	2219	2240
Carnoules d.	|	|	1614	...	|	|	1714	1728	|	|	1814	|	|	1914	|	2014	|	|	|	|	|	|	|
Les Arcs-Draguignan ▷ d.	1548	|	1642	...	1648	1717	1742	1749	1811	|	1842	|	1916	1942	2010	2042	|	2148	|	2217	|	2256	|
Fréjus ▷ d.	|	|	...	...	|	|	...	|	|	|	...	|	1931	...	|	...	|	|	|	|	|	|	|
St Raphaël-Valescure ▷ d.	1604	1625	...	...	1705	1734	...	1805	1829	1827	...	1905	1936	...	2028	...	2135	2205	2225	2234	2304	2312	2329
Cannes ▷ d.	1628	1650	...	...	1729	1759	...	1828	1853	1851	...	1929	2000	...	2052	...	2159	2229	2249	2258	2329	2337	2353
Antibes ▷ d.	1640	1702	...	...	1740	1810	...	1840	1903	1902	...	1940	2010	...	2103	...	2210	2240	2300	2310	2339	2349	0003
Nice Ville ▷ a.	1655	1717	...	...	1755	1825	...	1855	1919	1917	...	1955	2025	...	2117	...	2225	2255	2314	2325	2353	0004	0017
Nice Ville ▷ d.	...	1725	...	1759	...	...	...	...	...	...	...	...	...	...	...	...	...	...	...	...	...	...	...
Monaco-Monte Carlo ▷ d.	...	1746	...	1817	...	...	...	...	...	...	...	...	...	...	...	...	...	...	...	...	...	...	...
Menton ▷ d.	...	1757	...	1827	...	...	...	...	...	...	...	...	...	...	...	...	...	...	...	...	...	...	...
Ventimiglia ▷ a.	...	1808	...	1839	...	...	...	...	...	...	...	...	...	...	...	...	...	...	...	...	...	...	...

VENTIMIGLIA - NICE - TOULON - MARSEILLE 360

All *TGV* trains are [R]					*TGV*			*TGV*	4768		*TGV*		*TGV*	4758	*TGV*	*TGV*			*TGV*	4764	*TGV*		*TGV*
			17470		6172	17474		6854	4769	17478	5198		6174	4759	9864	6176		17482	6886	4765	6178	17486	6168
	⚒		▽	Ⓐ		Ⓐ ☆			★ J	△				★	b			Ⓐ ⊡	⊕	★	V		⑦ X
Ventimiglia ▷ d.	...	...	...	...	...	...	...	...	...	...	...	...	0847	...	...	...	...	...	...	...	...	...	...
Menton ▷ d.	...	...	...	...	...	...	...	...	...	...	...	...	0900	...	...	...	...	...	...	...	...	...	...
Monaco-Monte Carlo ▷ d.	...	...	...	...	...	...	...	...	...	...	...	...	0912	...	...	...	...	...	...	...	...	...	...
Nice Ville ▷ a.	...	...	...	...	...	...	...	...	...	...	...	...	0927	...	...	...	...	...	...	...	...	...	...
Nice Ville ▷ d.	...	...	0602	...	0639	0702	...	0732	0832	0837	0932	...	0941	1001	1032	1041	...	1232	1329	1336	1341	1432	1442
Antibes ▷ d.	...	...	0618	...	0656	0718	...	0750	0848	0857	0950	...	0959	1017	1049	1059	...	1249	1347	1351	1400	1448	1459
Cannes ▷ d.	...	...	0629	...	0707	0729	...	0801	0900	0908	1001	...	1010	1030	1101	1110	...	1302	1358	1403	1411	1500	1510
St Raphaël-Valescure ▷ d.	...	...	0651	...	0731	0751	...	0825	0925	0930	1026	...	1035	1053	1125	1135	...	1324	1422	1427	1436	1524	1535
Fréjus ▷ d.	...	...	0657	...	|	0756	...	|	|	0936	|	...	|	|	|	|	...	|	|	|	|	|	|
Les Arcs-Draguignan ▷ d.	0612	0642	0710	0714	|	0810	0814	|	0941	0950	|	...	1051	1109	1142	1151	1214	1340	|	1443	1453	1540	|
Carnoules d.	0639	0708	|	0741	|	|	0841	|	|	1010	|	...	|	|	|	|	1241	|	|	|	|	1559	|
Toulon a.	0709	0739	0745	0812	0817	0846	0912	0916	1017	1027	1115	...	|	1145	1215	|	1312	1414	1512	1519	|	1617	1621
Toulon 350 ▶ d.	0711	...	0747	...	0820	0849	...	0919	1019	1029	1117	...	|	1148	1218	|	...	1417	1515	1521	|	1619	1624
Marseille St Charles 350 ▶ a.	0805	...	0829	...	|	0929	...	0959	1059	1110	1159	...	|	1228	1259	|	...	1457	1557	1601	|	1700	|
Montpellier 355 a.	...	...	...	...	|	...	...	|	1251	...	|	...	|	1409	|	|	...	...	|	1741	|	...	|
Toulouse 321 a.	...	...	...	...	|	...	...	|	1517	...	|	...	|	1612	|	|	...	...	|	1945	|	...	|
Bordeaux 320 a.	...	...	...	...	|	...	...	|	...	...	|	...	|	1823	|	|	...	...	|	2150	|	...	|
Nantes 292 a.	...	...	...	...	|	...	...	|	...	...	|	...	|	...	|	|	...	...	|	...	|	...	|
Lyon Part-Dieu 350 a.	...	...	...	...	|	...	...	1155	...	...	1350	...	|	...	|	|	...	...	1750	...	|	...	|
Genève 345 a.	...	...	...	...	|	...	...	...	...	...	|	...	|	...	|	|	...	...	1942	...	|	...	|
Dijon 373 a.	...	...	...	...	|	...	...	...	...	...	1539	...	|	...	|	|	...	...	...	...	|	...	|
Strasbourg 384 a.	...	...	...	...	|	...	...	...	...	...	|	...	|	...	|	|	...	...	...	...	|	...	|
Metz 379 a.	...	...	...	...	|	...	...	...	...	...	1848	...	|	...	|	|	...	...	...	...	|	...	|
Lille Europe 11 a.	...	...	...	...	|	...	...	...	...	...	...	...	|	...	1736	|	...	...	...	...	|	...	|
Paris Gare de Lyon 350 a.	...	...	...	...	1211	...	...	...	...	...	...	...	1519	...	...	1615	...	...	...	...	1919	...	2011

	TGV	*TGV*	*EC*		*TGV*	*TGV*			*TGV*		4724	*TGV*			4394		*EC*		4330	*TGV*	4730		
	5184	6170	144	17490	6184	6876			6180	17494	4725	6186		17498	4395		160		4331	7988	4731		5770
		K	[R] ‡ M	Ⓐ				Ⓐ			[R] N	⑦ e		Ⓐ △	[R] S		[R] ‡ M		[R] D	⑤–⑦ F	[R] B ⊙		[R] P ◇
Ventimiglia ▷ d.	...	...	1521	...	...	...	...	...	...	...	...	...	...	...	...	...	1927	...	...	...	...	...	2017
Menton ▷ d.	...	...	1534	...	...	...	...	...	...	...	...	...	...	...	...	...	1942	...	...	...	...	...	2031
Monaco-Monte Carlo ▷ d.	...	...	1545	...	...	...	...	...	...	...	...	...	...	...	...	...	1955	...	...	...	...	...	2042
Nice Ville ▷ a.	...	...	1559	...	...	...	...	...	...	...	...	...	...	...	...	...	2012	...	...	...	...	...	2056
Nice Ville ▷ d.	1531	1539	...	1632	1641	1732	...	...	1741	1802	1832	1841	...	1941	2007	...	...	...	2034	2038	2057	...	2101
Antibes ▷ d.	1549	1559	...	1648	1659	1750	...	...	1758	1818	1849	1900	...	2001	2023	...	...	...	2052	2101	2116	...	2121
Cannes ▷ d.	1601	1610	...	1700	1710	1802	...	...	1810	1829	1902	1911	...	2011	2035	...	...	...	2105	2116	2129	...	2133
St Raphaël-Valescure ▷ d.	1626	1635	...	1725	1734	1827	...	...	1835	1852	1928	1935	...	2033	2100	...	...	...	2131	2143	2153	...	2158
Fréjus ▷ d.	|	|	...	|	|	|	...	...	|	|	|	|	...	2039	|	...	...	...	|	|	|	...	|
Les Arcs-Draguignan ▷ d.	1642	|	...	1742	|	|	...	1808	|	1908	2006	|	...	2053	2117	...	...	...	2147	|	2211	...	2223
Carnoules d.	|	|	...	|	|	|	...	1836	|	1928	|	|	...	2112	|	...	...	...	|	|	|	...	|
Toulon a.	1715	1720	...	1816	1822	1916	...	1906	1920	1946	2045	2020	...	2130	2153	...	...	...	2223	2235	2246	...	2259
Toulon 350 ▶ d.	1718	1723	...	1819	1825	1919	...	...	1923	1949	2048	2023	...	2132	2156	...	...	...	2226	2239	2249	...	2303
Marseille St Charles 350 ▶ a.	1759	|	...	1859	|	1959	...	...	|	2029	2141	|	...	2212	2238	...	...	...	2306	2318	2329	...	|
Montpellier 355 a.	|	|	...	...	|	|	...	...	|	...	|	|	...	...	|	...	...	...	|	|	|	...	|
Toulouse 321 a.	|	|	...	...	|	|	...	...	|	...	|	|	...	...	|	...	...	...	|	|	0515	...	|
Bordeaux 320 a.	|	|	...	...	|	|	...	...	|	...	0437	|	...	...	|	...	...	...	|	|	0810	...	|
Nantes 292 a.	|	|	...	...	|	|	...	...	|	...	0916r	|	...	...	|	...	...	...	|	|	...	...	|
Lyon Part-Dieu 350 a.	1950	|	...	...	|	2150	...	...	|	...	...	|	...	...	|	...	...	...	|	|	...	...	|
Genève 345 a.	|	|	...	...	|	|	...	...	|	...	...	|	...	...	|	...	...	...	|	|	...	...	|
Dijon 373 a.	|	|	...	...	|	2343	...	...	|	...	...	|	...	...	|	...	...	...	|	|	...	...	|
Strasbourg 384 a.	|	|	...	...	|	...	...	...	|	...	...	|	...	...	0759	...	...	...	|	|	...	...	|
Metz 379 a.	|	|	...	...	|	...	...	...	|	...	...	|	...	...	...	...	...	...	0745	|	...	...	|
Lille Europe 11 a.	2301	|	...	...	|	...	...	...	|	...	...	|	...	...	...	...	...	...	...	|	...	...	|
Paris Gare de Lyon 350 a.	...	2120	...	...	2211	...	...	...	2311	...	...	0017	...	...	...	...	...	...	...	0720	...	...	0746a

LOCAL TRAINS MARSEILLE - TOULON

Certain trains continue to / from Hyères (Table 352)

km		⚒		⚒		d	Ⓐ d		⚒				z	Ⓐ				Ⓐ			Ⓐ				w	d
0	**Marseille** d.	0603	0633	0703	0733	0833	0933	1103	1133	1223	1337	1433	1503	1533	1606	1627	1703	1733	1803	1833	1901	1937	2003	2033	2137	2303
27	Cassis d.	0625	0655	0725	0755	0855	0955	1130	1155	1255	1359	1455	1526	1555	1628	1655	1725	1755	1825	1855	1930	1959	2025	2055	2159	2325
37	La Ciotat d.	0632	0702	0732	0802	0902	1002	1137	1202	1302	1406	1502	1533	1602	1635	1702	1732	1802	1832	1902	1938	2006	2032	2102	2206	2332
51	Bandol d.	0643	0713	0743	0813	0913	1013	1149	1213	1313	1417	1513	1545	1613	1646	1713	1743	1813	1843	1913	1950	2017	2043	2113	2218	2343
67	**Toulon** a.	0659	0729	0759	0829	0929	1029	1205	1229	1329	1434	1529	1603	1629	1702	1729	1759	1829	1859	1931	2008	2034	2059	2129	2233	2359

	Ⓑ u	Ⓐ	⑥			⚒	⚒				s	z	Ⓐ	k	k	k			Ⓐ		Ⓐ					
Toulon d.	0455	0527	0541	0552	0624	0641	0711	0727	0755	0827	0927	1055	1155	1227	1255	1327	1533	1553	1634	1655	1727	1755	1856	1927	2027	2136
Bandol d.	0511	0542	0556	0606	0640	0656	0725	0742	0810	0842	0942	1111	1211	1242	1311	1342	1547	1608	1650	1711	1742	1811	1911	1942	2042	2151
La Ciotat d.	0523	0553	0608	0618	0652	0708	0737	0753	0822	0853	0953	1123	1223	1253	1323	1353	1559	1619	1702	1723	1753	1823	1923	1953	2053	2202
Cassis d.	0531	0601	0615	0625	0700	0715	0744	0801	0831	0901	1001	1131	1231	1301	1331	1401	1606	1626	1709	1731	1801	1831	1931	2001	2101	2210
Marseille a.	0555	0625	0639	0655	0725	0737	0805	0825	0855	0925	1025	1155	1255	1331	1355	1426	1633	1656	1735	1755	1825	1855	1955	2025	2125	2234

B – *CORAIL LUNÉA* – 🛏 1,2 cl. and [2] (reclining) Bordeaux - Nice and v.v. From Hendaye / to Irún on dates in Table **305**.
C – [12] Lille Europe (**5164**) - Charles de Gaulle (**9826**) - Nice; [12] Brussels (d 1021) - Nice.
D – *CORAIL LUNÉA* – 🛏 1,2 cl. and [2] (reclining) Luxembourg - Metz - Nice and v.v. For days of running see Table **379**.
E – ⑤⑥⑦ (also June 1; not Sept. 20). On June 20 Paris d. 2315. On ⑤ Sept. 18 - Nov. 6 Paris d. 2210. Departures from Paris on June 26, July 3, 10, 31 arrive up to 2 hours later.
F – ⑤⑥⑦ (also June 1, July 13, 14, Nov. 10, 11). Runs up to 75 minutes earlier on June 12, 19, 26, Oct. 2, Nov. 27, Dec. 4.
H – ⑤⑥⑦ June 26 - Aug. 30 (also June 1, July 14, Oct. 23, 24, 30, 31, Nov. 1, 2).
J – ⑤⑥⑦ June 26 - Aug. 30 (also June 1, July 14, Oct. 23, 24, 30, 31, Nov. 1, 2, 11).
K – July 5 - Aug. 30.
M – [12] and 🍸 Nice - Ventimiglia - Genova - Milano and v.v. (Table **90**).
N – 🛏 1,2 cl. and [2] (reclining) Nantes - Nice and v.v. For days of running see Table **292**. Timings from Nantes vary (see Table **292**).
P – *TRAIN BLEU* – 🛏 1,2 cl. and [2] (reclining) Paris Austerlitz - Nice - Ventimiglia and v.v. Train number **15771** on certain dates.
Q – ①②③④⑥ (not June 1, July 13, 14, Aug. 15, Oct. 31, Nov. 10, 11).
R – Mar. 30 - Sept. 17, also ⑤⑥ Sept. 18 - Dec. 12.
S – *CORAIL LUNÉA* – 🛏 1,2 cl. and [2] (reclining) Strasbourg - Nice and v.v. For days of running see Table **384**. Train **4294/5** and **4388/9** on certain dates.
T – Sept. 20 - Dec. 12.
U – Mar. 30 - Sept. 19.
V – Mar. 31 - Sept. 18, also ⑥⑦ Sept. 19 - Dec. 12.
W – ⑤ (daily July 5 - Aug. 30).
X – ⑦ (daily July 5 - Aug. 29), also June 1.

a – Paris **Austerlitz**.
b – To Brussels, arrive 1822 (Table **11**).
d – Subject to alteration on Ⓐ June 2 - 26, Nov. 9, 10, 12, 13.
e – Also June 1, July 14.
g – Also June 2, July 15; not June 1, July 13.

k – Subject to alteration on Ⓐ June 8 - 26, Sept. 28 - Oct. 2, Nov. 23 - Dec. 4.
n – Not June 1, July 14.
p – Lyon **Perrache**.
q – Also June 1, July 13, 14, Aug. 15, Oct. 31 (also Nov. 10, 11 Marseille - Cannes).
r – 1009 on June 28, Sept. 6.
s – Runs up to 4 minutes earlier on June 2 - 5.
u – Not June 9 - 12, 17 - 19.
w – Subject to alteration on June 10 - 12, 15.
y – On June 15 - 17 runs later (Bordeaux d. 1030, Nice a. 2056). On June 18, 19 Bordeaux d. 0957. On Sept. 21 - 25 runs later (Bordeaux d. 1030, Nice a. 2017).
z – Subject to alteration on June 2 - 5, 22 - 26.

TGV – [R], supplement payable, 🍸.

⊕ – Will not run Marseille - Nice or v.v. on Ⓐ June 8 - 26, Nov. 9, 10, 12, 13.
⊗ – On June 7, 14 depart Metz 0608. On July 8, 9, 28 - 30, Sept. 14 - 18 depart Dijon 0910.
⊡ – Will not run Marseille - Toulon or v.v. Ⓐ June 8 - 26, Sept. 28 - Oct. 2, Nov. 23 - Dec. 4.
⊙ – On ①-④ June 8 - 25, Sept. 28 - Oct. 1, Nov. 23 - Dec. 3 runs up to 45 minutes earlier. Train **14730** on certain dates.
☆ – Will not run Marseille - Toulon or v.v. on Ⓐ June 8 - 26, Nov. 9, 10, 12, 13.
◇ – Runs up to 45 minutes earlier on Ⓐ June 8 - 26, Nov. 23 - Dec. 4 (also Aug. 31 - Sept. 3, Sept. 21 - 24).
△ – Also calls at Cagnes sur Mer (11 minutes after Nice).
▽ – Also calls daily at La Ciotat (d. 0806). On ⑥ depart Toulon 0750, arrive Marseille 0834.
▷ – For local trains Les Arcs - Cannes - Nice - Ventimiglia see Table **361**.
▶ – For local trains Marseille - Toulon see separate panel. For complete *TGV* service Paris - Marseille / Toulon see Table **350**.
★ – *CORAIL TÉOZ*, [R], 🍸.
§ – Calls to pick up only.
‡ – Calls to set down only.

See Table 361 for local trains on the Riviera

361 LES ARCS - ST RAPHAEL - CANNES - NICE - MONACO - VENTIMIGLIA

Local trains

km			①–⑤	①–⑤		①–⑤	①–⑥	①–⑥		①–⑥			Ⓐ ◇	①–⑤		①–⑥	①–⑤		①–⑤	①–⑤		①–⑤			◇	①–⑥
0	**Les Arcs-Draguignan**	d.	...	...	...	...	...	...	...	...	...	0621	0638	...	...	...	...	...	0726	...	...	...	...	...	0847	...
23	Fréjus	d.	...	...	...	...	...	...	...	...	...	0634	0653	...	...	...	...	...	0740	...	...	...	...	...	0901	...
27	St Raphaël-Valescure	d.	...	...	...	...	...	0555	...	...	...	0639	0658	...	...	0710	...	...	0745	...	...	...	...	0842	0906	...
31	Boulouris sur Mer	d.	...	...	...	...	...	0559	...	...	...	0644	|	...	...	0714	...	...	0750	...	...	...	...	0846	|	...
**	Grasse	d.	...	...	...	...	0532	|	...	...	0640	|	|	...	0711	|	...	...	|	...	...	...	0837	|	|	...
60	**Cannes**	a.	...	...	...	...	0554	0625	...	...	0702	0718	0722	...	0733	0739	...	...	0823	...	...	...	0903	0920	0927	...
60	**Cannes**	d.	0434	0504	0534	...	0605	0627	0634	*0650*	0705	0720	0725	...	0735	0741	...	0806	0825	...	0837	...	0905	0922	0929	0936
69	Juan les Pins	d.	0444	0514	0544	...	0615	0636	0644	*0659*	0715	0728	|	...	0744	0751	...	0815	0833	...	0846	...	0915	0930	|	0946
71	Antibes	d.	0447	0517	0547	...	0618	0640	0647	*0702*	0718	0731	0736	...	0747	0755	...	0818	0836	...	0849	...	0918	0933	0940	0948
80	Cagnes sur Mer	d.	0458	0529	0559	...	0629	0648	0659	*0710*	0729	0738	|	0752	0759	0804	...	0829	0843	0851	0900	0921	0929	0940	|	0959
94	**Nice Ville**	a.	0513	0543	0613	...	0643	0703	0713	*0723*	0743	0750	0754	0804	0813	0818	...	0843	0855	0904	0914	0933	0943	0951	0955	1013
94	**Nice Ville**	d.	0516	0546	0616	0636	0646	0706	0716	0736	0746	...	...	0807	0816	...	0836	0846	...	0906	0916	0936	0946	...	...	1016
99	Villefranche sur Mer	d.	0523	0553	0623	|	0653	|	0723	|	0753	...	...	|	0823	...	|	0853	...	|	0923	|	0954	...	...	1023
101	Beaulieu sur Mer	d.	0526	0556	0626	0645	0656	0715	0726	0745	0756	...	...	0816	0826	...	0845	0856	...	0915	0926	0944	0957	...	...	1026
104	Eze	d.	0530	0600	0630	|	0700	|	0730	|	0800	...	...	|	0830	...	|	0900	...	|	0930	|	1001	...	...	1030
110	**Monaco-Monte Carlo**	d.	0539	0609	0639	0654	0709	0724	0739	0754	0810	...	...	0825	0841	...	0854	0909	...	0924	0939	0954	1010	...	...	1039
114	Cap Martin-Roquebrune	d.	0544	0614	0644	|	0716	|	0746	|	0816	...	...	|	0846	...	|	0914	...	|	0944	|	1016	...	...	1044
117	Menton	d.	0551	0621	0651	0704	0723	0734	0753	0804	0823	...	...	0835	0853	...	0904	0921	...	0934	0951	1004	1022	...	...	1051
127	**Ventimiglia**	a.	0603	0633	0703	...	0735	...	0805	...	0835	...	...	...	0905	...	...	0933	...	...	1003	1015	1034	...	...	1103

			①–⑤			Ⓐ ◇			①–⑤			①–⑥		①–⑤	Ⓐ ◇			①–⑥		①–⑤		①–⑥	◇	①–⑤	①–⑤	①–⑤
Les Arcs-Draguignan	d.	...	...	...	...	1046	...	...	...	...	1227	...	...	...	1349	...	...	...	...	...	...	1521	1548	...	...	...
Fréjus	d.	...	...	...	...	1101	...	...	...	...	1241	...	...	...	1404	...	...	...	...	...	...	1535	|	...	...	...
St Raphaël-Valescure	d.	...	...	...	1040	1106	...	...	...	...	1246	...	...	1340	1409	...	...	...	...	...	...	1540	1604	...	...	...
Boulouris sur Mer	d.	...	...	...	1044	|	...	...	...	...	1250	...	...	1344	|	...	...	...	...	...	...	1545	|	...	...	...
Grasse	d.	0937	...	1034	|	|	1100	...	...	1251	|	...	1337	|	|	...	1437	...	...	...	1537	|	|	...	...	...
Cannes	a.	1003	...	1103	1118	1126	1122	...	...	1313	1324	...	1403	1418	1429	...	1503	...	...	...	1602	1619	1625	...	...	...
Cannes	d.	1005	1036	1105	1120	1128	1135	...	1235	1315	1326	1335	1405	1420	1432	...	1505	...	1535	...	1605	1621	1628	...	1635	...
Juan les Pins	d.	1015	1045	1114	1127	|	1145	...	1245	1325	1334	1345	1414	1427	|	...	1514	...	1544	...	1614	1628	|	...	1645	...
Antibes	d.	1018	1048	1117	1131	1140	1148	...	1248	1328	1338	1348	1417	1431	1443	...	1517	...	1547	...	1617	1632	1640	...	1648	...
Cagnes sur Mer	d.	1029	1059	1128	1138	|	1159	...	1259	1339	1346	1359	1429	1439	|	...	1529	...	1559	...	1629	1639	|	1651	1659	1721
Nice Ville	a.	1043	1113	1143	1151	1155	1213	...	1313	1353	1359	1413	1443	1451	1457	...	1543	...	1613	...	1643	1651	1655	1703	1713	1734
Nice Ville	d.	1046	1116	...	...	...	1216	1246	1316	1356	...	1416	1446	...	...	1516	1546	1606	1616	1636	1646	...	...	1706	1716	1736
Villefranche sur Mer	d.	1054	1123	...	...	...	1223	1253	1323	1403	...	1423	1453	...	...	1523	1553	|	1623	|	1653	...	...	|	1723	|
Beaulieu sur Mer	d.	1057	1126	...	...	...	1226	1256	1326	1406	...	1426	1456	...	...	1526	1556	1615	1626	1645	1656	...	...	1714	1726	1745
Eze	d.	1101	1130	...	...	...	1230	1300	1330	1410	...	1430	1500	...	...	1530	1600	|	1630	|	1700	...	...	|	1730	|
Monaco-Monte Carlo	d.	1110	1139	...	...	...	1239	1309	1339	1419	...	1439	1509	...	...	1539	1610	1624	1640	1654	1711	...	...	1724	1739	1754
Cap Martin-Roquebrune	d.	1116	1144	...	...	...	1245	1314	1344	1424	...	1444	1514	...	...	1545	1616	|	1646	|	1716	...	...	|	1744	|
Menton	d.	1122	1151	...	...	...	1251	1321	1351	1431	...	1451	1521	...	...	1551	1623	1634	1653	1704	1723	...	...	1734	1751	1804
Ventimiglia	a.	1134	1203	...	...	...	1303	1333	1403	1443	...	1503	1533	...	...	1603	1635	...	1705	...	1735	...	...	...	1803	...

				Ⓑ		①–⑤			Ⓐ ◇		①–⑤				◇		①–⑥			①–⑤			Q ◇		⑤⑦ q ◇	h
Les Arcs-Draguignan	d.	...	1630	...	...	...	...	1721	1749	...	...	...	1821	...	1916	...	1921	...	...	...	...	...	2217	...	2256	...
Fréjus	d.	...	1644	...	...	...	...	1735	|	...	...	...	1836	...	1931	...	1937	...	...	...	...	...	|	...	|	...
St Raphaël-Valescure	d.	...	1649	...	...	...	...	1740	1805	...	...	...	1841	...	1936	...	1941	...	...	...	...	...	2234	...	2312	...
Boulouris sur Mer	d.	...	1653	...	...	...	...	1745	|	...	...	...	1845	...	|	...	1946	...	...	...	...	...	|	...	|	...
Grasse	d.	1637	|	...	...	...	1737	|	|	...	...	1837	|	...	|	1937	|	...	2037	...	2150	...	|	2237	|	...
Cannes	a.	1703	1719	...	...	...	1803	1819	1826	...	...	1903	1919	...	1957	2002	2019	...	2103	...	2212	...	2255	2303	2334	...
Cannes	d.	1705	1721	...	1736	...	1805	1821	1828	...	1836	1905	1921	1936	2000	2005	2021	2035	2105	2134	2214	2236	2258	2305	2337	2358
Juan les Pins	d.	1714	1729	...	1745	...	1815	1828	|	...	1845	1914	1929	1945	|	2014	2028	2045	2115	2144	2223	2245	|	2315	|	0008
Antibes	d.	1717	1732	...	1748	...	1818	1832	1840	...	1848	1917	1932	1948	2010	2017	2032	2048	2118	2147	2226	2247	2310	2318	2349	0011
Cagnes sur Mer	d.	1728	1738	1751	1759	1821	1829	1839	|	1851	1859	1928	1939	1959	|	2029	2039	2059	2129	2159	2237	2257	|	2329	|	0022
Nice Ville	a.	1743	1751	1803	1813	1833	1843	1851	1855	1903	1913	1943	1951	2013	2025	2043	2051	2113	2143	2213	2251	2310	2325	2343	0004	0036
Nice Ville	d.	1746	...	1806	1816	1836	1846	...	...	1906	1916	1946	...	2016	...	2046	...	2116	2146	2216	2253	2316	...	2346	...	0037
Villefranche sur Mer	d.	1753	...	|	1823	|	1853	...	...	|	1923	1953	...	2023	...	2053	...	2123	2153	2223	2300	2323	...	2353	...	0044
Beaulieu sur Mer	d.	1756	...	1814	1826	1844	1856	...	...	1914	1926	1956	...	2026	...	2056	...	2126	2156	2226	2303	2326	...	2356	...	0047
Eze	d.	1800	...	|	1830	|	1900	...	...	|	1930	2000	...	2030	...	2100	...	2130	2200	2230	2307	2330	...	0000	...	0051
Monaco-Monte Carlo	d.	1809	...	1824	1840	1854	1910	...	...	1924	1939	2009	...	2039	...	2110	...	2139	2210	2239	2316	2339	...	0009	...	0059
Cap Martin-Roquebrune	d.	1814	...	|	1846	|	1916	...	...	|	1944	2014	...	2044	...	2115	...	2144	2215	2244	2321	2344	...	0015	...	0104
Menton	d.	1821	...	1834	1853	1904	1923	...	...	1934	1951	2021	...	2051	...	2122	...	2150	2222	2251	2328	2351	...	0020	...	0110
Ventimiglia	a.	1833	...	...	1905	...	1935	...	...	1945	2003	2033	...	2103	...	2134	...	2203	2234	2303	2340	0003	...	...	...	...

				◇			Ⓐ ◇			①–⑤		①–⑤			①–⑤	◇		①–⑥		①–⑤		①–⑤			①–⑤	
Ventimiglia	d.	...	0454	...	0529	0554	...	...	0625	0640	0655	...	...	0725	...	...	0755	...	0820	...	0855	...	...	0955	1025	1055
Menton	d.	...	0506	...	0541	0606	...	...	0637	0651	0707	0717	...	0737	0747	...	0807	0817	0834	0847	0907	0915	...	1007	1037	1107
Cap Martin-Roquebrune	d.	...	0513	...	0548	0612	...	...	0644	|	0714	|	...	0744	|	...	0814	|	0841	|	0914	|	...	1014	1044	1114
Monaco-Monte Carlo	d.	...	0519	...	0555	0619	...	...	0650	0702	0720	0732	...	0750	0802	...	0820	0832	0847	0902	0920	0932	...	1020	1050	1120
Eze	d.	...	0527	...	0604	0627	...	...	0658	|	0729	|	...	0758	|	...	0829	|	0856	|	0928	|	...	1029	1058	1128
Beaulieu sur Mer	d.	...	0531	...	0608	0631	...	...	0702	0711	0733	0741	...	0802	0811	...	0832	0841	0900	0911	0932	0941	...	1032	1102	1132
Villefranche sur Mer	d.	...	0535	...	0611	0634	...	...	0706	|	0737	|	...	0806	|	...	0836	|	0903	|	0936	|	...	1036	1106	1136
Nice Ville	a.	...	0541	...	0618	0640	...	...	0712	0719	0743	0749	...	0812	0819	...	0842	0849	0909	0919	0942	0949	...	1042	1112	1142
Nice Ville	d.	0515	0542	0602	0620	0643	0702	0707	0715	0722	0746	0752	0806	0815	0822	0837	0845	0852a	0911	...	0945	...	1006	1045	1115	1145
Cagnes sur Mer	d.	0530	0557	|	0636	0658	|	0720	0729	0735	0801	0806	0818	0830	0835	0848	0900	0905a	0927	...	1000	...	1017	1100	1130	1200
Antibes	d.	0540	0608	0618	0647	0709	0718	0729	0740	...	0812	0817	0826	0840	...	0857	0911	...	0939	...	1011	...	1025	1111	1140	1210
Juan les Pins	d.	0543	0612	|	0650	0712	|	0732	0743	...	0815	0820	0829	0843	...	|	0914	...	0942	...	1014	...	1028	1114	1143	1213
Cannes	a.	0552	0620	0627	0700	0720	0727	0739	0752	...	0824	0830	0836	0852	...	0906	0922	...	0951	...	1023	...	1035	1122	1152	1222
Cannes	d.	0555	0623	0629	0711	...	0729	0747	...	...	0826	...	0838	...	...	0908	0925	...	...	...	1025	...	1037	1125	...	1224
Grasse	a.	0622	0655	|	|	...	|	0810	...	...	0852	...	|	...	...	|	0952	...	...	...	1048	...	|	1149	...	1249
Boulouris sur Mer	d.	...	...	|	0741	...	|	...	...	...	...	...	0913	...	...	|	...	...	...	...	...	...	1112	...	...	...
St Raphaël-Valescure	d.	...	...	0651	0745	...	0751	...	...	...	...	...	0917	...	...	0930	...	...	...	...	...	...	1118	...	...	...
Fréjus	d.	...	...	0657	...	...	0756	...	...	...	...	...	...	...	...	0936	...	...	...	...	...	...	1122	...	...	...
Les Arcs-Draguignan	a.	...	...	0708	...	...	0808	...	...	...	...	...	...	...	...	0948	...	...	...	...	...	...	1135	...	...	...

		①–⑤ △	①–⑥ △	Ⓐ ◇				①–⑤			◇				Ⓑ	⑥	①–⑤	Ⓐ ◇		①–⑤	①–⑥		①–⑤			◇
Ventimiglia	d.	...	1125	...	1155	...	...	1223	1255	1325	...	1355	1455	...	1526	...	1540	...	1555	...	...	1625	...	1655	...	...
Menton	d.	...	1137	...	1207	...	...	1235	1307	1337	...	1407	1507	...	1539	...	1551	...	1607	1617	...	1637	1647	1707	1717	...
Cap Martin-Roquebrune	d.	...	1144	...	1214	...	...	1242	1314	1344	...	1414	1514	...	1545	...	|	...	1614	|	...	1644	|	1714	|	...
Monaco-Monte Carlo	d.	...	1150	...	1220	...	...	1248	1320	1350	...	1420	1520	...	1551	...	1602	...	1620	1632	...	1650	1702	1720	1732	...
Eze	d.	...	1158	...	1228	...	...	1256	1328	1358	...	1429	1529	...	1600	...	|	...	1628	|	...	1658	|	1728	|	...
Beaulieu sur Mer	d.	...	1202	...	1232	...	...	1300	1332	1402	...	1432	1532	...	1604	...	1611	...	1632	1641	...	1702	1711	1732	1741	...
Villefranche sur Mer	d.	...	1206	...	1236	...	...	1304	1336	1406	...	1436	1536	...	1607	...	|	...	1636	|	...	1706	|	1736	|	...
Nice Ville	a.	...	1212	...	1242	...	...	1310	1342	1412	...	1442	1542	...	1613	...	1619	...	1642	1649	...	1712	1719	1742	1749	...
Nice Ville	d.	1206	1215	1232	1245	1306	...	1312	1345	1415	1432	...	1545	1601	1615	1615	1622	1632	1645	1652	1706	1715	1722	1745	1752	1802
Cagnes sur Mer	d.	1219	1230	|	1300	1318	...	1327	1400	1430	|	...	1600	1612	1630	1630	1635	|	1700	1705	1718	1730	1735	1800	1805	|
Antibes	d.	1226	1240	1249	1311	1326	...	1338	1411	1440	1448	...	1611	1619	1640	1640	...	1648	1710	...	1726	1740	...	1811	...	1818
Juan les Pins	d.	1229	1243	|	1314	1329	...	1341	1414	1443	|	...	1614	1622	1643	1643	...	|	1713	...	1729	1743	...	1814	...	|
Cannes	a.	1236	1252	1300	1322	1335	...	1349	1423	1452	1457	...	1622	1629	1652	1652	...	1658	1722	...	1735	1752	...	1822	...	1827
Cannes	d.	1238	...	1302	1324	1337	...	...	1428	1504	1500	...	1624	1631	...	...	...	1700	1725	...	1737	...	...	1825	...	1829
Grasse	a.	|	...	|	1352	|	...	...	1452	1527	|	...	1652	|	...	...	...	|	1752	...	|	...	...	1852	...	|
Boulouris sur Mer	d.	1313	...	|	...	1411	...	...	...	...	|	...	...	1707	...	...	...	|	...	...	1809	...	...	...	...	|
St Raphaël-Valescure	d.	1317	...	1324	...	1415	1441	...	...	...	1524	...	...	1712	...	...	...	1725	...	...	1814	...	...	...	...	1852
Fréjus	d.	...	...	|	...	...	1445	...	...	...	|	...	...	1716	...	...	...	|	...	...	1818	...	...	...	...	|
Les Arcs-Draguignan	a.	...	...	1338	...	...	1458	...	...	...	1538	...	...	1730	...	...	...	1740	...	...	1830	...	...	...	...	1906

Ⓐ – Mondays to Fridays, except holidays   Ⓑ – Daily except Saturdays   Ⓒ – Saturdays, Sundays and holidays

Local trains VENTIMIGLIA - MONACO - NICE - CANNES - ST RAPHAEL - LES ARCS 361

			①–⑤	①–⑥		①–⑤			Ⓐ		①–⑤				①–⑤	①–⑤			①–⑤	①–⑤				
	▽			n					◇			⊕				S				S		h		
Ventimiglia d.	...	1725	...	...	1755	...	1825	...	...	1855	...	1922	...	1955	2025	2025	2055	2125	2146	2146	...	2325	...	...
Menton d.	...	1737	1745	...	1807	1815	1837	1847	...	1907	1917	1934	...	2007	2037	2037	2107	2137	2158	2158	...	2337	...	...
Cap Martin-Roquebrune d.	...	1744	|	...	1814	|	1844	|	...	1914	|	1940	...	2014	2044	2044	2114	2144	2205	2205	...	2344	...	...
Monaco-Monte Carlo d.	...	1750	1802	...	1820	1832	1850	1902	...	1920	1932	1947	...	2020	2050	2050	2120	2150	2211	2211	2305	2350	...	...
Eze d.	...	1758	|	...	1828	|	1858	|	...	1928	|	1955	...	2029	2059	2059	2128	2159	2220	2220	2314	2359	...	...
Beaulieu sur Mer d.	...	1802	1811	...	1832	1841	1902	1911	...	1932	1941	1959	...	2032	2102	2102	2132	2203	2224	2224	2317	0003	...	...
Villefranche sur Mer d.	...	1806	|	...	1836	|	1906	|	...	1936	|	2002	...	2036	2106	2106	2136	2206	2228	2228	2321	0006	...	...
Nice Ville a.	...	1812	1819	...	1842	1849	1912	1919	...	1942	1949	2008	...	2042	2112	2112	2142	2212	2234	2234	2327	0012	...	...
Nice Ville d.	1806	1815	1822	1841	1845	...	1915	...	1941	1945	...	2011	...	2045	2115	2115	2145	2215	2245	2245	2330	0015	...	...
Cagnes sur Mer d.	1818	1830	1835	1852	1900	...	1930	...	1952	2000	...	2026	...	2059	2129	2129	2200	2231	2300	2300	2345	0031	...	...
Antibes d.	1826	1841	...	1901	1911	...	1940	...	2001	2011	...	2037	...	2110	2140	2140	2211	2242	2311	2311	2356	0042	...	...
Juan les Pins d.	1829	1844	...	|	1914	...	1943	...	|	2014	...	2040	...	2113	2143	2143	2214	2245	2314	2314	2359	0045	...	...
Cannes a.	1836	1852	...	1909	1922	...	1952	...	2009	2022	...	2048	...	2122	2152	2152	2222	2254	2322	2322	0007	0054	...	...
Cannes d.	1838	...	...	1912	1925	...	...	...	2011	2025	...	2050	...	2124	...	2154	2225	...	...	2325	...	...	...	...
Grasse a.	|	...	...	|	1952	...	...	...	|	2052	...	|	...	2146	...	|	2252	...	...	2352	...	...	...	...
Boulouris sur Mer d.	1913	...	...	|	...	...	...	...	|	...	...	2121	...	...	...	2227	...	...	...	...	...	...	...	...
St Raphaël-Valescure d.	1917	...	...	1935	...	...	...	...	2033	...	...	2125	...	...	...	2232	...	...	...	...	...	...	...	...
Fréjus d.	...	...	...	1940	...	...	...	...	2039	...	...	...	...	...	...	2235	...	...	...	...	...	...	...	...
Les Arcs-Draguignan a.	...	...	...	1955	...	...	...	...	2051	...	...	...	...	...	...	2248	...	...	...	...	...	...	...	...

Q – ①②③④⑥ (not June 1, July 13, 14, Nov. 10, 11).
S – June 15 - Sept. 11.

a – ①–⑤ only.
h – Not on Ⓐ Sept. 28 - Oct. 23.
n – Not June 1, July 14.
q – Also June 1, July 13, 14, Nov. 10, 11.

△ – On Aug. 1, Sept. 2, 19, Nov. 5 runs 6 minutes earlier.
▽ – Runs 3 - 4 minutes later on ⑥ May 16 - Sept. 26.
◇ – To / from Marseille (Table **360**).
⊕ – Runs 13 - 14 minutes later on Ⓐ June 8 - 26, Aug. 31 - Sept. 3, Nov. 23 - Dec. 4.
** – Grasse - Cannes = *17 km*.

BRIANÇON - GRENOBLE, LYON and MARSEILLE 362

Service is by 🚌 Sisteron - Veynes and v.v. Aug. 31 - Oct. 29

km																							5790	
		⚒		①	Ⓐ	Ⓐ										⑦		Ⓐ		Ⓐ	Ⓒ		🅁	
				g			u				Y				b	L							D§	
0	**Briançon** d.	...	...	0455	...	...	0612	...	0755	...	0913	...	1250	...	1500	...	...	1646	...	1745	1745	...	2030	...
13	L'Argentière les Écrins d.	...	...	0507	...	...	0625	...	0810	...	0929	...	1304	...	1513	...	...	1701	...	1800	1800	...	2045	...
28	Montdauphin-Guillestre d.	...	...	0518	...	...	0636	...	0821	...	0942	...	1316	...	1525	...	...	1713	...	1821	1820	...	2100	...
45	Embrun d.	...	...	0532	...	...	0654	...	0837	...	0959	...	1332	...	1547	...	...	1728	...	1837	1837	...	2117	...
82	**Gap** a.	...	...	0604	...	...	0727	...	0909	...	1037	...	1406	...	1628	...	...	1802	...	1912	1911	...	2154	...
82	**Gap** d.	0505	...	0606	0606	...	0730	...	0911	...	1040	...	1408	...	1632	1705	...	1805	...	...	1913	...	2157	...
109	Veynes-Dévoluy a.	0524	...	0625	0625	...	0752	...	0933	...	1108	...	1436	...	1655	1725	...	1833	...	...	1932	...	2223	...
109	Veynes-Dévoluy d.	0545	...	0627	0627	0633	▽	...	0935	...	1112	...	1440	...	1659	1727	...	1835	...	...	1934	...	2227	...
172	Die d.	|	...	0720	0720	|	...	...	|	...	1213	...	|	...	1752	|	...	|	...	...	|	...	2325	...
244	**Valence Ville** a.	|	...	0824	0824	|	...	...	|	...	1324	...	|	...	1855	|	...	|	...	...	|	...	0029	...
254	Valence TGV **350** a.	|	...	0838	0838	|	...	...	|	...	|	...	|	...	1907	|	...	|	...	...	|	...	|	...
261	Romans-Bourg de Peage a.	|	...	0848	0848	|	...	...	|	...	|	...	|	...	1916	|	...	|	...	...	|	...	|	...
	Lyon Part-Dieu 351 a.	|	...	...	...	|	...	...	|	...	1434	...	|	...	...	|	...	|	...	...	|	...	|	...
	Paris Austerlitz **351** a.	|	...	...	...	|	...	...	|	...	...	...	|	...	...	|	...	|	...	...	|	...	0646	...
159	Sisteron d.	0626	...	...	...	0719	...	...	1028	...	...	...	1525	...	...	1807	...	1917	...	...	2016	...	...	...
176	Château Arnoux - St Auban d.	0639	...	...	...	0736	...	...	1041	...	...	...	1539	...	...	1823	...	1930	...	...	2030	...	...	...
209	Manosque-Gréoux d.	0704	...	...	...	0803	...	...	1106	...	...	...	1605	...	...	1856	...	2002	...	...	2058	...	...	...
278	Aix en Provence ▷ d.	0751	...	...	...	0851	...	...	1151	...	...	...	1651	...	...	1953	...	2051	...	...	2151	...	...	...
315	**Marseille St Charles** ▷ a.	0822	...	...	...	0922	...	...	1222	...	...	...	1722	...	...	2024	...	2122	...	...	2222	...	...	...

		5799																						🚌
	Ⓐ	🅁		⚒	⑥	Ⓐ		⑥			Ⓒ		Ⓐ				Ⓐ	Ⓑ		Ⓑ	⑤	Ⓐ	Ⓑ	†
	n	D‡			t	x		v	Y			u			u				m				m	
Marseille St Charles ▷ d.	...	...	...	0636	0636	...	0836	...	...	1236	1236	...	...	...	...	1636	...	1734	...	1835	1835	...	...	...
Aix en Provence ▷ d.	...	...	...	0712	0712	...	0912	...	...	1312	1312	...	...	...	...	1712	...	1812	...	1912	1912	...	...	...
Manosque-Gréoux d.	...	...	...	0805	0805	...	0952	...	...	1401	1401	...	...	...	...	1756	...	1855	...	2003	2003	...	...	...
Château Arnoux - St Auban d.	...	...	...	0831	0831	...	1015	...	...	1432	1432	...	...	...	...	1824	...	1931	...	2031	2031	...	...	...
Sisteron d.	...	...	...	0845	0845	...	1029	...	...	1449	1449	...	...	...	...	1841	...	1945	...	2047	2047	...	...	...
Paris Austerlitz **351** d.	...	2205	...	|	|	...	|	...	...	|	|	...	...	...	...	|	...	|	...	|	|	...	...	...
Lyon Part-Dieu 351 d.	...	|	...	|	|	...	|	...	1111	|	|	...	...	...	...	|	...	|	...	|	|	...	...	...
Romans-Bourg de Peage d.	...	|	...	|	|	...	|	1040	|	|	|	...	...	...	...	|	1737	|	...	|	|	2018	2018	...
Valence TGV **365** d.	...	|	...	|	|	...	|	1049	|	|	|	...	...	...	...	|	1747	|	...	|	|	2027	2027	...
Valence Ville 365 d.	...	0414	...	|	|	...	|	1100	1224	|	|	...	...	...	...	|	1803	|	...	|	|	2039	2039	...
Die d.	...	0521	...	|	|	...	|	1215	1330	|	|	...	...	...	...	|	1907	|	...	|	|	2139	2139	...
Veynes-Dévoluy a.	...	0626	...	0926	0926	...	1109	1314	1428	1535	1535	...	...	...	▽	1931	1959	2030	...	2132	2132	2231	2231	...
Veynes-Dévoluy d.	...	0628	...	0934	0934	...	1111	1317	1439	1537	1537	...	...	...	1808	1933	2023	2038	...	2134	2134	2233	2233	...
Gap a.	...	0652	...	0955	0955	...	1130	1339	1501	1556	1556	...	...	...	1830	1956	2043	2058	...	2156	2156	2253	2253	...
Gap d.	0623	0655	...	...	1004	1050	1132	1341	1503	...	1558	1654	1733	...	1840	2001	...	...	2120	...	2200	2300	...	2300
Embrun d.	0655	0735	...	...	1039	1126	1205	1415	1542	...	1634	1729	1806	...	1916	2043	...	...	2200	...	2235	2331	...	2340
Montdauphin-Guillestre d.	0710	0755	...	...	1054	1143	1221	1431	1558	...	1650	1746	1822	...	1931	2059	...	...	2215	...	2252	2346	...	2355
L'Argentière les Écrins d.	0720	0811	...	...	1104	1155	1232	1444	1611	...	1702	1801	1837	...	1941	2113	...	...	2226	...	2304	2357	...	0005
Briançon a.	0733	0832	...	...	1117	1208	1245	1457	1627	...	1717	1815	1850	...	1954	2128	...	...	2238	...	2318	0010	...	0020

GAP - GRENOBLE *Service is by 🚌 Oct. 5 - 23*

km										
		⚒				⑥	Ⓑ			
					Qw		w			
	Briançon (see above) d.	...	0612	...	...	...	...	...	...	...
0	**Gap** d.	0530	0730	...	1131	1315	1330	1730	1930	...
27	Veynes-Dévoluy d.	0554	0754	...	1154	1354	1354	1754	2000	...
117	St Georges de Commiers d.	0720	0920	...	1320	1520	1520	1920	|	...
136	**Grenoble** a.	0744	0944	...	1344	1544	1544	1944	2144	...

							⑤		
	Q	w	w						
Grenoble d.	0813	1013	1213	1413	1613	1813	2013	...	...
St Georges de Commiers d.	0834	1034	1234	1434	1634	1834	2034	...	...
Veynes-Dévoluy d.	1008	1208	1408	1608	1808	2008	2213	...	...
Gap a.	1030	1230	1430	1630	1830	2030	...	...	...
Briançon (see above) a.	...	...	...	...	1954	...	...	...	...

LOCAL TRAINS MARSEILLE - AIX EN PROVENCE Journey time: 35 – 45 minutes

From Marseille St Charles: 0536 Ⓐ, 0544 ⚒, 0605 Ⓐ, 0644, 0705 Ⓐ, 0736 ⚒, 0744, 0804 Ⓐ, 0844, 1044, 1105 Ⓐ, 1205, 1305, 1336 Ⓐ, 1344, 1405 Ⓐ, 1423, 1505, 1536 Ⓒ, 1605, 1644 Ⓐ, 1744, 1805 Ⓐ, 1844 †, 1905, 1944, 2005 Ⓐ, 2036, 2044 Ⓐ, 2105, 2144, 2205 Ⓐ, 2305 **z**.

From Aix en Provence: 0511 Ⓐ, 0551 ⚒, 0611, 0631 ⚒, 0651 Ⓐ, 0731, 0831 Ⓐ, 0911, 1044, 1211, 1231, 1251 Ⓐ, 1311, 1411, 1431 Ⓐ, 1451, 1511, 1551 Ⓐ, 1611, 1631 Ⓐ, 1711, 1731, 1811, 1831 Ⓐ, 1851, 1931 Ⓐ, 1951 Ⓐ, 2031, 2111 †, 2131 Ⓐ, 2231, 2311 **z**.

D – *CORAIL LUNÉA* – 🛏 1, 2 cl., (2) (reclining).
L – ⑦ to June 28 (also June 1); ⑦ from Nov. 8 (also Nov. 4).
Q – Daily to Oct. 3; ⚒ from Oct. 5.
S – July 1 - Aug. 31.
Y – Subject to alteration June 1 - 7, 20, 21 and Ⓐ Oct. 19 - Nov. 13.

b – Not May 30, 31, June 6, 20.
g – Also June 2, July 15, Nov. 12; not June 1.
m – Not Oct. 21.
n – Not Oct. 22.
t – Not Aug. 15.

u – Subject to alteration Oct. 5 - 23.
v – Not June 20.
w – Subject to alteration Oct. 26 - 30, Nov. 2 - 6, 9 - 13.
x – Subject to alteration Oct. 19 - 23.
z – Subject to alteration Oct. 5 - 9, 12 - 16.
▷ – For local trains Marseille - Aix en Provence see below table.
▽ – To / from Grenoble (see panel below main table).
§ – Train number **15790** on certain dates.
‡ – Train number **15799** on certain dates.

🚌 BRIANÇON (station) - OULX (station)

Connects with TGV trains to / from Paris, Table **44**

Operator: Autocars ResAlp www.autocar-resalp.com. *To Dec. 18, 2009*

			S	
Briançon d.	0845	1055	1410	1645
Oulx a.	0950	1200	1510	1750

			S	
Oulx d.	0950	1305	1515	1925
Briançon a.	1055	1410	1620	2030

Also from Briançon 0740 🅁, from Oulx 2015 🅁, to reserve ✆ 04 92 20 47 50.

363 BELLEGARDE - ANNEMASSE - ÉVIAN LES BAINS

km		Ⓐ	①–⑥ x	⚒	b	TGV 6505 ⑦ S	†	①–⑥ y	TGV 6503 ⑥ F	c ⊖	🚌	①–⑥ x ▽	⚒ ⊕	①–⑥ x	①–⑥ x		Ⓐ §	Ⓒ §	①–⑥ x	Ⓐ	Ⓑ q	TGV 6511 ⑤ D	🚌		
	Paris Gare de Lyon **341** ... d.	...	...	...	...	0810	...	...	0910	...	...	...	...	...	...	...	...	...	...	...	...	1642	...	...	...
	Lyon Part-Dieu **345** ... d.	...	...	...	*0904*	|	...	...	|	*1104*	...	...	*1504*	...	...	...	*1704*	1704	...	...	...	|	1904	...	...
0	**Bellegarde** ▷ d.	0653	...	0834	1032	1107	1134	...	1210	1232	...	...	1632	...	...	...	1833	1836	...	1932	...	2024	2032	2132	2232
	Genève Eaux Vives **366a** .. d.	|	0732	|	|	|	|	1232	|	|	...	1632	|	1732	1802	1832	|	|	1932	|	...	|	|	|	|
38	Annemasse ▷ a.	0732	0743	0912	1107	1140	1212	1243	1242	1311	...	1643	1712	1743	1813	1843	1912	1912	1943	2012	...	2055	2112	2210	2315
38	Annemasse d.	...	0753	*0925**	1112	1145	...	1246	1252	1318	1520	1646	1718	1746	1818	1846	1918	1918	1946	2016	2034	2057	2118	2210	2317
68	Thonon les Bains d.	...	0828	*1010**	1140	1210	...	1315	1323	1347	1605	1715	1744	1815	1845	1915	1950	1950	2015	2041	2059	2122	2144	2245	2341
77	**Évian les Bains** a.	...	0837	*1025**	1148	1218	...	1324	1331	1355	1620	1722	1752	1824	1852	1924	1957	1957	2024	2049	2107	2130	2151	2300	2350

	Ⓐ	①–⑤ d		①–⑥ x	①–⑤ u	⑥	①–⑥ x		⚒	Ⓐ c	⑦	🚌 ⚒	b △	①–⑥ ▽	c	TGV 6510 ⑥ F	TGV 6508 ⑦ S	Ⓐ	⑦ Y	TGV 6512 ⑦ R		🚌 w	①–⑥ y		①–⑥ x ◇
Évian-les-Bains d.	0446	0532	0558	0632	0658	...	0732	0758	0858	*0928**	...	1058	1158	1334	1558	1633	1633	*1630**	1702	1723	1732	1750	1832	1903	1932
Thonon-les-Bains d.	0455	0542	0608	0642	0708	...	0741	0807	0908	*0940**	...	1110	1209	1345	1608	1645	1645	*1642**	1714	1734	1744	1803	1844	1914	1946
Annemasse a.	0519	0610	0636	0710	0736	...	0812	0836	0937	*1030**	...	1200	1236	1413	1636	1710	1711	*1732**	1741	1802	1811	1850	1911	1943	2014
Annemasse ▷ d.	0521	0617	0644	0717	0738	0738	0817	0844	...	1040	1040	...	1244	1417	1644	1721	1721	1744	1744	1806	1817	1850	1917	1945	2017
Genève Eaux Vives **366a** ... a.	|	0628	|	0728	|	|	0828	|	...	|	|	...	|	1428	|	|	|	|	|	|	1828	|	1928	|	2028
Bellegarde ▷ a.	0555	...	0718	...	0820	0820	...	0919	...	1120	1114	...	1318	...	1719	|	1751	1819	1819	1835	...	1935	...	2019	...
Lyon Part-Dieu **345** ... a.	...	...	*0847*	...	...	...	...	1107**v**	...	...	...	...	1447	...	*1847*	|	|	...	1953**z**	|	...	...	...	...	...
Paris Gare de Lyon **341** ... a.	...	...	...	...	...	...	...	...	...	...	...	...	...	...	...	2049	2048	...	...	2143	...	...	...	...	...

D – ⑤ July 10 - Sept. 18.
F – ⑥ July 11 - Aug. 22.
P – Daily to June 27; ①–⑥ June 29 - Aug. 29; daily from Aug. 31 (not July 14, Aug. 15, Oct. 25, Nov. 11).
R – ⑦ July 5 - Sept. 20 (also July 14).
S – ⑦ July 5 - Aug. 30 (also July 14).
Y – ⑦ to June 28/from Sept. 6.
b – Subject to alteration Bellegarde - Annemasse and v.v. on Ⓐ Sept. 7-25.
c – Subject to alteration on Ⓐ Sept. 7-25.
d – Not Sept. 10 Genève Eaux-Vives - Annemasse and v.v.
q – From Annecy (Table **367**).

u – Not July 20, Aug. 21, Nov. 17.
v – On Ⓐ change at Bellegarde, arrive Lyon Part Dieu 1102.
w – To July 4.
x – Not June 1, Aug. 1, Sept. 10.
y – Not June 1, Aug. 1, Sept. 10 Annemasse - Genève Eaux Vives and v.v.
z – Subject to alteration Amberieu - Lyon from Sept. 6.
TGV – Ⓡ, supplement payable, 🍷.
△ – Change at Bellegarde on Ⓐ. Subject to alteration Bellegarde - Lyon Ⓐ June 22 - July 6, Sept. 28 - Oct. 9, Nov. 30 - Dec. 4.
▷ – See also Table **365**.

▽ – Subject to alteration Sept. 7-11, 14-18.
◇ – Subject to alteration Aug. 4-10.
⊖ – Subject to alteration Lyon - Bellegarde on Ⓐ June 15 - July 10, Oct. 12-23.
⊕ – Subject to alteration on ①–④ Sept. 7-24 Bellegarde - Annemasse.
§ – From Lyon Perrache (depart 1650).
* – By 🚌.

Annemasse - Genève Eaux Vives and v.v. is by 🚌 Aug. 4-10.

364 GENÈVE and ANNECY - CHAMBÉRY - GRENOBLE - VALENCE

km		Ⓐ	⚒	⚒	⚒		Ⓐ	⚒	Ⓐ	Ⓐ	Ⓐ		Ⓐ		Ⓐ			⚒ s			⚒		Ⓐ	Ⓐ b
0	**Genève** **341 345** d.	...	...	...	...	...	...	...	...	0558	...	...	...	0658	...	...	...	...	...	1017	...	...	...	...
33	Bellegarde **341 345** d.	...	...	...	...	...	...	...	...	0628	...	...	...	0729	...	...	...	...	...	1049	...	...	...	...
66	Culoz **345** d.	...	...	...	...	...	...	...	...	0648	0658	...	...	0751	0756	...	...	...	...	|	...	...	...	1255
	Annecy **341 344** d.	...	...	...	...	0600	...	...	0638	...	|	0700	0716	...	|	0800	...	0836	0910	|	...	...	...	|
88	Aix les Bains **341 344** d.	...	...	...	...	0635	...	0701	0716	...	0722	0735	0754	...	0822	0835	...	0916	0952	1129	1200	...	*1300*	1316
102	**Chambéry** **341 344** a.	...	...	...	...	0646	...	0713	0728	...	0733	0746	0805	...	0837	0846	...	0926	1003	1140	1211	...	*1311*	1327
102	**Chambéry** d.	...	0506	...	0614	0649	0654	0720	...	...	...	0749	0815	...	...	0849	0914	...	...	1144	1215	1249	1315	...
116	Montmélian d.	...	0519	...	0625	|	0708	0733	...	...	...	|	0826	...	...	0900	0925	...	...	|	1227	|	1325	...
165	**Grenoble** a.	...	0553	...	0713	0735	0752	0821	...	...	...	0834	0912	...	...	0937	1012	...	...	1232	1312	1333	1412	...
165	**Grenoble** d.	0548	...	0638	...	...	0755	...	...	...	...	0838	...	...	...	...	1020	...	...	1238	...	1338	...	...
242	Romans-Bourg de Péage d.	0713	...	0754	...	...	0912	...	...	...	...	0938	...	...	...	...	1112	...	...	1345	...	1447	...	...
249	Valence TGV ⊙ d.	0723	...	0803	...	...	0921	...	...	...	...	0948	...	...	...	...	1122	...	...	1355	...	1457	...	...
259	**Valence Ville** ⊙ a.	0731	...	0810	...	...	0929	...	...	...	...	0957	...	...	...	...	1131	...	...	1408	...	1506	...	...

		⚒	L				⊡	Ⓐ	⚒			Ⓐ			Ⓐ		Ⓐ	⚒	⑦ P	Ⓐ		Ⓐ n	Ⓑ u	Ⓑ
Genève **341 345** d.	...	...	...	...	1417	...	...	...	...	1624	...	...	...	1658	...	...	...	...	...	1817	...	...	1944	...
Bellegarde **341 345** d.	...	...	...	...	1448	...	...	...	...	1655	...	...	...	1728	...	...	...	...	...	1849	...	...	2012	...
Culoz **345** d.	...	...	...	...	1513	...	...	...	...	|	...	...	...	1749	1759	...	...	...	1857	1915	...	...	2040	...
Annecy **341 344** d.	1300	...	1355	1500	|	...	1600	...	...	|	1700	...	1715	▬	|	1800	...	...	|	|	1900	...	|	2010
Aix les Bains **341 344** d.	1335	...	1435	1535	1535	...	1635	...	...	1735	1735	...	1758	...	1821	1835	...	...	1921	1933	1936	2025**z**	2100	2055
Chambéry **341 344** a.	1346	...	1446	1546	1546	...	1646	...	...	1746	1746	...	1809	**L**	1835	1846	...	...	1932	1943	1946	2036**z**	2110	2106
Chambéry d.	1349	1415	1449	1549	1549	1615	1648	1654	1715	1749	1749	1754	...	1815	...	1849	1854	1915	1934	...	1949	2039	...	2120
Montmélian d.	|	1427	|	|	|	1626	|	1706	1727	|	|	1808	...	1826	...	|	1907	1926	1946	...	2001	|	...	2131
Grenoble a.	1435	1512	1532	1632	1632	1712	1731	1751	1811	1834	1834	1853	...	1913	...	1934	1951	2012	2021	...	2036	2125	...	2205
Grenoble d.	...	...	1538	1638	1638	1715	1734	1753	...	1838	1838	...	...	...	...	1938	1954	...	...	...	2038	...	...	...
Romans-Bourg de Péage d.	...	...	1644	1744	1744	1828	1843	1900	...	1943	1943	...	...	...	...	2040	2101	...	...	...	2139	...	...	...
Valence TGV ⊙ d.	...	...	1653	1754	1754	1838	1853	1910	...	1953	1953	...	...	...	...	2049	2111	...	...	...	2149	...	...	...
Valence Ville ⊙ a.	...	...	1702	1802	1802	1846	1903	1918	...	2002	2002	...	...	...	...	2058	2119	...	...	...	2159	...	...	...

	Ⓐ	①–⑥		Ⓐ	⚒	⚒	Ⓐ			Ⓐ			Ⓐ		Ⓐ	Ⓐ	Ⓑ		⚒				Ⓐ	
Valence Ville ⊙ d.	...	...	...	...	...	...	...	0552	0603	0652	0703	0752	...	...	...	...	...	1100	1124	1155	1155	1300	...	...
Valence TGV ⊙ d.	...	...	...	...	...	...	...	0603	0615	0703	0715	0804	...	...	...	...	...	1111	1136	1210	1210	1310	...	...
Romans-Bourg de Péage d.	...	...	...	...	...	...	...	0611	0626	0712	0726	0815	...	...	...	...	...	1121	1145	1219	1219	1320	...	...
Grenoble a.	...	...	...	...	...	...	...	0720	0742	0822	0842	0916	...	...	...	...	...	1220	1303	1320	1320	1418	...	...
Grenoble d.	...	...	0535	0622	...	0645	0705	0725	0745	...	...	0925	1004	1105	...	1143	1205	1225	1305	1325	1325	1425	1505	1525
Montmélian d.	...	...	0625	0658	...	0732	0751	|	0832	...	...	|	1053	1154	...	|	1252	|	1352	|	|	|	1552	1600
Chambéry a.	...	...	0634	0707	...	0742	0800	0810	0842	...	...	1010	1102	1204	...	1228	1302	1310	1402	1410	1410	1509	1602	1610
Chambéry **341 344** d.	0606	0610	0645	0709	0727	*0750*	...	0814	0845	...	...	1014	...	1209	1213	...	...	1313	...	1414	1414	1520	...	1614
Aix les Bains **341 344** d.	0619	0623	0701	0722	0740	*0804*	...	0832	0856	...	...	1035	...	1224	1226	...	...	1334	...	1434	1430	1534	...	1634
Annecy **341 344** a.	0713	|	0751	|	0820	...	...	0908	...	...	...	1107	...	|	1313	...	...	1418	...	1514	|	1621	...	1714
Culoz **345** a.	...	0638	...	0738	...	...	...	...	...	...	...	...	...	1239	...	...	...	...	...	...	|	...	...	...
Bellegarde **341 345** a.	...	0705	...	0802	...	...	...	...	...	...	...	...	...	1305	...	...	...	...	...	...	1505	...	...	...
Genève 347 348 **341 345** a.	...	0732	...	0829	...	...	...	...	...	...	...	...	...	1332	...	...	...	...	...	...	1532	...	...	...

	Ⓐ	Ⓐ N	Ⓐ		Ⓐ	Ⓐ	†	⚒			Ⓐ	⚒			Ⓐ	Ⓐ				†	☆			⑦
Valence Ville ⊙ d.	...	...	...	1500	...	...	...	...	1600	1600	...	...	1638	...	1658	...	1738	...	1838	1852	1939	...	2038	2213
Valence TGV ⊙ d.	...	...	...	1512	...	...	...	...	1611	1611	...	...	1650	...	1710	...	1750	...	1849	1903	1950	...	2050	2224
Romans-Bourg de Péage d.	...	...	...	1521	...	...	...	...	1619	1619	...	...	1659	...	1718	...	1759	...	1859	1913	2001	...	2100	2235
Grenoble a.	...	...	...	1620	...	...	...	...	1718	1718	...	...	1820	...	...	...	1921	...	2021	2034	2056	...	2150	2328
Grenoble d.	1535	1605	...	1625	1635	...	1700	1705	1725	1725	1735	1805	1825	1845	...	1904	1925	1945	2026	2039	2101	...	2155	...
Montmélian d.	1623	1652	...	|	1722	...	1748	1751	|	|	1822	1852	1902	1934	...	1951	|	2032	2100	|	|	...	|	...
Chambéry a.	1632	1701	...	1712	1732	...	1757	1802	1810	1810	1832	1902	1912	1943	...	2002	2010	2042	2110	2123	2146	...	2241	...
Chambéry **341 344** d.	...	...	1705	1714	...	1749	...	...	1814	1814	...	...	1914	1949**r**	...	...	2014	...	2114	2130	...	2205	...	...
Aix les Bains **341 344** d.	...	...	1720	1730	...	1804	...	...	1828	1834	...	...	1933	1959**r**	...	...	2032	...	2134	2146	...	2218	...	...
Annecy **341 344** a.	...	...	|	1814	...	|	...	...	|	1920	...	...	2009	...	...	...	2104	...	2204	2224	...	2249	...	...
Culoz **345** a.	...	...	1740	...	...	1824	...	...	|	...	...	...	...	...	...	...	...	...	...	...	...	...	...	...
Bellegarde **341 345** a.	...	...	...	...	...	...	...	...	1901	...	...	...	...	...	...	...	...	...	...	...	...	...	...	...
Genève 347 348 **341 345** a.	...	...	...	...	...	...	...	...	1932	...	...	...	...	...	...	...	...	...	...	...	...	...	...	...

J – To July 10/from Aug. 24.
L – To May 31/from Sept. 7.
N – To May 20/from Sept. 7.
P – ⑦ to June 21/from Sept. 6.
b – By 🚌 June 15 - July 10.
n – Not July 20, Aug. 21, Nov. 17.
r – Not ⑥.
s – From St Gervais (Table **367**).

u – On Ⓑ June 21 - Sept. 6 runs Bellegarde (d. 1937) - Chambéry (a. 2034).
z – To June 19/from Sept. 7.
⊡ – To Avignon Centre (arrive 2027) on ⑤ to May 15/from Sept. 11.
☆ – From Avignon Centre on † to May 17/from Sept. 13, depart 1803 (Table **351**).
⊙ – Additional 🚌 runs 2-4 times per hour.

Engineering work Grenoble - Valence : May 21 - Sept. 6

All trains will be replaced by 🚌. Non-stop buses, journey 90 minutes:
From Grenoble: 0530 Ⓐ, 0615 Ⓐ **J**, 0645 ⚒, 0745 and hourly (2-hourly on †) to 1545, 1645, 1715 Ⓐ **J**, 1745, 1815 Ⓐ **J**, 1845, 1945, 2045 Ⓑ.
From Valence: 0550 Ⓐ, 0620 Ⓐ **J**, 0650 ⚒, 0720 Ⓐ **J**, 0750 and hourly (2-hourly on †) to 1550, 1650, 1720 Ⓐ **J**, 1750, 1850, 2050 Ⓑ.
Other buses run approx hourly Grenoble - Valence TGV.

(PARIS / LYON) - ANNECY / GENÈVE - ST GERVAIS 365

km	TGV trains convey 🍷			5705 5594						TGV 6561		TGV 6471		TGV 6467			TGV 6569				TGV 6573				
		Ⓐ	①-⑤ v	Ⓡ Z		①-⑥ s		⚒			⊗	⑥ B	①-⑥ v	⑥ D	①-⑤ x	⊗	Q	⊗		Ⓑ	Ⓑ	⚒ ⊗	①-⑤ v	G	⑥ D
	Paris Gare de Lyon **341** ... d.	...	...	2300a	...	...	...	...	...	0710	...	0810	...	0910	...	...	1110	...	...	...	1310	...	...	...	...
	Lyon Part-Dieu **345** ... d.	...	...	|	...	...	0704	...	...	|	0904	|	...	|	...	...	|	1304r	...	...	|	*1504*	...	...	...
	Chambéry **341/4 364** ... d.	...	...	0535	...	...	|	...	...	|	|	|	...	|	...	...	|	|	...	...	|	|	...	...	...
	Aix les Bains **364** ... d.	...	...	0559	...	...	|	...	...	|	|	|	...	|	...	...	|	|	...	...	|	|	...	...	...
0	**Annecy** ... ▲ d.	...	...	0708	...	...	|	...	...	|	|	|	...	|	...	...	|	|	...	1622	|	|	...	1722	1735
	Bellegarde ... ▽ d.	...	...	|	...	...	0828	0834	...	1007	1032	|	...	1210	...	1332	1407	1432	...	|	1607	1632	...	|	|
•23	**Genève Eaux-Vives** ▷ d.	0602x	0702x	|	0802	0902	...	|	...	...	|	|	1202	|	1402	|	...	|	...	|	...	|	1702x	|	|
•17	Annemasse ... ▷ a.	0613x	0713x	|	0813	0913	...	0912	...	...	1107	|	1213	1242	1413	1412	...	1512	...	|	...	1712	1713x	|	|
•17	Annemasse ... d.	0618	0718	|	0818	...	...	0918	...	...	1118	|	1218	1301	...	1418	...	1518	...	|	...	...	1718	|	|
39	La Roche sur Foron ... ▲ a.	0636	0734	0804	0836	...	...	0936	...	...	1136	|	1236	|	...	1436	...	1536	...	1703	...	...	1736	1812	1823
39	La Roche sur Foron ... d.	0640	0740	0831	0840	...	...	0940	...	...	1140	|	1240	|	...	1440	...	1540	...	1712	...	...	1740	1825	1854
61	Cluses (Haute-Savoie) ... d.	0706	0806	0851	0906	...	...	1005	...	...	1206	1237	1306	1350	...	1506	...	1606	...	1736	...	...	1806	1848	1919
80	Sallanches Megève ... d.	0720	0819	0905	0919	...	...	1019	...	...	1219	1253	1319	1406	...	1519	...	1620	...	1754	...	...	1819	1903	1934
86	**St Gervais** ... a.	0726	0825	0911	0925	...	...	1025	...	...	1225	1259	1325	1412	...	1525	...	1625	...	1800	...	...	1825	1909	1940

			TGV 6577						
	Ⓑ	①-⑤ x		d	△	①-⑥ c	Ⓐ	①-⑥ c	
Paris Gare de Lyon **341** ... d.	...	...	1504	...	...	...	...	...	...
Lyon Part-Dieu **345** ... d.	...	...	|	1704	1738	...	...	...	1904
Chambéry **341/4 364** ... d.	...	...	|	|	|	...	...	...	|
Aix les Bains **364** ... d.	...	...	|	|	|	...	...	...	|
Annecy ... ▲ d.	1826	...	|	|	1935	...	...	...	|
Bellegarde ... ▽ d.	|	...	1808	1833	|	...	...	...	2032
Genève Eaux-Vives . ▷ d.	|	1902	...	|	|	1932	...	2032	|
Annemasse ... ▷ a.	|	1913	...	1912	|	1943	...	2043	2112
Annemasse ... d.	|	...	...	1918	|	...	1958	...	2118
La Roche sur Foron ... ▲ a.	1902	...	...	1937	2012	...	2014	...	2137
La Roche sur Foron ... d.	1918	...	...	1940	...	...	2019	...	2140
Cluses (Haute-Savoie) ... d.	1940	...	...	2006	...	...	2042	...	2206
Sallanches Megève ... d.	1955	...	...	2019	...	...	2059	...	2219
St Gervais ... a.	2001	...	...	2025	...	...	2105	...	2225

		TGV 6564					TGV 6964				TGV 6568
			①-⑤ x	⚒	①-⑥	⚒	F		△	①-⑥ s	R
St Gervais ... d.	0530	...	...	0555	0630	0645	...	0730	...	...	...
Sallanches Megève ... d.	0536	...	...	0602	0636	0651	...	0736	...	...	...
Cluses (Haute-Savoie) ... d.	0551	...	...	0617	0651	0707	...	0751	...	...	...
La Roche sur Foron ... a.	0615	...	...	0639	0716	0731	...	0816	...	...	...
La Roche sur Foron ... ▲ d.	0619	...	...	0653	0719	0739	...	0820	...	...	...
Annemasse ... a.	0639	...	...	|	0739	|	...	0839	...	...	...
Annemasse ... ▷ d.	0644	...	0647	|	0747	|	...	...	0844	0847	...
Genève Eaux-Vives ▷ a.	|	...	0658	|	0758	|	...	...	|	0858	...
Bellegarde ... ▽ a.	0718	0749	...	|	...	|	...	...	0919	...	0948
Annecy ... ▲ a.	|	|	...	0733	...	0820	0830	...	|	...	|
Aix les Bains **364** ... a.	|	|	...	...	...	0914	0857	...	|	...	|
Chambéry **341/4 364** ... a.	|	|	...	...	...	0926	|	...	|	...	|
Lyon Part-Dieu **345** ... a.	0847	|	...	...	...	...	|	...	1102z	...	|
Paris Gare de Lyon **341** a.	...	1051	...	...	...	...	1207	...	...	...	1249

		TGV 6968					TGV 6572					TGV 6580	TGV 6490		TGV 6984				TGV 6584		TGV 6496				5596 5706
			①-⑤ v		①-⑥ y	⊗	⊡	⚒ ⊗			①-⑤ x	①-⑤ n	⑥ B		Ⓑ			①-⑤ x			⑥ D	Ⓑ			Ⓡ Z
St Gervais ... d.	0745	...	0830	...	1130	...	...	1330	1530	...	...	...	1610	1645	...	1730	...	...	...	...	1810	1827	...	...	2050
Sallanches Megève ... d.	0751	...	0836	...	1136	...	...	1336	1536	...	...	...	1621	1651	...	1736	...	...	...	...	1821	1833	...	...	2100
Cluses (Haute-Savoie) ... d.	0807	...	0850	...	1150	...	...	1351	1550	...	...	...	1638	1707	...	1751	...	...	...	...	1836	1849	...	...	2122
La Roche sur Foron ... a.	0830	...	0916	...	1216	...	...	1416	1616	...	...	...	|	1730	...	1816	...	...	...	...	|	1913	...	...	2139
La Roche sur Foron ... ▲ d.	0843	...	0918	...	1219	...	...	1419	1618	...	...	...	|	1743	...	1819	...	...	...	...	|	1919	...	...	2158
Annemasse ... a.	|	...	0939	...	1239	...	...	1439	1633	...	...	...	1711	|	...	1839	...	...	...	...	|	1938	...	...	|
Annemasse ... ▷ d.	|	...	0947	...	1247x	1244	...	1445	...	1644	1647	...	1721	|	...	1844	...	1847	...	...	|	...	1945	...	|
Genève Eaux-Vives . ▷ a.	|	...	0958	...	1258x	|	...	|	...	|	1658	...	|	|	...	|	...	1858	...	...	|	...	|	...	|
Bellegarde ... ▽ a.	|	...	...	...	...	1318	1348	1518	...	1719	...	1748	|	|	...	1924	1932	...	1948	...	|	...	2019	...	|
Annecy ... ▲ a.	0925	0935	...	...	...	|	|	...	...	|	...	|	|	1819	1832	...	|	...	|	...	1932	...	|	...	2232
Aix les Bains **364** ... a.	...	1001	...	...	...	|	|	...	...	|	...	|	|	...	1859	...	|	...	|	...	2029	...	|	...	2322
Chambéry **341/4 364** ... a.	...	1014	...	...	...	|	|	...	...	|	...	|	|	...	|	...	|	...	|	...	|	...	|	...	2337
Lyon Part-Dieu **345** ... a.	...	|	...	...	...	1447	|	...	...	1847	...	|	|	...	|	...	2047	...	|	...	|	...	*2147*	...	|
Paris Gare de Lyon **341** ... a.	...	1323	...	...	...	...	1649	...	...	...	...	2049	2049	...	2207	...	...	...	2249	...	2347	...	...	...	0617a

ANNECY - ANNEMASSE / GENÈVE Direct services

Subject to alteration on Nov. 3-6

	Ⓐ	Ⓐ	🚌 ⚒	Ⓐ	⚒	🚌 Ⓑ	Ⓐu	u	⚒	🚌 Ⓐ	🚌
Annecy ... d.	0603	0659	0733	0739	0903	1003	1103	1303	1703	1733	1833
La Roche sur Foron ... a.	0648	0732	|	0815	0935	1035	1135	1336	1735	|	1905
La Roche sur Foron ... d.	0650	0738	|	*0820*	0941	1035	1141	1341	1741	|	1905
Annemasse ... a.	0705	0755	|	*0839*	0955	|	1155	1355	1755	|	|
Genève Eaux-Vives ▷ a.	...	...	0853	...	...	1113	...	...	...	1848	1943

	Ⓐ	⚒	🚌 Ⓐ	Ⓐu	⚒u	🚌 Ⓑ		🚌 Ⓐ	Ⓐ	🚌
Genève Eaux-Vives ▷ d.	...	...	0843	...	...	1148	...	1813	...	2003
Annemasse ... d.	0602	0802	|	1002	1202	|	1600	|	1855	2020
La Roche sur Foron ... a.	0618	0818	0915	1018	1218	1222	1617	1848	1912	2050
La Roche sur Foron ... d.	0621	0825	0915	1021	1221	1222	1621	1848	1919	2050
Annecy ... a.	0652	0855	0952	1052	1252	1259	1652	1925	1959	2124

B – ⑥ June 27 - Aug. 29.
D – ⑥ July 11 - Aug. 29.
F – ⑥⑦ (daily July 4 - Aug. 28).
G – Daily to July 10; Ⓑ July 12 - Aug. 28; daily from Aug. 30.
Q – Daily to Sept. 13; ⑥⑦ Sept. 19 - Oct. 11; daily Oct. 17 - Nov. 22 (also Nov. 28, 29); daily from Dec. 5.
R – ⑥⑦ to June 14; daily June 20 - Aug. 30; ⑥⑦ Sept. 5 - Oct. 11; daily from Oct. 17.
Z – *CORAIL LUNÉA* - ⑤⑥⑦ (daily June 26 - Aug. 30). 🛏 1,2 cl. and (2) (reclining).
a – Paris **Austerlitz**.
c – Not June 1, Aug. 1, Sept. 10.
d – Starts from Lyon Perrache (depart 1650).
n – Not June 1, July 14.
r – Subject to alteration on June 10 - 12, Ⓐ June 22 - July 10, Sept. 14 - 25, Oct. 12 - 23, Nov. 23 - 27.
s – Not June 1, Sept. 10.
u – Subject to alteration Nov. 14 - 20 La Roche - Annemasse.
v – Not June 1.
x – ①-⑤ (not June 1, Sept. 10).
y – Not June 1, Aug. 15, Nov. 3 - 6, 9, 13, 16 - 20.
z – 1107 on ©.

TGV – Ⓡ, supplement payable, 🍷.
▲ – For connections Annecy - La Roche sur Foron and v.v. see panel below main table.
△ – To / from Évian les Bains (Table **363**).
▷ – For full service Genève Eaux-Vives - Annemasse and v.v. see Table **366a**.
▽ – Bellegarde - Annemasse : see also Table **363**. For connections Bellegarde - Genève see Table **345**.
⊗ – Subject to alteration Bellegarde - Annemasse and v.v. on Ⓐ Sept. 7 - 25.
⊡ – Arrive Paris 1710 on June 10 - 12.
• – Distance from La Roche sur Foron.

ENGINEERING WORK

Aug. 4 - 10
Services between Annemasse and Genève Eaux Vives will be operated by 🚌.

Nov. 3 - 6
Trains between La Roche sur Foron and Annecy are subject to alteration.

ST GERVAIS - CHAMONIX 365a

km		K	J				R								
0	**St Gervais** ... d.	0632	0651	0731	0832	0932	1032	1232	1332	1532	1632	1732	1832	1932	2032
9	Les Houches ... d.	0656	0718	0756	0856	0956	1056	1256	1356	1556	1656	1756	1856	1956	2056
20	**Chamonix** ... a.	0711	0732	0811	0911	1011	1111	1311	1411	1611	1711	1811	1911	2011	2111

	M	N			R			R			△				
Chamonix ... d.	0639	0655	0739	0839	0939	1039	1239	1339	1439	1539	1639	1739	1839	1939	...
Les Houches ... d.	0657	0717	0757	0857	0957	1057	1257	1357	1457	1557	1657	1757	1857	1957	...
St Gervais ... a.	0720	0740	0820	0920	1020	1120	1320	1420	1520	1620	1720	1820	1920	2020	...

J – To June 30 / from Sept. 1.
K – July 1 - Aug. 31.
M – © (daily July 3 - Sept. 1, Oct. 24 - Nov. 4).
N – Daily except when train in previous column runs (subject to alteration on Ⓐ Oct. 5 - 23).
R – June 13 - Sept. 13.
△ – Subject to alteration Oct. 5 - 23.

Many journeys continue to / from Le Châtelard or Martigny (Table **572**).

FRANCE

366 CHAMBÉRY - ALBERTVILLE - BOURG ST MAURICE

km	TGV trains convey 🍸	① g	🚌 ②–⑤ n	Ⓐ	🚌 ⚒	S	S	R	🚌 R	TGV 5190 ⑥ F△	TGV 6429 ⑥ S	⊗	S	R⊕	🚌 R		Ⓐ	🚌 R		E	🚌 Ⓑ h	⊡	🚌 ⑤⑦ w	5705 Ⓡ B
	Paris Gare de Lyon **341** d.	...	...	...	...	...	...	...	...	...	0850	...	...	...	...	...	...	...	...	...	...	...	...	2300a
	Lyon Part Dieu **344** d.	...	...	...	...	...	...	...	...	...	|	...	...	...	...	1441	...	...	...	1741	...	1941	...	|
	Aix les Bains **341/4** d.	...	...	...	...	...	...	...	...	...	|	...	...	...	...	|	...	...	...	|	...	|	...	|
0	**Chambéry** **367** d.	0618	0606	0645	0735	0818	1011	1011	...	1155	|	1205	1405	1405	...	1605	1720	...	1820	1910	2005	2105	2205	0545
14	Montmélian **367** d.	0629	0626	0658	0758	0829	|	|	...	|	|	1216	|	|	...	|	1731	...	1831	1922	2022	2116	|	|
26	St Pierre d'Albigny **367** d.	0638	0640	0710	0813	0837	|	|	...	|	|	1226	|	|	...	|	1740	...	1839	1932	2036	2125	|	|
62	Albertville a.	0702	0708	0733	0841	0900	1045	1045	...	1224	1231	1249	1438	1438	...	1638	1803	...	1902	1956	2058	2149	2250	0622
62	Albertville d.	0708	0708	...	0841	0913	1058	...	1055	1234	1241	1302	1451	...	1445	1651	...	1809	1915	2009	2058	2203	2250	0640
104	Moûtiers-Salins d.	0734	0746	...	0906	0939	1126	...	1123	1306	1314	1327	1517	...	1511	1716	...	1835	1941	2029	2123	2232	2315	0708
126	Aime la Plagne d.	0748	|	...	0924z	0953	1140	...	1141	1323	1331	1340	1531	...	1529	1731	...	1853	1955	2043	...	2246	...	0732
137	Landry d.	0756	|	...	0933z	1000	1148	...	1150	1332	1340	1348	1538	...	1537	1739	...	1902	2003	2051	...	2253	...	0743
146	**Bourg St Maurice** a.	0804	0815	...	0946z	1008	1156	...	1203	1339	1347	1355	1546	...	1550	1746	...	1915	2010	2058	...	2300	...	0751

	🚌 ⚒	C	Ⓐ			⊗	🚌 R	R⊕	S	🚌 R	R	S	TGV 6426 ⑥ S	TGV 5188 ⑥ F△		🚌 Ⓐ	Ⓐ	TGV 6438 ⑥ F	🚌 Ⓑ	🚌 Ⓑ R		🚌 ⑤⑦ w	🚌 ⑦ Y	5706 Ⓡ B
Bourg St Maurice d.	...	0535	...	0702	0810	1014	1157	...	1210	1359	...	1409	1449	1457	1606	...	...	1708	...	1712	1802	...	1900	2130
Landry d.	...	0543	...	0710	0818	1023	1204	...	1217	1406	...	1417	1500	1507	1614	...	...	1719	...	1719	1810	...	|	2139
Aime la Plagne d.	...	0552	...	0718	0826	1031	1212	...	1225	1415	...	1426	1510	1517	1622	...	...	1730	...	1728	1819	...	1925	2150
Moûtiers-Salins d.	0503	0607	*0642*r	0735	0841	1046	1232	...	1240	1435	...	1442	1533	1540	1636	1722	...	1748	1748	1748	1834	1928	1945	2212
Albertville a.	0536	0633	*0730*r	0800	0905	1112	1303	...	1301	1506	...	1507	1551	1600	1707	1805	...	1806	1819	1819	1857	2000	2015	2240
Albertville d.	0536	0646	0742	0808	0918	1125	...	1314	1314	...	1517	1517	1603	1612	1715	...	1815	1816	1819	1819	1911	2000	...	2259
St Pierre d'Albigny **367** d.	0557	0712	0806	0836	|	|	...	1333	1333	...	1536	1536	|	|	1738	...	1833	|	1847	1847	1933	|	...	|
Montmélian **367** d.	0612	0720	0814	0845	|	|	...	1341	1341	...	1544	1544	|	|	1746	...	1842	|	1902	1902	1941	|	...	|
Chambéry **367** a.	0635	0729	0824	0853	0950	1156	...	1351	1350	...	1553	1553	|	1648	1754	...	1853	|	1925	1925	1951	2050	...	2335
Aix les Bains **341/4** a.	0655	|	...	0911	...	...	...	...	...	...	...	...	|	...	|	...	...	|	...	...	...	...	...	|
Lyon Part Dieu **344** a.	...	0854	...	1026	...	...	...	...	...	...	...	...	|	...	1916	...	...	|	...	...	...	...	...	|
Paris Gare de Lyon **341** a.	...	...	...	...	...	...	...	...	...	...	...	...	2010	...	...	...	...	2207	...	...	...	...	...	0617a

B – *CORAIL LUNÉA* - ⑤⑥⑦ (daily June 26 - Aug. 27). 🛏 1,2 cl., 2 (reclining).
C – ⚒ (daily June 22 - Sept. 6).
E – Ⓑ (daily June 21 - Sept. 4).
F – ⑥ July 11 - Aug. 29.
R – To June 26 / from Aug. 31.
S – June 27 - Aug. 30.
Y – ⑦ to June 21 / from Sept. 6. To Grenoble, arrive 2150.

a – Paris **Austerlitz**.
g – Also July 15, Nov. 12.
h – Also Aug. 15.
n – Not June 2, July 14, Nov. 11.
r – By 🚌.
w – Also June 1, July 14; not July 12, Nov. 1
z – To June 26 / from Aug. 31.

TGV – Ⓡ, supplement payable, 🍸.
△ – To / from Lille (see panel on right).
⊡ – From Dijon on Ⓐ (Table **373**).
⊕ – Subject to alteration Ⓐ Sept. 28 - Oct. 23.
⊗ – Subject to alteration Sept. 7 - 25.

Lille - Bourg St Maurice	*TGV* 5190 ⑥F
Lille Europe d.	0651
Douai d.	0717
Arras d.	0735
TGV Haute Picardie d.	0759
Charles de Gaulle ✈ d.	0833
Marne la Vallée-Chessy d.	0848
Chambéry a.	1143
Bourg St Maurice a.	1339

Bourg St Maurice - Lille	*TGV* 5188 ⑥F
Bourg St Maurice d.	1457
Chambéry d.	1656
Marne la Vallée-Chessy a.	1946
Charles de Gaulle ✈ a.	2001
TGV Haute Picardie a.	2037
Arras a.	2057
Douai a.	2113
Lille Flandres a.	2137

366a GENÈVE EAUX-VIVES - ANNEMASSE

Certain journeys continue to / from St Gervais (Table **365**). *Service will be by* 🚌 *Aug. 4 - 10.*

km		①–⑤ v	①–⑤ v	①–⑤ v	①–⑤ v	①–⑥ △v		①–⑥ n	①–⑥ v	①–⑤ v	①–⑥ n	①–⑥ △v	①–⑤ v	①–⑤ v	①–⑤ v	①–⑤ n	①–⑥ △v	①–⑤ v	①–⑥ △v	①–⑥ △v	△	①–⑤ v	①–⑥ △v	①–⑥ v	
0	Genève Eaux-Vives d.	0532	0602	0632	0702	0732	0802	0832	0902	0932	1202	1232	1302	1332	1402	1432	1632	1702	1732	1802	1832	1902	1932	2032	...
6	Annemasse a.	0543	0613	0643	0713	0743	0813	0843	0913	0943	1213	1243	1313	1343	1413	1443	1643	1713	1743	1813	1843	1913	1943	2043	...

	①–⑤ v	①–⑤ v	①–⑤ △v	①–⑤ v	①–⑥ △v		①–⑥ △n	①–⑥ v	①–⑤ v	①–⑤ n	①–⑥ v	①–⑤ v	①–⑤ v	①–⑤ v	①–⑤ △n	①–⑥ v	①–⑤ v	①–⑥ v	①–⑥ v	△	①–⑤ v	①–⑥ △v	①–⑥ △v	
Annemasse d.	0517	0547	0617	0647	0717	0747	0817	0847	0917	0947	1217	1247	1317	1347	1417	1617	1647	1717	1747	1817	1847	1917	2017	...
Genève Eaux-Vives a.	0528	0558	0628	0658	0728	0758	0828	0858	0928	0958	1228	1258	1328	1358	1428	1628	1658	1728	1758	1828	1858	1928	2028	...

n – Not June 1.
v – Not June 1, Aug. 1, Sept. 10.
△ – To / from Évian les Bains (Table **363**).

273 PARIS - DREUX - GRANVILLE

Temporarily relocated from page 181

km		Ⓐ z	3411 Ⓐ	3413 Ⓒ	◇	16511 ⑦ n	Ⓐ	⚒ ◇	3421 ⚒	3423 †	◇	◇	3431 ⚒ ▽	3433 †	◇	3435 ⑤ f	⑥ t	3441 Ⓐ	3443 Ⓒ	3445 ⑤	Ⓐ	3453 Ⓒ	3451 Ⓐ	◇
0	**Paris Montparnasse** ⊖ **274** d.	...	0710	0837	0840	0925	0920	0940	1024	1024	1040	1240	1316	1322	1440	1515	1520	1629	1638	1726	1829	1930	1959	2140
17	Versailles Chantiers ▲ **274** d.	...	|	0849	0853	|	|	0953	|	|	1053	1253	|	|	1453	|	|	|	|	|	1841	1944	|	2153
82	**Dreux** d.	0456	0757	0925	0947	1012	1008	1047	1111	1111	1147	1347	|	|	1547	|	1607	1719	1724	|	1924	2023	2050	2247
118	Verneuil sur Avre d.	0528	|	0944	...	1041	1031	...	|	|	...	...	1420	1425	...	|	1637	1739	1743	|	1947	2042	2108	...
142	L'Aigle d.	0546	0826	0957	...	1059	1045	...	1140	1139	...	...	1433	1439	...	1627	1655	1752	1756	1847	2001	2055	2122	...
183	Surdon **271** d.	0616	0846	1017	...	1133	1113	...	|	|	...	...	1454	1459	...	|	1720	1813	1817	1910	2027	2115	2142	...
198	Argentan **271** d.	0627	0857	1028	...	1144	1124	...	1211	1208	...	...	1504	1510	...	1658	1730	1824	1828	1922	2037	2125	2152	...
226	Briouze d.	0650	0914	1044	...	1200	...	...	|	|	...	...	1521	1526	...	|	...	|	|	1941	...	2140	2208	...
243	Flers d.	0701	0925	1054	...	1211	...	...	1234	1230	...	...	1532	1537	...	1723	...	1847	1850	1954	...	2151	2219	...
272	Vire d.	0719	0942	1110	...	1227	...	...	1251	1246	...	...	1548	1555	...	1739	...	1904	1905	2010	...	2207	2234	...
298	Villedieu d.	0739	0956	1125	...	1242	...	...	1306	1300	...	...	1602	1609	...	1754	...	1920	1921	2025	...	2221	2249	...
313	Folligny **272** d.	0750	1006	1135	...	1254	...	...	|	|	...	...	|	|	...	|	...	|	|	2035	...	|	|	...
328	**Granville** **272** a.	0800	1016	1145	...	1304	...	...	1324	1319	...	...	1620	1626	...	1812	...	1938	1938	2045	...	2239	2307	...

	16510 ① g	Ⓐ	⑥ t	†	3410 ⑥ t	3410 Ⓐ	⚒ ◇	3412 †	◇	3420 △	◇	⑥ t	3430 ⚒	Ⓐ	3432 †	3440 ⚒	3442 †	⑤	H	3444 ⑦ e	◇	13272 ⑦ q	3450	3454 ⑦ e
Granville **272** d.	0444	...	...	...	0553	0558	...	0700	...	0907	...	...	1218	...	1353	1516	1519	1621	1637	1700	...	...	1859	1956
Folligny **272** d.	|	...	...	...	|	|	...	|	...	|	...	...	|	...	|	|	|	1633	1649	|	...	...	1909	2006
Villedieu d.	0502	...	...	...	0610	0615	...	0717	...	0925	...	...	1235	...	1410	1533	1539	1644	1700	1717	...	...	1921	2016
Vire d.	0517	...	...	...	0625	0630	...	0732	...	0941	...	...	1252	...	1425	1548	1555	1703	1719	1732	...	...	1936	2032
Flers d.	0535	...	...	...	0642	0647	...	0749	...	0959	...	...	1309	...	1443	1606	1611	1722	1738	1749	...	...	1954	2049
Briouze d.	0546	...	...	...	0653	0658	...	0800	...	|	...	...	1321	...	1454	|	|	1734	1750	1800	...	...	2006	2100
Argentan **271** d.	0604	0604	0625	0624	0710	0715	...	0817	...	1025	...	1150	1339	1421	1511	1634	1636	1755	1811	1817	...	1920	2023	2117
Surdon **271** d.	0614	0614	0635	0635	0720	0725	...	0827	...	1035	...	1200	1349	1431	1521	|	|	...	...	|	...	1931	2032	|
L'Aigle d.	0639	0639	0700	0706	0740	0745	...	0848	...	1056	...	1225	1410	1500	1542	1701	1702	...	...	1843	...	2000	2052	2144
Verneuil sur Avre d.	0653	0653	0713	0720	0754	0758	...	0901	...	1109	...	1243	|	1514	1555	|	|	...	...	|	...	2013	2106	|
Dreux d.	0716	0716	0737	0742	0814	0819	0849	0921	0949	|	1149	1314	|	1538	|	1733	1734	...	...	|	1949	2037	2126	2216
Versailles Chantiers ▲ **274** a.	0759	0759	|	|	|	|	0943	|	1043	|	1243	|	|	|	|	|	|	...	...	|	2043	2114	|	2250
Paris Montparnasse ⊖ **274** a.	0811	0811	0823	0830	0908	0911	0956	1008	1056	1215	1256	1405	1523	1625	1704	1819	1819	...	...	1959	2056	2125	2219	2303

H – ①–④ to July 6 (also July 15); ① July 20 - Aug. 24; ①–④ from Aug. 31 (not Nov. 11).
e – Also June 1, July 14, Nov. 11.
f – Not Oct. 9.
g – Also June 2, July 15; not June 1, July 13.
n – Also June 1, July 14; not July 12.
q – Also June 1, July 14.
t – Not Aug. 15.
z – On ②③④ July 7 - Aug. 27 (also July 13; not July 14) runs only to Argentan.
▲ – Local travel to / from Paris not permitted on certain trains (see Table **274** for local services).
△ – Subject to alteration Ⓐ Sept. 21 - Oct. 2.
▽ – Subject to alteration Sept. 14 - 18, Oct. 5 - 9.
◇ – Suburban train, 2nd class (approx hourly).
⊖ – Most trains use **Vaugirard** platforms (5 - 10 mins walk).

Rail / 🚌 Paris - Villedieu - Mont St Michel : see page 181.

Ⓐ – Mondays to Fridays, except holidays Ⓑ – Daily except Saturdays Ⓒ – Saturdays, Sundays and holidays

CHAMBÉRY - MODANE 367

km																							
						TGV				*TGV*				*TGV*				*TGV*					
					🚌	**9241**				**6403**				**9247**				**9249**					🚌
		Ⓐ								⑥					Ⓐ					Ⓐ	†		⑤⑦
			L			**M**	⊖		△	**E**				**M**				**M**					
	Paris Gare de Lyon **341** d.	...	...	...	...	0742	...	...	...	1158	...	...	...	1350	...	...	...	1524	...	...	...	...	...
	Lyon St Exupéry ✈ **342** d.	...	...	...	...	|	...	...	...	|	...	...	...	|	...	...	...	1720	...	...	...	...	...
	Lyon Part Dieu **344** d.	...	0631	...	...	|	...	...	...	|	...	...	1541	|	...	...	1641	|	...	...	...	...	...
	Aix les Bains **341/4** d.	...	|	...	...	|	...	...	...	|	...	...	|	1658	...	...	|	|	...	1953	...	...	...
0	**Chambéry** **366** d.	0641	0807	...	1005	1045	1210	...	1410	|	...	1610	1704	1711	1727	...	1800	1826	...	2008	2008	...	2205
14	Montmélian **366** d.	0653	0819	...	1023	|	1221	...	1422	|	...	1620	|	|	1737	...	1811	|	...	2018	2018	...	2223
26	St Pierre d'Albigny **366** d.	0702	0828	...	1038	|	1230	...	1431	|	...	1628	|	|	1747	...	1821	|	...	2026	2026	...	2238
71	St Jean de Maurienne d.	0744	0905	...	1134	1129	1311	...	1508	1549	...	1711	1757	|	1827	...	1857	|	...	2105	2105	...	2329
83	St Michel-Valloire d.	0754	0916	...	1150	|	1322	...	1520	1602	...	1722	1808	|	1836	...	1907	|	...	2114	2114	...	2343
99	**Modane** a.	0808	0930	...	1209	1150	1336	...	1536	1619	...	1736	1822	1813	1850	...	1921	1925	...	2127	2127	...	2359

									TGV		*TGV*										*TGV*	*TGV*		
									9240		**9242**	🚌									**6410**	**9248**		🚌
	Ⓐ	⑥				Ⓐ	Ⓒ							⚒			Ⓐ	†			⑥			⑤⑦
		t							**M**		**M**			▽			**c**				**F**	**M**		
Modane d.	0525	0525	0623	0705	...	0835	0835	...	0950	1029	1116	1220	...	1423	...	1624	1715	1715	...	1835	1853	1920	...	1921
St Michel-Valloire d.	0543	0543	0638	0725	...	0850	0850	...	|	1044	|	1237	...	1438	...	1639	1731	1731	...	1849	1909	|	...	1938
St Jean de Maurienne d.	0553	0553	0648	0751	...	0900	0900	...	1015	1056	1141	1253	...	1448	...	1650	1742	1742	...	1859	1920	|	...	1954
St Pierre d'Albigny **366** d.	0631	0631	0727	0832	...	0939	0939	...	|	1133	|	|	...	1527	...	1728	1820	1820	...	1939	|	|	...	2048
Montmélian **366** d.	0639	0639	0736	0841	...	0947	0947	...	|	1142	|	1408	...	1537	...	1738	1829	1829	...	1948	|	|	...	2108
Chambéry **366** a.	0647	0647	0745	0850	...	0956	0956	...	1052	1151	1220	1432	...	1545	...	1746	1838	1838	...	1956	|	2022	...	2130
Aix les Bains **341/4** a.	...	0702	|	...	...	|	...	...	|	|	|	...	...	...	...	...	1851	...	...	|	|	|	...	...
Lyon Part Dieu **344** a.	...	0843	0916	...	...	1116	...	...	|	1316	|	...	...	...	...	...	...	...	...	2116	|	|	...	...
Lyon St Exupéry ✈ **342** a.	...	...	...	...	...	...	...	...	|	...	|	...	...	...	...	...	...	...	...	...	|	2124	...	...
Paris Gare de Lyon **341** a.	...	...	...	...	...	...	...	...	1355	...	1515	...	...	...	...	...	...	...	...	...	2306	2319	...	...

E – ⑥ June 27 - Aug. 29.
F – ⑥ July 11 - Aug. 29.
L – ⚒ (daily June 22 - Sept. 6).
M – [12] and 🍷 Paris - Milano and v.v. (Table **44**). [R], special 'global' fares payable.

c – Depart Modane 1724 on Ⓐ Sept. 28 - Oct. 23.
t – Not Aug. 15.
TGV –[R], supplement payable, 🍷.
⊖ – Runs 30 minutes earlier on Ⓐ Sept. 28 - Oct. 23.

△ – Subject to alteration on Ⓐ Sept. 28 - Oct. 23.
▽ – Runs up to 14 minutes earlier on Ⓐ Sept. 28 - Oct. 23.

Via Mont Blanc road tunnel — 🚌 CHAMONIX - COURMAYEUR - AOSTA 368

From Apr. 20, 2009																		
		[R]§ ⚒	[R]‡ ⚒		[R]§	[R]‡	[R]§	[R]‡	[R]§	[R]‡	❖	[R]§ ⚒	[R]‡ ⚒	❖	[R]§	[R]§	[R]‡
St Gervais (rail station) d.	→	...	...	→	0815	...	...	...	...	...	→	...	...	→	...	...	...
Chamonix (rail station) d.	Apr. 20 -	0845	1615	June 27 -	0845	1010	1330	1500	1600	1745	Sept. 7 -	0845	1615	Dec. 20 - Apr. 18	0845	1500	1615
Courmayeur a.	June 26	0930	1700	Sept 6	0930	1055	1415	1545	1645	1830	Dec. 19	0930	1700	(not Dec. 25)	0930	1545	1700
Aosta (see below) a.		*1045*	*1830*		*1045*	*1200*	*1630*	*1730*	*1830*	*1930*		*1045*	*1830*		*1045*	*1730*	*1830*
		[R]§ ⚒	[R]‡ ⚒		[R]‡	[R]§	[R]‡	[R]§	[R]‡	[R]§	❖	[R]§ ⚒	[R]‡ ⚒	❖	[R]§	[R]‡	[R]§
Aosta (see below) d.	→	*0745*	*1335*	→	*0745*	*0945*	*1045*	*1335*	*1545*	*1645*	→	*0745*	*1335*	→	*0745*	*1045*	*1545*
Courmayeur d.	Apr. 20 -	0940	1510	June 27 -	0845	1045	1245	1445	1645	1745	Sept. 7 -	0940	1510	Dec. 20 - Apr. 18	0940	1300	1715
Chamonix (rail station) a.	June 26	1025	1555	Sept 6	0930	1130	1330	1530	1730	1830	Dec. 19	1025	1555	(not Dec. 25)	1025	1345	1800
St Gervais (rail station) a.		...	...		...	...	...	...	...	1900		...	...		...	...	...

§ – Operated by SAT, Le Fayet. ‡ – Operated by SAVDA, Aosta. ❖ – Subject to confirmation from Sept. 7, 2009.
Reservations by day before departure: Courmayeur (AG Mont Blanc ✆ 0165 841 305), Chamonix station (SAT ✆ 04 50 530 115), Aosta bus station (SAVDA ✆ 0165 262 027).

Connecting 🚌 service **Courmayeur - Pré St Didier - Aosta** (journey 60 minutes): Pré St Didier is 10 mins from Courmayeur. See also Table **586**. Operator: SAVDA, Aosta.
From Courmayeur: 0645, 0800, 0900, 0945, 1100, 1225, 1325, 1430 (⚒, schooldays only), 1530, 1630, 1730, 1830, 1945, 2145, 2245.
From Aosta: 0645, 0750, 0945, 1045, 1220, 1305 (⚒, schooldays only), 1335, 1445, 1545, 1645, 1745, 1845, 1945, 2045, 2145.
Service to June 30, 2009 (no service Dec. 25)

Narrow gauge. 2nd class only — CORSICAN RAILWAYS 369

May 18 - June 28, 2009

km																							
			⚒		⚒	⚒		⚒		⚒	⚒		Ⓐ			†		†		†		†	†	
0	**Bastia** d.	⚒	0640	...	0833	...	...	1520	...	1711	...	...	1828	...	†	0910	...	1023	...	1710	...	1820	...	...
21	Casamozza d.		0701	...	0901	...	...	1548	...	1732	...	...	1906	...		0938	...	1054	...	1738	...	1857	...	...
47	Ponte Leccia a.		0744	...	0934	...	...	1623	...	1805	...	...	1941	...		1013	...	1125	...	1814	...	1928	...	...
47	Ponte Leccia d.		0744	...	0938	0946	...	1623	...	1808	1815	...	1941	...		1013	...	1137	...	1814	...	1932	1939	...
99	Ile Rousse ▷ d.		|	...	|	1102	...	|	...	|	1930	...	|	...		|	...	1252	...	|	...	|	2054	...
120	**Calvi** ▷ a.		|	...	|	1135	...	|	...	|	2003	...	|	...		|	...	1325	...	|	...	|	2127	...
74	Corté d.		0826	...	1017	...	...	1702	...	1846	...	...	2015	...		1053	...	...	...	1853	...	2006	...	...
152	**Ajaccio Gare** a.		1023	...	1214	...	...	1859	...	2038	...	...	...	...		1246	...	...	...	2046	...	...	...	...

		⚒		⚒	⚒		⚒		⚒	⚒		⚒				†		†		†		†		
Ajaccio Gare d.	⚒	...	...	...	0632	...	0814	...	...	1506	...	1642	...	...	†	...	...	0855	...	...	...	1654	...	...
Corté d.		0639	...	...	0829	...	1017	...	...	1704	...	1844	...	...		...	...	1054	...	...	...	1853	...	...
Calvi ▷ d.		|	...	0710	|	...	|	...	1545	|	...	|	...	...		0820	...	|	...	1615	...	|	...	...
Ile Rousse ▷ d.		|	...	0748	|	...	|	...	1623	|	...	|	...	...		0858	...	|	...	1652	...	|	...	...
Ponte Leccia a.		0715	...	0859	0903	...	1054	...	1734	1738	...	1920	...	...		1009	...	1128	...	1803	...	1927	...	...
Ponte Leccia d.		0715	...	...	0908	...	1054	...	...	1742	...	1920	...	...		1016	...	1132	...	1820	...	1932	...	...
Casamozza d.		0750	...	...	0946	...	1127	...	...	1819	...	1955	...	...		1052	...	1205	...	1855	...	2005	...	...
Bastia a.		0822	...	...	1005	...	1153	...	...	1847	...	2014	...	...		1118	...	1231	...	1921	...	2031	...	...

Local service	⚒	⚒	⚒	⚒	⚒	⚒	⚒	⚒	⚒	⚒
Bastia d.	0622	0715	0900	1030	1215	1347	1439	1655	1717	1905
Casamozza a.	0652	0746	0930	1100	1245	1417	1510	1725	1749	1933

Local service	⚒	⚒	⚒	⚒	⚒	⚒	⚒	⚒	⚒	⚒
Casamozza d.	0702	0800	0951	1110	1310	1430	1555	1737	1753	2000
Bastia a.	0739	0830	1021	1140	1340	1501	1625	1807	1821	2028

Operator: Chemins de fer Corse (CFC) - operation is contracted to SNCF.
For Calvi - Ajaccio journeys change at Ponte Leccia (use both directions of the table).

▷ – Additional trains Calvi - Ile Rousse (*Tramway de la Balagne*):
From Calvi: 0750 ⚒, 0900 †, 0930 ⚒, 1100 †, 1150 ⚒, 1350 ⚒, 1400 †, 1620 ⚒, 1745 †, 1800 ⚒.
From Ile Rousse: 0840 ⚒, 1000 †, 1020 ⚒, 1150 †, 1240 ⚒, 1440 ⚒, 1510 †, 1710 ⚒, 1845.

370 PARIS - DIJON *TGV services*

Many *TGV* trains continue to Besançon or Belfort (Table **374**), Lausanne or Bern (Table **375**)

km	*TGV* trains convey 🍷	*TGV* 6751 ①–⑤ n	*TGV* 9281*	*TGV* 6755 ①–⑤ n	*TGV* 6757 ⑥⑦ e		*TGV* 6759	*TGV* 6711 ①–⑥ n	*TGV* 9269	*TGV* 6713 ⑤	*TGV* 9271 ⑦	*TGV* 6765 ①–⑤ n	*TGV* 6715 ⑥	*TGV* 6719 ⑤		*TGV* 9273*	*TGV* 6789	*TGV* 6769 B	*TGV* 6727 ⑥ K	*TGV* 9277	*TGV* 6731 ①–④ n	*TGV* 6773	*TGV* 6735 F	*TGV* 6775 ⑤	*TGV* 6777 ⑤⑦ e
0	**Paris Gare de Lyon** d.	0658	0758	0828	0824	...	1028	1124	1258	1410	1410	1428	1428	1458	...	1558	1658	1728	1732	1758	1858	1928	2028	2028	2127
212	Montbard d.	0806	|	|	0932	...	|	1232	|	|	|	|	|	1606	...	|	1806	|	|	|	2006	|	|	2133	|
284	**Dijon** a.	0840	0935	1005	1006	...	1205	1306	1437	1547	1547	1605	1605	1650	...	1735	1840	1905	1909	1935	2040	2107	2205	2207	2305

	TGV 6700 D	*TGV* 6704 ⑥	*TGV* 6784 ①–⑤ n		*TGV* 6756	*TGV* 9260	*TGV* 6710 ⑥		*TGV* 6714	*TGV* 9284	*TGV* 6762		*TGV* 6766 ①–⑤ n	*TGV* 6718 ⑥⑦ e	*TGV* 9268	*TGV* 6722 E	*TGV* 6726		*TGV* 6774	*TGV* 6776 Ⓑ	*TGV* 6734 ⑦ e		*TGV* 9288*	*TGV* 6770 ⑦ e	*TGV* 9274 ⑤⑦ e
Dijon d.	0620	0650	0652	...	0800	0924	0957	...	1052	1125	1152	...	1359	1457	1515	1621	1652	...	1758	1858	1918	...	2020	2121	2143
Montbard d.	|	0730	0730	...	|	|	|	...	1130	|	|	...	|	|	|	|	1730	...	|	|	1954	...	|	|	|
Paris Gare de Lyon a.	0800	0837	0837	...	0937	1103	1137	...	1237	1303	1331	...	1538	1637	1655	1759	1837	...	1938	2037	2103	...	2159	2303	2324

Lille - Dijon - Besançon	*TGV* 5130	*TGV* 5330 Q♠	*TGV* 5330 R♠
Lille Flandres d.	1842	...	...
Charles de Gaulle ✈ d.	1941	1121	1116
Marne la Vallée-Chessy § d.	2000	1056c	1131
Montbard d.	2106	1244	1244
Dijon a.	2139	1318	1318
Dole a.	2206	|	|
Besançon a.	2232	1405	1405

Besançon - Dijon - Lille	*TGV* 5152 ①–⑤ n	*TGV* 5156 ⑥⑦ e	*TGV* 5348 P♠
Besançon d.	0540	0652	1621
Dole d.	0605	0717	|
Dijon d.	0632	0744	1709
Montbard d.	0707	0819	1745
Marne la Vallée-Chessy § a.	0806	0918	1843
Charles de Gaulle ✈ a.	0820	0933	1858
Lille Europe a.	0915	1027	...

Melun - Marseille	*TGV* 6809 Ⓐ
Melun d.	0739
Sens d.	0814
Laroche Migennes d.	0837
Le Creusot TGV d.	0927
Lyon Part Dieu a.	1009
Marseille **350** a.	1156r

Marseille - Melun	*TGV* 6870 ①–④ n	*TGV* 6824 ⑤
Marseille **350** d.	1741	...
Lyon Part Dieu d.	1939	2056
Le Creusot TGV d.	2020	|
Laroche Migennes a.	2107	2219
Sens a.	2129	2242
Melun a.	2204	2316

B – Daily to July 5; Ⓑ July 6 - Aug. 30; daily from Aug. 31.
D – Ⓐ to July 3; ① July 6 - Aug. 17 (also July 15; not July 13); ①–⑤ from Aug. 24.
E – Ⓐ to July 3; ⑤ July 10 - Aug. 21; ①–⑤ from Aug. 24.
F – ①–④ to July 2 (not June 1); ④ July 9 - Aug. 20; ①–④ from Aug. 31.
K – July 11 - Aug. 29.
P – Daily from July 5.
Q – ① from July 6 (also July 15).
R – ②–⑦ from July 5 (not July 15).

c – Calls before Charles de Gaulle ✈.
e – Also June 1, July 14.
n – Not June 1, July 14.
r – 1215 July 6 - Aug. 28.
TGV – Ⓡ, supplement payable, 🍷.
♠ – To / from Caen and Cherbourg (Table **275**).
§ – Station for Disneyland Paris.
* – **9273** is **9285** on ⑤, **9281** is **9261** on ⑥, **9288** is **9272** on ⑥.

371 PARIS - SENS - AUXERRE and DIJON *For TGV see Table 370*

km		⚒	⚒	⚒			⚒			⚒		Ⓑ		Ⓐ	Ⓒ	Ⓑ	Ⓐ	Ⓒ	Ⓐ	Ⓒ	Ⓑ	Ⓐ	Ⓒ		Ⓐ
0	**Paris Bercy** d.	...	...	0620	0720	0820	0920	1020	1220	1320	1420	...	1520	1613	1620	...	1713	1720	1813	1820	...	1913	1920	2020	2220
113	Sens d.	...	...	0729	0818	0915	1021	1115	1315	1415	1515	...	1615	1715	1715	...	1815	1815	1915	1915	...	2015	2015	2115	2315
147	Joigny d.	...	...	0752	0834	0931	1038	1131	1331	1431	1531	...	1632	1731	1731	...	1831	1832	1931	1931	...	2032	2032	2131	2331
156	Laroche Migennes d.	0543	0743	0800	0844	0940	1046	1140	1340	1443	1540	1543	1643	1740	1740	1743	1843	1843	1940	1940	1943	2043	2043	2140	2338
175	**Auxerre** a.	|	|	0822	|	0953	|	1153	1353	|	1553	|	|	1753	1753	|	|	|	1953	1953	|	|	|	2153	*2359*f
197	Tonnerre d.	0610	0810	...	0910	...	1110	...	...	1510	...	1613	1710	...	...	1810	1910	1910	...	...	2010	2110	2110	...	...
243	Montbard d.	0638	0838	...	0938	...	1138	...	...	1538	...	1638	1738	...	...	1838	1938	1938	...	...	2038	2138	2138	...	...
315	**Dijon** a.	0716	0914	...	1014	...	1214	...	...	1614	...	1714	1814	...	...	1914	2014	2015	...	...	2114	2214	2214	...	...

	Ⓐ	⑥	Ⓐ	⑥	Ⓐ	⑥	⚒		⚒			Ⓑ		⑥t				Ⓑ	Ⓑ			Ⓑ			Ⓑ
Dijon d.	...	...	...	...	0546	0546	0646	...	0748	...	0946	1042	...	1225	...	1346	...	1546	1646	...	1746	1825	...	1946	2046
Montbard d.	...	...	...	...	0623	0623	0724	...	0824	...	1023	1124	...	1323	...	1423	...	1623	1723	...	1823	1923	...	2023	2123
Tonnerre d.	...	...	...	...	0649	0651	0751	...	0851	...	1051	1153	...	1351	...	1451	...	1651	1751	...	1851	1951	...	2051	2151
Auxerre d.	0450	0459	*0556*	0600	|	|	|	0809	|	1009	|	|	1209	|	1409	|	1609	|	|	1809	|	|	2009	|	|
Laroche Migennes d.	0515	0524	0615	0624	0714	0724	0818	0824	0924	1024	1124	1219	1224	1417	1424	1524	1624	1724	1818	1824	1924	2018	2024	2124	2218
Joigny d.	0522	0533	0622	0633	0720	0733	...	0833	0933	1033	1133	...	1233	...	1433	1533	1633	1733	...	1833	1933	...	2033	2133	...
Sens d.	0542	0550	0642	0651	0741	0751	...	0851	0951	1051	1151	...	1251	...	1451	1551	1651	1751	...	1851	1951	...	2051	2151	...
Paris Bercy a.	0643	0644	0744	0745	0843	0844	...	0944	1052	1144	1244	...	1344	...	1544	1646	1746	1846	...	1944	2044	...	2144	2244	...

CONNECTIONS LAROCHE MIGENNES - AUXERRE

	⚒	⚒	⚒	⚒	Ⓑ	⑥t		Ⓑ		⑦e		Ⓑ
Laroche Migennes d.	0723	0826	0853	1053	1226	1426	1653	1826	1853	2026	2053	2226
Auxerre a.	0743	0840	0914	1114	1244	1440	1714	1840	1914	2040	2114	2240

	a	⚒	⚒		⚒	Ⓑ		Ⓑ	Ⓑ	Ⓑ	
Auxerre d.	0650	0722	0850	1050	1250	1522	1650	1722	1850	1922	2050
Laroche Migennes a.	0708	0735	0908	1108	1308	1535	1710	1735	1908	1935	2108

LOCAL SERVICES PARIS - LAROCHE MIGENNES ❖

km							△	△	△		
0	**Paris Gare de Lyon** d.	0635	0835	1035	1235	1435	1635	1735	1835	1935	2035
45	Melun d.	0702	0902	1102	1302	1502	1701	1801	1901	2002	2101
60	Fontainebleau-Avon d.	0716	0916	1116	1316	1516	1716	1816	1916	2016	2116
79	Montereau d.	0735	0935	1135	1335	1535	1735	1835	1935	2035	2135
113	Sens d.	0822	1024	1219	1419	1619	1819	1919	2019	2119	2219
147	Joigny d.	0853	1053	1248	1448	1649	1848	1948	2048	2148	2249
156	**Laroche Migennes** a.	0900	1059	1256	1456	1656	1856	1956	2056	2156	2256

	Ⓐ					⑦e		⑦e		
Laroche Migennes d.	0642	0803	1003	1203	1403	1503	1603	1703	1803	2003
Joigny d.	0650	0810	1010	1210	1410	1510	1610	1710	1810	2010
Sens d.	0719	0841	1041	1241	1441	1541	1641	1741	1841	2041
Montereau d.	0748	0910	1110	1310	1510	1610	1710	1810	1910	2110
Fontainebleau-Avon d.	0808	0931	1131	1331	1531	1631	1731	1831	1931	2131
Melun d.	0820	0944	1144	1344	1544	1644	1744	1844	1944	2144
Paris Gare de Lyon a.	0850	1011	1211	1411	1611	1711	1811	1913	2011	2211

a – 8-9 minutes later on Ⓒ.
e – Also June 1, July 14, Nov. 11.
f – ⑤ only.
t – Not Aug. 15.

△ – On Ⓐ runs non-stop Paris - Montereau (journey 1 hour 55 mins to Laroche); slower trains run at 1743, 1843.
❖ – Also from Paris at 2235, from Laroche Migennes at 0403, 0503⑥, 0542Ⓐ, 0603Ⓒ, 0703⑥.

371a AUXERRE - AVALLON - AUTUN *2nd class only*

km		Ⓐ			⚒	⚒	⚒			
	Paris Bercy **371** d.	...	0820	...	...	1220	...	...	1813z	...
	Laroche Mig. **371** d.	0607	0940	...	...	1340	...	...	1940	...
0	**Auxerre** d.	0625	1000	...	1210	1410	...	1801	1955	...
17	Cravant-Bazarnes a.	0644	1016	...	1226	1426	...	1818	2013	...
17	Cravant-Bazarnes d.	0645	1021	1024	1232	1431	1434	1823	2018	2022
53	Clamecy a.	|	1104	|	*1324*c	1514	|	*1925*c	2103	|
86	Corbigny a.	|	1143x	|	|	...	|	|	2142	|
41	Sermizelles-Vézelay § d.	0719	...	1057	1305	...	1507	1854	...	2052
55	**Avallon** a.	0735	...	1113	1321	...	1523	1920	...	2108

	⚒			⑦x		⚒	⚒	⚒		N	Ⓑ	E
Avallon d.	0552	0659	...	...	1036	1246	...	1647	...	1839	...	1931
Sermizelles-Vézelay § d.	0609	0717	...	...	1100	1306	...	1704	...	1856	...	1948
Corbigny d.	|	|	0619	...	|	|	...	|	...	|	1807x	|
Clamecy d.	*0606*c	|	0659	0857	|	|	1242	|	1651	|	1843	|
Cravant-Bazarnes a.	0641	0744	0741	0938	1132	1339	1325	1737	1734	1929	1926	2016
Cravant-Bazarnes d.	0656	...	0751	0941	1144	...	1346	...	1744	...	1936	2017
Auxerre a.	0714	...	0807	0958	1200	...	1402	...	1759	...	1952	2036
Laroche Mig. **371** a.	...	...	0822	...	...	...	1422	...	1822	...	...	...
Paris Bercy **371** a.	...	...	0944	...	...	...	1544	...	1944	...	...	...

km		⚒	⚒		⑤	†
	Auxerre (see above) d.	...	...	...	1801	1801
0	**Avallon** d.	1118	1530	...	1927	1927
42	Saulieu d.	1213	1631	...	2022	2022
87	**Autun** a.	1309	1727	...	2118	2118
	Étang **374** a.	1332	1750	...	2136	2136

			Ⓐ	E
Étang **374** d.	0812	...	1430	...
Autun d.	0835	...	1450	1735
Saulieu d.	0930	...	1546	1830
Avallon a.	1024	...	1639	1924
Auxerre (see above) a.	1200	...	...	2036

E – ⑤–⑦ (also holidays).
N – ①②③④⑦ (also Aug. 15).
c – Change at Cravant-Bazarnes.
x – ⑦ and holidays (not Aug. 15).
z – 1820 on Ⓒ.

§ – Station is 9 km from Vézelay.

DIJON and LYON - PARAY LE MONIAL - MOULINS SUR ALLIER 372

km		Ⓐc			⚒		Ⓐ			
0	**Dijon** ▷ d.	...	...	...	...	...	...	1716	...	...
37	Beaune ▷ d.	...	...	...	...	...	...	1738	...	...
	Chalon sur Saône ▷ d.	0538	...	...	...	...	...	|	...	2009
52	Chagny ▷ d.	0551	...	...	...	...	...	1756	...	2021
81	**Montchanin** ▷ d.	0616	0706	1006	1206	1444	1705	1815	1906	2048
96	Montceau les Mines d.	0629	0720	1020	1221	1459	1721	1828	1920	2102
131	Paray le Monial d.	0702	0754	1054	1255	1533	1801	1900	1953	2135
142	Digoin d.	...	0804	1103	1304	1543	1811	1909	...	...
198	**Moulins sur Allier** a.	...	0856	1154	1350	1634	1902	1951	...	...
	Clermont Ferrand **330** a.	...	...	...	...	...	...	2100r	...	...

		Ⓐ	Ⓐ	Ⓒ					
Clermont Ferrand **330** d.	...	...	0616	0834	...	...	...	...	...
Moulins sur Allier d.	...	0555	0734	0942	1157	...	...	1648	1755
Digoin d.	...	0649	0816	1025	1249	...	...	1744	1846
Paray le Monial d.	0600	0700	0827	1035	1302	1602	...	1758	1901
Montceau les Mines d.	0636	0736	0859	1106	1338	1635	←	1833	1937
Montchanin ▷ d.	0650	0750	0911	1120	1357	1650	1709	1847	1951
Chagny ▷ d.	...	...	0932	1142	...	→	1731	...	...
Chalon sur Saône ▷ a.	...	...	|	|	...	...	1748	...	...
Beaune ▷ d.	...	...	0944	1154	...	...	...	...	...
Dijon ▷ a.	...	...	1010	1220	...	...	...	...	...

LYON - PARAY LE MONIAL - MOULINS SUR ALLIER

km				Ⓐ		Ⓐ
0	**Lyon Perrache** d.	1226	...	1654	1751	1849
4	**Lyon Part Dieu** d.	1239	...	|	1804	|
64	Lamure sur Azergues d.	1329	...	1757	1903	1959
128	Paray le Monial d.	1425	...	1854	2002	2051
139	Digoin d.	1434	...	...	2011	...
195	**Moulins sur Allier** a.	1520	...	...	2053	...
	Orléans **290** a.	|	...	...	2250	...
	Tours **290** a.	1755	...	...	...	...

	⚒	Ⓐc			†
Tours **290** d.	...	...	...	1213	...
Orléans **290** d.	...	...	0707	|	...
Moulins sur Allier d.	...	...	0901	1444	...
Digoin d.	...	...	0942	1526	...
Paray le Monial d.	0612	0708	0954	1537	2024
Lamure sur Azergues d.	0706	0805	1049	1631	2118
Lyon Part Dieu a.	|	|	1143	|	2205
Lyon Perrache a.	0810	0910	1158	1727	2217

c – Chalon - Paray le Monial - Lyon.
r – Change at Moulins sur Allier on † (a. 2102).
▷ – For connections Dijon and Chalon sur Saône - Montchanin see Table **374**.

DIJON - CHALON SUR SAÔNE - LYON 373

For *TGV* trains Paris - Mâcon Loché TGV and v.v. see Tables **340/1**. *Lyon - Grenoble times are subject to alteration on June 20, 21, 27, 28, July 17 - 19, Sept. 5, 6*

km					*TGV* **6801**	*TGV* **6813**				*TGV* **6811**					*TGV* **6781**	*TGV* **5148/9**						**4240 4241**		
		Ⓐ	⚒ ◇	Ⓐ	Ⓐ ♠	①⑥ z♥	Ⓐ	Ⓐ	Ⓒ	Ⓒ ♠	Ⓐ		Ⓐ C		Ⓐ	M §	Ⓐ			◇	Ⓐ	E	¶	
0	*Paris Gare de Lyon* **370** d.	...	...	...	...	...	...	...	...	...	...	...	...	...	0658	...	...	...	...	...	...	...	...	...
315	**Dijon** **372 374** d.	...	...	0533	0549	0614	...	0633	0633	0645	...	0718	0733	0833	0846	0916	0933	1018	1033	...	1123	1216	1208v	1223v
352	Beaune **372 374** d.	...	...	0553	|	|	...	0653	0653	|	...	0747	0753	0853	0907	|	0953	1047	1053	...	1152	|	1247	1253
367	Chagny **372** d.	...	...	0603	|	|	...	0703	0703	|	...	0758	0803	0903	|	|	1003	1058	1103	...	1202	|	1258	1303
382	**Chalon sur Saône** d.	...	...	0616	0623	0652	...	0716	0716	0721	...	0808	0816	0916	0924	0954	1016	1108	1116	...	1214	1251	1308	1316
440	Mâcon Ville d.	0553	0632	0646	0653	0722	0712	0746	0746	0752	0816	...	0846	0946	...	1024	1046	...	1146	1232	1246	1320	...	1346
478	Villefranche sur Saône ⊖ d.	0625	0705	0710	|	|	0739	0809	0814	|	0841	...	0909	1009	...	|	1109	...	1210	1304	1309	|	...	1409
512	**Lyon Part Dieu** a.	0651	|	0735	0727	0800	0805	0835	0839	0831	0905	...	0935	1035	...	1057	1135	...	1235	|	1335	1358	...	1435
	Grenoble **343** a.	...	|	0914	...	...	|	1014	1014	...	|	...	...	1214	...	...	1314	...	1413	|	1514	...	...	1614
512	**Lyon Perrache** a.	...	0733	...	...	...	0817	...	...	...	0917	...	...	...	...	...	...	...	...	1333	...	...	...	...

			4262 4263	*TGV* **5117/6**		*TGV* **6829**								*TGV* **6789**		**4264 4265**				**4266 4267**				
	Ⓐ		A△	B⊕		N	Ⓐ ◇		Ⓐ	◇	Ⓐ	Ⓐ C			Ⓐ	⑤ T		Ⓐ C		A	⚒	⑦ y		⑤⑦
Paris Gare de Lyon **370** d.	...	...	...	...	...	...	...	...	...	...	...	...	...	1658	...	...	...	...	...	...	...	...	...	...
Dijon **372 374** d.	1323	1423v	1455	1516	1533	1616s	...	1633	1650	...	1720	1733	1833	1843	1850	1907	1918	1933	2033	2048	2118	2133	2218	2318
Beaune **372 374** d.	1353	1453	|	|	1553	|	...	1653	1715	...	1748	1754	1853	1905	1916	|	1947	1953	2053	|	2147	2154	2247	2347
Chagny **372** d.	1403	1503	|	|	1603	|	...	1703	1725	...	1800	1804	1903	|	1925	|	1958	2003	2103	|	2158	2205	2258	2358
Chalon sur Saône d.	1416	1516	|	1552	1616	1651	...	1716	1734	...	1810	1815	1916	1921	1934	1945	2008	2016	2116	2124	2208	2217	2308	0008
Mâcon Ville d.	1447	1546	|	1623	1646	1722	1734	1746	...	1834	...	1846	1946	...	...	2015	...	2046	2146	2153	...	2250	...	...
Villefranche sur Saône ⊖ d.	1514	1608	|	|	1709	|	1804	1809	...	1904	...	1909	2010	...	...	|	...	2109	2214	|	...	2314	...	...
Lyon Part Dieu a.	1546	1635	1631	1701	1735	1757	|	1835	...	|	...	1935	2035	...	...	2055	...	2135	2237	2229	...	2337	...	...
Grenoble **343** a.	1733	1814	...	...	1914	...	|	2014	...	|	...	...	2214	...	...	...	...	...	|	|	...	|	...	...
Lyon Perrache a.	...	...	...	...	...	...	1833	...	...	1934	...	...	...	...	...	...	...	...	2251	2242	...	2351	...	...

		TGV **6784**			*TGV* **6786**		**4336 4337**				*TGV* **6852**				*TGV* **6850**			*TGV* **6792**	*TGV* **5170**		**4340 4341**			*TGV* **5198/9**
	Ⓐ	Ⓐ	① g	⚒	⑥	Ⓐ	A			Ⓐ ◇	①–⑤ ♠n	Ⓐ	◇		⑥⑦ ♠e	Ⓐ		Ⓐ	B⊗	Ⓐ	D		Ⓐ	M
Lyon Perrache d.	...	...	0508	...	...	0608	0635	...	...	0723	...	...	0823	...	...	...	...	...	...	...	...	...	1323	...
Grenoble **343** d.	...	...	|	...	...	|	|	...	0544	|	...	0642	|	0742	...	0842	0942	...	...	1042	...	1142	|	...
Lyon Part Dieu d.	...	...	0522	...	...	0622	0648	...	0722	|	0800	0822	|	0922	1000	1022	1122	...	1200	1222	1253	1322	|	1400
Villefranche sur Saône ⊖ d.	...	...	0549	...	...	0649	|	...	0749	0754	|	0849	0856	0949	|	1049	1149	...	|	1249	|	1349	1355	|
Mâcon Ville d.	...	...	0613	0613	...	0713	0725	...	0813	0824	0837	0913	0924	1013	1038	1113	1213	...	1238	1313	1337	1413	1426	1435
Chalon sur Saône d.	0534	0604	0645	0645	0708	0745	0754	0759	0845	...	0906	0945	...	1045	1107	1145	1245	1304	1310	1345	1406	1445	...	1505
Chagny **372** d.	0545	|	0655	0655	|	0755	|	0809	0855	...	|	0955	...	1056	|	1155	1255	|	|	1355	|	1455	...	|
Beaune **372 374** d.	0555	0622	0705	0705	0727	0804	|	0821	0905	...	|	1005	...	1106	|	1205	1305	1321	|	1405	|	1505	...	|
Dijon **372 374** a.	0620	0640	0724	0724	0747	0823	0827	0849	0924	...	0943	1024	...	1127	1143	1234	1338r	1348	1354	1434	1439	1534x	...	1539
Paris Gare de Lyon **370** a.	...	0837	...	...	0937	...	...	...	...	...	...	...	...	...	...	...	...	1537	...	...	...	...	...	...

				TGV **6794**									**4342 4343**						*TGV* **6880**		*TGV* **6876**		
	Ⓐ			⑦ e		Ⓑ		Ⓐ	Ⓐ	C		⚒ ◇	Ⓐ	A	C	Ⓑ ◇h		◇	Ⓐ	⑤⑦ b♥		N	Ⓐ	
Lyon Perrache d.	...	...	...	...	...	...	...	1623	1639	...	...	1723	1739	1759	...	1823	...	1923	...	...	...	...	2203	...
Grenoble **343** d.	1242	...	1344	...	...	1442	...	|	|	...	...	|	|	|	...	|	1742	|	1842	...	1942	...	|	...
Lyon Part Dieu d.	1422	...	1522	...	...	1622	...	|	1652	1722	...	|	1752	1812	1822	|	1922	|	2022	2126	2122	2156	2217	...
Villefranche sur Saône ⊖ d.	1449	...	1549	...	...	1649	...	1654	1719	1749	...	1754	1820	|	1849	1854	1949	1954	2048	|	2152	|	2247	...
Mâcon Ville d.	1513	...	1613	...	...	1712	...	1724	1744	1813	...	1824	1845	1855	1913	1924	2013	2023	2113	2202	2217	2235	2308	...
Chalon sur Saône d.	1545	1625	1645	1712	1725	1745	1749	...	...	1844	...	...	...	1923	1945	...	2045	...	2145	2232	2249	2304	...	...
Chagny **372** d.	1555	1639	1655	|	1740	1755	1803	...	...	1854	...	...	...	|	1955	...	2056	...	2155	|	2259	|	...	...
Beaune **372 374** d.	1605	1649	1705	1730	1749	1805	1815	...	...	1905	...	...	...	|	2005	...	2105	...	2205	|	2309	|	...	...
Dijon **372 374** a.	1624	1714	1724	1749	1814	1824	1844	...	...	1924	...	...	...	1956	2024	...	2124	...	2224	2305	2328	2343	...	...
Paris Gare de Lyon **370** a.	...	...	...	1938	...	...	...	...	...	...	...	...	...	...	...	...	...	...	...	...	...	...	...	...

A – (12) Metz - Dijon - Lyon and v.v.
B – (12) and 🍷 Dijon - Montpellier - Toulouse - Bordeaux and v.v.
C – To / from Chambéry (Table **344**).
D – June 14 - Sept. 21. (12) Cerbère - Montpellier - Dijon - Nancy - Metz; (12) Cerbère - Dijon (**4351**) - Strasbourg (Table **351**). Runs up to 7 minutes earlier Lyon - Dijon on Ⓐ Aug. 17 - Sept. 21.
E – June 13 - Sept. 20 (not July 6 - 10, 16, 17, 20, Sept. 14 - 18). (12) Metz - Nancy - Dijon - Montpellier - Portbou; (12) Strasbourg (**4251**) - Dijon - Portbou (Table **351**). Arrive Lyon 1405 on certain dates.
M – (12) and 🍷 Metz - Lyon - Marseille - Nice and v.v.
N – (12) and 🍷 Dijon - Lyon - Marseille - Nice and v.v.
T – (12) Metz - Lyon - Avignon - Montpellier (Table **351**).

b – Also June 1, July 14, Sept. 21 - 24, Nov. 23 - 26, 30, Dec. 1 - 3.
e – Also June 1, July 14.
g – Also June 2, July 15, Nov. 12; not June 1.
h – Also Aug. 15.
n – Not June 1, July 14.
r – 1324 on Ⓒ.
s – 1611 July 5 - Aug. 30 (also calling at Beaune 1633).

v – 10 minutes later on Ⓒ.
x – 1524 on Ⓒ.
y – Also June 1, July 14, Nov. 11.
z – Also June 2, July 7 - 10, 15 - 17, Sept. 15 - 18, Nov. 17 - 20; not June 1, July 13.

TGV – [R], supplement payable, 🍷.

♠ – To / from Marseille (Table **350**).
♥ – To / from Montpellier (Table **350**).
◇ – To / from Valence Ville (Table **351**).
¶ – Subject to alteration.
⊖ – Villefranche is also served by 🚌 service to Mâcon Loché TGV station, connecting with *TGV* trains to / from Paris (Tables **340/1**).
⊕ – On July 6 - 10, 16, 17, Sept. 14 - 18, Nov. 16 - 20 depart Dijon 1430, not calling at Chalon sur Saône or Mâcon. On July 28 - 30 depart Dijon 1506.
⊗ – On Sept. 21 - 25, Nov. 23 - Dec. 4 arrive Dijon 1424, not calling at Mâcon or Chalon sur Saône.
△ – On July 28 - 31, Aug. 4, 6, 10, 11, 13, 17 - 21, 25 - 28, 31, Sept. 1 - 4, 7 - 11, 21 - 25, 28 - 30, Oct. 1, 2 arrive Lyon Perrache 1701. On July 6 - 10, 16, 17, Sept. 14 - 18, Nov. 17 - 20, 24 - 27, 30, Dec. 1 - 4, 7 - 11 depart Dijon 1556, arrive Lyon Perrache 1733.
§ – On July 8, 9, 28 - 30, Sept. 14 - 18 depart Dijon 0910.

374 DIJON - MONTCHANIN - ÉTANG - AUTUN and NEVERS

Some trains 2nd class only

km			⚒	b	b	⚒	Ⓑ	Ⓑ		⑤	N
0	**Dijon** 372 373 d.	0603	0702	0903	1103	1329c	1603	1703	1803	1852	1903
37	Beaune 372 373 d.	0628	0726	0928	1128	1404	1628	1725	1831	1920	1929
81	Montchanin d.	0700	0754	1000	1200	1437	1659	|	1903	1951	2001
89	Le Creusot d.	0707	0802	1007	1207	1444	1707	1755	1911	1959	2008
111	**Étang** d.	0723	0816	1022	1222	1459	1722	1809	1926	2013	2023
179	Decize d.	0810	0855	1110	1309	1547	1810	1849	2015	2100	2110
216	**Nevers** a.	0837	0917	1137	1337	1618	1837	1911	2044	2127	2139
	Bourges **290** a.	...	0956	...	...	...	...	2007	...	...	...
	Vierzon **290** a.	...	1015	...	...	...	...	2026	...	...	...
	Tours **290** a.	...	1134	...	...	...	...	2154	...	...	...

	Ⓐ	Ⓐ		⚒z	†				Ⓑ	Ⓑ
Tours **290** d.	...	...	...	0703	...	...	...	...	...	1817
Vierzon **290** d.	...	...	...	0824	...	...	...	...	...	1937
Bourges **290** d.	...	...	...	0842	...	...	...	...	...	1957
Nevers d.	0517	0614	0716	0930	0930	1215	1519	1716	1817	2043
Decize d.	0544	0641	0745	0953	0957	1243	1547	1745	1845	2108
Étang d.	0633	0731	0834	1030	1040	1332	1635	1834	1935	2147
Le Creusot d.	0650	0748	0851	1044	1058	1348	1652	1851	1952	2201
Montchanin d.	0700	0800	0900	1051	1104	1400	1700	1900	2000	|
Beaune 372 373 d.	0730	0829	0930	1119	1131	1429	1730	1929	2030	2233
Dijon 372 373 a.	0754	0854	0954	1153	1154	1504r	1757x	1953	2054	2255

km		⚒	Ⓐ				Ⓐ	Ⓑh	⑥t		
0	**Chalon sur Saône** d.	0609	0708	0909	...	1609	1704	1806	1806	2009	...
15	Chagny d.	0622	0721	0921	...	1621	1717	1819	1819	2021	...
44	Montchanin d.	0647	0747	1012	...	1712	1814	1919	1919	2047	...
52	Le Creusot d.	...	...	1021	...	1724	1823	1931	1931	...	...
74	Étang a.	...	...	1046	...	1746	1847	1955	1955	...	...
89	**Autun** a.	...	...	...	...	...	...	2017	...	...	...

	Ⓐ	Ⓐ	⚒	⚒	⚒		⑤⑦v	Ⓐ		
Autun d.	...	...	...	...	...	...	1640	...	...	...
Étang d.	...	0603	0650	0750	1300	...	1704	1813	...	...
Le Creusot d.	...	0628	0716	0815	1326	...	1720	1830	...	...
Montchanin d.	0622	0634	0724	0823	1333	1709	1728	1839	1910	2010
Chagny d.	0710	...	0809*	0848	...	1731	1754	...	1936	2035
Chalon sur Saône a.	0726	...	0825	0905	...	1748	1806	...	1948	2048

CONNECTIONS ÉTANG - AUTUN

km		Ⓐ 🚌	⚒	a	🚌		Ⓐ a	⚒ 🚌		Ⓐ 🚌	u	Ⓑ 🚌	Ⓑ h
0	Étang d.	0638	0727	0812	1051	1250	1430	1504	1712	1726	1815	1852	2000
15	Autun a.	0659	0745	0830	1112	1308	1447	1525	1730	1747	1833	1911	2017

	⚒	⚒	⚒ 🚌	⚒ a	🚌	⑤⑦ v	⚒ a	⑤⑦ 🚌	①-④ n		⑤⑦ a
Autun d.	0609	0749	1217	1310	1603	1640	1733	1803	1808	1902	2119
Étang a.	0627	0806	1238	1332	1624	1657	1750	1824	1827	1920	2136

N – ①②③④⑦ only.
a – To/from Avallon (Table **371a**).
b – Depart Dijon 10 minutes earlier July 8, 9, 28 - 30, Sept. 14 - 18.
c – 1339 on ⑥. Subject to alteration July 6 - 10, 15 - 17, 20, Sept. 14 - 18.
h – Also Aug. 15.
n – Not June 1, July 14, Nov. 11.
r – 1454 on Ⓒ.
t – Not Aug. 15.
u – From July 4 depart 1829, arrive 1847
v – Also June 1, July 14, Nov. 10, 11.
x – 1759 on ⑥, 1801 on ⑦.
z – On ⑥ (not Aug. 15) Beaune d. 1128, Dijon a. 1147.
***** – Arrive 0749.

Additional 🚌 Étang - Autun: 2027 ⑤⑦.

375 DIJON - LAUSANNE and BERN

Special global fares are payable for international journeys. Certain trains continue beyond Lausanne to Aigle or Brig in Winter - see Table **42**

km				*TGV* 9281	*TGV* 9261				*TGV* 9269			*TGV* 9271		*TGV* 9273	*TGV* 9285		*TGV* 9287		*TGV* 9277				
		⚒		Ⓑ		Ⓐ	⑥ t			⚒	†	⑦			⑤		L				⑤⑦ v		
0	*Paris Gare de Lyon* **370** d.	...	...	0758	0758	...	...	...	1258	...	...	1410	...	1558	1558	...	1658	...	1758	...	...	...	...
315	**Dijon** 376 377 d.	...	...	0938	0938	...	*1136*	...	1440	...	...	1550	...	1738	1738	...	1846	...	1938	...	...	...	...
361	Dole 376 377 d.	0627	...	|	|	...	1220	...	1506	...	1555	|	...	1806	1806	1809	|	...	|	...	2141	...	...
393	Mouchard 376 d.	0646	...	1022	1022	...	1244	...	|	...	1616	|	...	|	|	1854	1935	...	2022	...	2200	...	...
417	Andelot 376 d.	0709	...	|	|	...	1313	...	|	...	|	|	...	|	|	1921	|	...	|	...	2218	...	...
438	Frasne d.	0723	...	1059	1102	1324	1327	...	1601	1608	1646	1707	...	1900	1900	1936	2010	...	2059	...	2233	...	...
454	Pontarlier 🏛 a.	0740	...	1110	|	1339	1342	...	|	1619	1700	|	...	|	1911	1952	2023	...	|	...	2243	...	...
462	Vallorbe 🏛 a.	...	...	|	1117	...	...	...	1616	...	...	1722	...	1916	|	...	|	...	2114	...	...	...	...
508	**Lausanne** a.	...	...	|	1152	...	...	...	1652	...	...	1758	...	1952	|	...	|	...	2152	...	...	...	...
518	Neuchâtel **511** a.	...	...	1156	...	...	...	...	...	...	...	...	...	...	1956	...	2107	...	...	...	...	...	...
561	**Bern 511** a.	...	...	1236	...	...	...	...	...	...	...	...	...	...	2036	...	2140	...	...	...	...	...	...

					TGV 9260		*TGV* 9284	*TGV* 9264					*TGV* 9268						*TGV* 9288	*TGV* 9272		*TGV* 9274	
	Ⓐ	⑥ t		E						Ⓒ	Ⓐ	⚒			Ⓒ	†	Ⓐ		Ⓑ			⑤⑦ w	
Bern 511 d.	...	...	...	...	...	...	0829	...	...	...	...	...	...	...	...	...	...	...	1723	...	...	...	...
Neuchâtel **511** d.	...	...	...	...	...	...	0900	...	...	...	...	...	...	...	...	...	...	...	1800	...	...	...	...
Lausanne d.	...	...	...	...	0703	...	|	0903	...	...	...	...	1303	...	...	...	...	...	|	1803	...	1922	...
Vallorbe 🏛 d.	...	...	...	...	0745	...	|	0940	...	...	...	...	1342	...	...	...	...	...	|	1840	...	2005	...
Pontarlier 🏛 d.	0555	0555	...	0747	|	...	0945	|	...	1220	1225	1346	|	...	1627	1718	1730	...	1845	|	...	|	...
Frasne d.	0611	0611	...	0800	0806	...	1007	1007	...	1236	1240	1357	1403	...	1641	1736	1748	...	1906	1906	...	2025	...
Andelot 376 d.	0626	0626	...	...	|	...	|	|	...	1250	...	...	|	...	1702	1751	1802	...	|	|	...	|	...
Mouchard 376 d.	0646	0646	...	...	0838	...	|	|	...	1319	...	...	|	...	1719	1816	...	...	1936	1936	...	2058	...
Dole 376 377 d.	0713	0711	...	...	|	...	1058	1058	...	1343	...	...	|	...	1739	1837	...	...	|	|	...	2117	...
Dijon 376 377 a.	0749	...	...	...	0921	...	1122	1122	...	...	...	...	1512	...	...	1907	...	...	2017	2017	...	2140	...
Paris Gare de Lyon **370** a.	...	...	...	...	1103	...	1303	1303	...	...	...	...	1655	...	...	...	...	...	2159	2159	...	2324	...

E – ②–⑤ (also ① from Nov. 16), not Aug. 21, Nov. 17.
L – Daily except ⑤.
t – Not Aug. 15.
v – Also June 1, July 14, Aug. 15, Nov. 11.
w – Also June 1, July 14.
TGV –Ⓡ, supplement payable, 🍷.

376 DIJON - DOLE - ST CLAUDE - OYONNAX

Some trains 2nd class

km			Ⓐ	Ⓑ h	Ⓒ	⑥ t	Ⓒ	Ⓐ	⑤ M	⑤⑦ w
0	**Dijon** 375 377 d.	...	...	...	0954	...	1700	1700	...	...
46	Dole 375 377 d.	...	*0627*	0931	1021	1258	1739	1735	...	2032
78	Mouchard 375 d.	...	*0646*	0955	1100	1327	1758	1758	...	2103
102	Andelot 375 a.	...	*0704*	1015	1117	1346	1816	1816	...	2123
102	Andelot d.	...	0712	1020	1122	1351	1821	1821	1924	2128
116	Champagnole d.	...	0737	1035	1135	1402	1832	1841	1935	2139
151	Morez a.	...	0821	1117	1218	1444	1915	1924	2017	2222
151	Morez d.	0644	0849	1121	1234	1517	1920	1928	2021	2226
174	**St Claude** a.	0708	0914	1146	1258	1542	1945	1953	2045	2250
207	Oyonnax (*see below*) a.	0743	...	1224	...	...	...	...	...	...

	① L	⚒		Ⓒ	⚒		†	†	N	⑤ f
Oyonnax (*see below*) d.	...	...	0747r	...	1410	...	...	1925	1951	1951
St Claude d.	0443	0616	0822	1207	1449	1637	1852	2000	2025	2048
Morez a.	0507	0642	0847	1232	1514	1702	1917	2025	2050	2113
Morez d.	0511	0650	0852	1246	1524	1706	1922	...	...	...
Champagnole d.	0553	0739	0933	1328	1606	1749	2004	...	...	...
Andelot a.	0605	0750	0945	1340	1619	1802	2015	...	...	...
Andelot 375 d.	0610	0759	0950	1345	1624	1812	2018	...	...	...
Mouchard 375 d.	0643c	0819	1015	1409	1653	1842	2044	...	...	...
Dole 375 377 a.	0703	0845	1038	1429	1717	1900	2106	...	...	...
Dijon 375 377 a.	...	...	...	1501	...	1926v	...	...	...	...

ST CLAUDE - OYONNAX

km		E		⑥	Ⓑ		⚒	†	†	⚒
0	St Claude d.	0523	0709	1146	1151	1527	1727	1800	2002	2027
33	Oyonnax a.	0557	0743	1220	1224	1600	1800	1833	2036	2101

	⚒			⚒	†			†	⚒	
Oyonnax d.	0747	1047	...	1410	1415	1650	...	1925	1951	2105
St Claude a.	0821	1120	...	1444	1449	1723	...	1959	2024	2138

🚌 OYONNAX / BELLEGARDE - BOURG EN BRESSE — *Bus service*

km	🚌	Ⓐ	Ⓐ			⚒	Ⓑ				Ⓑ
0	Oyonnax d.	...	0630	0918	1210	...	1310	1510	1650	...	1737
**	Bellegarde d.	0555	|	|	|	1225	|	|	|	1705	|
13	Brion Montréal la Cluse d.	0645	0655	0940	1230	1315	1330	1530	1715	1755	1805
49	Bourg en Bresse a.	...	0750	1025	1317	...	1417	1617	1802	...	1852

🚌	Ⓐ	Ⓐ	Ⓐ		⚒		Ⓑ		Ⓑ	
Bourg en Bresse d.	0625	...	0835	1240	...	1525	1735	...	1850	1935
Brion Montréal la Cluse d.	0705	0710	0920	1325	1340	1610	1820	1830	1935	2020
Bellegarde a.	|	0759	|	|	1429	|	|	1920	|	|
Oyonnax a.	0735	...	0940	1345	...	1635	1840	...	1955	2045

Additional 🚌 Oyonnax - Bourg en Bresse: From Oyonnax 0510 Ⓐ, 0610 ⚒, 0710 ⚒, 0715 §, 1105, 1315 §, 1605 Ⓐ, 1706 §, 1920 §.
From Bourg en Bresse 0745 ⚒, 0915 §, 1005 ⚒, 1040 ⚒ §, 1315 §, 1335 ⚒, 1645 Ⓐ, 1710, 1815 §, 2010 §, 2135.

E – ②–⑥ (not June 2, July 14, 15, Nov. 11, 12).
L – ① to June 29 / from Sept. 7 (also June 2, Nov. 12; not June 1).
M – ⑤ to July 3 / from Sept. 4 (also Nov. 10).
N – ①②③④⑥ (not June 1, July 14, Nov. 10, 11).
c – Arrives 0629.
f – Also Nov. 10.
h – Also Aug. 15.
r – ⚒ only.
t – Not Aug. 15.
v – ⑤–⑦ (also June 1, July 14, Nov. 10, 11).
w – Also Nov. 10.
§ – Journey 1 hour 25 mins.
****** – Bellegarde - Brion Montréal la Cluse = *28* km.

DIJON - BESANÇON - BELFORT 377

Some trains 2nd class only

Subject to alteration on Aug. 18, 19 Dijon - Dole and v.v.

km		⑥ t	Ⓐ d	Ⓐ	⚒	⚒	⚒	⚒	Ⓐ	Ⓒ	Ⓐ	*TGV* 6751 ①–⑤ n	Ⓒ	Ⓐ	*TGV* 6755 ①–⑤ n	*TGV* 6757 ⑥⑦ v	▷	⊖	⚒ ⊕	*TGV* 6759	⊖	⚒ ⊖	⊖	⚒ ⊖	4351 4350 A
	Paris Gare de Lyon **370** d.	...	...	...	...	...	...	...	...	...	...	0658	...	...	0828	0824	...	...	...	1028	...	...	...	...	...
0	**Dijon** **375 376** d.	...	0512	...	...	0602	0641	0705	0731	0734	0800	0843	0945	0948	1008	1009	1039	...	1136	1208	1215	...	1325	...	1450
46	Dole **375 376** d.	...	0544	...	...	0645	0714	0741	0804	0806	0832	0909	1016	1021	1034	1035	1110	...	1216	|	1252	...	1357	...	1516
91	**Besançon Viotte** a.	...	0617	...	...	0726	0742	0818	0832	0835	0900	0936	1047	1053	1101	1100	1138	...	1253	1256	1328	...	1424	...	1539
91	**Besançon Viotte** **384** d.	0611	0619	0647	0703	...	0744	...	0834	...	...	...	1049	...	...	...	...	1210	...	1301	...	1338	...	1520	1541
170	Montbéliard **384** d.	0713	0722	0744	0810	...	0844	...	0933	...	...	...	1147	...	...	...	...	1310	...	1352	...	1438	...	1621	1634
188	**Belfort** **384** a.	0727	0737	0759	0825	...	0858	...	0947	...	...	...	1202	...	...	...	...	1324	...	1405	...	1453	...	1635	1647

	Ⓐ		⑤	*TGV* 6765 ①–⑤ n		Ⓑ			Ⓐ	Ⓐ	⑦ e	⑥	*TGV* 6769 D	*TGV* 6769 ①–④ n	*TGV* 6727 ⑥ K	Ⓑ h		*TGV* 6773		⑤–⑦ b ▽	*TGV* 5130/1 L y	*TGV* 6775 ⑤	①–④ m	*TGV* 6777 ⑤⑦ s	⑤–⑦ b
Paris Gare de Lyon **370** ... d.	...	...	...	1428	...	...	...	...	...	...	...	...	1728	1728	1732	...	...	1928	...	...	...	2028	...	2128	...
Dijon **375 376** d.	1454	...	1551	1608	1615	1642	1716	1750	1814	1830	1836	1851	1908	1908	1911	1916	2004	2111	2117	2117	2142	2210	2219	2308	2329
Dole **375 376** d.	1527	...	1625	|	1648	1727	1750	1829	1847	1907	1909	1923	1934	1934	1939	1951	2035	2137	2148	2148	2208	2235	2251	2334	2358
Besançon Viotte a.	1558	...	1656	1703	1726	1806	1818	1906	1915	1944	1943	1951	1959	1959	2005	2018	2106	2205	2216	2216	2232	2301	2319	0001	0024
Besançon Viotte **384** d.	...	1630	...	...	1728	...	1820	1910	...	...	...	...	...	2006	...	2020	...	2208**c**	...	2235	...	...	...	...	...
Montbéliard **384** d.	...	1731	...	...	1827	...	1921	2019	...	...	...	...	...	2058	...	2118	...	2259**c**	...	2335	...	...	...	...	...
Belfort **384** a.	...	1746	...	...	1842	...	1935	2034	...	...	...	...	...	2112	...	2134	...	2313**c**	...	2350	...	...	...	...	...

	Ⓐ	*TGV* 6700 ① g	*TGV* 5152/3 ①–⑤ L n	Ⓐ	*TGV* 6754 ①–⑤ n			*TGV* 5156/7 ⑥⑦ L v	*TGV* 6756	*TGV* 6756 ①–⑤ n	⚒	⚒	Ⓐ		Ⓐ						*TGV* 6762 ⑥	*TGV* 6762	4251 4250 B	⚒	
Belfort **384** d.	...	...	...	...	...	0501	...	...	...	0552	...	0555	0625	0645	0729	...	...	0812	0917	...	0945	...	0958	...	...
Montbéliard **384** d.	...	...	...	...	...	0516	...	...	...	0606	...	0611	0640	0700	0744	...	...	0827	0933	...	0959	...	1011	...	...
Besançon Viotte **384** a.	...	...	...	...	...	0620	...	...	...	0656	...	0723	0740	0815	0844	...	...	0930	1032	...	1048	...	1103	...	...
Besançon Viotte d.	0508	0524	0540	0545	0556	...	0626	0652	0706	0706	0709	0728	0742	0817	...	0909	...	...	...	1037	1055	1055	1105	1227	...
Dole **375 376** d.	0535	0549	0605	0614	0623	...	0657	0717	0731	0731	0753	0756	0818	0900	...	0938	...	...	...	1109	|	|	1129	1305	...
Dijon **375 376** a.	0605	0613	0629	0642	0647	...	0734	0741	0757	0757	0823	0833	0849	0932	...	1011	...	...	...	1141	1145	1145	1153	1343	...
Paris Gare de Lyon **370** ... a.	...	0800	...	...	0837	...	...	...	0937	0937	...	...	...	...	...	...	...	...	...	...	1332	1332	...	...	...

	△	*TGV* 6766 ①–⑤ n	†	⚒ △	△			Ⓐ		*TGV* 6774			Ⓐ	*TGV* 6776 Ⓑ k	Ⓐ	Ⓒ	⚒	⚒	†	Ⓐ	Ⓑ h	†	*TGV* 6770 ⑦ s	Ⓐ	
Belfort **384** d.	1139	...	...	1216	1325	...	...	...	1536	1553	...	...	1624	...	1710	...	1740	...	1805	1814	...	1910	...	1934	2015
Montbéliard **384** d.	1153	...	...	1231	1340	...	...	...	1550	1607	...	...	1638	...	1725	...	1755	...	1820	1829	...	1925	...	1949	2030
Besançon Viotte **384** a.	1255	...	...	1343	1446	...	...	...	1652	1657	...	...	1750	...	1825	...	1909	...	1924	1934	...	2025	...	2049	2129
Besançon Viotte d.	...	1301	1308	1346	1448	...	1532	1638	...	1703	1710	1726	1752	1803	1827	1835	...	1914	...	...	2006	...	2034	...	2132
Dole **375 376** d.	...	1327	1338	1417	1525	...	1606	1714	...	1728	1745	1806	1830	1826	1906	1910	...	1959	...	...	2036	...	|	...	2202
Dijon **375 376** a.	...	1352	1409	1451	1559	...	1638	1748	...	1754	1817	1843	1906	1851	1936	1940	...	2032	...	...	2107	...	2118	...	2236
Paris Gare de Lyon **370** ... a.	...	1538	...	...	...	...	...	...	...	1938	...	...	...	2037	...	...	...	...	...	...	...	...	2303	...	...

A – June 14 - Sept. 21. (12) Cerbère (**4340**) - Dijon - Strasbourg.
B – June 13 - Sept. 20 (not July 19). (12) Strasbourg - Dijon (**4241**) - Portbou.
D – Daily to July 5; Ⓑ July 6 - Aug. 30; daily from Aug. 31.
K – ⑥ July 11 - Aug. 29.
L – (12) Lille - Charles de Gaulle ✈ - Besançon and v.v.

b – Also June 1, July 14, Nov. 10, 11.
c – ⑤⑦ (also June 1, July 14; not Sept. 20).
d – Not Aug. 19 Dijon - Dole.
e – Also June 1, July 14, Nov. 11.
g – Also June 2, July 15; not June 1, July 13.
h – Also Aug. 15.
k – Not Aug. 10, Sept. 20.
m – Not June 1, July 14, Nov. 10, 11.
n – Not June 1, July 14.
s – Also June 1, July 14; not Sept. 20.
t – Not Aug. 15.
v – Also June 1, July 14.
y – Not Aug. 10, 18, 19, Sept. 20.

TGV – Ⓡ, supplement payable, 🍸.

⊖ – Subject to alteration on Ⓐ Oct. 5 - 23.
⊕ – Dep. Dijon 1122, Dole 1204 on June 2 - 5, 8, July 15, 20. Subject to alteration on Ⓐ Oct. 5 - 23.
△ – Subject to alteration on Sept. 28 - Oct. 2, Oct. 26 - 30.
▽ – On ⑤ to July 3 (also June 1) Besançon d. 2219, Montbéliard d. 2318, Belfort a. 2334.
▷ – Depart Dijon 1034 on Ⓐ Oct. 5 - 23.

BESANÇON - LE LOCLE - LA CHAUX DE FONDS 378

2nd class

km		A		Ⓐ		⑥	⑦	A	Ⓐ		⑦e
0	**Besançon Viotte** d.	...	...	0713	1003	1225	1346	1356	1722	1824	2009
67	Morteau d.	0623	0725	0840	1122	1350	1502	1519	1855	1949	2130
80	Le Locle **512** a.	0640	0741	...	1140	...	...	1540	...	2007	...
88	**La Chaux de F 512** a.	0650	0751**c**	...	1149	...	...	1550	...	2017	...

	A	⚒		Ⓐ	⑥		A	⑥	†	
La Chaux de F 512 d.	0554	...	0810**r**	...	...	1610	1710	...	...	2041
Le Locle **512** d.	0601	...	0820	...	...	1620	1720	...	...	2051
Morteau d.	0618	0650	0842	1129	1227	1638	1738	1825	2010	2109
Besançon Viotte a.	...	0812	1001	1250	1348	1753	1858	1947	2126	...

A – ①–⑤ (not June 1).
c – *0758* on Ⓒ.
e – Also June 1, July 14, Nov. 11.
r – *0802* on Ⓒ.

METZ - NANCY - DIJON 379

km		*TGV* 5148	4240 4241 C ⊕	4240 4241 D ⊕	4262 4263 △	4264 4265 ⑤	4266 4267		4239 4238 R Ⓡ◇	4248 4249 T Ⓡ◇
0	**Luxembourg** **388** d.	...	...	...	...	...	...	...	1946	...
34	Thionville **388** d.	...	...	...	...	...	...	...	2019	...
64	**Metz** **388** d.	0611**r**	0820	0833	1136*	1530	1721	...	2041	2106
121	**Nancy** **388** d.	0651	0918	0930	1230	1630	1807	...	2134	2159
154	Toul d.	|	0940	0950	1250	1651	1828	...	2155	2221
198	Neufchâteau d.	|	1007	1015	1315	1716	1854	...	2220	2248
272	Culmont Chalindrey a.	|	|	|	|	|	1939	...	2307	2336
272	Culmont Chalindrey d.	|	|	|	|	|	1951	...	2326	2356
349	**Dijon** a.	0906	1149	1149	1443	1847	2036	...	|	|
	Lyon Part-Dieu **373** a.	1057	1358	1358	1631	2055	2229	...	|	|
	Lyon Perrache **373** a.	|	|	|	...	|	2242	...	|	|
	Avignon Centre **351** a.	|	1603	1603	...	2324	...	...	0412**x**	|
	Avignon TGV **350** a.	1213	|	|	...	|	...	...	|	|
	Montpellier **355** a.	|	1707	1707	...	0034	...	...	|	0628
	Perpignan **355** d.	|	1903	1903	...	...	...	...	|	0826
	Portbou **355** a.	|	2009	2009	...	...	...	...	|	0927
	Marseille **350** a.	1247	...	...	...	...	...	...	0532**x**	...
	Nice **360** a.	1528	...	...	...	...	...	...	0828**x**	...

	4330 4331 S Ⓡ◇		4348 4349 T Ⓡ◇		4336 4337		4340 4341 E	*TGV* 5198	4342 4343
Nice **360** d.	2034**z**	...	...	...	...	...	...	0932	...
Marseille **350** d.	2321**z**	...	...	...	...	...	...	1210	...
Cerbère **355** d.	|	...	2042	...	...	...	0625	|	...
Perpignan **355** d.	|	...	2133	...	...	...	0716	|	...
Montpellier **355** d.	|	...	2319	...	...	...	0907	|	...
Avignon TGV **350** d.	|	...	|	...	...	...	|	1245	...
Avignon Centre **351** d.	0021**z**	...	|	...	...	...	1019	|	...
Lyon Perrache **373** d.	|	...	|	...	0635	...	|	|	1759
Lyon Part-Dieu **373** d.	|	...	|	...	0648	...	1253	1400	1812
Dijon d.	|	...	|	...	0839	...	1505	1546	2007
Culmont Chalindrey a.	0507	...	0530	...	0923	...	|	|	|
Culmont Chalindrey d.	0523	...	0550	...	0937	...	|	|	|
Neufchâteau d.	0610	...	0639	...	1025	...	1635	|	2136
Toul d.	0635	...	0708	...	1050	...	1702	|	2201
Nancy **388** a.	0654	...	0729	...	1109	...	1722	1759	2220
Metz **388** a.	0745	...	0817	...	1206	...	1807	1848	2312
Thionville **388** a.	0815	...	...	...	...	...	...	...	...
Luxembourg **388** a.	0845	...	...	...	...	...	...	...	...

C – Ⓐ June 15 - Sept. 18 (not July 20).
D – Ⓒ June 13 - Sept. 20.
E – June 14 - Sept. 21.
R – Daily except Sept. 12, 19, 26, Oct. 3, 10, 17, Nov. 7, 14, 21, 28, Dec. 5, 12. On dates in note **x** train number is **4235/4295**.
S – Daily except Sept. 12, 19, 26, Oct. 3, 10, 17, Nov. 7, 14, 21, 28, Dec. 5, 12. On ①–④ to June 25/from Sept. 7 (not June 1, 2, Nov. 1 - 5) train number is **4388/4329**.
T – ⑤⑥⑦ to June 21 (also June 1), daily June 26 - Sept. 6, ⑤⑦ from Sept. 11 (also Sept. 12, 19, 26, Oct. 24, 31, Nov. 2 - 4).
r – 0608 on June 7, 14.
x – Departures from Luxembourg on ①–④ to June 25/from Sept. 7 (not June 1, 2, Nov. 1 - 5) arrive Avignon Centre 0446, Marseille 0556, Nice 0900.
z – On ①–④ to June 25/from Sept. 7 (not June 1, 2, Nov. 1 - 5) depart Nice 2007, Marseille 2253, Avignon Centre 0014. On June 12, 19, 26, Oct. 2, Nov. 27, Dec. 4 depart Nice 2011. On Aug. 31 - Sept. 3 depart Nice 2011, Marseille 2313.

TGV – Ⓡ, supplement payable, 🍸.

◇ – *CORAIL LUNÉA* – 🛏 1, 2 cl. and (2) (reclining).
△ – On July 28 - 31, Aug. 4, 6, 10, 11, 13, 17 - 21, 25 - 28, 31, Sept. 1 - 4, 7 - 11, 21 - 25, 28 - 30, Oct. 1, 2 arrive Lyon Perrache 1701. On July 6 - 10, 16, 17, Sept. 14 - 18, Nov. 17 - 20, 24 - 27, 30, Dec. 1 - 4, 7 - 11 runs 16 - 30 minutes later, arrive Lyon Perrache 1733.
⊕ – Not July 6 - 10, 16, 17, 20, Sept. 14 - 18 Dijon - Portbou.
* – 1134 on Ⓐ Oct. 13 - 23.

380 PARIS - TROYES - BELFORT - MULHOUSE

From November 13 timings may vary by ± 4 minutes

km	For TGV see Table **390**	1539			1541		1039		1041	1841		1545	1043	1043	1547		1045	1641	1047	11641	1741	1049	1643	1549	1645
		Ⓐ	⚒	Ⓐ	①–⑥	Ⓒ	①–⑥	Ⓐ	⑦	⚒			†	⚒		Ⓐ	Ⓑ	Ⓐ		Ⓐ			Ⓐ		
		S	c		n	c	n	c	e	▽	c											b		△	P
0	**Paris Est** d.	...	...	...	0642	...	0711	...	0812	0941	...	1213z	1243	1313z	1416z	...	1509	1611	1641	1711	1811	1841	1911	2013	2213
110	Nogent sur Seine d.	...	...	0650	0740	...	|	...	0910	1039	...	1308	|	|	1510	...	|	1712	|	1818	1911	|	2010	2108	2310
129	Romilly sur Seine d.	...	...	0702	0752	...	|	...	0924	1052	...	1320	|	|	1522	...	|	1726	|	1832	1924	|	2023	2120	2324
166	**Troyes** d.	0610	...	0722	0813	...	0835	...	0946	1114	...	1340	1408	1437	1544	...	1638	1748	1805	1853	1946	2009	2046	2142	2346
221	Bar sur Aube d.	|	...	0752	0845	...	|	...	1020	|	...	1412	|	|	1615	...	|	...	1840	...	2020	|	...	2214	...
262	Chaumont **382** d.	0655	...	0813	0907	...	0925	...	1045	1204	...	1433	1500	1527	1637	...	1728	...	1905	...	2045	2058	...	2236	...
296	Langres **382** d.	0715	...	▬	0927	...	|	...	1107	|	...	1453	|	|	1657	...	|	...	1926	...	2107	|	...	2256	...
307	Culmont Chalindrey **382** d.	0724	...	...	0935	...	|	...	1117	|	...	1501	|	|	1706	...	|	...	1937	...	2117	|	...	2304	...
	Dijon **379** a.	0828	...	...	...	...	|	...	|	|	...	...	|	|	▬	...	|	...	|	...	...	|	...	...	...
380	Vesoul d.	...	...	...	...	...	1028	...	1156	1307	...	...	1605	1629	...	...	1829	...	2015	...	...	2200	...	...	...
410	Lure d.	...	...	Ⓐ	...	...	1048	...	1217	...	...	...	1625	1649	†	...	1849	...	2035	...	...	2220	...	...	...
442	**Belfort** ▷ **384** d.	...	0659	0804	...	1057	1110	1155	1238	...	1355	...	1646	1712	1736	1802	1912	...	2059	...	...	2243	...	...	...
491	**Mulhouse** ▷ **384** a.	...	0738	0835	...	1136	...	1231	...	...	1434	...	...	1743a	1815	1848	1943x	...	2130	...	...	2311y	...	...	...

	1640	11640	1740	1940	1942		1742	1540	1040	1542				1042	1840	1544		1044	1548		1048	1046	1046		
	①–⑥	Ⓐ	Ⓐ	⑥	Ⓐ	⚒	⑦	①–⑥		Ⓐ	Ⓐ	†	⑥		Ⓑ		Ⓐ			Ⓒ	⑦	Ⓐ	⑥	Ⓑ	⑥
	n					c	d	n		S⊕	c	c	c				c			c	d	b		c	c
Mulhouse ▷ **384** d.	...	...	...	0349	0451q	0618	...	...	0745r	...	0855	0936	0955	1245s	...	...	1554	...	...	1659	...	1817r	...	1955	1955
Belfort ▷ **384** d.	...	...	...	0419	0521	0654	...	...	0820	...	0931	1024	1037	1322	...	...	1629	1650	...	1756	1819	1847	1847	2036	2052
Lure d.	...	...	...	0439	0541	▬	...	...	0842	...	▬	...	▬	1342	...	...	...	1712	...	...	1839	1907	1907	...	...
Vesoul d.	...	...	...	0459	0601		...	...	0902	...	...	...		1402	1520	...	...	1732	...	...	1858	1928	1928	...	...
Dijon **379** d.	...	...	...	|	|	...	...	...	|	0953	⊕	...	...	|	|	...	...	|	...	...	|	|	|	...	...
Culmont Chalindrey **382** d.	...	...	0528	0537	|	...	0713	0849	|	1047	1047	...	...	|	|	1649	...	|	1822	...	1936	2007	2007	...	...
Langres **382** d.	...	...	0539	0548	|	**1738**	0724	0859	|	1056	1056	...	**1642**	|	|	1659	...	|	1832	...	1947	|	|	...	...
Chaumont **382** d.	...	...	0601	0609	0703	Ⓐ	0746	0919	1004	1116	1116	...	⚒	1503	1624	1720	...	1834	1852	...	2008	2034	2034	...	...
Bar sur Aube d.	...	...	0622	0631	|		0807	0939	|	1137	1137	...	u	|	|	1741	...	|	1913	...	2031	|	|	...	...
Troyes d.	0509	0602	0656	0704	0751	0811	0840	1014	1050	1209	1209	...	1443	1550	1711	1812	...	1919	1945	...	2108	2120	2120	...	...
Romilly sur Seine d.	0530	0625	0716	0724	|	0832	0900	1035	|	1227	1227	...	1504	|	1731	1832	...	|	2006	...	2130	|	|	...	...
Nogent sur Seine d.	0543	0639	0729	0737	|	0846	0912	1048	|	1239	1239	...	1517	|	1744	1844	...	|	2018	...	2144	|	|	...	...
Paris Est a.	0645	0745	0830	0841	0916	0945	1015	1146	1218	1341	1341	...	1615	1714	1844	1944	...	2044	2115	...	2245	2245	2245	...	...

P – Ⓑ to Oct. 11; ⑦ from Oct. 18 (also Nov. 11; not June 28, July 5, 6, 9, 10, 12, 13, 15, 26).
S – From July 6.
a – Ⓐ only (subject to alteration Oct. 17 - Nov. 29).
b – Not July 13.
c – By 🚌 (or partly by 🚌) Aug. 17 - Nov. 28.
d – Also June 1, July 14, Nov. 11.
e – Also June 1, July 14.
n – Not June 1, July 14.
q – Depart 0429 on June 9, Aug. 18 - Oct. 16.
r – Subject to alteration Aug. 17 - Oct. 17.
s – Subject to alteration Aug. 17 - Oct. 18, Oct. 26 - 30.
u – Subject to alteration on Oct. 5 - 9, 12 - 16.
x – Subject to alteration Oct. 19 - Nov. 29.
y – Arrive 2319 Oct. 19 - Nov. 29.
z – 4 - 6 minutes earlier on Ⓐ June 22 - July 17, Oct. 19 - 23.
▷ – Local trains: 2nd class. Additional trains run.
▽ – Not on Ⓐ Sept. 14 - Oct. 2.
△ – On Ⓐ from Nov. 10, depart Paris 1947 and diverted Paris - Chaumont via Chalons en Champagne.
⊕ – On Ⓐ Oct. 5 - 16 runs 25 - 27 minutes earlier.

381 PARIS - CHÂLONS EN CHAMPAGNE - BAR LE DUC

km										2777							2785							
		Ⓐ	Ⓐ	Ⓐ	Ⓒ	⑥	Ⓐ	†				Ⓐ		Ⓐ	Ⓐ		Ⓑ		Ⓐ	⑤	Ⓒ	Ⓐ	⑤	†
				s	u	t	△		⊕	♥		⊗					♥x			f				w
0	**Paris Est** d.	0635	0735	0835	0835	1035	1035	1035	1235	1357	...	1435	1635	1735	...	1835	1927	...	1935	1935	2035	2135	2135	2235
95	Château Thierry d.	0730	0830	0930	0930	1123	1124	1123	1324	|	...	1522	1721	1830	...	1930	|	...	2030	2030	2122	2223	2222	2323
142	Épernay d.	0758	0858	0954	0958	1147	1147	1147	1352	|	...	1546	1751	1854	...	1958	|	...	2058	2058	2149	2247	2247	2348
	Champagne-Ardenne TGV d.	|	|	|	|	|	|	|	|	1440	...	|	|	|	...	|	2010	...	|	|	|	|	|	|
*172	**Châlons en Champagne** ▷ d.	0814	0915	1010	1015	1203	1203	1203	1409	1503	...	1604	1809	1910	1921	2015	2033	2037	2114	2116	2206	2303	2305	0004
205	Vitry le François ▷ d.	0832	0933	...	1033	1221	1221	...	1427	1521	1530	1622	1827	...	1939	2033	2052	2057	...	2134	...	...	2323	...
234	**St Dizier** ▷ a.	0851	*0959*	...	*1107*	1241	*1250*	...	1445	|	1550	1641	*1901*e	...	1957	2051	|	2116	...	2152	...	...	|	...
255	**Bar le Duc** ▷ a.	...	0958	...	1057	...	1247	...	...	1545	...	...	1851	...	...	...	2114	...	...	...	...	...	2349	...

				2778																	2784			
	Ⓐ	⚒	⚒	①–⑥	Ⓐ	G		⑦	⑦	⑥	⑥	Ⓐ	⑥⑦	Ⓐ		Ⓐ	Ⓐ		Ⓑ			Ⓐ	⑦	
				♥n				d	d							y	▽				♥		d	
Bar le Duc ▷ d.	...	...	...	0613	...	...	...	...	...	...	0940	...	...	...	1131	...	1341	...	...	...	1713	...	...	1937
St Dizier ▷ d.	...	...	0610	|	0637	0738	...	0934	...	0935	|	0940	1058	1122	|	1338	|	1538	...	1703	|	1738	1829	|
Vitry le François ▷ d.	...	...	0629	0638	0658	0758	...	0954	...	0954	1005	1001	1119	1141	1155	1400	1406	1559	...	1723	1738	1759	1850	2002
Châlons en Champagne ▷ d.	0519	0614	0649	0657	0715	0815	0815	1011	1022	...	1023	1019	1140	...	1212	...	1424	1616	1716	1742	1757	1816	1907	2019
Champagne-Ardenne TGV d.	|	|	...	0720	|	|	|	...	|	...	|	|	...	...	|	...	|	|	|	...	1819	|	|	|
Épernay d.	0537	0632	...	|	0731	0832	0832	...	1040	...	1040	1036	...	...	1229	...	1440	1632	1732	...	|	1832	1923	2035
Château Thierry d.	0600	0700	...	|	0800	0900	0900	...	1105	...	1105	1100	...	...	1258	...	1503	1700	1800	...	|	1900	1951	2100
Paris Est a.	0653	0753	...	0800	0853	0953	0953	...	1153	...	1153	1153	...	...	1353	...	1558	1753	1853	...	1900	1953	2041	2153

G – ①⑥⑦ (also June 2, July 14, Nov. 11; not June 1).
d – Also June 1, July 14, Nov. 11.
e – *1855* on Ⓒ.
f – Also June 1, July 13, Nov. 10.
n – Not June 1, July 14. From Commercy, depart 0551.
s – Not Nov. 9 - 20.
t – Not Aug. 15.
u – Not Nov. 11.
w – Depart 2134 on June 1; 2218 on June 28, July 5, 26, Aug. 15, 16, 23, Sept. 13, 20, Oct. 18, 25, Nov. 1, 8, 15.
x – To Commercy, arrive 2137.
y – Not Oct. 26 - 30, Nov. 3 - 6.
▷ – For other trains see Table **382**.
▽ – Subject to alteration Oct. 19 - Nov. 20.
△ – Dep. 1028 Oct. 12 - 16. Subject to alteration on Nov. 9, 12, 13, 16 - 20.
⊕ – Depart Paris 1227 on Oct. 12 - 16. Subject to alteration on Nov. 9, 11, 13, 16 - 20.
⊗ – Depart Paris 1427 on Oct. 12 - 16.
♥ – *TGV* train, 🅁, supplement payable, 🍷.
* – *188 km* via high-speed line.

382 REIMS - CHÂLONS EN CHAMPAGNE - METZ / NANCY / DIJON

Some 2nd class

km		Ⓑ	⑥§	Ⓐ	⑥u				⚒		⑦d
0	**Reims** ⊖ d.	...	...	0619	0751	...	...	...	...	1649	...
31	Épernay d.	...	0612	0646	0817	...	...	...	1620	1717	1822
61	**Châlons en Champ. 381** d.	...	0631	0704	0834	...	...	...	1637	1736	1841
94	Vitry le François **381** d.	...	0648	0721	0851	...	...	...	1655	1752	1857
143	Bar le Duc **381** d.	0710	0717	0749	0916	1010	1225	1608	1720	1821	1922
243	**Metz** (*see below*) a.	|	|	|	|	|	|	|	1812	|	2014
183	Commercy d.	0735	0738	0809	0936	1034	1247	1633	...	1842	...
209	Toul d.	0756	0755	0825	0952	1055	1303	1653	...	1859	...
242	**Nancy** a.	0818	0818	0846	1009	1117	1322	1718	...	1918	...

						Ⓑ	⑥	†	H	⑤
Nancy d.	0701	1002	1330	1600	1703	1801	1801	2034	2032	2041
Toul d.	0719	1023	1350	1624	1726	1823	1823	2055	2051	2100
Commercy d.	0733	1044	1410	1637	1747	1837	1838	2110	2106	2115
Metz (*see below*) d.	|	|	|	|	|	|	|	|	|	|
Bar le Duc **381** d.	0755	1106	1434	1659	1813	1858	1858	2132	2127	2137
Vitry le François **381** d.	0822	...	1501	...	...	1928	...	2159	...	2201
Châlons en Champ. 381 d.	0840	...	1519	...	...	1949	...	2217	...	2219
Épernay d.	0902	...	1535	...	...	2012	...	...	...	2236
Reims ⊖ a.	0922	...	...	...	...	2034	...	...	...	...

km		Ⓑ	⑥		Ⓑ	Ⓒ	Ⓐ		⑦	⑤	†
								N	e	f	
0	**Reims** ⊖ d.	0610	0854	1236	1640	1732	1748	1957	1957	1957	2126
58	**Châlons en Champ. 381** d.	0655	0934	1318	1720	1817	1825	2037	2039	2039	2211
91	Vitry le François **381** d.	0716	0955	1340	1741	1837	1844	2057	2058	2058	2230
120	St Dizier **381** d.	0736	1016	1400	1803	1855	1901	2117	2118	2118	2248
193	Chaumont **380** d.	0824	1102	1446	1853	...	...	2200	2202	2202	...
227	Langres **380** d.	0846	1123	1507	1914	...	...	2222	2222	2222	...
238	Culmont Chalindrey **380** a.	0855	1131	1515	1923	...	...	2230	2230	2230	...
238	Culmont Chalindrey **379** d.	0857	1133	1517	*1951*	...	...	...	2232	2232	...
315	**Dijon** **379** a.	0948	1226	1606	*2036*	...	...	...	2323	2323	...

	⚒	Ⓐ	①	⑥⑦	⑥			⑤⑦	Ⓑ	⑥
			g					e		
Dijon **379** d.	...	...	...	*0839*	...	...	1554	1704	1858	1941
Culmont Chalindrey **379** a.	...	...	...	*0923*	...	...	1658	1748	1946	2028
Culmont Chalindrey **380** d.	0538	0658	0925	0945	1222	...	1700	1755	1948	2030
Langres **380** d.	0548	0708	0935	0954	1232	...	1710	1806	1958	2040
Chaumont **380** d.	0609	0730	0955	1015	1252	...	1731	1826	2019	2059
St Dizier **381** d.	0655	0820	1039	1058	1340	1703	1820	1915	2104	2144
Vitry le François **381** d.	0716	0841	1101	1119	1400	1723	1842	1936	2125	2205
Châlons en Champ. 381 d.	0739	0904	1123	1140	...	1745	1903	1958	2144	2226
Reims ⊖ a.	0818	0942	1200	1220	...	1821	1941	2039	2223	2304

		E	⑤
Bar le Duc d.	0721	1229	1922
Metz a.	0814	1323	2016

		E	†	⚒
Metz d.	0829	1332	1830	1830
Bar le Duc a.	0923	1426	1927	1923

E – ①⑤ (also June 2, July 15, Nov. 10, 12; not June 1).
H – ①–④ (not holidays).
N – ①②③④⑥ (not June 1, July 13, 14, Oct. 31, Nov. 10, 11).
d – Also June 1, July 14, Nov. 11.
e – Also June 1, July 14, Nov. 10, 11.
f – Also Oct. 31.
g – Also June 2, July 14, 15, Nov. 11, 12; not Oct. 26, Nov. 2.
u – Not Aug. 15. Also † Bar le Duc - Nancy.
§ – Runs 20 minutes later on Aug. 15.

⊖ – Additional trains run Reims - Épernay and Reims - Châlons en Champagne.
Additional trains: Bar le Duc - Nancy 0603 Ⓐ, 1911; Nancy - Bar le Duc 1937 ⑥.

METZ and NANCY - STRASBOURG — 383

Some trains 2nd class

km					299									91									97			
		Ⓐ	⑥	Ⓐ	①–⑥	⚒	Ⓐ	Ⓐ		Ⓑ	⑥	⑥	†	S	Ⓐ	⚒	⑥	Ⓐ	†	Ⓑh	Ⓐ	†	R	⚒	Ⓐ	⚒
			t	⊖							▽t	t			△		t			◇◧						
	Luxembourg **388** d.	...	...	...	0543	...	...	...	...	...	...	...	...	1046	...	...	...	...	...	...	...	...	1610	...	...	...
0	**Metz** d.	...	...	...	0629	...	0748	...	0859	...	...	...	...	1132	...	1225	...	1334	1334	...	...	...	1653	...	1711	1742
	Nancy d.	...	...	0615	|	0715	|	0815	|	0915r	0915	1113	1113	|	1215	|	1315	|	|	1417	1615*	1612	|	1715	|	|
	Lunéville d.	...	...	0633	|	0733	|	0833	|	0932r	0934	1131	1130	|	1234	|	1332	|	|	1435	1634*	1629	|	1732	|	|
88	Sarrebourg d.	0620	0623	0656	|	0759	0845	0858	0956	1000	0959	1201	1201	|	1259	1328	1402	|	1431	1459	1658	1655	|	1758	1811	|
91	Réding d.	0626	0629	0700	0716	|	|	|	|	|	|	|	|	|	|	1333	|	1422	|	|	|	|	|	1802	1816	1829
114	Saverne d.	0643	0648	0715	0733	0815	0902	0915	1012	1017	1015	1217	1217	|	1315	1349	1417	1438	1448	1516	1714	1712	|	1815	1831	1845
159	**Strasbourg** a.	0719	0719	0739	0800	0839	0931	0937	1040	1039	1039	1239	1239	1250	1344	14152	1439	1505	1514	1539	1739	1735	1812	1840	1900	1908
	Mulhouse **385** a.	0816	...	0843	...	0945	...	...	...	...	1146	...	...	1352	1454	...	...	...	...	...	1846	...	1922	...	...	...
	Basel **385** a.	0840	...	0908	...	1009	...	...	...	...	1210	...	...	1420	1519	...	...	...	...	...	1910	...	1948	...	...	...

									2583		295
	Ⓑ	⚒	⑥	Ⓐ	†	Ⓐ	†	⑥	⑥	Ⓑ	†	Ⓑ
	h		t		◧			t	t	♥		M
Luxembourg **388** d.	...	...	...	...	...	...	...	...	...	...	...	2026
Metz d.	...	1824	...	...	...	1928	1932	1932	...	...	2051	2115
Nancy d.	1815	|	1915	1918	1920	|	|	|	2006	2045	|	|
Lunéville d.	1833	|	1933	1936	1937	|	|	|	2024	|	|	|
Sarrebourg d.	1858	1926	1956	1959	2000	|	|	2027	2047	2124	|	|
Réding d.	|	...	2000	|	|	2026	2019	|	|	|	|	|
Saverne d.	1916	...	2014	2015	2015	2044	2036	2045	2103	2142	2151	2213
Strasbourg a.	1941	...	2036	2037	2039	2108	2059	2108	2125	2204	2213	2238
Mulhouse **385** a.	2045	...	...	...	...	...	...	...	...	...	...	2344
Basel **385** a.	2109	...	...	...	...	...	...	...	...	...	...	0013

km		2584								296
		①–⑥	Ⓐ	⚒	Ⓐ	⑥	†	Ⓐ	⑥	Ⓑ
		♥n							t	M
	Basel **385** d.	...	...	...	0537	0537	...	...	...	0647
	Mulhouse **385** d.	...	...	...	0558	0558	...	0617	...	0713
	Strasbourg d.	0548	0558	0626	0706	0707	0706	0740	0739	0806
	Saverne d.	0612	0623	0650	0728	0729	0728	0802	0801	|
	Réding d.	|	0639	|	|	|	|	0817	0816	|
0	Sarrebourg d.	0631	0650	0705	0755	0754	0753	0821	0820	|
47	Lunéville d.	|	|	0731	|	|	|	0845	0844	|
80	**Nancy** a.	0709	|	0753	|	|	|	0904	0902v	|
	Metz a.	...	0741	...	0846	0846	0846	...	...	0927
	Luxembourg **388** a.	...	...	...	...	...	...	...	...	1014

								90						96								298
	Ⓐ	†		Ⓑ	Ⓐ	Ⓐ	⑥	⑥	R		Ⓐ	Ⓐ	†		R	⑥	Ⓐ	Ⓐ	†		Ⓑ	⑥	Ⓑ
	§		‡	⊡	‡	⊡		t					◧			t					h	t	
Basel **385** d.	0718	...	...	...	...	...	...	...	1304	...	...	1518	...	...	1604	...	...	1718	...	...	1818	...	...
Mulhouse **385** d.	0742	...	...	...	...	...	...	...	1334	...	...	1541	...	...	1635	...	...	1741	...	...	1841	...	...
Strasbourg d.	0842	0841	1002	1026	1143	1219	1220	1237	1436	1437	1535	1636	1636	1651	1737	1741	1741	1837	1837	1904	1937	1937	2000
Saverne d.	0903	0904	1027	1049	1205	1246	1251	1302	|	1503	1559	1701	1659	1714	|	1804	1806	1903	1900	1929	2003	2001	2023
Réding d.	|	|	|	|	1222	|	|	1320	|	|	1615	|	|	1730	|	|	|	1917	1914	|	|	|	2038
Sarrebourg d.	0920	0919	1051	1106	1231	1302	1307	1330	|	1519	1631	1719	1717	1742	|	1819	1821	1921	1919	1956	2019	2017	|
Lunéville d.	0941	0946	|	1133	|	1332	1333	|	|	1541	|	|	|	|	|	1847	1848	1944	1944	|	2048	2045	|
Nancy a.	1001	1004	|	1152	|	1352	1350	|	|	1602	|	1757	1757	|	|	1905	1906	2002	2003	|	2107	2106	|
Metz a.	...	...	1141	...	1327	...	...	1426	1553	...	1730	...	...	1830	1854	...	...	...	...	2043	...	...	2124
Luxembourg **388** a.	...	...	...	...	...	...	...	...	1645	...	...	...	...	...	1936	...	...	...	...	...	...	...	2215

Departures from Basel may be up to 4 mins earlier Aug. 17 - Sept. 11.

Departures from Nancy may be up to 5 mins earlier Sept. 28 - Nov. 13.

M – JEAN MONNET – ⟨12⟩ Brussels - Basel and v.v. (Table **40**).
R – ⟨12⟩ Brussels - Zürich and v.v. (Table **40**).
S – ⟨12⟩ Brussels - Zürich - Chur (Table **40**).
h – Also Aug. 15.
n – Not June 1, July 14.
r – Not on Ⓐ Sept. 28 - Nov. 20.
t – Not Aug. 15.

v – 0914 Oct. 3 - Nov. 7.
△ – Up to 40 mins earlier from Sept. 21.
▽ – On Sept. 14-25 arrive Basel 1223.
◇ – On Ⓐ Sept. 21 - Dec. 12 depart Nancy 1336, not calling at Lunéville.
⊡ – On Ⓐ Sept. 21-25, Nov. 23 - Dec. 4 arrive Nancy 40 minutes later, not calling at Lunéville.

⊖ – Runs up to 16 minutes earlier Sept. 28 - Nov. 13.
◧ – On † Oct. 4 - Nov. 11 runs up to 9 minutes earlier.
♥ – *TGV* train, Ⓡ, 🍷. To/from Paris (Table **390**).
§ – Arrive Nancy 1047 Sept. 28 - Nov. 20 (not calling at Lunéville).
‡ – Not Sept. 14-18.
* – Not Sept. 21 - Dec. 4.

STRASBOURG - BELFORT - BESANÇON - LYON — 384

Some trains 2nd class

🍷 on principal trains

km						4211	4251	TGV		4213		4215						4217		4219	4221		4293	4297
						4210	4241	5405/4		4212		4214						4216		4218	4220		4248	4296
		⚒		⚒	⑦	⚒	S							Ⓑ	⑥	Ⓑ	①–④	⑤⑦		P	⑤⑦		F	M
								⊕				△		h	t	h	m	d	⊙				Ⓡ	Ⓡ
0	**Strasbourg** 385 d.	...	...	...	...	0620	0816	0838	...	1013	...	1149	...	...	...	...	...	1531	...	1716	1819	...	2020	2100
43	Sélestat 385 d.	...	...	...	...	|	|	|	...	1034	...	|	...	...	...	...	...	|	...	|	|	...	2043	2123
65	Colmar 385 d.	...	...	...	...	0648	0847	0903	...	1047	...	|	...	...	...	...	...	1558	...	1744	|	...	2058	2138
106	Mulhouse 385 d.	...	...	...	...	0718	0919	0930	...	1118	...	1241	...	...	...	...	...	1630	...	1814	1911	...	2134	2210
155	**Belfort** a.	...	...	...	...	0745	0946	|	...	1146	...	|	...	...	...	...	...	|	...	1840	1936	...	2201	2239
155	**Belfort** 377 d.	...	...	...	...	0755	0958	|	...	1157	...	|	...	...	...	...	...	|	...	1850	1946	...	2212	2250
173	Montbéliard 377 d.	...	...	...	...	|	1011	1007	...	1211	...	1324	...	...	...	...	...	1709	...	1904	2001	...	2225	2304
252	**Besançon Viotte** 377 a.	...	...	...	...	0857	1103	1056	...	1303	...	1418	...	...	...	...	...	1803	...	1956	2054	...	2319	2358
252	**Besançon Viotte** d.	0607	0639	0722	0850	0859	1105	1058	1235x	1305	1340x	1420	...	1659	1707	1734	1806	1806	1830	1958	2057	...	2322	0001
292	Mouchard d.	0636	0712	0751	0920	|	|	|	1315	|	1422	|	...	1744	1744	1807	1832	|	1910	|	|	...	|	|
341	Lons-le-Saunier d.	0721	0754	0836	0958	1000	|	1156	1355	1408	1503	1520	...	1829	1826	1853	1911	1912	1957	2058	2156	...	|	|
405	Bourg-en-Bresse 353 d.	...	0837	...	1039	1040	|	1236	...	1445	...	|	...	1908	1908	1932v	...	|	...	2135	2233	...	|	|
465	**Lyon Part-Dieu** 353 a.	...	0920	...	1123	1123	1358	1316	...	1527	...	1639	...	...	...	...	...	2028	...	2216	2315	...	|	|
470	**Lyon Perrache** 353 a.	...	0932	...	1135	1137	|	|	...	...	...	...	...	...	...	...	...	2042	...	2230	2329	...	|	|
	Marseille **350** a.	...	...	...	...	...	|	1513	...	...	...	...	...	...	...	...	...	...	...	...	...	...	|	0556
	Nice **360** a.	...	...	...	...	...	|	...	...	...	...	...	...	...	...	...	...	...	...	...	...	...	|	0900
	Montpellier **355** a.	...	...	...	...	...	1707	...	...	...	...	...	...	...	...	...	...	...	...	...	...	...	0628	...
	Portbou **355** a.	...	...	...	...	...	2009	...	...	...	...	...	...	...	...	...	...	...	...	...	...	...	0927	...

						4310		4312		4314		4340	TGV			4316	4318	4318	4320			4322	4394	4348
						4311		4313		4315		4351	5430/1			4317	4319	4319	4321			4323	4395	4392
	⚒	⚒	⑦	Ⓐ	⑥	⚒			Ⓑ		⑥	T				⑤⑦	①–④	⑥	⑤⑦	⑥	⑤⑦	⑦	M	F
									h	▽	t		⊗			c‡	w	§	f‡		g	e	Ⓡ	Ⓡ
Cerbère **355** d.	...	...	...	...	...	...	...	...	...	...	...	0625	...	...	...	...	...	...	...	...	...	1650	...	2042
Montpellier **355** d.	...	...	...	...	...	...	...	...	...	...	...	0907	...	...	...	...	...	...	...	...	...	1937	...	2319
Nice **360** d.	...	...	...	...	...	...	...	...	...	...	...	|	...	...	...	...	...	...	...	...	...	|	2007	|
Marseille **350** d.	...	...	...	...	...	...	...	...	...	...	...	|	1246	...	...	...	...	...	...	...	...	|	2253	|
Lyon Perrache 353 d.	...	...	...	...	...	0707	...	0917	...	1235	...	|	|	...	1538	1654	1654	1732	1824	1919	2108	|	|	|
Lyon Part-Dieu 353 d.	...	...	...	...	...	0721	...	0931	...	1249	...	1253	1437	...	1550	1708	1708	1746	1838	1933	2122	2255	|	|
Bourg-en-Bresse 353 d.	0541	...	...	0655	...	0803	...	|	...	|	...	|	1525	...	1637	1753	1753	1833	|	2017	2218	2348	|	|
Lons-le-Saunier d.	0630	0727	0805	0812	0812	0841	1019	1048	1334	|	1416	|	1600	1610	1719	1830	1830	1912	1955	2059	2300	0030	|	|
Mouchard d.	0713	0811	0845	0856	0858	|	1056	|	1423	|	1503	|	|	1650	1803	|	|	|	|	2133	2337	0111	|	|
Besançon Viotte a.	0739	0840	0915	0925	0926	0939	1125	1145	1450z	1505	1532	1539	1659	1717	1836	1931	1931	2009	2051	2201	0006	0138	0448	0530
Besançon Viotte 377 d.	...	...	...	...	...	0941	...	1147	...	1506	...	1541	1701	...	...	1934	1933	2011	2054	...	...	0141	0451	0533
Montbéliard 377 d.	...	...	...	...	...	1033	...	|	...	1559	...	1634	1749	...	...	2027	2026	2103	2147	...	...	0240	0544	0627
Belfort 377 a.	...	...	...	...	...	|	...	1248	...	|	...	1647	|	...	...	|	2038	2116	2200	...	...	0253	0558	0640
Belfort d.	...	...	...	...	...	|	...	1258	...	|	...	1657	|	...	...	|	2048	2126	2210	...	...	0323	0610	0653
Mulhouse 385 a.	...	...	...	...	...	1110	...	1323	...	1636	...	1724	1825	...	...	2104	2113	2152	2237	...	...	0356	0637	0720
Colmar 385 a.	...	...	...	...	...	1137	...	1401s	...	|	...	1753	1850	...	...	2132	2141	2220	2305	...	...	0433	0715	0753
Sélestat 385 a.	...	...	...	...	...	|	...	|	...	|	...	|	|	...	...	2145	2154	2233	|	...	...	0450	0732	0806
Strasbourg 385 a.	...	...	...	...	...	1206r	...	1436s	...	1736	...	1827	1918	...	...	2207	2217	2255	2334	...	...	0520	0759	0834

F – *CORAIL LUNÉA* – ⑤⑥⑦ to June 28 (also June 1); daily June 29 - Sept. 6; ⑤⑥⑦ Sept. 11-27; ⑤⑦ from Oct. 2 (also Oct. 24, 31, Nov. 2-4). 🛏 1,2 cl. and ⟨2⟩ (reclining) Strasbourg - Dijon (**4293**) - Portbou and Cerbère - Dijon (**4392**) - Strasbourg
M – *ALSACE RIVIERA* – daily to Sept. 11; Ⓑ from Sept. 13. 🛏 1,2 cl. and ⟨2⟩ (reclining) Strasbourg - Nice and v.v. Train **4294/5** from Strasbourg, **4388/9** from Nice on certain dates.
P – ①②③④⑥ (not June 1, July 14, Aug. 15, Nov. 11).
S – June 13 - Sept. 20 (not July 19). ⟨12⟩ Strasbourg (**4251**) - Dijon (**4241**) - Portbou.
T – June 14 - Sept. 21. ⟨12⟩ Cerbère (**4340**) - Dijon (**4351**) - Strasbourg.

c – Also June 1, July 14, Nov. 11.
d – Also June 1, July 14, Aug. 15, Nov. 11.
e – Also June 1, July 14; not July 12.
f – Also June 1, July 14.
g – Not Aug. 14.
h – Also Aug. 15.
m – Not June 1, July 13, 14, Nov. 10, 11.
r – 1227 on Ⓐ Oct. 12-23.
s – From Oct. 12 arrive Colmar 1350, Strasbourg 1421.
t – Not Aug. 15.
v – ①–④ only.
w – Not June 1, July 14, Nov. 11.
x – Not Sept. 28 - Oct. 2, Oct. 26-30.

z – Not on Ⓐ Oct. 5-23.
TGV – Ⓡ, supplement payable, 🍷.
⊙ – 14-17 minutes later on ⑤⑦.
⊕ – Runs earlier on June 7, July 19, Oct 4 (Strasbourg d. 0813) and Ⓐ Sept. 28 - Oct. 9 (d. 0719).
⊗ – Runs later Lyon - Strasbourg (a. 2031) Ⓐ Oct. 12-23.
△ – Subject to alteration Sept. 28 - Oct. 2, Oct. 26-30 (arrives 2 hrs later).
▽ – Oct 5-23 Besançon d. 1612, Montbéliard 1704, Mulhouse 1754, Strasbourg a. 1913.
§ – On Oct. 10 arrive Strasbourg 2334.
‡ – On June 5, July 17 arrive Strasbourg 20-30 minutes later.

385 STRASBOURG - MULHOUSE - BASEL

See also Tables 390 and 384

For faster *TGV* trains Paris - Strasbourg - Mulhouse - Basel see Table **390**. For trains Strasbourg - Mulhouse - Belfort - Lyon see Table **384**.

km		Ⓐ	Ⓐ	Ⓐ	Ⓐ	⑥ t	Ⓐ	⑥ t	Ⓐ	⚒ ◇	†	Ⓐ	◇		⚒ ⊖	†	⚒ ◧	†			91 V	Ⓒ	Ⓐ ◇	Ⓑ	⑥
	Luxembourg 388 d.	...	...	...	...	...	...	...	...	...	...	...	...	...	...	...	...	...	...	...	1046	...	...	...	...
	Metz 383 d.	...	...	...	...	...	...	...	...	...	...	...	...	...	...	...	...	...	...	...	1132	...	...	...	...
0	**Strasbourg** d.	...	...	0520	0623	...	0653	0653	0723	0751	0753	0823	0853	...	0953	0953	1053	1053	1153	...	1253	1353	1353	1453	1453
43	Sélestat d.	...	...	0539	0642	...	0712	0720	0743	0810	0819	0842	0912	...	1012	1012	1112	1119	1212	...	1316	1412	1416	1512	1519
65	Colmar d.	...	...	0551	0655	...	0724	0733	0754	0823	0832	0854	0924	...	1024	1024	1124	1134	1224	...	1330	1424	1430	1524	1531
106	**Mulhouse** ▷ d.	0440	0530	0617	0715	0730	0746	0805	0818	0845	0856	0917	0947	...	1047	1049	1148	1205	1247	...	1355	1447	1456	1547	1553
140	**Basel** ▷ a.	0514	0555	0639	0739	0755	0808	0833	0840	0908	0918	0939	1009	...	1110	1111	1210	1227	1309	...	1420	1509	1519	1609	1614

	⚒	†	Ⓐ		Ⓒ	Ⓐ	⚒ ◇	†		97 R	Ⓐ	⑥	†	Ⓑ	◇	Ⓐ		†	Ⓐ	⑥	Ⓐ	†	Ⓒ	295 Ⓑ M	⑥ t
Luxembourg 388 d.	...	...	...	...	...	...	...	...	...	1610	...	...	...	...	...	...	...	...	...	...	...	...	...	2026	...
Metz 383 d.	...	...	...	...	...	...	...	...	...	1653	...	...	...	...	...	...	...	...	...	...	...	...	...	2115	...
Strasbourg d.	1553	1553	1623	1653	...	1723	1753	1753	...	1823	1853	1853	1853	1923	1953	2053	...	2123	...	2153	2153	2153	...	2253	2253
Sélestat d.	1612	1611	1642	1712	...	1742	1812	1812	...	1846	1912	1913	1920	1944	2012	2112	...	2151	...	2218	2212	2213	...	2312	2312
Colmar d.	1624	1623	1654	1724	...	1754	1825	1824	...	1900	1924	1927	1936	1957	2024	2125	...	2206	...	2231	2225	2228	...	2324	2325
Mulhouse ▷ d.	1647	1654	1717	1746	1804	1817	1848	1850	...	1924	1947	1955	2009	2021	2047	2148	...	2228	2252	2254	2245	2252	2305	2349	2346
Basel ▷ a.	1709	1716	1739	1810	1838	1839	1910	1912	...	1948	2009	2017	...	...	2109	2211	...	...	2326	2316	...	...	2339	0013	...

	⚒	Ⓐ	†	Ⓐ	⑥	Ⓐ ◇	Ⓐ	⑥	296 Ⓑ M	⚒ ◇	Ⓐ		⚒ ⊖	†	†	⚒ ◧	Ⓐ ◧	◧	⚒	†		90 W		Ⓑ	⑥
Basel ▷ d.	...	0518	0534	0537	0537	...	0618	0618	0648	0718	0748	0818	0918	0918	1004	1018	1048	1118	1218	...	...	1304	...	1418	1418
Mulhouse ▷ d.	0505	0542	0556	0558	0558	0617	0643	0642	0713	0742	0812	0843	0942	0941	1027	1043	1111	1141	1241	1238	...	1334	...	1441	1441
Colmar d.	0528	0602	0624	0625	0625	0646	0705	0708	0733	0801	0832	0902	1001	1005	1054	1102	1130	1201	1301	1306	...	1356	...	1501	1501
Sélestat d.	0541	0614	0636	0637	0636	0659	0717	0719	0744	0812	0843	0913	1012	1016	1105	1113	1141	1212	1313	1322	...	1410	...	1514	1512
Strasbourg a.	0603	0633	0704	0703	0704	0733	0740	0748	0803	0838	0904	0935	1034	1038	1134	1135	1203	1234	1335	1354	...	1433	...	1534	1541
Metz 383 a.	...	...	...	0846	0846	...	...	...	0927	...	...	...	...	...	...	...	...	...	...	...	...	1553	...	...	...
Luxembourg 388 a.	...	...	...	...	...	...	...	...	1014	...	...	...	...	...	...	...	...	...	...	...	...	1645	...	...	...

	⚒ ◇	†	Ⓐ	96 R		Ⓐ	Ⓐ ◇	Ⓒ	†	†	Ⓐ	◇	†	Ⓐ	†	⑥			†		Ⓐ	Ⓑ	Ⓑ		①–⑥
Basel ▷ d.	1518	1518	1548	1604	...	1648	1718	1718	1732	←	1748	1818	...	1918	1918	1918	2018	...	2125	2143	2226	2243	...	...	2345
Mulhouse ▷ d.	1541	1542	1611	1635	...	1711	1741	1741	1757	1810	1811	1841	1911	1942	1941	1941	2041	...	2149	2218	2252	2317	2323	...	0019
Colmar d.	1600	1602	1633	1656	...	1730	1800	1809	→	1832	1830	1900	1932	2001	2008	2010	2101	...	2213	...	...	...	2347	...	...
Sélestat d.	1614	1613	1645	1709	...	1741	1812	1820	...	1844	1842	1912	1944	2013	2023	2025	2112	...	2226	...	...	...	0000	...	...
Strasbourg a.	1633	1641	1704	1732	...	184	1833	1842	...	1904	1904	1933	2004	2036	2052	2052	2134	...	2249	...	...	...	0026	...	...
Metz 383 a.	...	...	...	1854	...	...	...	...	...	...	...	...	...	...	...	...	...	...	...	...	...	...	...	...	...
Luxembourg 388 a.	...	...	...	1936	...	...	...	...	...	...	...	...	...	...	...	...	...	...	...	...	...	...	...	...	...

M – JEAN MONNET – 12 Brussels - Basel and v.v.
R – IRIS – 12 Brussels - Basel - Zürich and v.v. (Table **40**).
V – VAUBAN – 12 Brussels - Basel - Zürich - Chur (Table **40**).
W – VAUBAN – 12 Zürich - Basel - Brussels (Table **40**).
t – Not Aug. 15.

◧ – Subject to alteration Sept. 14 - 25.
⊖ – Runs up to 22 minutes earlier on Ⓐ Sept. 14 - 25.
◇ – To / from Nancy on days in Table **383**.
▷ – Other local trains run.

Aug. 17 - Oct. 9
Timings may vary by a few minutes (departures from Basel may be up to 4 minutes earlier Aug. 17 - Sept. 11).

386 NANCY - ÉPINAL - REMIREMONT

km		⚒	Ⓐ	⚒	† L	⚒	⚒	⊕	†	⚒ ⊕		⚒	2571 ♥v		Ⓐ		Ⓐ		⚒		2573 Ⓒ ♥v	2573 Ⓐ ♥v	Ⓐ		H	⑤†
	Paris Est 390 d.	...	...	...	...	...	...	...	...	...	...	...	1212	...	...	...	...	...	...	...	1812	1812	...	...	...	...
0	**Nancy** d.	0605r	...	0705	0707	0720	0820	0905	1006	1119	1205	1303	1346	1405	1506	1605	1703	1720	1805	1904	1945	1950	2006	2105	2204	2255
74	Épinal a.	0705	...	0759	0800	0821	0914	1000	1100	1215	1301	1400	1427	1458	1600	1701	1800	1820	1901	2000	2026	2030	2112	2159	2300	2354
74	Épinal d.	...	0720	0801	0802	...	0916	1002	1102	1227	1303	...	1430	1500	*1616*	1703	1802	...	1903	2002	2029	2033	...	2201	...	...
100	**Remiremont** a.	...	0750	0825	0828	...	0942	1028	1128	1252	1332	...	1451	1524	*1645*	1728	1830	...	1929	2028	2052	2054	...	2225	...	...

	⚒	2574 Ⓐ ♥		⚒	⚒		2576 Ⓒ ♥z	Ⓐ ⊕	⊕	⚒ ⊕	⊕	Ⓐ		⚒	2578 ①–⑥ ♥n	⚒	†	Ⓒ	Ⓐ	Ⓒ L	2580 ⑦ ♥s	Ⓐ	⚒	† L	⚒	Ⓑ ◇
Remiremont d.	0530	0600	0626	0701	...	0833	0907	...	1038	...	1215	1418	...	1536	1603	...	1625	...	1729	1730	1805	...	1835	1839	1935	...
Épinal a.	0555	0622	0654	0729	...	0858	0928	...	1103	...	1245	1443	...	1600	1623	...	1654	...	1757	1758	1826	...	1902	1902	2000	...
Épinal d.	0600	0624	0659	0731	0800	0900	0931	1000	1104	1200	1247	...	1500	1602	1626	1656	1656	1726	1759	1800	1829	1830	1904	1904	2002	2110
Nancy a.	0659	0705	0758	0835	0854	0952	1011	1057	1159	1257	1342	...	1557	1658	1709	1752	1752	1825	1853	1857	1909	1930	1957	1957	2057	2203
Paris Est 390 a.	...	0845	...	...	...	...	1145	...	...	...	...	...	...	...	1845	...	...	...	...	...	2045	...	...	...	...	...

km		⚒	Ⓐ	⑥t	⚒	Ⓒ	Ⓐ
0	**Nancy** d.	0558c	...	...	...	...	1752
74	Épinal d.	0710	1025	1308	1440	1850	1850
132	Luxeuil les Bains d.	0759	1118	1352	1527	1936	1936
150	Lure 380 d.	0814	1131	1405	1541	1949	1949
182	**Belfort** 380 a.	0835	1149	1423	1601	2010	2010
200	Montbéliard 377 a.	...	...	...	1618	...	...

	⚒	⚒	†	⚒	⑤	⑦e
Montbéliard 377 d.	0548	...	...	1645	...	...
Belfort 380 d.	0603	1120	1633	1659	1940	1940
Lure 380 d.	0622	1140	1653	1724	2000	2000
Luxeuil les Bains d.	0635	1153	1706	1737	2013	2013
Épinal a.	0720	1241	1753	1825	2100	2100
Nancy a.	...	...	...	...	2159	2159

Additional trains: Nancy - Épinal 0620 ⚒, 1222 ⚒, 1620 Ⓐ, 1820 Ⓐ. Épinal - Nancy 0500 Ⓐ, 0624 ⑥ **t**, 0630 Ⓐ, 1233 ⚒, 1640 Ⓐ.

H – Not ⑤†.
L – To / from Luxembourg (Table **388**).
c – *0605* on ②–⑤ (not June 2, Nov. 11), change at Épinal.

e – Also June 1, July 14, Nov. 11.
n – Not July 14.
r – 0558 on ①⑥ (also June 2, Nov. 11).
s – Also July 14.
t – Not Aug. 15.
v – Depart Paris 9 - 11 minutes earlier July 11 - 14.
z – Not Nov. 11.
♥ – *TGV* train, 🄡, 🍸, supplement payable.
◇ – Depart 2101 on ⑤⑦ **e** (see panel below).
⊕ – Subject to alteration Sept. 14 - 25.

387 NANCY - ST DIÉ and STRASBOURG - ÉPINAL

km	*Also see below*	⚒	Ⓐ ▽	▽		Ⓐ		2591 ⑦ ♥e			2593 Ⓐ ♥	2595 ⑦ ♥e
	Paris Est 390 d.	...	...	...	...	...	...	1412	...	...	1812*	2012
0	**Nancy** d.	0628	0758	0901	1230	1259	1400	1546	1600	1756	1946	2145
33	Lunéville d.	0655	0825	0923	1250	1324	1422	1606	1620	1821	2007	2205
84	**St Dié** a.	0804	0915	1006	1345	1404	1509	1636	1714	1914	2036	2235

Also see below	2596 ①–⑥ ♥n	Ⓒ	Ⓐ ▽	Ⓒ	▽	Ⓐ	⚒			2598 ⑦ ♥u	
St Dié d.	0719	0853	0855	1059	1214	1449	1558	1640	1755	1923	1944
Lunéville d.	0751	0941	0945	1142	1311	1545	1640	1742	1842	1954	2039
Nancy a.	0809	1000	1006	1203	1332	1610	1702	1801	1902	2012	2102
Paris Est 390 a.	0945	...	...	...	...	...	...	...	...	2145	...

Additional trains: **Nancy - St Dié**: 0550 ⚒, 1201 Ⓐ, 1659 Ⓐ, 1726 Ⓐ, 1729 Ⓒ, 1853 †, 1857 ⚒, 1958 Ⓐ, 2000 Ⓒ, 2101 Ⓐ ▽.
St Dié - Nancy: 0521 Ⓐ, 0612 ⚒, 0637, 0729 Ⓐ, 1202 Ⓐ, 1545 †, 1853 Ⓐ.

km		⚒	Ⓐ	Ⓐ	†	⑥ t	⑥ t	†	Ⓐ	Ⓐ ▽	Ⓐ	†	⑥ t	⑦ e§	Ⓐ	Ⓐ	Ⓐ	⑥ t	⚒	†	Ⓐ	†	†
0	**Strasbourg** d.	...	...	0655	0815	0855	...	0955	0955	...	1205	...	1255	...	...	1555	...	...	1755	1755	...	...	1915
87	St Dié d.	0559	0733	0839	0942	1032	1037	1122	1132	1235	1350	1352	1436	1642	1650	1736	1825	1900	1926	1929	1942	1948	2048
147	**Épinal** a.	0705	0843	...	...	...	1144	...	...	1345	...	1500	...	1748	1808	...	1932	2008	...	...	2049	2053	...

	Ⓐ	Ⓐ	†	⚒	Ⓐ	⑥ t	†	Ⓐ	⑥ t	⚒ ▽	Ⓐ	⑥ t	†	†	Ⓐ	Ⓐ	†	⑥	⑥ t	Ⓐ	†	†	⚒
Épinal d.	0559	...	...	0735	...	...	1030	...	...	1239	...	...	1514	...	1652	...	...	1710	...	1825	1833	...	2042
St Dié d.	0708	0736	0813	0844	0851	0909	1135	1214	1216	1344	1538	1610	1619	1624	1759	1804	1800	1815	1831	1934	1940	2000	2151
Strasbourg a.	...	0901	0935	...	1026	1040	...	1351	1350	...	1717	1740	...	1755	...	1931	1941	...	2015	...	...	2123	...

e – Also June 1, July 14.
n – Not June 1, July 14.
t – Not Aug. 15.
u – Also July 14.

▽ – Subject to alteration on Sept. 14 - 18.
§ – Runs 16 - 21 minutes later to June 28.
* – 9 mins earlier July 11 - 13.

♥ – *TGV* train, 🄡, 🍸, supplement payable.

Engineering work: Strasbourg - St Dié is subject to alteration July 6 - Aug. 1, with 🚌 substitution.

LUXEMBOURG - METZ - NANCY — 388

Some trains 2nd class only

For *TGV* trains Luxembourg - Metz - Paris see Table **390**. For long distance trains to the south of France see Table **379**.

km					299																	91				
		⚒	⚒	†r	⚒s	⚒	†	⚒	⚒	⚒	Ⓐ	⚒	†	Ⓐ		Ⓐ	Ⓒ	Ⓐ	Ⓐ	Ⓒ	⑥⑦	S	Ⓐ		Ⓐ	
0	**Luxembourg** d.	...	0502	0529	0543	...	...	0614a	...	0655	...	0730	...	0755	0835	0846	0935	...	1034	...	...	1046	...	1135	...	1235
34	Thionville d.	...	0531	0555	0604	...	...	0642	...	0725	0738	0756	0806	0820	0900	0923	1000	1010	1101	...	1104	1111	...	1157	...	1300
46	Hagondange d.	...	0542	0607	|	...	...	0652	...	0734	0746	0806	0818	0831	0909	0934	1009	1019	1109	...	1113	|	...	1206	...	1309
64	**Metz** a.	...	0600	0621	0625	...	...	0706	...	0745	0758	0819	0836	0845	0921	0953	1022	1031	1120	...	1125	1129	...	1222	...	1321
64	**Metz** d.	0600	...	0628	...	0636	0656	0710	0729	...	0800	0824	0838	*0900*	0924	...	1024	1035	1124	1124	...	...	1157	1224	1259	1324
93	Pont-à-Mousson d.	0635	...	0649	...	0658	0727	0727	0749	...	0821	0845	0907	*0918*	0944	...	1044	1056	1144	1144	...	...	1218	1244	1320	1344
121	**Nancy** a.	0705	...	0705	...	0720	0759	0743	0806	...	0837	0902	0936	*0935*	1000	...	1100	1113	1200	1201	...	...	1235	1300	1337	1400

						97												295								
	Ⓐ				Ⓐ	R	Ⓐ	Ⓐ		Ⓐ		Ⓐ	Ⓐ			Ⓐ	Ⓒ	ⒷM	⑥⑦	⚒	†	†	Ⓐ	⚒	†	△
Luxembourg d.	1255	1330	1430	1535	...	1610	...	1615	1640	1655	1730	...	1755	1830	1931	2016	...	2026	...	...	2115	...	2145	2215	2235	...
Thionville d.	1319	1351	1453	1559	...	1631	...	1642	1707	1724	1759	...	1824	1900	1959	2040	...	2051	2104	2142	2142	...	2215	2245	2258	...
Hagondange d.	1331	1401	1503	1608	...	|	...	1653	1719	1733	1809	...	1835	1910	2007	2050	...	|	2113	2153	2153	...	2226	2253	2306	...
Metz a.	1343	1416	1518	1621	...	1650	...	1711	1731	1745	1822	...	1850	1921	2018	2108	...	2112	2125	2211	2211	...	2242	2304	2317	...
Metz d.	...	1421z	1524	1624	1633	...	1701	...	1733	*1800*	1825	1838	1900	1924	2021	2116	2116	...	...	2214	...	2224	...	...	...	2324
Pont-à-Mousson d.	...	1444z	1543	1644	|	...	1719	...	1754	*1818*	1847	1856	1921	1944	2040	2146	2145	...	...	2234	...	2245	...	...	...	2353
Nancy a.	...	1501z	1601	1701	1709	...	1738	...	1810	*1835*	1905	1913	1938	2000	2058	2216	2215	...	...	2251	...	2301	...	...	...	0023

															296											
	Ⓐ	Ⓐ	⚒	Ⓐ	⚒	⚒	⚒	Ⓐr	⚒	⑥⑦	†	Ⓐ	Ⓐ		ⒷM	Ⓐ	Ⓒ		Ⓐ	Ⓒ	Ⓐ			Ⓐ		Ⓐ
Nancy d.	...	...	...	0540	0620	0639	0657	0705	0720	...	0722	0749	...	0819	...	0852	0916	...	0953	1020	...	1122	...	1151	1220	1253
Pont-à-Mousson d.	...	...	...	0602	0638	0701	0715	|	0738	...	0754	0808	...	0836	...	0913	0933	...	1010	1036	...	1139	...	1208	1238	1310
Metz a.	...	...	...	0632	0657	0729	0734	0739	0758	...	0828	0828	...	0855	...	0933	0953	...	1032	1055	...	1158	...	1225	1257	1329
Metz d.	0534	0558	0622	0635	0700	0741	...	0746	0800	0810	...	...	0842	0900	0930	...	...	1019	...	1058	1100	1200	1219	...	1300	...
Hagondange d.	0546	0610	0641	0649	0713	0753	...	0800	0812	0822	...	...	0852	0912	|	...	...	1040	...	1114	1119	1213	1234	...	1314	...
Thionville d.	0557	0619	0653	0702	0724	0803	...	0810	0826	0830	...	...	0902	0923	0951	...	...	1051	...	1124	1129	1224	1247	...	1324	...
Luxembourg a.	0623	0646	0719	0730	0750	0830	...	...	0849	...	...	...	...	0945	1014	...	...	...	...	1150	1156	1247	1315	...	1345	...

				90										96								298				
			Ⓒ	T		Ⓐ	Ⓐ		Ⓐ	Ⓐ		Ⓑ	Ⓐ	R	⚒	†	Ⓐ	Ⓒ	Ⓐ			Ⓑs	Ⓐ	Ⓐ		
Nancy d.	1319	1418	1418	...	1520	...	*1552*	1619	...	*1651*	1720	1752	...	...	1820	1820	*1853*	1920	1920	...	2020	...	2053	2155	...	2251
Pont-à-Mousson d.	1336	1436	1436	...	1537	...	*1610*	1636	...	*1708*	1736	1810	...	...	1838	1837	*1913*	1937	1938	...	2037	...	2124	2212	...	2321
Metz a.	1355	1457	1457	...	1557	...	*1626*	1657	...	*1728*	1757	1829	...	...	1857	1857	*1931*	1957	1957	...	2057	...	2153	2233	...	2350
Metz d.	1400	1500	1500	1556	1600	1619	1639	1700	1718	1740	1800	...	1839	1856	1900	1900	1939	2000	2000	2020	2100	2128	...	...	2321	...
Hagondange d.	1413	1512	1512	|	1613	1634	1652	1715	1732	1751	1813	...	1850	|	1913	1913	1951	2013	2013	2039	2113	|	...	...	2338	...
Thionville d.	1424	1521	1523	1620	1624	1647	1707	1727	1742	1803	1824	...	1905	1917	1925	1925	2003	2024	2029	2049	2126	2150	...	...	2350	...
Luxembourg a.	1445	...	1544	1645	1650	1715	1730	1752	...	1830	1850	...	1930	1936	1949	1951	2032	2045	2050	...	2147	2215	...	...	0017	...

M – JEAN MONNET – (12) Brussels - Basel and v.v. (Table **40**).
R – IRIS – (12) Brussels - Basel - Zürich and v.v. (Table **40**).
S – VAUBAN – (12) Brussels - Basel - Zürich - Chur (Table **40**).
T – VAUBAN – (12) Zürich - Basel - Brussels (Table **40**).

a – Ⓐ only.
r – To / from Remiremont (Table **386**).
s – To / from Strasbourg (Table **383**).
z – ⑤⑥⑦ and holidays.

△ – On ⑤ Metz 2331, Pont-à-Mousson 0003, Nancy 0034.

Timings may vary on July 14, Nov. 11.
Trains may run up to 4 minutes earlier Sept. 2 - Oct. 9.

PARIS - REIMS - CHARLEVILLE MÉZIÈRES - SEDAN — 389

Some trains 2nd class only

km						*TGV* 2709		*TGV* 2713		*TGV* 2723		*TGV* 2733		*TGV* 2777			*TGV* 2743				*TGV* 2747				*TGV* 2753
		Ⓐ	Ⓐ	⑥	Ⓐ	①–⑥ n	⚒				◇‡		◇	B	Ⓐ	⚒			⚒	† ◇	Ⓑ	⑦ d	Ⓐ		⑤⑦ e
0	**Paris Est** d.	...	...	...	...	0757	...	0857	...	1127	...	1257	...	1357	...	...	1557	...	...	...	1727	...	...	...	1827
136	Champagne-Ardenne TGV ▷ d.	...	...	...	...	|	...	|	1001	|	...	|	...	1437	1447	...	|	...	...	...	|	...	...	1853	|
147	**Reims** ▷ a.	...	...	...	...	0842	...	0942	1008	1212	...	1342	...	...	1455	...	1642	...	...	...	1812	...	...	1901	1913
147	**Reims** d.	0631	0705	0706	0738	...	0858	...	1011	...	1228	1345	1407	...	1500	1622	...	1647r	1719	1729	...	1826	1827	1904	1917
186	Rethel d.	0655	0731	0730	0803	...	0923	...	1036	...	1254	|	1430	...	1525	1643	...	1709	1743	1751	...	1850	1854	1927	|
235	**Charleville-Mézières** a.	0726	0758	0758	0832	...	0950	...	1107	...	1320	1432	1458	...	1551	1714	...	1736	1813	1817	...	1915	1922	1954	2003
255	**Sedan** a.	0753	0821	0820	0857v	...	1012	...	1126	...	1341c	...	1519	...	1611	1737	...	1808	1846	1836	...	1937	1946	2015	...

	TGV 2751		*TGV* 2785			*TGV* 2757			*TGV* 2759		*TGV* 2765
	N ⊕		Ⓑ B	Ⓐ	†	⑤⑦ e	⑤⑦ x	⑤⑦ x	N	P	⑤⑦ e
Paris Est d.	1827	...	1927	...	...	2004	...	...	2057	...	2127
Champagne-Ardenne TGV ▷ d.	|	...	2007	2017	2019	|	...	2107	|	...	|
Reims ▷ a.	1913	...	...	2024	2026	2049	...	2115	2142	...	2213
Reims d.	1917	1937	...	2026	...	...	2104	2119	...	2152	2216
Rethel d.	1940	2003	...	2047	...	...	2125	2142	...	2214	2239
Charleville-Mézières a.	2006	2031	...	2113	...	...	2151	2208	...	2241	2306
Sedan a.	2029	2057	...	2132	...	...	2214	...	...	2311	2328

	TGV 2706		*TGV* 2778			*TGV* 2712		*TGV* 2714	
	①–⑤ n	⚒	①–⑥ Bn	Ⓐ	⑥	①–⑥ n	Ⓐ	Ⓐ	Ⓐ
Sedan d.	...	0532	...	0602	0607	...	...	0700	0707
Charleville-Mézières d.	...	0559	...	0628	0631	...	0659	0721	0739
Rethel d.	...	0628	...	0657	0703	...	0729	0750	0813
Reims a.	...	0655	...	0722	0728	...	0754	0811	0838
Reims ▷ d.	0645	0658	...	...	...	0745	0757	0815	...
Champ.-Ardenne TGV ▷ d.	|	0709	0720	...	...	|	0808	|	...
Paris Est a.	0730	...	0800	...	...	0830	...	0900	...

		TGV 2720		*TGV* 2722		*TGV* 2732				*TGV* 2738	*TGV* 2746		*TGV* 2752		*TGV* 2784			*TGV* 2756			*TGV* 2762			*TGV* 2766	
		Ⓒ u	⚒	①–⑥ n			⚒	⑥	Ⓑ ◇	Ⓑ	⑥	Ⓑ ◇	Ⓑ ⊗		B	⚒ z	Ⓑ ◇	⑤⑦ e	Ⓑ ◇				⑦ e	⑦ e	
Sedan d.	0737	0756	0848	...	1116	...	1210	1450	1457	...	...	1545	...	...	...	1630	1704	...	1746	1849	...	2012	2100	...	...
Charleville-Mézières d.	0801	0817	0910	...	1138	...	1230	1510	1517	...	1526	1606	1621	...	...	1706	1723	...	1814	1908	...	2035	2115	2126	...
Rethel d.	0833	0846	0938	...	1205	...	1306	1541	1547	...	|	1636	|	...	...	1736	1758	...	1844	1937	...	2104	...	|	...
Reims a.	0858	0909	0959	...	1228	...	1333	1602	1608	...	1611	1701	1709	...	...	1759	1824	...	1907	2000	...	2125	...	2211	...
Reims ▷ d.	0902	0915	...	1015	...	1245	...	...	...	1615	1615	...	1715	1755	...	1808	...	1845	1924	...	2015	...	...	2215	...
Champagne-Ardenne TGV ▷ d.	0912	|	...	|	...	|	...	...	...	|	|	...	|	1803	1819	1816	...	|	1934	...	|	...	...	|	...
Paris Est a.	...	1000	...	1100	...	1330	...	...	...	1700	1700	...	1800	...	1900	...	...	1930	...	...	2100	...	...	2300	...

B – To / from Bar le Duc (Table **381**).
N – ①②③④⑥ (not June 1, July 14).
P – ①②③④⑥ (not June 1, July 13, 14, Nov. 10, 11).
c – Ⓒ only.
d – Also June 1, July 14, Nov. 11.
e – Also June 1, July 14.

n – Not June 1, July 14.
r – 1650 on ⑥.
u – Starts from Reims on July 12, Oct. 11.
v – To July 3 / from Aug. 31.
x – Also June 1, July 13, 14, Nov. 10, 11.
z – Also Aug. 15.

TGV – Ⓡ, supplement payable, 🍸.
▷ – For full service see Table **391**.
⊕ – On July 11 terminates at Reims.
⊗ – On July 11 starts from Reims.
◇ – Subject to alteration on July 12.
‡ – Runs 40 - 55 mins later on July 20 - 24, Ⓐ Sept. 28 - Oct. 9.

CHARLEVILLE MÉZIÈRES - LONGWY and METZ — 389a

2nd class

km										
		⚒ m	Ⓐ	Ⓐ	⑥	◇	⚒ m	⚒	†	
	Reims 389 d.	...	0631	0705	0706	1407	...	1622	1729	1937
0	**Charleville-Mézières** 389 d.	...	0735	0807	0807	1503	...	1719	1822	2038
20	Sedan 389 a.	...	0753	0821	0820	1519	...	1737	1836	2057
20	Sedan d.	...	0755	0822	0821	1520	...	1738	1837	2058
69	Montmédy d.	...	0826	0854	0853	1553	...	1809	1908	2130
91	Longuyon 393 d.	0633	0847	0908	0906	1613	1810	1822	1922	2149
107	**Longwy** 393 a.	|	0859	|	|	1624	1822	|	|	2201
	Hayange d.	0704	...	0936	0935	...	...	1851	1950	...
170	**Metz** a.	0731	...	0958	0957	...	...	1912	2016	...

	Ⓐ	⚒ m	Ⓒ	⚒	Ⓑ △			⚒ m	
Metz d.	...	...	...	0704	...	...	...	1714	1835
Hayange d.	...	...	...	0731	...	...	...	1739	1859
Longwy 393 d.	0548	0619	0645	|	1013	...	1748	|	|
Longuyon 393 d.	0607	0632	0702	0800	1031	...	1805	1809	1927
Montmédy d.	0621	...	0717	0815	1045	...	1819	...	1941
Sedan a.	0651	...	0748	0847	1114	...	1848	...	2011
Sedan 389 d.	0707	...	0804	0848	1116	...	1849	...	2012
Charleville-Mézières 389 a.	0733	...	0819	0904	1133	...	1903	...	2027
Reims 389 a.	0838	...	...	0959	1228	...	2000	...	2125

m – (2) Longwy - Metz and v.v. (see both directions of table).
△ – Subject to alteration July 12, 27 - 31.
◇ – Subject to alteration on July 12.

390 TGV EST EUROPÉEN

PARIS - STRASBOURG - BASEL

For additional connections Strasbourg - Basel see Table **385**

km		TGV 9201 Ⓐ	TGV 2405 Ⓐ	TGV 9203 ⑥	TGV 9571	⊖		TGV 9211 ①–⑥ n	TGV 9213 ⑦ e	TGV 2419 Ⓑ	TGV 2421 ⑥	EC 91		TGV 9573	Ⓒ	Ⓐ	TGV 9215		TGV 2431 ⑤	TGV 2365 Ⓐ	TGV 2367 Ⓒ		TGV 9575 ⊙	
0	**Paris Est** d.	0624	0654	0654	0724	...	...	0824	0824	1024	1024	...	...	1124		...	1224	...	1324	1424	1424	...	1524	...
405	Saverne a.	|	|	|	|	...	...	|	|	|	1222	...	...	|		...	|	...	|	1624	|	...	|	...
450	**Strasbourg** a.	0843	0913	0913	0941	...	...	1043	1043	1243	1246	...	...	1341	...	...	1443	...	1543	1645	1644	...	1741	...
450	**Strasbourg** 385 d.	0847	...	0917	0945	0953	...	1047	1047	...	...	1253	...	1345	1353	1353	1447	...	...	1649	1648	1653	1745	1753
	Stuttgart Hbf **931** a.	|	...	|	1103	|	...	|	|	...	...	|	...	1503	|	|	|	...	...	|	|	|	1903	|
515	Colmar 385 d.	0914	...	0944	...	1024	...	|	1115	...	...	1330	...	...	1424	1430	|	...	...	1716	1715	1724	...	1824
556	Mulhouse 385 d.	0937	...	1006	...	1049	...	1132	1138	...	...	1355	...	...	1447	1456	1532	...	...	1735	1735	1746	...	1850
590	**Basel** 385 a.	0956	...	1026	...	1111	...	1152	1156	...	...	1420	...	...	1509	1519	1551	...	...	...	...	1810	...	1912
	Zürich HB **510** a.	...	...	...	...	...	...	1300	1300	...	...	1552	...	...	...	...	1700	...	...	...	...	...	...	...

	TGV 2443 N	TGV 2373 ⑤⑦ e	Ⓐ	⑥		TGV 2445 ⑤	TGV 2447 ⑦ e	TGV 9577 Ⓑ	TGV 2449 ⑥		TGV 9217		TGV 2457	Ⓐ	TGV 2375		TGV 2583 Ⓑ ◇	TGV 2467 Ⓑ	295 Ⓑ		TGV 2473 ⑤	TGV 2469* ⑦ e	TGV 2471 ⑦ J	
Paris Est d.	1624	1624	...	...	...	1654	1654	1724	1724	...	1754	...	1824	...	1924	...	1912	2024	...	...	2124	2124	2154	...
Saverne a.	|	|	...	...	...	|	1852	|	|	...	|	...	|	...	|	...	2140	|	...	...	|	|	|	...
Strasbourg a.	1843	1843	...	...	...	1913	1916	1941	1942	...	2011	...	2043	...	2143	...	2204	2243	...	...	2345	2345	0013	...
Strasbourg 385 d.	...	1847	1853	1853	...	...	...	1946	...	1953	2015	...	...	2053	2147	...	...	...	2253	...	...	...	...	...
Stuttgart Hbf **931** a.	...	|	|	|	...	...	...	2105	...	|	|	...	...	|	|	...	...	...	|	...	...	...	...	...
Colmar 385 d.	...	|	1924	1927	...	...	...	...	...	2024	|	...	...	2125	2214	...	...	...	2324	...	...	...	...	...
Mulhouse 385 d.	...	1927	1947	1955	...	...	...	...	...	2047	2057	...	...	2148	2232	...	...	...	2349	...	...	...	...	...
Basel 385 a.	...	...	2009	2017	...	...	...	...	...	2109	2115	...	...	2211	...	...	...	...	0013	...	...	...	...	...
Zürich HB **510** a.	...	...	...	...	...	...	...	...	...	...	2226	...	...	...	...	...	...	...	...	...	...	...	...	...

	TGV 2402 ① P	TGV 2584 ①–⑥ n◇	Ⓐ	TGV 2404 Ⓐ	Ⓐ	TGV 2350 Ⓐ	TGV 2406 ⑥	⚒	TGV 2410 Ⓑ	TGV 2352 ⑥	296 Ⓑ	TGV 9578 ①–⑥ b	TGV 2412 ⑦		TGV 9210 ①–⑥ n	TGV 9212 ⑦ e	TGV 9576 ⊙		TGV 2424 ①–⑥ n	TGV 2426 ⑦ e	TGV 9204 ⊕	⚒	†	TGV 9574 ①–④ n
Zürich HB **510** d.	...	...	...	...	...	...	...	...	...	...	...	...	...	...	0702	0702	...	...	...	...	...	...	...	...
Basel 385 d.	...	...	...	...	0518	...	...	0537	...	...	0647	...	...	...	0802	0802	...	0918	...	...	1102	1218	...	...
Mulhouse 385 d.	...	...	0505	...	0542	0553	...	0558	...	0622	0713	...	...	...	0830	0828	...	0941	...	...	1124	1241	1238	...
Colmar 385 d.	...	...	0528	...	0602	0612	...	0625	...	0643	0733	...	...	...	|	0847	...	1001	...	...	1144	1301	1306	...
Stuttgart Hbf **931** d.	...	...	|	...	|	|	...	|	...	|	|	0655	...	...	|	|	0855	|	...	...	|	|	|	1255
Strasbourg 385 a.	...	...	0603	...	0633	0639	...	0704	...	0709	0803	0813	...	...	0910	0912	1013	1038	...	...	1210	1335	1354	1413
Strasbourg d.	0515	0548	...	0615	...	0645	0645	...	0715	0715	...	0817	0816	...	0915	0915	1017	...	1111	1115	1215	...	...	1417
Saverne d.	|	0612	...	|	...	|	|	...	|	|	...	|	|	...	|	|	|	...	1135	|	|	...	...	|
Paris Est a.	0734	0845	...	0834	...	0904	0904	...	0934	0934	...	1034	1034	...	1134	1134	1234	...	1334	1334	1434	...	...	1634

	TGV 9574 ⑤–⑦ e	TGV 2356 ⑤–⑦ e	TGV 2440	TGV 9216	⚒	TGV 2448 ⑦ e	TGV 2446 ⑤	Ⓐ	TGV 2450 Ⓑ	Ⓐ	TGV 2452 Ⓐ	TGV 9572 ⑥	TGV 9572 ⑦ c	Ⓐ	TGV 2360 Ⓑ	TGV 2460 ⑥	TGV 9570 ①–⑤ b	TGV 9218 ①–⑤ b	TGV 9220 ⑥	TGV 9218 ⑦ c	TGV 2470 ⑤	TGV 2472 ⑦ e		TGV 2474 ⑦ e
Zürich HB **510** d.	...	...	...	1402	...	...	...	...	...	...	...	...	...	...	...	...	...	1802	1802	1802	...	...	...	...
Basel 385 d.	...	...	...	1502	1518	...	...	1548	...	1648	...	...	...	1748	...	...	...	1902	1902	1902	...	...	2018	...
Mulhouse 385 d.	...	1327	...	1529	1541	...	...	1611	...	1711	...	...	...	1811	1823	...	...	1924	1924	1929	...	...	2041	...
Colmar 385 d.	...	|	...	|	1600	...	...	1633	...	1730	...	...	...	1830	1842	...	...	|	1944	|	...	...	2101	...
Stuttgart Hbf **931** d.	1255	|	...	|	|	...	...	|	...	|	...	1655	1655	|	|	...	1855	|	|	|	...	...	|	...
Strasbourg 385 a.	1415	1407	...	1610	1633	...	...	1704	...	1804	...	1813	1815	1904	1909	...	2015	2010	2011	2011	...	...	2134	...
Strasbourg d.	1420	1420	1515	1615	...	1641	1644	...	1715	...	1816	1817	1820	...	1915	1915	2020	2020	2017	2017	2115	2115	...	2215
Saverne d.	|	|	|	|	...	1705	|	...	|	...	|	|	|	...	|	|	|	|	|	|	|	|	...	|
Paris Est a.	1637	1637	1734	1834	...	1904	1904	...	1934	...	2034	2034	2037	...	2134	2134	2237	2237	2234	2234	2334	2334	...	0034

PARIS - METZ - LUXEMBOURG

For additional connections Metz - Luxembourg see Table **388**

km		TGV 2601 ① g	TGV 2803 ①–⑥ n	TGV 2503 ☆	TGV 2809		TGV 2615		TGV 2621	TGV 2827		TGV 2831	TGV 2833 ⑦ e	TGV 2633 Ⓐ	TGV 2835 Ⓐ	TGV 2837 Ⓒ		TGV 2639 Ⓑ	298 Ⓑ	TGV 2643 Ⓐ	TGV 2843 ⑦ e	TGV 2647 ⑤⑦ e		
0	**Paris Est** d.	0639	0709	0812	0839	...	1039	...	1239	1409	...	1609	1739	1739	1839	1839	...	1939	...	2039	2039	2139	...	...
136	Champagne-Ardenne TGV d.	|	|	|	0921	...	|	...	|	|	...	|	|	|	|	|	...	|	...	|	|	|	...	...
236	Meuse TGV a.	|	|	0912	|	...	|	...	|	|	...	|	|	1838	|	1938	...	|	...	|	|	|	...	...
315	**Metz** a.	0802	0832	...	1008	...	1202	...	1403	1533	...	1732	1902	1908	2002	2008	...	2102	...	2202	2202	2302	...	...
315	**Metz** 388 d.	...	0835	...	1012	...	...	1219	...	1537	...	1736	1905	...	2005	2012	...	...	2128	...	2205	...	2321	...
345	Thionville 388 a.	...	0852	...	1028	...	...	1247	...	1554	...	1753	1922	...	2023	2028	...	...	2154	...	2222	...	2350	...
379	**Luxembourg** 388 a.	...	0915	...	1052	...	...	1315	...	1617	...	1815	1945	...	2045	2051	...	...	2215	...	2245	...	0017	...

	TGV 2650 Ⓐ	TGV 2652 Ⓐ	TGV 2857 ⑥	TGV 2855 Ⓐ	TGV 2861 ① g	Ⓐ	TGV 2660 ②–⑤ x	TGV 2863 ⑦ e	TGV 2662 ⑥		TGV 2865 ①–⑥ n	TGV 2664 ⑦ e	TGV 2869		TGV 2672	TGV 2676 Ⓑ	TGV 2881 ①–⑥ n	TGV 2881 ⑦ e	TGV 2545 Ⓑ ☆	TGV 2684 ⑤⑦ e		TGV 2891 ⑤⑦ e	TGV 2889 N	TGV 2893 ⑦ e
Luxembourg 388 d.	...	...	0640	0643	0810	0755	...	0807	...	...	1000	...	1308	1430	...	...	1712	1710	...	...	...	1902	1906	2013
Thionville 388 d.	...	...	0701	0704	0831	0820	...	0828	...	...	1021	...	1329	1453	...	...	1735	1731	...	...	...	1924	1928	2034
Metz 388 a.	...	...	0719	0721	0849	0845	...	0845	...	...	1038	...	1347	1518	...	...	1752	1749	...	...	...	1943	1945	2051
Metz d.	0625	0649	0725	0725	0855	...	0855	0849	0919	...	1042	1042	1353	...	1555	1655	1755	1755	...	1855	...	1948	1948	2055
Meuse TGV d.	|	0719	|	|	|	...	|	0919	0950	...	|	|	|	...	|	|	|	|	1847	|	...	|	|	|
Champagne-Ardenne TGV a.	|	|	|	|	|	...	|	|	|	...	|	|	|	...	|	|	|	|	|	|	...	2035	2035	|
Paris Est a.	0749	0819	0849	0849	1019	...	1019	1019	1049	...	1205	1205	1519	...	1720	1820	1920	1920	1946	2019	...	2119	2119	2219

J – ⑦ to June 28 / from Sept. 6 (also June 1).
N – ①②③④⑥ (not June 1, July 14).
P – ① to June 29 / from Aug. 31 (also June 2; not June 1).

b – Not June 1.
c – Also June 1.
e – Also June 1, July 14.
g – Also June 2, July 15; not June 1, July 13.
n – Not June 1, July 14.
r – Depart 1259 Mar. 15 - Aug. 23.
x – Also July 13; not June 2, July 14, 15.

ICE – 🅁 (Paris - Saarbrücken and v.v.); supplement payable.
TGV – 🅁, supplement payable, 🍸.
⊙ – To / from München (Table 32).
◇ – Via Nancy, calling also at Sarrebourg (Table 383).
⊡ – Calls at Meuse TGV (see Paris - Metz section).
⊕ – On Sept. 14 - 18, 21 - 25 runs up to 7 minutes earlier Basel - Strasbourg.

☆ – To / from Nancy.
⊖ – Runs up to 22 minutes earlier on Ⓐ Sept. 14 - 25.
* – On ⑦ July 5 - Aug. 30 (also July 14) train number is **2473**.

July 10 - 14, 20 - 26

Departures from Paris may be up to 10 minutes earlier.
Arrivals at Paris may be up to 10 minutes later. Other changes are possible.

Aug. 15 - Sept. 11

Strasbourg - Basel timings may vary by ± 3 minutes.

Sept. 2 - Oct. 9

Departures from Luxembourg will be 5 - 8 minutes earlier.
Arrivals at Luxembourg will be 5 - 6 minutes later.

TGV EST EUROPÉEN 390

PARIS - NANCY

Certain trains continue beyond Nancy to Épinal and Remiremont (Table **386**) or to Lunéville and St Dié (Table **387**). Train **2583/4** continues to / from Strasbourg.

km		TGV 2501 ①–⑥ n		TGV 2503 ⊡	TGV 2505 Ⓐ		TGV 2507 Ⓒ	TGV 2571		TGV 2509 Ⓐ	TGV 2591 ⑦ e		TGV 2513 ⑥	TGV 2515 Ⓑ	TGV 2517 Ⓐ		TGV 2573	TGV 2583 Ⓑ		TGV 2519 ①–⑥ n	TGV 2595 ⑦ e		TGV 2521 ⑦ e	
0	**Paris Est** d.	0712	...	0812	0905	...	1042	1212	...	1412	1412	...	1512	1612	1712	...	1812	1912	...	2012	2012	...	2112	...
330	**Nancy** a.	0842	...	0948	1035	...	1212	1342	...	1543	1543	...	1642	1742	1842	...	1942	2042	...	2142	2141	...	2242	...

	TGV 2531 Ⓐ	TGV 2584 ①–⑥ n	TGV 2596 ①–⑥ n	TGV 2533 ⑦ e		TGV 2576 Ⓒ	TGV 2535 Ⓐ		TGV 2537	TGV 2539 ①–④ n		TGV 2541 ⑤–⑦ e	TGV 2543 Ⓑ		TGV 2578 ①–⑥ n	TGV 2545 Ⓑ ⊡		TGV 2547 ⑤⑥	TGV 2580 ⑦ e		TGV 2549 Ⓐ	TGV 2598 ⑦ e	TGV 2551 ⑦ e	
Nancy d.	0615	0715	0815	0815	...	1015	1028	...	1215	1345	...	1515	1615	...	1715	1811	...	1915	1915	...	2015	2015	2115	...
Paris Est a.	0745	0845	0945	0945	...	1145	1200	...	1345	1515	...	1645	1745	...	1845	1946	...	2045	2045	...	2145	2145	2245	...

PARIS - SAARBRÜCKEN

🅁 on cross-border journeys and journeys within France

km	*ICE trains with* ✕	ICE 9551 ①–⑥ b	ICE 9553 ⑦ c	ICE 9553 ①–⑥ b		ICE 9555		ICE 9557 Ⓑ	ICE 9559	
0	**Paris Est** d.	0658	0901	0909	...	1309	...	1709	1905	...
304	Lorraine TGV d.	0815	1017	|	...	|	...	|	|	...
372	Forbach 🚘 d.	0849	1049	|	...	|	...	|	2049	...
383	**Saarbrücken** Hbf a.	0857	1057	1057	...	1457	...	1857	2057	...
	Frankfurt (Main) Hbf **919** a.	1058	1258	1258	...	1658	...	2058	2258	...

ICE trains with ✕	ICE 9558 ①–⑥ b	ICE 9556 ①–⑥ b	ICE 9556 ⑦ c		ICE 9554		ICE 9552 Ⓑ	ICE 9552 ⑥	ICE 9550 Ⓑ
Frankfurt (Main) Hbf **919** d.	0600	0901	0901	...	1301r	...	1658	1658	1901
Saarbrücken Hbf d.	0800	1101	1101	...	1501	...	1901	1901	2101
Forbach 🚘 d.	0810	|	1111	...	|	...	1911	1911	|
Lorraine TGV d.	|	|	|	...	|	...	|	1943	2140
Paris Est a.	0950	1249	1253	...	1650	...	2053	2057	2253

← **FOR NOTES SEE FOOT OF PREVIOUS PAGE**

STRASBOURG - NORTHERN and WESTERN FRANCE 391

	TGV 5420 ①–⑥ n	TGV 5420 ⑦ e	TGV 5486	TGV 5450 ⑦ e	TGV 5450 ①–⑥ n	TGV 5470	TGV 5452 ⑤–⑦ e	TGV 5422 ⊗	TGV 5452 ①–④ n	TGV 5454	TGV 5438 S	TGV 5488	TGV 5426 Ⓑ u
Strasbourg d.	0611	0620	0625	0741	0745	0856	1153	1206v	1420	1636r	1648	1756	1900
Lorraine TGV d.	0725	0732	0740	0852	0858	1008	1307	1326	1539	1748r	1759	1909	2012
Meuse TGV. d.	|	|	|	0911	0923	|	|	|	|	|	1823	|	|
Champagne-Ardenne TGV d.	0812	0812	0828	0944	0949	1049	1347	1407	1624	1832	1858	1948	2057
Marne la Vallée - Chessy a.	|	|	0856	1013	1018	1118	1416	|	1652	1908	|	2020	|
Massy TGV a.	|	|	0930	1058	1058	1157	1458	|	1728	1946	|	2058	|
Paris Charles de Gaulle ✈ a.	0843	0843	|	|	|	|	|	1437	|	|	1933	|	2128
Mantes la Jolie a.	|	|	|	|	|	|	|	|	|	|	2100	|	|
Rouen a.	|	|	|	|	|	|	|	|	|	|	2155c	|	|
Le Havre a.	|	|	|	|	|	|	|	|	|	|	2240c	|	|
TGV Haute Picardie a.	0914	0914	|	|	|	|	|	|	|	|	...	|	|
Arras a.	|	|	|	|	|	|	|	1520	|	|	...	|	|
Douai a.	|	|	|	|	|	|	|	1538	|	|	...	|	|
Lille Europe a.	0946	0946	|	|	|	|	|	1559	|	|	...	|	2223z
Le Mans a.	...	...	1020	|	|	1249	|	...	|	|	...	2151	...
Angers a.	...	...	1059	|	|	|	|	...	|	|	...	2236	...
Nantes a.	...	...	1140	|	|	|	|	...	|	|	...	2314	...
Laval a.	...	...	...	|	|	1333	|	...	|	|	...	...	...
Rennes a.	...	...	...	|	|	1410	|	...	|	|	...	...	...
St Pierre des Corps a.	...	...	...	1153	1153	...	1552	...	1821	2042	...	...	...
Futuroscope a.	...	...	...	1230	1230	...	|	...	|	|	...	...	...
Poitiers a.	...	...	...	1240	1240	...	1633	...	1902	2127	...	...	...
Angoulême a.	...	...	...	1326	1326	...	1719	...	1948	2216	...	...	...
Bordeaux St Jean a.	...	...	...	1428	1428	...	1823	...	2051	2318	...	...	...

	TGV 5400 ①–⑥ n	TGV 5440	TGV 5436 S	TGV 5478	TGV 5402 ⊕	TGV 5442 Ⓒ	TGV 5442 Ⓐ	TGV 5480	TGV 5416	TGV 5460	TGV 5444 ⑦ e	TGV 5446 ①–⑥ n	
Bordeaux St Jean d.	...	0633	...	...	...	1019	1030	...	...	...	1613	1708	...
Angoulême d.	...	0733	...	...	...	1123	1135	...	...	...	1714	1812	...
Poitiers d.	...	0820	...	...	...	1210	1225	...	...	...	1805	1902	...
Futuroscope d.	...	|	...	...	...	|	|	...	...	...	1815	1913	...
St Pierre des Corps d.	...	0902	...	...	...	1251	1307	...	...	...	1854	1949	...
Rennes d.	...	|	...	...	...	|	|	...	...	1710	|	|	...
Laval d.	...	|	...	...	...	|	|	...	...	1746	|	|	...
Nantes d.	...	|	...	0834	...	|	|	1520	...	|	|	|	...
Angers d.	...	|	...	0913	...	|	|	1600	...	|	|	|	...
Le Mans d.	...	|	...	0956	...	|	|	1640	...	1835	|	|	...
Lille Europe d.	0652	|	...	|	1121	|	|	|	1858	|	|	|	...
Douai d.	|	|	...	|	1142	|	|	|	|	|	|	|	...
Arras d.	|	|	...	|	1201	|	|	|	|	|	|	|	...
TGV Haute Picardie d.	|	|	...	|	1223	|	|	|	|	|	|	|	...
Le Havre d.	|	|	0720	|	|	|	|	|	|	|	|	|	...
Rouen d.	|	|	0804	|	|	|	|	|	|	|	|	|	...
Mantes la Jolie d.	|	|	0855	|	|	|	|	|	|	|	|	|	...
Paris Charles de Gaulle ✈ d.	0746	|	1040	|	1254	|	|	|	1953	|	|	|	...
Massy TGV d.	|	0958	|	1050	|	1349	1402	1730	|	1926	1947	2045	...
Marne la Vallée - Chessy d.	|	1039	|	1128	|	1429	1445	1808	|	2009	2029	2125	...
Champagne-Ardenne TGV a.	0816	1107	1113	1157	1324	1458	1513	1838	2023	2036	2057	2152	...
Meuse TGV a.	|	|	1147	|	|	|	|	|	|	|	2127	2219	...
Lorraine TGV a.	0857	1148	1208	1246	1405	1542	1555	1919	2104	2117	2148	2239*	...
Strasbourg a.	1010	1304	1333	1359	1517	1655	1717	2032	2217	2229	2302	2352*	...

S – From July 5.
c – On ⑦ (also July 14) arrive Rouen 2143, Le Havre 2228.
e – Also June 1, July 14.
f – Also June 1, July 13, 14, Nov. 10, 11.
m – Not June 1, July 13, 14, Nov. 10, 11.
n – Not June 1, July 14.
r – 3 minutes earlier on ⑤⑦ and holidays.
u – Depart Strasbourg 1859 on Sept. 4, 11, 18.
v – 1210 on Ⓒ.
z – 2227 on ⑦ (also June 1, July 14).
TGV – 🅁, supplement payable, 🍷.
⊕ – On Sept. 20 depart Lille 1138, not calling at Douai or Arras.
⊗ – On Sept. 20 arrive Lille 1530, not calling at Arras or Douai.
* – 4 - 5 minutes later on ⑤.

CONNECTING SERVICE

REIMS - CHAMPAGNE ARNENNE TGV :

Journey 8 - 10 minutes

From Reims :

0658 ⚒, 0741 Ⓒ, 0749 Ⓐ, 0757 Ⓐ, 0800 Ⓒ, 0902, 1023 Ⓐ, 1024 ⑥⑦ **e**, 1050, 1150, 1307, 1322 ⑤–⑦ **f**, 1342 Ⓐ, 1343 ⑥⑦ **e**, 1443 Ⓒ, 1458 Ⓐ, 1600 ①–④ **m**, 1755, 1808 Ⓑ, 1812 ⑥, 1820 ①–⑥ **n**, 1924, 2006, 2032 Ⓑ, 2045 ⑦ **e**, 2135 ⚒.

From Champagne-Ardenne TGV :

0818 ①–⑥ **n**, 0824 ⑦ **e**, 0838, 1001, 1101, 1117, 1210, 1339, 1359 ⑤–⑦ **f**, 1419, 1447, 1525, 1628 ①–④ **m**, 1848, 1853, 1959, 2017 Ⓑ, 2046 Ⓒ, 2050 Ⓐ, 2106, 2112 ⑦ **e**, 2202 ⚒.

CONNECTING 🚌 SERVICES

Bus services connect with the trains in Table **391** on the following routes :

Nancy - Lorraine TGV (journey 35 minutes)

Metz - Lorraine TGV (journey 25 minutes)

Verdun - Meuse TGV (journey 25 minutes)

For further details ✆ 03 87 78 67 09.

2nd class — CHÂLONS EN CHAMPAGNE - VERDUN 392

km		Ⓐd	Ⓒ	Ⓐb	Ⓐ	⑥t	H	⑦e	⑤f	
0	**Châlons en Champagne** d.	0820	1022	1222	1828	2027	2040	2040	2055	...
62	Ste Menehould d.	0906	1109	1311	1928	2114	2129	2127	2142	...
107	**Verdun** a.	0945	1148	1350	2008	2153	2210	2206	2222	...

	①g	⚒	⑦e		Ⓐu	Ⓐd			
Verdun d.	0503	0610	0641	...	1040	1539	...	1845	...
Ste Menehould d.	0542	0648	0720	...	1119	1618	...	1923	...
Châlons en Champagne a.	0631	0736	0807	...	1207	1706	...	2009	...

H – ①–④ (not June 1, July 13, 14, Nov. 10, 11).
b – Subject to alteration July 20 - Aug. 28, Sept. 14 - Oct. 9.
d – Subject to alteration Sept. 14 - 25.
e – Also June 1, July 14, Nov. 11.
f – Also Nov. 10. To Metz, arrive 2340.
g – Also June 2, July 15, Nov. 12; not June 1.
t – Not Aug. 15.
u – Subject to alteration July 20 - Aug. 28, Sept. 14 - Oct. 16.

392a VERDUN - METZ

km		Ⓐ	⚒		🚌 Ⓐ	Ⓒ	Ⓐr	Ⓐ	🚌 Ⓐ	Ⓐ	⑥	†	⑤f
0	**Verdun** d.	0633	...	1050	1205	...	1238	...	1700	1814	...	1927	2225
40	Conflans-Jarny d.	0718	0735	1130	1256	1318	1318	1642	1752	1854	1854	2006	2307
66	Hagondange 388 d.	|	0813	1203	|	1357	1356	1714	|	1925	1925	|	|
84	**Metz** 388 a.	0752	0829	1217	1335	1411	*1416*	1727	1840	1938	1938	2039	2340

	🚌 Ⓐ⊖	⚒	⚒r	†	🚌 Ⓐ	Ⓐ	†s	Ⓐ	⑥t	🚌 Ⓐ
Metz 388 d.	0715	0727	1230	1230	1420	1628	1656	1821	1828	1854
Hagondange 388 d.	|	0740	1246	1245	|	|	1714	|	1845	|
Conflans-Jarny d.	0759	0810	1325	1324	1504	1709	1757	1855	1929	1938
Verdun a.	0845	...	1400	...	1550	1744	1832	1929	2003	2024

f – ⑤ to Oct. 23 (also July 13, Nov. 10).
r – Subject to alteration on Ⓐ Oct. 12 - 23.
s – Depart Metz 1704 from Nov. 8.
t – Not Aug. 15.
⊖ – On ① (also June 2; not June 1) runs 55 mins earlier.

393 LONGWY - NANCY / LUXEMBOURG

Most trains 2nd class only

km		Ⓐ	⚒	Ⓐ	⑥t	Ⓐ	†	⑥t	†	Ⓐ	†
0	**Longwy** 389a d.	0539	0640	0839	1051	1218	1241	1658	1743	1826	1940
16	Longuyon 389a d.	0553	0654	0852	1104	1232	1255	1712	1757	1839	1953
57	Conflans-Jarny d.	0623	0724	0921	1135	1302	1324	1741	1827	1908	2023
100	Pont-à-Mousson d.	0653	0753	0949	1203	1331	1352	1809	1855	1937	2051
128	**Nancy** a.	0710	0812	1007	1221	1348	1409	1826	1912	1954	2109

	Ⓐ	Ⓐ	⑥t	†	⑥t	Ⓐ	†	Ⓐz	Ⓐ	⑥t	†	†
Nancy d.	0605	0848	0906	1006	1254	1402	1707	1735	1836	1856	1937	2246
Pont-à-Mousson d.	0625	0907	0923	1023	1311	1424	1724	1752	1854	1914	1955	2304
Conflans-Jarny d.	0655	0937	0952	1052	1340	1457	1754	1826	1924	1944	2025	2333
Longuyon 389a d.	0723	1007	1021	1120	1410	1525	1824	1856	1952	2014	2054	0003
Longwy 389a a.	0736	1020	1032	1132	1422	1537	1836	1908	2005	2027	2106	0016

km	★	Ⓐb	⚒	Ⓐ	⚒	Ⓐ	Ⓐ	⚒	Ⓐ	
0	**Longwy** d.	0622	0642	0725	0739	*0819*	1325	1843	1910	...
8	Rodange 🛃 d.	0630	0650	0737	0747	0824	1333	1904	1918	...
27	**Luxembourg** a.	0700	0720	0802	0816	0849	1359	1934	2010	...

★	⑥t	Ⓐh	Ⓐ	Ⓐ	Ⓐn	Ⓐ	Ⓐ	Ⓐ	⚒	Ⓐn	Ⓐ
Luxembourg d.	0550	*0733*	1201	1601	1626	1701	1726	1743	1801	1826	1901
Rodange 🛃 d.	0617	0831	1228	1628	1657	1729	1757	1810	1828	1857	1928
Longwy a.	0624	0838	1235	1635	1704	1736	1804	1817	1837	1904	1935

b – Change at Pétange.
h – To Nancy (upper table).
n – To Longuyon (arrive 16 minutes later).
t – Not Aug. 15.
z – Runs 12 - 13 mins later June 15 - Sept. 21.
★ – Also runs July 14, Nov. 11; no service June 23.

LONGWY - METZ Rail service: from Longwy 0619 ⚒, from Metz 1714 ⚒, journey 72 mins.
🚌 service (journey 55 mins):
From Longwy: 0505 Ⓐ, 0735, 0930 ⚒, 1240 ⚒, 1645 Ⓐ, 1845 †, 1920 ⑥, 1930 Ⓐ.
From Metz: 0620 Ⓐ, 0842 ⚒, 0850 †, 1220 ⚒, 1615 Ⓐ, 1805 ⚒, 2020 Ⓒ, 2115 Ⓐ.

394 METZ - FORBACH - SAARBRÜCKEN

Many trains 2nd class only

km		Ⓐ	Ⓐ	⑥t	⚒	⚒	†	Ⓐ◇	⑥t	†	⚒	⚒	▽	⊙	Ⓐ	Ⓐ		Ⓐ	Ⓐ	†	⑥t	Ⓐ		①–④m	⑤	†
0	**Metz** d.	0554	0642	0643	0741	0842	0842	0933	1042	1044	1216	1242	1345	1549	1642	1716	1747	1816	1834	1842	1919	1924	2019	2216	2339	2339
50	St Avold d.	0635	0718	0721	0812	0915	0914	1005	1113	1122	1252	1313	1417	1620	1713	1752	1818	1857	1912	1926	2006	2003	2050	2247	0010	0012
70	Forbach a.	0650	0734	0738	0826	0929	0927	1020	1127	1139	1308	1326	1432	1635	1726	1808	1832	1913	1924	1941	2022	2019	2104	2300	0024	0026
70	Forbach d.	0655	*0743*	0744	*0844*	0937	*0937*	1025	*1140*	1144	*1321*v	*1340*a	1437	1645	*1740*	...	*1844*	1918	*1938*	*1953*	2031	2024	*2117*r	*2314*	*0029*	0031
81	**Saarbrücken** a.	0705	*0752*	0752	*0853*	0945	*0945*	1033	*1149*	1152	*1330*v	*1349*a	1445	1654	*1749*	...	*1853*	1927	*1947*	*2002*	2040	2034	*2126*r	*2323*	*0038*	0039

	⚒△	⚒	⚒	Ⓐ	Ⓐ	Ⓒ	Ⓐ	†	⚒	Ⓐ	⑥t	⚒			Ⓐ	Ⓒ	Ⓐ	†	Ⓐ	⑥t	⚒	Ⓑh	⑦d	⚒▽	Ⓐ
Saarbrücken d.	0503	*0553*a	*0631*	0651	*0731*	0731	*0831*	*0917*	*0925*	*1131*	1153	...	1233	*1431*	*1631*	1631	...	...	1731	1753	...	*1831*	*1911*	1931	2240
Forbach a.	0512	*0602*a	*0640*	0700	*0740*	0740	*0840*	*0926*	*0934*	*1140*	1202	...	1242	*1440*	*1640*	1642	...	...	1739	1802	...	*1840*	*1920*	1940	2249
Forbach d.	0517	0607	0645	0707	0750	0745	0845	0931	0939	1145	...	1207	1244	1445	1645	1645	1707	1707	1744	...	1807	1847	1925	1945	...
St Avold d.	0533	0623	0659	0723	0805	0800	0900	0947	0952	1200	...	1223	1301	1459	1701	1700	1725	1724	1801	...	1823	1902	1940	1958	...
Metz a.	0610	0705	0734	0801	0837	0830	0932	1023	1023	1233	...	1301	1339	1530	1734	1731	1804	1810	1838	...	1858	1936	2014	2032	...

a – Ⓐ only.
d – Also July 14, Nov. 11.
h – Also Aug. 15.
m – Not holidays.
r – ⚒ only.
s – Subject to alteration Sept. 14 - 18.
t – Not Aug. 15.
v – Not ⑤.
◇ – Change at Forbach on ①.
△ – Change at Forbach on Ⓐ.
▽ – Change at Forbach on ⑤.
⊙ – Change at Forbach on ⑤–⑦.

METZ - SARREGUEMINES Journey 62 - 73 minutes:
From Metz: 1212 ⚒**s**, 1707 Ⓐ, 1820 ⑥**t**, 1919 Ⓑ**h**.
From Sarreguemines: 0621 ⚒, 0727 Ⓐ, 1210 ⚒**s**, 1714 †.

395 STRASBOURG - SAARBRÜCKEN

Some trains 2nd class only

km		Ⓐ	Ⓐ		⑥t	Ⓐ	†		⊕	Ⓐ⊕	⑥t		†	Ⓐ⊕	Ⓐ	⑥t	Ⓐ	⚒	Ⓐ	†	⑥t	Ⓐ	†	
0	**Strasbourg** d.	0554	0637	...	0752	0757	0845	...	1100	1222	1300	...	1430	1431	1530	1600	1626	1729	1830	1910	1930	1951	2010	...
71	Diemeringen d.	0646	0733	...	0848	0850	0943	...	1154	1323	1354	...	1522	1521	1622	1656	1729	1832	1929	2004	2023	2045	2112	...
97	Sarreguemines a.	0711	0752	...	0911	0911	1006	...	1217	1349	1418	...	1544	1544	1644	1720	1753	1856	1953	2023	2044	2105	2136	...
97	Sarreguemines 🛃 ▲ d.	0712	...	...	0912	0912	1023	...	1223	1355	1424	...	1555	...	1655	...	...	...	...	2026	2055	2126	...	...
115	**Saarbrücken** Hbf ▲ a.	0727	...	...	0927	0927	1042	...	1244	1415	1441	...	1615	...	1715	...	...	...	...	2043	2115	2143	...	...

	Ⓐ	Ⓐ	⚒	⚒		Ⓒ	Ⓐ⊕	⑥t	⚒⊕	†	Ⓐ⊕	⑤	①–④m	†	Ⓒ	Ⓐ	†	Ⓐ
Saarbrücken Hbf ▲ d.	0443	...	...	...	0745	1024	1124	1124	...	1224	1324	1511	1524	...	1714	...	...	1814
Sarreguemines 🛃 ▲ a.	0459	...	...	...	0802	1044	1144	1144	...	1244	1344	1529	1544	...	1732	...	...	1832
Sarreguemines d.	0501	0535	0605	0701	0805	1045	1145	1145	1245	1245	1345	1536	1553	1641	1742	1743	1824	1835
Diemeringen d.	0519	0554	0629	0730	0829	1106	1205	1207	1308	1308	1406	1557	1615	1704	1806	1807	1850	1858
Strasbourg a.	0625	0700	0735	0831	0927	1200	1304	1300	1404	1404	1505	1654	1711	1800	1900	1901	1952	2002

m – Not holidays.
t – Not Aug. 15.
⊕ – By 🚌 on Ⓐ Sept. 21 - Oct. 2 in revised timings.

▲ – Additional light rail service operates **Sarreguemines Bahnhof - Saarbrücken Hbf** (line **S1** continuing to / starting from Ludwigstrasse and Riegelsberg Süd). Journey time: 30 minutes.
From Sarreguemines: ⚒ hourly 0516 - 0016, † hourly 0716 - 0016. Runs every 30 minutes 0516 - 0916 and 1216 - 2116 on Ⓐ, 0816 - 1816 on ⑥, 1216 - 1816 on †.
From Saarbrücken: ⚒ hourly 0440 - 2340, † hourly 0740 - 2340. Runs every 30 minutes 0440 - 0840 and 1140 - 2040 on Ⓐ, 0740 - 1740 on ⑥, 1140 - 1740 on †.

396 STRASBOURG - WISSEMBOURG

66 km. Some 2nd class only

	Ⓐ	Ⓐ	Ⓒ		⑥t	Ⓐ		Ⓒ	Ⓐ		Ⓐ		
Strasbourg d.	0728	0809	0910	1055	1210	1224	1353	1555	1640	1719	1750	1825	1926
Haguenau d.	0803	0843	0942	1126	1242	1251	1429	1649	1706	1743	1822	1857	1953
Wissembourg a.	0831	0917	1017	1157	1318	1325	1457	1724	1738	1824	1849	1939	2026

	⑥t	Ⓐ	Ⓐ	Ⓒ	Ⓐ	⑥t				⚒	†
Wissembourg d.	0830	0846	0930	1036	1217	1238	1336	1541	1745	1859	2036
Haguenau d.	0901	0917	1003	1110	1303	1318	1402	1609	1822	1940	2103
Strasbourg a.	0935	0950	1035	1142	1330	1350	1425	1634	1855	2017	2137

Additional trains from Strasbourg: 0615 ⑥**t**, 0618 Ⓐ; from Wissembourg 0608 Ⓐ, 0640 ⚒, 0727 Ⓐ, 0744 ⑥. Strasbourg - Haguenau: 1 - 2 trains per hour. **t** – Not Aug. 15.

397 PRIVATE TOURIST RAILWAYS

CHEMIN DE FER DE LA MURE. Scenic electric railway

St Georges de Commiers - La Mure, *30 km*. **Days of running**: daily Apr. 1 - Oct. 31, 2009.

	D	B	C	B
St Georges de C. d.	0945	1200	1430	1700
La Mure a.	1135	1345	1620	1835

	B	B	D	C
La Mure d.	0945	1200	1430	1700
St Georges de C. a.	1115	1330	1605	1835

B – July 1 - Aug. 31. C – May 1 - Sept. 30. D – Apr. 1 - Oct. 31.
For SNCF connections see Table **362**. ✆ 04 76 735 734 www.trainlamure.com

VIVARAIS RAILWAY. Scenic steam (🚂) and diesel line

Days of running: Service suspended - no trains ran in 2008 and the line is unlikely to reopen in 2009.

Operator: Chemin de Fer du Vivarais, La Gare, 07300 Tournon sur Rhône, ✆ 04 75 08 20 30. Tournon station is a 20 - 30 minute walk from Tain-Hermitage-Tournon station (Table **351**).

TRAMWAY DU MONT BLANC *Tramway du Mont Blanc* ✆ 04.50.47.51.83, fax 04.50.78.32.75. The highest rack railway in France. www.compagniedumontblanc.fr

Summer Season June 13 - Sept. 20, 2009: runs from St Gervais Le Fayet (opposite SNCF station) to Nid d'Aigle (altitude 2380 metres), journey 70 - 75 minutes.
June 13 - July 7 and **Aug. 27 - Sept. 20**: from St Gervais Le Fayet 0745, 0910, 1015, 1140, 1340, 1440, returning from Nid d'Aigle at 0900, 1025, 1150, 1325, 1535, 1635.
July 8 - Aug. 26: from St Gervais Le Fayet 0715, 0910, 1015, 1045, 1140, 1310, 1340, 1410, 1540, 1640, 1710, returning at 0900, 1025, 1150, 1225, 1250, 1430, 1525, 1550, 1650, 1750, 1840.

Winter Season Dec. 20, 2008 - Apr. 26, 2009: runs from St Gervais Le Fayet (opposite SNCF station) to Bellevue (altitude 1800 metres), journey 60 minutes.
Depart St Gervais 0900, 1000 Ⓒ, 1100, 1300, 1430, returning from Bellevue 1000, 1100 Ⓒ, 1200, 1430, 1630.

CHAMONIX - MONTENVERS *Train du Montenvers* ✆ 04.50.53.12.54, fax 04.50.53.83.93. www.compagniedumontblanc.fr Journey 20 mins each way. Closed Oct. 12 - 23, 2009.
From Chamonix (200 metres from SNCF station) to Montenvers 'Mer de Glace' (altitude 1913 metres). A cable car (open until Oct. 4) takes visitors to the ice grotto inside the glacier.
June 1 - July 3 and **Aug. 24 - Oct. 11**: from Chamonix 0830 and every 30 minutes 0930 - 1700; returning from Montenvers every 30 minutes 0900 - 1730.
July 4 - Aug. 23: from Chamonix every 30 minutes 0800 - 1000, every 20 minutes 1000 - 1800. Return from Montenvers every 30 minutes 0800 - 1000, every 20 minutes 1000 - 1830.
Oct. 24 - Nov. 8: from Chamonix hourly 1000 - 1600, returning 1030 - 1630. **Nov. 9 - Dec. 18**: from Chamonix 1000, 1200, 1400, 1500, 1600, returning at 1130, 1330, 1430, 1530, 1630.

See page 32 for plan of central Paris

PARIS - PARIS AÉROPORTS ✈ 398

CHARLES DE GAULLE ✈ - PARIS

VAL shuttle train: air terminals - RER/TGV station.

Roissyrail (RER line B): Aéroport Charles de Gaulle 2 TGV - Paris Châtelet les Halles. Frequent service 0450-2400.

Journey time from Charles de Gaulle ✈:

Gare du Nord	35 minutes
Châtelet les Halles ★	38 minutes
St Michel Notre Dame	40 minutes
Antony (for Orly ✈, see middle panel)	58 minutes

★ Cross-platform interchange with *RER* for Gare de Lyon.

ORLY ✈ - PARIS (*VAL + RER B*)

VAL light rail: Orly Sud - Orly Ouest - Antony (7 minutes). Frequent service ① - ⑤: 0600 - 2230; ⑦: 0700 - 2300. Cross platform interchange with RER line B (below).

RER line B: Antony - Paris. Frequent service 0510-0010.

Journey time from Antony:

St Michel Notre Dame	20 minutes
Châtelet les Halles ☆	25 minutes
Gare du Nord	29 minutes

☆ Interchange with *RER* for Gare de Lyon.

ORLY ✈ - PARIS (*Orlyrail*)

🚌: Orly ✈ (Ouest and Sud) - Pont de Rungis Aéroport d'Orly station. Frequent shuttle service.

RER line C: Pont de Rungis Aéroport d'Orly - Paris. Every 15 minutes approx. 0500 - 2330 (0530 - 2400 from Paris).

Journey time from Pont de Rungis Aéroport d'Orly:

Paris Austerlitz	24 minutes
St Michel Notre Dame	27 minutes
Musée d'Orsay	31 minutes
Champ de Mars Tour Eiffel	39 minutes

SAVOIE SKI BUSES 399

SEE WINTER EDITIONS

AMIENS - ROUEN 268

Temporarily relocated from page 179

km		① g	Ⓐ	Ⓐ	⑥ t	†		Ⓐ △	Ⓐ 🚌	⑥ t	†		⑤	①–④ m		Ⓐ	†	⑥ t		Ⓐ	Ⓐ		Ⓒ	
	Lille Flandres **256** d.	...	...	0620	0805	...	...	...	...	...	...	...	...	...	...	...	...	...	...	1705	...	...	1805	...
0	**Amiens** d.	0542	...	0751	0933	0950	...	1215	...	1234	1450	...	1608	1613	...	1716	1722	1731	...	1828	1848	...	1940	...
31	Poix de Picardie d.	0601	...	0811	0951	1010	...	1234	...	1257	1509	...	1631	1636	...	1739	1745	1753	...	1845	1913	...	1958	...
52	Abancourt d.	0619	0722	0825	1004	1025	...	1247	...	1312	1522	...	1649	1648	...	1751	1800	1807	...	1857	1935	...	2010	...
73	Serqueux d.	0639	0738	0837	1018	1040	...	1300	1322	1327	1539	...	1705	1703	...	1807	1816	1827	...	1910	1949	...	2023	...
121	**Rouen Rive-Droite** a.	0722	0826	0909	1050	1115	...	...	1412	1408	1625	...	1740	...	...	1841	1850	1907	...	1941	...	...	2056	...

	Ⓐ	Ⓐ		⑥ t		†		Ⓐ 🚌	Ⓐ		Ⓐ 🚌	Ⓐ	⑥ t		①–④ 🚌 §	①–④ m	⑤			Ⓐ		⑤	†	
Rouen Rive-Droite d.	...	0704	...	0814	...	0916	...	1012	...	...	1135	...	1230	...	1535	...	1635	...	1814	1835	...	1917	1927	...
Serqueux d.	0622	0735	...	0848	...	0948	...	1102	1112	...	1300	1310	1310	...	1640	1715	1707	...	1846	1916	...	1949	2001	...
Abancourt d.	0637	0747	...	0903	...	1004	...	...	1126	...	...	1324	1324	...	...	1731	1722	...	1859	1929	...	2004	2016	...
Poix de Picardie d.	0655	0759	...	0915	...	1016	...	...	1139	...	...	1339	1339	...	...	1743	1734	...	1912	...	...	2016	2028	...
Amiens a.	0719	0816	...	0933	...	1033	...	...	1157	...	...	1401	1401	...	...	1801	1750	...	1929	...	...	2032	2048	...
Lille Flandres **256** a.	...	0937	...	1052	...	...	...	...	1327*	...	...	...	...	...	...	...	...	...	2058	...	...	...	...	...

g – Also June 2, July 15, Nov. 12; not June 1.
m – Not June 1, July 14, Nov. 11.
t – Not Aug. 15.
△ – May be affected by engineering work.
§ – Not June 1, July 14, Nov. 11. Runs 25 minutes later to July 2.

RENNES - REDON - NANTES 287

Temporarily relocated from page 188

km		⑥ t	⚒	Ⓐ J	Ⓐ K	Ⓒ	3832	Ⓐ	Ⓒ J	Ⓐ	8715 ☆		⑥	①–④ Kc	⑤ K	⑤	Ⓒ	⑤	⑤	Ⓐ	⑤	①–④ Jn	①–④ Kc	⑤ J	⑤ J	⑤ K
0	**Rennes** § d.	0625	...	0710	0740	0830	...	0847	1130	1223	1211	...	1245	1426	1426	...	*1430*	1537	1610	...	1647	*1644*	1644	...	1658	1705
72	Redon § a.	0711	...	|	|	0908	...	|	1228	|	1247	...	|	1501	1503	...	*1515*	|	1647	...	|	*1736*	1740	...	1753	1804
72	Redon ◇ d.	...	0750	|	|	...	0928	|	...	|	...	1303	|	1506	...	1507	1526	|	...	1658	|	1741	...	1745	...	...
106	Savenay ◇ d.	...	0817	|	|	...	|	|	...	|	...	1327	|	|	...	1530	1549	|	...	1722	|	1813	...	1816	...	...
145	**Nantes** ◇ a.	...	0840	0826	0854	...	1012	1002	...	1337	...	1350	1359	1550	...	1550	1610	1652	...	1745	1808	1835	...	1840	...	...

	†	Ⓐ	Ⓐ	† K	⑤ K	Ⓐ J	⑦ J	①–④ Kc	† J	⑥ t	† K	①–④ m	⑤	† J	† K	①–④ m	⑤⑥	⑤	①–④ m	①–④ Jn	①–④ Jn	⑤	⑥ t	† J	⑤ J
Rennes § d.	1729	1736	...	1735	1749	1750	...	1755	1803	1815	1824	1831	1835	1858	1900	1920	1921	...	1925	...	2020	2020	2034	2047	...
Redon § a.	|	|	...	1826	1848	1846	...	1856	1857	1855	1904	1916	1917	1939	1939	|	2019	...	2024	...	2107	2106	2111	2125	...
Redon ◇ d.	|	|	1832	...	...	...	1851	...	...	1901	...	1921	1922	1951	1947	|	...	2026	...	2026	...	...	...	2130	2144
Savenay ◇ d.	|	|	1904	...	...	...	1919	...	...	1928	...	1950	1949	2019	2016	|	...	2054	...	2052	...	...	...	2155	2211
Nantes ◇ a.	1848	1852	1932	...	...	...	1941	...	...	1950	...	2012	2012	2039	2036	2034	...	2116	...	2115	...	...	...	2216	2233

	Ⓐ J	Ⓒ J	† K	Ⓐ J	Ⓐ a	Ⓐ J⊕	⚒ K	†	⑥ J	⚒ K	Ⓑ	⑥ t	⑥ J	8730 R☆	Ⓐ	⑥ t	† J	Ⓐ		Ⓐ	⑥ u	†	⑥ u	⑤	①–④ m
Nantes ◇ d.	0612	...	...	0651	0725	0920	0920	1003	1008	1140	...	...	1227	...	1231	1312	...	1441	1450	...	1500	...	...	1520	1602
Savenay ◇ d.	0636	...	...	0715	|	0941	0941	1026	1030	1202	...	...	1249	...	|	1336	...	|	|	...	|	...	...	|	|
Redon ◇ a.	0701	..	...	0744	|	1010	1008	1053	1056	1227	...	...	1314	...	|	1403	...	|	1532	...	|	...	...	|	|
Redon § d.	*0716*	0736	0736	0754	|	1015	*1022*	1102	1102	...	1236	1241	...	1321	|	...	1408	|	...	1538	|	1540	1548	|	|
Rennes § a.	*0755*	0814	0814	0834	0843	1052	*1101*	1151	1151	...	1340	1340	...	1357	1347	...	1455	1555	...	1616	1616	1617	1626	1635	1718

	† J	①–④ Jn	①–④ Kc	⑤	Ⓒ t	Ⓒ K	† J	⑦ e	⑦ J	⑤	①–④ Kc	Ⓐ	⑥ t⊖	①–④ m	3854	⑥ t	⑤	⑥ Kt	①–④ m	⑤⑦ e	⑥ J	⑤	⑤⑦ b	①–④ m	⑥ t
Nantes ◇ d.	...	1622	1622	1622	1622	...	...	1723	...	1725	1728	1758	1802	...	1818	...	...	...	1903	1918	...	2022	2116	2126	2126
Savenay ◇ d.	...	1644	1643	1645	1643	...	...	1748	...	1748	1750	|	|	...	1841	...	...	...	|	|	...	2045	2141	2147	2147
Redon ◇ a.	...	1712	1710	1716	1712	...	...	1813	...	1817	1818	|	|	...	1908	...	...	...	|	|	...	2114	2207	2212	2212
Redon § d.	1646	*1719*	*1729*	*1737*	...	1729	1736	...	1818	...	...	|	|	1846	...	1919	1936	1936	|	|	2025	2119	2228	2227	2227
Rennes § a.	1742	*1807*	*1822*	*1811*	...	1823	1811	...	1855	...	...	1912	1916	1920	...	1955	2015	2015	2024	2035	2105	2155	2307	2305	2305

J – To July 4/from Aug. 31.
K – July 5 - Aug. 30.
R – ①–⑥. Train **8732** on Ⓐ July 6 - Aug. 28.
a – From Angers (depart 0620).
b – Also June 1, July 14, Nov. 11. From Bordeaux (train **3856**).
c – Not July 14.
e – Also June 1, July 14, Nov. 11.
m – Not June 1, July 14, Nov. 11.
n – Not June 1, Nov. 11.
t – Not Aug. 15.
u – Not June 13, Aug. 15.
§ – For other trains Rennes - Redon see Table **285**.
◇ – For other trains Redon - Nantes see Table **285**, for Savenay - Nantes see Tables **285** and **288**.
☆ – *TGV* train, [R]. Supplement payable.
⊕ – Not Sept. 28 - Oct. 2.
⊖ – From Tours (Table **289**).

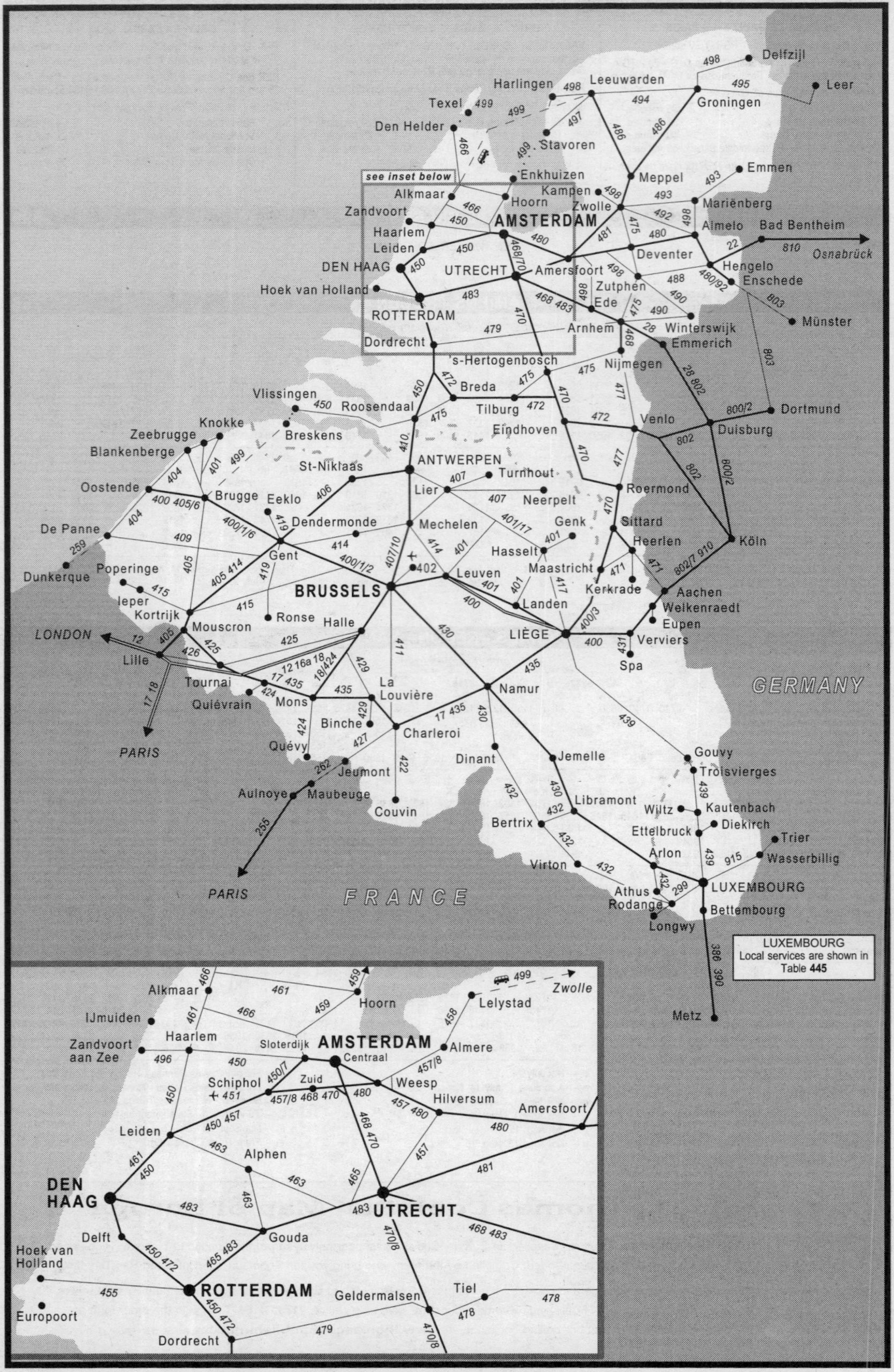
Delfzijl
Leer
Harlingen
Leeuwarden
Groningen
Texel
Den Helder
Stavoren
Enkhuizen
see inset below
Alkmaar
Hoorn
Kampen
Zwolle
Meppel
Emmen
Mariënberg
Zandvoort
AMSTERDAM
Almelo
Bad Bentheim
Osnabrück
Haarlem
Leiden
Deventer
Hengelo
Enschede
DEN HAAG
UTRECHT
Amersfoort
Zutphen
Hoek van Holland
Ede
Münster
ROTTERDAM
Arnhem
Winterswijk
Emmerich
Dordrecht
's-Hertogenbosch
Nijmegen
Breda
Vlissingen
Roosendaal
Tilburg
Dortmund
Venlo
Duisburg
Knokke
Eindhoven
Zeebrugge
Breskens
Blankenberge
ANTWERPEN
St-Niklaas
Turnhout
Lier
Oostende
Brugge
Eeklo
Neerpelt
Roermond
Dendermonde
Genk
Sittard
De Panne
Mechelen
Heerlen
Köln
Gent
Hasselt
Dunkerque
Poperinge
Maastricht
402
Leuven
BRUSSELS
Kerkrade
Aachen
Ieper
Landen
Welkenraedt
Kortrijk
Ronse
Eupen
LONDON
Mouscron
Halle
LIÈGE
Verviers
Lille
Spa
Tournai
La Louvière
Namur
GERMANY
Quiévrain
Mons
Binche
Charleroi
PARIS
Quévy
Dinant
Jemelle
Gouvy
Jeumont
Troisvierges
Aulnoye
Maubeuge
Couvin
Libramont
Wiltz
Kautenbach
Bertrix
Diekirch
Ettelbruck
Trier
Arlon
Wasserbilling
Virton
PARIS
FRANCE
Athus
LUXEMBOURG
Rodange
Bettembourg
Longwy
LUXEMBOURG
Local services are shown in Table 445
Metz
Zwolle
Alkmaar
Hoorn
Lelystad
IJmuiden
Haarlem
Almere
Zandvoort aan Zee
Sloterdijk
AMSTERDAM
Centraal
Schiphol
Zuid
Weesp
Hilversum
Amersfoort
Leiden
Alphen
DEN HAAG
UTRECHT
Delft
Gouda
Hoek van Holland
ROTTERDAM
Geldermalsen
Tiel
Europoort
Dordrecht

BELGIUM and LUXEMBOURG

Operator: Nationale Maatschappij der Belgische Spoorwegen/Société Nationale des Chemins de fer Belges (NMBS/SNCB), Société Nationale des Chemins de fer Luxembourgeois (CFL).

Services: All trains convey first and second classes of seating accommodation unless otherwise indicated. Trains for two or more different destinations are often linked together for part of their journeys, and passengers should be careful to join the correct portion of the train upon boarding.

Timings: Valid from **December 14, 2008** unless otherwise stated in the table, but minor alterations are expected from June 14. Local train services may be amended on and around the dates of public holidays (see page **2**), and passengers are advised to confirm their train times locally if planning to travel during these periods.

Reservations: Seat reservations are not available for journeys wholly within Belgium or Luxembourg. Reservations for some journeys *between* Belgium and Luxembourg can, however, be made at principal stations and appointed travel agents. *ICE* services to and from Germany require compulsory reservation.

Supplements: Supplements are not payable except for **International** journeys on *EC* trains.

OOSTENDE - BRUSSELS - LIÈGE - AACHEN 400

For *Thalys* trains Paris - Brussels - Köln / Oostende and v.v. – see Tables 16 / 21
For additional services Brugge - Brussels - Liège and v.v. – see Table 401

Services are liable to minor disruption owing to engineering work between Liège and Aachen

km			503		1504	504				505	*ICE* 11 [R]		506			507		508			509		510		*ICE* 15 [R]
		⚒		Ⓐ	H Ⓐ		Ⓐ	†	⚒		F	Ⓐ		Ⓐ			Ⓐ		Ⓐ			Ⓐ		Ⓐ	F
0	**Oostende 406** d.	...	...	...	0356	0438	...	...	...	0543	...	...	0643	...	...	0743	...	0843	...	...	0943	...	1043	...	...
22	Brugge ♣ **406** d.	...	...	...	0410	0453	...	...	...	0558	...	...	0658	...	...	0758	...	0858	...	...	0958	...	1058	...	...
62	Gent Sint-Pieters **406** d.	...	...	...	0452	0524	...	...	...	0624	...	...	0724	...	...	0824	...	0924	...	...	1024	...	1124	...	...
114	**Brussels Midi / Zuid** a.	...	...	...	0528	0555	...	...	...	0655	...	...	0755	...	...	0855	...	0955	...	...	1055	...	1155	...	...
114	**Brussels Midi / Zuid** d.	...	...	...	0530	0557	0624	...	...	0657	0718	0724	0757	0824	...	0857	0905	0957	1024	...	1057	1124	1157	1205	1218
116	Brussels Central d.	...	...	...	0534	0601	0628	...	...	0701	|	0728	0801	0828	...	0901	0909	1001	1028	...	1101	1128	1201	1209	|
118	Brussels Nord d.	...	...	...	0539	0606	0633	...	...	0706	0727	0733	0806	0833	...	0906	0914	1006	1033	...	1106	1133	1206	1214	1227
148	Leuven d.	...	...	...	0600	0625	|	...	...	0727	|	|	0826	|	...	0926	0932	1026	|	...	1126	|	1227	1232	|
218	**Liège Guillemins** a.	...	...	...	...	0703	0719	...	...	0800	0807	0819	0900	0919	...	1000	1019	1100	1119	...	1200	1219	1300	1319	1311
218	**Liège Guillemins 403** d.	...	...	0557	...	0705	0721	0726	0733	0805	0809	0821	0903	0921	0933	1005	1021	1105	1121	1133	1205	1221	1305	1321	1314
	Maastricht **403** a.	...	...	|	...	|	0750	|	|	|	|	0850	|	0950	|	|	1050	|	1150	|	|	1250	|	1350	|
242	Verviers Central d.	...	...	0628	...	0727	...	0751	0758	0827	|	...	0927	...	0958	1027	...	1127	...	1158	1227	...	1327	...	|
255	Welkenraedt d.	0601	0640	0640	...	0740	...	0803	0811	0840	|	...	0940	...	1011	1040	...	1140	...	1211	1240	...	1340	...	|
261	**Eupen** a.	|	0647	|	...	0747	...	|	|	0847	|	...	0947	...	|	1047	...	1147	...	|	1247	...	1347	...	|
274	**Aachen Hbf** a.	0616	...	0655	...	...	...	0818	0826	...	0836	...	...	...	1026	...	...	...	...	1226	...	...	...	...	1336
	Köln Hbf **802 910** a.	...	...	...	...	...	...	...	...	...	0915	...	...	...	...	...	...	...	...	...	...	...	...	...	1415

		511		512			513			514			515		516	*ICE* 17 [R]			517	518		519	520	521	522
			Ⓐ		Ⓐ			Ⓐ	Ⓐ		Ⓐ					F	Ⓐ								
Oostende 406 d.	...	1143	...	1243	...	...	1343	...	...	1443	...	...	1543	...	1643	...	...	...	1743	1843	...	1943	2043	2143	2239
Brugge ♣ **406** d.	...	1158	...	1258	...	...	1358	...	...	1458	...	...	1558	...	1658	...	...	...	1758	1858	...	1958	2058	2158	2254
Gent Sint-Pieters **406** d.	...	1224	...	1324	...	...	1424	...	...	1524	...	...	1624	...	1724	...	...	...	1824	1924	...	2024	2124	2224	2319
Brussels Midi / Zuid a.	...	1255	...	1355	...	...	1455	...	...	1555	...	...	1655	...	1755	...	...	...	1855	1955	...	2055	2155	2255	2355
Brussels Midi / Zuid d.	...	1257	1324	1357	1424	...	1457	1524	...	1557	1624	...	1657	...	1757	1818	1824	...	1857	1957	...	2057	2157	2257	2357
Brussels Central d.	...	1301	1328	1401	1428	...	1501	1528	...	1601	1628	...	1701	...	1801	|	1828	...	1901	2001	...	2101	2201	2301	0001
Brussels Nord d.	...	1306	1333	1406	1433	...	1506	1533	...	1606	1633	...	1706	...	1806	1827	1833	...	1906	2006	...	2106	2206	2306	0006
Leuven d.	...	1326	|	1426	|	...	1526	|	...	1626	|	...	1727	...	1827	|	|	...	1926	2026	...	2126	2226	2326	0026
Liège Guillemins a.	...	1400	1419	1500	1519	...	1600	1619	...	1700	1719	...	1800	...	1900	1911	1919	...	2000	2100	...	2200	2300	0019	0119
Liège Guillemins 403 d.	1333	1405	1421	1505	1521	1533	1605	1620	1638	1705	1721	1733	1805	...	1905	1914	1921	1928	2005	2105	2133	2205	2305	0021	0121
Maastricht **403** a.	|	|	1450	|	1550	|	|	1650	|	|	1750	|	|	...	|	|	1950	|	|	|	|	|	|	|	|
Verviers Central d.	1358	1427	...	1527	...	1558	1627	...	1708	1727	...	1758	1827	...	1927	|	...	1953	2027	2127	2158	2227	2327	0046	0146
Welkenraedt d.	1411	1440	...	1540	...	1611	1640	...	1724	1740	...	1811	1840	...	1940	|	...	2006	2040	2140	2211	2239	2339	0058	0158
Eupen a.	|	1447	...	1547	...	|	1647	...	|	1747	...	|	1847	...	1947	|	...	|	2047	2147	|	...	...	...	...
Aachen Hbf a.	1426	...	...	...	...	1626	...	...	1739	...	...	1826	...	...	...	1936	...	2021	...	...	2226	...	...	...	...
Köln Hbf **802 910** a.	...	...	...	...	...	...	...	...	...	...	...	...	...	...	...	2015	...	...	...	...	...	...	...	...	...

	527	528		529					530			531			*ICE* 16 [R]	532		533			534		535		
			Ⓐ		Ⓐ	†	⑥	Ⓐ		Ⓐ	Ⓐ			Ⓐ	F		Ⓐ			Ⓐ		Ⓐ			Ⓐ
Köln Hbf **802 910** d.	...	...	...	...	...	...	...	...	...	...	...	...	...	...	0844	...	...	...	...	...	...	...	...	...	...
Aachen Hbf d.	...	...	...	...	0622	0629	0634	...	...	0659	...	...	0835	...	0921	...	...	...	1034	...	...	...	...	1234	...
Eupen d.	...	...	...	0614	|	|	|	...	0714	|	...	0814	|	...	|	0914	...	1014	|	...	1114	...	1214	|	...
Welkenraedt d.	0404	0519	...	0622	0638	0646	0651	...	0722	0724	...	0822	0852	...	|	0922	...	1022	1051	...	1122	...	1222	1251	...
Verviers Central d.	0417	0532	...	0634	...	0658	0703	...	0734	0739	...	0834	0904	...	|	0934	...	1034	1103	...	1134	...	1234	1303	...
Maastricht **403** d.	|	|	...	|	...	|	|	0709	|	|	0809	|	|	0909	|	|	1009	|	|	1109	|	1209	|	|	1307
Liège Guillemins 403 a.	0440	0552	...	0654	...	0722	0726	0739	0754	0807	0839	0854	0927	0939	0946	0954	1039	1054	1126	1139	1154	1239	1254	1326	1339
Liège Guillemins d.	0443	0556	0639	0700	...	...	...	0741	0800	...	0841	0900	...	0941	0948	1000	1041	1100	...	1141	1200	1241	1300	...	1341
Leuven d.	0537	0637	|	0735	...	...	...	|	0837	...	|	0935	...	1030	|	1035	|	1135	...	|	1235	1330	1337	...	|
Brussels Nord d.	0551	0656	0729	0756	...	...	...	0829	0856	...	0929	0956	...	1048	1029	1056	1129	1156	...	1229	1256	1348	1356	...	1429
Brussels Central d.	0600	0700	0733	0800	...	...	...	0833	0900	...	0933	1000	...	1052	|	1100	1133	1200	...	1233	1300	1352	1400	...	1433
Brussels Midi / Zuid a.	0603	0703	0736	0803	...	...	...	0836	0903	...	0936	1003	...	1055	1035	1103	1136	1203	...	1236	1303	1355	1403	...	1436
Brussels Midi / Zuid d.	0605	0705	...	0805	...	...	...	...	0905	...	...	1005	...	...	...	1105	...	1205	...	...	1305	...	1405	...	...
Gent Sint-Pieters **406** d.	0639	0739	...	0839	...	...	...	...	0939	...	...	1039	...	...	...	1139	...	1239	...	...	1339	...	1439	...	...
Brugge ♣ **406** d.	0704	0804	...	0904	...	...	...	...	1004	...	...	1104	...	...	...	1204	...	1304	...	...	1404	...	1504	...	...
Oostende 406 a.	0717	0817	...	0917	...	...	...	...	1017	...	...	1117	...	...	...	1217	...	1317	...	...	1417	...	1517	...	...

	536		537			*ICE* 14 [R]	538		539			540			541		542	*ICE* 10 [R]	543		544	1544	1544	545	
		Ⓐ			Ⓐ	F		Ⓐ			Ⓐ		Ⓐ	Ⓐ				F				Ⓒ	H Ⓐ		
Köln Hbf **802 910** d.	...	...	...	...	...	1444	...	...	...	...	...	...	...	...	...	...	...	1943	...	...	...	...	...	...	...
Aachen Hbf d.	...	...	...	1434	...	1521	...	...	...	1634	...	...	1756	...	...	1832	...	2021	...	2034	...	...	...	...	2234
Eupen d.	1314	...	1414	|	...	|	1514	...	1612	|	...	1714	|	...	1814	|	1914	|	2014	|	2114	...	...	2210	|
Welkenraedt d.	1322	...	1422	1451	...	|	1522	...	1620	1651	...	1722	1812	...	1822	1849	1922	|	2022	2051	2122	...	...	2218	2251
Verviers Central d.	1334	...	1434	1503	...	|	1534	...	1634	1703	...	1734	...	...	1834	1901	1934	|	2034	2103	2134	...	...	2232	2303
Maastricht **403** d.	|	1409	|	|	1509	|	|	1609	|	|	1709	|	...	1809	|	|	|	|	|	|	|	...	...	|	|
Liège Guillemins 403 a.	1354	1439	1454	1526	1539	1542	1554	1639	1654	1726	1739	1754	...	1839	1854	1924	1954	2042	2054	2126	2154	...	...	2255	2326
Liège Guillemins d.	1400	1441	1500	...	1541	1544	1600	1641	1700	...	1741	1800	...	1841	1900	...	2000	2044	2100	...	2200	*2204*	...	2309	...
Leuven d.	1437	|	1537	...	|	|	1635	|	1737	...	|	1837	...	|	1937	...	2037	|	2135	...	2237	2302	2302	0004	...
Brussels Nord d.	1456	1529	1556	...	1629	1629	1656	1729	1756	...	1827	1856	...	1929	1956	...	2056	2129	2156	...	2256	2323	2323	0023	...
Brussels Central d.	1500	1533	1600	...	1633	|	1700	1733	1800	...	...	1900	...	1933	2000	...	2100	|	2200	...	2300	2327	2327	0027	...
Brussels Midi / Zuid a.	1503	1536	1603	...	1636	1635	1703	1736	1803	...	...	1903	...	1936	2003	...	2103	2135	2203	...	2303	2330	2330	0030	...
Brussels Midi / Zuid d.	1505	...	1605	...	...	...	1705	...	1805	...	...	1905	...	...	2005	...	2105	...	2205	...	2305	2336	2336	0037	...
Gent Sint-Pieters **406** d.	1539	...	1639	...	...	...	1739	...	1839	...	...	1939	...	...	2039	...	2139	...	2239	...	2339	0014	0014	0118	...
Brugge ♣ **406** d.	1604	...	1704	...	...	...	1804	...	1904	...	...	2004	...	...	2104	...	2204	...	2304	...	0000	0056	0056	0143	...
Oostende 406 a.	1617	...	1717	...	...	...	1817	...	1916	...	...	2017	...	...	2117	...	2217	...	2317	...	0012	0109	0109	0156	...

F – (12) and 🍷 Brussels - Köln Hbf - Frankfurt ✈ - Frankfurt Hbf and v.v.
H – From / to Hasselt – see Table **401**.

ICE – German high-speed train: special fares payable.
♣ – For Brugge - Zeebrugge and v.v. local service, see note ♣ on page 240.

401 KNOKKE / BLANKENBERGE - BRUSSELS - HASSELT, GENK and LIÈGE

For express services (Oostende -) Brugge - Brussels - Liège and v.v. – see Table 400

km	Ⓐ	Ⓐ	Ⓐ	ⒶG	ⒶO	Ⓐ	ⒶG	Ⓐ	Ⓐ	ⒶG	ⒶB	Ⓐ		Ⓐ	ⒶG	ⒶB	Ⓐ	Ⓐ	ⒶG	Ⓐ	Ⓐ	
	Knokke d.	...	...	...	...	...	...	...	...	...	...	0605		...	...	...	2005	...	...	...	2105	...
0	Blankenberge d.	...	...	...	...	...	...	...	...	...	0610	|		...	...	2010	|	...	...	2110	|	...
15	**Brugge** ♣ a.	...	...	...	...	...	...	...	...	...	0621	0624		...	...	2021	2024	...	...	2121	2124	...
15	**Brugge 406** ♣ d.	...	...	...	0410	...	...	0531	...	...	0631	0631		...	...	2031	2031	...	...	2131	2131	...
55	Gent Sint-Pieters **406** d.	...	...	...	0452	0503	...	0557	0608	...	0657	0657		2008	...	2057	2057	2108	...	2157	2157	...
	Denderleeuw d.	...	...	...	0510	0543	...	|	0643	...	|	|	▲	2043	...	|	|	2143	...	|	|	...
107	**Brussels Midi / Zuid** a.	...	...	...	0528	0606	...	0628	0706	...	0728	0728		2106	...	2128	2128	2206	...	2228	2228	...
107	**Brussels Midi / Zuid 400** d.	...	0508	0528	0530	0608	0628	0630	0709	0728	0730	0730	and	2108	2128	2130	2130	2208	2228	2230	2230	...
109	Brussels Central d.	...	0512	0532	0534	0612	0632	0634	0713	0732	0734	0734	at the	2112	2132	2134	2134	2212	2232	2234	2234	...
111	Brussels Nord d.	...	0518	0537	0539	0618	0637	0639	0718	0737	0739	0739	same	2118	2137	2139	2139	2218	2237	2239	2239	...
141	Leuven a.	...	0536	0555	0600	0636	0656	0700	0736	0755	0800	0800	minutes	2136	2155	2200	2200	2236	2255	2300	2300	...
141	Leuven d.	...	0538	0557	0610	0638	0658	0710	0738	0757	0810	0810	past	2138	2157	2210	2210	2238	2257	2310	2310	...
	Tienen d.	...	0551	0610	|	0651	0711	|	0751	0810	|	|	each	2151	2210	|	|	2251	2310	|	|	...
	Landen a.	...	0602	0620	|	0702	0720	|	0802	0820	|	|	hour	2202	2220	|	|	2302	2320	|	|	...
	Landen d.	0520	0604	0621	|	0704	0721	|	0804	0821	|	|	until	2204	2221	|	|	2304	2321	|	|	...
157	Aarschot **417** d.	|	|	|	0624	|	|	0726	|	|	0824	0824		|	|	2224	2224	|	|	2322	2324	...
175	Diest **417** d.	|	|	|	0635	|	|	0745	|	|	0835	0835		|	|	2235	2235	|	|	2342	2342	...
	Sint-Truiden d.	0529	0614	|	|	0714	|	|	0814	|	|	|		2214	|	|	|	2314	|	|	|	...
196	Hasselt **417** d.	0546	0631	|	0649	0731	|	0802	0831	|	0849	0849		2231	|	2249	2249	2331	|	2358	2358	...
	Genk a.	0603	0648	|	...	0748	|	...	0848	|	...	...		2248	|	...	...	2348	|	...	...	...
	Liège Guillemins 400 a.	...	...	0653	...	...	0754	...	...	0851	...	...		...	2251	...	...	...	2351	...	...	...

km		ⒶB	Ⓐ	Ⓐ	Ⓐ	Ⓒ	Ⓒ	Ⓒ	Ⓒ	Ⓒ	Ⓒ	ⒸB	Ⓒ	Ⓒ		ⒸB	Ⓒ	Ⓒ	ⒸB	Ⓒ	Ⓒ	Ⓒ
0	**Knokke** d.	...	2205	...	2305	...	...	...	...	...	...	...	0705	...		...	2105	...	...	2205	...	2305
	Blankenberge d.	2210	|	2310	|	...	...	...	...	...	...	0710	|	...		2110	|	...	2210	|	2310	|
22	**Brugge** ♣ a.	2221	2224	2321	2324	...	...	...	...	...	...	0721	0724	...		2121	2124	...	2221	2224	2321	2324
22	**Brugge 406** ♣ d.	2231	2231	...	...	0524	0524	...	0631	0631	...	0731	0731	...		2131	2131	...	2231	2231	...	...
62	Gent Sint-Pieters **406** d.	2257	2257	...	...	0557	0557	0611	0657	0657	0711	0757	0757	0811		2157	2157	2211	2257	2257	...	...
96	Denderleeuw d.	|	|	...	...	|	|	0643	|	|	0743	|	|	0843	▲	|	|	2243	|	|	...	...
119	**Brussels Midi / Zuid** a.	2328	2328	...	...	0628	0628	0704	0728	0728	0804	0828	0828	0904		2228	2228	2304	2328	2328	...	...
119	**Brussels Midi / Zuid 400** d.	...	...	...	...	0630	0630	...	0730	0730	...	0830	0830	...	and	2230	2230	...	...	...	...	...
121	Brussels Central d.	...	...	...	...	0634	0634	...	0734	0734	...	0834	0834	...	at the	2234	2234	...	...	...	...	...
123	Brussels Nord d.	...	...	...	...	0639	0639	...	0739	0739	...	0839	0839	...	same	2239	2239	...	...	...	...	...
152	Leuven a.	...	...	...	...	0658	0658	...	0758	0758	...	0858	0858	...	minutes	2258	2258	...	...	...	...	...
152	Leuven d.	...	...	...	...	0700	0700	...	0800	0800	...	0900	0900	...	past	2300	2300	...	...	...	...	...
170	Tienen d.	...	...	...	...	0711	0711	...	0811	0811	...	0911	0911	...	each	2311	2311	...	...	...	...	...
183	Landen a.	...	...	...	...	0721	0721	...	0821	0821	...	0921	0921	...	hour	2321	2321	...	...	...	...	...
183	Landen d.	...	...	...	...	*0729*	0732	...	*0829*	0833	...	*0929*	0932	...	until	*2329*	2332	...	...	...	...	...
	Aarschot **417** d.	...	...	...	...	|	|	...	|	|	...	|	|	...		|	|	...	...	...	...	...
	Diest **417** d.	...	...	...	...	|	|	...	|	|	...	|	|	...		|	|	...	...	...	...	...
194	Sint-Truiden d.	...	...	...	...	|	0741	...	|	0841	...	|	0941	...		|	2341	...	...	...	...	...
211	Hasselt **417** d.	...	...	...	...	|	0757	...	|	0857	...	|	0957	...		|	2357	...	...	...	...	...
227	**Genk** a.	...	...	...	...	|	0813	...	|	0913	...	|	1013	...		|	0013	...	...	...	...	...
	Liège Guillemins 400 a.	...	...	...	...	*0756*	...	...	*0856*	...	...	*0956*	...	...		*2356*	...	...	...	...	...	...

Ⓐ	Ⓐ	Ⓐ	Ⓐ	Ⓐ	Ⓐ	Ⓐ	ⒶB	ⒶG		Ⓐ	Ⓐ	ⒶB	ⒶG	Ⓐ	Ⓐ	ⒶG	Ⓐ	ⒶO	ⒶG	Ⓐ	Ⓐ	ⒶO
Liège Guillemins 400 d.	...	...	...	...	...	...	...	0508		...	...	...	2008	...	...	2106	...	...	2208	...	...	2309
Genk d.	...	...	...	...	⊠	...	...	|		1912	...	...	|	2012	...	|	2112	...	|	2212	...	|
Hasselt **417** d.	...	...	...	...	0430	⊡	⊡	|		1931	2011	2011	|	2031	2111	|	2131	2211	|	2231	2238	|
Sint-Truiden d.	...	...	...	...	0446	|	|	|		1947	|	|	|	2047	|	|	2147	|	|	2247	|	|
Diest **417** d.	...	...	...	...	|	⊡	⊡	|		|	2025	2025	|	|	2125	|	|	2225	|	|	2254	|
Aarschot **417** d.	...	...	...	...	|	0537	0537	|	▲	|	2039	2039	|	|	2139	|	|	2239	|	|	2312	|
Landen a.	...	...	...	...	0456	|	|	0539		1956	|	|	2039	2056	|	2139	2156	|	2239	2256	|	2338
Landen d.	...	...	...	...	0458	|	|	0540	and	1958	|	|	2040	2058	|	2140	2158	|	2240	...	|	2340
Tienen d.	...	...	...	...	0510	|	|	0552	at the	2010	|	|	2052	2110	|	2152	2210	|	2252	...	|	2351
Leuven a.	...	...	...	...	0522	0550	0550	0603	same	2022	2050	2050	2103	2122	2150	2203	2222	2250	2303	...	2326	0001
Leuven d.	...	...	...	...	0524	0600	0600	0605	minutes	2024	2100	2100	2105	2124	2200	2205	2224	2300	2305	...	...	0004
Brussels Nord d.	...	...	...	...	0545	0623	0623	0625	past	2045	2123	2123	2125	2145	2223	2225	2245	2323	2325	...	...	0023
Brussels Central d.	...	...	...	...	0549	0627	0627	0629	each	2049	2127	2127	2129	2149	2227	2229	2249	2327	2329	...	...	0027
Brussels Midi / Zuid 400 a.	...	...	...	...	0552	0630	0630	0632	hour	2052	2130	2130	2132	2152	2230	2232	2252	2330	2332	...	...	0030
Brussels Midi / Zuid d.	...	...	...	...	0556	0632	0632	...	until	2056	2132	2132	...	2156	2232	...	2256	2336	...	...	...	0037
Denderleeuw d.	...	...	...	...	0619	|	|	...		2119	|	|	...	2219	|	...	2319	2355	...	...	...	0056
Gent Sint-Pieters **406** d.	...	...	...	...	0652	0703	0703	...		2152	2203	2203	...	2252	2303	...	2352	0014	...	...	...	0118
Brugge 406 ♣ a.	...	...	...	...	...	0727	0727	...		...	2227	2227	...	...	2327	...	...	0051	...	...	...	0142
Brugge ♣ d.	0531	0538	0631	0638	...	0735	0738	...		...	2235	2238	...	...	...	...	...	...	...	...	...	...
Blankenberge a.	|	0549	|	0649	...	|	0749	...		...	|	2249	...	...	...	...	...	...	...	...	...	...
Knokke a.	0550	...	0650	...	...	0754	...	...		...	2254	...	...	...	...	...	...	...	...	...	...	...

Ⓒ	Ⓒ	Ⓒ	Ⓒ	Ⓒ	ⒸB	Ⓒ	Ⓒ	ⒸB	Ⓒ		Ⓒ	ⒸB	Ⓒ		Ⓒ	Ⓒ	Ⓒ		ⒸO	ⒸO		ⒸO
Liège Guillemins 400 d.	...	...	...	...	...	...	...	*0606*	...		...	*2006*	...	...	...	*2106*	...	...	...	*2206*	...	2309
Genk d.	...	...	...	...	...	...	0549	|	...		1949	|	...	...	2049	|	...	...	2149	|	...	|
Hasselt **417** d.	...	...	...	...	...	...	0607	|	...		2007	|	...	...	2107	|	...	...	2207	|	...	|
Sint-Truiden d.	...	...	...	...	...	...	0622	|	...		2022	|	...	...	2122	|	...	...	2222	|	...	|
Diest **417** d.	...	...	...	...	...	...	|	|	...		|	|	...	...	|	|	...	...	|	|	...	|
Aarschot **417** d.	...	...	...	...	...	...	|	|	...	▲	|	|	...	...	|	|	...	...	|	|	...	|
Landen a.	...	...	...	...	...	...	0630	*0633*	...		2030	*2033*	...	...	2130	*2133*	...	...	2230	*2233*	...	2338
Landen d.	...	...	...	...	...	...	0639	0639	...	and	2039	2039	...	...	2139	2139	...	...	2239	2239	...	2340
Tienen d.	...	...	...	...	...	...	0650	0650	...	at the	2020	2050	...	...	2150	2150	...	...	2250	2249	...	2351
Leuven a.	...	...	...	...	...	...	0700	0700	...	same	2100	2100	...	...	2200	2200	...	...	2300	2300	...	0001
Leuven d.	...	...	...	...	...	...	0702	0702	...	minutes	2102	2102	...	...	2202	2202	...	...	2302	2302	...	0004
Brussels Nord d.	...	...	...	...	...	...	0723	0723	...	past	2123	2123	...	...	2223	2223	...	...	2323	2323	...	0023
Brussels Central d.	...	...	...	...	...	...	0727	0727	...	each	2127	2127	...	...	2227	2227	...	...	2327	2327	...	0027
Brussels Midi / Zuid 400 a.	...	...	...	...	...	...	0730	0730	...	hour	2130	2130	...	...	2230	2230	...	...	2330	2330	...	0030
Brussels Midi / Zuid d.	...	...	0556	0632	0632	0656	0732	0732	0756	until	2132	2132	2156	...	2232	2232	2256	...	2336	2336	...	0037
Denderleeuw d.	...	...	0618	|	|	0718	|	|	0818		|	|	2218	...	|	|	2318	...	2355	2355	...	0056
Gent Sint-Pieters **406** d.	...	...	0649	0703	0706	0749	0803	0803	0849		2203	2203	2249	...	2303	2303	2349	...	0014	0014	...	0118
Brugge 406 ♣ a.	...	...	...	0727	0730	...	0827	0827	...		2227	2227	...	...	2328	2328	...	...	0051	0051	...	0142
Brugge ♣ d.	0631	0634	...	0735	0738	...	0835	0838	...		2235	2238	...	...	...	...	...	...	...	...	...	...
Blankenberge a.	|	0645	...	|	0749	...	|	0849	...		|	2249	...	...	...	...	...	...	...	...	...	...
Knokke a.	0650	...	...	0754	...	...	0854	...	...		2254	...	...	...	...	...	...	...	...	...	...	...

B – Passengers may be required to change trains at Brugge on some journeys.
G – From / to St Ghislain / Quiévrain and Mons – see Table **424**.
O – From / to Oostende – see Table **400**.

⊠ – Services from Genk depart at 0512, 0610, 0710, then 0812 and hourly to 1912 (then as shown).

⊡ – Services from Hasselt depart at 0502, 0601, 0703, 0811 and hourly until 1911 (then as shown); Diest depart 0518, 0617, 0719, 0826 and hourly until 1926 (then as shown).

▲ – Times may vary by up to 5 minutes on some journeys.

♣ – **Local service BRUGGE - ZEEBRUGGE and v.v.** Journey 16 minutes.

From **Brugge**:
to Zeebrugge Dorp station on Ⓐ (not June 28 - Aug. 31): 0541, 0609, 0709 and hourly until 2209.
to Zeebrugge Strand station on Ⓒ (daily June 28 - Aug. 31): 0709, 0909, 1109, 1309, 1509, 1709, 1909, 2109.

From **Zeebrugge**:
from Dorp station on Ⓐ (not June 28 - Aug. 31): 0602, 0633, 0733 and hourly until 2233.
from Strand station on Ⓒ (daily June 28 - Aug. 31): 0733, 0933, 1133, 1333, 1533, 1733, 1933, 2133.

BRUSSELS - BRUSSELS NATIONAAL AIRPORT ✈ - LEUVEN 402

km		Ⓐ	Ⓐ		Ⓐ	Ⓐ	Ⓐ	Ⓐ		Ⓐ Q	Ⓐ	Ⓐ	Ⓐ		Ⓐ Q	Ⓐ	Ⓐ		Ⓐ	Ⓐ Q	Ⓐ	Ⓐ	▲
	Gent Sint-P. **400/1** d.		...	...	...	...	0430	0515	...	...	...	0530	0615	...	...	...	0630	...	0715	...	...	0730	and
0	**Brussels Midi / Zuid 400/1** d.		0448	...	0500	0512	0536	0548	...	0600	0612	0636	0648	...	0658	0712	0736	...	0748	0758	0810	0836	at the
2	Brussels Central d.		0452	...	0504	0516	0540	0552	...	0604	0616	0640	0652	...	0702	0716	0740	...	0752	0802	0814	0840	same
4	Brussels Nord d.		0457	...	0509	0521	0545	0557	...	0609	0621	0645	0657	...	0709	0721	0745	...	0757	0809	0819	0845	minutes
6	Schaarbeek / Schaerbeek d.		|	...	|	|	|	|	...	|	|	|	|	...	|	|	|	...	|	|	|	|	past each
16	**Brussels Nationaal ✈** a.		0508	...	0524	0533	0556	0608	...	0624	0633	0656	0709	...	0726	0733	0756	...	0808	0826	0831	0856	hour
16	**Brussels Nationaal ✈** d.		0517	...	...	0539	...	0617	...	...	0639	...	0717	...	...	0739	...	...	0817	...	0839	...	until
36	Leuven **400/1** a.		0533	...	...	0552	...	0633	...	...	0652	...	0733	...	...	0752	...	...	0833	...	0852	...	

	Ⓐ	Ⓐ Q	Ⓐ	Ⓐ			Ⓐ	Ⓐ Q	Ⓐ	Ⓐ	▲	Ⓐ	Ⓐ Q	Ⓐ	Ⓐ			Ⓐ	Ⓐ Q		Ⓐ		
Gent Sint-P. **400/1** d.	1715	...	...	1730	...	...	1815	...	...	1830	and	2115	...	...	2130	...	...	2215	...	...	...	...	...
Brussels Midi / Zuid 400/1 d.	1748	1758	1812	1836	...	...	1848	1900	1912	1936	at the	2148	2200	2212	2236	...	...	2248	2300	...	2312	...	...
Brussels Central d.	1752	1802	1816	1840	...	...	1852	1904	1916	1940	same	2152	2204	2216	2240	...	...	2252	2304	...	2316	...	...
Brussels Nord d.	1759	1809	1821	1845	...	...	1857	1909	1921	1945	minutes	2157	2209	2221	2245	...	...	2257	2309	...	2321	...	...
Schaarbeek / Schaerbeek d.	|	|	|	|	...	...	|	|	|	|	past each	|	|	|	|	...	...	|	|	...	|	...	...
Brussels Nationaal ✈ a.	1810	1824	1833	1856	...	...	1908	1924	1933	1956	hour	2208	2224	2233	2256	...	...	2308	2324	...	2333	...	...
Brussels Nationaal ✈ d.	1817	...	1839	...	...	...	1917	...	1939	...	until	2217	...	2239	...	...	...	2317	...	...	2339	...	...
Leuven **400/1** a.	1833	...	1852	...	...	...	1933	...	1952	...		2233	...	2252	...	...	...	2333	...	...	2352	...	...

	Ⓒ	Ⓒ		Ⓒ	Ⓒ	Ⓒ	Ⓒ		Ⓒ Q		Ⓒ	Ⓒ	Ⓒ	Ⓒ Q	▲	Ⓒ	Ⓒ	Ⓒ	Ⓒ Q		Ⓒ		
Gent Sint-P. **400/1** d.		...	...	...	...	...	...	...	...	...	...	0530	...	...	and	...	2130	...	...	...	...	...	...
Brussels Midi / Zuid 400/1 d.		0450	...	0506	0523	0536	0550	...	0606	...	0623	0636	0650	0706	at the	2223	2236	2250	2306	...	2323	...	...
Brussels Central d.		0454	...	0510	0527	0540	0554	...	0610	...	0627	0640	0654	0710	same	2227	2240	2254	2310	...	2327	...	...
Brussels Nord d.		0459	...	0514	0532	0545	0559	...	0614	...	0632	0645	0659	0714	minutes	2232	2245	2259	2314	...	2332	...	...
Schaarbeek / Schaerbeek d.		|	...	0518	|	|	|	...	0618	...	|	|	|	0718	past each	|	|	|	2318	...	|	...	...
Brussels Nationaal ✈ a.		0510	...	0528	0543	0556	0610	...	0628	...	0643	0656	0710	0728	hour	2243	2256	2310	2328	...	2343	...	...
Brussels Nationaal ✈ d.		...	...	0537	...	...	...	...	0637	...	...	...	...	0737	until	...	...	...	2337	...	...	...	...
Leuven **400/1** a.		...	...	0551	...	...	...	...	0651	...	...	...	...	0751		...	...	...	2351	...	...	...	...

	Ⓐ	Ⓐ	Ⓐ Q	Ⓐ	Ⓐ	Ⓐ	Ⓐ Q	Ⓐ	Ⓐ	Ⓐ	Ⓐ Q	Ⓐ	Ⓐ	Ⓐ	Ⓐ Q	Ⓐ	Ⓐ	▲	Ⓐ	Ⓐ Q	Ⓐ	Ⓐ	Ⓐ
Leuven **400/1** d.		...	...	0527	...	0608	...	0627	...	0708	...	0727	...	0808	...	0827	...	and	2108	...	2127	...	2208
Brussels Nationaal ✈ a.		...	...	0543	...	0621	...	0643	...	0721	...	0743	...	0821	...	0843	...	at the	2121	...	2143	...	2221
Brussels Nationaal ✈ d.		0527	0536	0552	0604	0627	0636	0652	0702	0727	0736	0752	0804	0827	0836	0852	0904	same	2127	2136	2152	2204	2227
Schaarbeek / Schaerbeek a.		|	|	|	|	|	|	|	|	|	|	|	|	|	|	|	|	minutes	|	|	|	|	|
Brussels Nord a.		0539	0551	0603	0615	0639	0651	0703	0715	0739	0751	0803	0815	0839	0851	0903	0915	past each	2139	2151	2203	2215	2239
Brussels Central a.		0544	0556	0608	0620	0644	0658	0708	0720	0744	0758	0808	0820	0844	0858	0908	0920	hour	2144	2156	2208	2220	2244
Brussels Midi / Zuid 400/1 a.		0548	0600	0612	0624	0648	0702	0712	0724	0748	0802	0812	0824	0848	0902	0912	0924	until	2148	2200	2212	2224	2248
Gent Sint-P. **400/1** a.		...	...	0645	0728	...	...	0745	0828	...	...	0845	0928	...	...	0945	1028		...	...	2245	2328	...

	Ⓐ	Ⓐ	Ⓐ	Ⓐ	Ⓐ	Ⓐ	Ⓒ	Ⓒ	Ⓒ Q	Ⓒ	Ⓒ	▲	Ⓒ	Ⓒ Q	Ⓒ	Ⓒ	Ⓒ	Ⓒ Q	Ⓒ	Ⓒ	Ⓒ	Ⓒ	Ⓒ
Leuven **400/1** d.	...	2227	...	2308	...	2331		...	0509	...	...	and	...	2109	...	...	...	2209	...	...	...	2309	...
Brussels Nationaal ✈ a.	...	2243	...	2321	...	2347		...	0523	...	...	at the	...	2123	...	...	...	2223	...	...	...	2323	...
Brussels Nationaal ✈ d.	2237	2252	2304	2327	2336	2352		0517	0532	0550	0604	same	2117	2132	2150	2204	2217	2232	2250	2304	2317	2332	2350
Schaarbeek / Schaerbeek a.	|	|	|	|	|	|		|	0541	|	|	minutes	|	2142	|	|	|	2241	|	|	|	2342	|
Brussels Nord a.	2251	2303	2315	2339	2351	0003		0528	0545	0601	0615	past each	2128	2146	2201	2215	2228	2245	2301	2315	2328	2346	0001
Brussels Central a.	2256	2308	2320	2344	2356	0008		0533	0549	0606	0620	hour	2133	2150	2206	2220	2233	2249	2306	2320	2333	2350	0006
Brussels Midi / Zuid 400/1 a.	2300	2312	2324	2348	2400	0012		0537	0653	0610	0624	until	2137	2154	2210	2224	2237	2253	2310	2324	2337	2354	0010
Gent Sint-P. **400/1** a.	...	...	0028	...	...	...		...	...	...	0728		...	...	...	2328	...	...	...	...	...	...	...

Q – From / to Mons / Quévy / Quiévrain – see Table **424**.

▲ – Timings may vary by up to 4 minutes on some journeys.

LIÈGE - MAASTRICHT 403

km		Ⓐ p	⑥	Ⓒ	Ⓐ	Ⓒ	Ⓐ		Ⓒ	Ⓐ		Ⓒ	Ⓐ p	Ⓒ	Ⓐ	Ⓒ	Ⓐ	Ⓒ	Ⓐ	Ⓒ	Ⓐ	Ⓒ	Ⓐ
0	**Liège Guillemins** d.	0521	0618	0618	0621	0718	0721	and	1718	1719	...	1818	1832	1918	1921	2018	2021	2118	2123	2218	2221	2318	2321
19	Visé a.	0539	0635	0635	0639	0735	0739	hourly	1735	1739	...	1835	1849	1935	1939	2035	2039	2136	2139	2235	2238	2335	2338
32	**Maastricht** a.	0550	0650	...	0650	0750	0750	until	1750	1750	...	1850	1900	1950	1950	2050	2050j	2150	2150j	2250	2250j	2350	2350j

	Ⓐ	⑥		Ⓐ	Ⓒ		Ⓐ	Ⓒ		Ⓐ	Ⓒ		Ⓐ	Ⓒ		Ⓐ	Ⓒ		Ⓐ	Ⓒ			
Maastricht d.	0558j	0612	...	0709	0712g	...	0809	0812	and	2009	2012	...	2109j	2112	...	2209j	2212	...	2309j	2312	...	0009x	...
Visé d.	0608	0625	...	0722	0725	...	0822	0825	hourly	2018	2025	...	2122	2125	...	2222	2225	...	2322	2325	...	0021	...
Liège Guillemins a.	0624	0642	...	0739	0742	...	0839	0842	until	2039	2042	...	2139	2142	...	2239	2242	...	2339	2342	...	0039	...

g – ⑥ only.
j – Not Dec. 31.
p – Not Dec. 26.
x – Not Jan. 1.

KNOKKE - OOSTENDE - DE PANNE 404

De Lijn ✆ 059 56 53 53

Belgian Coastal Tramway

From **Knokke** (railway station):
In principle services operate daily 0630 – 2030, with enhanced frequency as follows:
November - Easter: every 20 minutes 1008 – 1748.
Easter - June: every 15 minutes 0858 – 1728.
July and August: every 10 minutes 0803 – 1833.
September and October: every 15 minutes 0858 – 1728.
Exact times are subject to minor variation.

From **De Panne** (railway station):
In principle services operate daily 0600 – 2000, with enhanced frequency as follows:
November - Easter: every 20 minutes 0849 – 1729.
Easter - June: every 15 minutes 0854 – 1739.
July and August: every 10 minutes 0829 – 1929.
September and October: every 15 minutes 0854 – 1739.
Exact times are subject to minor variation.

Knokke → Heist + *0h06* → Zeebrugge + *0h11* → Blankenberge + *0h23* → **Oostende** + *1h00* → Middelkerke + *1h25* → Nieuwpoort + *1h49* → Koksijde + *2h02* → **De Panne** + *2h21*
De Panne → Koksijde + *0h19* → Nieuwpoort + *0h32* → Middelkerke + *0h56* → **Oostende** + *1h19* → Blankenberge + *1h57* → Zeebrugge + *2h05* → Heist + *2h14* → **Knokke** + *2h21*

Connections into NMBS / SNCB rail services are available at Knokke (Table **401**), Zeebrugge (Table **401**), Blankenberge (Table **401**), Oostende (Tables **400/1**) and De Panne (Table **407**). De Panne railway station is situated in Adinkerke.

Dutch-language forms of some **French-language** Belgian names

Aarlen = **Arlon**
Aat = **Ath**
Bergen = **Mons**
Doornik = **Tournai**
Duinkerke = **Dunkerque** (France)
Hoei = **Huy**
Luik = **Liège**
Moeskroen = **Mouscron**
Namen = **Namur**
Nijvel = **Nivelles**
Rijsel = **Lille** (France)
's Gravenbrakel = **Braine le Comte**
Wezet = **Visé**

French-language forms of some **Dutch-language** Belgian names

Anvers = **Antwerpen**
Audenarde = **Oudenaarde**
Bruges = **Brugge**
Courtrai = **Kortrijk**
Dixmude = **Diksmuide**
Furnes = **Veurne**
Gand = **Gent**
Hal = **Halle**
La Panne = **De Panne**
Lierre = **Lier**
Louvain = **Leuven**
Malines = **Mechelen**
Menin = **Menen**
Ostende = **Oostende**
Renaix = **Ronse**
Roulers = **Roeselare**
Saint Nicolas = **Sint Niklaas**
Saint Trond = **Sint Truiden**
Termonde = **Dendermonde**
Tirlemont = **Tienen**
Tongres = **Tongeren**
Ypres = **Ieper**

Some other places outside Belgium

Aken / Aix la Chapelle = **Aachen**
Keulen / Cologne = **Köln**
Londen / Londres = **London**

405 LILLE - KORTRIJK - OOSTENDE and GENT

Lille - Mouscron and v.v. subject to alteration on French and Belgian public holidays

km		Ⓐ		Ⓐ	Ⓒ		Ⓐ	⚒	†		Ⓐ	⑥	†						⚒	†				
0	**Lille Flandres** § d.	...	...	...	...	...	...	0646	...	...	0805	0805	0810	...	0906	...	1008	...	1108	1108	...	1208	...	1305
10	Roubaix § d.	...	...	...	...	...	...	0658	...	...	0816	0818	|	...	|	...	1019	...	1119	|	...	1219	...	|
12	Tourcoing § d.	...	...	...	...	...	...	0721	...	...	0820	0821	|	...	|	...	1023	...	1123	|	...	1223	...	|
18	Mouscron d.	...	...	...	...	0627	...	0728	0730	...	0830	0830	0830	...	0930	...	1030	...	1130	1130	...	1230	...	1330
30	**Kortrijk 415** a.	...	...	...	...	0635	...	0736	0738	...	0838	0838	0838	...	0938	...	1038	...	1138	1138	...	1238	...	1338
30	**Kortrijk 414** d.	0443	0541	0548	0608	0637	0648	0742	0743	0748	0843	0843	0843	0848	0948	0943	1043	1048	1143	1143	1148	1243	1248	1348
	Brugge a.	0527	|	0627	0651	|	0727	|	|	0827	|	|	|	0927	1027	|	|	1127	|	|	1227	|	1327	1427
	Oostende a.	0547	|	0647	0747	|	0747	|	|	0847	|	|	|	0947	1047	|	|	1147	|	|	1247	|	1347	1447
72	**Gent Sint-Pieters 406 414** a.	...	0603	...	...	0702	...	0803	0803	...	0903	0903	0903	...	...	1003	1103	...	1203	1203	...	1303	...	...
	Antwerpen Centraal **406** a.	...	0654	...	...	0754	...	0854	0854	...	0954	0954	0954	...	...	1054	1154	...	1254	1254	...	1354	...	...

				Ⓒ												Ⓒ	Ⓐ		⚒	†		Ⓐ	†	⑥
	Lille Flandres § d.	...	1408	...	1508	...	...	1608	...	1706	...	1810	...	1905	...	2008	2013	...	2105	2109	...	2209	2204	2214
	Roubaix § d.	...	1420	...	|	...	...	1620	...	1718	...	1821	...	|	...	2020	|	...	|	2120	...	2220	|	|
	Tourcoing § d.	...	1424	...	|	...	...	1624	...	1722	...	1824	...	|	...	2024	|	...	|	2124	...	2224	|	|
	Mouscron d.	...	1430	...	1530	1530	...	1630	...	1730	...	1830	...	1930	...	2030	2030	...	2130	2130	...	2230	2230	2230
	Kortrijk 415 a.	...	1438	...	1538	1538	...	1638	...	1738	...	1838	...	1938	...	2038	2038	...	2138	2138	...	2238	2238	2238
	Kortrijk 414 d.	1343	1443	1448	1543	1543	1548	1643	1648	1751	1743	1843	1848	1943	1948	2043	2043	2048	2148	2148	2143	2243	2242	2242
	Brugge ◇ a.	|	|	1527	|	|	1627	|	1727	1830	|	|	1927	|	2027	|	|	2127	2227	2227	|	|	|	|
	Oostende ◇ a.	|	|	1547	|	|	1647	|	1747	1847	|	|	1947	|	2047	|	|	2147	2247	2247	|	|	|	|
	Gent Sint-Pieters 406 414 a.	1403	1503	...	1603	1603	...	1703	...	...	1803	1903	...	2003	...	2103	2103	...	...	...	2203	2303	2313	2313
	Antwerpen Centraal **406** a.	1454	1554	...	1654	1654	...	1754	...	...	1854	1954	...	2054	...	2154	2154	...	...	...	2254	2354	0017	0017

km		Ⓐ	Ⓐ	⑥	Ⓐ	Ⓐ	⚒	†	Ⓒ				Q		Ⓐ	Ⓒ					⚒	†		
	Antwerpen Centraal **406** d.	...	0458	...	...	...	0606	0606	...	0706	...	...	0806	...	0906	0906	...	...	1006	1106	...	...	...	1206
	Gent Sint-Pieters 406 414 d.	...	0549	0540	...	...	0657	0657	...	0757	...	...	0857	...	0957	0957	...	...	1057	1157	...	...	...	1257
0	**Oostende** ◇ d.	...	|	|	0514	0614	|	|	...	|	0714	0814	|	0914	|	|	...	1014	|	|	1114	1114	1214	|
22	Brugge ◇ d.	0507	|	|	0532	0628	|	|	0709	|	0734	0834	|	0934	|	|	...	1034	|	|	1134	1134	1234	|
75	**Kortrijk 414** a.	0554	0609	0611	0610	0707	0717	0717	0758	0817	0812	0912	0917	1012	1017	1017	...	1112	1117	1217	1212	1212	1312	1317
	Kortrijk 415 d.	...	0612	0612	...	...	0722	0722	...	...	0822	...	0922	...	1022	1022	...	...	1122	...	1222	1222	...	1322
	Mouscron a.	...	0620	0620	...	...	0730	0730	...	...	0830	...	0930	...	1030	1030	...	...	1130	...	1230	1230	...	1330
	Tourcoing § a.	...	|	|	...	...	0738	|	...	...	0837	...	0935	...	...	|	...	...	|	...	1238	|	...	1335
	Roubaix § a.	...	|	|	...	...	0741	|	...	...	0841	...	0939	...	...	|	...	...	|	...	1243	|	...	1339
	Lille Flandres § a.	...	0636	0636	...	...	0754	0758	...	...	0854	...	0951	...	...	1055	...	...	1154	...	1256	1252	...	1353

	Antwerpen Centraal **406** d.	...	1306	...	1406	1506	...	...	1606	...	...	1705	...	1805	1906	...	...	2006	...	2106	...	2206	2306	...
	Gent Sint-Pieters 406 414 d.	...	1357	...	1457	1557	...	...	1657	...	...	1757	...	1857	1957	...	...	2057	...	2157	...	2257	2357	...
	Oostende ◇ d.	1314	|	1414	|	|	1514	1614	|	...	1714	|	1814	|	|	1914	2014	|	2114	|	2214	|	|	...
	Brugge ◇ d.	1334	|	1434	|	|	1534	1634	|	...	1734	|	1834	|	|	1934	2034	|	2134	|	2234	|	|	...
	Kortrijk 414 a.	1412	1417	1512	1517	1617	1612	1712	1717	...	1812	1817	1912	1917	2017	2012	2112	2117	2212	2217	2317	2317	0029	...
	Kortrijk 415 d.	...	1422	...	1522	...	1622	...	1723	...	...	1823	...	1922	...	2022	...	2122	...	2222	...	...	...	...
	Mouscron a.	...	1430	...	1530	...	1630	...	1731	...	...	1831	...	1930	...	2030	...	2130	...	2230	...	...	...	...
	Tourcoing § a.	...	|	...	1535	...	1636	...	1738	...	...	1838	...	1935	...	|	...	|	...	...	...	...	...	...
	Roubaix § a.	...	|	...	1539	...	1641	...	1743	...	...	1842	...	1939	...	|	...	|	...	...	...	...	...	...
	Lille Flandres § a.	...	1455	...	1552	...	1653	...	1754	...	...	1854	...	1953	...	2055	...	2152	...	...	...	...	...	...

Q – Ⓐ (daily Dec. 9 - May 23, Sept. 29 - Dec. 12).
§ – Frequent services Lille Flandres - Lille Europe - Roubaix and Tourcoing are operated by the Lille *VAL* métro (Line 2) or by tram. For *TGV* trains see Table **250**.
◇ – For additional services between Oostende and Brugge see Tables **400**/**406**.

Engineering work Lille - Tourcoing Apr. 7 - May 29
Trains are replaced by 🚌 between Lille and Tourcoing or Mouscron. Departures from Lille are approximately 30 minutes earlier; arrivals at Lille are 30-40 minutes later.

406 OOSTENDE - GENT - ANTWERPEN

km		Ⓐ	Ⓐ	Ⓐ	Ⓐ	Ⓐ	Ⓐ	ⒶL	Ⓐ	▲	ⒶL	Ⓐ	Ⓐ	Ⓐ	ⒶL	Ⓒ	Ⓒ	Ⓒ	ⒸL	Ⓒ	▲	ⒸL	Ⓒ	ⒸL
0	**Oostende** § d.		...	...	0605	...	0701	...	0805	and	...	2105	...	2205	...		...	0539	...	0639	and	...	2139	...
22	Brugge § d.		...	...	0620	...	0716	...	0820	at the	...	2120	...	2220	...		...	0554	...	0654	at the	...	2154	...
	Kortrijk **405 414** d.		...	0541	|	0637	|	0742	|	same	2043	|	2143	|	2243		0541	|	0643r	|	same	2143	|	2242
62	**Gent Sint-Pieters** § d.		0505	0605	0647	0705	0747	0805	0847	minutes	2105	2147	2205	2247	2305		0605	0620	0705	0720	minutes	2205	2220	2325
89	Lokeren d.		0525	0625	0708	0725	0808	0825	0908	past	2125	2208	2225	2308	2325		0625	0640	0725	0740	past	2225	2240	2344
102	Sint-Niklaas d.		0535	0635	0718	0735	0818	0835	0918	each	2135	2218	2235	2218	2335		0635	0650	0735	0750	each	2235	2250	2353
125	Antwerpen Berchem a.		0549	0649	0734	0749	0834	0849	0934	hour	2149	2236	2250	2336	2349		0649	0707	0749	0807	hour	2249	2307	0012
127	**Antwerpen Centraal** a.		0554	0654	0739	0754	0839	0854	0939	until	2154	2241	2254	2341	2354		0654	0713	0754	0813	until	2254	2313	0017

	Ⓐ	ⒶL	Ⓐ	ⒶL	Ⓐ	ⒶL	Ⓐ	▲	ⒶL	Ⓐ	Ⓐ	Ⓐ	Ⓐ	Ⓒ	Ⓒ	ⒸL	Ⓒ	ⒸL	Ⓒ	▲	ⒸL	Ⓒ	Ⓒ	Ⓒ
Antwerpen Centraal d.		0458	0512	0606	0621	0706	0721	and	2106	2119	2206	2232	2306		0547	0606	0647	0706	0747	and	2106	2147	2206	2306
Antwerpen Berchem d.		0503	0517	0611	0626	0711	0726	at the	2111	2124	2211	2238	2311		0553	0611	0653	0711	0753	at the	2111	2153	2211	2311
Sint-Niklaas d.		0520	0535	0627	0644	0727	0744	same	2127	2144	2227	2304	2327		0612	0627	0712	0727	0812	same	2127	2212	2227	2327
Lokeren d.		0529	0544	0636	0653	0736	0753	minutes	2136	2153	2236	2321	2336		0621	0636	0721	0736	0821	minutes	2136	2221	2236	2336
Gent Sint-Pieters § a.		0548	0603	0655	0715	0755	0813	past	2155	2213	2255	2344	2355		0640	0655	0740	0755	0840	past	2155	2240	2255	2355
Kortrijk **405 414** a.		0609	|	0717	|	0817	|	each	2217	|	2317	...	0029		|	0717	|	0817	|	each	2217	|	2317	0029
Brugge § a.		...	0639	...	0740	...	0840	hour	...	2240	...	...	...		0712	...	0806	...	0906	hour	...	2306	...	...
Oostende § a.		...	0652	...	0755	...	0855	until	...	2255	...	...	...		0726	...	0821	...	0921	until	...	2321	...	...

L – For journeys from/to Lille – see Table **405**.
r – Journey at 06xx departs 0637; journey at 07xx departs 0742 on ⑥.
▲ – Timings may vary by up to 3 minutes on some journeys.
§ – For additional services Oostende - Gent see Table **400**; for additional services Brugge - Gent see Tables **400**/**401**.

407 ANTWERPEN and BRUSSELS - LIER - TURNHOUT and NEERPELT

km		Ⓐ	Ⓐ	Ⓐ	Ⓒ	Ⓐ	Ⓒ	Ⓐ	▲	Ⓐ	Ⓒ	Ⓐ	Ⓒ	Ⓐ	Ⓐ	Ⓒ	Ⓒ	Ⓐ	Ⓐ	Ⓒ	Ⓒ	Ⓐ	Ⓐ	Ⓒ
0	**Antwerpen Centraal** d.	0547	...	0613	0615	0647	0720	...		2013	2015	2047	2120	...	2113	2115	2220	...	2242	2215	2323	...	2334	2315
2	Antwerpen Berchem d.	0553	...	0619	0621	0653	0726	...	and	2019	2021	2053	2126	...	2119	2121	2226	...	2248	2221	2329	...	2340	2321
	Bruxelles Midi/Zuid d.	|	0537	|	|	|	|	0637	at	|	|	|	|	2037	|	|	|	2137	|	|	|	2237	|	|
	Mechelen d.	|	0605	|	|	|	|	0705	the	|	|	|	|	2105	|	|	|	2205	|	|	|	2305	|	|
14	Lier **414** d.	0606	0622	0629	0631	0706	0736	0722	same	2029	2031	2106	2136	2122	2129	2131	2236	2222	2302	2231	2339	2322	2354	2334
34	Herentals **414** d.	0622	0641	0645	0646	0722	0801	0741	minutes	2045	2046	2122	2201	2141	2145	2146	2301	2241	2326	2246	0001	2341	0018	2356
	Turnhout **414** a.	0639	0655	|	|	0738	0815	0755	past	|	|	2138	2215	2155	|	|	2315	2255	|	|	0015	2355	|	|
39	Olen d.	...	...	0650	0651	...	...	...	each	2050	2051	...	...	...	2150	2151	...	...	2331	2251	...	...	0023	0002
46	Geel d.	...	...	0656	0657	...	...	...	hour	2056	2057	...	...	...	2156	2157	...	...	2337	2257	...	...	0029	0008
55	Mol d.	...	...	0708	0708	...	...	...	until	2109	2108	...	...	...	2209	2208	...	...	2345	2308	...	...	0036	0014
79	**Neerpelt** a.	...	...	0726	0726	...	...	...		2126	2126	...	...	...	2226	2226	...	...	0003	2326	...	...	...	...

km		Ⓒ	Ⓐ	Ⓐ	Ⓒ	Ⓐ	Ⓐ	Ⓒ	Ⓐ	Ⓒ	Ⓐ	Ⓒ	Ⓒ	Ⓐ	Ⓐ	Ⓒ	▲	Ⓒ	Ⓐ	Ⓐ	Ⓒ	Ⓒ	Ⓐ	Ⓐ
	Neerpelt d.	...	0434	...	0534	0534	...	...	0631	0634	...	...	0734	0734	...	...		2034	2034	...	...	2134	2134	...
	Mol d.	0456	0457	...	0557	0557	...	...	0655	0657	...	...	0757	0757	...	...	and	2057	2057	...	...	2157	2157	...
	Geel d.	0504	0504	...	0604	0605	...	...	0703	0704	...	...	0804	0804	...	...	at	2104	2104	...	...	2204	2204	...
	Olen d.	0509	0510	...	0609	0610	...	...	0708	0709	...	...	0809	0810	...	...	the	2109	2110	...	...	2209	2210	...
0	Turnhout **414** d.	|	|	0458	|	|	0604	0645	|	|	0704	0745	|	|	0805	0845	same	|	|	2105	2145	|	|	2205
18	Herentals **414** d.	0515	0517	0521	0615	0617	0621	0704	0715	0715	0721	0804	0815	0817	0821	0904	minutes	2115	2117	2121	2204	2215	2224	2221
38	Lier **414** d.	0530	0532	0539	0630	0632	0639	0725	0731	0730	0739	0825	0830	0832	0839	0925	past	2130	2132	2139	2225	2230	2247	2239
55	Mechelen a.	|	|	0555	|	|	0655	|	|	|	0755	|	|	|	0855	|	each	|	|	2155	|	|	|	2255
79	Bruxelles Midi/Zuid a.	|	|	0623	|	|	0723	|	|	|	0823	|	|	|	0923	|	hour	|	|	2223	|	|	|	2323
	Antwerpen Berchem a.	0539	0541	...	0639	0641	...	0734	0741	0739	...	0824	0839	0841	...	0934	until	2139	2141	...	2234	2239	2302	...
	Antwerpen Centraal a.	0545	0547	...	0645	0647	...	0740	0747	0745	...	0840	0845	0847	...	0940		2145	2147	...	2240	2245	2307	...

▲ – Timings may vary by up to 3 minutes on some journeys.

GENT - DE PANNE 409

km			Ⓐ	Ⓐ	▲	Ⓐ		Ⓒ	▲	Ⓒ
	Brussels Nationaal ✈ 402 d.	Ⓐ	...	0552		2052	Ⓒ	...		...
	Brussels Midi/Zuid 401/2 d.		...	0614		2114		0556r		1956r
0	**Gent Sint-Pieters** d.		0552	0652		2152		0652		2052
30	Tielt d.		0617	0716	and	2216		0716	and	2116
47	Lichtervelde d.		0630	0730	hourly	2230		0730	hourly	2130
66	Diksmuide d.		0644	0744	until	2244		0744	until	2144
81	Veurne d.		0655	0755		2255		0755		2155
86	**De Panne** § a.		0701	0801		2301		0801		2201

		Ⓐ	Ⓐ	▲	Ⓐ		Ⓒ	▲	Ⓒ
De Panne § d.	Ⓐ	0456	0558		2059	Ⓒ	0659		2059
Veurne d.		0503	0605		2106		0706		2106
Diksmuide d.		0514	0616		2117		0717		2117
Lichtervelde d.		0534	0633	and	2133		0732	and	2132
Tielt d.		0545	0645	hourly	2145		0745	hourly	2144
Gent Sint-Pieters a.		0609	0709	until	2209		0809	until	2209
Brussels Midi/Zuid 401/2 a.		0646	0746		2246		0904r		2304r
Brussels Nationaal ✈ 402 a.		0708	0808		2308		...		...

r – Via Denderleeuw (Table **401**).

▲ – Timings may vary by up to 3 minutes on some journeys.

§ – Connection available into the **Belgian Coastal Tramway**. See Table **404** for details. De Panne railway station is situated in Adinkerke.

BRUSSELS - ANTWERPEN - ROOSENDAAL 410

For *Thalys* trains Paris - Brussels - Amsterdam and v.v. – see Table 18. Most services to/from Amsterdam convey 🍸.

km			Ⓐ	Ⓐ	Ⓐ	Ⓐ	Ⓐy	Ⓐ	Ⓐ	Ⓐ	Ⓐ	Ⓐ	Ⓐ	Ⓐ	Ⓐ	Ⓐ	Ⓐ	Ⓐ	Ⓐ	Ⓐ	Ⓐ	▲	Ⓐ	Ⓐ
	Charleroi Sud 411 d.	Ⓐ	...	...	...	...	...	0537	...	0607	...	0635	0705	...	0737	...	0807	...	0837	...	0907		...	1737
0	**Brussels Midi/Zuid** d.		0421	0455	0533	0555	0618	0628	0633	0655	0715	0728	0755	0816	0828	0833	0855	0918	0928	0933	0955	and	1818	1828
2	Brussels Central d.		0425	0459	0537	0559	0622	0632	0637	0659	0719	0732	0759	0820	0832	0837	0859	0922	0932	0937	0959	at	1822	1832
4	**Brussels Nord** d.		0430	0504	0542	0604	|	0637	0642	0704	|	0737	0804	|	0837	0842	0904	|	0937	0942	1004	the	|	1837
24	Mechelen **414** d.		0457	0522	0600	0622	0641	0654	0700	0722	0741	0754	0822	0841	0854	0900	0922	0941	0954	1000	1022	same	1841	1854
46	Antwerpen Berchem a.		0520	0537	0619	0637	|	0709	0719	0737	|	0809	0837	|	0909	0919	0937	|	1009	1019	1037	minutes	|	1909
48	**Antwerpen Centraal** a.		0536	0543	0625	0643	0657	0715	0725	0743	0757	0815	0843	0857	0915	0925	0943	0957	1015	1025	1043	past	1857	1915
48	**Antwerpen Centraal** ◧ d.		...	...	...	...	0700	...	...	...	0800	...	...	0900	...	...	...	1000	...	...	...	each	1900	...
89	**Roosendaal** 🏛 ◧ a.		...	...	...	...	0728	...	...	...	0828	...	...	0928	...	...	...	1028	...	...	...	hour	1928	...
	Rotterdam CS 450 a.		...	...	...	...	0806	...	...	...	0906	...	...	1006	...	...	...	1106	...	...	...	until	2006	...
	Amsterdam CS 450 a.		...	...	...	...	0906	...	...	...	1006	...	...	1106	...	...	...	1206	...	...	...		2106x	...

	Ⓐ	Ⓐ	Ⓐx	Ⓐ	Ⓐ	Ⓐx	Ⓐ	Ⓐx	Ⓐ	Ⓐ	Ⓐ	Ⓐ	Ⓐ		Ⓒ	Ⓒ	⑥z	Ⓒ	Ⓒ	Ⓒ	▲	Ⓒ	Ⓒ	Ⓒ
Charleroi Sud 411 d.	...	1807	...	1837	1907	...	2007	...	...	2107	...	2207	...	Ⓒ	...	...	...	0540	...	0640		...	1740	...
Brussels Midi/Zuid d.	1833	1855	1918	1927	1955	2018	2055	2118	2131	2155	2231	2255	2331		0505	0605	0615	0634	0715	0734	and	1815	1834	1915
Brussels Central d.	1837	1859	1922	1931	1959	2022	2059	2122	2135	2159	2235	2259	2335		0509	0609	0619	0638	0719	0738	at	1819	1838	1919
Brussels Nord d.	1842	1904	|	1936	2004	|	2104	|	2140	2204	2240	2304	2340		0514	0614	0624	0643	0724	0743	the	1824	1843	1924
Mechelen **414** d.	1900	1922	1941	1954	2022	2041	2122	2141	2158	2222	2258	2322	0003		0545	0645	0642	0705	0742	0805	same	1842	1905	1942
Antwerpen Berchem a.	1919	1937	|	2007	2037	|	2137	|	2230	2237	2330	2337	0031		0600	0700	|	0716	|	0816	minutes	|	1916	|
Antwerpen Centraal a.	1925	1943	1957	2015	2043	2057	2143	2157	2236	2243	2336	2343	0036		0606	0706	0657	0722	0757	0822	past	1857	1922	1957
Antwerpen Centraal ◧ d.	...	...	2000	...	...	2100	...	2200	...	...	...	...	...		...	...	0700	...	0800	...	each	1900	...	2000
Roosendaal 🏛 ◧ a.	...	...	2028	...	...	2128	...	2228	...	...	...	...	...		...	...	0728	...	0828	...	hour	1928	...	2028
Rotterdam CS 450 a.	...	...	2106	...	...	2206	...	2306	...	...	...	...	...		...	...	0806	...	0906	...	until	2006	...	2106
Amsterdam CS 450 a.	...	...	2206	...	...	2306	...	0006	...	...	...	...	...		...	...	0906	...	1006	...		2106	...	2206

	Ⓒ	Ⓒ	Ⓒ	Ⓒ	Ⓒ		Ⓒ	Ⓒ	Ⓒ	Ⓒ
Charleroi Sud 411 d.	1840	...	1980	...	2040	...	...	2140	...	2240
Brussels Midi/Zuid d.	1934	2015	2034	2115	2134	...	2215	2234	2305	2334
Brussels Central d.	1938	2019	2038	2119	2138	...	2219	2238	2309	2338
Brussels Nord d.	1943	2024	2043	2124	2143	...	2224	2243	2314	2343
Mechelen **414** d.	2005	2042	2105	2142	2205	...	2242	2305	2345	0005
Antwerpen Berchem a.	2016	|	2116	|	2216	...	|	2316	2400	0016
Antwerpen Centraal a.	2022	2057	2122	2157	2222	...	2257	2322	0006	0022
Antwerpen Centraal ◧ d.	...	2100	...	2200	...	...	2300	...	...	...
Roosendaal 🏛 ◧ a.	...	2128	...	2228	...	...	2328	...	...	...
Rotterdam CS 450 a.	...	2206	...	2306	...	...	0006	...	...	...
Amsterdam CS 450 a.	...	2306	...	0006	...	...	0106	...	...	...

		Ⓐ	Ⓐ	Ⓐ	Ⓐ	Ⓐ	Ⓐ	Ⓐ	Ⓐ	Ⓐ
Amsterdam CS 450 d.	Ⓐ	...	...	...	...	...	...	...	...	...
Rotterdam CS 450 d.		...	...	...	...	...	...	...	0555	...
Roosendaal 🏛 ◧ d.		...	...	...	...	...	...	...	0634	...
Antwerpen Centraal ◧ a.		...	...	...	...	...	...	...	0700	...
Antwerpen Centraal d.		0418	0517	0535	0545	0617	0635	0645	0703	0717
Antwerpen Berchem d.		0424	0523	0541	0551	0623	0641	0651	|	0723
Mechelen **414** d.		0455	0540	0602	0608	0640	0702	0708	0721	0740
Brussels Nord a.		0518	0556	0618	0623	0656	0718	0723	|	0756
Brussels Central a.		0523	0601	0623	0629	0701	0723	0728	0738	0801
Brussels Midi/Zuid a.		0527	0605	0627	0632	0670	0727	0732	0742	0805
Charleroi Sud 411 a.		...	0653	...	0723	0753	...	0823	...	0855

	Ⓐ	Ⓐ	Ⓐ	Ⓐ	Ⓐ	Ⓐ	Ⓐ	Ⓐ	Ⓐ	▲	Ⓐ	Ⓐ	Ⓐ	Ⓐ	Ⓐ	Ⓐ	Ⓐx	Ⓐ	Ⓐ	Ⓐx	Ⓐ	Ⓐx	Ⓐ	Ⓐ
Amsterdam CS 450 d.	...	...	0554	...	...	0654	...	...	...		1454	...	...	...	1554	...	1654	...	...	1754	...	1854	...	...
Rotterdam CS 450 d.	...	...	0655	...	...	0755	...	...	...	and	1555	...	...	...	1655	...	1755	...	...	1855	...	1955	...	...
Roosendaal 🏛 ◧ d.	...	...	0734	...	...	0834	...	...	...	at	1634	...	...	...	1734	...	1834	...	...	1934	...	2034	...	...
Antwerpen Centraal ◧ a.	...	...	0800	...	...	0900	...	...	...	the	1700	...	...	...	1800	...	1900	...	...	2000	...	2100	...	...
Antwerpen Centraal d.	0735	0745	0803	0817	0845	0903	0917	0935	0945	same	1703	1717	1735	1745	1803	1817	1903	1917	1924	2003	2017	2103	2117	2124
Antwerpen Berchem d.	0741	0751	|	0823	0851	|	0923	0941	0951	minutes	|	1723	1741	1751	|	1823	|	1923	1930	|	2023	|	2123	2130
Mechelen **414** d.	0802	0808	0821	0840	0908	0921	0940	1002	1008	past	1721	1740	1802	1808	1821	1840	1921	1940	2003	2021	2040	2121	2140	2203
Brussels Nord a.	0818	0823	|	0856	0923	|	0956	1018	1023	each	|	1756	1818	1823	|	1856	|	1956	2020	|	2056	|	2156	2220
Brussels Central a.	0823	0828	0838	0901	0928	0938	1001	1023	1028	hour	1738	1801	1823	1829	1838	1901	1938	2001	2025	2038	2101	2138	2201	2225
Brussels Midi/Zuid a.	0827	0832	0842	0905	0932	0942	1005	1027	1032	until	1742	1805	1827	1833	1842	1905	1942	2005	2029	2042	2105	2142	2205	2229
Charleroi Sud 411 a.	...	0923	...	0953	1023	...	1053	...	1123		...	1853	...	1923	...	1953	...	2053	...	...	2153	...	2253	...

	Ⓐx	Ⓐ	Ⓐ	Ⓐx	Ⓐ	Ⓐ			Ⓒ	Ⓒ	Ⓒ	Ⓒ	Ⓒ	Ⓒ	⑥	Ⓒ	Ⓒ	Ⓒ	▲	Ⓒ	Ⓒ	Ⓒ	Ⓒ	⑥
Amsterdam CS 450 d.	1954	...	...	2054	...	...	...	Ⓒ	...	...	...	...	...	...	0554	...	0654	...		1954	...	2054	...	2154
Rotterdam CS 450 d.	2055	...	...	2155	...	...	...		...	...	...	...	0555	...	0655	...	0755	...	and	2055	...	2155	...	2255
Roosendaal 🏛 ◧ d.	2134	...	...	2234	...	...	...		...	...	...	...	0634	...	0734	...	0834	...	at	2134	...	2234	...	2334
Antwerpen Centraal ◧ a.	2200	...	...	2300	...	...	...		...	...	...	...	0700	...	0800	...	0900	...	the	2200	...	2300	...	0000
Antwerpen Centraal d.	2203	2217	2224	2303	2317	2324	...		0453	0538	0554	0638	0703	0738	0803	0838	0903	0938	same	2203	2238	2303	2354	0003
Antwerpen Berchem d.	|	2223	2230	|	2323	2330	...		0458	0544	0600	0644	|	0744	|	0844	|	0944	minutes	|	2244	|	0000	|
Mechelen **414** d.	2221	2240	2303	2321	2340	0003	...		0523	0557	0623	0657	0720	0757	0820	0857	0920	0957	past	2220	2257	2320	0023	0020
Brussels Nord a.	|	2256	2320	|	2356	0024	...		0546	0617	0646	0717	0736	0817	0836	0917	0936	1017	each	2236	2317	2336	0046	0036
Brussels Central a.	2238	2301	2325	2338	0001	0029	...		0551	0622	0651	0722	0741	0822	0841	0922	0941	1022	hour	2241	2322	2341	0051	0041
Brussels Midi/Zuid a.	2242	2305	2329	2342	0005	0033	...		0555	0626	0655	0726	0745	0826	0845	0926	0945	1026	until	2245	2326	2345	0055	0045
Charleroi Sud 411 a.	...	2353	...	...	0115	...	...		...	0720	...	0820	...	0920	...	1020	...	1120		...	0020	...	...	...

x – Not Dec. 31.
y – Not Dec. 26.
z – Not holidays.

▲ – Timings may vary by up to 3 minutes on some journeys.

◧ – **Additional local services ANTWERPEN - ROOSENDAAL and v.v.**: Journey 50 minutes.
From **Antwerpen Centraal**: 0636⚒, 0736 and hourly until 2136.
From **Roosendaal**: 0737⚒, 0837 and hourly until 2237.

BRUSSELS - CHARLEROI 411

km			Ⓐ	Ⓐ	Ⓐ	Ⓐ	Ⓐ	▲	Ⓐ	Ⓐ	Ⓐ	Ⓐ	Ⓐ	Ⓐ	Ⓐ	Ⓐ	Ⓐ	Ⓐ	Ⓐ	Ⓐ		Ⓒ	Ⓒ		Ⓒ	
	Antwerpen C 410 d.	Ⓐ	...	0517	0545	0617	0645	and	1717	1745	1817	1845	1917	1945	2017	2045	2117	2145	2217	2317	Ⓒ	...	0538		2238	...
0	**Brussels Nord** d.		0525	0558	0625	0658	0725	at the	1758	1825	1858	1925	1958	2026	2058	2126	2158	2226	2258	2358		0535	0619	and	2319	...
2	Brussels Central d.		0529	0602	0629	0702	0729	same	1802	1829	1902	1929	2002	2030	2102	2130	2202	2230	2303	0002		0539	0623	each	2323	...
4	**Brussels Midi/Zuid** d.		0535	0607	0635	0707	0735	minutes	1807	1835	1907	1935	2007	2035	2107	2135	2207	2235	2307	0007		0545	0630	hour	2330	...
33	Nivelles d.		0600	0633	0700	0733	0800	past each	1833	1900	1933	2000	2033	2100	2133	2200	2233	2300	2333	0047		0614	0658	until	2358	...
56	Marchienne-au-Pont d.		0619	|	0719	|	0819	hour	|	1919	|	2019	|	2119	|	2219	|	2319	|	0111		0632	0716		0016	...
59	**Charleroi Sud** a.		0623	0653	0723	0753	0823	until	1853	1923	1953	2023	2053	2123	2153	2223	2253	2323	2353	0115		0636	0720		0020	...

			Ⓐ	Ⓐ	Ⓐ	Ⓐ	Ⓐ	Ⓐ	Ⓐ	Ⓐ	▲	Ⓐ	Ⓐ	Ⓐ	Ⓐ	Ⓐ						Ⓒ	Ⓒ		Ⓒ	Ⓒ
Charleroi Sud d.	...	Ⓐ	0433	0537	0607	0635	0705	0737	0807	0837	and	2107	2137	2207	2237	2307	...	...	...	...	Ⓒ	0540	0640		2240	2327
Marchienne-au-Pont d.	...		0438	0542	|	0640	|	0742	|	0842	at the	|	2142	|	2242	2312	...	...	...	...		0545	0645	and	2245	2332
Nivelles d.	...		0504	0601	0628	0659	0726	0801	0828	0901	same	2128	2201	2228	2301	2336	...	...	...	...		0603	0703	each	2303	2356
Brussels Midi/Zuid a.	...		0548	0625	0653	0723	0751	0825	0853	0925	minutes	2153	2225	2253	2325	0017	...	...	...	...		0629	0729	hour	2329	0036
Brussels Central a.	...		0558	0631	0658	0731	0758	0831	0858	0931	past each	2158	2230	2258	2330	0022	...	...	...	...		0637	0737	until	2337	0041
Brussels Nord a.	...		0602	0635	0702	0735	0802	0835	0902	0935	hour	2202	2234	2302	2334	0026	...	...	...	...		0641	0741		2341	0045
Antwerpen C 410 a.	...		0613	0715	0743	0815	0843	0915	0943	1015	until	2243	2315	2343	*0036*	...	...	...	...	...		0722	0822		0022	...

▲ – Timings may vary by up to 2 minutes on some journeys.

414 LEUVEN - MECHELEN and MECHELEN - GENT - KORTRIJK

km		Ⓐ	Ⓐ		Ⓒ	Ⓐ		Ⓒ	Ⓐ	▲	Ⓒ	Ⓐ	
0	**Mechelen 410** d.	...	...	...	...	0623	...	0705	0723		2205	2223	...
27	Dendermonde d.	0442	0542	...	0631	0644	...	0731	0744	and	2231	2244	...
57	**Gent Sint-P** a.	0506	0606	...	0657	0707	...	0757	0807	hourly	2257	2307	...
57	**Gent Sint-P 405** d.	0507	0608	...	0709	0709	...	0809	0809	until	2309	2309	...
99	**Kortrijk 405 415** a.	0540	0641	...	0742	0745	...	0842	0842		2342	2342	...

	Ⓐ	Ⓐn	Ⓒ	▲	Ⓐ	Ⓒ		Ⓐ	Ⓒ	
Kortrijk 405 415 d.	0415	0512	0518		2118	2118	...	2218	2218	...
Gent Sint-P 405 a.	0447	0546	0551	and	2151	2151	...	2252	2251	...
Gent Sint-P d.	0452	0548	0603	hourly	2153	2203	...	2258	2303	...
Dendermonde d.	0517	0617	0631	until	2218	2231	...	2323	2329	...
Mechelen 410 a.	0537	0637	0655		2237	2255	...	...	...	...

km		Ⓐ	Ⓐ	Ⓐ	Ⓐp	Ⓒ	and	Ⓐ	Ⓒ	Ⓐ	Ⓐ	Ⓒ	Ⓐ
0	Leuven d.	0515	0548	0615	0643	0635	hourly	2115	2135	2148	2215	2235	2248
24	Mechelen a.	0537	0617	0637	0713	0700	until	2137	2200	2217	2237	2300	2317

	Ⓐ	Ⓐ	Ⓐ	Ⓒ	Ⓐ	Ⓐ	and	Ⓐ	Ⓒ	Ⓐ
Mechelen d.	0543	0643	0652	0700	0723	0743	hourly	2243	2300	2323
Leuven a.	0613	0713	0720	0725	0745	0813	until	2313	2325	2345

n – Journeys after 0713 may run up to 5 minutes later.
p – Journeys after 0743 may run xx48.
▲ – Timings may vary by up to 5 minutes on some journeys.

415 BRUSSELS - ZOTTEGEM - KORTRIJK - POPERINGE

km			Ⓐ	Ⓒ	Ⓒ	Ⓐ	Ⓒ	Ⓐy	▲	Ⓒ	Ⓐ	Ⓒ	Ⓐ
0	**Brussels Nord** d.	...	0528	...	...	0632	0725	0732		2125	2132	2225	2232
2	Brussels Central d.	...	0532	...	...	0636	0729	0736		2129	2136	2229	2236
4	**Brussels Midi/Zuid** d.	...	0536	...	0635	0641	0735	0741		2135	2141	2235	2241
26	Denderleeuw d.	...	0553	...	0655	0701	0755	0801	and	2155	2201	2255	2301
46	**Zottegem** d.	...	0609	...	0715	0716	0815	0816		2215	2216	2315	2320
63	Oudenaarde 419 d.	...	0625	...	0729	0728	0829	0828	hourly	2229	2228	2329	2334
89	**Kortrijk 405 414** a.	...	0643	...	0745	0745	0845	0845		2245	2245	2345	2349
89	**Kortrijk** d.	0542	0644	0651	0751	0750	0851	0850	until	2251	2250	...	...
101	Menen d.	0555	0658	0704	0804	0803	0904	0903		2304	2303	...	...
123	**Ieper** d.	0613	0716	0722	0822	0821	0922	0921		2322	2321	...	...
133	**Poperinge** a.	0620	0723	0729	0829	0828	0929	0928		2329	2328	...	...

	Ⓐ	Ⓒ	Ⓒ	Ⓐ	▲	Ⓒ	Ⓐ	Ⓐ
Poperinge d.	0431	...	0531	0531r		2031	2031	2131
Ieper d.	0439	...	0539	0539r		2039	2039	2139
Menen d.	0457	...	0557	0557r		2057	2057	2157
Kortrijk a.	0509	...	0609	0609	and	2109	2109	2209
Kortrijk 405 414 d.	0515	0515	0615	0615		2115	2115	2215
Oudenaarde 419 d.	0533	0532	0632	0633	hourly	2132	2133	2233
Zottegem d.	0545	0547	0647	0646		2147	2146	2246
Denderleeuw d.	0601	0607	0707	0701	until	2207	2201	2305
Brussels Midi/Zuid a.	0619	0625	0725	0719		2225	2219	2323
Brussels Central a.	0624	...	0731	0724		2231	2224	2328
Brussels Nord a.	0628	...	0735	0728		2235	2228	2332

r – 05xx and 06xx journeys depart 5–7 minutes earlier.
y – A change of train is necessary at Kortrijk on 0732 departure from Brussels.
▲ – Timings may vary by up to 4 minutes on some journeys.

417 ANTWERPEN - HASSELT - LIÈGE

km		Ⓐ	Ⓐ	Ⓐ	Ⓐ	▲		Ⓐ	Ⓐ	Ⓐ	
0	**Antwerpen Centraal** d.		...	0531	0631		1931	2031	2131	2231	...
2	Antwerpen Berchem d.		...	0536	0636		1936	2036	2136	2236	...
14	Lier d.		...	0547	0647	and	1947	2047	2147	2247	...
41	Aarschot **401** d.		...	0613	0713	hourly	2013	2113	2213	2315	...
59	Diest **401** d.		...	0625	0725	until	2025	2125	2225	2325	...
80	**Hasselt 401** a.		...	0638	0738		2038	2138	2238	2338	...
80	**Hasselt** d.		0544	0646	0744		2044	2144	...	...	...
107	Tongeren d.		0607	0708	0807		2107	2205	...	...	...
135	**Liège Guillemins** a.		0640	0740	0840		2140	...	...	...	...

	Ⓒ	Ⓒ	Ⓒ		Ⓒ		Ⓒ		Ⓒ	Ⓒ	Ⓒ
Antwerpen Centraal d.		...	...	...	0643	and	1943	...	2043	2143	2243
Antwerpen Berchem d.		...	...	...	0648	at	1948	...	2048	2148	2248
Lier d.		...	...	...	0658	the	1958	...	2058	2158	2258
Aarschot **401** d.		...	...	...	0724	same	2024	...	2124	2224	2324
Diest **401** d.		...	...	...	0737	minutes	2037	...	2137	2241	2337
Hasselt 401 a.		...	...	...	0750	past	2050	...	2150	2256	2350
Hasselt d.		0558	0658	...	0758	each	2058	...	2158	2258	...
Tongeren d.		0618	0718	...	0818	hour	2118	...	2218	2318	...
Liège Guillemins a.		0652	0752	...	0852	until	2152	...	...	...	...

	Ⓐ	Ⓐ	Ⓐ	Ⓐ	Ⓐ	Ⓐ	Ⓐ	▲	Ⓐ	Ⓐ
Liège Guillemins d.		...	...	...	0620	0720	0820		2120	2220
Tongeren d.		...	...	0559	0654	0754	0854		2154	2253
Hasselt a.		...	...	0620	0716	0816	0916	and	2216	2315
Hasselt 401 d.		0400	0522	0622	0722	0822	0922	hourly	2222	...
Diest **401** d.		0416	0536	0636	0736	0836	0936	until	2236	...
Aarschot **401** d.		0429	0552	0652	0752	0852	0952		2252	...
Lier a.		0508	0613	0713	0813	0913	1013		2313	...
Antwerpen Berchem a.		0522	0624	0724	0826	0924	1024		2324	...
Antwerpen Centraal a.		0527	0629	0729	0831	0929	1029		2329	...

	Ⓒ		Ⓒ	Ⓒ		Ⓒ		Ⓒ		Ⓒ	
Liège Guillemins d.		...	...	0608	...	0708	and	2008	...	2108	...
Tongeren d.		...	...	0644	...	0744	at	2044	...	2144	...
Hasselt a.		...	...	0704	...	0804	the	2104	...	2204	...
Hasselt 401 d.		...	0610	0710	...	0810	same	2110	...	2210	...
Diest **401** d.		...	0624	0724	...	0824	minutes	2124	...	2224	...
Aarschot **401** d.		...	0641	0741	...	0841	past	2141	...	2241	...
Lier a.		...	0702	0802	...	0902	each	2202	...	2302	...
Antwerpen Berchem a.		...	0712	0812	...	0912	hour	2212	...	2312	...
Antwerpen Centraal a.		...	0717	0817	...	0917	until	2217	...	2317	...

▲ – Timings may vary by up to 3 minutes on some journeys.

419 GENT - RONSE and GENT - EEKLO

km		Ⓐ	Ⓐ	Ⓐ	Ⓐ		Ⓐ		Ⓐ				Ⓐ		Ⓐ		Ⓐ	Ⓐ	Ⓐ		Ⓐ		Ⓐ	
0	**Gent St-Pieters 400/1** d.	...	0555	0700	0727	0800	0900	1000	1100	...	1200	...	1300	1400	1500	1600	1623	1700	1723	1800	1900	2000	2100	2212
7	De Pinte d.	...	0603	0707	0734	0807	0907	1007	1107	...	1207	...	1307	1407	1507	1607	1630	1707	1730	1807	1907	2007	2107	2220
25	**Oudenaarde 415** a.	...	0625	0728	0757	0828	0928	1028	1128	...	1228	...	1328	1428	1528	1628	1649	1728	1754	1828	1928	2028	2128	2240
25	**Oudenaarde** d.	0540	0629	0738	0759	0838	0938	1038	1138	...	1238	...	1338	1438	1538	1638	1659	1738	1757	1838	1938	2038	2138	...
39	**Ronse** a.	0550	0639	0748	0809	0848	0948	1048	1148	...	1248	...	1348	1448	1548	1648	1709	1748	1807	1848	1948	2048	2148	...

	Ⓐ	Ⓐ	Ⓐ		Ⓐ	Ⓐ		Ⓐ			Ⓐ		Ⓐ		Ⓐ	Ⓐ			Ⓐ		Ⓐ		Ⓐ
Ronse d.	0508	0618	0647	0712	0748	0813	0912	1012	1112	...	1212	1312	1412	1512	1612	1648	...	1712	1812	1912	2012	2112	2202
Oudenaarde a.	0518	0628	0657	0722	0758	0823	0922	1022	1122	...	1222	1322	1422	1522	1622	1658	...	1722	1822	1922	2022	2122	2212
Oudenaarde 415 d.	0523	0631	0706	0731	0804	0831	0931	1031	1131	...	1231	1331	1431	1531	1631	1710	...	1731	1831	1931	2031	2131	2220
De Pinte d.	0543	0652	0727	0752	0826	0852	0952	1052	1152	...	1252	1352	1452	1552	1652	1732	...	1752	1852	1952	2052	2152	2241
Gent St-Pieters 400/1 a.	0549	0658	0734	0758	0833	0858	0958	1058	1158	...	1258	1358	1458	1559	1658	1739	...	1758	1858	1958	2058	2159	2247

km		Ⓐ	Ⓒ	Ⓐ	Ⓐ	Ⓒ	Ⓐ	Ⓐ	Ⓒ	Ⓐ	Ⓐ	Ⓒ	Ⓐ	Ⓐ	Ⓒ	Ⓐ	Ⓐ	Ⓒ	Ⓐ	Ⓐ	Ⓒ	Ⓐ	Ⓐ	Ⓐ	Ⓒ	Ⓐ
0	**Gent St-Pieters 400/1** d.	0636	0626	0711	0842	0826	0942	1042	1026	1142	1242	1226	1342	1442	1426	1542	1642	1626	1742	1759	1826	1842	1942	2042	2026	2142
7	Gent Dampoort d.	0646	0636	0721	0852	0836	0952	1052	1036	1152	1252	1236	1352	1452	1436	1552	1652	1636	1752	1809	1836	1852	1952	2052	2036	2152
27	**Eeklo** a.	0711	0701	0747	0917	0901	1017	1117	1101	1217	1317	1301	1417	1517	1501	1617	1717	1701	1817	1834	1901	1917	2017	2117	2101	2217

	Ⓐ	Ⓐ	Ⓐ	Ⓒ	Ⓐ	Ⓐ	Ⓒ	Ⓐ	Ⓐ	Ⓒ	Ⓐ	Ⓐ	Ⓒ	Ⓐ	Ⓐ	Ⓒ	Ⓐ	Ⓐ	Ⓒ	Ⓐ	Ⓐ	Ⓒ	Ⓐ	Ⓐ	Ⓒ	Ⓐ
Eeklo d.	0541	0626	0712	0717	0750	0842	0917	0942	1042	1117	1142	1242	1317	1342	1442	1517	1542	1625	1717	1741	1842	1917	1942	2042	2117	2142
Gent Dampoort d.	0609	0652	0739	0743	0818	0910	0943	1010	1110	1143	1210	1310	1343	1410	1510	1543	1610	1652	1743	1810	1910	1943	2010	2110	2143	2210
Gent St-Pieters 400/1 a.	0618	0701	0747	0752	0827	0919	0952	1019	1119	1152	1219	1319	1352	1419	1519	1552	1620	1701	1752	1819	1919	1952	2020	2119	2152	2219

422 CHARLEROI - COUVIN

km		Ⓐ	Ⓐ	Ⓒ	Ⓐ	Ⓐ	Ⓒ	Ⓐ	Ⓐ	Ⓒ	Ⓐ	Ⓐ	Ⓐ	Ⓒ	Ⓐ	Ⓒ	Ⓐ	Ⓐ	Ⓒ	Ⓐ	Ⓐ	Ⓐ	Ⓐ	Ⓒ	Ⓐ	
0	**Charleroi Sud 435** d.	0618	0713	0754	0814	0909	0954	1010	1114	1154	1207	1311	1405	1402	1541	1554	1613	1720	1754	1819	1853	1918	1952	1954	2107	2230
18	Berzée d.	0634	0729	0815	0830	0924	1015	1032	1130	1215	1223	1328	1421	1423	1557	1615	1629	1735	1815	1835	1909	1934	2008	2015	2123	2252
22	Walcourt d.	0639	0735	0822	0835	0929	1022	1038	1135	1222	1228	1333	1426	1430	1603	1622	1635	1741	1822	1840	1914	1945	2019	2022	2128	2300
35	Philippeville d.	0652	0750	0837	0847	0941	1037	1052	1147	1237	1242	1346	1438	1445	1615	1637	1641	1753	1837	1852	1929	1957	2025	2037	2141	2314
48	Mariembourg ▲ d.	0706	0800	0847	0858	0952	1047	1103	1155	1247	1252	1356	1449	1455	1625	1647	1700	1803	1847	1902	1939	2007	2035	2047	2151	2324
53	**Couvin** a.	0712	0808	0853	0904	0958	1053	1109	1204	1253	1258	1402	1455	1501	1631	1653	1706	1809	1853	1908	1945	2013	2041	2053	2157	2330

	Ⓐ	Ⓐ	Ⓒ	Ⓐ	Ⓐ	Ⓒw	Ⓐ	Ⓐ	Ⓒ	Ⓐ	Ⓒ	Ⓐ	Ⓐ	Ⓒ	Ⓐ	Ⓐ	Ⓒ	Ⓐ	Ⓒ	Ⓐ	Ⓐ	Ⓐ	Ⓒ	Ⓐ	Ⓐ	Ⓒ	Ⓐ
Couvin d.	0419	0448	0507	0553	0635	0707	0733	0830	0907	1034	1107	1151	1245	1259	1349	1501	1507	1532	1707	1711	1810	1911	1907	2000	2056	2059	2123
Mariembourg ▲ d.	0426	0455	0514	0600	0642	0714	0740	0837	0914	1041	1114	1158	1302	1306	1357	1508	1514	1539	1714	1718	1817	1918	1914	2014	2103	2106	2130
Philippeville d.	0437	0506	0525	0612	0653	0725	0751	0848	0925	1053	1125	1209	1314	1317	1408	1519	1525	1551	1725	1729	1828	1930	1925	2026	2114	2117	2142
Walcourt d.	0451	0518	0539	0626	0705	0739	0806	0900	0939	1105	1139	1221	1326	1331	1420	1531	1539	1603	1739	1741	1841	1942	1939	2038	2128	2131	2156
Berzée d.	0458	0525	0546	0630	0709	0746	0812	0906	0946	1111	1146	1228	1330	1338	1427	1538	1546	1610	1746	1748	1848	1946	1946	2042	2133	2138	2203
Charleroi Sud 435 a.	0519	0540	0606	0645	0725	0806	0827	0922	1006	1126	1206	1243	1345	1358	1442	1553	1606	1625	1806	1803	1903	2002	2006	2057	2154	2158	2224

w – Dec. 14 - June 21, Sept. 5 - Nov. 1.

▲ – Service available on certain dates Mariembourg - Treignes and v.v. Some trains operated by steam locomotive.
Operator: Chemin de Fer à Vapeur des 3 Vallées (CFV3V), Chaussée de Givet 49-51, 5660 Mariembourg. ✆ / fax +32 60 312 440.
Fuller details are shown in our *Tourist Railways* feature annually each July.

BRUSSELS - MONS - QUÉVY, QUIÉVRAIN and TOURNAI — 424

km	Ⓐ	Ⓐ	Ⓐ	Ⓐ	Ⓐ	Ⓐ	Ⓐ	AⒶ	Ⓐ		LⒶp	AⒶn	Ⓐ		LⒶ	AⒶ	Ⓐ	LⒶ	Ⓐ	AⒶ	LⒶ	LⒶ	
0	**Brussels Nord** d.	...	...	...	0453	...	0525	0553	...	...	0625	0653	...		2025	2053	...	2125	...	2153	2225	2325	...
2	Brussels Central d.	...	...	...	0457	...	0529	0557	...	...	0629	0659	...	▲	2029	2057	...	2129	...	2157	2229	2329	...
4	**Brussels Midi / Zuid** d.	...	...	...	0504	...	0534	0604	...	...	0634	0704	...	and at	2035	2104	...	2134	...	2204	2234	2334	...
33	Braine-le-Comte d.	...	...	...	0529	...	0554	0629	...	...	0654	0729	...	the same	2054	2129	...	2154	...	2229	2254	2357	...
39	Soignies d.	...	...	...	0535	...	0600	0635	...	...	0700	0735	...	minutes	2100	2135	...	2200	...	2235	2300	0003	...
64	**Mons** a.	...	...	...	0551	...	0614	0651	...	...	0714	0751	...	past each	2114	2151	...	2214	...	2251	2314	0019	...
64	**Mons 435** d.	...	0502	...	0553	0602	0616	0653	0702	...	0716	0753	0802	hour	2116	2153	2202	2216	2234	...	2316	0020	...
	Quévy a.	...	|	...	0608	|	|	0708	|	...	|	0808	|	until	|	2208	|	|	|	...	|	|	...
74	Saint-Ghislain a.	0432	0513	0532	...	0613	0628	...	0713	...	0730	...	0813		2130	...	2213	2228	2245	...	2328	0031	...
84	Quiévrain a.	0447	|	0547	...	|	0643	...	|	...	0746	...	|		2146	...	|	...	|	...	...	...	...
	Tournai 435 a.	...	0545	...	...	0645	...	...	0745	...	...	...	0845		...	...	2245	...	2315	...	...	...	...

km	Ⓒ	EⒸ	Ⓒ	EⒸ	Ⓒ		EⒸ	Ⓒ	EⒸ
	Brussels Nord d.	0546	...	0647	...		2147	...	2246
	Brussels Central d.	0550	...	0651	...		2151	...	2250
	Brussels Midi / Zuid d.	0554	...	0657	...	and at	2157	...	2254
	Braine-le-Comte d.	0618	...	0718	...	the same	2218	...	2318
	Soignies d.	0624	...	0724	...	minutes	2224	...	2324
	Mons a.	0641	...	0741	...	past each	2241	...	2341
0	**Mons 435** d.	0649	0654	0749	0754	hour	2249	2254	2349
15	Quévy a.	|	|	|	|	until	|	|	|
	Saint-Ghislain a.	0700	0705	0800	0805		2300	2305	2400
	Quiévrain a.	0726	|	0826	|		q	|	...
	Tournai 435 a.	...	0731	...	0831		...	2331	...

Ⓐ	LⒶ	AⒶ	LⒶ	Ⓐ	AⒶ	LⒶ	Ⓐ	AⒶ	LⒶ
Tournai 435 d.	...	...	...	0508	...	...	0608	...	...
Quiévrain d.	...	...	0514	|	...	0614	|	...	0714
St Ghislain d.	0427	...	0531	0547	...	0631	0640	...	0731
Quévy d.	|	0452	|	|	0552	|	|	0650	|
Mons 435 a.	0438	0507	0544	0558	0607	0644	0651	0705	0744
Mons d.	0439	0509	0546	...	0609	0646	...	0707	0746
Soignies d.	0501	0526	0601	...	0626	0701	...	0726	0801
Braine-le-Comte d.	0508	0533	0608	...	0633	0708	...	0733	0808
Brussels Midi / Zuid a.	0526	0556	0626	...	0656	0726	...	0753	0826
Brussels Central a.	0531	0603	0631	...	0701	0731	...	0801	0831
Brussels Nord a.	0535	0607	0635	...	0707	0735	...	0807	0835

	Ⓐ	AⒶ	LⒶ	Ⓐ	AⒶ		LⒶ	Ⓐ	AⒶ	Ⓐ	Ⓐ
Tournai 435 d.	0715	...	...	0815	...		...	2115	...	...	2215
Quiévrain d.	|	...	0814	|	...	▲	2114	|	...	2214	|
St Ghislain d.	0747	...	0831	0847	...	and at	2131	2147	...	2231	2247
Quévy d.	|	0747	|	|	0852	the same	|	|	2152	|	|
Mons 435 a.	0758	0802	0844	0858	0907	minutes	2144	2158	2207	2244	2259
Mons d.	...	0809	0846	...	0909	past each	2146	...	2209	2246	...
Soignies d.	...	0826	0901	...	0926	hour	2201	...	2226	2301	...
Braine-le-Comte d.	...	0833	0908	...	0933	until	2208	...	2233	2308	...
Brussels Midi / Zuid a.	...	0856	0926	...	0956		2226	...	2255	2330	...
Brussels Central a.	...	0901	0931	...	1001		2231	...	2303	2335	...
Brussels Nord a.	...	0907	0935	...	1007		2235	...	2307	2339	...

Ⓒ	EⒸ	EⒸ	Ⓒ	EⒸ	Ⓒ	EⒸ		Ⓒ	EⒸ	Ⓒ
Tournai 435 d.	...	...	0629	...	0729	...		2129	...	2235
Quiévrain d.	...	...	|	...	|	0734		|	2134	|
St Ghislain d.	0500	0600	0655	0700	0755	0800	and at	2155	2200	2301
Quévy d.	|	|	|	|	|	|	the same	|	|	|
Mons 435 a.	0511	0611	0706	0711	0806	0811	minutes	2206	2211	2312
Mons d.	0519	0619	...	0719	...	0819	past each	...	2219	...
Soignies d.	0537	0637	...	0737	...	0837	hour	...	2237	...
Braine-le-Comte d.	0543	0643	...	0743	...	0843	until	...	2243	...
Brussels Midi / Zuid a.	0604	0703	...	0803	...	0903		...	2303	...
Brussels Central a.	0609	0709	...	0809	...	0909		...	2309	...
Brussels Nord a.	0613	0713	...	0813	...	0913		...	2313	...

A – From / to Brussels Nationaal ✈ – see Table **402**.
E – From / to Leuven via Brussels Nationaal ✈ – see Table **402**.
L – From / to Liège – see Table **401**.
n – Variations: Brussels Nord d. 1753; Mons d. 1858; Quévy a. 1913. Brussels Nord d. 1453; Mons d. 1612; Quévy a. 1627.
p – Variations: Brussels Nord d. 1625, Quiévrain a. 1752.
q – Last arrival at Quiévrain is at 2126.
▲ – Timings may vary by up to 4 minutes on some journeys.

BRUSSELS - TOURNAI - MOUSCRON — 425

km		Ⓐ	Ⓐ	Ⓒr	▲	Ⓐ	Ⓒr	Ⓐ	Ⓒ	Ⓐ	Ⓒ
0	**Brussels Nord** d.	0452	0559	0612		2059	2112	2205	2212	2259	2326
2	Brussels Central d.	0456	0603	0616	and	2103	2116	2209	2216	2303	2330
4	**Brussels Midi / Zuid** d.	0501	0608	0621		2108	2121	2214	2221	2308	2334
55	Ath d.	0543	0644	0659	hourly	2144	2159	2249	2259	2344	0012
67	Leuze d.	0552	0653	0708		2153	2209	2258	2308	2353	0021
85	**Tournai** a.	0603	0704	0719	until	2204	2219	2309	2319	0004	0032
85	**Tournai 435** d.	0603	0706	0736r		2206	2236r	2311	2323	...	...
105	**Mouscron 435** a.	0622	0721	0751r		2221	2251r	2326	2338	...	...

	Ⓐ	Ⓐ	Ⓒ	Ⓐ	Ⓒt	Ⓐ	▲	Ⓒt	Ⓒ	Ⓐ
Mouscron 435 d.	...	0437	0524	0537	0609t	0639		2109t	2216	2239
Tournai 435 a.	...	0452	0539	0552	0624t	0654	and	2124t	2231	2254
Tournai d.	0425	0454	0541	0554	0641	0656		2141	2241	2256
Leuze d.	0437	0506	0553	0606	0653	0708	hourly	2153	2253	2309
Ath d.	0449	0516	0603	0616	0703	0718		2203	2303	2318
Brussels Midi / Zuid a.	0529	0552	0639	0652	0739	0752	until	2239	2339	2352
Brussels Central a.	0536	0557	0644	0658	0744	0757		2344	2344	2357
Brussels Nord a.	0540	0607	0648	0707	0748	0807		2348	2348	0001

r – On † Brussels departures 1312 – 2012 depart Tournai at xx22▲, arrive Mouscron xx37▲.
t – On † Brussels arrivals 1648 – 2248 depart Mouscron at xx24▲, arrive Tournai xx39▲.
▲ – Timings may vary by up to 4 minutes on some journeys.

TOURNAI - LILLE — 426

Subject to alteration on Belgian and French holidays

km	Ⓐ		Ⓐ	CⒶ	LⒶ	Ⓐ	LⒶ	LⒶ		LⒶ	LⒶ	LⒶ		LⒶ	Ⓐ	LⒶ	LⒶ	LⒶ	LⒶ		LⒶ	LⒶ	
	Mons **435** d.	...	0539	0629	0734	...	0834	0934	...	1034	1134	1234	...	1434	...	1534	1634	1734	1834	...	1934	2034	...
0	**Tournai** 🏛 § d.	...	0615	0654	0803	0838	0902	1002	...	1102	1220	1259	...	1459	1537	1559	1700	1803	1903	...	2004	2104	...
25	**Lille Flandres** a.	...	0646	0722	0832	0903	0920	1022	...	1120	1248	1328	...	1524	1610	1621	1726	1829	1927	...	2027	2126	...

Ⓒ		C†	C⑥	NⒸ	LⒸ	L⑥	L†	LⒸ	L†	L⑥		L⑥	L†	LⒸ	L†	L⑥	L†	L⑥	LⒸ		LⒸ	LⒸ	LⒸ	LⒸ
Mons **435** d.	...	0654	0654	0754	0854	0954	0954	1054	1154	1154	...	1254	1254	1354	1454	1454	1554	1554	1654	...	1754	1854	1954	2054
Tournai 🏛 § d.	...	0732	0732	0839	0932	1032	1032	1133	1232	1232	...	1334	1336	1432	1532	1532	1632	1632	1732	...	1832	1934	2032	2134
Lille Flandres a.	...	0750	0757	0900	0950	1050	1056	1151	1250	1256	...	1355	1354	1450	1550	1555	1654	1656	1756	...	1850	1957	2053	2152

Ⓐ		LⒶ	Ⓐ	LⒶ	Ⓐ		LⒶ	LⒶ	LⒶ	LⒶ		LⒶ	LⒶ	LⒶ	LⒶ		ⒶL	Ⓐ	LⒶ	LⒶ	LⒶ	LⒶ		
Lille Flandres d.	...	0618	0706	0732	0746	...	0842	0930	1031	1212	...	1341	1440	1534	1630	...	1737	1812	1839	1937	2044	2139	...	...
Tournai 🏛 § a.	...	0643	0735	0758	0814	...	0901	0956	1058	1241	...	1359	1458	1558	1658	...	1801	1840	1857	1958	2101	2158	...	...
Mons **435** a.	...	0726	...	0826	...	...	0926	1026	1126	1326	...	1426	1526	1626	1726	...	1826	...	1926	2026	2126	2226	...	...

Ⓒ	L⑥	L†	L⑥	LⒸ	LⒸ	LⒸ	L⑥	L†	LⒸ	L⑥	L†	LⒸ	L†	L⑥	L†	L⑥	L⑥	L†	L†	L⑥	LⒸ	N†	N⑥	Ⓒ
Lille Flandres d.	0700	0806	0807	0909	1007	1106	1205	1206	1309	1405	1408	1505	1606	1606	1703	1705	1805	1806	1901	1905	2012	2105	2109	2209
Tournai 🏛 § a.	0726	0827	0829	0927	1028	1124	1228	1224	1327	1428	1426	1523	1624	1627	1724	1728	1828	1824	1924	1928	2028	2128	2127	2227
Mons **435** a.	0806	0906	0906	1006	1106	1206	1306	1306	1406	1506	1506	1606	1706	1706	1806	1806	1906	1906	2006	2006	2106	2206	2206	2312

C – From / to Charleroi Sud – see Table **435**. L – From / to Liège – see Table **435**. N – From / to Namur – see Table **435**. § – Ticket point is Blandain.

CHARLEROI - JEUMONT — 427

km		Ⓐ	Ⓐ	Ⓐ	Ⓐ	Ⓐ	Ⓐ	Ⓐ	Ⓐ	
0	**Charleroi Sud 411 435** d.	0519	0710	0912	1012	1221	1610	1714	1812	...
31	**Jeumont** 🏛 a.	0559	0755	0952	1051	1300	1651	1754	1851	...

	Ⓐ	Ⓐ	Ⓐ	Ⓐ	Ⓐ	Ⓐ	Ⓐ	Ⓐ	
Jeumont 🏛 d.	0629	0809	1009	1109	1309	1708	1809	1909	...
Charleroi Sud 411 435 a.	0716	0853	1048	1148	1348	1747	1848	1948	...

Local services also operate within Belgium: Charleroi - Thuin (*15 km*) - Erquelinnes (*29 km*) and v.v.; approximately hourly on Ⓐ, every 2 hours on Ⓒ.

BRUSSELS - LA LOUVIÈRE - BINCHE — 429

km			Ⓐ	Ⓒ	▲	Ⓐ	Ⓒ		Ⓐ	
0	**Brussels Nord** d.	...	0532	0607		2132	2207	...	2232	...
2	Brussels Central d.	...	0536	0611		2136	2211	...	2236	...
4	**Brussels Midi / Zuid** d.	...	0541	0616	and at	2141	2216	...	2241	...
17	Halle d.	...	0552	|	the same	2152	|	...	2252	...
33	Braine-le-Comte a.	...	0604	0637	minutes	2204	2237	...	2304	...
33	Braine-le-Comte d.	...	0605	0639	past each	2205	2239	...	2305	...
52	**La Louvière Centre** a.	...	0622	0656	hour	2222	2256	...	2334	...
55	La Louvière Sud a.	...	0626	0702	until	2226	2302	...	2338	...
64	**Binche** a.	...	0640	0713		2240	2313	...	2350	...

	Ⓐ		Ⓒ	Ⓐ	▲	Ⓒ	Ⓐ	
Binche d.	0520	...	0547	0620		2147	2220	...
La Louvière Sud d.	0534	...	0558	0634		2158	2234	...
La Louvière Centre d.	0538	...	0558	0638	and at	2204	2238	...
Braine-le-Comte a.	0555	...	0621	0655	the same	2221	2255	...
Braine-le-Comte d.	0556	...	0613	0656	minutes	2223	2256	...
Halle d.	0609	...	|	0709	past each	|	2309	...
Brussels Midi / Zuid a.	0619	...	0644	0719	hour	2244	2319	...
Brussels Central a.	0624	...	0649	0724	until	2249	2324	...
Brussels Nord a.	0628	...	0653	0728		2253	2328	...

▲ – Timings may vary by up to 4 minutes on some journeys.

430 BRUSSELS - NAMUR - DINANT and LUXEMBOURG

km																										
												EC 91													EC 97	
		Ⓐ	Ⓒ	Ⓐ	Ⓐ	L	Ⓐ	Ⓐ		L		◆		L		L		L		L		L		L	◆	
0	**Brussels Midi / Zuid** . d.	...	...	...	0533	0603	0609	...	0633	0703	...	0733	...	0803	0833	0903	0933	1003	1033	1103	1133	1203	1233	1303	1309	...
2	Brussels Central .... d.	...	...	...	0537	0607	0613	...	0637	0707	...	0737	...	0807	0837	0907	0937	1007	1037	1107	1137	1207	1237	1307	1313	...
4	**Brussels Nord** .... d.	...	...	...	0542	0612	0618	...	0642	0712	...	0742	...	0812	0842	0912	0942	1012	1042	1112	1142	1212	1242	1312	1318	...
10	Brussels Luxembourg d.	...	...	...	0555	0625	0630	...	0655	0725	...	0755	...	0825	0855	0925	0955	1025	1055	1125	1155	1225	1255	1325	1330	...
33	Ottignies .... d.	...	...	...	0615	0645	|	...	0715	0745	...	0815	...	0845	0915	0945	1015	1045	1115	1145	1215	1245	1315	1345	|	...
48	Gembloux .... d.	...	...	...	0627	0657	|	...	0727	0757	...	0827	...	0857	0927	0957	1027	1057	1127	1157	1227	1257	1327	1357	|	...
65	**Namur** .... a.	...	...	...	0639	0709	0712	...	0739	0809	...	0839	...	0909	0939	1009	1039	1109	1139	1209	1239	1309	1339	1409	1412	...
65	**Namur** .... d.	0542	0611	0618	0641	0711c	0714	0718	0741	0811v	...	0841	...	0911v	0941	1011v	1041	1111v	1142	1211v	1241	1311v	1341	1411v	1414	...
	Dinant 428 .... a.	|	0639	0646	|	0739c	|	0746	|	0839v	...	|	...	0939v	|	1039v	|	1139v	|	1239v	|	1339v	|	1439v	|	...
94	Ciney .... d.	0602	...	...	0701	...	|	...	0801	...	...	0901	...	...	1001	...	1101	...	1201	...	1301	...	1401	...	|	...
117	Marloie .... d.	0617	...	...	0716	...	|	...	0816	...	...	0916	...	...	1016	...	1116	...	1216	...	1316	...	1416	...	|	...
123	Jemelle .... d.	0623	...	...	0723	...	|	...	0823	...	...	0923	...	...	1023	...	1123	...	1223	...	1323	...	1423	...	|	...
155	Libramont **428** .... d.	0646	...	...	0745	...	0811	...	0845	...	...	0945	...	...	1045	...	1145	...	1245	...	1345	...	1445	...	1510	...
201	Arlon .... d.	0719	...	...	0816	...	0840	...	0919	...	...	1016	...	...	1116	...	1219	...	1316	...	1419	...	1521	...	1540	...
229	**Luxembourg** .... a.	0736	...	...	0837	...	0901	...	0940	...	...	1036	...	...	1137	...	1240	...	1337	...	1445	...	1542	...	1600	...

km																										
														EC 295	EC 295											
			L	Ⓐ	Ⓐ		L	Ⓒ	Ⓐ	L	Ⓒ	Ⓐ	L	A	B	Ⓒ	Ⓐ	L	Ⓐ	Ⓐ			L		L	
	Brussels Midi / Zuid . d.	1333	1403	1409	...	1433	1503	1533	1533	1603	1633	1633	1703	1727	1733	1733	1733	1803	1809	...	1833	...	1903	1933	2003	2033
	Brussels Central .... d.	1337	1407	1413	...	1437	1507	1537	1537	1607	1637	1637	1707	1731	1737	1737	1737	1807	1813	...	1837	...	1907	1937	2007	2037
	Brussels Nord .... d.	1342	1412	1418	...	1442	1512	1542	1542	1612	1642	1642	1712	1736	1742	1742	1742	1812	1818	...	1842	...	1912	1942	2012	2042
	Brussels Luxembourg d.	1355	1425	1430	...	1455	1525	1555	1555	1626	1655	1654	1726	1748	1753	1755	1754	1825	1830	...	1855	...	1925	1955	2025	2055
	Ottignies .... d.	1415	1445	|	...	1515	1545	1615	1615	1646	1715	1715	1746	|	|	1815	1815	1845	|	...	1915	...	1945	2015	2045	2115
	Gembloux .... d.	1427	1457	|	...	1527	1557	1627	1629	1659	1727	1729	1758	|	|	1827	1828	1857	|	...	1927	...	1957	2027	2057	2127
	Namur .... a.	1439	1509	1512	...	1539	1609	1639	1640	1710	1739	1740	1810	1832	1832	1839	1840	1909	1912	...	1939	...	2009	2039	2109	2139
0	**Namur** .... d.	1441	1511v	1514	1518	1541	1611v	1641	1642	1711v	1741	1742	1811v	1834	1834	1841	1842	1911v	1914	1918	1941	...	2011v	2041	2111v	2141
27	**Dinant 428** .... a.	|	1539v	|	1546	|	1639v	|	|	1739v	|	|	1839v	|	|	|	|	1939v	|	1946	|	...	2039v	|	2139v	|
	Ciney .... d.	1501	...	|	...	1601	...	1701	1702	...	1801	1802	...	|	|	1901	1902	...	|	...	2001	...	...	2101	...	2201
	Marloie .... d.	1516	...	|	...	1616	...	1716	1717	...	1816	1817	...	|	|	1916	1917	...	|	...	2016	...	...	2116	...	2216
	Jemelle .... d.	1523	...	|	...	1623	...	1723	1725	...	1823	1825	...	|	|	1923	1925	...	1952	...	2023	...	...	2123	...	2223
	Libramont **428** .... d.	1545	...	1611	...	1646	...	1745	1748	...	1845	1848	...	|	|	1945	1948	...	2014	...	2045	...	...	2145	...	2245
	Arlon .... d.	1619	...	1641	...	1722	...	1819	1817	...	1920	1917	...	1956	1956	2019	2017	...	2044	...	2116	...	...	2216	...	2316
	Luxembourg .... a.	1640	...	1703	...	1742	...	1841	...	...	1947	...	...	2016	2016	2041	...	...	2103	...	2137	...	...	2237	...	2342

	L		Ⓐ L	Ⓒ		Ⓐ	Ⓒ		Ⓒ
Brussels Midi / Zuid .. d.	2103	2133	2203	2203	...	2233	2233	...	2333
Brussels Central .... d.	2107	2137	2207	2207	...	2237	2237	...	2337
Brussels Nord .... d.	2112	2142	2212	2212	...	2242	2242	...	2342
Brussels Luxembourg d.	2125	2154	2225	2225	...	2255	2255	...	2355
Ottignies .... d.	2145	2215	2245	2245	...	2315	2315	...	0022
Gembloux .... d.	2157	2227	2257	2257	...	2327	2327	...	0034
Namur .... a.	2209	2239	2309	2309	...	2339	2339	...	0046
Namur .... d.	2211v	2241	2318	...	...	2341	...	...	...
Dinant 428 .... a.	2239v	|	2346	...	...	|	...	...	...
Ciney .... d.	...	2301	...	...	...	0001	...	...	...
Marloie .... d.	...	2316	...	...	...	0016	...	...	...
Jemelle .... d.	...	2323	...	...	...	0022	...	...	...
Libramont **428** .... d.	...	2345	...	...	...	...	...	...	...
Arlon .... d.	...	0019	...	...	...	...	...	...	...
Luxembourg .... a.	...	0040	...	...	...	...	...	...	...

	Ⓐ	Ⓒ	Ⓐ		Ⓐ L	Ⓒ	Ⓐ	Ⓒ	L	Ⓐ	Ⓒ	L
Luxembourg .... d.	...	...	...	...	...	...	...	...	...	0520	...	...
Arlon .... d.	...	...	...	...	...	...	0443	...	...	0543	0546	...
Libramont **428** .... d.	...	...	...	...	...	...	0514	...	...	0614	0615	...
Jemelle .... d.	...	...	0436	...	...	...	0535	...	...	0635	0636	...
Marloie .... d.	...	...	0445	...	...	...	0544	...	...	0644	0645	...
Ciney .... d.	...	...	0501	...	...	...	0600	...	...	0700	0701	...
Dinant 428 .... d.	...	...	|	...	0514	...	|	...	0613x	|	|	0713x
Namur .... a.	...	...	0519	...	0542	...	0618	...	0642x	0718	0719	0742x
Namur .... d.	0411	0436	0521	...	0551	0551	0620	0621	0651	0720	0721	0751
Gembloux .... d.	0432	0449	0535	...	0605	0605	0634	0635	0705	0734	0735	0805
Ottignies .... d.	0452	0500	0547	...	0617	0617	0647	0648	0717	0747	0747	0817
Brussels Luxembourg .... a.	0525	0526	0605	...	0635	0635	0705	0705	0735	0805	0805	0835
Brussels Nord .... a.	0537	0537	0618	...	0648	0648	0718	0718	0748	0818	0818	0848
Brussels Central .... a.	0541	0542	0623	...	0653	0653	0723	0723	0753	0823	0823	0853
Brussels Midi / Zuid .... a.	0545	0546	0627	...	0657	0657	0727	0727	0757	0827	0827	0857

														EC 296												
	Ⓐ	Ⓒ	Ⓐ	Ⓐ	L		L		Ⓐ	Ⓐ	L		L	◆		L		L			L		L		L	
Luxembourg .... d.	0620	0620	...	0658	...	0719	...	0820	...	0858	...	0920	...	1024	...	...	1124	...	1224	...	...	1324	...	1420	...	1520
Arlon .... d.	0643	0646	...	0721	...	0747	...	0846	...	0923	...	0946	...	1046	...	...	1146	...	1246	...	...	1346	...	1446	...	1546
Libramont **428** .... d.	0714	0715	...	0748	...	0815	...	0915	...	0950	...	1015	...	1116	...	...	1215	...	1315	...	...	1415	...	1515	...	1615
Jemelle .... d.	0735	0736	...	0810	...	0836	...	0936	...	|	...	1036	...	1138	...	...	1236	...	1336	...	...	1436	...	1536	...	1636
Marloie .... d.	0744	0745	...	|	...	0845	...	0945	...	|	...	1045	...	1145	...	...	1245	...	1345	...	...	1445	...	1545	...	1645
Ciney .... d.	0800	0801	...	|	...	0901	...	1001	...	|	...	1101	...	1200	...	...	1301	...	1401	...	...	1501	...	1601	...	1701
Dinant 428 .... d.	|	|	0814	|	0814x	|	0914x	|	1014	|	1014x	|	1114x	|	...	1214x	|	1314x	|	...	1414x	|	1514x	|	1614x	|
Namur .... a.	0818	0819	0842	0846	0842x	0919	0942x	1019	1042	1046	1042x	1119	1142x	1218	...	1242x	1319	1342x	1419	...	1442x	1519	1542x	1619	1642x	1719
Namur .... d.	0820	0821	...	0848	0851	0921	0951	1021	...	1048	1051	1121	1151	1221	...	1251	1321	1351	1421	...	1451	1521	1551	1621	1651	1721
Gembloux .... d.	0834	0835	...	|	0905	0934	1005	1035	...	|	1105	1135	1205	1234	...	1305	1335	1405	1435	...	1505	1535	1605	1635	1705	1735
Ottignies .... d.	0847	0847	...	|	0917	0947	1017	1047	...	|	1117	1147	1217	1247	...	1317	1347	1417	1447	...	1517	1547	1617	1647	1717	1747
Brussels Luxembourg a.	0905	0905	...	0930	0935	1005	1035	1105	...	1130	1135	1205	1235	1305	...	1335	1405	1435	1505	...	1535	1605	1635	1705	1735	1805
Brussels Nord .... a.	0918	0918	...	0942	0948	1018	1048	1118	...	1142	1148	1218	1248	1318	...	1348	1418	1448	1518	...	1548	1618	1648	1718	1748	1818
Brussels Central .... a.	0923	0923	...	0947	0953	1023	1053	1123	...	1147	1153	1223	1253	1323	...	1353	1423	1453	1523	...	1553	1623	1653	1723	1753	1823
Brussels Midi / Zuid .. a.	0927	0927	...	0951	0957	1027	1057	1127	...	1151	1157	1227	1257	1327	...	1357	1427	1457	1527	...	1557	1627	1657	1727	1757	1827

					EC 90										EC 96											
	L	†	⚒	Ⓐ	◆	L	†	⚒	Ⓐ	Ⓐ	L		L		◆		L		Ⓐ	Ⓒ	Ⓐ	Ⓒ				
Luxembourg .... d.	...	1620	1620	...	1702	...	1720	1720	...	1758	...	1824	...	1920	1947	...	...	2020	...	...	2124	2124	...	2143	2258	2347
Arlon .... d.	...	1643	1646	...	1723	...	1743	1746	...	1823	...	1846	...	1946	2017	...	...	2046	...	...	2146	2146	...	2203	2320	0016
Libramont **428** .... d.	...	1714	1715	...	1751	...	1814	1815	...	1850	...	1915	...	2015	|	...	...	2115	...	...	2215	2215	...	...	...	...
Jemelle .... d.	...	1735	1736	...	|	...	1835	1836	...	|	...	1936	...	2036	|	...	...	2136	...	...	2236	2235	...	...	...	...
Marloie .... d.	...	1744	1745	...	|	...	1844	1845	...	|	...	1945	...	2045	|	...	...	2145	...	...	2245	...	...	...	...	...
Ciney .... d.	...	1800	1801	...	|	...	1900	1901	...	|	...	2001	...	2101	|	...	...	2201	...	...	2301	...	...	...	...	...
Dinant 428 .... d.	1714x	|	|	1814	|	1814x	|	|	1914	|	1914x	|	2014x	|	|	...	2114x	|	2214	2221	|	...	...	...	...	...
Namur .... a.	1742x	1818	1819	1842	1846	1842x	1918	1919	1942	1946	1942x	2019	2042x	2119	2139	...	2142x	2219	2242	2249	2319	...	...	...	...	...
Namur .... d.	1751	1820	1821	...	1848	1851	1920	1921	...	1948	1951	2021	2051	2121	2141	...	2151	2221	...	...	...	...	...	...	...	...
Gembloux .... d.	1805	1834	1835	...	|	1905	1934	1935	...	|	2005	2035	2105	2135	|	...	2205	2235	...	...	...	...	...	...	...	...
Ottignies .... d.	1817	1847	1847	...	|	1917	1947	1947	...	|	2017	2047	2117	2147	|	...	2217	2247	...	...	...	...	...	...	...	...
Brussels Luxembourg a.	1835	1905	1905	...	1930	1935	2005	2005	...	2030	2035	2105	2135	2205	2222	...	2235	2305	...	...	...	...	...	...	...	...
Brussels Nord .... a.	1848	1918	1918	...	1944	1948	2018	2018	...	2042	2048	2118	2148	2218	2235	...	2248	2318	...	...	...	...	...	...	...	...
Brussels Central .... a.	1853	1923	1923	...	1948	1953	2023	2023	...	2047	2053	2123	2153	2223	2241	...	2253	2323	...	...	...	...	...	...	...	...
Brussels Midi / Zuid .. a.	1857	1927	1927	...	1951	1957	2027	2027	...	2051	2057	2127	2157	2227	2245	...	2257	2327	...	...	...	...	...	...	...	...

◆ – **NOTES** (LISTED BY TRAIN NUMBERS)

90 – VAUBAN – [12] Zürich - Basel - Luxembourg - Brussels.
91 – VAUBAN – [12] Brussels - Luxembourg - Basel - Zürich - Chur.
96 – IRIS – [12] Chur - Zürich - Basel - Luxembourg - Brussels.
97 – IRIS – [12] Brussels - Luxembourg - Basel - Zürich.
296 – JEAN MONNET – Ⓑ: [12] Basel - Strasbourg - Luxembourg - Brussels.

A – JEAN MONNET – ①–⑤: [12] Brussels - Luxembourg - Strasbourg - Basel.
B – JEAN MONNET – ⑦: [12] Brussels - Luxembourg - Strasbourg - Basel.
L – Also conveys on Ⓐ: [12] Brussels - Namur - Liège and v.v. – see Table **435**.

c – Ⓒ only.
v – 7 minutes later on Ⓐ.
x – 7 minutes later on Ⓒ.

431 VERVIERS - SPA

16 km Journey time: 23 minutes

From **Verviers Central**: 0537Ⓐ, 0637Ⓐ, 0647Ⓒ, 0747, 0843Ⓒ, 0847Ⓐ, 0943, 1047, 1147, 1247, 1347, 1447, 1543, 1647, 1747, 1847, 1947, 2043, 2147.

From **Spa**: 0600Ⓐ, 0650Ⓒ, 0700Ⓐ, 0732Ⓐ, 0750, 0850 and hourly until 2150.

All trains continue beyond Spa to Spa-Géronstère (*1 km* from Spa).

ARDENNES LOCAL SERVICES — 432

Additional services operate on Ⓐ at peak times

km			Ⓐ	Ⓐ											Ⓐ		Ⓐ	Ⓐ		Ⓐ	Ⓒ	Ⓐ		Ⓐ			Ⓐ
0	**Libramont 430** d.	...	...	...	0651	0751	0851	0951	1051	1151	1251	1351	1451	1551	...	1651	...	...	1751	1820	1851	1854	1951	...	2051	2151	2251
12	Bertrix d.	0505	0532	0605	0706	0801	0906	1001	1106	1201	1306	1401	1506	1601	1606	1706t	...	1702	1801	1828	1906	1906	2001	2003	2059	2201	2259
	Dinant 430 a.	0608	0635	0708	0809	|	1009	|	1209	|	1409	|	1609	|	1709	1809	...	|	|	...	2009	2009	|	2105	...	|	...
57	Virton d.	...	...	...	...	0833	...	1033	...	1233	...	1433	...	1632	...	...	...	1733	1832	...	...	...	2036	...	...	2231	...
82	Rodange **445** d.	...	...	...	...	0905a	...	1107a	...	1258a	...	1459a	...	1656a	...	...	1750	1808	1858a	...	...	...	2103a	...	...	...	...
85	Athus **445** d.	...	...	...	...	0915a	...	1112a	...	1311a	...	1504a	...	1702a	...	...	1755	1815	1903a	...	...	...	2113a	...	...	...	...
100	**Arlon 430** a.	...	...	...	...	0932a	...	1129a	...	1328a	...	1521a	...	1718a	...	...	1812	1832	1920a	...	...	...	2130a	...	...	...	...

km			Ⓐ	Ⓒ	Ⓐ	Ⓐ										Ⓐ		Ⓐ		Ⓐ			Ⓐ		Ⓐ	Ⓐ	Ⓐ
	Arlon 430 d.	...	...	...	0627	...	0742a	...	0940a	...	1132a	...	1332a	...	1526a	1627	...	...	1727a	...	...	...	1925	1941a	...	2027	...
	Athus **445** d.	...	...	...	0647	...	0801a	...	0958a	...	1150a	...	1352a	...	1549a	1647	...	...	1754a	...	...	...	1942	1958a	...	2050	...
	Rodange **445** d.	...	...	...	0654	...	0808a	...	1007a	...	1207a	...	1407a	...	1607a	1659	...	...	1802a	...	...	...	...	2007a	...	2107	...
	Virton d.	0629	...	...	0725	...	0830	...	1029	...	1229	...	1429	...	1629	1720	...	...	1829	...	...	...	...	2029	...	2129	...
0	**Dinant 430** d.	|	0650	0651	|	0751	|	0851	|	1051	|	1251	|	1451	|	...	1651	1723	|	1825	1851	...	...	|	2051	|	2151
72	Bertrix d.	0701	0755	0801	0758	0854	0901	1001	1101	1201	1301	1401	1501	1601	1701	...	1801	1826	1901	1928	2001	...	...	2101	2154	2201	2254
	Libramont 430 a.	0709	0803	0809	0806	...	0909	1009	1109	1209	1309	1409	1509	1609	1709	...	1809	...	1909	...	2009	...	...	2109	...	2209	...

a – Ⓐ only.

t – Arrive 1659.

LIÈGE - NAMUR - CHARLEROI - TOURNAI — 435

For *Thalys* trains Liège - Paris and v.v. – see Table 17

km		Ⓐ	Ⓐ	L Ⓐ	Ⓐ	L Ⓐ	B Ⓐ	Ⓐ	L Ⓐ	B Ⓐ	Ⓐ	L Ⓐ	▲	B Ⓐ	Ⓐ	L Ⓐ	B Ⓐ	Ⓐ	Ⓐ	B Ⓐ	Ⓐ	Ⓐ	Ⓐ	Ⓐ
0	**Liège Guillemins** d.		...	...	...	...	0501	...	0547	0601	...	0647		1901	...	1947	2001	...	2047	2101	...	2147	2201	2247
29	Huy d.		...	...	...	...	0523	...	0608	0623	...	0708		1923	...	2008	2023	...	2108	2123	...	2208	2223	2307
40	Andenne d.		...	...	...	...	0533	...	|	0633	...	|	and at	1933	...	|	2033	...	|	2133	...	|	2233	2317
59	**Namur** d.		...	...	0449	...	0546	0549	0629	0646	0649p	0729	the same	1946	1949p	2029	2046	2049	2129	2146	2149	2229	2246	2332
76	Jemeppe-sur-Sambre d.		...	...	0504	...	...	0604	|	...	0704	|	minutes	...	2004	|	...	2104	|	...	2204	|	...	2347
81	Tamines d.		...	...	0512	...	...	0612	0648	...	0712	0748	past each	...	2012	2048	...	2112	2148	...	2212	2248	...	2355
96	**Charleroi Sud 422** d.		0419	...	0528	0558	...	0628	0702	...	0728	0802	hour until	...	2028	2102	...	2128	2202	...	2228	2302	...	0010
117	La Louvière Sud d.		0438	...	0547	0615	...	0647	0719	...	0747	0819		...	2047	2119	...	2147	2219	...	2247	2319	...	...
137	**Mons 424** a.		0500	0539	0600	0628	...	0700	0732	...	0800	0832		...	2100	2132	...	2200	2232	...	2300	2332	...	...
185	**Tournai 424 425** a.		0545	0602	0645	0652	...	0745	0757	...	0845	0857		...	2145	2157	...	2245	2315	...	...	...	...	...

	Ⓒ	L Ⓒ	L Ⓒ	L Ⓒ	▲	L Ⓒ	Ⓒ	Ⓒ	Ⓒ
Liège Guillemins d.		...	...	0650		1950	2050	2150	2250
Huy d.		...	...	0713		2013	2113	2213	2313
Andenne d.		...	...	0723	and at	2023	2123	2223	2323
Namur d.		...	0640	0740	the same	2040	2140	2240	2336
Jemeppe-sur-Sambre d.		...	0655	0755	minutes	2055	2155	2255	...
Tamines d.		...	0704	0804	past each	2104	2204	2304	...
Charleroi Sud 422 d.		0621	0721	0821	hour until	2121	2221	2319	...
La Louvière Sud d.		0639	0739	0839		2139	2239	...	...
Mons 424 a.		0652	0752	0852		2152	2252	...	...
Tournai 424 425 a.		0731	0831	0931		2231	2331	...	...

	Ⓐ	Ⓐ	Ⓐ	Ⓐ	B Ⓐ	Ⓐ	Ⓐ	B Ⓐ	Ⓐ	L Ⓐ
Tournai 424 425 d.		...	...	...	...	0508	0600	...	0608	0703
Mons 424 d.		0500	...	...	...	0600	0628	...	0700	0728
La Louvière Sud d.		0515	...	...	...	0615	0643	...	0715	0743
Charleroi Sud 422 d.		0534	...	0600	...	0640	0700	...	0734	0800
Tamines d.		0549	...	0613	...	0655	0713	...	0749	0813
Jemeppe-sur-Sambre d.		0557	...	|	...	0703	|	...	0757	|
Namur d.		0611	0614	0633	0714	0717	0733	0814	0811	0833
Andenne d.		...	0627	|	0728	...	|	0828	...	|
Huy d.		...	0639	0654	0739	...	0754	0839	...	0854
Liège Guillemins a.		...	0659	0713	0759	...	0813	0859	...	0913

	B Ⓐ	Ⓐ	L Ⓐ	▲	B Ⓐ	Ⓐ	L Ⓐ	B Ⓐ	Ⓐ	L Ⓐ	Ⓐ	Ⓐ	
Tournai 424 425 d.	...	0715	0803		...	2015	2103	...	2115	2203	2215	2303	...
Mons 424 d.	...	0800	0828		...	2059	2128	...	2200	2228	2259	2328	...
La Louvière Sud d.	...	0815	0843	and at	...	2113	2143	...	2215	2243	...	2343	...
Charleroi Sud 422 d.	...	0834	0900	the same	...	2138	2200	...	2234	2300	...	2358	...
Tamines d.	...	0849	0913	minutes	...	2153	2213	...	2249	2316	...	...	...
Jemeppe-sur-Sambre d.	...	0857	|	past each	...	2201	|	...	2257	2324	...	...	...
Namur d.	0914	0918q	0933	hour until	2214	2215q	2233	2314	2311	2340	...	...	...
Andenne d.	0928	...	|		2227	...	|	2327	...	2354	...	...	...
Huy d.	0939	...	0954		2239	...	2254	2339	...	0005	...	...	...
Liège Guillemins a.	0959	...	1013		2259	...	2313	2359	...	0025	...	...	...

	Ⓒ	Ⓒ	Ⓒ	Ⓒ	L Ⓒ	L Ⓒ	▲	L Ⓒ	L Ⓒ	L Ⓒ
Tournai 424 425 d.		...	...	0629	0729	0829		2029	2129	2235
Mons 424 d.		...	0608	0708	0808	0908		2108	2208	2312
La Louvière Sud d.		...	0622	0722	0822	0922	and at	2122	2222	...
Charleroi Sud 422 d.		...	0641	0741	0841	0941	the same	2141	2241	...
Tamines d.		...	0657	0757	0857	0957	minutes	2157	2257	...
Jemeppe-sur-Sambre d.		...	0706	0806	0906	1006	past each	2206	2306	...
Namur d.		0624	0724	0824	0924	1024	hour until	2224	2320	...
Andenne d.		0638	0738	0838	0938	1038		2238	...	...
Huy d.		0648	0748	0848	0948	1048		2248	...	...
Liège Guillemins a.		0710	0810	0910	1010	1110		2310	...	...

B – From/to Brussels – see Table **430**.
L – Most journeys run from/to Lille – see Table **426**.

p – Variations: Namur depart 0842, 0942, 1042, 1142, 1242, 1342, 1442.
q – Variations: Namur arrive 1611, 1711, 1811, 1911, 2011, 2111.

▲ – Timings may vary by up to 3 minutes on some journeys.

LIÈGE - LUXEMBOURG — 439

km									Ⓐ			
0	**Liège Guillemins** d.	0718	0918	1118	1318	1518	1618	1718	1829	1918	2118	2318
23	Rivage d.	0740	0940	1140	1340	1540	1642	1740	1900	1940	2140	2343
31	Aywaille d.	0748	0948	1148	1348	1548	1651	1748	1912	1948	2148	2352
58	Trois-Ponts d.	0811	1011	1211	1411	1611	1719	1811	1936	2011	2211	0015
70	Vielsalm d.	0823	1023	1223	1423	1623	1730	1823	1948	2023	2223	0027
81	**Gouvy** 🏛 d.	0835	1035	1235	1435	1635	1740	1835	1958	2035	2235	0036
91	Troisvierges **445** d.	0846	1046	1246	1446	1646	...	1846	...	2046	2246	...
99	Clervaux **445** d.	0854	1054	1254	1454	1654	...	1854	...	2054	2254	...
114	Kautenbach **445** d.	0908	1108	1308	1508	1708	...	1908	...	2108	2310	...
129	Ettelbruck **445** d.	0921	1121	1321	1521	1721	...	1921	...	2121	2322	...
141	Mersch **445** d.	0932	1132	1332	1532	1732	...	1932	...	2132	2332	...
160	**Luxembourg 445** a.	0945	1145	1345	1545	1745	...	1945	...	2145	2345	...

	Ⓐ	Ⓒ	Ⓐ								
Luxembourg 445 d.	...	...	...	0715	0915	1115	1315	1515	1715	1915	2115
Mersch **445** d.	...	...	...	0730	0930	1130	1330	1530	1730	1930	2130
Ettelbruck **445** d.	...	...	...	0741	0941	1141	1341	1541	1741	1941	2141
Kautenbach **445** d.	...	...	...	0753	0953	1153	1353	1553	1753	1953	2153
Clervaux **445** d.	...	...	...	0807	1007	1207	1407	1607	1807	2007	2207
Troisvierges **445** d.	...	...	...	0817	1017	1217	1417	1617	1817	2017	2217
Gouvy 🏛 d.	0607	0627	0703	0827	1027	1227	1427	1627	1827	2027	2227
Vielsalm d.	0618	0638	0713	0838	1038	1238	1438	1638	1838	2038	2238
Trois-Ponts d.	0631	0650	0726	0850	1050	1250	1450	1650	1850	2050	2250
Aywaille d.	0654	0713	0749	0913	1113	1313	1513	1713	1913	2113	2313
Rivage d.	0702	0721	0757	0921	1121	1321	1521	1721	1921	2121	2321
Liège Guillemins a.	0731	0742	0820	0942	1142	1342	1542	1742	1942	2142	2342

Additional journeys on Ⓐ: **Gouvy - Liège and v.v.**: 0509 from Gouvy, 1750 from Liège;
Gouvy - Luxembourg and v.v.: 0542, 0642 from Gouvy, 1615, 1815 from Luxembourg.

LUXEMBOURG – summary of services — 445

In principle, services shown below operate at the same minutes past each hour between 0800 and 2000, but variations are possible.
Only principal stations are listed, and additional services are available at peak times.

Luxembourg (xx15) → Mersch (xx30) → Ettelbruck (xx41) → Kautenbach (xx53) → Clervaux (xx07) → Troisvierges (xx15).

Luxembourg (xx20, also xx50⚒) → Bettembourg (xx31, also xx01⚒) → Noertzange (xx36, also xx06⚒) → Esch-sur-Alzette (xx44, also xx14⚒) → Pétange (xx06, also xx36⚒) → Rodange (xx12, also xx42⚒) → Athus (xx17).

Luxembourg (xx50, also xx20⚒) → Mersch (xx11, also xx41⚒) → Ettelbruck (xx28, also xx55⚒) → Kautenbach (xx42) → Wiltz (xx55).

Luxembourg (xx26) → Pétange (xx49) → Rodange (xx54).

Luxembourg (xx52) → Wasserbillig (xx32).

Luxembourg (xx47) → Kleinbettingen (xx05).

Bettembourg (xx34, also xx04⚒) → Dudelange-Centre (xx41, also xx11⚒) → Volmerange-les-Mines (xx48⚒, xx18⚒).

Ettelbruck (xx32⚒, xx43†, also xx10⚒) → Diekirch (xx37⚒, xx48†, also xx15⚒).

Troisvierges (xx45) → Clervaux (xx54) → Kautenbach (xx08) → Ettelbruck (xx21) → Mersch (xx32) → **Luxembourg** (xx45).

Athus (xx43) → Rodange (xx48, also xx18⚒) → Pétange (xx54, also xx24⚒) → Esch-sur-Alzette (xx18, also xx48⚒) → Noertzange (xx25, also xx55⚒) → Bettembourg (xx30, also xx00⚒) → **Luxembourg** (xx40, also xx10⚒).

Wiltz (xx05) → Kautenbach (xx19) → Ettelbruck (xx35, also xx05⚒) → Mersch (xx49, also xx19⚒) → **Luxembourg** (xx10, also xx40⚒).

Rodange (xx05) → Pétange (xx11) → **Luxembourg** (xx34).

Wasserbillig (xx27) → **Luxembourg** (xx08).

Kleinbettingen (xx15) → **Luxembourg** (xx33).

Volmerange-les-Mines (xx12⚒, xx42⚒) → Dudelange-Centre (xx18, also xx48⚒) → Bettembourg (xx26, also xx56⚒).

Diekirch (xx12†, xx23⚒, also xx45⚒) → Ettelbruck (xx17†, xx28⚒, also xx50⚒).

NETHERLANDS

SEE MAP PAGE 238

Operator: **NS** – Nederlandse Spoorwegen (www.ns.nl) – unless otherwise indicated.

Services: Trains convey first- and second-class seated accommodation, unless otherwise indicated in the tables. Some trains consist of portions for two or more destinations, and passengers should be careful to join the correct part of the train. The destination of each train portion is normally indicated beside the entrance doors. Train numbers of internal services are not announced or displayed on stations and are therefore not indicated in these tables. Sleeping cars (🛏) and couchettes (▬) are conveyed on international night trains only.

Validity: **December 14, 2008 - December 12, 2009.**

Holidays: Unless otherwise indicated, services marked ⚒ do not run on ⑦ or on Dec. 25, Jan. 1;
those marked Ⓐ do not run on ⑥⑦ or on Dec. 25, 26, Jan. 1, Apr. 13, 30, May 21, June 1;
those marked † run on ⑦ and on Dec. 25, Jan. 1;
those marked Ⓒ run on ⑥⑦ and on Dec. 25, 26, Jan. 1, Apr. 13, 30, May 21, June 1.
No trains, other than international services, will run between ± 2000 hours on Dec. 31 and ± 0100 on Jan. 1.

Tickets: There are ticket offices at all main stations. In addition, tickets to all destinations within the Netherlands are available from the ticket machines situated on every station. Tickets not bearing a pre-printed date must be date-stamped in the validating machines at platform entrances. Access to station platforms is strictly limited to persons in possession of a valid travel ticket, and high penalty fares are therefore charged for tickets bought from the conductor on board trains.

Reservations: Seat reservations are available only on international trains to, from, or via France and Germany

450 AMSTERDAM - DEN HAAG - ROTTERDAM - VLISSINGEN

For INTERNATIONAL TRAINS **Amsterdam** – **Brussels** – **Paris**, see Table **18**   For NIGHT NETWORK **Utrecht** – **Amsterdam** – **Rotterdam**, see Table **454**

km		H	G				Ⓐ	Ⓐ	⑥k	Ⓐ	L B	Ⓐ	Ⓐ	⚒	Ⓐ	Ⓐ	†	L B	⚒	Ⓐ	⚒		Ⓐ	Ⓐ⚡	
0	**Amsterdam** Centraal ... **458** d.	0010	0010	0028	0030	0132	...	...	...	...	...	...	...	0529	0539	0541	0545	0554	...	0559	0608	...	0611	0645	0629
5	Amsterdam Sloterdijk ... **458** d.	0016	0016	0034	0038	0139	...	...	...	...	...	...	...	|	0545	0548	|	|	...	|	0614	...	0617	|	|
17	**Schiphol** ✈ .... **457 458** d.	|	|	|	0051	|	...	...	...	...	...	...	...	0545	|	0601	0603	0610u	...	0613	|	...	0628	0702	0643
	Haarlem .... d.	0028	0029r	0044	|	0158	...	...	...	...	...	...	...	|	0559	|	|	|	...	|	0628	...	|	|	|
44	Leiden Centraal .... **457** d.	0048	0114e	...	0111	...	...	...	...	...	...	...	...	0605	0618	0620	0622	|	...	0634	0648	...	0650	|	0704
59	Den Haag Centraal .... a.	|	|	...	0126	...	...	...	...	...	...	...	...	|	|	0632	|	|	...	|	|	...	0702	|	|
	Den Haag Centraal ... **472** d.	|	|	...	...	...	...	...	...	0458	...	...	0528	|	|	...	|	*0628*	...	|	|	...	...	|	|
60	**Den Haag** HS .... **472** d.	0101	0142	...	...	...	...	...	...	0503	...	...	0533	0616	0631	...	0638	0635	...	0646	0701	...	...	|	0716
68	Delft .... **472** d.	0112	0155	...	...	...	...	...	...	0515	...	...	0549	|	0638	...	0648	|	...	|	0708	...	...	|	|
82*	**Rotterdam** Centraal ..... **472** d.	0128	0210	...	...	...	...	0448	0518	0533	0555	...	0604	0633	0653	...	0659	0655	...	0703	0723	0723	...	0728	0733
89	Rotterdam Lombardijen .... d.	...	...	...	...	...	...	0458	0528	0643	|	...	0614	|	0701	...	...	|	...	|	0731	0731	...	...	|
102	Dordrecht .... **472** d.	...	...	...	...	...	...	0515	0543	0557	0609	...	0628	0647	0715	...	...	0709	...	0716	0743	0743	...	...	0747
132	**Breda** .... **472** a.	...	...	...	...	...	...	0555t	0610	|	|	...	|	|	0740	...	...	|	...	...	0810	0810	...	...	|
140	**Roosendaal** .... a.	...	...	...	...	...	...	...	...	0626	0632	...	0658	0712	...	...	...	0732	...	...	...	...	...	...	0812
140	**Roosendaal** .... d.	...	...	...	...	...	0616	...	...	0629	...	0646	0700	0716	...	...	...	...	0746	...	...	...	...	...	0816
153	Bergen op Zoom .... a.	...	...	...	...	...	0625	...	...	0641	...	0655	0710	0725	...	...	...	...	0755	...	...	...	...	...	0825
190	Goes .... a.	...	...	...	...	...	0655	...	...	...	...	0722	...	0747	...	...	...	...	0822	...	...	...	...	...	0847
209	Middelburg .... a.	...	...	...	...	...	0709	...	...	...	...	0735	...	0758	...	...	...	...	0835	...	...	...	...	...	0858
215	**Vlissingen** .... a.	...	...	...	...	...	0718	...	...	...	...	0745	...	0808	...	...	...	...	0845	...	...	...	...	...	0908

		⚒	B				⚒	Ⓐ⚡		△		B						Ⓐ⚡				B		
Amsterdam Centraal .... **458** d.	0640	0641	0654	...	0659	0710	0711	0745	0729	0740	0741	0754	...	0759	0810	0811	and at the same minutes past each hour until	2045	2029	2040	2041	2054	...	2059
Amsterdam Sloterdijk .... **458** d.	0646	0647	|	...	|	0716	0717	|	|	0746	0747	|	...	|	0816	0817		|	|	2046	2047	|	...	|
Schiphol ✈ .... **457 458** d.	|	0658	0710u	...	0713	|	0728	0802	0743	|	0758	0810u	...	0813	|	0828		2102	2043	|	2058	2110u	...	2113
Haarlem .... d.	0658	|	|	...	|	0728	|	|	|	0758	|	|	...	|	0828	|		|	|	2058	|	|	...	|
Leiden Centraal .... **457** d.	0718	0720	|	...	0734	0748	0750	|	0804	0818	0820	|	...	0834	0848	0850		|	2104	2118	2120	|	...	2134
Den Haag Centraal .... a.	|	0732	|	...	|	|	0802	|	|	|	0832	|	...	|	|	0902		|	|	|	2132	|	...	|
Den Haag Centraal .... **472** d.	|	...	*0728*	...	|	|	...	|	|	|	...	*0828*	...	|	|	...		|	|	|	...	*2128*	...	|
Den Haag HS .... **472** d.	0731	...	0735	...	0746	0801	...	|	0816	0831	...	0835	...	0846	0901	...		|	2116	2131	...	2135	...	2146
Delft .... **472** d.	0738	...	|	...	|	0808	...	|	|	0838	...	|	...	|	0908	...		|	|	2138	...	|	...	|
Rotterdam Centraal ..... **472** d.	0753	...	0755	...	0803	0823	...	0828	0833	0853	...	0855	...	0903	0923	...		2128	2133	2153	...	2155	...	2203
Rotterdam Lombardijen .... d.	0801	...	|	...	|	0831	...	...	|	0901	...	|	...	|	0931	...		...	|	2201	...	|	...	|
Dordrecht .... **472** d.	0815	...	0809	...	0816	0843	...	...	0847	0911	...	0909	...	0916	0943	...		...	2147	2211	...	2209	...	2216
Breda .... **472** a.	0840a	...	|	...	...	0910	...	...	|	...	...	|	...	...	1010	...		...	|	...	...	|	...	...
Roosendaal .... a.	...	...	0832	...	...	...	...	...	0912	...	...	0932	...	...	...	...		...	2212	...	...	2232	...	...
Roosendaal .... d.	...	...	...	0846	...	...	...	...	0916	...	...	...	0946	...	...	...		...	2216	...	...	...	2246	...
Bergen op Zoom .... a.	...	...	...	0855	...	...	...	...	0925	...	...	...	0955	...	...	...		...	2225	...	...	...	2255	...
Goes .... a.	...	...	...	0922	...	...	...	...	0947	...	...	...	1022	...	...	...		...	2247	...	...	...	2322	...
Middelburg .... a.	...	...	...	0935	...	...	...	...	0958	...	...	...	1035	...	...	...		...	2258	...	...	...	2335	...
Vlissingen .... a.	...	...	...	0945	...	...	...	...	1008	...	...	...	1045	...	...	...		...	2308	...	...	...	2345	...

			Ⓐ⚡		†			⑥B				Ⓐ⚡							⑤⑥f	②⑦	E	C	D	H	C
Amsterdam Centraal .... **458** d.	2110	2111	2145	2129	2129	2140	2141	2154	2159	2210	2211	2245	2229	2240	2241	2259	2310	2311	2329	2329	2329	2340	2339	...	2341
Amsterdam Sloterdijk .... **458** d.	2116	2117	|	|	|	2146	2147	|	|	2216	2217	|	|	2246	2247	|	2316	2317	|	|	|	2346	2345	...	2347
Schiphol ✈ .... **457 458** d.	|	2128	2202	2143	2143	|	2158	2210u	2213	|	2228	2302	2243	|	2258	2313	|	2328	2343	2343	2343	|	|	...	2358
Haarlem .... d.	2128	|	|	|	|	2158	|	|	|	2228	|	|	|	2258	|	|	2328	|	|	|	|	2358	2355	...	|
Leiden Centraal .... **457** d.	2148	2150	|	2204	2204	2218	2220	|	2234	2248	2250	|	2304	2318	2320	2334	2348	2350	0004	0004	0004	0018	0022	...	0021
Den Haag Centraal .... a.	|	2202	|	|	|	|	2232	|	|	|	2302	|	|	|	2332	|	|	0002	|	|	|	|	|	...	0032
Den Haag Centraal .... **472** d.	|	...	|	|	|	|	...	*2228*	|	|	...	|	|	|	...	|	|	...	|	|	|	|	*0028*	0028	...
Den Haag HS .... **472** d.	2201	...	|	2216	2216	2231	...	2235	2246	2301	...	|	2316	2331	...	2346	0001	...	0016	0016	0016	0031	0042	0042	...
Delft .... **472** d.	2208	...	|	|	|	2238	...	|	|	2308	...	|	|	2338	...	|	0008	...	|	|	|	0038	0057	0057	...
Rotterdam Centraal ..... **472** d.	2223	...	2228	2233	2233	2253	...	2255	2303	2323	...	2328	2333	2353	...	0003	0023	...	0035	0035	0043	0050	0113	0115	...
Rotterdam Lombardijen .... d.	2231	...	...	|	|	2301	...	|	|	2331	...	...	|	0001	...	|	0031	...	|	0046	0052	...	0123	0124	...
Dordrecht .... **472** d.	2243	...	...	2247	2247	2311	...	2309	2316	2343	...	...	2347	0011	...	0018	0043	...	0048	0101	0107	...	0140	0142	...
Breda .... **472** a.	2310	...	...	|	|	...	...	|	...	0010	...	...	|	...	...	0034n	0110	...	|	|	|	...	...	...	...
Roosendaal .... a.	...	...	...	2312	2312	...	...	2332	...	...	...	...	0017	...	...	...	...	...	*0137*	0140	0147	...	...	...	...
Roosendaal .... d.	...	...	...	2316	2316	...	...	...	...	...	...	...	...	...	...	...	...	...	...	...	...	...	...	...	...
Bergen op Zoom .... a.	...	...	...	2325	2325	...	...	...	...	...	...	...	...	...	...	...	...	...	...	...	...	...	...	...	...
Goes .... a.	...	...	...	...	2347	...	...	...	...	...	...	...	...	...	...	...	...	...	...	...	...	...	...	...	...
Middelburg .... a.	...	...	...	...	2358	...	...	...	...	...	...	...	...	...	...	...	...	...	...	...	...	...	...	...	...
Vlissingen .... a.	...	...	...	...	0008	...	...	...	...	...	...	...	...	...	...	...	...	...	...	...	...	...	...	...	...

B – To Brussels (Table **410**).
C – ⑤⑥⑦ (also Dec. 25, Jan. 1, Apr. 13, 30, May 21, June 1).
D – ①–④ (not Dec. 25, Jan. 1, Apr. 13, 30, May 21, June 1).
E – ①③④ (not Dec. 25, Jan. 1, Apr. 13, 30, May 21, June 1).
G – ②–⑤ (not Dec. 26, Jan. 2, Apr. 14, May 1, 22, June 2).
H – ①⑥⑦ (also Dec. 26, Jan. 2, Apr. 14, May 1, 22, June 2).
L – ①–⑥ (not Dec. 25, 26, Jan. 1, Apr. 13, May 1, 21, June 1, July 21, Aug. 15, Nov. 11).

a – Ⓐ only.
e – Arrives 0102.
f – Also Apr. 13, 30, May 21, June 1.
k – Also Dec. 26, Apr. 13, 30, May 21, June 1.
n – Mornings of ⑤⑥⑦ only.
r – 0038 on ④⑤.
t – 0540 on ①④⑤.
u – Stops to pick up only.

△ – On Ⓐ the services from Amsterdam at 1340, 1440, 1540 and 1640 continue to Breda (arriving 1540, 1640, 1740 and 1840 respectively).
* – Amsterdam Centraal - Rotterdam Centraal via the high-speed line is 70 km.
⚡ – Via high-speed line. Supplement payable. **Expected to start running from July 2009 (to be confirmed).**

451 AMSTERDAM - SCHIPHOL ✈ all trains

From Amsterdam Centraal *17 km*

0002, 0030, 0045, 0145, 0245, 0345, 0445, 0502 **S**, 0505 **T**, 0529 ⚒, 0541 Ⓐ, 0545 †, 0559 Ⓐ, 0602, 0611 Ⓐ, 0629, 0632, 0641 ⚒, 0659, 0702, 0711 ⚒, 0729, 0732, 0741, 0759; then 0802–2329 at 02, 11, 29, 32, 41 and 59 minutes past each hour; 2341 **C**.

From Schiphol ✈ Journey time: 13–23 minutes

0008, 0018, 0029 **H**, 0100, 0200, 0300, 0400, 0500, 0537 Ⓒ, 0600, 0607, 0624 Ⓐ, 0629 Ⓐ, 0637, 0648, 0659 Ⓐ, 0707, 0716, 0729 ⚒, 0737, 0746, 0759 ⚒; then 0807–2329 at 07, 16, 29, 37, 46 and 59 minutes past each hour; 2346, 2359.

C – ⑤⑥⑦ (also Dec. 25, Jan. 1, Apr. 13, 30, May 21, June 1).
H – ①⑥⑦ (also Dec. 26, Jan. 2, Apr. 14, May 1, 22, June 2).

S – ①⑥ (also Dec. 26, Apr. 30, May 21).
T – ②–⑤ (not Dec. 25, 26, Jan. 1, Apr. 30, May 21).

VLISSINGEN - ROTTERDAM - DEN HAAG - AMSTERDAM 450

For INTERNATIONAL TRAINS **Paris – Brussels – Amsterdam**, see Table **18**   For NIGHT NETWORK **Rotterdam – Amsterdam – Utrecht**, see Table **454**

km		Ⓐ	Ⓐ		Ⓐ⚡		Ⓐ	⚒	⚒	Ⓐ		⚒	⚒	Ⓐ		Ⓐ⚡	⚒		Ⓐ				⚒	Ⓐ	
	Vlissingen d.	...	...	...	...	...	...	...	...	...	...	...	...	...	...	...	...	...	0545	...	...	...	0614	0614	...
	Middelburg d.	...	...	...	...	...	...	...	...	...	...	...	...	...	...	...	...	...	0552	...	...	...	0621	0621	...
	Goes d.	...	...	...	...	...	...	...	...	...	...	...	...	...	...	...	...	...	0605	...	...	...	0634	0634	...
	Bergen op Zoom d.	...	...	...	...	...	...	...	...	0534	...	...	...	0604	...	...	...	...	0632	...	...	...	0705	0705	...
	Roosendaal a.	...	...	...	...	...	...	...	...	0544	...	...	...	0614	...	...	...	...	0644	...	...	...	0716	0716	...
	Roosendaal d.	...	...	...	...	...	...	...	...	0547	...	...	...	0617	...	...	...	...	0647	...	...	...	...	0718	...
0	**Breda** 472 d.	...	...	...	...	...	...	...	...	|	...	...	0550a	|	...	...	...	0620v	|	...	...	0650a	...	|	...
29	Dordrecht 472 d.	*0436*	...	...	...	...	...	0537	...	0612	...	...	0622a	0643	0643	...	...	0652v	0712	0712	...	0722a	...	0742	0742
42	Rotterdam Lombardijen d.	*0449*	...	...	...	...	...	0550	...	|	...	...	0630a	|	|	...	...	0700v	|	|	...	0730a	...	|	|
49	**Rotterdam** Centraal 472 d.	0528	...	0532	0602	0558	...	0602	0611	0628	0628	...	0641	0658	0658	0702	...	0711	0728	0728	...	0741	...	0758	0758
64	Delft 472 d.	|	...	0547	|	|	...	0617	0624	|	|	...	0654	|	|	|	...	0724	|	|	...	0754	...	|	|
72	**Den Haag** HS 472 d.	0552	...	0600	|	0617	...	0630	0632	0647	0647	...	0702	0717	0717	|	...	0732	0747	0747	...	0802	...	0817	0817
	Den Haag Centraal 472 a.	|	...	0603	|	|	...	0633	|	|	|	...	|	|	|	|	...	|	|	|	...	|	...	|	|
	Den Haag Centraal d.	|	0558	...	|	|	0628	...	|	|	|	0658	|	|	|	|	0728	|	|	|	0758	|	...	|	|
88	Leiden Centraal 457 d.	0607	0613	...	|	0630	0643	...	0645	0700	0700	0713	0715	0730	0730	|	0743	0745	0800	0800	0813	0815	...	0830	0830
116	Haarlem d.	|	|	...	|	|	|	...	0706	|	|	|	0736	|	|	|	|	0806	|	|	|	0836	...	|	|
	Schiphol ✈ 457 458 d.	0624	0629	...	0628	0648	0659	...	|	0716	0716	0729	|	0746	0746	0728	0759	|	0816	0816	0829	|	...	0846	0846
130	Amsterdam Sloterdijk 458 a.	|	0643	...	|	|	0713	...	0715	|	|	0743	0745	|	|	|	0813	0815	|	|	0843	0845	...	|	|
135	**Amsterdam** Centraal 458 a.	0638	0650	...	0641	0703	0720	...	0722	0733	0733	0750	0752	0803	0803	0741	0820	0822	0833	0833	0850	0852	...	0903	0903

	Ⓐ⚡		L B			⚒			▽		Ⓐ⚡			B									Ⓐ⚡	
Vlissingen d.	...	...	...	...	...	0644	...	...	...	...	...	0715	...	...	...	...	0752	and at the same minutes past each hour until	...	...	...	...	2015	...
Middelburg d.	...	...	...	...	...	0651	...	...	...	...	...	0722	...	...	...	...	0759		...	...	...	...	2022	...
Goes d.	...	...	...	...	...	0704	...	...	...	...	...	0735	...	...	...	...	0811		...	...	...	...	2035	...
Bergen op Zoom d.	...	...	...	...	...	0735	...	...	...	...	...	0802	...	...	...	...	0833		...	...	...	...	2102	...
Roosendaal a.	...	...	...	...	...	0746	...	...	...	...	...	0814	...	...	...	...	0844		...	...	...	...	2114	...
Roosendaal d.	...	...	0730	...	...	0748	...	...	...	...	...	...	...	0830	...	...	0847		...	...	...	...	...	...
Breda 472 d.	...	0720v	|	...	...	|	...	...	0750a	...	...	...	0820	|	...	...	|		...	...	...	...	...	2120
Dordrecht 472 d.	...	0752	0754	...	←	0812	0812	...	0822	0842	...	...	0852	0854	...	←	0912		...	2122	2142	...	...	2152
Rotterdam Lombardijen d.	...	0800	|	...	0800	|	|	...	0830	|	...	...	0900	|	...	0900	|		...	2130	|	...	...	2200
Rotterdam Centraal 472 d.	0802	→	0808	...	0811	0828	0828	...	0841	0858	0902	...	→	0908	...	0911	0928		...	2141	2158	2202	...	→
Delft 472 d.	|	...	|	...	0824	|	|	...	0854	|	|	...	...	|	...	0924	|		...	2154	|	|	...	...
Den Haag HS 472 d.	|	...	0826	...	0832	0847	0847	...	0902	0917	|	...	...	0926	...	0932	0947		...	2202	2217	|	...	...
Den Haag Centraal 472 a.	|	...	*0833*	...	|	|	|	...	|	|	|	...	...	*0933*	...	|	|		...	|	|	|	...	...
Den Haag Centraal d.	|	...	|	0828	|	|	|	0858	|	|	|	...	...	|	0928	|	|		2158	|	|	|	...	...
Leiden Centraal 457 d.	|	...	|	0843	0845	0900	0900	0913	0915	0930	|	...	...	|	0943	0945	1000		2213	2215	2230	|	...	...
Haarlem d.	|	...	|	|	0906	|	|	|	0936	|	|	...	...	|	|	1006	|		|	2236	|	|	...	...
Schiphol ✈ 457 458 d.	0828	...	0849s	0859	|	0916	0916	0929	|	0946	0928	...	...	0949s	0959	|	1016		2229	|	2246	2228	...	...
Amsterdam Sloterdijk 458 a.	|	...	|	0913	0915	|	|	0943	0945	|	|	...	...	|	1013	1015	|		2243	2245	|	|	...	...
Amsterdam Centraal 458 a.	0841	...	0906	0920	0922	0933	0933	0950	0952	1003	0941	...	...	1006	1020	1022	1033		2250	2252	2303	2241	...	...

	B									B				C	C	E		B	⑥B	C	E	†	⚒		
Vlissingen d.	...	...	...	2052	...	...	...	2115	...	...	...	...	2152	...	...	...	2215	...	...	...	...	2252	...	...	2315
Middelburg d.	...	...	...	2059	...	...	...	2122	...	...	...	...	2159	...	...	...	2222	...	...	...	...	2259	...	...	2322
Goes d.	...	...	...	2111	...	...	...	2135	...	...	...	...	2211	...	...	...	2235	...	...	...	...	2311	...	...	2335
Bergen op Zoom d.	...	...	...	2133	...	...	...	2202	...	...	...	...	2233	...	...	...	2302	...	...	...	...	2333	2333	...	0002
Roosendaal a.	...	...	...	2144	...	...	...	2214	...	...	...	...	2244	...	...	...	2314	...	...	...	...	2344	2344	...	0014
Roosendaal d.	2130	...	...	2147	...	...	...	...	...	2230	...	...	2247	...	...	...	▬	2330	2330	...	...	2347	2349	...	▬
Breda 472 d.	|	...	...	|	...	...	...	...	2220	|	...	...	|	...	...	...	...	|	|	2320	2320	|	|	...	...
Dordrecht 472 d.	2154	...	←	2212	...	2222	2242	...	2252	2254	...	←	2312	...	2322	2322	...	2354	2354	2352	2352	0015	0015	...	...
Rotterdam Lombardijen d.	|	...	2200	|	...	2230	|	...	2300	|	...	2300	|	...	2330	2330	...	|	|	0000	0000	|	|	0020	...
Rotterdam Centraal 472 d.	2208	...	2211	2228	...	2241	2258	...	→	2308	...	2311	2328	...	2341	2341	...	0006	0008	0011	0011	0035	0035	0039	0102
Delft 472 d.	|	...	2224	|	...	2254	|	...	...	|	...	2324	|	...	2354	2354	...	...	|	0024	0024	...	...	0054	0115
Den Haag HS 472 d.	2226	...	2232	2247	...	2302	2317	...	...	2326	...	2332	2347	...	0002	0002	...	...	0026	0032	0041	...	...	0107	0123
Den Haag Centraal 472 a.	*2233*	...	|	|	...	|	|	...	...	*2333*	...	|	|	...	|	|	...	...	|	|	|	...	...	0110	|
Den Haag Centraal d.	|	2228	|	|	2258	|	|	...	...	|	2328	|	|	2358	|	|	0023	...	|	|	|	...	...	...	|
Leiden Centraal 457 d.	|	2243	2245	2300	2313	2315	2330	...	...	|	2343	2345	0000	0013	0015	0015	0039	...	|	0053	0107	...	...	...	0139
Haarlem d.	|	|	2306	|	|	2336	|	...	...	|	|	0006	|	|	0036	0044	|	...	|	0117	0141	...	...	...	|
Schiphol ✈ 457 458 d.	2249s	2259	|	2316	2329	|	2346	...	...	2349s	2359	|	0018	0029	|	|	0100	...	0049s	|	|	...	...	...	0200
Amsterdam Sloterdijk 458 a.	|	2313	2315	|	2343	2345	|	...	...	|	0013	0015	|	0043	0045	0057	|	...	|	0128	0153	...	...	...	|
Amsterdam Centraal 458 a.	2306	2320	2322	2333	2350	2352	0003	...	...	0006	0020	0022	0034	0050	0052	0102	0114	...	0106	0134	0200	...	...	...	0214

B – From Brussels (Table **410**).
C – ⑤⑥⑦ (also Dec. 25, Jan. 1, Apr. 13, 30, May 21, June 1).
E – ①–④ (not Dec. 25, Jan. 1, Apr. 13, 30, May 21, June 1).

a – Ⓐ only.
s – Stops to set down only.
v – ⚒ only.

▽ – From Breda at 0850 Ⓐ, 1550 Ⓐ, 1650 Ⓐ and 1750 Ⓐ. Other services in this pattern start from Dordrecht.
⚡ – Via high-speed line. Supplement payable. **Expected to start running from July 2009 (to be confirmed).**

UTRECHT - AMSTERDAM - DEN HAAG - ROTTERDAM Night Network 454

Timings may be amended when track maintenance work is taking place. Please check locally.

							Ⓒ		†	
Utrecht Centraal d.	...	0107	0207	0307	...	0407	0407	...	0507	...
Amsterdam Centraal a.	...	0142	0242	0342	...	0442	0442	...	0542	...
Amsterdam Centraal d.	0045	0145	0245	0345	...	0445	0445	...	0545	...
Schiphol ✈ d.	0103	0203	0303	0403	...	0502	0502	...	0603	...
Leiden Centraal d.	0122	0222	0322	0422	...	0522	0522	...	0622	...
Den Haag HS d.	0138	0238	0338	0438	...	0537	0538	...	0638	...
Delft d.	0146	0246	0346	0446	...	...	0546	...	0648	...
Rotterdam Centraal a.	0159	0259	0359	0459	...	...	0559	...	0659	...

								Ⓒ	
Rotterdam Centraal d.	...	0102	0202	0302	0402	...	0502	0502	...
Delft d.	...	0115	0215	0315	0415	...	0515	0515	...
Den Haag HS d.	0023	0123	0223	0323	0423	...	0523	0523	...
Leiden Centraal d.	0039	0139	0239	0339	0439	...	0539	0539	...
Schiphol ✈ d.	0100	0200	0300	0400	0500	...	0600	0600	...
Amsterdam Centraal a.	0114	0214	0314	0414	0514	...	0614	0614	...
Amsterdam Centraal d.	0117	0217	0317	0417	0517	...	...	0618	...
Utrecht Centraal a.	0152	0252	0352	0452	0552	...	...	0652	...

ROTTERDAM - HOEK VAN HOLLAND 455

For connections to shipping services, see Table **15a**

km		H	⑥⑦t	G		A	①m	Ⓐ	⚒	Ⓐ	⚒	Ⓐ		Ⓐ		Ⓐ						
0	**Rotterdam** Centraal d.	0013	0043	0059	...	0450	0513	0543	0613	0628	0643	0658	0713	0728	0743	0758	...	0813	0843	and every 30 minutes until	2313	2343
27	**Hoek van Holland** Haven a.	0042	0112	0130	...	0519	0542	0612	0642	0658	0712	0728	0742	0758	0812	0828	...	0842	0912		2342	0012

	H	G	△	H	G		Ⓐ	Ⓐ	Ⓐ	Ⓐ	⚒	Ⓐ	⚒	Ⓐ		Ⓐ						
Hoek van Holland Haven d.	0007	0013	0037	0107	0134	...	0537	0607	0637	0652	0707	0722	0737	0752	0807	0822	...	0837	0907	and every 30 minutes until	2307	2337
Rotterdam Centraal a.	0038	0047	0108	0138	0205	...	0608	0638	0708	0723	0738	0753	0808	0823	0838	0853	...	0908	0938		2338	0008

A – ②–⑤ (not Dec. 25, 26, Jan. 1, Apr. 30, May 21).
G – ②–⑤ (not Dec. 26, Jan. 2, Apr. 14, May 1, 22, June 2).
H – ①⑥⑦ (also Dec. 26, Jan. 2, Apr. 14, May 1, 22, June 2).

m – Not Apr. 13, June 1.
t – Also Apr. 14, May 1, 22, June 2.

△ – On ④ Hoek van Holland d. 0034, Rotterdam a. 0104.

457 LEIDEN - AMSTERDAM ZUID - HILVERSUM - UTRECHT and ALMERE - UTRECHT

For fast trains **Schiphol** ✈ - **Utrecht**, see Table **470**. For direct trains Leiden - Utrecht (via Alphen), see Table **463**.

km		Ⓐ	Ⓐ	Ⓐ	Ⓐ	⚒	Ⓐ	⚒	Ⓐ		⚒	
0	**Leiden** Centraal 450 d.	...	0518	...	...	...	...	0618	...	0648	...	...
27	Schiphol ✈ 450 458 d.	...	0541	...	0608	...	...	0638	...	0708	...	...
36	Amsterdam Zuid 458 d.	...	0548	...	0618	...	...	0648	...	0718	...	...
41	Duivendrecht 458 d.	...	0556	...	0626	...	...	0656	...	0726	...	...
49	Weesp 458 a.	...	0606	...	0636	...	...	0706	...	0736	...	...
49	Weesp 480 d.	...	0613	...	0643	...	...	0713	...	0743	...	...
	Almere Buiten d.	0541	|	0611	|	...	0641	|	0711	|	0741	...
	Almere Centrum d.	0549	|	0619	|	...	0649	|	0719	|	0749	...
58	Naarden-Bussum 480 d.	0605	0620	0635	0650	0650	0705	0720	0735	0750	0805	...
64	Hilversum 480 d.	0615	0631	0644	0701	0701	0714	0731	0744	0801	0814	...
81	**Utrecht** Centraal a.	0633	0651	0702	0721	0721	0732	0751	0802	0821	0832	...

				✣						⑤⑥j	E	†
Leiden Centraal d.	0718	0748	...	and at the same minutes past each hour until	2218	2248	...	2318	...	2348	2348	2348
Schiphol ✈ d.	0738	0808	...		2238	2308	...	2340	...	0014	0014	0014
Amsterdam Zuid d.	0748	0818	...		2248	2318	...	2348	...	0021	0021	0021
Duivendrecht d.	0756	0826	...		2256	2326	...	2356	...	0028	0028	0033
Weesp a.	0806	0836	...		2306	2336	...	0006	...	0038	0046	0046
Weesp d.	0813	0843	...		2313	2343	...	0013	...	0043	0047	0050
Almere Buiten d.	|	|	0841		|	|	2341	|	...	|	|	|
Almere Centrum d.	|	|	0849		|	|	2349	|	...	|	|	|
Naarden-Bussum d.	0820	0850	0905		2320	2350	0005	0020	...	0050	0054	0059
Hilversum d.	0831	0901	0914		2331	0001	0014	0031	...	0104	0105	0109
Utrecht Centraal a.	0851	0921	0932		2351	0021	0032	0051	...	0124	0124	0129

	②–⑦	①					Ⓐ		Ⓐ		⚒	
Utrecht Centraal d.	0028	0028	...	0513	0544	0609	0628	0638	0658	0708	0728	...
Hilversum d.	0046	0046	...	0533	0604	0630	0646	0659	0716	0729	0746	...
Naarden-Bussum d.	0052	0058	...	0544	0615	0640	0652	0709	0722	0739	0752	...
Almere Centrum a.	0107	0113	...	|	|	|	0711	|	0741	|	0811	...
Almere Buiten a.	0114	0119	...	|	|	|	0718	|	0748	|	0818	...
Weesp a.	...	...	...	0551	0622	0648	...	0716	...	0746	...	...
Weesp 458 d.	...	...	...	0553	0626	0653	...	0723	...	0753	...	...
Duivendrecht 458 d.	...	...	...	0604	0637	0704	...	0734	...	0804	...	...
Amsterdam Zuid 458 d.	...	...	...	0611	0644	0711	...	0741	...	0811	...	...
Schiphol ✈ 450 458 a.	...	...	...	0619	0650	0719	...	0747	...	0817	...	...
Leiden Centraal 450 a.	...	...	...	0642	0712	0742	...	0812	...	0842	...	...

				⊠								K
Utrecht Centraal d.	0738	0808	0828	and at the same minutes past each hour until	2138	2208	2228	2238	2308	2328	2338	2338
Hilversum d.	0759	0829	0846		2159	2229	2246	2259	2329	2346	2359	2359
Naarden-Bussum d.	0809	0839	0852		2209	2239	2252	2309	2339	2352	0009	0009
Almere Centrum a.	|	|	0911		|	|	2311	|	|	0011	|	|
Almere Buiten a.	|	|	0918		|	|	2318	|	|	0018	|	|
Weesp a.	0816	0846	...		2216	2246	...	2316	2346	...	0016	0016
Weesp d.	0823	0853	...		2223	2253	...	2323	2353	...	...	0023
Duivendrecht d.	0834	0904	...		2234	2304	...	2334	0004	...	...	0033
Amsterdam Zuid d.	0841	0911	...		2241	2311	...	2341	0011	...	...	0040
Schiphol ✈ a.	0847	0917	...		2247	2317	...	2347	0020	...	...	0047
Leiden Centraal a.	0912	0942	...		2312	2342	...	0012	...	...	...	...

E – ①–④ (not Dec. 25, Jan. 1, Apr. 13, 30, May 21, June 1).
K – ⑤⑥⑦ (also Dec. 25, Jan. 1, Apr. 13, 30, May 21, June 1).
j – Also Apr. 13, 30, May 21, June 1.

✣ – Additional journeys **Almere** Buiten - **Utrecht** Centraal: 0811 Ⓐ, 0911 ⚒, 1011 ⚒ and hourly until 1911 ⚒.
⊠ – Additional journeys **Utrecht** Centraal - **Almere** Buiten: 0758 ⚒, 0858 ⚒ and hourly until 1858 ⚒.

458 SCHIPHOL ✈ and AMSTERDAM - LELYSTAD

km		⑥⑦d	G			Ⓐ	Ⓐ	Ⓐ	⚒	ⒶL	⚒		ⒶL	⚒		ⒶL			ⒶL			ⒶL			ⒶL
0	**Schiphol** ✈ 450 457 d.	...	...	0026	...	...	0555	0626	...	0637	0656	...	0707	0726	...	0737	0756	...	0807	0826	...	0837	0856	...	0907
9	Amsterdam Zuid 457 d.	...	...	0034	...	...	0604	0634	...	|	0704	...	|	0734	...	|	0804	...	|	0834	...	|	0904	...	|
14	Duivendrecht 457 d.	...	...	0042	...	...	0612	0642	...	|	0712	...	|	0742	...	|	0812	...	|	0842	...	|	0912	...	|
	Amsterdam Sloterdijk 450 d.	0010	0010	|	...	...	|	|	0639	0653	|	0709	0723	|	0739	0753	|	0809	0823	|	0839	0853	|	0909	0923
	Amsterdam Centraal 450 a.	0016	0016	|	...	...	|	|	0646	0700	|	0716	0730	|	0746	0800	|	0816	0830	|	0846	0900	|	0916	0930
	Amsterdam Centraal 457 d.	0022	0026e	|	...	0606	|	|	0651	0703	|	0721	0733	|	0751	0803	|	0821	0833	|	0851	0903	|	0921	0933
22	Weesp 457 d.	0040	0048	0101	...	0621	0623	0653	0708	|	0723	0738	|	0753	0808	|	0823	0838	|	0853	0908	|	0923	0938	|
38	**Almere** Centrum d.	0052	0100	0114	...	...	0636	0706	0721	0726	0736	0751	0756	0806	0821	0826	0836	0851	0856	0906	0921	0926	0936	0951	0956
44	Almere Buiten d.	0059	0107	0121	...	...	0643	0713	0728	0732	0743	0758	0802	0813	0828	0832	0843	0858	0902	0913	0928	0932	0943	0958	1002
62	**Lelystad** Centrum a.	0113	0122	0138	...	...	0700	0728	...	0744	0757	0812h	0814	0827	0842h	0844	0857	0912h	0914	0927	0942h	0944	0957	1012h	1014

Schiphol ✈ 450 457 d.	0926	...	0937	0956	...	1007	and at the same minutes past each hour until	1856	...	1907	1926	...	1937	1956	...	2026	...	and at the same minutes past each hour until	2256	...	2326	...	2356
Amsterdam Zuid 457 d.	0934	...	|	1004	...	|		1904	...	|	1934	...	|	2004	...	2034	...		2304	...	2334	...	0004
Duivendrecht 457 d.	0942	...	|	1012	...	|		1912	...	|	1942	...	|	2012	...	2042	...		2312	...	2342	...	0012
Amsterdam Sloterdijk 450 d.	|	0939	0953	|	1009	1023		|	1909	1923	|	1939	1953	|	2009	|	2039		|	2310	|	2339	|
Amsterdam Centraal 450 a.	|	0946	1000	|	1016	1030		|	1916	1930	|	1946	2000	|	2016	|	2046		|	2316	|	2346	|
Amsterdam Centraal 457 d.	|	0951	1003	|	1021	1033		|	1921	1933	|	1951	2003	|	2021	|	2051		|	2321	|	2351	|
Weesp 457 d.	0953	1008	|	1023	1038	|		1923	1938	|	1953	2008	|	2023	2038	2053	2108		2323	2338	2353	0008	0024
Almere Centrum d.	1006	1021	1026	1036	1051	1056		1936	1951	1956	2006	2021	2026	2036	2051	2106	2121		2336	2351	0006	0021	0037
Almere Buiten d.	1013	1028	1032	1043	1058	1102		1943	1958	2002	2013	2028	2032	2043	2058	2113	2128		2343	2358	0013	0028	0044
Lelystad Centrum a.	1027	...	1044	1057	...	1114		1957	...	2014	2027	...	2044	2057	2112	2127	2142		2357	0012	0027	0042	0059

km		N			Ⓐ	⚒	†	Ⓐ	ⒶL		Ⓐ	ⒶL			ⒶL			ⒶL			ⒶL				
0	**Lelystad** Centrum d.	0000	...	0430	0450	0516	0516	0533	0545	0546c	0600	0615	0616c	0630	0645	0646c	0700	0715	0716c	0730	0745	0746h	...	0800	0815
18	Almere Buiten d.	0015	...	0445	0505	0530	0530	0548	0557	0602	0615	0627	0630	0645	0657	0700	0715	0727	0730	0745	0757	0800	...	0815	0827
24	**Almere** Centrum d.	0023	...	0453	0513	0538	0538	0556	0603	0608	0623	0633	0638	0653	0703	0708	0723	0733	0738	0753	0803	0808	...	0823	0833
40	Weesp 457 d.	0038	...	0509	0529	0555	0555	0609	|	0625	0637	|	0653	0707	|	0723	0737	|	0753	0807	|	0823	...	0837	|
53	**Amsterdam** Centraal 457 a.	|	...	|	|	0610	0612	|	0627	0642	|	0655	0708	|	0725	0738	|	0755	0808	|	0825	0838	...	|	0855
53	**Amsterdam** Centraal 450 d.	|	...	|	|	0616	...	|	0632	0646	|	0702	0716	|	0732	0746	|	0802	0816	|	0832	0846	...	|	0902
58	Amsterdam Sloterdijk 450 a.	|	...	|	|	0622	...	|	0639	0652	|	0709	0722	|	0739	0752	|	0809	0822	|	0839	0852	...	|	0909
	Duivendrecht 457 d.	0047	...	0518	0538	...	...	0618	|	...	0649	|	...	0718	|	...	0748	|	...	0818	|	...	...	0848	|
	Amsterdam Zuid 457 a.	0054	...	0524	0545	...	...	0626	|	...	0656	|	...	0726	|	...	0756	|	...	0826	|	...	...	0856	|
	Schiphol ✈ 450 457 a.	0103	...	0533	0555	...	...	0632	0651	...	0702	0721	...	0732	0751	...	0802	0821	...	0832	0851	...	...	0902	0921

																							K	
Lelystad Centrum d.	...	0830	0845	...	and at the same minutes past each hour until	1900	1915	...	1930	1945	...	...	2000	2016	2030	2046	and at the same minutes past each hour until	2230	2246	2300	2316	2330	2346
Almere Buiten d.	0830	0845	0857	0900		1915	1927	1930	1945	1957	2000	...	2015	2030	2045	2100		2245	2300	2315	2330	2345	0000
Almere Centrum d.	0838	0853	0903	0908		1923	1933	1938	1953	2003	2008	...	2023	2038	2053	2108		2253	2308	2323	2338	2353	0008
Weesp 457 d.	0853	0907	|	0923		1937	|	1953	2007	|	2023	...	2037	2053	2107	2123		2307	2323	2337	2353	0007	0023
Amsterdam Centraal 457 a.	0908	|	0925	0938		|	1955	2008	|	2025	2038	...	|	2108	|	2138		|	2338	|	0008	|	0040
Amsterdam Centraal 450 d.	0916	|	0932	0946		|	2002	2016	|	2032	2046	...	|	2116	|	2146		|	2346	|	0016	|	...
Amsterdam Sloterdijk 450 a.	0922	|	0939	0952		|	2009	2022	|	2039	2052	...	|	2122	|	2152		|	2352	|	0022	|	...
Duivendrecht 457 d.	...	0918	|	...		1948	|	...	2018	|	...	...	2048	...	2118	...		2318	...	2347	...	0017	...
Amsterdam Zuid 457 a.	...	0926	|	...		1956	|	...	2026	|	...	...	2056	...	2126	...		2326	...	2353	...	0023	...
Schiphol ✈ 450 457 a.	...	0932	0951	...		2002	2021	...	2032	2051	...	...	2102	...	2132	...		2332	...	2400	...	0032	...

G – ①–⑤ (not Apr. 14, May 1, 22, June 2).
K – ⑤⑥⑦ (also Dec. 25, Jan. 1, Apr. 13, 30, May 21, June 1).
L – Runs daily Schiphol - Amsterdam Centraal and v.v.

N – ②–⑦ (not Dec. 26, Jan. 2).
c – Ⓒ only.

d – Also Apr. 14, May 1, 22, June 2.
e – 0021 on ① (also Dec. 26, Jan. 2).
h – † only.

459 SCHIPHOL ✈ and AMSTERDAM - ENKHUIZEN

km					Ⓐ		Ⓐ		Ⓐ	Ⓒ	Ⓐ	Ⓐ	Ⓐ	⑥t										
0	**Amsterdam** Centraal 466 d.	0009	0038	...	0600	...	0631	...	...	0700	0709	...	0739	0739	...	0809	...	0839	and at the same minutes past each hour until	...	2309	...	2339	...
	Schiphol ✈ d.	|	|	...	|	0607	|	0637	0642	|	|	0712	|	|	0742	|	0812	|		2242	|	2312	|	2342
5	Amsterdam Sloterdijk 466 d.	0016	0044	...	0606	0622	0636	0652	0655	0706	0715	0725	0745	0744	0755	0815	0825	0845		2255	2315	2325	2345	2355
12	Zaandam 466 d.	|	0052	...	0613	...	0643	...	0704	0713	|	0734	|	0752	0804	|	0834	|		2304	|	2334	|	0007
44	Hoorn d.	0045	0122	...	0645	...	0716	...	0732	0745	0745	0802	0815	0823	0832	0845	0902	0915		2332	2345	0002	0015	0034
62	**Enkhuizen** a.	0107	0144	...	0707	...	0737	...	...	0807	0807	...	0837	0846	...	0907	...	0937		...	0007	...	0037	...

	⑥t	Ⓐ	Ⓐ	Ⓐ	Ⓐ	⚒	⚒	⚒	⚒	⚒											K	E	K	E
Enkhuizen d.	...	0440	...	0524	...	0554	...	0624a	...	0654	...	0724	...	0754	...	and at the same minutes past each hour until	2224	...	2254	...	2324	2324	2354	2354
Hoorn d.	0504	0505	0528	0550	0558	0620	0628	0650	0658	0720	0728	0750	0758	0820	0828		2250	2258	2320	2328	2350	2350	0020	0023
Zaandam 466 d.	0532	0534	0557	|	0627	|	0657	|	0727	|	0757	|	0827	|	0857		|	2327	|	2357	|	|	0047	0052
Amsterdam Sloterdijk 466 a.	0538	0540	0602	0615	0632	0646	0702	0715	0732	0745	0802	0815	0832	0845	0902		2315	2332	2345	0002	0015	0020	0052	0058
Schiphol ✈ a.	0552	0552	0617	|	0647	|	0717	|	0747	|	0817	|	0847	|	0917		|	2347	|	0017	|	|	|	|
Amsterdam Centraal 466 a.	...	...	...	0623	...	0653	...	0722	...	0752	...	0822	...	0852	...		2322	...	2352	...	0022	0028	0059	0105

E – ①–④ (not Dec. 25, Jan. 1, Apr. 13, 30, May 21, June 1).
K – ⑤⑥⑦ (also Dec. 25, Jan. 1, Apr. 13, 30, May 21, June 1).

a – Ⓐ only.
t – Also Dec. 26, Apr. 13, 30, May 21, June 1.

HAARLEM - ALKMAAR - HOORN 461

km					Ⓐ	Ⓐ	⑥t	Ⓐ	⑥t	Ⓐ	⚒	⚒												
0	**Haarlem** d.	0046	...	...	...	...	...	0643	...	0713	0743	0813	...	0843	0913	and every 30 minutes until	1913	1943	...	2013	2043	2143	2243	2343
11	Beverwijk d.	0103	...	...	...	...	...	0653	...	0723	0753	0823	...	0853	0923		1923	1953	...	2023	2053	2153	2253	2353
22	Castricum 466 d.	0117	0145	...	*0600*	*0620*	*0650*	0704	*0720*	0734	0804	0834	...	0904	0934		1934	2004	...	2034	2104	2204	2304	0004
34	**Alkmaar** 466 d.	0127	0157	...	0616	0645	0716	0716	0746	0746	0816	0846	...	0916	0946		1946	2016	...	2045	2116	2216	2316	0016
40	Heerhugowaard 466 a.	...	0204	...	0624	0653	0724	0724	0754	0754	0824	0854	...	0924	0954		1954	2024	...	*2058*	2124	2224	2324	0024
57	**Hoorn** a.	...	...	...	0640	0710	0740	0740	0810	0810	0840	0910	...	0940	1010		2010	2040	...	...	2140	2240	2340	0040

	⚒	Ⓐ	Ⓐ	⚒	⚒		†	⚒		†	⚒													
Hoorn d.	...	0551	0620	0650	0720	0750	...	0820	0850	...	0920	...	0950	1020	and every 30 minutes until	1920	1950	...	2050	2150	2250	2350	...	...
Heerhugowaard 466 d.	...	0605	0636	0706	0736	0806	*0830*	0836	0906	*0930*	0936	...	1006	1036		1936	2006	...	2106	2206	2306	0006	...	...
Alkmaar 466 d.	...	0614	0645	0715	0745	0815	0845	0845	0915	0945	0945	...	1015	1045		1945	2015	...	2115	2215	2315	0014	...	...
Castricum 466 d.	...	0626	0656	0726	0756	0826	0856	0856	0926	0956	0956	...	1026	1056		1956	2026	...	2126	2226	2326	...	...	...
Beverwijk d.	0625	0638	0708	0738	0808	0838	0908	0908	0938	1008	1008	...	1038	1108		2008	2038	...	2138	2238	2338	...	...	...
Haarlem a.	0644	0648	0718	0748	0818	0848	0918	0918	0948	1018	1018	...	1048	1118		2018	2048	...	2148	2248	2348	...	...	...

t – Also Dec. 26, Apr. 13, 30, May 21, June 1.

LEIDEN - ALPHEN - UTRECHT and ALPHEN - GOUDA 463

km				Ⓐ	⚒	⚒									
0	**Leiden** Centraal d.	0022	...	0552	0622	0652	0722	0752	0822	...	0852	0922	and every 30 minutes until	2322	2352
15	Alphen aan den Rijn △ d.	0038	...	0608	0638	0708	0738	0808	0838	...	0908	0938		2338	0008
34	Woerden d.	0057	...	0625	0654	0724	0754	0824	0854	...	0925	0955		2355	0025
50	**Utrecht** Centraal a.	0110	...	0638	0705	0735	0805	0835	0905	...	0938	1008		0008	0038

			Ⓐ	⚒	⚒										
Utrecht Centraal d.	0023	...	0556	0625	0655	...	0725	0755	and every 30 minutes until	2325	2355	...	...	...	...
Woerden d.	0040	...	0608	0638	0708	...	0738	0808		2338	0008	...	...	...	...
Alphen aan den Rijn △ d.	0057	...	0624	0654	0724	...	0754	0824		2354	0024	...	...	...	...
Leiden Centraal a.	0111	...	0637	0707	0737	...	0807	0837		0007	0037	...	...	...	...

△ – Connecting lightrail services run **Alphen - Gouda** and v.v. *17 km.* Journey: 20–21 minutes.
From Alphen at 0019, 0619 Ⓐ, 0649 ⚒, 0719 ⚒, 0749 ⚒, 0819, 0849 ⚒ and then at 19 and 49 ⚒ minutes past each hour until 1919, 1949 ⚒; then 2019, 2119, 2219 and 2319.
From Gouda at 0055, 0621 Ⓐ, 0651 Ⓐ, 0721 ⚒, 0751 ⚒, 0821 ⚒, 0851 and then at 21 ⚒ and 51 minutes past each hour until 2021 ⚒, 2051; then 2155, 2255 and 2351.

AMSTERDAM - GOUDA - ROTTERDAM 465

For fast trains **Amsterdam – Rotterdam** and v.v. via **Den Haag**, see Table **450**

km		Ⓐ	Ⓐ	⚒	⚒							K	J	K	④t	L
0	**Amsterdam** Centraal d.	0555	0625	0655	0725	...	0755	0825	and every 30 minutes until	2225	2255	2325	2325	2355	2355	2355
9	Duivendrecht d.	0610	0637	0707	0737	...	0807	0837		2237	2307	2337	2337	0007	0007	0007
27	Breukelen d.	0625	0655	0725	0755	...	0825	0855		2255	2325	2354	2354	0024	0026	0026
40	Woerden d.	0634	0704	0734	0804	...	0834	0904		2304	2334	0003	0003	0033	0040	0040
56	**Gouda** 483 d.	0646	0716	0746	0816	...	0846	0916		2316	2346	0016	0022	0046	0110r	0114r
70	Rotterdam Alexander 483 d.	0659	0729	0759	0829	...	0859	0929		2329	2359	0028	0033	0058	0122	0126
80	**Rotterdam** Centraal 483 a.	0709	0739	0809	0839	...	0909	0939		2339	0009	0041	0043	0111	0132	0136

	Ⓐ	Ⓐ	⚒	⚒												
Rotterdam Centraal 483 d.	0521	0550	0620	0650	...	0720	0750	and every 30 minutes until	2220	2250	...	2320	...	...	...	...
Rotterdam Alexander 483 d.	0531	0601	0631	0701	...	0731	0801		2231	2301	...	2331	...	...	...	...
Gouda 483 d.	0545	0615	0645	0715	...	0745	0815		2245	2315	...	2345	...	...	...	...
Woerden d.	0558	0628	0658	0728	...	0758	0828		2258	2328	...	2358	...	...	...	...
Breukelen d.	0608	0637	0707	0737	...	0807	0837		2307	2337	...	0007	...	...	...	...
Duivendrecht d.	0623	0653	0723	0753	...	0823	0853		2323	2353	...	0023	...	...	...	...
Amsterdam Centraal a.	0637	0706	0736	0806	...	0836	0906		2336	0006	...	0036	...	...	...	...

J – ①–④ (not Dec. 25, Jan. 1, Apr. 13, 30, May 21, June 1).
K – ⑤⑥⑦ (also Dec. 25, Jan. 1, Apr. 13, 30, May 21, June 1).
L – ①–③ (not Apr. 13, June 1).
r – Arrives 0052.
t – Not Dec. 25, Jan. 1, Apr. 30, May 21.

AMSTERDAM - ALKMAAR - DEN HELDER 466

km					Ⓐ	Ⓐ	Ⓐ	⚒	⑥t	Ⓐ	Ⓐ											K	Ⓒ	Ⓐ
	Arnhem **468** d.	...	...	...	...	...	...	...	...	...	...	0559a	0629v	0659v	...	0729	0759	and every 30 minutes until	2129	2159	...	2259	2259
	Utrecht Centraal **468** d.	...	0024	...	...	...	...	...	...	...	...	0640v	0710	0740	...	0810	0840		2210	2240	...	2340	2340
0	**Amsterdam** Centraal 459 d.	0028	0110	...	0518	...	0546	...	0616	0625	0642	0712	0742	0812	...	0842	0912		2242	2312	2346	0012	0012
5	Amsterdam Sloterdijk 459 d.	0034	0119	...	0524	...	0552	...	0622	0631	0649	0719	0749	0819	...	0849	0919		2249	2319	2352	0019	0019
12	Zaandam 459 d.	|	0124	...	0532	...	0559	...	0629	0638	0656	0726	0756	0826	...	0856	0926		2256	2326	2359	0026	0026
29	Castricum 461 d.	0117	0145	...	0600	...	0620	...	0650	0651	0708	0738	0808	0838	...	0908	0938		2308	2338	0025	0040	0042
41	**Alkmaar** 461 d.	0127	0157	...	0611	0620	0631	0650	0701	0704	0720	0750	0820	0850	...	0920	0950		2320	2350	0036	0051	0054
48	Heerhugowaard 461 d.	...	0204	...	...	0628	...	0658	...	...	0728	0758	0828	0858	...	0928	0958		2328	2358	...	0059	0103
83	**Den Helder** a.	...	...	...	...	0656	...	0726	...	...	0756	0826	0856	0926	...	0956	1026		2356	0026	...	0126	0131

	⑥⑦d		⚒	Ⓐ		Ⓐ	Ⓐ	Ⓒ	⚒	Ⓐ	⚒	⚒								J	K	K	J
Den Helder d.	0034	...	...	0504	...	0534	0604	...	0634	0646	0704	0716a	...	0734	0804	and every 30 minutes until	2134	2204	2234	...	...	2334	2334
Heerhugowaard 461 d.	0100	...	...	0530	...	0600	0630	...	0700	0712	0730	0742a	...	0800	0830		2200	2230	2300	...	...	0000	0000
Alkmaar 461 d.	0109	...	0455	0542	0558	0612	0642	0658	0712	0724	0742	0754	...	0812	0842		2212	2242	2312	2328	2328	0016	0016
Castricum 461 d.	...	...	0507	0551	0610	0621	0651	0710	0721	0736	0751	0806	...	0821	0851		2221	2251	2321	2340	2340	0029	0029
Zaandam 459 d.	...	...	0537	0606	0633	0636	0706	0733	0736	0752	0806	0822	...	0836	0906		2236	2306	2336	0000	0004	0054	0105
Amsterdam Sloterdijk 459 a.	...	...	0543	0612	0638	0642	0712	0738	0742	0757	0812	0827	...	0842	0912		2242	2312	2343	0005	0009	0101	0111
Amsterdam Centraal 459 a.	...	...	0548	0619	0646	0649	0719	0746	0749	0804	0819	0834	...	0849	0919		2249	2319	2349	0013	0016	0109	0117
Utrecht Centraal **468** a.	...	...	...	0649	...	0719	0749	...	0819	0835	0849	0904	...	0919	0949		2320	2350	0019	...	...	...	...
Arnhem **468** a.	...	...	...	0731	...	0801	0831	...	0901	...	0931	...	...	1002	1032		0002	0032	...	...	...	...	...

J – ①–④ (not Dec. 25, Jan. 1, Apr. 13, 30, May 21, June 1).
K – ⑤⑥⑦ (also Dec. 25, Jan. 1, Apr. 13, 30, May 21, June 1).
a – Ⓐ only.
d – Also Apr. 14, May 1, 22, June 2.
t – Also Dec. 26, Apr. 13, 30, May 21, June 1.
v – ⚒ only.

AMSTERDAM and SCHIPHOL ✈ - ARNHEM - NIJMEGEN 468

For INTERNATIONAL TRAINS **Amsterdam – Arnhem – Köln**, see Table **28**   For NIGHT NETWORK **Rotterdam – Amsterdam – Utrecht**, see Table **454**

km		H	G	③	H	⑦		Ⓐ	Ⓐ	Ⓐ	ⒶD	⑥t	⚒D	Ⓐ	⚒D	†	⚒	D	⚒	D	⚒	D	⚒	D
0	**Amsterdam** Centraal 470 d.	0022	0026	0026	0055	*0117*	...	...	0521	...	0622	...	0652	...	0722	...	...	0752	...	0822	...	0852	...	0922
5	Amsterdam Amstel 470 d.	0030	0035	0035	0103	|	...	...	0531	...	0630	...	0700	...	0730	...	...	0800	...	0830	...	0900	...	0930
	Schiphol ✈ 470 d.	|	|	|	|	|	...	...	|	...	|	...	|	0700	|	...	0730	|	0800	|	0830	|	0900	|
	Amsterdam Zuid 470 d.	|	|	|	|	|	...	...	|	...	|	...	|	0709	|	...	0739	|	0809	|	0839	|	0909	|
39	**Utrecht** Centraal 470 a.	0050	0055	0056	0137	*0152*	...	...	0611	...	0649	...	0719	0732	0749	...	0801	0819	0832	0849	0901	0919	0931	0949
39	**Utrecht** Centraal d.	0053	0056	0057	...	0200	...	0553	...	0623	0653	0653	0723	0737	0753	0753	0807	0823	0837	0853	0907	0923	0937	0953
79	Ede-Wageningen d.	0125	0133	0135	...	0230	...	0620	...	0650	0720	0721	0750	0802	0820	0821	0832	0850	0902	0920	0932	0950	1002	1020
96	**Arnhem** a.	0136	0148	0153	...	0241	...	0631	...	0701	0731	0732	0801	0815	0831	0832	0845	0902	0915	0932	0945	1002	1015	1032
96	**Arnhem** 475 d.	0141	0155	0159	...	0246	...	0638	...	0708	0738	0738	0808	0824	0838	0837	0854	0908	0924	0938	0954	1008	1024	1038
114	**Nijmegen** 475 a.	0156	0211	0215	...	0301	...	0651	...	0721	0751	0751	0821	0837	0851	0851	0907	0921	0937	0951	1007	1021	1037	1051

	⚒	D	⚒	D	⚒	D	⚒	D			D		D			D		D		D	D	D	D
Amsterdam Centraal 470 d.	...	0952	...	1022	...	1052	...	1122	...	...	1152	...	1222	and at the same minutes past each hour until	...	2052	...	2122	...	2152	2222	2252	2322
Amsterdam Amstel 470 d.	...	1000	...	1030	...	1100	...	1130	...	...	1200	...	1230		...	2100	...	2130	...	2200	2230	2300	2330
Schiphol ✈ 470 d.	0930	|	1000	|	1030	|	1100	|	...	1130	|	1200	|		2030	|	2100	|	...	|	|	|	|
Amsterdam Zuid 470 d.	0939	|	1009	|	1039	|	1109	|	...	1139	|	1209	|		2039	|	2109	|	...	|	|	|	|
Utrecht Centraal 470 a.	1001	1019	1031	1049	1102	1119	1131	1149	...	1201	1219	1231	1249		2101	2120	2131	2150	...	2220	2250	2320	2350
Utrecht Centraal d.	1007	1023	1037	1053	1107	1123	1137	1153	...	1207	1223	1237	1253		2107	2123	2137	2153	...	2223	2253	2323	2353
Ede-Wageningen d.	1032	1050	1102	1120	1132	1150	1202	1220	...	1232	1250	1302	1320		2132	2151	2202	2221	...	2251	2321	2351	0021
Arnhem a.	1045	1102	1115	1132	1145	1202	1215	1232	...	1245	1301	1315	1331		2145	2202	2215	2232	...	2302	2332	0002	0032
Arnhem 475 d.	1054	1108	1124	1138	1154	1208	1224	1238	...	1254	1308	1324	1338		2154	2208	2224	2238	...	2308	2338	0008	0039
Nijmegen 475 a.	1107	1121	1137	1151	1207	1221	1237	1251	...	1307	1321	1337	1351		2207	2221	2237	2251	...	2321	2351	0022	0056

D – From Den Helder (Table **466**).
G – ②④⑤ (not Dec. 26, Jan. 2, Apr. 14, May 1, 22, June 2).
H – ①⑥⑦ (also Dec. 26, Jan. 2, Apr. 14, May 1, 22, June 2).
t – Also Dec. 26, Apr. 13, 30, May 21, June 1.

468 NIJMEGEN - ARNHEM - SCHIPHOL ✈ and AMSTERDAM

For INTERNATIONAL TRAINS **Köln – Arnhem – Amsterdam**, see Table **28** For NIGHT NETWORK **Utrecht – Amsterdam – Rotterdam**, see Table **454**

km		Ⓐ	ⒶD	⚒D	Ⓐ	⚒D	D	Ⓐ	⚒	⚒D	D	Ⓐ	⚒	D	⚒	†D	⚒D	⚒	D	⚒	D	⚒	D	⚒
	Nijmegen 475 d.	...	0531	...	...	0609	...	0624	...	0639	...	0654	...	0709	0724	0730	0739	0754	0809	0824	0839	0854	0909	0924
	Arnhem 475 a.	...	0556	...	...	0623	...	0638	...	0653	...	0708	...	0723	0738	0753	0753	0808	0823	0838	0853	0908	0923	0938
	Arnhem d.	0546	0559	...	0616	0629	...	0646	0646	0659	...	0716	0716	0729	0746	0759	0759	0816	0829	0846	0859	0916	0929	0946
	Ede-Wageningen d.	0558	0610	...	0628	0640	...	0657	0657	0710	...	0727	0727	0740	0757	0810	0810	0827	0840	0857	0910	0927	0940	0957
	Utrecht Centraal a.	0625	0637	...	0653	0707	...	0723	0723	0737	...	0753	0753	0808	0823	0838	0837	0853	0908	0923	0938	0953	1008	1023
0	**Utrecht** Centraal 470 d.	0628	0640	0640	0658	0710	0710	0728	0728	0740	0740	0758	0758	0810	0828	0840	0840	0858	0910	0928	0940	0958	1010	1028
36	Amsterdam Zuid 470 a.	0652	|	|	0722	|	|	0752	0752	|	|	0822	0822	|	0852	|	|	0922	|	0952	|	1022	|	1052
45	**Schiphol** ✈ 470 a.	0659	|	|	0729	|	|	0759	0759	|	|	0829	0829	|	0859	|	|	0929	|	0959	|	1029	|	1059
	Amsterdam Amstel 470 a.	...	0701	0701	...	0731	0731	...	...	0801	0801	...	...	0831	...	0901	0901	...	0931	...	1001	...	1031	...
	Amsterdam Centraal 470 a.	...	0710	0710	...	0739	0739	...	...	0809	0809	...	...	0839	...	0909	0909	...	0939	...	1009	...	1039	...

	D	⚒	D	⚒				D		D			D		D		D	D		D			H
Nijmegen 475 d.	0939	0954	1009	1024	1039	...	1054	1109	1124	1139	and at	1954	2009	2024	2039	...	2109	2139	2209	2239	2309	...	...
Arnhem 475 a.	0953	1008	1023	1038	1053	...	1108	1123	1138	1153	the same	2008	2023	2038	2053	...	2123	2153	2223	2253	2323	...	...
Arnhem d.	0959	1016	1029	1046	1059	...	1116	1129	1146	1159	minutes	2016	2029	2046	2059	...	2129	2159	2229	2259	2329	...	...
Ede-Wageningen d.	1010	1027	1040	1057	1110	...	1127	1140	1157	1210	past each	2027	2040	2057	2110	...	2140	2210	2240	2310	2340	...	...
Utrecht Centraal a.	1038	1053	1108	1123	1138	...	1153	1207	1223	1237	hour until	2053	2108	2123	2138	...	2208	2238	2308	2338	0008	...	...
Utrecht Centraal 470 d.	1040	1058	1110	1128	1140	...	1158	1210	1228	1240		2058	2110	2128	2140	...	2210	2240	2310	2340	...	0025	0024
Amsterdam Zuid 470 a.	|	1122	|	1152	|	...	1222	|	1252	|		2122	|	2152	|	...	|	|	|	|	...	|	|
Schiphol ✈ 470 a.	|	1129	|	1159	|	...	1229	|	1259	|		2129	|	2159	|	...	|	|	|	|	...	|	|
Amsterdam Amstel 470 a.	1101	...	1131	...	1201	...	...	1231	...	1301		...	2131	...	2201	...	2231	2301	2331	0001	...	0050*	0100
Amsterdam Centraal 470 a.	1109	...	1139	...	1209	...	...	1239	...	1309		...	2139	...	2209	...	2239	2309	2339	0009	...	0100*	0108

D – To Den Helder (Table **466**). H – To Heerhugowaard (Table **466**). * – 6–8 minutes earlier on ①⑥⑦ (also Dec. 26, Jan. 2, Apr. 14, May 1, 22, June 2).

470 AMSTERDAM and SCHIPHOL ✈ - EINDHOVEN - MAASTRICHT

km		Ⓐ	Ⓐ	Ⓐ	Ⓐ	Ⓐ	Ⓐ	⚒	⚒	Ⓐ			⚒			⚒							
0	**Amsterdam** Centraal 468 d.	...	...	...	...	...	0607	...	...	0637	...	...	0707	...	...	0737	...	...	0807	...	0837	...	and at
6	Amsterdam Amstel 468 d.	...	...	...	...	...	0615	...	...	0645	...	...	0715	...	...	0745	...	...	0815	...	0845	...	the
40	**Utrecht** Centraal 468 a.	...	...	...	...	...	0634	...	...	0704	...	...	0735	...	...	0804	...	...	0835	...	0904	...	same
40	**Utrecht** Centraal d.	...	...	...	...	...	0638	...	...	0708	...	...	0738	...	...	0808	0808	...	0838	...	0908	...	minutes
88	's-Hertogenbosch d.	...	*0556*	...	*0626*	...	0708	...	...	0738	...	...	0808	...	...	0838	0838	...	0908	...	0938	...	past
120	**Eindhoven** a.	...	*0624*	...	*0654*	...	0727	...	...	0757	...	...	0827	...	...	0857	0857	...	0927	...	0957	...	each
120	**Eindhoven** d.	...	0632	...	0702	...	0732	0732	...	0802	0802	...	0832	0832	...	0902	0902	...	0932	...	1002	...	hour
149	Weert d.	...	0647	...	0717	...	0747	0747	...	0817	0817	...	0847	0847	...	0917	0917	...	0947	...	1017	...	until
173	Roermond d.	...	0703	...	0733	...	0803	0803	...	0833	0833	...	0903	0903	...	0933	0933	...	1003	...	1033	...	
197	Sittard a.	...	0718	⪡	0748	⪡	0818	0818	⪡	0849	0849	⪡	0918	0918	⪡	0948	0948	⪡	1018	⪡	1048	⪡	
197	Sittard d.	0630	0720	0722	0750	0752	0820	0820	0822	0850	0850	0852	0920	0920	0922	0950	0950	0952	1020	1022	1050	1052	
216	**Heerlen** a.	|	|	0737	|	0807	|	|	0837	|	|	0907	|	|	0937	|	|	1007	|	1037	|	1107	
219	**Maastricht** a.	0650	0734	...	0804	...	0834	0834	...	0904	0904	...	0934	0934	...	1004	1004	...	1034	...	1104	...	

										H
Amsterdam Centraal 468 d.	2107	...	2137	...	2207	...	2237	...	2307	...
Amsterdam Amstel 468 d.	2115	...	2145	...	2215	...	2245	...	2315	...
Utrecht Centraal 468 a.	2134	...	2204	...	2234	...	2304	...	2334	...
Utrecht Centraal d.	2138	...	2208	...	2238	...	2308	...	2338	...
's-Hertogenbosch d.	2208	...	2238	...	2308	...	2338	...	0008	...
Eindhoven a.	2227	...	2257	...	2327	...	2357	...	0028	...
Eindhoven d.	2232	...	2302	...	2332	...	0002	...	...	0034
Weert d.	2247	...	2317	...	2344	...	0019	...	...	0056
Roermond d.	2303	...	2333	...	0003	...	0034	...	...	...
Sittard a.	2318	⪡	2348	⪡	0018t	⪡	0049t	⪡	...	...
Sittard d.	2320	2322	2350	2354	0020t	0022t	0051t	0054t	...	...
Heerlen a.	|	2337	|	0011	|	0037t	|	0109t	...	...
Maastricht a.	2334	...	0008	...	0034t	...	0105t	...	...	...

	Ⓐ	Ⓐ	Ⓐ	Ⓐ	Ⓐ	Ⓐ	⚒	⚒	⚒	
Maastricht d.	...	...	...	0526	...	0556	...	...	0626	...
Heerlen d.	...	...	0523	|	0553	|	...	0623	|	...
Sittard a.	...	...	0538	0540	0608	0610	...	0638	0640	...
Sittard d.	...	...	⪢	0543	⪢	0613	...	⪢	0643	...
Roermond d.	...	...	...	0558	...	0629	...	...	0659	...
Weert d.	...	...	...	0612	...	0642	...	...	0712	...
Eindhoven a.	...	...	...	0630	...	0701	...	...	0729	...
Eindhoven d.	0534	0602	...	0632	...	0702	0702	...	0732	0732
's-Hertogenbosch d.	0553	0623	...	0653	...	0723	0723	...	0753	0753
Utrecht Centraal a.	0622	0652	...	0722	...	0752	0752	...	0822	0822
Utrecht Centraal 468 d.	0625	0655	...	0725	...	0755	0755	...	0825	0825
Amsterdam Amstel 468 a.	0644	0714	...	0744	...	0814	0814	...	0844	0844
Amsterdam Centraal 468 a.	0652	0722	...	0752	...	0822	0822	...	0852	0852

	⚒	⚒																						
Maastricht d.	...	0656	...	...	0726	...	0756	...	0826	and at	...	2056	...	2126	...	2156	...	2226	...	2256	...	2356	...	0010
Heerlen d.	0653n	|	...	0723r	|	0753	|	0823	|	the	2053	|	2123	|	2153	|	2223	|	2253	|	2353	|	0003	|
Sittard a.	0708	0710	...	0738	0740	0808	0810	0838	0840	same	2108	2110	2138	2140	2208	2210	2238	2240	2308	2310	0008	0010	0026	0030
Sittard d.	⪢	0713	...	⪢	0743	⪢	0813	⪢	0843	minutes	...	2113	...	2143	...	2213	...	2243	...	2313	...	0013	...	0032
Roermond d.	...	0729	...	...	0759	...	0829	...	0859	past	...	2129	...	2159	...	2229	...	2259	...	2329	...	0029k	...	0050
Weert d.	...	0742	...	...	0812	...	0842	...	0912	each	...	2142	...	2212	...	2242	...	2312	...	2342	...	0042k	...	...
Eindhoven a.	...	0759	...	...	0829	...	0859	...	0929	hour	...	2159	...	2229	...	2259	...	2329	...	2359	...	0100k	...	...
Eindhoven d.	...	0802	0802	...	0832	...	0902	...	0932	until	...	2202	...	2232	...	2302	...	2332	...	*0005*	...	...	...	...
's-Hertogenbosch d.	...	0823	0823	...	0853	...	0923	...	0953		...	2223	...	2253	...	2323	...	2353	...	*0037*	...	...	...	...
Utrecht Centraal a.	...	0852	0852	...	0922	...	0952	...	1022		...	2252	...	2322	...	2352	...	0022	...	...	...	...	...	...
Utrecht Centraal 468 d.	...	0855	0855	...	0925	...	0955	...	1025		...	2255	...	2325	...	2355	...	0025	...	...	...	...	...	...
Amsterdam Amstel 468 a.	...	0914	0914	...	0944	...	1014	...	1044		...	2314	...	2344	...	0014	...	0050z	...	...	...	...	...	...
Amsterdam Centraal 468 a.	...	0922	0922	...	0952	...	1022	...	1052		...	2322	...	2352	...	0022	...	0100z	...	...	...	...	...	...

SCHIPHOL ✈ - EINDHOVEN

	Ⓐ	Ⓐ	⚒						
Schiphol ✈ 468 ‡ d.	0614	0644	0644	0714	0744	and every	1914	1944	...
Amsterdam Zuid 468 ‡ d.	0623	0653	0653	0723	0753	30 minutes	1923	1953	...
Utrecht Centraal 468 ‡ a.	0646	0716	0716	0746	0816	until	1946	2016	...
Utrecht Centraal d.	0652	0722	...	0752	0822		1952	2022	...
's-Hertogenbosch d.	0721	0751	...	0821	0851		2021	2051	...
Eindhoven a.	0746	0816	...	0846	0916		2046	2116	...

	Ⓐ	Ⓐ	Ⓐ	⚒					
Eindhoven d.	0614	0644	0714	...	0744	0814	and every	1914	1944
's-Hertogenbosch d.	0638	0708	0738	...	0808	0838	30 minutes	1938	2008
Utrecht Centraal a.	0707	0737	0807	...	0837	0907	until	2007	2037
Utrecht Centraal 468 § d.	0713	0743	0813	0813	0843	0913		2013	2043
Amsterdam Zuid 468 § a.	0737	0807	0837	0837	0907	0937		2037	2107
Schiphol ✈ 468 § a.	0744	0814	0844	0844	0914	0944		2044	2114

H – ①⑥⑦ (also Dec. 26, Jan. 2, Apr. 14, May 1, 22, June 2).

k – 7–14 minutes later on the mornings of ②–⑤ (not Dec. 26, Jan. 2, Apr. 14, May 1, 22, June 2)

n – 0638 on ⑥ (also Dec. 26, Apr. 13, 30, May 21, June 1).

r – 0714 on †.

t – Up to 21 minutes later on the mornings of ①–⑤ (not Apr. 14, May 1, 22, June 2).

z – 6–8 minutes earlier on ①⑥⑦ (also Dec. 26, Jan. 2, Apr. 14, May 1, 22, June 2).

‡ – Additional trains Schiphol ✈ - Utrecht at 2014 and every 30 minutes until 2344.

§ – Additional trains Utrecht - Schiphol ✈ at 2113 and every 30 minutes until 2343.

⪡ – Detached from train in previous column at Sittard.

⪢ – Attached to train in next column at Sittard.

471 MAASTRICHT - HEERLEN - KERKRADE and AACHEN

km	See note ⊠				A	Ⓐ	Ⓐ	⚒	E	⚒	⚒						❖							
0	**Maastricht** d.	0015	0045	...	...	0515	0545	...	...	0615	0645	...	...	0715	0745	...	and at	2115	2145	...	2215	2245	2315	2345
11	Valkenburg d.	0027	0058	...	...	0527	0557	...	...	0627	0657	...	...	0727	0757	...	the same	2127	2157	...	2227	2257	2327	2357
24	**Heerlen** d.	0042	0114	...	0528	0545	0615	0615	0628	0645	0715	0715	0728	0745	0815	0828	minutes	2145	2215	2228	2245	2315	2345	0015
	Herzogenrath 802 a.	...	...	...	0543	|	|	|	0643	|	|	|	0743	|	|	0843	past each	|	|	2243	|	|	|	|
	Aachen Hbf 802 a.	...	...	...	0601	|	|	|	0701	|	|	|	0801	|	|	0901	hour until	|	|	2301	|	|	|	|
33	**Kerkrade** Centrum a.	...	...	...	...	0558	0628	0628	...	0658	0728	0728	...	0758	0828	...		2158	2228	...	2258	2328	2358	0028

km	See note ⊠			Ⓐ	Ⓐ	Ⓐ	⚒	⚒	A	⚒			E											
	Kerkrade Centrum d.	0031	...	...	...	0601	...	0631	...	0701	...	0731	...	0801	0831	...	0901	and at	2231	...	2301	2331	...	0001
0	**Aachen** Hbf 802 d.	|	...	|	|	|	|	|	0632	|	|	|	0732	|	|	0832	|	the same	|	2232	|	|	2332	|
14	Herzogenrath 802 d.	|	...	|	|	|	|	|	0650	|	|	|	0750	|	|	0850	|	minutes	|	2250	|	|	2350	|
24	**Heerlen** d.	0047	...	0517	0547	0617	0617	0647	0706	0717	0717	0747	0806	0817	0847	0906	0917	past each	2247	2306	2317	2347	0006	0017
	Valkenburg d.	0101	...	0531	0601	0631	0631	0701	...	0731	0731	0801	...	0831	0901	...	0931	hour until	2301	...	2331	0001	...	0031
	Maastricht a.	0114	...	0544	0614	0644	0644	0714	...	0744	0744	0814	...	0844	0914	...	0944		2314	...	2344	0014	...	0044

A – ①–⑤ (not Dec. 24, 25, 26, 31, Jan. 1, Apr. 10, 13, May 1, 21, June 1, 11).

E – ①–⑥ (not Dec. 25, 26, Jan. 1, Apr. 10, 13, May 1, 21, June 1, 11, Oct. 3).

❖ – On ⑦ Apr. 12 - Oct. 25 (also Apr. 13, May 1, 21, June 1, 11, Oct. 3) Heerlen d. 0826 (not 0828).

⊠ – Maastricht - Heerlen - Kerkrade and v.v. operated by **Veolia** (NS tickets valid).

DEN HAAG - EINDHOVEN - VENLO 472

km		N	N		Ⓐ	Ⓐ	Ⓐ	⑥t	Ⓐ	⚒	⚒										⚒	†	④–⑥
0	**Den Haag** Centraal 450 d.	...	...	...	...	0458	...	...	0551	0621	0651	...	0721	0751		2121	2151	...	2221	...	2251	2251	...
2	**Den Haag** HS 450 d.	...	0138	...	...	0503	...	*0538*	0556	0626	0656	...	0726	0756		2126	2156	...	2226	...	2256	2256	2346
10	Delft 450 d.	...	0146	...	...	0515	...	*0546*	0603	0633	0703	...	0733	0803		2133	2203	...	2233	...	2303	2303	|
24	**Rotterdam** Centraal 450 a.	...	0159	...	...	0531	...	*0559*	0615	0645	0715	...	0745	0815	and every	2145	2215	...	2245	...	2315	2315	0002
24	**Rotterdam** Centraal 450 d.	0102	0202	...	...	0533	0547	0617	0617	0647	0717	...	0747	0817	30 minutes	2147	2217	...	2247	...	2317	2317	0003
44	Dordrecht 450 d.	0116	0218	...	...	0557	0601	0631	0631	0701	0731	...	0801	0831	until	2201	2231	...	2301	...	2331	2331	0018
74	Breda 450 475 d.	0134	0236	...	...	...	0621	0651	0651	0721	0751	...	0821	0851		2221	2251	...	2321	...	2351	2351	0036
95	Tilburg 475 d.	0147	0250	...	...	...	0636	0706	0706	0736	0806	...	0836	0906		2236	2306	...	2336	2340	0006	0006	0050
132	**Eindhoven** a.	0219	0320	...	...	...	0700	0730	0730	0800	0830	...	0900	0930		2300	2330	...	2400	0009	0030	0030	0112
132	**Eindhoven** d.	...	...	...	0632	...	0702	0732	0732	0802	0832	0832	0902	0932		2302	2332	...	...	0018	0032	0032	...
145	Helmond d.	...	...	...	0641	...	0711	0741	0741	0811	0841	0841	0911	0941		2311	2341	...	...	0031	0042	0044	...
183	**Venlo** a.	...	...	...	0713	...	0743	0815	0815	0843	0913	0913	0943	1013		2343	0015	...	...	...	0113	0116	...

	N	N		Ⓐ	Ⓐ	Ⓐ	Ⓐ	⚒	⚒									K				
Venlo d.	...	...	...	...	...	0549	0619	...	0649	...	...	0719	0749		2119	2149	...	2219	2219	...	2249	...	2319
Helmond d.	...	...	...	...	...	0620	0650	...	0720	...	...	0750	0820		2150	2220	...	2250	2250	...	2320	...	2350
Eindhoven a.	...	...	...	...	...	0630	0700	...	0730	...	...	0800	0830		2200	2230	...	2300	2300	...	2330	...	2400
Eindhoven d.	0028	0128	...	0531	0602	0632	0702	0702	0732	0732	...	0802	0832		2202	2232	...	2302	2302	...	2332	...	...
Tilburg 475 d.	0056	0156	...	0557	0625	0655	0725	0725	0755	0755	...	0825	0855	and every	2225	2255	...	2325	2325	...	2355	...	...
Breda 450 475 d.	0114	0214	...	0610	0639	0709	0739	0739	0809	0809	...	0839	0909	30 minutes	2239	2309	...	2339	2339	...	0009	...	...
Dordrecht 450 d.	0138	0238	...	0629	0659	0729	0759	0759	0829	0829	...	0859	0929	until	2259	2329	...	2359	2359	0007	0029	...	...
Rotterdam Centraal 450 a.	0158	0254	...	0642	0712	0742	0812	0812	0842	0842	...	0912	0942		2312	2342	...	0012	0012	0033	0042	...	...
Rotterdam Centraal 450 d.	0202	0302	...	0646	0716	0746	0816	0816	0846	0846	...	0916	0946		2316	2346	...	...	0016	0039	...	0102	...
Delft 450 a.	0215	0315	...	0658	0728	0758	0828	0828	0858	0858	...	0925	0958		2328	2358	...	...	0029	0054	...	0117	...
Den Haag HS 450 a.	0222	0322	...	0705	0735	0805	0835	0835	0905	0905	...	0935	1005		2335	0005	...	...	0038	0105	...	0123	...
Den Haag Centraal 450 a.	...	...	...	0710	0740	0810	0840	0840	0910	0910	...	0940	1010		2340	0010	...	...	0043	0110	...	...	...

K – ⑤⑥⑦ (also Dec. 25, Jan. 1, Apr. 13, 30, May 21, June 1). N – ⑤⑥⑦ (also Jan. 1, Apr. 30). t – Also Apr. 13, 30, May 21, June 1.

ROOSENDAAL - 's-HERTOGENBOSCH - NIJMEGEN - ARNHEM - ZWOLLE 475

km		Ⓐ	Ⓐ	Ⓐ	⚒	Ⓐ	⚒	†	Ⓐ	⚒	†	⚒		†	⚒							H		
0	**Roosendaal** d.	...	...	...	...	0521	...	...	0551	...	...	0621	...	0645	0651	0721	0751		2121	2151	2221	...	2251	2321
23	Breda 472 d.	...	...	...	...	0540	...	...	0610	...	...	0640	...	0704	0710	0740	0810		2140	2210	2240	...	2310	2340
44	Tilburg 472 d.	...	...	...	...	0555	...	...	0625	...	...	0655	...	0725	0725	0755	0825		2155	2225	2255	...	2325	2355
67	**'s-Hertogenbosch** d.	...	...	...	...	0614	...	...	0644	...	...	0714	...	0744	0744	0814	0844		2214	2244	2314	...	2344	0012
86	Oss d.	...	...	...	...	0626	...	...	0656	...	...	0726	...	0756	0756	0826	0856	and every	2226	2256	2326	...	2356	—
110	**Nijmegen** 468 d.	...	*0531*	0615	...	0645	0645	*0709*	0715	...	0730	0745	...	0815	0815	0845	0915	30 minutes	2245	2315	2344	0003	0013	...
129	**Arnhem** 468 a.	...	*0556*	0635	...	0705	0705	*0723*	0735	...	0753	0805	...	0835	0835	0905	0935	until	2305	2335	0005	0020	0040	G
129	**Arnhem** d.	...	0600	0640	...	0710	0710	0730	0740	0740	...	0810	0810	0840	0840	0910	0940		2310	2340	...	0023	...	0051
145	Dieren d.	...	0619	0652	...	0722	0722	0749	0752	0752	...	0822	0822	0852	0852	0922	0952		2322	2352	...	0042	...	0109
159	Zutphen d.	0604	0634	0704	0704	0734	0734	0804	0804	0804	...	0834	0834	0904	0904	0934	1004		2334	0004	...	0054	...	0121
174	Deventer d.	0620	0650	0720	0720	0750	0750	0820	0820	0820	...	0850	0850	0920	0920	0950	1020		2350	0020	...	...	...	...
204	**Zwolle** a.	0644	0713	0744	0744	0814	0814	0844	0844	0844	...	0914	0914	0944	0944	1014	1044		0014	0044	...	...	...	...

	Ⓐ	Ⓐ	Ⓐ	Ⓐ	⚒		⚒										⑤⑥z	†	J		H	G		
Zwolle d.	...	...	...	...	...	...	0618a	...	0648a	0718v	...	0748	0818		2118	2148	2218	2218	2218	2248	...	...	2318	2350
Deventer d.	...	...	...	...	...	...	0644a	...	0714a	0744v	...	0814	0844		2144	2214	2244	2244	2244	2314	...	...	2344	0014
Zutphen d.	...	...	...	0548	...	...	0657	...	0727v	0757	...	0827	0857		2157	2227	2257	2257	2257	2327	...	...	2357	0027
Dieren d.	...	...	...	0600	...	...	0707	...	0737v	0807	...	0837	0907		2207	2237	2307	2307	2307	2337	...	...	0007	0037
Arnhem a.	...	...	...	0619	...	...	0720	...	0750v	0820	...	0850	0920	and every	2220	2250	2320	2320	2320	2350	...	...	0020	0050
Arnhem 468 d.	...	...	0558	0626	...	0656v	0726	...	0756	0826	...	0856	0926	30 minutes	2226	2256	2326	2326	2326	2356	...	...	*0038*	...
Nijmegen 468 d.	...	...	0619	0648	...	0718v	0748	...	0818	0848	...	0918	0948	until	2248	2318	2348	2348	2348	0015	0024	0041	*0056*	...
Oss d.	...	...	0634	0703	...	0733v	0803	...	0833	0903	...	0933	1003		2303	2333	0003	0003	0003	...	0044	0102	...	...
's-Hertogenbosch d.	...	0620	0650	0719	0719	0750	0819	0819	0849	0919	...	0949	1019		2319	2349	0019	0019	0030k	...	0102	0120	...	...
Tilburg 472 d.	*0557*	0637	0707	0737	0737	0807	0837	0837	0907	0937	...	1007	1037		2337	0007	0037	0038	0047	...	...	...	...	...
Breda 472 d.	0622	0652	0722	0752	0752	0822	0852	0852	0922	0952	...	1022	1052		2352	0022	0057	0101	0107	...	...	...	...	...
Roosendaal a.	0641	0711	0741	0811	0811	0842	0911	0911	0942	1011	...	1042	1111		0011	0042	0116	0119	0124	...	...	...	...	...

G – ②–⑤ (not Dec. 26, Jan. 2, Apr. 14, May 1, 22, June 2).
H – ①⑥⑦ (also Dec. 26, Jan. 2, Apr. 14, May 1, 22, June 2).
J – ①–④ (not Dec. 25, Jan. 1, Apr. 13, 30, May 21, June 1).
a – Ⓐ only.
k – Arrives 0018.
v – ⚒ only.
z – Also Apr. 13, 30, May 21, June 1.

NIJMEGEN - VENLO - ROERMOND 477

Operated by **Veolia** (NS tickets valid)

km					Ⓐ	Ⓐ		Ⓐ	⚒	Ⓐ	⚒	⚒		⚒										
0	**Nijmegen** d.	0008	...	...	...	...	...	0539	...	0609	...	0639	...	0709	...	...	0739	0809	and every	2239	2309	...	2338	...	...
24	Boxmeer d.	0031	...	...	...	...	...	0602	...	0632	...	0702	...	0732	...	...	0802	0832	30 minutes	2302	2332	...	0001	...	...
39	Venray d.	0045	...	...	...	...	...	0616	...	0646	...	0716	...	0746	...	...	0816	0846	until	2316	2346	...	0015	...	...
61	**Venlo** d.	0102	...	...	0534	0604	...	0634	0634	0704	0704	0734	0734	0804	0804	...	0834	0904		2334	0004	...	0030	...	...
84	**Roermond** a.	...	...	...	0557	0627	...	0657	0657	0727	0727	0757	0757	0827	0827	...	0857	0927		2357	0027	...	...	...	...

					Ⓐ	Ⓐ	⚒		Ⓐ	⚒	Ⓐ		⚒		⚒									
Roermond d.	0006	0036	...	...	...	...	...	...	0606	...	0636	...	0706	...	0736	...	...	0806	0836	and every	2236	2306	...	2336
Venlo d.	0028	0058	...	...	0500	0530	0600	...	0630	0630	0700	0700	0730	0730	0800	0800	...	0830	0900	30 minutes	2300	2330	...	2358
Venray d.	...	...	...	...	0517	0547	0617	...	0647	0647	0717	0717	0747	0747	0817	0817	...	0847	0917	until	2317	2347	...	...
Boxmeer d.	...	...	...	...	0530	0600	0630	...	0700	0700	0730	0730	0800	0800	0830	0830	...	0900	0930		2330	0000	...	...
Nijmegen a.	...	...	...	...	0550	0620	0650	...	0720	0720	0750	0750	0820	0820	0850	0850	...	0920	0950		2350	0020	...	...

ARNHEM - TIEL - GELDERMALSEN - UTRECHT and 's-HERTOGENBOSCH 478

km		B	Ⓐ	⚒	⚒														
0	**Tiel** d.	0552	0621	0651	0721	...	0751	0821	and every	1951	2021	...	2051	2105	2135	2205	2235	2305	2335
12	Geldermalsen a.	0604	0633	0703	0733	...	0803	0833	30 minutes	2003	2033	...	2103	2116	2146	2216	2247	2316	2347
38	**Utrecht** Centraal a.	0632	0702	0732	0802	...	0832	0902	until	2032	2102	...	2132	2147	2217	2247	2317	2347	0017

	Ⓐ	Ⓐ	Ⓐ	⚒															A
Utrecht Centraal d.	0528	0559	0628	0658	...	0728	0758	and every	1928	1958	...	2013	2043	2113	2143	2213	2243	2313	2343
Geldermalsen d.	0552	0622	0652	0722	...	0752	0822	30 minutes	1952	2022	...	2037	2107	2137	2207	2237	2307	2337	0007
Tiel a.	0605	0635	0705	0735	...	0805	0835	until	2005	2035	...	2049	2119	2149	2219	2249	2319	2349	0019

A – Daily except ③.
B – ①②③⑤ (not Dec. 26, Apr. 13, June 1).
E – ①–⑥ (not Dec. 25, 26, Jan. 1, Apr. 13, May 21, June 1).
c – Also May 1.
d – Also Apr. 30.

ARNHEM - TIEL and v.v. Operated by ***Syntus*** (NS tickets valid). 2nd class only. *44 km.* Journey time 37 – 39 minutes.
From Arnhem at 0031 ⑦ **c**, 0631 Ⓐ, 0701 Ⓐ, 0731 Ⓐ, 0801 Ⓐ, 0831 **E**, 0931, 1031 and hourly until 1531, then 1601 Ⓐ, 1631, 1701 Ⓐ, 1731, 1801 Ⓐ, 1831, 1931, 2031, 2131, 2231 and 2331.
From Tiel at 0618 Ⓐ, 0648 Ⓐ, 0718 Ⓐ, 0748 **E**, 0818 Ⓐ, 0848, 0948 and hourly until 1548, then 1618 Ⓐ, 1648, 1718 Ⓐ, 1748, 1818 Ⓐ, 1848, 1948, 2051, 2151, 2251 and 2351 ⑥ **d**.

GELDERMALSEN - 's-HERTOGENBOSCH and v.v. *22 km.* Journey time: 16 – 17 minutes.
From Geldermalsen at 0609 Ⓐ, 0639 Ⓐ, 0709 ⚒, 0739, 0809, 0839 and every 30 minutes until 2139, then 2239 and 2339.
From 's-Hertogenbosch at 0602 Ⓐ, 0632 Ⓐ, 0702 ⚒, 0732 ⚒, 0802, 0832 and every 30 minutes until 2202, then 2302.

DORDRECHT - GELDERMALSEN 479

Operated by **Arriva** (NS tickets valid); 2nd class only

km		Ⓐ	E	E						
0	**Dordrecht** d.	0437	0507	0537	0607	0637	and every	2337	0007	0037
10	Sliedrecht d.	0447	0517	0547	0617	0647	30 minutes	2347	0017	0047
24	Gorinchem d.	0502	0532	0602	0632	0702	until	0002	0032	0058
49	**Geldermalsen** a.	0533	0603	0633	0703	0733		0033	0103	...

	Ⓐ	E	E	E					
Geldermalsen d.	0539	...	0609	0639	...	0709	0739	and every	0039	0109
Gorinchem d.	0604	0604	0634	0704	0704	0734	0804	30 minutes	0104	0134
Sliedrecht d.	0616	0616	0646	0716	0716	0746	0816	until	0116	0146
Dordrecht a.	0625	0625	0655	0725	0725	0755	0825		0125	0155

E – ①–⑥ (not Dec. 25, 26, Jan. 1, Apr. 13, June 1).

480 AMSTERDAM and SCHIPHOL ✈ - AMERSFOORT - DEVENTER - ENSCHEDE

AMSTERDAM CENTRAAL - AMERSFOORT (all trains)

km			⑥⑦k	A		Ⓐ	Ⓐ	⚒	Ⓐ	⚒	⚒		⚒											
0	**Amsterdam** Centraal **458** d.	0006	0036	0043	...	0557	0606	0627	0636	0657	0706	0727	0736	0757	0806	0827	0836	0857	and at the same minutes past each hour until	2236	2257	2306	2328	2336
14	Weesp **457 458** d.	0024	0054	0100	...	|	0623	|	0653	|	0723	|	0753	|	0823	|	0853	|		2253	|	2323	|	2353
23	Naarden-Bussum **457** d.	0031	0101	0108	...	|	0630	|	0700	|	0730	|	0800	|	0830	|	0900	|		2300	|	2330	|	0000
29	Hilversum **457** d.	0040r	0111	0118	...	0619	0640	0649	0710	0719	0740	0749	0810	0819	0840	0849	0910	0919		2310	2319	2340	2349	0010
36	Baarn d.	0046r	0118	0125	...	|	0646	|	0716	|	0746	|	0816	|	0846	|	0916	|		2316	|	2346	|	0016
45	**Amersfoort** a.	0055r	0125	0133	...	0632	0655	0702	0725	0732	0755	0802	0825	0832	0855	0902	0925	0932		2325	2332	2355	0002	0025

				Ⓐ	Ⓐ	Ⓐ	Ⓐ		Ⓐ		⚒		⚒										K	
Amersfoort d.	0005	...	0435	0456	0536	0605	0628	0635	0658	0705	0728	0735	0758	0805	0828	0835	0858	and at the same minutes past each hour until	2235	2258	2305	2328	2335	2358
Baarn d.	0012	...	0442	0503	0543	0612	|	0642	|	0712	|	0742	|	0812	|	0842	|		2242	|	2312	|	2342	|
Hilversum **457** d.	0019	...	0449	0510	0550	0619	0641	0649	0711	0719	0741	0749	0811	0819	0841	0849	0911		2249	2311	2319	2341	2349	0011
Naarden-Bussum **457** d.	0029	...	0500	0519	0559	0628	|	0658	|	0728	|	0758	|	0828	|	0858	|		2258	|	2328	|	2358	|
Weesp **457 458** a.	0036	...	0507	0527	0606	0635	|	0705	|	0735	|	0805	|	0835	|	0905	|		2305	|	2335	|	0005	|
Amsterdam Centraal **458** a.	0056	...	0528	0548	0625	0652	0701	0722	0731	0752	0801	0822	0831	0852	0901	0922	0931		2322	2331	2352	0001	0022	0031

SCHIPHOL ✈ - AMERSFOORT - DEVENTER - ENSCHEDE

See table **481** for through journeys **Rotterdam / Den Haag - Amersfoort - Deventer - Enschede** and v.v.

km		Ⓐ	Ⓐ	Ⓐ	⚒	★	⚒			★				★		⊡	⊡						G	F
0	**Schiphol** ✈ **457** d.	...	0549	0619	...	0649	0719	0749	0819	0849	0919	0949	1019	1049	1119	1149	and at the same minutes past each hour until	2119	2149	2219	2249	2319	...	...
9	Amsterdam Zuid **457** d.	...	0558	0628	...	0658	0728	0758	0828	0858	0928	0958	1028	1058	1128	1158		2128	2158	2228	2258	2328	...	...
14	Duivendrecht **457** d.	...	0604	0634	...	0704	0734	0804	0834	0904	0934	1004	1034	1104	1134	1204		2134	2204	2234	2304	2334	...	...
37	Hilversum **457** d.	...	0622	0652	...	0722	0752	0822	0852	0922	0952	1022	1052	1122	1152	1222		2152	2222	2252	2322	2352	...	...
53	**Amersfoort** a.	...	0635	0705	...	0735	0805	0835	0905	0935	1005	1035	1105	1135	1205	1235		2205	2235	2305	2335	0005	...	...
			|	⚒		|	d	|		|		|		|		|			|		|	H		
53	**Amersfoort** d.	...	0641	0710	0710	0741	0810	0841	0910	0941	1010	1041	1110	1141	1210	1241		2210	2241	2310	2341	0010	0010	0010
96	Apeldoorn d.	0612	0707	0737	0737	0807	0837	0907	0937	1007	1037	1107	1137	1207	1237	1307		2237	2307	2337	0007	0037	0037	0037
111	**Deventer** d.	0627	0720	0750	0750	0820	0850	0920	0950	1020	1050	1120	1150	1220	1250	1320		2250	2320	2350	0020	0050	0057	0057
149	Almelo **492** d.	0700	0746	0816	0816	0846	0916	0946	1016	1046	1116	1146	1216	1246	1316	1346		2316	2346	0016	0046	0120	0127	0129
164	Hengelo **492** a.	0714	0757	0827	0827	0857	0927	0957	1027	1057	1127	1157	1227	1257	1327	1357		2327	2357	0027	0057	0130	0138	0141
172	**Enschede** **492** a.	0725	0805	0835	0835	*0915*	0935	1005	1035	*1115*	1135	1205	1235	*1315*	1335	1405		2335	0005	0036	0105	0138	0146	0148

	L	①m	Ⓐ	Ⓐ	⚒	⚒	⚒					★		♥	♥				★					
Enschede **492** d.	0454	0459	0526	0556	...	0626	0656	...	0726	0756	0826	*0855*	0926	0956	and at the same minutes past each hour until	1926	1956	2026	*2055*	2126	2156	2226	2245	...
Hengelo **492** d.	0505	0510	0535	0605	...	0635	0705	...	0735	0805	0835	0905	0935	1005		1935	2005	2035	2105	2135	2205	2235	2256	...
Almelo **492** d.	0518	0524	0549	0619	...	0649	0719	...	0749	0819	0849	0919	0949	1019		1949	2019	2049	2119	2149	2219	2249	2312	2332
Deventer d.	0545	0548	0615	0645	0645	0715	0745	0745	0815	0845	0915	0945	1015	1045		2015	2045	2115	2145	2215	2245	2315	...	0004
Apeldoorn d.	0557	0600	0627	0657	0657	0727	0757	0757	0827	0857	0927	0957	1027	1057		2027	2057	2127	2157	2227	2257	2327	...	0018
Amersfoort a.	0623	0623	0653	0723	0723	0753	0823	0823	0853	0923	0953	1023	1053	1123		2053	2123	2153	2223	2253	2323	2353	...	...
	|	|	Ⓐ	|	|	d	|	|		|		|		|			|		|		|		
Amersfoort d.	0625	0625	0655	0725	0725	0755	0825	0825	0855	0925	0955	1025	1055	1125		2055	2125	2155	2225	2255	2325	2355	...	...
Hilversum **457** d.	0638	0638	0708	0738	0738	0808	0838	0838	0908	0938	1008	1038	1108	1138		2108	2138	2208	2238	2308	2338	0008	...	...
Duivendrecht **457** a.	0657	0657	0726	0757	0757	0827	0857	0857	0927	0957	1027	1057	1127	1157		2127	2157	2227	2257	2327	2357	0027	...	...
Amsterdam Zuid **457** a.	0702	0702	0731	0802	0802	0832	0902	0902	0932	1002	1032	1102	1132	1202		2132	2202	2232	2302	2332	0002	0032	...	...
Schiphol ✈ **457** a.	0709	0709	0738	0809	0809	0839	0909	0909	0939	1009	1039	1109	1139	1209		2139	2209	2239	2309	2339	0009	0040	...	...

A – ①–⑤ (not Apr. 14, May 1, 22, June 2).
F – ④⑤ (not Dec. 26, Jan. 2, May 1, 22).
G – ②③ (not Apr. 14, June 2).
H – ①⑥⑦ (also Dec. 26, Jan. 2, Apr. 14, May 1, 22, June 2).
L – ②–⑤ (not Dec. 25, 26, Jan. 1, Apr. 30, May 21).

d – Daily.
k – Also Apr. 14, May 1, 22, June 2.
m – Not Apr. 13, June 1.
r – 10–12 minutes later on ②–⑤ (not Dec. 26, Jan. 2, Apr. 14, May 1, 22, June 2).

★ – *IC* train to / from Germany via Bad Bentheim (Table **22**).
⊡ – The services from Schiphol at 1249, 1449, 1649 and 1849 are *IC* trains to Germany via Bad Bentheim (see Table **22**; passengers for Enschede should change trains at Hengelo).
♥ – The services arriving Schiphol at 1309, 1509, 1709, 1909 and 2109 are *IC* trains from Germany via Bad Bentheim (see Table **22**; passengers from Enschede depart *1055 / 1255 / 1455 / 1655 / 1855* and change trains at Hengelo).

481 UTRECHT and SCHIPHOL ✈ - AMERSFOORT - ZWOLLE

For connecting trains **Amsterdam Centraal - Amersfoort** (also for other trains Schiphol ✈ - Amersfoort) see Table **480**

	Ⓐ	Ⓐ	Ⓐ	Ⓐ	⚒	Ⓐ	⚒	⚒	⚒	Ⓐ	⑥z	⚒		⚒		Ⓒ	Ⓐ	Ⓒ	†		Ⓐ	Ⓒ			Ⓒ
Rotterdam Centraal **483** d.	...	...	0603	...	...	...	...	0633	...	0703	0703	...	...	...	...	...	0733	0733	0733	...	0803	0803	...	...	...
Den Haag Centraal **483** d.	...	...	|	0606	...	...	...	|	0636	|	|	0706	...	...	...	...	|	|	|	0736	|	|	0806	...	...
Utrecht Centraal d.	0620	0620	0650	0650	0650	...	...	0720	0720	0747	0750	0750	0750	...	...	...	0817	0820	0820	0820	0847	0850	0850	...	...
Schiphol ✈ d.	|	|	|	|	|	0619	...	|	|	|	|	|	|	0719	...	0719z	|	|	|	|	|	|	|	0819	0819
Amsterdam Zuid d.	|	|	|	|	|	0628	...	|	|	|	|	|	|	0728	...	0728z	|	|	|	|	|	|	|	0828	0828
Duivendrecht d.	|	|	|	|	|	0634	...	|	|	|	|	|	|	0734	...	0734z	|	|	|	|	|	|	|	0834	0834
Amersfoort a.	0634	0634	0704	0704	0704	0705	...	0734	0734	0801	0804	0804	0804	0805	...	0805z	0831	0834	0834	0834	0901	0904	0904	0905	0905
Amersfoort d.	0638	0638	0710	0710	0710	0708	0708	0738	0738	0804	0810	0810	0810	0808	0808	0808	0834	0838	0838	0838	0904	0910	0910	0908	0908
Deventer **480** a.	|	|	0748	0748	0748	|	|	|	|	|	0848	0848	0848	|	|	|	|	|	|	|	|	0948	0948	|	|
Enschede **480** a.	|	|	0835	0835	0835	|	|	|	|	|	...	0935	0935	|	|	|	|	|	|	|	|	...	1035	|	|
Zwolle a.	0714	0714	...	...	...	0744	0744	0814	0814	0841	...	...	...	0844	0844	0844	0911	0914	0914	0914	0941	...	...	0944	0944
Leeuwarden **486** a.	|	0816	...	...	...	|	|	0914	|	0954	...	...	...	|	|	0954	1014	1014	1014	|	1054	...	...	|	1054
Groningen **486** a.	0814	...	...	...	...	0853	0853	...	0914	...	...	...	...	0953	0953	...	...	...	...	1014	...	...	...	1053	...

	Ⓐ	Ⓒ	Ⓒ		Ⓐ	Ⓒ			Ⓒ	Ⓐ	Ⓒ	⑥z							Ⓑr		⑥z				
Rotterdam Centraal **483** d.	0833	0833	0833	...	0903	0903	...	...	...	0933	0933	0933	...	1003	...	...	...	1033	1033	...	...	1103	...	...	...
Den Haag Centraal **483** d.	|	|	|	0836	|	|	0906	...	...	|	|	|	0936	|	1006	...	...	|	|	1036	1036	|	1106	...	...
Utrecht Centraal d.	0917	0920	0920	0920	0947	0950	0950	...	...	1017	1020	1020	1020	1050	1050	...	...	1120	1120	1120	1120	1150	1150	...	...
Schiphol ✈ d.	|	|	|	|	|	|	|	0919	0919	|	|	|	|	|	|	1019	1019	|	|	|	|	|	|	1119	1119
Amsterdam Zuid d.	|	|	|	|	|	|	|	0928	0928	|	|	|	|	|	|	1028	1028	|	|	|	|	|	|	1128	1128
Duivendrecht d.	|	|	|	|	|	|	|	0934	0934	|	|	|	|	|	|	1034	1034	|	|	|	|	|	|	1134	1134
Amersfoort a.	0931	0934	0934	0934	1001	1004	1004	1005	1005	1031	1034	1034	1034	1104	1104	1105	1105	1134	1134	1134	1134	1204	1204	1205	1205
Amersfoort d.	0934	0938	0938	0938	1004	1010	1010	1008	1008	1034	1038	1038	1038	1110	1110	1108	1108	1139	1139	1139	1139	1210	1210	1208	1208
Deventer **480** a.	|	|	|	|	|	1048	1048	|	|	|	|	|	|	1148	1148	|	|	|	|	|	|	1248	1248	|	|
Enschede **480** a.	|	|	|	|	|	1135	1135	|	|	|	|	|	|	1235e	1235	|	|	|	|	|	|	1335	1335	|	|
Zwolle a.	1011	1014	1014	1014	1041	...	...	1044	1044	1111	1114	1114	1114	...	...	1144	1144	1214	1214	1214	1214	...	...	1244	1244
Leeuwarden **486** a.	1114	1114	|	|	1154	...	...	|	1154	1214	1214	|	|	...	...	|	1254	1314	|	|	1314	...	...	|	1354
Groningen **486** a.	...	...	1114	1114	...	...	...	1153	...	...	...	1214	1214	...	...	1253	...	...	1314	1314	...	...	...	1353	...

		⑤f							⑥z		†						⑤⑦k		Ⓐ	Ⓒ	†			Ⓒ	Ⓐ
Rotterdam Centraal **483** d.	1133	1133	...	1203	...	...	...	1233	1233	...	...	1303	...	...	...	1333	1333	...	1403	1403	1403	...	...	...	1433
Den Haag Centraal **483** d.	|	|	1136	|	1206	...	...	|	|	1236	1236	|	1306	...	...	|	|	1336	|	|	|	1406	...	...	|
Utrecht Centraal d.	1220	1220	1220	1250	1250	...	...	1320	1320	1320	1320	1350	1350	...	...	1420	1420	1420	1447	1450	1450	1450	...	...	1517
Schiphol ✈ d.	|	|	|	|	|	1219	1219	|	|	|	|	|	|	1319	1319	|	|	|	|	|	|	|	1419	1419	|
Amsterdam Zuid d.	|	|	|	|	|	1228	1228	|	|	|	|	|	|	1328	1328	|	|	|	|	|	|	|	1428	1428	|
Duivendrecht d.	|	|	|	|	|	1234	1234	|	|	|	|	|	|	1334	1334	|	|	|	|	|	|	|	1434	1434	|
Amersfoort a.	1234	1234	1234	1304	1304	1305	1305	1334	1334	1334	1334	1404	1404	1405	1405	1434	1434	1434	1501	1504	1504	1504	1505	1505	1531
Amersfoort d.	1238	1238	1238	1310	1310	1308	1308	1338	1338	1338	1338	1410	1410	1408	1408	1438	1438	1438	1504	1510	1510	1510	1508	1508	1534
Deventer **480** a.	|	|	|	1348	1348	|	|	|	|	|	|	1448	1448	|	|	|	|	|	|	1548	1548	1548	|	|	|
Enschede **480** a.	|	|	|	1435g	1435	|	|	|	|	|	|	1535k	1535	|	|	|	|	|	|	...	1635	1635	|	|	|
Zwolle a.	1314	1314	1314	...	...	1344	1344	1414	1414	1414	1414	...	...	1444	1444	1514	1514	1514	1541	...	...	...	1544	1544	1611
Leeuwarden **486** a.	1414	|	|	...	...	|	1454	1514	|	|	1514	...	...	|	1554	1614	|	|	1654	...	...	...	|	1654	1714
Groningen **486** a.	...	1414	1414	...	...	1453	...	...	1514	1514	...	...	...	1553	...	...	1614	1614	...	...	...	...	1653	...	...

e – ②–⑥ (also Apr. 13, June 1; not Dec. 25, Jan. 1).
f – Not Dec. 26.
g – ①②③④⑦ (not Apr. 13, 30, May 21, June 1).
k – ⑤⑦ (also Dec. 25, Jan. 1; not Dec. 26).
r – Not Dec. 26, Apr. 13, 30 May 21, June 1.
z – ⑥ (also Dec. 26, Apr. 13, 30 May 21, June 1).

UTRECHT and SCHIPHOL ✈ - AMERSFOORT - ZWOLLE 481

For connecting trains **Amsterdam Centraal - Amersfoort** and v.v. (also for other trains Schiphol ✈ - Amersfoort and v.v.) see Table **480**

	Ⓒ	†		Ⓐ	Ⓒ			Ⓒ	Ⓑr	⑥z		Ⓐ	Ⓒ			Ⓒ	Ⓐ	Ⓒ		Ⓐ	Ⓒ			Ⓒ	Ⓐ
Rotterdam Centraal **483** d.	1433	1433	...	1503	1503	...	...	...	1533	1533	...	1603	1603	...	...	...	1633	1633	...	1703	1703	...	...	...	1733
Den Haag Centraal **483** d.	|	|	1436	|	|	1506	...	...	|	|	1536	|	|	1606	...	...	|	|	1636	|	|	1706	...	...	|
Utrecht Centraal d.	1520	1520	1520	1547	1550	1550	...	...	1617	1620	1620	1647	1650	1650	...	...	1717	1720	1720	1747	1750	1750	...	...	1817
Schiphol ✈ d.	|	|	|	|	|	|	1519	1519	|	|	|	|	|	|	1619	1619	|	|	|	|	|	|	1719	1719	|
Amsterdam Zuid d.	|	|	|	|	|	|	1528	1528	|	|	|	|	|	|	1628	1628	|	|	|	|	|	|	1728	1728	|
Duivendrecht d.	|	|	|	|	|	|	1534	1534	|	|	|	|	|	|	1634	1634	|	|	|	|	|	|	1734	1734	|
Amersfoort a.	1534	1534	1534	1601	1604	1604	1605	1605	1631	1634	1634	1701	1704	1704	1705	1705	1731	1734	1734	1801	1804	1804	1805	1805	1831
Amersfoort d.	1538	1538	1538	1604	1610	1610	1608	1608	1634	1638	1638	1704	1710	1710	1708	1708	1734	1738	1738	1804	1810	1810	1808	1808	1834
Deventer **480** a.	|	|	|	|	1648	1648	|	|	|	|	|	|	1748	1748	|	|	|	|	|	|	1848	1848	|	|	|
Enschede **480** a.	|	|	|	|	1735z	1735	|	|	|	|	|	|	1835	1835	|	|	|	|	|	|	1935	1935	|	|	|
Zwolle a.	1614	1614	1614	1641	...	...	1644	1644	1711	1714	1714	1741	...	...	1744	1744	1811	1814	1814	1841	...	...	1844	1844	1911
Leeuwarden **486** a.	1714	|	|	1754	...	...	|	1754	1814	1814	|	1854	...	...	|	1854	1914	1914	|	1954	...	...	|	1954	2014
Groningen **486** a.	...	1714	1714	...	...	...	1753	...	...	...	1814	...	...	...	1853	...	...	...	1914	...	...	...	1953	...	...

	Ⓒ	†		⑥z	Ⓐ	Ⓒ			Ⓒ	Ⓐ	Ⓒ	Ⓒ							p						
Rotterdam Centraal **483** d.	1733	1733	...	...	1803	1803	...	...	...	1833	1833	1833	...	1903	...	...	...	1933	1933	...	2003	...	...	...	2033
Den Haag Centraal **483** d.	|	|	1736	1736	|	|	1806	...	...	|	|	|	1836	|	1906	...	...	|	|	1936	|	2006	...	...	|
Utrecht Centraal d.	1820	1820	1820	1820	1847	1850	1850	...	...	1917	1920	1920	1920	1950	1950	...	...	2020	2020	2020	2050	2050	...	...	2120
Schiphol ✈ d.	|	|	|	|	|	|	|	1819	1819	|	|	|	|	|	|	1919	1919	|	|	|	|	|	2019	2019	|
Amsterdam Zuid d.	|	|	|	|	|	|	|	1828	1828	|	|	|	|	|	|	1928	1928	|	|	|	|	|	2028	2028	|
Duivendrecht d.	|	|	|	|	|	|	|	1834	1834	|	|	|	|	|	|	1934	1934	|	|	|	|	|	2034	2034	|
Amersfoort a.	1834	1834	1834	1834	1901	1904	1904	1905	1905	1931	1934	1934	1934	2004	2004	2005	2005	2034	2034	2034	2104	2104	2105	2105	2134
Amersfoort d.	1838	1838	1838	1838	1904	1910	1910	1908	1908	1934	1938	1938	1938	2010	2010	2008	2008	2038	2038	2038	2110	2110	2108	2108	2138
Deventer **480** a.	|	|	|	|	|	1948	1948	|	|	|	|	|	|	2048	2048	|	|	|	|	|	2148	2148	|	|	|
Enschede **480** a.	|	|	|	|	|	2035z	2035	|	|	|	|	|	|	2135	2135	|	|	|	|	|	2235p	2235	|	|	|
Zwolle a.	1914	1914	1914	1914	1941	...	...	1944	1944	2011	2014	2014	2014	...	...	2044	2044	2114	2114	2114	...	...	2144	2144	2214
Leeuwarden **486** a.	2014	|	|	2014	2054	...	...	|	2054	2114	2114	|	|	...	...	|	2154	2214	|	|	...	...	|	2254	2314
Groningen **486** a.	...	2014	2014	...	...	...	...	2053	...	...	...	2114	2114	...	...	2153	...	...	2214	2214	...	...	2253	...	...

	⑤f		B		Ⓒ		⚒	†				†		A								p	⑤⑥j	⑤⑥j	D
Rotterdam Centraal **483** d.	2033	...	...	2103	2103	...	...	...	...	2133	...	...	2203	2203	...	...	...	2233	...	2303	...	...	...	...	...
Den Haag Centraal **483** d.	|	2036	2036	|	|	2106	...	...	...	|	2136	2136	|	|	2206	...	...	|	2236	|	2306	...	...	...	...
Utrecht Centraal d.	2120	2120	2120	2150	2150	2150	...	...	...	2220	2220	2220	2250	2250	2250	...	...	2320	2320	2350	2350	...	...	...	...
Schiphol ✈ d.	|	|	|	|	|	|	2119	2119	2119	|	|	|	|	|	|	2219	2219	|	|	|	|	2319	2319	2319	2319
Amsterdam Zuid d.	|	|	|	|	|	|	2128	2128	2128	|	|	|	|	|	|	2228	2228	|	|	|	|	2328	2328	2328	2328
Duivendrecht d.	|	|	|	|	|	|	2134	2134	2134	|	|	|	|	|	|	2234	2234	|	|	|	|	2334	2334	2334	2334
Amersfoort a.	2134	2134	2134	2204	2204	2204	2205	2205	2205	2234	2234	2234	2304	2304	2304	2305	2305	2334	2334	0004	0004	0005	0005	0005	0005
Amersfoort d.	2138	2138	2138	...	2210	2210	2208	2208	2208	2238	2238	2238	2310	2310	2310	2308	2308	2338	2338	0010	0010	0008	0008	0008	0008
Deventer **480** a.	|	|	|	...	2248	2248	|	|	|	|	|	|	2348	2348	2348	|	|	|	|	0048	0048	|	|	|	|
Enschede **480** a.	|	|	|	...	...	2335	|	|	|	|	|	|	...	0036	0036	|	|	|	|	0138h	0138h	|	|	|	|
Zwolle a.	2214	2214	2214	...	...	...	2244	2244	2244	2314	2314	2314	...	...	...	2344	2344	0014	0014	...	...	0049	0049	0049	0101
Leeuwarden **486** a.	|	|	2314	...	...	...	|	|	2354	0015	|	0015	...	...	...	|	0101	...	...	...	...	...	|	0157	|
Groningen **486** a.	2314	2314	...	...	...	...	2353	0005	...	...	0014	...	...	...	...	0112	...	...	...	...	...	...	0157	...	0217

km		Ⓐ	Ⓐ	Ⓐ	Ⓐ	Ⓐ	Ⓐ	Ⓐ	⑥z	Ⓐ	⚒	Ⓐ	Ⓐ	⚒		⚒	⑥z	Ⓐ	⑥z	Ⓒ	⚒		Ⓐ	⑥z	
	Groningen **486** d.	...	...	...	...	0504	...	...	...	0545	...	...	0604	...	...	...	...	...	...	...	0644	...	...	...	0704
	Leeuwarden **486** d.	...	...	...	0500	|	...	0540	|	|	...	0605	|	...	...	...	...	0645	0636	...	|	...	0704	0704	|
0	**Zwolle** d.	...	0546	...	0616	0616	...	0641	0646	0646	0646	0711	0716	0716	...	...	...	0741	0746	0746	0746	0746	0811	0816	0816
	Enschede **480** d.	...	|	...	|	|	0526	|	|	|	|	|	|	|	...	0626	0626	|	|	|	|	|	|	|	|
	Deventer **480** d.	...	|	...	|	|	0615	|	|	|	|	|	|	|	...	0715	0715	|	|	|	|	|	|	|	|
67	**Amersfoort** a.	...	0623	...	0653	0653	0653	0720	0723	0723	0723	0750	0753	0753	...	0753	0753	0820	0823	0823	0823	0823	0850	0853	0853
67	**Amersfoort** d.	0610	0625	0640	0655	0655	0655	0721	0725	0725	0725	0751	0755	0755	0755	0755	0755	0821	0825	0825	0825	0825	0851	0855	0855
	Duivendrecht a.	|	|	|	0726	0726	|	|	|	|	|	|	0827	0827	0827	|	|	|	|	|	|	|	|	0927	0927
	Amsterdam Zuid a.	|	|	|	0731	0731	|	|	|	|	|	|	0832	0832	0832	|	|	|	|	|	|	|	|	0932	0932
	Schiphol ✈ a.	|	|	|	0738	0738	|	|	|	|	|	|	0839	0839	0839	|	|	|	|	|	|	|	|	0939	0939
88	**Utrecht** Centraal a.	0629	0640	0659	...	...	0710	0737	0740	0740	0740	0807	...	...	...	0810	0810	0837	0840	0840	0840	0840	0907	...	...
	Den Haag Centraal **483** a.	|	0725	|	...	...	0755	|	|	0825	0825	|	...	...	...	0855	|	|	|	|	0925	0925	|	...	...
	Rotterdam Centraal **483** a.	0712	...	0742	...	...	...	0827	0827	...	...	0857	...	...	...	...	0857	0927	0927	0927	...	...	0957	...	...

		Ⓒ	Ⓐ	†	⑥z		⚒	†			†	⑥z	Ⓑr		⚒	†			†						p
Groningen **486** d.	...	...	...	...	...	0744	...	...	0804	...	...	...	...	0844	...	...	0904	...	...	...	0944	...	1004	...	...
Leeuwarden **486** d.	...	...	0745	0734	0745	|	0804	0804	|	...	...	0845	0845	|	0904	0904	|	...	...	0945	|	1004	|	...	...
Zwolle d.	...	...	0841	0846	0846	0846	0911	0916	0916	...	...	0941	0946	0946	1011	1016	1016	...	...	1046	1046	1116	1116	...	...
Enschede **480** d.	0726	0726	|	|	|	|	|	|	|	0826	0826	|	|	|	|	|	|	0926	...	|	|	|	|	1026	1026
Deventer **480** d.	0815	0815	|	|	|	|	|	|	|	0915	0915	|	|	|	|	|	|	1015	1015	|	|	|	|	1115	1115
Amersfoort a.	0853	0853	0920	0923	0923	0923	0950	0952	0952	0953	0953	1020	1023	1023	1050	1053	1053	1053	1053	1123	1123	1153	1153	1153	1153
Amersfoort d.	0855	0855	0921	0925	0925	0925	0951	0955	0955	0955	0955	1021	1025	1025	1051	1055	1055	1055	1055	1125	1125	1155	1155	1155	1155
Duivendrecht a.	|	|	|	|	|	|	|	1027	1027	|	|	|	|	|	|	1127	1127	|	|	|	|	1227	1227	|	|
Amsterdam Zuid a.	|	|	|	|	|	|	|	1032	1032	|	|	|	|	|	|	1132	1132	|	|	|	|	1232	1232	|	|
Schiphol ✈ a.	|	|	|	|	|	|	|	1039	1039	|	|	|	|	|	|	1139	1139	|	|	|	|	1239	1239	|	|
Utrecht Centraal a.	0910	0910	0937	0940	0940	0940	1007	...	...	1010	1010	1037	1040	1040	1107	...	...	1110	1110	1140	1140	...	...	1210	1210
Den Haag Centraal **483** a.	0955	|	|	|	|	1025	|	...	...	1055	|	|	|	1125	|	...	...	1155	|	|	1225	...	...	1255	|
Rotterdam Centraal **483** a.	...	0957	1027	1027	1027	...	1057	...	...	...	1057	1127	1127	...	1157	...	...	...	1157	1227	...	...	...	...	1257

							D				†						†					E			⑤⑥j
Groningen **486** d.	...	...	1044	...	1104	...	...	...	...	1144	1144	...	1204	...	...	...	1244	1244	...	1304	...	...	...	...	1344
Leeuwarden **486** d.	...	1045	|	1104	|	...	...	...	1145	|	|	1204	|	...	...	1245	|	|	1304	|	...	...	...	1345	|
Zwolle d.	...	1146	1146	1216	1216	...	...	...	1246	1246	1246	1316	1316	...	...	1346	1346	1346	1416	1416	...	...	...	1446	1446
Enschede **480** d.	...	|	|	|	|	1126	1126	...	|	|	|	|	|	1226	1226	|	|	|	|	|	1326	1326	...	|	|
Deventer **480** d.	1115	|	|	|	|	1215	1215	1215	|	|	|	|	|	1315	1315	|	|	|	|	|	1415	1415	1415	|	|
Amersfoort a.	1153	1223	1223	1253	1253	1253	1253	1253	1323	1323	1323	1353	1353	1353	1353	1423	1423	1423	1453	1453	1453	1453	1453	1523	1523
Amersfoort d.	1155	1225	1225	1255	1255	1255	1255	1255	1325	1325	1325	1355	1355	1355	1355	1425	1425	1425	1455	1455	1455	1455	1455	1525	1525
Duivendrecht a.	|	|	|	1327	1327	|	|	|	|	|	|	1427	1427	|	|	|	|	|	1527	1527	|	|	|	|	|
Amsterdam Zuid a.	|	|	|	1332	1332	|	|	|	|	|	|	1432	1432	|	|	|	|	|	1532	1532	|	|	|	|	|
Schiphol ✈ a.	|	|	|	1339	1339	|	|	|	|	|	|	1439	1439	|	|	|	|	|	1539	1539	|	|	|	|	|
Utrecht Centraal a.	1210	1240	1240	...	...	1310	1310	1310	1340	1340	1340	...	...	1410	1410	1440	1140	1440	...	...	1510	1510	1510	1540	1540
Den Haag Centraal **483** a.	|	|	1325	...	...	1355	|	|	|	1425	|	...	...	1455	|	|	|	1525	...	...	1555	|	|	|	|
Rotterdam Centraal **483** a.	1257	1327	...	...	...	...	1357	1357	1427	...	1427	...	...	...	1457	1527	1527	...	...	...	...	1557	1557	1627	1627

		Ⓐ	Ⓒ			†	Ⓒ	Ⓐ	Ⓒ		Ⓐ	Ⓒ			†	Ⓒ	Ⓐ	Ⓒ		Ⓐ	Ⓒ			⑥z	Ⓒ
Groningen **486** d.	1344	...	...	1404	...	...	...	...	...	1444	...	...	1504	...	...	...	...	...	1544	...	...	1604	...	...	...
Leeuwarden **486** d.	|	1404	1404	|	...	...	...	1445	1445	|	1504	1504	|	...	...	...	1545	1545	|	1604	1604	|	...	...	...
Zwolle d.	1446	1511	1516	1516	...	...	...	1541	1546	1546	1611	1616	1616	...	...	...	1641	1646	1646	1711	1716	1716	...	...	...
Enschede **480** d.	|	|	|	|	1426	1426	...	|	|	|	|	|	|	1526	1526	...	|	|	|	|	|	|	1626	1626	...
Deventer **480** d.	|	|	|	|	1515	1515	1515	|	|	|	|	|	|	1615	1615	1615	|	|	|	|	|	|	1715	1715	1715
Amersfoort a.	1523	1550	1553	1553	1553	1553	1553	1620	1623	1623	1650	1653	1653	1653	1653	1653	1720	1723	1723	1750	1753	1753	1753	1753	1753
Amersfoort d.	1525	1551	1555	1555	1555	1555	1555	1621	1625	1625	1651	1655	1655	1655	1655	1655	1721	1725	1725	1751	1755	1755	1755	1755	1755
Duivendrecht a.	|	|	1627	1627	|	|	|	|	|	|	|	1727	1727	|	|	|	|	|	|	|	1827	1827	|	|	|
Amsterdam Zuid a.	|	|	1632	1632	|	|	|	|	|	|	|	1732	1732	|	|	|	|	|	|	|	1832	1832	|	|	|
Schiphol ✈ a.	|	|	1639	1639	|	|	|	|	|	|	|	1739	1739	|	|	|	|	|	|	|	1839	1839	|	|	|
Utrecht Centraal a.	1540	1607	...	...	1610	1610	1610	1637	1640	1640	1707	...	...	1710	1710	1710	1737	1740	1740	1807	...	...	1810	1810	1810
Den Haag Centraal **483** a.	1625	|	...	...	1655	|	|	|	|	1725	|	...	...	1755	|	|	|	|	1825	|	...	...	1855	|	|
Rotterdam Centraal **483** a.	...	1657	...	...	...	1657	1657	1727	1727	...	1757	...	...	...	1757	1757	1827	1827	...	1857	...	...	...	1857	1857

A – ①②③④⑥⑦ (also Dec. 26).
B – ①②③④⑥ (also Dec. 26; not Dec. 25, Jan. 1).
D – ①–④ (not Dec. 25, Jan. 1, Apr. 13, 30, May 21, June 1).
E – ②–⑥ (also Apr. 13, June 1; not Dec. 25, Jan. 1).

f – Not Dec. 26.
h – 8 – 10 minutes later on ②–⑤ (not Dec. 26, Jan. 2, Apr. 14, May 1, 22, June 2).
j – Also Apr. 13, 30, May 21, June 1.

p – ⑤⑥⑦ (also Dec. 25, Jan. 1, Apr. 13, 30, May 21, June 1).
r – Not Dec. 26, Apr. 13, 30 May 21, June 1.
z – ⑥ (also Dec. 26, Apr. 13, 30 May 21, June 1).

481 ZWOLLE - AMERSFOORT - SCHIPHOL ✈ and UTRECHT

For connecting trains **Amersfoort** - **Amsterdam Centraal** (also for other trains Amersfoort - Schiphol ✈) see Table **480**

		Ⓐ			Ⓐ	Ⓒ			†	Ⓒ							†	⚒	⚒		†	⚒			⚒
Groningen **486** d.	...	1644	1644	...	...	...	1704	...	...	...	...	1744	...	1804	...	...	...	...	1844	1844	...	...	1904	...	...
Leeuwarden **486** d.	1645	|	|	...	1704	1704	|	...	...	...	1745	|	1804	|	...	...	1845	1845	|	|	1904	1904	|	...	...
Zwolle d.	1746	1746	1746	...	1811	1816	1816	...	...	...	1846	1846	1916	1916	...	...	1941	1946	1946	1946	2011	2016	2016	...	...
Enschede **480** d.	|	|	|	...	|	|	|	1726	1726	...	|	|	|	|	1826	1826	|	|	|	|	|	|	|	1926	1926
Deventer **480** d.	|	|	|	...	|	|	|	1815	1815	1815	|	|	|	|	1915	1915	|	|	|	|	|	|	|	2015	2015
Amersfoort a.	1823	1823	1823	...	1850	1853	1853	1853	1853	1853	1923	1923	1953	1953	1953	1953	2020	2023	2023	2023	2050	2053	2053	2053	2053
Amersfoort d.	1825	1825	1825	...	1851	1855	1855	1855	1855	1855	1925	1925	1955	1955	1955	1955	2021	2025	2025	2025	2051	2055	2055	2055	2055
Duivendrecht a.	|	|	|	...	|	1927	1927	|	|	|	|	|	2027	2027	|	|	|	|	|	|	|	2127	2127	|	|
Amsterdam Zuid a.	|	|	|	...	|	1932	1932	|	|	|	|	|	2032	2032	|	|	|	|	|	|	|	2132	2132	|	|
Schiphol ✈ a.	|	|	|	...	|	1939	1939	|	|	|	|	|	2039	2039	|	|	|	|	|	|	|	2139	2139	|	|
Utrecht Centraal a.	1840	1840	1840	...	1907	...	...	1910	1910	1910	1940	1940	...	...	2010	2010	2037	2040	2040	2040	2107	...	...	2110	2110
Den Haag Centraal **483** a.	|	|	1925	...	|	...	...	1955	|	|	|	2025	...	...	2055	|	|	|	|	2125	|	...	...	2155	|
Rotterdam Centraal **483** a.	1927	1927	...	...	1957	...	...	...	1957	1957	2027	...	...	...	...	2057	2127	2127	2127	...	2157	...	...	...	2157

		⑤⑥j					⑤⑥j			D					⑤f			D	p						
Groningen **486** d.	...	1944	1944	...	2004	...	...	...	...	...	2044	...	2104	...	...	...	2144	...	...	...	2204	...	...	2234	...
Leeuwarden **486** d.	1945	|	|	2004	|	...	...	...	2045	2045	|	2104	|	...	...	...	|	2145	2145	2204	|	...	2234	|	...
Zwolle d.	2046	2046	2046	2116	2116	...	...	...	2146	2146	2146	2216	2216	...	...	...	2246	2246	2246	2316	2316	...	2346	2346	2349
Enschede **480** d.	|	|	|	|	|	2026	2026	...	|	|	|	|	|	2126	2126	...	|	|	|	|	|	2226	|	|	|
Deventer **480** d.	|	|	|	|	|	2115	2115	2115	|	|	|	|	|	2215	2215	2215	|	|	|	|	|	2315	|	|	|
Amersfoort a.	2123	2123	2123	2153	2153	2153	2153	2153	2223	2223	2223	2253	2253	2253	2253	2253	2323	2323	2323	2353	2353	2353	0028	0028	0045
Amersfoort d.	2125	2125	2125	2155	2155	2155	2155	2155	2225	2225	2225	2255	2255	2255	2255	2255	2325	2325	2325	2355	2355	2355	0030	0030	0049
Duivendrecht a.	|	|	|	2227	2227	|	|	|	|	|	|	2327	2327	|	|	|	|	|	|	0027	0027	|	|	|	|
Amsterdam Zuid a.	|	|	|	2232	2232	|	|	|	|	|	|	2332	2332	|	|	|	|	|	|	0032	0032	|	|	|	|
Schiphol ✈ a.	|	|	|	2239	2239	|	|	|	|	|	|	2339	2339	|	|	|	|	|	|	0040	0040	|	|	|	|
Utrecht Centraal a.	2140	2140	2140	...	...	2210	2210	2210	2240	2240	2240	...	...	2310	2310	2310	2340	2340	2340	...	...	0010	0046	0046	0112
Den Haag Centraal **483** a.	|	|	2225	...	...	2255	|	|	|	2325	2325	...	...	2355	|	|	0024	0024	|	...	...	...	...	...	...
Rotterdam Centraal **483** a.	2227	2227	...	...	...	...	2257	2257	2327	...	...	...	...	...	2357	2357	...	...	0027	...	...	...	...	...	...

← FOR NOTES SEE PREVIOUS PAGE

483 DEN HAAG and ROTTERDAM - GOUDA - UTRECHT

Many of these journeys are through services to / from **Deventer**, **Enschede**, **Leeuwarden** and / or **Groningen**. For details, see Table **481**

km					G	H	⑤–⑦		Ⓐ	Ⓐ	Ⓐ	⑥⑦	Ⓐ	Ⓐ	Ⓐ	⚒	⚒	⚒	⚒	⚒	⚒	⚒	⚒	
0	**Den Haag** Centraal d.	...	0006	0025	...	...	...	...	...	0525	...	...	0606	...	0621	...	0636	...	0651	...	0706	...	0721	...
	Rotterdam Centraal ... **465** d.	0003	|	|	0046	0050	0105	...	0521	|	0603	0605	|	0617	|	0633	|	0647	|	0703	|	0717	|	0733
	Rotterdam Alexander .. **465** d.	0011	|	|	0055	0101	|	...	0531	|	0611	|	|	0625	|	0641	|	0655	|	0711	|	0725	|	0741
28	Gouda **465** d.	0022	0025	0054	0107	0116	0121	...	0545	0551	0622	0621	0625	0637	0640	0652	0655	0707	0710	0722	0725	0737	0740	0752
60	**Utrecht** Centraal a.	0044	0047	...	...	...	0143	...	...	0625	0641	0642	0644	0656	0700	0711	0714	0726	0730	0741	0744	0756	0800	0811

		⚒	⚒						⚒	⚒			⚒	⚒								
Den Haag Centraal d.	0736	...	0751	...	0806	and at the	...	1006	...	1021	...	1036	...	1051	...	1106	...	1121	...	1136	...	1151
Rotterdam Centraal ... **465** d.	|	0747	|	0803	|	same minutes	1003	|	1017	|	1033	|	1047	|	1103	|	1117	|	1133	|	1147	|
Rotterdam Alexander ... **465** d.	|	0755	|	0811	|	past each	1011	|	1025	|	1041	|	1055	|	1111	|	1125	|	1141	|	1155	|
Gouda **465** d.	0755	0807	0810	0822	0825	hour until	1022	1025	1037	1040	1052	1055	1107	1110	1122	1125	1137	1140	1152	1155	1207	1210
Utrecht Centraal a.	0814	0826	0830	0841	0844		1041	1044	1056	1100	1111	1114	1126	1130	1141	1144	1156	1200	1211	1214	1226	1230

Den Haag Centraal d.	and at the	...	2006	...	2021	...	2036	...	2051	...	...	2106	...	2136	...	2206	...	2236	...	2306	...	2336
Rotterdam Centraal ... **465** d.	same minutes	2003	|	2017	|	2033	|	2047	|	...	2103	|	2133	|	2203	|	2233	|	2303	|	2333	|
Rotterdam Alexander ... **465** d.	past each	2011	|	2025	|	2041	|	2055	|	...	2111	|	2141	|	2211	|	2241	|	2311	|	2341	|
Gouda **465** d.	hour until	2022	2025	2037	2040	2052	2055	2107	2110	...	2122	2125	2152	2155	2222	2225	2252	2255	2322	2325	2352	2355
Utrecht Centraal a.		2041	2044	2056	2100	2111	2114	2126	2130	...	2141	2144	2211	2214	2241	2244	2311	2314	2341	2344	0011	0014

km		H	H		Ⓐ	Ⓐ	⚒	Ⓐ	⑥⑦	Ⓐ	Ⓐ	Ⓐ	Ⓐ	⚒	⚒	⚒	⑦	Ⓐ	⚒	⚒	⚒	⚒	⚒	⚒
0	**Utrecht** Centraal d.	0015	*0015*	...	0523	0600	0606	0603	0616	0630	0633	0645	0648	0700	0703	0715	0716	0718	0730	0733	0745	0748	0800	0803
32	Gouda **465** d.	0047	0046	...	0551	0620	0640	0623	0640	0650	0653	0705	0708	0719	0723	0735	0740	0738	0749	0753	0805	0808	0819	0823
46	Rotterdam Alexander .. **465** d.	|	0058	...	0604	|	|	0632	|	|	0702	|	0717	|	0732	|	|	0747	|	0802	|	0817	|	0832
56	**Rotterdam** Centraal ... **465** a.	|	0111	...	0618	|	|	0642	0656	|	0712	|	0727	|	0742	|	0756	0757	|	0812	|	0827	|	0842
	Den Haag Centraal a.	0113	...	...	...	0637	0705	...	...	0707	...	0725	...	0737	...	0755	...	...	0807	...	0825	...	0837	...

			⚒	⚒				⚒	⚒			⚒	⚒									
Utrecht Centraal d.	0815	0818	0830	0833	0845	0848	and at the	1030	1033	1045	1048	1100	1103	1115	1118	...	1130	1133	1145	1148	1200	1203
Gouda **465** d.	0835	0838	0849	0853	0905	0908	same minutes	1049	1053	1105	1108	1119	1123	1135	1138	...	1149	1153	1205	1208	1219	1223
Rotterdam Alexander ... **465** d.	|	0847	|	0902	|	0917	past each	|	1102	|	1117	|	1132	|	1147	...	|	1202	|	1217	|	1232
Rotterdam Centraal ... **465** a.	|	0857	|	0912	|	0927	hour until	|	1112	|	1127	|	1142	|	1157	...	|	1212	|	1227	|	1242
Den Haag Centraal a.	0855	...	0907	...	0925	...		1107	...	1125	...	1137	...	1155	...	...	1207	...	1225	...	1237	...

																				K	G
Utrecht Centraal d.	1215	1218	and at the	2045	2048	2100	2103	2115	2118	2130	2133	2145	2148	2215	2218	2245	2248	2315	2318	2345	2348	...
Gouda **465** d.	1235	1238	same minutes	2105	2108	2119	2123	2135	2138	2149	2153	2205	2208	2235	2238	2305	2308	2335	2338	0005	0008	0022
Rotterdam Alexander ... **465** d.	|	1247	past each	|	2117	|	2132	|	2147	|	2202	|	2217	|	2247	|	2317	|	2347	|	0017	0033
Rotterdam Centraal ... **465** a.	|	1257	hour until	|	2127	|	2142	|	2157	|	2212	|	2227	|	2257	|	2327	|	2357	|	0027	0044
Den Haag Centraal a.	1255	...		2125	...	2137	...	2155	...	2207	...	2225	...	2255	...	2325	...	2355	...	0024	...	...

G – ②–⑤ (not Dec. 26, Jan. 2, Apr. 14, May 1, 22, June 2). H – ①⑥⑦ (also Dec. 26, Jan. 2, Apr. 14, May 1, 22, June 2). K – ⑤⑥⑦ (also Dec. 25, Jan. 1, Apr. 13, 30, May 21, June 1).

486 ZWOLLE - GRONINGEN and LEEUWARDEN

For through journeys from / to **Rotterdam**, **Den Haag** and **Schiphol** ✈ via **Amersfoort**, see table **481**

km		⑥⑦c	G		Ⓐ	Ⓐ	⚒	Ⓐ	⚒		⚒	⚒			❖				K			†	⚒	†		
0	**Zwolle** d.	0052	0103	...	0547	0623	0647	0717	0723	0747	0817	0823	0847	0917	and at	2023	2047	2117	2123	2147	2217	2223	2247	2247	2317	2347
27	Meppel d.	0108	0125	...	0603	0639	0703	|	0739	0803	|	0839	0903	|	the same	2039	2103	|	2139	2203	|	2239	2303	2303	|	0004
47	Hoogeveen d.	0120	0137	...	0614	0651	0714	|	0751	0814	|	0851	0914	|	minutes	2051	2114	|	2151	2214	|	2251	2314	2314	|	0015
77	Assen d.	0139	0157	...	0634	0709	0734	0757	0809	0834	0857	0909	0934	0957	past each	2109	2134	2157	2209	2234	2257	2309	2334	2345	2357	0050
104	**Groningen** a.	0157	0217	...	0653	0731	0753	0814	0831	0853	0914	0931	0953	1014	hour until	2131	2153	2214	2231	2253	2314	2331	2353	0005	0014	0112

	L	②③		Ⓐ	Ⓐ	⚒	⚒		⚒				⚒		⊠						K					
Groningen d.	0504	0504	...	0545	0604	0625	0644	0704	0725	0744	...	0804	0825	0844	and at	2004	2025	2044	...	2104	2125	2144	2204	2234	...	2325
Assen d.	0522	0526	...	0601	0622	0644	0702	0722	0744	0800	...	0822	0844	0900	the same	2022	2044	2100	...	2122	2144	2200	2222	2253	...	2344
Hoogeveen d.	0541	0546	...	0617	0641	0703	|	0741	0803	|	...	0841	0903	|	minutes	2041	2103	|	...	2141	2203	|	2241	2312	...	0003
Meppel d.	0555	0558	...	|	0655	0715	|	0755	0815	|	...	0855	0915	|	past each	2055	2115	|	...	2155	2215	|	2255	2325	...	0020
Zwolle a.	0613	0613	...	0644	0714	0732	0744	0813	0832	0843	...	0913	0932	0843	hour until	2113	2132	2143	...	2213	2232	2243	2313	2342	...	0037

km		⑥⑦c		Ⓐ	Ⓐ	⚒	Ⓐ		⚒							
0	**Zwolle** d.	0055	...	0550	0620	0650	0720	0750	0820	0850	0920	and at	2220	2250	2320	2350
27	Meppel d.	0112	...	0607	0636	0707	|	0807	|	0907	|	the same	|	2307	2336	0008
41	Steenwijk d.	0121	...	0616	0645	0716	0743	0816	0843	0916	0943	minutes	2243	2316	2345	0017
65	Heerenveen d.	0136	...	0632	0700	0732	0759	0832	0856	0932	0956	past each	2256	2332	2358	0035
94	**Leeuwarden** a.	0157	...	0654	0723	0754	0816	0854	0914	0954	1014	hour until	2314	2354	0015	0101

	Ⓐ	Ⓐ	Ⓐ	⑥z	Ⓐ	⚒	†	⚒								
Leeuwarden d.	0500	0540	0605	0636	0645	0704	0734	0745	0804	0845	and at	2104	2145	2204	2234	2334
Heerenveen d.	0523	0600	0625	0657	0701	0725	0755	0801	0825	0901	the same	2125	2201	2225	2255	2356
Steenwijk d.	0542	0614	0641	0714	0715	0741	0812	0814	0841	0914	minutes	2141	2214	2241	2311	0012
Meppel d.	0553	0623	0651	0724	0725	0751	0822	|	0851	|	past each	2151	|	2251	2322	0023
Zwolle a.	0609	0639	0710	0740	0739	0809	0839	0839	0909	0939	hour until	2209	2239	2309	2339	0040

G – ②–⑤ (not Dec. 26, Jan. 2, Apr. 14, May 1, 22, June 2).
K – ⑤⑥⑦ (also Dec. 25, Jan. 1, Apr. 13, 30, May 21, June 1).
L – ①④⑤ (not Dec. 25, 26, Jan. 1, Apr. 13, 30, May 21, June 1).
c – Also Apr. 14, May 1, 22, June 2.
z – Also Dec. 26, Apr. 13, 30, May 21, June 1.
❖ – The services from Zwolle at 1623, 1723, 1823 and 1923 run daily.
⊠ – The services from Groningen at 1525, 1625, 1725, 1825 and 1925 run daily.

 For traffic arrangements on Dutch holiday dates, see page 248

OLDENZAAL - HENGELO - ZUTPHEN 488

Operated by **Syntus** (NS tickets valid) 2nd class only

km		J			Ⓐ	Ⓐ	E	E					E				E								H
0	**Oldenzaal** d.	0029	...	...	0559	0629	0659	0729	...	...	0759	0829	0829	and at	1959	2029	2029	...	2059	2129	2159	2229	2259	2329	2359
11	Hengelo d.	0044	...	...	0614	0644	0714	0744	...	...	0814	0840	0844	the same	2014	2040	2044	...	2114	2140	2214	2240	2314	2340	0014
26	Goor d.	0056	...	...	0629	0659	0729	0759	0759	...	0829	...	0859	minutes	2029	...	2059	...	2129	...	2229	...	2329	...	0029
39	Lochem d.	...	...	...	0638	0708	0738	0808	0808	...	0838	...	0908	past each	2038	...	2108	...	2138	...	2238	...	2338	...	0038
56	**Zutphen** a.	...	...	...	0653	0723	0753	0823	0823	...	0853	...	0923	hour until	2053	...	2123	...	2153	...	2253	...	2353	...	0054

	J			Ⓐ	Ⓐ	E	Ⓐ	E	E				E			E								H	H
Zutphen d.	0007	...	...	...	0607	...	0637	...	0707	...	...	0737	0807	...	and at	2007	...	2037	...	...	2137	...	2237	...	2337
Lochem d.	0019	...	...	...	0619	...	0649	...	0719	...	...	0749	0819	...	the same	2019	...	2049	...	...	2149	...	2249	...	2349
Goor d.	0028	...	...	0559	0629	0629	0659	0659	0729	0729	...	0759	0829	...	minutes	2029	...	2059	...	...	2159	..	2259	...	2359
Hengelo d.	...	...	...	0614	0644	0644	0714	0714	0744	0744	...	0814	0844	0844	past each	2044	2044	2114	...	2144	2214	2244	2314	2344	0014
Oldenzaal a.	...	...	...	0623	0653	0653	0723	0723	0753	0753	...	0823	0853	0853	hour until	2053	2053	2123	...	2153	2223	2253	2323	2353	0023

E – ①–⑥ (not Dec. 25, 26, Jan. 1, Apr. 13, May 21, June 1). H – ②–⑦ (also Apr. 13, June 1). J – ①③④⑤⑥⑦ (also Apr. 14, June 2).

ARNHEM and ZUTPHEN - WINTERSWIJK 490

Operated by **Syntus** (NS tickets valid) 2nd class only

km		Ⓐ	E								Ⓒ
0	**Arnhem** d.	0633	0733	...	0833	and	2132	...	2233	2333	2333
14	Zevenaar d.	0646	0746	...	0846	hourly	2146	...	2246	2346	2346
30	Doetinchem d.	0707	0807	...	0907	until	2207	...	2307	0006	0007
64	**Winterswijk** a.	0740	0840	...	0940		2240	...	2340	...	0040

	Ⓐ	E	E							
Winterswijk d.	0550	...	0650	...	...	0750	and	2250	...	...
Doetinchem d.	0623	0623	0723	0723	...	0823	hourly	2323	...	...
Zevenaar d.	0644	0644	0744	0744	...	0844	until	2344	...	...
Arnhem a.	0657	0657	0757	0757	...	0857		2357	...	...

☛ Additional journeys **Arnhem - Winterswijk**: 0703 Ⓐ, 0802 Ⓐ, 0902 Ⓐ, 1003 Ⓐ, 1103 Ⓐ, 1203 **E**, 1203 **E**, 1303 **E**, 1403 **E**, 1503 **E**, 1603 **E**, 1703 **E**, 1802 Ⓐ and 1903 Ⓐ.
Additional journeys **Winterswijk - Arnhem**: 0605 Ⓐ, 0620 Ⓐ, 0720 Ⓐ, 0820 Ⓐ, 0920 Ⓐ, 1020 Ⓐ, 1120 Ⓐ, 1220 **E**, 1320 **E**, 1420 **E**, 1520 **E**, 1620 **E**, 1720 **E** and 1820 Ⓐ.

km		⑥⑦c		Ⓐ	Ⓐ	⑥g	Ⓐ	Ⓒ			
0	**Zutphen** d.	0007	...	0701	0801	0807	0901	0907	1007	and	2307
22	Ruurlo d.	0023	...	0717	0817	0823	0917	0923	1023	hourly	2323
43	**Winterswijk** a.	0042	...	0736	0836	0842	0936	0942	1042	until	2342

	Ⓐ	Ⓐ	⑥g	L	L	L				⑤⑥f
Winterswijk d.	0615	0645	0651	0745	0845	0945	1051	and	2151	2251
Ruurlo d.	0633	0703	0709	0803	0903	1003	1109	hourly	2209	2309
Zutphen a.	0649	0719	0724	0819	0919	1019	1124	until	2224	2324

☛ Additional journeys **Zutphen - Winterswijk**: 0731 Ⓐ, 0831 Ⓐ, 0931 Ⓐ, 1037 Ⓐ, 1137 Ⓐ, 1237 **E**, 1337 **E**, 1437 **E**, 1537 **E**, 1637 **E**, 1737 **E** and 1837 Ⓐ.
Additional journeys **Winterswijk - Zutphen**: 0715 Ⓐ, 0815 Ⓐ, 0915 Ⓐ, 1021 Ⓐ, 1121 Ⓐ, 1221 **E**, 1321 **E**, 1421 **E**, 1521 **E**, 1621 **E**, 1721 **E** and 1821 Ⓐ.

E – ①–⑥ (not Dec. 25, 26, Jan. 1, Apr. 13, May 21, June 1).
L – Runs 5 – 6 minutes later on Ⓒ.
c – Also May 1; not Dec. 27.
f – Also Apr. 30; not Dec. 26.
g – Also Apr. 30.

ZWOLLE - ENSCHEDE 492

km		Ⓐ	⑥k	A	④⑤b	Ⓐ	Ⓐ	⚒	⚒	⚒		⚒		⚒					
0	**Zwolle** d.	...	...	...	...	0606	0636	0706	0736	0806	0836	0906	0936	1006	1036	1106	and	2306	2336
18	Raalte d.	...	...	...	...	0622	0652	0722	0752	0822	0852	0922	0952	1022	1052	1122	every 30	2322	2352
44	Almelo 480 d.	...	...	0619	0622	0649	0719	0749	0819	0849	0919	0949	1019	1049	1119	1149	minutes	2349	0019
59	Hengelo 480 d.	0613	0635	0636	0639	0705	0735	0805	0835	0905	0936	1005	1035	1105	1135	1205	until	0005	0035
67	**Enschede** 480 a.	0623	0645	0645	0648	0715	0745	0815	0845	0915	0946	1015	1045	1115	1145	1215		0015	0045

		⑥⑦c			Ⓐ	A	④⑤b	Ⓐ	⚒	⚒		⚒							
Enschede 480 d.	0017	0047	...	...	0515	0545	0550	0615	0645	0715	0745	0815	0845	0915	and	2245	2315	...	2345
Hengelo 480 d.	0028	0057	...	...	0526	0556	0601	0626	0656	0726	0756	0826	0856	0926	every 30	2256	2326	...	2356
Almelo 480 d.	0043	...	...	...	0543	0613	0616	0643	0713	0743	0813	0843	0913	0943	minutes	2313	2343	...	0013
Raalte d.	...	...	...	...	0610	0640	0642	0710	0740	0810	0840	0910	0940	1010	until	2340	0010	...	...
Zwolle a.	...	...	...	...	0627	0657	0657	0727	0757	0827	0857	0927	0957	1027		2357	0027	...	...

A – ①–③ (not Apr. 13, June 1).
b – Not Apr. 30, May 21.
c – Also Apr. 14, May 1, 22, June 2.
k – Also Dec. 26, Apr. 13, 30, May 21, June 1.

ZWOLLE - EMMEN 493

km		D		Ⓐ	Ⓐ	Ⓐ	⚒		⚒			⚒			e			e			A			B
0	**Zwolle** d.	0026	...	0556	0626	0656	0726	...	0756	0826	and at	1456	1526	...	1556	1626	and at	2056	2126	...	2156	2226	...	2326
23	Ommen d.	0044	...	0615	0644	0715	0744	...	0815	0844	the same	1515	1544	...	1615	1644	the same	2115	2144	...	2215	2244	...	2344
34	Mariënberg d.	0051	...	|	0651	|	0751	...	|	0851	minutes	|	1551	...	|	1651	minutes	|	2151	...	|	2251	...	2351
55	Coevorden d.	0107	...	0636	0707	0736	0807	...	0836	0907	past each	1536	1607	...	1636	1707	past each	2136	2207	...	2236	2307	...	0007
75	**Emmen** a.	0128	...	0651	0728	0751	0828	...	0851	0928	hour until	1551	1628	...	1651	1728	hour until	2151	2228	...	2251	2328	...	0028

	Ⓐ	Ⓐ	Ⓐ	⚒		⚒			⚒						e		e						B	
Emmen d.	0503	0533	0608	0633	...	0708	0733	and at	1508	1533	...	1608	...	1633	1708	and at	1908	1933	...	2033	2133	2233	2333	...
Coevorden d.	0522	0552	0624	0652	...	0724	0752	the same	1524	1552	...	1624	...	1652	1724	the same	1924	1952	...	2052	2152	2252	2352	...
Mariënberg d.	0538	0608	|	0708	...	|	0808	minutes	|	1608	...	|	...	1708	|	minutes	|	2008	...	2108	2208	2308	0008	...
Ommen d.	0546	0616	0645	0716	...	0745	0816	past each	1545	1616	...	1645	...	1716	1745	past each	1945	2016	...	2116	2216	2316	0016	...
Zwolle a.	0605	0635	0704	0735	...	0804	0835	hour until	1604	1635	...	1704	...	1735	1804	hour until	2004	2035	...	2135	2235	2335	0035	...

A – ④⑤⑥ (also Apr. 13, June 1; not Dec. 25, Jan. 1). D – ③–⑦ (also Apr. 14, June 2; not Dec. 26, Jan. 2). e – Not Dec. 25, Jan. 1, Apr. 12, May 31.
B – ②–⑥ (also Apr. 13, June 1; not Dec. 25, Jan. 1).

LEEUWARDEN - GRONINGEN 494

Operated by **Arriva** (NS tickets valid)

km				Ⓐ	Ⓐ	E	Ⓐ	E	Ⓐ	Ⓐ		E	Ⓐ			E	Ⓐ			E	Ⓐ			e
0	**Leeuwarden** d.	0004	...	0534	0604	0634	0659	0704	0734	0759	0804	0834	0859	...	0904	0934	0959	and at the same	1704	1734	1759	...	1804	1834
25	Buitenpost d.	0029	...	0559	0629	0659	0715	0729	0759	0815	0829	0859	0915	...	0929	0959	1015	minutes past	1729	1759	1815	...	1829	1859
54	**Groningen** a.	0053	...	0624	0653	0724	0734	0753	0824	0834	0853	0924	0934	...	0953	1024	1034	each hour until	1753	1824	1834	...	1853	1924

	Ⓐ		⑦r		⑦r		⑦r			
Leeuwarden d.	1859	1904	1934	2004	2034	2104	2134	2204	2304	...
Buitenpost d.	1915	1929	1959	2029	2059	2129	2159	2229	2329	...
Groningen a.	1934	1953	2024	2053	2124	2153	2224	2253	2353	...

	G	①m		Ⓐ	Ⓐ	E	Ⓐ	⑥k	Ⓐ	Ⓐ	Ⓐ	
Groningen d.	0004	0011	...	0534	0604	0634	0653	0704	0704	0734	0753	0804
Buitenpost d.	0029	0035	...	0559	0629	0659	0712	0729	0729	0759	0812	0829
Leeuwarden a.	0054	0059	...	0624	0654	0724	0729	0754	0756	0824	0829	0854

	E	Ⓐ			E	Ⓐ		E	Ⓐ			e	Ⓐ		e	Ⓐ		⑦r		⑦r		⑦r		
Groningen d.	0834	0853	...	0904	0934	0953	and at the same	1634	1653	1704	...	1734	1753	1804	1834	1853	1904	1934	2004	2034	2104	2134	2204	2304
Buitenpost d.	0859	0912	...	0929	0959	1012	minutes past	1659	1712	1729	...	1759	1812	1829	1859	1912	1929	1959	2029	2059	2129	2159	2229	2329
Leeuwarden a.	0924	0929	...	0954	1024	1029	each hour until	1724	1729	1754	...	1824	1829	1854	1924	1929	1954	2024	2054	2124	2154	2224	2254	2354

E – ①–⑥ (not Dec. 25, 26, Jan. 1, Apr. 13, June 1). e – Not Dec. 25, 26, Jan. 1, Apr. 12, May 31. m – Also Dec. 26, Jan. 2.
G – ②–⑦ (not Dec. 26, Jan. 2). k – Also Apr. 30, May 21. r – Also Dec. 25, Jan. 1, Apr. 13, June 1; not Dec. 21, 28, Apr. 12, May 31.

GRONINGEN - NIEUWESCHANS - LEER 495

Operated by **Arriva** ★

km				A	⑥k	Ⓐ	E	†	⚒		E		E		E		E		E							
0	**Groningen** d.	0019	...	0520	0541	0546	0620	0641	0646	0720	0746	0820	0846	0920	0946	and in the	1746	1820	1846	1920	...	2020	2120	2220	2320
34	Winschoten d.	0052	...	0555	0615	0621	0655	0715	0721	0755	0821	0855	0921	0955	1020	same pattern	1820	1855	1921	1955	...	2055	2155	2255	2355
46	Nieuweschans d.	0102	...	0608	...	0631	0705	...	0731	0808	0831	0905	0931	1008	...	**every two**	...	1905	1931	2008	...	2105	2205	2305	0005
57	Weener a.	...	...	0616	...	...	...	...	...	0816	...	...	...	1016	...	**hours**	...	...	...	2015	...	...	...	...	...
72	**Leer** (Ostfriesl) a.	...	...	0629	...	...	...	...	...	0829	...	...	...	1029	...	until	...	...	...	2029	...	...	...	...	...

				Ⓐ	E	Ⓐ	A	⑥k		E		E		E		E		E		E			E		
Leer (Ostfriesl) d.	...	...	...	...	...	...	0644	...	...	...	...	...	...	0923	0944z	...	and in the	...	...	1923	1944z	...	2123	2144z	...
Weener d.	...	...	...	...	...	...	0656	...	...	...	...	...	...	0935	0956z	...	same pattern	...	...	1935	1956z	...	2135	2156z	...
Nieuweschans d.	0022	0106	...	...	...	0645	0711	0711	...	0745	0811	0845	0911	0945	1011	...	**every two**	...	1911	1945	2011	2111	2145	2211	2322
Winschoten d.	0031	0115	...	0556	0620	0655	0720	0720	0720	0755	0820	0855	0920	0955	1020	1055	**hours**	1855	1920	1955	2020	2120	2155	2220	2331
Groningen a.	0106	0152	...	0634	0657	0734	0757	0757	0757	0834	0857	0934	0957	1034	1057	1134	until	1934	1957	2034	2057	2157	2234	2257	0006

A – ①–⑤ (not Dec. 25, 26, Jan. 1, Apr. 13, 30, May 21, June 1). k – Also Apr. 30, May 21. ★ – NS tickets are valid Groningen - Nieuweschans and v.v.
E – ①–⑥ (not Dec. 25, 26, Jan. 1, Apr. 13, June 1). z – ⑦ (also Dec. 25, 26, Jan. 1, Apr. 13, June 1).

496 AMSTERDAM - ZANDVOORT AAN ZEE

km					Ⓐ	⚒	⚒	Ⓒ	Ⓐ	†	⚒	†	⚒								
0	**Amsterdam** Centraal..... **450** d.	0015	...	...	...	*0608*	*0640*	*0710*	0715	*0740*	0745	*0810*	0815	0845	...	0915	0945	and at the same	2315	2345	...	...
5	Amsterdam Sloterdijk..... **450** d.	0021	...	...	...	*0614*	*0646*	*0716*	0721	*0746*	0751	*0816*	0821	0851	...	0921	0951	minutes past	2321	2351	...	...
19	Haarlem.................... **450** d.	0042	...	...	0558	0631	0701	0731	0731	0801	0801	0831	0831	0901	...	0931	1001		2331	0001	...	...
27	**Zandvoort** aan Zee.............a.	0053	...	...	0609	0642	0712	0742	0742	0812	0812	0842	0842	0912	...	0942	1012	each hour until	2342	0012	...	...

	H	G	H	G			Ⓐ	⚒	⚒													
Zandvoort aan Zee...............d.	0017	0017	0058	0058	...	...	0614	0647	0717	0747	...	0817	0847	and at the same	2217	2247	...	2317	2347	...	...	...
Haarlem.......................... **450** a.	0028	0028	0109	0110	...	...	0625	0658	0728	0758	...	0828	0858	minutes past	2228	2258	...	2328	2358	...	...	...
Amsterdam Sloterdijk...... **450** a.	*0045*	*0057*	*0128*	*0153*	...	...	0641	0711	0741	0811	...	0841	0911		2241	2311	...	2341	*0015*	...	...	...
Amsterdam Centraal...... **450** a.	*0052*	*0103*	*0135*	*0200*	...	...	0646	0717	0746	0817	...	0846	0918	each hour until	2246	2317	...	2346	*0022*	...	...	...

G – ②–⑤ (not Dec. 26, Jan. 2, Apr. 14, May 1, 22, June 2).

H – ①⑥⑦ (also Dec. 26, Jan. 2, Apr. 14, May 1, 22, June 2).

497 LEEUWARDEN - STAVOREN

Operated by **Arriva** (NS tickets valid); 2nd class only

km		Ⓐ	G	Ⓐ		G	G		G			G					t	⑤⑥h	
0	**Leeuwarden**.....d.	0530	0601	0632	0703	0703	0735	0803	0835	and at the same	1803	1835	1903	2003	2103	2203	2203	2320
22	Sneek...............d.	0552	0623	0654	0724	0725	0755	0825	0855	minutes past	1825	1855	1925	2025	2125	2224	2225	2341
51	Stavoren...........a.	0619	0650	0721	...	0752	...	0852	...	each hour until	1852	...	1952	2052	2152	...	2252	...

	Ⓐ	Ⓐ	G		Ⓐ	G	G		G			G					⑤⑥h	t
Stavoren............d.	...	0624	0658	...	0726	...	0758	...	...	0858	and at the same	...	1858	1958	2058	2158	2317	...
Sneek................d.	0629	0701	0729	0729	0801	0801	0829	0829	0901	0929	minutes past	1901	1929	2029	2129	2229	2346	2346
Leeuwarden......a.	0652	0723	0752	0752	0823	0823	0852	0852	0923	0952	each hour until	1923	2952	2052	2152	2252	0007	0007

G – ①–⑥ (not Dec. 25, 26, Jan. 1, Apr. 13, June 1).

h – Also Apr. 30, May 21; not Dec. 26.

t – Not Dec. 26, Apr. 13, June 1.

498 OTHER BRANCH LINES

ALMELO – MARIËNBERG Operated by **Connexxion** (NS tickets valid) *19 km* Journey time: 23 minutes

From Almelo:
0621 Ⓐ, 0644 Ⓐ, 0721 **E**, 0744 **E**, 0821 **E**, 0844 **E**, 0921 **E**, 0944 **E**, 1021 **E**, 1044 **E**, 1121, 1144 **E** and at 21 and 44 **E** minutes past each hour until 1721, 1744 **E**; then 1821 **E**, 1844 ⑦ **d**, 1921 **E**, 1944 ⑦ **d**, 2021 **E**, 2044 ⑦ **d**, 2121 **E** and 2144 ⑦ **d**.

From Mariënberg:
0649 Ⓐ, 0714 Ⓐ, 0749 **E**, 0814 **E**, 0849 **E**, 0914 **E**, 0949 **E**, 1014 **E**, 1049 **E**, 1114 **E**, 1149, 1214 **E**, 1249 and at 14 **E** and 49 minutes past each hour until 1714 **E**, 1749; then 1814 **E**, 1849 **E**, 1914 ⑦ **d**, 1949 **E**, 2014 ⑦ **d**, 2049 **E**, 2114 ⑦ **d**, 2149 **E** and 2214 ⑦ **d**.

AMERSFOORT – EDE-WAGENINGEN Operated by **Connexxion** (NS tickets valid) *34 km* Journey time: 37 minutes Amersfoort - Ede, 34 minutes Ede - Amersfoort.

From Amersfoort:
0015 **D**, 0045 ⑦ **z**, 0115 ⑦ **z**, 0515 Ⓐ, 0545 ⚒, 0615 ⚒, 0645 ⚒, 0715, 0745 and every 30 minutes until until 2345.

From Ede-Wageningen:
0001 **B**, 0031 **B**, 0055 **D**, 0131 ⑦ **z**, 0601 Ⓐ, 0631 ⚒, 0701 ⚒, 0731 ⚒, 0801, 0831 and every 30 minutes until 2331.

APELDOORN – ZUTPHEN *18 km* Journey time: 19 – 24 minutes

From Apeldoorn:
0010 **Q**, 0703 Ⓐ, 0733 Ⓐ, 0803 ⚒, 0833, 0903, 0933, 1003, 1033, 1103, 1140, 1210, 1240 and every 30 minutes until 2310.

From Zutphen:
0632 Ⓐ, 0702 Ⓐ, 0732 ⚒, 0802, 0832, 0902, 0932, 1002, 1032, 1102, 1136, 1206, 1236 and every 30 minutes until 2236; then 2336 **R**.

GRONINGEN – DELFZIJL Operated by **Arriva** (NS tickets valid) *38 km* Journey time: 37 – 40 minutes

From Groningen:
0024, 0533 Ⓐ, 0603 **G**, 0633, 0703 **S**, 0733, 0803 **G**, 0833 and at 03 **G** and 33 minutes past each hour until 1803 **G**, 1833; then 1903 Ⓐ, 1933, 2033, 2103 ④ **w**, 2133, 2233 and 2333.

From Delfzijl:
0015, 0104, 0515 ① **m**, 0615 Ⓐ, 0645 **G**, 0715, 0745 **S**, 0815, 0845 **G** and at 15 and 45 **G** minutes past each hour until 1815, 1845 **G**; then 1915, 1945 Ⓐ, 2015, 2115, 2215 and 2315.

LEEUWARDEN – HARLINGEN ¶ Operated by **Arriva** (NS tickets valid) *27 km* Journey time: 25 – 27 minutes 2nd class only

From Leeuwarden:
0459 Ⓐ, 0559 **G**, 0633 Ⓐ, 0659 **G**, 0733 **G**, 0759, 0833, 0859 and at 33 (▲) and 59 minutes past each hour until 1933, 1959; then 2059, 2159 and 2323.

From Harlingen Haven:
0528 Ⓐ, 0628 **G**, 0703 Ⓐ, 0728 **G**, 0803 **G**, 0828, 0903, 0928 and at 03 (●) and 28 minutes past each hour until 2003, 2028; then 2128, 2228 and 2352.

ZWOLLE – KAMPEN *13 km* Journey time: 10 minutes

From Zwolle:
0103 ⑥⑦ **e**, 0549 Ⓐ, 0619 Ⓐ, 0649 ⚒, 0719 ⚒, 0749 and at 19 ⚒ and 49 minutes past each hour until 1319 ⚒, 1349; then 1419, 1449 and every 30 minutes until 2349.

From Kampen:
0003, 0117 ⑥⑦ **e**, 0603 Ⓐ, 0633 Ⓐ, 0703 ⚒, 0733 ⚒, 0803, 0833 ⚒ and at 03 and 33 ⚒ minutes past each hour until 1303, 1333 ⚒; then 1403, 1433 and every 30 minutes until 2333.

B – ①②③④⑥⑦ (also Dec. 26, Jan. 2, May 1, 22).
D – ②–⑦ (not Dec. 26, Jan. 2).
E – ①–⑥ (not Dec. 25, 26, Jan. 1, Apr. 13, May 21, June 1).
G – ①–⑥ (not Dec. 25, 26, Jan. 1, Apr. 13, June 1).
Q – ①⑥⑦ (also Dec. 26, Jan. 2, Apr. 14, May 1, 22, June 2).
R – ⑤⑥⑦ (also Dec. 25, Jan. 1, Apr. 13, 30, May 21, June 1).
S – ⚒ (daily Apr. 27 - Sept. 26).

d – Also Dec. 25, 26, Jan. 1, Apr. 13, May 21, June 1.
e – Also Apr. 14, May 1, 22, June 2.
k – Also Apr. 30, May 21.
m – Not Apr. 13, June 1.
w – Not Dec. 25, Jan. 1, Apr. 30, May 21.
z – Also Dec. 27, Apr. 14, May 1, 22, June 2.

▲ – The services at 0933, 1033, 1133, 1533 and 1633 run on ①–⑥ **G** only.
● – The services at 1003, 1103, 1203, 1603 and 1703 run on ①–⑥ **G** only.
¶ – For ⛴ to / from Terschelling and Vlieland.

499 OTHER 🚌 and ⛴ LINES

ALKMAAR – HARLINGEN ¶ 🚌 *Connexxion Qliner* route **350 / 351** ★ Journey time: ± 1 hour 40 minutes

From Alkmaar rail station:
0524 Ⓐ, 0624 Ⓐ, 0724 ⚒, 0824, 0924 and hourly until 2124; also 2224 ⑦.

From Harlingen Veerbootterminal ¶:
0630 Ⓐ, 0730 Ⓐ, 0829 ⚒, 0929, 1029 and hourly until 2230.

ALKMAAR – LEEUWARDEN 🚌 *Connexxion Qliner* route **350** Journey time: ± 2 hours

From Alkmaar rail station:
0524 Ⓐ, 0624 ⚒, 0724 ⚒, 0824, 0924 and hourly until 2124; also 2224 ⑦.

From Leeuwarden rail station:
0601 Ⓐ, 0701 ⚒, 0800 ⑦, 0801 ⚒, 0900 ⑦, 0901 ⚒ and hourly until 2200 ⑦, 2201 ⚒.

DEN HELDER – TEXEL ⛴ *TESO*: ✆ +31 (0) 222 36 96 00 Journey time: 20 minutes

🚌 route **33**: Den Helder rail station (departs 20 minutes before ships sail) to Havenhoofd.
From Den Helder Havenhoofd: 0630 ⚒, 0730 ⚒ §, 0830, 0930 and hourly until 2130.

From Texel ('t Horntje ferryport): 0600 ⚒, 0700 ⚒ §, 0800, 0900 and hourly until 2100.
🚌 route **33**: Den Helder Havenhoofd (departs 5 minutes after ships arrive) to rail station.

ENKHUIZEN – STAVOREN ⛴ *Rederij V & O* ▲: ✆ +31 (0) 228 32 66 67 Journey time: 80 minutes Enkhuizen - Stavoren, 85 – 95 minutes Stavoren - Enkhuizen.

From Enkuizen Spoorhaven: 0830 **A**, 1230 **B**, 1630 **A**.

From Stavoren; 1005 **A**, 1405 **B**, 1805 **A**.

LELYSTAD – ZWOLLE 🚌 *Connexxion* route **330** Journey time: 64 – 68 minutes

From Lelystad rail station:
Ⓐ: 0607, 0637 and every 30 minutes until 1907; then 1935, 2035, 2135.
⑥: 0805, 0835 and every 30 minutes until 1935; then 2035, 2135.
⑦: 1235, 1335 and hourly until 2135.

From Zwolle rail station:
Ⓐ: 0556, 0626 and every 30 minutes until 1726; then 1759, 1831, 1901, 1931, 2001, 2101.
⑥: 0731, 0801 and every 30 minutes until 1901; then 2001, 2101.
⑦: 1201, 1301 and hourly until 2101.

VLISSINGEN – BRESKENS ⛴ *Veolia Transport Fast Ferries* ▲ Journey time: 20 minutes
0755, 0855 and hourly until 2055; ***also*** 0545 Ⓐ, 0655 Ⓐ, 0720 Ⓐ, 0820 Ⓐ, 1620 Ⓐ, 1720 Ⓐ, 2155 Ⓐ. Additional sailings operate May - September.

BRESKENS ferryport – **BRUGGE** rail station 🚌 *Veolia* route **42** Journey time: 83 minutes
0627 Ⓐ, 0727 ⚒, 0827 ⚒, 0927, 1027 and hourly until 2027.

BRUGGE rail station – **BRESKENS** ferryport 🚌 *Veolia* route **42** Journey time: 78 minutes
0657 ⚒, 0757 ⚒, 0857, 0957 and hourly until 1957; then 2057 ⚒.

BRESKENS – VLISSINGEN ⛴ *Veolia Transport Fast Ferries* ▲ Journey time: 20 minutes
0825, 0925 and hourly until 2125; ***also*** 0615 Ⓐ, 0725 Ⓐ, 0750 Ⓐ, 0850 Ⓐ, 1650 Ⓐ, 1750 Ⓐ, 2225 Ⓐ. Additional sailings operate May - September.

A – Daily Apr. 18 – 29, May 1 - Sept. 27, Oct. 17 – 25 (also Oct. 3, 4, 10, 11)
B – Daily May 1 - Sept. 27.

▲ – Conveys foot passengers, cycles and mopeds only.
¶ – For ⛴ to / from Terschelling and Vlieland.
§ – Runs daily April 1 - Sept. 30.

★ – Change at Kop Afsluitdijk on all services. Additional direct services run May 31 - Aug. 22: From Alkmaar at 1254 ①⑤⑥⑦, 1754 ⑦. From Harlingen Haven at 1459 ①⑤⑥⑦, 2000 ⑦.

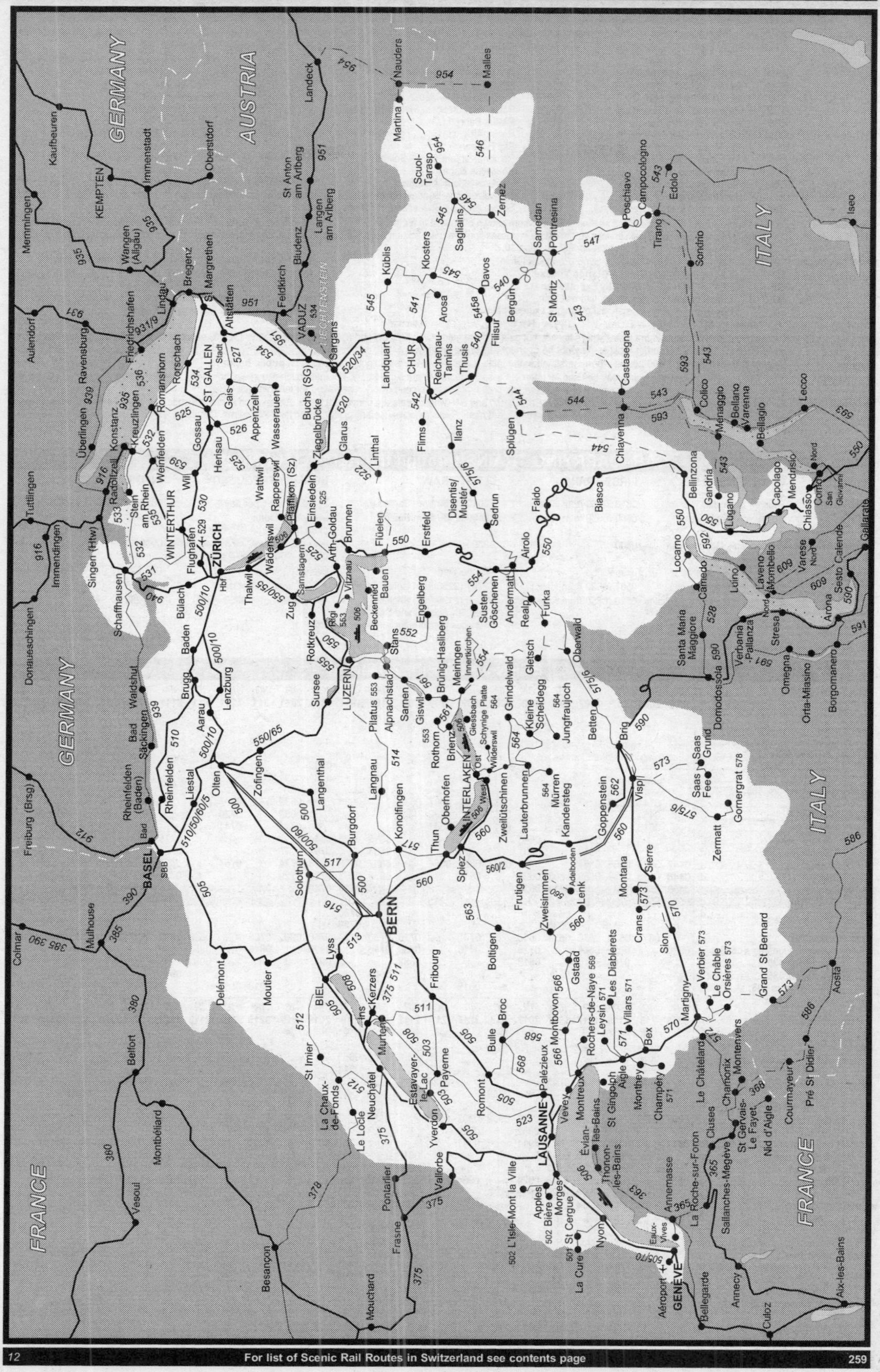
FRANCE
GERMANY
AUSTRIA
ITALY
LIECHTENSTEIN
BASEL
ZÜRICH
BERN
LUZERN
LAUSANNE
GENÈVE
INTERLAKEN
CHUR
ST GALLEN
WINTERTHUR
BIEL
VADUZ
KEMPTEN
Schaffhausen
Konstanz
Friedrichshafen
Lindau
Bregenz
St Margrethen
Buchs (SG)
Sargans
Landquart
Klosters
Davos
Arosa
Thusis
Filisur
Bergün
Samedan
St Moritz
Pontresina
Poschiavo
Tirano
Zernez
Scuol-Tarasp
Landeck
Nauders
Malles
Brunnen
Flüelen
Erstfeld
Göschenen
Andermatt
Airolo
Faido
Biasca
Bellinzona
Locarno
Lugano
Chiasso
Domodossola
Brig
Visp
Zermatt
Sierre
Sion
Martigny
Montreux
Vevey
Aigle
Bex
Gstaad
Zweisimmen
Spiez
Thun
Brienz
Meiringen
Fribourg
Neuchâtel
Yverdon
Vallorbe
Pontarlier
Solothurn
Olten
Aarau
Baden
Zug
Nyon
Chamonix
Annecy
Besançon
Mulhouse
Colmar
Belfort
Aosta
Milano

SWITZERLAND

Operators: There are numerous operators of which Schweizerische Bundesbahnen (SBB)/Chemins de fer Fédéraux (CFF)/Ferrovie Federali Svizzere (FFS) is the principal. Bus services are provided by PostAuto/Autopostale (PA). Table headings show the operators' initials; abbreviations used in the European Timetable are:

AB	Appenzeller Bahnen	MGB	Matterhorn Gotthard Bahn	SGV	Schifffahrtsgesellschaft des Vierwaldstättersees
BAM	Bière - Apples - Morges	MOB	Montreux - Oberland Bernois	SMC	Sierre - Montana - Crans
BLM	Bergbahn Lauterbrunnen - Mürren	MThB	Mittelthurgau Bahn	SNCF	Société Nationale des Chemins de Fer Français
BLS	BLS Lötschbergbahn	NStCM	Nyon-St Cergue-Morez	SOB	Schweizerische Südostbahn
BOB	Berner Oberland Bahnen	PA	PostAuto / Autopostale / AutoDaPosta	SPB	Schynige Platte Bahn
BRB	Brienz - Rothorn Bahn	PB	Pilatus Bahn	THURBO	an alliance of MThB and SBB
CGN	Compagnie Générale de Navigation	RA	RegionAlps	TMR	Transports de Martigny et Régions
CP	CarPostal Suisse	RB	Rigi Bahnen	TPC	Transports Publics du Chablais
FART	Ferrovie Autolinee Regionali Ticinesi	RBS	Regionalverkehr Bern - Solothurn	TPF	Transports Publics Fribourgeois
FS	Ferrovie dello Stato	RhB	Rhätische Bahn	URh	Untersee und Rhein
GGB	Gornergrat Bahn	RM	Regionalverkehr Mittelland	WAB	Wengernalpbahn
JB	Jungfraubahn	SBB	Schweizerische Bundesbahnen	ZB	Zentralbahn
MIB	Meiringen - Innertkirchen Bahn	SBS	Schweizerische Bodensee-Schifffahrtsgesellschaft	ZSG	Zürich Schifffahrtsgesellschaft

Services: All trains convey first and second class seating, **except** where shown otherwise in footnotes or by a '1' or '2' in the train column, or where the footnote shows sleeping and/or couchette cars only. For most local services you **must** be in possession of a valid ticket before boarding your train. Some international trains convey sleeping cars (🛏) and/or couchette cars (🛏), descriptions of which appear on page **10**.

Train Categories:

CIS	Italian high-speed **Cisalpino** tilting (*Pendolino*) train.	*CNL*	**City Night Line** quality international overnight hotel train.
TGV	French high-speed **Train à Grande Vitesse**.	*IC*	**InterCity** quality internal express train.
ICE	German high-speed **InterCity Express** train.	*ICN*	**InterCity Neigezug** high-speed tilting train.
EC	**EuroCity** quality international express train.	*IR*	**InterRegio** fast inter-regional trains.
EN	**EuroNight** quality international overnight express train.	*RE*	**RegioExpress** semi-fast regional trains.

Catering: ✕ – Restaurant; (✕) – Bistro; (🍸) – Bar coach; 🍸 – Minibar.
Details of catering is shown in the tables where known, but as a general guide *CIS*, *ICE*, *EC* and *ICN* trains convey ✕ or (✕), *IC* services convey ✕ or (🍸), and *TGV* and *IR* trains convey (🍸) or 🍸. Catering facilities may not be open for the whole journey.

Timings: Valid until **December 12, 2009** unless otherwise stated in the table. Local services are subject to alteration on **public holidays**.

Supplements: *TGV*, *CIS* and *ICE* high-speed trains may be used for internal Swiss journeys without supplement. For international journeys however, *TGV* services are priced as 'global' fare and *CIS* services are subject to the payment of a supplement; both types require compulsory reservation for international travel.

Reservations: Seat reservations may be made on all *ICE*, *CIS*, *TGV*, *EC*, *IC*, *ICN* and *EN* (where seats are conveyed) trains. Reservation is recommended for travel in first class observation cars. Fares in Switzerland are calculated according to distance and many Swiss railways use artificially inflated tariff-kilometres. Distances shown in tables below, however, are actual kilometres.

CAR-CARRYING TRAINS through the ALPINE TUNNELS

BLS, MGB, RhB, SBB

TUNNEL	CAR TERMINALS	FIRST TRAIN*	LAST TRAIN*	NORMAL FREQUENCY	INFORMATION ✆
ALBULA:	Thusis - Samedan	0810 (0750 from Samedan)	2010 (1750 from Samedan)	7 – 10 services per day	081 288 47 16, 081 288 55 11
FURKA:	Oberwald - Realp	0600 (0630 from Realp)	2100 (2130 from Realp)	every 60 minutes more frequent on ①⑤⑥⑦.	027 927 76 66, 027 927 76 76
LÖTSCHBERG:	Kandersteg - Goppenstein	0600	2300	every 30 minutes, more frequent 0730 – 1900 on ⑤⑥⑦ and mid-June – mid-Oct.	0900 55 33 33
OBERALP:	Andermatt - Sedrun	unspecified	unspecified	every 60 minutes	027 927 77 07, 027 927 77 40
SIMPLON:	Brig - Iselle (Italy)	0531 (0620 from Iselle)	2201 (2250 from Iselle)	11 – 12 services per day	0900 300 300
VEREINA:	Selfranga (Klosters) - Sagliains	0520 (0550 from Sagliains)	2050 (2120 from Sagliains) Dec. 9 - Apr. 30 and Dec. 1 - 13, services continue for a further 2 hours	every 30 minutes 0850 – 1920	081 288 37 37

* – Not necessarily daily.

500 BERN and BIEL - ZÜRICH

SBB

km		IR 1903	IR 2005	IC 707	IR 2107	IR 1909	ICN 509 ✕	IR 2009 Ⓐ	IC 809 ✕	IR 3209	IC 709 ✕ F	IR 2109	IR 1911	ICN 1511 ✕	IR 2011	IC 811 ✕	IR 3211	IC 711 ✕	IR 2111	EN 314 L	IR 1915	ICN 515 ✕	IR 2015	IC 815 ✕
	Genève Aéroport ✈ **505** d.	...	...	...	...	...	...	...	...	...	...	...	...	...	...	...	...	...	...	...	...	...	...	...
	Genève **505** d.	...	...	...	...	...	...	...	...	...	...	...	...	...	...	...	...	0536	...	...	...	0614	...	...
	Lausanne **505** d.	...	...	...	...	...	...	...	...	...	...	...	...	0539	...	...	...	0620	...	...	...	|	...	...
	Brig **560** d.	...	...	...	...	...	...	...	...	...	...	...	...	|	...	0547	...	|	...	0439s	...	|	...	0649
	Interlaken Ost **560** d.	...	...	...	...	...	...	...	...	...	...	...	...	|	...	|	...	|	...	|	...	|	...	|
0	**Bern** d.	0421	0441	0530	...	...	...	0539	0602	0607	0632	...	0636	|	0639	0702	0707	0732	...	0620s	0736	|	0739	0802
23	Burgdorf d.	|	0454	|	...	...	...	0552	|	0620	|	...	|	|	0652	|	0720	|	...	|	|	|	0752	|
47	Langenthal d.	|	0513	|	...	...	...	0611	|	0641	|	...	|	|	0711	|	0741	|	...	|	|	|	0811	|
	Biel/Bienne d.	|	|	|	0515	...	0543	|	|	|	|	0615	|	0644	|	|	|	|	0715	|	|	0746	|	|
	Solothurn d.	|	|	|	0533	...	0601	|	|	|	|	0633	|	0702	|	|	|	|	0733	|	|	0801	|	|
67	**Olten** a.	0447	0525	0555	0557	...	0618	0623	0628	0654	|	0657	0702	0718	0724	|	0754	|	0757	0745s	0802	0818	0824	|
67	**Olten** d.	0448	0535	0557	0559	0603	0620	...	0631	...	|	0659	0703	0720	0729	|	...	|	0759	|	0803	0820	0829	|
80	Aarau d.	0458	0545	|	|	0614	0630	...	|	...	|	|	0714	0730	|	|	...	|	|	|	0814	0830	|	|
90	Lenzburg d.	0506	0554	|	|	|	|	...	|	...	|	|	|	|	|	|	...	|	|	|	|	|	|	|
	Brugg d.	|	|	|	|	0630	|	...	|	...	|	|	0730	|	|	|	...	|	|	|	0830	|	|	|
	Baden a.	|	|	|	|	0638	|	...	|	...	|	|	0738	|	|	|	...	|	|	|	0838	|	|	|
122	**Zürich HB** a.	|	0618	0628	0630	0654	0656	...	0702	...	0728	0730	0754	0756	0802	0758	...	0828	0830	0842	0854	0856	0902	0858
	Zürich Flughafen ✈ **530/5** a.	0530	...	0650	0646	...	0720	...	0716	...	0750	0746	...	0820	...	0816	...	0850	0846	...	...	0920	...	0916
	St Gallen **530** a.	...	...	0753	|	...	0815	...	|	...	0853	|	...	0915	...	|	...	0953	|	...	...	1015	...	|
	Konstanz **535** a.	...	...	...	0754	...	...	...	|	...	...	0854	...	...	...	|	...	...	0954	...	...	...	...	|
	Romanshorn **535** a.	...	...	...	...	...	...	...	0818	...	...	...	...	...	...	0918	...	...	...	...	...	...	...	1018

km		IR 3215	IC 715 ✕	IR 2115	IR 1917	ICN 1517 ✕	IR 2017	IC 817 (✕)	IR 3217	IC 717 ✕	IR 2117	IR 1919	ICN 519 ✕	IR 2019	IC 819 ✕	IR 3219	IC 719 ✕	IR 2119	IR 1921	ICN 1521 ✕	IR 2021	IC 821 (✕)	IR 3221	IC 721 ✕
	Genève Aéroport ✈ **505** d.	...	0636	...	...	...	...	...	...	0736	...	...	0805	...	...	...	0836	...	...	...	...	...	...	0936
	Genève **505** d.	...	0645	...	...	...	...	...	...	0745	...	...	0814	...	...	...	0845	...	...	...	...	...	...	0945
	Lausanne **505** d.	...	0720	...	...	0745	...	...	...	0820	...	...	|	...	...	...	0920	...	...	0945	...	...	...	1020
	Brig **560** d.	...	|	...	...	|	...	0749	...	|	...	...	|	...	0849	...	|	...	...	|	...	0949	...	|
	Interlaken Ost **560** d.	...	|	...	...	|	...	|	...	|	...	...	|	...	|	...	|	...	...	|	...	|	...	|
	Bern d.	0807	0832	...	0836	|	0839	0902	0907	0932	...	0936	|	0939	1002	1007	1032	...	1036	|	1039	1102	1107	1132
	Burgdorf d.	0820	|	...	|	|	0852	|	0920	|	...	|	|	0952	|	1020	|	...	|	|	1052	|	1120	|
	Langenthal d.	0841	|	...	|	|	0911	|	0941	|	...	|	|	1011	|	1041	|	...	|	|	1111	|	1141	|
0	**Biel/Bienne** d.	|	|	0815	|	0846	|	|	|	|	0915	|	0946	|	|	|	|	1015	|	1046	|	|	|	|
25	Solothurn d.	|	|	0833	|	0901	|	|	|	|	0933	|	1001	|	|	|	|	1033	|	1101	|	|	|	|
60	**Olten** a.	0854	|	0857	0902	0918	0924	|	0954	|	0957	1002	1018	1024	|	1054	|	1057	1102	1118	1124	|	1154	|
60	**Olten** d.	...	|	0859	0903	0920	0929	|	...	|	0959	1003	1020	1029	|	...	|	1059	1103	1120	1129	|	...	|
73	Aarau d.	...	|	|	0914	0930	|	|	...	|	|	1014	1030	|	|	...	|	|	1114	1130	|	|	...	|
	Lenzburg d.	...	|	|	|	|	|	|	...	|	|	|	|	|	|	...	|	|	|	|	|	|	...	|
91	Brugg d.	...	|	|	0930	|	|	|	...	|	|	1030	|	|	|	...	|	|	1130	|	|	|	...	|
100	Baden a.	...	|	|	0938	|	|	|	...	|	|	1038	|	|	|	...	|	|	1138	|	|	|	...	|
122	**Zürich HB** a.	...	0928	0930	0954	0956	1002	0958	...	1028	1030	1054	1056	1102	1058	...	1128	1130	1154	1156	1202	1158	...	1228
	Zürich Flughafen ✈ **530/5** a.	...	0950	0946	...	1020	...	1016	...	1050	1046	...	1120	...	1116	...	1150	1146	...	1220	...	1216	...	1250
	St Gallen **530** a.	...	1053	|	...	1115	...	|	...	1153	|	...	1215	...	|	...	1253	|	...	1315	...	|	...	1353
	Konstanz **535** a.	...	...	1054	...	...	...	|	...	...	1154	...	...	...	|	...	...	1254	...	...	...	|	...	...
	Romanshorn **535** a.	...	...	...	...	...	...	1118	...	...	...	...	...	...	1218	...	...	...	...	...	...	1318	...	...

F – From Fribourg. L – LUNA – Roma - Zürich. s – Stops to set down only.

SBB — BERN and BIEL - ZÜRICH — 500

	IR	IR	ICN	IR		IC	IR	IC	IR	IR	ICN	IR		IC	IR	IC	IR	IR	ICN	IR		IC	IR	IC
	2121	**1923**	**523**	**2023**		**823**	**3223**	**723**	**2123**	**1925**	**1525**	**2025**		**825**	**3225**	**725**	**2125**	**1927**	**527**	**2027**		**827**	**3227**	**727**
			✕			✕		✕			✕			(✕)		✕			✕			✕		✕
Genève Aéroport ✈ **505** d.	...	...	1005	...	...	...	...	1036	...	...	...	...	...	...	...	1136	...	...	1205	...	...	...	...	1236
Genève **505** d.	...	...	1014	...	...	...	...	1045	...	...	...	...	...	...	...	1145	...	...	1214	...	...	...	...	1245
Lausanne **505** d.	...	...	|	...	...	...	...	1120	...	...	1145	...	...	...	...	1220	...	...	|	...	...	...	...	1320
Brig **560** d.	...	...	|	...	...	1049	...	|	...	...	|	...	...	1149	...	|	...	...	|	...	...	1249	...	|
Interlaken Ost **560** d.	...	...	|	...	...	|	...	|	...	...	|	...	...	|	...	|	...	...	|	...	...	|	...	|
Bern d.	...	1136	|	1139	...	1202	1207	1232	...	1236	|	1239	...	1302	1307	1332	...	1336	|	1339	...	1402	1407	1432
Burgdorf d.	...	|	|	1152	...	|	1220	|	...	|	|	1252	...	|	1320	|	...	|	|	1352	...	|	1420	|
Langenthal d.	...	|	|	1211	...	|	1241	|	...	|	|	1311	...	|	1341	|	...	|	|	1411	...	|	1441	|
Biel/Bienne d.	1115	|	1146	|	...	|	|	|	1215	|	1246	|	...	|	|	|	1315	|	1346	|	...	|	|	|
Solothurn d.	1133	|	1201	|	...	|	|	|	1233	|	1301	|	...	|	|	|	1333	|	1401	|	...	|	|	|
Olten a.	1157	1202	1218	1224	...	|	1254	|	1257	1302	1318	1324	...	|	1354	|	1357	1402	1418	1424	...	|	1454	|
Olten d.	1159	1203	1220	1229	...	|	...	|	1259	1303	1320	1329	...	|	...	|	1359	1403	1420	1429	...	|	...	|
Aarau d.	|	1214	1230	|	...	|	...	|	|	1314	1330	|	...	|	...	|	|	1414	1430	|	...	|	...	|
Lenzburg d.	|	|	|	|	...	|	...	|	|	|	|	|	...	|	...	|	|	|	|	|	...	|	...	|
Brugg d.	|	1230	|	|	...	|	...	|	|	1330	|	|	...	|	...	|	|	1430	|	|	...	|	...	|
Baden a.	|	1238	|	|	...	|	...	|	|	1338	|	|	...	|	...	|	|	1438	|	|	...	|	...	|
Zürich HB a.	1230	1254	1256	1302	...	1258	...	1328	1330	1354	1356	1402	...	1358	...	1428	1430	1454	1456	1502	...	1458	...	1528
Zürich Flughafen ✈ **530/5** a.	1246	...	1320	...	...	1316	...	1350	1346	...	1420	...	...	1416	...	1450	1446	...	1520	...	...	1516	...	1550
St Gallen **530** a.	|	...	1415	...	...	|	...	1453	|	...	1515	...	...	|	...	1553	|	...	1615	...	...	|	...	1653
Konstanz **535** a.	1354	...	...	...	...	|	...	...	1454	...	...	...	...	|	...	...	1554	...	...	...	...	|	...	...
Romanshorn **535** a.	...	...	...	...	...	1418	...	...	...	...	...	...	...	1518	...	...	...	...	...	...	...	1618	...	...

	IR	IR	ICN	IR	IC	IR	IC	IR	IR	ICN	IR		IC	IR	IC	IR	IR	ICN	IR		IC	IR	IC	IR
	2127	**1929**	**1529**	**2029**	**829**	**3229**	**729**	**2129**	**1931**	**531**	**2031**		**831**	**3231**	**731**	**2131**	**1935**	**1535**	**2035**		**835**	**3235**	**735**	**2135**
			✕		✕		✕			✕			✕		✕			✕			(✕)		✕	
Genève Aéroport ✈ **505** d.	...	...	...	...	...	...	1336	...	...	1405	...	...	...	...	1436	...	...	...	...	...	...	...	1536	...
Genève **505** d.	...	...	...	...	...	...	1345	...	...	1414	...	...	...	...	1445	...	...	...	...	...	...	...	1545	...
Lausanne **505** d.	...	...	1345	...	...	...	1420	...	...	|	...	...	...	...	1520	...	...	1545	...	...	...	...	1620	...
Brig **560** d.	...	...	|	...	1349	...	|	...	...	|	...	...	1449	...	|	...	...	|	...	...	1549	...	|	...
Interlaken Ost **560** d.	...	...	|	...	|	...	|	...	...	|	...	...	|	...	|	...	...	|	...	...	|	...	|	...
Bern d.	...	1436	|	1439	1502	1507	1532	...	1536	|	1539	...	1602	1607	1632	...	1636	|	1639	...	1702	1707	1732	...
Burgdorf d.	...	|	|	1452	|	1520	|	...	|	|	1552	...	|	1620	|	...	|	|	1652	...	|	1720	|	...
Langenthal d.	...	|	|	1511	|	1541	|	...	|	|	1611	...	|	1641	|	...	|	|	1711	...	|	1741	|	...
Biel/Bienne d.	1415	|	1446	|	|	|	|	1515	|	1546	|	...	|	|	|	1615	|	1646	|	...	|	|	|	1715
Solothurn d.	1433	|	1501	|	|	|	|	1533	|	1601	|	...	|	|	|	1633	|	1701	|	...	|	|	|	1733
Olten a.	1457	1502	1518	1524	|	1554	|	1557	1602	1618	1624	...	|	1654	|	1657	1702	1718	1724	...	|	1754	|	1757
Olten d.	1459	1503	1520	1529	|	...	|	1559	1603	1620	1629	...	|	...	|	1659	1703	1720	1729	...	|	...	|	1759
Aarau d.	|	1514	1530	|	|	...	|	|	1614	1630	|	...	|	...	|	|	1714	1730	|	...	|	...	|	|
Lenzburg d.	|	|	|	|	|	...	|	|	|	|	|	...	|	...	|	|	|	|	|	...	|	...	|	|
Brugg d.	|	1530	|	|	|	...	|	|	1630	|	|	...	|	...	|	|	1730	|	|	...	|	...	|	|
Baden a.	|	1538	|	|	|	...	|	|	1638	|	|	...	|	...	|	|	1738	|	|	...	|	...	|	|
Zürich HB a.	1530	1554	1556	1602	1558	...	1628	1630	1654	1656	1702	...	1658	...	1728	1730	1754	1756	1802	...	1758	...	1828	1830
Zürich Flughafen ✈ **530/5** a.	1546	...	1620	...	1616	...	1650	1646	...	1720	...	...	1716	...	1750	1746	...	1820	...	...	1816	...	1850	1846
St Gallen **530** a.	|	...	1715	...	|	...	1753	|	...	1815	...	...	|	...	1853	|	...	1915	...	...	|	...	1953	|
Konstanz **535** a.	1654	...	...	...	|	...	...	1754	...	...	...	...	|	...	...	1855	...	...	...	...	|	...	...	1954
Romanshorn **535** a.	...	...	...	...	1718	...	...	...	...	...	...	...	1818	...	...	...	...	...	...	...	1918	...	...	...

	IR	ICN	IR	IC	IR		IC	IR	IR	ICN	IR	IC	IR	IC	IR	IR	ICN		IR	IC	IR	IC	IR	IR
	1937	**537**	**2037**	**837**	**3237**		**737**	**2137**	**1939**	**1539**	**2039**	**839**	**3239**	**739**	**2139**	**1941**	**541**		**2041**	**841**	**3241**	**741**	**2141**	**1943**
		✕		✕			✕			✕		(✕)		✕			✕			✕		✕		
Genève Aéroport ✈ **505** d.	...	1605	...	...	...	...	1636	...	...	...	...	...	...	1736	...	...	1805	...	...	...	...	1836	...	...
Genève **505** d.	...	1614	...	...	...	...	1645	...	...	...	...	...	...	1745	...	...	1814	...	...	...	...	1845	...	...
Lausanne **505** d.	...	|	...	...	...	...	1720	...	...	1745	...	...	...	1820	...	...	|	...	...	...	...	1920	...	...
Brig **560** d.	...	|	...	1649	...	...	|	...	...	|	...	1749	...	|	...	...	|	...	...	1849	...	|	...	...
Interlaken Ost **560** d.	...	|	...	|	...	...	|	...	...	|	...	|	...	|	...	...	|	...	...	|	...	|	...	...
Bern d.	1736	|	1739	1802	1807	...	1832	...	1836	|	1839	1902	1907	1932	...	1936	|	...	1939	2002	2007	2032	...	2036
Burgdorf d.	|	|	1752	|	1820	...	|	...	|	|	1852	|	1920	|	...	|	|	...	1952	|	2020	|	...	|
Langenthal d.	|	|	1811	|	1841	...	|	...	|	|	1911	|	1941	|	...	|	|	...	2011	|	2041	|	...	|
Biel/Bienne d.	|	1746	|	|	|	...	|	1815	|	1846	|	|	|	|	1915	|	1946	...	|	|	|	|	2015	|
Solothurn d.	|	1801	|	|	|	...	|	1833	|	1901	|	|	|	|	1933	|	2001	...	|	|	|	|	2033	|
Olten a.	1802	1818	1824	|	1854	...	|	1857	1902	1918	1924	|	1954	|	1957	2002	2018	...	2024	|	2054	|	2057	2102
Olten d.	1803	1820	1829	|	...	...	|	1859	1903	1920	1929	|	...	|	1959	2003	2020	...	2029	|	...	|	2059	2103
Aarau d.	1814	1830	|	|	...	...	|	|	1914	1930	|	|	...	|	|	2014	2030	...	|	|	...	|	|	2114
Lenzburg d.	|	|	|	|	...	...	|	|	|	|	|	|	...	|	|	|	|	...	|	|	...	|	|	|
Brugg d.	1830	|	|	|	...	...	|	|	1930	|	|	|	...	|	|	2030	|	...	|	|	...	|	|	2130
Baden a.	1838	|	|	|	...	...	|	|	1938	|	|	|	...	|	|	2038	|	...	|	|	...	|	|	2138
Zürich HB a.	1854	1856	1902	1858	...	...	1928	1930	1954	1956	2002	1958	...	2028	2030	2054	2056	...	2102	2058	...	2128	2130	2154
Zürich Flughafen ✈ **530/5** a.	...	1920	...	1916	...	...	1950	1946	...	2020	...	2016	...	2050	2046	...	2120	...	...	2116	...	2150	...	...
St Gallen **530** a.	...	2015	...	|	...	...	2053	|	...	2115	...	|	...	2153	|	...	2215	...	...	|	...	2253	...	...
Konstanz **535** a.	...	...	...	|	...	...	...	2054	...	...	...	|	...	...	2154	...	...	...	...	|	...	...	...	...
Romanshorn **535** a.	...	...	...	2018	...	...	...	...	...	...	...	2118	...	...	...	...	...	...	...	2218	...	...	...	...

	ICN	IR	IC	IR	IR	IC	IR		ICN	IR	IC	IR	IC	IR		IC	ICN	RE	IR	IC	IC	ICN	IR	IC
	1543	**2043**	**843**	**3243**	**2143**	**743**	**1945**		**545**	**2045**	**845**	**3245**	**745**	**1947**		**847**	**1547**	**3647**	**3247**	**747**	**849**	**1549**	**3249**	**803**
	✕		(✕)			✕			✕															⑥⑦y
Genève Aéroport ✈ **505** d.	...	...	...	...	...	1936	...	...	2005	...	...	...	2036	...	...	...	...	...	...	2136	...	...	...	...
Genève **505** d.	...	...	...	...	...	1945	...	...	2014	...	...	...	2045	...	...	...	...	...	...	2145	...	...	...	...
Lausanne **505** d.	1945	...	...	...	...	2020	...	...	|	...	...	...	2120	...	...	...	2145	...	...	2220	...	...	...	...
Brig **560** d.	|	...	1949	...	...	|	...	...	|	...	...	...	|	...	...	...	|	...	...	|	...	...	...	...
Interlaken Ost **560** d.	|	...	|	...	...	|	...	...	|	...	...	...	|	...	...	...	|	...	...	|	...	...	...	...
Bern d.	|	2039	2102	2107	...	2132	...	...	|	2137	2202	2207	2232	...	...	2302	|	...	2307	2332	0002	...	0007	0102
Burgdorf d.	|	2052	|	2120	...	|	...	...	|	2152	|	2222	|	...	...	|	|	...	2322	|	|	...	0022	|
Langenthal d.	|	2111	|	2141	...	|	...	...	|	2211	|	2242	|	...	...	|	|	...	2342	|	|	...	0042	|
Biel/Bienne d.	2046	|	|	|	2115	|	...	...	2146	|	|	|	|	...	...	|	2246	...	|	|	|	2346	|	|
Solothurn d.	2101	|	|	|	2133	|	...	...	2203	|	|	|	|	...	...	|	2305	...	|	|	|	0005	|	|
Olten a.	2118	2124	|	2154	2157	2158	...	...	2219	2224	2228	2254	2258	...	...	|	2330	...	2354	2358	0028	0030	0054	0128
Olten d.	2120	...	|	...	...	2200	2203	...	2220	...	2230	...	2300	2303	...	|	2335	2336	...	0000	0033	0035	...	0133
Aarau d.	2130	...	|	...	...	|	2214	...	2230	...	|	...	|	2314	...	|	2345	2347	...	0009	|	0045	...	0143
Lenzburg d.	|	...	|	...	...	|	|	...	|	...	|	...	|	|	...	|	|	|	...	0018	|	0052	...	|
Brugg d.	|	...	|	...	...	|	2230	...	|	...	|	...	|	2330	...	|	|	0003	...	|	|	|	...	|
Baden a.	|	...	|	...	...	|	2238	...	|	...	|	...	|	2338	...	|	|	0013	...	|	|	|	...	|
Zürich HB a.	2156	...	2158	...	...	2231	2254	...	2256	...	2301	...	2331	2354	...	2358	0010	0042	...	0033	0104	0112	...	0207j
Zürich Flughafen ✈ **530/5** a.	2220	...	2216	...	...	...	...	...	2320	...	2316	...	...	...	...	...	0027	...	...	...	...	...	...	...
St Gallen **530** a.	2317	...	|	...	...	...	...	...	0018	...	|	...	...	...	...	...	0125	...	...	...	...	...	...	...
Konstanz **535** a.	...	...	|	...	...	...	...	...	...	...	|	...	...	...	...	...	...	...	...	...	...	...	...	...
Romanshorn **535** a.	...	...	2318	...	...	...	...	...	...	...	0018	...	...	...	...	...	...	...	...	...	...	...	...	...

j – Arrive 0215 on ⑦.

y – Also Jan. 1.

500 ZÜRICH - BIEL and BERN SBB

	IR 2006	IC 706	IR 2106	IR 3208	IR 2008	IC 808 ✕	ICN 508 ✕	IR 1908		IR 2108	IC 708 ✕	IC 1008 🍷 Ⓐ	IR 3210		IR 2010	IC 810 (✕)	ICN 1510 ✕	IR 1910	IR 2110	IC 710 ✕	IC 1012 🍷 Ⓐ	IR 3212	IR 2012	IC 812 ✕
Romanshorn **535** d.	...	...	...	...	...	...	...	...	...	...	...	...	...	...	...	0538	...	...	...	...	...	...	...	0638
Konstanz **535** d.	...	...	...	...	...	...	...	...	...	...	...	...	...	...	...	|	...	...	0602	...	...	...	...	|
St Gallen **530** d.	...	...	...	...	...	...	...	...	...	...	0511	...	...	...	...	|	0544	...	|	0611	...	...	...	|
Zürich Flughafen ✈ **530/5** d.	...	...	...	...	...	...	...	...	...	...	0613	...	...	...	...	0640	0643	...	0710	0713	...	...	...	0743
Zürich HB d.	...	0521	...	...	0558	0600	0604	0606	...	0630	0632	0647	...	...	0658	0700	0704	0706	0730	0732	0747	...	0758	0800
Baden d.	...	|	...	...	|	|	|	0622	...	|	|	|	...	...	|	|	|	0722	|	|	|	...	|	|
Brugg d.	...	|	...	...	|	|	|	0632	...	|	|	|	...	...	|	|	|	0732	|	|	|	...	|	|
Lenzburg d.	...	0542	...	...	|	|	|	|	...	|	|	|	...	...	|	|	|	|	|	|	|	...	|	|
Aarau d.	...	0548	...	...	|	|	0630	0647	...	|	|	|	...	...	|	|	0730	0747	|	|	|	...	|	|
Olten a.	...	0558	...	...	0629	|	0639	0656	...	0701	|	|	...	...	0729	|	0739	0756	0801	|	|	...	0829	|
Olten d.	0536	0603	0603	0606	0636	|	0641	0658	...	0703	|	|	0706	...	0736	|	0741	0758	0803	|	|	0806	0836	|
Solothurn d.	|	|	0628	|	|	|	0659	|	...	0728	|	|	|	...	|	|	0759	|	0828	|	|	|	|	|
Biel/Bienne a.	|	|	0645	|	|	|	0713	|	...	0745	|	|	|	...	|	|	0813	|	0845	|	|	|	|	|
Langenthal d.	0549	|	...	0618	0649	|	|	|	...	...	|	|	0718	...	0749	|	|	|	...	|	|	0818	0849	|
Burgdorf d.	0607	|	...	0638	0707	|	|	|	...	...	|	|	0738	...	0807	|	|	|	...	|	|	0838	0907	|
Bern a.	0621	0629	...	0653	0721	0657	|	0725	...	...	0729	0745	0753	...	0821	0757	|	0825	...	0829	0845	0853	0921	0857
Interlaken Ost **560** a.	...	|	...	...	...	|	|	...	...	...	|	...	...	...	...	|	|	...	...	|	...	...	...	|
Brig **560** a.	...	|	...	...	...	0811	|	...	...	...	|	...	...	...	...	0911	|	...	...	|	...	...	...	1011
Lausanne **505** a.	...	0740	...	...	...	...	|	...	...	...	0840	...	...	...	...	...	0915	...	...	0940	...	...	...	...
Genève **505** a.	...	0815	...	...	...	...	0846	...	...	...	0915	...	...	...	...	...	...	...	...	1015	...	...	...	...
Genève Aéroport ✈ **505** a.	...	0824	...	...	...	...	0855	...	...	...	0924	...	...	...	...	...	...	...	...	1024	...	...	...	...

	ICN 512 ✕	IR 1912	IR 2112	IC 712 ✕	IR 3216	IR 2016	IC 816 (✕)	ICN 1516 ✕	IR 1916		IR 2116	IC 716 ✕	IR 3218	IR 2018	IC 818 ✕	ICN 518 ✕	IR 1918		IR 2118	IC 718 ✕	IR 3220	IR 2020	IC 820 ✕	ICN 1520 ✕
Romanshorn **535** d.	...	...	...	...	...	...	0741	...	...	...	...	...	...	...	0841	...	...	...	...	...	...	...	0941	...
Konstanz **535** d.	...	...	0702	...	...	...	|	...	...	...	0803	...	...	...	|	...	...	...	0903	...	...	...	|	...
St Gallen **530** d.	0642	...	|	0711	...	...	|	0748	...	...	|	0811	...	...	|	0848	...	...	|	0911	...	...	|	0948
Zürich Flughafen ✈ **530/5** d.	0739	...	0810	0813	...	...	0840	0843	...	...	0910	0913	...	...	0940	0943	...	...	1010	1013	...	...	1040	1043
Zürich HB d.	0804	0806	0830	0832	...	0858	0900	0904	0906	...	0930	0932	...	0958	1000	1004	1006	...	1030	1032	...	1058	1100	1104
Baden d.	|	0822	|	|	...	|	|	|	0922	...	|	|	...	|	|	|	1022	...	|	|	...	|	|	|
Brugg d.	|	0832	|	|	...	|	|	|	0932	...	|	|	...	|	|	|	1032	...	|	|	...	|	|	|
Lenzburg d.	|	|	|	|	...	|	|	|	|	...	|	|	...	|	|	|	|	...	|	|	...	|	|	|
Aarau d.	0830	0847	|	|	...	|	|	0930	0947	...	|	|	...	|	|	1030	1047	...	|	|	...	|	|	1130
Olten a.	0839	0856	0901	|	...	0929	|	0939	0956	...	1001	|	...	1029	|	1039	1056	...	1101	|	...	1129	|	1139
Olten d.	0841	0858	0903	|	0906	0936	|	0941	0958	...	1003	|	1006	1036	|	1041	1058	...	1103	|	1106	1136	|	1141
Solothurn d.	0859	|	0928	|	|	|	|	0959	|	...	1028	|	|	|	|	1059	|	...	1128	|	|	|	|	1159
Biel/Bienne a.	0913	|	0945	|	|	|	|	1013	|	...	1045	|	|	|	|	1113	|	...	1145	|	|	|	|	1213
Langenthal d.	|	|	...	|	0918	0949	|	|	|	...	...	|	1018	1049	|	|	|	...	...	|	1118	1149	|	|
Burgdorf d.	|	|	...	|	0938	1007	|	|	|	...	...	|	1038	1107	|	|	|	...	...	|	1138	1207	|	|
Bern a.	|	0925	...	0929	0953	1021	0957	|	1025	...	...	1029	1053	1121	1057	|	1125	...	...	1129	1153	1221	1157	|
Interlaken Ost **560** a.	|	...	...	|	...	...	|	|	...	...	...	|	...	...	|	|	...	...	...	|	...	...	|	|
Brig **560** a.	|	...	...	|	...	...	1111	|	...	...	...	|	...	...	1211	|	...	...	...	|	...	...	1311	|
Lausanne **505** a.	|	...	...	1040	...	...	...	1115	...	...	...	1140	...	...	...	|	...	...	...	1240	...	...	...	1315
Genève **505** a.	1046	...	...	1115	...	...	...	...	...	...	...	1215	...	...	...	1246	...	...	...	1315	...	...	...	...
Genève Aéroport ✈ **505** a.	1055	...	...	1124	...	...	...	...	...	...	...	1224	...	...	...	1255	...	...	...	1324	...	...	...	...

	IR 1920	IR 2120	IC 720 ✕	IR 3222	IR 2022	IC 822 ✕	ICN 522 ✕	IR 1922		IR 2122	IC 722 ✕	IR 3224	IR 2024	IC 824 (✕)	ICN 1524 ✕	IR 1924	IR 2124	IC 724 ✕	IR 3226	IR 2026	IC 826 ✕	ICN 526 ✕	IR 1926	IR 2126
Romanshorn **535** d.	...	...	...	...	...	1041	...	...	...	...	...	...	...	1141	...	...	...	...	...	...	1241	...	...	...
Konstanz **535** d.	...	1003	...	...	...	|	...	...	...	1103	...	...	...	|	...	...	1203	...	...	...	|	...	...	1303
St Gallen **530** d.	...	|	1011	...	...	|	1048	...	...	|	1111	...	...	|	1148	...	|	1211	...	...	|	1248	...	|
Zürich Flughafen ✈ **530/5** d.	...	1110	1113	...	...	1140	1143	...	...	1210	1213	...	...	1240	1243	...	1310	1313	...	...	1340	1343	...	1410
Zürich HB d.	1106	1130	1132	...	1158	1200	1204	1206	...	1230	1232	...	1258	1300	1304	1306	1330	1332	...	1358	1400	1404	1406	1430
Baden d.	1122	|	|	...	|	|	|	1222	...	|	|	...	|	|	|	1322	|	|	...	|	|	|	1422	|
Brugg d.	1132	|	|	...	|	|	|	1232	...	|	|	...	|	|	|	1332	|	|	...	|	|	|	1432	|
Lenzburg d.	|	|	|	...	|	|	|	|	...	|	|	...	|	|	|	|	|	|	...	|	|	|	|	|
Aarau d.	1147	|	|	...	|	|	1230	1247	...	|	|	...	|	|	1330	1347	|	|	...	|	|	1430	1447	|
Olten a.	1156	1201	|	...	1229	|	1239	1256	...	1301	|	...	1329	|	1339	1356	1401	|	...	1429	|	1439	1456	1501
Olten d.	1158	1203	|	1206	1236	|	1241	1258	...	1303	|	1306	1336	|	1341	1358	1403	|	1406	1436	|	1441	1458	1503
Solothurn d.	|	1228	|	|	|	|	1259	|	...	1328	|	|	|	|	1359	|	1428	|	|	|	|	1459	|	1528
Biel/Bienne a.	|	1245	|	|	|	|	1313	|	...	1345	|	|	|	|	1413	|	1445	|	|	|	|	1513	|	1545
Langenthal d.	|	...	|	1218	1249	|	|	|	...	...	|	1318	1349	|	|	|	...	|	1418	1449	|	|	|	...
Burgdorf d.	|	...	|	1238	1307	|	|	|	...	...	|	1338	1407	|	|	|	...	|	1438	1507	|	|	|	...
Bern a.	1225	...	1229	1253	1321	1257	|	1325	...	...	1329	1353	1421	1357	|	1425	...	1429	1453	1521	1457	|	1525	...
Interlaken Ost **560** a.	...	...	|	...	...	|	|	...	...	...	|	...	...	|	|	...	...	|	...	...	|	|	...	...
Brig **560** a.	...	...	|	...	...	1411	|	...	...	...	|	...	...	1511	|	...	...	|	...	...	1611	|	...	...
Lausanne **505** a.	...	...	1340	...	...	...	|	...	...	...	1440	...	...	...	1515	...	...	1540	...	...	...	|	...	...
Genève **505** a.	...	...	1415	...	...	...	1446	...	...	...	1515	...	...	...	...	...	...	1615	...	...	...	1646	...	...
Genève Aéroport ✈ **505** a.	...	...	1424	...	...	...	1455	...	...	...	1524	...	...	...	...	...	...	1624	...	...	...	1655	...	...

	IC 726 ✕	IR 3228	IR 2028	IC 828 (✕)	ICN 1528 ✕	IR 1928	IR 2128	IC 728 ✕	IR 3230	IR 2030	IC 830 ✕	ICN 530 ✕	IR 1930		IR 2130	IC 730 ✕	IR 3232	IR 2032	IC 832 (✕)	ICN 1532 ✕	IR 1932	IR 2132	IC 732 ✕	IR 3236
Romanshorn **535** d.	...	...	...	1341	...	...	...	...	...	...	1441	...	...	...	...	...	...	...	1541	...	...	...	...	...
Konstanz **535** d.	...	...	...	|	...	...	1403	...	...	...	|	...	...	...	1503	...	...	...	|	...	...	1603	...	...
St Gallen **530** d.	1311	...	...	|	1348	...	|	1411	...	...	|	1448	...	...	|	1511	...	...	|	1548	...	|	1611	...
Zürich Flughafen ✈ **530/5** d.	1413	...	...	1440	1443	...	1510	1513	...	...	1540	1543	...	...	1610	1613	...	...	1640	1643	...	1710	1713	...
Zürich HB d.	1432	...	1458	1500	1504	1506	1530	1532	...	1558	1600	1604	1606	...	1630	1632	...	1658	1700	1704	1706	1730	1732	...
Baden d.	|	...	|	|	|	1522	|	|	...	|	|	|	1622	...	|	|	...	|	|	|	1722	|	|	...
Brugg d.	|	...	|	|	|	1532	|	|	...	|	|	|	1632	...	|	|	...	|	|	|	1732	|	|	...
Lenzburg d.	|	...	|	|	|	|	|	|	...	|	|	|	|	...	|	|	...	|	|	|	|	|	|	...
Aarau d.	|	...	|	|	1530	1547	|	|	...	|	|	1630	1647	...	|	|	...	|	|	1730	1747	|	|	...
Olten a.	|	...	1529	|	1539	1556	1601	|	...	1629	|	1639	1656	...	1701	|	...	1729	|	1739	1756	1801	|	...
Olten d.	|	1506	1536	|	1541	1558	1603	|	1606	1636	|	1641	1658	...	1703	|	1706	1736	|	1741	1758	1803	|	1806
Solothurn d.	|	|	|	|	1559	|	1628	|	|	|	|	1659	|	...	1728	|	|	|	|	1759	|	1828	|	|
Biel/Bienne a.	|	|	|	|	1613	|	1645	|	|	|	|	1713	|	...	1745	|	|	|	|	1813	|	1845	|	|
Langenthal d.	|	1518	1549	|	|	|	...	|	1618	1649	|	|	|	...	...	|	1718	1749	|	|	|	...	|	1818
Burgdorf d.	|	1538	1607	|	|	|	...	|	1638	1707	|	|	|	...	...	|	1738	1807	|	|	|	...	|	1838
Bern a.	1529	1553	1621	1557	|	1625	...	1629	1653	1721	1657	|	1725	...	...	1729	1753	1821	1757	|	1825	...	1829	1853
Interlaken Ost **560** a.	|	...	...	|	|	...	...	|	...	...	|	|	...	...	...	|	...	...	|	|	...	...	|	...
Brig **560** a.	|	...	...	1711	|	...	...	|	...	...	1811	|	...	...	...	|	...	...	1911	|	...	...	|	...
Lausanne **505** a.	1640	...	...	...	1715	...	...	1740	...	...	...	|	...	...	...	1840	...	...	...	1915	...	...	1940	...
Genève **505** a.	1715	...	...	...	...	...	...	1815	...	...	...	1846	...	...	...	1915	...	...	...	...	...	...	2015	...
Genève Aéroport ✈ **505** a.	1724	...	...	...	...	...	...	1824	...	...	...	1855	...	...	...	1924	...	...	...	...	...	...	2024	...

SBB — ZÜRICH - BIEL and BERN — 500

km (via hsl)		IR 2036	IC 836	ICN 536	IR 1936	IR 2136	IC 736	IR 3238	IR 2038	IC 838	ICN 1538	IR 1938		IR 2138	IC 738	IR 3240	IR 2040	IC 840	ICN 1540	ICN 540	IR 1940	IR 2140	IC 740	IR 3242
			✕	✕			✕			✕	✕				✕			✕	✕ ⚒	✕ †			✕	
	Romanshorn **535** d.	...	1641	...	...	...	...	...	...	1741	...	...	...	...	...	...	...	1841	...	...	...	...	...	...
	Konstanz **535** d.	...	|	...	...	1703	...	...	...	|	...	...	...	1803	...	...	...	|	...	...	...	1903	...	...
	St Gallen **530** d.	...	|	1648	...	|	1711	...	...	|	1748	...	...	|	1811	...	...	|	1848	1848	...	|	1911	...
	Zürich Flughafen ✈ **530/5** d.	...	1740	1743	...	1810	1813	...	...	1840	1843	...	...	1910	1913	...	...	1940	1943	1943	...	2010	2013	...
	Zürich HB d.	1758	1800	1804	1806	1830	1832	...	1858	1900	1904	1906	...	1930	1932	...	1958	2000	2004	2004	2006	2030	2032	...
	Baden d.	|	|	|	1822	|	|	...	|	|	|	1922	...	|	|	...	|	|	|	|	2022	|	|	...
	Brugg d.	|	|	|	1832	|	|	...	|	|	|	1932	...	|	|	...	|	|	|	|	2032	|	|	...
	Lenzburg d.	|	|	|	|	|	|	...	|	|	|	|	...	|	|	...	|	|	|	|	|	|	|	...
	Aarau d.	|	|	1830	1847	|	|	...	|	|	1930	1947	...	|	|	...	|	|	2030	2030	2047	|	|	...
	Olten a.	1829	|	1839	1856	1901	|	...	1929	|	1939	1956	...	2001	|	...	2029	|	2039	2039	2056	2101	|	...
0	**Olten** d.	1836	|	1841	1858	1903	|	1906	1936	|	1941	1958	...	2003	|	2006	2036	|	2041	2041	2058	2103	|	2106
	Solothurn d.	|	|	1859	|	1928	|	|	|	|	1959	|	...	2028	|	|	|	|	2059	2059	|	2128	|	|
	Biel/Bienne a.	|	|	1913	|	1945	|	|	|	|	2013	|	...	2045	|	|	|	|	2113	2113	|	2145	|	|
	Langenthal d.	1849	|	|	|	...	|	1918	1949	|	|	|	...	...	|	2018	2049	|	...	|	|	...	|	2118
	Burgdorf d.	1907	|	|	|	...	|	1938	2007	|	|	|	...	...	|	2038	2107	|	...	|	|	...	|	2138
62	**Bern** a.	1921	1857	|	1925	...	1929	1953	2021	1957	|	2025	...	...	2029	2053	2121	2057	...	|	2125	...	2129	2153
	Interlaken Ost **560** a.	...	|	|	...	...	|	...	...	|	|	...	...	...	|	...	...	...	...	|	...	...	|	...
	Brig **560** a.	...	2011	|	...	...	|	...	...	2111	|	...	...	...	|	...	...	...	...	|	...	...	|	...
	Lausanne **505** a.	...	...	|	...	...	2040	...	...	...	2115	...	...	...	2140	...	...	...	...	|	...	...	2240	...
	Genève **505** a.	...	...	2046	...	...	2115	...	...	...	...	...	...	...	2215	...	...	...	...	2246	...	...	2324	...
	Genève Aéroport ✈ **505** a.	...	...	2055	...	...	2124	...	...	...	...	...	...	...	2224	...	...	...	...	2255	...	...	2333	...

km (via hsl)		IR 2042	IC 842	ICN 1542	IR 1942	EN 313		IR 2142	IC 742	IC 844	IR 2044	ICN 1544	IR 1944	IC 744		IC 846	IR 2046	ICN 1546	IR 1946	IC 746	IC 800	IR 2002	IC 802	
			(✕)			L			✕ F	✕												⑥⑦q	⑥⑦q	
	Romanshorn **535** d.	...	1941	...	...	...	...	...	...	2041	...	...	...	...	...	2141	...	...	...	...	...	...	...	...
	Konstanz **535** d.	...	|	...	...	...	...	2003	...	|	...	...	...	...	...	|	...	...	...	...	...	...	...	...
	St Gallen **530** d.	...	|	1948	...	...	...	|	2011	|	...	2048	...	2111	...	|	...	2144	...	...	...	...	...	...
	Zürich Flughafen ✈ **530/5** d.	...	2040	2043	...	...	...	2110	2113	2140	...	2143	...	2213	...	2240	...	2243	...	...	...	...	...	...
	Zürich HB d.	2058	2100	2104	2106	2123	...	2130	2132	2200	...	2204	2206	2232	...	2300	...	2304	2306	2332	0000	...	0100	...
	Baden d.	|	|	|	2122	|	...	|	|	|	...	|	2222	|	...	|	...	|	2322	|	|	...	|	...
	Brugg d.	|	|	|	2132	|	...	|	|	|	...	|	2232	|	...	|	...	|	2332	|	|	...	|	...
	Lenzburg d.	|	|	|	|	|	...	|	|	|	...	|	|	|	...	|	...	|	|	|	|	...	|	...
	Aarau d.	|	|	2130	2147	|	...	|	|	|	...	2230	2247	|	...	|	...	2330	2347	|	|	...	|	...
	Olten a.	2129	|	2139	2155	|	...	2201	|	2232	...	2239	2255	2302	...	2332	...	2339	2355	0002	0032	...	0131	...
0	**Olten** d.	2137	|	2141	...	2159u	...	2203	|	2235	2237	2241	...	2304	...	2335	2337	2341	...	0004	0033	0037	0135	...
	Solothurn d.	|	|	2159	...	|	...	2228	|	|	|	2258	...	|	...	|	|	0005	...	|	|	|	|	...
58	**Biel/Bienne** a.	|	|	2213	...	|	...	2245	|	|	|	2314	...	|	...	|	|	0022	...	|	|	|	|	...
	Langenthal d.	2149	|	|	...	|	...	...	|	|	2249	|	...	|	...	|	2349	|	...	|	|	0049	|	...
	Burgdorf d.	2209	|	|	...	|	...	...	|	|	2309	|	...	|	...	|	0009	|	...	|	|	0109	|	...
	Bern a.	2223	2157	|	...	2304u	...	...	2229	2302	2323	|	...	2332	...	0002	0023	|	...	0032	0100	0123	0202	...
	Interlaken Ost **560** a.	...	...	|	...	|	...	...	...	...	...	|	...	...	...	...	...	|	...	...	...	...	...	...
	Brig **560** a.	...	...	|	...	0058u	...	...	...	...	...	|	...	...	...	...	...	|	...	...	...	...	...	...
	Lausanne **505** a.	...	...	2315	...	...	...	...	...	...	...	0015	...	...	...	...	...	0124c	...	...	...	...	...	...
	Genève **505** a.	...	...	...	...	...	...	...	...	...	...	...	...	...	...	...	...	...	...	...	...	...	...	...
	Genève Aéroport ✈ **505** a.	...	...	...	...	...	...	...	...	...	...	...	...	...	...	...	...	...	...	...	...	...	...	...

F – To Fribourg.
L – LUNA – Zürich - Roma.
c – ⑥⑦ only.
q – Also Jan. 1.
u – Stops to pick up only.

NStCM. Narrow gauge. 2nd class only — NYON - ST CERGUE - LA CURE — 501

km																															
		j	k	j	j		j	j					j			j		j		j		j		j		j					m
0	**Nyon** d.	0528	0553	...	0628	0653	0728	0753	0817	0917	1017	1117	1153	1217	1317	1353	1417	1453	1517	1553	1617	1653	1717	1753	1817	1853	1917	1953	2130	2253	0017
19	St Cergue a.	0606	0625	0638	0701	0725	0758	0825	0848	0948	1048	1148	1225	1248	1348	1425	1448	1525	1548	1625	1648	1725	1748	1825	1848	1925	1948	2025	2159	2324	0048
27	La Cure a.	0620	0651	0651	...	0742	0813	...	0912	1004	1104	1204	...	1312	1404	...	1504	...	1604	...	1704	...	1804	...	1904j	...	2004	...	...	...	...

	j		j	⚒	j	j		j						j			j			j			j			j				
La Cure d.	...	...	0622	0653	...	0745	0815	...	0915	1015	1115	1215	...	...	1315	1415	...	1515	1615	...	...	1715	...	1815	...	1915	2015	...	...	...
St Cergue d.	0540	0608	0645	0708	0732	0808	0832	0908	0932	1032	1132	1232	...	1308	1332	1432	1508	1532	1632	1708	...	1732	1808	1832	1908	1932	2032	2208	2332	...
Nyon a.	0610	0643	0718	0743	0805	0843	0905	0943	1005	1105	1205	1305	...	1343	1405	1505	1543	1605	1705	1743	...	1805	1843	1905	1943	2005	2105	2243	0005	...

j – Ⓐ (not Sept. 21).
k – ⑥ (also Sept. 21; not Aug. 1).
m – ⑥⑦ (not Apr. 11, Aug. 2).

BAM. Narrow gauge. 2nd class only — MORGES - BIÈRE and L'ISLE MONT LA VILLE — 502

km																									
		⚒		⚒		⚒		⚒			⚒		⚒		⚒			⚒		⚒				F⁄	
0	**Morges** d.	0621	0702	0746	0846	0946	1046	1136	...	1216	1316	1403	1503	1603	1646	1736	...	1816	1846	1946	2036	2207	2336	0132	...
12	Apples a.	0633	0717	0801	0901	1001	1101	1151	...	1231	1331	1418	1518	1618	1701	1751	...	1831	1901	2001	2051	2222	2351	0147	...
19	**Bière** a.	0646	0730	0814	0914	1014	1114	1204	...	1244	1344	1431	1531	1631	1714	1804	...	1844	1914	2014	2104	2235	0004	0200	...

	⚒		⚒	Ⓐ		⚒		⚒			⚒		⚒		⚒		⚒			⚒				F⁄	
Bière d.	0545	0625	0653	0709	0753	0853	0953	1053	1126	...	1222	1306	1353	1453	1553	1653	1726	...	1811	1853	1953	2126	2253	0026	...
Apples d.	0555	0635	0704	0719	0803	0903	1003	1103	1136	...	1232	1316	1403	1503	1603	1703	1736	...	1821	1903	2003	2136	2303	0036	...
Morges a.	0615	0655	0724	0736	0823	0923	1023	1123	1156	...	1251	1336	1423	1523	1623	1723	1756	...	1841	1923	2023	2156	2323	0056	...

km																									
			⚒		Ⓐ🚌	Ⓒ	Ⓐ🚌	Ⓒ		Ⓐ🚌	Ⓒ		Ⓐ		⚒	A🚌	B	A🚌	C	A🚌	B	C	C	F	
0	Apples d.	0602	0635	0719	0903	0903	1103	1103	1233	1420	1420	1620	1703	1753	1833	1903	1903	2003	2003	2053	2053	2224	2353	0150	...
11	L'Isle Mont la Ville d.	0614	0647	0731	0917	0917	1117	1117	1247	1434	1434	1634	1717	1805	1846	1917	1917	2017	2017	2107	2107	2238	0007	0204	...

		⚒			Ⓐ🚌	Ⓒ	Ⓐ🚌	Ⓒ		Ⓐ🚌	Ⓒ			Ⓐ		⚒	A🚌	B	A🚌	C	A🚌	B	C	F	
L'Isle Mont la Ville d.	0618	0648	0746	...	0946	0946	1119	1119	1259	1446	1446	1646	...	1719	1805	1846	1946	1946	2036	2036	2119	2119	2246	0019	...
Apples a.	0632	0702	0801	...	1001	1001	1134	1134	1314	1501	1501	1701	...	1734	1819	1901	2001	2001	2051	2051	2134	2134	2301	0034	...

A – ①②③④ (also Sept. 21; not Dec. 25, Jan. 1, Apr. 13, May 21, June 1).
B – ⑤⑥⑦ (also Dec. 25, Jan. 1, Apr. 13, May 21, June 1).
C – ⑤⑥ (not Dec. 26, Jan. 2, Apr. 10, Aug. 1).
F – ⑥⑦ (not Dec. 27, Jan. 3, Apr. 11, Aug. 2).
⁄ – Supplement payable.

SBB — YVERDON - FRIBOURG — 503

km										
		Ⓐ		Ⓐ						
0	**Yverdon** d.	0520	0601	0620	...	0701	and	2101	2201	...
18	Estavayer-le-Lac d.	0538	0619	0638	...	0719	hourly	2119	2219	...
28	Payerne d.	0553	0630	0653	...	0730	until	2130	2230	...
50	**Fribourg** a.	0621	0658	0721	...	0758		2158	2259	...

		Ⓐ	Ⓒ				G	⑤⑥	
Fribourg d.	0601a	0701	0703	0803	and	2203	2303	2342	...
Payerne d.	0630	0730	0730	0830	hourly	2230	2330	0009	...
Estavayer-le-Lac d.	0640	0740	0740	0840	until	2240	2340	0019	...
Yverdon a.	0657	0757	0757	0857		2257	2357	0036	...

G – ①②③④⑦ only.
a – Ⓐ only.

505 GENÈVE - LAUSANNE - BIEL, BASEL and BERN SBB

km		ICN 509	IR 2509	ICN 1609	ICN 1511	IR 2511	ICN 611	IR 1711	IC 711	IR 2515	ICN 515	ICN 1615	RE 2615	IC 715	RE 2917	IR 2517	ICN 617	ICN 1517	RE 2617	IC 717	IR 2519	ICN 519	ICN 1619	RE 2619	IC 719	IR 2521
					✕		✕		✕		✕	✕					✕	✕		✕	🍷	✕	✕		✕	🍷
								B							Ⓐ											
0	Genève A ✈ 570 d.	...	...	...	...	...	...	...	...	...	...	...	0612	0636	...	0701	0705	...	...	0736	0801	0805	...	...	0836	0901
6	**Genève 570** d.	...	...	...	...	0456	...	0521	0536	0610	0614	...	0621	0645	0649	0710	0714	...	0720	0745	0810	0814	...	0821	0845	0910
27	Nyon **570** d.	...	...	...	...	0510	...	0537	0550	|	0627	...	0637	|	0705	|	0727	...	0736	|	|	0827	...	0837	|	|
53	Morges **570** d.	...	...	...	...	0528	...	0600	0605	|	0641	...	0700	|	0724	|	0741	...	0759	|	|	0841	...	0900	|	|
66	**Lausanne 570** a.	...	...	...	...	0540	...	0612	0615	0643	|	...	0712	0718	0737	0743	|	...	0812	0818	0843	|	...	0912	0918	0943
	Lausanne 508 d.	...	0445t	...	0539	0545	...	...	0620	0645	|	0645	...	0720	...	0745	|	0745	...	0820	0845	|	0845	...	0920	0945
	Yverdon d.	...	|	...	0604	|	...	...	|	|	0704	0707	...	|	...	|	0804	0807	...	|	|	0904	0907	...	|	|
	Neuchâtel d.	...	|	...	0624	|	...	...	|	|	0724	0727	...	|	...	|	0824	0827	...	|	|	0924	0927	...	|	|
	Biel/Bienne a.	...	|	...	0641	|	...	...	|	|	0741	0743**k**	...	|	...	|	0841	0843**k**	...	|	|	0941	0943**k**	...	|	|
	Biel/Bienne d.	0543	|	0549	0644	|	0649	...	|	|	0746	0749	...	|	...	|	0849	0846	...	|	|	0946	0949	...	|	|
	Moutier d.	|	|	0608	|	|	0708	...	|	|	|	0808	...	|	...	|	0908	|	...	|	|	|	1008	...	|	|
	Delémont d.	|	|	0623	|	|	0723	...	|	|	|	0823	...	|	...	|	0923	|	...	|	|	|	1023	...	|	|
	Basel a.	|	|	0653	|	|	0753	...	|	|	|	0853	...	|	...	|	0953	|	...	|	|	|	1053	...	|	|
87	Palézieux **508** d.	|	0501t	...	|	0601	...	...	|	0701	|	...	...	|	...	0801	...	|	...	|	0901	|	...	...	|	1001
106	Romont d.	|	0516t	...	|	0616	...	...	|	0716	|	...	...	|	...	0816	...	|	...	|	0916	|	...	...	|	1016
132	Fribourg d.	|	0534	...	|	0634	...	...	0704	0734	|	...	...	0804	...	0834	...	|	...	0904	0934	|	...	...	1004	1034
163	**Bern** a.	|	0556	...	|	0656	...	...	0726	0756	|	...	...	0826	...	0856	...	|	...	0926	0956	|	...	...	1026	1056
	Olten **500** a.	0618	|	...	0718	|	...	...	|	|	0818	...	...	|	...	|	...	0918	...	|	|	1018	...	...	|	|
	Luzern **565** a.	|	0700	...	|	0800	...	...	|	0900	|	...	...	|	...	1000	...	|	...	|	1100	|	...	...	|	1200
	Zürich HB **500** a.	0656	...	...	0756	...	...	...	0828	...	0856	...	...	0928	...	...	...	0956	...	1028	...	1056	...	...	1128	...
	Zürich Flug ✈ **530** a.	0720	...	...	0820	...	...	...	0850	...	0920	...	...	0950	...	...	...	1020	...	1050	...	1120	...	...	1150	...
	St Gallen **530** a.	0815	...	...	0915	...	...	...	0953	...	1015	...	...	1053	...	...	...	1115	...	1153	...	1215	...	...	1253	...

km		ICN 621	ICN 1521	RE 2621	IC 721	IR 2523	ICN 523	ICN 1623	RE 2623	IC 723	IR 2525	ICN 625	ICN 1525	RE 2625	IC 725	IR 2527	ICN 527	ICN 1627	RE 2627	IC 727	IR 2529	ICN 629	ICN 1529	RE 2629	IC 729	IR 2531
		✕	✕		✕	🍷	✕	✕		✕	🍷	✕	✕		✕	🍷	✕	✕		✕	🍷	✕	✕		✕	🍷
	Genève A ✈ 570 d.	0905	...	...	0936	1001	1005	...	...	1036	1101	1105	...	...	1136	1201	1205	...	...	1236	1301	1305	...	...	1336	1401
	Genève 570 d.	0914	...	0921	0945	1010	1014	...	1021	1045	1110	1114	...	1121	1145	1210	1214	...	1221	1245	1310	1314	...	1321	1345	1410
	Nyon **570** d.	0927	...	0937	|	|	1027	...	1037	|	|	1127	...	1137	|	|	1227	...	1237	|	|	1327	...	1337	|	|
	Morges **570** d.	0941	...	1000	|	|	1041	...	1100	|	|	1141	...	1200	|	|	1241	...	1300	|	|	1341	...	1400	|	|
	Lausanne 570 a.	|	...	1012	1018	1043	|	...	1112	1118	1143	|	...	1212	1218	1243	|	...	1312	1318	1343	|	...	1412	1418	1443
0	**Lausanne 508** d.	|	0945	...	1020	1045	|	1045	...	1120	1145	|	1145	...	1220	1245	|	1245	...	1320	1345	|	1345	...	1420	1445
39	Yverdon d.	1004	1007	...	|	|	1104	1107	...	|	|	1204	1207	...	|	|	1304	1307	...	|	|	1404	1407	...	|	|
75	Neuchâtel d.	1024	1027	...	|	|	1124	1127	...	|	|	1224	1227	...	|	|	1324	1327	...	|	|	1424	1427	...	|	|
105	**Biel/Bienne** a.	1041	1043**k**	...	|	|	1141	1143**k**	...	|	|	1241	1243**k**	...	|	|	1341	1343**k**	...	|	|	1441	1443**k**	...	|	|
105	**Biel/Bienne** d.	1049	1046	...	|	|	1146	1149	...	|	|	1249	1246	...	|	|	1346	1349	...	|	|	1449	1446	...	|	|
129	Moutier d.	1108	|	...	|	|	|	1208	...	|	|	1308	|	...	|	|	|	1408	...	|	|	1508	|	...	|	|
140	Delémont d.	1123	|	...	|	|	|	1223	...	|	|	1323	|	...	|	|	|	1423	...	|	|	1523	|	...	|	|
179	**Basel** a.	1153	|	...	|	|	|	1253	...	|	|	1353	|	...	|	|	|	1453	...	|	|	1553	|	...	|	|
	Palézieux **508** d.	...	|	...	|	1101	|	...	...	|	1201	...	|	...	|	1301	|	...	...	|	1401	...	|	...	|	1501
	Romont d.	...	|	...	|	1116	|	...	...	|	1216	...	|	...	|	1316	|	...	...	|	1416	...	|	...	|	1516
	Fribourg d.	...	|	...	1104	1134	|	...	...	1204	1234	...	|	...	1304	1334	|	...	...	1404	1434	...	|	...	1504	1534
	Bern a.	...	|	...	1126	1156	|	...	...	1226	1256	...	|	...	1326	1356	|	...	...	1426	1456	...	|	...	1526	1556
	Olten **500** a.	...	1118	...	|	|	1218	...	...	|	|	...	1318	...	|	|	1418	...	...	|	|	...	1518	...	|	|
	Luzern **565** a.	...	|	...	|	1300	|	...	...	|	1400	...	|	...	|	1500	|	...	...	|	1600	...	|	...	|	1700
	Zürich HB **500** a.	...	1156	...	1228	...	1256	...	...	1328	...	...	1356	...	1428	...	1456	...	...	1528	...	...	1556	...	1628	...
	Zürich Flug ✈ **530** a.	...	1220	...	1250	...	1320	...	...	1350	...	...	1420	...	1450	...	1520	...	...	1550	...	...	1620	...	1650	...
	St Gallen **530** a.	...	1315	...	1353	...	1415	...	...	1453	...	...	1515	...	1553	...	1615	...	...	1653	...	...	1715	...	1753	...

km		ICN 531	ICN 1631	RE 2631	IC 731	IC 2535	ICN 635	ICN 1535	RE 2635	IC 735	IR 2537	ICN 537	ICN 1637	RE 2637	IC 737	IR 2539	ICN 639	ICN 1539	RE 2639	IC 739	RE 2941	IR 2541	ICN 541	ICN 1641	RE 2641	IC 741
		✕	✕		✕	🍷	✕	✕		✕	🍷	✕	✕		✕	🍷	✕	✕		✕			✕	✕		✕
																					Ⓐ					
	Genève A ✈ 570 d.	1405	...	1412	1436	...	1505	...	...	1536	1601	1605	...	...	1636	1701	1705	...	...	1736	...	1801	1805	...	...	1836
	Genève 570 d.	1414	...	1421	1445	...	1514	...	1521	1545	1610	1614	...	1621	1645	1710	1714	...	1721	1745	1749	1810	1814	...	1821	1845
	Nyon **570** d.	1427	...	1437	|	...	1527	...	1537	|	|	1627	...	1637	|	|	1727	...	1737	|	1805	|	1827	...	1837	|
0	Morges **570** d.	1441	...	1500	|	...	1541	...	1600	|	|	1641	...	1700	|	|	1741	...	1800	|	1824	|	1841	...	1900	|
	Lausanne 570 a.	|	...	1512	1518	...	|	...	1612	1618	1643	|	...	1712	1718	1743	|	...	1812	1818	1837	1843	|	...	1912	1918
	Lausanne 508 d.	|	1445	...	1520	1545	|	1545	...	1620	1645	|	1645	...	1720	1745	|	1745	...	1820	...	1845	|	1845	...	1920
39	Yverdon d.	1504	1507	...	|	|	1604	1607	...	|	|	1704	1707	...	|	|	1804	1807	...	|	...	|	1904	1907	...	|
	Neuchâtel d.	1524	1527	...	|	|	1624	1627	...	|	|	1724	1727	...	|	|	1824	1827	...	|	...	|	1924	1927	...	|
	Biel/Bienne a.	1541	1543**k**	...	|	|	1641	1643**k**	...	|	|	1741	1743**k**	...	|	|	1841	1843**k**	...	|	...	|	1941	1943**k**	...	|
	Biel/Bienne d.	1546	1549	...	|	|	1649	1646	...	|	|	1746	1749	...	|	|	1849	1846	...	|	...	|	1946	1949	...	|
	Moutier d.	|	1608	...	|	|	1708	|	...	|	|	|	1808	...	|	|	1908	|	...	|	...	|	|	2008	...	|
	Delémont d.	|	1623	...	|	|	1723	|	...	|	|	|	1823	...	|	|	1923	|	...	|	...	|	|	2023	...	|
	Basel a.	|	1653	...	|	|	1753	|	...	|	|	|	1853	...	|	|	1953	|	...	|	...	|	|	2053	...	|
	Palézieux **508** d.	|	...	...	|	1601	...	|	...	|	1701	|	...	...	|	1801	...	|	...	|	...	1901	|	...	...	|
	Romont d.	|	...	...	|	1616	...	|	...	|	1716	|	...	...	|	1816	...	|	...	|	...	1916	|	...	...	|
	Fribourg d.	|	...	...	1604	1634	...	|	...	1704	1734	|	...	...	1804	1834	...	|	...	1904	...	1934	|	...	...	2004
	Bern a.	|	...	...	1626	1656	...	|	...	1726	1756	|	...	...	1826	1856	...	|	...	1926	...	1956	|	...	...	2026
	Olten **500** a.	1618	...	...	|	|	...	1718	...	|	|	1818	...	...	|	|	...	1918	...	|	...	|	2018	...	...	|
	Luzern **565** a.	|	...	...	|	1800	...	|	...	|	1900	|	...	...	|	2000	...	|	...	|	...	2100	|	...	...	|
	Zürich HB **500** a.	1656	...	...	1728	...	...	1756	...	1828	...	1856	...	...	1928	...	...	1956	...	2028	...	...	2056	...	...	2128
	Zürich Flug ✈ **530** a.	1720	...	...	1750	...	...	1820	...	1850	...	1920	...	...	1950	...	...	2020	...	2050	...	...	2120	...	...	2150
	St Gallen **530** a.	1815	...	...	1853	...	...	1915	...	1953	...	2015	...	...	2053	...	...	2115	...	2153	...	...	2215	...	...	2253

	IR 2543	ICN 643	ICN 1543	RE 2643	IC 743	IR 2545	ICN 545	ICN 1645	RE 2645	IC 745	IR 2547	ICN 647	ICN 1547	RE 2647	IC 747	IR 2689	ICN 1647	RE 11638	IR 2691	ICN 1649	IR 2699	RE 2601	IR 2501	RE 2603	
		✕	✕		✕		✕	✕		✕					✕										
																							⑥⑦r	⑥⑦p	
Genève Aéroport ✈ 570 d.	1901	1905	...	...	1936	2001	2005	...	...	2036	2047	2105	...	...	2136	2147	...	2206	2247	...	2347	0012	...	...	...
Genève 570 d.	1910	1914	...	1921	1945	2010	2014	...	2021	2045	2056	2114	...	2121	2145	2156	...	2221	2256	...	2356	0021	...	0118	...
Nyon **570** d.	|	1927	...	1937	|	|	2027	...	2037	|	2110	2127	...	2137	|	2210	...	2237	2310	...	0010	0037	...	0137	...
Morges **570** d.	|	1941	...	2000	|	|	2041	...	2100	|	2128	2141	...	2200	|	2228	...	2300	2328	...	0028	0100	...	0200	...
Lausanne 570 a.	1943	|	...	2012	2018	2043	|	...	2112	2118	2140	|	...	2212	2218	2240	...	2312	2340	...	0040	0112	...	0212	...
Lausanne 508 d.	1945	|	1945	...	2020	2045	|	2045	...	2120	2145	|	2145	...	2220	2245	2245	...	2345	2345	...	...	0132	...	...
Yverdon d.	|	2004	2007	...	|	|	2104	2107	...	|	|	2204	2207	...	|	|	2307	...	|	0007	...	...	|	...	...
Neuchâtel d.	|	2024	2027	...	|	|	2124	2127	...	|	|	2224	2227	...	|	|	2327	...	|	0027	...	...	|	...	...
Biel/Bienne a.	|	2041	2043**k**	...	|	|	2141	2143**k**	...	|	|	2241	2243**k**	...	|	|	2343	...	|	0043	...	...	|	...	...
Biel/Bienne d.	|	2049	2046	...	|	|	2146	2149	...	|	|	2249	2246	...	|	|	2349	...	|	...	...	...	|	...	...
Moutier d.	|	2108	|	...	|	|	|	2208	...	|	|	2308	|	...	|	|	0008	...	|	...	...	...	|	...	...
Delémont d.	|	2123	|	...	|	|	|	2223	...	|	|	2323	|	...	|	|	0018	...	|	...	...	...	|	...	...
Basel a.	|	2153	|	...	|	|	|	2253	...	|	|	2353	|	...	|	|	...	...	|	...	...	...	|	...	...
Palézieux **508** d.	2001	...	|	...	|	2101	|	...	...	|	2201	...	|	...	|	2301	...	...	0001	...	...	...	0148	...	...
Romont d.	2016	...	|	...	|	2116	|	...	...	|	2216	...	|	...	|	2316	...	...	0016	...	...	...	0203	...	...
Fribourg d.	2034	...	|	...	2104	2134	|	...	...	2204	2234	...	|	...	2304	2334	...	...	0034	...	...	...	0220	...	...
Bern a.	2056	...	|	...	2126	2156	|	...	...	2226	2256	...	|	...	2326	2356	...	...	0056	...	...	...	...	...	...
Olten **500** a.	|	...	2118	...	2158	|	2219	...	...	2258	|	...	2330	...	2358	...	...	...	...	...	...	...	...	...	...
Luzern **565** a.	2200	...	|	...	|	2300	|	...	...	|	2400	...	|	...	|	...	...	...	...	...	...	...	...	...	...
Zürich HB **500** a.	...	...	2156	...	2231	...	2256	...	...	2331	...	...	0010	...	0033	...	...	...	...	...	...	...	...	...	...
Zürich Flughafen ✈ **530** a.	...	...	2220	...	...	...	2320	...	...	...	...	...	0027	...	...	...	...	...	...	...	...	...	...	...	...
St Gallen **530** a.	...	...	2317	...	...	...	0018	...	...	...	...	...	0125	...	...	...	...	...	...	...	...	...	...	...	...

B – To Brig.
k – Connects with train in previous column.
p – Also Jan. 1, May 22.
r – Also Dec. 25, 26, Jan. 1, 2, Apr. 10, 13, May 21, June 1.
t – ① (also Apr. 14, June 2; not Apr. 13, June 1).

SBB BERN, BASEL and BIEL - LAUSANNE - GENÈVE 505

	RE 2602	RE 2604	ICN 1604	ICN 504 Ⓐ	IR 2504	IC 704 ✕	RE 2606	ICN 1506	ICN 606 ✕	IR 2506	IC 706 ✕	RE 2608	ICN 1608 ✕	ICN 508 ✕	IR 2508 🍷	IC 708 ✕	RE 2610	ICN 1510 ✕	ICN 610 ✕	IR 2510 🍷	IC 710 ✕	RE 2612	ICN 1612 ✕	ICN 512 ✕	IR 2512 🍷
St Gallen **530** d.	...	...	...	...	...	...	...	...	...	...	...	...	...	...	...	0511	...	0544	...	...	0611	...	...	0642	...
Zürich Flughafen ✈ **530** d.	...	...	...	...	...	...	...	...	...	...	...	...	...	...	...	0613	...	0643	...	...	0713	...	...	0739	...
Zürich HB **500** d.	...	...	...	...	...	...	...	...	...	...	0521	...	...	0604	...	0632	...	0704	...	...	0732	...	...	0804	...
Luzern **565** d.	...	...	...	...	...	...	...	...	...	...	|	...	...	|	0600	|	...	|	...	0700	|	...	...	|	0800
Olten **500** d.	...	...	...	...	...	...	...	...	...	...	|	...	...	0641	|	|	...	0741	...	|	|	...	...	0841	|
Bern d.	...	...	...	...	0504	0534	...	...	...	0604	0634	...	...	|	0704	0734	...	|	...	0804	0834	...	...	|	0904
Fribourg d.	...	...	...	...	0526	0555	...	...	...	0626	0655	...	...	|	0726	0755	...	|	...	0826	0855	...	...	|	0926
Romont d.	...	...	...	...	0544	|	...	...	...	0644	|	...	...	|	0744	|	...	|	...	0844	|	...	...	|	0944
Palézieux **508** d.	...	...	...	...	0559	|	...	...	...	0659	|	...	...	|	0759	|	...	|	...	0859	|	...	...	|	0959
Basel d.	...	...	...	...	|	|	...	...	...	|	|	...	0603	|	|	|	...	|	0703	|	|	...	0803	|	|
Delémont d.	...	...	...	...	|	|	...	...	0542	|	|	...	0642	|	|	|	...	|	0742	|	|	...	0842	|	|
Moutier d.	...	...	...	...	|	|	...	...	0552	|	|	...	0652	|	|	|	...	|	0752	|	|	...	0852	|	|
Biel/Bienne a.	...	...	...	...	|	|	...	...	0610**k**	|	|	...	0710	0713**k**	|	|	...	0813	0810**k**	|	|	...	0910	0913**k**	|
Biel/Bienne d.	...	...	0513	0519	|	|	...	0613	0619	|	|	...	0716	0719	|	|	...	0816	0819	|	|	...	0916	0919	|
Neuchâtel d.	...	...	0531	0537	|	|	...	0631	0637	|	|	...	0734	0737	|	|	...	0834	0837	|	|	...	0934	0937	|
Yverdon d.	...	...	0551	0557	|	|	...	0650	0657	|	|	...	0754	0757	|	|	...	0854	0857	|	|	...	0954	0957	|
Lausanne 508 a.	...	...	0612**z**	|	0615	0640	...	0715	|	0715	0740	...	0815	|	0815	0840	...	0915	|	0915	0940	...	1015	|	1015
Lausanne 570 d.	0448	0548	...	|	0617	0642	0648	...	|	0717	0742	0748	...	|	0817	0842	0848	...	|	0917	0942	0948	...	|	1017
Morges **570** d.	0500	0600	...	0619	|	|	0700	...	0719	|	|	0800	...	0819	|	|	0900	...	0919	|	|	1000	...	1019	|
Nyon **570** d.	0523	0623	...	0633	|	|	0723	...	0733	|	|	0823	...	0833	|	|	0923	...	0933	|	|	1023	...	1033	|
Genève 570 a.	0539	0639	...	0646	0650	0715	0739	...	0746	0750	0815	0839	...	0846	0850	0915	0939	...	0946	0950	1015	1039	...	1046	1050
Genève Aéroport ✈ **570** d.	0548	...	...	0655	0659	0724	...	...	0755	0759	0824	...	...	0855	0859	0924	...	...	0955	0959	1024	...	...	1055	1059

	IC 712 ✕	RE 2614	ICN 1516 ✕	ICN 614 ✕	IR 2516 🍷	IC 716 ✕	RE 2618	ICN 1618 ✕	ICN 518 ✕	IR 2518 🍷	IC 718 ✕	RE 2620	ICN 1520 ✕	ICN 620 ✕	IR 2520 🍷	IC 720 ✕	RE 2622	ICN 1622 ✕	ICN 522 ✕	IR 2522 🍷	IC 722 ✕	RE 2624	ICN 1524 ✕	ICN 624 ✕	IR 2524 🍷
St Gallen **530** d.	0711	...	0748	...	...	0811	...	...	0848	...	0911	...	0948	...	...	1011	...	...	1048	...	1111	...	1148	...	...
Zürich Flughafen ✈ **530** d.	0813	...	0843	...	...	0913	...	...	0943	...	1013	...	1043	...	...	1113	...	...	1143	...	1213	...	1243	...	...
Zürich HB **500** d.	0832	...	0904	...	...	0932	...	...	1004	...	1032	...	1104	...	...	1132	...	...	1204	...	1232	...	1304	...	...
Luzern **565** d.	|	...	|	...	0900	|	...	...	|	1000	|	...	|	...	1100	|	...	...	|	1200	|	...	|	...	1300
Olten **500** d.	|	...	0941	...	|	|	...	...	1041	|	|	...	1141	...	|	|	...	...	1241	|	|	...	1341	...	|
Bern d.	0934	...	|	...	1004	1034	...	...	|	1104	1134	...	|	...	1204	1234	...	...	|	1304	1334	...	|	...	1404
Fribourg d.	0955	...	|	...	1026	1055	...	...	|	1126	1155	...	|	...	1226	1255	...	...	|	1326	1355	...	|	...	1426
Romont d.	|	...	|	...	1044	|	...	...	|	1144	|	...	|	...	1244	|	...	...	|	1344	|	...	|	...	1444
Palézieux **508** d.	|	...	|	...	1059	|	...	...	|	1159	|	...	|	...	1259	|	...	...	|	1359	|	...	|	...	1459
Basel d.	|	...	|	0903	|	|	...	1003	|	|	|	...	|	1103	|	|	...	1203	|	|	|	...	|	1303	|
Delémont d.	|	...	|	0942	|	|	...	1042	|	|	|	...	|	1142	|	|	...	1242	|	|	|	...	|	1342	|
Moutier d.	|	...	|	0952	|	|	...	1052	|	|	|	...	|	1152	|	|	...	1252	|	|	|	...	|	1352	|
Biel/Bienne a.	|	...	1013	1010**k**	|	|	...	1110	1113**k**	|	|	...	1213	1210**k**	|	|	...	1310	1313**k**	|	|	...	1413	1410**k**	|
Biel/Bienne d.	|	...	1016	1019	|	|	...	1116	1119	|	|	...	1216	1219	|	|	...	1316	1319	|	|	...	1416	1419	|
Neuchâtel d.	|	...	1034	1037	|	|	...	1134	1137	|	|	...	1234	1237	|	|	...	1334	1337	|	|	...	1434	1437	|
Yverdon d.	|	...	1054	1057	|	|	...	1154	1157	|	|	...	1254	1257	|	|	...	1354	1357	|	|	...	1454	1457	|
Lausanne 508 a.	1040	...	1115	|	1115	1140	...	1215	|	1215	1240	...	1315	|	1315	1340	...	1415	|	1415	1440	...	1515	|	1515
Lausanne 570 d.	1042	1048	...	|	1117	1142	1148	...	|	...	1242	1248	...	|	1317	1342	1348	...	|	1417	1442	1448	...	|	1517
Morges **570** d.	|	1100	...	1119	|	|	1200	...	1219	...	|	1300	...	1319	|	|	1400	...	1419	|	|	1500	...	1519	|
Nyon **570** d.	|	1123	...	1133	|	|	1223	...	1233	...	|	1323	...	1333	|	|	1423	...	1433	|	|	1523	...	1533	|
Genève 570 a.	1115	1139	...	1146	1150	1215	1239	...	1246	...	1315	1339	...	1346	1350	1415	1439	...	1446	1450	1515	1539	...	1546	1550
Genève Aéroport ✈ **570** d.	1124	...	...	1155	1159	1224	...	...	1255	...	1324	1348	...	1355	1359	1424	...	...	1455	1459	1524	...	...	1555	1559

	IC 724 ✕	RE 2626	ICN 1626 ✕	ICN 526 ✕	IR 2526 🍷	IC 726 ✕	RE 2628	ICN 1528 ✕	ICN 628 ✕	IR 2528 🍷	IC 728 ✕	RE 2630	ICN 1630 ✕	ICN 530 ✕	IR 2530	IC 730 ✕	RE 2632	ICN 1532 ✕	ICN 632 ✕	IR 2532 🍷	IC 732 ✕	RE 2636	ICN 1636 ✕	ICN 536 ✕	IR 2536
St Gallen **530** d.	1211	...	...	1248	...	1311	...	1348	...	...	1411	...	...	1448	...	1511	...	1548	...	...	1611	...	...	1648	...
Zürich Flughafen ✈ **530** d.	1313	...	...	1343	...	1413	...	1443	...	...	1513	...	...	1543	...	1613	...	1643	...	...	1713	...	...	1743	...
Zürich HB **500** d.	1332	...	...	1404	...	1432	...	1504	...	...	1532	...	...	1604	...	1632	...	1704	...	...	1732	...	...	1804	...
Luzern **565** d.	|	...	...	|	1400	|	...	|	...	1500	|	...	...	|	1600	|	...	|	...	1700	|	...	...	|	1800
Olten **500** d.	|	...	...	1441	|	|	...	1541	...	|	|	...	...	1641	|	|	...	1741	...	|	|	...	...	1841	|
Bern d.	1434	...	...	|	1504	1534	...	|	...	1604	1634	...	...	|	1704	1734	...	|	...	1804	1834	...	...	|	1904
Fribourg d.	1455	...	...	|	1526	1555	...	|	...	1626	1655	...	...	|	1726	1755	...	|	...	1826	1855	...	...	|	1926
Romont d.	|	...	...	|	1544	|	...	|	...	1644	|	...	...	|	1744	|	...	|	...	1844	|	...	...	|	1944
Palézieux **508** d.	|	...	...	|	1559	|	...	|	...	1659	|	...	...	|	1759	|	...	|	...	1859	|	...	...	|	1959
Basel d.	|	...	1403	|	|	|	...	|	1503	|	|	...	1603	|	|	|	...	|	1703	|	|	...	1803	|	|
Delémont d.	|	...	1442	|	|	|	...	|	1542	|	|	...	1642	|	|	|	...	|	1742	|	|	...	1842	|	|
Moutier d.	|	...	1452	|	|	|	...	|	1552	|	|	...	1652	|	|	|	...	|	1752	|	|	...	1852	|	|
Biel/Bienne a.	|	...	1510	1513**k**	|	|	...	1613	1610**k**	|	|	...	1710	1713**k**	|	|	...	1813	1810**k**	|	|	...	1910	1913**k**	|
Biel/Bienne d.	|	...	1516	1519	|	|	...	1616	1619	|	|	...	1716	1719	|	|	...	1816	1819	|	|	...	1916	1919	|
Neuchâtel d.	|	...	1534	1537	|	|	...	1634	1637	|	|	...	1734	1737	|	|	...	1834	1837	|	|	...	1934	1937	|
Yverdon d.	|	...	1554	1557	|	|	...	1654	1657	|	|	...	1754	1757	|	|	...	1854	1857	|	|	...	1954	1957	|
Lausanne 508 a.	1540	...	1615	|	1615	1640	...	1715	|	1715	1740	...	1815	|	1815	1840	...	1915	|	1915	1940	...	2015	|	2015
Lausanne 570 d.	1542	1548	...	|	1617	1642	1648	...	|	1717	1742	1748	...	|	1817	1842	1848	...	|	1917	1942	1948	...	|	2017
Morges **570** d.	|	1600	...	1619	|	|	1700	...	1719	|	|	1800	...	1819	|	|	1900	...	1919	|	|	2000	...	2019	|
Nyon **570** d.	|	1623	...	1633	|	|	1723	...	1733	|	|	1823	...	1833	|	|	1923	...	1933	|	|	2023	...	2033	|
Genève 570 a.	1615	1639	...	1646	1650	1715	1739	...	1746	1750	1815	1839	...	1846	1850	1915	1939	...	1946	1950	2015	2039	...	2046	2050
Genève Aéroport ✈ **570** d.	1624	...	...	1655	1659	1724	...	...	1755	1759	1824	...	...	1855	1859	1924	...	...	1955	1959	2024	...	...	2055	2059

	IC 736 ✕	RE 2638	ICN 1538 ✕	ICN 638 ✕	IR 2538	IC 738 ✕	RE 2640	ICN 1640 ✕	ICN 1540 ✕ ⚒	ICN 540 ✕ †	IR 2540	IC 740	RE 2642	ICN 642	ICN 1542	IR 2542	IC 742	RE 2644	ICN 1644	ICN 1544	IR 2648	ICN 646	IR 2546	ICN 1546	RE 2600 ⑥⑦p
St Gallen **530** d.	1711	...	1748	...	...	1811	...	...	1848	1848	...	1911	...	...	1948	...	2011	...	...	2048	...	...	...	2144	...
Zürich Flughafen ✈ **530** d.	1813	...	1843	...	...	1913	...	...	1943	1943	...	2013	...	...	2043	...	2113	...	...	2143	...	...	...	2243	...
Zürich HB **500** d.	1832	...	1904	...	...	1932	...	...	2004	2004	...	2032	...	...	2104	...	2132	...	...	2204	...	...	...	2304	...
Luzern **565** d.	|	...	|	...	1900	|	...	...	|	|	2000	|	...	...	|	2100	|	...	...	|	...	...	2300	|	...
Olten **500** d.	|	...	1941	...	|	|	...	...	2041	2041	|	|	...	...	2141	|	|	...	...	2241	...	...	|	2341	...
Bern d.	1934	...	|	...	2004	2034	...	...	|	|	2104	2134	...	...	|	2204	2234	...	...	|	2308	...	0008	|	...
Fribourg d.	1955	...	|	...	2026	2055	...	...	|	|	2126	2155	...	...	|	2226	2254	...	...	|	2330	...	0034	|	...
Romont d.	|	...	|	...	2044	|	...	...	|	|	2144	|	...	...	|	2244	...	...	...	|	2348	...	0052**j**	|	...
Palézieux **508** d.	|	...	|	...	2059	|	...	...	|	|	2159	|	...	...	|	2259	...	...	...	|	0003	...	0107**j**	|	...
Basel d.	|	...	|	1903	|	|	...	2003	|	|	|	|	...	2103	|	|	...	...	2203	|	|	2303	|	|	...
Delémont d.	|	...	|	1942	|	|	...	2042	|	|	|	|	...	2142	|	|	...	...	2242	|	|	2337	|	|	...
Moutier d.	|	...	|	1952	|	|	...	2052	|	|	|	|	...	2152	|	|	...	...	2252	|	|	...	|	|	...
Biel/Bienne a.	|	...	2013	2010**k**	|	|	...	2110	2113**k**	2113**k**	|	|	...	2210	2213**k**	|	...	...	2310	2314	|	...	|	0022	...
Biel/Bienne d.	|	...	2016	2019	|	|	...	2116	...	2119	|	|	...	2219**e**	2216	|	...	...	...	2316	|	...	|	0025**c**	...
Neuchâtel d.	|	...	2034	2037	|	|	...	2134	...	2137	|	|	...	2237**e**	2234	|	...	...	...	2334	|	...	|	0043**c**	...
Yverdon d.	|	...	2054	2057	|	|	...	2154	...	2157	|	|	...	2257**e**	2254	|	...	...	...	2354	|	...	|	0103**c**	...
Lausanne 508 a.	2040	...	2115	|	2115	2140	...	2215	...	|	2215	2240	...	|	2315	2315	...	...	...	0015	0019	...	0122**j**	0124**c**	...
Lausanne 570 d.	2042	2048	...	|	2120	2142	2148	...	...	|	2220	2245	2248	|	...	2320	...	2348	...	...	0021	...	...	...	0130
Morges **570** d.	|	2100	...	2119	2132	|	2200	...	...	2219	2232	2254	2300	2319**e**	...	2332	...	0000	...	...	0033	...	...	...	0142
Nyon **570** d.	|	2123	...	2133	2150	|	2223	...	...	2233	2250	2310	2323	2333**e**	...	2350	...	0023	...	...	0051	...	...	...	0205
Genève 570 a.	2115	2139	...	2146	2204	2215	2239	...	...	2246	2304	2324	2339	2346**e**	...	0004	...	0039	...	...	0105	...	...	...	0224
Genève Aéroport ✈ **570** d.	2124	...	...	2155	2213	2224	...	...	...	2255	2313	2333	...	2355**e**	...	...	...	...	...	...	...	...	...	...	...

c – ⑥⑦ only.
e – † only.
j – ⑤⑥⑦ only.
k – Connects with train in previous column(s).
p – Also Jan. 1, May 22.
z – Arrive 0615 on Ⓐ.

✕ – Restaurant (✕) – Bistro (🍷) – Bar coach 🍷 – Minibar

506 SWISS LAKES

LAC LÉMAN

June 14 - September 13 — Operator: CGN

⚒					S				S	W				S					W					S	S			W	S
...	...	...	...	...	1015	...	...	...	1425	1450	...	...	...	1840	d. Genève ⊗ ... a.	...	...	...	1440	...	...	...	...	1805	1920	...	...	...	2200
...	...	...	...	...	1101	...	...	...	|	1538	...	...	...	1937	d. Coppet ... d.	...	...	...	1350	...	...	...	...	|	1830	...	...	...	2108
...	...	...	...	...	1135	...	...	...	1550	1550	...	...	1812	|	d. Nyon ... d.	...	...	1212	1240	...	...	...	...	1645	1800	...	...	...	2043
...	...	...	1030	...	1205	...	...	...	1610	1632	...	...	1835	2010	d. Yvoire ... d.	...	...	1152	1310	...	...	1510	...	1620	1730	...	...	2015	2020
...	...	...	1051	...	|	...	...	...	...	|	...	...	1925	▬	d. Thonon-les-Bains .. d.	...	...	1058	|	...	...	1422	...	...	|	...	...	|	▬
0700	0820	1005	1120	1145	|	1315	1445	1615	...	|	1800	1920	|	2045	d. Evian-les-Bains ... d.	0815	1000	|	|	1135	1305	1345	1435	...	|	1605	1750	|	1915
|	|	|	|	|	1315	|	|	|	...	1750	|	|	|	|	d. Morges ... d.	|	|	|	1119	|	|	...	|	...	1609	|	|	1920	|
0735	0855	1040	1140	1220	1350	1351	1520	1650	...	1825	1835	1955	2020	2120	a. Lausanne-Ouchy .. d.	0740	0925	1000	1045	1100	1230	...	1400	...	1535	1530	1715	1845	1840

	S					S						S					S					S				S			
...	0920	...	1055	...	...	1230	1400	1415	...	...	...	1530	1700	1840	d. Lausanne-Ouchy .. a.	...	1220	...	...	1347	...	1520	1652	...	1750	1820	...	2002	2000
...	|	1005	1200	1205	...	|	1505	|	1405	...	1605	1635	|	|	d. Vevey-Marché ... d.	1000	1132	...	1202	1246	1359	1435	1551	1559	1645	1732	...	1905	1934
...	|	1010	|	1210	...	|	|	|	1410	...	1610	1640	|	|	d. Vevey-La Tour ... d.	|	|	...	|	|	|	|	|	|	|	|	...	|	|
...	|	1040	1220	1240	...	|	1525	|	1440	...	1640	1702	|	1915	d. Montreux ... d.	0940	1111	...	|	1225	|	1415	1530	|	1620	1710	...	1844	1920
...	|	1047	...	1247	...	|	...	|	1447	...	1647	...	|	...	d. Territet ... d.	|	|	...	|	...	|	|	...	|	1605	...	...	|	...
...	|	1055	...	1255	...	|	...	|	1455	...	1655	...	|	...	d. Château-de-Chillon .. d.	|	1100	...	|	...	|	1403	...	|	1555	...	...	1833	...
...	|	1103	...	1303	...	|	...	|	1503	...	1703	...	|	...	d. Villeneuve ... d.	0923	1052	...	|	...	|	1355	...	|	1545	...	...	1825	...
...	1015	|	...	|	...	1320	...	1505	|	...	1730	...	1750	...	d. St Gingolph ... d.	|	|	...	1138	...	1338	|	...	1538	|	...	...	|	...
...	1030	1125	...	1325	...	1333	...	1520	1525	...	1745	...	1803	...	d. Bouveret ... d.	0900	1030	...	1125	...	1325	1333	...	1525	1520	...	...	1803	...
...	...	1138	...	1338	...	...	...	...	1538	...	...	...	...	...	a. St Gingolph ... d.	...	1015	...	...	...	...	1320	...	...	1505	...	...	1750	...

THUNERSEE

May 31 - September 13 — Operator: BLS

X					S					R			X					S				R
0833	0933	1033	...	1133	1238	1404	1504	1638	...	1833	d. Thun ... a.	1124	1323	1424	...	1524	1627	1724	1901	1956	...	2112
0844	0944	1044	...	1144	1249	1415	1515	1650	...	1844	d. Hünibach ... d.	1113	1311	1413	...	1513	1615	1711	1849	1944	...	2100
0857	0957	1057	...	1157	1302	1428	1528	1703	...	1857	d. Oberhofen ... d.	1100	1257	1400	...	1459	1603	1656	1838	1931	...	2047
0911	1011	1111	...	1211	1316	|	1542	1717	...	1911	d. Gunten ... d.	1044	1244	1344	...	1444	1547	1640	|	1915	...	2033
0923	1023	1123	...	1223	1328	1505	1554	1728	...	1923	d. Spiez ... d.	1034	1233	1334	...	1434	1536	1630	1804	1905	...	2023
0934	1034	1134	...	1234	1340	1516	1605	1739	...	1934	d. Faulensee ... d.	1021	1220	1321	...	1421	1522	1617	1751	1852	...	2010
0949	1049	1149	...	1249	1355	1531	1620	1754	...	1949	d. Merligen ... d.	1006	1206	1306	...	1406	1506	1602	1736	1837	...	|
0956	1056	1156	...	1256	1403	1538	1627	1801	...	1956	d. Beatenbucht ... d.	0959	1159	1259	...	1358	1459	1555	1729	1830	...	1957
1045	1145	1245	...	1345	1445	1627	1716	1848	...	...	a. Interlaken West ... d.	0909	1109	1209	...	1309	1409	1509	1640	1740	...	...

VIERWALDSTÄTTERSEE

May 21 - September 13 — Operator: SGV

			S			S															S		S			S		
0743	0812	...	0912	1012	...	1112	1212	1312	...	1412	1612	1718	1812	d. Luzern (Bahnhofquai) ... a.	0938	1047	1247	1345	1347	1447	1547	1647	...	1720	1847	1947	2047
|	0822	...	0922	1022	...	1122	1222	1322	...	1422	1622	|	1822	d. Verkehrshaus Lido ... d.	|	1035	1235	|	1337	1435	1535	1635	...	|	1835	1935	2035
|	|	...	|	|	...	|	|	|	...	|	|	|	|	d. Kehrsiten-Bürgenstock ... d.	0910	|	|	1315	|	|	|	|	...	|	|	|	|
0810	0844	...	0944	1044	...	1144	1244	1344	...	1444	1644	1744	1844	d. Hertenstein ... d.	0858	1014	1214	|	|	1414	1514	1614	...	|	1814	1914	2014
0848p	0853	...	0953	1053	...	1153	1253	1353	...	1553	1653	1753	1853	d. Weggis ... d.	0848	1005	1205	|	1312	1405	1505	1605	...	|	1805	1905	2005
0831	0911	...	1011	1111	...	1211	1311	1411	...	1511	1711	1811	1911	d. Vitznau ... d.	0833	0949	1149	1249	1256	1349	1449	1549	...	|	1749	1849	1949
...	0928	...	1028	1128	...	1228	1328	1428	...	1528	1728	1859	1928	d. Beckenried ... d.	...	0905	1132	1232	...	1332	1432	1532	...	1630	1732	1832	1932
...	0945	...	1045	1145	...	1245	1345	1445	...	1545	1745	1915	...	d. Gersau ... d.	...	0849	1115	1215	...	1315	1415	1515	...	1615	1715	1815	...
...	1002	...	1102	1202	...	1302	1402	1502	...	1602	1802	1932	...	d. Treib ... d.	...	0834	1058	1158	...	1258	1358	1458	...	1558	1658	1758	...
...	1011	1017	1111	1211	1217	1311	1411	1511	1517	1611	1811	1939	...	d. Brunnen ... d.	...	0825	1050	1150	...	1250	1350	1450	...	1550	1650	1750	...
...	1021	1027	1121	1221	1227	1321	1421	1521	1527	1621	1821	...	...	d. Rütli ... d.	...	...	1036	1136	...	1236	1336	1436	1516	1536	1636	1736	...
...	1032	|	|	|	1238	|	|	1532	|	|	1832	...	...	d. Sisikon ... d.	...	...	1024	|	...	1224	|	|	1458	|	|	|	...
...	1039	|	|	|	1245	1339	|	1539	|	|	1839	...	...	d. Tellsplatte ... d.	...	...	1016	|	...	1216	|	|	1451	|	|	|	...
...	|	1042	1136	1236	|	|	1436	|	1542	1636	1850	...	...	d. Bauen ... d.	...	...	1006	1121	...	|	1321	1421	1440	1521	1621	1721	...
...	|	1050	1143	1243	|	|	1443	|	1550	1643	1858	...	...	d. Isleten-Isenthal ... d.	...	...	0958	1113	...	|	1313	1413	|	1513	1613	1713	...
...	1055	1101	1155	1255	1259	1355	1455	1555	1601	1655	1909	...	...	a. Flüelen ... d.	...	...	0946	1100	...	1200	1300	1400	1421	1500	1600	1700	...

	†												Sz	Sz			†													Sz
0845	0920	0945	1015	1045	1145	1245	1345	1400	1445	1545	1600	1815	1920	...	d. Luzern (Bahnhofquai) . a.	1202	1152	1215	1311	1338	1523	1547	1553	1711	1747	1802	1823	2030	2145	2234
0855	0930	0955	1025	1055	1155	1255	1355	1410	|	1555	1610	|	|	...	d. Verkehrshaus Lido ... d.	1152	|	1205	1301	|	1513	1536	1543	1701	1736	1752	1813	|	2135	|
|	|	|	1107	|	|	|	|	1454	|	|	1703	|	|	...	a. ..Küssnacht am Rigi .. d.	|	|	1111	|	|	|	|	1458	|	|	1707	|	|	|	|
0926	0953	1032	...	1126	1232	1326	1432	...	1521	1633	...	1854	|	...	d. Kehrsiten-Bürgenstock d.	1120	|	...	1228	1310	1427	1516	...	1627	1715	...	1727	1956	2104	|
0934	1001	1040	...	1134	1240	1334	1440	...	1529	1641	...	1902	|	2140	d. Kehrsiten Dorf ... d.	1111	|	...	1220	1301	1418	1507	...	1618	|	...	1718	1947	...	|
|	1017	1056	...	|	|	|	1456	...	1545	1656	...	1926	|	|	d. Hergiswil ... d.	1046	|	...	1205	|	|	|	...	|	|	...	|	|	...	|
0948	1026	1105	...	1148	1254	1348	1505	...	1554	1704	...	1933	2000	2155	d. Stansstad ... d.	1038	1116	...	1157	1249	1406	1456	...	1606	1657	...	1706	1935	...	2155
|	|	|	...	|	1302	|	|	...	|	...	...	...	2010	2205	d. Hergiswil ... d.	|	|	...	|	1240	|	1447	...	*1545*	|	...	1656	1926	...	...
1009	1047	1127	...	1209	1327	1409	1527	...	1615	...	...	...	...	...	a. Alpnachstad ... d.	1015	1055	...	1135	1215	1343	1422	...	1545	1635	...	...	...	...	...

ZÜRICHSEE

June 1 - September 30 — Operator: ZSG

			†											†			⚒					†		
0930	0955	1030	1100	1130	...	1230	1330	1430	1530	1630	1730	d. Zürich (Bürkliplatz) ... a.	1315	1315	1415	1515	1615	1707	1715	1815	1915	1924	2015	2155
|	|	1058	1131	|	...	1258	|	1458	|	1658	|	d. Erlenbach ... d.	1245	|	|	1445	|	|	1645	|	1845	|	|	|
0956	1029	|	|	1156	...	|	1356	|	1556	|	1756	d. Thalwil ... d.	|	1246	1348	|	1548	1632	|	1748	|	1855	1948	2120
1003	|	|	|	1203	...	|	1403	|	1603	|	1803	d. Oberrieden ... d.	|	|	1339	|	1539	1623	|	1739	|	1846	1939	|
|	1116	1138	1208	|	...	1338	|	1538	|	1738	1854	d. Wädenswil ... d.	1206	1209	|	1406	|	1542	1606	|	1806	|	|	2029
1113	1200	1219	...	1313	...	1419	1513	1619	1713	1819	1940	a. Rapperswil ... d.	1125	...	1230	1325	1430	1455	1525	1630	1725	1730	1830	1945

BRIENZERSEE

May 31 - September 13 — Operator: BLS

	Q		Q	m			Q		Q	m
0910	1110	1210	1410	1610	d. Interlaken Ost ... a.	1155	1400	1510	1710	1915
0925	1135	1225	1435	1627	d. Bönigen ... d.	1129	1343	1444	1653	1850
0953	1157	1257	1457	1658	d. Iseltwald ... d.	1107	1319	1425	1621	1828
1018	1216	1314	1516	1726	d. Giessbach ... d.	1050	1255	1357	1602	1810
1030	1230	1330	1530	1740	a. Brienz ... d.	1040	1245	1345	1545	1800

Q – Daily. Normally operated by historic Steamship on ⑥⑦ (daily July 6 - Aug. 30).
R – ②–⑥ June 2 - Sept. 5 (not Aug. 1). Normally operated by historic Steamship.
S – Normally operated by historic Steamship.
W – Daily. Normally operated by historic Steamship June 28 - Sept. 6.
X – † (daily July 6 - Aug. 30; also Sept. 6, 13).

b – Via Bauen.
m – July 5 - Aug. 30.
p – Via Vitznau.
x – † (daily July 1 - Aug. 24).
z – ⑤ July 3 - Aug. 28.
⊗ – Genève has landing stages at: Mont-Blanc, Jardin-Anglais, Pâquis and Eaux-Vives. Services do not call at all landing stages.

Operators:

BLS – Schifffahrt Berner Oberland: ✆ +41 (0)33 334 52 11. (www.bls.ch)
CGN – Compagnie Générale de Navigation: ✆ +41 (0)848 811 848. (www.cgn.ch)
SGV – Schifffahrtsgesellschaft Vierwaldstättersee: ✆ +41 (0)41 367 67 67. (www.lakelucerne.ch)
ZSG – Zürich Schifffahrtsgesellschaft: ✆ +41 (0)44 487 13 33. (www.zsg.ch)

Table 510 notes

♦ – **NOTES** (LISTED BY TRAIN NUMBER)

6 – [12] and ✕ Chur - Basel - Köln - Dortmund (- Hamburg ⑧).
7 – [12] and ✕ (①–⑥, Hamburg -) Dortmund - Basel - Chur.
90 – VAUBAN – [12] Zürich - Basel - Luxembourg - Brussels.
91 – VAUBAN – [12] Brussels - Luxembourg - Basel - Zürich - Chur.
96/7 – IRIS – [12] Zürich - Basel - Luxembourg - Brussels and v.v.
100 – ①–⑥ (also Apr. 12, May 31; not Apr. 13, June 1): [12] and ✕ Chur - Zürich - Basel - Hamburg.
101 – [12] and ✕ Hamburg - Basel - Zürich - Chur.
102 – ⑦ (also Apr. 13, June 1; not Apr. 12, May 31): [12] and ✕ Chur - Zürich - Basel - Hamburg - Kiel.
162/3 – TRANSALPIN – [12] and ✕ Wien - Innsbruck - Basel and v.v.
270/1 – [12] and ✕ Zürich - Basel - Frankfurt (Main) and v.v.
272 – ①–⑥ (also Apr. 12, May 31; not Dec. 25, Apr. 13, June 1): [12] and ✕ Zürich - Basel - Hamburg.
371 – [12] and ✕ Karlsruhe - Basel - Zürich.
372 – ⑦ (also Dec. 25, Apr. 13, June 1; not Apr. 12, May 31): [12] and ✕ Zürich - Basel - Berlin Ost.
458/9 – *City Night Line* – For days of running and composition – see Table **73**.
478/9 – *City Night Line* KOMET – For days of running and composition – see Table **73**.
9210 – [12] and (🍸) Zürich - Basel - Paris Est. Runs as train **9212** on some dates.
9211 – [12] and (🍸) Paris Est - Basel - Zürich (- Chur, ⑥ Dec. 20 - Mar. 28). Runs as train **9213** or **9221** on some dates.
9215 – [12] and (🍸) Paris Est - Basel - Zürich.
9216 – [12] and (🍸) Zürich - Basel - Paris Est.
9217 – [12] and (🍸) Paris Est - Basel - Zürich.
9218 – [12] and (🍸) (⑥ Dec. 20 - Mar. 28, Chur -) Zürich - Basel - Paris Est. Runs as train **9220** or **9222** on some dates.

H – [12] and ✕ Zürich - Basel - Hamburg and v.v.
Z – [12] and ✕ Zürich - Basel - Hamburg - Kiel and v.v.

e – † only.
q – ⑥⑦ (also Jan. 1).
r – ⑥ Dec. 20 - Mar. 28.
s – Stops to set down only.
u – Stops to pick up only.

BLS PAYERNE - MURTEN - KERZERS (- LYSS) 508

TEMPORARILY RELOCATED ON PAGE 274

SBB BASEL - ZÜRICH 510

km		IR 2057	IR 1953	IC 553	IR 2059	IR 1759	IC 759	IR 1955	IC 559	IR 2061	IR 1761	IC 761	CNL 479	IR 1961	IC 561	IR 2065	IR 1765	ICE 371	CNL 458	EC 163	IC 565	IR 2067	IR 1767	IC 767	IR 1967	IC 567	IR 2069	IR 1769
				(✕)		✕						✕	◆	🍸	🍸		✕	✕ ◆	◆	✕ ◆	(✕)					(✕)		
0	Basel SBB d.	0440	0514	0533	0540	0547	0607	0614	0633	0640	0647	0707	0710s	0714	0733	0740	0747	0807	0810s	0814	0833	0840	0847	0907	0914	0933	0940	0947
17	Rheinfelden d.	0452	0526	|	0551	|	|	0626	|	0651	|	|	|	0726	|	0751	|	|	|	0826	|	0851	|	|	0926	|	0951	|
	Liestal d.	|	|	|	|	0556	|	|	|	|	0656	|	|	|	|	|	0756	|	|	|	|	|	0856	|	|	|	|	0956
	Aarau d.	|	|	|	|	0623	|	|	|	|	0723	|	|	|	|	|	0823	|	|	|	|	|	0923	|	|	|	|	1023
	Lenzburg d.	|	|	|	|	0630	|	|	|	|	0730	|	|	|	|	|	0830	|	|	|	|	|	0930	|	|	|	|	1030
57	Brugg d.	0520	0600	|	0620	|	|	0700	|	0720	|	|	|	0800	|	0820	|	|	|	0900	|	0920	|	|	1000	|	1020	|
66	Baden d.	0529	0608	|	0629	|	|	0708	|	0729	|	|	0759s	0808	|	0829	|	|	0858s	0908	|	0929	|	|	1008	|	1029	|
88	Zürich HB a.	|	0624	0626	|	0652	0700	0724	0726	|	0752	0800	0820	0824	0826	|	0852	0900	0917	0924	0926	|	0952	1000	1024	1026	|	1052
	Zürich Flug ✈ 530/5 a.	0556	...	|	0656	|	...	...	|	0756	|	...	...	...	|	0856	|	...	...	...	|	0956	|	...	...	|	1056	|
	Chur 520 a.	...	...	0752	...	0843	...	...	0852	...	0943	...	...	...	0952	...	1043	...	...	...	1052	...	1143	...	...	1152	...	1243

	ICE 271	IR 1969	IC 569	IR 2071	IR 1771	IC 771	IR 1971	IC 571	IR 2073	IR 1773	TGV 9211	IR 1973	IC 573	IR 2075	IR 1775	IC 777	IR 1975	IC 575	IR 2077	IR 1777	EC 7	IR 1977	IC 577	IR 2079	IR 91	ICE 73	IR 1979
	✕ ◆		(✕)					🍸			(🍸) ◆	🍸	🍸				🍸	(✕)			✕ ◆		(✕)		◆	✕ Z	
Basel SBB d.	1007	1014	1033	1040	1047	1107	1114	1133	1140	1147	1207	1214	1233	1240	1247	1307	1314	1333	1340	1347	1407	1414	1433	1440	1447	1507	1514
Rheinfelden d.	|	1026	|	1051	|	|	1126	|	1151	|	|	1226	|	1251	|	|	1326	|	1351	|	|	1426	|	1451	|	|	1526
Liestal d.	|	|	|	|	1056	|	|	|	|	1156	|	|	|	|	1256	|	|	|	|	1356	|	|	|	|	1456	|	|
Aarau d.	|	|	|	|	1123	|	|	|	|	1223	|	|	|	|	1323	|	|	|	|	1423	|	|	|	|	1523	|	|
Lenzburg d.	|	|	|	|	1130	|	|	|	|	1230	|	|	|	|	1330	|	|	|	|	1431	|	|	|	|	1530	|	|
Brugg d.	|	1100	|	1120	|	|	1200	|	1220	|	|	1300	|	1320	|	|	1400	|	1420	|	|	1500	|	1520	|	|	1600
Baden d.	|	1108	|	1129	|	|	1208	|	1229	|	|	1308	|	1329	|	|	1408	|	1429	|	|	1508	|	1529	|	|	1608
Zürich HB a.	1100	1124	1126	|	1152	1200	1224	1226	|	1252	1300	1324	1326	|	1352	1400	1424	1426	|	1452	1500	1524	1526	|	1552	1600	1624
Zürich Flug ✈ 530/5 a.	...	...	|	1156	|	...	...	|	1256	|	|	...	|	1356	|	...	...	|	1456	1513	|	...	|	1556	|	...	...
Chur 520 a.	...	...	1252	...	1343	...	...	1352	...	1443	1425r	...	1452	...	1543	...	...	1552	...	...	1643	...	1652	...	1743	...	...

	IC 579	IR 2081	EC 101	TGV 9215	IR 1981	IC 581	IR 2085	IR 1785	ICE 75	IR 1985	IC 585	IR 2087	IR 1787	IC 787	IR 1987	IC 587	IR 2089	IR 1789	ICE 77	IR 1989	IC 589	IR 2091	IR 1791	IC 791	IR 97	IC 591	IR 1792
	🍸		✕ ◆	(🍸) ◆		🍸			✕ H		🍸			✕		(✕)			✕ H		(✕)			✕	◆		(✕)
Basel SBB d.	1533	1540	1547	1607	1614	1633	1640	1647	1707	1714	1733	1740	1747	1807	1814	1833	1840	1847	1907	1914	1933	1940	1947	2007	2014	2033	2047
Rheinfelden d.	|	1551	|	|	1626	|	1651	|	|	1726	|	1751	|	|	1826	|	1851	|	|	1926	|	1951	|	|	2026	|	|
Liestal d.	|	|	1556	|	|	|	|	1656	|	|	|	|	1756	|	|	|	|	1856	|	|	|	|	1956	|	|	|	2056
Aarau d.	|	|	1623	|	|	|	|	1723	|	|	|	|	1823	|	|	|	|	1923	|	|	|	|	2023	|	|	|	2123
Lenzburg d.	|	|	1630	|	|	|	|	1730	|	|	|	|	1830	|	|	|	|	1930	|	|	|	|	2030	|	|	|	2130
Brugg d.	|	1620	|	|	1700	|	1720	|	|	1800	|	1820	|	|	1900	|	1920	|	|	2000	|	2020	|	|	2100	|	|
Baden d.	|	1629	|	|	1708	|	1729	|	|	1808	|	1829	|	|	1908	|	1929	|	|	2008	|	2029	|	|	2108	|	|
Zürich HB a.	1626	|	1652	1700	1724	1726	|	1752	1800	1824	1826	|	1852	1900	1924	1926	|	1952	2000	2024	2026	|	2052	2100	2124	2126	2152
Zürich Flug ✈ 530/5 a.	|	1656	|	...	...	|	1756	|	...	...	|	1856	|	...	...	|	1956	|	...	...	|	2056	|	...	...	...	|
Chur 520 a.	1752	...	1843	...	...	1852	...	1943	...	...	1952	...	2045	...	...	2052	...	2145	...	...	2152	...	2245	...	...	...	2345

	ICE 79	IR 1993	TGV 9217	IR 1795	IC 795	IR 1995	IR 1799	IC 797	IR 1997	IR 1999	IR 1951
	✕ H		(🍸) ◆								q
Basel SBB d.	2107	2114	2133	2147	2207	2214	2247	2307	2314	0014	0114
Rheinfelden d.	|	2126	|	|	|	2226	|	|	2326	0026	0126
Liestal d.	|	|	|	2156	|	|	2256	|	|	|	|
Aarau d.	|	|	|	2223	|	|	2323	|	|	|	|
Lenzburg d.	|	|	|	2230	|	|	2330	|	|	|	|
Brugg d.	|	2200	|	|	|	2300	|	|	0000	0100	0200
Baden d.	|	2208	|	|	|	2308	|	|	0008	0108	0208
Zürich HB a.	2200	2224	2226	2252	2259	2324	2352	2400	0024	0124	0224
Zürich Flug ✈ 530/5 a.	...	...	...	...	...	...	...	...	...	...	...
Chur 520 a.	...	...	...	...	...	...	...	...	...	...	...

	IR 1756	IR 1956	ICE 78	IR 1758	IC 558	IR 2058	IR 1958	TGV 9210	IR 1760	IR 2060	IC 560
			✕ H	✕				(🍸) ◆			(✕)
Chur 520 d.	...	...	...	...	...	...	...	...	0513	...	0606
Zürich Flug ✈ 530/5 d.	...	...	...	...	...	0604	...	...	|	0704	|
Zürich HB d.	0508	0536	0602	0608	0634	|	0636	0702	0708	|	0734
Baden d.	|	0552	|	|	|	0633	0652	|	|	0733	|
Brugg d.	|	0601	|	|	|	0642	0702	|	|	0742	|
Lenzburg d.	0529	|	|	0629	|	|	|	|	0729	|	|
Aarau d.	0537	|	|	0637	|	|	|	|	0737	|	|
Liestal d.	0602	|	|	0702	|	|	|	|	0802	|	|
Rheinfelden d.	|	0635	|	|	|	0717	0734	|	|	0810	|
Basel SBB a.	0612	0651	0657	0712	0727	0734	0747	0757	0812	0823	0827

km		IR 1960	ICE 76	IR 1764	IR 2062	IC 562	IR 1962	IC 766	IR 1766	IR 2066	IC 566	IR 1966	ICE 74	IR 1768	IR 2068	IC 568	IR 1968	EC 102	EC 100	IR 1770	IR 2070	IC 570	IR 90	ICE 72	IR 1772	IR 2072	IC 572	IR 1972
			✕ Z	✕		(✕)	🍸				(✕)		✕ Z			🍸	🍸	✕ ◆	✕ ◆			🍸	◆	✕ H			(✕)	
	Chur 520 d.	...	...	...	...	0709	...	0713	...	...	0809	...	...	0816	...	0909	...	0916	0916	...	...	1009	...	...	1016	...	1109	...
	Zürich Flug ✈ 530/5 d.	...	...	...	0804	|	...	|	...	0904	|	...	...	|	1004	|	...	|	|	...	1104	|	...	...	|	1204	|	...
0	Zürich HB d.	0736	0802	0808	|	0834	0836	0902	0908	|	0934	0936	1002	1008	|	1034	1036	1102	1102	1108	|	1134	1136	1202	1208	|	1234	1236
	Baden d.	0752	|	|	0833	|	0852	|	|	0933	|	0952	|	|	1033	|	1052	|	|	|	1133	|	1152	|	|	1233	|	1252
	Brugg d.	0802	|	|	0842	|	0902	|	|	0942	|	1002	|	|	1042	|	1102	|	|	|	1142	|	1202	|	|	1242	|	1302
32	Lenzburg d.	|	|	0829	|	|	|	|	0929	|	|	|	|	1029	|	|	|	|	|	1129	|	|	|	|	1229	|	|	|
41	Aarau d.	|	|	0837	|	|	|	|	0937	|	|	|	|	1037	|	|	|	|	|	1137	|	|	|	|	1237	|	|	|
77	Liestal d.	|	|	0902	|	|	|	|	1002	|	|	|	|	1102	|	|	|	|	|	1202	|	|	|	|	1302	|	|	|
	Rheinfelden d.	0834	|	|	0910	|	0934	|	|	1010	|	1034	|	|	1110	|	1134	|	|	|	1210	|	1234	|	|	1310	|	1334
91	Basel SBB a.	0847	0857	0912	0923	0927	0947	0957	1012	1023	1027	1047	1057	1112	1123	1127	1147	1157	1157	1212	1223	1227	1247	1257	1312	1323	1327	1347

	EC 6	IR 1774	IR 2074	IC 574	IR 1974	TGV 9216	IR 1776	IR 2076	IC 576	IR 96	IC 778	IR 1778	IR 2078	IC 578	IR 1978	IC 780	IR 1780	IR 2080	IC 580	IR 1980	ICE 372	ICE 272	IR 1782	IR 2082	IC 582	IR 1982	TGV 9218	IR 1784
	✕ ◆			(✕)		(🍸) ◆			(✕)	◆				🍸					✕		✕ ◆	✕ ◆			(✕)		(✕) ◆	
Chur 520 d.	1116	...	...	1209	...	...	1216	...	1309	...	...	1316	...	1409	...	...	1416	...	1509	...	...	...	...	...	1609	...	1633r	1616
Zürich Flug ✈ 530/5 d.	|	...	1304	|	...	...	|	1404	|	...	...	|	1504	|	...	...	|	1604	|	...	...	...	...	1704	|	...	|	|
Zürich HB d.	1302	1308	|	1334	1336	1402	1408	|	1434	1436	1502	1508	|	1534	1536	1602	1608	|	1634	1636	1702	1702	1708	|	1734	1736	1802	1808
Baden d.	|	|	1333	|	1352	|	|	1433	|	1452	|	|	1533	|	1552	|	|	1633	|	1652	|	|	|	1733	|	1752	|	|
Brugg d.	|	|	1342	|	1402	|	|	1442	|	1502	|	|	1542	|	1602	|	|	1642	|	1702	|	|	|	1742	|	1802	|	|
Lenzburg d.	|	1329	|	|	|	|	1429	|	|	|	|	1529	|	|	|	|	1629	|	|	|	|	|	1729	|	|	|	|	1829
Aarau d.	|	1337	|	|	|	|	1437	|	|	|	|	1537	|	|	|	|	1637	|	|	|	|	|	1737	|	|	|	|	1837
Liestal d.	|	1402	|	|	|	|	1502	|	|	|	|	1602	|	|	|	|	1702	|	|	|	|	|	1802	|	|	|	|	1902
Rheinfelden d.	|	|	1410	|	1434	|	|	1510	|	1534	|	|	1610	|	1634	|	|	1710	|	1734	|	|	|	1810	|	1834	|	|
Basel SBB a.	1357	1412	1423	1427	1447	1457	1512	1523	1527	1547	1557	1612	1623	1627	1647	1657	1712	1723	1727	1747	1757	1757	1812	1823	1827	1847	1857	1912

	IR 2086	IC 586	EC 162	ICE 270	IR 1786	IR 2088	IC 588	IR 1988	CNL 459	IC 790	IR 1788	IR 2090	IC 590	IR 1990	CNL 478	IC 792	IR 1790	IR 2092	IC 592	IR 1992	IR 794	IR 1792	IR 1994	IC 796	IR 1794	IR 1996	IR 1798	IR 1752
		(✕)	✕ ◆	✕ ◆			(✕)		◆	✕					◆		✕											q
Chur 520 d.	...	1709	...	...	1716	...	1809	...	...	...	1816	...	1909	...	...	...	1916	...	2009e	...	2013	...	...	2113	...	...	...	...
Zürich Flug ✈ 530/5 d.	1804	|	...	...	|	1904	|	...	...	...	|	2004	|	...	...	...	|	2104	|	...	|	...	...	|	...	...	...	...
Zürich HB d.	|	1834	1836	1902	1908	|	1934	1936	1944	2002	2008	|	2034	2036	2042	2102	2108	|	2134	2136	2202	2208	2236	2302	2308	2336	0008	0108
Baden d.	1833	|	1852	|	|	1933	|	1952	1958u	|	|	2033	|	2052	2058u	|	|	2133	|	2152	|	|	2252	|	|	2352	|	|
Brugg d.	1842	|	1902	|	|	1942	|	2002	|	|	|	2042	|	2102	|	|	|	2142	|	2202	|	|	2302	|	|	0002	|	|
Lenzburg d.	|	|	|	|	1929	|	|	|	|	|	2029	|	|	|	|	|	2129	|	|	|	|	2229	|	|	2329	|	0029	0129
Aarau d.	|	|	|	|	1937	|	|	|	|	|	2037	|	|	|	|	|	2137	|	|	|	|	2237	|	|	2337	|	0037	0137
Liestal d.	|	|	|	|	2002	|	|	|	|	|	2102	|	|	|	|	|	2202	|	|	|	|	2302	|	|	0002	|	0102	0202
Rheinfelden d.	1910	|	1934	|	|	2010	|	2034	|	|	|	2110	|	2134	|	|	|	2210	|	2234	|	|	2334	|	|	0034	|	|
Basel SBB a.	1923	1927	1947	1957	2012	2023	2027	2047	2051u	2057	2112	2123	2127	2147	2151u	2157	2212	2223	2227	2247	2257	2312	2347	2357	0012	0047	0112	0212

FOR NOTES SEE OPPOSITE PAGE

511 BERN and FRIBOURG - NEUCHÂTEL

BLS, TPF*

km		⚒	Ⓐ								▲															
0	**Bern** d.	...	0554	0608	...	0654	...	0708	...	0754	and at	1908	...	1954	...	2008	...	2108	...	...	2208	2234	2308	2334	0010	...
22	Kerzers d.	...	0611	0631	...	0711	...	0731	...	0811	the same	1931	...	2011	...	2031	...	2135	...	...	2231	2301	2331	0001	0037	...
	Fribourg d.	0533	|	|	0633	|	...	|	0733	|	minutes	|	1933	|	...	|	2033	|	2133	...	|	|	|	|	|	...
	Murten d.	0600	|	|	0700	|	...	|	0800	|	past each	|	2000	|	...	|	2100	|	2200	...	|	|	|	|	|	...
30	Ins d.	0611	0617	0638	0711	0717	...	0738	0811	0817	hour	1938	2011	2017	...	2038	2111	2142	2211	...	2238	2313	2338	0013	0044	...
43	**Neuchâtel** a.	0624	0627	0657	0724	0727	...	0757	0824	0827	until	1957	2024	2027	...	2057	2127	2158	2224	...	2257	2326	2357	0026	0059	...

km				⚒z											▲											
	Neuchâtel d.	0601	0633	0636	0701	0733	0736	0801	0830	0836	0901	0933	0936	1001	and at	1933	1936	2001	2036	2101	2136	2201	2236	2301	2336	0009
0	Ins d.	0617	0643	0650	0717	0743	0750	0817	0840	0850	0917	0943	0950	1017	the same	1943	1950	2017	2050	2121	2150	2217	2250	2317	2352	0025
10	Murten d.	|	|	0701	|	|	0801	|	|	0901	|	|	1001	|	minutes	|	2001	|	2101	|	2201	|	2301	|	|	|
32	**Fribourg** a.	|	|	0728	|	|	0827	|	|	0927	|	|	1027	|	past each	|	2027	|	2127	|	2227	|	2327	|	|	|
	Kerzers d.	0630	0649	...	0730	0749	...	0830	0849	...	0930	0949	...	1030	hour	1949	...	2030	...	2134	...	2230	...	2330	0000	0038
	Bern a.	0652	0706	...	0752	0806	...	0856	0906	...	0952	1006	...	1052	until	2006	...	2052	...	2156	...	2252	...	2352	0026	0103

z – Not Aug. 1.

▲ – Variations: 1033, 1133 from Fribourg; 0936, 1036 from Neuchâtel, run only Murten - Ins - Neuchâtel and v.v. on Oct. 4.

* – Operators: BLS, Bern - Ins - Neuchâtel; TPF, Fribourg - Ins.

512 BIEL and NEUCHÂTEL - LA CHAUX DE FONDS - LE LOCLE

SBB

km		Ⓐ	Ⓐ																								⑤⑥
0	**Biel/Bienne** d.	0509	...	0614	...	0650	...	0717	...	...	0750	and at	1917	...	...	1950	...	...	2017	...	2117	...	2217	...	2319	...	2350
28	St Imier d.	0541	...	0641	...	0731	...	0744	...	...	0831	the same	1944	...	...	2031	...	...	2052	...	2152	...	2252	...	2352	...	0028
	Neuchâtel d.	|	0528	|	0631	|	...	|	0731	0737	|	minutes	|	1931	1937	|	...	2031	|	2037	|	2137	|	2237	|	2337	|
44	La Chaux de Fonds d.	0558	0602	0655	0705**t**	0747	...	0758	0802	0818	0847	past each	1958	2002	2018	2047	...	2059	2110	2115	2210	2215	2310	2315	0010	0015	0044
52	**Le Locle** a.	...	0610	...	0713**t**	...	...	...	0810	0827	...	hour until	...	2010	2027	...	...	...	...	2123	...	2223	...	2323	...	0023	...

km																											
0	**Le Locle** d.	0546	...	0630	0650	...	0724**r**	...	0750	...	...	0832	and at	1850	...	...	1932	1950	...	2032	...	2132	...	2232	...	2332	...
8	La Chaux de Fonds d.	0557	0559	0642	0701	0702	0742	...	0801	0802	0813	0842	the same	1901	1902	1913	1942	2001	2002	2042	2051	2142	2151	2242	2251	2342	2351
37	**Neuchâtel** a.	0626	|	0719	0729	|	0819	...	0829	|	|	0919	minutes	1929	|	|	2019	2030	|	2119	|	2219	|	2319	|	0019	|
	St Imier d.	...	0613	...	...	0716	...	...	...	0816	0830	...	past each	...	1916	1930	...	...	2016	...	2109	...	2209	...	2309	...	0009
	Biel/Bienne a.	...	0640	...	...	0741	...	...	...	0841	0909	...	hour until	...	1941	2009	...	...	2041	...	2141	...	2241	...	2343	...	0041

r – 0732 on ©.

t – 3 minutes later on ©.

513 BERN - BIEL

SBB

km																									⑥⑦j
0	**Bern** d.	0530	...	0600	0612	0630	0642	and at the same minutes	2000	2012	2030	2042	...	2100	2112	2130	2200	2212	2230	2300	2312	2330	0012	0015	0112
23	Lyss d.	0553	...	0623	0630	0653	0700	past each	2023	2030	2053	2100	...	2123	2130	2153	2223	2230	2253	2323	2330	2353	0030	0038	0134
34	**Biel/Bienne** a.	0606	...	0636	0638	0706	0708	hour until	2036	2038	2106	2108	...	2136	2138	2206	2236	2238	2306	2336	2338	0006	0038	0051	0142

																							⑥⑦j
Biel/Bienne d.	0518	...	0551	0554	0621	0624	and at the same minutes	1951	1954	2021	2024	...	2051	2054	2121	2124	2154	2221	2224	2254	2321	2324	2354	0026
Lyss d.	0530	...	0600	0607	0630	0637	past each	2000	2007	2030	2037	...	2100	2107	2130	2137	2207	2230	2237	2307	2330	2337	0007	0035
Bern a.	0554	...	0618	0630	0648	0700	hour until	2018	2030	2048	2100	...	2118	2130	2148	2200	2230	2248	2300	2330	2348	2400	0030	0053

j – Also Jan. 1.

514 BERN - LUZERN via Langnau

BLS

For faster services Bern - (Olten -) Luzern see Tables 505/565

km												
0	**Bern** § d.	0537**a**	0612	0637	0712	and at	2137	2212	2237	2312	2342	0012
21	Konolfingen § d.	0553**a**	0634	0653	0734	the same	2153	2234	2253	2334	2356	0034
38	Langnau § d.	0606	0652	0706	0752	minutes	2206	2252	2306	2352	0008	0052
75	Wolhusen d.	0645	...	0745	...	past each	2245	...	2345	...	...	...
96	**Luzern** a.	0703	...	0803	...	hour until	2303	...	0010	...	...	...

Luzern d.	0557	0657	...	and at	2057	...	2157	...	...	2316	0016
Wolhusen d.	0615	0715	...	the same	2115	...	2215	...	...	2344	0040
Langnau § d.	0654	0754	0808	minutes	2154	2208	2254	2308	0008	0022	0118
Konolfingen § d.	0708	0808	0826	past each	2208	2226	2308	2326	0026	...	...
Bern § a.	0726	0826	0848	hour until	2226	2248	2326	2348	0048	...	...

a – Ⓐ only.

Additional services operate Bern - Langnau and v.v.

516 BERN - SOLOTHURN

Narrow gauge. RBS

km																								
0	**Bern RBS** d.	0605	0635	and at the same minutes past	1905	1935	...	2005	...	2041	2111	2141	...	2211	2241	2311	...	2341	...	0011	...	...	...
34	Solothurn a.	0642	0712	each hour until	1942	2012	...	2042	...	2124	2154	2224	...	2254	2324	2354	...	0024	...	0054	...	...	...

Solothurn d.	0548	...	0618	0648	and at the same minutes past	1918	1948	...	2005	...	2035	2107	...	2137	2207	...	2237	2307	...	2337	...	...	...
Bern RBS a.	0625	...	0655	0725	each hour until	1955	2025	...	2050	...	2120	2150	...	2220	2250	...	2320	2350	...	0020	...	...	...

517 SOLOTHURN - BURGDORF - THUN

BLS

km																											
0	**Solothurn** d.	0601	0701	...	0801	0901	...	1001	1101	...	1201	1301	...	1401	1501	...	1601	1701	...	1801	...	1901	...	...	...	...	...
5	Biberist d.	0606	0706	...	0806	0906	...	1006	1106	...	1206	1306	...	1406	1506	...	1606	1706	...	1806	...	1906	...	...	...	...	...
21	**Burgdorf** a.	0627	0727	...	0827	0927	...	1027	1127	...	1227	1327	...	1427	1527	...	1627	1727	...	1827	...	1927	...	...	...	...	...
21	**Burgdorf** d.	0630	0730	*0747*	0830	0930	*0947*	1030	1130	*1147*	1230	1330	*1347*	1430	1530	*1547*	1630	1730	*1747*	1830	*1847*	1930	*1947*	*2047*	*2147*	*2247*	*2347*
28	Hasle-Rüegsau d.	0639	0739	0801	0839	0939	1001	1039	1139	1201	1239	1339	1401	1439	1539	1601	1639	1739	1801	1839	1901	1939	2001	2101	2201	2301	0001
46	Konolfingen a.	0700	0800	0822	0900	1000	1022	1100	1200	1222	1300	1400	1422	1500	1600	1622	1700	1800	1822	1900	1922	2000	2022	2122	2222	2322	0022
46	Konolfingen d.	0701	0801	0835	0901	1001	1035	1101	1201	1235	1301	1401	1435	1501	1601	1635	1701	1801	1835	1901	1935	2001	2035	2135	2235	2335	0035
61	**Thun** a.	0718	0818	0856	0918	1018	1056	1118	1218	1256	1318	1418	1456	1518	1618	1656	1718	1818	1856	1918	1956	2018	2056	2156	2255	2355	0055

	Ⓐ																										
Thun d.	0532	0639	0739	0839	0903	0939	1039	1103	1139	1239	1303	1339	1439	1503	1539	1639	1703	1739	1803	1839	1903	1939	2009	2109	2209	2309	0009
Konolfingen a.	0553	0658	0758	0858	0924	0958	1058	1124	1158	1258	1324	1358	1458	1524	1558	1658	1724	1758	1824	1858	1924	1958	2030	2130	2230	2330	0030
Konolfingen d.	0600	0700	0800	0900	0935	1000	1100	1135	1200	1300	1335	1400	1500	1535	1600	1700	1735	1800	1835	1900	1935	2000	2035	2135	2235	2335	0035
Hasle-Rüegsau d.	0620	0720	0820	0920	0957	1020	1120	1157	1220	1320	1357	1420	1520	1557	1620	1720	1757	1820	1857	1920	1957	2020	2057	2157	2257	2357	0057
Burgdorf a.	0629	0729	0829	0929	*1012*	1029	1129	*1212*	1229	1329	*1412*	1429	1529	*1612*	1629	1729	*1812*	1829	*1912*	1929	*2012*	2029	*2112*	*2212*	*2312*	*0012*	0106
Burgdorf d.	0632	0732	0832	0932	...	1032	1132	...	1232	1332	...	1432	1532	...	1632	1732	...	1832	...	1932	...	...	...	...	...	...	...
Biberist a.	0650	0750	0850	0950	...	1050	1150	...	1250	1350	...	1450	1550	...	1650	1750	...	1850	...	1950	...	...	...	...	...	...	...
Solothurn a.	0657	0757	0857	0957	...	1057	1157	...	1257	1357	...	1457	1557	...	1657	1757	...	1857	...	1957	...	...	...	...	...	...	...

X – ⑦ (also Dec. 25, 26, Jan. 1, 2, Apr. 10, 13, May 21, June 1, Aug. 1).

h – Change at Hasle-Rüegsau.

Additional services operate:

Solothurn - Burgdorf: 0436Ⓐ, 0518⚒, 0636⚒, 0736⚒, 1236⚒, 1336⚒, 1636, 1736, 1836, 2015, 2115, 2215, 2315, 0015**X**.
Burgdorf - Thun: 0451⚒, 0517Ⓐ, 0547Ⓐ**h**, 0551†, 0647**h**, 0847**h**, 1047**h**, 1247**h**, 1447**h**, 1647**h**.

Thun - Burgdorf: 0503⚒**h**, 0603**h**, 0703**h**, 0803**h**, 1003**h**, 1203**h**, 1403**h**, 1603**h**.
Burgdorf - Solothurn: 0502Ⓐ, 0532Ⓐ, 0555⚒, 0632©, 0655⚒, 1155⚒, 1255⚒, 1555, 1655, 1755, 1855, 2015, 2115, 2215, 2315.

SBB — ZÜRICH - SARGANS - CHUR — 520

km		IR	IC		IR	IR	IC	IC	IR	IR	IC		IR	IC	EC	IR	IC		IR	IC		IR	IC		TGV	IR	IC
		1755	**553**		**10759**	**1759**	**559**	**169**	**10761**	**1761**	**561**		**1765**	**565**	**163**	**1767**	**567**		**1769**	**569**		**1771**	**571**		**9221**	**1773**	**573**
			(✕)			✕	🍷				🍷		✕	(✕)	✕		(✕)			(✕)			🍷		(🍷)		🍷
					y			F	Ⓒ						◆										◆		
	Basel SBB **510** d.	...	0533	...	...	0547	0633	...	...	0647	0733	...	0747	0833	0814	0847	0933	...	0947	1033	...	1047	1133	...	1207	1147	1233
0	**Zürich HB** d.	0612	0637	...	0707	0712	0737	0740	0807	0812	0837	...	0912	0937	0940	1012	1037	...	1112	1137	...	1212	1237	...	1300s	1312	1337
12	Thalwil d.	0622	|	...	|	0722	|	|	|	0822	|	...	0922	|	|	1022	|	...	1122	|	...	1222	|	...	|	1322	|
24	Wädenswil d.	0632	|	...	|	0732	|	|	|	0832	|	...	0932	|	|	1032	|	...	1132	|	...	1232	|	...	|	1332	|
33	Pfäffikon d.	0641	|	...	0731	0741	|	|	|	0841	|	...	0941	|	|	1041	|	...	1141	|	...	1241	|	...	|	1341	|
57	Ziegelbrücke d.	0659	|	...	|	0759	|	|	|	0859	|	...	0959	|	|	1059	|	...	1159	|	...	1259	|	...	|	1359	|
90	**Sargans 534** d.	0721	0733	0748	|	0821	0833	0837	0904	0921	0933	0948	1021	1033	1037	1121	1133	1148	1221	1233	1248	1321	1333	1348	1405	1421	1433
106	Buchs **534** a.	|	|	0759	|	|	|	0850	|	|	|	0959	|	|	1050	|	|	1159	|	|	1259	|	|	1359	|	|	|
103	Landquart d.	0736	0743	...	0814	0834	0843	...	0914	0934	0943	...	1034	1043	...	1134	1143	...	1234	1243	...	1334	1343	...	1415	1434	1443
116	**Chur** a.	0745	0752	...	0823	0843	0852	...	0923	0943	0952	...	1043	1052	...	1143	1152	...	1243	1252	...	1343	1352	...	1425	1443	1452
	St Moritz **540** a.	...	*0958*	...	...	...	*1058*	...	...	...	*1158*	...	...	*1258*	...	...	*1358*	...	...	*1458*	...	...	*1558*	...	...	...	*1658*

	EC	IR	IC		EC	IC		IR	IC		EC	IC	EC	IR	IC		IR	IC		IR	IC		IR	EN	IR	EN	IR
	161	**1775**	**575**		**7**	**577**		**91**	**579**		**101**	**581**	**165**	**1785**	**585**		**1787**	**587**		**1789**	**589**		**1791**	**465**	**1793**	**467**	**1797**
			(✕)		✕	(✕)			🍷		✕	🍷			🍷			(✕)			(✕)						
	◆				◆			◆			◆		◆											◆		◆	
Basel SBB **510** d.	...	1247	1333	...	1407	1433	...	1447	1533	...	1547	1633	...	1647	1733	...	1747	1833	...	1847	1933	...	1947	*2033*	2047	*2133*	...
Zürich HB d.	1340	1412	1437	...	1512	1537	...	1612	1637	...	1712	1737	1740	1812	1837	...	1912	1937	...	2012	2037	...	2112	2140	2212	2240	2312
Thalwil d.	|	1422	|	...	1522	|	...	1622	|	...	1722	|	|	1822	|	...	1922	|	...	2022	|	...	2122	|	2222	|	2322
Wädenswil d.	|	1432	|	...	1532	|	...	1632	|	...	1732	|	|	1832	|	...	1932	|	...	2032	|	...	2132	|	2232	|	2332
Pfäffikon d.	|	1441	|	...	1541	|	...	1641	|	...	1741	|	|	1841	|	...	1941	|	...	2041	|	...	2141	|	2241	|	2341
Ziegelbrücke d.	|	1459	|	...	1559	|	...	1659	|	...	1759	|	|	1859	|	...	1959	|	...	2059	|	...	2159	|	2259	|	2359
Sargans 534 d.	1437	1521	1533	1548	1621	1633	1648	1721	1733	1748	1821	1833	1837	1921	1933	1948	2021	2033	2048	2121	2133	2143	2221	2237	2321	2337	0025
Buchs **534** a.	1450	|	|	1559	|	|	1659	|	|	1759	|	|	1850	|	|	1959	|	|	2059	|	|	2154	|	2250	|	2350	|
Landquart d.	...	1534	1543	...	1634	1643	...	1734	1743	...	1834	1843	...	1934	1943	...	2036	2043	...	2136	2143	...	2236	...	2336	...	0040
Chur a.	...	1543	1552	...	1643	1652	...	1743	1752	...	1843	1852	...	1943	1952	...	2045	2052	...	2145	2152	...	2245	...	2345	...	0049
St Moritz **540** a.	...	...	*1758*	...	...	*1858*	...	...	*1958*	...	...	*2058*	...	...	*2159*	...	...	*2259*	...	...	...	...	...	...	...	...	...

	EN	IR		IC	IR	EN	IC	IR		IC	IR		IC	EC		IC	IR	EC	IC	EC		IC	IR		IC	IR	
	466	**1760**		**560**	**1762**	**464**	**562**	**766**		**566**	**1768**		**568**	**100**		**570**	**1772**	**164**	**572**	**6**		**574**	**1776**		**576**	**1778**	
				(✕)			(✕)			(✕)			🍷	✕		🍷			(✕)	✕		(✕)			(✕)		
	◆			⚒		◆								◆				◆		◆							
St Moritz **540** d.	...	...	...	...	...	...	...	...	...	...	...	...	*0704*	...	...	*0804*	...	...	*0904*	...	...	*1004*	...	...	*1104*	...	...
Chur d.	...	0513	...	0606	0613	...	0709	0713	...	0809	0816	...	0909	0916	...	1009	1016	...	1109	1116	...	1209	1216	...	1309	1316	...
Landquart d.	...	0523	...	0615	0623	...	0719	0723	...	0819	0826	...	0919	0926	...	1019	1026	...	1119	1126	...	1219	1226	...	1319	1326	...
Buchs **534** d.	0510	|	0607	|	|	0710	|	|	0801	|	|	0901	|	|	1001	|	|	1110	|	|	1201	|	|	1301	|	|	1401
Sargans 534 d.	0524	0539	0622	0625	0639	0724	0728	0739	0812	0828	0839	0912	0928	0939	1012	1028	1039	1124	1128	1139	1212	1228	1239	1312	1328	1339	1412
Ziegelbrücke d.	|	0601	...	0647	0701	|	|	0801	...	|	0901	...	|	1001	...	|	1101	|	|	1201	...	|	1301	...	|	1401	...
Pfäffikon d.	|	0619	...	|	0719	|	|	0819	...	|	0919	...	|	1019	...	|	1119	|	|	1219	...	|	1319	...	|	1419	...
Wädenswil d.	|	0628	...	|	0728	|	|	0828	...	|	0928	...	|	1028	...	|	1128	|	|	1228	...	|	1328	...	|	1428	...
Thalwil d.	|	0638	...	|	0738	|	|	0838	...	|	0938	...	|	1038	...	|	1138	|	|	1238	...	|	1338	...	|	1438	...
Zürich HB a.	0620	0647	...	0723	0747	0820	0823	0847	...	0923	0947	...	1023	1047	...	1123	1147	1220	1223	1247	...	1323	1347	...	1423	1447	...
Basel SBB **510** a.	*0727*	0812	...	0827	...	...	0927	0957	...	1027	1112	...	1127	1157	...	1227	1312	...	1327	1357	...	1427	1512	...	1527	1612	...

	IC	IR	EC	IC	IR		IC	IR	TGV	EC	IC	IR		IC	IR	IR	IC	IC	IR	IR		IC	IR		IR		IR
	578	**1780**	**160**	**580**	**782**		**582**	**1784**	**9222**	**162**	**586**	**1786**		**588**	**1788**	**10790**	**168**	**590**	**1790**	**10792**		**592**	**794**		**796**		**1796**
	🍷			✕			(✕)		(🍷)	✕	(✕)	✕		(✕)				🍷	✕			🍷					
			◆						◆	◆						Ⓒz	F			Ⓒy		†					
St Moritz **540** d.	*1204*	...	...	*1304*	...	...	*1404*	...	...	...	*1504*	...	...	*1604*	...	...	...	*1704*	...	...	...	*1804*	*1804*	...	*1904*	...	*2004*
Chur d.	1409	1416	...	1509	1516	...	1609	1616	1633	...	1709	1716	...	1809	1816	1837	...	1909	1916	1937	...	2009	2013	...	2113	...	2213
Landquart d.	1419	1426	...	1519	1526	...	1619	1626	1645	...	1719	1726	...	1819	1826	1847	...	1919	1926	1947	...	2019	2023	...	2123	...	2223
Buchs **534** d.	|	|	1510	|	|	1601	|	|	|	1710	|	|	1801	|	|	|	1910	|	|	|	2010	|	|	2120	|	2201	|
Sargans 534 d.	1428	1439	1524	1528	1539	1612	1628	1639	1655	1724	1728	1739	1812	1828	1839	|	1924	1928	1939	1958	2025	2028	2039	2135	2139	2212	2239
Ziegelbrücke d.	|	1501	|	|	1601	...	|	1701	|	|	|	1801	...	|	1901	|	|	|	2001	|	...	|	2101	...	2201	...	2301
Pfäffikon d.	|	1519	|	|	1619	...	|	1719	|	|	|	1819	...	|	1919	1930	|	|	2019	|	...	|	2119	...	2219	...	2319
Wädenswil d.	|	1528	|	|	1628	...	|	1728	|	|	|	1828	...	|	1928	|	|	|	2028	|	...	|	2128	...	2228	...	2328
Thalwil d.	|	1538	|	|	1638	...	|	1738	|	|	|	1838	...	|	1938	|	|	|	2038	|	...	|	2138	...	2238	...	2338
Zürich HB a.	1523	1547	1620	1623	1647	...	1723	1747	1802u	1820	1823	1847	...	1923	1947	1953	2020	2023	2047	2053	...	2123	2147	...	2247	...	2347
Basel SBB **510** a.	1627	1712	...	1727	...	...	1827	1912	1857	1947	1927	2012	...	2027	2112	...	...	2127	2212	...	...	2227	2257	...	2357	...	...

◆ – **NOTES** (LISTED BY TRAIN NUMBER)

6 – 🚃12 and ✕ Chur - Basel - Köln - Dortmund (- Hamburg Ⓑ).
7 – 🚃12 and ✕ (①–⑥, Hamburg -) Dortmund - Basel - Chur.
91 – VAUBAN – 🚃12 Brussels - Luxembourg - Basel - Zürich - Chur.
100 – 🚃12 and ✕ Chur - Zürich - Basel - Hamburg (- Kiel, ⑦, also Apr. 13, June 1; not Apr. 12, May 31, train number **102**).
101 – 🚃12 and ✕ Hamburg - Basel - Zürich - Chur.
160/1 – VORARLBERG – 🚃12 Zürich - Innsbruck - Wien and v.v.
162/3 – TRANSALPIN – 🚃12 and ✕ Wien - Innsbruck - Basel and v.v.
164/5 – KAISERIN ELISABETH – 🚃12 and ✕ Salzburg - Innsbruck - Zürich and v.v.
464/5 – ZÜRICHSEE – 🛏 1, 2 cl., ▬ 2 cl. and 🚃2 Graz - Innsbruck - Feldkirch - Zürich and v.v.; 🛏 1, 2 cl. and ▬ 2 cl. Zagreb (**414/5**) - Villach - Zürich and v.v.; 🚃2 Beograd (**414/5**) - Zagreb - Zürich and v.v.; 🚃12 Buchs - Zürich and v.v.
466/7 – WIENER WALZER – 🛏 1, 2 cl., ▬ 2 cl. and 🚃2 [reclining] Wien - Zürich and v.v.; ▬ 2 cl. and 🚃2 Budapest - Wien - Zürich and v.v.; 🛏 1, 2 cl. and ▬ 2 cl. Praha - Linz - Zürich and v.v.; 🚃12 Buchs - Zürich and v.v.
9221/2 – ⑥ Dec. 20 - Mar. 28: 🚃12 and (🍷) Paris Est - Basel - Zürich - Chur and v.v.

F – 🚃12 From/to Feldkirch.
s – Stops to set down only.
u – Stops to pick up only.
y – May 16 - Oct. 18.
z – Dec. 14 - May 17, Oct. 24 - Dec. 12.

SBB — ZIEGELBRÜCKE - LINTHAL — 522

km									EXTRA SERVICES ▶▶▶	Ⓒ	Ⓒ
0	Ziegelbrücke d.	0605	and	1905	2005	2105	2205	2305		0921	1121
11	Glarus d.	0620	hourly	1920	2020	2120	2220	2320		0939	1139
16	Schwanden d.	0628	until	1928	2027	2127	2227	2327		0946	1146
27	Linthal ▲ a.	0646		1946	2052y	2152y	2252y	2352j		0959	1159

								EXTRA SERVICES ▶▶▶	Ⓒ	Ⓒ
Linthal ▲ d.	0515d	0612	and	2012	*2104*y	*2204*y	*2304*y		1601	1801
Schwanden d.	0534	0631	hourly	2031	2131	2231	2331		1614	1814
Glarus d.	0543	0641	until	2041	2141	2241	2341		1623	1823
Ziegelbrücke a.	0557	0655		2055	2155	2255	2355		1637	1837

d – ⚒ only.
j – ⑤⑥⑦ (also Dec. 25, Jan. 1, Apr. 13, May 21, June 1). Connection by 🚌.
y – Connection by 🚌.

▲ – 🚌 service **Linthal - Flüelen** Bahnhof (Table **550**) and v.v. operates **June 27 - September 27, 2009** over the Klausenpass. Ⓡ. Journey time: 2 hours 25 minutes. **NO WINTER SERVICE.**
From **Linthal**: 0805Ⓒ, 0905, 1010, 1505, 1705Ⓒ. From **Flüelen**: 0550Ⓒ, 0730, 0930, 1500Ⓒ, 1530.
Operator: PostAuto Zentralschweiz, Luzern. ✆ (Luzern) 058 448 06 22, fax: 058 667 34 33.

SBB — LAUSANNE - PALÉZIEUX - PAYERNE — 523

Subject to alteration 2235 - 0530 May 2 - June 27 (not May 30) Lausanne - Palézieux and v.v.; replacement 🚌 services will operate

km																	Ⓐ										✗Z		
0	**Lausanne 505** d.	0524	0624	0724	...	0824	0924	1024	1124	1224	...	1324	1424	1524	1624	...	1700	1724	1824	1924	2024	2124	...	2316	0002	...	0116	...	...
21	Palézieux **505** d.	0541	0641	0741	...	0841	0941	1041	1141	1241	...	1341	1441	1541	1641	...	1718	1741	1841	1941	2041	2141	...	2340	0025	...	0139	...	...
38	Moudon d.	0600	0700	0800	...	0900	1000	1100	1200	1300	...	1400	1500	1600	1700	...	1733	1800	1900	2000	2100	2200	...	2359	...	...	...	...	...
58	Payerne **508** a.	0619	0722	0821	...	0919	1019	1119	1219	1321	...	1419	1519	1619	1721	...	1752	1819	1921	2019	2119	2219	...	0018	...	...	...	...	...

			Ⓐ																											
Payerne **508** d.	0539	0639	0708	...	0738	...	0839	...	0939	1039	...	1139	1238	...	1339	1439	1539	...	1639	1736	...	1839	1939	...	2039	2139	...	2239	...	...
Moudon d.	0559	0659	0725	...	0759	...	0859	...	0959	1059	...	1159	1259	...	1359	1459	1559	...	1659	1759	...	1859	1959	...	2059	2159	...	2259	...	...
Palézieux **505** d.	0618	0718	0742	...	0818	...	0918	...	1018	1118	...	1218	1318	...	1418	1518	1618	...	1718	1818	...	1918	2018	...	2118	2218	...	2318	...	...
Lausanne 505 a.	0636	0736	0800	...	0836	...	0936	...	1036	1136	...	1236	1336	...	1436	1536	1636	...	1736	1836	...	1936	2036	...	2136	2236	...	2336	...	...

Z – ⑥⑦ (also Jan. 1).
✗ – Supplement payable.

525 ARTH GOLDAU - ST GALLEN - ROMANSHORN

SBB, SOB*

km																											
				IR			*IR*			*IR*	*IR*	*IR*	*IR*	*IR*	*IR*	*IR*		*IR*	*IR*	*IR*	*IR*	*IR*	*IR*	*IR*		
				2401			**2405**			**2407**	**2409**	**2411**	**2415**	**2417**	**2419**	**2421**		**2423**	**2425**	**2427**	**2429**	**2431**	**2435**	**2437**		
			⚒		Ⓐ						**V**	**V**	**V**	**V**	**V**	**V**		**V**	**V**	**V**	**V**	**V**	**V**	**V**		
	Luzern **550**	d.	...	...	...	...	...	...	...	...	...	0740	0840	0940	1040	1140	1240	...	1340	1440	1540	1640	1740	1840	1940	...	...
0	**Arth Goldau**	d.	...	...	...	0523	...	...	...	...	...	0813	0913	1013	1113	1213	1313	...	1413	1513	1613	1713	1813	1913	2013	2114	2214
20	Biberbrugg ◐	d.	...	...	...	0547	0550	...	0650	0750	...	0835	0935	1035	1135	1235	1335	...	1435	1535	1635	1735	1835	1935	2035	2136	2236
26	Samstagern ◐	d.	...	...	...	...	0557	...	0657	0757	...	|	|	|	|	|	|	...	|	|	|	|	|	|	|	2144	2244
34	Pfäffikon	d.	...	...	...	...	0615	...	0715	0815	...	0854	0954	1054	1154	1254	1354	...	1454	1554	1654	1754	1854	1954	2054	2158	2258
38	Rapperswil	a.	...	...	...	...	0622	...	0722	0822	...	0859	0959	1059	1159	1259	1359	...	1459	1559	1659	1759	1859	1959	2059	2202	2302
38	Rapperswil	d.	...	...	0602**d**	...	...	0703	...	...	0803	0903	1003	1103	1203	1303	1403	...	1503	1603	1703	1803	1903	2003	2103	2203	2303
66	Wattwil	d.	...	...	0630**d**	...	...	0730	...	...	0830	0930	1030	1130	1230	1330	1430	...	1530	1630	1730	1830	1930	2030	2130	2230	2330
89	Herisau	d.	0546	*0608*	0651	...	...	0751	...	...	0851	0951	1051	1151	1251	1351	1451	...	1551	1651	1751	1851	1951	2051	2151	2253	2353
97	**St Gallen**	a.	0554	*0617*	0658	...	...	0758	...	...	0858	0958	1058	1158	1258	1358	1458	...	1558	1658	1758	1858	1958	2058	2158	2301	0001
97	**St Gallen 532**	d.	0601	0631	0701	...	...	0801	...	...	0901	1001	1101	1201	1301	1401	1501	...	1601	1701	1801	1901	2001	2101	2201	2302	0002
119	**Romanshorn 532**	a.	0627	0657	0727	...	...	0827	...	...	0927	1027	1127	1227	1327	1427	1527	...	1627	1727	1827	1927	2027	2127	2227	2329	0029

						IR	*IR*	*IR*	*IR*	*IR*	*IR*	*IR*	*IR*	*IR*	*IR*	*IR*	*IR*	*IR*	*IR*		*IR*					
						2408	**2410**	**2412**	**2416**	**2418**	**2420**	**2422**	**2424**	**2426**	**2428**	**2430**	**2432**	**2436**	**2438**		**2442**					
						V	**V**	**V**	**V**	**V**	**V**	**V**	**V**	**V**	**V**	**V**	**V**	**V**	**V**							
Romanshorn 532	d.	...	...	0532**d**	...	0634	0734	0834	0934	1034	1134	1234	1334	1434	1534	1634	1734	1834	1934	...	*2034*	...	*2134*	...	*2234*	...	2334
St Gallen 532	a.	...	...	0556**d**	...	0659	0759	0859	0959	1059	1159	1259	1359	1459	1559	1659	1759	1859	1959	...	*2059*	...	*2159*	...	*2259*	...	2359
St Gallen	d.	...	...	0557	...	0702	0802	0902	1002	1102	1202	1302	1402	1502	1602	1702	1802	1902	2002	...	2102	...	2202	...	2302	...	0002
Herisau	d.	...	...	0606	...	0710	0810	0910	1010	1110	1210	1310	1410	1510	1610	1710	1810	1910	2010	...	2110	...	2211	...	2311	...	0011
Wattwil	d.	...	...	0630	...	0732	0832	0932	1032	1132	1232	1332	1432	1532	1632	1732	1832	1932	2032	...	2132	...	2232	...	2332	...	0032
Rapperswil	a.	...	...	0657	...	0757	0857	0957	1057	1157	1257	1357	1457	1557	1657	1757	1857	1957	2057	...	2157	...	2257	...	2357	...	...
Rapperswil	d.	0548	0636	0700	...	0800	0900	1000	1100	1200	1300	1400	1500	1600	1700	1800	1900	2000	...	2103	...	2203	...	2303	...	0003	...
Pfäffikon	d.	0556	0647	0706	...	0806	0906	1006	1106	1206	1306	1406	1506	1606	1706	1806	1906	2006	...	2107	...	2207	...	2307	...	0007	...
Samstagern ◐	d.	0608	0658	0715	...	|	|	|	|	|	|	|	|	|	|	|	|	|	...	2118	...	2218	...	2319	...	0019	...
Biberbrugg ◐	d.	0616	0706	0724	...	0824	0924	1024	1124	1224	1324	1424	1524	1624	1724	1824	1924	2024	...	2125	...	2225	...	...	...	...	...
Arth Goldau	a.	0642	0729	0745	...	0846	0946	1046	1146	1246	1346	1446	1546	1646	1746	1846	1946	2046	...	2150	...	2250	...	...	...	...	...
Luzern **550**	a.	...	...	...	...	0920	1020	1120	1220	1320	1420	1520	1620	1720	1820	1920	2020	2120	...	...	...	...	...	...	...	...	...

d – ⚒ only.

V – VORALPEN EXPRESS – 12 Luzern - Rapperswil - St Gallen - Romanshorn and v.v. Also conveys (🍷) or 🍷 on most services.

◐ – For service to Einsiedeln see panel below.

* – Operated by SOB, except Rapperswil - Wattwil (SBB).

km													
							and						
0	**Wädenswil**	d.	0559	0629**j**	0659**j**	0734	0804	every	2204	2234	2304	2334	0004
6	Samstagern	d.	0611	0637**j**	0711	0741	0811	30	2211	2241	2320	2341	0020
11	Biberbrugg. ●	d.	0620	0650	0720	0750	0820	minutes	2220	2250	2327	2350	0027
17	**Einsiedeln** ●	a.	0627	0657	0727	0757	0827	until	2227	2257	2333	2357	0033

								and				
Einsiedeln ●	d.	0518	0600	0630	0659	0730	0800	every	2230	2300	2330	...
Biberbrugg ●	d.	0524	0607	0637	0707	0737	0807	30	2237	2307	2337	...
Samstagern	d.	0534	0615	0645	0715	0745	0815	minutes	2245	2315	2345	...
Wädenswil	a.	0543	0624	0654	0724	0754	0824	until	2254	2324	2354	...

● – Additional services run Biberbrugg - Einsiedeln and v.v.

j – 4–5 minutes later on ©.

526 GOSSAU - APPENZELL - WASSERAUEN

Narrow gauge. AB

km																												
			⚒																									
0	**Gossau**	d.	0548	0647	0717	0747	0817	0847	0917	0947	1017	1047	1117	1147	1247	1347	1447	1517	1547	1617	1647	1717	1747	1847	1947	2047	2147	2312
5	Herisau	a.	0553	0653	0723	0753	0823	0853	0923	0953	1023	1053	1123	1153	1253	1353	1453	1523	1553	1623	1653	1723	1753	1853	1953	2053	2153	2318
5	Herisau	d.	0554**a**	0654	0724	0754**p**	0824	0854	0924	0954	1024**p**	1054	1124	1154	1254	1354	1454	1524	1554	1624	1654	1724	1754	1854	1954	2054	2154	2319
15	Urnäsch	d.	0608**a**	0708	0738	0808**p**	0838	0908	0938	1008	1038**p**	1108	1138	1208	1308	1408	1508	1538	1608	1638	1708	1738	1808	1908	2008	2108	2208	2333
26	**Appenzell**	d.	0630**a**	0730	0800	0830**p**	0900	0930	1000	1030	1100**p**	1130	1200	1230	1330	1430	1530	1600	1630	1657	1730	1800	1833	1927	2027	2127	2227	2350
32	**Wasserauen**	a.	0641**a**	0741	0811	0841**p**	0911	0941	1011	1041	1111**p**	1141	1211**a**	1241	1341	1441	1541	1611**q**	1641	1711**q**	1741	1811**a**	1844	*1941***y**	*2041***y**	*2141***y**	...	...

																										🚌**p**	
Wasserauen	d.	...	...	0645**a**	0749	0819	0849**p**	0919	0949	1019	1049**p**	1119	1149**a**	1219	1310	1419	1519	1549**q**	1619	1649**q**	1719	1749**a**	1819	1849	*1942***y**	*2042***y**	2142	...
Appenzell	d.	0603**a**	0633	0703**a**	0803	0833	0903**p**	0933	1003	1033	1103**p**	1133	1203	1233	1333	1433	1533	1603	1633	1703	1733	1803	1833	1903	2003	2103	2153	2203
Urnäsch	d.	0620**a**	0650	0720**a**	0820	0850	0920**p**	0950	1020	1050	1120**p**	1150	1220	1250	1350	1450	1550	1620	1650	1720	1750	1820	1850	1920	2020	2120	...	2220
Herisau	a.	0636**a**	0706	0736**a**	0836	0906	0936**p**	1006	1036	1106	1136**p**	1206	1236	1306	1406	1506	1606	1636	1706	1736	1806	1836	1906	1936	2036	2136	...	2236
Herisau	d.	0637	0707	0737	0837	0907	0937	1007	1037	1107	1137	1207	1237	1307	1407	1507	1607	1637	1707	1737	1807	1837	1907	1937	2037	2137	...	2237
Gossau	a.	0643	0713	0743	0843	0913	0943	1013	1043	1113	1143	1213	1243	1313	1413	1513	1613	1643	1713	1743	1813	1843	1913	1943	2043	2143	...	2243

a – Ⓐ only. **p** – May 17 - Oct. 25. **q** – Apr. 10 - Nov. 8. **y** – Connection by 🚌.

527 ST GALLEN - APPENZELL

Narrow gauge rack railway. AB

km																											
			⚒	⚒	Ⓐ	🚌©			⚒			and				q								Ⓐ	🚌	🚌	🚌**z**
0	**St Gallen**	d.	0607	0637**a**	0707	0723	0737**d**	0807	0837	0907	0937	every	1637	1707	1737	1752	1807	1837	1907	1937	2007	2037	2107	2137	2230	2330	0030
7	Teufen	d.	0624	0654**a**	0724	0735	0754**d**	0824	0854	0924	0954	30	1654	1724	1754	1808	1824	1854	1924	1954	2024	2054	2124	2154	2242	2342	0042
14	Gais ▲	d.	0640	0710	0740	0746	0810	0840	0910	0940	1010	minutes	1710	1740	1810	1820	1840	1910	1940	2010	2039	2109	2139	2210	2252	2352	0052
20	**Appenzell**	a.	0651	0721	0751	0757	0821	0851	0921	0951	1021	until	1721	1751	1821**p**	1831	1851	1921	1951	2021	*2057***y**	*2121***y**	...	2221	2307	0002	0102

		⚒	Ⓐ	⚒	Ⓐ		⚒						and			©	Ⓐ							🚌	🚌	🚌
Appenzell	d.	0508	0608	0638	0658	0708	0738	0808**a**	0838	0908**d**	0938	1008	every	1638	1708	1738	1738	1808	1838	1908	1938	2008	2038	2108	2155	2246
Gais ▲	d.	0520	0620	0650	0708	0720	0750	0820	0850	0920	0950	1020	30	1650	1720	1750	1755	1820	1850	1920	1950	2020	2050	2117	2204	2258
Teufen	d.	0534	0633	0703	0721	0733	0803	0833	0903	0933	1003	1033	minutes	1703	1733	1803	1808	1833	1903	1933	2003	2033**a**	2103	2127	2215	2308
St Gallen	a.	0555	0650	0720	0738	0750	0820	0850	0920	0950	1020	1050	until	1720	1750	1820	1825	1850	1920	1950	2020	2050**a**	2120	2140	2228	2321

a – Ⓐ only.

d – ⚒ only.

p – © (daily Dec. 24 - Jan. 4, July 6 - Aug. 9; also May 20, 22).

q – Ⓐ Dec. 15 - 23, Jan. 5 - July 3, Aug. 10 - Dec. 11 (not May 20, 22).

x – Not Aug. 1.

y – Connection by 🚌.

z – ⑥⑦ (not Apr. 11).

▲ – Rail service **Gais - Altstätten Stadt** and v.v. *8 km.* Journey time: 22 minutes. **Operator**: AB.
From **Gais**: 0552Ⓐ🚌, 0652Ⓐ, 0700⑥**x**🚌, 0700†, 0800, 0851 and hourly until 1751, 1911🚌, 2011🚌.
From **Altstätten Stadt**: 0617Ⓐ🚌, 0717Ⓐ, 0725⑥**x**🚌, 0725†, 0828 and hourly until 1828, 1928🚌, 2028🚌.

A bus connects Altstätten Stadt with Altstätten SBB station (Table **534**). Journey time: 6 minutes.

528 LOCARNO - DOMODOSSOLA

FART

km													
					h		**P**	**C**	**h**	**P**	**j**		
						🍷	🍷	🍷		🍷			
0	**Locarno**	d.	0650	0813	0915	1042	1213	1412	1455	1542	1556	1746	1850
20	Camedo 🏛	d.	0726	0849	0949	1117	1249	1446**u**	1530	1618	1635	1826	1929
26	Re ⊗	d.	0743	0905	1005	1135	1304	1504	1545	1633	1650	1844	1944
34	S M Maggiore §⊗	d.	0755	0917	1017	1148	1316	1516	1557	1645	1701	1856	1956
53	**Domodossola**	a.	0837	0956	1056	1230	1356	1556	1636	1725	1741	1936	2036

			j	**P**	**j**	**C**	**P**	**h**				
				🍷	🍷	🍷	🍷		🍷	🍷		
Domodossola	d.	0535**a**	0825	0925	0945	1025	1125	1158	1405	1525	1805	2025
S. M. Maggiore §⊗	d.	0614**a**	0905	1005	1025	1105	1204	1238	1445	1605	1845	2104
Re ⊗	d.	0624	0917	1017	1037	1117	1216	1250	1457	1617	1857	2116
Camedo 🏛	d.	0640	0933	1034	1056	1136	1232	1306	1514	1637	1913	2132
Locarno	a.	0718	1010	1110	1146	1210	1308	1348	1552	1715	1948	2208

C – Conveys observation cars (supplement payable).

P – Conveys observation cars Mar. 22 - Oct. 18 (supplement payable).

a – ①–⑤ only.

h – Mar. 22 - Oct. 18.

j – † Mar. 22 - June 7; daily June 14 - Sept. 6; ⑦ Sept. 13 - Oct. 18 (also Apr. 25, June 2).

u – Stops to pick up only.

⊗ – Request stop.

§ – Full name is Santa Maria Maggiore.

529 ZÜRICH - ZÜRICH FLUGHAFEN ✈

Journey time: 9 - 13 minutes

Additional services are available at peak times

From **Zürich HB:**
0502, 0520, 0539, 0547, 0601, 0607, 0609, 0617, 0627, 0637, 0639, 0647, 0655, 0707, 0709, 0717, 0727, 0737, 0739, 0747, 0755, 0801, 0807, 0809, 0817, 0827, 0837, 0839, 0847, 0855, and at xx01, xx07, xx09, xx17, xx27, xx37, xx39, xx47, xx55 minutes past each hour until 2001, 2007, 2009, 2017, 2027, 2037, 2039, 2047, 2055, then 2107, 2109, 2117, 2127, 2139, 2147, 2207, 2209, 2217, 2227, 2239, 2247, 2307, 2309, 2327, 0017.

From **Zürich Flughafen:**
0503, 0546, 0602, 0613, 0620, 0632, 0633, 0639, 0643, 0702, 0709, 0713, 0720, 0732, 0739, 0743, 0802, 0809, 0813, 0820, 0832, 0839, 0843, 0847, 0902, 0910, 0913, 0920, 0932, 0940, 0943, 0947, 0951, and at xx02, xx10, xx13, xx20, xx32, xx40, xx43, xx47, xx51 minutes past each hour until 2002, 2010, 2013, 2020, 2032, 2040, 2043, 2047, 2051, then 2102, 2110, 2113, 2120, 2132, 2140, 2143, 2202, 2213, 2220, 2232, 2240, 2243, 2302, 2320, 2340, 2343, 0010, 0041.

SBB ZÜRICH - ST GALLEN 530

km		IC 705	ICN 507	IC 707		ICN 509	EC 191	IC 709	ICN 1511	IC 711		ICN 515	EC 193	IC 715	ICN 1517	IC 717	ICN 519	IC 719		ICN 1521	IC 721	ICN 523	EC 195	IC 723
			✕	✕		✕	✕	✕	✕	✕		✕	✕	✕	✕	✕	✕	✕		✕	✕	✕	✕	✕
							M	F					M										M	
	Genève Aéroport ✈ **505** d.	...	...	...	...	...	...	...	...	...	...	...	...	0636	...	0736	0805	0836	...	...	0936	1005	...	1036
	Genève **505** d.	...	...	...	...	...	...	...	...	0536	...	0614	...	0645	...	0745	0814	0845	...	...	0945	1014	...	1045
	Lausanne **505** d.	...	...	...	...	...	...	...	0539	0620	...	|	...	0720	0745	0820	|	0920	...	0945	1020	|	...	1120
	Biel **500** d.	...	...	...	...	0543	...	...	0644	|	...	0746	...	|	0846	|	0946	|	...	1046	|	1146	...	|
	Bern **500** d.	...	...	0530	...	|	...	0632	|	0732	...	|	...	0832	|	0932	|	1032	...	|	1132	|	...	1232
0	**Zürich HB 535** d.	0539	0609	0639	...	0709	0716	0739	0809	0839	...	0909	0916	0939	1009	1039	1109	1139	...	1209	1239	1309	1316	1339
10	**Zürich Flughafen** ✈ **535** d.	0552	0622	0652	...	0722	0728	0752	0822	0852	...	0922	0928	0952	1022	1052	1122	1152	...	1222	1252	1322	1328	1352
30	Winterthur **535** d.	0607	0637	0707	...	0737	0742	0807	0837	0907	...	0937	0942	1007	1037	1107	1137	1207	...	1237	1307	1337	1342	1407
57	Wil **539** d.	0625	0654	0725	...	0754	|	0825	0854	0925	...	0954	|	1025	1054	1125	1154	1225	...	1254	1325	1354	|	1425
78	Gossau d.	0645	0710	0745	...	0807	|	0845	0907	0945	...	1007	|	1045	1107	1145	1207	1245	...	1307	1345	1407	|	1445
87	**St Gallen** a.	0653	0717	0753	...	0815	0818	0853	0915	0953	...	1015	1018	1053	1115	1153	1215	1253	...	1315	1353	1415	1418	1453

	ICN 1525	IC 725	ICN 527	IC 727	ICN 1529	IC 729	ICN 531	IC 3831		IC 731	ICN 1535	EC 197	IC 735	ICN 537	IC 737	ICN 1539	IC 739		ICN 541	IC 741	ICN 1543	IR 3841	ICN 545	ICN 1547
	✕	✕	✕	✕	✕	✕	✕			✕	✕	✕	✕	✕	✕	✕	✕		✕				✕	
								Ⓐ				M												
Genève Aéroport ✈ **505** d.	...	1136	1205	1236	...	1336	1405	...	...	1436	...	...	1536	1605	1636	...	1736	...	1805	1836	...	...	2005	...
Genève **505** d.	...	1145	1214	1245	...	1345	1414	...	...	1445	...	...	1545	1614	1645	...	1745	...	1814	1845	...	...	2014	...
Lausanne **505** d.	1145	1220	|	1320	1345	1420	|	...	...	1520	1545	...	1620	|	1720	1745	1820	...	|	1920	1945	...	|	2145
Biel **500** d.	1246	|	1346	|	1446	|	1546	...	...	|	1646	...	|	1746	|	1846	|	...	1946	|	2046	...	2146	2246
Bern **500** d.	|	1332	|	1432	|	1532	|	...	...	1632	|	...	1732	|	1832	|	1932	...	|	2032	|	...	|	|
Zürich HB 535 d.	1409	1439	1509	1539	1609	1639	1709	1733	...	1739	1809	1816	1839	1909	1939	2009	2039	...	2109	2139	2209	2239	2309	0017
Zürich Flughafen ✈ **535** d.	1422	1452	1522	1552	1622	1652	1722	1745	...	1752	1822	1828u	1852	1922	1952	2022	2052	...	2122	2152	2222	2252	2322	0029
Winterthur **535** d.	1437	1507	1537	1607	1637	1707	1737	1800	...	1807	1837	1842u	1907	1937	2007	2037	2107	...	2137	2207	2237	2307	2337	0044
Wil **539** d.	1454	1525	1554	1625	1654	1725	1754	|	...	1825	1854	|	1925	1954	2025	2054	2125	...	2154	2225	2254	2325	2354	0100
Gossau d.	1507	1545	1607	1645	1707	1745	1807	|	...	1845	1907	|	1945	2007	2045	2107	2145	...	2207	2245	2310	2345	0011	0118
St Gallen a.	1515	1553	1615	1653	1715	1753	1815	1839	...	1853	1915	1919u	1953	2015	2053	2115	2153	...	2215	2253	2317	2353	0018	0125

		IC 708	ICN 1510	IC 710	ICN 512	IR 3810	IC 712	ICN 1516	IC 716	ICN 518		IC 718	ICN 1520	IC 720	EC 196	ICN 522	IC 722	ICN 1524		IC 724	ICN 526	IC 726	ICN 1528	IC 728
		Ÿ	✕	✕	✕		✕	✕	✕	✕		✕	✕	✕	✕	✕	✕	✕		✕	✕	✕	✕	✕
						R									M									
St Gallen d.	0432	0511	0544	0611	0642	0644	0711	0748	0811	0848	...	0911	0948	1011	1042	1048	1111	1148	...	1211	1248	1311	1348	1411
Gossau d.	0439	0519	0551	0619	0650	0652	0719	0756	0819	0856	...	0919	0956	1019	|	1056	1119	1156	...	1219	1256	1319	1356	1419
Wil **539** d.	0456	0539	0610	0639	0706	0711	0739	0810	0839	0910	...	0939	1010	1039	|	1110	1139	1210	...	1239	1310	1339	1410	1439
Winterthur **535** d.	0515	0558	0628	0658	0725	0733	0758	0828	0858	0928	...	0958	1028	1058	1119	1128	1158	1228	...	1258	1328	1358	1428	1458
Zürich Flughafen ✈ **535** a.	0529	0611	0641	0711	0737	|	0811	0841	0911	0941	...	1011	1041	1111	1132	1141	1211	1241	...	1311	1341	1411	1441	1511
Zürich HB 535 a.	...	0623	0653	0723	0751	0759	0823	0853	0923	0953	...	1023	1053	1123	1144	1153	1223	1253	...	1323	1353	1423	1453	1523
Bern **500** a.	...	0729	|	0829	|	...	0929	|	1029	|	...	1129	|	1229	...	|	1329	|	...	1429	|	1529	|	1629
Biel **500** a.	...	|	0813	|	0913	...	|	1013	|	1113	...	|	1213	|	...	1313	|	1413	...	|	1513	|	1613	|
Lausanne **505** a.	...	0840	0915	0940	|	...	1040	1115	1140	|	...	1240	1315	1340	...	|	1440	1515	...	1540	|	1640	1715	1740
Genève **505** a.	...	0915	...	1015	1046	...	1115	...	1215	1246	...	1315	...	1415	...	1446	1515	...	...	1615	1646	1715	...	1815
Genève Aéroport ✈ **505** a.	...	0924	...	1024	1055	...	1124	...	1224	1255	...	1324	...	1424	...	1455	1524	...	...	1624	1655	1724	...	1824

	ICN 530	IC 730	EC 194	ICN 1532	IC 732	ICN 536		IC 736	ICN 1538	IC 738	ICN 1540	ICN 540	IC 740	EC 192	ICN 1542	IC 742	ICN 1544	IC 744		EC 190	ICN 1546	ICN 548	ICN 500	
	✕	✕	✕	✕	✕	✕		✕	✕	✕	✕	✕	✕	✕		✕	✕	✕		✕				
			M								⚒	†		M		F				M				
St Gallen d.	1448	1511	1542	1548	1611	1648	...	1711	1748	1811	1848	1848	1911	1942	1948	2011	2048	2111	...	2142	2144	2244	2344	...
Gossau d.	1456	1519	|	1556	1619	1656	...	1719	1756	1819	1856	1856	1919	|	1956	2019	2056	2119	...	|	2151	2251	2351	...
Wil **539** d.	1510	1539	|	1610	1639	1710	...	1739	1810	1839	1910	1910	1939	|	2010	2039	2110	2139	...	|	2210	2310	0010	...
Winterthur **535** d.	1528	1558	1619	1628	1658	1728	...	1758	1828	1858	1928	1928	1958	2019	2028	2058	2128	2158	...	2219	2228	2328	0028	...
Zürich Flughafen ✈ **535** a.	1541	1611	1632	1641	1711	1741	...	1811	1841	1911	1941	1941	2011	2032	2041	2111	2141	2211	...	2232	2241	2341	0041	...
Zürich HB 535 a.	1553	1623	1644	1653	1723	1753	...	1823	1853	1923	1953	1953	2023	2044	2053	2123	2153	2223	...	2244	2253	2353	0053	...
Bern **500** a.	|	1729	...	|	1829	|	...	1929	|	2029	|	|	2129	...	|	2229	|	2332	...	...	|	...	...	...
Biel **500** a.	1713	|	...	1813	|	1913	...	|	2013	|	2113	2113	|	...	2213	...	2314	...	...	...	0022	...	...	...
Lausanne **505** a.	|	1840	...	1915	1940	|	...	2040	2115	2140	...	|	2240	...	2315	...	0015	...	...	...	0124c	...	...	...
Genève **505** a.	1846	1915	...	...	2015	2046	...	2115	...	2215	...	2246	2324	...	...	...	...	...	...	...	...	...	...	...
Genève Aéroport ✈ **505** a.	1855	1924	...	...	2024	2055	...	2124	...	2224	...	2255	2333	...	...	...	...	...	...	...	...	...	...	...

F – From / to Fribourg.
M – (12) Zürich - München and v.v.
R – Ⓐ: (12) Rorschach - Zürich.
c – ⑥⑦ only.
u – Stops to pick up only.

SBB WINTERTHUR - SCHAFFHAUSEN 531

Winterthur d.	0542	0606	0619	0642	and at the same minutes past each hour until	1606	1619	1642	1706	1719	1742	1806	1819	1842	1906	1919	1942	2006	2019	2042	2106	2142	2208	2242	2342
Schaffhausen a.	0614	0638	0644	0714		1638	1644	1714	1738	1744	1814	1838	1844	1914	1938	1944	2014	2038	2044	2114	2138	2214	2238	2314	0014

km						Ⓐ		Ⓐz																	
0	Schaffhausen d.	0521	0544	0614	0621	0631	0643	0701	0714	0721	0744	...	0814	0821	0846	and at the same minutes past each hour until	2014	2021	2046	2121	2146	2221	2246	2321	2346
30	Winterthur a.	0554	0619	0642	0654	0659	0719	0729	0742	0754	0819	...	0842	0854	0919		2042	2054	2119	2154	2219	2254	2319	2354	0023

z – Not Aug. 1.

SBB, THURBO* SCHAFFHAUSEN - ROMANSHORN - RORSCHACH 532

km		⚒																							
0	**Schaffhausen 939/40** d.	...	...	...	0531	...	0601	0631	and at the same minutes past each hour until	1701	1731	1801	1831	1901	1931	2001	...	2031	2101	...	2131	2201	...	2301	0006
20	Stein am Rhein d.	...	...	0527	0557	...	0627	0657		1727	1757	1827	1857	1927	1957	2025	...	2057	2125	...	2157	2225	...	2327	0030
46	**Kreuzlingen** a.	...	...	0556	0626	...	0656	0726		1756	1826	1856	1926	1956	2026	...	...	2126	...	...	2226	...	...	2356	0056
46	**Kreuzlingen** d.	0500	0530	0600	0630	...	0700	0730		1800	1830	1900	1930	2000	2030	...	2100	2130	...	2200	2230	...	2300	...	...
47	Kreuzlingen Hafen d.	0502	0532	0602	0632	...	0702	0732		1802	1832	1902	1932	2002	2032	...	2102	2132	...	2202	2232	...	2302	...	...
65	**Romanshorn** a.	0525	0555	0625	0655	...	0725	0755		1825	1855	1925	1955	2025	2055	...	2125	2155	...	2225	2255	...	2325	...	...
65	**Romanshorn** d.	0528	0604d	0628	0704d	...	0732	0804		1832	1904	1932	...	2032	...	...	2132	...	...	2232	...	...	2332	...	...
	St Gallen **525** a.	|	0629d	|	0729d	...	|	0829		|	1929	|	...	|	...	...	|	...	...	|	...	...	|	...	...
73	Arbon a.	0536	...	0636	...	...	0741	...		1841	...	1941	...	2041	...	...	2141	...	...	2241	...	...	2341	...	...
79	Rorschach Hafen a.	0543	...	0643	...	...	0748	...		1848	...	1948	...	2048	...	...	2148	...	...	2248	...	...	2348	...	...
80	**Rorschach** a.	0547	...	0647	...	...	0752	...		1852	...	1952	...	2052	...	...	2152	...	...	2252	...	...	2352	...	...

Rorschach d.	...	0507	...	0607	...	0707	...	...	0807	...	and at the same minutes past each hour until	1807	...	1907	...	...	2007	...	...	2107	...	...	2207	2307	...
Rorschach Hafen d.	...	0508	...	0608	...	0708	...	...	0808	...		1808	...	1908	...	...	2008	...	...	2108	...	...	2208	2308	...
Arbon d.	...	0517	...	0617	...	0717	...	...	0817	...		1817	...	1917	...	...	2017	...	...	2117	...	...	2217	2317	...
St Gallen **525** d.	...	|	...	|	0631d	|	0731d	...	|	0831		|	1831	|	...	1931	|	...	...	|	...	...	|	|	...
Romanshorn a.	...	0527	...	0627	0657d	0727	0757d	...	0827	0857		1827	1857	1927	...	1957	2027	...	...	2127	...	...	2227	2327	...
Romanshorn d.	...	0532	0602	0632	0702	0732	0802	...	0832	0902		1832	1902	1932	...	2002	2032	...	2102	2132	...	2202	2232	2332	0032
Kreuzlingen Hafen d.	...	0554	0624	0654	0724	0754	0824	...	0854	0924		1854	1924	1954	...	2024	2054	...	2124	2154	...	2224	2254	2354	0054
Kreuzlingen a.	...	0556	0626	0656	0726	0756	0826	...	0856	0926		1856	1926	1956	...	2026	2056	...	2126	2156	...	2226	2256	2356	0056
Kreuzlingen d.	0531	0601	0631	0701	0731	0801	0831	...	0901	0931		1901	1931	...	...	2031	...	...	2131	...	...	2231	...	...	...
Stein am Rhein d.	0600	0630	0700	0730	0800	0830	0900	...	0930	1000		1930	2000	...	2030	2100	...	2130	2200	...	2230	2257	...	...	...
Schaffhausen 939/40 a.	0626	0656	0726	0756	0826	0856	0926	...	0956	1026		1956	2026	...	2056	2126	...	2156	2226	...	2256	...	...	...	...

d – ⚒ only.

* – SBB operate Romanshorn - Rorschach; THURBO operate Schaffhausen - Romanshorn.

533 SCHAFFHAUSEN - KREUZLINGEN

Valid April 5 - October 18 (no winter service) URh

		✕A		✕B		✕A		✕A	
Schaffhausen d.	...	0910	...	1110	...	1310	...	1510	...
Stein am Rhein d.	...	1115	...	1315	...	1515	...	1715	...
Kreuzlingen Hafen a.	...	1350	...	1550	...	1750	...	1950y	...

		✕A		✕A		✕A		✕C	
Kreuzlingen Hafen d.	...	0900	...	1100	...	1400	...	1600	...
Stein am Rhein d.	...	1130	...	1330	...	1630	...	1830	...
Schaffhausen a.	...	1245	...	1445	...	1745	...	1945y	...

A – © Apr. 5-19; daily Apr. 25 - Oct. 4.
B – † Apr. 26 - June 28; daily July 4 - Sept. 13, Oct. 3-18 (also May 1, June 11, Sept. 20, 27).
C – † Apr. 26 - June 28; daily July 4 - Sept. 13, Sept. 20 - Oct. 4 (also May 1, June 11, Oct. 3).
y – Not Aug. 8.

534 ST GALLEN - BUCHS - CHUR

SBB

km		RE 3803	RE 3805	RE 3807	EC 191 M	RE 3809	RE 3811	EC 193 M	RE 3815	RE 3817	RE 3819	RE 3821	EC 195 M	RE 3823	RE 3825	RE 3827	RE 3829	RE 3833	IR 1787	EC 197 M	RE 3835	RE 3837	IR 1791		
0	**St Gallen** d.	0600	0703	0803	0819	0903	1003	1019	1103	1203	1303	1403	1419	1503	1603	1703	1803	1903	...	1919	2003	2103	...	2204	2305
16	Rorschach d.	0621	0721	0821	|	0921	1021	|	1121	1221	1321	1421	|	1521	1621	1721	1821	1921	...	|	2021	2121	...	2222	2322
27	**St Margrethen** d.	0631	0731	0831	0840	0931	1031	1040	1131	1231	1331	1431	1440	1531	1631	1731	1831	1931	...	1940	2031	2131	...	2232	2332
39	Altstätten **527** d.	0642	0742	0842	...	0942	1042	...	1142	1242	1342	1442	...	1542	1642	1742	1842	1942	...	...	2042	2142	...	2243	2343
65	**Buchs 520** ⊖ d.	0701	0801	0901	...	1001	1101	...	1201	1301	1401	1501	...	1601	1701	1801	1901	2001	...	...	2101	2201	...	2306	0006
81	Sargans **520** ⊖ d.	0713	0813	0913	...	1013	1113	...	1213	1313	1413	1513	...	1613	1713	1813	1913	2012	2021	...	2113	2212	2221	2318	0022
93	Landquart **520** d.	0728	0828	0928	...	1028	1128	...	1228	1328	1428	1528	...	1628	1728	1828	1928	...	2036	...	2128	...	2236	...	...
107	**Chur 520** a.	0738	0838	0938	...	1038	1138	...	1238	1338	1438	1538	...	1638	1738	1838	1938	...	2045	...	2138	...	2245	...	...

		IR 1760	RE 3812	RE 3816	RE 3818	RE 3820	EC 196 M	RE 3822	RE 3824	RE 3826	RE 3828	RE 3830	EC 194 M	RE 3832	RE 3834	RE 3836	RE 3838	EC 192 M	RE 3840	RE 3842	EC 190 M	IR 794	RE 3844	IR 796	
Chur 520 d.	...	0513	...	0622	0722	0822	...	0922	1022	1122	1222	1322	...	1422	1522	1622	1722	...	1822	1922	...	2013	...	2113	...
Landquart **520** d.	...	0523	...	0633	0733	0833	...	0933	1033	1133	1233	1333	...	1433	1533	1633	1733	...	1833	1933	...	2023	...	2123	...
Sargans **520** ⊖ d.	...	0537	0541	0648	0748	0848	...	0948	1048	1148	1248	1348	...	1448	1548	1648	1748	...	1848	1948	...	2037	2048	2137	2143
Buchs 520 ⊖ d.	...	...	0600	0701	0801	0901	...	1001	1101	1201	1301	1401	...	1501	1601	1701	1801	...	1901	2001	...	...	2101	...	2157
Altstätten **527** d.	0551	...	0615	0717	0817	0917	...	1017	1117	1217	1317	1417	...	1517	1617	1717	1817	...	1917	2017	...	...	2117	...	2214
St Margrethen d.	0605	...	0626	0729	0829	0929	1020	1029	1129	1229	1329	1429	1520	1529	1629	1729	1829	1920	1929	2029	2120	...	2129	...	2227
Rorschach d.	0619	...	0637	0740	0840	0940	|	1040	1140	1240	1340	1440	|	1540	1640	1740	1840	|	1940	2040	|	...	2140	...	2239
St Gallen a.	0638	...	0656	0756	0856	0956	1041	1056	1156	1256	1356	1456	1541	1556	1656	1756	1856	1941	1956	2056	2141	...	2156	...	2258

⊖ – 🚌 services to **VADUZ (LIECHTENSTEIN)**

[line 12]	⚒	⚒																			⚒		⚒
Buchs (Bahnhof) d.	0533	0603	...	0633	...	0703	0733	...	0803	0833	and at the same minutes	2003	2033	...	2103	...	2133	...	2203	...	2233	...	2303
Vaduz Post d.	0550	0620	...	0650	...	0720	0750	...	0820	0850	past each	2020	2050	...	2120	...	2150	...	2220	...	2250	...	2318
Sargans (Bahnhof) a.	0621	0651	...	0721	...	0751	0821	...	0851	0921	hour until	2051	2121	...	...	...	2221	...	...	...	2321	...	...

[line 12]	⚒																	⑤⑥j				
Sargans (Bahnhof) d.	0606	...	0636	...	0706	0736	...	0806	0836	...	0906	0936	and at the same minutes	2106	2136	...	2226	...	2346	...	...	...	...
Vaduz Post d.	0638	...	0708	...	0738	0808	...	0838	0908	...	0938	1008	past each	2138	2208	...	2256	...	0016	...	...	...	...
Buchs (Bahnhof) a.	0655	...	0725	...	0755	0825	...	0855	0925	...	0955	1025	hour until	2155	2225	...	...	...	...	...	...	...	...

🚌 [line 14] **Feldkirch** (Bahnhof) - **Vaduz** (Post) and v.v. Journey time: 36 minutes. Service shown operates on Ⓐ; a reduced service operates on ©.
Operator: Liechtenstein Bus Anstalt LBA, Städtle 38, 9490 Vaduz. ✆ +423 236 63 10, fax +423 236 63 11.

From **Feldkirch**: 0620, 0650, 0720, 0750 and hourly until 1550, then 1620, 1650, 1720, 1750, 1820, 1850.

From **Vaduz**: 0630, 0702, 0732 and hourly until 1532, then 1602, 1632, 1702, 1732, 1802, 1832, 1902.

M – (12) and ✕ Zürich - München and v.v.
j – Not Dec. 26, Jan. 2, Apr. 10, May 1.

535 ZÜRICH - KONSTANZ and ROMANSHORN

SBB

km		IC 807 (✕)	IR 2107	IC 809 ✕	IR 2109	IC 811 ✕	IR 2111	IC 815 ✕	IR 2115	IC 817 (✕)	IR 2117	IC 819 ✕	IR 2119	IC 821 (✕)	IR 2121	IC 823 ✕	IR 2123	IC 825 (✕)	IR 2125	IC 827 ✕	IR 2127	IC 829 ✕	IR 2129	IC 831 ✕	IR 2131
	Brig **560** d.	...	...	...	...	0547	...	0649	...	0749	...	0849	...	0949	...	1049	...	1149	...	1249	...	1349	...	1449	...
	Interlaken Ost **560** d.	...	...	...	...	|	...	|	...	|	...	|	...	|	...	|	...	|	...	|	...	|	...	|	...
	Bern **500** d.	...	...	0602	...	0702	...	0802	...	0902	...	1002	...	1102	...	1202	...	1302	...	1402	...	1502	...	1602	...
	Biel **500** d.	...	0515	|	0615	|	0715	|	0815	|	0915	|	1015	|	1115	|	1215	|	1315	|	1415	|	1515	|	1615
0	**Zürich HB 530** d.	0607	0637	0707	0737	0807	0837	0907	0937	1007	1037	1107	1137	1207	1237	1307	1337	1407	1437	1507	1537	1607	1637	1707	1737
10	**Zürich Flug ✈ 530** d.	0618	0648	0718	0748	0818	0848	0918	0948	1018	1048	1118	1148	1218	1248	1318	1348	1418	1448	1518	1548	1618	1648	1718	1748
30	Winterthur **530** d.	0635	0705	0735	0805	0835	0905	0935	1005	1035	1105	1135	1205	1235	1305	1335	1405	1435	1505	1535	1605	1635	1705	1735	1805
46	Frauenfeld d.	0647	0717	0747	0817	0847	0917	0947	1017	1047	1117	1147	1217	1247	1317	1347	1417	1447	1517	1547	1617	1647	1717	1747	1817
64	Weinfelden **539** ▲ d.	0700	0730	0800	0830	0900	0930	1000	1030	1100	1130	1200	1230	1300	1330	1400	1430	1500	1530	1600	1630	1700	1730	1800	1830
	Kreuzlingen ▲ a.	|	0750	|	0850	|	0950	|	1050	|	1150	|	1250	|	1350	|	1450	|	1550	|	1650	|	1750	|	1850
	Konstanz ▲ a.	|	0754	|	0854	|	0954	|	1054	|	1154	|	1254	|	1354	|	1454	|	1554	|	1654	|	1754	|	1854
86	**Romanshorn** a.	0718	...	0818	...	0918	...	1018	...	1118	...	1218	...	1318	...	1418	...	1518	...	1618	...	1718	...	1818	...

	IC 835 (✕)	IR 2135	IC 837 ✕	IR 2137	IC 839 (✕)	IR 2139	IC 841 ✕		IC 843	IC 845
Brig **560** d.	1549	...	1649	...	1749	...	1849	...	1949	...
Interlaken Ost **560** d.	|	...	|	...	|	...	|	...	|	...
Bern **500** d.	1702	...	1802	...	1902	...	2002	...	2102	2202
Biel **500** d.	|	1715	|	1815	|	1915	|	...	|	|
Zürich HB 530 d.	1807	1837	1907	1937	2007	2037	2107	...	2207	2307
Zürich Flug ✈ 530 d.	1818	1848	1918	1948	2018	2048	2118	...	2218	2318
Winterthur **530** d.	1835	1905	1935	2005	2035	2105	2135	...	2235	2335
Frauenfeld d.	1847	1917	1947	2017	2047	2117	2147	...	2247	2347
Weinfelden **539** ▲ d.	1900	1930	2000	2030	2100	2130	2200	...	2300	0000
Kreuzlingen ▲ a.	|	1950	|	2050	|	2150	|	...	|	|
Konstanz ▲ a.	|	1954	|	2054	|	2154	|	...	|	|
Romanshorn a.	1918	...	2018	...	2118	...	2218	...	2318	0018

	IC 810 (✕)	IR 2110	IC 812 ✕	IR 2112	IC 816 (✕)	IR 2116	IC 818 ✕	IR 2118	IC 820 ✕	IR 2120
Romanshorn d.	0538	...	0638	...	0741	...	0841	...	0941	...
Konstanz ▲ d.	|	0602	|	0702	|	0803	|	0903	|	1003
Kreuzlingen ▲ d.	|	0607	|	0707	|	0807	|	0907	|	1007
Weinfelden **539** ▲ d.	0559	0629	0659	0729	0759	0829	0859	0929	0959	1029
Frauenfeld d.	0612	0642	0713	0742	0812	0842	0912	0942	1012	1042
Winterthur **530** d.	0625	0655	0728	0755	0825	0855	0925	0955	1025	1055
Zürich Flughafen ✈ 530 a.	0638	0708	0741	0808	0838	0908	0938	1008	1038	1108
Zürich HB 530 a.	0651	0721	0753	0821	0851	0921	0951	1021	1051	1121
Biel **500** d.	|	0845	|	0945	|	1045	|	1145	|	1245
Bern **500** a.	0757	...	0857	...	0957	...	1057	...	1157	...
Interlaken Ost **560** a.	|	...	|	...	|	...	|	...	|	...
Brig **560** a.	0911	...	1011	...	1111	...	1211	...	1311	...

km		IC 822 ✕	IR 2122	IC 824 (✕)	IR 2124	IC 826 ✕	IR 2126	IC 828 (✕)	IR 2128	IC 830 ✕	IR 2130	IC 832 (✕)	IR 2132	IC 836 ✕	IR 2136	IC 838 ✕	IR 2138	IC 840 ✕	IR 2140	IC 842 (✕)	IR 2142	IC 844 ✕		IC 846	IC 848
	Romanshorn d.	1041	...	1141	...	1241	...	1341	...	1441	...	1541	...	1641	...	1741	...	1841	...	1941	...	2041	...	2141	2238
0	**Konstanz** ▲ d.	|	1103	|	1203	|	1303	|	1403	|	1503	|	1603	|	1703	|	1803	|	1903	|	2003	|	...	|	|
1	Kreuzlingen ▲ d.	|	1107	|	1207	|	1307	|	1407	|	1507	|	1607	|	1707	|	1807	|	1907	|	2007	|	...	|	|
24	Weinfelden **539** ▲ d.	1059	1129	1159	1229	1259	1329	1359	1429	1459	1529	1559	1629	1659	1729	1759	1829	1859	1929	1959	2029	2059	...	2159	2259
	Frauenfeld d.	1112	1142	1212	1242	1312	1342	1412	1442	1512	1542	1612	1642	1712	1742	1812	1842	1912	1942	2012	2042	2112	...	2212	2312
	Winterthur **530** d.	1125	1155	1225	1255	1325	1355	1425	1455	1525	1555	1625	1655	1725	1755	1825	1855	1925	1955	2025	2055	2125	...	2225	2325
	Zürich Flug ✈ 530 a.	1138	1208	1238	1308	1338	1408	1438	1508	1538	1608	1638	1708	1738	1808	1838	1908	1938	2008	2038	2108	2138	...	2238	2338
	Zürich HB 530 a.	1151	1221	1251	1321	1351	1421	1451	1521	1551	1621	1651	1721	1751	1821	1851	1921	1951	2021	2051	2121	2151	...	2251	2351
	Biel **500** d.	|	1345	|	1445	|	1545	|	1645	|	1745	|	1845	|	1945	|	2045	|	2145	|	2245	|	...	|	...
	Bern **500** a.	1257	...	1357	...	1457	...	1557	...	1657	...	1757	...	1857	...	1957	...	2057	...	2157	...	2302	...	0002	...
	Interlaken Ost **560** a.	|	...	|	...	|	...	|	...	|	...	|	...	|	...	|	...	...	...	...	...	...	...	...	...
	Brig **560** a.	1411	...	1511	...	1611	...	1711	...	1811	...	1911	...	2011	...	2111	...	...	...	...	...	...	...	...	...

▲ – Additional services operate **Weinfelden - Kreuzlingen - Konstanz and v.v.** journey time: 30–36 minutes.
From **Weinfelden**: 0602, 0702, 0802, 0902, 1002, 1202, 1302, 1502, 1602, 1702, 2002, 2102, 2202, 2302, 0002.
From **Konstanz**: 0524, 0621, 0721, 0821, 0918, 1321, 1418, 1521, 1621, 1721, 1818, 1918, 2021, 2121, 2221, 2321.

SBS 🚢 ROMANSHORN - FRIEDRICHSHAFEN car ferry service 536

Journey time: 41 minutes. ✕ available 0836 - 2136 from Romanshorn; 0841 - 2241 from Friedrichshafen. 🍸 on other sailings. Operator: SBS ✆ 071 466 78 88

From **Romanshorn**: 0936 and hourly until 1636.
From **Friedrichshafen**: 0941 and hourly until 1641.

Services shown operate daily. Additional hourly service available on certain dates from 0536 - 0836 and 1736 - 2136 from Romanshorn; 0541 - 0841 and 1741 - 2041, 2241 from Friedrichshafen.

THURBO WEINFELDEN - WIL 539

km		Ⓐv		Ⓐv		Ⓐv		and		y
0	Weinfelden **535** d.	0457	0532	0557	0632	0657	0732	hourly	2232	2332
19	Wil **530** a.	0520	0555	0622	0655	0722	0755	until	2255	2355

	Ⓐv		Ⓐv		Ⓐv		and		z
Wil **530** d.	0525	0601	0625	0701	0732	0801	hourly	2301	0011
Weinfelden **535** a.	0550	0624	0650	0724	0757	0824	until	2324	0034

v – Not May 1.
y – ⑤⑥ (also Dec. 31, Apr. 9, 12, 30, May 20, 21, 31).
z – ⑥⑦ (also Jan. 1, Apr. 10, 13, May 1, 21, 22, June 1).

Additional services operate Ⓐ (not May 1): Weinfelden depart 1602, 1702, 1802; Wil depart 1632, 1732, 1832.

RhB. Narrow gauge CHUR - ST MORITZ 540

For *Glacier Express* services see Table **575**

km		⊗ 2⚒		◐	◐🍸	**961** ♦Ⓡ✓	**1325** ♦	**951** ♦Ⓡ✓	**953** ♦Ⓡ✓		◐🍸‡	◐🍸	◐🍸‡	◐⊡‡	◐🍸‡	◐🍸	p	◐🍸‡	◐⊡	◐	◐⊡‡	◐‡	◐‡	◐	S
0	**Chur 575** d.	0458	...	0648	0758	...	...	0830	0858	...	0858	0958	1058	1158	1258	1358	1431	1458	1558	1658	1758	1858	1956	2056	...
10	Reichenau-Tamins **575** d.	0509	...	0701	0808	...	...	0838u	0908u	...	0908	1008	1108	1208	1308	1408	|	1508	1608	1708	1808	1908	2007	2107	...
27	Thusis d.	0536	...	0730	0830	...	...	|	0930u	...	0930	1030	1130	1230	1330	1430	1504	1530	1630	1730	1830	1930	2033	2133	...
41	Tiefencastel d.	0552	...	0747	0847	...	...	0917u	0947u	...	0947	1047	1147	1247	1347	1447	1528	1547	1647	1747	1847	1947	2050	2150	...
51	**Filisur 545a** d.	0612	...	0802	0902	0917	...	|	1002u	...	1002	1102	1202	1302	1402	1502	1542	1602	1702	1802	1902	2002	2105	2205	...
59	Bergün/Bravuogn d.	0630	...	0814	0914	0929u	...	|	1014u	...	1014	1114	1214	1314	1414	1514	1556	1614	1714	1814	1914	2014	2117	2217	...
72	Preda d.	0646x	...	0830	0930	|	...	|	1030u	...	1030	1130	1230	1330	1430	1530	|	1630	1730	1830	1930	2030	2134	2234	...
84	**Samedan** a.	0702	...	0847	0946	|	...	|	1046	...	1046	1146	1246	1346	1446	1546	1631	1646	1746	1847	1947	2047	2149	2249	...
84	**Samedan 546** d.	...	0712	0850	0950	1008u	1011	|	1050	...	1050	1150	1250	1350	1450	1550	1632	1650	1750	1850	1950	2050	2151	2251	2341
89	Pontresina **546/7** a.	...	|	|	|	1014	|	1027	1057	...	|	|	|	|	|	|	|	|	|	|	|	|	|	|	|
87	Celerina **546/7** d.	...	0715	0853	0953	...	|	...	...	...	1053	1153	1253	1353	1453	1553	1635	1653	1753	1853	1953	2053	2154	2254	2344
89	**St Moritz 546/7** a.	...	0719	0858	0958	...	1018	...	...	...	1058	1158	1258	1358	1458	1558	1639	1658	1758	1858	1958	2058	2159	2259	2348

	Ⓐ	S⚒	⚒◐	†◐	◐	◐‡	◐⊡	◐🍸	◐🍸	◐🍸‡	◐⊡	◐⊡	◐🍸‡	◐🍸‡	**950** ♦Ⓡ✓	**1360** ♦	**960** ♦Ⓡ✓	**954** ♦Ⓡ✓		◐🍸‡	◐⊡‡	◐	◐⊡‡		q
St Moritz 546/7 d.	...	0500	0540	0557	0704	0804	0904	1004	1104	1204	1304	1404	1504	1604	...	1635	...	...	...	1704	1804	1904	2004	2104	2120
Celerina **546/7** d.	...	0503	0543	0600	0707	0807	0907	1007	1107	1207	1307	1407	1507	1607	...	|	...	...	...	1707	1807	1907	2007	2107	|
Pontresina **546/7** d.	...	|	|	|	|	|	|	|	|	|	|	|	|	|	1624	|	1638	1702	...	|	|	|	|	|	|
Samedan 546 a.	...	0507	0548	0605	0711	0811	0911	1011	1111	1211	1311	1411	1511	1611	|	1642	1644	1708	...	1711	1811	1911	2011	2111	2127
Samedan d.	0500	...	0550	0605	0717	0817	0917	1017	1117	1217	1317	1417	1517	1617	|	...	1648	1717	...	1717	1817	1917	2017	...	2130
Preda d.	|	...	0604	0620	0730	0830	0930	1030	1130	1230	1330	1430	1530	1630	|	...	|	1730s	...	1730	1830	1930	2030	...	|
Bergün/Bravuogn d.	0529	...	0621	0637	0747	0847	0947	1047	1147	1247	1347	1447	1547	1647	|	...	1732s	1747s	...	1747	1847	1948	2048	...	2205
Filisur 545a d.	0542	...	0634	0650	0801	0901	1001	1101	1201	1301	1401	1501	1601	1701	|	...	1744	1800s	...	1801	1901	2001	2101	...	2221s
Tiefencastel d.	0556	...	0651	0704	0815	0915	1015	1115	1215	1315	1415	1515	1615	1715	1732s	...	...	1815s	...	1815	1915	2015	2115	...	2235s
Thusis d.	0612	...	0711	0721	0833	0933	1033	1133	1233	1333	1433	1533	1633	1733	1751s	...	...	1831s	...	1833	1933	2033	2133	...	2251s
Reichenau-Tamins **575** d.	0633	...	|	0747	0853	0953	1053	1153	1253	1353	1453	1553	1653	1753	|	...	...	1852s	...	1853	1953	2055	2155	...	|
Chur 575 a.	0645	...	0741	0759	0903	1003	1103	1203	1303	1403	1503	1603	1703	1803	1828	...	...	1903	...	1903	2003	2109	2209	...	2325

♦ – **NOTES** (LISTED BY TRAIN NUMBER)

950/1 – BERNINA EXPRESS – May 16 - Oct. 18: 🚃 [observation cars] and 🍸 Tirano - Pontresina - Chur and v.v.
953/4 – BERNINA EXPRESS – Dec. 14 - May 15, Oct. 19 - Dec. 12: 🚃 [observation cars] Chur - Pontresina - Tirano and v.v.
960/1 – BERNINA EXPRESS – May 16 - Oct. 18: 🚃 [observation cars] and 🍸 Tirano - Pontresina - Davos and v.v.
1325 – ENGADIN STAR – May 16 - Oct. 18: 🚃 Landquart - Klosters - St Moritz.
1360 – ENGADIN STAR – Ⓒ (daily May 16 - Oct. 18): 🚃 St Moritz - Klosters - Landquart.

S – 🚃 St Moritz - Klosters and v.v.
p – ⑥ Dec. 20 - Mar. 28.
q – ⑤ Jan. 9 - Mar. 6.
s – Stops to set down only.
u – Stops to pick up only.
x – Stops on request only.

⊗ – Mixed train. Times subject to variation.
‡ – Conveys ✕ on some dates.
⊡ – Conveys 🍸 on some dates.
◐ – Conveys 🚃 [observation cars] Dec. 20 - Apr. 13, Ⓡ, ✓.
✓ – Supplement payable.

RhB. Narrow gauge CHUR - AROSA 541

km		⚒			y		y		and				z
0	**Chur** d.	0519	0625	0808	0852	0908	0952	1008	and	1908	2004	2104	2255
18	Langwies d.	0600	0709	0849	0931	0949	1031	1049	hourly	1949	2043	2145	2336x
26	Arosa a.	0618	0727	0909	0948	1009	1048	1109	until	2009	2103	2205	2353

	⚒	Ⓐ	Ⓒ				w		and			y
Arosa d.	0556	0628	0651	0748	0848	0948	1027	1048	and	1948	2108	2359
Langwies d.	0613	0644	0708	0804	0904	1004	1049	1104	hourly	2004	2123	0016x
Chur a.	0656	0726	0752	0852	0952	1052	1139	1152	until	2052	2207	0059

w – ⑥ Jan. 3 - Feb. 28.
x – Stops on request only.
y – Ⓒ Jan. 2 - Mar. 1.
z – Operated by 🚌 ①②③④⑦ Apr. 14 - Nov. 26 (not May 20, 21, 31).

PA 🚌 CHUR - FLIMS 542

🚌 **Chur** (Bahnhof) - **Flims Dorf** (Post), ± 35 minutes, and **Flims Waldhaus** (Post), ± 40 minutes.

From **Chur**:
Ⓐ: 0603, 0640, 0658, 0758, 0858, 0958, 1058, 1120, 1158, 1245, 1258, 1358, 1458, 1558, 1620, 1658, 1720, 1740, 1758, 1820, 1858, 2000, 2100, 2200, 2300.
Ⓒ: 0603⑥, 0658, 0758 and hourly until 1658, 1720⑥, 1758, 1858, 2000, 2100, 2200, 2300.

From **Flims Waldhaus** (± 5 minutes from Flims Dorf):
Ⓐ: 0516, 0613, 0659, 0700, 0714 and hourly until 1114, 1149, 1214, 1259, 1314 and hourly until 1814, 1843, 1918, 2018, 2113, 2213, 2313.
Ⓒ: 0516⑥, 0613, 0714 and hourly until 1814, 1918, 2018, 2113, 2213, 2313.

AP, FNM, PA, RhB* BERNINA and POSCHIAVO 🚌 services 543

TIRANO - APRICA and EDOLO

	⚒	⚒	⚒	⚒	⚒	⚒y	⚒	⚒	⚒	⚒
Tirano Stazione d.	...	...	1030	...	...	1205	...	1430	1655	...
Aprica S Pietro a.	0647	0907	1115	1125	1232	1250	1402	1510	1740	1842
Edolo a.	0730	0935	...	1153	1300	...	1430	...	...	1910

	⚒	⚒z	⚒	⚒	⚒	⚒	⚒	⚒	⚒	⚒
Edolo d.	0615	...	0830	1050	...	1200	1325	...	...	1755
Aprica d.	0643	0700	0858	1118	1120	1228	1353	1515	1745	1838
Tirano Stazione a.	...	0745	...	...	1200	...	...	1600	1825	...

ST MORITZ and TIRANO - LUGANO

	P Ⓡ		B Ⓡ
St Moritz Bahnhof ◧ d.	1220	...	...
Tirano d.	|	...	1425
Chiavenna Stazione d.	1410	...	|
Menaggio ◐ d.	1505x	...	◐
Lugano Stazione a.	1610s	...	1730
Lugano Via S. Balestra a.	1620	...	1740

	B Ⓡ		Q Ⓡ
Lugano Via S. Balestra d.	0945	...	1120
Lugano Stazione ◐ d.	1000	...	1140u
Menaggio d.	◐	...	1230x
Chiavenna Stazione d.	|	...	1400
Tirano a.	1255	...	|
St Moritz Bahnhof ◧ a.	...	...	1525

B – Bernina Express service. Runs Apr. 3 - Oct. 18.
P – Palm Express service. Runs daily Dec. 19 - Jan. 4; ⑤⑥⑦ Jan. 9 - June 7; daily June 12 - Oct. 18; ⑤⑥⑦ Oct. 23 - Dec. 12.
Q – Palm Express service. Runs ①⑥⑦ Dec. 14 - 15; daily Dec. 20 - Jan. 5; ①⑥⑦ Jan. 10 - June 8; daily June 13 - Oct. 19; ①⑥⑦ Oct. 24 - Dec. 12.
s – Stops to set down only.
u – Stops to pick up only.
x – Calls only if advance reservation is made.
y – Depart 1245 on schooldays.
z – Depart 0655 on schooldays.

◧ – 🏛 is at Castasegna.
◐ – 🏛 is at Gandria.

* – Operators:
Tirano - Aprica: Automobilistica Perego (AP): ✆ (0342) 701 200; fax (0342) 704 400;
Aprica - Edolo: FNM Autoservizi, Reservation: ✆ (02) 96 19 23 10; fax (02) 96 19 23 99;
Tirano - Lugano: RhB, Reservation: ✆ Poschiavo (081) 288 54 54; fax (081) 288 54 47;
St Moritz - Lugano: PA, Reservation: ✆ St Moritz (081) 833 94 40; fax (081) 833 94 45.

544 🚌 CHUR - BELLINZONA and CHIAVENNA — PA

km			[R]j	V[R]h	V[R]		Yk	[R]	V[R]h		[R]	V[R]h		[R]	V[R]		[R]	Yk	V[R]h		[R]		[R]⟋g	[R]⟋f
0	**Chur** Bahnhof **540** d.	...	0808	0813	0913	...	...	1008	1113	...	1208	1313	...	1408	1513	...	1608	...	1713	...	1808	...	...	...
40	Thusis Bahnhof **540** d.	0735	0835u	0840u	0940u	0935	...	1035u	1140u	1135	1235u	1340u	1335	1435u	1540u	1535	1635u	...	1740u	1735	1835u	1935	2240	2340
64	Splügen Post d.	0809	0904	0904	1004	1009	1020	1104	1204	1209	1304	1404	1409	1504	1604	1609	1704	1715	1804	1809	1904	2007	2320	0020
	San Bernardino Posta a.	0829	0923	0923	1023	1029	|	1123	1223	1229	1323	1423	1429	1523	1623	1629	1723	|	1823	1829	1923	2027	...	...
	Chiavenna Stazione ◐ a.	|	|	|	|	|	1215	|	|	|	|	|	|	|	|	|	|	1910	|	|	|	|	...	...
179	**Bellinzona** Stazione a.	*0950*	1020	1013	1113	*1150*	...	1220	1313	*1350*	1420	1513	*1550*	1620	1713	*1750*	1820	...	1913	*1950*	2020	*2150*	...	...

		Yk		V[R]h	V[R]		V[R]	V[R]		V[R]h	V[R]		V[R]	Yk	V[R]j	V[R]h		V[R]h	V[R]		V[R]	[R]⟋g	[R]⟋e
Bellinzona Stazione d.	...	*0707*	...	*0807*	0845	0940	*1007*	1045	1140	*1207*	1245	1340	*1407*	1445	...	1540	1545	*1607*	1645	1740	*1807*	1840r	...	...
Chiavenna Stazione ◐ d.	...	|	0750	|	|	|	|	|	|	|	|	|	|	|	1430	|	|	|	|	|	|	|	...	...
San Bernardino Posta d.	...	0823	|	0923	0935	1033	1123	1135	1233	1323	1335	1433	1523	1535	|	1633	1635	1723	1735	1833	1923	1935	...	...
Splügen Post d.	0745	0845	0940	0945	0953	1053	1145	1153	1253	1345	1353	1453	1545	1553	1625	1653	1653	1745	1753	1853	1945	1953	2332	0032
Thusis Bahnhof **540** d.	0825	0925	...	1025	1020s	1125s	1225	1220s	1325s	1425	1420s	1525s	1625	1620s	...	1725s	1720s	1825	1820s	1925s	2021	2020s	2359	0059
Chur Bahnhof **540** a.	...	...	...	...	1045	1150	...	1245	1350	...	1445	1550	...	1645	...	1750	1745	...	1845	1950	...	2045	...	...

V – San Bernardino Route Express.
Y – Splügen Pass service.
e – ⑥⑦ (also Dec. 27, Apr. 11).
f – ①②③④⑦ (also Dec. 26, Apr. 10).
g – ⑤⑥ (not Dec. 26, Apr. 10).
h – June 13 - Oct. 18.
j – Dec. 14 - June 12, Oct. 19 - Dec. 12.
k – June 13 - Oct. 11.
r – Depart 1845 on ⚒.
s – Stops to set down only.
u – Stops to pick up only.
◐ – 🚌 is at Splügen Pass.
⟋ – Supplement payable.
Reservations: ✆ Chur (058) 386 31 66.

545 LANDQUART - KLOSTERS - DAVOS / SCUOL TARASP — Narrow gauge. RhB

Valid March 16 - November 22. Engineering work Ardez - Scuol-Tarasp and v.v.; connections by 🚌

km		⊗ Ⓐ	⚒	Ⓐ					E				ⒸL		A								
	Chur d.	...	...	*0550*	...	...	0720	0752	...	...	0820	0852	...	...	0920	...	1020			1720	...	1820	...
0	**Landquart** d.	0451	0525	0615	0647	0747	0749k	0809	0820	0847	0849k	0909	0920	0947	0949k	1047	1049k	and at	1747	1749k	1847	1849k	...
21	Küblis d.	0511x	0555	0644	0713	0811	0815	...	0847	0911	0915	...	0947	1011	1015	1111	1115	the same	1811	1815	1911	1915	...
30	Klosters Dorf d.	0524x	0609	0658	0726	|	0828	...	|	|	0928	...	|	|	1028	|	1128	minutes	|	1828	|	1928	...
32	**Klosters** 🚗 d.	0529	0617	0702	0734	0828	0834	...	0903	0928	0934	...	1003	1028	1034	1128	1134	past each	1828	1834	1928	1934	...
	Sagliains **546** 🚗 §a.	|	|	|	0754	|	0853	...	...	|	0953	...	...	|	1053	|	1153	hour	|	1853	|	1953	2004
	Ardez 🚌 a.	|	|	|	0808	|	0904	...	...	|	1004	...	...	|	1104	|	1204	until	|	...	|	...	2014
	Scuol-Tarasp 546 🚌 a.	|	|	|	*0828*	|	*0928*	...	...	|	*1017*	...	...	|	*1128*	|	*1228*		|	...	|	...	*2028*
47	Davos Dorf d.	0550	0640	0725	...	0850	...	...	...	0950	...	...	...	1050	...	1150	...		1850	...	1950	...	...
50	**Davos Platz 545a** a.	0556	0647	0729	...	0855	...	...	...	0955	...	...	...	1055	...	1155	...		1855	...	1955	...	...

								🚌 y
Chur d.	*1920*	...	*1952*	...	*2052*	*2152*	...	...
Landquart d.	1947	...	2047	...	2147	2247	...	0043
Küblis d.	2013	...	2113	...	2213	2313	...	0112
Klosters Dorf d.	2025	...	2125	...	2225	2325	...	0127
Klosters 🚗 d.	2030	2033	2130	2133	2230	2330	...	0132
Sagliains **546** 🚗 § a.	|	2054	|	2154	|	|	...	|
Ardez 🚌 a.	|	2108	|	2208	|	|	...	|
Scuol-Tarasp 546 🚌 a.	|	*2122*	|	*2222*	|	|	...	|
Davos Dorf d.	2053	...	2153	...	2253	2353	...	0147
Davos Platz 545a a.	2057	...	2157	...	2257	2357	...	0153

	⚒		Ⓐ						
Davos Platz 545a d.	0454	0550	0627	0702	...	0802	...	0902	...
Davos Dorf d.	0457	0553	0630	0705	...	0805	...	0905	...
Scuol-Tarasp 546 🚌 d.	|	|	|	|	*0730*	|	*0830*	|	*0930*
Ardez 🚌 d.	|	|	|	|	0745	|	0850	|	0950
Sagliains **546** 🚗 § d.	|	|	|	|	0803	|	0903	|	1003
Klosters 🚗 d.	0520	0617	0654	0729	0825	0832	0925	0932	1025
Klosters Dorf d.	0523	0620	0657	0732	0828	|	0928	|	1028
Küblis d.	0538	0634	0712	0746	0843	0848	0943	0948	1043
Landquart a.	0607	0706	0738	0813	0910	0913k	1010	1013k	1110
Chur a.	0638	0730a	*0806*	...	0938	...	1038	...	1138

km											G			Lq							🚌		🚌
	Davos Platz 545a d.	1002	...	1102	...	...	1202		...	1702	...	...	1802	...	...	1902	...	2002	...	2102	...	...	...
	Davos Dorf d.	1005	...	1105	...	...	1205	and at	...	1705	...	...	1805	...	...	1905	...	2005	...	2105	...	...	...
0	**Scuol-Tarasp 546** 🚌 d.	|	*1030*	|	...	*1130*	|	the same	*1630*	|	...	*1730*	|	...	*1830*	|	*1930*	|	*2036*	|	...	*2130*	...
	Ardez 🚌 d.	|	1050	|	...	1150	|	minutes	1650	|	...	1750	|	...	1850	|	1950	|	2046	|	...	2145	...
17	Sagliains **546** 🚗 §d.	|	1103	|	...	1203	|	past each	1703	|	...	1803	|	...	1903	|	2003	|	2103	|	...	2203	...
39	**Klosters** 🚗 d.	1032	1125	1132	...	1225	1232	hour	1725	1732	1754	1825	1832	1854	1925	1932	2024	2029	2124	2129	...	2229	...
	Klosters Dorf d.	|	1128	|	...	1228	|	until	1728	|	|	1828	|	|	1928	|	▬	2032	▬	2132	...	2232	...
	Küblis d.	1048	1143	1148	...	1243	1248		1743	1748	1813	1843	1848	1913	1943	1948	🚌	2046	🚌	2146	...	2246	...
	Landquart a.	1113k	1210	1213k	...	1310	1313		1810	1813k	1836	1910	1913k	1936	2010	2013k	2045	2113	2145	2213	2242	2313	2342
	Chur a.	...	1238	...	...	1338	...		1838	...	...	1938	...	...	2038j	...	2109	...	2209	...	2306	...	0014

A – RE AQUALINO – (12) Disentis/Mustér - Scuol-Tarasp.
E – ENGADIN STAR – May 16 - Oct. 18: (12) Landquart - Klosters - St Moritz.
G – ENGADIN STAR – Ⓒ (daily May 16 - Oct. 18): (12) St Moritz - Klosters - Landquart.
L – (12) Landquart - St Moritz and v.v.
a – Ⓐ only.
j – By connecting train on Ⓐ.
k – Connects with train in previous column.
q – Ⓒ May 16 - Oct. 18.
x – Stops on request only.
y – ⑥⑦ (also Apr. 10, May 21; not Apr. 11).
§ – Sagliains station can only be used for changing trains.
⊗ – Mixed train. Times subject to variation.
🚗 – Car-carrying shuttle available (see page 260).

545a DAVOS - FILISUR — Narrow gauge. RhB

For *Glacier Express* services see Table **575**

km		⚒						961 ♦[R]⟋									p						
0	**Davos Platz 545** d.	0605	...	0731	...	0831	...	0850u	...	0931	...	...	1031	and hourly	1931	...	2031	...	...	...	...	...	...
16	**Filisur 540** a.	0630	...	0756	...	0856	...	0917u	...	0956	...	...	1056	until	1956	...	2056	...	...	...	...	...	...

	⚒									960 ♦[R]⟋								p				
Filisur 540 d.	0635	...	0804	and hourly	1604	...	...	1704	...	1744s	...	1804	...	1904	...	2004	...	2107	...	...	...	...
Davos Platz 545 a.	0700	...	0829	until	1629	...	...	1729	...	1809s	...	1829	...	1929	...	2029	...	2132	...	...	...	...

♦ – **NOTES** (LISTED BY TRAIN NUMBER)
960/1 – BERNINA EXPRESS – May 16 - Oct. 18: (12) [observation cars] and 🍸 Tirano - Pontresina - Davos and v.v.
p – May 16 - Oct. 18.
s – Stops to set down only.
u – Stops to pick up only.
⟋ – Supplement payable.

508 PAYERNE - MURTEN - KERZERS (- LYSS) — BLS

km		⚒		⚒					
0	Payerne **523** ⊡ d.	0556	0634	0701	0734	and at the same minutes	2134	2236	0006
11	Avenches ⊡ d.	0609	0648	0710	0748	past each	2148	2248	0017
18	Murten ⊡ a.	0616	0656	0717	0756	hour until	2156	2256	0024

	Ⓐ	⚒	†	⚒				
Murten ⊡ d.	0514	0602	0603	0643	0703	and at the same minutes	2203	2342
Avenches ⊡ d.	0522	0611	0611	0649	0711	past each	2211	2350
Payerne **523** ⊡ a.	0534	0624	0624	0657	0724	hour until	2224	0002

km		Ⓐ		Ⓐ		Ⓐ		Ⓐ					Ⓐ		Ⓐ		Ⓐ							
0	Murten d.	0547	0617	0647	0717	0747	0817	0847	0917	and hourly	1617	...	1647	1717	1747	1817	1847	1917	...	2017	2117	2217	2317	0025
8	Kerzers ▲ a.	0556	0626	0656	0726	0756	0826	0856	0926	until	1626	...	1656	1726	1756	1826	1856	1926	...	2026	2126	2226	2326	0034

	Ⓐ	Ⓐ	Ⓐ		Ⓐ		Ⓐ					Ⓐ		Ⓐ		Ⓐ							
Kerzers ▲ d.	0504	0534	0604	0634	0704	0734	0804	0834	and hourly	1634	...	1704	1734	1804	1834	1904	1934	...	2034	2138	2234	2334	0040
Murten a.	0513	0543	0613	0643	0713	0743	0813	0843	until	1643	...	1713	1743	1813	1843	1913	1943	...	2043	2147	2243	2342	0049

⊡ – Additional services operate at peak times.

▲ – **Rail service KERZERS - LYSS and v.v.:** *17 km*, journey 20 minutes.
From **Kerzers**: 0606 and hourly until 2306. From **Lyss**: 0532, 0632 and hourly until 2232, then 0011.

PONTRESINA / ST MORITZ - SCUOL TARASP — 546

Narrow gauge. RhB

km		⚒ S	⚒	⚒	⚒	†	† P																y	E	
0	**St Moritz 540/7** d.	0500	0540	...	0604	0557	...	...	0704	...	0804	...	...	0904	...	1004	...	...	1104		...	1604	...	1635	...
	Pontresina 540/7 d.	|	|	...	|	|	0557	0702	|	0802	|	...	0902	|	1002	|	...	1102	|	and at	1602	|	1638	|	1702
5	Samedan **540** a.	0507	0548	...	0610	0605	0603	0708	0711k	0808	0811k	...	0908	0911k	1008	1011k	...	1108	1111k	the same	1608	1611k	1644	1642	1708
5	Samedan d.	0507	...	0555	0611	...	0617	0714	...	0814	...	...	0914	...	1014	...	...	1114	...	minutes	1614	...	...	1646	1714
15	Zuoz d.	0521	...	0608	0624	...	0630	0727	...	0827	...	...	0927	...	1027	...	...	1127	...	past each	1627	...	...	1659	1727
32	Zernez ⊖ d.	0540	...	0638	...	...	0649	0747	...	0849	...	...	0949	...	1049	...	...	1149	...	hour	1649	...	...	1720	1749
38	Susch d.	0546	...	0644	...	...	0655	0753	...	0855	...	...	0955	...	1055	...	...	1155	...	until	1655	...	...	...	1755
40	Sagliains **545** § a.	0550	...	0647	...	...	0700	0757	...	0900	...	...	1000	...	1100	...	...	1200	...		1700	...	...	...	1800
57	**Scuol-Tarasp 545** a.	...	...	0709x	...	...	...	0819x	...	0925x	...	...	1025x	...	1125x	...	...	1225x	...		1725x	...	...	...	1825x

		M									
St Moritz 540/7 d.	1704	1735	...	1804	...	1904	...	2004	...	2104	...
Pontresina 540/7 d.	|	|	1802	|	1902	|	2002	|	2102	|	2202j
Samedan **540** a.	1711k	1742	1808	1811k	1908	1911k	2008	2011k	2108	2111k	2208j
Samedan d.	...	1746	1814	...	1914	...	2014	—	2114	—	2214
Zuoz d.	...	1759	1827	...	1927	...	2027	...	2127	...	2227
Zernez ⊖ d.	...	1820	1849	...	1949	...	2047	...	2147	...	2247
Susch d.	...	...	1855	...	1955	...	2053	...	2153	...	2253
Sagliains **545** § a.	...	...	1900	...	2000	...	2057	2059	2157	2159	2257
Scuol-Tarasp 545 a.	...	...	1925x	...	2025x	...	...	2119x	...	2219x	2317x

	⚒	⚒						F	y		
Scuol-Tarasp 545 d.	...	0607v	0642v	0738v	...	0834v	...	...	...	0934v	...
Sagliains **545** § d.	...	|	0702	0758	0803	0856	...	...	...	0956	...
Susch d.	...	0631	0705	...	0805	0858	...	...	...	0958	...
Zernez ⊖ d.	...	0638	0713	...	0813	0908	...	0933	...	1008	...
Zuoz d.	0634	0657	0734	...	0834	0927	...	0956	...	1027	...
Samedan a.	0649	0711	0749	...	0849	0942	...	1006	...	1042	...
Samedan **540** d.	0650	0712	0751	...	0851	0949	0950	1011	1008	1043r	1050
Pontresina 540/7 a.	0656	|	0757	...	0857	0956	|	|	1014	1049r	|
St Moritz 540/7 a.	...	0719	...	...	...	...	0958	1018	...	...	1058

	L															K
Scuol-Tarasp 545 d.	...	1034v	...		1834v	...	1934v	...	...	2038v	...	...	2138v	...	...	...
Sagliains **545** § d.	...	1056	...	and at	1856	...	1956	...	...	2058	2103	...	2158	2203	...	2257
Susch d.	...	1058	...	the same	1858	...	1958	...	...	...	2105	...	...	2205	...	2259
Zernez ⊖ d.	1033	1108	...	minutes	1908	...	2008	...	...	...	2113	...	...	2213	...	2307
Zuoz d.	1056	1127	...	past each	1927	...	2027	...	...	...	2134	...	...	2234	...	2327
Samedan a.	1109	1142	...	hour	1942	...	2042	...	...	...	2149	...	...	2249	...	2340
Samedan **540** d.	1111	1149	1150	until	1949	1950	...	2050	2051	...	2151	2151	...	2251	2251	2341
Pontresina 540/7 a.	|	1156	|		1956	|	...	|	2057	...	2157	|	...	2257	|	|
St Moritz 540/7 a.	1118	...	1158		...	1958	...	2058	...	...	...	2159	...	...	2259	2348

⊖ – 🚌 service **Zernez - Malles and v.v.** (journey 1 h 35 minutes):
From **Zernez posta**: 0715, 0815 **y**, 0915, 1015 **y**, 1115, 1215 **y**, 1315, 1415 **y**, 1515, 1615 **y**, 1715, 1815 **y**.
From **Malles / Mals bahnhof**: 0703 **y**, 0803 **y**, 0903, 1003 **y**, 1103, 1203 **y**, 1303, 1403 **y**, 1503, 1603 **y**, 1703, 1803 **y**, 1903.
Operator: AutoDaPosta (PA), Agentura Scuol, CH-7550 Scuol. ✆ +41 (0)81 864 16 83, fax +41 (0)81 864 91 48.

E – ENGADIN STAR – © (daily May 16 - Oct. 18): (12) St Moritz - Landquart.
F – ENGADIN STAR – May 16 - Oct. 18: (12) Landquart - St Moritz.
K – (12) Klosters (d. 2232) - St Moritz.
L – ©: (12) Landquart - St Moritz.
M – © May 16 - Oct. 18: (12) St Moritz - Landquart.
P – (12) Pontresina - Klosters (a. 0725).
S – (12) St Moritz - Klosters (a. 0615).
j – ⑧ (also Aug. 1).
k – Connects with train in previous column.
r – By connecting train May 16 - Oct. 18 (6 minutes later).
v – Mar. 16 - Nov. 22 replaced by 🚌 Scuol-Tarasp - Ardez (between Scuol-Tarasp and Sagliains; depart up to 8 minutes earlier).
x – Mar. 16 - Nov. 22 replaced by 🚌 Ardez (between Sagliains and Scuol-Tarasp) - Scuol-Tarasp (arrive up to 12 minutes later).
y – May 16 - Oct. 18.
§ – Sagliains station can only be used for changing trains.

ST MORITZ - TIRANO — 547

Narrow gauge. RhB — May 16 - October 18

km		🚌	⊗	⊗				y	971 ♦🅁⚡	y	961 ♦🅁⚡	951 ♦🅁⚡	y				973 ♦🅁⚡						977 ♦🅁⚡		
0	**St Moritz** d.	...	...	...	...	0745	0845	0915	0941	1003	...	...	1043	1045	1145	...	1145	...	1245	1345	1445	1545	1545	...	1645
2	Celerina Staz ⊡ d.	...	...	...	...	0748	0848	|	|	|	...	...	|	1048	1148	...	1148u	...	1248	1348	1448	1548	1548u	...	1648
6	**Pontresina** a.	...	...	...	...	0755	0855	|	0950	1012	...	...	1052	1055	1155	...	|	...	1255	1355	1455	1555	|	...	1655
6	**Pontresina 540** d.	...	...	...	0704	0809	0904	0927	0956	—	1023	1035	1055	1109	...	...	1204u	...	1304	1409	1504	...	1609u	...	1704
12	Morteratsch ⊡ d.	...	...	...	0713	0818	0913	0935	1005	...	|	|	1103	1118	...	...	1213	...	1313	1418	1513	...	1618	...	1713
17	Bernina Diavolezza ⊡ d.	...	...	...	0723	0828	0923	0941	1013	...	1039	|	1111	1128	...	...	1223	...	1323	1428	1523	...	1628	...	1723
18	Bernina Lagalb ⊡ d.	...	...	...	0725	0830	0925	0943	|	...	|	|	1113	1130	...	...	1225	...	1325	1430	1525	...	1630	...	1725
22	Ospizio Bernina d.	...	...	...	0734	0839	0934	0957	1024	...	1049	|	1120	1139	...	...	1234	...	1334	1439	1534	...	1639	...	1734
27	Alp Grüm d.	...	...	...	0746	0853	0946	...	1037	...	1104	1114s	1139	1155	...	...	1249	...	1347	1454	1546	...	1653	...	1746
44	**Poschiavo** a.	...	...	...	0827	0935	1027	...	1115s	...	1141	1157s	1219	1239	...	...	1329s	...	1427	1535	1627	...	1735s	...	1827
44	**Poschiavo** d.	0610	0626	0736	0829	0938	1029	...	|	1117	1143	|	1226	1241	...	...	|	1332	1441	1548	1629	...	|	1737	1829
48	Le Prese d.	0616	0634x	0744x	0837	0946	1037	...	1124s	1124	1150	1206s	1233	1249	...	...	1341s	1341	1449	1546	1637	...	1746s	1746	1837
51	Miralago ⊡ d.	0620	0639	0749	0843	0952	1043	...	|	|	|	|	|	1255	...	...	1347s	1347	1455	1552	1643	...	1752s	1752	1843
54	Brusio ⊡ d.	0624	0647	0757	0851	1000	1051	...	1137s	1137	|	|	1245	1303	...	...	1355s	1355	1503	1600	1651	...	1800s	1800	1851
58	Campocologno 🛃 d.	0629	0657	0807	0903	1012	1103	...	1146s	1148	1212	1227s	1254	1315	...	...	1406s	1412	1517	1610	1703	...	1810s	1812	1903
61	**Tirano** a.	0638	0712	0823	0912	1021	1112	...	1157	1157	1220	1235	1306	1324	...	...	1419	1419	1526	1622	1712	...	1820	1820	1912

		⊗ Ⓐ		⊗		⊗		🚌 ⑤h	🚌	
St Moritz d.	1745	...	1845	...	1945	...	2020	...	...	...
Celerina Staz ⊡ d.	1748	...	1848	...	1948	...	2023	...	...	...
Pontresina a.	1755	...	1855	...	1955	...	2030	m	...	...
Pontresina 540 d.	...	1809	—	1904	—	2009	...	2057	...	...
Morteratsch ⊡ d.	...	1818	...	1913	...	2018	...	|	...	...
Bernina Diavolezza ⊡ d.	...	1828	...	1921	...	2026	...	|	...	...
Bernina Lagalb ⊡ d.	...	1830	...	1924	...	2029	...	|	...	...
Ospizio Bernina d.	...	1839x	...	1933x	...	2038x	...	|	...	...
Alp Grüm d.	...	1849x	🚌	1942x	...	2047x	...	|	...	...
Poschiavo a.	...	1935	Ⓐ	2029	🚌	2134	...	2135	...	...
Poschiavo d.	...	...	1937	...	2032	...	...	...	2137	...
Le Prese d.	...	...	1943s	...	2038s	...	...	...	2143s	...
Miralago ⊡ d.	...	...	1947s	...	2042s	...	...	...	2147s	...
Brusio ⊡ d.	...	...	1951s	...	2046s	...	...	...	2151s	...
Campocologno 🛃 d.	...	...	1955s	...	2050s	...	...	...	2155s	...
Tirano a.	...	...	2005	...	2100	...	...	...	2205	...

		⊗ Ⓐ	🚌					970 ♦🅁⚡		
Tirano d.	...	...	0650	...	...	0740	0850	0850	...	0940
Campocologno 🛃 d.	...	...	0657	...	...	0752	0901	0901u	...	0952
Brusio ⊡ d.	...	...	0702	...	...	0800	0909	0909u	...	1000
Miralago ⊡ d.	...	...	0707	...	...	0807	0916	0916u	...	1007
Le Prese d.	...	...	0711	...	...	0813	0922	0922u	...	1013
Poschiavo a.	...	...	0728	...	...	0823	0931	|	...	1023
Poschiavo d.	...	0628	—	0733	...	0825	...	0933u	...	1025
Alp Grüm d.	...	0705x	...	0815	...	0907	...	1015	...	1114
Ospizio Bernina d.	...	0714x	...	0824	...	0916	...	1024	...	1123
Bernina Lagalb ⊡ d.	...	0722	...	0832	...	0924	...	1032	...	1131
Bernina Diavolezza ⊡ d.	...	0724	...	0834	...	0926	...	1034	...	1133
Morteratsch ⊡ d.	...	0734	...	0844	...	0936	...	1044	...	1143
Pontresina 540 a.	...	0750	...	0858	...	0950	...	1056s	...	1156
Pontresina d.	0720	...	0756	0901	...	0952	...	|	1101	1202
Celerina Staz ⊡ d.	0725	...	0801	0906	...	0957	...	1106s	1106	1207
St Moritz a.	0731	...	0807	0912	...	1003	...	1112	1112	1213

	z				972 ♦🅁⚡				950 ♦🅁⚡	960 ♦🅁⚡		y		974 ♦🅁⚡			⊗		⊗			🚌 ⑤h	⊗	⊗	
Tirano d.	1000	1032	1140	1245	1245	...	1338	...	1404	1431	1449	...	...	1449	...	1540	1650	...	1740	...	...	...	1850	1940	...
Campocologno 🛃 d.	1010	1042	1152	1256	1256u	...	1348	...	1412u	1439	1457	...	...	1457	...	1552	1701	...	1752	...	...	...	1901	1952	...
Brusio ⊡ d.	1018	1050	1200	1304	1304u	...	1356	...	|	1447	1506	...	...	1506u	...	1600	1709	...	1800	...	...	...	1909	2000	...
Miralago ⊡ d.	|	1057	1207	1311	1311u	...	1403	...	|	|	|	...	...	|	...	1607	1716	...	1807	...	...	...	1916	2007	...
Le Prese d.	1030	1103	1213	1317	1317u	...	1409	...	1433u	1500	1519	...	...	1519u	...	1613	1722	...	1812x	...	...	...	1922	2012x	...
Poschiavo a.	1042	1113	1226	1326	|	...	1419	...	|	1508	1528	...	...	1528	...	1623	1732	...	1823	...	...	...	1932	2023	...
Poschiavo d.	1045	1115	1239	...	1332u	...	1425	...	1444u	1509	...	...	...	1535	...	1625	1734	...	1825	...	...	1915	...	...	...
Alp Grüm d.	1132	1211	1318	...	1415	...	1507	...	|	1548	...	1600	...	1616	...	1707	1811x	...	1902x	...	...	|	...	...	...
Ospizio Bernina d.	1141	1220	1335	...	1424	...	1516	...	|	1557	...	1608	...	1625	...	1716	1820x	...	1911x	...	...	|	...	...	...
Bernina Lagalb ⊡ d.	|	1228	1343	...	1432	...	1524	...	|	|	...	1617	...	|	...	1724	1828	...	1919	...	...	|	...	...	...
Bernina Diavolezza ⊡ d.	1151	1230	1345	...	1434	...	1526	...	|	|	...	1620	...	1635	...	1726	1830	...	1921	...	...	|	...	...	...
Morteratsch ⊡ d.	1200	1240	1354	...	1444	...	1536	...	|	|	...	1629	...	1645	...	1736	1840	...	1931	...	...	|	...	...	...
Pontresina 540 a.	1213	1255	1407	...	1457s	...	1550	...	1605	1628	...	1644	...	1658s	...	1750	1857	...	1950	...	...	2000	...	...	...
Pontresina d.	1215	1301	1409	...	|	1501	1556	...	...	...	...	1654	...	|	1701	1756	...	1901	...	1956	...	n	...	...	...
Celerina Staz ⊡ d.	1220	1306	1414	...	1506s	1506	1601	...	...	...	...	|	...	|	|	1801	...	1906	...	2001	...	...	...	...	...
St Moritz a.	1226	1312	1420	...	1512	1512	1607	...	...	...	...	1703	...	1711	1711	1807	...	1912	...	2007	...	...	...	...	...

♦ – **NOTES** (LISTED BY TRAIN NUMBER)

950/1 – BERNINA EXPRESS – (12) [observation cars] and 🍸 Chur - Pontresina - Tirano and v.v.
960/1 – BERNINA EXPRESS – (12) [observation cars] and 🍸 Davos - Pontresina - Tirano and v.v.
970/7 – BERNINA EXPRESS – (12) [observation cars] Tirano - St Moritz and v.v.
971/4 – BERNINA EXPRESS – (12) [observation cars] St Moritz - Tirano and v.v. Conveys 🍸 June 1 - Sept. 30.
972/3 – BERNINA EXPRESS – (12) [observation cars] Tirano - St Moritz and v.v.

h – May 29 - Oct. 16 (also May 20).
m – From Samedan (d. 2050).
n – To Samedan (a. 2008).
s – Stops to set down only.
u – Stops to pick up only.
x – Stops on request only.
y – June 27 - Sept. 27.
z – © (daily June 29 - Aug. 30).

◐ – Conveys (12) [observation cars], 🅁, ⚡.
⊗ – Mixed train. Times subject to variation.
⊡ – Request stop.
⚡ – Supplement payable.

550 LUZERN and ZÜRICH - LOCARNO, CHIASSO and MILANO

SBB, FS

	RE 14063	EC 131 ⊡		CIS 151 ⊙✕	IR 2257 △		CIS 13 ⊙✕ ♦	IR 2159 △	IR 2409 (🍷) R	IR 2259 z	ICN 667 ✕	IR 2163 △ y	IR 2163 q	IR 2411 (🍷) R	IR 2263 x	CIS 15 ⊙✕ M	IR 2165 △🍷		IR 2415 (🍷) R	ICN 671 ✕	IR 2267 △	IR 2417 (🍷) R	CIS 10017 ⊡	CIS 17 ⊙✕	IR 2169 △ W	
Basel SBB **565** d.	...	...	...	...	...	...	...	0603	...	...	...	0703	...	...	...	...	0803	...	...	0903	...	...	...	...	1003	...
Olten **565** d.	...	...	...	...	...	...	...	0630	...	...	...	0730	...	...	...	...	0830	...	...	0930	...	...	...	...	1030	...
Luzern 565 d.	...	...	...	...	...	...	...	0718	0740	...	...	0818	0820	0840	...	...	0918	...	0940	1018	...	1040	...	...	1118	...
Küssnacht am Rigi d.	...	...	...	...	...	...	...	|	0758	...	...	|	|	0858	...	...	|	...	0958	|	...	1058	...	...	|	...
Zürich HB d.	...	...	...	...	0609	...	0701	|	|	0731	0809	|	|	|	0831	0901	|	...	|	|	1009	|	1109	...	|	...
Zug d.	...	...	...	...	0631	...	0727	|	|	0757	0831	|	|	|	0857	0927	|	...	|	|	1031	|	1131	...	|	...
Arth-Goldau a.	...	...	...	...	0646k	...	0745	0745k	0811	0813	0846	0845	0849	0911	0913	0945	0945k	...	1011	1045	1046k	1111	1146	...	1145k	...
Arth-Goldau d.	...	...	...	...	0652	...	0750	0752	—	0815	0850	0852	0852	—	0915	0950	0952	...	—	1050	1052	—	1150	...	1152	...
Schwyz d.	...	...	...	...	0700	...	|	0800	...	|	|	0900	0900	...	|	|	1000	...	...	|	1100	...	|	...	1200	...
Brunnen d.	...	...	...	...	0704	...	|	0804	...	|	|	0904	0904	...	|	|	1004	...	...	|	1104	...	|	...	1204	...
Flüelen d.	...	...	...	...	0716	...	|	0816	...	|	|	0916	0916	...	|	|	1016	...	...	|	1116	...	|	...	1216	...
Erstfeld d.	...	...	...	...	0724	...	|	0824	...	|	|	0924	0924	...	|	|	1024	...	...	|	1124	...	|	...	1224	...
Göschenen d.	...	...	...	...	0750	...	|	0850	...	0902	|	0950	0950	...	1002	|	1050	...	...	|	1150	...	|	...	1250	...
Airolo d.	...	...	0657	...	0801	...	|	0901	...	0913	|	1001	1001	...	1013	|	1101	...	...	|	1201	...	|	...	1301	...
Faido d.	...	...	0715	...	0819	...	|	0919	...	|	|	1019	1019	...	|	|	1119	...	*IR*	|	1219	...	|	...	1319	...
Biasca d.	0552j	0652	0738	...	0840	...	|	0940	...	|	|	1040	1040	...	1052	|	1140	...	**133**	|	1240	...	|	...	1340	...
Bellinzona a.	0605j	0705	0751	...	0853	...	0921	0953	...	1005	1023	1053	1053	...	1105	1121	1153	...		1223	1253	...	1323	...	1353	...
Bellinzona ▲ d.	0607	0707	0757	...	0854	0857	0923	0954	0957	1009	1025	1054	1054	1057	1109	1123	1154	1157	1209	1225	1254	1257	1325	...	1354	1357
Locarno ▲ a.	|	|	|	...	0913	|	|	1013	|	|	|	1113	1113	|	|	|	1213	|	|	|	1313	|	|	...	1413	|
Lugano a.	0635	0735	0827	...	...	0927	0944	...	1027	1035	1046	...	...	1127	1135	1144	...	1227	1235	1246	...	1327	|	...	...	1427
Lugano d.	0637	0737	0828	0848	...	0928	0948	...	1028	1037	...	...	...	1128	1137	1148	...	1228	1237	...	...	1328	1346	1348	...	1428
Capolago-Riva San Vitale d.	|	|	0842	|	...	0942	|	...	1042	|	...	...	...	1142	|	|	...	1242	|	...	...	1342	...	|	...	1442
Mendrisio d.	0652	0752	0848	|	...	0948	|	...	1048	1053	...	...	...	1148	1153	|	...	1248	1252	...	...	1348	...	|	...	1448
Chiasso a.	0659	0759	0856	|	...	0956	|	...	1056	1059	...	...	...	1156	1159	|	...	1256	1259	...	...	1356	...	|	...	1456
Chiasso 🏛 d.	...	0804	0859	|	...	0959	|	...	1059	...	...	...	...	1159	...	|	...	1259	1304	...	...	1359	...	|	...	1459
Como San Giovanni § a.	...	0809	0903	0914	...	1003	1014	...	1103	...	...	...	...	1203	...	1214	...	1303	1309	...	...	1403	...	1414	...	1503
Milano Centrale § a.	...	0855	...	0950	...	...	1050	...	...	...	...	...	...	...	...	1250	...	...	1350	...	...	...	...	1450	...	...

	IR 2419 (🍷) R	ICN 675 ✕	IR 2271 △	IR 2421 (🍷) R	CIS 19 ⊙✕ M	IR 2173 △ W	IR 2423 (🍷) R	ICN 679 ✕	IR 2275 △	IR 2425 (🍷) R	CIS 10021 ⊡	CIS 21 ⊙✕	IR 2177 △		IR 2427 (🍷) R	ICN 683 ✕	IR 2279 △	IR 2429 (🍷) R	CIS 23 ⊙✕ Ma	CIS 23 ⊙✕ Mc	IR 2181 △	IR 2431 (🍷) R	ICN 687 ✕	IR 2283 △	IR 2435 (🍷) R	CIS 10025 ⊡
Basel SBB **565** d.	...	1103	...	...	...	1203	...	1303	...	...	...	...	1403	...	...	1503	...	...	...	...	1603	...	1703	...	...	...
Olten **565** d.	...	1130	...	...	...	1230	...	1330	...	...	...	...	1430	...	...	1530	...	...	...	...	1630	...	1730	...	...	...
Luzern 565 d.	1140	1218	...	1240	...	1318	1340	1418	...	1440	...	...	1518	...	1540	1618	...	1640	...	...	1718	1740	1818	...	1840	...
Küssnacht am Rigi d.	1158	|	...	1258	...	|	1358	|	...	1458	...	...	|	...	1558	|	...	1658	...	...	|	1758	|	...	1858	...
Zürich HB d.	|	|	1209	|	1309	|	|	|	1409	|	1509	...	|	...	|	|	1609	|	1701	1709	|	|	|	1809	|	1909
Zug d.	|	|	1231	|	1331	|	|	|	1431	|	1531	...	|	...	|	|	1631	|	1727	1731	|	|	|	1831	|	1931
Arth-Goldau a.	1211	1245	1246k	1311	1346	1345k	1411	1445	1446k	1511	1546	...	1545k	...	1611	1645	1646k	1711	1745	1746	1745k	1811	1845	1846k	1911	1946
Arth-Goldau d.	—	1250	1252	—	1350	1352	—	1450	1452	—	1550	...	1552	...	—	1650	1652	—	1750	1750	1752	...	1850	1852	...	1950
Schwyz d.	...	|	1300	...	|	1400	...	|	1500	...	|	...	1600	...	...	|	1700	...	|	|	1800	...	|	1900	...	|
Brunnen d.	...	|	1304	...	|	1404	...	|	1504	...	|	...	1604	...	...	|	1704	...	|	|	1804	...	|	1904	...	|
Flüelen d.	...	|	1316	...	|	1416	...	|	1516	...	|	...	1616	...	...	|	1716	...	|	|	1816	...	|	1916	...	|
Erstfeld d.	...	|	1324	...	|	1424	...	|	1524	...	|	...	1624	...	...	|	1724	...	|	|	1824	...	|	1924	...	|
Göschenen d.	...	|	1350	...	|	1450	...	|	1550	...	|	...	1650	...	...	|	1750	...	|	|	1850	...	|	1950	...	|
Airolo d.	...	|	1401	...	|	1501	...	|	1601	...	|	...	1701	...	...	|	1801	...	|	|	1901	...	|	2001	...	|
Faido d.	*EC*	|	1419	...	|	1519	...	|	1619	...	|	...	1719	...	*EC*	|	1819	...	|	|	1919	...	|	2019	...	|
Biasca d.	**171**	|	1440	...	|	1540	...	|	1640	...	|	...	1740	...	**175**	|	1840	...	|	|	1940	...	|	2040	...	|
Bellinzona a.	⊡	1423	1453	...	1523	1553	...	1623	1653	...	1723	...	1753	...	⊡	1823	1853	...	1921	1923	1953	...	2023	2053	...	2123
Bellinzona ▲ d.	1409	1425	1454	1457	1525	1554	1557	1625	1654	1657	1725	...	1754	1757	1809	1825	1854	1857	1923	1925	1954	...	2025	2054	...	2125
Locarno ▲ a.	|	|	1513	|	|	1613	|	|	1713	|	|	...	1813	|	|	|	1913	|	|	|	2013	...	|	|	...	|
Lugano a.	1435	1446	...	1527	1546	...	1627	1646	...	1727	1746	...	...	1827	1835	1846	...	1927	1944	1946	...	...	2046	2126	...	2146
Lugano d.	1437	...	...	1528	1548	...	1628	...	...	1728	...	1748	...	1828	1837	1848	...	1928	1948	1948	...	...	2048	2127	...	...
Capolago-Riva San Vitale d.	|	...	...	1542	|	...	1642	...	...	1742	...	|	...	1842	|	|	...	1942	|	|	...	...	|	2142	...	...
Mendrisio d.	1452	...	...	1548	|	...	1648	...	...	1748	...	|	...	1848	1852	|	...	1948	|	|	...	...	|	2149	...	...
Chiasso a.	1459	...	...	1556	|	...	1656	...	...	1756	...	|	...	1856	1859	1908	...	1956	|	|	...	...	2108	2158	...	...
Chiasso 🏛 d.	1504	...	...	1559	|	...	1659	...	...	1759	...	|	...	1859	1904	...	...	1959	|	|	...	...	...	...	...	...
Como San Giovanni § a.	1509	...	...	1603	1614	...	1703	...	...	1803	...	1814	...	1903	1909	...	...	2003	2014	2014	...	...	...	...	...	...
Milano Centrale § a.	1555	...	...	...	1650	...	...	...	...	...	...	1850	...	...	1950	...	...	...	2050	2050	...	...	...	...	...	...

	CIS 25 ⊙✕	IR 2187 △	IR 2437 (🍷) R	IC 2287 n	ICN 691 ✕	IR 2289 △	ICN 693	IR 2191	IR 2197	IR 2293 △	IR 2295
Basel SBB **565** d.	...	1803	...	...	1903	...	...	2003	...	...	...
Olten **565** d.	...	1830	...	...	1930	...	...	2030	...	...	...
Luzern 565 d.	...	1918	1940	...	2018	...	...	2118	2218	...	...
Küssnacht am Rigi d.	...	|	1958	...	|	...	...	|	|	...	...
Zürich HB d.	...	|	|	1931	|	2009	2109	|	|	2209	2309
Zug d.	...	|	|	1957	|	2031	2131	|	|	2231	2331
Arth-Goldau a.	...	1945k	2011	2013	2045	2046k	2146	2145k	2245	2246	2346
Arth-Goldau d.	...	1952	...	2015	2050	2052	2150	2154	...	2254	*2355*
Schwyz d.	...	2000	...	|	|	2100	|	2202	...	|	*0003*
Brunnen d.	...	2004	...	|	|	2104	|	2206	...	|	*0006*
Flüelen d.	...	2016	...	|	|	2116	|	2217	...	|	*0016*
Erstfeld d.	...	2024	...	|	|	2124	|	2227	...	2316	*0025*
Göschenen d.	...	2050	...	2102	|	2150	|	...	...	2340	...
Airolo d.	...	2101	...	2113	|	2201	|	...	...	2351	...
Faido d.	...	2119	...	|	|	2219	|	...	...	0009	...
Biasca d.	...	2140	...	2152	|	2240	|	...	...	0030	...
Bellinzona a.	...	2153	...	2205	2223	2253	2323	...	...	0042	...
Bellinzona ▲ d.	...	2154	...	2209	2225	...	2325	...	...	0043	...
Locarno ▲ a.	...	|	...	|	|	...	|	...	...	|	...
Lugano a.	...	2226	...	2235	2246	...	2346	...	...	0114	...
Lugano d.	2148	2227	...	2237	2248	...	2348	...	...	0116	...
Capolago-Riva San Vitale d.	|	2242	...	|	|	...	|	...	...	0130	...
Mendrisio d.	|	2249	...	2253	2302	...	0002	...	...	0138	...
Chiasso a.	|	2258	...	2259	2310	...	0010	...	...	0146	...
Chiasso 🏛 d.	|	...	...	...	...	...	...	...	...	...	...
Como San Giovanni § a.	2214	...	...	...	...	...	...	...	...	...	...
Milano Centrale § a.	2250	...	...	...	...	...	...	...	...	...	...

	ICN 650 ✕	IR 2164	IR 2166 △	ICN 654 ✕	IR 2408 (🍷) R	IR 2272 △	ICN 658 ✕	IR 2410 (🍷) R	IR 2170 △		CIS 12 ⊙✕
Milano Centrale § d.	...	...	...	...	...	...	...	...	...	...	0710
Como San Giovanni § d.	...	...	...	...	...	...	...	...	...	0725j	0745
Chiasso 🏛 a.	...	...	...	...	...	...	...	...	...	0731j	|
Chiasso d.	0448	...	...	0548	...	0611	0641	...	0711	0733	|
Mendrisio d.	0457	...	...	0557	...	0620	0650	...	0720	0742	|
Capolago-Riva San Vitale d.	|	...	...	|	...	|	|	...	|	0745	|
Lugano a.	0510	...	...	0610	...	0635	0705	...	0735	0800	0810
Lugano d.	0512	...	...	0612	...	0637	0712	...	0737	0800	...
Locarno ▲ d.	|	...	...	|	...	|	|	...	|	|	...
Bellinzona ▲ a.	0534	...	...	0634	...	0705	0734	...	0805	0830	...
Bellinzona d.	0536	...	0606	0636	...	0706	0736	...	0806	0839	...
Biasca d.	|	...	0618	|	...	0718	0735	...	0818	0855	...
Faido d.	|	...	0640	|	...	0740	|	...	0840	...	...
Airolo d.	|	...	0658	|	...	0758	|	...	0858	...	...
Göschenen d.	|	...	0708	|	...	0808	|	...	0908	...	...
Erstfeld d.	|	0627	0733	|	...	0833	|	...	0933	...	...
Flüelen d.	|	0636	0742	|	...	0842	|	...	0942	...	...
Brunnen d.	|	0651	0754	|	...	0854	|	...	0954	...	...
Schwyz d.	|	0656	0758	|	...	0858	|	...	0958	...	...
Arth-Goldau a.	0709	0706k	0806	0809k	...	0906	0909k	...	1006	...	...
Arth-Goldau d.	0713	0714	0814	0813	0848	0913	0914	0948	1014	...	...
Zug d.	0729	|	|	0829	|	0929	|	|	|	...	...
Zürich HB a.	0751	|	|	0851	|	0951	|	|	|	...	...
Küssnacht am Rigi d.	...	|	|	...	0859	...	|	0959	|	...	...
Luzern 565 a.	...	0741	0841	...	0920	...	0941	1020	1041	...	...
Olten **565** a.	...	0827	0927	...	...	...	1027	...	1127	...	...
Basel SBB **565** a.	...	0853	0953	...	...	...	1053	...	1153	...	...

♦ – **NOTES** (LISTED BY TRAIN NUMBER)

13 – [12] and ✕ Zürich - Milano - Firenze.

B – [12] and ✕ Basel - Milano.

M – [12] and ✕ Zürich - Milano.

R – VORALPEN EXPRESS – [12] Luzern - St Gallen - Romanshorn and v.v.

W – [12] Basel - Locarno and v.v. May 1 - Oct. 25 also conveys [1] [observation car] and runs as WILHELM TELL EXPRESS Flüelen - Locarno and v.v. Ⓡ

a – ①–⑤ only.

c – ⑥⑦ only.

j – Ⓐ (also Jan. 2, Apr. 10; not May 1).

k – Connects with train in previous column(s).

n – ⑤ (not Dec. 26, Jan. 2, Apr. 10).

p – ①–⑤ Dec. 15 - June 12 (not Dec. 25, 26, Jan. 1, 6, Apr. 13, May 1, June 2).

q – June 14 - Dec. 12.

x – Apr. 4 - Nov. 1.

y – Dec. 14 - June 13.

z – ⑥ (also ⑦ July 5 - Nov. 1).

⊙ – *CISALPINO Pendolino* train. Ⓡ inclusive of supplement for international journeys; may be used for Swiss internal journeys without reservation.

⊡ – Operated by *CISALPINO*. Ⓡ for international journeys; may be used for Swiss internal journeys without reservation.

△ – Also conveys [1] [observation car].

▲ – For additional services Locarno - Bellinzona and v.v. – see panel on page 277.

FS, SBB — MILANO, CHIASSO and LOCARNO - ZÜRICH and LUZERN — 550

km		CIS		IR	ICN	EC		IR	CIS		IR	ICN		IR	CIS	CIS		IR	ICN		IR	CIS		IR	ICN	IR
		10012		2276	662	132		2174	14		2280	666		2178	16	10016		2282	670		2182	18		2286	674	170
		⊡		△	✕	⊡		△	⊙✕		△	✕		△	⊙✕	⊡		△	✕		△	⊙✕		△	✕	
								W	M					W								M				
0	**Milano Centrale** § d.	...	...	...	...	0800	...	...	0910	...	...	...	...	...	1110	...	...	...	...	...	...	1310	...	...	...	1410
47	Como San Giovanni § d.	...	0755	...	...	0850	0855	...	0945	0955	...	...	1055	...	1145	...	1155	...	...	1255	...	1345	1355	...	...	1451
51	**Chiasso** 🏛 a.	...	0801	...	...	0856	0901	...	|	1001	...	...	1101	...	|	...	1201	...	...	1301	...	|	1401	...	...	1456
51	**Chiasso** d.	...	0803	...	0852	0900	0903	...	|	1003	...	...	1103	...	|	...	1203	...	...	1303	...	|	1403	...	...	1500
58	Mendrisio d.	...	0812	...	|	0907	0912	...	|	1012	...	...	1112	...	|	...	1212	...	...	1312	...	|	1412	...	...	1507
63	Capolago-Riva San Vitale d.	...	0815	...	|	|	0915	...	|	1015	...	...	1115	...	|	...	1215	...	...	1315	...	|	1415	...	...	|
77	**Lugano** a.	...	0830	...	0910	0922	0930	...	1010	1030	...	...	1130	...	1210	...	1230	...	...	1330	...	1410	1430	...	...	1522
77	**Lugano** d.	0812	0830	...	0912	0924	0930	...	1012	1030	...	1112	1130	...	...	1212	1230	...	1312	1330	...	1412	1430	...	1512	1524
	Locarno ▲ d.	|	|	0846	|	|	|	0946	|	|	1046	|	|	1146	...	|	|	1246	|	|	1346	|	|	1446	|	|
106	Bellinzona ▲ a.	0834	0900	0904	0934	0950	1000	1004	1034	1100	1104	1134	1200	1204	...	1234	1300	1304	1334	1400	1404	1434	1500	1504	1534	1550
106	Bellinzona d.	0836	▬	0906	0936	▬	...	1006	1036	▬	1106	1136	▬	1206	...	1236	▬	1306	1336	▬	1406	1436	▬	1506	1536	▬
125	Biasca d.	|	...	0918	|	...	...	1018	|	...	1118	|	...	1218	...	|	...	1318	|	...	1418	|	...	1518	|	...
151	Faido d.	|	...	0940	|	...	...	1040	|	...	1140	|	...	1240	...	|	...	1340	|	...	1440	|	...	1540	|	...
171	Airolo d.	|	...	0958	|	...	...	1058	|	...	1158	|	...	1258	...	|	...	1358	|	...	1458	|	...	1558	|	...
187	Göschenen d.	|	...	1008	|	...	...	1108	|	...	1208	|	...	1308	...	|	...	1408	|	...	1508	|	...	1608	|	...
216	Erstfeld d.	|	...	1033	|	...	...	1133	|	...	1233	|	...	1333	...	|	...	1433	|	...	1533	|	...	1633	|	...
225	Flüelen d.	|	*IR*	1042	|	*IR*	...	1142	|	*IR*	1242	|	*IR*	1342	...	|	*IR*	1442	|	*IR*	1542	|	*IR*	1642	|	*IR*
237	Brunnen d.	|	**2412**	1054	|	**2416**	...	1154	|	**2418**	1254	|	**2420**	1354	...	|	**2422**	1454	|	**2424**	1554	|	**2426**	1654	|	**2428**
240	Schwyz d.	|	(🍷)	1058	|	(🍷)	...	1158	|	(🍷)	1258	|	(🍷)	1358	...	|	(🍷)	1458	|	(🍷)	1558	|	(🍷)	1658	|	(🍷)
248	**Arth-Goldau** a.	1009**k**	**R**	1106	1109**k**	**R**	...	1206	1209**k**	**R**	1306	1309**k**	**R**	1406	...	1409**k**	**R**	1506	1509**k**	**R**	1606	1609**k**	**R**	1706	1709**k**	**R**
248	**Arth-Goldau** d.	1013	1048	1113	1114	1148	...	1214	1213	1248	1313	1314	1348	1414	...	1413	1448	1513	1514	1548	1614	1613	1648	1713	1714	1748
264	Zug d.	1029	|	1129	|	|	...	|	1229	|	1329	|	|	|	...	1429	|	1529	|	|	|	1629	|	1729	|	|
293	**Zürich HB** a.	1051	|	1151	|	|	...	|	1251	|	1351	|	|	|	...	1451	|	1551	|	|	|	1651	|	1751	|	|
*	Küssnacht am Rigi d.	...	1059	...	|	1159	...	|	...	1259	...	|	1359	|	...	...	1459	...	|	1559	|	...	1659	...	|	1759
*	**Luzern 565** a.	...	1120	...	1141	1220	...	1241	...	1320	...	1341	1420	1441	...	...	1520	...	1541	1620	1641	...	1720	...	1741	1820
	Olten **565** a.	...	...	...	1227	...	...	1327	...	...	...	1427	...	1527	...	...	...	...	1627	...	1727	...	...	...	1827	...
	Basel SBB **565** a.	...	...	...	1253	...	...	1353	...	...	...	1453	...	1553	...	...	...	...	1653	...	1753	...	...	...	1853	...

		IR	CIS	CIS	RE	IR		IR	ICN	EC		IR	CIS		IR	EC	CIS		IR	CIS		IR	CIS	CIS		EC
		2188	20	10020	14078	2288		2290	678	172		2192	22		2294	174	10156		2196	24		2298	158	10158		178
		△	⊙✕	⊡				△	✕	⊡		△	⊙✕		△	⊡	⊡		△	⊙✕		△	⊙✕	⊡		⊡
					j	m							♦			z				♦						v
Milano Centrale § d.	...	...	1510	...	...	...	...	...	...	1610	...	...	1710	...	...	1735	...	...	...	1910	...	...	2010	...	...	0010
Como San Giovanni § d.	1455	...	1545	...	...	...	1555	...	...	1650	1655	...	1745	1755	...	1820	...	1855	...	1945	1955	...	2045	...	2055	0050
Chiasso 🏛 a.	1501	...	|	...	...	...	1601	...	...	1656	1701	...	|	1801	...	1826	...	1901	...	|	2001	...	|	...	2101	0056
Chiasso d.	1503	...	|	...	1600	1600	1603	...	...	1700	1703	...	|	1803	...	1840	...	1903	...	|	2003	...	|	...	2103	0100
Mendrisio d.	1512	...	|	...	1607	1608	1612	...	...	1707	1712	...	|	1812	...	1848	...	1912	...	|	2012	...	|	...	2112	0107
Capolago-Riva San Vitale d.	1515	...	|	...	|	|	1615	...	...	|	1715	...	|	1815	...	|	...	1915	...	|	2015	...	|	...	2115	|
Lugano a.	1530	...	1610	...	1622	1623	1630	...	...	1722	1730	...	1810	1830	...	1904	...	1930	...	2010	2030	...	2110	...	2130	0122
Lugano d.	1530	...	...	1612	1624	1625	1630	...	1712	1724	1730	...	1812	1830	...	...	1912	1930	...	2012	2030	...	...	2112	2130	0124
Locarno ▲ d.	|	1546	...	|	|	|	|	1646	|	|	|	1746	|	|	1846	...	|	|	1946	|	|	2046	...	|	|	|
Bellinzona ▲ a.	1600	1604	...	1634	1650	1651	1700	1704	1734	1750	1802	1804	1834	1900	1904	...	1934	2000	2004	2034	2100	2104	...	2134	2200	0150
Bellinzona d.	...	1606	...	1636	▬	1654	...	1706	1736	▬	...	1806	1836	▬	1906	...	1936	...	2006	2036	...	2106	...	2136	...	...
Biasca d.	...	1618	...	|	...	1707	...	1718	|	...	...	1818	|		1918	...	|	...	2018	|	...	2118	...	|	...	...
Faido d.	...	1640	...	|	...	|	...	1740	|	...	...	1840	|	...	1940	...	|	...	2040	|	...	2140	...	|	...	...
Airolo d.	...	1658	...	|	...	1745	...	1758	|	...	...	1858	|	...	1958	...	|	...	2058	|	...	2158	...	|	...	...
Göschenen d.	...	1708	...	|	...	1757	...	1808	|	...	...	1908	|	...	2008	...	|	...	2108	|	...	2208	...	|	...	...
Erstfeld d.	...	1733	...	|	...	|	...	1833	|	...	...	1933	|	...	2033	...	|	...	2133	|	...	2233	...	|	...	...
Flüelen d.	...	1742	...	|	*IR*	|	...	1842	|	*IR*	...	1942	|	*IR*	2042	...	|	...	2142	|	...	2242	...	|	...	...
Brunnen d.	...	1754	...	|	**2430**	|	...	1854	|	**2432**	...	1954	|	**2436**	2054	...	|	...	2154	|	...	2254	...	|	...	...
Schwyz d.	...	1758	...	|	(🍷)	|	...	1858	|	(🍷)	...	1958	|	(🍷)	2058	...	|	...	2158	|	...	2258	...	|	...	...
Arth-Goldau a.	...	1806	...	1809**k**	**R**	1844**k**	...	1906	1909**k**	**R**	...	2006	2009**k**	**R**	2106	...	2109**k**	...	2206	2209**k**	...	2306	...	2309**k**	...	...
Arth-Goldau d.	...	1814	...	1813	1848	1846	...	1913	1914	1948	...	2014	2013	2048	2113	...	2114	...	2214	2213	...	2313	...	2314	...	...
Zug d.	...	|	...	1829	|	1903	...	1929	|	|	...	|	2029	|	2129	...	|	...	|	2229	...	2329	...	|	...	...
Zürich HB a.	...	|	...	1851	|	1928	...	1951	|	|	...	|	2051	|	2151	...	|	...	|	2251	...	2351	...	|	...	...
Küssnacht am Rigi d.	...	|	...	...	1859	...	...	...	|	1959	...	|	...	2059	...	...	|	...	|	...	...	...	...	|	...	...
Luzern 565 a.	...	1841	...	...	1920	...	...	...	1941	2020	...	2041	...	2120	...	...	2141	...	2241	...	...	...	...	2341	...	...
Olten **565** a.	...	1927	...	...	...	...	...	...	2027	...	...	2127	...	...	...	...	2227	...	2327	...	...	...	...	0027	...	...
Basel SBB **565** a.	...	1953	...	...	...	...	...	...	2053	...	...	2153	...	...	...	...	2253	...	2353	...	...	...	...	0056	...	...

▲ – Additional services **BELLINZONA - LOCARNO and v.v.**:

km									j			j											
0	Bellinzona d.	0500	0530	and at the same minutes past each hour until	1600	1630	...	1700	1716	1730	1800	1816	1830	...	1900	1930	and at the same minutes past each hour until	2300	2330	...	0000	0046	...	...
21	Locarno a.	0527	0557		1627	1657	...	1727	1742	1757	1827	1842	1857	...	1927	1957		2327	2357	...	0024	0110	...	...

										j			j										
Locarno d.	0533	...	0603	0633	and at the same minutes past each hour until	1603	1633	...	1703	1717	1733	1803	1817	1833	...	1903	1933	and at the same minutes past each hour until	2303	2333	...	0014	0044	0114
Bellinzona a.	0557	...	0627	0657		1627	1657	...	1727	1742	1757	1827	1842	1857	...	1927	1957		2327	2357	...	0036	0106	0136

§ – Additional services **MILANO PORTA GARIBALDI - COMO SAN GIOVANNI and v.v.** (2nd class only):

	⚒							
Milano Porta Garibaldi d.	0608	0638	0738	0838	and at the same minutes past each hour until	2038	2138	2238
Monza d.	0625	0655	0755	0855		2055	2155	2255
Como San Giovanni a.	0708	0738	0838	0938		2138	2238	2338

Como San Giovanni d.	0723	0823	0923	and at the same minutes past each hour until	1923	2023	2123	2223
Monza d.	0805	0905	1005		2005	2105	2205	2305
Milano Porta Garibaldi a.	0826	0922	1022		2022	2122	2222	2322

♦ – **NOTES** (LISTED BY TRAIN NUMBER)

24 – 🚃12 and ✕ Firenze - Milano - Zürich.

B – 🚃12 and ✕ Milano - Basel.

M – 🚃12 and ✕ Milano - Zürich.

R – VORALPEN EXPRESS – 🚃12 Romanshorn - St Gallen - Luzern.

W – 🚃12 Basel - Locarno and v.v. May 1 - Oct. 25 also conveys 🚃1 [observation car] and runs as WILHELM TELL EXPRESS Locarno - Flüelen. Ⓡ

j – Ⓐ (also Jan. 2, Apr. 10; not May 1).

k – Connects with train in previous column(s).

m – ⑦ July 5 - Nov. 1.

v – ①⑦ (also Apr. 14).

z – Not Apr. 13.

⊙ – *CISALPINO Pendolino* train. Ⓡ inclusive of supplement for international journeys; may be used for Swiss internal journeys without reservation.

⊡ – Operated by *CISALPINO*. Ⓡ for international journeys; may be used for Swiss internal journeys without reservation.

△ – Also conveys 🚃1 [observation car].

▲ – For additional services Locarno - Bellinzona and v.v. see panel.

* – Other distances: Arth-Goldau *0*, Küssnacht am Rigi *12 km*, Luzern *28 km*.

552 LUZERN - STANS - ENGELBERG

Narrow gauge rack railway. ZB

km		⚒						T			T											🚌			🚌			🚌		🚌
0	**Luzern 561** ..... d.	0609	0623	0641	0711	0741	0811	0834	0841	0911	0934	0941	1011		1941	2011	...	2041	...	2111	2141	...	2211	2241	...	2341	...
9	Hergiswil **561** .. d.	0625	0635	0655	0725	0755	0825	|	0855	0925	|	0955	1025	and	1955	2025	...	2055	...	2126	2155	...	2226	2255	...	2355	...
11	Stansstad .... d.	0629	0639	0659	0730	0759	0830	|	0859	0930	|	0959	1030	hourly	1959	2030	...	2059	...	2130	2159	...	2230	2259	...	2359	...
15	Stans .... d.	0633	0643	0704	0735	0803	0835	0852	0903	0935	0952	1003	1035	until	2003	2035	...	2105	...	2133	2205	...	2233	2305	...	0005	...
19	Dallenwil .... d.	0640	...	0708a	0740	...	0840	|	...	0940	|	...	1040		...	2040	...	2109	2111	...	2209	2211	...	2309	2311	0009	0011
34	**Engelberg** ...... a.	0712	...	...	0812	...	0912	0923	...	1012	1023	...	1112		...	2112	...	...	2132	...	...	2232	...	...	2332	...	0032

				Ⓐ										T			T						🚌		🚌		🚌	
Engelberg ....d.	...	...	...	...	0645	...	0745	...		1545	...	...	1628	1645	...	1728	1745	...		2045	...	2145	...	2245	...	2345	...
Dallenwil..........d.	0550	0607	...	0709	0718	0749a	0818	...	and	1618	...	...	|	1718	1749	|	1818	...	and	2118	...	2206	2212	2306	2312	0006	0012
Stans................d.	0555	0613	0655	0717	0725	0755	0825	0855	hourly	1625	1655	...	1707	1725	1755	1807	1825	1855	hourly	2125	2155	...	2225	...	2317	...	0018
Stansstad ....d.	0600	0617	0700	0721	0730	0800	0830	0900	until	1630	1700	...	|	1730	1800	|	1830	1900	until	2130	2200	...	2230	...	2321	...	0022
Hergiswil **561** ...d.	0604	0624	0705	0725	0734	0805	0834	0905		1634	1705	...	|	1734	1805	|	1834	1905		2134	2205	...	2234	...	2324	...	0025
Luzern 561 ......a.	0615	0636	0719	0734	0749	0819	0849	0919		1649	1719	...	1726	1749	1819	1826	1849	1919		2149	2219	...	2249	...	...	...	...

T – TITLIS EXPRESS – © Dec. 14 - Mar. 29; ⑥⑦ July 4 - Oct. 11.

a – Ⓐ only.

553 MOUNTAIN RAILWAYS IN CENTRAL SWITZERLAND

2nd class only. RB

km			p		S							p	q
0	Arth-Goldau.... d.	0800	0910	1010	1015	1110	1210	1310	1410	1510	1610	1710	1810
9	Rigi Kulm .... a.	0845	0947	1047	1205	1147	1247	1347	1447	1547	1647	1747	1847

		p					S				p	q
Rigi Kulm .... d.	0900	1004	1104	1204	1304	1404	1405	1504	1604	1704	1804	1904
Arth-Goldau. a.	0948	1048	1148	1248	1348	1448	1535	1548	1648	1748	1848	1948

km		Dec. 14 to May 20	m		and hourly until		m	m			May 21 to Sept. 13			r					V	r		and hourly until		
0	Rigi Kulm .... d.		0910	1000		1700	1800	1900	...	...		0915	1000	1050	1100	1200	1300	1400	1410	1430	1500		2000	2240
7	Vitznau........... a.		0949	1040		1740	1840	1940	...	...		0955	1040	1140	1140	1240	1340	1440	1505	1515	1540		2040	2320

	Dec. 14 to May 20	m		and hourly until		m	m			May 21 to Sept. 13				r	T			and hourly until					
Vitznau..................... d.		0835	0915		1615	1715	1815	...	...		0835	0915	1015	1050	1055	...	1115		1915	...	2205	...	...
Rigi Kulm .... a.		0905	0945		1645	1745	1845	...	...		0905	0945	1045	1120	1240	...	1145		1945	...	2235	...	...

ALPNACHSTAD - PILATUS KULM. Narrow gauge rack railway. *5 km*. Journey time: 30 minutes uphill, 40 minutes downhill. **Operator**: PB, ✆ 041 329 11 11.
Services run daily ***early May - Nov. 22*** (weather permitting). **NO WINTER SERVICE** (December - April).

From **Alpnachstad**: 0815 **j**, 0855, 0935, 1015, 1055, 1135, 1215, 1300, 1340, 1420, 1500, 1550, 1630 **j**, 1710 **k**, 1750 **x**, 1830 **x**.

From **Pilatus Kulm**: 0850 **j**, 0930, 1010, 1050, 1130, 1210, 1255, 1335, 1415, 1455, 1545, 1625, 1705 **j**, 1745 **k**, 1825 **x**, 1910 **x**.

BRIENZ - BRIENZER ROTHORN. Narrow gauge rack railway. *8 km*. Most services operated by steam train. Journey time: 55–60 minutes uphill, 60–70 minutes downhill.
Operator: BRB, ✆ 033 952 22 22. Service valid **May 24 - Oct. 26, 2008 (also May 17, 18)**, and is subject to demand and weather conditions on the mountain. A reduced service operates until June 6. Extra trains may run at busy times. **No winter service** (November - April).

From **Brienz**: 0737, 0837, 0937, 1005, 1040, 1145, 1245, 1345, 1445, 1545, 1620.

From **Brienzer Rothorn**: 0834, 0936, 1038, 1110, 1215, 1315, 1415, 1515, 1615, 1650, 1725.

S – 🚂 Steam train. Runs ⑥ July 4 - Sept. 26 from Arth-Goldau; ⑦ July 5 - Sept. 20 from Rigi Kulm. Supplement payable (from Arth-Goldau only, CHF 10).
T – 🚂 Steam train. Runs ⑦ July 5 - Sept. 13 from Vitznau. Supplement payable (CHF 10).
V – 🚂 Steam train. Runs ⑥ July 4 - Sept. 12 from Rigi Kulm.

j – Until Oct. 24.
k – May 21 - Aug. 29.
m – May 1 - 20.

p – ⑥⑦ Dec. 14 - 21; daily Dec. 22 - Mar. 22; © Mar. 28 - Apr. 26; daily May 1 - Oct. 30; ⑥⑦ Oct. 31 - Dec. 12 (also Dec. 8).
q – Daily Dec. 20 - Jan. 4; ⑤⑥⑦ May 1 - June 21; daily June 27 - Aug. 30; ⑤⑥⑦ Sept. 4 - Oct. 25 (also May 21, June 1, 11).
r – † May 24 - June 28; daily July 1 - Aug. 23 (also May 21, Aug. 30, Sept. 6, 13).
t – ①–⑥ May 22 - June 30, Aug. 24 - Sept. 12.
x – June 28 - Aug. 29.

554 🚌 MEIRINGEN - ANDERMATT

Service June 20 - October 4, 2009 (no winter service) PA

	R	R	R		R	R	R	R	R	R	R
Meiringen Bahnhof.......... d.	...	...	...	...	0920	...	1100	1300	1330	1520	...
Susten Passhöhe.......... d.	...	...	1010	...	|	...	|	|	1440	|	...
Göschenen Bahnhof.... d.	0810	...	1049	...	|	...	|	|	1519	|	...
Grimsel Passhöhe............ d.	|	...	|	...	1050	...	1220	1404	|	1630	...
Oberwald Bahnhof .... a.	|	...	|	...	1116	...	1250	...	|	1654	...
Oberwald Bahnhof .... d.	|	1005	|	...	1125	1320	...	...	|	...	1715
Furka Passhöhe............... d.	|	1044	|	...	|	1415	...	...	|	...	1751
Realp Post .... d.	0854	...	|	...	|	1441	...	...	|	...	1817
Andermatt Bahnhof......... a.	...	...	1104	...	1520	1500	...	...	1534	...	1835

	R	R	R	R	R	R	R	R	R k	R	R
Andermatt Bahnhof...... d.	...	...	0830	...	0915	...	1140	...	1535	...	1545
Realp Post.................... d.	...	0854	|	...	|	...	|	...	|	...	1609
Furka Passhöhe............ d.	...	0950	|	1100	|	...	|	...	|	...	1636
Oberwald Bahnhof .... a.	...	...	1020	1131	1210	...	1510	...	|	...	1706
Oberwald Bahnhof .... d.	0745	...	1030	...	...	1336	...	...	|	1700	...
Grimsel Passhöhe......... d.	0811	...	1130	...	...	1408	...	1530	|	1732	...
Göschenen Bahnhof. d.	...	...	|	...	...	|	...	|	1551	|	...
Susten Passhöhe ...... d.	...	...	|	...	...	|	...	|	1631	|	...
Meiringen Bahnhof....... a.	...	...	1230	...	...	1512	...	1634	1731	1836	...

k – Runs 30 minutes later on ①–⑤.

555 ZÜRICH FLUGHAFEN ✈ - ZÜRICH - LUZERN

SBB

km																Ⓐ			Ⓐ				Ⓐ			
0	**Zürich Flughafen ✈ 530/5** ...... d.	...	...	...	...	...	...	...	0847	...	and at	1547	...	...	...	1647	...	...	1747	...	...	...	1847	...	1947
10	**Zürich HB 530/5** .... d.	0535	0604	0635	0704	0735	0804	0835	0904	0935	the same	1604	1635	...	1641	1704	1735	1741	1804	1835	...	1841	1904	1935	2004
22	Thalwil.................................. d.	0545	0614	0645	0714	0745	0814	0845	0914	0945	minutes	1614	1645	...	1654	1714	1745	1754	1814	1845	...	1854	1914	1945	2014
39	Zug....................................... d.	0602	0629	0702	0729	0802	0829	0902	0929	1002	past each	1629	1702	...	1712	1729	1802	1812	1829	1902	...	1912	1929	2002	2029
49	Rotkreuz................................ d.	0610	|	0710	|	0810	|	0910	|	1010	hour	|	1710	...	1721	|	1810	1821	|	1910	...	1921	|	2010	|
67	**Luzern** .... a.	0625	0649	0725	0749	0825	0849	0925	0949	1025	until	1649	1725	...	1739	1749	1825	1839	1849	1925	...	1939	1949	2025	2049

										w
Zürich Flughafen ✈ 530/5 ...... d.	...	2047	...	...	...	...	...	...	...	...
Zürich HB 530/5...................... d.	2035	2104	2135	2204	2235	2304	2335	0007	...	0230
Thalwil.................................... d.	2045	2114	2145	2214	2245	2314	2345	0017	...	|
Zug .... d.	2102	2129	2202	2229	2302	2329	0002	0035	...	0302
Rotkreuz.................................. d.	2110	|	2210	|	2310	|	0010	0046	...	0309
Luzern .... a.	2125	2149	2225	2249	2325	2349	0025	0107	...	0330

					Ⓐ				Ⓐ	
Luzern .... d.	0455	0528	...	0610	0620	0635	...	0710	0720	0735
Rotkreuz.................................. d.	0513	0549	...	|	0636	0648	...	|	0736	0748
Zug.. d.	0526	0558	...	0631	0648	0658	...	0731	0748	0758
Thalwil .... d.	0542	0616	...	0646	0705	0716	...	0746	0805	0816
Zürich HB 530/5...................... a.	0555	0625	...	0656	0719	0725	...	0756	0819	0825
Zürich Flughafen ✈ 530/5.... a.	0613	...	...	...	...	...	...	0813	...	...

																								w
Luzern .... d.	0810	0835	and at	1510	1535	...	1610	1635	1710	1735	1810	1835	1910	1935	...	2010	2035	2110	2135	2210	2235	2310	2335	...	0101
Rotkreuz.................................. d.	|	0848	the same	|	1548	...	|	1648	|	1748	|	1848	|	1948	...	|	2048	|	2148	|	2248	|	2348	...	|
Zug .... d.	0831	0858	minutes	1531	1558	...	1631	1658	1731	1758	1831	1858	1931	1958	...	2031	2058	2131	2158	2231	2258	2331	2358	...	0128
Thalwil.................................... d.	0846	0916	past each	1546	1616	...	1646	1716	1746	1816	1846	1916	1946	2016	...	2046	2116	2146	2216	2246	2316	2346	0016	...	|
Zürich HB 530/5...................... a.	0856	0925	hour	1556	1625	...	1656	1725	1756	1825	1856	1925	1956	2025	...	2056	2125	2156	2225	2256	2325	2356	0025	...	0153
Zürich Flughafen ✈ 530/5 ...... a.	0913	...	until	1613	...	...	1713	...	1813	...	1913	...	2013	...	...	...	...	...	...	...	...	...	...	...	...

w – ⑥⑦ (also Dec. 25, 26, Jan. 1, 2, Apr. 10, 13, May 21, June 1).

SBB

BASEL - BERN - INTERLAKEN and BRIG

km		IC 953	IC 806	ICE 1055	IC 955	IC 808	CIS 51	IC 959	IC 810	ICE 1061	IC 961	IC 812	IC 1063	ICE 5	IC 816	IC 1067	IC 967	IC 818	IC 1069	IC 969	IC 820	IC 1071	ICE 373	IC 822	CIS 57	IC 973	IC 824	IC 1075	ICE 375
			(✕)		✕	✕	⊙✕	(✕)	(✕)		✕	✕		✕	(✕)	(✕)	✕	✕	✕	✕	✕	✕	✕	✕	⊙✕	(✕)	(✕)	✕	✕
							M							♦									B		T				B
	Romanshorn **535** ... d.	...	...	...	...	...	...	...	0538	...	...	0638	...	...	0741	...	...	0841	...	...	0941	...	...	1041	...	...	1141	...	...
	Zürich Flug ✈ **535**. d.	...	...	...	...	...	...	...	0640	...	...	0743	...	...	0840	...	...	0940	...	...	1040	...	...	1140	...	...	1240	...	...
	Zürich HB **500** .... d.	...	...	...	...	0600	...	...	0700	...	...	0800	...	...	0900	...	...	1000	...	...	1100	...	...	1200	...	...	1300	...	...
0	**Basel SBB** .... d.	...	...	0524	0601	|	0628	0701	|	0728	0801	|	0828	0901	|	0928	1001	|	1028	1101	|	1128	1201	|	1228	1301	|	1328	1401
14	Liestal .... d.	...	...	0534	|	|	0638	|	|	0738	|	|	0838	|	|	0938	|	|	1038	|	|	1138	|	|	1238	|	|	1338	|
39	Olten .... d.	...	...	0600	0629	|	0700	0729	|	0800	0829	|	0900	0929	|	1000	1029	|	1100	1129	|	1200	1229	|	1300	1329	|	1400	1429
101	**Bern** .... a.	...	...	0627	0656	0657k	0727	0756	0757k	0827	0856	0857k	0927	0956	0957k	1027	1056	1057k	1127	1156	1157k	1227	1256	1257k	1327	1356	1357k	1427	1456
101	**Bern** .... d.	0604	0607	0635	0704	0707	0735	0804	0807	0835	0904	0907	0935	1004	1007	1035	1104	1107	1135	1204	1207	1235	1304	1307	1335	1404	1407	1435	1504
132	Thun .... d.	0622	0625	0654	0722	0725	0754	0822	0825	0854	0922	0925	0954	1022	1025	1054	1122	1125	1154	1222	1225	1254	1322	1325	1354	1422	1425	1454	1522
142	**Spiez** .... a.	0631	0634	0702	0731	0734	0802	0831	0834	0902	0931	0934	1002	1031	1034	1102	1131	1134	1202	1231	1234	1302	1331	1334	1402	1431	1434	1502	1531
142	**Spiez** .... d.	0632	0636	0703	0733	0736	0805	0833	0836	0903	0933	0936	1005	1033	1036	1103	1133	1136	1205	1233	1236	1303	1333	1336	1405	1433	1436	1503	1533
	Interlaken West...... d.	0652	|	0723	0752	|	|	0852	|	0923	0952	|	|	1052	|	1123	1152	|	|	1252	|	1323	1352	|	|	1452	|	1523	1552
	Interlaken Ost ...... a.	0657	|	0728	0757	|	|	0857	|	0928	0957	|	|	1057	|	1128	1157	|	|	1257	|	1328	1357	|	|	1457	|	1528	1557
197	Visp .... d.	...	0703	...	...	0803	0832	...	0903	...	...	1003	1032	...	1103	...	...	1203	1232	...	1303	...	...	1403	1432	...	1503	...	...
206	**Brig** .... a.	...	0711	...	...	0811	0840	...	0911	...	...	1011	1040	...	1111	...	...	1211	1240	...	1311	...	...	1411	1440	...	1511	...	...
	Milano C **590** .... a.	...	...	...	...	...	1035	...	...	...	...	...	...	...	...	...	...	...	...	...	...	...	...	...	1640	...	...	...	...

	IC 826	IC 1077	IC 977	IC 828	IC 1079	IC 979	IC 830	IC 1081	IC 981	IC 832	CIS 59	ICE 277	IC 836	IC 1085	ICE 987	IC 838	IC 1087	ICE 279	IC 1089	IC 1091	IC 991	IC 1093	IC 1095	IC 1097	EN 313	IC 993	IC 995	ICE 947	IC 949
	✕	✕	✕	(✕)	(✕)	(✕)	✕	✕	✕	(✕)	⊙✕	✕	✕	(✕)		✕	✕	✕	✕			🍷			Ⓡ ⟋	✕			
											M	B						B	①–⑥	⑦			①–⑥	⑦	♦				L
Romanshorn **535** ....d.	1241	...	...	1341	...	...	1441	...	...	1541	...	...	1641	...	...	1741	...	...	...	...	...	...	...	...	...	...	...	...	...
Zürich Flug ✈ **535**..d.	1340	...	...	1440	...	...	1540	...	...	1640	...	...	1740	...	...	1840	...	...	...	...	...	...	...	...	...	...	...	...	...
Zürich HB **500** ....d.	1400	...	...	1500	...	...	1600	...	...	1700	...	...	1800	...	...	1900	...	...	...	...	...	...	...	...	2123	...	...	...	...
Basel SBB................d.	|	1428	1501	|	1528	1601	|	1628	1701	|	1728	1801	|	1828	1901	|	1928	2001	2028	2028	2101	2128	...	...	|	2201	2301	...	...
Liestal ....d.	|	1438	|	|	1538	|	|	1638	|	|	1738	|	|	1838	|	|	1938	|	2038	2038	|	2138	...	...	|	|	|	...	...
Olten ....d.	|	1500	1529	|	1600	1629	|	1700	1729	|	1800	1829	|	1900	1929	|	2000	2029	2100	2100	2129	2200	...	...	2159u	2229	2330	...	...
Bern..........................a.	1457k	1527	1556	1557k	1627	1656	1657k	1727	1756	1757k	1827	1856	1857k	1927	1956	1957k	2027	2056	2127	2127	2156	2227	...	...	|	2256k	2357	...	...
Bern..........................d.	1507	1535	1604	1607	1635	1704	1707	1735	1804	1807	1835	1904	1907	1935	2004	2007	2035	2107	2135	2135	2207	...	2235	2235	2304u	2308	...	0008	0108
Thun...........................d.	1525	1554	1622	1625	1654	1722	1725	1754	1822	1825	1854	1922	1925	1954	2022	2025	2054	2125	2154	2154	2225	...	2254	2254	2324u	2326	...	0028	0133
Spiez ....a.	1534	1602	1631	1634	1702	1731	1734	1802	1831	1834	1902	1931	1934	2002	2031	2034	2102	2134	2202	2202	2234	...	2302	2302	|	2335	...	0038	0143
Spiez ....d.	1536	1605	1633	1636	1703	1733	1736	1805	1833	1836	1905	1933	1936	2003	2033	2036	2104	2135	2204	2205	2235	...	2305	2305	2335u	2336	...	0038	0143
Interlaken West.......d.	|	|	1652	|	1723	1752	|	|	1852	|	|	1952	|	2023	2049	|	|	2152	|	|	2252	...	|	|	|	2354	...	0052	0200
Interlaken Ost........a.	|	|	1657	|	1728	1757	|	|	1857	|	|	1957	|	2028	2054	|	|	2156	|	|	2256	...	f	|	|	2359	...	0059	0206
Visp............................d.	1603	1632	...	1703	...	...	1803	1832	...	1903	1932	...	2003	...	...	2103	f	...	2232	|	...	...	2335	f	|	...	...	...	...
Brig.............................a.	1611	1640	...	1711	...	...	1811	1840	...	1911	1940	...	2011	...	...	2111	2209	...	2240	2301	...	...	2343	0009	0058u	...	...	...	...
Milano C **590** ....a.	...	...	...	...	...	...	...	...	...	...	2135	...	...	...	...	...	...	...	...	...	...	...	...	...	...	...	...	...	...

km		IC 952	EN 314	IC 1058	ICE 278	IC 811	IC 1060	IC 956	IC 815	IC 1064	ICE 276	IC 817	IC 1066	IC 962	IC 819	CIS 50	ICE 374	IC 821	IC 1070	IC 968	IC 823	IC 1072	ICE 370	IC 825	IC 1074	IC 974	IC 827	CIS 52	IC 978
		✕	Ⓡ ⟋	✕	✕	✕	(✕)	(✕)	✕	✕	✕	(✕)	(✕)	✕	✕	⊙✕	✕	(✕)	(✕)	✕	✕	✕	✕	(✕)	✕	(✕)	✕	⊙✕	✕
			♦		B						B					M	B						B					T	
	Milano C **590** .... d.	...	...	...	...	...	...	...	...	...	...	...	...	...	...	0725	...	...	...	...	...	...	...	...	...	...	...	1120	...
	Brig .... d.	...	0439s	...	...	0547	...	...	0649	0720	...	0749	...	...	0849	0920	...	0949	...	...	1049	1120	...	1149	...	...	1249	1320	...
	Visp .... d.	...	|	...	...	0554	...	...	0657	0728	...	0757	...	...	0857	0928	...	0957	...	...	1057	1128	...	1157	...	...	1257	1328	...
0	**Interlaken Ost** ...... d.	...	|	0521	0601	f	0627	0701	|	|	0801	|	0831	0901	|	|	1001	|	1031	1101	|	|	1201	|	1231	1301	|	|	1401
2	Interlaken West...... d.	...	|	0526	0606	|	0632	0706	|	|	0806	|	0836	0906	|	|	1006	|	1036	1106	|	|	1206	|	1236	1306	|	|	1406
18	**Spiez** .... a.	...	0544s	0548	0622	0624	0652	0722	0724	0753	0822	0824	0852	0922	0924	0953	1022	1024	1052	1122	1124	1153	1222	1224	1252	1322	1324	1353	1422
	Spiez .... d.	0520	|	0550	0623	0625	0654	0723	0725	0754	0823	0825	0854	0923	0925	0954	1023	1025	1054	1123	1125	1154	1223	1225	1254	1323	1325	1354	1423
	Thun .... d.	0530	0554s	0601	0633	0636	0704	0733	0736	0804	0833	0836	0904	0933	0936	1005	1033	1036	1104	1133	1136	1204	1233	1236	1304	1333	1336	1404	1433
	Bern .... a.	0552	0620s	0623	0652	0654k	0723	0752	0754k	0823	0852	0854k	0923	0952	0954k	1023	1052	1054k	1123	1152	1154k	1223	1252	1254k	1323	1352	1354k	1423	1452
	Bern .... d.	0604	|	0634	0704	0702	0734	0804	0802	0834	0904	0902	0934	1004	1002	1034	1104	1102	1134	1204	1202	1234	1304	1302	1334	1404	1402	1434	1504
	Olten .... d.	0631	0745s	0705	0731	|	0805	0831	|	0905	0931	|	1005	1031	|	1105	1131	|	1205	1231	|	1305	1331	|	1405	1431	|	1505	1531
	Liestal .... d.	|	|	0721	|	|	0821	|	|	0921	|	|	1021	|	|	1121	|	|	1221	|	|	1321	|	|	1421	|	|	1521	|
	Basel SBB .... a.	0655	|	0732	0755	|	0832	0855	|	0932	0955	|	1032	1055	|	1132	1155	|	1232	1255	|	1332	1355	|	1432	1455	|	1532	1555
	Zürich HB **500** .... a.	...	0842	...	...	0758	...	...	0858	...	...	0958	...	...	1058	...	...	1158	...	...	1258	...	...	1358	...	...	1458	...	...
	Zürich Flug ✈ **535**. a.	...	...	...	...	0816	...	...	0916	...	...	1016	...	...	1116	...	...	1216	...	...	1316	...	...	1416	...	...	1516	...	...
	Romanshorn **535** ... a.	...	...	...	...	0918	...	...	1018	...	...	1118	...	...	1218	...	...	1318	...	...	1418	...	...	1518	...	...	1618	...	...

	IC 829	IC 1078	ICE 376	IC 831	IC 1080	IC 982	IC 835	ICE 1082	IC 986	IC 837	IC 1086	IC 988	IC 839	IC 1088	IC 990	IC 841	IC 1092	IC 992	IC 843	CIS 56	ICE 994	IC 1096	ICE 996	IC 851		ICE 998	IC 853	IC 1098	
	✕	✕	✕	✕	✕	(✕)	(✕)		✕	✕	✕	✕	(✕)	(✕)	(✕)	✕	✕	✕	(✕)	⊙✕									
			♦																	M				z			y	⑤⑥	
Milano C **590** ....d.	...	...	...	...	...	...	...	...	...	...	...	...	...	...	...	...	...	...	...	1825	...	...	...	...	...	...	...	...	...
Brig............................d.	1349	...	...	1449	1520	...	1549	...	...	1649	1720	...	1749	...	...	1849	1920	...	1949	2020	...	2120	...	2220	...	...	2226	...	...
Visp............................d.	1357	...	...	1457	1528	...	1557	...	...	1657	1728	...	1757	...	...	1857	1928	...	1957	2028	...	2128	...	2228	...	...	|	...	...
Interlaken Ost........d.	|	1431	1501	|	|	1601	|	1631	1701	|	|	1801	|	1831	1901	|	|	2001	|	|	2101	|	2201	|	...	2301	|	2333	...
Interlaken West.......d.	|	1436	1506	|	|	1606	|	1636	1706	|	|	1806	|	1836	1906	|	|	2006	|	|	2106	|	2206	|	...	2306	|	2338	...
Spiez ....a.	1424	1452	1522	1524	1553	1622	1624	1652	1722	1724	1753	1822	1824	1852	1922	1924	1953	2022	2024	2053	2122	2153	2222	2253	...	2322	2322	2354	...
Spiez ....d.	1425	1454	1523	1525	1554	1623	1625	1654	1723	1725	1754	1823	1825	1854	1923	1925	1954	2023	2025	2054	2123	2154	2223	2254	...	2323	2325	2355	...
Thun............................d.	1436	1504	1533	1536	1604	1633	1636	1704	1733	1736	1804	1833	1836	1904	1933	1936	2004	2033	2036	2105	2133	2204	2233	2304	...	2333	2336	0005	...
Bern...........................a.	1454k	1523	1552	1554k	1623	1652	1654k	1723	1752	1754k	1823	1852	1854k	1923	1952	1954k	2023	2052	2054k	2123	2152	2223	2252	2323	...	2352	2354	0024	...
Bern...........................d.	1502	1534	1604	1602	1634	1704	1702	1734	1804	1802	1834	1904	1902	1934	2004	2002	2034	2104	2102	2134	2204	...	2304	...	...	...	...	...	...
Olten ....a.	|	1605	1631	|	1705	1731	|	1805	1831	|	1905	1931	|	2005	2031	|	2105	2131	|	2205	2231	...	2331	...	...	...	...	...	...
Liestal ....a.	|	1621	|	|	1721	|	|	1821	|	|	1921	|	|	2021	|	|	2121	|	|	2221	|	...	|	...	...	...	...	...	...
Basel SBB..................a.	|	1632	1655	|	1732	1755	|	1832	1855	|	1932	1955	|	2032	2055	|	2132	2155	|	2232	2255	...	2355	...	...	...	...	...	...
Zürich HB **500** ....a.	1558	...	...	1658	...	...	1758	...	...	1858	...	...	1958	...	...	2058	...	...	2158	...	...	...	...	...	...	...	...	...	...
Zürich Flug ✈ **535**..a.	1616	...	...	1716	...	...	1816	...	...	1916	...	...	2016	...	...	2116	...	...	2216	...	...	...	...	...	...	...	...	...	...
Romanshorn **535** .....a.	1718	...	...	1818	...	...	1918	...	...	2018	...	...	2118	...	...	2218	...	...	2318	...	...	...	...	...	...	...	...	...	...

♦ – **NOTES** (LISTED BY TRAIN NUMBER)

5 – 🚃12 and ✕ (①, also Apr. 14, June 2; not Apr. 13, June 1, Hamburg -) Frankfurt - Basel - Interlaken.

313 – LUNA – 🛏 1, 2 cl. and 🛌 2 cl. Zürich - Brig - Roma Termini. Also conveys 🚃12 Zürich - Brig (without supplement).

314 – LUNA – 🛏 1, 2 cl. and 🛌 2 cl. Roma Termini - Brig - Zürich. Also conveys 🚃12 Brig - Zürich (without supplement).

376 – 🚃12 and ✕ Interlaken - Basel - Frankfurt.

B – 🚃12 and ✕ Interlaken - Basel - Berlin Ost and v.v.

L – MOONLINER – ⑥⑦ (also Jan. 1).

M – 🚃12 and ✕ Basel - Milano and v.v.

T – 🚃12 and ✕ Basel - Milano - Trieste and v.v.

f – Via Frutigen.

k – Connects with train in previous column.

p – ①–⑥ June 15 - Dec. 12.

q – ⑦ June 14 - Dec. 6.

s – Stops to set down only.

u – Stops to pick up only.

y – ⑦ Dec. 14 - June 7.

z – ①–⑥ Dec. 15 - June 13.

⟋ – Supplement payable.

⊙ – *CISALPINO Pendolino* train: Ⓡ inclusive of supplement for international journeys; may be used for Swiss internal journeys without reservation. *A change of trains may be necessary at Domodossola (between Brig and Milano).*

561 LUZERN - INTERLAKEN

ZB. Narrow gauge rack railway

km																											
		Ⓐ	P				⚒				P						P									P	
0	**Luzern 552** d.	...	...	...	0537	0606	0637	0655	0708	0737	0755	0808	0837	0855	0908	0937	0955	1008	1037	1055	1108	1137	1155	1208	1237	1255	1308
9	Hergiswil **552** d.	...	...	...	0553	0623	0653	0706	0723	0753	0806	0823	0853	0906	0923	0953	1006	1023	1053	1106	1123	1153	1206	1223	1253	1306	1323
13	Alpnachstad d.	...	...	...	0558	0628	0658	|	0728	0758	|	0828	0858	|	0928	0958	|	1028	1058	|	1128	1158	|	1228	1258	|	1328
15	Alpnach Dorf d.	...	...	...	0601	0631	0701	0711	0731	0801	0811	0831	0901	0911	0931	1001	1011	1031	1101	1111	1131	1201	1211	1231	1301	1311	1331
21	Sarnen d.	...	...	...	0609	0639	0709	0720	0739	0809	0820	0839	0909	0920	0939	1009	1020	1039	1109	1120	1139	1209	1220	1239	1309	1320	1339
23	Sachseln d.	...	...	...	0614	0644	0714	|	0744	0814	|	0844	0914	|	0944	1014	|	1044	1114	|	1144	1214	|	1244	1314	|	1344
29	Giswil d.	...	...	...	0626	0651	0721	0730	0751	0821	0830	0851	0921	0930	0951	1021	1030	1051	1121	1130	1151	1221	1230	1251	1321	1330	1351
36	Lungern § d.	...	...	...	0639	...	▬	0744	...	▬	0844	...	▬	0944	▬	▬	1044	...	▬	1144	...	▬	1244	...	▬	1344	...
40	Brünig Hasliberg d.	...	...	...	0656	...	...	0756	...	...	0856	...	...	0956	...	...	1056	...	...	1156	...	...	1256	...	...	1356	...
45	**Meiringen ●** a.	...	...	...	0711	...	...	0812	...	...	0912	...	...	1012	...	...	1112	...	...	1212	...	...	1312	...	...	1412	...
45	**Meiringen ●** d.	0547	0614	0647	0720	...	0744	0821	...	0844	0921	...	0944	1021	...	1044	1121	...	1144	1221	...	1244	1321	...	1344	1421	...
58	**Brienz** d.	0559	0626	0701	0734	...	0800	0838	...	0900	0938	...	1000	1038	...	1100	1138	...	1200	1238	...	1300	1338	...	1400	1438	...
65	Oberried d.	0609	0638	0713	0744	...	0812	|	...	0912	|	...	1012	|	...	1112	|	...	1212	|	...	1312	|	...	1412	|	...
74	**Interlaken Ost** a.	0622	0651	0724	0755	...	0824	0855	...	0924	0955	...	1024	1055	...	1124	1155	...	1224	1255	...	1324	1355	...	1424	1455	...

					P									P						P							
Luzern 552 d.	1337	1355	1408	1437	1455	1508	1537	1555	1608	1637	1655	1708	1737	1755	1808	1837	1855	1908	1937	1955	2008	2037	2108	2137	2208	2311	0030
Hergiswil **552** d.	1353	1406	1423	1453	1506	1523	1553	1606	1623	1653	1706	1723	1753	1806	1823	1853	1906	1923	1953	2006	2023	2053	2123	2153	2223	2326	0043
Alpnachstad d.	1358	|	1428	1458	|	1528	1558	|	1628	1658	|	1728	1758	|	1828	1858	|	1928	1958	|	2028	2058	2128	2158	2228	2330	0048
Alpnach Dorf d.	1401	1411	1431	1501	1511	1531	1601	1611	1631	1701	1711	1731	1801	1811	1831	1901	1911	1931	2001	2011	2031	2101	2131	2201	2231	2332	0050
Sarnen d.	1409	1420	1439	1509	1520	1539	1609	1620	1639	1709	1720	1739	1809	1820	1839	1909	1920	1939	2009	2020	2039	2109	2139	2209	2239	2340	0057
Sachseln d.	1414	|	1444	1514	|	1544	1614	|	1644	1714	|	1744	1814	|	1844	1914	|	1944	2014	|	2044	2114	2144	2214	2244	2344	0100
Giswil d.	1421	1430	1451	1521	1530	1551	1621	1630	1651	1721	1730	1751	1821	1830	1851	1921	1930	1951	2021	2030	2051	2121	2152	2221	2251	2351	0108
Lungern § d.	▬	1444	...	▬	1544	...	▬	1644	...	▬	1744	...	▬	1844	...	...	1944	...	▬	2044	▬	...	2206	▬	...	...	...
Brünig Hasliberg d.	...	1456	...	...	1556	...	...	1656	...	...	1756	...	...	1856	...	...	1956	...	...	2101	...	...	2217	...	...	...	...
Meiringen ● a.	...	1512	...	...	1612	...	...	1712	...	...	1812	...	...	1912	...	...	2012	...	...	2116	...	...	2232	...	...	...	...
Meiringen ● d.	1444	1521	...	1544	1621	...	1644	1721	...	1744	1821	...	1844	1921	...	...	...	...	2018	...	2118	...	...	2237	...	...	...
Brienz d.	1500	1538	...	1600	1638	...	1700	1738	...	1800	1838	...	1900	1935	...	...	...	...	2032	...	2132	...	...	2249	...	...	...
Oberried d.	1512	|	...	1612	|	...	1712	|	...	1812	|	...	1912	1944	...	...	...	...	2042	...	2142	...	...	2259	...	...	...
Interlaken Ost a.	1524	1555	...	1624	1655	...	1724	1755	...	1824	1855	...	1924	1956	...	...	...	...	2055	...	2155	...	...	2311	...	...	...

		⚒		P				Ⓐ		P										P						P	
Interlaken Ost d.	...	...	...	...	...	...	...	0627	...	0704	0733	...	0804	...	0833	...	0904	...	0933	1004	...	1033	1104	1133	...	1204	1233
Oberried d.	...	...	...	...	...	...	...	0639	...	0714	0746	...	|	...	0846	...	|	...	0946	|	...	1046	|	1146	...	|	1246
Brienz d.	...	...	...	...	...	...	...	0650	...	0725	0757	...	0825	...	0857	...	0925	...	0957	1025	...	1057	1125	1157	...	1225	1257
Meiringen ● a.	...	...	...	...	...	...	...	0703	...	0735	0809	...	0835	...	0909	...	0935	...	1009	1035	...	1109	1135	1209	...	1235	1309
Meiringen ● d.	...	...	...	0546	...	...	0646	▬	...	0746	▬	...	0846	...	▬	...	0946	...	▬	1046	...	▬	1146	▬	...	1246	▬
Brünig Hasliberg d.	...	...	...	0557	...	...	0657	...	...	0757	...	...	0857	...	...	...	0957	...	...	1057	...	...	1157	...	...	1257	...
Lungern § d.	...	...	...	0610	...	...	0710	...	...	0810	...	...	0910	...	...	...	1010	...	...	1110	...	...	1210	...	...	1310	...
Giswil d.	0506	0536	0606	0627	0636	0706	0729	0736	0806	0829	0836	0906	0929	0936	1006	...	1029	1036	1106	1129	1136	1206	1229	1236	1306	1329	1336
Sachseln d.	0515	0545	0615	0634	0645	0715	|	0745	0815	|	0845	0915	|	0945	1015	...	|	1045	1115	|	1145	1215	|	1245	1315	|	1345
Sarnen d.	0520	0550	0620	0640	0650	0720	0740	0750	0820	0840	0850	0920	0940	0950	1020	...	1040	1050	1120	1140	1150	1220	1240	1250	1320	1340	1350
Alpnach Dorf d.	0525	0555	0625	0645	0655	0725	0745	0755	0825	0845	0855	0925	0945	0955	1025	...	1045	1055	1125	1145	1155	1225	1245	1255	1325	1345	1355
Alpnachstad d.	0530	0600	0630	|	0700	0730	|	0800	0830	|	0900	0930	|	1000	1030	...	|	1100	1130	|	1200	1230	|	1300	1330	|	1400
Hergiswil **552** d.	0538	0608	0638	0654	0708	0738	0754	0808	0838	0854	0908	0938	0954	1008	1038	...	1054	1108	1138	1154	1208	1238	1254	1308	1338	1354	1408
Luzern 552 a.	0552	0622	0652	0704	0722	0752	0804	0822	0852	0904	0922	0952	1004	1022	1052	...	1104	1122	1152	1204	1222	1252	1304	1322	1352	1404	1422

								P						P								P					
Interlaken Ost d.	...	1304	...	1333	1404	1433	...	1504	1533	...	1604	1633	...	1704	1733	...	1804	1833	...	1904	1933	2008	...	2105	2200	2315	...
Oberried d.	...	1314	...	1346	|	1446	...	|	1546	...	|	1646	...	|	1746	...	|	1846	...	|	1946	2020	...	2117	2211	2326	...
Brienz d.	...	1325	...	1357	1425	1457	...	1525	1557	...	1625	1657	...	1725	1757	...	1825	1857	...	1925	1957	2031	...	2129	2221	2336	...
Meiringen ● a.	...	1335	...	1409	1435	1509	...	1535	1609	...	1635	1709	...	1735	1809	...	1835	1909	...	1935	2009	2043	...	2141	2233	2348	...
Meiringen ● d.	...	1346	...	▬	1446	▬	...	1546	▬	...	1646	▬	...	1746	▬	...	1846	▬	...	1946	▬	...	2051	▬	▬	...	...
Brünig Hasliberg d.	...	1357	...	...	1457	...	...	1557	...	...	1657	...	...	1757	...	...	1857	...	...	1957	...	...	2102	...	...	...	...
Lungern § d.	...	1410	...	...	1510	...	...	1610	...	...	1710	...	...	1810	...	...	1910	...	...	2010	...	...	2115	...	...	...	...
Giswil d.	1406	1429	1436	1506	1529	1536	1606	1629	1636	1706	1729	1736	1806	1829	1836	1906	1929	1936	2006	2029	2106	...	2136	2206	2306	...	...
Sachseln d.	1415	|	1445	1515	|	1545	1615	|	1645	1715	|	1745	1815	|	1845	1915	|	1945	2015	|	2115	...	2145	2215	2315	...	...
Sarnen d.	1420	1440	1450	1520	1540	1550	1620	1640	1650	1720	1740	1750	1820	1840	1850	1920	1940	1950	2020	2040	2120	...	2150	2220	2320	...	...
Alpnach Dorf d.	1425	1445	1455	1525	1545	1555	1625	1645	1655	1725	1745	1755	1825	1845	1855	1925	1945	1955	2025	2045	2125	...	2155	2225	2325	...	...
Alpnachstad d.	1430	|	1500	1530	|	1600	1630	|	1700	1730	|	1800	1830	|	1900	1930	|	2000	2030	|	2130	...	2200	2230	2330	...	...
Hergiswil **552** d.	1438	1454	1508	1538	1554	1608	1638	1654	1708	1738	1754	1808	1838	1854	1908	1938	1954	2008	2038	2054	2138	...	2208	2238	2338	...	...
Luzern 552 a.	1452	1504	1522	1552	1604	1622	1652	1704	1722	1752	1804	1822	1852	1904	1922	1952	2004	2022	2052	2104	2152	...	2222	2252	2352	...	...

P – GOLDENPASS PANORAMIC – Conveys [1] [observation car] and [12]. Also conveys ✕ on most services (Reservation recommended for observation car).

p – ⚒ Dec. 15 - May 16; daily May 17 - Aug. 23; ①–⑥ Aug. 24 - Dec. 12.

q – © May 16 - Aug. 23.

§ – Buses depart from Lungern **Dorfkapelle**.

● – Rail service **Meiringen - Innertkirchen** and v.v. Narrow gauge. 2nd class only. *5 km*. Journey time: 11 minutes. **Operator**: MIB. Trains run from **Meiringen MIB** (300 metres from SBB station).

From **Meiringen MIB**: 0617Ⓐ, 0642Ⓐ, 0717Ⓐ, 0742, 0817⚒, 0842, 0942, 1042, 1117Ⓐ, 1142, 1217⚒, 1242, 1317 **p**, 1342, 1417 **q**, 1442, 1517 **q**, 1542, 1617 **p**, 1642, 1717Ⓐ, 1742, 1817Ⓐ, 1842, 1917.

From **Innertkirchen**: 0557Ⓐ, 0628Ⓐ, 0700Ⓐ, 0728, 0800, 0828⚒, 0900, 1000, 1100, 1128Ⓐ, 1200, 1228⚒, 1300, 1328 **p**, 1400, 1428 **q**, 1500, 1528 **q**, 1600, 1628 **p**, 1700, 1728Ⓐ, 1800, 1828Ⓐ, 1900.

562 SPIEZ - BRIG (via Lötschberg pass)

BLS

km																									
		RE **3253**	*RE* **3255** T	*RE* **3257**	*RE* **3259**	*RE* **3261**		*CNL* **1179** ♦		*RE* **3263**	*RE* **3265**	*RE* **3267**	*RE* **3269**	*RE* **3271**	*RE* **3273**		*RE* **3275**	*RE* **3277**	*RE* **3279**	*RE* **3281**	*IC* **1087** B	*RE* **3285**		*IC* **1097** ⑦	*RE* **3251**
	Bern d.	...	...	0740	0840	0940	...	...	...	1040c	1140e	1240e	1340e	1440e	1540e	...	1640	1740	1840	1940	2035	...	...	2235	...
0	**Spiez** d.	0612	0712	0812	0912	1012	...	1047**s**	...	1112	1212	1312	1412	1512	1612	...	1712	1812	1912	2012	2105	2212	...	2305	0012
14	Frutigen ● d.	0625	0725	0825	0925	1025	...	1059**s**	...	1125	1225	1325	1425	1525	1625	...	1725	1825	1925	2025	2117	2225	...	2317	0025
31	Kandersteg 🚗 d.	0642	0742	0842	0942	1042	...	1116**s**	...	1142	1242	1342	1442	1542	1642	...	1742	1842	1942	2042	2133	2242	...	2333	0042
48	Goppenstein 🚗 d.	0657	0757	0857	0957	1057	...	1130**s**	...	1157	1257	1357	1457	1557	1657	...	1757	1857	1957	2057	2145	2257	...	2345	0053
74	**Brig** a.	0724	0824	0924	1024	1124	...	1156	...	1224	1324	1424	1524	1624	1724	...	1824	1924	2024	2124	2209	2324	...	0009	0120

	RE **3256**	*IC* **811** R	*RE* **3256**	*RE* **3258**	*RE* **3260**		*RE* **3262**	*RE* **3264**	*RE* **3266**	*RE* **3268**	*RE* **3270**	*RE* **3272**	*RE* **3274**	*RE* **3276**	*RE* **3278**		*CNL* **1178** ♦		*RE* **3280**	*RE* **3282**	*RE* **3284**	*RE* **3286**	*RE* **3288**	
Brig d.	0536	0547	...	0636	0736	...	0836	0936	1036	1136	1236	1336	1436	1536	1636	...	1700	...	1736	1836	1936	2040	2207	...
Goppenstein 🚗 d.	0601	|	←	0701	0801	...	0901	1001	1101	1201	1301	1401	1501	1601	1701	...	1723**u**	...	1801	1901	2001	2105	2234	...
Kandersteg 🚗 d.	0612	|	0612	0712	0812	...	0912	1012	1112	1212	1312	1412	1512	1612	1712	...	1738**u**	...	1812	1912	2012	2116	2246	...
Frutigen ● d.	→	0613	0632	0732	0832	...	0932	1032	1132	1232	1332	1432	1532	1632	1732	...	1757**u**	...	1832	1932	2032	2132	2303	...
Spiez a.	...	0624	0647	0747	0847	...	0947	1047	1147	1247	1347	1447	1547	1647	1747	...	1813**u**	...	1847	1947	2047	2147	2319	...
Bern a.	...	0654	0720	0820	0920	...	1020c	1120e	1220e	1320e	1420e	1520e	1620	1720	1820	...	...	...	1920	...	...	...	...	...

♦ – **NOTES** (LISTED BY TRAIN NUMBER)

1178/9 – *City Night Line* KOMET – For days of running and composition – see Table **73**.

B – [12] and ✕ Basel - Brig.
R – [12] and ✕ Brig - Romanshorn.
T – From Thun.

c – © only.
e – † only.
s – Stops to set down only.
u – Stops to pick up only.

🚗 – Car-carrying shuttle available (see page 260).

● – 🚌 **SERVICE FRUTIGEN - ADELBODEN and v.v.:** 20 km, journey 30 minutes.
Operator: AFA, 3715 Adelboden. ✆ +41 (0)33 673 74 74, fax +41 (0)33 673 74 70.
From **Frutigen:** 0615Ⓐ, 0631, 0708Ⓐ, 0731 and hourly until 1831, then 1900Ⓐ, 1931, 2031, 2130, 2230, 2330.
From **Adelboden:** 0535Ⓐ, 0550, 0622Ⓐ, 0650 and hourly until 1750, then 1830Ⓐ, 1850, 1950, 2050, 2150, 2228.

BLS SPIEZ - ZWEISIMMEN 563

km		⚒	†	⚒	†	†	⚒		Ⓒ	†	⚒	G		⚒	†			⚒	†	⚒	†	G	⚒	†	⚒	†	†	⚒
	Interlaken Ost **560** ... d.	...		...			...	...	...			0908	...	...			...	...		...		1308	...		...		1508	1508
0	**Spiez 560** d.	0605	0608	0707	0712	0735	0740	0812	0845	0912	0914	0935	1012	1107	1112	1135	...	1209	1212	1309	1312	1335	1409	1412	1508	1512	1535	1541
11	Erlenbach im Simmental . d.	0624	0627	0723	0728	0750	0756	0828	|	0928	0929	0949	1028	1122	1128	1150	...	1227	1228	1326	1328	1349	1426	1428	1525	1528	1550	1555
26	Boltigen d.	0642	0645	0741	0746	0810	0811	0846	0909	0946	0947	1009	1046	1146	1146	1209	...	1245	1246	1345	1346	1408	1444	1446	1544	1546	1610	1610
35	**Zweisimmen** a.	0652	0655	0751	0756	0819	0820	0856	0919	0956	0957	1019	1056	1156	1156	1219	...	1255	1256	1355	1356	1419	1454	1456	1554	1556	1619	1619

	⚒	†	Ⓐ		G							
Interlaken Ost **560** .. d.	...		...	...	1708	...	...	...	...	...	...	...
Spiez 560 d.	1607	1612	1642	1712	1742	1814	1912	2012	2107	2207	2307	...
Erlenbach im Simmental . d.	1627	1628	1655	1728	1755	1828	1930	2030	2122	2222	2322	...
Boltigen d.	1645	1646	1710	1746	1811	1846	1947	2047	2140	2240	2340	...
Zweisimmen a.	1655	1656	1720	1756	1820	1856	1957	2057	2150	2250	2350	...

	Ⓐ	⚒	†	Ⓐ	⚒	†	Ⓐ					
Zweisimmen d.	0541	0556	0559	0634	0657	0701	0732	...	0801	0900	0937	1001
Boltigen d.	0548	0606	0609	0645	0706	0710	0741	...	0810	0909	0947	1010
Erlenbach im Simmental d.	0605	0625	0628	0701	0725	0729	0757	...	0829	0929	1003	1029
Spiez 560 a.	0619	0640	0643	0718	0740	0744	0812	...	0843	0946	1021	1045
Interlaken Ost **560** a.	...	...	...	...	...	...	...	...	...	...	...	...

	†	⚒	G			⚒	†			⚒	†	⚒	†	G			Ⓒ										
Zweisimmen d.	1101	1107	1138	...	1200	1259	1301	1337	...	1359	1401	1458	1501	1536	...	1600	1636	1701	1738	...	1801	1903	2003	2108	2208	2308	...
Boltigen d.	1110	1116	1147	...	1210	1308	1310	1346	...	1409	1410	1507	1510	1545	...	1610	1645	1710	1746	...	1810	1912	2012	2117	2217	2317	...
Erlenbach im Simmental . d.	1129	1134	1203	...	1228	1327	1329	1402	...	1427	1429	1526	1529	1604	...	1628	|	1729	1806	...	1829	1931	2031	2135	2235	2335	...
Spiez 560 a.	1144	1150	1221	...	1245	1346	1344	1421	...	1443	1443	1541	1544	1621	...	1643	1711	1742	1821	...	1843	1946	2046	2150	2250	2350	...
Interlaken Ost **560** .. a.	...	...	1250	...	...	...	...	1450	...	...	...	...	...	1650	...	...	...	...	1850	...	...	...	...	...	...	...	...

G – GOLDEN PASS PANORAMIC – Ⓡ for groups.

Narrow gauge rack railway. BOB, WAB, JB INTERLAKEN - KLEINE SCHEIDEGG - JUNGFRAUJOCH 564

km						j	v			j	j			j	j			j	j			j	j			j	
0	**Interlaken Ost** d.	0635	0635	0705	0705	0735	0735	0805	0805	0835	0835	0905	0905	0935	0935	1005	1005	1035	1035	1105	1105	1135	1135	1205	1205	1235	1305
3	Wilderswil ▲ d.	0640	0640	0710	0710	0740	0740	0810	0810	0840	0840	0910	0910	0940	0940	1010	1010	1040	1040	1110	1110	1140	1140	1210	1210	1240	1310
8	Zweilütschinen d.	0646	0647	0716	0717	0746	0747	0816	0817	0846	0847	0916	0917	0946	0947	1016	1017	1046	1047	1116	1117	1146	1147	1216	1217	1246	1316
12	**Lauterbrunnen ●** a.	0655	|	0725	|	0755	|	0825	|	0855	|	0925	|	0955	|	1025	|	1055	|	1125	|	1155	|	1225	|	1255	1325
	change trains		|		|		|		|	j	|		|		|		|	j	|		|		|		|	j	
12	**Lauterbrunnen** d.	0659	|	0739	|	0804	|	0830	|	0913	|	0939	|	1004	|	1030	|	1113	|	1139	|	1204	|	1230	|	1313	1339
16	Wengen a.	0712	|	0753	|	0818	|	0844	|	0927	|	0953	|	1018	|	1044	|	1127	|	1153	|	1218	|	1244	|	1327	1353
16	Wengen d.	0715	|	0759	|	0824j	|	0849	|	0934	|	0959	|	1024j	|	1049	|	1134	|	1159	|	1224j	|	1249	|	1334	1359
19	Grindelwald a.	|	0709	|	0739	|	0809	|	0839	|	0909	|	0939	|	1009	|	1039	|	1109	|	1139	|	1209	|	1239	|	|
	change trains	|	|	|	|	|	j	|	|	|	j	|	|	|	j	|	|	|	j	|	|	|	j	|		|	|
19	Grindelwald d.	|	0717	|	0747	|	0817	|	0847	|	0917	|	0947	|	1017	|	1047	|	1117	|	1147	|	1217	|	1247	|	|
20	Grindelwald Grund . d.	|	0725	|	0755	|	0825	|	0855	|	0925	|	0955	|	1025	|	1055	|	1125	|	1155	|	1225	|	1255	|	|
23	**Kleine Scheidegg** a.	0739	0750	0824	0820	0849j	0850	0914	0920	1002	0950	1024	1020	1049j	1050	1114	1120	1202	1150	1224	1220	1249j	1250	1314	1320	1402	1424

				j			j	j			j	j			v			⚒	⚒								
Interlaken Ost d.	1305	1405	1405	1435	1505	1505	1535	1535	1605	1605	1635	1635	1705	1705	1735	1805	1805	1835	1835	1905	1905	2005	2005	2101	2105	2201	2205
Wilderswil ▲ d.	1310	1410	1410	1440	1510	1510	1540	1540	1610	1610	1640	1640	1710	1710	1740	1810	1810	1840	1840	1910	1910	2010	2010	2106	2110	2206	2210
Zweilütschinen d.	1317	1416	1417	1447	1516	1517	1546	1547	1616	1617	1646	1647	1716	1717	1746	1816	1817	1846	1847	1916	1917	2016	2017	2112	2116	2212	2216
Lauterbrunnen ● a.	|	1425	|	|	1525	|	1555	|	1625	|	1655	|	1725	|	1755	1825	|	1855	|	1925	|	2025	|	2121	|	2221	|
change trains	|	|	|	|	|	|	|	|	|	|	|	|	|	|	|	|	|	|	|	|	|	|	|	|	|	|	|
Lauterbrunnen d.	|	1430	|	|	1539	|	1604	|	1630	|	1713	|	1739	|	1804	1830	|	1904	|	1930	|	2030	|	2130	|	2230	|
Wengen a.	|	1444	|	|	1553	|	1618	|	1644	|	1727	|	1753	|	1818	1844	|	1918	|	1944	|	2044	|	2144	|	2244	|
Wengen d.	|	1449	|	|	1559	|	1624k	|	1649	|	...	|	1759j	|	...	...	|	...	|	...	|	...	|	...	|	...	|
Grindelwald a.	1339	|	1439	1509	|	1539	|	1609	|	1639	...	1709	|	1739	...	...	1839	...	1909	...	1939	...	2039	...	2135	...	2235
change trains		|		j	|		|	j	|				|	j					j								
Grindelwald d.	1347	|	1447	1517	|	1547	|	1617	|	1647	...	...	|	1747	...	...	1847	...	1917	...	...	...	...	...	...	...	...
Grindelwald Grund.. d.	1355	|	1455	1525	|	1555	|	1625	|	1655	...	...	|	1755	...	...	1852	...	1922	...	...	...	...	...	...	...	...
Kleine Scheidegg a.	1420	1514	1520	1550	1624	1620	1649k	1650k	1714	1720	...	...	1824j	1820	...	...	...	...	...	...	...	...	...	...	...	...	...

												j		t				j				j				j	
Kleine Scheidegg d.	...	...		...	...	...	...	...	...	...	...	...	0744t	0803	0831	0833	0856j	0903	0925	0933	0944j	1003	1031	1033	1056j	1103	1125
Grindelwald Grund.. d.	...	...		...	...	...	...	0708	...	0738	...	0808	|	0838	|	0908	|	0938	|	1008	|	1038	|	1108	|	1138	|
Grindelwald a.	...	...		...	...	...	...	0712	...	0742	...	0812	|	0842	|	0912	|	0942	|	1012	|	1042	|	1112	|	1142	|
change trains			⚒							v			|	j	|		|	j	|		|	j	|		|	j	|
Grindelwald d.	0519	...	0546	...	0619	...	...	0719	...	0749	...	0819	|	0849	|	0919	|	0950	|	1019	|	1049	|	1119	|	1149	|
Wengen a.	|	...	|	...	|	...	...	|	...	|	...	|	0815t	|	0904	|	0929j	|	0953	|	1015j	|	1104	|	1129j	|	1153
Wengen d.	|	0512	|	0606	|	0641	0713	|	0737	|	0802	|	0828	|	0911	|	0937	|	1002	|	1028	|	1111	|	1137	|	1202
Lauterbrunnen a.	|	0528	|	0623	|	0657	0729	|	0754	|	0819	|	0845	|	0928	|	0954	|	1019	|	1045	|	1128	|	1154	|	1219
change trains	|		|		|	v		|	j	|		|	j	|		|	j	|		|	j	|			j	|	
Lauterbrunnen ● d.	|	0534	|	0633	|	0703	0733	|	0803	|	0833	|	0903	|	0933	|	1003	|	1033	|	1103	|	1133	|	1203	|	1233
Zweilütschinen d.	0540	0544	0611	0643	0643	0713	0743	0743	0813	0813	0843	0843	0913	0913	0943	0943	1013	1013	1043	1043	1113	1113	1143	1143	1213	1213	1243
Wilderswil ▲ d.	0546	0549	0617	0649	0649	0719	0749	0749	0819	0819	0849	0849	0919	0919	0949	0949	1019	1019	1049	1049	1119	1119	1149	1149	1219	1219	1249
Interlaken Ost a.	0550	0554	0622	0654	0654	0724	0754	0754	0824	0824	0854	0854	0924	0924	0954	0954	1024	1024	1054	1054	1124	1124	1154	1154	1224	1224	1254

							j				j				j				j			j					
Kleine Scheidegg d.	1133	1231	1233	1325	1333	1344j	1403	1431	1433	1456j	1503	1525	1533	1544j	1603	1631	1633	1656j	1703	1725	1733	1833	1830j	...	...	...	...
Grindelwald Grund.. d.	1208	|	1308	|	1408	|	1438	|	1508	|	1538	|	1608	|	1638	|	1708	|	1738	|	1808	1908	|	...	...	...	...
Grindelwald a.	1212	|	1312	|	1412	|	1442	|	1512	|	1542	|	1612	|	1642	|	1712	|	1742	|	1812	1912	|	...	...	...	...
change trains		|		|		|	j	|		|	j	|		|	j	|		|	v	|			|				
Grindelwald d.	1219	|	1319	|	1419	|	1449	|	1519	|	1549	|	1619	|	1649	|	1719	|	1749	|	1819	1919	|	2019	...	2119	...
Wengen a.	|	1304	|	1353	|	1415j	|	1504	|	1529j	|	1553	|	1615j	|	1704	|	1729j	|	1753	|	|	1858j	|	...	|	...
Wengen d.	|	1311	|	1402	|	1428	|	1511	|	1537	|	1602	|	1628	|	1711	|	1737	|	1802	|	|	1902	|	2002	|	2108
Lauterbrunnen a.	|	1328	|	1419	|	1445	|	1528	|	1554	|	1619	|	1645	|	1728	|	1754	|	1819	|	|	1919	|	2019	|	2125
change trains	|		|		|	j	|		|	j	|		|	j	|		|	v	|		|	|		|		|	
Lauterbrunnen ● d.	|	1333	|	1433	|	1503	|	1533	|	1603	|	1633	|	1703	|	1733	|	1803	|	1833	|	|	1933	|	2033	|	2133
Zweilütschinen d.	1243	1343	1343	1543	1443	1513	1513	1543	1543	1613	1613	1643	1643	1713	1713	1743	1743	1813	1813	1843	1843	1940	1944	2040	2044	2140	2144
Wilderswil ▲ d.	1249	1349	1349	1449	1449	1519	1519	1549	1549	1619	1619	1649	1649	1719	1719v	1749	1749	1819	1819	1849	1849	1946	1950	2046	2050	2146	2150
Interlaken Ost a.	1254	1354	1354	1454	1454	1524	1524	1554	1554	1624	1624	1654	1654	1724	1724v	1754	1754	1824	1824	1854	1854	1950	1954	2050	2054	2150	2154

At times of heavy snowfall (November 1 - April 30) the Eigergletscher - Jungfraujoch service is subject to cancellation

km				t		t		t			t		t		t			t		t			t	
0	**Kleine Scheidegg** d.	0800	0830	0900	0930	1000	1030	1100	1130	...	1200	1230	1300	1330	1400	1430	...	1500	1530	1630	...	1730	1840	...
2	Eigergletscher d.	0810	0840	0910	0940	1010	1040	1110	1140	...	1210	1240	1310	1340	1410	1440	...	1510	1540	1640	...	1740	1850	...
9	**Jungfraujoch** a.	0852	0922	0952	1022	1052	1122	1152	1222	...	1252	1322	1352	1422	1452	1522	...	1552	1622	1716	...	...	...	...

	t		t			t			t		t			t		t			t			t	
Jungfraujoch d.	0900	0930	1000	...	1030	1100	1130	...	1200	1230	1300	1330	...	1400	1430	1500	1530	...	1600	1640	...	1750	...
Eigergletscher d.	0940	1010	1040	...	1110	1140	1210	...	1240	1310	1340	1410	...	1440	1510	1540	1610	...	1640	1710	...	1817	...
Kleine Scheidegg a.	0950	1020	1050	...	1120	1150	1220	...	1250	1320	1350	1420	...	1450	1520	1550	1620	...	1650	1720	...	1825	...

h – June 20 - Sept. 27.
j – Dec. 14 - Apr. 13, May 2 - Oct. 25.
k – Jan. 25 - Apr. 13, May 2 - Oct. 25.
m – Dec. 20 - Apr. 13, May 16 - Oct. 18.
t – May 2 - Oct. 25.
v – ①–⑥ (also ⑦ Dec. 14 - Apr. 12, May 3 - Oct. 25).

Additional trains run between Lauterbrunnen, Wengen and Jungfraujoch and between Grindelwald and Jungfraujoch.

● – Cableway operates **Lauterbrunnen - Grütschalp**, and narrow gauge railway **Grütschalp - Mürren**, *total: 5 km*. **Operator**: BLM. Journey time: 20 minutes allowing for the connection.
From **Lauterbrunnen**: 0610, 0631, 0701, 0731, 0801 and every 30 minutes◆ until 1831, then 1931, 2031 **m**.
From **Mürren**: 0606, 0636, 0706 and every 30 minutes◆ until 1906, then 2006 **m**.
◆ – Additional services available Dec. 20 - Apr. 13, May 16 - Oct. 18.

▲ – Narrow gauge rack railway operates **May 21 - Oct. 25 Wilderswil - Schynige Platte**. *7 km*. Journey time: 52 minutes. **Operator**: SPB, ✆ 033 828 73 51. Service may be reduced In bad weather.
From **Wilderswil**: 0725, 0805 **h**, 0845, 0925, 1005, 1045, 1125, 1205 **h**, 1245, 1325, 1405, 1445, 1525, 1605 **h**, 1645.
From **Schynige Platte**: 0821, 0901 **h**, 0941, 1021, 1101, 1141, 1221 **h**, 1301, 1341, 1421, 1501, 1541, 1621, 1701 **h**, 1753.

565 BASEL, OLTEN and BERN - LUZERN SBB

km		IR 2451	RE 3557	IR 2509	IR 2159	IR 2453	RE 3559	IR 2511	IR 2163		IR 2455	RE 3561	IR 2515	IR 2165	IR 2457	RE 3565	IR 2517		ICN 671	IR 2459	RE 3567	IR 2519	IR 2169	IR 2461	RE 3569	IR 2521	ICN 675
					△ L			🍷	L y				🍷	△ L			🍷		🍴 G			🍷	△ L			🍷	🍴 G
	Genève Aéroport ✈ **505** d.	...	...	...	...	...	...	...	...	...	...	...	...	...	...	...	0701	...	...	...	...	0801	...	...	...	0901	...
	Genève **505** d.	...	...	...	...	...	...	0456	...	...	...	...	0610	...	...	...	0710	...	...	...	...	0810	...	...	...	0910	...
	Lausanne **505** d.	...	...	0445r	...	...	...	0545	...	...	...	...	0645	...	...	...	0745	...	...	...	...	0845	...	...	...	0945	...
0	**Basel SBB** d.	...	...	|	0603	0617	...	|	0703	...	0717	...	|	0803	0817	...	|	...	0903	0917	...	|	1003	1017	...	|	1103
14	Liestal d.	...	...	|	|	0626	...	|	|	...	0726	...	|	|	0826	...	|	...	|	0926	...	|	|	1026	...	|	|
21	Sissach d.	...	...	|	|	0633	...	|	|	...	0733	...	|	|	0833	...	|	...	|	0933	...	|	|	1033	...	|	|
39	**Olten** a.	...	...	|	0628	0647	...	|	0728	...	0747	...	|	0828	0847	...	|	...	0928	0947	...	|	1028	1047	...	|	1128
39	**Olten** d.	0549	0606	|	0630	0649	0706	|	0730	...	0749	0806	|	0830	0849	0906	|	...	0930	0949	1006	|	1030	1049	1106	|	1130
	Bern d.	|	|	0600	|	|	|	0700	|	...	|	|	0800	|	|	|	0900	...	|	|	|	1000	|	|	|	1100	|
47	Zofingen d.	0558	0612	0628	|	0658	0712	0728	|	...	0758	0812	0828	|	0858	0912	0928	...	|	0958	1012	1028	|	1058	1112	1128	|
69	Sursee d.	0611	0632	0641	|	0711	0732	0741	|	...	0811	0832	0841	|	0911	0932	0941	...	|	1011	1032	1041	|	1111	1132	1141	|
95	**Luzern** a.	0630	0656	0700	0705	0730	0756	0800	0805	...	0830	0856	0900	0905	0930	0956	1000	...	1005	1030	1056	1100	1105	1130	1156	1200	1205

	IR 2463	RE 3571	IR 2523	IR 2173	IR 2465	RE 3573	IR 2525	ICN 679	IR 2467	RE 3575	IR 2527	IR 2177	IR 2469	RE 3577	IR 2529	ICN 683	IR 2471	RE 3579	IR 2531	IR 2181	IR 2473	RE 3581	IR 2535	ICN 687	IR 2475	RE 3585	IR 2537
			🍷	△ L			🍷	🍴 G			🍷	△ L			🍷	🍴 C			🍷	△ L			🍷	🍴 C			🍷
Genève Aéroport ✈ **505** d.	...	...	1001	...	...	...	1101	...	...	...	1201	...	...	...	1301	...	...	...	1401	...	...	...	...	...	...	...	1601
Genève **505** d.	...	...	1010	...	...	...	1110	...	...	...	1210	...	...	...	1310	...	...	...	1410	...	...	...	...	...	...	...	1610
Lausanne **505** d.	...	...	1045	...	...	...	1145	...	...	...	1245	...	...	...	1345	...	...	...	1445	...	...	...	1545	...	...	...	1645
Basel SBB d.	1117	...	|	1203	1217	...	|	1303	1317	...	|	1403	1417	...	|	1503	1517	...	|	1603	1617	...	|	1703	1717	...	|
Liestal d.	1126	...	|	|	1226	...	|	|	1326	...	|	|	1426	...	|	|	1526	...	|	|	1626	...	|	|	1726	...	|
Sissach d.	1133	...	|	|	1233	...	|	|	1333	...	|	|	1433	...	|	|	1533	...	|	|	1633	...	|	|	1733	...	|
Olten a.	1147	...	|	1228	1247	...	|	1328	1347	...	|	1428	1447	...	|	1528	1547	...	|	1628	1647	...	|	1728	1747	...	|
Olten d.	1149	1206	|	1230	1249	1306	|	1330	1349	1406	|	1430	1449	1506	|	1530	1549	1606	|	1630	1649	1706	|	1730	1749	1806	|
Bern d.	|	|	1200	|	|	|	1300	|	|	|	1400	|	|	|	1500	|	|	|	1600	|	|	|	1700	|	|	|	1800
Zofingen d.	1158	1212	1228	|	1258	1312	1328	|	1358	1412	1428	|	1458	1512	1528	|	1558	1612	1628	|	1658	1712	1728	|	1758	1812	1828
Sursee d.	1211	1232	1241	|	1311	1332	1341	|	1411	1432	1441	|	1511	1532	1541	|	1611	1632	1641	|	1711	1732	1741	|	1811	1832	1841
Luzern a.	1230	1256	1300	1305	1330	1356	1400	1405	1430	1456	1500	1505	1530	1556	1600	1605	1630	1656	1700	1705	1730	1756	1800	1805	1830	1856	1900

	IR 2187	IR 2477	RE 3587	IR 2539	ICN 691	IR 2479	RE 3589	IR 2541	IR 2191	IR 2481	RE 3591	IR 2543	IR 2193	IR 2483	RE 3593	IR 2545	IR 2195	IR 2485	RE 3595	IR 2547	IR 2199	IR 2487	RE 3597	IR 2151	IR 2489	IR 2153	
	△ C				🍴 C				E				△				△									⑥⑦ q	
Genève Aéroport ✈ **505** d.	...	...	...	1701	...	...	...	1801	...	...	...	1901	...	...	...	2001	...	...	...	2047	...	...	...	...	...	...	...
Genève **505** d.	...	...	...	1710	...	...	...	1810	...	...	...	1910	...	...	...	2010	...	...	...	2056	...	...	...	...	...	...	...
Lausanne **505** d.	...	...	...	1745	...	...	...	1845	...	...	...	1945	...	...	...	2045	...	...	...	2145	...	...	...	...	...	...	...
Basel SBB d.	1803	1817	...	|	1903	1917	...	|	2003	2017	...	|	2103	2117	...	|	2203	2217	...	|	2303	2317	...	0003	0017	0101	...
Liestal d.	|	1826	...	|	|	1926	...	|	|	2026	...	|	|	2126	...	|	|	2226	...	|	|	2326	...	|	0026	0110	...
Sissach d.	|	1833	...	|	|	1933	...	|	|	2033	...	|	|	2133	...	|	|	2233	...	|	|	2333	...	|	0033	0116	...
Olten a.	1828	1847	...	|	1928	1947	...	|	2028	2047	...	|	2128	2147	...	|	2228	2247	...	|	2328	2347	...	0028	0047	0128	...
Olten d.	1830	1849	1906	|	1930	1949	2006	|	2030	2049	2106	|	2130	2149	2206	|	2230	2249	2306	|	2330	2349	0006	0033	...	0136	...
Bern d.	|	|	|	1900	|	|	|	2000	|	|	|	2100	|	|	|	2200	|	|	|	2300	|	|	|	|	...	|	...
Zofingen d.	|	1858	1912	1928	|	1958	2012	2028	|	2058	2112	2128	|	2158	2212	2228	|	2256	2312	2328	|	2356	0012	|	...	0143	...
Sursee d.	|	1911	1932	1941	|	2011	2032	2041	|	2111	2132	2141	|	2211	2232	2241	|	...	2332	2341	|	...	0034	0051	...	0157	...
Luzern a.	1905	1930	1956	2000	2005	2030	2056	2100	2105	2130	2156	2200	2205	2230	2256	2300	2305	...	2356	2400	0005	...	0058	0110	...	0215	...

km (via hsl)		RE 3554	IR 2452	IR 2160	IR 2508	RE 3558	IR 2454	IR 2162	IR 2510	RE 3560	IR 2456	IR 2164	IR 2512	RE 3562	IR 2458	IR 2166	IR 2516	RE 3566	IR 2460	ICN 658		IR 2518	RE 3568	IR 2462	IR 2170	IR 2520	RE 3570
								△	🍷			E	🍷			△ B	🍷			🍴 C		🍷			△ C	🍷	
	Luzern d.	0457	0530	0554	0600	0604	0630	0654	0700	0704	0730	0754	0800	0804	0830	0854	0900	0904	0930	0954	...	1000	1004	1030	1054	1100	1104
	Sursee d.	0521	0548	|	0618	0626	0648	|	0718	0726	0748	|	0818	0826	0848	|	0918	0926	0948	|	...	1018	1026	1048	|	1118	1126
0	Zofingen d.	0543	0602	|	0632	0645	0702	|	0732	0745	0802	|	0832	0845	0902	|	0932	0945	1002	|	...	1032	1045	1102	|	1132	1145
63	**Bern** a.	|	|	|	0700	|	|	|	0800	|	|	|	0900	|	|	|	1000	|	|	|	...	1100	|	|	|	1200	|
	Olten a.	0552	0610	0627	|	0652	0710	0727	|	0752	0810	0827	|	0852	0910	0927	|	0952	1010	1027	...	|	1052	1110	1127	|	1152
	Olten d.	...	0612	0629	|	...	0712	0729	|	...	0812	0829	|	...	0912	0929	|	...	1012	1029	...	|	...	1112	1129	|	...
	Sissach d.	...	0627	|	|	...	0727	|	|	...	0827	|	|	...	0927	|	|	...	1027	|	...	|	...	1127	|	|	...
	Liestal d.	...	0634	|	|	...	0734	|	|	...	0834	|	|	...	0934	|	|	...	1034	|	...	|	...	1134	|	|	...
	Basel SBB a.	...	0644	0653	|	...	0744	0753	|	...	0844	0853	|	...	0944	0953	|	...	1044	1053	...	|	...	1144	1153	|	...
	Lausanne **505** a.	...	...	...	0815	...	...	...	0915	...	...	...	1015	...	...	...	1115	...	...	...	...	1215	...	...	...	1315	...
	Genève **505** a.	...	...	...	0850	...	...	...	0950	...	...	...	1050	...	...	...	1150	...	...	...	...	...	...	...	...	1350	...
	Genève Aéroport ✈ **505** a.	...	...	...	0859	...	...	...	0959	...	...	...	1059	...	...	...	1159	...	...	...	...	...	...	...	...	1359	...

	IR 2464	ICN 662	IR 2522	RE 3572	IR 2466	IR 2174	IR 2524	RE 3574	IR 2468	ICN 666	IR 2526	RE 3576	IR 2470	IR 2178		IR 2528	RE 3578	IR 2472	ICN 670	IR 2530	RE 3580	IR 2474	IR 2182	IR 2532	RE 3582	IR 2476	ICN 674
		🍴 C	🍷			△ L	🍷			🍴 G	🍷			△🍷 L		🍷			🍴 G	🍷			△ L	🍷			🍴 G
Luzern d.	1130	1154	1200	1204	1230	1254	1300	1304	1330	1354	1400	1404	1430	1454	...	1500	1504	1530	1554	1600	1604	1630	1654	1700	1704	1730	1754
Sursee d.	1148	|	1218	1226	1248	|	1318	1326	1348	|	1418	1426	1448	|	...	1518	1526	1548	|	1618	1626	1648	|	1718	1726	1748	|
Zofingen d.	1202	|	1232	1245	1302	|	1332	1345	1402	|	1432	1445	1502	|	...	1532	1545	1602	|	1632	1645	1702	|	1732	1745	1802	|
Bern a.	|	|	1300	|	|	|	1400	|	|	|	1500	|	|	|	...	1600	|	|	|	1700	|	|	|	1800	|	|	|
Olten a.	1210	1227	|	1252	1310	1327	|	1352	1410	1427	|	1452	1510	1527	...	|	1552	1610	1627	|	1652	1710	1727	|	1752	1810	1827
Olten d.	1212	1229	|	...	1312	1329	|	...	1412	1429	|	...	1512	1529	...	|	...	1612	1629	|	...	1712	1729	|	...	1812	1829
Sissach d.	1227	|	|	...	1327	|	|	...	1427	|	|	...	1527	|	...	|	...	1627	|	|	...	1727	|	|	...	1827	|
Liestal d.	1234	|	|	...	1334	|	|	...	1434	|	|	...	1534	|	...	|	...	1634	|	|	...	1734	|	|	...	1834	|
Basel SBB a.	1244	1253	|	...	1344	1353	|	...	1444	1453	|	...	1544	1553	...	|	...	1644	1653	|	...	1744	1753	|	...	1844	1853
Lausanne **505** a.	...	...	1415	...	...	...	1515	...	...	...	1615	...	...	...	...	1715	...	...	...	1815	...	...	...	1915	...	...	...
Genève **505** a.	...	...	1450	...	...	...	1550	...	...	...	1650	...	...	...	...	1750	...	...	...	1850	...	...	...	1950	...	...	...
Genève Aéroport ✈ **505** a.	...	...	1459	...	...	...	1559	...	...	...	1659	...	...	...	...	1759	...	...	...	1859	...	...	...	1959	...	...	...

	IR 2536	RE 3586	IR 2478	IR 2188	IR 2538	RE 3588	IR 2480		ICN 678	IR 2540	RE 3590	IR 2482	IR 2192	IR 2542	RE 3592	IR 2484		IR 2544	RE 3594	IR 2486	IR 2196	IR 2546	RE 3596	IR 2488		RE 3598	IR 2150
	🍷			△🍷 L					🍴 G				△ L								△ L						⑥⑦ q
Luzern d.	1800	1804	1830	1854	1900	1904	1930	...	1954	2000	2004	2030	2054	2100	2104	2130	...	2200	2204	...	2254	2300	2304	...	...	0004	0049
Sursee d.	1818	1826	1848	|	1918	1926	1948	...	|	2018	2026	2048	|	2118	2126	2148	...	2218	2226	...	|	2318	2326	...	...	0026	0108
Zofingen d.	1832	1845	1902	|	1932	1945	2002	...	|	2032	2045	2102	|	2132	2145	2202	...	2232	2245	2302	|	2332	2345	0005	...	0045	0121
Bern a.	1900	|	|	|	2000	|	|	...	|	2100	|	|	|	2200	|	|	...	2300	|	|	|	2400	|	|	...	|	|
Olten a.	|	1852	1910	1927	|	1952	2010	...	2027	|	2052	2110	2127	|	2152	2210	...	...	2252	2310	2327	|	2352	0012	...	0052	0128
Olten d.	|	...	1912	1929	|	...	2012	...	2029	|	...	2112	2129	|	...	2212	...	...	...	2312	2329	|	...	0013	...	...	0136
Sissach d.	|	...	1927	|	|	...	2027	...	|	|	...	2127	|	|	...	2227	...	...	...	2327	|	|	...	0027	...	...	|
Liestal d.	|	...	1934	|	|	...	2034	...	|	|	...	2134	|	|	...	2234	...	...	...	2334	|	|	...	0034	...	...	|
Basel SBB a.	|	...	1944	1953	|	...	2044	...	2053	|	...	2144	2153	|	...	2244	...	...	...	2344	2353	|	...	0044	...	...	0159
Lausanne **505** a.	2015	...	...	...	2115	...	...	...	...	2215	...	...	...	2315	...	...	...	...	...	...	...	0122j	...	...	...	...	...
Genève **505** a.	2050	...	...	...	2204	...	...	...	...	2304	...	...	...	0004	...	...	...	...	...	...	...	...	...	...	...	...	...
Genève Aéroport ✈ **505** a.	2059	...	...	...	2213	...	...	...	...	2313	...	...	...	...	...	...	...	...	...	...	...	...	...	...	...	...	...

B – 🚃 12 Bellinzona - Basel.
C – 🚃 12 Basel - Chiasso and v.v.
E – 🚃 12 Basel - Erstfeld and v.v.
G – 🚃 12 Basel - Lugano and v.v.
L – 🚃 12 Basel - Locarno and v.v.

j – ⑤⑥⑦ only.
q – Also Jan. 1.
r – ① (also Apr. 14, June 2; not Apr. 13, June 1).
y – Dec. 14 - June 13.

△ – Also conveys 🚃 1 [observation car].

LENK - ZWEISIMMEN - MONTREUX — 566

Narrow gauge. MOB

km		Ⓐ		Ⓐ																Ⓐ		Ⓐ					⑤⑥
0	**Lenk** d.	0611	0634	0703	0737	0837	0937	1003	1037	1103	1137	1237	1303	1337	1437	1537	1603	1637	1737	1803	1845	1903	1937	2037	2137	2237	2326
13	**Zweisimmen** a.	0629	0652	0721	0755	0855	0955	1021	1055	1121	1155	1255	1321	1355	1455	1555	1621	1655	1755	1821	1901	1921	1955	2055	2155	2255	2344

km						2111			3115			2119	2221	3123				2129	2127				2131				
						🍸 G			🍸 G★			(🍸) C	🍸 G	🍸 G★				(🍸) 🅁 T	🍸 G★			Ⓐ	(🍸) C				
0	**Zweisimmen** d.	0411	0518	0605	0700	0826	0905	0934	1026	1105	...	1226	1305	1426	...	1505	1515	...	1626	...	1705	1724	1826	1905	2005	2105	2155
9	Saanenmöser d.	0426	0532	0619	0714	0841	0919	0947	1041	1119	...	1241	1319	1441	...	1519	1530	...	1641	...	1719	1738	1841	1919	2019	2119	2208
11	Schönried d.	0431	0537	0624	0719	0846	0924	0952	1046	1124	...	1246	1324	1446	...	1524	1535	...	1646	...	1724	1743	1846	1924	2024	2124	2212
16	**Gstaad** d.	0440	0547	0634	0730	0856	0935	1000	1056	1135	...	1256	1335	1456	...	1535	1544	...	1656	...	1735	1752	1856	1935	2035	2135	2222
19	Saanen d.	0444	0551	0639	0735	0901	0940	...	1101	1140	...	1301	1340	1501	...	1540	1548	...	1701	...	1740	1756	1901	1940	2040	2140	2226s
23	Rougemont d.	0450	0556	0645	0741	0906	0946	...	1106	1146	...	1306	1346	1506	...	1546	...	...	1706	...	1746	...	1906	1946	2046	2146	2231s
29	Château d'Oex d.	0503	0610	0706	0806	0916	1006	...	1116	1206	...	1316	1406	1516	...	1606	...	...	1716	...	1806	...	1916	2006	2106	2206	2240
40	**Montbovon** d.	0522	0631	0723	0826	0931	1026	...	1131	1226	...	1331	1426	1531	...	1626	...	1711	1731	...	1826	...	1931	2026	2130	2233	...
51	Les Avants § d.	0544	0652	0743	0847	0952	1047	...	1152	1247	...	1352	1447	1552	...	1647	...	|	1752	...	1847	...	1952	2047	2150	2253	...
55	Chamby ⊙ § d.	0555	0659	0750	0854	1000	1054	...	1200	1254	...	1400	1454	1600	...	1654	...	|	1800	...	1854	...	2000	2054	2157	2300	...
58	Chernex § d.	0601	0704	0756	0900	1005	1100	...	1205	1300	...	1405	1500	1605	...	1700	...	|	1805	...	1900	...	2005	2100	2202	2305	...
62	**Montreux** § a.	0610	0713	0805	0910	1013	1110	...	1213	1310	...	1413	1510	1613	...	1710	...	1810	1813	...	1910	...	2013	2110	2211	2315	...

							2216		2118	3118	2222				3126		2228	2128				2134				
	Ⓐ	Ⓐ	Ⓒ					(🍸) C		(🍸) 🅁 T	🍸 C★	🍸 G				🍸 G		(🍸) C	🍸 G		Ⓐ		🍸 G★				
Montreux § d.	...	...	...	0540	0635	0745	...	0847	...	0925	0945	1045	1145	...	1245	1345	...	1445	1545	1645	...	...	1745	1845	1945	2045	2145
Chernex § d.	...	...	...	0550	0645	0755	...	0855	...	|	0955	1055	1155	...	1255	1355	...	1455	1555	1655	...	...	1755	1855	1955	2059	2201
Chamby ⊙ § d.	...	...	...	0556	0650	0800	...	0900	...	|	1000	1100	1200	...	1300	1400	...	1500	1600	1700	...	...	1800	1900	2000	2104	2206
Les Avants § d.	...	...	...	0604	0658	0807	...	0912	...	|	1007	1112	1207	...	1312	1407	...	1512	1607	1712	...	...	1807	1912	2008	2112	2214
Montbovon d.	...	...	...	0622	0722	0828	...	0932	...	1012	1028	1132	1228	...	1332	1428	...	1532	1628	1732	...	...	1828	1932	2032	2132	2234
Château d'Oex d.	...	0541	0550	0639	0737	0843	...	0949	...	...	1043	1149	1243	...	1349	1443	...	1549	1643	1749	...	...	1843	1949	2049	2149	2249
Rougemont d.	...	0555	0603	0651	0750	0853	...	1003	...	...	1053	1203	1253	...	1403	1453	...	1603	1653	1803	...	...	1853	2003	2103	2203	2303
Saanen d.	0514	0601	0620	0657	0756	0859	...	1009	...	...	1059	1209	1259	...	1409	1459	1552	1609	1659	1809	1821	...	1859	2009	2109	2209	2309
Gstaad d.	0519	0606	0625	0703	0803	0905	1005	1014	...	...	1105	1214	1305	...	1414	1505	1557	1614	1705	1814	1827	...	1905	2014	2114	2214	2314
Schönried d.	0528	0614	0634	0711	0812	0914	1014	1023	...	...	1114	1223	1314	...	1423	1514	1606	1623	1714	1823	1836	...	1914	2023	2123	2223	2323
Saanenmöser d.	0533	0618	0639	0715	0817	0918	1019	1028	...	...	1118	1228	1318	...	1428	1518	1611	1628	1718	1828	1841	...	1918	2028	2128	2228	2328
Zweisimmen a.	0547	0631	0653	0729	0834	0932	1034	1043	...	...	1132	1243	1332	...	1443	1532	1625	1643	1732	1843	1854	...	1932	2043	2143	2243	2343

	Ⓐ		Ⓐ																	Ⓐ		Ⓐ					⑤⑥
Zweisimmen d.	0548	0611	0634	0703	0803	0903	0937	1003	1037	1103	1137	...	1203	1303	1403	1503	1537	1603	1703	1737	1803	1825	1903	2003	2103	2203	2303
Lenk a.	0606	0629	0652	0721	0821	0921	0956	1021	1056	1121	1156	...	1221	1321	1421	1521	1556	1621	1721	1756	1821	1842	1921	2021	2121	2221	2321

§ – ADDITIONAL SERVICES LES AVANTS - MONTREUX and v.v. (2nd class only):

	Ⓐ	Ⓐ		q		q		Ⓐ			
Les Avants d.	0710	0815	...	1323	...	1720	...	1800	...	2320	...
Chamby ⊙ d.	0717	0822	...	1330	...	1728	...	1807	...	2327	...
Chernex d.	0723	0834	...	1335	...	1734	...	1812	...	2332	...
Montreux a.	0736	0844	...	1345	...	1744	...	1824	...	2342	...

	Ⓐ	Ⓐ		q		q		Ⓐ			
Montreux d.	0643	0740	...	1216	...	1606	...	1714	...	2251	2345
Chernex d.	0653	0757	...	1226	...	1617	...	1724	...	2304	2355s
Chamby ⊙ d.	0658	0804	...	1231	...	1622	...	1729	...	2309	0000s
Les Avants a.	0706	0811	...	1238	...	1629	...	1736	...	2316	0007

C – GOLDEN PASS CLASSIC – 🚃12 and (🍸).
G – GOLDEN PASS PANORAMIC – conveys 🚃12 [observation cars].
T – TRAIN DU CHOCOLAT – ①③④ May 4 - July 2; daily July 3 - Aug. 31; ①③④ Sept. 2 - 30: conveys 🚃1 only.

q – Ⓐ Dec. 15 - 19, Jan. 5 - Apr. 3, Apr. 20 - July 3, Aug. 24 - Oct. 9, Oct. 26 - Dec. 11 (not Feb. 16 - 20, May 22, Sept. 21).
s – Stops to set down only.

★ – Also conveys VIP accommodation. 🅁
⊙ – Chamby is a request stop.

MONTBOVON - BULLE - PALÉZIEUX — 568

Narrow gauge. 2nd class only. TPF

km																								611		🚌
		Ⓐ		⚒																				🅁 F w		
0	**Montbovon** d.	...	0540a	0640	0723	0840	...	0940	1040	1140	...	1240	1340	1440	...	1540	1640	1740	...	1840	1940	2040	...	2130	...	2140
13	Gruyères d.	...	0558a	0658	0745	0858	...	0958	1058	1158	...	1258	1358	1458	...	1558	1658	1758	...	1858	1958	2058	...	|	...	2158
17	**Bulle** ▲ a.	...	0608a	0708	0753	0908	...	1008	1108	1208	...	1308	1408	1508	...	1608	1708	1808	...	1908	2008	2108	...	2204	...	2208
17	**Bulle** d.	0513	0613	0713	0813	0913	...	1013	1113	1213	...	1313	1413	1513	...	1613	1713	1813	...	1913	2013	2113	...	...	...	...
37	Châtel-St Denis a.	0541	0641	0741	0841	0941	...	1041	1141	1241	...	1341	1441	1541	...	1641	1741	1841	...	1941	2041	2141	...	...	...	...
37	Châtel-St Denis d.	0544	0644	0744	0844	0944	...	1044	1144	1244	...	1344	1444	1544	...	1644	1744	1844	...	1944	2044	2144	...	...	...	...
44	**Palézieux** a.	0555	0655	0755	0855	0955	...	1055	1155	1255	...	1355	1455	1555	...	1655	1755	1855	...	1955	2055	2155	...	...	...	...

																	610					🚌		
	Ⓐ	⚒															🅁 F w							
Palézieux d.	...	...	0605a	0705	0805d	0905	1005	...	1105	1205	1305	1405	...	1505	1605	1705	...	...	1805	1905	...	2005	...	2105	2205
Châtel-St Denis a.	...	...	0616a	0716	0816d	0916	1016	...	1116	1216	1316	1416	...	1516	1616	1716	...	...	1816	1916	...	2016	...	2116	2216
Châtel-St Denis d.	...	...	0619a	0719	0819d	0919	1019	...	1119	1219	1319	1419	...	1519	1619	1719	...	...	1819	1919	...	2019	...	2119	2219
Bulle a.	...	...	0647a	0747	0847d	0947	1047	...	1147	1247	1347	1447	...	1547	1647	1747	...	...	1847	1947	...	2047	...	2147	2247
Bulle ▲ d.	0452	0552	0652	0756	0852	0952	1052	...	1152	1252	1352	1452	...	1552	1652	1752	...	1830	1852	1952	...	...	2052	...	...
Gruyères d.	0459	0559	0659	0803	0859	0959	1059	...	1159	1259	1359	1459	...	1559	1659	1759	...	|	1859	1959	...	...	2059	...	...
Montbovon a.	0518	0620	0720	0824	0920	1020	1120	...	1220	1320	1420	1520	...	1620	1720	1820	...	1904	1920	2020	...	...	2120	...	...

F – TRAIN FONDUE – 🚃1 [observation car], 🚃12 and ✕ Montbovon - Bulle and v.v. 🅁.
a – Ⓐ only.
d – ⚒ only.
q – Not June 11, Dec. 8.
w – ⑥ Jan. 10 - Apr. 25, Oct. 31 - Nov. 28 (not Jan. 24, Feb. 7, 28, Mar. 7, 28, Apr. 11, 18, Nov. 14).
x – Not Aug. 1.

▲ – Local TPF rail services **Bulle - Broc** (*5 km*, journey time 11 minutes), **Bulle - Romont** (*18 km*, journey time 22 minutes); TPF 🚌 service **Bulle - Fribourg** (*28 km*, journey time 32 minutes, line **346**). Other services available (some via Sorens) journey time 45 – 60 minutes, line **336**.

From **Bulle**: 0619Ⓐ, 0713⚒, 0813, 0913⚒, 1013, 1113Ⓐ, 1154Ⓐ, 1213Ⓒ, 1313, 1413Ⓐ, 1513, 1554Ⓐ, 1613⑥**x**, 1713, 1813, 1913.
From **Broc**: 0632Ⓐ, 0732⚒, 0832, 0932⚒, 1032, 1132Ⓐ, 1232Ⓒ, 1249Ⓐ, 1332, 1432Ⓐ, 1532, 1632⚒, 1732, 1832, 1932.
From **Bulle**: 0546Ⓐ, 0646, 0746⚒, 0846, 1046, 1204, 1318Ⓐ, 1418, 1518Ⓐ, 1618, 1718, 1818, 1918.
From **Romont**: 0619Ⓐ, 0719, 0819⚒, 0919, 1119, 1247, 1347Ⓐ, 1447, 1547Ⓐ, 1647, 1747, 1847, 1947.
From **Bulle** (Gare) 🚌 service: 0556Ⓐ **q**, 0626, 0656Ⓐ **q**, 0726, 0756Ⓐ **q**, 0826 and hourly until 1226, 1256Ⓐ **q**, 1326 and hourly until 1626, 1656Ⓐ **q**, 1726, 1756Ⓐ **q**, 1826, 1926, 2026, 2056, 2145, 2245, 2345⑤⑥.
From **Fribourg** (Gare) 🚌 service: 0602Ⓐ **q**, 0632Ⓐ **q**, 0702, 0732Ⓐ **q**, 0802 and hourly until 1202, 1232Ⓐ **q**, 1302 and hourly until 1602, 1632Ⓐ **q**, 1702, 1732Ⓐ **q**, 1802, 1832Ⓐ **q**, 1902, 2002, 2102, 2202, 2302.

MONTREUX - CAUX - ROCHERS DE NAYE — 569

Narrow gauge rack railway. 2nd class only. MOB

No service between Caux and Rochers de Naye during bad weather

km									B																
0	**Montreux** d.	0545	0645	0745	...	0847	0946	1046	1046	...	1146	1246	...	1346	1446	1546	...	1646	1746	...	1846	1946	2046	2146	2246
3	Glion ▲ d.	0558	0658	0758	...	0900	1000	1100	1102	...	1200	1300	...	1400	1500	1600	...	1700	1800	...	1900	2000	2100	2200	2258s
5	Caux a.	0609	0709	0809	...	0911	1011	1111	1116	...	1211	1311	...	1411	1511	1611	...	1711	1811	...	1911	2011	2111	2211	2311
10	**Rochers de Naye** a.	...	...	...	...	0941p	1041p	1141p	1208	...	1241p	1341p	...	1441p	1541p	1641p	...	1741r	1841t	...	...	...	...	...	...

														B											
Rochers de Naye d.	...	...	...	...	...	0946p	1046p	...	1146p	1246p	...	1346p	1446p	1520	...	1546p	1646p	...	1746r	1846t	...	...	...	...	...
Caux d.	0612	0712	...	0812	0916	1016	1116	...	1216	1316	...	1416	1516	1555	...	1616	1716	...	1816	1916	...	2016	2116	2216	...
Glion ▲ d.	0625	0725	...	0825	0929	1029	1129	...	1229	1329	...	1429	1529	1616	...	1629	1729	...	1829	1929	...	2029	2129	2229	...
Montreux a.	0637	0737	...	0837	0941	1041	1141	...	1241	1341	...	1441	1541	1630	...	1641	1741	...	1841	1941	...	2041	2141	2241	...

B – BELLE EPOQUE – Ⓒ July 4 - Aug. 30. Runs only in good weather.
p – Daily Dec. 14 - Oct. 30; Ⓒ Oct. 31 - Dec. 12.
r – May 31 - Sept. 27.
s – Stops to set down only.
t – June 29 - Aug. 30.

▲ – Funicular railway operates daily except in summer **Glion - Territet** and v.v. **Operator**: MVR, ✆ 0900 245 245. Engineering work is currently taking place – contact operator for schedule.

570 GENÈVE - LAUSANNE - SION - BRIG SBB

km		IR 1709	IR 1411	IR 1711	EC 35 ⊡ M	IR 1711	IR 1415	IR 1715	IR 1417	IR 1717	EC 37 ⊡🍷 V	IR 1717		IR 1419	IR 1719	IR 1421	IR 1721	IR 1423	IR 1723	IR 1425	EC 125 ⊡ M	IR 1425	TGV 9261 (🍷) ◆	IR 1725	IR 1427	IR 1727
0	Genève A ✈ 505 d.	...	...	...	...	...	0547	0627	0647	0724	0733	...	...	0747	0827	0847	0927	0947	1027	1047	...	...	...	1127	1147	1227
6	**Genève 505** d.	...	...	0521	0545	...	0556	0636	0656	0733	0742	...	...	0756	0836	0856	0936	0956	1036	1056	1107	...	...	1136	1156	1236
27	Nyon 505 d.	...	...	0537	|	...	0610	0650	0710	0747	|	...	...	0810	0850	0910	0950	1010	1050	1110	|	...	...	1150	1210	1250
53	Morges 505 d.	...	...	0600	|	...	0628	0705	0728	0802	|	...	...	0828	0905	0928	1005	1028	1105	1128	|	...	...	1205	1228	1305
66	**Lausanne 505** a.	...	...	0612	0617	...	0640	0715	0740	0812	|	←	...	0840	0915	0940	1015	1040	1115	1140	1140	←	...	1215	1240	1315
66	**Lausanne** ▲ d.	...	0545	→	0620	0624	0645	0720	0745	→	0820u	0824	...	0845	0920	0945	1020	1045	1120	→	1146	1150	1157	1220	1245	1320
84	Vevey ▲ d.	...	0559	...	|	0638	0659	0734	0759	...	|	0838	...	0859	0934	0959	1034	1059	1134	...	|	1204	|	1234	1259	1334
92	**Montreux** ▲ d.	...	0605	...	0639	0644	0705	0740	0805	...	0839	0844	...	0905	0940	1005	1040	1105	1140	...	1205	1210	1217	1240	1305	1340
105	Aigle ▲ d.	...	0616	...	|	0655	0716	0751	0816	...	|	0855	...	0916	0951	1016	1051	1116	1151	...	|	1221	1230	1251	1316	1351
114	Bex d.	...	0623	...	|	|	0723	|	0823	...	|	|	...	0923	|	1023	|	1123	|	...	|	1227	|	|	1323	|
118	St Maurice d.	...	0628	...	|	|	0728	|	0828	...	|	|	...	0928	|	1028	|	1128	|	...	|	1232	|	|	1328	|
133	Martigny d.	...	0638	...	|	0712	0738	0808	0838	...	|	0912	...	0938	1008	1038	1108	1138	1208	...	|	1243	1249	1308	1338	1408
158	**Sion** d.	0624	0654	...	0714	0728	0754	0824	0854	...	0914	0928	...	0954	1024	1054	1124	1154	1224	...	1243	1258	1306	1324	1354	1424
174	Sierre d.	0634	0704	...	|	0738	0804	0834	0904	...	|	0938	...	1004	1034	1104	1134	1204	1234	...	1253	1308	1317	1334	1404	1434
184	Leuk d.	0642	0712	...	|	|	0812	0842	0912	...	|	|	...	1012	1042	1112	1142	1212	1242	...	|	|	1326	1342	1412	1442
203	Visp d.	0655	0722	...	|	0755	0824	0855	0924	...	|	0955	...	1024	1055	1124	1155	1224	1255	...	|	1324	1338	1355	1424	1455
212	**Brig** a.	0702	0730	...	0740	0802	0830	0902	0930	...	0940	1002	...	1030	1102	1130	1202	1230	1302	...	1314	1330	1345	1402	1430	1502
368	*Milano C 590* a.	...	...	...	0935	...	...	...	...	...	1135	...	...	...	...	...	...	...	...	...	1535	...	...	...	...	...

	IR 1429	IR 1729	IR 1431	IR 1731	IR 1435	EC 127 ⊡ M	IR 1435	IR 1735	IR 1437	TGV 9267 (🍷) ◆	IR 1737	IR 1439	IR 1739	IR 1441	EC 129 ⊡ M	IR 1441	IR 1741	IR 1443	TGV 9273 (🍷) ◆	IR 1743	IR 1445	IR 1745	EN 311 ◆	IR 1749	IR 1449	
Genève A ✈ 505 d.	1247	1327	1347	1427	1447	...	...	1527	1547	...	1627	1647	1727	1747	...	...	1827	1847	...	1927	1947	2027	2127	2227	2312	...
Genève 505 d.	1256	1336	1356	1436	1456	1510	...	1536	1556	...	1636	1656	1736	1756	1807	...	1836	1856	...	1936	1956	2036	2136	2236	2321	...
Nyon 505 d.	1310	1350	1410	1450	1510	|	...	1550	1610	...	1650	1710	1750	1810	|	...	1850	1910	...	1950	2010	2050	2150	2250	2337	...
Morges 505 d.	1328	1405	1428	1505	1528	|	...	1605	1628	...	1705	1728	1805	1828	|	...	1905	1928	...	2005	2028	2105	2205	2305	0001	...
Lausanne 505 a.	1340	1415	1440	1515	1540	1543	←	1615	1640	...	1715	1740	1815	1840	|	←	1915	1940	...	2015	2040	2115	2215	2315	0012	...
Lausanne ▲ d.	1345	1420	1445	1520	→	1546	1550	1620	1645	1657	1720	1745	1820	→	1846u	1850	1920	1945	1957	2020	2045	2120	2220	2320	0024	...
Vevey ▲ d.	1359	1434	1459	1534	...	|	1604	1634	1659	|	1734	1759	1834	...	|	1904	1934	1959	|	2034	2059	2134	2234	2334	0038	...
Montreux ▲ d.	1405	1440	1505	1540	...	1605	1610	1640	1705	1717	1740	1805	1840	...	1905	1910	1940	2005	2015	2040	2105	2140	2240	2340	0044	...
Aigle ▲ d.	1416	1451	1516	1551	...	|	1621	1651	1716	1727	1751	1816	1851	...	|	1921	1951	2016	2026	2051	2116	2151	2251	2351	0055	...
Bex d.	1423	|	1523	|	...	|	1627	|	1723	...	|	1823	|	...	|	1927	|	2023	|	2058	2123	2158	2258	2358	0102	...
St Maurice d.	1428	|	1528	|	...	|	1632	|	1728	...	|	1828	|	...	|	1932	|	2028	|	2103	2128	2203	2303	0003	0107	...
Martigny d.	1438	1508	1538	1608	...	|	1643	1708	1738	...	1808	1838	1908	...	|	1943	2008	2038	2045	2114	2138	2214	2314	0014	0117	...
Sion d.	1454	1524	1554	1624	...	1643	1658	1724	1754	...	1824	1854	1924	...	1943	1958	2024	2054	2103	2127	2154	2229	2329	0029	0131	...
Sierre d.	1504	1534	1604	1634	...	1653	1708	1734	1804	...	1834	1904	1934	...	1953	2008	2034	2104	2116	...	2204	2239	2339	0039	...	...
Leuk d.	1512	1542	1612	1642	...	|	|	1742	1812	...	1842	1912	1942	...	|	|	2042	2112	2126	...	2212	2247	2347	0047	...	...
Visp d.	1524	1555	1624	1655	...	|	1724	1755	1824	...	1855	1924	1955	...	|	2024	2055	2124	2141	...	2224	2259	2359	0059	...	...
Brig a.	1530	1602	1630	1702	...	1714	1730	1802	1830	...	1902	1930	2002	...	2014	2030	2102	2130	2147	...	2230	2305	0005	0105	...	...
Milano C 590 a.	...	...	...	...	...	1935	...	...	...	...	...	...	...	...	2235	...	...	...	...	...	...	...	...	...	...	...

	IR 1402	IR 1702	IR 1404	IR 1706	IR 1406	IR 1708	IR 1408	EN 316 ◆	IR 1410	IR 1712	IR 1412	IR 1714	IR 1414	IR 1718	IR 1418	EC 120 ⊡ M	IR 1418	IR 1720	TGV 9268 (🍷) ◆	IR 1420	IR 1722	IR 1422	IR 1724	IR 1424	IR 1726	IR 1426
Milano C 590 d.	...	...	...	...	...	...	...	...	...	...	...	...	...	...	...	0825	...	...	...	...	...	...	...	...	...	...
Brig d.	...	...	0428	...	0528	0600	0628	0657	0728	0757	0828	0857	0928	0957	1028	1046	...	1057	1101	1128	1157	1228	1257	1328	1357	1428
Visp d.	...	...	0436	...	0536	0608	0636	0707	0736	0807	0836	0907	0936	1007	1036	|	...	1107	1111	1136	1207	1236	1307	1336	1407	1436
Leuk d.	...	...	0447	...	0547	0619	0647	0718	0747	0818	0847	0918	0947	1018	|	|	...	1118	1123	1147	1218	1247	1318	1347	1418	|
Sierre d.	...	...	0455	...	0555	0626	0655	0726	0755	0826	0855	0926	0955	1026	1051	1106	...	1126	1132	1155	1226	1255	1326	1355	1426	1451
Sion d.	...	0426	0506	0532	0606	0637	0706	0737	0806	0837	0906	0937	1006	1037	1102	1117	...	1137	1143	1206	1237	1306	1337	1406	1437	1502
Martigny d.	...	0440	0520	0545	0620	0651	0720	0751	0820	0851	0920	0951	1020	1051	1116	|	...	1151	1157	1220	1251	1320	1351	1420	1451	1516
St Maurice d.	...	0451	0531	0556	0631	|	0731	|	0831	|	0931	|	1031	|	1126	|	...	|	|	1231	|	1331	|	1431	|	1526
Bex d.	...	0456	0536	0601	0636	|	0736	|	0836	|	0936	|	1036	|	1131	|	...	|	|	1236	|	1336	|	1436	|	1531
Aigle ▲ d.	...	0503	0543	0608	0643	0708	0743	0808	0843	0908	0943	1008	1043	1108	1138	|	...	1208	1215	1243	1308	1343	1408	1443	1508	1538
Montreux ▲ d.	...	0514	0554	0619	0654	0719	0754	0819	0854	0919	0954	1019	1054	1119	1149	1155	...	1219	1227	1254	1319	1354	1419	1454	1519	1549
Vevey ▲ d.	...	0521	0601	0626	0701	0726	0801	0826	0901	0926	1001	1026	1101	1126	1156	|	...	1226	|	1301	1326	1401	1426	1501	1526	1556
Lausanne ▲ a.	...	0535	0615	0640	0715	0740	0815	0840	0915	0940	1015	1040	1115	1140	1210	1214	←	1240	1245	1315	1340	1415	1440	1515	1540	1610
Lausanne 505 d.	0520	0540	0620	0645	0720	0745	0820	0845	0920	0945	1020	1045	1120	1145	→	1217	1220	1245	...	1320	1345	1420	1445	1520	1545	→
Morges 505 d.	0532	0550	0632	0654	0732	0754	0832	0854	0932	0954	1032	1054	1132	1154	...	|	1232	1254	...	1332	1355	1432	1454	1532	1554	
Nyon 505 d.	0550	0605	0650	0710	0750	0810	0850	0910	0950	1010	1050	1110	1150	1210	...	|	1250	1310	...	1350	1410	1450	1510	1550	1610	
Genève 505 a.	0604	0619	0704	0724	0804	0824	0904	0924	1004	1024	1104	1124	1204	1224	...	1250	1304	1324	...	1404	1424	1504	1524	1604	1624	
Genève A ✈ 505 a.	0613	0628	0713	0733	0813	0833	0913	0933	1013	1033	1113	1133	1213	1233	...	...	1313	1333	...	1413	1433	1513	1533	1613	1633	

	EC 122 ⊡ M	IR 1426	IR 1728	IR 1428	TGV 9272 (🍷) ◆	IR 1730	IR 1430	EC 124 ⊡ M	IR 1430	IR 1732	TGV 9274 (🍷) ◆	IR 1432	IR 1736	EC 40 ⊡ M	IR 1736	IR 1436	IR 1738	IR 1438	IR 1740	IR 1440	IR 2540	EC 42 ⊡🍷 V	IR 1442	IR 2542	IR 1444	IR 2648
Milano C 590 d.	1225	...	...	...	...	...	...	1425	...	...	...	...	...	1625	...	...	...	...	...	...	...	1920	...	...	...	...
Brig d.	1446	...	1457	1528	1541	1557	1628	1646	...	1657	...	1728	1757	1820	...	1828	1857	1928	1957	2028	...	2123	2128	...	2228	...
Visp d.	|	...	1507	1536	1549	1607	1636	|	...	1707	...	1736	1807	|	...	1836	1907	1936	2007	2036	...	|	2136	...	2236	...
Leuk d.	|	...	1518	1547	1602	1618	|	|	...	1718	...	1747	|	|	...	1847	1918	1947	2018	2047	...	|	2147	...	2247	...
Sierre d.	1506	...	1526	1555	1611	1626	1651	1706	...	1726	...	1755	1822	|	...	1855	1926	1955	2026	2055	...	|	2155	...	2255	...
Sion d.	1517	...	1537	1606	1626	1637	1702	1717	...	1737	...	1806	1833	1847	...	1906	1937	2006	2035	2106	...	2151	2206	...	2306	...
Martigny d.	|	...	1551	1620	1642	1651	1716	|	...	1751	...	1820	1847	|	...	1920	1951	2020	▬	2120	...	|	2220	...	2320	...
St Maurice d.	|	...	|	1631	|	|	1726	|	...	|	...	1831	|	|	...	1931	|	2031	...	2131	...	|	2231	...	2331	...
Bex d.	|	...	|	1636	|	|	1731	|	...	|	...	1836	|	|	...	1936	|	2036	...	2136	...	|	2236	...	2336	...
Aigle ▲ d.	|	...	1608	1643	1714	1708	1738	|	...	1808	1835	1843	1904	|	...	1943	2008	2043	...	2143	...	|	2243	...	2343	...
Montreux ▲ d.	1555	...	1619	1654	1727	1719	1749	1755	...	1819	1849	1854	1915	1921	...	1954	2019	2054	*IR*	2154	...	2224	2254	...	2354	...
Vevey ▲ d.	|	...	1626	1701	|	1726	1756	|	...	1826	|	1901	1922	|	...	2001	2026	2101	**2538**	2201	...	|	2301	...	0001	...
Lausanne ▲ a.	1614	←	1640	1715	1745	1740	1810	1814s	←	1840	1908	1915	1936	1940	←	2015	2040	2115		2215	...	2240	2315	...	0015	...
Lausanne 505 d.	1620	1620	1645	1720	...	1745	→	|	1820	1845	...	1920	→	1945	1948	2020	2045	...	2120	...	2220	2242	...	2320	...	0021
Morges 505 d.	|	1632	1654	1732	...	1754	...	|	1832	1854	...	1932	...	|	1957	2032	2054	...	2132	...	2232	|	...	2332	...	0033
Nyon 505 d.	|	1650	1710	1750	...	1810	...	|	1850	1910	...	1950	...	|	2013	2050	2110	...	2150	...	2250	|	...	2350	...	0051
Genève 505 a.	1653	1704	1724	1804	...	1824	...	1853	1904	1924	...	2004	...	2018	2027	2104	2124	...	2204	...	2304	2315	...	0004	...	0105
Genève A ✈ 505 a.	...	1713	1733	1813	...	1833	...	...	1913	1933	...	2013	...	...	2038	2113	2133	...	2213	...	2313	2324	...	...	...	...

◆ – **NOTES** (LISTED BY TRAIN NUMBER)

311 – LUNA – 🛏12 Genève Aéroport - Brig; 🛏 1,2 cl. and ▬ 2 cl. Genève - Roma.
316 – LUNA – 🛏12 Brig - Genève Aéroport; 🛏 1,2 cl. and ▬ 2 cl. Roma - Genève.
9261 – ⑥ Dec. 20 - Mar. 28, July 11 - Aug. 29 (also Dec. 25, Jan. 1): 12 and (🍷) Paris - Brig.
9267 – ⑦ Dec. 21 - Mar. 29, July 5 - Aug. 30: 12 and (🍷) Paris - Aigle.
9268 – ⑥ Dec. 20 - Mar. 28, July 11 - Aug. 29 (also Dec. 25, Jan. 1): 12 and (🍷) Brig - Paris.
9272 – ⑥ Dec. 20 - Mar. 28, July 11 - Aug. 29 (also Dec. 25, Jan. 1): 12 and (🍷) Brig - Paris.
9273 – ③⑤ Dec. 19 - Jan. 2; ⑤ Jan. 9 - Mar. 27, July 10 - Aug. 28: 12 and (🍷) Paris - Brig.
9274 – ⑦ Dec. 21 - Mar. 29, July 5 - Aug. 30: 12 and (🍷) Aigle - Paris.

M – 12 and ✕ Genève - Milano and v.v.
V – 12 and ✕ Genève Aéroport - Milano - Venezia and v.v.

s – Stops to set down only.
u – Stops to pick up only.

⊙ – *CISALPINO Pendolino* train: Ⓡ inclusive of supplement for international journeys; may be used for Swiss internal journeys without reservation.
⊡ – Operated by *CISALPINO*. Ⓡ for international journeys; may be used for Swiss internal journeys without reservation. From June 14 service will be operated by *CISALPINO Pendolino* train (note ⊙).

▲ – Additional local services operate hourly **Lausanne - Montreux - Villeneuve** and v.v. calling at all stations including Territet and Veytaux-Chillon; **Lausanne** depart xx00, **Villeneuve** depart xx24. Bus connections are available between Villeneuve and Aigle.

2nd class only — Local services from VEVEY, AIGLE and BEX — 571

VEVEY - BLONAY. Narrow gauge. *6 km.* Journey time: 14–16 minutes. **Operator**: MOB.

From **Vevey**: 0639, 0709, 0739, 0809, 0839, 0909, 0939, 1009⚒, 1039, 1109⚒, 1139, 1209⚒, 1239, 1309⚒, 1339, 1409⚒, 1439, 1509⚒, 1546, 1609⚒, 1639, 1709Ⓐ, 1739, 1809Ⓐ, 1839, 1909Ⓐ, 1939, 2009, 2043, 2143, 2243, 2343, 0043⑥⑦.

From **Blonay**: 0600, 0632, 0700, 0732, 0800, 0832, 0900, 0932⚒, 1000, 1032⚒, 1100, 1132⚒, 1200, 1232⚒, 1300, 1332⚒, 1400, 1432⚒, 1500, 1532⚒, 1600, 1632Ⓐ, 1700, 1732Ⓐ, 1800, 1832Ⓐ, 1900, 1932, 2000, 2100, 2200, 2300, 2359⑤⑥.

AIGLE - LEYSIN. Narrow gauge rack railway. *6 km.* Journey time: 29–39 minutes. **Operator**: TPC.

From **Aigle**: 0550⚒, 0620©, 0720Ⓐ, 0756, 0900, 0956 and hourly until 2056, then 2256.

From **Leysin** Grand Hotel: 0525, 0624Ⓐ, 0653©, 0753, 0857, 0953 and hourly until 2153, then 2327.

AIGLE - LES DIABLERETS. Narrow gauge. *23 km.* Journey time: 45–55 minutes. **Operator**: TPC.

From **Aigle**: 0618, 0720, 0828, 0955, 1059, 1140Ⓐ, 1155©, 1240Ⓐ, 1255©, 1355, 1459, 1555, 1659, 1755, 1855, 2055, 2159.

From **Les Diablerets**: 0513Ⓐ, 0611©, 0622Ⓐ, 0713, 0813, 0948, 1045, 1148, 1250, 1332Ⓐ, 1348©, 1445, 1548, 1645, 1748, 1904, 2048, 2145.

AIGLE - CHAMPÉRY. Narrow gauge rack railway. 2nd class only. **Operator**: TPC.

km																											
		⚒			⚒				⚒		⚒		⚒					⚒								⑥y	
0	**Aigle** d.	0518	0618	0720	0807	0822	0922	1022	1105	1120	1155	1224	1255	1320	1422	1520	1624	1705	1720	1824	1855	1955	2055	2153	2255	...	2355
11	Monthey Ville d.	0547	0645	0748	0826	0848	0948	1048	1124	1148	1214	1248	1314	1348	1448	1548	1647	1724	1748	1848	1921	2021	2114	2213	2314	2330	0014
23	**Champéry** a.	0620	0720	0821	...	0921	1021	1130	...	1221	...	1321	...	1421	1521	1628	1720	...	1821	1921	1954	2054	...	2245	...	0003	...

		⚒		⚒					⚒		⚒		⚒						⚒						z		⑦y
Champéry d.	...	0533	0600c	0631a	0700d	0734	0834	0934	...	1034	...	1134	...	1301	1334	1434	1534	1631	...	1734	1834	1934	2034	2134	2246	...	0004
Monthey Ville d.	0540	0617	0641	0712	0742	0814	0914	1014	1042	1112	1127	1216	1231	1342	1414	1512	1616	1712	1727	1816	1916	2016	2116	2216	2321	2317	0039
Aigle a.	0600	0637	0701	0732	0802	0834	0934	1034	1102	1132	1147	1236	1251	1402	1434	1532	1636	1732	1747	1836	1936	2036	2136	2236	...	2337	...

BEX - VILLARS. *12 km.* Journey time: 40–46 minutes. All trains call at Bex (Place du Marché), and Bévieux (*3 km* and 10 minutes from Bex). **Operator**: TPC.

From **Bex**: 0631, 0739, 0839, 0939, 1039, 1149, 1239, 1339, 1457, 1549, 1639, 1743, 1843, 1934, 2105.

From **Villars**: 0542, 0644, 0733, 0833, 0933, 1033, 1143, 1233, 1333, 1433, 1543, 1633, 1738, 1838, 1947, 2042.

a – Ⓐ only.
c – © only.
d – ⚒ only.
y – Also Aug. 1.
z – Change at Monthey En Place for connection to Aigle.

2nd class only. SNCF, TMR — MARTIGNY - CHAMONIX — 572

Narrow gauge rack railway. Through journeys operate as MONT BLANC EXPRESS. Passengers may be required to change trains at Vallorcine

km		Ⓐ	N					P	P			P			P		R	P	S		T			
0	**Martigny** d.	...	...	0547	0647	0801	0901	...	1001	1101	1201	1201	1301	...	1401	1501	1501	1601	1643	...	1701	1801	1901	2012
7	Salvan d.	0512	...	0603	0705	0817	0917	...	1017	1117	1217	1217	1317	...	1417	1517	1517	1617	1659	...	1717	1817	1917	2028
9	Les Marécottes d.	0516	...	0607	0710	0821	0921	...	1021	1121	1221	1221	1321	...	1421	1521	1521	1621	1703	...	1721	1821	1921	2032
14	Finhaut d.	0528	...	0620	0723	0834	0934	...	1034	1134	1234	1234	1334	...	1434	1534	1534	1634	1716	...	1734	1834	1934	2045*
18	Le Châtelard Frontière 🏛 d.	0540	...	0632	0735	0847	0947	...	1047	1147	1245	1247	1347	...	1447	1545	1547	1647	1728	1747	1747	1847	1947	2056*
21	**Vallorcine** a.	...	...	...	0753x	0853	0953	...	1053	1153	...	1253	1353	...	1453	...	1553	1653	...	1753	1753	1853	1953	...
					K														Q					
21	**Vallorcine** d.	...	0617	0700	0800	0900	1000	1030	1100	1200	...	1300	1400	1500	1500	1600	1600	1657	1721	1800	1800	1900	2000	...
28	Argentière Haute Savoie d.	...	0633	0716	0816	0916	1016	1049	1116	1216	...	1317	1416	1516	1516	1616	1616	1714	1738	1816	1816	1916	2016	...
32	Les Tines d.	...	0642	0726	0826	0926	1026	1058	1126	1226	...	1326	1426	1526	1526	1626	1626	1725	1747	1826	1826	1926	2026	...
36	**Chamonix** a.	...	0651	0733	0833	0933	1033	1107	1133	1233	...	1333	1433	1533	1533	1633	1633	1733	1756	1833	1833	1933	2033	...
	St Gervais **365a** a.	...	0740	0820	0920	1020r	1120	...	...	1320	...	1420	1520	1620	1620	1720	1720	1820	...	1920	1920	2020	...	...

	Ⓐ		K	L			P	P			P			P	S	E		P	Q		P			
St Gervais **365a** d.	...	...	0632	0651	0731	0832	...	0932	1032	...	...	1232	1332	1332	...	...	1532	1532	...	...	1632	1732	1832	1932
Chamonix d.	...	...	0716	0737	0816	0916	0945	1016	1116	...	1216	1316	1416	1416	...	1516	1616	1616	1643	...	1716	1816	1916	2016
Les Tines d.	...	...	0727	0747	0827	0927	0954	1027	1127	...	1227	1327	1427	1427	...	1527	1627	1627	1652	...	1726	1827	1927	2027
Argentière Haute Savoie d.	...	...	0736	0756	0836	0936	1004	1036	1136	...	1236	1336	1436	1436	...	1536	1636	1636	1702	...	1737	1836	1936	2036
Vallorcine a.	...	...	0752	...	0852	0952	1022	1052	1152	...	1252	1352	1452	1452	...	1552	1652	1652	1720	...	1752	1852	1952	2052
				D												T								
Vallorcine d.	...	...	...	0759x	0859	0959	...	1059	1159	...	1259	1359	...	1459	...	1559	...	1659	...	1759	1759	1859	1959	...
Le Châtelard Frontière 🏛 d.	0545	0638	...	0807	0907	1007	...	1107	1207	1307	1307	1407	...	1507	1550	1607	...	1707	...	1807	1807	1907	2007	...
Finhaut d.	0555	0648	...	0817	0917	1017	...	1117	1217	1317	1317	1417	...	1517	1600	1617	...	1717	...	1817	1817	1917	2017	...
Les Marécottes d.	0608	0700	...	0829	0929	1029	...	1129	1229	1329	1329	1429	...	1529	1612	1629	...	1729	...	1829	1829	1929	2029	...
Salvan d.	0612	0704	...	0834	0934	1034	...	1134	1234	1334	1334	1434	...	1534	1617	1634	...	1734	...	1834	1834	1934	2034	...
Martigny a.	...	0726	...	0855	0955	1055	...	1155	1255	1355	1355	1455	...	1555	1638	1655	...	1755	...	1855	1855	1955	2054	...

D – Daily from Le Châtelard Frontière.
E – To Aug. 31 / from Sept. 22.
K – July 1 - Aug. 31.
L – Dec. 14 - June 30, Sept. 1 - Dec. 12.
N – Ⓐ to July 2; Ⓐ Sept. 2 - Oct. 2; Ⓐ Nov. 5 - Dec. 11.
P – Dec. 14 - Mar. 29, June 13 - Sept. 13.
Q – ①②④⑤ (daily June 13 - Sept. 13).
R – Mar. 16 - June 19, Sept. 14 - Dec. 12.
S – ①②④⑤ June 2 - 10, 12 - 26, Aug. 24 - Oct. 20, Nov. 2 - Dec. 11.
T – Daily except dates in note **S**.
r – June 13 - Sept. 13.
x – July 1 - 31.
* – Runs if passengers are present at Les Marécottes.

Engineering work Oct 5 - 23: trains will be replaced by 🚌 between Vallorcine and Chamonix.

In the event of deep snow or very bad weather, certain trains may be suspended between Vallorcine and Argentière.

SION VALLEY RESORTS — 573

MARTIGNY - ORSIÈRES▲ and LE CHÂBLE: *19 km*, 26 minutes to both resorts. ▲ – A change of train is necessary at Sembrancher. **Operator**: RA.

From **Martigny**: 0813, 0913, 1013, 1130, 1213, 1313, 1413, 1523, 1613©, 1647, 1723, 1823, 1913, 2013, 2123⑤⑥.

From **Orsières and Le Châble**: 0548Ⓐ, 0648, 0809, 0909, 1009, 1057, 1209, 1309, 1409, 1519, 1609, 1643©, 1719, 1819, 1909, 2048⑤⑥.

LE CHÂBLE - VERBIER: 🚌 service. Journey time: ± 25 minutes. **Operator**: PA.

From **Le Châble Gare**: 0655, 0730Ⓐ, 0750⑥**q**, 0852, 0950, 1100©, 1100Ⓐ**r**, 1245, 1405, 1500**m**, 1610, 1718, 1800**j**, 1812**p**, 1905, 1955**w**, 2050**w**, 2155**n**.
From **Verbier Post**: 0618⚒, 0720, 0840⚒, 0920, 1025, 1215, 1335, 1435**m**, 1525, 1645, 1747, 1840, 1930, 2020**w**.

MARTIGNY - AOSTA: 🚌 service via Grand St Bernard tunnel. Service runs daily throughout the year. Journey time: ± 2 hours. **Operator**: TMR / SAVDA.

From **Martigny Gare**: 0825, 1655. From **Aosta Stazione**: 0805, 1625 (🚌 to Orsières arrive 1805, then train forward depart 1819, Martigny arrive 1845).

SION - CRANS-SUR-SIERRE: 🚌 service. Journey time: ± 45 minutes. **Operator**: PA.

From **Sion Gare**: 0645⚒, 0745, 0845⚒, 1000, 1045⚒, 1150, 1230⚒ 1345, 1545, 1650, 1800, 1910.

From **Crans-sur-Sierre Post**: 0645, 0745⚒, 0835, 0935⚒, 1050, 1135⚒, 1245, 1345⚒, 1545, 1645, 1805, 1900.

SIERRE - CRANS-sur-SIERRE - MONTANA: 🚌 service. Principal stop in **Crans-sur-Sierre** is Hotel Scandia (± 40 minutes from Sierre, ± 8 minutes from Montana. **Operator**: SMC.

From **Sierre Gare**: 0745, 0845, 0945⚒**z**, 1045⚒**z**, 1130, 1230⚒**z**, 1340, 1440⚒**z**, 1540, 1658, 1745, 1940, 2030, 2207.

From **Montana Gare**: 0607⚒**z**, 0642, 0743†**y**, 0839⚒**z**, 1003, 1043⚒**z**, 1133⚒**z**, 1230, 1334⚒**z**, 1438, 1603, 1638, 1733⚒**z**, 1818, 1907, 2048.

BRIG - SAAS-FEE: 🚌 service. Journey time: 50–70 minutes. All services call at **Visp** (Bahnhof Süd) ± 20 minutes from Brig, and **Saas Grund** (Post) ± 15 minutes from Saas Fee.

From **Brig (Bahnhof)**: 0515, 0615, 0645, 0715 and every 30 minutes until 1115, then 1140, 1215, 1251, 1315, 1345 and every 30 minutes until 1845, then 1945, 2045, 2215⑤⑥**x**.

From **Saas-Fee**: 0602, 0635, 0702, 0731, 0802, 0826, and at xx02 and xx26 each hour until 1926, then 2026, 2330⑤⑥**x**.

Operator: PA. Seat reservation **compulsory** from Saas Fee to Brig on journeys 0802 - 1802. Reserve seats at least two hours before departure: ✆ 027 958 11 45.

j – Daily Dec. 14 - June 26, Sept. 21 - Dec. 12.
m – Daily Dec. 15 - Apr. 25; ⚒ Apr. 27 - Dec. 12.
n – ⑤⑥ Dec. 19 - Apr. 18 (not Dec. 26, Jan. 2).
p – June 27 - Sept. 20.
q – Not Aug. 1, 15.
r – 35 minutes later on ③ schooldays.
w – Dec. 20 - Apr. 19.
x – Not Dec. 26, Jan. 2, Apr. 10, Aug. 1.
y – Also Mar. 19, June 11, Aug. 15, Dec. 8; not Apr. 10.
z – Also Apr. 10; not Mar. 19, June 11, Aug. 15, Dec. 8.

575 GLACIER EXPRESS — MGB, RhB*

Glacier Express through services (compulsory reservation). **No service Oct. 19 - Dec. 12.** For local services see Table **576**. Narrow gauge rack railway

km		WINTER SERVICE ▶▶▶	900 ⊡ W ✕	910 ⊡ ✕	SUMMER SERVICE ▶▶▶	902 ★ S ✕🍷	904 ★ ✕	906 ★ ✕🍷	908 ★ ✕
0	**Zermatt** d.		...	1000		0900	0913	1000	1013
21	St Niklaus △ d.		...	1037		0937	|	|	|
36	Visp △ d.		1005	1107		1007	1025	1107	1125
45	**Brig** △ d.		1017	1117		1017	1040	1117	1140
62	Fiesch △ d.		1043	1143		1043	|	|	|
86	Oberwald △ d.		1111	1212		1111	|	|	|
113	**Andermatt** a.	**Dec. 14**	1136	1236	**May 16**	1136	1202	1237	1300
113	**Andermatt** d.	**to**	1156	1256	**to**	1156	1223	1248	1308
132	Sedrun △ d.	**May 15**	|	|	**Oct. 18**	1241	|	|	|
142	**Disentis/Mustér** ▽ a.		1258	1356		1306	1322	1352	1411
	Chur ▽ a.		1438	1537		1437	1438	1537	1538
	Thusis ▽ a.		...	1628		|	1528	|	|
	Tiefencastel ▽ a.		...	1647		1550	1547	1651	1652
	Filisur 545a ▽ a.		...	1701		1611	1601	|	|
	Davos Platz **545a** a.		...	|		1648	|	|	|
	Bergün/Bravuogn ▽ a.		...	1713		...	1613	|	|
	Samedan 546 ▽ a.		...	1746		...	1646	1802	1803
	Celerina **546/7** ▽ a.		...	1753		...	1653	|	|
	St Moritz 546/7 a.		...	1758		...	1658	1811	1811

	WINTER SERVICE ▶▶▶	901 ⊡ W ✕	903 ⊡ ✕	SUMMER SERVICE ▶▶▶	905 ★ ✕🍷	907 ★ ✕	909 ★ ✕	911 ★ S ✕🍷
St Moritz 546/7 d.		...	0904		0918	0919	1004	...
Celerina **546/7** △ d.		...	0907		|	|	1007	...
Samedan 546 △ d.		...	0917		0929	0930	1017	...
Bergün/Bravuogn △ d.		...	0947		|	|	1047	...
Davos Platz **545a** d.		...	|		|	|	|	0950
Filisur 545a △ d.	**Dec. 14**	...	1001	**May 16**	|	|	1101	1030
Tiefencastel △ d.	**to**	...	1015	**to**	1032	1032	1115	1048
Thusis △ d.	**May 15**	...	1033	**Oct. 18**	|	|	1133	|
Chur △ d.		1015	1115		1138	1139	1214	1215
Disentis/Mustér △ d.		1139	1239		1252	1307	1338	1352
Sedrun ▽ a.		|	|		|	|	|	1406
Andermatt a.		1249	1349		1350	1411	1434	1457
Andermatt d.		1302	1354		1355	1419	1455	1519
Oberwald ▽ a.		1325	1420		|	|	|	1542
Fiesch ▽ a.		1355	1451		|	|	|	1615
Brig ▽ a.		1423	1523		1523	1541	1624	1643
Visp ▽ a.		1437	1537		1537	1603	1638	1707
St Niklaus ▽ a.		...	|		|	|	|	1753
Zermatt a.		...	1652		1652	1711	1752	1831

All Glacier Express trains convey (12) [observation cars]. Reservations for ✕ are obligatory in advance through Railgourmino swissAlps AG, ✆ Chur (081) 300 15 15 (meals are served between 1100 and 1330 at your seat). Further information: www.glacierexpress.ch

S – June 13 - Oct. 18.
W – Dec. 25 - Jan. 4, Feb. 1 - May 15.
⊡ – Ⓡ (reservation fee including supplement: 10 CHF).
★ – Ⓡ (reservation fee including supplement: 30 CHF).

△ – Calls to pick up only.
▽ – Calls to set down only.
* – For operators see foot of page.

576 *Local Services* ZERMATT - BRIG - ANDERMATT (- GÖSCHENEN) - DISENTIS - CHUR — MGB, RhB*

Narrow gauge rack railway. For *Glacier Express* through services see Table **575**

ZERMATT - BRIG

km											
0	**Zermatt** d.	0539	0613	0739		1839	1913	2013	2113	2213	...
8	Täsch d.	0551	0625	0751	and	1851	1925	2025	2125	2225	...
21	St Niklaus d.	0617	0653	0817	every	1917	1953	2053	2153	2249	...
29	Stalden-Saas d.	0638	0713	0838	hour	1938	2012	2112	2212	2310	...
36	Visp a.	0647	0724	0847	until	1947	2022	2122	2222	2320	...
36	Visp d.	0652	0726	0852	△	1952	2025	2125	2225	2321	...
45	**Brig** a.	0703	0736	0903		2003	2035	2135	2235	2329	...

Brig d.	0510	0553		1453	1608	1653	1753	1853	1953	2053
Visp a.	0520	0604	and	1504	1620	1704	1804	1904	2004	2104
Visp d.	0529	0610	every	1510	1625	1710	1810	1910	2010	2110
Stalden-Saas d.	0539	0620	hour	1520	1636	1720	1820	1920	2020	2120
St Niklaus d.	0556	0638	until	1538	1655	1738	1838	1938	2038	2138
Täsch d.	0622	0702	▽	1602	1721	1802	1902	2002	2102	2202
Zermatt a.	0633	0714		1614	1734	1814	1914	2014	2114	2214

VISP - BRIG - ANDERMATT

km									①–⑥	⑦	
	Visp d.	...	0708	0808		1908	2008	2108	2236	2255	...
0	**Brig** d.	0623	0723	0823	and	1923	2023	2123	2250	2310	...
7	Mörel d.	0633	0733	0833	every	1933	2033	2133	2259	2319	...
10	Betten d.	0639	0739	0839	hour	1939	2039	2139	2305	2325	...
17	Fiesch d.	0658	0758	0858	until	1958	2058	2157	2323	2343	...
41	Oberwald 🚗 d.	0744	0844	0944		2044	2144	*2239*z	...	...	...
59	Realp ▲ 🚗 § d.	0805	0905	1005		2105	2205t	...	...	...	...
68	**Andermatt** a.	0820	0920	1020		2120	2220t	...	...	...	...

							t			y
Andermatt d.	...	...	0737	0837		1837	1910	1937	2037	...
Realp ▲ 🚗 § d.	...	...	0750	0850	and	1850	1922	1950	2050	...
Oberwald 🚗 d.	*0612*z	0713	0813	0913	every	1913	1942	2013	2113	*2239*z
Fiesch d.	0657	0757	0857	0957	hour	1957	2027	2057	2157	2326
Betten d.	0717	0816	0916	1016	until	2016	2048	2116	2216	2344
Mörel d.	0724	0824	0924	1024		2024	2055	2124	2224	2351
Brig a.	0733	0833	0933	1033		2033	2103	2133	2233	0001
Visp a.	0748	0850	0950	1050		2050	...	2150	...	...

ANDERMATT - DISENTIS

km		🚌									n			w		n	m								🚌	
0	**Andermatt** 🚗 d.	...	0727	...	0827	...	0927	1027	...	1127	1227	...	1327	1355	...	1427	1434	...	1527	1627	...	1727	1827	...	...	...
10	Oberalppass d.	...	0750	...	0850	...	0950	1050	...	1150	1250	...	1350	1415	...	1450	1453	...	1550	1650	...	1750	1850	...	...	...
19	Sedrun 🚗 d.	0705	0817	...	0917	...	1017	1117	...	1217	1317	...	1417	...	...	1517	1517	...	1617	1717	...	1817	1917	...	2001	...
29	**Disentis/Mustér** a.	0728	0836	...	0936	...	1036	1136	...	1236	1336	...	1436	...	...	1536	1536	...	1636	1736	...	1836	1936	...	2022	...

	v	r							m	n		n	m									🚌	🚌		
Disentis/Mustér d.	0711	0714	0814	...	0914	1014	...	1114	1220	1214	...	1314	...	1414	...	1514	1614	...	1714	1814	...	1919	2021	...	...
Sedrun 🚗 d.	0731	0731	0831	...	0931	1031	...	1131	1240	1231	...	1331	...	1431	...	1531	1631	...	1731	1831	...	1936	2039	...	...
Oberalppass d.	0753	0753	0853	...	0953	1053	...	1153	1301	1253	...	1353	1455	1453	...	1553	1653	...	1753	1853	...	...	...	...	...
Andermatt 🚗 a.	0822	0822	0922	...	1022	1122	...	1222	...	1322	...	1422	1422	1522	...	1622	1722	...	1822	1922	...	...	...	...	...

DISENTIS - CHUR

km			⚒								
0	**Disentis/Mustér** d.	0545	0615	0645	0745	and	1745	1845	1945	2045	...
12	Trun d.	0601	0630	0701	0801	every	1801	1901	2001	2101	...
30	Ilanz d.	0624	0653	0724	0824	hour	1824	1924	2024	2124	...
49	Reichenau-Tamins d.	0650	0720	0750	0850	until	1850	1950	2050	2150	...
59	**Chur** a.	0704	0734	0804	0902		1902	2002	2104	2204	...

	⚒									
Chur d.	0611	0656	0756	0856	and	1756	1856	1959	2059	2259
Reichenau-Tamins d.	0625	0705	0805	0905	every	1805	1905	2013	2113	2310
Ilanz d.	0653	0733	0833	0933	hour	1833	1933	2042	2142	2336
Trun d.	0714	0753	0853	0953	until	1853	1953	2101	2201	2355
Disentis/Mustér a.	0731	0811	0911	1011		1911	2011	2119	2219	0012

GÖSCHENEN - ANDERMATT

km					and						
0	**Göschenen** d.	0753	0812	0853	hourly	1812	1853	1912	2012	2112	2153
4	**Andermatt** a.	0803	0822	0903	until	1822	1903	1922	2022	2122	2203

					and					
Andermatt d.	0725	0748	0828	0848	hourly	1828	1848	1948	2048	2128
Göschenen a.	0739	0803	0842	0903	until	1842	1903	2003	2103	2142

m – May 16 - Oct. 18.
n – Not May 16 - Oct. 18.
r – May 16 - Dec. 12.
t – ⑤ Dec. 19 - Apr. 3, May 22 - Oct. 16.
v – Dec. 14 - May 15.

w – Dec. 14 - Apr. 13.
y – On ⑦ runs 20 minutes later Fiesch - Brig.
z – Connection by 🚌.
§ – Realp is a request stop.

△ – Additional services Zermatt - Visp: 1113, 1213, 1613, 1713, 1813.
▽ – Additional services Visp - Zermatt: 0843, 0943, 1043, 1243, 1843.
▲ – 🚂 service (summer only, not daily) runs Realp - Furka - Gletsch. Operator: Dampfbahn Furka-Bergstrecke ✆ 0848 000 144.
🚗 – Car-carrying shuttle available (see page 260).
* – For operators see foot of page.

578 ZERMATT - GORNERGRAT — Narrow gauge rack railway. GGB

Journey 33 minutes, *9 km*. Additional winter-sports journeys run Dec. 21 - Apr. 17 between Riffelalp and Gornergrat. *Services are liable to be suspended in bad weather*

Dec. 14 - Apr. 26, May 30 - Oct. 18, Nov. 28 - Dec. 12

From Zermatt: 0710, 0800, 0824, 0848, 0912*, 0936*, 1000*, 1024*, 1048*, 1112*, 1136, 1200, 1224, 1248, 1312, 1336, 1400, 1424, 1448, 1512, 1536, 1600, 1624, 1712, 1800, 1912 **p**.
From Gornergrat: 0755, 0843, 0907, 0931, 0955, 1019, 1043, 1107, 1131, 1155, 1219, 1243, 1307, 1331, 1355, 1419, 1443, 1507, 1531, 1555, 1619, 1643, 1707, 1755, 1843, 1957 **p**.

Apr. 27 - May 29, Oct. 19 - Nov. 27

From Zermatt: 0710 **r**, 0824, 0936 **r**, 1024, 1136, 1224, 1336, 1424, 1536 **r**, 1624, 1712 **r**, 1800 **r**.
From Gornergrat: 0755 **r**, 0931, 1019 **r**, 1131, 1219, 1331, 1419, 1531, 1619 **r**, 1707, 1755 **r**, 1843 **r**.

p – Dec. 14 - Apr. 19, June 13 - Sept. 27.
r – Apr. 27 - May 29, Oct. 19 - Nov. 1.
* – Duplicated by non-stop journeys Dec. 21 - Apr. 19 (journey 29 minutes).

 * – Operators: MGB, Zermatt - Andermatt / Göschenen - Disentis; RhB, Disentis - Chur.

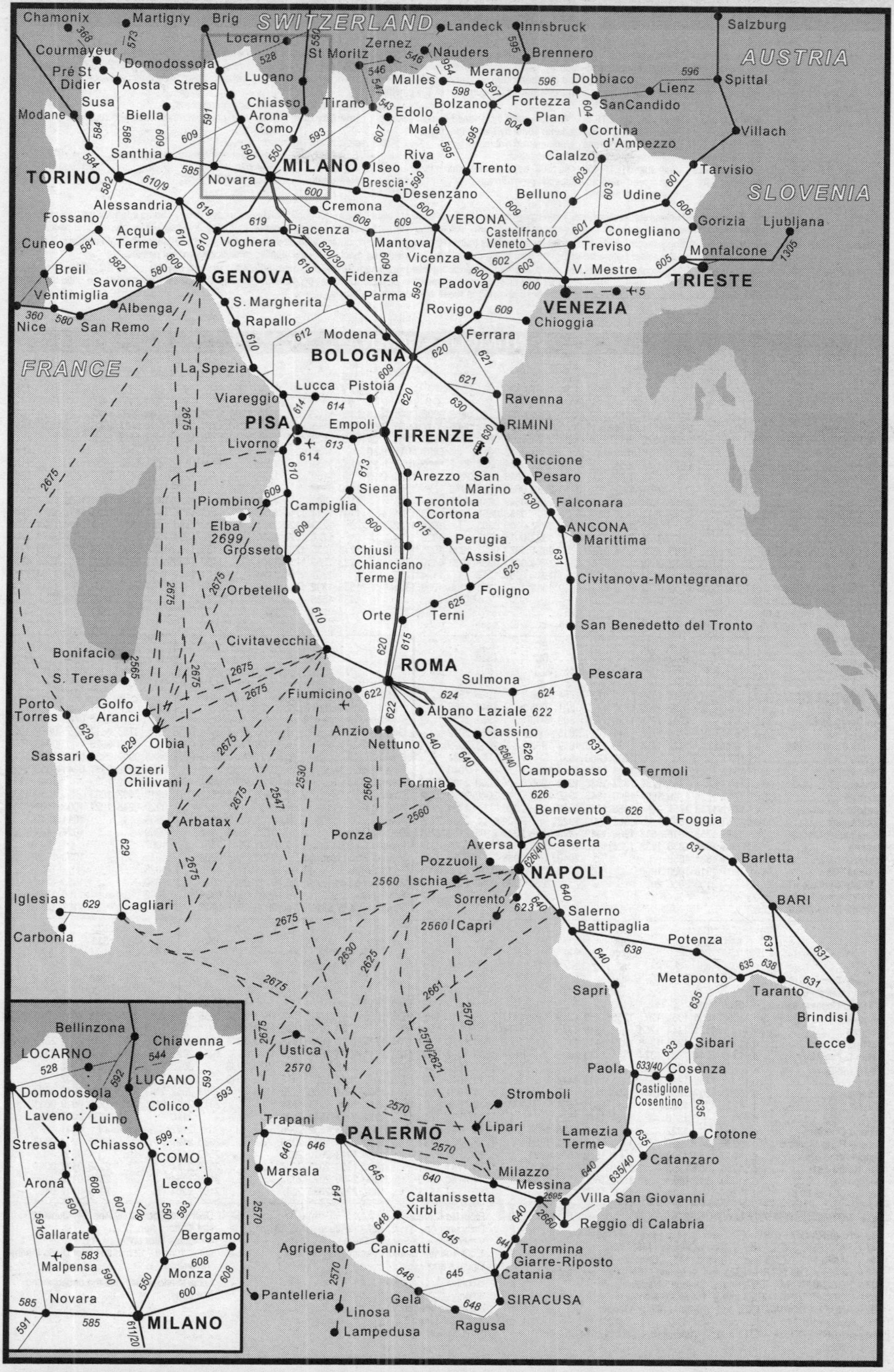
SWITZERLAND
AUSTRIA
SLOVENIA
FRANCE
Chamonix
Martigny
Brig
Landeck
Innsbruck
Salzburg
Locarno
Courmayeur
Domodossola
Zernez
St Moritz
Nauders
Brennero
Pré St Didier
Aosta
Stresa
Lugano
Malles
Merano
Dobbiaco
Spittal
Lienz
Susa
Modane
Biella
Chiasso
Arona
Como
Tirano
Edolo
Bolzano
Fortezza
SanCandido
Plan
Malé
Cortina d'Ampezzo
Villach
Santhia
TORINO
Novara
MILANO
Iseo
Riva
Trento
Calalzo
Tarvisio
Brescia
Desenzano
Belluno
Udine
Alessandria
Cremona
Fossano
Acqui Terme
Voghera
Piacenza
Mantova
VERONA
Castelfranco Veneto
Conegliano
Gorizia
Ljubljana
Cuneo
Treviso
Monfalcone
Vicenza
Breil
Fidenza
Padova
V. Mestre
TRIESTE
Savona
GENOVA
Ventimiglia
Parma
VENEZIA
Albenga
S. Margherita
Rovigo
Nice
San Remo
Chioggia
Rapallo
Modena
Ferrara
BOLOGNA
La Spezia
Lucca
Pistoia
Ravenna
Viareggio
PISA
Empoli
FIRENZE
RIMINI
Livorno
Riccione
San Marino
Pesaro
Arezzo
Siena
Piombino
Campiglia
Terontola Cortona
Falconara
Elba
ANCONA
Marittima
Perugia
Grosseto
Chiusi Chianciano Terme
Assisi
Civitanova-Montegranaro
Orbetello
Foligno
Orte
Terni
San Benedetto del Tronto
Civitavecchia
Bonifacio
ROMA
S. Teresa
Sulmona
Pescara
Fiumicino
Porto Torres
Golfo Aranci
Albano Laziale
Anzio
Olbia
Nettuno
Cassino
Sassari
Ozieri Chilivani
Campobasso
Termoli
Formia
Arbatax
Benevento
Foggia
Ponza
Aversa
Caserta
Pozzuoli
NAPOLI
Barletta
Ischia
Sorrento
Salerno
Iglesias
Cagliari
Battipaglia
BARI
Carbonia
Capri
Potenza
Metaponto
Taranto
Sapri
Brindisi
Lecce
Sibari
Paola
Cosenza
Castiglione Cosentino
Ustica
Stromboli
Lipari
Trapani
PALERMO
Lamezia Terme
Crotone
Catanzaro
Marsala
Milazzo
Messina
Villa San Giovanni
Caltanissetta Xirbi
Reggio di Calabria
Agrigento
Canicattì
Taormina Giarre-Riposto
Catania
Pantelleria
Gela
SIRACUSA
Linosa
Ragusa
Lampedusa
Bellinzona
Chiavenna
LOCARNO
LUGANO
Colico
Laveno
Luino
Lecco
Gallarate
Bergamo
Malpensa
Monza
Novara
MILANO

ITALY

Operator: Trenitalia, a division of Ferrovie dello Stato SpA (FS), unless otherwise noted.

Services: All trains convey First and Second classes of travel unless otherwise shown by a figure "2" at the top of the column, or in a note in the Table heading. Overnight sleeping car (🛏) or couchette (▬) trains do not necessarily convey seating accommodation or may convey only second class seats - refer to individual footnotes. Excelsior sleeping cars offer en-suite facilities. Descriptions of sleeping and couchette cars appear on page **10**. Refreshment services (✕ or 🍷) where known, may only be available for part of the journey, and may be added to or taken away from trains during the currency of the timetable.

Train Categories: There are 9 categories of express train:

AV	**Alta Velocità**	premium fare ETR 500 services using high-speed lines.
CIS	**Cisalpino**	services from / to Switzerland; some by Pendolino train.
EC	**EuroCity**	international express; supplement payable.
EN	**EuroNight**	higher standard of overnight express.
ES	**Eurostar Italia**	high speed (ETR 450 / 460 / 500) services at premium fare.
ESc	**Eurostar City**	high speed services at special premium fare.
IC	**InterCity**	internal day express.
ICN	**InterCityNight**	internal night express.
ICp	**InterCity** Plus	internal express with new coaches; supplement payable.

Other services are classified:

E	**Espresso**	semi-fast or international services.
*ES*L*	**ES* LINK**	🚌 link.
R	**Regionale**	Local train.

Timings: Valid **until June 13, 2009** unless stated otherwise. Trains may be cancelled or altered at holiday times – for public holiday dates see page 2. Some international trains which are not available for local travel are not shown in this section; these include some *City Night Line* services running between Germany and Italy – see International pages.

Tickets: Seat reservations are strongly recommended for travel on all express trains. Reservations are compulsory on all services indicated by 🅁 under the train number. Rail tickets must be date-stamped by the holder before boarding the train using the self-service validating machines – this applies to all tickets except passes.

Supplements: Supplements are calculated according to class of travel and total distance travelled (minimum 10km, maximum 3000km), and are payable on all *EC*, *ICp* and *IC* trains, regardless of the number of changes of train. A higher fare (including supplement) is payable for travel by *AV*, *ES*, *ESc* and *CIS* trains. Some trains are only available to passengers holding long distance tickets and the restrictions applying to these are noted in the tables.

580 VENTIMIGLIA - GENOVA

km		ICp 503 🅁🍷 ♦	ICp 651 🅁🍷 ⚒		⚒		ICp 515 🅁✕	2	Ⓒ 2	Ⓐ 2	ICp 657 🅁🍷	C2		⚒ T	EC 139 🅁🍷 ♦	† T	Ⓐ	2	† C2	⚒ T2	† 2	m 2	†	ICp 693 🅁🍷 ♦	Ⓒ	Ⓐ	⚒
0	**Ventimiglia** 🏛 **581** d.	...	0445	0507	0517	...	0633	0646	0750	0750	0858	0908	0948	1048	1058	1107	...	1150	1206	1206	1220	1354a	1420	1458	...	...	1526
5	Bordighera d.	...	0452	0514	0524	...	0640	0655	0757	0757	0905	0917	0956	1055	1105	1115	...	1157	1216	1216	1229	1401a	1427	1505	...	...	1533
16	**San Remo 581** d.	...	0502	0522	0533	...	0650	0704	0806	0806	0915	0928	1006	1104	1115	1128	...	1205	1226	1226	1237	1409a	1435	1515	...	...	1542
24	Taggia-Arma d.	...	0508	0528	0539	...	|	0710	0812	0812	|	0937	1015	1110	|	1136	...	1212	1233	1233	1243	1414	1441	|	...	...	1548
39	Imperia Porto Maurizio d.	...	0521	0541	0551	...	0707	0722	0824	0824	0932	—	1032	1123	1132	1154	...	1229	...	—	1255	1432	1453	1532	...	...	1600
41	Imperia Oneglia d.	...	|	0545	0555	...	|	0732	0828	0828	|	...	1036	1129	|	1159	...	1236	...	...	1259	1437	1458	|	...	...	1605
46	Diano Marina d.	...	|	0551	0601	...	0715	0738	0835	0835	0940	...	1042	...	1140	—	...	1242	...	...	1305	1443	1504	1540	...	...	1612
61	Alassio d.	...	0541	0604	0626	...	0730	0756	0849	0849	0956	⚒	1056	...	1156	Ⓒ	...	1302	...	...	1329	1502	1523	1556	1609	1609	1639
67	**Albenga** d.	...	0549	0611	0636	0657	0738	0803	0855	0855	1004	1015	1104	...	1204	1214	1214	1312	...	1413	1336	1512	1531	1604	1616	1616	1649
76	Loano d.	...	|	0622	0651	0711	|	0817	0905	0905	|	1024	1122	...	|	1223	1223	1321	...	1422	1350	1521	1546	|	1624	1624	1704
79	Pietra Ligure d.	...	|	0626	0655	0716	|	0822	0915	0915	|	1028	1130	...	|	1228	1228	1330	...	1426	1354	1531	1551	|	1628	1628	1708
85	Finale Ligure Marina d.	...	0603	0634	0704	0725	0752	0831	0923	0923	1018	1035	1138	...	1218	1235	1235	1338	...	1433	1403	1538	1602	1618	1635	1635	1716
108	**Savona** d.	0552	0619	0655	0726	0747	0807	0900k	0941	0958	1033	1110	1201	...	1233	1253	1255	1408	...	1452	1433	1601	1618	1633	1655	1655	1732
120	Varazze d.	|	|	0704	0735	0759	|	0913k	0956	1013	|	1124	1215	...	|	1301	1304	1423	...	1501	1447	1615	...	|	1704	1704	*1754*
151	**Genova** Piazza Principe § a.	0631	0702	0744	0815	0844	0849	1002	1052	1101	1106	1209	1301	...	1306	1332	1344	1509	...	1532	1541	1701	...	1706	1732	1747	*1839*
	Milano Centrale **610** a.	|	0855	0945	...	...	|	...	...	...	1255	...	...	...	1450	1535	...	...	...	1737	...	...	...	1850	1938	...	...
	Pisa Centrale **610** a.	0856	...	...	...	...	1057	...	...	...	...	...	...	...	...	...	...	...	...	...	...	...	...	...	...	...	...
	Roma Termini **610** a.	1214	...	...	...	...	1414	...	...	...	...	...	...	...	...	...	...	...	...	...	...	...	...	...	...	...	...

	P	†	ICp 1537 🅁 Ⓒ	ICp 669 🅁 Ⓐ	†	⚒	⚒ 2	EC 147 🅁🍷 ♦		ICp 1539 🅁 †	2	
Ventimiglia 🏛 **581** d.	1554	...	1645	1658	1723	1723	1754	1858	...	1935	1951	...
Bordighera d.	1601	...	1652	1705	1730	1730	1801	1905	...	1942	1958	...
San Remo 581 d.	1610	...	1702	1715	1739	1739	1809	1915	...	1952	2006	...
Taggia-Arma d.	1616	...	1708	1721	1744	1744	1815	|	...	1958	2012	...
Imperia Porto Maurizio d.	1629	...	1722	1734	1756	1756	1832	1932	...	2011	2029	...
Imperia Oneglia d.	1634	...	|	|	1800	1800	1837	|	...	|	2034	...
Diano Marina d.	1641	...	|	|	1806	1806	1843	1940	...	|	2040	...
Alassio d.	1702	...	1741	1756	1832	1838	1902	1956	...	2039	2102	2224
Albenga d.	1710	1725	1749	1804	1840	1846	1910	2004	2010	2048	2113	2232
Loano d.	1721	1736	1757	|	1856	1859	1918	|	2020	|	2121	2240
Pietra Ligure d.	1730	1747	1807	|	1900	1909	1922	|	2024	|	2130	2244
Finale Ligure Marina d.	1738	1755	1815	1818	1909	1919	1929	2018	2031	2105	2138	2251
Savona d.	1758v	1820	1830	1833	1928	1935	1955	2033	2049	2123	2201	2312
Varazze d.	1812v	1831	1838	|	...	...	2010	|	2058	|	2215	2325
Genova P P § a.	1901	1918	1906	1906	...	...	2056	2106	2136	2214	2301	0009
Milano Centrale **610** a.	...	2130	2050	2050	...	...	...	2250	2335	2359	...	...
Pisa Centrale **610** a.	...	...	...	...	...	...	...	...	...	...	...	...
Roma Termini **610** a.	...	...	...	...	...	...	...	...	...	...	...	...

	⚒ 2		2	⚒ 2	2	⚒	†	ICp 692 🅁🍷 ♦	q 2	
Roma Termini **610** d.	...	...	...	...	...	...	...	...	...	...
Pisa Centrale **610** d.	...	...	...	...	...	...	...	...	...	...
Milano Centrale **610** d.	...	...	...	...	...	...	0625	0700	...	0820
Genova P P § d.	0523	0608	0644	0715	...	0753	0842	0855	0859	1026
Varazze d.	0606	0653	0729	0808	...	0839	0926	|	0946	1057
Savona d.	0621	0710	0745	0823	0848	0907	0938	0928	1007	1110
Finale Ligure Marina d.	0637	0729	0801	...	0905	0926	0957	0941	1038	1123
Pietra Ligure d.	0643	0737	0807	...	0914	0932	1003	|	1045	1131
Loano d.	0648	0742	0812	...	0919	0937	1009	|	1050	1136
Albenga d.	0655	0804	0821	...	0929	0948	1024	1003	1103	1144
Alassio d.	0702	0812	0829	...	0936	...	...	1011	1110	...
Diano Marina d.	0725	0834	0851	...	0959	...	...	1024	1141	...
Imperia Oneglia d.	0731	0841	0857	...	1007	...	...	|	1148	...
Imperia Porto Maurizio d.	0735	0845	0904	...	1011	...	...	1033	1153	...
Taggia-Arma d.	0746	0856	0916	...	1023	...	...	|	1204	...
San Remo 581 d.	0752	0905	0926	...	1030	...	...	1050	1211	...
Bordighera d.	0801	0917	0939	...	1042	...	...	1100	1221	...
Ventimiglia 🏛 **581** a.	0808	0926	0948	...	1050	...	...	1107	1231	...

	ICp 650 🅁 Ⓐ	ICp 1536 🅁 Ⓒ	2		EC 144 🅁🍷 ♦	⚒ 2	†	T		Ⓐ 2	Ⓒ 2	x2		EC 160 🅁🍷 ♦	⚒ 2	† 2	⚒ 2	Ⓐ	Ⓒ	ICp 660 🅁🍷	2	Ⓐ	Ⓒ	ICp 538 🅁✕		ICp 668 🅁🍷	ICp 542 🅁🍷 ♦
Roma Termini **610** d.	...	...	...	...	...	...	...	...	...	...	...	...	...	...	...	...	...	...	...	...	...	...	...	1546	...	...	1746
Pisa Centrale **610** d.	...	...	...	...	...	...	...	...	...	...	...	...	...	...	...	...	...	...	...	...	...	...	...	1900	...	...	2102
Milano Centrale **610** d.	0905	0905	...	...	1110	...	...	...	...	...	...	...	1420	1510	...	...	...	...	1625	1700	...	...	1825	|	2025	2105	|
Genova Piazza Principe § d.	1055	1055	1059	1217	1255	1259	1259	...	1417	...	...	1459	1625	1655	1717	1738	1746	1817	1830	1855	1859	2017	2038	2112	2231	2255	2323
Varazze d.	|	1121	1144	1258	|	1345	1345	...	1458	...	...	1544	1655	|	1758	1819	1828	1858	1904	|	1944	2058	2112	|	2310	|	|
Savona d.	1129	1132	1213	1308	1329	1411	1411	...	1508	1540	1538	1613	1705	1729	1813	1829	1841	1912	1914	1929	2008	2108	2122	2146	2333	2329	0003
Finale Ligure Marina d.	1141	1144	1235	1324	1341	1433	1433	...	1524	1600	1602	1635	1723	1741	1836	1844	1900	1932	1932	1941	2031	2124	2142	2158	2351	2341	...
Pietra Ligure d.	|	1150	1241	1331	|	1439	1439	...	1530	1613	1613	1641	1731	|	1842	1850	1908	1938	1938	|	2038	2131	2148	|	2357	|	...
Loano d.	|	1156	1246	1336	|	1444	1444	...	1535	1619	1619	1646	1736	|	1847	1855	1913	1943	1943	|	2044	2136	2153	|	0002	|	...
Albenga d.	1203	1207	1254	1347	1403	1453	1453	...	1544	1631	1631	1653	1744	1803	1854	1905	1925	1951	1951	2003	2052	2147	2201	2212	0012	0003	...
Alassio d.	1211	1215	1301	...	1411	1501	1501	...	1555	1638	1638	1703	1755c	1811	1901	1917	1934	...	...	2011	2101	2155	2209	2220	0020	0011	...
Diano Marina d.	|	|	1316	...	1424	1516	1525	...	...	1708	1708	1719	...	1824	1917	1941	2000	...	...	|	2116	...	...	2233	0035	0024	...
Imperia Oneglia d.	|	|	1322	...	|	1522	1536	1604	...	1714	1714	1725	...	|	1923	1952	2006	...	...	|	2122	...	...	|	0041	|	...
Imperia Porto Maurizio d.	1230	1241	1328	...	1433	1531	1542	1609	...	1718	1721	1733	...	1833	1931	1957	2010	...	...	2030	2127	...	...	2242	|	0033	...
Taggia-Arma d.	1242	1253	1343	...	|	1543	1553	1621	...	1729	1734	1745	...	|	1943	2010	2021	...	...	2042	2138	...	...	|	0055	|	...
San Remo 581 d.	1250	1302	1350r	...	1450	1550	1600	1628	...	1735	1741	1751	...	1850	1950	2017	2027	...	...	2050	2144	...	...	2258	0101	0050	...
Bordighera d.	1300	1312	1400r	...	1500	1600	1610	1638	...	1744	1750	1800	...	1900	2000	2027	2037	...	...	2100	2154	...	...	2308	0110	0100	...
Ventimiglia 🏛 **581** a.	1307	1320	1409r	...	1507	1607	1617	1646	...	1752	1757	1811	...	1907	2007	2035	2047	...	...	2107	2204	...	...	2315	0117	0107	...

♦ – **NOTES** (LISTED BY TRAIN NUMBER)

139 – RIVIERA DEI FIORI – 🚃12 and 🍷 Nice - Genova (**140**).- Milano.
147 – SANREMO – 🚃12 and 🍷 Nice - Genova (**148**) - Milano.
144 – SANREMO – 🚃12 and 🍷 Milano (**143**) - Genova - Nice.
160 – RIVIERA DEI FIORI – 🚃12 and 🍷 Milano (**159**) - Genova - Nice.
503 – BOCCANEGRA – 🚃12 and 🍷 Savona - Napoli.
542 – BOCCANEGRA – 🚃12 and 🍷 Roma - Savona.
692 – ANDREA DORIA – 🚃12 and 🍷 Milano (**691**) - Genova - Ventimiglia.
693 – ANDREA DORIA – 🚃12 and 🍷 Ventimiglia - Genova (**694**) - Milano.

C – From / to Cuneo.
P – Daily until Apr. 11; Ⓐ Apr. 14 - June 13: 🚃12 Ventimiglia - La Spezia - Parma.
T – 🚃12 Torino - Cuneo - Ventimiglia - Imperia Oneglia and v.v.

a – Ⓐ only.
c – Ⓒ only.
k – 8 minutes later on Ⓐ.
m – Apr. 12 - June 13.

q – Daily until Apr. 11; Ⓐ Apr. 14 - June 13.
r – Not Ⓒ from Apr. 12.
v – 4 minutes later until Apr. 11.
x – On Ⓒ runs 8 – 12 minutes later Diano Marina - Ventimiglia.

§ – Local services may use the underground platforms.

CUNEO - NICE, VENTIMIGLIA and SAN REMO — 581

2nd class only

km		f	d	⚒	†		T	d			Ld	Lc	T	d		c		d	c	b			y				🚌
	Torino P.N. **582** d.	...	...	...	...	...	...	...	...	...	0730	0730	0835	...	...	...	...	...	...	...	...	...	...	...	...	...	...
0	**Cuneo** d.	...	...	0602	0604	...	0655	0740	0833	...	0904	0904	1012	1034	...	1204	1304	1402	1504	...	1604	1704	...	1807	1905	2010	2205
29	Limone ▦ d.	...	...	0639	0641	...	0742	0810	0910	...	0939	0939	1049	1110	...	1242	1347	1435	1550	...	1644	1747	...	1849	1943	2047	2249
47	Tende d.	0610	...	0658	0700	...	0802	...	0928	...	0957	0957	1107	...	1210	1306	1405	...	1608	...	1722	1809	...	1916	2006	...	...
75	Breil sur Roya a.	0647	...	0732	0734	...	0834	...	0957	...	1025	1025	1137	...	1249	1346	1441	...	1643	...	1802	1844	...	1945	2034	...	...
75	Breil sur Roya d.	0651	0649	0734	0736	0738	0841	...	...	1008	1026	1026	1139	...	1250	1348	1443	...	1645	1716	1813	1846	1936	1947	2036	...	...
*	**Nice Ville** a.	0755	|	|	|	0841	|	...	...	1112	|	|	|	...	1355	|	|	...	|	1825	1917	|	2038	|	|	...	...
96	**Ventimiglia** a.	...	0716	0759	0801	...	0905	...	...	...	1045	1045	1203	...	...	1420	1510	...	1718	...	...	1910	...	2020	2101	...	...
96	**Ventimiglia 580** d.	...	...	...	...	...	0908	...	...	...	1048	1107	1206	...	...	...	...	...	...	...	...	...	...	...	...	...	...
112	**San Remo 580** a.	...	...	...	...	...	0927	...	...	...	1103	1127	1225	...	...	...	...	...	...	...	...	...	...	...	...	...	...

	🚌	d	d	d	c						c		T			d	c	T	d	L						
San Remo 580 d.	...	...	...	...	...	...	...	...	...	...	...	...	1143	...	...	...	...	...	...	1628	...	...	...	...	...	...
Ventimiglia 580 a.	...	...	...	...	...	...	...	...	...	...	...	...	1200	...	...	...	...	...	...	1646	...	...	...	...	...	...
Ventimiglia d.	...	...	0540	...	0645	...	0816	0907	...	...	1050	...	1204	...	1348	...	...	1556	...	1649	...	1756	...	1947	...	...
Nice Ville d.	...	...	|	...	|	0721	|	|	0905	...	|	...	|	1236	|	...	...	|	...	|	1704	|	1755	|	1920	...
Breil sur Roya a.	...	...	0602	...	0711	0828	0840	0934	1003	...	1115	...	1229	1340	1417	...	...	1620	...	1713	1808	1822	1905	2017	2025	...
Breil sur Roya d.	...	...	0604	...	0713	...	0842	0936	1005	...	1117	...	1231	1347	1419	...	...	1622	...	1715	...	1824	1923	2035	...	...
Tende d.	...	...	0637	...	0803	...	0910	1020	1049	...	1156	...	1305	1428	1455	...	...	1700	...	1750	...	1859	2007	2108	...	...
Limone ▦ d.	0600	0642	0703	0817	0826	...	0938	1048	...	1120	1217	...	1325	1452	1515	1600	1616	1724	1749	1812	...	1918	2028	2127	...	...
Cuneo a.	0644	0720	0738	0855	0903	...	1011	1126	...	1155	1257	...	1357	1526	1550	1640	1656	1754	1827	1846	...	1957	2100	2200	...	...
Torino P.N. **582** a.	...	...	...	...	...	...	...	...	...	...	...	...	...	...	...	...	...	1925	...	2030	...	...	...	...	...	...

L – [12] Torino - Imperia Oneglia and v.v.
T – From/to Taggia-Arma.

b – ⑦ (also French public holidays).
c – ⑦ (also Italian public holidays).

d – ①–⑥ (not Italian public holidays).
f – ①–⑥ (not French public holidays).
y – ⑦ July 5 - Aug. 30 (also July 14, Aug. 15).

* – Nice - Breil sur Roya: *44 km*.

TORINO - CUNEO and SAVONA — 582

Most trains 2nd class only

km		⚒	†z	†	⚒	⚒	V	†	⚒	⚒	†z	⑥y	L	†V	⚒V	†z	⚒		⚒	†	†	⚒	†	⚒		†	⚒	†	⚒
0	**Torino P N** d.	...	0545	...	0600	...	0620	0655	0700	...	0725	0725	0730	0800	0800	0835	0835	...	0900	0940	...	1030	1035	1100	1135	...	1200	1235	1235
52	Savigliano d.	...	|	...	0646	...	0717	0744	0750	...	0810	0810	0825	0849	0853	0923	0923	...	0953	1028	...	1123	1121	1150	1222	...	1253	1323	1322
64	Fossano d.	0602	0625	0636	0655	0707	0727	0755	0801	0808	0822	0822	0836	0857	0903	0932	0935	...	1002	1037	1040	1134	1130	1200	1232	1240	1303	1332	1332
90	**Cuneo** a.	|	|	|	0723	|	|	0829	0829	|	|	|	0902	|	|	|	1000	...	|	1058	|	1157	|	|	1255	|	|	|	1355
83	Mondovi d.	0621	0639	0654	...	0726	0741	...	...	0826	0840	0840	...	0911	0919	0945	...	...	1018	...	1059	...	1144	1216	...	1259	1325	1345	...
103	Ceva d.	0644	0654	0712	...	0742	0756	...	...	0846	0900	0900	...	0926	0933	1000	...	...	1033	...	1118	...	1200	1232	...	1318	1339	1400	...
153	**Savona** a.	0744	0742	0809	...	0843	0845	...	...	0940	0949	0949	...	1019	1026	1046	...	...	1122	...	1215	...	1248	1320	...	1415	1425	1447	...

	⚒	†	†	⚒	⚒V	†V	⚒	⚒		†	⚒	†		⚒	⚒		†	⚒	⚒	†	⚒		†	⚒	⚒				
Torino P N d.	1300	1325	...	1330	1400	1400	1435	1500	1535	...	1600	...	1635	1700	1725	1735	...	1800	1835	1835	1900	1935	2000	2000	2100	2135	2235	2340	...
Savigliano d.	1353	1415	...	1421	1453	1453	1522	1552	1623	...	1650	...	1723	1747	1802	1823	...	1846	1922	1922	1953	2023	2046	2049	2150	2223	2328	0028	...
Fossano d.	1403	1425	1430	1432	1503	1503	1533	1602	1632	1640	1659	1728	1732	1756	1812	1833	1845	1855	1932	1931	2003	2032	2055	2058	2159	2232	2338	0038	...
Cuneo a.	|	1449	|	1455	|	|	1555	|	1654	|	|	|	1755	|	1835	1855	|	|	1955	|	|	2055	|	|	|	2255	2400	0100	...
Mondovi d.	1419	...	1449	...	1518	1518	...	1619	...	1658	1715	1741	...	1815	...	...	1906	1909	...	1943	2019	...	2113	2116	2217	...	...	...	...
Ceva d.	1434	...	1508	...	1533	1532	...	1633	...	1718	1731	1758	...	1832	...	...	1928	1932	...	1958	2033	...	2133	2136	2235	...	...	...	...
Savona a.	1522	...	1606	...	1625	1628	...	1734	...	1821	1823	1852	...	1920	...	...	2023	2022	...	2046	2122	...	2226	2230	...	...	...	...	...

	⚒		⚒	⚒	⚒	⚒	†	⚒	⚒	⚒	†		⚒	⚒	†	⚒	Ⓒ	Ⓐ	†	⚒	†	†	†z	⚒	†		⚒	⚒	†
Savona d.	...	...	...	...	0515	...	...	0548	...	0626	0628	...	0724	...	0725	0748	...	...	0911	0942	0942	...	1111	...	1140	...	1240	...	1311
Ceva d.	...	...	0535	...	0613	...	...	0652	...	0729	0729	...	0831	...	0835	0847	...	...	0958	1030	1036	...	1158	...	1237	...	1327	...	1358
Mondovi d.	...	...	0551	...	0626	...	...	0705	...	0746	0746	...	0845	...	0853	0905	...	...	1012	1044	1055	...	1211	...	1257	...	1346	...	1412
Cuneo d.	0435	0500	|	0600	|	0648	0705	|	0725	|	|	0813	|	0836	|	|	0903	0905	|	|	|	1103	|	1203	|	1303	|	1403	|
Fossano d.	0458	0524	0607	0625	0640	0710	0728	0718	0749	0802	0802	0836	0857	0902	0909	0922	0925	0928	1027	1059	1112	1127	1227	1227	1315	1331	1403	1427	1429
Savigliano d.	0508	0534	0617	0635	0648	0719	0737	0727	0758	0811	0811	0846	...	0911	...	...	0936	0937	1037	1110	...	1137	1237	1237	...	1340	1412	1437	1438
Torino P N a.	0600	0625	0710	0730	0735	0755	0825	0815	0835	0900	0900	0935	...	1000	...	...	1025	1035	1125	1205t	...	1225	1325	1325	...	1425	1500	1525	1525

	⚒	†		⚒	⚒	†	⚒	†		†	⚒	†		†z	⚒	†	L			†z	⑥	Ⓐ	⑥	†	⚒	⚒	⚒	†z
Savona d.	1340	1341	...	1442	...	1500	1538	1540	...	1621	1638	1703	...	1713	1735	1745	...	1838	...	1854	1854	...	...	...	2036	...	2116	2136
Ceva d.	1432	1437	...	1530	...	1549	1627	1634	...	1709	1725	1754	...	1812	1830	1838	...	1928	...	1946	1946	...	...	...	2129	...	2215	2224
Mondovi d.	1446	1456	...	1547	...	1605	1642	1653	...	1723	1740	1809	...	1826	1844	1857	...	1943	...	2001	2001	...	...	...	2146	...	2228	2238
Cuneo d.	|	|	1503	|	1603	|	|	|	1703	|	|	|	1756	|	|	|	1902	|	2003	|	|	2105	2105	2105	|	2205	|	|
Fossano d.	1501	1514	1527	1602	1627	1627	1659	1710	1727	1738	1758	1826	1826	1839	1859	1915	1927	1959	2027	2015	2015	2129	2129	2141	2201	2229	2240	2251
Savigliano d.	1510	...	1537	1611	1636	1636	1708	...	1737	1747	1807	...	1836	1848	1908	...	1938	2008	2037	2024	2024	2138	2138	2150	2210	2239	2248	2259
Torino P N a.	1600	...	1625	1700	1725	1725	1800	...	1830	1835	1900	...	1925	1930	2000	...	2030	2100	2125	2110	2110	2239t	2230	2235	2300	2335	2345	2345

ADDITIONAL SERVICES FOSSANO - CUNEO and v.v. (2nd class only):

	⚒	†	⚒		⚒	†	⚒	†	⚒	⚒	†	⚒		⚒	†		⚒	⚒	⚒	⚒	†		⚒		
Fossano d.	0625	0735	0749	...	0907	0925	1107	1134	1207	1307	1336	1407	...	1507	1535	...	1606	1707	1800	1900	1935	...	2007	2107	...
Cuneo a.	0647	0758	0811	...	0930	0947	1130	1157	1229	1330	1359	1429	...	1529	1558	...	1630	1730	1830	1930	1959	...	2029	2130	...

	⚒	⚒		†	⚒		†	⚒	⚒	†	⚒	⚒		†	⚒	†	⚒		⚒	⚒		⚒	†		
Cuneo d.	0403	0700	...	1000	1132	...	1200	1231	1331	1401	1431	1531	...	1600	1631	1657	1731	...	1810	1914	...	2031	2205	...	...
Fossano a.	0425	0728	...	1022	1155	...	1222	1253	1353	1424	1453	1555	...	1622	1653	1718	1753	...	1832	1944	...	2053	2227	...	...

L – [2] Torino - Ventimiglia - Imperia Oneglia and v.v.
V – From/to Ventimiglia.

t – Torino **Porta Susa**.
y – From May 30.

z – Apr. 12 - May 3 and from May 31.

MILANO MALPENSA AEROPORTO ✈ — 583

FNM *Malpensa Express*

45 km, journey 40 minutes (50 minutes by 🚌). All rail services call at Milano Nord Bovisa (7 minutes from Cadorna, 33 minutes from Malpensa). Special fare payable.

From **Milano Nord Cadorna**: 0410🚌, 0457, 0527, 0557, 0627, 0657 and every 30 minutes until 2057, then 2127, 2157, 2227, 2257, 2327🚌.

Operator: Ferrovie Nord Milano, Piazzale Cadorna 14, 20123 Milano. ✆ + 39 02 85 111, fax: + 39 02 85 11 708.

From **Malpensa Aeroporto**: 0553, 0623, 0653, 0723, 0753 and every 30 minutes until 2153, then 2223, 2253, 2323, 2353, 0023🚌, 0130🚌.

584 MODANE - OULX - TORINO

Local trains are 2nd class only

Additional connections operate Susa - Bussolena by 🚌 (all journeys on † are by 🚌). Timings in *italics*: change at Bussoleno.

km		†	⚒	⚒	⚒	⚒	†	⚒	⚒	†	⚒	†	⚒	⚒	*EC* 9241 [R] P	⚒	†	⚒	Ⓐ	©	⚒	Ⓐ	Ⓐ	©
0	**Modane** 🏛 d.	...	...	...	...	...	...	...	...	...	...	...	...	...	1155	...	...	...	...	...	...	...	...	...
20	Bardonecchia d.	0513	0555	...	0650	...	0713	0810	...	0913	1005	1108	...	*1152*	1220	*1302*	1313	1405	*1502*	1513	...	1632	...	1713
31	Oulx ▲ d.	0526	0606	...	0701	...	0727	0823	...	0926	1017	1121	...	*1205*	1230	*1315*	1326	1417	*1514*	1527	...	1644	...	1726
⊖	Susa d.	|	|	0618	|	0737	|	|	0944	|	|	|	1155	1232	|	1342	|	|	1543	|	1643	|	1738	|
61	Bussoleno d.	0556	0637	0643	0733	0749	0757	0854	0954	0955	1053	1152	1205	1242	|	1352	1355	1452	1553	1557	1653	1715	1748	1755
106	**Torino Porta Nuova** a.	0645	0715	0742	0810	0840	0845	0945	1045	1045	1145	1240	1255	1340	|	1445	1445	1545	1645	1645	1745	1805	1840	1845
107	**Torino Porta Susa** a.	...	...	...	...	...	...	...	...	...	...	...	...	...	1317	...	...	...	...	...	...	...	...	...
	Milano Centrale **585** a.	...	...	...	...	...	...	...	...	...	...	...	...	...	1455	...	...	...	...	...	...	...	...	...

	Ⓐ	†	⚒	*EC* 9247 [R] P	Ⓐ	©	*EC* 9249 [R] P	⚒	Ⓐ	©
Modane 🏛 d.	...	...	...	1820	...	...	1930	...	...	...
Bardonecchia d.	1740	1805	...	1847	*1900*	1923	1957	2019	*2058*	2113
Oulx ▲ d.	1750	1816	...	1857	*1913*	1937	2007	2031	*2111*	2126
Susa d.	|	|	1843	|	1943	|	|	|	2143	|
Bussoleno d.	1818	1844	1853	|	1953	2006	|	2100	2153	2155
Torino Porta Nuova a.	1915	1915	1945	|	2045	2055	|	2150	2245	2245
Torino Porta Susa a.	...	...	...	1945	...	...	2055	...	...	...
Milano Centrale **585** a.	...	...	...	2120	...	...	2225	...	...	...

	⚒	⚒		*EC* 9240 [R] P	⚒	†	⚒	†	*EC* 9242 [R] P
Milano Centrale **585** d.	...	...	...	0640	...	...	...	...	0810
Torino Porta Susa d.	...	...	...	0811	...	...	...	...	0940
Torino Porta Nuova d.	0610	0655	0720	|	0815	0835	0910	0915	|
Bussoleno d.	0701	0749	0810	|	0911	0906	0957	1004	|
Susa a.	|	0758	|	|	0920	|	|	|	|
Oulx ▲ d.	0732	...	0838	0900	...	0930	1024	1035	1030
Bardonecchia d.	0742	...	0852	0912	...	0940	1034	1050	1040
Modane 🏛 a.	...	...	...	0938	...	...	...	...	1105

	⚒	⚒		⚒	†	⚒	⚒	©	Ⓐ	⚒	Ⓐ	©	Ⓐ	*EC* 9248 [R] P	Ⓐ	Ⓐ	©	Ⓐ	Ⓐ	©	Ⓐ	⚒	©	Ⓐ
Milano Centrale **585** d.	...	...	...	...	...	...	...	...	...	...	...	...	...	1610	...	...	...	...	...	...	...	...	...	...
Torino Porta Susa d.	1020	...	...	...	...	...	...	...	...	...	...	...	...	1735	...	...	...	...	...	...	...	...	...	...
Torino Porta Nuova d.	|	1100	1130	1215	1315	1315	1420	1520	1520	1615	1700	1715	1715	|	1755	1815	1815	1845	1915	1915	1940	2020	2130	2130
Bussoleno d.	1111	1154	1220	1310	1405	1415	1519	1610	1616	1711	1738	1816	1816	|	1834	1907	1906	1936	2006	2006	2030	2111	2223	2226
Susa a.	1120	1203r	|	1320	|	|	1528	|	1625	1720	|	|	1825	|	|	1916	|	|	2015	|	|	2120	|	2235
Oulx ▲ § d.	*1148*	...	1248	*1346*	1433	1445	...	1640	*1653*	...	1807	1849	...	1825	1905	...	1934	2009	...	2034	2058	...	2250	*2322**
Bardonecchia § d.	*1200*	...	1300	*1400*	1445	1457	...	1652	*1705*	...	1817	1902	...	1840	1916	...	1947	2022	...	2047	2110	...	2302	*2341**
Modane 🏛 a.	...	...	...	...	...	...	...	...	...	...	...	...	...	1905	...	...	...	...	...	...	...	...	...	...

P – 🚃12 and ✕ Paris - Milano and v.v. (Table **44**). Special 'global' fares payable.
r – 1215 on ⑥.
▲ – Station for the resorts of Cesana, Claviere and Sestriere.
⊖ – Bussoleno - Susa: *8 km*.
* – By 🚌.

585 TORINO - MILANO

km				*ESc* 9707 [R]		*ESc* 9711 [R] T		*AV* 9491 [R]✕ R		*AV* 9661 [R]✕ Ⓐ		*ESc* 9715 [R]🍷			*AV* 9663 [R]✕			*EC* 9241 [R]✕ P		*ESc* 9733 [R]🍷			*AV* 9667 [R]✕ Ⓐ
0	**Torino Porta Nuova 586** d.	0450	0550	0605	0650	0708	...	0715	0750	0755	0850	0925	...	1050	1118	1150	1250	...	1350	1405	1450	1550	1650	1655
6	**Torino Porta Susa 586** d.	0459	0559	0615u	0659	0718u	...	0726u	0759	0807u	0859	0935u	...	1103	1130u	1159	1259	1320	1359	1415u	1459	1559	1659	1707u
29	Chivasso **586** d.	0516	0616	|	0714	|	...	|	0816	|	0916	|	...	1120	|	1216	1316	|	1416	|	1516	1616	1716	|
60	Santhià d.	0533	0633	|	0734	|	...	|	0833	|	0933	|	...	1143	|	1233	1333	|	1433	|	1533	1633	1733	|
79	Vercelli d.	0546	0646	0656	0746	0800	...	|	0846	|	0946	1023	...	1200	|	1246	1346	|	1446	1456	1546	1646	1746	|
101	Novara d.	0603	0703	0714	0801	0815	...	|	0903	|	1003	1040	...	1214	|	1303	1403	|	1503	1514	1603	1703	1803	|
153	**Milano Centrale** a.	0645	0745	0750	0842	0850	...	0841p	0945	0917	1045	1120	...	1250	1240	1345	1445	1455	1545	1550	1645	1745	1845	1817
	Verona Porta Nuova **600** a.	...	...	0927	...	1027	...	...	...	...	...	1257	...	...	...	...	...	...	...	1727	...	...	...	...
	Venezia Santa Lucia **600** a.	...	...	1040	...	1140	...	...	...	...	...	1410	...	...	...	...	...	...	...	1840	...	...	...	...

			AV 9669 [R]✕	*EC* 9247 [R]✕ P		*EC* 9249 [R]✕ P			
Torino Porta Nuova 586 d.	1750	1850	1927	...	1950	...	2055	2150	2250
Torino Porta Susa 586 d.	1759	1859	1939u	1947	1959	2057	2104	2159	2259
Chivasso **586** d.	1816	1916	|	|	2016	|	2121	2216	2316
Santhià d.	1833	1933	|	|	2033	|	2138	2233	2333
Vercelli d.	1846	1946	|	2028	2046	|	2151	2246	2346
Novara d.	1903	2003	|	2043	2103	|	2207	2303	0003
Milano Centrale a.	1945	2044	2049	2120	2145	2225	2248	2345	0045
Verona Porta Nuova **600** a.	...	...	...	...	...	...	...	...	...
Venezia Santa Lucia **600** a.	...	...	...	...	...	...	...	...	...

				EC 9240 [R]✕ P		*AV* 9660 [R]✕ Ⓐ	*EC* 9242 [R]✕ P		
Venezia Santa Lucia **600** d.	...	...	...	...	...	...	...	...	...
Verona Porta Nuova **600** d.	...	...	...	...	...	...	...	...	...
Milano Centrale d.	0015	0515	0600	0640	0715	0743	0810	0815	0915
Novara d.	0059	0559	0645	0714	0759	|	0844	0859	0959
Vercelli d.	0116	0614	0700	0728	0814	|	0857	0914	1014
Santhià d.	0127	0625	0713	|	0825	|	|	0925	1025
Chivasso **586** d.	0148	0644	0730	|	0844	|	|	0944	1044
Torino Porta Susa 586 a.	0206	0700	0748	0809	0900	0853s	0937	1000	1100
Torino Porta Nuova 586 a.	...	0710	0800	...	0910	0905	...	1010	1115

		ESc 9712 [R]🍷				*AV* 9664 [R]✕		*EC* 9248 [R]✕ P			*ESc* 9728 [R]		*AV* 9666 [R]✕ Ⓐ	*ESc* 9732 [R]		*AV* 9668 [R]✕	Ⓐ		*AV* 9494 [R]✕ R			*ESc* 9746 [R] T		
Venezia Santa Lucia **600** d.	...	0850	...	...	...	...	...	...	...	...	1420	...	...	1520	...	...	...	...	...	...	...	1850	...	...
Verona Porta Nuova **600** d.	...	1002	...	...	...	...	...	...	...	...	1532	...	...	1632	...	...	...	...	...	...	...	2002	...	...
Milano Centrale d.	1115	1140	1215	1315	1415	1443	1515	1610	1615	...	1710	1715	1743	1810	1815	1843	1848	1915	1917p	2015	2115	2150	2215	2301
Novara d.	1159	1214	1259	1359	1459	|	1559	|	1659	...	1748	1759	|	1848	1859	|	1929	1959	|	2059	2159	2228	2259	0012
Vercelli d.	1214	1230	1314	1414	1514	|	1614	|	1714	...	1801	1814	|	1901	1914	|	1943	2014	|	2114	2214	2241	2314	...
Santhià d.	1225	|	1325	1425	1525	|	1625	|	1725	...	|	1825	|	|	1925	|	1955	2025	|	2125	2225	|	2325	...
Chivasso **586** d.	1244	|	1344	1444	1544	|	1644	|	1744	...	|	1844	|	|	1944	|	2013	2044	|	2144	2244	|	2344	...
Torino Porta Susa 586 a.	1300	1309s	1400	1500	1600	1553s	1700	1733	1800	...	1843s	1900	1853s	1943s	2000	1953s	2034	2100	2027s	2200	2300	2323s	2400	...
Torino Porta Nuova 586 a.	1310	1320	1410	1510	1610	1605	1710	...	1810	...	1855	1910	1905	1955	2010	2005	...	2110	2040	2210	2310	2335	0010	...

P – 🚃12 and 🍷 Paris Gare de Lyon - Milano and v.v. Special 'global' fares payable.
R – 🚃12 ✕ 🍷 Torino - Milano - Bologna - Roma and v.v.
T – 🚃12 Torino - Venezia - Trieste and v.v.
p – Milano **Porta Garibaldi**.
s – Calls to set down only.
u – Calls to pick up only.

586 TORINO - AOSTA - PRÉ ST DIDIER

Most trains 2nd class only

km				⚒	⚒			†			⚒	†	⚒				Ⓐ	Ⓐ		⚒	†	⚒		⚒	†	†	
0	**Torino Porta Nuova 585** d.	...	...	...	0625	0735	0825	0930	...	1125	*1150*	*1150*	*1225*	1325	1425	...	*1450*	...	1625	*1650*	1725	1725	1825	1920	1920	2025	2225
6	Torino Porta Susa **585** d.	...	...	...	0634	0744	0835	0941	...	1136	*1159*	*1159*	*1235*	1334	1433	...	*1459*	...	1636	*1659*	1734	1734	1834	1928	1928	2034	2234
29	Chivasso **585** d.	...	...	...	0706	0806	0900	1011	...	1200	1219	1253	*1303*	1400	1500	...	1520	...	1703	1720	1803	1758	1902	2000	2006	2101	2300
62	Ivrea d.	...	0624	0650	0747	0836	0925	1037	...	1225	1304	1338	1338	1425	1529	...	1610	1637	1728	1805	1834	1834	1928	2025	2037	2126	2326
79	Pont Saint Martin d.	...	0642	0712	0801	0853	0944	1051	...	1239	1323	1352	1354	1439	1544	...	▬	1652	1742	1833	1848	1850	1942	2046	2054	2147	2340
91	Verrès d.	...	0701	0728	0812	0910	0955	1108	...	1251	1333	1409	1409	1450	1556	...	...	1707	1753	1850	1859	1901	1953	2057	2112	2158	2351
104	Chatillon-Saint Vincent d.	...	0714	0741	0826	0922	1008	1122	...	1311	1344	1421	1421	1509	1615	...	...	1718	1811	1902	1912	1914	2013	2115	2125	2211	0004
129	**Aosta** a.	...	0735	0811	0853	0940	1032	1142	...	1332	1408	1444	1452	1532	1635	...	...	1750	1832	1924	1933	1935	2034	2136	2144	2232	0025
	change trains				d			†	⚒		d				©	Ⓐ	©				†	⚒					
129	**Aosta** d.	0642	0744	...	0903	...	1041	1147	1240	1337	1439	...	...	1541	1642	1711	1744	...	1846	...	1948	1946	...	...	...	...	...
161	**Pré St Didier** ▲ a.	0733	0835	...	0954	...	1132	1238	1327	1428	1530	...	...	1632	1733	1758	1835	...	1937	...	2039	2039	...	...	...	...	...

CONTINUED ON NEXT PAGE

PRÉ ST DIDIER - AOSTA - TORINO 586

			⚒					⚒	†									Ⓒ	Ⓐ		Ⓒ	Ⓐ	Ⓒ	Ⓐ	Ⓒ	
Pré St Didier ▲ d.	...	...	0639	...	0741	0900	1038	1140	1144	...	...	...	1334	1436	1538	...	...	1639	1702		1741	1837	1843	1943	1945	2047
Aosta a.	...	...	0726	...	0828	0947	1125	1227	1231	...	...	...	1421	1523	1625	...	...	1726	1753		1828	1928	1930	2030	2032	2134
change trains								━	d	⚒		⚒			†	⚒		d	⚒	Ⓐ	†	⚒	d		d	⚒
Aosta d.	0510	0625	...	0737	0836	1034	1148	...	1236	1336	...	1415	1429	1536	1637	1637	...	1735	1759	...	1833	1846	1937	...	2037	2141
Chatillon-Saint Vincent d.	0530	0646	...	0759	0858	1055	1210	...	1255	1358	...	1435	1451	1557	1657	1657	...	1756	1823	...	1853	1914	1957	...	2059	2200
Verrès d.	0542	0701	...	0812	0910	1108	1222	...	1309	1409	...	1450	1505	1611	1709	1707	...	1809	1833	...	1912	1927	2010	...	2112	2210
Pont Saint Martin d.	0552	0712	...	0822	0921	1118	1239	...	1322	1425	...	1503	1515	1621	1720	1721	...	1820	1850	...	1922	1942	2020	...	2123	2223
Ivrea d.	0606	0724	...	0835	0936	1131	1257	...	1337	1447	...	1517	1528	1636	1740	1742	...	1833	1909	...	1941	2004	2036	...	2137	2236
Chivasso **585** d.	0647	0808	...	0906	1007	1206	1335	1344	1407	1534	1544	...	1602	1710	1811	1833	1844	1905	1953	2027	2015	2048	2106	...	2208	2318
Torino Porta Susa **585** a.	0709	0825	...	0923	1030	1233	...	1400	1425	...	1600	...	1621	1725	1830	...	1900	1922	...	2051	2034	...	2124	...	2225	2339
Torino Porta Nuova 585 a.	0720	0835	...	0935	1040	1245	...	1410	1435	...	1610	...	1635	1740	1840	...	1910	1935	...	2100	2045	...	2135	...	2235	2350

d – Daily.

▲ – A connecting 🚌 service is available Pré St Didier - Courmayeur and v.v. (see Table **368**).

BRIG - STRESA - MILANO 590

For night trains from Genève / Basel to Roma and Venezia see Table **82**

km							*EC* **35**		*CIS* **51**		*EC* **37**	*IR* **2715**		*EC* **125**		*CIS* **57**				*EC* **127**				*CIS* **59**	*EC* **129**	
		2y	2	2	2 ⚒	2 †	⊡	2	⊙✕	2	⊡🍸 V		2	⊡	2	⊙✕ T		2 ⚒	2	⊡	2		2	⊙✕	⊡	2
	Genève Aéroport **570** d.	...	...	...	...	...	...	...	...	...	0733	...	...	...	...	...	...	...	...	...	...	...	...	...	...	...
	Genève **570** d.	...	...	...	...	...	0545	...	...	...	0742	...	...	1107	...	...	...	...	...	1510	...	...	...	...	1807	...
	Lausanne **570** d.	...	...	...	...	...	0620	...	...	...	0820	...	...	1146	...	...	...	...	...	1546	...	...	...	...	1846	...
	Basel **560** d.	...	...	...	...	...	|	...	0628	...	|	...	...	|	...	1228	...	...	...	|	...	...	...	1728	|	...
	Bern **560** d.	...	...	...	...	...	|	...	0735	...	|	...	...	|	...	1335	...	...	...	|	...	...	...	1835	|	...
0	**Brig** 🏛 d.	...	...	...	...	...	0744	...	0844	...	0944	1044	...	1320	...	1444	...	...	...	1720	...	...	...	1944	2020	...
42	**Domodossola** 🏛 § a.	...	...	...	...	...	0812	...	0912	...	1012	1112	...	1350	...	1512	...	...	...	1750	...	...	...	2012	2050	...
42	**Domodossola** d.	0555	0605	0655	0728	0750	0817	0825	0917	0948	1017	...	1255	1405	1357	1517	1525	1605	1655	1805	1810	1855	1957	2017	2105	2155
72	Verbania-Pallanza d.	0617	0627	0716	0747	0817	|	0846	|	1014	|	...	1316	1423	1433	|	1546	1633	1716	1823	1836	1915	2023	|	2123	2223
77	Baveno d.	|	0632	|	|	0822	|	|	|	1019	|	...	|	|	1438	|	|	1638	|	|	1841	|	2028	|	|	2228
81	Stresa d.	0624	0638	0723	0755	0827	0839	0853	|	1024	|	...	1323	1431	1443	|	1553	1642	1723	1831	1845	1923	2039	|	2131	2232
98	Arona d.	0637	0657	0736	0808	0851	|	0906	|	1049	|	...	1336	1445	1502	|	1606	1700	1736	1845	1903	1936	2059	|	2145	2251
124	Gallarate d.	0658	0731	0758	0832	0922	|	0928	1003	1128	1104	...	1358	1503	1532	1603	1628	1731	1758	1903	1932	1958	2127	2103	2203	2321
150	Rho d.	|	0800	|	0900	0944	|	|	|	1149	|	...	|	|	1559	|	|	1800	|	|	1959	|	2149	|	|	2345
165	**Milano Porta Garibaldi** a.	0733	0815	0835	0915	0957	|	|	|	1207	|	...	|	|	1613	|	|	1813	|	|	2013	|	2202	|	|	2357
167	**Milano Centrale** a.	...	...	...	...	...	0935	1004	1035	...	1135	...	1435	1535	...	1640	1705	...	1835	1935	...	2035	...	2135	2235	...

			CIS **50**		*EC* **120**			*CIS* **52**	*EC* **122**			*IR* **2730**	*EC* **124**				*EC* **40**			*CIS* **56**			*EC* **42**			
		2	⊙✕	2	⊡	⚒	†	⊙✕ T	⊡		2	⑥	⊡	2	2		⊡	2		⊙✕			⊡🍸 V	2	2	
Milano Centrale d.	...	...	0725	0755	0825	...	...	1120	1225	...	1325	...	1425	...	1525	...	1625	...	1725	1825	...	...	1920	1925	...	2125
Milano Porta Garibaldi d.	0505	0617	|	|	|	0900	0900	|	|	1246	|	...	|	1447	|	1600	|	1647	|	|	1755	1835	|	|	2047	|
Rho d.	0522	0630	|	|	|	0912	0912	|	|	1300	|	...	|	1500	|	|	|	1701	|	|	|	|	|	|	2100	|
Gallarate d.	0551	0654	0758	0832	0858	0931	0931	1158	1258	1327	1400	...	1458	1527	1600	1636	|	1727	1802	|	1831	1914	|	2002	2128	2200
Arona d.	0618	0724	|	0853	0916	0959	1007	|	1316	1348	1421	...	1516	1555	1621	1711	|	1754	1824	|	1911	1935	|	2021	2157	2221
Stresa d.	0637	0743	|	0906	0929	1018	1027	|	1329	1408	1434	...	1529	1613	1634	1732	1721	1812	1837	1921	1930	1955	|	2034	2216	2234
Baveno d.	0642	0747	|	|	|	1023	1031	|	|	1412	|	...	|	1617	|	1736	|	1816	|	|	1935	1959	|	|	2220	|
Verbania-Pallanza d.	0647	0752	|	0914	0936	1028	1037	|	1336	1417	1442	...	1536	1622	1642	1741	|	1821	1845	|	1940	2004	|	2042	2225	2242
Domodossola a.	0718	0818	0843	0935	0955	1105	1108	1243	1355	1437	1505	...	1555	1643	1705	1810	1743	1850	1905	1943	2000	2025	2043	2105	2253	2305
Domodossola 🏛 § d.	...	...	0848	...	1010	...	...	1248	1410	...	...	1510	1610	...	...	...	1748	...	...	1948	...	...	2048	...	...	...
Brig 🏛 a.	...	...	0916	...	1040	...	...	1316	1440	...	...	1539	1640	...	...	...	1816	...	...	2016	...	...	2116	...	...	...
Bern **560** a.	...	...	1023	...	|	...	...	1423	|	...	...	...	|	...	...	...	|	...	...	2123	...	...	|	...	...	...
Basel **560** a.	...	...	1132	...	|	...	...	1532	|	...	...	...	|	...	...	...	|	...	...	2232	...	...	|	...	...	...
Lausanne **570** a.	...	...	...	...	1214	...	...	...	1614	...	...	...	1814	...	...	...	1940	...	...	...	...	...	2240	...	...	...
Genève **570** a.	...	...	...	...	1250	...	...	...	1653	...	...	...	1853	...	...	...	2018	...	...	...	...	...	2315	...	...	...
Genève Aéroport **570** a.	...	...	...	...	...	...	...	...	...	...	...	...	...	...	...	...	...	...	...	...	...	...	2324	...	...	...

Local service BRIG - DOMODOSSOLA and v.v. (2nd class only):

km		Ⓐ		🚌	⑥z		🚌 Ⓐ		🚌	⑥z	Ⓒ		🚌	🚌	⑥z	🚌	🚌	Ⓐ			🚌		🚌		🚌	
0	**Brig** d.	0607	0705*	...	0820	0830*	...	1005*	...	1018	1107	1140*	...	*1305*r	1420	*1430*r	*1605*r	1707	1807	1905*	...	2030*	...	2205*	...	0016
23	Iselle di Trasquera § d.	0627	0725	0730	|	0852	0900	1028	1030	|	1127	1200	1210	1330	|	1505	1630	1727	1827	1926	1935	2053	2100	2226	2230	0036
42	**Domodossola** a.	0645	...	0800	0849	...	0928	...	1058	1047	1145	...	1238	1358	1449	1533	1658	1745	1845	...	2003	...	2128	...	2258	0054

		Ⓐ		⚒	🚌 Ⓐ		🚌		🚌		⑥	🚌		🚌		🚌		🚌		🚌		🚌		🚌		
Domodossola d.	0357	0515	0615	0705	0830	...	1000	...	1140	...	1215	1245	...	1435	...	1600	...	1735	...	1905	...	2030	...	2200	...	...
Iselle di Trasquera § d.	0420	0539	0639	0727	0858	0915	1028	1040	1208	1215	1239	1313	1340	1503	1515	1628	1640	1803	1815	1933	1940	2058	2115	2228	2240	...
Brig a.	0434	0553	0653	0742	...	0935*	...	1101*	...	1235*	1253	...	1400*	...	1535*	...	1702*	...	1835*	...	2003*	...	2135*	...	2303*	...

T – 🚃12 and ✕ Basel - Milano - Venezia Mestre - Trieste and v.v.
V – 🚃12 and ✕ Genève Aéroport - Milano - Venezia Santa Lucia and v.v.
r – Connection by train from Brig Autoquai (see note *).
y – An additional journey runs one hour earlier to Milano Centrale.

z – *IR* train (1, 2 class).
§ – Ticket point is **Iselle**.
* – Brig Autoquai (allow 8 minutes walk from Brig station).

⊙ – *CISALPINO Pendolino* train. 🅁 inclusive of supplement. Due to technical difficulties, a change of train may be necessary at Domodossola.
⊡ – Operated by *CISALPINO*. 🅁 inclusive of supplement.

DOMODOSSOLA and ARONA - NOVARA 591

2nd class only except where shown

km		⚒		ⒸS	Ⓐ		⚒				⚒	Ⓒ	Ⓒ		🚌 Ⓐ	⚒				⚒	⚒	⚒			†			
0	**Domodossola** d.	0523	...	0618	0618	...	0615	...	0653	...	0755	...	...	...	1100	...	...	...	1236	1340	...	...	...	1557	...	...	1747	1902
38	Omegna d.	0618	...	|	|	...	0657	...	0759	...	0850	...	...	...	1201	...	...	...	1337	1431	...	...	...	1645	...	...	1842	1943
44	Pettenasco d.	0625	...	|	|	...	0704	...	0805	...	0857	...	...	...	1208	...	...	...	1344	|	...	...	...	1651	...	...	1850	1950
47	Orta-Miasino d.	0629	...	|	|	...	0708	...	0809	...	0901	...	...	...	1212	...	...	...	1354	1442	...	...	...	1655	...	...	1855	1959
60	Borgomanero d.	0642	...	|	|	...	0723	...	0821	...	0916	...	...	...	1232	1253	...	...	1409	1458	...	...	...	1714	...	...	1908	2017
	Arona d.	|	0637	0704	0704	...	|	0756	|	...	|	1002	1205	...	...	|	...	1400	|	|	...	...	1636	|	...	1845	|	|
	Oleggio d.	|	0700	0721	0721	...	|	0818	|	...	|	1022	1228	...	...	|	...	1424	|	|	...	...	1658	|	...	1911	|	|
90	**Novara** a.	0713	0719	0733	0734	0735	0752	0836	0854	0907	0951	1040	1246	1313	...	1328	1423	1441	1450	1533	1605	1706	1717	1753	1909	1931	1942	2046
157	Alessandria a.	...	...	0822	...	0822	...	...	...	1021	...	...	...	1429	...	...	1534	...	...	...	1718	1820	...	...	2018	...	...	...

km		⚒	⚒				🚌	b	d			⚒			⚒		Ⓐ					Ⓐ	Ⓐ				n	ⒸS
	Alessandria d.	...	...	...	...	...	...	...	...	...	...	...	1240	...	1355	...	...	1535	...	...	1643	...	...	1741	...	...	2040	2118
0	**Novara** d.	0538	0553	0634	0653	0805	...	0912	1002	1223	1254	1350	1402	1412	1506	1519	1632	1648	1732	1739	1753	1822	1832	1853	1920	1926	2152	2203
17	Oleggio d.	|	0610	|	0722	|	...	0928	1023	|	1311	|	...	1441	...	|	|	...	|	1759	...	|	1846	...	|	1942	...	2218
37	**Arona** a.	|	0635	|	0742	|	...	0952	1047	|	1334	|	...	1504	...	|	|	...	|	1823	...	|	1906	...	|	2004	...	2231
	Borgomanero d.	0608	...	0722	...	0839	0845	...	...	1252	...	1425	...	...	...	1556	1700	...	1809	...	...	1912	|	...	2003	...	...	|
	Orta-Miasino d.	0630	...	0736	...	...	0907	...	...	1306	...	1443	...	...	...	1612	1713	...	1825	...	...	1932	|	...	2017	...	...	|
	Pettenasco d.	0635	...	0741	...	...	0913	...	...	1311	...	1448	...	...	...	1617	1718	...	1830	...	...	1937	|	...	2021	...	...	|
	Omegna d.	0658	...	0800	...	...	0920	...	...	1323	...	1458	...	...	...	1624	1725	...	1843	...	...	1944	|	...	2027	...	...	|
93	**Domodossola** a.	0744	...	0850	...	...	1011	...	...	1413	...	1548	...	...	...	1716	1805	...	1936	...	...	2018	2007	...	2113	...	...	2314

S – From May 30.
b – By 🚌 on Ⓐ (depart Novara 0910, arrive Arona 1007).
d – By 🚌 on Ⓐ (depart Novara 1010, arrive Arona 1107).
n – On ⑦ from May 31 depart Alessandria 2047, arrive Novara 2135.

592 BELLINZONA - LUINO
2nd class only

km											
0	**Bellinzona 550** d.	0554	0754	...	0950	*1154*	...	*1354*	*1554*	*1754*	...
9	Cadenazzo d.	0606	0806	...	1006	1206	...	1406	1606	1806	...
27	Pino-Tronzano 🏛 d.	0627	0827	...	1027	1227	...	1427	1627	1827	...
40	**Luino 608** a.	0644	0844	...	1044	1244	...	1444	1644	1844	...

Luino 608 d.	0705	...	1115	1315	...	1515	...	1715	1915	...
Pino-Tronzano 🏛 d.	0722	...	1131	1331	...	1531	...	1731	1931	...
Cadenazzo a.	0744	...	1152	1352	...	1552	...	1752	1952	...
Bellinzona 550 a.	0754	...	*1204*	*1404*	...	*1604*	...	1800	2008	...

Operator: FS – Ferrovie dello Stato / FFS – Ferrovie Federali Svizzere.

593 MILANO - COLICO - TIRANO

km																								
		2 ⚒		2 †	2 ▷	2 ⚒	2 †			⚒				2 Ⓐ			2 ⚒				2	🚌	▷	2
0	**Milano Centrale** ▷ d.	...	0620	0625p	0650p	0720	0720	0820	1020	1125	1220	...	1420	1520p	1620	1720	1750	1820	1920	2020	2125	...	2150p	2250
12	Monza ▷ d.	...	0634	0643	0709	0734	0734	0834	1034	1138	1234	...	1434	1534	1634	1734	1804	1834	1934	2034	2139	...	2209	2306
50	Lecco ▷ d.	...	0702	0718	0750	0801	0802	0902	1102	1208	1302	...	1502	1602	1702	1802	1836	1902	2001	2102	2209	...	2250	2347
72	Varenna-Esino d.	...	0724	0753	...	...	0824	0924	1124	...	1324	...	1524	...	1724	1824	...	|	2024	2124	2240	...	...	...
75	Bellano-Tartavalle Terme d.	...	0733	0802	...	...	0833	0933	1133	...	1333	...	1533	...	1733	1833	...	1933	2033	2133	2245	...	...	...
89	**Colico** a.	...	0747	0823	...	...	0847	0947	1147	...	1347	...	1547	...	1747	1847	...	1947	2047	2147	2300	2305	...	...
116	Chiavenna ▲ a.	...	|	0848	...	...	|	|	|	...	|	...	|	...	|	|	...	|	|	|	...	|	...	...
130	Sondrio a.	0652	0821	...	...	...	0921	1021	1221	...	1422	...	1622	...	1821	1921	...	2021	2121	2221	...	2347	...	...
156	**Tirano** a.	0734	0850	...	...	...	1007	1050	1250	...	1450	...	1650	...	1850	...	...	2050	2150	...	...	...	...	...

	2 ▽			2 ⚒		⚒						2 Ⓐ	2 ⚒		2 †	2 †	2 ⚒		2 †	2 ⚒	2 ▽	2	🚌	2
Tirano d.	...	...	0610	...	0710	...	0910	1110	...	1310	1510	...	...	1710	...	1810	...	1910	1952	...	...	...	...	2125
Sondrio d.	...	0528	0638	...	0738	...	0938	1138	...	1338	1538	...	...	1738	...	1838	...	1938	2038	...	...	2123	...	2202
Chiavenna ▲ d.	...	|	|	...	|	...	|	|	...	|	|	...	...	|	1802	|	...	|	|	...	...	|	...	...
Colico d.	...	0601	0716	...	0816	...	1016	1216	...	1416	1616	...	...	1816	1837	1916	...	2016	2116	2116	...	2203	...	...
Bellano-Tartavalle Terme d.	...	0616	0732	...	0832	...	1032	1232	...	1432	1632	...	...	1832	1901	1932	...	2032	2132	2132	...	2219	...	...
Varenna-Esino d.	...	0621	0737	...	0837	...	1037	1237	...	1437	1637	...	...	1837	1906	1937	...	2037	2137	2137	...	2224	...	...
Lecco ▽ d.	0610	0653	0759	0826	0859	0957	1059	1259	...	1459	1659	1729	1757	1859	1946	1959	1959	2059	2159	2159	2210	2248	2305	...
Monza ▽ d.	0652	0727	0827	0857	0927	1027	1127	1327	...	1527	1727	1757	1827	1927	2014	2027	2027	2127	2227	2227	2252	2322r	0013	...
Milano Centrale ▽ a.	0710p	0740	0840	0910	0940	1040	1140	1340	...	1540	1740	1810	1840p	1940	2030p	2040	2040	2140	2240	2240	2310p	2335r	0044	...

p – Milano **Porta Garibaldi**.
r – From Mar. 30.

▷ – Local trains run Milano Porta Garibaldi - Lecco hourly 0650 - 2150.
▽ – Local trains run Lecco - Milano Porta Garibaldi hourly 0610 - 2210.

▲ – **Local service COLICO - CHIAVENNA**: Journey 28 – 35 minutes, 2nd class only.
From **Colico**: 0550, 0707, 0810 ⚒, 0846 ⚒, 1002, 1046 ⚒, 1202, 1246 ⚒, 1402, 1446 ⚒, 1602, 1646 ⚒, 1802, 1852 ⚒, 2002.
From **Chiavenna**: 0626, 0745 ⚒, 0843 ⚒, 0850 †, 0928 ⚒, 1043, 1128 ⚒, 1243, 1328 ⚒, 1443, 1528 ⚒, 1643, 1728 ⚒, 1845, 1930 ⚒, 2040.

595 INNSBRUCK - BOLZANO / BOZEN - VERONA - BOLOGNA

km																									
		ES 9311 🅁🍷		2 ⚒	2	2	2 ⚒	2	2 Ⓐ	1871 2 L	2	*IC* 717 ♦	2 Ⓒ	2 Ⓒ	2 ⑥v	2	*EC* 81 🅁✕	2	2	2	2	2 ⚒	*EC* 85 🅁✕ ♦	2	2
	München Hbf **951** d.	...	...	...	...	...	...	...	...	...	...	...	...	...	...	...	0730	...	...	...	...	...	0931	...	...
0	**Innsbruck Hbf** ▷ d.	...	...	...	0516	...	0546	0616	...	0700	0716	...	...	...	0816	0816	0927	...	0916	...	1016	...	1127	1116	1216
18	Matrei ▷ d.	...	...	...	0534	...	0604	0634	...	0718	0734	...	...	...	0834	0834	|	...	0934	...	1034	...	|	1134	1234
23	Steinach in Tirol ▷ d.	...	...	...	0539	...	0609	0639	...	0723	0739	...	...	...	0839	0839	|	...	0939	...	1039	...	|	1139	1239
37	**Brennero** 🏛 ▷ a.	...	...	...	0555	...	0624	0655	...	0737	0755	...	...	...	0855	0855	|	...	0955	...	1055	...	|	1155	1255
					2		2d	▬		|	2⚒				⑥v	2	|		2		2		|	2	2
37	**Brennero** 🏛 d.	...	...	...	0605	...	0638		...	0739	0804	...	...	0838	0908	0938	|	...	1038	...	1138	...	|	1238	1308
60	Vipiteno / Sterzing d.	...	...	...	0626	...	0657	...	...	0758	0823	...	...	0857	0927	0957	|	...	1057	...	1157	...	|	1257	1327
78	Fortezza / Franzensfeste d.	...	...	0542	0646	...	0715	...	...	0815	0841	...	...	0915	0945	1015	1046	...	1115	...	1215	...	1246	1315	1345
89	Bressanone / Brixen d.	...	...	0554	0656	...	0725	...	...	...	0851	...	...	0925	0955	1025	1056	...	1125	...	1225	...	1256	1325	1355
99	Chiusa / Klausen d.	...	...	0602	0704	...	0733	2	...	...	0859	...	...	0933	1003	1033	|	...	1133	...	1233	...	|	1333	1403
127	**Bolzano / Bozen** a.	...	...	0626	0728	...	0759	⚒	...	...	0925	...	...	0959	1029	1059	1129	...	1159	...	1259	...	1329	1359	1429
127	**Bolzano / Bozen** d.	...	0500	0630	0731	0737	▬	0831	0907	...	▬	0931	0937	...	1031	▬	...	1137	▬	1231	...	1304	1331	...	1431
143	Ora / Auer d.	...	0512	0642	0743	0755	...	0843	0925	...	...	0943	0955	...	1043	...	...	1155	...	1243	...	1322	|	...	1443
165	Mezzocorona d.	...	0526	0655	0756	0816	...	0856	0942	...	...	0958	1016	...	1056	...	...	1216	...	1256	...	1343	|	...	1456
182	**Trento** ▲ d.	...	0540	0712	0810	0832	...	0910	0957	...	...	1012	1032	...	1110	...	...	1232	...	1310	...	1355	1403	...	1510
206	Rovereto d.	...	0554	0726	0825	0846	...	0925	1012	...	...	1028	1046	...	1125	...	...	1246	2	1325	...	...	1419	...	1525
274	**Verona Porta Nuova** a.	...	0647	0818	0917	0952	Ⓒ	1017	...	...	...	1111	1159	...	1217	...	...	1352	⚒	1417	...	...	1457	...	1617
274	**Verona Porta Nuova** d.	0601	0659	...	...	...	0959	...	...	...	1147	1131	...	...	...	1259	...	...	1415	1457	...	...	1511	...	1659
388	**Bologna Centrale** a.	0705	0832	...	...	...	1132	...	...	...	1332	1315	...	...	...	1432	...	...	1604	1634	...	...	1611	...	1832
	Milano Centrale **600** a.	|	...	...	...	...	...	...	...	...	...	...	...	...	...	...	...	...	...	...	...	...	...	...	...
	Venezia Santa Lucia **600** a.	|	...	...	...	...	...	...	...	...	...	...	...	...	...	...	...	...	...	...	...	...	...	...	...
	Firenze SMN **620** a.	0814	...	...	...	...	...	...	...	...	...	...	...	...	...	...	...	...	...	...	...	...	...	...	...
	Roma Termini **620** a.	1000	...	...	...	...	...	...	...	...	...	...	...	...	...	...	...	...	...	...	...	...	...	...	...
	Napoli Centrale **620** a.	...	...	...	...	...	...	...	...	...	...	...	...	...	...	...	...	...	...	...	...	...	...	...	...

	2	*EC* 87 🅁✕	2	2	*ES* 9313 🅁✕	2	2	1875 2 L⑤f	*EC* 89 *EC* 92 🅁🍷	2	2	*E* 1595 ♦	2	2	1873 2 L	*EC* 83 🅁🍷	2	2	2	*E* 925 *E* 837 Q	2	2	*E* 1601 ♦	*EN* 485 🅁 ♦	*EN* 363 🅁 B
München Hbf **951** d.	...	1130	...	...	...	...	...	...	1330	...	...	...	...	...	...	1530	...	...	...	...	...	...	...	2103	2103
Innsbruck Hbf ▷ d.	...	1327	...	1316	...	1416	...	1503	1527	...	1516	...	1616	...	1701	1727	...	1715	1816	...	1916	2016	...	2305	2305
Matrei ▷ d.	...	|	...	1334	...	1434	...	1521	|	...	1534	...	1634	...	1719	|	...	1734	1834	...	1934	2034	...	|	|
Steinach in Tirol ▷ d.	...	|	...	1339	...	1439	...	1526	|	...	1539	...	1639	...	1724	|	...	1739	1839	...	1939	2039	...	|	|
Brennero 🏛 ▷ a.	...	|	...	1355	...	1455	...	1540	|	...	1555	...	1655	...	1740	|	...	1755	1855	...	1955	2055	...	2342	2342
		|		2		2		|	|		2		2		|	|		2	2		2	2		|	|
Brennero 🏛 d.	1338	|	...	1438	...	1508	1538	1543	|	...	1638	...	1708	1738	1743	|	...	1838	1908	...	2008	2108	...	2357	2357
Vipiteno / Sterzing d.	1357	|	...	1457	...	1527	1557	1603	|	...	1657	...	1727	1757	1804	|	...	1857	1927	...	2027	2127	...	|	|
Fortezza / Franzensfeste d.	1415	1446	...	1515	...	1545	1615	1621	1646	...	1715	...	1745	1815	1821	1846	...	1915	1945	...	2045	2145	2154	0029	0029
Bressanone / Brixen d.	1425	1456	...	1525	...	1555	1625	...	1656	...	1725	...	1755	1825	...	1856	...	1925	1955	...	2055	2155	2205	0038	0038
Chiusa / Klausen d.	1433	|	...	1533	...	1603	1633	...	|	...	1733	...	1803	1833	...	|	...	1933	2003	...	2103	2203	|	|	|
Bolzano / Bozen a.	1500	1529	...	1559	...	1629	1659	...	1729	...	1759	...	1829	1859	...	1929	...	1959	2029	...	2129	2229	2236	0107	0107
Bolzano / Bozen d.	...	1531	1537	...	1606	1631	...	...	1731	1737	...	1837	1831	...	...	1931	1937	...	2031	2050	...	2231r	2301	0109	0109
Ora / Auer d.	...	|	1555	...	|	1643	...	...	|	1755	...	1854	1843	...	...	|	1955	...	2043	2103	...	2248r	2314	|	|
Mezzocorona d.	...	|	1616	...	|	1656	...	...	|	1816	...	1915	1856	...	...	|	2016	...	2056	2124	...	2310r	2330	|	|
Trento ▲ d.	...	1603	1632	...	1649	1710	...	...	1803	1832	...	1929	1910	...	...	2003	2032	...	2110	2139	...	2323r	2348	0142	0142
Rovereto d.	...	1619	1646	...	1705	1725	...	...	1819	1846	...	1945	1925	...	...	2019	2046	...	2125	2155	...	...	0006	|	|
Verona Porta Nuova a.	...	1657	1759	...	1747	1817	...	...	1901	1952	...	2032	2017	...	...	2101	2152	...	2217	2237	...	...	|	0237	0237
Verona Porta Nuova d.	...	1659	...	...	1800	1848	...	...	1915	...	...	2052	2106	...	...	...	...	...	...	2240	...	...	|	0305	0440
Bologna Centrale a.	...	|	...	...	1902	2032	...	...	|	...	...	2228	2234	...	...	...	...	...	...	0058	...	...	|	0435	|
Milano Centrale **600** a.	...	|	...	...	|	...	...	...	2035	...	...	|	...	...	...	...	...	...	...	|	...	...	|	|	|
Venezia S.L. **600** a.	...	1810	...	...	|	...	...	...	...	...	...	|	...	...	...	...	...	...	...	|	...	...	|	|	0638
Firenze SMN **620** a.	...	...	...	...	2009	...	...	...	...	...	...	2344c	...	...	...	...	...	...	...	|	...	...	|	0618	...
Roma Termini **620** a.	...	...	...	...	2159	...	...	...	...	...	...	...	...	...	...	...	...	...	...	0609t	...	...	0837t	0905	...
Napoli Centrale **620** a.	...	...	...	...	...	...	...	...	...	...	...	...	...	...	...	...	...	...	...	0926	...	...	...	...	...

FOR NOTES SEE NEXT PAGE

ADDITIONAL TRAINS INNSBRUCK - BRENNERO — 2nd class

	⚒	⚒	⚒	⚒	⚒	⚒	⚒			
Innsbruck Hbf d.	0846	1045	1246	1446	1646	1846	1946	2116	2216	2316
Matrei d.	0904	1104	1304	1504	1704	1904	2004	2134	2234	2334
Steinach in Tirol d.	0908	1108	1308	1508	1708	1908	2009	2138	2239	2339
Brennero 🏛 a.	...	...	...	...	...	...	2023	...	2255	2355

			⚒		⚒	⚒	⚒	⚒	⚒	⚒
Brennero 🏛 d.	0535	0605	0635	0705	...	...	...	...	...	...
Steinach in Tirol d.	0552	0622	0652	0722	0852	1052	1252	1452	1652	1852
Matrei d.	0557	0627	0657	0727	0857	1057	1257	1457	1657	1857
Innsbruck Hbf a.	0613	0643	0713	0743	0914	1113	1313	1513	1713	1913

BOLOGNA - VERONA - BOLZANO / BOZEN - INNSBRUCK 595

						E 1602		*E*824 *E*924		*EC* 188				*E* 1594		*EC*93 *EC*88				*EC* 82					
	2	2	2	2	2		2		2	[R]🍷	2	2	2		2	[R]🍷	2	2	2	[R]✕	2		2	2	2
	⚒	L (1870)		⑥y		♦	⚒	R	⚒h					♦				†						⚒	⚒
Napoli Centrale **620** d.	...	...	...	...	...	...	...	1845	...	...	...	...	...	2259	...	...	...	...	...	...	...	...	...	...	...
Roma Termini **620** d.	...	...	...	...	...	2157t	...	2205t	...	...	...	...	...	|	...	...	...	...	...	...	...	...	...	...	...
Firenze SMN **620** d.	...	...	...	...	...	|	...	|	...	...	...	...	...	|	...	...	...	...	...	...	...	...	...	...	...
Venezia Santa Lucia **600** d.	...	...	...	...	...	|	...	|	...	...	...	...	...	|	...	...	...	...	...	...	...	...	...	...	...
Milano Centrale **600** d.	...	...	...	...	...	|	...	|	...	...	...	...	...	|	...	0705	...	...	...	...	...	...	...	...	...
Bologna Centrale d.	...	...	...	...	...	|	...	0400	0503	...	...	...	0604	0535	0643	|	0748	...	...	...	...	0948x	...	...	1048
Verona Porta Nuova a.	...	...	...	...	...	|	...	0610	0655	...	...	...	0744	0802	0823	0836	0926	...	...	...	...	1122x	...	...	1226
Verona Porta Nuova d.	...	...	...	*0525*	...	|	0609	0620	...	0659	...	0747	▬	0805	...	0859	▬	0947	...	...	...	1147	...	1209	...
Rovereto d.	...	...	...	*0612*	...	0626	0715	0721	...	0741	*0751*z	0837	...	0857	...	0941	...	1037	...	...	*1150*a	1237	...	1315	...
Trento ▲ d.	...	...	*0558*z	*0628*	...	0644	0731	0739	...	0758	*0807*z	0853	...	0913	...	0958	...	1053	...	...	*1207*a	1253	...	1331	...
Mezzocorona d.	...	...	*0613*z	*0641*	...	0657	0744	0752	...	|	*0818*z	0905	...	0926	...	|	...	1105	...	...	*1218*a	1305	...	1344	...
Ora / Auer d.	...	...	*0634*z	*0704*	...	0713	0805	0810	...	|	*0839*z	0919	...	0945	...	|	2	1119	...	...	*1235*a	1319	...	1405	...
Bolzano / Bozen a.	...	...	*0652*z	*0722*	...	0732	0822	0843	...	0830	*0856*z	0930	2	1006	...	1030	©	1131	...	...	*1252*a	1330	...	1422	...
Bolzano / Bozen d.	0600	...	0700	0729	0800	0809	...	...	...	0832	0901	0932	1000	...	...	1032	1100	...	1200	1232	1300	1332	1400	...	...
Chiusa / Klausen d.	0625	...	0725	0754	0825	|	...	...	...	|	0925	0955	1025	...	...	|	1125	...	1225	|	1325	1355	1425	...	...
Bressanone / Brixen d.	0634	...	0734	0802	0834	0843	...	...	...	0901	0934	1004	1034	...	...	1101	1134	...	1234	1301	1334	1404	1434	...	...
Fortezza / Franzensfeste d.	0645	0720	0745	0812	0845	0856	...	...	...	0915	0945	1015	1045	...	...	1115	1145	...	1245	1315	1345	1415	1445	...	...
Vipiteno / Sterzing d.	0703	0739	0803	0833	0903	...	...	...	...	|	1003	1033	1103	...	...	|	1203	...	1303	|	1403	1433	1503	...	...
Brennero 🏢 a.	0722	0758	0822	0852	0922	...	...	...	...	|	1022	1052	1122	...	...	|	1222	...	1322	|	1422	1452	1522	...	...
	2d	|	2	2	2					|		2	2			|	2d		2	|		2	2		
Brennero 🏢 ▷ d.	0735	0805	0905	0905	1005	...	...	...	...	|	...	1105	1205	...	...	|	1305	...	1405	|	...	1505	1605	...	...
Steinach in Tirol ▷ d.	0752	0822	0922	0922	1022	...	...	...	...	|	...	1122	1222	...	...	|	1322	...	1422	|	...	1522	1622	...	...
Matrei ▷ d.	0757	0827	0927	0927	1027	...	...	...	...	1018	...	1127	1227	...	...	|	1327	...	1427	|	...	1527	1627	...	...
Innsbruck Hbf ▷ a.	0814	0843	0943	0943	1043	...	...	...	...	1034	...	1143	1243	...	...	1232	1343	...	1443	1432	...	1543	1643	...	...
München Hbf **951** a.	...	...	...	...	...	...	...	...	...	1225	...	...	...	...	...	1427	...	...	...	1626	...	...	...	...	...

	EC 84		*ES* 9310				*EC* 86			1874			1872					*ES* 9312				*IC* 718		*EN* 358	*EN* 484
	[R]✕	2	[R]✕		2	2	[R]✕	2		2	2	2	2		2	2		[R]✕	2	2				[R]	[R]
	♦					Ⓐ				L⑦k			Ln			Ⓐ			Ⓐb	⚒		♦		B	♦
Napoli Centrale **620** d.	...	...	...	...	...	...	...	...	...	...	...	...	...	...	...	...	...	...	...	...	...	...	...	...	...
Roma Termini **620** d.	...	...	0900	...	...	...	...	...	...	...	...	...	...	...	...	...	...	1555	...	...	...	...	...	...	1910
Firenze SMN **620** d.	...	...	1049	...	...	...	...	...	...	...	...	...	...	...	...	...	...	1749	...	...	...	...	...	...	2153
Venezia Santa Lucia **600** d.	...	...	|	...	...	...	1320	...	...	...	...	...	...	...	...	...	...	|	...	...	...	...	...	2251	|
Milano Centrale **600** d.	...	...	|	...	...	...	|	...	...	...	...	...	...	...	...	...	...	|	...	...	...	...	...	|	|
Bologna Centrale d.	1117	...	1154	1148	...	...	|	...	1348	...	...	...	...	1548	...	...	1748	1858	...	*1848*r	1948	1956	2118	|	2305
Verona Porta Nuova a.	1245	...	1259	1324	...	...	1438	...	1522	...	...	...	...	1722	...	...	1922	1954	...	*2035*r	2122	2146	2248	0025	0031
Verona Porta Nuova d.	1259	...	1311	1343	...	1409	1459	...	1547	...	...	*1609*a	...	1747	...	1809	1947	...	2009	2109	2147	2207	...	0101	0101
Rovereto d.	1341	...	1351	1437	...	1515	1541	*1550*a	1637	...	*1651*a	*1715*a	...	1837	...	1915	2037	...	2115	2215	2237	2251	...	|	|
Trento ▲ d.	1358	*1411*a	1406	1453	...	1531	1558	*1607*a	1653	...	*1707*a	*1731*a	...	1853	...	1931	2053	...	2131	2231	2253	2308	...	|	|
Mezzocorona d.	|	*1423*a	|	1505	...	1544	|	*1618*a	1705	...	*1718*a	*1744*a	...	1905	...	1944	2105	...	2144	2244	2305	2320	...	|	|
Ora / Auer d.	|	*1439*a	|	1519	...	1605	|	*1635*a	1719	...	*1735*a	*1805*a	...	1919	...	2005	2119	...	2205	2305	2319	2334	...	|	|
Bolzano / Bozen a.	1430	*1455*a	1448	1530	...	1622	1630	*1652*a	1730	...	*1752*a	*1822*a	...	1930	...	2022	2130	...	2222	2322	2331	2350	...	|	|
Bolzano / Bozen d.	1432	1500	...	1532	1600	...	1632	1700	1732	...	1800	1832	...	1932	2000	*2030*	2132	...	*2258*	...	...	...	...	|	|
Chiusa / Klausen d.	|	1525	...	1555	1625	...	|	1722	1755	...	1825	1855	...	1955	2025	*2055*	2155	...	*2322*	...	...	...	...	|	|
Bressanone / Brixen d.	1501	1534	...	1604	1634	...	1701	1730	1804	...	1834	1904	...	2004	2034	*2104*	2204	...	*2331*	...	...	...	...	|	|
Fortezza / Franzensfeste d.	1515	1545	...	1615	1645	...	1715	1741	1815	1841	1845	1915	1945	2015	2045	*2121*	2215	...	*2340*	...	...	...	...	|	|
Vipiteno / Sterzing d.	|	1603	...	1633	1703	...	|	1801	1833	1856	1903	1933	2003	2033	2103	...	2233	...	...	...	...	...	...	|	|
Brennero 🏢 a.	|	1622	...	1652	1722	...	|	1822	1852	1913	1922	1952	2021	2052	2122	...	2252	...	...	...	...	...	...	0341	0341
	|			2	2		|		2	|		2	|	2			2							|	|
Brennero 🏢 ▷ d.	|	...	...	1705	1805	...	|	...	1905	1918	...	2005	2023	2105	...	...	2305	...	...	...	...	...	...	0356	0356
Steinach in Tirol ▷ d.	|	...	...	1722	1822	...	|	...	1922	1933	...	2022	|	2122	...	...	2322	...	...	...	...	...	...	|	|
Matrei ▷ d.	|	...	...	1727	1827	...	|	...	1927	1938	...	2027	|	2127	...	...	2327	...	...	...	...	...	...	|	|
Innsbruck Hbf ▷ a.	1632	...	...	1743	1843	...	1832	...	1943	1954	...	2043	2056	2143	...	...	2343	...	...	...	...	...	...	0430	0430
München Hbf **951** a.	1827	...	...	...	...	...	2027	...	...	...	...	...	...	...	...	...	...	...	...	...	...	...	...	0630	0630

♦ – **NOTES** (LISTED BY TRAIN NUMBER)

84 – MICHELANGELO – (12) and ✕ Rimini - Bologna - Innsbruck - München. Runs as train **1284** on ©.

85 – MICHELANGELO – (12) and ✕ München - Innsbruck - Bologna - Rimini.

484/5 – LUPUS – 🛏 1, 2 cl. (Excelsior), 🛏 1, 2 cl., ▬ 2 cl. and (2) Roma (**234/5**) - Bologna - München and v.v. Supplement payable.

717 – ADIGE – (12) Bolzano - Verona - Mantova (d. 1205) - Modena (d. 1253) - Bologna - Lecce.

718 – ADIGE – (12) Lecce - Bologna - Modena (d. 2023) - Mantova (d. 2115) - Verona - Bolzano.

1594 – ⑤ Dec. 19 - Mar. 20, ⑤ June 19 - Sept. 11 (from Reggio): 🛏 1,2 cl. (T2), ▬ 2 cl. and (2) Reggio di Calabria - Bolzano.

1595 – ⑥ Dec. 20 - Mar. 21, ⑥ June 20 - Sept. 12. 🛏 1,2 cl. (T2), ▬ 2 cl. and (2) Bolzano - Reggio di Calabria.

1601 – ⑥ Jan. 10 - Feb. 7; ⑥⑦ Feb. 14 - Mar. 22. 🛏 1, 2 cl. (Excelsior), 🛏 1,2 cl. (T2), 🛏 1,2 cl., ▬ 2 cl. (4 berth) San Candido (**1600**) - Fortezza - Bolzano - Roma Tiburtina.

1602 – ⑤ Jan. 9 - Feb. 6; ⑤⑥ Feb. 13 - Mar. 21 (from Roma): 🛏 1, 2 cl. (Excelsior), 🛏 1,2 cl. (T2), 🛏 1,2 cl. and ▬ 2 cl. (4 berth) Roma Tiburtina - Bolzano - Fortezza (**1603**) - San Candido. After Roma calls to set down only.

B – 🛏 1, 2 cl. (Excelsior), 🛏 1, 2 cl., ▬ 2 cl. and (2) Venezia - Verona (**484/5**) - München Hbf and v.v.

L – (2) Innsbruck - San Candido - Lienz and v.v. (Table **596**).

Q – ①②④⑤⑥⑦ (also Jan. 7, June 3; not Dec. 25, Jan. 8, June 4). 🛏 1, 2 cl. (Excelsior), 🛏 1, 2 cl. (T2), 🛏 1, 2 cl., ▬ 2 cl. (4 / 6 berth) and (2) Bolzano - Bologna - Lecce; 🛏 1, 2 cl., ▬ 2 cl. (4 berth) and (2) Bolzano - Bologna (**837**) - Napoli.

R – From Lecce and Napoli ①③④⑤⑥⑦ (also Jan. 6, June 2; not Jan. 7, June 3). 🛏 1, 2 cl. (Excelsior), 🛏 1, 2 cl. (T2), 🛏 1, 2 cl. ▬ 2 cl. (4 / 6 berth) and (2) Lecce - Bologna - Bolzano; 🛏 1, 2 cl., ▬ 2 cl. (4 berth) and (2) Napoli (**824**) - Bologna (**924**) - Bolzano.

OTHER TRAIN NAMES: **81/188** VAL GARDENA / GRODNERTAL, **82/83** PAGANINI, **86/87** TIEPOLO, **88/89** LEONARDO DA VINCI.

a – Ⓐ only.
b – Runs on Ⓑ Trento - Bolzano; daily Bolzano - Fortezza.
c – Firenze **Campo di Marte**.
d – Daily.
f – Also Apr. 30, May 20, June 10; not May 1, 22, June 12.
h – Change at Poggio Rusco (0557 / 0603).
k – Also Jan. 6, Apr. 13; not Jan. 4, Apr. 12, May 31.
n – On ⑥ Dec. 20 - Mar. 28 runs 16 minutes later Brennero - Innsbruck (train **1876**).
r – Ⓑ (not Apr. 12).
t – Roma **Tiburtina**.
v – Also runs on † Bolzano - Verona.
x – © only.
y – Connection Verona - Bolzano runs on ⚒.
z – ⚒ only.

▷ – For additional trains Innsbruck - Brennero and v.v. see foot of page 294. Austrian holiday dates apply Innsbruck - Brennero and v.v.

▲ – **TRENTO - MALÉ - MARILLEVA**

To Malé *56 km* 70–90 mins, to Marilleva *65 km*, 90–100 mins

⚒: 19 departures to Malé, 14 to Marilleva.
†: 15 departures to Malé, 10 to Marilleva.

Operator: Trentino transporti S.p.A, Via Innsbruck 65, 38100 Trento. ✆ +39 0 461 821000, fax +39 0 461 031407.

2nd class except where shown — FORTEZZA / FRANZENSFESTE - SAN CANDIDO / INNICHEN - LIENZ 596

km					1871	1603														1875				1873		
		⚒	⚒			A				⚒			⚒				⚒			⑤f		⚒			◇	
	Innsbruck Hbf **595** d.	...	...	...	0700	...	...	...	...	...	...	...	...	...	...	...	...	...	...	1503	...	...	...	1701	...	...
	Brennero 🏢 **595** d.	...	...	...	0739	...	...	...	...	...	...	...	...	...	...	...	...	...	...	1543	...	...	...	1743	...	...
0	**Fortezza / Franzensfeste** d.	...	0650	...	0815	0919	0950	...	1050	...	1150	1250	...	1350	...	1450	...	1550	...	1621	1650	...	1751	1821	1850	...
33	Brunico / Bruneck d.	...	0730	...	0852	1007	1030	...	1130	...	1230	1330	...	1430	...	1530	...	1630	...	1704	1730	...	1830	1905	1930	...
61	Dobbiaco / Toblach d.	...	0801	...	0925	1042	1101	...	1201	...	1301	1401	...	1501	...	1601	...	1701	...	1740	1801	...	1901	1941	2001	...
65	**San Candido / Innichen** a.	...	0806	...	0931	1048	1106	...	1206	...	1306	1406	...	1506	...	1606	...	1706	...	1747	1806	...	1906	1947	2006	...
65	**San Candido / Innichen** 🏢 d.	0640	...	0909	0933	...	...	1109	...	1209	...	...	1409	...	1509	...	1609	...	1709	1753	...	1822	...	1949	...	2009
78	Sillian 🏢 d.	0653	...	0922	0946	...	...	1122	...	1222	...	...	1422	...	1522	...	1622	...	1722	1806	...	1835	...	2003	...	2022
108	**Lienz** a.	0725	...	0953	1017	...	...	1153	...	1253	...	...	1453	...	1553	...	1653	...	1753	1836	...	1906	...	2033	...	2052

A – ⑤ Jan. 9 - Feb. 6; ⑤⑥ Feb. 13 - Mar. 21 (from Roma): 🛏 1, 2 cl. (Excelsior), 🛏 1, 2 cl. (T2), 🛏 1, 2 cl., ▬ 2 cl. (4 berth) Roma Tiburtina - Bolzano - Fortezza (**1603**) - San Candido. Calls to set down only.

f – Also Apr. 30, May 20, June 10; not May 1, 22, June 12.

◇ – Additional journeys Fortezza - San Candido: 1950, 2020.

Certain journeys are operated by SAD

596 LIENZ - SAN CANDIDO / INNICHEN - FORTEZZA / FRANZENSFESTE

2nd class except where shown

	1870																	1874			1872			1600	
					Ⓐ			⚒			⚒				⚒			⑦k	⚒					A	
Lienz d.	0515	...	*0706*	...	...	...	*0957*	1106	...	...	1306	...	1406	...	1506	...	*1606*	1624	1706	...	1735	...	*1845*	...	...
Sillian d.	0545	...	*0737*	...	...	...	*1038*	1139	...	...	1339	...	1439	...	1539	...	*1639*	1655	1739	...	1807	...	*1918*	...	...
San Candido / Innichen 🏛 a.	0558	...	*0750*	...	...	...	*1051*	1152	...	...	1352	...	1452	...	1552	...	*1652*	1708	1752	...	1820	...	*1931*	...	...
San Candido / Innichen 🏛 d.	0600	0655	0755	0849	0933	0955	1055	...	1155	1255	...	1355	...	1455	...	1555	1655	1711	...	1755	1825	1855	1955	2008	2055
Dobbiaco / Toblach d.	0606	0701	0801	0858	0939	1001	1101	...	1201	1301	...	1401	...	1501	...	1601	1701	1717	...	1801	1831	1901	2001	2013	2101
Brunico / Bruneck d.	0637	0732	0831	0932	1007	1032	1132	...	1232	1332	...	1432	...	1532	...	1632	1732	1802	...	1832	1905	1932	2032	2103	2133
Fortezza / Franzensfeste a.	0719	0810	0910	1010	1040	1110	1210	...	1310	1410	...	1510	...	1610	...	1710	1810	1840	...	1910	1944	2010	2110	2140	2210
Brennero 🏛 **595** a.	0758	...	...	...	...	...	...	...	...	...	...	...	...	...	...	...	...	1913	...	...	2021	...	...	...	...
Innsbruck Hbf **595** a.	0843	...	...	...	...	...	...	...	...	...	...	...	...	...	...	...	...	1954	...	...	2056r	...	...	...	...

A – ⑥ Jan. 10 - Feb. 7; ⑥⑦ Feb. 14 - Mar. 22. 1,2 cl. (Excelsior), 1,2 cl. (T2), 1,2 cl., 2 cl. (4 berth) San Candido - Fortezza (**1601**) - Bolzano - Roma Tiburtina. Calls to pick up only.

k – Also Jan. 6, Apr. 13; not Jan. 4, Apr. 12, May 31.

r – 2112 on ⑥ Dec. 20 - Mar. 28 (train **1876**).

Certain journeys are operated by SAD

597 BOLZANO / BOZEN - MERANO / MERAN

2nd class only

km		⚒				⚒§	Ⓒ	Ⓐ§	⚒§		⚒§		⚒§		⚒§		⚒§		⚒§		⚒§		⚒§		⚒§		
	Brennero **595** d.	...	0538	0638	...	...	0838	...	...	0938	...	1038	...	1138	...	1238	...	1338	...	1438	...	1538	...	1638	...	1738	1838
0	**Bolzano / Bozen** d.	0631	0702	0802	0903	0935	1002	1003	1035	1102	1135	1202	1235	1302	1335	1402	1435	1502	1535	1602	1635	1702	1735	1802	1835	1902	2002
32	Merano / Meran a.	0714	0744	0844	0944	1014	1044	1044	1117	1144	1214	1244	1314	1344	1414	1444	1514	1544	1614	1644	1714	1744	1814	1844	1914	1944	2044

	⚒		⚒		⚒§		⚒§	Ⓒ	⚒§		⚒§		⚒§		⚒§		⚒§		⚒§		⚒§		⚒§	n	⚒§		
Merano / Meran d.	0611	0716	0746	0816	0846	0916	0946	1016	1046	1116	1146	1216	1246	1316	1346	1416	1446	1516	1546	1616	1646	1716	1746	1816	1846	1916	2016
Bolzano / Bozen a.	0658	0758	0826	0859	0926	0958	1026	1058	1126	1158	1226	1258	1326	1358	1426	1459	1526	1558	1626	1658	1726	1757	1826	1857	1926	1958	2058
Brennero **595** a.	0822	0922	...	1022	...	1122	...	1222	...	1322	...	1422	...	1522	...	1622	...	1722	...	1822	...	1922	...	...	...	...	...

n – To Fortezza (arrive 1950) and San Candido (arrive 2106).

§ – Operated by SAD (for contact details see Table **598**).

Additional journeys: from Bolzano / Bozen 0550 ⚒, 0736 ⚒§, 0835 ⚒§, 1935 ⚒§, 2035, 2202 ⚒§; from Merano / Meran 0644 ⚒§, 0703 Ⓐ, 1946 Ⓐ§, 2046 ⚒§, 2146.

598 MERANO / MERAN - MALLES / MALS

2nd class only SAD

km																									
0	Merano / Meran d.	0542	0635	0718	0746	0816	0916	0946	1016	1116	1146	1216	1316	1346	1416	1516	1546	1616	1716	1746	1816	1916	1946	2046	2246
60	Malles / Mals **546 / 954** a.	0700	0754	0838	0855	0938	1038	1055	1138	1238	1255	1338	1438	1455	1538	1638	1655	1738	1838	1855	1938	2038	2055	2155	2355

Malles / Mals **546 / 954** d.	0547	0611	0703	0720	0820	0903	0920	1020	1103	1120	1220	1303	1320	1420	1503	1520	1620	1703	1720	1820	1903	1920	2020	2120	...
Merano / Meran a.	0702	0732	0813	0843	0943	1013	1043	1143	1213	1243	1343	1413	1443	1543	1613	1643	1743	1813	1843	1943	2013	2043	2143	2234	

Trains call at Silandro / Schlanders 46–54 minutes after leaving Merano, 24–28 minutes after leaving Malles.

Ferrovia della Val Venosta Operator: Servizi Autobus Dolomiti (SAD), Via Conciapelli 60, I-39100 Bolzano. ✆ +39 0471 97 12 59, fax +39 0471 97 00 42.

599 ITALIAN LAKES (LAGO MAGGIORE, GARDA, COMO)

Lago Maggiore: ⛴ services link Arona, Stresa, Baveno, Laveno, Luino and Locarno throughout the year on an irregular schedule. For details contact the operator below:
Operator: Navigazione sul Lago Maggiore, Viale F. Baracca 1, 28041 Arona, Italy. ✆ + 39 0322 233 200. Fax: + 39 0322 249 530.

Lago di Garda: ⛴ services link Desenzano, Peschiera, Garda, Salo, Gardone and Riva, (April to September only), on an irregular schedule. For details contact the operator below:
Operator: Navigazione sul Lago di Garda, Piazza Matteotti, 25015 Desenzano del Garda, Italy. ✆ + 39 30 91 41 321, 2, 3. Fax: + 39 30 91 44 640.

Lago di Como: ⛴ services link Como, Bellagio, Menaggio, Varenna, Bellano and Colico (April to September only) on an irregular schedule. For details contact the operator below:

Hydrofoil service **April 5 - May 30, 2009**:

	⚒	†	⚒	†	⚒	⚒	†	⚒		⚒			
Como d.	0733	0845	0920	1110	1215	1330	1400	1420	1615	1710	1810	1910	...
Tremezzo d.	0819r	0924	1004	1148	1252	1419	1445	1507	1652	1757	1858	1947	...
Bellagio d.	0813r	0931	1021r	1155	1259	1439r	1452	1514	1658	1804	1905	1953	...
Menaggio d.	0808	0939	1014	1202	1306	1430	1500	1521	1704	1812	1913	1959	...
Bellano d.	...	0949	...	1211	1318	1455	1516	...	1713	1821	1929	2011	...
Colico a.	...	1022	...	1238	1345	1528	1549	...	1740	...	1959	2034	...

	⚒		⚒	⚒	†		⚒	†		⚒	†	⚒	⑥h
Colico d.	0604	0622	...	...	1024	1345	...	...	1604	1741	1741	...	1959
Bellano d.	0628	0653	...	...	1104	1413	...	...	1644	1806	1806	...	|
Menaggio d.	0641	0703	0808	1014	1114	1424	1522	1557	1655	1814	1814	1843	2030
Bellagio d.	0647	0712	0814	1023	1123	1431	1531	1610	1704	1820	1820	1852	2039
Tremezzo d.	0653	0718	0820	1029	1129	1438	1537	1618	1710	1826	1826	1858	|
Como a.	0730	0805	0857	1115	1211	1518	1624	1705	1800	1857	1905	1940	2117

h – Not holidays.

r – Via Menaggio.

Operator: Navigazione Lago di Como, Via Per Cernobbio 18, 22100 Como, Italy. ✆ +39 (0) 31 579 211, fax: +39 (0) 31 570 080.

600 MILANO - VERONA - VENEZIA

km			*EN*			*ESc*		*EC*	*ESc*		*ESc*	*ES*		*ESc*	*ESc*		*ESc*	*ESc*		*EC*	*ESc*			*ESc*
			363			**9701**		**93**	**9703**		**9707**	**9401**		**9711**	**9713**		**9791**	**9715**		**37**	**9719**			**9723**
			R		2	R 🍷		R 🍷	R 🍷		R 🍷	R 🍷		R 🍷	R 🍷	2	R 🍷	R 🍷		R ✕	R 🍷			R 🍷
			♦		⚒			♦			T			V		†	Ⓒ	T		♦	Ⓐ	Ⓐ	†	
0	**Milano Centrale** d.	0015	...	...	...	0635	0625	0705	0735	0725	0805	0835	0825	0905	0935	0920p	1035	1135	...	1205	1235	1225	1305p	1335
4	Milano Lambrate d.	0022	...	...	...	|	0633	|	|	0733	|	|	0833	|	|	0932	|	|	1130	|	|	1233	1325	|
34	Treviglio d.	0049	...	...	...	|	0655	|	|	0755	|	|	0855	|	|	0955	|	|	1155	|	|	1255	1344	|
83	Brescia d.	0136	...	...	0601	0723	0735	0753	0823	0835	0853	|	0935	0953	1023	1030	1123	1223	1235	1253	1323	1335	1429	1423
111	Desenzano-Sirmione d.	0152	...	...	0626	0737	0751	0808	|	0851	0907	|	0951	|	1037	1046	|	|	1250	|	1337	1351	1445	|
125	Peschiera del Garda § d.	0202	...	...	0635	|	0801	0819	0843	0901	|	|	1001	1013	|	1055	1143	1243	1301	1313	|	1401	1454	1443
148	**Verona Porta Nuova** a.	0223	...	...	0654	0757	0820	0836	0857	0915	0927	|	1020	1027	1057	1110	1157	1257	1316	1327	1357	1420	1511	1457
148	**Verona Porta Nuova** d.	...	0440	0555	0702	0759	...	...	0859	0918	0929	|	...	1029	1059	1113	1159	1259	1318	1329	1359	...	1514	1459
200	Vicenza d.	...	0520	0646	0747	0826	...	...	0926	0959	0956	|	...	1056	1126	1147	1226	1326	1359	1356	1426	...	1557	1526
230	Padova **620** d.	...	0554	0713	0815	0842	...	...	0942	1020	1012	1028	...	1112	1142	1208	1242	1342	1420	1412	1442	...	1616	1542
258	**Venezia Mestre 620** a.	...	0625	0748	0838	0858s	...	...	0958s	1038	1028s	1044s	...	1128s	1158s	1236	1258s	1358s	1443	1428	1458s	...	1642	1558s
258	**Venezia Mestre 620** d.	...	0628	0750	0840	|	...	...	|	1040	|	|	...	|	|	1238	|	|	1445	1430	|	...	1644	|
267	**Venezia Santa Lucia 620** a.	...	0638	0802	0852	0910	...	...	1010	1049	1040	1055	...	1140	1210	1249	1310	1410	1455	1440	1510	...	1656	1610
	Trieste Centrale **605** a.	...	...	...	...	...	...	...	...	...	...	...	...	1358	...	...	...	...	...	...	...	...	...	...

		ESc		*ESc*	*EC*		*ESc*	*ESc*		*CIS*	*ES*		*ESc*		*ESc*		*ESc*	*ESc*		*ESc*		*ESc*		
		9727		**9729**	**87**		**9733**	**9735**		**57**	**9403**		**9741**		**9743**		**9793**	**9745**		**9749**		**9753**		
		R		R 🍷	R ✕		R 🍷	R 🍷		R ✕	R ✕		R		R		R	R		R		R 🍷		
					♦		T			♦			♦	⚒			Ⓒ	Ⓐ				♦		
Milano Centrale d.	1325	1435	1425	1505	...	1525	1605	1635	1625	1705	1735	1725	1805	1800	1835	1825	1905	1905	1925	2005	2025	2105	2125	2230
Milano Lambrate d.	1333	|	1433	|	...	1533	|	|	1633	|	|	1733	|	1812	|	1833	|	|	1933	|	2033	|	2133	2238
Treviglio d.	1355	|	1455	|	...	1553	|	|	1655	|	|	1755	|	1831	|	1855	|	|	1955	|	2053	|	2153	2258
Brescia d.	1435	1523	1535	1553	...	1635	1653	1723	1735	1753	|	1835	1853	1902	1923	1935	1953	1953	2035	2053	2135	2157	2235	2335
Desenzano-Sirmione d.	1451	1537	1551	|	...	1651	1707	|	1751	1807	|	1851	|	...	1937	1951	|	|	2051	2107	2151	2213	2251	2351
Peschiera del Garda § d.	1501	|	1601	1613	...	1701	|	1743	1801	|	|	1901	1913	...	|	2001	2013	2013	2101	|	2201	2223	2301	0001
Verona Porta Nuova a.	1520	1557	1620	1627	...	1720	1727	1757	1820	1827	|	1915	1927	...	1957	2020	2027	2027	2120	2127	2215	2244	2320	0020
Verona Porta Nuova d.	...	1559	...	1629	1659	...	1729	1759	...	1829	|	1918	1929	...	1959	...	2029	2029	...	2129	2218	2247	...	...
Vicenza d.	...	1626	...	1656	1726	...	1756	1826	...	1856	|	1952	1956	...	2026	...	2056	2056	...	2156	2252	2320	...	...
Padova **620** d.	...	1642	...	1712	1742	...	1812	1842	...	1912	1928	2012	...	...	2042	...	2112	2118	...	2212	2310	2338	...	...
Venezia Mestre 620 a.	...	1658s	...	1728s	1758	...	1828s	1858s	...	1928	1944s	2038	...	...	2058s	...	2128s	2138s	...	2228s	2339	2356	...	...
Venezia Mestre 620 d.	...	|	...	|	1800	...	|	|	...	1945	|	2040	...	...	|	...	|	|	...	|	2341	...	...	...
Venezia Santa Lucia 620 a.	...	1710	...	1740	1810	...	1840	1910	...	|	1955	2051	...	...	2110	...	2140	2150	...	2240	2352	...	...	...
Trieste Centrale **605** a.	...	...	...	...	...	...	...	...	...	2118	...	...	...	...	...	...	...	...	...	...	...	...	...	...

FOR NOTES SEE NEXT PAGE

VENEZIA - VERONA - MILANO 600

				ESc 9702 🄡🍷 ♦	*ESc* 9704 🄡		*ES* 9400 🄡✕	*ESc* 9706 🄡 ♦		*ESc* 9708 🄡 Ⓐ	*CIS* 52 🄡✕ ♦	*ESc* 9712 🄡 T		*ESc* 9792 🄡🍷 Ⓒ	*ESc* 9714 🄡🍷			*ESc* 9718 🄡🍷		*ESc* 9722 🄡🍷		*EC* 86 🄡✕ ♦	*ESc* 9726 🄡	*ESc* 9728 🄡 T
		2 Ⓒ	Ⓐ																					
Trieste Centrale **605** d.	...	...	...	...	...	...	...	...	...	...	0635	...	...	...	...	...	...	...	...	...	...	...	...	...
Venezia Santa Lucia 620 d.	...	0514	0514	...	0620	...	0705	...	...	0750	|	0850	...	0950	1050	...	1109	1150	...	1250	...	1320	1350	1420
Venezia Mestre 620 a.	...	0524	0524	...	|	...	|	...	...	|	0815	|	...	|	|	...	1120	|	...	|	...	1330	|	|
Venezia Mestre 620 d.	...	0526	0526	0542	0632u	...	0716u	...	...	0802u	0832	0902u	...	1002u	1102u	...	1122	1202u	...	1302u	...	1332	1402u	1432u
Padova **620** d.	...	0547	0547	0604	0649	...	0734	...	...	0819	0849	0919	...	1019	1119	...	1145	1219	...	1319	...	1349	1419	1449
Vicenza d.	...	0605	0605	0622	0705	...	|	0805	...	0835	0905	0935	...	1035	1135	...	1205	1235	...	1335	...	1405	1435	1505
Verona Porta Nuova a.	...	0637	0643	0650	0730	...	|	0830	...	0900	0930	1000	...	1100	1200	...	1237	1300	...	1400	...	1438	1500	1530
Verona Porta Nuova d.	0540	0640	0646	0653	0732	0740	|	0832	0840	0902	0932	1002	...	1102	1202	1206	1240	1302	1340	1402	1440	...	1502	1532
Peschiera del Garda § d.	0557	0654	0700	0708	0747	0757	|	0847	0857	|	|	1017	...	1117	|	1222	1257	1317	1357	|	1457	...	1517	1546
Desenzano-Sirmione d.	0607	0705	0711	0719	|	0807	|	|	0907	0922	0952	|	...	|	1222	|	1307	|	1407	1422	1507	...	|	|
Brescia d.	0627	0727	0733	0740	0809	0827	|	0909	0927	0939	1009	1039	...	1139	1239	1249	1327	1339	1427	1439	1527	...	1539	1609
Treviglio d.	0705	0803	0815	|	|	0903	|	|	1003	|	|	|	...	|	|	1325	1403	|	1503	|	1603	...	|	|
Milano Lambrate d.	0728	0815	0837	|	|	0929	|	|	1031	|	|	|	...	|	|	1349	1435	|	1529	|	1629	...	|	|
Milano Centrale a.	0735	0835	0845	0825	0855	0935	0925	0955	...	1025	1055	1125	...	1225	1325	1355	1445	1425	1535	1525	1635	...	1625	1655

		ESc 9730 🄡🍷	*ESc* 9732 🄡 T		*EC* 42 🄡✕ ♦		*ESc* 9738 🄡		*ESc* 9740 🄡	*EC* 92 🄡🍷 ♦	2 †	*ES* 9402 🄡✕		2 †	*ESc* 9744 🄡	*ESc* 9746 🄡🍷 V		*ESc* 9750 🄡🍷			⚒	†	*EN* 358 🄡 ♦	
Trieste Centrale **605** d.	...	...	...	...	...	...	...	...	...	...	...	...	...	...	...	1625	...	...	...	...	...	...	...	...
Venezia Santa Lucia 620 d.	...	1450	1520	1504	1620	...	1650	1705	1720	...	1742	1805	...	1809	1820	1850	...	1950	1904	...	2034	2109	2251	...
Venezia Mestre 620 a.	...	|	|	1513	1630	...	|	1716	|	...	1752	|	...	1821	|	1900	...	|	1916	...	2046	2120	2301	...
Venezia Mestre 620 d.	...	1502u	1532u	1515	1632	...	1702u	1718	1732u	...	1754	1816u	...	1823	1832u	1902	...	2002u	1918	...	2048	2122	2304	...
Padova **620** d.	...	1519	1549	1541	1649	...	1719	1741	1749	...	1816	1834	...	1856	1849	1719	...	2019	1954	...	2124	2142	2328	...
Vicenza d.	...	1535	1605	1608	1705	...	1735	1808	1805	...	1834	|	...	1917	1905	1935	...	2035	2021	...	2151	2202	2347	...
Verona Porta Nuova a.	...	1600	1630	1642	1730	...	1800	1842	1830	...	1919	|	...	1956	1930	2000	...	2100	2116	...	2240	2240	0025	...
Verona Porta Nuova d.	1540	1602	1632	1645	1732	1740	1802	1845	1832	1915	1922	|	1940	2007	1932	2002	2040	2102	...	2140	...	2243	...	...
Peschiera del Garda § d.	1557	|	1647	1658	1747	1757	|	1858	1847	|	1946	|	1957	2030	|	2017	2057	|	...	2157	...	2300	...	...
Desenzano-Sirmione d.	1607	1622	|	1707	|	1807	1822	1907	|	|	1959	|	2007	2039	1952	|	2107	2122	...	2207	...	2310	...	...
Brescia d.	1627	1639	1709	1727	1809	1827	1839	1927	1909	|	2014	|	2027	2057	2009	2039	2127	2139	...	2227	...	2332	...	...
Treviglio d.	1703	|	|	1803	|	1903	|	2003	|	|	...	|	2103	2134	|	|	2203	|	...	2303	...	0001	...	...
Milano Lambrate d.	1731	|	|	1829	|	1932	|	2032	|	|	...	|	2129	2153	|	|	2229	|	...	2329	...	0022	...	...
Milano Centrale a.	1740	1725	1755	1835	1900	1940	1925	2040	1955	2035	...	2025	2135	2210p	2055	2125	2235	2225	...	2335	...	0030	...	...

♦ – **NOTES** (LISTED BY TRAIN NUMBER)

37 – [12] and ✕ Genève Aéroport - Milano - Venezia. Operated by *CISALPINO*.
42 – [12] and ✕ Venezia - Milano - Genève Aéroport. Operated by *CISALPINO*.
52 – [12] and ✕ Trieste - Venezia Mestre - Milano - Basel. *CISALPINO Pendolino* train; supplement payable.
57 – [12] and ✕ Basel - Milano - Venezia Mestre - Trieste. *CISALPINO Pendolino* train; supplement payable.
86 – TIEPOLO – [12] and ✕ Venezia - Verona - Innsbruck - München.
87 – TIEPOLO – [12] and ✕ München - Innsbruck - Verona - Venezia.
92 – LEONARDO DA VINCI – [12] and 🍷 München (**89**) - Verona - Milano.
93 – LEONARDO DA VINCI – [12] and 🍷 Milano - Verona (**88**) - München.
358 – 🛏 1, 2 cl. (Excelsior), 🛏 1, 2 cl., ▬ 2 cl. and [2] Venezia - Verona (**484**) - München.
363 – 🛏 1, 2 cl. (Excelsior), 🛏 1, 2 cl., ▬ 2 cl. and [2] München (**485**) - Verona - Venezia.
9702 – [12] and 🍷 Venezia Mestre - Milano; 🛏 1, 2 cl. and ▬ 2 cl. (4 berth) Wien (**235**) - Venezia Mestre - Milano.
9706 – [12] Udine (**9705**) - Treviso - Vicenza - Milano.
9741 – [12] Milano - Vicenza - Treviso (**9742**) - Udine.
9753 – [12] and 🍷 Milano - Venezia Mestre; 🛏 1, 2 cl. and ▬ 2 cl. (4 berth) Milano - Venezia Mestre (**234**) - Wien.

T – [12] and 🍷 Torino - Milano - Venezia and v.v.
V – [12] and 🍷 Torino - Milano - Venezia Santa Lucia - Trieste and v.v.
p – Milano **Porta Garibaldi**.
s – Calls to set down only.
u – Stops to pick up only.
§ – Station for Gardaland Park. Free shuttle bus available.

VENEZIA - UDINE - VILLACH 601

km		*E* 1236 ♦	*E* 1238 ♦	*ESc* 9753 *EN* 234 J	*EN* 234 ♦	Ⓐp	q		*ICN* 774 ♦	2 †C		⚒	2 ⚒C	⚒	†			2 ⚒	2 B		⚒	2 C	*EC* 30 🄡✕ ♦			2 C
	Roma Termini **620** d.	1650	1720	...	1910	...	...	...	2236t	...	...	...	...	...	...	...	...	...	...	...	...	...	...	...	...	...
	Firenze SMN **620** d.	2055c	2055c	...	2153	...	...	...	0148c	...	...	...	...	...	...	...	...	...	...	...	...	...	...	...	...	...
	Bologna Centrale **620** d.	2220	2220	...	2320	...	...	...	0318	...	...	...	...	...	...	...	...	...	...	...	...	...	...	...	...	...
	Milano Centrale **600** d.	|	|	2105	|	...	...	...	|	...	...	...	...	...	...	...	...	...	...	...	...	...	...	...	...	...
0	**Venezia Santa Lucia** d.	|	|	|	|	0526	0526	0547	0604	0643	0704	0718	0804	0904	0904	1004	1204	1304	1326	1404	1504	1526	1548	1604	1704	1726
9	**Venezia Mestre** a.	0011	0011	2356	0102	0536	0536	0558	0614	0654	0714	0729	0814	0914	0914	1014	1214	1314	1337	1414	1514	1537	1558	1614	1714	1737
9	**Venezia Mestre** d.	0036	0036	0130	0130	0538	0538	0600	0616	0656	0716	0731	0816	0916	0916	1016	1216	1316	1339	1416	1516	1539	1600	1616	1716	1739
30	Treviso Centrale d.	|	|	|	|	0558	0558	0622	0636	0719	0735	0753	0840	0935	0937	1035	1235	1338	1407	1435	1538	1622	1617	1635	1737	1807
57	Conegliano **603** d.	|	|	|	|	0618	0617	0644	0656	0746	0754	0819	0903	0954	1003	1054	1254	1356	1435	1454	1557	1647	1635	1654	1757	1837
74	Sacile d.	|	|	|	|	0642	0630	0657	0712	...	0807	0837	...	1007	1020	1107	1307	1414	...	1507	1610	...	|	1707	1810	...
87	Pordenone d.	|	|	|	|	0653	0641	0710	0724	...	0817	0849	...	1017	1031	1117	1317	1423	...	1517	1620	...	1655	1717	1820	...
136	**Udine** a.	0155	0155	|	|	0730	0722	0751	0805	...	0853	0931	...	1053	1112	1153	1353	1502	...	1553	1656	...	1734	1753	1856	...
136	**Udine** d.	0157	0157	|	|	0734	0734	...	...	...	0856	0934	...	...	...	1156r	1356	...	...	1556	1659	...	1737	1756	1859v	...
	Trieste Centrale **606** a.	|	|	|	|	0846	0856	...	...	...	1004	1050	...	...	...	1304r	1504	...	...	1704	1807	...	|	1904	2007v	...
230	Tarvisio Boscoverde 🏛 a.	0304	0304	0339	0339	...	...	...	...	...	...	...	...	...	...	...	...	...	...	...	...	...	1840	...	...	...
258	**Villach Hbf** a.	0341	0341	0415	0415	...	...	...	...	...	...	...	...	...	...	...	...	...	...	...	...	...	1913	...	...	...

		2	2 B		*ESc* 9742 🄡 U	*ES* 9392 🄡✕	2	*EN* 236 H			
Roma Termini **620** d.	...	...	...	...	...	1550	...	...	...	...	...
Firenze SMN **620** d.	...	...	...	...	...	1737	...	...	...	...	...
Bologna Centrale **620** d.	...	...	...	...	...	1840	...	...	...	...	...
Milano Centrale **600** d.	...	...	...	...	1805	|	...	...	...	...	...
Venezia Santa Lucia d.	1804	1904	1943	2004	|	|	2056	2105	2204	2304	2356
Venezia Mestre a.	1814	1914	1953	2014	|	2015	2106	|	2214	2315	0006
Venezia Mestre d.	1816	1916	1955	2016	|	2031	2108	2118u	2216	2317	0008
Treviso Centrale d.	1835	1938	2017	2035	2049	2057	2129	2142	2235	2338	0027
Conegliano **603** d.	1854	1956	2038	2054	2107	2117	2149	2205	2254	0000	0046
Sacile d.	1907	2009	...	2107	2120	|	2202	|	2307	0013	0059
Pordenone d.	1917	2019	...	2117	2129	2138	2214	2228	2317	0023	0109
Udine a.	1953	2055	...	2153	2159	2206	2256	2304	2353	0058	0145
Udine d.	1956	...	...	2156	...	...	...	2306	0003	...	...
Trieste Centrale **606** a.	2104	...	...	2304	...	...	...	|	0131	...	...
Tarvisio Boscoverde 🏛 a.	...	...	...	...	...	...	...	0005	...	...	...
Villach Hbf a.	...	...	...	...	...	...	...	0042	...	...	...

	EN 235 ♦	*EN* 235 *ESc* 9702 K	*E* 1237 ♦	*E* 1239 ♦		*ESc* 9705 🄡 U	*ES* 9391 🄡✕		*EN* 237 H
Villach Hbf d.	0003	0003	0045	0045	...	...	...	...	0445
Tarvisio Boscoverde 🏛 d.	0041	0041	0123	0123	...	...	...	...	0533
Trieste Centrale **606** d.	|	|	|	|	...	...	...	0502v	|
Udine a.	|	|	0217	0217	...	...	...	0623v	0633
Udine d.	|	|	0219	0219	0510	0540	0552	0628	0636
Pordenone d.	|	|	|	|	0547	0609	0620	0705	0713
Sacile d.	|	|	|	|	0559	0620	|	0715	|
Conegliano **603** d.	|	|	|	|	0615	0631	0640	0727	0738
Treviso Centrale d.	|	|	|	|	0642	0650	0659	0746	0801
Venezia Mestre a.	0252	0252	0332	0332	0713	|	0721	0805	0821s
Venezia Mestre d.	0311	0542	0357	0357	0714	|	0747	0807	|
Venezia Santa Lucia a.	|	|	|	|	0726	|	|	0817	0834
Milano Centrale **600** a.	|	0825	|	|	...	0955	|	...	...
Bologna Centrale **620** a.	0448	...	0541	0541	...	...	0921	...	...
Firenze SMN **620** a.	0618	...	0705c	0705c	...	...	1023	...	...
Roma Termini **620** a.	0905	...	1045	1045	...	...	1210	...	...

FOR NOTES SEE NEXT PAGE

601 VILLACH - UDINE - VENEZIA

	2 B			2 †		2 ⚒C	2 †C	†	⚒	2 B		EC 31 🅁✕ ◆	⚒		2		⚒	2 B		Ⓐ	2 B		2 C	ICN 771 ◆	
Villach Hbf d.	...	...	...	...	...	...	...	...	...	...	...	1047	...	...	...	...	...	...	...	...	...	...	...	...	...
Tarvisio Boscoverde d.	...	...	...	...	...	...	...	...	...	...	...	1121	...	...	...	...	...	...	...	...	...	...	...	...	...
Trieste Centrale **606** d.	...	0558x	0656	...	0856	...	...	...	...	...	1056	|	1126	1256	...	1456	...	...	1656	1755	...	1856	...	...	2042
Udine a.	...	0728	0804	...	1004	...	...	...	...	...	1204	1214	1253	1404	...	1607	...	...	1804	1903	...	2004	...	...	2204
Udine d.	...	0742	0807	0911	1007	...	...	1043	1102	...	1207	1217	1258	1407	1502	1607	1702	...	1807	1906	...	2007	...	2122	2207
Pordenone d.	...	0819	0844	0948	1044	...	...	1123	1139	...	1244	1254	1335	1444	1539	1644	1739	...	1844	1944	...	2044	...	2158	2244
Sacile d.	...	0830	0854	0959	1054	...	...	1137	1149	...	1254	|	1345	1454	1549	1654	1749	...	1854	1954	...	2054	...	2210	2254
Conegliano **603** d.	0823	0849	0906	1011	1106	1116	1139	1155	1201	1219	1306	1324	1403	1506	1601	1706	1801	1820	1906	2005	2035	2106	2208	2223	2306
Treviso Centrale d.	0846	0915	0925	1030	1125	1138	1202	1222	1222	1241	1325	1349	1422	1525	1622	1725	1822	1847	1925	2023	2102	2125	2230	2242	2325
Venezia Mestre a.	0914	0937	0944	1052	1144	1202	1230	1244	1244	1304	1344	1409	1444	1544	1644	1744	1844	1915	1944	2044	2130	2144	2254	2302	2344
Venezia Mestre d.	0916	0939	0946	1054	1146	1205	1232	1246	1246	1306	1346	1411	1446	1546	1646	1746	1846	1917	1946	2046	2132	2146	2256	2304	2346
Venezia Santa Lucia a.	0928	0949	0956	1105	1156	1216	1243	1256	1256	1317	1356	1420	1456	1556	1656	1756	1856	1928	1956	2056	2143	2156	2307	2313	2356
Milano Centrale **600** a.	...	...	...	...	...	...	...	...	...	...	...	...	...	...	...	...	...	...	...	...	...	...	...	|	...
Bologna Centrale **620** a.	...	...	...	...	...	...	...	...	...	...	...	...	...	...	...	...	...	...	...	...	...	...	...	0217	...
Firenze SMN **620** a.	...	...	...	...	...	...	...	...	...	...	...	...	...	...	...	...	...	...	...	...	...	...	...	|	...
Roma Termini **620** a.	...	...	...	...	...	...	...	...	...	...	...	...	...	...	...	...	...	...	...	...	...	...	...	0656t	...

◆ – NOTES (LISTED BY TRAIN NUMBER)

30/1 – ALLEGRO JOHANN STRAUSS – [12] and ✕ Venezia - Wien Süd and v.v.

234 – ALLEGRO TOSCA – 🛏 1,2 cl. (Excelsior), 🛏 1,2 cl., ▬ 2 cl. and [2] Roma - Venezia Mestre - Villach - Wien Süd. Supplement payable.

235 – ALLEGRO TOSCA – 🛏 1,2 cl. (Excelsior), 🛏 1,2 cl., ▬ 2 cl. and [2] Wien Süd - Villach - Venezia Mestre - Roma. Supplement payable.

771 – MARCO POLO – 🛏 1,2 cl., ▬ 2 cl. (4 berth) and [2] Udine - Venezia Santa Lucia - Napoli.

774 – MARCO POLO – 🛏 1,2 cl., ▬ 2 cl. (4 berth) and [2] Napoli - Roma Tiburtina - Venezia Santa Lucia - Udine.

1236 – ALLEGRO ROSSINI – ⑥ Apr. 4 - Sept. 26 (from Roma): 🛏 1,2 cl. (Excelsior), 🛏 1,2 cl., ▬ 2 cl. and [2] Roma - Wien Süd. Supplement payable.

1237 – ALLEGRO ROSSINI – ⑤ Apr. 3 - Sept. 25 (from Wien): 🛏 1,2 cl. (Excelsior), 🛏 1,2 cl., ▬ 2 cl. and [2] Wien Süd - Roma. Supplement payable.

1238 – ALLEGRO ROSSINI – Dec. 20, 21, 27 - 30, Jan. 2 - 4, Apr. 5, 13, May 1, 21, June 1, 11 (from Roma): 🛏 1,2 cl. (Excelsior), 🛏 1,2 cl., ▬ 2 cl. and [2] Roma - Wien Süd. Supplement payable.

1239 – ALLEGRO ROSSINI – Dec. 19, 20, 26 - 29, Jan. 1 - 3, Apr. 4, 12, 30, May 20, 31, June 10 (from Wien): 🛏 1,2 cl. (Excelsior), 🛏 1,2 cl., ▬ 2 cl. and [2] Wien Süd - Roma. Supplement payable.

B – [2] Venezia - Ponte nelle Alpi - Belluno and v.v.
C – [2] Venezia - Ponte nelli Alpi - Calalzo and v.v.
H – ALLEGRO DON GIOVANNI – 🛏 1,2 cl., ▬ 2 cl. and [2] Venezia - Villach - Salzburg - Wien Westbf and v.v. Supplement payable.
J – ALLEGRO TOSCA – 🛏 1,2 cl. and ▬ 2 cl. (4 berth) Milano (**9753**) - Venezia Mestre - Wien Süd. Supplement payable.
K – ALLEGRO TOSCA – 🛏 1,2 cl. and ▬ 2 cl. (4 berth) Wien Süd - Venezia Mestre (**9702**) - Milano. Supplement payable.
U – [12] Milano (**9706/41**) - Treviso - Udine and v.v.
c – Firenze **Campo di Marte**.
p – Dec. 14 - June 5.
q – ⑥ Dec. 20 - June 6; ⚒ June 8 - Dec. 12.
r – ①⑥⑦ and holidays.
s – Calls to set down only.
t – Roma **Tiburtina**.
u – Calls to pick up only.
v – Ⓐ until June 5; ⚒ from June 8.
x – Depart 0604 on †.

602 VICENZA - TREVISO

2nd class only except where shown

km		⚒	⚒		⚒	⚒	⚒z	†			†	⚒	⚒	⚒		⚒		†	⚒	⚒z			ESc 9741 🅁U		⚒
0	**Vicenza** d.	0546	0615	0654	0810	0839	0918	0918	...	1120	1330	1404	1507	1550	1630	1700	...	1730	1800	1900	1928	...	1958	...	2007
24	Cittadella d.	0611	0640	0718	0835	0904	0943	0943	...	1145	1355	1429	1532	1615	1655	1721	...	1756	1824	1924	1952	...	2017	...	2031
36	Castelfranco Veneto d.	0634	0702	0743	0850	0929	1004	1004	...	1207	1410	1452	1548	1635	1711	1737	...	1811	1840	1945	2008	...	2029	...	2047
60	**Treviso Centrale** a.	0656	0727	0808	...	0951	1027	1027	...	1230	1433	1516	1610	1658	1732	1756	...	1835	1905	2007	2030	...	2046	...	2110

	⚒	⚒	⚒		ESc 9706 🅁U	⚒		⚒	†	⚒	†		⚒z		⚒		⚒z	⚒			⚒		Ⓐz	†	
Treviso Centrale d.	0528	0547	0613	...	0653	0702	0731	...	0938	1009	1138	...	1240	1332	1432	1538	1640	1711	1750	...	1838	...	2012	2046	...
Castelfranco Veneto d.	0547	0614	0637	...	0714	0726	0756	0942	1004	1038	1207	...	1304	1400	1456	1601	1705	1741	1812	...	1902	...	2037	2116	...
Cittadella d.	0600	0629	0652	...	0729	0746	0811	0959	1020	1052	1222	...	1317	1415	1510	1617	1719	1757	1827	...	1917	...	2053	2132	...
Vicenza a.	0626	0656	0719	...	0803	0814	0837	1025	1046	1120	1249	...	...	1440	1537	1645	1745	1822	1855	...	1944	...	2123	2200	...

U – [12] Milano - Vicenza - Treviso (**9705/42**) - Udine and v.v.
z – Not Apr. 9 - 14.

603 CONEGLIANO and PADOVA - BELLUNO and CALALZO

2nd class only except where shown

km		E 1606 H	b	⚒	†		⚒	⚒				⚒z												Ⓐ			
	Venezia SL **601** d.	...	...	...	0643	...	0804	...	...	...	...	...	1226	1326	...	...	1526	...	...	...	1726	...	...	1826	1943	...	...
0	**Conegliano 601** d.	...	0627	...	0746	...	0903	...	...	...	...	1240	1337	1435	...	...	1647	...	1747	...	1837	...	...	|	2038	...	...
14	Vittorio Veneto d.	...	0643	...	0811	...	0917	...	...	...	...	1257	1353	1456	...	...	1703	...	1807	...	1853	...	...	|	2051	...	...
	Padova d.	...	|	0600	|	0649	|	...	0933	...	1134	|	|	|	1250	1345	|	1534	|	1705	|	...	1812	|	|	1916	2120
	Castelfranco Veneto d.	...	|	0629	|	0725	|	...	1002	...	1203	|	|	|	1322	1425	|	1614	|	1733	|	...	1846	|	|	1950	2155
	Montebelluna d.	...	|	0643	|	0747	|	...	1020	...	1217	|	|	|	1336	1443	|	1627	|	1751	|	...	1908	1932	|	2008	2207
	Feltre d.	...	|	0733	|	0834	|	...	1054	...	1250	|	|	|	1425	1531	|	1711	|	1827	|	...	1943	2017	|	2041	2241
	Belluno d.	0619	|	0816	|	0908	|	...	1125	1156	1325	|	|	|	1513	1601	|	1753r	|	1909	|	...	2018	2048	|	2114	2312
41	Ponte nelle Alpi a.	|	0718	0824	0846	0917	0948	...	...	1204	1333	1328	1427	1526	1523	...	1734	1802	1843	*1926*	1924	...	...	...	2122	2121	...
41	Ponte nelle Alpi d.	|	0726	0826	0856	0920e	0957	0953	...	1205	1334	1335	*1429*	1527	1531	...	1742	1808	1845	...	1932	1952	...	...	2124	2127	...
	Belluno § a.	|	|	|	|	|	|	1001	...	|	|	1343	*1436*	1534	|	...	|	|	1853	...	|	2000	...	...	2132	|	...
78	**Calalzo ▲** a.	0730	0805	0915	0936	1003e	1046	...	...	1254	1422	...	...	...	1614	...	1825	1850	...	...	2018	...	...	...	...	2212c	...

km									⚒	†				⚒z												E 1607 L	
0	**Calalzo ▲** d.	...	...	0638	...	0813	...	...	0941	1007	...	1229	1313	...	...	...	1506	...	1622	...	1723	...	1852	...	1930	2056	2036
	Belluno § d.	...	0604	|	0732	|	...	1015	|	|	1126	|	|	1408	...	1542	|	...	|	1725	|	1917	|	1941	|	|	|
37	Ponte nelle Alpi a.	...	0612	0721	0739	0853	...	1023	1024	1048	1134	1313	1401	1416	...	1550	1552	...	1703	1733	1806	1926	1930	1949	2019	|	2115
37	Ponte nelle Alpi d.	...	0613	0723	0741	0857	...	...	1033	1056	1135	1315	...	1428	1429	...	1559	1557	1704	1735	1807	...	1931	1951	2020	|	2127
44	**Belluno** d.	0608	|	0735	|	0909	1018	...	|	|	|	1326	...	|	1437	...	|	1605	1713	|	1816	...	1939	|	2027	2144	|
75	Feltre d.	0643	|	0809	|	0945	1055	...	|	|	|	1400	...	|	1507	...	|	1638	1750	|	1848	...	2016	|	...	...	|
110	Montebelluna d.	0728	|	0848	|	1019	1129	...	|	|	|	1444	...	|	1542	...	|	1714	1828	|	1926	...	2057	|	...	...	|
127	Castelfranco Veneto d.	0744	|	0902	|	1035	1143	...	|	|	|	1504	...	|	1604	...	|	1733	1846	|	1943	...	2113	|	...	...	|
158	**Padova** a.	0818	|	0936	|	1110	1217	...	|	|	|	1538	...	|	1643	...	|	1808	1917	|	2017	...	2148	|	...	...	|
	Vittorio Veneto d.	...	0644	...	0810	...	...	...	1101	1124	1204	...	...	1456	...	...	1628	...	...	1806	...	...	...	2018	...	...	2153
	Conegliano 601 a.	...	0659	...	0822	...	...	...	1115	1138	1218	...	...	1511	...	...	1646	...	...	1818	...	...	...	2033	...	...	2206
	Venezia SL **601** a.	...	0805	...	0928	...	...	...	1216	1243	1317	...	...	...	...	...	...	...	...	1928	...	...	...	2143	...	...	2307

H – Dec. 19 - 22, 25 - 29, Jan. 1 - 5; ⑤ Jan. 9 - Mar. 20, June 19 - July 17; daily July 24 - Sept. 4 (from Roma): 🛏 1,2 cl. (Excelsior), 🛏 1,2 cl. (T2), 🛏 1,2 cl. and ▬ 2 cl. (4 berth) Roma Tiburtina - Belluno - Calalzo-Cortina.
L – Dec. 20 - 23, 26 - 30, Jan. 2 - 6; ⑥ Jan. 10 - Mar. 21, ⑥ June 20 - July 18; daily July 25 - Sept. 5: 🛏 1,2 cl. (Excelsior), 🛏 1,2 cl. (T2), 🛏 1,2 cl. and ▬ 2 cl. (4 berth) Calalzo-Cortina - Belluno - Roma Tiburtina.

b – From Treviso, depart 0605.
c – 2223 on ⑥ Jan. 10 - Mar. 21.
e – † only.
r – Arrive 1740.
z – Not Apr. 9 - 14.
§ – See other direction of table for further connections.
▲ – Full name of station is Calalzo-Pieve di Cadore-Cortina.

Note - connections at Ponte nelle Alpi may be shown in previous column.

VAL GARDENA / GRÖDNERTAL and CORTINA 🚌 services — 604

Service **445**	⚒		y	y				y	
San Candido / Innichen d.	...	0750	0841	0911	1111	...	1411	1511	1811
Dobbiaco / Toblach ♣ d.	0659	0759	0850	0920	1120	...	1420	1520	1820
Cortina a.	0749	0849	...	...	1210	...	1510	...	1910

Service **445**	⚒		y	y				y		
Cortina d.	0755	0855	...	...	...	1320	1555	...	1915	...
Dobbiaco / Toblach ♣ d.	0840	0940	1040	1110	...	1402	1640	1710	2000	...
San Candido / Innichen a.	0849	0949	1049	1119	...	1411	1649	1719	...	...

♣ – Dobbiaco town. Services also call at Dobbiaco railway station en route between Dobbiaco town and Cortina (5 minutes from town stop).

y – Until Oct. 5.

Service **350**	⚒									
Bolzano / Bozen ♦ d.	0642	0824	1052	*1115*	1224	*1315*	1524	1724	*1815*d	1924
Ponte Gardena / Waidbruck d.	0715	0855	1123	1155	1255	1355	1555	1755	1855	1955
Ortisei / St Ulrich ▲ d.	0745	0925	1155	1225	1325	1425	1625	1825	1925	2025
Santa/St Cristina ▲ d.	0755	0935	1205	1235	1335	1435	1635	1835	1935	2035
Selva / Wolkenstein ▲ d.	0804	0944	1214	1244	1344	1444	1644	1844	1944	2044
Plan ▲ a.	0807	0947	1217	1247	1347	1447	1647	1847	1947	2047

Service **350**	⚒									
Plan ▲ d.	0609	0705	0839	1039	...	1309	...	1509	...	1739
Selva / Wolkenstein ▲ d.	0612	0708	0842	1042	...	1312	...	1512	...	1742
Santa/St Cristina ▲ d.	0621	0717	0851	1051	...	1321	...	1521	...	1751
Ortisei / St Ulrich ▲ d.	0633	0729	0903	1103	...	1333	...	1533	...	1803
Ponte Gardena / Waidbruck d.	0701	0757	0933	1133	...	1401	...	1601	...	1833
Bolzano / Bozen ♦ a.	0730j	0828	1004	1204	...	1432	...	1632	...	1904

♦ – Bolzano / Bozen town. Services also call at railway station (2 minutes from town stop).
d – ⚒ only.
▲ – Extra buses run Ortisei/St Ulrich - Plan and v.v. in summer.
j – Bolzano / Bozen railway station only (not town).

Timings shown above are valid **September 10, 2008 - June 19, 2009.**
Operator: Servizi Autobus Dolomiti, Via Conciapelli 60, 39100, Bolzano / Bozen. ✆: + 39 0471 450111 Fax: + 39 0471 970042.

🚌 service **30 Cortina - Calalzo**. 35 km. Journey time: 55 minutes. Timings are valid **September 15, 2008 - June 9, 2009.**

From **Cortina Autostazione** (Bus Station): 0535⚒, 0625⚒, 0650⚒, 0700†, 0832⚒, 0900†, 0930⚒, 1115, 1220⚒, 1240⚒, 1315⚒, 1402, 1505, 1605⚒, 1705, 1755⚒, 1920, 1940.

From **Calalzo Stazione** (FS rail station): 0625⚒, 0658, 0740⚒, 0830, 0935⚒, 1015†, 1055⚒, 1215⚒, 1305, 1400⚒, 1455, 1620, 1755⚒, 1810†, 1900⚒, 2025⚒, 2035†.

Operator: Dolomitibus, via Col Da Ren 14, 32100, Belluno, Italy. ✆ +39 00 437 217 111, fax +39 00 437 940 522.

VENEZIA - TRIESTE — 605

km			*ICN* 773 ♦	*ICN* 777 ♦	2 ⚒				*ESc* 9711 Ⓡ T		†	⚒						*CIS* 57 Ⓡ✕ ♦		*ICp* 707 Ⓡ✕ M		*EN* 241 Ⓡ ♦⊖		*ES* 9397 Ⓡ✕ ♦	
	Roma Termini **620** d.	...	2236t	...	...	...	...	...	...	...	...	...	...	...	...	...	...	...	...	1444	...	...	...	1750	...
0	**Venezia Santa Lucia** d.	0011	|	...	0728	0911	0948	...	1152	1211	1311	1311	1411	1511	1611	1711	1811	...	1936	|	...	2120	...	|	2257
9	**Venezia Mestre** d.	0023	0532	0703	0741	0923	1000	...	1203	1223	1323	1323	1423	1523	1623	1723	1823	1945	1949	2111	...	2132	...	2219	2312
42	Santa Dona di Piave-Jesolo d.	0047	0558	0732	0808	0947	1024	...	1233	1247	1347	1347	1447	1547	1647	1747	1847	|	2016	2134	...	2156	...	|	2346
69	Portogruaro-Caorle d.	0108	0616	0801	0831	1008	1045	...	1252	1308	1408	1408	1508	1608	1708	1808	1908	2020	2037	2150	...	2214	...	2259	0010
83	Latisana-Lignano d.	0119	0628	0817	0844	1019	1056	...	1304	1319	1419	1419	1519	1619	1719	1819	1919	|	2050	2202	...	2226	...	2310r	0022
101	San Giorgio di Nogaro d.	0132	0640	0833	0857	1032	1109	...	|	1332	1432	1438	1532	1632	1732	1832	1932	|	2104	|	...	|	...	|	0037
112	Cervignano-Aquileia-Grado d.	0140	0650	0845	0905	1040	1117	...	1322	1340	1440	1446	1540	1640	1740	1840	1940	|	2112	2219	...	2243	...	|	0044
129	Monfalcone **606** d.	0153	0704	0901	0919	1053	1130	...	1336	1353	1453	1459	1553	1653	1753	1853	1953	2055	2125	2234	...	2258	...	2341	0057
157	**Trieste Centrale 606** a.	0216	0728	0928	0942	1116	1153	...	1358	1418	1516	1522	1616	1719	1816	1916	2016	2118	2148	2258	...	...	...	0003	0120

	2		*EN* 240 Ⓡ ♦⊖			*CIS* 52 Ⓡ✕ ♦		*ICp* 702 Ⓡ✕ M	*ES* 9394 Ⓡ✕ ♦									*ESc* 9746 Ⓡ T			Ⓑv		*ICN* 778 ♦	2 Ⓐ	*ICN* 772 ♦
Trieste Centrale 606 d.	...	0430	...	0532	...	0635	0641	0704	0749	0818	0918	...	1144	1244	1344	1444	1544	1625	1644	1744	1844	1918	1946	2021	2154
Monfalcone **606** d.	...	0453	0544	0555	...	0658	0705	0729	0812	0841	0941	...	1207	1307	1407	1507	1607	1652	1707	1807	1907	1941	2012	2048	2220
Cervignano-Aquileia-Grado d.	...	0505	0556	0607	...	|	0718	0742	|	0853	0953	...	1219	1319	1419	1519	1619	1707	1719	1819	1919	1954	2026	2101	2233
San Giorgio di Nogaro d.	...	0514	|	0616	...	|	0725	|	|	0902	1002	...	1228	1328	1428	1528	1628	|	1728	1828	1928	2003	2035	2110	2242
Latisana-Lignano d.	...	0526	0614	0629	...	|	0743	0802	0841r	0915	1015	...	1241	1341	1441	1541	1641	1726	1741	1841	1941	2021	2050	2129	2256
Portogruaro-Caorle d.	0512	0537	0625	0640	...	0737	0753	0813	0851	0926	1026	...	1252	1352	1452	1552	1652	1736	1752	1852	1952	2032	2103	2141	2308
Santa Dona di Piave-Jesolo d.	0536	0557	0642	0703	...	|	0815	0830	|	0946	1046	...	1312	1412	1512	1612	1712	1753	1812	1912	2012	2059	2121	...	2325
Venezia Mestre a.	0611	0622	0704	0728	...	0815	0849	0854	0930	1011	1111	...	1337	1439	1537	1637	1737	1822	1837	1937	2037	2136	2149	...	2349
Venezia Santa Lucia a.	0624	0634	0716	0740	...	...	0902	|	|	1024	1124	...	1349	1449	1549	1649	1749	1833	1849	1949	2049	2149	...	...	|
Roma Termini **620** a.	...	...	...	...	...	...	...	1516	1410	...	...	...	...	...	...	...	...	...	...	...	...	...	...	...	0656t

♦ – **NOTES** (LISTED BY TRAIN NUMBER)

52 – [12] and ✕ Trieste - Venezia Mestre - Milano - Basel. *CISALPINO Pendolino* train; supplement payable.
57 – [12] and ✕ Basel - Milano - Venezia Mestre - Trieste. *CISALPINO Pendolino* train; supplement payable.
240 – VENEZIA – 🛏 1,2 cl., ▬ 2 cl. and [2] Budapest - Zagreb - Ljubljana - Venezia; ▬ 2 cl. Beograd (**412**) - Zagreb - Venezia. Conveys 🛏 1,2 cl. and [2] (also ▬ 2 cl. May 29 - Sept. 18) București (**1821**) - Arad (**354**) - Budapest - Venezia.
241 – VENEZIA – 🛏 1,2 cl., ▬ 2 cl. and [2] Venezia - Ljubljana - Zagreb - Budapest; ▬ 2 cl. Venezia - Zagreb (**413**) - Beograd. Conveys 🛏 1,2 cl. and [2] (also ▬ 2 cl. May 31 - Sept. 20) Venezia - Budapest (**355**) - Arad (**1822**) - București.
772 – MARCO POLO – 🛏 1,2 cl., ▬ 2 cl. (4 berth) and [12] Trieste - Venezia Mestre (**771**) - Napoli.
773 – MARCO POLO – 🛏 1,2 cl., ▬ 2 cl. (4 berth) and [12] Napoli (**774**) - Venezia Mestre - Trieste.
777 – TERGESTE – ▬ 2 cl. (4 berth) and [12] Lecce (**776**) - Venezia Mestre - Trieste.
778 – TERGESTE – ▬ 2 cl. (4 berth) and [12] Trieste - Venezia Mestre (**779**) - Lecce.
9394 – [12] and ✕ Trieste - Venezia Mestre (**9393**) - Roma.
9397 – [12] and ✕ Roma (**9398**) - Venezia Mestre - Trieste.

M – MIRAMARE – [12] and ✕ Trieste - Venezia Mestre (**703/6**) - Roma and v.v.
T – [12] Torino - Venezia - Trieste and v.v.
r – ⑥⑦ June 1 - Sept. 14.
t – Roma **Tiburtina**.
v – Not Apr. 12, 24, 30, June 1.
⊖ – Ⓡ and special fares payable for journeys to / from Slovenia.

UDINE - TRIESTE — 606

Most services 2nd class only

km		⚒		⚒		⚒	Ⓐz	y			⚒	†	q	r		s		p	⚒m			Ⓐ	†		b	⑥m	
	Venezia SL **601** d.	...	...	...	...	...	0526	0526	...	0704	0718	...	1004	...	...	...	1204	...	...	...	1404	...	...	...	1504	1504	...
0	**Udine 601** d.	0552	...	0630	0655	0730	0734	0734	...	0856	0934	1000	1156	1207	...	1245	1356	1420	1420	...	1556	1627	1629	...	1659	1704	...
33	Gorizia Centrale d.	0628	...	0654	0733	|	0801	0805	...	0920	1003	1036	1220	1234	...	1318	1420	1452	1458	...	1620	1700	1705	...	1723	1736	...
55	Monfalcone **605** d.	0655	...	0717	0759	0813	0823	0828	...	0941	1025	1101	1241	1305	...	1343	1441	1516	1523	...	1641	1722	1730	...	1744	1800	...
83	**Trieste Centrale 605** a.	0721	...	0740	0828	0836	0846	0856	...	1004	1050	1130	1304	1329	...	1409	1504	1540	1552	...	1704	1750	1759	...	1807	1829	...

		†	⑥m	Ⓐ			Ⓒ	Ⓐz	⑥			
Venezia SL **601** d.	1604	...	1704	1704	...	1804	...	...	...	2004	2204	...
Udine 601 d.	1756	1814	1859	1859	...	1956	2021	2036	2036	2156	0003	...
Gorizia Centrale d.	1820	1839	1923	1923	...	2020	2054	2109	2109	2220	0038	...
Monfalcone **605** d.	1841	1900	1944	1944	...	2041	2116	2131	2131	2241	0103	...
Trieste Centrale 605 a.	1904	1923	2007	2007	...	2104	2142	2157	2157	2304	0131	...

	⚒	⚒	†			⚒	†		†	
Trieste Centrale 605 d.	0502	0558	0604	...	0656	0735	0735	0856	0956	...
Monfalcone **605** d.	0527	0623	0629	...	0719	0803	0758	0919	1024	...
Gorizia Centrale d.	0551	0648	0653	...	0740	0826	0818	0940	1048	...
Udine 601 a.	0623	0728	0728	...	0804	0857	0843	1004	1123	...
Venezia SL **601** a.	0817	0949	0949	...	0956	...	...	1156	...	...

		⚒	†			⚒	b			⑦	⑥	Ⓐm	Ⓐz	Ⓐ			⑥	Ⓐ		Ⓐ			⚒		⑥	Ⓑ	
Trieste Centrale 605 d.	1056	1126	1208	...	1256	1330	1411	...	1456	1551	1559	1602	1603	1631	...	1656	1722	1734	...	1755	1856	...	1935	2042	2216	2221	...
Monfalcone **605** d.	1119	1154	1237	...	1319	1400	1434	...	1519	1618	1622	1630	1628	1659	...	1719	1750	1757	...	1818	1919	...	2003	2108	2239	2244	...
Gorizia Centrale d.	1140	1219	1301	...	1340	1425	|	...	1540	1641	1643	1653	1651	1722	...	1740	1814	|	...	1839	1940	...	2027	2131	2300	2305	...
Udine 601 a.	1204	1253	1338	...	1404	1504	1517	...	1604	1710	1709	1723	1724	1755	...	1804	1849	1837	...	1903	2004	...	2058	2204	2324	2329	...
Venezia SL **601** a.	1356	1456	...	...	1556	...	...	...	1756	...	...	...	...	...	...	1956	2056	...	...	2056	2156	...	...	2356	...	...	...

b – ⚒ to June 6; Ⓐ from June 8.
m – From June 8.
p – Daily until June 6; † from June 7.
q – ①⑥⑦ and holidays.
r – ②③④⑤ (not holidays).
s – Daily until June 6; ⚒ from June 8.
y – ⑥ to June 6; ⚒ from June 8.
z – Dec. 15 - June 5.

607 FERROVIE NORD MILANO services

BRESCIA - EDOLO : *103 km* Journey: approximately 120 – 150 minutes 2nd class only

From **Brescia**: 0556⚒, 0703†, 0903, 1103, 1303, 1503, 1703, 1754Ⓐ, 1903.

From **Edolo**: 0550⚒, 0643⚒, 0750, 0950, 1150, 1350, 1550, 1750, 1950†.

Subject to alteration July 1 - August 31

MILANO - COMO LAGO : *46 km* Journey: 52 – 65 minutes 2nd class only

From **Milano Cadorna**: Hourly 0640 – 2040 (also 0610⚒, 0710⚒, 0800Ⓐ, 0900, 1210⚒, 1310⚒, 1400†, 1410Ⓐ, 1510Ⓐ, 1610Ⓐ, 1710Ⓐ, 1810, 1910⚒, 2010⚒, 2110).

From **Como Lago**: Hourly 0617 – 2117 (also 0547⚒, 0647⚒, 0747⚒, 0836⚒, 0936Ⓐ, 1247⚒, 1347⚒, 1447Ⓐ, 1547Ⓐ, 1647Ⓐ, 1747, 1836†, 1847⚒, 1947).

MILANO - VARESE - LAVENO : *72 km* Journey: 87 – 107 mins 2nd class only

From **Milano Cadorna**: 0605⚒, 0635, 0705Ⓐ, 0750, 0850, 0935, 1035, 1135, 1205⚒, 1235Ⓒ, 1250, 1350, 1435Ⓒ, 1450Ⓐ, 1535, 1605Ⓐ, 1650, 1720Ⓐ, 1750, 1820Ⓐ, 1850, 1920Ⓐ, 1935Ⓒ, 2020Ⓐ.

From **Laveno Mombello**: 0537Ⓐ, 0607, 0637, 0707, 0737, 0807Ⓐ, 0837, 0937, 1037, 1137, 1237, 1307⚒, 1337, 1437, 1537, 1637, 1737, 1807Ⓐ, 1837, 1937, 2037.

Additional journeys run Milano Cadorna - Varese (journey 64 minutes).

Operator: Ferrovie Nord Milano, Piazzale Cadorna 14, 20123 Milano.
✆ + 39 02 20 222 www.lenord.it For 🚌 Edolo - Tirano see Table **543**.

608 MILANO local services

MILANO - BERGAMO : Some services 2nd class only

km																									
		Ⓐ		Ⓐ	Ⓒ	Ⓐ	Ⓒ		Ⓐ		Ⓐ					Ⓐ	Ⓒ	Ⓐ	Ⓒ	Ⓐ	Ⓒ				
0	**Milano Centrale** ◇ ....d.	0525**p**	0610	0710	0710	0810	0810	0910	1003**p**	1110	1210**p**	1310	1410	1510	1610	1710	1710	1810	1810	1910	1910	2010	2110	2210	2345
34	Treviglio Ovest..........d.	0608	|	|	0750	|	0850	0950	▽	1150	1306	1350	1450	1550	1650	|	1750	|	1850	|	1950	2050	2150	2250	|
56	**Bergamo**....................a.	0630	0658	0758	0813	0858	0913	1013	1107	1213	1328	1413	1513	1613	1713	1758	1813	1858	1913	1958	2013	2113	2213	2313	0033

	⚒	Ⓒ	Ⓐ		Ⓐ			Ⓐ								Ⓒ	Ⓐ							
Bergamo.....................d.	0453	0547	0602	0647	0720	0732	0802	0832	0947	1053	1147	1247	1347	1447	1602	1647	1702	1747	1847	...	1947	2047	2147	2247	...
Treviglio Ovest..........d.	▽	0605	|	0705	|	0747	|	0847	1005	▽	1205	1305	1405	1505	|	1705	|	1805	1905	...	2005	2105	2205	2305	...
Milano Centrale ◇ .....a.	0557**p**	0650	0650	0750	0820**p**	0830	0850	0950**p**	1050	1157**p**	1250	1350	1450	1550	1650	1750	1750	1850	1950	...	2050	2150	2250	2350	...

Additional trains run approx hourly Milano Porta Garibaldi - Bergamo via Monza, journey 64 minutes, *43 km*.

MILANO - LUINO : *91 km* 2nd class only

	⚒	⚒	⚒	⚒				Ⓐ		⚒	
Milano P G ....d.	0515	0656	*0830*	*1230*	*1330*	*1530*	*1730*	1745	*1830*	1856	*2202***v**
Gallarate **590**.........d.	0601	0735	0913	1313	1413	1613	1813	1826	1913	1937	2256
Laveno Mombello...d.	0650	0820	0952	1349	1449	1649	1849	1904	1951	2014	2328
Luino 592 ....a.	0707	0835	1008	1408	1508	1708	1908	1919	2008	2032	2347

	⚒	⚒		Ⓒ	⚒		⚒			⚒	
Luino 592 ....d.	0632	0723	0852	1252	1352	1452	1552	1652	1752	1952	2052
Laveno Mombello...d.	0649	0738	0912	1312	1412	1512	1612	1712	1812	2016	2112
Gallarate **590**.........a.	0725	0804	0947	1347	1447	1547	1647	1747	1847	2047	2147
Milano P G ....a.	0804	0846	*1030*	*1430*	*1530*	*1630*	*1730*	*1830*	*1930*	*2130*	*2255***v**

Additional journeys (change at Gallarate): from **Milano PG** 0530†, 0730†, 0930†, 1130†, 1430⚒, 1630⚒, 1930; from **Luino** 0552Ⓐ, 0752†, 1052†, 1852†, 2152Ⓒ.

MILANO - CREMONA - MANTOVA :

km												
							⚒		Ⓐ	Ⓒ		
0	**Milano C** ....d.	0620	0815	1022**n**	1215	1415	1620	1720	1850	1848**n**	2020	...
60	Codogno......d.	0704	0904	1104	1304	1504	1708	1804	1930	1930	2104	...
88	Cremona......d.	0735	0926	1126	1326	1524	1729	1823	1949	1949	2124	...
151	**Mantova**.....a.	0832	1017	1217	1413	1617	1815	1917	2045	2045	2217	...

			⚒							2†	
Mantova..................d.	0520	0612	0647	0943	1143	1437	1543	1737	1943	1953	...
Cremona ....d.	0618	0658	0734	1030	1230	1525	1630	1835	2030	2056	...
Codogno ....a.	0641	0720	0754	1051	1254	1546	1653	1853	2053	2136	2151
Milano C ....a.	0745	0801**n**	0840	1145	1345	1640	1749**n**	1950	2145	...	2245

NOTES – SEE FOOT OF PAGE

609 Local services in NORTHERN and CENTRAL ITALY

2nd class only

ALESSANDRIA - ACQUI TERME : *34 km* Journey 28 – 38 minutes

From **Alessandria**: 0619⚒, 0700⚒, 0752†**m**, 0911, 1136, 1243, 1337⚒, 1609†, 1641Ⓐ, 1741, 1937.

From **Acqui Terme**: 0617⚒, 0700, 0723⚒, 0946, 1320, 1510, 1546⚒, 1727†**r**, 1820⚒, 2021†**m**.

BOLOGNA - PORRETTA TERME : *59 km* Journey 60 – 72 minutes

From **Bologna Centrale**: 0552⚒, 0630⚒, 0704, 0804⚒, 0904, 1004⚒, 1104, 1204, 1304, 1404, 1504, 1604, 1704, 1734⚒, 1804, 1834Ⓐ, 1904, 1934Ⓐ, 2004, 2104.

From **Porretta Terme**: 0500⚒, 0550, 0608⚒, 0640, 0718, 0750⚒, 0822, 0922⚒, 1022, 1122⚒, 1222, 1322, 1422, 1522, 1622, 1722, 1821, 1921, 2021, 2050Ⓐ, 2122Ⓐ.

Subject to alteration July 1 - August 31

CAMPIGLIA - PIOMBINO : *16 km* Journey 22 – 30 minutes

From **Campiglia Marittima**: 0603⚒, 0710⚒, 1016⑥**k**, 1016†**s**, 1330Ⓐ, 1339⑥, 1533, 1647, 1737Ⓐ, 1737†**h**, 1804, 1839⑥**z**, 1839†**h**, 1930†**z**, 2100†**z**.

From **Piombino Marittima**: 0638⚒, 0746⚒, 0926, 1053⑥**k**, 1053†**s**, 1132⑥**z**, 1132†**h**, 1520⚒, 1609, 1725, 1812Ⓐ, 1812†**h**, 1841, 2010†**z**.

GENOVA - ACQUI TERME : *58 km* Journey 65 – 81 minutes

From **Genova Piazza Principe**:
⚒: 0612, 0714, 0902, 1021Ⓐ, 1222, 1322, 1422, 1548, 1712Ⓐ, 1747, 1822Ⓐ, 1922, 2043.
†: 0612, 0736, 0907, 1039, 1206, 1342, 1437, 1607, 1747, 1922, 2043.

From **Acqui Terme**:
⚒: 0520, 0610, 0703, 0740, 0851Ⓐ, 1025, 1215, 1316, 1414, 1554, 1716, 1817, 2049.
†: 0602, 0736, 0900, 1034, 1203, 1334, 1601, 1748, 1916, 2049.

Subject to alteration July 1 - August 31

PORRETTA TERME - PISTOIA : *40 km* Journey 48 – 55 minutes

From **Porretta Terme**: 0540⚒, 0647⚒, 0719†, 0720⚒, , 0817, 0926⚒, 1021, 1324, 1428, 1521, 1727, 1921.

From **Pistoia**: 0515⚒, 0614, 0705†, 0712⚒, 0825⚒, 0921, 1224, 1316, 1422, 1621, 1721, 1926.

ROVIGO - CHIOGGIA : *57 km*

		†z	⚒	†b	⚒	†	⚒	⚒e	†	⚒	⚒	†c	⚒
Rovigo...... d.	0622	0748	0810	0917	1017	1217	1249	1421	1455	1617	1817	1817	1943
Adria.......... d.	0657	0821	0835	0945	1045	1246	1322	1450	1523	1648	1843	1844	2016
Chioggia... a.	0739	0855	0911	1021	1120	1321	1356	1532	1558	1724	1920	1920	2050

	⚒	†	⚒	⚒	†q	⚒	†	⚒	⚒e	†	⚒	c	⚒
Chioggia... d.	0651	0744	0756	0938	1030	1244	1337	1444	1609	1615	1739	1937	2100
Adria.......... d.	0724	0820	0836	1014	1107	1321	1413	1517	1647	1652	1814	2013	2129
Rovigo...... a.	0751	0847	0902	1045	1134	1347	1440	1545	1713	1718	1845	2043	2148

SANTHIÀ - ARONA : *65 km* Journey 60 – 73 minutes

From **Santhià**: 0640⚒, 0840, 0908†, 1240⚒, 1352, 1443Ⓐ, 1640Ⓐ, 1744, 1845.

From **Arona**: 0655, 1120†, 1155⚒, 1347⚒, 1511, 1730, 1810Ⓐ, 1845†, 1908†, 1955.

Trains call at Borgomanero approximately 45 mins from Santhia and 15 mins from Arona.

SANTHIÀ - BIELLA SAN PAOLO : *27 km* Journey 20 – 35 minutes

From **Santhià**: 0637⚒, 0737⚒, 0755†, 0837⚒, 0900†, 0940†, 0951⚒, 1152⚒, 1237, 1355⚒, 1437, 1552⚒, 1637, 1737⚒, 1837†, 1846⚒, 1925Ⓐ, 1959, 2048, 2142.

From **Biella**: 0548, 0624⚒, 0711Ⓐ, 0723⚒, 0750†, 0802⚒, 0851†, 0902⚒, 0944⚒, 1145, 1301⚒, 1350⚒, 1353†, 1500⚒, 1545, 1702⚒, 1748†, 1801⚒, 1832⚒, 1952, 2042.

Subject to alteration July 1 - August 31

SIENA - CHIUSI-CHIANCIANO TERME : *89 km* Journey 71 – 94 minutes

From **Siena**: 0557⚒, 0601†, 0801†, 0806⚒, 1004†, 1216⚒, 1328⚒, 1357⚒, 1404†, 1448, 1601†, 1604⚒, 1659⚒, 1743⚒, 1804†, 1815⚒, 1927⚒, 2004†, 2019⚒.

From **Chiusi**: 0430⚒, 0605⚒, 0627†, 0707⚒, 0832†, 0914⚒, 1031†, 1038⚒, 1232†, 1350⚒, 1510⚒, 1632†, 1707⚒, 1832†, 1843⚒, 1928⚒, 2031†, 2038⚒, 2132.

SIENA - GROSSETO : *102 km* Journey 77 – 107 minutes

From **Siena**: 0602⚒, 0753, 1218, 1329, 1543, 1744, 1839, 1943.

From **Grosseto**: 0500, 0620⚒, 0722, 0940, 1336†, 1340⚒, 1547⚒, 1645, 1758, 1953.

TRENTO - CASTELFRANCO VENETO - VENEZIA :

km											
				⚒	⚒		⚒				
0	**Trento**..........................d.	*0705*	0805	*0905*	*1005*	*1105*	*1205*	*1305*	*1505*	*1605*	*1705*
31	Levico Terme................d.	*0755*	0855	*0955*	*1055*	*1155*	*1255*	*1355*	*1555*	*1655*	*1755*
44	Borgo Valsugana Centro..d.	*0809*	0909	*1009*	*1109*	*1209*	*1309*	*1409*	*1609*	*1709*	*1809*
97	Bassano del Grappa....a.	*0903*	1006	*1106*	*1206*	*1306*	*1406*	*1506*	*1706*	*1806*	*1906*
97	Bassano del Grappa....d.	0908	1008	1121	1223	1342	1431	1533	1740	1812	1922
116	Castelfranco Veneto ....d.	0926	1028	1147	1242	1405	1449	1604	1805	1834	1941
148	Venezia Mestre.............a.	1001	1108	1232	1332	1459	1532	1659	1901	1932	2032
157	**Venezia Santa Lucia**......a.	1014	1122	1246	1346	1513	1546	1713	1914	1946	2046

			†	⚒		⚒				
Venezia Santa Lucia......d.	0543	0727	0827	0857	1127	1327	1427	1627	1727	1927
Venezia Mestre.............d.	0611	0741	0841	0911	1141	1341	1441	1642	1741	1941
Castelfranco Veneto ....d.	0651	0836	0926	1011	1227	1433	1540	1744	1832	2032
Bassano del Grappa....a.	0712	0859	0951	1035	1250	1457	1602	1807	1855	2053
Bassano del Grappa....d.	*0717*	0915	1015	*1115*	*1315*	*1515*	*1615*	1815	*1915*	2108
Borgo Valsugana Centro..d.	*0825*	1025	1126	*1225*	*1425*	*1626*	*1730*	1925	*2025*	2205
Levico Terme................d.	*0844*	1044	1144	*1244*	*1444*	*1644*	*1744*	1944	*2044*	2218
Trento..........................a.	*0927*	1127	1227	*1327*	*1527*	*1727*	*1827*	2027	*2127*	2257

VERONA PORTA NUOVA - MANTOVA - MODENA :

km													
		⚒	⚒		⚒	A	⚒		⚒				
0	**Verona P N** d.	0631	0758	0856	0931	1131	1230	1357	1545	1658	1743	1900	1959
37	Mantova ....d.	0725	0843	0934	1020	1205	1330	1445	1635	1745	1834	1949	2050
56	Suzzara......d.	0748	0906	0953	1041	|	1354	1509	1656	1810	1900	2009	2114
98	**Modena** ....a.	0835	0952	1027	1126	1251	1445	1552	1738	1901	1948	2102	2156

	⚒		⚒	⚒				⚒			⚒	†	A
Modena..... d.	0605	0658	0813	0906	...	1329	1422	1522	1630	1741	1837	...	2023
Suzzara ..... d.	0656	0747	0905	0954	...	1421	1508	1608	1720	1834	1922	...	|
Mantova .... d.	0724	0825	0933	1010	1221	1446	1530	1642	1739	1901	1948	1948	2115
Verona P N . a.	0813	0920	1020	...	1306	1533	1603	1734	*1836*	1949	2042	2042	2146

NOTES FOR TABLES 608/9

A – ADIGE – 🍽 Bolzano - Verona - Bologna - Lecce and v.v. (*IC* **717/8**).

b – Until June 2.

c – 40 minutes later on † from June 7.

e – Not Apr. 9 - 14.

h – From Apr. 12.

k – Until May 30 (not Apr. 25).

m – From May 31.

n – Milano **Lambrate**.

p – Milano **Porta Garibaldi**.

q – 22 minutes earlier from June 7.

r – 1739 to Mar. 8.

s – Until Apr. 5.

v – Milano Porta Garibaldi **Passante**.

x – Not Apr. 25.

z – From June 6.

◇ – Services from Centrale also call at Lambrate (8 mins from Centrale).

▽ – Via Monza.

TORINO and MILANO - GENOVA - PISA - ROMA 610

km			*IC* **501** 🍷 ⚒	*ES* **9305** Ⓡ 🍷		*ICp* **503** Ⓡ 🍷 ♦		*ICp* **645** Ⓡ		2	†A	*ICp* **517** Ⓡ Ⓐ	⚒	*ICp* **691** Ⓡ 🍷 ♦	*ICp* **515** Ⓡ ✕ ♦	2		†F	⚒F	2 ⚒	2 †	2	*ICp* **1533** Ⓡ 🍷 ©	*ICp* **647** Ⓡ Ⓐ	A	2
0	**Torino Porta Nuova 619**	d.	...	...	...	...	...	...	...	...	0520	...	0635	...	...	...	...	...	...	...	...	...	0720	...	...	...	0820
56	Asti **619**	d.	...	...	...	...	...	...	...	...	0606	...	0713	...	...	...	...	...	...	...	...	...	0806	...	...	...	0906
91	Alessandria **619**	d.	...	...	...	...	...	...	...	...	0628	...	0732	...	...	...	...	...	...	...	...	...	0833	...	...	...	0930
112	Novi Ligure	d.	...	...	...	...	...	...	...	...	0650	...	0745	...	...	...	...	...	...	...	...	...	0850	...	...	...	0943
	Milano Centrale	d.	...	...	...	...	...	...	0605	...	|	0625	|	0625	0700	...	...	...	...	...	0720	0720	|	0805	0810	0820	|
	Pavia	d.	...	...	...	...	...	...	0635	...	|	0700	|	0700	0735	...	...	...	...	...	0753	0753	|	0835	0835	0855	|
	Voghera **619**	d.	...	...	...	...	...	...	|	...	|	0716	|	0716	0751	...	...	...	...	...	0811	0811	|	0851	0851	0911	|
	Tortona **619**	d.	...	...	...	...	...	...	0700	...	|	0729	|	0729	|	...	...	...	...	...	0824	0824	|	|	|	0923	|
166	**Genova Piazza Principe 619**	a.	...	...	...	...	...	...	0744	...	0749	0822	0830	0836	0842	...	...	...	...	...	0908	0910	0943	0942	0942	1014	1032
166	**Genova Piazza Principe**	d.	...	...	...	0605	0637	0711	0747	...	0752	...	...	|	...	0852	...	...	...	...	0911	0913	...	0947	0947	...	1035
169	Genova Brignole	d.	...	...	0600	0614	0645	0720	0758	...	0803	...	...	0847	...	0900	...	...	...	...	0920	0922	...	0958	0958	...	1041
194	Santa Margherita-Portofino	d.	...	...	|	0647	|	0757	0822	...	0834	...	...	...	...	|	...	...	...	...	0957	1000	...	1022	1030	...	...
196	Rapallo	d.	...	...	|	0652	0711	0801	0827	...	0838	...	...	...	...	0923	...	...	...	...	1002	1005	...	1027	1036	...	...
205	Chiavari	d.	...	...	|	0701	0721	0809	0836	...	0846	...	...	...	...	0932	...	...	...	...	1011	1014	...	1036	1045	...	...
212	Sestri-Levante	d.	...	0515	|	0710	0729	0816	0844	...	0856	...	...	...	...	|	...	...	...	...	1025	1027	...	1044	1053	...	...
235	Levanto	d.	...	|	|	0730	|	0836	0858	...	0924	...	...	...	...	|	...	...	...	...	1054	1053	...	1058	1111	...	...
249	Riomaggiore	d.	...	|	|	|	|	0856	|	...	0949	...	...	...	...	|	...	...	...	...	1121	1123	...	|	|	...	...
256	**La Spezia Centrale**	d.	...	0546	0651	0749	0759	0908	0919	...	1002	...	...	...	...	1006	...	...	...	...	1132	1132	...	1119	1138	...	...
272	Sarzana	d.	...	0559	|	▬	|	0921	|	...	1016	...	...	...	...	|	←	...	1057	1057	...	...	...	|	|	...	...
282	Carrara-Avenza	d.	...	0608	|	...	|	0929	|	...	1024	...	...	...	...	|	1024	...	1104	1105	...	...	...	1137	|	...	...
289	Massa Centro	d.	...	0616	|	...	0825	0936	0947	...	→	...	...	...	...	|	1030	...	1111	1112	...	...	...	1145	1205	...	...
310	Viareggio	d.	...	0630	|	...	0839	0956	1002	...	...	...	...	...	...	1038	1050	...	1130	1136	...	...	...	1206	1223	...	...
331	**Pisa Centrale**	d.	0545	0649	0732	0745	0859	1015	1021	...	...	...	...	...	...	1100	1121j	1145	1147	1201	...	...	...	1224	1248	...	...
	Firenze SMN **614**	a.	|	|	|	|	|	...	|	...	...	...	...	...	...	|	|	|	...	...	...	...	...	|	|	...	...
351	**Livorno Centrale**	d.	0604	0706	0746	0804	0915	...	1038	...	...	...	...	...	...	1116	1137j	1204	...	...	...	...	...	1242	1305	...	...
374	Rosignano	d.	0621	|	|	0821	|	...	...	...	...	...	...	...	...	|	...	1221	...	...	...	...	...	|	|	...	...
385	Cecina	d.	0630	0729	|	0830	0936	...	...	...	...	...	...	...	...	1138	...	1230	...	...	...	...	...	1306	1339	...	...
420	Campiglia Marittima	d.	0653	0748	|	0853	0954	...	...	...	...	...	...	...	...	|	...	1253	...	...	...	...	...	1325	1400	...	...
437	Follonica	d.	0704	0758	|	0904	|	...	...	...	...	...	...	...	...	|	...	1304	...	...	...	...	...	1336	1411	...	...
479	Grosseto	d.	0732	0819	|	0932	1028	...	...	...	...	...	...	...	...	1228	...	1332	...	...	...	...	...	1400	1433	...	...
517	Orbetello	d.	0754	0837	|	0954	|	...	...	...	...	...	...	...	...	|	...	1354	...	...	...	...	...	...	...	...	...
556	Tarquinia	d.	0827	|	|	1027	|	...	...	...	...	...	...	...	...	|	...	1427	...	...	...	...	...	...	...	...	...
586	**Civitavecchia**	d.	0841	0917	|	1041	1122	...	...	...	...	...	...	...	...	1322	...	1441	...	...	...	...	...	...	...	...	...
595	Santa Marinella	d.	0848	|	|	1048	|	...	...	...	...	...	...	...	...	|	...	1448	...	...	...	...	...	...	...	...	...
617	Ladispoli-Cerveteri	d.	0904	|	|	1104	|	...	...	...	...	...	...	...	...	|	...	1504	...	...	...	...	...	...	...	...	...
660	**Roma Ostiense**	a.	0937	1000	|	1137	1200	...	...	...	...	...	...	...	...	1400	...	1537	...	...	...	...	...	...	...	...	...
667	**Roma Termini**	a.	0950	1014	0959	1150	1214	...	...	...	...	...	...	...	...	1414	...	1550	...	...	...	...	...	...	...	...	...
	Napoli Centrale **640**	a.	...	1236	...	...	1436	...	...	...	...	...	...	...	...	...	...	...	...	...	...	...	...	...	...	...	...

km			Ⓐ	*ICp* **649** Ⓡ ♦	*ICp* **519** Ⓡ 🍷 ♦		*EC* **143** Ⓡ 🍷 ♦	*ICp* **523** Ⓡ 🍷 ♦	2	*ICp* **653** Ⓡ			†	⚒	*ESc* **9799** Ⓡ 🍷	*ICp* **655** Ⓡ	2	*ICp* **529** Ⓡ ⚒	A	*EC* **159** Ⓡ 🍷 ♦	*ICp* **533** Ⓡ 🍷	2	G	*ICp* **605** Ⓡ	*ICp* **537** Ⓡ		©A
	Torino Porta Nuova 619	d.	...	...	0905	...	...	1105	1120	...	...	...	...	...	1305	...	1320	1405	...	...	1505	1520	...	...	1605	...	...
	Asti **619**	d.	...	...	0943	...	...	1143	1206	...	...	...	...	...	1343	...	1406	1443	...	...	1543	1606	...	...	1643	...	...
	Alessandria **619**	d.	...	...	1002	...	...	1202	1233	...	...	...	...	...	1402	...	1433	1502	...	...	1602	1633	...	...	1702	...	...
	Novi Ligure	d.	...	...	|	...	...	|	1249	...	...	...	...	...	|	...	1450	1515	...	...	|	1648	...	...	1715	...	...
0	**Milano Centrale**	d.	0850	0905	|	...	1110	|	|	1205	...	...	1225	1225	|	1405	|	|	1420	1510	|	|	...	1600	|	...	1625
39	Pavia	d.	0915	0935	|	...	1135	|	|	1235	...	...	1300	1300	|	1435	|	|	1455	1535	|	|	...	1635	|	...	1659
65	Voghera **619**	d.	0933	|	|	...	1151	|	|	|	...	...	1316	1316	|	1451	|	|	1512	1551	|	|	...	1651	|	...	1715
82	Tortona **619**	d.	...	1000	|	...	|	|	|	1300	...	...	1328	1328	|	|	|	|	1523	|	|	|	...	|	|	...	1726
154	**Genova Piazza Principe 619**	a.	...	1042	1049	...	1242	1249	1334	1342	...	...	1418	1434	1449	1542	1536	1553	1613	1642	1649	1734	...	1742	1753	...	1816
	Genova Piazza Principe	d.	...	...	1052	...	...	1252	1336	1347	...	1411	|	|	1452	1547	1539	1556	...	...	1652	1736	...	1748	1802	1811	...
	Genova Brignole	d.	...	...	1100	...	...	1300	1342	1358	...	1420	1427	1442	1500	1558	1548	1602	...	...	1700	1742	...	1758	1808	1820	...
	Santa Margherita-Portofino	d.	...	...	|	...	...	|	...	1422	...	1456	...	...	|	|	1626	...	...	...	|	▬	...	1822	...	1849	...
	Rapallo	d.	...	...	1123	...	...	|	...	1427	...	1500	...	...	1523	1627	1630	...	...	...	|	...	...	1827	...	1853	...
	Chiavari	d.	...	...	|	...	...	|	...	1436	...	1508	...	...	1532	1636	1638	...	...	...	1729	...	...	1836	...	1901	...
	Sestri-Levante	d.	...	...	|	...	...	1334	...	1444	...	1518	...	...	|	1644	1648	...	...	...	|	...	...	1844	...	1911	...
	Levanto	d.	...	...	|	...	...	|	...	1458	...	1538	...	...	|	1658	1724	...	...	...	|	...	...	1858	...	1931	...
	Riomaggiore	d.	...	...	|	...	...	|	...	|	...	1552	...	...	|	|	1751	...	...	...	|	...	...	|	...	1953	...
	La Spezia Centrale	d.	...	...	1206	...	...	1406	...	1518	...	1602	...	...	1606	1718	1802	...	...	...	1806	...	...	1919	...	2002	...
	Sarzana	d.	...	...	|	...	...	|	...	...	...	1616	...	...	|	▬	1816	...	...	...	|	...	...	|	...	2017	...
	Carrara-Avenza	d.	...	...	|	...	...	1423	...	...	...	1624	...	...	|	...	1824	...	...	...	|	...	...	1940	...	2025	...
	Massa Centro	d.	...	...	1226	...	...	|	...	...	...	1630	...	...	1627	...	1830	...	...	...	1826	...	...	|	...	2033	...
	Viareggio	d.	...	...	1240	...	...	1441	...	...	...	1652	...	...	|	...	1852	...	...	...	1840	⑤⑥	...	1957	...	2057	...
	Pisa Centrale	d.	...	...	1300	1345	...	1500	...	...	1545	1722	...	...	1700	1745	1919	...	...	...	1900	1956	1956	2015	...	2122	...
	Firenze SMN **614**	a.	...	...	|	|	...	|	...	...	|	|	...	...	|	|	...	...	...	...	|	|	|	|	...	|	...
	Livorno Centrale	d.	...	...	1316	1404	...	1516	...	...	1604	1738	...	...	1716	1804	...	...	...	...	1916	2014	2014	2030	...	2140	...
	Rosignano	d.	...	...	|	1421	...	|	...	...	1621	...	...	...	|	1821	...	...	...	...	|	2031	2031	...	...	...	...
	Cecina	d.	...	...	|	1430	...	|	...	...	1630	...	...	...	|	1830	...	...	...	...	1939	2040	2040	...	...	...	...
	Campiglia Marittima	d.	...	...	|	1453	...	1553	...	...	1653	...	...	...	|	1853	...	...	...	...	1956	2103	2103	...	...	...	...
	Follonica	d.	...	...	1403	1504	...	|	...	...	1704	...	...	...	1803	1904	...	...	...	...	2007	2114	2114	...	...	...	...
	Grosseto	d.	...	...	1428	1532	...	1628	...	...	1732	...	...	...	1828	1932	...	...	...	...	2034	2142	2142	...	...	...	...
	Orbetello	d.	...	...	|	1554	...	|	...	...	1754	...	...	...	|	1954	...	...	...	...	2052	2204	2204	...	...	...	...
	Tarquinia	d.	...	...	|	1627	...	|	...	...	1827	...	...	...	|	2027	...	...	...	...	|	2236	2236	...	...	...	...
	Civitavecchia	d.	...	...	1522	1641	...	1722	...	...	1841	...	...	...	1922	2041	...	...	...	...	2131	2250	2250	...	...	...	...
	Santa Marinella	d.	...	...	|	1648	...	|	...	...	1848	...	...	...	|	2048	...	...	...	...	|	2257	2257	...	...	...	...
	Ladispoli-Cerveteri	d.	...	...	|	1704	...	|	...	...	1904	...	...	...	|	2104	...	...	...	...	|	2312	2312	...	...	...	...
	Roma Ostiense	a.	...	...	1600	1737	...	1800	...	...	1937	...	...	...	2000	2137	...	...	...	...	2214	2339	2339	...	...	...	...
	Roma Termini	a.	...	...	1614	1750	...	1814	...	...	1950	...	...	...	2014	2150	...	...	...	...	2228	2354	2357t	...	...	...	...
	Napoli Centrale **640**	a.	...	...	...	...	...	2036	...	...	...	...	...	...	2236	...	...	...	...	...	...	...	...	...	...	...	...

♦ – **NOTES** (LISTED BY TRAIN NUMBER)

143 – SANREMO – 🛏12 and 🍷 Milano - Genova (**144**) - Nice.
159 – RIVIERA DEI FIORI – 🛏12 and 🍷 Milano - Genova (**160**) - Nice.
503 – BOCCANEGRA – 🛏12 Savona - Napoli.
515 – TIRRENO – 🛏12 and ✕ Ventimiglia - Genova - Roma.
519 – CARIGNANO – 🛏12 and 🍷 Torino - Roma.
523 – CAPODIMONTE – 🛏12 and 🍷 Torino - Salerno.
649 – MAMELI – 🛏12 Milano - Genova (**650**) - Ventimiglia. Train numbers **1535/6** on ©.
691 – ANDREA DORIA – 🛏12 and 🍷 Milano - Genova (**692**) - Ventimiglia.

A – To Albenga.
F – FRECCIA DELLA VERSILIA – 🛏12 Bergamo - Fidenza - Aulla - Pisa.
G – ①②③④⑦ only.
j – 7 minutes later on ⚒.
t – Roma **Tiburtina**.

610 TORINO and MILANO - GENOVA - PISA - ROMA

	Ⓐ	⚒	*E* 1941 ♦	*ICp* 659 [R] 🍷 ♦	*ICp* 539 [R] ✕ ♦		2	*ICp* 661 [R]	*ICp* 541 [R]	ⒸA	Ⓐ	2 ⑤q	*ICp* 663 [R]	*ICp* 543 [R] Ⓑp	2	*ICp* 665 [R] 🍷	V	*ICN* 761 ♦	*ICp* 667 [R] 🍷 ♦	2	*E* 809 ♦		2	*ICp* 1571 [R] †	
Torino Porta Nuova 619 d.	...	...	1655	...	1705	...	1720	...	1805	...	...	...	...	1905	1920	...	...	2050	...	2120	2155	...	2225	...	...
Asti **619** d.	...	...	1730	...	1743	...	1806	...	1843	...	...	...	...	1943	2006	...	...	2126	...	2206	2237	...	2317	...	...
Alessandria **619** d.	...	...	1750	...	1802	...	1831	...	1902	...	...	...	...	2002	2033	...	...	2146	...	2230	2300	...	2339	...	...
Novi Ligure d.	...	...	|	...	|	...	1847	...	1915	...	...	...	...	|	2049	...	...	2159	...	2247	|	...	2355	...	...
Milano Centrale d.	1625	1635	|	1700	|	1705	|	1800	|	1825	1825	1853g	1905	|	|	2010	2025	|	2105	|	|	2225	|	...	...
Pavia d.	1700	1712	|	1736	|	|	|	1835	|	1902	1904	|	1935	|	|	2035	2059	|	2135	|	|	2300	|	...	...
Voghera **619** d.	1716	1733	|	1751	|	|	|	1851	|	1918	1922	|	1951	|	|	2055	2115	|	2151	|	|	2316	|	...	...
Tortona **619** d.	1729	1745	|	|	|	|	|	1903	|	1930	1936	|	|	|	|	|	2127	|	|	|	|	2329	|	...	...
Genova Piazza Principe 619 a.	1818	...	1837	1842	1849	|	1934	1945	1953	2025	2028	|	2042	2049	2135	2148	2217	2237	2242	2333	2350	0030	0052	...	...
Genova Piazza Principe d.	|	...	1840	...	1852	|	1937	1948	1957	...	|	|	|	2052	2137	2151	...	2240	...	2334	2353	...	0054	...	...
Genova Brignole d.	1829	...	1849	...	1900	|	1948	1958	2003	...	2037	|	2051	2100	2143	2200	...	2249	...	2340	0002	...	0100	...	...
Santa Margherita-Portofino d.	...	...	|	...	|	|	2031	2022	...	...	...	|	...	|	...	2221	...	|	...	...	|	...	...	...	...
Rapallo d.	...	...	|	...	1923	w	2035	2027	...	...	...	w	...	2123	...	2226	...	|	...	...	0028	...	...	...	...
Chiavari d.	...	...	|	...	1932	|	2045	2036	...	...	...	|	...	2133	...	2235	...	|	...	...	0038	...	...	...	...
Sestri-Levante d.	...	...	|	...	|	|	2054	2044	...	...	...	|	...	2141	...	2246	...	|	...	...	|	...	...	...	...
Levanto d.	...	...	|	...	|	|	2126	2058	...	...	...	|	...	|	...	2300	...	|	...	...	|	...	...	...	...
Riomaggiore d.	...	...	|	...	|	|	2156	|	...	...	...	|	...	|	...	|	...	|	...	...	|	...	...	...	...
La Spezia Centrale d.	...	...	1955	...	2006	|	2204	2119	...	...	...	|	...	2212	...	2319	...	2358	...	...	0127	...	...	...	...
Sarzana d.	...	...	|	...	|	2044	...	|	...	...	...	2241	...	2225	...	...	...	|	...	...	|	...	...	...	...
Carrara-Avenza d.	...	...	|	...	|	2052	...	|	...	...	...	2249	...	2234	...	...	...	|	...	...	|	...	...	...	...
Massa Centro d.	...	...	|	...	|	2059	...	2141	...	...	...	2257	...	2241	...	...	...	|	...	...	|	...	...	...	...
Viareggio d.	...	...	|	...	2038	2119	...	2156	...	...	...	2318	...	2254	...	...	...	0030	...	...	|	...	...	...	...
Pisa Centrale d.	...	...	2047	...	2056	2138	...	2215	...	...	...	2337	...	2313	...	...	...	0050	...	...	0219	...	...	...	...
Firenze SMN **614** a.	...	...	|	...	2200	|	...	|	...	...	...	|	...	|	...	...	...	|	...	...	|	...	...	...	...
Livorno Centrale d.	...	...	2104	...	...	2153	...	2230	...	...	...	2353	...	2329	...	...	...	0107	...	...	0240	...	...	0527	...
Rosignano d.	...	...	|	...	...	...	...	...	...	...	...	...	...	...	...	...	...	|	...	...	|	...	...	|	...
Cecina d.	...	...	|	...	...	...	...	...	...	...	...	...	...	...	...	...	...	|	...	...	|	...	...	0550	...
Campiglia Marittima d.	...	...	|	...	...	...	...	...	...	...	...	...	...	...	...	...	...	|	...	...	|	...	...	0612	...
Follonica d.	...	...	|	...	...	...	...	...	...	...	...	...	...	...	...	...	...	|	...	...	|	...	...	0628	...
Grosseto d.	...	...	2210	...	...	...	...	...	...	...	...	...	...	...	...	...	...	0217	...	...	0358	...	...	0655	...
Orbetello d.	...	...	...	...	...	...	...	...	...	...	...	...	...	...	...	...	...	|	...	...	|	...	...	0713	...
Tarquinia d.	...	...	...	...	...	...	...	...	...	...	...	...	...	...	...	...	...	|	...	...	|	...	...	|	...
Civitavecchia d.	...	...	...	...	...	...	...	...	...	...	...	...	...	...	...	...	...	|	...	...	0455	...	...	0752	...
Santa Marinella d.	...	...	...	...	...	...	...	...	...	...	...	...	...	...	...	...	...	|	...	...	|	...	...	|	...
Ladispoli-Cerveteri d.	...	...	...	...	...	...	...	...	...	...	...	...	...	...	...	...	...	|	...	...	|	...	...	|	...
Roma Ostiense a.	...	...	...	...	...	...	...	...	...	...	...	...	...	...	...	...	...	|	...	...	|	...	...	0831	...
Roma Termini a.	...	...	...	...	...	...	...	...	...	...	...	...	...	...	...	...	...	|	...	...	0551	...	...	0844	...
Napoli Centrale **640** a.	...	...	...	...	...	...	...	...	...	...	...	...	...	...	...	...	...	0558f	...	...	0911	...	...	1114	...

	2		*E* 806 ♦	2	*ICp* 648 [R]	*ICp* 500 [R]	*ICp* 652 [R] 🍷 ♦	V	*ICp* 502 [R]	⚒	*ICp* 654 [R]	*ICN* 768 ♦		*E* 1940 ♦		*ICp* 504 [R] ⚒	*ICp* 656 [R]	2	*ICp* 506 [R] ✕ ♦	*ICp* 658 [R] 🍷 ♦	P	2	2 †		*ICp* 662 [R]
Napoli Centrale **640** d.	...	...	2108	...	...	...	...	...	...	...	...	...	...	...	...	...	...	...	...	...	...	...	...	...	...
Roma Termini d.	...	...	2350	...	...	...	...	...	...	...	...	...	...	...	...	...	...	...	...	...	...	...	...	0609	...
Roma Ostiense d.	...	...	|	...	...	...	...	...	...	...	...	...	...	...	...	...	...	...	...	...	...	...	...	0619	...
Ladispoli-Cerveteri d.	...	...	|	...	...	...	...	...	...	...	...	...	...	...	...	...	...	...	...	...	...	...	...	0649	...
Santa Marinella d.	...	...	|	...	...	...	...	...	...	...	...	...	...	...	...	...	...	...	...	...	...	...	...	0705	...
Civitavecchia d.	...	...	0052	...	...	...	...	...	...	...	...	...	...	...	...	...	...	...	...	...	...	...	...	0715	...
Tarquinia d.	...	...	|	...	...	...	...	...	...	...	...	...	...	...	...	...	...	...	...	...	...	...	...	0729	...
Orbetello d.	...	...	|	...	...	...	...	...	...	...	...	...	...	...	...	...	...	0559a	...	...	...	...	...	0802	...
Grosseto d.	...	...	0154	...	...	...	...	...	...	...	...	...	...	...	...	...	...	0628	...	...	...	0755	...	0828	...
Follonica d.	...	...	|	...	...	...	...	...	...	...	...	...	...	...	...	...	...	0654	...	...	...	0826	...	0854	...
Campiglia Marittima d.	...	...	|	...	...	...	...	...	...	...	...	...	...	...	...	...	...	0707	...	...	...	0840	...	0905	...
Cecina d.	...	...	|	...	...	...	...	...	...	...	...	...	...	...	...	...	...	0732	...	...	...	0908	...	0928	...
Rosignano d.	...	...	|	...	...	...	...	...	...	...	...	...	...	...	...	...	...	0740	...	...	...	0916	...	0936	...
Livorno Centrale d.	...	...	0311	...	...	...	...	...	...	...	0526	0542	...	0534s	0550	0632	...	0811	...	...	...	0937	...	1000	...
Firenze SMN **614** d.	...	...	|	...	...	...	...	...	...	...	|	|	...	|	|	|	...	|	0751	...	...	|	...	|	...
Pisa Centrale d.	...	...	0328	...	...	...	...	...	...	...	0544	0600	...	0552s	0608	0649	...	0826	0902	...	...	0957	...	1015	...
Viareggio d.	...	...	|	...	...	...	...	...	...	...	0601	0618	...	|	0626	0706	...	...	0919	...	...	▬	...	...	...
Massa Centro d.	...	...	|	...	...	...	...	...	...	...	0616	|	...	|	0650	0719	...	...	|	...	...	...	...	...	...
Carrara-Avenza d.	...	...	|	...	...	...	...	...	...	...	|	|	...	|	0656	0726	...	...	|	...	...	...	...	...	...
Sarzana d.	...	...	|	...	...	...	...	...	...	0606	|	0642	...	|	0705	0735	...	...	|	...	...	...	...	...	...
La Spezia Centrale d.	...	...	0416	...	0502	...	...	...	...	0627	0640	0701	...	0708s	|	0750	...	...	0953	...	1000	...	...	...	1040
Riomaggiore d.	...	...	|	...	|	...	...	...	...	|	|	|	...	|	|	|	...	...	|	...	1009	...	...	...	|
Levanto d.	...	...	|	...	0525	...	...	...	...	0644	0701	|	...	|	|	|	...	...	|	...	1023	...	...	...	1101
Sestri-Levante d.	...	0434	|	...	0541	...	...	...	...	0701	0716	|	...	|	|	0818	...	...	|	...	1043	...	...	...	1116
Chiavari d.	...	0445	0510	...	0552	...	...	...	...	0711	0724	|	...	|	|	0827	...	...	1027	...	1053	...	...	...	1124
Rapallo d.	...	0453	0520	...	0601	...	...	...	...	0721	0733	|	...	|	w	0836	...	...	1036	...	1101	...	...	...	1133
Santa Margherita-Portofino d.	...	0457	|	...	0607	...	...	...	...	0726	0739	|	...	|	|	|	...	...	|	...	1105	...	...	...	|
Genova Brignole d.	...	0536	0555	0617	0635	0657	...	...	0757	0804	0810	0835	...	0853s	|	0902	0910	...	1102	...	1142	...	...	...	1210
Genova Piazza Principe a.	...	0542	0601	|	0641	|	...	...	|	0810a	0816	0841	...	0859s	|	0908	|	...	1108	...	...	⚒	...	...	1216
Genova Piazza Principe 619 d.	0543	0545	0604	0625	0644	0708	0719	0758	0808	...	0819	0844	...	0902s	|	0912	0919	...	1112	1119	...	1125	1145	...	1219
Tortona **619** d.	|	0634	|	|	|	|	|	0844	|	...	0859	|	...	|	|	|	|	...	|	|	...	1233	1233	...	|
Voghera **619** d.	|	0646	|	|	0734	|	0808	0856	|	...	0912	|	...	|	|	|	1008	...	|	1208	...	1246	1246	...	1308
Pavia d.	|	0707	|	|	0751	|	0825	0912	|	...	0928	|	...	|	|	|	1025	...	|	1225	...	1302	1302	...	1325
Milano Centrale a.	|	0740	|	|	0820	|	0855	0945	|	...	0955	|	...	|	1025	|	1055	...	|	1255	...	1335	1335	...	1355
Novi Ligure d.	0635	...	|	0707	...	0741	...	...	0841	...	...	0925	...	|	...	|	...	...	|	...	...	...	...	...	...
Alessandria **619** d.	0657	...	0705	0726	...	0757	...	...	0857	...	...	0941	...	0946s	...	0957	...	...	1157	...	...	...	...	...	...
Asti **619** d.	0720	...	0731	0751	...	0816	...	...	0916	...	...	1002	...	1008s	...	1016	...	...	1216	...	...	...	...	...	...
Torino Porta Nuova 619 a.	0810	...	0820	0840	...	0855	...	...	0955	...	...	1045	...	1110	...	1055	...	...	1255	...	...	...	...	...	...

♦ – **NOTES** (LISTED BY TRAIN NUMBER)

506 – DONATELLO – [12] and ✕ Firenze (**505**) - Pisa - Torino.
539 – DONATELLO – [12] and ✕ Torino - Pisa (**540**) - Firenze.
652 – MAZZINI – ⚒: [12] and 🍷 Ventimiglia (**651**) - Genova - Milano.
658 – CRISTOFORO COLOMBO – [12] and 🍷 Ventimiglia (**657**) - Genova - Milano.
659 – CRISTOFORO COLOMBO – [12] and 🍷 Milano - Genova (**660**) - Ventimiglia.
667 – MAZZINI – [12] and 🍷 Milano - Genova (**668**) - Ventimiglia.
761 – SCILLA – 🛏 1, 2 cl., ▬ 2 cl. and [12] Torino - Reggio; ▬ 2 cl. (4 berth) and [2] Torino - Lamezia (**763**) - Reggio.
768 – SCILLA – 🛏 1, 2 cl., ▬ 2 cl. and [12] Reggio - Torino; ▬ 2 cl. (4 berth) and [2] Reggio (**766**) - Lamezia - Torino.
806 – 🛏 1, 2 cl. (Excelsior), 🛏 1, 2 cl. (T2), 🛏 1, 2 cl., ▬ 2 cl. (4/6 berth) and [2] Napoli - Torino.
809 – 🛏 1, 2 cl. (Excelsior), 🛏 1, 2 cl. (T2), 🛏 1, 2 cl., ▬ 2 cl. (4/6 berth) and [2] Torino - Napoli.
1940 – TRENO DEL SOLE – 🛏 1, 2 cl. and ▬ 2 cl. (4 berth) Palermo - Torino; 🛏 1, 2 cl. and ▬ 2 cl. (4 berth) Siracusa (**1942**) - Messina - Torino.
1941 – TRENO DEL SOLE – 🛏 1, 2 cl. and ▬ 2 cl. (4 berth) Torino - Palermo; 🛏 1, 2 cl. and ▬ 2 cl. (4 berth) Torino - Messina (**1945**) - Siracusa.

A – To Albenga.
P – [12] Parma - Aulla - La Spezia - Genova. Runs up to 7 minutes later Sestri-Levante - Genova on ②③.
V – From / to Ventimiglia.

a – Ⓐ only.
f – Napoli **Campi Flegrei**.
g – Milano **Porta Garibaldi**.
p – Not Apr. 12, 25, and days before holidays.
q – Also Apr. 30, June 1; not May 1, 29.
s – Stops to set down only.
w – Via Fidenza and Aulla.

ROMA - PISA - GENOVA - MILANO and TORINO 610

	2	ICp 514 [R] 🍷	EC 140 [R] 🍷 ♦	2	Ⓐ	⚒	†	ICp 606 [R]			ICp 516 [R] 🍷 ♦	A		ICp 518 [R] Ⓐ	ICp 664 [R] 🍷			ICp 520 [R] 🍷	ICp 694 [R] 🍷 ♦		ICp 524 [R] ⚒		ICp 666 [R]			⚒
Napoli Centrale **640** d.	...	...	...	...	...	...	...	...	...	...	0730	...	...	...	...	...	...	0924	...	...	...	...	...	...	...	...
Roma Termini d.	...	0735	...	...	...	...	...	...	...	...	0946	...	...	...	...	1009	...	1146	...	...	...	...	...	1209	...	...
Roma Ostiense d.	...	0745	...	...	...	...	...	...	...	...	0957	...	...	...	...	1019	...	1157	...	...	...	...	...	1219	...	...
Ladispoli-Cerveteri d.	...	|	...	...	...	...	...	...	...	...	|	...	...	...	...	1049	...	|	...	...	...	...	...	1249	...	...
Santa Marinella d.	...	|	...	...	...	...	...	...	...	...	|	...	...	...	...	1105	...	|	...	...	...	...	...	1305	...	...
Civitavecchia d.	...	0825	...	...	...	...	...	...	...	...	1037	...	...	...	...	1115	...	1237	...	...	...	...	...	1315	...	...
Tarquinia d.	...	|	...	...	...	...	...	...	...	...	|	...	...	...	...	1129	...	|	...	...	...	...	...	1329	...	...
Orbetello d.	...	0901	...	...	...	...	...	...	...	...	|	...	...	...	...	1202	...	|	...	...	...	...	...	1402	...	...
Grosseto d.	...	0922	...	...	...	...	...	...	...	...	1130	...	...	...	...	1228	...	1329	...	...	...	...	...	1428	...	...
Follonica d.	...	0944	...	...	...	...	...	...	...	...	1151	...	...	...	...	1254	...	|	...	...	...	...	...	1454	...	...
Campiglia Marittima d.	...	0955	...	...	...	...	...	...	...	...	|	...	...	...	...	1305	...	1358	...	...	...	...	...	1505	...	...
Cecina d.	...	1016	...	...	...	...	...	...	...	...	|	...	...	...	...	1328	...	|	...	...	...	...	...	1528	...	...
Rosignano d.	...	|	...	...	...	...	...	...	...	...	|	...	...	...	...	1336	...	|	...	...	...	...	...	1536	...	...
Livorno Centrale d.	...	1042	...	...	...	...	...	1126	1223	...	1242	...	...	...	1326	1400	1423	1442	...	...	...	...	...	1600	1623	...
Firenze SMN **614** d.	...	|	...	...	...	...	...	|	|	...	|	...	...	...	|	|	|	|	...	...	...	...	...	|	|	...
Pisa Centrale d.	...	1100	...	...	...	1033	1110	1144	1241	...	1300	...	...	...	1344	1415	1441	1500	...	...	...	...	...	1615	1641	...
Viareggio d.	...	1117	...	...	...	1053	1131	1202	1301	...	|	...	...	...	1402	...	1501	1517	...	...	...	...	...	▬	1701	...
Massa Centro d.	...	1131	...	...	...	1111	1149	|	1319	...	1327	...	←	...	1416	...	1519	|	...	...	...	...	...	...	1719	...
Carrara-Avenza d.	...	|	...	...	...	1121	1155	1219	1327	...	|	...	1327	...	|	...	1527	1533	...	...	...	←	...	...	1726	...
Sarzana d.	...	|	...	...	...	1144	1204	|	→	...	|	...	1336	...	|	...	1536	|	...	...	...	1537	...	...	1735	...
La Spezia Centrale d.	...	1153	...	...	...	1223	1223	1240	▬	...	1353	...	1401	...	1440	...	→	1553	...	...	...	1601	1640	...	→	...
Riomaggiore d.	...	|	...	...	...	1231	1231	|	...	...	|	...	1409	...	|	...	▬	|	...	...	...	1609	|	...	▬	...
Levanto d.	...	|	...	...	...	1245	1245	1301	...	...	|	...	1423	...	1501	...	...	|	...	...	...	1633	1701	...	...	...
Sestri-Levante d.	...	|	...	...	...	1305	1305	1316	...	...	|	...	1444	...	1516	...	...	1622	...	...	...	1704	1716	...	...	...
Chiavari d.	...	1227	...	...	...	1315	1315	1324	...	...	1427	...	1454	...	1524	...	...	|	...	...	...	1714	1724	...	...	...
Rapallo d.	...	|	...	...	...	1323	1323	1333	←	←	1436	...	1502	...	1533	...	...	|	...	...	...	1722	1733	...	...	...
Santa Margherita-Portofino d.	...	|	...	...	...	1327	1327	1339	⚒	†	|	...	1506	...	1539	...	2	|	...	...	...	1727	1739	←	...	...
Genova Brignole d.	1217	1302	...	1325	1336	1413	1413	1410	1416	1416	1502	...	1545	1557	1610	...	1617	1702	...	...	1757	1812	1810	1816	†	1917
Genova Piazza Principe a.	|	1308	...	|	|	→	→	1416	1422	1422	1508	...	1551	|	1616	...	|	1708	...	...	|	→	1816	1822	A	|
Genova Piazza Principe 619 d.	1225	1312	1319	1333	1345	...	...	1419	1425	1425	1512	1546	...	1608	1619	...	1625	1712	1719	1745	1808	...	1819	1825	1935	1925
Tortona **619** d.	|	|	|	|	1433	...	...	|	|	|	|	1634	...	|	1700	...	|	|	|	1833	|	...	1859	|	2026	2026
Voghera **619** d.	|	|	1408	|	1446	...	...	1508	|	|	|	1647	...	|	|	...	|	|	1808	1846	|	...	|	|	2038	2038
Pavia d.	|	|	1425	|	1502	...	...	1525	|	|	|	1703	...	|	1725	...	|	|	1825	1902	|	...	1925	|	2055	2055
Milano Centrale a.	|	|	1450	|	1535	...	...	1555	|	|	|	1737	...	|	1755	...	|	|	1850	1938	|	...	1955	|	2130	2130
Novi Ligure d.	1309	|	...	1414	...	...	...	...	1509	1509	|	...	...	1641	...	...	1709	|	...	...	1841	...	...	1909	...	...
Alessandria **619** d.	1329	1357	...	1429	...	...	...	...	1529	1529	1557	...	...	1657	...	...	1729	1757	...	...	1857	...	...	1929	...	...
Asti **619** d.	1351	1416	...	1451	...	...	...	...	1551	1551	1616	...	...	1716	...	...	1751	1816	...	...	1916	...	...	1951	...	...
Torino Porta Nuova 619 a.	1440	1455	...	1540	...	...	...	...	1640	1640	1655	...	...	1755	...	...	1840	1855	...	...	1955	...	...	2040	...	...

	ESc 9798 [R] 🍷	ICp 670 [R] ♦	2		⑦t	ICp 1534 [R] 🍷 Ⓒ	ICp 672 [R]		F		ICp 538 [R] 🍴 ♦	EC 148 [R] 🍷 ♦	A				ES 9308 [R] 🍷	2		ICp 542 [R] 🍷 ♦		IC 546 🍷 Ⓑp	IC 1572 ⑥q		2	2
Napoli Centrale **640** d.	1124	...	...	...	...	...	...	...	...	...	1324	...	...	...	...	...	...	...	...	...	...	1724	1724	...	...	...
Roma Termini d.	1346	...	...	...	...	...	...	1409	...	...	1546	...	...	1609	...	...	1800	...	...	1746	1809	1946	1946	2009	2109	2209
Roma Ostiense d.	1357	...	...	...	...	...	...	1419	...	...	1557	...	...	1619	...	...	|	...	...	1757	1820	1957	1957	2019	2120	2220
Ladispoli-Cerveteri d.	|	...	...	...	...	...	...	1449	...	...	|	...	...	1649	...	...	|	...	...	|	1849	|	|	2049	2151	2257
Santa Marinella d.	|	...	...	...	...	...	...	1505	...	...	|	...	...	1705	...	...	|	...	...	|	1905	|	|	2105	2207	2312
Civitavecchia d.	1437	...	...	...	...	...	...	1515	...	...	1637	...	...	1715	...	...	|	...	...	1837	1915	2038	2037	2115	2216	2321
Tarquinia d.	|	...	...	...	...	...	...	1529	...	...	|	...	...	1729	...	...	|	...	...	|	1929	|	|	2129	2229	2333e
Orbetello d.	|	...	...	...	...	...	...	1602	...	...	|	...	...	1802	...	...	|	...	...	|	2002	2113	2113	2202	2302	0006e
Grosseto d.	1529	...	...	...	...	1604	1610	1628	...	1650	1729	...	...	1828	...	...	|	...	...	1934	2028	2131	2131	2228	2329	0033e
Follonica d.	1551	...	...	...	...	1625	1632	1654	...	1714	|	...	...	1854	...	...	|	...	...	|	2054	2153	2153	2254	...	...
Campiglia Marittima d.	|	...	...	...	...	1636	1643	1705	...	1725	|	...	...	1905	...	←	|	...	...	2001	2105	2205	2205	2305	...	...
Cecina d.	|	...	...	...	...	1655	1702	1728	...	1752	1816	...	...	1927	...	1927	|	...	...	2018	2128	2222	2222	2328	...	...
Rosignano d.	|	...	...	...	...	|	|	1736	...	1800	|	...	...	→	...	1936	|	...	...	|	2136	|	|	2336	...	...
Livorno Centrale d.	1642	...	...	...	1705	1718	1726	1800	...	1828	1842	...	...	▬	1850	2000	2013	...	...	2044	2200	2247	2245	0001	...	...
Firenze SMN **614** d.	|	...	...	...	|	|	|	|	...	|	|	...	...	...	|	|	|	...	...	|	|	|	...	|	...	...
Pisa Centrale d.	1700	...	...	...	1722	1736	1744	1815	1820	1846	1900	...	...	...	1909	2015	2027	...	...	2102	2220	2304	...	0015	...	...
Viareggio d.	1717	...	...	...	1740	1753	1802	...	1837	1906	1917	...	...	...	1928	▬	|	...	...	2119	▬	2321	...	...	...	...
Massa Centro d.	1731	...	...	...	1757	1813	1816	...	1856	1925	|	...	...	←	1945	...	|	...	...	2134	...	2334	...	...	...	...
Carrara-Avenza d.	|	...	...	←	1803	1820	|	...	1902	1932	|	...	...	1932	1952	...	|	...	...	|	...	2340	...	...	...	...
Sarzana d.	|	...	...	1736	1812	|	|	...	1909	→	|	...	...	1940	2002	...	|	...	...	|	2	2349	...	...	...	...
La Spezia Centrale d.	1753	...	1713	1801	|	1840	1840	...	▬	...	1953	...	...	2001	|	...	2107	...	2116	2200	2222	0006	...	...	...	...
Riomaggiore d.	|	...	1722	1809	|	|	|	...	...	...	|	...	...	2009	|	...	|	...	2124	|	2231	|	...	...	...	...
Levanto d.	|	...	1746	1823	|	1901	1901	...	...	...	|	...	...	2022	|	...	|	...	2138	|	2248	|	...	...	...	...
Sestri-Levante d.	|	...	1817	1844	|	1916	1916	...	...	...	|	...	...	2042	|	...	|	...	2159	2228	2308	0040	...	...	...	...
Chiavari d.	|	...	1828	1854	|	1924	1924	...	...	...	2027	...	...	2052	|	...	|	...	2209	2236	2315	...	...	...	...	...
Rapallo d.	1833	...	1840	1902	w	1933	1933	...	...	...	2036	...	...	2103	w	*ICp*	|	...	2216	2245	2323	...	...	...	...	...
Santa Margherita-Portofino d.	|	...	1845	1906	|	1939	1939	...	2	...	|	...	...	2107	|	**1540**	|	...	2220	|	2327	...	...	...	...	...
Genova Brignole d.	1902	...	1935	1945	|	2010	2010	...	2024	...	2102	...	...	2154	|	[R]	2159	2224	2257	2313	0016	...	...	...	...	...
Genova Piazza Principe a.	1908	...	1941	1951	|	2016	2016	...	|	...	2108	...	...	2200	|	†	...	|	...	2319	...	...	...	...	...	...
Genova Piazza Principe 619 d.	1912	1919	1944	...	|	2019	2019	...	2032	...	...	2119	2149	...	|	2227	...	2232	...	...	...	...	...	...	...	...
Tortona **619** d.	|	2000	2032	...	|	|	|	...	|	...	...	|	2236	...	|	|	...	|	...	...	...	...	...	...	...	...
Voghera **619** d.	|	|	2045	...	|	2108	2108	...	|	...	...	2208	2247	...	|	2316	...	|	...	...	...	...	...	...	...	...
Pavia d.	|	2025	2102	...	|	2125	2125	...	|	...	...	2225	2303	...	|	2333	...	|	...	...	...	...	...	...	...	...
Milano Centrale a.	|	2050	2140	...	2202g	2155	2155	...	|	...	...	2250	2335	...	2320	2359	...	|	...	...	...	...	...	...	...	...
Novi Ligure d.	|	...	...	...	...	...	...	...	2114	...	...	...	...	...	...	...	...	2313	...	...	...	...	...	...	...	...
Alessandria **619** d.	1957	...	...	...	...	...	...	...	2134	...	...	...	...	...	...	...	...	2331	...	...	...	...	...	...	...	...
Asti **619** d.	2016	...	...	...	...	...	...	...	2155	...	...	...	...	...	...	...	...	2351	...	...	...	...	...	...	...	...
Torino Porta Nuova 619 a.	2055	...	...	...	...	...	...	...	2240	...	...	...	...	...	...	...	...	0040	...	...	...	...	...	...	...	...

♦ – **NOTES** (LISTED BY TRAIN NUMBER)

140 – RIVIERA DEI FIORI – [12] and 🍷 Nice (**139**) - Genova - Milano.
148 – SANREMO – [12] and 🍷 Nice (**147**) - Genova - Milano.
516 – CAPODIMONTE – [12] and 🍷 Salerno - Torino.
538 – TIRRENO – [12] and 🍴 Napoli - Ventimiglia.
542 – BOCCANEGRA – [12] and 🍷 Roma - Genova - Savona.
670 – MAMELI – [12] Ventimiglia (**669**) - Genova - Milano. Train number **1537/8** on Ⓒ.
694 – ANDREA DORIA – [12] and 🍷 Ventimiglia (**693**) - Genova - Milano.

A – From Albenga.
F – FRECCIA DELLA VERSILIA – [12] Pisa - Aulla - Fidenza - Bergamo.

e – † only.
g – Milano **Porta Garibaldi**.
p – Not Apr. 12, 25, and days before holidays.
q – Also Apr. 12, 25, and days before holidays.
t – Also Apr. 13, June 2; not Apr. 12, May 31.
w – Via Aulla, Fidenza.

612 PARMA and FIDENZA - SARZANA and LA SPEZIA

Most services 2nd class only

km																											
		⚒				⚒	H	Y	BX	c		⚒		⚒	⚒	⚒	⚒			⚒		F	Ⓐ	⑤j		⚒	†
	Milano Centrale d.	...	...	...	...	...	...	0650	...	...	...	...	...	...	...	...	...	...	...	...	1705	...	...	1853g	...	...	...
0	**Parma** d.	...	...	0512	0617	...	0752	|	...	1116	...	...	1306	...	1345	...	...	*1455*	1638	1715	|	1901	1950	|	2050	2251	2251
*	**Fidenza** d.	...	...	|	|	0736	|	0834	0913	|	...	1242	|	1342	|	...	1447	|	|	|	1843	|	|	2033	|	|	|
23	Fornovo d.	...	...	0530	0638	0753	0819	0900	0930	1136	...	1310	1328	1409	1411	...	1514	*1521*	1709	1743	1905	1919	2014	2103	2113	2310	2313
61	Borgo Val di Taro d.	...	0547	0605	0725	...	0851	0934	0959	1210	1310	...	1409	...	1453	...	...	*1602*	1743	1827	1942	2004	...	2136	2157	2342	2346
79	Pontremoli d.	0545	0603	0628	0745	...	0907	0950	1017	...	1326	...	1426	...	1509	1548	...	1643	1801	...	1959	2023	...	2157	2215	2359	0002
100	Aulla Lunigiana d.	0607	0623	0653	0811	...	0926	1011	1039	...	1352	...	1452	...	...	1613	...	1707	1827	...	2022	2052	...	2219	2235	...	0025
108	San Stefano di Magra d.	0614	0631	0659	0818	...	0933	1019	1047	...	1359	...	1500	...	...	1620	...	1714	1834	...	2032	2059	...	2227	2242	...	0032
116	**Sarzana** a.	|	0640	|	|	...	|	1032	1056	...	|	...	|	...	...	|	...	|	|	...	2043	|	...	2240	|	...	|
	Pisa C 610 a.	|	0737	|	|	...	|	1137	1201	...	|	...	|	...	...	|	...	|	|	...	2135	|	...	2334	|	...	|
	Livorno 610 a.	|	...	|	|	...	|	1157	...	...	|	...	|	...	...	|	...	|	|	...	2153	|	...	2353	|	...	|
120	**La Spezia Centrale** a.	0632	...	0720	0835	...	0946	...	...	...	1418	...	1518	...	...	1638	...	1735	1851	...	...	2113	...	...	2259	...	0048

	⚒	⚒	⚒				H	v	c	⚒		⚒		⚒	⚒		⚒	⚒	⑦w	k	V		B		G	J	
La Spezia Centrale d.	...	...	...	0540	0627	...	0752	1016	1016	...	1220	...	1320	1445	...	1525	1707	...	...	1817	1835	1902	...	...	2102	2108	...
Livorno 610 d.	...	...	...	|	|	0550	|	|	|	...	|	...	|	|	...	|	|	...	1705	|	|	|	...	1850	|	|	...
Pisa C 610 a.	...	...	...	|	|	0608	|	|	|	...	|	...	|	|	...	|	|	...	1722	|	|	|	1820	1909	|	|	...
Sarzana d.	...	...	...	|	|	0705	|	|	|	...	|	...	|	|	...	|	|	...	1812	|	|	|	1910	2002	|	|	2100
San Stefano di Magra d.	...	...	...	0553	0645	0715	0810	1032	1032	...	1236	...	1341	1503	...	1543	1729	...	1823	1834	1852	1919	1924	2013	2113	2119	2126
Aulla Lunigiana d.	...	...	...	0600	0653	0723	0818	1041	1041	...	1245	...	1352	1510	...	1550	1736	...	1830	1842	1859	...	1934	2022	2122	2126	2133
Pontremoli d.	0500	0605	...	0627	0718	0743	0837	1107	1107	...	1314	...	1416	1535	1541	1614	1758	...	1852	1906	1924	...	1957	2043	2144	2145	2156
Borgo Val di Taro d.	0516	0620	...	0642	0736	0759	0853	1124	1125	...	1330	...	1434	...	1603	1630	1817	1907	1907	1922	1945	...	2014	2059	2201	2201	...
Fornovo d.	0600	0700	0703	0722	0818	0839	0926	...	1205	1209	1412	1414	1520	...	1640	1710	...	1948	1951	2015	2021	...	2045	2135	2231	2231	...
Fidenza a.	|	|	0731	|	|	0904	|	...	|	1237	|	1442	|	...	|	|	...	|	2013	|	|	...	2103	2154	|	|	...
Parma a.	0630	0723	...	0745	0840	|	0940	...	1225	...	1434	...	1542	...	1702	1732	...	2015	|	2037	2037	...	...	|	2250	2250	...
Milano Centrale a.	...	...	...	...	...	1025	...	...	...	...	...	...	...	...	...	...	...	...	2202g	...	...	...	...	2320	...	...	...

B – FRECCIA DELLA VERSILIA – (12) Bergamo - Pisa and v.v.
F – (12) Bologna - Parma - La Spezia - Genova.
G – Dec. 14 - Apr. 11: (12) Ventimiglia - La Spezia - Parma.
H – (12) Parma - La Spezia - Genova and v.v.
J – From Apr. 14: (12) (Ⓐ Ventimiglia -) Savona - La Spezia - Parma.
X – Pisa a. 1147 on †.
Y – Pisa a. 1124, Livorno a. 1143 on †.

c – © from Feb. 28.
g – Milano **Porta Garibaldi**.
j – Also Apr. 30, June 1; not May 1, 29.
k – ⚒ (also † until Apr. 11).
v – Ⓐ from Feb. 23.
w – Also Apr. 13, June 2; not Apr. 12, May 31.

* – Fidenza - Fornovo is *25 km*.

613 FIRENZE - SIENA, PISA, PISA AEROPORTO ✈ and LIVORNO

Most services 2nd class only

km																												
		⚒		⚒						⚒	D					†	⚒	⚒		⚒							⚒	
0	**Firenze SMN 614** d.	0430	0535	...	0610	0628	0637	0727	...	0732	0751	0757	0810	0805	0827	0850	0857	0910	0927	1010	1027	1037	1057	...	1110	1127	1157	1210
34	Empoli d.	0506	0602	0627	0647	0655	0714	0759	0806	0808	0820	0830	0840	0845	0859	0927	0930	0940	0959	1040	1059	1114	1130	...	1140	1159	1230	1240
	Poggibonsi d.	|	|	0705	|	0729	|	|	0848	|	|	|	0915	|	|	|	|	1015	|	1115	|	|	|	...	1215	|	|	1315
	Siena a.	|	|	0731	|	0752	|	|	0914	|	|	|	0938	|	|	|	|	1038	|	1138	|	|	|	...	1238	|	|	1338
81	**Pisa Centrale 614** ¶ d.	0555	0643	...	0732	...	0802	0834	...	0901t	0859	0906	...	0925	0934	1013	1020t	...	1034	...	1134	1202	1206	...	...	1234	1306	...
	Pisa Aeroporto ✈ ¶ a.	|	|	...	...	...	0807	|	...	0906	...	...	...	0930	|	...	1025	...	|	...	|	1207	...	...	...	|	...	...
101	**Livorno** a.	0612	0656	...	...	...	...	0849	...	...	...	...	...	...	0949	...	...	...	1049	...	1149	...	...	...	...	1249	...	...

km																												
					⚒	⚒								⚒					⚒	⚒z						Ⓐ		
	Firenze SMN 614 d.	1227	...	1257	1310	1327	...	1337	1357	1410	...	1427	1457	1510	1527	...	1537	1557	1610	1627	1657	1710	1727	1737	1757	1810	1827	1857
0	Empoli d.	1259	1308	1330	1340	1359	1408	1414	1430	1440	...	1459	1530	1540	1559	1608	1614	1630	1640	1659	1730	1740	1759	1814	1830	1840	1859	1930
38	Poggibonsi d.	|	1349	|	1415	|	1449	|	|	1515	...	|	|	1615	|	1649	|	|	1715	|	|	1815	|	|	|	1915	|	|
63	**Siena** a.	|	1414	|	1438	|	1514	|	|	1538	...	|	|	1638	|	1714	|	|	1738	|	|	1838	|	|	|	1938	|	|
	Pisa Centrale 614 ¶ d.	1334	...	1406	...	1434	...	1504	1506	...	...	1534	1606	...	1634	...	1659	1706	...	1734	1806	...	1834	1904	1906	...	1934	2006
	Pisa Aeroporto ✈ ¶ a.	|	...	...	...	|	...	|	...	...	...	|	...	...	|	...	...	...	...	|	...	...	|	|	...	...	|	...
	Livorno a.	1349	...	...	...	1449	...	1520	...	...	...	1549	...	...	1649	...	...	...	...	1749	...	...	1849	1922	...	...	1949	...

						⚒							
Firenze SMN 614 d.	1910	1927	1957	...	2010	2027	2037	2057	2127	...	2157	2307	0037
Empoli d.	1940	1959	2030	...	2040	2059	2114	2130	2159	2208	2233	2343	0114
Poggibonsi d.	2015	|	|	...	2115	|	|	|	|	2249	|	|	|
Siena a.	2038	|	|	...	2138	|	|	|	|	2314	|	|	|
Pisa Centrale 614 ¶ d.	...	2034	2109	...	...	2131	2202	2209	2234	...	2322	0032	0159
Pisa Aeroporto ✈ ¶ a.	...	|	|	...	...	...	2207	|	|	...	|	|	...
Livorno a.	...	2049	2124	...	...	...	...	2224	2249	...	2337	0047	...

			⚒					⚒	†	⚒	
Livorno d.	...	0521	...	0620	...	...	...	0711	...	...	0730
Pisa Aeroporto ✈ ¶ d.	...	|	...	|	...	0641	...	|	...	...	|
Pisa Centrale 614 ¶ d.	0415	0539	...	0638	...	0654	...	0729	0729	...	0754
Siena d.	|	|	0550	|	0627	|	0639	|	|	0702	|
Poggibonsi d.	|	|	0615	|	0649	|	0703	|	|	0728	|
Empoli d.	0452	0618	0653	0709	0723	0731	0752	0802	0802	0820	0831
Firenze SMN 614 a.	0527	0652	0728	0737	0750	0803	0828	0833	0833	0855	0903

km																												
		⚒				⚒	†	⚒		⚒			⚒		⚒	⚒			⚒							⚒	†	⚒
	Livorno d.	...	0811	...	...	0911	0911	...	...	1011	...	...	...	1111	...	...	...	1211	...	...	1311	...	...	1343	1411	...	1435	...
0	Pisa Aeroporto ✈ ¶ d.	...	|	...	...	|	|	...	...	|	...	1042	...	|	...	1143	...	|	...	1243	|	...	...	|	|	...	|	...
2	**Pisa Centrale 614** ¶ d.	...	0829	...	...	0929	0929	...	...	1029	1054	1101	...	1129	...	1154	...	1229	...	1254	1329	...	1354	1401	1429	...	1454	1454
	Siena d.	0732	|	0818	0847	|	|	0918	...	|	|	|	1041	|	1118	|	1141	|	1218	|	|	1318	|	|	|	1418	|	|
	Poggibonsi d.	0809	|	0846	0909	|	|	0946	...	|	|	|	1112	|	1146	|	1212	|	1246	|	|	1346	|	|	|	1446	|	|
	Empoli d.	0852	0902	0921	0940	1002	1017	1021	...	1102	1131	1147	1152	1202	1221	1231	1252	1302	1321	1331	1402	1421	1431	1447	1502	1521	1531	1531
	Firenze SMN 614 a.	...	0933	0950	1010	1033	1046	1050	...	1133	1203	1223	...	1233	1250	1303	...	1333	1350	1403	1433	1450	1503	1523	1533	1550	1603	1603

	⚒					⚒									⚒	†		⚒				⚒	D				
Livorno d.	1511	...	1543	...	1611	...	...	1711	...	...	...	1811	...	...	...	...	1911	...	...	2006	...	...	...	...	2111	...	...
Pisa Aeroporto ✈ ¶ d.	|	...	|	...	|	...	...	|	...	...	1753	|	...	...	...	...	|	...	...	|	...	...	...	...	|	...	2220
Pisa Centrale 614 ¶ d.	1529	...	1601	...	1629	...	1654	1729	...	...	1801	1829	...	1854	1901	1913	1929	...	1954	2029	...	2042	2056	2101	2129	...	2230
Siena d.	|	1518	|	...	|	1618	|	|	1718	...	|	|	1818	|	|	|	|	1918	|	|	2018	|	|	|	|	2118	|
Poggibonsi d.	|	1546	|	...	|	1646	|	|	1746	...	|	|	1846	|	|	|	|	1946	|	|	2046	|	|	|	|	2146	|
Empoli d.	1602	1621	1647	...	1702	1721	1731	1802	1821	...	1847	1902	1921	1931	1947	1953	2002	2021	2031	2102	2121	2116	2132	2147	2202	2221	2315
Firenze SMN 614 a.	1633	1650	1723	...	1733	1750	1803	1833	1850	...	1923	1933	1950	2003	2023	2024	2033	2050	2103	2133	2150	2155	2200	2223	2233	2250	2350

D – DONATELLO – (12) and ✕ Firenze (**505/540**) - Pisa (**506/539**) - Torino and v.v.

t – Arrives 10 minutes earlier.
z – Daily from May 31.

¶ – For complete service Pisa - Pisa Aeroporto see Table **614** (page 303).

614 FIRENZE - LUCCA - VIAREGGIO and PISA

Most services 2nd class only

km																									
		⚒	⚒	⚒									†	⚒									⚒	
0	**Firenze SMN 613** d.	0510	...	...	...	0610	0708	...	0808	...	0908	...	1008	...	...	1208	...	and at	1908	...	2008	...	2115	2208
17	Prato Centrale d.	0533	...	...	...	0634	0729	...	0829	...	0929	...	1029	...	...	1229	...	the same	1929	...	2029	...	2138	2229
34	Pistoia d.	0551	...	...	...	0652	0745	...	0845	...	0945	...	1045	...	...	1245	...	minutes	1945	...	2045	...	2153	2245
47	Montecatini Centro d.	0604	...	...	...	0706	0805	...	0905	...	1005	...	1105	...	...	1305	...	past each	2005	...	2105	...	2205	2305
78	Lucca ⊡ d.	0651	0653	0708	0742	0755	0831	0842	0931	0942	1031	1042	1131	1242	1312	1331	1342	hour	2031	2042	2131	2142	2231	2331
101	**Viareggio** a.	0711	|	|	|	|	0849	|	0949	|	1049	|	1149	|	|	1349	|	until	2049	|	2149	|	2249	2349
	Pisa Centrale 613 ⊡ a.	...	0716	0740	0812	0825	...	0912	...	1012	...	1107	...	1312	1342	...	1412		...	2112	...	2212	...	...

⊡ – Additional services operate Lucca - Pisa Centrale on ⚒.

PISA and VIAREGGIO - LUCCA - FIRENZE — 614

Most services 2nd class only

km																									
		⚒																					⚒		
0	**Pisa Centrale 613** . ⊡ d.	0620	...	...	0704	0750	...	0850	...	0950	...	...	1250	...	1343	...	1450	...	and at	1950	...	2050	...	2150	...
	Viareggio d.	|	0630	0714	|	|	0811	|	0911	|	1011	1211	|	1311	|	1411	|	1511	the same	|	2011	|	2111	|	2211
24	Lucca ⊡ d.	0645	0650	0731	0736	0822	0832	0917	0932	1017	1032	1232	1317	1332	1408	1432	1517	1532	minutes	2017	2032	2117	2132	2217	2232
	Montecatini Centro d.	...	0718	0758	...	...	0857	...	0957	...	1057	1257	...	1357	...	1457	...	1557	past each	...	2057	...	2158	...	2257
	Pistoia d.	...	0732	0812	...	...	0912	...	1012	...	1112	1312	...	1412	...	1512	...	1612	hour	...	2112	...	2214	...	2312
	Prato Centrale d.	...	0747	0828	...	...	0928	...	1028	...	1130	1328	...	1428	...	1528	...	1628	until	...	2128	...	2230	...	2328
	Firenze SMN 613 a.	...	0806	0852	...	...	0952	...	1100	...	1159	1352	...	1452	...	1552	...	1652		...	2152	...	2252	...	2350

⊡ – Additional services operate Pisa Centrale - Lucca on ⚒.

¶ – **Full service PISA Centrale - PISA Aeroporto ✈ and v.v.**: *2 km*, journey 5 minutes. Most services 2nd class only.

From **Pisa Centrale**: 0620, 0720, 0750, 0802, 0850, 0901⚒, 0925, 0950, 1020⚒, 1050, 1120, 1202⚒, 1220, 1250, 1320, 1350, 1420, 1450, 1520, 1550, 1620, 1650, 1720, 1742, 1820, 1850, 1920, 1950, 2020, 2050, 2120, 2202.

From **Pisa Aeroporto**: 0641, 0735, 0818, 0835, 0915, 0942⚒, 1005, 1042, 1105, 1135, 1143⚒, 1235, 1243⚒, 1305, 1335, 1405, 1435, 1505, 1535, 1605, 1635, 1705, 1735, 1753, 1835, 1905, 1935, 2005, 2035, 2105, 2135, 2220.

FIRENZE - PERUGIA - FOLIGNO and ROMA — 615

Faster express trains Firenze - Arezzo - Chiusi - Roma are shown in Table 620

km		*ICN* 771	*ES* 9321				*ICp* 579		*EN* 235							*IC* 585					*ICp* 703				*IC* 591	
			[R] 🍷			2	[R] ✕	2				2				🍷					[R] ✕	2	2		✕	2
		♦	⚒	⚒	†	⚒	⚒	⚒	♦	⚒	†	⚒				♦		⚒			♦		⚒		♦	
0	**Firenze SMN** d.	...	...	...	...	...	0550	...	0630	0645	0709	...	0802	0913	...	1027r	...	1102	1113	1213	1227r	1313	...	1413	1427r	1513
88	Arezzo d.	0458	...	...	...	...	0630	...	|	0746	0814	...	0914	1014	...	1106	...	1147	1214	1314	1306	1414	...	1514	1506	1614
106	Castiglion Fiorentino d.	|	...	...	...	...	|	...	|	0759	0827	...	0927	1027	...	|	...	1203	1227	1327	|	1427	...	1527	|	1627
122	Terontola d.	0520	...	...	...	0625	0650	0709	|	0812	0840	0840	0940	1040	...	|	...	1221	1240	1340	|	1440	1445	1540	|	1640
134	Passignano ▲ d.	|	...	...	...	0638	|	0720	|	|	|	0853	0951	|	...	|	...	1234	|	1351	|	|	1458	1551	|	|
165	**Perugia** a.	|	...	...	...	0718	|	0750	|	|	|	0932	1018	|	...	|	...	1301	|	1419	|	|	1533	1619	|	|
165	**Perugia 625** d.	|	0645	0700	0723	0723	|	0751	|	|	|	0934	1020	|	...	|	1118	1303	|	1421	|	|	1540	1621	|	|
176	Ponte San Giovanni d.	|	0654	0710	0733	0734	|	0805	|	|	|	0947	1031	|	...	|	1131	1312	|	1430	|	|	1549	1630	|	|
189	Assisi **625** d.	|	0704	0721	0745	0752	|	0823	|	|	|	0958	1042	|	...	|	1144	1329	|	1441	|	|	1600	1642	|	|
200	Spello d.	|	|	0730	0754	0801	|	0832	|	|	|	1007	1051	|	...	|	1153	1339	|	1457	|	|	1609	1650	|	|
205	**Foligno 625** a.	|	0715	0735	0800	0807	|	0837	|	|	|	1014	1056	|	...	|	1200	1345	|	1502	|	|	1615	1656	|	|
133	Castiglion del Lago d.	|	|	...	|	...	|	...	|	0820	0848	...	...	1048	...	|	|	...	1248	...	|	1448	...	...	|	1648
151	Chiusi ▼ d.	0541	|	...	|	...	0710	...	0732	0838	0903	...	...	1101	...	1145	|	...	1301	...	1345	1515	...	...	1545	1715
191	Orvieto d.	|	|	...	|	...	0731	...	0757	0905	0930	...	...	1127	...	1209	|	...	1327	...	1409	1542	...	...	1609	1742
233	Orte **625** d.	|	0816	...	0936	...	|	...	|	0943	1005	...	...	1202	...	1238	1317	...	1402	...	1438	1617	...	...	1638	1817
311	Roma Tiburtina **625** a.	0656	0849s	...	1011	...	|	...	|	1050	1040	...	...	1244	...	|	1352	...	1437	...	|	1652	...	...	|	1852
316	**Roma Termini 625** a.	...	0859	...	1019	...	0824	...	0905	1100	1051	...	...	1254	...	1316	1403	...	1448	...	1516	1703	...	...	1716	1903

		ES 9333		*IC* 705			*IC* 595					*ICp* 597
		[R] 🍷		✕			🍷					[R]
				♦			♦					♦
Firenze SMN d.	...	...	1613	1627r	1713	1813	1827r	1913	2013	...	2113	2138
Arezzo d.	...	...	1714	1706	1814	1914	1906	2014	2114	...	2214	2223
Castiglion Fiorentino d.	...	...	1727	|	1827	1927	|	2027	2127	...	2227	|
Terontola d.	...	...	1740	|	1840	1940	1927	2040	2140	...	2240	2249
Passignano ▲ d.	...	...	1751	|	|	1951	|	|	2151	...	|	|
Perugia a.	...	...	1819	|	|	2019	|	|	2222	...	|	2316
Perugia 625 d.	1718	1803	1821	|	|	2021	|	|	2227	...	|	2318
Ponte San Giovanni d.	1732	1812	1831	|	|	2030	|	|	2236	...	|	2327
Assisi **625** d.	1745	1822	1843	|	|	2041	|	|	2247	...	|	2336
Spello d.	1754	|	1853	|	|	2050	|	|	2256	...	|	|
Foligno 625 a.	1759	1835	1900	|	|	2056	|	|	2302	...	|	2350
Castiglion del Lago d.	|	|	...	|	1848	...	|	2048	...	...	2248	...
Chiusi ▼ d.	|	|	...	1745	1915	...	1945	2115	...	...	2301	...
Orvieto d.	|	|	...	1809	1942	...	2009	2142	...	...	2327	...
Orte **625** d.	1917	1943	...	1838	2017	...	2038	2217	...	...	0002	...
Roma Tiburtina **625** a.	1952	2014s	...	|	2052	...	|	2252	...	...	0037	...
Roma Termini 625 a.	2003	2024	...	1916	2103	...	2116	2303	...	...	0048	...

		ICp 580								*IC* 582
		[R]	2			2				🍷
	⚒	♦	⚒			⚒				♦
Roma Termini 625 d.	...	...	...	0557	...	...	0657	...	0755	0841
Roma Tiburtina **625** d.	...	...	...	0605	...	...	0705	...	0803	|
Orte **625** d.	...	...	...	0642	...	...	0742	...	0840	0922
Orvieto d.	...	...	...	0716	...	...	0816	...	|	0950
Chiusi ▼ d.	...	...	...	0755	...	...	0855	...	|	1013
Castiglion del Lago d.	...	...	...	0811	...	...	0912	...	|	|
Foligno 625 d.	0526	0600	0640	|	...	0736	|	0918	0956	|
Spello d.	0532	|	0645	|	...	0742	|	0924	1008	|
Assisi **625** d.	0541	0612	0653	|	...	0751	|	0933	1017	|
Ponte S. Giovanni d.	0553	0629	0711	|	...	0804	|	0946	1032	|
Perugia 625 a.	0601	0638	0720	|	...	0812	|	0954	1043	|
Perugia d.	0603	0640	0722	|	...	0814	|	0955	...	|
Passignano ▲ d.	0639	|	0754	|	...	0854	|	1026	...	|
Terontola d.	0656	0710	0807	0820	...	0909	0921	1037	...	|
Castiglion Fiorentino d.	0709	|	...	0833	...	...	0942	|	...	|
Arezzo d.	0727	0735	...	0845	...	...	0957	1100	...	1053
Firenze SMN a.	0835	0817	...	0947	...	...	1047	1147	...	1133r

			IC 704				*IC* 586			*ES* 9328	*ICp* 706			*ICp* 1554		*IC* 592	*ICp* 1588		*ICp* 594				*EN* 234		*ES* 9336	*ICN* 774
			✕				✕			[R] 🍷	[R] ✕		2	[R]		🍷	[R]		[R] ✕	2		2		2	[R] 🍷	
			♦			⚒	♦				♦		⚒	♦		♦	♦		Ⓑ p	⚒		⚒	♦		Ⓑ p	♦
Roma Termini 625 d.	0915	...	1044	1105	...	1157	1244	1257	...	1332	1444	1500	...	...	...	1644	...	1657	1755	...	...	...	1910	1857	2000	...
Roma Tiburtina **625** d.	0913	...	|	1113	...	1205	|	1305	...	1340u	|	1508	...	1532	...	|	1658	1705	|	...	...	...	|	1905	2008u	2236
Orte **625** d.	0950	...	1122	1150	...	1242	1322	1342	...	1411	1522	1546	...	|	...	1722	|	1742	|	...	...	...	|	1942	2045	|
Orvieto d.	1024	...	1150	1224	...	|	1350	1416	...	|	1550	1620	...	1657	...	1750	1801	1816	1848	...	...	...	2002	2016	|	|
Chiusi ▼ d.	1055	...	1213	1255	...	|	1413	1455	...	|	1613	1655	...	1720	...	1813	1827	1855	1912	...	...	...	2025	2055	|	0007
Castiglion del Lago d.	1111	...	|	1311	...	|	|	1511	...	|	|	1711	...	|	...	|	|	1911	|	...	...	...	|	2111	|	|
Foligno 625 d.	|	1103	|	|	1303	1351	|	|	1503	1515	|	|	1625	|	1703	|	|	|	|	1820	1903	1934	|	|	2154	|
Spello d.	|	1109	|	|	1309	1402	|	|	1509	|	|	|	1630	|	1709	|	|	|	|	1830	1909	1940	|	|	|	|
Assisi **625** d.	|	1118	|	|	1318	1412	|	|	1518	1531	|	|	1643	|	1718	|	|	|	|	1843	1918	1949	|	|	2206	|
Ponte San Giovanni d.	|	1130	|	|	1331	1431	|	|	1530	1550	|	|	1656	|	1731	|	|	|	|	1856	1931	2001	|	|	2217	|
Perugia 625 a.	|	1139	|	|	1339	1440	|	|	1538	1558	|	|	1705	|	1739	|	|	|	|	1905	1940	2011	|	|	2226	|
Perugia d.	|	1141	|	|	1341	...	|	|	1539	...	|	|	1707	|	1741	|	|	|	|	...	1942	2020	|	|	...	|
Passignano ▲ d.	|	1208	|	|	1409	...	|	|	1609	...	|	|	1752	|	1809	|	|	|	|	...	2009	2049	|	|	...	|
Terontola d.	1120	1220	|	1320	1420	...	|	1520	1620	...	|	1720	1804	|	1820	|	1844	1920	1931	...	2020	2100	|	2120	...	0025
Castiglion Fiorentino d.	1133	1233	|	1333	1433	...	|	1533	1633	...	|	1733	...	|	1833	|	|	1933	|	...	2033	...	|	2133	...	|
Arezzo d.	1145	1245	1253	1345	1445	...	1453	1545	1645	...	1653	1745	...	1755	1845	1853	1912	1945	1957	...	2045	...	|	2145	...	0047
Firenze SMN a.	1247	1347	1333r	1447	1547	...	1533r	1647	1747	...	1733r	1847	...	1854r	1947	1933r	2015r	2047	2038	...	2147	...	2130	2247	...	0145c

♦ – **NOTES** (LISTED BY TRAIN NUMBER)

234/5 – ALLEGRO TOSCA – 🛏 1,2 cl. (Excelsior), 🛏 1,2 cl., ▬ 2 cl. and [2] Roma - Wien Süd and v.v.; 🛏 1,2 cl. (Excelsior), 🛏 1,2 cl., ▬ 2 cl. and [2] Roma - Bologna (**484/5**) - München and v.v. Supplement payable.

580/97 – TACITO – [12] Terni - Milano and v.v.

582/95 – VESUVIO – [12] and 🍷 Napoli - Milano and v.v.

585/92 – BRERA – [12] and 🍷 Milano - Napoli and v.v.

586/91 – PARTENOPE – [12] and ✕ Napoli - Milano and v.v.

703 – MIRAMARE – [12] and ✕ Trieste (**702**) - Venezia Mestre - Napoli.

704/5 – MATILDE SERAO – [12] and ✕ Napoli - Venezia and v.v.

706 – MIRAMARE – [12] and ✕ Roma (**707**) - Venezia Mestre - Trieste.

771/4 – MARCO POLO – 🛏 1,2 cl., ▬ 2 cl. (4 berth) and [2] Napoli - Udine and v.v.; 🛏 1,2 cl., ▬ 2 cl. (4 berth) and [2] Napoli - Venezia Mestre (**772/3**) - Trieste and v.v.

1554 – CARACCIOLO – ⑦ (also Apr. 13, June 2; not Apr. 12, May 31): [12] Salerno - Milano.

1588 – ASPROMONTE – ⑦ (also Apr. 13, June 2, 7; not Apr. 12, May 31): [12] Reggio - Milano.

c – Firenze **Campo di Marte**.
p – Not Apr. 12, 25, and days before holidays.
r – Firenze **Rifredi**.
s – Stops to set down only.
u – Stops to pick up only.

▲ – Passignano sul Trasimeno.
▼ – Chiusi - Chianciano Terme.

Additional local services are available on ⚒ Firenze - Chiusi and v.v. serving Arezzo, Castiglion Fiorentino, Terontola-Cortona and Castiglion del Lago.

619 MILANO and TORINO - BOLOGNA

Trains with intermediate stops only. Express services shown on Tables 620, 630

km		E 907 ♦	ES 9409 [R]✕	ESc 9775 [R] A	ESc 9761 [R]🍷 ♦	IC 585 🍷	R	†L	⚒L	ES 9459 [R]✕ ♦	ICp 1589 [R] ♦	P	A	ESc 9763 [R]🍷 ♦	ICp 553 [R]✕ ♦	ICp 1545 [R]🍷 ♦	A	IC 591 ✕	†	ESc 9777 [R]🍷 A	A	ICp 1549 [R] ♦	E 823 ♦	ESc 9779 [R]🍷 ♦	ICp 1557 [R] ♦	A
0	**Milano Centrale** d.	...	0545	0600	0700	0705	...	0650	0650	...	0735	0730	...	...	0915	0950	...	1100	...	1200	...	1210	1220	...	1400	...
	Torino P N 610 d.	2250	|	|	|	|	...	|	|	...	|	|	0605	0745	|	|	...	|	...	|	...	|	|	1150	|	...
	Asti **610** d.	2332	|	|	|	|	...	|	|	...	|	|	0651	0819	|	|	...	|	...	|	...	|	|	1230	|	...
	Alessandria **610** d.	2356	|	|	|	|	...	|	|	...	|	|	0716	0839	|	|	...	|	...	|	...	|	|	1250	|	...
	Tortona **610** d.	0014	|	|	|	|	0649	|	|	...	|	|	0750	|	|	|	...	|	...	|	...	|	|	|	|	...
	Voghera **610** d.	0027	|	|	|	|	0703	|	|	...	|	|	0803	0905	|	|	...	|	...	|	...	|	|	1315	|	...
72	Piacenza d.	0105	0629	0645	0740	0750	0754	0805	0810	...	0842	0835	0852	0940	0956	|	1052	1151	1208	1248	1252	1259	1317	1351	1449	1452
107	Fidenza d.	|	0650	|	|	|	0816	0830	0832	0846	0907	0858	0915	|	|	|	1115	|	1232	|	1315	|	|	|	1506	1515
129	Parma d.	|	0703	0713	|	0814	0830	...	...	0901	0921	0911	0930	|	1023	1100	1130	1217	1245	1313	1330	1325	|	1418	1518	1529
157	Reggio Emilia d.	|	0719	0730	|	0829	0847	...	...	|	0938	0927	0947	|	1038	|	1146	1235	1303	1330	1347	1341	|	1433	1533	1545
182	Modena d.	|	0734	0745	|	0842	0901	...	...	0923	0953	0941	1001	|	1053	1130	1200	1248	1319	1345	1401	1355	|	1447	1547	1600
219	**Bologna Centrale** a.	0234	0758	0814	0852	0904	0928	...	...	0950	1022	1012	1028	1052	1114	1150	1228	1309	1346	1411	1428	1421	1445	1511	1612	1628
	Roma Termini **620** a.	...	1058	...	...	1316	...	...	...	1236	1441t	...	...	...	...	...	...	1716	...	...	...	...	2006t	...	1958t	...
	Napoli C **640** a.	...	...	...	...	1550	...	...	...	...	1722	...	...	...	...	...	...	...	...	...	...	...	...	...	2248p	...

km		IC 595 🍷		ESc 9781 [R]🍷 ♦		E 1921 ♦	ESc 9783 [R]🍷 ♦	L	ICp 597 [R] ♦	A		ESc 9785 [R]🍷 A	R	⑤y	E 1991 ♦	ICN 751 ♦	IC 549 ✕ R		E 923 ♦	ESc 9787 [R]🍷 v		ICN 781 ♦	E 833 ♦	E 901 ♦	ICN 785 ♦	E 1911 ♦
	Milano Centrale d.	1500	...	1600	...	1620	1700	1705	1745	...	1820	1900	...	1853g	1943g	2000	2005	...	2040	2100	...	2100	2200	...	2300	2320
0	**Torino P N 610** d.	|	1420	|	...	|	|	|	|	1620	|	|	...	|	|	|	|	1820	|	|	...	|	|	2105	|	|
56	Asti **610** d.	|	1506	|	...	|	|	|	|	1706	|	|	...	|	|	|	|	1906	|	|	...	|	|	2139	|	|
91	Alessandria **610** d.	|	1533	|	...	|	|	|	|	1733	|	|	...	|	|	|	|	1933	|	|	...	|	|	2206	|	|
113	Tortona **610** d.	|	1550	|	...	|	|	|	|	1750	|	|	1850	|	|	|	|	1950	|	|	...	|	|	2222	|	|
130	Voghera **610** d.	|	1603	|	...	|	|	|	|	1803	|	|	1903	|	|	|	|	2003	|	|	...	|	|	2235	|	|
188	Piacenza d.	1548	1643	1645	1652	1705	1745	1812	1845	1852	1912	1945	1952	2004	|	2044	2051	2054	2139	2145	2152	2204	2254	2314	2346	0011
	Fidenza d.	1605	...	|	1715	|	|	1835	|	1915	1937	|	2015	2028	|	|	2112	2119	2158	|	2215	|	2319	|	|	|
	Parma d.	1617	...	1713	1729	1736	1813	...	1911	1928	1951	2013	2030	...	|	|	2124	2131	2217	2211	2230	2243	2333	2351	0018	0101
	Reggio Emilia d.	1631	...	1730	1745	1753	1830	...	1926	1944	2008	2030	2046	...	|	|	2139	2147	2234	2226	2247	2303	2351	0010	0038	|
	Modena d.	1644	...	1745	1759	1808	1845	...	1941	1959	2022	2045	2100	...	2207	|	2152	2201	2250	2241	2304	2318	0008	0027	0055	|
	Bologna Centrale a.	1704	...	1811	1828	|	1911	...	2004	2028	2052	2111	2128	...	2228	2200	2218	2225	2314	2306	2337	2352	0039	0054	0124	|
	Roma Termini **620** a.	2116	...	...	...	2315t	...	...	...	...	...	...	...	...	...	...	...	...	...	...	...	...	0452t	...	...	0723t
	Napoli C **640** a.	2342	...	...	...	...	...	...	...	...	...	...	...	...	...	...	...	...	...	...	...	...	0734	...	...	1012

	E 900 ♦	ICN 780 ♦	E 1910 ♦			ICN 784 ♦	E 830 ♦	E 906 ♦		ESc 9776 [R] Ⓐ	E 926 ♦	IC 550 ✕ R	L	ICN 752 ♦	A	ESc 9778 [R]🍷 A	E 1920 ♦	A	ICp 580 [R] ♦		ESc 9780 [R]🍷 ♦	E 834 ♦	A	IC 582 🍷	A
Napoli C **640** d.	...	...	2030	...	...	...	2150	...	...	...	...	...	...	...	...	...	...	...	...	...	...	...	...	...	...
Roma Termini **620** d.	...	...	2306	...	...	...	0047t	...	...	...	...	...	...	0428t	...	...	0515t	...	...	...	...	0613t	...	0841	...
Bologna Centrale d.	0325	0412	|	0452	0530	0548	0557	0618	0627	0643	0702	0741	...	0756	0830	0856	|	0930	0956	...	1056	1108	1130	1247	1330
Modena d.	|	0435	|	0521	0556	0612	0623	0639	0653	0706	0730	0801	...	|	0856	0915	0927s	0956	1015	...	1115	|	1156	1308	1356
Reggio Emilia d.	|	0453	|	0536	0611	0629	0641	0654	0708	0720	0747	0816	...	|	0910	0929	0944s	1010	1029	...	1130	|	1210	1322	1410
Parma d.	|	0512	0521	0553	0628	0648	0702	0713	0724	0736	|	0833	...	|	0929	0945	0958s	1027	1044	...	1145	|	1227	1337	1427
Fidenza d.	|	|	|	0607	0642	|	|	|	0739	|	|	0845	0907	|	0945	|	|	1040	|	...	|	|	1240	1355	1440
Piacenza d.	0446	0554	0602	0638	0708	0730	0814	0752	0817	0808	0832	0908	0932	0919	1006	1015	1030s	1110	1117	1117	1217	1228	1306	1418	1506
Voghera **610** d.	0524	|	|	0721	|	|	|	0833	0859	|	|	|	|	|	...	|	|	...	|	1159	|	|	...	|	...
Tortona **610** d.	0537	|	|	0736	|	|	|	0847	0912	|	|	|	|	|	...	|	|	...	|	1212	|	|	...	|	...
Alessandria **610** d.	0554	|	|	0800	|	|	|	0905	...	|	|	|	|	|	...	|	|	...	|	1229	|	|	...	|	...
Asti **610** d.	0625	|	|	0822	|	|	|	0927	...	|	|	|	|	|	...	|	|	...	|	1251	|	|	...	|	...
Torino P N 610 a.	0705	|	|	0910	|	|	|	1010	...	|	|	|	|	|	...	|	|	...	|	1340	|	|	...	|	...
Milano Centrale a.	...	0705	0725	...	0800	0820	0920	...	...	0910	0920	1000	1025	1005	...	1100	1130	...	1200	...	1300	1320	...	1500	...

	A	ESc 9782 [R]🍷 ♦	A	ESc 9784 [R]🍷 A		ICp 1550 [R] ⑦j	IC 586 ✕	A	ESc 9786 [R]🍷 ♦		R	ICp 568 [R]✕ ♦	ESc 9766 [R]🍷 ♦	R	L⑦j	ES 9460 [R]✕ ♦	A	ICp 1554 [R] ♦	IC 592 🍷	P	A	L	ES 9498 [R]✕	IC 1588 ♦	ESc 9788 [R]🍷 A
Napoli C **640** d.	...	...	...	...	...	...	1024	...	...	...	...	...	...	...	...	...	...	1259p	1424	...	...	...	...	1442	...
Roma Termini **620** d.	...	...	...	...	...	...	1244	...	...	...	...	...	...	...	...	1545	...	1532t	1644	...	...	...	1822	1658t	...
Bologna Centrale d.	1430	1456	1530	1556	...	1606	1703	1730	1756	...	1830	1856	1908	...	...	1810	1930	2017	2056	2003	2030	...	2110	2137	2156
Modena d.	1456	1515	1556	1615	...	1628	1725	1756	1815	...	1856	1915	|	...	...	1834	1956	2041	2115	2030	2056	...	2131	2205	2215
Reggio Emilia d.	1510	1530	1610	1630	...	1643	1745	1810	1830	...	1910	1929	|	...	...	|	2010	2054	2130	2057	2110	...	2145	2219	2230
Parma d.	1527	1546	1627	1645	...	1659	1800	1827	1845	...	1927	1945	|	...	...	1910	2027	2109	2145	2117	2127	...	2202	2235	2245
Fidenza d.	1540	|	1640	|	...	|	|	1840	|	...	1940	|	|	←	2016	1926	2040	2124	|	2132	2140	2204	2215	2246	|
Piacenza d.	1606	1623	1706	1717	1717	1727	1823	1910	1917	1917	2006	2020	2016	2027	2040	...	2106	2150	2220	2158	2206	2227	2238	2304	2315
Voghera **610** d.	...	1657	...	|	1759	|	|	...	|	1957	→	|	2049	2108	|	...	...	|	|	|	...	|	|	|	|
Tortona **610** d.	...	|	...	|	1812	|	|	...	|	2009	...	|	|	2120	|	...	...	|	|	|	...	|	|	|	|
Alessandria **610** d.	...	1724	...	|	1829	|	|	...	|	2029	...	|	2117	...	|	...	...	|	|	|	...	|	|	|	|
Asti **610** d.	...	1744	...	|	1851	|	|	...	|	2049	...	|	2139	...	|	...	...	|	|	|	...	|	|	|	|
Torino P N 610 a.	...	1825	...	|	1940	|	|	...	|	2140	...	|	2215	...	|	...	...	|	|	|	...	|	|	|	|
Milano Centrale a.	...	...	...	1800	...	1815	1905	...	2000	...	...	2105	...	...	2202g	...	...	2240	2300	2310	...	2320	2320	2350	2359

♦ – **NOTES** (LISTED BY TRAIN NUMBER)

553/68 – MURGE – [12] and ✕ Milano - Taranto (**554/67**) - Metaponto (**555/66**) - Crotone and v.v.
580/97 – TACITO – [12] Terni - Milano and v.v.
751/2 – TOMMASO CAMPANELLA – 🛏 1,2 cl., ▬ 2 cl. and [12] Reggio - Milano and v.v.; ▬ 2 cl. (4 berth) and [2] Reggio (**750/3**) - Lamezia - Milano and v.v.
780/1 – FRECCIA SALENTINA – 🛏 1,2 cl. (Excelsior), 🛏 1,2 cl. (T2), 🛏 1,2 cl.; ▬ 2 cl. (4 berth) and [12] Lecce - Milano and v.v.
784/5 – FRECCIA DEL LEVANTE – ▬ 2 cl. and [12] Crotone (**782/7**) - Metaponto (**783/6**) - Taranto - Milano; 🛏 1,2 cl. (Excelsior), 🛏 1,2 cl. (T2), 🛏 1,2 cl., ▬ 2 cl. and [12] Taranto - Milano.
823 – FRECCIA DEL SUD – ①③⑤⑦: ▬ 2 cl. and [2] Milano - Catania - Agrigento; [2] Milano - Catania (**827**) - Siracusa.
830 – ②④⑦: ▬ 2 cl. and [2] Salerno - Milano.
833 – ①③⑤: ▬ 2 cl. and [2] Milano - Salerno.
834 – FRECCIA DEL SUD – ②④⑥⑦: ▬ 2 cl. and [2] Agrigento - Catania - Milano; [2] Siracusa (**836**) - Catania - Milano.
900 – ⑦; also Apr. 13, June 2; not Apr. 12, May 31 (from Bari): 🛏 1,2 cl. (T2), ▬ 2 cl. and [2] Bari - Torino.
901/6 – FRECCIA ADRIATICA – 🛏 1,2 cl. (T2), 🛏 1,2 cl., ▬ 2 cl. and [2] Torino - Lecce and v.v.; ▬ 2 cl. and [2] Torino - Bari (**903/10**) - Taranto (**904/9**) - Metaponto (**905/8**) - Catanzaro Lido and v.v.
907 – ⑤; also Apr. 30; not May 1 (from Torino): 🛏 1,2 cl. (T2), ▬ 2 cl. and [2] Torino - Bari.
923/6 – 🛏 1,2 cl. (T2), ▬ 2 cl. (4/6 berth) and [2] Milano - Lecce and v.v.
1545 – GARGANO – ⑥ (not Apr. 25, May 2): [12] and 🍷 Milano - Lecce.
1549 – APULIA – ⑤ (not May 1): [12] Milano - Bari.
1554 – CARACCIOLO – ⑦ (also Apr. 13, June 2; not Apr. 12, May 31): [12] Salerno - Milano.
1557 – CARACCIOLO – ⑤ (not May 1): [12] Milano - Salerno.
1588 – ASPROMONTE – ⑦ (also Apr. 13, June 2; not Apr. 12, May 31): [12] Reggio - Milano.
1589 – ASPROMONTE – ⑥ (not Apr. 25, May 2): [12] Milano - Reggio.
1910/1 – 🛏 1,2 cl. (Excelsior), 🛏 1,2 cl. (T2), 🛏 1,2 cl., ▬ 2 cl. (4 berth) and [2] Napoli - Milano and v.v.
1920/1 – TRINACRIA – 🛏 1,2 cl. (T2), 🛏 1,2 cl. and ▬ 2 cl. (4/6 berth) Milano - Palermo and v.v.; 🛏 1,2 cl. (T2), 🛏 1,2 cl. and ▬ 2 cl. (4/6 berth) Milano - Messina (**1923**) - Siracusa and v.v.
1991 – MONGIBELLO – Apr. 10, 14, 30, May 4, 29, June 3; ①⑤ from June 8: 🛏 1,2 cl. (T2), ▬ 2 cl. and [2] Milano - Siracusa; ▬ 2 cl. (4 berth) and [2] Milano - Messina (**1993**) - Palermo.
9459 – [12] and ✕ Bergamo (**9458**) - Treviglio - Roma.
9460 – [12] and ✕ Roma - Bergamo.
9761 – [12] and 🍷 Milano - Lecce.
9763/6 – [12] and 🍷 Torino - Lecce and v.v.
9779/82 – [12] and 🍷 Torino - Bari and v.v.
9780/1 – [12] and 🍷 Milano - Pescara and v.v.
9783/6 – [12] and 🍷 Pescara - Milano and v.v.

A – From/to Ancona.
L – [12] Milano - Aulla - Livorno and v.v.
P – ⑥⑦ (also Apr. 13, May 1, June 2; not Apr. 12, May 2): [2] Milano - Pescara and v.v.
R – From/to Rimini.

g – Milano **Porta Garibaldi**.
j – Also Apr. 13, June 2; not Apr. 12, May 31.
p – Napoli **Piazza Garibaldi**.
s – Stops to set down only.
t – Roma **Tiburtina**.
v – ①②③④⑦ (not Apr. 12, 25, and days before holidays).
y – Also Apr. 30, June 1; not May 1, 29.

VENEZIA and MILANO - BOLOGNA - FIRENZE - ROMA 620

km		*E*	*E*	*ICN*	*E*	*ICp*	*EN*	*EN*		*E*	*EN*	*ES*		*ES*	*ES*		*ES*		*ES*		*IC*	*IC*	*ES*		*ES*
		833	**837**	**771**	**1911**	**579**	**235**	**313**		**1239**	**1237**	**9423**		**9389**	**9311**		**9409**		**9463**		**585**	**713**	**9391**		**9459**
						R ✕	⊡	⊡		⊡	⊡	R ✕		R ✕	R 🍷		R ✕		R ✕		🍷	🍷	R ✕		R ✕
		♦	♦	Z	Z	⚒	♦	♦		♦	♦			Ⓐ	♦					⚒		♦	♦		♦
0	**Venezia Santa Lucia 600** d.	...	...	2330	...	...	...	...	...	...	...	...	...	0556	...	...	...	0557	0636	0657	...	0715	...	0720	...
9	**Venezia Mestre 600** d.	...	...	0021	...	...	0311	...	...	0357	0357	...	...	0607u	...	...	...	0609	0647u	0709	...	0728	0747	0734	...
37	Padova **600** d.	...	...	0045	...	...	|	...	...	0421	0421	...	0535	0624	...	...	...	0633	0704	0733	...	0750	0803	0807	...
81	Rovigo d.	...	...	0119	...	...	|	...	...	0448	0448	...	0607	|	...	...	...	0707	0728	0810	...	0821	0834	0843	...
113	Ferrara d.	...	...	0141	...	...	0419	...	...	0509	0509	...	0631	|	...	...	...	0731	0749	0831	...	0842	0854	0902	...
	Milano C 619/30 d.	2200	...	|	2320	...	|	...	...	|	|	...	|	|	...	...	0545	|	|	|	0705	|	|	|	...
160	**Bologna C 619/30** a.	0039	...	0217	|	...	0448	...	...	0541	0541	...	0704	|	...	...	0758	0804	0821	0904	0904	0912	0921	0938	...
160	**Bologna C** d.	0044	0115	0222	|	...	0515	0524s	...	0546	0546	0637	...	|	0709	...	0802	...	0825	...	0908	...	0925	...	0954
241	Prato d.	|	|	|	|	...	|	|	...	|	|	0725	...	|	|	...	|	...	|	...	1016	...	|	...	|
255	Firenze Campo di Marte d.	|	|	|	|	...	|	0641s	...	0733	0733	|	...	|	|	...	|	...	|	...	1027r	...	|	...	1052r
257	**Firenze SMN** a.	|	|	|	|	...	0618	|	...	|	|	0739	...	|	0814	...	0904	...	0923	...	|	...	1023	...	|
257	**Firenze SMN** d.	|	|	|	|	0550	0630	|	...	|	|	0749	...	|	0824	...	0918	...	0933	...	|	...	1033	...	|
345	Arezzo d.	|	|	0458	|	0630	|	|	...	|	|	|	...	|	|	...	|	...	|	...	1106	...	|	...	|
408	Chiusi-Chianciano Terme d.	|	|	0541	|	0710	0732	|	...	|	|	|	...	|	|	...	|	...	|	...	1145	...	|	...	|
568	Roma Tiburtina a.	0452	0609	0656	0723	|	|	|	...	|	|	|	...	|	|	...	|	...	|	...	|	...	|	...	|
573	**Roma Termini** a.	|	|	|	|	0824	0905	0912	...	1045	1045	0929	...	0955	1000	...	1058	...	1110	...	1316	...	1210	...	1236
	Napoli Centrale **640** a.	0734	0926	1000	1012	...	...	...	...	...	...	1105	...	...	...	...	...	...	...	...	1550	...	...	...	...

		ES	*ICp*	*ICp*		*ES*	*ES*	*CIS*		*IC*		*ES*		*ES*	*E*		*IC*				*IC*	*IC*	*E*	*ES*	
		9467	**1589**	**703**		**9393**	**9469**	**13**		**591**		**9395**		**9473**	**823**		**705**				**595**	**715**	**1921**	**9399**	
		R ✕	R	R ✕		R ✕	R ✕	R ✕		✕		R ✕		R ✕			✕				🍷			R ✕	
			Z	♦		♦	Ⓒ	♦							Z							♦	Z		
Venezia Santa Lucia 600 d.	0757	0843	...	...	...	...	1043	...	1057	...	...	1143	1157	1243	...	1257	1309	1357	...	1457	...	1527	...	1543	1557
Venezia Mestre 600 d.	0809	0854u	...	0920	...	0954	1054u	...	1109	...	...	1154u	1209	1254u	...	1309	1322	1409	...	1509	...	1541	...	1554u	1609
Padova **600** d.	0833	0911	...	0941	...	1011	1111	...	1133	...	...	1211	1233	1311	...	1333	1341	1433	...	1533	...	1602	...	1611	1633
Rovigo d.	0907	|	...	1008	...	1034	|	...	1207	...	...	1234	1307	|	...	1405	1410	1507	...	1607	...	1625	...	1634	1707
Ferrara d.	0931	|	...	1028	...	1054	|	...	1231	...	...	1254	1331	|	...	1433	1428	1531	...	1631	...	1643	...	1653	1731
Milano C 619/30 d.	|	|	0735	|	...	|	|	1115	|	1100	...	|	|	|	1220	|	|	|	...	|	1500	|	1620	|	|
Bologna C 619/30 a.	1004	1021	1022	1054	...	1121	1221	1258	1304	1309	...	1321	1404	1421	1445	1504	1454	1604	...	1704	1704	1712	|	1721	1804
Bologna C d.	...	1025	1032	1102	...	1125	1225	1302	...	1313	...	1325	...	1425	1455	...	1508	...	...	...	1708	...	|	1725	...
Prato d.	...	|	1131	1216	...	|	|	|	...	1416	...	|	...	|	1633	...	1616	...	...	...	1816	...	|	|	...
Firenze Campo di Marte d.	...	|	1203	1227r	...	|	|	|	...	1427r	...	|	...	|	1658	...	1627r	...	...	...	1827r	...	2035	|	...
Firenze SMN a.	...	1123	|	|	...	1223	1323	1415	...	|	...	1423	...	1523	|	...	|	...	...	...	|	...	|	1823	...
Firenze SMN d.	...	1133	|	|	...	1233	1333	...	...	|	...	1433	...	1533	|	...	|	...	...	...	|	...	|	1833	...
Arezzo d.	...	|	|	1306	...	|	|	...	...	1506	...	|	...	|	|	...	1706	...	...	...	1906	...	|	|	...
Chiusi-Chianciano Terme d.	...	|	1306	1345	...	|	|	...	...	1545	...	|	...	|	|	...	1745	...	...	...	1945	...	|	|	...
Roma Tiburtina a.	...	|	1441	|	...	|	|	...	...	|	...	|	...	|	2006	...	|	...	...	...	|	...	2315	|	...
Roma Termini a.	...	1310	|	1516	...	1410	1510	...	...	1716	...	1610	...	1710	...	...	1916	...	...	...	2116	...	...	2010	...
Napoli Centrale **640** a.	...	...	1722	1750	...	...	...	...	...	1938	...	...	...	...	...	...	2138	...	...	...	2342	...	...	...	...

	ES		*ES*		*ICp*	*ES*		*E*		*ICN*	*E*	*E*	*ICN*			Alta Velocità (*AV*) services via high-speed line ▶▶▶▶	*AV*	*AV*	*AV*	*AV*	*AV*	*AV*	*AV*	*AV*
	9481		**9313**		**597**	**9485**		**1931**		**751**	**1595**	**1991**	**779**				**9421**	**9501**	**9425**	**9503**	**9425**	**9505**	**9427**	**9507**
	R ✕		R ✕		R	R ✕											R ✕	R ✕	R ✕	R ✕	R ✕	R ✕	R ✕	R ✕
			B		♦			Z		Z	Z	Z	♦				①–⑥	Ⓐ	①–⑥	Ⓐ	①–⑥	Ⓐ		Ⓐ
Venezia Santa Lucia 600 d.	1643	1657	...	1757	...	1836	1857	1909	1957	...	...	...	...	...	...		...	...	...	...	...	...	...	...
Venezia Mestre 600 d.	1654u	1709	...	1809	...	1847u	1909	1925	2009	...	...	...	2211	...	...		...	...	...	...	...	...	...	...
Padova **600** d.	1711	1733	...	1833	...	1903	1933	1949	2033	...	...	...	2236	...	...		...	...	...	...	...	...	...	...
Rovigo d.	|	1807	...	1907	...	1930	2007	2022	2107	...	...	...	2316	...	...		...	...	...	...	...	...	...	...
Ferrara d.	|	1831	...	1931	...	1951	2031	2047	2131	...	...	...	2336	...	...		...	...	...	...	...	...	...	...
Milano C 619/30 d.	|	|	...	|	1745	|	|	|	|	2000	...	1943g	...	...	...		...	0615	0630	0645	...	0715	0730	0745
Bologna C 619/30 a.	1821	1904	...	2004	2004	2021	2104	2120	2204	2200	...	2228	...	...	...		...	|	0735	|	...	|	0835	|
Bologna C d.	1825	...	1906	...	2008	2025	...	2148	...	2208	2233	2233	...	...	...		...	|	0739	|	...	|	0839	|
Prato d.	|	...	|	...	2059	|	...	|	...	|	|	|	...	...	...		...	|	|	|	...	|	|	|
Firenze Campo di Marte d.	|	...	|	...	|	|	...	2247	...	2325	2344	2355	...	...	...		...	|	|	|	...	|	|	|
Firenze SMN a.	1923	...	2009	...	2116	2123	...	...	...	...	...	...	...	...	...		...	|	0839	|	←	|	0939	|
Firenze SMN d.	1933	...	2019	...	2138	2133	...	...	...	...	...	...	...	...	...		0640	|	→	|	0849	|	→	|
Arezzo d.	|	...	|	...	2221	|	...	...	...	...	...	...	...	...	...		0714	|	...	|	|	|	...	|
Chiusi-Chianciano Terme d.	|	...	|	...	...	|	...	...	...	...	...	...	...	...	...		|	|	...	|	|	|	...	|
Roma Tiburtina a.	|	...	|	...	...	|	...	...	...	...	...	...	...	...	...		|	|	...	|	|	|	...	|
Roma Termini a.	2110	...	2159	...	...	2310	...	...	...	...	...	...	...	...	...		0829	0945	...	1015	1029	1045	...	1115
Napoli Centrale **640** a.	...	...	...	...	...	...	...	...	...	...	...	...	...	...	...		1005	...	...	...	1205	...	...	...

km (via hsl)		*AV*	*AV*	*AV*	*AV*	*AV*	*AV*	*AV*	*AV*	*AV*	*AV*	*AV*	*AV*	*AV*	*AV*	*AV*	*AV*	*AV*	*AV*	*AV*	*AV*	*AV*	*AV*	*AV*	*AV*
		9427	**9509**	**9429**	**9491**	**9431**	**9433**	**9641**	**9435**	**9437**	**9439**	**9511**	**9441**	**9643**	**9443**	**9513**	**9445**	**9515**	**9447**	**9517**	**9449**	**9519**	**9451**	**9453**	**9521**
		R ✕	R ✕	R ✕	R ✕	R ✕	R ✕	R ✕	R ✕	R ✕	R ✕	R 🍷	R ✕	R ✕	R ✕	R ✕	R ✕	R ✕	R ✕	R ✕	R ✕	R ✕	R ✕	R ✕	R ✕
			⚒		♦			Ⓐ				Ⓐ	♦		♦	Ⓑ		Ⓑ		Ⓑ		Ⓐ		Ⓑ	⑤
	Venezia Santa Lucia 600 d.	...	...	...	...	...	...	1043	...	...	...	...	...	1443	...	...	...	...	...	...	...	...	...	...	...
	Venezia Mestre 600 d.	...	...	...	...	...	...	1054u	...	...	...	...	...	1454u	...	...	...	...	...	...	...	...	...	...	...
	Padova **600** d.	...	...	...	...	...	...	1111	...	...	...	...	...	1511	...	...	...	...	...	...	...	...	...	...	...
	Rovigo d.	...	...	...	...	...	...	|	...	...	...	...	...	|	...	...	...	...	...	...	...	...	...	...	...
	Ferrara d.	...	...	...	...	...	...	|	...	...	...	...	...	|	...	...	...	...	...	...	...	...	...	...	...
0	**Milano C 619/30** d.	...	0815	0830	0845g	0930	1030	|	1130	1230	1330	1415	1430	|	1530	1615	1630	1715	1730	1815	1830	1845	1930	2030	2015
213	**Bologna C 619/30** a.	...	|	0935	1005	1035	1135	1221	1235	1335	1435	|	1535	1621	1635	|	1735	|	1835	|	1935	1950	2035	2135	|
——	**Bologna C** d.	...	|	0939	1009	1039	1139	1225	1239	1339	1439	|	1539	1625	1639	|	1739	|	1839	|	1939	1952	2039	2139	|
	Prato d.	...	|	|	|	|	|	|	|	|	|	|	|	|	|	|	|	|	|	|	|	|	|	2226	|
	Firenze Campo di Marte d.	...	|	|	|	|	|	|	|	|	|	|	|	|	|	|	|	|	|	|	|	|	|	|	|
	Firenze SMN a.	←	|	1039	1109	1139	1239	1323	1339	1439	1539	|	1639	1723	1739	|	1839	|	1939	|	2039	|	2139	2242	|
0	**Firenze SMN** d.	0949	|	1049	1119	1149	1249	1333	1349	1449	1549	|	1649	1733	1749	|	1849	|	1949	|	2049	|	2149	...	|
	Arezzo d.	|	|	|	|	|	|	|	|	|	|	|	|	|	|	|	|	|	|	|	|	|	|	...	|
	Chiusi-Chianciano Terme d.	|	|	|	|	|	|	|	|	|	|	|	|	|	|	|	|	|	|	|	|	|	|	...	|
	Roma Tiburtina a.	|	|	|	|	|	|	|	|	|	|	|	|	|	|	|	|	|	|	|	|	2211	|	...	|
261	**Roma Termini** a.	1129	1145	1229	1259	1329	1429	1510	1529	1629	1729	1745	1829	1910	1929	1945	2029	2045	2129	2145	2229	|	2329	...	2345
	Napoli Centrale **640** a.	1305	...	1405	...	...	1605	1646	...	1805	1905	...	2005	2046	2105	...	2205	...	2305	...	...	2335	...	...	...

♦ – **NOTES** (LISTED BY TRAIN NUMBER)

13 – [12] and ✕ Zürich - Milano - Firenze. *CISALPINO Pendolino* train; supplement payable.
235 – ALLEGRO TOSCA – 🛏 1,2 cl. (Excelsior), 🛏 1,2 cl., ▬ 2 cl. and [2] Wien Süd - Villach - Venezia Mestre - Roma; 🛏 1,2 cl. (Excelsior), 🛏 1,2 cl., ▬ 2 cl. and [2] München (**485**) - Bologna - Roma.
313 – LUNA – 🛏 1,2 cl. and ▬ 2 cl. Zürich - Brig - Roma; 🛏 1,2 cl. and ▬ 2 cl. Genève (**311**) - Brig - Roma.
597 – TACITO – [12] Milano - Terni.
703 – MIRAMARE – [12] and ✕ Trieste (**702**) - Venezia Mestre - Napoli.
713 – ADRIATICO – [12] and 🍷 Venezia - Bari.
715 – MANIN – [12] Venezia - Pescara.
779 – TERGESTE – ▬ 2 cl. (4 berth) and [12] Trieste (**778**) - Venezia Mestre - Lecce; 🛏 1,2 cl. (Excelsior), 🛏 1,2 cl. (T2), 🛏 1,2 cl. and [12] Venezia Santa Lucia (**1599**) - Mestre - Lecce.
833 – ①③⑤: ▬ 2 cl. and [2] Milano - Salerno.
837 – ①②④⑤⑥⑦, also June 3; not June 4 (from Bolzano): 🛏 1,2 cl., ▬ 2 cl. (4 berth) and [2] Bolzano (**925**) - Bologna - Napoli.
1237 – ALLEGRO ROSSINI – ⑤ Apr. 3 - Sept. 25 (from Wien): 🛏 1,2 cl. (Excelsior), 🛏 1,2 cl., ▬ 2 cl. and [2] Wien Süd - Roma.
1239 – ALLEGRO ROSSINI – Apr. 4, 12, 30, May 20, 31, June 10 (from Wien): 🛏 1,2 cl. (Excelsior), 🛏 1,2 cl., ▬ 2 cl. and [2] Wien Süd - Roma.

9311 – [12] and 🍷 Verona - Roma.
9391 – [12] and ✕ Udine - Venezia Mestre - Roma.
9393 – [12] and ✕ Trieste (**9394**) - Venezia Mestre - Roma.
9441 – [12] and ✕ Milano - Napoli - Salerno.
9443 – [12] and ✕ Milano - Napoli - Salerno.
9459 – [12] and ✕ Bergamo (**9458**) - Treviglio - Roma.
9491 – [12] and 🍷 Torino - Roma.

B – [12] and ✕ Bolzano - Bologna - Roma.
Z – For days of running and composition see Table **640**.

g – Milano **Porta Garibaldi**.
r – Firenze **Rifredi**.
s – Stops to set down only.
u – Stops to pick up only.

⊡ – Supplement payable.

620 ROMA - FIRENZE - BOLOGNA - MILANO and VENEZIA

km			E 1992	ICN 752				E 1930	E 1920	ICp 580	ICp 578	ES 9462	ICp 580			E 834	ES 9310		ES 9388		IC 582	IC 714	ES 9470		IC 704
										R	R ✕	R ✕	R				R ✕		R ✕		🍷	🍷	R ✕		✕
		⚒	Z	Z				Z	Z	♦			♦			Z	B				Z	♦			
	Napoli Centrale **640** d.	...	...	...	...	...	...	...	...	...	...	...	...	...	...	...	...	...	...	...	...	...	...	...	0824
0	**Roma Termini** d.	...	...	...	...	...	...	...	...	...	0635	0650	...	...	...	...	0900	...	0950	...	0841	...	1050	...	1044
5	Roma Tiburtina d.	...	...	0428	...	...	...	...	0515s	...	|	|	...	...	...	0613	|	...	|	...	|	...	|	...	|
165	Chiusi-Chianciano Terme d.	...	...	|	...	...	...	...	|	...	0809	|	...	...	...	|	|	...	|	...	1013	...	|	...	1213
229	Arezzo d.	...	...	|	...	...	...	...	|	0735	0857	|	...	...	...	|	|	...	|	...	1053	...	|	...	1253
316	**Firenze SMN** a.	...	...	|	...	...	...	...	|	0817	0938	0827	...	...	...	|	1039	...	1127	...	|	...	1227	...	|
316	**Firenze SMN** d.	...	...	|	...	...	...	...	|	0829	...	0837	...	...	...	|	1049	...	1137	...	|	...	1237	...	|
319	Firenze Campo di Marte d.	...	0559	0638	...	...	...	0753s	0724s	|	...	|	←	...	...	0918	|	...	|	...	1136r	...	|	...	1336r
333	Prato d.	...	|	|	...	...	...	|	|	0842	...	|	0844	...	...	0942	|	...	|	...	1145	...	|	...	1345
413	**Bologna C** a.	...	0719	0752	...	...	...	0928s	|	→	...	0934	0952	...	...	1100	1150	...	1234	...	1243	...	1334	...	1453
413	**Bologna C 619/30** d.	0602	0724	0756	0756	...	0900	|	|	...	...	0938	0956	1000	...	1108	...	1156	1238	...	1247	1256	1338	1356	1504
632	**Milano C 619/30** a.	|	1005g	1005	|	...	|	|	1130	...	...	|	1200	|	...	1320	...	|	|	...	1500	|	|	|	|
	Ferrara d.	0637	...	...	0830	...	0930	1019s	...	...	...	|	...	1031	...	...	...	1230	1307	...	...	1323	|	1430	1533
	Rovigo d.	0659	...	...	0854	...	0954	1042s	...	...	...	|	...	1054	...	...	...	1254	1326	...	...	1341	|	1454	1551
	Padova **600** d.	0738	...	...	0929	...	1029	1117s	...	...	...	1051	...	1129	...	...	...	1329	1351	...	...	1410	1451	1529	1619
	Venezia Mestre 600 a.	0801	...	...	0951	...	1051	1137s	...	...	...	1106s	...	1151	...	...	...	1351	1406s	...	...	1436	1506s	1551	1637
	Venezia Santa Lucia 600 a.	0813	...	...	1003	...	1103	1150	...	...	...	1117	...	1203	...	...	...	1403	1417	...	...	1449	1517	1603	1649

	ES 9474		ES 9390	CIS 24		IC 586		ES 9478		ES 9460	ICp 706	ES 9392		ES 9312		ES 9482		ICp 1554		ES 9398	IC 592	IC 716	ES 9498	ICp 1588	ES 9486
	R ✕		R ✕	R ✕		✕		R ✕		R ✕	R ✕	R ✕		R 🍷		R ✕		R		R ✕	🍷		R ✕	R	R ✕
				♦						♦	♦	♦		♦		Ⓒ		Z		♦		♦		Z	Ⓒ
Napoli Centrale **640** d.	...	...	...	...	...	1024	...	...	...	...	...	...	...	...	...	...	...	1259p	...	...	1424	...	...	1442	...
Roma Termini d.	1250	...	1350	...	...	1244	...	1450	...	1545	1444	1550	...	1555	...	1650	...	|	...	1750	1644	...	1822	|	1850
Roma Tiburtina d.	|	...	|	...	...	|	...	|	...	|	|	|	...	|	...	|	...	1532	...	|	|	...	|	1658	|
Chiusi-Chianciano Terme d.	|	...	|	...	...	1413	...	|	...	|	1613	|	...	|	...	|	...	1720	...	|	1813	...	|	1827	|
Arezzo d.	|	...	|	...	...	1453	...	|	...	|	1653	|	...	|	...	|	...	1755	...	|	1853	...	|	1912	|
Firenze SMN a.	1427	...	1527	...	...	|	...	1627	...	|	|	1727	...	1739	...	1827	...	|	...	1927	|	...	1955	|	2027
Firenze SMN d.	1437	...	1537	1554	...	|	...	1637	...	|	|	1737	...	1749	...	1837	...	|	...	1937	|	...	2005	|	2037
Firenze Campo di Marte d.	|	...	|	|	...	1536r	...	|	...	1719r	1736r	|	...	|	...	|	...	1857r	...	|	1936r	...	|	2008	|
Prato d.	|	...	|	|	...	1545	...	|	...	|	|	|	...	|	...	|	...	1912	...	|	1945	...	|	2029	|
Bologna C a.	1534	...	1634	1648	...	1659	...	1734	...	1806	1828	1834	...	1854	...	1934	...	2013	...	2034	2052	...	2106	2127	2134
Bologna C 619/30 d.	1538	1556	1638	1654	1656	1703	...	1738	1756	...	1832	1840	1856	...	...	1938	1956	2017	...	2038	2056	2106	2110	2137	2138
Milano C 619/30 a.	|	|	|	1855	|	1905	...	|	|	...	|	|	|	...	...	|	|	2240	...	|	2300	|	2320	2350	|
Ferrara d.	|	1630	1707	...	1730	...	...	|	1830	...	1914	1907	1930	...	...	|	2030	...	...	2107	...	2133	...	...	|
Rovigo d.	|	1654	1726	...	1754	...	...	|	1854	...	1935	1926	1954	...	...	|	2056	...	...	2126	...	2150	...	...	|
Padova **600** d.	1651	1729	1751	...	1829	...	...	1851	1929	...	2016	1959	2029	...	...	2051	2129	...	...	2151	...	2219	...	...	2251
Venezia Mestre 600 a.	1706s	1751	1806s	...	1851	...	...	1906s	1951	...	2045	2015	2051	...	...	2106s	2151	...	...	2206	...	2237	...	...	2306s
Venezia Santa Lucia 600 a.	1717	1803	1817	...	1903	...	...	1917	2003	...	...	...	2103	...	...	2117	2203	...	...	...	...	2250	...	...	2317

	EN 1236	EN 1238	ICp 594		EN 314	EN 234	E 824	ICN 774	ICN 776	E 1910	E 1594	E 830				AV 9424	AV 9500	AV 9426	AV 9502	AV 9426	AV 9504	AV 9506	AV 9428	AV 9508
	⊡	⊡	R ✕		⊡	⊡										R ✕	R ✕	R ✕	R ✕	R ✕	R ✕	R 🍷	R ✕	R ✕
	♦	♦	Ⓑ v		♦	♦	♦	Z	♦	Z	Z	♦				①–⑥	Ⓐ		Ⓐ		Ⓐ	Ⓐ		⚒
Napoli Centrale **640** d.	...	...	...	...	...	...	1845	1957	...	2030	2259	2150	...	...		...	...	...	...	...	...	0625	...	...
Roma Termini d.	1650	1720	1755	...	1956	1910	|	|	...	2306	|	|	...	...	**Alta**	...	0615	0630	0645	...	0715	|	0730	0815
Roma Tiburtina d.	|	|	|	...	|	|	2205	2236	...	|	|	0047u	...	...	**Velocità**	...	|	|	|	...	|	0749	|	|
Chiusi-Chianciano Terme d.	|	|	1912	...	|	2025	2350	0007	...	|	|	|	...	...	(*AV*)	...	|	|	|	...	|	|	|	|
Arezzo d.	|	|	1957	...	|	|	0032	0047	...	|	|	|	...	...		...	|	|	|	...	|	|	|	|
Firenze SMN a.	|	|	2038	...	|	2130	|	|	...	|	|	|	...	...	services	...	|	0809	|	←	|	|	0909	|
Firenze SMN d.	|	|	...	...	|	2153	|	|	...	|	|	|	...	...	via high-	0709	|	→	|	0819	|	|	0919	|
Firenze Campo di Marte d.	2055	2055	...	...	2157u	|	|	0148	...	|	|	|	...	...	speed line	|	|	...	|	|	|	|	|	|
Prato d.	|	|	...	...	|	|	|	|	...	|	|	|	...	...		0725	|	...	|	|	|	|	|	|
Bologna C a.	2203	2203	...	...	|	2255	0300	0313	...	|	0528	0552	...	...	▶▶▶▶	0820	|	...	|	0920	|	1008	1020	|
Bologna C 619/30 d.	2220	2220	...	2235	2318u	2320	...	0318	...	|	...	0557	...	...		0824	|	...	|	0924	|	1010	1024	|
Milano C 619/30 a.	|	|	...	|	...	|	...	|	...	0725	...	0920	...	...		0929	0945	...	1015	1029	1045	1115	1129	1145
Ferrara d.	2256	2256	...	2307	...	2350	...	0349	0516	...	...	...	...	...		...	...	...	...	...	...	...	...	...
Rovigo d.	2319	2319	...	2328	...	|	...	0411	0538	...	...	...	...	...		...	...	...	...	...	...	...	...	...
Padova **600** d.	2349	2349	...	2400	...	0041	...	0450	0621	...	...	...	...	...		...	...	...	...	...	...	...	...	...
Venezia Mestre 600 a.	0011	0011	...	...	...	0102	...	0508	0643	...	...	...	...	...		...	...	...	...	...	...	...	...	...
Venezia Santa Lucia 600 a.	...	...	...	...	...	...	...	0526	...	...	...	...	...	...		...	...	...	...	...	...	...	...	...

km (via hsl)		AV 9430	AV 9640	AV 9432	AV 9434	AV 9436	AV 9438	AV 9440	AV 9510	AV 9442	AV 9494	AV 9512	AV 9494	AV 9444	AV 9514	AV 9446	AV 9642	AV 9516	AV 9448	AV 9518	AV 9450	AV 9644	AV 9452	AV 9454	AV 9456
		R ✕	R ✕	R ✕	R ✕	R ✕	R ✕	R ✕	R ✕	R ✕	R ✕	R ✕	R ✕	R ✕	R 🍷	R ✕	R ✕	R 🍷	R ✕	R ✕	R ✕	R ✕	R ✕	R ✕	R ✕
						♦			Ⓑ y		♦	Ⓐ	♦		Ⓑ		Ⓐ	Ⓑ		Ⓑ	Ⓑ	Ⓐ		Ⓑ	
	Napoli Centrale **640** d.	0654	0716	0754	0854	0954	...	1154	...	1254	...	...	...	1354	...	...	1516	...	1554	...	1654	1716	1754	1816	1854
0	**Roma Termini** d.	0830	0850	0930	1030	1130	1230	1330	1415	1430	1500	1515	...	1530	1615	1630	1650	1715	1730	1815	1830	1850	1930	1950	2030
	Roma Tiburtina d.	|	|	|	|	|	|	|	|	|	|	|	...	|	|	|	|	|	|	|	|	|	|	|	|
	Chiusi-Chianciano Terme d.	|	|	|	|	|	|	|	|	|	|	|	...	|	|	|	|	|	|	|	|	|	|	|	2127
	Arezzo d.	|	|	|	|	|	|	|	|	|	|	|	...	|	|	|	|	|	|	|	|	|	|	2107	2157
261	**Firenze SMN** a.	1009	1027	1109	1209	1309	1409	1509	|	1609	1639	|	←	1709	|	1809	1827	|	1909	|	2009	2027	2109	2138	2229
	Firenze SMN d.	1019	1037	1119	1219	1319	1419	1519	|	1619	→	|	1649	1719	|	1819	1837	|	1919	|	2019	2037	2119	...	2239
	Firenze Campo di Marte d.	|	|	|	|	|	|	|	|	|	...	|	|	|	|	|	|	|	|	|	|	|	|	...	|
	Prato d.	|	|	|	|	|	|	|	|	|	...	|	|	|	|	|	|	|	|	|	|	|	|	...	2255
——	**Bologna C** a.	1120	1134	1220	1320	1420	1520	1620	|	1720	...	|	1754	1820	|	1920	1934	|	2020	|	2120	2134	2220	...	2342
0	**Bologna C 619/30** d.	1124	1138	1224	1324	1424	1524	1624	|	1724	...	|	1758	1824	|	1924	1938	|	2024	|	2124	2138	2224	...	...
213	**Milano C 619/30** a.	1229	|	1329	1429	1529	1629	1729	1745	1829	...	1845	1913g	1929	1945	2029	|	2045	2129	2145	2229	|	2329	...	...
	Ferrara d.	...	|	...	...	...	...	...	...	...	...	...	...	...	...	...	|	...	...	...	...	|	...	...	...
	Rovigo d.	...	|	...	...	...	...	...	...	...	...	...	...	...	...	...	|	...	...	...	...	|	...	...	...
	Padova **600** d.	...	1251	...	...	...	...	...	...	...	...	...	...	...	...	...	2051	...	...	...	...	2251	...	...	...
	Venezia Mestre 600 a.	...	1306s	...	...	...	...	...	...	...	...	...	...	...	...	...	2106s	...	...	...	...	2306s	...	...	...
	Venezia Santa Lucia 600 a.	...	1317	...	...	...	...	...	...	...	...	...	...	...	...	...	2117	...	...	...	...	2317	...	...	...

♦ – **NOTES** (LISTED BY TRAIN NUMBER)

24 – (12) and ✕ Firenze - Milano - Zürich.

234 – ALLEGRO TOSCA – 🛏 1,2 cl. (Excelsior), 🛏 1,2 cl., ▬ 2 cl. and (2) Roma - Venezia Mestre - Villach - Wien Süd; 🛏 1,2 cl. (Excelsior), 🛏 1,2 cl., ▬ 2 cl. and (2) Roma - Bologna (**484**) - München.

314 – LUNA – 🛏 1,2 cl. and ▬ 2 cl. Roma - Brig - Zürich; 🛏 1,2 cl. and ▬ 2 cl. Roma - Brig (**316**) - Genève.

580 – TACITO – (12) Terni - Milano.

706 – MIRAMARE – (12) and ✕ Roma - Venezia Mestre (**707**) - Trieste.

714 – ADRIATICO – (12) and 🍷 Bari - Venezia.

716 – MANIN – (12) Pescara - Venezia.

776 – TERGESTE – ▬ 2 cl. (4 berth) and (12) Lecce - Venezia Mestre (**777**) - Trieste; 🛏 1,2 cl. (Excelsior), 🛏 1,2 cl. (T2), 🛏 1,2 cl. and (12) Lecce - Venezia Mestre (**1598**) - Venezia Santa Lucia.

824 – ①③④⑤⑥⑦ (also June 2; not June 3): 🛏 1,2 cl., ▬ 2 cl. (4 berth) and (2) Napoli - Bologna (**924**) - Bolzano.

830 – ②④⑦: ▬ 2 cl. and (2) Salerno - Milano.

1236 – ALLEGRO ROSSINI – ⑥ Apr. 4 - Sept. 26: 🛏 1,2 cl. (Excelsior), 🛏 1,2 cl., ▬ 2 cl. and (2) Roma - Wien Süd.

1238 – ALLEGRO ROSSINI – Apr. 5, 13, May 1, 21, June 1, 11: 🛏 1,2 cl. (Excelsior), 🛏 1,2 cl., ▬ 2 cl. and (2) Roma - Wien Süd.

9312 – (12) and 🍷 Roma - Verona.

9392 – (12) and ✕ Roma - Venezia Mestre - Udine.

9398 – (12) and ✕ Roma - Venezia Mestre (**9397**) - Trieste.

9436 – (12) and ✕ Salerno - Napoli - Milano.

9460 – (12) and ✕ Roma - Bergamo.

9494 – (12) and ✕ Roma - Torino.

B – (12) and ✕ Roma - Bologna - Bolzano.

Z – For days of running and composition see Table **640**.

g – Milano **Porta Garibaldi**.

p – Napoli **Piazza Garibaldi**.

r – Firenze **Rifredi**.

s – Stops to set down only.

u – Stops to pick up only.

v – Not Apr. 12, 25, and days before holidays.

y – Not Apr. 13, May 1, June 2.

⊡ – Supplement payable.

FERRARA and BOLOGNA - RAVENNA - RIMINI 621

2nd class only except where shown

For express services Bologna - Faenza - Rimini see Table 630

km																									
		⚒			⚒	⚒	⚒			⚒	†		⚒		†n	m		z					⚒	z	
0	**Ferrara 620** d.	...	0557	...	...	0717	...	...	...	0817	0816	...	0913	...	1010	1031	...	...	...	1215	...	...	1309	...	...
	Bologna C 630 d.	...	|	...	0650	|	...	...	0758	|	|	...	|	0906	|	|	1106	...	...	|	...	1306	|	...	1406
	Imola d.	...	|	...	0712	|	...	...	0823	|	|	...	|	0935	|	|	1136	...	...	|	...	1336	|	...	1436
	Castelbolognese d.	...	|	...	0719	|	...	...	0832	|	|	...	|	0942	|	|	1142	...	...	|	...	1342	|	...	1442
	Lugo d.	...	|	...	0734	|	...	...	0846	|	|	...	|	1000	|	|	1200	...	...	|	...	1400	|	...	1501
74	**Ravenna** a.	...	0715	...	0803	0830	...	...	0913	0928	0921	...	1025	1025	1115	1129	1225	...	...	1324	...	1425	1432	...	1525
74	**Ravenna** d.	0635	...	0733	...	...	0832	...	0922	0933	...	...	...	...	1121	1131	...	1239	...	...	1336	...	...	1435	1535
95	Cervia d.	0656	...	0756	...	...	0900	...	0943	1002	...	...	...	...	1138	1148	...	1304	...	...	1400	...	...	1502	1557
103	Cesenatico d.	0703	...	0802	...	...	0906	...	0956	1009	...	...	...	...	1145	1155	...	1310	...	...	1406	...	...	1508	1603
124	**Rimini 630** a.	0732	...	0836	...	...	0936	...	1017	1036	...	...	...	...	1214	1228	...	1337	...	...	1437	...	...	1535	1631

																							ICN 779 ◆	
				⚒	⚒k			†	⚒			⚒	†	⚒	Ⓐ									
Ferrara 620 d.	1414	...	...	...	...	...	1615	...	...	...	...	1701	...	...	...	1814	...	...	2014	...	...	...	2338	...
Bologna C 630 d.	|	...	...	1506	...	1606	|	...	...	...	1706	|	...	...	1755	|	1806	1906	|	2006	...	2206	|	...
Imola d.	|	...	...	1536	...	1635	|	...	...	...	1734	|	...	...	|	|	1835	1935	|	2034	...	2236	|	...
Castelbolognese d.	|	...	...	1542	...	1642	|	...	...	...	1742	|	...	...	1821	|	1842	1942	|	2042	...	2242	|	...
Lugo d.	|	...	...	1600	...	1700	|	...	...	...	1800	|	...	...	1834	|	1900	2000	|	2100	...	2256	|	...
Ravenna a.	1529	...	...	1625	...	1725	1725	...	...	...	1825	1814	...	...	1855	1926	1925	2025	2124	2125	...	2320	0029	...
Ravenna d.	...	1535	...	...	1647	...	...	1730	1735	...	...	...	1835	1835	...	...	1935	...	...	...	2135	...	0031	...
Cervia d.	...	1557	...	...	1710	...	...	1758	1758	...	...	...	1856	1900	...	...	1959	...	...	...	2157	...	|	...
Cesenatico d.	...	1603	...	...	1717	...	...	1805	1805	...	...	...	1908	1907	...	...	2005	...	...	...	2204	...	|	...
Rimini 630 a.	...	1631	...	...	1751	...	...	1836	1836	...	...	...	1933	1933	...	...	2035	...	...	...	2233	...	0111	...

km																									
		ICN 776 ◆		z	⚒			⚒	†		⚒	⚒	⚒	†				⚒	†	†		⚒			
	Rimini 630 d.	0333	...	0518	...	...	0620	...	...	0651	0736	...	...	...	0820	...	0921	...	1020	...	...	...	...	...	1230
	Cesenatico d.	|	...	0550	...	...	0646	...	...	0722	0803	...	...	...	0852	...	0955	...	1054	...	...	...	...	...	1257
	Cervia d.	|	...	0557	...	...	0657	...	...	0728	0809	...	...	...	0859	...	1001	...	1100	...	...	...	...	...	1303
	Ravenna a.	0411	...	0615	...	...	0719	...	...	0748	0829	...	...	...	0920	...	1020	...	1118	...	...	...	...	...	1324
0	**Ravenna** d.	0413	0503	...	0620	0630	...	0726	0735	0754	...	0835	0840	0931	0935	...	...	1031	...	1134	1135	1226	1235	...	...
28	Lugo d.	|	0528	...	|	0659	...	|	|	0812	...	0901	|	|	1000	...	...	|	...	|	1200	|	1300	...	...
42	Castelbolognese d.	|	0544	...	|	0716	...	|	|	|	...	0916	|	|	1016	...	...	|	...	|	1216	|	1316	...	...
50	Imola d.	|	0551	...	|	0724	...	|	|	|	...	0923	|	|	1023	...	...	|	...	|	1223	|	1323	...	...
84	**Bologna C 630** a.	|	0620	...	|	0748	...	|	|	0852	...	0954	|	|	1053	...	...	|	...	|	1254	|	1354	...	...
	Ferrara 620 a.	0514	...	...	0739	...	...	0846	0848	...	...	...	0950	1049	...	...	...	1142	...	1248	...	1347	...	...	...

			z		⚒		r	⚒k	q	Ⓐ			x		z		⚒	†		x				
Rimini 630 d.	...	...	1320	...	...	1420	...	1520	1551	...	1615	...	1720	...	...	...	1820	1838	...	1920	...	2020		...
Cesenatico d.	...	...	1353	...	...	1454	...	1549	1624	...	1702	...	1751	...	...	...	1852	1907	...	1952	...	2052		...
Cervia d.	...	...	1359	...	...	1501	...	1558	1633	...	1709	...	1757	...	...	...	1859	1914	...	1958	...	2059		...
Ravenna a.	...	...	1421	...	...	1521	...	1622	1652	...	1729	...	1820	...	...	...	1920	1932	...	2020	...	2120		...
Ravenna d.	1350	1335	...	...	1444	1531	1538	...	1702	1635	1736	1735	...	1835	1824	...	...	1935	1950	...	2035	...	2134	...
Lugo d.	|	1400	...	...	|	1600	|	...	|	1700	|	1800	...	1900	|	...	...	2000	|	...	2100	...	|	...
Castelbolognese d.	|	1416	...	...	|	1616	|	...	|	1716	|	1816	...	1917	|	...	...	2016	|	...	2116	...	|	...
Imola d.	|	1423	...	...	|	1623	|	...	|	1723	|	1822	...	1923	|	...	...	2023	|	...	2123	...	|	...
Bologna C 630 a.	|	1454	...	...	|	1654	|	...	|	1752	|	1854	...	1952	|	...	...	2054	|	...	2154	...	|	...
Ferrara 620 a.	1505	...	...	...	1608	...	1658	...	1812	...	1849	...	...	...	1936	...	...	...	2103	...	...	...	2241	...

◆ – **NOTES** (LISTED BY TRAIN NUMBER)

776 – TERGESTE – 2 cl. (4 berth) and (12) Lecce - Venezia Mestre (**777**) - Trieste; 1,2 cl. (Excelsior), 1,2 cl. (T2), 1,2 cl. and (12) Lecce - Mestre (**1598**) - Venezia Santa Lucia.

779 – TERGESTE – 2 cl. (4 berth) and (12) Trieste (**778**) - Venezia Mestre - Lecce; 1,2 cl. (Excelsior), 1,2 cl. (T2), 1,2 cl. and (12) Venezia Santa Lucia (**1599**) - Mestre - Lecce.

k – Jan. 7 - May 30.
m – From June 8.
n – Until June 7.
q – From June 7.
r – Until June 2.
x – ⚒ (daily from June 7).
z – ⚒ (daily from June 3).

ROMA AIRPORTS ✈ and other local services 622

ROMA FIUMICINO AIRPORT ✈

Leonardo Express rail service Roma Termini - Roma Fiumicino ✈. *26 km* Journey time: 31 minutes. Special fare payable.

From **Roma Termini**: 0552, 0622, 0652, and every 30 minutes until 2252.

From **Roma Fiumicino**: 0636, 0706, 0736, and every 30 minutes until 2336.

Additional rail service (2nd class only) operates from Roma Tiburtina **and** Roma Ostiense - Roma Fiumicino ✈. *26 km* Journey times: Tiburtina - ✈ 41 – 42 minutes; Ostiense - ✈ 27 minutes.

From **Roma Tiburtina** (Ostiense 15 minutes later):
0505, 0533, 0548⚒, 0603, 0618⚒, 0633, 0648⚒, and every 15 minutes (30†) until 2033, then 2103, 2133, 2203, 2233.

From **Roma Fiumicino** ✈:
0557, 0627, 0642⚒, 0657, 0712⚒, 0727, 0742⚒, 0757, and every 15 minutes (30†) until 2127, then 2157, 2227, 2257, 2327.

A reduced service operates mid-July - mid-Aug.

ROMA CIAMPINO AIRPORT ✈

Frequent services operate Roma Termini - Ciampino and v.v., journey approximately 15 minutes. There is a 🚌 service between Ciampino station and airport.

ROMA - ANZIO and v.v. *57 km* Journey time: 56 – 68 minutes. 2nd class only. All services continue to Nettuno (*3 km* and 4 – 6 minutes from Anzio).

From **Roma Termini**:
⚒: 0505, 0607, 0710, 0807, 0907 and hourly until 1407, then 1428, 1507, 1607, 1709, 1807, 1907, 1930, 2007, 2107, 2148.
†: 0710, 0807, 0907, 1107, 1307, 1407, 1607, 1807, 2007, 2148.

From **Anzio**:
⚒: 0452, 0558, 0632, 0658, 0733, 0754, 0836, 0937 and hourly until 1837, then 1935, 2037, 2150.
†: 0632, 0733, 0836, 0937, 1237, 1437, 1637, 1837, 1935, 2150.

ROMA - CIAMPINO - ALBANO LAZIALE and v.v. *29 km* Journey time: 40 – 58 minutes. 2nd class only.

From **Roma Termini**: 0534⚒, 0720, 0837, 1000⚒, 1210, 1306⚒, 1406, 1506⚒, 1606, 1706⚒, 1806, 1906⚒, 2006, 2106⚒.

From **Albano Laziale**: 0632⚒, 0702⚒, 0739⚒, 0820, 1019⚒, 1023†, 1119⚒, 1335, 1420⚒, 1520⚒, 1524†, 1620⚒, 1720⚒, 1724†, 1820⚒, 1920⚒, 1924†, 2020⚒, 2120⚒, 2124†, 2213⚒.

All trains call at Ciampino, Marino Laziale and Castel Gandolfo approximately 15, 30 and 35 minutes from Roma, 6, 11 and 30 minutes from Albano Laziale respectively.

623 NAPOLI - SORRENTO, BAIANO and SARNO

2nd class only · Circumvesuviana Ferrovia

Services depart from Napoli Porta Nolana station and call at Napoli Piazza Garibaldi ▲ 2 minutes later.

NAPOLI (Porta Nolana) - SORRENTO and v.v. Journey: 55 - 68 minutes. *45 km.* All services call at Ercolano, Pompei Villa di Misteri, Castellammare di Stabia, Vico Equense and Meta.

From **Napoli:** 0509⚒, 0539, 0609⚒, 0640, 0644⚒, 0709, 0739⚒, 0811, 0822, 0839, 0909, 0939 and every 30 minutes until 1309, 1341, 1409, 1439, 1511, 1522⚒, 1539, 1609, 1639, 1709, 1741, 1809, 1839, 1911, 1939, 2009, 2039, 2109, 2139, 2209, 2242.

From **Sorrento:** 0501, 0537, 0607⚒, 0625, 0655, 0722, 0738⚒, 0755, 0826, 0852⚒, 0907, 0937 and every 30 minutes until 1307, 1325, 1356, 1422, 1455, 1526, 1552⚒, 1607, 1637, 1707, 1725, 1756, 1822, 1855, 1926, 2007, 2037, 2107, 2137, 2225.

NAPOLI (Porta Nolana) - BAIANO and v.v. Journey 60 minutes.

From **Napoli:** 0517⚒, 0548, 0618⚒, 0648, 0718, 0748, 0818, 0848⚒, 0918, 0948⚒, 1018, 1048⚒, 1118, 1148⚒, 1218, 1318, 1348⚒, 1418†, 1430⚒, 1448⚒, 1518, 1548Ⓐ, 1618, 1648Ⓐ, 1718†, 1730⚒, 1748Ⓐ, 1818, 1848Ⓐ, 1918, 1948, 2018, 2048.

From **Baiano:** 0502, 0532⚒, 0602, 0632⚒, 0700, 0730, 0802, 0832, 0902, 0932, 1002, 1032⚒, 1102, 1132⚒, 1202, 1232⚒, 1302, 1332⚒, 1402, 1430, 1502, 1532⚒, 1602, 1632⚒, 1702, 1730Ⓐ, 1802, 1832Ⓐ, 1902, 1932Ⓐ, 2002, 2032Ⓐ, 2102.

NAPOLI (Porta Nolana) - SARNO and v.v. Journey 65 minutes. All services call at Poggiomarino (49 minutes from Napoli, 12 minutes from Sarno).

From **Napoli:** 0502⚒, 0532, 0602⚒, 0632, 0722, 0802, 0832⚒, 0902, 0932⚒, 1002, 1032⚒, 1102, 1132⚒, 1202, 1232, 1302, 1332⚒, 1402, 1432⚒, 1502, 1532Ⓐ, 1602, 1632Ⓐ, 1702, 1732Ⓐ, 1802, 1832Ⓐ, 1902, 1932, 2002, 2042, 2102**p**.

From **Sarno:** 0453, 0519⚒, 0549, 0619⚒, 0649, 0719, 0741, 0759, 0819, 0849, 0919, 0949, 1019⚒, 1049, 1119⚒, 1149, 1219⚒, 1249, 1349, 1419, 1449, 1519⚒, 1549, 1619⚒, 1649, 1719Ⓐ, 1749, 1819Ⓐ, 1849, 1919Ⓐ, 1949, 2019Ⓐ, 2049.

p – To Poggiomarino only.

▲ – Adjacent to **Napoli Centrale** main line station - connection is by moving walkway. Operator: Circumvesuviana Ferrovia ✆ +39 081 77 22 444, fax +39 081 77 22 450.

Frequent 🚌 services operate along the Amalfi Coast between Sorrento and Salerno. Up to 20 services on ⚒, less frequent on †. Change of buses at Amalfi is necessary. Operator: SITA, Via Campegna 23, 80124 Napoli. ✆ +39 081 610 67 11, fax +39 081 239 50 10.

624 ROMA - PESCARA

2nd class only

km					⚒	Ⓐ				⚒	
0	**Roma Tiburtina** ▲ d.	...	0751	1046	1157	1250	1426	1626	1832j	1942	2048
40	Tivoli ▲ d.	...	0844	1147	1236	|	1508		1910	2045	2132
108	Avezzano d.	0608	0951	1256	1349	1433	1618	1816	2025	2209	2242
172	**Sulmona 626** d.	0729	1050	1410	...	1537	1716	1912	2131	...	...
226	Chieti a.	0831	1130	1515	...	1631	1805	2003	2215	...	...
240	**Pescara C** a.	0849	1149	1533	...	1655	1825	2021	2233	...	...

				Ⓐ		⚒					
Pescara C d.	...	...	0620	0645	0920	1242	1409	1600	...	1758	1904
Chieti d.	...	...	0637	0709	0940	1300	1427	1617	...	1823	1921
Sulmona 626 d.	...	0554	0728	0828	1025	1402	1514	1714	1740	1925	2010
Avezzano d.	0457	0651	0820	0924	1129	*1521*	1615	...	1901	...	2110
Tivoli ▲ d.	0610	0759	|	|	1235	...	1713	...	2029	...	2221
Roma Tiburtina ▲ a.	0658	0844t	1000	1100	1308	...	1750r	...	2125	...	2300

j – Depart 1838 on †.
r – Arrive 1800 on ⚒.
t – Roma **Termini**.
▲ – Additional services operate Roma Tiburtina - Tivoli and v.v., journey 55–60 minutes.

625 ROMA - FOLIGNO - ANCONA

km		2 ⚒	2 ⚒	2 ⚒	*ICp* 580 R T	2 ⚒	2 ⚒			*ES* 9324 R 🍷		2 ⚒	2 ⚒	⚒	⚒		*ES* 9328 R 🍷		*ES* 9330 R 🍷		*ES* 9332 R ✕ R	2 ⚒	Ⓑq		*ES* 9334 R 🍷	*ES* 9336 R Ⓑh		
0	**Roma Termini 615** d.	...	...	...	...	...	...	0550	0755	0936	...	...	...	1130	1157	1304	1332	1357	1535	1557	1738	...	1757	1830	1932	2000	2030	2236
5	**Roma Tiburtina 615** d.	...	...	...	...	...	...	0558	0803	|	...	...	...	1139	1205	1312	1340u	1405	|	1605	|	...	1805	1838	1940u	2008u	2039	2244
83	**Orte 615** d.	...	...	...	...	...	...	0635	0840	|	...	...	...	1215	1242	1350	1411	1442	|	1642	|	...	1842	1917	|	2045	2115	2321
112	Terni d.	...	...	...	0515	0541	...	0656	0901	1027	...	...	...	1236	1303	1409	1430	1506	1624	1707	1822	...	1917	1953	2032	2108	2146	2342
141	Spoleto d.	...	...	...	0540	0616	...	0718	0930	|	...	...	...	1306	1332	1434	1454	1530	|	1743	|	...	1940	2021	2055	2138	2208	0011
167	**Foligno** a.	...	...	...	0557	0636	...	0738	0951	1058	...	...	...	1326	1349	1449	1510	1547	1659	1803	1851	...	1957	2038	2109	2152	2225	0030
167	**Foligno 615** d.	...	...	0550	0600	0640	0645	0740	0956	1100	1103	...	...	1328	1351	1450	1515	1549	1701	1806	1853	1903	2000	2042	2111	2154	2228	...
	Assisi 615 a.	...	...	|	0611	0652	|	|	1016	|	1117	...	...	|	1411	1504	1529	|	|	|	|	1917	2014	|	|	2204	|	...
	Perugia 615 a.	...	...	|	0638	0720	|	|	1043	|	1139	...	...	|	1440	1528	1558	|	|	|	|	1940	2040	|	|	2226	|	...
224	**Fabriano** d.	0500	0600	0643	...	...	0743	0845	...	1142	...	1208	...	1419	...	...	...	1659	1744	1910	1933	...	...	2141	2156	...	2332	...
268	Jesi d.	0542	0642	0733	...	...	0830	0922	...	1210	...	1248	1426	1512	...	...	...	1736	1812	1949	|	...	...	2212	2227	...	0009	...
286	Falconara Marittima **630** d.	0557	0706	0747	...	...	0851	0938	...	1222	...	1306	1443	1529	...	...	...	1752	1825	2006	2011	...	...	2224	2240	...	0023	...
295	**Ancona 630** a.	0608	0718	0800	...	...	0905	0955	...	1231	...	1319	1455	1540	...	...	...	1803	1835	2019	*2035**	...	...	2238	2250	...	0035	...
	Ancona Marittima a.	0618	0729a	0809	...	...	0914	...	...	...	...	1329a	1505	...	...	...	...	...	...	...	...	...	...	...	...	...	...	...

		⚒	*ES* 9321 R 🍷 ⚒	*ES* 9323 R 🍷	†	2 ⚒	*ES* 9325 R ✕ R	2 ⚒				*ES* 9327 R 🍷	2 ⚒		2 Ⓐ	2	*ES* 9331 R 🍷		2 ⚒	*ES* 9333 R 🍷	2 Ⓐ		2 ⚒	2	2		2 ⚒	2	*ICp* 597 R T
Ancona Marittima d.	...	...	...	...	...	...	...	0645	...	...	...	1226a	...	1404	...	...	...	1535	...	1617	...	1721a	1821a	...	...	1938	...	...
Ancona 630 d.	0336	...	...	0624	...	...	*0722**	0655	0808	...	1108	1235	1408	1414	...	1523	...	1544	...	1626	1650	1730	1830	...	1908	1947	2128	...
Falconara Marittima **630** d.	0347	...	...	0634	...	...	0748	0706	0818	...	1118	1247	1418	1426	...	1533	...	1556	...	1638	1703	1741	1841	...	1919	1959	2139	...
Jesi d.	0359	...	...	0645	...	...	|	0725	0832	...	1129	1304	1432	1443	...	1543	...	1614	...	1657	1718	1759	1902	...	1933	2020	2155	...
Fabriano d.	0435	...	...	0716	...	...	0825	0813	0914	...	1206	1352	1514	1534	...	1614	...	1658	...	1741	1811	1852	2002	...	2017	2100	2249	...
Perugia 615 d.	|	0603	0645	|	0723	0751	|	...	|	1118	|	|	|	...	1621	|	1718	|	1803	...	|	...	...	2021	|	...	|	2318
Assisi 615 d.	|	0624	0704	|	0745	0823	|	...	|	1144	|	|	|	...	1642	|	1745	|	1822	...	|	...	...	2041	|	...	|	2336
Foligno 615 a.	0519	0639	0715	0758	0800	0837	0901	...	1001	1200	1248	1459	1610	...	1656	1658	1759	1756	1835	...	1908	...	...	2056	2105	...	2340	2350
Foligno d.	0531	0641	0718	0759	0803	...	0903	...	1003	1203	1250	1507	1611	...	...	1659	1801	...	1837	...	1909	...	...	...	2106	...	...	2354
Spoleto d.	0557	0659	0735	|	0824	...	|	...	1019	1221	1305	1531	1628	...	...	|	1822	...	1854	...	1925	...	...	...	2123	...	...	0010
Terni d.	0623	0731	0758	0833	0909	...	0936	...	1049	1255	1328	1558	1658	...	...	1732	1855	...	1916	...	1952	...	...	...	2145	...	...	0035
Orte 615 d.	0654	0800	0816	|	0936	...	|	...	1117	1317	|	...	1718	...	...	|	1917	...	1943	...	2015	...	...	...	2208	...	...	...
Roma Tiburtina 615 a.	0728	0837	0849s	|	1011	...	|	...	1152	1352	1414s	...	1752	...	...	|	1952	...	2014s	...	2108	...	...	...	2245	...	...	...
Roma Termini 615 a.	0738	...	0859	0924	1019	...	1024	...	1203	1403	1424	...	1803	...	...	1824	2003	...	2024	...	2118	...	...	...	2256	...	...	...

R – [12] and ✕ Roma - Rimini and v.v.
T – TACITO – [12] Terni - Perugia - Milano and v.v.
a – Ⓐ only.
h – Not Apr. 12, 25, and days before holidays.
q – Not Apr. 12.
s – Stops to set down only.
u – Stops to pick up only.
* – By 🚌 from/to Falconara Marittima.

626 ROMA - CASERTA - NAPOLI and FOGGIA

km		⚒	Cr	*E* 833 B	2 ⚒	2 ⚒		C	*E* 837 Z	2 †	*ES* 9351 R ✕	2 ⚒	2		Cr	*ICp* 677 R ✕	C		2	⚒r	*ES* 9353 R ✕	⚒	2	C	
0	**Roma Termini** d.	...	...	0501t	...	...	...	0615	0617t	...	0800	...	0725	...	...	0801	0915	...	...	...	1400	...	1315	...	...
138	Cassino d.	...	...	|	0657	...	...	0738	0759	...	|	...	0938	...	...	0935	1036	...	1317	...	|	...	1449	...	...
	Sulmona 624 d.	...	...	|	|	...	...	|	|	...	|	0632	|	...	...	|	|	...	|	...	|	...	|	...	...
	Castel di Sangro d.	...	...	|	|	...	...	|	|	...	|	0748	|	...	...	|	|	...	|	...	|	...	|	...	...
	Pescolanciano-Chiauci d.	...	...	|	|	...	...	|	|	...	|	|	|	...	...	|	|	...	|	...	|	...	|	...	...
	Campobasso d.	0518r	0550	|	|	0624r	...	|	|	0710r	|	|	|	...	0828	|	|	...	|	1219	|	1311r	|	1415r	...
	Carpinone d.	0559r	0632	|	|	0718r	...	|	|	0754r	|	0839	|	...	0922	|	|	...	|	1307	|	1400r	|	1500	...
	Isernia d.	0609	0641	|	|	0736	...	0822	|	0805	|	0849	|	...	0932	|	1118	...	|	1319	|	1412	|	1510	...
170	Vairano-Caianello d.	0648	...	|	0727	0814	...	...	|	0851	|	0931	1010	...	...	0952	...	...	1347	1404	|	1457	1510	...	...
216	Caserta d.	0714	...	|	0816	0842	...	...	0853	0920	0915	1005	1055	...	...	1021	...	...	1431	...	1518	1530	1542	...	...
	Napoli Centrale a.	0748	...	0734	0858	0916	...	...	0926	0952	|	1047	...	...	...	|	...	...	1512	...	|	1603	...	...	...
279	Benevento d.	...	...	...	...	...	...	...	...	...	1004	...	...	...	...	1109	...	...	...	...	1600	...	...	...	...
380	**Foggia 631** a.	...	...	...	...	...	...	...	...	...	1105	...	...	...	...	1230	...	...	...	...	1705	...	...	...	...
	Bari Centrale **631** a.	...	...	...	...	...	...	...	...	...	1214	...	...	...	...	1357	...	...	...	...	1815	...	...	...	...
	Lecce **631** a.	...	...	...	...	...	...	...	...	...	1346	...	...	...	...	...	...	...	...	...	1937	...	...	...	...

FOR NOTES SEE OPPOSITE PAGE

ROMA - CASERTA - NAPOLI and FOGGIA 626

km		2 ⚒	⚒C	†C	*ES* 9355 🅁✕	*ES* 9385 🅁🍷 T	🚌 2 †		†C	⚒C	2	2 †	2 ⚒	⚒	*ES* 9357 🅁✕		†C	2	C	⚒C	†C	2 ⚒	*E* 891 Z		*E* 951 F	*ICN* 789 H
	Roma Termini d.	1401	1415	1420	1600	1638	...	...	...	...	...	1647	1647	1715	1800	...	1728	1815	...	1940	1942	*1947*	2225	...	2330	2358
	Cassino d.	|	1543	1545	|	|	...	...	...	...	...	1844	1854	1847	|	...	1855	1950	...	|	|	2155	|	...	0108	0140
0	**Sulmona 624** d.	|	|	|	|	|	1425	...	...	...	1544	|	|	|	|	...	|	|	...	|	|	|	|	...	|	|
77	Castel di Sangro d.	|	|	|	|	|	1605	...	...	...	1700	|	|	|	|	...	|	|	...	|	|	|	|	...	|	|
106	Pescolanciano-Chiauci d.	|	|	|	|	|	|	...	...	...	1731	|	|	|	|	...	|	|	...	|	|	|	|	...	|	|
	Campobasso d.	|	|	|	|	|	|	...	1628r	1630r	|	|	|	|	|	1803r	|	|	1943r	|	|	|	|	...	|	|
119	Carpinone d.	|	|	|	|	|	1705	...	1715	1714	1744	|	|	|	|	1853r	|	|	2030	|	|	|	|	...	|	|
130	Isernia d.	|	1627	1627	|	|	1725	...	1725	1723	1757	|	|	|	|	1904	1942	|	2040	2145	2147	|	|	...	|	|
176	Vairano-Caianello d.	|	...	...	|	|	1810	...	...	...	1839	1913	1926	1910	|	1958	...	2013	...	...	...	2219	|	...	|	|
222	Caserta d.	1617	...	...	1716	1825	1835	...	...	...	1921	1957	2010	1942	1915	2028	...	2044	...	...	...	2306	0036	...	0155	0236
256	**Napoli Centrale** a.	|	...	...	|	|	1916	...	...	...	2002	...	...	...	|	2100	...	2126	...	...	...	2337	...	...	|	|
	Benevento d.	1724	...	...	1756	1918	...	...	...	...	...	...	...	...	|	...	...	...	...	...	...	...	...	...	|	0330
	Foggia 631 a.	...	...	...	1858	2044	...	...	...	...	...	...	...	...	2051	...	...	...	...	...	...	...	...	...	n	0453
	Bari Centrale **631** a.	...	...	...	2020	2204	...	...	...	...	...	...	...	...	2159	...	...	...	...	...	...	...	...	...	|	0635
	Lecce **631** a.	...	...	...	...	...	...	...	...	...	...	...	...	...	2321	...	...	...	...	...	...	...	...	...	0845	0820

km		2 †	2 ⚒	2 ⚒	2	C		2 ⚒	2 ⚒	C	2	*ES* 9350 🅁✕		C	🚌 2 †	⚒r	C	*ES* 9352 🅁✕		⚒	2	2	C		⚒C	†Cr
	Lecce **631** d.	...	...	...	...	...	...	...	...	...	...	...	...	...	...	...	...	0539	...	...	...	...	...	...	...	...
	Bari Centrale **631** d.	...	...	...	...	...	...	...	...	...	...	0535	...	...	...	...	...	0701	...	...	...	...	...	...	...	...
	Foggia 631 d.	...	...	...	...	...	...	...	...	...	...	0655	...	...	...	...	...	0807	...	...	...	...	...	...	...	...
	Benevento d.	...	...	0515	...	...	...	...	...	...	...	0801	...	...	...	...	...	|	...	...	...	...	...	...	...	...
	Napoli Centrale d.	...	...	|	...	...	...	0551	...	...	0750	|	...	...	0830	...	...	|	...	1214	...	...	...	1415	...	...
	Caserta d.	0510	0510	0605	0612	...	...	0622	0714	...	0827	0839	...	...	0910	...	...	0944	...	1244	1313	1340	...	1445	...	...
	Vairano-Caianello d.	0556	0557	|	0647	...	...	0655	0748	...	0911	|	...	...	0943	...	...	|	...	1317	1359	1411	...	1521	...	...
	Isernia d.	|	|	|	|	0642	...	0735	|	0823	|	|	...	0933	1030	1050	1119	|	...	1413	|	|	1511	1603	1628	1628
0	Carpinone d.	|	|	|	|	|	...	0750	|	0834	|	|	...	|	1048	1101	1130	|	...	1424r	|	|	|	1615r	1640	1640
48	**Campobasso** d.	|	|	|	|	|	...	|	|	0918r	|	|	...	|	|	1153	1215r	|	...	1522r	|	|	|	1709r	1730r	1730
	Pescolanciano-Chiauci d.	|	|	|	|	|	...	0805	|	...	|	|	...	|	|	...	...	|	...	...	|	|	|	...	...	...
	Castel di Sangro d.	|	|	|	|	|	...	0844	|	...	|	|	...	|	1155	...	...	|	...	...	|	|	|	...	...	...
	Sulmona 624 d.	|	|	|	|	|	...	1003	|	...	|	|	...	|	1330	...	...	|	...	...	|	|	|	...	...	...
	Cassino a.	0624	0630	|	0710	0729	...	...	0811	...	0950	|	...	1013	...	...	...	|	...	...	1431	1435	1553	...	...	...
	Roma Termini a.	0838	0835	0816	0848	0853	...	...	0945	...	...	1000	...	1140	...	...	...	1100	...	...	1646	1625	1716	...	...	...

			2 ⚒	2 †		*ES* 9354 🅁✕	⚒C	†C	⚒	†Cr	*E* 824 Z	C	*ICp* 678 🅁✕			*ES* 9384 🅁🍷 R	⚒Cr	†Cr	*ES* 9356 🅁✕	*E* 830 A		*ICN* 752 Z	*E* 892 Z	*ICN* 788 H	*E* 956 G	
	Lecce **631** d.	...	...	...	...	1222	...	...	...	...	...	...	...	...	...	...	...	...	1714	...	...	...	...	2228	2048	...
	Bari Centrale **631** d.	...	...	...	...	1344	...	...	...	...	...	...	1513	...	...	1707	...	...	1846	...	...	...	...	0015	|	...
	Foggia 631 d.	...	...	...	...	1454	...	...	...	...	...	...	1654	...	...	1822	...	...	1955	...	...	...	...	0159	n	...
	Benevento d.	...	...	...	...	1559	...	...	...	...	...	...	1818	...	...	1951	...	...	2108	...	...	...	...	0327	|	...
	Napoli Centrale d.	1527	1535	1547	...	|	...	...	1730	...	1845	...	|	1943	...	|	...	...	|	2150	...	...	...	|	|	...
	Caserta d.	1602	1614	1624	...	1639	...	...	1800	...	1917	...	1911	2014	...	2036	...	...	2146	2224	...	0158	0347	0418	0426	...
	Vairano-Caianello d.	1647	1658	1709	...	|	...	...	1841	...	|	...	1941	2042	...	|	...	...	|	|	...	|	|	|	|	...
	Isernia d.	1801	|	|	...	|	1724	1726	1922	1943	|	2041	|	2124	...	|	2146	2148	|	|	...	|	|	|	|	...
	Carpinone d.	1815	|	|	...	|	|	|	1933r	1954	|	|	|	2135r	...	|	|	|	|	|	...	|	|	|	|	...
	Campobasso d.	|	|	|	...	|	|	|	2028r	2046	|	|	|	2220r	...	|	2240	2245	|	|	...	|	|	|	|	...
	Pescolanciano-Chiauci d.	1828	|	|	...	|	|	|	...	...	|	|	|	...	...	|	...	...	|	|	...	|	|	|	|	...
	Castel di Sangro d.	1901	|	|	...	|	|	|	...	...	|	|	|	...	...	|	...	...	|	|	...	|	|	|	|	...
	Sulmona 624 d.	2018	|	|	...	|	|	|	...	...	|	|	|	...	...	|	...	...	|	|	...	|	|	|	|	...
	Cassino a.	...	1734	1743	...	|	1805	1804	...	...	2013	2125	2005	...	...	|	...	...	|	|	...	|	|	|	|	...
	Roma Termini a.	...	...	...	...	1800	1925	1928	...	...	2158t	2250	2137	...	...	2238	...	...	2300	0038t	...	0417t	0617	0629	0635	...

A – ②④⑦: 🛏 2 cl. and [2] Salerno - Napoli - Milano.
B – ②④⑥ (previous night from Milano): 🛏 2 cl. and [2] Milano - Napoli - Salerno.
C – [12] Roma - Isernia - Campobasso and v.v.
F – Not May 1: [2] Roma - Taranto - Lecce; [2] Roma - Metaponto (**953**) - Catanzaro Lido.
G – Not Apr. 30: [2] Lecce - Taranto - Roma; [2] Catanzaro Lido (**954**) - Metaponto - Roma.
H – TAVOLIERE – 🛏 1, 2 cl., 🛏 2 cl. (4 berth) and [12] Lecce - Roma and v.v.
R – ⑦ (also Apr. 13, June 2; not Apr. 12, May 31): [12] and 🍷 Taranto - Roma.
T – ⑤ (also Apr. 30; not May 1): [12] and 🍷 Roma - Taranto.
Z – For days of running and composition – see Table **640**.
n – Via Taranto.
r – Until May 31.
t – Roma **Tiburtina**.

SARDINIA 629

Some trains 2nd class only

km		†S	⚒S	⚒	†	⚒	†	†		⚒		⚒	⚒	†P	⚒P	⚒		†S	⚒S		†	⚒	⚒C	†	...		⚒	†			
0	Cagliari d.	0630	0640	0700	0901	1000	1010	1140	...	1200	...	1330	1400	1444	1453	1530	...	1636	1640	...	1654	1700	1740	1754	...	1830	1900	1930	...	2040	...
17	Decimomannu d.	0641	0651	0711	0915	1010	1027	1153	...	1215	...	1350	1417	1456	1507	1544	...	|	|	...	1711	1713	1754	1806	...	1844	1914	1949	...	2052	...
95	Oristano d.	0740	0754	0819	1040	1115	1139	1306	...	1314	1320	1514	1535	1607	1607	1642	...	1736	1736	...	1824	1825	1854	1916	...	2000	2030	2103	...	2158	...
154	Macomer d.	0826	0845	...	1146	1209	...	...	...	...	1417	...	...	1705	1705	...	...	1823	1820	...	1917	1926	1946	...	...	...	...	...	...	...	...
214	Ozieri-Chilivani a.	0919	0926	...	...	...	...	...	...	...	1507	...	...	1753	1753	...	...	1906	...	...	...	...	2035	...	...	...	...	...	...	...	...

km			⚒	†	†		†S	⚒S	y		⚒	P	†S	⚒
0	Ozieri-Chilivani d.	...	0711	...	0738	0853	0925	0934	1029	1521d	...	1758	1915	2040
47	Sassari d.	0700	0759	0801	0827	0935	1006	1013	1111	1605d	1745	1843	2003	2123
66	Porto Torres d.	0718	0814	0819	...	...	...	...	...	1623	1803	1900	...	...
67	Porto Torres M a.	0720	0816	0821	...	...	...	...	...	1625	1805	1903	...	...

	†S		†	⚒	†P	⚒P	⚒	S	⚒	†S	⚒P		
Porto Torres M d.	...	0730	...	...	0920	0926	...	...	1647d	...	1820	1915	...
Porto Torres d.	...	0733	...	...	0923	0929	...	...	1650d	...	1823	1919	...
Sassari d.	0654	0748	0800	0803	0940	0947	1330	1430	1708	1847	1844	1935	1940
Ozieri-Chilivani a.	0734	...	0841	0844	1027	1034	1411	1512	1749	1935	1931	...	2027

km		⚒	⚒	†	⚒	†	⚒		⚒	⚒				C
0	Ozieri-Chilivani d.	...	0640	0745	0851	0924	0937	...	...	1413	1518	1800	1913	2037
71	Olbia d.	0648	0747	0853	0951	1030	1043	1310	1415	1521	1617	1909	2011	2141
92	Golfo Aranci a.	0711	...	...	...	...	...	1334	1440	...	*1648*	...	2037	...

	†	†C	⚒C	⚒	†	⚒		⚒					
Golfo Aranci d.	...	...	0724	...	...	...	1340	1525	...	1747	...	2044	...
Olbia d.	0630	0744	0749	0822	0920	0928	1403	1550	1647	1811	1925	2104	...
Ozieri-Chilivani a.	0736	0845	0848	0929	1022	1036	*1510*	...	1751	*1937*	2032	...	...

km		⚒	†	⚒	⚒		⚒	†	⚒S		†S	†C	⚒C		†P	⚒P		⚒	†	⚒	†	⚒	S		⚒	⚒	†	⚒		⚒P	†S
0	Ozieri-Chilivani d.	...	...	...	...	...	...	...	...	...	0741	0847	0850	...	1034	1041	...	...	...	...	...	...	1517	...	...	...	...	...	...	1941	1942
60	Macomer d.	...	...	...	...	...	0655	...	0808	...	0827	0933	0946	...	1120	1127	...	...	...	...	1427	...	1607	...	1724	...	...	...	...	2027	2028
120	Oristano d.	0530	0542	0600	0642	...	0753	0753	0852	...	0913	1022	1035	...	1208	1212	...	1413	1445	1449	1522	1610	1657	...	1826	1914	1948	2032	...	2122	2118
197	Decimomannu d.	0643	0648	0714	|	...	0850	0854	|	...	1003	1117	1131	...	1312	1308	...	1509	1550	1555	1636	1725	1756	...	1948	2018	2055	2149	...	2213	2219
214	Cagliari a.	0704	0705	0728	0746	...	0906	0910	0946	...	1018	1132	1145	...	1329	1323	...	1524	1611	1609	1658	1738	1810	...	2001	2033	2116	2102	...	2229	2234

km		⚒																				†							
0	Cagliari d.		0520	0543	...	0620	0644	...	0748	0848	0920	1120	1220	1340	1420	...	1520	...	1720	1820	1920	2047		0728	1128	1435	1640	1723	1838	1952	2047
17	Decimomannu d.		0534	0557	...	0634	0704	...	0808	0906	0935	1133	1234	1355	1440	...	1533	...	1740	1840	1940	2105		0747	1147	1452	1658	1741	1856	2011	2105
46	Villamassargia ⊡ a.		|	0631	0641	0706	0735	0741	0835	0933	0959	1156	1259	1421	1505	1510	1558	1604	1805	1905	2005	2128		0809	1209	1516	1720	1810	1919	2034	2128
	Carbonia Stato a.		0605	|	0655	|	|	0755	|	|	1015	|	|	|	1524	|	1614	|	1824	|	|	|		|	|	|	|	|	|	|	|
55	Iglesias a.		...	0649	...	0719	0749	...	0845	0941	...	1205	1315	1435	...	1517	...	1613	...	1917	2017	2138		0819	1219	1526	1730	1820	1929	2044	2138

km		⚒																				†							
	Iglesias d.		...	0630	0700	...	0730	0800	...	0900	...	1030	...	1254	1347	1454	...	1654	...	1854	...	1954		0620	0830	1339	1545	1740	1845	1941	2054
0	Carbonia Stato d.		0620	|	|	0716	|	|	0828	|	1021	|	1243	|	|	|	1540	|	1648	|	1848	|		|	|	|	|	|	|	|	|
22	Villamassargia ⊡ d.		0634	0639	0709	0733	0739	0809	0842	0909	1035	1040	1257	1302	1356	1507	1601	1702	1707	1902	1907	2007		0628	0838	1347	1553	1748	1853	1948	2103
	Decimomannu d.		...	0703	0736	...	0803	0837	0901	0936	...	1107	...	1325	1426	1534	1625	...	1729	...	1927	2032		0652	0900	1410	1616	1811	1922	2012	2132
	Cagliari a.		...	0724	0754	...	0824	0857	0916	0956	...	1124	...	1338	1441	1547	1646	...	1747	...	1942	2045		0709	0919	1428	1634	1829	1940	2032	2152

C – Cagliari - Olbia / Golfo Aranci and v.v.
P – Cagliari - Porto Torres and v.v.
S – Cagliari - Sassari and v.v.
d – ⚒ only. y – Runs 14 minutes later on ⚒.
⊡ – Full name is Villamassargia-Domusnovas.

Narrow gauge services on Sardinia are operated by Ferrovie della Sardegna (FdS), Via Cugia 1, 09129 Cagliari. ✆ +39 070 342341. Cagliari - Sorgono (166km), Macomer - Bosa Marina (45km), Mandas - Arbatax (160km), Macomer - Nuoro (63km), Sassari - Alghero San Agostino (35km), Sassari - Palau Marina (150km), Sassari - Sorso (11km). Services operate to differing frequencies; some lines have an occasional tourist service only. Fuller details are shown in our *Tourist Railways* feature annually each July.

630 MILANO - BOLOGNA - RIMINI - ANCONA

km		E 901 ♦	ICN 785 ♦	E 925 ♦	E 907 ♦	2 ⚒	2 †	2 ⚒	ES 9325 [R] ✕ R	2 ⚒		2 ⚒	ESc 9775 [R] 🍷		ESc 9761 [R] 🍷	IC 713 🍷		2 ⑥⑦q	ESc 9763 [R] 🍷	ⓒ	Ⓐ	ICp 553 [R] ✕	ICp 1545 [R] 🍷 ⑥p		ESc 9765 [R] 🍷	IC 717 ♦
	Torino Porta Nuova 619 . d.	2105	...	...	2250	...	...	...	...	...	...	...	...	...	...	...	...	...	0745	...	...	...	...	...	...	...
	Venezia Santa Lucia 620 d.	|	...	...	|	...	...	...	...	...	...	...	...	...	...	0715	...	...	|	...	...	...	...	...	...	...
0	**Milano Centrale 619/20** ... d.	|	2300	...	|	...	...	...	...	...	...	...	0600	...	0700	|	...	0730	|	...	...	0915	0950	...	1105	...
219	**Bologna Centrale 619/20** a.	0054	0124	...	0234	...	...	...	...	...	...	...	0814	...	0852	0912	...	1012	1052	...	...	1114	1150	...	1252	...
219	**Bologna Centrale** .... d.	0059	0130	0139	0239	...	...	...	...	...	0638	...	0820	0838	0856	0920	...	1017	1056	1038	1038	1120	1154	1238	1256	1320
254	Imola .... d.	|	|	|	|	...	...	...	...	...	0701	...	|	0902	|	|	...	1042	|	1101	1104	|	|	1301	|	|
261	Castelbolognese .... d.	|	|	|	|	...	...	...	...	...	0708	...	|	0909	|	|	...	|	|	1108	1121	|	|	1308	|	|
269	Faenza .... d.	|	|	|	|	...	...	...	...	...	0717	...	0851	0917	|	0951	...	1052	|	1115	1136	1151	|	1317	|	1351
284	Forlì .... d.	|	|	|	|	...	...	...	...	...	0728	...	0901	0932	|	1001	...	1103	|	1125	1157	1201	1226	1332	|	1401
302	Cesena .... d.	|	|	|	|	...	...	...	...	...	0741	...	0913	0945	|	1013	...	1114	|	1142	1214	1213	1239	1345	|	1413
331	**Rimini** ● .... d.	0202	0237	0245	|	0550	0600	0625	0650	0717	0807	...	0936	1007	0953	1036	...	1134	1155	1207	1247	1236	1303	1407	1353	1436
340	Riccione .... d.	|	|	|	|	0600	0608	0636	|	0727	0817	...	0947	1017	|	1047	...	1144	|	1217	1256	|	1312	1417	|	1447
349	Cattolica .... d.	|	|	|	|	0610	0615	0646	|	0737	0826	...	0955f	1026	|	1056	...	1151	|	1226	1306	|	1320	1427	|	1456
364	Pesaro .... d.	|	|	|	|	0621	0626	0656	0710	0749	0838	0855	1010	1038	1017	1110	...	1203	|	1238	1319	1302	1332	1438	|	1510
376	Fano .... d.	|	|	|	|	0629	0634	0704	|	0757	0846	0904	|	1046	|	|	...	|	|	1246	1327	|	|	1446	|	|
398	Senigallia .... d.	|	|	|	|	0643	0648	0719	|	0811	0901	0919	1028	1101	|	1128	...	1223	|	1301	1341	|	|	1501	|	1528
415	Falconara Marittima 625 .... d.	|	|	|	|	0659	0702	0735	0739	0830	0911	0933	|	1111	|	|	...	|	|	1311	1357	|	|	1511	|	|
423	**Ancona 625** .... a.	0257	0333	0341	0440	0712	0717	0749	...	0843	0924	0947	1047	1124	1051	1147	...	1243	1255	1324	1410	1334	1405	1524	1441	1547
	Ancona Marittima 625 .... a.	|	|	|	|	0721	...	0758	...	0852	...	0956	...	...	|	|	...	|	|	...	...	|	|	...	|	|
	Pescara Centrale 631 . a.	0422	0459	0523	0624	...	...	...	...	...	...	...	...	...	1205	1325	...	1436	1417	...	...	1509	1541	...	1605	1725
	Bari Centrale 631 .... a.	0749	0826	0915	1040	...	...	...	...	...	...	...	...	...	1451	1640	...	...	1713	...	...	1841	1900	...	1853	2047
	Lecce 631 .... a.	0955	...	1120	...	...	...	...	...	...	...	...	...	...	1621	...	...	...	1843	...	...	...	2040	...	2023	2225

	2 ⚒		ESc 9777 [R] 🍷		ESc 9767 [R] 🍷 ♦	ICp 1549 [R] ⑤m	ESc 9779 [R] 🍷			2 Ⓐ	EC 85 ✕ ♦		ES 9769 [R] 🍷	IC 715		ESc 9781 [R] 🍷		ESc 9783 [R] 🍷			ESc 9785 [R] 🍷		IC 549 ✕	E 923 ♦	ICN 781 ♦	ICN 779 ♦
Torino Porta Nuova 619 .. d.	...	...	...	...	...	...	1150	...	...	...	...	...	...	...	...	...	...	...	...	1620	...	...	...	...	...	...
Venezia Santa Lucia 620 . d.	...	...	...	...	...	...	|	...	...	...	...	...	...	1527	...	...	...	...	...	|	...	...	...	...	...	2211v
Milano Centrale 619/20 .... d.	...	...	1200	...	1305	1210	|	...	...	...	...	...	1505	|	...	1600	...	1700	...	|	1900	...	2000	2040	2100	|
Bologna Centrale 619/20 . a.	...	...	1411	...	1452	1421	1511	...	...	...	...	...	1652	1712	...	1811	...	1911	...	2033	2111	...	2200	2314	2352	r
Bologna Centrale .... d.	...	1338	1420	1438	1456	1430	1520	1538	...	...	1620	1638	1656	1720	1738	1818	1838	1920	1938	2038	2120	2138	2222	2319	2357	|
Imola .... d.	...	1401	|	1501	|	|	|	1603	...	...	|	1659	|	|	1805	|	1903	|	2002	2101	|	2202	|	|	|	|
Castelbolognese .... d.	...	1408	|	1508	|	|	|	1610	...	...	|	1706	|	|	1812	|	1910	|	2009	2108	|	2209	|	|	|	|
Faenza .... d.	...	1417	1451	1517	|	|	1551	1619	...	...	1651	1717	|	1751	1820	1851	1917	1951	2017	2117	2151	2217	2251	|	|	|
Forlì .... d.	...	1428	1501	1532	|	|	1601	1630	...	...	1701	1732	|	1801	1831	1901	1928	2001	2028	2128	2201	2229	2301	|	0034	|
Cesena .... d.	...	1441	1513	1545	|	|	1613	1642	...	...	1713	1745	|	1813	1845	1913	1941	2013	2044	2141	2213	2246	2313	|	|	|
Rimini ● .... d.	1443	1507	1536	1607	1553	1558	1636	1713	...	1700	1743	1807	1753	1836	1911	1936	2007	2036	2113	2207	2236	2319	2336	0030	0104	0113
Riccione .... d.	1455	1516	1547	1617	|	|	1647	1724	...	1710	...	1816	|	|	1920	1947	2017	2047	...	2217	|	...	...	0041	|	|
Cattolica .... d.	1504	1523	1555f	1626	|	|	|	1734	...	1720	...	1826	|	1850	1930	|	2026	|	...	2226	2250	...	...	|	|	|
Pesaro .... d.	1516	1534	1610	1638	|	|	1703	1746	...	1730	...	1836	|	1903	1942	2003	2038	2103	...	2238	2303	...	...	0101	|	|
Fano .... d.	1524	1542	1619	1646	|	|	1712	...	...	1738	...	1846	|	1912	1950	2012	2046	|	...	2246	2312	...	...	|	|	|
Senigallia .... d.	1539	1557	1632	1701	|	|	1725	...	...	1753	...	1901	|	|	2005	2025	2101	|	...	2301	2325	...	...	|	|	|
Falconara Marittima 625 .... d.	1551	1607	1644	1711	|	|	|	...	...	1810	...	1914	|	1935	2023	|	2111	2130	...	2311	|	...	...	|	|	|
Ancona 625 .... a.	1605	1619	1700	1724	1641	1703	1747	...	...	1830	...	1924	1842	1947	2037	2047	2124	2141	...	2324	2347	...	...	0137	0202	0209
Ancona Marittima 625 ..... a.	1614a	...	...	...	|	|	|	...	...	|	...	|	|	|	...	|	...	|	...	...	...	...	...	|	|	|
Pescara Centrale 631 .. a.	...	...	...	...	1805	1834	1925	...	...	2055	...	...	1957	2125	...	2225	...	2315	...	...	...	...	...	0256	0329	0338
Bari Centrale 631 .... a.	...	...	...	...	2055	2230	2235	...	...	...	...	...	2304	...	...	...	...	...	...	...	...	...	...	0618	0645	0705
Lecce 631 .... a.	...	...	...	...	...	...	...	...	...	...	...	...	...	...	...	...	...	...	...	...	...	...	...	0810	0830	0902

	E 900 ♦	E 924 ♦	ICN 780 ♦	ICN 776 ♦	ICN 784 ♦	E 906 ♦	E 926 ♦	IC 550 ✕		ESc 9778 [R] 🍷			Ⓐ	ESc 9780 [R] 🍷	ⓒ	EC 84 ✕ ♦	EC 1284 ✕ ♦	IC 714 🍷			ESc 9760 [R] 🍷 ♦		ESc 9782 [R] 🍷	ESc 9762 [R] 🍷		ESc 9784 [R] 🍷
Lecce 631 .... d.	...	1805	1907	1927	...	2125	2205	...	...	...	...	...	...	...	...	...	...	...	...	...	...	...	...	0704	...	...
Bari Centrale 631 .... d.	1955	2022	2100	2124	2259	2338	2359	...	...	...	...	...	...	...	...	...	...	0510	...	...	0649	...	0710	0834	...	...
Pescara Centrale 631 .. d.	2350	0001	0029	0100	0204	0241	0321	...	...	...	...	...	...	0635	...	...	...	0820	...	...	0953	...	1028	1119	...	...
Ancona Marittima 625 ..... d.	|	|	|	|	|	|	|	...	...	...	...	...	...	|	...	...	...	|	...	...	|	...	|	|	...	...
Ancona 625 .... d.	0124	0133	0158	0233	0330	0406	0445	...	0545	0620	0635	0740	0800	0815	0835	...	...	1015	1035	...	1115	1135	1210	1240	1246	1310
Falconara Marittima 625 ..... d.	|	|	|	|	|	|	|	...	0555	|	0646	0751	0811	0826	0845	...	...	|	1043	...	|	1145	|	|	1257	1319
Senigallia .... d.	|	|	|	|	|	|	|	...	0607	0637	0700	0805	0821	|	0855	...	...	|	1053	...	|	1159	1227	|	1307	1330
Fano .... d.	|	|	|	|	|	|	|	...	0621	0649	0714	0819	0835	|	0909	...	...	1042	1107	...	|	1213	1242	|	1321	1342
Pesaro .... d.	|	|	|	|	|	|	|	...	0631	0659	0724	0828	0843	0852	0918	...	...	1052	1116	...	|	1223	1252	1316	1330	1352
Cattolica .... d.	|	|	|	|	|	|	|	...	0642	|	0735	0839	0854	|	0929	...	...	1105	1127	...	|	1234	|	|	1341	|
Riccione .... d.	|	|	|	|	|	|	|	...	0650	|	0745	0845	0904	0910	0939	...	...	|	1136	...	|	1244	1310	|	1351	1410
Rimini ● .... d.	|	0230	0256	0333	0427	0502	0541	0613	0703	0722	0800	0900	0930	0926	0953	0953	1003	1126	1155	...	1209	1300	1326	1339	1403	1426
Cesena .... d.	|	|	|	|	0448	|	|	0637	0721	0745	0818	0918	0953	0945	1011	1018	1022	1145	1213	...	|	1318	1345	|	1421	1445
Forlì .... d.	|	|	|	|	0501	|	|	0649	0734	0757	0831	0931	1007	0957	1023	1029	1033	1157	1226	...	|	1331	1357	|	1434	1457
Faenza .... d.	|	|	|	|	|	|	|	0700	0744	0807	0842	0942	1020	1007	1034	1040	1044	1207	1238	...	|	1342	1407	|	1444	1507
Castelbolognese .... d.	|	|	|	|	|	|	|	|	0750	|	0850	0950	1032	|	1041	|	|	|	1250	...	|	1349	|	|	1450	|
Imola .... d.	|	|	|	|	|	|	|	|	0756	|	0857	0957	1051	|	1055	|	|	|	1257	...	|	1356	|	|	1456	|
Bologna Centrale .... a.	0320	0330	0408	r	0543	0612	0652	0736	0822	0846	0922	1022	1122	1046	1122	1113	1113	1246	1322	...	1304	1422	1446	1504	1522	1546
Bologna Centrale 619/20 . d.	0325	...	0412	|	0548	0618	0702	0741	...	0856	...	...	...	1056	...	...	...	1256	...	...	1308	...	1456	1508	...	1556
Milano Centrale 619/20 .... a.	|	...	0705	|	0820	|	0920	1000	...	1100	...	...	...	1300	...	...	...	|	...	...	1455	...	|	1700	...	1800
Venezia Santa Lucia 620 . a.	|	...	...	0643v	...	|	...	...	...	...	...	...	...	...	...	...	...	1449	...	...	...	...	|	...	...	...
Torino Porta Nuova 619 .. a.	0705	...	...	...	...	1010	...	...	...	...	...	...	...	...	...	...	...	...	...	...	...	...	1825	...	...	...

	2 ⚒	2 ⚒	ICp 1550 [R] ⑦n	2 Ⓐ		ESc 9786 [R] 🍷	ESc 9764 [R] 🍷	2 ⚒	ICp 568 [R] ✕ ♦	ICp 1546 [R] ⑦n			2 ⑥⑦q	IC 718 ♦	ESc 9766 [R] 🍷	2 ⚒	2 Ⓐ	IC 716		ESc 9788 [R] 🍷	ESc 9768 [R] 🍷	2 Ⓐ	ES 9332 [R] ✕ R	2 ⚒		
Lecce 631 .... d.	...	...	...	...	...	...	...	...	...	0940	...	...	...	1020	1128	...	...	...	...	...	1337	...	...	...	...	...
Bari Centrale 631 .... d.	...	...	0910	...	...	...	1105	...	1113	1120	...	...	...	1203	1258	...	...	...	...	...	1507	...	...	...	...	...
Pescara Centrale 631 .. d.	...	...	1230	...	...	1320	1350	...	1435	1444	...	...	1505	1530	1550	...	...	1630	...	...	1750	...	...	...	...	...
Ancona Marittima 625 ...... d.	1314	1334	|	1412	...	|	|	1545a	|	|	...	...	|	|	|	1713a	1735	|	...	...	|	1917	...	2003	...	...
Ancona 625 .... d.	1323	1343	1358	1421	1435	1500	1515	1554	1620	1627	1635	...	1658	1708	1715	1722	1744	1810	1835	1900	1913	1926	...	2012	2035	...
Falconara Marittima 625 ..... d.	1334	1355	|	1433	1447	1511	|	1606	|	|	1644	...	1708	|	|	1734	1756	1822	1845	1911	|	1938	2020	2025	2046	...
Senigallia .... d.	1348	1412	|	1450	1457	|	|	1620	|	|	1656	...	1719	1724	|	1752	1812	1833	1859	1922	|	1952	|	2039	2100	...
Fano .... d.	1403	1427	|	1505	1511	1530	|	1634	|	|	1710	...	1733	|	|	1806	1828	|	1913	1936	|	2007	|	2053	2115	...
Pesaro .... d.	1413	1435	|	1513	1520	1540	|	1642	1652	1703	1718	...	1744	1743	|	1815	1836	1852	1923	1946	1946	2017	2044	2101	2125	...
Cattolica .... d.	...	1446	|	1524	1531	1551f	|	1653	|	1715	1729	...	1756	1756	|	...	1848	|	1934	1958f	|	...	|	2112	2136	...
Riccione .... d.	...	1456	|	1534	1541	1602	|	1702	|	1724	1740	...	1806	1807	|	...	1858	1910	1943	2007	|	...	|	2122	2145	...
Rimini ● .... d.	...	1510	1451	1548	1555	1626	1609	1715	1726	1734	1755	...	1832	1826	1809	...	1912	1926	1955	2026	2007	...	2108	2130	2200	...
Cesena .... d.	...	...	|	...	1613	1645	|	...	1745	1752	1813	...	1850	1845	|	...	...	1945	2013	2045	|	...	...	...	2220	...
Forlì .... d.	...	...	|	...	1626	1657	|	...	1757	1805	1826	...	1904	1857	|	...	...	1957	2026	2057	|	...	...	...	2233	...
Faenza .... d.	...	...	|	...	1638	1707	|	...	1807	|	1838	...	1915	1907	|	...	...	2007	2043	2107	|	...	...	...	2244	...
Castelbolognese .... d.	...	...	|	...	1650	|	|	...	|	|	1850	...	|	|	|	...	...	|	2051	|	|	...	...	...	2250	...
Imola .... d.	...	...	|	...	1657	|	|	...	|	|	1856	...	1928	|	|	...	...	|	2057	|	|	...	...	...	2256	...
Bologna Centrale .... a.	...	...	1600	...	1722	1746	1706	...	1846	|	1922	...	1958	1946	1904	...	...	2048	2122	2146	2059	...	...	...	2322	...
Bologna Centrale 619/20 . d.	...	...	1606	...	...	1756	1710	...	1856	|	...	...	2003	...	1908	...	...	2106	...	2156	2103	...	...	...	...	...
Milano Centrale 619/20 .... a.	...	...	1815	...	...	2000	1900	...	2105	2135	...	...	2310	...	|	...	...	|	...	2359	2255	...	...	...	...	...
Venezia Santa Lucia 620 . a.	...	...	...	...	...	...	...	...	...	...	...	...	...	...	|	...	...	2250	...	...	...	...	...	...	...	...
Torino Porta Nuova 619 .. a.	...	...	...	...	...	...	...	...	...	...	...	...	...	...	2215	...	...	...	...	...	...	...	...	...	...	...

FOR NOTES SEE OPPOSITE PAGE

ANCONA - BARI - LECCE — 631

	2 ⚒	2	*E* 923 ♦	*ICN* 789 ♦	*ICN* 781 ♦	*E* 951 ♦	*ICN* 779 ♦	2 ⚒	*E* 903 A	*E* 901 ♦		*ICN* 785 ♦	*E* 925 ♦	2	2 ⚒	*E* 907 ♦	2 ⚒	*ES* 9351 [R] ✕	2 ⚒	2 ⚒	2	2 ⚒	*ICp* 677 [R] ✕	*ESc* 9761 [R] 🍷	2 ⚒	2 ⚒
Torino Porta Nuova **619** ..d.	...	...	...	...	...	...	...	...	2105	2105	...	...	...	...	...	2250	...	...	...	...	...	...	...	...	...	...
Venezia Santa Lucia **620**.d.	...	...	...	...	...	...	2211v	...	|	|	...	...	...	...	...	|	...	...	...	...	...	...	...	...	...	...
Milano C **619/20/30**.......d.	...	...	2040	...	2100	...	|	...	|	|	...	2300	...	...	...	|	...	...	...	...	...	...	...	0700	...	...
Bologna C **619/20/30**.....d.	...	...	2319	...	2357	...	r	...	0059	0059	...	0130	0139	...	...	0239	...	...	...	...	...	...	...	0856	...	...
Ancona 625/30 ....d.	...	...	0137	...	0205	...	0212	...	0259	0259	...	0336	0343	...	...	0443	...	...	...	0625	0730	...	...	1054	...	...
Civitanova-Montegranaro ....d.	...	...	|	...	|	...	|	...	|	|	...	|	|	...	...	0512	...	...	...	0704	0805	...	...	|	...	...
San Benedetto del Tronto ...d.	...	...	|	...	|	...	|	...	|	|	...	|	0437	...	...	0538	...	...	...	0738	0839	...	...	|	...	...
Pescara Centrale...............a.	...	...	0256	...	0329	...	0338	...	0422	0422	...	0459	0523	...	...	0624	...	...	...	0835	0931	...	...	1205	...	...
Pescara Centrale...............d.	...	...	0300	...	0332	...	0341	...	0425	0425	...	0502	0526	...	...	0627	...	...	...	▬	▬	...	...	1208	...	...
Termoli ....d.	...	...	0403	...	|	...	0445	...	0530	0530	...	0608	0636	...	...	0744	...	...	...	...	...	...	...	|	...	...
Roma Termini **626**...........d.	...	...	|	2358	|	...	|	...	|	|	...	|	|	...	...	|	...	0800	...	...	...	...	0801	|	...	...
Foggia 626 ....a.	...	...	0450	0453	0524	...	0540	...	0625	0625	...	0700	0743	...	...	0837	...	1105	...	...	...	...	1230	1347	...	...
Foggia ....d.	...	...	0453	0508	0530	...	0544	...	0633	0633	...	0704	0747	...	...	0843	...	1114	...	...	...	...	1244	1350	...	...
Barletta..............................d.	...	...	0533	0544	0606	...	0621	...	0707	0707	...	0745	0821	...	...	0938	...	1143	...	2	...	...	1316	|	...	...
Bari Centrale ....a.	...	...	0618	0635	0645	...	0705	...	0749	0749	...	0826	0915	...	...	1040	...	1214	...	⚒	2	...	1357	1451	...	...
Bari Centrale ▲................d.	0505	0537	0623	0639	0649	...	0709	0714	0804	0805	...	0849	0930	0935	1015	...	1148	1218	1249	1317	1420	1405	...	1455	1545	1606
Gioia del Colle.....................d.	|	|	|	|	|	...	|	0803	0835	|	...	0933	|	|	1058	...	|	|	|	1406	1503	|	...	|	|	1647
Taranto 638 ▲ ....a.	|	|	|	|	|	0657	|	0845	0914	|	...	1009	|	|	1141	...	|	|	|	1454	1543	|	...	|	|	1731
Crotone **635**...................a.	|	|	|	|	|	|	|	...	1245	|	...	1400	|	|	...	...	|	|	|	...	...	|	...	|	|	...
Monopoli.............................d.	0537	0609	0652	0702	0715	|	0742	...	...	0837	...	...	0959	1009	...	...	1221	1241	1323	...	...	1430	...	|	1608	...
Fasano ....d.	0545	0617	0702	0713	0725	|	0754	...	...	0848	...	...	1010	1018	...	...	1231	1250	1331	...	...	1440	...	|	1616	...
Ostuni.................................d.	0559	0631	0715	0728	0738	|	0808	...	...	0902	...	...	1023	1033	...	...	1247	1302	1342	...	...	1451	...	1532	1630	...
Brindisi ▲ ....d.	0626	0658	0740	0753	0804	0814	0832	...	...	0926	...	...	1049	1140	...	...	1333	1324	1407	...	...	1516	...	1557	1656	...
Lecce ....a.	0658	0730	0810	0820	0830	0845	0902	...	...	0955	...	...	1120	1220	...	...	1403	1346	1440	...	...	1547	...	1621	1727	...

	IC 713 🍷	2 ⑥⑦q	*ESc* 9763 [R] 🍷	2 ⚒	2	*ES* 9353 [R] ✕	2	*ICp* 553 [R] ✕	*ICp* 1545 [R] ⑥p	*ESc* 9765 [R] 🍷	2	2	*ES* 9355 [R] ✕	*IC* 717 ♦	*ESc* 9767 [R] 🍷	*ICp* 1549 [R] ⑤m	2 ⚒	*ES* 9385 [R] 🍷 ⑤m	*ESc* 9779 [R] 🍷	*E* 981 ♦	*ES* 9357 [R] ✕	*ESc* 9769 [R] 🍷	2	*IC* 715	*ESc* 9781 [R] 🍷	*ESc* 9783 [R] 🍷
Torino Porta Nuova **619** ..d.	...	...	0745	...	...	...	...	...	...	...	...	...	...	...	...	...	...	...	1150	...	...	...	...	...	...	...
Venezia Santa Lucia **620**.d.	0715	...	|	...	...	...	...	...	...	...	...	...	...	...	...	...	...	...	|	...	...	...	...	1527	...	...
Milano C **619/20/30**.......d.	|	0730	|	...	...	...	...	0915	0950	1105	...	...	...	...	1305	1210	...	...	|	...	...	1505	...	|	1600	1700
Bologna C **619/20/30**.....d.	0920	1017	1056	...	...	...	...	1120	1154	1256	...	...	...	1320	1456	1430	...	...	1520	...	...	1656	...	1720	1818	1920
Ancona 625/30 ....d.	1150	1246	1258	...	...	...	...	1337	1408	1444	...	...	...	1550	1644	1708	...	...	1750	...	...	1845	...	1950	2050	2144
Civitanova-Montegranaro ....d.	1216	1320	|	...	...	...	...	1406	1433	|	...	...	...	1616	|	|	...	...	1816	...	...	|	...	2020	2116	2208
San Benedetto del Tronto ...d.	1248	1352	|	...	...	...	...	1429	1458	1530	...	...	...	1648	1730	|	...	...	1846	...	...	|	...	2046	2146	2236
Pescara Centrale...............a.	1325	1436	1417	...	...	...	...	1509	1541	1605	...	...	...	1725	1805	1834	...	...	1925	...	...	1957	...	2125	2225	2315
Pescara Centrale...............d.	1328	...	1420	...	...	...	...	1512	1544	1608	...	...	...	1728	1808	1839	...	...	1928	...	...	2000	...	▬	...	...
Termoli ....d.	1428	...	1516	...	...	...	...	1620	1642	1700	...	...	...	1828	|	1941	...	...	2028	...	...	2103	...	...	...	...
Roma Termini **626**...........d.	|	...	|	...	...	1400	...	|	|	|	...	...	1600	|	|	|	...	1638	|	...	1800	|	...	...	...	...
Foggia 626 ....a.	1528	...	1604	...	...	1705	...	1723	1739	1747	...	...	1858	1921	1946	2054	...	2044	2119	...	2051	2154	...	...	...	...
Foggia ....d.	1531	...	1607	...	...	1714	...	1727	1742	1750	...	...	1907	1924	1949	2106	...	2053	2122	...	2100	2157	...	...	...	...
Barletta..............................d.	1603	...	1638	...	...	1745	...	1801	1815	|	...	...	1938	1959	|	2139	...	2125	2154	...	|	2229	...	...	...	...
Bari Centrale ....a.	1640	...	1713	...	...	1815	...	1841	1900	1853	...	...	2020	2047	2055	2230	...	2204	2235	...	2159	2304	...	2	...	...
Bari Centrale ▲................d.	...	...	1717	1726	1738	1819	1824	1907	1905	1857	1935	1944	...	2051	2105	...	2058	2213	...	2256	2203	...	2310	2320	...	...
Gioia del Colle.....................d.	...	...	|	1808	|	|	1905	1939	|	|	|	2026	...	|	2139	...	|	2245	...	2345	|	...	|	0008	...	...
Taranto 638 ▲ ....a.	...	...	|	1855	|	|	1951	2014	|	|	|	2112	...	|	2217	...	|	2319	...	0029	|	...	|	0051	...	...
Crotone **635**...................a.	...	...	|	...	|	|	...	2359	|	|	|	...	...	|	...	...	|	...	...	...	|	...	|	...	...	...
Monopoli.............................d.	...	...	|	...	1812	|	...	...	1928	1920	2011	...	...	2114	...	...	2132	...	...	...	|	...	2342	...	...	...
Fasano ....d.	...	...	1745	...	1822	|	...	...	1938	|	2019	...	...	2124	...	...	2141	...	...	...	|	...	2350	...	...	...
Ostuni.................................d.	...	...	|	...	1835	|	...	...	1951	|	2033	...	...	2137	...	...	2155	...	...	...	|	...	0004	...	...	...
Brindisi ▲ ....d.	...	...	1818	...	1924k	1913	...	...	2014	1959	2100	...	...	2200	...	...	2219	...	...	...	2257	...	0028	...	...	...
Lecce ....a.	...	...	1843	...	1955	1937	...	...	2040	2023	...	...	...	2225	...	...	2250	...	...	...	2321	...	0100	...	...	...

♦ – **NOTES FOR TABLES 630/1** (LISTED BY TRAIN NUMBER)

84 – MICHELANGELO – Ⓐ: [12] and ✕ Rimini - Bologna - München. Supplement payable.
85 – MICHELANGELO – [12] and ✕ München - Bologna - Rimini. Supplement payable.
568 – MURGE – [12] and ✕ Crotone (**566**) - Metaponto (**567**) - Taranto - Milano.
717/8 – ADIGE – [12] Bolzano - Verona - Bologna - Lecce and v.v.
776 – TERGESTE – ▬ 2 cl. (4 berth) and [12] Lecce - Venezia Mestre (**777**) - Trieste; 🛏 1,2 cl. (Excelsior), 🛏 1,2 cl. (T2), 🛏 1,2 cl. and [12] Lecce - Venezia Mestre (**1598**) - Venezia Santa Lucia.
779 – TERGESTE – ▬ 2 cl. (4 berth) and [12] Trieste (**778**) - Venezia Mestre - Lecce; 🛏 1,2 cl. (Excelsior), 🛏 1,2 cl. (T2), 🛏 1,2 cl. and [12] Venezia Santa Lucia (**1599**) - Venezia Mestre - Lecce.
780/1 – FRECCIA SALENTINA – 🛏 1,2 cl. (Excelsior), 🛏 1,2 cl. (T2), 🛏 1,2 cl., ▬ 2 cl. (4 berth) and [12] Lecce - Milano and v.v.
784 – FRECCIA DEL LEVANTE – ▬ 2 cl. and [12] Crotone (**782**) - Metaponto (**783**) - Taranto - Milano; 🛏 1,2 cl. (Excelsior), 🛏 1,2 cl. (T2), 🛏 1,2 cl., ▬ 2 cl. and [12] Taranto - Milano.
785 – FRECCIA DEL LEVANTE – ▬ 2 cl. and [12] Milano - Taranto (**786**) - Metaponto (**787**) - Crotone; 🛏 1,2 cl. (Excelsior), 🛏 1,2 cl. (T2), 🛏 1,2 cl., ▬ 2 cl. and [12] Milano - Taranto.
789 – TAVOLIERE – 🛏 1,2 cl., ▬ 2 cl. (4 berth) and [12] Roma - Lecce.
900 – ⑦; also Apr. 13, June 2; not Apr. 12, May 31 (from Bari): 🛏 1,2 cl. (T2), ▬ 2 cl. and [2] Bari - Torino.
901 – FRECCIA ADRIATICA – 🛏 1,2 cl. (T2), 🛏 1,2 cl., ▬ 2 cl. and [2] Torino - Lecce; ▬ 2 cl. and [2] Torino (**901**) - Bari (**903**) - Taranto (**904**) - Metaponto (**905**) - Catanzaro Lido.
906 – FRECCIA ADRIATICA – 🛏 1,2 cl. (T2), 🛏 1,2 cl., ▬ 2 cl. and [2] Lecce - Torino; ▬ 2 cl. and [2] Catanzaro Lido (**908**) - Metaponto (**909**) - Taranto (**910**) - Bari (**906**) - Torino.
907 – ⑤; also Apr. 30; not May 1 (from Torino): 🛏 1,2 cl. (T2), ▬ 2 cl. and [2] Torino - Bari.
923 – 🛏 1,2 cl. (T2), ▬ 2 cl. (4/6 berth) and [2] Milano - Lecce.
924 – ①③④⑤⑥⑦ (also June 2; not June 3): 🛏 1,2 cl. (Excelsior), 🛏 1,2 cl. (T2), 🛏 1,2 cl., ▬ 2 cl. (4/6 berth) and [2] Lecce - Bologna - Bolzano.
925 – ①②④⑤⑥⑦, also June 3; not June 4 (from Bolzano): 🛏 1,2 cl. (Excelsior), 🛏 1,2 cl. (T2), 🛏 1,2 cl., ▬ 2 cl. (4/6 berth) and [2] Bolzano - Bologna - Lecce.
926 – 🛏 1,2 cl. (T2), ▬ 2 cl. (4/6 berth) and [2] Lecce - Milano.
951 – Not May 1 (from Roma): [2] Roma - Taranto - Lecce; [2] Roma - Metaponto (**953**) - Catanzaro Lido.
981 – Ⓐ: [2] Bari - Taranto (**982**) - Metaponto (**983**) - Villa S G - Reggio di Calabria.
1284 – MICHELANGELO – Ⓒ: [12] and ✕ Rimini - Bologna - München. Supplement payable.
9760/7 – [12] and 🍷 Taranto - Bari - Milano and v.v.

A – FRECCIA ADRIATICA – ▬ 2 cl. and [2] Torino (**901**) - Bari - Taranto (**904**) - Metaponto (**905**) - Catanzaro Lido.
R – [12] and 🍷 Roma - Rimini and v.v.

a – Ⓐ only.
f – From June 1.
k – Arrive 1903.
m – Also Apr. 30; not May 1.
n – Also Apr. 13, June 2; not Apr. 12, May 31.
p – Not Apr. 25, May 2.
q – Also Apr. 13, May 1, June 2; not Apr. 12, May 2.
r – Via Ravenna.
v – Venezia **Mestre**.

▲ – For additional services Taranto - Brindisi/Bari and v.v. – see below.
● – For 🚌 service Rimini - San Marino and v.v. – see below.

▲ – LOCAL SERVICES TARANTO - BRINDISI/BARI and v.v. 2nd class only

TARANTO - BRINDISI and v.v.: 70 km, journey 61 – 84 minutes.

From **Taranto**: 0516⚒, 0536⚒, 0624, 0851⚒, 1205⚒, 1247⚒, 1355⚒, 1437⚒, 1616⚒, 1817, 1906.

From **Brindisi**: 0541⚒, 0704⚒, 0813⚒, 1143⚒, 1324, 1409⚒, 1434⚒, 1630, 1728⚒, 1803⚒, 2025.

TARANTO - BARI and v.v. (additional services): 115 km, journey 83 – 110 minutes.

From **Taranto**: 0442⚒, 0504†, 0634, 0708⚒, 0815⚒, 1023†, 1231⚒, 1531⚒, 1907†.

From **Bari**: 0350, 0546⚒, 0647⚒, 0811†, 1605†.

● – 🚌 service available **Rimini - San Marino and v.v.**, 27 km, journey 40 – 50 minutes. Departures from Rimini (FS railway station). Operator: F.lli Benedettini s.a. ✆ +378 90 67 48.

631 LECCE - BARI - ANCONA

	ESc 9780	*IC* 714	*ES* 9350	*ESc* 9760			*ES* 9352	*ESc* 9782		*E* 990		*ESc* 9762	*ICp* 1550			*ESc* 9764	*ICp* 568	*ICp* 1546		*IC* 718			*ESc* 9766	*ES* 9354		
	R 🍷	🍷	R ✕	R 🍷	2	2	R ✕	R 🍷	2		2	R 🍷	R	2		R 🍷	R ✕	R	2		2	2	R 🍷	R ✕	2	2
						⚒			⚒	♦	⚒		⑦n	⚒				⑦n	⑥⑦q	♦	⚒				⚒	⚒
Lecce d.	...	...	...	...	0456	...	0539	...	0546	...	0605	0704	...	0800	...	...	...	0940	...	1020	1040	1055	1128	1222	1230	...
Brindisi ▲ d.	...	...	...	...	0527	...	0603	...	0623	...	0635	0728	...	0824	...	...	...	1005	...	1047	1110	1129	1152	1245	1302	...
Ostuni d.	...	...	...	...	0550	...	|	...	0647	...	0658	|	...	|	...	...	...	1025	...	1107	1132	1156	|	|	1328	...
Fasano d.	...	...	...	...	0604	...	|	...	0700	...	0712	|	...	|	...	...	...	1038	...	1120	1145	1229	1221	|	1343	...
Monopoli d.	...	...	...	...	0613	...	|	...	0709	...	0721	0802	...	0900	...	...	...	1048	...	1130	1155	1238	|	|	1352	...
Crotone **635** d.	...	...	...	...	|	...	|	...	|	...	|	|	...	|	...	...	...	|	...	|	|	|	|	|	|	...
Taranto 638 ▲ d.	...	...	...	0532	|	0547	|	...	|	0608	|	|	...	|	...	...	0941	|	...	|	|	|	|	|	|	1336
Gioia del Colle d.	...	...	...	0607	|	0624	|	...	|	0657	|	|	...	|	...	...	1013	|	...	|	|	|	|	|	|	1419
Bari Centrale ▲ a.	...	...	...	0640	0651	0709	0657	...	0745	0746	0758	0830	...	0930	...	...	1048	1116	...	1159	1223	1313	1254	1340	1430	1502
Bari Centrale d.	...	0510	0535	0649	...	...	0701	0710	...	...	...	0834	0910	▬	...	1105	1113	1120	...	1203	...	...	1258	1344	▬	...
Barletta d.	...	0547	0614	0720	...	...	|	0753	...	...	...	|	0954	...	...	|	1149	1200	...	1248	...	...	1329	1414	...	...
Foggia a.	...	0623	0646	0752	...	...	0758	0833	...	...	...	0937	1031	...	...	1207	1224	1234	...	1328	...	...	1404	1445	...	...
Foggia 626 d.	...	0627	0655	0756	...	...	0807	0836	...	...	...	0940	1035	...	...	1210	1227	1239	...	1331	...	...	1407	1454	...	...
Roma Termini **626** a.	...	|	1000	|	...	...	1100	|	...	...	...	|	|	*ESc*	...	|	|	|	...	|	...	...	|	1800	*IC*	...
Termoli d.	...	0719	...	0850	...	...	...	0928	...	...	...	1026	1128	**9786**	...	|	1334	1344	...	1426	...	...	1456	...	**716**	...
Pescara Centrale a.	...	0817	...	0950	...	...	...	1025	...	...	...	1116	1227	R 🍷	...	1347	1432	1441	...	1527	...	...	1547	...		...
Pescara Centrale d.	0635	0820	...	0953	...	...	...	1028	...	...	...	1119	1230	1320	...	1350	1435	1444	1505	1530	...	...	1550	...	1630	...
San Benedetto del Tronto d.	0713	0900	...	|	...	...	...	1111	...	...	...	1152	|	1400	...	1425	1521	1527	1545	1611	...	...	|	...	1711	...
Civitanova-Montegranaro d.	0738	0927	...	|	...	...	...	1138	...	...	...	|	|	1427	...	|	1545	1556	1616	1638	...	...	|	...	1738	...
Ancona 625/30 a.	0812	1012	...	1112	...	...	...	1207	...	...	...	1237	1354	1457	...	1512	1617	1624	1655	1705	...	...	1712	...	1807	...
Bologna C **619/20/30** a.	1046	1246	...	1304	...	...	...	1446	...	...	...	1504	1600	1746	...	1706	1846	|	1958	1946	...	...	1904	...	2048	...
Milano C **619/20/30** a.	1300	|	...	1455	...	...	...	|	...	...	...	1700	1815	2000	...	1900	2105	2135	2310	...	...	...	|	...	|	...
Venezia Santa Lucia **620** a.	...	1449	...	...	...	...	...	|	...	...	...	...	...	...	...	...	...	...	...	...	...	...	|	...	2250	...
Torino Porta Nuova **619** a.	...	...	...	...	...	...	...	1825	...	...	...	...	...	...	...	...	...	...	...	...	...	...	2215	...	...	...

	ESc 9768			*ICp* 678			*ES* 9384				*ES* 9356			*E* 900	*E* 924		*ICN* 780	*ICN* 776	*E* 956		*ICN* 784		*E* 906	*E* 908	*E* 926	*ICN* 788
	R 🍷	2	2	R ✕	2	2	R 🍷	2	2	2	R ✕	2	2			2				2						
			⚒		⚒	†	⑦n			⚒		⚒		♦	♦	⚒	♦	♦	♦		♦		♦	A	♦	♦
Lecce d.	1337	1345	...	...	1430	...	...	1530	...	1645	1714	1745	...	...	1805	...	1907	1927	2048	1950	...	...	2125	...	2205	2228
Brindisi ▲ d.	1402	1418	...	...	1506	...	...	1603	...	1710	1738	1815	...	...	1834	...	1932	1956	2123	2033	...	...	2154	...	2236	2252
Ostuni d.	1421	1441	...	...	1528	...	...	1627	...	|	1758	1839	...	...	1856	...	1955	2019	|	2057	...	...	2215	...	2258	2314
Fasano d.	|	1455	...	...	1541	...	...	1640	...	|	1810	1853	...	...	1910	...	2009	2033	|	2111	...	...	2228	...	2311	2327
Monopoli d.	|	1504	...	...	1551	...	...	1649	...	1746	1819	1902	...	...	1922	...	2020	2045	|	2125	...	...	2240	...	2321	2337
Crotone **635** d.	|	|	...	...	|	...	...	|	...	|	|	|	...	...	|	...	|	|	|	|	1730	...	|	1802	|	|
Taranto 638 ▲ d.	|	|	1426	...	|	1522	1550	|	1641	|	|	|	1805	...	|	1905	|	|	2236	|	2120	...	|	2156	|	|
Gioia del Colle d.	|	|	1510	...	|	1601	1625	|	1721	|	|	|	1850	...	|	1948	|	|	...	|	2204	...	|	2237	|	|
Bari Centrale ▲ a.	1503	1543	1556	...	1630	1645	1658	1727	1805	1815	1842	1940	1937	...	1958	2031	2053	2119	...	2200	2241	...	2315	2314	2352	0008
Bari Centrale d.	1507	...	...	1513	...	...	1707	...	...	...	1846	...	...	1955	2022	...	2100	2124	...	...	2259	...	2338	2338	2359	0015
Barletta d.	|	...	...	1602	...	...	1738	...	...	...	1917	...	...	2043	2116	...	2138	2211	...	...	2332	...	0011	0011	0044	0102
Foggia a.	1608	...	...	1636	...	...	1813	...	...	...	1946	...	...	2130	2155	...	2221	2256	...	...	0010	...	0046	0046	0125	0143
Foggia 626 d.	1612	...	...	1654	...	...	1822	...	...	...	1955	...	...	2136	2159	...	2225	2300	...	...	0013	...	0050	0050	0130	0159
Roma Termini **626** a.	|	...	...	2137	...	...	2238	...	...	...	2300	...	...	|	|	...	|	|	...	...	|	...	|	|	|	0629
Termoli d.	|	...	...	...	...	...	...	...	...	...	...	...	...	2238	2255	...	2320	2357	...	...	|	...	|	|	0220	...
Pescara Centrale a.	1747	...	...	...	...	...	...	...	...	...	...	...	...	2347	2359	...	0026	0057	...	...	0201	...	0238	0238	0319	...
Pescara Centrale d.	1750	...	...	...	...	...	...	...	...	...	...	...	...	2350	0001	...	0029	0100	...	...	0204	...	0241	0241	0321	...
San Benedetto del Tronto d.	|	...	...	...	...	...	...	...	...	...	...	...	...	0030	0040	...	|	|	...	...	|	...	|	|	|	...
Civitanova-Montegranaro d.	|	...	...	...	...	...	...	...	...	...	...	...	...	0054	|	...	|	|	...	...	|	...	|	|	|	...
Ancona a.	1910	...	...	...	...	...	...	...	...	...	...	...	...	0122	0130	...	0155	0229	...	...	0327	...	0403	0403	0443	...
Bologna C **619/20/30** a.	2059	...	...	...	...	...	...	...	...	...	...	...	...	0320	0330	...	0408	r	...	...	0543	...	0612	0612	0652	...
Milano C **619/20/30** a.	2255	...	...	...	...	...	...	...	...	...	...	...	...	|	...	...	0705	|	...	...	0820	...	|	|	0920	...
Venezia Santa Lucia **620** a.	...	...	...	...	...	...	...	...	...	...	...	...	...	|	...	...	...	0643v	...	...	...	...	|	|	...	...
Torino Porta Nuova **619** a.	...	...	...	...	...	...	...	...	...	...	...	...	...	0705	...	...	...	...	...	...	...	...	1010	1010	...	...

♦ – **NOTES** (LISTED BY TRAIN NUMBER)

718 – ADIGE – [12] Lecce - Bologna - Verona - Bolzano.
776 – TERGESTE – ▬ 2 cl. (4 berth) and [12] Lecce - Venezia Mestre (**777**) - Trieste; 🛏 1,2 cl. (Excelsior), 🛏 1,2 cl. (T2), 🛏 1,2 cl. and [12] Lecce - Venezia Mestre (**1598**) - Venezia Santa Lucia.
780 – FRECCIA SALENTINA – 🛏 1,2 cl. (Excelsior), 🛏 1,2 cl. (T2), 🛏 1,2 cl., ▬ 2 cl. (4 berth) and [12] Lecce - Milano.
784 – FRECCIA DEL LEVANTE – ▬ 2 cl. and [12] Crotone (**782**) - Metaponto (**783**) - Taranto - Milano; 🛏 1,2 cl. (Excelsior), 🛏 1,2 cl. (T2), 🛏 1,2 cl., ▬ 2 cl. and [12] Taranto - Milano.
788 – TAVOLIERE – 🛏 1,2 cl., ▬ 2 cl. (4 berth) and [12] Lecce - Roma.
900 – ⑦; also Apr. 13, June 2; not Apr. 12, May 31 (from Bari): 🛏 1,2 cl. (T2), ▬ 2 cl. and [2] Bari - Torino.
906 – FRECCIA ADRIATICA – 🛏 1,2 cl. (T2), 🛏 1,2 cl., ▬ 2 cl. and [2] Lecce - Torino; ▬ 2 cl. and [2] Catanzaro Lido (**908**) - Metaponto (**909**) - Taranto (**910**) - Bari (**906**) - Torino.
924 – ①③④⑤⑥⑦ (also June 2; not June 3): 🛏 1,2 cl. (Excelsior), 🛏 1,2 cl. (T2), 🛏 1,2 cl., ▬ 2 cl. (4/6 berth) and [2] Lecce - Bologna - Bolzano.
926 – 🛏 1,2 cl. (T2), ▬ 2 cl. (4/6 berth) and [2] Lecce - Milano.
956 – Not Apr. 30: [2] Lecce - Taranto - Roma; [2] Catanzaro Lido (**954**) - Metaponto - Roma.
990 – Ⓐ (from Reggio): [2] Reggio di Calabria (**986**) - Villa S G - Metaponto (**989**) - Taranto - Bari.

A – FRECCIA ADRIATICA – ▬ 2 cl. and [2] Catanzaro Lido - Metaponto (**909**) - Taranto (**910**) - Bari (**906**) - Torino.
n – Also Apr. 13, June 2; not Apr. 12, May 31.
q – Also Apr. 13, May 1, June 2; not Apr. 12, May 2.
r – Via Ravenna.
v – Venezia **Mestre**.
▲ – For additional services Taranto - Brindisi/Bari and v.v. – see page 311.

633 ROMA and LAMEZIA - PAOLA - COSENZA - SIBARI

km		2	2	2	2	2	2	2	*ICp* 511/2 R	2	2
		⚒	©			⚒		⚒	S	Ⓑy	
	Roma Termini **640** d.	...	...	...	...	...	...	...	1420	...	...
	Napoli Centrale **640** d.	...	0648	...	0854	...	1250	...	1648	...	1842
	Lamezia Terme **640** d.	...	|	...	|	...	|	...	|	...	|
0	**Paola 640** ▲ d.	...	1100	...	1300	...	1700	...	2025	...	2251
21	Castiglione-Cosentino ▲ a.	...	1116	...	1318	...	1723	...	2048	...	2308
26	**Cosenza** ▲ a.	...	1125	...	1325	...	1730	...	2055	...	2315
——	**Cosenza** d.	1045	...	1243	...	1417	...	1817	2110	2117	...
0	Castiglione-Cosentino d.	1051	...	1249	...	1423	...	1823	|	2123	...
60	**Sibari** a.	1145	...	1353	...	1522	...	1915	2158	2219	...

	2	2	*ICp* 535/6 R	2	2	2	2	2	2	2
		⚒	S	©	⚒		Ⓐ	⚒	⚒	
Sibari d.	...	0715	1000	...	1310	...	1505	...	1710	...
Castiglione-Cosentino a.	...	0812	|	...	1401	...	1601	...	1802	...
Cosenza a.	...	0818	1055	...	1407	...	1607	...	1807	...
Cosenza ▲ d.	0530	...	1110	1225	...	1425	...	1622	...	1825
Castiglione-Cosentino ▲ d.	0537	...	1117	1232	...	1434	...	1629	...	1832
Paola 640 ▲ a.	0550	...	1135	1250	...	1450	...	1643	...	1850
Lamezia Terme **640** a.	|	...	|	|	...	|	...	...	...	|
Napoli Centrale **640** a.	1010	...	1512	1712	...	1910	...	...	...	2302
Roma Termini **640** a.	...	...	1733	...	...	...	...	...	...	...

S – SILA – [2] Roma (**507/30**) - Sibari (**513/34**) - Crotone and v.v.
y – Also Apr. 25.

▲ – **Additional services PAOLA - COSENZA and v.v.** 2nd class only.
From **Paola**: 0630⚒, 0700⚒, 0727⚒, 0730†, 0752⚒, 0830⚒, 0900⚒, 0935⚒, 0945†, 1136†, 1202⚒, 1230⚒, 1330⚒, 1400⚒, 1430, 1530⚒, 1600⚒, 1730⚒, 1830, 1930⚒, 2050†, 2110⚒, 2200⚒, 2230.
From **Cosenza**: 0555⚒, 0625⚒, 0650, 0725⚒, 0750⚒, 0825⚒, 0855, 0950⚒, 1030†, 1125⚒, 1155⚒, 1250, 1325⚒, 1350⚒, 1450⚒, 1525⚒, 1605†, 1622⚒, 1700⚒, 1750, 1850⚒, 1950, 2025, 2125, 2220⚒.

REGGIO DI CALABRIA - SIBARI - TARANTO 635

Most services 2nd class only

km		*E* 986		*ICp* 566 [R]		*ICp* 534 [R]																				*ICN* 782
		◆	⚒	◆	⚒	◆	⚒	†	⚒	⚒	⚒	†	⚒	⚒	⚒	⚒	†	⚒	†	⚒	Ⓐ	⚒	⚒	⚒	†	◆
0	**Reggio di Calabria** d.	2340	...	...	...	...	...	0630	0637	...	...	0825	0837	...	...	...	1025	1037	...	...	...	1237	...	...	...	...
30	Melito di Porto Salvo d.	|	...	...	...	...	...	0706	0702	...	...	0902	0902	...	...	...	1102	1102	...	...	...	1302	...	...	...	...
96	Locri d.	|	...	...	...	...	...	0812	0810	...	...	1007	1007	...	...	...	1210	1210	...	...	...	1409	...	...	...	...
101	Siderno d.	|	...	...	...	...	...	0818	0818	...	...	1012	1013	...	...	...	1215	1219	...	...	...	1420	...	...	...	...
112	Roccella Jonica d.	|	...	...	...	...	...	0831	0833	...	...	1024	1027	...	...	...	1231	1234	...	...	...	1434	...	...	...	...
160	Soverato d.	|	...	...	...	...	...	0923	0910	...	...	1113	1114	...	...	...	1317	1310	...	...	...	1506	...	...	...	...
178	Catanzaro Lido a.	|	...	...	...	...	...	0940	0925	...	...	1130	1130	...	...	...	1335	1325	...	...	...	1525	...	...	...	...
	Catanzaro Lido ▲ d.	|	...	...	0540	...	...	0950	0930a	...	...	1140	1140	1135	...	1230	1345	1340	1346	1346	...	...	1530	...	...	...
	Catanzaro ▲ d.	|	...	...	|	...	...	0959	|	...	...	1153	1153	|	...	|	1353	1353	|	|	...	...	|	...	...	...
	Lamezia Terme ▲ a.	0117	...	...	|	...	...	1037	|	...	...	1237	1237	|	...	|	1430	1437	|	|	...	...	|	...	...	...
238	**Crotone** d.	|	...	0605	0627	0800	...	...	1022a	...	...	...	...	1221	...	1320	...	...	1436	1442	...	...	1617	...	1650	1730
325	Rossano d.	|	...	0710	0734	0912	...	...	1117a	...	...	...	...	1337	...	1438	...	...	1546	1557	...	...	1733	...	1806	1849
336	Corigliano Calabro d.	|	...	0721	0744	0927	...	...	1127a	...	...	...	...	1346	...	1447	...	...	1555	1608	...	...	1743	...	1815	1901
351	**Sibari** a.	0313	...	0731	0757	0944	...	...	1139a	...	...	...	...	1356	...	1458	...	...	1605	1620	...	...	1755	...	1825	1915
351	**Sibari** d.	0333	0510	0734	...	...	1003	...	...	1155	1245	...	...	...	1400	...	...	...	...	...	1645	...	1758	1830	...	1918
366	Trebisacce d.	|	0525	0749	...	...	1019	...	...	1216	1258	...	...	...	1415	...	...	...	...	...	1701	...	1810	1846	...	1933
430	Metaponto **638** d.	0455	0630	0847	...	...	1130	...	...	1321	1359	...	...	...	1520	...	...	...	...	...	1804	...	1918	1944	...	2023
473	**Taranto 631/8** a.	0550	0716	0924	...	...	*1226*	...	...	1402	1446	...	...	...	1602	...	...	...	...	...	1843	...	2006	2024	...	2100
	Bari Centrale **631** a.	0746	...	1048	...	...	...	...	...	...	...	...	...	...	...	...	...	...	...	...	...	...	...	...	...	2241

	E 908		*E* 954	*ICN* 766				*ICN* 750		*E* 890
	◆	⚒	◆	◆	†	⚒	⚒	◆	⚒	◆
Reggio di Calabria d.	...	1437	...	1610	1625	1637	...	1710	1837	1910
Melito di Porto Salvo d.	...	1502	...	1633	1700	1702	...	1733	1902	1938
Locri d.	...	1609	...	1740	1806	1809	...	1840	2006	2104
Siderno d.	...	1614	...	1747	1810	1819	...	1847	2012	2113
Roccella Jonica d.	...	1633	...	1803	1824	1832	...	1903	2033	2131
Soverato d.	...	1710	...	1847	1913	1911	...	1944	2115a	2214
Catanzaro Lido a.	...	1725	...	1902	1930	1925	...	2000	2130a	2230
Catanzaro Lido ▲ d.	1710	...	1815	1917	1940	...	1935	2015	...	2245
Catanzaro ▲ d.	|	...	|	1928	1953	...	|	2025	...	2256
Lamezia Terme ▲ a.	|	...	|	2003	2030	...	|	2100	...	2335
Crotone d.	1802	...	1916	...	...	...	2026	...	...	...
Rossano d.	1916	...	2033	...	...	...	2138	...	...	...
Corigliano Calabro d.	1928	...	2045	...	...	...	2147	...	...	...
Sibari a.	1939	...	2055	...	...	...	2158	...	...	...
Sibari d.	1942	...	2058	...	...	...	...	...	...	...
Trebisacce d.	2002	...	2115	...	...	...	...	...	...	...
Metaponto **638** d.	2054	...	2220	...	...	...	...	...	...	...
Taranto 631/8 a.	2138	...	...	...	...	...	...	...	...	...
Bari Centrale **631** a.	2314	...	...	...	...	...	...	...	...	...

		E 893						*E* 953	*ICN* 753	
	⚒	◆	⚒	†	⚒	⚒	⚒	◆	◆	⚒
Bari Centrale **631** d.	...	...	...	...	...	...	...	...	...	...
Taranto 631/8 d.	...	...	...	...	...	0508	...	...	...	0645
Metaponto **638** d.	...	...	...	...	...	0553	...	0615	...	0737
Trebisacce d.	...	...	...	...	...	0654	...	0709	...	0845
Sibari a.	...	...	...	...	...	0703	...	0727	...	0900
Sibari d.	...	...	...	...	0602	0705	...	0739	...	...
Corigliano Calabro d.	...	...	...	...	0612	0722	...	0800	...	...
Rossano d.	...	...	...	...	0620	0735	...	0812	...	...
Crotone d.	...	...	...	...	0735	0859	...	0931	...	...
Lamezia Terme ▲ d.	...	0545	0713	...	|	|	0913	|	0940	...
Catanzaro ▲ d.	...	0627	0752	...	|	|	0952	|	1022	...
Catanzaro Lido ▲ a.	...	0635	0800	...	0825	0957	1000	1025	1030	...
Catanzaro Lido d.	0610	0650	0810	0808	...	...	1010	...	1045	...
Soverato d.	0624	0710	0824	0825	...	...	1023	...	1058	...
Roccella Jonica d.	0705	0810	0904	0914	...	...	1102	...	1138	...
Siderno d.	0717	0832	0916	0927	...	...	1116	...	1150	...
Locri d.	0722	0839	0925	0933	...	...	1122	...	1156	...
Melito di Porto Salvo d.	0828	1008	1028	1044	...	...	1228	...	1252	...
Reggio di Calabria a.	0853	1040	1053	1120	...	...	1253	...	1315	...

km		*ICN* 763		*E* 904	*ICN* 786																	*ICp* 513 [R]		*ICp* 554 [R]	*E* 982
		◆	⚒	◆	◆	⚒	†	⚒	⚒	†	⚒	⚒	⚒	†	⚒	⚒	†		⚒	⚒	⚒	Ⓐ	◆		◆	◆
	Bari Centrale **631** d.	...	...	0804	0849	...	...	...	...	...	...	...	...	...	...	...	...	...	...	...	...	...	...	...	1907	2256
	Taranto 631/8 d.	...	...	0931	1031	...	...	...	...	...	1147	...	...	...	...	1438	...	...	1709	...	1816	1931	...	...	2032	0048
	Metaponto **638** d.	...	...	1011	1111	...	...	...	...	...	1238	...	...	...	...	1519	...	...	1802	...	1920	2024	...	...	2118	0215
	Trebisacce d.	...	...	1057	1215	...	...	...	...	...	1339	...	...	...	...	1616	...	...	1913	...	2031	2134	...	...	2210	|
	Sibari a.	...	...	1110	1226	...	...	...	...	...	1353	...	...	...	...	1631	...	...	1930	...	2050	2148	...	...	2224	0308
	Sibari d.	...	...	1113	1229	...	...	...	...	...	...	1400	1532	...	...	...	...	1710	...	1955	...	...	2213	...	2227	0328
	Corigliano Calabro d.	...	...	1128	1245	...	...	...	...	...	...	1410	1545	...	...	...	...	1721	...	2005	...	...	2224	...	2244	|
	Rossano d.	...	...	1139	1257	...	...	...	...	...	...	1418	1554	...	...	...	...	1734	...	2013	...	...	2234	...	2256	|
	Crotone d.	...	...	1248	1400	...	...	...	...	...	...	1534	1713	...	...	...	...	1845	...	2135	...	...	2335	...	2359	|
0	Lamezia Terme ▲ d.	1040	...	|	...	1313	1313	...	1513	1513	...	|	|	1708	1713	...	...	|	...	...	...	...	...	...	...	0511
38	Catanzaro ▲ d.	1117	...	|	...	1352	1352	...	1552	1552	...	|	|	1747	1752	...	...	|	...	...	...	...	...	...	...	|
47	Catanzaro Lido ▲ a.	1125	...	1345	...	1400	1400	...	1600	1600	...	1625	1805	1755	1800	...	...	1930	...	...	...	...	...	...	...	|
	Catanzaro Lido d.	1140	1210	...	...	1410	1410	1512	1610	1610	...	...	...	1805	1810	...	1845	...	...	...	...	...	...	...	...	|
	Soverato d.	1155	1224	...	...	1424	1427	1529	1629	1632	...	...	...	1822	1824	...	1914	...	...	...	...	...	...	...	...	|
	Roccella Jonica d.	1233	1304	...	...	1505	1515	1617	1705	1720	...	...	...	1916	1905	...	2015	...	...	...	...	...	...	...	...	|
	Siderno d.	1246	1316	...	...	1520	1527	1629	1717	1732	...	...	...	1928	1917	...	2027	...	...	...	...	...	...	...	...	|
	Locri d.	1254	1321	...	...	1525	1532	1634	1723	1741	...	...	...	1934	1923	...	2033	...	...	...	...	...	...	...	...	|
	Melito di Porto Salvo d.	1350	1429	...	...	1628	1635	1755	1828	1847	...	...	...	2052	2028	...	2144	...	...	...	...	...	...	...	...	|
	Reggio di Calabria a.	1415	1453	...	...	1653	1712	1833	1853	1923	...	...	...	2128	2053	...	2210	...	...	...	...	...	...	...	...	0655

◆ – **NOTES** (LISTED BY TRAIN NUMBER)

513 – SILA – [2] Roma (**507**) - Paola (**511**) - Cosenza (**512**) - Sibari - Crotone.
534 – SILA – [2] Crotone - Sibari (**535**) - Cosenza (**536**) - Paola (**530**) - Roma.
554 – MURGE – [12] Milano (**553**) - Taranto - Metaponto (**555**) - Crotone.
566 – MURGE – [12] Crotone - Metaponto (**567**) - Taranto (**568**) - Milano.
750 – TOMMASO CAMPANELLA – ▬ 2 cl. (4 berth) and [2] Reggio di Calabria - Lamezia (**752**) - Milano.
753 – TOMMASO CAMPANELLA – ▬ 2 cl. (4 berth) and [2] Milano (**751**) - Lamezia - Reggio di Calabria.
763 – SCILLA – ▬ 2 cl. (4 berth) and [2] Torino (**761**) - Lamezia - Reggio di Calabria.
766 – SCILLA – ▬ 2 cl. (4 berth) and [2] Reggio di Calabria - Lamezia (**768**) - Torino.
782 – FRECCIA DEL LEVANTE – ▬ 2 cl. and [12] Crotone - Metaponto (**783**) - Taranto (**784**) - Milano.
786 – FRECCIA DEL LEVANTE – ▬ 2 cl. and [12] Milano (**785**) - Taranto - Metaponto (**787**) - Crotone.
890 – 🛏 1, 2 cl., ▬ 2 cl. and [2] Reggio di Calabria - Lamezia (**894/8**) - Roma.
893 – 🛏 1, 2 cl., ▬ 2 cl. and [2] Roma (**895**) - Lamezia - Reggio di Calabria.
904 – FRECCIA ADRIATICA – ▬ 2 cl. and [2] Torino (**901**) - Bari (**903**) - Taranto - Metaponto (**905**) Catanzaro Lido.
908 – FRECCIA ADRIATICA – ▬ 2 cl. and [2] Catanzaro Lido - Metaponto (**909**) - Taranto (**910**) - Bari (**906**) - Torino.
953 – Not May 1 (from Roma): [2] Roma (**951**) - Metaponto - Catanzaro Lido.
954 – Not Apr. 30: [2] Catanzaro Lido - Metaponto (**956**) - Roma.
982 – Ⓐ: [2] Bari (**981**) - Taranto - Metaponto (**983**) - Villa S G - Reggio di Calabria.
986 – Ⓐ: [2] Reggio di Calabria - Villa S G - Metaponto (**989**) - Taranto (**990**) - Bari.

a – Ⓐ only.

▲ – **LAMEZIA TERME - CATANZARO LIDO and v.v. (additional services)**: Journey 50–75 minutes. All trains call at Catanzaro; 33–56 minutes from Lamezia Terme, 10–15 minutes from Catanzaro Lido. 2nd class only.
From **Lamezia Terme**: 0613, 0813⚒, 1113⚒, 1213, 1413⚒, 1613⚒, 1813⚒, 1913, 2113⚒.
From **Catanzaro Lido**: 0640⚒, 0740, 0840, 0940⚒, 1240⚒, 1440⚒, 1540⚒, 1640, 1740⚒, 1840⚒, 1940⚒, 2140⚒.

NAPOLI - POTENZA - TARANTO 638

km		*E* 951	2	2	*ICp* 675 [R] ✕	2	2	2	2	2	2	*ES* 9363 [R] 🍷
		◆	⚒	†		⚒	⚒				Ⓐ	
	Roma T **640** d.	2330	...	...	0627	...	...	...	...	...	...	1545
0	**Napoli C 640** d.	|	...	...	0848	...	...	1355p	...	1624	1658	1742p
26	Pompei d.	|	...	...	|	...	...	1436	...	1654	1731	|
54	Salerno d.	0243	0930	0930	0926	...	1354	1459	1635	1719	1754	1819
74	Battipaglia d.	0307	0951	0953	0943	...	1419	1521	1657	1735	1810	1837
166	**Potenza** Centrale d.	0440	1122	1142	1057	1415	1619	1707	1837	1923	...	1954
273	Metaponto **635** d.	0609	...	...	1218	1554	...	*1912*d	...	2042	...	2119
317	**Taranto 635** a.	0650	...	...	1252	1636	...	...	...	2124	...	2153

	2	2	2	*ES* 9360 [R] 🍷	*ES* 9380 [R] 🍷	2	2	*ICp* 676 [R] ✕	2	2	*E* 956
	⚒	⚒	†	⚒	†					⚒	◆
Taranto 635 d.	...	...	...	0616	0736	1005	...	1400	*1408*d	...	2244
Metaponto **635** d.	...	...	...	0650	0811	1044	...	1436	*1501*d	...	0005
Potenza Centrale d.	0520	0613	0617	0811	0931	1217	1410	1559	1753	1843	0133
Battipaglia d.	0651	0751	0751	0925	1101	1344	1554	1717	1951	2034	0304
Salerno d.	0712	0808	0808	0942	1121	1405	1613	1735	2008	2053	0322
Pompei a.	0733	0829	0829	|	1137	1435	...	|	...	...	|
Napoli C 640 a.	0811	0909	0909	1018p	1200p	1506	...	1812	...	...	|
Roma T **640** a.	...	...	...	1216	1400	...	...	2033	...	...	0635

◆ – **NOTES** (LISTED BY TRAIN NUMBER)

951 – Not May 1 (from Roma): ▬ 2 cl. and [2] Roma - Taranto - Lecce; [2] Roma - Metaponto (**953**) - Catanzaro Lido.
956 – Not Apr. 30: ▬ 2 cl. and [2] Lecce - Taranto - Roma; [2] Catanzaro Lido (**954**) - Metaponto- Roma.

d – ⚒ only.
p – Napoli **Piazza Garibaldi**.

640 ROMA - NAPOLI - SICILY

km		E 1993 M	E 1991 ♦	2 ⚒	E 1595 ♦	2 ⚒	ICN 751 ♦	2	ICN 761 ♦		2	E 833 ♦	2	ES 9371 [R] 🍷	2	E 809 ♦	2 ⚒	E 837 ♦	ICp 675 [R] ✕ ♦	ICp 723 [R] 🍷 ♦	ICp 721 [R] 🍷 U	2 ⚒	2 †	ICN 771 ♦	E 1911 ♦
	Torino P N **610** d.	...	...	...	...	...	...	...	2050	...	...	...	...	...	...	2155	...	...	...	...	...	...	...	...	...
	Milano C **619/20** d.	1943	1943	...	...	...	2000	...	|	...	...	2200	...	...	...	|	...	...	...	...	...	...	...	...	2320
	Venezia S L **620** d.	|	|	...	...	...	|	...	|	...	...	|	...	...	...	|	...	...	...	...	...	...	...	2330	|
	Bologna C **620** d.	2233	2233	...	2233	...	2208	...	|	...	...	0044	...	...	...	|	...	0115	...	...	...	...	...	0222	|
0	**Roma Termini 620** d.	|	|	...	|	...	|	...	|	...	...	0501t	0541	0645	...	0612	...	0617t	0627	0719	0719	...	...	0713t	0735t
62	Latina d.	|	|	...	|	...	|	...	|	...	...	0540	0618	|	...	0650	...	|	0658	0758	0758	...	...	|	|
129	Formia d.	|	|	...	|	...	|	...	|	...	...	0626	0709	|	...	0753	...	|	0737	0840	0840	...	...	0855	|
195	Aversa d.	|	|	...	|	...	|	...	|	...	...	0712	0755	|	...	0846	...	|	0811	0912	0912	...	...	|	|
	Caserta **626** d.	|	|	...	|	...	0446	...	|	...	...	|	|	|	...	|	...	|	|	|	|	...	...	|	|
214	**Napoli Centrale 620/6** a.	|	|	...	|	...	|	...	0558f	...	...	0734	0823	0838p	...	0911	...	0926	0836	0930	0930	...	...	1000	1012
214	**Napoli Centrale** d.	|	|	...	|	...	|	0550	0602f	...	0648	0754	▬	0842p	0854	...	...	...	0848	0942	0942	...	...	...	...
240	Pompei d.	|	|	...	|	...	|	0618	|	...	0717	0825	...	|	0923	...	...	...	|	|	|	...	...	...	...
268	Salerno d.	|	|	...	0527	...	0540	0643	0657	...	0742	0854	...	0919	0944	...	...	...	0926	1019	1019	...	...	...	...
288	Battipaglia d.	|	|	...	|	...	0558	0701	0715	...	0801	▬	...	|	1001	...	...	...	0941	|	|	...	...	...	...
318	Agropoli d.	|	|	...	0559	...	0618	0724	0733	...	0824	...	...	|	1024	...	...	...	...	|	|	...	...	...	...
349	Ascea d.	|	|	...	0623	...	0647	0750	0756	...	0848	...	...	|	1050	...	...	...	...	|	|	...	...	...	...
395	Sapri d.	|	|	...	0654	...	0717	0840	0831	...	0928	...	...	1028	1126	...	...	...	...	|	|	...	...	...	...
407	Maratea d.	|	|	...	|	...	0728	0856	0842	...	0938	...	...	|	1141	...	...	...	...	|	|	...	...	...	...
455	Belvedere Marittimo d.	|	|	...	|	...	|	0947	|	...	1009	...	...	|	1221	...	...	...	...	|	|	...	...	...	...
489	Paola d.	0723	0723	...	0749	...	0820	1015	0933	...	1057	...	...	1118	1300	...	...	...	...	1218	1218	...	...	...	...
	Cosenza a.	|	|	...	|	...	|	...	|	...	1125c	...	...	|	1325	...	...	...	...	|	|	...	...	...	...
546	**Lamezia Terme C** a.	0800	0800	...	0824	...	0900	...	1015	...	▬	...	...	1152	...	...	...	...	...	1250	1250	...	...	...	...
546	**Lamezia Terme C** d.	0803	0803	...	0854	...	0908	...	1025	...	...	...	...	1155	...	...	...	...	...	1253	1253	...	...	...	...
638	Gioia Tauro d.	|	|	...	0942	...	0956	...	1107	...	...	...	...	1235	...	...	...	...	...	|	|	...	...	...	...
675	Villa San Giovanni a.	0915	0915	...	1015	...	1027	...	1138	...	...	...	...	1304	...	...	...	...	...	1355	1355	...	...	...	...
675	Villa San Giovanni d.	1005	1005	...	1037	...	1030	...	1141	...	...	...	...	1307	...	...	...	...	...	1407	1407	...	...	...	...
	Reggio di Calabria a.	|	|	...	1055	...	1050	...	1203	...	2	2	2	1320	...	...	...	...	...	|	|	...	...	...	...
684	**Messina Centrale** a.	1040	1040	...	...	...	...	...	...	...	⚒	†	⚒	...	...	...	...	...	...	1513	1513	...	...	...	...
684	**Messina Centrale** d.	1130	1138	1205	...	1215	...	...	...	...	1310	1350	1410	...	...	...	1420	...	...	1526	1538	1535	1535	...	...
	Taormina-Giardini d.	|	1219	1316	...	|	...	...	...	...	1403	1453	1513	...	...	...	|	...	...	|	1618	|	|	...	...
	Giarre-Riposto **644** d.	|	1236	1336	...	|	...	...	...	...	1420	1516	1528	...	...	...	|	...	...	|	1635	|	|	...	...
	Catania Centrale a.	|	1305	1402	...	|	...	...	...	...	1444	1545	1550	...	...	...	|	...	...	|	1658	|	|	...	...
	Catania Centrale d.	|	1311	1420	...	|	...	...	...	...	...	...	...	...	...	...	|	...	...	|	1703	|	|	...	...
	Augusta d.	|	1413	1516	...	|	...	...	...	...	...	...	...	...	...	...	|	...	...	|	1806	|	|	...	...
	Siracusa 648 a.	|	1445	1543	...	|	...	...	...	...	...	...	...	...	...	...	|	...	...	|	1825	|	|	...	...
720	Milazzo d.	1155	...	...	...	1257	...	...	...	...	...	...	...	...	...	...	1447	...	...	1551	...	1608	1608	...	...
849	Cefalù d.	1346	...	...	...	1522	...	...	...	...	...	...	...	...	...	...	1650	...	...	1747	...	1831	1830	...	...
879	Termini Imerese **645/7** d.	1411	...	...	...	1545	...	...	...	...	...	...	...	...	...	...	1710	...	...	1812	...	1903	1859	...	...
916	**Palermo C 645/7** a.	1440	...	...	...	1615	...	...	...	...	...	...	...	...	...	...	1736	...	...	1835	...	1929	1935	...	...

km (via hsl)		2 ⚒	2 Ⓐ	2 †z	IC 1571 ♦	ICp 589 [R] ①–⑥	IC 501 🍷 ♦	ES 9373 [R] 🍷 ⚒	2	2	2 ⚒	ICp 729 [R] 🍷 V	ICp 727 [R] 🍷 ♦	ICp 1573 [R] ⑦	2 ⚒	ICp 503 [R] ✕ ♦		IC 585 🍷	2	ES 9375 [R] ✕	ICp 589 [R]	2	ICp 507 [R] ♦	ICp 1589 [R] ♦	2
	Torino P N **610** d.	...	...	...	...	...	...	...	...	...	...	...	...	...	...	...	...	...	...	...	...	...	...	...	...
	Milano C **619/20** d.	...	...	...	...	...	...	...	...	...	...	...	...	...	...	...	...	0705	...	...	...	...	...	0735	...
	Venezia S L **620** d.	...	...	...	...	...	...	...	...	...	...	...	...	...	...	...	...	|	...	...	...	...	...	|	...
	Bologna C **620** d.	...	...	...	...	...	...	...	...	...	...	...	...	...	...	...	...	0908	...	...	...	...	...	1032	...
0	**Roma Termini 620** d.	...	...	...	0900	0927	1027	1045	...	1049	...	1128	1128	1145	...	1227	...	1337	1249	1345	1327	...	1420	1445t	1449
	Latina d.	...	...	...	0934	0958	1058	|	...	1127	...	1158	1158	1216	...	1258	...	1414	1327	|	1358	...	1458	1517	1527
	Formia d.	...	...	...	1009	1035	1135	|	...	1213	...	1235	1235	1253	...	1335	...	1451	1413	|	1433	...	1535	1556	1613
	Aversa d.	...	...	...	1048	1113	1213	|	...	1259	...	1312	1312	1326	...	1413	...	1525	1459	|	1513	...	1613	1653	1701
	Caserta **626** d.	...	...	...	|	|	|	|	...	|	...	|	|	|	...	|	...	|	|	|	|	...	|	|	|
216	**Napoli Centrale 620/6** a.	...	...	...	1114	1136	1236	1238p	...	1323	...	1330	1330	1346	...	1436	...	1550	1530	1538p	1536	...	1636	1722	1728
	Napoli Centrale d.	...	...	...	...	1148	...	1242p	1250	▬	...	1342	1342	1358	1350	...	...	...	▬	1542p	1548	1634	1648	1734	...
	Pompei d.	...	...	...	...	|	...	|	1319	...	...	|	|	|	1418	...	...	...	...	|	|	1715	|	|	...
	Salerno d.	...	...	...	...	1231	...	1315	1342	...	...	1419	1419	1435	1442	...	...	...	...	1615	1626	1743	1731	1811	...
	Battipaglia d.	...	...	...	...	1247	...	|	1401	...	...	|	|	1453	1501	...	...	...	...	|	1644	1801	1747	|	...
	Agropoli d.	...	...	...	...	|	...	|	1425	...	...	|	|	|	1523	...	...	...	...	|	|	1825	1803	|	...
	Ascea d.	...	...	...	...	|	...	|	1453	...	...	|	|	|	1549	...	...	...	...	|	|	1853	1828	1901	...
	Sapri d.	...	...	...	...	1353	...	1420	1541	...	...	1527	1527	1559	1630	...	...	...	...	1720	1745	1930	1901	1936	...
	Maratea d.	...	...	...	...	1403	...	|	1551	...	...	|	|	1609	...	...	...	...	...	|	1755	...	|	|	...
	Belvedere Marittimo d.	...	...	...	...	|	...	|	1627	...	...	|	|	|	...	...	...	...	...	|	|	...	|	|	...
	Paola d.	...	...	...	...	1453	...	1509	1700	...	...	1618	1618	1705	...	...	...	...	...	1808	1845	...	2006	2043	...
	Cosenza a.	...	...	...	...	|	...	|	1730	...	...	|	|	|	...	...	...	...	...	|	|	...	|	|	...
	Lamezia Terme C a.	...	...	...	...	1529	...	1539	...	...	...	1650	1650	1744	...	...	...	...	...	1839	1922	...	2040	2123	...
	Lamezia Terme C d.	...	...	...	...	1532	...	1542	...	...	...	1653	1653	1747	...	...	...	...	...	1842	1925	...	2043	2126	...
	Gioia Tauro d.	...	...	...	...	1615	...	1623	...	...	...	|	|	1830	...	...	...	...	...	1923	2010	...	2123	2207	...
	Villa San Giovanni a.	...	...	...	...	1644	...	1650	...	...	...	1755	1755	1901	...	...	...	...	...	1950	2042	...	2151	2235	...
	Villa San Giovanni d.	...	...	...	...	1647	...	1653	...	...	...	1807	1807	1904	...	...	...	...	...	1953	2045	...	2154	2238	...
	Reggio di Calabria a.	...	...	...	...	1700	...	1705	...	2	...	|	|	1920	...	...	...	...	2	2005	2100	...	2208	2250	...
	Messina Centrale a.	...	...	...	...	...	...	...	...	...	...	1913	1913	...	...	...	...	...	⚒	...	...	...	...	...	...
	Messina Centrale d.	1600	1715	1720	...	...	...	...	...	1830	1835	1926	1940	...	...	...	...	...	2145	...	...	...	...	...	...
	Taormina-Giardini d.	1646	|	1817	...	...	...	...	...	|	1927	|	2025	...	...	...	...	...	2227	...	...	...	...	...	...
	Giarre-Riposto **644** d.	1704	|	1834	...	...	...	...	...	|	1944	|	2042	...	...	...	...	...	2243	...	...	...	...	...	...
	Catania Centrale a.	1730	|	1859	...	...	...	...	...	|	2008	|	2107	...	...	...	...	...	2305	...	...	...	...	...	...
	Catania Centrale d.	1732	|	1901	...	...	...	...	...	|	2010	|	2110	...	...	...	...	...	...	...	...	...	...	...	...
	Augusta d.	1838	|	1947	...	...	...	...	...	|	2104	|	2206	...	...	...	...	...	...	...	...	...	...	...	...
	Siracusa 648 a.	1900	|	2010	...	...	...	...	...	|	2130	|	2230	...	...	...	...	...	...	...	...	...	...	...	...
	Milazzo d.	...	1739	...	...	...	...	...	...	1853	...	1951	...	...	...	...	...	...	...	...	...	...	...	...	...
	Cefalù d.	...	1931	...	...	...	...	...	...	2104	...	2130	...	...	...	...	...	...	...	...	...	...	...	...	...
	Termini Imerese **645/7** d.	...	1957	...	...	...	...	...	...	2132	...	2153	...	...	...	...	...	...	...	...	...	...	...	...	...
	Palermo C 645/7 a.	...	2020	...	...	...	...	...	...	2155	...	2220	...	...	...	...	...	...	...	...	...	...	...	...	...

♦ – **NOTES** (LISTED BY TRAIN NUMBER)

501 – CARDUCCI – ⚒: [12] and 🍷 Sestri Levante - Napoli.
503 – BOCCANEGRA – [12] and 🍷 Savona - Genova - Napoli.
507 – SILA – [12] Roma - Reggio; [2] Roma - Paola (**511**) - Cosenza (**512**) - Sibari (**513**) - Crotone.
675 – JONIO – [12] and ✕ Roma - Taranto.
723 – PELORITANO – [12] and 🍷 Roma - Palermo.
727 – ARCHIMEDE – [12] and 🍷 Roma - Siracusa.
751 – TOMMASO CAMPANELLA – 🛏 1, 2 cl., ▬ 2 cl. and [12] Milano - Reggio; ▬ 2 cl. (4 berth) and [2] Milano - Lamezia (**753**) - Reggio.
761 – SCILLA – 🛏 1, 2 cl., ▬ 2 cl. and [12] Torino - Reggio; ▬ 2 cl. (4 berth) and [2] Torino - Lamezia (**763**) - Reggio.
771 – MARCO POLO – 🛏 1, 2 cl., ▬ 2 cl. (4 berth) and [2] Udine - Napoli; 🛏 1, 2 cl., ▬ 2 cl. (4 berth) and [12] Trieste (**772**) - Venezia - Napoli.
809 – 🛏 1, 2 cl. (Excelsior), 🛏 1, 2 cl. (T2), 🛏 1, 2 cl., ▬ 2 cl. (4/6 berth) and [2] Torino - Napoli.
833 – ①③⑤: ▬ 2 cl. and [2] Milano - Salerno.
837 – ①②④⑤⑥⑦, also June 3; not June 4 (from Bolzano): 🛏 1, 2 cl., ▬ 2 cl. (4 berth) and [2] Bolzano (**925**) - Bologna - Napoli.
1571 – CARDUCCI – †: [12] Livorno - Napoli.
1589 – ASPROMONTE – ⑥ Jan. 10 - June 13 (not Apr. 25, May 2): [12] Milano - Reggio.
1595 – ⑥ Dec. 20 - Mar. 21, June 20 - Sept. 12 (from Bolzano): 🛏 1,2 cl. (T2), ▬ 2 cl. and [2] Bolzano - Reggio.
1911 – 🛏 1,2 cl. (Excelsior), 🛏 1, 2 cl. (T2), 🛏 1,2 cl., ▬ 2 cl. (4 berth) and [2] Milano - Napoli.
1991 – MONGIBELLO – Apr. 10, 14, 30, May 4, 29, June 3; ①⑤ from June 8: 🛏 1, 2 cl. (T2), ▬ 2 cl. and [2] Milano - Siracusa.

M – MONGIBELLO – Apr. 10, 14, 30, May 4, 29, June 3; ①⑤ from June 8: ▬ 2 cl. (4 berth) and [2] Milano (**1991**) - Messina - Palermo.
U – PELORITANO – [12] Roma (**723**) - Messina - Siracusa.
V – ARCHIMEDE – [12] Roma (**727**) - Messina - Palermo.

c – © only.
f – Napoli **Campi Flegrei**.
p – Napoli **Piazza Garibaldi** (situated under Centrale).
t – Roma **Tiburtina**.
z – Not Apr. 12.

ROMA - NAPOLI - SICILY 640

km		*ICp* 703	*ES* 9363	*ICp* 521			*IC* 591	*ES* 9377			*ICp* 523	*IC* 705	*E* 1925				*E* 823	*E* 853	*ICp* 1557	*ESc* 9799	*IC* 595	*E* 1939	*E* 891		*E* 1921
		R ✕	R 🍷	R 🍷	2	2	✕	R ✕	2	2	R 🍷	✕		2	2	2			R	R 🍷	🍷			2	
		◆	◆							⚒			◆	⚒	⚒	⚒	◆	◆	⑤y			◆	◆		◆
	Torino P N **610** d.	...	...	...	...	...	...	...	...	...	1105	...	...	...	...	...	...	...	...	1305	...	...	...	...	...
	Milano C **619/20** d.	...	...	...	...	...	...	...	...	...	|	...	...	...	...	...	1220	...	1400	|	1500	...	...	...	1620
	Venezia S L **620** d.	0920**z**	...	...	...	...	...	...	...	...	|	1309	...	...	...	...	|	...	|	|	|	...	...	...	|
	Bologna C **620** d.	1102	...	...	...	...	...	...	...	...	|	1508	...	...	...	...	1455	...	1616	|	1708	...	...	...	|
	Roma Termini 620 d.	1537	1545	1627	...	1649	1738	1700	...	...	1827	1939	1958	...	...	...	2011**t**	2013	2016**t**	2027	2137	2118	2225	...	2320**t**
	Latina d.	1614	|	1658	...	1727	1808	|	...	...	1858	2008	2029	...	...	...	|	|	2105	2058	2208	2150	2301	...	|
	Formia d.	1651	|	1733	...	1813	1843	|	...	...	1935	2043	2105	...	...	...	|	|	2143	2135	2243	2226	2346	...	|
	Aversa d.	1725	|	1813	...	1901	1917	|	...	...	2009	2116	|	...	...	...	|	|	|	2209	2318	|	|	...	|
	Caserta **626** d.	|	|	|	...	|	|	|	...	...	|	|	|	...	...	...	2228	2228	|	|	|	|	0036	...	|
	Napoli Centrale 620/6 a.	1750	1738**p**	1836	...	1928	1938	1821	...	...	2036	2138	2158	...	...	...	|	|	2248**p**	2236	2342	2317	|	...	|
	Napoli Centrale d.	...	1742**p**	1848	1842	...	...	1830	1950	...	2048	...	2210	...	...	...	|	|	2252**p**	...	...	2329	|	...	|
	Pompei d.	...	|	|	1919	...	...	|	2019	...	|	...	|	...	...	...	|	|	|	...	...	|	|	...	|
	Salerno d.	...	1819	1931	1942	...	...	1859	2041	...	2123	...	2249	...	...	...	|	|	2328	...	...	|	|	...	|
	Battipaglia d.	...	1835	1947	2001	...	...	|	2101	...	...	...	|	...	...	...	|	|	...	...	...	|	|	...	|
	Agropoli d.	...	...	|	2021	...	...	|	2125	...	...	...	|	...	...	...	|	|	...	...	...	|	|	...	|
	Ascea d.	...	...	|	2048	...	...	|	2153	...	...	...	|	...	...	...	|	|	...	...	...	|	|	...	|
	Sapri d.	...	...	2051	2122	...	...	|	2230	...	...	...	|	...	...	...	|	|	...	...	...	|	0248	...	|
	Maratea d.	...	...	2102	2132	...	...	|	...	...	...	...	|	...	...	...	|	|	...	...	...	|	|	...	|
	Belvedere Marittimo d.	...	...	|	2210	...	...	|	...	...	...	...	|	...	...	...	|	|	...	...	...	|	|	...	|
0	Paola d.	...	...	2151	2251	...	...	2032	...	...	...	...	|	...	...	...	0137	0137	...	...	...	|	0350	...	|
26	Cosenza a.	...	...	|	2315	...	...	|	...	...	...	...	|	...	...	...	|	|	...	...	...	|	|	...	|
—	**Lamezia Terme C** a.	...	...	2227	...	...	...	2059	...	...	...	...	|	...	...	...	0218	0218	...	...	...	|	0427	...	|
	Lamezia Terme C d.	...	...	2230	...	...	...	2102	...	...	...	...	|	...	...	...	0221	0221	...	...	...	|	0430	...	|
	Gioia Tauro d.	...	...	2313	...	...	...	|	...	...	...	...	|	...	...	...	|	|	...	...	...	|	0521	...	|
	Villa San Giovanni a.	...	...	2340	...	...	...	2158	...	...	...	...	0255	...	...	...	0335	0335	...	...	...	0420	0607	...	0620
0	Villa San Giovanni d.	...	...	2343	...	...	...	2201	...	...	...	...	0310	...	...	...	0350	0350	...	...	...	0435	0610	...	0700
15	**Reggio di Calabria** a.	...	...	2355	...	...	...	2214	...	...	...	...	|	...	...	...	|	|	...	...	...	|	0630	...	|
—	**Messina Centrale** a.	...	...	...	...	...	...	...	...	...	...	...	0435	...	...	...	0520	0520	...	...	...	0600	...	...	0735
0	**Messina Centrale** d.	...	...	...	...	...	...	...	...	0430	...	...	0459	0525	0530	0540	0545	0545	...	...	...	0623	...	0705	0834
47	Taormina-Giardini d.	...	...	...	...	...	...	...	...	|	...	...	|	0603	|	|	0630	0630	...	...	...	0716	...	|	|
65	Giarre-Riposto **644** d.	...	...	...	...	...	...	...	...	|	...	...	|	0623	|	|	0647	0647	...	...	...	0738	...	|	|
95	**Catania Centrale** a.	...	...	...	...	...	...	...	...	|	...	...	|	0643	|	|	0712	0712	...	...	...	0802	...	|	|
95	**Catania Centrale** d.	...	...	...	...	...	...	...	...	|	...	...	|	0647	|	|	0755	0755	...	...	...	0815	...	|	|
151	Augusta d.	...	...	...	...	...	...	...	...	|	...	...	|	0749	|	|	0851	0851	...	...	...	0917	...	|	|
182	**Siracusa 648** a.	...	...	...	...	...	...	...	...	|	...	...	|	0817	|	|	0920	0920	...	...	...	0940	...	|	|
	Milazzo d.	...	...	...	...	...	...	...	...	0456	...	...	0524	...	0557	0611	...	...	...	...	...	...	...	0728	0859
	Cefalù d.	...	...	...	...	...	...	...	...	0702	...	...	0719	...	0803	0822	...	...	...	...	...	...	...	0915	1109
	Termini Imerese **645/7** d.	...	...	...	...	...	...	...	...	0729	...	...	0742	...	0835	0852	...	...	...	...	...	...	...	0937	1130
	Palermo C 645/7 a.	...	...	...	...	...	...	...	...	0755	...	...	0810	...	0900	0930	...	...	...	...	...	...	...	1000	1155

	E 1923	*E* 985	*E* 895	*E* 1941	*E* 1945	*E* 951	*E* 1935	*E* 1931	*E* 1933	
	Z	◆	◆	◆	R	◆	B	◆	T	
Torino P N **610** d.	...	...	...	1655	1655	...	...	...	...	...
Milano C **619/20** d.	1620	...	...	|	|	...	...	...	...	...
Venezia S L **620** d.	|	...	...	|	|	...	1909	1909	1909	...
Bologna C **620** d.	|	...	...	|	|	...	2148	2148	2148	...
Roma Termini 620 d.	2320**t**	...	2300	|	|	2330	|	|	|	...
Latina d.	|	...	|	|	|	|	|	|	|	...
Formia d.	|	...	|	|	|	|	|	|	|	...
Aversa d.	|	...	|	|	|	|	|	|	|	...
Caserta **626** d.	|	...	|	|	|	0155	|	|	|	...
Napoli Centrale 620/6 a.	|	...	|	|	|	|	|	|	|	...
Napoli Centrale d.	|	...	|	|	|	|	|	|	|	...
Pompei d.	|	...	|	|	|	|	|	|	|	...
Salerno d.	|	...	0210	|	|	0243	0440**s**	0440**s**	0440**s**	...
Battipaglia d.	|	...	|	|	|	0305	|	|	|	...
Agropoli d.	|	...	|	|	|	...	|	|	|	...
Ascea d.	|	...	|	|	|	...	|	|	|	...
Sapri d.	|	...	0339	|	|	...	0555**s**	0555**s**	0555**s**	...
Maratea d.	|	...	|	|	|	...	|	|	|	...
Belvedere Marittimo d.	|	...	|	|	|	...	|	|	|	...
Paola d.	|	...	0438	|	|	...	0649**s**	0649**s**	0649**s**	...
Cosenza a.	|	...	|	|	|	...	|	|	|	...
Lamezia Terme C a.	|	...	0536	0541**s**	0541**s**	...	0726**s**	0726**s**	0726**s**	...
Lamezia Terme C d.	|	0511	0538	0544**s**	0544**s**	...	0729**s**	0729**s**	0729**s**	...
Gioia Tauro d.	|	0604	0722	0622**s**	0622**s**	...	0812**s**	0812**s**	0812**s**	...
Villa San Giovanni a.	0620	0639	0758	0655**s**	0655**s**	...	0845**s**	0845**s**	0845**s**	...
Villa San Giovanni d.	0700	0642	0813	0705	0705	...	0900	|	|	...
Reggio di Calabria a.	|	0655	0830	|	|	...	0924	|	|	...
Messina Centrale a.	0735	...	...	0835	0835	...	...	1035**s**	1035**s**	...
Messina Centrale d.	0838	...	...	0904**s**	0857	...	...	1057**s**	1105	...
Taormina-Giardini d.	0915**s**	...	...	|	0936**s**	...	...	1137**s**	|	...
Giarre-Riposto **644** d.	0929**s**	...	...	|	0957**s**	...	...	1152**s**	|	...
Catania Centrale a.	0956**s**	...	...	|	1020**s**	...	...	1216**s**	|	...
Catania Centrale d.	1002**s**	...	...	|	1024**s**	...	...	1230**s**	|	...
Augusta d.	1106**s**	...	...	|	1120**s**	...	...	1325**s**	|	...
Siracusa 648 a.	1130	...	...	|	1145	...	...	1355	|	...
Milazzo d.	...	...	...	0928**s**	...	...	...	...	1131	...
Cefalù d.	...	...	...	1126**s**	...	...	...	...	1323	...
Termini Imerese **645/7** d.	...	...	...	1145**s**	...	...	...	...	1343	...
Palermo C 645/7 a.	...	...	...	1215	...	...	...	...	1415	...

Alta Velocità (*AV*) – services via high-speed line

km (via hsl)		*AV* 9601	*AV* 9421		*AV* 9423	*AV* 9425		*AV* 9427	*AV* 9429
		R ✕ Ⓐ	R ✕ ◆		R ✕	R ✕ ①–⑥		R ✕	R ✕
	Milano Centrale d.	...	...	...	...	0630	...	0730	0830
	Venezia Santa Lucia d.	...	...	...	...	|	...	|	|
	Bologna Centrale d.	...	...	...	...	0739	...	0839	0939
0	Roma Termini d.	0725	0844	...	0944	1044	...	1144	1244
216	Napoli Centrale a.	0846	1005	...	1105	1205	...	1305	1405
	Napoli Centrale d.	...	...	...	...	...	...	...	...
	Salerno d.	...	...	...	...	...	...	...	...

	AV 9433	*AV* 9641		*AV* 9437	*AV* 9439		*AV* 9621	*AV* 9441	
	R ✕	R ✕ Ⓐ		R ✕	R ✕		R ✕ Ⓐ	R ✕	
Milano Centrale d.	1030	...	...	1230	1330	...	...	1430	...
Venezia Santa Lucia d.	|	1043	...	|	|	...	...	|	...
Bologna Centrale d.	1139	1225	...	1339	1439	...	...	1539	...
Roma Termini d.	1444	1525	...	1644	1744	...	1825	1844	...
Napoli Centrale a.	1605	1646	...	1805	1905	...	1946	2005	...
Napoli Centrale d.	...	...	...	...	...	...	...	2017	...
Salerno d.	...	...	...	...	...	...	...	2054	...

	AV 9643		*AV* 9443	*AV* 9445		*AV* 9447		*AV* 9519	
	R ✕		R ✕	R ✕		R ✕		R ✕ Ⓐ	
Milano Centrale d.	...	...	1530	1630	...	1730	...	1845	...
Venezia Santa Lucia d.	1443	...	|	|	...	|	...	|	...
Bologna Centrale d.	1625	...	1639	1739	...	1839	...	1952	...
Roma Termini d.	1925	...	1944	2044	...	2144	...	2213**t**	...
Napoli Centrale a.	2046	...	2105	2205	...	2305	...	2335	...
Napoli Centrale d.	...	...	2117	...	...	...	...	...	...
Salerno d.	...	...	2153	...	...	...	...	...	...

For **Alta Velocità** (*AV*) services north of Roma – see Table **620**.

◆ – **NOTES** (LISTED BY TRAIN NUMBER)

703 – MIRAMARE – [12] and ✕ Trieste (**702**) - Venezia Mestre - Napoli.

823 – FRECCIA DEL SUD – ①③⑤⑦: ▬ 2 cl. and [2] Milano - Catania - Agrigento; [2] Milano - Catania (**827**) - Siracusa.

853 – FRECCIA DEL SUD – ②④⑥: [2] Roma - Catania - Agrigento; [2] Roma - Catania (**857**) - Siracusa.

891 – ⑤ Jan. 9 - June 12 (also Apr. 30; not May 1): ▬ 2 cl. and [2] Roma - Reggio.

895 – 🛏 1, 2 cl., ▬ 2 cl. and [2] Roma - Reggio; 🛏 1, 2 cl., ▬ 2 cl. and [2] Roma - Lamezia (**893**) - Reggio.

951 – Not May 1: [2] Roma - Taranto - Lecce; [2] Roma - Metaponto (**953**) - Catanzaro Lido.

985 – ①–⑥, not Apr. 12 and days after holidays (from Bari): [2] Bari (**981**) - Taranto (**982**) - Metaponto (**983**) - Reggio.

1921 – TRINACRIA – 🛏 1, 2 cl. (T2), 🛏 1, 2 cl. and ▬ 2 cl. (4/6 berth) Milano - Palermo; [2] Messina - Palermo.

1925 – IL GATTOPARDO – 🛏 1, 2 cl. (Excelsior), 🛏 1, 2 cl. (T2), 🛏 1, 2 cl., ▬ 2 cl. (4 berth) and [2] Roma - Palermo.

1931 – FRECCIA DELLA LAGUNA – 🛏 1, 2 cl. and ▬ 2 cl. (4 berth) Venezia - Siracusa.

1939 – BELLINI – 🛏 1, 2 cl. (Excelsior), 🛏 1, 2 cl. (T2), 🛏 1, 2 cl., ▬ 2 cl. (4 berth) and [2] Roma - Siracusa.

1941 – TRENO DEL SOLE – 🛏 1, 2 cl. and ▬ 2 cl. (4 berth) Torino - Palermo; [2] Messina - Palermo.

9363 – [12] and 🍷 Roma - Taranto.

9421 – ①–⑥: [12] and ✕ Firenze - Napoli.

B – FRECCIA DELLA LAGUNA – 🛏 1, 2 cl. and ▬ 2 cl. (4 berth) Venezia (**1931**) - Villa SG - Reggio.

R – TRENO DEL SOLE – 🛏 1, 2 cl. and ▬ 2 cl. (4 berth) Torino (**1941**) - Messina - Siracusa.

T – FRECCIA DELLA LAGUNA – 🛏 1, 2 cl. and ▬ 2 cl. (4 berth) Venezia (**1931**) - Messina - Palermo.

Z – TRINACRIA – 🛏 1, 2 cl. (T2), 🛏 1, 2 cl. and ▬ 2 cl. (4/6 berth) Milano (**1921**) - Messina - Siracusa.

p – Napoli **Piazza Garibaldi** (situated under Centrale).

s – Stops to set down only.

t – Roma **Tiburtina**.

y – ⑤ (also Apr. 30; not May 1).

z – Venezia **Mestre**.

640 SICILY - NAPOLI - ROMA

	E 894 ♦	E 892 ♦	E 1922 Z	E 1920 ♦		E 854 X	E 834 Y	2	E 956 ♦	E 1924 ♦	E 986 ♦	2	2 ①–⑥	IC 582 🍷	E 1938 ♦	2	ICp 516 [R] 🍷	IC 704 ✕	2	ICp 520 [R] 🍷	2	ES 9360 [R] 🍷 ♦	IC 586 ✕	ES 9372 [R] ✕	ESc 9798 [R] 🍷	ES 9380 [R] 🍷 ♦
Palermo C 645/7 d.	...	...	...	1700	...	...	...	1805	...	1840	...	2030	...	...	...	...	...	...	...	...	...	...	...	...	...	...
Termini Imerese **645/7** d.	...	...	...	1728	...	...	...	1834	...	1907	...	2103	...	...	...	...	...	...	...	...	...	...	...	...	...	...
Cefalù d.	...	...	...	1748	...	...	...	1900	...	1932	...	2131	...	...	...	...	...	...	...	...	...	...	...	...	...	...
Milazzo d.	...	...	...	1942	...	...	...	2059	...	2116	...	2302	...	...	...	...	...	...	...	...	...	...	...	...	...	...
Siracusa 648 d.	...	...	1715	|	...	1740	1740	|	...	|	...	|	...	...	2025	...	...	...	...	...	...	...	...	...	...	...
Augusta d.	...	...	1741	|	...	1805	1805	|	...	|	...	|	...	...	2048	...	...	...	...	...	...	...	...	...	...	...
Catania Centrale a.	...	...	1840	|	...	1900	1900	|	...	|	...	|	...	...	2144	...	...	...	...	...	...	...	...	...	...	...
Catania Centrale d.	...	...	1844	|	...	1920	1920	|	...	|	...	|	...	...	2204	...	...	...	...	...	...	...	...	...	...	...
Giarre-Riposto **644** d.	...	...	1909	|	...	1947	1947	|	...	|	...	|	...	...	2232	...	...	...	...	...	...	...	...	...	...	...
Taormina-Giardini d.	...	...	1928	|	...	2006	2006	|	...	|	...	|	...	...	2250	...	...	...	...	...	...	...	...	...	...	...
Messina Centrale a.	...	...	2010	2010	...	2100	2100	2130	...	2140	...	2328	...	...	2335	...	...	...	...	...	...	...	...	...	...	...
Messina Centrale d.	...	...	2030	2030	...	2120	2120	...	...	2200	...	...	...	...	2355	...	...	...	...	...	...	...	...	...	...	...
Reggio di Calabria d.	2035	2140	|	|	...	|	|	...	...	|	2340	...	...	...	|	...	...	...	...	...	...	...	...	0646	...	...
Villa San Giovanni a.	2051	2154	2155	2155	...	2245	2245	...	...	2325	2355	...	...	...	0120	...	...	...	...	...	...	...	...	0659	...	...
Villa San Giovanni d.	2120	2157	2220	2220	...	2310	2310	...	...	2340	2358	...	...	...	0145	...	...	...	...	...	...	...	...	0702	...	...
Gioia Tauro d.	2205	2242	|	|	...	|	|	...	...	|	0030	...	...	...	|	...	...	...	...	...	...	...	...	|	...	...
Lamezia Terme C a.	2330	2340	|	|	...	0014	0014	...	...	|	0114	...	...	...	|	...	...	...	...	...	...	...	...	0758	...	...
Lamezia Terme C d.	0022	2343	|	|	...	0017	0017	...	...	|	...	...	...	...	|	...	...	...	...	...	...	...	...	0801	...	...
Cosenza d.	|	|	|	|	...	|	|	...	...	|	...	...	...	...	|	...	...	...	...	...	0530	...	...	|	...	...
Paola d.	0111	0033	|	|	...	0100	0100	...	...	|	...	...	...	...	|	...	...	...	...	...	0553	...	...	0831	...	...
Belvedere Marittimo d.	|	|	|	|	...	|	|	...	...	|	...	...	...	...	|	...	...	...	...	...	0622	...	...	|	...	...
Maratea d.	|	|	|	|	...	|	|	...	...	|	...	...	...	...	|	...	...	...	...	...	0706	...	...	|	...	...
Sapri d.	0211	0130	|	|	...	|	|	...	...	|	...	...	...	...	|	...	...	...	0615	...	0720	...	...	|	...	...
Ascea d.	|	|	|	|	...	|	|	...	...	|	...	...	...	...	|	...	...	...	0649	...	0813	...	...	|	...	...
Agropoli d.	|	|	|	|	...	|	|	...	...	|	...	...	...	...	|	...	...	...	0717	...	0840	...	...	|	...	...
Battipaglia d.	|	|	|	|	...	|	|	...	0304	|	...	...	...	...	|	...	...	...	0742	...	0902	0925	...	|	...	1101
Salerno d.	0346	0255	|	|	...	|	|	...	0322	|	...	...	...	...	|	...	0643	...	0801	...	0922	0942	...	1005	...	1121
Pompei d.	|	|	|	|	...	|	|	...	|	|	...	...	...	...	|	...	|	...	0822	...	0940	|	...	|	...	1138
Napoli Centrale a.	0440	|	|	|	...	|	|	...	|	0448	...	...	...	...	0619	...	0718	...	0902	...	1010	1018p	...	1030	...	1200p
Napoli Centrale 620/6 d.	0452	|	|	|	...	|	|	...	|	0500	...	...	0530	0614	0631	0637	0730	0824	...	0924	...	1022p	1024	1039	1124	1204p
Caserta **626** d.	|	0347	|	|	...	|	|	...	0426	|	...	...	|	|	|	|	|	|	...	|	...	|	|	|	|	|
Aversa d.	0510	|	|	|	...	|	|	...	|	|	...	...	0547	0636	|	0657	0746	0842	...	0946	...	|	1044	|	1146	|
Formia d.	0547	0440	|	|	...	|	|	...	0523	0554	...	...	0633	0715	0734	0746	0825	0915	...	1023	...	|	1120	|	1223	|
Latina d.	0632	0530	|	|	...	|	|	...	0558	0640	...	...	0709	0750	0817	0834	0859	0950	...	1059	...	|	|	|	1259	|
Roma Termini 620 a.	0708	0617	0505t	0505t	...	0605	0608t	...	0635	0723	...	...	0753	0823	0856	0918	0933	1023	...	1133	...	1216	1223	1200	1333	1400
Bologna C 620 a.	...	...	|	|	...	...	1100	...	...	...	...	...	...	1243	...	...	|	1453	...	|	...	...	1659	...	|	...
Venezia SL 620 a.	...	...	|	|	...	...	|	...	...	...	...	...	...	|	...	...	|	1649	...	|	...	...	|	...	|	...
Milano C 619/20 a.	...	...	1130	1130	...	...	1320	...	...	...	...	...	...	1500	...	...	|	...	...	|	...	...	1905	...	|	...
Torino PN 610 a.	...	...	...	...	...	...	...	...	...	...	...	...	...	...	...	...	1655	...	...	1855	...	...	...	...	2055	...

	ICp 522 [R] 🍷	2 ⚒	2 ⚒	ICp 1554 [R] ♦	ES 9374 [R] ✕	ICp 538 [R] ✕	IC 592 🍷	ICp 1588 [R] ♦	2 ⚒	2 †	2	ICp 530 [R] ♦	2 ⚒	2 ⚒	2	ICp 728 [R] 🍷 ♦	ICp 722 [R] U	2	IC 546 🍷 ♦	IC 1572 ♦	2	2 z	2 z	ES 9376 [R] 🍷 ⑧y	2 †	
Palermo C 645/7 d.	...	...	0405	...	...	...	...	...	...	...	...	...	...	0605	...	0730	...	...	...	...	...	0825	...	...	0841	...
Termini Imerese **645/7** d.	...	...	0431	...	...	...	...	...	...	...	...	...	...	0632	...	0756	...	...	...	...	...	0849	...	...	0920	...
Cefalù d.	...	...	0455	...	...	...	...	...	...	...	...	...	...	0701	...	0823	...	...	...	...	...	0916	...	...	0955	...
Milazzo d.	...	...	0718	...	...	...	...	...	...	...	...	...	...	0855	...	0955	...	...	...	...	...	1059	...	...	1214	...
Siracusa 648 d.	...	0505	|	...	...	...	...	...	...	...	...	...	0630	|	...	|	0800	...	...	...	...	|	0850	...	|	...
Augusta d.	...	0526	|	...	...	...	...	...	...	...	...	...	0653	|	...	|	0822	...	...	...	...	|	0916	...	|	...
Catania Centrale a.	...	0607	|	...	...	...	...	...	...	...	...	...	0744	|	...	|	0905	...	...	...	...	|	1000	...	|	...
Catania Centrale d.	...	0612	|	...	...	...	...	...	...	...	...	...	0747	|	...	|	0908	...	...	...	...	|	1003	...	|	...
Giarre-Riposto **644** d.	...	0636	|	...	...	...	...	...	...	...	...	...	0807	|	...	|	0934	...	...	...	...	|	1025	...	|	...
Taormina-Giardini d.	...	0701	|	...	...	...	...	...	...	...	...	...	0821	|	...	|	0950	...	...	...	...	|	1044	...	|	...
Messina Centrale a.	...	0750	0752	...	...	...	...	...	...	...	...	...	0920	0920	...	1025	1030	...	...	...	...	1125	1135	...	1250	...
Messina Centrale d.	...	▬	...	...	...	...	...	...	...	...	...	...	...	...	...	1040	1040	...	...	...	...	▬	...	...	...	...
Reggio di Calabria d.	0652	...	...	...	0855	...	...	0925	...	...	...	0930	...	...	...	|	|	...	...	...	...	...	...	1355	...	...
Villa San Giovanni a.	0707	...	...	...	0906	...	...	0939	...	...	...	0945	...	...	...	1150	1150	...	...	...	...	...	...	1406	...	...
Villa San Giovanni d.	0710	...	...	...	0909	...	...	0942	...	...	...	0948	...	...	...	1210	1210	...	...	...	...	...	...	1409	...	...
Gioia Tauro d.	0740	...	...	...	0935	...	...	1010	...	...	...	1019	...	...	...	|	|	...	...	...	...	...	...	1435	...	...
Lamezia Terme C a.	0820	...	...	...	1012	...	...	1053	...	...	...	1100	...	...	...	1306	1306	...	...	...	...	...	...	1512	...	...
Lamezia Terme C d.	0823	...	...	...	1015	...	...	1056	...	...	...	1103	...	...	...	1309	1309	...	...	...	...	2	...	1515	...	...
Cosenza d.	|	...	...	...	|	...	...	|	...	...	...	|	...	...	...	|	|	...	...	...	1225c	1425	...	|	...	...
Paola d.	0900	...	...	...	1047	...	...	1133	...	...	...	1205	...	...	1157	1344	1344	...	...	...	1253	1453	...	1547	...	...
Belvedere Marittimo d.	|	...	...	...	|	...	...	|	...	...	...	|	...	...	1228	|	|	...	...	...	1322	1527	...	|	...	...
Maratea d.	0950	...	...	...	|	...	...	|	...	...	...	|	...	...	1312	|	|	...	...	...	1404	1610	...	|	...	...
Sapri d.	1001	...	...	...	1135	...	...	1226	...	...	1245	1301	...	...	1325	1433	1433	...	...	...	1421	1622	...	1635	...	...
Ascea d.	|	...	...	...	|	...	...	1255	...	...	1325	1337	...	...	1403	|	|	...	...	...	1459	1703	...	|	...	...
Agropoli d.	|	...	...	...	|	...	...	|	...	...	1356	1359	...	...	1437	|	|	...	...	...	1532	1731	...	|	...	...
Battipaglia d.	1106	...	...	...	|	...	...	|	...	...	1425	1420	...	...	1501	|	|	...	...	...	1602	1757	...	|	...	...
Salerno d.	1128	...	...	1207	1244	...	...	1356	...	...	1444	1436	...	...	1512	1544	1544	...	...	...	1622	1820	...	1742	...	...
Pompei d.	|	2	...	1230	|	...	...	|	...	...	1502	|	...	...	1541	|	|	...	...	...	1643	1841	...	|	...	...
Napoli Centrale a.	1212	①–⑥	...	1255p	1318p	...	...	1430	...	...	1534	1512	...	...	1612	1618	1618	...	...	...	1712	1910	...	1815p	...	...
Napoli Centrale 620/6 d.	1224	1230	...	1259p	1322p	1324	1424	1442	1430	1430	...	1524	...	...	...	1630	1630	1638	1724	1724	...	...	...	1822p	...	...
Caserta **626** d.	|	|	...	|	|	|	|	|	|	|	...	|	...	...	...	|	|	|	|	|	...	...	...	|	...	...
Aversa d.	1246	1252	...	|	|	1346	1442	1459	1452	1502	...	1546	...	...	...	1646	1646	1653	1746	1746	...	...	...	|	...	...
Formia d.	1323	1344	...	1401	|	1423	1515	1542	1544	1551	...	1623	...	...	...	1726	1726	1744	1823	1823	...	...	...	|	...	...
Latina d.	1359	1430	...	1438	|	1459	1550	1618	1630	1637	...	1659	...	...	...	1759	1759	1830	1859	1859	...	...	...	|	...	...
Roma Termini 620 a.	1433	1511	...	1527t	1516	1533	1623	1653t	1713	1720	...	1733	...	...	...	1833	1833	1913	1933	1933	...	...	...	2016	...	...
Bologna C 620 a.	...	...	...	2013	...	...	2052	2127	...	...	...	...	...	...	...	...	...	...	...	...	...	...	...	...	...	...
Venezia SL 620 a.	...	...	...	|	...	...	|	|	...	...	...	...	...	...	...	...	...	...	...	...	...	...	...	...	...	...
Milano C 619/20 a.	...	...	...	2240	...	...	2300	2350	...	...	...	...	...	...	...	...	...	...	...	...	...	...	...	...	...	...
Torino PN 610 a.	...	...	...	...	...	...	...	...	...	...	...	...	...	...	...	...	...	...	...	...	...	...	...	...	...	...

♦ – **NOTES** (LISTED BY TRAIN NUMBER)

530 – SILA – [12] Reggio - Roma; [2] Crotone (**534**) - Sibari (**535**) - Cosenza (**536**) - Paola - Roma.
546 – CARDUCCI – ⑧ (not Apr. 12, 25, and days before holidays): [12] and 🍷 Napoli - Sestri Levante.
728 – PELORITANO – [12] and 🍷 Palermo - Roma.
892 – ⑦ Dec. 14 - June 7 (also June 2; not Apr. 12, May 31): ▬ 2 cl. and [2] Reggio - Roma.
894 – 🛏 1, 2 cl., ▬ 2 cl. and [2] Reggio - Roma; 🛏 1, 2 cl., ▬ 2 cl. and [2] Reggio (**890**) - Lamezia - Roma.
956 – Not Apr. 30 (from Lecce): [2] Lecce - Roma; [2] Catanzaro Lido (**954**) - Metaponto - Roma.
986 – Ⓐ: [2] Reggio - Metaponto (**989**) - Taranto (**990**) - Bari.
1554 – CARACCIOLO – ⑦ (also Apr. 13, June 2; not Apr. 12, May 31): [12] Salerno - Milano.
1572 – CARDUCCI – ⑥ (also Apr. 12, 25, and days before holidays): [12] Napoli - Livorno.
1588 – ASPROMONTE – ⑦ Dec. 14 - June 7 (also Apr. 13, June 2; not Apr. 12, May 31): [12] Reggio - Milano.
1920 – TRINACRIA – 🛏 1, 2 cl. (T2), 🛏 1,2 cl. and ▬ 2 cl. (4/6 berth) Palermo - Milano; [2] Palermo - Messina.
1924 – IL GATTOPARDO – 🛏 1, 2 cl. (Excelsior), 🛏 1, 2 cl. (T2), 🛏 1,2 cl., ▬ 2 cl. (4 berth) and [2] Palermo - Roma.
1938 – BELLINI – 🛏 1, 2 cl. (Excelsior), 🛏 1, 2 cl. (T2), 🛏 1,2 cl., ▬ 2 cl. (4 berth) and [2] Siracusa - Roma.

9360 – ⚒: [12] and 🍷 Taranto - Roma.
9380 – †: [12] and 🍷 Taranto - Roma.

U – PELORITANO – [12] Siracusa - Messina (**728**) - Roma.
X – FRECCIA DEL SUD – ①③⑤: [2] Agrigento - Catania - Roma; [2] Siracusa (**856**) - Catania - Roma.
Y – FRECCIA DEL SUD – ②④⑥⑦: ▬ 2 cl. and [2] Agrigento - Catania - Milano; [2] Siracusa (**836**) - Catania - Milano.
Z – TRINACRIA – 🛏 1, 2 cl. (T2), 🛏 1, 2 cl. and ▬ 2 cl. (4/6 berth) Siracusa - Messina (**1920**) - Milano.

c – Ⓒ only.
p – Napoli **Piazza Garibaldi** (situated under Centrale).
t – Roma **Tiburtina**.
y – Not Apr. 12, 25, and days before holidays.
z – Not Apr. 12.

SICILY - NAPOLI - ROMA 640

	E 824 ♦	*ICp* 676 [R] ✕ ♦	2	*ICp* 730 [R] V	*ICp* 724 [R] 🍷 ♦	*ICN* 774 ♦		*ICp* 590 [R]	*E* 1910 ♦	2 ⚒	2 ⚒	*E* 806 ♦	2 †	*ES* 9378 [R] 🍷	*E* 830 ♦	2	*E* 1594 ♦	2 ⚒	2 ⚒	*ICN* 768 ♦		*E* 1942 R	*E* 1940 ♦		*ICN* 752 ♦
Palermo C 645/7 d.	...	...	...	1020	...	...	...	...	...	1135	...	...	...	...	...	...	...	...	1305	...	...	...	1430	...	...
Termini Imerese **645/7** d.	...	...	...	1046	...	...	...	...	...	1201	...	...	...	...	...	...	...	...	1333	...	...	...	1456	...	...
Cefalù d.	...	...	...	1110	...	...	...	...	...	1224	...	...	...	...	...	...	...	...	1404	...	...	...	1523	...	...
Milazzo d.	...	...	...	1250	...	...	...	...	...	1441	...	...	...	...	...	...	...	...	1604	...	...	...	1707	...	...
Siracusa 648 d.	...	...	...	│	1045	...	...	...	...	│	...	...	...	...	...	...	...	...	│	...	...	1450	│	...	...
Augusta d.	...	...	...	│	1105	...	...	...	...	│	...	...	...	...	...	...	...	...	│	...	...	1515	│	...	...
Catania Centrale a.	...	...	...	│	1155	...	...	...	...	│	...	...	...	...	...	...	...	...	│	...	...	1601	│	...	...
Catania Centrale d.	...	...	...	│	1200	...	...	...	...	│	1350	...	1350	...	...	...	...	1422	│	...	...	1604	│	...	...
Giarre-Riposto **644** d.	...	...	...	│	1224	...	...	...	...	│	1414	...	1418	...	...	...	...	1448	│	...	...	1630	│	...	...
Taormina-Giardini d.	...	...	...	│	1242	...	...	...	...	│	1444	...	1441	...	...	...	...	1514	│	...	...	1648	│	...	...
Messina Centrale a.	...	...	...	1320	1325	...	...	...	...	1510	1527	...	1545	...	...	...	...	1605	1625	...	...	1725	1730	...	...
Messina Centrale d.	...	...	...	1335	1335	...	...	...	...	▬	...	...	▬	...	...	...	...	...	...	...	...	1750	1750	...	...
Reggio di Calabria d.	...	...	...	│	│	...	...	1455	...	...	...	...	...	1645	...	...	1615	...	...	1820	...	│	│	...	1935
Villa San Giovanni a.	...	...	...	1440	1440	...	...	1509	...	...	...	...	...	1657	...	...	1630	...	...	1837	...	1910	1910	...	1948
Villa San Giovanni d.	...	...	...	1505	1505	...	...	1512	...	...	...	...	...	1700	...	...	1653	...	...	1840	...	1935	1935	...	1951
Gioia Tauro d.	...	...	...	│	│	...	...	1540	...	...	...	...	...	1728	...	...	1732	...	...	1913	...	│	│	...	2021
Lamezia Terme C a.	...	...	...	1602	1602	...	...	1623	...	...	...	...	...	1807	...	...	1820	...	...	2000	...	2039	2039	...	2107
Lamezia Terme C d.	...	...	...	1605	1605	...	...	1626	...	...	...	...	...	1810	...	...	1855	...	...	2025	...	2042	2042	...	2130
Cosenza d.	...	...	...	│	│	...	...	│	...	...	...	...	2	│	...	1825	│	...	...	│	...	│	│	...	│
Paola d.	...	...	...	1640	1640	...	...	1704	...	...	...	...	1653	1845	...	1853	1937	...	...	2104	...	2118	2118	...	2215
Belvedere Marittimo d.	...	...	...	│	│	...	...	│	...	...	...	...	1726	│	...	1925	│	...	...	│	...	│	│	...	│
Maratea d.	...	...	...	│	│	...	...	1754	...	...	...	...	1811	│	...	2010	│	...	...	2150	...	│	│	...	2305
Sapri d.	...	...	...	│	│	...	...	1805	...	...	...	...	1821	1934	...	2020	2034	...	...	2205	...	2212	2212	...	2322
Ascea d.	...	...	...	│	│	...	...	│	...	...	...	...	1906	│	...	2101	2108	...	...	2236	...	│	│	...	2353
Agropoli d.	...	...	...	│	│	...	...	│	...	...	...	...	1937	│	...	2138	2130	...	...	2303	...	│	│	...	0022
Battipaglia d.	...	1717	...	│	│	...	...	1916	...	...	...	...	2002	│	...	2202	│	...	...	2328	...	│	│	...	0047
Salerno d.	...	1735	...	1842	1842	...	...	1933	...	...	...	...	2022	2042	2035	2221	2208	...	...	2344	...	2329	2329	...	0104
Pompei d.	...	│	...	│	│	...	...	│	...	...	...	...	2041	│	2102	│	│	...	...	│	...	│	│	...	│
Napoli Centrale a.	...	1812	...	1918	1918	...	...	2012	...	2	...	...	2110	2118p	2138	2302	2247	...	...	│	...	│	│	...	│
Napoli Centrale 620/6 d.	1845	1824	1830	1930	1930	1957	...	2024	2030	2048	...	2108	...	2122p	2150	...	2259	...	...	│	...	│	│	...	│
Caserta **626** d.	1917	│	│	│	│	│	...	│	│	│	...	│	...	│	2224	...	│	...	...	0037	...	│	│	...	0158
Aversa d.	│	1846	1852	1946	1946	│	...	2044	│	2106	...	2129	...	│	│	...	│	...	...	│	...	│	│	...	│
Formia d.	│	1923	1944	2021	2021	2113	...	2123	│	2154	...	2211	...	│	2318u	...	│	...	...	│	...	│	│	...	│
Latina d.	│	1959	2030	2059	2059	2151	...	2159	│	2245	...	2257	...	│	2356u	...	│	...	...	│	...	│	│	...	│
Roma Termini 620 a.	2158t	2033	2112	2133	2133	2231t	...	2233	2245	2330	...	2336	...	2315	0038t	...	│	...	...	│	...	│	│	...	0417t
Bologna C **620** a.	0300	...	...	...	...	0313	...	...	│	...	...	│	...	...	0552	...	0528	...	...	│	...	│	│	...	0752
Venezia S L **620** a.	...	...	...	...	...	0526	...	...	│	...	...	│	...	...	│	...	...	...	...	│	...	│	│	...	│
Milano C **619/20** a.	...	...	...	...	...	...	...	...	0725	...	...	│	...	...	0920	...	...	...	...	│	...	│	│	...	1005
Torino P N **610** a.	...	...	...	...	...	...	...	...	...	...	...	0820	...	...	...	...	...	...	...	1045	...	1110	1110	...	...

	E 1992 ♦	*E* 1990 M		2 Ⓐ	*E* 1934 B	*E* 1930 ♦	*E* 1932 T	2 ⚒		
Palermo C 645/7 d.	...	1500	...	1525	...	...	1600	...	...	...
Termini Imerese **645/7** d.	...	1527	...	1556	...	...	1626	...	...	...
Cefalù d.	...	1553	...	1615	...	...	1651	...	...	...
Milazzo d.	...	1751	...	1800	...	...	1844	...	...	...
Siracusa 648 d.	1530	│	...	│	...	1555	│	1700	...	...
Augusta d.	1552	│	...	│	...	1620	│	1725	...	...
Catania Centrale a.	1640	│	...	│	...	1715	│	1818	...	...
Catania Centrale d.	1645	│	...	│	...	1733	│	1821	...	...
Giarre-Riposto **644** d.	1715	│	...	│	...	1758	│	1851	...	...
Taormina-Giardini d.	1736	│	...	│	...	1818	│	1911	...	...
Messina Centrale a.	1825	1815	...	1835	...	1905	1910	2000	...	...
Messina Centrale d.	1845	1845	...	...	...	1925	1925	...	...	...
Reggio di Calabria d.	│	│	...	...	2025	│	│	...	...	...
Villa San Giovanni a.	2010	2010	...	...	2040	2050	2050	...	...	...
Villa San Giovanni d.	2040	2040	...	...	2115	2115	2115	...	...	...
Gioia Tauro d.	│	│	...	...	2147	2147	2147	...	...	...
Lamezia Terme C a.	2145	2145	...	...	2230	2230	2230	...	...	...
Lamezia Terme C d.	2148	2148	...	...	2233	2233	2233	...	...	...
Cosenza d.	│	│	...	...	│	│	│	...	...	...
Paola d.	2223	2223	...	...	2313	2313	2313	...	...	...
Belvedere Marittimo d.	│	│	...	...	│	│	│	...	...	...
Maratea d.	│	│	...	...	│	│	│	...	...	...
Sapri d.	│	│	...	...	0006	0006	0006	...	...	...
Ascea d.	│	│	...	...	│	│	│	...	...	...
Agropoli d.	│	│	...	...	│	│	│	...	...	...
Battipaglia d.	│	│	...	...	│	│	│	...	...	...
Salerno d.	0027	0027	...	...	0126	0126	0126	...	...	...
Pompei d.	│	│	...	...	│	│	│	...	...	...
Napoli Centrale a.	│	│	...	...	│	│	│	...	...	...
Napoli Centrale 620/6 d.	│	│	...	...	│	│	│	...	...	...
Caserta **626** d.	│	│	...	...	│	│	│	...	...	...
Aversa d.	│	│	...	...	│	│	│	...	...	...
Formia d.	│	│	...	...	│	│	│	...	...	...
Latina d.	│	│	...	...	│	│	│	...	...	...
Roma Termini 620 a.	│	│	...	...	│	│	│	...	...	...
Bologna C **620** a.	0719	0719	...	...	0928	0928	0928	...	...	...
Venezia S L **620** a.	│	│	...	...	1150	1150	1150	...	...	...
Milano C **619/20** a.	1005n	1005n	...	...	...	...	...	...	...	...
Torino P N **610** a.	...	...	...	...	...	...	...	...	...	...

Alta Velocità (*AV*) – services via high-speed line

km (via hsl)		*AV* 9506 [R] ✕ Ⓐ		*AV* 9430 [R] ✕	*AV* 9640 [R] ✕ Ⓐ		*AV* 9432 [R] ✕	*AV* 9604 [R] ✕ Ⓐ	*AV* 9434 [R] ✕
	Salerno d.	...	...	0606	...	...	...	...	...
	Napoli Centrale a.	...	...	0642	...	...	...	...	...
0	Napoli Centrale d.	0625	...	0654	0716	...	0754	0816	0854
216	Roma Termini a.	0747t	...	0815	0837	...	0915	0937	1015
	Bologna Centrale a.	1008	...	1120	1134	...	1220	...	1320
	Venezia Santa Lucia a.	│	...	│	1317	...	│	...	│
	Milano Centrale a.	1115	...	1229	...	...	1329	...	1429

	AV 9436 [R] ✕		*AV* 9440 [R] ✕	*AV* 9442 [R] ✕		*AV* 9444 [R] ✕	*AV* 9642 [R] ✕ Ⓐ		*AV* 9448 [R] ✕
Salerno d.	0906	...	...	...	...	...	...	...	...
Napoli Centrale a.	0942	...	...	...	...	...	...	...	...
Napoli Centrale d.	0954	...	1154	1254	...	1354	1516	...	1554
Roma Termini a.	1115	...	1315	1415	...	1515	1637	...	1715
Bologna Centrale a.	1420	...	1620	1720	...	1820	1934	...	2020
Venezia Santa Lucia a.	│	...	│	│	...	│	2117	...	│
Milano Centrale a.	1529	...	1729	1829	...	1929	...	...	2129

	AV 9450 [R] ✕ Ⓑ	*AV* 9644 [R] ✕ Ⓐ		*AV* 9452 [R] ✕	*AV* 9454 [R] ✕ ♦		*AV* 9456 [R] ✕		
Salerno d.	...	...	...	...	...	...	...	...	...
Napoli Centrale a.	...	...	...	...	...	...	...	...	...
Napoli Centrale d.	1654	1716	...	1754	1816	...	1854	...	...
Roma Termini a.	1815	1837	...	1915	1937	...	2015	...	...
Bologna Centrale a.	2120	2134	...	2220	...	...	2342	...	...
Venezia Santa Lucia a.	│	2317	...	│	...	...	...	...	...
Milano Centrale a.	2229	...	...	2329	...	...	...	...	...

For **Alta Velocità** (*AV*) services north of Roma – see Table **620**.

♦ – **NOTES** (LISTED BY TRAIN NUMBER)

676 – JONIO – [12] and ✕ Taranto - Roma.
724 – ARCHIMEDE – [12] and 🍷 Siracusa - Roma.
752 – TOMMASO CAMPANELLA – 🛏 1, 2 cl., ▬ 2 cl. and [12] Reggio - Milano; ▬ 2 cl. (4 berth) and [2] Reggio (**750**) - Lamezia - Milano.
768 – SCILLA – 🛏 1, 2 cl., ▬ 2 cl. and [12] Reggio - Torino; ▬ 2 cl. (4 berth) and [2] Reggio (**766**) - Lamezia - Torino.
774 – MARCO POLO – 🛏 1, 2 cl., ▬ 2 cl. (4 berth) and [2] Napoli - Udine; 🛏 1, 2 cl., ▬ 2 cl. (4 berth) and [12] Napoli - Venezia Mestre (**773**) - Trieste.
806 – 🛏 1, 2 cl. (Excelsior), 🛏 1,2 cl. (T2), 🛏 1, 2 cl., ▬ 2 cl. (4/6 berth) and [2] Napoli - Torino.
824 – ①③④⑤⑥⑦ (not June 2, 3): 🛏 1, 2 cl., ▬ 2 cl. (4 berth) and [2] Napoli - Bologna (**924**) - Bolzano.
830 – ②④⑦: ▬ 2 cl. and [2] Salerno - Milano.
1594 – ⑤ Dec. 19 - Mar. 20, June 19 - Sept. 11: 🛏 1,2 cl. (T2), ▬ 2 cl. and [2] Reggio - Bolzano.
1910 – 🛏 1,2 cl. (Excelsior), 🛏 1,2 cl. (T2), 🛏 1,2 cl., ▬ 2 cl. (4 berth) and [2] Napoli - Milano.
1930 – FRECCIA DELLA LAGUNA – 🛏 1, 2 cl. and ▬ 2 cl. (4 berth) Siracusa - Venezia.
1940 – TRENO DEL SOLE – 🛏 1, 2 cl. and ▬ 2 cl. (4 berth) Palermo - Torino; [2] Palermo - Messina.
1992 – MONGIBELLO – Apr. 9, 13, 29, May 3, 28, June 2; ④⑦ from June 7: 🛏 1, 2 cl. (T2), ▬ 2 cl. and [2] Siracusa - Milano.
9454 – Ⓑ: [12] and ✕ Napoli - Firenze.

B – FRECCIA DELLA LAGUNA – 🛏 1, 2 cl. and ▬ 2 cl. (4 berth) Reggio - Villa S G (**1930**) - Venezia.
M – MONGIBELLO – Apr. 9, 13, 29, May 3, 28, June 2; ④⑦ from June 7: ▬ 2 cl. (4 berth) and [2] Palermo - Messina (**1992**) - Milano.
R – TRENO DEL SOLE – 🛏 1, 2 cl. and ▬ 2 cl. (4 berth) Siracusa - Messina (**1940**) - Torino.
T – FRECCIA DELLA LAGUNA – 🛏 1, 2 cl. and ▬ 2 cl. (4 berth) Palermo - Messina (**1930**) - Venezia.
V – ARCHIMEDE – [12] Palermo - Messina (**724**) - Roma.

n – Milano **Porta Garibaldi**.
p – Napoli **Piazza Garibaldi** (situated under Centrale).
t – Roma **Tiburtina**.
u – Stops to pick up only.

644 CATANIA - RANDAZZO - RIPOSTO
Ferrovia Circumetnea

Winter service valid from September 15, 2008. No service on †

km		⚒	⚒	⚒	⚒	⚒	⚒	⚒	⚒	⚒	⚒	⚒	⚒	⚒	⚒
0	**Catania ▲** ..d.	...	0648	0748	...	0930	...	1113	1209	1315	1436	1642	1822	1915	2006
20	Paternò ....d.	...	0720	0821	...	1006	...	1147	1244	1349	1510	1716	1855	1949	2038
36	Adrano ....d.	...	0753	0856	...	1037	...	1218	1317	1425	1544	1747	1924	2019	...
52	Bronte ....d.	...	0822	0926	...	1108	...	1247	1352	1457	1613	1816	1953	2047	...
71	Randazzo.....d.	0746	0854	0957	1000	1138	1155	1325	1422	1527	1645	1847	2023	2117	...
109	Giarre **640**...a.	0853	...	...	1106	...	1302	1430	...	...	1750	...	...	...	...
111	**Riposto** ....a.	0857	...	...	1109	...	1305	1433	...	...	1753	...	...	...	...

	⚒	⚒	⚒	⚒	⚒		⚒	⚒	⚒	⚒	⚒	⚒	⚒	⚒
Riposto.....d.	...	...	...	0653	0830	...	1014	...	...	1236	1339	1436	...	1805
Giarre **640** d.	...	...	...	0658	0834	...	1018	...	...	1241	1343	1440	...	1809
Randazzo .d.	0520	0616	0654	0820	1001	...	1130	1216	1320	1426	1457	1552	1711	1921
Bronte ....d.	0551	0648	0724	0851	1032	...	...	1248	1352	1456	...	...	1741	1952
Adrano.......d.	0619	0716	0752	0919	1101	...	...	1316	1423	1522	...	...	1810	2018
Paternò.....d.	0650	0745	0822	0949	1131	...	...	1348	1455	1551	...	...	1840	2049
Catania ▲a.	0724	0816	0854	1020	1202	...	...	1420	1527	1623	...	...	1912	2119

▲ – Catania Borgo station. The Metropolitana di Catania operates a metro service Borgo - Porto and v.v. (3.8 km) via Catania Centrale station. Weekdays only, every 15 minutes 0700–2045.

645 PALERMO and AGRIGENTO - CATANIA
2nd class only except where shown

km		⚒	⚒	⚒	⚒	⚒			⚒		⚒	⚒		†	⚒	⚒		A		⚒	G			
0	**Palermo C 647**..........d.	...	...	0555	0635	...	0808	...	1205	...	...	...	1435	...	...	...	...	...	...	...	1722	...	1846	...
37	Termini Imerese **647**.........d.	...	...	0622	0704	...	0837	...	1231	...	...	...	1502	...	...	...	...	...	...	...	1752	...	1915	...
70	Roccapalumba Alia **647**........d.	...	...	0649	0745	...	0911	...	1301	...	...	1437	1531	1535	...	1535	...	...	...	1740	1823	...	1951	...
	Agrigento C 647 ....d.	...	...	|	|	0813	|	1225	|	...	1314	|	1647	|	...	|	...	1500	...	|	|	1850	|	...
	Aragona-Caldare **647**........d.	...	...	|	|	0832	|	1247	|	...	1331	|	...	|	...	|	...	1517	...	|	|	1907	|	...
	Canicattì **648**..............d.	...	...	|	|	0916	|	1323	|	...	1409	|	...	|	...	|	...	1607	...	|	|	1941	|	...
	Caltanissetta Xirbi **648**.........a.	...	...	0739	0850	|	1000	|	1352	...	|	1530	...	1620	...	1625	...	|	...	1836	1912	|	2040	...
	Caltanissetta C **648**..........d.	0542	0655	0754	0906	0948	|	1353	1410	←	1445	1546	...	|	1620	1641	←	1642	...	1855	1925	2006	...	...
127	Caltanissetta Xirbi **648**.........d.	0551	0705	...	...	0955	1002	1403	...	1403	...	...	...	1621	1632	...	1632	1653	...	...	...	2014	...	...
154	Enna ....d.	0613	0742	...	...	...	1028	→	...	1426	...	...	...	1643	→	...	1654	1726	...	...	...	2038	...	...
243	**Catania Centrale** ....a.	0733	0857	...	...	...	1148	...	...	1540	...	...	...	1800	...	...	1810	1850	...	...	...	2150	...	...

km		⚒	⚒	⚒	G ⚒	⚒	†	†	†	B	Ⓐ	⚒		†	⚒	⚒	†		⚒	†	†			
	Catania Centrale ....d.	...	...	0550	...	...	...	0715	...	0735	...	1040	...	1335	1335	1415	...	...	1605	...	1605	1828	...	...
	Enna ....d.	...	...	0712	...	...	...	0833	...	0905	...	1204	...	1451	1451	1539	...	...	1727	...	1727	1946	...	...
0	Caltanissetta Xirbi **648**.........a.	...	...	0734	...	...	...	0855	...	0933	...	1228	...	1517	1517	1601	...	...	1748	...	1748	2009	...	...
6	Caltanissetta C **648**..........d.	0600	0620	0743	0803	0804	0851	0909	←	0949	1120	1240	...	1527	1531	|	1620	...	|	1735	1806	2023	...	...
	Caltanissetta Xirbi **648**.........d.	0615	|	...	0818	|	0903	|	0903	|	1135	...	...	|	|	1604	1632	...	1750	1751	...	...	2050	...
35	Canicattì **648**..............d.	|	0653	...	|	0836	→	0945	|	1035	|	...	...	1613	1613	|	|	...	|	|	...	...	|	...
65	Aragona-Caldare **647**........d.	|	0724	...	|	0909	...	1014	|	1115	|	...	...	1644	1644	|	|	...	|	|	...	...	|	...
78	**Agrigento C 647** ....a.	|	0741	...	|	0929	...	1030	|	1130	|	...	...	1700	1700	|	|	...	|	|	...	...	|	...
	Roccapalumba Alia **647**........d.	0711	...	...	0912	...	...	...	1002	...	1225	...	...	...	...	1703	1727	...	1845	1845	...	...	2139	...
	Termini Imerese **647**.........d.	0736	...	...	0943	...	...	...	1029	...	1301	...	...	...	...	1731	1756	...	1911	1911	...	...	2212	...
	Palermo C 647..........a.	0800	...	...	1017	...	...	...	1100	...	1330	...	...	...	...	1800	1824	...	1940	1940	...	...	2245	...

A – FRECCIA DEL SUD – On ②④⑥⑦ (train number **834**) [couchette] 2 cl. and [2] Agrigento - Milano. On ①③⑤ (train number **854**) [2] Agrigento - Roma.
B – FRECCIA DEL SUD – On ①②④⑥ (train number **823**) [couchette] 2 cl. and [2] Milano - Agrigento. On ③⑤⑦ (train number **853**) [2] Roma - Agrigento.
G – [2] Palermo - Gela and v.v.

CATANIA - GELA and v.v. 2nd class only, *137 km*, journey 2½ hours (approximately).
From **Catania**: 0555 ⚒, 0922 ⚒, 1223 ⚒, 1322 ⚒, 1440 ⚒, 1742 ⚒.
From **Gela**: 0545 ⚒, 0700 ⚒, 0910 ⚒, 1235 ⚒, 1325 ⚒, 1428 ⚒, 1730 ⚒.

646 PALERMO - TRAPANI
2nd class only

km		⚒	⚒	⚒	†	⚒	⚒	†k	†k	⚒	⚒	†	†	⚒	⚒	⚒	⚒	⚒	†	⚒	†	⚒	⚒			⚒
0	**Palermo Centrale**.............d.	...	...	...	...	...	0638	0740	...	...	0929	0938	...	...	1129	...	1329	...	1429	1429	...	..	...	...	1829	1929
73	Castellammare del Golfo ...d.	...	0644	...	...	...	0836	0922	...	1037	1110	1118	...	...	1259	...	1514	...	1558	1558	...	...	...	1923	2004	2107
79	Alcamo Diramazione..........d.	...	0652	0700	...	...	0844	0930	0939	1044	1117	1125	1134	...	1311	1313	1522	1528	1607	1607	1610	...	...	1930	2012	2114
121	Castelvetrano..................d.	0624	0730	|	0828	0828	0920	|	1022	1124	|	|	1212	1316	|	1404	|	1604	1648	1647	|	1715	1815	2013	|	2150
144	Mazara del Vallo.............d.	0642	0754	|	0847	0851	0939	|	1045	1146	|	|	1239	1339	|	1428	|	1623	1711	...	|	1734	1838	2031	|	...
165	Marsala.........................d.	0703	0813	|	0911	0913	0958	|	1102	1205	|	|	1255	1401	|	1451	|	1647	1730	...	|	1759	1903	2055	|	...
196	**Trapani**.........................a.	0735	0840	0745	0937	0940	1022	1009	1137	1234	1158	1205	1326	1435	1350	1520	1604	1713	1757	...	1651	1833	1928	2125	2048	...

km		⚒	⚒	⚒	†k	⚒	⚒	⚒	†k	†	†	⚒	⚒		⚒	⚒			⚒	†				⚒		
0	**Trapani**.........................d.	0500	0523	0618	0706	0605	0838	0843	0840	1012	1125	1215	1155	1246	1330	1423	1426	...	1700	1701	1600	1820	1932	1938	2028	...
	Marsala.........................d.	|	|	|	|	0635	|	0912	0910	|	1152	|	1228	1319	1402	1450	|	...	|	|	1626	1845	|	2005	2054	...
	Mazara del Vallo.............d.	|	|	|	|	0705	|	0940	0928	|	1210	|	1244	1338	1427	1509	|	...	|	|	1644	1903	|	2032	2109	...
	Castelvetrano..................d.	|	|	|	|	0731	|	1001	0950	|	1235	|	1304	1403	1447	1529	|	...	|	|	1707	1922	|	2052	2130	...
47	Alcamo Diramazione..........d.	0537	0601	0655	0747	0809	0918	1045	1027	1052	...	1255	1343	1440	...	...	1506	...	1739	1740	1745	2002	2013	...	...	...
53	Castellammare del Golfo ...d.	0544	...	0702	0754	0816	0926	1052	...	1059	...	...	1350	...	...	...	1513	...	...	...	1753	...	2022	...	...	...
126	**Palermo Centrale**.............a.	0727	...	0837	0936	...	...	1237	...	1237	...	...	1537	...	...	...	...	...	...	...	2006	...	2200	...	...	...

k – Not Apr. 12.

647 PALERMO - AGRIGENTO
2nd class only

km		⚒	k			⚒		⚒	†	⚒		⚒	
0	**Palermo C 645**.......... d.	0735	0835	1035	1235	1335	1435	1535	1635	1635	1740	1835	2015
37	Termini-Imerese **645**.. d.	0803	0901	1101	1301	1402	1502	1601	1702	1702	1806	1901	2046
70	Roccapalumba-Alia **645**. d.	0836	0936	1129	1329	1434	1533	1635	1732	1736	1835	1938	2116
125	Aragona-Caldare **645**. d.	0928	1028	1224	1429	1521	1628	1725	1828	1828	1933	2038	2203
139	**Agrigento C 645**....... a.	0947	1045	1245	1447	1547	1647	1745	1845	1845	1950	2055	2221

	⚒	⚒	⚒	k			⚒				
Agrigento C 645 .... d.	0450	0538	0653	0825	1057	1325	1410	1525	1607	1808	2005
Aragona-Caldare **645**. d.	0508	0556	0710	0843	1114	1343	1430	1545	1629	1829	2023
Roccapalumba-Alia **645** d.	0605	0650	0806	0936	1209	1436	1533	1634	1736	1920	2117
Termini-Imerese **645**. d.	0635	0721	0830	1004	1235	1504	1604	1703	1803	1946	2145
Palermo C 645....... a.	0700	0750	0855	1030	1300	1530	1630	1730	1830	2011	2213

k – Not Apr. 12.

648 SIRACUSA - CALTANISSETTA
2nd class only

km		⚒G	†G	⚒		†	⚒		⚒	⚒	⚒		
0	**Siracusa 640**..................d.	...	...	0520	1000	...	...	1255	...	1400	1745	...	2028
62	Pozzallo...........................d.	...	...	0629	1112	...	...	1357	...	1514	1842	...	2129
92	Modica ....d.	...	...	0715	1154	...	...	1442	1352	1546	1928	2000	2210
112	Ragusa............................d.	...	...	0742	1221	...	...	1507	1418	...	...	2023	...
153	Vittoria ....d.	...	...	0824	1303	...		...	1505	...	...	2106	...
183	Gela ....d.	0620	0708	0850	1330	1420	1420	...	1533	...	...	2135	...
218	Licata ....d.	0656	0738	...	...	1453	1453	...	1612	...	...	...	...
264	Canicattì **645**..................d.	0737	0824	...	...	1540	1540	...	1659	...	...	...	...
293	**Caltanissetta C 645**.......d.	0803	0851	...	...	1612	1617	...	1733	...	...	...	...
296	Caltanissetta Xirbi **645**....a.	0810	0858	...	...	1619	...	...	1742	...	...	...	...

	⚒	⚒	⚒	†	⚒	⚒			G	
Caltanissetta Xirbi **645**.d.	...	...	...	...	...	...	...	...	1918	...
Caltanissetta C 645....d.	...	...	...	...	0545	...	...	...	1926	...
Canicattì **645** ....d.	...	...	...	...	0616	...	...	...	2002	...
Licata ....d.	...	...	...	...	0655	...	...	...	2044	...
Gela ....d.	...	...	...	0700	0733	1250	1415	1721	2116	...
Vittoria ....d.	...	...	...	0731	0803	1324	1446	1752	...	...
Ragusa..........................d.	...	...	0806	0821	0900	1420	1539	1843	...	...
Modica ....d.	0520	0622	0828	0844	0920	1441	1608	1904	...	...
Pozzallo........................d.	0550	0653	0901	0927	...	1513	1640	1937	...	...
Siracusa 640 ....a.	0655	0755	1005	1021	...	1620	1740	2045	...	...

G – [2] Palermo - Gela and v.v.

MALTA

Bus services are operated by ATP (www.atp.com.mt) on behalf of the Government's Transport Department ADT (www.maltatransport.com) and operate frequently throughout Malta.

649 PRINCIPAL BUS SERVICES
Approx frequency (in minutes) shown in *italics*

Routes from Valletta: 1/2/4/6 Vittoriosa (*15*), 3 Senglea (*20-30*), 8 Airport (*30*), 10-13 Birzebugia (*10-15*), 17-21 Zabbar / Marsascala (*20-30*), 27/127 Marsaxlokk (*30*), 32/34 Zurrieq (*15-20*), 45/145 Cirkewwa for Gozo ferry (*20*), 49/58-59 Mosta / Bugibba (*10*), 55-56 Naxxar (*15-20*), 62/64/66/67/68 Sliema / St Julians (*5*), 80/81/84 Rabat / Dingli (*15*), 88 Zebbug (*15*), 89 Siggiewi (*20-30*).

Routes from Sliema: 65 Mosta / Rabat (*30*), 645 Bugibba / Cirkewwa for Gozo ferry (*30*), 652 Bugibba / Golden Bay (*30*). **Gozo**: service 25 Victoria - Mgarr connects with ferries.

SCENIC RAIL ROUTES OF EUROPE

The following is a list of some of the most scenic rail routes of Europe, detailed timings for most of which can be found within the timetable. Routes marked * are the Editor's personal choice. This list does not include specialised mountain and tourist railways.

Many more scenic lines are clearly marked on the Thomas Cook New Rail Map of Europe - see the back of this book for details.

Types of scenery : C-Coastline, F-Forest, G-Gorge, L-Lake, M-Mountain, R-River.

ALBANIA

Elbasan - Pogradec	ML G R

AUSTRIA

Bruck an der Mur - Villach	R
Gmunden - Stainach Irdning*	ML
Innsbruck - Brennero	M
Innsbruck - Garmisch Partenkirchen*	M
Innsbruck - Schwarzach-St Veit	M G
Klagenfurt - Unzmarkt	M
Landeck - Bludenz*	M
Linz - Krems	R
St Pölten - Mariazell*	M
Salzburg - Villach*	M G
Selzthal - Hieflau - Steyr	M G R
Wiener Neustadt - Semmering - Graz	M

BELGIUM and LUXEMBOURG

Liège - Luxembourg*	R
Liège - Marloie	R
Namur - Dinant	R

BULGARIA

Septemvri - Dobriniste	M
Sofija - Burgas	M
Tulova - Gorna Orjahovitza	M

CROATIA and BOSNIA

Rijeka - Ogulin	M
Ogulin - Split	M
Sarajevo - Ploče	M G R

CZECH REPUBLIC

Karlovy Vary - Mariánské Lázně	R F
Karlovy Vary - Chomutov	R
Praha - Děčín	R

DENMARK

Struer - Thisted	C

FINLAND

Kouvola - Joensuu	L F

Many other lines run through scenic areas.

FRANCE

Aurillac - Neussargues	M G
Bastia - Ajaccio	M
Chambéry - Bourg St Maurice	M
Chambéry - Modane	ML
Chamonix - Martigny*	M G
Clermont Ferrand - Béziers	M G
Clermont Ferrand - Nîmes*	M G R
Gap - Briançon	ML
Genève - Aix les Bains	M R
Grenoble - Veynes - Marseille	M
Marseille - Ventimiglia	C
Mouchard - Besançon - Montbéliard	R
Nice - Digne	M
Nice / Ventimiglia - Cuneo*	M G
Perpignan - Latour de Carol*	M G
Portbou - Perpignan	C
Sarlat - Bergerac	R
Toulouse - Latour de Carol	M
Valence - Veynes	M

GERMANY

Arnstadt - Meiningen	M
Bonn - Siegen	R
Dresden - Děčín	G R
Freiburg - Donaueschingen	G F
Garmisch Partenkirchen - Kempten	M
Heidelberg - Neckarelz	R
Koblenz - Mainz*	G R
München - Lindau	M
Murnau - Oberammergau	ML
Naumburg - Saalfeld	R

GERMANY - continued

Niebüll - Westerland	C
Nürnberg - Pegnitz	G R
Offenburg - Konstanz	M F
Pforzheim - Nagold / Wildbad	F
Plattling - Bayerisch Eisenstein	F
Rosenheim - Freilassing - Berchtesgaden	ML
Rosenheim - Wörgl	M
Stuttgart - Singen	F
Titisee - Seebrugg	L F
Trier - Koblenz - Giessen	R
Ulm - Göppingen	M
Ulm - Tuttlingen	R

GREAT BRITAIN and IRELAND

Alnmouth - Dunbar	C
Barrow in Furness - Maryport	C
Coleraine - Londonderry	C
Dun Laoghaire - Wicklow	C
Edinburgh - Aberdeen	C
Exeter - Newton Abbot	C
Glasgow - Oban / Mallaig*	ML
Inverness - Kyle of Lochalsh*	M C
Liskeard - Looe	R
Llanelli - Craven Arms	M
Machynlleth - Pwllheli	M C
Perth - Inverness	M
Plymouth - Gunnislake	R
Rosslare - Waterford	C R
St Erth - St Ives	C
Sheffield - New Mills	M
Shrewsbury - Aberystwyth	M R
Skipton - Settle - Carlisle	M R

GREECE

Korinthos - Patras	C
Diakoptó - Kalávrita	M G

HUNGARY

Budapest - Szob	R
Eger - Szilvásvárad	M
Székesfehérvár - Balatonszentgyörgy	L
Székesfehérvár - Tapolca	L

ITALY

Bologna - Pistoia	M
Bolzano - Merano	M
Brennero - Verona*	M
Brig - Arona	ML
Domodossola - Locarno*	M G
Firenze - Viareggio	M
Fortezza - San Candido	M
Genova - Pisa	C
Genova - Ventimiglia	C
Lecco - Tirano	ML
Messina - Palermo	C
Napoli - Sorrento	C
Roma - Pescara	M
Salerno - Reggio Calabria	C
Taranto - Reggio Calabria	C
Torino - Aosta	M

NORWAY

Bergen - Oslo*	ML
Bodø - Trondheim	ML
Dombås - Åndalsnes	M
Drammen - Larvik	C
Lillestrom - Kongsvinger	R
Myrdal - Flåm*	M C
Oslo / Røros - Trondheim	ML
Stavanger - Kristiansand	M

POLAND

Jelenia Góra - Walbrzych	M
Kraków - Zakopane	M
Olsztyn - Elk	L
Olsztyn - Morag	L
Tarnów - Krynica	M

PORTUGAL

Guarda - Entroncamento	M R
Pampilhosa - Guarda	M
Porto - Coimbra	C R
Porto - Pocinho*	R
Porto - Valença	M C
Regua - Vila Real	M G
Tua - Mirandela*	M G R

ROMANIA

Braşov - Ploeşti	M
Caransebeş - Craiova	M G R
Feteşti - Constanţa	R
Oradea - Cluj Napoca	R

SERBIA and MONTENEGRO

Priboj - Bar	ML

SLOVAKIA

Banská Bystrica - Brezno - Košice	M
Žilina - Poprad Tatry	M

SLOVENIA

Jesenice - Sežana	M R
Maribor - Zidani Most	M
Trieste - Ljubljana - Zagreb	G R

SPAIN

Algeciras - Ronda	M R
Barcelona - Latour de Carol	M
Bilbao - San Sebastián	M
Bilbao - Santander	M
Ferrol - Gijón*	C
Granada - Almería	M
Huesca - Canfranc	M G R
León - Monforte de Lemos	M
León - Oviedo	M
Lleida - La Pobla de Segur	ML
Madrid - Aranda - Burgos	ML
Málaga - Bobadilla	G
Santander - Oviedo	M C
Zaragoza - València	M R

SWEDEN

Bollnäs - Ånge - Sundsvall	ML
Borlänge - Mora	ML F
Borlänge - Ludvika - Frövi	ML F
Narvik - Kiruna	M F
Östersund - Storlien	L F

Many other lines run through scenic areas.

SWITZERLAND

Andermatt - Göschenen	G
Basel - Delémont - Moutier	M R
Chur - Arosa	M G
Chur - Brig - Zermatt*	M
Chur - St Moritz*	M G
Davos - Filisur	M G
Davos - Landquart	M
Interlaken Ost - Jungfraujoch*	M
Interlaken Ost - Luzern	ML
Interlaken West - Spiez	L
Lausanne - Brig	ML R
Lausanne - Neuchâtel - Biel	ML
Montreux - Zweisimmen - Lenk	ML G
Rorschach - Kreuzlingen	L
St Moritz - Scuol Tarasp	M
St Moritz - Tirano*	M
Spiez - Zweisimmen	G
Thun - Brig*	ML
Zürich / Luzern - Chiasso	ML
Zürich - Chur	ML

Many other lines run through scenic areas.

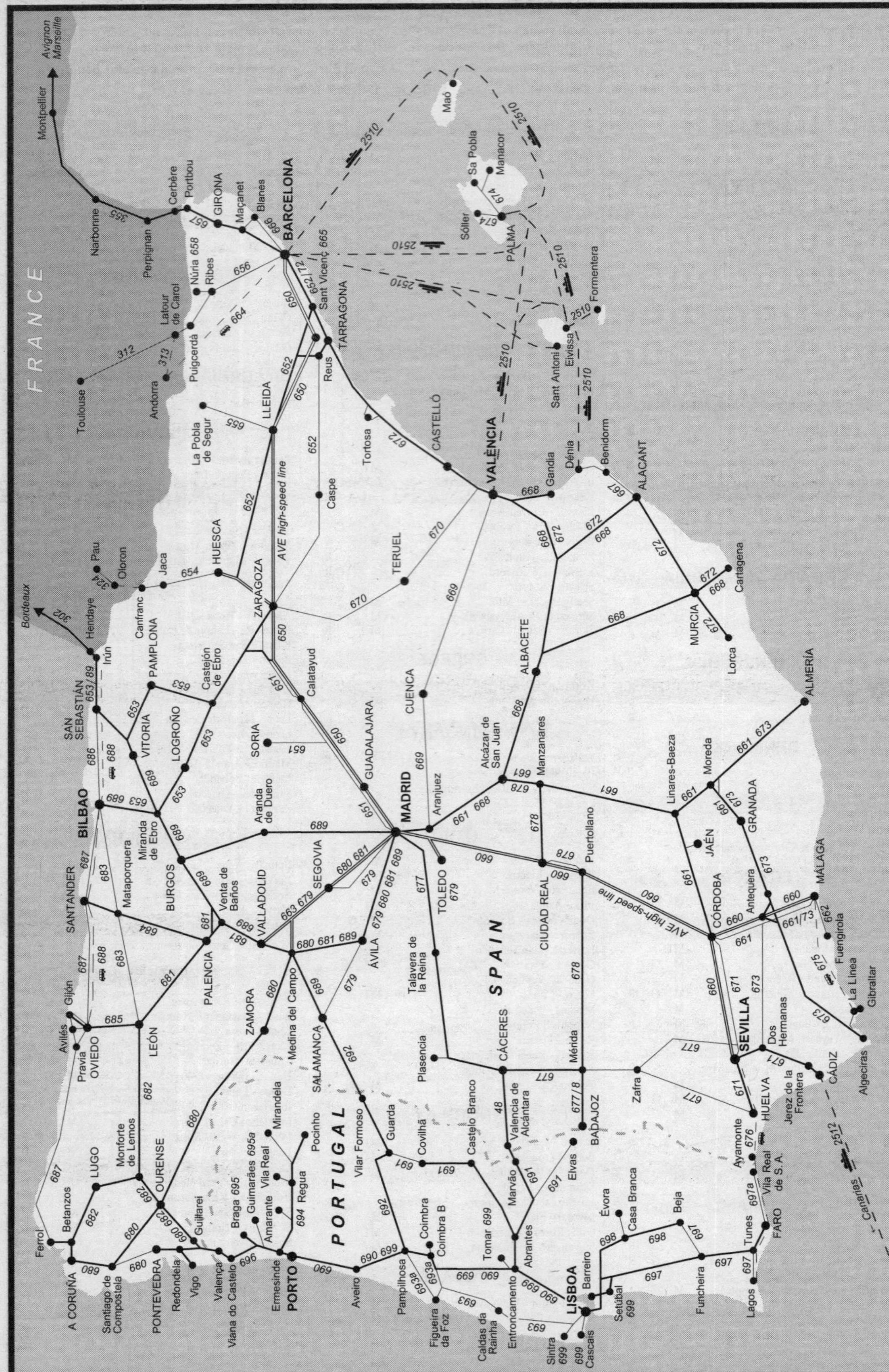
FRANCE
SPAIN
PORTUGAL
Bordeaux
Avignon
Marseille
Montpellier
Narbonne
Perpignan
Cerbère
Portbou
Toulouse
Pau
Oloron
Hendaye
Irún
Andorra
Latour de Carol
Puigcerdà
Núria
Ribes
GIRONA
Maçanet
Blanes
BARCELONA
Sant Vicenç
TARRAGONA
Reus
LLEIDA
La Pobla de Segur
Caspe
Tortosa
CASTELLÓ
VALÈNCIA
Gandia
Dénia
Benidorm
ALACANT
Cartagena
MURCIA
Lorca
ALMERÍA
Palma
Sóller
Sa Pobla
Manacor
Maó
Eivissa
Sant Antoni
Formentera
HUESCA
Jaca
Canfranc
PAMPLONA
ZARAGOZA
AVE high-speed line
TERUEL
Calatayud
CUENCA
Aranjuez
Castejón de Ebro
LOGROÑO
VITORIA
SAN SEBASTIÁN
BILBAO
Miranda de Ebro
BURGOS
SORIA
GUADALAJARA
MADRID
TOLEDO
Alcázar de San Juan
Manzanares
ALBACETE
CIUDAD REAL
Puertollano
Linares-Baeza
Moreda
GRANADA
JAÉN
CÓRDOBA
Antequera
MÁLAGA
Fuengirola
SEVILLA
Dos Hermanas
Jerez de la Frontera
CÁDIZ
Algeciras
La Línea
Gibraltar
HUELVA
Ayamonte
Zafra
Mérida
BADAJOZ
CÁCERES
Plasencia
Talavera de la Reina
ÁVILA
SEGOVIA
Aranda de Duero
VALLADOLID
Venta de Baños
PALENCIA
Mataporquera
SANTANDER
Gijón
Avilés
Pravia
OVIEDO
LEÓN
ZAMORA
Medina del Campo
SALAMANCA
Vilar Formoso
Guarda
Covilhã
Castelo Branco
Valencia de Alcántara
Marvão
Elvas
Abrantes
Tomar
Entroncamento
LISBOA
Barreiro
Setúbal
Sintra
Cascais
Caldas da Rainha
Figueira da Foz
Pampilhosa
Coimbra
Coimbra B
Aveiro
PORTO
Ermesinde
Amarante
Guimarães
Braga
Vila Real
Regua
Pocinho
Mirandela
Viana do Castelo
Valença
Guillarei
Vigo
Redondela
PONTEVEDRA
Santiago de Compostela
A CORUÑA
Ferrol
Betanzos
LUGO
Monforte de Lemos
OURENSE
Évora
Casa Branca
Beja
Funcheira
Tunes
Lagos
FARO
Vila Real de S. A.
Canarias

SPAIN

Operator: **Renfe Operadora** – unless otherwise indicated.

Services: On long-distance trains first class is known as *Preferente* and second class as *Turista*; a 'super-first class' – *Club* – is additionally available on *AVE* and some *Avant* trains. Unless otherwise indicated (by '2' in the train column or [2] in the notes), all trains convey both first- and second-class seating accommodation.

🍸 indicates a buffet car (*cafetería*) or a mobile trolley service. ✕ indicates a full restaurant car service or the availability of hot meals served from the buffet car. Meals are served free of extra charge to holders of *Club* and *Preferente* tickets on all *AVE* trains and to holders of *Preferente* tickets on *Alaris*, *Altaria*, *Alvia*, *Euromed*, and *Trenhotel* services. Note that catering services may not be available throughout a train's journey, particularly in the case of trains with multiple origins / destinations.

▬ indicates coaches equipped with couchettes: for occupancy of these a standard supplement is payable in addition to the normal *Turista* fare. 🛏 indicates sleeping-cars with single, double, and 3- or 4-berth compartments. The *Turista* fare is payable plus a sleeping-car supplement corresponding to the type and standard of accommodation. ***Trenhotel*** services additionally convey *Gran Clase* accommodation: *de luxe* single- and double-occupancy compartments with *en suite* shower and toilet. *Preferente* fare is payable for travel in *Gran Clase* plus a sleeping-car supplement corresponding to the type and standard of accommodation.

Train categories:
- ☐ ***Alaris***: Fast tilting trains.
- ☐ ***Altaria*** (*Alta*): Talgo trains which can change gauge and run on the high-speed lines as well as the broad-gauge system.
- ☐ ***Alta Velocidad Española*** (*AVE*): High-speed trains running on the standard-gauge lines.
- ☐ ***Alvia***: The newest high-speed gauge-changing trains.
- ☐ ***Arco***: Quality day express trains.
- ☐ ***Avant*** (*Av*): Medium-distance high-speed trains on the standard-gauge lines.
- ☐ ***Diurno*** (*D*): Ordinary long-distance day trains.
- ☐ ***Estrella*** (*Estr*): Night trains, conveying 🛏, ▬, [1] and [2] as indicated.
- ☐ ***Euromed*** (*Em*): Trains similar of similar construction to *AVE* but running on the broad-gauge Barcelona - València - Alacant route.
- ☐ ***Talgo***: Quality express trains using light, articulated stock.
- ☐ ***Trenhotel*** (*Hotel*): Quality night express trains (see Services, above)

Local (*Media Distancia*) and suburban (*Cercanías*) trains are shown without an indication of category except for some fast ***Tren Regional Diesel*** (*TRD*) and ***R-598*** services.

Reservations: Reservations are **compulsory** for all journeys by services for which a **train category** (e.g. *D*, *IC*, *TRD*) is shown in the timing column. A reservation fee paid to the conductor on board the train costs more than one bought in advance. Advance purchase of tickets is also available for travel by services for which a train number is shown.

Supplements: Higher fares, incorporating a supplement, are payable for travel by *Alaris*, *Altaria*, *Alvia*, *Arco*, *AVE*, *Euromed*, *InterCity*, *Talgo*, and *Trenhotel* services. 'Global' fares – i.e. inclusive of meals and accommodation – are payable for travel by the international hotel trains from Barcelona to Milano / Paris / Zürich and v.v., and Madrid - Paris and v.v.

Timings: Timings have been compiled from the latest information supplied by operators.

High-speed services — MADRID - ZARAGOZA - BARCELONA — 650

km		*Av*	*AVE*	*Av*	*AVE*	*AVE*	*AVE*	*AVE*	*Alvia*	*AVE*	*AVE*	*AVE*	*Av*	*Av*	*AVE*	*Alvia*	*AVE*	*AVE*	*Av*	*AVE*	*Av*	*AVE*	*AVE*	*Alvia*	*AVE*
		8077	**3053**	**8087**	**3063**	**3071**	**3271**	**3073**	**601**	**3081**	**3083**	**3093**	**8507**	**8127**	**3103**	**605**	**3113**	**3123**	**8547**	**3133**	**8167**	**3143**	**3151**	**609**	**3153**
		E	**C**		**D**	**C**	**B**			①–⑥						**N**						Ⓑ	Ⓑ **h**		
	Sevilla **660** d.	...	...	...	...	...	...	...	...	...	...	...	...	...	...	...	...	...	...	...	...	...	...	...	...
	Málaga **660** d.	...	...	...	...	...	...	...	...	...	...	...	...	...	...	...	...	...	...	...	...	...	...	...	...
0	**Madrid** Puerta de Atocha d.	...	0545	...	0630	0700	0720	0730	0740	0800	0830	0930	...	...	1030	1035	1130	1230	...	1330	...	1430	1500	1505	1530
64	Guadalajara - Yebes d.	...	|	...	|	|	|	|	0806	|	|	0954	...	...	|	|	|	|	...	1354	...	|	|	|	|
221	Calatayud d.	...	|	...	|	|	|	0828	0851	|	|	|	1035	...	|	|	1228	|	1340	|	...	|	|	|	1628
	Logroño **653** a.	...	|	...	|	|	|	|	|	|	|	|	|	...	|	|	|	|	|	|	...	|	|	|	|
	Pamplona / Iruña **653** a.	...	|	...	|	|	|	|	1055	|	|	|	|	...	|	1334	|	|	|	|	...	|	|	1814	|
	Hendaye **653** a.	...	|	...	|	|	|	|	1304	|	|	|	|	...	|	...	|	|	|	|	...	|	|	...	|
307	**Zaragoza** Delicias d.	...	0705	...	0749	|	|	0855	...	|	0949	1055	1105	...	1149	...	1255	1349	1410	1455	...	1548	|	...	1655
	Huesca **654** a.	...	|	...	|	|	|	|	...	|	|	|	...	...	|	...	|	|	...	|	...	|	|	...	|
447	Lleida d.	0705	0752	0805	|	|	|	0940	...	|	|	1140	...	1205	|	...	1340	|	...	1540	1605	|	|	...	1740
526	Camp de Tarragona d.	0738	0823	0838	|	|	|	1013	...	|	|	1213	...	1238	|	...	1413	|	...	1613	1638	|	|	...	1811
621	**Barcelona** Sants a.	0822	0904	0922	0927	0943	1003	1054	...	1043	1127	1254	...	1317	1327	...	1454	1527	....	1654	1717	1727	1738	...	1854

	AVE	*AVE*	*Av*	*AVE*	*AVE*	*AVE*	*AVE*	*Alvia*	*AVE*	*Alvia*	*AVE*	*Alvia*	*AVE*	*Av*	*AVE*	*AVE*	*AVE*	*Alvia*	*Av*	*Alvia*	*AVE*	*AVE*	*AVE*	*AVE*	*AVE*
	3161	**3363**	**8187**	**3163**	**3171**	**3173**	**3181**	**620**	**3941**	**537**	**3183**	**701**	**3191**	**8217**	**3393**	**3991**	**3193**	**237**	**8607**	**801**	**3201**	**3291**	**3203**	**3211**	**3213**
	Ⓑ				Ⓑ **p**		Ⓑ **q**	**J**		**W**		**A**						**F**		**G**	**f**	**P**		Ⓑ	**M**
Sevilla **660** d.	...	...	...	...	...	...	...	...	1600	...	...	...	...	...	...	...	...	...	...	...	...	...	...	...	...
Málaga **660** d.	...	...	...	...	...	...	...	...	|	...	...	...	...	...	...	1650	...	...	...	...	...	...	...	...	...
Madrid Puerta de Atocha d.	1600	1605	...	1630	1700	1730	1800	...	|	...	1830	1835	1900	...	1905	|	1930	...	...	1935	2000	2020	2030	2100	2130
Guadalajara - Yebes d.	|	|	...	|	|	1754	|	...	|	...	|	1901	|	...	1929	|	|	...	...	2001	|	|	|	|	2154
Calatayud d.	|	|	...	|	|	|	|	...	|	...	|	1948	|	...	2009	|	2028	...	2045	2048	|	|	|	|	2234
Logroño **653** a.	|	|	...	|	|	|	|	...	|	...	|	2158	|	...	|	|	|	1910	|	|	|	|	|	|	|
Pamplona / Iruña **653** a.	|	|	...	|	|	|	|	...	|	1755	|	...	|	...	|	|	|	|	|	2305	|	|	|	|	|
Hendaye **653** a.	|	|	...	|	|	|	|	...	|	|	|	...	|	...	|	|	|	|	|	...	|	|	|	|	|
Zaragoza Delicias d.	|	1727	...	1749	|	1855	|	1906	1934	1948	1949	...	|	...	2036	2040	2055	2105	2115	...	|	2138	2149	|	2300
Huesca **654** a.	|	1810**v**	...	|	|	|	|	|	|	|	|	...	|	...	2120	|	|	|	...	...	|	...	|	|	|
Lleida d.	|	...	1805	|	|	1940	|	2000	2022	2046	|	...	|	2105	...	2124	2140	2203	...	...	|	...	|	|	2345
Camp de Tarragona a.	|	...	1838	|	|	2013	|	2031	2056	2120	|	...	|	2138	...	2152	2213	2233	...	...	|	...	|	|	0014
Barcelona Sants a.	1838	...	1917	1927	1938	2054	2043	2115	2139	2205	2127	...	2143	2217	...	2233	2254	2320	...	...	2238	...	2327	2338	...

	AVE	*AVE*	*AVE*	*AVE*	*Alvia*	*Av*	*Alvia*	*AVE*	*AVE*	*AVE*	*AVE*	*Av*	*Alvia*	*Alvia*	*AVE*	*AVE*	*AVE*	*Alvia*	*AVE*	*Av*	*Alvia*	*AVE*	*AVE*	*AVE*	*AVE*
	3052	**3060**	**3260**	**3062**	**802**	**8066**	**538**	**3072**	**3270**	**3070**	**3272**	**8496**	**534**	**702**	**3082**	**3940**	**3080**	**238**	**3092**	**8096**	**623**	**3090**	**3102**	**3990**	**3112**
	T	**C**	**C**	**R**	**Z**	**E**	**H W**		**B**	**C**			**V W**	**L**			①–⑥	**F**			**K**	Ⓑ			
Barcelona Sants d.	...	0600	0630	...	...	0610	0640	0700	0720	0730	...	...	0740	...	0800	0815	0830	0848	0900	0910	0920	0930	1000	1030	1100
Camp de Tarragona d.	...	|	|	0636	...	0649	0719	|	|	|	...	...	0819	...	0836	0851	|	0927	|	0954	0957	|	1036	1106	|
Lleida d.	...	|	|	0705	...	0720	0750	|	|	|	...	...	0850	...	0905	0920	|	1006	|	1025	1026	|	1105	1135	|
Huesca **654** d.	...	|	|	|	...	...	|	|	|	|	0810	...	|	...	|	|	|	|	|	...	|	|	|	|	|
Zaragoza Delicias d.	0700	0734	|	0754	...	...	0844	0832	|	|	0855	0900	0942	...	0954	1009	|	1058	1032	...	1114	|	1154	1227	1232
Irún **653** d.	|	|	|	|	...	...	|	|	|	|	|	|	|	...	|	|	|	|	|	...	...	|	|	|	|
Pamplona / Iruña **653** d.	|	|	|	|	0645	...	1026	|	|	|	|	|	1131	...	|	|	|	|	|	...	...	|	|	|	|
Logroño **653** d.	|	|	|	|	|	...	...	|	|	|	|	|	...	0752	|	|	|	1241	|	...	...	|	|	|	|
Calatayud d.	0725	|	|	|	|	...	...	|	|	|	0920	0930	...	0952	1019	|	|	...	|	...	...	|	|	|	|
Guadalajara - Yebes d.	0803	|	|	0853	|	...	...	|	|	|	0958	...	...	1038	|	|	|	...	|	...	...	|	1253	|	|
Madrid Puerta de Atocha a.	0835	0857	0908	0923	0950	...	...	0957	1003	1013	1029	...	...	1106	1123	|	1113	...	1157	...	...	1213	1323	|	1357
Málaga **660** a.	...	...	...	...	...	...	...	...	...	...	...	...	...	...	...	|	...	...	...	...	...	...	...	1615	...
Sevilla **660** a.	...	...	...	...	...	...	...	...	...	...	...	...	...	...	...	1352	...	...	...	...	...	...	...	...	...

	Alvia	*Av*	*AVE*	*AVE*	*AVE*	*Av*	*Alvia*	*AVE*	*AVE*	*AVE*	*Av*	*AVE*	*AVE*	*AVE*	*AVE*	*Av*	*Av*	*AVE*	*AVE*	*AVE*	*AVE*	*Alvia*	*AVE*	*Av*	*AVE*
	602	**8536**	**3122**	**3132**	**3142**	**8146**	**606**	**3152**	**3150**	**3162**	**8166**	**3160**	**3172**	**3170**	**3182**	**8186**	**8606**	**3180**	**3592**	**3192**	**3190**	**610**	**3202**	**8206**	**3212**
	X			Ⓑ			Ⓑ **g**		Ⓑ **h**			Ⓑ		Ⓑ **q**				**y**			**f**				
Barcelona Sants d.	...	...	1200	1300	1400	1410	...	1500	1530	1600	1610	1630	1700	1730	1800	1810	...	1830	...	1900	1930	...	2000	2010	2100
Camp de Tarragona d.	...	...	1236	|	1436	1449	...	|	|	1636	1649	|	|	|	1836	1849	...	|	...	|	|	...	2036	2049	2136
Lleida d.	...	...	1305	|	1505	1520	...	|	|	1705	1720	|	|	|	1905	1920	...	|	...	|	|	...	2105	2120	2205
Huesca **654** d.	...	...	|	|	|	...	...	|	|	|	...	|	|	|	|	...	...	|	1935**v**	|	|	...	|	...	|
Zaragoza Delicias d.	...	1300	1354	1432	1554	...	...	1632	|	1754	...	|	1832	|	1954	...	2005	|	2020	2032	|	...	2154	...	2254
Irún **653** d.	...	|	|	|	|	...	...	|	|	|	...	|	|	|	|	...	|	|	|	|	|	1735	|	...	|
Pamplona / Iruña **653** d.	1115	|	|	|	|	...	1445	|	|	|	...	|	|	|	|	...	|	|	|	|	|	1934	|	...	|
Logroño **653** d.	|	|	|	|	|	...	|	|	|	|	...	|	|	|	|	...	|	|	|	|	|	|	|	...	|
Calatayud d.	1308	1330	1419	|	|	...	|	|	|	1819	...	|	|	|	|	...	2035	|	|	|	|	2133	2219	...	|
Guadalajara - Yebes d.	1355	...	|	|	1653	...	|	|	|	|	...	|	|	|	2053	...	...	|	|	|	|	2221	|	...	|
Madrid Puerta de Atocha a.	1424	...	1523	1557	1723	...	1748	1757	1808	1923	...	1908	1957	2008	2123	...	...	2108	2141	2157	2213	2250	2323	...	0017
Málaga **660** a.	...	...	...	...	...	...	...	...	...	...	...	...	...	...	...	...	...	...	...	...	...	...	...	...	...
Sevilla **660** a.	...	...	...	...	...	...	...	...	...	...	...	...	...	...	...	...	...	...	...	...	...	...	...	...	...

A – Ⓑ (not Oct. 11, Dec. 6).
B – ①–④ (not June 24, Aug. 1–30, Sept. 24, Oct. 12, Nov. 9, Dec. 8).
C – ①–⑤ (not June 24, Aug. 3–28, Sept. 11, 24, Oct. 12).
D – ①–⑥ (not June 24, Aug. 1–29).
E – ①–⑤ (not June 24).
F – [12] Barcelona - Bilbao and v.v.
G – Ⓑ (also July 4, 11).
H – ①–⑤ (not July 6–10, 31, Aug. 31, Sept. 11).
J – FINISTERRE – [12] and 🍸 Vigo - Barcelona.
K – COVADONGA – [12] and 🍸 Barcelona - Vigo.
L – ①–⑥ (not Oct. 12, Dec. 7).
M – Ⓑ (not Oct. 11, Dec. 7).
N – ①–⑥ (also July 5, 12; not Aug. 3–30).
P – Ⓑ (not Aug. 1–29, Oct. 11, Dec. 7).
R – ①–⑥ (not Oct. 12, Dec. 8).
T – ①–⑥ (not Aug. 2–30, Oct. 12, Dec. 8).
V – ⑥⑦.
W – [12] Barcelona - Irún and v.v.
X – ⑦ (daily June 14 - Aug. 2, Aug. 31 - Dec. 12).
Z – ①–⑥ (also July 5, 12; not Oct. 12, Dec. 7, 8).
f – Not June 24, Aug. 1–29, Sept. 24, Oct. 11.
g – Also July 4, 11; not Oct. 11, Dec. 5, 7.
h – Not June 24, Aug. 2–28, Sept. 24, Oct. 11.
p – Not Aug. 2–28.
q – Not June 24, Aug. 2–28.
v – ⑤⑦ (also Oct. 12, Nov. 9; not Oct. 11, Nov. 8).
y – Not Aug. 1–29.
☛ *AVE* trains convey ✕ and 🍸. *Alvia* trains convey 🍸. *Avant* trains (*Av*) are *Turista* class only.

651 MADRID - SORIA and ZARAGOZA

km	For high-speed trains see Table 650																								Estr
						17308			17012					17302				17406			17304		370			
		2	2		2	2		2	2	2		2	2		2	2	2		2	2	2	C			
		①–⑤	⑥⑦		①–⑤			⑥⑦		①–⑥			⑤			⑦	⑤		⑦						
0	**Madrid** Chamartín d.	...	...	...	0700	0815	...	0915	1030	...	...	...	1548	...	...	...	1715	...	...	1915	2025	2200	...	...	...
55	Guadalajara d.	...	...	...	0739	0853	...	0952	1105	...	...	1528	1626	...	...	1751	1751	...	...	1955	2105	2242	...	...	...
138	Sigüenza d.	...	...	...	0842	0945	...	1055	1158	...	...	1631	1720	...	...	1854	1854	...	...	2052	2207	2335	...	...	...
248	**Soria** a.	...	...	...	|	1112	...	|	|	...	...	...	1850	...	...	|	...	...	...	2215	|	|	...	...	...
178	Arcos de Jalón d.	0650	0855	...	0910	...	...	1124	1223	1255	...	...	...	...	1735j	1922	...	...	...	...	2236	0004	...	...	...
241	Calatayud d.	0736	0939	...	...	...	...	...	1259	1341	...	...	...	...	1825	...	...	...	2100	...	...	0043	...	...	...
339	**Zaragoza** Delicias a.	0855	1102	...	...	...	...	...	1400	1452	...	...	...	...	1945	...	...	...	2220	...	...	0151	...	...	...

For high-speed trains see Table 650	Estr																								
	373			17305		17303											17307	17309	17011	17311					
	C	2		2	2	2		2		2	2		2	2	2		2	2	2	2	2	2			
		①–⑤		①–⑤	⑥⑦	⑥⑦		①–⑤		⑥⑦			b	⑤			⑦	①–⑥		⑦					
Zaragoza Delicias d.	0312	...	...	...	...	...	...	0745	...	0915	...	...	...	...	1510	...	...	...	1725	...	...	2020	...	...	...
Calatayud d.	0427	...	...	...	...	...	...	0909	...	1035	...	...	...	...	1626	...	...	...	1823	...	...	2139	...	...	...
Arcos de Jalón d.	0508	0621	...		0840	...	...	0957	...	1125	1230	...	...	...	1715f	...	...	...	1900	...	1935o	2228	...	...	...
Soria d.	|	|	...	0740	|	0845	...	...	...	...	|	...	...	...	...	...	1645	1740	|	1825	|	...	...	...	...
Sigüenza d.	0536	0652	...	0900	0911	1006	...	...	...	...	1301	...	1645	1700	...	...	1813	1903	1925	1947	2005	...	...	...	...
Guadalajara a.	0628	0753	...	0949	1012	1054	...	...	...	...	1402	...	1746	1801	...	...	1903	1954	2015	2039	2103	...	...	...	...
Madrid Chamartín a.	0721	0833	...	1028	1052	1135	...	...	...	...	...	...	...	1840	...	...	1945	2035	2055	2123	2143	...	...	...	...

☛ **FOR NOTES**, SEE TABLE **653** BELOW.

652 ZARAGOZA - BARCELONA

km	For high-speed trains see Table 650	Hotel	Hotel		Estr	Hotel									Talgo									Estr
		995	945		930	921			15650						530									370
		F 🍷	B 🍷	2	A	G 🍷	2	2	2	2	2	2	2	2	M	2	2	2	2	2	2	2	2	C
		¶	¶		🍷	¶			①–⑤			⑥⑦			🍷		①–⑤	①–⑥	⑦					
	Madrid Chamartín **651** d.	...	...	...	...	...	...	...	...	...	...	...	...	...	...	...	...	...	...	...	...	...	...	2200
0	**Zaragoza** Delicias d.	0500	0520	...	0352	0632	...	...	0627	...	...	0905	...	1218	...	1445	...	1508	...	...	1648	...	2029	2101	0156
114	Caspe d.	|	|	...	|	|	...	0720	|	...	...	|	...	1345	...	|	...	|	...	...	1813	...	2200	|	|
★	Lleida d.	|	|	...	0600	0730	0715	|	0836	...	...	1121	1310	|	1545	1651	...	1720	1748	1748	|	...	...	2322	|
239	Reus d.	|	|	0643	0715	|	|	0911	...	1110	1210	...	1437	1540	1714	1803	1841	...	|	|	2003	2118	...	...	0507
257	Tarragona **672** d.	0624t	0644t	0700	0734	0804t	|	0925	...	1125	1225	...	1454	1557	1729	1816	1857	...	|	|	2020	2134	...	...	0532
282	Sant Vicenç de Calders **672** d.	|	|	0719	|	|	0845	0945	...	1145	1245	...	1515	1618	1747	|	1917	...	1913	1923	2040	2200	...	...	0600
342	**Barcelona** Sants **672** a.	0725	0745	0809	0859	0845	0935	1035	...	1235	1335	...	1605	1705	1835	1921	2009	...	2005	2017	2136	2302	...	...	0736
345	Barcelona Pass. de Gràcia a.	...	...	0815	...	...	0944	1045	...	1244	1344	...	1614	1714	1844	...	2015	...	2012	2023	2143	2307	...	...	|
	Cerbère **657** a.	...	...	|	...	...	|	|	...	|	|	...	|	|	|	...	|	...	|	|	|	|	...	...	1035
350	**Barcelona** França a.	...	...	0823	...	...	0952	1055	...	1252	1353	...	1623	1722	1852	...	2024	...	2020	2032	2152	2316	...	...	...

For high-speed trains see Table 650											Talgo									Hotel		Hotel	Estr	Hotel	Estr
											533	15657								922		996	933	946	373
	2	2	2	2	2	2	2	2	2	2	N	2	2	2	2	2	2	2	2	G 🍷	2	F 🍷	A	B 🍷	C
	①–⑥	①–⑤	⑦		⑥						🍷			⑧z						¶		¶	🍷	¶	
Barcelona França d.	...	...	...	0617	...	0650	0717	0847	0946	1147	...	...	1347	...	1546	1648	1717	1847	2018	...	2118	...	...	...	...
Portbou **657** d.	...	...	...	|	...	|	|	|	|	|	...	...	|	...	|	|	|	|	|	...	|	...	...	...	1940
Barcelona Pass. de Gràcia d.	...	...	...	0626	...	0659	0726	0856	0956	1156	...	...	1355	...	1556	1656	1726	1855	2026	...	2126	...	...	...	|
Barcelona Sants **672** d.	...	...	...	0633	...	0706	0733	0903	1003	1203	1230	...	1403	...	1603	1703	1733	1903	2033	2050	2133	2145	2200	2205	2220
Sant Vicenç de Calders **672** d.	...	...	...	0718	...	0807	0818	0948	1047	1248	|	...	1447	...	1648	1747	1818	1947	2118	|	2222	|	|	|	2317
Tarragona **672** d.	...	...	...	0739	...	|	0839	1009	1108	1308	1327	...	1509	...	1708	1809	1837	|	2139	2133t	2243	2226t	2300	2246t	2341
Reus d.	...	...	...	0754	...	|	0855	1028	1123	1326	1341	...	1529	...	1724	1827	1852	|	2154	|	2258	|	2314	|	2356
Lleida d.	...	0620	...	...	0925	0955	...	|	...	1455	1441	1500	1646	1820	|	1953	|	2111	...	2219	...	|	0015	|	|
Caspe d.	0655	|	0828	...	|	...	...	1237	...	...	|	|	...	|	1920	...	2047	...	...	|	...	|	|	|	|
Zaragoza Delicias a.	0823	0851	0956	...	1153	...	...	1411	...	...	1643	1720	...	2025	2100	...	...	...	...	2325	...	2345	0218	0005	0307
Madrid Chamartín **651** a.	...	...	...	...	...	...	...	...	...	...	...	...	...	...	...	...	...	...	...	...	...	...	...	...	0721

☛ **FOR NOTES**, SEE TABLE **653** BELOW.

653 ZARAGOZA - IRÚN and BILBAO

km						Alvia	Alvia	Alvia	Alvia	Alvia						Talgo	Talgo					Alvia	Alvia		Hotel	Estr
		18069	18071	16023	16023	538	601	534	238	623	18021		18073	16025	16025	533	533	18023	16017	18075	18077	701	801	18079	922	933
		2 P	2	2	2	D		E	Q	H	2		2	2	2	N	N	2	2	2	2	🍷	🍷	2	G 🍷	A
		①	①–⑥	①–⑥	①–⑥	🍷	🍷	🍷	🍷	🍷						🍷	🍷	⑤				⑧r	⑧q	⑧	¶	🍷
	Barcelona Sants **652** d.	...	...	...	...	0640	...	0740	0848	0920	...	...	...	...	...	1230	1230	...	...	...	...	...	...	...	2050	2200
	Madrid Pta de Atocha **650** d.	...	...	...	...	|	0740	|	|	|	...	...	...	...	...	|	|	...	...	...	...	1835	1935	...	|	|
0	**Zaragoza** Delicias d.	...	0638	...	...	0844	|	0942	1058	1116	1140	...	1425	...	...	1648	1648	1628	...	1748	1924	|	|	2117	2325	0220
94	Castejón de Ebro ★ d.	...	0732	0737	...	|	1005	|	|	1212	1251	...	1533	1540	...	1745	1755	1723	...	1849	2031	|	|	2224	0044	0320
182	**Pamplona / Iruña** d.	...	|	0837	0857	1028	1057	1133	|	1307	1357	...	|	1634	1637	1842	|	1846	1940	|	|	|	2305	...	|	|
234	Altsasu **689** d.	...	|	...	0928y	|	|	|	|	|	...	...	|	...	1716y	1916	|	...	2015y	|	|	|	...	...	|	|
275	Vitoria / Gasteiz **689** d.	...	|	...	1000	|	|	|	|	1400	...	...	|	...	1752	|	|	...	2045	|	|	|	...	...	|	|
321	San Sebastián / Donostia d.	...	|	...	...	1218s	1240	1325	|	|	...	...	|	...	...	2043	|	...	...	|	|	|	...	...	|	|
337	**Irún** **689** a.	...	|	...	...	1243	1259	1348	|	|	...	...	|	...	...	2105	|	...	...	|	|	|	...	...	|	|
339	Hendaye **689** a.	...	|	...	...	...	1304	...	|	|	...	...	|	...	...	2116	|	...	...	|	|	|	...	...	|	|
171	**Logroño** d.	0736	0838a	...	...	...	...	...	1243	|	...	...	1629	...	...	...	1846	...	...	1954	2134c	2158	...	...	0132	0419
242	Miranda de Ebro **689** d.	0832	...	...	...	...	...	...	1339	1421	...	...	...	...	...	...	1953	...	...	...	...	...	...	...	...	...
347	**Bilbao** Abando **689** a.	...	...	...	...	...	...	...	1516	...	...	...	...	...	...	...	2141	...	...	...	...	...	...	...	...	...

		Alvia		Alvia				Talgo	Talgo						Alvia	Alvia	Alvia		Alvia					Estr	Hotel	
	18070	802	18072	702	16007	18074		530	530	16022	18076	16021		18020	620	537	237	18022	610	16011	16011	18078	18017	930	921	
		R	2	R	2	2		M	M	2	2	2	2	2	J		Q	2		2	2	2	2 P	A	G 🍷	
	①–⑤	🍷		🍷	①–⑥			🍷	🍷	①–⑥			c		🍷	🍷	🍷	⑦	🍷				⑦	🍷	¶	
Bilbao Abando **689** d.	...	...	...	...	...	...	...	...	1005	...	...	...	...	...	...	...	1645	...	...	...	...	...	...	...	...	...
Miranda de Ebro **689** d.	...	...	...	...	...	...	...	...	1151	...	...	...	...	...	1556	...	1814	...	...	...	...	...	2130	...	...	...
Logroño d.	...	...	0730a	0752	...	...	...	...	1246	...	1337	...	1645	...	|	...	1910	...	...	...	...	2005	2230	0157	0404	...
Irún **689** d.	...	...	|	|	...	...	...	1030	|	...	|	...	|	...	|	1550	|	...	1735	...	...	|	...	|	|	...
San Sebastián / Donostia d.	...	...	|	|	...	...	...	1045	|	...	|	...	|	...	|	1610	|	...	1751	...	...	|	...	|	|	...
Vitoria / Gasteiz **689** d.	...	...	|	|	0750	...	...	|	|	...	|	1530	|	...	1617	|	|	...	|	1905	...	|	...	|	|	...
Altsasu **689** d.	...	...	|	|	0820y	...	...	1202	|	...	|	1601y	|	...	|	|	|	...	|	1936y	...	|	...	|	|	...
Pamplona / Iruña d.	...	0645	|	|	0852	...	...	1231	|	1313	|	1635	|	1645	1710	1755	|	1905	1934	2008	2010	|	...	|	|	...
Castejón de Ebro d.	0625	0735	0830	|	...	1030	...	1345	1345	1421	1433	...	1739	1747	1809	|	|	2006	|	...	2105	2106	...	0251	0457	...
Zaragoza Delicias a.	0733	|	0940	|	...	1138	...	1440	1440	...	1535	...	...	1850	1904	1948	2100	2100	|	...	...	2215	...	0350	0629	...
Madrid Pta de Atocha **650** a.	...	0950	...	1106	...	...	...	|	|	...	...	...	...	...	|	|	|	...	2250	...	...	...	...	|	|	...
Barcelona Sants **652** a.	...	...	...	...	...	...	...	1921	1921	...	...	...	...	...	2115	2205	2320	...	...	...	...	...	...	0859	0845	...

A – PÍO BAROJA – ⑧: 🛏, couchette and [1] Gijón - Barcelona and v.v. On ⑤⑦ conveys through cars from / to Salamanca (Table **689**).
B – ANTONIO MACHADO – 🛏 and [2] Barcelona - Zaragoza - Sevilla - Cádiz and v.v.
C – COSTA BRAVA – 🛏 1, 2 cl., couchette 2 cl. and [2] Madrid - Barcelona - Portbou and v.v.
D – ①–⑤ (not July 6–10, 31, Aug. 31, Sept. 11).
E – ⑥⑦.
F – GIBRALFARO – 🛏 and [2] Barcelona - Zaragoza - Córdoba - Málaga and v.v.
G – GALICIA – 🛏 and [1] (reclining) Barcelona - A Coruña and Vigo and v.v.
H – COVADONGA – [12] and 🍷 Barcelona - Vigo.
J – FINISTERRE – [12] and 🍷 Vigo - Barcelona.
M – MIGUEL DE UNAMUNO – [12] Bilbao, Irún and Salamanca - Barcelona.
N – MIGUEL DE UNAMUNO – [12] Barcelona - Bilbao, Hendaye and Salamanca.
P – To / from Valladolid.
Q – [12] Barcelona - Bilbao and v.v.
R – ①–⑥ (not Oct. 12, Dec. 7).

a – ①–⑤.
b – Not ⑤.
c – ⑤⑥⑦.
f – ⑤ (only).
j – ⑤⑦ only.
o – ⑦ only.
q – Also July 5, 12.
r – Not Oct. 11, Dec. 6.
s – Stops to set down only.
t – Camp de Tarragona.
y – Altsasu Pueblo (*230 km*).
z – On ⑦ depart Lleida 1815, arrive Zaragoza 2028.

¶ – Via high speed line.
★ – Calatayud - Castejón: *140 km*.
Lleida - Reus: *90 km*.
Lleida - Sant Vicenç: *106 km*.
Zaragoza - Lleida: *189 km*.

2nd class (except *AVE* trains) — ZARAGOZA - HUESCA - CANFRANC — 654

km		*Av* 8677 ①–⑤			*TRD* 15646		*Av* 8747		*AVE* 3363 C	*Av* 8787	*AVE* 3393	*TRD* 18504 B
	Madrid ◇ **650** ...d.	...	...	...	...	...	...	...	1605	...	1905	...
0	**Zaragoza** Delicias d.	0702	0740	...	1026	...	1413	1513	1727	1806	2036	2040
58	Tardienta d.	0730	0836	...	1116	...	1441	1559	|	1834	2107	2127
80	**Huesca** d.	0744	0900	...	1135	...	1455	1617	1810	1848	2120	2139
115	Ayerbe d.	...	0947	...	1208	...	...	1655	...	...	...	...
174	Sabiñánigo d.	...	1050	...	1310	...	...	1806	...	...	...	...
190	Jaca ‡ d.	...	1108	...	1327	...	...	1827	...	...	...	...
215	**Canfranc 324** ... ‡ a.	...	1140	...	...	...	...	1859	...	...	...	...

	TRD 18511 B	*Av* 8687 ①–⑤	*AVE* 3272			*Av* 8757		*TRD* 15647	*Av* 8797	*AVE* 3592 C	
Canfranc 324 ... ‡ d.	...	...	...	0650	...	...	...	...	...	...	1755
Jaca ‡ d.	...	...	...	0720	...	...	...	1535	...	...	1825
Sabiñánigo d.	...	...	...	0737	...	...	...	1552	...	...	1845
Ayerbe d.	...	...	...	0839	...	...	...	1654	...	...	1948
Huesca d.	0705	0755	0810	0932	...	1525	...	1735	1903	1935	2033
Tardienta d.	0719	0809	0822	0950	...	1539	...	1751	1917	|	2048
Zaragoza Delicias a.	0811	0837	0850	1042	...	1607	...	1833	1945	2015	2142
Madrid ◇ **650** ..a.	...	...	1029	...	...	...	...	...	...	2141	...

A – ①–⑤ (not Dec. 6).
B – From / to València.
C – ⑥⑦ (also Oct. 12, Nov. 9; not Oct. 11, Nov. 8).
‡ – 🚌 Jaca bus station (± *2 km* from rail station) - Canfranc and v.v.: daily at 1455 from Jaca, 1300 from Canfranc; journey 30 minutes; operated by *Mancobús*.
◇ – Madrid Puerta de Atocha.

FGC 2nd class — LLEIDA - LA POBLA DE SEGUR — 655

km											
0	**Lleida** d.	0600	0715	0905	...	1145	1345	1515	1750	...	2030
27	Balaguer d.	0623	0744	0934	...	1214	1419	1544	1819	...	2059
77	Tremp d.	...	...	1039	...	...	1524	...	...	...	2204
90	**La Pobla de Segur** ...a.	...	...	1055	...	...	1540	...	...	...	2220

La Pobla de Segur ...d.	...	0640	...	...	...	1256	...	...	...	1805
Tremp d.	...	0655	...	...	...	1311	...	...	...	1820
Balaguer d.	0630	0800	0945	...	1225	1416	...	1600	1830	1925
Lleida a.	0659	0830	1014	...	1254	1446	...	1629	1859	1955

2nd class — BARCELONA - PUIGCERDÀ - LATOUR DE CAROL — 656

km											
0	**Barcelona** Sants d.	0700	0757	0917	1106	1206	1406	1516	1706	1857	2015
33	Granollers - Canovelles .. d.	0741	0836	0952	1148	1241	1447	1553	1747	1933	2051
74	Vic d.	0819	0922	1034	1234	1319	1522	1626	1822	2010	2129
90	Torelló d.	0834	0939	1051	1249	1335	1535	1644	1838	2029	2144
110	Ripoll d.	0855	1005	1112	1311	1357	1555	1706	1902	2053	2205
124	Ribes de Freser ..... **658** a.	0914	1023	1134	...	1416	...	1727	1923	2114	...
145	La Molina a.	0951	...	1202	...	1445	...	1755	1955	2139	...
159	Puigcerdà a.	*1015*	...	*1235*	...	*1518*	...	*1828*	*2028*	*2212*	...
163	**Latour de Carol** 🏛 **312** a.	*1030*	...	*1250*	...	*1533*	...	*1843*	...	...	...

	Ⓐ									
Latour de Carol 🏛 **312** d.	...	...	*0754*	*1015*	...	*1258*	...	*1608*	...	*1826*
Puigcerdà d.	...	*0618*	*0809*	*1030*	...	*1313*	...	*1623*	...	*1841*
La Molina d.	...	0653	0844	1105	...	1348	...	1658	...	1916
Ribes de Freser ..... **658** d.	...	0724	0916	1137	...	1420	...	1729	...	1948
Ripoll d.	0634	0745	0938	1157	1329	1440	1639	1751	1832	2007
Torelló d.	0654	0806	0958	1217	1356	1505	1706	1819	1858	2031
Vic d.	0708	0821	1013	1233	1413	1520	1724	1838	1912	2046
Granollers - Canovelles .. d.	0742	0857	1051	1308	1506	1600	1808	1912	1953	2118
Barcelona Sants a.	0819	0937	1128	1346	1549	1637	1858	1949	2036	2158

🚌 – Puigcerdà - Latour de Carol. From mid - June the bus will operate Ribes de Freser or Ripoll - Puigcerdà - Latour de Carol.

BARCELONA - GIRONA - PORTBOU — 657

For hotel trains Barcelona - Paris and v.v., see Table **45**; Barcelona - Zürich and v.v., see Table **49**; Barcelona - Milano and v.v., see Table **90**

km		2 ①–⑤	2 ⑥	2 ①–⑤	2 ⑥⑦ q	*Estr* 370 D	*Talgo* 73 🍷 T	2 ①–⑤	2 ⑥⑦	2 ①–⑤	2 ⑥⑦	2 ①–⑤	2 ⑥⑦	2 ①–⑤	2 ⑥⑦	2 ①–⑤	2 ⑥⑦	2 ①–⑤	2 ⑦	2 ①–⑤	2 ⑥	2 ⑦	2	
0	**Barcelona** Sants **666** d.	0616	0646	0716	0746	0753	0845f	0816	0846	0916	0946	1016	1046	1116	1146	1246	1246	1316	1346	1416	1416	1446	1516	...
3	Barcelona Passeig de Gràcia d.	0620	0650	0720	0751	|	|	0821	0850	0920	0951	1021	1050	1120	1151	1251	1250	1320	1351	1421	1421	1451	1520	...
31	Granollers Centre d.	0649	0719	0755	|	0829	|	|	0919	0949	|	|	1119	1149	|	|	1319	1349	|	|	|	|	1549	...
72	Maçanet - Massanes **666** d.	0726	0756	0836	0848	|	|	0918	0959	1026	1048	1118	1156	1226	1248	1348	1356	1426	1448	1518	1518	1548	1626	...
86	Caldes de Malavella d.	0737	0807	0847	0859	0906	|	0929	1010	1037	1059	1129	1207	1237	1259	1359	1407	1437	1459	1529	1529	1559	1637	...
102	**Girona** d.	0752	0822	0902	0911	0925	0955	0941	1025	1052	1111	1141	1222	1252	1311	1411	1422	1452	1511	1541	1541	1611	1652	...
118	Flaçà d.	0807	0837	0917	0923	0938	|	0953	1040	1107	1123	1153	1237	1307	1323	1423	1437	1507	1523	1553	1553	1623	1707	...
143	Figueres d.	0830	0900	0940	0940	0958	1025	1010	1103	1130	1140	1210	1300	1330	1340	1439	1500	1530	1540	1609	1610	1640	1730	...
162	Llançà d.	0845	0915	0955	0953	1016	|	1023	1118	1145	1153	1223	1315	1345	1353	...	1515	1545	1553	...	1623	1653	1745	...
169	**Portbou** 🏛 a.	0855	0925	1005	1000	1025	1048	1030	1128	1155	1200	1230	1325	1355	1400	...	1525	1555	1600	...	1630	1700	1755	...
171	**Cerbère** 🏛 **355** a.	0900	0930	1010	...	1035	1111	...	1133	1200	...	...	1330	1400	...	...	1530	1600	...	...	...	...	1800	...

	2	*Talgo* 460 🍷 A	2	2 ①–⑤	2 ①–⑤	2	2 ①–⑤	2	2 ⑦	2 ①–⑤	2 ⑥⑦
Barcelona Sants **666** d.	1616	1642	1716	1816	1846	1916	1946	2016	2046	2116	2146
Barcelona Passeig de Gràcia d.	1621	|	1720	1821	1851	1920	1951	2021	2051	2121	2151
Granollers Centre d.	|	|	1749	|	|	1949	|	|	|	|	|
Maçanet-Massanes **666** d.	1718	|	1826	1918	1948	2026	2051	2118	2152	2221	2253
Caldes de Malavella d.	1729	|	1837	1929	1959	2037	2102	2129	2203	2232	2304
Girona d.	1741	1748	1852	1941	2011	2059	2114	2141	2214	2242	2314
Flaçà d.	1753	|	1907	1953	2023	2114	2126	2153	2226	...	...
Figueres d.	1809	1815	1930	2010	2039	2137	2142	2209	2242	...	...
Llançà d.	...	|	1945	2023	...	2152	...	...	...	...	...
Portbou 🏛 a.	...	1837	1955	2030	...	2202	...	...	...	...	...
Cerbère 🏛 **355** a.	...	1902	2000	...	...	...	...	...	...	...	...

	2 ①–⑤	2 ①–⑤	2 ①–⑥	2 ⑦	2 ①–⑥	2 ⑦	2 ①–⑥
Portbou 🏛 **355** d.	...	...	...	...	0659	...	...
Llançà d.	...	...	...	...	0708	...	...
Figueres d.	...	0605	0640	...	0724	0740	0817
Flaçà d.	...	0621	0656	...	0746	0756	0833
Girona d.	0611	0635	0710	0710	0802	0810	0847
Caldes de Malavella d.	0621	0645	0721	0721	0816	0821	0857
Maçanet - Massanes **666** d.	0632	0656	0732	0732	0827	0832	0908
Granollers Centre d.	|	|	|	|	0902	|	|
Barcelona Passeig de Gràcia a.	0734	0804	0834	0834	0934	0934	1004
Barcelona Sants **666** a.	0739	0809	0839	0839	0939	0939	1009

	2	2	*Talgo* 463 🍷 N	2	2	2	2	2	2 ⑥⑦	2 Ⓑ	2 ⑥	2 ①–⑤	2 ⑥⑦	2 ①–⑤	*Talgo* 70 🍷 T	2 ⑦	2 ⑦	2 ①–⑤	2 ⑥⑦	*Estr* 373 D	2 ⑥⑦	2 ①–⑤		
Portbou 🏛 **355** d.	0829	...	0952	1029	1126	1229	1326	1429	1526	1559	1629	...	1726	1727	1753	1756	1829	1859	1931	1940	2030	2036	...	...
Llançà d.	0838	...	|	1038	1133	1238	1333	1438	1533	1608	1638	...	1733	1736	|	1803	1838	1908	1940	1950	2038	2044	...	...
Figueres d.	0854	0947	1013	1054	1147	1254	1347	1454	1547	1624	1654	1717	1747	1752	1812	1817	1854	1924	1956	2005	2051	2058	...	...
Flaçà d.	0916	1003	|	1116	1203	1316	1403	1516	1603	1646	1716	1733	1803	1814	|	1833	1916	1946	2018	2023	2108	2114	...	...
Girona d.	0932	1017	1042	1132	1217	1332	1417	1532	1617	1702	1732	1747	1817	1830	1838	1847	1932	2002	2034	2042	2122	2128	...	...
Caldes de Malavella d.	0946	1027	|	1146	1227	1346	1427	1546	1627	1716	1746	1757	1827	1844	|	1857	1946	2016	2048	2055	2134	2139	...	...
Maçanet-Massanes **666** d.	0957	1038	|	1157	1238	1357	1438	1557	1638	1727	1757	1808	1838	1901	|	1908	1957	2027	2059	|	2145	2150	...	...
Granollers Centre d.	1032	|	|	1232	|	1432	|	1632	|	1802	1832	|	|	1934	|	|	2032	2102	2138	2131	2218	2222	...	...
Barcelona Passeig de Gràcia a.	1104	1134	|	1304	1334	1504	1534	1704	1734	1834	1904	1904	1934	2004	|	2004	2104	2134	2208	|	2247	2252	...	...
Barcelona Sants **666** a.	1109	1139	1146	1309	1339	1509	1539	1709	1739	1839	1909	1909	1939	2009	1959f	2009	2109	2139	2213	2202	2252	2256	...	...

A – MARE NOSTRUM – 🚃12 Lorca - Montpellier.
D – COSTA BRAVA – 🛏 1, 2 cl., 🛏 2 cl. and 🚃2 Madrid - Barcelona - Portbou and v.v.
N – MARE NOSTRUM – 🚃12 Montpellier - Cartagena.
T – CATALÁN TALGO – 🚃12 Barcelona - Montpellier and v.v.
f – Barcelona França.

2nd class — VALL DE NÚRIA — 658

Ribes Enllaç - **Queralbs** - **Núria** rack railway — *Nov. 28, 2008 - Oct. 31, 2009*

High Season ⑥⑦ (daily Dec. 20 - Jan. 6, Apr. 4 - 13, June 20 - Sept. 13). See Note ⊖.
From Ribes: 0830, 0920, 1010, 1100, 1150, 1240, 1330, 1420, 1510, 1600, 1650, 1740.
From Núria: 0830, 0920, 1010, 1100, 1150, 1240, 1330, 1420, 1510, 1600, 1650, 1740, 1830.

Low Season ①–⑤ (except dates above). No service Nov. 1 - 27.
From Ribes: 0930, 1110, 1250, 1455, 1640, 1730, 1830⑤, 2030⑤.
From Núria: 0830, 1020, 1200, 1400, 1545, 1730, 1820, 1920⑤, 2115⑤.

Journey times **Ribes** – **Queralbs** (*6 km*) 20 minutes, **Ribes** – **Núria** (*12 km*) 40 minutes.
Operator: Ferrocarrils de la Generalitat de Catalunya (FGC) ✆ +34 972 73 20 30.
⊖ – Also June 1, Oct. 12. Reduced service Dec. 25. Extra evening services run on ⑤.

2nd class — AEROPORT ✈ BARCELONA — 659

Local rail service *Cercanías* (suburban) line **C2**.
Aeroport ✈ - Barcelona Sants – Barcelona Passeig de Gràcia
Journey time: 22 minutes Sants, 27 minutes Passeig de Gràcia

From Aeroport:
0608, 0638, 0708, 0738 and every 30 minutes until 2308, 2338.

From Barcelona Sants:
0535, 0609, 0639, 0709 and every 30 minutes until 2239, 2309.

660 MADRID - CÓRDOBA - SEVILLA and MÁLAGA — High-speed services

km		AVE	AVE	AVE	AVE	AVE	AVE	AVE	Alta	AVE	Alta	AVE	AVE	Alta	AVE	AVE	AVE	AVE	AVE	AVE	AVE	AVE	AVE	AVE
		2260	**2062**	**2070**	**2270**	**2072**	**2080**	**2280**	**9366**	**2090**	**9218**	**2092**	**2100**	**9320**	**2102**	**2110**	**3940**	**2112**	**2120**	**2122**	**2130**	**3990**	**2140**	**2142**
		①–⑤	①–⑤	①–⑤			①–⑥	①–⑥					①–⑥		①–⑥									
		p					p	p																
	Barcelona Sants **650** d.	...	...	...	...	...	...	...	...	...	...	...	...	...	...	...	0815	...	...	...	...	1030	...	...
0	**Madrid** Puerta de Atocha d.	0630	0635	0700	0730	0735	0800	0830	0840	0900	0905	0935	1000	1005	1035	1100	|	1130	1200	1235	1300	|	1400	1435
171	Ciudad Real d.	0719	|	|	|	|	|	|	0941	0951	1007	1026	|	1103	|	|	1205	|	|	1326	1351	|	|	|
210	Puertollano d.	0734	|	|	|	|	|	|	0957	1007	1023	1044	|	1120	|	|	1221	|	|	1342	1407	|	|	|
345	**Córdoba** d.	0820	0825	0844	|	|	0944	1014	1043	1052	1110	1127	1144	1209	1219	1244	1306	1314	1344	1427	1452	1513	1544	1619
470	**Sevilla** a.	0905	|	0930	0950	|	1030	1100	|	1135	|	|	1230	1318	|	1330	1352	|	1430	|	1535	|	1630	|
	Cádiz **671** a.	...	|	...	...	|	...	...	|	...	|	|	...	1503	|	...	...	|	...	|	...	|	...	|
	Huelva **671** a.	...	|	...	...	|	...	...	|	...	|	|	...	...	|	...	...	|	...	|	...	|	...	|
419	Puente Genil - Herrera ¶ a.	...	0848	...	...	|	...	...	|	...	|	|	...	...	|	...	...	|	...	1448	...	1534	...	|
455	Antequera - Santa Ana § a.	...	0901	...	...	|	...	...	1122	...	1148	|	...	...	|	...	...	|	...	1501	...	1547	...	|
	Algeciras **673** a.	...	|	...	...	|	...	...	1405	...	|	|	...	...	|	...	...	|	...	|	...	|	...	|
	Granada **673** a.	...	|	...	...	|	...	...	...	...	1342	|	...	...	|	...	...	|	...	|	...	|	...	|
513	**Málaga** María Zambrano a.	...	0930	...	...	1014	...	...	...	...	...	1223	...	...	1315	...	...	1410	...	1530	...	1615	...	1715

	AVE	Alta	AVE	AVE	AVE	Alta	AVE	AVE	Alta	AVE	AVE	Alta	AVE	AVE	AVE	AVE	AVE	AVE	AVE	AVE	Hotel	Hotel	AVE	
	2150	**9330**	**2152**	**2160**	**2360**	**9332**	**2162**	**2170**	**9234**	**2172**	**2180**	**9386**	**2182**	**2190**	**2390**	**2192**	**2200**	**2202**	**2210**	**2212**	**996**	**946**	**2220**	
	⑧		⑤⑦		⑤⑦									⑧		⑤⑦	⑧				A	B		
	p		w		m									p		w					✕	✕		
Barcelona Sants **650** d.	...	...	...	...	...	...	...	...	...	...	...	...	...	...	...	...	...	...	...	...	2145	2205	...	...
Madrid Puerta de Atocha d.	1500	1505	1535	1600	1630	1620	1635	1700	1705	1735	1800	1805	1835	1900	1930	1935	2000	2035	2100	2135	|	|	2200	...
Ciudad Real d.	|	|	|	|	|	1733	|	1751	|	1826	|	|	|	1951	|	|	|	|	|	2226	|	|	2251	...
Puertollano d.	|	|	|	|	|	1750	|	1807	|	1844	|	|	|	2007	|	|	|	|	|	2242	|	|	2307	...
Córdoba d.	|	1706	|	1744	1814	1837	1819	1852	1909	1927	1944	2011	|	2052	2114	2119	|	|	2244	2327	0708	0728	2352	...
Sevilla a.	1720	|	|	1830	1900	1944	|	1935	|	|	2030	|	|	2135	2200	|	2220	|	2330	|	|	0839	0035	...
Cádiz **671** a.	...	|	|	...	...	2137	|	...	|	|	...	|	|	...	...	|	...	|	...	|	|	1026	...	...
Huelva **671** a.	...	|	|	...	...	...	|	...	|	|	...	2221	|	...	...	|	...	|	...	|	|	...	...	...
Puente Genil - Herrera ¶ a.	...	|	|	...	...	...	|	...	|	1948	...	...	|	...	...	|	...	|	...	2348	0737	...	...	...
Antequera - Santa Ana § a.	...	|	|	...	...	...	|	...	|	2001	...	...	|	...	...	|	...	|	...	0001	0754	...	...	...
Algeciras **673** a.	...	2033	|	...	...	...	|	...	|	|	...	...	|	...	...	|	...	|	...	|	|	...	...	...
Granada **673** a.	...	...	|	...	...	...	|	...	2141	|	...	...	|	...	...	|	...	|	...	|	|	...	...	...
Málaga María Zambrano a.	...	...	1810	...	...	...	1915	...	...	2030	...	...	2110	...	...	2215	...	2305	...	0030	0825	...	...	...

	AVE	AVE	AVE	AVE	AVE	AVE	AVE	AVE	AVE	AVE	Alta	AVE	Alta	AVE	Alta	AVE	Alta	AVE	AVE	AVE	Alta	AVE	AVE	AVE
	2261	**2061**	**2263**	**2073**	**2271**	**2071**	**2083**	**2281**	**2081**	**2093**	**9365**	**2091**	**9315**	**2101**	**9367**	**2113**	**9219**	**2111**	**2123**	**2121**	**9323**	**2131**	**2143**	**2141**
	①–⑤	①–⑤	①–⑤			①–⑥	①–⑤	①–⑥			①–⑥	①–⑥									⑦			⑧
	p					p		p			j										h			p
Málaga María Zambrano d.	...	...	0635	0710	...	...	0800	...	...	0900	...	...	...	...	...	1100	...	...	1200	...	...	...	1400	...
Granada **673** d.	...	...	|	|	...	...	|	...	...	|	...	...	...	...	...	|	0945	...	|	...	...	...	|	...
Algeciras **673** d.	...	...	|	|	...	...	|	...	...	|	...	...	...	...	0830	|	|	...	|	...	...	...	|	...
Antequera - Santa Ana § d.	...	...	0701	|	...	...	|	...	...	0926	...	...	...	...	|	|	|	...	|	...	...	...	1426	...
Puente Genil - Herrera ¶ d.	...	...	0714	|	...	...	|	...	...	|	...	...	...	...	|	|	|	...	|	...	...	...	1439	...
Huelva **671** d.	...	...	|	|	...	...	|	...	...	|	0745	...	...	...	|	|	|	...	|	...	1120	...	|	...
Cádiz **671** d.	...	...	|	|	...	...	|	...	...	|	|	...	0740	...	|	|	|	...	|	...	|	...	|	...
Sevilla d.	0615	0645	|	|	0715	0745	|	0815	0845	|	|	0945	0925	1045	|	|	|	1145	|	1245	|	1345	|	1445
Córdoba d.	0658	0729	0739	|	0803	|	0856	0858	0929	0959	1002	1028	1037	1129	1144	1156	1213	1229	1256	1328	1341	|	1504	1529
Puertollano d.	0740	|	0821	|	0845	|	|	|	|	1041	|	1110	1125	|	|	|	|	|	|	1413	|	|	1546	|
Ciudad Real d.	0755	|	0837	|	0859	|	|	|	|	1057	|	1124	1141	|	|	|	|	|	|	1427	|	|	1602	|
Madrid Puerta de Atocha a.	0850	0915	0932	0940	0955	1005	1040	1045	1115	1150	1210	1220	1241	1315	1357	1340	1429	1415	1440	1520	1550	1605	1655	1715
Barcelona Sants **650** a.	...	...	...	...	...	...	...	...	...	...	...	...	...	...	...	...	...	...	...	...	...	...	...	...

	AVE	AVE	AVE	AVE	AVE	AVE	AVE	AVE	AVE	AVE	Alta	Alta	AVE	AVE	AVE	AVE	AVE	Alta	AVE	Hotel	Hotel	AVE	AVE	
	2153	**2151**	**2163**	**3941**	**2361**	**2161**	**3991**	**2173**	**2171**	**2183**	**9331**	**9333**	**2181**	**2391**	**2193**	**2191**	**2203**	**9237**	**2201**	**995**	**945**	**2213**	**2211**	
			⑤⑦			⑤⑦							⑧	⑧	⑤⑦					A	B			
			w			m								p	w					✕	✕			
Málaga María Zambrano d.	1500	...	1600	...	...	...	1650	1700	...	1805	...	...	...	...	1900	...	2000	...	...	2045	...	2100	...	...
Granada **673** d.	|	...	|	...	...	...	|	|	...	|	...	...	...	...	|	...	|	1800	...	|	...	|	...	...
Algeciras **673** d.	|	...	|	...	...	...	|	|	...	|	1515	...	...	...	|	...	|	|	...	|	...	|	...	...
Antequera - Santa Ana § d.	|	...	|	...	...	...	1715	1726	...	|	1749	...	...	...	|	...	|	1950	...	2111	...	2126	...	...
Puente Genil - Herrera ¶ d.	|	...	|	...	...	...	1728	1739	...	|	|	...	...	...	|	...	|	|	...	2126	...	2139	...	...
Huelva **671** d.	|	...	|	...	...	...	|	|	...	|	|	...	...	...	|	...	|	|	...	|	...	|	...	...
Cádiz **671** d.	|	...	|	...	...	...	|	|	...	|	|	1615	...	...	|	...	|	|	...	|	1900	|	...	...
Sevilla d.	|	1545	|	1600	1615	1645	|	|	1745	|	|	1800	1845	1915	|	1945	|	|	2045	|	2055	|	2145	...
Córdoba d.	1556	1629	|	1645	1700	1729	1753	1804	1829	|	1834	1907	1929	|	2002	2029	|	2031	2129	2158	2210	2204	2228	...
Puertollano d.	|	|	|	1727	1742	|	|	|	|	|	1922	1954	|	|	|	|	|	2120	|	|	|	2247	2312	...
Ciudad Real d.	|	|	|	1741	1756	|	|	|	|	|	1939	2010	|	|	|	|	|	2138	|	|	|	2303	2326	...
Madrid Puerta de Atocha a.	1740	1815	1840	|	1850	1915	|	1948	2015	2040	2050	2120	2115	2135	2145	2215	2235	2250	2315	|	|	2355	0020	...
Barcelona Sants **650** a.	...	...	...	2139	...	...	2233	...	...	...	...	...	...	...	...	...	...	...	...	0725	0745	...	...	...

A – GIBRALFARO – 🛏 and ② Barcelona - Córdoba - Málaga and v.v.
B – ANTONIO MACHADO – 🛏 and ② Barcelona - Cádiz and v.v.
h – Also Aug. 15, Oct. 12, Dec. 7, 8.
j – Not Aug. 15, Oct. 12, Dec. 7, 8.
m – Not July 19 - Sept. 12, Oct. 11, Dec. 6.
p – Not July 19 - Sept. 12.
w – Not Oct. 11, Dec. 6.
§ – ± *17 km* from Antequera.
¶ – ± *8 km* from Puente Genil.
☛ All trains convey 🍷. *AVE* trains also convey ✕.

Madrid – Puertollano — *Avant* high-speed shuttle services — *Turista* class; 🍷

	8260		8080		8100		8130		8140		8150	8160		8170		8180		8190	8390	8200		8210		8220
	A								A		B	⑤t				⑧			A	⑧		B		⑧
Madrid Puerta de Atocha d.	0640	...	0815	...	1015	...	1315	...	1415	...	1545	1615	...	1715	...	1815	...	1915	1945	2015	...	2115	...	2215
Ciudad Real d.	0736	...	0911	...	1111	...	1411	...	1511	...	1641	1711	...	1811	...	1911	...	2011	2041	2111	...	2211	...	2311
Puertollano a.	0753	...	0928	...	1128	...	1428	...	1528	...	1658	1728	...	1828	...	1928	...	2028	2058	2128	...	2228	...	2328

	8261		8271	8071	8471	8081		8101		8121		8151		8161		8171		8181		8191		8201		8211
	A		B	A	A							B		A				⑤⑦t				⑧		
Puertollano d.	0625	...	0700	0715	0745	0815	...	1015	...	1215	...	1515	...	1615	...	1715	...	1815	...	1915	...	2015	...	2115
Ciudad Real d.	0642	...	0717	0732	0802	0832	...	1032	...	1232	...	1532	...	1632	...	1732	...	1832	...	1932	...	2032	...	2132
Madrid Puerta de Atocha a.	0738	...	0813	0828	0858	0928	...	1128	...	1328	...	1628	...	1728	...	1828	...	1928	...	2028	...	2128	...	2228

A – ①–⑤ (not June 11). B – ①–⑥ (not June 11). t – Also June 10; not June 12.

Málaga – Córdoba – Sevilla — *Avant* high-speed shuttle services — *Turista* class; 🍷

	8654	8664	8664	8694		8744	8764	8784	8804
	A	A					A		
Málaga María Zambrano d.	...	0645	...	0910	...	1430	1615	1810	2015
Antequera - Santa Ana § d.	...	0711	...	0936	...	1456	1641	1836	2041
Puente Genil - Herrera ¶ d.	...	0726	...	0950	...	1510	1655	1850	2055
Córdoba a.	...	0750	...	1015	...	1535	1720	1915	2120
Córdoba d.	0650	0755	0755	1020	...	1540	1725	1920	2125
Sevilla a.	0735	0840	0840	1105	...	1625	1810	2005	2210

	8075	8085	8095	8095	8125	8155	8175	8195	8215	
	A	A		⑥⑦			A			
Sevilla d.	0650	0800	0920	0920	1230	1540	1755	1935	2135	...
Córdoba a.	0735	0845	1005	1005	1315	1625	1840	2020	2220	...
Córdoba d.	0740	0850	...	1010	1320	1630	1845	2025	...	...
Puente Genil - Herrera ¶ d.	0803	0913	...	1033	1343	1653	1908	2048	...	...
Antequera - Santa Ana § d.	0817	0927	...	1047	1357	1707	1922	2102	...	...
Málaga María Zambrano a.	0845	0955	...	1115	1425	1735	1950	2130	...	...

A – ①–⑤ (not May 1). § – ± *17 km* from Antequera. ¶ – ± *8 km* from Puente Genil.

662 MÁLAGA - TORREMOLINOS - FUENGIROLA — 2nd class

km				⚒		⚒			
0	**Málaga** María Zambrano d.	0519	0549	0619	0649	0719	0749	and	2219
8	Aeropuerto ✈ d.	0534	0604	0634	0704	0734	0804	every	2234
16	**Torremolinos** d.	0546	0616	0646	0716	0746	0816	30	2246
20	Benalmádena d.	0553	0623	0653	0723	0753	0823	minutes	2253
31	**Fuengirola** a.	0609	0639	0709	0739	0809	0839	until	2309

		⚒		⚒						
Fuengirola d.	0617	0647	0717	0747	0817	and	2217	2247	2317	...
Benalmádena d.	0630	0700	0730	0800	0830	every	2230	2300	2330	...
Torremolinos d.	0637	0707	0737	0807	0837	30	2237	2307	2337	...
Aeropuerto ✈ d.	0649	0719	0749	0819	0849	minutes	2249	2319	2349	...
Málaga María Zambrano a.	0703	0743	0813	0843	0913	until	2303	2333	0003	...

MADRID - GRANADA, ALMERÍA and MÁLAGA 661

For other trains Madrid – Córdoba – Granada / Málaga and v.v. via the AVE high-speed line, see Table **660**

km		*Hotel*	*Hotel*	*Estr*					*Talgo*			*Arco*	*Arco*	*Arco*					*Talgo*		*R-598*			
		897	**996**	**940**	**17008**	**13021**	**13097**	**13068**	**276**	**18030**	**13058**	**697**	**697**	**697**	**13035**	**17804**		**13073**	**278**	**18034**	**18914**	**18032**	**17000**	
		✕	✕	🍷	2	2	2	2	🍷	2	2	2 🍷	2 🍷	2 🍷	2	2	2	2	🍷	2	2	2	2	
		R	**S**	**P**	①–⑤	**D**		**A**			⑤⑥	**N**	**G**	**H**	**D**	**B**		**D**		①–⑤	⑧			
0	**Madrid** Chamartín § d.	...	...	...	...	...	...	...	0800	0842	...	...	...	...	...	...	...	...	1514	1540	...	1818	2040	...
8	**Madrid** Atocha Cercanías § d.	...	...	...	...	...	...	...	0818	0900	...	...	...	...	...	...	...	...	1532	1553	...	1832	2055	...
	Madrid Puerta de Atocha § d.	...	...	...	0732	...	...	...	|	|	...	...	...	...	...	1328	...	...	|	|	1740	|	|	...
57	Aranjuez § d.	...	...	...	0809	...	...	...	|	0934	...	...	...	...	...	1409	...	...	|	1632	|	1908	2129	...
	Barcelona Sants **672** d.	2130	2145	...	|	...	...	...	|	|	...	0800	0800	0800	...	|	...	...	|	|	|	|	|	...
	València Nord **668** d.	0051	|	...	|	...	...	...	|	|	...	1128	1128	1128	...	|	...	...	|	|	|	|	|	...
157	Alcázar de San Juan **678** d.	0401	|	...	0900	...	...	...	0937	1030	...	1455	1455	1455	...	1501	...	...	1653	1724	1853	2002	2228	...
	Bilbao Abando **689** d.	|	|	2125	...	...	...	...	|	|	...	|	|	|	...	|	...	...	|	|	|	|	...	...
206	Manzanares **678** d.	|	|	0535	...	...	...	...	|	1059	...	1518	1518	1518	...	1527	...	...	1719	1753	1915	2030	...	...
323	Linares - Baeza a.	0538	|	0650	...	...	...	...	1118	1223	...	1636	1636	1636	...	...	...	...	1837	1912	2035	2155	...	...
323	Linares - Baeza d.	0548	|	0651	...	...	...	...	1120	1224	...	1646	1655	1655	...	...	1730	...	1838	1913	2035	2156	...	...
441	Moreda d.	|	|	|	...	...	...	...	|	|	...	|	1836	1836	...	...	1917	...	|	|	|	|	...	...
499	**Granada** **673** a.	0835	|	|	...	...	...	...	|	|	...	|	|	1930	...	...	2006	...	|	|	|	|	...	...
466	Guadix **673** d.	...	|	|	...	...	...	...	1304	|	...	|	1858	...	...	...	...	...	2025	|	|	|	...	...
565	**Almería** **673** a.	...	|	|	...	...	...	...	1418	|	...	|	2018	...	...	...	...	...	2136	|	|	|	...	...
¶	**Jaén** d.	...	|	|	...	0805	1000	...	...	1308	...	|	...	...	1650	...	...	1840	...	1958	2121	2241	...	...
371	Andújar d.	...	|	|	...	0846	1040	...	...	...	...	1721	...	...	1738	...	...	1922	...	...	...	...	...	...
450	**Córdoba** a.	...	0705	0824	...	0936	1136	...	...	...	...	1815	...	...	1830	...	...	2011	...	...	...	...	...	...
450	**Córdoba** d.	...	0708	0824	...	...	...	1215	...	...	1645	1825	...	...	...	...	...	...	...	...	...	...	...	...
501	Montilla d.	...	|	|	...	...	...	1252	...	...	1729	1900	...	...	...	...	...	...	...	...	...	...	...	...
527	Puente Genil d.	...	0739**p**	0938	...	...	...	1314	...	...	1751	1919	...	...	...	...	...	...	...	...	...	...	...	...
574	Bobadilla **673** d.	...	|	1013	...	...	...	1352	...	...	1827	1954	...	...	...	...	...	...	...	...	...	...	...	...
643	**Málaga** María Zambrano **673** a.	...	0825	1115	...	...	...	...	...	...	...	2116	...	...	...	...	...	...	...	...	...	...	...	...

			R-598	*R-598*		*Talgo*		*Arco*	*Arco*	*Arco*										*Talgo*		*Hotel*	*Hotel*	*Estr*
	18047	**18031**	**18915**	**18917**	**18033**	**277**	**13093**	**694**	**694**	**694**	**17041**		**18035**	**17801**	**13047**	**18037**	**13071**	**13067**	**13069**	**279**	**13027**	**894**	**995**	**941**
	2	2	2	2	2	🍷	2	2 🍷	2 🍷	2 🍷	2	2	2	2	2	2	2	2	2	🍷	2	✕	✕	🍷
	①–⑤	①–⑤	①–⑤	⑦	①–⑥			**H**	**G**	**N**	**C**			**B**	**D**	⑦	**D**	**A**	⑤⑥			**R**	**T**	**Q**
Málaga María Zambrano **673** d.	...	...	...	...	...	...	...	...	...	0710	...	...	...	...	...	...	...	...	...	...	...	...	2045	2235
Bobadilla **673** d.	...	...	...	...	...	...	...	...	...	0802	...	...	...	...	...	...	...	1600	1915	...	...	...	|	2328
Puente Genil d.	...	...	...	...	...	...	...	...	...	0832	...	...	...	...	...	...	...	1635	1954	...	...	...	2126**p**	2359
Montilla d.	...	...	...	...	...	...	...	...	...	0853	...	...	...	...	...	...	...	1657	2015	...	...	...	|	|
Córdoba a.	...	...	...	...	...	...	...	...	...	0934	...	...	...	...	...	...	...	1736	2054	...	...	...	2155	0057
Córdoba d.	...	...	...	...	...	...	0800	...	...	1000	...	...	...	...	1447	...	1623	...	...	...	2012	...	2158	0058
Andújar d.	...	...	...	...	...	...	0858	...	...	1051	...	...	...	...	1543	...	1718	...	...	...	2103	...	|	|
Jaén d.	...	0603	0645	0838	0838	...	0945	...	...	|	...	...	1538	...	1634	1717	1812	...	...	...	2154	...	|	|
Almería **673** d.	...	|	|	|	|	0715	...	0740	...	|	...	...	|	...	...	|	...	...	...	1605	...	...	|	|
Guadix **673** d.	...	|	|	|	|	0813	...	0907	...	|	...	...	|	...	...	|	...	...	...	1718	...	...	|	|
Granada **673** d.	...	|	|	|	|	|	...	|	0845	|	...	1335	|	...	...	|	...	...	...	|	...	2155	|	|
Moreda d.	...	|	|	|	|	|	...	0931	0937	|	...	1425	|	...	...	|	...	...	...	|	...	|	|	|
Linares - Baeza a.	...	0642	0725	0918	0920	0958	...	1105	1110	1123	...	1558	1617	...	...	1758	...	...	...	1910	...	0028	|	0215
Linares - Baeza d.	...	0642	0725	0919	0921	0959	...	1147	1147	1147	...	...	1618	...	...	1759	...	...	...	1911	...	0040	|	0216
Manzanares **678** d.	...	0758	0843	1038	1038	|	...	1308	1308	1308	1520	...	1747	1809	...	1926	...	...	...	2034	...	|	|	0333
Bilbao Abando **689** a.	...	|	|	|	|	|	...	|	|	|	|	...	|	|	...	|	...	...	...	|	...	|	|	1229
Alcázar de San Juan **678** d.	0551	0830	0909	1105	1108	1141	...	1353	1353	1353	1550	...	1817	1836	...	1955	...	...	...	2101	...	0230	|	...
València Nord **668** a.	|	|	|	|	|	|	...	1650	1650	1650	|	...	|	|	...	|	...	...	...	|	...	0505	|	...
Barcelona Sants **672** a.	|	|	|	|	|	|	...	2050	2050	2050	|	...	|	|	...	|	...	...	...	|	...	0929	0725	...
Aranjuez § d.	0644	0924	|	|	1200	|	...	...	...	...	1652	...	1920	1927	...	2044	...	...	...	|	...	...	...	...
Madrid Puerta de Atocha § a.	0720	|	1028	1221	|	|	...	...	...	...	|	...	|	2006	...	|	...	...	...	|	...	...	...	...
Madrid Atocha Cercanías § a.	...	1008	...	...	1237	1305	...	...	...	...	1728	...	1959	...	...	2127	...	...	...	2218	...	...	...	...
Madrid Chamartín § a.	...	1022	...	...	1251	1320	...	...	...	...	1742	...	2013	...	...	2141	...	...	...	2236	...	...	...	...

A – ①②③④⑦.
B – To / from Badajoz (Table **678**).
C – From Ciudad Real.
D – To / from Sevilla.
G – GARCÍA LORCA – ①④⑥.
H – GARCÍA LORCA – ③⑤⑦.
N – GARCÍA LORCA – (2) Barcelona - Málaga and v.v.; (2) Barcelona - Córdoba - Sevilla and v.v. (Table **671**).
P – PICASSO – June 19, 26, 30, July 3, 10, 14, 17, 24, 30, Aug. 7, 14, 21, 24, 26, 28, Sept. 4: 🛏, 🛏 and (12) Bilbao - Málaga (Table **689**).
Q – PICASSO – June 21, 28, July 1, 5, 12, 15, 19, 26, Aug. 1, 9, 16, 23, 25, 27, 31, Sept. 6: 🛏, 🛏 and (12) Málaga - Bilbao (Table **689**).
R – ALHAMBRA – 🛏 and (1) (reclining) Barcelona - Granada and v.v.
p – Puente Genil - **Herrera**.
¶ – Linares - Jaen: *59 km*. Jaen - Andújar: *54 km*.
§ – Madrid - Alcázar and v.v.: see also Table **667**.

2nd class MÁLAGA - TORREMOLINOS - FUENGIROLA Table relocated to page 324 662

High-speed services MADRID - VALLADOLID 663

km		*AVE*	*Alvia*	*Alvia*	*Alvia*	*Alvia*	*Avant*	*Avant*	*Alvia*		*Alvia*	*AVE*	*Talgo*	*Talgo*	*Alvia*	*Avant*	*Alvia*	*Alvia*	*Avant*	*Alvia*	*Alvia*	*Alvia*	*Avant*	
		4069	**4071**	**4073**	**4087**	**4087**	**8089**	**8109**	**4111**		**4133**	**4149**	**151**	**151**	**4141**	**8159**	**4167**	**4167**	**8179**	**4183**	**4181**	**4201**	**8219**	
		①–⑤	①–⑥	①–⑥	①–⑥		①–⑤	⑥⑦					①–⑥	①–⑥				⑧	⑤ **y**		⑧			
		m	**f**	**f**			2 **q**	2 **t**								2			2		**h**	**h**	2	
	Alacant Terminal **668** d.	...	...	...	...	...	...	...	...	...	...	...	...	...	1035**n**	...	...	...	...	1400	...	...	...	...
0	**Madrid** Chamartín d.	0635	0650	0740	0800	0800	0830	1030	1100	...	1330	1400	1420	1420	1440	1530	1610	1610	1730	1805	1830	2015	2100	...
68	Segovia Guiomar ¶ d.	|	|	|	0833	0833	0901	1101	|	...	|	|	1453	1453	1516	1601	1643	1643	1801	1841	|	|	2131	...
	A Coruña **680** a.	|	|	|	|	|	|	|	|	...	|	|	2208	|	|	|	|	|	|	|	|	|	|	...
	Pontevedra **680** a.	|	|	|	|	|	|	|	|	...	|	|	...	2226	|	|	|	|	|	|	|	|	|	...
180	**Valladolid** Campo Grande a.	0737	0801	0851	0917	0917	0940	1140	1211	...	1441	1456	...	...	1559	1640	1732	1732	1840	1924	1945	2125	2210	...
	Gijón Cercanías **681** a.	...	1155	|	|	|	...	...	1605	...	|	...	...	...	2002	...	|	|	...	|	2339	...	...	...
	Santander **681** a.	...	...	1207	|	|	...	...	...	...	1755	...	...	...	...	...	|	|	...	2242	...	...	...	...
	Bilbao Abando **689** a.	...	...	...	1252	|	...	...	...	...	...	...	...	...	...	...	|	2111	...	...	...	...	...	...
	Hendaye **689** a.	...	...	...	...	1354	...	...	...	...	...	...	...	...	...	...	2200	...	...	...	...	...	...	...

	Avant	*Alvia*	*AVE*	*Avant*	*Alvia*	*Alvia*	*Alvia*	*Alvia*	*Alvia*	*Avant*	*AVE*	*Alvia*	*Alvia*		*Avant*	*Talgo*	*Talgo*	*Avant*	*Alvia*	*Alvia*		*Alvia*	*Alvia*	
	8278	**4060**	**4088**	**8108**	**4072**	**4070**	**4086**	**4086**	**4100**	**8168**	**4178**	**4142**	**4140**		**8198**	**152**	**152**	**8218**	**4166**	**4166**		**4180**	**4182**	
	①–⑤	①–⑥	①–⑤	⑥⑦		①–⑥		①–⑥								⑧	⑧	⑤ **y**		⑧		⑧	⑧	
	2 **q**	**j**	**m**	2 **r**		**f**				2								2				**h**	**b**	
Irún **689** d.	...	...	...	...	...	...	0815	...	...	...	...	...	...	...	...	...	...	...	1620	...	...	...	...	...
Bilbao Abando **689** d.	...	...	...	...	...	...	|	0855	...	...	...	...	...	...	...	...	...	...	|	1710	...	...	...	...
Santander **681** d.	...	...	...	...	0705	...	|	|	...	...	...	1405	...	...	...	...	...	...	|	|	...	...	1920	...
Gijón Cercanías **681** d.	...	...	...	...	|	0715	|	|	1025	...	...	|	1400	...	...	...	...	...	|	|	...	1815	|	...
Valladolid Campo Grande d.	0645	0804	0830	0920	1021	1114	1237	1237	1420	1530	1700	1718	1801	...	1935	...	...	2020	2048	2048	...	2210	2237	...
Pontevedra **680** d.	|	|	|	|	|	|	|	|	|	|	|	|	|	...	|	1250	...	|	|	|	...	|	|	...
A Coruña **680** d.	|	|	|	|	|	|	|	|	|	|	|	|	|	...	|	|	1310	|	|	|	...	|	|	...
Segovia Guiomar ¶ d.	|	|	|	0958	1106	|	1322	1322	|	1608	|	|	1846	...	2013	2033	2033	2058	2133	2133	...	|	|	...
Madrid Chamartín a.	0755	0920	0932	1030	1143	1229	1357	1357	1540	1640	1756	1833	1923	...	2045	2108	2108	2130	2208	2208	...	2325	2352	...
Alacant Terminal **668** a.	...	...	...	...	1550	...	...	...	...	...	...	...	2338**p**	...	...	...	...	...	...	...	...	...	...	...

b – Not Oct. 11.
f – Not Oct. 12.
h – Not Oct. 11, Dec. 7.
j – Not Oct. 11, Dec. 8.
m – Not Aug. 3 – 30.
n – Not ⑦.
p – Not ⑥.
q – Not June 11.
r – Also June 11.
t – Also May 1.
y – Also Apr. 30; not May 1.
☛ All trains convey 🍷. *AVE* trains also convey ✕.
¶ – *4 km* from city centre.
AV – ***Avant*** high-speed services. Single class. 🍷.

664 🚌 BARCELONA - ANDORRA

From **Barcelona** Nord bus station: 0615, 1030, 1300Ⓑ, 1500, 1900.
From **Andorra la Vella** bus station: 0600, 1030, 1500, 1800Ⓑ, 1915.

Journey 3 hrs 15 mins. Operator: Alsina Graells, Barcelona (ALSA) ✆ +34 902 42 22 42.
Additional slower services also operate.

From **Barcelona** Sants railway station: 0615, 0815, 1115, 1315, 1545, 1815, 2015, 2315.
From **Andorra la Vella** bus station: 0615, 0815, 1115, 1315, 1515, 1815, 2015, 2215.

Journey 3 hours (continues to / from Barcelona ✈). Operator: Autocars Nadal ✆ +376 805 151.

665 SITGES — 2nd class

Local rail service **Barcelona - Sitges - Sant Vicenç de Calders**.
From Barcelona Sants: 0606, 0636 and every 30 minutes until 2206; then 2306.
From Sant Vicenç: 0600, 0615, 0632Ⓐ, 0643Ⓐ, 0658, 0732, 0751, 0816, 0831, 0903, 0933 and every 30 minutes until 2103; then 2200.

Additional trains operate **Barcelona - Sitges** and v.v.

Journey times: **Barcelona** – **Sitges** (*34 km*) 30 minutes,
Barcelona – **Sant Vicenç** (*60 km*) 57 minutes.

666 BARCELONA - MATARÓ, BLANES and MAÇANET — 2nd class

Cercanías (suburban) line **C1**. For faster services Barcelona - Maçanet via Granollers, see Table **657**.
Approximate journey times (in mins) to / from **Barcelona** Sants: Mataró (43), Arenys de Mar (55), Calella (71), Pineda de Mar (74), Malgrat de Mar (80), Blanes (85), Maçanet-Massanes (98).

Barcelona Sants – **Mataró** and v.v. *35 km*
Ⓐ: 4–6 trains per hour.
From Barcelona 0555–2311; from Mataró 0526–2234.
Ⓒ: 2–4 trains per hour.
From Barcelona 0612–2300; from Mataró 0559–2220.

Barcelona Sants – **Blanes** *67 km*
0612, 0642 and every 30 mins. until 2042, then 2124, 2158, 2233.
Blanes - **Barcelona** Sants
0603, 0633, 0653, 0703, 0733 and every 30 mins. until 2103, 2144.

Barcelona Sants – Blanes – **Maçanet - Massanes** *82 km*
0612, 0712 and hourly until 1912, then 2042, 2158.
Maçanet - Massanes – Blanes – **Barcelona** Sants
0620, 0650, 0720, 0820 and hourly until 2020, then 2130.

667 ALACANT - BENIDORM - DÉNIA — 2nd class

By tram (route L1)									N
Alacant Mercado ⊙ d.	0544	0614	every	1944	2014	2044	2114	2144	2325**z**
El Campello d.	0609	0639	30	2009	2039	2109	2139	2209	2350
La Vila Joiosa d.	0638	0708	minutes	2038	2108	2138	2208	2238	0017
Benidorm a.	0653	0723	until	2053	2123	2153	2223	2253	0034
By train (route L9)									
Benidorm d.	0659	...		2059	...	2159	...	...	...
Altea d.	0714	...	every	2114	...	2211	...	...	...
Calpe d.	0730	...	hour	2130	...	...	...	...	...
Teulada d.	0745	...	until	2145	...	...	...	...	...
Gata d.	0754	...		2154	...	...	...	...	...
Dénia a.	0808	...		2208	...	...	...	...	...

By train (route L9)									
Dénia d.	...	...	...	0620	...		2020	...	...
Gata d.	...	...	...	0635	...		2035	...	...
Teulada d.	...	...	...	0644	...	every	2044	...	...
Calpe d.	...	...	...	0659	...	hour	2059	...	...
Altea d.	...	0616	...	0716	...	until	2116	...	2216
Benidorm a.	...	0629	...	0729	...		2129	...	2229
By tram (route L1)	P								
Benidorm d.	0126	0635	0705	0735	0805	every	2135	2205	...
La Vila Joiosa d.	0142	0653	0723	0753	0823	30	2153	2223	...
El Campello d.	0212	0723	0753	0823	0853	minutes	2223	2253	...
Alacant Mercado ⊙ a.	0238**z**	0748	0818	0848	0918	until	2248	2318	...

N – ④⑤⑥ July 3 - Aug. 30 (2008 dates).
P – ⑤⑥⑦ July 4 - Aug. 31 (2008 dates).
z – **Alacant** Puerta del Mar.
⊙ – ± 900 m from Alacant Renfe station.
Operator: Tram Metropolitano / FGV ✆ 900 72 04 72
www.fgvalicante.com

668 MADRID - CARTAGENA, ALACANT and VALÈNCIA

km		*Hotel* 894	18024 2	*Alaris* 1074	2	*Alvia* 1076	*Alta* 220	*Alaris* 1084	*Alaris* 1094	*Alvia* 1096	18081	*Alta* 222	*Alaris* 1414	*Alvia* 4072	*Arco* 694	*Alta* 228	*Alaris* 1144	*Alvia* 1146	18040 33040	*Alaris* 1454	2	*Alvia* 1166	*Alta* 224	*Alaris* 1174	18044
		✕ C	①–⑤	✕ G	⑥⑦	🍷 D	🍷 E	✕ K	✕	🍷	2	🍷	✕	🍷 S	🍷 A	🍷 Ⓑ h	✕ Ⓑ	🍷	2	✕	⑤⑦	🍷	🍷	✕	2 ⑤
0	**Madrid** Chamartín ‡ d.	...	...	0640	...	0654	0713	0740	0842	0900	...	0940	1100	1203	...	1234	1340	1400	1419	1500	...	1600	1629	1640	1639
8	**Madrid** Atocha Cercanías ‡ d.	...	...	0700	...	0712	0731	0800	0900	0918	...	1000	1120	1220	...	1253	1400	1418	1433	1518	...	1618	1647	1700	1653
	Madrid Pta de Atocha ‡ d.	...	...	|	...	|	|	|	|	|	...	|	|	|	...	|	|	|	|	|	...	|	|	|	|
57	Aranjuez ‡ d.	...	...	|	...	|	|	|	|	|	...	|	|	1251	...	|	|	|	1509	|	...	|	|	|	1724
	Badajoz **678** d.	...	...	|	...	|	|	|	|	|	...	|	|	|	0715	|	|	|	|	|	...	|	|	|	|
	Ciudad Real **678** d.	...	0551**y**	|	...	|	|	|	|	|	0918	|	|	|	1157	|	|	|	|	|	...	|	|	|	|
157	Alcázar de San Juan ‡ a.	...	0657**y**	|	...	0824	0848	|	|	|	1029	|	|	1334	1315	|	|	|	1608	1629	...	|	|	|	1824
157	Alcázar de San Juan d.	0230	0700	|	0800	0825	0849	|	|	|	1032	|	|	1336	1353	|	|	|	1609	1630	...	|	|	|	1828
288	**Albacete** d.	0327	0820	0903	0922	0924	0947	1003	1103	1124	1145	1210	1323	1431	1453	1505	1602	1626	1728	1724	1733	1828	1856	1902	1941
354	Hellín d.	|	|	|	|	|	1022	|	|	|	|	|	|	|	|	|	|	|	...	|	|	|	|	|	...
458	Alcantarilla d.	|	|	|	|	|	1133	|	|	|	|	|	|	|	|	|	|	|	...	|	|	|	|	|	...
466	Murcia **672** d.	|	|	|	|	|	1143	|	|	|	|	1351	|	|	|	1644	|	|	...	|	|	|	2047	|	...
531	**Cartagena** **672** a.	|	|	|	|	|	...	|	|	|	|	1442	|	|	|	1726	|	|	...	|	|	|	2132	|	...
424	Elda - Petrer d.	|	|	|	|	1025	...	|	|	1222	1259	...	|	1530	|	...	|	1726	...	|	|	1930	...	|	...
464	**Alacant** Terminal a.	|	|	|	|	1055	...	|	|	1250	1328	...	|	1558	|	...	|	1753	...	|	|	1959	...	|	...
435	Xátiva **672** d.	|	0935	|	1047	...	...	1054	|	...	...	...	1414	...	1553	...	|	...	...	1817	1915	...	...	|	...
491	**València** Nord △ **672** a.	0505	1016	1027	1125	...	...	1128	1225	...	...	...	1447	...	1650	...	1725	...	...	1849	2000	...	...	2025	...
	Barcelona Sants **672** a.	0929	...	...	...	...	...	...	|	...	...	...	...	...	2050	...	...	...	...	...	...	...	...	|	...
553	Gandia △ a.	...	...	...	...	...	...	...	1323	...	...	...	...	...	...	...	...	...	...	...	...	...	...	2121**v**	...

	Alaris 1184	*Alvia* 1186	*Talgo* 74	*Alaris* 1194	18032	*Alta* 226	*Alvia* 4140	*Alaris* 1504	17000	*Alaris* 11504
	✕	🍷 Ⓑ t	🍷 Q	✕	2	🍷 Ⓑ t	🍷 N	✕ Ⓑ f	2	✕ ⑤
Madrid Chamartín ‡ d.	1740	1800	1813	1840	1818	1900	1943	2000	2040	2056
Madrid Atocha Cercanías ‡ d.	1800	1818	1828	1900	1832	1918	2000	2018	2055	2115
Madrid Pta de Atocha ‡ d.	|	|	|	|	|	|	|	|	|	|
Aranjuez ‡ d.	|	|	|	|	1907	|	|	|	2129	|
Alcázar de San Juan ‡ a.	|	|	1937	|	1957	2033	2114	|	2228	|
Alcázar de San Juan d.	|	|	1938	|	2010**b**	2034	2116	|	...	|
Albacete d.	2002	2026	2036	2103	2124**b**	2135	2211	2223	...	2324
Hellín d.	|	|	|	|	...	2210	|	|	...	|
Alcantarilla d.	|	|	|	|	...	|	|	|	...	|
Murcia **672** d.	|	|	|	|	...	2317	|	|	...	|
Cartagena **672** a.	|	|	|	|	...	0013	|	|	...	|
Elda - Petrer d.	|	2125	2144	|	...	...	2313	|	...	|
Alacant Terminal a.	|	2150	2212	|	...	...	2338	|	...	|
Xátiva **672** d.	|	...	...	2154	...	...	...	|	...	|
València Nord △ **672** a.	2125	...	...	2227	...	...	...	2345	...	0048
Barcelona Sants **672** a.	...	...	...	...	...	...	...	...	...	...
Gandia △ a.	...	...	...	...	...	...	...	...	...	...

	Hotel 897	18047 2		18041 2	*Alta* 221	18049 2	*Alaris* 1065	*Alvia* 1077	*Alaris* 1075	*Alaris* 1085
	✕ C	①–⑤		①–⑤	🍷 L	⑥⑦	✕ G	🍷 H	✕ T	✕ B
Gandia △ d.	...	...	...	...	...	...	...	...	...	...
Barcelona Sants **672** d.	2130	...	...	...	...	...	...	...	...	...
València Nord △ **662** d.	0051	...	...	...	...	...	0650	...	0750	0850
Xátiva **672** d.	|	...	...	...	...	...	0721	...	|	|
Alacant Terminal d.	|	...	...	...	...	...	|	0700	|	|
Elda - Petrer d.	|	...	...	...	...	...	|	0727	|	|
Cartagena **672** d.	|	...	...	...	0530	...	|	|	|	|
Murcia **672** d.	|	...	...	...	0611	...	|	|	|	|
Alcantarilla d.	|	...	...	...	|	...	|	|	|	|
Hellín d.	|	...	...	...	|	...	|	|	|	|
Albacete d.	0243	0427**e**	...	0627	0750	0724**z**	0813	0826	0913	1013
Alcázar de San Juan a.	0346	0550**e**	...	0735	|	0834**z**	|	|	|	|
Alcázar de San Juan ‡ d.	...	0551	...	0736	|	0835	|	|	|	|
Aranjuez ‡ d.	...	0644	...	0832	|	0934	|	|	|	|
Madrid Pta de Atocha ‡ a.	...	0720	...	|	|	|	|	|	|	|
Madrid Atocha Cercanías ‡ a.	...	...	...	0912	1004	1014	1023	1034	1123	1223
Madrid Chamartín ‡ a.	...	...	...	0928	1021	1028	1037	1048	1138	1237

A – GARCÍA LORCA – [2] Badajoz - Alcázar - Barcelona and v.v.
B – ①–⑤ (daily June 14 - Sept. 20).
C – 🛏 and [2] Granada - Alcázar - Barcelona and v.v.
D – ①–⑥ May 17 - Oct. 10; ①–⑤ Oct. 13 - Dec. 12 (not Nov. 9, Dec. 8).
E – ①–⑤ (not Aug. 1–30, Oct. 12, Nov. 9).
G – ①–⑥ (not Oct. 12, Nov. 9, Dec. 7, 8).
H – ①–⑥ (not Oct. 12, Nov. 9, Dec. 8).
J – Ⓑ (daily May 17 - Oct. 10).
K – [12] Madrid - València - Castelló de la Plana (- Benicàssim June 16 - Oct. 12) and v.v. (Table **672**).
L – ①–⑥ (not Aug. 1–30, Oct. 12, Nov. 9).
N – Ⓑ. [12] Gijón - Alacant.

P – ①–⑥. [12] Alacant - Gijón.
Q – ⑥. [12] A Coruña and Pontevedra - Alacant.
R – ⑦. [12] Alacant - A Coruña and Pontevedra.
S – From / to Santander.
T – [12] Madrid - València - Castelló de la Plana and v.v. (Table **672**).

b – Not ⑥.
e – ① only.
f – Not Oct. 11, Nov. 8, Dec. 6, 7.
g – Also May 14; not May 15.
h – Daily Aug. 1–30; not Dec. 7.

r – Also Oct. 12, Nov. 9, Dec. 8; not Oct. 11, Nov. 8, Dec. 6.
t – Not Dec. 7.
v – ⑤ only.
x – ⑦ only.
y – ① only.
z – ⑥ only.

‡ – See also Table **661**.
△ – See next page.

VALÈNCIA, ALACANT and CARTAGENA - MADRID — 668

	Talgo 85 ♀ R	Alta 223 ♀	Alvia 4141 ♀ P	Alaris 1415 ✕	Alvia 1127 ♀	Arco 697 ♀ A	Alta 229 ♀ Ⓑ	Alvia 4183 ♀ S	Alaris 1445 ✕ Ⓑ	2 ⑤⑦	Alaris 1155 ✕ K	Alta 1167 ♀ J	18043 33043 2	Alaris 1165 ✕	Alta 225 ♀	18083 2	Alaris 1175 ✕	18045 2 ⑦	Alvia 1187 ♀	18027 2	Alaris 1185 ✕	Alta 227 ♀ Ⓑt	Alvia 1207 ♀ Ⓑt	Alaris 1505 ✕ Ⓑf	Alaris 11505 ✕ ⑦r
Gandia △ d.	...	...	...	...	...	...	...	...	...	...	...	...	...	1540	...	...	...	...	...	...	...	...	...	...	...
Barcelona Sants **672** d.	...	...	...	...	...	0800	...	...	...	...	...	...	...	│	...	...	...	...	...	...	...	...	...	...	...
València Nord △ **672** d.	...	...	...	1125	...	1128	...	...	1420	1433	1550	...	...	1650	...	...	1750	...	...	1805	1850	...	...	2020	2120
Xàtiva **672** d.	...	...	...	1156	...	1224	...	...	│	1515	│	...	...	│	...	...	1821	...	...	1841	│	...	...	2052	│
Alacant Terminal d.	0935	...	1035	│	1205	│	...	1400	│	│	│	1605	...	│	...	1700	│	...	1805	│	│	...	2000	│	│
Elda-Petrer d.	1002	...	1057	│	1232	│	...	1426	│	│	│	1631	...	│	...	1728	│	...	1832	│	│	...	2023	│	│
Cartagena **672** d.	│	0850	│	│	│	│	1215**x**	│	│	│	│	│	...	│	1555	│	│	...	│	│	│	1820	│	│	│
Murcia **672** d.	│	0936	│	│	│	│	1258	│	│	│	│	│	...	│	1643	│	│	...	│	│	│	1905	│	│	│
Alcantarilla d.	│	0945	│	│	│	│	│	│	│	│	│	│	...	│	│	│	│	...	│	│	│	│	│	│	│
Hellín d.	│	1049	│	│	│	│	│	│	│	│	│	│	...	│	│	│	│	...	│	│	│	2024	│	│	│
Albacete d.	1109	1127	1158	1249	1329	1337	1446	1523	1541	1702	1712	1730	1740	1813	1833	1844	1913	1916	1931	1958	2012	2103	2118	2145	2242
Alcázar de San Juan a.	1204	1232	│	│	│	1437	│	1615	│	...	│	│	1853	│	│	1957	2006	2022	│	2125	│	2200	2210	│	│
Alcázar de San Juan ‡ d.	1205	1233	│	│	│	1510	│	1616	│	...	│	│	1854	│	│	2007	2007	2023	│	2128**x**	│	2201	2211	│	│
Ciudad Real **678** a.	│	│	│	│	│	1621	│	│	│	...	│	│	│	│	│	2115	│	│	│	2240**x**	│	│	│	│	│
Badajoz **678** a.	│	│	│	│	│	2145	│	│	│	...	│	│	│	│	│	...	│	│	│	...	│	│	│	│	│
Aranjuez ‡ d.	│	│	│	│	│	...	│	1700	│	...	│	│	1953	│	│	...	│	2123	│	...	│	│	│	│	│
Madrid Pta de Atocha ‡ a.	│	│	│	│	│	...	│	│	│	...	│	│	│	│	│	...	│	│	│	...	│	│	│	│	│
Madrid Atocha Cercanías ‡ a.	1320	1359	1415	1500	1542	...	1704	1733	1751	...	1920	1940	2034	2021	2045	...	2126	2156	2142	...	2222	2317	2325	2353	0051
Madrid Chamartín ‡ a.	1335	1415	1432	1514	1556	...	1718	1748	1805	...	1934	1955	2048	2035	2100	...	2140	2210	2156	...	2236	2332	2339	0007	0105

FOR NOTES SEE PREVIOUS PAGE

△ – *Cercanías* (suburban) line **C1**: **Valencia** - **Gandia** and v.v. 2nd class. Journey time: 54–60 minutes.

From **València** Nord
Ⓐ: 0611, 0641 and every 30 minutes until 1941; then 1956, 2033, 2041, 2111, 2141, 2211, 2241.
Ⓒ: 0641, 0741 and hourly until 2241.

From **Gandia**
Ⓐ: 0605, 0640, 0655, 0710, 0725, 0740, 0755, 0825, 0840, 0855, 0915, 0925, 0955 and every 30 minutes until 2225.
Ⓒ: 0655, 0755 and hourly until 2055; then 2225.

MADRID - CUENCA - VALÈNCIA — 669

2nd class

km		14160	18760 ①–⑤	18160		18162		18164		18766
0	**Madrid** Puerta de Atocha d.	...	...	0850	...	1223	...	1600	...	1940
49	Aranjuez **661 668** d.	...	0610	0925	...	1257	...	1635	...	2017
201	**Cuenca** d.	0740	0837	1140**r**	...	1450	...	1852	...	2225
327	Requena d.	0927	...	1322	...	1631	...	2037	...	...
399	**València** Sant Isidre ◧ a.	1049	...	1445	...	1752	...	2150	...	...

	18761	18161	18763 ①–⑤	14501	18765	14161	18771 ⑦	18769 ①–⑥	14163
València Sant Isidre ◧ d.	...	0814	...	1232	...	1514	...	...	1814
Requena d.	...	0947	...	1344	...	1651	...	...	1940
Cuenca d.	0705	1138	1320	1552	1620	1841	1848	1855	2135
Aranjuez **661 668** d.	0908	1327	1536	...	1819	...	2052	2052	...
Madrid Puerta de Atocha a.	0947	1404	1620	...	1901	...	2129	2129	...

r – Arrives 1119.

◧ – *Renfe* rail tickets to / from València are valid on *MetroValencia* services between Sant Isidre and either Plaça d'Espanya (on Line 1) or Bailén (on Line 5) – both are adjacent to València Nord main railway station. Allow at least 15 minutes for the transfer.

VALÈNCIA - TERUEL - ZARAGOZA — 670

2nd class

km		18500			*TRD* * 18502			*TRD* * 18504 H		
0	**València** Nord d.	...	...	...	0942	...	...	1547	...	1847
34	Sagunt d.	...	...	...	1010	...	...	1614	...	1917
65	Segorbe d.	...	...	...	1037	...	...	1641	...	1947
171	**Teruel** d.	0645	...	...	1208	...	...	1819	...	2137
242	Calamocha d.	0740	...	...	1252	...	...	1907	...	...
305	Cariñena d.	0846	...	...	1335	...	...	1957	...	...
359	**Zaragoza** Delicias a.	0937	...	...	1414	...	...	2035	...	...
361	**Zaragoza** El Portillo a.	0941	...	...	1419	...	...	2044	...	...

			TRD * 18511 H			*TRD* * 18513			18515
Zaragoza El Portillo d.	...	...	0807	...	...	1558	...	...	1907
Zaragoza Delicias d.	...	...	0812	...	...	1603	...	...	1912
Cariñena d.	...	...	0849	...	...	1639	...	...	1954
Calamocha d.	...	...	0937	...	...	1730	...	...	2101
Teruel d.	0800	...	1024	...	...	1815	...	...	2155
Segorbe d.	0938	...	1153	...	...	1948	...	...	...
Sagunt d.	1012	...	1222	...	...	2020	...	...	...
València Nord a.	1042	...	1251	...	...	2049	...	...	...

H – To / from Huesca (Table **654**).

* – Reservation on these trains is not compulsory, but is recommended on ⑤⑦.

CÓRDOBA - SEVILLA - HUELVA and CÁDIZ — 671

km		13000 2 ①–⑤ f	13002 2 ①–⑥ f	13030 2 ①–⑤ f	*Hotel* 946 ✕ A	13004 2	13037 2	13006 2 ①–⑤ f	13021 2 J	13021 2	13008 2 ①–⑤ f	*Alta* 9320	13010 2	13032 2	13012 2 ①–⑤ f	13039 2	13014 2	13028 2	13016 2	*Alta* 9332	13035 2 J	*Arco* 697 G	13018 2	13095 2	*Alta* 9386	13073 2 J
	Madrid Pta de Atocha **660** d.	...	...	...	...	...	...	...	...	...	...	1005	...	...	...	...	...	...	...	1620	...	...	...	...	1805	...
0	**Córdoba** **660** d.	...	...	0715	0728	...	...	...	0938	...	...	1209	...	1335	...	...	...	1610	...	1837	1832	1840	...	...	2011	2013
51	Palma del Río d.	...	...	0744	│	...	...	...	1009	...	...	│	...	1404	...	...	...	1640	...	│	1901	│	...	...	│	2042
129	**Sevilla** **660** a.	...	...	0831	0839	...	...	...	1058	...	...	1318	...	1456	...	...	...	1730	...	1944	1949	1955	...	...	│	2134
129	**Sevilla** **673** § d.	0635	0755	...	0845	0900	0910	1005	...	1100	1210	1323	1405	...	1535	1640	1700	...	1808	1948	...	...	2005	2030	│	2135
204	La Palma del Condado d.	│	│	...	│	│	1010	│	...	│	│	│	│	...	│	1739	│	...	│	│	...	...	│	2127	2153**s**	│
244	**Huelva** a.	│	│	...	│	│	1045	│	...	│	│	│	│	...	│	1815	│	...	│	│	...	...	│	2200	2221	│
145	Dos Hermanas **673** § d.	0650	0808	...	│	0913	...	1018	...	1113	1223	│	1420	...	1550	...	1713	...	1821	│	...	...	2018	...	...	2148
162	Utrera § d.	0700	│	...	│	0924	...	│	...	│	1235	│	│	...	1601	...	│	...	1832	│	...	...	│	...	...	2159
236	Jerez de la Frontera d.	0745	0857	...	0946	1011	...	1109	...	1208	1320	1416	1515	...	1646	...	1808	...	1919	2051	...	...	2116	...	...	2241
250	Puerto de Santa María d.	0755	0907	...	0956	1021	...	1119	...	1218	1330	1429	1525	...	1656	...	1818	...	1929	2101	...	...	2126	...	...	2251
271	San Fernando-Bahía Sur d.	0819	0932	...	1014	1042	...	1143	...	1238	1353	1448	1549	...	1714	...	1839	...	1951	2119	...	...	2150	...	...	2311
284	**Cádiz** a.	0834	0947	...	1026	1056	...	1156	...	1251	1406	1503	1604	...	1729	...	1852	...	2004	2137	...	...	2203	...	...	2325

	13001 2 ①–⑤ f	13023 2 ①–⑤ f	*Arco* 694 G	13041 2	13003 2 ①–⑥ f	*Alta* 9365 ①–⑥ p	13025 2	*Alta* 9315	13005 2	*Alta* 9323 ⑦ q	13007 2 ①–⑤ f	13009 2	13047 2 J	13011 2 ①–⑤ f	13071 2 J	13013 2 ①–⑤ f	13043 2	13015 2	*Alta* 9333	13027 2 J	13017 2	13031 2	13049 2	*Hotel* 945 ✕ A	13019 2	13033 2
Cádiz d.	0545	...	...	...	0645	...	...	0740	0850	...	1000	1105	...	1300	...	1355	...	1500	1615	1700	1800	...	...	1900	1910	2015
San Fernando-Bahía Sur d.	0559	...	...	...	0700	...	...	0751	0901	...	1012	1116	...	1311	...	1410	...	1515	1631	1713	1812	...	...	1913	1921	2029
Puerto de Santa María d.	0619	...	...	...	0724	...	...	0809	0921	...	1034	1135	...	1331	...	1434	...	1540	1649	1733	1832	...	...	1933	1941	2048
Jerez de la Frontera d.	0630	...	...	...	0735	...	...	0822	0931	...	1044	1145	...	1341	...	1444	...	1551	1702	1743	1842	...	...	1943	1951	2058
Utrera § d.	0715	...	...	...	0817	...	...	│	│	...	│	│	...	1421	...	│	...	1632	│	│	│	...	...	│	2036	2144
Dos Hermanas **673** § d.	0727	...	...	...	0829	...	...	│	1024	...	1134	1235	...	1433	...	1535	...	1644	│	1831	1935	...	...	│	2048	2156
Huelva d.	│	...	...	0710	│	0745	...	│	│	1120	│	│	...	│	...	│	1425	│	│	│	│	...	1850	│	│	│
La Palma del Condado d.	│	...	...	0739	│	0811	...	│	│	1147	│	│	...	│	...	│	1458	│	│	│	│	...	1922	│	│	│
Sevilla **673** § a.	0741	...	...	0844	0843	│	...	0922	1040	│	1147	1248	...	1447	...	1548	1557	1657	1755	1845	1948	...	2020	2043	2103	2210
Sevilla **660** d.	...	0750	0820	...	...	│	0900	0925	...	│	...	...	1325	...	1500	...	...	...	1800	1848	...	2015	...	2055	...	...
Palma del Río d.	...	0840	│	...	...	│	0949	│	...	│	...	...	1414	...	1548	...	...	...	│	1939	...	2104	...	│	...	...
Córdoba **660** a.	...	0911	0937	...	...	1001	1026	1035	...	1340	...	...	1445	...	1621	...	...	...	1906	2010	...	2135	...	2207	...	...
Madrid Pta de Atocha **660** a.	...	...	...	...	...	1210	...	1241	...	1550	...	...	...	...	...	...	...	...	2120	...	...	...	...	...	...	...

A – ANTONIO MACHADO – 🛏 and 2 Barcelona - Córdoba - Cádiz and v.v.
G – GARCÍA LORCA – 2 Barcelona - València - Sevilla and v.v.
J – From / to Jaén.
f – Not Aug. 15, Oct. 12, Nov. 1, Dec. 8.
p – Not Aug. 15, Oct. 12, Dec. 7, 8.
q – Also Aug. 15, Oct. 12, Dec. 7, 8.
s – Stops to set down only.
§ – Frequent suburban services operate Sevilla - Utrera and v.v.

672 BARCELONA - VALÈNCIA - ALACANT - CARTAGENA

km		2	Alaris 1075 🍷	2 ①–⑤	2 ①–⑥	Em 1071 🍷 ①–⑥	2 ⑥	Arco 697 🍷 F	2	Em 1091 🍷 P	18093 2	Em 1101 🍷	18093 2	Alaris 1111 🍷	2	2 ⑤⑦	Talgo 463 🍷 J	Alaris 1155 🍷	2	2	Em 1341 🍷 A	Talgo 165 🍷	2	Em 1161 🍷	2
	Portbou **657** d.	...	...	...	...	...	...	...	...	...	...	...	...	...	...	...	0952	...	...	...	...	...	...	...	...
0	**Barcelona** França d.	...	...	...	0548	...	...	...	0746	...	0919	...	...	...	1047	...	|	...	...	1318	...	...	1446	...	1618
5	Barcelona Passeig de Gràcia d.	...	...	...	0556	...	...	...	0755	...	0927	...	...	...	1055	...	|	...	...	1326	...	...	1456	...	1626
8	**Barcelona** Sants **652** d.	...	...	...	0603	0700	...	0800	0803	0900	0933	1000	...	1100	1103	...	1200	...	...	1333	1430	1500	1503	1600	1633
68	Sant Vicenç de Calders **652** d.	...	...	...	0648	|	...	|	0848	|	1017	|	...	|	1147	...	|	...	...	1416	|	|	1547	|	1716
82	Altafulla - Tamarit d.	...	...	...	0658	|	...	|	|	|	1028	|	...	|	1158	...	|	...	...	1426	|	|	1558	|	1727
93	**Tarragona** **652** d.	...	...	...	0707	0754	...	0856	0909	0955	1039	1055	...	1155	1207	...	1254	...	...	1435	1524	1555	1608	1657	1738
103	Port Aventura d.	...	...	...	0720	|	...	|	0917	|	1047	|	...	|	1216	...	|	...	...	1443	|	|	1616	|	1747
105	Salou d.	...	...	...	0724	|	...	0907	0922	|	1051	|	...	1204	1219	...	1307	...	...	1447	|	1606	1620	|	1751
163	L'Aldea - Amposta d.	...	...	...	0807	|	...	0940	1006	|	1138	|	←	1237	1302	...	1335	...	...	1532	|	1633	1710	|	1836
176	Tortosa' d.	...	...	0645	0817	|	0751	|	1015	|	1149	|	1151	|	1312	...	|	...	1330	1542	|	|	1720	|	1847
202	Vinaròs d.	...	...	0720	...	|	0828	0956	...	|	→	|	1227	1253	▬	...	1350	...	1404	▬	|	1648	▬	|	▬
208	Benicarló - Peñíscola d.	...	...	0726	...	|	0833	1002	...	|	...	|	1233	1259	...	...	1355	...	1410	...	|	1654	...	|	...
268	Benicàssim d.	...	...	0804	...	|	0914	|	...	|	...	|	1310	1329	...	...	1419	1442c	1448	...	|	1719	...	|	...
280	Castelló de la Plana d.	...	0650	0815	...	0915	0922	1036	...	1117	...	1215	1319	1338	2	...	1427	1455	1457	...	1643	1727	...	1812	2
353	**València** Nord a.	...	0740	0907	...	0959	1019	1121	...	1159	...	1300	1412	1430	①–④	...	1515	1540	1553	2	1730	1821	...	1859	⑤
	València Nord **668** d.	0704	0750	...	...	1005	...	1128	...	...	...	1306	...	1435	1433	1515	1520	1550	...	1620	...	1827	...	1905	1935
409	Xátiva **668** d.	0738	|	...	...	|	...	1224	...	...	...	|	...	|	1513	1551	1607	|	...	1657	...	1906	...	|	2017
	Madrid Chamartín **668** a.	|	1138	...	...	|	...	|	...	...	...	|	...	|	|	|	|	1934	...	|	...	|	...	|	|
	Badajoz **678** a.	|	▬	...	...	|	...	2145	...	...	...	|	...	|	|	|	|	...	...	|	...	|	...	|	|
	Granada **661** a.	|	...	...	...	|	...	1930	...	...	...	|	...	|	|	|	|	...	...	|	...	|	...	|	|
	Almería **661** a.	|	...	...	...	|	...	2028	...	...	...	|	...	|	|	|	|	...	...	|	...	|	...	|	|
	Málaga **661** a.	|	...	...	...	|	...	2116	...	...	...	|	...	|	|	|	|	...	...	|	...	|	...	|	|
	Sevilla **671** a.	|	...	...	...	|	...	1955	...	...	...	|	...	|	|	|	|	...	...	|	...	|	...	|	|
495	Elda - Petrer d.	0837	...	...	...	|	...	...	...	...	...	|	...	|	1616	1648	1701	...	...	1753	...	1946	...	|	2107
536	**Alacant** a.	0903	...	...	...	1140	...	...	...	...	...	1500	...	1645	1651	1717	1724	...	...	1819	...	2014	...	2040	2132
	Alacant § d.	0908	...	...	...	...	...	...	...	...	...	...	...	...	...	...	1734	...	...	1824	...	2024	...	...	...
614	Murcia § a.	1028	2	...	...	...	...	...	...	...	...	...	...	...	...	...	1849	...	...	1935	...	2136	2	...	...
	Murcia **668** § d.	...	1208	...	...	...	...	...	...	...	...	...	...	...	...	...	1905	...	...	1944	...	2144	2155	...	...
677	**Lorca** Sutullena § a.	...	|	...	...	...	...	...	...	...	...	...	...	...	...	...	|	...	...	|	...	2250	|	...	...
679	**Cartagena** **668** § a.	...	1258	...	...	...	...	...	...	...	...	...	...	...	...	...	1952	...	...	2033	...	...	2245	...	...

	Talgo 1171 🍷	2 ⑦	Em 1181 🍷	2	Alaris 1391 🍷	2	Em 1401 🍷 ⑧p	2	Hotel 897 🍴 B	
Barcelona França d.	...	...	...	1748	...	1917	...	2046	...	...
Barcelona Passeig de Gràcia d.	...	...	...	1756	...	1925	...	2056	...	...
Barcelona Sants **652** d.	1700	...	1800	1803	1930	1933	2030	2103	2130	...
Sant Vicenç de Calders **652** d.	|	...	|	1848	|	2017	|	2147	|	...
Altafulla - Tamarit d.	|	...	|	1900	|	2029	|	2159	|	...
Tarragona **652** d.	1755	...	1854	1909	2025	2040	2123	2208	2224	...
Port Aventura d.	|	...	|	1923	|	2050	|	2219	|	...
Salou d.	1807	...	|	1928	2038	2055	|	2223	2238	...
L'Aldea - Amposta d.	1841	...	|	2017	2112	2142	|	2306	|	...
Tortosa d.	|	...	|	2028	|	2153	|	2316	|	...
Vinaròs d.	1858	1903	|	...	2129	2228	|	...	|	...
Benicarló - Peñíscola d.	1904	1908	|	...	2135	...	|	...	|	...
Benicàssim d.	1933	1948	|	...	2203	...	|	...	|	...
Castelló de la Plana d.	1941	1957	2013	...	2212	...	2241	...	2359	...
València Nord a.	2025	2052	2059	...	2303	...	2325	...	0049	...
València Nord **668** d.	2031	...	2105	...	...	...	...	...	0051	...
Xátiva **668** d.	2121	...	|	...	...	...	...	...	|	...
Granada **661** a.	|	...	|	...	...	...	...	...	0835	...
Elda - Petrer d.	2158	...	|	...	...	...	...	...	...	...
Alacant a.	2221	...	2240	...	...	...	...	...	...	...
Alacant § d.	2236	...	...	...	...	...	...	...	...	...
Murcia § a.	2343	...	...	...	...	...	...	...	...	...
Murcia **668** § d.	...	...	...	...	...	...	...	...	...	...
Lorca Sutullena § a.	...	...	...	...	...	...	...	...	...	...
Cartagena **668** § a.	...	...	...	...	...	...	...	...	...	...

	2 ①–⑥	Hotel 894 🍴 B	Em 1362 🍷 Z	2	2	Em 1282 🍷	2 ①–⑥	2	
Cartagena **668** § d.	...	...	...	...	...	...	...	...	...
Lorca Sutullena § d.	...	...	...	...	...	...	...	...	...
Murcia **668** § a.	...	...	...	...	...	...	...	...	...
Murcia § d.	...	...	...	...	...	...	0555	...	...
Alacant § a.	...	...	...	...	...	...	0718	...	...
Alacant d.	...	...	...	...	...	0655	0721	...	...
Elda - Petrer d.	...	...	...	...	...	|	0753	...	...
Granada **661** d.	...	2155	...	...	...	|	|	...	...
Xátiva **668** d.	...	|	...	...	...	|	0847	...	...
València Nord **668** a.	...	0505	...	...	...	0827	0933	...	...
València Nord d.	...	0511	0640	...	...	0835	...	...	...
Castelló de la Plana d.	...	0606	0717	...	...	0918	...	...	...
Benicàssim d.	...	|	|	...	...	|	...	...	...
Benicarló - Peñíscola d.	...	|	|	...	...	|	...	...	...
Vinaròs d.	...	|	|	0710	...	|	...	...	...
Tortosa d.	0615	|	|	0748	0918	|	...	1045	...
L'Aldea - Amposta d.	0626	|	|	0800	0930	|	...	1055	...
Salou d.	0707	0740	|	0843	1013	|	...	1142	...
Port Aventura d.	0710	|	|	0845	1023	|	...	1145	...
Tarragona **652** d.	0721	0755	0836	0856	1032	1040	...	1156	...
Altafulla - Tamarit d.	|	|	|	0904	1038	|	...	|	...
Sant Vicenç de Calders **652** d.	0743	|	|	0917	1057	|	...	1216	...
Barcelona Sants **652** a.	0835	0929	0947	1005	1146	1142	...	1305	...
Barcelona Passeig de Gràcia a.	0844	...	...	1014	1151	...	...	1315	...
Barcelona França a.	0853	...	...	1023	1200	...	...	1325	...

	Talgo 1102 🍷 L	2	Em 1112 🍷	Alaris 1084 🍷	2	Talgo 460 🍷 K	Alaris 1142 🍷	2	Em 1152 🍷 ⑧	Em 1162 🍷 ⑧	2	Arco 694 🍷 G	18096 2	Talgo 264 🍷	2	Em 1182 🍷	18096 2	2 ⑧	Em 1392 🍷 Q	Alaris 1202 🍷	2 ⑧	Talgo 1212 🍷 ⑦y	14202 2	Alaris 1184 🍷	2 ⑦
Cartagena **668** § d.	...	...	...	...	...	...	...	...	...	...	...	...	...	1300	...	...	...	...	...	...	...	...	1650	...	...
Lorca Sutullena § d.	...	...	...	...	...	0820	...	...	...	...	...	...	...	|	...	...	...	...	...	...	...	...	|	...	...
Murcia **668** § a.	...	...	...	...	...	0920	...	...	...	...	...	...	...	1344	...	...	...	...	...	...	...	...	1741	...	...
Murcia § d.	0635	...	...	...	...	0945	...	...	...	...	...	...	...	1404	...	...	...	...	...	...	...	1647	1747	...	...
Alacant § a.	0746	...	...	...	...	1059	...	...	...	...	...	...	...	1503	...	...	...	...	...	...	...	1758	1858	...	...
Alacant d.	0806	...	0925	...	...	1109	...	...	...	1420	...	...	...	1523	...	1616	...	1728	...	1820v	...	1818	1902	...	1933
Elda - Petrer d.	0831	...	|	...	...	1135	...	...	...	|	...	...	...	1547	...	|	...	1803	...	|	...	1846	1930	...	2010
Sevilla **671** d.	|	...	|	...	...	|	...	...	...	|	...	0820	...	|	...	|	...	|	...	|	...	|	|	...	|
Málaga **661** d.	|	...	|	...	...	|	...	...	...	|	...	0710	...	|	...	|	...	|	...	|	...	|	|	...	|
Almería **661** d.	|	...	|	...	...	|	...	...	...	|	...	0740	...	|	...	|	...	|	...	|	...	|	|	...	|
Granada **661** d.	|	...	|	...	...	|	...	...	...	|	...	0845	...	|	...	|	...	|	...	|	...	|	|	...	|
Badajoz **678** d.	|	...	|	...	...	|	...	...	...	|	...	0715	...	|	...	|	...	|	...	|	...	|	|	...	|
Madrid Chamartín **668** d.	|	...	|	0800	...	|	...	...	...	|	...	|	...	|	...	|	...	|	...	|	...	|	|	1740	|
Xátiva **668** d.	0916	...	|	1054	...	1213	...	...	...	|	...	1553	...	1626	...	|	...	1852	...	|	...	1933	2024	|	2102
València Nord **668** a.	0953	...	1055	1128	...	1257	...	...	...	1555	...	1650	...	1707	...	1800	...	1932	...	1950v	...	2019	2106	2125	2138
València Nord d.	1000	1035	1105	1133	...	1308	1405	...	1505	1605	...	1655	1700	1715	...	1805	...	...	1935	2005	2010	2035	...	2130	...
Castelló de la Plana d.	1043	1134	1144	1222	...	1352	1451	...	1546	1647	...	1744	1759	1801	...	1845	...	...	2016	2048	2104	2120	...	2215	...
Benicàssim d.	1050	1142	|	1229c	...	1401	1500	...	|	|	...	|	1807	1809	...	|	←	...	|	2056	2112	2129	...	...	...
Benicarló - Peñíscola d.	1119	1226	|	...	...	1426	1533	...	|	|	...	1815	1847	1831	...	|	1848	...	|	2123	2149	2157	...	...	...
Vinaròs d.	1125	1232	|	...	...	1431	1539	...	|	|	...	1820	→	1836	...	|	1855	...	|	2129	2155	2203	...	...	...
Tortosa d.	|	1307	|	...	1324	|	|	1554	|	|	1725	|	...	|	1850	|	1936	...	|	|	2230	|	...	...	...
L'Aldea - Amposta d.	1140	...	|	...	1336	1447	1555	1605	|	|	1735	1836	...	1851	1903	|	1950	...	|	2144	2241	2219	...	...	...
Salou d.	1215	...	|	...	1413	1520	1630	1645	|	|	1818	1914	...	1927	1943	|	2039	...	|	2213	...	2255	...	...	...
Port Aventura d.	|	...	|	...	1416	|	|	1647	|	|	1821	|	...	|	|	|	2041	...	|	|	...	|	...	...	...
Tarragona **652** d.	1234	...	1309	...	1428	1539	1641	1658	1710	1811	1830	1928	...	1940	1957	2010	2100	...	2137	2242	...	2306	...	...	...
Altafulla - Tamarit d.	|	...	|	...	1435	|	|	1706	|	|	1838	|	...	|	2005	|	2108	...	|	|	...	|	...	...	...
Sant Vicenç de Calders **652** d.	|	...	|	...	1447	|	|	1718	|	|	1849	1947	...	|	2017	|	2118	...	|	|	...	|	...	...	...
Barcelona Sants **652** a.	1339	...	1409	...	1535	1637	1739	1805	1809	1910	1935	2050	...	2041	2105	2113	2205	...	2237	2346	...	2358	...	...	...
Barcelona Passeig de Gràcia a.	...	...	...	...	1544	|	...	1814	...	...	1944	...	...	...	2111	...	2214	...	...	...	...	...	...	...	...
Barcelona França a.	...	...	...	...	1552	|	...	1822	...	...	1953	...	...	...	2120	...	2222	...	...	...	...	...	...	...	...
Cerbère **657** a.	...	...	...	...	...	1902	...	...	...	...	...	...	...	...	...	...	...	...	...	...	...	...	...	...	...

A – ⑧ (daily July 25 - Sept. 9).
B – ALHAMBRA – 🛏 and [1] (reclining) Barcelona - Granada and v.v.
F – GARCÍA LORCA – Daily: [2] Barcelona - Badajoz, Málaga and Sevilla. ①④⑥: [2] Barcelona - Almería. ③⑤⑦: [2] Barcelona - Granada.
G – GARCÍA LORCA – Daily: [2] Badajoz, Málaga and Sevilla - Barcelona. ③⑤⑦: [2] Almería - Barcelona. ①④⑥: [2] Granada - Barcelona.
J – MARE NOSTRUM – [12] Montpellier - Cartagena.
K – MARE NOSTRUM – [12] Lorca - Montpellier.
L – Murcia - València ①–⑥. València - Barcelona daily.

P – Daily (①–⑥ July 26 - Sept. 6; not Nov. 11, Dec. 8).
Q – Daily (⑧ July 25 - Sept. 5; not Nov. 10, Dec. 7).
Z – ①–⑥ (not Oct. 10, Dec. 7).

c – June 16 - Oct. 12.
p – Not Oct. 9, Dec. 6, 7.
v – ①–⑥.
y – Also Oct. 12, Dec. 8; not Oct. 11, Dec. 6.

§ – Additional local trains operate between these stations.

2nd class — SEVILLA and ALGECIRAS - MÁLAGA, GRANADA and ALMERÍA — 673

For trains **Sevilla** – **Málaga** and v.v. via **Córdoba**, see Table **660**

km		*R-598* 13920	13061 C	*R-598* 13900	13063		*Alta* 9367	*R-598* 13902	*R-598* 13926		*R-598* 13904	13077		*R-598* 13910 ⑤⑦	*R-598* 13922	*Alta* 9331	13065	*R-598* 13906	*R-598* 13924	*Alta* 9234	13079 D	*R-598* 13908		
0	**Sevilla** ¶ d.	0700	...	0735	...	...	...	1105	1150	...	1300	...	...	1510	1605	...	...	1705	1740	...	...	2010	...	...
15	Dos Hermanas ¶ d.	0713u	...	0749u	...	...	...	1119u	1203u	...	1314u	...	...	1524u	1618u	...	...	1719u	1753u	...	...	2024u	...	...
	Algeciras d.	|	...	|	0705	...	0830	|	|	...	|	1215	...	|	|	1515	1550	|	|	...	1850	|	...	...
	San Roque - La Línea d.	|	...	|	0719	...	|	|	|	...	|	1229	...	|	|	|	1603	|	|	...	1903	|	...	...
	Ronda d.	|	0712	|	0857	...	1000	|	|	...	|	1411	...	|	|	1646	1735	|	|	...	2047	|	...	...
	Madrid Pta de Atocha **660** d.	|	|	|	|	...	1357	|	|	...	|	|	...	|	|	2050	|	|	|	1705	...	|	...	...
167	Bobadilla **661** d.	|	0800	0913	0948	...	...	1247	|	...	1439	1508	...	1646	|	...	1835	1844	|	|	...	2149	...	...
236	**Málaga** M. Zambrano **661** a.	|	0909	1014	|	...	...	1341	|	...	1539	|	...	1740	|	...	|	1939	|	|	...	2246	...	...
183	Antequera d.	0843	...	...	1004	...	...	...	1337	...	...	1524	...	...	1747	...	1848	...	1943	2014	...	...	...	...
290	**Granada** a.	1000	...	...	1133	...	...	...	1459	...	...	1649	...	...	1909	...	2017	...	2102	2141	...	...	...	...
290	**Granada** **661** d.	1004	...	...	...	...	...	...	1503	...	...	...	...	...	1913	...	...	...	2106	...	...	...	...	...
372	Guadix **661** d.	1107	...	...	...	...	...	...	1600	...	...	...	...	...	2016	...	...	...	2203	...	...	...	...	...
471	**Almería** **661** a.	1221	...	...	...	...	...	...	1717	...	...	...	...	...	2124	...	...	...	2311	...	...	...	...	...

km		13074 D	*R-598* 13901	13064	*R-598* 13941		*Alta* 9219	*R-598* 13903	*Alta* 9366	*R-598* 13943		*R-598* 13905	13076		*R-598* 13907	*R-598* 13945	*Alta* 9330	13062	13057 C	*R-598* 13909 ⑤⑦	*R-598* 13911	*R-598* 13947		
0	**Almería** **661** d.	...	...	...	0600	...	...	...	...	0925	...	...	...	...	...	1420	...	...	...	...	...	1805	...	...
99	Guadix **661** d.	...	...	...	0717	...	...	...	...	1037	...	...	...	...	...	1530	...	...	...	...	...	1923	...	...
181	**Granada** **661** a.	...	...	...	0814	...	...	...	...	1129	...	...	...	...	...	1627	...	...	...	...	...	2019	...	...
181	**Granada** d.	...	...	0715	0818	...	0945	...	...	1133	...	...	1355	...	...	1632	...	1720	...	...	...	2023	...	...
288	Antequera d.	...	...	0841	0942	...	1108	...	...	1247	...	...	1520	...	...	1752	...	1850	...	...	...	2145	...	...
	Málaga M. Zambrano **661** d.	...	0740	|	|	...	|	1040	...	|	...	1405	|	...	1635	|	...	|	1843	1905	2013	|	...	...
304	Bobadilla **661** d.	...	0834	0857	|	...	|	1132	...	|	...	1455	1538	...	1725	|	...	1902	1948	1956	2106	|	...	...
	Madrid Pta de Atocha **660** d.	...	|	|	|	...	1439	|	0840	|	...	|	|	...	|	|	1505	|	|	|	|	|	...	...
376	Ronda d.	0750	|	0958	|	...	...	|	1228	|	...	|	1636	...	|	|	1902	1959	2042	|	|	|	...	...
468	San Roque - La Línea d.	0924	|	1130	|	...	...	|	|	|	...	|	1820	...	|	|	|	2128	...	|	|	|	...	...
480	**Algeciras** a.	0939	|	1146	|	...	...	|	1405	|	...	|	1836	...	|	|	2033	2141	...	|	|	|	...	...
456	Dos Hermanas ¶ a.	...	0956s	...	1109s	...	...	1255s	...	1413s	...	1621s	...	...	1851s	1930s	...	...	...	2120s	2231s	2316s	...	...
471	**Sevilla** ¶ a.	...	1010	...	1127	...	...	1310	...	1430	...	1639	...	...	1907	1945	...	...	...	2137	2245	2332	...	...

C – ①-⑥ (not Aug. 15, Oct. 12, Dec. 8). **s** – Stops to set down only. **u** – Stops to pick up only. ¶ – Frequent suburban services run Sevilla - Dos Hermanas and v.v.
D – ①-⑤ (not Aug. 15, Oct. 12, Dec. 8).

SFM 2nd class — PALMA DE MALLORCA - INCA - SA POBLA and MANACOR — 674

km			Ⓐ	Ⓐ	Ⓐ	Ⓐ	Ⓐ	Ⓐ	and at	Ⓐ	Ⓐ	Ⓐ	Ⓐ			©	©	©	©	and at	©	©	©	©	
									the same											the same					
0	**Palma** d.	Ⓐ	0544	0609	0644	0709	0744	0809	minutes	2044	2109	2124	2209	...	©	0604	0634	0704	0734	minutes	2034	2104	2134	2204	...
7	Marratxi d.		0559	0619	0659	0719	0759	0819	past	2059	2119	2139	2219	...		0619	0649	0719	0749	past	2049	2119	2149	2219	...
29	**Inca** d.		0624	0644	0724	0744	0824	0844	each	2124	2144	2204	2244	...		0644	0714	0744	0814	each	2114	2144	2214	2244	...
***	sa Pobla a.		0641	|	0741	|	0841	|	hour	2141	|	2221	|	...		|	0731	|	0831	hour	2131	|	2231	|	...
64	**Manacor** a.		...	0715	...	0815	...	0915	until	...	2215	...	2315	...		0715	...	0815	...	until	...	2215	...	2315	...

		Ⓐ	Ⓐ	Ⓐ	Ⓐ	Ⓐ	and at	Ⓐ	Ⓐ	Ⓐ	Ⓐ	Ⓐ			©	©	©	©	©	and at	©	©	©	©	©
							the same													the same					
Manacor d.	Ⓐ	...	0622	...	0722	...	minutes	2022	...	2122	...	2222	...	©	0622	0722	...	0822	...	minutes	2022	...	2122	...	2222
sa Pobla d.		...	|	0656	|	0756	past	|	2056	|	2156	|	...		|	|	0806	|	0906	past	|	2106	|	2206	|
Inca d.		0634	0654	0714	0754	0814	each	2054	2114	2154	2214	2254	...		0654	0754	0824	0854	0924	each	2054	2124	2154	2224	2254
Marratxi d.		0658	0718	0738	0818	0838	hour	2118	2138	2218	2238	2318	...		0718	0818	0848	0918	0948	hour	2118	2148	2218	2248	2318
Palma a.		0713	0728	0753	0828	0853	until	2128	2153	2228	2253	2328	...		0733	0833	0903	0933	1003	until	2133	2203	2233	2303	2333

Operator: Serveis Ferroviaris de Mallorca (SFM) ✆ +34 971 752 245. *** – *19 km* Inca - sa Pobla.

PALMA DE MALLORCA - SÓLLER
0800, 1010, 1050, 1215, 1330, 1510, 1930.
28 km Journey time: 55 minutes.

SÓLLER - PALMA DE MALLORCA
0700, 0910, 1050, 1215, 1400, 1830, 1900 ©.
Operator: Ferrocarril de Sóller (FS) ✆ +34 971 752 051.

A connecting tram service operates **Sóller** - **Port de Sóller**.
5 km. Journey time: 15–20 minutes.
From Sóller: 0700, 0800, 0900, 1000, 1100, 1200, 1300, 1400, 1500, 1600, 1700, 1800, 1900, 2020.
From Port de Sóller: 0730, 0825, 0930, 1025, 1130, 1230, 1325, 1430, 1530, 1630, 1700, 1730, 1800, 1830, 1930, 2040.

MÁLAGA and ALGECIRAS - LA LÍNEA (for Gibraltar) — 675

There are no cross-border bus services: passengers to/from Gibraltar must cross the frontier on foot (walking-time about 5 minutes) and transfer to/from Gibraltar local bus services

MÁLAGA bus stn – **LA LÍNEA** bus station (for **Gibraltar**)
From Málaga: 0700, 1015 ▽, 1400, 1715, 1915 ⑦.
From La Línea: 0715, 1030, 1415 ▽, 1745, 2045 ⑦.
Journey time: 3 hours. Operator: Automóviles Portillo, Málaga ✆ +34 902 143 144.
▽ – Journey operated by Alsina Graells (see Table **664** for contact details).

ALGECIRAS bus station - **LA LÍNEA** bus station (for **Gibraltar**)
From Algeciras: Ⓐ: every 30 mins 0700–2130, also 2230.
⑥: every 45 mins 0700–2115, also 2230. †: every 45 mins 0800–2130, also 2230.
From La Línea: Ⓐ: 0700 then every 30 mins 0745–2215, also 2315.
⑥: every 45 mins 0700–2200, also 2315. †: 0700 then every 45 mins 0845–2215, also 2315.
Journey time: 45 mins. Operator: Transportes Generales Comes SA, Algeciras ✆ +34 956 653 456.

DAMAS ☆ — SEVILLA - AYAMONTE - FARO - LAGOS — 676

		⚒	©	Ⓐ	Ⓐ	Ⓐ	⑥	Ⓑ		Ⓐ	⚒	†	†	⚒	
Sevilla Plaza de Armas d.	*0730*	0930	1100	1130	...	1230	*1330*	*1330*	1530	*1630*	*1730*	*1800*	1900	1930	...
Huelva d.	0900	1100	1230	1300	1345	1400	1515	1530	1700	1800	1930	1930	2030	2100	...
Ayamonte a.	1000	1200	1330	1400	1445	1500	1615	1630	1800	1900	2030	2030	2130	2200	...

	Ⓐ		Ⓐ	©	Ⓐ	⚒		⚒	⑥	Ⓐ	†	Ⓐ			
Ayamonte d.	*0715*	*0845*	0930	0945	1030	...	*1145*	*1400*	1500	1530	1615	1630	1730	...	1930
Huelva d.	0830	1000	1100	1100	1130	1200	1300	1500	1600	1630	1730	1730	1830	1900	2030
Sevilla Plaza de Armas a.	1000	1130	1230	1230	...	1330	1430	1630	1730	1800	1900	1900	...	2030	2200

Ayamonte - Vila Real de Santo António Guadiana
Journey time: 10 minutes ◇ *Subject to alteration*
July 1 - Sept. 30: from Ayamonte (ES) every 30 mins 0930 - 2100; from Vila Real (PT) every 30 mins 0800 - 2000.
Oct. 1 - June 30: from Ayamonte (ES) every 40 mins 0940 ⚒ - 1900 ⚒ (also 2000 ⚒); on ⑦ hourly 1030 - 1830.
from Vila Real (PT) every 40 mins 0900 ⚒ - 1900 ⚒;
on ⑦ hourly 1000 - 1600, then 1700 or 1730.

INTERNATIONAL bus SERVICE Joint EVA △ / DAMAS ☆ service *for international journeys only* No service Dec. 25, Jan. 1.

Sevilla, Plaza de Armas d.	Summer	0630	0800	1330	1615	Winter	0730	1615
Huelva d.	service	0745	0915	1445	1730	service	0845	1730
Ayamonte ES d.		|	1000	|	1815		0930	1815
Vila Real de Santo António PT a.	June 2 -	|	0925	|	1740	from	0855	1740
Faro, Av. da República a.	Sept. 15	0820	1040	1520	1855	Sept. 16	1010	1855
Albufeira, Alto dos Caliços a.	2008	0900	1125	1600	1940	2008	1055	1940
Portimão, Largo do Dique a.	→	|	1200	|	2015	→	1130	2015
Lagos, Rossio de S. João a.		0945	1230	1645	2045		1200	2045

Lagos, Rossio de S. João d.	Summer	0615	0730	1230	1445	Winter	0630	1345
Portimão, Largo do Dique d.	service	|	0800	|	1515	service	0700	1415
Albufeira, Alto dos Caliços d.		0700	0835	1315	1550		0735	1450
Faro, Av. da República d.	June 2 -	0740	0920	1355	1635	from	0820	1535
Vila Real de Santo António PT d.	Sept. 15	|	1035	|	1750	Sept. 16	0935	1650
Ayamonte ES a.	2008	|	1200	|	1915	2008	1100	1815
Huelva a.	→	1015	1245	1630	2000	→	1145	1905
Sevilla, Plaza de Armas a.		1130	1400	1745	2115		1300	2015

☆ – DAMAS, Huelva ✆ +34 959 256 900. www.damas-sa.es
△ – EVA, Faro ✆ +351 289 899 700. www.eva-bus.com
◇ – Empresa de Transportes do Rio Guadiana, Vila Real ✆ +351 281 543 152. Services after 1700 in winter are subject to modification.

ES – Spain (Central European Time). PT – Portugal (West European Time).
Sevilla Plaza de Armas bus station is ± 2 km from Sevilla (Santa Justa) rail station.
Huelva bus station is ± 1 km from the rail station.
Ayamonte bus station is ± 1.5 km from the ferry terminal.

677 MADRID - CÁCERES - BADAJOZ

km																									
			R-598			*R-598*			*TRD*	*R-598*							*TRD*		*Talgo*		*TRD*			*Hotel*	
			17904	**18772**		**17902**	**18774**		**17014**	**17900**				**17804**		**17702**	**17016**	**17824**	**194**	**17704**	**17018**	**17706**	**17708**	**332**	
		2	2	2f	2	2	2p	2	2	2	2	2	2	2	2	2	2	2	🍷	2	2	2	2	R ✕	
		①⑥	①–⑤	①–⑤	①–⑤	⑥⑦	⑥⑦	⑥⑦			**P**	⑦					**B**	⑤⑦		①–⑤	Ⓑ	①–⑥	⑦	**A**	
0	**Madrid** Puerta de Atocha d.	...	...	...	...	...	...	...	0740	0955	...	...	...	1328	...	1430	1525	1525	1640	1755	1907	2007	2050	2225	...
138	Talavera de la Reina d.	...	...	...	...	...	...	...	0902	1121	...	...	...	|	...	1605	1653	1706	1803	1925	2034	2135	2222	0008	...
270	Plasencia a.	...	...	...	...	...	...	...	1022	1242	...	...	...	◧	...	...	1820	1838	|	...	2148	...	...	|	...
	Plasencia d.	...	0538	...	...	0720	...	...	1025	1245	...	...	...	|	...	...	...	...	|	...	2151	...	...	|	...
335	**Cáceres** d.	...	0644	...	...	0830	...	...	1141	1350	...	...	1900	|	...	...	...	...	2004	...	2301	...	...	0151	...
401	Mérida a.	...	0751	...	...	0938	...	...	1245	1458	...	...	2006	2012	...	...	...	...	2101	...	0006	...	...	...	...
401	Mérida **678** d.	...	0755	0800	0900	0945	0945	1100	...	1503	1510	...	...	2024	2042	...	...	...	2113	...	...	...	...	...	...
461	**Badajoz** **678** a.	...	0840	|	0946	1025	|	1146	...	1540	|	...	...	2115	|	...	...	...	2153	...	...	...	...	...	...
467	Zafra d.	0550	...	0901	...	...	1046	...	...	...	1604	...	...	...	2137	...	...	...	...	...	...	...	...	...	...
641	Sevilla a.	|	...	1221	...	...	1404	...	...	...	...	...	...	...	...	...	...	...	...	...	...	...	...	...	...
513	Fregenal de la Sierra d.	0641	...	...	...	...	...	...	...	...	...	1440	...	...	...	...	...	...	...	...	...	...	...	...	...
652	Huelva a.	0935	...	...	...	...	...	...	...	...	...	1735	...	...	...	...	...	...	...	...	...	...	...	...	...

	Hotel		*TRD*	*TRD*			*Talgo*								*TRD*			*R-598*		*TRD*			*R-598*		
	335	**17705**	**17021**	**17023**			**197**						**17707**	**17801**	**17027**	**17801**		**17907**		**17025**	**17817**	**18779**	**17909**		
	R ✕	2	2	2	2	2	🍷	2	2	2	2	2	2	2	2	2	2	2		2	2	2	2	2	
	A		①–⑤	⑥	①–⑤	①–⑤		①–⑤	⑥⑦	⑥⑦	⑥⑦	⑦					**P**			**B**	⑤⑦			⑤⑦	
Huelva d.	...	...	...	...	...	...	...	...	...	...	...	0950	...	...	...	...	...	...	...	...	...	...	...	1900	...
Fregenal de la Sierra d.	...	...	...	...	...	...	...	...	...	...	...	1245	...	...	...	...	...	...	...	...	...	...	...	2158	...
Sevilla d.	...	...	...	...	...	...	...	...	...	...	...	...	...	...	...	...	...	...	...	...	...	1550	...	|	...
Zafra d.	...	...	...	...	0655	...	...	...	0845	...	...	...	...	...	...	...	1402	...	...	...	...	1913	...	2246	...
Badajoz **678** d.	...	...	...	...	|	0700	0735	...	|	0855	...	...	...	1240	...	...	|	1420	...	...	...	|	1958	...	...
Mérida **678** a.	...	...	...	...	0745	0748	0808	...	0935	0943	...	...	...	1326	...	←	1452	1456	...	...	...	2008	2037	...	...
Mérida d.	...	...	0545	0620	...	...	0820	0905	...	...	0950	...	...	1328	1335	1328	...	1500	...	...	...	...	2045	...	...
Cáceres d.	0508	...	0646	0721	...	...	0925	1010	...	...	1055	...	...	→	1436	|	...	1602	...	...	...	...	2155	...	...
Plasencia a.	|	...	0757	0835	...	...	|	...	...	...	...	...	...	...	1543	|	...	1702	...	...	...	...	2315	...	...
Plasencia d.	|	...	0800	0850	...	...	|	...	...	...	...	...	...	...	1545	◧	...	1705	...	1911	1944	...	...	...	...
Talavera de la Reina d.	0714	0905	0922	1018	...	...	1125	...	...	...	...	...	1430	...	1710	|	...	1820	...	2031	2115	...	...	...	...
Madrid Puerta de Atocha a.	0858	1038	1055	1200	...	...	1251	...	...	...	...	...	1600	...	1845	2006	...	1956	...	2212	2258	...	...	...	...

A – LUSITANIA *Hotel Train* – 🛏 *Gran Clase* (1, 2 berths), 🛏 *Preferente* (1, 2 berths), 🛏 1, 2 cl. (T4), (12) and ✕ Madrid - Cáceres - Lisboa and v.v. Special fares apply.
B – ①②③④⑥.
P – From / to Puertollano (Table **678**).
f – Not Aug. 15, Oct. 12, Dec. 8.
p – Also Aug. 15, Oct. 12, Dec. 8.
◧ – Via Ciudad Real (Table **678**).

678 ALCÁZAR DE SAN JUAN - BADAJOZ

km										
								Arco		**18027**
							17804	**697**	**18083**	**V**
		2	2	2	2	2	2	2	2	2
		①–⑤		⑥	①–⑥	**Z**		**G**	**C**	⑦
	Madrid Pta de Atocha **661/8** d.	...	...	...	...	...	1328	...	...	...
	Albacete **661** d.	...	...	...	...	...	|	1337	1844	1958
0	**Alcázar de San Juan** **661** d.	...	0750	...	1240	...	1501	1510	2007	2128
50	Manzanares **661** d.	...	0819	...	1309	...	1528	1540	2037	2157
114	Ciudad Real **660** d.	...	0857	...	1347	...	1612	1637	2115	2240
153	Puertollano **660** d.	...	...	...	...	1132	1647	1718	...	...
265	Cabeza del Buey d.	0610	...	0740	...	1316	1831	1911	...	...
392	Mérida **677** a.	0750	...	0924	...	1457	2012	2047	...	...
451	**Badajoz** **677** a.	*0840*	...	*1025*	...	*1540*	2115	2145	...	...

	18024		*Arco*					
	V	**18081**	**694**	**17041**	**17801**			
	2	2	2	2	2	2	2	2
	①	**C**	**G**			**Z**	Ⓑ	Ⓑ
Badajoz **677** d.	...	...	0715	...	1240	*1420*	...	...
Mérida **677** d.	...	...	0756	...	1328	1506	...	2050
Cabeza del Buey d.	...	...	0927	...	1503	1645	...	2233
Puertollano **660** d.	...	...	1106	...	1643	1841	...	...
Ciudad Real **660** d.	0551	0918	1157	1441	1726	...	2150	...
Manzanares **661** d.	0629	0958	1244	1520	1809	...	2227	...
Alcázar de San Juan **661** a.	0657	1029	1315	1549	1835	...	2257	...
Albacete **661** a.	0819	1144	1452	|	|	...	...	...
Madrid Pta de Atocha **661/8** a.	...	...	...	1728r	2006	...	...	...

C – COSTA DE LA MANCHA – (2) Alacant - Ciudad Real and v.v.
G – GARCÍA LORCA – (2) Barcelona - Badajoz and v.v.
V – (2) València - Ciudad Real and v.v.
Z – To / from Zafra (Table **677**).
r – Madrid Atocha Cercanías.

679 MADRID - TOLEDO, SEGOVIA and SALAMANCA

2nd class

km		*AV*	*AV*	*AV*	*AV*	*AV*	*AV*	*AV*	*AV*	*AV*	*AV*	*AV*	*AV*
		8062	**8072**	**8292**	**8302**	**8102**	**8322**	**8132**	**8152**	**8172**	**8182**	**8192**	**8212**
		A	**A**			**D**					**B**		
0	**Madrid** △ d.	0650	0750	0920	1020	1050	1220	1350	1550	1750	1850	1950	2150
75	**Toledo** a.	0720	0820	0950	1050	1120	1250	1420	1620	1820	1920	2020	2220

	AV	*AV*	*AV*	*AV*	*AV*	*AV*	*AV*	*AV*	*AV*	*AV*	*AV*	*AV*
	8273	**8073**	**8283**	**8093**	**8103**	**8123**	**8133**	**8153**	**8173**	**8183**	**8193**	**8213**
	A	**B**	**C**							**D**		
Toledo d.	0650	0730	0800	0930	1030	1230	1330	1530	1730	1830	1930	2130
Madrid △ a.	0720	0800	0832	1000	1100	1300	1400	1600	1800	1900	2000	2200

km		*AV*	*AV*	*AV*		*AV*	*AV*	*AV*	*AV*		*AV*	
		8089	**8109**	**8129**		**8159**	**8169**	**8179**	**8199**		**8219**	
		A										
0	**Madrid** Chamartín d.	0830	1030	1200	...	1530	1630	1730	1915	...	2100	...
68	**Segovia** Guiomar ¶ a.	0900	1100	1231	...	1600	1701	1800	1946	...	2130	...

	AV	*AV*	*AV*	*AV*	*AV*		*AV*	*AV*	*AV*	*AV*	*AV*
	8078	**8278**	**8088**	**8098**	**8108**		**8158**	**8168**	**8188**	**8198**	**8218**
	A	**A**	**A**	**D**	**D**						
Segovia Guiomar ¶ d.	0700	0723	0800	0905	0958	...	1525	1608	1820	2013	2058
Madrid Chamartín a.	0732	0755	0832	0937	1030	...	1557	1640	1852	2045	2130

km		①–⑤							①–⑤		
0	**Madrid** Atocha C. d.	0733	...	1001	1202	1401	1602	1802	2002	...	...
8	Madrid Chamartín d.	0747	...	1016	1216	1415	1616	1816	2016	...	...
108	**Segovia** a.	0935	...	1204	1402	1603	1757	2003	2213	...	...

	①–⑤							①–⑤		
Segovia d.	0755	...	1055	1255	1455	1650	1855	2055	...	...
Madrid Chamartín a.	0938	...	1237	1437	1637	1837	2037	2236	...	...
Madrid Atocha C. a.	0951	...	1250	1450	1650	1850	2050	2249	...	...

km			*TRD*	*TRD*	*TRD*	*TRD*	*TRD*	*TRD*	*TRD*	*TRD*	
			18901	**18903**	**18905**	**18907**	**18913**	**18919**	**18909**	**18911**	
							①–⑥	⑤⑥⑦			
0	**Madrid** Chamartín ◧ d.	...	0845	1105	1340	1545	1707	1843	2000	2113	...
122	Ávila ◧ d.	0710	1015	1238	1514	1715	1840	2014	2132	2245	...
233	**Salamanca** a.	0841	1122	1349	1625	1825	1951	2129	2237	2350	...

	TRD	*TRD*	*TRD*	*TRD*	*TRD*	*TRD*		*TRD*	*TRD*	
	18910	**18900**	**18912**	**18902**	**18918**	**18904**		**18906**	**18908**	
	①–⑥				⑤⑥⑦					
Salamanca d.	0545	0747	0958	1225	1455	1542	1640	1800	2002	...
Ávila ◧ d.	0652	0855	1112	1335	1612	1650	1815	1910	2113	...
Madrid Chamartín ◧ a.	0830	1028	1244	1509	1721	1822	...	2045	2245	...

A – ①–⑤ (not Oct. 12, Nov. 9, Dec. 7, 8).
B – ①–⑤ (not Aug. 3 – 28, Oct. 12, Nov. 9, Dec. 8).
C – ①–⑤ (not Oct. 12, Nov. 9, Dec. 8).
D – ⑥⑦ (Also Oct. 12, Nov. 9, Dec. 7, 8).
△ – Madrid Puerta de Atocha.
◧ – See also Tables **680**, **681**, **689**.
¶ – 4 km from city centre. For long-distance high-speed services calling at Segovia Guiomar, see Table **663**.
AV – ***Avant*** high-speed services. Single class. 🍷.

MADRID - ZAMORA - VIGO, PONTEVEDRA and A CORUÑA — 680

For services to / from A Coruña via León, see Table **682**

km		2 ①-⑥	R-598 12412 2 ①-⑤	Hotel 851 ✕ C	R-598 12414 2	Hotel 851 ✕ D	R-598 12022 2	2	2 ①-⑤	R-598 12418 2	2	2 ①-⑤	2 ①-⑤	Hotel 922 🍷 G	2 ⑥	2 ⑥⑦	R-598 12422 2 ①-⑤	R-598 12424 2	2	R-598 12428 2	2 ①-⑤	2	R-598 12430 2 ①-⑤	
0	**Madrid** Chamartín ... **681 689** d.	...	...	2230	...	2230	...	...	...	...	...	...	...	...	...	...	...	...	...	...	...	...	...	...
121	Ávila ... **681 689** d.	...	...	0003	...	0003	...	...	...	...	...	...	...	...	...	...	...	...	...	...	...	...	...	...
	Irún **689** ... d.	...	...	|	...	|	...	...	...	...	...	...	...	...	...	...	...	...	...	...	...	...	...	...
	Barcelona Sants **652** ... d.	...	...	|	...	|	...	...	...	...	...	...	...	2050	...	...	...	...	...	...	...	...	...	...
	Miranda de Ebro **681 689** ... d.	...	...	|	...	|	...	...	...	...	...	...	...	|	...	...	...	...	...	...	...	...	...	...
207*	Medina del Campo... **681 689** d.	...	...	0053	...	0053	...	...	...	...	...	...	...	|	...	...	...	...	...	...	...	...	...	...
297	**Zamora** ... d.	...	...	0149	...	0149	...	...	...	...	...	...	...	|	...	...	...	...	...	...	...	...	...	...
404	Puebla de Sanabria ... d.	...	...	0314	...	0314	...	...	...	...	...	0635	...	|	0745	...	...	...	...	...	...	...	...	...
547	**Ourense** ... d.	...	...	0520	...	0540	0657	...	...	...	...	0827	0841	0920	0933	0947	...	...	...	...	...	1430	...	...
641	Guillarei ... d.	...	...	|	...	0655	|	...	...	...	...	...	1015	1048	...	1120	...	...	...	...	...	|	...	...
	Vigo ... d.	...	0535	|	0630	|	|	0705	0803	0855	0940	...	|	|	...	|	1040	1215	1305	1400	1420	|	1520	...
666	Redondela ... d.	...	0545	|	|	0720	|	0720	0816	|	0953	...	1035	1109	...	1140	|	1225	1319	|	1431	|	|	...
678	**Vigo** ... a.	...	|	|	|	0733s	|	|	|	|	|	...	1051	1120	...	1151	|	|	|	|	|	|	|	...
684	**Pontevedra** ... d.	...	0606	|	0656	0825	|	0744	0832	0927	1017	...	...	...	...	...	1108	1245	1343	1427	1450	|	1550	...
717	Vilagarcía de Arousa ... d.	...	0626	|	0718	...	|	0811	...	0948	1041	...	...	...	...	...	1128	1306	1406	1447	...	|	1610	...
677	Santiago de Compostela ... d.	0635	0705	0723	0756	...	0830	0901	...	1021	1124	...	...	...	...	...	1204	1340	1448	1520	...	1618	1643	...
751	**A Coruña** ... a.	0731	0749	0819	0845	...	0915	1007	...	1106	1218	...	...	...	...	...	1246	1428	1547	1603	...	...	1728	...

	2	2	R-598 12434 2	R-598 12436 2	Arco 283 2 B	Arco 283 2 A	2	2 ⑦	2 ①-⑤	R-598 12440 2	Talgo 85 🍷 K⑦	Talgo 151 🍷 ①-⑥	2 ⑦	R-598 12442 2	Talgo 85 🍷 H⑦	Talgo 151 🍷 ①-⑥	2	2	Alvia 623 🍷 X	2 ①-⑤	2 ⑦	2	2 J	
Madrid Chamartín ... **681 689** d.	...	...	...	...	...	...	...	...	...	...	1355	1420	...	...	1355	1420	...	...	...	...	...	1430	...	...
Ávila ... **681 689** d.	...	...	...	...	...	...	...	...	...	...	1526	|	...	...	1526	|	...	...	...	...	...	1602	...	...
Irún **689** ... d.	...	...	...	...	...	0845	...	...	...	...	|	◧	...	...	|	◧	...	...	...	...	...	|	...	...
Barcelona Sants **652** ... d.	...	...	...	...	...	|	...	...	...	...	|	|	...	...	|	|	...	...	0920	...	...	|	...	...
Miranda de Ebro **681 689** ... d.	...	...	...	...	1118	1118	...	...	...	...	|	|	...	...	|	|	...	...	1422	...	...	|	...	...
Medina del Campo... **681 689** d.	...	...	...	...	|	|	...	...	...	...	1619	1600	...	...	1619	1600	...	...	|	...	...	1646	1806	...
Zamora ... d.	...	...	...	...	|	|	...	...	...	...	1707	1649	...	...	1707	1649	...	...	|	...	...	...	1907	...
Puebla de Sanabria ... d.	...	...	...	...	|	|	...	1750	...	...	1820	1800	...	...	1820	1800	...	...	|	...	...	...	2029	...
Ourense ... d.	...	1527	...	...	1818	1830	...	1945	...	...	2003	1945	...	...	2009	2000	2022	2039	2113	...	...	...	...	...
Guillarei ... d.	...	1650	...	...	1938	|	...	...	...	...	|	|	...	...	2120	2112	2145	|	|	...	...	...	...	...
Vigo ... d.	1545	|	1705	1815	|	|	1845	...	1930	1955	|	|	2025	2100	|	|	|	|	|	2213	2230	...	...	...
Redondela ... d.	1558	1711	|	|	1959	|	1901	...	1942	|	|	|	2037	|	2140s	2131s	2208	|	2252	2226	2245	...	...	...
Vigo ... a.	|	1724	|	|	2010	|	|	...	|	|	|	|	|	|	2154	2144	2224	|	2305	|	|	...	...	...
Pontevedra ... d.	1619	...	1732	1846	...	|	1923	...	1959	2023	|	|	2058	2126	2243	2226	...	|	...	2247	2307	...	...	...
Vilagarcía de Arousa ... d.	1645	...	1752	1906	...	|	1946	...	...	2043	|	|	2121	2147	...	...	...	|	...	2311	2328	...	...	...
Santiago de Compostela ... d.	1730	...	1826	1938	...	2010	2030	...	...	2117	2132	2123	2201	2227	...	...	...	2231	...	2352	0007	...	...	...
A Coruña ... a.	1829	...	1909	2022	...	2108	2129	...	...	2205	2226	2208	...	2310	...	...	...	...	...	...	...	...	...	...

km		2 J	18010 2 ①-⑥	2 ①-⑥	R-598 12411 2 ①-⑤	2 ①-⑤	2	Alvia 620 🍷 Y	R-598 12413 2	2 ①-⑤	2 ⑥	R-598 12417 2	Arco 280 2 A	Arco 280 2 B	Talgo 74 🍷 H⑥	R-598 12419 2 ①-⑤	Talgo 74 🍷 K⑥	2	R-598 12423 2 ①-⑤	2 ⑥⑦	Talgo 152 🍷 Ⓑ	R-598 12425 2	2	Talgo 152 🍷 Ⓑ
0	**A Coruña** ... d.	...	...	...	0540	...	...	...	0655	...	...	0750	0800	...	...	0822	0900	0927	1030	...	...	1150	1225	1310
74	Santiago de Compostela ... d.	...	...	0545	0626	0645	...	...	0738	...	0807	0837	0904	...	...	0908	0954	1021	1114	...	...	1234	1318	1357
116	Vilagarcía de Arousa ... d.	...	...	0637	0702	|	...	...	0812	...	|	0907	|	...	...	0937	|	1103	1144	...	...	1303	1400	|
149	**Pontevedra** ... d.	...	...	0655	0722	|	...	...	0832	0845	|	0927	|	...	0845	0956	|	1131	1203	...	1250	1323	1426	|
	Vigo ... d.	...	...	|	|	|	0640	0755	|	|	|	|	|	0910	0930	|	|	|	|	...	1337	|	|	|
167	Redondela ... d.	...	...	0720	0741	|	0652	0806	0853	0907	|	|	|	0921	0941	|	|	1155	|	...	1349	|	1452	|
179	**Vigo** ... a.	...	...	0737	0752	|	|	|	0905	0921	|	0958	|	|	|	1029	|	·1210	1231	...	|	1354	1505	|
192	Guillarei ... d.	...	...	...	...	|	0714	|	...	...	|	...	|	0939	0959	...	|	...	...	...	1408	...	...	|
	Ourense ... d.	...	...	...	...	0836	0841	0927	...	...	0957	...	1100	1100	1138	...	1138	...	...	1510	1546	...	...	1546
	Puebla de Sanabria ... d.	0715	...	...	...	...	...	|	...	...	...	...	|	|	1320	...	1320	...	...	1718	1728	...	...	1728
	Zamora ... d.	0832	...	...	...	...	...	|	...	...	...	...	|	|	1430	...	1430	...	...	...	1847	...	...	1847
	Medina del Campo... **681 689** d.	0927	1040	...	...	...	...	|	...	...	...	...	|	|	1533	...	1533	...	...	...	1938	...	...	1938
	Miranda de Ebro **681 689** ... a.	...	|	...	...	...	...	1555	...	...	...	...	1740	1740	|	...	|	...	...	...	|	...	...	|
	Barcelona Sants **652** ... a.	...	|	...	...	...	...	2115	...	...	...	...	|	...	|	...	|	...	...	...	|	...	...	|
	Hendaye **689** ... a.	...	|	...	...	...	...	...	...	...	...	...	2035	...	|	...	|	...	...	...	◧	...	...	◧
	Ávila ... **681 689** d.	...	1125	...	...	...	...	...	...	...	...	...	...	...	1620	...	1620	...	...	...	|	...	...	|
	Madrid Chamartín ... **681 689** a.	...	1309	...	...	...	...	...	...	...	...	...	...	...	1752	...	1752	...	...	...	2108	...	...	2108

	2 ①-⑤	R-598 12429 2	2	2	2 ①-④	R-598 12431 2	2	Hotel 921 🍷 G	2 ⑤	R-598 12435 2	2	R-598 12437 2	2 ①-⑤	2	R-598 12023 2		Hotel 852 ✕ D	2	R-598 12441 2	Hotel 852 ✕ C	2 ①-⑤	2 ⑦		
A Coruña ... d.	...	1355	...	...	...	1445	1523	...	...	1655	...	1750	...	1850	1945	...	...	2000	2050	2145	2210	2230	...	...
Santiago de Compostela ... d.	...	1439	...	1455	...	1528	1621	...	...	1738	...	1833	...	1944	2032	...	...	2057	2133	2235	2302	2327	...	...
Vilagarcía de Arousa ... d.	...	1513	...	|	...	1559	1707	...	...	1808	...	1902	...	2030	|	...	...	2141	2205	|	...	...	...	...
Pontevedra ... d.	1510	1532	...	|	...	1619	1731	...	...	1828	...	1923	2025	2100	|	...	2130	2205	2226	|	...	...	...	...
Vigo ... d.	|	|	1447	|	...	|	|	1823	...	|	2012	|	|	|	|	...	2220u	|	|	|	...	...	...	...
Redondela ... d.	1527	|	1459	|	...	|	1753	1834	...	|	2024	|	2043	2127	|	...	2236	2227	|	|	...	...	...	...
Vigo ... a.	1540	1603	|	|	...	1648	1805	|	...	1859	|	1954	2056	2140	|	...	|	2242	2259	|	...	...	...	...
Guillarei ... d.	...	...	1521	|	...	...	...	1853	...	...	2046	...	...	...	|	...	2258	...	...	|	...	...	...	...
Ourense ... d.	...	...	1646	1640	1725	...	...	2002	2010	...	2221	...	...	...	2201	...	0035	...	...	0035	...	...	...	...
Puebla de Sanabria ... d.	...	...	...	...	1939	...	...	|	2215	...	...	...	...	...	...	...	0233	...	...	0233	...	...	...	...
Zamora ... d.	...	...	...	...	...	...	...	|	...	...	...	...	...	...	...	...	0400	...	...	0400	...	...	...	...
Medina del Campo... **681 689** d.	...	...	...	...	...	...	...	|	...	...	...	...	...	...	...	...	0540	...	...	0540	...	...	...	...
Miranda de Ebro **681 689** ... a.	...	...	...	...	...	...	...	|	...	...	...	...	...	...	...	...	|	...	...	|	...	...	...	...
Barcelona Sants **652** ... a.	...	...	...	...	...	...	...	0845	...	...	...	...	...	...	...	...	|	...	...	|	...	...	...	...
Hendaye **689** ... a.	...	...	...	...	...	...	...	...	...	...	...	...	...	...	...	...	|	...	...	|	...	...	...	...
Ávila ... **681 689** d.	...	...	...	...	...	...	...	...	...	...	...	...	...	...	...	...	0625	...	...	0625	...	...	...	...
Madrid Chamartín ... **681 689** a.	...	...	...	...	...	...	...	...	...	...	...	...	...	...	...	...	0805	...	...	0805	...	...	...	...

A – CAMINO DE SANTIAGO – (12) and 🍷 Irún / Hendaye - Miranda de Ebro - Ourense - A Coruña and v.v.
B – CAMINO DE SANTIAGO – (2) Bilbao - Miranda de Ebro - Ourense - Vigo and v.v.
C – RÍAS GALLEGAS *Hotel Train* – 🛏 and (2) Madrid - A Coruña and v.v.
D – RÍAS GALLEGAS *Hotel Train* – 🛏 and (2) Madrid - Pontevedra and v.v.
G – GALICIA – 🛏 and (2) (reclining) Barcelona - Vigo and v.v.
H – (12) Alacant - Pontevedra and v.v.
J – (2) Valladolid - Puebla de Sanabria and v.v.
K – (12) Alacant - A Coruña and v.v.

X – COVADONGA – (12) and 🍷 Barcelona - Vigo.
Y – FINISTERRE – (12) and 🍷 Vigo - Barcelona.

s – Stops to set down only.
u – Stops to pick up only.

◧ – Via high-speed line.
* – *153 km* Madrid - Medina del Campo via high-speed line.

681 MADRID - LEÓN

km			Alvia	Alvia		Arco	Alvia			Alvia	Alvia	Alvia				Alvia	Alvia				Alvia	Hotel	Hotel	Estr
		18009	**4071**	**4073**	**18101**	**283**	**4111**	**18215**	**18001**	**4133**	**623**	**4141**	**18003**	**18217**	**18105**	**4183**	**4181**	**18791**	**18791**	**18005**	**4201**	**751**	**922**	**933**
		2	①–⑥	①–⑥	2		🍷	2	2	🍷	🍷	🍷	2	2	2	🍷	🍷	2	2	2	🍷	Ⓑ	🍷	
		①–⑥	f	f		B					E	X			T	R	Ⓑh	⑤	⑤		h	A	G	P
0	**Madrid** Chamartín ... **680 689** d.	...	0650	0740	...	...	1100	...	1130	1330	...	1440	1430	...	...	1805	1830	1645	...	1814	2015	2230	...	...
121	Ávila .... **680 689** d.	...	◧	◧	...	...	◧	...	1309	◧	...	◧	1602	...	...	◧	◧	1823	...	1950	◧	0002	...	...
207	Medina del Campo... **680 689** d.	0655	|	|	...	...	|	...	1354	|	...	|	1647	...	...	|	|	1913	...	2035	|	0051	...	...
249	**Valladolid** C. Grande ..... **689** d.	0737	0803	0853	0935	...	1213	1235	1421	1443	...	1601	1714	1755	1810	1926	1947	1940	...	2100	2127	0122	...	...
286	Venta de Baños .... **689** d.	0804	|	|	1008	...	|	1308	1445	|	...	|	1738	1825	1843	|	|	2002	...	2124	|	|	...	...
	Barcelona Sants **652** .... d.	|	|	|	|	...	|	|	|	|	0920	|	|	|	|	|	|	|	...	|	|	|	2050	2200
	Irún **689** .... d.	|	|	|	|	0845	|	|	|	|	|	|	|	|	|	|	|	|	...	|	|	|	|	|
	Bilbao Abando **689** .... d.	|	|	|	|	0915	|	|	|	|	|	|	|	|	|	|	|	|	...	|	|	|	|	|
	Miranda de Ebro.......... **689** d.	|	|	|	|	1118	|	|	|	|	1422	|	|	|	|	|	|	|	...	|	|	|	|	|
	Burgos Rosa de Lima.. **689** d.	|	|	|	|	1213	|	|	|	|	1521	|	|	|	|	|	|	|	...	|	|	|	0319	0613
297	Palencia .... **689** d.	0815	0836	0926	1020	1300	1245	1320	1455	1516	1610	1634	1748	1836	1855	1959	2016	2014	2020	2134	2201	0157	0406	0707
	Santander **684** .... a.	|	|	1207	1334	|	|	|	|	1755	|	|	|	|	2216	2242	|	|	2330	|	|	|	|	|
420	**León** .... a.	0927	0936	...	...	1405	1344	1440	1604	...	1713	1737	1856	2000	...	...	2118	2127	...	2244	2305	0258	0510	0814
	Gijón Cercanías **685** .... a.	...	1155	...	...	|	1605	...	...	...	|	2002	...	...	...	...	2339	|	...	...	...	|	|	1110
	Ponferrada **682** .... a.	...	...	...	...	1542	...	...	...	...	1846	...	...	...	...	...	...	2325	...	...	...	0428	0642	...
	Vigo **682** .... a.	...	...	...	...	2010	...	...	...	...	2305	...	...	...	...	...	...	...	...	...	...	|	1120	...
	A Coruña **682** .... a.	...	...	...	...	2108	...	...	...	...	...	...	...	...	...	...	...	...	...	...	...	|	1120	...
	Ferrol **682** .... a.	...	...	...	...	...	...	...	...	...	...	...	...	...	...	...	...	...	...	...	...	0913	...	...

	Alvia		Alvia	Alvia		Alvia	Alvia		Arco		Alvia	Alvia							Alvia	Alvia		Estr	Hotel	Hotel
	4060	**18002**	**4072**	**4070**		**4100**	**620**	**18004**	**280**	**18214**	**4142**	**4140**	**18102**	**18006**	**18216**	**18104**	**18790**	**18790**	**4180**	**4192**	**18008**	**930**	**921**	**752**
	①–⑥	2	🍷	①–⑥	2	🍷	🍷	2		2	🍷	🍷	2	2	2	2	2	2	Ⓑ	Ⓑ	2	🍷	🍷	Ⓑ
	p		R	f	⑥⑦		F		C			Y			⑦	①–⑥	⑦	⑦	h	b		P	G	A
Ferrol **682** .... d.	...	...	...	...	...	...	...	...	...	...	...	...	...	...	...	...	...	...	...	...	...	...	...	2100
A Coruña **682** .... d.	...	...	...	...	...	...	...	...	0800	...	...	...	...	...	...	...	...	...	...	...	...	...	1805	|
Vigo **682** .... d.	...	...	...	...	...	...	0755	...	0910	...	...	...	...	...	...	...	...	...	...	...	...	...	1823	|
Ponferrada **682** .... d.	...	...	...	...	...	...	1142	...	1321	...	...	...	...	...	...	...	...	1700	...	...	...	...	2247	0145
Gijón Cercanías **685** .... d.	...	...	...	0715	...	1025	|	...	|	...	...	1400	...	...	...	...	...	|	1815	...	...	1940	|	|
León .... d.	0630	0713	...	0937	...	1247	1312	1320	1454	1500	...	1624	...	1652	1737	...	...	1908	2035	...	2050	2212	0025	0324
Santander **684** .... d.	|	|	0705	|	0820	|	|	|	|	|	1405	|	1415	|	|	1655	1720	|	|	1920	|	|	|	|
Palencia .... **689** d.	0730	0818	0947	1040	1141	1348	1416	1426	1557	1622	1644	1727	1732	1757	1849	2017	2019	2025	2136	2203	2208	2328	0130	0426
Burgos Rosa de Lima.. **689** d.	|	|	|	|	|	|	1501	|	1644	|	|	|	|	|	|	|	|	|	|	|	|	0011	0217	|
Miranda de Ebro.......... **689** a.	|	|	|	|	|	|	1555	|	1740	|	|	|	|	|	|	|	|	|	|	|	|	|	|	|
Bilbao Abando **689** .... a.	|	|	|	|	|	|	|	|	1957	|	|	|	|	|	|	|	|	|	|	|	|	|	|	|
Hendaye **689** .... a.	|	|	|	|	|	|	|	|	2035	|	|	|	|	|	|	|	|	|	|	|	|	|	|	|
Barcelona Sants **652** .... a.	|	|	|	|	|	|	2115	|	...	|	|	|	|	|	|	|	|	|	|	|	|	0859	0845	|
Venta de Baños .... **689** d.	|	0825	|	|	1152	|	...	1436	...	1633	|	|	1741	1807	1858	2028	2029	2035	|	|	2218	...	...	|
Valladolid C. Grande ..... **689** d.	0804	0849	1021	1114	1220	1420	...	1458	...	1705	1718	1801	1809	1828	1922	2100	2052	2100	2210	2237	2246	...	...	0500
Medina del Campo... **680 689** a.	|	0917	|	|	...	|	...	1523	...	...	|	|	...	1853	1951	...	...	2132	|	|	2323	...	...	0526
Ávila .... **680 689** a.	◧	1001	◧	◧	...	◧	...	1608	...	...	◧	◧	...	1938	2037	...	...	2216	◧	◧	...	...	...	0623
Madrid Chamartín ... **680 689** a.	0920	1139	1143	1229	...	1540	...	1742	...	...	1833	1923	...	2121	2214	...	...	2352	2325	2352	...	...	...	0805

☛ **FOR NOTES**, SEE TABLE **682** BELOW.

682 LEÓN - VIGO, FERROL and A CORUÑA

km			R-598				Hotel	Hotel							Arco	Arco				Alvia	Arco				Hotel
			12021				**922**	**922**							**283**	**283**				**623**	**723**			**18791**	**751**
		2	2	2	2	2	🍷		2	2	2	2	2	2	2	🍷	2	2	2			2	2	2	Ⓑ
		①–⑤	①–⑤	①–⑤	①–⑤	⑥⑦	G	G	⑥⑦	⑥⑦	①–⑤	⑦			B	B				E	✤	T	⑤	⑤	A
	Madrid Chamartín ‡ d.	...	...	...	...	...	...	...	...	...	...	...	...	...	...	...	...	...	...	...	...	...	...	1645	2230
	Barcelona Sants... ‡ d.	...	...	...	...	...	2050	2050	...	...	...	...	...	...	...	...	...	...	...	0920	...	...	...	|	|
	Irún .... ‡ d.	...	...	...	...	...	|	|	...	...	...	...	...	...	...	0845	...	...	...	|	...	...	...	|	|
	Bilbao Abando...... ‡ d.	...	...	...	...	...	|	|	...	...	...	...	...	...	0915	|	...	...	...	|	...	...	...	|	|
0	**León** .... d.	...	...	...	...	...	0514	0514	...	...	0710	...	...	...	1407	1407	...	...	...	1715	...	2005	...	2128	0300
52	Astorga.......... d.	...	...	...	...	...	0545	0545	...	...	0749	...	...	...	1444	1444	...	...	...	1746	...	2045	...	2209	0331
128	**Ponferrada** .... d.	...	...	0600	...	...	0643	0643	0700	...	0901	...	...	...	1543	1543	...	...	1751	1847	...	2155	...	2325	0429
238	Monforte de Lemos..... a.	...	...	0743	...	...	0815	0815	0841	...	...	...	...	...	1715	1715	...	...	1930	2028	...	...	...	...	0556
	Monforte de Lemos..... d.	...	...	0748	0752	...	0840	0834	0844	0853	...	1123	...	...	1730	1730	1825	...	1934	2032	2055	...	2138	...	0611
285	Ourense .... **680** d.	...	...	0841	|	...	|	0920	0947	|	...	1209	...	...	1818	1830	|	...	2022	2113	|	...	2220	...	|
416	**Vigo** .... **680** a.	...	...	1051	|	...	|	1120	1151	|	...	...	...	...	2010	|	|	...	2224	2305	|	...	...	...	|
309	Lugo.......... d.	...	...	...	0852	...	0934	...	...	0955	...	...	...	...	...	|	1924	...	...	...	2157	...	...	...	0706
	Ferrol .... d.	0700	0915	...	|	0935	|	...	...	|	...	...	1430	1710	...	▲	|	2020	...	...	|	...	...	...	|
402	Betanzos - Infesta.......d.	0753	1000	...	1012	1029	1051	...	...	1124	...	...	1530	1758	...	|	2057	2119	...	...	2324	...	...	...	0825
445	**Ferrol** .... a.	|	|	...	|	|	|	...	...	|	...	...	|	|	...	|	|	|	...	...	|	...	...	...	0913
428	**A Coruña** .... **680** a.	0820	1022	...	1039	1055	1120	...	...	1150	...	...	1556	1826	...	2108	2124	2147	...	...	2354	...	...	...	...

					Arco	Alvia	R-598		Arco	Arco									Hotel	Hotel				Hotel	
					720	**620**	**12020**		**280**	**280**			**18790**						**921**	**921**				**752**	
	2	2	2	2			2	2	🍷	2	2	2	2	2	2	2	2			🍷	2	2	2	Ⓑ	
	①–⑤	⑥	①–⑤		✤	F	①–⑤		C	C	⑥⑦	①–⑥	⑦				⑦		G	G				A	
A Coruña .... **680** d.	...	...	0625	...	0650	...	0725	0827	0800	...	1056	...	...	1440	...	...	...	...	...	1805	1840	1858	2029	...	...
Ferrol .... d.	...	...	|	...	|	...	|	|	|	...	|	...	...	|	...	...	...	...	...	|	|	|	|	2100	...
Betanzos - Infesta.......d.	...	...	0655	...	0714	...	0752	0857	|	...	1125	...	...	1510	...	...	...	...	...	1829	1909	1927	2059	2155	...
Ferrol .... a.	...	...	0748	...	|	...	0832	|	▲	...	1215	...	...	1559	...	...	...	...	...	|	|	2012	2147	|	...
Lugo.......... d.	...	...	...	...	0829	...	...	1022	|	...	...	...	...	...	...	...	...	...	...	1937	2036	...	...	2308	...
Vigo .... **680** d.	...	...	...	0640	|	0755	...	|	|	0910	...	...	...	...	1447	...	...	...	1823	|	|	...	...	|	...
Ourense .... **680** d.	...	0805	...	0843	|	0927	...	|	1100	1100	...	...	...	...	1648	...	1740	...	2002	|	|	...	...	|	...
Monforte de Lemos......a.	...	0850	...	0928	0940	1005	...	1121	1140	1140	...	...	...	...	1734	...	1824	...	2045	2036	2137	...	...	0000	...
Monforte de Lemos......d.	...	...	...	0933	...	1010	...	...	1150	1150	...	...	...	...	1739	...	...	...	2110	2110	...	...	...	0015	...
Ponferrada.......... d.	0712	...	...	1113	...	1142	...	...	1321	1321	...	1700	1700	...	1940	1945	...	...	2247	2247	...	...	...	0145	...
Astorga.......... d.	0823	...	...	...	...	1242	...	...	1420	1420	...	1825	1825	...	...	2105	...	...	2348	2348	...	...	...	0243	...
León .... a.	0900	...	...	...	...	1310	...	...	1452	1452	...	1903	1903	...	...	2144	...	...	0020	0020	...	...	...	0322	...
Bilbao Abando...... ‡ a.	...	...	...	...	...	|	...	...	|	1957	...	...	|	...	...	...	...	...	|	|	...	...	...	|	...
Hendaye .... ‡ a.	...	...	...	...	...	|	...	...	2035	...	...	...	|	...	...	...	...	...	|	|	...	...	...	|	...
Barcelona Sants.... ‡ a.	...	...	...	...	...	2115	...	...	...	...	...	...	|	...	...	...	...	...	0845	0845	...	...	...	|	...
Madrid Chamartín.. ‡ a.	...	...	...	...	...	...	...	...	...	...	...	...	2352	...	...	...	...	...	...	...	...	...	...	0805	...

A – ATLÁNTICO *Hotel Train* – Ⓑ: 🛏, 🛌 and ⟨1⟩ Madrid - Ferrol and v.v.
B – CAMINO DE SANTIAGO – ⟨12⟩ and 🍷 Irún - A Coruña. ⟨2⟩ Bilbao - Vigo.
C – CAMINO DE SANTIAGO – ⟨12⟩ and 🍷 A Coruña - Hendaye. ⟨2⟩ Vigo - Bilbao.
E – COVADONGA – ⟨12⟩ and 🍷 Barcelona - Vigo.
F – FINISTERRE – ⟨12⟩ and 🍷 Vigo - Barcelona.
G – GALICIA – 🛏 and ⟨1⟩ (reclining) Barcelona - A Coruña and Vigo and v.v. 🍷 Barcelona - A Coruña and v.v.
P – PÍO BAROJA – Ⓑ: 🛏, 🛌 and ⟨12⟩ Barcelona - Gijón and v.v.
R – ⟨12⟩ Alacant - Madrid - Santander and v.v.

T – ①②③④⑥⑦.
X – From Alacant on ①–⑥.
Y – To Alacant on Ⓑ.

b – Not Oct. 11.
f – Not Oct. 12.
h – Not Oct. 11, Dec. 7.
p – Not Oct. 12, Dec. 8.

▲ – Via Santiago (Table **680**).
‡ – See Table **681** (above).
◧ – Via high-speed line (Table **663**).
✤ – For through journeys from Train **623** via Monforte de Lemos, Train number **1623** applies. For through journeys to Train **620** via Monforte de Lemos, Train number **1620** applies.

683 LEÓN - BILBAO

FEVE narrow-gauge

1400 →	1445 →	1535 →	1636 →	1717 →	1801 →	1935 →	2042 →	2130
León	La Vecilla	Cistierna	Guardo	Vado Cervera	Mataporquera	Espinosa	Balmaseda	**Bilbao** Concordia
2148	← 2059	← 2018	← 1921	← 1841	← 1800	← 1623	← 1519	← 1430

PALENCIA - SANTANDER 684

km		Alvia 4073 🍷 A	2		Alvia 4133	2	2 C	Alvia 4183 🍷 E	2 ⑤
	Madrid Chamartín **681 689** d.	0740	...	...	1330	...	...	1805	...
	Valladolid C. Grande **681 689** d.	0853	0935	...	1443	1455	1810	1926	...
0	**Palencia** d.	0926	1020	...	1516	1537	1855	1959	2020
98	Aguilar de Campoo d.	1027	1136	...	|	1701	2007	2101	2131
110	Mataporquera **683** d.	|	1146	...	|	1712	2016	|	2141
129	Reinosa § d.	1052	1202	...	|	1730	2036	2127	2156
188	Torrelavega § d.	1141	1300	...	1730	1826	2140	2217	2257
218	**Santander** § a.	1207	1334	...	1755	1900	2216	2242	2330

	2 ①–⑤	Alvia 4072 🍷 E	2 ⑥⑦	Alvia 4142 🍷	2	2 ①–⑥	2 ⑦	Alvia 4182 🍷 B	
Santander § d.	...	0705	0820	1405	1415	1655	1720	1920	...
Torrelavega § d.	...	0730	0854	1430	1450	1730	1747	1945	...
Reinosa § d.	0715	0819	0957	|	1551	1833	1842	2034	...
Mataporquera **683** d.	0734	|	1013	|	1607	1849	1857	|	...
Aguilar de Campoo d.	0744	0843	1028	|	1619	1859	1904	2058	...
Palencia a.	0859	0945	1140	1642	1731	2016	2018	2201	...
Valladolid C. Grande **681 689** a.	0943	1019	1220	1716	1809	2100	2052	2235	...
Madrid Chamartín **681 689** a.	...	1143	...	1833	...	...	...	2352	...

A – ①–⑥ (not June 13, Oct. 12).
B – ⑧ (not June 12, Oct. 11).
C – ①②③④⑥⑦.
E – From / to Alacant.
§ – Additional local services operate between these stations.

LEÓN - OVIEDO - GIJÓN 685

km		Estr 933 A	Alvia 4071 ①–⑥ f		2	Alvia 4111 🍷	Alvia 4141 🍷 C	2 ⑧	Alvia 4181 🍷 ⑧h	
	Barcelona Sants **681** d.	2200	...	...	...	...	...	...	...	...
	Madrid Chamartín **681** d.	|	0650	...	...	1100	1440	...	1830	...
0	**León** d.	0816	0938	...	1315	1344	1739	1939	2120	...
109	Pola de Lena § a.	|	|	...	1449	|	1858	2122	|	...
140	**Oviedo** ▽ § a.	1026	1126	...	1523	1532	1930	2203	2310	...
172	**Gijón** Cercanias § a.	1110	1155	...	1553	1605	2002	2243	2339	...

	2 ①–⑤	Alvia 4070 ①–⑥ f	Alvia 4100 🍷	2	Alvia 4140 🍷 B		Alvia 4180 🍷 ⑧h	Estr 930 A	
Gijón Cercanias § d.	0650	0715	1025	1300	1400	...	1815	1940	...
Oviedo ▽ § d.	0729	0743	1054	1336	1428	...	1843	2010	...
Pola de Lena § d.	0807	|	1125	1418	1500	...	|	|	...
León a.	1008	0935	1245	1601	1622	...	2033	2210	...
Madrid Chamartín **681** a.	...	1229	1540	...	1923	...	2325	|	...
Barcelona Sants **681** a.	...	...	...	...	...	...	...	0859	...

A – ⑧ PÍO BAROJA: 🛏, 🛌 and (12) Barcelona - Gijón and v.v.
B – To Alacant on ⑧.
C – From Alacant on ①–⑥.
f – Not June 12, Oct. 12.
h – Not Oct. 11, Dec. 7.

▽ – **OVIEDO – AVILÉS** and v.v. ***Renfe Cercanías*** (suburban) service. *31 km.* Journey time: ± 38 minutes.
From Oviedo: Approximately 1 train each hour 0550 Ⓐ, 0616 Ⓐ, then 0716 until 2216. **From Avilés**: Approximately 1 train each hour 0641 Ⓐ, 0741 Ⓐ, then 0841 until 2311.
Additional services on Ⓐ.

§ – **GIJÓN – OVIEDO – POLA de LENA** and v.v. ***Renfe Cercanías*** (suburban) service. *63 km.* Journey time: ± 78 minutes.
From Pola de Lena: Approximately 1–2 trains each hour from 0630 until 2200. **From Gijón**: Approximately 1–2 trains each hour from 0600 until 2230.

EuskoTren (narrow gauge) SAN SEBASTIÁN - BILBAO 686

					Ⓐ	Ⓐd				
Hendaye **689** d.		0847c	1947c		...	...	...		...	...
San Sebastián ⊡ Amara d.	F	0918	2018	S	0547	0647	0747		1947	2047
Zarautz d.	A	0945	2045	L	0620	0720	0820	and	2020	2120
Zumaia d.	S	0953	2053	O	0629	0729	0829	hourly	2029	2129
Eibar d.	T	1036	2136	W	0713	0813	0913		2113	2213
Durango d.	→	1101	2201	→	0742	0842	0942	until	2142	2245
Bilbao Bolueta ⊖ a.		1135	2235		0821	0921	1021		2221	...
Bilbao Atxuri § a.		1139	2239		0825	0925	1025		2225	...

						Ⓐ	Ⓐ			
Bilbao Atxuri § d.		0934	2034		...	0557	0657		1957	2057
Bilbao Bolueta ⊖ d.	F	0939	2039	S	...	0601	0701	and	2001	2101
Durango d.	A	1012	2112	L	0539	0641	0741	hourly	2041	2141
Eibar d.	S	1035	2135	O	0613	0713	0813		2113	2213
Zumaia d.	T	|	|	W	0700	0800	0900	until	2200	...
Zarautz d.	→	1122	2222	→	0708	0808	0908		2208	...
San Sebastián ⊡ Amara a.		1147	2247		0739	0839	0939		2239	...
Hendaye **689** a.		1215c	2315c		...	...	...		...	...

c – © only.
d – Daily Eibar - Bilbao.
⊡ – San Sebastián / Donostia.
§ – Bilbao Atxuri ⇆ Bilbao Concordia: ± *1000 m.* Linked by tram approx every 10 minutes, journey 6 minutes. Bilbao Concordia is adjacent to Bilbao Abando (*Renfe*).
⊖ – Metro interchange.
Operator: EuskoTren. 2nd class, narrow gauge.
Distance: San Sebastian - Bilbao *108* km.

FEVE (narrow gauge) BILBAO - SANTANDER - OVIEDO - FERROL 687

		Ⓐ			S	ⒶW	S		S	
Bilbao Concordia § d.	...	...	...	0802	...	...	...	1302	...	1930
Marrón d.	...	0720	...	0940	...	...	...	1434	...	2106
Treto d.	...	0731	...	0950	...	...	...	1444	...	2116
Santander a.	...	0828	...	1100	...	...	...	1558	...	2215
Santander ▽ d.	...	...	0910	...	...	...	...	1610	...	...
Torrelavega ▽ d.	...	...	0937	...	...	...	...	1638	...	...
Cabezón de la Sal ▽ d.	...	...	1007	...	...	...	...	1707	...	...
Unquera d.	...	...	1044	...	...	...	...	1743	...	...
Llanes d.	0755	...	1113	...	1400	1430	1725	1813	2020	...
Ribadesella d.	0832	...	1153	...	1436	1507	1804	1852	2055	...
Oviedo a.	1029	...	1340	...	1629	1707	...	2040	2254	...

		Ⓐ		ⒶW	S		S		S	
Oviedo d.	...	...	0905	1035	1035	...	1435	1535	...	1855
Ribadesella d.	...	0710	1100	1241	1241	...	1635	1735	1853	2054
Llanes d.	...	0745	1139	1317	1317	...	1710	1814	1928	2130
Unquera d.	...	...	1208	...	...	...	...	1843	▬	...
Cabezón de la Sal ▽ d.	...	...	1249	...	...	...	...	1924	...	...
Torrelavega ▽ d.	...	...	1316	...	...	...	...	1949	...	...
Santander ▽ a.	...	...	1346	...	...	...	...	2017	Ⓐ	...
Santander d.	0800	...	1400	...	...	1900	...	...	2035	...
Treto d.	0900	...	1503	...	...	2000	...	...	2133	...
Marrón d.	0911	...	1514	...	...	2011	...	...	2143	...
Bilbao Concordia § a.	1046	...	1646	...	...	2146	...	...	...	...

Oviedo △ d.	...	...	0747	...	...	...	...	1447	...	1847
Gijón Cercanías △ d.	...	0732	|	0932	...	1132	1432	|	1832	|
Avilés △ d.	...	0814	|	1018	...	1218	1518	|	1918	|
Pravia △ d.	...	0844	0847	1048	...	1248	1548	1552	1948	2000
Luarca d.	...	...	0956	▬	...	...	...	1703	...	2119
Navia d.	...	...	1021	...	...	...	...	1728	...	2140
Ribadeo d.	0650	...	1112	...	1445	...	...	1817	...	...
Viveiro d.	0756	...	1220	Ⓐ	1553	...	...	1923	...	...
Ortigueira d.	0833	...	1257	1500	1630	...	...	2000	...	...
Ferrol a.	0949	...	1409	1611	1740	...	...	2111	...	...

							Ⓐ			
Ferrol d.	...	...	...	0810	...	1030	1345	1518	...	1845
Ortigueira d.	...	...	...	0923	...	1143	1456	1631	...	1959
Viveiro d.	...	...	...	0959	...	1219	▬	1707	...	2035
Ribadeo d.	...	...	...	1110	...	1325	...	1818	...	2148
Navia d.	0640	...	...	1158	...	...	...	1907	...	...
Luarca d.	0707	...	...	1223	...	...	...	1932	...	...
Pravia △ d.	0829	0848	1148	1331	1348	...	1648	2049	2048	...
Avilés △ d.	|	0926	1226	|	1428	...	1728	|	2128	...
Gijón Cercanías △ a.	|	1008	1308	|	1508	...	1808	|	2208	...
Oviedo △ a.	0929	...	...	1428	...	...	...	2148	...	...

S – July 1 - Aug. 31.
W – Sept. 1 - June 30.
▽ – Additional trains run Santander - Cabezón de al Sal and v.v.
△ – Additional trains run Oviedo / Gijón - Pravia and v.v.
§ – Bilbao Concordia is adjacent to Bilbao Abando (*Renfe*).
Operator: FEVE. 2nd class, narrow gauge.

ALSA ★ 🚌 IRÚN - BILBAO - SANTANDER - GIJÓN 688

🚌	▽ ①–⑥			▼ ⑧	▼ ⑥	①–⑥	⑦				▼ ⑧	⑥		①–⑤	▽ ⑧		▼				▽ ⑤⑦		⑦	
Irún RENFE rail station d.	...	...	...	0645	...	0745	...	...	0845	...	...	...	1100	1215	...	1345	1445	...	1645	1830	...	2045	2115	2355
San Sebastián / Donostia d.	...	...	...	0710	...	0810	...	...	0910	...	...	...	1125	1240	...	1410	1510	...	1710	1855	...	2110	2140	0020
Bilbao TermiBus § d.	0600	...	0700	0830	0830	0930	0930	1015	1030	1130	1230	1230	1330	1400	1430	1530	1630	1730	1830	2030	2100	2230	2300	0145
Santander § d.	0715	0830	0830	0950	0950	1100	1115	1145	1215	1300	1350	1400	1530	...	1545	1700	1750	1900	2000	2200	2215	2350	0020	0330
Oviedo a.	1000*	1145	...	1205	1205	...	...	...	1530	...	1605	...	1845	...	1800	...	2005	2145	2300	...	0030	...	...	0600
Gijón a.	0930	1215	...	1235	1235	...	...	...	1600	...	1635	...	1915	...	1830	...	2035	2215	2330	...	0100	...	...	0700

🚌		①–⑥			①–⑥	⑦	▼	▽ ①–⑥	⑦	①–⑥	▽ ①–⑥		⑤⑦	▼ ⑧	▼ ⑥			▼ ①–④	▼ ⑤⑦			▽ ⑧		▽ ⑤
Gijón d.	0014	...	...	...	...	...	0715	...	0815	0815	0915	1115	...	1315	1315	...	1515	1615	1615	...	1715	1915	2015	2115
Oviedo d.	0100	...	...	...	...	...	0745	...	0845	0845	0945	1145	...	1345	1345	...	1545	1645	1645	...	1745	1945	2045	2145
Santander § d.	0345	0545	0700	0800	0930	0930	1005	1200	1200	1230	1200	1500	1530	1605	1605	1700	1900	1905	1905	...	2030	2200	2340	2359
Bilbao TermiBus § d.	0515	0730	0840	0930	1130	1130	1120	1315	1400	1415	1315	1630	1730	1720	1720	1830	2045	2020	2020	2045	2200	2315	...	0115
San Sebastián / Donostia a.	0640	0840	1000	...	1240	...	1230	...	1600	1615	...	...	1840	...	1830	1940	2155	2130	...	2155	2310	...	...	...
Irún RENFE rail station a.	0700	0910	1030	...	1310	...	1305	...	1630	1645	...	...	1910	...	1905	2010	2225	2205	...	2225	2340	...	...	...

▼ – *Clase Supra* luxury coach.
▽ – *Eurobús* luxury coach.
§ – Additional services operate Bilbao - Santander and v.v.
★ – ALSA: ✆ +34 913 270 540 www.alsa.es
* – Calls after Gijon.

689 MADRID and SALAMANCA - BILBAO and IRÚN

km		16007 ①–⑥ N 2	2 ①–⑤	18401 2 ①–⑥	16203 2	Estr 941 🍷 P	17201 2	TRD 18302 2 ①–⑤	Alvia 601 🍷	Talgo 530 🍷 U ✤	Alvia 4087 🍷	Alvia 4087 🍷 ①–⑥	TRD 18314 2 ⑥	2 Y	18061 2	16003 2	D 410 2 🍷 ✤	D 410 2 ✤	17203 2	2	16021 2	16021 2 N	Alvia 620 🍷 B	2 ①–⑤
△																								
0	**Madrid** Chamartín ...... **680 681** d.	...	...	...	...	...	...	...	0740**p**	...	0800	0800	...	...	0830	...	...	...	...	...	...	...	...	...
**	Aranda de Duero .... d.	...	...	...	...	...	...	...	|	...	|	|	...	...	|	...	...	...	...	...	...	...	...	...
121	Ávila .... **680 681** d.	...	...	...	...	0704	0715	...	|	...	|	|	...	...	0959	...	...	...	1048	...	...	...	...	...
	Salamanca .... d.	...	...	...	...	|	|	0715	|	0800	|	|	0813	...	|	...	1030	1030	|	...	...	...	...	...
207	Medina del Campo...... **680 681** d.	...	...	...	...	0747	0803	0806	|	0853	|	|	0908	0928	1044	...	1120	1120	1137	...	...	...	...	...
250	**Valladolid** Campo Grande. **681** d.	...	...	0700	...	0817	0831	0841	|	0925	0919	0919	0942	1014	1111	...	1151	1151	1208	1235	...	...	...	...
286	Venta de Baños .... **681** d.	...	...	0726	...	|	...	...	|	|	|	|	...	...	1134	...	1215	1215	...	1308	...	...	...	...
298	Palencia .... **681** d.	...	...	0739	...	|	...	...	⊡	|	|	|	...	...	1147	...	|	|	...	1318	...	...	1416	...
371	**Burgos** Rosa de Lima .... **681** d.	...	...	0830	...	0923	...	...	|	1037	1022	1022	...	...	1235	...	1304	1304	...	...	...	...	1501	...
460	Miranda de Ebro .... **653** d.	...	0720	▬	0900	1013	...	...	|	1151	1117	1120	...	...	1340	...	1425	1440	...	...	1501	...	1556	1715
565	**Bilbao** Abando .... **653** a.	...	|	**16001**	|	1229	...	...	|	|	|	1252	...	...	|	...	|	1632	...	...	|	...	|	|
	Barcelona Sants **653** .... a.	...	|	2	|	...	...	...	|	1921	|	...	...	...	|	...	|	...	...	...	|	...	2115	|
494	Vitoria / Gasteiz .... **653** d.	0750	0746	0928	0927	...	...	...	|	...	1140	...	...	...	1412	1417	1503	...	...	...	1528	1530	...	1742
537	Altsasu .... **653** d.	0820**n**	...	0954	...	...	...	...	|	...	|	...	...	...	...	1445	1528	...	...	...	...	1601**n**	...	...
624	**San Sebastián / Donostia** ▲ **653** d.	...	...	1110	...	...	...	...	1240	...	1324	...	...	...	...	1600	1644	...	...	...	...	...	...	...
641	**Irún** .... ▲ **653** a.	...	...	1135	...	...	...	...	1259**s**	...	1348	...	...	...	...	1623	1704	...	...	...	...	...	...	...
643	Hendaye .... ▲ **653** a.	...	...	...	...	...	...	...	1304	...	1354	...	...	...	...	...	1713	...	...	...	...	...	...	...

	TRD 18306 2	Arco 280 D	Arco 280 2 E	17221 2	18063 2	16005 2	16011 2 N	Talgo 201 Ⓑ j	Alvia 4167 🍷	Alvia 4167 🍷 Ⓑ	TRD 18316 2 ⑦	17225 2 Ⓑ	18017 2 K	18065 2 Ⓑ	TRD 18312 2 ①–⑥	18719 2 ①–⑥	TRD 18324 2 ⑦	2 ⑦	Estr 930 🍷 C ✤	Hotel 921 🍷 G	17111 2 ⑤	18007 2 Ⓑ	Estr 310 🍷 S	
Madrid Chamartín .... **680 681** d.	...	...	...	...	1313	...	...	1430	1610	1610	...	...	...	1730	...	...	...	...	...	...	1932	2030	...	...
Aranda de Duero .... d.	...	...	...	...	|	...	...	1633	|	|	...	...	...	|	...	...	...	...	...	...	|	|	...	...
Ávila .... **680 681** d.	...	...	...	1410	1445	...	...	|	|	|	...	1720	...	1910	...	...	...	...	...	...	2128	2159	...	...
Salamanca .... d.	1350	...	...	|	|	...	...	|	|	|	1705	|	...	|	2010	...	2049	...	2105	...	|	|	0005	...
Medina del Campo....... **680 681** d.	1448	...	...	1458	1530	...	...	|	|	|	1758	1808	...	1955	2105	...	2149	...	2200	...	2222	2244	0057	...
Valladolid Campo Grande.. **681** d.	1515	...	...	1538	1557	...	...	|	1734	1734	1837	1847	1900	2022	2139	2200	2223	2232	2229	...	2252	2311	0130	...
Venta de Baños .... **681** d.	1537	...	...	...	1618	...	...	|	|	|	...	...	1921	2046	...	2233	...	2305	|	...	...	2338	|	...
Palencia .... **681** d.	1543	1557	1557	...	1629	...	...	|	|	|	...	...	1935	2059	...	2243	...	2315	2328	0130	...	2348	|	...
Burgos Rosa de Lima .... **681** d.	...	1644	1644	...	1717	...	...	1740	1837	1837	...	...	2023	2146	...	...	...	...	0011	0217	...	...	0254	...
Miranda de Ebro .... **653** d.	...	1750	1832	...	1818	...	...	...	1935	1939	...	...	2125	2248	...	...	...	...	|	|	...	...	0355	...
Bilbao Abando .... **653** a.	...	|	2000	...	|	...	...	...	|	2111	...	...	...	|	...	...	...	...	|	|	...	...	|	...
Barcelona Sants **653** .... a.	...	|	...	...	|	...	...	...	|	...	...	...	...	|	...	...	...	...	0859	0845	...	...	|	...
Vitoria / Gasteiz .... **653** d.	...	1813	...	...	1845	1900	1905	...	1956	...	...	...	...	2315	...	...	...	...	...	...	...	...	0424	...
Altsasu .... **653** d.	...	1839	...	...	...	1929	1936**n**	...	|	...	...	...	...	...	...	...	...	...	...	...	...	...	|	...
San Sebastián / Donostia ▲ **653** d.	...	2005	...	...	...	2050	...	...	2135	...	...	...	...	...	...	...	...	...	...	...	...	...	0634	...
Irún .... ▲ **653** a.	...	2027**s**	...	...	...	2108	...	...	2157**s**	...	...	...	...	...	...	...	...	...	...	...	...	...	0658	...
Hendaye .... ▲ **653** a.	...	2035	...	...	...	...	...	...	2203	...	...	...	...	...	...	...	...	...	...	...	...	...	0710	...

km		Hotel 922 G 🍷	18000 2 ①–⑥	TRD 18300 2 ①–⑤	2 ①–⑤	Estr 933 🍷 C ✤	18702 2 r ①–⑤	TRD 18304 2 ⑥	18010 2 ①–⑥	18069 2 L	17218 2	16000 2 ①–⑥	16023 ①–⑥ N 2	Alvia 4086 🍷	Alvia 4086 🍷 ①–⑥	17202 2	Arco 283 2 E	Arco 283 D	TRD 18308 2	17220 2	18012 2	Alvia 623 🍷 A	2 ⑦	2 Y
0	**Irún** .... ▲ **653** d.	...	...	...	...	...	...	...	...	...	...	0640	...	0815	...	...	...	0845	...	...	...	...	...	...
17	**San Sebastián / Donostia** ▲ **653** d.	...	...	...	...	...	...	...	...	...	...	0657	...	0832	...	...	...	0902	...	...	...	...	...	...
104	Altsasu .... **653** d.	...	...	...	...	...	...	...	...	...	...	0814	0928**n**	|	...	...	...	1017	...	...	...	...	...	...
147	Vitoria / Gasteiz .... **653** d.	...	...	...	...	...	...	...	0726	...	...	0845	1000	1009	...	...	...	1040	...	...	1340	...	...	...
	Barcelona Sants **653** .... d.	2050	...	...	...	2200	...	...	|	...	...	...	...	|	...	...	...	|	...	...	|	0920	...	...
	Bilbao Abando .... **653** d.	|	...	...	...	|	...	...	|	...	...	...	...	|	0855	...	0915	|	...	...	|	|	...	...
180	Miranda de Ebro .... **681** d.	|	...	...	...	|	...	...	0749	0837	...	...	...	1034	1034	...	1118	1118	...	...	1403	1422	...	...
270	**Burgos** Rosa de Lima .... **681** d.	0319	...	...	...	0613	...	...	0849	0942	...	...	...	1127	1127	...	1213	1213	...	...	1501	1521	...	...
353	Palencia .... **681** d.	0404	0630	...	0733	0707	0900	...	0940	1037	...	...	...	|	|	...	1258	1258	1315	...	1552	1608	...	...
355	Venta de Baños .... **681** d.	...	0640	...	0744	|	0910	...	0950	1056	...	...	...	|	|	...	...	...	1324	...	1602	...	...	...
391	**Valladolid** Campo Grande. **681** d.	...	0701	0726	0815	0756	0943	0945	1011	1120	1125	...	...	1237	1237	1315	...	...	1348	1415	1623	...	1725	1735
434	Medina del Campo...... **680 681** d.	...	0729	0803	...	0825	...	1018	1040	...	1204	...	...	|	|	1348	...	...	1417	1454	1654	...	1750	1805
504	**Salamanca** .... a.	...	|	0859	...	0916	...	1118	|	...	|	...	...	|	|	|	...	...	1515	|	|	...	|	...
	Ávila .... **680 681** d.	...	0814	...	...	...	...	...	1125	...	1255	...	...	|	|	1437	...	...	...	1545	1739	...	1837	...
	Aranda de Duero .... d.	...	|	...	...	...	...	...	|	...	...	...	...	|	|	...	...	...	...	...	|	...	|	...
	Madrid Chamartín ...... **680 681** a.	...	0943	...	...	...	...	...	1309	...	...	...	...	1357	1357	...	...	...	...	...	1924	...	2026**a**	...

	2 ①–⑤	D 413 2 ✤	D 413 2 🍷 ✤	TRD 18318 2 ⑦	16002 2	17200 2	Alvia 4166 🍷 Ⓑ	Alvia 4166 🍷	Alvia 610 🍷	16025 2 N	18014 2	TRD 18310 2	Talgo 200 Ⓑ j	2 Ⓑ	18408 2 Ⓑ	Talgo 533 🍷 U ✤	16017 2 N	16208 2	Estr 940 🍷 Q	16004 2	16004 2	Estr 313 🍷 T		
Irún .... ▲ **653** d.	...	...	1320	...	1517	...	...	1620	1735	...	...	...	...	...	...	...	...	...	...	1937	...	2200	...	...
San Sebastián / Donostia ▲ **653** d.	...	...	1337	...	1535	...	...	1639	1751	...	...	...	...	...	...	...	...	...	...	1956	...	2220	...	...
Altsasu .... **653** d.	...	...	1448	...	1652	...	...	|	|	1716**n**	...	...	...	...	...	...	2015**n**	...	...	2114	...	|	...	...
Vitoria / Gasteiz .... **653** d.	1430	...	1515	...	1721	...	...	1817	|	1752	1755	...	...	1850	...	...	2045	2055	...	2142	2150	0015	...	...
Barcelona Sants **653** .... d.	|	...	|	...	...	...	...	|	|	...	|	...	...	|	...	1230	...	|	...	...	|	|	...	...
Bilbao Abando .... **653** d.	|	1400	|	...	...	...	1710	|	|	...	|	...	...	|	...	|	...	|	2125	...	|	|	...	...
Miranda de Ebro .... **681** d.	1457	1602	1602	...	...	...	1844	1844	|	...	1816	...	...	1917	1920	2005	...	2122	2257	...	2214	0040	...	...
Burgos Rosa de Lima .... **681** d.	...	1704	1704	...	...	...	1940	1940	|	...	1917	...	1955	...	2024	2106	...	...	2353	...	...	0159	...	...
Palencia .... **681** d.	...	|	|	...	...	...	|	|	⊡	...	2013	...	|	...	2120	|	...	...	|	...	...	|	...	...
Venta de Baños .... **681** d.	...	1748	1748	...	...	...	|	|	|	...	2023	...	|	...	2130	|	...	...	|	...	...	|	...	...
Valladolid Campo Grande.. **681** d.	...	1813	1813	1850	...	1946	2048	2048	|	...	2050	2055	|	...	2200	2217	...	...	0058	...	...	0320	...	...
Medina del Campo....... **680 681** d.	...	1844	1844	1924	...	2024	|	|	|	...	2114	2130	|	...	...	2244	...	...	0126	...	...	0353	...	...
Salamanca .... a.	...	1937	1937	2021	...	|	|	|	|	...	|	2225	|	...	...	2334	...	...	|	...	...	0448	...	...
Ávila .... **680 681** d.	...	...	...	...	...	2114	|	|	|	...	2202	...	|	...	...	...	...	...	0210	...	...	...	...	...
Aranda de Duero .... d.	...	...	...	...	...	...	|	|	|	...	|	...	2059	...	...	...	...	...	...	...	...	...	...	...
Madrid Chamartín .... **680 681** a.	...	...	...	...	...	...	2208	2208	2250**p**	...	2342	...	2305	...	...	...	...	...	...	...	...	...	...	...

A – COVADONGA – (12) and 🍷 Barcelona - Palencia - Vigo.
B – FINISTERRE – (12) and 🍷 Vigo - Palencia - Barcelona.
C – PÍO BAROJA – ⑤⑦: 🛏, ▬ and (1) Salamanca - Barcelona and v.v. ✤.
D – CAMINO DE SANTIAGO – (12) and 🍷 A Coruña - Ourense - Miranda de Ebro - Irún / Hendaye and v.v.
E – CAMINO DE SANTIAGO – (2) Vigo - Ourense - Miranda de Ebro - Bilbao and v.v.
G – GALICIA – 🛏 and (1) (reclining) Barcelona - A Coruña and Vigo and v.v.
K – To Logroño on ⑥.
L – From Logroño on ①.
N – To / from Pamplona (Table **653**).
P – PICASSO – June 21, 28, July 1, 5, 12 (one day later from Ávila): 🛏, ▬ and (12) Málaga - Bilbao (Table **661**).
Q – PICASSO – June 19, 26, 30, July 3, 10, 14: 🛏, ▬ and (12) Bilbao - Málaga (Table **661**).
S – SUREX – 🛏, ▬ and (12) Lisboa - Hendaye.

T – SUREX – 🛏, ▬ and (12) Irún - Lisboa.
U – MIGUEL DE UNAMUNO – (12) Salamanca - Barcelona and v.v. ✤.
Y – (2) Puebla de Sanabria - Valladolid and v.v.

a – Continues to Madrid Atocha (arrive 2042).
j – Not Dec. 7.
n – Altsasu Pueblo.
p – Madrid Puerta de Atocha.
r – From Reinosa (Table **684**).
s – Stops to set down only.

✤ – Subject to confirmation.
⊡ – Runs via Pamplona (Table **653**).

* – Train number from Vitoria.
** – Madrid - Aranda: *168 km*. Aranda - Burgos: *115 km*.
§ – Train number to Vitoria.
△ – Via Ávila.

▲ – **SAN SEBASTIÁN - IRÚN** and v.v. *Renfe Cercanías* (suburban) service. *17 km.* Journey time: ± 23 minutes.
From San Sebastián: Approximately 2–3 trains each hour from 0630 until 2300. **From Irún**: Approximately 2–3 trains each hour from 0522 until 2222.

▲ – **SAN SEBASTIÁN** (Amara) - **IRÚN** (Colón, near Renfe station) - **HENDAYE** (SNCF station) and v.v. *EuskoTren* (narrow-gauge) service. *22 km.* Journey time: ± 37 minutes.
From San Sebastián: 0555 Ⓐ, 0615 Ⓑ, 0645 Ⓐ, 0715, 0745 and every 30 minutes until 2145 then 2315 ⑥ **s**; also at 1148 Ⓒ **n**, 2248 Ⓒ **n**. On ⑦ also hourly 0015–0615 (2-hourly winter).
From Hendaye (A): 0647 Ⓐ, 0703 Ⓑ, 0733 Ⓐ, 0803, 0833 and every 30 minutes until 2233 then 0003 ⑦ **s**; also at 0847 Ⓒ **n**, 1947 Ⓒ **n**. On ⑦ also hourly 0103–0703 (2-hourly winter).
A – 4 minutes later from Irún. n – Non-stop journey, not calling at Irún (journey 27–29 minutes). From / to Bilbao (Table **686**). s – Summer only (late-June to mid-Sept).

PORTUGAL

SEE MAP PAGE 320

Operator: CP – Comboios de Portugal (www.cp.pt).

Train categories: ***Alfa Pendular*** – *AP* – high-quality tilting express trains. ***Intercidades*** – *IC* – high-quality express trains linking the main cities of Portugal to Lisboa and Porto. ***Interregional*** – *IR* – 'semi-fast' links usually calling at principal stations only. ***Regional*** and ***Suburbano*** – local stopping trains (shown without train numbers).
Higher fares are payable for travel by *AP* and *IC* trains, also the international **Sud Expresso** service (Lisboa - Hendaye / Irún - Lisboa), and there is an additional supplement for travel by *AP* trains. The **Lusitânia** *Hotel Train* service (Lisboa - Madrid and v.v.) is shown in Table **48**, special fares apply. The Porto - Vigo trains are classified *IN*.

Services: All services shown with a train number convey first and second class accommodation (on *Alfa Pendular* trains termed, respectively, *Conforto* and *Turística*) unless otherwise indicated. *Regional* and *Suburbano* trains convey second-class seating only.
AP, *IC*, *IR* and international trains convey a buffet car (*carruagem-bar*) and there is an at-seat service of meals to passengers in 1st class on *AP* and certain *IC* trains. Sleeping- (🛏) and couchette (▬) cars are of the normal European types described on page 10.

Reservations: Reservations are compulsory for travel by *AP* and *IC* trains, also the *Sud Expresso* and *Lusitania*. Seat reservation is not normally available on other services.

Timings: Valid from **December 14, 2008**. Timings do not usually change on set dates in Portugal, and amendments may come into effect at short notice.

LISBOA - COIMBRA - PORTO 690

Reservations compulsory on all *AP* and *IC* trains. For local trains Entroncamento - Coimbra / Coimbra - Aveiro / Aveiro - Porto see Table **699**

km		AP 121	AP 131	IC 521	AP 123	IC 511	IC 523	AP 182	IC 525	AP 125	IC 513	IR 821	AP 133	IC 527	AP 135	310 311	AP 127	IC 621	AP 184	IC 515	AP 137	IC 529	AP 129	IC 531
		Ⓐ		①–⑥	①–⑥					⚒		⑤			Ⓑ	S								
			△		n	◇					◇	f	△		h△	🅁		☆		◇	△			
	Faro **697** d.	...	...	...	...	...	...	0655	...	...	...	...	...	...	...	...	...	...	1455	...	...	...	...	...
0	**Lisboa** Sta Apolónia ▷ d.	0600	0700	0730	0800	0830	0930	|	1130	1200	1230	...	1400	1530	1600	1606	1700	1730	|	1828	1900	1930	2000	2130
7	**Lisboa** Oriente ▷ d.	0609	0709	0739	0809	0839	0939	1009	1139	1209	1239	...	1409	1539	1609	1614	1709	1739	1809	1837	1909	1939	2009	2139
31	Vila Franca de Xira ▷ d.	|	|	0752	|	0852	0952	|	1152	|	1252	...	|	1552	|	|	|	1752	|	1850	|	1952	|	2152
75	Santarém ▷ d.	|	|	0814	0840	0915	1013	|	1213	|	1313	...	|	1613	|	|	|	1813	|	1913	|	2013	2040	2213
107	**Entroncamento** ▷ d.	|	|	0833	0900	0936	1033	|	1233	|	1333	1358	|	1633	|	1719	|	1833	|	1934	|	2033	2100	2233
131	Fátima ⊙ d.	|	|	|	|	0949	|	|	|	|	1347	1414	|	|	|	1733	|	|	|	1947	|	|	|	|
171	Pombal d.	|	|	0906	0929	1013	1109	|	1306	|	1410	1438	|	1706	|	1757	|	1909	|	2011	|	2106	2129	2309
199	Alfarelos d.	|	|	|	|	1027	|	|	1320	|	1424	1456	|	1720	|	|	|	|	|	2025	|	|	|	|
218	**Coimbra** B ▶ d.	0746	0846	0931	0952	1041	1134	1146	1333	1346	1438	1510	1546	1733	1746	1826	1846	1933	1946	2039	2046	2131	2152	2334
232	Pampilhosa d.	|	|	|	|	1053	|	|	1343	|	1453	1521	|	1743	|	1841	|	|	|	2051	|	|	|	|
273	Aveiro d.	0811	0911	1000	1016	...	1200	1211	1401	1411	...	1552	1611	1801	1811	...	1911	2000	2011	...	2111	2200	2216	0000
318	Espinho d.	|	|	1024	1037	...	1224	|	1423	|	...	1623	|	1823	|	...	|	2024	|	...	|	2224	2237	0024
334	Vila Nova de Gaia d.	0838	0939	1033	1046	...	1233	1238	1433	1438	...	1633	1639	1833	1838	...	1938	2034	2038	...	2139	2233	2246	0033
337	**Porto** Campanhã ▽ a.	0844	0944	1039	1052	...	1239	1244	1439	1444	...	1639	1644	1839	1844	...	1944	2039	2044	...	2144	2239	2252	0039

		AP 180	AP 130	IC 520	AP 120	312 313	IC 510	IC 620	AP 122	IC 522	AP 124	IC 524	AP 132	IC 512	IC 526	AP 186	AP 126	IC 528	AP 128	AP 134	IC 514	IC 530	IR 820	AP 136
	①–⑥			①–⑥	①–⑥	S			⚒		Ⓑ								Ⓑ				⑦	Ⓑ
			△	n	n	🅁	◇	☆			b		△	◇						△	◇			h△
Porto Campanhã ▽ d.	0123	0547	0647	0652	0745	...	...	0852	0947	1052	1147	1252	1347	...	1452	1547	1647	1652	1745	1847	...	1952	1956	2047
Vila Nova de Gaia d.	0128	0552	0652	0657	0750	...	...	0857	0952	1057	1152	1257	1352	...	1457	1552	1652	1657	1750	1852	...	1957	2002	2052
Espinho d.	0141	|	|	0708	0800	...	...	0908	|	1108	|	1308	|	...	1508	|	|	1708	1800	|	...	2008	2012	|
Aveiro d.	0216	0621	0721	0732	0821	...	...	0931	1021	1131	1221	1331	1421	...	1529	1621	1721	1731	1821	1921	...	2031	2042	2121
Pampilhosa d.	0247	|	|	|	|	0838	0907	|	|	1148	|	|	|	1507	1546	|	|	|	|	|	2007	|	2106	|
Coimbra B ▶ d.	0300	0645	0745	0800	0845	0851	0919	0957	1045	1158	1245	1357	1445	1519	1557	1645	1745	1757	1845	1945	2019	2057	2117	2145
Alfarelos d.	0315	|	|	|	|	|	0933	|	|	1211	|	|	|	1533	1610	|	|	|	|	|	2033	|	2131	|
Pombal d.	0334	|	|	0825	0908	0919	0948	1022	|	1225	|	1423	|	1548	1625	|	|	1823	1908	|	2048	2123	2147	|
Fátima ⊙ d.	0403	|	|	|	|	0942	1012	|	|	|	|	|	|	1612	|	|	|	|	|	|	2112	|	|	|
Entroncamento ▷ d.	0421	|	|	0858	0938	0956	1025	1058	|	1258	|	1458	|	1625	1658	|	|	1858	1938	|	2125	2158	2225	|
Santarém ▷ d.	0446	|	|	0917	0958	|	1045	1117	|	1317	|	1517	|	1645	1717	|	|	1917	1958	|	2145	2217	2245	|
Vila Franca de Xira ▷ d.	0524	|	|	0940	|	|	1109	1140	|	1340	|	1540	|	1709	1740	|	|	1940	|	|	2209	2240	2322	|
Lisboa Oriente ▷ a.	0542	0822	0922	0952	1029	1054	1121	1152	1222	1352	1422	1552	1622	1721	1752	1822	1922	1952	2029	2122	2221	2252	2341	2322
Lisboa Sta Apolónia ▷ a.	0553	|	0930	1000	1038	1103	1130	1200	1230	1400	1430	1600	1630	1730	1800	|	1930	2000	2038	2130	2230	2300	2349	2330
Faro **697** a.	...	1155	...	...	...	...	...	...	...	...	...	...	...	...	...	2155	...	...	...	...	...	...	...	...

S – SUD EXPRESSO – see Table **692**.
b – Not public holidays.
f – If ⑤ is a public holiday runs previous day.
h – Not Apr. 10, May 1, Oct. 5, Dec. 25.
n – Not Apr. 11, Oct. 5.
⊙ – Fátima station is *20* km from Fátima.
◇ – Lisboa - Guarda and v.v. (Table **692**).
☆ – Lisboa - Porto - Guimarães and v.v. (Table **695a**).
△ – Lisboa - Porto - Braga and v.v. (Table **695**).
▷ – For other fast trains see Table **691**, for local trains see Table **699**.
▽ – Local services run Porto Campanhã - Porto São Bento.
▶ – Local trains run Coimbra B - Coimbra and v.v. (journey 4 mins).

LISBOA - ABRANTES - ELVAS and COVILHÃ 691

km				IC 541			IC 543				IC 545
		⚒									
0	**Lisboa** Sta Apolónia ▷ d.	...	...	0818	...	...	1318	1618	...	...	1918
7	**Lisboa** Oriente ▷ d.	...	...	0826	...	...	1327	1628	...	...	1926
31	Vila Franca de Xira ▷ d.	...	...	0843	...	...	1340	1644	...	...	1943
75	Santarém ▷ d.	...	...	0909	...	...	1404	1713	...	...	2009
107	**Entroncamento** ▷ d.	...	0746	0931	0949	1150	1424	1753	1845	1943	2035
135	Abrantes d.	...	0821	0958	1029	1224	1445	1826	1920	2015	2056
175	Torre das Vargens d.	...	|	|	1110	|	|	|	2002	|	|
240	Marvão Beirã 🏛 a.	...	|	|	*1221*v	|	|	|	*2112*v	|	|
217	Portalegre ⊖ d.	...	|	|	1203	|	|	|	2056	|	|
266	**Elvas** ⊙ a.	...	|	|	1318	|	|	|	2211	|	|
199	Ródão d.	...	0930	1049	...	1322	1536	1939	...	2119	2147
229	Castelo Branco a.	...	1001	1114	...	1352	1601	2008	...	2150	2212
229	Castelo Branco d.	0619	*1009*	1130	...	*1438*	1618	*2013*	...	...	2228
283	Fundaõ d.	0724	*1112*	1211	...	*1546*	1657	*2116*	...	...	2309
301	**Covilhã** a.	0748	*1136*	1230	...	*1610*	1717	*2140*	...	...	2328

			IC 540				IC 542	IC 544	
	①–⑥								
Covilhã d.	*0430*r	...	0709	*0843*	*1250*	...	1456	1758	1825
Fundaõ d.	*0449*r	...	0725	*0903*	*1310*	...	1512	1814	1845
Castelo Branco a.	*0550*r	...	0808	*1005*	*1412*	...	1555	1857	1947
Castelo Branco d.	0555	...	0824	1015	1424	...	1611	1913	...
Ródão d.	0625	...	0850	1049	1454	...	1637	1939	...
Elvas ⊙ d.	|	0453	|	|	|	1400	|	|	...
Portalegre ⊖ d.	|	0609	|	|	|	1516	|	|	...
Marvão Beirã 🏛 d.	|	*0554*v	|	|	|	*1459*v	|	|	...
Torre das Vargens d.	|	0710	|	|	|	1615	|	|	...
Abrantes d.	0723	0746	0941	1153	1559	1651	1728	2030	...
Entroncamento ▷ d.	0804	0820	1002	1221	1629	1725	1751	2056	...
Santarém ▷ d.	0830	...	1022	...	...	...	1810	2116	...
Vila Franca de Xira ▷ d.	0915	...	1049	...	...	...	1838	2140	...
Lisboa Oriente ▷ a.	0932	...	1101	...	...	...	1851	2151	...
Lisboa Sta Apolónia ▷ a.	0941	...	1111	...	...	...	1900	2200	...

r – ⚒ only.
v – Change at Torre das Vargens.
▷ – For other fast trains see Table **690**, for local trains see Table **699**.
△ – From Covilhã 0535, 1140, 1618; from Guarda 0710, 1322, 1820.
⊙ – *16 km* from Badajoz (no rail service across the border).
⊖ – Station is *10 km* from Portalegre.

For the LUSITANIA Lisboa - Madrid night train via Marvão Beirã see Table **45**.

COVILHÃ - GUARDA *Currently replaced by* 🚌 △

km								
0	Covilhã d.	0553	1140	1618	Guarda d.	0725	1337	1830
46	Guarda a.	0708	1255	1733	Covilhã a.	0838	1450	1942

(LISBOA -) COIMBRA - GUARDA - VILAR FORMOSO 692

km			IC 511		IC 513		310/1		IC 515	
		⚒				Ⓑ	S			⑤r
	Lisboa Sta Apolónia **690** d.	...	0830	...	1230	...	1606	...	1828	...
	Lisboa Oriente **690** d.	...	0839	...	1239	...	1614	...	1837	...
0	**Coimbra** d.	0704	*1030*	1200	*1353*	1602	*1750*	1828	*1951*	...
2	**Coimbra** B d.	0708	1041	1206	1438	1606	1826	1835	2039	...
16	Pampilhosa d.	0721	1054	1218	1453	1619	1842	1853	2052	...
51	Santa Comba Dão d.	0803	1120	1251	1526	1654	1909	1938	2118	...
83	Nelas d.	0835	1140	1319	1547	1726	1936	2010	2138	...
95	Mangualde d.	0845	1148	1330	1555	1736	1945	2020	2146	...
171	**Guarda** a.	0945	1240	1438	1651	1845	2040	2125	2239	2250
218	Vilar Formoso 🏛 PT d.	...	*1345*	...	*1823*	*1933*	2125	...	...	2324
220	Fuentes d'Oñoro 🏛 ES d.	...	...	...	...	...	2232	...	...	...
346	**Salamanca** a.	...	...	...	...	...	0002	...	...	...

			313		IC 510		IC 512			IC 514
	①	⚒	S	⚒				①–⑥	⑦n	
Salamanca d.	...	...	0455	...	...	...	...	...	...	...
Fuentes d'Oñoro 🏛 ES d.	...	...	0640	...	...	...	...	...	...	...
Vilar Formoso 🏛 PT d.	...	...	0610	0632	...	...	*1207*	...	...	*1645*
Guarda d.	0029	0500	0639	0715	0722	1040	1322	1623	1623	1813
Mangualde d.	0126	0557	0734	...	0814	1148	1414	1739	1739	1908
Nelas d.	0134	0607	0743	...	0822	1157	1422	1751	1751	1916
Santa Comba Dão d.	0201	0638	0805	...	0841	1226	1441	1820	1820	1938
Pampilhosa d.	0230	0714	0838	...	0907	1305	1507	1853	1853	2007
Coimbra B a.	0242	0728	0849	...	0917	1319	1517	1905	1905	2017
Coimbra a.	...	0734	*0859*	...	*0945*	1324	*1545*	1910	*1923*	*2028*
Lisboa Oriente **690** a.	...	...	1054	...	1121	...	1721	...	2131	2221
Lisboa Sta Apolónia **690** a.	...	...	1103	...	1130	...	1730	...	2141	2230

S – SUD EXPRESSO – 🛏 1, 2 cl., ▬ 2 cl. and (2) Lisboa - Hendaye / Irún - Lisboa (Table **46**); ✖ Lisboa - Vilar Formosa and v.v. 🅁. Not Dec. 24, 31. Only for passengers making international journeys (unless space is available).
n – Also Oct. 5; not Oct. 4.
r – If ⑤ is a public holiday will run instead on ④.
ES – Spain (Central European Time).
PT – Portugal (West European Time).

693 LISBOA - CALDAS DA RAINHA - FIGUEIRA DA FOZ / COIMBRA

Linha do Oeste

km										IR 805					IR 807	IR 809				IR 901			
		①–⑥	Ⓐ	Ⓐ	Ⓒ	Ⓐ	Ⓐ	Ⓒn			Ⓐ	Ⓐ	Ⓒn				Ⓐ	Ⓐ	Ⓒn		Ⓐ	Ⓐ	⑦n
0	**Lisboa** Oriente ▷ d.	0507s	0538	...	0555s	...	...	...	...	...	...	...	...	...	...	...	1717	...	...	...	1947	...	...
7	Entrecampos ▷ d.	0518	0547	...	0606	0707	...	...	...	1034*	1037	...	...	...	1434*	1634*	1727	...	...	1844*	1957	...	...
9	Sete Rios ▷ d.	0523	0551	...	0611	0711	...	...	...	1037	1041	...	...	...	1437	1637	1731	...	...	1847	2001	...	...
22	Agualva - Cacém ⊙ ▷ d.	0540	0613	...	0629	0733	...	0739	...	1054	1103	...	1116	...	1454	1654	1753	...	1810	1909	2023	...	2102
26	Mira Sintra - Meleças ▷ d.	0545	0618	0635	0635	0738	0747	0747	...	1100	1108	1122	1122	...	1500	1700	1758	1818	1818	1915	2028	2109	2109
72	Torres Vedras d.	0645	...	0735	0735	...	0851	0851	...	1146	...	1223	1223	...	1546	1743	...	1916	1916	2005	...	2207	2207
95	Bombarral d.	0710	...	0800	0800	...	0917	0917	...	1206	...	1247	1247	...	1606	1806	...	1941	1941	2026	...	2232	2232
114	**Caldas da Rainha** a.	0732	...	0822	0822	...	0939	0939	...	1218	...	1309	1309	...	1618	1818	...	2003	2003	2038	...	2254	2254

				IR 804				IR 806		IR 808				IR 900									
	⑥r	Ⓐ	Ⓐ		Ⓒr	Ⓐ	Ⓐ				Ⓒr	Ⓐ	Ⓐ		Ⓒr	Ⓐ	Ⓐ		⑥	⑦r	Ⓐ	Ⓐ	Ⓑ
Caldas da Rainha d.	0517	0517	...	0658	0737	0737	...	0828	...	1109	1339	1339	...	1509	1741	1741	...	...	1900	1900	1900	...	2132
Bombarral d.	0538	0538	...	0711	0759	0759	...	0841	...	1121	1400	1400	...	1521	1805	1805	...	...	1921	1921	1921	...	2153
Torres Vedras d.	0603	0603	...	0736	0824	0824	...	0906	...	1145	1426	1426	...	1545	1831	1831	...	...	1946	1946	1946	...	2222
Mira Sintra - Meleças ▷ d.	0710	0708	0729	0822	0931	0931	0949	0952	...	1232	1532	1531	1549	1632	1935	1934	1939	...	2050	2050	2047	2109	2322
Agualva - Cacém ⊙ ▷ a.	0715	...	0733	0827	0936	...	0953	0957	...	1237	1537	...	1553	1637	1939	...	1943	...	2055	2055	...	2113	2327
Sete Rios ▷ a.	...	...	0756	0850	...	...	1016	1020	...	1300	...	...	1616	1700	...	...	2006	...	2113	...	...	2136	2347
Entrecampos ▷ a.	...	...	0759	0853*	...	...	1020	1023*	...	1303*	...	...	1620	1703*	...	...	2009	...	2117	...	...	2140	2352
Lisboa Oriente ▷ a.	...	...	0810	...	...	...	...	...	...	...	...	...	...	...	...	...	2020	...	2127s	...	...	...	0002s

km		IR 801		IR 803		
		①–⑥				
0	**Caldas da Rainha** d.	0620	0850	1322	1620	1858
13	São Martinho do Porto d.	0628	0904	1335	1628	1911
47	Marinha Grande d.	0659	0943	1414	1659	1950
57	Leiria d.	0710	0951	1423	1708	1959
104	Bifurcação de Lares ▽ a.	|	1047	1512	|	2050
111	**Figueira da Foz** a.	*0847*z	1055	1526	*1856*x	2100
118	Alfarelos ▽ d.	0800	...	...	1800	...
138	**Coimba** B ▽ a.	0816	...	...	1817	...
140	**Coimbra** ▽ a.	*0826*	...	...	1827	...

		IR 800			IR 802
	①–⑥				Ⓑ
Coimbra ▽ d.	...	*0845*	...	...	1900
Comiba B ▽ d.	...	0904	...	...	1910
Alfarelos ▽ d.	...	0921	...	...	1928
Figueira da Foz d.	0618	*0908*z	1106	1604	*1915*z
Bifurcação de Lares ▽ d.	0632	|	1116	1612	|
Leiria d.	0711	1015	1206	1707	2022
Marinha Grande d.	0722	1026	1217	1718	2032
São Martinho do Porto d.	0758	1054	1252	1754	2101
Caldas da Rainha a.	0812	1105	1306	1808	2111

- **n** – From Monte Abraão (depart 8 minutes earlier).
- **r** – To Monte Abraão (arrive 9 minutes later).
- **s** – Lisboa **Santa Apolónia**.
- **x** – Not ⑥. Change at Verride.
- **z** – Change at Verride.
- ▷ – For suburban services see Table **699**.
- ▽ – See Table **693a** for connections to / from Coimbra.
- ⊙ – Connections to / from Lisboa Rossio every 20 minutes (see Table **699**).
- * – Terminal platforms (Entrecampos - Poente).

693a FIGUEIRA DA FOZ - COIMBRA

km		⚒	⚒	Ⓐ						Ⓐ							
0	**Figueira da Foz** d.	0632	0710	0741	0811	0908	1025	1118	1315	1410	1515	1615	1710	1815	1915	2010	2228
8	Bifurcação de Lares d.	0644	0721	0753	0822	0919	1036	1129	1326	|	1527	1626	1721	1826	1929	2021	2239
22	Alfarelos d.	0702	0740	0810	0842	0942	1055	1147	1346	1431	1546	1646	1741	1846	1949	2041	2258
42	**Coimbra** B a.	0730	0807	0828	0911	1010	1122	1215	1414	1459	1614	1714	1808	1914	2016	2110	2325
44	**Coimbra** a.	0739	0816	0837	0925	1019	1131	1224	1423	1508	1623	1723	1817	1923	2028	2121	2334

	▽	▽	▽
Figueira da Foz d.	0637	1242	1925
Pampilhosa d.	0806	1409	2056
Coimbra B a.	0820	1424	2110
Coimbra B d.	0821	1425	*2133*
Comibra a.	0826	1429	*2137*

	⚒	⚒								Ⓐ		Ⓑ	Ⓐ				
Coimbra d.	0535	0642	0753	0912	0953	...	1251	1353	1451	1654	1706	1750	1835	1951	2222	0019	...
Coimbra B d.	0544	0652	0802	0923	1002	...	1259	1402	1500	1703	1715	1759	1846	2000	2231	0027	...
Alfarelos d.	0611	0719	0821	0949	1030	...	1326	1431	1526	1721	1742	1826	1907	2017	2258	0055	...
Bifurcação de Lares d.	0631	0738	0837	1007	1053	...	1344	1449	1545	|	1801	1845	|	2036	2316	0113	...
Figueira da Foz a.	0645	0750	0847	1018	1105	...	1355	1500	1556	1743	1812	1856	1928	2048	2327	0124	...

	▽	▽	▽
Coimbra d.	*0627*	1246	1928
Coimbra B a.	*0631*	1250	1932
Coimbra B d.	0655	1252	1934
Pampilhosa d.	0711	1309	1951
Figueira da Foz a.	0837	1436	2119

For main line trains calling at Alfarelos see Table **690**. Other trains : Coimbra - Alfarelos Table **699**, Figuerira da Foz - Bif. de Lares Table **693**.

▽ – Rail service currently suspended.

694 PORTO - RÉGUA - POCINHO

km	*Numbered trains : IR*			861	863	867	869	873	877	961	
		Ⓐ									
0	**Porto** São Bento d.	0630	...	...	0915	...	1319	...	...	1920	...
3	**Porto** Campanhã d.	0635	...	0725	0920	1115	1324	1520	1715	1925	2156
12	Ermesinde d.	0647	...	0736	0929	1124	1333	1529	1726	1938	2206
50	Caíde d.	0723	0727	0810	1003	1203	1407	1603	1804	2012	2240
59	Livração ▷ d.	...	0740	0820	1012	1212	1416	1612	1812	2021	2254
64	Marco de Canaveses d.	...	0747	0827	1019	1219	1423	1619	1819	2028	2301
107	**Régua** ▷ a.	...	0844	0915	1106	1305	1510	1707	1908	2119	2358
	Pocinho (below) a.	...	...	1039	...	...	...	...	2033	...	...

		862	864	866	870	874	878	962		
Pocinho (below) d.	...	...	...	...	...	...	...	...	...	...
Régua ▷ d.	0605	0730	0858	1045	1243	1449	1659	1901	2032	...
Marco de Canaveses d.	0703	0815	0944	1132	1331	1536	1745	1946	2132	...
Livração ▷ d.	0709	0821	0950	1138	1337	1542	1751	1952	2138	...
Caíde d.	0727	0833	1002	1150	1349	1554	1803	2004	2155	2213
Ermesinde d.	0803	0905	1035	1222	1421	1626	1838	2039	...	2259
Porto Campanhã a.	0814	0915	1045	1230	1430	1635	1850	2049	...	2310
Porto São Bento a.	...	...	...	1236	...	...	1855	2055	...	2315

km	*Numbered trains : IR*	861	△	865		871		875	△	877	
	Porto Campanhã d.	0725	...	...	...	...	...	...	...	1715	...
0	**Régua** d.	0916	...	1116	...	1531	...	1729	...	1909	...
23	Pinhão d.	0943	...	1142	...	1557	...	1755	...	1935	...
36	Tua a.	0957	1026	1156	...	1612	...	1810	1815	1949	...
90	Mirandela a.	|	1213	|	...	|	...	|	2010	|	...
68	**Pocinho** a.	1039	...	1240	...	1658	...	1854	...	2033	...

	860	△	868		872	876		▽	960	
					⚒	†				
Pocinho d.	0654	...	1113	...	1318	1528	...	...	1731	1905
Mirandela d.	|	0937	|	...	|	|	...	1614	|	|
Tua d.	0736	1126	1157	...	1400	1612	...	1802	1815	1950
Pinhaõ d.	0751	...	1213	...	1416	1628	...	...	1831	2005
Régua a.	0816	...	1238	...	1441	1654	...	...	1856	2030
Porto Campanhã a.	...	...	...	...	...	...	...	...	...	...

▷ NARROW-GAUGE BRANCHES. *Both branches are currently operated by* 🚌 *in the following timings:*

23 km	Ⓐ					Ⓐ		
Livração d.	0610	0715	0830	1215	1620	1820	2050	...
Amarante a.	0650	0755	0910	1250	1700	1900	2130	...
	Ⓐ						Ⓐ	
Amarante d.	0520	0620	0735	1050	1250	1700	1900	2050
Livração a.	0600	0700	0815	1130	1325	1740	1940	2130

26 km	①–⑤				
Régua d.	0706	0846	1120	1520	1920
Vila Real a.	0800	0939	1213	1613	2015
	①–⑤				
Vila Real d.	0700	0944	1351	1755	1915
Régua a.	0755	1038	1445	1850	2010

△ – By taxi Tua - Cachão and v.v. ▽ – By taxi.

🚂 steam-hauled tourist train:
⑥ May 30 - Oct. 3, 2009
Régua d. 1446 → Pinhão d. 1543 → Tua a. 1605.
Tua d. 1706 → Pinhão d. 1746 → Régua 1822.

695 PORTO - BRAGA

km						AP 131								AP 133				AP 135					AP 137			
		△	△	Ⓐ						△					△	△	Ⓐ	Ⓑh						Ⓐ		
	Lisboa Sta Ap. **690**. d.	...	...	...	...	0700	...	...	...	...	...	...	...	1400	...	...	...	1600	...	...	...	...	1900	...	...	...
0	**Porto** São Bento ▷ d.	0645	0745	0825	0845	|	0945	1045	1145	1245	1345	1445	1545	|	1645	1745	1825	|	1845	1925	1945	2045	|	2145	2245	0025
3	**Porto** Campanhã ▷ d.	0650	0750	0830	0850	0946	0950	1050	1150	1250	1350	1450	1550	1646	1650	1750	1830	1846	1850	1930	1950	2050	2146	2150	2250	0030
12	Ermesinde ▷ d.	0702	0802	0842	0902	|	1002	1102	1202	1302	1402	1502	1602	|	1702	1802	1841	|	1902	1942	2002	2102	|	2202	2302	0042
26	Trofa ▷ d.	0718	0818	0859	0918	|	1018	1118	1218	1318	1418	1518	1618	|	1718	1818	1854	|	1918	1959	2018	2118	|	2218	2318	0055
35	Famalicão ▷ d.	0729	0829	0908	0929	1018	1029	1129	1229	1329	1429	1529	1629	1718	1729	1829	1901	1918	1929	2008	2029	2129	2218	2229	2329	0104
42	Nine ▷ d.	0737	0837	0913	0937	|	1037	1137	1237	1337	1437	1537	1637	|	1737	1837	1906	|	1937	2013	2037	2137	|	2237	2337	0109
57	**Braga** a.	0758	0858	0925	0958	1031	1058	1158	1258	1358	1458	1558	1658	1731	1758	1858	1916	1931	1958	2025	2058	2158	2231	2258	2358	0129

		AP 130												AP 132							AP 134				AP 136	
			Ⓐ		Ⓐ	Ⓒ	Ⓐ								▽				Ⓐ			Ⓐ			Ⓑh	d
Braga d.	0530	0604	0608	0630	0705	0730	0744	0805	0830	0930	1030	1130	1230	1304	1330	1430	1530	1630	1713	1730	1804	1815	1830	1930	2004	2030
Nine ▷ d.	0550	|	0620	0650	0717	0750	0754	0817	0850	0950	1050	1150	1250	|	1350	1450	1550	1650	1723	1750	|	1827	1850	1950	|	2050
Famalicão ▷ d.	0558	0619	0626	0658	0723	0758	0759	0823	0858	0958	1058	1158	1258	1319	1358	1458	1558	1658	1728	1758	1819	1833	1858	1958	2019	2058
Trofa ▷ d.	0610	|	0635	0710	0735	0810	0807	0835	0910	1010	1110	1210	1310	|	1410	1510	1610	1710	1736	1810	|	1842	1910	2010	|	2110
Ermesinde ▷ d.	0629	|	0649	0729	0749	0829	0819	0849	0929	1029	1129	1229	1329	|	1429	1529	1629	1729	1748	1829	|	1857	1929	2029	|	2129
Porto Campanhã ▷ a.	0641	0645	0701	0741	0801	0841	0831	0901	0941	1041	1141	1241	1341	1345	1441	1541	1641	1741	1756	1841	1845	1910	1941	2041	2045	2141
Porto São Bento ▷ a.	0645	|	0705	0745	0805	0845	0835	0905	0945	1045	1145	1245	1345	|	1445	1545	1645	1745	1800	1845	|	1915	1945	2045	|	2145
Lisboa Sta Ap. **690**. a.	...	0930	...	...	...	...	...	...	...	...	...	...	...	1630	...	...	...	...	...	...	2130	...	...	...	2330	...

- **d** – Additional journeys run at 2130 Ⓒ, 2230 Ⓐ, 2326.
- **h** – Not Apr. 10, May 1, Oct. 5, Dec. 25.
- ▷ – For other trains see Table **696**.
- ▽ – Additional journey : 1308 Ⓐ (journey time 1 hour).
- △ – Additional journeys : 0625 Ⓐ, 0725 Ⓐ, 1225 Ⓐ, 1625 Ⓐ, 1725 Ⓐ (journey time 1 hour).

PORTO - GUIMARÃES 695a

60 km

											IC **621**
				Ⓐ				Ⓐ	Ⓐ		
Lisboa Sta Ap. **690** ... d.	...	...	...	...	...	...	...	...	...	...	...	1730
Porto São Bento .... ▷ d.	0715	0815	1015	1115	1215	1415	1615	1715	1815	1915	2015	|
Porto Campanhã .... ▷ d.	0720	0820	1020	1120	1220	1420	1620	1720	1820	1920	2020	2041
Ermesinde .... ▷ d.	0732	0832	1032	1132	1232	1432	1632	1732	1832	1932	2032	|
Trofa .... ▷ d.	0748	0850	1050	1150	1250	1450	1650	1750	1848	1950	2050	2101
Guimarães .... a.	0833	0933	1133	1233	1333	1533	1733	1833	1933	2033	2133	2140

		IC **620**										
									Ⓐ			
Guimarães .... d.	0654	0743	0754	0854	0954	1154	1354	1554	1709	1809	1954	2054
Trofa .... ▷ d.	0740	0825	0840	0940	1040	1240	1440	1640	1759	1900	2040	2140
Ermesinde .... ▷ d.	0758	|	0858	0958	1058	1258	1458	1658	1819	1919	2058	2158
Porto Campanhã .... ▷ a.	0810	0845	0910	1010	1110	1310	1510	1710	1831	1931	2110	2210
Porto São Bento ..... ▷ a.	0815	|	0915	1015	1115	1315	1515	1715	1835	1935	2115	2215
Lisboa Sta Ap. **690** ... a.	...	1200	...	...	...	...	...	...	...	...	...	...

▷ – See also Tables **695** and **696**.

Additional trains: **Porto - Guimarães** 0615, 2115 Ⓒ, 2215 Ⓐ, 2315; **Guimarães - Porto** 0554 Ⓐ, 1909 Ⓐ, 2254.

PORTO - VIANA DO CASTELO - VALENÇA - VIGO 696

km		*IR* **851**	*IN* **421**		*IR* **853**	*IR* **855**	*IN* **423**		*IR* **857**	
		Ⓐ							Ⓐ	
0	**Porto** Campanhã .... ▷ d.	0555	0755	...	1245	1555	1755	...	2005	...
12	Ermesinde .... ▷ d.	0605	0807	...	1255	1607	1807	...	2016	...
23	Trofa .... ▷ d.	0618	0826	...	1310	1624	1827	...	2033	...
32	Famalicão .... ▷ d.	0629	0836	...	1321	1635	1837	...	2044	...
39	**Nine** .... ▷ d.	0636	0843	...	1328	1642	1844	...	2051	...
51	Barcelos .... d.	0646	0858	...	1338	1653	1854	...	2105	...
82	**Viana do Castelo** .... d.	0734	0930	...	1414	1728	1931	...	2139	...
116	Vila Nova de Cerveira .... d.	0808	1003	...	1445	1758	2001	...	2209	...
130	**Valença** .... PT d.	0820	1017	...	1457	1811	2015	...	2222	...
134	Tui .... ES d.	...	1135	...	...	...	2130	...	...	...
162	Redondela **681** .... d.	...	1159	...	...	...	2156	...	...	...
174	**Vigo 681** .... a.	...	1214	...	...	...	2212	...	...	...

			IN **420**	*IR* **850**		*IR* **852**	*IR* **854**	*IN* **422**	
	Ⓐ								
Vigo 681 .... d.	...	...	0740	...	...	...	...	1942	...
Redondela **681** .... d.	...	...	0754	...	...	...	...	1957	...
Tui .... ES d.	...	...	0829	...	...	...	...	2037	...
Valença .... PT d.	0548	...	0737	0951	...	1414	1742	1945	...
Vila Nova de Cerveira .... d.	0602	...	0750	1004	...	1427	1757	2000	...
Viana do Castelo .... d.	0643	...	0825	1037	...	1459	1832	2032	...
Barcelos .... d.	0730	...	0859	1113	...	1534	1913	2104	...
Nine .... ▷ d.	0745	...	0913	1124	...	1546	1925	2115	...
Famalicão .... ▷ d.	0752	...	0921	1132	...	1554	1933	2123	...
Trofa .... ▷ d.	0801	...	0930	1141	...	1603	1942	2132	...
Ermesinde .... ▷ d.	0824	...	0946	1157	...	1619	1957	2146	...
Porto Campanhã .... ▷ a.	0835	...	0955	1210	...	1630	2010	2155	...

ADDITIONAL LOCAL TRAINS

	Ⓐ	Ⓒ	Ⓐ		Ⓐ			Ⓐ	Ⓒ	Ⓑ
Porto São Bento **695** .... d.	*0625*	*0645*	*0825*	*0945*	*1245*	*1345*	*1625*a	*1825*	*1845*	*2045*
Nine .... d.	0717	0742	0918	1059	1355	1455	1729	1924	2006	2142
Barcelos .... d.	0731	0756	0932	1114	1410	1509	1743	1937	2023	2156
Viana do Castelo .... a.	0817	0842	1018	1158	1454	1556	1829	2021	2108	2240
Viana do Castelo .... d.	*0824*	*0846*	*1036*	...	...	*1606*	*1831*	...	...	...
Vila Nova de Cerveira .... d.	*0909*	*0931*	*1121*	...	...	*1651*	*1915*	...	...	...
Valença .... d.	*0925*	*0947*	*1137*	...	...	*1707*	*1931*	...	...	...

		Ⓐ		Ⓐ	Ⓒ	Ⓐ			
Valença .... d.	...	*0623*	...	*1102*	*1123*	...	*1503*	...	*1826*
Vila Nova de Cerveira .... d.	...	*0639*	...	*1120*	*1139*	...	*1519*	...	*1842*
Viana do Castelo .... a.	...	*0724*	...	*1205*	*1224*	...	*1604*	...	*1929*
Viana do Castelo .... d.	0536	0733	0934	1211	1229	1313	1610	1729	1937
Barcelos .... d.	0619	0818	1019	1255	1313	1409	1654	1813	2024
Nine .... a.	0634	0833	1034	1310	1328	1424	1709	1828	2039
Porto São Bento **695** ...... a.	*0745*	*0945*	*1145*	*1405*	*1445*	*1545*	*1800*a	*1945*	*2145*

a – Ⓐ only. ▷ – See also Table **695**. ES – Spain (Central European Time). PT – Portugal (West European Time).

LISBOA - PINHAL NOVO - TUNES - FARO 697

km ∆				*AP* **180**	*IC* **570**		*IC* **572**	*IC* **574**		*AP* **186**	*IC* **576**
											E
	Porto Campanhã **690** .. d.	...	...	0547	...	...	...	...	...	1547	...
	Coimbra B **690** .... d.	...	...	0645	...	...	...	...	...	1645	...
0	**Lisboa** Oriente .... ⊙ d.	...	...	0840	1020	...	1320	1720	...	1840	1920
7	Entrecampos .... ⊙ d.	...	...	0851	1030	...	1330	1730	...	1851	1930
18	Pragal .... ⊙ d.	...	...	|	1044	...	1344	1744	...	|	1944
	Barreiro .... d.	...	0643	|	|	...	|	|	1807	|	|
47	Pinhal Novo .... ⊙ d.	...	0655	0930	1106	...	1406	1806	1821	1931	2006
60	Setúbal .... d.	...	0707	|	1114	...	1414	1818	1830	|	2021
110	Alcácer do Sal .... d.	...	0753	|	1154	...	1447	1851	1920	|	2054
134	Grândola .... d.	...	0809	|	1208	...	1502	1907	1935	|	2108
**	**Beja** .... d.	0755	|	|	|	1417	|	|	|	|	|
196	Funcheira .... d.	0851	0857	|	1241	1513	1538	1940	2047r	|	2141
280	**Tunes** .... ▷ d.	...	1014	1127	1344	...	1649	2043	2155	2128	2245
285	Albufeira .... ▷ d.	...	1020	1133	1349	...	1654	2048	2201	2134	2251
302	Loulé .... ▷ d.	...	1034	1146	1401	...	1711	2100	2215	2147	2303
318	**Faro** .... ▷ a.	...	1048	1155	1411	...	1721	2110	2228	2155	2313

		AP **182**	*IC* **670**		*IC* **672**		*AP* **184**		*IC* **674**	*IC* **676**
										F
Faro .... ▷ d.	0548	0655	0920	...	1320	...	1455	1553	1700	1858
Loulé .... ▷ d.	0603	0706	0931	...	1322	...	1506	1607	1711	1909
Albufeira .... ▷ d.	0617	0719	0944	...	1349	...	1518	1621	1723	1921
Tunes .... ▷ d.	0622	0725	0952	...	1356	...	1524	1626	1729	1928
Funcheira .... d.	0730	|	1107	1110	1458	1518	|	1742	1831	2047
Beja .... a.	|	|	|	1210	|	1616	|	|	|	|
Grândola .... d.	0824	|	1140	...	1531	...	|	1831	1906	2123
Alcácer do Sal .... d.	0840	|	1153	...	1545	...	|	1851	1920	2137
Setúbal .... d.	0934	|	1225	...	1617	...	|	1943	1952	2212
Pinhal Novo .... ⊙ d.	0945	0923	1233	...	1625	...	1723	1956	2005	2224
Barreiro .... a.	0957	|	|	...	|	...	|	2008	|	|
Pragal .... ⊙ a.	...	|	1250	...	1643	...	|	...	2023	2243
Entrecampos .... ⊙ a.	...	0957	1303	...	1656	...	1757	...	2036	2256
Lisboa Oriente .... ⊙ a.	...	1004	1312	...	1705	...	1804	...	2045	2305
Coimbra B **690** .... a.	...	1145	...	...	...	...	1945	...	...	...
Porto Campanhã **690** . a.	...	1244	...	...	...	...	2044	...	...	...

LOCAL TRAINS LAGOS - TUNES - FARO

			⚒		⚒						
0	**Lagos** .... d.	0611	0655	0826	1037	1253	1410	1624	1810	1915	2016
18	Portimão .... d.	0629	0713	0849	1055	1311	1428	1642	1828	1933	2034
29	Silves .... d.	0644	0728	0904	1111	1326	1443	1657	1848	1949	2048
42	Algoz .... d.	0700	0744	0921	1127	1342	1459	1717	1904	2009	2110
46	**Tunes** .... a.	0706	0750	0927	1133	1348	1504	1723	1909	2014	2115
46	**Tunes** .... ▷ d.	0707	0755	0933	1138	1355	1505	1728	1910	2015	*2155*
52	Albufeira .... ▷ d.	0718	0802	0944	1146	1402	1517	1735	1921	2022	*2201*
69	Loulé .... ▷ d.	0733	0819	1003	1204	1417	1533	1751	1942	2042	*2215*
85	**Faro** .... ▷ a.	0751	0837	1018	1219	1432	1548	1806	1957	2057	*2228*

		⚒				⚒					⑤v
Faro .... ▷ d.	0712	0927	1055	1300	1617	1730	1827	1910	2010	...	...
Loulé .... ▷ d.	0733	0944	1112	1317	1634	1751	1844	1927	2027	...	...
Albufeira .... ▷ d.	0749	1003	1132	1332	1654	1807	1900	1943	2048	...	...
Tunes .... ▷ a.	0754	1008	1137	1337	1659	1812	1905	1949	2053	...	...
Tunes .... d.	0755	1013	1139	1349	1701	1813	1910	1950	2054	2200	2250
Algoz .... d.	0801	1019	1145	1354	1707	1818	1916	1957	2100	2205	2255
Silves .... d.	0817	1035	1201	1410	1723	1834	1931	2015	2115	2221	2311
Portimão .... d.	0832	1055	1216	1428	1738	1849	1950	2034	2130	2236	2326
Lagos .... a.	0850	1113	1234	1446	1756	1907	2008	2052	2148	2255	2345

E – ⑤ (daily June 1 - Aug. 31), also Apr. 9; not Apr. 10.
F – ⑦ (daily June 1 - Aug. 31), also Oct. 5; not Oct. 4.
r – Arrive 2027.
v – If ⑤ is a public holiday runs instead on ④.
⊙ – See Table **698** for other fast trains, Table **699** for local services. Trains also call at Sete Rios.
▷ – Also see other section of table above or below.
** – Beja - Funcheira: *62 km*
∆ – Via Setúbal (subtract *9* km for direct trains).

FARO - VILA REAL DE SANTO ANTÓNIO 697a

							Ⓐ				Ⓐ	
0	**Faro** .... d.	0734	0925	1225	1434	1625	1730	1825	1925	2125	2235	2325
10	Olhão .... d.	0745	0941	1240	1445	1641	1741	1841	1941	2141	2246	2336
32	Tavira .... d.	0816	1010	1308	1511	1710	1810	1910	2010	2210	2314	0004
56	**Vila Real** § .... a.	0845	1039	1339	1540	1739	1839	1939	2039	2239	2343	0033

		Ⓐ								
Vila Real § .... d.	0547	0617	0716	0941	1141	1310	1543	1741	1841	2041
Tavira .... d.	0613	0648	0746	1013	1213	1340	1613	1813	1913	2113
Olhão .... d.	0637	0714	0813	1040	1241	1407	1640	1840	1940	2140
Faro .... a.	0648	0724	0824	1051	1252	1418	1651	1851	1951	2151

§ – Vila Real de Santo António. (± *1 500 m* from bus station / ferry terminal).

Additional journeys on Ⓐ:
Faro - Tavira 0758, 1025, 1130, 1323, 1525; Tavira - Faro 0913, 1119, 1312, 1513, 1711.

LISBOA - PINHAL NOVO - ÉVORA and BEJA 698

km				*IC* **690**	*IC* **592**		*IC* **694**			*IC* **696**	*IC* **594**
			b								
0	**Lisboa** Oriente ...... ⊙ d.	...	...	0810	0910	...	1410	...	...	1810	1910
7	Entrecampos .... ⊙ d.	...	...	0821	0921	...	1421	...	...	1821	1921
18	Pragal .... ⊙ d.	...	...	0835	0935	...	1435	...	...	1835	1935
47	**Pinhal Novo** .... ⊙ d.	...	0706	0858	0958	...	1458	...	...	1901	2001
88	Vendas Novas .... d.	...	0748	0924	1024	...	1524	...	...	1934	2036
	Évora .... d.	0616	|	|	|	1200	|	1524	1745	|	|
122	Casa Branca .... a.	0636	0819	0949	1049	1220	1549	1544	1805	1959	2101
122	Casa Branca .... d.	0641	0819	0950	1050	1225	1550	1553	1812	2000	2102
148	Évora .... a.	|	|	1008	|	|	1608	|	|	2018	|
185	**Beja** .... a.	0735	0915	...	1131	1323	...	1650	1905	...	2143

	IC **598**	*IC* **590**			*IC* **692**			*IC* **698**	*IC* **596**	
							d			
Beja .... d.	...	0814	0930	1256	...	1618	1720	...	1914	1946
Évora .... d.	0636	|	|	|	1338	|	|	1838	|	|
Casa Branca .... a.	0656	0856	1023	1351	1356	1714	1810	1855	1958	2038
Casa Branca .... d.	0657	0857	1028	1358	1357	1718	1811	1856	1959	2043
Évora .... a.	|	|	1049	1419	|	1739	|	|	|	2104
Vendas Novas .... d.	0721	0923	...	...	1421	...	1839	1920	2023	...
Pinhal Novo .... ⊙ d.	0751	0951	...	...	1451	...	1920	1951	2051	...
Pragal .... ⊙ a.	0813	1013	...	...	1513	...	...	2013	2113	...
Entrecampos .... ⊙ a.	0826	1026	...	...	1526	...	...	2026	2126	...
Lisboa Oriente ..... ⊙ a.	0835	1036	...	...	1535	...	...	2036	2135	...

b – From Barreiro, depart 0651. d – To Barreiro, arrive 1935. ⊙ – See Table **697** for other fast trains and Table **699** for local services. *IC* trains also call at Sete Rios.

699 OTHER LOCAL SERVICES

LISBOA - ESTORIL - CASCAIS

26 km (Estoril *24 km*)

																					*	*			
Lisboa Cais do Sodre .d.	Ⓐ	0530	every	0700	every	1000	every	1700	every	2030	every	2200	every	0130	Ⓒ	0530	every	0730	0800	every	1920	1940	2000	every	0130
Estoril .d.		0606	30	0728	15	1029	20	1729	15	2059	20	2236	30	0206		0606	30	0806	0829	20	1949	2016	2036	30	0206
Cascais .a.		0610	mins	0732	mins	1033	mins	1733	mins	2103	mins	2240	mins	0210		0610	mins	0810	0833	mins	1953	2020	2040	mins	0210

																				*	*			
Cascais .d.	Ⓐ	0530	0600	0630	0648	every	2048	2108	2130	every	0130	Ⓒ	0530	every	0700	every	0803	every	1903	1923	1943	2000	every	0130
Estoril .d.		0534	0604	0634	0652	15-20 ◧	2052	2112	2134	30	0134		0534	30	0707	20	0807	20	1907	1927	1947	2004	30	0134
Lisboa Cais do Sodre .a.		0610	0640	0703	0720	mins	2121	2141	2210	mins	0210		0610	mins	0743	mins	0836	mins	1936	1956	2023	2040	mins	0210

◧ – Every 15 minutes 0648 - 0948, every 20 minutes 1008 - 1648, every 15 minutes 1703 - 1948, every 20 minutes 2008 - 2108. * – Every 30 mins 1900 - 2000 October - early May.

LISBOA ROSSIO - SINTRA

27 km

Lisboa Rossio .. d.	Ⓐ	0621	every	2201	every	0131	Ⓒ	0601	every	0121
Monte Abraão .... d.		0639	20	2219	30	0149		0619	20	0139
Agualva - Cacém d.		0646	mins	2226	mins	0156		0626	mins	0146
Sintra .... a.		0700	△	2240		0210		0640	⊖	0200

Sintra .... d.	Ⓐ	0556	every	2156	every	0056	Ⓒ	0516	every	2116	every	0046
Agualva - Cacém. d.		0610	20	2210	30	0110		0530	20	2130	30	0100
Monte Abraão .... d.		0618	mins	2218	mins	0118		0538	mins	2138	mins	0108
Lisboa Rossio .. a.		0636	▽	2236		0136		0556		2156		0126

△ – Every 10 minutes 0611 - 0941, 1641 - 2021. ▽ – Every 10 minutes 0546 - 0916, 1616 - 1936 (also at 0506, 0526). ⊖ – Every 30 minutes 2121 - 0121.

LISBOA ORIENTE - MIRA SINTRA-MELEÇAS

See also Table 693

Lisboa Oriente ....d.	Ⓐ	0538	▲		▲	Ⓒ	0638		0008
Roma Areeiro ....d.		0545	0605		2255		0645	every	0015
Entrecampos ....d.		0547	0607	every	2257		0647	30	0017
Sete Rios ....d.		0551	0611	10-20	2301		0651	mins	0021
Monte Abraão ....d.		0605	0625	mins	2315		0705		0035
Agualva - Cacém ....d.		0613	0633	△	2323		...		...
Mira Sintra - Meleças ...a.		0618	0638		2328		...		...

Mira Sintra - Meleças ... d.	Ⓐ	0639	0649		2209	2239	2309	Ⓒ	...		...
Agualva - Cacém .... d.		0643	0653	every	2213	2243	2313		...		...
Monte Abraão .... d.		0651	0701	10-20	2221	2251	2321		0551		2321
Sete Rios .... d.		0706	0716	mins	2236	2306	2336		0606	every	2336
Entrecampos .... d.		0709	0719		2240	2310	2339		0609	30	2339
Roma Areeiro .... d.		0711	0722		2242	2312	2341		0611	mins	2341
Lisboa Oriente .... a.		0720	▼		▼	...	2350		0620		2350

△ – Every 30 minutes 2155 - 2255 (also to Cacém 2325, 2355, 0025).
▲ – From Oriente every 30 mins 0538 - 0938, 1638 - 1938 (also every 30 mins 0717 - 0847, 1647 - 1947). Connections Oriente to Roma Areeiro also run every 30 mins 0657 - 2327.
▼ – Through journeys Mira Sintra Meleças to Oriente: every 30 mins 0639 - 0839, 1609 - 1939 (also every 30 mins 0629 - 0859, 1629 - 1929). Connections Roma Areeiro to Oriente also run every 30 mins 0619 - 2219. Additional journeys Cacém - Oriente run 0513 - 0624.

LISBOA - PINHAL NOVO - SETÚBAL

Operator: Fertagus. CP tickets not valid.

Roma Areeiro .... d.	Ⓐ	0542		2242	2357	0042	Ⓒ	0642		2342
Entrecampos .... d.		0544	and	2244	2359	0044		0644	and	2344
Sete Rios .... d.		0548	every	2248	0003	0048		0648	every	2348
Pragal .... d.		0559	hour	2259	0014	0059		0659	hour	2359
Pinhal Novo .... d.		0627	until	2327	0042	0127		0727	until	0027
Setúbal .... a.		0640		2340	0055	0140		0740		0040

Setúbal .... d.	Ⓐ	0547	0657		1857	1927	2017		0017	Ⓒ	0557		2257
Pinhal Novo .... d.		0601	0711	and	1911	1941	2031	and	0031		0611	and	2311
Pragal .... d.		0629	0739	every	1939	2009	2059	every	0059		0639	every	2339
Sete Rios .... d.		0640	0750	hour	1950	2020	2110	hour	0110		0650	hour	2350
Entrecampos .... d.		0643	0753	until	1953	2023	2113	until	0113		0653	until	2353
Roma Areeiro .... a.		0645	0755		1955	2025	2115		0115		0655		2355

Additional journeys on Ⓐ: from Roma Areeiro 1812, 1912, 2012, from Setúbal 0627, 0727, 0827. *Fertagus* trains operate every 10 - 20 mins (30 evenings and Ⓒ) Roma Areeiro - Pragal - Coina.

Catamaran LISBOA - BARREIRO

Soflusa / Transtejo

From Lisboa Terreiro do Paço: By ⛴ journey time 20 minutes. *10* km

Ⓐ: 0545, 0610, 0640; every 5–10 minutes 0655–0920; 0940, 1005; every 30 minutes 1020–1550; 1615, 1630; every 10–15 minutes 1650–2040; 2105, 2130, 2200, 2230, 2300, 2330, 0000, 0030, 0100, 0130, 0230.

Ⓒ: 0545, 0610, 0640, 0710, 0740, 0805, 0830, 0855, 0920 and every 30 minutes until 2120, 2200, 2230, 2300, 2330, 0000, 0030, 0100, 0130, 0230.

From Barreiro Barcos: By ⛴ journey time 20 minutes. *10* km

Ⓐ: 0515, 0545, 0615; every 5–10 minutes 0630–0925; 0940, every 30 minutes 0955–1455; 1525, 1545, 1600; every 10–15 minutes 1620–2000; 2015, 2040, 2100, 2130, 2200, 2230, 2300, 2330, 0000, 0030, 0100, 0200.

Ⓒ: 0515, 0545, 0615, 0645, 0715, 0740, 0805, 0830, 0855 and every 30 minutes until 2055, 2130, 2200, 2230, 2300, 2330, 0000, 0030, 0100, 0200.

BARREIRO - SETÚBAL

See also Tables **697** and **698**

0	**Barreiro** .... d.	0625	and	2325	0029
15	Pinhal Novo .... d.	0644	hourly	2344	0048
28	**Setúbal** .... a.	0655	until	2355	0059

	Ⓒ			
Setúbal .... d.	0548	0648	and	2348
Pinhal Novo ...... d.	0600	0700	hourly	0000
Barreiro .... a.	0618	0718	until	0018

Additional journeys on Ⓐ:
From Barreiro: 0555, 0655, 0756, 0855, 1655, 1755, 1855, 1955.
From Setúbal: 0510, 0618, 0718, 0818, 0918, 1718, 1818, 1918, 2021.
All journeys continue beyond Setúbal to Praias do Sado A (8 minutes).

LISBOA - ENTRONCAMENTO - TOMAR

km			Ⓐ	⚒		⑥	Ⓐ		Ⓐ	Ⓐ		Ⓐ		Ⓐ			Ⓐ§		Ⓐ§				Ⓐ	
0	**Lisboa** Santa Apolónia ..... ▷ d.	0015	0548	0648	0748	0806	0848	0948	1048	1148	1248	1348	1448	1548	1618	1648	1718	1748	1818	1848	1948	2048	2148	2248
7	**Lisboa** Oriente .... ▷ d.	0024	0556	0656	0756	0814	0856	0956	1056	1156	1256	1356	1456	1556	1628	1656	1726	1756	1826	1856	1956	2056	2156	2256
31	Vila Franca de Xira .... d.	0042	0615	0715	0815	0835	0913	1015	1113	1215	1313	1415	1515	1615	1644	1715	1742	1815	1842	1915	2015	2115	2213	2313
75	Santarém .... d.	0119	0658	0758	0858	0920	0950	1058	1152	1258	1350	1458	1552	1706	1713	1758	1819	1858	1918	1958	2058	2152	2250	2350
107	Entroncamento .... d.	0145	0724	0824	0923	0941	1016	1124	1218	1324	1416	1524	1617	1731	1737	1824	1841	1923	1940	2024	2128	2218	2316	0016
130	**Tomar** .... a.	...	0755	0855	0950	...	...	1155	1245	...	1443	1555	1651	1758	...	1855	1902	1954	2001	2055	2155	2251	2343	0043

	⚒	Ⓐ	Ⓐ§		Ⓐ§		⚒		Ⓐ			Ⓐ		Ⓐ					Ⓐ	Ⓑ	⑥	Ⓐ	
Tomar .... d.	...	0515	0557	0614v	0657	0710v	...	0802	...	1009	1109v	...	1315	...	1509	1609	1702	1802	1913	2002	*2002*	...	2210
Entroncamento .... d.	0421	0543	0618	0641	0719	0741	0804	0836	0924	1036	1141	1236	1343	1436	1542	1637	1736	1836	1942	2036	2035	2143	2242
Santarém .... d.	0446	0608	0639	0706	0740	0806	0830	0901	0949	1101	1207	1302	1408	1502	1607	1702	1801	1901	2007	2101	2101	2205	2307
Vila Franca de Xira .... d.	0524	0646	0707	0744	0816	0844	0915	0946	1031	1146	1245	1346	1446	1546	1645	1746	1845	1946	2045	2146	2146	2246	2345
Lisboa Oriente .... ▽ a.	0542	0703	0723	0803	0831	0903	0932	1002	1048	1202	1302	1402	1503	1602	1702	1802	1902	2002	2102	2202	2202	2302	0002
Lisboa Santa Apolónia .... ▽ a.	0553	0711	0731	0811	0841	0911	0941	1011	1057	1211	1311	1411	1511	1611	1711	1811	1911	2011	2111	2211	2211	2311	0010

▷ – Additional local trains Santa Apolónia - Oriente: hourly 0536 - 0136 (on Ⓐ also runs every 30 minutes 0536 - 0936, 1636 - 2036).
▽ – Additional local trains Oriente - Santa Apolónia: hourly 0615 - 0115 (on Ⓐ also runs every 30 minutes 0615 - 1015, 1715 - 2115).
v – ⚒ only.
§ – *IR* train.

ENTRONCAMENTO - COIMBRA

km		Ⓐ			⚒						Ⓐ		Ⓑ
0	**Entroncamento** ... d.	0442	0542	0659	0742	0842	1142	1242	1542	1742	1845	1959	2132
24	Fátima ⊙ .... d.	0503	0603	0720	0809	0903	1203	1309	1603	1809	1913	2020	2153
64	Pombal .... d.	0535	0635	0751	0842	0941	1234	1342	1635	1842	1945	2052	2225
91	Alfarelos .... d.	0558	0658	0815	0905	1004	1257	1405	1658	1905	2009	2120	2248
111	Coimbra B .... a.	0624	0718	0841	0925	1030	1317	1424	1718	1924	2032	2139	2314
111	Coimbra B .... d.	0631	0723	0849	0932	1035	1325	1430	*1742*	1935	*2041*	2147	...
113	**Coimbra** .... a.	0635	0729	0853	0936	1039	1329	1434	*1746*	1939	*2046*	2151	...

	①–⑥	Ⓐ					Ⓐ			Ⓑ
Coimbra .... d.	*0635*	0716	0837	1039	1329	1623	1723	1817	1914	2013
Coimbra B .... a.	*0639*	0720	0841	1043	1333	1627	1727	1821	1918	2017
Coimbra B .... d.	0650	0725	0853	1049	1338	1632	1735	1826	1925	2022
Alfarelos .... d.	0707	0747	0910	1116	1411	1658	1758	1858	1958	2049
Pombal .... d.	0731	0827	0934	1140	1435	1722	1831	1922	2022	2112
Fátima ‡ .... d.	0802	0900	1005	1212	1507	1754	1905	1954	2054	2152
Entroncamento .. a.	0824	0920	1032	1232	1527	1814	1928	2014	2114	2213

⊙ – Station is *20 km* from Fátima.

AVEIRO - COIMBRA

km					Ⓐ			Ⓐ					
0	**Aveiro** .... d.	0649	0749	0949	1049	1133	1223	1349	1449	1533	1749	1949	2149
41	Pampilhosa .... d.	0725	0825	1025	1126	1210	1300	1425	1525	1610	1825	2025	2226
55	Coimbra B .... a.	0740	0840	1040	1140	1224	1314	1440	1540	1624	1840	2040	2240
57	**Coimbra** .... a.	0745	0845	1047	1146	1230	1318	1446	1545	1632	1846	2046	2246

		⚒								
Coimbra .... d.	0635	0745	0845	1056	1338	1446	1638	1846	1946	2210
Coimbra B .... d.	0640	0750	0850	1101	1348	1451	1646	1850	1951	2215
Pampilhosa .... d.	0655	0805	0905	1116	1404	1505	1702	1905	2006	2231
Aveiro .... a.	0732	0843	0943	1153	1441	1543	1739	1943	2043	2308

Additional trains: **Aveiro - Coimbra**: 0549 ⚒, 0849 Ⓐ, 1633 Ⓐ, 1849 Ⓐ, 2049 Ⓐ. **Coimbra - Aveiro**: 0545 Ⓐ, 1004 Ⓐ, 1146 Ⓐ, 1240 Ⓐ, 1545 Ⓐ, 1738 Ⓐ, 2046 Ⓐ.

Suburban trains run **Porto - Espinho - Aveiro** approx. hourly.

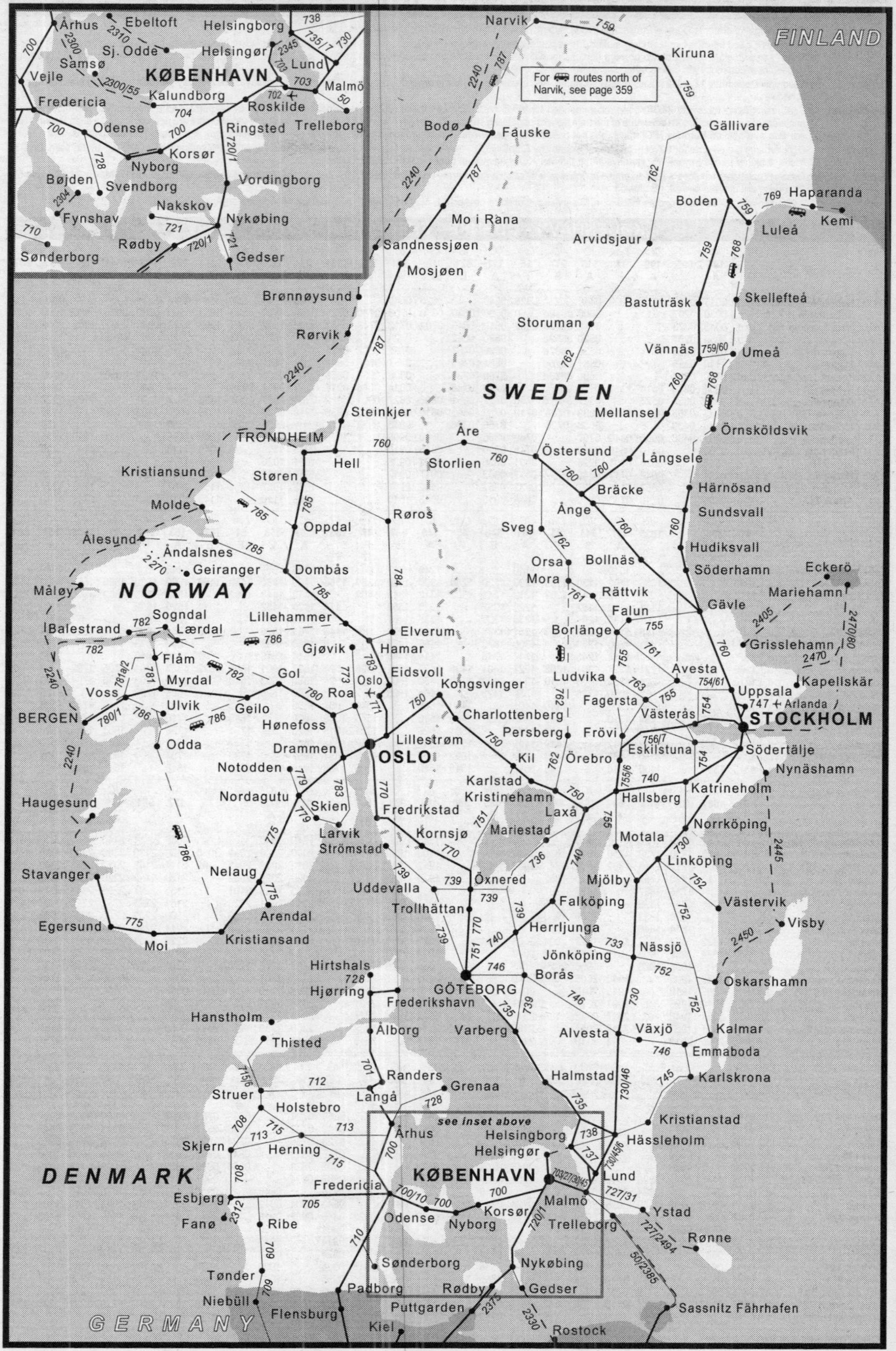
FINLAND
For routes north of Narvik, see page 359
Narvik
Kiruna
Gällivare
Bodø
Fauske
Mo i Rana
Boden
Haparanda
Kemi
Luleå
Arvidsjaur
Sandnessjøen
Mosjøen
Brønnøysund
Skellefteå
Bastuträsk
Storuman
Rørvik
Vännäs
Umeå
SWEDEN
Mellansel
Steinkjer
Örnsköldsvik
TRONDHEIM
Åre
Hell
Storlien
Östersund
Långsele
Kristiansund
Støren
Bräcke
Härnösand
Molde
Røros
Ånge
Sundsvall
Oppdal
Sveg
Ålesund
Hudiksvall
Åndalsnes
Orsa
Bollnäs
Geiranger
Dombås
Mora
Söderhamn
Eckerö
Måløy
NORWAY
Rättvik
Mariehamn
Falun
Gävle
Sogndal
Lillehammer
Balestrand
Lærdal
Elverum
Borlänge
Grisslehamn
Hamar
Gjøvik
Flåm
Avesta
Kapellskär
Eidsvoll
Ludvika
Gol
Oslo
Roa
Myrdal
Kongsvinger
Uppsala
Voss
Fagersta
Arlanda
Ulvik
Geilo
Västerås
Charlottenberg
STOCKHOLM
BERGEN
Hønefoss
Persberg
Frövi
Lillestrøm
Eskilstuna
Odda
Drammen
OSLO
Kil
Örebro
Södertälje
Notodden
Nynäshamn
Karlstad
Nordagutu
Kristinehamn
Hallsberg
Katrineholm
Haugesund
Skien
Laxå
Fredrikstad
Mariestad
Norrköping
Larvik
Kornsjø
Strömstad
Motala
Linköping
Stavanger
Nelaug
Öxnered
Mjölby
Uddevalla
Falköping
Västervik
Trollhättan
Arendal
Egersund
Herrljunga
Visby
Moi
Kristiansand
Jönköping
Nässjö
Hirtshals
Borås
GÖTEBORG
Oskarshamn
Hjørring
Frederikshavn
Hanstholm
Ålborg
Varberg
Alvesta
Växjö
Kalmar
Thisted
Emmaboda
Randers
Halmstad
Karlskrona
Grenaa
Struer
Langå
Holstebro
Kristianstad
see inset above
Århus
Helsingborg
Hässleholm
Skjern
Herning
Helsingør
DENMARK
KØBENHAVN
Lund
Fredericia
Esbjerg
Malmö
Ystad
Odense
Korsør
Fanø
Ribe
Nyborg
Trelleborg
Rønne
Sønderborg
Nykøbing
Tønder
Padborg
Rødby
Gedser
Niebüll
Puttgarden
Sassnitz Fährhafen
Flensburg
Kiel
Rostock
GERMANY
Ebeltoft
Sj. Odde
Samsø
Vejle
Kalundborg
Roskilde
Ringsted
Korsør
Bøjden
Svendborg
Vordingborg
Nakskov
Fynshav
Sønderborg

DENMARK

Operators: The principal operator is Danske Statsbaner (DSB). Arriva Tog (AT) operate many local services in Jutland.

Services: InterCity (*IC*) and InterCityLyn (*Lyn*) trains offer *Business* (1st class), *Standard* (2nd class), and on some services *Hvilepladser* ('quiet' seats) and *Familiepladser* ('family' seats). These services often consist of two or more portions for different destinations and care should be taken to join the correct portion. Other trains convey 1st and 2nd (standard) classes of accommodation unless otherwise shown.

Timings: Valid until **December 12, 2009** unless otherwise stated. Alterations may be made on and around the dates of public holidays (see **Holiday periods** below for known changes to schedules).

Reservations: Seat reservations (currently 20 DKK) are recommended for travel on *IC* and *Lyn* trains (especially at peak times) and may be purchased a maximum of two months and a minimum of 15 minutes before departure of the train from its *originating* station. Passengers may board the train without a reservation but are not guaranteed a seat. Reservations are also available on EuroCity (*EC*) trains. It is not possible to reserve seats on other types of train. Special reservation rules may apply during holiday periods.

Supplements: Supplements are payable for travel to and from Germany by EuroCity (*EC*) trains; also for journeys København – Høje Taastrup – Nykøbing Falster and v.v. by *EC* train. On DSB trains, a higher fare is payable for journeys in the Greater København area between 0100 and 0500 hours.

Holiday periods: Danske Statsbaner services will be amended as follows: a ⑤ service will operate on Apr. 8, May 7, 20, June 4; a ⑥ service will operate on Apr. 9, 10, 12, May 8, 21, 31, June 5; a ⑦ service will operate on Apr. 13, June 1.
Arriva services will be amended as follows: a ⑥ service will operate on Apr. 11, May 30, June 5; a ⑦ service will operate on Apr. 9, 10, 12, 13, May 8, 21, 31, June 1.

700 KØBENHAVN - ODENSE - FREDERICIA - ÅRHUS

km		*IC*	*IC*	*IC*	*Lyn*	*IC*	*IC*	*Lyn*	*IC*	*IC*	*Lyn*	*IC*	*IC*	*IR*	*Lyn*	*IC*	*IC*	*Lyn*	*IC*	*IC*	*IR*	*Lyn*	*IC*	*IC*
		191	**805**	**109**	**11**	**113**	**917**	**15**	**117**	**821**	**19**	**121**	**925**	**1631**	**23**	**125**	**829**	**27**	**129**	**933**	**1643**	**29**	**133**	**837**
		A		**A**	**F**	**A**	**S**	**F**	**A**	**E**	**F**	**A**	**S**		**F**	**A**	**E**	**F**	**A**	**S**		**F**	**A**	**E**
				①–⑤	①–⑥	①–⑥		①–⑥			①–⑥			⑤**z**				①–⑥			⑤**z**			
0	**København Lufthavn** ... d.	0011	0140	...	...	0440	...	0528	0540	...	0620	0640	...	...	0728	0740	...	...	0840	...	...	...	0940	...
11	**København H 721** .... § d.	0030	0207	...	...	0500	0530**d**	0550	0600	0630	0650	0700	0730	0725	0750	0800	0830	0850	0900	0930	0925	0950	1000	1030
31	Høje Taastrup **721** ..... § d.	0043	0223	...	...	0512	0543**d**	0602	0612	0643	0702	0712	0743	0743	0802	0812	0843	0902	0912	0943	0942	1002	1012	1043
42	Roskilde **721** .... § d.	0055	0237	...	...	0520	0552**d**	|	0620	0652	|	0720	0752	0755	|	0820	0852	|	0920	0952	0955	|	1020	1052
75	Ringsted **721** .... d.	0120	0258	...	...	0535	0607**d**	|	0635	0707	|	0735	0807	0825	|	0835	0907	|	0935	1007	1015	|	1035	1107
104	Slagelse .... d.	0140	0315	...	...	0551	0625**d**	|	0651	0725	|	0751	0825	0844	|	0851	0925	|	0951	1025	1038	|	1051	1125
119	Korsør .... d.	0150	0324	...	...	0600	0633**d**	|	0700	0733	|	0800	0833	0855	|	0900	0933	|	1000	1033	1050	|	1100	1133
143	Nyborg .... d.	0204	0338	0514	...	0614	0646**d**	|	0714	0746	|	0814	0846	0917	|	0914	0946	|	1014	1046	1106	|	1114	1146
171	**Odense** .... a.	0220	0357	0527	...	0627	0701**d**	0706	0727	0801	0806	0827	0901	0932	0906	0927	1001	1006	1027	1101	1122	1106	1127	1201
171	**Odense 729** .... d.	0223	0358	0530	0610	0633	0703	0710	0730	0803	0810	0830	0903	0935	0910	0930	1003	1010	1030	1103	1134	1110	1130	1203
221	Middelfart **710** .... d.	0250	0430	0556	|	0658	0728	|	0756	0828	|	0856	0928	|	|	0956	1028	|	1056	1128	|	|	1156	1228
231	**Fredericia** .... a.	0302	0438	0605	0640	0707	...	0740	0805	...	0840	0905	...	1010	0940	1005	...	1040	1105	...	1211	1140	1205	...
231	**Fredericia 705/10/5** ..... d.	0303	...	0610	0645	0710	...	0745	0810	...	0845	0910	...	...	0945	1010	...	1045	1110	...	...	1145	1210	...
257	Vejle **715** .... d.	0318	...	0626	0701	0726	...	0801	0826	...	0901	0926	...	...	1001	1026	...	1101	1126	...	...	1201	1226	...
288	Horsens .... d.	0334	...	0642	0717	0742	...	0817	0842	...	0917	0942	...	...	1017	1042	...	1117	1142	...	...	1217	1242	...
317	Skanderborg **713** .... d.	0349	...	0657	0732	0757	...	0832	0857	...	0932	0957	...	...	1032	1057	...	1132	1157	...	...	1232	1257	...
340	**Århus 713** .... a.	0406	...	0710	0745	0810	...	0845	0910	...	0945	1010	...	...	1045	1110	...	1145	1210	...	...	1245	1310	...

	Lyn	*EC*		*IR*	*IC*	*IC*	*Lyn*	*IC*	*IC*	*Lyn*	*IC*	*IC*	*Lyn*	*IR*	*IC*	*IC*	*Lyn*	*IR*	*IC*	*IC*	*Lyn*	*IR*	*IC*	*IC*
	41	**386**		**1635**	**137**	**941**	**43**	**141**	**845**	**45**	**145**	**949**	**47**	**1651**	**149**	**853**	**51**	**1679**	**153**	**957**	**55**	**1655**	**157**	**861**
	F				**A**	**S**	**F**	**A**	**E**	**F**	**A**	**S**	**F**		**A**	**E**	**F**	**E**	**A**	**S**	**F**		**A**	**E**
		♦		⑤**z**										⑤**z**				⑤**x**				⑤**x**		
København Lufthavn .... d.	...	...	...	...	1040	...	...	1140	...	...	1240	...	...	...	1340	...	...	...	1440	...	...	...	1540	...
København H 721 ...... § d.	1050	...	...	1056	1100	1130	1150	1200	1230	1250	1300	1330	1350	1356	1400	1430	1450	1456	1500	1530	1550	1556	1600	1630
Høje Taastrup **721** ...... § d.	1102	...	...	|	1112	1143	1202	1212	1243	1302	1312	1343	1402	|	1412	1443	1502	|	1512	1543	1602	|	1612	1643
Roskilde **721** .... § d.	|	...	...	1114	1120	1152	|	1220	1252	|	1320	1352	|	1414	1420	1452	|	1514	1520	1552	|	1614	1620	1652
Ringsted **721** .... d.	|	...	...	|	1135	1207	|	1235	1307	|	1335	1407	|	|	1435	1507	|	|	1535	1607	|	|	1635	1707
Slagelse .... d.	|	...	...	1146	1151	1225	|	1251	1325	|	1351	1425	|	1445	1451	1525	|	1546	1551	1625	|	1646	1651	1725
Korsør .... d.	|	...	...	|	1200	1233	|	1300	1333	|	1400	1433	|	|	1500	1533	|	|	1600	1633	|	|	1700	1733
Nyborg .... d.	|	...	...	|	1214	1246	|	1314	1346	|	1414	1446	|	|	1514	1546	|	|	1614	1646	|	|	1714	1746
Odense .... a.	1206	...	...	1221	1227	1301	1306	1327	1401	1406	1427	1501	1506	1521	1527	1601	1606	1622	1627	1701	1706	1722	1727	1801
Odense 729 .... d.	1210	...	...	1224	1230	1303	1310	1330	1403	1410	1430	1503	1510	1524	1530	1603	1610	...	1630	1703	1710	1724	1730	1803
Middelfart **710** .... d.	|	...	...	|	1256	1328	|	1356	1428	|	1456	1528	|	|	1556	1628	|	...	1656	1728	|	|	1756	1828
Fredericia .... a.	1240	...	...	1256	1305	...	1340	1405	...	1440	1505	...	1540	1557	1605	...	1640	...	1705	...	1740	1757	1805	...
Fredericia 705/10/5 ...... d.	1245	1255	...	1259	1310	...	1345	1410	...	1445	1510	...	1545	1559	1610	...	1645	...	1710	...	1745	1759	1810	...
Vejle **715** .... d.	1301	1310	...	1315	1326	...	1401	1426	...	1501	1526	...	1601	1615	1626	...	1701	...	1726	...	1801	1815	1826	...
Horsens .... d.	1317	|	...	1333	1342	...	1417	1442	...	1517	1542	...	1617	1634	1642	...	1717	...	1742	...	1817	1834	1842	...
Skanderborg **713** .... d.	1332	|	...	1350	1357	...	1432	1457	...	1532	1557	...	1632	1651	1657	...	1732	...	1757	...	1832	1851	1857	...
Århus 713 .... a.	1345	1350	...	1406	1410	...	1445	1510	...	1545	1610	...	1645	1706	1710	...	1745	...	1810	...	1845	1906	1910	...

	Lyn	*IR*	*IC*	*IC*	*Lyn*	*IC*	*IC*	*Lyn*	*EN*	*EC*	*IC*	*IC*	*Lyn*		*IC*	*IC*	*IC*	*Lyn*	*IC*	*IC*	*IC*	*IC*	*IC*	
	59	**1661**	**161**	**965**	**63**	**165**	**869**	**65**	**483**	**380**	**169**	**973**	**69**		**175**	**173**	**877**	**73**	**177**	**981**	**179**	**885**	**189**	
	F		**A**	**S**	**F**	**A**	**E**	**F**	Ⓡ		**A**	**S**			**A**	**A**								
		⑤**x**							♦ ⊡	♦					⑥	Ⓑ		⑤–⑦						
København Lufthavn .... d.	...	...	1640	...	...	1740	...	...	...	...	1840	...	...	...	1940	1940	...	...	2040	...	2140	...	2309	...
København H 721 ...... § d.	1650	1656	1700	1730	1750	1800	1830	1850	1853	...	1900	1930	1950	...	2000	2000	2030	2050	2100	2130	2200	2230	2330	...
Høje Taastrup **721** ...... § d.	1702	|	1712	1743	1802	1812	1843	1902	1907	...	1912	1943	2002	...	2012	2012	2043	2102	2112	2143	2212	2243	2343	...
Roskilde **721** .... § d.	|	1714	1720	1752	|	1820	1852	|	|	...	1920	1952	|	...	2020	2020	2052	|	2120	2152	2220	2252	2352	...
Ringsted **721** .... d.	|	|	1735	1807	|	1835	1907	|	1931	...	1935	2007	|	...	2035	2035	2107	|	2135	2207	2235	2307	0010	...
Slagelse .... d.	|	1746	1751	1825	|	1851	1925	|	|	...	1951	2025	|	...	2051	2051	2125	|	2151	2225	2251	2325	0027	...
Korsør .... d.	|	|	1800	1833	|	1900	1933	|	|	...	2000	2033	|	...	2100	2100	2133	|	2200	2233	2300	2333	0036	...
Nyborg .... d.	|	|	1814	1846	|	1914	1946	|	|	...	2014	2046	|	...	2114	2114	2146	|	2214	2246	2314	2346	0049	...
Odense .... a.	1806	1822	1827	1901	1906	1927	2001	2006	2021	...	2027	2101	2106	...	2127	2127	2201	2206	2227	2301	2327	0001	0107	...
Odense 729 .... d.	1810	1824	1830	1903	1910	1930	2003	2010	...	...	2030	2103	2110	...	2130	2130	2203	2210	2230	2303	2330	0003	0109	...
Middelfart **710** .... d.	|	|	1856	1928	|	1956	2028	|	...	...	2056	2128	|	...	2156	2156	2228	|	2256	2328	2356	0029	0135	...
Fredericia .... a.	1840	1857	1905	...	1940	2005	...	2040	...	...	2105	...	2140	...	2203	2205	...	2240	2305	...	0005	0041	0147	...
Fredericia 705/10/5 ...... d.	1845	1859	1910	...	1945	2010	...	2045	...	2106	2110	...	2145	...	2208	2210	...	2245	2308	...	0010	...	0149	...
Vejle **715** .... d.	1901	1915	1926	...	2001	2026	...	2101	...	2120	2126	...	2201	...	2226	2225	...	2301	2326	...	0026	...	0204	...
Horsens .... d.	1917	1934	1942	...	2017	2042	...	2117	...	2137	2142	...	2217	...	2245	2244	...	2317	2345	...	0042	...	0220	...
Skanderborg **713** .... d.	1932	1951	1957	...	2032	2057	...	2132	...	2153	2157	...	2232	...	2300	2259	...	2332	0000	...	0057	...	0235	...
Århus 713 .... a.	1945	2006	2010	...	2045	2110	...	2145	...	2207	2210	...	2245	...	2314	2314	...	2345	0014	...	0113	...	0251	...

	IC		*Lyn*	*IC*	*IC*	*IC*	*Lyn*	*Lyn*	*IC*		*Lyn*	*IC*	*EN*	*IC*	*Lyn*	*IC*	*EC*	*IC*	*Lyn*	*IC*	*IC*	*IR*	*Lyn*	*IC*
	190		**2**	**800**	**802**	**804**	**906**	**6**	**108**		**10**	**908**	**482**	**112**	**14**	**812**	**381**	**116**	**18**	**916**	**120**	**1658**	**24**	**820**
	A										**A**	**S**	Ⓡ	**A**	**F**	**E**		**A**	**F**	**S**	**A**		**F**	**E**
		①–⑤	①–⑤	①–⑥	①–⑤		①–⑤	①–⑤	①–⑥		①–⑤		♦ ⊡		①–⑥		♦					⑥**k**		
Århus 713 729 .... d.	0156	...	0414	...	...	...	...	0546	0559**g**	...	0627	...	...	0659	0727	...	0753	0759	0827	...	0859	0903	0927	...
Skanderborg **713** .... d.	0210	...	0428	...	...	...	...	0601	0613**g**	...	0642	...	...	0713	0742	...	0808	0813	0842	...	0913	0919	0942	...
Horsens .... d.	0225	...	0443	...	...	...	...	0616	0628**g**	...	0656	...	...	0728	0756	...	0824	0828	0856	...	0928	0936	0956	...
Vejle **715** .... d.	0243	...	0500	...	...	...	...	0632	0646**g**	...	0713	...	...	0746	0813	...	0841	0846	0913	...	0946	1956	1013	...
Fredericia 715 .... a.	0302	...	0516	...	...	...	...	0648	0702**g**	...	0729	...	...	0802	0829	...	0856	0902	0929	...	1002	1012	1029	...
Fredericia 705 710 .... d.	0306	0445	0521	0526	0540	0616	...	0653	0707	...	0734	...	...	0807	0834	...	...	0907	0934	...	1007	1014	1034	...
Middelfart **710** .... d.	0314	0452	|	0534	0548	0624	0651	|	0716	...	|	0746	...	0816	|	0846	...	0916	|	0946	1016	1023	|	1046
Odense .... a.	0341	0518	0553	0559	0615	0652	0716	0724	0743	...	0804	0812	...	0843	0904	0912	...	0943	1004	1012	1043	1048	1104	1112
Odense 729 .... d.	0347	0523	0556	0601	0630	0659	0720	0729	0746	...	0808	0816	0822	0846	0908	0916	...	0946	1008	1016	1046	1050	1108	1116
Nyborg .... d.	0403	0538	0610	0616	0646	0714	0735	|	0801	...	|	0830	|	0901	|	0930	...	1001	|	1030	1101	1106	|	1130
Korsør .... d.	0416	0551	|	0629	0659	0727	|	|	0814	...	|	0843	|	0914	|	0943	...	1014	|	1043	1114	|	|	1143
Slagelse .... d.	0425	0601	|	0639	0709	0737	0755	|	0824	...	|	0853	|	0924	|	0953	...	1024	|	1053	1124	1128	|	1153
Ringsted **721** .... a.	0444	0618	|	0655	0726	0752	|	|	0838	...	|	0909	0916	0938	|	1009	...	1038	|	1109	1138	1144	|	1209
Roskilde **721** .... § a.	0505	0639	|	0711	0744	0812	|	|	0855	...	|	0925	|	0955	|	1025	...	1055	|	1125	1155	1202	|	1225
Høje Taastrup **721** ...... § a.	0516	0647	0700	0719	0753	0823	|	0834	0905	...	0912	0934	0943	1005	1012	1034	...	1105	1109	1134	1205	1215	1209	1234
København H 721 ...... § a.	0536	0703	0715	0736	0810	0839	0843	0848	0919	...	0926	0950	0959	1019	1026	1050	...	1119	1123	1150	1219	1231	1223	1250
København Lufthavn ...... a.	0559	...	0739	...	...	...	...	...	0939	...	...	...	...	1039	...	...	...	1139	...	...	1239	...	...	...

FOR NOTES SEE FACING PAGE

ÅRHUS - FREDERICIA - ODENSE - KØBENHAVN 700

	IC	IR	Lyn	IC	IC	Lyn	IC	IC	IR	Lyn	IC	IC	Lyn	IC	IC	EC	Lyn	IC	IC	IR	Lyn	IC	IC	IR
	124	**1632**	**26**	**924**	**128**	**28**	**828**	**132**	**1640**	**40**	**932**	**136**	**42**	**836**	**140**	**387**	**44**	**940**	**144**	**1646**	**46**	**844**	**148**	**1654**
	A		F	S	A	F	E	A		F	S	A	F	E	A		F	S	A		F	E	A	
		⑤z							⑤z							♦				⑤w				⑤z
Århus 713 729 d.	0959	...	1027	...	1059	1127	...	1159	...	1227	...	1259	1327	...	1359	1411	1427	...	1459	1503	1527	...	1559	1603
Skanderborg **713** d.	1013	...	1042	...	1113	1142	...	1213	...	1242	...	1313	1342	...	1413	|	1442	...	1513	1519	1542	...	1613	1618
Horsens d.	1028	...	1056	...	1128	1156	...	1228	...	1256	...	1328	1356	...	1428	|	1456	...	1528	1538	1556	...	1628	1635
Vejle **715** d.	1046	...	1113	...	1146	1213	...	1246	...	1313	...	1346	1413	...	1446	1459	1513	...	1546	1558	1613	...	1646	1655
Fredericia 715 a.	1102	...	1129	...	1202	1229	...	1302	...	1329	...	1402	1429	...	1502	1515	1529	...	1602	1616	1629	...	1702	1712
Fredericia 705 710 d.	1107	1112	1134	...	1207	1234	...	1307	1312	1334	...	1407	1434	...	1507	...	1534	...	1607	...	1634	...	1707	1714
Middelfart **710** d.	1116	|	|	1146	1216	|	1246	1316	|	|	1346	1416	|	1446	1516	...	|	1546	1616	...	|	1646	1716	1723
Odense a.	1143	1150	1204	1212	1243	1304	1312	1343	1348	1404	1412	1443	1504	1512	1543	...	1604	1612	1643	...	1704	1712	1743	1750
Odense 729 d.	1146	1152	1208	1216	1246	1308	1316	1346	1350	1408	1416	1446	1508	1516	1546	...	1608	1616	1646	...	1708	1716	1746	1752
Nyborg d.	1201	1210	|	1230	1301	|	1330	1401	1408	|	1430	1501	|	1530	1601	...	|	1630	1701	...	|	1730	1801	1808
Korsør d.	1214	|	|	1243	1314	|	1343	1414	|	|	1443	1514	|	1543	1614	...	|	1643	1714	...	|	1743	1814	|
Slagelse d.	1224	|	|	1253	1324	|	1353	1424	1439	|	1453	1524	|	1553	1624	...	|	1653	1724	...	|	1752	1824	1830
Ringsted **721** a.	1238	|	|	1309	1338	|	1409	1438	1455	|	1509	1538	|	1609	1638	...	|	1709	1738	...	|	1809	1838	1845
Roskilde **721** § a.	1255	1300	|	1325	1355	|	1425	1455	1513	|	1525	1555	|	1625	1655	...	|	1725	1755	...	|	1825	1855	1903
Høje Taastrup **721** § a.	1305	1315	1309	1334	1405	1409	1434	1505	|	1510	1534	1605	1610	1634	1705	...	1710	1734	1805	...	1810	1834	1905	1916
København H 721 § a.	1319	1331	1323	1350	1419	1423	1450	1519	1537	1523	1550	1619	1623	1650	1719	...	1723	1750	1819	...	1823	1850	1919	1933
København Lufthavn a.	1339	...	...	...	1439	...	...	1539	...	...	...	1639	...	...	1738	...	...	...	1839	...	...	...	1939	...

	IR	Lyn	IC	IC	IR	Lyn	IC	IC	IR	Lyn	IC	IC	IR	Lyn	IC	IC	Lyn	IC	IC	Lyn	IC	IC	IC	IC
	1650	**50**	**948**	**152**	**1648**	**54**	**852**	**156**	**1680**	**56**	**956**	**160**	**1662**	**60**	**860**	**164**	**64**	**964**	**168**	**68**	**868**	**172**	**176**	**180**
		F	S	A		F	E	A	E	A	S	A		F	E	A	A	S	A		E	A	A	A
	⑤v				⑦t				⑤x				⑤z							⑦				
Århus 713 729 d.	1603	1627	...	1659	1703	1727	...	1759	...	1827	...	1859	1903	1927	...	1959	2027	...	2059	2127	...	2159	2259	0001
Skanderborg **713** d.	1620	1642	...	1713	1719	1742	...	1813	...	1842	...	1913	1918	1942	...	2013	2042	...	2113	2142	...	2213	2313	0015
Horsens d.	1638	1656	...	1728	1735	1756	...	1828	...	1856	...	1928	1935	1956	...	2028	2056	...	2128	2156	...	2228	2328	0031
Vejle **715** d.	1659	1713	...	1746	1754	1813	...	1846	...	1913	...	1946	1956	2013	...	2046	2113	...	2146	2213	...	2246	2346	0050
Fredericia 715 a.	1716	1729	...	1802	1810	1829	...	1902	...	1929	...	2002	2012	2029	...	2102	2129	...	2202	2229	...	2302	0005	0107
Fredericia 705 710 d.	...	1734	...	1807	1813	1834	...	1907	...	1934	...	2007	2014	2034	...	2107	2134	...	2207	2234	...	2307	0010	0112
Middelfart **710** d.	...	|	1746	1816	1822	|	1846	1916	1923	|	1946	2016	2023	|	2046	2116	|	2146	2216	|	2246	2316	0019	0120
Odense a.	...	1804	1812	1843	1849	1904	1912	1943	1951	2004	2012	2043	2050	2104	2112	2143	2204	2212	2246	2304	2312	2346	0049	0151
Odense 729 d.	...	1808	1816	1846	1851	1908	1916	1946	1953	2008	2016	2046	2052	2108	2116	2146	2208	2216	2249	2308	2316	2349	0055	...
Nyborg d.	...	|	1830	1901	1907	|	1930	2001	2009	|	2030	2101	2108	|	2130	2201	|	2230	2304	|	2331	0004	0111	...
Korsør d.	...	|	1843	1914	|	|	1943	2014	|	|	2043	2114	|	|	2143	2214	|	2243	2317	|	2347	0017	0125	...
Slagelse d.	...	|	1853	1924	1929	|	1953	2024	2031	|	2053	2124	2129	|	2153	2224	|	2253	2327	|	2356	0027	0135	...
Ringsted **721** a.	...	|	1909	1938	1944	|	2009	2038	2047	|	2109	2138	2144	|	2209	2238	|	2309	2344	|	0011	0043	0152	...
Roskilde **721** § a.	...	|	1925	1955	2002	|	2025	2055	2110	|	2125	2155	2202	|	2225	2255	|	2325	0001	|	0030	0101	0209	...
Høje Taastrup **721** § a.	...	1909	1934	2005	2016	2012	2034	2105	2119	2109	2134	2205	2216	2212	2234	2305	2312	2334	0011	0015	0038	0110	0219	...
København H 721 § a.	...	1923	1950	2019	2033	2026	2050	2119	2134	2123	2150	2219	2233	2226	2250	2319	2326	2350	0026	0032	0053	0127	0236	...
København Lufthavn a.	...	1948	...	2039	...	...	...	2139	...	2148	...	2239	...	2247	...	2339	2347	...	0046	0059	...	0147	0254	...

A – From / to Aalborg on some days (see Table **701**).
E – From / to Esbjerg (Table **705**).
F – From / to Frederikshavn on some days. A change of train may be necessary at Aalborg (see Table **701**).
S – From / to Sønderborg (Table **710**).
d – ①–⑥ only.
g – ⑥ only.
k – Jan. 17 - June 20, Aug. 22 - Dec. 12 (not Apr. 9, 10, 12, May 8, 21, 23, 30, June 5, 6).
t – Jan. 11 - June 21, Aug. 23 - Dec. 6 (not Apr. 13, June 7).
v – Jan. 16 - Apr. 17, Oct. 16 - Dec. 11.
w – Jan. 16 - June 19, Aug. 14 - Dec. 11 (not Apr. 8, May 20, 22, June 4).
x – Jan. 16 - June 19, Aug. 14 - Dec. 11 (not Apr. 8, May 22, June 4).
z – Apr. 24 - June 19, Aug. 21 - Oct. 9 (not May 20, 22, June 4).
§ – *IC* and *Lyn* trains are not available for local journeys. Frequent local trains run between Roskilde and København.
⊡ – For passengers making international journeys only.
♦ – For days of running and composition see Table **710**.

2nd class only (*IC* & *Lyn* 1st & 2nd class) ÅRHUS - AALBORG - FREDERIKSHAVN 701

km		IC				Lyn		IC			IC		IC	Lyn	IC	Lyn		IC	Lyn		IC	Lyn	IC	Lyn	IC	Lyn	IC
		191				**7**		**105**			**107**		**109**	**11**	**113**	**15**		**117**	**19**		**121**	**23**	**125**	**27**	**129**	**29**	**133**
			①–⑤		①–⑤	①–⑤	①–⑤	①–⑤	⑥⑦	①–⑥	①–⑤	⑥⑦		①–⑥		①–⑥	⑦		①–⑥	⑦							z
0	**Århus 712 729** d.	0410	...	...	0453	0530	...	0543	0543	...	0625	0653**g**	0716	0752	0816	0852	...	0916	0952	...	1016	1052	1116	1152	1216	1252	1316
46	Langå **712** d.	0440	...	...	0523	|	...	0613	0613	...	0652	0717**g**	0743	|	0843	|	...	0943	|	...	1043	|	1143	|	1243	|	1343
59	Randers d.	0450	...	...	0534	0602	...	0622	0624	...	0701	0727**g**	0754	0825	0854	0925	...	0954	1025	...	1054	1125	1154	1225	1254	1325	1354
91	Hobro d.	0507	...	...	0553	0620	...	0638	0643	...	0717	0743**g**	0811	0842	0911	0942	...	1011	1042	...	1111	1142	1211	1242	1311	1342	1411
140	**Aalborg** a.	0550	...	...	0634	0651	...	0718	0724	...	0756	0821**g**	0851	0913	0951	1013	...	1051	1113	...	1151	1213	1251	1313	1351	1413	1451
140	**Aalborg** d.	...	0605	0626	...	...	0656	...	...	0726	0758	0826	...	0926	...	1026	1026	...	1126**h**	1126	...	1226**h**	...	1326**h**	...	1426**t**	...
188	Hjørring **729** d.	...	0645	0709**j**	...	...	0748	...	...	0809**j**	0847	0909	...	1009	...	1109	1109	...	1209**h**	1209	...	1309**h**	...	1409**h**	...	1509**t**	...
225	**Frederikshavn** a.	...	0719	0737**j**	...	...	0820	...	...	0838	0917	0934	...	1037	...	1134	1134	...	1237**h**	1237	...	1334**h**	...	1437**h**	...	1537**t**	...

		Lyn	IC		Lyn		IC		Lyn		IC	Lyn	IC	Lyn	IC	Lyn	IC	Lyn	IC		Lyn	IC	Lyn		IC		IC
		41	**137**		**43**		**141**		**45**		**145**	**47**	**149**	**51**	**153**	**55**	**157**	**59**	**161**		**63**	**165**	**63**		**169**		**173/5**
	⑤		⑥⑦	①–⑤		①–⑤	⑤–⑦	①–④		①–⑤										⑥	Ⓑ		Ⓑ	⑥		⑥⑦	
Århus 712 729 d.	1316	1352	1416	1416	1452	...	1516	1516	1552	...	1616	1652	1716	1752	1816	1852	1916	1952	2016	...	2052	2116	2152	...	2216	...	2320
Langå **712** d.	1346	|	1443	1446	|	...	1543	1546	|	...	1643	|	1743	|	1843	|	1943	|	2043	...	|	2143	|	...	2243	...	2348
Randers d.	1356	1425	1454	1456	1525	...	1554	1556	1625	...	1654	1725	1754	1825	1854	1925	1954	2025	2054	...	2125	2154	2225	...	2254	...	2358
Hobro d.	1416	1442	1511	1516	1542	...	1611	1616	1642	...	1711	1742	1811	1842	1911	1942	2011	2042	2111	...	2142	2211	2242	...	2311	...	0015
Aalborg a.	1458	1513	1551	1558	1613	...	1651	1658	1713	...	1751	1813	1851	1913	1951	2013	2051	2113	2151	...	2213	2251	2313	...	2354	...	0058
Aalborg d.	...	1526**t**	...	...	1626**v**	1643	...	...	1726	1743	...	1826	...	1926	...	2026	...	2126	...	2226	2226	...	2326	2326	...	0026	...
Hjørring **729** d.	...	1609**t**	...	...	1709**v**	1745	...	...	1809	1845	...	1909	...	2009	...	2109	...	2209	...	2309	2309	...	0009	0009	...	0109	...
Frederikshavn a.	...	1637**t**	...	...	1741**v**	1817	...	...	1837	1917	...	1934	...	2037	...	2134	...	2237	...	2334	2334	...	0037	0037	...	0137	...

	Lyn	IC	Lyn	IC	Lyn		IC	Lyn		IC			Lyn	IC	Lyn	IC	Lyn	IC	Lyn	IC	Lyn	IC	Lyn	IC	Lyn	IC	Lyn
	10	**112**	**14**	**116**	**18**		**120**	**24**		**124**			**26**	**128**	**28**	**132**	**40**	**136**	**42**	**140**	**44**	**144**	**46**	**148**	**50**	**152**	**54**
	①–⑤	①–⑥	①–⑥		①–⑥	⑦		①–⑥	⑦	⑥⑦	①–⑤	①–⑤															
Frederikshavn d.	...	...	0437**a**	...	0542	0542	...	0639	0639	...	...	0742	0742**c**	...	0839	...	0942	...	1039	...	1142**h**	...	1239	...	1341**h**	...	1439**v**
Hjørring **729** d.	...	...	0506**a**	...	0611	0611	...	0711	0711	...	...	0813	0811**c**	...	0911	...	1011	...	1111	...	1211**h**	...	1311	...	1411**h**	...	1511**v**
Aalborg a.	...	...	0549**a**	...	0655	0655	...	0755	0755	...	...	0853	0855**c**	...	0955	...	1055	...	1155	...	1255**h**	...	1355	...	1455**h**	...	1555**v**
Aalborg d.	0459	0515	0559	0615	0659	...	0715	0759	...	0815	0815	...	0859	0915	0959	1015	1059	1115	1159	1215	1259	1315	1359	1415	1459	1515	1559
Hobro d.	0530	0555	0630	0655	0730	...	0755	0830	...	0855	0900	...	0930	0955	1030	1055	1130	1155	1230	1255	1330	1355	1430	1455	1530	1555	1630
Randers d.	0546	0612	0646	0712	0746	...	0812	0846	...	0912	0921	...	0946	1012	1046	1112	1146	1212	1246	1312	1346	1412	1446	1512	1546	1612	1646
Langå **712** d.	|	0622	|	0722	|	...	0822	|	...	0922	0932	...	|	1022	|	1122	|	1222	|	1322	|	1422	|	1522	|	1622	|
Århus 712 a.	0620	0651	0720	0751	0820	...	0851	0920	...	0951	1003	...	1020	1051	1120	1151	1220	1251	1320	1351	1420	1451	1520	1551	1620	1651	1720

	IC			Lyn	IC			Lyn	IC			Lyn	IC	IC	Lyn		IC	Lyn		IC		IC		IC			IC
	156			**56**	**160**			**60**	**164**			**64**	**166**	**168**	**68**		**172**	**72**		**176**		**180**		**184**			**190**
	z	⑤	①–⑤		z	⑤	①–⑤			①–⑤		Ⓑ	①–④	⑤–⑦	Ⓑ	⑥		①–⑤	⑥⑦					y	⑤⑥		
Frederikshavn d.	...	...	1456	1537**h**	...	...	1556	1639**h**	...	1657	1741	...	...	...	1839**v**	1839	...	1942	1942	...	2039	...	2144	...	...	2244	...
Hjørring **729** d.	...	...	1544	1611**h**	...	...	1644	1711**h**	...	1744	1811	...	...	...	1911**v**	1911	...	2011	2011	...	2111	...	2211	...	...	2311	...
Aalborg a.	...	...	1629	1655**h**	...	...	1729	1755**h**	...	1829	1855	...	...	...	1955**v**	1955	...	2055	2055	...	2155	...	2255	...	...	2355	...
Aalborg d.	1615	1615	...	1659	1715	1715	...	1759	1815	...	...	1859	1915	1915	1959	...	2015	2059	...	2115	...	2215	...	2315	2315	...	0010
Hobro d.	1655	1700	...	1730	1755	1800	...	1830	1855	...	...	1930	1955	1955	2030	...	2055	2130	...	2155	...	2255	...	2355	0000	...	0051
Randers d.	1712	1721	...	1746	1812	1821	...	1846	1912	...	...	1946	2012	2012	2046	...	2112	2146	...	2212	...	2312	...	0012	0021	...	0108
Langå **712** d.	1722	1732	...	|	1822	1832	...	|	1922	...	...	|	2022	2022	|	...	2122	|	...	2222	...	2322	...	0022	0032	...	0117
Århus 712 a.	1751	1803	...	1820	1851	1903	...	1920	1951	...	...	2020	2051	2051	2120	...	2151	2220	...	2251	...	2354	...	0054	0103	...	0149

a – ①–⑤ only.
c – ⑥⑦ only.
g – ⑥ only.
h – Connection on ⑤.
j – 3–5 minutes later ①–⑤.
t – Connection on Ⓑ.
v – Connection on ①–⑤.
y – ①②③④⑦.
z – ①②③④⑥⑦.

DENMARK

703 HELSINGØR - KØBENHAVN - KØBENHAVN LUFTHAVN (KASTRUP) ✈ - MALMÖ

km												and at											
0	**Helsingør** § d.	0012j	0112j	0212j	0312j	...	...	...	0435	0455	0515	the same	1855	1915	1935	1952	and	2252	...	2312	2332	2352
43	Østerport ⊡ § d.	0055	0155	0255	0355	0425	0445	0505	0515	0535	0555	minutes	1935	1955	2015	2035	every	2335	...	2355	0015	0035
46	**København H 700/20/1** ⊡ § d.	0103	0203	0303	0403	0433	0453	0513	0523	0543	0603	past each	1943	2003	2023	2043	20	2343	...	0003	0023	0043
58	Køb Lufthavn (Kastrup) ✈ ⊡ a.	0116	0216	0316	0416	0445	0505	0525	0536	0556	0616	hour	1956	2016	2036	2056	minutes	2356	...	0016	0036	0056
94	**Malmö C** a.	0138	0238	0338	0438	...	...	...	0558	0618	0638	until	2018	2038	2058	2118	until	0018	...	0038	...	...

										and at												
Malmö C d.	0022	0122	0222	0322	0422	...	0502	0522	0542	the same	1822	1842	1902	1922	and	2322	...	...	...	...	...
Køb Lufthavn (Kastrup) ✈ ⊡ d.	0044	0144	0244	0344	0444	0504	0524	0544	0604	minutes	1844	1904	1924	1944	every	2344	...	0004	0024	...	...
København H 700/20/1 ⊡ § d.	0059	0159	0259	0359	0459	0519	0539	0559	0619	past each	1859	1919	1939	1959	20	2359	...	0019	0039	...	...
Østerport ⊡ § a.	0106	0206	0306	0406	0506	0526	0546	0606	0626	hour	1906	1926	1946	2006	minutes	0006	...	0026	0046	...	...
Helsingør § a.	0148j	0248j	0348j	0448j	0544	0604	0624	0644	0704	until	1944	2004	2024	2048	until	0048	...	0108	0128	...	...

j – ⑥⑦ only. ⊡ – Additional services operate Østerport - Kastrup and v.v. § – Additional services operate ①–⑤ København H - Helsingør and v.v.

704 KØBENHAVN - KALUNDBORG

km		①–⑤	①–⑥	①–⑤	⑥⑦	①–⑤		①–⑤		①–⑤		①–⑤		①–⑤		①–⑤		①–⑤		①–⑤	①–⑤		①–⑤	①–⑤		①–⑤	①–⑤
0	**København H** d.	0450	0538	0641	0734	0734	0834	0853	0934	0953	1034	1053	1134	1153	1234	1253	1334	1353	1434	1453	1514	1534	1553	1614	1634	1653	1714
20	Høje Taastrup d.	0504	0554	0655	0749	0749	0849	0905	0949	1006	1049	1106	1149	1206	1249	1306	1349	1406	1449	1506	1529	1549	1606	1629	1649	1706	1729
31	Roskilde d.	0512	0606	0706	0802	0803	0902	0915	1002	1015	1102	1115	1202	1215	1302	1315	1402	1415	1502	1515	1538	1602	1615	1638	1702	1715	1738
67	Holbæk a.	0543	0638	0743	0832	0838	0932	0940	1032	1040	1132	1140	1232	1240	1332	1340	1432	1440	1532	1540	1608	1632	1640	1708	1732	1740	1808
67	Holbæk d.	0544	0659	0746	0841	0841	0941c	0941	1041c	1041	1141c	1141	1241c	1241	1341c	1341	1441c	1441	1541c	1541	1609	1641c	1641	1709	1741c	1741	1809
111	Kalundborg a.	0624	0742	0830	0918	0918	1018c	1018	1118c	1118	1218c	1218	1318c	1318	1418c	1418	1518c	1518	1618c	1618	1647	1718c	1718	1747	1818c	1818	1847

		①–⑤								
København H d.	1734	1814	1834	1934	2034	2134	2234	2334	0034	...
Høje Taastrup d.	1749	1829	1849	1949	2049	2149	2249	2349	0049	...
Roskilde d.	1802	1838	1902	2002	2102	2202	2302	0002	0102	...
Holbæk a.	1832	1908	1932	2032	2132	2232	2332	0032	0132	...
Holbæk d.	1841	1909	1941	2041	2141	2241	2341	0041	0141	...
Kalundborg a.	1918	1948	2018	2118	2218	2318	0018	0118	0218	...

	①–⑤	①–⑥	①–⑤	①–⑤	⑥	①–⑤	①–⑤	①–⑤	⑥⑦	①–⑤	①–⑤	⑥⑦
Kalundborg d.	0439	0504	0523	0559	0602	0610	0629	0654	0655	0728	0753	0757
Holbæk a.	0509	0542	0601	0643	0638	0651	0659	0732	0731	0802	0833	0833
Holbæk d.	0510	0543	0602	0644	0639	0717	0703	0734	0734	0804	0834	0841
Roskilde a.	0541	0613	0634	0716	0710	0750	0735	0805	0805	0833	0905	0911
Høje Taastrup a.	0554	0626	0642	0726	0723	0804	0744	0815	0818	0844	0917	0924
København H a.	0611	0642	0659	0743	0740	0822	0801	0832	0835	0901	0933	0941

	①–⑤		①–⑤		①–⑤		①–⑤		①–⑤		①–⑤		⑥⑦	①–⑤	⑥⑦	①–⑤	⑥⑦	①–⑤	⑥⑦	①–⑤	⑥⑦	①–⑤					
Kalundborg d.	0853	0853c	0953	0953c	1053	1053c	1153	1153c	1253	1253c	1353	1353c	1453	1453	1553	1553	1653	1653	1753	1753	1853	1853	1953	2053	2153	2253	...
Holbæk a.	0934	0935c	1035	1035c	1135	1135c	1235	1235c	1335	1335c	1436	1435c	1535	1535	1635	1639	1735	1739	1835	1839	1935	1939	2035	2135	2235	2335	...
Holbæk d.	0935	0941	1037	1041	1137	1141	1237	1241	1337	1341	1437	1441	1541	1541	1641	1641	1741	1741	1841	1841	1941	1941	2041	2141	2241	2341	...
Roskilde a.	1000	1011	1102	1111	1202	1211	1302	1311	1402	1411	1504	1511	1611	1617	1711	1717	1811	1817	1911	1917	2011	2011	2111	2211	2311	0011	...
Høje Taastrup a.	1009	1024	1113	1124	1213	1224	1313	1324	1413	1424	1513	1524	1624	1638	1724	1738	1824	1838	1924	1938	2024	2024	2124	2224	2324	0024	...
København H a.	1023	1041	1127	1141	1227	1241	1327	1341	1427	1441	1527	1541	1641	1654	1741	1754	1841	1854	1941	1954	2041	2041	2141	2241	2341	0041	...

c – ⑥⑦ only.

705 FREDERICIA - ESBJERG

2nd class only (*IC* & *Lyn* 1st & 2nd class)

km		*IC* 191									*IC* 821				*IC* 829				*IC* 869			*IC* 877			EXTRA TRAIN	*IR* 1679
				①–⑤	①–⑥	①–⑤	①–⑤	①–⑤	⑥⑦	①–⑥																⑤x
	København **700** d.	0030	...	...	...	...	...	...	...	...	0630	...	...	...	0830	...		...	1830	...	...	2030	...	...		1456
	Odense **700** d.	0223	...	...	...	...	...	...	...	...	0803	...	...	...	1003	...		...	2003	...	...	2203	...	...		1624
	Middelfart **700** d.	0250	...	...	...	...	...	...	...	...	0829	...	...	...	1029	...	and in	...	2029	...	...	2229	...	...		|
	Århus **700** d.	|	...	...	...	...	...	0613	...	0630	|	0730	...	0830	|	0930	the same	1830	|	1930	2030	|	2130	...		|
0	**Fredericia 700/10** d.	0301	0314	0417	0524	0551	0614	0722	0720	0758	|	0902	...	0958	|	1058	pattern	1958	|	2058	2208	|	2308	0010		|
20	Kolding **710** d.	...	0330	0432	0539	0608	0630	0736	0736	0813	0844	0917	...	1013	1044	1113	until	2013	2044	2113	2223	2244	2323	0025		1707
33	Lunderskov **710** d.	...	0339	0442	0548	0618	0639	0743	0745	0823	|	0927	...	1023	|	1123		2023	|	2123	2233	|	2333	0035		|
44	Vejen d.	...	0348	0451	0558	0627	0648	0751	0755	0832	0901	0936	...	1032	1101	1132		2032	2101	2132	2242	2301	2342	0044		1724
72	Bramming **709** a.	...	0412	0515	0622	0653	0713	0812	0819	0857	0915	1000	...	1057	1115	1157		2057	2115	2157	2307	2315	0007	0108		1749
88	**Esbjerg** a.	...	0424	0528	0634	0705	0726	0824	0832	0909	0928	1013	...	1109	1128	1209		2109	2128	2209	2319	2328	0019	0120		1802

			Lyn 806				*IC* 812				*IC* 820			*IC* 828		*IC* 860			*IC* 868			*IC* 176		EXTRA TRAIN	*IR* 1680
	①–⑤		①–⑤	①–⑤	①–⑥	①–⑤																			⑤x
Esbjerg d.	0448	0541	0557	0620	0648	0715	0741	0748	0848	...	0941	0948	1048	1141		1941	1948	2048	2141	2148	2248	...	...		1822
Bramming **709** d.	0459	0552	0608	0632	0700	0727	0753	0801	0900	...	0953	1000	1100	1153		1953	2000	2100	2153	2200	2300	...	...		1834
Vejen d.	0522	0613	0625	0656	0725	0752	0812	0825	0925	...	1012	1025	1125	1212	and in	2012	2025	2125	2212	2225	2325	...	...		1851
Lunderskov **710** d.	0531	0620	|	0705	0733	0800	|	0833	0933	...	|	1033	1133	|	the same	|	2033	2133	|	2233	2333	...	...		|
Kolding **710** d.	0541	0629	0641	0715	0743	0811	0832	0843	0943	...	1032	1043	1143	1232	pattern	2032	2043	2143	2232	2243	2343	...	...		1908
Fredericia 700/10 a.	0557	0643	|	0730	0759	0826	|	0859	0959	...	|	1059	1159	|	until	|	2059	2159	|	2259	2359	0010	...		|
Århus **700** a.	...	0801a	|	...	0934	...	|	1034	1134	...	|	1234	1334	|		|	2234	...	|	...	...	|	...		|
Middelfart **700** a.	...	...	|	...	...	...	0846	...	...	...	1046	...	...	1246		2046	...	...	2246	...	...	0019	...		1922
Odense **700** a.	...	...	0720	...	...	...	0912	...	...	...	1112	...	...	1312		2112	...	...	2312	...	...	0049	...		1945
København **700** a.	...	...	0848	...	...	...	1050	...	...	...	1250	...	...	1450		2250	...	...	0053	...	...	0236	...		2134

a – ①–⑤ only.
x – Jan. 16 - June 19, Aug. 14 - Dec. 11 (not Apr. 8, May 22, June 4).

Additional services operate Fredericia - Esbjerg and v.v. on ①–⑤.

708 ESBJERG - SKJERN and SKJERN - STRUER

2nd class only. Operator: *AT*

km										and each								⑥	†	⑥					†	
0	**Esbjerg 705** ⊗ d.	Ⓐ	0427	0532	0618	0712	0834	0933	1023	train every	1733	1823	2035	2235	2335	...	Ⓒ	0521	0656	0735	0935	and every	1935	2135	2218	2335
17	Varde ⊗ d.		0447	0552	0641	0736	0854	0953	1043	two hours	1753	1847	2055	2255	2354	...		0541	0716	0755	0955	two hours	1955	2201	2239	2354
60	**Skjern 713** a.		0524	0629	0722	0813	0931	1030	1122	until	1831	1925	2132	2333	...	...		0618	0753	0832	1032	until	2032	2238	...	...

km																	⑥	†	⑥	†	⑥						
0	**Skjern 713** d.	Ⓐ	0436	0526	0630	0723	0832	0932	1032		1732	1936	2136	...	Ⓒ	0441	0624	0624	0802	0836	1036		2036	...	2318	...
23	Ringkøbing a.		0454	0545	0650	0743	0855	0955	1055	and	1755	1955	2155	...		0459	0643	0643	0821	0855	1055	and every	2055	...	2337	...
23	Ringkøbing d.		0455	0549	0651	0744	0856	0956	1056	hourly	1756	1956	2200	...		0501	0656	0656	0822	0856	1056	two hours	2056	...	2338	...
71	Holstebro a.		0540	0634	0731	0831	0934	1034	1134	until	1834	2034	2238	...		0549	0734	0734	0900	0934	1134	until	2134	...	0016	...
71	Holstebro **715** d.		0546	0639	...	0849	0935	1035	1135		1835	2035	2239	...		0559	0735	0735	0913	0935	1135		2135	...	0017	...
86	**Struer 715** a.		0605	0656	...	0904	0949	1049	1149		1849	2049	2253	...		0612	0749	0749	0933	0949	1149		2149	...	0030	...

														⑥		†	⑥							
Struer 715 d.	Ⓐ	0445	0525	0620	...	0832	0933		1633	1820	2020	2220	...	Ⓒ	0501	...	0634	0720	...	0920		1920	2133	...	...
Holstebro **715** a.		0500	0537	0638	...	0847	0948	and	1648	1834	2034	2234	...		0515	...	0648	0734	...	0934	and every	1934	2149	...	...
Holstebro d.		0507	0542	0656	0746	0849	0949	hourly	1649	1835	2035	2239	...		0516	...	0649	0735	...	0935	two hours	1935	...	2210	...
Ringkøbing a.		0547	0625	0741	0831	0931	1031	until	1731	1914	2114	2318	...		0555	...	0731	0814	...	1014	until	2014	...	2250	...
Ringkøbing d.		0551	0625	0745	0832	0932	1032		1732	1914	2114	2318	...		0556	...	0734	0814	...	1014		2014	...	2251	...
Skjern 713 a.		0611	0649	0805	0852	0952	1052		1752	1934	2134	2338	...		0616	...	0755	0834	...	1034		2034	...	2311	...

									and each								⑥	†	⑥						
Skjern 713 d.	Ⓐ	0539	0632	0654	0814	0900	0959	1054	train every	1559	1654	1800	1938	2138	2343	Ⓒ	0625	0806	0838	1038	and every	2038	...	2324	...
Varde ⊗ d.		0621	0711	0740	0857	0953	1042	1132	two hours	1642	1732	1842	2015	2215	0020		0705	0843	0915	1115	two hours	2115	2222	0001	...
Esbjerg 705 ⊗ a.		0641	0734	0803	0917	1013	1102	1155	until	1702	1755	1902	2035	2235	0040		0725	0903	0935	1135	until	2135	2242	0021	...

⊗ – Additional services operate Esbjerg - Varde and v.v.

ESBJERG - RIBE - TØNDER - NIEBÜLL — 709

Operator: *AT*. 2nd class only — Valid until July 3

km																									
																	⑥								
0	**Esbjerg 705** ⊗ d.	Ⓐ	0513	0611	0659	0722	0807	0907	1007	and	1707	1807	1907	2007	2207	2309	Ⓒ	0507	...	0707	and	1907	2007	2207	2309
16	Bramming **705** ⊗ d.		0528	0627	0718	0736	0822	0921	1021	hourly	1721	1821	1921	2021	2221	2323		0521	...	0721	hourly	1921	2021	2221	2323
33	Ribe ⊗ d.		0546	0656	0736	0758	0841	0943	1044	until	1744	1843	1944	2043	2244	2343		0544	...	0744	until	1944	2043	2244	2343
80	**Tønder** a.		0639	0745	...	...	0929	1031	1131		1831	...	2031	...	2331	...		0631	...	0831		2031	...	2331	...

																⑥								
Tønder d.	Ⓐ	...	0606	0645	...	0830	0933	1035	and	1835	...	2035	...	...	2335	Ⓒ	...	0637r	0837	and	2037	...	...	2337
Ribe ⊗ d.		0608	0658	0738	0819	0924	1025	1125	hourly	1925	2025	2125	2225	2355	0025		0625	0725	0925	hourly	2125	2225	2355	0025
Bramming **705** ⊗ a.		0626	0716	0757	0840	0942	1043	1142	until	1942	2042	2142	2242	0012	0042		0643	0742	0942	until	2142	2242	0012	0042
Esbjerg 705 ⊗ a.		0644	0735	0814	0855	0956	1057	1156		1956	2056	2156	2256	0026	0056		0656	0756	0956		2156	2256	0026	0056

km		Ⓐ	⚒	⑥				Ⓐ	Ⓒ	Ⓐ		h
0	**Tønder** ▲ ⊡ d.	0722	0834	0934	1034	1234	1434	1534	1634	1734	1834	2034
17	Niebüll **821** ▲ ⊡ a.	0741	0853	0953	1053	1253	1453	1553	1653	1753	1853	2053

	Ⓐ	⚒				Ⓐ	Ⓒ	Ⓐ		h	
Niebüll **821** ▲ ⊡ d.	0701	0806	1006	1206	1406	1506	1606	1706	1806	2006	...
Tønder ▲ ⊡ a.	0719	0825	1025	1225	1425	1525	1625	1725	1825	2025	...

h – Apr. 4 - July 3.
r – ⑥ only.

⊗ – Additional services operate Esbjerg - Ribe and v.v.

▲ – Bus service operates Niebüll - Tønder and v.v. up to 4 times daily on ⚒. Operator: Autokraft Niebüll. ✆ +49 0 46 61 87 75, fax +49 0 46 61 80 89.

⊡ – Operated by Nord-Ostsee-Bahn GmbH, Kiel. ✆ +49 (0) 180 10 180 11.

FREDERICIA - SØNDERBORG and FLENSBURG (- HAMBURG) — 710

km		IC 191	IC 190		Lyn 2				IC 917		IC 117			EC 381	IC 925		IC 125			IC 933		IC 133			IC 941		IC 141	
							①–⑤			①–⑥				♦														
	København **700** d.	0030	...	...	...	...	...	...	0530d	...	0600	...	...	...	0730	...	0800	...	...	0930	...	1000	...	...	1130	...	1200	...
	Odense **700** d.	0223	...	...	...	...	...	...	0703	...	0730	...	...	...	0903	...	0930	...	...	1103	...	1130	...	...	1303	...	1330	...
	Århus **700** d.	|	0156	...	0414	...	0449	...	|	0630	|	...	0730	0753	|	0830	|	...	0930	|	1030	|	...	1130	|	1230	|	...
0	**Fredericia 700** d.	0301	0302	0314	0516	0542	0609	0611	|	0758	0805	0817	0902	0858	|	0958	1005	1017	1058	|	1158	1205	1217	1258	|	1358	1405	1417
	Middelfart **700** d.	...	...	|	...	|	▬	|	0729	|	...	|	|	|	0929	|	...	|	|	1129	|	...	|	|	1329	|	...	|
20	Kolding **705** d.	...	...	0330	...	0556	...	0627	0744	0813	...	0831	0917	0910	0944	1013	...	1031	1113	1144	1213	...	1231	1313	1344	1413	...	1431
33	Lunderskov **705** d.	...	...	0338	...	0604	...	0636	0752	0822	...	0840	0926	|	0952	1022	...	1040	1122	1152	1222	...	1240	1322	1352	1422	...	1440
60	Vojens d.	...	...	...	...	0628	①–⑤	0706	0815	▬	...	0903	▬	|	1015	...	...	1103	▬	1215	...	...	1303	▬	1415	...	...	1503
95	Tinglev d.	...	...	...	...	0648	0651	0731	0839	...	...	0930	...	|	1039	...	...	1130	...	1239	...	...	1330	...	1439	...	...	1530
136	**Sønderborg** a.	...	...	...	...	0729	|	|	0918	...	...	|	...	|	1118	...	...	|	...	1318	...	...	|	...	1518	...	...	|
110	Padborg 🏛 **823** a.	...	...	...	...	...	0705	0742	...	0754	...	0941	0945	1000	...	...	...	1141	1154	...	...	...	1341	1345	...	...	...	1541
122	**Flensburg** 🏛 **823** a.	...	...	...	...	...	...	...	...	0807	...	...	0958	1022	...	...	...	...	1207	...	...	...	...	1358	...	...	...	...
302	*Hamburg Hbf* **823** a.	...	...	...	...	...	...	...	...	1014	...	...	1214	1232	...	...	...	...	1414	...	...	...	...	1614	...	...	...	...

		IC 145	EC 387	IC 949		IC 149			IC 957		IC 157			IC 965		IC 165			EN 483 Ⓡ		IC 973	IC 173/5				IC 981	IC 189	
			♦																♦ ⊡									
København **700** d.	...	1300	...	1330	...	1400	...	...	1530	...	1600	...	...	1730	...	1800	...	...	1853	...	1930	2000	...	...	...	2130	2330	...
Odense **700** d.	...	1430	...	1503	...	1530	...	...	1703	...	1730	...	...	1903	...	1930	...	...	2023	...	2103	2130	...	...	...	2303	0109	...
Århus **700** d.	1330	|	1411	|	1430	|	...	1530	|	1630	|	...	1730	|	1830	|	...	...	|	1930	|	|	2030	...	2130	|	|	...
Fredericia 700 d.	1458	1505	1524	|	1558	1605	1617	1658	|	1758	1805	1817	1858	|	1958	2005	2017	...	|	2058	|	2205	2208	2217	2308	|	0147	0153
Middelfart **700** d.	|	...	|	1529	|	...	|	|	1729	|	...	|	|	1929	|	...	|	...	|	|	2129	▬	|	|	|	2329	...	|
Kolding **705** d.	1513	...	1537	1544	1613	...	1631	1713	1744	1813	...	1831	1913	1944	2013	...	2031	...	2106	2113	2144	...	2223	2231	2323	2344	...	0206
Lunderskov **705** d.	1522	...	|	1552	1622	...	1640	1722	1752	1822	...	1840	1922	1952	2022	...	2040	...	|	2122	2152	...	2232	2240	2332	2352	...	0214
Vojens d.	▬	...	|	1615	...	...	1703	▬	1815	...	...	1903	▬	2015	...	...	2103	...	|	...	2215	...	...	2303	...	0015	...	0231
Tinglev d.	...	...	|	1639	...	...	1730	...	1839	...	...	1930	...	2039	...	...	2130	...	|	...	2239t	2242	...	2328	...	0039	...	0252
Sønderborg a.	...	...	|	1718	...	...	|	...	1918	...	...	|	...	2118	...	...	|	...	...	...	2318	|	...	|	...	0118	...	0330
Padborg 🏛 **823** a.	1545	...	1632	...	...	...	1741	1745	...	...	...	1941	1945	...	...	...	2141	2145	2158	...	...	2256	...	2340	...	...	...	...
Flensburg 🏛 **823** a.	1558	...	1652	...	...	...	...	1758	...	...	...	...	1958	...	...	...	...	2158	2231	...	...	...	...	...	...	...	...	...
Hamburg Hbf **823** a.	1814	...	1853	...	...	...	...	2014	...	...	...	...	2237z	...	...	...	...	...	...	...	...	...	...	...	...	...	...	...

	Lyn 906		IC 908	EN 482 Ⓡ			IC 812		IC 916			IC 820		IC 924			IC 828	EC 386		IC 132	IC 932			IC 836		IC 940		
	①–⑤	①–⑤		♦ ⊡	①–⑥	①–⑤												♦										
Hamburg Hbf **823** d.	...	...	...	...	...	...	...	...	...	*0620z*	...	...	...	...	0843	...	...	0930	...	...	...	1043	...	...	...	...	1243	...
Flensburg 🏛 **823** d.	...	...	...	0549	0701	...	...	...	...	0901	...	...	...	...	1101	...	...	1132	...	...	...	1301	...	...	...	...	1501	...
Padborg 🏛 **823** d.	...	0530	...	0620	0711	0717	...	...	...	0911	0917	...	...	...	1111	1117	...	1150	...	...	...	1311	1317	...	...	...	1511	1517
Sønderborg d.	0503	|	0559	|	▬	|	...	...	0759	▬	|	...	...	0959	▬	|	...	|	...	...	1159	▬	|	...	...	1359	▬	|
Tinglev d.	0545	0548v	0641	|	...	0729	...	...	0841	...	0929	...	...	1041	...	1129	...	|	...	...	1241	...	1329	...	...	1441	...	1529
Vojens d.	0606	0615	0706	|	①–⑥	0754	...	...	0902	...	0954	...	...	1102	...	1154	...	|	...	...	1302	...	1354	...	...	1502	...	1554
Lunderskov **705** d.	0625	0637	0722	|	0733	0814	...	0833	0920	0933	1014	...	1033	1120	1133	1214	...	|	1233	...	1320	1333	1414	...	1433	1520	1533	1614
Kolding **705** d.	0635	0646	0732	0721	0743	0824	0832	0843	0932	0943	1024	1032	1043	1132	1143	1224	1232	1241	1243	...	1332	1343	1424	1432	1443	1532	1543	1624
Middelfart **700** a.	0651	|	0746	|	|	|	0846	|	0946	|	|	1046	|	1146	|	|	1246	|	|	...	1346	|	|	1446	|	1546	|	|
Fredericia 700 a.	|	0702	|	|	0759	0838	|	0859	|	0959	1038	|	1059	|	1159	1238	|	1254	1302	1307	|	1359	1438	|	1459	|	1559	1638
Århus **700** a.	|	...	|	|	0934	...	|	1034	|	1134	...	|	1234	|	1334	...	|	1350	1434	|	|	1534	...	|	1634	|	1734	...
Odense **700** a.	0716	...	0812	0818	...	...	0912	...	1012	...	...	1112	...	1212	...	...	1312	...	...	1343	1412	...	...	1512	...	1612	...	...
København **700** a.	0843	...	0950	0959	...	...	1050	...	1150	...	...	1250	...	1350	...	...	1450	...	...	1519	1550	...	...	1650	...	1750	...	...

	IC 844		IC 948				IC 852		IC 956			IC 860		EC 380	IC 964				IC 868		IC 177		IC 976	IC 176	IC 179		IC 189	IC 190
														♦														
Hamburg Hbf **823** d.	...	...	...	...	1443	...	...	...	...	1643	...	...	...	1730	...	...	1849	...	...	...	...	...	...	...	...	...	...	...
Flensburg 🏛 **823** d.	...	...	...	...	1701	...	...	...	...	1901	...	...	...	1939	...	...	2101	...	...	...	...	...	...	...	...	...	...	...
Padborg 🏛 **823** d.	...	...	...	...	1711	1717	...	...	...	1911	1917	...	...	1958	...	...	2111	2117	...	...	...	2217	...	...	...	...	...	...
Sønderborg d.	...	...	1559	...	...	|	...	...	1759	▬	|	...	...	|	1959	...	▬	|	...	...	...	|	2159	...	...	2345	...	...
Tinglev d.	...	...	1641	...	...	1729	...	...	1841	...	1929	...	...	|	2041	...	...	2129	...	...	...	2229	2241	...	...	0023	...	...
Vojens d.	...	...	1702	...	...	1754	...	...	1902	...	1954	...	...	|	2102	...	...	2154	...	...	...	...	2302	...	...	0044	...	...
Lunderskov **705** d.	...	1633	1720	1733	...	1814	...	1833	1920	1933	2014	...	2033	|	2120	2133	...	2214	...	2233	...	...	2320	...	...	0105	...	...
Kolding **705** d.	1632	1643	1732	1743	...	1824	1832	1843	1932	1943	2024	2032	2043	2051	2132	2143	IC	2224	2232	2243	...	...	2332	...	...	0113	...	...
Middelfart **700** a.	1646	|	1746	|	...	|	1846	|	1946	|	|	2046	|	|	2146	|	**173/5**	|	2246	|	...	...	|	...	...	|	...	...
Fredericia 700 a.	|	1659	|	1759	...	1838	|	1859	|	1959	2038	|	2059	2104	|	2159	2208	2238	|	2259	2308	...	2345	0010	0010	0126	0149	0306
Århus **700** a.	|	1834	|	1934	...	...	|	2034	|	2134	...	|	2234	2207	|	...	2314	...	|	...	0014	...	...	|	0113	...	0251	|
Odense **700** a.	1712	...	1812	...	...	...	1912	...	2012	...	...	2112	...	...	2212	...	...	...	2312	...	...	...	...	0049	...	...	...	0341
København **700** a.	1850	...	1950	...	...	...	2050	...	2150	...	...	2250	...	...	2350	...	...	...	0053	...	...	...	...	0236	...	...	...	0536

♦ – **NOTES** (LISTED BY TRAIN NUMBER)

380/1 – (12) and 🍷 (Until Feb. 28, Berlin -) Hamburg - Århus and v.v.
386/7 – (12) and 🍷 Århus - Fredericia - Hamburg and v.v.
482 – *City Night Line* HANS CHRISTIAN ANDERSEN – 🛏 1, 2 cl., ▬ 2 cl., (2) [reclining] and ✕ (⑥ Dec. 27 - Apr. 18, Innsbruck -) München - København; 🛏 1, 2 cl., ▬ 2 cl. (4/6 berth), (2) [reclining] and ✕ Basel - Frankfurt - København; 🛏 1, 2 cl., ▬ 2 cl., (2) [reclining] and 🍷 Amsterdam - Köln - København.
483 – *City Night Line* HANS CHRISTIAN ANDERSEN – 🛏 1, 2 cl., ▬ 2 cl., (2) [reclining] and ✕ København - München (- Innsbruck, ⑤ Dec. 26 - Apr. 17 from København); 🛏 1, 2 cl., ▬ 2 cl. (4/6 berth), (2) [reclining] and ✕ København - Frankfurt - Basel; 🛏 1, 2 cl., ▬ 2 cl., (2) [reclining] and 🍷 København - Köln - Amsterdam.

d – ①–⑥ only.
t – Arrive 4 minutes earlier.
v – Arrive 0541.
z – Change at Neumünster (see Table **823**).

⊡ – For passengers making international journeys only.

712 ÅRHUS - VIBORG - STRUER

2nd class only (**IC** & **Lyn** 1st & 2nd class). Operator: *AT*

km		Ⓐ											z			Ⓒ ⑥		⑥				†		
	København 700 ..... d.	...	...	...	...	...	...	...		...	...	...	...	...	...	...	...	...	...	...	...	...	...	
0	**Århus 700** ⊗ d.	0517	0617	0726	0826	0926	1026	1226		1726	1826	2026	2126	2226	2326	0455	0626	0726	0826	0926	1026	1126	1226	
46	Langå **700** ⊗ a.	0548	0648	0758	0858	0958	1058	1258	and	1758	1858	2058	2158	2258	2358	0527	0658	0758	0858	0958	1058	1158	1258	and
46	Langå ⊗ d.	0553	0653	0803	0903	1003	1103	1303	hourly	1803	1903	2103	2203	2307	0003	0531	0703	0803	0903	1003	1103	1203	1303	hourly
86	Viborg ⊗ d.	0633	0731	0838	0938	1038	1138	1338	until	1838	1941	2141	2238	2341	0036	0607	0740	0841	0941	1041	1141	1241	1341	until
116	Skive d.	0703	0800	0903	1003	1103	1203	1403		1903	2005	2204	2305	0005	0059	0632	0805	0905	1005	1105	1205	1305	1405	
148	**Struer** a.	0729	0825	0929	1029	1129	1229	1429		1929	2031	...	2331	0031	0124	0701	0831	0931	1031	1131	1231	1331	1431	

			⑥x				725 ①–⑤	1625 ⑥x	757	765 ⑤†w
København 700 ...... d.	...	...	...	...	...	DSB	0800	0800	1600	1800
Århus 700 ⊗ d.	1826	2026	2126	2226	2326	*IC*	1126	1126	1926	2126
Langå **700** ⊗ a.	1858	2058	2158	2258	2358	services	1158	1158	1958	2158
Langå ⊗ d.	1903	2103	2203	2307	0003	►►►►	1203	1203	2003	2203
Viborg ⊗ d.	1941	2141	2238	2341	0036		1238	1241	2041	2238
Skive d.	2005	2204	2305	0005	0059		1303	1305	2105	2305
Struer a.	2031	...	2331	0031	0124		1328	1331	2131	2331

	Ⓐ								▲	
Struer d.	0440	0510	0540	0610	0636	0701	0758	0901		1701
Skive d.	0506	0536	0606	0636	0702	0733	0833	0933	and	1733
Viborg ⊗ d.	0532	0602	0632	0702	0729	0802	0902	1002	hourly	1802
Langå ⊗ a.	0606	0636	0706	0736	0803	0833	0933	1033	until	1833
Langå **700** ⊗ d.	0610	0640	0710	0740	0808	0838	0938	1038		1838
Århus 700 ⊗ a.	0642	0712	0742	0812	0840	0910	1010	1110		1910
København 700 .. a.	...	...	...	...	...	...	...	...		...

						Ⓒ ⑥				▲		t						728 ①–⑤	1628 ⑥⑦	1652 ⑤y	752 ⑦v	768 ①–⑤	1668 ⑦v	
Struer d.	1732	1935	2035	...	2232	0535	0635	0739	0935		1735	1835	1935	2035	...	2232	DSB	0831	0835	1431	1435	1832	1835	...
Skive d.	1801	2004	2104	2209	2302	0603	0704	0805	1004	and	1804	1904	2004	2104	2209	2302	*IC*	0901	0904	1501	1504	1904	1904	...
Viborg ⊗ d.	1824	2029	2129	2235	2326	0631	0729	0829	1029	hourly	1829	1929	2029	2129	2235	2326	services	0924	0929	1524	1529	1929	1929	...
Langå ⊗ a.	1903	2100	2200	2306	0002	0702	0800	0900	1100	until	1900	2000	2100	2200	2306	0002	►►►►	1003	1000	1603	1603	2000	2000	...
Langå **700** ⊗ d.	1908	2108	2208	2311	0008	0708	0808	0908	1108		1908	2008	2108	2208	2311	0008		1008	1008	1608	1608	2008	2008	...
Århus 700 ⊗ a.	1940	2140	2240	2343	0040	0740	0840	0940	1140		1940	2040	2140	2240	2343	0040		1040	1040	1640	1640	2040	2040	...
København 700 ...... a.	...	...	...	...	...	...	...	...	...		...	...	...	...	...	...		1419	1419	2019	2019	0026	0026	...

t – Apr. 9, 10, 12, May 8, 21, 31 only.
v – Not Apr. 9, 10, 12, May 8, 21, 31.
w – Also Apr. 8, May 7, 20; not Apr. 9, 10, 12, May 8, 21, 31.
x – Also Apr. 9, 10, 12, May 8, 21, 31.
y – Also Apr. 8, May 7, 20.

z – ①②③④ (not Apr. 8, May 7, 20).

▲ – Additional service on Apr. 9, 10, 12, May 8, 21, 31 only: Struer d. 1435, Skive d. 1504, Viborg d. 1529, Langå d. 1608, Århus a. 1640.

⊗ – Additional services operate Århus - Viborg and v.v.

See **Table 715** below for direct services Struer - Herning - København and v.v.

713 ÅRHUS - HERNING - STRUER

2nd class only. Operator: *AT*

km		Ⓐ															Ⓒ ⑥									
0	**Århus 700** ⊗ d.	0504	0604	0715	0841	0915	and at	1641	1715	1741	1841	1941	2041	2141	2241	2341	0541	0741	and	1741	1841	1941	2041	2141	2241	2341
23	Skanderborg **700** ⊗ d.	0524	0624	0736	0904	0936	the same	1704	1736	1804	1904	2004	2104	2204	2304	0004	0604	0804	every	1804	1904	2004	2104	2204	2304	0004
53	Silkeborg ⊗ d.	0558	0653	0807	0937	1007	minutes	1737	1807	1837	1937	2037	2137	2237	2337	0032	0637	0837	two	1837	1937	2037	2137	2237	2337	0039
94	**Herning** ⊗ a.	0638	0735	0847	1017	1047	past	1817	1847	1917	2017	2117	2217	2317	0017	0110	0717	0917	hours	1917	2017	2117	2217	2317	0017	0117
94	**Herning 715** d.	0656	0748	0850	...	1050	each hour	...	1850	...	2040	...	2240	...	...	...	0740	0940	until	1940	...	...	2240	...	...	...
136	**Skjern** a.	0737	0828	0927	...	1127	until	...	1927	...	2117	...	2317	...	...	...	0817	1017		2017	...	...	2317	...	...	...

	Ⓐ														Ⓒ ⑥		⑥	†	†	⑥				Ⓒ		
Skjern d.	0559	0650	0741	0838	0938	1138	...	and at	1738	...	...	1943	...	2143	...	...	0622	...	0809	0843	1043	and	2043	...	2321	...
Herning 715 a.	0638	0727	0818	0918	1018	1218	...	the same	1818	...	...	2021	...	2221	...	...	0700	...	0847	0921	1121	every	2121	...	2359	...
Herning ⊗ d.	0647	0752	0821	0921	1021	1221	1251	minutes	1821	1851	1951	2051	2151	2251	0551	0651	0751	0751	0851	0951	1151	two	2151	2251	0000	...
Silkeborg ⊗ d.	0731	0832	0906	1006	1106	1306	1332	past	1906	1932	2032	2132	2232	2332	0632	0732	0832	0832	0932	1032	1232	hours	2232	2332	0041	...
Skanderborg **700** ⊗ a.	0759	0859	0934	1034	1134	1334	1359	each hour	1934	1959	2059	2159	2259	2359	0659	0759	0859	0859	0959	1059	1259	until	2259	2359	0108	...
Århus 700 ⊗ a.	0820	0920	0954	1054	1154	1359	1420	until	1954	2020	2120	2220	2320	0020	0720	0820	0920	0920	1020	1120	1320		2320	0020	0129	...

⊗ – Additional services operate Århus - Herning and v.v.

715 FREDERICIA - STRUER - THISTED

2nd class only (**IC** & **Lyn** 1st & 2nd class)

km		*IC* 791	①–⑤	①–⑥	①–⑤	①–⑤	①–⑤	*IC* 113 ①–⑥		*IC* 117		*IC* 721	*IC* 125		*IC* 729	*IC* 133		*IC* 737 ①–⑤	*IC* 1637 ⑥⑦	*IC* 141		①–④	*IC* 745	①–⑤	*IC* 149	
	København 700 ..... d.	0030	...	...	...	...	...	0500	...	0600	...	0700	0800	...	0900	1000	...	1100	1100	1200	...	...	1300	...	1400	...
	Odense 700 d.	0223	...	...	...	...	...	0633	...	0730	...	0830	0930	...	1030	1130	...	1230	1230	1330	...	...	1430	...	1530	...
0	**Fredericia 700** d.	0303	...	0508	...	0558	...	0710	0713	0810	0813	0910	1010	1013	1110	1210	1213	1310	1310	1410	1413	...	1510	...	1610	1613
26	Vejle **700** d.	0319	...	0530	...	0625	...	0724	0734	0824	0834	0934	1024	1032	1134	1224	1234	1334	1334	1424	1434	...	1534	...	1624	1634
99	Herning a.	0411	...	0632	...	0733	...	...	0834	...	0934	1034	...	1134	1234	...	1334	1434	1434	...	1534	...	1634	...	...	1734
99	Herning **713** d.	0412	0549	0643	0656	...	0754	...	0835	...	0935**d**	1035	...	1135	1235	...	1335	1435	1435	...	1535	1609	1635	1709	...	1735
140	Holstebro **708** d.	0447	0626	0718	0738	...	0834	...	0906	...	1006**d**	1106	...	1206	1306	...	1406	1506	1506	...	1606	1649	1706	1749	...	1806
155	**Struer 708** a.	0459	0639	0735	0756	...	0847	...	0919	...	1019**d**	1119	...	1219	1319	...	1419	1519	1519	...	1619	1706	1719	1806	...	1819
229	*Thisted 716* a.	...	...	...	...	...	...	...	...	...	...	...	...	...	...	...	...	1651	1653	...	...	...	...	...	...	...

	IC 753	*IC* 755 ①–④	*IC* 157	⑤–⑦	*IC* 761	*IC* 165	Ⓑ	*IC* 769	*IC* 173 Ⓑ	Ⓑ	*IC* 777
København 700 ...... d.	1500	1600	1600	...	1700	1800	...	1900	2000	...	2100
Odense 700 d.	1630	1730	1730	...	1830	1930	...	2030	2130	...	2230
Fredericia 700 d.	1710	1810	1810	1813	1910	2010	2013	2110	2210	2213	2308
Vejle **700** d.	1734	1834	1824	1834	1934	2024	2034	2134	2224	2234	2334
Herning a.	1834	1934	...	1934	2034	...	2134	2234	...	2334	0034
Herning **713** d.	1835	1935	...	1935	2035	...	2135	2235	...	2335	0035
Holstebro **708** d.	1906	2006	...	2006	2106	...	2206	2306	...	0006	0106
Struer 708 a.	1919	2019	...	2019	2119	...	2219	2319	...	0019	0119
Thisted 716 a.	...	...	...	...	2257	...	...	...	...	...	...

	Lyn 706 ①–⑤	①–⑤	*Lyn* 710 ①–⑤	①–⑤	⑥	①–⑤	*Lyn* 14	①–⑤	*IC* 716	①–⑤	①–⑤
Thisted 716 d.	...	...	...	...	...	...	...	...	...	...	...
Struer 708 d.	0434	0513	0533	...	0545	0551	...	0610	0644	0704	0720
Holstebro **708** d.	0451	0528	0546	...	0559	0606	...	0630	0701	0717	0739
Herning **713** a.	0521	0605	0615	←	0630	0643	...	0710	0733	0748	0811
Herning d.	0524	→	0617	0632	0632	0656	...	...	0738	...	...
Vejle **700** d.	0625	...	0708	0733	0733	0803	0813	...	0835	...	...
Fredericia 700 a.	0641	...	0725	0753	0753	0823	0829	...	0853	...	...
Odense 700 a.	0724	...	0804	...	...	...	0904	...	0943	...	...
København 700 .. a.	0848	...	0926	...	...	...	1026	...	1119	...	...

	①–⑤	⑥	*IC* 120	*IC* 1624 ⑥⑦	*IC* 724 ①–⑤		*IC* 128	*IC* 732		*IC* 136	*IC* 740		*IC* 144	*IC* 748	①–④		*IC* 152	*IC* 756		*IC* 160	*IC* 764 ①–⑤	*IC* 1664 ⑥⑦	Ⓑ	*IC* 168		*IC* 776
Thisted 716 d.	...	...	...	0727	0728	...	...	...	...	...	...	...	...	...	...	...	...	...	...	...	1723	1727	...	...	...	...
Struer 708 d.	0741	0751	...	0851	0851	0951	...	1051	1151	...	1251	1351	...	1451	1502	1551	...	1651	1751	...	1851	1851	1951	...	2051	2151
Holstebro **708** d.	0800	0805	...	0905	0905	1005	...	1105	1205	...	1305	1405	...	1505	1522	1605	...	1705	1805	...	1905	1905	2005	...	2105	2205
Herning **713** a.	0835	0835	...	0935	0935	1035	...	1135	1235	...	1335	1435	...	1535	1558	1635	...	1735	1835	...	1935	1935	2035	...	2135	2235
Herning d.	0836	0836	...	0936	0936	1036	...	1136	1236	...	1336	1436	...	1536	...	1636	...	1736	1836	...	1936	1936	2036	...	2136	2236
Vejle **700** d.	0935	0935	0946	1035	1035	1135	1146	1235	1335	1346	1435	1535	1546	1635	...	1735	1746	1835	1935	1946	2035	2035	2135	2146	2235	2333
Fredericia 700 a.	0953	0953	1002	1053	1053	1153	1202	1253	1353	1402	1453	1553	1602	1653	...	1753	1802	1853	1953	2002	2053	2053	2153	2202	2253	2353
Odense 700 a.	...	...	1043	1143	1143	...	1243	1343	...	1443	1543	...	1643	1743	...	...	1843	1943	...	2043	2143	2143	...	2246	...	0049
København 700 ...... a.	...	...	1219	1319	1319	...	1419	1519	...	1619	1719	...	1819	1919	...	...	2019	2119	...	2219	2319	2319	...	0026	...	0236

d – ①–⑥ only.

716 STRUER - THISTED

2nd class only (**IC** 1st & 2nd class). Operator: *AT* (**IC** trains: *DSB*)

km		Ⓐ							*IC* 737 K			*IC* 761 K			Ⓒ ⑥					*IC* 1637 K			*IC* 761 K	
0	Struer d.	0450	0548	0800	1033	1233	1333	1433	1533	1654	1931	2135	2335	...	0545	0723	0935	1135	1335	1535	1723	1935	2135	2335
74	Thisted a.	0612	0727	0921	1151	1351	1454	1556	1651	1820	2049	2257	0053	...	0703	0841	1053	1253	1453	1653	1841	2053	2257	0053

	Ⓐ		*IC* 724 K							*IC* 764 K				Ⓒ ⑥	*IC* 1624 K					*IC* 1664 K				
Thisted d.	0514	0616	0728	0824	1000	1200	1357	1459	1618	1723	1858	2200	...	0512	0727	0903	1103	1303	1503	1727	1903	...	2200	...
Struer a.	0635	0733	0847	0941	1120	1320	1520	1620	1743	1843	2018	2318	...	0631	0847	1023	1223	1423	1623	1847	2023	...	2318	...

K – From / to København (Table **715**).

KØBENHAVN - RØDBY - PUTTGARDEN (- HAMBURG) 720

EC services only. For local trains see Table 721
Valid March 28 - August 9

km		*EC* 2908 B	*EC* 2910 q		*EC* 2906	*EC* 2904 x		*EC* 2902		*EC* 2900 y
0	**København H** d.	0726	0926	...	1126	1326	...	1526	...	1726
20	Høje Taastrup ● d.	0738	0938	...	1138	1338	...	1538	...	1738
91	Næstved ● d.	0832	1032	...	1232	1432	...	1632	...	1832
147	Nykøbing (Falster) ● d.	0912	1112	...	1312	1512	...	1712	...	1912
183	Rødby ⛴ ▲ a.	0934	1134	...	1334	1534	...	1734	...	1934
202	**Puttgarden** ⛴ ▲ a.	1035	1235	...	1435	1635	...	1835	...	2035
291	*Lübeck* **825** a.	1136	1336	...	1536	1736	...	1936	...	2136
353	*Hamburg Hbf* **825** a.	1216	1416	...	1616	1816	...	2016	...	2216

	EC 2901 z	*EC* 2903		*EC* 2905	*EC* 2911 q		*EC* 2907 B		*EC* 2909 x
Hamburg Hbf **825** d.	0725	0928	...	1328	1528	...	1728	...	1928
Lübeck **825** d.	0806	1006	...	1406	1606	...	1806	...	2006
Puttgarden ⛴ ▲ d.	0910	1110	...	1510	1710	...	1910	...	2110
Rødby ⛴ ▲ d.	1005	1205	...	1605	1805	...	2005	...	2205
Nykøbing (Falster) ● a.	1029	1229	...	1629	1829	...	2029	...	2229
Næstved ● a.	1118	1318	...	1717	1918	...	2118	...	2314
Høje Taastrup ● a.	1216	1416	...	1813	2008	...	2208	...	0007
København H a.	1231	1431	...	1827	2022	...	2222	...	0019

B – (12) and 🍸 København - Berlin Ost and v.v.
q – ⑤⑥ May 29 - June 6; daily June 13 - Aug. 30 (not Aug. 24 - 27).
x – June 19 - Aug. 23.
y – Apr. 3 - Oct. 25.
z – Apr. 4 - Oct. 26.
▲ – Through trains are conveyed by ⛴ Rødby - Puttgarden and v.v. ✕ on board ship. Passengers to/from Rødby or Puttgarden may be required to leave or join the train on board the train-ferry. See **Table 2375** for other available sailings.
● – From København stops to pick up only; to København stops to set down only.

KØBENHAVN - NYKØBING - RØDBY and NAKSKOV 721

Valid March 28 - July 6

km		4207 ①–⑤	4611 ①–⑤	①–⑤	⑥⑦	①–⑤	⑥⑦	①–⑤	4625 F	4609 G	①–⑤		⑥⑦	①–⑤	⑥⑦	①–⑤	⑥⑦	4739 ①–⑤		4641 ⑥⑦	①–⑤	⑥⑦	①–⑤	⑥⑦
0	**København H 700** d.	...	...	0534	0534	0634	0703	0704	0803	0803	0840	...	0903	0942	1003	1042	1103	1142	...	1203	1242	1303	1342	1403
20	Høje Taastrup **700** d.	...	...	0548	0548	0646	0717	0718	0817	0817	0854	...	0917	0956	1017	1056	1117	1156	...	1217	1256	1317	1356	1417
31	Roskilde **700** d.	...	...	0604	0604	0655	0727	0730	0827	0830	0902	...	0927	1004	1027	1104	1127	1204	...	1227	1304	1327	1404	1427
64	Ringsted **700** ● d.	...	...	|	|	|	|	|	|	|	0925	...	|	1025	|	1125	|	1225	...	|	1325	|	1425	|
	Køge d.	...	...	0623	0620	0715	0745	0813	0845	0848	|	...	0945	|	1045	|	1145	|	...	1245	|	1345	|	1445
91	Næstved ● d.	...	0551	0650	0700	0750	0816	0850	0916	0920	0953	...	1016	1053	1116	1153	1216	1253	...	1316	1353	1416	1453	1516
118	Vordingborg d.	...	0610	0708	0718	0811	0834	0907	0934	0938	1011	...	1034	1111	1134	1211	1234	1311	...	1334	1411	1434	1511	1534
147	Nykøbing (Falster) .. ⊙ ⊡ d.	0503	0643	0731	0742	0835	0903	0930	0958	1000	1037	...	1059	1137	1158	1237	1259	1338	...	1403	1437	1458	1534	1558
183	Rødby a.	0530	0705	...	...	...	0927j	...	...	...	...	...	...	...	...	...	...	1402	...	1427	...	...	...	...

	①–⑤	①–⑤	⑥⑦	①–⑤	4757 ①–⑤	4657 J	①–⑤	①–⑤		①–⑤	⑥⑦	4663 y	①–⑤					🚌						
København H 700 d.	1442	1503	1503	1538	1603	1603	1620	1642	...	1703	1703	1726	1745	...	1803	1903	2003	...	2103	2203	2303	...	0003	...
Høje Taastrup **700** d.	1456	1517	1517	1553	1617	1617	1635	1654	...	1717	1717	1738	1759	...	1817	1917	2017	...	2117	2217	2317	...	0017	...
Roskilde **700** d.	1504	1526	1527	1602	1626	1627	1644	|	...	1726	1727	|	1810	...	1827	1927	2027	...	2127	2227	2327	...	0027	...
Ringsted **700** ● d.	1525	1545	|	1621	1645	|	1702	|	...	1745	|	|	1831	...	|	|	|	...	|	|	|	...	|	...
Køge d.	|	|	1545	|	|	1645	|	|	...	|	1745	|	|	...	1845	1945	2045	...	2145	2245	2345	...	0045	...
Næstved ● d.	1553	1613	1616	1649	1713	1716	1729	1745	...	1813	1816	1832	1859	...	1916	2016	2116	...	2216	2316	0016	...	0113	...
Vordingborg d.	1611	1632	1634	1707	1732	1734	1747	1801	...	1831	1834	1847	1916	...	1934	2034	2134	...	2234	2334	0034	...	0131	...
Nykøbing (Falster) .. ⊙ ⊡ d.	1634	1658	1659	1731	1800	1758	1809	1822	...	1858	1858	1912	1939	...	1958	2059	2158	2205	2257	2357	0057	...	0154	...
Rødby a.	...	...	...	...	1827	...	...	...	...	...	...	1934	...	...	...	...	...	2245	...	...	...	...	...	...

	4704 ①–⑤	⑥⑦	①–⑤	①–⑤	①–⑤	①–⑤	⑥	①–⑤	4714 ①–⑤	①–⑤		①–⑤	⑥⑦	①–⑤	①–⑤	4730 ①–⑤	⑥⑦	①–⑤	⑥⑦		①–⑤	⑥⑦	①–⑤	4642 ⑥⑦
Rødby d.	0415	...	...	...	...	...	...	...	0555	...	...	...	...	...	...	0722	...	...	...	...	...	...	...	1016j
Nykøbing (Falster) .. ⊙ ⊡ d.	0440	0443	0516	...	0543	...	0543	0605	0624	...	...	0639	0643	...	0706	0747	0749	0812	0843	...	0915	0947	1012	1043
Vordingborg d.	0503	0508	0538	...	0606	...	0608	0627	0645	...	...	0658	0708	0710	0731	0810	0811	0838	0908	...	0939	1012	1038	1108
Næstved ● d.	0523	0529	0558	0547	0625	0616	0629	0645	0703	0700	...	0715	0731	0729	0750	0830	0831	0859	0931	...	0959	1031	1059	1129
Køge d.	|	0558	|	0625	|	0655	0704	|	|	0737	...	|	0804	|	|	|	0904	|	1004	...	|	1104	|	1204
Ringsted **700** ● d.	0550	|	0625	|	0651	|	|	0712	0733	|	...	|	|	0756	0818	0857	|	0933	|	...	1030	|	1130	|
Roskilde **700** d.	0608	0621	0645	0651	|	0719	0721	0732	0749	0806	...	0803	0821	0823	0838	0917	0921	0953	1021	...	1049	1121	1149	1221
Høje Taastrup **700** a.	0616	0630	0653	0705	0714	0731	0729	0740	0757	0819	...	0811	0829	0837	0848	0925	0929	1001	1029	...	1057	1129	1157	1229
København H 700 a.	0630	0646	0710	0722	0730	0747	0745	0757	0814	0835	...	0827	0845	0853	0905	0942	0945	1016	1045	...	1113	1145	1213	1245

km		①–⑤	4646 H	4748 L	⑥⑦	①–⑤	⑥⑦	①–⑤	4656 ①–⑤	⑥⑦	4660 ⑥⑦	①–⑤		①–⑤	⑥⑦			⑥	4676 ①–⑤	4678 K			🚌 x	
0	Rødby d.	...	...	...	...	...	...	...	1419	...	1508	...	...	...	...	...	...	...	1905	...	...	...	2150	...
	Nykøbing (Falster) . ⊙ ⊡ d.	1112	1147	1212	1243	1312	1347	1412	1447	1447	1547	1548	1643	1735	1747	...	1840	1947	1947	1947	2043	2147	2235	2248
	Vordingborg d.	1138	1212	1238	1308	1338	1412	1438	1511	1511	1612	1611	1708	1802	1812	...	1908	2012	2012	2012	2108	2212	...	2312
	Næstved ● d.	1159	1231	1259	1329	1359	1431	1459	1531	1531	1631	1631	1729	1831	1831	...	1929	2031	2031	2031	2129	2231	...	2331
	Køge d.	|	1304	|	1404	|	1504	|	1604	1604	1704	1704	1804	1904	1904	...	2004	2104	2104	2104	2204	2304	...	0004
	Ringsted **700** ● d.	1230	|	1330	|	1430	|	1530	|	|	|	|	|	|	|	...	|	|	|	|	|	|	...	|
	Roskilde **700** d.	1249	1321	1349	1421	1449	1521	1549	1621	1621	1721	1721	1821	1921	1921	...	2021	2121	2121	2121	2221	2321	...	0021
	Høje Taastrup **700** a.	1257	1329	1357	1429	1457	1529	1557	1629	1629	1729	1729	1829	1929	1929	...	2029	2129	2129	2129	2229	2329	...	0029
	København H 700 a.	1313	1345	1413	1445	1513	1545	1613	1645	1645	1745	1745	1845	1945	1945	...	2045	2145	2145	2145	2245	2345	...	0045

F – ⑥⑦. To Gedser (arrive 1033).
G – ①–⑤. To Gedser (arrive 1033).
H – ⑥. From Gedser (depart 1106).
J – ⑦. To Gedser (arrive 1830).
K – ⑦. From Gedser (depart 1908).
L – ①–⑤. From Gedser (depart 1106).
j – Mar. 29 only.
x – Mar. 28 - June 18.
y – Mar. 30 - Apr. 2.
z – Connection by 🚌.
● – Connecting 🚌 services operate Ringsted - Næstved and v.v.
⊙ – Trains run approximately hourly (more frequent on ①–⑤) Nykøbing (Falster) - Nakskov and v.v., journey 45 minutes (A/S Lollandbanen).
⊡ – 🚌 connection Nykøbing (Falster) Railway Station - Gedser Market Place and v.v. *25 km*, journey 35 minutes.

KØBENHAVN - YSTAD - RØNNE 727

km				B	A		C					D		E					y		G		
0	**København H** d.	Jan. 11	0639	1007	1339	1707	2039	...	May 1	0639	1007	1339	1707	2039	...	June 26	0639	1007	1339	1707	2039	...	...
11	Kastrup ✈ d.	to	0652	1020	1352	1720	2052	...	to	0652	1020	1352	1720	2052	...	to	0652	1020	1352	1720	2052	...	...
76	**Ystad** a.	Apr. 30	0755	1132	1451	1825	2150	...	June 25	0757	1133	1457	1827	2152	...	Aug. 31	0757	1133	1457	1827	2152	...	...
	Ystad ⛴ d.	▶▶▶▶	*0830*	*1200*	*1530*	*1900*	*2230*	...	▶▶▶▶	*0830*	*1200*	*1530*	*1900*	*2230*	...	▶▶▶▶	*0830*	*1200*	*1530*	*1900*	*2230*	...	...
	Rønne ⛴ a.		*0945*	*1315*	*1645*	*2015*	*2345*	...		*0945*	*1315*	*1645*	*2015*	*2345*	...		*0945*	*1315*	*1645*	*2015*	*2345*	...	...

			B	A		C				z	F		E				x			G		
Rønne ⛴ d.	Jan. 11	*0645*	*1015*	*1345*	*1715*	*2045*	...	May 1	*0645*	*1015*	*1345*	*1715*	*2045*	...	June 26	*0645*	*1015*	*1345*	*1715*	*2045*	...	...
Ystad ⛴ a.	to	*0800*	*1130*	*1500*	*1830*	*2200*	...	to	*0800*	*1130*	*1500*	*1830*	*2200*	...	to	*0800*	*1130*	*1500*	*1830*	*2200*	...	...
Ystad d.	Apr. 30	0815	1145	1516	1845	2218	...	June 25	0815	1145	1516	1845	2218	...	Aug. 31	0817	1147	1518	1847	2220	...	...
Kastrup ✈ a.	▶▶▶▶	0917	1246	1617	1947	2317	...	▶▶▶▶	0917	1246	1617	1947	2317	...	▶▶▶▶	0917	1246	1617	1947	2317	...	...
København H a.		0931	1300	1631	2001	2331	...		0931	1300	1631	2001	2331	...		0931	1300	1631	2001	2331	...	...

A – ⑤ Feb. 6 - Mar. 6; ⑤⑦ Mar. 7 - 29; ⑤⑥⑦ Apr. 3 - 30 (also Apr. 13, 27; not Apr. 10, 11).
B – ⑥ Apr. 3 - 30 (also Apr. 5, 13).
C – ⑦ Apr. 3 - 30 (also Apr. 8, 12, 27).
D – ④⑤⑥⑦ (also May 4, 6, 18, June 22; not May 14, June 1).
E – ⑤⑦ (also May 11; not May 1).
F – ①④⑤⑥⑦ (also May 6, 18; not May 14).
G – ①④⑤⑥⑦ June 26 - Aug. 9; ⑤⑦ Aug. 10 - 31 (also Aug. 15, 31; not June 29, Aug. 3).
x – Not Aug. 21, 28.
y – Not Aug. 17, 24.
z – Not May 15, 29, June 5, 12, 19.

728 BRANCH LINES in Denmark — 2nd class only

ÅRHUS - GRENAA: *69 km*

	y	y			and						
Århus..........d.	0514	0614	...	0714	hourly	2214	...	2320	...	...	...
Grenaa..........a.	0626	0726	...	0828	until	2328	...	0035	...	...	...

	①–⑤	z	y	y		and			and		
Grenaa..........d.	0502	0532	0632	0732	0832	hourly	1832	1933	hourly	2233	2338
Århus..........a.	0614	0644	0744	0844	0945	until	1945	2045	until	2345	0052

ODENSE - SVENDBORG: *48 km*

	①–⑥			①–⑥	and		①–⑥		and			
Odense........d.	0534	0634	0734	0804	hourly	1534	1604	1634	hourly	2234	2351	...
Svendborg...a.	0617	0717	0817	0846	until	1617	1646	1717	until	2317	0035	...

	①–⑤	①–⑥			①–⑥	and		①–⑥		and		
Svendborg...d.	0522	0622	0722	0822	0852	hourly	1722	1752	1822	hourly	2322	0039
Odense........a.	0605	0705	0805	0905	0934	until	1805	1834	1905	until	0005	0131

HJØRRING - HIRTSHALS: Nordjyske Jernbaner A/S — *18 km* — Journey 22 minutes

From **Hjørring**: *Subject to alteration on and around holidays*

①–⑤: 0456, 0553, 0618, 0645, 0714, 0746, 0816, 0912, 1012, 1112**x**, 1129**w**, 1212, 1312, 1412, 1512, 1612, 1642, 1712, 1742, 1812, 1912**x**, 1948**w**, 2112, 2318.

⑥: 0712, 0812, 0912, 1012, 1112**x**, 1129**w**, 1212**x**, 1312, 1412, 1612, 1712, 1912**x**, 1948**w**, 2112, 2318.

⑦: 0812, 0912, 1012**w**, 1112**x**, 1129**w**, 1212**x**, 1312, 1412, 1612, 1712, 1812, 1912**x**, 1948**w**, 2112, 2318.

From **Hirtshals / Color Line**: *Subject to alteration on and around holidays*

①–⑤: 0523, 0619, 0646, 0712, 0747, 0817, 0843, 0943, 1043, 1143**x**, 1215**w**, 1243, 1343, 1443, 1543, 1643, 1713, 1743, 1813, 1843, 2014, 2143, 2344.

⑥: 0743, 0843, 0943, 1043, 1143**x**, 1215**w**, 1243**x**, 1343, 1443, 1643, 1743, 1843, 2014, 2143, 2344.

⑦: 0843, 0943, 1043**w**, 1143**x**, 1215**w**, 1243**x**, 1343, 1443, 1643, 1743, 1843, 2014, 2143, 2344.

w – June 27 - Aug. 9.
x – Jan. 11 - June 26, Aug. 10 - Dec. 12.
y – ①–⑥ (not Apr. 9, 10, 12, May 8, 21, 31).
z – ①–⑤ (not Apr. 9, 10, 12, May 8, 21, 31).

ICELAND

There are no railways in Iceland but bus services serve all major settlements (some are only served in summer, particularly in the eastern part of the country). Principal bus services enabling a circuit around the country are shown below - see the right hand column for operating dates of each journey. See www.bsi.is and www.austurleid.is for further information.

729 PRINCIPAL BUS SERVICES — *Sept. 2008 - Sept. 2009*

Clockwise direction	*depart / arrive*	*Anti-clockwise direction*	*depart / arrive*	*Days of operation (applies to both directions)*
Reykjavik - Akureyri △:	d. 0830 a. 1430 *	Akureyri - Reykjavik △:	d. 0830 a. 1430 *	Daily May 1 - Sept. 30; ①–⑥ Oct. 1 - Apr. 30.
	d. 1500 a. 2100		d. 1500 a. 2100	⑦ Oct. 1 - Apr. 30.
	d. 1700 a. 2300		d. 1700 a. 2300	⑤ Oct. 1 - Apr. 30, ⑤⑦ May 1 - June 14; daily June 15 - Aug. 31; ⑤⑦ Sept. 1 - 30.
Akureyri - Egilsstadir:	d. 0800 a. 1155	Egilsstadir - Akureyri:	d. 1300 a. 1645	Daily June 1 - Aug. 31. Limited winter service (4 per week ⊖).
Egilsstadir - Hofn:	d. 0745 a. 1100	Hofn - Egilsstadir:	d. 1700 a. 2015	Daily June 1 - Aug. 31. No winter service.
Hofn - Reykjavik:	d. 1100 a. 1855	Reykjavik - Hofn:	d. 0830 a. 1615	Daily June 1 - Sept. 15.
	d. 1200 a. 1905		d. 1230 a. 1930	②⑤⑦ Sept. 16 - May 31.

Blue Lagoon: departures several times per day from Reykjavik, also infrequent departures from Kevlavik Airport to Blue Lagoon.

Egilsstadir - Seydisfjördur (for Smyril ferry, Table **2285**) June 1 - Aug. 31: depart Egilsstadir 0950 Ⓐ, 1300 ③⑥⑦ **b**, 1345 ④, 1705 Ⓐ; depart Seydisfjördur 0820 Ⓐ, 1220 ③⑥⑦ **b**, 1250 ④, 1610 Ⓐ. A limited service operates in winter.

Reykjavik - Thingvellir - Geysir: depart Reykjavik June 15 - Aug. 31, arriving back at 1645 (2008 schedule).

b – June 28 - Aug. 10.

⊖ – From Akureyri 0845 ②③, 1200 ⑦, 1300 ⑤, from Egilsstadir 1400 ②③, 1615 ⑦, 1715 ⑤.

* 1415 June 1 - Aug. 31.

△ – Additional journey runs via interior *Kjolur* route via Geysir and Gulfoss daily June 18 - Sept. 4: Reykjavik 0800 → Akureyri 1700; Akureyri 0800 → Reykjavik 1700. Reservation compulsory.

SWEDEN

SEE MAP PAGE 339

Operators: Most services are operated by **Statens Järnvägar** - Swedish State Railways (*SJ*). There is, however, a number of other operators which run services shown within the European Timetable; these are indicated by their initials in the relevant table heading, or at the top of each train column where more than one operator runs services on the same route.
AEX – Arlanda Express (A-Train AB). *MER* – MerResor. *Øtåg* – Øresundståg. *ST* – Svenska Tågkompaniet AB. *VEO* – Veolia Transport.
The Regional Public Transport Authority is responsible for many local services, known collectively as Länstrafik (*LT*). Those shown within these pages are abbreviated as follows:
LTAC – Länstrafiken Västerbotten. *Skåne* – Skånetrafiken. *V* – Västtrafik. *VTAB* – Värmlandstrafik.

Services: Trains convey first and second classes of accommodation, unless otherwise shown. The fastest trains are classified *X2000* (high-speed trains). Sleeping cars (🛏) are of two basic types with a range of supplements: older cars (those without showers) have one berth in first class, two or three berths in second class. Newer cars either have compartments with shower and WC (one or two berth, first class only) or have shower and WC available in the car (one or two berths in first class, two berths in second class). Couchette cars (▬) have six berths and are second class only. Refreshment services (✕, 🍸, Bistro or Shop) may be available for part of the journey only.

Timings: Valid until **June 14 - August 15, 2009** except where indicated otherwise. Alterations may be made on and around the dates of public holidays.

Tickets: Through journeys between Länstrafik and Statens Järnvägar, Veolia Transport or Svenska Tågkompaniet are possible with a combined ticket known as 'Tågplus'. Similarly, Arlanda Express may be combined with Statens Järnvägar journeys. However, Veolia Transport and Svenska Tågkompaniet have their own fare structures and tickets cannot be combined with those of Statens Järnvägar.

Reservations: Seat reservation is compulsory on all *X2000* and night trains, and for through journeys to København (excluding local and *Skåne* services). Reserved seats are not labelled and, if occupied, must be claimed by presenting the seat ticket on the train.

Supplements: Special supplements are payable for travel on *X2000* high-speed trains.

730 STOCKHOLM - MALMÖ - KØBENHAVN

km		*X2000*		*X2000*	*X2000*		*X2000*			*X2000*			*VEO*	*X2000*		*VEO*	*VEO*		*X2000*		*X2000*	*X2000*		*X2000*	*X2000*
		509	**69**	**519**	**521**	**221**	**523**	**221**	**223**	**525**	**223**	**225**	**7103**	**527**		**7103**	**7103**		**529**	**229**	**531**	**533**		**535**	**537**
		🅁 ✕	🅁	🅁 ✕	🅁 ✕		🅁 ✕			🅁 ✕			🅁 ✕	🅁 ✕		🅁 ✕	🅁 ✕		🅁 ✕		🅁 ✕	🅁 ✕		🅁 ✕	🅁 ✕
		⚒ q	◆	Ⓐ z	⚒	Ⓐ	Ⓐ	Ⓐ	⑥		⑥	Ⓐ	◆ m	A		◆ p	◆ n							B	
0	**Stockholm** Central ‡ d.	...	...	0521	0621	0706	0721	...	0800	0821	...	0825	0855	0921	...	0946	0946	...	1021	1040	1121	1221	...	1321	1421
15	Flemingsberg ‡ d.	...	...	|	|	0717	|	...	0811	|	...	0836	|	|	...	|	|	...	1032	1051	|	|	...	1332	1432
36	Södertälje Syd ‡ d.	...	...	0539	0639	0728	|	...	0822	0839	...	0847	|	0940	...	|	|	...	|	1102	1139	1239	...	|	|
	Katrineholm **740 754** d.	...	...	|	|	|	0814	←	|	|	←	|	|	|	...	|	|	...	|	|	|	|	...	|	|
103	Nyköping d.	...	...	|	|	0808	|	0810	0902	|	0904	0927	|	|	...	|	|	...	|	1142	|	|	...	|	|
162	**Norrköping 754** a.	...	0529**s**	0633	0733	→	0835	0848	→	0933	0942	1005	1027	1035	...	1136	1139	...	1133	1225	1233	1333	...	1433	1533
162	**Norrköping** d.	...	|	0635	0735	...	0837	0850	...	0935	0944	1007	1027	1037	...	1136	1139	...	1135	1227	1235	1335	...	1435	1535
209	Linköping d.	...	0558**s**	0700	0800	...	0902	0917	...	1000	1010	1033	1111	1102	...	1215	1215	...	1200	1253	1300	1400	...	1500	1600
241	**Mjölby 755** d.	...	|	|	0815	...	|	...	...	1015	...	...	|	|	...	|	|	...	1215	...	|	1415	...	|	1615
277	Tranås d.	...	|	0730	|	...	|	...	...	|	...	...	|	|	...	|	|	...	|	...	|	|	...	|	|
329	**Nässjö** d.	...	0702**s**	0753	0853	...	0953	...	...	1053	...	...	|	1153	...	|	|	...	1253	...	1353	1453	...	1553	1653
416	Alvesta d.	0627	0746**s**	0827	0927	...	1027	...	...	1127	...	...	|	1227	...	|	|	...	1327	...	1427	1527	...	1627	1727
514	Hässleholm **745/6** a.	0702	0841**s**	0902	1002	...	1102	...	...	1202	...	...	1343**s**	1302	...	1446**s**	1451**s**	...	1402	...	1502	1602	...	1702	1802
581	Lund **745/6** § a.	0731	0920**s**	0931	1031	...	1131	...	...	1231	...	...	1423**s**	1331	...	1525**s**	1538**s**	...	1431	...	1531	1631	...	1731	1831
597	**Malmö 745/6** a.	0746**s**	0955	0946	1046**s**	...	1146	...	...	1246**s**	...	...	1440	1346	...	1543	1557	...	1446	...	1546	1646	...	1746	1846**s**
597	**Malmö 703** d.	|	...	...	|	...	...	...	...	|	...	...	...	...	...	...	...	...	|	...	...	|	...	...	|
633	København (Kastrup) ✈ **703** a.	0819**s**	...	...	1118**s**	...	...	...	...	1328**s**	...	...	...	...	...	...	...	...	1518**s**	...	...	1718**s**	...	...	1918**s**
645	**København H 703** a.	0832	...	...	1132	...	...	...	...	1342	...	...	...	...	...	...	...	...	1531	...	...	1730	...	...	1932

◆ – **NOTES** (LISTED BY TRAIN NUMBER)

69 – ④⑤†: 🛏, ▬ and 2nd class seats Storlien (**10077**) - Stockholm - Malmö; 🍸 Norrköping - Malmö.

7103 – ③ June 22 - Aug. 24 (from Narvik): ▬, 2nd class seats and ✕ (also panorama car) Narvik - Stockholm - Malmö. Train number **17103** from Aug. 10.

A – ⑤ (⚒ June 29 - Aug. 15).
B – ⑤† (daily June 29 - Aug. 15).
m – July 6 - Aug. 9.
n – June 23 - July 5.
p – Aug. 10 - 23.
q – June 14 - 27.
s – Stops to set down only.
z – Not June 29 - Aug. 15.

STOCKHOLM - MALMÖ - KØBENHAVN 730

	237	539	203		541	203	241	271	513	543		291	253	505		263	545	263	245		251		5	
		X2000			X2000				X2000	X2000				X2000			X2000							
		R ✕			R ✕				R ✕	R ✕				R ✕			R ✕						R	
		Ⓑ	④⑤†			④⑤†	Ⓑ	Ⓐz	♦	Ⓑw		⑥	Ⓐn	Ⓑx		Ⓐm		Ⓐm	Ⓑ				♦	
Stockholm Central ‡ d.	1440	1521	1545	...	1615	...	1640	1644	1721	1721	...	1725	1730	1740	...	1745	1821	...	1840	...	2145	...	2155	...
Flemingsberg ‡ d.	1451	1532	|	...	|	...	1651	1655	1732	1732	...	1736	1741	|	...	1756	|	...	1851	...	2156	...	|	...
Södertälje Syd ‡ d.	1502	|	1605	...	1634	...	1702	|	|	|	...	1748	1753	1758	...	1808	1839	...	1902	...	2208	...	2220u	...
Katrineholm **740 754** d.	|	|	|	...	|	...	|	|	|	|	...	|	|	|	...	|	|	...	|	...	|	...	|	...
Nyköping d.	1542	|	|	...	|	...	1742	|	|	|	...	1829	1842	|	...	1850	|	...	1942	...	2249	...	|	...
Norrköping 754 a.	1625	1633	1710	...	1730	...	1827	1807	1833	1833	...	1907	1920	|	...	1928	1933	←	2025	...	2327	...	|	...
Norrköping d.	1627	1635	1713	...	1733	...	1829	1807	1835	1835	...	1909	1922	|	...	1938	1935	1938	2027	...	2329	...	|	...
Linköping d.	1653	1700	1742	...	1800	...	1855	1835	1900	1900	...	1937	1947	|	...	→	2000	2006	2053	...	2355	...	|	...
Mjölby 755 d.	...	|	1802	...	1815	...	...	...	|	|	...	...	...	|	...	...	2015	...	...	...	...	...	|	...
Tranås d.	...	|	|	...	|	←	...	...	1929	1929	...	...	...	|	...	...	|	...	...	...	...	...	|	...
Nässjö d.	...	1753	1900	...	1853	1900	...	...	1953	1955	...	...	...	|	...	...	2053	...	...	...	...	...	|	...
Alvesta d.	...	1827	→	...	1928	1944	...	...	...	2029	...	...	...	2033	...	...	2127	...	...	...	...	...	|	...
Hässleholm **745/6** a.	...	1902	...	...	2004	2026	...	...	...	2104	...	...	...	2108	...	...	2202	...	...	...	...	...	0445s	...
Lund **745/6** § a.	...	1931	...	...	2034	2102	...	...	...	2133	...	...	...	2137	...	...	2231	...	...	...	...	...	0604s	...
Malmö 745/6 a.	...	1946	...	...	2049	2117	...	...	...	2148s	...	...	...	2155s	...	...	2246	...	...	...	...	...	0620	...
Malmö 703 d.	...	...	...	...	...	...	...	...	...	|	...	...	...	|	...	...	...	...	...	...	...	...	...	...
København (Kastrup) ✈ **703** a.	...	...	...	...	...	...	...	...	...	2218s	...	...	...	2228s	...	...	...	...	...	...	...	...	...	...
København H 703 a.	...	...	...	...	...	...	...	...	...	2232	...	...	...	2242	...	...	...	...	...	...	...	...	...	...

	218	260	220	520	222	512	224	522	224		524	516	226	526	526		528	230	530		532	234	504	534
				X2000		X2000		X2000			X2000	X2000		X2000	X2000		X2000		X2000		X2000		X2000	X2000
				R ✕		R ✕		R ✕			R ✕	R ✕		R ✕	R ✕		R ✕		R ✕		R ✕		R ✕	R ✕
	Ⓐ	Ⓐm	Ⓐ	Ⓐt	Ⓐ	♦	⑥	Ⓐ	⑥		Ⓐz	♦		†	⚒		⚒	⑥			L	Ⓑ	†	⚒
København H 703 d.	...	...	...	...	...	...	...	...	...	...	...	...	...	...	0619	...	...	...	...	...	...	...	1016	1019
København Kastrup ✈ **703** d.	...	...	...	...	...	...	...	...	...	...	...	...	...	...	0631u	...	...	...	...	...	...	...	1029u	1031u
Malmö 703 a.	...	...	...	...	...	...	...	...	...	...	...	...	...	...	|	...	...	...	...	...	...	...	|	|
Malmö 745/6 d.	...	...	...	...	...	...	...	0514	...	...	0614	...	...	0714	0714u	...	0814	...	0914	...	1014	...	1114u	1114u
Lund **745/6** § d.	...	...	...	...	...	...	...	0528	...	...	0628	...	...	0728	0728	...	0828	...	0928	...	1028	...	1128	1128
Hässleholm **745/6** d.	...	...	...	...	...	...	...	0557	...	...	0657	...	...	0757	0757	...	0857	...	0957	...	1057	...	1157	1157
Alvesta **746** d.	...	...	...	...	...	...	...	0634	...	...	0734	...	...	0834	0834	...	0934	...	1034	...	1134	...	1234	1234
Nässjö d.	...	...	...	...	...	0642	...	0708	...	...	0808	0808	...	0908	0908	...	1008	...	1108	...	1208	...	1308	1308
Tranås d.	...	...	...	...	...	0703	...	|	...	...	|	|	...	|	|	...	|	...	|	...	|	...	|	|
Mjölby 755 d.	...	...	...	...	...	|	...	0744	...	...	|	|	...	0944	0944	...	|	...	1144	...	|	...	1344	1344
Linköping d.	0506	0528	0615	0638	0700	0740	0754	0800	...	...	0900	0900	0905	1000	1000	...	1058	1105	1200	...	1258	1303	1400	1400
Norrköping a.	0532	0554	0641	0700	0726	0802	0820	0822	...	...	0922	0922	0931	1022	1022	...	1120	1131	1222	...	1320	1331	1422	1422
Norrköping 754 d.	0534	0556	0643	0702	0728	0804	0822	0824	←	...	0924	0924	0933	1024	1024	...	1122	1133	1224	...	1322	1333	1424	1424
Nyköping d.	0617	0645	0724	|	0808	|	0900	|	0903	...	|	|	1013	|	|	...	|	1213	|	...	|	1413	|	|
Katrineholm **740 754** a.	|	|	|	|	|	|	→	|	|	...	|	|	|	|	|	...	|	|	|	...	|	|	|	|
Södertälje Syd ‡ a.	0656	0725	0805	0757	0847	|	...	0918	0942	...	|	|	1052	1118	1118	...	1216	1252	|	...	1416	1452	1518	1518
Flemingsberg ‡ a.	0706	0736	0816	0808	0856	0906	...	|	0952	...	1025	1025	1102	|	|	...	1227	1302	1326	...	|	1502	|	|
Stockholm Central ‡ a.	0720	0750	0831	0820	0909	0920	...	0939	1005	...	1039	1039	1115	1139	1139	...	1239	1315	1339	...	1437	1515	1539	1539

	236	536	238	7100	538	262	540	254	242	542		544	246	204	206	546	10066		548	550	554		6	
		X2000		VEO	X2000		X2000			X2000		X2000				X2000			X2000	X2000	X2000			
		R ✕		R ✕	R ✕		R ✕			R ✕		R ✕				R ✕	R		R ✕	R ✕	R ✕		R	
	⑥		Ⓑ	♦		Ⓐt	Ⓑ	⑥	Ⓑ			Ⓑ	Ⓑ	⑤†	④		♦		†z	Ⓑ	Ⓑp		♦	
København H 703 d.	...	...	...	...	1219	...	...	...	...	1419	...	...	...	...	...	1619	...	...	...	1818	2019	...	...	...
København Kastrup ✈ **703** d.	...	...	...	...	1231u	...	...	...	...	1431u	...	...	...	...	...	1631u	...	...	...	1831u	2031u	...	...	...
Malmö 703 a.	...	...	...	...	|	...	...	...	...	|	...	...	...	...	...	|	...	...	...	|	|	...	...	...
Malmö 745/6 d.	...	1214	...	1208	1314u	...	1414	...	...	1514u	...	1614	...	1617	1617	1714u	1717	...	1814	1914u	2114u	...	2308	...
Lund **745/6** § d.	...	1228	...	1226u	1328	...	1428	...	...	1528	...	1628	...	1632	1632	1728	1736u	...	1828	1928	2128	...	2323u	...
Hässleholm **745/6** d.	...	1257	...	1306u	1357	...	1457	...	...	1557	...	1657	...	1706	1706	1757	1813u	...	1857	1957	2203	...	0001u	...
Alvesta **746** d.	...	1334	...	|	1434	...	1534	...	...	1634	...	1734	...	1758	1758	1834	1904u	...	1934	2034	2239	...	|	...
Nässjö d.	...	1408	...	|	1508	...	1608	...	...	1708	...	1808	...	1840	1840	1908	1949u	...	2008	2108	...	...	|	...
Tranås d.	...	|	...	|	|	...	|	...	...	|	...	|	...	|	|	|	|	...	|	|	...	...	|	...
Mjölby 755 d.	...	|	...	|	1544	...	|	...	...	1744	...	|	...	|	|	1944	|	...	|	|	...	...	|	...
Linköping d.	1408	1458	1503	1536	1600	...	1658	1705	1705	1800	...	1858	1905	1940	1940	2000	2050u	...	2057	2157	...	...	|	...
Norrköping a.	1434	1520	1529	1607	1622	...	1720	1731	1731	1822	...	1920	1931	2006	2006	2022	|	...	2120	2219	...	...	|	...
Norrköping 754 d.	1436	1522	1531	1609	1624	...	1722	1733	1733	1824	...	1922	1933	2009	2009	2024	2125u	...	2122	2221	...	...	|	...
Nyköping d.	1516	|	1613	|	|	1713	|	1814	1814	|	...	|	2013	|	|	|	...	...	|	|	...	...	|	...
Katrineholm **740 754** a.	|	|	|	|	|	|	|	|	|	|	...	|	|	|	|	|	...	...	|	|	...	...	|	...
Södertälje Syd ‡ a.	1557	|	1652	|	1718	1800	|	1857	1857	1918	...	|	2052	|	|	2118	...	...	|	2315	...	...	0638s	...
Flemingsberg ‡ a.	1607	1624	1702	|	|	1811	1827	1907	1907	|	...	2027	2102	|	|	|	...	...	|	2326	...	...	|	...
Stockholm Central ‡ a.	1620	1639	1715	1800	1739	1824	1839	1920	1920	1939	...	2039	2115	2135	2143	2139	...	...	2235	2339	...	...	0705	...

♦ – **NOTES** (LISTED BY TRAIN NUMBER)

5/6 – Ⓑ: sleeper, couchette and (2) Stockholm - Malmö and v.v.
512 – Ⓐ (not June 29 - Aug. 15): (12) and ✕ Jönköping - Nässjö - Stockholm.
513 – Ⓑ (not June 28 - Aug. 15): (12) and ✕ Stockholm - Nässjö - Jönköping.
516 – ⑥ (not June 29 - Aug. 15): (12) and ✕ Jönköping - Nässjö - Stockholm.
7100 – ⑤ June 22 - Aug. 24 (from Malmö): couchette, (2), ✕ (also panorama car) Malmö - Stockholm - Narvik.
10066 – ④⑤†: sleeper, couchette and (2) Malmö - Stockholm (**76**) - Storlien; ✕ Malmö - Stockholm.

L – ⑤⑥ (daily June 29 - Aug. 15).
m – June 14 - 28.
n – June 29 - Aug. 15.
p – June 14 - 26.
s – Stops to set down only.
t – Not June 29 - Aug. 9.
u – Stops to pick up only.
w – June 28 - Aug. 15.
x – Not June 27 - Aug. 15.
z – Not June 29 - Aug. 15.

‡ – Most trains on this table do not convey passengers for local journeys between Stockholm and Södertälje Syd and v.v. Local trains run every 30 minutes Stockholm Central - Södertälje Hamn - Södertälje Centrum and v.v. (journey 42 mins). 🚌 Södertälje Syd - Södertälje Centrum runs every 30 minutes.

§ – From Malmö stops to pick up only, to Malmö stops to set down only. Frequent local trains run between Lund and Malmö.

MALMÖ - YSTAD 731

Operator: *Skåne*

65 km. Journey time: 45 minutes. 2nd class only

From **Malmö**:
0019②③④⑤⑥†, 0119Ⓒ, 0545⚒, 0619Ⓐ, 0645Ⓐ, 0719, 0745Ⓐ, 0819, 0919, 1019, 1119, 1219, 1319, 1419, 1445Ⓐ, 1519, 1545Ⓐ, 1619, 1645Ⓐ, 1719, 1745Ⓐ, 1819, 1845Ⓐ, 1919, 2019, 2119, 2219, 2319.

From **Ystad**:
0510Ⓐ, 0540Ⓐ, 0610⚒, 0640Ⓐ, 0710⚒, 0740Ⓐ, 0810, 0840Ⓐ, 0910, 1010, 1110, 1210, 1310, 1410, 1440Ⓐ, 1510, 1540Ⓐ, 1610, 1640Ⓐ, 1710, 1740Ⓐ, 1810, 1840Ⓐ, 1910, 1940Ⓐ, 2010, 2110, 2210, 2310, 0010Ⓒ.

Table 760 (continued from page 354)

STOCKHOLM - GÄVLE and v.v. (additional services):

	Ⓐ				Ⓑ		⑥		Ⓐ		Ⓑ	
Stockholm C. d.	0930	...	1130	...	1530	...	1630	...	1730	...	1930	...
Arlanda C ✈ ◧ d.	0948	...	1148	...	1548	...	1648	...	1748	...	1948	...
Uppsala **761** d.	1007	...	1207	...	1607	...	1707	...	1807	...	2007	...
Gävle 755 a.	1054	...	1258	...	1658	...	1758	...	1858	...	2058	...

	Ⓐ		⚒		Ⓑ		Ⓑ		⑥		Ⓑ	
Gävle 755 d.	0626	...	0906	...	1306	...	1502	...	1534	...	1702	...
Uppsala **761** a.	0721	...	0951	...	1351	...	1551	...	1631	...	1751	...
Arlanda C ✈ ◧ a.	0739	...	1009	...	1409	...	1609	...	1652	...	1809	...
Stockholm C. a.	0800	...	1030	...	1430	...	1630	...	1716	...	1830	...

SUNDSVALL - ÖSTERSUND and v.v. (local services):

Operator: *VEO*

		Ⓐ	Ⓐ	⑥	†	Ⓐ	⚒	†	
Sundsvall d.	0510	0742	1015	1316	1406	1410	1635	1800	2340
Ånge d.	0633	0855	1127	1441	1518	1518	1749	1913	0052
Bräcke d.	0648	0912	1144	1503	1535	1535	1806	1930	...
Östersund a.	0739	0958	1230	1549	1616	1616	1852	2025	...

	Ⓐ	Ⓐ	⑥	Ⓑ	⑥	Ⓑ	Ⓑ		
Östersund d.	...	0754	0812	1122a	1220	1325	1640	2046	...
Bräcke d.	...	0836	0901	1213a	1306	1412	1727	2133	...
Ånge d.	0610	0854	0924	1232	1324	1435	1748	2152	...
Sundsvall a.	0724	1002	1046	1346	1447	1553	1909j	2306	...

a – Ⓐ only.
j – Arrive 1902 on Ⓐ.

733 SKÖVDE - JONKÖPING - NÄSSJÖ

2nd class only except where shown

km																													
		Ⓐq	ⒶSz	Ⓐ	⑥Sz	⑥	Ⓐ		Ⓐ	Ⓐ		⑥	⑥				Ⓐ	⚒		Ⓐ	†	Ⓑ			†	†		Ⓒ	Ⓐ
0	**Skövde 740** .. d.	*0450*	...	*0557*	...	0656	0658	...	0754	...	0854	0925	...	1054	...	1254	1355	...	1454	1532	1552	...	1702	...	1800	...	1856	2230	2230
	Göteborg .... d.	|	...	|	...	|	|	...	|	0657	|	|	0902	|	...	|	|	1302	|	|	|	1502	|	...	|	1707	|	|	|
30	Falköping **740** d.	0511	...	0621	...	0716	0718	...	0812	0820	0916	0943	1020	1114	...	1316	1413	1420	1514	1548	1610	1616	1725	...	1818	1828	1916	2250	2250
100	Jönköping ...... a.	0551	...	0707	...	0756	0758	...	...	0902	1001	...	1100	1159	...	1401	...	1500	1601	...	...	1702	1810	...	...	1911	2001	2332	2332
100	Jönköping ...... d.	0553	0610	0710	0735	0800	0802	...	...	0904	1010	...	1102	1201	...	1407	...	1509	1607	...	...	1708	1812	...	...	1914	2003	2334	2334
143	**Nässjö 730** ... a.	0624	0637	0741	0802	0838	0838	...	...	0942	1041	...	1140	1235	...	1441	...	1548r	1642	...	...	1741	1843	...	...	1945	2041	0005	0021

	Ⓐq	Ⓐ	Ⓐ	⑥	⚒	Ⓐ	⑥		Ⓐ	Ⓐ			⑥			Ⓑ	Ⓐ	†			Ⓐq	†	†			ⒷSy			
Nässjö 730 ..... d.	0500	0545	0702	0724	0824	...	...	0921	1017	...	1120	...	1206	1317	1523	1617	...	...	1721	...	1819	1819	...	1921	...	2002	2120	...	...
Jönköping .... a.	0530	0622	0737	0759	0900	...	...	0953	1050	...	1156	...	1245	1350	1559	1658	...	...	1752	...	1851	1851	...	1954	...	2032	2152	...	...
Jönköping .... d.	0533	0625	0740	0801	0902	...	...	1001	1102	...	1201	...	1304	1401	1601	1702	...	...	1754	...	1857	1853	...	2003	...	...	2154	...	...
Falköping **740** . a.	0618	0706	0833	0842	0945	0950	1019	1045	1143	1211	1245	...	1344	1445	1646	1742	1754	1756	1842	...	1941	1942	1950	2044	...	...	2235	2243	...
Göteborg ..... a.	|	|	|	|	1057	|	|	|	1257	|	|	...	1457	|	|	1857	|	|	|	...	|	2057	|	|	...	...	...	|	...
Skövde 740 .... a.	0638	0735	0854	0902	...	1008	1037	1106	...	1229	1306	...	...	1506	1706	...	1815	1814	1902	...	2001	...	2008	2106	...	...	...	2301	...

S – *X2000*: (12) and ✕ Stockholm - Nässjö - Jönköping and v.v. 🅁 and special supplement payable. Train numbers **512/3/6**.

q – Not July 6 - Aug. 9.
r – Arrive 1543 on ⑤⑥.
y – Not June 28 - Aug. 15.
z – Not June 29 - Aug. 15.

735 GÖTEBORG - MALMÖ - KØBENHAVN

Local services are amended July 6 - August 9. A replacement 🚌 service will operate Laholm - Ängelholm and v.v.; journey times are extended

km			Øtåg	Øtåg	X2000	Øtåg	Øtåg		Øtåg	X2000	Øtåg		Øtåg	Øtåg	X2000	Øtåg	Øtåg			Øtåg	Øtåg				Øtåg	Øtåg
		5			**481**			**601**		**487**		**609**			**485**			**10603**	**603**			**661**	**10605**	**605**		
		🅁			🅁✕					🅁✕					🅁✕											
		♦⊡	Ⓐ	⚒	Ⓐp	Ⓐ	Ⓐ	Ⓐ		⑥p	Ⓐp	⑥		Ⓐ			Ⓐ	Ⓒ	Ⓐ		Ⓐ	⑤p	Ⓒ	Ⓐ		Ⓐ
	Oslo Sentral **770** .... d.	2132	...	...	...	...	...	...	...	...	...	...	...	...	...	...	...	...	...	...	...	...	...	...	...	...
0	**Göteborg** .... d.	0230	...	0542a	0627	0642	0712	0727	0742d	0757	0842	0927	0942	1042	1132	1142	1242	1327	1327	1342	1442	1457	1527	1527	1542	1612
28	Kungsbacka .... d.	|	...	0600a	|	0700	0730	|	0800d	|	0900	|	1000	1100	|	1200	1300	|	|	1400	1500	1515u	|	|	1600.	1630
76	Varberg .... d.	|	...	0621a	0702	0721	0751	0803	0821d	0831	0921	1003	1021	1121	1202	1221	1321	1403	1403	1421	1521	1538	1603	1603	1621	1651
106	Falkenberg .... d.	|	...	0636a	0717	0736	0806	|	0836d	0849	0936	|	1036	1136	1218	1236	1336	|	|	1436	1536	1555	|	|	1636	1706
150	**Halmstad** .... d.	|	0604	0704	0736	0804	0827	0835	0904	0907	1004	1035	1104	1204	1240	1304	1404	1435	1435	1504	1604	1617	1635	1635	1704	1725
*	Hässleholm .... a.	0445s	|	|	0830	|	...	|	|	0958	|	|	|	|	1332	|	|	|	|	|	|	1718	|	|	|	...
173	Laholm .... d.	|	0615	0715	|	0815	...	|	0915	|	1015r	|	1115	1215	|	1315	1415	|	|	1515	1615	|	|	|	1715	...
185	Båstad .... d.	|	0623	0723	|	0823	...	|	0923	|	1023r	|	1123	1223	|	1323	1423	|	|	1523	1623	|	|	|	1723	...
210	Ängelholm .... d.	|	0645	0745	|	0845	...	|	0945	|	1045r	|	1145	1245	|	1345	1445	|	|	1545	1645	|	|	|	1745	...
237	**Helsingborg** .... a.	|	0704	0804	|	0904	...	0930	1004	|	1104r	1134	1204	1304	|	1404	1504	1533	1533	1604	1704	|	1734	1734	1804	...
237	**Helsingborg 737** .... d.	|	0710	0810	|	0910	...	0938	1010	|	1110r	1138	1210	1310	|	1410	1510	1538	1538	1610	1710	|	1738	1738	1810	...
259	Landskrona **737** .... d.	|	0722	0822	|	0922	...	|	1022	|	1122r	|	1222	1322	|	1422	1522	|	|	1622	1722	|	|	|	1822	...
290	Lund **737** .... a.	0604s	0737	0837	0900s	0937	...	1002s	1037	1028s	1137r	1202s	1237	1337	1400s	1437	1537	1603s	1609s	1637	1737	1800s	1803s	1809s	1837	...
306	**Malmö 737** .... a.	0620	0752	0852	0915s	0952	...	1019s	1052	1043s	1152r	1219s	1252	1352	1415s	1452	1552	1617	1623s	1652	1752	1815	1820	1823s	1852	...
306	**Malmö 701** .... d.	...	0802	0902	|	1002	...	|	1102	|	1202r	|	1302	1402	|	1502	1602	...	|	1702	1802	...	...	|	1902	...
342	København (Kastrup) ✈ **703** . a.	...	0823	0923	0947s	1023	...	1047s	1123	1127s	1223r	1250s	1323	1423	1447s	1523	1623	...	1647s	1723	1823	...	...	1849s	1923	...
354	**København H 703** .... a.	...	0837	0937	1002	1037	...	1100	1137	1141	1237r	1304	1337	1437	1502	1537	1637	...	1701	1737	1837	...	...	1901	1937	...

	Øtåg	Øtåg	X2000	Øtåg	Øtåg	Øtåg		Øtåg	Øtåg	X2000	Øtåg
			495				**607**			**445**	
			🅁✕							🅁✕	
	Ⓐ	Ⓐ	Ⓑ		Ⓐ	Ⓐ			Ⓐ	SⒷ	
Oslo Sentral **770** .... d.	...	...	...	...	...	...	...	...	...	...	...
Göteborg .... d.	1642	1712	1727	1742	1812	1842	1927	1942	2042	2132	2242
Kungsbacka .... d.	1700	1730	|	1800	1830	1900	|	2000	2100	2150	2300
Varberg .... d.	1721	1751	1801	1821	1851	1921	2003	2021	2125	2209	2321
Falkenberg .... d.	1736	1806	1819	1836	1906	1936	|	2036	2138	2225	2336
Halmstad .... d.	1804	1827	1839	1904	1927	2004	2035	2104	2204	2244	2357
Hässleholm .... a.	|	...	1931	|	...	|	|	|	|	...	...
Laholm .... d.	1815	...	|	1915	...	2015	|	2115	2215	...	...
Båstad .... d.	1823	...	|	1923	...	2023	|	2123	2223	...	...
Ängelholm .... d.	1845	...	|	1945	...	2045	|	2145	2245	...	...
Helsingborg .... a.	1904	...	|	2004	...	2104	2130	2204	2304	...	...
Helsingborg 737 .... d.	1910	...	|	2010	...	2110	2138	2210	2310	...	...
Landskrona **737** .... d.	1922	...	|	2022	...	2122	|	2222	2322	...	...
Lund **737** .... a.	1937	...	2000s	2037	...	2137	2203s	2237	2337	...	...
Malmö 737 .... a.	1952	...	2015s	2052	...	2152	2219s	2252	2352	...	...
Malmö 701 .... d.	2002	...	|	2102	...	2202	|	2302	...	...	...
København (Kastrup) ✈ **703** .. a.	2023	...	2047s	2123	...	2223	2247s	2323	...	...	...
København H 703 .... a.	2037	...	2102	2137	...	2237	2302	2337	...	...	...

	X2000	Øtåg	Øtåg	Øtåg	Øtåg	X2000	Øtåg	Øtåg	X2000	Øtåg
	412					**426**			**484**	
	🅁✕					🅁✕			🅁✕	
	SⒶp	Ⓐ	Ⓐ	Ⓐ	⚒	S⑥	Ⓐ	Ⓐ	Ⓐ	
København H 703 ...... d.	...	...	...	...	...	...	...	0523	0529	0623d
København (Kastrup) ✈ **703** d.	...	...	...	...	...	...	...	0536	0542u	0636d
Malmö 701 .... a.	...	...	...	...	...	...	...	0558	|	0658d
Malmö 737 .... d.	...	...	...	...	0508a	...	...	0608	0617u	0708d
Lund **737** .... d.	...	...	...	...	0522a	...	...	0622	0629u	0722d
Landskrona **737** .... d.	...	...	...	...	0538a	...	...	0638	|	0738d
Helsingborg 737 .... a.	...	...	...	...	0550a	...	...	0650	|	0750d
Helsingborg .... d.	...	...	...	...	0553a	...	...	0653	|	0753d
Ängelholm .... d.	...	...	...	...	0613a	...	...	0713	|	0813d
Båstad .... d.	...	...	...	...	0637a	...	...	0737	|	0837d
Laholm .... d.	...	...	...	...	0644a	...	...	0744	|	0844d
Hässleholm .... d.	...	...	...	...	|	...	...	|	0700	|
Halmstad .... d.	0520	0532	0602	0628	0702	0720	0732	0802	0750	0902
Falkenberg .... d.	0538	0549	0619	0645	0719	0739	0749	0819	0808	0919
Varberg .... d.	0554	0604	0634	0700	0734	0754	0804	0834	0822	0934
Kungsbacka .... d.	0613	0627	0657	0724	0757	0813	0827	0857	|	0957
Göteborg .... a.	0631	0647	0717	0747	0817	0832	0847	0917	0905	1017
Oslo Sentral **770** .... a.	...	...	...	...	...	...	...	...	...	...

	X2000		Øtåg	Øtåg		Øtåg	Øtåg		Øtåg	Øtåg	X2000	Øtåg		Øtåg	Øtåg			Øtåg	Øtåg	X2000	Øtåg	Øtåg	Øtåg		Øtåg	
	486	**600**			**608**			**602**			**492**		**660**			**604**	**10604**			**496**				**610**		**6**
	🅁✕										🅁✕									🅁✕						🅁
	⑥	Ⓐ	Ⓐ		⑥	Ⓐp			Ⓐ			Ⓐ	†	Ⓐ		Ⓐ	Ⓒ	Ⓐ	Ⓐ	Ⓑ	p	Ⓐ				♦⊡
København H 703 .... d.	0657	0659	0723	0823	0859	0923r	1023	1059	1123	1223	1257	1323	1441	...	1423	1459	...	...	1523	1557	1623	1723	1823	1859	2023	...
København (Kastrup) ✈ **703** . d.	0709u	0711u	0736	0836	0911u	0936r	1036	1111u	1136	1236	1309u	1336	1455u	...	1436	1511u	...	...	1536	1609u	1636	1736	1836	1911u	2036	...
Malmö 701 .... a.	|	|	0758	0858	|	0958r	1058	|	1158	1258	|	1358	|	...	1458	|	...	...	1558	|	1658	1758	1858	|	2058	...
Malmö 737 .... d.	0745u	0737u	0808	0908	0942u	1008r	1108	1142u	1208	1308	1345u	1408	|	...	1508	1537u	1542	...	1608	1645u	1708	1808	1908	1942u	2108	2308
Lund **737** .... d.	0757u	0749u	0822	0922	0954u	1022r	1122	1154u	1222	1322	1357u	1422	|	...	1522	1551u	1556u	...	1622	1657u	1722	1822	1922	1954u	2122	2323u
Landskrona **737** .... d.	|	|	0838	0938	|	1038r	1138	|	1238	1338	|	1438	|	...	1538	|	|	...	1638	|	1738	1838	1938	|	2138	|
Helsingborg 737 .... a.	|	0821	0850	0950	1021	1050r	1150	1221	1250	1350	|	1450	|	...	1550	1620	1620	...	1650	|	1750	1850	1950	2020	2150	|
Helsingborg .... d.	|	0825	0853	0953	1025	1053r	1153	1225	1253	1353	|	1453	|	...	1553	1624	1624	...	1653	|	1753	1853	1953	2025	2153	|
Ängelholm .... d.	|	|	0913	1013	|	1113r	1213	|	1313	1413	|	1513	|	...	1613	|	|	...	1713	|	1813	1913	2013	|	2213	|
Båstad .... d.	|	|	0937	1037	|	1137r	1237	|	1337	1437	|	1537	|	...	1637	|	|	...	1737	|	1837	1937	2037	|	2237	|
Laholm .... d.	|	|	0944	1044	|	1144r	1244	|	1344	1444	|	1544	|	...	1644	|	|	...	1744	|	1844	1944	2044	|	2244	|
Hässleholm .... d.	0830	|	|	|	|	|	|	|	|	|	1428	|	1532	...	|	|	|	...	|	1728	|	|	|	|	|	0001u
Halmstad .... d.	0920	0923	1002	1102	1123	1202	1302	1320	1402	1502	1521	1602	1628	1632	1702	1723	1723	1732	1802	1818	1902	2002	2102	2124	2256	|
Falkenberg .... d.	0937	|	1019	1119	|	1219	1319	1338	1419	1519	1538	1619	1652	1649	1719	|	|	1749	1819	1837	1919	2019	2119	|	...	|
Varberg .... d.	0952	0953	1034	1134	1153	1234	1334	1353	1434	1534	1554	1634	1707	1704	1734	1753	1753	1804	1834	1852	1934	2034	2134	2154	...	|
Kungsbacka .... d.	|	|	1057	1157	|	1257	1357	|	1457	1557	|	1657	1731s	1727	1757	|	|	1827	1857	|	1957	2057	2157	|	...	|
Göteborg .... a.	1032	1030	1117	1217	1230	1317	1417	1432	1517	1617	1632	1717	1752	1747	1817	1830	1830	1847	1917	1932	2017	2117	2217	2232	...	0227
Oslo Sentral **770** .... a.	...	...	...	...	...	...	...	...	...	...	...	...	...	...	...	...	...	...	...	...	...	...	...	...	...	0700

♦ – **NOTES** (LISTED BY TRAIN NUMBER)

5 – Ⓑ: 🛏 and 🛌 Oslo (**3/10003**) - Göteborg - Malmö; 🛏, 🛌 and (2) Oslo (**3/10003**) - Göteborg (**6**) - Stockholm.

6 – Ⓑ: 🛏 and 🛌 Malmö - Göteborg (**4/10004**) - Oslo; 🛏, 🛌 and (2) Stockholm (**5**) - Göteborg (**4/10004**) - Oslo.

S – (12) and ✕ Stockholm - Göteborg - Halmstad and v.v.

a – Ⓐ only.
d – ⚒ only.
p – Not July 6 - Aug. 9.
r – From Aug. 10.
s – Stops to set down only.
u – Stops to pick up only.

⊡ – (2) available Malmö - Oslo and v.v. by changing train portions at Göteborg.

X2000 - High speed train. Special supplement payable.

* – Halmstad - Hässleholm: *91 km*.

HALLSBERG - MARIESTAD - LIDKÖPING - HERRLJUNGA 736

Operator: *V* 2nd class only

km		Ⓐ	Ⓐ	Ⓐ	Ⓐ	⑥	Ⓒ	Ⓐ	Ⓐ	†	⑥	Ⓐ	⑥	†	†	Ⓐ	Ⓐ	†	⑥	⑥	Ⓐ	†	Ⓐ	†	Ⓐ	
0	**Hallsberg 740** ...... d.	...	...	...	...	...	...	0851	...	...	1025	...	...	1228	...	...	1443	...	...	1626	1639	...	...	1850	1950	...
30	Laxå **740** .... d.	...	...	...	...	...	...	0909	...	...	1042	...	...	1246	...	...	1500	...	...	1644	1657	...	...	1907	2008	...
92	Mariestad .... d.	...	0540	0650	...	...	0835	1001	...	...	1139	...	...	1334	1405	1435	1554	1630	1640	1736	1756	1815	...	1958	2058	...
146	Lidköping .... a.	...	0620	0741	...	...	0915	1049	...	...	1227	...	...	...	1453	1515	1642	1710	1720	1824	1844	1903	...	2046	2146	...
146	Lidköping .... d.	0538	0622	...	0756	0800	0915	...	1105	1205	...	1300	1312	...	1500	1518	1715	1720	1720	...	...	1905	2006	...	...	...
201	**Herrljunga 740** .... a.	0623	0702	...	0844	0847	0957	...	1154	1255	...	1349	1359	...	1550	1600	1802	1759	1802	...	...	1954	2052	...	...	...
	Göteborg **740** .... a.	...	0757	...	...	...	1047	...	...	...	...	...	...	...	...	1647	...	1847	1852	...	...	...	...	...	...	...

	Ⓐ	Ⓐ	⑥	Ⓐ	Ⓐ	Ⓐ	†	⑥	Ⓐ	Ⓐ	⑥	⑥	Ⓐ	†	Ⓐ	†	†	Ⓒ	Ⓐ	†	⚒	Ⓐ	⑥	†	†	Ⓐ
Göteborg **740** ..... d.	...	...	...	...	...	...	...	...	0932	...	...	1102	...	1132	...	...	...	...	...	...	1712	...	1912	1912	...	...
Herrljunga 740 ...... d.	...	...	...	0703	...	0911	...	0959	1018	...	...	1146	1159	1218	...	1302	...	1600	1602	...	1802	1858	1958	2000	2100	2108
Lidköping .... a.	...	...	...	0753	...	1000	...	1046	1058	...	...	1225	1247	1304	...	1349	...	1647	1649	...	1843	1949	2038	2038	2147	2155
Lidköping .... d.	0500	0530	0717	...	0757	...	1018	1048	1058	...	...	1225	...	1304	1334	...	1517	...	1703	1712	1845	...	2038	2047	...	...
Mariestad .... d.	0550	0621	0807	...	0845	...	1111	1136	1138	1218	1227	1305	...	1344	1424	...	1607	...	1758	1800	1923	...	2118	2125	...	...
Laxå **740** .... d.	0638	...	0855	...	...	...	1200	...	...	1308	1316	...	...	...	1513	...	1655	...	1848	...	...	...	...	...	...	...
Hallsberg 740 .... a.	0655	...	0912	...	...	...	1218	...	...	1325	1333	...	...	...	1533	...	1713	...	1905	...	...	...	...	...	...	...

KØBENHAVN - LUFTHAVN (KASTRUP) ✈ - MALMÖ - HELSINGBORG 737

Operator: *Skåne* (Ø – *Øtåg*)

Subject to alteration August 3 - 9

km		Ⓐ2	ØⒶ	Ⓐ2	Ⓐy2	ØⒶ	ØⒶz	2	Ⓐy2	Ø⚒	Ⓐ	Ⓒ2	Ⓐ2	ØⒶ		2	Ø	2	Ø⚒	2	Ø	2	Ø⚒	2	Ø
	København H **703** .... d.	...	...	...	...	0523	...	...	...	0623	...	...	...	0723	...	...	0823	...	0923	...	1023	...	1123	...	1223
	Lufthavn (Kastrup) **703** .... d.	...	...	...	...	0536	...	...	...	0636	...	...	...	0736	...	...	0836	...	0936	...	1036	...	1136	...	1236
0	**Malmö 703 735** .... d.	0438	0508	0538	0603	0608	0634	0638	0703	0708	0734	0738	0740	0808	...	0838	0908	0938	1008	1038	1108	1138	1208	1238	1308
16	Lund **735** .... d.	0451	0522	0551	0617	0622	0648	0651	0717	0722	0748	0751	0754	0822	...	0851	0922	0951	1022	1051	1122	1151	1222	1251	1322
48	Landskrona **735** .... d.	0515	0538	0615	0645	0638	0704	0715	0745	0738	0804	0815	0815	0838	...	0915	0938	1015	1038	1115	1138	1215	1238	1315	1338
69	**Helsingborg 735** .... a.	0532	0550	0632	0702	0650	0718	0732	0802	0750	0818	0832	0832	0850	...	0932	0950	1032	1050	1132	1150	1232	1250	1332	1350

	2	Ø⚒		Ⓐy2		Ø	Ⓐz	Ⓒ2	Ⓐ2	Ⓐz2		Ø⚒	zⒶ	2	Ⓐz2		Ø	Ⓐ	2	Ⓐ2z		ØⒶ	2	Ø	2
København H **703** .... d.	...	1323	...	...	...	1423	...	...	...	...	...	1523	...	...	...	...	1623	...	...	...	...	1723	...	1823	...
Lufthavn (Kastrup) **703** ..... d.	...	1336	...	...	...	1436	...	...	...	...	...	1536	...	...	...	...	1636	...	...	...	...	1736	...	1836	...
Malmö 703 735 .... d.	1338	1408	1438	1503	...	1508	1534	1538	1540	1603	...	1608	1634	1638	1703	...	1708	1734	1738	1803	...	1808	1838	1908	1938
Lund **735** .... d.	1351	1422	1451	1517	...	1522	1548	1551	1554	1617	...	1622	1648	1651	1717	...	1722	1748	1751	1817	...	1822	1851	1922	1951
Landskrona **735** .... d.	1415	1438	1515	1545	...	1538	1604	1615	1615	1645	...	1638	1704	1715	1745	...	1738	1804	1815	1845	...	1838	1915	1938	2015
Helsingborg 735 .... a.	1432	1450	1532	1602	...	1550	1618	1632	1632	1702	...	1650	1718	1732	1802	...	1750	1818	1832	1902	...	1850	1932	1950	2032

	ØⒶ	2	Ø	2	ØⒶ	2	Ø⚒	⚒2	H	
København H **703** .... d.	1923	...	2023	...	2123	...	2223	...	...	...
Lufthavn (Kastrup) **703** ..... d.	1936	...	2036	...	2136	...	2236	...	...	...
Malmö 703 735 .... d.	2008	2038	2108	2138	2208	2238	2311	2338	0100	...
Lund **735** .... d.	2022	2051	2122	2151	2222	2251	2325	2351	0114	...
Landskrona **735** .... d.	2040	2115	2138	2215	2240	2315	2343	0015	0138	...
Helsingborg 735 .... a.	2052	2132	2150	2232	2252	2332	2355	0032	0155	...

	ØⒶ	Ⓐ2	2y	Ⓒ2	ØⒶ	Ⓐ2	Ⓐz	⚒2	ØⒶ	2
Helsingborg 735 .... d.	0506	0527	0553	0553	0610	0627	0645	0653	0710	0727
Landskrona **735** .... d.	0520	0545	0611	0611	0622	0645	0658	0711	0722	0745
Lund **735** .... d.	0539	0610	0636	0636	0639	0710	0716	0736	0739	0810
Malmö 703 735 .... a.	0552	0623	0649	0649	0652	0723	0729	0749	0752	0823
Lufthavn (Kastrup) **703** ... a.	0623	...	...	...	0723	...	...	...	0823	...
København H **703** .... a.	0637	...	...	...	0737	...	...	...	0837	...

	Ⓐ	Ⓐy2	Ø⚒	2	Ⓐy2	Ø⚒	2		Ø	2	Ø⚒	2	Ø	2	Ø⚒	2	Ø	2	Ⓐz2	Ø⚒		Ⓐ2	Ⓒ2	Ⓐy2	Ø
Helsingborg 735 .... d.	0745	0753	0810	0827	0853	0910	0927	...	1010	1027	1110	1127	1210	1227	1310	1327	1410	1427	1453	1510	...	1527	1527	1553	1610
Landskrona **735** .... d.	0758	0811	0822	0845	0911	0922	0945	...	1022	1045	1122	1145	1222	1245	1322	1345	1422	1445	1511	1522	...	1545	1545	1611	1622
Lund **735** .... d.	0816	0836	0839	0910	0936	0939	1010	...	1039	1110	1139	1210	1239	1310	1339	1410	1439	1510	1536	1539	...	1608	1610	1636	1639
Malmö 703 735 .... a.	0829	0849	0852	0923	0949	0952	1023	...	1052	1123	1152	1223	1252	1323	1352	1423	1452	1523	1549	1552	...	1620	1623	1649	1652
Lufthavn (Kastrup) **703** ..... a.	...	...	0923	...	...	1023	...	...	1123	...	1223	...	1323	...	1423	...	1523	...	...	1623	...	...	...	...	1723
København H **703** .... a.	...	...	0937	...	...	1037	...	...	1137	...	1237	...	1337	...	1437	...	1537	...	...	1637	...	...	...	...	1737

		Ⓐz	2		Ø⚒	Ⓐ2	Ⓒ2	Ⓐz		Ⓐy2	Ø	2	ØⒶ	2	Ø	2	ØⒶ	2		Ø	2	ØⒶ	⚒2		H
Helsingborg 735 .... d.	1627	1645	1653	...	1710	1727	1727	1745	...	1753	1810	1827	1910	1927	2010	2027	2110	2127	...	2210	2227	2310	2327	...	0027
Landskrona **735** .... d.	1645	1658	1711	...	1722	1745	1745	1758	...	1811	1822	1845	1922	1945	2022	2045	2122	2145	...	2222	2245	2322	2345	...	0045
Lund **735** .... d.	1710	1716	1736	...	1739	1808	1810	1816	...	1836	1839	1910	1939	2010	2039	2110	2139	2210	...	2239	2310	2339	0010	...	0108
Malmö 703 735 .... a.	1723	1729	1749	...	1752	1820	1823	1829	...	1849	1852	1923	1952	2023	2052	2123	2152	2223	...	2252	2323	2355	0023	...	*0130*
Lufthavn (Kastrup) **703** ..... a.	...	...	...	...	1823	...	...	...	...	...	1923	...	2023	...	2123	...	2223	...	...	2323	...	...	...	...	...
København H **703** .... a.	...	...	...	...	1837	...	...	...	...	...	1937	...	2037	...	2137	...	2237	...	...	2337	...	...	...	...	...

H – ②③④⑤⑥† only. **y** – June 14 - Aug. 2, Aug. 10 - 23. **z** – June 14 - Aug. 23. **Ø** – Operated by *Øtåg*.

HÄSSLEHOLM - HELSINGBORG 738

Operator: *Skåne* Journey 55 – 65 minutes *77 km*

From **Hässleholm**: 0525Ⓐ, 0622⚒, 0722, 0822, and hourly until 2222, then 2322⚒.

From **Helsingborg**: 0536Ⓐ, 0636, 0736, and hourly until 2236, then 2336⚒.

VARBERG and GÖTEBORG - UDDEVALLA - STRÖMSTAD 739

2nd class only except where shown

km				V							*X2000* 475 V									V	V		V				
		†	Ⓐ	⚒	Ⓐ	⚒	⑥		⑥	Ⓐ		Ⓑ	†		⑥	Ⓐt	Ⓐv	Ⓑ	Ⓒ	Ⓑ			†	†	Ⓐ	⚒	†
0	**Varberg 735** .... d.	0200	...	...	0613	0705a	0742	...	0949	0954	...	...	1142	...	1342	1348	1400	1444a	1548	...	...	1644a	...	1825	1842	1952	2144
84	Borås **746** .... a.	0310	...	...	0727	0827a	0854	...	1104	1105	...	...	1253	...	1453	1458	1510	1558a	1704	...	...	1758a	...	1941	1953	2103	2258
	Borås .... d.	...	0600	...	—	0831	—	1005	—	...	...	1202	—	1403	—	—	...	1603	—	...	...	1803	...	2000	2009	—	...
127	Herrljunga **740** .... a.	...	0637	...	...	0908	...	1042	...	...	...	1239	...	1440	...	...	...	1640	...	...	...	1840	...	2037	2046	...	...
	Herrljunga .... d.	...	0644r	...	...	0918	...	1118c	...	...	1255	1318	...	1518	...	...	...	1718	...	...	...	1917	...	2116	...	...	...
191	Vänersborg .... d.	...	0733r	...	...	1004	...	1204c	...	...	1338	1403	...	1604	V	...	...	1808	V	...	...	2005	...	2202	...	...	...
195	Öxnered **750** .... d.	...	0739r	...	V	1010	V	1210c	V	...	|	1412	V	1610	Ⓐ	V	...	1815	Ⓐ	...	...	2011	...	2208	...	V	...
	Göteborg .... ▲ d.	...	|	0647	0847	|	1047	|	1247	...	|	|	1447	|	1547	1647	...	|	1717	1747	1847	|	1947	|	...	2047	...
217	Uddevalla C .... ▲ a.	...	0755r	0758	0958	1026	1158	1226c	1358	...	1400	1429	1558	1626	1701	1758	...	1830	1836	1858	1958	2027	2058	2223	...	2158	...
	Uddevalla C .... d.	...	...	0813	1013	...	1213	...	...	...	1414	...	1609	...	...	1813	...	...	...	...	2003	...	...	...	...	...	...
309	**Strömstad** .... a.	...	...	0933	1133	...	1333	...	...	...	1534	...	1733	...	...	1937	...	...	...	...	2123	...	...	...	...	...	...

km					V	V	V		V	V		V			V			V		V	V		*X2000* 478	V		V	
		Ⓐ	⑥	Ⓐ	Ⓐ	⚒	⚒	⚒	Ⓒ	⚒	†		Ⓒ				Ⓒ		Ⓑ		Ⓑ		V	Ⓒ	†		†
0	**Strömstad** .... d.	...	...	...	...	...	0637	...	0637g	...	...	0830	...	...	1030	...	...	1230	...	1430	...	...	1631	...	...	1836	...
92	Uddevalla C .... a.	...	...	...	...	...	0758	...	0758g	...	...	0955	...	...	1155	...	...	1355	...	1555	...	...	1752	...	...	1957	...
	Uddevalla C .... ▲ d.	...	...	0524r	0611	0709	0805a	0803	0809	0909	0933	1009	...	1133	1209	1330	...	1409	1533	1609	1709	1736	1807	1809	1933	2009	...
180	**Göteborg** .... ▲ a.	...	...	|	0722	0822	0922a	|	0922	1022	|	1122	...	|	1322	|	...	1522	|	1722	1822	|	|	1922	|	2122	...
	Öxnered **750** .... d.	...	...	0540r	...	—	...	0819	—	...	0949	—	...	1149	...	1349	...	—	1549	...	—	1753	|	...	1949	...	...
	Vänersborg .... d.	...	...	0547r	...	...	...	0825	...	...	0955	...	...	1155	...	1355	...	...	1555	...	...	1759	1832	...	1955	...	...
	Herrljunga **746** .... a.	...	...	0633r	...	...	...	0910	...	...	1040	⚒	...	1241	...	1445	...	...	1643	...	...	1845	1916	...	2041	...	...
	Herrljunga .... d.	...	...	0647	...	...	...	0916	...	...	1116	1116	...	1316	...	1516	...	...	1716	...	...	1923	...	...	2116	...	...
	Borås **746** .... a.	...	...	0724	...	†	...	0953	⑥	...	1153	1153	...	1353	...	1557	...	Ⓐ	1757	...	†	1958	...	...	2151	...	...
	Borås .... d.	0628	0658	0727	...	0900	...	1001a	1043	...	...	1200a	1258	...	...	1600a	1643	1700	1800a	...	1842	2000a	...	...	2158	...	0040
	Varberg 735 .... a.	0740	0813	0837	...	1010	...	1115a	1158	...	...	1310a	1413	...	...	1716a	1754	1811	1913a	...	1952	2115a	...	...	2310	...	0150

V – [12] and ✕ Stockholm - Herrljunga - Uddevalla - Strömstad and v.v.

a – Ⓐ only. **c** – Ⓒ only. **g** – ⑥ only.

r – Not July 6 - Aug. 9. **t** – Not July 13 - 26. **v** – July 13 - 26.

▲ – Additional services available Göteborg - Uddevalla and v.v.

740 STOCKHOLM - HALLSBERG - GÖTEBORG

For Stockholm - Hallsberg - Karlstad / Oslo and v.v. services see Table 750

km		2 Ⓐ	2 Ⓐ	2 Ⓐk	2 Ⓐj	2 Ⓐk	10077 R ♦	10073 R ♦	X2000 421 R✕ Ⓐ	159 ⚒y	2 †	623 🍷 Ⓐ	X2000 423 R✕ Ⓐz	97 R ♦	2 ⚒	X2000 425 R✕ ⚒	X2000 415 R✕ †	VEO 7101 R✕ ♦	163 x	X2000 427 R✕ ⚒z	2 ⚒	X2000 475 R✕ ♦	X2000 429 R✕	167	2 ⑥	X2000 433 R✕
0	**Stockholm** C **730** d.	...	...	...	...	...	...	...	0610	...	...	0630	0714	...	...	0810	0810	0759	0707d	0914	...	0955	1010	0907	...	1210
15	Flemingsberg ‡ d.	...	...	...	...	...	...	...	|	...	...	0641	0725	...	...	|	|	|	|	0925	...	|	|	|	...	|
36	Södertälje Syd ‡ d.	...	...	...	...	...	...	...	0628	...	...	0653	|	...	...	0828	0828	|	|	0936	...	1015	1028	|	...	1228
108	Flen **730** d.	...	...	...	...	...	...	...	|	...	...	0729	|	...	...	|	|	|	V	|	...	|	|	V	...	|
131	Katrineholm **730** d.	...	...	...	...	...	...	...	0706	...	...	0743	|	...	...	0906	|	|	|	|	...	|	1106	|	...	1306
197	**Hallsberg 755/6** a.	...	...	...	...	...	...	...	|	...	...	0817	0830	0838s	...	|	0926	0955	|	|	...	1113	|	|	...	|
	Örebro C **755/6** d.	...	...	...	...	...	0551g	0551	|	0710	...	...	|	|	...	|	|	|	0910	|	...	|	|	1110	...	|
197	**Hallsberg** d.	...	...	...	...	...	0608s	0608s	|	0733	...	...	0832	|	...	|	0928	0955	0933	|	...	1116	|	1133	...	|
227	Laxå **736** d.	...	...	...	...	...	|	|	|	0748	...	...	|	|	...	|	|	|	0948	|	...	|	|	1148	...	|
272	Töreboda d.	...	...	...	...	...	|	|	|	0809	...	...	|	|	...	|	|	|	1009	|	...	|	|	1209	...	|
311	**Skövde** d.	0450	0557	0635	0653	0653	0708s	0708s	0811	0832	0832	...	0915	0930s	...	1011	1011	1102s	1032	1115	1132g	1200	1211	1232	...	1411
341	Falköping d.	0508	0615	0650	0713	0713	|	|	|	0850	0850	...	|	|	0950	|	|	|	1050	|	1150	|	|	1250	1350	|
375	Herrljunga **736/9** a.	0528	0636	0708	0732	0732	0742s	0742s	0835	0906	0908	...	|	1003s	1008	|	|	|	1106	|	1208	1224	|	1306	1408	1435
	Borås a.	|	|	|	|	|	|	|	|	|	|	...	|	|	|	|	|	|	|	|	|	...	|	|	|	|
410	Alingsås a.	0549	0657	0729	0753	0754	|	|	|	0927	0928	...	|	|	1028	1046s	1046s	|	1127	|	1228	...	1246s	1327	1428	|
455	**Göteborg** a.	0617	0732	0802	0822	0832	0837	0837	0917	0957	0957	...	1017	1052	1057	1117	1117	1222	1157	1217	1257	...	1317	1357	1457	1517
	Oslo S **770** a.	...	...	...	...	...	...	...	...	...	...	...	...	...	...	...	...	...	...	...	...	...	...	...	...	...

	171	633 Ⓐ	X2000 435 R✕ Ⓐz	2	X2000 437 R✕	175	637	X2000 439 R✕ Ⓑw	2	639 Ⓑn	649 Ⓐm	X2000 411 R✕	179	641 Ⓐr	631 Ⓑp	10641 Ⓐq	X2000 443 R✕ Ⓑv	X2000 405 R✕ Ⓑt	2 †	X2000 445 R✕	183	X2000 447 R✕ R	2 ⚒	X2000 449 R✕ Ⓑz	5 R ♦	651
Stockholm C **730** d.	1107	1225	1315	...	1410	1307	1425	1515	...	1530	1530	1610	1507	1625	1625	1625	1710	1736	...	1810	1707	1910	...	2010	2155	2210
Flemingsberg ‡ d.	|	1236	1326	...	|	|	1436	|	...	1541	1541	|	|	1636	1636	1636	|	|	...	|	|	1921	...	|	|	2221
Södertälje Syd ‡ d.	|	1248	|	...	1428	|	1448	|	...	1553	1553	1628	|	1647	1648	1648	1728	|	...	1828	|	|	...	2028	2220u	2233
Flen **730** d.	V	1324	|	...	|	V	1525	|	...	1630	1630	|	V	1725	1725	1725	|	|	...	|	V	|	...	|	|	2315
Katrineholm **730** d.	|	1338	|	...	1506	|	1539	|	...	1644	1644	1706	|	1738	1739	1739	|	|	...	1906	|	2006	...	2106	|	2329
Hallsberg 755/6 a.	|	1412	1431	...	|	|	1613	1628	...	1719	1719	|	|	1808	1813	1813	1826	|	...	|	|	|	...	2130	|	0003
Örebro C **755/6** d.	1310	...	|	...	|	1510	...	|	...	...	...	|	1710	...	...	...	|	|	...	|	1910	|	...	|	|	...
Hallsberg d.	1333	...	1433	...	|	1533	...	1630	...	...	...	|	1733	...	...	...	1828	|	...	|	1933	|	...	2132	2340u	...
Laxå **736** d.	1348	...	|	...	|	1548	...	|	...	...	...	|	1748	...	...	...	|	|	...	|	1948	|	...	|	|	...
Töreboda d.	1409	...	|	...	|	1609	...	|	...	...	...	|	1809	...	...	...	|	|	...	|	2009	|	...	|	|	...
Skövde d.	1432	...	1516	1532	1611	1632	...	1713	1732g	...	...	1811	1832	...	...	...	1911	|	...	2011	2032	2111	2137	2215	|	...
Falköping d.	1450	...	|	1550	|	1650	...	|	1750	...	...	|	1850	...	...	...	|	|	1950	|	2050	|	2155	|	|	...
Herrljunga **736/9** a.	1506	...	|	1608	|	1706	...	1737	1808	...	...	1835	1906	...	...	...	|	|	2008	2035	2106	|	2213	|	|	...
Borås a.	|	...	|	|	|	|	...	|	|	...	...	|	|	...	...	...	|	|	|	|	|	|	|	|	|	...
Alingsås a.	1527	...	|	1628	1646s	1727	...	|	1828	...	...	|	1927	...	...	...	1947s	|	2028	|	2127	2147s	2233	|	|	...
Göteborg a.	1557	...	1617	1657	1717	1757	...	1817	1857	...	...	1917	1957	...	...	...	2017	2022	2057	2117	2157	2217	2302	2317	0200	...
Oslo S **770** a.	...	...	...	...	...	...	...	...	...	...	...	...	...	...	...	...	...	...	...	...	...	...	...	...	0700*	...

	2 Ⓒ	6 R ♦	618 Ⓐ	620 Ⓐ	X2000 420 R✕ Ⓐf	X2000 400 R✕ Ⓐh	622 Ⓐo	632 Ⓐm	164 ⚒	X2000 412 R✕ Ⓐ	2 Ⓐ	X2000 424 R✕ N	168	628 ⚒	X2000 426 R✕ ⚒	X2000 416 R✕ †	2 ⑥	X2000 428 R✕ ⚒z	630	172	X2000 430 R✕	2 Ⓐ	X2000 432 R✕ e	176	634 636 Ⓒ	X2000 434 R✕
Oslo S **770** d.	...	2132§	...	...	...	...	...	...	...	...	...	...	...	...	...	...	...	...	...	...	...	...	...	...	...	...
Göteborg d.	0032	0250	...	...	0507	0600	...	...	0602	0642	0657	0742	0802	...	0842	0842	0902	0942	...	1002	1042	1102	1142	1202	...	1242
Alingsås d.	0059	|	...	...	0534u	|	...	...	0630	|	0730	0807u	0830	...	|	0907	0930	1007u	...	1030	1107u	1130	|	1230	...	|
Borås d.	|	|	...	...	|	|	...	...	|	|	|	|	|	...	|	|	|	|	...	|	|	|	|	|	...	|
Herrljunga **736/9** d.	0118	|	...	...	0548	|	...	...	0652	0720	0750	|	0852	...	0920	|	0950	|	...	1052	|	1150	|	1252	...	1320
Falköping d.	0137	|	...	...	0604	|	...	...	0711	|	0809	|	0911	...	|	|	1009	|	...	1111	|	1211	|	1311	...	|
Skövde d.	0155	|	...	...	0622	|	...	...	0729	0747	▬	0847	0929	...	0947	0947	...	1047	...	1129	1147	1229	1242	1329	...	1347
Töreboda d.	...	|	...	...	|	|	...	...	0746	|	...	|	0946	...	|	|	...	|	...	1146	|	...	|	1346	...	|
Laxå **736** d.	...	|	...	...	|	|	...	...	0808	|	...	|	1008	...	|	|	...	|	...	1208	|	...	|	1408	...	|
Hallsberg a.	...	0509s	...	...	0704	|	...	...	0825	|	**624**	|	1025	...	|	|	...	|	...	1225	|	...	|	1425	...	|
Örebro C **755/6** a.	...	|	...	...	|	|	...	...	0848	|	⑥	|	1048	...	|	|	...	|	...	1248	|	...	|	1448	...	|
Hallsberg 755/6 d.	...	|	0522	0627	0707	|	0712	0728	|	|	0835	|	|	0941	|	|	...	|	1142	|	|	...	|	|	1341	|
Katrineholm **730** a.	...	|	0556	0700	0732	|	0745	0800	|	0851	0908	|	|	1016	1051	1051	...	|	1217	|	1251	...	|	|	1416	1451
Flen **730** a.	...	|	0611	0715	|	|	0814	0814	V	|	0922	|	V	1029	|	|	...	|	1230	V	|	...	|	V	1429	|
Södertälje Syd ‡ a.	...	0638s	0649	0751	|	|	0850	0850	|	0929	0958	|	|	1105	1129	1129	...	1224	1306	|	1329	...	1424	|	1505	1529
Flemingsberg ‡ a.	...	|	0702	0802	0821	|	0902	0902	|	|	1010	1032	|	1116	|	|	...	|	1317	|	|	...	|	|	1516	|
Stockholm C **730** a.	...	0705	0716	0816	0835	0846	0915	0915	1052	0950	1024	1045	1252	1130	1150	1150	...	1245	1330	1452	1350	...	1445	1652	1530	1550

	2 ⚒	X2000 436 R✕ Ⓑz	638 Ⓑ	180	X2000 438 R✕	2	VEO 7102 R✕ ♦	X2000 440 R✕ Ⓑr	194	2 Ⓐk	644	X2000 442 R✕ Q	98 R ♦	646 Ⓐr	2 Ⓑ	X2000 444 R✕ Ⓑz	10648 Ⓑ	188	X2000 446 R✕	X2000 478 R✕ ♦	76 R ♦	10072 R ♦	152 2	X2000 450 R✕ Ⓑz	2	2 P
Oslo S **770** d.	...	...	...	...	...	...	...	...	...	...	...	...	...	...	...	...	...	...	...	...	...	...	...	...	...	...
Göteborg d.	1302	1342	...	1402	1442	1502	1532	1542	1602	1627	...	1642	1700	...	1707	1742	...	1802	1842	...	1900	1900	2002	2042	2132	2302
Alingsås d.	1330	1407u	...	1430	|	1530	|	1607u	1630	1700	...	|	|	...	1737	1810u	...	1830	|	...	|	|	2030	|	2200	2329
Borås d.	|	|	...	|	|	|	|	|	|	|	...	|	|	...	|	|	...	|	|	...	|	|	|	|	|	|
Herrljunga **736/9** d.	1350	|	...	1452	|	1550	|	|	1652	1732	...	|	1744u	...	1757	|	...	1852	1920	1925	1946u	1946u	2050	|	2220	2349
Falköping d.	1410	|	...	1511	|	1611	|	|	1711	1754	...	|	|	...	1820	|	...	1911	|	|	|	|	2111	|	2243	0009
Skövde d.	...	1447	...	1529	1542	1629g	1649u	1647	1729	1815	...	1745	1820u	...	1840a	1847	...	1929	1947	1952	2017u	2017u	2130	2145	2301	0029
Töreboda d.	...	|	...	1546	|	...	|	|	1746	...	...	|	|	...	...	|	...	1946	|	|	|	|	...	|	...	...
Laxå **736** d.	...	|	...	1610	|	...	|	|	1808	...	...	|	|	...	...	|	...	2008	|	|	|	|	...	|	...	...
Hallsberg a.	...	|	...	1630	|	...	1744	|	1825	...	...	|	1915u	...	...	1930	...	2025	|	2035	2110u	2110u	...	2226	...	...
Örebro C **755/6** a.	...	|	...	1652	|	...	|	|	1848	...	...	|	...	...	...	|	...	2048	|	|	...	2130	...	|	...	...
Hallsberg 755/6 d.	...	|	1541	|	|	...	1744	|	|	...	1744	|	...	1849	...	1932	2005	|	|	2037	...	...	...	2228	...	...
Katrineholm **730** d.	...	|	1614	|	1646	...	|	|	|	...	1819	1851	...	1919	...	|	2045	|	2051	|	...	...	...	|	...	...
Flen **730** d.	...	|	1629	V	|	...	|	|	V	...	1832	|	...	1932	...	|	2059	V	|	|	...	...	...	|	...	...
Södertälje Syd ‡ a.	...	1623	1705	|	1724	...	|	|	|	...	1908	1929	...	2007	...	|	2147	|	2129	2135	...	...	...	2326	...	...
Flemingsberg ‡ a.	...	|	1716	|	|	...	|	1832	|	...	1919	|	...	2018	...	2037	2159	|	|	|	...	...	...	|	...	...
Stockholm C **730** a.	...	1645	1731	1852	1745	...	1945	1845	2052	...	1932	1950	...	2031	...	2050	2213	2252	2150	2156	...	...	...	2346	...	...

♦ – **NOTES** (LISTED BY TRAIN NUMBER)

5 – Ⓑ: 🛏, ▬ and [2] Stockholm - Göteborg - Malmö; 🛏, ▬ and [2] Stockholm - Göteborg (**4/10004**) - Oslo.

6 – Ⓑ: (from Malmö): 🛏, ▬ and [2] Malmö - Göteborg - Stockholm; 🛏, ▬ and [2] Oslo (**3/10003**) - Göteborg - Stockholm.

76 – Ⓑ: 🛏, ▬ and [2] Göteborg - Stockholm - Storlien; ✕ and [Bio] Göteborg - Stockholm; ✕ Sundsvall - Storlien.

97/8 – 🛏, ▬ and [2] Luleå (**91/2**) - Gävle - Göteborg and v.v.; 🍷 Gävle - Göteborg and v.v.

475/8 – [12] Stockholm - Herrljunga - Uddevalla - Strömstad and v.v.; ✕ Stockholm - Uddevalla and v.v.

7101 – † June 22 - Aug. 24 (from Narvik): ▬, [2], ✕ (also panorama car) Narvik - Stockholm - Göteborg.

7102 – ① June 22 - Aug. 24: ▬, [2], ✕ (also panorama car) Göteborg - Stockholm - Narvik.

10072 – ⑥: 🛏, ▬ and [2] Göteborg - Stockholm - Storlien; ✕ and [Bio] Göteborg - Stockholm; ✕ Sundsvall - Storlien.

10073 – ⑥ (from Storlien, one day later from Örebro): 🛏, ▬ and [2] Storlien - Stockholm - Göteborg; ✕ and [Bio] Storlien - Sundsvall; ✕ Örebro - Göteborg.

10077 – Ⓑ (from Storlien, one day later from Örebro): 🛏, ▬ and [2] Storlien - Stockholm - Göteborg; ✕ and [Bio] Storlien - Sundsvall; ✕ Örebro - Göteborg.

X2000 – High speed train. Special supplement payable.

[Bio] – Cinema / bistro car.

N – ①②③④ June 14 - 21.
P – ①②③④† only.
Q – Ⓑ (daily from June 19).
R – ①②③④† June 14 - 18.
V – Via Västerås – see Table **756**.

a – Ⓐ only.
d – ⚒ only.
e – June 14 only.
f – Not July 6 - Aug. 2.
g – ⑥ only.
h – Not July 29 - Aug. 9.
j – July 6 - Aug. 9.
k – Not July 6 - Aug. 9.
m – June 29 - Aug. 2.
n – Not June 28 - Aug. 1.
‡ – Most trains on this table do not convey passengers for local journeys between Stockholm and Södertälje Syd or v.v. Local trains run every 30 minutes Stockholm Central - Södertälje Hamn - Södertälje Centrum and v.v. (journey 42 mins). 🚌 Södertälje Syd - Södertälje Centrum runs every 30 minutes.

o – Not June 29 - Aug. 2.
p – June 28 - Aug. 1.
q – Aug. 3 - 15.
r – June 14 - 28.
s – Stops to set down only.
t – June 14 - 26.
u – Stops to pick up only.
v – Not June 27 - Aug. 9.
w – Not July 4 - Aug. 2.
x – Runs as train **193** on †.
y – Runs as train **157** on ⑥.
z – June 14 - 21.
***** – Arrive 0800 July 6 - Aug. 8.
§ – Depart 1939 July 5 - Aug. 7.

Operator: Øtåg

KØBENHAVN - MALMÖ - KRISTIANSTAD - KARLSKRONA 745

km		Ⓐ	Ⓐ	⚒		Ⓐ	Ⓒ	Ⓐ		⚒	†	Ⓐ		⚒	†	Ⓐ			Ⓐ		Ⓑ	⑥	Ⓐ		Ⓑ
0	**København H 703/30** d.	...	...	0543	0643	0743	0743	0803	0843	0943	0943	1003	1043	1143	1143	1203	1243	1343	1403	1443	1543	1543	1603	1643	1743
12	Kastrup ✈ 703/30 d.	...	...	0556	0656	0756	0756	0816	0856	0956	0956	1016	1056	1156	1156	1216	1256	1356	1416	1456	1556	1556	1616	1656	1756
47	**Malmö 703** a.	...	...	0618	0718	0818	0818	0838	0918	1018	1018	1038	1118	1218	1218	1238	1318	1418	1438	1518	1618	1618	1638	1718	1818
47	**Malmö 730/46** d.	...	0528	0628	0728	0828	0828	0848	0928	1028	1028	1048	1128	1228	1228	1248	1328	1428	1448	1528	1628	1628	1648	1728	1828
63	Lund 730/46 d.	...	0542	0642	0742	0842	0842	0902	0942	1042	1042	1102	1142	1242	1242	1302	1342	1442	1502	1542	1642	1642	1702	1742	1842
81	Eslöv 746 d.	...	0552	0652	0752	0852	0852	0912	0952	1052	1052	1112	1152	1252	1252	1312	1352	1452	1512	1552	1652	1652	1712	1752	1852
130	Hässleholm 730/46 a.	...	0616	0716	0816	0916	0916	0936	1016	1116	1116	1136	1216	1316	1316	1336	1416	1516	1536	1616	1716	1716	1736	1816	1916
130	Hässleholm d.	0516	0618	0718	0818	0918	0918	...	1018	1118	1118	...	1218	1318	1318	...	1418	1518	...	1618	1718	1718	...	1818	1918
160	**Kristianstad** a.	0537	0637	0737	0837	0937	0937	...	1037	1137	1137	...	1237	1337	1337	...	1437	1537	...	1637	1737	1737	...	1837	1937
160	**Kristianstad** d.	0546	0646	0746	0846	0946	...	...	1046	1146	...	...	1246	1346	...	...	1446	1546	...	1646	1746	...	...	1846	1946
191	Sölvesborg d.	0607	0707	0807	0907	1007	...	...	1107	1207	...	...	1307	1407	...	...	1507	1607	...	1707	1807	...	...	1907	2007
222	Karlshamn d.	0632	0732	0832	0932	1032	...	...	1132	1232	...	...	1332	1432	...	...	1532	1632	...	1732	1832	...	...	1932	2032
260	Ronneby d.	0700	0800	0900	1000	1100	...	...	1200	1300	...	...	1400	1500	...	...	1600	1700	...	1800	1900	...	...	2000	2100
290	**Karlskrona** a.	0722	0822	0922	1022	1122	...	...	1222	1322	...	...	1422	1522	...	...	1622	1722	...	1822	1922	...	...	2022	2122

	⑥	Ⓐ		Ⓑ	⑥	Ⓑ			⚒	Ⓒ
København H 703/30 d.	1743	1803	1843	1943	1943	2003	2043	2143	2243	0003
Kastrup ✈ 703/30 d.	1756	1816	1856	1956	1956	2016	2056	2156	2256	0016
Malmö 703 a.	1818	1838	1918	2018	2018	2038	2118	2218	2318	0038
Malmö 730/46 d.	1828	1848	1928	2028	2028	2048	2128	2228	2328	0053
Lund 730/46 d.	1842	1902	1942	2042	2042	2102	2142	2242	2342	0113
Eslöv 746 d.	1852	1912	1952	2052	2052	2112	2152	2252	2352	0126
Hässleholm 730/46 a.	1916	1936	2016	2116	2116	2136	2216	2316	0016	0155
Hässleholm d.	1918	...	2018	2118	2118	...	2218	2318	0018	0157
Kristianstad a.	1937	...	2037	2137	2137	...	2237	2337	0037	0216
Kristianstad d.	...	...	2046	2146	...	...	2246	...	...	...
Sölvesborg d.	...	...	2107	2207	...	...	2307	...	...	...
Karlshamn d.	...	...	2132	2232	...	...	2332	...	...	...
Ronneby d.	...	...	2200	2300	...	...	0000	...	...	...
Karlskrona a.	...	...	2222	2322	...	...	0022	...	...	...

	Ⓐ	Ⓐ	Ⓒ	⚒	†	Ⓐ	Ⓐ	⑥		⚒
Karlskrona d.	...	0438	...	0538	...	...	0638	...	0738	...
Ronneby d.	...	0502	...	0602	...	...	0702	...	0802	...
Karlshamn d.	...	0530	...	0630	...	...	0730	...	0830	...
Sölvesborg d.	...	0552	...	0652	...	...	0752	...	0852	...
Kristianstad a.	...	0614	...	0714	...	...	0814	...	0914	...
Kristianstad d.	0520	0623	0623	0723	0723	...	0823	0823	0923	...
Hässleholm a.	0541	0640	0640	0740	0740	...	0840	0840	0940	...
Hässleholm 730/46 d.	0542	0642	0642	0742	0742	0824	0842	0842	0942	1024
Eslöv 746 d.	0606	0706	0706	0806	0806	0847	0906	0906	1006	1047
Lund 730/46 d.	0617	0717	0717	0817	0817	0857	0917	0917	1017	1057
Malmö 730/46 a.	0632	0732	0732	0832	0832	0912	0932	0932	1032	1112
Malmö 703 d.	0642	0742	0742	0842	0842	0922	0942	0942	1042	1122
Kastrup ✈ 703/30 a.	0703	0803	0803	0903	0903	0943	1003	1003	1103	1143
København H 703/30 a.	0717	0817	0817	0917	0917	0957	1017	1017	1117	1157

	Ⓐ	Ⓒ		Ⓐ			Ⓐ	⚒	†		Ⓑ			Ⓐ	Ⓑ	⑥		Ⓐ	Ⓑ	⑥		Ⓐ	Ⓑ	⑥	
Karlskrona d.	0838	...	0938	...	1038d	1138	...	1238	...	1338	...	1438	1538	...	1638	...	1738	...	1838	...	1938	...	2038	...	2138
Ronneby d.	0902	...	1002	...	1102d	1202	...	1302	...	1402	...	1502	1602	...	1702	...	1802	...	1902	...	2002	...	2102	...	2202
Karlshamn d.	0930	...	1030	...	1130d	1230	...	1330	...	1430	...	1530	1630	...	1730	...	1830	...	1930	...	2030	...	2130	...	2230
Sölvesborg d.	0952	...	1052	...	1152d	1252	...	1352	...	1452	...	1552	1652	...	1752	...	1852	...	1952	...	2052	...	2152	...	2252
Kristianstad a.	1014	...	1114	...	1214d	1314	...	1414	...	1514	...	1614	1714	...	1814	...	1914	...	2014	...	2114	...	2214	...	2314
Kristianstad d.	1023	1023	1123	...	1223	1323	...	1423	1423	1523	...	1623	1723	...	1823	1823	1923	...	2023	2023	2123	...	2223	2223	2323
Hässleholm a.	1040	1040	1140	...	1240	1340	...	1440	1440	1540	...	1640	1740	...	1840	1840	1940	...	2040	2040	2140	...	2240	2240	2341
Hässleholm 730/46 d.	1042	1042	1142	1224	1242	1342	1424	1442	1442	1542	1624	1642	1742	1824	1842	1842	1942	2024	2042	2042	2142	2224	2242	2242	2342
Eslöv 746 d.	1106	1106	1206	1247	1306	1406	1447	1506	1506	1607	1647	1706	1806	1847	1906	1906	2006	2047	2106	2106	2206	2247	2306	2306	0006
Lund 730/46 d.	1117	1117	1217	1257	1317	1417	1457	1517	1517	1617	1657	1717	1817	1857	1917	1917	2017	2057	2117	2117	2217	2257	2317	2317	0017
Malmö 730/46 a.	1132	1132	1232	1312	1332	1432	1512	1532	1532	1632	1712	1732	1832	1912	1932	1932	2032	2112	2132	2132	2232	2312	2332	2332	0032
Malmö 703 d.	1142	1142	1242	1322	1342	1442	1522	1542	1542	1642	1722	1742	1842	1922	1942	1942	2042	2122	2142	2142	2242	2322	...	...	...
Kastrup ✈ 703/30 a.	1203	1203	1303	1343	1403	1503	1543	1603	1603	1703	1743	1803	1903	1943	2003	2003	2103	2143	2203	2203	2303	2343	...	...	...
København H 703/30 a.	1217	1217	1317	1357	1417	1517	1557	1617	1617	1717	1757	1817	1917	1957	2017	2017	2117	2157	2217	2217	2317	2357	...	...	...

d – ⚒ only.

KØBENHAVN - MALMÖ and GÖTEBORG - KALMAR and KARLSKRONA 746

km		Øtåg	Øtåg	Øtåg		Øtåg	Øtåg	Øtåg		Øtåg	Øtåg	Øtåg				Øtåg	Øtåg	Øtåg	Øtåg	Øtåg		Øtåg		Øtåg	Øtåg	X2000		Øtåg
		Ⓐ	Ⓐ	Ⓐ			Ⓐ		⚒	Ⓐ		Ⓐ	Ⓒ	Ⓐ		Ⓐ	Ⓒ	Ⓐ		Ⓐ			Ⓑ		Ⓑ	K		
0	**København 703** d.	...	...	0603	...	0703	0803	0903	...	1003	1103	1203	...	...	...	1303	1303	1403	1503	1603	...	1703	...	1903	2003	2019	...	2103
12	Kastrup ✈ 703 d.	...	...	0616	...	0716	0816	0916	...	1016	1116	1216	...	...	...	1316	1316	1416	1516	1616	...	1716	...	1916	2016	2031u	...	2116
47	**Malmö 703** a.	...	...	0638	...	0738	0838	0938	...	1038	1138	1238	...	...	...	1338	1338	1438	1538	1638	...	1738	...	1938	2038	|	...	2138
47	**Malmö 730/45** d.	...	0548	0648	...	0748	0848	0948	...	1048	1148	1248	...	...	...	1348	1348	1448	1548	1648	...	1748	...	1948	2048	2114u	...	2148
63	Lund 730/45 d.	...	0602	0702	...	0802	0902	1002	...	1102	1202	1302	...	...	...	1402	1402	1502	1602	1702	...	1802	...	2002	2102	2128u	...	2202
80	Eslöv 745 d.	...	0612	0712	...	0812	0912	1012	...	1112	1212	1312	...	...	...	1412	1412	1512	1612	1712	...	1812	...	2012	2112	|	...	2212
130	Hässleholm 730/45 d.	...	0639	0739	...	0839	0939	1039	...	1139	1239	1339	...	...	...	1439	1439	1539	1639	1739	...	1839	...	2039	2139	2203	...	2239
181	Älmhult d.	...	0702	0802	...	0902	1002	1102	...	1202	1302	1402	...	...	...	1502	1502	1602	1702	1802	...	1902	...	2102	2202	|	...	2302
	Göteborg ▲ d.	...	|	|	...	|	|	|	0907	|	|	|	1212	1212	...	|	|	|	|	|	1607	|	1807	|	|	|	...	|
	Borås ▲ d.	...	|	|	...	|	|	|	1004	|	|	|	1307	1307	...	|	|	|	|	|	1704	|	1902	|	|	|	...	|
	Limmared d.	...	|	|	...	|	|	|	1032	|	|	|	1335	1335	...	|	|	|	|	|	1734	|	1930	|	|	|	...	|
	Värnamo d.	...	|	|	...	|	|	|	1111	|	|	|	1419	1419	...	|	|	|	|	|	1816	|	2009	|	|	|	...	|
228	Alvesta 730 a.	...	0721	0821	...	0921	1021	1121	1137	1221	1321	1421	1445	1445	...	1521	1521	1621	1721	1821	1842	1921	2035	2121	2221	2239	...	2321
228	Alvesta ▲ d.	0601	0722	0826	...	0934	1027	1134	1144	1235	1334	1427	1447	1447	...	1534	1534	1642	1734	1827	1845	1934	2044	2134	2225	2241	...	2322
245	**Växjö** ▲ d.	0628	0733	0836	...	0946	1037	1146	1158	1300	1346	1437	1500	1500	...	1546	1546	1657	1746	1837	1859	1946	2102	2146	2236	2252	...	2335
302	Emmaboda a.	0703	0805	...	...	1020	...	1220e	1229	1333t	1420	...	1531	1531	...	1621	1621	1729t	1820	...	1930	2020b	2133	2220	...	...	...	0008
302	Emmaboda ● d.	0706	0806	...	...	1022	...	1230e	1231	1340t	1422	...	1532	1552	...	1624	1629	1731t	1827	...	1932	2028b	2135	2222	...	...	...	0010
330	Nybro d.	0722	0821	...	...	1036	...	1244e	1246	1354t	1436	...	1547	1609	...	1638	1643	1745t	1841	...	1947	2042b	2150	2236	...	...	...	0024
359	**Kalmar** a.	0737	0836	...	...	1051	...	1300e	1302	1414t	1452	...	1603	1625	...	1653	1658	1801t	1856	...	2003	2057b	2206	2251	...	...	...	0039

km		Øtåg	X2000		Øtåg	Øtåg	Øtåg		Øtåg	Øtåg	Øtåg	Øtåg	Øtåg			Øtåg	Øtåg	Øtåg	Øtåg			Øtåg	Øtåg		Øtåg	Øtåg	Øtåg	Øtåg
		Ⓐ	V		Ⓐ	⚒		⚒	⚒		Ⓐ	⚒	†	Ⓒ	Ⓐ	Ⓐ		Ⓑ		Ⓐ	Ⓒ	Ⓐ		Ⓑ	Ⓐ		Ⓑt	Ⓐ
	Kalmar d.	...	...	...	...	0554a	0707	0804	...	0909	...	1055	1109	1157	1157	...	1309	1345r	1501	1553	1556	...	1701	1753	...	1903	1956	2106
	Nybro d.	...	...	...	...	0610a	0723	0820	...	0925	...	1111	1125	1213	1213	...	1325	1402r	1517	1609	1614	...	1717	1813	...	1919	2014	2122
	Emmaboda ● a.	...	...	...	...	0623a	0737	0834	...	0938	...	1124	1138	1228	1228	...	1338	1416r	1530	1624	1629	...	1730	1827	...	1932	2028	2135
	Emmaboda d.	...	...	...	...	0626a	0739	0835	...	0940	...	1126	1140	1230	1230	...	1340	1420r	1540	1626	1631	...	1740	1829	...	1940	2030	2140
	Växjö ▲ d.	0518	0602	...	0614	0658	0811	0906	0920	1012	1120	1208	1212	1302	1302	1320	1412	1513	1612	1704	1702	1720	1812	1904	1920	2012	2102	2212
	Alvesta ▲ a.	0532	0613	...	0624	0710	0824	0919	0931	1025	1131	1219	1225	1315	1315	1331	1425	1524	1625	1715	1715	1731	1825	1915	1931	2025	2115	2225
0	Alvesta 730 d.	0533	0627	...	0631	0712	0833	0927	0933	1033	1133	1233	1233	1324	1344	1333	1433	1533	1633	1717	1717	1733	1833	1921	1933	2035	...	...
49	Värnamo d.	|	|	...	|	|	|	0954	|	|	|	|	|	1356	1420	|	|	|	|	1748	1746	|	|	1947	|	|	...	...
110	Limmared d.	|	|	...	|	|	|	1032	|	|	|	|	|	1435	1458	|	|	|	|	1830	1830	|	|	2027	|	|	...	...
149	Borås ▲ a.	|	|	...	|	|	|	1100	|	|	|	|	|	1503	1526	|	|	|	|	1859	1859	|	|	2055	|	|	...	...
222	**Göteborg** ▲ a.	|	|	...	|	|	|	1157	|	|	|	|	|	1602	1622	|	|	|	|	1957	1957	|	|	2152	|	|	...	...
	Älmhult d.	0553	|	...	0653	0732	0853	...	0953	1053	1153	1253	1253	...	...	1353	1453	1553	1653	...	...	1753	1853	...	1953	2055	...	...
	Hässleholm 730/45 a.	0616	0702	...	0716	0755	0916	...	1016	1116	1216	1316	1316	...	...	1416	1516	1616	1716	...	...	1816	1916	...	2016	2118	...	...
	Eslöv 745 a.	0646	|	...	0746	0820	0946	...	1046	1146	1246	1346	1346	...	...	1446	1546	1646	1746	...	...	1846	1946	...	2046	2146	...	...
	Lund 730/45 a.	0657	0731s	...	0757	0831	0957	...	1057	1157	1257	1357	1357	...	...	1457	1557	1657	1757	...	...	1857	1957	...	2057	2157	...	...
	Malmö 730/45 a.	0712	0746s	...	0812	0846	1012	...	1112	1212	1312	1412	1412	...	...	1512	1612	1712	1812	...	...	1912	2012	...	2112	2212	...	...
	Malmö 703 d.	0722	|	...	0822	0902	1022	...	1122	1222	1322	1422	1422	...	...	1522	1622	1722	1822	...	...	1922	2022	...	2122	2222	...	...
	Kastrup ✈ 703 a.	0743	0819s	...	0843	0923	1043	...	1143	1243	1343	1443	1443	...	...	1543	1643	1743	1843	...	...	1943	2043	...	2143	2243	...	...
	København 703 a.	0757	0832	...	0857	0937	1057	...	1157	1257	1357	1457	1457	...	...	1557	1657	1757	1857	...	...	1957	2057	...	2157	2257	...	...

● – CONNECTING SERVICES **Emmaboda - Karlskrona and v.v.:**

km		Ⓐ	⑥	Ⓐ	†	⚒	†			Ⓑ	⑥	Ⓑ	
0	Emmaboda d.	0708	0841	0943	1025	1129	1234	1425	1632	1832	1937	2140	...
57	Karlskrona a.	0751	0925	1026	1108	1212	1317	1508	1715	1915	2025	2225	...

	⑥	Ⓑ	⚒	†	⚒	†		Ⓑ	⑥	†	Ⓐ	
Karlskrona a.	0748	0851	1034	1142	1252	1333	1534	1735	1844	1935	2047	...
Emmaboda d.	0831	0933	1118	1225	1335	1416	1618	1818	1927	2018	2130	...

K – Ⓑ June 14 - 26: [1 2] København - Växjö; ✕ København - Alvesta. [R] and special supplement payable. Train number **554**.

V – ⚒ June 14 - 27: [1 2] and ✕ Växjö - København. [R] and special supplement payable. Train number **509**.

a – Ⓐ only.
b – Ⓑ only.
e – † only.
r – Ⓐ (not July 6 - Aug. 9).

s – Stops to set down only.
t – Not Ⓐ July 6 - Aug. 9.
u – Stops to pick up only.

▲ – Additional trains run Göteborg - Borås and v.v., and Alvesta - Växjö and v.v.

747 STOCKHOLM - STOCKHOLM ARLANDA ✈

Arlanda Express. Operator: A-Train AB (*AEX*)

Journey time: 20 minutes. All services stop at Arlanda Södra (17 minutes from Stockholm, 2 minutes from Arlanda Norra). Södra serves terminals 2, 3 and 4; Norra serves terminal 5.

From **Stockholm Central:** 0435, 0505, 0520, 0535, 0550, 0605, 0620, 0635, 0650 and at the same minutes past each hour until 2205, 2220, 2235, 2305, 2335, 0005, 0035.

From **Arlanda Norra:** 0505, 0535, 0550, 0605, 0620, 0635, 0650 and at the same minutes past each hour until 2205, 2220, 2235, 2250, 2305, 2335, 0005, 0035, 0105.

Minor alterations to schedules are possible at peak times

750 STOCKHOLM - HALLSBERG - KARLSTAD - OSLO

km		VTAB 2 Ⓐ	623 Ⓐ	VTAB 2 Ⓐ	625 ✕ ⚒	629 †	627 ⑥	VTAB 2	VTAB 2 Ⓐ	633 🍷 Ⓐ	VTAB 2 Ⓐ	637 ⑥	637 Ⓑ	VTAB 2 ⑥	639 Ⓑx	VTAB 2 ①–④	VTAB 2 ⑤	631 Ⓑv	X2000 459 [R] ✕ Ⓑw	VTAB 2 †	647 🍷	VTAB 2 Ⓑ		4 [R] ♦
0	**Stockholm** C **730/40** d.	...	0630	...	0829	1025	1025	...	...	1225	...	1425	1425	...	1530	...	...	1625	1715	...	1915	...	...	2155
15	Flemingsberg **730/40** d.	...	0641	...	0840	1036	1036	...	...	1236	...	1436	1436	...	1541	...	...	1636	|	...	1926	...	...	|
36	Södertälje Syd **730/40** d.	...	0653	...	0852	1048	1048	...	...	1248	...	1438	1448	...	1553	...	...	1648	1733u	...	1938	...	...	2220u
108	Flen **730/40** d.	...	0729	...	0928	1124	1124	...	...	1324	...	1525	1525	...	1630	...	...	1725	|	...	2014	...	...	|
131	Katrineholm **730/40** d.	...	0743	...	0942	1138	1138	...	...	1338	...	1539	1539	...	1644	...	...	1739	1811	...	2028	...	...	|
197	**Hallsberg 740** a.	...	0817	...	1016	1212	1212	...	...	1412	...	1613	1613	...	1719	...	...	1813	|	...	2102	...	...	|
197	**Hallsberg** d.	...	0820	...	1020	1215	1215	...	...	1415	...	1615	1615	...	1722	...	...	1815	1837u	...	2105	...	...	2340u
263	Degerfors d.	...	0851	...	1052	1245	1245	...	...	1448	...	1645	1645	...	1804	...	...	1846	1902	...	2135	...	...	|
289	Kristinehamn d.	0602	0907	...	1109	1303	1308	...	...	1505	1603	1707	1707	...	1819	1844	1844	1903	1918	...	2153	...	...	|
329	**Karlstad 751** a.	0632	0928	...	1131	1329	1329	...	...	1526k	1632	1730	1730	...	1842	1910	1910	1929	1940	...	2215	...	...	|
329	**Karlstad** d.	0642	...	0933	1135	...	...	1345	1534	1559	1712	...	1732	1750	...	1914	1914	...	1944	1957	...	2220	...	|
349	Kil d.	0658	...	0950	1149	...	...	1359	1547	1612	1729	...	1753	1804	...	1932	1932	...	2000	2011	...	2234	...	|
397	Arvika d.	0746	...	1024	1217	...	...	1435	1622	...	1808	...	1826	1841	...	2030t	2007	...	2026	2048	...	2311	...	|
432	Charlottenberg 🏛 a.	0812	...	1046	1237	...	...	1459	1645	...	1834	...	1846	1907	...	2054	...	...	...	2114	...	2337	...	|
474	Kongsvinger a.	...	...	1114	1306	...	...	...	1712	...	...	...	1915	...	...	...	...	...	...	...	...	...	...	|
574	**Oslo** Sentral a.	...	...	1230	1436	...	...	...	1831	...	...	...	2041	...	...	...	...	...	...	...	...	...	...	0700r

	622 Ⓐm	632 Ⓐq	X2000 452 [R] ✕ Ⓐm	X2000 454 [R] ✕ ⑥m	VTAB 2 Ⓐ	628 ⚒	VTAB 2 Ⓐ	VTAB 2 Ⓐ	VTAB 2 †	VTAB 2 ⑥	630 Ⓐ	630 Ⓒ		634 ✕ ⑥	638 🍷 Ⓑ	VTAB 2 Ⓐ	VTAB 2 Ⓒ	644 🍷	VTAB 2 Ⓐ	10648 Ⓑ	VTAB 2 Ⓐ	VTAB 2 Ⓐ		3 [R] ♦
Oslo Sentral d.	...	...	...	...	...	...	...	...	...	...	0725	...	...	0928	...	1329	...	...	...	1549	...	1929	...	2132n
Kongsvinger d.	...	...	...	...	...	...	...	...	...	...	0849	...	...	1047	...	1439	...	...	...	1717	...	2052	...	|
Charlottenberg 🏛 d.	...	...	...	...	0621	...	0720	0817	0834	0847	0917	...	...	1115	...	1507	1507	...	1625	1745	2033	2128	...	|
Arvika d.	...	...	0553	0634	0649	...	0756	0841	0903	0916	0941	...	...	1136	...	1535	1536	...	1653	1808	2059	2156	...	|
Kil d.	...	...	0620	0700	0726	...	0832	0917	0939	0959	1010	...	...	1210	1341a	1610	1612	...	1730	1834	2132	2233	...	|
Karlstad 751 a.	...	...	0634	0712	0739	...	0845	0930	0952	1012	1023	...	...	1224	1400a	1625	1625	...	1743	1848	2145	2246	...	|
Karlstad d.	0600	0615	0638	0715	0744	0823	...	...	...	...	1025	1025	...	1226	1420	...	...	1632	1755	1850	...	...	...	|
Kristinehamn d.	0623	0639	0657	0734	0810	0850	...	...	...	...	1047	1047	...	1251	1444	...	...	1654	1821	1917	...	...	...	|
Degerfors d.	0638	0654	0710	0747	...	0909	...	...	...	...	1110	1110	...	1305	1505	...	...	1708	...	1933	...	...	...	|
Hallsberg a.	0710	0725	|	0815	...	0939	...	...	...	...	1140	1140	...	1338	1538	...	...	1740	...	2003	...	...	...	0509s
Hallsberg 740 d.	0712	0728	|	0817	...	0941	...	...	...	...	1142	1142	...	1341	1541	...	...	1744	...	2005	...	...	...	|
Katrineholm **730/40** a.	0745	0800	|	0841	...	1014	...	...	...	...	1215	1215	...	1414	1614	...	...	1817	...	2045	...	...	...	|
Flen **730/40** a.	0814	0814	|	|	...	1028	...	...	...	...	1229	1229	...	1428	1628	...	...	1831	...	2059	...	...	...	|
Södertälje Syd **730/40** a.	0850	0850	|	0918s	...	1104	...	...	...	...	1305	1305	...	1504	1704	...	...	1907	...	2147	...	...	...	0638s
Flemingsberg **730/40** a.	0902	0902	|	|	...	1116	...	...	...	...	1317	1317	...	1516	1716	...	...	1919	...	2159	...	...	...	|
Stockholm C **730/40** a.	0915	0915	0850	0939	...	1130	...	...	...	...	1330	1330	...	1530	1731	...	...	1932	...	2213	...	...	...	0705

♦ – **NOTES** (LISTED BY TRAIN NUMBER)

3 – Ⓑ June 14 - Aug. 30: 🛏, ▬ and [2] Oslo - Göteborg (**6**) - Stockholm; 🛏 and ▬ Oslo - Göteborg (**5**) - Malmö. Train number **10003** July 5 - Aug. 7.

4 – Ⓑ June 14 - Aug. 30: 🛏, ▬ and [2] Stockholm (**5**) - Göteborg - Oslo; 🛏 and ▬ Malmö (**6**) - Göteborg - Oslo.

a – Ⓐ only.
k – Connects into train in previous column.
m – Not June 29 - Aug. 2.
n – Depart 1939 July 5 - Aug. 7.
q – June 29 - Aug. 2.
r – Arrive 0800 July 6 - Aug. 8.
s – Stops to set down only.
t – Arrive 2007.
u – Stops to pick up only.
v – June 28 - Aug. 1.
w – Not June 27 - Aug. 1.
x – Not June 28 - Aug. 1.
X2000 – High speed train. Special supplement payable.

751 KARLSTAD - GÖTEBORG

A replacement 🚌 service will operate July 6 - August 9 Trollhättan - Göteborg and v.v.; journey times are extended

km		Ⓐ	Ⓐ	⑥	Ⓐ	Ⓒ	⑥	†	Ⓐ	⚒	†	†	Ⓐ
0	**Karlstad 750** d.	...	0603	0700	0904	0904	1231	1310	1348	1559	1559	1757	1859
19	Kil d.	...	0621	0717	0919	0919	1246	1325	1402	1615	1615	1815	1913
70	Säffle d.	...	0654	0748	0956	0951	1318	1357	1434	1648	1654	1846	1944
87	Åmål d.	*0532*	0707	0758	1007	1002	1329	1408	1445	1658	1705	1857	1955
128	Mellerud d.	*0556*	0733	0824	1033	1029	1355	1433	1510	1723	1731	1924	2021
169	Öxnered a.	0627	0800	0847	1056	1053	1417	1457	1533	1748	1754	1955	2044
179	Trollhättan a.	0633	0807	0856	1103	1103	1424	1504	1540	1802	1802	2002	2051
251	**Göteborg** a.	0729	0852	0953	1151	1151	1510	1549	1629	1853	1853	2047	2136

	Ⓐ	⑥	Ⓒ	Ⓐ	⑥	†	Ⓐ	⚒	†	†	Ⓐ
Göteborg d.	0707	0807	1007	1108	1306	1407	1507	1708	1708	1910	1910
Trollhättan d.	0756	0856	1056	1155	1350	1453	1555	1751	1751	1958	1958
Öxnered d.	0805	0904	1104	1204	1358	1502	1605	1800	1800	2007	2007
Mellerud d.	0827	0926	1127	1226	1426	1524	1626	1822	1822	2028	2032
Åmål d.	0852	0953	1152	1251	1451	1549	1651	1846	1846	2053	2101
Säffle d.	0905	1013	1204	1304	1504	1601	1708	1859	1908	2105	2113
Kil a.	0937	1046	1237	1339	1536	1635	1748	1941	1941	2138	2147
Karlstad 750 a.	0959	1100	1258	1400	1551	1650	1804	1956	1956	2152	2203

752 SECONDARY LINES in South - East Sweden

KLT 🚌 *service is subject to alteration* — 2nd class only except where shown

km	Operator: *KLT*	Ⓐ	⚒						†	⚒				Ⓑ
0	Västervik d.	0541	0646	0747	...	1107	1407	...	1609	1609	...	1840	...	1940
116	Linköping a.	0730	0830	0930	...	1245	1546	...	1752	1754	...	2020	...	2132

Operator: *KLT*	Ⓐ	⚒			F	⑤						Ⓑ
Linköping d.	0545	0912	1112	...	1412	1412	1612	...	1733	1933	...	2109
Västervik a.	0727	1052	1252	...	1550	1554	1800	...	1920	2123	...	2250

km	Operator: *KLT*	Ⓐ‡	Ⓐ‡	⑥‡	‡		‡	‡		‡	‡	Ⓑ‡		Ⓑ‡
0	Linköping d.	...	0539	...	0812	...	1035	1305	...	1551	1712	1911	...	2114
123	Hultsfred d.	0618	0718	0718	0959	...	1226	1452	...	1726	1853	2052	...	2250
159	Berga a.	0642	0742	0742	1023	...	1249	1516	...	1749	1916	2115	...	...
159	Berga d.	0647	0749	0749	1028	...	1254	1524	...	1754	1921	2120	...	...
235	Kalmar **746** a.	0744	0850	0850	1126	...	1351	1621	...	1850	2023	2216	...	...

Operator: *KLT*	Ⓐ‡	Ⓐ‡	⑥‡	‡	‡		‡	‡	‡		Ⓑ‡	Ⓑ‡
Kalmar **746** d.	...	0550	...	0750	1025	...	1246	1427	1646	...	1925	2115
Berga a.	...	0647	...	0847	1123	...	1347	1524	1746	...	2023	2215
Berga d.	...	0652	...	0852	1128	...	1352	1529	1751	...	2028	2220
Hultsfred d.	0547	0717	0717	0916	1154	...	1416	1554	1816	...	2052	2244
Linköping a.	0725	0850	0850	1054	1345	...	1550	1733	1952	...	2226	...

km	*KLT* 🚌 service	⚒			†	⚒						Ⓑ	Ⓑ	Ⓑ
0	Berga d.	0745	0853	1028	1128	1140	1255	1353	1527	1755	1920	2023	2120	2220
29	Oskarshamn a.	0815	0923	1058	1158	1210	1325	1423	1600	1825	1953	2053	2151	2250

KLT 🚌 service	⚒					⚒				Ⓑ	Ⓑ	Ⓑ
Oskarshamn d.	0715	0815	0953	1050	1220	1315	1450	1715	1845	1950	2045	2145
Berga a.	0745	0845	1023	1120	1250	1345	1520	1745	1915	2020	2115	2215

km	Operator: *MER*		Ⓐ				Ⓒ		Ⓐ				⑤†	
0	Nässjö d.	...	0703	...	0919	...	1316	...	1525	...	1721	...	1916	...
83	Hultsfred a.	...	0818	...	1037	...	1431	...	1639	...	1839	...	2030	...

Operator: *MER*		Ⓐ								⑤†		
Hultsfred d.	...	0628	...	0929	...	1327	...	1729	...	1923	...	...
Nässjö a.	...	0743	...	1043	...	1440	...	1845	...	2040	...	...

F – Daily except ⑤.
‡ – Also conveys 1st class.
⊡ – Operator: *VEO*.

754 NORRKÖPING - VÄSTERÅS - UPPSALA

2nd class only

km		Ⓐ	Ⓐ	Ⓐz	⚒	⚒			Ⓐz	Ⓑ	Ⓐz		Ⓑ
0	**Norrköping 730** d.	...	0633	0747	0832	1033	1233	1433	1534	1632	1736	1833	2033
48	Katrineholm **730** d.	...	0658	0813	0900	1100	1300	1500	1600	1700	1801	1900	2100
71	Flen **730** d.	...	0713	0826	0913	1113	1313	1513	1613	1713	1816	1913	2116
112	Eskilstuna d.	0652	0752	0908	0952	1152	1352	1552	1652	1752	1852	1952	2152
160	**Västerås** a.	0725	0825	0940	1025	1225	1425	1625	1725	1825	1925	2025	2225
160	**Västerås** d.	0727	0827	...	1027	1227	1427	1627b	1727	1827	...	2027r	...
199	Sala **761** a.	0753	0850	...	1050	1250	1450	1650b	1753	1850	...	2050r	...
	Uppsala **760/1** a.	...	...	...	...	...	...	...	...	...	...	...	...

	Ⓐz	⚒			⚒	Ⓑ	Ⓐz		Ⓐ	Ⓑ	Ⓐz	Ⓐz
Uppsala **760/1** d.	...	...	...	...	...	...	...	...	1711	...	...	2111
Sala **761** d.	...	0707a	0910d	1110	1310	1510	1607	1710b	1807	1910	2110	2207
Västerås a.	...	0733a	0933d	1133	1333	1533	1633	1733b	1833	1933	2133	2233
Västerås d.	0635	0735	0935	1135	1335	1535	1635	1735	1835	1935	2135	...
Eskilstuna d.	0709	0809	1009	1209	1409	1609	1709	1809	1907	2009	2207	...
Flen **730** d.	0744	0844	1044	1244	1444	1644	1744	1844	...	2044	...	...
Katrineholm **730** d.	0800	0900	1100	1300	1500	1658	1758	1900	...	2100	...	...
Norrköping 730 a.	0825	0925	1125	1325	1525	1723	1823	1925	...	2125	...	...

a – Ⓐ only.
b – Ⓑ only.
d – ⚒ only.
r – † (also Ⓐ June 14-28).
z – June 14-28.

MJÖLBY - HALLSBERG - ÖREBRO - GÄVLE 755

Operator: *ST*

A replacement 🚌 service will operate July 11 - August 9 Mjölby - Motala and v.v.; journey times are extended

km		Ⓐ	Ⓐq	Ⓐ	Ⓐ	⚒	Ⓐ	Ⓐ	Ⓐ	⑥	⚒	†		Ⓐ	⑥	Ⓐq			Ⓐq	Ⓑ	Ⓑ	⑥	98 ®G	Ⓑ	Ⓑ	Ⓑ	
0	**Mjölby 730** d.	...	...	...	...	...	...	0554	...	...	0812	...	1012	...	...	...	1212	1412	...	...	1612	1612	...	1812	...	2011	...
27	Motala d.	...	...	...	...	...	...	0611	...	...	0829	...	1029	...	...	...	1229	1429	...	...	1629	1629	...	1829	...	2028	...
96	**Hallsberg** a.	...	...	...	...	...	...	0657	...	...	0911	...	1111	...	...	...	1307	1506	...	...	1714	1714	...	1913	...	2114	...
	Hallsberg 756 d.	...	...	...	...	0519	0640	0718	0812r	...	0924	...	1123	...	...	...	1317	1517	1640	...	1722	1722	1915u	1940	1946	2124	...
121	**Örebro C 756** a.	...	...	...	...	0538	0659	0737	0831r	...	0943	...	1143	...	...	...	1336	1536	1659	...	1741	1741	|	1959	2005	2143	...
	Örebro C d.	...	...	...	...	0540	0700	0748	0900	0900	0947	...	1145	1300	1300	...	1342	1541	1700	1706	1747	...	1937u	2001	2017	...	...
146	Frövi d.	...	...	...	...	0554	0714	0803	0914	0914	1001	...	1159	1314	1314	...	1356	1555	1714	1720	1801	...	|	2015	2031	...	...
204	Kopparberg d.	...	...	...	...	0640	|	0846	|	|	1044	...	1242	|	|	...	1439	1659	1758	|	1844	...	|	2103	|	...	...
232	Grängesberg d.	...	...	...	...	0659	|	0911	|	|	1103	...	1310	|	|	...	1458	1718	1817	|	1914	...	|	2128	|	...	...
247	Ludvika d.	...	...	...	0626	0711	|	0922	|	|	1117	...	1325	|	|	...	1511	1729	1831	|	1926	...	|	2139	|	...	...
295	**Borlänge** a.	...	...	...	0704	0754	|	0951	|	|	1150	...	1357	|	|	...	1545	1758	1909	|	1955	...	|	2208	|	...	...
	Borlänge 761 d.	0518	0600	...	0709	0810	|	1013	|	|	1216	1216	1416	|	|	1510	1616	1810	1915	|	2016	...	|	2217	|	...	...
317	Falun **761** d.	0539	0631	...	0740	0828	|	1032	|	|	1235	1235	1435	|	|	1528	1634	1833	1945	|	2034	...	|	2233	|	...	...
	Fagersta d.	|	|	0600	|	|	0806	|	1006	1005	|	|	|	1405	1405	|	|	|	...	1804	|	...	|	...	2122	...	...
	Avesta Krylbo d.	|	|	0634	|	|	0838	|	1035	1032	|	|	|	1432	1440	|	|	|	...	1830	|	...	2137u	...	2149	...	...
371	Storvik d.	0613	0710	0714	0815	0909	0921	1111	1122	1126	1312	1312	1511	1515	1520	1611	1711	1917	...	1909	2111	...	|	...	2232	...	...
385	Sandviken d.	0624	0721	0725	0828	0920	0932	1122	1133	1138	1323	1323	1522	1526	1531	1622	1722	1929	...	1920	2122	...	|	...	2247	...	...
408	**Gävle 760** a.	0646	0736	0746	0849	0936	0946	1137	1148	1152	1338	1338	1537	1546	1546	1649	1744	1945	...	1940	2137	...	2238	...	2301	...	...

km		Ⓐ	Ⓐ	Ⓐ	⑥	97 ®G	⑥	Ⓐq	⑥	Ⓑ	Ⓐ	⚒	⚒	†	†		Ⓐ	Ⓐ	Ⓒ	Ⓐ		Ⓑ	Ⓑ	Ⓐq	Ⓑ	Ⓑ	Ⓑ
0	**Gävle 760** d.	...	0421	...	...	0515	...	...	0616	0616a	0720	0812	0818	...	1014	1022	1212	1222	1222	1415	1422	1620	1626	1722	1822	2022	2028
23	Sandviken d.	...	0437	...	...	|	...	...	0632	0632a	0741	0829	0835	...	1031	1039	1229	1239	1239	1431	1439	1638	1643	1739	1839	2039	2045
37	Storvik d.	...	0452	...	...	|	...	...	0642	0642a	0751	0838	0845	...	1040	1049	1239	1249	1249	1440	1449	1648	1653	1749	1849	2049	2055
95	Avesta Krylbo d.	...	0537	...	...	0610s	...	...	|	|	|	0920	|	...	1121	|	1321	|	|	1525	|	|	1737	|	|	|	2148
130	Fagersta d.	...	0600	...	...	|	0745	...	|	|	|	0946	|	...	1148	|	1348	|	|	1557	|	|	1803	|	|	|	2214
	Falun **761** d.	...	|	0509e	...	|	|	0609	0726	0726a	0830	|	0924	...	|	1126	|	1326	1326	|	1526	1725	|	1830	1926	2126	...
	Borlänge 761 a.	...	|	0530e	...	|	|	0626	0743	0743a	0850	|	0941	...	|	1143	|	1343	1343	|	1543	1743	|	1856	1943	2143	...
	Borlänge d.	...	|	0531	0531	|	|	0650	0800	0800a	...	|	1000	1000	|	1200	|	1400	1400	|	1600b	1800	|	...	2000	...	...
	Ludvika d.	...	|	0604	0604	|	|	0718	0829	0829a	...	|	1028	1028	|	1228	|	1429	1429	|	1628b	1828	|	...	2029	...	...
	Grängesberg d.	...	|	0620	0620	|	|	0729	0842	0842a	...	|	1039	1039	|	1241	|	1441	1441	|	1639b	1850	|	...	2040	...	...
	Kopparberg d.	...	|	0640	0640	|	|	0749	0902	0905a	...	|	1104	1100	|	1303	|	1506	1506	|	1659b	1910	|	...	2100	...	...
202	Frövi d.	0555	0643	0725	0725	|	0829	0834	0946	0949a	...	1033	1148	1145	1231	1350	1431	1554	1554	1642	1746b	1954	1844	...	2152	...	...
228	**Örebro C** a.	0610	0700	0740	0740	0816s	0844	0849	1001	1004a	...	1051	1203	1200	1246	1405	1447	1609	1610	1659	1800b	2009	1859	...	2210	...	...
	Örebro C 756 d.	0615	0704	0741	0823	|	...	0853	1019	1019	...	...	1213	1213	...	1415	1448	*1625*j	1625	1735	1808b	2025	1903	...	2216	...	...
252	**Hallsberg 756** a.	0634	0722	0800	0843	0838s	...	0912	1038	1038	...	...	1232	1232	...	1434	1506	*1644*j	1644	1754	1827b	2044	1922	...	2235	...	...
	Hallsberg d.	0648	...	...	0853	...	...	...	1052	1052	...	...	1245	1245	...	1445	...	*1652*j	1653	...	1843b	2055	...	...	...	...	...
	Motala d.	0727	...	...	0931	...	...	...	1132	1130	...	...	1328	1328	...	1527	...	*1731*j	1736	...	1931b	2143	...	...	...	...	...
	Mjölby 730 a.	0743	...	...	0947	...	...	...	1148	1146	...	...	1348	1348	...	1547	...	*1747*j	1752	...	1948b	2211	...	...	...	...	...

G – 🛏, 🛌 and (2) Luleå (**91/2**) - Gävle - Göteborg and v.v.; ✕ Gävle - Göteborg and v.v.

a – Ⓐ only.
b – Ⓑ only.
e – ① only.

j – Through train July 6 - 10 (no change necessary).
q – Not July 6 - Aug. 9.

r – Not July 20 - Aug. 9
s – Stops to set down only.
u – Stops to pick up only.

STOCKHOLM - VÄSTERÅS - ÖREBRO - HALLSBERG 756

km		159 Ⓐ	Ⓐ	Ⓐj	163 ⚒	167	171	175	Ⓐ	179	Ⓐj	Ⓐ	792 Ⓐ	Ⓐj	183	Ⓐj	756 Ⓐ	756 †k	187	Ⓑ	20072 V	772 G	772 ⑤	⑥	Y	⑤⑥
0	**Stockholm** C ⊡ d.	...	0600	0637	0707	0907	1107	1307	1407	1507	1537	1607	1637	1656	1707	1737	1807	1807	1907	2007	2130	2207	2207	2207	2307	2337
72	Enköping ⊡ d.	...	0638	0718	0748	0948	1148	1348	1445	1548	1618	1645	1718	|	1748	1818	1845	1845	1948	2048	|	2245	2248	2245	2348	0015
107	**Västerås** ⊡ d.	0608	0653	0736	0808	1008	1208	1408	1500	1608	1636	1700	1738	1745	1808	1836	1902	1902	2008	2106	2221	2302	2308	2300	0006	0030
141	Köping d.	0627	...	...	0827	1027	1227	1427	...	1627	...	...	1757	...	1827	...	1919j	1919	2027	...	...	2319	2327	...	...	...
159	Arboga **757** d.	0641	...	...	0841	1041	1241	1441	...	1641	...	...	1811	...	1841	...	1931j	1931	2041	...	...	2331	2341	...	...	...
205	**Örebro** a.	0704	...	...	0905	1104	1304	1504	...	1704	...	...	1835	...	1904	...	1952j	1952	2104	...	...	2352	0005	...	...	...
205	**Örebro 755** ▲ d.	0710	...	...	0910	1110	1310	1510	...	1710	...	...	1838	...	1910	...	1955j	1955	2107	...	...	2355	0008	...	...	...
230	**Hallsberg 755** ▲ a.	0730	...	...	0930	1130	1330	1530	...	1730	...	...	1858	...	1930	...	2015j	2015	2127	...	...	0015	0028	...	...	...
	Göteborg a.	0957	...	...	1157	1357	1557	1757	...	1957	...	...	...	...	2157	...	...	...	...	...	...	...	...	...	...	...

	20073 V	Ⓐj	Ⓐ	711 Ⓐ	781 Ⓐj	Ⓐ	715 ⚒	Ⓐj		10719 ⑥	719 Ⓐ	164 ⚒	723 †	168	172		176	Ⓐj	Ⓐ	180	Ⓐ	194	188		76 ®◆	10072 ®◆
Göteborg d.	...	...	...	...	...	...	...	...	...	...	...	0602	...	0802	1002	...	1202	...	...	1402	...	1602	1802	...	1900	1900
Hallsberg 755 ▲ d.	...	...	...	0533	0558	...	0633a	...	...	0723	0745	0828	0845	1028	1228	...	1428	...	...	1632	...	1828	2028	...	2110u	2110
Örebro 755 ▲ a.	...	...	...	0553	0618	...	0653a	...	...	0743	0805	0848	0905	1048	1248	...	1448	...	...	1652	...	1848	2048	...	|	|
Örebro d.	...	...	...	0556	0621	...	0656a	...	...	0746	0808	0856	0907	1056	1256	...	1456	...	...	1656	...	1856	2056	...	2130u	2130
Arboga **757** d.	...	...	...	0619	|	...	0721a	...	...	0810	0830	0921	0930	1121	1321	...	1521	...	...	1721	...	1921	2121	...	|	|
Köping d.	...	...	...	0631	|	...	0731a	...	...	0821	0839	0931	0939	1131	1331	...	1531	...	...	1731	...	1931	2131	...	|	|
Västerås ⊡ d.	0450	0559	0622	0652	0714	0722	0752	0822	...	0852	0859	0952	0959	1152	1352	...	1552	1622	1659	1752	1859	1952	2152	...	2228	2228
Enköping ⊡ d.	|	0613	0639	0709	|	0739	0809	0839	...	0909	0913	1009	1013	1209	1409	...	1609	1639	1713	1809	1913	2009	2209	...	...	...
Stockholm C ⊡ a.	0550	0652	0722	0752	0804	0822	0852	0922	...	0952	0952	1052	1052	1252	1452	...	1652	1722	1752	1852	1952	2052	2252	...	...	...

G – ①②③④† only.
V – ⑥ (from Stockholm, one day later from Västerås): (2) Stockholm - Västerås and v.v.; 🛏 and 🛌 Stockholm (**20072/3**) - Västerås (**10072/3**) - Storlien and v.v.
Y – ①②③④ only.

a – Ⓐ only.
j – Not June 29 - Aug. 9.
k – June 14 - Aug. 9.
u – Stops to pick up only.

◆ – For days of running and composition see Tables **740/60**.
▲ – Additional services operate Hallsberg - Örebro and v.v.
⊡ – Additional services operate Stockholm - Västerås and v.v.

STOCKHOLM - ESKILSTUNA - ARBOGA 757

A replacement 🚌 service will operate August 10 - October 25 Södertälje Syd - Läggesta / Strängnäs and v.v.; journey times are extended

km		Ⓐ	Ⓐ	⑥						Ⓐ	Ⓐ			Ⓐz	Ⓐ		Ⓐ		Ⓐ	Ⓒ		Y	⑤⑥	
0	**Stockholm** C d.	0625	0725	0751	0851	1051	...	1251	1451	1551	1630	1651	...	1725	1751	1851	1951	...	2151	2151	...	2250	2321	...
36	Södertälje Syd d.	0646	0746	0812	0912	1112	...	1312	1512	1612	1653	1712	...	1748	1812	1912	2012	...	2212	2212	...	2312	2342	...
67	Läggesta ● d.	0705	0805	0830	0930	1130	...	1330	1530	1630	1713	1730	...	1807	1830	1930	2030	...	2230	2230	...	2330	2359	...
83	Strängnäs d.	0719	0819	0840	0940	1140	...	1340	1540	1640	1726	1740	...	1824	1840	1940	2040	...	2240	2240	...	2340	0010	...
115	Eskilstuna a.	0739	0834	0855	0955	1155	...	1355	1555	1655	1742	1755	...	1840	1855	1955	2055	...	2255	2255	...	2355	0025	...
115	Eskilstuna d.	0800	...	...	1000	1200	...	1400	1600	...	...	1800	...	...	...	2000	...	...	2300	...	...	...	...	...
141	Kungsör d.	0813	...	...	1013	1213	...	1413	1613	...	...	1813	...	...	...	2013	...	...	2313	...	...	...	...	...
159	**Arboga 756** a.	0825	...	...	1025	1225	...	1425	1625	...	...	1825	...	...	...	2025	...	...	2325	...	...	...	...	...
	Örebro **756** a.	...	...	...	...	...	...	...	...	...	...	...	...	...	...	...	...	...	...	...	...	...	...	...

	Ⓐ	Ⓐ	Ⓐz	Ⓐ		⑥	Ⓐ	Ⓐ		⑥	⚒	⚒	†						Ⓐ					
Örebro **756** d.	...	...	...	...	...	...	...	...	...	...	...	...	...	...	...	...	...	...	...	...	...	...	...	...
Arboga 756 d.	...	...	...	0625	...	...	...	0725	...	...	...	0935	...	1135	...	1335	1535	...	...	1735	1935	...	2135	...
Kungsör d.	...	...	...	0635	...	...	...	0735	...	...	...	0944	...	1144	...	1344	1544	...	...	1744	1944	...	2144	...
Eskilstuna a.	...	...	...	0651	...	...	...	0751	...	...	...	1000	...	1200	...	1400	1600	...	...	1800	2000	...	2200	...
Eskilstuna d.	0515	0615	0642	0655	...	0705	0715	0755	...	0805	0905	1005	1005	1205	...	1405	1605	...	1705	1803	2005	...	2205	...
Strängnäs d.	0529	0631	|	0711	...	0719	0731	0811	...	0819	0919	1019	1019	1219	...	1419	1619	...	1719	1817	2019	...	2219	...
Läggesta ● d.	0538	0641	|	0721	...	0728	0741	0821	...	0828	0928	1028	1028	1228	...	1428	1628	...	1728	1827	2028	...	2228	...
Södertälje Syd d.	0558	0703	|	0744	...	0747	0801	0843	...	0847	0947	1047	1047	1247	...	1447	1647	...	1747	1847	2047	...	2247	...
Stockholm C a.	0620	0724	0735	0809	...	0809	0824	0905	...	0909	1009	1109	1109	1309	...	1509	1709	...	1809	1909	2109	...	2309	...

Y – ①②③④ only.

z – June 14 - 28.

● – Summer only narrow gauge service operates Läggesta nedre - Mariefred. Operator: Östra Södermanlands Järnväg ✆ +46 (0)159 210 00, fax +46 (0)159 210 06.

759 NARVIK - KIRUNA - LULEÅ - UMEÅ

km		7011 ⚒	7003 2†	91 ♦	17087 ♦	95 2	10091 ♦	VEO 7101/3 ♦	7006 ♦	10093 ♦	7007 ♦	[bus]
0	**Narvik** d.	...	...	...	...	1042	...	1110	...	1435	...	1927
40	Riksgränsen 🏛 d.	...	...	...	...	1132	...	1159	...	1526	...	2014
47	Vassijaure ◇ d.	...	...	...	...	1139	...	|	...	|	...	2026
67	Björkliden d.	...	...	...	...	1201	...	1234	...	1600	...	2045
76	Abisko Östra d.	...	...	...	...	1225	...	1303	...	1625	...	2100
169	**Kiruna** d.	0544	0830	...	...	1350	...	1459	...	1735	...	2224
269	Gällivare **762** d.	0647	0939	...	...	1506	...	1617	...	1840	...	...
437	**Boden 760** § a.	0836	1144	...	...	1714	...	1852	...	2036	2041	...
*	**Luleå 760/8** § a.	0902	1218	1635	1635	1748	1809	|	2003	|	2105	...
437	**Boden 759** § d.	...	...	1725	1725	...	1850	1900	2028	2056	...	...
483	Älvsbyn d.	...	...	1753	1753	...	1918	|	...	2123	...	...
611	Bastuträsk **768** d.	...	...	1917	1917	...	2041	|	...	2246	...	...
722	Vännäs d.	...	...	|	2029	...	2149	2211	...	2356	...	...
753	**Umeå 768** a.	...	...	2048	...	...	...	...	...	...	...	...

	[bus]	7004 ♦	94 ♦	10094 ♦	7005 ♦	VEO 7100 ♦v	VEO 7100 ♦w	96 2	10092 ♦	92 ♦	17084 ♦	VEO 7102 ♦	7000 7010 ⚒	7002 †
Umeå d.	...	...	...	...	...	...	...	...	...	0647	...	...	...	...
Vännäs d.	...	...	0306	0306	...	0457	0457	...	0643	|	0718	0835	...	...
Bastuträsk **768** d.	...	...	0415	0415	...	|	|	...	0802	0843	0843	|	...	...
Älvsbyn d.	...	...	0536	0536	...	|	|	...	0939	1013	1013	|	...	...
Boden 759 § a.	...	...	0614	0614	0629	0753	0753	...	1026	1051	1051	1309	...	...
Luleå 760/8 § d.	...	0540	|	|	0655	|	|	1020	1110	1145	1145	|	1700	1840
Boden 760 § d.	...	0609	0634	0634	...	0810	0837	1101	...	...	...	1309	1729	1906
Gällivare **762** d.	...	...	0838	0838	...	1056	1127	1306	...	...	...	1525	1916	2103
Kiruna d.	0707	...	0946t	1115t	...	1230	1300	1416	...	...	...	1702	2020	2203
Abisko Östra d.	0823	...	1104	1227	...	1352	1503	1526	...	...	...	1845	...	...
Björkliden d.	0837	...	1121	1244	...	1413	1524	1541	...	...	...	1906	...	...
Vassijaure ◇ d.	0856	...	|	|	...	|	|	1602	...	...	...	|	...	...
Riksgränsen 🏛 d.	0909	...	1151	1317	...	1450	1600	1615	...	...	...	1936	...	...
Narvik a.	1000	...	1239	1403	...	1615	1730	1704	...	...	...	2030	...	...

760 UMEÅ and STORLIEN - GÄVLE - STOCKHOLM

km		X2000 561 R✕ Ⓐn	10093 R ♦	X2000 563 R✕ Ⓐ	X2000 567 R✕	X2000 571 R✕		X2000 579 R✕	X2000 583 R✕ Ⓑ	X2000 587 R✕		10077 R ♦	69 R ♦	10073 R ♦		91 R ♦	97 R ♦	17087 R ♦	X2000 423 R✕ Ⓐz	10091 R ♦		VEO 7101 ♦	VEO 7103 ♦	
	Umeå 768 d.	...	...	...	...	...	...	...	...	...	...	...	...	...	...	2058	2058	...	...	...	...	...	...	...
	Vännäs d.	...	2356	...	...	...	...	...	...	...	...	...	...	...	...	2137	2137	2137	...	2154	...	2211	2211	...
	Långsele d.	...	0231	...	...	...	...	...	...	...	...	...	...	...	...	0010	0010	0010	...	0026	...	|	|	...
0	**Storlien** 🏛 ▲ d.	...	|	...	...	...	...	...	...	1323j	...	1737	1737	1737	...	|	|	|	...	|	...	|	|	...
48	Duved ▲ d.	...	|	...	...	...	...	...	...	1401j	...	1827	1827	1827	...	|	|	|	...	|	...	|	|	...
57	Åre ▲ d.	...	|	...	...	...	...	...	...	1412j	...	1840	1840	1840	...	|	|	|	...	|	...	|	|	...
162	**Östersund** ▲ a.	...	|	...	...	...	...	...	...	1527j	...	2007	2007	2007	...	|	|	|	...	|	...	|	|	...
162	**Östersund 762** ⊖ d.	...	|	...	0600a	0805c	...	...	...	1530	...	2050	2050	2050	...	|	|	|	...	|	...	|	|	...
233	Bräcke ⊖ d.	...	0409	...	0638a	0844c	...	...	...	1636	...	2143	2143	2143	...	|	|	|	...	0205	...	|	|	...
263	Ånge ⊖ d.	...	0426	...	0656a	0902c	...	...	...	1655	...	2209	2209	2209	...	0157	0157	0157	...	|	...	0255	0327	...
432	Bollnäs d.	...	0618	...	|	|	...	...	...	|	...	|	|	|	...	0342	0342	0342	...	0412	...	|	|	...
	Härnösand **768** d.	...	|	...	|	|	...	...	...	|	...	|	|	|	...	|	|	|	...	|	...	|	|	...
*	**Sundsvall 768** ⊖ a.	...	|	...	0808a	1007c	...	...	...	1803	...	2315	2315	2315	...	|	|	|	...	|	...	|	|	...
	Sundsvall d.	0508	|	0612	0811	1011	...	1411	1611	1811	...	2325	2325	2325	...	|	|	|	...	|	...	|	|	...
	Hudiksvall d.	0556	|	0658	0858	1058	...	1458	1658	1859	...	0032	0032	0032	...	|	|	|	...	|	...	|	|	...
	Söderhamn d.	0625	|	0725	0925	1125	...	1525	1725	1925	...	|	|	|	...	|	|	|	...	|	...	|	|	...
531	**Gävle 755** a.	0703	0721s	0803	1003	1203	...	1603	1806	2003	...	0153	0153	0153	...	0451	0451	0451	...	0524	...	0542	0646	...
	Gävle ⊗ d.	0706	|	0806	1006	1206	...	1606	1806	2006	...	0153	0153	0153	...	0506	0515	0515	0525	0526	...	0542	0646	...
	Uppsala **761** ⊗ a.	0751s	0824s	0851s	1051s	1251s	...	1651s	1851s	2051s	...	0249	0249	|	...	0601	|	|	0621	0627s	...	0646	0832	...
	Arlanda C ✈ ◧ ⊗ a.	0809	|	0909	1109	1309	...	1709	1911	2109	...	0312	0312	|	...	|	|	|	|	|	...	|	|	...
	Stockholm C. ⊗ a.	0830	0912	0930	1130	1330	...	1730	1932	2130	...	0337s	0337s	0550	...	0645	|	|	0700	0715	...	0744	0927	...
	Göteborg **740** a.	...	...	...	...	...	...	...	...	...	...	0837	|	0837	...	...	1052	1052	1017	...	...	1222	1557r	...
	Malmö **730** a.	...	...	...	...	...	...	...	...	...	...	...	0955	...	...	...	...	...	...	...	...	...	...	...

km		X2000 560 R✕ Ⓐ	X2000 564 R✕	X2000 572 R✕	X2000 576 R✕	X2000 580 R✕ Ⓑ	X2000 20582 R✕ Ⓐh	X2000 582 R✕ Ⓐz		94 R ♦	10094 R ♦	X2000 584 R✕		VEO 7100 ♦	10092 R ♦	92 R ♦		VEO 7102 ♦	98 R ♦	17084 R ♦		10072 R ♦	76 R ♦	10066 R ♦
	Malmö **730** d.	...	...	...	...	...	...	...	...	...	...	...	...	1208	...	...	...	...	...	...	...	...	...	1717
	Göteborg **740** d.	...	...	...	...	...	...	...	...	...	...	...	...	|	...	...	...	1532	1700	1700	...	1900	1900	|
0	**Stockholm C.** ⊗ d.	0630	0830	1230	1430	1630	1716	1721	...	1812	1812	1830	...	1822	2012	2042	...	2027	|	|	...	2130	2352u	2352u
39	Arlanda C ✈ ◧ ⊗ d.	0648	0848	1248	1448	1648	1736	1739	...	|	|	1848	...	|	|	|	...	|	|	|	...	|	0021	0021
69	Uppsala **761** ⊗ d.	0707u	0907u	1307u	1507u	1707u	1758u	1758u	...	1858u	1858u	1907u	...	1859	2101u	2124u	...	2104	|	|	...	|	0040u	0040u
182	**Gävle** ⊗ a.	0754	0954	1354	1554	1754	1847	1847	...	|	|	1954	...	2006	2154	2222	...	2204	2238	2238	...	0113	0137	0137
182	**Gävle 755** d.	0757	0957	1357	1557	1757	1850	1850	...	1953u	1953u	1957	...	2006	2157	2258	...	2204	2258	2258	...	0137	0137	0137
260	Söderhamn d.	0834	1034	1434	1634	1835	1937	1937	...	|	|	2034	...	|	|	|	...	|	|	|	...	0234	0234	0234
314	Hudiksvall d.	0900	1100	1500	1700	1901	2003	2003	...	|	|	2100	...	|	|	|	...	|	|	|	...	|	|	|
402	**Sundsvall** a.	0949	1149	1552	1749	1950	2052	2052	...	|	|	2155	...	|	|	|	...	|	|	|	...	0358	0358	0358
—	**Sundsvall 768** ⊖ d.	...	1152	...	1754g	1953	...	...	...	|	|	...	...	|	|	|	...	|	|	|	...	0405	0405	0405
*	Härnösand **768** a.	...	|	...	|	|	...	...	...	|	|	...	...	|	|	|	...	|	|	|	...	|	|	|
	Bollnäs d.	...	|	...	|	|	...	...	...	2054	2054	...	...	|	2252	2356	...	|	2356	2356	...	|	|	|
	Ånge ⊖ d.	...	1302	...	1859g	2059	...	...	...	2241	2241	...	...	2316	|	0134	...	0154	0134	0134	...	0514	0514	0514
0	Bräcke ⊖ d.	...	1319	...	1916g	2123	...	...	...	2300	2300	...	...	|	0104	|	...	|	|	|	...	0537	0537	0537
	Östersund 762 ⊖ a.	...	1403	...	1955g	2226	...	...	...	|	|	...	...	|	|	|	...	|	|	|	...	0652	0652	0652
	Östersund ▲ d.	...	1408y	...	...	...	...	...	...	|	|	...	...	|	|	|	...	|	|	|	...	0700	0700	0700
	Åre ▲ d.	...	1541y	...	...	...	...	...	...	|	|	...	...	|	|	|	...	|	|	|	...	0838	0838	0838
	Duved ▲ d.	...	1551y	...	...	...	...	...	...	|	|	...	...	|	|	|	...	|	|	|	...	0856	0856	0856
	Storlien 🏛 ▲ a.	...	1629y	...	...	...	...	...	...	|	|	...	...	|	|	|	...	|	|	|	...	0950	0950	0950
131	Långsele d.	...	...	...	...	...	...	...	...	0031	0031	...	...	|	0409	0333	...	|	0333	0333	...	...	...	...
341	Vännäs a.	...	...	...	...	...	...	...	...	0306	0306	...	...	0447	0643	0613	...	0835	0613	0613	...	...	...	...
372	**Umeå 768** a.	...	...	...	...	...	...	...	...	...	...	...	...	...	...	0637	...	...	0637	...	...	...	...	...

♦ – **NOTES FOR TABLES 759/760** (LISTED BY TRAIN NUMBER)

69 – ④⑤†: [sleeper], [couchette] and [2] Storlien (**10077**) - Stockholm - Malmö; [bar] Norrköping - Malmö.
76 – ⑧ (from Göteborg): [sleeper], [couchette] and [2] Göteborg - Stockholm - Storlien; ✕ and [Bio] Göteborg - Stockholm; ✕ Sundsvall - Storlien. Conveys ④⑤†: [sleeper], [couchette] and [2] Malmö (**10066**) - Stockholm - Storlien.
91 – June 14-29: [sleeper], [couchette], [2] and [bar] Luleå - Stockholm.
92 – June 14-30: [sleeper], [couchette], [2] and [bar] Stockholm - Luleå.
94 – June 14 - July 4 (from Stockholm): [sleeper], [couchette], [2] and ✕ Stockholm - Narvik; [sleeper], [couchette] and [2] Stockholm - Boden (**7005**) - Luleå; [2] Luleå (**7004**) - Boden - Narvik.
97 – June 14 - July 24, Aug. 4-15: [sleeper], [couchette] and [2] Luleå (**91/10091**) - Gävle - Göteborg; ✕ Gävle - Göteborg.
98 – June 14 - July 23, Aug. 4-15: [sleeper], [couchette] and [2] Göteborg - Gävle (**92/10092**) - Luleå; ✕ Göteborg - Gävle.
7004/7 – [2] Narvik (**94/10093/10094/20093**) - Boden - Luleå and v.v.
7005/6 – [sleeper], [couchette] and [2] Stockholm (**94/10093/10094/20093**) - Boden - Luleå and v.v.
7100 – ⑤ June 22 - Aug. 24 (from Malmö): [couchette], [2], ✕ (also panorama car) Malmö - Stockholm - Narvik.
7101 – † June 22 - Aug. 24 (from Narvik): [couchette], [2], ✕ (also panorama car) Narvik - Stockholm - Göteborg.
7102 – ① June 22 - Aug. 24 (from Göteborg): [couchette], [2], ✕ (also panorama car) Göteborg - Stockholm - Narvik.
7103 – ③ June 22 - Aug. 24 (from Narvik): [couchette], [2] and ✕ (also panorama car) Narvik - Stockholm - Malmö. July 6 - Aug. 9 runs as shown to Gävle, then Uppsala a. 0752, Stockholm a. 0832, Malmö a. 1440. Train number **17103** from Aug. 10.
10066 – ④⑤†: [sleeper], [couchette] and [2] Malmö - Stockholm (**76**) - Storlien; ✕ Malmö - Stockholm.
10072 – ⑥ (from Göteborg): [sleeper], [couchette] and [2] Göteborg - Stockholm - Storlien; [sleeper] and [couchette] (also [2] by changing trains at Västerås) Stockholm (**20072**) - Västerås - Storlien; ✕ and [Bio] Göteborg - Stockholm; ✕ Sundsvall - Storlien.
10073 – ⑥ (from Storlien): [sleeper], [couchette] and [2] Storlien - Stockholm - Göteborg; [sleeper] and [couchette] (also [2] by changing trains at Västerås) Storlien - Västerås (**20073**) - Stockholm; ✕ and [Bio] Storlien - Sundsvall; ✕ Örebro - Göteborg.
10077 – ⑧ (from Storlien): [sleeper], [couchette] and [2] Storlien - Stockholm - Göteborg; ✕ and [Bio] Storlien - Sundsvall; ✕ Örebro - Göteborg. Conveys ④⑤†: [sleeper], [couchette] and [2] Storlien - Stockholm (**69**) - Malmö.
10091 – June 30 - Aug. 15 (from Luleå): [sleeper], [couchette], [2] and ✕ Luleå - Stockholm.
10092 – July 1 - Aug. 15 (from Stockholm): [sleeper], [couchette], [2] and ✕ Stockholm - Luleå.
10093 – [sleeper], [couchette], [2] and ✕ Narvik - Stockholm; [sleeper], [couchette] and [2] Luleå (**7006**) - Boden - Stockholm; [2] Narvik - Boden (**7007**) - Luleå. Runs as train **20093** on ①②③④†.
10094 – July 5 - Aug. 15 (from Stockholm): [sleeper], [couchette], [2] and ✕ Stockholm - Narvik; [sleeper], [couchette] and [2] Stockholm - Boden (**7005**) - Luleå; [2] Luleå (**7004**) - Boden - Narvik.
17084 – July 24 - Aug. 2: [sleeper], [couchette] and [2] Göteborg (**98**) - Gävle (**92/10092**) - Vännäs - Luleå; ✕ Göteborg - Gävle.
17087 – July 25 - Aug. 3: [sleeper], [couchette] and [2] Luleå - Vännäs (**91/10091**) - Gävle (**97**) - Göteborg; ✕ Gävle - Göteborg.

a – Ⓐ only.
c – Ⓒ only.
g – ⑥ only.
h – June 22-28.
j – Not June 14.
k – Connection on ⑥.
n – June 14-28.
r – Arrive 1543 from Aug. 10.
s – Stops to set down only.
t – Arrive 0941.
u – Stops to pick up only.
v – ⑥ July 6 - Aug. 15.
w – ⑥ June 23 - July 5.
y – Not Aug. 15.
z – June 14-21.

§ – *VEO* [bus] service Boden - Luleå and v.v. (jouney 45 minutes): From Luleå: 0715, 1215, 1810. From Boden: 0805, 1325, 1905. *Operates only when VEO train services run.*

◇ – Ticket point.
▲ – For Östersund - Storlien - Trondheim services see panel below.
⊖ – For Sundsvall - Östersund local services see panel on page 347.
⊗ – For additional services Stockholm - Gävle and v.v. see panel on page 347.
◧ – From Stockholm stops to pick up only; to Stockholm stops to set down only.
* – Ånge - Sundsvall: *94 km*; Boden - Luleå: *36 km*; Härnösand - Sundsvall: *68 km*.

ÖSTERSUND - TRONDHEIM and v.v.: Operator: *VEO*

km		2	2		2	2
0	**Östersund** d.	0800	1621	**Trondheim** d.	0820k	1640
105	Åre d.	0921	1738	Storlien 🏛 d.	1012	1832
114	Duved d.	0929	1746	Duved d.	1048	1908
162	Storlien 🏛 a.	1007	1824	Åre d.	1104	1921
268	**Trondheim** a.	1155k	2012	**Östersund** a.	1216	2033

STOCKHOLM - BORLÄNGE - MORA 761

km		ST		ST		ST			ST			ST					ST				ST				ST			
			10		40			16 10016		20	44		54	22	24	46		58	596	28		598 10590	48	32	36		10038	38
		Ⓐ	Ⓐz	⚒	Ⓐ	⑥	D	E		Ⓑz	⑥	Ⓑ	Ⓑx	Ⓐz	F	†	⚒	⑤z	†y	Ⓐ		Ⓐz		⑥	A	Ⓑ	B	C
0	**Stockholm** C. **760** d.	...	0614	...	0744	...	0855	0944	...	1144	1144	...	1144	1244	1344	1344	...	1444	1544	1544	...	1655	1744	...	1944	...	2211	2214
37	Arlanda C ✈ ◧ d.	...	0634	...	0804	...	0915	1004	...	1204	1204	...	1204	1304	1404	1404	...	1504	1604	1604	...	1715	1804	...	2004	...	2232	2234
66	Uppsala **754/60** d.	...	0656	...	0827	...	0935	1027	...	1227	1227	...	1227	1328	1427	1427	...	1533	1627	1627	...	1736u	1827	...	2027	...	2257	2257
128	Sala d.	...	0745	...	0902	...	|	1102	...	1302	1302	...	1302	|	1502	1502	...	1611	1700	1702	...	|	1902	...	2102	...	2331	2331
161	Avesta Krylbo d.	...	0804	...	0920	...	1023	1120	...	1320	1320	...	1320	1420	1520	1520	...	1638	1716	1728	...	1834	1920	...	2120	...	2351	2351
226	**Borlänge** a.	...	0851	...	1008	...	1100	1208	...	1408	1408	...	1408	1506	1608	1608	...	1734	1750	1815	...	1920	2008	...	2208	...	0032	0032
	Borlänge ● d.	0638	0853	0901	1015	1020	1103	1210	1220	1410	1412	1418	1425	...	1610	1612	1620	1749	1752	1817	1820	|	2012	2016	2210	2220	0034	0034
250	Falun **755** ● a.	|	0910	|	|	|	1123	1228	|	1428	|	|	|	...	1628	|	|	|	1812	1835	|	1959	|	2036	2228	|	0052	0052
269	Leksand d.	0710	...	0932	1053	1051	...	...	1251	...	1450	1449	1502	...	...	1652	1651	1831	...	...	1851	...	2051	...	...	2251	...	...
289	Rättvik d.	0726	...	0947	1113	1113	...	...	1311	...	1510	1512	1525	...	...	1712	1712	1852	...	...	1912	...	2114	...	...	2307	...	...
329	**Mora** ♣ a.	0749	...	1010	1139	1136	...	...	1334	...	1536	1535	1549	...	...	1738	1735	1919	...	...	1935	...	2140	...	...	2330	...	...
330	Mora Strand ♣ a.	0755	...	1015	...	1143	...	...	1341	...	...	1544	...	...	...	...	1742	...	...	...	1942	...	...	...	...	2336	...	...

		ST			ST		ST				ST				ST		ST						ST			ST		ST
	11		591 10591	41		595		19	43	10019		23		45		27		31	59	55	33	47		35	49		39	
	Ⓐz	Ⓐ	Ⓐz	Ⓐ	⑥	⑥z	Ⓑ	Ⓐz	⑥	†	⚒	⚒	D	Ⓑ	⑥	⑥		Ⓑ	†z	Ⓑx	⑥	⑥	Ⓑ	Ⓑz	†	⚒	Ⓐz	Ⓑ
Mora Strand ♣ d.	...	0515	...	...	0627	...	0820	...	...	...	1029	...	...	...	1227	...	1425	...	...	...	...	...	1627	...	...	1827	...	2029
Mora ♣ d.	...	0520	...	0624	0632	...	0825	...	0820	...	1033	...	...	1223	1232	...	1430	...	1442	1606	...	1621	1632	...	1821	1832	...	2034
Rättvik d.	...	0543	...	0649	0655	...	0848	...	0845	...	1056	...	...	1248	1255	...	1453	...	1509	1630	...	1646	1655	...	1846	1855	...	2057
Leksand d.	...	0558	...	0709	0710	...	0903	...	0903	...	1111	...	...	1309	1310	...	1508	...	1530	1649	...	1709	1710	...	1909	1910	...	2112
Falun **755** ● d.	0520	|	0617	|	|	0732	|	...	|	0932	|	1132	1236	|	|	1332	|	1532	|	|	1724	|	|	1732	|	|	1932	|
Borlänge ● a.	0542	0630	0638	0748	0742	0750	0941	...	0943	0950	1145	1150	1254	1348	1342	1350	1542	1550	1610	1719	1742	1748	1742	1750	1948	1942	1950	2144
Borlänge d.	0548	...	0640	0752	...	0752	...	0952	0952	0952	...	1152	1256	1352	...	1352	...	1552	1622	1752	...	1752	...	1752	1952	...	1952	...
Avesta Krylbo d.	0633	...	0715	0839	...	0839	...	1042	1039	1039	...	1239	1338	1439	...	1439	...	1639	1716	1839	...	1839	...	1839	2039	...	2039	...
Sala a.	0653	...	|	0858	...	0858	...	1101	1058	1058	...	1258	|	1458	...	1458	...	1658	1736	1858	...	1858	...	1858	2058	...	2058	...
Uppsala **754/60** a.	0731	...	0802s	0933	...	0933s	...	1133s	1133	1133	...	1333	1434s	1533	...	1533	...	1733	1815	1933	...	1933	...	1933	2133	...	2133	...
Arlanda C ✈ ◧ a.	0752	...	0822	0953	...	0953	...	1153	1153	1153	...	1353	1453	1553	...	1553	...	1753	1836	1953	...	1953	...	1953	2153	...	2153	...
Stockholm C. **761** a.	0816	...	0845	1016	...	1016	...	1216	1216	1216	...	1416	1516	1616	...	1616	...	1816	1900	2018	...	2018	...	2018	2216	...	2216	...

A – Ⓑ (not Ⓐ June 29 - Aug. 9).
B – ①②③④† from Aug. 9.
C – Ⓑ June 14 - 28; ⑤ from Aug. 9.
D – ①②③④ (not June 29 - Aug. 9).
E – Ⓒ (also Ⓐ June 29 - Aug. 9).
F – ⑥ (also Ⓐ except June 29 - Aug. 9).
s – Stops to set down only.
u – Stops to pick up only.
x – June 29 - Aug. 9.
y – Not June 22 - Aug. 8.
z – Not June 29 - Aug. 9.
♣ – Local journeys are not permitted between Mora and Mora Strand.
● – Additional services operate Borlänge - Falun and v.v.
◧ – From Stockholm calls to pick up only; to Stockholm calls to set down only.

KRISTINEHAMN - MORA - ÖSTERSUND - GÄLLIVARE 762

INLANDSBANAN **2009 service (Summer only)**

km		A	🚌A	C	
0	**Kristinehamn 750** d.	0900	...	...	...
40	Nykroppa d.	0940	0945	...	...
66	**Persberg** d.	...	1010	...	...
—	Vansbro d.	...	1245	...	...
0	**Mora 761** d.	...	1340	1440	...
14	Orsa d.	...	...	1454	...
137	Sveg d.	...	...	1718	...
321	**Östersund 760** a.	...	...	2036	...

	C		🚌B	
Östersund 760 d.	0720	...	...	...
Sveg d.	1048	...	...	...
Orsa d.	1258	...	...	...
Mora 761 d.	1312	...	1345	...
Vansbro d.	...	...	1433	...
Persberg d.	...	...	1635	...
Nykroppa d.	...	...	|	...
Kristinehamn 750 a.	...	...	1740	...

km		D	
0	**Östersund 760** d.	0715	...
115	Ulriksfors d.	0904	...
244	Vilhelmina d.	1138	...
312	Storuman d.	1256	...
384	Sorsele d.	1420	...
473	Arvidsjaur d.	1555	...
646	Jokkmokk d.	1931	...
746	**Gällivare 759** a.	2145	...

	E	
Gällivare 759 d.	0650	...
Jokkmokk d.	0843	...
Arvidsjaur d.	1241	...
Sorsele d.	1416	...
Storuman d.	1518	...
Vilhelmina d.	1651	...
Ulriksfors d.	1846	...
Östersund 760 a.	2027	...

All rail services operated by Railbus.
A – ①–⑤ June 22 - July 31.
B – Ⓑ June 22 - July 31.
C – June 8 - Aug. 30 (not June 19, 20).
D – June 8 - Aug. 29 (not June 19, 20).
E – June 9 - Aug. 30 (not June 19, 20).
– Steam trains operate ⑤⑥ July 10 - Aug. 8 Arvidsjaur - Slagnäs and v.v. (*53 km*); depart 1745, arrive back 2200. ✆ +46 (0)70 356 72 47.
Operator: Inlandsbanan AB, Box 561, 831 27, Östersund. ✆ +46 (0)63 19 44 00, fax +46 (0)63 19 44 06.

VÄSTERÅS - LUDVIKA 763

Operator: *ST* 2nd class only

km		⚒	Ⓐ	Ⓐ	⑥	Ⓐq		⚒	†	Ⓐq			Ⓐq		Ⓐq			Ⓐ	Ⓐ	Ⓐq	Ⓑ	Ⓐ	
0	**Västerås** d.	0615	0715	0815	0815	0915	...	1015	1015	1115	...	1215	1315	1415	1515	1615	...	1715	1815	1915	2015	2115	...
80	Fagersta C d.	0713	0812	0916	0912	1012	...	1113	1112	1212	...	1312	1412	1514	1612	1713	...	1812	1913	2012	2114	2212	...
129	**Ludvika** a.	0755	...	0958	...	...	...	1155	...	...	...	...	...	1556	...	1755	...	...	1955	...	2157	...	...

	Ⓐ	⚒	Ⓐq	⚒	Ⓐq	Ⓑ	⑥	Ⓐq	⚒	†		Ⓐq			Ⓐ		Ⓐq		Ⓑ		Ⓐ		Ⓐ
Ludvika d.	...	0605	...	0805	...	1005	...	...	1205	...	...	...	...	...	...	1605	...	...	1805	...	...	...	2005
Fagersta C d.	0548	0648	0748	0848	0948	1048	1048	1148	1248	1248	...	1348	...	1448	1548	1648	1748	...	1848	...	1948	...	2048
Västerås a.	0645	0745	0846	0945	1045	1145	1145	1245	1345	1345	...	1445	...	1545	1645	1745	1845	...	1945	...	2045	...	2145

q – Not July 6 - Aug. 9.

🚌 SUNDSVALL - UMEÅ - LULEÅ - HAPARANDA 768

Operator: *LTAC* **Subject to alteration from June 14**

			Ⓑ				Ⓐ			
Sundsvall ‡ d.	...	...	...	0805	1005	1205	...	1405	1605	...
Härnösand § d.	...	...	...	0900	1100	1300	...	1500	1700	...
Örnsköldsvik § d.	...	...	...	1035	1235	1435	...	1635	1835	...
Umeå § a.	...	...	...	1205	1405	1605	...	1805	2005	...
Umeå § d.	0545	0800	1000	1215	1415	1615	1725	1815	2015	...
Skellefteå § d.	0810	1030	1225	1420	1620	1820	2000	2020	2220	...
Piteå § d.	0930	1150	1350	1535	1735	1935	2125	2135	2335	...
Luleå § a.	1025	1240	1440	1625	1825	2025	2220	2225	0025	...
Haparanda § a.	1310	1530	1740	1850	2050	2250	0100	...	...	...

							Ⓐ		†	Ⓐ
Haparanda § d.	...	0520	0720	...	1120	1200	1335	1610	1810	1810
Luleå § d.	0545	0750	0950	1150	1350	1500	1620	1855	2045	2055
Piteå § d.	0640	0845	1045	1245	1445	1605	1725	1955	2140	2155
Skellefteå § d.	0755	1000	1200	1400	1600	1740	1850	2120	2300	2310
Umeå § a.	0950	1155	1355	1555	1755	1950	2100	2330	0120	0130
Umeå § d.	1005	1205	1405	1605	1805	...	...	...	...	...
Örnsköldsvik § d.	1140	1340	1540	1740	1940	...	...	...	...	...
Härnösand § d.	1310	1510	1710	1910	2110	...	...	...	...	...
Sundsvall ‡ a.	1355	1555	1755	1955	2155	...	...	...	...	...

§ – Bus station.
‡ – All buses originate / terminate at Sundsvall bus station (journey 5 – 10 minutes).

🚌 LULEÅ - HAPARANDA and TORNIO - KEMI 769

Information: Länstrafiken Norrbotten* ✆ +46 020 47 00 47

Luleå - Haparanda valid August 18, 2008 - June 13, 2009; Tornio - Kemi valid June 1 - August 12, 2009

	Ⓐ	Ⓒ				Ⓑ			Ⓐ		⑥	Ⓐ
Luleå Bus Station § d.	0820	0830	1050	1310	...	1510	1635	1835	1930	2035	2240	2240
Haparanda Bus Station ▲ § d.	1035	1050	1310	1530	...	1740	1850	2050	2150	2250	0055	0100

	Ⓐ			Ⓐ				Ⓐ	Ⓒ		
Haparanda Bus Station ▲ § d.	0440	0520	0720	0910	...	1120	1200	1335	1400	1610	1810
Luleå Bus Station § a.	0700	0740	0940	1140	...	1340	1425	1600	1625	1835	2035

	Ⓐ	⚒	Ⓐ	Ⓐ	Ⓐ	⚒	Ⓐ		Ⓐ	Ⓐ	⑥	Ⓐ	Ⓐ	Ⓐ	Ⓐ	⑥	Ⓐ	⑦x	Ⓐ	Ⓐ	Ⓐ	Ⓐ	Ⓐ	Ⓐ	Ⓐ	Ⓐ	Ⓐ	⑦x	Ⓐ
Tornio Bus Station ▲ ‡ d.	0510	0525	0615	0700	0715	0810	0910	1005	1105	1205	1235	1315	1405	1415	1435	1440	1500	1500	1505	1515	1605	1650	1700	1705	1815	1855	1915	1915	2020
Kemi Railway Station **790** ● ‡ a.	|	|	|	|	0800	|	|	|	|	|	|	|	|	|	|	|	|	|	|	|	|	|	1723	1740	|	1918	|	|	|
Kemi Bus Station ● ‡ a.	0558	0555	0650	0725	0755	0855	0950	1030j	1155	1240	1310	1350	1450	1450	1500	1510	1525	1525	1545	1600	1640	1715	1725	1738	1900	1920	1950	1950	2055

	①	②-⑥	Ⓐ	Ⓐ	Ⓐ	Ⓐ	Ⓐ	⚒	Ⓐ	Ⓐ	Ⓐ	⑥	Ⓐ	Ⓐ	Ⓐ	Ⓐ	Ⓐ	Ⓐ	Ⓐ	Ⓐ	⑥	Ⓐ	①-④	⑤		⑥⑦	Ⓐ	Ⓐ	⑥
Kemi Bus Station ● ‡ d.	0000	0115	0615	0645	0715	0745	0815	0910	0925	1000	1125	1125	1215	1315	1345	1415	1430	1510	1530	1605	1630	1640	1715	1725	1820	1850	1900	2100	2245
Kemi Railway Station **790** ● ‡ d.	|	|	|	0646	|	|	|	0915	0920	|	|	|	|	|	1346	|	1432	|	1525	1606	|	|	|	|	1835	1851	|	|	|
Tornio Bus Station ▲ ‡ a.	0030	0150	0650	0715	0750	0820	0850	0950	0955	1050	1150	1200	1250	1350	1430	1450	1500	1550	1605	1645	1705	1715	1750	1800	1905	1925	1935	2135	2315

j – 5 minutes later on Ⓒ.
x – Runs †. However, runs on the last day only when there are two consecutive holidays.
‡ – Finnish time.
§ – Swedish time.
▲ – Walking distance between Haparanda Bus Station and Tornio Bus Station is approximately 800 metres.
● – Walking distance between Kemi Railway and Bus stations is approximately 200 metres.
* – Tornio - Kemi is operated by Veljekset Salmela; ✆ +358 16 446 666.

NORWAY

SEE MAP PAGE 339

Operator: Norges Statsbaner (NSB).

Services: All trains convey second class seating accommodation. Many services, as identified in the notes, also convey *NSB Komfort* accommodation (see below). Sleeping-cars (🛏) have one-, two-, and three-berth compartments; passengers may reserve a berth in any category with either a first or second-class ticket. Most long distance express trains convey a bistro car (✗) serving hot and cold meals, drinks and snacks. 🍸 indicates that drinks and light refreshments are available from automatic vending machines.

Timings: NSB services are valid **June 14 - Dec. 12, 2009.**

Reservations: Seat reservation is highly recommended on long-distance routes Oslo - Kristiansand - Stavanger (Table **775**), Oslo - Bergen (Table **780**), Oslo - Trondheim / Åndalsnes (Table **785**) and Trondheim - Bodø (Table **787**).

Supplements: A supplement is payable (90 NOK) to use *NSB Komfort* accommodation, a dedicated area provided on many trains with complimentary tea / coffee and newspapers.

770 OSLO - HALDEN - GÖTEBORG

Most trains convey NSB Komfort and 🍸

July 6 - Aug. 9 (also June 14, Nov. 13 – 15, 23 – 29) trains are replaced by 🚌 Trollhättan - Göteborg and v.v. Earlier departures / later arrivals at Göteborg (up to 36 minutes).

km	*Norwegian train number*	103	105	107	109	109	111	113	115	117	117	119	121	141	123	143	125	125	127	129	131	133	135	137	139
	Swedish train number		391			393					395							397	399						
		Ⓐ	①–⑤	⚒e		⑥	⚒e		⚒e		Ⓑ	A		Ⓐw	Ⓐ	Ⓐw		⑥	Ⓑ		Ⓑ		Ⓑ	Ⓑn	
0	**Oslo** Sentral .... d.	0600	0700	0800	0900	0900	1000	1100	1200	1300	1300	1400	1500	1530	1600	1632	1700	1700	1800	1900	2000	2100	2200	2300	2359
60	Moss .... d.	0643	0744	0843	0943	0943	1043	1143	1243	1343	1343	1443	1543	|	1644	|	1743	1743	1843	1943	2043	2143	2243	2343	0050
94	Fredrikstad .... d.	0709	0810	0910	1009	1009	1109	1209	1309	1409	1409	1509	1609	1637	1711	1739	1810	1810	1909	2010	2109	2209	2309	0009	0117
109	Sarpsborg .... d.	0729	0825	0925	1024	1024	1124	1224	1324	1424	1424	1523	1623	1653	1725	1753	1825	1825	1924	2025	2125	2225	2323	0023	0130
137	**Halden** .... a.	0749	0845	0945	1044	1044	1144	1244	1344	1444	1444	1543	1643	1719	1746	1818	1845	1845	1944	2045	2145	2245	2343	0043	0150
137	**Halden** ★ .... d.	...	0851	...	...	1050	...	...	...	...	1450	...	...	...	...	...	...	1848	1953	...	...	...	...	...	...
268	Öxnered **751** .... a.	...	1004	...	...	1204	...	...	...	...	1604	...	...	...	...	...	...	2002	2107	...	...	...	...	...	...
278	Trollhättan **751** .... a.	...	1011	...	...	1211	...	...	...	...	1611	...	...	...	...	...	...	2009	2114	...	...	...	...	...	...
350	**Göteborg 751** .... a.	...	1052	...	...	1253	...	...	...	...	1654	...	...	...	...	...	...	2052	2156	...	...	...	...	...	...

Swedish train number								390			392					394					396		398		
Norwegian train number	102	104	142	106	144	108	110	112	112	114	116	116	118	120	122	124	124	126	128	130	132	132	134	136	138
	Ⓐ	Ⓐ	Ⓐw	A	Ⓐw		A	①–⑤		⚒e	⑥		⚒		Ⓐe	Ⓑ		B		Ⓑ	⑥		Ⓑ	C	
Göteborg 751 .... d.	...	...	...	...	...	...	...	0643	...	...	0845	...	...	...	...	1245	...	...	...	...	1639	...	1746	...	...
Trollhättan **751** .... d.	...	...	...	...	...	...	...	0729	...	...	0929	...	...	...	...	1328	...	...	...	...	1724	...	1831	...	...
Öxnered **751** .... d.	...	...	...	...	...	...	...	0736	...	...	0936	...	...	...	...	1335	...	...	...	...	1731	...	1838	...	...
Halden ★ .... a.	...	...	...	...	...	...	...	0849	...	...	1049	...	...	...	...	1448	...	...	...	...	1847	...	1951	...	...
Halden .... d.	0400	0500	0532	0558	0632	0658	0800	0900	0900	1000	1100	1100	1200	1300	1400	1500	1500	1600	1700	1800	1900	1900	2000	2100	2200
Sarpsborg .... d.	0422	0522	0553	0620	0653	0720	0822	0923	0923	1022	1122	1122	1222	1322	1422	1521	1521	1621	1723	1823	1922	1922	2023	2123	2223
Fredrikstad .... d.	0437	0537	0607	0634	0707	0734	0837	0937	0937	1037	1137	1137	1237	1337	1437	1535	1535	1635	1737	1837	1937	1937	2037	2137	2237
Moss .... d.	0503	0603	0633	0701	0733	0801	0903	1003	1003	1103	1203	1203	1303	1403	1503	1601	1601	1701	1803	1903	2003	2003	2103	2203	2303
Oslo Sentral .... a.	0545	0645	0715	0745	0815	0845	0945	1045	1045	1145	1245	1245	1345	1445	1545	1645	1645	1745	1845	1945	2045	2045	2145	2245	2345

A – Ⓐ (⚒ to June 26 and from Aug. 17).
B – Ⓐ (Ⓑ to June 26 and from Aug. 17).
C – Daily to June 21; ⑥ June 27 - Aug. 15 (also June 28); daily from Aug. 17.

e – Not June 22 - Aug. 16.
n – Not June 22 – 26, June 29 - Aug. 16.
w – Not June 29 - Aug. 7.

★ – ▦ at Kornsjø (*km169*).

771 OSLO - OSLO ✈ GARDERMOEN

See also Table 783

Operated by NSB Gardermobanen AS.
Special fares apply.
✆ +47 23 15 90 00
fax +47 23 15 90 01.

Daily services (journey time: 22 minutes)
Trains call at Lillestrøm 10 minutes from Oslo
From Oslo Sentral every 20 minutes 0445 - 0005.
From Gardermoen every 20 minutes 0536 - 0056.

Additional services on Ⓑ (journey time: 19 minutes)
Non-stop services
From Oslo Sentral every 20 minutes: 0615 - 2235 on Ⓐ, 1115 - 2315 on ⑦.
From Gardermoen every 20 minutes: 0646 - 2306 on Ⓐ, 1146 - 2346 on ⑦.

773 OSLO - GJØVIK

All trains convey NSB Komfort and 🍸

km		E					Ⓐ				ⒶG	Ⓐh	
0	**Oslo** S..... ‡ d.	0707	0907	1107	1307	1507	1613	1707	1907	2107	2232	2307	0007
56	Roa........ ‡ d.	0805	1004	1203	1403	1605	1711	1809	2004	2205	2341	0008	0107
70	Jaren .... ‡ d.	0821	1020	1219	1419	1621	1728	1824	2020	2220	2357	0024	0123
99	Eina .... d.	0845	1044	1243	1442	1644	1755	1847	2044	2243	0020	0047	0146
110	Raufoss ...... d.	0855	1054	1253	1452	1654	1806	1857	2054	2253	0030	0057	0156
122	**Gjøvik** .... a.	0905	1104	1303	1502	1704	1816	1907	2104	2303	0040	0107	0206

	Ⓐ◇	⑥⑦k	Ⓐ	Ⓐ								
Gjøvik ..... d.	0433	0533	0549	0633	0738	0937	1136	1332	1535	1734	1937	2134
Raufoss ... d.	0444	0544	0600	0644	0749	0948	1147	1343	1546	1745	1948	2145
Eina .... d.	0454	0554	0610	0654	0759	0958	1157	1353	1556	1756	1958	2155
Jaren .... ‡ d.	0517	0617	0633r	0717	0822	1021	1220	1417	1620	1823	2021	2219
Roa....... ‡ d.	0533	0633	0650r	0734	0838	1037	1236	1434	1637	1839	2037	2236
Oslo S.. ‡ a.	0629	0731	0750r	0834	0935	1133	1334	1532	1734	1935	2134	2333

E – Ⓐ (also June 14; daily from Aug. 17).
G – June 22 - Aug. 14.
h – Not June 22 - Aug. 14.
k – Not June 20 - Aug. 16.
r – June 29 - Aug. 14 Jaren d. 0640, Roa d. 0657, Oslo a. 0801.
◇ – Runs 16 – 19 minutes later June 29 - Aug. 14.
‡ – Additional trains operate Oslo - Jaren and v.v.

775 OSLO - KRISTIANSAND - STAVANGER

Service until Oct. 18. All services are operated by 🚌 between Sandnes and Stavanger.

km				73			77	79	81	81	
		769	771	773	773	775	777	779		781	705
		Ⓐ	⚒	⚒		Ⓑ				⑤⑦	Ⓑ
		✗⊡	✗⊡	✗⊡	✗⊡	✗⊡	✗⊡	✗⊡	✗⊡	✗⊡	♣✗
0	**Oslo** Sentral .... § d.	...	...	0711	...	...	1111	1507	1709	1709	2247
41	Drammen .... § d.	...	...	0748u	...	...	1148u	1544u	1745u	1745u	2337u
87	Kongsberg .... § d.	...	...	0821	...	...	1222	1621	1817	1817	0017
134	Nordagutu .... d.	...	...	0856	...	...	1256	1657	1851	1851	0055x
151	Bø .... d.	...	...	0910	...	...	1311	1711	1905	1905	0111
209	Neslandsvatn .... d.	...	...	0954	...	...	1357	1755	1950	1950	|
225	Gjerstad .... d.	...	...	1007	...	...	1412	1809	2003	2003	0211x
270	Nelaug .... d.	...	...	1040	...	...	1449	1845	2036	2036	0246x
353	**Kristiansand** .... a.	...	...	1138	...	...	1555	1943	2134	2134	0354
353	**Kristiansand** .... d.	0520	0805	1146	1146	1415	1610	1950	...	2200	0412
465	Moi .... d.	0643	0928	1310	1310	1542	1741	2117	...	2330	0542x
514	Egersund .... ◇ d.	0725	1003	1348	1348	1620	1818	2155	...	0017	0622
573	Sandnes .... ◇ a.	0806	1045	1437	1437	1708	1908	2236	...	0057	0708
587	**Stavanger** .... ◇ a.	*0838**	*1115**	*1512**	*1512**	*1737**	*1937**	*2307**	...	*0123**	*0738**

			776	778	780	782	784	784	786	
	70	72	76		80	82		84		706
	Ⓐm	D		Ⓐ		Ⓑ		⑤	Ⓑ	Ⓑ
	✗⊡	✗⊡	✗⊡	✗⊡	✗⊡	✗⊡	✗⊡	✗⊡	✗⊡	♣✗
Stavanger .... ◐ d.	...	...	*0550**	*0845**	*1015**	*1345**	*1540**	*1540**	*1915**	*2210**
Sandnes .... ◐ d.	...	...	0616	0917	1047	1417	1617	1617	1947	2240
Egersund .... ◐ d.	...	...	0704	1004	1130	1502	1705	1705	2029	2331
Moi .... d.	...	...	0739	1039	1207	1541	1742	1742	2105	0011
Kristiansand .... a.	...	...	0902	1205	1340	1709	1905	1905	2228	0140
Kristiansand .... d.	0530	0740	0910	...	1405	1717	...	1913	...	0215
Nelaug .... d.	0626	0839	1009	...	1508	1815	...	|	...	0330x
Gjerstad .... d.	0656	0912	1044	...	1543	1849	...	|	...	0404x
Neslandsvatn .... d.	0709	0925	1056	...	1556	1902	...	|	...	|
Bø .... d.	0752	1013	1140	...	1642	1952	...	2131	...	0504
Nordagutu .... d.	0806	1027	1156	...	1659	2006	...	|	...	0519x
Kongsberg .... ¶ d.	0844	1104	1237	...	1737	2040	...	2220	...	0600
Drammen .... ¶ a.	0918s	1146s	1314s	...	1818s	2118s	...	2254s	...	0640s
Oslo Sentral .... ¶ a.	0956	1226	1356	...	1856	2156	...	2334	...	0726

Nelaug - Arendal

km		Ⓐm	D	⑦	⚒					Ⓑ	
0	Nelaug .... d.	0630	0845	1015	1045	...	1510	1845	...	2040	...
36	Arendal .... a.	0705	0920	1050	1120	...	1545	1920	...	2115	...

	Ⓐm	D				Ⓑ	⑥		Ⓑ	
Arendal .... d.	0545	0800	0930	...	1410	1735	1800	...	1955	...
Nelaug .... a.	0620	0835	1005	...	1445	1810	1835	...	2030	...

D – ①–⑥ June 20 - Aug. 8; ⑥ from Aug. 15.

m – Not June 22 - Aug. 7.
s – Stops to set down only.
u – Stops to pick up only.
x – Stops on request.
y – Not ⑥⑦ June 27 - Aug. 16.
z – Not ⑥ June 27 - Aug. 15.

* – By 🚌 Sandnes - Stavanger and v.v.
▲ – All services operated by 🚌 Sandnes - Stavanger and v.v.
♣ – Conveys 🛏 and ▭2. Reservation recommended.
⊡ – Reservation recommended. Conveys *NSB Komfort*.

§ – Additional local trains **Oslo** S - **Drammen** (39 minutes) - **Kongsberg** (79 – 81 minutes): 0617 ⚒, 0717 **z**, 0817 ⚒, 0917 **y**, 1017, 1117 **y**, 1217, 1317 **y**, 1417, 1517 **y**, 1617, 1717 **y**, 1817, 1917 **y**, 2017, 2217 and 0017.

¶ – Additional local trains **Kongsberg** - **Drammen** (44 – 49 minutes) - **Oslo** S (85 – 88 minutes): 0453 Ⓐ, 0553 ⚒**z**, 0653 ⚒, 0750 ⚒**z**, 0853, 0953 ⚒**z**, 1053, 1150 **y**, 1253, 1353 **y**, 1453, 1550 **y**, 1650, 1751 **y**, 1853, 1953 Ⓐ, 2053 and 2253.

◇ – Additional local trains **Egersund** - **Sandnes** (50 – 54 minutes) - **Stavanger** ▲ (78 – 82 minutes): 0536 Ⓐ, 0604 Ⓐ, 0636 ⚒, 0706 Ⓐ, 0736 ⚒, 0836 ⚒, 0936, 1036, 1136, 1236, 1336, 1438, 1536, 1604 Ⓐ, 1636, 1736, 1836, 1936, 2036, 2136, 2236 and 2336.

◐ – Additional local trains **Stavanger** ▲ - **Sandnes** (27 – 32 minutes) - **Egersund** (76 – 82 minutes): 0501 Ⓐ, 0601 ⚒, 0701 ⚒, 0801 ⚒, 0901, 1001, 1101, 1201, 1301, 1401, 1431 Ⓐ, 1456, 1526 Ⓐ, 1556, 1701, 1801, 1901, 2001, 2101, 2201, 2301 Ⓑ, 2331.

PORSGRUNN - NORDAGUTU - NOTODDEN — 779

No service on ©

km		Ⓐ	Ⓐh	Ⓐ	Ⓐh	Ⓐ	Ⓐh	Ⓐ	Ⓐh
0	**Porsgrunn** 783 d.	...	0639	0751	0951	*1115**	1425	1551	1705
9	Skien 783 d.	0544	0648	0800	1000	1220	1434	1600	1714
43	Nordagutu d.	0613	0723	0832	1034	1258**e**	1508	1634	1748
62	**Notodden** a.	0633	0743	0851	1054	1318	1528	1654	1808

	Ⓐ	Ⓐh	Ⓐ	Ⓐh	Ⓐ	Ⓐh	Ⓐ	Ⓐh
Notodden d.	0643	0812	0954	1124	1428	1554	1708	1847
Nordagutu d.	0704	0833	1015	1145	1449	1615	1729	1908
Skien 783 a.	0734	0904	1044	1214	1519	1645	1759	1940
Porsgrunn 783 a.	0743	0913	*1143**	*1239*	1528	1658	*1843**	*2043**

e – Arrives 1250.
h – Not June 22 - Aug. 14.
* – By 🚌 to / from Skien.

OSLO - BERGEN — 780

km		609 M R	61 ✕⊡	601 ✕⊡	1829 S	1817 Ⓑ	607 ⑦E R	603 ⑤F R	63 ✕⊡		605 Ⓑ NR
0	**Oslo** Sentral 783 d.	0635	0811	1033	...	...	1227	1433	1607	...	2309
41	Drammen △ 783 d.	0716	0848	1115	...	...	1305	1512	1644	...	2354
112	Hønefoss d.	0816	0938	1225	...	...	1414	1619	1737	...	0056
208	Nesbyen d.	|	1049	1341	...	...	1532	1744	1847	...	0223
225	Gol d.	0935	1101	1354	...	...	1545	1800	1900	...	0239
250	Ål d.	0955	1124	1419	1439	...	1608	1832	1921	...	0305
275	Geilo d.	1015	1145	1442	1503	...	1630	1855	1942	...	0328
286	Ustaoset d.	|	1156	1454	1514	...	1643	1905	1953	...	0341
324	Finse d.	1110	1225	1526	1550	...	1717	1937	2021	...	0417
354	**Myrdal** 781 a.	1141	1253	1551	1621	...	1746	2006	2045	...	0445
403	**Voss** 781 a.	1311	1341	1637	1701	1753	1834	2048	2128	...	0532
443	Dale ▽ 781 a.	|	|	1709**n**	...	1824	1903**x**	|	2156**x**	...	0608
480	Arna ▽ 781 a.	1410	1441	1740	...	1857	1935	2155	2228**x**	...	0644
489	**Bergen** 781 a.	1422	1452	1752	...	1905	1945	2204	2235	...	0656

	62 ✕⊡	1828 S		602 ✕⊡		604 ⑤⑦ FR	64 ✕⊡	610 M R		606 Ⓑ NR
Bergen 781 d.	0758	...	...	1028	...	1458	1558	1610	...	2258
Arna △ 781 d.	0806	...	...	1037	...	1506	1606	1618	...	2307
Dale △ 781 d.	0836**x**	...	...	1107**x**	...	|	|	|	...	2344**x**
Voss 781 d.	0907	...	...	1139	...	1608	1710	1733	...	0015
Myrdal 781 d.	0950	1003	...	1225	...	1657	1752	1828	...	0105
Finse d.	1017	1042	...	1254	...	1730	1818	1900	...	0138
Ustaoset d.	1046	1122	...	1326	...	1800	1845	|	...	0209
Geilo d.	1058	1142	...	1339	...	1812	1857	1946	...	0224
Ål d.	1121	1200	...	1400	...	1833	1919	2007	...	0246
Gol d.	1141	...	...	1423	...	1858	1938	2028	...	0308
Nesbyen d.	1152	...	...	1436	...	1909	1949	2041	...	0321
Hønefoss d.	1304	...	...	1554	...	2023	2059	2200	...	0442
Drammen ▽ 783 a.	1353	...	...	1652	...	2125	2157	2303	...	0539
Oslo Sentral 783 a.	1432	...	...	1732	...	2212	2236	2350	...	0626

E – From Oct. 4.
F – From Oct. 2.
M – Until Sept. 27.
N – Conveys 🛏, 2 and ✕.
R – Reservation recommended.
S – Daily July 13 - Aug. 16; ⑥⑦ Aug. 22 - Sept. 27.
n – ⑥⑦ (daily from Sept. 26). Stops on request only.
x – Stops on request only.
⊡ – Reservation recommended. Conveys *NSB Komfort*.
△ – Trains stop to pick up ony.
▽ – Trains call to set down only.

MYRDAL - VOSS - BERGEN and MYRDAL - FLÅM — 781

Service until Sept. 27

km		⑦		Ⓐ	605 Ⓑ ✕◇	Ⓐ	Ⓐ	Ⓐe	⚒			Ⓐe	609 ◇	61 ✕◇			601 ①–⑤ ✕◇	601 ⑥⑦ ✕◇	B	C	Ⓑ			⑤	63 ✕◇
	Oslo Sentral 780 d.	...	...	...	2309	...	...	...	...	...	...	...	0635	0811	...	...	1033	1033	...	...	...	...	...	...	1607
0	**Myrdal** d.	...	...	...	0445	...	...	...	...	0955	1110	...	1220	1258	...	1450	1555	1556	1615	1624	...	1710	...	1940	2047
18	Mjølfjell d.	...	...	...	|	...	...	0742	...	1010**x**	1128**x**	...	|	|	...	|	|	|	|	|	...	1737	...	1955**x**	|
49	**Voss** a.	...	...	...	0532	...	...	0816	...	1044	1206	...	1311	1341	...	1540	1637	1637	1657	1701	...	1814	...	2025	2128
49	**Voss** d.	...	...	0515	0537	0617	0720	0835	0835	1050	...	1250	1312	1343	1435	1552	1640	1640	...	...	1753	...	1920	...	2130
89	Dale d.	0128	...	0543	0608	0646	0749	0907	0907	1122	...	1318	|	|	1503	1623	|	1709**z**	...	...	1824	...	1950	...	2156**z**
104	Vaksdal d.	0143	...	0559	0626	0705	0805	0924	0924	1140	...	1336	|	|	1522	1639	|	|	...	...	1840	...	2009	...	|
126	Arna ‡ d.	0200	...	0617	0644**s**	0727	0826	0946	0946	1157	...	1356	1410**s**	1441**s**	1543	1657	1740**s**	1740**s**	...	...	1857	...	2026	...	2228**z**
135	**Bergen** ‡ a.	0208	...	0625	0656	0735	0835	0954	0954	1205	...	1405	1422	1452	1552	1705	1752	1752	...	...	1905	...	2034	...	2235

	⑦		Ⓐe		Ⓐ	62 ✕◇		602 ✕◇	Ⓐ				Ⓐ	64 ✕◇	610 ◇	Ⓐ		⑤	Ⓐ			Ⓑ		⑥	606 Ⓑ ✕◇
Bergen ‡ d.	0035	...	...	...	0657	0758	0840	1028	1110	...	1310	...	1510	1558	1610	1628	1710	1710	1810	1928	...	2128	...	2258	2258
Arna ‡ d.	0044	...	...	...	0707	0806**u**	0848	1037**u**	1118	...	1318	...	1518	1606**u**	1618**u**	1636	1718	1718	1818	1936	...	2136	...	2306	2307**u**
Vaksdal d.	0101	...	...	...	0726	|	0905	|	1140	...	1336	...	1539	|	|	1656	1740	1740	1840	1953	...	2153	...	2324	2326**x**
Dale d.	0118	...	...	...	0748	0836**x**	0924	1107**y**	1156	...	1355	...	1554	|	|	1712	1756	1756	1857	2009	...	2212	...	2340	2344**x**
Voss a.	...	...	...	...	0820	0905	0953	1135	1226	...	1425	...	1625	1708	1726	1743	1825	1825	1932	2039	...	2240	...	0010	0013
Voss d.	...	...	0700	0830	0830	0907	0958	1139	...	1350	1432	...	...	1710	1733	...	...	1840	...	...	...	...	...	...	0015
Mjølfjell d.	...	...	0732	0902**x**	0902**x**	|	1029**x**	|	...	1419**x**	1506	...	...	|	|	...	...	1911**x**	...	...	...	...	...	...	|
Myrdal a.	...	...	...	0920	0920	0947	1046	1220	...	1435	1523	...	...	1750	1822	...	...	1928	...	...	...	...	...	...	0101
Oslo Sentral 780 a.	...	...	...	...	...	1432	...	1732	...	...	...	...	...	2236	2350	...	...	...	...	...	...	...	...	...	0626

Myrdal - Flåm ⊗

km										A		
0	Myrdal d.	0939	1055	1211	1327	1443	1559	1715	1829	1941	2055	...
20	Flåm a.	1035	1150	1305	1425	1540	1655	1810	1925	2035	2145	...

									A		
Flåm d.	0835	0945	1100	1220	1335	1450	1605	1725	1835	1945	...
Myrdal a.	0927	1043	1159	1315	1431	1547	1703	1817	1929	2040	...

A – Until Aug. 30.
B – Daily until July 12; ①–⑤ from Aug. 17.
C – Daily July 13 - Aug. 16; ⑥⑦ Aug. 22 - Sept. 27.
e – Not June 22 - Aug. 14.
s – Stops to set down only.
u – Stops to pick up only.
x – Stops on request.
y – Stops on request to pick up only.
z – Stops on request to set down only.
‡ – Additional local services operate.
◇ – Reservation recommended. See also Table **780**.
⊗ – **Operator**: Flåm Utvikling AS. ✆ +47 57 63 21 00. 30 % discount available for rail pass holders.

May 1 - Sept. 30, 2009 ⛴ FLÅM - GUDVANGEN and 🚌 GUDVANGEN - VOSS — 781a

	⛴	🚌		⛴ B	🚌 B		⛴ C	🚌 C		⛴	🚌
Flåm d.	0900	...	...	1100	...	...	1320	...	...	1510	...
Gudvangen a.	1110	...	...	1310	...	...	1530	...	...	1720	...
Gudvangen d.	...	1140	...	...	1320	...	...	1540	...	...	1745
Voss a.	...	1255	...	...	1435	...	...	1655	...	...	1900

	🚌 Ⓐ	⛴ C	🚌	⛴	🚌	⛴ B	🚌 D	⛴ C	🚌 Ⓑ	🚌 Ⓐ	⛴ A
Voss d.	0845	...	1000	...	1045	...	1430	...	1525	1610	...
Gudvangen a.	0935**e**	...	1110	...	1133**e**	...	1530	...	1615**e**	1710	...
Gudvangen d.	...	1030	...	1130	...	1320	...	1600	...	...	1720
Flåm a.	...	1240	...	1340	...	1530	...	1810	...	...	1930

A – Until May 17 and from Sept. 28.
B – June 20 - Aug. 20.
C – May 18 - Sept. 27.
D – ①–⑥ (daily June 27 - Aug. 15).
e – Bus stop on E16 main road.
🚌 operators : Sogn Billag ✆ +47 57 67 66 00. Skyss ✆ +47 5523 9550.
⛴ operator : Fylkesbaatane i Sogn og Fjordane ✆ +47 5775 7000.

May 1 - Sept. 30, 2009 ⛴ / 🚌 GOL and FLÅM - BALESTRAND - BERGEN — 782

	⛴ A	⛴ ①–⑥	⛴ A	🚌 J	⛴ ⑦E	⛴	🚌	🚌	🚌 J	🚌	🚌
Gol skysstasjon d.	...	...	...	...	...	...	...	1325	...	...	1900
Sogndal ⊕ d.	...	...	...	0750	...	...	...	|	1430	...	|
Kaupangersenteret d.	...	...	...	0805	...	...	...	|	1445	...	|
Øvre Årdal ◇ d.	...	*0530*a	...	0745	...	...	1430	|	1430	1850	|
Lærdal d.	...	*0605*a	...	0845	...	...	|	1525	1525	|	2105
Kaupangersenteret d.	...	*0640*a	...	|	...	...	1540**v**	1600	|	2000	2140
Sogndal ⊕ d.	...	0705	...	|	1040	...	1555**v**	1620	|	2015	2205
Flåm d.	0600	|	←	0930	|	1530	...	|	1620	...	|
Leikanger d.	0715	0730	0730	|	1110	1630	...	1645	|	...	2230
Balestrand d.	→	0750	0800	|	1130	1655	...	1735	|	...	2310
Voss a.	...	|	...	1035	|	|	...	...	1730	...	...
Bergen ⊡ a.	...	1140*	...	1230	1515	2040	...	...	1915	...	...

	⛴ A	🚌	🚌 J	⛴	🚌	🚌	⛴ ⑥	🚌 J	⛴ Ⓑn	🚌	🚌 ⑤⑦
Bergen ⊡ d.	...	...	0855	0800	...	...	1415	1535	1630	...	...
Voss d.	...	...	1045	|	...	...	|	1725	|	...	...
Balestrand d.	0830	1005	|	1150	1310	...	1820	|	2020	2120**b**	...
Leikanger d.	0900	1045	|	1220	1350	...	1835	|	2045	2200**b**	...
Flåm a.	1030	|	1155	1325	|	...	|	1835	|	|	...
Sogndal ⊕ d.	...	1130	|	...	1430	1430	1900	|	2120	2230	2230
Kaupangersenteret d.	...	1145	|	...	1445	1445	...	|	...	2245	2245
Lærdal a.	...	1225	1250	...	1525	|	...	1920	...	2325	|
Øvre Årdal ◇ a.	...	|	1345	...	|	1605	...	2040	...	|	0010
Kaupangersenteret a.	...	|	1320	...	|	...	...	2000	...	|	...
Sogndal ⊕ a.	...	|	1335	...	|	...	...	2015	...	|	...
Gol skysstasjon a.	...	1415	...	...	1715	...	...	...	...	0120	...

A – ①–⑤ June 22 - Aug. 21.
E – Until June 14 and Aug. 23 - Sept. 27.
J – Two routes: 🚌 Sogndal - Lærdal - Bergen and v.v.; 🚌 Øvre Årdal - Lærdal - Bergen and v.v.
a – Ⓐ. By 🚌 to Sogndal.
b – Ⓑ only.
n – Not ⑦ June 21 - Aug. 16.
v – 20 minutes later on ⑥⑦.
* – *1150* on ⑥ (change boats at Sollibotn, d. *1005*).
◇ – Øvre Årdal Farnes.
⊕ – 🚌: Sogndal skysstasjon. ⛴: Sogndal kai.
⊡ – 🚌: Bus station. ⛴: Strandkaiterminal.
🚌 operator : Sogn Billag ✆ +47 57 67 66 00.
⛴ operator : Fylkesbaatane i Sogn og Fjordane ✆ +47 57 75 70 00.

783 LILLEHAMMER - OSLO - SKIEN

All trains convey *NSB Komfort* and 🍷

km		Ⓐ	Ⓐ	Ⓐ	Ⓒv‡	Ⓐ	Ⓑt	⑥z	⑥z	Ⓐ◇	Ⓑt	⑥z	⚒h		Ⓐ	Ⓒ	Ⓐ	⑦v	Ⓐ		Ⓑ		Ⓑ		Ⓑh	
0	**Lillehammer** 785 d.	...	0402	0523	0523	0618	0717	0717	0819	0820	0913	0913	1018	1110	1211	1315	1315	1414	1414	1509	1620	1714	1811	1920	2012	2114
58	**Hamar** 785 a.	...	0447	0608	0608	0703	0804	0804	0904	0905	1003	1003	1104	1156	1258	1405	1405	1501	1501	1602	1706	1803	1857	2005	2104	2202
58	**Hamar** 785 d.	...	0450	0612	0612	0706	0806	0806	0907	0907	1007	1007	1107	1203	1307	1407	1407	1503	1503	1604	1708	1807	1908	2008	2107	2205
117	Eidsvoll d.	...	0535	0656	0656	0756	0856	0856	0956	0956	1056	1056	1156	1256	1356	1456	1456	1556	1556	1656	1756	1856	1956	2056	2156	2256
133	Oslo ✈ ● 771 785 d.	...	0546	0708	0708	0808	0908	0908	1008	1008	1108	1108	1208	1308	1408	1508	1508	1608	1608	1708	1808	1908	2008	2108	2208	2308
164	Lillestrøm 771 785 d.	...	0601	0723	0723	0823	0923	0923	1023	1023	1123	1123	1223	1323	1423	1523	1523	1623	1623	1723	1823	1923	2023	2123	2223	2323
185	**Oslo** Sentral 771 785 a.	...	0612	0734	0734	0834	0934	0934	1034	1034	1134	1134	1234	1334	1434	1534	1534	1634	1634	1734	1834	1934	2034	2134	2234	2334
185	**Oslo** Sentral d.	0537	0643	0743	0743	0843	0943	0943	1043	1043	1143	1143	1243	1343	1443	1543	1543	1643	1643	1743	1843	1943	2043	2143	2243	2343
225	Drammen d.	0616	0722	0822	0822	0922	1022	1022	1122	1122	1222	1222	1322	1422	1522	1622	1622	1722	1722	1822	1922	2022	2122	2222	2322	0022
259	Holmestrand d.	0640	0746	0846	0846	0946	1046	1046	1146	1146	1246	1246	1346	1446	1546	1646	1646	1746	1746	1846	1946	2046	2146	2246	2346	0046
273	Skoppum d.	0651	0757	0857	0857	0957	1057	1057	1157	1157	1257	1257	1357	1457	1557	1657	1657	1757	1757	1857	1957	2057	2157	2257	2357	0057
289	Tønsberg d.	0717	0815	0915	0915	1015	1115	1115	1215	1215	1315	1315	1415	1515	1615	1715	1715	1815	1815	1915	2015	2115	2215	2310	0010	0110
313	**Sandefjord** d.	0737	0837	0937	0937	1037	1137	1137	1237	1237	1337	1337	1437	1538	1638	1738	1738	1837	1837	1937	2037	2137	2236	2331	0031	0131
332	Larvik a.	0750	0850	0950	0950	1050	1150	1150	1250	1250	1350	1350	1450	1551	1651	1751	1751	1850	1850	1950	2050	2150	2249	2344	0044	0144
332	Larvik d.	*0752**	*0852**	0955	*0952**	*1052**	*1152**	1152	*1252**	*1252**	*1352**	1352	*1452**	*1552**	*1652**	*1752**	1802	*1852**	1855	1955	*2052**	2152	2251	2346	0046	0146
366	Porsgrunn 779 d.	*0815**	*0915**	1032	*1015**	*1115**	*1215**	1228	*1315**	*1315**	*1415**	1428	*1515**	*1615**	*1715**	*1815**	1839	*1915**	1931	2033	*2115**	2228	2326	0021	0121	0221
375	**Skien** 779 a.	*0833**	*0933**	1040	*1033**	*1133**	*1233**	1236	*1333**	*1333**	*1433**	1436	*1533**	*1633**	*1733**	*1836**	1847	*1933**	1939	2041	*2133**	2236	2334	0029	0129	0229

	Ⓐ	⚒z	Ⓐ	Ⓐ		⚒z	Ⓐ	Ⓒ	⚒h	Ⓐ	Ⓒ	Ⓑ	⑥	Ⓑ	Ⓑv	⚒	⑦	Ⓐ	⑦	⚒	⑦	Ⓑh		Ⓑ	Ⓑ	
Skien 779 d.	0339	0437	0503	0538	0632	0738	*0825**	0837	*0925**	*1025**	1032	*1125**	*1225**	1231	*1325**	*1425**	1438	*1520**	1532	*1620**	1638	*1725**	*1825**	*1925**	*2025**	...
Porsgrunn 779 d.	0348	0446	0513	0547	0647	0748	*0843**	0847	*0943**	*1043**	1042	*1143**	*1243**	1241	*1343**	*1443**	1448	*1543**	1542	*1643**	1648	*1743**	*1843**	*1943**	*2043**	...
Larvik a.	0422	0520	0547	0622	0722	0822	*0910**	0922	*1010**	*1110**	1116	*1210**	*1310**	1316	*1410**	*1510**	1522	*1610**	1616	*1710**	1722	*1810**	*1910**	*2010**	*2110**	...
Larvik d.	0424	0522	0549	0624	0724	0824	0924	0924	1024	1124	1124	1224	1324	1324	1424	1524	1524	1624	1624	1724	1724	1824	1924	2024	2124	...
Sandefjord d.	0439	0537	0604	0639	0738	0838	0938	0938	1038	1138	1138	1238	1338	1338	1438	1537	1537	1637	1637	1737	1737	1838	1938	2038	2138	...
Tønsberg d.	0501	0559	0626	0701	0801	0901	1001	1001	1101	1201	1201	1301	1401	1401	1501	1601	1601	1701	1701	1801	1801	1901	2001	2101	2201	...
Skoppum d.	0513	0611	0638	0713	0813	0913	1013	1013	1113	1213	1213	1313	1413	1413	1513	1613	1613	1713	1713	1813	1813	1913	2013	2113	2213	...
Holmestrand d.	0524	0622	0653	0724	0824	0924	1024	1024	1124	1224	1224	1324	1424	1424	1524	1624	1624	1724	1724	1824	1824	1924	2024	2124	2224	...
Drammen d.	0553	0653	0720	0751	0851	0951	1051	1051	1151	1251	1251	1351	1451	1451	1551	1651	1651	1751	1751	1851	1851	1951	2051	2151	2251	...
Oslo Sentral a.	0630	0732	0758	0828	0928	1028	1128	1128	1230	1328	1328	1428	1528	1528	1628	1728	1728	1828	1828	1928	1928	2028	2128	2228	2328	...
Oslo Sentral 771 785 d.	0637	0737	...	0837	0937	1037	1137	1137	1237	1337	1337	1437	1537	1537	1637	1737	1737	1837	1837	1937	1937	2037	2137	...	2337	2337
Lillestrøm 771 785 d.	0649	0749	...	0849	0949	1049	1149	1149	1249	1349	1349	1449	1549	1549	1649	1749	1749	1849	1849	1949	1949	2049	2149	...	2349	2349
Oslo ✈ ● 771 785 d.	0705	0805	...	0905	1005	1105	1205	1205	1305	1405	1405	1505	1605	1605	1705	1805	1805	1905	1905	2005	2005	2105	2205	...	0005	0005
Eidsvoll d.	0716	0816	...	0916	1016	1116	1216	1216	1316	1416	1416	1516	1616	1616	1716	1816	1816	1916	1916	2016	2016	2116	2216	...	0016	0016
Hamar 785 a.	0800	0902	...	1000	1100	1200	1300	1300	1403	1500	1500	1600	1704	1704	1800	1900	1900	2007	2007	2102	2102	2200	2305	...	0100	0100
Hamar 785 d.	0805	0905	...	1004	1106	1202	1303	1303	1407	1505	1505	1606	1709	1709	1806	1902	1902	2009	2009	2105	2105	2203	2307	...	0104	0104
Lillehammer 785 a.	0854	0950	...	1053	1154	1248	1350	1350	1458	1556	1556	1655	1758	1758	1902	1955	1955	2101	2101	2150	2150	2248	2352	...	0149	0149

h – Not June 22 - Aug. 16.
t – Also ⑥ June 27 - Aug. 15.
v – Not ⑦ June 28 - Aug. 16.
z – Not ⑥ June 27 - Aug. 15.
* – By 🚌.
◇ – Change trains at Oslo.
‡ – On ⑦ Larvik d. *1005**, Porsgrunn d. *1028**, Skien a. *1048**.
● – Oslo Lufthavn Gardermoen.

784 HAMAR - RØROS - TRONDHEIM

km		Ⓐ	⑥	Ⓐ	E	Ⓑ	Ⓐ	Ⓒ		G	Ⓑ
0	**Hamar** d.	...	...	0810	1009	1209	...	...	1608	1811	2014
32	Elverum d.	...	...	0833	1034	1234	...	...	1633	1834	2039
64	Rena d.	...	...	0855	1059	1256	...	...	1655	1859	2101
120	Koppang d.	...	...	0937	1141	1338	...	...	1737	1941	2143
273	**Røros** a.	...	...	1130	1335	1529	...	...	1930	2131	2334
273	**Røros** d.	0505	0705	...	...	...	1535	1630	1937	...	...
384	Støren 785 d.	0640	0835	...	...	...	1709	1802	2108	...	...
435	**Trondheim** S 785 a.	0735	0930	...	...	...	1800	1855	2200	...	...

	Ⓐ	E	Ⓐ		Ⓒ		G	⑦		Ⓐ	⑦
Trondheim S 785 d.	...	...	0540	0950	0950	...	...	1350	...	1615	2040
Støren 785 d.	...	...	0640	1041	1041	...	...	1444	...	1709	2134
Røros a.	...	...	0815	1212	1212	...	...	1615	...	1845	2305
Røros d.	0427	0619	0824	...	1218	1218	1411	1622	1622	...	...
Koppang d.	0617	0809	1017	...	1417	1417	1606	1817	1817	...	...
Rena d.	0659	0854	1059	...	1459	1459	1654	1859	1859	...	...
Elverum d.	0721	0916	1121	...	1521	1521	1716	1921	1921	...	...
Hamar a.	0746	0941	1146	...	1546	1546	1741	1946	1946	...	...

E – ①–⑥ to June 20; ⑥ June 27 - Aug. 15; ①–⑥ from Aug. 17.
G – Ⓑ to June 21; ⑦ June 28 - Aug. 9; Ⓑ from Aug. 16.

785 OSLO - LILLEHAMMER - ÅNDALSNES and TRONDHEIM

km		407	41	2351	313	2343	45	2355	47	2347	329	405
		Ⓐe		♥	Ⓐ	ⒶL		★	Ⓑ	ⒷL	Ⓑ	Ⓑ
		R	R	R		R	R	R	R	R		R
		✕⊡	✕⊡	🍷	🍷⊡	🍷	✕⊡	🍷	✕⊡	🍷	🍷⊡	✕N
0	**Oslo** Sentral 783 d.	...	0807	...	1037	...	1417	...	1607	...	1837	2305
21	Lillestrøm 783 d.	...	0819**u**	...	1049	...	1430**u**	...	1619**u**	...	1849	2327**u**
52	Oslo ✈ ⊖ 783 d.	...	0833**u**	...	1105	...	1445**u**	...	1633**u**	...	1905	2346**u**
127	**Hamar** 783 d.	...	0929	...	1202	...	1537	...	1730	...	2009	0045
185	**Lillehammer** 783 d.	...	1015	...	1248	1301	1623	...	1813	...	2109	0139
243	Ringebu d.	...	1058	...	...	1344	1705	...	1855	...	2152	0233
267	Vinstra d.	...	1113	...	...	1402	1722	...	1912	...	2209	0251
298	Otta d.	...	1138	...	...	1428	1747	...	1934	...	2233	0320
344	Dombås d.	...	1210	1215	...	1500	1824	1828	2006	2008	2306	0402
458	**Åndalsnes** a.	...	|	1349	...	1619	|	2002	|	2124	...	|
430	Oppdal d.	0645	1312	...	...	...	1926	...	2106	...	...	0512
502	Støren 784 d.	0735	1401	...	...	...	2017	...	2155	...	...	0608
553	**Trondheim** S 784 a.	0830	1448	...	...	...	2100	...	2243	...	...	0700

	308	2340	316	2352	42	2344	44	2356	46	406
	⚒	ⒶL		♠		ⒷL	Ⓑ	♣		Ⓑ
		R		R	R	R	R	R	R	R
	🍷⊡	🍷	🍷⊡	🍷	✕⊡	🍷	✕⊡	🍷	✕⊡	✕N
Trondheim S 784 d.	...	...	...	...	0825	...	1405	...	1525	2305
Støren 784 d.	...	...	...	...	0909	...	1449	...	1609	2355
Oppdal d.	...	...	...	...	1003	...	1541	...	1700	0056
Åndalsnes d.	...	0742	...	0913	|	1445	|	1611	|	|
Dombås d.	0513	0904	...	1055	1104	1613	1644	1756	1803	0210
Otta d.	0545	0934	...	...	1137	...	1714	...	1834	0249
Vinstra d.	0609	0957	...	...	1158	...	1741	...	1856	0313
Ringebu d.	0625	1013	...	...	1216	...	1757	...	1919	0332
Lillehammer 783 d.	0717	1059	1110	...	1300	...	1846	...	2005	0419
Hamar 783 d.	0806	...	1208	...	1350	...	1930	...	2049	0512
Oslo ✈ ⊖ 783 d.	0908	...	1308	...	1443**s**	...	2015**s**	...	2143**s**	0606**s**
Lillestrøm 783 d.	0923	...	1323	...	1501**s**	...	2031**s**	...	2201**s**	0626**s**
Oslo Sentral 783 a.	0934	...	1334	...	1513	...	2042	...	2212	0643

🚌 ✣	⚒		C	B		Ⓐ	Ⓐ	C		Ⓑ¶	Ⓑ¶
Åndalsnes d.	0730	0950	1400	1415	...	1630	1700	2010	2015	2130	2130
Molde a.	0900	1120	|	1540	...	|	1830	|	2135	2255	|
Ålesund a.	...	...	1610	...	...	1840	...	2220	...	...	2345

🚌 ✣	Ⓐ	H	A	Ⓑ	Ⓑ	A	D			
Ålesund d.	...	...	0645	...	1220	1345	...	...	...	2100
Molde d.	0620	0720	|	1305	|	|	1450	2015	2200	|
Åndalsnes a.	0740	0855	0900	1425	1435	1600	1610	2130	2315	2320

🚌			Ⓐ				⑤⑦		Ⓑ		
Oppdal skysstasjon d.	0530	...	1050	...	1315	...	1810	...	2130	...	...
Kristiansund a.	0905	...	1430	...	1635	...	2130	...	0040	...	...

🚌	⚒		Ⓐ					⑤⑦		
Kristiansund d.	0630	...	1040	...	...	1315	...	1635	...	2040
Oppdal skysstasjon a.	0940	...	1420	...	...	1640	...	2010	...	0005

A – 20 minutes later from Aug. 31.
B – 30 minutes **earlier** from Aug. 31.
C – 15–20 minutes **earlier** from Aug. 31.
D – 10 minutes later from Aug. 31.
H – From Aug. 31 Molde d. 0800, Åndalsnes a. 0920.
L – From Aug. 31.
N – Conveys 🛏 and 🛏2.
R – Reservation recommended.
e – Not June 22 - Aug. 14.
s – Stops to set down only.
u – Stops to pick up only.
⊡ – Conveys *NSB Komfort*.
✣ – Subject to confirmation.
⊖ – Oslo Lufthavn Gardermoen (see also Table **771**).
¶ – From Aug. 31. By Taxi (only available for passengers from train **2347**). Runs on request only – please inform the on train staff.
♥ – From Aug. 31 runs with train number **2341** and arrives Åndalsnes 1332.
★ – From Aug. 31 runs with train number **2345** and arrives Åndalsnes 1944.
♠ – From Aug. 31 departs Åndalsnes 0933 and runs with train number **2342**.
♣ – From Aug. 31 departs Åndalsnes 1630 and runs with train number **2346**.

786 SOUTHWEST NORWAY 🚌 LINKS

BERGEN - TRONDHEIM (Operator: NOR-WAY Bussekspress ✆ +47 815 44 444)
Bergen ⊡ d. 1630 → Oppdal a. 0435 → Trondheim a. 0645.
Trondheim d. 2000 → Oppdal d. 2210 → Bergen ⊡ a. 0945.

BERGEN - ÅLESUND (Operator: NOR-WAY Bussekspress ✆ +47 815 44 444)
Bergen ⊡ d. 0800 → Ålesund a. 1735 (1720 on ⑥).
Ålesund d. 1100 → Bergen ⊡ a. 2020.

BERGEN - LILLEHAMMER (Operator: NOR-WAY Bussekspress ✆ +47 815 44 444)
Bergen ⊡ d. 0855 → Voss d. 1045 → Flåm d. 1155 → Lillehammer skysstasjon a. 1745.
Lillehammer skysstasjon d. 1035 → Flåm d. 1620 → Voss a. 1730 → Bergen ⊡ a. 1915.

BERGEN - KRISTIANSAND (Operator: NOR-WAY Bussekspress ✆ +47 815 44 444)
Bergen ⊡ d. 0730 → Odda d. 1115 → Haukeli a. 1250, d. 1445 → Kristiansand a. 1855.
Kristiansand d. 0845 → Haukeli a. 1250, d. 1445 → Odda a. 1630 → Bergen ⊡ a. 1955.

BERGEN - ODDA ★ 🚌/⛴ *Journey time: 3 hrs 15 m – 3 hrs 40 m.*
From Bergen ⊡ at 0730, 1130, 1430 Ⓑ, 1730 ⑦ and 2030 Ⓑ.
From Odda ⊡ at 0535 ⚒, 1230, 1635 and 2035 Ⓑ.

GEILO - ODDA ★ *Journey time: 3 hrs 25 m. Summer services only: May 1 - Sept. 30, 2009.*
From Geilo railway station at 1150. From Odda ⊡ at 0720, 1230 Ⓑ **S**.

VOSS - ULVIK ★ *Journey time: 50 – 65 minutes.*
From Voss at 0845 Ⓐ, 1005 ⚒ **V**, 1140 Ⓐ, 1530 Ⓐ **z**, 1645 ⑥ **R**, 1735 Ⓑ and 2135 Ⓑ.
From Ulvik ⊡ at 0725 Ⓐ, 0855 ⚒ **V**, 1410 Ⓐ **z**, 1525 Ⓑ **V** and 1810 Ⓑ.

R – Until Sept. 26.
S – June 22 - Aug. 16 only. Journey time: 3 hrs 50 m.
V – Daily until Oct. 2.
z – Also ⑥ from Oct. 3.
⊡ – Bus station.
★ – Operator: Skyss ✆ +47 5523 9550.

TRONDHEIM - BODØ and NARVIK 787

km		1781 Ⓐh 🍷	1783 Ⓐ 🍷	475 ✕N	🚌 ◇	473 ⑥ 🍷	473 Ⓐ 🍷R	1785 Ⓐh 🍷	471 ✕R	1791 Ⓐ 🍷	🚌 ◇	479 Ⓑh 🍷R	477 Ⓑ 🍷R
0	**Trondheim** S § d.	...	...	2335	...	...	...	...	0740	...	...	...	1558
33	Værnes ✈ ‡... § d.	...	...	0005	...	...	...	...	0815	...	...	...	1631u
34	Stjørdal......... § d.	...	...	0010	...	...	...	...	0820	...	...	...	1637u
126	Steinkjer .... § d.	...	...	0129	...	...	...	...	0943	...	...	...	1801u
220	Grong..............d.	...	...	0240	...	...	...	...	1053	...	...	...	1907
406	Mosjøen ....d.	...	...	0457	...	0650	0650	...	1309	...	...	1645	2120
498	Mo i Rana.........d.	...	...	0608	...	0754	0800	...	1420	...	...	1747	2225
648	Rognan.............d.	0542	0642	0802	...	...	0954	1145	1615	1740	...	1936	...
	Bodø ⊖........d.	|	|	|	0700	...	|	|	|	|	1615	|	...
674	Fauske ....a.	0603	0703	0825	0815	...	1014	1206	1637	1800	1730	1956	...
674	Fauske ....d.	0603	0703	0830	0855	...	1016	1206	1645	1808	1810	2001	...
	Narvik ⊡ ......a.	|	|	|	1330	...	|	|	|	|	2300	|	...
729	**Bodø**...............a.	0642	0742	0910	...	...	1055	1253	1725	1847	...	2040	...

	478 🍷R	470 Ⓐh 🍷	1792 ⒶV 🍷	1784 Ⓐh 🍷	🚌 ◇	472 ✕R	1790 Ⓐ 🍷	474 Ⓑ 🍷R	🚌 ◇	476 ✕N
Bodø............d.	...	0748	0748	1015	...	1215	1605	1727	...	2110
Narvik ⊡ ...d.	...	|	|	|	0700	|	|	|	1610	|
Fauske ....a.	...	0828	0828	1100	1200	1255	1643	1806	2110	2148
Fauske ....d.	...	0828	0828	1100	1215	1258	1645	1807	2130	2152
Bodø ⊖.....a.	...	|	|	|	1325	|	|	|	2240	|
Rognan..........d.	...	0848	0848	1120	...	1320	1705	1832	...	2214
Mo i Rana......d.	0820	1032	...	...	...	1531	...	2017	...	0015
Mosjøen.........d.	0928	1136	...	...	...	1641	...	2118	...	0140
Grong ....d.	1146	...	...	...	...	1905	...	...	...	0426
Steinkjer ..... § d.	1250	...	...	...	...	2016	...	...	...	0540
Stjørdal....... § d.	1404	...	...	...	...	2134	...	...	...	0704
Værnes ✈ ‡ § d.	1406	...	...	...	...	2136	...	...	...	0706
Trondheim . § a.	1439	...	...	...	...	2210	...	...	...	0740

Local services Trondheim - Steinkjer and v.v.

km	▶	Ⓐ	⚒	z		z		Ⓐh	w	Ⓐh		w	Ⓑ
0	**Trondheim** S ...d.	0610	0710	0910	1110	1310	1510	1539	1710	1810	1910	2110	2310
31	Hell ● ....d.	0643	0743	0943	1143	1343	1543	1613	1743	1843	1943	2143	2343
33	Værnes ✈ ‡ ● ..d.	0645	0745	0945	1145	1345	1545	1615	1745	1845	1945	2145	2345
34	Stjørdal............d.	0652	0752	0952	1152	1352	1552	1620	1752	1852	1952	2152	2349
126	**Steinkjer**.........a.	0816	0916	1116	1319	1516	1716	1744	1916	2016	2116	2313	0107

▶	Ⓐ	z		z		z		w	Ⓐh	
Steinkjer.......d.	0528	0728	0925	1128	1328	1528	1728	1925	2028	2128
Stjørdal............d.	0652	0852	1052	1252	1452	1652	1852	2052	2152	2252
Værnes ✈ ‡ ● d.	0654	0854	1054	1254	1454	1654	1854	2054	2154	2254
Hell ● ....d.	0657	0857	1057	1257	1457	1657	1857	2057	2157	2257
Trondheim S.a.	0732	0932	1132	1332	1532	1732	1932	2132	2229	2332

N – Conveys 🛏 and 🛏. Reservation recommended.
R – Reservation recommended.
V – June 22 - Aug. 14.

h – Not June 22 - Aug. 14.
u – Stops to pick up only.
w – Not June 27, July 4, 11, 18, 25, Aug. 1, 8.
z – Daily to June 26; ①–⑤ June 29 - Aug. 7; daily from Aug. 10.

● – Trains stop on request.
⊡ – Bus station.
⊖ – Bodø Busstorget.
‡ – Station for Trondheim Airport.
§ – See also panel below main table.
◇ – Operator: Cominor. ✆ +47 7692 3500.

▶ – **Additional services** Trondheim - Stjørdal - Steinkjer and v.v.:
From Trondheim at 0510Ⓐh, 0810Ⓐh, 1010Ⓐh, 1210Ⓐ, 1410Ⓐ, 1439Ⓐh and 1610Ⓐ.
From Steinkjer at 0600Ⓐh, 0628Ⓐ, 0657Ⓐh, 0828Ⓐ, 1028Ⓐh, 1228Ⓐh, 1428Ⓐ, 1628Ⓐh and 1828Ⓐ.

LAPLAND 🚌 LINKS 789

Narvik – Tromsø – Alta

Operator: Cominor

km		①–⑤	①–⑥			Ⓑ	Ⓑ		⑦	
0	**Narvik** bus station ......d.	0520	...	...	...	1250	1250	1530	1840	...
	Narvik rail station ....d.	|	...	...	...	1257	1257	|	1847	...
181	Nordkjosbotn ....d.	0820	0820	...	...	1615	1615	1845	2150	...
252	**Tromsø** Prostneset .d.	0925	0925	...	1600	|	1725	1945	2250	...
241	Lyngseidet..................d.	...	...	...	1745	1745	...	...	...	...
465	**Alta**...........................a.	...	...	...	2230	2230	...	...	...	...

km		①–⑤				①–⑥	①–⑤	⑥	⑦	⑦	⑦
0	**Alta**...........................d.	...	...	...	...	1045	1045	1045	...	1400	1400
224	Lyngseidet..................d.	...	...	...	...	1545	1545	1545	...	1910	1910
293	**Tromsø** Prostneset .d.	0615	1000	...	1600	|	1725	1800	1900	|	2050
	Nordkjosbotn ....d.	0730	1105	...	1705	1705	...	...	2010	2010	...
	Narvik rail station ....a.	1025	1410	...	|	|	...	...	|	|	...
	Narvik bus station ......a.	1030	1415	...	2010	2010	...	...	2310	2310	...

Alta – Hammerfest – Karasjok – Kirkenes

Operator: FFR Veolia Transport

km		①–⑤	①–⑤	①–⑤ ◇	①③	⑤⑦	①–④	①–④ ◇	⑥R	⑤⑦	⑤⑦ ◇
0	**Alta**...........................d.	...	0635	...	...	...	1430	...	1445	1500	...
	Hammerfest ....d.	...	|	0710	...	...	|	1500	|	|	1540
87	Skaidi ....a.	...	0800	0805	...	...	1605	1600	1605	1635	1635
87	Skaidi ....d.	...	0810	0810	...	...	1615	1615	1610	1645	1645
	Hammerfest ....a.	...	0900	|	...	...	1705	|	1700	1745	|
112	Olderfjord ....d.	...	▬	0845	...	...	...	1650	...	...	1720
212	Honningsvåg ★.......a.	...	...	1025	...	...	...	1830	...	...	1900
174	Lakselv.......................d.	...	...	1010	...	...	...	1755	...	...	1835
248	Karasjok ....d.	...	⑦	1125	1200	1410	...	1910	...	...	1950
429	Tanabru.......................d.	0830	1130	...	1500	1715	...	...	...	...	...
571	**Kirkenes**...................a.	1050	1350	...	1720	1935	...	...	...	...	...

km		①–⑤ ◇	①–⑤	⑥R	⑥S	Q	①–④ ◇	①–④	⑤⑦ ◇	Ⓑ
	Kirkenes...................d.	...	...	...	...	0805	...	...	...	1510
	Tanabru.......................d.	...	...	...	...	1035	...	...	...	1800
	Karasjok ....d.	0515	...	...	...	1310	1350	...	1430	▬
	Lakselv.......................d.	0725	...	...	...	...	1520	...	1605	...
	Honningsvåg ★.......d.	0640	...	...	1400	...	1440	...	1510	...
	Olderfjord ....d.	0845	...	...	1650	...	1650	...	1720	⑤⑦
0	Hammerfest ....d.	|	0810	0840	|	...	|	1615	|	1635
57	Skaidi ....a.	0905	0905	0935	1710	...	1710	1710	1740	1735
57	Skaidi ....d.	0915	0915	0935	1720	...	1720	1720	1750	1750
	Hammerfest ....a.	1010	|	|	1815	...	1815	|	1845	|
144	**Alta**...........................a.	...	1035	1055	...	...	...	1840	...	1915

Rovaniemi – Muonio – Tromsø

Operator: Eskelisen Lapin Linjat

km		◐	C	
0	**Rovaniemi** bus station d.	0800	1130	...
157	Kittilä ....d.	1040	1335	...
238	Muonio ....d.	1300	1505	...
327	Karesuvanto ....d.	1435	1625	...
440	Kilpisjärvi ⊡ .... FI d.	1625	1810	...
535	Nordkjosbotn .... NO d.	...	1830	...
608	**Tromsø** Prostneset .... a.	...	1930	...

	D	◐	
Tromsø Prostneset .. d.	0730	...	...
Nordkjosbotn ...... NO d.	0830	...	...
Kilpisjärvi ⊡ .... FI d.	1110	1315	...
Karesuvanto ....d.	1240	1515	...
Muonio ....d.	1410	1700	...
Kittilä..........................d.	1535	1835	...
Rovaniemi bus station a.	1740	2040	...

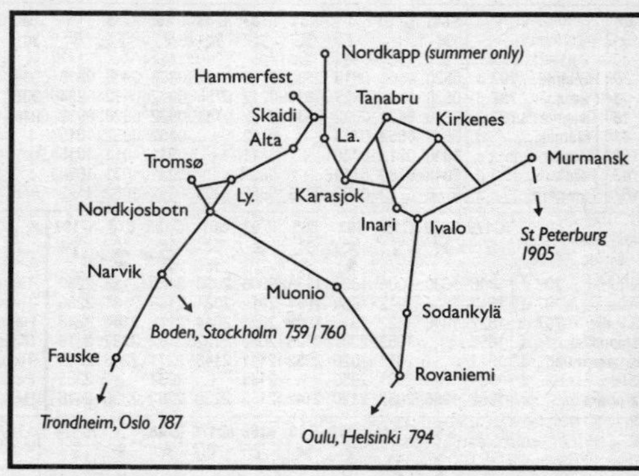

Rovaniemi – Karasjok, Nordkapp, Tanabru, Kirkenes and Murmansk

km	Operator:	G	G ⊖	S	G/M ①③⑤	E	E H	P ①–⑥	E	G/L Ⓑ	G A
0	**Rovaniemi** bus station d.	0800	...	...	...	1145	1145	1520	1720	2000	2255
	Rovaniemi rail station d.	0820	...	...	...	1100	1100	1525	1645k	2010	2300
130	Sodankylä...................d.	1020	...	...	...	1345	1345	1730	1915	2200	0105
305	Ivalo .... FI d.	1250	1300	...	1530	1625	1625	1935	2130	0015	0310
345	Inari...................... FI d.	...	1340	...	|	1700	1700	...	2205	...	...
461	Karasjok............ NO a.	...	...	...	|	1755	1755	...	|	...	...
536	Lakselv, Statoil........ a.	...	...	...	|	...	1855	...	|	...	...
735	**Nordkapp** .... a.	...	...	...	|	...	2220	...	|	...	...
	Tanabru .... NO a.	...	...	...	|	...	...	...	2355r	...	...
	Kirkenes, Europris NO d.	...	...	1500	|	...	...	...	...	...	...
	Murmansk .... RU a.	...	...	2100v	2300	...	...	...	...	...	...

Operator:	P ⑥	G A	E	G ①–⑤	G/L ①–⑥	E J	E	S	G/M ①③⑤	G	G
Murmansk .... RU d.	...	...	...	...	...	...	...	0700v	0830	...	...
Kirkenes .... NO a.	...	...	...	...	...	...	...	1100	|	...	...
Tanabru.......... NO d.	...	...	0330t	...	...	...	...	...	|	...	...
Nordkapp ....d.	...	...	|	...	...	0100	...	...	|	...	...
Lakselv, Statoil ....d.	...	...	|	...	...	0810	...	...	|	...	...
Karasjok............. NO d.	...	...	|	...	...	0915	0915	...	|	...	...
Inari....................... FI d.	...	...	0715	1105	...	1210	1210	...	|	1415	...
Ivalo .... FI d.	0530	0615	0820	1140	1215	1320	1320	...	1400	1450	1615
Sodankylä...................d.	0755	0900	1045	...	1500	1550	1550	...	...	...	1845
Rovaniemi rail station . a.	0945	1045	1225	...	1715	1730	1730	...	...	...	2030
Rovaniemi bus station a.	0950	1050	1230	...	1710	1735	1735	...	...	...	2035

Operator codes:
E – Eskelisen Lapin Linjat.
G – Gold Line.
L – Liikenne O. Niemelä.
M – Murmanskavtotrans.
P – Pikakuljetus Rovaniemi.
S – Pasvikturist AS.

A – ①–⑤ to May 29 and from Aug. 17.
C – June 1 - Sept. 19.
D – June 2 - Sept. 20.
H – June 1 - Aug. 22.
J – June 2 - Aug. 23.
N – June 8 - Aug. 23.
P – June 9 - Aug. 24.
Q – ①③⑤⑦.
R – Until Oct. 24.
S – June 13 - Aug. 22.

k – 1725 May 31 - Sept. 6.
r – ③④⑤⑦ (daily May 31 - Sept. 20).
t – ①④⑤⑥ (daily June 1 - Sept. 19).
v – Murmansk Vorovskogo gate.

⊖ – Runs one hour later on ⑥⑦.
⊡ – Trekking centre (Retkeilykeskus).
◇ – Two routes: Hammerfest - Olderfjord - Karasjok and v.v.; Hammerfest - Olderfjord - Honningsvåg and v.v.
◐ – Operator: Gold Line.

★ – **Honningsvåg - Nordkapp** and v.v.
34 km. Journey 45 minutes.
Summer service May 4 - Sept. 6, 2009.
From Honningsvåg (Nordkapphuset) at 1045 and 2130 **N**.
From Nordkapp at 0015 **P** and 1315.

FI – Finland (East European Time).
NO – Norway (Central European Time).
RU – Russia (Moskva Time).

FINLAND

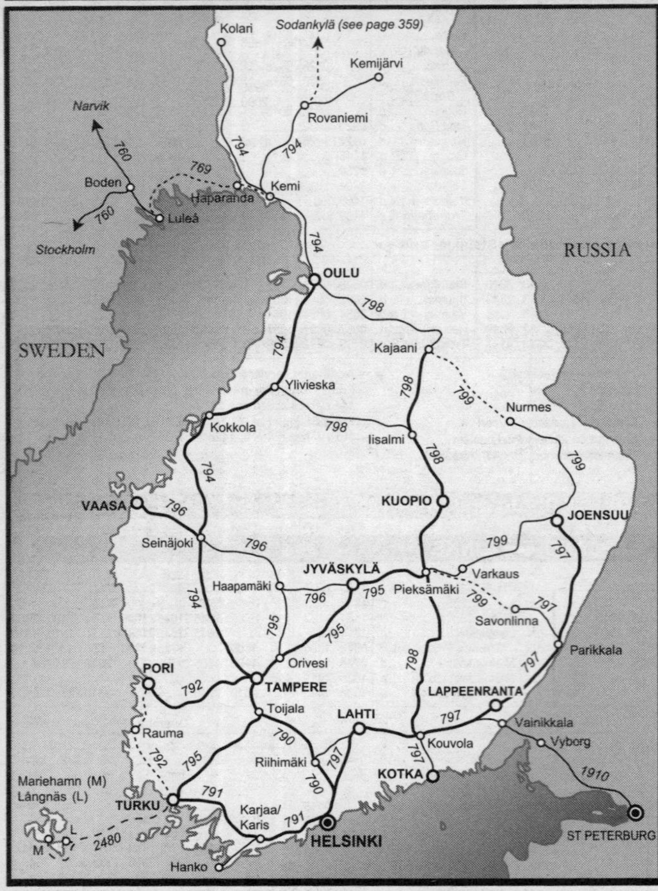

Operator: VR – VR-Yhtymä Oy (www.vr.fi).

Tickets and train types: For all except purely local journeys, tickets are always sold for travel by a specific train or combination of trains. There are four different pricing-scales, corresponding to each of the following train types (in descending order of cost):

- **S 220 Pendolino** (e.g. *S* **123**) – high-speed tilting trains (220 km/h), with 1st (*Business*) and 2nd class seats. Reservation compulsory.
- **InterCity** (e.g. *IC* **124**) – quality fast trains between major centres, with 1st and 2nd class seats, all reservable.
- **Express**, *pikajunat* (train number only shown, e.g. **128**) – other fast trains, with 2nd class seats, all reservable. Night expresses convey sleeping-cars and 2nd class seats only (marked ★ in the tables).
- **Regional**, *taajamajunat* (no train number shown) – stopping-trains, normally with 2nd class seats only.

S 220, InterCity and Express tickets include a seat reservation when purchased in advance.

Rail tickets are **not** valid on 🚌 services (except Kemi - Tornio). However, special combined train / bus fares are available on certain routes.

Services: ✕ indicates a train with a restaurant car.

Trains marked 🍷 convey a buffet car or a *MiniBistro* trolley service.

Complimentary light meals are served to holders of Plus and Business Plus tickets.

A supplement is payable for travel in sleeping-cars (🛏) in addition to the appropriate **Regional** fare – 2nd class for a berth in a 2- or 3-person cabin, 1st class for occupancy of a single-berth cabin. Sleeper supplements cost up to 50% more on peak nights in mid-winter. Seated passengers on night express trains pay the 2nd class **Express** fare.

Timings: Timings are valid, unless otherwise indicated, **May 31 - Sept. 6, 2009.**

In these tables Ⓐ = ①–⑤, ⚒ = ①–⑥.

Changes to the normal service pattern are likely to occur on and around the dates of public holidays. On June 19 services operate as on ⑥ (except for trains **863**, **870**, **873** and **874** which do not run). On June 20 an amended ⑦ service operates (many long distance trains do not run – please check locally if travelling on June 20).

790 HELSINKI - TAMPERE

For through journeys to / from **Oulu** and **Rovaniemi**, see table **794**. For through journeys to / from **Jyväskylä** and **Pieksämäki**, see table **795**.

km		*S* 841	*IC* 161		*S* 41	*IC* 83	*IC* 43	*IC* 165	*IC* 85		*S* 845	*IC* 847	*IC* 169	*IC* 171		*S* 87	*IC* 849	*IC* 173	*S* 89	*IC* 175		*S* 853	*IC* 855	*S* 91	*IC* 177		*IC* 57
		✕ ⚒	Ⓐ	2 ⚒	✕ Ⓐ	✕	✕	🍷 ⚒	🍷	2	✕	✕	🍷	🍷	2	✕	✕	🍷	✕ Ⓑ	🍷	2	✕	✕	✕	🍷	2	✕ Ⓑ
0	**Helsinki**.... **797** d.	0530	0606	0619	0630	0706	0730	0806	0906	0919	0930	1006	1106	1206	1219	1230	1306	1406	1430	1506	1519	1530	1606	1630	1706	1719	1730
3	Pasila........ **797** d.	0536	0612	0624	0636	0712	0736	0812	0912	0924	0936	1012	1112	1212	1224	1236	1312	1412	1436	1512	1524	1536	1612	1636	1712	1724	1736
16	Tikkurila ⊙ **797** d.	0546	0622	0632	0646	0722	0746	0822	0922	0932	0946	1022	1122	1222	1232	1246	1322	1422	1446	1522	1532	1546	1622	1646	1722	1732	1746
71	Riihimäki......... d.	0613	0652	0713	|	0752	|	0852	0952	1013	|	1052	1152	1252	1313	|	1352	1452	|	1552	1613	|	1652	|	1752	1813	|
108	Hämeenlinna... d.	0630	0711	0736	|	0811	|	0911	1011	1036	|	1111	1211	1311	1336	|	1411	1511	|	1611	1636	|	1711	|	1811	1836	|
147	Toijala............. d.	0648	0731	0759	|	0831	|	0931	1031	1059	|	1131	1231	1331	1359	|	1431	1531	|	1631	1659	|	1731	|	1831	1859	|
187	**Tampere**......... a.	0706	0752	0822	0756	0852	0902	0952	1052	1122	1056	1152	1252	1352	1422	1356	1452	1552	1556	1652	1722	1656	1752	1756	1852	1922	1902

	IC 179	*S* 859	*IC* 181	863	865	*IC* 93	867	*IC* 185	873	*IC* 189
	🍷	✕	🍷	✕ ★	✕ ★	🍷	✕ ★	✕ E	✕ ★	🍷
Helsinki .... **797** d.	1806	1830	1906	1852	1926	2006	2023	2100	2123	2230
Pasila .... **797** d.	1812	1836	1912	1859	1934	2012	2031	2106	2131	2236
Tikkurila ⊙ **797** d.	1822	1846	1922	1911	1948	2022	2044	2116	2144	2246
Riihimäki...........d.	1852	|	1952	2001	2026	2052	2122	2152	2222	2316
Hämeenlinna.....d.	1911	|	2011	2026	2052	2111	2148	2211	2248	2335
Toijala...............d.	1931	|	2031	2053	|	2131	|	2231	|	2355
Tampere ....a.	1952	1956	2052	2120	2142	2152	2238	2252	2336	0016

	864	866	*IC* 160	870	*IC* 162	874	872	*S* 80	*S* 40	*IC* 164		*S* 82	*S* 42
	✕ ★	✕ ★	Ⓐ	✕ ★	✕ Ⓐ	✕ ★	✕ ★	✕ Ⓐ	✕ Ⓐ	🍷 ⚒	2	✕ ⚒	✕ ⚒
Tampere................d.	0405	0440	0533	0548	0604	0611	0636	0657	0702	0707	0732	0757	0802
Toijala.....................d.	0434	0507	0554	0615	0626	0638	0737	|	|	0728	0755	|	|
Hämeenlinna..........d.	0502	0534	0615	0642	0647	0705	0804	|	|	0749	0818	|	|
Riihimäki ....d.	0531	0600	0635	0708	0707	0732	0832	|	|	0809	0852	|	|
Tikkurila ⊙...... **797** a.	0610	0635	0702	0746	0737	|	0942	0810	0815	0837	0928	0910	0915
Pasila............... **797** a.	0622	0647	0711	0758	0746	0828	0953	0819	0824	0846	0936	0919	0924
Helsinki.......... **797** a.	0630	0654	0717	0806	0752	0836	1000	0825	0830	0852	0941	0925	0930

	IC 166	*S* 84	*IC* 844	*IC* 188	*S* 46	*IC* 86	*IC* 170	*IC* 48		*IC* 174	*IC* 176	*IC* 850	*S* 852	*IC* 88	*S* 62	*IC* 180		*IC* 854	*S* 90	*IC* 182		*S* 856	*IC* 184	*IC* 858	*IC* 92	*S* 860	*S* 94
	🍷 ⚒	✕ ⚒	✕ ⚒	🍷 ⑦	✕	🍷	🍷	✕	2	🍷	🍷	✕	✕	🍷	✕	🍷	2	✕	✕	🍷	2	✕	🍷	✕	🍷	✕ Ⓑ	✕
Tampere ....d.	0807	0902	0907	0907	1002	1007	1107	1207	1237	1307	1407	1507	1602	1607	1702	1707	1737	1807	1902	1907	1937	2002	2007	2102	2107	2202	2302
Toijala...............d.	0828	|	0928	0928	|	1028	1128	1228	1300	1328	1428	1528	|	1628	|	1728	1800	1828	|	1928	2000	|	2028	|	2128	2221	2321
Hämeenlinna.....d.	0849	|	0949	0949	|	1049	1149	1249	1323	1349	1449	1549	|	1649	|	1749	1823	1849	|	1949	2023	|	2049	|	2149	2239	2339
Riihimäki ....d.	0909	|	1009	1009	|	1109	1209	1309	1352	1409	1509	1609	|	1709	|	1809	1852	1909	|	2009	2052	|	2109	|	2209	2256	2356
Tikkurila ⊙ **797** a.	0937	1015	1037	1037	1115	1137	1237	1337	1428	1437	1537	1637	1715	1737	1815	1837	1928	1937	2015	2037	2128	2115	2137	2221	2237	2321	0021
Pasila .... **797** a.	0946	1024	1046	1046	1124	1146	1246	1346	1436	1446	1546	1646	1724	1746	1824	1846	1936	1946	2024	2046	2136	2124	2146	2230	2246	2330	0030
Helsinki .... **797** a.	0952	1030	1052	1052	1130	1152	1252	1352	1441	1452	1552	1652	1730	1752	1830	1852	1941	1952	2030	2052	2141	2130	2152	2236	2252	2336	0036

Additional regional trains Helsinki - Riihimäki and v.v. ⊠

				⚒								
Helsinki ....d.	0036	0136	...	0548	...	0648	and	2248	...	2336	...
Pasila ....d.	0041	0141	...	0553	...	0653	hourly	2253	...	2341	...
Tikkurila ⊙ .....d.	0058	0158	...	0602	...	0702	until	2302	...	2358	...
Riihimäki.........a.	0150	0250	...	0646	...	0746		2346	...	0050	...

			Ⓐ	Ⓒ							
Riihimäki.........d.	0414	...	0514	0514	...	0614	and	2214	...	2314	...
Tikkurila ⊙ .....d.	0505	...	0558	0605	...	0658	hourly	2258	...	0005	...
Pasila ....a.	0520	...	0607	0620	...	0707	until	2307	...	0020	...
Helsinki..........a.	0525	...	0612	0625	...	0712		2312	...	0025	...

E – ①②③④⑦.

⊙ – For Helsinki ✈ Vantaa.
⊠ – 2nd class only.

★ – Overnight train to / from northern Finland. Conveys 🛏 and 2nd class seats.
For through cars and days of running see Table **794**.

HELSINKI - TURKU and HANKO — 791

km		IC 121	IC 159	S 123		IC 125	S 127	IC 129		IC 131	IC 133	IC 135		IC 137		IC 139		IC 141		143	S 145		IC 147	IC 149		IC 153
		🍷	🍷 Ⓐ	🍴 ⚒		🍷	🍴 ⚒	🍷	2 ⚒	🍷	🍷	🍷	2	🍷	2 Ⓐ	🍷	2 Ⓐ	🍷	2	2	🍴	2 Ⓑ	🍷 Ⓑ	🍷		
0	**Helsinki** d.	0546	0634	0738	...	0903	1003	1103	1133	1203	1303	1403	1433	1503	1533	1603	1633	1703	1733	1803	1903	1933	2003	2103	...	2303
3	Pasila d.	0552	0640	0745	...	0909	1009	1109	1138	1209	1309	1409	1438	1509	1538	1609	1638	1709	1738	1809	1909	1938	2009	2109	...	2309
87	Karjaa / Karis ★ d.	0645	0736	0834	...	1003	1103	1203	1239	1303	1403	1503	1539	1603	1639	1703	1739	1803	1839	1903	2003	2039	2103	2203	...	0006
138	Salo d.	0712	0803	0857	...	1030	1130	1230	...	1330	1430	1530	...	1630	...	1730	...	1830	...	1930	2030	...	2130	2230	...	0033
194	**Turku** a.	0744	0833	0925	...	1100	1200	1300	...	1400	1500	1600	...	1700	...	1800	...	1900	...	2000	2100	...	2200	2300	...	0103
197	Turku satama a.	0753	...	...	...	...	...	...	...	...	...	...	...	...	...	*1819*	...	1912	...	2012	...	...	...	...	...	...

		IC 122		IC 124			S 126	IC 128	IC 130		S 132	IC 134	IC 136		S 138	IC 140	IC 142		IC 144	IC 146	IC 148		IC 150	IC 152	154
	2 Ⓐ	🍷 Ⓐ	2 Ⓐ	🍷	2 ⚒	2 ⑦	🍴 ⚒	🍷 Ⓐ	🍷		🍴 ⚒	🍷	🍷	2 ⚒	🍴	🍷	🍷	2	🍷	🍷	🍷	2	🍷	🍷	2
Turku satama d.	...	...	...	...	...	...	...	0738	0815	...	...	...	...	...	...	...	...	...	...	...	...	...	...	1945	2045
Turku d.	...	0544	...	0638	...	...	0735	0755	0855	...	1000	1100	1200	...	1300	1400	1500	...	1600	1700	1800	...	1900	2000	2100
Salo d.	...	0616	...	0710	...	...	0805	0830	0932	...	1032	1132	1232	...	1332	1432	1532	...	1632	1732	1832	...	1932	2032	2132
Karjaa / Karis ★ d.	0600	0643	0650	0737	0752	0800	0828	0900	1000	...	1100	1200	1300	1304	1400	1500	1600	1615	1700	1800	1900	1918	2000	2100	2200
Pasila a.	0707	0736	0753	0826	0853	0916	0913	0951	1051	...	1151	1251	1351	1407	1451	1551	1651	1722	1751	1851	1951	2022	2051	2151	2251
Helsinki a.	0712	0742	0759	0832	0858	0921	0919	0957	1057	...	1157	1257	1357	1412	1457	1557	1657	1727	1757	1857	1957	2027	2057	2157	2257

★ – **KARJAA / KARIS - HANKO** and v.v. *50 km*. Journey time: 40 minutes (55–60 minutes by 🚌). 2nd class only. **Karjaa - Hanko** at 0743, 0835 Ⓐ 🚌, 1010, 1220 🚌, 1310, 1410 ⚒ 🚌, 1510, 1610 Ⓐ 🚌, 1710, 1745 Ⓐ 🚌, 1910 and 2210. **Hanko - Karjaa** at 0540 Ⓐ 🚌, 0640, 0720 Ⓐ 🚌, 0910, 1050 Ⓐ 🚌, 1210, 1410, 1435 🚌, 1610, 1810, 1900 Ⓐ 🚌 and 2110.

792 — TAMPERE and TURKU - PORI

2nd class only

km		⚒									
0	**Tampere** d.	0807	...	1215	1415	1615	1815	2205	...	...	...
135	**Pori** a.	0937	...	1345	1556	1748	1948	2335	...	...	...

	⚒									
Pori d.	0520	0715	...	1015	...	1415	1615	1815	...	...
Tampere a.	0650	0850	...	1145	...	1545	1747	1945	...	...

km		🚌	🚌	🚌	🚌	🚌	🚌	🚌	Ⓑ 🚌	🚌	🚌
0	**Turku** bus station d.	0815	1100	1500	1500	...	1630	1800	...	1830	2030
93	Rauma bus station d.	0945	1230	1640	|	1710	1805	|	1915	2010	2155
144	**Pori** bus station a.	1035	1320	...	1720	1815	...	2020	2020	...	2240

	🚌	⚒ 🚌	🚌	🚌	🚌	🚌	🚌	Ⓑ 🚌	🚌	🚌
Pori bus station d.	0600	0805	0830	...	1230	...	1720	1920	1930	...
Rauma bus station d.	0645	0910	|	1040	1320	1535	1810	2025	|	2210
Turku bus station a.	0820	...	1050	1220	1450	1700	1940	...	2150	2345

TAMPERE - OULU, KOLARI and ROVANIEMI — 794

km		873				S 841	S 241			IC 43	IC 243	801		S 845	IC 847	703	S 61	IC 849	IC 173	S 853	IC 855	IC 57	S 859	863	865		867
		★ T	🚌 Ⓐ	🚌 Ⓐ	2	🍴 ⚒	🍴 ⚒	2	🚌 ⚒	🍴	🍴	2 🍴 K	🚌	🍴	🍴	2 🍴 J	‡ 🍴 Ⓑ	🍴	🍷 Ⓑ	🍴	🍴	🍴 Ⓑ V	🍴	★ A	★	🚌 Ⓐ	★ ⑤
	Helsinki **793** d.	2123	...	...	...	0530	...	...	...	0730	...	...	...	0930	1006	...	1230	1306	1406	1530	1606	1730	1830	1852	1926	...	2023
0	**Tampere** d.	0025	...	...	...	0709	...	...	...	0905	...	...	...	1100	1200	...	1400	1500	1600	1700	1802	1905	2000	2136	2211	...	2308
75	Parkano d.	0121	...	...	...	|	...	...	...	0943	...	...	...	|	1238	...	|	1538	1638	1736	1842	1948	|	|	2310	...	|
159	Seinäjoki d.	0232	...	...	...	0815	*0825*z	...	...	1020	*1035*z	...	...	1207	1330	...	1514	1624	1720	1812	1932	2030	2109	2353	0019	...	0107
292	Kokkola d.	0450	...	...	0644	...	1023	...	...	—	1233	...	...	1329	1509	...	...	1810	...	1952	2112	...	2232	0159	0233	...	0411
371	Ylivieska d.	0554	...	...	0735	...	1113	...	...	...	1324	...	...	1414	1601	...	...	1902	...	2036	2204	...	2315	0314	0333	...	0506
493	**Oulu** a.	0727	...	...	0849	...	1222	...	...	🚌	1442	...	...	1517	1713	...	...	2013	...	2146	2323	...	0018	0438	0504	...	0624
493	**Oulu** d.	0755	...	...	...	...	...	1237	...	Ⓐ	...	1449	...	...	...	1727	...	2023b	...	...	...	...	...	0458	0522	...	0635
599	Kemi a.	0909	...	0920	...	...	...	1345	...	1432	...	1552	...	...	...	1829	...	2126b	...	...	...	...	...	0615	0630	0646	0746
808	**Kolari** a.	|	...	1305	...	...	...	|	...	1805	...	|	...	...	...	|	...	|	...	...	...	...	...	0927	|	1015	|
713	**Rovaniemi** a.	1041	1135	...	...	...	...	1507	1520	...	...	1711	1720	...	...	1948	...	2246b	...	...	...	...	...	...	0753	...	0932
796	Kemijärvi ⊡ a.	...	1250	...	...	...	...	...	1645	...	...	...	1835	...	...	...	...	...	...	...	...	...	...	...	0945	...	...

	S 40	S 42	IC 844	S 246	S 46	IC 248	IC 48			IC 850	S 852	S 62		708	IC 854		810	S 856	IC 858	S 860		864		866	870	872	874
	🍴 Ⓐ	🍴 ⚒	🍴 ⚒ V	🍴 ⚒	🍴	🍴	🍴	🚌 Ⓐ	🚌 Ⓐ X	🍴	🍴	🍴	🚌 ⚒	2 🍴 J	🍴	🚌	2 🍴 P	🍴	🍴	🍴 Ⓑ	2	★ ⑦	🚌 Ⓐ	★ U	★ B	★ D	★
Kemijärvi ⊡ d.	...	...	...	...	...	...	...	...	0525	...	...	...	0840	...	...	1115	...	...	...	...	...	...	...	...	...	...	1900
Rovaniemi d.	...	...	...	...	...	...	...	...	0645	0715r	...	...	0950	1007	...	1230	1250	...	...	...	1630	1717	...	1800	...	...	2110
Kolari d.	...	...	...	...	...	...	...	0415	...	|	...	...	...	|	...	...	|	...	...	...	|	|	1605	|	1845	1845	|
Kemi d.	...	...	...	...	...	...	...	0725	...	0837r	...	...	...	1125	...	...	1410	...	...	...	1753	1855	1918	1939	2150	2150	2234
Oulu a.	...	...	...	...	...	...	...	...	...	0937r	...	...	...	1225	...	...	1519	...	...	...	1857	2023	...	2058	2302	2302	2343
Oulu d.	...	...	...	0448	...	0624	...	...	...	0942	1132	...	...	...	1232	...	...	1525	1533	1730	1907	2028	...	2127	2324	2324	2352
Ylivieska d.	...	...	...	0556	...	0737	...	...	...	1059	1239	...	...	...	1346	...	...	1635	1655	1837	2034	2222	...	2313	0052	0052	0113
Kokkola d.	...	*0430*z	*0505*z	0639	...	0827	...	...	...	1148	1326	...	...	...	1443	...	...	1718	1747	1927	2130	2323	...	0014	0201	0201	0235
Seinäjoki d.	0550	0650	0738	*0840*z	0850	*1025*z	1038	...	...	1338	1447	1545	...	...	1638	...	...	1850	1938	2050	...	0115	...	0212	0355	0355	0413
Parkano d.	0623	0723	0821	...	|	...	1116	...	...	1416	|	|	...	...	1716	...	...	|	2017	|	...	|	...	0307	|	|	|
Tampere a.	0656	0756	0858	...	0959	...	1158	...	...	1457	1557	1656	...	...	1758	...	...	1957	2059	2154	...	0314	...	0401	0541	0541	0551
Helsinki **793** a.	0830	0930	1052	...	1130	...	1352	...	...	1652	1730	1830	...	...	1952	...	...	2130	2236	2336	...	0630	...	0654	0806	1000	0836

A – ③⑤⑥ June 10 - Sept. 5.
B – ⑥ June 13 - Sept. 5.
D – ④⑦ June 11 - Sept. 6.
J – From / to Kajaani (Table **798**).
K – From Kouvola (on ⚒) and Kuopio (Table **798**).
P – To Pieksämäki (Table **798**).

T – Also conveys 🛏 Turku (**933**) - Tampere - Rovaniemi.
U – Also conveys 🛏 Rovaniemi - Tampere (**904**) - Turku.
V – From / to Vaasa (Table **796**).
X – From Aug. 17.
b – Ⓑ only.

r – ⚒ only.
z – By 🚌 Seinäjoki - Kokkola and v.v.
★ – Conveys 🛏, [2] and 🍴.
⊡ – 🚌 services operate to / from the bus station.
‡ – Train **87** Helsinki - Tampere.

TURKU - TAMPERE - PIEKSÄMÄKI — 795

km		S 81 §	IC 905	IC 83	IC 165		909	IC 85	IC 847	911	S 87	IC 849	IC 917	IC 173	S 89		S 853	921	923	S 91	S 859	IC 927	IC 927	931	IC 93	933
		K 🍴 Ⓐ	🍷	🍴	🍷 ⚒	2	2	🍷	🍴	2 🍴	🍴	🍴	🍷	🍷	🍴 Ⓑ	2	🍴	2 🍴	2	🍴	🍴	🍴	K 🍴 Ⓑ	2	🍷 Ⓑ	R
0	Turku satama d.	...	...	...	...	...	0836	...	...	...	...	...	...	...	...	...	...	...	...	...	...	...	...	1950	...	2050
3	**Turku** d.	...	0700	...	...	...	0905	...	...	1005	...	...	1305	...	...	...	...	1505	1605	...	...	1805	1805	2005	...	2105
69	Loimaa d.	...	0741	...	...	...	0944	...	...	1044	...	...	1344	...	...	...	...	1544	1644	...	...	1844	1844	2044	...	2147
	Helsinki **790** d.	0630	|	0706	0806	...	|	0906	1006	|	1230	1306	|	1406	1430	...	1530	|	|	1630	1830	|	|	|	2006	|
131	Toijala d.	|	0825	0831	0931	...	1025	1031	1131	1125	|	1431	1425	1531	|	...	|	1625	1725	|	|	1925	1925	2125	2131	2234
171	**Tampere** a.	0756	0847	0852	0952	...	1047	1052	1152	1147	1356	1452	1447	1552	1556	...	1656	1647	1747	1756	1956	1947	1947	2147	2152	2300
171	**Tampere** d.	0805	...	0905	...	1005	...	1105	...	1205	1405	...	1505	...	1605	1615	...	1705	...	1805	...	2005	2005	...	2205	...
213	Orivesi d.	|	...	0930	...	1031	...	|	...	1230	|	...	1530	...	|	1641	...	1730	...	1832	...	2030	2030	...	2232	...
285	Haapamäki a.	|	...	|	...	1124	...	|	...	|	|	...	|	...	|	1734	...	|	...	|	...	|	|	...	|	...
269	Jämsä d.	0858	...	1006	...	...	...	1205	...	1306	1500	...	1606	...	1656	...	...	1806	...	1906	...	2106	2106	...	2307	...
326	Jyväskylä d.	0927	...	1045	...	...	...	1235	...	1345	1527	...	1645	...	1730	...	...	1840	...	1946	...	2136	2140	...	2337	...
406	**Pieksämäki** a.	1009	...	1134	...	...	...	...	...	1434	...	...	1734	...	1812	...	...	1934	...	2028	...	...	2231	...	...	...

	904	S 80	906	S 82	S 84	IC 86	IC 912		916	IC 48		IC 176	IC 922	IC 850	IC 88	924		928	IC 854	S 90		S 856	IC 92	IC 934	936	S 94
	T	🍴 Ⓐ	2 Ⓐ	🍴 ⚒	K 🍴 ⚒	🍷	🍷		2 🍴	🍴	2	🍷	🍴	🍴	🍷	2		2 🍴	🍴	🍴	2	🍴	🍷	🍷	2 ⑦	🍴
Pieksämäki d.	...	...	...	0530	0643	...	...	...	0924	...	...	...	1228	...	...	...	...	1528	...	...	...	...	1828	...	...	2053
Jyväskylä d.	...	0530	...	0630	0730	0822	...	...	1022	...	...	...	1322	...	1425	...	...	1622	...	1735	...	...	1922	...	...	2137
Jämsä d.	...	0557	...	0657	0757	0856	...	...	1054	...	...	...	1354	...	1458	...	...	1654	...	1804	...	...	1954	...	...	2204
Haapamäki d.	...	|	...	|	|	|	...	...	|	...	1221	...	|	...	|	...	...	|	...	|	1821	...	|	...	...	|
Orivesi d.	...	|	...	|	0827	0931	...	...	1129	...	1317	...	1429	...	|	...	...	1729	...	|	1917	...	2029	...	...	|
Tampere a.	...	0650	...	0750	0850	0955	...	...	1153	...	1342	...	1453	...	1553	...	...	1753	...	1853	1942	...	2053	...	...	2253
Tampere d.	0556	0657	0711	0757	0902	1007	1011	...	1211	1207	...	1407	1511	1507	1607	1611	...	1811	1807	1902	...	2002	2107	2111	2211	2302
Toijala d.	0623	|	0735	|	|	1028	1035	...	1235	1228	...	1428	1535	1528	1628	1635	...	1835	1828	|	...	|	2128	2135	2235	2321
Helsinki **790** a.	|	0825	|	0925	1030	1152	|	...	|	1352	...	1552	|	1652	1752	|	...	|	1952	2030	...	2130	2252	|	|	0036
Loimaa d.	0706	...	0813	...	...	...	1113	...	1313	...	...	...	1613	...	...	1713	...	1916	...	...	...	...	...	2215	2313	...
Turku a.	0750	...	0850	...	...	...	1150	...	1355	...	...	...	1655	...	...	1750	...	1955	...	...	...	...	...	2252	2350	...
Turku satama a.	0802	...	...	...	...	...	...	...	...	...	...	...	...	...	...	1819	...	*2012*	...	...	...	...	...	...	...	...

K – To / from Kuopio (Table **798**).
R – [2] Turku - Tampere; 🛏 Turku - Tampere (**873**) - Rovaniemi.
T – [2] Tampere - Turku; 🛏 Rovaniemi (**866**) - Tampere (**904**) - Turku.
§ – Train **41** Helsinki - Tampere.

796 JYVÄSKYLÄ - SEINÄJOKI - VAASA

km		⚒2	⚒2	2		2	2	2	2	IC57 Ⓑ✕	2
0	**Jyväskylä** d.	...	0733	...	...	1033	...	...	1633	...	...
78	Haapamäki d.	...	0844	...	...	1144	...	...	1744	...	...
151	Alavus d.	...	0953	...	...	1253	...	...	1853	...	...
	Helsinki **793/4** d.	...	|	...	...	|	...	...	|	1730	...
196	Seinäjoki a.	...	1025	...	...	1325	...	...	1925	2030	...
196	Seinäjoki d.	0820	1038	1038	...	1340	1638	1816	1943	2045	2115
270	**Vaasa** a.	0915	1136	1136	...	1438	1736	1918	2045	2137	2213

	⚒2	IC844 ⚒✕	⑦2	2		2	2	2	Ⓑ2	2	Ⓑ2
Vaasa d.	0553	0622	0742	0930	...	1222	1453	1520	1808	1808	1935
Seinäjoki a.	0642	0720	0840	1028	...	1320	1439	1618	1906	1906	2033
Seinäjoki d.	...	0738	...	1034	...	...	...	1634	1942	...	...
Helsinki **793/4** a.	...	1052	...	|	...	...	...	|	|	...	...
Alavus d.	...	...	...	1107	...	...	...	1707	2015	...	...
Haapamäki d.	...	...	...	1215	...	...	...	1815	2122	...	...
Jyväskylä a.	...	...	...	1327	...	...	...	1927	2233	...	...

797 HELSINKI - KOUVOLA - SAVONLINNA and JOENSUU

km		2	S1 ✕	2	IC71 J✕	2	IC3 ✕	2	2	IC73 K✕	IC107 🍷 Ⓐ	IC5 ✕	2	IC109 🍷	2	S7 B✕	IC77 J✕	IC77§ ✕ Ⓑ	2	IC111 🍷 Ⓑ	2	IC11 ✕	2	S79 C✕	IC113 ✕	2	2 Ⓑd
0	**Helsinki** 790 d.	0641	0712	0741	0800	0841	1000	1041	1141	1100	1212	1300	1341	1412	1441	1512	1600	1600	1641	1712	1741	1800	1841	1912	2012	2141	2241
3	Pasila 790 d.	0646	0718	0746	0806	0846	1006	1046	1146	1106	1218	1306	1346	1418	1446	1518	1606	1606	1646	1718	1746	1806	1846	1918	2018	2146	2246
16	Tikkurila ⊙ 790 d.	0655	0728	0755	0816	0855	1016	1055	1155	1116	1228	1316	1355	1428	1455	1528	1616	1616	1655	1728	1755	1816	1855	1928	2028	2155	2255
104	Lahti d.	0741	0802	0841	0902	0941	1102	1141	1241	1202	1308	1402	1441	1508	1541	1602	1702	1702	1743	1808	1841	1902	1941	2002	2108	2241	2342
166	**Kouvola** a.	▬	0843	▬	0943	...	1143	▬	...	1243	1348	1443	▬	1548	...	1643	1743	1743	1828a	1848	...	1943	▬	2043	2148	...	0027
166	**Kouvola** d.	...	0845	...	...	...	1145	...	...	...	1350	1445	...	...	...	1647	...	1751	▬	...	...	1945	...	...	2150	...	...
252	Lappeenranta d.	2	0931	2	...	...	1231	2	...	...	1438	1531	2	...	...	1741	...	1842	2	...	...	2036	2	...	2240	...	...
288	Imatra d.	⚒	0957		...	...	1257		...	...	...	1557		...	...	1804	...	1909	Ⓑ	...	...	2102		...	2304	...	...
352	Parikkala d.	0725	1042	1045	...	...	1338	1341	...	...	...	1638	1641	...	...	|	...	1953	1956	...	...	2143	2146	...	...	...	...
411	**Savonlinna** a.	0819	|	1139	...	...	|	1435	...	...	...	|	1735	...	...	|	...	|	2050	...	...	|	2240	...	...	...	...
482	**Joensuu** a.	...	1151	...	...	...	1453	...	...	...	...	1748	...	...	...	1949	...	2103	...	...	...	2253	...	...	...	...	...

	2 ⚒e	IC102 🍷 Ⓐ	2	IC104 ✕ ⚒	2 ⚒	S2 ✕ ⚒	S70 J✕ ⚒	2	IC4 ✕	2	IC74 J✕	2	IC6 ✕	2	IC68 K✕	2	S8 ✕	IC118 🍷 Ⓐ	S76 K✕	IC114 🍷	2	IC10 ✕	IC66 K✕ Ⓑ	IC78 J✕	2	IC12 ✕	2
Joensuu d.	...	...	...	...	...	0507	...	...	0607r	...	...	...	0904	...	...	...	1222	...	...	...	...	1523	...	...	...	1814	...
Savonlinna d.	...	...	...	...	0517	|	...	...	|	...	...	0917	|	...	...	1236	|	...	...	...	1536	|	...	...	1829	|	...
Parikkala d.	...	...	...	...	0610	0616	...	...	0720r	...	...	1010	1016	...	...	1329	1336	...	...	...	1629	1636	...	...	1922	1927	...
Imatra d.	...	...	...	0556	▬	0653	...	...	0801	...	...	▬	1057	...	...	▬	1417	...	...	...	▬	1717	...	...	▬	2012	...
Lappeenranta d.	...	...	...	0622	...	0716	...	...	0827	...	...	...	1123	...	...	...	1443	1530	...	...	...	1743	...	...	...	2038	...
Kouvola a.	...	...	...	0710	2	0803	...	...	0915	...	...	2	1211	...	...	2	1531	1618	...	...	2	1831	...	...	2	2126	...
Kouvola d.	0454	0612	0630a	0712		0805	0817	...	0917	...	1117		1217	...	1428		1533	1620	1633	1728		1833	1928	2033		2133	...
Lahti d.	0540	0654	0717	0754	0817	0848	0900	0917	1000	1117	1200	1217	1300	1417	1512	1517	1618	1705	1718	1812	1823	1918	2012	2118	2123	2218	2323
Tikkurila ⊙ 790 a.	0627	0732	0806	0832	0905	0922	0932	1005	1044	1205	1244	1305	1344	1505	1550	1605	1650	1744	1750	1850	1909	2002	2050	2202	2209	2302	0009
Pasila 790 a.	0635	0741	0815	0841	0914	0931	0941	1014	1054	1214	1254	1314	1354	1514	1559	1614	1659	1754	1759	1859	1918	2012	2059	2212	2218	2312	0018
Helsinki 790 a.	0640	0748	0821	0848	0919	0937	0948	1019	1100	1219	1300	1319	1400	1519	1606	1619	1706	1800	1806	1906	1923	2018	2106	2218	2223	2318	0023

Regional trains **RIIHIMÄKI - KOUVOLA - KOTKA** ⊠

km		⚒e	⚒e							Ⓐ											Ⓑ			Ⓑ		Ⓑ	
0	**Riihimäki** d.	...	0613	0713	...	0813	0913	1013	1113	1113	...	1213	1313	1413	...	1513	1613	...	1713	1813	1813	1913	2013	...	2213	...	0013
59	Lahti d.	...	0650	0754	...	0854	0954	1054	1154	1205	...	1254	1354	1450	...	1554	1654	...	1754	1849	1850	1954	2054	...	2254	2342	0054
121	**Kouvola** d.	0630	0735	*0843**	0850	...	...	...	*1243**	1252	1252	...	...	1535a	1542	...	*1743**	1754	...	...	1935	...	*2148**	2155	...	0027	...
173	**Kotka** satama a.	0715	...	...	0935	...	...	...	...	1337	1337	...	...	...	1627	...	...	1839	...	...	...	...	...	2240	...	...	...

	Ⓐ	Ⓐ	⑥e	⚒e		⚒e					Ⓐ							Ⓒ🚌									Ⓑ
Kotka satama d.	...	...	...	...	...	0724	...	...	...	1021	1021	...	...	...	...	...	1435	...	...	...	1635	...	...	...	1916	...	2248
Kouvola d.	...	*0454*	*0454*	...	...	0810	0825r	...	...	1107	1109	*1117**	...	...	...	...	1521	1545	1625a	...	1721	*1833**	...	...	2002	*2133**	2334
Lahti d.	0452	0544	0628	0706	0806	...	0911	1006	1106	...	1206v	1206	1306	1406	1506	1606	*1616**	1700	1711	1806	*1810**	1928	2006	2106	*2116**	2228	...
Riihimäki a.	0533	0624	0708	0746	0846	...	0946	1046	1146	...	1246	1246	1346	1446	1546	1646	...	...	1746	1846	...	2008	2046	2146	...	2308	...

B – Conveys on Ⓑ 🛏12 Helsinki - Kouvola (**75**) - Kuopio (Table **798**).
C – 🛏12 Helsinki - Kuopio (- Kajaani Ⓑ).
K – To / from Kuopio (Table **798**).
J – To / from Kajaani (Table **798**).

a – Ⓐ only.
d – Runs daily Helsinki - Lahti.
e – Not Oct. 31.
r – ⚒ only.
v – Arrives 1154.

§ – Train **9** from Kouvola.
* – Connection by *S* or *IC* train (higher fare payable).
⊙ – For Helsinki ✈ Vantaa.
⊠ – 2nd class only.

798 KOUVOLA - KUOPIO - OULU

km		2 ⚒	2 ⚒	801 2✕ ⚒	801 2✕	S81* ✕ Ⓐ	IC71 ✕	703 2✕	IC73 ✕	705 2✕	2	707 2✕	707 2✕ Ⓑ	S75‡ ✕ Ⓑ	🚌 ⒷJ	IC77 ✕	709 2✕ Ⓑ	S79 ✕	S79 ✕ Ⓑ	IC927 T✕ Ⓑ
	Helsinki **797** d.	...	...	...	...	0630	0800	...	1100	...	...	*1412*	*1412*	1512	...	1600	*1712*	1912	1912	...
0	**Kouvola** d.	...	...	0625	...	◇	0956	...	1258	...	...	1556	1556	1652	...	1757	1856	2050	2050	...
113	Mikkeli d.	...	...	0752	...	|	1108	...	1406	...	...	1708	1708	1754	...	1913	2005	2147	2147	...
184	Pieksämäki d.	...	...	0839	...	1011	1154	...	1453	...	...	1754	1754	1836	...	1959	2052	2227	2227	2233
273	**Kuopio** d.	...	...	0947e	0947	1058	1254	...	1543	1548	...	1852	1856	1924	2000	2053	2145	2317	2320	2323
358	Iisalmi d.	...	0545	1048	1048	...	1353	...	...	1650	1654	...	1958	...	2125	2151	...	...	0015	...
512	Ylivieska a.	...	0727	|	|	...	|	...	...	|	1829	...	|	...	...	|	...	...	|	...
441	Kajaani d.	0620	|	1144	1144	...	1442	1512	...	1746e	...	...	2056e	...	...	2240	...	...	0100	...
484	Paltamo d.	0652	|	1215	1215	...	...	1543	...	1818	...	...	2129	...	...	...	...	...	...	...
633	**Oulu** a.	0834	*0849*	1355	1355	...	...	1724	...	1956	...	...	2314	...	...	...	...	...	...	...
	Rovaniemi **794** a.	...	...	1711	1629	...	...	1948	...	...	...	...	...	...	...	...	...	...	...	...

	700 2✕ ⚒	S70 ✕ ⚒	S84 ✕ ⚒		IC74 ✕		704 2✕ ⚒	IC68 ✕	S76 ✕	706 2✕	IC66 ✕ Ⓑ	2	708 2✕	IC78 ✕	810 2✕	S94 ✕	714 2✕ Ⓑ		2 Ⓑ	2 Ⓑ
Rovaniemi **794** d.	...	...	...	...	...	...	...	...	...	...	...	...	1007	...	1250	...	...	...	...	...
Oulu d.	...	...	...	...	...	...	0712	...	...	1005	...	...	1237	...	1529	...	...	...	*1907*	2019
Paltamo d.	...	...	...	...	...	...	0849	...	...	1146	...	...	1415	...	1705	...	...	...	|	2200
Kajaani d.	...	0352	...	...	0617	...	0920	...	...	1220	...	...	1446	1517	1747	...	...	...	|	2229
Ylivieska d.	...	|	...	...	|	...	|	...	...	|	...	1428	...	|	|	...	...	...	2040	...
Iisalmi d.	...	0440	...	...	0712	...	1015	...	...	1315	...	1605	...	1613	1840	...	...	...	2220	...
Kuopio d.	0408	0540	0555	...	0813	...	1112	1128	1358	1419	1612	...	...	1726v	1950v	...	...	...	...	...
Pieksämäki d.	0513	0632	0643	...	0909	...	...	1224	1449	1526e	1708	...	...	1832e	2044	2053	2104	...	...	...
Mikkeli d.	0600	0713	|	...	0956	...	...	1310	1530	1613	1755	...	...	1915	...	|	2151	...	...	...
Kouvola a.	0704	0807	◇	...	1059	...	...	1415	1623	1717	1913	...	...	2017	...	◇	2255	...	...	...
Helsinki **797** a.	*0848*	0948	1030	...	1300	...	...	1606	1806	*1906*	2106	...	...	2218	...	0036	...	...	...	...

J – From June 1.
T – From Turku (Table **795**).

e – Arrives 9 – 11 minutes earlier.
v – Arrives 14 minutes earlier.

* – Train **41** Helsinki - Tampere.
‡ – Train **7** Helsinki - Kouvola.
◇ – Via Tampere (Table **795**).

799 PIEKSÄMÄKI - JOENSUU - NURMES - KAJAANI

2nd class only

km		🚌 Ⓐ			🚌 Ⓐ		🚌	🚌 ⚒		Ⓑ	🚌 Ⓑ	
0	**Pieksämäki** d.	0655	...	1158	1235	1456	1640	1800	1839	2102	2240	...
49	Varkaus d.	0750	...	1233	1310	1530	1725	1835	1912	2137	2315	...
183	**Joensuu** ⊙ a.	1000	...	1403	...	1700	1920	...	2043	2310	...	...

		🚌 ⚒			🚌 Ⓐ	🚌 ⑥	🚌 Ⓐ	🚌 ⑦		Ⓑ
Joensuu ⊙ d.	0652	0910	...	1228	...	...	1500	1515	1612	1836
Varkaus d.	0828	1120	...	1407	1605	1715	1720	1725	1749	2014
Pieksämäki a.	0901	1155	...	1440	1650	1750	1755	1800	1821	2046

km		🚌 ⚒		🚌 ⑦	🚌 ⚒	🚌 ⚒	🚌		🚌 Ⓐ	🚌 Ⓑ	🚌 Ⓑ	🚌 ⑦
0	**Joensuu** ⊙ d.	0900	1202	1210	1405	1520	1630	1810	2115	2115	2315	2315
104	Lieksa ⊙ a.	|	1321	|	|	1705	|	1929	2245	|	0040	|
160	Nurmes ⊙ a.	1055	1408	1400	1610	...	1830	2016	...	2335	...	0135
274	**Kajaani** bus station a.	1255	...	1600	1805	...	2030	...	...	...	...	...

	🚌 ⚒		🚌 ⚒	🚌 ⑦	🚌 Ⓑ	🚌	🚌	🚌 Ⓐ		🚌
Kajaani bus station d.	...	...	0540	...	...	1040	...	...	...	1710
Nurmes ⊙ d.	...	0640	0750	0915	...	1235	...	...	1550	1905
Lieksa ⊙ d.	0510	0726	|	1005	1005	|	1250	1410	1636	1950
Joensuu ⊙ a.	0645	0845	1010	1150	1150	1430	1435	1600	1755	2130

🚌 (◇) **PIEKSÄMÄKI** – **SAVONLINNA** (bus station) at 1020 ⚒ and 1520.
🚌 (◇) **SAVONLINNA** (bus station) – **PIEKSÄMÄKI** at 0655 ⚒ and 1230.

⊙ – 🚌 timings are at the bus station.
◇ – *123 km.* Journey time: 1 hr 50 m - 2 hrs 5 m.

GERMANY

Operator: Principal operator is Deutsche Bahn Aktiengesellschaft (DB). Many regional services are run by independent operators – these are specified in the table heading (or by footnotes for individual trains).

Services: Trains convey first- and second-class seating accommodation unless otherwise shown (by '2' in the column heading, a footnote or a general note in the table heading). Overnight sleeping car (🛏) and couchette (▬) trains do not necessarily convey seating accommodation - refer to individual footnotes for details. Any light refreshment service on overnight trains (🍷) may only be available to couchette and sleeping car passengers. Descriptions of sleeping and couchette cars appear on page 10.

There are various categories of trains in Germany. The type of train is indicated by the following letter codes above each column (or by a general note in the table heading):

ICE	**InterCity Express**	German high-speed (230–320 km/h) train. Higher fares payable.
EC	**EuroCity**	International express train.
IC	**InterCity**	Internal express train.
THA	**Thalys**	International high-speed train. Special fares.
TGV	**Train à Grande Vitesse**	French high-speed (320 km/h) train.
RJ	**Railjet**	Austrian high-speed train.
IRE	**InterRegio Express**	Regional express train.
RE	**Regional Express**	Semi-fast train.
RB	**Regional Bahn**	Stopping train.
CNL	**City Night Line**	Quality overnight express train. Most services convey *Deluxe* sleeping cars (1/2 berth) with en-suite shower and WC, *Economy* sleeping cars (1/2/4 berth), couchettes (4/6 berth) and reclining seats. *Talgo* type trains operate on the routes München - Hamburg / Berlin and convey *Deluxe* sleeping cars, special 2 berth couchettes (*Kajütte*) and reclining seats. Most trains convey ✕. Reservation compulsory. See also page 10.
EN	**Euro Night**	International overnight express train. See also page 10.
D	**Durchgangszug**	Or **Schnellzug** – other express train (day or night).
S-Bahn		Suburban stopping train.

Other operators:

ALX	**Arriva-Länderbahn-Express**	Operated by Arriva / Regentalbahn AG - Die Länderbahn. Runs trains on the route Hof - Regensburg - München - Oberstdorf / Lindau.
X	**InterConnex**	Long-distance routes operated by Veolia Verkehr GmbH. **DB tickets are not valid.**

Timings: Valid **June 14 - December 12**, 2009 (except where shown otherwise in the table heading).

Many long distance trains operate on selected days only for part of the journey. These are often indicated in the train composition footnote by showing the dated journey segment within brackets. For example '[12] Leipzig - Hannover (- Dortmund ⑦)' means that the train runs daily (or as shown in the column heading) between Leipzig and Hannover, but only continues to Dortmund on Sundays. Additional footnotes / symbols are often used to show more complex running dates, e.g. '[12] (München ▢ -) Nürnberg - Hamburg' means that the train runs only on dates in note ▢ between München and Nürnberg, but runs daily (or as shown in the column heading) between Nürnberg and Hamburg.

International overnight trains that are not intended for internal German journeys are not usually shown in the German section. Please refer to the International section for details of these services. A number of other overnight trains run over long distances without making a public stop making it difficult to show them clearly in the relevant German tables. For ease of reference these trains have been summarised in an additional table below.

Engineering work may occasionally disrupt services at short notice (especially at weekends and during holiday periods), so it is advisable to check timings locally before travelling. The locations of known service alterations are summarised in the shaded panel below.

Supplements: A 'Sprinter' supplement (€16 in first class, €11 in second class) is payable for travel by limited stop *ICE **SPRINTER*** trains **1090–1097**. Special 'global' fares are payable for international journeys on *Thalys* trains. A variable supplement (*Aufpreis*) is payable for travel by overnight *CNL* and *EN* trains, the cost of which depends on the type of accommodation required (sleeper, couchette or reclining seat). Please note that it is not possible for single travellers to book a berth in a shared sleeping compartment on *CNL* trains. However, holders of 2nd class tickets are able to book a *CNL Economy* single berth compartment.

Reservations: Reservation is compulsory for travel by *CNL*, *Thalys* and other trains marked Ⓡ. Seat reservations are also available on *ICE*, *EC* and *IC* trains (€5 first class, €4 second class).

Holidays: Oct. 3 is the only national German public holiday during this timetable period (trains marked ⚒ do not run). In addition there are other regional holidays as follows: Aug. 15 – Mariä Himmelfahrt (Assumption); Oct. 31 – Reformationstag (Reformation Day); Nov. 18 – Buß und Bettag. On these days the regional service provided is usually that applicable on ⑦ (please refer to individual footnotes for details).

ENGINEERING WORK SUMMARY

- **Stralsund - Pasewalk**: Until July 2. Most southbound *IC / EC* trains run up to 26 minutes earlier.
- **Stuttgart - Schwäbisch-Gmünd - Aalen**: Until Oct. 15. *IC* services between Stuttgart and Nürnberg are diverted via Backnang. Regional trains replaced by 🚌 Schwäbisch Gmünd - Aalen until July 26 (replaced by 🚌 Schorndorf - Schwäbisch Gmünd from July 27).
- **Amsterdam** (via Oberhausen): June 12–14, Aug. 9. *ICE* trains are diverted, not calling at Arnhem, Oberhausen, Duisburg or Düsseldorf. A change of train at Eindhoven may be required.
- **Hannover - Hamburg**: June 14 - July 19. Most *IC* services in Table **902** do not operate between Hannover and Hamburg. *ICE* services in Table **900** continue to run, but with journey times extended by up to 25 minutes (earlier departures / later arrivals at Hamburg).
- **Northeim - Hannover**: June 14, 15, 20, 21, 22 most *IC* services do not call at Northeim, Kreiensen, Alfeld and Elze. July 11, 12 most *IC* services do not call at Kreiensen, Alfeld and Elze.
- **Nordhausen - Halle**: June 14 - Aug. 1. All trains replaced by 🚌 Sangerhausen - Lutherstadt Eisleben and v.v. with journey times extended by up to 35 minutes (earlier departures from Halle).
- **Berlin**. June 20 - July 3. Services via the Berlin Stadtbahn (Spandau - Zoo - Hbf - Ostbahnhof) are subject to alteration including earlier departures / later arrivals. Certain *IC* and overnight trains operate to / from / via Berlin Gesundbrunnen. See note ▲ in Table **810** for further details.
- **Basel - Freiburg**: June 27, 28. Trains **104/5**, **2100/2/3/5** do not operate Basel - Freiburg and v.v.
- **Köln - Düsseldorf - Essen - Dortmund**: July 18–26. Certain trains do not call at Bochum and journeys may be extended by a few minutes.
- **Köln - Bonn - Koblenz**: July 19. Trains diverted, not calling at Bonn Hbf, Remagen or Andernach. Certain trains (mainly those from / to Hamburg) call at Köln Messe/Deutz instead of Köln Hbf. Extended journey times.
- **Aalen - Donauwörth**: July 27 - Oct. 15. Trains replaced by 🚌 between Goldshöfe and Nördlingen resulting in extended journey times.
- **Bamberg - Nürnberg**: Aug. 1 - Sept. 14. Trains replaced by 🚌 between Bamberg and Forchheim. A limited train service operates between Forchheim and Nürnberg. *ICE* services from / to Berlin will operate every two hours to / from Bamberg with replacement express 🚌 services operating between Bamberg and Erlangen / Nürnberg. Direct *ICE* trains run every two hours between Berlin and München via Erfurt and Würzburg (extended journey times).
- **Münster - Rheine**: Oct. 26 - Nov. 22. *IC* trains diverted with journeys extended by up to 45 minutes. Later arrivals / earlier departures at Rheine and stations north thereof. Regional services replaced by 🚌 with extended journey times.

Overnight Trains Summary

		CNL 482	*D* 50482	*CNL* 472	*D* 50472	*EN* 447	*CNL* 457	*CNL* 40447	*CNL* 1259	*CNL* 459	*CNL* 478
		Ⓡ✕	Ⓡ	Ⓡ🍷	Ⓡ	Ⓡ🍷	Ⓡ🍷	Ⓡ🍷	Ⓡ✕	Ⓡ🍷	Ⓡ✕
		H	M	A	N	J	K	B	S	C	⊖ L
München Hbf	d.	1900**h**	1900**h**	...	...	...	...	...	...	...	...
Ingolstadt Hbf	d.	1947**h**	1947**h**	...	...	...	...	...	...	...	...
Nürnberg Hbf	d.	2135	2135	...	...	...	...	...	...	...	...
Würzburg Hbf	d.	2233	2233	...	...	...	...	...	...	...	...
Zürich HB	d.	|	|	...	...	...	...	...	1944	1944	2042
Basel SBB **912**	d.	|	|	1804	1804	...	...	...	2107	2107	2207
Karlsruhe Hbf **912**	d.	|	|	2018	2018	...	...	...	2305	2305	0011
Frankfurt (Main) Süd	d.	|	|	2218	2218	...	...	...	0055	0055	|
Fulda	d.	2343	2343	|	|	...	...	...	|	|	|
Erfurt Hbf	a.	|	|	|	|	...	...	...	0414	0520	|
Weimar	a.	|	|	|	|	...	...	...	0458	0540	|
Leipzig Hbf	a.	|	|	|	|	...	...	...	|	0641	|
Amsterdam Centraal **28**	d.	|	|	|	|	1901	1901	1901	|	|	|
Köln Hbf **800**	d.	|	|	|	|	2228	2228	2228	|	|	|
Dortmund Hbf	d.	|	|	|	|	2356	2356	2356	|	|	|
Hamm (Westf)	d.	|	|	|	|	0014	0014	0014	|	|	|
Bielefeld Hbf	d.	|	|	|	|	0043	0043	0043	|	|	|
Berlin Hbf	a.	|	|	|	|	|	0421**p**	|	0718	|	|
Berlin Ostbahnhof	a.	|	|	|	|	|	0430**p**	|	...	|	|
Warszawa Centralna **24**	a.	|	1035	|	1035	1035	|	|	...	|	|
Dresden Hbf	a.	|	...	|	...	...	0707	|	...	0807	|
Praha hlavní **1100**	a.	|	...	|	...	...	0956	|	...	1052	|
Hamburg Hbf	a.	0356**f**	...	0356**f**	...	...	...	0356**f**	...	...	0906**z**
Neumünster	a.	0442**f**	...	0442**f**	...	...	...	0442**f**	...	...	...
Flensburg	a.	0547**f**	...	0547**f**	...	...	...	0547**f**	...	...	...
København H **710**	a.	0959**e**	...	0959**e**	...	...	...	0959**e**	...	...	...

		CNL 479	*CNL* 458	*CNL* 1258	*CNL* 483	**446** **483**	*EN* 446	*CNL* 456	*CNL* 40483	**446** **473**	*CNL* 473
		Ⓡ✕	Ⓡ🍷	Ⓡ✕	Ⓡ✕	Ⓡ	Ⓡ🍷	Ⓡ🍷	Ⓡ🍷	Ⓡ	Ⓡ🍷
		⊖ L	C	S	H	M	J	K	B	N	A
København H **710**	d.	...	...	...	1853	...	...	...	1853	...	1853
Flensburg	d.	...	...	...	2233	...	...	...	2233	...	2233
Neumünster	d.	...	...	...	2335	...	...	...	2335	...	2335
Hamburg Hbf	d.	1918	...	...	0031	...	...	...	0031	...	0031
Praha hlavní **1100**	d.	|	1829	...	|	...	...	1829	|	...	|
Dresden Hbf	d.	|	2115	...	|	...	...	2051	|	...	|
Warszawa Centralna **24**	d.	|	|	...	|	1755	1755	|	|	1755	|
Berlin Ostbahnhof	d.	|	|	...	|	|	|	0022**q**	|	|	|
Berlin Hbf	d.	|	|	2222	|	|	|	0032**q**	|	|	|
Bielefeld Hbf	a.	|	|	|	|	|	0356	0356	0356	|	|
Hamm (Westf)	a.	|	|	|	|	|	0429	0429	0429	|	|
Dortmund Hbf	a.	|	|	|	|	|	0450	0450	0450	|	|
Köln Hbf **800**	a.	|	|	|	|	|	0614*	0614*	0614*	|	|
Amsterdam Centraal **28**	a.	|	|	|	|	|	1029	1029	1029	|	|
Leipzig Hbf	d.	|	2253	|	|	|	...	...	...	|	|
Weimar	d.	|	0005	0047	|	|	...	...	...	|	|
Erfurt Hbf	d.	|	0117	0117	|	|	...	...	...	|	|
Fulda	a.	|	|	|	0450**r**	0450**r**	...	...	...	|	|
Frankfurt (Main) Süd	a.	|	0359	0359	|	|	...	...	...	0654	0654
Karlsruhe Hbf **912**	a.	0437	0540	0540	|	|	...	...	...	0818	0818
Basel SBB **912**	a.	0654	0755	0755	|	|	...	...	...	1037	1037
Zürich HB	a.	0834**t**	0917	0917	|	|	...	...	...	...	...
Würzburg Hbf	a.	...	...	...	0534**v**	0534**v**	...	...	...	...	...
Nürnberg Hbf	a.	...	...	...	0645**x**	0645**x**	...	...	...	...	...
Ingolstadt Hbf	a.	...	...	...	0807	0807	...	...	...	...	...
München Hbf	a.	...	...	...	0857	0857	...	...	...	...	...

A – AURORA – 🛏 1, 2 cl. and ▬ 2 cl. Basel - København and v.v.
B – BOREALIS – 🛏 1, 2 cl., ▬ 2 cl. and [2] Amsterdam - København and v.v.
C – CANOPUS – 🛏 1, 2 cl., ▬ 2 cl. and [2] Praha - Zürich and v.v.
H – HANS CHRISTIAN ANDERSEN – 🛏 1, 2 cl., ▬ 2 cl. and [2] München - København and v.v.
J – JAN KIEPURA – 🛏 1, 2 cl., ▬ 2 cl. and [2] Warszawa - Amsterdam and v.v.; 🛏 1, 2 cl. Moskva - Amsterdam and v.v.
K – KOPERNIKUS – 🛏 1, 2 cl., ▬ 2 cl. and [2] Praha - Köln - Amsterdam and v.v.
L – KOMET – 🛏 1, 2 cl., ▬ 2 cl. and [2] Zürich - Hamburg and v.v.
M – 🛏 1, 2 cl. and ▬ 2 cl. München - Warszawa and v.v.; 🛏 1, 2 cl. München - Moskva and v.v.
N – 🛏 1, 2 cl. and ▬ 2 cl. Basel - Warszawa and v.v.; 🛏 1, 2 cl. Basel - Moskva and v.v.
S – SIRIUS – 🛏 1, 2 cl., ▬ 2 cl. and [2] Berlin - Halle - Zürich and v.v.

e – 1026 on ⑦ July 5 - Sept. 13.
f – 8–11 minutes later on ①–⑥ June 22 - July 20 (also June 28). On July 5, 12, 19 arrives Hamburg 0406, Neumünster 0511, Flensburg 0639. On ⑦ July 26 - Sept. 13 arrives Neumünster 0502, Flensburg 0639.
h – On ⑥⑦ München d. 1915, Ingolstadt d. 2013.
p – June 20 - July 3 calls at Berlin Gesundbrunnen (not Hbf or Ostbf).
q – June 20 - July 3, Aug. 1, 2, 3 calls at Berlin Gesundbrunnen (d. 0042), not Ostbf or Hbf.

r – 0509 on ①⑦.
t – 0820 on ⑥⑦.
v – 0549 on ①⑦.
x – ②–⑦ only.
z – 0845 on †.
***** – Not July 5.
⊖ – Daily until Nov. 1; ④–⑦ from Nov. 5.

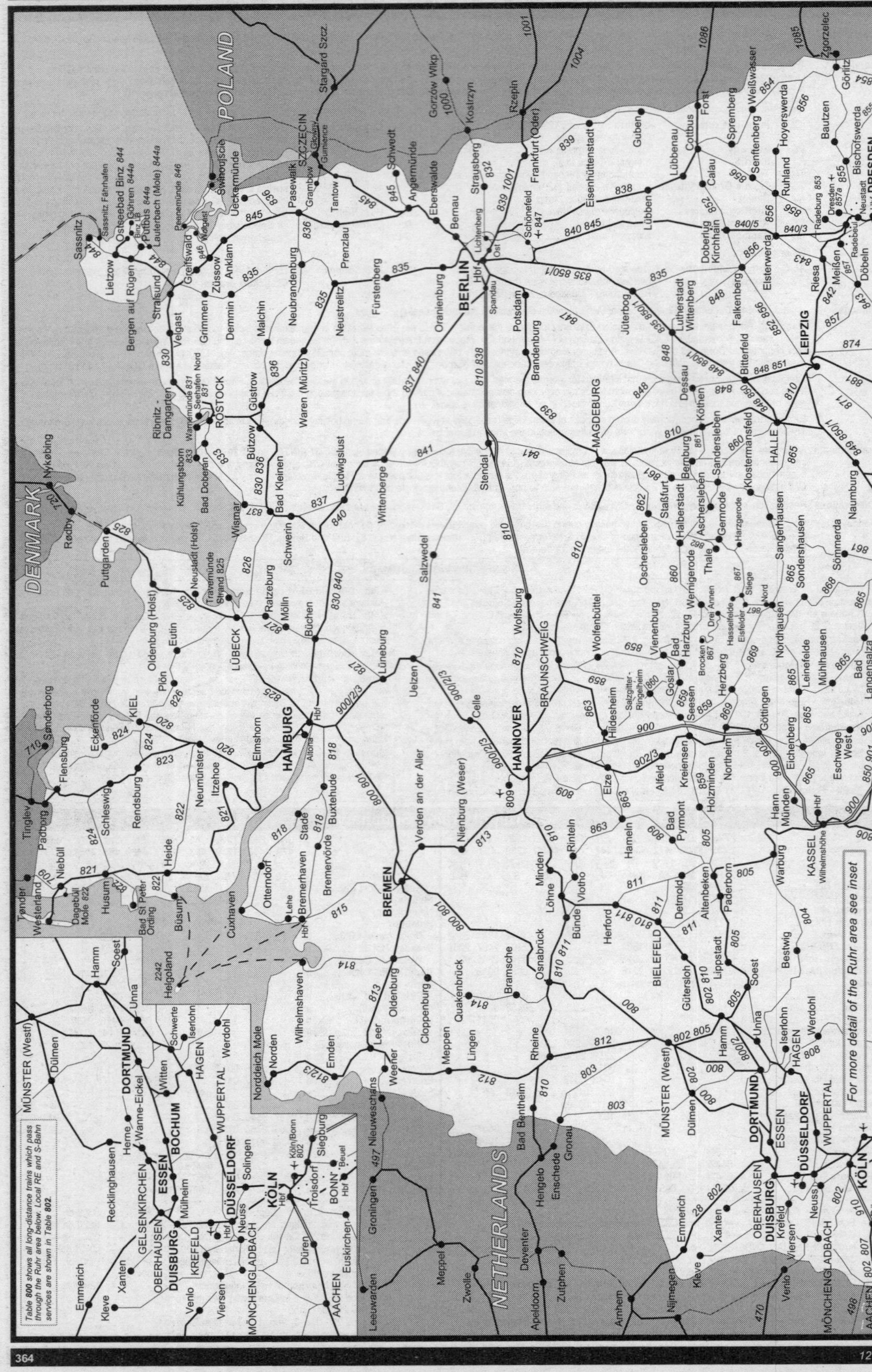
DENMARK
POLAND
NETHERLANDS
Table 800 shows all long-distance trains which pass through the Ruhr area below. Local RE and S-Bahn services are shown in Table 802.
For more detail of the Ruhr area see inset
HAMBURG
BERLIN
BREMEN
HANNOVER
LEIPZIG
DRESDEN
HALLE
MAGDEBURG
ROSTOCK
KIEL
LÜBECK
BRAUNSCHWEIG
BIELEFELD
KASSEL
DORTMUND
ESSEN
DUISBURG
DÜSSELDORF
KÖLN
BOCHUM
SZCZECIN
Flensburg
Schleswig
Rendsburg
Neumünster
Itzehoe
Elmshorn
Husum
Heide
Westerland
Niebüll
Puttgarden
Rødby
Nykøbing
Stralsund
Greifswald
Bergen auf Rügen
Sassnitz
Wismar
Schwerin
Güstrow
Neubrandenburg
Neustrelitz
Pasewalk
Angermünde
Eberswalde
Frankfurt (Oder)
Cottbus
Potsdam
Brandenburg
Stendal
Wolfsburg
Uelzen
Lüneburg
Celle
Göttingen
Hildesheim
Osnabrück
Münster (Westf)
Oldenburg
Emden
Wilhelmshaven
Bremerhaven
Cuxhaven
Helgoland
Paderborn
Hamm
Soest
Erfurt
Bitterfeld
Dessau
Lutherstadt Wittenberg
Riesa
Görlitz
Zgorzelec
Rzepin
Kostrzyn
Gorzów Wlkp
Stargard Szcz.
Świnoujście
Groningen
Leeuwarden
Zwolle
Deventer
Hengelo
Enschede
Arnhem
Nijmegen
Venlo
Aachen
Mönchengladbach
Krefeld
Wuppertal
Hagen
Bonn
Siegburg
Düren

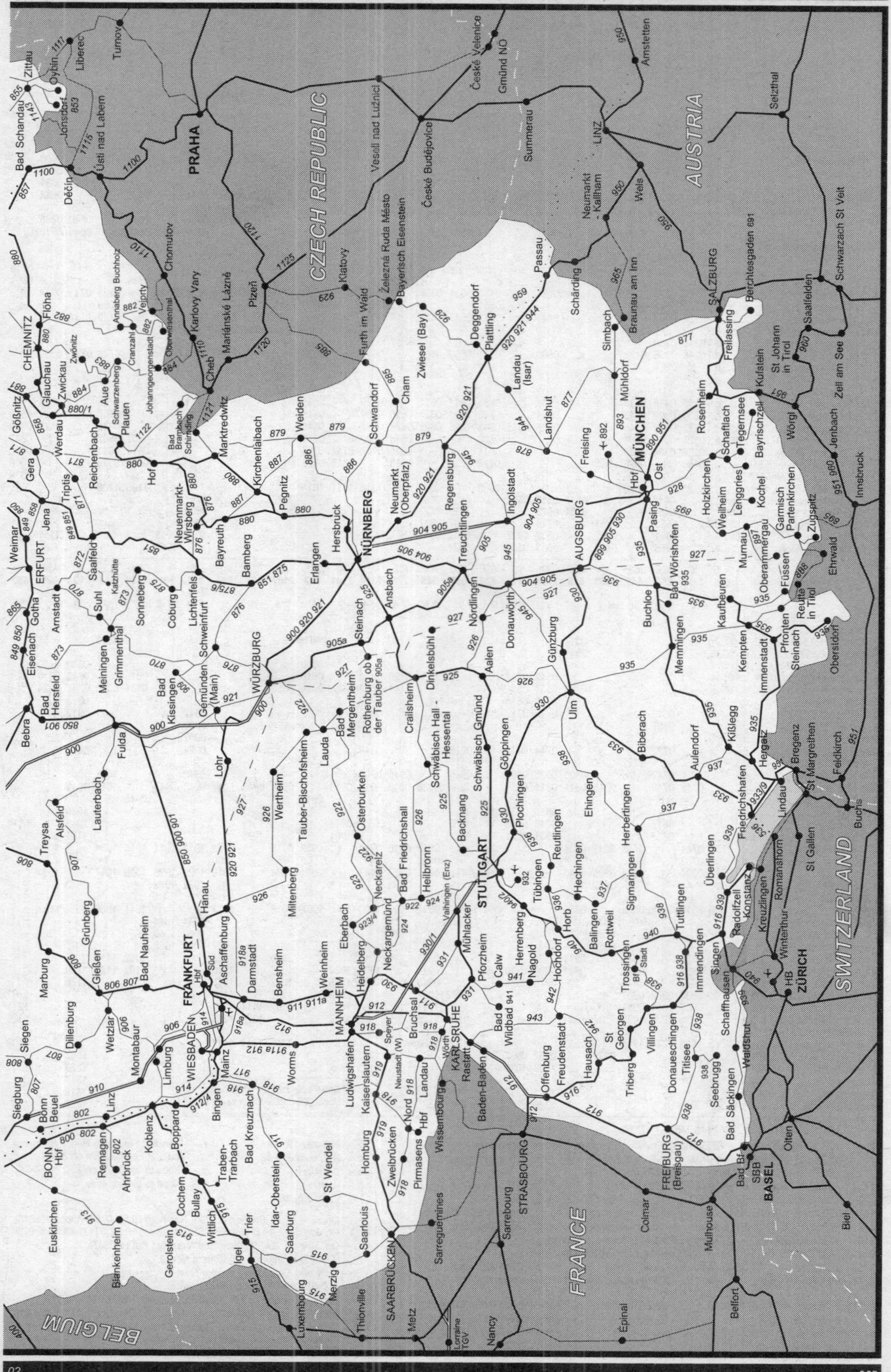
BELGIUM
FRANCE
SWITZERLAND
AUSTRIA
CZECH REPUBLIC
FRANKFURT
STUTTGART
MÜNCHEN
NÜRNBERG
WÜRZBURG
AUGSBURG
MANNHEIM
KARLSRUHE
WIESBADEN
SAARBRÜCKEN
STRASBOURG
BASEL
ZÜRICH
SALZBURG
LINZ
PRAHA
CHEMNITZ
ERFURT
BONN
Luxembourg
Trier
Koblenz
Mainz
Bingen
Bad Kreuznach
Darmstadt
Heidelberg
Heilbronn
Pforzheim
Offenburg
FREIBURG (Breisgau)
Konstanz
Lindau
Friedrichshafen
Ulm
Kempten
Memmingen
Ingolstadt
Regensburg
Passau
Landshut
Rosenheim
Kufstein
Innsbruck
Garmisch-Partenkirchen
Bamberg
Bayreuth
Hof
Plauen
Zwickau
Gera
Jena
Weimar
Gotha
Eisenach
Fulda
Gießen
Marburg
Siegen
Limburg
Koblenz
Hanau
Aschaffenburg
Schweinfurt
Coburg
Ansbach
Treuchtlingen
Donauwörth
Aalen
Tübingen
Reutlingen
Sigmaringen
Tuttlingen
Singen
Schaffhausen
Villingen
Donaueschingen
Mulhouse
Colmar
Metz
Nancy
Belfort
Épinal
Plzeň
Cheb
Karlovy Vary
Děčín
Ústí nad Labem
České Budějovice
Bad Schandau
Zittau
Liberec

800 KOBLENZ - KÖLN - DORTMUND - HAMBURG

km	See notes ▲ and ⊗	ICE 949	IC 2020	ICE 841	ICE 1020	IC 2241	IC 2128	IC 2128	ICE 541	IC 2214	IC 2314	IC 2145	IC 2355	ICE 853	ICE 843	IC 2331	CNL 40478	CNL 418	ICE 608	ICE 1095	ICE 553	ICE 543	ICE 828	IC 2212	IC 2143
		①		①	①–⑤	①–⑥	①	②–⑤	①–⑥	V		①–⑥	①	①–⑥		⊡	Q Ⓡ	Q Ⓡ		①–④	①–⑥		①–⑤		①–⑥
				✕	✕	B 🍷	🍷		✕	✕	✕♦	🍷	🍷♦	✕	✕	N 🍷	🍷♦	🍷♦	K 🍷	Ⓡ ⚡ ✕	✕	✕	🍷	✕♦	🍷
	Basel SBB 🏛 **912** d.	...	...	...	...	...	...	...	...	...	...	...	...	...	...	...	2207	...	2326		...	...	...	...	...
	Karlsruhe Hbf **912** d.	...	...	...	...	...	...	...	...	...	...	...	...	...	...	...	0011	...	0129	...	...	...	...	...	...
	München Hbf **904 930** d.	...	...	...	...	...	...	...	...	...	...	...	...	...	...	...	|	2244	|	...	...	...	...	...	...
	Stuttgart Hbf **930** d.	...	...	...	...	...	...	...	...	...	...	...	...	...	...	...	|	0126b	|	...	...	...	...	...	...
	Nürnberg Hbf **920** d.	...	...	...	...	...	...	...	...	...	...	...	...	...	...	...	|	|	|	...	...	...	...	...	...
	Frankfurt (Main) Hbf **910/2** d.	...	2314	...	...	...	...	...	...	...	...	...	...	...	...	...	|	|	0315	...	...	...	0510	...	...
	Frankfurt Flughafen ✈ § d.	...	2328	...	...	...	...	...	...	...	...	...	...	...	...	...	|	|	0346r	...	...	...	0524	...	...
	Mainz Hbf **912** d.	...	2347	...	...	...	...	...	...	...	...	...	...	...	...	...	|	|	0408	...	...	...	|	...	...
0	**Koblenz** Hbf d.	...	0047	...	...	...	...	...	...	...	...	...	...	...	...	...	0445s	0445s	0503	...	0547	...	|	0606	...
18	Andernach d.	...	0059	...	...	...	...	...	...	...	...	...	...	...	...	...	|	|	|	...	|	...	|	0619	...
39	Remagen d.	...	0111	...	...	...	...	...	...	...	...	...	...	...	...	...	|	|	|	...	|	...	|	0631	...
59	**Bonn** Hbf d.	...	0125	...	...	...	...	...	...	...	...	...	...	...	...	...	0521s	0521s	0544	...	0625	...	|	0644	...
	Köln/Bonn Flughafen ✈ d.	...	|	...	...	...	...	...	...	...	...	...	...	...	...	...	|	|	|	...	|	...	0629	|	...
93	**Köln** Hbf a.	...	0148	...	...	...	...	...	...	...	...	...	...	...	...	...	0545s	0545s	0605	...	0646	...	0640	0705	...
93	**Köln** Hbf d.	0151	0210	0329	...	...	0411	...	0429	0511	0511	0513	...	0549	0529	0542	|	|	0609	0616	0649	0626	0645	0710	0711
94	**Köln** Messe/Deutz d.	|	|	|	...	...	|	...	|	|	|	|	...	|	|	|	|	|	|	|	|	|	|	|	|
	Solingen Hbf d.	|	|	|	...	...	|	...	|	|	|	0531	...	|	|	|	|	|	|	|	|	|	|	|	0731
	Wuppertal Hbf d.	|	|	|	...	...	|	...	|	|	|	0543	...	0617	|	|	|	|	|	|	0717	|	|	|	0743
	Hagen Hbf d.	|	|	|	...	...	|	...	|	|	|	0601	...	0635	|	|	|	|	|	|	0735	|	|	|	0801
133	**Düsseldorf** Hbf d.	0215	0234	0353	...	...	0434	...	0453	0534	0534	|	0546	|	0553	0605	0613s	0613s	0633	0639u	|	0653	0711	0734	|
140	Düsseldorf Flughafen ✈ d.	0222	0241	0400	...	...	|	...	0501	|	|	|	0553	|	0600	0613	|	|	|	|	|	0700	|	|	|
157	**Duisburg** Hbf d.	0232	0252	0410	...	...	0447	...	0511	0547	0547	|	0604	|	0610	0624	0628s	0628s	0646	0651u	|	0710	0724	0747	|
165	Oberhausen Hbf d.	|	|	|	...	...	|	...	|	|	|	|	|	|	|	0632	0637	0637	|	|	|	|	|	|	|
167	Mülheim (Ruhr) Hbf d.	0240	0300	|	...	...	|	...	|	|	|	|	|	|	|	|	...	...	|	|	|	|	|	|	|
176	**Essen** Hbf d.	0248	0308	0423	...	...	0500	...	0524	0600	0600	|	0618	|	0623	|	...	...	0700	0703u	|	0723	0735j	0800	|
	Gelsenkirchen Hbf d.	|	|	|	...	...	|	...	|	|	|	|	|	|	|	0644	...	...	|	|	|	|	...	|	|
	Wanne-Eickel Hbf d.	|	|	|	...	...	|	...	|	|	|	|	|	|	|	0650	...	...	|	|	|	|	...	|	|
	Recklinghausen Hbf d.	|	|	|	...	...	|	...	|	|	|	|	|	|	|	0658	...	...	|	|	|	|	...	|	|
192	Bochum Hbf d.	0259	0318	0435	...	...	0511	...	0535	0611	0611	|	0629	|	0635	|	...	...	0711	|	|	0735	...	0811	|
210	**Dortmund** Hbf a.	0309	0329	0445	...	...	0521	...	0546	0621	0621	0620	0639	|	0646	|	...	...	0721	|	|	0746	...	0821	0820
210	**Dortmund** Hbf **805** d.	0312	0332	0448	...	...	0525	0525	0548	0625	0625	0628	0642	|	0648	|	...	...	0725	|	|	0748	...	0825	0828
	Hamm (Westf) **805** a.	0328	0352	0504	...	...	|	|	0606	|	|	0643	0702	0702	0707	|	...	...	|	|	0802	0807	...	|	0843
	Hamm (Westf) d.	0330	0354	0506	...	...	|	|	0611	|	|	0645	0707	0711	0711	|	...	...	|	|	0811	0811	...	|	0845
	Hannover Hbf **810** a.	0458	|	0628	...	...	|	|	0728	|	|	0818	|	0828	0828	|	...	...	|	|	0928	0928	...	|	1018
	Leipzig Hbf **810** a.	|	|	|	...	...	|	|	|	|	|	1119	|	|	|	|	...	...	|	|	|	|	...	|	1319
	Berlin Hbf ▲ **810** a.	0655	|	0820	...	...	|	|	0909	|	|	...	1316	1011	1011	|	...	...	|	|	1108	1108	...	|	...
266	Münster (Westf) Hbf **801** d.	...	0417	...	...	0538	0557	0557	...	0657	0657	...	...	...	...	0727	...	...	0757	|	...	...	...	0857	...
316	Osnabrück Hbf **801** d.	...	0453	...	...	0601	0623	0623	...	0723	0723	...	...	...	...	...	...	...	0823	|	...	...	...	0923	...
438	**Bremen** Hbf **801** d.	...	0555*	...	0717	...	0724	0724	...	0817	0817	...	...	...	...	...	...	...	0917	|	...	...	...	1017	...
553	**Hamburg** Hbf **801** a.	...	0651*	...	0812	...	0832	0832	...	0912	0912	...	...	...	...	...	...	...	1012	0945	...	...	...	1111	...
560	**Hamburg** Altona a.	...	0705*	...	0826	...	0853	0853	...	0927	...	...	...	...	...	...	...	...	...	0959	...	...	...	...	...

See notes ▲ and ⊗	ICE 826	IC 2357	ICE 855	ICE 845	IC 2333	ICE 616	IC 2320	IC 2120	ICE 824	ICE 555	ICE 545	ICE 226	IC 2310	IC 2141	ICE 822	IC 2157	ICE 857	ICE 847	IC 331	IC 331	ICE 1124	ICE 614	IC 2028	ICE 820	ICE 557
		①–⑥			⊖	◇	V		①–⑤						①–⑥				①–⑥		⑦			①–⑤	
	🍷	🍷	T ✕	✕	N 🍷	🍷	✕	✕♦	D 🍷	✕	A ✕	🍷♦	✕♦	🍷	🍷	🍷♦	✕	✕	🍷♦	🍷♦	🍷	🍷	🍷	🍷	✕
Basel SBB 🏛 **912** d.	...	...	...	...	...	...	...	...	...	...	...	...	...	...	...	...	...	...	...	...	...	...	...	...	...
Karlsruhe Hbf **912** d.	...	...	...	...	...	...	...	...	...	...	...	...	...	...	...	...	...	...	...	...	...	...	...	...	...
München Hbf **904 930** d.	0032g	...	...	...	...	0317	...	...	...	...	...	...	...	...	0451g	...	...	...	...	...	...	0523	...	0551	...
Stuttgart Hbf **930** d.	0305	...	...	...	...	0551	...	...	...	...	...	...	...	...	|	...	...	...	...	...	...	0751	...	|	...
Nürnberg Hbf **920** d.	|	...	...	...	...	|	...	...	...	...	...	...	...	...	0600	...	...	...	...	...	...	|	0530	0700	...
Frankfurt (Main) Hbf **910/2** d.	0544	...	...	...	...	|	0542	0542	0702	...	...	0729	0638	...	0810	...	...	...	...	...	0816	|	0742	0910	...
Frankfurt Flughafen ✈ § d.	0607	...	...	...	...	0709	0557	0557	0714	...	...	0743	0657	...	0824	...	...	...	...	...	0831	0909	0757	0924	...
Mainz Hbf **912** d.	|	...	...	...	...	|	0618	0618	|	...	...	|	0717	...	|	...	...	...	...	...	|	|	0820	|	...
Koblenz Hbf d.	|	...	0643	...	...	|	0712	0712	|	...	...	|	0812	...	|	...	...	...	0842	...	|	|	0912	|	...
Andernach d.	|	...	0657	...	...	|	|	|	|	...	...	|	|	...	|	...	...	...	0855	...	|	|	|	|	...
Remagen d.	|	...	|	...	...	|	|	|	|	...	...	|	|	...	|	...	...	...	0907	...	|	|	|	|	...
Bonn Hbf d.	|	...	0722	...	...	|	0744	0744	|	0825e	...	|	0844	...	|	...	...	...	0921	...	|	|	0944	|	...
Köln/Bonn Flughafen ✈ d.	|	...	|	0712	...	|	|	|	|	|	...	|	|	...	|	...	...	...	|	...	|	|	|	|	...
Köln Hbf a.	|	...	0742	|	...	0805	0805	0805	|	0846e	...	0840	0905	...	|	...	...	...	0942	...	|	1005	1005	|	...
Köln Hbf d.	|	0715	0749	|	0748	0811	0811	0811	|	0849	0828	0848	0911	0913	|	0905	0949	...	0948	0948	|	1011	1011	|	1049
Köln Messe/Deutz d.	0717	|	|	0730	|	|	|	|	0824	|	|	|	|	|	0917	|	|	...	|	|	0945	|	|	1017	|
Solingen Hbf d.	|	|	|	|	|	|	0830	0830	|	|	|	|	|	0931	|	|	|	...	|	|	|	|	1030	|	|
Wuppertal Hbf d.	|	|	0817	|	|	|	0843	0843	|	0917	|	|	|	0943	|	|	1017	...	|	|	|	|	1043	|	1117
Hagen Hbf d.	|	|	0835	|	|	|	0901	0901	|	0935	|	|	|	1001	|	|	1035	...	|	|	|	|	1101	|	1135
Düsseldorf Hbf d.	0739	0746	|	0753	0811	0834	|	|	0846	|	0853	0915	0934	|	0939	0946	|	0953	1011	1011	1016	1034	|	1039	|
Düsseldorf Flughafen ✈ d.	|	0753	|	0800	|	|	|	|	0853	|	0900	|	|	|	|	0953	|	1000	|	|	|	|	|	|	|
Duisburg Hbf d.	0751	0804	|	0810	0825	0847	|	|	0905	|	0910	0927	0947	|	0951	1004	|	1010	1025	1025	1029	1047	|	1051	|
Oberhausen Hbf d.	|	|	|	|	0832	|	|	|	|	|	|	0933	|	|	|	|	|	|	1032	1032	|	|	|	|	|
Mülheim (Ruhr) Hbf d.	|	|	|	|	|	|	|	|	|	|	|	...	|	|	|	|	|	|	|	|	|	|	|	|	|
Essen Hbf d.	0804j	0818	|	0823	|	0859	|	|	0917j	|	0923	...	1000	|	1002j	1018	|	1023	|	|	1041	1059	|	1102j	|
Gelsenkirchen Hbf d.	|	|	|	|	0844	|	|	|	...	|	|	...	|	|	...	|	|	|	1044	1044	|	|	|	...	|
Wanne-Eickel Hbf d.	|	|	|	|	0850	|	|	|	...	|	|	...	|	|	...	|	|	|	1050	1050	|	|	|	...	|
Recklinghausen Hbf d.	|	|	|	|	0858	|	|	|	...	|	|	...	|	|	...	|	|	|	1058	1058	|	|	|	...	|
Bochum Hbf d.	0816c	0829	|	0835	|	0911	|	|	...	|	0935	...	1011	|	...	1029	|	1035	|	|	1052	1111	|	...	|
Dortmund Hbf a.	0827c	0839	|	0846	|	0921	0920	0920	...	|	0946	...	1021	1020	...	1039	|	1046	|	|	1102	1121	1120	...	|
Dortmund Hbf **805** d.	...	0842	|	0848	|	...	0926	0926	...	|	0948	...	1025	1028	...	1042	|	1048	|	|	...	...	1126	...	|
Hamm (Westf) **805** a.	...	0902	0902	0907	|	...	|	|	...	1002	1007	...	|	1043	...	1102	1102	1107	|	|	...	...	|	...	1202
Hamm (Westf) d.	...	0907	0911	0911	|	...	|	|	...	1011	1011	...	|	1045	...	1107	1111	1111	|	|	...	...	|	...	1211
Hannover Hbf **810** a.	...	|	1028	1028	|	...	|	|	...	1128	1128	...	|	1218	...	|	1228	1228	|	|	...	...	|	...	1328
Leipzig Hbf **810** a.	...	|	|	|	|	...	|	|	...	|	|	...	|	1519	...	|	|	|	|	|	...	...	|	...	|
Berlin Hbf ▲ **810** a.	...	1516	1211	1211	|	...	|	|	...	1308	1308	...	|	...	...	1716	1411	1411	|	|	...	...	|	...	1508
Münster (Westf) Hbf **801** d.	...	...	...	...	0927	...	0957	0957	...	...	...	...	1057	...	...	...	...	...	1127	1127	...	...	1157	...	...
Osnabrück Hbf **801** d.	...	...	...	...	...	...	1023	1023	...	...	...	...	1123	...	...	...	...	...	...	...	...	...	1223	...	...
Bremen Hbf **801** d.	...	...	...	...	...	...	1117	1117	...	...	...	...	1217						...	...	...	...	1317	...	...
Hamburg Hbf **801** a.	...	...	...	...	...	...	1211	1212	...	...	...	...	1312						...	...	...	...	1412	...	...
Hamburg Altona a.	...	...	...	...	...	...	1226	...	...	...	...	...	...						...	...	...	...	1426	...	...

See Table ***802*** *for Rhein-Ruhr local RE and S-Bahn services*

♦ – **NOTES** (LISTED BY TRAIN NUMBER)

226 – ICE INTERNATIONAL – [12] and 🍷 Frankfurt - Arnhem - Utrecht - Amsterdam.
331 – [12] and 🍷 (Luxembourg ①–⑥ -) Köln - Münster - Emden. Runs with train number **231** and continues to Norddeich Mole on ①②③④⑥ from Oct. 26.
418 – POLLUX – 🛏 1, 2 cl., ▬ 2 cl., [2] and 🍷 München - Amsterdam.
2120 – Until Oct. 25. FEHMARN – [12] and ✕ Frankfurt - Lübeck - Puttgarden.
2157 – [12] and 🍷 Köln - Kassel - Erfurt - Halle - Berlin (- Stralsund ⑧). Train number **2257** on ⑥.
2212 – RÜGEN – [12] and ✕ Koblenz - Hamburg - Rostock - Stralsund - Ostseebad Binz.
2310 – NORDFRIESLAND – [12] and ✕ Frankfurt - Köln - Westerland.
2314 – Until Oct. 25. DEICHGRAF – [12] and ✕ Köln - Westerland.
2355 – STRELASUND – [12] Düsseldorf - Kassel - Erfurt - Halle - Berlin - Ostseebad Binz.
40478 – PEGASUS – 🛏 1, 2 cl., ▬ 2 cl., [2] (reclining) and 🍷 Zürich - Amsterdam.

A – From Aachen Hbf (d. 0740), Düren (d. 0758) on ①–⑥.
B – To Berlin (Table **810**).
D – From Darmstadt Hbf (d. 0637).
K – To Kiel (Table **820**).

N – To Norddeich Mole (Table **812**).
Q – Daily until Nov. 1; ④–⑦ from Nov. 5.
T – From Trier (Table **915**). ✕ from Köln.
V – From Oct. 26.

b – Not July 10 - Oct. 5.
c – ⑥⑦ from July 18.
e – ①–⑥ only.
g – ① only.
j – From July 18.

r – Frankfurt Flughafen Regionalbahnhof (calls at Fernbahnhof on July 4).
s – Stops to set down only.
u – Stops to pick up only.

* – On June 14, 21 Bremen d. 0703, Hamburg Hbf a. 0756, Altona a. 0816. On July 5, 12, 19 Bremen d. 0652, Hamburg Hbf a. 0743, Altona a. 0756.
◇ – On June 21, July 5 starts from Augsburg Hbf (d. 0357).
⊡ – ①④⑤⑥⑦ until Oct. 26; ① from Nov. 2.
⊖ – Daily until Oct. 31; ①–⑥ from Nov. 2.
⚡ – *ICE* ***SPRINTER***. Supplement payable.
§ – Frankfurt Flughafen Fernbahnhof. See also Tables **910** and **912**.
▲ – Berlin timings are subject to alteration June 20 - July 3. See Table **810**.
⊗ – Timings Köln - Düsseldorf - Dortmund are subject to alteration July 18 – 26 (certain trains do not call at Bochum). Koblenz - Köln timings also subject to change on July 19 (trains do not call at Andernach, Remagen or Bonn).

KOBLENZ - KÖLN - DORTMUND - HAMBURG 800

See notes ▲ and ⊠	ICE	ICE	IC	IC	ICE	IC	IC	IC	IC	ICE	ICE	IC	ICE	ICE	ICE	ICE	ICE	ICE	ICE	IC	ICE	IC	IC	ICE	ICE
	547	547	1118	1112	128	1112	2116	2049	2359	859	849	333	612	1126	1026	726	559	549	126	2114	600	2047	2151	951	941
	①–⑤		①–④	⑤		⑤			⑤⑦					①⑦	②–⑥	①–⑥			E		⑥	Ⓑ			
	✕	✕	¶	🍷	A🍷	🍷	✕♦	🍷	🍷♦	✕	✕	🍷♦	🍷	✕♦	✕♦	🍷	✕	✕	A🍷	✕	🍷	🍷	🍷	✕	✕
Basel SBB 🏛 **912** d.	...	...	...	...	...	...	...	...	...	...	...	...	...	...	...	...	...	...	...	...	...	...	...	...	...
Karlsruhe Hbf **912** d.	...	...	...	...	...	...	...	...	...	...	...	...	...	...	...	...	...	...	...	...	1107	...	...	...	...
München Hbf **904 930** d.	...	...	...	...	...	...	...	...	...	...	...	...	0723	0614g	...	0755	...	...	...	...	|	...	...	...	...
Stuttgart Hbf **930** d.	...	...	0714	0714	...	...	0737	...	...	...	...	...	0951	|	...	|	...	...	...	0937	|	...	...	...	...
Nürnberg Hbf **920** d.	...	...	|	|	...	...	|	...	...	...	...	...	|	0729g	0729	0900	...	...	...	|	|	...	...	...	...
Frankfurt (Main) Hbf **910/2** d.	...	...	|	|	0928	...	|	...	...	...	...	...	|	0942	0942	1110	...	...	1128	|	|	...	...	...	...
Frankfurt Flughafen ✈ § d.	...	...	|	|	0943	...	|	...	...	...	...	...	1109	0957	0957	1124	...	...	1143	|	1209	...	...	...	...
Mainz Hbf **912** d.	...	...	0848p	0848p	|	...	0920y	...	...	...	...	...	|	1020	1020	|	...	...	|	1120y	|	...	...	...	...
Koblenz Hbf d.	...	...	0943y	0943y	|	...	1012	...	...	...	...	1042	|	1112	1112	|	...	...	|	1212	|	...	...	...	...
Andernach d.	...	...	0956y	0956y	|	...	|	...	...	...	...	1055	|	|	|	|	...	...	|	|	|	...	...	...	...
Remagen d.	...	...	|	|	|	...	|	...	...	...	...	1107	|	|	|	|	...	...	|	|	|	...	...	...	...
Bonn Hbf d.	...	...	1022	1022	|	...	1044	...	...	...	...	1121	|	1144	1144	|	1223e	...	|	1244	|	...	...	...	...
Köln/Bonn Flughafen ✈ d.	1012	...	|	|	|	...	|	...	...	...	...	|	|	|	|	|	|	1212	|	|	|	...	...	...	...
Köln Hbf a.	|	...	1042	1042	1040	...	1105	...	...	...	...	1142	1205	1205	1205	|	1242e	|	1240	1305	1305	...	...	...	...
Köln Hbf d.	|	...	1045	1045	1048	...	1111	1113	1120	1149	...	1148	1211	1211	1211	|	1249	|	1248	1311	1311	1313	...	1349	...
Köln Messe/Deutz d.	1030	...	|	|	|	...	|	|	|	|	...	|	|	|	|	1217	|	1230	|	|	|	|	...	|	...
Solingen Hbf d.	|	...	|	|	|	...	|	1131	|	|	...	|	|	|	|	|	|	|	|	|	1331	1331	...	|	...
Wuppertal Hbf d.	|	...	|	|	|	...	|	1143	|	1217	...	|	|	1243	1243	|	1317	|	|	|	1343	1343	...	1417	...
Hagen Hbf d.	|	...	|	|	|	←	|	1201	|	1235	...	|	|	1301	1301	|	1335	|	|	|	1401	1401	...	1435	...
Düsseldorf Hbf d.	1053	1053	1106	1106	1114	1117	1134	|	1146	|	1153	1211	1234	|	|	1239	|	1253	1314	1334	|	|	1346	|	1353
Düsseldorf Flughafen ✈ d.	1100	1100	...	→	|	|	|	|	1153	|	1200	|	|	|	|	|	|	1300	|	|	|	|	1353	|	1400
Duisburg Hbf d.	1110	1110	...	...	1126	1131	1147	|	1204	|	1210	1225	1247	|	|	1251	|	1310	1328	1347	|	|	1404	|	1410
Oberhausen Hbf d.	|	|	...	...	1133	|	|	|	|	|	|	1232	|	|	|	|	|	|	1333	|	|	|	|	|	|
Mülheim (Ruhr) Hbf d.	|	|	...	...	...	1138	|	|	|	|	|	|	|	|	|	|	|	|	...	|	|	|	|	|	|
Essen Hbf d.	1123	1123	...	...	...	1146	1200	|	1218	|	1223	|	1259	|	|	1304t	|	1323	...	1400	|	|	1418	|	1423
Gelsenkirchen Hbf d.	|	|	...	...	...	|	|	|	|	|	|	1244	|	|	|	|	|	|	...	|	|	|	|	|	|
Wanne-Eickel Hbf d.	|	|	...	...	...	|	|	|	|	|	|	1250	|	|	|	|	|	|	...	|	|	|	|	|	|
Recklinghausen Hbf d.	|	|	...	...	...	|	|	|	|	|	|	1258	|	|	|	|	|	|	...	|	|	|	|	|	|
Bochum Hbf d.	1135	1135	...	...	...	1157	1211	|	1229	|	1235	|	1311	|	|	1316r	|	1335	...	1411	|	|	1429	|	1435
Dortmund Hbf a.	1146	1146	...	...	...	1208	1221	1220	1239	|	1246	|	1321	1320	1320	1330r	|	1346	...	1421	1420	1420	1439	|	1446
Dortmund Hbf **805** d.	1148	1148	...	...	...	1210	1225	1228	1242	|	1248	|	...	1326	1326	...	|	1348	...	1425	...	1428	1442	|	1448
Hamm (Westf) **805** a.	1207	1207	...	...	...	1232	|	1243	1302	1302	1307	|	...	|	|	...	1402	1407	...	|	...	1443	1502	1502	1507
Hamm (Westf) d.	1211	1211	...	...	...	1234	|	1245	1307	1311	1311	|	...	|	|	...	1411	1411	...	|	...	1445	1507	1511	1511
Hannover Hbf **810** a.	1328	1328	...	...	...	1359	|	1418	|	1428	1428	|	...	|	|	...	1528	1528	...	|	...	1618	|	1628	1628
Leipzig Hbf **810** a.	|	|	...	...	...	|	|	1719	|	|	|	|	...	|	|	...	|	|	...	|	...	1919	|	|	|
Berlin Hbf ▲ **810** a.	1508	1508	...	...	...	1551	|	...	1916	1611	1611	|	...	|	|	...	1710	1710	...	|	...	...	2116	1811	1811
Münster (Westf) Hbf **801** d.	...	...	...	...	...	...	1257	...	...	...	...	1327	...	1357	1357	...	...	...	...	1457	...	...	...	...	...
Osnabrück Hbf **801** d.	...	...	...	...	...	...	1323	...	...	...	...	...	...	1423	1423	...	...	...	...	1523	...	...	...	...	...
Bremen Hbf **801** d.	...	...	...	...	...	...	1417	...	...	...	...	...	...	1517	1517	...	...	...	...	1617	...	...	...	...	...
Hamburg Hbf **801** a.	...	...	...	...	...	...	1511	...	...	...	...	...	...	1612	1612	...	...	...	...	1712	...	...	...	...	...
Hamburg Altona a.	...	...	...	...	...	...	...	...	...	...	...	...	...	...	...	...	...	...	...	1727	...	...	...	...	...

See notes ▲ and ⊠	IC	ICE	IC	ICE	ICE	ICE	ICE	IC	IC	IC	ICE	ICE	IC	IC	ICE	ICE	IC	IC	IC	IC	ICE	IC	ICE	ICE	ICE
	335	610	2024	722	651	641	124	1920	1916	2112	1128	508	2045	2153	953	943	2014	2004	2006	1808	518	2026	628	653	643
								⑦	⑤		⑤	⑥	Ⓑ	Ⓑ	Ⓑ		①–⑤	⑦	⑥	⑦					
	🍷♦	🍷	✕♦	🍷	✕	✕	A🍷		S🍷	✕	🍷	🍷	🍷	🍷♦	✕	✕	🍷♦	🍷♦	🍷♦	♦	🍷		🍷	✕	✕
Basel SBB 🏛 **912** d.	...	...	...	...	...	...	...	...	...	...	...	1112	...	...	...	...	...	...	...	...	...	...	...	...	...
Karlsruhe Hbf **912** d.	...	...	...	...	...	...	...	...	...	...	...	1307	...	...	...	...	...	1221	1221	...	...	...	...	...	...
München Hbf **904 930** d.	...	0923	...	0955	...	...	...	...	0841	...	1055	|	...	...	...	...	...	|	|	...	1123	...	1155	...	...
Stuttgart Hbf **930** d.	...	1151	...	...	...	...	...	...	1114	1137	|	|	...	...	...	...	1209	|	|	...	1351	...	...	...	...
Nürnberg Hbf **920** d.	...	|	0928	1100	...	...	...	...	|	|	1200	|	...	...	...	...	|	|	|	...	|	...	1300	...	...
Frankfurt (Main) Hbf **910/2** d.	...	|	1144	1310	...	...	1329	1201b	|	|	1410	|	...	...	...	...	|	|	|	...	|	1344	1510	...	...
Frankfurt Flughafen ✈ § d.	...	1309	1157	1324	...	...	1343	1215b	|	|	1424	1409	...	...	...	...	|	|	|	...	1509	1357	1524	...	...
Mainz Hbf **912** d.	...	|	1220	|	...	...	|	b	1248p	1320y	|	|	...	...	...	...	1342p	1342p	1342p	...	|	1420	|	...	...
Koblenz Hbf d.	1242	|	1312	|	...	...	|	1343	1343y	1412	|	|	...	...	...	...	1442	1442	1442	...	|	1512	|	...	...
Andernach d.	1255	|	|	|	...	...	|	1356	1356y	|	|	|	...	...	...	...	1455	1455	1455	...	|	|	|	...	...
Remagen d.	1307	|	|	|	...	...	|	1408	1408y	|	|	|	...	...	...	...	1507	1507	1507	...	|	|	|	...	...
Bonn Hbf d.	1321	|	1344	|	1425	...	|	1422	1422y	1444	|	|	...	...	...	...	1521	1521	1521	...	|	1544	|	...	...
Köln/Bonn Flughafen ✈ d.	|	|	|	|	|	...	|	|	|	|	|	|	...	...	...	...	|	|	|	...	|	|	|	...	1612
Köln Hbf a.	1342	1405	1405	|	1446	...	1440	1442	1443	1505	|	1505	...	...	...	...	1542	1542	1542	...	1605	1605	|	...	|
Köln Hbf d.	1348	1411	1411	|	1449	...	1448	1445	1445	1511	|	1511	1513	...	1549	...	1548	1548	1548	1539	1611	1611	|	1649	|
Köln Messe/Deutz d.	|	|	|	1417	|	...	|	|	|	|	1517	|	|	...	|	...	|	|	|	|	|	|	1617	|	1630
Solingen Hbf d.	|	|	1430	|	|	...	|	|	|	|	|	1531	1531	...	|	...	|	|	|	|	|	1630	|	|	|
Wuppertal Hbf d.	|	|	1443	|	1517	...	|	|	|	|	|	1543	1543	...	1617	...	|	|	|	|	|	1643	|	1717	|
Hagen Hbf d.	|	|	1501	|	1535	...	|	|	|	|	|	1601	1601	...	1635	...	|	|	|	|	|	1701	|	1735	|
Düsseldorf Hbf d.	1411	1434	|	1439	|	1453	1514	1518	1518	1534	1540	|	|	1546	|	1553	1611	1611	1611	1617	1634	|	1639	|	1653
Düsseldorf Flughafen ✈ d.	|	|	|	|	|	1500	|	|	|	|	|	|	|	1553	|	1600	|	|	|	|	|	|	|	|	1700
Duisburg Hbf d.	1425	1447	|	1451	|	1510	1528	1532	1532	1547	1552	|	|	1604	|	1610	1625	1625	1625	1630	1647	|	1651	|	1710
Oberhausen Hbf d.	1432	|	|	|	|	|	1533	|	|	|	|	|	|	|	|	|	1632	1632	|	|	|	|	|	|	|
Mülheim (Ruhr) Hbf d.	|	|	|	|	|	|	...	|	|	|	|	|	|	|	|	|	|	|	1633	|	|	|	|	|	|
Essen Hbf d.	|	1459	|	1502j	|	1523	...	1544	1544	1600	1603j	|	|	1618	|	1623	|	|	1641	1643	1659	|	1702j	|	1723
Gelsenkirchen Hbf d.	1444	|	|	...	|	|	...	|	|	|	...	|	|	|	|	|	1644	1644	|	|	|	|	...	|	|
Wanne-Eickel Hbf d.	1450	|	|	...	|	|	...	|	|	|	...	|	|	|	|	|	1650	1650	|	|	|	|	...	|	|
Recklinghausen Hbf d.	1458	|	|	...	|	|	...	|	|	|	...	|	|	|	|	|	1658	1658	|	|	|	|	...	|	|
Bochum Hbf d.	|	1511	|	...	|	1535	...	1555	1555	1611	...	|	|	1629	|	1635	|	|	1652	|	1711	|	...	|	1735
Dortmund Hbf a.	|	1521	1520	...	|	1546	...	1605	1605	1621	...	1620	1620	1639	|	1646	|	|	1703	1700	1721	1720	...	|	1746
Dortmund Hbf **805** d.	|	...	1526	...	|	1548	...	1608	1608	1625	...	...	1628	1642	|	1648	|	|	...	1702	...	1726	...	|	1748
Hamm (Westf) **805** a.	|	...	|	...	1602	1607	...	1628	1632	|	...	...	1643	1702	1702	1707	|	|	...	|	...	|	...	1802	1807
Hamm (Westf) d.	|	...	|	...	1611	1611	...	1631	1634	|	...	...	1645	...	1711	1711	|	|	...	|	...	|	...	1811	1811
Hannover Hbf **810** a.	|	...	|	...	1728	1728	...	1758	1758	|	...	...	1818	...	1828	1828	|	|	...	|	...	|	...	1928	1928
Leipzig Hbf **810** a.	|	...	|	...	|	|	...	|	|	|	...	...	2119	...	|	|	|	|	...	|	...	|	...	...	|
Berlin Hbf ▲ **810** a.	|	...	|	...	1908	1908	...	1951	1955	|	...	...	...	...	2011	2011	|	|	...	|	...	|	...	2108	2108
Münster (Westf) Hbf **801** d.	1527	...	1557	...	...	...	...	...	...	1657	...	...	...	...	...	...	1727	1727	...	1738	...	1757	...	...	...
Osnabrück Hbf **801** d.	...	...	1623	...	...	...	...	...	...	1723	...	...	...	...	...	...	...	...	...	1813	...	1823	...	...	...
Bremen Hbf **801** d.	...	...	1717	...	...	...	...	...	...	1817	...								...	1907	...	1917	...	...	...
Hamburg Hbf **801** a.	...	...	1812	...	...	...	...	...	...	1912	...								...	2006	...	2012	...	...	...
Hamburg Altona a.	...	...	1826	...	...	...	...	...	...	1927	...								...	...	...	2026	...	...	...

*See Table **802** for Rhein-Ruhr local RE and S-Bahn services*

♦ – **NOTES** (LISTED BY TRAIN NUMBER)

333/5 – [12] and 🍷 Luxembourg - Koblenz - Emden - Norddeich Mole.
1026 – [12] and ✕ Regensburg - Frankfurt - Köln - Kiel.
1126 – [12] and ✕ (München ① -) Frankfurt - Köln - Kiel.
1808 – [12] Köln - Hamburg - Westerland.
2004 – BODENSEE – [12] and 🍷 Konstanz - Mannheim - Emden.
2006 – BODENSEE – [12] and 🍷 Konstanz - Mannheim - Dortmund.
2014 – [12] and 🍷 Stuttgart - Mannheim - Emden.
2024 – [12] and ✕ Passau - Regensburg - Frankfurt - Köln - Hamburg.
2116 – [12] and ✕ Stuttgart - Heidelberg - Köln - Hamburg - Stralsund (- Greifswald ①–⑤).
2153 – [12] and 🍷 Düsseldorf - Kassel - Erfurt - Halle.
2359 – [12] and 🍷 Köln - Kassel - Erfurt - Halle - Berlin - Stralsund.

A – To Amsterdam (Table **28**).
E – Until Oct. 25.
S – From Salzburg (Table **890**).

b – From Aug. 30 departs Frankfurt (Main) Hbf 1215, Frankfurt Flughafen 1228 and calls additionally at Mainz Hbf (d. 1248).
e – ①–⑥ only.
g – ① only.
j – From July 18.
p – From Aug. 24.
r – ⑥ only.
t – ⑥ until July 11; ①–⑥ from July 18.
y – 2–6 minutes later until Aug. 23.

¶ – Train number **1918** on ③. Conveys 🍷 on ①.
§ – Frankfurt Flughafen Fernbahnhof. See also Tables **910** and **912**.
▲ – Berlin timings are subject to alteration June 20 - July 3. See Table **810**.
⊠ – Timings Köln - Düsseldorf - Dortmund are subject to alteration July 18 – 26 (certain trains do not call at Bochum). Koblenz - Köln timings also subject to change on July 19 (trains do not call at Andernach, Remagen or Bonn).

800 KOBLENZ - KÖLN - DORTMUND - HAMBURG

See notes ▲ and ⊠	IC 2012	ICE 506	EC 100	EC 102	IC 2012	IC 2155	ICE 122	ICE 955	ICE 945	IC 337	ICE 516	IC 2022	ICE 624	ICE 655	ICE 645	IC 118	ICE 914	EC 6	IC 2041	ICE 606	ICE 104	ICE 622	ICE 957	ICE 947	EC 114
			①–⑥	⑦		⑦		Ⓑ									①–⑤		⑦	①–⑥			Ⓑ		
	🍷♦	🍷	✕♦	✕♦	🍷♦	🍷♦	A🍷	✕	✕	🍷♦	🍷	🍷	🍷	✕	✕	🍷♦	🍷	✕♦	🍷	🍷	🍷♦	🍷	✕	✕	✕♦
Basel SBB 🚌 912 d.	...	...	1218	1218	...	...	...	...	...	...	...	...	...	...	...	...	...	1418	...	...	1512	...	...	...	...
Karlsruhe Hbf 912 d.	...	1507	1412	1412	...	...	...	...	...	...	...	...	...	...	...	...	...	1612	...	...	1707	...	...	...	...
München Hbf 904 930 d.	...	|	|	|	...	...	...	...	...	...	1323	...	1355	...	...	...	...	|	...	...	|	1455	...	...	1340
Stuttgart Hbf 930 d.	1314	|	|	|	...	...	...	...	...	...	1551	...	|	...	...	1512	...	|	...	...	|	|	...	...	1610t
Nürnberg Hbf 920 d.	|	|	|	|	...	...	...	...	...	...	|	...	1500	...	...	|	...	|	...	...	|	1600	...	...	|
Frankfurt (Main) Hbf 910/2 d.	|	|	|	|	...	...	1629	...	...	...	|	1542	1710	...	...	|	1717	|	...	...	|	1810	...	...	|
Frankfurt Flughafen ✈ § d.	|	1609	|	|	...	...	1643	...	...	...	1709	1557	1724	...	...	|	1732	|	...	...	1809	1824	...	...	|
Mainz Hbf 912 d.	1448z	|	1520z	1520z	...	...	|	...	...	...	|	1620	|	...	...	1648	|	1720z	...	...	|	|	...	...	1742y
Koblenz Hbf d.	1543	|	1612	1612	...	...	|	...	...	1642	|	1712	|	...	...	1743	|	1812	...	...	|	|	...	...	1843
Andernach d.	1556	|	|	|	...	...	|	...	...	1655	|	|	|	...	...	1756	|	|	...	...	|	|	...	...	1856
Remagen d.	1608	|	|	|	...	...	|	...	...	1707	|	|	|	...	...	1808	|	|	...	...	|	|	...	...	1908
Bonn Hbf d.	1622	|	1644	1644	...	...	|	...	...	1721	|	1744	|	...	...	1822	|	1844	...	...	|	|	...	...	1922
Köln/Bonn Flughafen ✈ d.	|	|	|	|	...	...	|	...	...	|	|	|	|	...	1812b	|	|	|	...	...	|	|	...	...	|
Köln Hbf a.	1642	1705	1705	1705	...	...	1740	...	...	1742	1805	1805	|	...	|	1842	|	1905	...	...	1905	|	...	...	1942
Köln Hbf d.	1648	1711	1711	1711	...	...	1748	1749	...	1745	1811	1811	|	1849	|	1845	|	1911	1913	1913	1917	|	1949	...	1948
Köln Messe/Deutz d.	|	|	|	|	...	...	|	|	...	|	|	|	1817	|	1830b	|	1852	|	|	|	|	1922	|	...	|
Solingen Hbf d.	|	1731	|	|	...	...	|	|	...	|	1829	|	|	|	|	|	|	|	1931	1931	|	|	|	...	|
Wuppertal Hbf d.	|	1743	|	|	...	...	|	1817	...	|	1843	|	|	1917	|	|	|	|	1943	1944	|	|	2017	...	|
Hagen Hbf d.	|	1801	|	|	...	...	|	1835	...	|	1901	|	|	1935	|	|	|	|	2001	2002	|	|	2035	...	|
Düsseldorf Hbf d.	1714	|	1734	1734	...	1746	1813	|	1753	1816c	|	1834	1839	|	1853	1913	1917	1934	|	|	1940	1944	|	1953	2012
Düsseldorf Flughafen ✈ d.	|	|	|	|	...	1753	|	|	1800	|	|	|	|	|	1900	|	|	|	|	|	|	|	|	2000	|
Duisburg Hbf d.	1727	|	1747	1747	...	1804	1826	|	1810	1829	|	1847	1851	|	1910	1926	1930	1947	|	|	1953	1957	|	2010	2025
Oberhausen Hbf d.	|	|	|	|	...	|	1833	|	|	1836	|	|	|	|	|	|	|	|	|	|	1958	|	|	|	|
Mülheim (Ruhr) Hbf d.	1734h	|	|	|	...	|	...	|	|	|	|	|	|	|	|	|	|	|	|	|	...	|	|	|	2033
Essen Hbf d.	1740	|	1800	1800	...	1818	...	|	1823	|	|	1900	1904	|	1923	1938	1942	2000	|	|	...	2010	|	2023	2041
Gelsenkirchen Hbf d.	|	|	|	|	...	|	...	|	|	1848	|	|	|	|	|	1948	|	|	|	|	...	|	|	|	|
Wanne-Eickel Hbf d.	|	|	|	|	...	|	...	|	|	|	|	|	|	|	|	|	|	|	|	|	...	|	|	|	|
Recklinghausen Hbf d.	|	|	|	|	...	|	...	|	|	1859	|	|	|	|	|	1959	|	|	|	|	...	|	|	|	|
Bochum Hbf d.	1753	|	1811	1811	...	1829	...	|	1835	|	|	1911	1916	|	1935	|	1952	2011	|	|	...	2026	|	2035	2051
Dortmund Hbf a.	1805	1820	1821	1821	←	1839	...	|	1846	|	1920	1921	1929	|	1946	|	2003	2021	2020	2021	...	2038	|	2046	2102
Dortmund Hbf 805 d.	→	...	1825	1825	1828	1842	...	|	1848	|	...	1925	...	|	1948	|	...	2025b	2028	...	...	...	|	2048	...
Hamm (Westf) 805 a.	...	...	|	|	1843	1902	...	1902	1907	|	...	|	...	2002	2007	|	...	|	2043	...	...	...	2102	2107	...
Hamm (Westf) d.	...	...	|	|	1845	...	...	1911	1911	|	...	|	...	2011	2011	|	...	|	2045	...	...	...	2111	2111	...
Hannover Hbf 810 a.	...	...	|	|	2018	...	...	2028	2028	|	...	|	...	2128	2128	|	...	|	2218	...	...	...	2228	2228	...
Leipzig Hbf 810 a.	...	...	|	|	2323v	...	...	|	|	|	...	|	...	|	|	|	...	|	...	...	...	...	|	|	...
Berlin Hbf ▲ 810 a.	...	...	|	|	...	...	...	2221	2221	|	...	|	...	2309	2309	|	...	|	...	...	...	...	0019	0019	...
Münster (Westf) Hbf 801 d.	...	...	1857	1857	...	...	...	...	...	1928	...	1957	...	...	...	2029	...	2057b	...	...	...	...	...	...	...
Osnabrück Hbf 801 d.	...	...	1923	1923	...	...	...	...	...	...	...	2023	...	...	...	...	...	2123b	...	...	...	...	...	...	...
Bremen Hbf 801 d.	...	...	2017	2017	...	...	...	...	...	...	...	2117	...	...	...	...	...	2221b	...	...	...	...	...	...	...
Hamburg Hbf 801 a.	...	...	2112	2112	...	...	...	...	...	...	...	2212	...	...	...	...	...	2314b	...	...	...	...	...	...	...
Hamburg Altona a.	...	...	2126	...	...	...	...	...	...	...	...	2226	...	...	...	...	...	2329b	...	...	...	...	...	...	...

See notes ▲ and ⊠	ICE 26	ICE 514	ICE 928	ICE 926	ICE 120	ICE 657	ICE 647	IC 2339	IC 2318	IC 2318	ICE 1002	ICE 502	ICE 528	ICE 924	ICE 810	ICE 24	ICE 512	ICE 526	CNL 457	IC 1910	IC 2110	ICE 500	ICE 524	ICE 22	ICE 1122
			⑦	⑥	Ⓑ	⑦	⑦	Ⓑ		Ⓑ	⑥	Ⓑ	Ⓑ	⑥	Ⓑ			Ⓑ	Ⓡ	⑦	Ⓑ				
	W✕	🍷	🍷	🍷	A🍷	✕	✕	🍷			🍷	🍷	🍷	G🍷	🍷	W✕	🍷	🍷	🍷♦		✕	🍷	🍷	W✕	🍷
Basel SBB 🚌 912 d.	...	...	...	...	...	...	...	...	...	...	...	...	...	...	...	...	...	...	...	...	...	1912	...	...	...
Karlsruhe Hbf 912 d.	...	...	...	...	...	...	...	...	...	...	1908	1908	...	...	...	...	...	...	...	...	...	2101	...	...	...
München Hbf 904 930 d.	...	1523	1555	1555	...	...	...	...	...	...	|	|	1650	1650	...	...	1723	1755	...	1612	...	|	1855	...	...
Stuttgart Hbf 930 d.	...	1751	|	|	...	...	...	...	1741	1741	|	|	|	|	...	...	1951	|	...	1914	1937	|	|	...	...
Nürnberg Hbf 920 d.	1527	|	1700	1700	...	...	...	...	|	|	|	|	1800	1800	...	1727	|	1900	...	|	|	|	2000	1927	...
Frankfurt (Main) Hbf 910/2 d.	1742	|	1910	1910	1928	...	...	...	|	|	|	|	2010	2010	2016	1942	|	2110	...	|	|	|	2210	2146	2310
Frankfurt Flughafen ✈ § d.	1757	1909	1924	1923	1943	...	...	...	|	|	2009	2009	2024	2024	2031	1957	2109	2124	...	|	|	2209	2224	2159	2324
Mainz Hbf 912 d.	1820	|	|	|	|	...	...	...	1920z	1920z	|	|	|	|	|	2020	|	|	...	2048z	2120z	|	|	2220	|
Koblenz Hbf d.	1912	|	|	|	|	...	...	1943	2012	2012	|	|	|	|	|	2112	|	|	...	2143	2212	|	|	2312	|
Andernach d.	|	|	|	|	|	...	...	1955	|	|	|	|	|	|	|	|	|	|	...	2156	|	|	|	|	|
Remagen d.	|	|	|	|	|	...	...	2007	|	|	|	|	|	|	|	|	|	|	...	2208	|	|	|	|	|
Bonn Hbf d.	1945	|	|	|	|	2025	...	2021	2044	2044	|	|	|	|	|	2144	|	|	...	2222	2244	|	|	2344	|
Köln/Bonn Flughafen ✈ d.	|	|	|	2027	|	|	...	|	|	|	|	|	|	|	2139	|	|	|	...	|	|	|	2330	|	|
Köln Hbf a.	2005	2005	|	2040	2040	2046	...	2042	2105	2105	2105	2105	|	|	|	2205	2205	|	...	2242	2305	2312	|	0005	0036
Köln Hbf d.	2011	2011	|	2048	2048	2049	...	2045	...	2111	2111	2111	|	|	|	2211	2211	|	2228	2245	...	2317	|	0011	0041
Köln Messe/Deutz d.	|	|	2017	|	|	|	...	|	...	|	|	|	2117	2117	2152	|	|	2223	|	|	...	|	2345	|	|
Solingen Hbf d.	2030	|	|	|	|	|	...	|	...	|	|	2131	|	|	|	2230	|	|	|	|	...	|	|	|	|
Wuppertal Hbf d.	2043	|	|	|	|	2117	...	|	...	|	|	2143	|	|	|	2243	|	|	2314	|	...	|	|	|	|
Hagen Hbf d.	2101	|	|	|	|	2135	...	|	...	|	|	2201	|	|	|	2301	|	|	|	|	...	|	|	|	|
Düsseldorf Hbf d.	|	2034	2039	2113	2113	|	2053	2116c	...	2134	2134	|	2139	2139	2213	|	2234	2244	2202*	2309	...	2340	0007	0036	0105
Düsseldorf Flughafen ✈ d.	|	|	|	|	|	|	2100	|	...	|	|	|	|	|	|	|	|	|	|	|	...	2348	|	|	0112
Duisburg Hbf d.	|	2047	2052	2126	2126	|	2110	2129	...	2147	2147	|	2151	2151	2226	|	2247	2256	2147*	2322	...	2357	0020	0049	0121
Oberhausen Hbf d.	|	|	|	|	2133	|	|	|	...	|	|	|	|	|	|	|	|	|	2139*	|	...	|	|	|	|
Mülheim (Ruhr) Hbf d.	|	|	|	|	...	|	|	2137	...	|	|	|	|	|	|	|	|	|	|	2330	...	|	|	|	|
Essen Hbf d.	|	2059	2104	2138	...	|	2123	2145	...	2200	2200	|	2204	2204	2238	|	2259	2309	|	2339	...	0009	0032	0101	0133
Gelsenkirchen Hbf d.	|	|	|	|	...	|	|	|	...	|	|	|	|	|	|	|	|	|	|	|	...	|	|	|	|
Wanne-Eickel Hbf d.	|	|	|	|	...	|	|	|	...	|	|	|	|	|	|	|	|	|	|	|	...	|	|	|	|
Recklinghausen Hbf d.	|	|	|	|	...	|	|	|	...	|	|	|	|	|	|	|	|	|	|	|	...	|	|	|	|
Bochum Hbf d.	|	2111	2115	2148	...	|	2135	2156	...	2211	2211	|	2216	2216	2249	|	2311	2326	|	2350	...	0020	0043	0111	0143
Dortmund Hbf a.	2120	2121	2130	2159	...	|	2146	2207	...	2221	2221	2220	2228	2228	2300	2320	2321	2338	|	2400	...	0030	0053	0122	0154
Dortmund Hbf 805 d.	...	2125	2132	...	...	|	2148	...	...	2225v	2228	2228	...	...	...	...	2325	...	2356	...	...	...	...	...	...
Hamm (Westf) 805 a.	...	|	2147	...	...	2202	2207	...	...	|	2248	2248	...	...	...	...	|	...	|	...	...	...	...	...	...
Hamm (Westf) d.	...	|	2149	...	...	2211	2211	...	...	|	2250	2250	...	...	...	...	|	...	0014	...	...	...	...	...	...
Hannover Hbf 810 a.	...	|	2317	...	...	2328	2328	...	...	|	0026	0026	...	...	...	...	|	...	|	...	...	...	...	...	...
Leipzig Hbf 810 a.	...	|	...	...	...	|	|	...	...	|	...	...	...	...	...	...	|	...	|	...	...	...	...	...	...
Berlin Hbf ▲ 810 a.	...	|	...	...	...	0112	0112	...	...	|	...	...	...	...	...	...	|	...	0421k	...	...	...	...	...	...
Münster (Westf) Hbf 801 d.	...	2201	...	...	...	...	...	...	...	2254v	...	...	...	...	...	...	2357	...	...	...	...	...	...	...	...
Osnabrück Hbf 801 d.	...	2227	...	...	...	...	...	...	...	...	...	...	...	...	...	...	...	...	...	...	...	...	...	...	...
Bremen Hbf 801 d.	...	2323	...	...	...	...	...	...	...	...	...	...	...	...	...	...	...	...	...						
Hamburg Hbf 801 a.	...	0020	...	...	...	...	...	...	...	...	...	...	...	...	...	...	...	...	...						
Hamburg Altona a.	...	0034	...	...	...	...	...	...	...	...	...	...	...	...	...	...	...	...	...						

*See Table **802** for Rhein - Ruhr local RE and S-Bahn services*

♦ – **NOTES** (LISTED BY TRAIN NUMBER)

6 – [12] and ✕ Chur - Zürich - Basel - Karlsruhe - Dortmund (- Hamburg Ⓑ).
100/2 – [12] and ✕ Chur - Zürich - Basel - Köln - Hamburg (- Kiel ⑦).
104 – ICE INTERNATIONAL – [12] and 🍷 Basel - Köln - Arnhem - Utrecht - Amsterdam.
114 – WÖRTHERSEE – [12] and ✕ Klagenfurt - Villach - Salzburg - Dortmund.
118 – [12] and 🍷 Innsbruck - Bregenz - Lindau - Ulm - Stuttgart - Münster. On ①–⑤ until Aug. 21 does not call at Mainz and departs Koblenz 1746. On ⑥⑦ until Aug. 23 departs Mainz 1652.
337 – [12] and 🍷 Luxembourg - Trier - Koblenz - Emden.
457 – KOPERNIKUS – 🛏 1, 2 cl., ▬ 2 cl. and [2] Amsterdam - Dresden - Praha (Table **28**); 🛏 1, 2 cl., ▬ 2 cl. and [2] (*CNL* **40447** – BOREALIS) Amsterdam - København (Table **50**); 🛏 1, 2 cl., ▬ 2 cl. and [2] (*EN* **447** – JAN KIEPURA) Amsterdam - Warszawa (Table **24**); conveys 🛏 1, 2 cl. Amsterdam - Warszawa - Moskva (Table **24**). For overnight journeys only.
2012 – ALLGÄU – [12] and 🍷 Oberstdorf - Ulm - Köln - Hannover (- Magdeburg ⑤⑦) (- Leipzig ⑦).
2155 – [12] and 🍷 Düsseldorf - Kassel - Erfurt.

A – To Amsterdam (Table **28**).
G – From Garmisch (d. 1518).
W – [12] and ✕ Wien - Passau - Regensburg - Dortmund.

b – Ⓑ only.
c – Arrives 10 minutes earlier.
h – Not ⑤.
k – June 20 - July 3 calls at Berlin Gesundbrunnen (a. 0419) and Lichtenberg (a. 0430), **not** Berlin Hbf.
t – 1613 on ⑥⑦.
v – ⑦ only.
y – Not ①–⑤ July 13 - Aug. 21. Departs 1746 on ⑥⑦ until Aug. 23.
z – 3–4 minutes later until Aug. 23.

* – Calls before Köln.
§ – Frankfurt Flughafen Fernbahnhof ✈. See also Tables **910** and **912**.
▲ – Berlin timings are subject to alteration June 20 - July 3. See Table **810**.
⊠ – Timings Köln - Düsseldorf - Dortmund are subject to alteration July 18 – 26 (certain trains do not call at Bochum). Koblenz - Köln timings also subject to change on July 19 (trains do not call at Andernach, Remagen or Bonn).

HAMBURG - DORTMUND - KÖLN - KOBLENZ 800

km	See notes ▲ and ⊠	ICE 523	ICE 1123	ICE 948	ICE 23	CNL 456	ICE 711	ICE 925	ICE 525	ICE 501	IC 2319	IC 2338	ICE 813	ICE 527	ICE 25	ICE 513	ICE 815	EC 115	ICE 529	ICE 503	EC 7	EC 7	IC 119	ICE 646	ICE 656
		①–⑤	⑥	①		R	①–⑤	⑥⑦	①–⑤		①–⑥	①–⑥	①–⑤	①–⑥			①–⑥				①–⑥			①–⑤	①–⑤
		🍷	🍷	✕	W✕	🍷◆	◆	🍷	🍷	🍷		🍷	🍷	G🍷	W✕	🍷	🍷	✕◆	🍷	🍷	✕◆	✕◆	🍷◆	✕	✕
	Hamburg Altona d.	...	...	...	...	...	...	...	...	...	...	...	...	...	...	...	...	...	...	...	0428	...	...	...	...
	Hamburg Hbf 801 d.	...	...	...	...	...	...	...	...	...	...	...	...	...	...	...	...	...	...	...	0442	...	...	...	...
	Bremen Hbf 801 d.	...	...	...	...	...	...	...	...	...	...	...	...	...	...	...	...	...	...	...	0540	...	...	...	...
	Osnabrück Hbf 801 d.	...	...	...	...	...	...	...	...	...	...	...	...	...	...	...	...	...	...	...	0637	...	...	...	...
	Münster (Westf) Hbf 801 d.	...	...	...	...	...	...	...	...	...	0504**g**	...	...	...	...	0601	...	0631	...	...	0704	...	0727	...	...
	Berlin Hbf ▲ 810 d.	...	...	0036	...	0032**k**	...	...	...	...	|	...	...	...	...	|	...	|	...	...	|	...	|	0427	0427
	Leipzig Hbf 810 d.	...	...	|	...	|	...	...	...	...	|	...	...	...	...	|	...	|	...	...	|	...	|	|	|
	Hannover Hbf 810 d.	...	...	0231	...	|	...	...	...	...	|	...	...	0410**g**	...	|	...	|	...	0540	|	...	|	0621	0621
	Hamm (Westf) a.	...	...	0359	...	0429	...	...	...	...	|	...	...	0548**g**	...	|	...	|	...	0713	|	...	|	0748	0748
0	Hamm (Westf) 805 d.	...	...	0401	...	|	...	...	...	...	|	...	...	0551**g**	...	|	...	|	...	0715	|	...	|	0752	0754
	Dortmund Hbf 805 a.	...	...	0418	...	0450	...	...	...	...	0533**g**	...	...	0616**g**	...	0633	...	|	...	0732	0733	...	|	0809	|
	Dortmund Hbf d.	0401	0421	0421	0433	|	0502	0501	0523	0537	0538	0552	0559	0623	0636	0638	0652	|	0723**c**	0737	0738	0738	|	0812	|
	Bochum Hbf d.	0413	0433	0433	0445	|	0513	0513	0535	|	0549	0603	0611	0635	|	0649	0704	|	0735**c**	|	0749	0749	|	0825	|
	Recklinghausen Hbf d.	|	|	|	|	|	|	|	|	|	|	|	|	|	|	|	|	0700	|	|	|	|	0757	|	|
	Wanne-Eickel Hbf d.	|	|	|	|	|	|	|	|	|	|	|	|	|	|	|	|	0709	|	|	|	|	0806	|	|
	Gelsenkirchen Hbf d.	|	|	|	|	|	|	|	|	|	|	|	|	|	|	|	|	0715	|	|	|	|	0812	|	|
	Essen Hbf d.	0423	0445	0444	0456	|	0524	0523	0553	|	0600	0615	0623	0650	|	0700	0715	|	0753**j**	|	0800	0800	0823	0836	|
	Mülheim (Ruhr) Hbf d.	|	|	|	|	|	|	|	|	|	|	0623	|	|	|	|	|	|	|	|	|	|	0831	|	|
	Oberhausen Hbf d.	|	|	|	|	0737*	|	|	|	|	|	|	|	|	|	|	|	0727	|	|	|	|	|	|	|
	Duisburg Hbf d.	0437	0459	0457	0508	0715*	0536	0537	0608	|	0613	0631	0637	0703	|	0713	0729	0735	0808	|	0813	0813	0838	0849	|
	Düsseldorf Flughafen ✈ d.	|	|	0507	|	|	|	|	|	|	|	|	|	|	|	|	|	|	|	|	|	|	|	0859	|
	Düsseldorf Hbf d.	0453	0513	0518	0523	0654*	0551	0553	0622	|	0627	0648	0653	0722	|	0727	0748	0752	0822	|	0827	0827	0852	0908	|
48	**Hagen** Hbf d.	|	|	|	|	|	|	|	|	0557	|	|	|	|	0657	|	|	|	|	0757	|	|	|	|	0824
75	Wuppertal Hbf d.	|	|	|	|	0539	|	|	|	0614	|	|	|	|	0714	|	|	|	|	0814	|	|	|	|	0841
93	Solingen Hbf d.	|	|	|	|	|	|	|	|	0627	|	|	|	|	0727	|	|	|	|	0827	|	|	|	|	|
120	**Köln** Messe/Deutz a.	0513	0533	|	|	|	0610	0613	0642	|	|	|	|	0742	|	|	0808	|	0842	|	|	|	|	0928	|
121	**Köln** Hbf a.	|	|	0540**t**	0546	0614	|	|	|	0646	0649	0713	0716	|	0746	0749	|	0815	|	0846	0850	0850	0915	|	0909
	Köln Hbf d.	|	|	0543**t**	0553	...	|	|	|	0654	0653	0718	0720	|	0753	0754	|	0818	|	0854	0853	0853	0918	|	...
	Köln/Bonn Flughafen ✈ a.	0529	0545	0604	|	...	|	0629	|	|	|	|	|	|	|	|	0819	|	|	|	|	|	|	0942	...
	Bonn Hbf d.	|	|	...	0614	...	|	|	|	|	0714	0736	|	|	0814	|	|	0837	|	|	0914	0914	0937	...	...
	Remagen d.	|	|	...	|	...	|	|	|	|	|	0750	|	|	|	|	|	0851	|	|	|	|	0951	...	...
	Andernach d.	|	|	...	|	...	|	|	|	|	|	0802	|	|	|	|	|	0903	|	|	|	|	1003	...	...
	Koblenz Hbf a.	|	|	...	0646	...	|	|	|	|	0746	0816	|	|	0846	|	|	0915	|	|	0946	0946	1015	...	...
	Mainz Hbf 912 a.	|	|	...	0738	...	0744**r**	|	|	|	0837	...	|	|	0938	|	|	1013**h**	|	|	1037	1037	1111**z**	...	...
	Frankfurt Flughafen ✈ § a.	0634	0634	...	0759	...	|	0734	0734	0751	|	...	0827	0834	0959	0851	0926	|	0934	0951	|	|	|	...	...
	Frankfurt (Main) Hbf 910/2 a.	0648	0648	...	0813	...	|	0748	0748	|	|	...	0841	0848	1013	|	0941	|	0948	|	|	|	|	...	...
	Nürnberg Hbf 920 a.	0859	0859	...	1028	...	|	0959	0959	|	...	...	...	1059	1228	|	...	|	1159	|	|	|	|	...	...
	Stuttgart Hbf 930 a.	|	|	...	...	...	0923	|	|	|	1018	...	...	|	...	1008	...	1153	|	|	|	|	1246	...	...
	München Hbf 904 930 a.	1004	1004	...	...	...	...	1104	1104	|	...	...	...	1204	...	1230	...	1416	1304	|	|	|	...	...	...
	Karlsruhe Hbf 912 a.	...	...	...	...	...	...	...	...	0858	...	...	...	...	...	...	...	...	...	1056	1147	1147	...	...	...
	Basel SBB 🏛 912 a.	...	...	...	...	...	...	...	...	1047	...	...	...	...	...	...	...	...	...	...	1337	1337	...	...	...

See notes ▲ and ⊠	ICE 621	ICE 1094	ICE 121	ICE 515	ICE 27	IC 2005	IC 2015	ICE 946	ICE 956	ICE 105	IC 2013	EC 101	IC 2013	ICE 644	ICE 654	ICE 625	IC 2023	ICE 517	IC 336	ICE 944	ICE 954	IC 2156	IC 2044	ICE 507	IC 2113
		①–④	①–⑥			⑤⑥	①–④	①–⑥	①–⑥											①–⑥	①–⑥	①–⑥	①–⑥	⑦	
	🍷	R ⚡	A🍷	🍷	W✕	🍷◆	🍷◆	✕	✕	A🍷	🍷◆	✕◆	🍷◆	✕	✕	🍷	🍷	🍷	🍷◆	✕	✕	🍷◆	🍷	🍷	✕
Hamburg Altona d.	...	0558	...	0523	...	...	...	...	...	...	...	0632	...	...	...	...	0732	...	...	...	...	...	...	...	0832
Hamburg Hbf 801 d.	...	0612	...	0537	...	...	...	...	...	...	...	0646	...	...	...	...	0746	...	...	...	...	...	...	...	0846
Bremen Hbf 801 d.	...	|	...	0637	...	...	...	...	...	...	...	0744	...	...	...	...	0844	...	...	...	...	...	...	...	0944
Osnabrück Hbf 801 d.	...	|	...	0732	...	...	...	...	...	...	...	0837	...	...	...	...	0937	...	...	...	...	...	...	...	1037
Münster (Westf) Hbf 801 d.	...	|	...	0801	...	0832	0832	...	...	...	...	0904	...	...	...	...	1004	...	1032	...	...	...	...	...	1104
Berlin Hbf ▲ 810 d.	...	|	...	|	...	|	|	0537	0537	...	...	|	...	0650	0650	...	|	...	|	0748	0748	...	...	...	|
Leipzig Hbf 810 d.	...	|	...	|	...	|	|	|	|	...	0436**g**	|	...	|	|	...	|	...	|	|	|	...	0640	...	|
Hannover Hbf 810 d.	...	|	...	|	...	|	|	0731	0731	...	0740	|	...	0831	0831	...	|	...	|	0931	0931	...	0940	...	|
Hamm (Westf) a.	...	|	...	|	...	|	|	0848	0848	...	0912	|	...	0948	0948	...	|	...	|	1048	1048	...	1112	...	|
Hamm (Westf) 805 d.	...	|	...	|	...	|	|	0852	0854	...	0914	|	...	0952	0954	...	|	...	|	1052	1054	1056	1114	...	|
Dortmund Hbf 805 a.	...	|	...	0833	...	|	|	0909	|	...	0932	0933	←	1009	|	...	1033	...	|	1109	|	1115	1132	...	1133
Dortmund Hbf d.	0816**c**	|	...	0837	0838	|	|	0912	|	...	→	0938	0952	1012	|	1023**v**	1036	1038	|	1112	|	1118	1137	1137	1138
Bochum Hbf d.	0829**c**	|	...	|	0849	|	|	0925	|	...	...	0949	1003	1025	|	1035**v**	|	1049	|	1125	|	1130	|	|	1149
Recklinghausen Hbf d.	|	|	...	|	|	0900	0900	|	|	...	...	|	|	|	|	|	|	|	1100	|	|	|	|	|	|
Wanne-Eickel Hbf d.	|	|	...	|	|	0909	0909	|	|	...	...	|	|	|	|	|	|	|	1109	|	|	|	|	|	|
Gelsenkirchen Hbf d.	|	|	...	|	|	0915	0915	|	|	...	...	|	|	|	|	|	|	|	1115	|	|	|	|	|	|
Essen Hbf d.	0840	0853**s**	...	|	0900	|	|	0936	|	...	...	1000	1014	1036	|	1053	|	1100	|	1136	|	1141	|	|	1200
Mülheim (Ruhr) Hbf d.	|	|	...	|	|	|	|	|	|	...	...	|	1022	|	|	|	|	|	|	|	|	|	|	|	|
Oberhausen Hbf d.	|	|	0900	|	|	0927	0927	|	|	1000	...	|	|	|	|	|	|	|	1127	|	|	|	|	|	|
Duisburg Hbf d.	0855	|	0908	|	0913	0934	0934	0949	|	1008	...	1013	1032	1049	|	1108	|	1113	1134	1149	|	1155	|	|	1213
Düsseldorf Flughafen ✈ d.	|	|	|	|	|	|	|	0959	|	|	...	|	|	1059	|	|	|	|	|	1159	|	1206	|	|	|
Düsseldorf Hbf d.	0913	0916**s**	0923	|	0927	0948	0948	1005	|	1022	...	1027	1050	1108	|	1122	|	1127	1148	1205	|	1212	|	|	1227
Hagen Hbf d.	|	|	|	0857	|	|	|	...	0924	|	...	|	|	|	1024	|	1057	|	|	...	1124	...	1157	1157	|
Wuppertal Hbf d.	|	|	|	0914	|	|	|	...	0941	|	...	|	|	|	1041	|	1114	|	|	...	1141	...	1214	1214	|
Solingen Hbf d.	|	|	|	0926	|	|	|	...	|	|	...	|	|	|	|	|	1127	|	|	...	|	...	1226	1227	|
Köln Messe/Deutz a.	0935	|	0943	|	|	|	|	...	|	|	...	|	|	1128	|	1142	|	|	|	...	|	...	|	|	|
Köln Hbf a.	|	0941	|	0946	0949	1012	1012	...	1009	1045	...	1049	1112	|	1109	|	1146	1149	1212	...	1209	...	1245	1246	1250
Köln Hbf d.	|	...	|	0954	0953	1018	1018	...	...	1054	...	1053	1118	|	1112**e**	|	1153	1154	1218	...	...	...	...	1254	1253
Köln/Bonn Flughafen ✈ a.	|	...	|	|	|	|	|	...	...	|	...	|	|	1142	|	|	|	|	|	...	...	...	...	|	|
Bonn Hbf d.	|	...	|	|	1014	1036	1036	...	...	|	...	1114	1137	...	1132**e**	|	1214	|	1236	...	...	...	...	|	1314
Remagen d.	|	...	|	|	|	1050	1050	...	...	|	...	|	1151	...	...	|	|	|	1250	...	...	...	...	|	|
Andernach d.	|	...	|	|	|	1102	1102	...	...	|	...	|	1203	...	...	|	|	|	1302	...	...	...	...	|	|
Koblenz Hbf a.	|	...	|	|	1046	1115	1115	...	...	|	...	1146	1215	...	...	|	1246	|	1316	...	...	...	...	|	1346
Mainz Hbf 912 a.	|	...	|	|	1138	1212**r**	1212**r**	...	...	|	...	1237	1311**z**	...	...	|	1338	|	...	...	...	...	...	|	1437
Frankfurt Flughafen ✈ § a.	1034	...	1043	1051	1159	|	|	...	...	1151	...	|	|	...	...	1234	1359	1251	...	...	...	...	...	1351	|
Frankfurt (Main) Hbf 910/2 a.	1048	...	1102	|	1213	|	|	...	...	|	...	|	|	...	...	1248	1413	|	...	...	...	...	...	|	|
Nürnberg Hbf 920 a.	1259	...	...	|	1428	|	|	...	...	|	...	|	|	...	...	1459	...	|	...	...	...	...	...	|	|
Stuttgart Hbf 930 a.	|	...	...	1208	...	|	1358	...	...	|	...	|	1446	...	...	|	...	1408	...					|	1622
München Hbf 904 930 a.	1404	...	...	1430	...	|	...	...	...	|	...	|	...	...	...	1604	...	1631	...					|	...
Karlsruhe Hbf 912 a.	...	...	...	...	...	1334	...	...	...	1251	...	1347	...	...	...	...	...	...	...					1456	...
Basel SBB 🏛 912 a.	...	...	...	...	...	...	...	...	...	1447	...	1537	...	...	...	...	...	...	...					...	...

*See Table **802** for Rhein-Ruhr local RE and S-Bahn services*

◆ – **NOTES** (LISTED BY TRAIN NUMBER)

7 – [12] and ✕ (Hamburg ①–⑥ -) Dortmund - Basel - Zürich - Chur.
101 – [12] and ✕ Hamburg - Köln - Karlsruhe - Basel - Zürich - Chur.
115 – WÖRTHERSEE – [12] and ✕ Münster - Salzburg - Villach - Klagenfurt.
119 – [12] and 🍷 Münster - Ulm - Linau - Bregenz - Innsbruck.
336 – [12] and 🍷 Emden - Münster - Koblenz - Trier - Luxembourg.
456 – KOPERNIKUS – 🛏 1, 2 cl., ▬ 2 cl. and [2] Praha - Dresden - Amsterdam (Table **28**); 🛏 1, 2 cl., ▬ 2 cl. and [2] (*CNL* **40483** – BOREALIS) København - Amsterdam (Table **50**); 🛏 1, 2 cl., ▬ 2 cl. and [2] (*EN* **446** – JAN KIEPURA) Warszawa - Amsterdam (Table **24**); conveys 🛏 1, 2 cl. Moskva - Warszawa - Amsterdam (Table **24**). For overnight journeys only.
711 – [12] Dortmund - Wiesbaden (Table **910**) - Stuttgart.
2005 – BODENSEE – [12] and 🍷 Emden - Mannheim - Konstanz.
2013 – ALLGÄU – [12] (Leipzig ① -) (Magdeburg ①–⑥ -) Hannover - Köln - Oberstdorf.
2015 – [12] and 🍷 Emden - Mannheim - Stuttgart.
2156 – [12] and 🍷 Erfurt - Kassel - Düsseldorf.

A – From Amsterdam (Table **28**).
G – To Garmisch on ⑥ (a. 1341).

W – [12] and ✕ Dortmund - Köln - Regensburg - Passau - Wien.

c – ⑥⑦ only.
e – ①–⑥ only.
g – ① only.
h – Not ①–⑤ July 13 - Aug. 21. Arrives 1009 on ⑥⑦ July 5 - Aug. 23 (also June 14, 21, 28).
j – ⑥⑦ until July 12; daily from July 18.
k – June 20 - July 4 (also Aug. 1, 2, 3) calls at Berlin Lichtenberg (d. 0024) and Berlin Gesundbrunnen (d. 0042), **not** Berlin Hbf.

r – From Aug. 24.
s – Stops to set down only.
t – Not July 27, Aug. 3.
v – ⑦ only.
z – 4 minutes earlier until Aug. 23.

***** – Arrival times. Calls after Köln.

⚡ – *ICE* ***SPRINTER***. Supplement payable. Conveys ✕.
§ – Frankfurt Flughafen Fernbahnhof. See also Tables **910** and **912**.
▲ – Berlin timings are subject to alteration June 20 - July 3. See Table **810**.
⊠ – Timings Dortmund - Düsseldorf - Köln are subject to alteration July 18 – 26 (certain trains do not call at Bochum). Köln - Koblenz timings also subject to change on July 19 (trains do not call at Bonn, Remagen or Andernach).

800 HAMBURG - DORTMUND - KÖLN - KOBLENZ

See notes ▲ and ⊠	ICE 123	IC 1911	IC 1111	ICE 642	ICE 652	ICE 629	IC 2025	ICE 519	IC 334	ICE 721	ICE 942	ICE 952	IC 2154	IC 2046	IC 2115	ICE 125	IC 1913	IC 1913	IC 1913	ICE 640	ICE 650	ICE 723	IC 2027	IC 2327	ICE 611
		⑤	⑦			Ⓑ				⑥⑦			①–⑥				Ⓑ	⑦	⑤			Ⓑ			
	A 🍷			🍴	🍴	🍷		🍷	🍷♦	🍷	🍴	🍴	🍷	🍷	🍴♦	A 🍷	‡		🍷	🍴	🍴	🍷	🍴♦	🍴♦	🍷
Hamburg Altona d.	...	...	...	...	...	...	0932	...	...	...	...	...	...	...	...	...	...	...	...	...	...	...	1132	...	...
Hamburg Hbf 801 d.	...	...	...	...	...	...	0946	...	...	...	...	...	...	...	1046	...	...	...	...	...	...	...	1146	1146	...
Bremen Hbf 801 d.	...	...	...	...	...	...	1044	...	...	...	...	...	...	...	1144	...	...	...	...	...	...	...	1244	1244	...
Osnabrück Hbf 801 d.	...	...	...	...	...	...	1137	...	...	...	...	...	...	...	1237	...	...	...	...	...	...	...	1337	1337	...
Münster (Westf) Hbf 801 d.	...	...	...	...	...	...	1204	...	1232	...	...	...	...	...	1304	...	...	...	...	...	...	...	1404	1404	...
Berlin Hbf ▲ **810** d.	...	...	...	0850	0850	...	|	...	|	...	0948	0948	0639	...	|	...	...	1010	...	1050	1050	...	|	|	...
Leipzig Hbf **810** d.	...	...	...	|	|	...	|	...	|	...	|	|	|	0840e	|	...	...	|	...	|	|	...	|	|	...
Hannover Hbf **810** d.	...	...	...	1031	1031	...	|	...	|	...	1131	1131	|	1140	|	...	...	1158	1158	1231	1231	...	|	|	...
Hamm (Westf) a.	...	...	...	1148	1148	...	|	...	|	...	1248	1248	1252	1312	|	...	...	1323	1323	1348	1348	...	|	|	...
Hamm (Westf) 805 d.	...	...	...	1152	1154	...	|	...	|	...	1252	1254	1256	1314	|	...	...	1325	1325	1352	1354	...	|	|	...
Dortmund Hbf 805 a.	...	...	...	1209	|	...	1233	...	|	...	1309	|	1315	1332	1333	...	...	1347	1347	1409	|	...	1433	1433	...
Dortmund Hbf d.	...	1152	1152	1212	|	1223v	1236	1238	|	1257	1312	|	1318	1337	1338	...	...	1352	1352	1412	|	...	1436	1436	1438
Bochum Hbf d.	...	1204	1204	1225	|	1235v	|	1249	|	1309	1325	|	1330	|	1349	...	...	1403	1403	1425	|	...	|	|	1449
Recklinghausen Hbf d.	...	|	|	|	|	|	|	|	1300	|	|	|	|	|	|	...	...	|	|	|	|	...	|	|	|
Wanne-Eickel Hbf d.	...	|	|	|	|	|	|	|	1309	|	|	|	|	|	|	...	...	|	|	|	|	...	|	|	|
Gelsenkirchen Hbf d.	...	|	|	|	|	|	|	|	1315	|	|	|	|	|	|	...	...	|	|	|	|	...	|	|	|
Essen Hbf d.	...	1214	1214	1236	|	1253	|	1300	|	1324	1336	|	1341	|	1400	...	...	1414	1414	1436	|	1453	|	|	1500
Mülheim (Ruhr) Hbf d.	...	1222	1222	|	|	|	|	|	|	|	|	|	|	|	|	...	...	1422	1422	|	|	|	|	|	|
Oberhausen Hbf d.	1226	|	|	|	|	|	|	|	1327	|	|	|	|	|	|	1426	...	|	|	|	|	|	|	|	|
Duisburg Hbf d.	1234	1230	1230	1249	|	1308	|	1313	1334	1338	1349	|	1355	|	1413	1434	...	1430	1430	1449	|	1508	|	|	1513
Düsseldorf Flughafen ✈ d.	|	|	|	1259	|	|	|	|	|	|	1359	|	1406	|	|	|	...	|	|	1459	|	|	|	|	|
Düsseldorf Hbf d.	1248	1251	1251	1305	|	1322	|	1327	1348	1353	1408	|	1412	|	1427	1448	1451	1451	1451	1505	|	1522	|	|	1527
Hagen Hbf d.	|	|	|	...	1224	|	1257	|	|	|	|	1324	...	1357	|	|	|	|	|	...	1424	|	1457	1457	|
Wuppertal Hbf d.	|	|	|	...	1241	|	1314	|	|	|	|	1341	...	1414	|	|	|	|	|	...	1441	|	1514	1514	|
Solingen Hbf d.	|	|	|	...	|	|	1327	|	|	|	|	|	...	1426	|	|	|	|	|	...	|	|	1527	1527	|
Köln Messe/Deutz a.	|	|	|	...	|	1342	|	|	|	|	1428	|	...	|	|	|	|	|	|	...	|	1542	|	|	|
Köln Hbf a.	1312	1315	1315	...	1309	|	1346	1349	1412	1416	|	1409	...	1445	1450	1512	1515	1515	1515	...	1509	|	1546	1546	1549
Köln Hbf d.	1320	1318	1318	...	1312	|	1353	1354	1418	1428	|	...	...	...	1453	1520	1518	1518	1518	...	...	|	1553	1553	1554
Köln/Bonn Flughafen ✈ a.	|	|	|	...	|	|	|	|	|	1439	1445	...	...	...	|	|	|	|	|	...	...	|	|	|	|
Bonn Hbf d.	|	1337	1337	...	1332	|	1414	|	1436	|	...	...	...	...	1514	|	1537	1537	1537	...	...	|	1614	1614	|
Remagen d.	|	1351	1351	...	...	|	|	|	1450	|	...	...	...	...	|	|	1551	1551	1551	...	...	|	|	|	|
Andernach d.	|	1403	1403	...	...	|	|	|	1502	|	...	...	...	...	|	|	1603	1603	1603	...	...	|	|	|	|
Koblenz Hbf a.	|	1415	1415	...	...	|	1446	|	1516	|	...	...	...	...	1546	|	1615	1615	1615	...	...	|	1646	1646	|
Mainz Hbf **912** a.	|	1511t	1511t	...	...	|	1538	|	...	|	...	...	...	...	1637	|	1711z	1711z	1711z	...	...	|	1738	1738	|
Frankfurt Flughafen ✈ § a.	1414	|	|	...	...	1434	1559	1451	...	1534	...	...	...	...	|	1614	|	|	|	...	...	1634	1759	1759	1651
Frankfurt (Main) Hbf **910/2** a.	1430	|	|	...	...	1448	1613	|	...	1548	...	...	...	...	|	1630	|	|	|	...	...	1648	1813	1813	|
Nürnberg Hbf **920** a.	...	|	|	...	...	1659	...	|	...	1759	...	...	...	...	|	...	|	|	|	...	...	1859	2028	2028	|
Stuttgart Hbf **930** a.	...	1646	1646	...	...	|	...	1608	...	|	...	...	...	...	1825	...	1846	1846	1846	...	...	|	...	...	1808
München Hbf **904 930** a.	...	...	...	...	...	1804	...	1830	...	1904	...	...	...	...	...	...	...	...	2123	...	...	2004	...	...	2030
Karlsruhe Hbf **912** a.	...	...	...	...	...	...	...	...	...	...	...	...	...	...	...	...	...	...	...	...	...	...	...	...	...
Basel SBB 🏛 **912** a.	...	...	...	...	...	...	...	...	...	...	...	...	...	...	...	...	...	...	...	...	...	...	...	...	...

See notes ▲ and ⊠	IC 332	IC 332	ICE 940	ICE 950	IC 2152	ICE 725	ICE 725	IC 2048	IC 2311	ICE 127	IC 1915	ICE 548	ICE 548	ICE 558	ICE 727	ICE 1025	ICE 1125	ICE 613	IC 330	ICE 848	ICE 858	IC 2150	ICE 729	IC 2140	IC 2213
		Ⓑ			⑤⑦	⑦				G	⑤⑦		Ⓑ		Ⓑ		⑤								
	🍷♦	🍷♦	🍴	🍴	🍷♦	🍷	🍷	🍷	🍴♦	A 🍷	¶	🍴	🍴	🍴	🍷	🍴♦	🍴♦	🍷	🍷♦	🍴	🍴	🍷♦	🍷	🍷	🍴♦
Hamburg Altona d.	...	...	...	...	...	...	...	...	...	...	...	...	...	...	...	...	...	...	...	...	...	...	...	...	...
Hamburg Hbf 801 d.	...	...	...	...	...	...	...	...	1246	...	...	...	...	...	...	1346	1346	...	...	...	...	...	...	...	1446
Bremen Hbf 801 d.	...	...	...	...	...	...	...	...	1344	...	...	...	...	...	...	1444	1444	...	...	...	...	...	...	...	1544
Osnabrück Hbf 801 d.	...	...	...	...	...	...	...	...	1437	...	...	...	...	...	...	1537	1537	...	...	...	...	...	...	...	1637
Münster (Westf) Hbf 801 d.	1431	1431	...	...	...	...	...	...	1504	...	...	...	...	...	...	1603	1603	...	1631	...	...	...	...	...	1704
Berlin Hbf ▲ **810** d.	|	|	1148	1148	0839f	...	...	...	|	...	1208	1250	1250	1250	...	|	|	...	|	1348	1348	1039	...	...	|
Leipzig Hbf **810** d.	|	|	|	|	|	...	...	1040	|	...	|	|	|	|	...	|	|	...	|	|	|	|	...	1240	|
Hannover Hbf **810** d.	|	|	1331	1331	|	...	...	1340	|	...	1358	1431	1431	1431	...	|	|	...	|	1531	1531	|	...	1540	|
Hamm (Westf) a.	|	|	1448	1448	1452	...	...	1512	|	...	1524	1548	1548	1548	...	|	|	...	|	1648	1648	1652	...	1712	|
Hamm (Westf) 805 d.	|	|	1452	1454	1456	...	...	1514	|	...	1526	1552	1552	1554	...	|	|	...	|	1652	1654	1656	...	1714	|
Dortmund Hbf 805 a.	|	|	1509	|	1515	...	...	1532	1533	...	1547	1609	1609	|	...	1633	1633	...	|	1709	|	1715	...	1732	1733
Dortmund Hbf d.	|	|	1512	|	1518	1522	...	1537	1538	...	1552	1612	1612	|	...	1636	1636	1638	|	1712	|	1718	...	1737	1738
Bochum Hbf d.	|	|	1525	|	1530	1536	...	|	1549	...	1603	1625	1625	|	...	|	|	1649	|	1725	|	1730	...	|	1749
Recklinghausen Hbf d.	1459	1459	|	|	|	|	...	|	|	...	|	|	|	|	...	|	|	|	1659	|	|	|	...	|	|
Wanne-Eickel Hbf d.	1508	1508	|	|	|	|	...	|	|	...	|	|	|	|	...	|	|	|	1708	|	|	|	...	|	|
Gelsenkirchen Hbf d.	1514	1514	|	|	|	|	...	|	|	...	|	|	|	|	...	|	|	|	1714	|	|	|	...	|	|
Essen Hbf d.	|	|	1536	|	1541	1553	1553	|	1600	...	1614	1636	1636	|	1653	|	|	1700	|	1736	|	1741	1753	|	1800
Mülheim (Ruhr) Hbf d.	|	|	|	|	|	|	|	|	|	...	1622	|	|	|	|	|	|	|	|	|	|	|	|	|	|
Oberhausen Hbf d.	1526	1526	|	|	|	|	|	|	|	1626	|	|	|	|	|	|	|	|	1726	|	|	|	|	|	|
Duisburg Hbf d.	1533	1533	1549	|	1555	1608	1608	|	1613	1634	1630	1649	1649	|	1708	|	|	1713	1734	1749	|	1755	1808	|	1813
Düsseldorf Flughafen ✈ d.	|	|	1559	|	1606	|	|	|	|	|	|	1659	1659	|	|	|	|	|	|	1759	|	1807	|	|	|
Düsseldorf Hbf d.	1548	1548	1605	|	1612	1622	1622	|	1627	1648	1651	1705	1708	|	1722	|	|	1727	1748	1805	|	1815	1821	|	1827
Hagen Hbf d.	|	|	...	1524	...	|	|	1557	|	|	|	...	|	1624	|	1657	1657	|	|	...	1724	...	|	1757	|
Wuppertal Hbf d.	|	|	...	1541	...	|	|	1614	|	|	|	...	|	1641	|	1714	1714	|	|	...	1741	...	|	1814	|
Solingen Hbf d.	|	|	...	|	...	|	|	1626	|	|	|	...	|	|	|	|	|	|	|	...	|	...	|	1826	|
Köln Messe/Deutz a.	|	|	...	|	...	1642	1642	|	|	|	|	...	1728	|	1742	|	|	|	|	...	|	...	1841	|	|
Köln Hbf a.	1612	1612	...	1609	...	|	|	1645	1649	1712	1715	...	|	1709	|	1746	1746	1749	1812	...	1809	...	|	1845	1849
Köln Hbf d.	...	1618	...	...	...	|	|	...	1653	1720	1718	...	|	...	|	1753	1753	1754	1818	...	...	...	|	...	1853
Köln/Bonn Flughafen ✈ a.	...	|	...	...	...	|	|	...	|	|	|	...	1744	...	|	|	|	|	|	...	...	...	|	...	|
Bonn Hbf d.	...	1636	...	...	...	|	|	...	1714	|	1737	...	...	...	|	1814	1814	|	1836	...	...	...	|	...	1914
Remagen d.	...	1650	...	...	...	|	|	...	|	|	1751	...	...	...	|	|	|	|	1850	...	...	...	|	...	|
Andernach d.	...	1702	...	...	...	|	|	...	|	|	1803	...	...	...	|	|	|	|	1902	...	...	...	|	...	|
Koblenz Hbf a.	...	1716	...	...	...	|	|	...	1746	|	1815	...	...	...	|	1846	1846	|	1916	...	...	...	|	...	1946
Mainz Hbf **912** a.	...	...	...	...	...	|	|	...	1837	|	1911t	...	...	...	|	1938	1938	|	...	...	...	...	|	...	2037
Frankfurt Flughafen ✈ § a.	...	...	...	...	...	1734	1734	...	|	1814	|	...	...	...	1834	1959	1959	1851	...	...	...	...	1934	...	|
Frankfurt (Main) Hbf **910/2** a.	...	...	...	...	...	1748	1748	...	|	1830	|	...	...	...	1848	2013	2013	|	...	...	...	...	1948	...	|
Nürnberg Hbf **920** a.	...	...	...	...	...	1959	1959	...	|	...	|	...	...	...	2059	2224	2224	|	...	...	...	...	2159	...	|
Stuttgart Hbf **930** a.	...	...	...	...	...	|	|	...	2022	...	2046	...	...	...	|	|	...	2008	...	...	...	...	|	...	2222
München Hbf **904 930** a.	...	...	...	...	...	2105	2105							...	2204	2348	...	2232	...	...	...	...	2307	...	...
Karlsruhe Hbf **912** a.	...	...	...	...	...	...	...							...	...	...	...	...	...	...	...	...	...	...	...
Basel SBB 🏛 **912** a.	...	...	...	...	...	...	...							...	...	...	...	...	...	...	...	...	...	...	...

*See Table **802** for Rhein - Ruhr local RE and S-Bahn services*

♦ – **NOTES** (LISTED BY TRAIN NUMBER)

330 – NORDERNEY – [12] and 🍷 Norddeich Mole - Emden - Koblenz - Luxembourg.
332 – [12] and 🍷 Norddeich Mole - Emden - Köln (- Luxembourg Ⓑ).
334 – [12] and 🍷 Norddeich Mole - Emden - Koblenz - Luxembourg.
1025 – Daily except ⑤. [12] and 🍴 Kiel - Köln - Frankfurt - München.
1125 – [12] and 🍴 Kiel - Köln - Frankfurt - Regensburg.
2027 – ⑦ June 14 - Sept 27 (not July 19, 26, Aug. 2, 9); ①②③④⑥⑦ from Oct. 5. [12] and 🍴 Hamburg - Köln - Regensburg - Passau.
2115 – [12] and 🍴 (Greifswald ①–⑤ -) Stralsund - Hamburg - Köln - Stuttgart.
2150 – [12] and 🍷 (Stralsund ①–⑥ -) Berlin - Halle - Erfurt - Kassel - Düsseldorf. Train number **2250** on ⑦.
2152 – [12] and 🍷 (Berlin ⑤ -) Halle - Erfurt - Kassel - Düsseldorf.
2213 – RÜGEN – [12] and 🍴 Ostseebad Binz - Stralsund - Rostock - Köln - Stuttgart.
2311 – NORDFRIESLAND – [12] and 🍴 Westerland - Köln - Heidelberg - Stuttgart.
2327 – ①–⑥ until Oct. 3 (also July 19, 26, Aug. 2, 9, Oct. 4); ⑤ from Oct. 9. LÜBECKER BUCHT – [12] and 🍴 Puttgarden - Lübeck - Hamburg - Köln - Frankfurt - Regensburg - Passau.

A – From Amsterdam (Table **28**).
G – Until Oct. 25.

e – ①–⑥ only.
f – ⑤ only.
t – From Aug. 28.
v – ⑦ only.
z – 4 minutes earlier until Aug. 23.

‡ – Train number **1119** on ①③④. Conveys 🍷 on ①③⑤.
¶ – Conveys 🍷 on ⑦.
§ – Frankfurt Flughafen ✈ Fernbahnhof See also Tables **910** and **912**.
▲ – Berlin timings are subject to alteration June 20 - July 3. See Table **810**.
⊠ – Timings Dortmund - Düsseldorf - Köln are subject to alteration July 18 – 26 (certain trains do not call at Bochum). Köln - Koblenz timings also subject to change on July 19 (trains do not call at Bonn, Remagen or Andernach).

HAMBURG - DORTMUND - KÖLN - KOBLENZ 800

See notes ▲ and ⊠	IC 1113	IC 1917	ICE 129	ICE 546	ICE 546	ICE 556	ICE 556	IC 2029	ICE 615	IC 2332	IC 2334	ICE 846	ICE 856	IC 2356	ICE 605	ICE 605	IC 2142	IC 2215	IC 2315	ICE 227	ICE 544	ICE 744	ICE 554	IC 2321	IC 2121
	⑤	⑦			①–⑥		①–⑤		◇	E	G					Ⓑ	Ⓑ	R			①–⑥	⑦		R	
	🍷	🍷	A🍷	✕	✕	✕	✕	🍷	🍷	🍷	🍷	✕	T✕	🍷♦	🍷	🍷	🍷	✕	✕♦	A🍷	✕	✕	✕	✕	✕♦
Hamburg Altona ... d.	...	...	...	...	...	...	...	1532	...	...	...	...	...	...	...	...	...	1632	...	...	...	...	...	1732	...
Hamburg Hbf ... **801** d.	...	...	...	...	...	...	...	1546	...	...	...	...	...	...	...	...	...	1646	1646	...	...	...	...	1746	1746
Bremen Hbf ... **801** d.	...	...	...	...	...	...	...	1644	...	...	...	...	...	...	...	...	...	1744	1744	...	...	...	...	1844	1844
Osnabrück Hbf ... **801** d.	...	...	...	...	...	...	...	1737	...	...	...	...	...	...	...	...	...	1837	1837	...	...	...	...	1937	1937
Münster (Westf) Hbf ... **801** d.	...	...	...	...	...	...	...	1804	...	1832	1832	...	...	...	...	...	...	1904	1904	...	...	...	...	2004	2004
Berlin Hbf ▲ **810** ... d.	1408	1408	...	1450	1450	1450	1450	|	...	|	|	1548	1548	1239	...	...	...	|	|	...	1650	1650	1650	|	|
Leipzig Hbf **810** ... d.	|	|	...	|	|	|	|	|	...	|	|	|	|	|	...	...	1440	|	|	...	|	|	|	|	|
Hannover Hbf **810** ... d.	1558	1558	...	1631	1631	1631	1631	|	...	|	|	1731	1731	|	...	...	1740	|	|	...	1831	1831	1831	|	|
Hamm (Westf) ... a.	1724	1724	...	1748	1748	1748	1748	|	...	|	|	1848	1848	1852	...	...	1912	|	|	...	1948	1948	1948	|	|
Hamm (Westf) ... **805** d.	1726	1726	...	1752	1752	1754	1754	|	...	|	|	1852	1854	1856	...	...	1914	|	|	...	1952	1952	1954	|	|
Dortmund Hbf ... **805** a.	1747	1747	...	1809	1809	|	|	1833	...	|	|	1909	|	1915	...	...	1932	1933	1933	...	2009	2009	|	2033	2033
Dortmund Hbf ... d.	1752	1752	...	1812	1812	|	|	1836	1838	|	|	1912	|	1918	1923	1923	1937	1938	1938	...	2012	2012	|	2036	2036
Bochum Hbf ... d.	1803	1803	...	1825	1825	|	|	|	1849	|	|	1925	|	1930	1937	1937	|	1949	1949	...	2025	2025	|	|	|
Recklinghausen Hbf ... d.	|	|	...	|	|	|	|	|	|	1900	1900	|	|	|	|	|	|	|	|	...	|	|	|	|	|
Wanne-Eickel Hbf ... d.	|	|	...	|	|	|	|	|	|	1909	1909	|	|	|	|	|	|	|	|	...	|	|	|	|	|
Gelsenkirchen Hbf ... d.	|	|	...	|	|	|	|	|	|	1915	1915	|	|	|	|	|	|	|	|	...	|	|	|	|	|
Essen Hbf ... d.	1814	1814	...	1836	1836	|	|	|	1900	|	|	1936	|	1941	1949	1949	|	2000	2000	...	2036	2036	|	|	|
Mülheim (Ruhr) Hbf ... d.	1822	1822	...	|	|	|	|	|	|	|	|	|	|	|	|	|	|	|	|	...	|	|	|	|	|
Oberhausen Hbf ... d.	|	|	1826	|	|	|	|	|	|	1927	1927	|	|	|	|	|	|	|	|	2026	|	|	|	|	|
Duisburg Hbf ... d.	1830	1830	1834	1849	1849	|	|	|	1913	1934	1934	1949	|	1955	2005	2005	|	2013	2013	2034	2049	2049	|	|	|
Düsseldorf Flughafen ✈ ... d.	|	|	|	1859	1859	|	|	|	|	|	|	1959	|	2007	|	|	|	|	|	|	2059	2059	|	|	|
Düsseldorf Hbf ... d.	1851	1851	1848	1905	1908	|	|	|	1927	1948	1948	2008	|	2015	2022	2022	|	2027	2027	2048	2108	2108	|	|	|
Hagen Hbf ... d.	|	|	|	...	|	1824	1824	1857	|	|	|	|	1924	...	|	|	1957	|	|	|	|	|	2024	2057	2057
Wuppertal Hbf ... d.	|	|	|	...	|	1841	1841	1914	|	|	|	|	1941	...	|	|	2014	|	|	|	|	|	2041	2114	2114
Solingen Hbf ... d.	|	|	|	...	|	|	|	1927	|	|	|	|	|	...	|	|	2026	|	|	|	|	|	|	2127	2127
Köln Messe/Deutz ... a.	|	|	|	...	1932	|	|	|	|	|	|	|	|	...	2042	2042	|	|	|	|	|	2128	|	|	|
Köln Hbf ... a.	1915	1915	1912	...	|	1909	1909	1946	1949	2012	2012	2034	2009	...	|	|	2045	2049	2049	2112	2133	|	2109	2146	2146
Köln Hbf ... d.	...	1918	1920	...	|	1912**q**	1912	1953	1958	...	...	...	2018	...	|	|	...	2053	2053	2120	...	|	...	2153	2153
Köln/Bonn Flughafen ✈ ... a.	...	|	|	...	1945	|	|	|	|	...	...	...	|	...	|	|	...	|	|	|	...	2142	...	|	|
Bonn Hbf ... d.	...	1937	|	...	...	1932**q**	1937	2014	|	...	...	...	2041	...	|	|	...	2114	2114	|	...	...	...	2214	2214
Remagen ... d.	...	1951	|	...	...	...	|	|	|	...	...	...	|	...	|	|	...	|	|	|	...	...	...	|	|
Andernach ... d.	...	2003	|	...	...	...	|	|	|	...	...	...	2105	...	|	|	...	|	|	|	...	...	...	|	|
Koblenz Hbf ... a.	...	2015	|	...	...	...	2011	2046	|	...	...	...	2115	...	|	|	...	2146	2146	|	...	...	...	2246	2246
Mainz Hbf **912** ... a.	...	2111**t**	|	...	...	...	...	2140	|	...	...	...	...	...	|	|	...	2238	2238	|	...	...	...	2338	2338
Frankfurt Flughafen ✈ § ... a.	...	|	2014	...	...	...	...	2159	2055	...	...	...	...	...	2151	2151	...	2258	2258	2218	...	...	...	2359	2359
Frankfurt (Main) Hbf **910/2**. a.	...	|	2030	...	...	...	...	2213	|	...	...	...	...	...	|	|	...	2310	2310	2234	...	...	...	0013	0013
Nürnberg Hbf **920** ... a.	...	|	...	...	...	...	...	0038	|	...	...	...	...	...	|	|	...	...	...	...	...	...	...	...	...
Stuttgart Hbf **930** ... a.	...	|	...	...	...	...	...	...	2208	...	...	...	...	...	|	|	...	...	...	...	...	...	...	...	...
München Hbf **904 930** ... a.	...	|	...	...	...	...	...	...	0034	...	...	...	...	...	|	|	...	...	...	...	...	...	...	...	...
Karlsruhe Hbf **912** ... a.	...	2224	...	...	...	...	...	...	...	...	...	...	...	...	2300	2300	...	...	...	...	...	...	...	...	...
Basel SBB 🚌 **912** ... a.	...	...	...	...	...	...	...	...	...	...	...	...	...	...	...	0058**b**	...	...	...	...	...	...	...	...	...

See notes ▲ and ⊠	ICE 617	IC 2330	ICE 844	ICE 854	ICE 854	IC 2354	IC 2144	IC 2307	ICE 542	ICE 552	CNL 419	CNL 40419	ICE 609	ICE 842	ICE 852	IC 2352	IC 2146	IC 2242	IC 2309	IC 2309	ICE 540	ICE 540	ICE 840	IC 2240	IC 2021
		N		Ⓑ	⑦	⑦	Ⓑ				Q Ⓡ	Q Ⓡ			⑦	⑦	⑦	Ⓑ		⑤–⑦	L	⑤⑥	⑦	⑦	
	🍷	🍷	✕	✕	✕			✕	✕	✕	🍷♦	🍷♦	K✕	✕	✕	♦		B	¶	¶				B	
Hamburg Altona ... d.	...	...	...	...	...	...	...	1832	...	...	...	...	...	...	...	...	...	...	2032	2032	...	...	...	...	2232
Hamburg Hbf ... **801** d.	...	...	...	...	...	...	...	1846	...	...	...	...	1946	...	...	...	...	...	2046	2046	...	...	...	...	2246
Bremen Hbf ... **801** d.	...	...	...	...	...	...	...	1944	...	...	...	...	2044	...	...	...	...	...	2144	2144	...	...	...	...	2347
Osnabrück Hbf ... **801** d.	...	...	...	...	...	...	...	2037	...	...	...	...	2137	...	...	...	...	2201	2239	2239	...	...	...	2359	0045
Münster (Westf) Hbf ... **801** d.	...	2032	...	...	...	...	...	2104	...	...	...	...	2203	...	...	...	...	2225	2304	2304	...	...	...	0024	0115
Berlin Hbf ▲ **810** ... d.	...	|	1748	1748	1748	1440	...	|	1850	1850	...	...	|	1948	1948	1639	...	...	|	|	2105	2105	2148	...	|
Leipzig Hbf **810** ... d.	...	|	|	|	|	|	1640	|	|	|	...	...	|	|	|	|	1840	...	|	|	|	|	|	...	|
Hannover Hbf **810** ... d.	...	|	1931	1931	1931	|	1940	|	2031	2031	...	...	|	2131	2131	|	2140	...	|	|	2300	2300	2340	...	|
Hamm (Westf) ... a.	...	|	2048	2048	2048	2052	2110	|	2148	2148	...	...	|	2248	2248	2252	2310	...	|	|	0023	0023	0109	...	0135
Hamm (Westf) ... **805** d.	...	|	2052	2054	2054	2056	2112	|	2152	2154	...	...	|	2252	2254	2256	2312	...	|	|	0025	0025	0111	...	0137
Dortmund Hbf ... **805** a.	...	|	2110	|	|	2115	2132	2133	2209	|	...	...	2233	2309	|	2315	2332	...	2333	2333	0042	0047	0127	...	0154
Dortmund Hbf ... d.	2038	|	2112	|	|	2118	2137	2138	2212	|	...	...	2238	2312	|	2318	2337	...	...	2338	0044	0049	0130	...	0203
Bochum Hbf ... d.	2049	|	2125	|	|	2130	|	2149	2225	|	...	...	2250	2325	|	2330	|	...	...	2350	0056	0102	0142	...	0215
Recklinghausen Hbf ... d.	|	2100	|	|	|	|	|	|	|	|	...	...	|	|	|	|	|	...	...	|	|	|	|	...	|
Wanne-Eickel Hbf ... d.	|	2109	|	|	|	|	|	|	|	|	...	...	|	|	|	|	|	...	...	|	|	|	|	...	|
Gelsenkirchen Hbf ... d.	|	2115	|	|	|	|	|	|	|	|	...	...	|	|	|	|	|	...	...	|	|	|	|	...	|
Essen Hbf ... d.	2100	|	2136	|	|	2141	|	2200	2236	|	...	...	2300	2336	|	2341	|	...	...	0000	0106	0113	0153	...	0228
Mülheim (Ruhr) Hbf ... d.	|	|	|	|	|	|	|	|	|	|	...	...	|	|	|	|	|	...	...	|	|	|	|	...	|
Oberhausen Hbf ... d.	|	2127	|	|	|	|	|	|	|	|	2248	2248	|	|	|	|	|	...	...	|	|	|	|	...	|
Duisburg Hbf ... d.	2113	2134	2151	|	|	2156	|	2213	2249	|	2256**u**	2256**u**	2313	2349	|	2355	|	...	...	0013	0119	0127	0206	...	0241
Düsseldorf Flughafen ✈ ... d.	|	|	2201	|	|	2208	|	|	2259	|	|	|	|	2359	|	0006	|	...	...	|	0129**n**	0139**c**	0216	...	0252
Düsseldorf Hbf ... d.	2127	2148	2209	|	|	2216	|	2227	2308	|	2312**u**	2312**u**	2327	0007	|	0014	|	...	...	0027	0138	0147	0224	...	0302
Hagen Hbf ... d.	|	|	|	2124	2124	|	2157	|	|	2224	|	|	|	|	2324	|	2357	...	...	|	|	|	|	...	|
Wuppertal Hbf ... d.	|	|	|	2141	2141	|	2214	|	|	2241	|	|	|	|	2341	|	0014	...	...	|	|	|	|	...	|
Solingen Hbf ... d.	|	|	|	|	|	|	2226	|	|	|	|	|	|	|	|	|	0026	...	...	|	|	|	|	...	|
Köln Messe/Deutz ... a.	|	|	|	|	|	|	|	|	|	|	|	|	|	|	|	|	|	...	...	|	|	|	|	...	|
Köln Hbf ... a.	2149	2212	2231	2209	2209	2240	2245	2249	2330	2309	|	|	2349	0029	0009	0035	0045	...	...	0049	0201	0209	0246	...	0336
Köln Hbf ... d.	2154	...	...	...	2218	...	...	2253	...	2318**q**	2346**u**	2346**u**	2353	...	...	...	...	...	...	...	0214	...	...	...	0352
Köln/Bonn Flughafen ✈ ... a.	|	...	...	...	|	...	...	|	...	|	|	|	|	...	...	...	...	...	...	...	0226	...	...	...	0404
Bonn Hbf ... d.	|	...	...	...	2237	...	...	2314	...	2339**q**	0007**u**	0007**u**	0014	...	...	...	...	...	...	...	...	...	...	...	|
Remagen ... d.	|	...	...	...	|	...	...	2328	...	...	|	|	|	...	...	...	...	...	...	...	...	...	...	...	|
Andernach ... d.	|	...	...	...	|	...	...	2341	...	...	|	|	|	...	...	...	...	...	...	...	...	...	...	...	|
Koblenz Hbf ... a.	|	...	...	...	2311	...	...	2354	...	...	0044**u**	0044**u**	0046	...	...	...	...	...	...	...	...	...	...	...	0512
Mainz Hbf **912** ... a.	|	...	...	...	...	...	...	...	...	...	|	|	0141	...	...	...	...	...	...	...	...	...	...	...	0627
Frankfurt Flughafen ✈ § ... a.	2256	...	...	...	...	...	...	...	...	...	|	|	0202**r**	...	...	...	...	...	...	...	...	...	...	...	0646
Frankfurt (Main) Hbf **910/2**. a.	|	...	...	...	...	...	...	...	...	...	|	|	0217	...	...	...	...	...	...	...	...	...	...	...	0702
Nürnberg Hbf **920** ... a.	|	...	...	...	...	...	...	...	...	...	|	|	|	...	...	...	...	...	...	...	...	...	...	...	...
Stuttgart Hbf **930** ... a.	0052**j**	...	...	...	...	...	...	...	...	...	0419**z**	|	|	...	...	...	...	...	...	...	...	...	...	...	...
München Hbf **904 930** ... a.	...	...	...	...	...	...	...	...	...	...	0716	|	|	...	...	...	...	...	...	...					
Karlsruhe Hbf **912** ... a.	...	...	...	...	...	...	...	...	...	...	...	0437	0337	...	...	...	...	...	...						
Basel SBB 🚌 **912** ... a.	...	...	...	...	...	...	...	...	...	...	...	0654	0547	...	...	...	...	...	...						

*See Table **802** for Rhein-Ruhr local RE and S-Bahn services*

♦ – **NOTES** (LISTED BY TRAIN NUMBER)

419 – POLLUX – 🛏 1, 2 cl., ▬ 2 cl., (2) (reclining) and 🍷 Amsterdam - München.
2121 – Until Oct. 25. FEHMARN – (12) and ✕ Puttgarden - Lübeck - Frankfurt.
2315 – Until Oct. 25. DEICHGRAF – (12) and ✕ Westerland - Stuttgart.
2352 – (12) Stralsund - Berlin - Halle - Erfurt - Kassel - Köln.
2356 – STRELASUND – (12) and 🍷 (Ostseebad Binz ①–⑥ -) Stralsund - Berlin - Halle - Erfurt - Kassel - Düsseldorf.
40419 – PEGASUS – 🛏 1, 2 cl., ▬ 2 cl., (2) (reclining) and 🍷 Amsterdam - Zürich.

A – From Amsterdam (Table 28).
B – From Berlin (Table **810**).
E – Daily until Oct. 25; ⑤⑦ from Oct. 30. From Emden (Table **812**).
G – ①–④ from Oct. 26. From Norddeich Mole (Table **812**).
K – From Kiel (Table 820).
L – ①②③④⑦.
N – ③–⑦ until Oct. 25; ⑦ from Nov. 1. From Norddeich Mole (Table **812**).
Q – Daily until Nov. 2; ①⑤⑥⑦ from Nov. 6.

R – From Oct. 26.
T – To Trier (Table **915**). ✕ Berlin - Köln.

b – Basel **Badischer Bahnhof**.
c – Not June 27, July 4.
j – 0040 on the mornings of ①⑦ (also July 11, 18, 25).
n – Not June 29.
q – Ⓑ only.
r – Frankfurt Flughafen ✈ Regionalbahnhof.
t – From Aug. 30.
u – Stops to pick up only.
z – Not July 10 - Oct. 5.

◇ – On June 20, July 4 terminates at Augsburg Hbf (a. 2352).

¶ – Conveys 🍷 on ⑦.
§ – Frankfurt Flughafen Fernbahnhof. See also Tables **910** and **912**.
▲ – Berlin timings are subject to alteration June 20 - July 3. See Table **810**.
⊠ – Timings Dortmund - Düsseldorf - Köln are subject to alteration July 18 – 26 (certain trains do not call at Bochum). Köln - Koblenz timings also subject to change on July 19 (trains do not call at Bonn, Remagen or Andernach).

801 Local services MÜNSTER - OSNABRÜCK - BREMEN - HAMBURG

See Table **800** for fast trains

Münster (Westf) Hbf - **Osnabrück** Hbf and v.v. Operated by WestfalenBahn. Journey time: 36 minutes.
From Münster (Westf) Hbf at 0004 Ⓒ, 0504 Ⓐ, 0604 ⚒, 0634 Ⓐ, 0704, 0734 Ⓐ, 0804, 0904 and hourly until 1604, then 1634 Ⓐ, 1704, 1734 Ⓐ, 1804, 1904, 2004, 2104, 2204 and 2304.
From Osnabrück Hbf at 0019 Ⓒ, 0519 Ⓐ, 0549 Ⓐ, 0619 ⚒, 0719, 0749 Ⓐ, 0819, 0919 and hourly until 1619, then 1649 Ⓐ, 1719, 1749 Ⓐ, 1819, 1919, 2019, 2119, 2219 and 2319.

Osnabrück Hbf - **Bremen** Hbf and v.v. *RE* services. Journey time: 72–74 minutes. Certain trains continue to / start from Bremerhaven (see Table **815**).
From Osnabrück Hbf at 0421 ¶ ⚒, 0538 ⚒, 0638 ⚒, 0738, 0838, 0938, 1038, 1138, 1238 ⚒, 1338 Ⓑ, 1438, 1538, 1638, 1738, 1838, 1938 Ⓑ, 2038 and 2138.
From Bremen Hbf 0506 ⚒, 0606 ⚒, 0706 ⚒, 0806, 0906, 1006, 1106, 1206, 1306, 1406, 1506, 1606 ⚒, 1706, 1806 Ⓑ, 1906, 2006 Ⓑ, 2106 and 2253.

Bremen Hbf - **Hamburg** Hbf and v.v. *metronom* (operated by metronom Eisenbahngesellschaft). Journey time: 72–81 minutes.
From Bremen Hbf at 0513, 0618 Ⓐ, 0628 Ⓒ, 0645 ⚒, 0728, 0828, 0928, 1028, 1128, 1228, 1328, 1428, 1528, 1628, 1728, 1828, 1928, 2028, 2128 and 2228.
From Hamburg Hbf at 0015 ⑦, 0515 ⚒, 0615, 0715, 0815, 0915, 1015, 1115, 1215, 1315, 1415, 1515, 1615, 1652 Ⓐ, 1715, 1815, 1915, 2015, 2115, 2215 † and 2315.

¶ – Arrives Bremen 0548.

802 RHEIN – RUHR LOCAL SERVICES

RE / RB services

Services in this table (pages 372 – 374) are shown route by route. Sub-headings indicate the route number and principal stations served.

RE1 Aachen - Köln - Düsseldorf - Duisburg - Dortmund - Hamm ⊡ *RE6* Düsseldorf - Duisburg - Dortmund - Bielefeld - Minden ⊡

km																							⑤⑥	
0	**Aachen** Hbf.. **807 910** d.	...	...	...	...	0451e	...	0551	...	0651	...		...	1751	...	1851	...	1951	...	2051	2151	2251	2351	2351
31	Düren .... **807** d.	...	...	...	...	0517e	...	0617	...	0717	...		...	1817	...	1917	...	2017	...	2117	2217	2317	0017	0017
70	**Köln** Hbf ...... **807 910** a.	...	...	...	...	0544e	...	0644	...	0744	...		...	1844	...	1944	...	2044	...	2144	2244	2344	0044	0044
70	**Köln** Hbf .... d.	...	...	...	...	0551	...	0651	...	0751	...		...	1851	...	1951	...	2051	...	2151	2251	2351	0051	...
71	**Köln** Messe/Deutz ...... d.	...	...	...	...	0554	...	0654	...	0754	...	and at	...	1854	...	1954	...	2054	...	2154	2254	2354	0054	...
83	Leverkusen Mitte .... d.	...	...	...	...	0605	...	0705	...	0805	...		...	1905	...	2005	...	2105	...	2205	2305	0005	0105	...
110	**Düsseldorf** Hbf .... d.	0423c	...	0523	...	0623	0654e	0723	0754r	0823	0854	the same	1854	1923	...	2023	...	2123	...	2223	2323	0023	0123	...
117	Düsseldorf Flughafen ✈ d.	0429c	...	0529	...	0629	0702e	0729	0802r	0829	0902		1902	1929	...	2029	...	2129	...	2229	2329	0029	0129	...
134	**Duisburg** Hbf .... d.	0439	...	0539	...	0639	0715e	0739	0815r	0839	0915	minutes	1915	1939	...	2039	...	2139	...	2239	2339	0039	0139	...
144	Mülheim (Ruhr) Hbf...... d.	0445	...	0545	...	0645	0721e	0745	0821r	0845	0921		1921	1945	...	2045	...	2145	...	2245	2345	0045	0145	...
153	**Essen** Hbf .... d.	0453	...	0553	...	0653	0729e	0753	0829r	0853	0929	past each	1929	1953	...	2053	...	2153	...	2253	2353	0053	0153	...
169	Bochum Hbf................ d.	0505	...	0605	...	0705	0743e	0805	0843r	0905	0943		1943	2005	...	2105	...	2205	...	2305	0005	0105	0205	...
187	**Dortmund** Hbf............ d.	0517	0555	0617	0655	0717	0755	0817	0855	0917	0955	hour until	1955	2017	2055	2117	2155	2217	*2255*	2317	0017	0117	0217	...
218	**Hamm** (Westf) ..... **810** d.	0546	0615	0640	0715	0745	0815	0840	0915	0945	1015		2015	2040	2115	2145	2215	2245	2322	2345	0045	0145	0245	...
268	Gütersloh Hbf ...... **810** d.	...	0649	...	0749	...	0849	...	0949	...	1049		2049	...	2149	...	2249	...	2355	...	...	...	...	...
285	**Bielefeld** Hbf....... **810** a.	...	0658	...	0758	...	0858	...	0958	...	1058		2058	...	2158	...	2258	...	0008	...	...	...	...	...
299	Herford .... **810** a.	...	0707r	...	0807	...	0907	...	1007	...	1107		2107	...	2207r	...	2307b	...	...	...	...	...	...	...
309	Löhne .... **810** a.	...	0713r	...	0813	...	0913	...	1013	...	1113		2113	...	2213r	...	2313b	...	...	...	...	...	...	...
315	Bad Oeynhausen . **810** a.	...	0718r	...	0818	...	0918	...	1018	...	1118		2118	...	2218r	...	2318b	...	...	...	...	...	...	...
330	**Minden** (Westf).... **810** a.	...	0730r	...	0830	...	0930	...	1030	...	1130		2130	...	2230r	...	2330b	...	...	...	...	...	...	...

				⚒																			⑤⑥	
Minden (Westf) ..... **810** d.	...	...	...	0528e	...	0628r	...	0728r	...	0828	...		1728	...	1828	...	1928	...	2028	...	2128	...	...	2228r
Bad Oeynhausen ... **810** d.	...	...	...	0539e	...	0639r	...	0739r	...	0839	...		1739	...	1839	...	1939	...	2039	...	2139	...	...	2239r
Löhne .... **810** d.	...	...	...	0544e	...	0644r	...	0744r	...	0844	...		1744	...	1844	...	1944	...	2044	...	2144	...	...	2244r
Herford .... **810** d.	...	...	...	0550e	...	0650r	...	0750r	...	0850	...		1750	...	1850	...	1950	...	2050	...	2150	...	...	2250r
Bielefeld Hbf........ **810** d.	...	...	...	0559	...	0659	...	0759	...	0859	...	and at	1759	...	1859	...	1959	...	2059	...	2159	...	...	2259
Gütersloh Hbf .... **810** d.	...	...	...	0608	...	0708	...	0808	...	0908	...		1808	...	1908	...	2008	...	2108	...	2208	...	...	2308
Hamm (Westf)....... **810** d.	0416	0516	0616	0644	0720	0744	0816	0844	0920	0944	1016	the same	1844	1920	1944	2016	2044	2116	2144	2216	2244	2316	2316	2344
Dortmund Hbf............ d.	0445	0545	0645	0706	0745	0806	0845	0906	0945	1006	1045		1906	1945	2004	2045	2104	2145	2204	2245	2304	2345	2345	0004
Bochum Hbf................. d.	0456	0556	0656	0719	0756	0819	0856	0919	0956	1019	1056	minutes	1919	1956	...	2056	...	2156	...	2256	...	2356	2356	...
Essen Hbf .... d.	0509	0609	0709	0732	0809	0832	0909	0932	1009	1032	1109		1932	2009	...	2109	...	2209	...	2309	...	0009	0009	...
Mülheim (Ruhr) Hbf....... d.	0516	0616	0716	0738	0816	0838	0916	0938	1016	1038	1116	past each	1938	2016	...	2116	...	2216	...	2316	...	0016	0016	...
Duisburg Hbf .... d.	0524	0624	0724	0748	0824	0848	0924	0948	1024	1048	1124		1948	2024	...	2124	...	2224	...	2324	...	0021	0024	...
Düsseldorf Flughafen ✈ d.	0532	0632	0732	0757	0832	0857	0932	0957	1032	1057	1132	hour until	1957	2032	...	2132	...	2232	...	2332	...	...	0032	...
Düsseldorf Hbf .... d.	0540	0640	0740	0805	0840	0905	0940	1005	1040	1105	1140		2005	2040	...	2140	...	2240	...	2340	...	...	0040	...
Leverkusen Mitte .... d.	0555	0655	0755	...	0855	...	0955	...	1055	...	1155		...	2055	...	2155	...	2255	...	2355	...	...	0055	...
Köln Messe/Deutz .... d.	0608	0708	0808	...	0908	...	1008	...	1108	...	1208		...	2108	...	2208	...	2308	...	0008	...	...	0108	...
Köln Hbf .... a.	0611	0711	0811	...	0911	...	1011	...	1111	...	1211		...	2111	...	2211	...	2311	...	0011	...	...	0111	...
Köln Hbf .... **807 910** d.	0615	0715	0815	...	0915	...	1015	...	1115	...	1215		...	2115	...	2215	...	2315	...	0015	...	...	0115	...
Düren .... **807** d.	0639	0739	0839	...	0939	...	1039	...	1139	...	1239		...	2139	...	2239	...	2339	...	0039	...	...	0139	...
Aachen Hbf... **807 910** a.	0707	0807	0907	...	1007	...	1107	...	1207	...	1307		...	2207	...	2307	...	0007	...	0107	...	...	0207	...

RE2 Mönchengladbach - Duisburg - Essen - Gelsenkirchen - Münster ⊡ *RB33* Aachen - Mönchengladbach - Duisburg ⊡ *RB42* Essen - Münster

km		Ⓐ	⚒			⚒																⊖		
0	**Aachen** Hbf............... d.	...	*0413*	...	*0513*	*0513*	...	0538r	*0613*	...	0638		*1813*	...	1838	*1913*	...	1938	*2013*	...	2038	*2113*	...	2238
62	**Mönchengladbach** Hbf d.	...	0521	...	0621	0621	...	0637	0721	...	0737		1921	...	1937	2021	...	2037	2121	...	2137	2221	...	2337
71	Viersen .... d.	...	0531	...	0631	0631	...	0645	0731	...	0745	and at	1931	...	1945	2031	...	2045	2131	...	2145	2231	...	2345
86	Krefeld Hbf .... d.	...	0542	...	0642	0642	...	0659	0742	...	0759		1942	...	1959	2042	...	2059	2142	...	2159	2242	...	2359
107	**Duisburg** Hbf .... d.	...	0601	...	0701	0701	...	0724	0801	...	0824	the same	2001	...	2024	2101	...	2124	2201	...	2224	2301	...	0024
117	Mülheim (Ruhr) Hbf...... d.	...	0607	...	0707	0707	...	...	0807	...	...		2007	...	...	2107	...	...	2207	...	...	2307	...	...
126	**Essen** Hbf .... d.	0515	0615	0648	0713	0715	0748	...	0815	0848	...	minutes	2015	2048	...	2115	2148	...	2215	2248	...	2316	2348	...
134	Gelsenkirchen Hbf ...... d.	0524	0624	0656	...	0724	0756	...	0824	0856	...		2024	2056	...	2124	2156	...	2224	2256	...	2324	2356	...
139	Wanne-Eickel Hbf .... d.	0529	0629	0701	...	0729	0801	...	0829	0901	...	past each	2029	2101	...	2129	2201	...	2229	2301	...	2329	0001	...
149	Recklinghausen Hbf .... d.	0537	0637	0709	...	0737	0809	...	0837	0909	...		2037	2109	...	2137	2209	...	2237	2309	...	2337	0009	...
164	Haltern am See .... d.	0549	0649	0719	...	0749	0819	...	0849	0919	...	hour until	2049	2119	...	2148	2219	...	2248	2319	...	2348	0019	...
177	Dülmen .... d.	0559	0659	0728	...	0759	0828	...	0859	0928	...		2059	2128	...	...	2228	...	...	2328	...	...	0028	...
206	**Münster** (Westf) Hbf.... a.	0621	0721	0749	...	0821	0849	...	0921	0949	...		2121	2149	...	...	2249	...	...	2349	...	...	0049	...

	⚒	⚒	⚒	⚒																				
Münster (Westf) Hbf..... d.	0411	...	0511	0537e	...	...	0611	0637r	...	0711	0737r	...	0811	0837	...	0911		2037	...	2111	...	...	2211	2311
Dülmen .... d.	0432	...	0532	0558e	...	...	0632	0658r	...	0732	0758r	...	0832	0858	...	0932		2058	...	2132	...	...	2232	2332
Haltern am See .... d.	0441	0508	0541	0608	...	...	0641	0708	...	0741	0808	...	0841	0908	...	0941	and at	2108	...	2141	2208	...	2241	2341
Recklinghausen Hbf..... d.	0451	0521	0551	0621	...	...	0651	0721	...	0751	0821	...	0851	0921	...	0951		2121	...	2151	2221	...	2251	2351
Wanne-Eickel Hbf .... d.	0500	0529	0600	0629	...	...	0700	0729	...	0800	0829	...	0900	0929	...	1000	the same	2129	...	2200	2229	...	2300	0000
Gelsenkirchen Hbf .... d.	0504	0534	0604	0634	...	...	0704	0734	...	0804	0834	...	0904	0934	...	1004		2134	...	2204	2234	...	2304	0004
Essen Hbf .... d.	0515	0545	0615	0645	0645	...	0714	0745	...	0814	0845	...	0914	0945	...	1014	minutes	2145	...	2214	2245	...	2314	0014
Mülheim (Ruhr) Hbf....... d.	...	0551	...	0651	0651	...	...	0751	...	...	0851	...	...	0951	...	...		2151	...	...	2251	...	...	...
Duisburg Hbf .... d.	...	0559	...	0659	0659	0736	...	0759	0836	...	0859	0936	...	0959	1036	...	past each	2159	2236	...	2259	2336	...	...
Krefeld Hbf .... d.	...	0619	...	0719	0719	0800	...	0819	0900	...	0919	1000	...	1019	1100	...		2219	2300	...	2319	0000	...	...
Viersen .... d.	...	0633	...	0733	0733	0813	...	0833	0913	...	0933	1013	...	1033	1113	...	hour until	2233	2313	...	2333	0013	...	...
Mönchengladbach Hbf a.	...	0642	...	0742	0742	0820	...	0842	0920	...	0942	1020	...	1042	1120	...		2242	2320	...	2342	0020	...	...
Aachen Hbf.................. a.	...	*0745*	...	*0845*	*0845*	0920	...	*0945*	1020	...	*1045*	1120	...	*1145*	1220	...		*2345*	0020	...	*0045*	...	...	...

RE3 Düsseldorf - Duisburg - Gelsenkirchen - Dortmund - Hamm ⊡

km											
0	**Düsseldorf** Hbf .... d.	0545e	0645r	0745	0845		1845	1945	2045		2345
7	Düsseldorf Flughafen ✈ d.	0552e	0652r	0752	0852		1852	1952	2052		2352
24	**Duisburg** Hbf .... a.	0603e	0703r	0803	0903	and	1903	2003	2103	and	0003
24	**Duisburg** Hbf .... d.	0610	0710	0810	0910		1910	2010	2110		0010
32	Oberhausen Hbf .... d.	0618	0718	0818	0918	hourly	1918	2018	2118	hourly	0018
48	Gelsenkirchen Hbf ...... d.	0631	0731	0831	0931		1931	2031	2131		0031
53	Wanne-Eickel Hbf .... d.	0636	0736	0836	0936	until	1936	2036	2136	until	0036
57	Herne .... d.	0640	0740	0840	0940		1940	2040	2140		0040
78	**Dortmund** Hbf............ a.	0657	0757	0857	0957		1957	2057	2157		0057
109	**Hamm** (Westf) Hbf....... a.	0730e	0830e	0930e	1030r		2030e	2130e	*2245*		*0145*

Hamm (Westf) Hbf.... d.	0529e	0629e	0729e	0829r		1729r	1829e	*1920*	*2016*	*2116*
Dortmund Hbf......... d.	0603	0703	0803	0903		1803	1903	2003	2103	2203
Herne .... d.	0620	0720	0820	0920	and	1820	1920	2020	2120	2220
Wanne-Eickel Hbf .... d.	0624	0724	0824	0924		1824	1924	2024	2124	2224
Gelsenkirchen Hbf ... d.	0629	0729	0829	0929	hourly	1829	1929	2029	2129	2229
Oberhausen Hbf....... d.	0643	0743	0843	0943		1843	1943	2043	2144	2243
Duisburg Hbf .... a.	0648	0748	0848	0948	until	1848	1948	2048	2150	2248
Duisburg Hbf .... d.	0652	0752	0852	0952		1852	1952	2052	2152	2252
Düsseldorf Flughafen . d.	0702	0802	0902	1002		1902	2002	2102	2202	2302
Düsseldorf Hbf .... a.	0710	0810	0910	1010		1910	2010	2110	2210	2310

b – Ⓑ only.
c – Ⓒ only.
e – Ⓐ only.
r – ⚒ only.
⊖ – Change trains at Essen on ①②③④⑥⑦ (through train on ⑤).
⊡ – See note and shaded panel on page 373.

RE4 Aachen - Mönchengladbach - Düsseldorf - Wuppertal - Dortmund ⊡ *RE13* Venlo - Mönchengladbach - Düsseldorf - Wuppertal - Hamm ⊡

km			⚒	⚒	Ⓐ		⚒																		
0	**Aachen** Hbf .... **471** d.	0253	0413	...	...	0513	...	0613	...	0713	...		...	1713	...	1813	...	1913	...	2013	...	2113	...	2238
14	Herzogenrath .... **471** d.	0307	0427	...	...	0527	...	0627	...	0727	...		...	1727	...	1827	...	1927	...	2027	...	2127	...	2253
58	Rheydt Hbf .... d.	0341	0503	...	...	0603	...	0703	...	0803	...		...	1803	...	1903	...	2003	...	2103	...	2203	...	2330
	Venlo 🏛 .... d.	|	|	0504	0504	|	0604	|	0704	|	0804	and at	1704	|	1804	|	1904	|	2004	|	2104	|	2204	|
	Kaldenkirchen .... d.	|	|	0510	0510	|	0610	|	0710	|	0810		1710	|	1810	|	1910	|	2010	|	2110	|	2210	|
	Viersen .... d.	|	|	0527	0527	|	0627	|	0727	|	0827	the same	1727	|	1827	|	1927	|	2027	|	2127	|	2227	|
62	**Mönchengladbach** Hbf d.	0349	0510	0545j	0545j	0610	0645j	0710	0745j	0810	0845j		1745j	1810	1845j	1910	1945j	2010	2045j	2110	2145j	2210	2235	2336
79	Neuss Hbf .... d.	0403	0524	0557	0557	0624	0657	0724	0757	0824	0857	minutes	1757	1824	1857	1924	1957	2024	2057	2124	2157	2224	...	...
90	**Düsseldorf** Hbf .... a.	0413	0534	0608	0608	0634	0708	0734	0808	0834	0908		1808	1834	1908	1934	2008	2034	2108	2134	2208	2234	...	...
90	**Düsseldorf** Hbf .... d.	f	0540e	...	0614	0640r	0714	0740	0814	0840	0914	past each	1814	1840	1914	1940	2014	2040	...	2140	...	2240	...	...
117	**Wuppertal** Hbf .... d.	...	0602e	...	0631	0702r	0731	0802	0831	0902	0931		1831	1902	1931	2002	2031	2102	...	2202	...	2302	...	...
144	**Hagen** Hbf .... d.	...	0630e	...	0658	0730r	0758	0830	0858	0930	0958	hour until	1858	1930	1955	2030	2055	2130	...	2230	...	2330	...	...
159	Witten .... d.	...	0641e	...	|	0741r	|	0841	|	0941	|		|	1941	|	2041	|	2141	...	2241	...	2341	...	...
175	**Dortmund** Hbf .... d.	...	0651e	...	|	0751r	|	0851	|	0951	|		|	1951	|	2051	|	2151	...	2251	...	2351	...	...
	Schwerte (Ruhr) .... d.	...	...	...	0708	...	0808e	...	0908r	...	1008		1908	...	2031	...	2131	...	...	...	...	...	...	...
	Unna .... d.	...	...	...	0720	...	0820e	...	0920r	...	1020		1920	...	2043	...	2143	...	...	...	...	...	...	...
	Hamm (Westf) .... d.	...	...	...	0734	...	0834e	...	0934r	...	1034		1934	...	2056	...	2157	...	...	...	...	...	...	...

km		⚒	⚒																					
0	**Hamm** (Westf) .... d.	...	...	...	...	0622e	...	0722e	...	0822e	...	0922r	...	1022		1722	...	1822	...	1922	...	...	...	...
19	Unna .... d.	...	...	...	...	0635e	...	0735e	...	0835e	...	0935r	...	1035		1735	...	1835	...	1935	...	...	...	...
35	Schwerte (Ruhr) .... d.	...	...	...	...	0648e	...	0748e	...	0848e	...	0948r	...	1048		1748	...	1848	...	1948	...	...	...	...
	Dortmund Hbf .... d.	...	...	...	0609e	|	0709r	|	0809	|	0909	|	1009	|	and at	|	1809	|	1909	|	2009	...	2109	2209
	Witten .... d.	...	...	...	0619e	|	0719r	|	0819	|	0919	|	1019	|		|	1819	|	1919	|	2019	...	2119	2219
48	**Hagen** Hbf .... d.	...	...	0602e	0632e	0702r	0732r	0802	0832	0902	0932	1002	1032	1102	the same	1802	1832	1902	1932	2002	2032	...	2132	2232
75	**Wuppertal** Hbf .... d.	...	...	0626e	0658e	0726r	0758r	0826	0858	0926	0958	1026	1058	1126		1826	1858	1926	1958	2026	2058	...	2158	2258
102	**Düsseldorf** Hbf .... a.	...	...	0645e	0719e	0745r	0819r	0845	0919	0945	1019	1045	1119	1145	minutes	1845	1919	1945	2019	2045	2119	...	2219	2319
102	**Düsseldorf** Hbf .... d.	0548	0622	0648r	0722	0748	0822	0848	0922	0948	1022	1048	1122	1148		1848	1922	1948	2022	2048	2122	2148	2222	2322
113	Neuss Hbf .... d.	0601	0636	0701r	0736	0801	0836	0901	0936	1001	1036	1101	1136	1201	past each	1901	1936	2001	2036	2101	2136	2201	2236	2336
130	**Mönchengladbach** Hbf d.	0625j	0649	0725j	0749	0825j	0849	0925j	0949	1025j	1049	1125j	1149	1225j		1925j	1949	2025j	2049	2125j	2149	2225j	2249	2349
139	Viersen .... d.	0633	|	0733	|	0833	|	0933	|	1033	|	1133	|	1233	hour until	1933	|	2033	|	2133	|	2233	|	|
157	Kaldenkirchen .... d.	0652	|	0752	|	0852	|	0952	|	1052	|	1152	|	1252		1952	|	2052	|	2152	|	2252	|	|
167	**Venlo** 🏛 .... a.	0657	|	0757	|	0857	|	0957	|	1057	|	1157	|	1257		1957	|	2057	|	2157	|	2257	|	|
	Rheydt Hbf .... d.	...	0654	...	0754	...	0854	...	0954	...	1054	...	1154	...		...	1954	...	2054	...	2154	...	2254	2354
	Herzogenrath .... **471** d.	...	0729	...	0829	...	0929	...	1029	...	1129	...	1229	...		...	2029	...	2129	...	2229	...	2329	0029
	Aachen Hbf .... **471** a.	...	0745	...	0845	...	0945	...	1045	...	1145	...	1245	...		...	2045	...	2145	...	2245	...	2345	0045

RE5 Koblenz - Bonn - Köln - Düsseldorf - Duisburg - Emmerich ⊡

km				Ⓐ	◐	⚒															◐	◐		◐	◐
0	**Koblenz** Hbf .... d.	...	...	0516	0526	0616	0716	0816	0916	1016	1116	1216	1316	1416	1516	1616	1716	1816	1916	2016	2026	2126	...	2226	2326
18	Andernach .... d.	...	...	0526	0543	0626	0726	0826	0926	1026	1126	1226	1326	1426	1526	1626	1726	1826	1926	2026	2043	2143	...	2243	2343
29	Bad Breisig .... d.	...	...	0533	0554	0633	0733	0833	0933	1033	1133	1233	1333	1433	1533	1633	1733	1833	1933	2033	2054	2154	...	2254	2354
39	Remagen .... d.	...	...	0542	0611j	0642	0742	0842	0942	1042	1142	1242	1342	1442	1542	1642	1742	1842	1942	2042	2111j	2211j	...	2311j	0011j
59	**Bonn** Hbf .... d.	...	...	0601	0632	0701	0801	0901	1001	1101	1201	1301	1401	1501	1601	1701	1801	1901	2001	2101	2132	2232	...	2332	0032
93	**Köln** Hbf .... a.	...	...	0628	0701	0728	0828	0928	1028	1128	1228	1328	1428	1528	1628	1728	1828	1928	2028	2128	2201	2301	...	0001	0101
93	**Köln** Hbf .... ♥ d.	...	0631r	0631	▬	0731	0831	0931	1031	1131	1231	1331	1431	1531	1631	1731	1831	1931	2031	2131	...	...	2351	...	...
106	Leverkusen Mitte .... d.	...	0645r	0645	...	0745	0845	0945	1045	1145	1245	1345	1445	1545	1645	1745	1845	1945	2045	2145	...	...	0005	...	...
133	**Düsseldorf** Hbf .... d.	...	0703r	0703	...	0803	0903	1003	1103	1203	1303	1403	1503	1603	1703	1803	1903	2003	2103	2203	...	...	0023	...	...
140	Düsseldorf Flughafen ✈ d.	...	0710r	0710	...	0810	0910	1010	1110	1210	1310	1410	1510	1610	1710	1810	1910	2010	2110	2210	...	...	0029	...	...
157	**Duisburg** Hbf .... d.	0620	0720	0720	0820	0820	0920	1020	1120	1220	1320	1420	1520	1620	1720	1820	1920	2020	2120	2220	...	...	0044	...	...
165	Oberhausen Hbf .... d.	0628	0728	0728	0828	0828	0928	1028	1128	1228	1328	1428	1528	1628	1728	1828	1928	2028	2128	2228	...	...	0051	...	...
192	Wesel .... d.	0659	0755	0755	0855	0855	0955	1055	1155	1255	1355	1455	1555	1655	1755	1855	1955	2055	2155	2255	...	...	0119	...	...
226	**Emmerich** .... a.	0725	0821	0821	0925	0925	1021	1125	1221	1325	1421	1525	1621	1725	1821	1925	2021	2125	2227	2327	...	...	0152	...	...

	Ⓐ	◐	⚒		⚒														◐		◐	◐			
Emmerich .... d.	...	...	0433e	0533	0533	0636	0740	0836	0940	1036	1140	1236	1340	1436	1540	1636	1740	1836	...	1940	...	...	2036	2140	2234
Wesel .... d.	...	...	0506e	0606	0606	0706	0806	0906	1006	1106	1212	1306	1412	1506	1612	1706	1812	1906	...	2012	...	...	2106	2206	2307
Oberhausen Hbf .... d.	...	...	0534e	0634	0634	0734	0834	0934	1034	1134	1234	1334	1434	1534	1634	1734	1834	1934	...	2034	...	...	2134	2234	2335
Duisburg Hbf .... d.	...	...	0542	0640	0642	0742	0842	0942	1042	1142	1242	1342	1442	1542	1642	1742	1842	1942	...	2042	...	...	2140	2240	2341
Düsseldorf Flughafen ✈ d.	...	...	0551	▬	0651	0751	0851	0951	1051	1151	1251	1351	1451	1551	1651	1751	1851	1951	...	2051	...	...	2202	2302	▬
Düsseldorf Hbf .... d.	...	...	0558	...	0658	0758	0858	0958	1058	1158	1258	1358	1458	1558	1658	1758	1858	1958	...	2058	...	...	2210	2310	...
Leverkusen Mitte .... d.	...	...	0614	...	0714	0814	0914	1014	1114	1214	1314	1414	1514	1614	1714	1814	1914	2014	...	2114	...	...	...	...	⑤⑥
Köln Hbf .... ★ a.	...	...	0629	...	0729	0829	0929	1029	1129	1229	1329	1429	1529	1629	1729	1829	1929	2029	...	2129	...	...	...	...	d ◐
Köln Hbf .... d.	0532	0556	0632	0732	0732	0832	0932	1032	1132	1232	1332	1432	1532	1632	1732	1832	1932	2032	2056	2138	2156	2256	...	...	2356
Bonn Hbf .... d.	0558	0627	0658	0758	0758	0858	0958	1058	1158	1258	1358	1458	1558	1658	1758	1858	1958	2058	2127	2208	2227	2327	...	...	0027
Remagen .... d.	0615	0654j	0715	0815	0815	0915	1015	1115	1215	1315	1415	1515	1615	1715	1815	1915	2015	2115	2154j	2233	2254j	2354j	...	...	0054j
Bad Breisig .... d.	0623	0703	0723	0823	0823	0923	1023	1123	1223	1323	1423	1523	1623	1723	1823	1923	2023	2123	2203	...	2303	0003	...	...	0103
Andernach .... d.	0630	0714	0730	0830	0830	0930	1030	1130	1230	1330	1430	1530	1630	1730	1830	1930	2030	2130	2214	...	2314	0014	...	...	0114
Koblenz Hbf .... a.	0642	0731	0742	0842	0842	0942	1042	1142	1242	1342	1442	1542	1642	1742	1842	1942	2042	2142	2231	...	2331	0031	...	...	0131

RE7 Krefeld - Köln - Wuppertal - Hagen - Hamm - Münster (- Rheine: Table 812) ⊡

km		Ⓐ									
0	**Krefeld** Hbf .... d.	...	...	0535r	0635		1935	2035	2135	2235	2335
19	Neuss Hbf .... d.	...	...	0553r	0653		1953	2053	2153	2253	2353
57	**Köln** Hbf .... a.	...	...	0618r	0718	and	2018	2118	2218	2318	0018
57	**Köln** Hbf .... ♥ d.	...	0521e	0621r	0721		2021	2121	2221	2352	0052
85	Solingen Hbf .... d.	...	0543e	0643r	0743	hourly	2043	2143	2243	0020	0120
103	**Wuppertal** Hbf .... d.	...	0556e	0656r	0756		2056	2156	2256	0037	0137
130	**Hagen** Hbf .... d.	0521	0621	0721	0821	until	2121	2221	2321	...	...
143	Schwerte (Ruhr) .... d.	0531	0631	0731	0831		2131	2231	2331	...	...
159	Unna .... d.	0543	0643	0743	0843		2143	2243	2343	...	...
178	**Hamm** (Westf) .... d.	0559	0659	0759	0859		2159	2259	0010z	...	...
214	**Münster** (Westf) Hbf .... d.	0622	0722	0822	0922		2229	2329	0040	...	...

	⚒	⚒k								
Münster (Westf) Hbf . d.	...	...	0529e	0634		2034	...	...	2134	2234
Hamm (Westf) .... d.	...	0501	0601	0701		2101	...	...	2201	2301
Unna .... d.	...	0514	0614	0714		2114	...	...	2214	2314
Schwerte (Ruhr) .... d.	...	0527	0627	0727	and	2127	...	...	2227	2327
Hagen Hbf .... d.	0439e	0539	0639	0739		2139	...	...	2237	2337
Wuppertal Hbf .... d.	0504e	0604	0704	0804	hourly	2204	2221	2321	...	...
Solingen Hbf .... d.	0515e	0615	0715	0815		2215	2238	2338	...	...
Köln Hbf .... ★ a.	0538e	0638	0738	0838	until	2238	2305	0005	...	...
Köln Hbf .... d.	0542	0642	0742	0842		2242	2342	...	...	...
Neuss Hbf .... d.	0607	0707	0807	0907		2307	0007	...	...	...
Krefeld Hbf .... a.	0625	0725	0825	0925		2325	0025	...	...	...

RE10 Düsseldorf - Krefeld - Kleve

km		⚒	Ⓐ			Ⓐ				
0	**Düsseldorf** Hbf .... d.	0609	0639	0709		1939	2009	2109	2209	2309
27	**Krefeld** Hbf .... d.	0637	0707	0737	and at	2007	2037	2137	2237	2337
57	Geldern .... d.	0702	0732	0802	the same	2032	2102	2202	2302	0002
66	Kevelaer .... d.	0709	0739	0809	minutes	2039	2109	2209	2309	0009
72	Weeze .... d.	0715	0745	0815	past each	2045	2115	2215	2315	0015
79	Goch .... d.	0721	0751	0821	hour until	2051	2121	2221	2321	0021
92	**Kleve** .... a.	0734	0804	0834		2104	2134	2234	2334	0034

	⚒		Ⓐ		Ⓐ				
Kleve .... d.	0525	0619	0649		1749	1819	1919		2219
Goch .... d.	0538	0635	0705	and at	1805	1835	1935		2235
Weeze .... d.	0545	0645	0715	the same	1815	1845	1945	and	2245
Kevelaer .... d.	0551	0651	0721	minutes	1821	1851	1951	hourly	2251
Geldern .... d.	0558	0658	0728	past each	1828	1858	1958	until	2258
Krefeld Hbf .... d.	0626	0726	0756	hour until	1856	1926	2026		2326
Düsseldorf Hbf .... a.	0652	0752	0822		1922	1952	2052		2352

d – Runs daily Köln - Remagen.
e – Ⓐ only.
f – To Düsseldorf Flughafen Terminal ✈ (a. 0425).
j – Arrives 8 – 10 minutes earlier.
k – Runs daily Köln - Krefeld.
r – ⚒ only.
z – Arrives 2357.
⊡ – See shaded panel for a summary of the principal Rhein – Ruhr *RE* routes.
♥ – Trains also call at Köln Messe/Deutz (3 minutes after Köln Hbf).
★ – Trains also call at Köln Messe/Deutz (4 minutes before Köln Hbf).
◐ – Operated by TransRegio Deutsche Regionalbahn GmbH.

	RE1	*RE2*	*RE3*	*RE4*	*RE5*	*RE6*	*RE7*	*RE13*	*RB33*
Aachen Hbf	●	...	...	●	...	...	...	...	●
Köln Hbf	●	...	...	|	●	...	●	...	|
Mönchengladbach Hbf	|	●	...	●	|	...	|	●	●
Düsseldorf Hbf	●	|	●	●	●	●	|	●	|
Duisburg Hbf	●	●	●	|	●	●	|	|	●
Essen Hbf	●	●	|	|	...	●	|	|	...
via Gelsenkirchen	|	●	●	|	...	|	|	|	...
via Wuppertal and Hagen	|	|	|	●	...	|	●	●	...
Dortmund Hbf	●	|	●	●	...	●	|	|	...
Hamm (Westf)	●	|	●	...	...	●	●	●	...
Münster (Westf) Hbf	...	●	...	...	...	...	●	...	...

802 RHEIN – RUHR LOCAL SERVICES *RE / RB services*

RB8 / 27 Mönchengladbach - Köln - Königswinter - Koblenz

km		Ⓐ	⚒	⚒		⚒						▲								Ⓑq				
0	**Mönchengladbach** ⊖ d.	0440	0503e	0540	0603e	0640	0703e	0740	0803e	0840	...		1340	...	1440	1503e		1740	1803e	1840	1903e	*1940*	*2040*	*2140*
3	Rheydt Hbf ⊖ d.	0444	0507e	0544	0607e	0644	0707e	0744	0807e	0844	...		1344	...	1444	1507e		1744	1807e	1844	1907e	*1944*	*2044*	*2144*
22	Grevenbroich ⊖ d.	0502	0528e	0602	0628e	0702	0728e	0802	0828e	0902	...	and at	1402	...	1502	1528e	and at	1802	1828e	1902	1928e	*2002*	*2102*	*2202*
56	**Köln** Hbf ⊖ a.	0535	0600e	0635	0700e	0735	0800e	0835	0900e	0935	...		1435	...	1535	1600e		1835	1900e	1935	2000e	*2035*	*2135*	*2235*
56	**Köln** Hbf **807** d.	0538	0601t	0638	0701t	0738	0801t	0838	0901t	0938	1001t	the same	1438	1501t	1538	1601t	the same	1838	1901t	1938	2001t	2101	2201	2301
57	**Köln** Messe/Deutz d.	0541	0604t	0641	0704t	0741	0804t	0841	0904t	0941	1004t		1441	1504t	1541	1604t		1841	1904t	1941	2004t	2104	2204	2304
71	Köln/Bonn Flughafen ✈ d.	0550	|	0650	|	0750	|	0850	|	0950	|	minutes	1450	|	1550	|	minutes	1850	|	1950	|	|	|	|
83	Troisdorf **807** d.	0601	0623	0701	0723	0801	0823	0901	0923	1001	1023		1501	1523	1601	1623		1901	1923	2001	2023	2123	2223	2323
92	**Bonn** Beuel d.	0611	0633	0711	0733	0811	0833	0911	0933	1011	1033	past each	1511	1533	1611	1633	past each	1911	1933	2011	2033	2133	2233	2333
100	Königswinter d.	0620	0643	0720	0743	0820	0843	0920	0943	1020	1043		1520	1543	1620	1643		1920	1943	2020	2043	2143	2243	2343
105	Bad Honnef d.	0626	0649	0726	0749	0826	0849	0926	0949	1026	1049	hour until	1526	1549	1626	1649	hour until	1926	1949	2026	2049	2149	2249	2349
115	Linz (Rhein) d.	0637	0702	0735	0802	0835	0902	0935	1002	1035	1102		1535	1602	1635	1702		1935	2002	2035	2102	2202	2302	0002
122	Bad Hönningen d.	0642	0709	0740	0809	0840	0909	0940	1009	1040	1109		1540	1609	1640	1709		1940	2009	2040j	2109	2209	2309	...
138	Neuwied d.	0655	0724	0752	0824	0852	0924	0952	1024	1052	1124		1552	1624	1652	1724		1952	2024	2052j	2124	2224	2324	...
◊153	**Koblenz** Hbf a.	0716	0740	0816	0840	0913	0940	1013	1040	1113	1140		1613	1640	1713	1740		2013	2040	2113j	2140	2240	2340	...

	⚒			Ⓐ		Ⓐ	⑥k		⚒													Ⓑq		
Koblenz Hbf d.	...	...	0515r	0536	0618r	0636	0648	0718	0748	0818	0848		1218	1248	1318	1348	1418		1818	1848	1918	1948	2018	2118
Neuwied d.	...	...	0532r	0558	0632r	0658	0708	0732	0808	0832	0908		1232	1306	1332	1408	1432		1832	1908	1932	2008	2032	2132
Bad Hönningen d.	...	...	0546r	0612	0646r	0712	0719	0746	0819	0846	0919	and at	1246	1317	1346	1419	1446	and at	1846	1919	1946	2019	2046	2146
Linz (Rhein) d.	0453	...	0553	0619	0653	0719	0724	0753	0824	0853	0924		1253	1322	1353	1424	1453		1853	1924	1953	2024	2053	2153
Bad Honnef d.	0503	...	0603	0629	0703	0729	0733	0803	0833	0903	0933	the same	1303	1333	1403	1433	1503	the same	1903	1933	2003	2033	2103	2203
Königswinter d.	0509	...	0609	0635	0709	0735	0739	0809	0839	0909	0939		1309	1339	1409	1439	1509		1909	1939	2009	2039	2109	2209
Bonn Beuel d.	0518	...	0618	0646	0718	0746	0749	0818	0849	0918	0949	minutes	1318	1349	1418	1449	1518	minutes	1918	1949	2018	2049	2118	2218
Troisdorf **807** d.	0528	...	0628	0659	0728	0759	0759	0828	0859	0928	0959		1328	1359	1428	1459	1528		1928	1959	2028	2059	2128	2228
Köln/Bonn Flughafen ✈ d.	|	...	|	0708	|	0808	0808	|	0908	|	1008	past each	|	1408	|	1508	|	past each	|	2008	|	2108	|	|
Köln Messe/Deutz d.	0550	0619	0650	0719	0750	0819	0819	0850	0919	0950	1019		1350	1419	1450	1519	1550		1950	2019	2050	2119	2150	2250
Köln Hbf **807** a.	0553	0622	0653	0722	0753	0822	0822	0853	0922	0953	1022	hour until	1353	1422	1453	1522	1553	hour until	1953	2022	2053	2122	2153	2253
Köln Hbf ⊖ d.	0559e	0625	0659e	0725	0759e	0825	0825	...	0925	...	1025		...	1425	1459e	1525	1559e		1959e	2025	...	2125	*2225*	*2325*
Grevenbroich ⊖ d.	0630e	0655	0730e	0755	0830e	0855	0855	...	0955	...	1055		...	1455	1530e	1555	1630e		2030e	2055	...	2155	*2255*	*2355*
Rheydt Hbf ⊖ d.	0651e	0715	0751e	0815	0851e	0915	0915	...	1015	...	1115		...	1515	1551e	1615	1651e		2051e	2115	...	2215	*2315*	*0015*
Mönchengladbach ⊖ a.	0656e	0720	0756e	0820	0856e	0920	0920	...	1020	...	1120		...	1520	1556e	1620	1656e		2056e	2120	...	2220	*2320*	*0020*

S-Bahn 13 Köln - Köln/Bonn Flughafen ✈ - Troisdorf

				Ⓒ		Ⓒ	Ⓐ		Ⓐ	Ⓒ	Ⓐ			Ⓐ	Ⓒ	Ⓐ							
Köln Hbf d.	0011	0041	0241	0241	0341	0341	0421	0441	0501	0511	0521	0541	and at the same	2001	2011	2021	2041	2111	2141	2211	2241	2311	2341
Köln Messe/Deutz d.	0013	0043	0243	0243	0343	0343	0423	0443	0503	0513	0523	0543	minutes past	2003	2013	2023	2043	2113	2143	2213	2243	2313	2343
Köln/Bonn Flughafen ✈ d.	0026	0056	0255	0256	0355	0356	0436	0456	0516	0526	0536	0556	each hour until	2016	2026	2036	2056	2126	2156	2226	2256	2326	2356
Troisdorf a.	0036	0108	...	0308	...	0408	0448	0508	0528	0536	0548	0608		2028	2036	2048	2108	2136	2208	2236	2308	2336	0008

					Ⓒ		Ⓒ		Ⓐ	Ⓒ	Ⓐ			Ⓐ	Ⓒ	Ⓐ							
Troisdorf d.	0023	0053	0123	...	0303	...	0403	...	0513	0523	0533	0553	and at the same	2013	2023	2033	2053	2123	2153	2223	2253	2323	2353
Köln/Bonn Flughafen ✈ d.	0034	0104	0134	...	0314	0314	0414	0414	0524	0534	0544	0604	minutes past	2024	2034	2044	2104	2134	2204	2234	2304	2334	0004
Köln Messe/Deutz a.	0046	0116	0146	...	0326	0326	0426	0426	0536	0546	0556	0616	each hour until	2036	2046	2056	2116	2146	2216	2246	2316	2346	0016
Köln Hbf a.	0049	0119	0149	...	0329	0329	0429	0429	0539	0549	0559	0619		2039	2049	2059	2119	2149	2219	2249	2319	2349	0019

Dortmund - Unna - Soest ⊠

km			Ⓒ		⚒		⚒	Ⓐ			Ⓐ			Ⓐ									
0	**Dortmund** Hbf **805** d.	0007	0107	...	0507	...	0607	0637	...	0707	0737	and at the same	1907	1937	...	2007	...	2107	...	2207	...	2307	...
23	Unna d.	0032	0132	...	0532	...	0632	0702	...	0732	0802	minutes past	1932	2002	...	2032	...	2132	...	2232	...	2332	...
53	**Soest** **805** a.	0055	0155	...	0555	...	0655	0725	...	0755	0825	each hour until	1955	2025	...	2055	...	2155	...	2255	...	2355	...

		Ⓒ		⚒	Ⓐ	⚒	Ⓐ			Ⓐ			Ⓐ										
Soest **805** d.	0003	0103	...	0503	0533	0603	0633	...	0703	0733	and at the same	1803	1833	...	1903	...	2003	...	2103	...	2203	...	2303
Unna d.	0027	0127	...	0527	0557	0627	0657	...	0727	0757	minutes past	1827	1857	...	1927	...	2027	...	2127	...	2227	...	2327
Dortmund Hbf **805** a.	0051	0151	...	0551	0621	0651	0721	...	0751	0821	each hour until	1851	1921	...	1951	...	2051	...	2151	...	2251	...	2351

RB 53 Dortmund - Schwerte - Iserlohn

km		Ⓐ	Ⓐ	Ⓐ		Ⓐ		Ⓐ			Ⓐ		Ⓐ		Ⓐ		Ⓐ		Ⓐ		Ⓐ			b
0	**Dortmund** Hbf d.	0523	0553	0623	0653	0723	0753	0823	0853	and at the same	1523	1553	1623	1653	1723	1753	1823	1853	1923	1953	2023	2053	2153	2323
18	Schwerte (Ruhr) d.	0545	0615	0645	0715	0745	0815	0842	0915	minutes past	1542	1615	1645	1715	1745	1815	1842	1915	1942	2015	2042	2115	2215	2344
38	**Iserlohn** a.	0608	0638	0708	0738r	0808	0838	...	0938	each hour until	...	1638	1708	1738	1808	1838	...	1938	...	2038	...	2138	2238	...

	Ⓐ	Ⓐ	Ⓐ		Ⓐ		Ⓐ		Ⓐ			Ⓐ		Ⓐ		Ⓐ		Ⓐ		Ⓐ			
Iserlohn d.	...	0523	...	0617e	0647	0717r	0747	0817	...	0917	and at the same	...	1617	1647	1717	1747	1817	...	1917	...	2017	2117	2217
Schwerte (Ruhr) d.	0520	0550	0620	0650	0720	0750	0820	0850	0920	0950	minutes past	1620	1650	1720	1750	1820	1850	1920	1950	2020	2050	2150	2250
Dortmund Hbf a.	0539	0609	0639	0709	0739	0809	0839	0909	0939	1009	each hour until	1639	1709	1739	1809	1839	1909	1939	2009	2039	2109	2209	2309

RB30 BONN - REMAGEN (*20 km*) - AHRBRÜCK (*48 km*) and v.v.

From Bonn Hbf at 0749 ⚒, 0849 and hourly until 2049.
Trains depart Remagen 22 minutes later. Journey time from Bonn: 67 minutes.

From Ahrbrück at 0704 ⚒, 0804 and hourly until 2004 (also 2117 and 2217 to Remagen only).
Journey time to Remagen 43 minutes, Bonn 64 minutes.

RB31 DUISBURG - MOERS - XANTEN and v.v. (45 km, journey time: 45 minutes)

From Duisburg Hbf at: 0556 ⚒, 0710 ⚒, 0810, 0910 and hourly until 2310.
From Xanten at: 0500 ⚒, 0600 ⚒, 0700, 0800 and hourly until 2200.
Trains call at Moers 18 minutes from Duisburg, 28 minutes from Xanten.

OTHER USEFUL S-BAHN LINKS

Services operate every 20 minutes (every 30 minutes evenings and weekends)

Service	*Route (journey time in minutes)*
S3	Oberhausen Hbf - Mülheim Hbf (8) - Essen Hbf (17).
S7	Düsseldorf Flughafen Terminal ✈ - Düsseldorf Hbf (12) - Solingen Hbf (34).
S9	Essen Hbf - Wuppertal Hbf (47).

b – To Bestwig (Table **804**).
e – Ⓐ only.
j – Linz - Koblenz on † only
k – Not Oct. 3.
q – Also Oct. 3.
r – ⚒ only.
t – 2 minutes later on Ⓐ.
◊ – Via Koblenz-Lützel (*159 km* via Koblenz-Ehrenbreitstein).
▲ – On Ⓐ the 1040 and 1140 from Mönchengladbach depart Linz 2 mins later, Bad Hönningen 4 mins later, Neuwied 5 mins later and arrive Koblenz 5 mins later.
⊖ – Additional trains Mönchengladbach Hbf - Köln Hbf and v.v.
From Mönchengladbach at 0440 ⑥ **k**, 0540 †, 0640 †, 1840 ⑥ **k**, 2240, 2340.
From Köln Hbf at 0025, 0525 ⚒, 0725 Ⓒ, 0825 †, 0925 †, 2125 ⑥ **k**.
⊠ – Operated by **eurobahn** Keolis Deutschland GmbH & Co. KG (2nd class only).

803 DORTMUND and MÜNSTER - ENSCHEDE *2nd class only*

km	△	Ⓐ	⚒						⑦	Ⓐ
0	**Dortmund** Hbf d.	0552	0652	0752r	0852	and	1852	1952	1952	2052
44	Dülmen d.	0640	0740	0840r	0940	hourly	1940	2040	2040	2140
61	Coesfeld (Westf) d.	0705	0801	0901	1001	until	2001	2053	2101	2153
96	Gronau (Westf) d.	0739	0839	0939	1039		2039	...	2139	...
103	**Enschede** a.	0750	0850	0950	1050		2050	...	2150	...

△	Ⓐ	⚒	⚒	⚒					
Enschede d.	...	...	0556e	0656	0756	and	1856	1956	2056
Gronau (Westf) d.	...	0525e	0621	0708	0821	hourly	1921	2007	2107
Coesfeld (Westf) d.	0506	0603	0703	0803	0903	until	2003	...	...
Dülmen d.	0520	0617	0717	0817	0917		2017	...	...
Dortmund Hbf a.	0607	0707	0807	0907	1007		2107	...	...

km	♥	Ⓐ	Ⓐ	⚒						⑤⑥
0	**Münster** (Westf) Hbf d.	0508	0608	0708	...	0808	and	2108	2208	2308
56	Gronau (Westf) d.	0604	0709	0809	0809	0909	hourly	2209	2309	0009
63	**Enschede** a.	*0620*	0720	0820	0820	0920	until	2220	2320	0020

♥	⚒	Ⓐ	⑥k					⑤⑥	⑤⑥
Enschede d.	...	*0626*	0626	0726t	0826	and	2126	2226	2326
Gronau (Westf) d.	0544	0644	0644	0744	0844	hourly	2144	2244	2344
Münster (Westf) Hbf a.	0644	0744	0744	0844	0944	until	2244	2344	0044

e – Ⓐ only.
k – Not Oct. 3.
r – ⚒ only.
t – ①–⑥ only.
△ – Operated by Prignitzer Eisenbahn GmbH. German holiday dates apply.
♥ – Operated by DB (*RB* services). German holiday dates apply.

RE services — HAGEN - KASSEL — 804

km		⚒	Ⓐ	⑥k	⚒	Ⓐ	⑥k														Ⓒ			d
0	**Hagen** Hbf ... **802** d.	...	0509	...	...	0603	0613	0713	0813	0913	1013	1113	1213	1313	1413	1513	1613	1713	1813	1913	2013	2013	2113	2213	*2321*
14	Schwerte (Ruhr) ... **802** d.	...	0519	...	...	0615	0623	0723	0823	0923	1023	1123	1223	1323	1423	1523	1623	1723	1823	1923	2023	2023	2123	2223	2349
57	Arnsberg (Westf) ... d.	...	0549	...	...	0649	0656	0756	0856	0956	1056	1156	1256	1356	1456	1556	1656	1756	1856	1956	2056	2056	2156	2256	0020
77	Meschede ... d.	...	0608	...	...	0709	0716	0816	0916	1016	1116	1216	1316	1416	1516	1616	1716	1816	1916	2016	2116	2116	2216	2316	0039
86	Bestwig ... d.	...	0615	0623	...	0717	0723	0823	0923	1023	1123	1223	1323	1423	1523	1623	1723	1823	1923	2023	2122	2123	2222	2322	0046
100	Brilon Wald ... d.	...	0629	0638	...	0734	0738	0838	0938	1038	1138	1238	1338	1438	1538	1638	1738	1838	1938	2038	...	2138	...	...	...
152	Warburg (Westf) ... a.	...	0714	0720	...	0820	0820	0920	1020	1120	1220	1320	1420	1520	1620	1720	1820	1920	2020	2120	...	2220	...	...	...
152	Warburg (Westf) ... **805** d.	0601	0720	0721	0801	...	...	0921	...	1121	...	1321	...	1521	...	1721	...	1921	...	*2139*	...	...	...	...	...
205	**Kassel** Hbf ... a.	0656	0759	0759	0856	...	...	0959	...	1159	...	1359	...	1559	...	1759	...	1959	...	*2234*	...	...	...	...	...
209	**Kassel** Wilhelmshöhe .. **805** a.	...	0809	0809	...	...	...	1009	...	1209	...	1409	...	1609	...	1809	...	2009	...	...	...	...	...	...	...

	⚒	⚒	⚒		Ⓐ	⑥k		Ⓐ	⚒															⚒	†
Kassel Wilhelmshöhe ... **805** d.	...	...	...	...	...	...	...	...	...	...	0748	...	0948	...	1148	...	1348	...	1548	...	1748	...	1948	...	...
Kassel Hbf ... d.	...	...	...	...	*0517*	*0517*	...	0619	...	...	0758	...	0958	...	1158	...	1358	...	1558	...	1758	...	1958	2029	2259
Warburg (Westf) ... **805** a.	...	...	...	...	*0610*	*0610*	...	0714	...	...	0835	...	1035	...	1235	...	1435	...	1635	...	1835	...	2035	2123	2353
Warburg (Westf) ... d.	...	...	0532z	...	0632	0638	...	...	0738	...	0838	0938	1038	1138	1238	1338	1438	1538	1638	1738	1838	1938	2038	...	...
Brilon Wald ... d.	...	...	0622	...	0719	0722	...	...	0822	...	0922	1022	1122	1222	1322	1422	1522	1622	1722	1822	1922	2022	2122	...	...
Bestwig ... d.	0436	0536	0636	0636	0736	0736	0736	...	0836	0836	0936	1036	1136	1236	1336	1436	1536	1636	1736	1836	1936	2036	2136	...	...
Meschede ... d.	0443	0543	0643	0643	0743	0743	0743	...	0843	0843	0943	1043	1143	1243	1343	1443	1543	1643	1743	1843	1943	2043	2143	...	...
Arnsberg (Westf) ... d.	0503	0603	0703	0703	0803	0803	0803	...	0903	0903	1003	1103	1203	1303	1403	1503	1603	1703	1803	1903	2003	2103	2203	...	...
Schwerte (Ruhr) ... **802** d.	0535	0635	0735	0735	0835	0835	0835	...	0935	0935	1035	1135	1235	1335	1435	1535	1635	1735	1835	1935	2035	2135	2235	...	...
Hagen Hbf ... **802** a.	0546	0646	0746	0746	0846	0846	0846	...	0946	0946	1046	1146	1246	1346	1446	1546	1646	1746	1846	1946	2046	2146	2246	...	...

d – From Dortmund Hbf (d. 2323). **k** – Not Oct. 3. **z** – 0538 on ⑥.

RE / *RB* services except where shown — DORTMUND and MÜNSTER - PADERBORN - KASSEL — 805

km		Ⓐ ◇	⑥k ◇		*IC* **2355** ①–⑥ ◐ 🍷	Ⓐ ◇	Ⓒ ◇		*IC* **2357** 🍷	Ⓐ ◇	Ⓒ ◇		*IC* **2157** § 🍷	Ⓐ ◇	Ⓒ ◇		*IC* **2359** ⑤⑦ 🍷	Ⓐ ◇	Ⓒ ◇		*IC* **2151** 🍷	Ⓐ ◇	Ⓒ ◇		*IC* **2153** Ⓑ 🍷
	Köln Hbf **800** ... d.	...	...	...	...	...	...	...	0715e	...	...	...	0905	...	...	...	1120	...	...	...	...	...	...	...	...
	Düsseldorf Hbf **800** ... d.	...	...	...	0546g	...	...	...	0746e	...	...	...	0946	...	...	...	1146	...	...	...	1346	...	...	...	1546
0	**Dortmund** Hbf ... **802** d.	...	...	...	0642	...	...	...	0842	...	...	...	1042	...	...	...	1242	...	...	...	1442	...	...	...	1642
	Münster (Westf) Hbf.. **802** d.	0510	0510	0634	|	0710	0710	0834	|	0910	0910	1034	|	1110	1110	1234	|	1310	1310	1434	|	1510	1510	1634	|
31	Hamm (Westf) ... **802** a.	0537	0537	0659	0702	0737	0737	0859	0902	0937	0937	1059	1102	1137	1137	1259	1302	1337	1337	1459	1502	1537	1537	1659	1702
31	Hamm (Westf) ... d.	0546	0552	...	0707	0746	0752	...	0907	0946	0952	...	1107	1146	1152	...	1307	1346	1352	...	1507	1546	1552	...	1707
57	Soest ... **802** d.	0602	0608	...	0722	0802	0808	...	0922	1002	1008	...	1122	1202	1208	...	1322	1402	1408	...	1522	1602	1608	...	1722
77	Lippstadt ... d.	0614	0620	...	0733	0814	0820	...	0933	1014	1020	...	1133	1214	1220	...	1333	1414	1420	...	1533	1614	1620	...	1733
109	**Paderborn** Hbf . ⊖ **809 811** d.	0642	0642	...	0749	0842	0842	...	0949	1042	1042	...	1149	1242	1242	...	1349	1442	1442	...	1549	1642	1642	...	1749
126	Altenbeken ... ⊖ **809 811** d.	0654	0654	...	0804	0854	0854	...	1004	1054	1054	...	1204	1254	1254	...	1404	1454	1454	...	1604	1654	1654	...	1804
163	Warburg (Westf) ... **804** d.	0716	0716	...	0826	0916	0916	...	1026	1116	1116	...	1226	1316	1316	...	1426	1516	1516	...	1626	1716	1716	...	1826
220	**Kassel** Wilhelmshöhe .. **804** a.	*0809*	*0809*	...	0857	*1009*	*1009*	...	1057	*1209*	*1209*	...	1257	*1409*	*1409*	...	1457	*1609*	*1609*	...	1658	*1809*	*1809*	...	1858
	Erfurt Hbf **850** ... a.	...	...	...	1032	...	...	...	1232	...	...	...	1432	...	...	...	1632	...	...	...	1832	...	...	...	2032
	Halle (Saale) Hbf **850** ... a.	...	...	...	1156	...	...	...	1356	...	...	...	1556	...	...	...	1756	...	...	...	1956	...	...	...	2200
	Berlin Hbf **850** ... a.	...	...	...	1316	...	...	...	1516	...	...	...	1716	...	...	...	1916	...	...	...	2116	...	...	...	...
	Stralsund **845** ... a.	...	...	...	1624	...	...	...	...	...	...	...	2040b	...	...	...	2224	...	...	...	...	...	...	...	...

	Ⓐ ◇	Ⓒ ◇	*IC* **2155** ⑦ 🍷	◇	◇	◇	◇	◇	⑤⑥ ◇	◇
Köln Hbf **800** ... d.	...	...	...	...	...	...	...	...	...	...
Düsseldorf Hbf **800** ... d.	...	...	1746	...	...	...	...	...	...	...
Dortmund Hbf ... **802** d.	...	...	1842	...	...	...	...	...	...	...
Münster (Westf) Hbf .. **802** d.	1710	1710	|	1840z	1910	*2034*	*2134*	*2234*	*2234*	2310
Hamm (Westf) ... **802** a.	1737	1737	1902	1906z	1937	*2059*	*2159*	*2259*	*2259*	2337
Hamm (Westf) ... d.	1746	1752	1907	1916	1952	2107	2207	2307	2307	0007
Soest ... **802** d.	1802	1808	1922	1932	2008	2123	2223	2323	2323	0023
Lippstadt ... d.	1814	1820	1933	1944	2020	2135	2235	2335	2335	0035
Paderborn Hbf .. ⊖ **809 811** d.	1842	1842	1949	2009	2058t	2200	2300	2359	0002	0100
Altenbeken ... ⊖ **809 811** d.	1854	1854	2004	...	2110	...	...	...	0014	...
Warburg (Westf) ... **804** d.	1916	1916	2026	...	2132	...	...	...	0036	...
Kassel Wilhelmshöhe ... **804** a.	*2009*	*2009*	2057	...	*2234*h	...	...	...	...	...
Erfurt Hbf **850** ... a.	...	...	2232	...	...	...	...	...	...	...
Halle (Saale) Hbf **850** ... a.	...	...	...	...	...	...	...	...	...	...
Berlin Hbf **850** ... a.	...	...	...	...	...	...	...	...	...	...
Stralsund **845** ... a.	...	...	...	...	...	...	...	...	...	...

	⚒ ◇	◇	Ⓐ ◇	Ⓒ ◇	Ⓒ ◇	Ⓐ ◇	Ⓒ ◇	Ⓐ ◇	*IC* **2156** ①–⑥ 🍷	
Stralsund **845** ... d.	...	...	...	...	...	...	...	...	...	...
Berlin Hbf **850** ... d.	...	...	...	...	...	...	...	...	...	...
Halle (Saale) Hbf **850** ... d.	...	...	...	...	...	...	...	...	...	...
Erfurt Hbf **850** ... d.	...	...	...	...	...	...	...	...	0725	...
Kassel Wilhelmshöhe **804** d.	...	...	...	...	...	...	*0748*	*0748*	0900	...
Warburg (Westf) ... **804** d.	...	...	0624	0639k	...	...	0839	0839	0934	...
Altenbeken ... ⊖ **809 811** d.	...	...	0647	0702k	...	...	0902	0902	0956	...
Paderborn Hbf ⊖ **809 811** d.	0513	0621	0721r	0716	0816	0821	0916	0921	1010	...
Lippstadt ... d.	0536	0644	0744	0736	0836	0844	0936	0944	1026	...
Soest ... **802** d.	0548	0656	0756	0748	0848	0856	0948	0956	1037	...
Hamm (Westf) ... a.	0606	0714	0814	0806	0906	0914	1006	1014	1052	...
Hamm (Westf) ... **802** d.	0620	0720	0820	0820	0920	0920	1020	1020	1056	1059
Münster (Westf) Hbf **802** a.	0647	0747	0847	0847	0947	0947	1047	1047	|	1122
Dortmund Hbf ... **802** a.	...	...	...	...	...	...	...	...	1115	...
Düsseldorf Hbf **800** ... a.	...	...	...	...	...	...	...	...	1212	...
Köln Hbf **800** ... a.	...	...	...	...	...	...	...	...	...	...

	Ⓒ ◇	Ⓐ ◇	*IC* **2154** ①–⑥ 🍷		Ⓒ ◇	Ⓐ ◇	*IC* **2152** ⑤⑦ 🍷		Ⓒ ◇	Ⓐ ◇	*IC* **2150** ‡ 🍷		Ⓒ ◇	Ⓐ ◇	*IC* **2356** ◐ 🍷		Ⓒ ◇	Ⓐ ◇	*IC* **2354** 🍷		◇	*IC* **2352** ⑦ 🍷	◇	①–⑥ ◇	◇
Stralsund **845** ... d.	...	...	...	...	...	...	...	...	...	...	0739e	...	...	...	0939	...	...	...	...	...	...	1339	...	...	...
Berlin Hbf **850** ... d.	...	...	0639	...	...	...	0839f	...	...	...	1039	...	...	...	1239	...	...	...	1440	...	...	1639	...	...	...
Halle (Saale) Hbf **850** ... d.	...	...	0800	...	...	...	1000	...	...	...	1200	...	...	...	1400	...	...	...	1600	...	...	1800	...	...	...
Erfurt Hbf **850** ... d.	...	...	0924	...	...	...	1124	...	...	...	1324	...	...	...	1524	...	...	...	1724	...	...	1924	...	...	...
Kassel Wilhelmshöhe ... **804** d.	*0948*	*0948*	1100	...	*1148*	*1148*	1300	...	*1348*	*1348*	1500	...	*1548*	*1548*	1700	...	*1748*	*1748*	1900	...	*1948*	2100	...	...	...
Warburg (Westf) ... **804** d.	1039	1039	1134	...	1239	1239	1334	...	1439	1439	1534	...	1639	1639	1734	...	1839	1839	1934	...	2039	2134	2139y	2139	...
Altenbeken ... ⊖ **809 811** d.	1102	1102	1156	...	1302	1302	1356	...	1502	1502	1556	...	1702	1702	1756	...	1902	1902	1956	...	2102	2156	2202y	2202	...
Paderborn Hbf .. ⊖ **809 811** d.	1116	1121	1210	...	1316	1321	1410	...	1516	1521	1610	...	1716	1721	1810	...	1916	1921	2010	...	2116	2210	2216	2215	2311
Lippstadt ... d.	1136	1144	1226	...	1336	1344	1426	...	1536	1544	1626	...	1736	1744	1826	...	1936	1944	2026	...	2139	2226	2239	...	2334
Soest ... **802** d.	1148	1156	1237	...	1348	1356	1437	...	1548	1556	1637	...	1748	1756	1837	...	1948	1956	2037	...	2151	2237	2251	...	2346
Hamm (Westf) ... a.	1206	1214	1252	...	1406	1414	1452	...	1606	1614	1652	...	1806	1814	1852	...	2006	2014	2052	...	2209	2252	2309	...	0004
Hamm (Westf) ... **802** d.	1220	1220	1256	1259	1420	1420	1456	1458	1620	1620	1656	1659	1820	1820	1856	1859	2020	2020	2056	2058	*2259*	2256	*2316*	...	*0010*
Münster (Westf) Hbf .. **802** a.	1247	1247	|	1322	1447	1447	|	1522	1647	1647	|	1722	1847	1847	|	1922	2047	2047	|	2122	*2329*	|	|	...	*0040*
Dortmund Hbf ... **802** a.	...	...	1315	...	...	...	1515	...	...	...	1715	...	...	...	1915	...	...	...	2115	...	...	2315	*2343*	...	...
Düsseldorf Hbf **800** ... a.	...	...	1412	...	...	...	1612	...	...	...	1815	...	...	...	2015	...	...	...	2214w	...	...	0012	...	...	...
Köln Hbf **800** ... a.	...	...	...	...	...	...	...	...	...	...	...	...	...	...	...	...	...	...	2240w	...	...	0035	...	...	...

Paderborn - Holzminden ⊡

km		Ⓐ	⑥k	Ⓐ	Ⓐ	⚒						Ⓒ
0	**Paderborn** Hbf ... d.	0453	0553	0553	0607	0653	0753	and	2053	2206	2315
17	Altenbeken ... d.	0507	0606	0606	0621	0707	0807	hourly	2107	2219	2329
66	**Holzminden** ... a.	0553	0651	0658	0720	0753	0853	until	2153	2302	0012

	Ⓐ	⚒	Ⓐ	⚒					Ⓒ
Holzminden ... d.	0450	0604	0618	0704	0804	and	2104	2204	2316
Altenbeken ... d.	0537	0652	0707	0752	0852	hourly	2152	2252	0001
Paderborn Hbf ... a.	0551	0705	0720	0805	0905	until	2205	2305	0015

b – Ⓑ only.
e – ①–⑥ only.
f – ⑤ only.
g – ① only.
h – Kassel **Hbf**.
k – ⑥ (not Oct. 3).
r – Arrives 0700.
t – Arrives 2044.
w – ⑦ only.
y – ⑤⑥ only.
z – On Ⓒ Münster d. *1834*, Hamm a. *1859*.

§ – Train number **2257** on ⑥.
‡ – Train number **2250** on ⑦.
◐ – To / from Ostseebad Binz (Table **844**).
◇ – Operated by **eurobahn** Keolis Deutschland GmbH & Co. KG (2nd class only).
⊖ – See panel below for Holzminden connections.
⊡ – Operated by Nord West Bahn (2nd class only).

806 FRANKFURT - GIESSEN - KASSEL

See Table **900** for faster *ICE* services Frankfurt - Kassel - Hannover - Hamburg and v.v.

km	See note ▲	*RE* 4120	*RE* 4100	*IC* 2378	*RE* 4102	*IC* 2376	*RE* 4104	*IC* 2374	*RE* 4106	*IC* 2372	*RE* 4108	*IC* 2370	*IC* 2270	*RE* 4110	*IC* 2276	*RE* 4112	*IC* 2274	*RE* 4114	*IC* 2272	*IC* 2282	*IC* 2172	*RE* 4116	*RE* 4118	*IC* 1874	*RE* 25034
		†	⚒	①–⑥	4122			⊖				T	⑤⑦		¶				①–⑤	⑥	⑦	⑤–⑦	①–④	⑦	
				🍷		N🍷		🍷		🍷		K🍷	K🍷		🍷		🍷		🍷	A🍷	S🍷				
	Karlsruhe Hbf **911** d.	...	...	...	...	0647e	...	0854	...	1054	...	1253	1253	...	1454	...	1654	...	1854	...	...	...	...	...	...
	Heidelberg Hbf **911** d.	...	...	...	...	0724e	...	0924	...	1124	...	1324	1324	...	1524	...	1724	...	1924	...	1924	...	...	2124	...
0	**Frankfurt (Main)** Hbf **807** d.	0509	0522	0623	0718t	0823	0922	1023	1122	1223	1322	1423	1423	1522	1623	1722	1823	1922	2023	2023	2023	2122	2122	2223	2228
34	Friedberg (Hess) **807** d.	0532	0545	0646	0745	0846	0945	1046	1145	1246	1345	1446	1446	1545	1646	1745	1846	1945	2046	2046	2046	2145	2145	2246	2251
38	Bad Nauheim **807** d.	0536	|	|	|	|	|	|	|	|	|	|	|	|	|	|	|	|	|	|	|	|	|	|	2255
66	**Gießen** **807** d.	0604	0604	0705	0804	0905	1004	1105	1204	1305	1404	1505	1505	1604	1705	1804	1905	2004	2105	2105	2105	2204	2204	2305	2322
96	Marburg (Lahn) d.	0621	0621	0721	0821	0921	1021	1121	1221	1321	1421	1521	1521	1621	1721	1821	1921	2021	2121	2121	2121	2221	2221	2321	2350
118	Stadtallendorf d.	0636	0636	|	0836	|	1036	|	1236	|	1436	|	|	1636	|	1836	|	2036	|	|	|	2236	2236	|	0009
138	Treysa d.	0651	0651	0746	0851	0946	1051	1146	1251	1346	1451	1546	1546	1651	1746	1851	1946	2051	2146	2146	2146	2250	2250	2346	0026
166	Wabern d.	0707	0707	0804	0907	1004	1107	1204	1307	1404	1507	1604	1604	1707	1804	1907	2004	2107	2204	2204	2204	2308	...	0004	...
196	**Kassel** Wilhelmshöhe ‡ a.	0727	0727	0826	0927	1026	1127	1226	1327	1426	1527	1626	1626	1727	1826	1927	2027	2127	2226	2226	2226	2328	...	0026	...
200	**Kassel** Hbf ‡ a.	0734	0734	|	0934	|	1134	|	1334	|	1534	|	|	1734	|	1934	|	2135	...	...	...	2335	...	...	...
	Hannover Hbf **902** a.	...	...	0956	...	1156	...	1356	...	1556	...	1756	1756	...	1956	...	2156f	...	...	...	...	...	...	...	...
	Hamburg Hbf **902** ▲ a.	...	...	1127	...	1328	...	1529	...	1730	...	1927	1927	...	2126	...	2327v	...	...	...	...	...	...	...	...
	Stralsund **830** ▲ a.	...	...	...	...	1630	...	...	...	2032	...	...	2230	...	...	...	...	...	...	...	...	...	...	...	...

See note ▲	*RE* 25045	*RE* 4121	*RE* 4101	*IC* 2273	*RE* 4125	*RE* 4103	*IC* 2275	*RE* 25007	*RE* 4105	*IC* 2277	*RE* 4107	*IC* 2279	*RE* 4109	*IC* 2371	*RE* 4111	*RE* 4127	*IC* 2373	*RE* 4113	*IC* 2375	*RE* 4115	*IC* 2377	*RE* 4117	*IC* 2379	*IC* 1899	*RE* 4129
		①–⑤	⑥n	①–⑥	①–⑤	⑥⑦	①–⑤								⑥⑦	①–⑤							⑤	⑦	
				🍷			S			🍷		🍷		K🍷			🍷		🍷		O🍷		🍷	B	
Stralsund **830** ▲ d.	...	...	...	...	...	...	...	...	...	...	...	0527e	...	...	...	...	0927	...	...	...	1327	...	1527	...	...
Hamburg Hbf **902** ▲ d.	...	...	...	...	...	...	...	...	...	0628e	...	0827e	...	1028	...	...	1228	...	1428	...	1628	...	1828	...	...
Hannover Hbf **902** d.	...	...	...	...	...	...	0600	...	...	0800e	...	1000e	...	1200	...	...	1400	...	1600	...	1800	...	2000	2101	...
Kassel Hbf ‡ d.	...	0401	0423	...	0613	0615	|	...	0823	|	1023	|	1223	|	1423	1423	|	1623	|	1823	|	2023	|	|	2222
Kassel Wilhelmshöhe ‡ d.	...	0406	0429	0531	0619	0621	0731	...	0829	0931	1029	1131	1229	1331	1429	1429	1531	1629	1731	1829	1931	2029	2131	2204	2227
Wabern d.	...	0424	0448	0551	0644	0646	0751	...	0848	0951	1048	1151	1248	1351	1448	1448	1551	1648	1753	1848	1951	2048	2151	2225	2250
Treysa d.	...	0440	0505	0609	0705	0705	0809	0815	0905	1009	1105	1209	1305	1409	1505	1505	1609	1705	1809	1905	2009	2105	2209	2243	2309
Stadtallendorf d.	...	0455	0519	|	0719	0719	|	0829	0919	|	1119	|	1319	|	1519	1519	|	1719	|	1919	|	2119	|	2300	2323
Marburg (Lahn) d.	0408	0512	0535	0635	0735	0735	0835	0849	0935	1035	1135	1235	1335	1435	1535	1535	1635	1735	1835	1935	2035	2135	2235	2314	2339
Gießen **807** d.	0439	0536	0553	0653	0753	0753	0853	0922	0953	1053	1153	1253	1353	1453	1553	1553	1653	1753	1853	1953	2053	2153	2253	2332	0006
Bad Nauheim **807** d.	0505	0554	|	|	|	|	|	0938	|	|	|	|	|	|	|	|	|	|	|	|	|	|	|	2351	0029
Friedberg (Hess) **807** d.	0510	0600	0612	0711	0812	0812	0912	0942	1012	1111	1212	1311	1412	1511	1612	1612	1712	1812	1912	2012	2111	2212	2311	2356	0034
Frankfurt (Main) Hbf **807** a.	0536	0625	0634	0733	0836	0834	0933	1007	1034	1133	1234	1333	1434	1533	1634	1636	1733	1834	1933	2034	2133	2234	2333	0019	0057
Heidelberg Hbf **911** a.	...	...	...	0830	...	...	1030	...	...	1230	...	1430	...	1630	...	...	1830	...	2032b	...	2247z	...	...	...	...
Karlsruhe Hbf **911** a.	...	...	...	0902	...	...	...	...	...	1301	...	1501	...	1701	...	...	1901	...	2105a	...	2322z	...	...	...	...

A – From Saarbrücken (Table **919**).
B – From Berlin (Table **810**).
K – From / to Konstanz (Table **916**).
N – To Ostseebad Binz (Table **844**) on ⑥.
O – From Ostseebad Binz (Table **844**).
S – From / to Stuttgart (Table **930**).
T – ①②③④⑥.

a – ①–⑤ only.
b – ⑧ only.
e – ①–⑥ only.
f – ⑤⑦ only.
n – Not Oct. 3.
t – 0722 on ©.
v – ⑦ only.

z – ⑤⑦ only. On ⑦ Heidelberg a. 2230, Karlsruhe a. 2304.

⊖ – On ⑤ runs with train number **2174** and continues to Rostock (Table **830**).
¶ – On ⑦ runs with train number **2288** and continues to Rostock (Table **830**).
‡ – See also Tables **804** / **901**.
▲ – **June 14 - July 19** all services are subject to alteration Hannover - Hamburg and v.v. Most *IC* trains in this table do not operate north of Hannover during this period (see Table **900** for alternative services).

807 AACHEN - KÖLN - SIEGEN - GIESSEN - FRANKFURT

RE / *RB* services

km																									
				©	⑥k	Ⓐ	Ⓐ	Ⓐ		⚒															
0	**Aachen** Hbf **802 910** d.	...	...	...	...	...	...	...	...	0510e	...	0610e	...	0710e	...	0810r	...	0910	1010	...	1110	...	1210	...	1310
31	Düren **802** d.	...	...	...	...	...	...	...	...	0544e	...	0644e	...	0744e	...	0844r	...	0944	1044	...	1144	...	1244	...	1344
70	**Köln** Hbf **802 910** a.	...	...	...	...	...	...	...	...	0612e	...	0712e	...	0812e	...	0912r	...	1012	1112	...	1212	...	1312	...	1412
70	**Köln** Hbf **802 910** d.	...	...	0341	...	...	0431	...	...	0623	...	0723	...	0823	...	0923	...	1023	1123	...	1223	...	1323	...	1423
71	**Köln** Messe/Deutz **802 910** d.	...	...	0343	...	...	0433	...	...	0626	...	0726	...	0826	...	0926	...	1026	1126	...	1226	...	1326	...	1426
91	Troisdorf **802** d.	...	...	0409	...	...	0454	...	...	0640	...	0740	...	0840	...	0940	...	1040	1140	...	1240	...	1340	...	1440
95	Siegburg/Bonn **910** d.	...	...	0414	...	...	0459	...	...	0645	...	0745	...	0845	...	0945	...	1045	1145	...	1245	...	1345	...	1445
102	Hennef (Sieg) d.	...	...	0420	...	...	0506	...	...	0650	...	0750	...	0850	...	0950	...	1050	1150	...	1250	...	1350	...	1450
114	Eitorf d.	...	...	0431	...	...	0517	...	...	0659	...	0759	...	0859	...	0959	...	1059	1159	...	1259	...	1359	...	1459
136	Au (Sieg) d.	...	...	0455	0509	0515	0539	0545	...	0717	...	0817	...	0917	...	1017	...	1117	1217	...	1317	...	1417	...	1517
142	Wissen (Sieg) d.	...	...	▬	0516	0522	▬	0552	...	0722	...	0822	...	0922	...	1022	...	1122	1222	...	1322	...	1422	...	1522
154	Betzdorf (Sieg) d.	...	...	...	0530	0536	...	0606	...	0733	...	0833	...	0933	...	1033	...	1133	1233	...	1333	...	1433	...	1533
171	**Siegen** a.	...	...	...	0555	0601	...	0631	...	0752	...	0852	...	0952	...	1052	...	1152	1252	...	1352	...	1452	...	1552
												|				|			|			|		
		Ⓐ	Ⓐ		⚒	Ⓐ	⑥k	Ⓐ		⑥k				Ⓐ							©				
171	**Siegen** d.	...	0457	...	0559	0606	0644	0654	...	0802	...	0854	...	1002	...	1054	...	1202	1254	...	1402	...	1454	...	1602
203	Dillenburg d.	0424	0527	0531r	0623	0633	0718	0728	0733	0827	0833r	0918	0933	1027	1033r	1118	1133	1227	1318	1333	1427	1433r	1518	1533	1627
209	Herborn d.	0432	0532	0539r	0628	0643	0723	0734	0740	0833	0840r	0923	0940	1033	1040r	1123	1140	1233	1323	1340	1433	1440r	1523	1540	1633
231	Wetzlar **906** d.	0454	0552	0601r	0648	0709	0737	0752	0802	0848	0902r	0937	1002	1048	1102r	1137	1202	1248	1337	1402	1448	1502r	1537	1602	1648
244	**Gießen** **906** a.	0505	|	0611r	0658	0722	0747	0802	0814	0858	0914r	0947	1014	1058	1114r	1147	1214	1258	1347	1414	1458	1514r	1547	1614	1658
244	**Gießen** **806** d.	0514	|	0619v	0705	*0728*	*0753*	0809	0822	0905	0922	*0953*	1022	1105	1122	*1153*	1222	1305	*1353*	1422	1505	1522	*1553*	1622	1705
272	Bad Nauheim **806** d.	0538	|	0638	0723	*0755*	|	0826	0838	0926	0938	|	1038	1126	1138	|	1238	1326	|	1438	1526	1538	|	1638	1726
276	Friedberg (Hess) **806** d.	0542	|	0642	0728	*0800*	*0812*	0830	0842	0930	0942	*1012*	1042	1130	1142	*1212*	1242	1330	*1412*	1442	1530	1542	*1612*	1642	1730
310	**Frankfurt** (Main) Hbf **806** a.	0607	0640	0707	0754	*0826*	*0834*	0855	0907	0953	1007	*1034*	1107	1153	1207	*1234*	1307	1353	*1434*	1507	1553	1607	*1636*	1707	1753

Aachen Hbf **802 910** d.	1410	...	1510	1610	1710	...	1810	1910	...	...	...
Düren **802** d.	1444	...	1544	1644	1744	...	1844	1944	...	...	...
Köln Hbf **802 910** a.	1512	...	1612	1712	1812	...	1912	2012	...	...	...
Köln Hbf **802 910** d.	1523	...	1623	1723	1823	...	1923	2023	2123	2223	2323
Köln Messe/Deutz **802 910** d.	1526	...	1626	1726	1826	...	1926	2026	2126	2226	2326
Troisdorf **802** d.	1540	...	1640	1740	1840	...	1940	2040	2140	2240	2340
Siegburg/Bonn **910** d.	1545	...	1645	1745	1845	...	1945	2045	2145	2245	2345
Hennef (Sieg) d.	1550	...	1650	1750	1850	...	1950	2050	2150	2250	2350
Eitorf d.	1559	...	1659	1759	1859	...	1959	2059	2159	2259	2359
Au (Sieg) d.	1617	...	1717	1817	1917	...	2017	2117	2217	2317	0017
Wissen (Sieg) d.	1622	...	1722	1822	1922	...	2022	2122	2224	2324	0024
Betzdorf (Sieg) d.	1633	...	1733	1833	1933	...	2033	2133	2239	2339	0039
Siegen a.	1652	...	1752	1852	1952	...	2052	2152	2302	0002	0102
	|			|	▬		|	▬	|		
Siegen d.	1654	...	1802	1854	...	...	2054	...	2307	...	...
Dillenburg d.	1718	1733	1827	1918	1933	*2027*e	2118	2233e	2331	...	...
Herborn d.	1723	1740	1833	1923	1940	*2035*e	2123	2240e	2336	...	...
Wetzlar **906** d.	1737	1802	1848	1937	2002	*2057*e	2137	2302e	2350	...	...
Gießen **906** a.	1747	1814	1858	1947	2014	*2108*e	2147	2314e	2400	...	...
Gießen **806** d.	*1753*	1822	1905	*1953*	2022	2117	*2153*	2322	*0006*	...	...
Bad Nauheim **806** d.	|	1838	1926	|	2038	2140	|	2345	*0029*	...	...
Friedberg (Hess) **806** d.	*1812*	1842	1930	*2012*	2042	2143	*2212*	2349	*0034*	...	...
Frankfurt (Main) Hbf **806** a.	*1834*	1907	1953	*2034*	2107	2209	*2234*	0011	*0057*	...	...

			⚒		Ⓐ	Ⓐ		⚒	
Frankfurt (Main) Hbf **806** d.	0032	...	*0522*	...	...	0630	*0718*t	0802	0850j
Friedberg (Hess) **806** d.	0055	...	*0545*	...	...	0659	*0745*	0827	0915
Bad Nauheim **806** d.	0059	...	|	...	...	0703	|	0832	0919
Gießen **806** a.	0122	...	*0603*	...	...	0725	*0803*	0853	0935
Gießen **906** d.	▬	...	0613	...	0652	0740	0809	0909	0940
Wetzlar **906** d.	...	...	0622	...	0703	0750	0818	0918	0950
Herborn d.	...	...	0635	...	0727	0812	0833	0932	1012
Dillenburg d.	...	...	0640	...	0736	0823	0839	0937	1023
Siegen a.	...	...	0705	...	0804	...	0906	1001	...
			|				|		
	⚒				d			d	
Siegen d.	0454	0608	0707	0707	0808	...	0908	1008	...
Betzdorf (Sieg) d.	0515	0626	0726	0726	0826	...	0926	1026	...
Wissen (Sieg) d.	0527	0636	0736	0736	0836	...	0936	1036	...
Au (Sieg) d.	0535	0642	0742	0742	0842	...	0942	1042	...
Eitorf d.	0556	0659	0759	0759	0859	...	0959	1059	...
Hennef (Sieg) d.	0609	0709	0809	0809	0909	...	1009	1109	...
Siegburg/Bonn **910** d.	0614	0714	0814	0814	0914	...	1014	1114	...
Troisdorf **802** d.	0619	0719	0819	0819	0919	...	1019	1119	...
Köln Messe/Deutz **802 910** d.	0634	0734	0834	0834	0934	...	1034	1134	...
Köln Hbf **802 910** a.	0637	0737	0837	0837	0937	...	1037	1137	...
Köln Hbf **802 910** d.	0647e	0747e	0847	...	0947	...	1047	1147	...
Düren **802** d.	0715e	0815e	0915	...	1015	...	1115	1215	...
Aachen Hbf **802 910** a.	0748e	0848e	0948	...	1048	...	1148	1248	...

d – Daily from Siegen.
e – Ⓐ only.
j – 0852 on †.
k – Not Oct. 3.
r – ⚒ only.
t – *0722* on ©.
v – 0622 on ©.

RE / RB services — FRANKFURT - GIESSEN - SIEGEN - KÖLN - AACHEN — 807

			Ⓒ			Ⓑ						Ⓑh	Ⓐ	Ⓐ	Ⓒ					Ⓑh			Ⓐ	◇	
Frankfurt (Main) Hbf ..... **806** d.	*0922*	0952	1002	1052	*1122*	1202	1252	*1322*	1402	1452	*1522*	1601	1701	1630	1652	*1722*	1801	1852	*1922*	2002	2052	*2122*	2152	2228	*2326*
Friedberg (Hess) .... **806** d.	*0945*	1015	1027	1115	*1145*	1227	1315	*1345*	1427	1515	*1545*	1626	|	1656	1715	*1745*	1826	1915	*1945*	2027	2115	*2145*	2215	2251	*2348*
Bad Nauheim.............. **806** d.	|	1019	1032	1119	|	1232	1319	|	1432	1519	|	1631	1727	1700	1719	|	1831	1919	|	2032	2119	|	2219	2255	|
Gießen .... **806** a.	*1003*	1035	1053	1135	*1203*	1253	1335	*1403*	1453	1535	*1603*	1659	|	1725	1735	*1803*	1859	1935	*2003*	2053	2135	*2203*	2242	2318	*0010*
Gießen .... **906** d.	1009	1040r	1109	1140	1209	1309	1340	1409	1509	1540	1609	1709	|	1740	1740	1809	1909	1940	2009	2109	2140	2209	2248	2324	0030
Wetzlar .... **906** d.	1018	1050r	1118	1150	1218	1318	1350	1418	1518	1550	1618	1718	1750	1755	1750	1818	1918	1950	2018	2118	2150	2218	2258	2335	0041
Herborn .... d.	1033	1112r	1132	1212	1233	1332	1412	1433	1532	1612	1633	1732	1807	1817	1812	1833	1932	2012	2033	2132	2212	2233	2320	2357	0102
Dillenburg .... d.	1039	1123r	1137	1223	1239	1337	1423	1439	1537	1623	1639	1737	1812	1825	1823	1839	1937	2023	2039	2137	2223	2239	2328	0005	0111
Siegen .... a.	1106	...	1201	...	1306	1401	...	1506	1601	...	1706	1801	1839	...	...	1906	2001	...	2106	2201	▬	2306	▬	...	...
	|		d		|	d		|			|	d				|			|	d		Ⓐ	⑥k		
Siegen .... d.	1108	...	1208	...	1308	1408	...	1508	1608	...	1708	1808	...	...	...	1908	2008	...	2108	2208	...	2313	2359	...	...
Betzdorf (Sieg) .... d.	1126	...	1226	...	1326	1426	...	1526	1626	...	1726	1826	...	...	...	1926	2026	...	2126	2226	...	2336	0023	...	...
Wissen (Sieg)..................... d.	1136	...	1236	...	1336	1436	...	1536	1636	...	1736	1836	...	...	...	1936	2036	...	2136	2236	...	2348	0034	...	...
Au (Sieg)............................ d.	1142	...	1242	...	1342	1442	...	1542	1642	...	1742	1842	...	...	...	1942	2042	...	2142	2242	2320	2357	0043	...	...
Eitorf.................................. d.	1159	...	1259	...	1359	1459	...	1559	1659	...	1759	1859	...	...	...	1959	2059	...	2159	2259	2339	...	...	...	...
Hennef (Sieg) .... d.	1209	...	1309	...	1409	1509	...	1609	1709	...	1809	1909	...	...	...	2009	2109	...	2209	2309	2353	...	...	...	...
Siegburg/Bonn .... **910** d.	1214	...	1314	...	1414	1514	...	1614	1714	...	1814	1914	...	...	...	2014	2114	...	2214	2314	2359	...	...	...	...
Troisdorf .... **802** d.	1219	...	1319	...	1419	1519	...	1619	1719	...	1819	1919	...	...	...	2019	2119	...	2219	2319	0003	...	...	...	...
Köln Messe/Deutz..**802 910** d.	1234	...	1334	...	1434	1534	...	1634	1734	...	1834	1934	...	...	...	2034	2134	...	2234	2334	0027	...	...	...	...
Köln Hbf ....**802 910** a.	1237	...	1337	...	1437	1537	...	1637	1737	...	1837	1937	...	...	...	2037	2137	...	2237	2337	0029	...	...	...	...
Köln Hbf ....**802 910** d.	1247	...	1347	...	1447	1547	...	1647	1747	...	1847	1947	...	...	...	*2047*e	...	...	...	...	...	...	...	...	...
Düren .... **802** d.	1315	...	1415	...	1515	1615	...	1715	1815	...	1915	2015	...	...	...	*2115*e	...	...	...	...	...	...	...	...	...
Aachen Hbf...........**802 910** a.	1348	...	1448	...	1548	1648	...	1748	1848	...	1948	2048	...	...	...	*2148*e	...	...	...	...	...	...	...	...	...

d – Daily from Siegen.
e – Ⓐ only.
h – Also Oct. 3.
k – Not Oct. 3.
r – ⚒ only.
◇ – Change trains at Gießen on ①–④.

ABELLIO Rail NRW — ESSEN - HAGEN - SIEGEN — 808

km																									
		Ⓐ	Ⓐ	Ⓐ	Ⓐ	Ⓒ		⚒		⚒		⚒			⚒		Ⓐ		Ⓐ		Ⓐ				
0	**Essen** Hbf.... ⊡ d.	...	...	...	...	...	0634e	...	0734e	...	0834r	...	0934		...	1634	...	1734	...	1834	...	1934	...	...	...
16	Bochum Hbf.. ⊡ d.	...	...	...	...	...	0647e	...	0747e	...	0847r	...	0947	and at	...	1647	...	1747	...	1847	...	1947	...	...	...
30	Witten Hbf .... ⊡ d.	...	...	...	...	...	0657e	...	0757e	...	0857r	...	0957		...	1657	...	1757	...	1857	...	1957	...	...	...
45	**Hagen** Hbf.... ⊡ a.	...	...	...	...	...	0709e	...	0809e	...	0909r	...	1009	the same	...	1709	...	1809	...	1909	...	2009	...	...	...
45	**Hagen** Hbf........d.	...	...	0540	0610	0615	0715	0740	0815	0840	0915	0940	1015		1640	1715	1740	1815	1840	1915	1940	2015	2115	2215	2315
75	Altena (Westf) ...d.	...	...	0605	0636	0640	0740	0805	0840	0905	0940	1005	1040	minutes	1705	1740	1805	1840	1905	1940	2005	2040	2140	2240	2340
84	Werdohl............d.	...	...	0614	0645	0649	0749	0814	0849	0914	0949	1014	1049		1714	1749	1814	1849	1914	1949	2014	2049	2149	2249	2349
106	Finnentrop ....d.	0502	0558	0631	0703	0707	0807	0831	0907	0931	1007	1031	1107	past each	1731	1807	1831	1907	1931	2007	2031	2107	2207	2307	0007
119	Lennestadt ♥ ...d.	0515	0610	0643	0715	0718	0818	0843	0918	0943	1018	1043	1118		1743	1818	1843	1918	1943	2018	2043	2119	2219	2319	0019
141	Kreuztal ....d.	0537	0633	0706	0738	0739	0837	0906	0937	1006	1037	1106	1137	hour until	1806	1837	1906	1937	2006	2037	2106	2142	2242	2342	0042
152	**Siegen** ....a.	0550	0644	0719	0750	0749	0849	0919	0949	1019	1049	1119	1149		1819	1849	1919	1949	2020	2049	2119	2154	2254	2354	0054

	⚒	Ⓐ		⚒		Ⓐ		Ⓐ			⚒			⚒		Ⓐ		Ⓐ		Ⓐ				
Siegen ....d.	...	0402	...	0506	...	0543	0612	0636	0712	...	0743	0812		1543	1612	1643	1712	1743	1812	1843	1912	2011	2111	2211	2311
Kreuztal ....d.	...	0413	...	0517	...	0555	0622	0648	0722	...	0754	0822	and at	1554	1622	1654	1722	1754	1822	1854	1922	2022	2122	2222	2323
Lennestadt ♥ ....d.	...	0436	...	0540	...	0618	0641	0711	0741	...	0817	0841		1617	1641	1717	1741	1817	1841	1917	1941	2045	2145	2245	2347
Finnentrop ....d.	0453	0453	...	0553	0553	0631	0653	0730	0753	...	0830	0853	the same	1630	1653	1730	1753	1830	1853	1930	1953	2058	2158	2258	2400
Werdohl.............d.	0510	0510	...	0610	0610	0647	0710	0747	0810	...	0847	0910		1647	1710	1747	1810	1847	1910	1947	2010	2115	2215	2315	...
Altena (Westf) ....d.	0519	0519	...	0619	0619	0656	0719	0756	0819	...	0856	0919	minutes	1656	1719	1756	1819	1856	1919	1956	2019	2124	2224	2324	...
Hagen Hbf.........a.	0546	0546	...	0646	0646	0723	0746	0823	0846	...	0923	0946		1723	1746	1823	1846	1923	1946	2023	2046	2151	2251	2351	...
Hagen Hbf..... ⊡ d.	...	...	...	0651e	...	...	0751e	...	0851r	...	...	0951	past each	...	1751	...	1851	...	1951	...	...	...	...	...	...
Witten Hbf ..... ⊡ d.	...	...	...	0702e	...	...	0802e	...	0902r	...	...	1002		...	1802	...	1902	...	2002	...	...	...	...	...	...
Bochum Hbf... ⊡ d.	...	...	...	0714e	...	...	0814e	...	0914r	...	...	1014	hour until	...	1814	...	1914	...	2014	...	...	...	...	...	...
Essen Hbf..... ⊡ a.	...	...	...	0729e	...	...	0829e	...	0929r	...	...	1029		...	1829	...	1929	...	2029	...	...	...	...	...	...

Additional services Essen - Hagen and v.v.

	⚒									
Essen Hbf.................. d.	0508	0608	0708	and	1908	2008	2108	2208	2308	...
Bochum Hbf.................. d.	0522	0622	0722	hourly	1922	2022	2122	2222	2322	...
Witten Hbf.................... d.	0533	0633	0733	until	1933	2033	2133	2233	2333	...
Hagen Hbf.................. a.	0546	0646	0746		1946	2046	2146	2246	2346	...

	⚒								
Hagen Hbf...................... d.	0517	0617	0717	and	1917	2017	2117	2217	2317
Witten Hbf......................... d.	0531	0631	0731	hourly	1931	2031	2131	2231	2331
Bochum Hbf........................ d.	0541	0641	0741	until	1941	2041	2141	2241	2341
Essen Hbf........................ a.	0556	0656	0756		1956	2056	2156	2256	2356

e – Ⓐ only.
r – ⚒ only.
⊡ – See also panel below main table.
♥ – Lennestadt - Altenhundem.

S-Bahn 5 — PADERBORN - HAMELN - HANNOVER - HANNOVER FLUGHAFEN ✈ — 809

km																									
						Ⓑ	⑥		⚒	†				⚒	†				⚒	†				⚒	†
0	**Paderborn** Hbf ..... **805 811** d.	...	...	...	...	0512e	...	...	0614	...	...	0714	...	0814	...	...	0914	...	1014	...	...	1114	...	1214	...
17	Altenbeken........... **805 811** d.	...	...	...	...	0524e	...	...	0626	...	...	0726	...	0826	...	...	0926	...	1026	...	...	1126	...	1226	...
56	Bad Pyrmont.......................d.	...	...	0505r	...	0602e	0605	0635e	0702	0705	0735e	0802	...	0902	0905	...	1002	...	1102	1105	...	1202	...	1302	1305
75	Hameln ....a.	...	...	0519r	...	0616e	0619	0649e	0716	0719	0749e	0816	...	0916	0919	...	1016	...	1116	1119	...	1216	...	1316	1319
75	Hameln ....d.	0420e	0450e	0520	0550r	0620	0620	0650r	0720	0720	0750r	0820	0850r	0920	0920	0950r	1020	1050r	1120	1120	1150r	1220	1250r	1320	1320
133	**Hannover** Hbf.....................a.	0503e	0533e	0603	0633r	0703	0703	0733r	0803	0803	0833r	0903	0933r	1003	1003	1033r	1103	1133r	1203	1203	1233r	1303	1333r	1403	1403
133	**Hannover** Hbf.....................d.	0505	0535	0605	0635	0705	0705	0735	0805	0805	0835	0905	0935	1005	1005	1035	1105	1135	1205	1205	1235	1305	1335	1405	1405
148	**Hannover** Flughafen ✈.......a.	0523	0553	0623	0653	0723	0723	0753	0823	0823	0853	0923	0953	1023	1023	1053	1123	1153	1223	1223	1253	1323	1353	1423	1423

				⚒	†				⚒	†				Ⓐ	Ⓒ					Ⓐ	Ⓒ				⑤–⑦
Paderborn Hbf.......**805 811** d.	...	1314	...	1414	...	...	1514	...	1614	...	...	1714	...	1814	...	...	1914	...	2014	...	...	2114	...	...	...
Altenbeken ....**805 811** d.	...	1326	...	1426	...	...	1526	...	1626	...	...	1726	...	1826	...	...	1926	...	2026	...	...	2126	...	...	...
Bad Pyrmont........................ d.	1335e	1402	...	1502	1505	...	1602	1635e	1702	1705	...	1802	1835e	1902	1905	...	2002	...	2102	2105	...	2202	...	2305	2305
Hameln .... a.	1349e	1416	...	1516	1519	...	1616	1649e	1716	1719	...	1816	1849e	1916	1919	...	2016	...	2116	2119	...	2216	...	2319	2319
Hameln .... d.	1350r	1420	1450r	1520	1520	1550r	1620	1650r	1720	1720	1750e	1820	1850e	1920	1920	1950e	2020	2050e	2120	2120	...	2220	...	2320	2320
Hannover Hbf .... a.	1433r	1503	1533r	1603	1603	1633r	1703	1733r	1803	1803	1833e	1903	1933e	2003	2003	2033e	2103	2133e	2203	2203	...	2303	...	0003	0003
Hannover Hbf .... d.	1435	1505	1535	1605	1605	1635	1705	1735	1805	1805	1835	1905	1935	2005	2005	2035	2105	2135	2205	2205	2235	2305	2335	...	0005
Hannover Flughafen ✈ .... a.	1453	1523	1553	1623	1623	1653	1723	1753	1823	1823	1853	1923	1953	2023	2023	2053	2123	2153	2223	2223	2253	2323	2353	...	0022

		①⑥⑦	Ⓐ	⚒		⚒					†	⚒				†	⚒				†	⚒			
Hannover Flughafen ✈ .... d.	0006	0036	...	...	0506	0536	0536	0606	0636	0706	0736	0736	0806	0836	0906	0936	0936	1006	1036	1106	1136	1136	1206	1236	1306
Hannover Hbf .... a.	0023	0053	...	...	0523	0553	0553	0623	0653	0723	0753	0753	0823	0853	0923	0953	0953	1023	1053	1123	1153	1153	1223	1253	1323
Hannover Hbf .... d.	...	0100	0455	...	0525e	0555	...	0625r	0655	0725r	0755	0755	0825r	0855	0925r	0955	0955	1025r	1055	1125r	1155	1155	1225r	1255	1325r
Hameln............................... a.	...	0144	0540	...	0610e	0640	...	0710r	0740	0810r	0840	0840	0910r	0940	1010r	1040	1040	1110r	1140	1210r	1240	1240	1310r	1340	1410r
Hameln............................... d.	...	...	0544g	0544	0611e	0644	...	0711e	0744	...	0841	0844	...	0944	...	1041	1044	...	1144	...	1241	1244	1311e	1344	...
Bad Pyrmont....................... d.	...	...	0600g	0600	0625e	0700	...	0725e	0800	...	0855	0900	...	1000	...	1055	1100	...	1200	...	1255	1300	1325e	1400	...
Altenbeken ....**805 811** d.	...	...	0634g	0634	...	0734	...	...	0834	...	...	0934	...	1034	...	...	1134	...	1234	...	...	1334	...	1434	...
Paderborn Hbf.......**805 811** a.	...	...	0646g	0646	...	0746	...	...	0846	...	...	0946	...	1046	...	...	1146	...	1246	...	...	1346	...	1446	...

	†	⚒				†	⚒				Ⓒ	Ⓐ				Ⓒ	Ⓐ								
Hannover Flughafen ✈ .... d.	1336	1336	1406	1436	1506	1536	1536	1606	1636	1706	1736	1736	1806	1836	1906	1936	1936	2006	2036	2106	2136	2206	2236	2306	2336
Hannover Hbf .... a.	1353	1353	1423	1453	1523	1553	1553	1623	1653	1723	1753	1753	1823	1853	1923	1953	1953	2023	2053	2123	2153	2223	2253	2323	2353
Hannover Hbf .... d.	1355	1355	1425r	1455	1525r	1555	1555	1625r	1655	1725r	1755	1755	1825e	1855	1925e	1955	1955	2025e	2055	2125e	2155	...	2255	...	2355
Hameln............................... a.	1440	1440	1510r	1540	1610r	1640	1640	1710r	1740	1810r	1840	1840	1910e	1940	2010e	2040	2040	2110e	2140	2210e	2240	...	2340	...	0040
Hameln............................... d.	1441	1444	...	1544	1611e	1641	1644e	...	1744	1811e	1841	1844	...	1944	...	2041	2044	...	2144	...	2241	...	2341	...	...
Bad Pyrmont....................... d.	1455	1500	...	1600	1625e	1655	1700e	...	1800	1825e	1855	1900	...	2000	...	2055	2100	...	2200	...	2255	...	2355	...	...
Altenbeken ....**805 811** d.	...	1534	...	1634	...	...	1734e	...	1834	...	...	1934	...	2034	...	...	2134	...	2234	...	...	...	...	...	...
Paderborn Hbf.......**805 811** a.	...	1546	...	1646	...	...	1746e	...	1846	...	...	1946	...	2046	...	...	2146	...	2246	...	...	...	...	...	...

e – Ⓐ only.
g – ① only.
r – ⚒ only.

810 HAMM and BAD BENTHEIM - HANNOVER - BERLIN and LEIPZIG

km	km	See note ▲	CNL 457	ICE 1741	ICE 949	ICE 649	IC 2031	RE 14201	ICE 841	ICE 841	IC 2147	RE 14003	IC 2241	ICE 541	ICE 541	ICE 876	IC 2033	RE 14203	EC 341	ICE 1092	IC 2145	ICE 843	ICE 853	ICE 696	IC 2145
			Ⓡ	①–⑤	①	①–⑤	①–⑥	⚒⊖	①	①–⑥	①–⑤	⚒⊖	①–⑥	①–⑥		①–⑥			①–⑥	①–⑤	①–⑥		①–⑥	①	①–⑥
			🍷♦	R					✕	✕	🍷		M🍷	✕	✕	✕♦	🍷		♦	D⚡ ✕	🍷	✕	✕	L✕	🍷
		Bonn Hbf **800** d.	...	...	...	...	...	...	...	...	...	...	...	...	...	...	...	...	...	...	...	...	...	...	...
		Köln/Bonn Flughafen ✈ **800** d.	...	...	...	...	...	...	...	...	...	...	...	...	...	...	...	...	...	...	...	...	...	...	...
		Köln Hbf **800** d.	2228	...	0151	...	...	...	0329	...	...	...	...	0429	...	...	...	...	...	...	0513	0529	0549	...	...
		Wuppertal Hbf **800** d.	2314	...	|	...	...	...	|	...	...	...	...	|	...	...	...	...	...	...	0543	|	0617	...	...
		Hagen Hbf **800** d.	|	...	|	...	...	...	|	...	...	...	...	|	...	...	...	...	...	...	0601	|	0635	...	...
		Düsseldorf Hbf **800 802** d.	2202	...	0215	...	...	...	0353	...	...	...	...	0453	...	...	...	...	...	...	|	0553	|	...	...
		Dortmund Hbf **800 802** d.	2356	...	0312	...	...	...	0448	...	...	...	...	0548	...	...	...	...	...	...	0628	0648	|	...	...
0		**Hamm** (Westf) **802** d.	0014	...	0330	...	...	...	0506	...	...	...	...	0611	...	...	...	...	...	...	0645	0711	0711	...	...
50		Gütersloh Hbf **802** d.	|	...	0351	...	...	...	0526	...	...	...	...	|	...	...	...	...	...	...	0705	|	|	...	...
67		**Bielefeld** Hbf **802** d.	0043	...	0403	...	...	0424	0537	...	...	...	...	0638	...	...	...	0624	...	...	0717	0737	0737	...	...
81		Herford **802** d.	|	...	0413	...	...	0433	|	...	...	...	...	|	...	...	...	0633	...	...	0727	|	|	...	...
		Schiphol ✈ **22** d.	|	...	|	...	...	|	|	...	...	...	...	|	...	...	...	|	...	...	|	|	|	...	...
		Bad Bentheim 🏛 **811** d.	|	...	|	...	...	|	|	...	...	...	...	|	...	...	...	|	...	...	|	|	|	...	...
		Rheine **811** d.	|	...	|	...	...	|	|	...	...	...	...	|	...	...	...	|	...	...	|	|	|	...	...
		Osnabrück Hbf **811** d.	|	...	|	...	...	|	|	...	...	0515	0604	|	...	...	...	|	...	...	|	|	|	...	...
		Bünde (Westf) **811** d.	|	...	|	...	...	|	|	...	...	0539	0626	|	...	...	...	|	...	...	|	|	|	...	...
91		Löhne (Westf) **802** d.	|	...	|	...	...	0440	|	...	...	0550	|	|	...	...	...	0640	...	...	|	|	|	...	...
97		Bad Oeynhausen **802** d.	|	...	|	...	...	0445	|	...	...	0555	0639	|	...	...	...	0645	...	...	0737	|	|	...	...
112		Minden (Westf) **802** d.	|	...	0430	...	...	0507**t**	0600	...	...	0607	0649	|	...	...	...	0707**t**	...	...	0749	|	|	...	...
		Basel SBB **912** d.	|	...	|	...	...	|	|	...	...	|	|	|	...	...	...	|	...	...	|	|	|	...	...
		Stuttgart Hbf **930** d.	|	...	|	...	...	|	|	...	...	|	|	|	...	...	...	|	...	...	|	|	|	...	...
		Frankfurt (Main) Hbf **900** d.	|	...	|	...	...	|	|	...	...	|	|	|	...	0510**g**	...	|	...	0614	|	|	|	...	...
		Oldenburg (Oldb) **813** d.	|	...	|	...	...	|	|	...	...	|	|	|	...	|	0535**e**	|	...	|	|	|	|	...	...
		Bremen Hbf **813** d.	|	...	|	...	...	|	|	...	...	|	|	|	...	|	0609	|	...	|	|	|	|	...	...
177		**Hannover** Hbf a.	|	...	0458	...	...	0550	0628	...	...	0650	0718	0728	...	|	0714	0750	...	|	0818	0828	0828	...	←
177		**Hannover** Hbf d.	|	...	0501	0527	0536	0555	0631	0631	0636	0655	0721	0731	0731	|	0736	0755	...	|	→	0831	0831	...	0836
212		Peine d.	|	...	|	|	|	0624	|	|	|	0724	|	|	|	|	|	0824	...	|	...	|	|	...	|
238	0	**Braunschweig** Hbf ‡ d.	|	...	|	0601	0610	0641	|	|	0711	0741	|	|	|	0800	0810	0841	...	|	...	|	|	0900	0911
274		Helmstedt ‡ d.	|	...	|	|	0632	*0720*a	|	|	|	...	|	|	|	|	0832	...	...	|	...	|	|	|	|
322		**Magdeburg** Hbf ‡ a.	|	...	|	|	0657	...	|	|	0755	...	|	|	|	|	0857	...	...	|	...	|	|	|	0955
322		**Magdeburg** Hbf ‡ d.	|	0626	|	|	0703	...	|	|	0803	...	|	|	|	|	0903	...	...	|	...	|	|	|	1003
372		Köthen ‡ d.	|	0655	|	|	0732	...	|	|	0832	...	|	|	|	|	|	...	...	|	...	|	|	|	1032
408		**Halle (Saale)** Hbf ‡ d.	|	0718	|	|	0755	...	|	|	0855	...	|	|	|	|	0952	...	...	|	...	|	|	|	1055
426		Leipzig/Halle Flughafen ✈ ‡ a.	|	0729	|	|	0805	...	|	|	0905	...	|	|	|	|	1003	...	...	|	...	|	|	|	1105
446		**Leipzig** Hbf ‡ a.	|	0743	|	|	0819	...	|	|	0919	...	|	|	|	|	1017	...	...	|	...	|	|	|	1119
	32	Wolfsburg d.	|	...	0534	0620	...	...	0705	0705	...	...	0755	|	|	0818	...	...	...	|	...	0905	0905	0918	...
	107	Stendal **838** d.	|	...	0605	0647	...	...	0733	0733	...	...	0826	|	|	|	...	...	0848	|	...	|	|	|	...
	141	Rathenow **838** d.	|	...	|	|	...	...	|	|	...	...	0843	|	|	|	...	...	|	|	...	|	|	|	...
	199	**Berlin** Spandau ▲ **838** a.	|	...	0641	0722	...	...	0806	0806	...	...	0905	0854	0854	0911	...	...	0923	0938	...	0956	0956	1010	...
	215	**Berlin** Hbf ▲ **838** a.	0421**z**	...	0655	0736	...	...	0820	0820	...	...	0920	0909	0909	0925	...	...	0937	0952	...	1011	1011	1025	...
	220	**Berlin** Ostbahnhof ▲ **838** a.	0430**z**	...	0706	0748	...	...	0832	0832	...	...	0931	0919	0919	0937	...	...	0948**v**	1002	...	1022	1022	1035	...

See note ▲	RE 14005	IC 2243	ICE 543	ICE 553	ICE 874	IC 2035	RE 14205	IC 2143	ICE 845	ICE 855	ICE 694	IC 2143	RE 14007	IC 141	ICE 545	ICE 555	ICE 872	IC 2037	RE 14207	IC 2141	ICE 847	ICE 857	ICE 692	IC 2141	RE 14009
		¶		①–⑥				①–⑥				①–⑥													
		🍷	✕	K✕	✕♦	🍷		🍷	✕	✕♦	✕	🍷		🍷	A✕	✕	✕	N🍷		🍷	✕	✕	✕	🍷	
Bonn Hbf **800** d.	...	...	...	0625	...	...	...	...	...	0722	...	...	...	...	...	0825**e**	...	...	...	...	...	...	...	...	...
Köln/Bonn Flughafen ✈ **800** d.	...	...	...	|	...	...	...	...	0712	|	...	...	...	...	...	|	...	...	...	...	...	...	...	...	...
Köln Hbf **800** d.	...	...	0626	0649	...	...	...	0711	|	0749	...	...	...	...	0828	0849	...	...	...	0913	...	0949	...	...	...
Wuppertal Hbf **800** d.	...	...	|	0717	...	...	...	0743	|	0817	...	...	...	...	|	0917	...	...	...	0943	...	1017	...	...	...
Hagen Hbf **800** d.	...	...	|	0735	...	...	...	0801	|	0835	...	...	...	...	|	0935	...	...	...	1001	...	1035	...	...	...
Düsseldorf Hbf **800 802** d.	...	...	0653	|	...	...	...	|	0753	|	...	...	...	...	0853	|	...	...	...	|	0953	|	...	...	...
Dortmund Hbf **800 802** d.	...	...	0748	|	...	...	...	0828	0848	|	...	...	...	...	0948	|	...	...	...	1028	1048	|	...	...	...
Hamm (Westf) **802** d.	...	...	0811	0811	...	...	...	0845	0911	0911	...	...	...	...	1011	1011	...	...	...	1045	1111	1111	...	...	...
Gütersloh Hbf **802** d.	...	...	|	|	...	...	...	0905	|	|	...	...	...	...	|	|	...	...	...	1105	|	|	...	...	...
Bielefeld Hbf **802** d.	...	...	0838	0838	...	...	0824	0917	0937	0937	...	...	...	...	1038	1038	...	...	1024	1117	1137	1137	...	...	...
Herford **802** d.	...	...	|	|	...	...	0833	0927	|	|	...	...	...	...	|	|	...	...	1033	1127	|	|	...	...	...
Schiphol ✈ **22** d.	...	...	|	|	...	...	|	|	|	|	...	...	...	0649	|	|	...	...	|	|	|	|	...	...	...
Bad Bentheim 🏛 **811** d.	*0557*a	0721**e**	|	|	...	...	|	|	|	|	...	...	*0757*r	0928	|	|	...	...	|	|	|	|	...	...	*0957*
Rheine **811** d.	0638	0735**e**	|	|	...	...	|	|	|	|	...	...	0838	0942	|	|	...	...	|	|	|	|	...	...	1038
Osnabrück Hbf **811** d.	0716	0804	|	|	...	...	|	|	|	|	...	...	0916	1008	|	|	...	...	|	|	|	|	...	...	1116
Bünde (Westf) **811** d.	0738	0826	|	|	...	...	|	|	|	|	...	...	0938	|	|	|	...	...	|	|	|	|	...	...	1138
Löhne (Westf) **802** d.	0750	|	|	|	...	...	0840	|	|	|	...	...	0950	|	|	|	...	...	1040	|	|	|	...	...	1150
Bad Oeynhausen **802** d.	0755	0839	|	|	...	...	0845	0937	|	|	...	...	0955	1039	|	|	...	...	1045	1137	|	|	...	...	1155
Minden (Westf) **802** d.	0807	0849	|	|	...	...	0907**t**	0949	|	|	...	...	1007	1049	|	|	...	...	1107**t**	1149	|	|	...	...	1207
Basel SBB **912** d.	|	|	|	|	...	...	|	|	|	|	...	...	|	|	|	|	0608	...	|	|	|	|	...	...	|
Stuttgart Hbf **930** d.	|	|	|	|	...	...	|	|	|	|	0651	...	|	|	|	|	|	...	|	|	|	|	0851	...	|
Frankfurt (Main) Hbf **900** d.	|	|	|	|	0713	...	|	|	|	|	0813	...	|	|	|	|	0913	...	|	|	|	|	1013	...	|
Oldenburg (Oldb) **813** d.	|	|	|	|	|	0735	|	|	|	|	|	...	|	|	|	|	|	0935	|	|	|	|	|	...	|
Bremen Hbf **813** d.	|	|	|	|	|	0809	|	|	|	|	|	...	|	|	|	|	|	1009	|	|	|	|	|	...	|
Hannover Hbf a.	0850	0918	0928	0928	|	0914	0950	1018	1028	1028	|	←	1050	1118	1128	1128	|	1114	1150	1218	1228	1228	|	←	1250
Hannover Hbf d.	0855	0921	0931	0931	|	0936	0955	→	1031	1031	|	1036	1055	1121	1131	1131	|	1136	1155	→	1231	1231	|	1236	1255
Peine d.	0924	|	|	|	|	|	1024	...	|	|	|	|	1124	|	|	|	|	|	1224	...	|	|	|	|	1324
Braunschweig Hbf ‡ d.	0941	|	|	|	1000	1010	1041	...	|	|	1100	1111	1141	|	|	|	1200	1210	1241	...	|	|	1300	1311	1341
Helmstedt ‡ d.	...	|	|	|	|	1032	...	...	|	|	|	|	...	|	|	|	|	1232	...	...	|	|	|	|	—
Magdeburg Hbf ‡ a.	...	|	|	|	|	1057	...	...	|	|	|	1155	...	|	|	|	|	1257	...	...	|	|	|	1355	...
Magdeburg Hbf ‡ d.	...	|	|	|	|	1103	...	...	|	|	|	1203	...	|	|	|	|	1303	...	...	|	|	|	1403	...
Köthen ‡ d.	...	|	|	|	|	|	...	...	|	|	|	1232	...	|	|	|	|	|	...	...	|	|	|	1432	...
Halle (Saale) Hbf ‡ d.	...	|	|	|	|	1152	...	...	|	|	|	1255	...	|	|	|	|	1352	...	...	|	|	|	1455	*IC*
Leipzig/Halle Flughafen ✈ ‡ a.	...	|	|	|	|	1203	...	...	|	|	|	1305	...	|	|	|	|	1403	...	...	|	|	|	1505	**1931**
Leipzig Hbf ‡ a.	...	|	|	|	|	1217	...	...	|	|	|	1319	...	|	|	|	|	1417	...	...	|	|	|	1519	⑤
Wolfsburg d.	...	0955	|	|	1018	...	...	...	1105	1105	|	...	...	1155	|	|	1218	...	...	...	1305	1305	|	...	**U**
Stendal **838** d.	...	1026	|	|	|	...	...	...	|	|	|	...	...	1226	|	|	|	...	...	...	|	|	|	...	1407
Rathenow **838** d.	...	1043	|	|	|	...	...	...	|	|	|	...	...	1243	|	|	|	...	...	...	|	|	|	...	|
Berlin Spandau ▲ **838** a.	...	1105	1053	1053	1111	...	...	...	1156	1156	1207	...	...	1305	1253	1253	1311	...	...	...	1356	1356	1405	...	1448
Berlin Hbf ▲ **838** a.	...	1120	1108	1108	1125	...	...	...	1211	1211	1221	...	...	1320	1308	1308	1325	...	...	...	1411	1411	1419	...	1458
Berlin Ostbahnhof ▲ **838** a.	...	1131	1119	1119	1137	...	...	...	1222	1222	1231	...	...	1332	1319	1319	1337	...	...	...	1422	1422	1430	...	...

♦ – **NOTES** (LISTED BY TRAIN NUMBER)

341 – WAWEL – (12) Hamburg - Uelzen - Berlin - Cottbus - Forst 🏛 - Wrocław - Kraków.

457 – KOPERNIKUS – 🛏 1, 2 cl., ▬ 2 cl. and (2) Amsterdam - Köln - Berlin - Dresden - Praha (Table **28**); 🛏 1, 2 cl., ▬ 2 cl. and (2) (*EN* **447** – JAN KIEPURA) Amsterdam - Köln - Berlin - Warszawa (Table **24**); conveys 🛏 1, 2 cl. Amsterdam - Moskva (Table **24**). For overnight journeys only.

855 – (12) and ✕ Trier - Koblenz - Berlin.

874 – (12) and ✕ (Basel Bad. Bf ① -) Karlsruhe - Mannheim - Frankfurt - Berlin.

876 – (12) and ✕ (Frankfurt ① -) Kassel - Berlin.

A – From Aachen Hbf (d. 0740) and Düren (d. 0758) on ①–⑥.

D – From Darmstadt Hbf (d. 0543).

K – From Koblenz Hbf (d. 0547).

L – From Kassel (Table **900**).

M – From Münster (Table **800**).

N – From Norddeich Mole (Table **813**).

R – To Dresden (Table **842**).

U – From Uelzen (Table **841**).

a – ①–⑤ only.

e – ①–⑥ only.

g – ① only.

r – ⚒ only.

t – Arrives 10 minutes earlier.

v – Not June 20 - July 3.

z – June 20 - July 3 calls at Berlin Gesundbrunnen (a. 0419) and Lichtenberg (a. 0430), **not** Hbf or Ostbahnhof.

¶ – Train number **2343** on ⑦.

⊖ – Runs daily Hannover - Braunschweig.

⚡ – *ICE SPRINTER*. Ⓡ and supplement payable.

‡ – See panel on page 379 for additional local services.

▲ – **June 20 - July 3** Berlin timings are subject to alteration as follows:
ICE trains from the Hannover direction do not call at Berlin Spandau and arrive Berlin Hbf / Ostbahnhof up to 32 minutes later.
ICE trains from the Frankfurt direction terminate at Berlin Hbf.
IC trains from the Stendal direction, which normally terminate at Berlin Ostbahnhof, are diverted to Berlin Gesundbrunnen (not calling at Hbf / Ostbahnhof).
For other services see individual notes.

HAMM and BAD BENTHEIM - HANNOVER - BERLIN and LEIPZIG — 810

See note ▲	*IC* 143	*ICE* 547	*ICE* 557	*ICE* 278	*IC* 2039	*RE* 14209	*IC* 1112	*IC* 2049	*ICE* 849	*ICE* 859	*ICE* 690	*IC* 2049	*RE* 14011	*IC* 145	*IC* 245	*ICE* 549	*ICE* 559	*ICE* 276	*IC* 2131	*IC* 2239	*RE* 14211	*IC* 2047	*ICE* 941	*ICE* 951	*ICE* 598
							⑤							Ⓑ	⑥					z		Ⓑ			¶
	🍷	✕	✕	A✕	🍷		T🍷	🍷	✕	✕	✕	🍷		S🍷	🍷	✕	✕	A✕	L🍷	R		🍷	✕	✕	✕
Bonn Hbf **800** d.	...	...	...	...	...	...	1022	...	...	...	...	...	...	...	...	...	1223e	...	...	...	...	...	...	...	...
Köln/Bonn Flughafen ✈ **800** d.	...	1012a	...	...	...	...	|	...	...	...	...	...	...	...	...	1212	|	...	...	...	...	...	...	...	...
Köln Hbf **800** d.	...	|	1049	...	...	...	1045	1113	...	1149	...	...	...	...	...	|	1249	...	...	...	...	1313	...	1349	...
Wuppertal Hbf **800** d.	...	|	1117	...	...	...	|	1143	...	1217	...	...	...	...	...	|	1317	...	...	...	...	1343	...	1417	...
Hagen Hbf **800** d.	...	|	1135	...	...	...	|	1201	...	1235	...	...	...	...	...	|	1335	...	...	...	...	1401	...	1435	...
Düsseldorf Hbf **800 802** d.	...	1053	|	...	...	...	1117	|	1153	|	...	...	...	...	...	1253	|	...	...	...	...	|	1353	|	...
Dortmund Hbf **800 802** d.	...	1148	|	...	...	...	1210	1228	1248	|	...	...	...	...	...	1348	|	...	...	...	...	1428	1448	|	...
Hamm (Westf) **802** d.	...	1211	1211	...	...	...	1234	1245	1311	1311	...	...	...	...	...	1411	1411	...	...	...	...	1445	1511	1511	...
Gütersloh Hbf **802** d.	...	|	|	...	...	...	1255	1305	|	|	...	...	...	...	...	|	|	...	...	...	...	1505	|	|	...
Bielefeld Hbf **802** d.	...	1238	1238	...	...	1224	1306	1317	1337	1337	...	...	...	...	...	1438	1438	...	...	...	1424	1517	1537	1537	...
Herford **802** d.	...	|	|	...	...	1233	1315	1327	|	|	...	...	...	...	...	|	|	...	...	...	1433	1527	|	|	...
Schiphol ✈ **22** d.	0849	|	|	...	...	|	|	|	|	|	...	...	...	1049	1049	|	|	...	...	...	|	|	|	|	...
Bad Bentheim 🏛 **811** d.	1128	|	|	...	...	|	|	|	|	|	...	...	*1157*	1328	1328	|	|	...	...	...	|	|	|	|	...
Rheine **811** d.	1142	|	|	...	...	|	|	|	|	|	...	...	1238	1342	1342	|	|	...	...	...	|	|	|	|	...
Osnabrück Hbf **811** d.	1208	|	|	...	...	|	|	|	|	|	...	...	1316	1408	1408	|	|	...	...	...	|	|	|	|	...
Bünde (Westf) **811** d.	1229	|	|	...	...	|	|	|	|	|	...	...	1338	|	|	|	|	...	...	...	|	|	|	|	...
Löhne (Westf) **802** d.	|	|	|	...	...	1240	|	|	|	|	...	...	1350	|	|	|	|	...	...	...	1440	|	|	|	...
Bad Oeynhausen **802** d.	|	|	|	...	...	1245	|	1337	|	|	...	...	1355	1439	1439	|	|	...	...	...	1445	1537	|	|	...
Minden (Westf) **802** d.	1249	|	|	...	...	1307t	|	1349	|	|	...	...	1407	1449	1449	|	|	...	...	...	1507t	1549	|	|	...
Basel SBB **912** d.	|	|	|	0812	...	|	|	|	|	|	...	...	|	|	|	|	|	1012	...	...	|	|	|	|	...
Stuttgart Hbf **930** d.	|	|	|	|	...	|	|	|	|	|	1051	...	|	|	|	|	|	|	...	...	|	|	|	|	1251
Frankfurt (Main) Hbf **900** d.	|	|	|	1113	...	|	|	|	|	|	1213	...	|	|	|	|	|	1313	...	...	|	|	|	|	1413
Oldenburg (Oldb) **813** d.	|	|	|	|	1135	|	|	|	|	|	|	...	|	|	|	|	|	|	1335	...	|	|	|	|	|
Bremen Hbf **813** d.	|	|	|	|	1209	|	|	|	|	|	|	...	|	|	|	|	|	|	1409	...	|	|	|	|	|
Hannover Hbf a.	1318	1328	1328	|	1314	1350	1359	1418	1428	1428	|	←	1450	1518	1518	1528	1528	|	1514	...	1550	1618	1628	1628	|
Hannover Hbf d.	1321	1331	1331	|	1336	1355	1402	→	1431	1431	|	1436	1455	1521	1521	1531	1531	|	1536	...	1555	→	1631	1631	|
Peine d.	|	|	|	|	|	1424	|	...	|	|	|	|	1524	|	|	|	|	|	|	...	1624	...	|	|	|
Braunschweig Hbf ‡ d.	|	|	|	1400	1410	1441	|	...	|	|	1500	1511	1541	|	|	|	|	1600	1610	...	1641	...	|	|	1700
Helmstedt ‡ d.	|	|	|	|	1432	...	|	...	|	|	|	|	...	|	|	|	|	|	1632	...	...	...	|	|	|
Magdeburg Hbf ‡ a.	|	|	|	|	1457	...	|	...	|	|	|	1555	...	|	|	|	|	|	1657	...	...	...	|	|	|
Magdeburg Hbf ‡ d.	|	|	|	|	1503	...	|	...	|	|	|	1603	...	|	|	|	|	|	1700	1703	...	...	|	|	|
Köthen ‡ d.	|	|	|	|	|	...	|	...	|	|	|	1632	...	|	|	|	|	|	|	1732	...	...	|	|	|
Halle (Saale) Hbf ‡ d.	|	|	|	|	1552	...	|	...	|	|	|	1655	...	|	|	|	|	|	|	1755	...	...	|	|	|
Leipzig/Halle Flughafen ✈ ‡ a.	|	|	|	|	1603	...	|	...	|	|	|	1705	...	|	|	|	|	|	|	1805	...	...	|	|	|
Leipzig Hbf ‡ a.	|	|	|	|	1617	...	|	...	|	|	|	1719	...	|	|	|	|	|	|	1819	...	...	|	|	|
Wolfsburg d.	1355	|	|	1418	...	...	1438	...	1505	1505	|	...	...	1555	1555	|	|	1618	|	...	...	...	1705	1705	|
Stendal **838** d.	1426	|	|	|	...	...	|	...	|	|	|	...	...	1626	1626	|	|	|	|	...	...	...	|	|	|
Rathenow **838** d.	1443	|	|	|	...	...	|	...	|	|	|	...	...	1643	1643	|	|	|	|	...	...	...	|	|	|
Berlin Spandau ▲ **838** a.	1505	1453	1453	1511	...	...	1541	...	1556	1556	1607	...	...	1705	1706	1655	1655	1711	|	...	...	...	1756	1756	1805
Berlin Hbf ▲ **838** a.	1520	1508	1508	1525	...	...	1551	...	1611	1611	1621	...	...	1715	1721	1710	1710	1725	1827	...	...	...	1811	1811	1819
Berlin Ostbahnhof ▲ **838** a.	1531	1519	1519	1537	...	...	...	...	1622	1622	1631	...	...	...	1732	1721	1721	1737	1838	...	...	...	1822	1822	1830e

See note ▲	*IC* 2047	*RE* 14013	*IC* 147	*ICE* 641	*ICE* 651	*ICE* 374	*IC* 2133	*RE* 14213	*IC* 1920	*IC* 1916	*IC* 2045	*ICE* 943	*ICE* 953	*ICE* 596	*IC* 2045	*RE* 14015	*IC* 149	*ICE* 643	*ICE* 653	*ICE* 370	*IC* 2135	*RE* 14215	*ICE* 1090	*IC* 2012	*ICE* 945
	Ⓑ								⑦	⑤	Ⓑ		Ⓑ		Ⓑ								Ⓑ		
	🍷		🍷	✕	✕	A✕	🍷		F	T🍷	🍷	✕	✕	✕	🍷		🍷	✕	✕	A✕	N🍷		✕⚡	G🍷	✕
Bonn Hbf **800** d.	...	...	...	...	1425	...	...	...	1422	1422	...	...	...	...	...	...	...	...	...	...	...	...	...	1622	...
Köln/Bonn Flughafen ✈ **800** d.	...	...	...	...	|	...	...	...	|	|	...	...	...	...	...	...	...	1612	...	...	...	...	...	|	...
Köln Hbf **800** d.	...	...	...	...	1449	...	...	...	1445	1445	1513	...	1549	...	...	...	...	|	1649	...	...	...	...	1648	...
Wuppertal Hbf **800** d.	...	...	...	...	1517	...	...	...	|	|	1543	...	1617	...	...	...	...	|	1717	...	...	...	...	|	...
Hagen Hbf **800** d.	...	...	...	...	1535	...	...	...	|	|	1601	...	1635	...	...	...	...	|	1735	...	...	...	...	|	...
Düsseldorf Hbf **800 802** d.	...	...	...	1453	|	...	...	...	1518	1518	|	1553	|	...	...	...	...	1653	|	...	...	...	...	1714	1753
Dortmund Hbf **800 802** d.	...	...	...	1548	|	...	...	...	1608	1608	1628	1648	|	...	...	...	...	1748	|	...	...	...	...	1828	1848
Hamm (Westf) **802** d.	...	...	...	1611	1611	...	...	...	1631	1634	1645	1711	1711	...	...	...	...	1811	1811	...	...	...	...	1845	1911
Gütersloh Hbf **802** d.	...	...	...	|	|	...	...	...	1655	1655	1705	|	|	...	...	...	...	|	|	...	...	...	...	1905	|
Bielefeld Hbf **802** d.	...	...	...	1638	1638	...	...	1624	1706	1706	1717	1737	1737	...	...	...	...	1838	1838	...	...	1824	...	1917	1937
Herford **802** d.	...	...	...	|	|	...	...	1633	1715	1715	1727	|	|	...	...	...	...	|	|	...	...	1833	...	1927	|
Schiphol ✈ **22** d.	...	...	1249	|	|	...	...	|	|	|	|	|	|	...	...	...	1449	|	|	...	...	|	...	|	|
Bad Bentheim 🏛 **811** d.	...	*1357*	1528	|	|	...	...	|	|	|	|	|	|	...	...	*1557*	1728	|	|	...	...	|	...	|	|
Rheine **811** d.	...	1438	1542	|	|	...	...	|	|	|	|	|	|	...	...	1638	1742	|	|	...	...	|	...	|	|
Osnabrück Hbf **811** d.	...	1516	1608	|	|	...	...	|	|	|	|	|	|	...	...	1716	1808	|	|	...	...	|	...	|	|
Bünde (Westf) **811** d.	...	1538	1629	|	|	...	...	|	|	|	|	|	|	...	...	1738	|	|	|	...	...	|	...	|	|
Löhne (Westf) **802** d.	...	1550	|	|	|	...	...	1640	|	|	|	|	|	...	...	1750	|	|	|	...	...	1840	...	|	|
Bad Oeynhausen **802** d.	...	1555	|	|	|	...	...	1645	|	|	1737	|	|	...	...	1755	1839	|	|	...	...	1845	...	1937	|
Minden (Westf) **802** d.	...	1607	1649	|	|	...	...	1707t	|	|	1749	|	|	...	...	1807	1849	|	|	...	...	1907t	...	1949	|
Basel SBB **912** d.	...	|	|	|	|	1212	...	|	|	|	|	|	|	...	...	|	|	|	|	1412	...	|	...	|	|
Stuttgart Hbf **930** d.	...	|	|	|	|	|	...	|	|	|	|	|	|	1451	...	|	|	|	|	|	...	|	1651	|	|
Frankfurt (Main) Hbf **900** d.	...	|	|	|	|	1513	...	|	|	|	|	|	|	1613	...	|	|	|	|	1713	...	|	1813	|	|
Oldenburg (Oldb) **813** d.	...	|	|	|	|	|	1535	|	|	|	|	|	|	|	...	|	|	|	|	|	1735	|	|	|	|
Bremen Hbf **813** d.	...	|	|	|	|	|	1609	|	|	|	|	|	|	|	...	|	|	|	|	|	1809	|	|	|	|
Hannover Hbf a.	←	1650	1718	1728	1728	|	1714	1750	1758	1758	1818	1828	1828	|	←	1850	1918	1928	1928	|	1914	1950	|	2018	2028
Hannover Hbf d.	1636	1655	1721	1731	1731	|	1736	1755	1801	1801	→	1831	1831	|	1836	1855	1921	1931	1931	|	1936	1955	|	→	2031
Peine d.	|	1724	|	|	|	|	|	1824	|	|	...	|	|	|	|	1924	|	|	|	|	|	2024	|	...	|
Braunschweig Hbf ‡ d.	1711	1741	|	|	|	1800	1810	1841	|	|	...	|	|	1900	1911	1941	|	|	|	2000	2010	2041	|	...	|
Helmstedt ‡ d.	|	...	|	|	|	|	1832	...	|	|	...	|	|	|	|	...	|	|	|	|	2032	...	|	...	|
Magdeburg Hbf ‡ a.	1755	...	|	|	|	|	1857	...	|	|	...	|	|	|	1955	...	|	|	|	|	2057	...	|	...	|
Magdeburg Hbf ‡ d.	1803	...	|	|	|	|	1903	...	|	|	...	|	|	|	2003	...	|	|	|	|	2103	...	|	...	|
Köthen ‡ d.	1832	...	|	|	|	|	|	...	|	|	...	|	|	|	2032	...	|	|	|	|	2132	...	|	...	|
Halle (Saale) Hbf ‡ d.	1855	...	|	|	|	|	1952	...	|	|	...	|	|	|	2055	...	|	|	|	|	2155	...	|	...	|
Leipzig/Halle Flughafen ✈ ‡ a.	1905	...	|	|	|	|	2003	...	|	|	...	|	|	|	2105	...	|	|	|	|	2205	...	|	...	|
Leipzig Hbf ‡ a.	1919	...	|	|	|	|	2017	...	|	|	...	|	|	|	2119	...	|	|	|	|	2219	...	|	...	|
Wolfsburg d.	...	...	1755	|	|	1818	...	...	1837	1837	...	1905	1905	|	...	...	1955	|	|	2018	...	...	|	...	2105
Stendal **838** d.	...	...	1826	|	|	|	...	...	|	|	...	|	|	|	...	...	2026	|	|	|	...	...	|	...	2133
Rathenow **838** d.	...	...	1843	|	|	|	...	...	|	|	...	|	|	|	...	...	2043	|	|	|	...	...	|	...	|
Berlin Spandau ▲ **838** a.	...	...	1905	1853	1853	1911	...	...	1941	1941	...	1956	1956	2005	...	...	2105	2053	2053	2111	...	...	2138	...	2206
Berlin Hbf ▲ **838** a.	...	...	1920	1908	1908	1925	...	...	1951	1955	...	2011	2011	2019	...	...	2120	2108	2108	2128	...	...	2148	...	2221
Berlin Ostbahnhof ▲ **838** a.	...	...	1931	1919	1919	1937	...	...	...	...	...	2022	2022	2030	...	...	2131	2119	2119	2138	...	...	...	...	2232

A – From Interlaken via Bern (Table **560**).
F – From Frankfurt via Koblenz (Tables **800/912**).
G – ALLGÄU – (12) and 🍷 Oberstdorf - Stuttgart - Koblenz - Hannover (- Magdeburg ⑤⑦) (- Leipzig ⑦).
L – OSTFRIESLAND – (12) and 🍷 Emden - Magdeburg - Berlin (- Cottbus Ⓑ).
N – From Norddeich Mole on dates in Table **813**.
R – From Warnemünde (via Rostock and Schwerin) daily until Aug. 30, also ⑤⑦ Sept. 4 - Oct. 25. See also Tables **830**, **837** and **841**.
S – To Szczecin (Table **845**).
T – From Stuttgart via Koblenz (Tables **800/912**).

a – ①–⑤ only.
e – ①–⑥ only.
t – Arrives 10 minutes earlier.

z – Not Sept. 5, 12, 19, 26, Oct. 3, 10, 17, 24.

¶ – Train number **998** on ⑦.

▲ – **June 20 - July 3** Berlin timings are subject to alteration as follows: *ICE* trains from the Hannover direction do not call at Berlin Spandau and arrive Berlin Hbf / Ostbahnhof up to 32 minutes later. *ICE* trains from the Frankfurt direction terminate at Berlin Hbf. *IC* trains from the Stendal direction, which normally terminate at Berlin Ostbahnhof, are diverted to Berlin Gesundbrunnen (not calling at Hbf / Ostbahnhof).

⚡ – *ICE* ***SPRINTER***. Ⓡ and supplement payable.

‡ – See panel below main table for additional *RE* / *RB* services.

	Ⓐ			Ⓐ		Ⓐ
Braunschweig Hbf d.	0617	0717	then hourly on Ⓐ,	2017	2117	2217
Helmstedt d.	0645	0745	every **two** hours	2045	2145	2245
Magdeburg Hbf a.	0729	0829	on Ⓒ until	2129	2229	2329

	Ⓐ	Ⓐ	①–⑤	⑥⑦			
Magdeburg Hbf d.	0407	0504	0555	0607	0707	and	2207
Köthen d.	0447	0545	0633	0647	0747	hourly	2247
Halle (Saale) Hbf a.	0515	0615	0702	0715	0815	until	2315

Halle (Saale) Hbf d.	0512	0523	and at the same	2212	2223	2326
Leipzig/Halle Flughafen ✈ d.	0524	|	minutes past	2224	|	2337
Leipzig Hbf a.	0538	0559	each hour until	2238	2259	2351

810 HAMM and BAD BENTHEIM - HANNOVER - BERLIN and LEIPZIG

See note ▲	ICE	IC	ICE	RE	IC	IC	ICE	ICE	ICE	IC	RB	RE	IC	ICE	ICE	ICE	RE	ICE	RE	ICE	ICE	ICE	ICE	ICE	ICE
	955	**2012**	**594**	**14017**	**241**	**241**	**645**	**655**	**870**	**2137**	**36041**	**14217**	**2041**	**947**	**957**	**592**	**14019**	**928**	**14219**	**647**	**657**	**372**	**1743**	**502**	**1002**
	Ⓑ	⑤⑦	⑥		Ⓑ	⑤⑦				Ⓑ			⑦		Ⓑ			⑦		⑦	⑦	⑦	⑦	Ⓑ	⑥
	✕	🍷◆	✕		🍷	🍷	✕	✕	✕	🍷x			🍷	✕	✕	✕		🍷◆		✕	✕	Z✕		K🍷	K🍷
Bonn Hbf **800** d.	...	...	...	...	...	...	...	...	...	...	...	...	...	...	...	...	...	...	...	...	2025	...	...	...	...
Köln/Bonn Flughafen ✈ **800** d.	...	...	...	...	...	...	1812b	...	...	...	...	...	...	...	...	...	...	...	...	...	|	...	...	...	...
Köln Hbf **800** d.	1749	...	...	...	...	...	|	1849	...	...	...	...	1913	...	1949	...	...	2017d	...	...	2049	...	...	2111	2111
Wuppertal Hbf **800** d.	1817	...	...	...	...	...	|	1917	...	...	...	...	1943	...	2017	...	...	|	...	...	2117	...	...	2143	|
Hagen Hbf **800** d.	1835	...	...	...	...	...	|	1935	...	...	...	...	2001	...	2035	...	...	|	...	...	2135	...	...	2201	|
Düsseldorf Hbf **800 802** d.	|	...	...	...	...	...	1853	|	...	...	...	...	|	1953	|	...	...	2039	...	2053	|	...	...	|	2134
Dortmund Hbf **800 802** d.	|	...	...	...	...	...	1948	|	...	...	...	...	2028	2048	|	...	...	2132	...	2148	|	...	...	2228	2228
Hamm (Westf) **802** d.	1911	...	...	...	...	...	2011	2011	...	...	...	...	2045	2111	2111	...	...	2149	...	2211	2211	...	...	2250	2250
Gütersloh Hbf **802** d.	|	...	...	...	...	...	|	|	...	...	...	...	2105	|	|	...	...	2209	...	|	|	...	...	2310	2310
Bielefeld Hbf **802** d.	1937	...	...	...	...	...	2038	2038	...	...	...	2024	2117	2137	2137	...	...	2220	2224	2238	2238	...	...	2320	2320
Herford **802** d.	|	...	...	...	...	...	|	|	...	...	...	2033	2127	|	|	...	...	|	2233	|	|	...	...	2330	2330
Schiphol ✈ **22** d.	|	...	...	...	1649	1649	|	|	...	...	...	|	|	|	|	...	...	|	|	|	|	...	...	|	|
Bad Bentheim 🏛 **811** d.	|	...	...	*1757*	1928	1928	|	|	...	...	...	|	|	|	|	...	*1957*	|	|	|	|	...	...	|	|
Rheine **811** d.	|	...	...	1838	1942	1942	|	|	...	...	...	|	|	|	|	...	2038	|	|	|	|	...	...	|	|
Osnabrück Hbf **811** d.	|	...	...	1916	2008	2008	|	|	...	...	...	|	|	|	|	...	2116	|	|	|	|	...	...	|	|
Bünde (Westf) **811** d.	|	...	...	1938	2029	2029	|	|	...	...	...	|	|	|	|	...	2138	|	|	|	|	...	...	|	|
Löhne (Westf) **802** d.	|	...	...	1950	|	|	|	|	...	...	...	2040	|	|	|	...	2150	|	2240	|	|	...	...	|	|
Bad Oeynhausen **802** d.	|	...	...	1955	|	|	|	|	...	...	...	2045	2137	|	|	...	2155	|	2245	|	|	...	...	|	|
Minden (Westf) **802** d.	|	...	...	2007	2049	2049	|	|	...	...	...	2107t	2149	|	|	...	2207	2247	2257	|	|	...	...	2346	2346
Basel SBB **912** d.	|	...	...	|	|	|	|	|	1612	...	...	|	|	|	|	...	|	|	...	|	|	1812	...	|	|
Stuttgart Hbf **930** d.	|	...	1651	|	|	|	|	|	|	...	...	|	|	|	|	1851	|	|	...	|	|	|	...	|	|
Frankfurt (Main) Hbf **900** d.	|	...	1813	|	|	|	|	|	1913	...	...	|	|	|	|	2013	|	|	...	|	|	2113	...	|	|
Oldenburg (Oldb) **813** d.	|	...	|	|	|	|	|	|	|	1935r	...	|	|	|	|	|	|	|	...	|	|	|	...	|	|
Bremen Hbf **813** d.	|	...	|	|	|	|	|	|	|	2009r	...	|	|	|	|	|	|	|	...	|	|	|	...	|	|
Hannover Hbf a.	2028	←	|	2050	2118	2118	2128	2128	|	2114r	...	2150	2218	2228	2228	|	2250	2317	...	2328	2328	|	...	0026	0026
Hannover Hbf d.	2031	2036	|	2055	...	2121	2131	2131	|	2136	...	2155	...	2231	2231	|	2255	...	...	2331	2331	|	2350	...	...
Peine d.	|	|	|	2124	...	|	|	|	|	2157	...	2224	...	|	|	|	2324	...	...	|	|	|	|	...	...
Braunschweig Hbf ‡ d.	|	2111	2100	2141	...	|	|	|	2200	2213	...	2241	...	|	|	2300	2341	...	...	|	|	2359	0026	...	...
Helmstedt ‡ d.	|	|	|	...	...	|	|	|	|	2235	...	...	...	|	|	|	...	...	...	|	|	|	|	...	...
Magdeburg Hbf ‡ a.	|	2155	|	...	...	|	|	|	|	2300	...	...	...	|	|	|	...	...	...	|	|	|	0113	...	...
Magdeburg Hbf ‡ d.	|	2203w	|	...	...	|	|	|	|	...	2308	...	...	|	|	|	...	...	...	|	|	|	...	...	...
Köthen ‡ d.	|	2234w	|	...	...	|	|	|	|	...	2348	...	...	|	|	|	...	...	...	|	|	|	...	...	...
Halle (Saale) Hbf ‡ d.	|	2257w	|	...	...	|	|	|	|	...	0016	...	...	|	|	|	...	...	...	|	|	|	...	...	...
Leipzig/Halle Flughafen ✈ ‡ a.	|	2308w	|	...	...	|	|	|	|	...	*0042*	...	...	|	|	|	...	...	...	|	|	|	...	...	...
Leipzig Hbf ‡ a.	|	2323w	|	...	...	|	|	|	|	...	*0058*	...	...	|	|	|	...	...	...	|	|	|	...	...	...
Wolfsburg d.	2105	...	2118	...	...	2155	|	|	2218	...	...	...	...	2305	2305	2318	...	...	...	0005	0005	0018	...	...	...
Stendal **838** d.	2133	...	|	...	...	2226	|	|	|	...	...	...	...	2333n	2333n	|	...	...	...	|	|	|	...	...	...
Rathenow **838** d.	|	...	|	...	...	2243	|	|	|	...	...	...	...	|	|	|	...	...	...	|	|	|	...	...	...
Berlin Spandau ▲ **838** a.	2206	...	2211	...	...	2305	2254	2254	2311	...	...	...	...	0004	0004	0011	...	...	...	0057	0057	0111	...	...	...
Berlin Hbf ▲ **838** a.	2221	...	2226	...	...	2320	2309	2309	2325	...	...	...	...	0019	0019	0027	...	...	...	0112	0112	0125	...	...	...
Berlin Ostbahnhof ▲ **838** a.	2232	...	2237	...	...	2330	2319	2319	2337	...	...	...	...	0030	0030	0038	...	...	...	0122	0122	0136	...	...	...

km	See note △	CNL	ICE	ICE	RE	ICE	ICE	ICE	RE	IC	IC	ICE	RE	IC	ICE	ICE	ICE	IC	ICE	RE	IC	ICE	ICE	ICE	IC
		456	**948**	**527**	**14002**	**503**	**656**	**646**	**14202**	**2136**	**242**	**373**	**14004**	**2013**	**593**	**956**	**946**	**2013**	**1091**	**14204**	**2134**	**375**	**654**	**644**	**240**
		🅁	①	①	⚒		①–⑤	①–⑤	⚒⊖	①–⑤	①–⑥	①–⑤		①–⑥	⑥⑦	①–⑥	①–⑥		①–⑤						①–⑥
		🍷◆	✕	◆		K🍷	✕	✕			🍷	A✕		◆	✕	✕	✕	🍷◆	⚡✕		🍷◆	A✕	✕	✕	🍷
0	**Berlin** Ostbahnhof △ **838** d.	0022	0026	...	...	...	0417	0417	...	...	...	0421	...	...	0520	0525	0525	...	...	...	...	0621	0640	0640	0626
5	**Berlin** Hbf △ **838** d.	0032	0036	...	...	...	0427	0427	...	...	...	0432	...	...	0531	0537	0537	...	0608	...	...	0632	0650	0650	0637
21	**Berlin** Spandau △ **838** d.	|	0051	...	...	...	0442	0442	...	...	...	0448	...	...	0546	0552	0552	...	0618	...	...	0647	0705	0705	0651
79	Rathenow **838** d.	|	|	...	...	...	|	|	...	...	...	|	...	...	|	|	|	...	|	...	...	|	|	|	0716
113	Stendal **838** d.	|	0126	...	...	...	0518	0518	...	...	...	|	...	...	|	0626	0626	...	|	...	...	|	|	|	0734
188	Wolfsburg d.	|	0155	...	...	...	0546	0546	...	...	...	0540	...	...	0640	0655	0655	...	|	...	...	0740	|	|	0805
	Leipzig Hbf ‡ d.	|	|	...		...	|	|	...	...	...	|	...	0436g	|	|	|	...	|	...	0540a	|	|	|	|
	Leipzig/Halle Flughafen ✈ ‡ d.	|	|	...	...	...	|	|	...	...	...	|	...	0450g	|	|	|	...	|	...	0553a	|	|	|	|
	Halle (Saale) Hbf ‡ d.	|	|	...	...	...	|	|	...	...	...	|	...	0503g	|	|	|	...	|	...	0607a	|	|	|	|
	Köthen ‡ d.	|	|	...	...	...	|	|	...	...	...	|	...	0524g	|	|	|	...	|	...	0628a	|	|	|	|
	Magdeburg Hbf ‡ a.	|	|	...	...	...	|	|	...	...	...	|	...	0556g	|	|	|	...	|	...	0656a	|	|	|	|
	Magdeburg Hbf ‡ d.	|	|	...	...	...	|	|	...	0501	...	|	...	0600	|	|	|	...	|	...	0700	|	|	|	|
	Helmstedt ‡ d.	|	|	...	...	...	|	|	...	0528	...	|	...	0628	|	|	|	...	|	0646a	0728	|	|	|	|
	Braunschweig Hbf ‡ d.	|	|	...	0420	...	|	|	0520	0551	...	0558	0620	0651	0658	|	|	...	|	0720	0751	0758	|	|	|
	Peine d.	|	|	...	0437	...	|	|	0537	0606	...	|	0637	|	|	|	|	...	|	0737	|	|	|	|	|
263	**Hannover** Hbf a.	|	0228	...	0505	...	0618	0618	0605	0627	...	|	0705	0723	|	0728	0728	←	|	0805	0823	|	0828	0828	0837
263	**Hannover** Hbf d.	|	0231	0410	0509	0540	0621	0621	0609	0645j	0640	|	0709	→	|	0731	0731	0740	|	0809	0845	|	0831	0831	0840
	Bremen Hbf **813** a.	|	|	|	|	|	|	|	|	0751j	|	|	|	...	|	|	|	|	|	|	0951	|	|	|	|
	Oldenburg (Oldb) **813** a.	|	|	|	|	|	|	|	|	0822j	|	|	|	...	|	|	|	|	|	|	1022	|	|	|	|
	Frankfurt (Main) Hbf **900** a.	|	|	|	|	|	|	|	|	...	|	0844	|	...	0944	|	|	|	0942	|	...	1044	|	|	|
	Stuttgart Hbf **930** a.	|	|	|	|	|	|	|	|	...	|	|	|	...	1108	|	|	|	1108	|	...	|	|	|	|
	Basel SBB **912** a.	|	|	|	|	|	|	|	|	...	|	1147	|	...	...	|	|	|	...	|	...	1347	|	|	|
328	Minden (Westf) **802** d.	|	0302	0447	0555	0612	0651	0651	0702	...	0712	...	0752	...	...	|	|	0812	...	0902t	...	...	|	|	0912
343	Bad Oeynhausen **802** d.	|	|	|	0607	|	|	|	0714	...	0722	...	0804	...	...	|	|	0822	...	0914	...	...	|	|	|
349	Löhne (Westf) **802** d.	|	|	|	0611	|	|	|	0719	...	|	...	0811	...	...	|	|	|	...	0919	...	...	|	|	|
359	Bünde (Westf) **811** d.	|	|	|	0622	|	|	|	|	...	|	...	0821	...	...	|	|	|	...	|	...	...	|	|	0932
396	**Osnabrück** Hbf **811** d.	|	|	|	0647	|	|	|	|	...	0753	...	0847	...	...	|	|	|	...	|	...	...	|	|	0953
444	Rheine **811** d.	|	|	|	0723	|	|	|	|	...	0821	...	0923	...	...	|	|	|	...	|	...	...	|	|	1021
465	Bad Bentheim 🏛 **811** a.	|	|	|	*0803*	|	|	|	|	...	0834	...	*1003*	...	...	|	|	|	...	|	...	...	|	|	1034
655	*Schiphol* ✈ **22** a.	|	|	|	...	|	|	|	|	...	1109	...	...	...	...	|	|	|	...	|	...	...	|	|	1309
	Herford **802** d.	|	0320	0504	...	0632	0710	0710	0727	...	...	...	...	...	...	|	|	0833	...	0927	...	...	|	|	...
	Bielefeld Hbf **802** d.	0356	0330	0514	...	0641	0720	0720	0736	...	...	...	...	...	...	0822	0822	0842	...	0936	...	...	0922	0922	...
	Gütersloh Hbf **802** d.	|	0340	0524	...	0651	|	|	...	...	...	...	...	...	...	|	|	0852	...	...	...	...	|	|	...
	Hamm (Westf) **802** a.	0429	0359	0548	...	0713	0748	0748	...	...	...	...	...	...	...	0848	0848	0912	...	...	...	...	0948	0948	...
	Dortmund Hbf **800 802** a.	0450	0418	0616	...	0732	|	0809	...	...	...	...	...	...	...	|	0909	0932	...	...	...	...	|	1009	...
	Düsseldorf Hbf **800 802** a.	0654	0514	0719	...	|	|	0905	...	...	...	...	...	...	...	|	1005	1045	...	...	...	...	|	1105	...
	Hagen Hbf **800** a.	|	|	|	...	0755	0822	|	...	...	...	...	...	...	...	0922	...	|	...	...	...	...	1022	|	...
	Wuppertal Hbf **800** a.	0539	|	|	...	0812	0839	|	...	...	...	...	...	...	...	0939	...	|	...	...	...	...	1039	|	...
	Köln Hbf **800** a.	0614	0540	0742d	...	0846	0909	|	...	...	...	...	...	...	...	1009	...	1112	...	...	...	...	1109	|	...
	Köln/Bonn Flughafen ✈ **800** d.	...	0604	...	...	...	...	0942	...	...	...	...	...	...	...	...	...	|	...	...	...	...	|	1142	...
	Bonn Hbf **800** a.	...	...	...	...	...	...	...	...	...	...	...	...	...	...	...	...	1135	...	...	...	...	1132e	...	...

◆ – **NOTES** (LISTED BY TRAIN NUMBER)

456 – KOPERNIKUS – 🛏 1, 2 cl., 🛌 2 cl. and 🚃2 Praha - Dresden - Berlin - Köln - Amsterdam (Table **28**); 🛏 1, 2 cl., 🛌 2 cl. and 🚃2 (*EN* **446** – JAN KIEPURA) Warszawa - Berlin - Köln - Amsterdam (Table **24**); conveys 🛏 1, 2 cl. Moskva - Amsterdam (Table **24**). For overnight journeys only. June 20 - July 4 (also Aug. 1, 2, 3) calls at Berlin Lichtenberg (d. 0024) and Gesundbrunnen (d. 0042), **not** Ostbahnhof or Hbf.

527 – WETTERSTEIN – 🚃12 and 🍷 Hannover - Köln messe/Deutz - Frankfurt - Nürnberg - München.

928 – 🚃12 and 🍷 München - Köln Messe/Deutz - Hannover.

2012 – ALLGÄU – 🚃12 and 🍷 Oberstdorf - Stuttgart - Köln - Hannover (- Magdeburg ⑤⑦) (- Leipzig ⑦).

2013 – ALLGÄU – 🚃12 and 🍷 (Leipzig ① -) (Magdeburg ①–⑥ -) Hannover - Köln - Stuttgart - Oberstdorf.

2134 – 🚃12 and 🍷 (Leipzig ①–⑤ -) Magdeburg - Oldenburg - Emden.

A – 🚃12 and ✕ Berlin - Basel - Bern - Interlaken.
K – 🚃12 and 🍷 Karlsruhe - Köln - Hannover and v.v.
Z – From Zürich (Table **510**).

a – ①–⑤ only.
b – Ⓑ only.
d – Köln **Messe/Deutz**.
e – ①–⑥ only.

g – ① only.
j – From July 20.
n – Not July 13–15.
r – ⑦ June 14 - July 12; Ⓑ from July 19.
t – Arrives 10 minutes earlier.
w – ⑦ only.
x – Conveys 🍷 on ⑤⑦ only.

⊖ – Runs daily Braunschweig - Hannover.
⚡ – *ICE* ***SPRINTER***. 🅁 and supplement payable.
‡ – See panels on pages 379 and 381 for additional local services.

▲ – **June 20 - July 3** Berlin timings are subject to alteration as follows:
ICE trains from the Hannover direction do not call at Berlin Spandau and arrive Berlin Hbf / Ostbahnhof up to 32 minutes later.
ICE trains from the Frankfurt direction terminate at Berlin Hbf.
IC trains from the Stendal direction, which normally terminate at Berlin Ostbahnhof, are diverted to Berlin Gesundbrunnen (not calling at Hbf / Ostbahnhof).

△ – **June 20 - July 3** Berlin timings are subject to alteration as follows:
ICE trains to Hannover and beyond depart Berlin Hbf / Ostbahnhof up to 31 minutes **earlier** and do not call at Berlin Spandau.
ICE trains to Frankfurt and beyond start from Berlin Hbf (departure time may be a few minutes later).
IC trains to Stendal and beyond, which normally start from Berlin Ostbahnhof, are re-timed to start from Berlin Gesundbrunnen (not calling at Ostbahnhof / Hbf).

LEIPZIG and BERLIN - HANNOVER - BAD BENTHEIM and HAMM — 810

See note △	RE 14006	IC 2044	ICE 595	ICE 954	ICE 944	IC 2044	RE 14206	IC 2238	IC 2132	ICE 871	ICE 652	ICE 642	IC 148	IC 248	RE 14008	IC 2046	ICE 597	ICE 952	ICE 942	IC 2046	IC 1913	IC 1913	RE 14208	IC 2130	ICE 277
		①–⑥		①–⑥	①–⑥	①–⑥		R					①–⑥	⑦		①–⑥					⑦	⑤			
		🍷	🍴	🍴	🍴	🍷			O 🍷	🍴	🍴	🍴	S 🍷	🍷		🍷	🍴	🍴	🍴	🍷	T	L 🍷		🍷	A 🍴
Berlin Ostbahnhof △ **838** d.	...	...	0726	0738	0738	...	...	...	0721	0821	0840	0840	...	0826	...	...	0926	0938	0938	...	...	...	...	...	1020
Berlin Hbf △ **838** d.	...	...	0737	0748	0748	...	...	...	0732	0832	0850	0850	0839	0837	...	...	0937	0948	0948	...	1010	...	...	...	1031
Berlin Spandau △ **838** d.	...	...	0751	0803	0803	...	...	...	|	0847	0905	0905	0851	0851	...	...	0951	1003	1003	...	1020	...	...	...	1047
Rathenow **838** d.	...	...	|	|	|	...	...	...	|	|	|	|	0914	0916	...	...	|	|	|	...	|	...	...	...	|
Stendal **838** d.	...	...	|	|	|	...	...	...	|	|	|	|	0935	0935	...	...	|	|	|	...	|	...	...	...	|
Wolfsburg d.	...	...	|	0855	0855	...	...	...	|	0940	|	|	1005	1005	...	...	|	1055	1055	...	1121	...	...	...	1140
Leipzig Hbf ‡ d.	...	0640	|	|	|	...	...	0740	|	|	|	|	|	|	...	0840	|	|	|	...	|	...	...	0942	|
Leipzig/Halle Flughafen ✈ ‡ d.	...	0653	|	|	|	...	...	0753	|	|	|	|	|	|	...	0853	|	|	|	...	|	...	...	0955	|
Halle (Saale) Hbf ‡ d.	...	0707	|	|	|	...	...	0807	|	|	|	|	|	|	...	0907	|	|	|	...	|	...	...	1009	|
Köthen ‡ d.	...	0728	|	|	|	...	...	0828	|	|	|	|	|	|	...	0928	|	|	|	...	|	...	...	|	|
Magdeburg Hbf ‡ a.	...	0756	|	|	|	...	...	0855	0858	|	|	|	|	|	...	0956	|	|	|	...	|	...	...	1056	|
Magdeburg Hbf ‡ d.	...	0800	|	|	|	...	...	...	0901	|	|	|	|	|	...	1000	|	|	|	...	|	...	...	1100	|
Helmstedt ‡ d.	...	|	|	|	|	...	...	...	0928	|	|	|	|	|	...	|	|	|	|	...	|	...	...	1128	|
Braunschweig Hbf ‡ d.	0820	0851	0858	|	|	...	0920	...	0951	0958	|	|	|	|	1020	1051	1058	|	|	...	|	...	1120	1151	1158
Peine d.	0837	|	|	|	|	...	0937	...	|	|	|	|	|	|	1037	|	|	|	|	...	|	...	1137	|	|
Hannover Hbf a.	0905	0923	|	0928	0928	←	1005	...	1023	|	1028	1028	1037	1037	1105	1123	|	1128	1128	←	1155	...	1205	1223	|
Hannover Hbf d.	0909	→	|	0931	0931	0940	1009	...	1045	|	1031	1031	1040	1040	1109	→	|	1131	1131	1140	1158	1158	1209	1245	|
Bremen Hbf **813** a.	|	...	|	|	|	|	|	...	1151	|	|	|	|	|	|	...	|	|	|	|	|	|	|	1351	|
Oldenburg (Oldb) **813** a.	|	...	|	|	|	|	|	...	1222	|	|	|	|	|	|	...	|	|	|	|	|	|	|	1422	|
Frankfurt (Main) Hbf **900** a.	|	...	1144	|	|	|	|	...	...	1244	|	|	|	|	|	...	1344	|	|	|	|	|	|	...	1444
Stuttgart Hbf **930** a.	|	...	1308	|	|	|	|	...	...	|	|	|	|	|	|	...	1508	|	|	|	|	|	|	...	|
Basel SBB **912** a.	|	...	...	|	|	|	|	...	...	1547	|	|	|	|	|	...	...	|	|	|	|	|	|	...	1747
Minden (Westf) **802** d.	0952	...	...	|	|	1012	1102t	...	...	...	|	|	1112	1112	1152	...	...	|	|	1212	|	|	1302t	...	...
Bad Oeynhausen **802** d.	1004	...	...	|	|	1022	1114	...	...	...	|	|	1122	1122	1204	...	...	|	|	1222	|	|	1314	...	...
Löhne (Westf) **802** d.	1011	...	...	|	|	|	1119	...	...	...	|	|	|	|	1211	...	...	|	|	|	|	|	1319	...	...
Bünde (Westf) **811** d.	1021	...	...	|	|	|	|	...	...	...	|	|	|	|	1221	...	...	|	|	|	|	|	|	...	...
Osnabrück Hbf **811** d.	1047	...	...	|	|	|	|	...	...	...	|	|	1153	1153	1247	...	...	|	|	|	|	|	|	...	...
Rheine **811** d.	1123	...	...	|	|	|	|	...	...	...	|	|	1221	1221	1323	...	...	|	|	|	|	|	|	...	...
Bad Bentheim 🏛 **811** a.	*1203*	...	...	|	|	|	|	...	...	...	|	|	1234	1234	*1403*	...	...	|	|	|	|	|	|	...	...
Schiphol ✈ **22** a.	...	...	...	|	|	|	|	...	...	...	|	|	1509	1509	...	...	...	|	|	|	|	|	|	...	...
Herford **802** d.	...	...	...	|	|	1033	1127	...	...	...	|	|	...	...	...	...	...	|	|	1233	1244	1244	1327	...	...
Bielefeld Hbf **802** d.	...	...	...	1022	1022	1042	1136	...	...	...	1122	1122	...	...	...	...	...	1222	1222	1242	1253	1253	1336	...	...
Gütersloh Hbf **802** d.	...	...	...	|	|	1052	...	...	...	...	|	|	...	...	...	...	...	|	|	1252	1303	1303	...	...	...
Hamm (Westf) **802** a.	...	...	...	1048	1048	1112	...	...	...	...	1148	1148	...	...	...	...	...	1248	1248	1312	1323	1323	...	...	...
Dortmund Hbf **800 802** a.	...	...	...	|	1109	1132	...	...	...	...	|	1209	...	...	...	...	...	|	1309	1332	1347	1347	...	...	...
Düsseldorf Hbf **800 802** a.	...	...	...	|	1205	|	...	...	...	...	|	1305	...	...	...	...	...	|	1405	|	1442	1442	...	...	...
Hagen Hbf **800** a.	...	...	...	1122	...	1155	...	...	...	...	1222	...	...	...	...	...	...	1322	|	1355	|	|	...	...	...
Wuppertal Hbf **800** a.	...	...	...	1139	...	1212	...	...	...	...	1239	...	...	...	...	...	...	1339	|	1412	|	|	...	...	...
Köln Hbf **800** a.	...	...	...	1209	...	1245	...	...	...	...	1309	...	...	...	...	...	...	1409	|	1445	1515	1515	...	...	...
Köln/Bonn Flughafen ✈ **800** d.	...	...	...	...	...	...	...	...	...	...	|	...	...	...	...	...	...	...	1445	...	|	|	...	...	...
Bonn Hbf **800** a.	...	...	...	...	...	...	...	...	...	...	1332	...	...	...	...	...	...	...	...	...	1535	1535	...	...	...

See note △	ICE 650	ICE 640	IC 146	RE 14010	IC 2048	ICE 599	ICE 950	ICE 940	IC 2048	IC 1915	RE 14210	IC 2038	ICE 279	ICE 558	ICE 548	IC 144	RE 14012	IC 2140	ICE 691	ICE 858	ICE 848	IC 2140	IC 1113	IC 1917	RE 14212
										⑤⑦													⑤	⑦	
	🍴	🍴	🍷		🍷	🍴	🍴	🍴	🍷	T ¶		🍷	A 🍴	🍴	🍴	🍷		🍷	🍴	🍴	🍴	🍷	🍷	K 🍷	
Berlin Ostbahnhof △ **838** d.	1040	1040	1026	...	...	1126	1138	1138	...	...	...	...	1221	1240	1240	1226	...	...	1326	1338	1338	...	...	...	...
Berlin Hbf △ **838** d.	1050	1050	1037	...	...	1137	1148	1148	...	1208	...	...	1232	1250	1250	1236	...	...	1337	1348	1348	...	1408	1408	...
Berlin Spandau △ **838** d.	1105	1105	1051	...	...	1151	1203	1203	...	1220	...	...	1247	1305	1305	1251	...	...	1351	1403	1403	...	1420	1420	...
Rathenow **838** d.	|	|	1116	...	...	|	|	|	...	|	...	...	|	|	|	1316	...	...	|	|	|	...	|	|	...
Stendal **838** d.	|	|	1135	...	...	|	|	|	...	|	...	...	|	|	|	1335	...	...	|	|	|	...	|	|	...
Wolfsburg d.	|	|	1205	...	...	|	1255	1255	...	1321	...	...	1340	|	|	1405	...	...	|	1455	1455	...	1521	1521	...
Leipzig Hbf ‡ d.	|	|	|	...	1040	|	|	|	...	|	...	1142	|	|	|	|	...	1240	|	|	|	...	|	|	...
Leipzig/Halle Flughafen ✈ ‡ d.	|	|	|	...	1053	|	|	|	...	|	...	1155	|	|	|	|	...	1253	|	|	|	...	|	|	...
Halle (Saale) Hbf ‡ d.	|	|	|	...	1107	|	|	|	...	|	...	1209	|	|	|	|	...	1307	|	|	|	...	|	|	...
Köthen ‡ d.	|	|	|	...	1128	|	|	|	...	|	...	|	|	|	|	|	...	1328	|	|	|	...	|	|	...
Magdeburg Hbf ‡ a.	|	|	|	...	1156	|	|	|	...	|	...	1256	|	|	|	|	...	1356	|	|	|	...	|	|	...
Magdeburg Hbf ‡ d.	|	|	|	...	1200	|	|	|	...	|	...	1300	|	|	|	|	...	1400	|	|	|	...	|	|	...
Helmstedt ‡ d.	|	|	|	...	|	|	|	|	...	|	...	1328	|	|	|	|	...	|	|	|	|	...	|	|	...
Braunschweig Hbf ‡ d.	|	|	|	1220	1251	1258	|	|	...	|	1320	1351	1358	|	|	|	1420	1451	1458	|	|	...	|	|	1520
Peine d.	|	|	|	1237	|	|	|	|	...	|	1337	|	|	|	|	|	1437	|	|	|	|	...	|	|	1537
Hannover Hbf a.	1228	1228	1237	1305	1323	|	1328	1328	←	1355	1405	1423	|	1428	1428	1437	1505	1523	|	1528	1528	←	1554	1554	1605
Hannover Hbf d.	1231	1231	1240	1309	→	|	1331	1331	1340	1358	1409	1445	|	1431	1431	1440	1509	→	|	1531	1531	1540	1558	1558	1609
Bremen Hbf **813** a.	|	|	|	|	...	|	|	|	|	|	|	1551	|	|	|	|	|	...	|	|	|	|	|	|	|
Oldenburg (Oldb) **813** a.	|	|	|	|	...	|	|	|	|	|	|	1622	|	|	|	|	|	...	|	|	|	|	|	|	|
Frankfurt (Main) Hbf **900** a.	|	|	|	|	...	1544	|	|	|	|	|	...	1644	|	|	|	|	...	1744	|	|	|	|	|	|
Stuttgart Hbf **930** a.	|	|	|	|	...	1708	|	|	|	|	|	...	|	|	|	|	|	...	1908	|	|	|	|	|	|
Basel SBB **912** a.	|	|	|	|	...	...	|	|	|	|	|	...	1947	|	|	|	|	...	...	|	|	|	|	|	|
Minden (Westf) **802** d.	|	|	1312	1352	...	...	|	|	1412	|	1502t	...	...	|	|	1512	1552	...	...	|	|	1612	|	|	1702t
Bad Oeynhausen **802** d.	|	|	|	1404	...	...	|	|	1422	|	1514	...	...	|	|	1522	1604	...	...	|	|	1622	|	|	1714
Löhne (Westf) **802** d.	|	|	|	1411	...	...	|	|	|	|	1519	...	...	|	|	|	1611	...	...	|	|	|	|	|	1719
Bünde (Westf) **811** d.	|	|	1332	1421	...	...	|	|	|	|	|	...	...	|	|	|	1621	...	...	|	|	|	|	|	|
Osnabrück Hbf **811** d.	|	|	1353	1447	...	...	|	|	|	|	|	...	...	|	|	1553	1647	...	...	|	|	|	|	|	|
Rheine **811** d.	|	|	1421	1523	...	...	|	|	|	|	|	...	...	|	|	1621	1723	...	...	|	|	|	|	|	|
Bad Bentheim 🏛 **811** a.	|	|	1434	*1603*	...	...	|	|	|	|	|	...	...	|	|	1634	*1803*	...	...	|	|	|	|	|	|
Schiphol ✈ **22** a.	|	|	1709	...	...	...	|	|	|	|	|	...	...	|	|	1909	...	...	...	|	|	|	|	|	|
Herford **802** d.	|	|	...	...	...	...	|	|	1433	1444	1527	...	...	|	|	...	...	...	...	|	|	1633	1644	1644	1727
Bielefeld Hbf **802** d.	1322	1322	...	...	...	...	1422	1422	1442	1453	1536	...	...	1522	1522	...	...	...	...	1622	1622	1642	1653	1653	1736
Gütersloh Hbf **802** d.	|	|	...	...	...	...	|	|	1452	1503	...	...	...	|	|	...	...	...	...	|	|	1652	1703	1703	...
Hamm (Westf) **802** a.	1348	1348	...	...	...	...	1448	1448	1512	1524	...	...	...	1548	1548	...	...	...	...	1648	1648	1712	1724	1724	...
Dortmund Hbf **800 802** a.	|	1409	...	...	...	...	|	1509	1532	1547	...	...	...	|	1609	...	...	...	...	|	1709	1732	1747	1747	...
Düsseldorf Hbf **800 802** a.	|	1505	...	...	...	...	|	1605	|	1642	...	...	...	|	1705	...	...	...	...	|	1805	|	1842	1842	...
Hagen Hbf **800** a.	1422	...	...	...	...	...	1522	...	1555	|	...	...	...	1622	|	...	...	...	...	1722	...	1755	|	|	...
Wuppertal Hbf **800** a.	1439	...	...	...	...	...	1539	...	1612	|	...	...	...	1639	|	...	...	...	...	1739	...	1812	|	|	...
Köln Hbf **800** a.	1509	...	...	...	...	...	1609	...	1645	1715	...	...	...	1709	|	...	...	...	...	1809	...	1845	1915	1915	...
Köln/Bonn Flughafen ✈ **800** d.	...	...	...	...	...	...	...	...	...	|	...	...	...	...	1744b	...	...	...	...	...	...	...	...	|	...
Bonn Hbf **800** a.	...	...	...	...	...	...	...	...	...	1735	...	...	...	...	...	...	...	...	...	...	...	...	...	1935	...

A – To Interlaken via Bern (Table **560**).
K – To Karlsruhe (Tables **800** / **912**).
L – To München via Stuttgart (Tables **800** / **912** / **930**).
O – OSTFRIESLAND – 🚌12 and 🍷 (Cottbus ①–⑥ -) Berlin - Oldenburg (- Norddeich Mole ⊡).
R – Daily except Sept. 6, 13, 20, 27, Oct. 4, 11, 18, 25. To Warnemünde (via Schwerin and Rostock) daily until Aug. 30, also ⑤⑥ Sept. 4 - Oct. 24. See also Tables **841**, **837** and **830**.

S – From Szczecin (Table **845**).
T – To Stuttgart (Tables **800** / **912**).

b – Ⓑ only.
t – Arrives 10 minutes earlier.

¶ – Conveys 🍷 on ⑦.
⊡ – Daily until Oct. 25; ⑤⑦ from Oct. 30.
⊕ – Runs 12 – 14 minutes later on ⑦.
❖ – Later service (daily): Leipzig Hbf d. 2338, Leipzig/Halle Flughafen d. 2353, Halle (Saale) Hbf a. 0005.

△ – **June 20 - July 3** Berlin timings are subject to alteration as follows:
ICE trains to Hannover and beyond depart Berlin Hbf / Ostbahnhof up to 31 minutes **earlier** and do not call at Berlin Spandau.
ICE trains to Frankfurt and beyond start from Berlin Hbf (departure may be a few minutes later).
IC trains to Stendal and beyond, which normally start from Berlin Ostbahnhof, are re-timed to start from Berlin Gesundbrunnen (not calling at Ostbahnhof / Hbf).

‡ – See panel below main table for additional *RE* / *RB* services.

						❖
Leipzig Hbf d.	0451	0505	and at the same	2151	2205	2238
Leipzig/Halle Flughafen ✈ d.	0506	|	minutes past	2206	|	2253
Halle (Saale) Hbf a.	0518	0541	each hour until	2218	2241	2305

Halle (Saale) Hbf d.	0010	...	0543	and	2143	...	2245
Köthen d.	0039	...	0612	hourly	2212	...	2314
Magdeburg Hbf a.	0123	...	0651	until	2251	...	2353

		Ⓐ			①–⑥	⊕
Magdeburg Hbf d.	0530	0630	then hourly on Ⓐ,	1930	2030	2200
Helmstedt d.	0614	0714	every **two** hours	2014	2114	2245
Braunschweig Hbf a.	0642	0742	on Ⓒ until	2042	2142	2314

810 LEIPZIG and BERLIN - HANNOVER - BAD BENTHEIM and HAMM

See note △	IC 2036	ICE 873	ICE 556	ICE 546	IC 142	RE 14014	IC 2142	ICE 693	ICE 856	ICE 846	IC 2142	RE 14214	IC 2034	ICE 875	ICE 554	ICE 544	ICE 744	IC 140	EC 340	RE 14016	ICE 695	IC 2144	ICE 854	ICE 844	IC 2144
							⑧				⑧					①–⑥	⑦		⑧		⑥	⑧	⑧		⑧
	N🍷	🍴	Q🍴	🍴	🍷		🍷	🍴	🍴◆	🍴	🍷		🍷	🍴	🍴	🍴	🍴	🍷	◆		🍴	🍷	R🍴	🍴	
Berlin Ostbahnhof △ 838 d.	...	1421	1440	1440	1426	...	...	1526	1538	1538	...	...	...	1621	1640	1640	1640	1626	1723	...	1723	...	1738	1738	...
Berlin Hbf △ 838 d.	...	1432	1450	1450	1437	...	...	1537	1548	1548	...	...	...	1633	1650	1650	1650	1637	1735	...	1735	...	1748	1748	...
Berlin Spandau △ 838 d.	...	1449	1505	1505	1451	...	...	1551	1603	1603	...	...	...	1649	1705	1705	1705	1651	1750	...	1751	...	1803	1803	...
Rathenow 838 d.	...				1516	...	...				...	...	...					1716		...		...			...
Stendal 838 d.	...				1535	...	...				...	...	...					1735	1824	...		...			...
Wolfsburg d.	...	1540			1605	...	...		1655	1655	...	...	...	1740				1805	...	...		...	1855	1855	...
Leipzig Hbf ‡ d.	1342					...	1440				...	...	1542						...	...		1640			...
Leipzig/Halle Flughafen ✈ ‡ d.	1355					...	1453				...	...	1555						...	...		1653			...
Halle (Saale) Hbf ‡ d.	1409					...	1507				...	...	1609						...	...		1707			...
Köthen ‡ d.						...	1528				...	...							...	...		1728			...
Magdeburg Hbf ‡ a.	1456					...	1556				...	...	1656						...	...		1756			...
Magdeburg Hbf ‡ d.	1500					...	1600				...	...	1700						...	...		1800			...
Helmstedt ‡ d.	1528					...					...	...	1728						...	...					...
Braunschweig Hbf ‡ d.	1551	1558				1620	1651	1658			...	1720	1751	1758					...	1820	1858	1851			...
Peine d.						1637					...	1737							...	1837					...
Hannover Hbf a.	1623		1628	1628	1637	1705	1723		1728	1728	←	1805	1823		1828	1828	1828	1837	...	1905		1923	1928	1928	←
Hannover Hbf d.	1645		1631	1631	1640	1709	→		1731	1731	1740	1809	1845		1831	1831	1831	1840	...	1909		→	1931	1931	1940
Bremen Hbf **813** a.	1751						...						1951						...			...			
Oldenburg (Oldb) **813** a.	1822						...						2022						...			...			
Frankfurt (Main) Hbf **900** a.	...	1844					...	1944					...	2044					...		2142	...			
Stuttgart Hbf **930** a.	...						...	2108					...						...		2308	...			
Basel SBB **912** a.	...	2147					...	...					...	2355					...		...	...			
Minden (Westf) 802 d.	...	...			1712	1752	...	...			1812	1902t	...	...				1912	...	1952	...	...			2012
Bad Oeynhausen 802 d.	...	...				1804	...	...			1822	1914	...	...				1922	...	2004	...	...			2022
Löhne (Westf) 802 d.	...	...				1811	...	...				1919	...	...					...	2011	...	...			
Bünde (Westf) 811 d.	...	...			1732	1821	...	...					...	...					...	2021	...	...			
Osnabrück Hbf 811 d.	...	...			1753	1847	...	...					...	...				1953	...	2047	...	...			
Rheine 811 d.	...	...			1821	1923	...	...					...	...				2021	...	2123	...	...			
Bad Bentheim 🏛 811 a.	...	...			1834	*2003*	...	...					...	...				2034	...	*2203*	...	...			
Schiphol ✈ **22** a.	...	...			2109	...	...	...					...	...				2309	...	...	...	...			
Herford 802 d.	...	...			...	...	...	...			1833	1927	...	...				...	...	...	...	...			2032
Bielefeld Hbf 802 d.	...	...	1722	1722	...	...	...	...	1822	1822	1842	1936	...	...	1922	1922	1922	...	...	...	...	...	2022	2022	2041
Gütersloh Hbf 802 d.	...	...			...	...	...	...			1852	...	...	...				...	...	...	...	...			2051
Hamm (Westf) 802 a.	...	...	1748	1748	...	...	...	...	1848	1848	1912	...	...	...	1948	1948	1948	...	...	...	...	...	2048	2048	2110
Dortmund Hbf **800 802** a.	...	...		1809	...	...	...	...		1909	1932	...	...	...		2009	2009	...	...	...	...	...		2110	2132
Düsseldorf Hbf **800 802** a.	...	...		1905	...	...	...	...		2005		...	...	...		2105	2105	...	...	...	...	...		2207	
Hagen Hbf **800** a.	...	...	1822		...	...	...	...	1922		1955	...	...	...	2022			...	...	...	...	...	2122		2155
Wuppertal Hbf **800** a.	...	...	1839		...	...	...	...	1939		2012	...	...	...	2039			...	...	...	...	...	2139		2212
Köln Hbf **800** a.	...	...	1909		...	...	...	...	2009	2034	2045	...	...	...	2109	2133		...	...	...	...	...	2209	2231	2245
Köln/Bonn Flughafen ✈ **800** d.	...	...		1945e	...	...	...	...		...	...	...	...	...	...	...	2142	...	...	...	...	...		...	...
Bonn Hbf **800** a.	...	...	1932b	...	...	...	...	...	2039	...	...	...	...	...	...	...	...	...	...	...	...	...	2235w	...	...

See note △	ICE 1093	RE 14216	IC 2032	ICE 877	ICE 552	ICE 542	IC 2242	RE 14018	IC 1899	IC 2146	ICE 697	ICE 852	ICE 842	ICE 832	ICE 862	IC 2146	IC 1932	IC 1930	IC 2030	ICE 879	IC 2240	ICE 540	ICE 1740	ICE 840	ICE 850
	⑧								⑦	⑧	⑧	⑦		B	⑤C	⑦	⑦	⑦	⑧	⑦	⑤⑦		A	⑦	⑦
	🍴⚡		🍷	🍴◆	🍴	🍴	🍷◆		◆	🍷	🍴◆	🍴	🍴	🍴	🍴		◆	U🍷	¶	🍴◆	M🍷	🍴	D	🍴	🍴
Berlin Ostbahnhof △ 838 d.	1754	...	...	1821	1840	1840	1826	...	...	...	1926	1938	1938	1938	1938	...	...	...	...	2021	2026	2054	...	2138	2138
Berlin Hbf △ 838 d.	1805	...	...	1833	1850	1850	1837	...	1909	...	1937	1948	1948	1948	1948	...	...	2026	...	2032	2037	2105	...	2148	2148
Berlin Spandau △ 838 d.	1819	...	...	1849	1905	1905	1851	...	1920	...	1951	2003	2003	2003	2003	...	2007	2035	...	2047	2051	2120	...	2203	2203
Rathenow 838 d.		...	...				1916	...		...						...			...		2114		...		
Stendal 838 d.		...	...				1935	...		...						...		2116	...		2134	2153	...	2236	2236
Wolfsburg d.		...	...	1940			2005	...	2021	...		2055	2055	2055	2055	...		▬	...	2140	2205	2221	...	2304	2304
Leipzig Hbf ‡ d.		...	1742					...		1840						...		...	1940				2010		
Leipzig/Halle Flughafen ✈ ‡ d.		...	1755					...		1853						...		...	1953				2024		
Halle (Saale) Hbf ‡ d.		...	1809					...		1907						...		...	2007				2037		
Köthen ‡ d.		...						...		1928						...		*RE*	2028				2058		
Magdeburg Hbf ‡ a.		...	1856					...		1956						...		**14218**	2056				2127		
Magdeburg Hbf ‡ d.		...	1900					...		2000						...			2100				2200w		
Helmstedt ‡ d.		...	1928					...								...			2128						
Braunschweig Hbf ‡ d.		1920	1951	1958				2020		2051	2058					...		2120	2151	2158			2248w		
Peine d.		1937						2037								...		2137							
Hannover Hbf a.		2005	2023		2028	2028	2037	2105	2055	2123		2128	2128	2128	2128	←	2142	2205	2223		2237	2256	2320w	2335	2335
Hannover Hbf d.		2009	2045		2031	2031	2040	2109	2101	→		2131	2131	2145	2145	2140	2145	2209	...		2240w	2300	...	2340	2345
Bremen Hbf **813** a.			2151							...				2244	2247		2244		...				...		0045
Oldenburg (Oldb) **813** a.			2222b							...				...	2331j		2315		...				...		0123
Frankfurt (Main) Hbf **900** a.	2142		...	2244					0019	...	2344k			...	...		...		...	0058			...		...
Stuttgart Hbf **930** a.	2308		...	...					...	...	...			...	...		...		...	...			...		...
Basel SBB **912** a.	...		...	...					...	...	...			...	...		...		...	...			...		...
Minden (Westf) 802 d.	...	2102t	...	...			2112	2152	...	...	...			...	...	2212	...	2302t	...	...	2312w		...	0011	...
Bad Oeynhausen 802 d.	...	2114	...	...			2122	2204	...	...	...			...	...	2222	...	2314	...	...	2322w		...		...
Löhne (Westf) 802 d.	...	2119	...	...				2211	...	...	...			...	...		...	2319	...	...			...		...
Bünde (Westf) 811 d.	...		...	...			2135	2221	...	...	...			...	...		...		...	...	2335w		...		...
Osnabrück Hbf 811 d.	...		...	...			2159	2246	...	...	...			...	...		...		...	...	2358w		...		...
Rheine 811 d.	...		...	...			...	*2346*	...	...	...			...	...		...		...	...	...		...		...
Bad Bentheim 🏛 811 a.	...		...	...			...	...	...	...	...			...	...		...		...	...	...		...		...
Schiphol ✈ **22** a.	...		...	...			...	...	...	...	...			...	...		...		...	...	...		...		...
Herford 802 d.	...	2127	...	...			...	...	...	...	...			...	...	2232	...	2327	...	...	...	2344	...	0029	...
Bielefeld Hbf 802 d.	...	2136	...	...	2122	2122	...	...	...	...	...	2222	2222	...	...	2241	...	2336	...	...	...	2354	...	0039	...
Gütersloh Hbf 802 d.	...	...	...	...			...	...	...	...	...			...	...	2251	...	...	...	...	...	0004	...	0049	...
Hamm (Westf) 802 a.	...	...	...	...	2148	2148	...	...	...	...	...	2248	2248	...	...	2310	...	...	...	...	...	0023	...	0109	...
Dortmund Hbf **800 802** a.	...	...	...	...		2209	...	...	...	...	...		2309	...	...	2332	...	...	...	...	...	0042*	...	0127	...
Düsseldorf Hbf **800 802** a.	...	...	...	...		2305	...	...	...	...	...		0005	...	...		...	...	...	...	...	0136*	...	0222	...
Hagen Hbf **800** a.	...	...	...	...	2222		...	...	...	...	...	2322		...	...	2355	...	...	...	...	...		...		...
Wuppertal Hbf **800** a.	...	...	...	...	2239		...	...	...	...	...	2339		...	...	0012	...	...	...	...	...		...		...
Köln Hbf **800** a.	...	...	...	...	2309	2330	...	...	...	...	...	0009	0029	...	...	0045	...	...	...	...	...	0201*	...	0246	...
Köln/Bonn Flughafen ✈ **800** d.	...	...	...	...		...	...	...	...	...	...	...	...	...	...	...	...	...	...	...	...	0226*	...	...	...
Bonn Hbf **800** a.	...	...	...	...	2339b	...	...	...	...	...	...	...	...	...	...	...	...	...	...	...	...	...	...	...	...

◆ – **NOTES** (LISTED BY TRAIN NUMBER)

340 – WAWEL – 🛏 Kraków - Forst 🏛 - Cottbus - Berlin - Uelzen - Hamburg. June 21 - July 3 does not call at Berlin Ostbahnhof and departs Berlin Hbf 1741.
697 – 🛏 and 🍴 Berlin - Kassel (- Frankfurt ⑤⑦).
856 – 🛏 and 🍴 Berlin - Koblenz - Trier.
877/9 – 🛏 and 🍴 Berlin - Mannheim - Karlsruhe.
1899 – 🛏 Berlin - Kassel - Gießen - Frankfurt.
1932 – 🛏 Stralsund - Berlin Spandau - Bremen - Oldenburg.
2242 – 🛏 and 🍷 Berlin - Osnabrück (- Münster ⑧). Train number **2342** on ⑥.

A – ①②③④⑦.
B – ①②③④⑥ from July 20.
C – From July 24.
D – From Dresden (Table **842**). Conveys 🍴 on ⑦.

M – To Münster (Table **800**).
N – To Norddeich Mole (Table **813**).
Q – To Koblenz Hbf (a. 2011) on ①–⑤.
R – To Koblenz Hbf (a. 2311) on ⑦.
U – To Uelzen (Table **841**).

b – ⑧ only.
e – ①–⑥ only.
j – From Oct. 2.
k – ⑤⑦ only.
t – Arrives 10 minutes earlier.
w – ⑦ only.

¶ – Conveys 🍷 on ⑦.

* – On the mornings of ⑥⑦ Dortmund a. 0047, Düsseldorf a. 0145 and terminates at Köln Hbf, a. 0209.
⚡ – *ICE* ***SPRINTER***. 🅁 and supplement payable.
‡ – See panel on page 381 for additional local services.

△ – **June 20 - July 3** Berlin timings are subject to alteration as follows: *ICE* trains to Hannover and beyond depart Berlin Hbf / Ostbahnhof up to 31 minutes **earlier** and do not call at Berlin Spandau. *ICE* trains to Frankfurt and beyond start from Berlin Hbf (departure may be a few minutes later). *IC* trains to Stendal and beyond, which normally start from Berlin Ostbahnhof, are re-timed to start from Berlin Gesundbrunnen (not calling at Ostbahnhof / Hbf).

BIELEFELD - PADERBORN and BAD BENTHEIM — 811

Nord West Bahn; Westfalenbahn

Bielefeld Hbf - **Paderborn** Hbf via Hövelhof (*44 km*). Operated by Nord West Bahn. Journey time: 62 – 75 minutes.

From Bielefeld at 0432 Ⓐ, 0528 Ⓐ, 0539 ⑥ **k**, 0616 Ⓐ, 0639 ⑥ **k**, 0739 ⚒, 0839 ⚒, 0939, 1039 ⚒, 1139, 1239 ⚒, 1339, 1439 ⚒, 1539, 1639 ⚒, 1739, 1839 Ⓐ, 1939, 2039 Ⓐ, 2139 and 2239 Ⓐ.

From Paderborn at 0504 Ⓐ, 0513 ⑥ **k**, 0604 Ⓐ, 0613 ⑥ **k**, 0628 Ⓐ, 0713 ⚒, 0813 ⚒, 0913, 1013 ⚒, 1113, 1213 ⚒, 1313, 1413 ⚒, 1513, 1613 ⚒, 1713, 1813 Ⓐ, 1913, 2013 Ⓐ, 2113 and 2213 Ⓐ.

km	⊖	⚒		⚒							⑤–⑦
0	**Bielefeld** Hbf .... d.	0750	0850	0950	1050	1250	1450	1650	1850	2050	2250
11	Oerlinghausen .... d.	0803	0903	1003	1103	1303	1503	1703	1903	2103	2303
31	Detmold .... a.	0820	0920	1020	1120	1320	1520	1720	1920	2120	2320
60	Altenbeken .... a.	...	0946	...	1146	...	1546	1746	1946	...	2345

⊖	Ⓐ	⚒		⚒							
Altenbeken .... d.	0610	0713**a**	0813	...	1013	1213	...	1613	1813	2013	...
Detmold .... d.	0637	0740	0840	0940	1040	1240	1440	1640	1840	2040	2240
Oerlinghausen .... d.	0655	0801	0901	1001	1101	1301	1501	1701	1901	2101	2301
Bielefeld Hbf .... a.	0706	0812	0912	1012	1112	1312	1512	1712	1912	2112	2312

km	⊡	Ⓐ	⚒					Ⓒ	F ⊖	
	Bielefeld Hbf **810** ... d.	*0509*	*0609*	*0709*	and	*2109*	*2209*	*2209*	2250	...
0	Herford .... d.	0530	0633	0733		2133	2233	2233	|	...
28	Detmold .... d.	0559	0702	0802	hourly	2202	2258	2302	2320	...
57	Altenbeken ‡ .... a.	0624	0727	0827		2227	...	2327	2345	...
74	**Paderborn** Hbf ‡ .... a.	0638	0741	0841	until	2241	...	2341	2358	...

⊡	Ⓐ	⚒							F ⊖	
Paderborn Hbf ‡ ... d.	...	0518	...	0621	and	2021	2121	...	2232	...
Altenbeken ‡ .... d.	...	0530	...	0633		2033	2133	...	2245	...
Detmold .... d.	0458	0558	...	0701	hourly	2101	2201	...	2322	...
Herford .... a.	0524	0624	...	0727		2127	2227	...	2350	...
Bielefeld Hbf **810** a.	*0548*	*0648*	...	*0748*	until	*2148*	2248	...	0007	...

km	⊡ See also Table **810**	⚒	⚒							
0	**Bielefeld** Hbf .... d.	0509	0609	...	0709		2109	2209	2309	...
14	Herford .... a.	0520	0620	...	0720	and	2120	2220	2320	...
14	Herford .... d.	0533	0633	...	0733		2133	2233	2333	...
28	Bünde (Westf) .... d.	0546	0646	...	0746	hourly	2146	2246	2346	...
65	**Osnabrück** Hbf .... d.	0614	0714	...	0814		2214	2314	0012	...
113	**Rheine** .... a.	0646	0746	...	0846	until	2246	2346	...	...
134	Bad Bentheim .... a.	0703	0803	...	0903		2303	...	...	...

⊡ See also Table **810**	⚒	⚒								
Bad Bentheim .... d.	...	...	0557**a**	0657**r**	0757**r**	0857		1957	2057	2157
Rheine .... d.	...	0514	0614**a**	0714**r**	0814	0914	and	2014	2114	2214
Osnabrück Hbf .... d.	0448	0548	0648	0748	0848	0948		2048	2148	2248
Bünde (Westf) .... d.	0513	0613	0713	0813	0913	1013	hourly	2113	2213	2313
Herford .... a.	0527	0627	0727	0827	0927	1027		2127	2227	2327
Herford .... d.	0537	0637	0737	0837	0937	1037	until	2137	2237	2337
Bielefeld Hbf .... a.	0548	0648	0748	0848	0948	1048		2148	*2248*	2348

F – ⑤–⑦ only.
a – Ⓐ only.
k – Not Oct. 3.
r – ⚒ only.
‡ – See also Tables **805/9**.
⊖ – 2nd class only. Operated by Nord West Bahn.
⊡ – Operated by WestfalenBahn.

MÜNSTER - EMDEN - NORDDEICH — 812

RE services except where shown

km	See note ▲	Ⓐ	⚒	⚒		*IC* 2331 A 🍷			*IC* 2333 H 🍷			*IC* 231 C L🍷	*IC* 331 E 🍷◆	*IC* 2132 D 🍷	Ⓒ	Ⓐ		*IC* 333 L🍷			*IC* 335 L🍷			*IC* 2014 ①–⑤ 🍷◆	*IC* 2004 ⑦ 🍷◆
	Köln Hbf **800** .... d.	...	...	...	...	0542	...	...	0748	...	...	0948	0948	...	...	...	...	1148	...	...	1348	...	...	1548	1548
0	**Münster** (Westf) Hbf. § d.	0502	...	0602	0702	0731	0805	0905	0931	1005	1105	1131	1131	...	1205	1205	1305	1331	1405	1505	1531	1605	1705	1731	1731
39	Rheine .... § d.	0534	0534	0634	0734	0756	0834	0934	0956	1034	1134	1156	1156	...	1234	1234	1334	1356	1434	1534	1556	1634	1734	1756	1756
70	Lingen (Ems) .... d.	0556	0556	0656	0756	0815	0856	0956	1015	1056	1156	1215	1215	...	1256	1256	1356	1415	1456	1556	1615	1656	1756	1815	1815
91	Meppen .... d.	0611	0611	0711	0811	0828	0911	1011	1029	1111	1211	1229	1229	...	1311	1329**h**	1411	1429	1511	1611	1629	1711	1811	1829	1829
137	Papenburg (Ems) .... d.	0643	0643	0743	0843	0855	0943	1043	1056	1143	1243	1256	1256	...	1343	1403	1443	1456	1543	1643	1656	1743	1843	1856	1856
154	Leer (Ostfriesl) ..... **813** d.	0656	0656	0756	0856	0918**j**	0956	1056	1109	1156	1256	1309	1309	1319	1356	1415	1456	1509	1556	1656	1709	1756	1856	1909	1909
180	**Emden** Hbf .... **813** a.	0713	0713	0813	0913	0934	1013	1113	1125	1213	1313	1325	1325	1336	1413	1432	1513	1525	1613	1713	1725	1813	1913	1925	1925
180	**Emden** Hbf .... **813** d.	*0735*	*0735*	*0843*	...	0937	*1043*	...	1141	*1243*	...	1328	...	1341	*1443*	*1443*	...	1527**v**	*1643*	...	1728	*1843*	...	...	...
209	Norden .... **813** d.	*0807*	*0807*	*0907*	...	1003	*1107*	...	1205	*1307*	...	1353	...	1409	*1507*	*1507*	...	1550**v**	*1707*	...	1753	*1907*	...	...	...
215	**Norddeich** .... **813** a.	*0813*	*0813*	*0913*	...	1009	*1113*	...	1211	*1313*	...	1359	...	1415	*1513*	*1513*	...	1557**v**	*1713*	...	1759	*1913*	...	...	...
	Norddeich Mole .. **813** a.	*0817*	*0817*	*0918*	...	1014	*1118*	...	1217	*1318*	...	1404	...	1421	*1518*	*1518*	...	1604**v**	*1718*	...	1804	*1918*	...	...	...

See note ▲	*IC* 2036 🍷◆			*IC* 337 L🍷		Ⓑ t		¶	¶
Köln Hbf **800** .... d.	...	...	...	1745	...	...	...	...	...
Münster (Westf) Hbf .. § d.	...	1805	1905	1931	2005	2105	2205	2311	0011
Rheine .... § d.	...	1834	1934	1956	2034	2134	2234	2343	0043
Lingen (Ems) .... d.	...	1856	1956	2015	2056	2156	2256	...	...
Meppen .... d.	...	1911	2011	2029	2111	2211	2311	...	...
Papenburg (Ems) .... d.	...	1943	2043	2056	2143	2243	2343	...	...
Leer (Ostfriesland) **813** d.	1925	1956	2056	2109	2156	2256	2356	...	...
Emden Hbf .... **813** a.	1942	2013	2113	2125	2213	2313	0013	...	...
Emden Hbf .... **813** d.	1945	*2043*	...	...	*2243*	...	...	...	...
Norden .... **813** d.	2008	*2107*	...	...	*2307*	...	...	...	...
Norddeich .... **813** a.	2015	*2113*	...	...	*2313*	...	...	...	...
Norddeich Mole ... **813** a.	2021	...	...	...	...	...	...	...	...

See note ▲	Ⓐ	⚒	⚒	⚒	*IC* 2015 ①–④ 🍷◆	*IC* 2005 ⑤⑥ 🍷◆	Ⓐ	Ⓒ		*IC* 2037 🍷◆	*IC* 336 L🍷
Norddeich Mole .... **813** d.	...	...	...	...	...	...	...	...	...	0737	...
Norddeich .... **813** d.	...	...	...	0532	...	...	...	...	*0642*	0740	...
Norden .... **813** d.	...	...	...	0538	...	...	...	...	*0648*	0747	...
Emden Hbf .... **813** a.	...	...	...	0602	...	...	...	...	*0716*	0812	...
Emden Hbf .... **813** d.	...	0450	0550	0604	0634	0634	0642	0650	0750	0814	0834
Leer (Ostfriesland) .... **813** d.	...	0506	0606	0621	0653	0653	0658	0706	0806	0831	0853
Papenburg (Ems) .... d.	...	0516	0616	...	0704	0704	0709	0716	0816	...	0904
Meppen .... d.	...	0550	0650	...	0731	0731	0750	0750	0850	...	0931
Lingen (Ems) .... d.	...	0604	0704	...	0744	0744	0804	0804	0904	...	0944
Rheine .... § d.	0528	0628	0729	...	0804	0804	0829	0829	0929	...	1004
Münster (Westf) Hbf .... § a.	0554	0654	0756	...	0829	0829	0856	0856	0956	...	1029
Köln Hbf **800** .... a.	...	...	...	...	1012	1012	...	...	...	...	1212

See note ▲			*IC* 334 L🍷			Ⓐ	*IC* 332 🍷◆	Ⓐ	Ⓒ		*IC* 330 L🍷			*IC* 2135 D 🍷	*IC* 2332 E 🍷	*IC* 2334 K 🍷			*IC* 2330 B 🍷			Ⓑ t	¶		
Norddeich Mole ... **813** d.	...	*0840*	0953	...	*1040*	...	1136	...	...	*1240*	1354	...	*1440*	1539	...	1558	...	*1640*	1754	...	*1840*	...	...	2040	...
Norddeich .... **813** d.	...	*0842*	0956	...	*1042*	...	1139	...	...	*1242*	1402	...	*1442*	1542	...	1602	...	*1642*	1802	...	*1842*	...	...	2042	...
Norden .... **813** d.	...	*0848*	1004	...	*1048*	...	1146	...	...	*1248*	1409	...	*1448*	1549	...	1609	...	*1648*	1809	...	*1848*	...	...	2048	...
Emden Hbf .... **813** a.	...	*0916*	1026	...	*1116*	...	1218	...	...	*1316*	1431	...	*1516*	1611	...	1631	...	*1716*	1831	...	*1916*	...	...	2116	...
Emden Hbf .... **813** d.	0850	0950	1034	1050	1150	1224	1234	...	1250	1350	1434	1450	1550	1619	1634	1634	1650	1750	1834	1850	1950	2050	...	2118	2214
Leer (Ostfriesland) . **813** d.	0906	1006	1053	1106	1206	1241	1253	...	1306	1406	1453	1506	1606	1636	1653	1653	1706	1806	1853	1906	2006	2106	...	2135	2229
Papenburg (Ems) .... d.	0916	1016	1104	1116	1216	1251	1304	←	1316	1416	1504	1516	1616	...	1704	1704	1716	1816	1904	1916	2016	2116	...	▬	2239
Meppen .... d.	0950	1050	1131	1150	1250	1325	1331	1337	1350	1450	1531	1550	1650	...	1731	1731	1750	1850	1931	1950	2050	2150	...	...	2313
Lingen (Ems) .... d.	1004	1104	1144	1204	1304	→	1344	1351	1404	1504	1544	1604	1704	...	1744	1744	1804	1904	1944	2004	2104	2204	...	...	2327
Rheine .... § d.	1029	1129	1204	1229	1327	...	1404	1429**j**	1429	1529	1604	1629	1729	...	1804	1804	1829	1929	2004	2029	2129	2229	2252	2352	2349
Münster (Westf) Hbf .. § a.	1056	1156	1229	1256	1356	...	1429	1456	1456	1556	1629	1656	1756	...	1829	1829	1856	1956	2029	2056	2156	2256	2325	0025	...
Köln Hbf **800** .... a.	...	...	1412	...	...	...	1612	...	...	...	1812	...	...	...	2012	2012	...	...	2212	...	...	...	...	...	...

Additional trains Münster - Rheine and v.v.

	¶		¶			¶		¶	¶
Köln Hbf **802** .... d.	...	0621**r**	...	0821	each train runs every	...	1821	...	...
Münster (Westf) Hbf ..... d.	0735	0824	0935	1024	**two** hours	1935	2024	2135	2235
Rheine .... a.	0808	0851	1008	1051	until	2008	2051	2208	2308

	¶ ⚒	Ⓐ			¶		¶			¶
Rheine .... d.	0452	0606	0617	0706	0752	0906	0952	each train runs every	1906	1952
Münster (Westf) Hbf . a.	0525	0632	0650	0732	0825	0932	1025	**two** hours	1932	2025
Köln Hbf **802** .... a.	...	0838	...	0938	...	1138	...	until	2138	...

◆ – **NOTES** (LISTED BY TRAIN NUMBER)

331 – BORKUM – [12] and 🍷 (Luxembourg ★ -) Köln - Emden.
332 – [12] and 🍷 Norddeich Mole - Köln (- Luxembourg Ⓑ).
2004/5 – BODENSEE – [12] and 🍷 Konstanz - Karlsruhe - Koblenz - Köln - Emden and v.v.
2014/5 – [12] and 🍷 Stuttgart - Koblenz - Köln - Emden and v.v.
2036/7 – [12] and 🍷 Leipzig - Hannover - Bremen - Norddeich Mole and v.v.

A – ①④⑤⑥⑦ until Oct. 26; ① from Nov. 2.
B – ③–⑦ until Oct. 25; ⑦ from Nov. 1.
C – ①②③④⑥ from Oct. 26.
D – Daily until Oct. 25; ⑤⑦ from Oct. 30. See Table **813** for further details.
E – Daily until Oct. 25; ⑤⑦ from Oct. 30.
H – Daily until Oct. 31; ①–⑥ from Nov. 2.
K – ①–④ from Oct. 26.
L – From / to Luxembourg (Table **915**).

h – Arrives 1310.
j – Arrives 11 – 12 minutes earlier.
r – ⚒ only.
t – Also Oct. 3.
v – On ⑦ Aug. 30 - Oct. 25 Emden d. 1535, Norden d. 1607, Norddeich a. 1613, Norddeich Mole a. 1618.

★ – ①–⑥ until Oct. 24; ⑤ from Oct. 30.
¶ – Operated by WestfalenBahn.
§ – See panel below main table for additional trains.

▲ – **Oct. 26 - Nov. 22** all services Münster - Rheine and v.v. are subject to alteration. During this period *IC* trains are diverted (northbound trains run up to 45 minutes later Rheine - Emden - Norddeich Mole; southbound trains run up to 45 minutes **earlier** Norddeich Mole - Emden - Rheine). Regional trains are replaced by 🚌 between Münster and Rheine with extended journey times.

813 NORDDEICH - EMDEN - BREMEN - HANNOVER

km		RE 4401	RB 14801 Ⓐ	ICE 531 ① ✕	ICE 531 W ✕	RE 4403	RE 14531 ⚒	IC 2033 ①–⑥ 🍷	IC 2033 ⑦	RE 4407	ICE 533 ①–⑥ ✕	RE 4407	RE 14533	IC 2035 🍷	RE 4411	ICE 535 L ✕	RE 4411	IC 2037 🍷	RE 4415	ICE 537 L ✕	RE 4415	RE 14535	IC 2039 🍷	RE 4419	ICE 539 L ✕	RE 4419
◧	**Norddeich Mole** 812 d.	...	...	...	...	...	...	...	...	...	...	...	...	...	...	...	...	0737	0840	...	...	...	...	1040	...	...
0	**Norddeich** 812 d.	...	...	...	...	...	...	...	...	...	...	...	0532r	...	0642	...	...	0740	0842	...	...	0922	...	1042	...	...
6	Norden 812 d.	...	...	...	...	...	...	...	...	...	...	...	0538r	...	0648	...	...	0747	0848	...	...	0928	...	1048	...	...
35	**Emden** Hbf 812 d.	...	...	...	...	...	0418	...	...	0518	...	...	0604	...	0718	...	...	0814	0918	...	...	1018	...	1118	...	...
61	Leer (Ostfriesland) 812 a.	...	...	...	...	...	0435	...	...	0535	...	...	0621	...	0735	...	...	0831	0935	...	...	1035	...	1135	...	...
61	Leer (Ostfriesland) d.	...	...	...	...	...	0442	...	...	0542	...	...	0632	...	0742	...	...	0841	0942	...	...	1042	...	1142	...	...
101	Bad Zwischenahn d.	...	...	...	...	...	0510	...	...	0613	...	...	0707	...	0813	...	...	0918	1013	...	...	1112	...	1213	...	...
116	**Oldenburg** (Oldb) a.	...	...	...	...	...	0521	...	...	0623	...	...	0719	...	0823	...	...	0930	1023	...	...	1123	...	1223	...	...
116	**Oldenburg** (Oldb) d.	...	0409	0447	...	...	...	0535	...	0635	0642h	...	...	0735	0835	...	...	0935	1035	...	...	...	1135	1235	...	...
147	Delmenhorst d.	...	0438	|	...	...	...	0553	...	0654	|	...	...	0753	0854	...	...	0953	1054	...	...	...	1153	1254	...	...
161	**Bremen** Hbf a.	...	0451	0512	...	...	...	0603	...	0705	0709h	←	...	0803	0905	...	←	1003	1105	...	←	...	1203	1305	...	←
161	**Bremen** Hbf ◇ d.	0418	...	0514	0514	0518	...	0609	0609	→	0714	0718	...	0809	→	0914	0918	1009	→	1114	1118	...	1209	→	1314	1318
196	Verden (Aller) ◇ d.	0443	...	|	|	0543	...	0629	0629	...	|	0743	...	0829	...	|	0943	1029	...	|	1143	...	1229	...	|	1343
227	Nienburg (Weser) ◇ d.	0505	...	|	|	0605	...	0647	0647	...	|	0805	...	0847	...	|	1005	1047	...	|	1205	...	1247	...	|	1405
283	**Hannover** Hbf ◇ a.	0538	...	0614	0614	0638	...	0714	0714	...	0814	0838	...	0914	...	1014	1038	1114	...	1214	1238	...	1314	...	1414	1438
	Magdeburg Hbf **810** a.	...	...	|	|	...	...	0857	0857	...	|	...	...	1057	...	|	...	1257	...	|	...	...	1457	...	|	...
	Berlin Hbf **810** a.	...	...	|	|	...	...	|	|	...	|	...	...	|	...	|	...	|	...	|	...	...	|	...	|	...
	Leipzig Hbf **810** a.	...	...	|	|	...	...	1017	1017	...	|	...	...	1217	...	|	...	1417	...	|	...	...	1617	...	|	...
	Nürnberg Hbf **900** a.	...	...	0928	0928	...	...	...	...	...	|	...	...	...	...	1329	...	...	...	|	...	...	...	...	|	...
	München Hbf **900** a.	...	...	1041	1041	...	...	...	...	...	1304	...	...	...	...	1443	...	...	...	1707	...	...	...	...	1903	...

	IC 2131 B 🍷	RE 4423	ICE 631 L ✕	RE 4423	RE 14537	IC 2133 🍷	RE 4427	ICE 633 Y ✕	RE 4427	IC 2135 ★ 🍷	IC 2135 🍷	RE 4431	ICE 635 Z ✕	ICE 635 ⑦ ✕	RE 4431	RE 14539	IC 2137 P ¶	RE 4433	RE 4435	ICE 637 ⑦ ✕	RE 4435	RB 14837	RE 4437	RE 14541 14839	RE 4439	RB 14841
Norddeich Mole 812 d.	...	1240	...	...	...	...	1440	...	...	1539	...	1640	...	...	...	...	...	...	1840	...	...	...	...	...	2040	...
Norddeich 812 d.	...	1242	...	...	...	...	1442	...	...	1542	...	1642	...	...	...	...	...	...	1842	...	...	...	...	...	2042	...
Norden 812 d.	...	1248	...	...	...	...	1448	...	...	1549	...	1648	...	...	...	...	...	...	1848	...	...	...	...	...	2048	...
Emden Hbf 812 d.	1219	1318	...	...	1418	...	1518	...	...	1619	...	1718	...	...	...	1818	...	...	1918	...	...	...	...	2018	2118	...
Leer (Ostfriesland) 812 a.	1236	1335	...	...	1435	...	1535	...	...	1636	...	1735	...	...	...	1835	...	...	1935	...	...	...	...	2035	2135	...
Leer (Ostfriesland) d.	1242	1342	...	...	1442	...	1542	...	...	1641	...	1742	...	...	...	1842	...	...	1942	...	...	...	...	2042	2142	...
Bad Zwischenahn d.	1321	1413	...	...	1512	...	1613	...	...	1718	...	1813	...	...	...	1912	...	...	2013	...	...	...	...	2112	2213	...
Oldenburg (Oldb) a.	1331	1423	...	...	1523	...	1623	...	...	1730	...	1823	...	...	...	1923	...	...	2023	...	...	...	...	2123	2223	...
Oldenburg (Oldb) d.	1335	1435	...	...	...	1535	1635	...	...	1735	1735	1835	...	...	...	...	1935	...	2035	...	...	2109	...	2137	2235	2340
Delmenhorst d.	1353	1454	...	...	...	1553	1654	...	...	1753	1753	1854	...	...	...	...	1953	...	2054	...	...	2138	...	2204	2254	0009
Bremen Hbf a.	1403	1505	...	←	...	1603	1705	...	←	1803	1803	1905	...	...	←	...	2003	...	2105	...	←	2151	...	2221	2305	0022
Bremen Hbf ◇ d.	1409	→	1514	1518	...	1609	→	1714	1718	1809	1809	→	1914	1914	1918	...	2009	2018	→	2114	2118	...	2218	...	2311	...
Verden (Aller) ◇ d.	1429	...	|	1543	...	1629	...	|	1743	1829	1829	...	|	|	1943	...	2029	2043	...	|	2143	...	2243	...	2343	...
Nienburg (Weser) ◇ d.	1447	...	|	1605	...	1647	...	|	1805	1847	1847	...	|	|	2005	...	2047	2105	...	|	2205	...	2305	...	0005	...
Hannover Hbf ◇ a.	1514	...	1614	1638	...	1714	...	1814	1838	1914	1914	...	2014	2014	2038	...	2114	2138	...	2213	2238	...	2338	...	0038	...
Magdeburg Hbf **810** a.	1657	...	|	...	...	1857	...	|	...	2057	2057	...	|	|	...	...	2300	...	...	...	...	...	...	...	...	...
Berlin Hbf **810** a.	1827	...	|	...	...	|	...	|	...	|	|	...	|	|	...	...	...	...	...	...	...	...	...	...	...	...
Leipzig Hbf **810** a.	...	...	|	...	...	2017	...	|	...	2219	2219	...	|	|	...	...	...	...	...	...	...	...	...	...	...	...
Nürnberg Hbf **900** a.	...	...	|	...	...	...	...	|	...	...	...	...	2324	2324	...	...	...	...	...	...	...	...	...	...	...	...
München Hbf **900** a.	...	...	2102	...	...	...	...	2302	...	...	...	...	...	0038	...	...	...	...	...	...	...	...	...	...	...	...

	RE 4400	RE § 14530 ⚒	RE ‡ 14532	RE 4402	RE 4404	IC 2136 ①–⑥ L	RE 14534	RE 4406	ICE 636 ①–⑤ L ✕	RE 4406	IC 2134 🍷	RE 4410	ICE 634 L ✕	RE 4410	IC 2132 C 🍷	IC 2132 ★ C 🍷	RE 4414	ICE 632 L ✕	RE 4414	IC 2130 🍷	RE 14536	RE 4418	ICE 630 L ✕	RE 4418	IC 2038 🍷	RE 14538
München Hbf **900** d.	...	...	...	...	...	...	...	...	...	...	...	...	0517a	...	...	...	...	0650	...	...	...	...	0915	...	...	...
Nürnberg Hbf **900** d.	...	...	...	...	...	...	...	...	...	...	...	...	0631	...	...	...	...	|	...	...	...	...	1032	...	...	...
Leipzig Hbf **810** d.	...	...	...	...	...	...	...	...	...	...	0540a	...	|	...	...	...	...	|	...	0942	...	...	|	...	1142	...
Berlin Hbf **810** d.	...	...	...	...	...	...	...	...	...	...	|	...	|	...	0732	0732	...	|	...	|	...	...	|	...	|	...
Magdeburg Hbf **810** d.	...	...	...	...	...	0501a	...	...	...	...	0700	...	|	...	0901	0901	...	|	...	1100	...	...	|	...	1300	...
Hannover Hbf ◇ d.	0021	...	...	0521	0617	0645	...	0721	0745	...	0845	0921	0945	...	1045	1045	1121	1145	...	1245	...	1321	1345	...	1445	...
Nienburg (Weser) ◇ d.	0055	...	...	0555	0655	0713	...	0755	|	...	0913	0955	|	...	1113	1113	1155	|	...	1313	...	1355	|	...	1513	...
Verden (Aller) ◇ d.	0115	...	...	0615	0715	0730	...	0815	|	...	0930	1015	|	...	1130	1130	1215	|	...	1330	...	1415	|	...	1530	...
Bremen Hbf ◇ a.	0139	...	...	0641	0742	0751	...	0843	0844	←	0951	1039	1044	←	1151	1151	1241	1244	←	1351	...	1441	1444	←	1551	...
Bremen Hbf d.	...	0444	0543	0654	...	0755	...	→	...	0854	0955	→	...	1054	1155	1155	→	...	1254	1355	...	→	...	1454	1555	...
Delmenhorst d.	...	0455	0556	0704	...	0806	...	...	...	0904	1006	...	...	1104	1206	1206	...	...	1304	1406	...	...	...	1504	1606	...
Oldenburg (Oldb) a.	...	0518	0623	0723	...	0822	...	...	...	0923	1022	...	...	1123	1222	1222	...	...	1323	1422	...	...	...	1523	1622	...
Oldenburg (Oldb) d.	...	0532	0626	0732	...	...	0832	...	...	0932	1032	...	...	1132	...	1224	...	...	1332	...	1432	...	...	1532	...	1632
Bad Zwischenahn d.	...	0545	0638	0745	...	...	0845	...	...	0945	1044	...	...	1145	...	1236	...	...	1345	...	1445	...	...	1545	...	1645
Leer (Ostfriesland) a.	...	0615	0707	0815	...	...	0915	...	...	1015	1115	...	...	1215	...	1307	...	...	1415	...	1515	...	...	1615	...	1715
Leer (Ostfriesland) 812 d.	...	0625	0715	0825	...	...	0925	...	...	1025	1120	...	...	1225	...	1319	...	...	1425	...	1522	...	...	1625	...	1722
Emden Hbf 812 d.	...	0643	0735	0843	...	...	0942	...	...	1043	1137	...	...	1243	...	1341	...	...	1443	...	1538	...	...	1643	...	1738
Norden 812 d.	...	0707	0807	0907	...	...	...	...	...	1107	...	...	...	1307	...	1409	...	...	1507	...	...	...	...	1707	...	...
Norddeich 812 a.	...	0713	0813	0913	...	...	...	...	...	1113	...	...	...	1313	...	1415	...	...	1513	...	...	...	...	1713	...	...
Norddeich Mole 812 a.	...	0717	0817	0918	...	...	...	...	...	1118	...	...	...	1318	...	1421	...	...	1518	...	...	...	...	1718	...	...

	RE 4422	ICE 538 Y ✕	RE 4422	IC 2036 🍷	RE 4426	ICE 536 ✕	RE 4426	IC 2034 🍷	RE 14540	RE 4430	ICE 776 Ⓑ F ✕	RE 4430	IC 2032 🍷	IC 2032 Ⓑ 🍷	RE 14542 Ⓑ	RE 4434	ICE 832 ⊡ ✕	IC 1932 ⑦ H	RE 4440	RE 4440 ⑥	ICE 862 ⑤ L ✕	RE 4436	ICE 732 Y ✕	ICE 732 ⑦ ✕	RE 4438	ICE 850 ⑦ ✕
München Hbf **900** d.	...	1052	...	...	...	1251	...	...	...	...	...	...	...	...	...	...	...	...	...	...	...	...	1820	1820	...	...
Nürnberg Hbf **900** d.	...	|	...	...	...	|	...	...	...	...	...	...	...	...	...	...	...	...	...	...	...	...	1933	1933	...	...
Leipzig Hbf **810** d.	...	|	...	1342	...	|	...	1542	...	...	...	...	1742	1742	...	...	...	...	...	...	...	...	|	|	...	...
Berlin Hbf **810** d.	...	|	...	|	...	|	...	|	...	...	...	...	|	|	...	...	1948	2007s	...	...	1948	...	|	|	...	2148v
Magdeburg Hbf **810** d.	...	|	...	1500	...	|	...	1700	...	...	...	...	1900	1900	...	...	|	|	...	...	|	...	|	|	...	|
Hannover Hbf ◇ d.	1521	1545	...	1645	1721	1745	...	1845	...	1921	1949	...	2045	2045	...	2121	2145	2145	...	...	2145	2221	2251	2251	2321	2345
Nienburg (Weser) ◇ d.	1555	|	...	1713	1755	|	...	1913	...	1955	|	...	2113	2113	...	2155	|	|	...	...	|	2255	|	|	2355	|
Verden (Aller) ◇ d.	1615	|	...	1730	1815	|	...	1930	...	2015	|	...	2130	2130	...	2215	|	|	...	...	|	2315	|	|	0015	|
Bremen Hbf ◇ a.	1639	1645	←	1751	1839	1845	←	1951	...	2039	2048	←	2151	2151	...	2241	2244	2244	...	...	2247	2339	2349	2349	0039	0045
Bremen Hbf d.	→	...	1654	1755	→	...	1854	1955	...	→	2050t	2056	...	2155	...	...	...	2247	2254	2254	2258j	...	...	2352	...	0047
Delmenhorst d.	...	...	1704	1806	...	...	1904	2006	...	...	|	2106	...	2206	...	...	...	2258	2304	2304	2311j	...	...	|	...	0101
Oldenburg (Oldb) a.	...	...	1723	1822	...	...	1923	2022	...	...	2115t	2125	...	2222	...	...	...	2315	2323	2323	2331j	...	...	0017	...	0123
Oldenburg (Oldb) d.	...	...	1732	1832	...	...	1932	...	2032	...	...	2132	...	...	2232	...	...	...	...	2332	...	...	...	...	...	...
Bad Zwischenahn d.	...	...	1745	1844	...	...	1945	...	2045	...	...	2145	...	...	2245	...	...	...	...	2345	...	...	...	...	...	...
Leer (Ostfriesland) a.	...	...	1815	1915	...	...	2015	...	2115	...	...	2215	...	...	2315	...	...	...	...	0015	...	...	...	...	...	...
Leer (Ostfriesland) 812 d.	...	...	1825	1925	...	...	2025	...	2122	...	...	2225	...	...	2322	...	...	...	...	0025	...	...	...	...	...	...
Emden Hbf 812 d.	...	...	1843	1945	...	...	2043	...	2138	...	...	2243	...	...	2338	...	...	...	...	0041	...	...	...	...	...	...
Norden 812 d.	...	...	1907	2008	...	...	2107	...	...	...	...	2307	...	...	...	...	...	...	...	...	...	...	...	...	...	...
Norddeich 812 a.	...	...	1913	2015	...	...	2113	...	...	...	...	2313	...	...	...	...	...	...	...	...	...	...	...	...	...	...
Norddeich Mole 812 a.	...	...	1918	2021	...	...	...	...	...	...	...	...	...	...	...	...	...	...	...	...	...	...	...	...	...	...

B – OSTFRIESLAND – (12) and 🍷 Emden - Magdeburg - Berlin (- Cottbus Ⓑ).
C – OSTFRIESLAND – (12) and 🍷 (Cottbus ①–⑥ -) Berlin - Magdeburg - Oldenburg (- Norddeich Mole ★).
F – From Frankfurt (Table **900**).
H – From Stralsund (Table **845**).
L – From July 20.
P – ⑦ June 14 - July 12; Ⓑ from July 19.
W – ① June 15 - July 13; ①–⑤ from July 20.
Y – ⑦ June 14 - July 12; daily from July 19.
Z – ⑥⑦ June 14 - July 12; daily from July 18.

a – ①–⑤ only.
h – From Sept. 28.
j – From Oct. 2.
r – ⚒ only.
s – Berlin **Spandau**.
t – ①–⑤ from Sept. 28.
v – 2131 on June 21, 28.

⊡ – ①②③④⑥ from July 20.
★ – Daily until Oct. 25; ⑤⑦ from Oct. 30.
§ – Train number *RB* **14800** Bremen - Oldenburg.
‡ – Train number *RB* **14802** Bremen - Oldenburg.
¶ – Conveys 🍷 on ⑤⑦.
◧ – Norddeich Mole is 300 metres from Norddeich.
◇ – Additional *RE* trains Bremen - Verden - Nienburg - Hannover and v.v.:
From Bremen Hbf at 0618 and every two hours until 1818.
From Hannover Hbf at 0821 and every two hours until 2021.

Nord West Bahn — OSNABRÜCK - OLDENBURG - WILHELMSHAVEN — 814

km		⚒	Ⓐ	n		Ⓐ										B							⚒		†
0	**Osnabrück** Hbf d.	...	0442	0602	...	0626	0702	0802	0902	1002	1102	1202	1302	1402	1502	...	1602	1702	1802	1902	2002	2102	...	2253	2253
20	Bramsche d.	...	0500	0617	...	0641	0717	0817	0917	1017	1117	1217	1317	1417	1517	...	1617	1717	1817	1917	2017	2117	...	2313	2313
50	Quakenbrück d.	...	0540	0640	...	0710	0740	0840	0940	1040	1140	1240	1340	1440	1540	...	1640	1740	1840	1940	2040	2140	...	2340	2340
72	Cloppenburg d.	...	0556	0656	...	0740	0756	0856	0956	1056	1156	1256	1356	1456	1556	...	1656	1756	1856	1956	2056	2156	...	2356	2356
113	**Oldenburg** (Oldb) a.	...	0629	0729	...	0819	0829	0929	1029	1129	1229	1329	1429	1529	1629	...	1729	1829	1929	2029	2129	2229	...	0029	0029
113	**Oldenburg** (Oldb) d.	0535	0635	0735	0735	...	0835	0935	1035	1135	1235	1335	1435	1535	1635	1706	1735	1835	1935	2035	2135	2235	2335	...	0039
143	Varel (Oldb) d.	0558	0658	0758	0758	...	0858	0958	1058	1158	1258	1358	1458	1558	1658	1729	1758	1858	1958	2058	2158	2258	2358	...	0103
165	**Wilhelmshaven** a.	0618	0718	0818	0818	...	0918	1018	1118	1218	1318	1418	1518	1618	1718	1748	1818	1918	2018	2118	2218	2318	0018	...	0122

	Ⓐ	⚒	Ⓐ	⚒	Ⓐ							Ⓐ		Ⓑ									ⒸA		
Wilhelmshaven d.	...	0444	...	0544	*0613*	0644	0744	0844	0944	1044	1144	...	1244	1344	...	1444	1544	1644	1744	1844	1944	2044	2044	2144	2244
Varel (Oldb) d.	...	0502	...	0602	*0631*	0702	0802	0902	1002	1102	1202	...	1302	1402	1402	1502	1602	1702	1802	1902	2002	2102	2102	2202	2302
Oldenburg (Oldb) a.	...	0525	...	0625	*0653*	0725	0825	0925	1025	1125	1225	...	1325	1425	1425	1525	1625	1725	1825	1925	2025	2125	2125	2225	2325
Oldenburg (Oldb) d.	0412	0529	0557	0629	0657	0729	0829	0929	1029	1129	1229	1257	1329	1429	1429	1529	1629	1729	1829	1929	2029	...	2129	2229	...
Cloppenburg d.	0444	0606	0633	0706	0733	0806	0906	1006	1106	1206	1306	1333	1406	1506	1506	1606	1706	1806	1906	2006	2106	...	2206	2302	...
Quakenbrück d.	0459	0621	0650	0721	0750	0821	0921	1021	1121	1221	1321	1350	1421	1521	1521	1621	1721	1821	1921	2021	2121	...	2221	2321	...
Bramsche d.	0521	0642	0710	0742	0810	0842	0942	1042	1142	1242	1342	1412	1442	1542	1542	1642	1742	1842	1942	2042	2142	...	2242	2342	...
Osnabrück Hbf a.	0540	0658	0727	0758	0827	0858	0958	1058	1158	1258	1358	1427	1458	1558	1558	1658	1758	1858	1958	2058	2158	...	2258	2358	...

A – From Until Oct. 25. **B** – From Bremen Hbf (d. 1631). **n** – Not Nov. 1, 8, 15, 22, 29, Dec. 6. **Operator**: Nord West Bahn GmbH. ✆ +49 (0) 1805 60 01 61.

RE / RB services — BREMEN - BREMERHAVEN - CUXHAVEN — 815

km			⚒					Ⓐ	ⒸN			Ⓐ			Ⓐ			Ⓐ	ⒸN			Ⓐ			Ⓐ
	Osnabrück Hbf **800/1** d.	...	...	...	0538**r**	...	...	0638	...	0738	...	...	0938	...	...	1138	...	...	...	1338**b**	...	1438	1538	...	1638
0	**Bremen** Hbf d.	0004	0534	0634	0656	...	0734	0756	0757	0856	0934	...	1056	1134	...	1256	1334	...	1357	1456	1534	1556	1656	1734	1756
21	Osterholz-Scharmbeck d.	0021	0552	0652	0710	...	0752	0810	0811	0910	0952	...	1110	1152	...	1310	1352	...	1411	1510	1552	1610	1710	1752	1810
63	**Bremerhaven** Hbf d.	0056	0627	0727	0732	0736	0827	0832	0837	0932	1027	1036	1132	1227	1236	1332	1427	1436	1437	1532	1627	1632	1732	1827	1832
66	**Bremerhaven** Lehe d.	0101	0632	0732	0737	0742	0832	0837	0843	0937	1032	1042	1137	1232	1242	1337	1432	1442	1443	1537	1632	1637	1737	1832	1837
106	**Cuxhaven** a.	...	*0727*	...	...	0827	...	*0927*	0922	*1027*	...	1127	*1227*	...	1327	*1427*	...	1527	1522	*1627*	...	*1727*	*1827*	...	*1927*

			Ⓐ		Ⓑ			Ⓐ	Ⓐ	†	
Osnabrück Hbf **800/1** d.	1738	...	...	...	1938	...	...	2038	...	...	...
Bremen Hbf d.	1856	1934	...	2034	2056	...	2134	2156	...	2157	2304
Osterholz-Scharmbeck d.	1910	1952	...	2052	2110	...	2152	2210	...	2211	2322
Bremerhaven Hbf d.	1932	2027	2036	2127	2132	2136	2227	2232	2236	2238	2357
Bremerhaven Lehe d.	1937	2032	2042	2132	2137	2142	2232	2237	2242	2244	0002
Cuxhaven a.	*2027*	...	2127	...	...	2227	...	...	2327	2323	...

	⚒	⚒	Ⓐ	⚒		⚒	Ⓐ		
Cuxhaven d.	...	...	*0509*	...	...	0639	...	...	*0739*
Bremerhaven Lehe d.	0407	0528	0554	0623	0628	0719	0723	0728	0823
Bremerhaven Hbf d.	0412	0533	0559	0628	0633	0724	0728	0733	0828
Osterholz-Scharmbeck d.	0446	0608	0634	0650	0708	...	0750	0808	0850
Bremen Hbf a.	0504	0626	0656	0703	0726	...	0803	0826	0903
Osnabrück Hbf **800/1** a.	...	...	...	0820	...	...	0920	...	1020

	Ⓐ			ⒸN	Ⓐ			Ⓐ			Ⓐ			C	Ⓐ			Ⓐ			Ⓐ	⑤F		Ⓐ	⑤⑥
Cuxhaven d.	*0839*	...	*0939*	1033	1039	...	*1139*	1239	...	*1339*	1439	...	*1539*	1633	*1639*	...	*1739*	1839	...	*1939*	2039	...	*2139*	2239	...
Bremerhaven Lehe d.	0923	0928	1023	1112	1119	1128	1223	1319	1328	1423	1519	1528	1623	1712	1723	1728	1823	1919	1928	2023	2119	...	2228	2319	2328
Bremerhaven Hbf d.	0928	0933	1028	1118	1124	1133	1228	1324	1333	1428	1524	1533	1628	1718	1728	1733	1828	1924	1933	2028	2124	2128	2233	2324	2333
Osterholz-Scharmbeck d.	0950	1008	1050	1143	...	1208	1250	...	1408	1450	...	1608	1650	1743	1750	1808	1850	...	2008	2050	...	2155	2308	...	0008
Bremen Hbf a.	1003	1026	1103	1158	...	1226	1303	...	1426	1503	...	1626	1703	1758	1803	1826	1903	...	2026	2103	...	2210	2326	...	0026
Osnabrück Hbf **800/1** a.	1120	...	1220	...	...	...	1420	...	...	1620	...	...	1820	...	1920	...	2020	...	...	2220	...	...	...	...	...

C – ⑥⑦ until Nov. 1; ⑦ from Nov. 8. **F** – Until Oct. 30. **N** – Until Nov. 1. **b** – Ⓑ only. **r** – ⚒ only.

metronom; EVB — HAMBURG - CUXHAVEN and BREMERHAVEN — 818

Hamburg - Buxtehude - Cuxhaven ⊖

km		Ⓐ‡	⚒	‡	Ⓐ‡	Ⓐ	⚒	⚒		⚒		⚒		⚒		⚒		⚒					Ⓐ	Ⓒ	‡
0	**Hamburg** Hbf § d.	0448	...	0528	0558	...	...	0707	0807	0907	1007	1107	1207	1307	1407	1506	1607	1707	1807	1907	2007	2107	2207	2310	2328
12	**Hamburg** Harburg § d.	0501	...	0541	0611	0624	...	0724	0824	0924	1024	1124	1224	1324	1424	1524	1624	1724	1824	1924	2024	2124	2224	2327	2341
33	**Buxtehude** § d.	0526	...	0606	0636	0638	...	0738	0838	0938	1038	1138	1238	1338	1438	1538	1638	1738	1838	1938	2038	2138	2238	2341	0006
54	Stade § d.	0547	0551	0627	...	0656	0656	0756	0856	0956	1056	1156	1256	1357	1456	1556	1656	1756	1856	1956	2056	2156	2256	2359	0027
102	Otterndorf d.	...	0633	...	...	0738	0738	0838	0938	1038	1138	1238	1338	1441	1538	1638	1738	1838	1938	2038	2138	2238	2338	0041	...
116	**Cuxhaven** a.	...	0645	...	...	0750	0750	0850	0950	1050	1150	1250	1350	1453	1550	1650	1750	1850	1950	2050	2150	2250	2350	0053	...

	Ⓐ	⚒	Ⓐ	⚒	†	‡	⚒				⚒		⚒		⚒		⚒			Ⓒ	Ⓐ	‡	Ⓒ	Ⓐ	‡
Cuxhaven d.	0434	0510	0551	0610	0636	...	0652	0752	0910	1010	1110	1210	1310	1410	1510	1610	1710	1810	1910	2010	2039	...	2210	2239	...
Otterndorf d.	0446	0521	0603	0621	0648	...	0704	0804	0921	1021	1121	1221	1321	1421	1521	1621	1721	1821	1921	2021	2050	...	2221	2250	...
Stade § d.	0527	0603	0645	0703	0731	0735	0747	0846	1003	1103	1203	1303	1403	1503	1603	1703	1803	1903	2003	2103	2131	2135	2303	2331	2335
Buxtehude § d.	0546	0621	0702	0721	...	0755	0805	0903	1021	1121	1221	1321	1421	1521	1621	1721	1821	1921	2021	2121	...	2155	2321	...	2355
Hamburg Harburg § a.	0600	0637	0718	0736	...	0820	0820	0918	1037	1137	1237	1337	1437	1536	1637	1736	1837	1937	2037	2137	...	2220	2337	...	0020
Hamburg Hbf § a.	*0614*	0656	0736	0758	...	0834	0838	0938	1058	1158	1258	1358	1458	1558	1658	1758	1858	1958	2058	2158	...	2234	2354	...	0034

Buxtehude - Bremerhaven △

km		⚒		Ⓐ	Ⓐ	Ⓒ	⚒f		⚒f		Ⓐ	⑥n	Ⓐ	Ⓒ	⑥n	Ⓐ		⑥n	Ⓐ		⑥n	Ⓐ	Ⓒ	Ⓐ	e
0	**Buxtehude** d.	...	0537**a**	0637	0717	0737**z**	0837	0937**g**	1037	1137**g**	*1237*	1242	1337	1342	1442	*1452*	1542**e**	1642	*1652*	1742**e**	1842	1852	1942	1952	2142
39	Bremervörde a.	...	0620**a**	0722	0820	0820**z**	0920	1020**g**	1120	1220**g**	*1320*	1325	1420	1425	1525	*1535*	1625**e**	1725	*1735*	1825**e**	1925	1935	2025	2035	2225
39	Bremervörde d.	0535	0635	0735	0835	0835	...	1035	...	1235	1335	...	...	1435	...	1540	1640	...	1740	1840	...	1940	2040	...	...
78	**Bremerhaven** Hbf a.	0621	0721	0821	0921	0921	...	1121	...	1321	1421	...	...	1521	...	1621	1721	...	1821	1921	...	2021	2121	...	...

	Ⓐ	⚒	†	⚒		Ⓐ	⑥n	Ⓐ	Ⓒ	Ⓐ	⑥n	Ⓐ	Ⓒ	Ⓐ	⑥n		⚒e		⑥n	Ⓐ		Ⓐ		⚒	†
Bremerhaven Hbf ⊡ d.	...	0539**a**	...	0639	0739	0839	...	...	0939	1039	...	...	1139	1239	...	1339	...	1539	...	1639	1739	1839	1939	2039	2139
Bremervörde ⊡ a.	...	0622**a**	...	0722	0822	0922	...	...	1022	1122	...	...	1222	1322	...	1422	...	1622	...	1722	1822	1922	2022	2122	2222
Bremervörde d.	0525	0625	0630	0725	0825**g**	0925	0930	1025	1030	1125	1130	1225	1230	1325	1330	1430**e**	1530	1630**e**	1730	*1740*	1830**e**	1940	2030**c**	...	...
Buxtehude a.	0610	0710	0715	0810	0910**g**	1010	1015	1110	1115	1210	1215	1310	1315	1410	1415	1515**e**	1615	1715**e**	1815	*1825*	1915**e**	2025	2115**c**	...	...

a – Ⓐ only.
c – Ⓒ only.
e – 10 minutes later on Ⓐ.
f – 5 minutes later on ⑥.
g – 5 minutes later on Ⓒ.
n – Not Oct. 3.
z – 5 minutes later on †.
‡ – Hamburg S-Bahn (2nd class only).
§ – Additional S-Bahn trains operate.
⊖ – Operated by metronom Eisenbahngesellschaft mbH.
△ – Operated by Eisenbahnen und Verkehrsbetriebe Elbe-Weser GmbH (EVB).
⊡ – **Additional trains** Bremerhaven Hbf - Bremervörde: 2239 ⑥, 2339 Ⓐ.

RE services except where shown — HAMBURG - KIEL — 820

km			⚒						ICE 608 B⊕ 🍷	ICE 76 w Z ✕	ICE 1026 1126 A ✕	ICE 74 Z◧ ✕	ICE 892 Ⓑ M ✕	ICE 974 Ⓑ S◧ ✕	EC 102 ⑦ C ✕
0	**Hamburg** Hbf **823** d.	0028	0520	0620	and	2220	2323	also	1015	1538	1615	1738	1856	2040	2115
37	Elmshorn **823** d.	0100	0552	0650	hourly	2250	2353		|	|	|	|	|	|	|
73	Neumünster **823** d.	0132	0618	0716	until	2316	0019		1103	1626	1703	1828	1948	2128	2203
111	**Kiel** Hbf a.	0158	0639	0736		2336	0039		1121	1644	1721	1846	2007	2147	2220

	⑥n	Ⓐ							ICE 973 ①–⑥ S△ ✕	ICE 73 Z ✕	ICE 791 ①–⑥ M ✕	ICE 1025 1125 A ✕		ICE 673 w K ✕	ICE 609 B ✕
Kiel Hbf d.	0355	0405	0521	0621	0721	and	2321	also	0612	0712	0753	1238	...	1712	1838
Neumünster **823** d.	0420	0425	0542	0642	0742	hourly	2342		0631	0730	0813	1257	...	1730	1857
Elmshorn **823** d.	0453	0457	0609	0709	0809	until	0009		|	|	|	|	...	|	|
Hamburg Hbf **823** a.	0530	0530	0637	0737	0837		0037		0720	0820	0903	1343	...	1819	1943

A – (12) Frankfurt - Köln - Kiel and v.v.
B – (12) Basel - Karlsruhe - Frankfurt - Köln - Kiel and v.v.
C – (12) Chur - Zürich - Basel - Karlsruhe - Köln - Kiel.
K – (12) Kiel - Hannover - Frankfurt - Karlsruhe (- Basel ⑥).
M – (12) Berlin - Kiel and v.v.
S – (12) Kiel - Hannover - Frankfurt - Stuttgart and v.v.
Z – (12) Kiel - Hannover - Frankfurt - Karlsruhe - Basel - Zürich and v.v.

n – Not Oct. 3.
w – From July 20.

⊕ – Runs 17–20 minutes later July 18–26.
◧ – Runs 8–15 minutes later June 14 - July 19.
△ – Runs 21–22 minutes **earlier** June 14 - July 19.

821 HAMBURG - WESTERLAND

DB; NOB

km		◇	◇ Ⓐ	◇	◇ Ⓒ	◇	◇ Ⓐ	◇	◇	◇	◇	◇ S	IC● 2314 S ✕	◇ W	◇	IC● 2074 ⑥⑦ D✕	IC● 2072 ①–⑤ D✕	◇	◇	◇ ①–⑤	◇ ⑥⑦	IC● 2310 F✕	◇	IC● 2170 P J🍷	IC● 2170 Z J🍷
	Köln Hbf **800** d.	...	...	...	...	...	...	...	...	...	...	...	0511	...	...	...	...	...	...	...	...	0911	...	...	...
	Berlin Hbf **840** d.	...	...	...	...	...	...	...	...	...	...	...	|	...	...	0823	0823	...	...	...	...	|	...	...	...
	Hamburg Hbf ... **820** d.	...	...	...	...	...	*0500‡*	...	*0620**	*0720**	*0820**	*0850‡*	0915	*0920**	*1020**	1049	1049	*1120**	*1220**	*1243**	*1250‡*	1315	*1420**	1449	1502
0	**Hamburg** Altona d.	...	...	...	...	...	0524	...	0637	0733	0833	0910	|	0933	1033	|	|	1133	1233	1303	1310	|	1433	|	|
30	Elmshorn **820** d.	...	...	...	...	...	0545	...	0657	0755	0855	0932	|	0955	1055	|	|	1155	1255	1322	1332	|	1455	|	|
64	Itzehoe a.	...	...	...	...	...	0610	...	0721	0819	0919	0956	1001	1019	1119	1141	1141	1219	1319	1344	1356	1401	1519	1541	1548
64	Itzehoe d.	...	0456	...	0538	...	0610	...	0722	0820	0920	0957	1016	1020	1120	1143	1143	1220	1320	1345	1357	1416	1520	1543	1550
123	Heide (Holst) a.	...	0540	...	0622	...	0656	...	0756	0856	0956	1033	1052	1056	1156	1218	1218	1256	1356	1420	1432	1453	1556	1618	1623
123	Heide (Holst) d.	...	0549	...	0623	...	0702	...	0802	0902	1002	1034	1054	1102	1202	1220	1220	1302	1402	1421	1433	1455	1602	1620	1625
157	Husum a.	...	0615	...	0649	...	0728	...	0828	0928	1028	1058	1117	1128	1228	1242	1242	1328	1429	1446	1458	1518	1628	1642	1646
157	Husum d.	0558	...	0630	...	0658	0730	0730	0830	0930	1030	1100	1119	1130	1230	1244	1244	1330	1430	1448	1500	1520	1630	1644	1648
197	Niebüll a.	0628	...	0658	...	0728	0758	0758	0858	0958	1058	1128	1145	1158	1258	1310	1310	1358	1458	1514	1528	1546	1658	1710	1711
197	Niebüll d.	0631	...	0701	...	0731	0801	0801	0901	1001	1101	1131	1201	1201	1301	1331	1331	1401	1501	1517	1531	1601	1701	1731	1731
237	**Westerland** (Sylt) a.	0705	...	0735	...	0805	0835	0835	0937	1035	1135	1207	1234	1235	1337	1404	1406	1435	1535	1551	1605	1634	1735	1804	1804

	◇	◇	◇	◇	◇	IC 1808 ⑦	◇	◇	◇ ⊖		
Köln Hbf **800** d.	...	...	...	...	...	1539	...	...	...	...	...
Berlin Hbf **840** d.	...	...	...	...	...	|	...	...	...	...	...
Hamburg Hbf ... **820** d.	*1520**	*1620**	*1720**	*1820**	*1920**	2009	*2020**	*2120**	*2220**	*2240‡*	*2340‡*
Hamburg Altona d.	1533	1633	1733	1833	1933	|	2033	2133	2233	2302	0002
Elmshorn **820** d.	1555	1655	1755	1855	1955	|	2055	2155	2255	2329	0029
Itzehoe a.	1619	1719	1819	1919	2019	2054	2119	2219	2319	2358	0058
Itzehoe d.	1620	1720	1820	1920	2020	2109	2120	2220	2320	...	...
Heide (Holst) a.	1656	1756	1856	1956	2056	2143	2203	2303	0003	...	...
Heide (Holst) d.	1702	1802	1902	2002	2102	2145	2204	2304	0004	...	...
Husum a.	1728	1828	1928	2028	2128	2212	2230	2330	0030	...	...
Husum d.	1730	1830	1930	2030	2130	2219	2232	*2333*	...	...	...
Niebüll a.	1758	1858	1958	2058	2158	2244	2300	*0001*	...	...	...
Niebüll d.	1801	1901	2001	2101	2201	2247	2301	*0002*	...	...	...
Westerland (Sylt) a.	1835	1935	2035	2135	2235	2314	2335	*0034*	...	...	...

	◇	◇		◇ Ⓐ	◇ Ⓐ	◇	◇ R	◇	◇	◇
Westerland (Sylt) d.	0000	0100	...	...	0423	...	0522	0622	0722	0822
Niebüll a.	0030	0130	...	...	0453	...	0559	0659	0759	0859
Niebüll d.	0031	0131	...	...	0454	...	0601	0701	0801	0901
Husum a.	0101	0201	...	...	0522	...	0629	0729	0830	0929
Husum d.	...	...	...	0425	...	0525	0631	0731	0831	0931
Heide (Holst) a.	...	...	...	0450	...	0550	0656	0756	0856	0956
Heide (Holst) d.	...	...	...	0452	...	0552	0702	0802	0902	1002
Itzehoe a.	...	...	...	0536	...	0636	0736	0836	0936	1036
Itzehoe d.	...	...	...	0537	...	0637	0737	0837	0937	1037
Elmshorn **820** d.	...	...	...	0602	...	0702	0802	0902	1002	1102
Hamburg Altona a.	...	...	...	0624	...	0724	0824	0924	1024	1124
Hamburg Hbf **820** a.	...	...	...	*0637**	...	*0737**	*0837**	*0937**	*1037**	*1137**
Berlin Hbf **840** a.	...	...	...	...	...	...	...	...	...	...
Köln Hbf **800** a.	...	...	...	...	...	...	...	...	...	...

	IC 2001 ①	IC● 2311 H✕	◇	◇	◇	IC● 2171 ⑤–⑦ L🍷	IC● 2181 N 🍷	◇	◇ ⑥⑦ S	◇ ①–⑤ S	◇ W	IC● 2315 S G✕	◇	◇	IC● 2073 ①–⑤ D✕	IC● 2075 ⑥⑦ D✕	◇	◇	◇	◇	◇		◇	◇	◇
Westerland (Sylt) d.	0856	0926	0952	1022	1122	1156	1156	1222	1252	1252	1322	1326	1422	1522	1552	1552	1622	1722	1822	1922	2022	...	2122	...	2255
Niebüll a.	0929	0959	1029	1059	1159	1229	1229	1259	1329	1329	1359	1359	1459	1559	1629	1629	1659	1759	1859	1959	2059	...	2159	...	2326
Niebüll d.	0931	1013	1031	1101	1201	1245	1245	1301	1331	1331	1401	1413	1501	1601	1645	1645	1701	1801	1901	2001	2101	...	2201	...	2329
Husum a.	0955	1039	1059	1130	1230	1310	1310	1330	1357	1359	1429	1439	1529	1629	1710	1710	1730	1829	1929	2029	2129	...	2229	...	2358
Husum d.	0957	1041	1101	1131	1231	1312	1312	1331	1358	1400	1431	1441	1531	1631	1712	1712	1731	1831	1931	2031	2131	...	...	2244	...
Heide (Holst) a.	1018	1102	1129	1156	1256	1333	1333	1356	1420	1422	1456	1502	1556	1656	1733	1733	1756	1856	1956	2056	2156	...	...	2309	...
Heide (Holst) d.	1020	1104	1131	1202	1302	1335	1335	1402	1421	1423	1502	1504	1602	1702	1735	1735	1802	1902	2002	2102	2202	...	...	2310	...
Itzehoe a.	|	1139	1205	1236	1336	1412	1412	1436	1455	1458	1536	1539	1636	1736	1812	1812	1836	1936	2036	2146	2246	...	...	2354	...
Itzehoe d.	|	1155	1206	1237	1337	1414	1414	1437	1456	1459	1537	1555	1637	1737	1814	1814	1837	1937	2037	2147	2247	2323	...	...	...
Elmshorn **820** d.	|	|	1228	1302	1402	|	|	1502	|	|	1602	|	1702	1803	|	|	1902	2002	2102	2214	2314	2353	...	...	...
Hamburg Altona a.	1134	|	1249	1324	1424	|	|	1524	1538	1543	1624	|	1724	1824	|	|	1924	2024	2124	2235	2335	0020	...	...	...
Hamburg Hbf ... **820** a.	...	1243	*1311‡*	*1337**	*1437**	1511	1511	*1537**	*1601‡*	*1601‡*	*1637**	1643	*1737**	*1837**	1909	1909	*1937**	*2037**	*2137**	*2252*	*0001‡*	*0037**	...	...	...
Berlin Hbf **840** a.	...	|	...	...	...	...	...	...	...	...	...	|	...	...	2121	2121	...	...	...	...	...	...	...	...	...
Köln Hbf **800** a.	...	1649	...	...	...	...	...	...	...	...	...	2049	...	...	...	...	...	...	...	...	...	...	...	...	...

D – SYLTER STRAND. From / to Dresden on dates in Table **840**.
F – NORDFRIESLAND – [12] and ✕ Frankfurt - Koblenz - Köln - Westerland.
G – DEICHGRAF – [12] and ✕ Westerland - Köln - Koblenz - Frankfurt.
H – NORDFRIESLAND – [12] and ✕ Westerland - Köln - Koblenz - Heidelberg - Stuttgart.
J – WATTENMEER – [12] and 🍷 (Frankfurt ⑥⑦ -) Hannover - Westerland.
L – WATTENMEER – [12] and 🍷 Westerland - Hannover - Frankfurt.
N – ①–④ until Oct. 26; ① from Nov. 2. WATTENMEER – [12] and 🍷 Westerland - Hannover - Göttingen.
P – Daily July 20 - Oct. 25; ④–⑦ from Oct. 29.
R – Change trains at Husum on Ⓒ.
S – Until Oct. 25.
W – From Oct. 26.
Z – Until July 19.

* – Change trains at Elmshorn.
‡ – S-Bahn connection Hamburg Hbf - Hamburg Altona and v.v.
⊖ – On ⑦ until Oct. 25 Itzehoe a. 2317, d. 2318, Heide a. 0004, d. 0005, Husum a. 0033.
● – From Apr. 4 conveys [2] to / from Dagebüll Mole (Table **822**).
◇ – Operated by Nord-Ostsee-Bahn GmbH.

822 SCHLESWIG-HOLSTEIN BRANCH LINES

Neumünster - Heide - Büsum ☒

km		⚒		⚒	⑥k		Ⓐ																		
0	Neumünster d.	...	...	...	0537	...	0537	...	0737	...	0937	...	1137	...	1337	...	1537	...	1737	...	1937	...	...	...	2137
63	Heide a.	...	...	...	0646	...	0710	...	0846	...	1046	...	1246	...	1446	...	1646	...	1846	...	2046	...	...	...	2246
63	Heide d.	0451	...	0601	0701	0701	...	0801	0901	1001	1101	1201	1301	1401	1501	1601	1701	1801	1901	2001	2101	...	2208	...	...
87	Büsum a.	0517	...	0627	0727	0727	...	0827	0927	1027	1127	1227	1327	1427	1527	1627	1727	1827	1927	2027	2127	...	2234	...	...

	⚒	⚒		⚒	⑥k																			
Büsum d.	...	0521	...	0631	0631	...	0731	0831	0931	1031	1131	1231	1331	1431	1531	1631	1731	1831	1931	2031	2131	...	2238	...
Heide a.	...	0547	...	0657	0657	...	0757	0857	0957	1057	1157	1257	1357	1457	1557	1657	1757	1857	1957	2057	2157	...	2304	...
Heide d.	0517	...	...	...	0717	0717	...	0917	...	1117	...	1317	...	1517	...	1717	...	1917	...	2117	...	...	2317	...
Neumünster a.	0625	...	...	...	0825	0825	...	1025	...	1228	...	1425	...	1625	...	1825	...	2025	...	2225	...	...	0025	...

Husum - Bad St Peter Ording ◇

km		⚒								
0	Husum d.	0437	0537	and hourly until	1837	1937	2037	2137	2237	...
21	Tönning d.	0502	0602		1902	2002	2102	2202	2302	...
43	Bad St Peter Ording a.	0528	0628		1928	2028	2128	2228	2328	...

	⚒								
Bad St Peter Ording d.	0534	0634	and hourly until	1934	2034	2134	2234	2334	...
Tönning d.	0605	0705		2005	2105	2205	2305	0005	...
Husum a.	0624	0724		2024	2124	2224	2324	0024	...

Niebüll - Dagebüll Mole ⊡

km	*Until Oct. 25*	◐					★	★		★	★	⑤–⑦
	Hamburg Hbf a.	...	...	...	...	...	0915	1049	...	1315	1449r	...
	Niebüll a.	...	...	...	...	...	1145	1310	...	1546	1710	...
0	Niebüll neg d.	0625	0805	0905	1035	1135	1205	1325	1425	1605	1725	1910
14	Dagebüll Mole a.	0644	0824	0924	1054	1150	1220	1345	1451	1624	1740	1929

Until Oct. 25	◧		★		★	★		★		⑤–⑦	🚌 ①–④
Dagebüll Mole d.	0705	0825	0935	1100	1200	1335	1435	1605	1835	1935	1935
Niebüll neg a.	0724	0844	0954	1119	1226	1354	1454	1629	1854	1954	1955
Niebüll d.	...	...	1013	...	1245	1413	...	1645	...	...	...
Hamburg Hbf a.	...	...	1243	...	1511	1643	...	1909	...	...	...

km	*From Oct. 26*	Ⓐ	🚌 Ⓒ	⚒		🚌 Ⓐ					🚌 ♥	⑤⑦
0	Niebüll neg d.	0635	0705	0805	0905	1035	1135	1320	1410	1720	1805	1910
14	Dagebüll Mole a.	0654	0720	0824	0920	1055	1154	1335	1429	1735	1825	1929

From Oct. 26	Ⓐ	🚌 Ⓒ	⚒		🚌 Ⓐ					🚌 ♥	⑤⑦
Dagebüll Mole d.	0705	0725	0825	0923	1100	1200	1340	1435	1740	1835	1935
Niebüll neg a.	0724	0740	0844	0938	1120	1219	1355	1454	1755	1855	1954

k – Not Oct. 3.
r – 1502 until July 19.
♥ – ①②③④⑥ (not Dec. 12).
◐ – By 🚌 on ⑥⑦ (Niebüll d. 0705, Dagebüll Mole a. 0720).
◧ – By 🚌 on ⑥⑦ (Dagebüll Mole d. 0725, Niebüll a. 0740).

★ – Conveys [2] (*IC*) from / to Hamburg and beyond (see Table **821**).
☒ – **Operator**: Schleswig-Holstein-Bahn GmbH.
◇ – **Operator**: Nord-Ostsee-Bahn GmbH.
⊡ – **Operator**: Norddeutsche Eisenbahngesellschaft Niebüll GmbH.
✆ +49 (0) 4661 98088 90. Niebüll neg station is situated a short distance from the Niebüll DB station forecourt.

823 HAMBURG - NEUMÜNSTER - FLENSBURG - PADBORG

RE / RB services except where shown

km																									
		①–⑥	CNL 482 ℝ▲ A🍷	⚒	C	Ⓐ				ICE 386 🍷									ICE 380 ◇🍷				IC 1888 ⑦ M🍷			IC 1870 ⑦ ◇
0	**Hamburg** Hbf .... 820 d.	2323p	...	...	0520z	0520	0620	0720	0843	0930	0920	1043	1120	1243	1320	1443	1520	1643	1730r	1720	1843	1920	2032	2050	2120	2233
37	Elmshorn .... 820 d.	2353p	...	...	0552z	0552	0650	0750	0910	|	0950	1110	1150	1310	1350	1510	1550	1710	|	1750	1910	1950	|	2117	2150	|
73	Neumünster .... 820 d.	0033	0444	0533	0635	0657	0733	0835	0933	1022	1035	1133	1235	1333	1435	1533	1635	1733	1822	1835	1933	2033	2122	2143	2233	2321
112	Rendsburg .... 824 d.	0104	|	0604	0709	0727	0804	0909	1004	1049	1109	1204	1309	1404	1509	1604	1709	1804	1854	1909	2004	2104	2150	2217	2304	2349
136	Schleswig .... 824 d.	0120	|	0620	0725	0743	0821	0925	1020	1105	1125	1220	1325	1420	1525	1620	1725	1820	1910	1925	2020	2120	2205	2233	2320	0005
174	**Flensburg** .... a.	0148	0547	0648	0752	0810	0852	0952	1045	1125	1152	1245	1352	1445	1552	1645	1752	1845	1931	1952	2045	2148	2226	2258	2348	0027
174	**Flensburg** .... 710 d.	...	0549	0701	...	...	0901	...	1101	1132	...	1301	...	1501	...	1701	...	1901	1939	...	2101	...	...	...	...	...
186	**Padborg** 🏛 .... 710 a.	...	0600	0711	...	...	0911	...	1111	1142	...	1311	...	1511	...	1711	...	1911	1950	...	2111	...	...	...	...	...
	Århus 700 .... a.	...	...	...	...	...	...	...	...	1350	...	...	...	...	...	...	...	...	2207	...	...	...	...	...	...	...

	⚒	E						ICE 381 ◇🍷		IC 1871 ⑤ ◇🍷		IC 1807 ⑤					ICE 387 🍷							CNL 483 ℝ A🍷	Ⓑ
Århus 700 .... d.	...	...	...	...	...	...	...	0753	...	...	...	...	...	...	...	...	1411	...	...	...	...	...	...	...	...
Padborg 🏛 .... 710 d.	...	...	...	...	0754	...	0945	1010	...	...	1154	...	...	1345	...	1545	1640	...	1745	...	1945	...	2145	2218	...
Flensburg .... 710 a.	...	...	...	...	0807	...	0958	1022	...	...	1207	...	...	1358	...	1558	1652	...	1758	...	1958	...	2158	2231	...
Flensburg .... d.	0410	0510	0609	0710	0809	0910	1009	1024	1110	1201	1209	1256	1310	1409	1510	1609	1654	1710	1809	1910	2008	2110	...	2233	2310
Schleswig .... 824 d.	0438	0538	0634	0738	0834	0938	1034	1045	1138	1223	1234	1317	1338	1434	1538	1634	1716	1738	1834	1938	2038	2138	...	|	2338
Rendsburg .... 824 d.	0457	0557	0651	0757	0851	0957	1051	1103	1157	1241	1251	1334	1357	1451	1557	1651	1733	1757	1851	1957	2057	2157	...	|	2357
Neumünster .... 820 a.	0526	0626	0721	0826	0921	1027	1121	1130	1226	1308	1321	1358	1428	1521	1626	1721	1759	1826	1921	2026	2126	2226	...	2333	0026
Elmshorn .... 820 a.	0607	0707	0745	0907	0945	1107	1145	|	1307	1337	1345	|	1507	1545	1707	1745	|	1907	1945	2107	2207	2307	...	...	...
Hamburg Hbf .... 820 a.	0637	0737	0814	0937	1014	1137	1214	1232	1337	1408	1414	1448	1537	1614	1737	1814	1853	1937	2014	2137	2237	2337	...	...	...

A – HANS CHRISTIAN ANDERSEN – 🛏 1, 2 cl., 🛌 2 cl. and (2) München - København and v.v. For Basel cars (train number **472/3** – AURORA) and Amsterdam via Köln cars (train number **40447/40483** – BOREALIS) see overnight trains summary on page 363. For overnight journeys only.
C – ⑥⑦ to July 4; ⑥ July 11 - Sept. 12; ⑥⑦ from Sept. 19.
E – ①–⑥ (daily to July 4 and from Sept. 14).
M – From München (Table **900**).

p – Previous day.
r – 1736 June 20 - July 3.
z – ⑥ (not Oct. 3).

◇ – From/to Berlin (Table **840**).

▲ – 7–11 minutes later on ①–⑥ June 22 - July 20 (also June 28). On ⑦ July 5 - Sept. 13 Neumünster d. 0504 (0513 on July 5, 12, 19); Flensburg a. 0639, d. 0641, Padborg a. 0707.

824 KIEL - HUSUM and FLENSBURG

RB services

km		△ ①–⑥	⚒	e								
0	**Kiel** Hbf............d.	0001	0344	0501	0556e	0701	and hourly until	2001	2101	2201	2301
40	Rendsburg . **823** d.	0034	0431	0534	0634	0734		2034	2134	2234	2334
65	Schleswig .. **823** d.	0052	0449	0552	0652	0752		2052	2152	2252	2352
102	**Husum**..............a.	0124	0521	0624	0724	0824		2124	2224	2324	0024

	△ ⚒								Ⓑ
Husum ....d.	0422	0529	...	0635	and hourly until	2035	2135	2235	2335
Schleswig .... **823** d.	0454	0601	...	0707		2107	2207	2307	0007
Rendsburg .... **823** d.	0514	0621	...	0727		2127	2227	2327	0027
Kiel Hbf........................a.	0549	0654e	...	0800		2200	2300	2400	0100

km		Ⓐ	⚒								
0	**Kiel** Hbf...........d.	0406	0520	0642	0742	and hourly until	2042	2142	2242	2342	...
29	Eckernförde .....d.	0432	0554	0710	0809		2109	2209	2309	0011	...
50	Süderbrarup ....d.	0450	0614	0729	0829		2129	2229	2329	0031	...
81	**Flensburg**.......a.	0519	0642	0756	0856		2156	2256	2358	0058	...

	⚒								
Flensburg ....d.	0445	0547	...	0703	and hourly until	2103	2203	...	2323
Süderbrarup ....d.	0514	0614	...	0729		2129	2229	...	2350
Eckernförde ....d.	0532	0632	...	0749		2149	2249	...	0011
Kiel Hbf........................a.	0604	0700	...	0816		2216	2316	...	0038

e – ①–⑥ (daily to July 4 and from Sept. 14).

△ – Kiel - Husum operator: Nord-Ostsee-Bahn GmbH. ✆ +49 (0) 180 10 180 11.

825 HAMBURG - LÜBECK - PUTTGARDEN

RB / RE services except where shown

km																									
							EC 31 J R				ICE 33 R🍷						IC 2120 G F			EC 35 R				EC 237 Q R		
0	**Hamburg** Hbf .... d.	0026	0511	0611	...	0711	0725	0811	...	0911	0928	1011	...	1111	1211	...	1233	...	1311	1328	1411	...	1511	1528	1611	...
40	Bad Oldesloe .... d.	0049	0534	0634	...	0734	|	0834	...	0934	|	1034	...	1134	1234	...	|	...	1334	|	1434	...	1534	|	1634	...
63	**Lübeck** Hbf .... a.	0106	0551	0651	...	0751	0804	0851	...	0951	1004	1051	...	1151	1251	...	1310	...	1352	1404	1451	...	1551	1604	1651	...
															H	H	|	G								
63	**Lübeck** Hbf .... d.	...	0611	0711	0711	0811	0806	0911	0911	1011	1006	1111	1111	1211	1311	1311	1313	1318	1411	1406	1511	1511	1611	1606	1711	1711
93	Neustadt (Holst) ...... a.	...	0651	0751	|	0851	|	0951	|	1051	|	1153	|	1251	1353	|	|	1401	1451	|	1553	|	1651	|	1753	|
115	Oldenburg (Holst) ...... d.	...	...	...	0811	...	0838	...	1011	...	1038	...	1211	...	...	1411	1410	...	...	1438	...	1611	...	1638	...	1811
151	**Puttgarden** 🏛 .... a.	...	...	...	0839	...	0904	...	1039	...	1105	...	1239	...	...	1439	1435	...	...	1505	...	1639	...	1705	...	1839
	København H 720 .. a.	...	...	...	...	...	1231v	...	...	...	1431v	...	...	...	...	...	...	...	...	1827v	...	...	...	2022v	...	...

		ICE 37 ¶ B R				EC 39 L R		ICE 584 Ⓑ M			
Hamburg Hbf .... d.	1711	1728	1811	...	1911	1928	2011	2103	2111	2211	2326
Bad Oldesloe .... d.	1734	|	1834	...	1934	|	2034	|	2134	2234	2349
Lübeck Hbf .... a.	1751	1804	1851	...	1951	2004	2051	2139	2151	2251	0006
Lübeck Hbf .... d.	1811	1806	1911	1911	2011	2006	2111	...	2211	2311	...
Neustadt (Holst) ..... a.	1851	|	1953	|	2051	|	2149	...	2245	2345	...
Oldenburg (Holst) ...... d.	...	1838	...	2011	...	2038	2220b	...	...	0014	...
Puttgarden 🏛 .... a.	...	1905	...	2039	...	2105	2248b	...	...	0042	...
København H 720 .. a.	...	2222v	...	...	...	0019	...	...	...	...	...

			⚒	ICE 583 ①–⑥ M						IC 2327 A	
København H 720 d.	...	...	...	...	...	...	...	...	...	...	...
Puttgarden 🏛 .... d.	...	...	...	...	0521r	0622	...	...	...	0907	0922
Oldenburg (Holst)... d.	...	...	...	...	0547r	0648	...	...	...	0933	0948
Neustadt (Holst) d.	...	...	0517	...	0617	|	0709	0821	0917	|	|
Lübeck Hbf .... a.	...	...	0550	...	0650	0750	0750	0855	0950	1032	1055
			d								
Lübeck Hbf .... d.	0415	0510	0610	0617	0710	...	0810	0910	1010	1036	...
Bad Oldesloe .... d.	0431	0527	0627	|	0727	...	0827	0927	1027	|	...
Hamburg Hbf .... a.	0508	0551	0651	0654	0751	...	0851	0951	1051	1115	...

		ICE 38 B R				EC 238 Q R				EC 36 R		IC 2121 G F	H		EC 34 L R				ICE 32 R🍷				EC 30 G R			
København H 720 .. d.	...	0726z	...	...	...	0926z	...	...	...	1126z	...	...	...	...	1326z	...	...	...	1526z	...	...	...	1726z	...	...	...
Puttgarden 🏛 .... d.	...	1042	...	1122	...	1242	...	1322	...	1442	...	1507	1522	...	1642	...	1722	...	1842	...	1922	...	2042	...	2113	...
Oldenburg (Holst) ...... d.	...	1106	...	1148	...	1306	...	1348	...	1506	...	1533	1548	...	1706	...	1748	...	1906	...	1948	...	2106	...	2139	...
Neustadt (Holst) ..... d.	1013	|	1113	|	1213	|	1313	|	1413	|	1513	|	|	1613j	|	1713	|	1813	|	1913	|	2013	|	2113	2213	2313
Lübeck Hbf .... a.	1055	1136	1155	1255	1255	1336	1355	1455	1455	1536	1555	1629	1655	1655	1736	1754	1854	1854	1936	1955	2055	2055	2136	2155	2248	2348
Lübeck Hbf .... d.	1110	1138	1210	...	1310	1338	1410	...	1510	1538	1610	1633	...	1710	1738	1810	...	1910	1938	2010	...	2110	2138	2210	2310	0010
Bad Oldesloe .... d.	1127	|	1227	...	1327	|	1427	...	1527	|	1627	|	...	1727	|	1827	...	1927	|	2027	...	2127	|	2227	2327	0027
Hamburg Hbf .... a.	1151	1216	1252	...	1351	1416	1451	...	1551	1616	1651	1715	...	1751	1816	1851	...	1951	2016	2051	...	2151	2216	2251	2351	0051

Lübeck - Travemünde

km		Ⓐ🚌	🚌			●	
0	**Lübeck** Hbf ....d.	0605	0705	...	0801	and hourly until	2201	...
18	Travemünde Skandinavienkai ⊡ ...a.	0638	0738	...	0818		2218	...
21	**Travemünde** Strand ....a.	0644	0744	...	0823		2223	...

	Ⓐ🚌	🚌			♥			
Travemünde Strand ....d.	0613	0713	...	0831	and hourly until	2231	...	...
Travemünde Skandinavienkai ⊡ d.	0619	0719	...	0836		2236	...	...
Lübeck Hbf ....a.	0652	0752	...	0853		2253	...	...

A – ①–⑥ until Oct. 3 (also July 19, 26, Aug. 2, 9, Oct. 4); ⑤ from Oct. 9. LÜBECKER BUCHT – (12) Puttgarden - Köln - Frankfurt - Passau.
B – (12) and 🍷 Berlin - Hamburg - København and v.v.
F – FEHMARN – (12) Frankfurt - Köln - Puttgarden and v.v.
G – Until Oct. 25.
H – From Oct. 26.
J – Until Oct. 26.
L – June 19 - Aug. 23.
M – From/to München (Table **900**).

Q – Daily until Aug. 30; ⑥⑦ Sept 5 - 27.
R – Reservation recommended.

b – Neustadt - Puttgarden on Ⓑ (not Oct. 2).
d – Daily from Lübeck
j – 1621 until Oct. 25.
r – ⚒ only.
v – 11–20 minutes earlier from Aug. 10.
z – 16 minutes later from Aug. 10.

● – On June 15, 22, Sept. 21, 28 services from Lübeck 0801 - 1301 are replaced by 🚌 (arrivals are up to 21 minutes later).
♥ – On June 15, 22, Sept. 21, 28 services from Travemünde Strand 0831 - 1331 are replaced by 🚌 (departures are up to 18 minutes earlier).
¶ – June 20 - July 3 Hamburg d. 1736, Lübeck a. 1809, d. 1811, Oldenburg d. 1843, then as shown.
⊡ – For sailings to/from Trelleborg (Table **2390**) and Helsinki (Table **2485**).

826 KIEL - LÜBECK - BAD KLEINEN

RE / RB services

km																									
				ⒶS				S				S				P			N				H		
0	**Kiel** Hbf d.	...	0444	...	...	0544	0644	...	each train runs every **two** hours until	1344	1444	...	...	1544	1644	...	1744	1844	...	1944	2044	2144	...	2244	2344
33	Plön d.	...	0516	...	...	0616	0716	...		1416	1516	...	...	1616	1716	...	1816	1916	...	2016	2116	2216	...	2316	0016
47	Eutin d.	...	0530	...	...	0630	0730	...		1430	1530	...	...	1630	1730	...	1830	1930	...	2030	2130	2230	...	2330	0030
80	**Lübeck** Hbf a.	...	0558	...	...	0656	0756	...		1456	1556	...	...	1656	1756	...	1856	1956	...	2056	2156	2256	...	2357	0058
80	**Lübeck** Hbf d.	0504	...	0601	...	0704	...	0801		1504	...	1601	...	1704	...	1801	1904	...	2001	2104	...	...	2301	...	...
119	Grevesmühlen d.	0538	...	0638	...	0741	...	0838		1541	...	1638	...	1741	...	1838	1941	...	2038	2141	...	...	2338	...	...
142	**Bad Kleinen** a.	0553	...	0656	...	0755	...	0856		1555	...	1656	...	1755	...	1856	1955	...	2056	2155	...	...	2356	...	...

				⚒	ⒶH		Ⓐ		N			S			S				S			S			
Bad Kleinen d.	...	...	...	...	0432	...	0518	0602	0703	...	0802	0903	...	each train runs every **two** hours until	1703	...	1802	...	1903	...	2002	2103	...	2202	...
Grevesmühlen d.	...	...	...	...	0446	...	0540	0617	0722	...	0817	0922	...		1722	...	1817	...	1922	...	2017	2122	...	2221	...
Lübeck Hbf a.	...	...	...	...	0525	...	0622	0654	0756	...	0854	0956	...		1756	...	1854	...	1956	...	2054	2156	...	2256	...
Lübeck Hbf d.	0018	...	0400	0500	...	0603	...	0703	...	0803	0903	...	1003		...	1803	1903	...	...	2003	2103	...	2201	...	2301
Eutin d.	0049	...	0428	0528	...	0628	...	0728	...	0828	0928	...	1028		...	1828	1928	...	...	2028	2128	...	2229	...	2329
Plön d.	0105	...	0444	0544	...	0644	...	0744	...	0844	0944	...	1044		...	1844	1944	...	...	2044	2144	...	2244	...	2344
Kiel Hbf a.	0145	...	0515	0615	...	0715	...	0815	...	0915	1015	...	1115		...	1915	2015	...	...	2115	2215	...	2315	...	0015

H – From / to Schwerin (Table **830**). **N** – To / from Neubrandenburg (Table **836**). **P** – To Pasewalk (Table **836**). **S** – To / from Szczecin (Table **836**).

827 LÜBECK - BÜCHEN - LÜNEBURG

RB services

km		Ⓐ							
0	**Lübeck** Hbf d.	0505	0605	0702	0810	and at the same minutes past each hour until	2010	2110	2324
9	Lübeck Flughafen ✈ d.	0513	0613	0711	0818		2018	2118	2332
22	Ratzeburg d.	0528	0627	0730	0830		2030	2130	2344
31	Mölln (Lauenburg) d.	0535	0634	0737	0837		2037	2137	2352
50	Büchen a.	0548	0646	0749	0849		2049	2149	0004
50	Büchen d.	0556	0656	0756	0905		2105	2205	...
79	**Lüneburg** a.	0619	0719	0819	0927		2127	2227	...

	Ⓐ	Ⓐ	Ⓒ							
Lüneburg d.	0526	0628	0628	0728	0825	0933	and at the same minutes past each hour until	1933	2033	2245
Büchen a.	0548	0650	0650	0750	0847	0955		1955	2055	2308
Büchen d.	0556	0655	0710	0810	0910	1010		2010	2110	2324
Mölln (Lauenburg) d.	0608	0707	0722	0822	0922	1022		2022	2122	2336
Ratzeburg d.	0616	0715	0731	0831	0931	1031		2031	2131	2345
Lübeck Flughafen ✈ d.	0625	0724	0740	0840	0940	1040		2040	2140	2354
Lübeck Hbf a.	0633	0732	0748	0848	0948	1048		2048	2148	0002

830 HAMBURG - ROSTOCK - STRALSUND

km	See note ▲	*RE* 33203	*RE* 33205	*RE* 33090	*RE* 33001	*RE* 33207	*IC* 2186	*RE* 33023	*RE* 33005	*RE* 33209	*IC* 2184	*RE* 33007	*RE* 33211	*IC* 2182	*IC* 2238	*RE* 33009	*RE* 33213	*IC* 2212	*RE* 33011	*RE* 33215	*IC* 2376	*RE* 33013	*RE* 33217	*IC* 2116	*IC* 2174
			①–⑤	①–⑤			①	①–⑤			①–⑥				B										⑤
				L							🍷♦			♦	♦			🍴♦			🍷♦			🍴♦	🍷♦
	Hamburg Altona d.	...	...	...	...	...	0528	...	...	...	...	...	...	...	...	...	...	...	...	...	...	...	...	...	...
0	**Hamburg** Hbf d.	...	...	...	...	...	0541	*0525*	0636	...	0744	0837	...	0942	...	1030	...	1117	1230	...	1344	1430	...	1516	1542
47	Büchen d.	...	...	...	0504a	...	|	*0559*t	0704	...	|	0905	...	|	...	1058	...	|	1304	...	|	1458	...	|	|
123	**Schwerin** Hbf a.	...	...	...	0549a	...	0635	*0652*	0749	...	0835	0950	...	1035	...	1149	...	1208	1349	...	1435	1549	...	1608	1635
123	**Schwerin** Hbf **836 837** d.	...	...	0412	0551	...	0637	0704	0751	...	0837	0951	...	1037	1055	1151	...	1210	1351	...	1437	1551	...	1610	1637
140	Bad Kleinen ... **836 837** d.	...	...	0426	0602	...	|	0718	0802	...	|	1002	...	|	1109	1202	...	|	1402	...	|	1602	...	|	|
181	Bützow **836** d.	...	...	...	0629	...	0710	0747	0829	...	0910	1029	...	1110	1135	1229	...	1243	1429	...	1511	1629	...	1643b	1710
211	**Rostock** Hbf a.	...	...	...	0652	...	0732	0810	0852	...	0932	1052	...	1132	1154	1252	...	1306	1452	...	1532	1652	...	1704	1732
211	**Rostock** Hbf d.	0453	0553	...	...	0700	0738	...	...	0900	0938	...	1100	1138k	...	...	1300	1317	...	1500	1538	...	1700	1717	...
240	Ribnitz-D'garten West d.	0516	0616	...	...	0723	0759	...	...	0921	0959	...	1121	1159k	...	...	1321	1339	...	1521	1559	...	1721	1739	...
265	Velgast d.	0541	0638	...	...	0741	0816	...	...	0941	1016	...	1141	1216k	...	...	1341	1355	...	1541	1616	...	1741	1754	...
283	**Stralsund** a.	0556	0656	...	...	0756	0830	...	...	0956	1030	...	1156	1230k	...	...	1356	1412	...	1556	1630	...	1756	1812	...
	Ostseebad Binz **844** a.	|	|	...	...	|	0932	...	...	|	1132	...	|	...	...	...	|	1516	...	|	1741h	...	|	...	...
	Sassnitz **844** a.	0655	0755	...	...	0855	...	...	...	1055	...	...	1255	...	...	...	1455	...	...	1655	...	...	1855	...	...

See note ▲	*RE* 33015	*RE* 33219	*IC* 2372	*RE* 33017	*RE* 33221	*IC* 2188	*IC* 2270	*RE* 33019	*IC* 2288	*RE* 33021	*RB* 33287
						①–④	⑤⑦		⑦		
			A 🍷				🍷♦		🍷♦		
Hamburg Altona d.	...	...	...	...	...	1921	...	...	...	...	...
Hamburg Hbf d.	1636	...	1744	1836	...	1944	1944	2036	2146	2250	*0004*r
Büchen d.	1704	...	|	1904	...	|	|	2104	2210	2318	0058
Schwerin Hbf a.	1749	...	1835	1949	...	2035	2035	2149	2241	0003	0147
Schwerin Hbf **836 837** d.	1751	...	1837	1951	...	2037	2037	2151	2247	0004	...
Bad Kleinen ... **836 837** d.	1802	...	|	2002	...	|	|	2202	|	0015	...
Bützow **836** d.	1829	...	1910	2029	...	2110	2110	2229	2320	0041	...
Rostock Hbf a.	1852	...	1932	2052	...	2132	2132	2252	2341	0102	...
Rostock Hbf d.	...	1900	1938	...	2100	...	2139	...	...	...	...
Ribnitz-Damgarten West d.	...	1921	1959	...	2121	...	2159	...	...	...	...
Velgast d.	...	1941	2016	...	2141	...	2216	...	...	...	...
Stralsund a.	...	1956	2032	...	2156	...	2230	...	...	...	...
Ostseebad Binz **844** a.	...	|	...	...	|	...	...	...	...	...	...
Sassnitz **844** a.	...	2055	...	...	2255	...	...	...	...	...	...

See note ▲	*RE* 33000	*RE* 33030	*IC* 2189	*RE* 33002	*RE* 33204	*IC* 2279	*RE* 33206	*RE* 33004	*IC* 2115
	①–⑤		①–⑥		①–⑤	①–⑥			
			🍷			A 🍷			🍴♦
Sassnitz **844** d.	...	...	...	...	0403	...	0505	...	...
Ostseebad Binz **844** d.	...	...	...	...	|	...	|	...	...
Stralsund d.	...	...	...	...	0455	0527	0600	...	0727
Velgast d.	...	...	...	...	0509	0541	0615	...	0741
Ribnitz-Damgarten West d.	...	...	...	...	0525	0555	0632	...	0755
Rostock Hbf a.	...	...	...	...	0547	0616	0654	...	0819
Rostock Hbf d.	...	...	0500	0507	...	0625	...	0707	0825
Bützow **836** d.	...	...	0521	0528	...	0646	...	0728	0846
Bad Kleinen **836 837** d.	...	...	0547	0553	...	|	...	0753	|
Schwerin Hbf **836 837** a.	...	...	0600	0604	...	0721	...	0804	0921
Schwerin Hbf d.	0400	0501	0604	0615	...	0723	...	0807	0923
Büchen d.	0450	0555	0636	0702	...	|	...	0854	|
Hamburg Hbf a.	0518	0624	0701	0729	...	0819	...	0924	1019
Hamburg Altona a.	...	...	0715	...	...	...	...	...	...

See note ▲	*RE* 33208	*RE* 33006	*IC* 2373	*RE* 33210	*RE* 33008	*IC* 2213	*RE* 33212	*RE* 33010	*IC* 2239	*IC* 2377	*RE* 33214	*RE* 33012	*IC* 2379	*RE* 33216	*RE* 33014	*IC* 2183	*IC* 2183	*RE* 33218	*RE* 33016	*IC* 2185	*RE* 33220	*RE* 33018	*RB* 33286	*RE* 33222	*RE* 33095
									C							⑦	⑤			⑦					
			A 🍷			🍴♦			♦	🍷♦			🍷♦			H 🍴	🍷			H					L
Sassnitz **844** d.	0705	...	...	0905	...	...	1105	...	...	...	1305	...	...	1505	...	...	...	...	...	...	1905	...	...	2103	...
Ostseebad Binz **844** d.	|	...	...	|	...	1029	|	...	...	1229	|	...	...	|	...	1629	...	1706	...	...	|	...	...	|	...
Stralsund d.	0800	...	0927	1000	...	1127	1200	...	...	1327	1400	...	1527	1600	...	1727	1727	1800	...	1927	2000	...	...	2200	...
Velgast d.	0815	...	0941	1015	...	1141	1215	...	...	1341	1415	...	1541	1615	...	1741	1741	1815	...	1941	2015	...	...	2215	...
Ribnitz-Damgarten West d.	0833	...	0955	1032	...	1155	1232	...	...	1400	1432	...	1555	1632	...	1800	1800	1832	...	1955	2032	...	...	2232	...
Rostock Hbf a.	0854	...	1019	1054	...	1219	1254	...	...	1419	1454	...	1619	1654	...	1820	1820	1854	...	2019	2054	...	...	2254	...
Rostock Hbf d.	...	0907	1025	...	1107	1243	...	1307	1405	1425	...	1507	1625	...	1707	1825	1825	...	1907	2025	...	2107	...	*2307*	...
Bützow **836** d.	...	0928	1046	...	1128	1304	...	1328	1427	1446	...	1528	1646	...	1728	1846	1846	...	1928	2046	...	2128	...	*2328*	...
Bad Kleinen ... **836 837** d.	...	0953	|	...	1153	|	...	1353	1449	|	...	1553	|	...	1753	|	|	...	1953	|	...	2153	...	*2353*	0002
Schwerin Hbf **836 837** a.	...	1004	1121	...	1204	1337	...	1404	1500	1521	...	1604	1721	...	1804	1921	1921	...	2004	2121	...	2204	...	*0004*	0015
Schwerin Hbf d.	...	1012	1123	...	1212	1339	...	1407	...	1523	...	1607	1723	...	1807	1923	1923	...	2007	2123	...	...	2211	...	...
Büchen d.	...	1057	|	...	1257	|	...	1454	...	|	...	1658	|	...	1854	|	|	...	2054	|	...	...	2314	...	...
Hamburg Hbf a.	...	1127	1216	...	1327	1431	...	1524	...	1616	...	1727	1816	...	1924	2016	2016	...	2124	2216	...	...	*0018*s	...	...
Hamburg Altona a.	...	...	...	...	...	...	...	...	...	...	...	...	...	...	...	...	...	...	...	...	...	...	...	...	...

♦ – **NOTES** (LISTED BY TRAIN NUMBER)

2115/6 – [12] and 🍴 (Greifswald ①–⑤ -) Stralsund - Köln - Koblenz - Heidelberg - Stuttgart and v.v.
2174 – [12] and 🍷 Karlsruhe - Frankfurt - Hannover - Hamburg - Rostock.
2182 – [12] (Kassel ①–⑤ -) (Hannover ①–⑥ -) Hamburg - Stralsund.
2184 – ARKONA – [12] and 🍷 (Hannover ①–⑤ -) Hamburg - Ostseebad Binz.
2212 – RÜGEN – [12] and 🍴 Koblenz - Köln - Hamburg - Ostseebad Binz.
2213 – RÜGEN – [12] and 🍴 Ostseebad Binz - Hamburg - Köln - Koblenz - Heidelberg - Stuttgart.
2238/9 – WARNOW – [12] Leipzig - Magdeburg - Stendal - Rostock - Warnemünde and v.v.
2270 – SCHWARZWALD – [12] and 🍷 Konstanz - Karlsruhe - Frankfurt - Hannover - Hamburg - Stralsund.
2288 – [12] and 🍷 Karlsruhe - Frankfurt - Hannover - Hamburg - Rostock.
2376 – [12] and 🍷 (Karlsruhe ①–⑥ -) Frankfurt - Hannover - Hamburg - Stralsund (- Ostseebad Binz ⑥).
2377 – ARKONA – [12] and 🍷 Ostseebad Binz - Hamburg - Hannover - Frankfurt (- Karlsruhe ⑤⑦).
2379 – [12] and 🍷 Stralsund - Hamburg - Hannover (- Göttingen ⑤⑦) (- Frankfurt ⑤).

A – [12] and 🍷 Stralsund - Hamburg - Hannover - Frankfurt - Karlsruhe and v.v.
B – Daily until Aug. 30; ⑤⑥ Sept. 4 - Oct. 24. Continues to Warnemünde (a. 1228).
C – Daily until Aug. 30; ⑤⑦ Sept. 4 - Oct. 25. Starts from Warnemünde (d. 1348).

H – To Hannover (Table **902**).
L – To / from Lübeck (Table **826**).

a – ①–⑤ only.
b – Ⓑ only.
h – ⑥ only.
k – On ⑥ until Oct. 24 departs Rostock 1149, Ribnitz 1216, Velgast 1237, arrives Stralsund 1249.
r – *S-Bahn* connection. Change trains at Aumühle (a. *0036*, d. 0038).
s – *S-Bahn* connection. Change trains at Aumühle (a. 2333, d. *2346*).
t – *0553* on ①.

▲ – **June 14 - July 19** all services are subject to alteration Hannover - Hamburg and v.v. During this period, most *IC* services that normally operate from / to Hannover (and south thereof) will start from / terminate at Hamburg Hbf (and will operate with a different train number).

ROSTOCK - WARNEMÜNDE and SEEHAFEN NORD — 831

S-Bahn

Rostock Hbf - Rostock Seehafen Nord and v.v. *12 km*. Journey time: 18 minutes. **Rostock Überseehafen ferry terminal** is situated just over 1 km from Seehafen Nord station.
From Rostock Hbf at 0434 Ⓐ, 0534 Ⓐ, 0634, 0734 Ⓐ, 0834, 0934, 1034, 1134, 1234, 1334, 1434, 1534, 1634, 1734, 1834, 1934, 2034 and 2134.
From Rostock Seehafen Nord at 0506 Ⓐ, 0603 Ⓐ, 0706, 0806 Ⓐ, 0906, 1006, 1106, 1206, 1306, 1403, 1503, 1603, 1706, 1806, 1906, 2006, 2106 and 2206.

Rostock Hbf - Warnemünde and v.v. *13 km*. Journey time: 21 minutes.

From Rostock Hbf on Ⓐ at 0001, 0401, 0431, 0446, 0501, 0516, 0531, 0546, 0556 and every 10 minutes until 0816, 0831 and every 15 minutes until 1416, 1426 and every 10 minutes until 1716, 1731 and every 15 minutes until 2016, 2036, 2101, 2141, 2201, 2231 and 2301.
From Rostock Hbf on © at 0001, 0431, 0501, 0531, 0601, 0631, 0701, 0716 and every 15 minutes until 2016, 2036, 2101, 2141, 2201, 2231 and 2301.

From Warnemünde on Ⓐ at 0037, 0407, 0432, 0507, 0522, 0532 and every 10 minutes until 0822, 0837 and every 15 minutes until 1422, 1432 and every 10 minutes until 1722, 1737 and every 15 minutes until 2037, 2107, 2137, 2207, 2237 and 2307.
From Warnemünde on © at 0037, 0432, 0507, 0532, 0552, 0607, 0637, 0707, 0737, 0752 and every 15 minutes until 2037, 2107, 2137, 2207, 2237 and 2307.

BERLIN - KOSTRZYN — 832

Niederbarnimer Eisenbahn (2nd class only)

km									
0	**Berlin** Lichtenberg ..... d.	0534	0634	each train	1934	2034	...	...	...
23	Strausberg ..... d.	0552	0652	runs every	1952	2052	...	...	...
80	**Kostrzyn** 🚌 ..... a.	0652	0743	two hours until	2052	2143	...	...	...

Kostrzyn 🚌 ..... d.	0503	...	0558	0705	each train	1958	2105	...
Strausberg ..... d.	0611	...	0711	0811	runs every	2111	2211	...
Berlin Lichtenberg ... a.	0628	...	0728	0828	two hours until	2128	2228	...

WISMAR - ROSTOCK — 833

RE services

km		Ⓐ								
0	**Wismar** ..... d.	0442	0542	...	0642	and	2042	...	2142	...
22	Neubukow ..... d.	0511	0611	...	0711	hourly	2111	...	2211	...
41	Bad Doberan ▲ ..... d.	0530	0630	...	0730	until	2130	...	2230	...
57	**Rostock** Hbf ..... a.	0551	0651	...	0751		2151	...	2250	...

	Ⓐ								
Rostock Hbf ..... d.	0412	0509	...	0606	and	2106	...	2206	...
Bad Doberan ▲ ..... d.	0432	0532	...	0632	hourly	2132	...	2225	...
Neubukow ..... d.	0451	0551	...	0651	until	2151	...	...	...
Wismar ..... a.	0515	0615	...	0715		2215	...	...	...

▲ – **BAD DOBERAN - OSTSEEBAD KÜHLUNGSBORN WEST**. All services worked by steam locomotive. 2nd class only. Journey time: 40 minutes.
Operator: Mecklenburgische Bäderbahn Molli GmbH, Am Bahnhof, 18209 Bad Doberan. ✆ +49 (0) 38203 4150, Fax +49 (0) 38203 41512. **Service until Nov. 1**.
From **Bad Doberan** at 0835 Ⓐ, 0936, 1036, 1136, 1236, 1343, 1436, 1536, 1636, 1745 and 1845.
From **Ostseebad Kühlungsborn West** at 0643 Ⓐ, 0828, 0935, 1035, 1135, 1235, 1335, 1435, 1535, 1635 and 1735.

ROSTOCK and STRALSUND - BERLIN - LUTHERSTADT WITTENBERG — 835

RE services

km			◐	①–⑤					ICE 1709 E M		◐		ICE 1711 G M					◐			X 80004 ⊠ L				◐
	Warnemünde **831** ..... d.	...	...	...	...	...	...	...	0658	...	...	...	0902	...	...	...	...	...	...	...	1415	...	...	...	...
0	**Rostock** Hbf ..... d.	...	...	0437	...	...	...	0633	0724	...	...	0833	0924	...	...	1033	...	...	1233	...	1432	...	1453	...	...
34	Güstrow ..... d.	...	...	0502	...	...	...	0658	|	...	...	0858	|	...	...	1058	...	...	1258	...	1456	...	|	...	...
85	Waren (Müritz) ..... d.	...	...	0533	...	...	...	0731	0806	...	...	0931	1006	...	...	1131	...	...	1331	...	1527	...	1535	...	...
	Stralsund ..... d.	...	...	|	...	0502	0602e	|	|	0702	0802	|	|	0902	1002	|	1102	1202	|	1302	|	1402	|	1502	1602
	Grimmen ..... d.	...	...	|	...	0523	0623e	|	|	0723	0823	|	|	0923	1023	|	1123	1223	|	1323	|	1423	|	1523	1623
	Demmin ..... d.	...	...	|	...	0546	0646e	|	|	0746	0846	|	|	0946	1046	|	1146	1246	|	1346	|	1446	|	1546	1646
	Neubrandenburg ..... d.	0427f	0527	|	...	0630	0730	|	|	0830	0930	|	|	1030	1130	|	1230	1330	|	1430	|	1530	|	1630	1730
121	**Neustrelitz** Hbf ..... a.	0455f	0556	0558	...	0658	0757	0756	0833	0858	0956	0956	1033	1058	1156	1156	1258	1356	1356	1458	1551	1556	1600	1658	1756
121	**Neustrelitz** Hbf ..... d.	0502	...	0602	...	0702	...	0802	0835	0902	...	1002	1035	1102	...	1202	1302	...	1402	1502	1552	...	1602	1702	...
141	Fürstenberg (Havel) ..... d.	0515	...	0616	...	0716	...	0816	|	0916	...	1016	|	1116	...	1216	1316	...	1416	1516	|	...	1616	1716	...
162	Gransee ..... d.	0532	...	0633	...	0731	...	0833	|	0931	...	1033	|	1131	...	1233	1331	...	1433	1531	|	...	1633	1731	...
191	Oranienburg ..... d.	0550	...	0650	...	0750	...	0850	|	0950	...	1050	|	1150	...	1250	1350	...	1450	1550	|	...	1650	1750	...
223	**Berlin** Hbf ..... a.	0615	...	0715	...	0815	...	0915	0942	1015	...	1115	1145	1215	...	1315	1415	...	1515	1615	1703	...	1715	1815	...
223	**Berlin** Hbf ..... △ d.	0617	...	0717	0717	0817	...	0917	0952	1017	...	1117	1152	1217	...	1317	1417	...	1517	1617	...	...	1717	1817	...
276	Luckenwalde ..... d.	0655	...	0754	0754	0855	...	0954	|	1055	...	1154	|	1255	...	1354	1455	...	1554	1655	...	...	1754	1855	...
289	Jüterbog ..... d.	0703	...	0802	0802	0903	...	1002	|	1103	...	1202	|	1303	...	1402	1503	...	1602	1703	...	...	1802	1903	...
	Falkenberg (Elster) ..... a.	0746	...	|	|	0946	...	|	|	1146	...	|	|	1346	...	|	1546	...	|	1746	...	...	|	1946	...
321	**Lutherstadt Wittenberg** △ a.	...	...	0829	0829	...	...	1029	1033	...	...	1229	1233	...	...	1429	...	...	1629	...	...	...	1829	...	...

			⑥⑦				◐ Ⓑ			◐
Warnemünde **831** ..... d.	...	...	1817	...	...	...	...	...	...	...
Rostock Hbf ..... d.	1633	...	1837	...	1833	...	...	2033	...	...
Güstrow ..... d.	1658	...	|	...	1858	...	...	2058	...	...
Waren (Müritz) ..... d.	1731	...	1922	...	1931	...	...	2131	...	...
Stralsund ..... d.	|	1702	|	1802	|	1902	2002	|	2102	...
Grimmen ..... d.	|	1723	|	1823	|	1923	2023	|	2123	...
Demmin ..... d.	|	1746	|	1846	|	1946	2046	|	2146	...
Neubrandenburg ..... d.	|	1830	|	1930	|	2030	2130	|	2230	2252
Neustrelitz Hbf ..... a.	1756	1858	1947	1956	1956	2058	2156	2156	▬	2327
Neustrelitz Hbf ..... d.	1802	1902	1948	...	2002	2102	...	2202	...	▬
Fürstenberg (Havel) ..... d.	1816	1916	2002	...	2016	2116	...	2216	...	...
Gransee ..... d.	1833	1931	|	...	2033	2131	...	2233	...	...
Oranienburg ..... d.	1850	1950	2034	...	2050	2150	...	2252	...	...
Berlin Hbf ..... a.	1915	2015	2059	...	2115	2215	...	2317	...	H
Berlin Hbf ..... △ d.	1917	2017	...	...	2117	2217	...	...	2321	0015
Luckenwalde ..... d.	1954	2055	...	...	2154	2305	...	...	0006	0100
Jüterbog ..... d.	2002	2103	...	...	2202	2312	...	...	0014	0108
Falkenberg (Elster) ..... a.	|	2146	...	...	|	2356	...	...	...	|
Lutherstadt Wittenberg .. △ a.	2029	...	...	...	2229	...	...	...	...	0124c

km		①–⑤	◐		H			⑥⑦		◐
	Lutherstadt Wittenberg △ d.	...	...	...	0526	...	...	...	0728	...
0	**Falkenberg** (Elster) ..... d.	...	...	...	|	...	0609	...	|	...
49	Jüterbog ..... d.	...	...	0453	0554	...	0653	...	0756	...
62	Luckenwalde ..... d.	...	...	0501	0601	...	0701	...	0803	...
115	**Berlin** Hbf ..... △ a.	...	...	0541	0641	...	0741	...	0841	...
115	**Berlin** Hbf ..... d.	0443	...	0543	0643	...	0743	0814	0843	...
147	Oranienburg ..... d.	0508	...	0608	0708	...	0808	0839	0908	...
176	Gransee ..... d.	0526	...	0627	0726	...	0827	|	0926	...
197	Fürstenberg (Havel) ..... d.	0543	...	0643	0743	...	0843	0911	0943	...
218	**Neustrelitz** Hbf ..... a.	0555	...	0655	0755	...	0855	0923	0955	...
218	**Neustrelitz** Hbf ..... d.	0604	0601	0700	0801	0803	0900	0924	1001	1003
253	**Neubrandenburg** ..... d.	|	0633	0733	|	0833	0933	|	|	1033
295	Demmin ..... d.	|	0709	0809	|	0909	1009	|	|	1109
319	Grimmen ..... d.	|	0729	0829	|	0929	1029	|	|	1129
342	**Stralsund** ..... a.	|	0751	0851	|	0951	1051	|	|	1151
	Waren (Müritz) ..... d.	0631	...	...	0831	...	...	0950	1031	...
	Güstrow ..... d.	0702	...	...	0902	...	...	|	1102	...
	Rostock Hbf ..... a.	0724	...	...	0924	...	...	1035	1124	...
	Warnemünde **831** ..... a.	...	...	...	...	...	...	1058	...	...

				X 80003 ⊠ L		◐							◐ Ⓑd		ICE 1706 B M		Ⓑd			◐ Ⓑ		⊡		⑤⑥	
Lutherstadt Wittenberg .. △ d.	...	0926	...	...	...	1126	...	...	1326	...	...	1526	...	...	1722	1726	...	...	1926	...	...	...	2126	...	...
Falkenberg (Elster) ..... d.	0810	|	...	...	1009	|	...	1209	|	...	1409	|	...	1609	|	|	...	1809	|	...	2009	2009	|	...	2209
Jüterbog ..... d.	0853	0954	...	...	1053	1154	...	1253	1354	...	1453	1554	...	1653	|	1754	...	1853	1954	...	2053	2053	2154	...	2253
Luckenwalde ..... d.	0901	1001	...	...	1101	1201	...	1301	1401	...	1501	1601	...	1701	|	1801	...	1901	2001	...	2101	2101	2201	...	2300
Berlin Hbf ..... △ a.	0941	1041	...	...	1141	1241	...	1341	1441	...	1541	1641	...	1741	1805	1841	...	1941	2041	...	2141	2141	2245	...	2345
Berlin Hbf ..... d.	0943	1043	...	1058	1143	1243	...	1343	1443	...	1543	1643	...	1743	1812	1843	...	1943	2043	...	...	2143	...	2249	...
Oranienburg ..... d.	1008	1108	...	|	1208	1308	...	1408	1508	...	1608	1708	...	1808	|	1908	...	2008	2108	...	...	2208	...	2313	...
Gransee ..... d.	1027	1126	...	|	1227	1326	...	1427	1526	...	1627	1726	...	1827	|	1926	...	2027	2126	...	...	2227	...	2332	...
Fürstenberg (Havel) ..... d.	1043	1143	...	|	1243	1343	...	1443	1543	...	1643	1743	...	1843	|	1943	...	2043	2143	...	...	2243	...	2348	...
Neustrelitz Hbf ..... a.	1055	1155	...	1205	1254	1355	...	1454	1555	...	1655	1755	...	1855	1921	1955	...	2055	2155	...	...	2255	...	0000	...
Neustrelitz Hbf ..... d.	1100	1157	1203	1206	1300	1401	1403	1500	1601	1603	1700	1801	1803	1900	1923	2001	2003	2100	2201	2203	...	2303	...	0001	...
Neubrandenburg ..... d.	1133	|	1233	|	1333	|	1433	1533	|	1633	1733	|	1833	1933	|	|	2033	2133	|	2228	...	2330	...	0028	...
Demmin ..... d.	1209	|	1309	|	1409	|	1509	1609	|	1709	1809	|	1909	2009	|	|	2109	2209	|	...	...	...	...	...	...
Grimmen ..... d.	1229	|	1329	|	1429	|	1529	1629	|	1729	1829	|	1929	2029	|	|	2129	2229	|	...	...	...	...	...	...
Stralsund ..... a.	1251	|	1351	|	1451	|	1551	1651	|	1751	1851	|	1951	2051	|	|	2151	2251	|	...	...	...	...	...	...
Waren (Müritz) ..... d.	...	1223	...	1231	...	1431	...	...	1631	...	...	1831	...	...	1950	2031	...	...	2231	...	...	...	...	...	...
Güstrow ..... d.	...	|	...	1302	...	1502	...	...	1702	...	...	1902	...	...	|	2102	...	...	2302	...	...	...	...	...	...
Rostock Hbf ..... a.	...	1304	...	1324	...	1524	...	...	1724	...	...	1924	...	...	2030	2124	...	...	2324	...	...	...	...	...	...
Warnemünde **831** ..... a.	...	...	...	1357	...	...	...	...	...	...	...	...	...	...	2044	...	...	...	...	...	...	...	...	...	...

B – Ⓑ only. Train number **1726** Aug. 2 - Sept. 14.
E – ①–⑤ only. Train number **1729** Aug. 3 - Sept. 14.
G – ⑥ only. Train number **309** Aug. 1 - Sept. 12.
H – To / from Halle (Table **848**) on ⑥⑦.
L – From / to Leipzig (Table **851**).
M – (12) and ✕ Warnemünde - Leipzig - Nürnberg - München and v.v.

c – ⑥⑦ only.
d – Runs daily Neustrelitz - Neubrandenburg.
e – ①–⑥ only.
f – 14 minutes earlier on June 16, 17.

⊡ – ①②③④⑦.
△ – See Tables **850/1** for other *ICE* / *IC* services Berlin - Lutherstadt Wittenberg and v.v.
⊠ – Operated by Veolia Verkehr GmbH. **DB tickets not valid**.
◐ – Operated by Ostseeland Verkehr GmbH.

836 LÜBECK and SCHWERIN - PASEWALK - SZCZECIN and UECKERMÜNDE

DB (*RE* services); OLA ‡

km			‡	Ⓐ		‡	Ⓐ	©	‡		‡		‡Ⓐ	‡		‡		‡		‡		‡	‡⑤		‡⑦
0	**Lübeck** Hbf .... 826 d.	...	...	...	...	...	0601	...	...	0801	...	1001	...	...	1201	...	1401	...	1601	...	1801	...	...	2001	...
	Schwerin Hbf 830/7 d.	...	...	0444	...	0551	|	0640	0751	|	0951	|	...	1151	|	1351	|	1551	|	1751	|	1951	1951	|	2151
62	Bad Kleinen 826 830/7 d.	...	...	0504	...	0602	0704	0704	0802	0904	1002	1104j	...	1202	1304	1402	1504	1602	1704	1802	1904	2002	2002	2104	2202
103	Bützow .... 830 d.	...	...	0535	...	0632	0735	0735	0832	0935	1032	1137	...	1232	1335	1432	1535	1632	1735	1832	1935	2032	2032	2135	2232
117	Güstrow .... a.	...	...	0544	...	0641	0744	0744	0841	0944	1041	1146	...	1241	1344	1441	1544	1641	1744	1841	1944	2041	2041	2144	2241
117	Güstrow .... d.	...	...	0558	...	0705	0758	0758	0905	0958	1105	1158	...	1305	1358	1505	1558	1705	1758	1905	1958	2105	2105	2158	2305
146	Teterow .... d.	...	...	0622	...	0730	0822	0822	0930	1022	1130	1222	...	1330	1422	1530	1622	1730	1822	1930	2022	2130	2130	2222	2328
160	Malchin .... d.	...	0535a	0633	...	0741	0833	0833	0941	1033	1141	1233	...	1341	1433	1541	1633	1741	1833	1941	2033	2141	2141	2233	2340
204	**Neubrandenburg** .... a.	...	0611a	0709	...	0826	0909	0909	1026	1109	1226	1309	...	1426	1509	1626	1709	1826	1909	2026	2109	2226	2226	2309	0015
204	**Neubrandenburg** .... d.	0516a	0612	0712	0712	0832	0912	0912	1032	1112	1232	1312	...	1432	1512	1632	1712	1832	1912	2032	2132	...	2232	...	...
257	**Pasewalk** .... a.	0600a	0701	0800	0800	0916	1000	1000	1116	1200	1316	1400	...	1516	1600	1716	1800	1916	2003	2116	2217	...	2315	...	...
257	**Pasewalk** .... ◧ d.	0603	0723	0801	0801	0923	1001	1001	1123	1201	1323	1401	1404	1523	1601	1723	1801	1927	2004	2123	...	...	2328	...	...
287	Ueckermünde ...... ◧ a.	|	0754	|	|	0954	|	|	1154	|	1354	|	1438	1554	|	1754	|	1958	|	2154	...	...	|	...	...
284	Grambow .... d.	0626	...	0825	0825	...	1025	1025	...	1225	...	1424	...	...	1625	...	1824	...	2027	...	...	...	2351	...	...
294	Szczecin Gumience ▦ d.	0637	...	0836	0836	...	1036	1036	...	1238	...	1438	...	...	1638	...	1836	...	2038	...	...	...	0002	...	...
299	**Szczecin** Główny .... a.	0643	...	0842	0842	...	1042	1042	...	1244	...	1444	...	...	1644	...	1842	...	2044	...	...	...	0007	...	...

	‡⑥	‡	Ⓐ	‡	Ⓐ		‡	‡Ⓐ		‡		‡		‡		‡	‡Ⓐ		‡		‡		‡	‡⑦	
Szczecin Główny .... d.	0013	...	...	...	0454	...	...	...	0654	...	0854	...	1054	...	1254	...	...	1454	...	1654	...	1854	...	...	2054
Szczecin Gumience ▦ d.	0020	...	...	...	0501	...	...	...	0701	...	0901	...	1101	...	1301	...	...	1501	...	1701	...	1901	...	...	2101
Grambow .... d.	0030	...	...	...	0511	...	...	...	0711	...	0911	...	1111	...	1311	...	...	1511	...	1711	...	1911	...	...	2111
Ueckermünde ...... ◧ d.	|	...	...	...	|	...	0556r	0654	|	0802	|	1002	|	1202	|	1402	1452	|	1602	|	1802	|	2004	2004	|
Pasewalk .... ◧ a.	0051	...	...	...	0533	...	0628r	0726	0733	0834	0933	1034	1133	1234	1333	1438	1524	1533	1634	1733	1834	1933	2036	2036	2133
Pasewalk .... d.	0052	...	...	...	0541	...	0643	...	0741	0843	0941	1043	1141	1243	1341	1443	...	1541	1643	1741	1843	1945	2043	2043	2145
Neubrandenburg .... a.	0130	...	...	...	0628	...	0728	...	0828	0928	1028	1128	1228	1328	1428	1528	...	1628	1728	1828	1928	2028	2128	2128	2231
Neubrandenburg .... d.	...	...	0446	0528	0638	0638	0735	...	0838	0935	1038	1135	1238	1335	1438	1535	...	1638	1735	1838	1935	2038	...	2135	...
Malchin .... d.	...	...	0520	0609	0716	0716	0809	...	0916	1009	1116	1209	1316	1409	1516	1609	...	1716	1809	1916	2009	2116	...	2209	...
Teterow .... d.	...	...	0532	0620	0728	0728	0820	...	0928	1020	1128	1220	1328	1420	1528	1620	...	1728	1820	1928	2020	2128	...	2220	...
Güstrow .... a.	...	...	0556	0648	0756	0756	0848	...	0956	1048	1156	1248	1356	1448	1556	1648	...	1756	1848	1956	2048	2156	...	2248	...
Güstrow .... d.	...	0508	0609	0708	0809	0809	0908	...	1009	1108	1209	1308	1409	1508	1609	1708	...	1809	1908	2009	2108	2209	...	2308	...
Bützow .... 830 d.	...	0517	0619	0717	0819	0819	0917	...	1019	1117	1219	1317	1419	1517	1619	1717	...	1819	1917	2019	2117	2219	...	2317	...
Bad Kleinen 826 830/7 a.	...	0553	0649	0753	0849	0849	0953	...	1049	1153	1249	1353	1457	1553	1649	1753	...	1849	1953	2049	2153	2249	...	2353	...
Schwerin Hbf 830/7 a.	...	0604	|	0804	|	|	1004	...	|	1204	|	1404	|	1604	|	1804	...	|	2004	|	2204	2303	...	0004	...
Lübeck Hbf .... 826 a.	...	...	0756	...	0956	0956	...	...	1156	...	1356	...	1556	...	1756	...	...	1956	...	2156	...	...	...	...	...

a – Ⓐ only.
j – 1057 until Aug. 30 (also ⑤⑥ Sept. 4 - Oct. 24).
r – ⚒ (not Oct. 31).

‡ – Operated by Ostseeland Verkehr (OLA).
◧ – Additional trains Pasewalk - Ueckermünde and v.v. (operated by OLA ‡): **From Pasewalk** at 0515 ⚒ r and 0611 Ⓐ. **From Ueckermünde** at 2202.

837 WISMAR - SCHWERIN - BERLIN

RE services except where shown

km		Ⓐ		①–⑥ ◇	Ⓐ ◇			Ⓐ ◇					◇		*IC* 2239 A L			Ⓐ ◇		◇	◇			◇		Ⓐ
0	**Wismar** .... d.	0427	...	0539	...	0644	0732	...	0844	0933	1044	1133	1244	1333	...	1430	1533	...	1644	1733	1844	...	1933	2044	2140	2244
16	Bad Kleinen .... a.	0444	...	0554	...	0659	0748	...	0859	0948	1059	1148	1259	1348	...	1445p	1548	...	1659	1748	1859	...	1948	2059	2155	2300
16	Bad Kleinen .... 830/6 d.	0445	...	0557	...	0701	0758	...	0901	0958	1101	1158	1301	1358	1449	1501	1558	...	1701	1758	1901	...	1958	2101	2157	2302
32	**Schwerin** Hbf . 830/6 a.	0458	...	0609	...	0713	0810	...	0913	1010	1113	1210	1313	1410	1500	1513	1610	...	1713	1810	1913	...	2010	2113	2209	2314
32	**Schwerin** Hbf .... d.	▶	0517	0610	0648	0714	0817	0846	0914	1017	1114	1217	1314	1417	1502	1514	1617	1648	1714	1811	1914	...	2017	2114	▬	...
72	Ludwigslust .... a.	...	0547	0639	0712	0746	0847	0910	0946	1047	1146	1247	1346	1447	1524	1546	1647	1712	1746	1841	1946	...	2047	2146	...	...
72	Ludwigslust .... 840 d.	...	0548	0648	...	...	0848	...	...	1048	...	1248	...	1448	1526	...	1648	...	...	1849	...	...	...	2148	C	...
116	Wittenberge .... 840 d.	...	0612	0712	...	...	0912	...	...	1112	...	1312	...	1512	1545	...	1712	...	...	1913	...	2112	...	2212	2302	...
207	Nauen .... d.	...	0705	0805	...	...	1005	...	...	1205	...	1409	...	1605	...	...	1805	...	...	2006	...	2205	...	...	2355	...
229	**Berlin** Spandau . 840 d.	...	0720	0820	...	...	1020	...	...	1220	...	1424	...	1620	...	...	1820	...	...	2020	...	2220	...	...	0010	...
241	**Berlin** Hbf .... 840 a.	...	0729	0829	...	...	1029	...	...	1229	...	1433	...	1629	...	...	1829	...	...	2029	...	2229	...	...	0025	...

	①–⑥		①–⑥ ◇		Ⓐ			Ⓐ ◇		*IC* 2238 B L						◇			Ⓐ ◇			◇				
Berlin Hbf .... 840 d.	...	0426	0521	...	...	...	0730	...	...	...	0930	...	1131	...	1330	...	1530	...	...	1730	...	...	1930	2030	2130	2230
Berlin Spandau ... 840 d.	...	0436	0531	...	...	...	0740	...	...	...	0940	...	1140	...	1340	...	1541	...	...	1740	...	...	1940	2040	2140	2240
Nauen .... d.	...	0452	0545	...	...	...	0754	...	...	...	0954	...	1154	...	1354	...	1555	...	...	1754	...	...	1954	2054	2154	2254
Wittenberge .... 840 d.	...	0548	0650	...	...	...	0850	...	...	1012	1050	...	1250	...	1450	...	1650	...	...	1850	...	...	2049	2150	2249	2349
Ludwigslust .... 840 a.	...	0611	0713	...	...	...	0913	...	...	1030	1113	...	1313	...	1513	...	1713	...	...	1913	...	...	...	2213	▬	...
Ludwigslust .... d.	0514a	0612	0714	...	0740	0812	0914	0938	1012	1032	1114	1212	1314	1412	1514	1612	1714	1812	1845	1914	2012	2054	...	2214	...	...
Schwerin Hbf .... a.	0544a	0645	0744	...	0806	0845	0944	1004	1045	1053	1144	1245	1344	1445	1544	1645	1744	1845	1909	1944	2045	2125	...	2244	...	...
Schwerin Hbf ... 830/6 d.	0545	0647	0745	0745	...	0847	0945	...	1047	1055	1145	1247	1345	1447	1545	1647	1745	1847	...	1945	2047	2145	...	...	2251	...
Bad Kleinen ...... 830/6 a.	0558	0659	0758	0758	...	0859	0958	...	1059	1106p	1158	1259	1358	1459	1558	1659	1758	1859	...	1958	2059	2158	...	...	2304	...
Bad Kleinen .... d.	0604	0701	0804	0804	...	0901	1004	...	1111	...	1204	1301	1404	1501	1604	1701	1804	1901	...	2004	2101	2204	...	...	2305	...
Wismar .... a.	0619	0717	0819	0819	...	0916	1019	...	1126	...	1219	1316	1419	1516	1619	1716	1819	1916	...	2019	2116	2219	...	...	2320	...

A – Daily until Aug. 30; ⑤⑦ Sept. 4 - Oct. 25.
B – Daily until Aug. 30; ⑤⑥ Sept. 4 - Oct. 24.
C – To Cottbus (Table **838**).

L – [12] Leipzig - Magdeburg - Stendal - Rostock - Warnemünde and v.v.

a – Ⓐ only.
p – Connects with train in previous column.

◇ – Connects at Ludwigslust with fast *ICE*, *EC* or *IC* train to / from Berlin (see Table **840**).
▶ – Continues to Berlin on ①④⑤ (see next column).

838 STENDAL - BERLIN - LÜBBEN - COTTBUS

RE services except where shown

km				⚒				*EC* 341 A										*IC* 2131 Ⓑ E 🍷							W
0	**Stendal** .... 810 d.	...	0448	0516	...	0616	...	0848e	0803	...	1003	...	1203	...	1403	...	1603	...	...	1803	...	2003	...	2219	...
34	Rathenow .... 810 a.	...	0504	0557*	...	0657*	...	|	0845*	...	1045*	...	1245*	...	1445*	...	1645*	...	...	1845*	...	2045*	...	2300*	...
34	Rathenow .... 810 d.	0405a	0505	...	0605	0705	0805	|	0905	1005	1107	1205	1307	1405	1507	1605	1707	...	1805	1907	2005	2105	2205	2307	...
92	**Berlin** Spandau ... 810 d.	0449a	0548	...	0648	0749	0848	0925e	0949	1049	1149	1249	1349	1448	1549	1648	1749	...	1849	1949	2048	2149	2249	2347	0010
104	**Berlin** Zoo .... d.	0458a	0557	...	0658	0758	0857	|	0958	1058	1158	1258	1358	1457	1558	1657	1758	...	1858	1958	2057	2158	2258	2356	0020
108	**Berlin** Hbf .... 810 d.	0503a	0603	...	0703	0803	0903	0941	1003	1103	1203	1303	1403	1503	1603	1703	1803	1831	1903	2003	2103	2203	2303	2400	0040
113	**Berlin** Ostbahnhof 810 d.	0513	0613	...	0713	0813	0913	0951	1013	1113	1213	1313	1413	1513	1613	1713	1813	1841	1913	2013	2113	2213	2313	...	0049
146	Königs Wusterhausen . d.	0539	0639	...	0739	0839	0939	|	1039	1139	1239	1339	1439	1539	1639	1739	1839	|	1939	2039	2139	2239	2339	...	0113
192	Lübben (Spreewald) .... d.	0609	0707	...	0807	0907	1007	1043	1107	1207	1307	1407	1507	1609	1707	1807	1907	1932	2008	2107	2218	2318	0018	...	0149
203	Lübbenau (Spreew) ..... d.	0620	0715	...	0815	0915	1015	1053	1115	1215	1315	1415	1515	1620	1715	1815	1915	1942	2015	2115	2225	2326	0025	...	0157
233	**Cottbus** .... a.	0646	0746	...	0844	0944	1044	1111	1144	1244	1344	1444	1544	1644	1744	1844	1944	2000	2044	2144	2249	...	0048	...	0216

		⚒	Ⓐ			*IC* 2132 ①–⑥ N 🍷											*EC* 340 B								
Cottbus .... d.	...	...	...	0416	0516	0600	0616	0716	0816	0916	1016	1116	1216	1316	1416	1516	1600	1616	1716	1816	1916	2016	2112	...	2310
Lübbenau (Spreew) ...... d.	0041	...	...	0441	0541	0620	0641	0741	0841	0941	1041	1141	1241	1341	1441	1541	1620	1641	1741	1841	1941	2041	2135	...	2333
Lübben (Spreewald) ..... d.	0048	...	...	0448	0548	0629	0648	0748	0848	0948	1048	1148	1248	1348	1448	1548	1630	1648	1748	1848	1948	2048	2142	...	2340
Königs Wusterhausen .. d.	0119	...	...	0519	0619	|	0719	0819	0919	1019	1119	1219	1319	1419	1519	1619	|	1719	1819	1919	2019	2119	2221	...	0019
Berlin Ostbahnhof 810 d.	0147	...	...	0548	0648	0721	0748	0848	0948	1048	1148	1248	1348	1448	1548	1648	1723	1748	1848	1948	2048	2148	2248	...	0048
Berlin Hbf .... 810 d.	0159a	...	...	0558	0658	0728	0758	0858	0958	1058	1158	1258	1358	1458	1558	1658	1735	1758	1858	1958	2058	2158	2258	0015	0100
Berlin Zoo .... d.	0204a	...	0504	0604	0704	...	0804	0904	1004	1104	1204	1304	1404	1504	1604	1704	|	1804	1904	2004	2104	2204	2304	0021	0104
Berlin Spandau .... 810 d.	...	...	0513	0613	0713	...	0813	0913	1013	1113	1213	1313	1413	1514	1613	1714	1750b	1813	1913	2013	2113	2213	2313	0029	...
Rathenow .... 810 a.	...	...	0554	0654	0754	...	0849	0955	1049	1154	1249	1354	1449	1554	1654	1754	|	1854	1954	2054	2155	2249	2356	0102	...
Rathenow .... 810 d.	...	0542*	...	0710*	...	...	0910*	...	1110*	...	1310*	...	1510*	...	1710*	...	|	1905*	...	2105*	...	...	2357	...	...
Stendal .... 810 a.	...	0621	...	0749	...	...	0949	...	1149	...	1349	...	1549	...	1749	...	1824b	1944	...	2144	...	...	0013	...	...

A – WAWEL – [12] (Hamburg ①–⑥ -) Berlin - Cottbus - Forst ▦ - Wrocław - Katowice - Kraków.
B – WAWEL – [12] Kraków - Katowice - Wrocław - Forst ▦ - Cottbus - Berlin (- Hamburg Ⓑ).
E – OSTFRIESLAND – [12] Emden - Oldenburg - Bremen - Hannover - Magdeburg - Cottbus.
N – OSTFRIESLAND – [12] Cottbus - Magdeburg - Hannover - Bremen - Oldenburg (- Norddeich Mole ⊡).
W – From Wittenberge (Table **837**).

a – Ⓐ only.
b – Ⓑ only.
e – ①–⑥ only.

* – By 🚌 Großwudicke - Rathenow and v.v.
⊡ – Daily until Oct. 25; ⑤⑦ from Oct. 30.

RE services — MAGDEBURG - BERLIN - FRANKFURT (ODER) - COTTBUS — 839

km				Ⓐ	Ⓒ									P 🍷					E ♣					
0	**Magdeburg** Hbf ... d.	...	...	*0446*v	0458	...	0603	...	0706	...	and at the same minutes past each hour until	1606	...	1700	1706	...	1806	...	1854	1906	2006	2104	2204	*2317*
79	**Brandenburg** Hbf ... d.	0422	0500	0600	0600	0622*	0700	0722*	0800	0822		1700	1722	1742	1800	1822	1900	1922	|	2000	2100	2156	2256	0021
114	Potsdam Hbf ... d.	0451	0522	0622	0622	0652	0722	0752	0822	0852		1722	1752	1800	1822	1852	1922	1952	2007	2022	2122	2222	2322	0052
123	Berlin Wannsee ... d.	0457	0528	0628	0628	0658	0728	0758	0828	0858		1728	1758	1809	1828	1858	1928	1958	2015	2028	2128	2228	2328	0058
138	**Berlin** Zoo ... d.	0510	0542	0642	0642	0712	0742	0812	0842	0912		1742	1812	|	1842	1912	1942	2012	2032	2042	2142	2242	2342	0112
142	**Berlin** Hbf ... d.	0515	0548	0648	0648	0718	0748	0818	0848	0918		1748	1818	1831	1848	1918	1948	2018	|	2048	2148	2248	2348	0118
147	**Berlin** Ostbahnhof ... **1001** d.	0523	0559	0659	0659	0729	0759	0829	0859	0929		1759	1829	1841	1859	1929	1959	2029	2048	2059	2159	2259	2359	0128
194	Fürstenwalde (Spree) ... d.	*0608*	0632	0732	0732	0807	0832	0907	0932	1007		1832	1907	|	1932	2007	2032	2107	...	2137	2237	2337	0037	...
228	**Frankfurt (Oder)** ... **1001** a.	*0630*	0702	0802	0802	0826	0902	0926	1002	1026		1902	1926	⊖	2002	2026	2102	2126	...	2207	2307	0007	0107	...
	Cottbus (see below) ... a.	*0751*	...	...	...	...	...	...	...	...		...	...	2000**b**	...	2129	...	2250	...	2315	0029	...	...	...

	Ⓒ							N 🍷	C ♣															⑤⑥
Cottbus (see below) ... d.	...	...	...	...	0341	...	0441	0600e	...	0511	0543	...	...	and at the same minutes past each hour until	...	...	...	...	1908	...	2108	...	...	...
Frankfurt (Oder) ... **1001** d.	...	...	0351	...	0451	0533	0554	⊖	...	0633	0654	0733	0754		1833	1854	1933	1954	2029	2126	2224	...	2323	2323
Fürstenwalde (Spree) ... d.	...	...	0419	...	0519	0550	0624	|	...	0650	0724	0750	0824		1850	1924	1950	2024	2050	2153	2251	...	2350	2350
Berlin Ostbahnhof ... **1001** d.	0129	...	0459	0530	0559	0629	0659	0721	0706	0729	0759	0829	0859		1929	1959	2029	2059	2129	2229	2327	2330	0029	0029
Berlin Hbf ... d.	0141	...	0511	0541	0611	0641	0711	0732	|	0741	0811	0841	0911		1941	2011	2041	2111	2141	2241	...	2341	0041	0041
Berlin Zoo ... d.	0147	...	0517	0547	0617	0647	0717	|	0725	0747	0817	0847	0917		1947	2017	2047	2116	2147	2247	...	2347	0047	0047
Berlin Wannsee ... d.	0200	...	0530	0600	0630	0700	0730	0749	0736	0800	0830	0900	0930		2000	2030	2100	...	2200	2300	...	0000	0100	0100
Potsdam Hbf ... d.	0208	...	0538	0608	0638	0708	0738	0757	0744	0808	0838	0908	0938		2008	2038	2108	...	2208	2308	...	0008	0108	0108
Brandenburg Hbf ... d.	0237	...	0600	0637	0700	0737	0800	0816	|	0837	0900	0937	1000		2037	2100	2140	...	2237	2338	...	0037	0137	0138
Magdeburg Hbf ... a.	...	...	0653	...	0753	...	0853	0858	0904	...	0953	...	1053		...	2153	2238	...	...	0031	...	...	...	0223

km		Ⓐ	Ⓐ							
0	**Frankfurt (Oder)** ... d.	0404	0434	0534	and hourly until	1934	2028	2131	2209	2309
23	Eisenhüttenstadt ... d.	0424	0454	0554		1954	2049	2152	2230	2331
48	Guben ... d.	0446	0516	0616		2016	2106	2214	2252	2353
86	**Cottbus** ... a.	0521	0551	0651		2051	2129	2250	2315	0029

					Ⓐ					
Cottbus ... d.	0341	0441	0511	0543	0608	0708	and hourly until	1908	2108	2308
Guben ... d.	0405	0508	0548	0607	0644	0744		1944	2143	2344
Eisenhüttenstadt ... d.	0426	0529	0610	0628	0704	0805		2005	2203	0005
Frankfurt (Oder) ... a.	0448	0551	0631	0650	0724	0824		2024	2222	0024

C – ⑥⑦ only.
E – ⑤–⑦ only.
N – *IC* **2132**. To Norddeich (Tables **810**/**813**).
P – *IC* **2131**. From Emden (Tables **813**/**810**).

b – Ⓑ only.
e – ①–⑥ only.
v – Change trains at Genthin (a. *0527*, d. 0537).
⊖ – Via Lübben (Table **838**).

♣ – *HARZ-BERLIN-EXPRESS.* [2] Berlin - Halberstadt - Thale and v.v. (Table **862**); [2] Berlin - Halberstadt - Vienenburg and v.v. (Table **860**). Operated by Veolia Verkehr Sachsen-Anhalt GmbH. **DB tickets not valid.**
* – 4 minutes later on Ⓐ.

HAMBURG - BERLIN - DRESDEN — 840

km		*CNL* **457**	*EC* **171**	*ICE* **1607***	*ICE* **701**	*EC* **173**	*ICE* **1507***	*EC* **341**	*ICE* **705**	*ICE* **1609***	*EC* **175**	*ICE* **1509***	*ICE* **709**	*ICE* **109***	*EC* **177**	*ICE* **803**	*ICE* **38 381**	*EC* **379**	*ICE* **1513***	*ICE* **807**	*IC* **1871**	*ICE* **1515***	*EC* **179**	*ICE* **901**	*IC* **2071**
				①	②–⑥	⊖	①–⑤	①–⑥	Ⓑ	⑥	⊖	①–⑥									⑤				
		A	✕♦	✕M	✕	✕♦	✕M	♦	✕	✕M	✕♦	✕♦	✕	✕♦	✕♦	✕	B 🍷	✕♦	✕M	✕	F 🍷	✕M	✕♦	✕	✕
0	**Hamburg** Altona ... d.	...	...	0546	0546	0614	0651	0642	0752	0752	0819	...	0952	1037	...	1152	...	...	1254	1352	...	1431	...	1552	1617
7	**Hamburg** Hbf ... **830** d.	...	...	0600	0600	0628	0708	0705	0806	0806	0833	0908	1006	1051	...	1206	1239	...	1308	1406	1411	1453	...	1606	1631
54	Büchen ... **830** d.	...	...	|	|	0656	|	|	|	|	0856	|	|	|	...	|	|	...	|	|	1433	|	...	|	1656
122	Ludwigslust ... **837** d.	...	...	0644	0644	0722	|	◐	|	|	0922	|	|	|	...	|	|	...	1351	|	1459	|	...	|	1722
167	Wittenberge ... **837** d.	...	...	0701	0701	0741	|	|	|	|	0941	|	|	|	...	|	|	...	1408	|	|	|	...	|	1741
280	**Berlin** Spandau ... **837** d.	...	...	0738	0738	0824	|	0925	0937	0937	1024	|	1137	|	...	1337	|	...	|	1537	1558	|	...	1737	1824
292	**Berlin** Hbf ... **837** a.	...	...	0746	0746	0832	0844	0937	0945	0945	1032	1044	1145	1231	...	1346	1427	...	1452	1545	1608	1631	...	1745	1832
292	**Berlin** Hbf ... **845** d.	0500**o**	0635	0752	...	0835	0858	...	...	0952	1035	1058	...	1258	1235	...	▽	1435	1458	...	...	1658	1635	...	1835
	Leipzig Hbf **851** ... a.	|	|	0905	...	|	1005	...	...	1105	|	1205	...	1405	|	...	...	|	1605	...	...	1805	|	...	|
	Elsterwerda .. **843 845** d.	|	0801	...	...	|	...	...	...	...	|	...	...	...	1401	...	...	|	...	...	...	...	1801	...	2001
485	**Dresden** Neustadt ... a.	|	0842	...	...	1042	...	...	...	...	1242	...	...	...	1442	...	...	1642	...	...	...	...	1842	...	2042
489	**Dresden** Hbf ... **843** a.	0707	0853	...	...	1053	...	...	...	...	1253	...	...	...	1453	...	...	1653	...	...	...	...	1853	...	2057

	ICE **1517***	*ICE* **905**	*ICE* **1519**	*IC* **2073**	*IC* **2075**	*IC* **1877**	*ICE* **909**	*ICE* **1521**	*ICE* **1005**	*ICE* **1007**
	Ⓑ		Ⓑ	①–⑤	⑥⑦	④	⑤⑦	⑦	①–⑥	⑤⑦
	✕E	✕	✕	T✕	T✕		✕	✕	‡✕	§✕
Hamburg Altona ... d.	1652	1750	1853	...	...	1952	1952	...	2102	2152
Hamburg Hbf ... **830** d.	1708	1804	1908	1921	1921	2006	2006	2121	2121	2206
Büchen ... **830** d.	|	|	|	1945	1945	|	|	|	|	|
Ludwigslust ... **837** d.	|	1846	|	2011	2011	|	|	2204	2204	|
Wittenberge ... **837** d.	|	|	|	2030	2030	|	|	2222	2222	|
Berlin Spandau ... **837** d.	|	1939	2040	2113	2113	2142	|	2300	2258	2335
Berlin Hbf ... **837** a.	1844	1947	2048	2121	2121	2156	2142	2309	2313	2350
Berlin Hbf ... **845** d.	1858	1952**h**	2058	2128	2128**h**	...	2152**f**	2312	...	...
Leipzig Hbf **851** ... a.	2005	2105**h**	2210	|	|	...	2307**f**	0029	...	...
Elsterwerda ... **843 845** d.	...	...	...	|	|	...	...	...	...	...
Dresden Neustadt ... a.	...	...	...	2329	2329**h**	...	...	...	...	...
Dresden Hbf ... **843** a.	...	...	...	2337	2337**h**	...	...	...	...	...

	ICE **1006**	*ICE* **1004**	*ICE* **1518***	*ICE* **908**	*ICE* **1616**	*IC* **2072**	*IC* **2074**	*IC* **2070**	*ICE* **904**	*ICE* **1614***	*ICE* **1614***
	⊙	①–⑤	①–⑤	⑥⑦	①–⑤	①–⑤	⑥⑦			①–⑥	⑦
	✕	✕	✕M	✕	✕	T✕	T✕	✕	✕	✕♦	✕
Dresden Hbf ... **843** d.	...	...	...	...	...	0604	0604**k**	0704	...	...	...
Dresden Neustadt ... d.	...	...	...	...	...	0614	0614**k**	0714	...	...	...
Elsterwerda .. **843 845** d.	...	...	...	...	...	0652	0652**k**	0752	...	...	...
Leipzig Hbf **851** ... d.	...	...	0548	0548**k**	0651	|	|	|	...	0851	...
Berlin Hbf ... **845** a.	...	...	0700	0700**k**	0811	0820	0820**k**	0919	...	1006	...
Berlin Hbf ... **837** d.	0517	0555	0713	0713	0817	0823	0823	...	0925	1017	1017
Berlin Spandau . **837** d.	0527	0605	0723	0723	0827	0832	0832	...	|	1027	1027
Wittenberge ... **837** d.	0606	0644	|	|	|	0914	0914	...	|	|	|
Ludwigslust ... **837** d.	0624	0701	|	|	|	0934	0934	...	|	|	|
Büchen ... **830** d.	|	|	|	|	|	1001	1001	...	|	|	|
Hamburg Hbf ... **830** a.	0706	0745	0852	0852	0956	1023	1023	...	1101	1156	1156
Hamburg Altona ... a.	...	0759	0915	0915	1014	...	...	...	1119	1216	1216

	EC **178**	*ICE* **1514***	*ICE* **808**	*ICE* **1512***	*EC* **176**	*ICE* **804**	*ICE* **108***	*EC* **378**	*ICE* **37 380**	*ICE* **800**	*ICE* **1508***	*EC* **174**	*EC* **340**	*ICE* **1606***	*ICE* **706**	*ICE* **1506***	*EC* **172**	*ICE* **1604***	*IC* **1870**	*EC* **170**	*ICE* **1504***	*ICE* **702**	*ICE* **1502***	*ICE* **700**	*CNL* **456**
		⊡		Ⓑ			Ⓑ				Ⓑ		Ⓑ	⑥	Ⓑ	⑤⑦		Ⓑ	⑦		⑤–⑦	①–④	①–⑥	⑦	
	✕♦	✕M	✕	✕M	✕♦	✕	✕♦	✕♦	B 🍷	✕	✕♦	✕♦	✕♦	✕M	✕	✕M	✕♦	✕M	F	✕♦	✕M	✕	✕M	✕	A
Dresden Hbf ... **843** d.	0904	...	...	...	1104	...	...	1304	...	...	...	1504	...	...	...	...	1704	...	...	1904	...	...	...	...	2051
Dresden Neustadt ... d.	0914	...	...	...	1114	...	...	1314	...	...	...	1514	...	...	...	...	1714	...	...	1914	...	...	...	...	|
Elsterwerda ... **843 845** d.	|	...	...	...	|	...	...	1352	...	...	...	|	...	...	...	...	|	...	...	1952	...	...	...	...	|
Leipzig Hbf **851** ... d.	|	0951	...	1151	|	...	1351	|	...	...	1551	|	...	1651	...	1751	|	1851	...	|	1951	...	2151	...	|
Berlin Hbf ... **845** a.	1119	1100	...	1302	1320	...	1500	1518	◇	...	1700	1720	...	1805	...	1900	1920	2007	...	2120	2100	...	2300	...	2334**o**
Berlin Hbf ... **837** d.	...	1125	1217	1316	1324	1417	1503	...	1526	1618	1716	1724	1735	1817	1817	1916	1924	2017	2022	...	2126	2126	2305	2305	...
Berlin Spandau ... **837** d.	...	|	1227	|	1333	1427	|	...	|	1627	|	1733	1750	1827	1827	|	1933	2027	2032	...	2135	2135	2315	2315	...
Wittenberge ... **837** d.	...	|	|	|	1419	|	1549	...	|	|	|	1819	|	|	|	|	2019	|	2118	...	|	|	|	|	...
Ludwigslust ... **837** d.	...	|	|	|	1438	|	1608	...	|	|	|	1838	◐	|	|	|	2038	|	2137	...	|	|	|	|	...
Büchen ... **830** d.	...	|	|	|	1504	|	|	...	|	|	|	1905	|	|	|	|	2105	|	|	...	|	|	|	|	...
Hamburg Hbf ... **830** a.	...	1301	1356	1452	1526	1556	1649	...	1718	1756	1852	1927	2024	1956	1956	2052	2132	2157	2224	...	2305	2305	0043	0043	...
Hamburg Altona ... a.	...	1316	1414	1506	1540	1623	1706	...	...	1818	...	1943	2039	2015	2015	2113	2146	2214	...	...	2321	2321	0057	0057	...

♦ – **NOTES** (LISTED BY TRAIN NUMBER)

108/9 – [12] and ✕ Innsbruck - München - Nürnberg - Jena - Leipzig - Hamburg and v.v. See also note ▲.
170/1 – [12] and ✕ Budapest - Bratislava - Praha - Děčín - Berlin and v.v.
172/3 – VINDOBONA – [12] and ✕ Wien - Břeclav - Praha - Děčín - Berlin - Hamburg and v.v.
174/5 – [12] and ✕ Budapest - Bratislava - Praha - Děčín - Berlin - Hamburg and v.v.
176 – [12] and ✕ Brno - Praha - Děčín - Berlin - Hamburg.
177 – [12] and ✕ Berlin - Děčín - Praha - Wien.
178 – [12] and ✕ Praha - Děčín - Berlin.
179 – [12] and ✕ Berlin - Děčín - Praha - Brno.
340/1 – WAWEL – [12] Kraków - Forst 🏛 - Cottbus - Berlin - Hamburg and v.v.
378 – [12] and ✕ Wien - Praha - Děčín - Berlin - Stralsund (- Ostseebad Binz on dates in Table **844**).
379 – [12] and ✕ (Ostseebad Binz on dates in Table **844** -) Stralsund - Berlin - Děčín - Praha - Brno.
1508/9 – [12] and ✕ München - Nürnberg - Jena - Leipzig - Kiel and v.v. See also note ▲.
1614 – [12] and ✕ Nürnberg - Jena - Leipzig - Hamburg. See also note ▲.

A – KOPERNIKUS – 🛏 1, 2 cl., 🛏 2 cl. and [2] ([R]) Praha - Berlin - Köln - Amsterdam and v.v. (see overnight trains summary on page 363). Conveys [2] (*D* **60456/7**) Praha - Berlin and v.v.
B – [12] (37/8) Berlin - Hamburg - Puttgarden - København and v.v.; [12] (380/1) Berlin - Hamburg - Flensburg - Århus and v.v. June 20 - July 3 operates from / to Berlin Gesundbrunnen (not calling at Berlin Ostbahnhof or Hbf).
E – [12] and ✕ Hamburg - Leipzig - Jena - Nürnberg - München (see also note ▲); conveys [12] (1717) Hamburg - Berlin - Leipzig - Erfurt (see Table **850**).

F – To / from Flensburg (Table **823**).
M – [12] and ✕ Hamburg - Leipzig - Jena - Nürnberg - München and v.v. See also note ▲.
T – SYLTER STRAND – To / from Westerland (Table **821**).

f – ⑤ only.
h – ⑦ only.
k – ⑥ only.
o – Berlin **Ostbahnhof** (diverted to Berlin Lichtenberg June 19 - July 3, also train **456** on July 31, Aug. 1, 2).

◐ – Via Stendal.
▽ – To Berlin Ostbf (a. 1438).
◇ – From Berlin Ostbf (d. 1516).
‡ – Train number **1015** on ⑤.
§ – Train number **1623** on ⑤.
⊙ – Train number **1016** on ⑥.
⊡ – Train number **1714*** on ⑥⑦.

⊖ – On June 14 does **not** run Hamburg - Berlin.
▲ – A different routing will apply south of Leipzig Aug. 1 - Sept. 14.
* – A different train number applies **Aug. 1 - Sept. 14** as follows: **1607** runs as **1667**; **1507** runs as **1567**; **1609** runs as **1669**; **1509** runs as **1569**; **109** runs as **1571**; **1513** runs as **1573**; **1515** runs as **1575**; **1517** runs as **1577**; **1518** runs as **1578**; **1614** runs as **1674**; **1514/1714** run as **1574**; **1512** runs as **1572**; **108** runs as **1570**; **1508** runs as **1568**; **1606** runs as **1666**; **1506** runs as **1586**; **1604** runs as **1684**; **1504** runs as **1564**; **1502** runs as **1562**.

841 MAGDEBURG - STENDAL - UELZEN and WITTENBERGE

RE / RB services except where shown

km		⚒	Ⓐ	Ⓐ	Ⓒ				①–⑥		*IC* 2238 D R															*EC* 340 Ⓑ W
0	**Magdeburg** Hbf .... d.	0357	...	0508	0603	0603	0608	0708	0757	0808	0857	0903	0908	1008	1103	1108	1208	1303	1308	1408	1503	1508	1608	1703	1708	...
58	Stendal .... a.	0442	...	0556	0642	0642	0656	0756	0833	0858	0933	0942	0956	1056	1142	1156	1256	1342	1356	1456	1542	1556	1656	1742	1756	...
58	Stendal .... d.	0446	0458	0558	0644	0644	0658a	0758	0834	...	0935	0944	0958	...	1144	1158	1258a	1344	1358	1503a	1544	1558	1658a	1744	1758	1826
113	**Wittenberge** .... a.	|	0537	0637	|	|	0737a	0837	0909	...	1010	|	1037	...	|	1237	1337a	|	1437	1541a	|	1637	1737a	|	1837	|
116	Salzwedel .... a.	0526	...	...	0713	0719	...	...	...	...	...	1013	...	...	1213	...	...	1413	...	...	1613	...	...	1813	...	1851
116	Salzwedel .... d.	0536	...	...	0714	0720	...	...	...	...	...	1014	...	...	1214	...	...	1414	...	...	1614	...	...	1814	...	1853
167	**Uelzen** .... a.	0608	...	...	0745	0751	...	...	...	...	...	1045	...	...	1245	...	...	1445	...	...	1645	...	...	1845	...	1929

						IC 1930 ⑦B		Ⓑ			⑥k
Magdeburg Hbf .... d.	1808	1903	1908	...	2008	...	2108	...	2212	2318	2318
Stendal .... a.	1856	1942	1956	...	2056	...	2156	...	2300	0006	0006
Stendal .... d.	1858	1944	...	2007	2101	2123	2218	2215	...	...	0019
Wittenberge .... a.	1937	|	...	|	2140	|	2257	|	...	...	|
Salzwedel .... a.	...	2013	...	2047	...	2150	...	2254	...	...	0057
Salzwedel .... d.	...	2014	...	...	...	2152	...	...	...	...	...
Uelzen .... a.	...	2045	...	...	...	2216	...	...	...	...	...

	Ⓐ		Ⓐ		①–⑥			⚒		*EC* 341 G W	
Uelzen .... d.	...	...	...	...	...	...	...	0620	...	0756	...
Salzwedel .... a.	...	...	...	...	...	...	...	0652	...	0818	...
Salzwedel .... d.	...	...	0458	...	0533	0600	...	0654	...	0820	...
Wittenberge .... d.	...	...	|	0516a	|	|	0616a	|	0716	|	0816a
Stendal .... a.	...	...	0540	0555a	0604	0640	0655a	0723	0755	0846	0855a
Stendal .... d.	0354	0457	0543	0557	0607	0644	0657	0725	0757	...	0857
Magdeburg Hbf .... a.	0440	0544	0622	0644	0649	0725	0744	0802	0844	...	0944

			①–⑥						*IC* 1931 ⑤B					*IC* 2239 E R										Ⓐ		
Uelzen .... d.	0821	...	...	...	...	1102	...	...	1250	1302	...	...	1502	...	...	...	1702	...	...	1902	...	...	2103	...	...	...
Salzwedel .... a.	0858	...	...	...	...	1133	...	...	1321	1333	...	...	1533	...	...	...	1733	...	...	1933	...	...	2134	...	...	...
Salzwedel .... d.	0902	...	...	...	...	1134	...	...	1323	1334	...	...	1534	...	...	...	1734	...	...	1934	2016	...	2135	2219	...	...
Wittenberge .... d.	|	0916	1016	...	1116	|	...	1316	|	|	1421a	1516	|	1552	1616a	1716	|	1821a	1916	|	|	2057	|	|	2227	0001
Stendal .... a.	0943	0955	1055	...	1155	1207	...	1355	1404	1409	1457a	1555	1607	1624	1655a	1755	1807	1857a	1955	2007	2055	2136	2213	2302	2308	0042
Stendal .... d.	...	0957	1057	1057	1157	1211	1257	1357	...	1411	1458	1557	1611	1626	1657	1757	1811	1858	1957	2011	2057	2137	2214	...	2312	...
Magdeburg Hbf .... a.	...	1044	1144	1144	1244	1251	1344	1444	...	1451	1545	1644	1651	1701	1744	1844	1851	1945	2044	2051	2144	2224	2302	...	2359	...

B – From / to Berlin (Table **810**).
D – Daily until Aug. 30; ⑤⑥ Sept. 4 - Oct. 24.
E – Daily until Aug. 30; ⑤⑦ Sept. 4 - Oct. 25.
G – ①–⑥ only.

R – WARNOW – [12] Leipzig - Halle - Magdeburg - Schwerin - Rostock - Warnemünde and v.v.
W – WAWEL – [12] Kraków - Wrocław - Forst 🛃 - Cottbus - Berlin - Hamburg and v.v.

a – Ⓐ only.
k – Also Oct. 2, 30; not Dec. 12.

842 LEIPZIG - DRESDEN

km		◧	◧ ①–⑤ v	◧ ⑥⑦ t		*RE* 17441		*RE* 17443 ⚒r	*RE* 17445	*CNL* 459 [R] R🍷	*D* 61459 F	*RE* 17447 ⚒r	*ICE* 1741 ①–⑤ J	*RE* 17449	*ICE* 1553 ①–⑤ G✕	*RE* 17451 ⚒r	*ICE* 1543 ✕	*RE* 17453	*ICE* 1555 ①–⑥ ✕	*RE* 17455 ⚒r	*ICE* 1545 ⚒ ✕	*ICE* 1745 † ✕	*RE* 17457
	Frankfurt Flughafen Fernbf ✈ **850** d.	...	...	...	...	...	...	...	...	...	...	...	...	...	...	...	...	...	...	...	0811	...	...
	Frankfurt (Main) Hbf **850** .... d.	...	...	...	...	...	...	...	...	0055z	...	...	...	...	0517g	...	0618e	...	0720	...	|	0822	...
0	**Leipzig** Hbf .... d.	0010	0010	0120	...	...	...	0458	0558	|	0651	0658	0751	0758	0851	0858	0951	0958	1051	1058	1151	1151	1158
26	Wurzen .... d.	0038	0038	0151	...	...	...	0519	0619	|	|	0719	|	0819	|	0919	|	1019	|	1119	|	|	1219
53	Oschatz .... d.	...	0057	0211	...	...	...	0538	0638	|	|	0738	|	0838	|	0938	|	1038	|	1138	|	|	1238
66	Riesa .... d.	...	...	...	...	0448	...	0548	0648	0721	0723	0748	0823	0848	0923	0948	1023	1048	1123	1148	1223	1223	1248
102	Coswig .... **843 856 857** d.	...	...	...	...	0518	...	0619	0719	|	|	0819	|	0919	|	1019	|	1119	|	1219	|	|	1319
116	**Dresden** Neustadt ▲ .... **856 857** a.	...	...	...	...	0531	...	0634	0734	0801	0801	0831	0859	0934	1000	1031	1059	1134	1200	1231	1259	1259	1334
120	**Dresden** Hbf .... **843 856 857** a.	...	...	...	...	0538	...	0641	0741	0807	0807	0840	0906	0941	1007	1040	1106	1141	1207	1240	1306	1306	1341

	ICE 1557 ①–⑥ S✕	*ICE* 1597 ⑦ W✕	*RE* 17459 ⚒r	*ICE* 1547 ✕	*RE* 17461	*ICE* 1559 W✕	*RE* 17463	*ICE* 1549 ✕	*RE* 17465	*ICE* 1651 W✕	*RE* 17467	*ICE* 1641 ✕	*RE* 17469	*ICE* 1653 W✕	*RE* 17471 Ⓑ	*ICE* 1643 ✕	*RE* 17473	*ICE* 1602 ‡Ⓑ M✕	*RE* 17475	*ICE* 1645 ✕	◧	*ICE* 1657 ⑤⑦ W✕	*RE* 17477
Frankfurt Flughafen Fernbf ✈ **850** d.	...	0901	...	1011	...	1103	...	1211	...	1303	...	1411	...	1503	...	1611	...	...	...	1811	...	1903	...
Frankfurt (Main) Hbf **850** .... d.	0921	0921	...	|	...	1119	...	|	...	1319	...	|	...	1520	...	|	...	...	...	|	...	1919	...
Leipzig Hbf .... d.	1251	1251	1258	1351	1358	1451	1458	1551	1558	1651	1658	1751	1758	1851	1858	1951	1958	2051	2058	2151	2208	2256	2306
Wurzen .... d.	|	|	1319	|	1419	|	1519	|	1619	|	1719	|	1819	|	1919	|	2019	|	2119	|	2236	|	2327
Oschatz .... d.	|	|	1338	|	1438	|	1538	|	1638	|	1738	|	1838	|	1938	|	2038	|	2138	|	...	|	2346
Riesa .... d.	1323	1323	1348	1423	1448	1523	1548	1623	1648	1723	1748	1823	1848	1923	1948	2023	2048	2123	2148	2223	...	2328	2356
Coswig .... **843 856 857** d.	|	|	1419	|	1519	|	1619	|	1719	|	1819	|	1919	|	2019	|	2119	|	2219	|	...	|	0028
Dresden Neustadt ▲ .... **856 857** a.	1400	1401	1431	1459	1534	1600	1631	1659	1734	1800	1831	1859	1934	2000	2031	2059	2131	2200	2231	2259	...	0001	0041
Dresden Hbf .... **843 856 857** a.	1407	1407	1440	1506	1541	1607	1640	1706	1741	1807	1840	1906	1941	2007	2040	2106	2138	2207	2238	2306	...	0009	0048

	◧ ①–⑤ v	◧ †h	*RE* 17440 ⚒r	*ICE* 1644 ①–⑤ ✕	*RE* 17442	*ICE* 1605* ①–⑥ M✕	*RE* 17444 ⚒r	*ICE* 1642 ①–⑥ ✕	*RE* 17446	*ICE* 1652 W✕	*RE* 17448 ⚒r	*ICE* 1640 ✕	*RE* 17450	*ICE* 1650 W✕	*RE* 17452 ⚒r	*ICE* 1548 ✕	*RE* 17454	*ICE* 1558 W✕	*RE* 17456 ⚒r	*ICE* 1546 ✕	*RE* 17458	*ICE* 1556 W✕	*RE* 17460
Dresden Hbf .... **843 856 857** d.	...	...	0412	0444	0520	0554	0620	0654	0720	0754	0820	0854	0920	0954	1020	1054	1120	1154	1220	1254	1320	1354	1420
Dresden Neustadt ▲ .... **856 857** d.	...	...	0419	0452	0527	0602	0627	0702	0727	0802	0827	0902	0927	1002	1027	1102	1127	1202	1227	1302	1327	1402	1427
Coswig .... **843 856 857** d.	...	...	0431	|	0539	|	0639	|	0739	|	0839	|	0939	|	1039	|	1139	|	1239	|	1339	|	1439
Riesa .... d.	...	...	0501	0525	0609	0636	0709	0736	0809	0836	0909	0936	1009	1036	1109	1136	1209	1236	1309	1336	1409	1436	1509
Oschatz .... d.	0406	0500	0510	|	0618	|	0718	|	0818	|	0918	|	1018	|	1118	|	1218	|	1318	|	1418	|	1518
Wurzen .... d.	0425	0519	0530	|	0638	|	0738	|	0838	|	0938	|	1038	|	1138	|	1238	|	1338	|	1438	|	1538
Leipzig Hbf .... a.	0453	0548	0553	0557	0703	0707	0801	0807	0901	0907	1001	1007	1101	1107	1201	1207	1301	1307	1401	1407	1501	1507	1601
Frankfurt (Main) Hbf **850** .... a.	...	...	...	|	...	...	...	|	...	1236	...	|	...	1436	...	|	...	1636	...	|	...	1836	...
Frankfurt Flughafen Fernbf ✈ **850** a.	...	...	...	0948	...	...	...	1148	...	1255	...	1348	...	1455	...	1548	...	1655	...	1748	...	1855	...

	ICE 1544 ①–⑤ ✕	*ICE* 1744 ⑦ ✕	*RE* 17462	*ICE* 1554 W✕	*ICE* 1594 Ⓑ S✕	*RE* 17464	*ICE* 1542 ①–⑤ ✕	*ICE* 1742 ⑦ ✕	*RE* 17466	*ICE* 1552 ✕	*RE* 17468	*ICE* 1740 H	*RE* 17470 Ⓑ	*ICE* 1550 ⑦ ✕	*RE* 17472		*D* 61458 E	*CNL* 458 [R] R🍷		◧		*RE* 17474	*RE* 17476
Dresden Hbf .... **843 856 857** d.	1454	1454	1520	1554	1554	1620	1654	1654	1720	1754	1820	1854	1920	1954	2020	...	2115	2115	...	...	...	2220	2320
Dresden Neustadt ▲ .... **856 857** d.	1502	1502	1527	1602	1602	1627	1702	1702	1727	1802	1827	1902	1927	2002	2027	...	2126	2126	...	...	...	2227	2327
Coswig .... **843 856 857** d.	|	|	1539	|	|	1639	|	|	1739	|	1839	|	1939	|	2039	...	|	|	...	...	...	2239	2339
Riesa .... d.	1536	1536	1609	1636	1636	1709	1736	1736	1809	1836	1909	1936	2009	2036	2109	...	2203	2203	...	...	...	2309	0009
Oschatz .... d.	|	|	1618	|	|	1718	|	|	1818	|	1918	|	2018	|	2118	...	|	|	...	...	...	2318	...
Wurzen .... d.	|	|	1638	|	|	1738	|	|	1838	|	1938	|	2038	|	2138	...	|	|	...	2220	...	2338	...
Leipzig Hbf .... a.	1607	1607	1701	1707	1707	1801	1807	1807	1901	1907	2001	2005	2101	2107	2201	...	2240	|	...	2248	...	2359	...
Frankfurt (Main) Hbf **850** .... a.	1940	|	...	2036	2036	...	2146	|	...	2254	...	...	...	0051	...	...	...	0359z	...	...	...	...	...
Frankfurt Flughafen Fernbf ✈ **850** a.	...	1948	...	2055	...	...	...	2149	...	...	...	...	...	...	...	...	...	...	...	...	...	...	...

E – [2] Praha - Erfurt.
F – [2] Fulda - Praha.
G – [12] and ✕ (Frankfurt ① -) Eisenach - Dresden. Train number **1753** on ②–⑤ Aug. 4 - Sept. 11.
H – ①②③④⑦. [12] Dresden - Leipzig - Magdeburg (- Hannover ⑦). Conveys ✕ on ⑦.
J – From Magdeburg (Table **810**).
M – [12] and ✕ München - Nürnberg - Leipzig - Dresden and v.v.
R – CANOPUS – 🛏 1, 2 cl., 🛏 2 cl., [2] (reclining) and 🍷 Praha - Karlsruhe - Basel - Zürich and v.v.
S – From / to Saarbrücken (Table **919**).
W – From / to Wiesbaden (Table **912**).

e – ①–⑥ only.
g – ① only.

h – Also Oct. 31, Nov. 18.
r – Not Oct. 31, Nov. 18.
t – Also Nov. 18.
v – Not Nov. 18.
z – Frankfurt (Main) **Süd**.

* – Train number **1665** Aug. 1 - Sept. 14.
‡ – Train number **1662** Aug. 2 - Sept. 14.
◧ – *S-Bahn*.
▲ – On certain dates services may not call at Dresden Neustadt. Please check locally before travelling.

RE / RB services except where shown — (BERLIN -) ELSTERWERDA - CHEMNITZ and DRESDEN — 843

See Tables **851** / **874** for Berlin - Chemnitz via Leipzig. See Table **840** for direct *EC* and *IC* services Berlin - Dresden and v.v.

km							*EC* 171						*EC* 171						*EC* 179		*IC* 2071			
					Ⓐ	Ⓐ	✕						✕				Ⓐ		✕		✕			
	Berlin Hbf **845** d.	...	...	...	0422	...	0635	...	0728	...	0929	...	1235	...	1329	...	1429	...	1635	...	1835	...	1929	...
0	**Elsterwerda** d.	...	0452a	0603a	0614	0703	0759	0803	0932	1003	1132	1203	1359	1403	1532	1603	1631	1703a	1759	1803	1959	2003	2132	2214
24	Riesa a.	...	0518a	0629a	...	0729	...	0829	...	1029	...	1229	...	1429	...	1629	...	1729a	...	1829	...	2029	...	2240
24	Riesa d.	0441	0541	0641	...	0741	...	0841	...	1041	...	1241	...	1441	...	1641	...	1741	...	1841	...	2041	...	2241
50	Döbeln Hbf d.	0506	0606	0706	...	0806	...	0906	...	1106	...	1306	...	1506	...	1706	...	1806	...	1906	...	2106	...	2306
91	**Chemnitz** Hbf a.	0553	0653	0753	...	0853	...	0953	...	1153	...	1353	...	1553	...	1753	...	1853	...	1953	...	2153	...	2353

				IC 2072		*IC* 2070						*EC* 378								*EC* 170				
	Ⓐ			G✕		✕						✕				Ⓐ				✕	Ⓑ		Ⓐ	
Chemnitz Hbf d.	0405	...	0505	...	0605	...	0805	...	1005	...	1205	...	1405	...	1505	...	1605	...	1805	...	1905	2005	2105	2205
Döbeln Hbf d.	0446	...	0546	...	0646	...	0846	...	1046	...	1246	...	1446	...	1546	...	1646	...	1846	...	1946	2046	2146	2246
Riesa a.	0511	...	0611	...	0711	...	0911	...	1111	...	1311	...	1511	...	1611	...	1713	...	1913	...	2011	2111	2211	2311
Riesa d.	0516a	...	0616a	...	0716	...	0932	...	1132	...	1316	...	1516	...	1632a	...	1732	...	1916	...	2032v	2132c	2232	...
Elsterwerda a.	0539a	0546	0639a	0652	0739	0752	0955	1035	1155	1235	1339	1352	1539	1635	1655a	1734	1755	1835	1939	1952	2055v	2155c	2255	...
Berlin Hbf **845** a.	...	0733	...	0820	...	0919	...	1232	...	1432	...	1518	...	1832	...	1933	...	2032	...	2120	...	...	...	...

Elsterwerda - Dresden

km		Ⓐ	Ⓐ	Ⓐ						⑥⑦
0	Elsterwerda-Biehla d.	0440	0540	0640	0740	0940	and every	2140	2340	2340
2	**Elsterwerda** d.	0445	0545	0645	0745	0945	**two** hours	2145	2343	2345
41	Coswig **842 856/7** d.	0525	0625	0725	0825	1025	until	2225	...	0025
59	**Dresden** Hbf **842 856/7** a.	0546	0646	0746	0846	1046		2246	...	0046

		Ⓐ					
Dresden Hbf **842 856/7** d.	0509	0609	0709	0909	and every	1909	2109
Coswig **842 856/7** d.	0533	0633	0733	0933	**two** hours	1933	2133
Elsterwerda a.	0612	0712	0812	1012	until	2012	2212
Esterwerda-Biehla a.	0619	0719	0819	1019		2019	2219

G – ①–⑥ only. Train number **2074** on ⑥. **a** – Ⓐ only. **c** – ⑥⑦ (also Nov. 18). **v** – ①–⑤ (not Nov. 18).

RE / RB services except where shown — STRALSUND - OSTSEEBAD BINZ / SASSNITZ — 844

km											*IC* 2186					*CNL* 1259	*IC* 2184								
		Ⓐ			Ⓐ	Ⓐ					①		A		A	⑥J 🅁♦	①–⑥ H🍸		A		A		A		A
	Hamburg Hbf **830** d.	...	...	...	...	...	...	...	...	...	0541	...	...	...	...	...	0744	...	...	...	...	...	...	...	...
	Rostock Hbf **830** d.	...	...	0453	...	0553	...	...	0700	...	0738	...	...	0900	...	...	0938	...	...	1100	...	...	...	1300	...
0	**Stralsund** d.	0504	...	0604	...	0704	0704	...	0804	...	0841	0904	...	1004	...	...	1041	1104	...	1204	...	1304	...	1404	...
29	Bergen auf Rügen d.	0533	...	0633	...	0733	0733	...	0833	...	0905	0933	...	1033	...	1044	1105	1133	...	1233	...	1333	...	1433	...
39	Lietzow (Rügen) d.	0542	...	0642	0644	0742	0742	0744	0842	0844	|	0942	0944	1042	1044	|	|	1142	1144	1242	1244	1342	1344	1442	1444
	Ostseebad Binz a.	|	...	|	0657	|	|	0757	|	0857	0932	0955	|	|	1057	1117	1132	1155	|	|	1257	1355	|	|	1457
51	**Sassnitz** a.	0556	...	0655	...	0755	0755	...	0855	...	...	...	0957	1055	...	...	...	...	1157	1255	...	...	1357	1455	...

	IC 2212					*IC* 2355	*IC* 2376					*EC* 378												
	✕♦		A		A	🍸♦	⑥ 🍸♦					✕♦												Ⓑ
Hamburg Hbf **830** d.	1117	...	...	...	...	...	1344	...	...	...	...	...	...	...	...	...	...	...	...	...	...	...	...	...
Rostock Hbf **830** d.	1317	...	...	1500	...	...	1538	...	...	1700	...	...	...	...	1900	...	...	...	...	...	2100	...	...	...
Stralsund d.	1425	1504	...	1604	...	1637	1657	1704	...	1804	...	1830	1904	...	2004	...	2104	...	...	...	2204	...	...	2311
Bergen auf Rügen d.	1451	1533	...	1633	...	1706	1721	1733	...	1833	...	1854	1933	...	2033	...	2133	...	←	...	2233	...	...	2339
Lietzow (Rügen) d.	|	1542	1544	1642	1644	|	|	1742	1744	1842	1844	|	1942	1944	2042	2044	2141	2144	2146	...	2242	2244	...	...
Ostseebad Binz a.	1516	1555	|	|	1657	1732	1741	1755	|	|	1857	1917	1955	|	|	2057	→	|	2158	...	|	2257	...	...
Sassnitz a.	...	...	1557	1655	...	...	...	...	1757	1855	...	...	...	1957	2055	...	...	2157	...	...	2255	...	...	...

km												*IC* 2356					*IC* 2213		*EC* 379						*IC* 2377
		Ⓐ				Ⓐ	⚒r					①–⑥ ♦	A		A		✕♦		✕♦	A			A		🍸♦
	Sassnitz d.	0403	...	0505	...	...	0605	...	0705	...	0805	...	...	0905	1003	...	...	...	...	...	1105	...	1203	...	...
0	**Ostseebad Binz** d.	|	...	|	...	0603	|	0703	|	0803	|	0843	0903	|	|	1006	1029	...	1042	1103	|	...	|	1206	1229
12	Lietzow (Rügen) d.	0417	...	0520	...	0616	0620	0716	0720	0816	0820	|	0916	0920	1017	1020	|	...	|	1116	1120	...	1217	1220	|
22	Bergen auf Rügen d.	0425	...	0528	...	...	0628	...	0728	...	0828	0910	...	0928	...	1028	1053	...	1108	...	1128	...	...	1228	1253
51	**Stralsund** a.	0454	...	0557	...	...	0657	...	0757	...	0857	0934	...	0957	...	1057	1119	...	1130	...	1157	...	...	1257	1319
	Rostock Hbf **830** a.	0547	...	0654	...	...	...	...	0854	...	...	...	...	1054	...	...	1219	...	...	...	1254	...	...	...	1419
	Hamburg Hbf **830** a.	...	...	...	...	...	...	...	...	...	...	...	...	...	...	...	1431	...	...	...	...	...	...	...	1623

									IC 2183			*IC* 1852			*CNL* 1258									
	A		A		A		A		⑦ H✕			⑦ B			⑥K 🅁♦									
Sassnitz d.	...	1305	1403	...	...	1505	1603	...	...	1703	...	...	1803	...	...	...	1905	2003	...	...	2103	...	2203	...
Ostseebad Binz d.	1303	|	|	1406	1503	|	|	1606	1629	|	1706	1757	|	1806	1820	1903	|	|	2006	2103	|	...	|	2206
Lietzow (Rügen) d.	1316	1320	1417	1420	1516	1520	1617	1620	|	1717	1720	|	1817	1820	|	1917	1920	2017	2020	2116	2120	...	2217	2220
Bergen auf Rügen d.	...	1328	...	1428	...	1528	...	1628	1652	...	1728	1818	...	1828	1842	...	1928	...	2028	...	2128	...	...	2228
Stralsund a.	...	1357	...	1457	...	1557	...	1657	1719	...	1757	1845	...	1857	...	...	1957	...	2057	...	2157	...	...	2257
Rostock Hbf **830** a.	...	1454	...	...	...	1654	...	...	1820	...	1854	...	...	...	...	...	2054	...	...	...	2254	...	...	...
Hamburg Hbf **830** a.	...	...	...	...	...	...	...	...	2016	...	...	...	...	...	...	...	...	...	...	...	...	...	...	...

♦ – **NOTES** (LISTED BY TRAIN NUMBER)

378 – Daily until Sept. 12; ⑤⑥ Sept. 18 - Oct. 24. (12) and ✕ Wien - Praha - Berlin - Ostseebad Binz.

379 – Daily until Sept. 13; ⑥⑦ Sept. 19 - Oct. 25. (12) and ✕ Ostseebad Binz - Berlin - Praha - Brno. Until July 2 Ostseebad Binz d. 1022, Bergen auf Rügen d. 1043, Stralsund a. 1105.

1258/9 – SIRIUS – 🛏 1, 2 cl., ▬ 2 cl., (2) (reclining) Ostseebad Binz - Basel - Zürich and v.v.

2212 – RÜGEN – (12) and ✕ Koblenz - Köln - Hamburg - Ostseebad Binz.

2213 – RÜGEN – (12) and ✕ Ostseebad Binz - Hamburg - Köln - Stuttgart.

2355 – STRELASUND – (12) and 🍸 (Düsseldorf ① -) (Dortmund ①–⑥ -) Erfurt - Halle - Berlin - Ostseebad Binz.

2356 – STRELASUND – (12) and 🍸 Ostseebad Binz - Berlin - Halle - Erfurt - Kassel - Düsseldorf. Until July 2 Ostseebad Binz d. 0826, Bergen auf Rügen d. 0846, Stralsund a. 0908.

2376 – (12) and 🍸 Karlsruhe - Frankfurt - Hannover - Hamburg - Ostseebad Binz.

2377 – ARKONA – (12) and 🍸 Ostseebad Binz - Hamburg - Hannover - Frankfurt (- Karlsruhe on dates in Table **911**).

A – Daily until Oct. 9; ①–⑤ from Oct. 12.
B – To Berlin (Table **845**).
H – From / to Hannover (Table **902**).
J – ⑥ July 4 - Aug. 22 (previous day from Zürich).
K – ⑥ July 4 - Aug. 22.
r – Not Oct. 31.

OLA ● — BERGEN AUF RÜGEN - PUTBUS - LAUTERBACH and RÜGENSCHE BÄDERBAHN — 844a

km		Ⓐ	Ⓒ		h			h	
0	**Bergen** auf Rügen d.	0536	0636	0736	0836	each train runs	1736	1836	1936
10	**Putbus** a.	0545	0645	0745	0845	every **two**	1745	1845	1945
12	**Lauterbach** Mole a.	0550	0650	0750	...	hours until	1750	...	1950

	Ⓐ	Ⓒ		h			h	
Lauterbach Mole d.	0605	0705	0805	...	each train runs	1756	...	2005
Putbus d.	0612	0712	0812	0912	every **two**	1802	1912	2012
Bergen auf Rügen a.	0621	0721	0821	0921	hours until	1811	1921	2021

Rügensche Bäderbahn. Operated by Eisenbahn-Bau- und Betriebsgesellschaft Pressnitztalbahn mbH, Bahnhofstraße 1a - 18586 Göhren. **Valid until Oct. 3, 2009**.

km											w
0	**Lauterbach** Mole d.	...	...	...	1101h	1301h	1501h	...	1701h	1901h	...
2	**Putbus** a.	...	...	...	1108h	1308h	1508h	...	1708h	1908h	...
2	**Putbus** d.	0748	...	0948	1148	1348	1548	...	1748	1948	...
14	Binz Lokalbahn ▲ ‡ d.	0820	0924	1020	1220	1420	1620	1724	1820	2020	2224
22	Sellin (Rügen) Ost ‡ d.	0849	0953	1049	1249	1449	1649	1753	1849	2049	2253
27	**Göhren** (Rügen) ‡ a.	0904	1008	1104	1304	1504	1704	1808	1904	2104	2308

										w
Göhren (Rügen) ‡ d.	0828	0932	1132	1332	1532	1628	1732	1828	1932	2128
Sellin (Rügen) Ost ‡ d.	0847	0951	1151	1351	1551	1647	1751	1847	1951	2147
Binz Lokalbahn ▲ ‡ d.	0913	1020	1220	1420	1620	1713	1820	1916	2020	2213
Putbus a.	...	1046	1246	1446	1646	...	1846	1942	2046	...
Putbus d.	...	1050h	1250h	1450h	1650h	...	1850h	...	...	...
Lauterbach Mole a.	...	1056h	1256h	1456h	1656h	...	1856h	...	...	...

h – Until Aug. 30.
w – June 27 - Aug. 29 only.
● – Ostseeland Verkehr GmbH.
▲ – 2½ km from Ostseebad Binz DB station.
‡ – Additional trains Binz - Göhren and v.v. **From Binz** at 1124, 1324 and 1524. **From Göhren** at 1028, 1228 and 1428.

845 ELSTERWERDA - BERLIN - STRALSUND

RE / RB services except where shown

km		①–⑤	IC 2115 ①–⑤ J✕	¶				CNL 1259 ⑥X [R]T	①–⑤		⑥⑦ Z	◧		①–⑤		IC 2351 H 🍷	⑥⑦		①–⑤		IC 2353 K 🍷				IC 2355 G 🍷
0	**Elsterwerda** 840 d.	...	...	...	...	0425r	...	...	0546	...	...	...	0624	0734	...	...	...	0835	...	...	...	1035	...	...	...
20	Doberlug-Kirchhain d.	...	...	...	...	0454	...	...	0601	...	...	...	0643	0749	...	...	...	0854	...	...	...	1054	...	...	...
140	**Berlin** Hbf 840 a.	...	...	...	...	0632	...	0718	0733	...	...	...	0832	0933	...	...	...	1032	...	...	...	1232	...	...	...
140	**Berlin** Hbf d.	...	...	...	0534	0634	...	|	0734	0734	0809	0759	0834	0934	0934	0938	...	1034	...	1134	1138	1234	...	1334	1338
166	Bernau (b. Berlin) d.	...	...	...	0553	0653	...	|	0753	0753	0829	0836	0853	0953	0953	0959	...	1053	...	1153	1159	1253	...	1353	1359
188	Eberswalde Hbf d.	...	...	0507	0608	0707	...	|	0807	0807	0844	0850	0907	1007	1007	1015	...	1107	...	1207	1215	1307	...	1407	1415
214	Angermünde a.	...	...	0525	0626	0725	...	|	0825	0825	0859	0905	0925	1025	1025	1029	...	1125	...	1225	1229	1325	...	1425	1429
214	Angermünde d.	...	...	0533	0634	0733	0737	|	0834	0834	0900	0910	0933	1034	1034	1031	1034	1133	1134	1234	1231	1333	1334	1434	1431
237	Schwedt (Oder) a.	...	...	|	0657	|	|	|	0857	0857	|	|	|	1057	1057	|	|	|	|	1257	|	|	|	1457	|
	Tantow (ticket point) d.	...	...	|	...	|	0813	|	...	...	|	0939	|	...	...	|	1110	|	1210	...	|	|	1410	...	|
	Szczecin Gumience 🏛 d.	...	...	|	...	|	0829	|	...	...	|	0955	|	...	...	|	1126	|	1226	...	|	|	1426	...	|
	Szczecin Głowny a.	...	...	|	...	|	0834	|	...	...	|	1001	|	...	...	|	1132	|	1232	...	|	|	1432	...	|
251	Prenzlau d.	...	...	0600	...	0800	...	|	...	...	0924	...	1000	...	...	1054	...	1200	...	...	1254	1400	...	...	1454
276	**Pasewalk** a.	...	...	0616	...	0816	...	|	...	...	|	...	1016	...	...	1108	...	1216	...	...	1308	1416	...	...	1508
276	**Pasewalk** d.	0428	...	0621	...	0821	...	|	...	...	|	...	1021	...	...	1110	...	1221	...	...	1310	1417	...	...	1510
319	Anklam d.	0501	...	0652	...	0851	...	|	...	...	|	...	1051	...	...	1136	...	1251	...	...	1336	1451	...	...	1536
335	Züssow 846 d.	0514	...	0705	...	0905	...	0945	...	...	1014	...	1105	...	...	1148	...	1305	...	...	1348	1505	...	...	1548
353	Greifswald 846 d.	0530	0702	0722	...	0922	...	0959	...	...	1028	...	1122	...	...	1201	...	1322	...	...	1401	1522	...	...	1601
384	**Stralsund** 846 a.	0553	0724	0746	...	0944	...	...	...	...	1051	...	1144	...	...	1224	...	1344	...	...	1424	1544	...	...	1624

				EC 378 B✕			IC 145 Ⓑ A	①–⑤		IC 2157 Ⓑ L 🍷			①–⑤		IC 2359 ⑤⑦ L		⑤⑥	①–⑤	⑥⑦	⑦	⑤–⑦ b	⑥⑦	①–⑤ ♥	①–⑥	
Elsterwerda 840 d.	1235	...	...	1352	1435	...	...	1534	...	...	1635	...	1734	...	...	1835	1835	1934	...	...	...	2035	2035	...	...
Doberlug-Kirchhain d.	1254	...	...	|	1454	...	...	1549	...	...	1654	...	1749	...	...	1854	1854	1949	...	...	...	2054	2054	...	...
Berlin Hbf 840 a.	1432	...	...	1518	1632	...	...	1733	...	...	1832	...	1933	...	...	2032	2032	2133	...	...	...	2232	2234	...	...
Berlin Hbf d.	1434	...	1534	1537	1634	...	1728	1734	1734	1752	1834	...	1934	1934	1938	2034	2034	2134	2134	...	...	2234	2235	...	2334
Bernau (b. Berlin) d.	1453	...	1553	1559	1653	...	1750	1756	1756	1813	1853	...	1953	1953	1959	2053	2053	2153	2153	...	...	2253	2253	...	2353
Eberswalde Hbf d.	1507	...	1607	1615	1707	...	1805	1813	1813	1828	1907	...	2007	2007	2015	2107	2107	2207	2207	...	...	2311	2311	...	0011
Angermünde a.	1525	...	1625	1629	1725	...	1821	1832	1832	1843	1925	...	2025	2025	2029	2125	2125	2225	2225	...	...	2330	2330	...	...
Angermünde d.	1533	1534	1634	1630	1733	1743	1839	1834	1834	1845	1933	1951	2034	2034	2031	2133	2133	*2234*	2234	2233	2234	2334	2334	2334	...
Schwedt (Oder) a.	|	|	1657	|	|	|	|	1857	1857	|	|	|	2057	2057	|	|	|	*2257*	2257	|	|	2357	2357	|	...
Tantow (ticket point) d.	|	1610	...	|	|	1822	|	...	...	|	|	2031	...	...	|	|	|	...	...	|	2310	...	...	|	...
Szczecin Gumience 🏛 d.	|	1626	...	|	|	1838	1929	...	...	|	|	2048	...	...	|	|	|	...	...	|	2326	...	...	|	...
Szczecin Głowny a.	|	1632	...	|	|	1848	1935	...	...	|	|	2058	...	...	|	|	|	...	...	|	2332	...	...	|	...
Prenzlau d.	1600	...	...	1653	1800	...	...	...	...	1908	2000	...	...	...	2054	2200	2200	...	...	2301	...	...	...	0002	...
Pasewalk a.	1616	...	...	1707	1816	...	...	...	...	1921	2016	...	...	...	2108	2216	2216	...	...	2317	...	...	...	0018	...
Pasewalk d.	1620	...	...	1708	1820	...	...	...	...	1923	2021	...	...	...	2110	...	2221	...	...	2318	...	...	...	...	...
Anklam d.	1651	...	...	1734	1851	...	...	...	...	1951	2052	...	...	...	2136	...	2251	...	...	2349	...	...	...	...	...
Züssow 846 d.	1705	...	...	1746	1905	...	...	...	...	2003	2106	...	...	...	2148	...	2305	...	...	0002	...	...	...	...	...
Greifswald 846 d.	1722	...	...	1759	1922	...	...	...	...	2017	2122	...	...	...	2201	...	2322	...	...	0018	...	...	...	...	...
Stralsund 846 a.	1744	...	...	1822	1944	...	...	...	...	2040	2144	...	...	...	2224	...	2344	...	...	0039	...	...	...	...	...

km		Ⓒ	Ⓐ	①			Ⓐ			IC 148 ①–⑥ A			IC 2150 ①–⑥ D⊠				IC 2356 E⊠				EC 379 C⊠		Ⓐ		
	Stralsund 846 d.	...	...	0319	...	...	...	...	0416	...	...	0616	0739	...	...	0816	0939	...	1016	...	1139	...	...	1216	...
	Greifswald 846 d.	...	...	0354	...	...	...	...	0438	...	...	0638	0759	...	...	0838	0959	...	1038	...	1159	...	...	1238	...
	Züssow 846 d.	...	...	0407	...	...	...	...	0454	...	...	0654	0813	...	...	0854	1013	...	1054	...	1213	...	...	1254	...
	Anklam d.	...	...	0418	...	...	...	...	0506	...	...	0706	0825	...	...	0906	1025	...	1106	...	1225	...	...	1306	...
	Pasewalk a.	...	...	0441	...	...	...	...	0534	...	...	0734	0848	...	...	0934	1048	...	1136	...	1248	...	...	1336	...
	Pasewalk d.	...	...	0442	0442	...	...	...	0544	...	...	0744	0850	...	...	0944	1050	...	1144	...	1250	...	...	1344	...
	Prenzlau d.	...	...	0457	0457	...	...	...	0600	...	...	0800	0907	...	...	1000	1107	...	1200	...	1307	...	...	1400	...
0	**Szczecin** Głowny d.	...	...	|	|	...	...	0517	|	0610	...	|	|	...	0913	|	|	...	|	1224	|	...	...	|	1424
5	Szczecin Gumience 🏛 d.	...	...	|	|	...	...	0525	|	0617	...	|	|	...	0920	|	|	...	|	1234	|	...	...	|	1434
24	Tantow (ticket point) d.	...	...	|	|	...	...	0541	|	0635u	...	|	|	...	0941	|	|	...	|	1251	|	...	...	|	1451
	Schwedt (Oder) d.	...	...	|	|	0506	0506	|	|	|	0706	|	|	0906	|	|	|	1106	|	|	|	1306	1306	|	|
64	Angermünde a.	...	...	0523	0523	0529	0529	0616	0628	0705	0729	0828	0927	0929	1015	1028	1127	1129	1226	1325	1328	1329	1329	1426	1525
	Angermünde d.	...	0434	...	...	0533	0533	...	0634	0720	0734	0834	0929	0934	...	1034	1129	1134	1233	...	1330	1334	1334	1433	...
	Eberswalde Hbf d.	0449	0454	...	...	0552	0552	...	0654	0744	0754	0854	0946	0954	...	1054	1146	1154	1252	...	1346	1354	1354	1452	...
	Bernau (b. Berlin) d.	0509	0509	...	...	0609	0609	...	0709	0800	0809	0909	1003	1009	...	1109	1203	1209	1307	...	1403	1409	1409	1507	...
	Berlin Hbf a.	0527	0527	...	...	0627	0627	...	0726	0821	0827	0927	1023	1027	...	1127	1223	1227	1325	...	1423	1427	1427	1525	...
	Berlin Hbf 840 d.	0529	0529	...	...	...	0629	...	0728	...	...	0929	...	...	...	1129	...	...	1329	...	...	...	1429	1529	...
	Doberlug-Kirchhain d.	0713	0713	...	...	...	0814	...	0913	...	...	1113	...	...	...	1313	...	...	1513	...	...	...	1614	1713	...
	Elsterwerda 840 a.	0732	0732	...	...	...	0831	...	0932	...	...	1132	...	...	...	1332	...	...	1532	...	...	...	1631	1732	...

	IC 2352 N ⊠		Ⓐ			IC 2350 Ⓑ R⊠		Ⓐ			IC 1932 ⑦ M	IC 2358 ⑥ ⊠	⊡	IC 2116 ①–⑤ J✕		IC 1852 ⑦ O	CNL 1258 ⑥V [R]T	△	⑥⑦ Z		⑤–⑦ b		①–⑤	⑥⑦	● 2
Stralsund 846 d.	1339	...	...	1417	...	1539	...	...	1616	...	1711	1739	...	1814	1825	1859	...	...	1912	...	...	2016	...	...	2303
Greifswald 846 d.	1359	...	...	1438	...	1559	...	...	1638	...	1731	1759	...	1833	1846	1919	1921	...	1932	...	...	2038	...	...	2328
Züssow 846 d.	1413	...	...	1454	...	1613	...	...	1654	...	|	1813	...	...	1901	|	1934	...	1952	...	...	2054	...	...	2342
Anklam d.	1425	...	...	1506	...	1625	...	...	1706	...	1754	1825	...	...	1913	1942	|	...	|	...	...	2106	...	...	...
Pasewalk a.	1448	...	...	1534	...	1648	...	...	1736	...	1817	1848	...	...	1941	2005	|	...	|	...	...	2134	...	...	...
Pasewalk d.	1450	...	...	1544	...	1650	...	...	1744	...	1819	1850	...	...	1944	2007	|	...	|	...	...	2144	...	...	...
Prenzlau d.	1507	...	...	1600	...	1707	...	...	1800	...	1836	1907	...	...	2000	2024	|	...	2041	...	...	2200	...	...	...
Szczecin Głowny d.	|	...	...	|	1624	|	...	...	|	1753	|	|	...	...	|	|	|	2006	|	...	2128	|	...	...	...
Szczecin Gumience 🏛 d.	|	...	...	|	1634	|	...	...	|	1800	|	|	...	...	|	|	|	2013	|	...	2135	|	...	...	...
Tantow (ticket point) d.	|	...	...	|	1651	|	...	...	|	1820	|	|	...	...	|	|	|	2029	|	...	2151	|	...	...	...
Schwedt (Oder) d.	|	1506	1506	|	|	|	1706	1706	|	|	|	|	1906	...	|	|	|	|	|	2106	|	|	2303	2303	...
Angermünde a.	1527	1529	1529	1626	1725	1727	1729	1729	1826	1854	1856	1927	1929	...	2028	2045	|	2057	2105	2129	2225	2228	2326	2326	...
Angermünde d.	1529	1534	1534	1633	...	1729	1734	1734	1833	...	1858	1929	1934	...	2033	2047	|	2058	2109	2134	...	2234	2334	2334	...
Eberswalde Hbf d.	1546	1554	1554	1652	...	1746	1754	1754	1852	...	1914	1946	1954	...	2052	2104	|	2114	2126	2154	...	2254	2354	2354	...
Bernau (b. Berlin) d.	1603	1609	1609	1707	...	1803	1809	1809	1907	...	1931	2003	2009	...	2107	2121	|	2132	2141	2209	...	2309	0009	0009	...
Berlin Hbf a.	1623	1627	1627	1725	...	1823	1827	1827	1925	...	1943g	2022	2027	...	2125	2140	|	2206	2159	2227	...	2327	0022g	0027	...
Berlin Hbf 840 d.	...	...	1629	1729	...	...	...	1829	1929	...	...	...	...	...	2129	...	2222	...	...	...	...	...	...	...	...
Doberlug-Kirchhain d.	...	...	1814	1913	...	...	...	2014	2113	...	...	...	...	...	2313	...	...	...	...	...	...	...	...	...	...
Elsterwerda 840 a.	...	...	1831	1932	...	...	...	2031	2132	...	...	...	...	...	2332	...	...	...	...	...	...	...	...	...	...

A – 🚃12 Amsterdam - Berlin - Angermünde - Szczecin and v.v.
B – 🚃12 and ✕ Wien - Praha - Dresden - Stralsund (- Ostseebad Binz ⊖).
C – 🚃12 and ✕ (Ostseebad Binz ⊖ -) Stralsund - Dresden - Praha - Brno.
D – 🚃12 and 🍷 Stralsund - Berlin - Halle - Erfurt - Kassel - Düsseldorf.
E – STRELASUND – 🚃12 and 🍷 (Ostseebad Binz ①–⑥ -) Stralsund - Berlin - Halle - Erfurt - Kassel - Düsseldorf.
G – STRELASUND – 🚃12 and 🍷 (Düsseldorf ① -) (Dortmund ①–⑥ -) Erfurt - Halle - Berlin - Ostseebad Binz.
H – Daily until Nov. 2; ①⑤⑦ from Nov. 6. From Halle on dates in Table **850**.
J – 🚃12 and ✕ Greifswald - Rostock - Hamburg - Köln - Stuttgart and v.v.
K – 🚃12 and 🍷 (Kassel ① -) Erfurt - Halle - Berlin - Stralsund.
L – 🚃12 Köln - Kassel - Erfurt - Halle - Berlin - Stralsund.
M – 🚃12 Stralsund - Berlin Spandau (a. 1958) - Hannover - Bremen - Oldenburg.
N – Daily until Nov. 2; ①⑤⑦ from Nov. 6. 🚃12 and 🍷 Stralsund - Berlin - Halle - Erfurt (- Kassel - Köln ⑦).

O – From Ostseebad Binz (Table **844**).
R – 🚃12 and 🍷 Stralsund - Berlin - Halle - Erfurt (- Fulda - Würzburg ⑦).
T – SIRIUS – 🛏 1, 2 cl., ━ 2 cl., 🚃2 (reclining) Ostseebad Binz - Basel - Zürich and v.v. For Overnight journeys only.
V – ⑥ July 4 - Aug. 22.
X – ⑥ July 4 - Aug. 22 (previous day from Zürich).
Z – Until Oct. 4.
b – Also Nov. 11.
g – Berlin **Gesundbrunnen**.
r – 0435 on ⑥⑦.
u – Stops to pick up only.
● – Operated by Usedomer Bäderbahn.

¶ – Change trains at Angermünde on ②–⑥.
◧ – Also calls at Berlin Zoo (d. 0753) and Berlin Ostbahnhof (d. 0811). From Potsdam Hbf on ①–⑤ (d. 0727).
△ – Also calls at Berlin Ostbahnhof (a. 2155) and Berlin Zoo (a. 2212). To Potsdam Hbf on ①–⑤ (a. 2233).
⊡ – On ⑦ until Oct. 4 runs 3 minutes **earlier** Angermünde - Berlin.
♥ – Change trains at Berlin Südkreuz (a. 2225, d. 2228).
⊖ – See Table **844** for running dates to / from Ostseebad Binz.
⊠ – Until July 2 runs up to 26 minutes **earlier** Stralsund - Pasewalk.

Usedomer Bäderbahn (2nd class only)

STRALSUND - ZÜSSOW - ŚWINOUJŚCIE

Service until Oct. 4 **846**

km		Ⓐ														
0	**Stralsund** **845** d.	...	0522a	...	0722	...	0922	then	1522	...	1722	...	1922	...	2202	2303
31	Greifswald **845** d.	...	0547a	...	0747	...	0947	hourly from	1547	...	1747	...	1947	...	2225	2328
49	Züssow **845** d.	...	0607a	0707	0807	0907	1007	Züssow	1607	1707	1807	1907	2007	2107	2239	2343
67	Wolgast d.	0530	0630	0730	0830	0930	1030	and every	1630	1730	1830	1930	2030	2130	2259	0002
77	Zinnowitz ▲ d.	0548	0648	0748	0848	0952	1052	two hours	1652	1752	1848	1948	2048	2148	2319	...
104	Seebad Heringsdorf d.	0630	0730	0830	0938	1038	1138	from	1738	1838	1930	2030	2130	2230	2353	...
106	Seebad Ahlbeck d.	0634	0734	0834	0943	1043	1143	Stralsund	1743	1843	1934	2034	2134	2234	...	...
110	**Świnoujście** Centrum ‡ a.	0639	0739	0839	0948	1048	1148		1748	1848	1939	2039	2139	2239	...	...

	Ⓐ		Ⓐe	©d												
Świnoujście Centrum ‡ d.	0418	0518	0554	0618	0718	0818	0905	1005	then	1605	1705	1805	1918	2018	2218	2244
Seebad Ahlbeck d.	0424	0524	0600	0624	0724	0824	0913	1013	hourly to	1613	1713	1813	1924	2024	2224	2250
Seebad Heringsdorf d.	0433	0533	0609	0633	0733	0833	0920	1020	Züssow	1620	1720	1820	1933	2033	2233	2254
Zinnowitz ▲ d.	0511	0611	0648	0711	0811	0910	1009	1109	and every	1709	1809	1911	2011	2111	2311	...
Wolgast d.	0531	0631	0731j	0731	0831	0931	1031	1131	two hours	1731	1831	1929	2031	2131	2326	...
Züssow **845** a.	0550	0650	0750	0750	0850	0950	1050	1150	to	1750	1850	1948	2050	2150	...	...
Greifswald **845** a.	0611	...	0811	0811	...	1011	...	1211	Stralsund	1811	...	2003	...	2211	...	...
Stralsund **845** a.	0638	...	0838	0838	...	1038	...	1238		1838	...	2028	...	2238	...	...

a – Ⓐ only.
d – Runs daily July 18 - Aug. 30.
e – Not July 20 - Aug. 28.
j – Arrives 0703.

▲ – **Zinnowitz - Peenemünde** and v.v. (*12 km*, journey 14 minutes):
From Zinnowitz at 0431 Ⓐ, 0512 Ⓐ, 0612, 0659 Ⓐ **e**, 0712 © **d**, 0812, 0912 and hourly until 2112.
From Peenemünde at 0452 Ⓐ, 0530 Ⓐ, 0630, 0717 Ⓐ **e**, 0730 © **d**, 0830, 0930 and hourly until 2130.

‡ – A frequent ferry service operates from the harbour to the Polish mainland and Świnoujście PKP station.

RE services

BERLIN SCHÖNEFELD ✈ - BERLIN - DESSAU

847

km			Ⓐ																	Ⓐ	①–④		s		s
0	**Berlin** Schönefeld ✈ ‡ d.	0425a	0525	0625r	0725	0825	0925	1025	1125	1225	1325	1425	1525	1625	1725	1825	1925	2025	2125	2225	2225		0655		2255
19	**Berlin** Ostbahnhof ‡ d.	0443	0543	0643	0743	0843	0943	1043	1143	1243	1343	1443	1543	1643	1743	1843	1943	2043	2143	2243	2243		0713	and	2313
24	**Berlin** Hbf ‡ d.	0454	0554	0654	0754	0854	0954	1054	1154	1254	1354	1454	1554	1654	1754	1854	1954	2054	2154	2254	2254	also	0725	hourly	2325
28	**Berlin** Zoo ‡ d.	0500	0600	0700	0800	0900	1000	1100	1200	1300	1400	1500	1600	1700	1800	1900	2000	2100	2200	2259	2300		0730	until	2330
43	**Berlin** Wannsee d.	0516	0616	0716	0816	0916	1016	1116	1216	1316	1416	1516	1616	1716	1816	1916	2016	2116	2216	...	2316		...		...
95	Belzig d.	0603	0703	0803	0901	1003	1101	1203	1303	1403	1503	1603	1703	1803	1901	2003	2101	2203	2303	...	0001		...		...
139	Roßlau (Elbe) **848** d.	0636	0736	0836	...	1036	...	1236c	1336a	1436	1536a	1636	1736a	1836	...	2036	...	2236	2336q	...	...		...		...
144	**Dessau** Hbf **848** a.	0643	0743	0843	...	1043	...	1243c	1343a	1443	1543a	1643	1743a	1843	...	2043	...	2243	2343q	...	...		...		...

	Ⓐ																	Ⓐ					v		v
Dessau Hbf **848** d.	...	...	0517e	0617a	0717	0817a	0917c	1017a	1117c	...	1317	1417a	1517	1617a	1717	1817a	1917c	2017	2117c	2317	...		...		...
Roßlau (Elbe) **848** d.	...	...	0525e	0625a	0725	0825a	0925c	1025a	1125c	...	1325	1425a	1525	1625a	1725	1825a	1925c	2025	2125c	2325	...		...		...
Belzig d.	0402	0502	0602	0702	0802	0902	1002	1102	1202	1302	1402	1502	1602	1702	1802	1902	2002	2102	2202	0002	...		...		...
Berlin Wannsee d.	0446	0546	0646	0746	0846	0946	1046	1146	1246	1346	1446	1546	1646	1746	1846	1946	2046	2146	2246	0046	...		...		...
Berlin Zoo ‡ d.	0501	0601	0701	0801	0901	1001	1101	1201	1301	1402	1502	1602	1701	1802	1901	2002	2101	2201	2301	0101	...		0528	and	2128
Berlin Hbf ‡ d.	0507	0607	0707	0807	0907	1007	1107	1207	1307	1408	1507	1608	1707	1808	1907	2008	2107	2207	2307	0107	...	also	0534	hourly	2135
Berlin Ostbahnhof ‡ d.	0518	0618	0718	0818	0918	1018	1118	1218	1318	1418	1518	1618	1718	1818	1918	2018	2118	2218	2316	0116	...		0545	until	2145
Berlin Schönefeld ✈ ‡ a.	0536	0636r	0736	0836	0936	1036	1136	1236	1336	1436	1536	1636	1736	1836	1936	2036	2136	2236	...	...	...		0602		2202

a – Ⓐ only.
c – © only.
e – ①–⑥ only.
q – ⑦ only.
r – ⚒ only.
s – To Berlin Spandau (arrives 13 minutes after Berlin Zoo).
v – From Berlin Spandau (departs 11 – 12 minutes before Berlin Zoo).
‡ – S-Bahn trains also operate early morning to late evening (every 20 minutes – route **S9** – journey time approximately 40 minutes Berlin Schönefeld ✈ - Berlin Hbf and v.v.).

RE / RB services

MAGDEBURG - DESSAU - LEIPZIG and HALLE

848

km		©	©																						
0	**Magdeburg** Hbf d.	...	...	...	...	...	...	0512	...	...	0612r	...	...	0712	...	...	0812	...	...	0912	...	...	1012	...	...
	Falkenberg (Elster) d.	B	...	...	...	...	...	|	0524k	...	|	0624a	...	|	0724	...	|	...	...	|	0924	...	|	...	...
	Lutherstadt Wittenberg ★ d.	0127	...	0406a	0445	0511	0541	|	0611k	0645	|	0711	0745	|	0811	0845	|	0911	0945	|	1011	1045	|	1111	1145
56	Roßlau (Elbe) **847** d.	|	...	0438a	|	0543	|	0605	0643k	|	0705r	0743	|	0805	0843	|	0859	0943	|	1005	1043	|	1059	1143	|
61	**Dessau** Hbf **847** a.	0158	...	0445a	|	0549	|	0613	0649k	|	0713r	0749	|	0813	0849	|	0907	0949	|	1013	1049	|	1107	1149	|
61	**Dessau** Hbf d.	0159	...	0452	|	0552	|	0614	0652	|	0714	0752	|	...	0852	|	0914	0952	|	...	1052	|	1114	1152	|
87	Bitterfeld ★ a.	0214	...	0516	0516	0615	0612	0632	0715	0716	0732	0815	0816	...	0915	0916	0931	1015	1016	...	1115	1116	1131	1215	1216
87	Bitterfeld ★ d.	0215	0220	0520	0520	0617	0620	0632	0720	0720	0732	0820	0820	...	0920	0920	0932	1020	1020	...	1120	1120	1132	1220	1220
	Halle (Saale) Hbf ★ a.	0233	|	0544	|	0641	|	|	0744	|	|	|	0844	...	0944	|	|	|	1044	...	1144	|	|	|	1244
120	**Leipzig** Hbf ★ a.	...	0250	...	0549	...	0649	0658	...	0749	0758	0849	...	...	...	0949	0958	1049	...	...	...	1149	1158	1249	...

km																									
	Magdeburg Hbf d.	1112	...	...	1212	...	...	1312	...	...	1412	...	...	1512	...	...	1612	...	...	1712	...	...	1812	...	...
0	**Falkenberg** (Elster) d.	|	...	...	|	1224	...	|	...	...	|	...	...	|	1524	...	|	...	...	|	1724	...	|	1819a	...
54	Lutherstadt Wittenberg ★ d.	|	1211	1245	|	1311	1345	|	1411	1445	|	1511	1545	|	1611	1645	|	1711	1745	|	1811	1845	|	1911	1945
86	Roßlau (Elbe) **847** d.	1205	1243	|	1259	1343	|	1405	1443	|	1459	1543	|	1605	1643	|	1659	1743	|	1805	1843	|	1859	1943	|
91	**Dessau** Hbf **847** a.	1213	1249	|	1307	1349	|	1413	1449	|	1507	1549	|	1613	1649	|	1707	1749	|	1813	1849	|	1907	1949	|
91	**Dessau** Hbf d.	...	1252	|	1314	1352	|	...	1452	|	1514	1552	|	...	1652	|	1714	1752	|	...	1852	|	1914	1952	|
117	Bitterfeld ★ a.	...	1315	1316	1331	1415	1416	...	1515	1516	1531	1615	1616	...	1715	1716	1731	1815	1816	...	1915	1916	1931	2015	2016
117	Bitterfeld ★ d.	...	1320	1320	1332	1420	1420	...	1520	1520	1532	1620	1620	...	1720	1720	1732	1820	1820	...	1920	1920	1932	2020	2020
147	**Halle** (Saale) Hbf ★ a.	...	1344	|	|	|	1444	...	1544	|	|	|	1644	...	1744	|	|	|	1844	...	1944	|	|	|	2044
	Leipzig Hbf ★ a.	...	...	1349	1358	1449	...	...	...	1549	1558	1649	...	...	...	1749	1758	1849	...	...	...	1949	1958	2049	...

Magdeburg Hbf d.	1912	...	...	2012	...	...	2112	...	...	2312
Falkenberg (Elster) d.	|	1924	...	|	...	...	|	2124	...	|
Lutherstadt Wittenberg ★ d.	|	2011	2054	|	...	2145	|	2211	2245	|
Roßlau (Elbe) **847** d.	2005	2043	|	2053	...	|	2205	2243	|	0005
Dessau Hbf **847** a.	2013	2049	|	2100	...	|	2213	2249	|	0013
Dessau Hbf d.	...	...	|	2102	2152	|	...	2252	|	...
Bitterfeld ★ a.	...	...	2123	2125	2215	2216	...	2315	2316	...
Bitterfeld ★ d.	...	...	2131	2127	2220	2220	...	2320	2320	...
Halle (Saale) Hbf ★ a.	...	...	2156	|	2244	|	...	|	2344	...
Leipzig Hbf ★ a.	...	...	...	2157	...	2249	...	2349	...	...

		Ⓐ	Ⓐ	Ⓐ	©				Ⓐ	⚒r
Leipzig Hbf ★ d.	...	0410	...	...	...	...	...	0510	...	...
Halle (Saale) Hbf ★ d.	...	|	0415	...	0427	...	0515	|	...	0547a
Bitterfeld ★ a.	...	0439	0439	...	0451	...	0539	0539	...	0611a
Bitterfeld ★ d.	...	0443	0443	...	0452	...	0543	0543	...	0613a
Dessau Hbf a.	...	|	0508	...	|	...	|	0608	...	0638a
Dessau Hbf **847** d.	0434	|	0511	*0517*	|	0542	|	0611	*0617*	0640
Roßlau (Elbe) **847** d.	0442	|	0518	0529	|	0550	|	0618	0629	0648
Lutherstadt Wittenberg ★ d.	|	0515	0548	|	0524	|	0615	0649	|	|
Falkenberg (Elster) a.	|	...	0638	|	R	|	...	...	|	|
Magdeburg Hbf a.	0537	...	...	0620	...	0645	...	...	0720	0745

Leipzig Hbf ★ d.	0610	...	...	...	0710	0801	0810	...	...	...	0910	1001	1010	...	...	...	1110	1201	1210	...	...	...	1310	1401	1410
Halle (Saale) Hbf ★ d.	|	0615	...	0715	|	|	|	0815	...	0915	|	|	|	1015	...	1115	|	|	|	1215	...	1315	|	|	|
Bitterfeld ★ a.	0639	0639	...	0739	0739	0825	0839	0839	...	0939	0939	1025	1039	1039	...	1139	1139	1225	1239	1239	...	1339	1339	1425	1439
Bitterfeld ★ d.	0643	0643	...	0743	0743	0827	0843	0843	...	0943	0943	1027	1043	1043	...	1143	1143	1227	1243	1243	...	1343	1343	1427	1443
Dessau Hbf a.	|	0708	...	|	0808	0846	|	0908	...	|	1008	1046	|	1108	...	|	1208	1248	|	1308	...	|	1408	1448	|
Dessau Hbf **847** d.	|	0711	0742	|	0811	0851	|	0911	0942	|	1011	1051	|	1111	1142	|	1211	1251	|	1311	1342	|	1411	1451	|
Roßlau (Elbe) **847** d.	|	0718	0750	|	0818	0858	|	0918	0950	|	1018	1058	|	1118	1150	|	1218	1258	|	1318	1350	|	1418	1458	|
Lutherstadt Wittenberg ★ d.	0715	0751	|	0815	0849	|	0915	0949	|	1015	1051	|	1115	1149	|	1215	1249	|	1315	1351	|	1415	1449	|	1515
Falkenberg (Elster) a.	...	0838	|	...	...	|	...	...	|	...	1138	|	...	...	|	...	...	|	...	1438	|	...	...	|	...
Magdeburg Hbf a.	...	...	0845	...	...	0945	...	...	1045	...	...	1145	...	...	1245	...	...	1345	...	...	1445	...	...	1545	...

																							⑤–⑦		
Leipzig Hbf ★ d.	...	...	...	1510	1601	1610	...	...	...	1710	1801	1810	...	...	...	1910	2001	2010	...	...	2110	2211	...	2310	...
Halle (Saale) Hbf ★ d.	1415	1446a	1515	|	|	|	1615	1646a	1715	|	|	|	1815	...	1915	|	|	|	2015	2115	|	|	...	|	2315
Bitterfeld ★ a.	1439	1511a	1539	1539	1625	1639	1639	1711a	1739	1739	1825	1839	1839	...	1939	1939	2025	2039	2039	2139	2139	2237	...	2339	2339
Bitterfeld ★ d.	1443	1513a	1543	1543	1627	1643	1643	1713a	1743	1743	1827	1843	1843	...	1943	1943	2027	2043	2043	2143	2143	2237	...	2343	2343
Dessau Hbf a.	1508	1538a	|	1608	1648	|	1708	1738a	|	1808	1848	|	1908	...	|	2008	2046	|	2108	|	2208	2255	...	0008	|
Dessau Hbf **847** d.	1511	1542	|	1611	1651	|	1711	1742	|	1811	1851	|	1911	1942	|	2011v	2048	|	2111	|	2211g	2257	2311	...	|
Roßlau (Elbe) **847** d.	1518	1550	|	1618	1658	|	1718	1750	|	1818	1858	|	1918	1950	|	2018v	2055	|	2118	|	2218g	2305	2318	...	|
Lutherstadt Wittenberg ★ d.	1554	|	1615	1651	|	1715	1754	|	1815	1849	|	1915	1951	|	2015	2049v	|	2115	2151	2215	2249g	|	2349	...	0015
Falkenberg (Elster) a.	1641	|	...	1738a	|	...	1841	|	...	...	|	...	2038	|	...	...	|	...	2238b	...	...	|	...	...	...
Magdeburg Hbf a.	...	1645	...	...	1745	...	...	1845	...	...	1945	...	...	2045	...	...	2145	...	...	...	...	2359	...	...	...

B – From Berlin (Table **835**).
R – To Rostock via Berlin (Table **835**).
a – Ⓐ only.
b – Ⓑ only.
g – ①–④ only.
k – ①–⑥ only.
r – ⚒ (not Oct. 31).
v – ⚒ only.
★ – See Tables **850** and **851** for *ICE* and *IC* services Lutherstadt Wittenberg - Bitterfeld - Halle / Leipzig and v.v.

849 Local services LEIPZIG and HALLE - EISENACH and SAALFELD *RB services*

See Tables **850** and **851** for faster *IC* and *ICE* services

km																									
		Ⓐ		Ⓐ				Ⓐ	Ⓒ																H
0	**Halle** (Saale) Hbf d.	0420	...	...	0522	...	0622	...	...	0722	...	0822	...		1822	...	1922	...	2022	...	2122	...	2222	...	2326
32	Weißenfels d.	0453	...	...	0553	...	0653	...	...	0753	...	0853	...		1853	...	1953	...	2053	...	2153	...	2253	...	2358
46	Naumburg (Saale) Hbf d.	0503	0503	...	0603	0613	0703	0707	0713	0803	...	0903	0913	each train	1903	1913	2003	...	2103	...	2203	...	2303	2307	0008
59	Großheringen d.	0513	0513	0519	0613	|	0713	|	|	0813	0822	0913	|		1913	|	2013	2022	2113	2122	2213	2222	2313	|	0018
	Jena Paradies d.	|	|	0546	|	0648	|	0740	0748	|	0848	|	0948	runs every	|	1948	|	2048	|	2148	|	2248	|	2340	|
	Göschwitz (Saale) d.	|	|	0551	|	0654	|	0754r	0754	|	0854	|	0954		|	1954	|	2054	|	2154	|	2254	|	2345	|
	Rudolstadt (Thür) d.	|	|	0618	|	0721	|	0821	0821	|	0921	|	1021	**two hours**	|	2021	|	2121	|	2221	|	2321	|	...	|
	Saalfeld (Saale) a.	|	|	0627	|	0730	|	0830	0830	|	0930	|	1030		|	2030	|	2132	|	2233	|	2330	|	...	|
87	Weimar d.	0540	0540	...	0640	...	0740	...	...	0840	...	0940	...	until	1940	...	2040	...	2140	...	2240	...	2340	...	0042
108	**Erfurt** Hbf d.	0559	0559	...	0659	...	0801	...	...	0859	...	1001	...		2001	...	2059	...	2206r	...	2312t	...	2359	...	0059
136	Gotha d.	0624	0624	...	0724	...	0827	...	...	0924	...	1027	...		2027	...	2124	...	2230	...	2341	...	0024	...	...
165	**Eisenach** a.	0647	0647	...	0747	...	0850	...	...	0947	...	1050	...		2050	...	2147	...	2253	...	0004	...	0047	...	...

km																								
			Ⓐ																		L				
	Eisenach d.	0406a	...	0507	...	0607	...	0709	...	0811	...	0907		...	1707	...	1811	...	1907	...	2011	...	2107	...	...
	Gotha d.	0430a	...	0531	...	0631	...	0733	...	0835	...	0931		...	1731	...	1835	...	1931	...	2035	...	2131	2231	...
	Erfurt Hbf d.	0454	...	0600	...	0700	...	0800	...	0900	...	1000	each train	...	1800	...	1900	...	2000	...	2100	...	2200	2300	...
	Weimar d.	0511	...	0620	...	0720	...	0820	...	0920	...	1020		...	1820	...	1920	...	2020	...	2120	...	2220	2320	...
0	**Saalfeld** (Saale) d.	|	0508	|	0618	|	0724	|	0824	|	0930	|	runs every	1730	|	1824	|	1930	|	2024	|	2132	|	|	2235
10	Rudolstadt (Thür) d.	|	0518	|	0628	|	0733	|	0833	|	0939	|		1739	|	1833	|	1939	|	2033	|	2141	|	|	2244
42	Göschwitz (Saale) d.	|	0544	|	0658	|	0801	|	0901	|	1005	|	**two hours**	1805	|	1901	|	2005	|	2101	|	2207	|	|	2311
47	**Jena** Paradies d.	|	0549	|	0703	|	0806	|	0906	|	1011	|		1811	|	1906	|	2011	|	2106	|	2214	|	|	2316
75	Großheringen d.	0534	|	0644	0730	0744	|	0844	0932	0944	|	1044	until	|	1844	1932	1944	2037	2044	2132	2144	|	2244	2344	...
	Naumburg (Saale) Hbf d.	0545	0625	0654	...	0754	0839	0854	...	0954	1045	1054		1845	1854	...	1954	...	2054	...	2154	2249	2254	2354	...
	Weißenfels d.	0556	0636	0705	...	0805	...	0905	...	1005	...	1105		...	1905	...	2005	...	2105	...	2204	...	2305	0005	...
	Halle (Saale) Hbf a.	0629	0707	0737	...	0837	...	0937	...	1037	...	1137		...	1937	...	2037	...	2137	...	2240	...	2337	0037	...

Leipzig - Weißenfels and v.v. ⊠

From Leipzig Hbf at 0419 Ⓐ, 0445 Ⓒ, 0519 Ⓐ, 0619 Ⓐ, 0647 Ⓒ, 0747 Ⓐ, 0847, 0947 Ⓐ, 1047, 1147 Ⓐ, 1247, 1347 Ⓐ, 1447, 1547 Ⓐ, 1647, 1747 Ⓐ, 1847, 1947 Ⓐ, 2047 and 2317.
From Weißenfels at 0426, 0526 Ⓐ, 0626, 0726 Ⓐ, 0826, 0926 Ⓐ, 1026, 1126 Ⓐ, 1226, 1326 Ⓐ, 1426, 1526 Ⓐ, 1626, 1726 Ⓐ, 1826, 1926 Ⓐ, 2026 and 2205.

Eisenach - Bebra and v.v. ❖

From Eisenach at 0452 Ⓐ, 0530 Ⓐ, 0614 ⚒, 0712 ⚒, 0812, 0912 ⚒, 1012, 1112 Ⓐ, 1212, 1331 Ⓐ, 1412, 1512 Ⓐ, 1612, 1712 Ⓐ, 1812, 1912 Ⓐ, 2012, 2112 Ⓐ and 2212 Ⓒ.
From Bebra at 0506 Ⓐ, 0606 ⚒, 0659 Ⓐ, 0706 Ⓒ, 0806 ⑥, 0906, 1006 Ⓐ, 1106, 1206 Ⓐ, 1306 Ⓒ, 1315 Ⓐ, 1418 Ⓐ, 1506, 1606 Ⓐ, 1706, 1806 Ⓐ, 1906, 2006 Ⓐ and 2118.

H – From Leipzig Hbf (d. 2317).
L – To Leipzig Hbf (a. 2245).

a – Ⓐ only.
r – Arrives 9 – 10 minutes earlier.
t – Arrives 2257.

⊠ – Journey 40 – 46 minutes.
❖ – Journey 35 – 41 minutes. 2nd class only. Operated by CANTUS Verkehrsgesellschaft.

850 BERLIN and LEIPZIG - ERFURT - KASSEL and FRANKFURT

Alternative regional services: Table **835** Berlin - Lutherstadt Wittenberg. Table **848** Lutherstadt Wittenberg - Halle. Table **849** Leipzig / Halle - Erfurt - Eisenach - Bebra.

km		IC 1850	IC 1850	ICE 1646	ICE 1646	ICE 1656	ICE 1644		IC 2156	ICE 1654	IC 2154	ICE 1642	IC 2154	ICE 1607 1727	ICE 1652	IC 2152	ICE 1640	IC 2152	ICE 1609 1709	ICE 1650	IC 2150	ICE 1548	IC 2150	ICE 1711	ICE 1558
		①	①–⑤	①	①–⑤	①–⑥	①–⑥		①–⑥		①–⑥	①–⑥	①–⑥					⑤⑦			◐		◐		
								◇						⊖					⊖					⊖	
				✕	✕	✕	✕		🍷	✕	🍷	✕	🍷	✕	✕	🍷	✕	🍷	✕	✕	🍷	✕	🍷	✕	✕
	Stralsund **845** d.	...	...	...	...	...	...	...	...	...	...	...	...	...	...	...	...	...	...	...	0739e	...	...	...	...
	Berlin Hbf **851** d.	0041	...	...	...	...	...	...	...	0548e	0639	...	...	0752	...	0839e	...	...	0952	...	1039	...	...	1152	...
	Lutherstadt Wittenberg **851** d.	0124	...	...	...	...	...	...	...	0633e	0721	...	...	0835	...	0921e	...	...	1035	...	1121	...	...	1235	...
	Bitterfeld **851** d.	0141	...	...	...	...	...	...	...	0649e	0738	...	...	|	...	0938e	...	...	|	...	1138	...	...	|	...
	Halle (Saale) Hbf d.	0203	...	...	...	...	...	...	...	|	0800	...	...	|	...	1000	...	...	|	...	1200	...	...	|	...
	Dresden Hbf **842** d.	|	...	...	...	...	0444a	...	...	|	|	0654	...	|	0754	|	0854	...	|	0954	|	1054	...	|	1154
0	**Leipzig** Hbf **851** d.	0235	...	0404	...	0501	0601	...	...	0715	|	0811	...	0905	0915	|	1011	...	1105	1115	|	1211	...	1305	1315
40	Weißenfels d.	|	...	|	...	|	|	...	...	|	0825	|	...	...	|	1025	|	...	...	|	1225	|	...	...	|
54	Naumburg (Saale) Hbf **851** d.	|	...	0438	...	0538	0640	...	...	|	0835	|	..	...	|	1035	|	...	...	|	1235	|	...	...	|
95	Weimar **858** d.	0336	...	0502	...	0602	0704	...	...	0808	0900	0905	←	...	1008	1100	1105	←	...	1208	1300	1305	←	...	1408
117	**Erfurt** Hbf **858** d.	0353	...	0518	0518	0618	0719	...	0725	0822	0914	0920	0924	...	1022	1114	1120	1124	...	1222	1314	1320	1324	...	1422
144	Gotha d.	0411	...	0535	0535	0636	0735	...	0742	0839	→	|	0942	...	1039	→	|	1142	...	1239	→	|	1342	...	1439
173	**Eisenach** d.	0426	...	0551	0551	0652	0752	...	0758	0855	...	0952	0958	...	1055	...	1152	1158	...	1255	...	1352	1358	...	1455
	Bebra **901** d.	0503	0503	|	|	|	|	...	0823	|	...	|	1023	...	|	...	|	1223	...	|	...	|	1423	...	|
	Kassel Wilhelmshöhe **901** a.	|	|	|	|	|	|	...	0858	|	...	|	1058	...	|	...	|	1258	...	|	...	|	1458	...	|
	Düsseldorf Hbf **800** a.	|	|	|	|	|	|	...	1212	|	...	|	1412	...	|	...	|	1612	...	|	...	|	1815	...	|
230	Bad Hersfeld **901** d.	0514	0514	0619	0619	0720	0819	...	...	|	...	1019	...	...	|	...	1219	...	...	|	...	1419	...	...	|
272	Fulda **900/1** d.	0541	0541	0644	0644	0744	0844	...	...	0944	...	1044	...	...	1144	...	1244	...	...	1344	...	1444	...	...	1544
353	Hanau Hbf **900/1** d.	0623	0623	|	|	|	|	...	...	|	...	|	...	...	|	...	|	...	...	|	...	|	...	...	|
372	**Frankfurt** (Main) Süd a.	|	|	0737	0737	|	0935	0943	...	|	...	1135	...	...	|	...	1335	...	...	|	...	1535	...	...	|
376	**Frankfurt** (Main) Hbf **900/1** a.	0642	0642	*0744*f	*0744*f	0836	*0944*r	0953	...	1036	...	*1144*f	...	...	1236	...	*1344*f	...	...	1436	...	*1544*f	...	...	1636
	Frankfurt Flughafen ✈ § a.	...	...	0750	0750	0855	0948	...	...	1055	...	1148	...	...	1255	...	1348	...	...	1455	...	1548	...	...	1655
	Mainz Hbf **912** a.	...	...	...	...	0916	...	...	...	1116j	...	...	...	...	1316j	...	...	...	...	1516	...	...	...	...	1716j
	Wiesbaden Hbf **912** a.	...	...	...	...	0933	...	...	...	1133j	...	...	...	...	1333j	...	...	...	...	1533	...	...	...	...	1733j

	IC 2356	ICE 1546	IC 2356	ICE 1613	ICE 1556	IC 1858	IC 2354	ICE 1544	ICE 1744	IC 2354	ICE 1615	ICE 1554	ICE 1594	IC 1856	IC 1854	IC 2352	ICE 1542	IC 1742	IC 2352	ICE 1617	ICE 1552	IC 2350	IC 2350	ICE 1717	ICE 1717
						⑦		①–⑤	⑦				Ⓑ	⑦	⑦		①–⑤	⑦	⑦			Ⓑ	⑦	Ⓑ	⑦
	O		O	⊖		T	B			B	⊖		R							⊖			L	H	H
	🍷	✕	🍷	✕	✕	🍷	🍷	✕	✕	🍷	✕	✕	✕			🍷	✕	✕	🍷	✕	✕	🍷	🍷	✕	✕
Stralsund **845** d.	0939	...	...	...	...	...	...	...	...	...	...	...	...	...	...	1339t	...	...	...	...	...	1539	1539	...	...
Berlin Hbf **851** d.	1239	...	...	1352	...	...	1440	...	...	...	1552	...	...	...	...	1639	...	...	...	1752	...	1839	1839	1858	1858
Lutherstadt Wittenberg **851** d.	1321	...	...	1435	...	...	1521	...	...	...	1635	...	...	...	...	1721	...	...	...	1835	...	1921	1921	|	|
Bitterfeld **851** d.	1338	...	...	|	...	...	1538	...	...	...	|	...	...	...	...	1738	...	...	...	|	...	1938	1938	|	|
Halle (Saale) Hbf d.	1400	...	...	|	...	...	1600	...	...	...	|	...	...	1700	...	1800	...	...	...	|	...	2002	2002	|	|
Dresden Hbf **842** d.	|	1254	...	|	1354	...	|	1454	1454	...	|	1554	1554	|	...	|	1654	1654	...	|	1754	|	|	|	|
Leipzig Hbf **851** d.	|	1411	...	1505	1515	1543	|	1611	1611	...	1705	1715	1715	|	1743	|	1811	1811	...	1905	1915	|	|	2011	2011
Weißenfels d.	1425	|	...	...	|	|	1625	|	|	...	...	|	|	1722	|	1825	|	|	...	...	|	2025	2025	|	|
Naumburg (Saale) Hbf **851** d.	1435	|	...	...	|	1618	1635	|	|	...	...	|	|	1733	1818	1835	|	|	...	...	1951	2035	2035	2047	2047
Weimar **858** d.	1500	1505	←	...	1608	1645	1700	1705	1705	←	...	1808	1808	1812	1845	1900	1905	1905	←	...	2015	2103	2103	2111	2111
Erfurt Hbf **858** d.	1514	1520	1524	...	1622	1706	1714	1720	1720	1724	...	1822	1822	1827	1906	1914	1920	1920	1924	...	2030	2118	2120	2127	2129
Gotha d.	→	|	1542	...	1639	1730	→	|	|	1742	...	1839	1839	1846	1930	→	|	|	1942	...	2047	...	2138	...	|
Eisenach d.	...	1552	1558	...	1655	1746	...	1752	1752	1758	...	1855	1855	1901	1946	...	1952	1952	1958	...	2103	...	2153	...	2158
Bebra **901** d.	...	|	1623	...	|	|	...	|	|	1823	...	|	|	|	|	...	|	|	2023	...	|	...	→	...	|
Kassel Wilhelmshöhe. **901** a.	...	|	1658	...	|	|	...	|	|	1858	...	|	|	|	|	...	|	|	2058	...	|	...	...	...	|
Düsseldorf Hbf **800** a.	...	|	2015	...	|	|	...	|	|	2214w	...	|	|	|	|	...	|	|	0012	...	|	...	...	...	|
Bad Hersfeld **901** d.	...	1619	...	...	|	|	...	1819	1819	...	...	|	|	|	|	...	2020	2020	...	...	|	...	...	...	2227
Fulda **900/1** d.	...	1644	...	...	1744	1838	...	1844	1844	...	...	1944	1944	1953	2038	...	2044	2044	...	...	2159x	...	...	...	2251
Hanau Hbf **900/1** d.	...	|	...	...	|	|	...	|	|	...	...	|	|	|	|	...	2125	2125	...	...	2240	...	...	...	2335
Frankfurt (Main) Süd a.	...	1735	...	...	|	|	...	|	1935	...	...	|	|	|	|	...	2138	2138	...	...	|	...	...	...	|
Frankfurt (Main) Hbf **900/1** a.	...	*1744*f	...	...	1836	1932	...	1940	*1944*f	...	...	2036	2036	2052	2142	...	2146	*2152*h	...	...	2254	...	...	...	2349
Frankfurt Flughafen ✈ § a.	...	1748	...	...	1855	...	...	...	1948	...	...	2055	...	...	...	...	...	2149	...	...	...	...	...	...	...
Mainz Hbf **912** a.	...	...	...	...	1916	...	...	...	...	...	...	2116	...	...	...	...	...	...	...	...	...	...	...	...	...
Wiesbaden Hbf **912** a.	...	...	...	...	1933	...	...	...	...	...	...	2133	...	...	...	...	...	...	...	...	...	...	...	...	...

FOR NOTES SEE NEXT PAGE →

FRANKFURT and KASSEL - ERFURT - LEIPZIG and BERLIN 850

Alternative regional services: Table **835** Berlin - Lutherstadt Wittenberg. Table **848** Lutherstadt Wittenberg - Halle. Table **849** Leipzig / Halle - Erfurt - Eisenach - Bebra.

	IC	ICE	ICE	ICE	ICE	ICE	D	CNL	IC	CNL
	2350	**1737**	**1757**	**905**	**1550**	**1519**	**61458**	**458**	**61258**	**1258**
	⑦	⑥♥	⑥	**1619**	⑦	Ⓑ		Ⓡ		Ⓡ
	L	⊖		⊖		⊖	**P**	**A**		**Y**
	🍷	✕		✕	✕	✕	2	🍷	2	✕
Stralsund **845** d.	...	...	...	...	...	...	...	...	...	...
Berlin Hbf **851** d.	...	1858	1858	1952	...	2058	...	...	2222	2222
Lutherstadt Wittenberg **851** d.	...	|	|	2035	...	2140	...	...	2310	2310**u**
Bitterfeld **851** d.	...	1958	1956	|	...	|	...	...	2327	|
Halle (Saale) Hbf d.	...	|	2016	|	...	|	...	...	2351	2351**u**
Dresden Hbf **842** d.	...	|	|	|	1954	|	2115	2115	|	|
Leipzig Hbf **851** d.	...	2020	|	2105	2112	2210	2253	2253	|	|
Weißenfels d.	...	|	|	...	|	...	|	|	|	|
Naumburg (Saale) Hbf **851** d.	...	2050	2057**v**	...	2147	...	2339	|	0021	|
Weimar **858** d.	...	...	2121	...	2210	...	0005	0005**u**	0047	0047**u**
Erfurt Hbf **858** d.	...	...	2136	...	2225	...	0020	0117**u**	0101	0117**u**
Gotha d.	←	...	...	...	2242	...	...	|	...	|
Eisenach d.	2202	...	...	...	2258	...	...	|	...	|
Bebra **901** d.	|	...	...	...	|	...	...	|	...	|
Kassel Wilhelmshöhe **901** a.	|	...	...	...	|	...	...	|	...	|
Düsseldorf Hbf **800** a.	|	...	...	...	|	...	...	|	...	|
Bad Hersfeld **901** d.	2234	...	...	...	2326	...	...	|	...	|
Fulda **900/1** d.	2302	...	...	...	2351	...	...	|	...	|
Hanau Hbf **900/1** d.	...	...	...	...	0034	...	...	|	...	|
Frankfurt (Main) Süd a.	...	...	...	...	0044	...	...	0359	...	0359
Frankfurt (Main) Hbf **900/1** a.	...	...	...	...	0051	...	...	...	...	...
Frankfurt Flughafen ✈ § a.	...	...	...	...	...	...	...	...	...	...
Mainz Hbf **912** a.	...	...	...	...	...	...	...	...	...	...
Wiesbaden Hbf **912** a.	...	...	...	...	...	...	...	...	...	...

km		CNL	IC	CNL	D	ICE	ICE	ICE	IC	IC
		1259	**61259**	**459**	**61459**	**1616**	**1516**	**1516**	**2351**	**2351**
		Ⓡ		Ⓡ		①–⑤	①–⑤		①–⑥	**N**
		Z		**A**	**P**	⊖	‡	‡		
		✕	2	🍷	2	✕	✕	✕	🍷	🍷
	Wiesbaden Hbf **912** d.	...	...	...	...	...	...	...	...	...
	Mainz Hbf **912** d.	...	...	...	...	...	...	...	...	...
0	**Frankfurt** Flughafen ✈ § d.	...	...	...	...	...	...	...	...	...
	Frankfurt (Main) Hbf **900/1** d.	...	...	...	...	...	...	...	...	...
11	**Frankfurt** (Main) Süd d.	0055	...	0055	...	...	...	...	...	...
—	Hanau Hbf **900/1** d.	|	...	|	...	...	...	...	...	...
	Fulda **900/1** d.	|	...	|	0341	...	...	...	...	...
	Bad Hersfeld **901** d.	|	...	|	0410	...	...	...	...	...
	Düsseldorf Hbf **800** d.	|	...	|	|	...	...	...	...	...
0	**Kassel** Wilhelmshöhe **901** d.	|	...	|	|	...	...	...	...	...
54	Bebra **901** d.	|	...	|	|	...	...	...	...	...
99	**Eisenach** d.	|	...	|	0449	...	0602	...	...	...
128	Gotha d.	|	...	|	0505	...	0617	...	...	...
155	**Erfurt** Hbf **858** d.	0414**s**	0444	0520**s**	0525	...	0635	0635	...	...
177	Weimar **858** d.	0458**s**	0500	0540**s**	0542	...	0652	0652	...	...
218	Naumburg (Saale) Hbf **851** d.	|	0527	|	0608	...	0715	0715	...	...
232	Weißenfels d.	|	|	|	|	...	|	|	...	...
	Leipzig Hbf **851** a.	|	|	0641	0641	0651	0747	0747	...	...
	Dresden Hbf **842** a.	|	|	0807	0807	|	|	|	...	...
264	**Halle** (Saale) Hbf d.	0557**s**	0559	...	...	|	|	|	0801	0801
294	Bitterfeld **851** d.	|	0619	...	...	0709	|	|	0820	0820
331	Lutherstadt Wittenberg **851** d.	0634**s**	0636	...	...	0725	|	|	0836	0836
429	**Berlin** Hbf **851** a.	0718	0718	...	...	0811	0900	0900	0916	0916
	Stralsund **845** a.	...	...	...	...	...	...	...	...	1224

	ICE	ICE	ICE	IC	ICE	IC	ICE	ICE	IC	ICE	ICE	IC	ICE	ICE	ICE	IC	ICE	IC	ICE	ICE	IC	ICE	IC	ICE	ICE
	1553	**1553**	**1614**	**2353**	**1543**	**2353**	**1555**	**1612**	**2355**	**1545**	**1745**	**2355**	**1557**	**1597**	**1610**	**2357**	**1547**	**2357**	**1559**	**1608**	**2157**	**1549**	**2157**	**1651**	**1606**
	①	②–⑤	①–⑥	①	①–⑥		①–⑥	①–⑥	①–⑥	⚒	†		①–⑥	⑦											**1706**
		¶	⊖					⊖	**D**			**D**	**R**		⊖	**C**		**C**		⊖	◧		◧		⊖
	✕	✕	✕	🍷	✕	🍷	✕	✕	🍷	✕	✕	🍷	✕	✕	✕	🍷	✕	🍷	✕	✕	🍷	✕	🍷	✕	✕
Wiesbaden Hbf **912** d.	...	...	...	...	...	...	...	...	...	...	...	...	...	0824	...	...	...	...	1024**n**	...	...	...	...	1224**n**	...
Mainz Hbf **912** d.	...	...	...	...	...	...	...	...	...	...	...	...	...	0842	...	...	...	...	1042	...	...	...	...	1242	...
Frankfurt Flughafen ✈ § d.	...	...	...	...	...	...	...	...	...	0811	...	...	...	0901	...	...	1011	...	1103	...	...	1211	...	1303	...
Frankfurt (Main) Hbf **900/1** d.	0517	...	...	...	0618	...	0720	...	...	*0813***f**	0822	...	0921	0921	...	...	*1013***f**	...	1119	...	...	*1213***f**	...	1319	...
Frankfurt (Main) Süd d.	|	...	...	...	|	...	|	...	...	0822	|	...	|	|	...	...	1022	...	|	...	...	1222	...	|	...
Hanau Hbf **900/1** d.	|	...	...	...	0634	...	|	...	...	|	|	...	|	|	...	...	|	...	|	...	...	|	...	|	...
Fulda **900/1** d.	0611	...	...	...	0715	...	0813	...	...	0915	0915	...	1013	1013	...	...	1115	...	1213	...	...	1315	...	1413	...
Bad Hersfeld **901** d.	0635	...	...	...	0739	...	|	...	...	0939	0939	...	|	|	...	...	1139	...	|	...	...	1339	...	|	...
Düsseldorf Hbf **800** d.	|	...	...	...	|	...	|	...	0546**g**	|	|	...	|	|	...	0746**e**	|	...	|	...	0946	|	...	|	...
Kassel Wilhelmshöhe **901** d.	|	...	...	0700	|	...	|	...	0900	|	|	...	|	|	...	1100	|	...	|	...	1300	|	...	|	...
Bebra **901** d.	|	...	...	0736	|	...	|	...	0936	|	|	...	|	|	...	1136	|	...	|	...	1336	|	...	|	...
Eisenach d.	0702	0702	...	0800	0807	...	0902	...	1000	1007	1007	...	1102	1102	...	1200	1207	...	1302	...	1400	1407	...	1502	...
Gotha d.	0718	0718	...	0816	|	←	0918	...	1016	|	|	←	1118	1118	...	1216	|	←	1318	...	1416	|	←	1518	...
Erfurt Hbf **858** d.	0735	0735	...	0832	0838	0843	0935	...	1032	1038	1038	1043	1135	1135	...	1232	1238	1243	1335	...	1432	1438	1443	1535	...
Weimar **858** d.	0750	0750	...	→	0852	0900	0949	...	→	1052	1052	1100	1149	1149	...	→	1252	1300	1349	...	→	1452	1500	1549	...
Naumburg (Saale) Hbf **851** d.	0814	0814	...	...	|	0925	|	...	...	|	|	1125	|	|	...	...	|	1325	|	...	...	|	1525	|	...
Weißenfels d.	|	|	...	...	|	0935	|	...	...	|	|	1135	|	|	...	...	|	1335	|	...	...	|	1534	|	...
Leipzig Hbf **851** a.	0846	0846	0851	...	0945	|	1041	1051	...	1145	1145	|	1241	1241	1251	...	1345	|	1441	1451	...	1545	|	1641	1651
Dresden Hbf **842** a.	1007	1007	|	...	1106	|	1207	|	...	1306	1306	|	1407	1407	|	...	1506	|	1607	|	...	1706	|	1807	|
Halle (Saale) Hbf d.	...	...	|	...	...	0959	...	|	...	...	...	1159	...	...	|	...	...	1359	...	|	...	...	1559	...	|
Bitterfeld **851** d.	...	...	|	...	...	1020	...	|	...	...	...	1220	...	...	|	...	...	1420	...	|	...	...	1620	...	|
Lutherstadt Wittenberg **851** d.	...	...	0922	...	...	1036	...	1122	...	...	...	1236	...	...	1322	...	...	1436	...	1522	...	...	1636	...	1722
Berlin Hbf **851** a.	...	...	1006	...	...	1116	...	1205	...	...	...	1316	...	...	1405	...	...	1516	...	1605	...	...	1716	...	1805
Stralsund **845** a.	...	...	...	...	...	1424	...	...	...	...	...	1624	...	...	...	...	...	...	...	...	...	...	2040**b**	...	...

	IC	ICE	IC	IC	ICE	ICE	IC	ICE	IC	IC	IC	ICE	IC		ICE	ICE	IC	ICE	ICE	IC	ICE	ICE	ICE	ICE	ICE
	2359	**1641**	**2359**	**2259**	**1653**	**1604**	**2151**	**1643**	**2151**	**1859**	**2204**	**1655**	**2153**		**1645**	**1502**	**2153**	**1657**	**1600**	**2155**	**592**	**1747**	**1647**	**1659**	**1659**
	⑤⑦		⑤⑦	①–④		**1704**				⑤	①–④	Ⓑ	Ⓑ			**1722**	Ⓑ	Ⓑ	⑤⑦	⑦		⑦	①–⑥	Ⓑ	⑤⑦
						⊖						⊖		◇		⊖			⊖						
	🍷	✕	🍷	🍷	✕	✕	🍷	✕	🍷	🍷	🍷	✕	🍷		✕	✕	🍷	🍷	✕	🍷		✕	✕	✕△	✕△
Wiesbaden Hbf **912** d.	...	...	...	...	1424**j**	...	...	...	...	...	...	1624**j**	...	...	...	...	...	1824**j**	...	...	...	...	...	2024**k**	2024**k**
Mainz Hbf **912** d.	...	...	...	...	1442**j**	...	...	...	...	...	...	1642**j**	...	...	...	...	...	1842	...	...	...	...	...	2042**k**	2042**k**
Frankfurt Flughafen ✈ § d.	...	1411	...	...	1503	...	...	1611	...	...	...	1703	...	...	1811	...	...	1903	...	...	...	2011	...	2103	2103
Frankfurt (Main) Hbf **900/1** d.	...	*1413***f**	...	...	1520	...	...	*1613***f**	...	1615	1617	1720	...	1807	*1813***r**	...	...	1919	...	...	2013	|	2022	2119	2119
Frankfurt (Main) Süd d.	...	1422	...	...	|	...	...	1622	...	|	|	|	...	1817	1822	...	...	|	...	...	|	2022	|	|	|
Hanau Hbf **900/1** d.	...	|	...	...	|	...	...	|	...	|	1637	|	...	...	|	...	...	|	...	...	2027	2037	2037	|	|
Fulda **900/1** d.	...	1515	...	...	1613	...	...	1715	...	1721	1721	1813	...	...	1915	...	...	2013	...	...	...	2118	2118	2213	2213
Bad Hersfeld **901** d.	...	1539	...	...	|	...	...	1739	...	1749	1749	|	...	...	1939	...	...	|	...	...	...	2142	2142	|	|
Düsseldorf Hbf **800** d.	1146	|	...	...	|	...	1346	|	...	|	|	|	1546	...	|	...	...	|	...	1746	...	|	|	|	|
Kassel Wilhelmshöhe **901** d.	1500	|	...	...	|	...	1700	|	...	|	|	|	1900	...	|	...	...	|	...	2100	...	|	|	|	|
Bebra **901** d.	1536	|	...	...	|	...	1736	|	...	|	1800	|	1936	...	|	...	...	|	...	2136	...	|	|	|	|
Eisenach d.	1600	1607	...	...	1702	...	1800	1807	...	|	...	1902	2000	...	2007	...	...	2101	...	2200	...	2210	2210	2301	2301
Gotha d.	1616	|	←	...	1718	...	1816	|	←	1831	...	1918	2016	...	|	...	←	2118	...	2216	...	2227	2227	2316	2316
Erfurt Hbf **858** d.	1632	1638	1643	1643	1735	...	1832	1838	1843	1855	...	1935	2032	...	2038	...	2043	2135	...	2232	...	2244	2244	2331	2335
Weimar **858** d.	→	1652	1700	1700	1749	...	→	1852	1900	1912	...	1949	→	...	2052	...	2100	2151	...	...	...	2258	2258	...	2349
Naumburg (Saale) Hbf **851** d.	...	|	1725	1725	|	...	...	|	1925	1938	...	|	...	...	|	...	2128	2213	...	...	...	2322	2322	...	0012
Weißenfels d.	...	|	1734	1734	|	...	...	|	1935	1948	...	|	...	...	|	...	2138	|	...	...	...	|	|	...	|
Leipzig Hbf **851** a.	...	1745	|	|	1841	1851	...	1945	|	2018	...	2041	...	...	2145	2151	|	2245	2301	...	...	0035	0035	...	0044
Dresden Hbf **842** a.	...	1906	|	|	2007	|	...	2106	|	...	...	|	...	...	2306	|	|	0009**y**	|	...	...	|	|	...	...
Halle (Saale) Hbf d.	...	...	1759	1759	...	|	...	...	1959	...	...	|	...	...	...	|	2200	...	|	...	...	2350*	2350*	...	...
Bitterfeld **851** d.	...	...	1820	1820	...	|	...	...	2020	...	...	|	...	...	...	|	...	...	|	...	...	...	...	...	...
Lutherstadt Wittenberg **851** d.	...	...	1836	1836	...	1922	...	...	2036	...	...	2122	...	...	...	|	...	...	2332	...	...	...	...	...	...
Berlin Hbf **851** a.	...	...	1916	1916	...	2007	...	...	2116	...	...	2204	...	...	...	2300	...	...	0014	...	...	...	...	...	...
Stralsund **845** a.	...	...	2224	...	...	...	...	...	...	...	...	...	...	...	...	...	...	...	...	...	...	...	...	...	...

A – CANOPUS – 🛏 1, 2 cl., ▬ 2 cl., (2) (reclining) and 🍷 Praha - Karlsruhe - Basel - Zürich and v.v.
B – (12) and 🍷 Berlin - Kassel - Dortmund (- Köln ⑦).
C – (12) and 🍷 (Köln - Düsseldorf ①–⑥ -) Dortmund - Kassel - Erfurt - Berlin.
D – STRELASUND – (12) and 🍷 (Düsseldorf ① -) (Dortmund ①–⑥ -) Erfurt - Berlin - Ostseebad Binz.
H – From / to Hamburg (Table **840**).
L – To Gemünden (a. 2332) and Würzburg (a. 2356).
N – ①–⑥ until Nov. 2; ①⑤ from Nov. 6.
O – From Ostseebad Binz on ①–⑥ (Table **844**).
P – From / to Praha (Table **1100**).
R – To / from Saarbrücken (Table **919**).
T – To Stuttgart (Tables **911**/**930**).
Y – SIRIUS – 🛏 1, 2 cl., ▬ 2 cl., (2) (reclining) and ✕ (Ostseebad Binz ♠ -) Berlin - Basel - Zürich.
Z – SIRIUS – 🛏 1, 2 cl., ▬ 2 cl., (2) (reclining) and ✕ Zürich - Basel - Berlin. On ⑤ July 3 - Aug. 21 conveys 🛏 1, 2 cl., ▬ 2 cl. and (2) (reclining) Zürich - Basel - Ostseebad Binz.

a – ①–⑤ only.
b – Not ⑥.
e – ①–⑥ only.
f – Change trains at Fulda (see Table **900**).
g – ① only.
h – Change trains at Hanau (see Table **900**).
j – From Aug. 24.
k – Not ⑦ June 14 - Aug. 23.
n – 7 minutes later until Aug. 23.
r – ⑥ only (change trains at Fulda).
s – Stops to set down only.
t – Daily until Nov. 2; ①⑤⑦ from Nov. 6.
u – Stops to pick up only.
v – Arrives 2047.
w – ⑦ only.

x – Arrives 2151.
y – Leipzig - Dresden on ⑤⑦ only.

§ – Frankfurt Flughafen Fernbahnhof.
◇ – Frankfurt S-Bahn.
⊖ – See Table **851** for further details.
* – Arrival time (calls before Leipzig).
◧ – Train number **2257** on ⑥.
◐ – Train number **2250** on ⑦.
‡ – Train number **1576** Aug. 1 - Sept. 14.
¶ – Train number **1753** Aug. 4 - Sept. 11.
♠ – ⑥ July 4 - Aug. 22.
♥ – Aug. 1 - Sept. 12 runs with train number **1579** and departs Leipzig 2019.
△ – ✕ on ①–⑤ only.

851 BERLIN - LEIPZIG - SAALFELD - NÜRNBERG

Alternative regional services: Table **835** Berlin - Lutherstadt Wittenberg. Table **848** Lutherstadt Wittenberg - Leipzig. Table **849** Leipzig / Halle - Saalfeld. Table **875** Lichtenfels - Nürnberg.

Subject to alteration Aug. 1 - Sept. 14. See note ⊠.

km		*RB* 16841	*ICE* 1501	*RB* 16843	*ICE* 1603	*ICE* 1644	*ICE* 1503	*RE* 3481	*ICE* 1654	*ICE* 1605	*IC* 2154	*ICE* 1505	*RE* 3483	*ICE* 1727	*X* 80002	*IC* 2152	*ICE* 1507	*ICE* 1707	*ICE* 1707	*RE* 3485	*ICE* 1709	*ICE* 1609	*IC* 2150	*ICE* 1509	*ICE* 1719
		①–⑤	①–⑤		①–⑤	①–⑥	①–⑥		①–⑥	①–⑥	①–⑥			¶			①–⑤	⑥	⑥⑦		Ⓑ	⑥	**2250**	①–⑥	⑦
			✕		✕	✕	✕	◧	✕⊖	✕D	🍷⊖	✕	◧	✕	△	🍷⊖	✕	G✕	✕	◧	R✕	✕	🍷⊖	K✕	✕
	Hamburg Hbf **840** d.	...	...	...	...	...	...	...	...	...	...	...	...	0600**g**	...	...	0708	...	...	...	...	0806	...	0908	...
0	**Berlin** Hbf **850** d.	...	...	...	...	...	...	...	0548	...	0639	0652	...	0752	0757	0839**e**	0858	0858	...	...	0952	0952	1039	1058	1058
98	Lutherstadt Wittenberg **850** d.	...	...	...	...	...	...	...	0633	...	0721	0736	...	0835	|	0921**e**	|	|	...	...	1035	1035	1121	|	|
135	Bitterfeld **850** d.	...	...	...	...	...	...	...	0649	...	0738	|	...	|	|	0938**e**	|	|	...	...	|	|	1138	|	|
168	**Leipzig** Hbf a.	...	...	...	...	...	...	...	0705	...	|	0805	...	0905	0916	|	1005	1005	...	...	1105	1105	|	1205	1205
168	**Leipzig** Hbf **850** d.	...	...	...	0501	0601	...	...	...	0711	|	0816	...	0911	...	|	1016	1016	1016	...	1111	1111	|	1216	1216
	Halle (Saale) Hbf **850** d.	...	...	...	|	|	0602	...	...	|	0800	|	...	|	...	1000	|	|	|	...	|	|	1200	|	|
222	Naumburg (Saale) Hbf **850** d.	...	...	...	0545	0638	0645	...	...	|	0833	0851	...	|	...	1033	1051	1051	1051	...	|	|	1233	1251	1251
261	**Jena** Paradies d.	...	...	...	0608	...	0711	...	...	0806	...	0917	...	1006	...	...	1117	1117	1117	...	1206	1206	...	1317	1317
308	**Saalfeld** (Saale) d.	0434	...	0525	0634	...	0741	0752	...	|	...	0946	0952	|	...	...	1146	1146	1146	1152	|	|	...	1346	1346
372	Kronach d.	0532	...	0628	|	...	|	0841	...	|	...	|	1041	|	...	...	|	|	|	1241	|	|	...	|	|
395	Lichtenfels d.	0555	0628	0650	0729	...	0832	0853	...	0926	...	|	1053	1126	...	...	|	|	|	1253	1326	1326	...	|	|
427	**Bamberg** d.	...	0647	...	0746	...	0849	...	...	0943	...	|	...	1143	...	...	|	|	|	...	1343	1343	...	|	|
465	Erlangen d.	...	0708	...	|	...	0908	...	...	1003	...	|	...	1203	...	...	|	|	|	...	1403	1403	...	|	|
489	**Nürnberg** Hbf a.	...	0725	...	0820	...	0925	...	...	1020	...	1125	...	1220	...	...	1325	1325	1325	...	1420	1420	...	1525	1525
	Augsburg Hbf **904** a.	...	|	...	|	...	1032	...	...	|	...	|	...	1332	...	...	|	|	|	...	|	|	...	|	|
	München Hbf **904** a.	...	0839	...	0938	...	1110*	...	...	1137	...	1240	...	1412*	...	...	1439	1439	1439	...	1539	1539	...	1640	1640

	RE 3487	*ICE* 1711	*IC* 2356	*ICE* 109	*RE* 3489	*ICE* 1613	*IC* 2354	*ICE* 1513	*RE* 3491	*ICE* 1615	*IC* 2352	*ICE* 1515	*X* 80004	*ICE* 1617	*ICE* 1617	*IC* 2350	*ICE* 1517	*ICE* 1737	*ICE* 905	*ICE* 1619	*ICE* 1519	*ICE* 909	*CNL* 1201	*CNL* 1201	*ICE* 1521
															⑤⑦	Ⓑ	Ⓑ	⑥	⑦	①–⑥	Ⓑ	⑤	Ⓡ⑥	Ⓡ Ⓑ	⑦
	◧	R✕	🍷⊖	E✕	◧	✕	🍷⊖	✕	◧	✕	🍷⊖	✕	R△	✕	✕	🍷⊖	♣✕	✕	✕	✕	✕	✕	B✕	B✕	✕
Hamburg Hbf **840** d.	...	...	...	1051	...	...	...	1308	...	...	...	1453	...	...	...	...	1708	...	1804	...	1908	2006	...	...	2121
Berlin Hbf **850** d.	...	1152	1239	1258	...	1352	1440	1458	...	1552	1639	1658	1706	1752	1752	1839	1858	1858	1952	1952	2058	2152	2212	2212	2312
Lutherstadt Wittenberg **850** d.	...	1235	1321	|	...	1435	1521	|	...	1635	1721	|	|	1835	1835	1921	|	|	2035	2035	2140	2238	|	|	2354
Bitterfeld **850** d.	...	|	1338	|	...	|	1538	|	...	|	1738	|	|	|	|	1938	|	1958	|	|	|	|	|	|	|
Leipzig Hbf a.	...	1305	|	1405	...	1505	|	1605	...	1705	|	1805	1832	1905	1905	|	2005	2015	2105	2105	2210	2307	|	|	0029
Leipzig Hbf **850** d.	...	1311	|	1416	...	1511	|	1616	...	1711	|	1816	▬	...	1911	|	2011	2020	▬	...	...	...	|	|	...
Halle (Saale) Hbf **850** d.	...	|	1400	|	...	|	1600	|	...	|	1800	|	*RE*	...	|	2002	|	|	*RE*	...	...	...	0053**u**	0053**u**	...
Naumburg (Saale) Hbf **850** d.	...	|	1433	1451	...	|	1633	1651	...	|	1833	1851	**3493**	...	|	2033	2052	2052	**3495**	...	...	...	|	|	...
Jena Paradies d.	...	1406	...	1517	...	1606	...	1717	...	1806	...	1917		...	2006	...	2117	2117		...	...	...	|	|	...
Saalfeld (Saale) d.	1352	|	...	1546	1552	|	...	1746	1752	|	...	1946	1952	...	|	...	2146	2146	2152	...	...	...	|	|	...
Kronach d.	1441	|	...	|	1641	|	...	|	1841	|	...	|	2041	...	|	...	|	|	2247	...	...	...	|	|	...
Lichtenfels d.	1453	1526	...	|	1653	1726	...	|	1853	1926	...	|	2053	...	2126	...	2236	2236	2310	...	...	...	|	|	...
Bamberg d.	...	1543	...	|	...	1743	...	|	...	1943	...	2051	...	...	2143	...	2253	2253	...	...	...	...	|	|	...
Erlangen d.	...	1603	...	|	...	1803	...	|	...	2003	...	|	...	...	2203	...	2315	2315	...	...	...	...	|	|	...
Nürnberg Hbf a.	...	1620	...	1725	...	1820	...	1925	...	2020	...	2125	...	...	2220	...	2334	2334	...	...	...	...	|	|	...
Augsburg Hbf **904** a.	...	1731	...	|	...	1934	...	|	...	2134	...	|	...	...	|	...	|	|	...	...	...	...	|	0554**s**	...
München Hbf **904** a.	...	1811*	...	1838	...	2012*	...	2040	...	2215*	...	2240	...	...	2340**h**	...	0049	0049	...	...	...	...	0637	0639	...

	ICE 1518	*ICE* 1518	*CNL* 1200	*ICE* 1616	*ICE* 1516	*RB* 16842	*ICE* 1614	*X* 80003	*RE* 3480	*ICE* 1514	*ICE* 1714	*ICE* 1714	*IC* 2353	*ICE* 1612	*RE* 3482	*ICE* 1712	*ICE* 1512	*IC* 2355	*ICE* 1610	*RE* 3484	*ICE* 108	*IC* 2357	*ICE* 1608	*RE* 3486	*ICE* 1508
	①	①–⑥	Ⓡ	①–⑤		①–⑥	①–⑥			①–⑤	⑥	⑥⑦		①–⑥		⑥	Ⓑ								Ⓑ
		§✕	A✕	✕	✕		✕	W△		✕	✕	✕	🍷⊖	✕	◧	✕	✕	🍷⊖	✕	◧	E✕	🍷⊖	✕	◧	K✕
München Hbf **904** d.	0014	...	2304	...	...	...	...	...	...	0431*	0516	...	...	0530*	...	0720	0720	...	0743*	...	0921	...	0945*	...	1120
Augsburg Hbf **904** d.	0054	...	2345**u**	...	...	...	...	...	...	0513	|	...	...	0615	...	|	|	...	0822	...	|	...	1024	...	|
Nürnberg Hbf d.	0222	...	|	...	...	...	0520	...	...	0635	0635	...	...	0737	...	0834	0834	...	0937	...	1036	...	1137	...	1234
Erlangen d.	0242	...	|	...	...	...	0540	...	...	|	|	...	...	0757	...	|	|	...	0957	...	|	...	1157	...	|
Bamberg d.	0303	...	|	...	...	...	0601	...	...	|	|	...	...	0816	...	|	|	...	1016	...	|	...	1216	...	|
Lichtenfels d.	0321	...	|	...	...	0543	0621	...	0704	|	|	...	...	0833	0904	|	|	...	1033	1104	|	...	1233	1304	|
Kronach d.	|	...	|	...	...	0607	|	...	0717	|	|	...	...	|	0917	|	|	...	|	1117	|	...	|	1317	|
Saalfeld (Saale) d.	0414	...	|	...	...	0709	0717	...	0808	0815	0815	...	...	|	1008	1015	1015	...	|	1208	1215	...	|	1408	1415
Jena Paradies d.	0442	...	|	...	...	...	0744	...	...	0844	0844	...	...	0954	...	1044	1044	...	1154	...	1244	...	1354	...	1444
Naumburg (Saale) Hbf **850** d.	0505	...	|	...	0715	...	|	...	...	0908	0908	...	0925	|	...	1108	1108	1125	|	...	1308	1325	|	...	1508
Halle (Saale) Hbf **850** a.	|	...	0500**s**	...	|	...	|	...	...	|	|	...	0956	|	...	|	|	1156	|	...	|	1356	|	...	|
Leipzig Hbf **850** a.	0540	...	|	...	0747	...	0841	...	...	0941	0941	...	|	1046	...	1141	1141	|	1246	...	1341	|	1446	...	1541
Leipzig Hbf d.	0548	0548	|	0651	0751	...	0851	0926	...	0951	0951	0951	|	1051	...	1151	1151	|	1251	...	1351	|	1451	...	1551
Bitterfeld **850** d.	|	|	|	0709	|	...	|	|	...	|	|	|	1020	|	...	|	|	1220	|	...	|	1420	|	...	|
Lutherstadt Wittenberg **850** d.	|	|	|	0725	|	...	0922	|	...	|	|	|	1036	1122	...	|	|	1236	1322	...	|	1436	1522	...	|
Berlin Hbf **850** a.	0700	0700	0741	0811	0900	...	1006	1050	...	1100	1100	1100	1116	1205	...	1300	1302	1316	1405	...	1500	1516	1605	...	1700
Hamburg Hbf **840** a.	0852	0852	...	0956	...	...	1156	...	...	1301	1301	1301	...	...	...	...	1452	...	...	...	1649**b**	...	...	...	1852

	ICE 1708	*IC* 2157	*ICE* 1706	*ICE* 1606	*RE* 3488	*ICE* 1716	*ICE* 1506	*IC* 2259	*ICE* 1704	*ICE* 1604	*X* 80005	*RE* 3490	*ICE* 1724	*ICE* 1504	*IC* 2151	*ICE* 1602	*ICE* 1655	*RE* 3492	*ICE* 1502	*ICE* 1722	*IC* 2153	*ICE* 1600	*RE* 3494	*ICE* 1500	*ICE* 1647
	⑥	**2257**	Ⓑ	⑥		Y	⑤⑦	**2359**	⑥	Ⓑ			①–④	⑤–⑦		Ⓑ	Ⓑ		①–⑥	⑦	Ⓑ	⑤⑦			**1747**
	H✕	🍷⊖	W✕	✕	◧	✕	✕	Ⓑ🍷	✕	✕	△	◧	✕	✕	🍷⊖	D✕	✕⊖	◧	✕	✕	⊖	✕		✕	⊖
München Hbf **904** d.	1120	...	1225	1225	...	1320	1320	⊖	1341*	1341*	...	...	1520	1520	...	1621	...	...	1720	1720	...	1745*	...	1920	...
Augsburg Hbf **904** d.	|	...	|	|	...	|	|	...	1419	1419	...	...	|	|	...	|	...	...	|	|	...	1822	...	|	...
Nürnberg Hbf d.	1234	...	1337	1337	...	1434	1434	...	1537	1537	...	...	1636	1636	...	1737	...	...	1836	1836	...	1937	...	2035	...
Erlangen d.	|	...	1357	1357	...	|	|	...	1557	1557	...	...	|	|	...	1757	...	...	|	|	...	1957	...	2054	...
Bamberg d.	|	...	1416	1416	...	|	|	...	1616	1616	...	...	|	|	...	1816	...	...	|	|	...	2016	...	2114	...
Lichtenfels d.	|	...	1433	1433	1504	|	|	...	1633	1633	...	1704	|	|	...	1833	...	1904	|	|	...	2033	2103	2132	...
Kronach d.	|	...	|	|	1517	|	|	...	|	|	...	1717	|	|	...	|	...	1917	|	|	...	|	2118	|	...
Saalfeld (Saale) d.	1415	...	|	|	1608	1615	1615	...	|	|	...	1808	1815	1815	...	|	...	2008	2015	2015	...	2127	2208	2225	...
Jena Paradies d.	1444	...	1554	1554	...	1644	1644	...	1754	1754	...	...	1844	1844	...	1954	...	...	2044	2044	...	2156	...	2252	...
Naumburg (Saale) Hbf **850** d.	1508	1525	|	|	...	1708	1708	1725	|	|	...	...	1908	1908	1925	|	...	...	2108	2108	2128	2219	...	2316	2322
Halle (Saale) Hbf **850** a.	|	1556	|	|	...	|	|	1756	|	|	...	...	|	|	1956	|	...	...	|	|	2200	|	...	|	2350
Leipzig Hbf **850** a.	1541	|	1646	1646	...	1741	1741	|	1846	1846	...	...	1941	1941	|	2046	...	...	2141	2141	...	2251	...	2349	...
Leipzig Hbf d.	1551	|	1651	1651	...	1751	1751	|	1851	1851	1855	...	1951	1951	|	...	2051	...	2151	2151	...	2301	...	...	...
Bitterfeld **850** d.	|	1620	|	|	...	|	|	1820	|	|	|	...	|	|	2020	...	|	...	|	|	...	|	...	...	...
Lutherstadt Wittenberg **850** d.	|	1636	1722	1722	...	|	|	1836	1922	1922	|	...	|	|	2036	...	2122	...	|	|	...	2332	...	...	...
Berlin Hbf **850** a.	1700	1716	1805	1805	...	1900	1900	1916	2005	2007	2015	...	2100	2100	2116	...	2204	...	2300	2300	...	0014	...	...	...
Hamburg Hbf **840** a.	...	...	...	1956	...	...	2052	...	...	2157	...	...	...	2305	...	...	...	...	0043	...	...	...	...	...	...

A – CAPELLA – 🛏 1 cl., ▬ 2 cl., (2) (reclining) and ✕ München - Fürth (Bay) Hbf (d. 0109**u**) - Potsdam Hbf (a. 0658) - Berlin Wannsee (a. 0709) - Berlin Zoo (a. 0730) - Berlin Ostbahnhof (a. 0752).
B – CAPELLA – 🛏 1 cl., ▬ 2 cl., (2) (reclining) and ✕ Berlin Ostbahnhof (d. 2203) - Berlin Zoo (d. 2220) - Berlin Wannsee (d. 2254) - Potsdam Hbf (d. 2304) - Fürth (Bay) Hbf (a. 0424**s**) - München.
D – To / from Dresden (Table **842**).
E – From / to Innsbruck (Table **951**).
G – To Garmisch (a. 1622).
H – From Garmisch (d. 0925).
K – To / from Kiel (Table **820**).
R – From Warnemünde via Rostock (Table **835**).
W – To Warnemünde via Rostock (Table **835**).
Y – ①②③④⑥.

b – Not ⑥.
e – ①–⑥ only.
g – ① only.

h – ⑦ only.
s – Stops to set down only.
u – Stops to pick up only.

¶ – Train number **1607** on ①.
§ – Train number **908** on ⑥.
⊖ – See Table **850** for further details.
♣ – Conveys (12) (*ICE* **1717**) Hamburg - Berlin - Leipzig - Naumburg - Erfurt (Table **850**).
◧ – (12) Saalfeld - Lichtenfels - Bayreuth / Hof and v.v.
△ – *InterConnex*. Operated by Veolia Verkehr GmbH. **DB tickets are not valid**.
* – Earlier arrival / later departure possible by changing trains at Nürnberg (see Table **904**).

⊠ – **Engineering work** Aug. 1 - Sept. 14 between Bamberg and Nürnberg will affect all *ICE* services between Leipzig and Nürnberg (also overnight trains *CNL* **1200/1**). During this period *ICE* services will operate every two hours via Jena to / from Bamberg. A replacement 🚌 service will operate between Bamberg and Elangen / Nürnberg. Direct *ICE* trains will run every two hours via Erfurt and Würzburg (extended journey times). Full details can be found on page 41.

COTTBUS - LEIPZIG 852

RE / RB services

km			⚒									
0	**Cottbus** ●	d.	0502	0702	0902	1102	1302	1502	1702	1902	1959	2300
24	Calau (Niederl) ●	d.	0519	0719	0919	1119	1319	1519	1719	1919	2017	2319
46	Finsterwalde ●	d.	0532	0732	0932	1132	1332	1532	1732	1932	2031	2333
56	Doberlug-Kirchhain ●	d.	0540	0740	0940	1140	1340	1540	1740	1940	2038	2340
79	Falkenberg (Elster) ●	a.	0556	0756	0956	1156	1356	1556	1756	1956	2106	0006
79	Falkenberg (Elster) 856	d.	0557	0757	0957	1157	1357	1557	1757	1957	...	...
97	Torgau 856	d.	0611	0811	1011	1211	1411	1611	1811	2011	...	...
124	Eilenburg 856	d.	0640	0840	1040	1240	1440	1640	1840	2040	...	...
149	**Leipzig** Hbf 856	a.	0700	0900	1100	1300	1500	1700	1900	2100	...	...

				⚒							
Leipzig Hbf 856	d.	...	*0607*	0707	0907	1107	1307	1507	1707	1907	2107
Eilenburg 856	d.	...	*0628*	0728	0928	1128	1328	1528	1728	1928	2128
Torgau 856	d.	...	*0650*	0750	0950	1150	1350	1550	1750	1950	2150
Falkenberg (Elster) 856	a.	...	*0705*	0803	1003	1203	1403	1603	1803	2003	2203
Falkenberg (Elster) ♥	d.	0526	0726	0804	1004	1204	1404	1604	1804	2004	2204
Doberlug-Kirchhain ♥	d.	0549	0749	0820	1020	1220	1420	1620	1820	2020	2220
Finsterwalde ♥	d.	0556	0756	0827	1027	1227	1427	1627	1827	2027	2227
Calau (Niederl) ♥	d.	0611	0811	0840	1040	1240	1440	1640	1840	2040	2240
Cottbus ♥	a.	0631	0831	0858	1058	1258	1458	1658	1858	2058	2258

● – Additional trains Cottbus - Falkenberg at 0556 Ⓐ, 0759, 1159, 1359, 1559 and 1759.

♥ – Additional trains Falkenberg - Cottbus at 0626 Ⓐ, 0851, 1251, 1451, 1651 and 1851.

STEAM TRAINS IN SACHSEN 853

km			Ⓐe							⊡	
	Dresden Hbf (S-Bahn) **857**	d.	*0430*	...	*0800*	*1000*	*1230*	*1400*	*1630*	*1800*	...
0	Radebeul Ost	d.	0456	...	0826	1026	1256	1426	1656	1826	...
8	Moritzburg	d.	0525	...	0853	1055	1323	1455	1723	1853	...
16	Radeburg	a.	0546	...	...	1116	...	1516	...	...	...

		Ⓐe								⊡
Radeburg	d.	0611	...	...	...	1139	...	1539	...	...
Moritzburg	d.	0634	...	0903	...	1203	1333	1603	1733	1903
Radebeul Ost	a.	0701	...	0930	...	1230	1400	1630	1800	1930
Dresden Hbf (S-Bahn) **857**	a.	*0727*	...	*0957*	...	*1257*	*1427*	*1657*	*1827*	*1957*

km					🍷	Ⓒd		🍷		Ⓒd		🍷		Ⓒd		🍷			Ⓒ🍷		🍷	🍷	🍷	🍷	🍷	🍷
0	Zittau	d.	High season	0847	0905	0946	...	1105	...	1146	...	1305	...	1346	...	1505	...	...	1705	Low season	0905	...	...	1334	...	...
9	Bertsdorf	d.	until Nov. 1	0939	0939	1019	1028	1139	1139	1219	1228	1339	1339	1419	1428	1539	1539	1628	1739	♣	0939	1037	1139	1405	1452	1547
12	Kurort Oybin	a.	→	|	0951	|	1040	1151	|	|	1240	1351	|	|	1440	1551	|	|	1751	→	0951	|	1151	1417	|	1559
13	Kurort Jonsdorf	a.		0951	...	1031	...	...	1151	1231	...	...	1351	1431	...	...	1551	1640	...		...	1049	...	...	1504	...

				🍷	Ⓒd			🍷	Ⓒd			🍷	Ⓒd			🍷		Ⓒ🍷		🍷	🍷	🍷	🍷	🍷	🍷
Kurort Jonsdorf	d.	High season	1002	...	1051	...	1202	...	1251	...	1403	...	1451	...	1602	...	1723	...	Low season	...	1101	...	...	1515	...
Kurort Oybin	d.	until Nov. 1	|	1006	|	1052	|	1206	|	1252	|	1406	|	1452	|	1606	|	1806	♣	1006	|	1206	1430	|	1612
Bertsdorf	d.	→	1014	1018	1104	1104	1214	1218	1304	1304	1414	1418	1504	1504	1614	1618	1740	1818	→	1017	1112	1219	1441	1527	1624
Zittau	a.		...	1048	1134	...	...	1248	1334	...	...	1448	1534	...	...	1648	1809	1848		...	...	1247	...	...	1653

Operators: Radebeul service – BVO Bahn GmbH, Betriebsleitung Lößnitzgrundbahn, Am Bahnhof 1, 01468 Moritzburg. ✆ +49 (0) 35207 89290. www.loessnitzgrundbahn.de
Zittau service – SOEG - Sächisch Oberlausitzer Eisenbahngesellschaft mbH, Bahnhofstraße 41, 02763 Zittau. ✆ +49 (0) 3583 540540. www.soeg-zittau.de

d – Diesel train. e – Not June 29 - Aug. 7, Oct. 12–23, Nov. 18. ⊡ – Until Nov. 1. ♣ – Nov. 28 - Dec. 12 (no service Nov. 2–27).

SEUSSLITZ - DRESDEN - BAD SCHANDAU 853a

April 4 - November 1, 2009

Special dates: May 1 "Steamship Parade", May 14 "Riverboat - Shuffle", Aug. 15 "Steamship - Fest". Contact the operator for service details on these dates.

		A	B			A	A	A	A		A	A	C
Seußlitz	d.	...	...	...	...	...	...	...	...	...	...	1315	...
Meißen	d.	...	...	...	...	...	...	...	...	...	...	1445	1615
Radebeul	d.	...	...	...	...	...	...	...	...	...	...	1630	1800
Dresden ⊡	d.	...	0830	0900	1000	1030	...	1200	1330	1400	1600	1800	1930
Pillnitz	d.	...	1020	1050	1130	1200	...	1330	1500	1530	1730	...	...
Pirna	d.	0930	1130	1200	...	1300	1430	...	1600	...	...	...	...
Königstein	d.	1130	1400	1430	...	1500	1630	...	1800	...	...	...	...
Bad Schandau	a.	1215	...	...	...	1600	1715	...	1845	...	...	...	...

		A		A	C	A		A	B		A	A	A
Bad Schandau	d.	...	...	0930	...	...	...	1215	...	...	...	1630	1730
Königstein	d.	...	...	1000	...	...	...	1245	1430	1500	...	1700	1800
Pirna	d.	...	...	1115	...	...	...	1400	1600	1630	...	1815	1915
Pillnitz	d.	...	1145	1200	...	1345	1545	...	1645	1715	1745	1900	...
Dresden ⊡	d.	0945	1245	1300	1415	1445	1645	...	1800	1830	1845	2000	...
Radebeul	d.	1045	...	...	1515	...	...	...	...	...	...	...	...
Meißen	d.	1145	...	...	1615	...	...	...	...	...	...	...	...
Seußlitz	a.	1245	...	...	...	...	...	...	...	...	...	...	...

A – Apr. 25 - Oct. 25.
B – ④⑤⑥ Apr. 25 - Oct. 24.
C – May 2 - Oct. 4.
⊡ – Dresden Terrassenufer.

Operator: Sächsische Dampfschiffahrts GmbH & Co. Conti Elbschiffahrts KG. Hertha-Lindner Straße 10, D-01067 Dresden. ✆ +49 (0) 351 866 090, Fax +49 (0) 351 866 09 88.

COTTBUS - GÖRLITZ - ZITTAU 854

ODEG ★ 2nd class only

km			Ⓐe	Ⓐe	Ⓐ								Ⓐe											⚒e	Ⓐe		
0	**Cottbus**	d.	...	...	0458	...	0603	0703	0803	0903	1003	1103	1103	1203	1303	1403	1503	1603	1703	1803	1903	2007	2103	2103	2203	...	2305
24	Spremberg	d.	...	...	0516	...	0622	0722	0822	0922	1022	1121	1122	1222	1322	1422	1522	1622	1722	1822	1921	2026	2122	2122	2222	...	2324
42	Weißwasser	d.	...	0435	0535	0535	0635	0735	0835	0935	1035	...	1135	1235	1335	1435	1535	1635	1735	1835	...	2043	2135	2135	2235	...	2344
72	Horka	d.	...	0500	0600	0600	0700	0800	0900	1000	1100	...	1200	1300	1400	1500	1600	1700	1800	1900	...	2104	2200	2200	2300	...	0005
93	**Görlitz**	a.	...	0515	0615	0615	0715	0815	0915	1015	1115	...	1215	1315	1415	1515	1615	1715	1814	1915	...	2119	2215	2215	2315	...	0020
93	**Görlitz**	d.	0417	0520	0620	0620	0720	0820	0920	1022	1120	...	1220	1317	1420	1520	1617	1720	1820	1920	...	2121	...	2220	...	...	...
127	**Zittau**	a.	0456	0554	0654	0654	0754	0854	0954	1056	1154	...	1254	1356	1454	1554	1656	1754	1854	1959	...	2155	...	2254	...	...	...

		Ⓐ		Ⓒz	Ⓐe							Ⓐe														Ⓐe
Zittau	d.	...	...	...	0404	...	0501	0601	0701	0801	0901	1005	...	1101	1201	1304	1401	1501	1604	1701	...	...	1908	...	2102	2201
Görlitz	a.	...	...	...	0438	...	0540	0640	0740	0840	0940	1041	...	1140	1240	1338	1440	1540	1638	1740	...	...	1942	...	2141	2240
Görlitz	d.	0340	...	0440	0444	...	0544	0644	0744	0844	0944	1045	...	1144	1244	1344	1444	1544	1644	1744	...	...	1944	...	2144	2244
Horka	d.	0354	...	0454	0458	...	0558	0658	0758	0858	0958	1059	...	1158	1258	1358	1458	1558	1658	1758	...	...	1958	...	2158	2258
Weißwasser	d.	0420	...	0520	0520	...	0620	0720	0820	0920	1020	1120	...	1220	1320	1420	1520	1620	1720	1820	...	...	2020	...	2220	2319
Spremberg	d.	0433	...	0535	0535	...	0638	0738	0838	0938	1038	1138	1138	1238	1338	1438	1538	1638	1738	1838	1938	...	2036	...	2238	...
Cottbus	a.	0451	...	0553	0553	...	0657	0757	0857	0957	1057	1157	1157	1257	1357	1457	1557	1657	1757	1857	1957	...	2054	...	2257	...

e – Not Nov. 18.
z – Also Nov. 18.

★ – Ostdeutsche Eisenbahn GmbH, Reichenbacher Str. 1, 02827 Görlitz. ✆ +49 (0) 30 514 88 88 88. www.odeg.info

DRESDEN - GÖRLITZ and ZITTAU 855

RE / RB services

km				⚒r																							
0	**Dresden** Hbf	d.	0534	0609	0637	0709	0727	0809	0909	1009	1109	1209	1309	1327	1409	1509	1609	1709	1727	1809	1909	2009	2109	2210	2210	2313	2337
4	Dresden Neustadt	d.	0541	0616	0645	0716	0732	0816	0916	1016	1116	1216	1316	1332	1416	1516	1616	1716	1732	1816	1916	2016	2116	2217	2217	2320	2345
41	Bischofswerda	d.	0622	0646	0721	0745	|	0846	0945	1046	1145	1246	1345	|	1446	1545	1646	1745	|	1846	1945	2046	2145	2256	2259	2349	0021
79	Ebersbach (Sachs)	d.	0702	|	|	0814	|	|	1014	|	1214	|	1414	|	|	1614	|	1814	|	|	2014	|	2214	2332	|	0018	|
83	Neugersdorf	d.	0706	|	|	0819	|	|	1019	|	1219	|	1419	|	|	1619	|	1819	|	|	2019	|	2219	2335	|	0022	|
105	**Zittau**	a.	0729	|	|	0838	|	|	1038	|	1238	|	1438	|	|	1638	|	1838	|	|	2038	|	2238	2358	|	0041	|
	Liberec **1117**	a.	...	|	|	0918	|	|	...	|	1318	|	...	|	|	1718	|	...	|	|	2118	|	...	...	|	...	|
	Bautzen	d.	...	0658	0736	T	0812	0858	...	1058	...	1258	...	1412	1458	T	1658	...	1812	1858	...	2058	...	...	2314	...	0036
	Löbau (Sachs)	d.	...	0712	0755	...	|	0912	...	1112	...	1312	...	|	1512	...	1712	...	|	1912	...	2112	...	...	2333	...	0055
	Görlitz	a.	...	0727	0815	...	0840	0927	...	1127	...	1327	...	1440	1527	...	1727	...	1840	1927	...	2127	...	...	2353	...	0115
	Wrocław Gł **1085**	a.	...	...	...	...	1100	...	...	...	...	...	...	1700	...	...	...	...	2100	...	...	...	...	...	...	...	...

km			⚒r			⚒r																					
	Wrocław Gł **1085**	d.	...	...	...	...	...	...	0705	...	...	...	...	...	...	1305	...	...	...	...	...	...	1805	...	...	...	...
0	**Görlitz**	d.	...	...	0535	0630	...	0832	0921	...	1032	...	1232	...	1432	1521	...	1632	...	1832	...	1945	2021	...	2145	2233	...
24	Löbau (Sachs)	d.	...	...	0550	0645	...	0847	|	...	1047	...	1247	...	1447	|	...	1647	...	1847	...	2006	|	...	2206	2254	...
46	Bautzen	d.	...	...	0604	0700	...	0901	0949	...	1101	...	1301	T	1501	1549	...	1701	...	1901	...	2024	2049	T	2224	2312	...
	Liberec **1117**	d.	...	...	|	|	...	|	|	0838	|	...	|	1238	|	|	...	|	1638	|	...	|	|	2036	|	|	...
	Zittau	d.	0356	0515	|	|	0719	|	|	0919	|	1119	|	1319	|	|	1519	|	1719	|	1919	|	|	2119	|	|	2225
	Neugersdorf	d.	0419	0535	|	|	0739	|	|	0939	|	1139	|	1339	|	|	1539	|	1739	|	1939	|	|	2139	|	|	2248
	Ebersbach (Sachs)	d.	0424	0539	|	|	0743	|	|	0943	|	1143	|	1343	|	|	1543	|	1743	|	1943	|	|	2143	|	|	2252
65	Bischofswerda	d.	0503	0609	0616	0713	0814	0914	|	1014	1114	1214	1314	1414	1514	|	1614	1714	1814	1914	2014	2040	|	2214	2240	2328	2332
102	Dresden Neustadt	a.	0536	0637	0644	0741	0841	0941	1025	1041	1141	1241	1341	1441	1541	1625	1641	1741	1841	1941	2041	2113	2125	2241	2313	...	0005
106	**Dresden** Hbf	a.	0547	0644	0651	0748	0848	0948	1032	1048	1148	1248	1348	1448	1548	1632	1648	1748	1848	1948	2048	2122	2132	2248	2320	...	0014

T – To / from Tanwald on ⑥⑦ (also Czech holidays). See Table **1141**.

r – Not Oct. 31, Nov. 18.

856 DRESDEN and LEIPZIG - RUHLAND - COTTBUS and HOYERSWERDA

RE services

km	km												⊠										
	0	**Dresden** Hbf .. **842 843 857** d.	...	...	0540	...	...	0646	0740	...	...	0844		1740	...	...	1844	1940	...	...	2044	...	2140	...
	4	**Dresden** Neustadt. **842 857** d.	...	...	|	...	...	0653	|	...	...	0853		|	...	...	1853	|	...	...	2053	...	|	...
	18	Coswig .... **842 843 857** d.	...	...	0604	...	...	0704	0804	...	...	0904		1804	...	...	1904	2004	...	...	2104	...	2204	...
0		**Leipzig** Hbf .... **852** d.	...	...	|	...	0607	|	|	...	0807	|	each train	|	...	1807	|	|	...	2007	|	...	|	2316
25		Eilenburg .... **852** d.	...	...	|	...	0628	|	|	...	0828	|		|	...	1828	|	|	...	2028	|	...	|	2340
52		Torgau .... **852** d.	...	...	|	...	0650	|	|	...	0850	|	runs every	|	...	1850	|	|	...	2050	|	...	|	0000
70		Falkenberg (Elster) .... **852** d.	0411a	...	|	0611a	0709	|	|	0811a	0909	|		|	1811a	1909	|	|	2011a	2109	|	...	|	0015
94		Elsterwerda-Biehla ◇ ....d.	0431a	E	|	0631a	0733	|	|	0831a	0933	|	two hours	|	1831a	1933	|	|	2031a	2133	|	...	|	...
120	73	Ruhland ....a.	0452a	0555	0656	0652a	0754	0757	0856	0852a	0954	0957		1856	1852a	1954	1957	2056	2052a	2154	2157	...	2249	...
120	73	Ruhland ....d.	0507	0600	0657	0707	0802	0802	0857	0907	1002	1002	until	1857	1907	2002	2002	2057	2107	2202	2202	...	2257	...
145		Hoyerswerda ★ ....a.	|	|	0720	|	0825	|	0920	|	1025	|		1920	|	2025	|	2120	|	2225	|	...	2320	...
	86	Senftenberg.........................d.	0518	0610	...	0718	...	0812	...	0918	...	1012		...	1918	...	2012	...	2118	...	2212	2348	...	...
	120	**Cottbus** .... **852** a.	0550	0643	...	0750	...	0842	...	0950	...	1042		...	1950	...	2042	...	2150	...	2243	0019	...	...

											⊡													
Cottbus....................... **852** d.	0417	...	0514	...	0608	...	0714	...	0808	...		1513	...	1608	...	1714	...	1808	...	1914	...	2008	...	2208
Senftenberg .... d.	0446	...	0544	...	0640	...	0744	...	0840	...		1544	...	1640	...	1744	...	1840	...	1944	...	2040	...	2241
Hoyerswerda ★................ d.	|	0438	|	0531	|	0638	|	0731	|	0838		|	1531	|	1638	|	1731	|	1838	|	1931	|	2038	|
Ruhland.................................. a.	0457	0501	0553	0555	0651	0701	0753	0755	0851	0901	each train	1553	1555	1651	1701	1753	1755	1851	1901	1953	1955	2051	2101	2252
Ruhland.................................. d.	0505a	0502	0559	0602	0705a	0702	0759	0802	0905a	0902		1559	1602	1705a	1702	1759	1802	1905a	1902	1959	2002	2105a	2102	2253
Elsterwerda-Biehla ◇ .... d.	0528a	|	|	0625	0728a	|	|	0825	0928a	|	runs every	|	1625	1728a	|	|	1825	1928a	|	|	2025	2128a	|	L
Falkenberg (Elster)..... **852** d.	0550a	|	|	0655	0750a	|	|	0855	0950a	|		|	1655	1750a	|	|	1855	1950a	|	|	2055	2150a	|	...
Torgau .... **852** d.	...	|	|	0711	...	|	|	0911	...	|	two hours	|	1711	...	|	|	1911	...	|	|	2111	...	|	...
Eilenburg.................. **852** d.	...	|	|	0740	...	|	|	0940	...	|		|	1740	...	|	|	1940	...	|	|	2140	...	|	...
Leipzig Hbf............... **852** a.	...	|	|	0800	...	|	|	1000	...	|	until	|	1800	...	|	|	2000	...	|	|	2203	...	|	...
Coswig ....**842 843 857** d.	...	0550	0646	...	...	0750	0847	...	...	0950		1647	...	...	1750	1847	...	...	1950	2047	...	...	2150	...
Dresden Neustadt ..**842 847** a.	...	|	0659	...	...	|	|	...	...	|		|	...	...	|	|	...	...	|	|	...	...	|	...
Dresden Hbf ...**842 843 857** a.	...	0613	0706	...	...	0812	0902	...	...	1012		1702	...	...	1812	1902	...	...	2012	2102	...	...	2213	...

E – From Elsterwerda (d. 0531).
L – To Elsterwerda (a. 2319).

a – ①–⑤ only.
e – Not Nov. 18.
h – Also Nov. 18.

t – Not June 29 - Aug. 7, Oct. 12–23, Nov. 18.
w – ⑥⑦ (also Nov. 18; daily June 27 - Aug. 9 and Oct. 10–25).

⊠ – The 1211 and 1411 from Falkenberg run daily throughout.
⊡ – The 1208 and 1408 from Cottbus run daily throughout.
◇ – See Table **843** for connections from / to Elsterwerda.

★ – **Hoyerswerda - Görlitz** and v.v. *73 km*. Journey time: 59–63 minutes (70–84 minutes for trains marked ‡). 2nd class only.
Operated by Ostdeutsche Eisenbahn GmbH (ODEG).
From Hoyerswerda at 0524 Ⓐ **e**, 0622 Ⓐ **e**, 0724 Ⓒ **h**, 0832 Ⓐ **e**, 1032, 1230, 1430, 1632, 1730 ⑦, 1832, 2032 and 2232.
From Görlitz at 0517 Ⓐ **e**, 0617 Ⓒ **h**, 0635 ‡ Ⓐ **e**, 0824, 1024, 1223 **w**, 1235 ‡ Ⓐ **t**, 1423 **w**, 1435 ‡ Ⓐ **t**, 1624, 1815 ‡ ⑦, 1824 ①–⑥, 2024.

857 BAD SCHANDAU - DRESDEN - MEISSEN - LEIPZIG

RB / S-Bahn services

km	*S-Bahn*																						
0	**Bad Schandau** ⊡ .... **1100** d.	0011	...	...	...	0441e	0511	0541e	0611	0641		1741	1811	1841	1911	1941	2011	...	2111	...	2211	...	2311
23	Pirna ....d.	0035	...	...	0435	0505	0535	0605	0635	0705	and at	1805	1835	1905	1935	2005	2035	2105	2135	2205	2235	2305	2335
40	**Dresden** Hbf **842/3 856 1100** d.	0058	...	0430	0500	0530	0600	0630	0700	0730	the same	1830	1900	1930	2000	2030	2100	2130	2200	2230	2300	2330	0000
44	**Dresden** Neustadt .. **842 856** d.	...	...	0437	0507	0537	0607	0637	0707	0737	minutes	1837	1907	1937	2007	2037	2107	2137	2207	2237	2307	2337	0007
50	Radebeul Ost ....d.	...	...	0446	0516	0546	0616	0646	0716	0746	past each	1846	1916	1946	2016	2046	2116	2146	2216	2246	2316	2346	0016
58	Coswig .... **842/3 856** d.	...	...	0458	0528	0558	0628	0658	0728	0758	hour until	1858	1928	1958	2028	2058	2128	2158	2228	2258	2328	2358	0028
68	**Meißen**..................................a.	...	...	0507	0537	0607	0637	0707	0737	0807		1907	1937	2007	2037	2107	2137	2207	2237	2307	2337	0007	0037

S-Bahn					Ⓐe																			
Meißen...................................d.	...	0020	...	...	...	...	0450	0520	...	0550	0620		1850	1920	...	1950	2020	2050	2120	2150	2220	2250	2320
Coswig .... **842/3 856** d.	...	0031	...	...	...	0430	0500	0530	...	0600	0630	and at	1900	1930	...	2000	2030	2100	2130	2200	2230	2300	2330
Radebeul Ost.........................d.	...	0042	...	...	...	0440	0510	0540	...	0610	0640	the same	1910	1940	...	2010	2040	2110	2140	2210	2240	2310	2340
Dresden Neustadt ... **842 856** d.	...	0051	...	...	...	0450	0520	0550	...	0620	0650	minutes	1920	1950	...	2020	2050	2120	2150	2220	2250	2320	2350
Dresden Hbf . **842/3 856 1100** d.	0015	0058	0103	...	0430	0500	0530	0600	...	0630	0700	past each	1930	2000	...	2030	2100	2130	2200	2230	2300	2330	2357
Pirna......................................d.	0039	...	0126	...	0454	0524	0554	0624	...	0654	0724	hour until	1954	2024	...	2053	2124	2153	2224	2253	2324	2353	...
Bad Schandau ⊡ .... **1100** a.	0101k	...	...	...	0516	0546	0616e	0646	...	0716	0746		2016	2046	...	...	2146	...	2246	...	2346	...	...

km											
0	**Meißen**.............d.	...	...	0724e	0924	1124	1324	1524	1724	1924	2124
21	Nossen.............d.	...	0555e	0755	0955	1155	1355	1555	1755	1955	2155
29	Roßwein............d.	...	0605e	0805	1005	1205	1405	1605	1805	2005	2205
40	Döbeln Hbf ....d.	0526	0626	0826	1026	1226	1426	1626	1826	2026	2226
53	Leisnig...............d.	0539	0639	0839	1039	1239	1439	1639	1839	2039	2239
68	Großbothen ....d.	0557	0657	0857	1057	1257	1457	1657	1857	2057	2257
75	Grimma ob Bf....d.	0604	0704	0904	1104	1304	1504	1704	1904	2104	2304
106	**Leipzig** Hbf ......a.	0641	0736	0936	1136	1336	1541	1741	1936	2136	2336

	Ⓐe										
Leipzig Hbf ....d.	...	0615	0815	1015	1215	1415	1615	1815	1915	2115	2317
Grimma ob Bf ....d.	...	0648	0848	1048	1248	1448	1648	1848	1948	2148	2350
Großbothen...............d.	...	0656	0856	1056	1256	1456	1656	1856	1956	2156	2358
Leisnig.....................d.	...	0710	0910	1110	1310	1510	1710	1910	2010	2210	0012
Döbeln Hbf................d.	0524	0724	0924	1124	1324	1524	1724	1924	2024	2224	0025
Roßwein ....d.	0538	0738	0938	1138	1338	1538	1738	1938	2038e	2238	...
Nossen ....d.	0550	0750	0950	1150	1350	1550	1750	1950	2048e	2248	...
Meißen ....a.	0615	0815	1015	1215	1415	1615	1815	2015	...	...	...

e – Ⓐ (not Nov. 18).
k – ②–⑥ only.

⊡ – A frequent ferry services links the railway station with Bad Schandau town centre. **Operator**: Oberelbische Verkehrsgesellschaft Pirna - Sebnitz mbH. ✆ +49 (0) 3501 7920.
Depart Bad Schandau, Bahnhof 0700 and every 30 minutes until 2100 (10 minute journey). Depart Bad Schandau, Elbkai 0650 and every 30 minutes until 2050 (5 minute journey).

857a DRESDEN - DRESDEN FLUGHAFEN ✈

S-Bahn

km								
0	**Dresden** Hbf ....d.	0418	0448	and at the same	2248	2318	...	...
4	**Dresden** Neustadt ......d.	0425	0455	minutes past	2255	2325	...	...
15	**Dresden** Flughafen ✈ a.	0440	0510	each hour until	2310	2340	...	...

Dresden Flughafen ✈ ....d.	0446	0516	and at the same	2316	2346	...	...	...
Dresden Neustadt ....a.	0459	0529	minutes past	2329	2359	...	...	...
Dresden Hbf.......................a.	0507	0537	each hour until	2337	0007	...	...	...

858 CHEMNITZ / ZWICKAU - GERA - ERFURT

RB / RE services

km		⑥	Ⓐ	G	Ⓐ	⚒r▶	⚒rG	G	▶	G	▶	G	▶	G	▶	G	▶	G	▶	L	Ⓒ	▶		
0	**Chemnitz** Hbf............... **880** d.	...	...	...	...	0625	...	...	0825	...	1025	...	1225	...	1425	...	1625	...	1825	...	*1859*	2025	...	...
32	Glauchau (Sachs)........... **880** d.	...	...	...	...	0652	...	...	0852	...	1052	...	1252	...	1452	...	1652	...	1852	...	1926	2052	...	...
	Zwickau (Sachs) Hbf .. **881** d.	...	...	...	...	|	0657	...	|	0858	|	1058	|	1258	|	1458	|	1658	|	1858	|	|	2058	...
	Werdau .... **881** d.	...	...	...	...	|	0706	...	|	0906	|	1106	|	1306	|	1506	|	1706	|	1906	|	|	2106	...
48	Gößnitz .... **881** a.	...	...	...	...	0713	0721	...	0913	0921	1113	1121	1313	1321	1513	1521	1713	1721	1913	1920	1946	2113	2121	...
48	Gößnitz ....d.	...	...	...	...	▬	0727	...	▬	0927	▬	1127	▬	1327	▬	1527	▬	1727	▬	1927	1946	▬	2127	...
83	**Gera** Hbf ....a.	...	...	...	...	...	0756	...	...	0956	...	1156	...	1356	...	1556	...	1756	...	1956	2024	...	2156	...
83	**Gera** Hbf ....d.	0437	0445	0601	0623	0702	0802	0802	0902	1002	1102	1202	1302	1402	1502	1602	1702	1802	1902	2002	...	2133	2202	2337
123	Göschwitz (Saale).................d.	0508	0518	0628	0650	0729	0829	0829	0929	1029	1129	1229	1329	1429	1529	1629	1729	1829	1929	2029	...	2210	2229	0013
128	**Jena** West...........................d.	0513	0523	0634	0657	0736	0836	0836	0936	1036	1136	1236	1336	1436	1536	1636	1736	1836	1936	2036	...	2215	2236	0018
151	Weimar......................... **850** d.	0534	0546	0650	0715	0752	0852	0852	0952	1052	1152	1252	1352	1452	1552	1652	1752	1852	1952	2052	...	2237	2252	0039
172	**Erfurt** Hbf...................... **850** a.	*0557*	0602	0705	0729	0806	0906	0906	1006	1106	1206	1306	1406	1506	1606	1706	1806	1906	2006	2106	...	*2257*	2305	*0059*

			⚒r	⚒r	Ⓐ	⑥	Ⓒ		G	G		G		G		G		G		G		G		
Erfurt Hbf....................... **850** d.	0031	0437	...	...	*0516*	*0600*	...	0645	0750	0850	0950	1050	1150	1250	1350	1450	1550	1650	1750	1850	1950	2050	2150	*2300*
Weimar.......................... **850** d.	0050	0456	...	...	0546	0621	...	0659	0806	0906	1006	1106	1206	1306	1406	1506	1606	1706	1806	1906	2006	2106	2206	2323
Jena West.............................d.	0110	0517	...	...	0607	0644	...	0723	0823	0923	1023	1123	1223	1323	1423	1523	1623	1723	1823	1923	2023	2123	2223	2345
Göschwitz (Saale)..................d.	0115	0522	...	...	0612	0649	...	0728	0828	0928	1028	1128	1228	1328	1428	1528	1628	1728	1828	1928	2028	2128	2228	2350
Gera Hbf ....a.	...	0554	...	...	0647	0724	...	0754	0854	0954	1054	1154	1254	1354	1454	1554	1654	1754	1854	1954	2054	2154	2254	0025
Gera Hbf ....d.	...	...	0600	...	...	...	0729	0800	▬	1000	▬	1200	▬	1400	▬	1600	▬	1800	▬	2000	▬	...	...	...
Gößnitz.................................a.	...	...	0629	◀	...	...	0809	0829	◀	1029	◀	1229	◀	1429	◀	1629	◀	1829	◀	2029	◀	...	...	...
Gößnitz........................... **881** d.	...	...	0633	0637	...	...	0809	0833	0837	1033	1037	1233	1237	1433	1437	1633	1637	1833	1837	2033	2037	...	...	...
Werdau .... **881** d.	...	...	0649	|	...	...	|	0849	|	1049	|	1249	|	1449	|	1649	|	1849	|	2049	|	...	...	...
Zwickau (Sachs) Hbf ... **881** a.	...	...	0656	|	...	...	|	0856	|	1056	|	1256	|	1456	|	1656	|	1856	|	2056	|	...	...	...
Glauchau (Sachs)............ **880** d.	...	...	...	0702	...	...	0830	...	0902	...	1102	...	1302	...	1502	...	1702	...	1902	...	2102	...	...	...
Chemnitz Hbf................ **880** a.	...	...	...	0730	...	...	*0859*	...	0930	...	1130	...	1330	...	1530	...	1730	...	1930	...	2130	...	...	...

G – To / from Göttingen (Table **865**).
L – To Leinefelde (Table **865**).

r – Not Oct. 31.

▶ – Attached to train in the next column at Gößnitz.
◀ – Detached from train in previous column at Gößnitz.

RB services BRAUNSCHWEIG - BAD HARZBURG - GOSLAR - HERZBERG and HOLZMINDEN 859

BRAUNSCHWEIG - GOSLAR and BAD HARZBURG

km		Ⓐ								Ⓒ	Ⓐ			Ⓐ		Ⓐ							Ⓑt			
0	**Braunschweig** Hbf... d.	0513	0626	0708	0826	0908	1026	1108	1226	1308	1322	1426	1508	1551	1626	1639	1708	1826	1908	2026	2108	...	2220	...	...	...
12	Wolfenbüttel .... d.	0522	0636	0717	0836	0917	1036	1117	1236	1317	1331	1436	1517	1601	1636	1650	1717	1836	1917	2036	2117	...	2230	...	...	...
39	Vienenburg **860** .... d.	0547	0702	0742	0902	0942	1102	1142	1302	1342	1356	1502	1542	1626	1702	1714	1742	1902	1942	2102	2142	...	2254	...	...	...
47	**Bad Harzburg 860** a.	|	0710	|	0910	|	1110	|	1310	|	|	1510	|	1634	1710	|	|	1910	|	2110	|	...	|	...	...	...
58	**Goslar 860** .... a.	0600	*0726*r	0754	...	0954	...	1154	*1338*	1354	1408	...	1554	*1658*	...	1727	1754	...	1954	...	2154	...	2307	...	...	...

km		Ⓐ	Ⓐ	⚒	⚒	⚒							Ⓒ	Ⓐ												
0	**Goslar 860** .... d.	0445	0523	...	0627	...	0808	*0828*r	1008	...	1208	...	1409	1423	*1428*	1608	...	1808	*1828*	2008	...	...	2221	...	...	...
	Bad Harzburg 860 d.	|	0541	0541	|	0651	|	0851	|	1051	|	1251	|	|	1451	|	1651	|	1851	|	2051	...	|	...	...	...
13	Vienenburg **860** .... d.	0457	0556	0556	0639	0701	0820	0901	1020	1101	1220	1301	1422	1435	1501	1620	1701	1820	1901	2020	2101	...	2233	...	...	...
40	Wolfenbüttel .... d.	0521	0620	0620	0702	0725	0845	0925	1045	1125	1245	1325	1446	1500	1525	1645	1725	1845	1925	2045	2125	...	2258	...	...	...
52	**Braunschweig** Hbf... a.	0530	0629	0629	0711	0734	0855	0934	1055	1134	1255	1334	1455	1509	1534	1655	1734	1855	1934	2055	2134	...	2308	...	...	...

BRAUNSCHWEIG - SEESEN - HERZBERG

km		Ⓐ	Ⓐ			⚒			⚒			⚒			Ⓐ			Ⓐ			Ⓐ			Ⓐ		B
0	**Braunschweig** Hbf... d.	0504	0604	0704	0804	0804	0904	1004	1004	1104	1204	1204	1304	1404	1404	1504	1604	1604	1704	1804	1804	1904	2004	2004	...	2204
31	Salzgitter-Ringelheim d.	0529	0629	0729	0829	0829	0929	1029	1029	1129	1229	1229	1329	1429	1429	1529	1629	1629	1729	1829	1829	1929	2029	2029	...	2229
52	Seesen .... d.	0545	0645	0745	0844	0845	0945	1044	1045	1145	1244	1245	1345	1444	1445	1545	1644	1645	1745	1844	1845	1945	2044	2045	...	2244
71	Osterode (Harz) Mitte . d.	0607	0707	0807	...	0907	1007	...	1107	1207	...	1309	1407	...	1507	1607	...	1707	1807	...	1907	2007	...	2107	...	...
83	**Herzberg** (Harz) .... a.	0621	0721	0821	...	0921	1021	...	1121	1221	...	1325	1421	...	1521	1621	...	1721	1821	...	1921	2021	...	2121	...	...

	ⒶB	Ⓐ	Ⓐ	ⒸB	Ⓐ	Ⓒ	⚒			⚒			⚒			Ⓐ			Ⓐ			Ⓐ			Ⓐ	
Herzberg (Harz) .... d.	...	0534	0634	...	0730	0734	0834	...	0934	1034	...	1134	1234	...	1334	1434	...	1534	1634	...	1734	1834	...	1934	2034	...
Osterode (Harz) Mitte . d.	...	0547	0647	...	0745	0747	0847	...	0947	1047	...	1147	1247	...	1347	1447	...	1547	1647	...	1747	1847	...	1947	2047	...
Seesen .... d.	0513	0613	0713	0713	0813	0813	0913	0913	1013	1113	1113	1213	1313	1313	1413	1513	1513	1613	1713	1713	1813	1913	1913	2013	2113	2113
Salzgitter-Ringelheim . d.	0529	0629	0729	0729	0829	0829	0929	0929	1029	1129	1129	1229	1329	1329	1429	1529	1529	1629	1729	1729	1829	1929	1929	2029	2129	2129
Braunschweig Hbf.... a.	0551	0651	0751	0751	0851	0851	0951	0951	1051	1151	1151	1251	1351	1351	1451	1551	1551	1651	1751	1751	1851	1951	1951	2051	2151	2151

BAD HARZBURG - SEESEN - KREIENSEN - HOLZMINDEN

km		Ⓐ	Ⓐ	Ⓐ	⚒	⚒		Ⓑ			Ⓑ				Ⓐ			Ⓒ	Ⓐ		Ⓐ		Ⓐ		†	B
0	**Bad Harzburg 860** ... d.	...	...	0618	...	0714	0820	0820	...	1020	1020	...	1220	1323	1420	...	1620	1620	...	1723	1723	1820	...	2020	...	...
11	Goslar **860** .... d.	0532	...	0631	...	0731	0833	0833	...	1033	1033	...	1233	1341	1433	...	1633	1633	...	1741	1741	1833	...	2033	...	...
34	Seesen .... d.	0550	...	0650	...	0751	0851	0851	...	1051	1051	...	1251	1359	1451	...	1651	1651	...	1759	1759	1851	1959	2051	...	2249
48	Bad Gandersheim ..... d.	0600	...	0700	...	0802	0902	0902	...	1102	1102	...	1302	1410	1502	...	1702	1702	...	1810	1810	1902	2010	2102	...	2300
54	**Kreiensen** .... a.	0607	...	0707	...	0809	0909	0909	...	1109	1109	...	1309	1416	1509	...	1709	1709	...	1816	1816	1909	2016	2109	...	2307
54	**Kreiensen** .... d.	...	0627	0708	0754	...	...	0923	0923	...	1123	1123	1323	...	1523	1649	...	1723	1749	...	1829	1923	...	2123	2238	...
98	**Holzminden** .... a.	...	0700	0742	0828	...	...	0957	0957	...	1157	1157	1357	...	1557	1723	...	1757	1823	...	1902	1957	...	2157	2312	...

	ⒶB	Ⓐ	Ⓐ	Ⓐ	ⒸB	Ⓐ	⑥k	Ⓐ						⑥k			⚒		Ⓐ		Ⓐ	Ⓒ	Ⓐ		†	
Holzminden .... d.	...	...	0530	...	...	0629	0654	0710	0759	0959	1159	...	1359	1359	...	1559	1559	...	1654	...	1754	1759	1834	1959	2034	...
Kreiensen .... a.	...	...	0604	...	...	0703	0728	0744	0833	1033	1233	...	1433	1433	...	1633	1633	...	1728	...	1828	1833	1908	2033	2108	...
Kreiensen .... d.	0457	0535	...	0646	0657	...	0746	0746	0846	1046	1246	1346	...	1446	1446	...	1646	1646	1749	1749	1846	1846	1938	2046	2138	2138
Bad Gandersheim ..... d.	0502	0540	...	0651	0702	...	0751	0751	0851	1051	1251	1351	...	1451	1451	...	1651	1651	1754	1754	1851	1851	1943	2051	2143	2143
Seesen .... d.	0512	0551	...	0702	0712	...	0802	0802	0902	1102	1302	1402	...	1502	1502	...	1702	1702	1805	1805	1902	1902	1954	2102	2155	2155
Goslar **860** .... a.	...	0610	...	0721	...	...	0821	0821	0921	1121	1321	1421	...	1521	1521	...	1721	1721	1824	1824	1921	1921	...	2121	2213	2213
Bad Harzburg 860 ... a.	...	0634	...	0738	...	...	0840	0840	0934	1134	1338	1440	...	1534	1534	...	1738	1738	1840	1840	1934	1934	...	2134	...	...

B – [12] Braunschweig - Seesen - Kreiensen and v.v.
k – Not Oct. 3.
r – ⚒ only.
t – Also Oct. 3.

DB (*RE* services); *Harz Elbe Express* ◇ HANNOVER - BAD HARZBURG - HALLE 860

km			Ⓐ			Ⓐ	Ⓐ	Ⓒ	⚒		⚒														⑤–⑦	①–④
0	**Hannover** Hbf.......... d.	0019	...	...	...	...	...	...	...	...	0546	0651	...	0747	0855	...	0947	1055	...	1147	1255	...	1347	1449	...	...
36	**Hildesheim** Hbf .... d.	0050	...	...	...	...	...	...	...	...	0614	0721	...	0814	0921	...	1014	1121	...	1214	1321	...	1414	1521	...	...
70	Salzgitter-Ringelheim d.	▬	...	...	...	...	...	...	...	...	0643	0744	...	0843	0944	...	1043	1144	...	1243	1344	...	1443	1544	...	...
89	Goslar **859** .... d.	...	...	...	...	0523	0611	...	...	0643a	0658	0759	...	0858	0959	...	1058	1159	...	1258	1359	...	1458	1559	...	...
100	**Bad Harzburg 859** ... a.	...	...	...	...	0535	|	...	...	|	0711	0809	...	0911	1009	...	1111	1209	...	1311	1409	...	1511	1609	...	...
100	**Bad Harzburg 859** ... d.	...	...	...	...	0541	|	...	0651	|	...	0815	*0851*	...	1015	*1051*	...	1215	*1251*	...	1415	*1451*	...	1615	*1651*	*1651*
108	Vienenburg **859** .... d.	...	...	...	...	0548	0623	...	0658	0707	...	0824	0907	...	1024	1107	...	1224	1307	...	1424	1507	...	1624	1707	1707
124	Ilsenburg .... d.	...	...	0449a	0531	▬	0633	0625	...	0725	...	0835	0925	...	1035	1125	...	1235	1325	...	1435	1525	...	1635	1725	1725
133	Wernigerode .... d.	...	...	0501a	0542	...	0643	0636	...	0736	...	0842	0936	...	1042	1136	...	1242	1336	...	1442	1536	...	1642	1736	1736
157	**Halberstadt** .... a.	...	...	0519a	0602	Ⓐ	0656	0652	...	0753	...	0854	0953	...	1054	1153	...	1254	1353	...	1454	1553	...	1654	1753	1753
157	**Halberstadt** .... d.	0349r	0444	0524	m	0607	0658	0658	...	0801	...	0858	1001	...	1058	1201	...	1258	1401	...	1458	1601	...	1658	A	1801
190	Aschersleben .... d.	0415	0515	0553	...	0639	0718	0723	...	0829	...	0918	1029	...	1118	1229	...	1318	1429	...	1518	1629	...	1718	...	1829
201	Sandersleben (Anh) ... d.	0429	0528	0606	...	0649	0725	0733	...	0846	...	0925	1046	...	1125	1246	...	1325	1446	...	1525	1646	...	1725	...	1846
219	Könnern .... ⊡ d.	0442	0544	0621	...	0701	0736	0745	...	0900	...	0936	1100	...	1136	1300	...	1336	1500	...	1536	1700	...	1736	...	1900
248	**Halle** (Saale) Hbf .... a.	0511	0616	0653	...	0729	0754	0805	...	0929	...	0954	1129	...	1154	1329	...	1354	1529	...	1554	1729	...	1754	...	1929

Hannover Hbf .... d.	1547	1655	...	1747	1855	...	1947	2045	2045	2147	2219	2319
Hildesheim Hbf......... d.	1614	1721	...	1814	1921	...	2014	2109	2109	2214	2250	2350
Salzgitter-Ringelheim . d.	1643	1744	...	1843	1944	...	2043	2131	2131	2243	▬	...
Goslar **859** .... d.	1658	1759	...	1858	1959	...	2058	2147	2152	2257	...	...
Bad Harzburg 859 .... a.	1711	1809	...	1911	2009	...	2111	|	2204	...	...	...
Bad Harzburg 859 .... d.	▬	1815	*1851*	...	2015	*2051*	...	|	...	...	...	...
Vienenburg **859** .... d.	...	1824	1907	...	2024	2107	...	2157	...	...	...	...
Ilsenburg.................. d.	...	1835	1925	...	2037	2125	...	2208	...	...	2303	...
Wernigerode .... d.	...	1842	1936	...	2044	2136	...	2216	...	...	2314	...
Halberstadt.............. a.	...	1854	1953	...	2056	2153	...	2228	...	...	2331	...
Halberstadt.............. d.	1801	1858	2001	...	2105	...	...	2229	...	...	...	...
Aschersleben .... d.	1829	1918	2029	...	2126	...	...	2247	...	...	...	...
Sandersleben (Anh).... d.	1846	1925	2046	...	2133	...	...	2254	...	...	...	...
Könnern............... ⊡ d.	1900	1936	2100	...	2144	...	...	2304	...	...	...	...
Halle (Saale) Hbf.... ⊡ a.	1929	1954	2129	...	2202	...	...	2321	...	...	...	...

	Ⓐ	Ⓐ	Ⓐ	Ⓒ	Ⓐ		Ⓒ	Ⓐ	
Halle (Saale) Hbf .... d.	...	...	...	...	0426	...	...	0517	0602
Könnern .... ⊡ d.	...	...	...	...	0444	...	...	0545	0621
Sandersleben (Anh) .... d.	...	...	...	...	0455	...	...	0606	0631
Aschersleben .... d.	...	...	...	...	0503	...	...	0624	0639
Halberstadt .... a.	...	...	...	...	0531	...	...	0653	0657
Halberstadt .... d.	...	0441	...	...	0543	...	0543	▬	0703
Wernigerode.................... d.	...	0502	...	...	0559	...	0600	...	0717
Ilsenburg .... d.	...	0518	...	...	0609	...	0615	...	0725
Vienenburg **859** .... d.	...	0532	...	...	0623	...	0628	0702	0738
Bad Harzburg 859........... a.	...	|	...	...	|	...	...	0710	0746
Bad Harzburg 859........... d.	...	|	0540	...	|	0643	...	...	0752
Goslar **859** .... d.	0457	0542	0554	0605	0640	0657	...	...	0808
Salzgitter-Ringelheim........ d.	0511	...	0608	0616	0652	0711	...	...	0819
Hildesheim Hbf .... d.	0543	...	0639	0640	0720	0744	...	...	0843
Hannover Hbf................. a.	0609	...	0706	0706	0747	0811	...	...	0906

		Ⓒ	Ⓐ			Ⓐ	Ⓒ																			m
Halle (Saale) Hbf........ d.	...	0623	0623	0809	0832	0832	...	1009	...	1032	1209	...	1232	1409	...	1432	1609	...	1632	1809	...	1832	2009	2032	2236	...
Könnern............... ⊡ d.	...	0651	0701z	0824	0859	0859	...	1024	...	1059	1224	...	1259	1424	...	1459	1624	...	1659	1824	...	1859	2024	2105	2305	...
Sandersleben (Anh).... d.	...	0705	0713	0834	0913	0913	...	1034	...	1113	1234	...	1313	1434	...	1513	1634	...	1713	1834	...	1913	2034	2119	2319	...
Aschersleben .... d.	...	0718	0729	0841	0929	0929	...	1041	...	1129	1241	...	1329	1441	...	1529	1641	...	1729	1841	...	1929	2041	2136	2348	...
Halberstadt.............. a.	...	0746	0757	0900	0957	0957	B	1100	...	1157	1300	...	1357	1500	...	1557	1700	...	1757	1900	...	1957	2100	2203	0016	...
Halberstadt.............. d.	...	0803	0803	0903	▬	1003	1003	1103	...	1203	1303	...	1403	1503	...	1603	1703	...	1803	1903	...	2003	2103	*2230*	...	0021
Wernigerode .... d.	...	0820	0820	0917	...	1020	1020	1117	...	1220	1317	...	1420	1517	...	1620	1717	...	1820	1917	...	2020	2117	*2247*	...	0038
Ilsenburg.................. d.	...	0835	0835	0925	...	1035	1035	1125	...	1235	1325	...	1435	1525	...	1635	1725	...	1835	1925	...	2037	2125	*2258*	...	0048
Vienenburg **859** .... d.	...	0848	0848	0938	...	1048	1048	1138	...	1248	1338	...	1448	1538	...	1648	1738	...	1848	1938	...	2050	2138	...	...	▬
Bad Harzburg 859 .... a.	...	*0910*	*0910*	0946	...	*1110*	*1110*	1146	...	*1310*	1346	...	*1510*	1546	...	*1710*	1746	...	*1910*	1946	...	*2110*	2146	...	...	...
Bad Harzburg 859 .... d.	0846	...	...	0952	1046	...	...	1152	1246	...	1352	1446	...	1552	1646	...	1752	1846	...	1952	2046	▬	2206	...	...	...
Goslar **859**................ d.	0900	...	...	1008	1100	...	...	1208	1300	...	1408	1500	...	1608	1700	...	1808	1900	...	2008	2100	...	2218	...	...	...
Salzgitter-Ringelheim . d.	0914	...	...	1019	1114	...	...	1219	1314	...	1419	1514	...	1619	1714	...	1819	1914	...	2019	2114	...	...	...	...	...
Hildesheim Hbf......... d.	0944	...	...	1043	1144	...	...	1243	1344	...	1443	1544	...	1643	1744	...	1843	1944	...	2043	2144	2207	...	...	...	2307
Hannover Hbf .... a.	1011	...	...	1106	1211	...	...	1306	1411	...	1506	1611	...	1706	1811	...	1906	2011	...	2106	2211	2238	...	...	...	2338

A – To Berlin via Magdeburg (see Tables **862** and **839**).
B – From Berlin via Magdeburg (see Tables **839** and **862**).

a – Ⓐ only.
k – Not Oct. 3, 31.
m – To / from Magdeburg (Table **862**).

r – ⚒ only.
z – Arrives 0650.

◇ – *Harz Elbe Express* (*HEX*). Operated by Veolia Verkehr Sachsen-Anhalt GmbH.

⊡ – **Bernburg - Könnern** and v.v. (*16 km*, journey 25 minutes) ◇.
From Bernburg (trains marked ◧ continue to Halle): 0512 Ⓐ, 0628 Ⓐ, 0649 ⑥ **k** ◧, 0730 Ⓐ ◧, 0830 Ⓒ, 0933 ◧, 1133 ◧ and every two hours until 1933 ◧, then 2033.
From Könnern (trains marked ◐ start from Halle, departing 29 – 35 minutes earlier): 0546 Ⓐ, 0656 Ⓐ, 0743 Ⓒ ◐, 0805 Ⓐ ◐, 0904 Ⓒ, 1001 ◐, 1201 ◐ and every two hours until 2001 ◐, then 2237 ◐.

861 MAGDEBURG - SANGERHAUSEN - ERFURT and DESSAU - ASCHERSLEBEN

RE / RB services

Magdeburg - Erfurt and Aschersleben

km		Ⓐ		Ⓐ	Ⓐ	Ⓐ			⑥								Ⓐ	Ⓒ	Ⓐ							
0	**Magdeburg** Hbf d.	...	...	...	0400	0511	0611	0711	0711	0811	0911	1011	1111	1211	1311	1411	1457	1511	1533	1611	1711	1811	1911	2011	2111	2244
37	Staßfurt d.	...	...	...	0432	0547	0642	0748	0748	0842	0949	1042	1148	1242	1348	1442	1535	1548	1606	1642	1748	1842	1948	2042	2148	2326
44	Güsten d.	...	...	...	0440	0555	0649	0757	0802	0849	0956	1049	1155	1249	1355	1449	1543	1555	1613	1649	1755	1849	1955	2053	2155	2334
	Aschersleben a.	...	...	...	0452	0606	|	0808	|	|	1007	|	1206	|	1406	|	|	1606	1624	|	1806	|	2006	|	2206	2345
60	Sandersleben d.	...	...	0549	▬	...	0702	▬	0815	0902	▬	1102	▬	1302	▬	1502	1555	▬	▬	1702	▬	1902	▬	2105	▬	...
66	Hettstedt d.	...	...	0556	...	...	0709	...	0822	0909	...	1109	...	1309	...	1509	1602	...	...	1709	...	1909	...	2112	...	...
75	Klostermansfeld d.	...	...	0605	...	...	0719	...	0832	0919	...	1119	...	1319	...	1519	1611	Ⓒ	Ⓐ	1719	...	1919	⑤⑦	2122	...	...
97	**Sangerhausen** d.	0517	0544**t**	0627	0647	...	0740	0840	0857	0940	1040	1140	1240	1340	1440	1540	1631	1640	1640	1740	1840	1940	2040	2142	2148	...
142	Sömmerda d.	0552	0631	0702	0729	...	0829	0929	...	1029	1129	1229	1329	1429	1529	1629	...	1729	1729	1829	1929	2029	2129	...	2231	...
167	**Erfurt** Hbf a.	0609	0652	0719	0750	...	0850	0950	...	1050	1150	1250	1350	1450	1552	1652	...	1750	1752	1850	1950	2050	2150	...	2252	...

	Ⓐ	Ⓐ	Ⓒ	Ⓐ	Ⓐ	Ⓐ		Ⓒ	Ⓐ											⑥	Ⓐ					
Erfurt Hbf d.	...	...	...	...	...	0509	...	0608	0617	0708	0808	0908	1008	1108	1208	1308	1408	1508	1608	...	1641	1708	1808	1908	2008	2208
Sömmerda d.	...	...	...	...	...	0529	...	0629	0638	0729	0829	0929	1029	1129	1229	1329	1429	1529	1629	...	1659	1729	1829	1929	2029	2231
Sangerhausen d.	...	...	...	0510	...	0617	0617	0713	0730	0817	0916	1017	1116	1217	1316	1417	1516	1617	1721**j**	1737	1736	1817	1916	2017	2116	2314
Klostermansfeld d.	...	...	...	0530	...	0636	0636	...	▬	0836	▬	1036	▬	1236	▬	1436	▬	1636	▬	1759	...	1836	▬	2036	▬	...
Hettstedt d.	...	...	...	0540	...	0646	0646	...	...	0846	...	1046	...	1246	...	1446	...	1646	...	1809	...	1846	...	2046	...	...
Sandersleben d.	...	...	...	0553	...	0653	0653	...	...	0853	...	1053	...	1253	...	1453	...	1653	...	1817	...	1853	...	2054	...	...
Aschersleben d.	0447	0526	0547	|	0621	|	|	...	0747	|	0947	|	1147	|	1347	|	1544**g**	|	1747	|	...	|	1947	|	2147	...
Güsten d.	0458	0538	0558	0605	0633	0705	0705	...	0758	0905	0959	1105	1158	1305	1358	1505	1556**g**	1705	1758	1829	...	1905	1958	2107	2158	...
Staßfurt d.	0507	0546	0607	0613	0643	0713	0713	...	0807	0913	1007	1113	1207	1313	1408	1513	1607	1713	1807	1843	...	1913	2007	2114	2207	...
Magdeburg Hbf a.	0541	0624	0641	0641	0716	0742	0742	...	0841	0941	1041	1141	1241	1341	1442	1541	1641	1741	1841	1911	...	1941	2041	2142	2247	...

Dessau - Aschersleben

km		Ⓐ	Ⓒ	Ⓐ		Ⓐ		Ⓒ	Ⓐ			Ⓐ					Ⓐ	Ⓒ								
0	**Dessau** Hbf d.	0419	0457	0526	0603	0650	...	0711	0731	0803	0903	1003	1103	1203	1306	1403	1503	1503	1603	1703	1803	1903	2003	2105	...	2303
21	Köthen a.	0442	0520	0554	0626	0714	...	0734	0752	0826	0926	1026	1126	1226	1329	1426	1526	1526	1626	1726	1826	1926	2026	2127	...	2326
21	Köthen d.	0451	0522	0554	0627	0716	...	0735	0755	0827	0935	1027	1135	1227	1335	1427	1531	1535	1627	1735	1827	1935	2035	2135	...	2327
42	Bernburg d.	0512	0544	0615	0649	0737	...	0756	0817	0849	0956	1049	1156	1249	1356	1449	1553	1556	1649	1756	1849	1956	2052	2156	...	2349
54	Güsten d.	0522	0554	0626	0700	0747	0757	0808	0827	0900	1008	1100	1208	1300	1408	1500	1603	1608	1700	1808	1900	2008	2102	2208	...	0000
66	**Aschersleben** a.	0533	0606	0634	0712	...	0808	0820	0836	0912	1020	1112	1220	1312	1420	1512	1613	1620	1712	1820	1912	2020	2113	2220	...	0012

		Ⓐ	Ⓒ	Ⓐ		Ⓒ			Ⓐ		Ⓐ					Ⓐ	Ⓒ	Ⓐ								
Aschersleben d.	0433	0517	0559	0559	0647	0738	0747	...	0847	0938	1047	1138	1247	1338	1447	1535	1538	...	1647	1738	1847	1938	...	2045	...	2138
Güsten d.	0444	0529	0610	0610	0659	0750	0758	0805	0859	0950	1059	1150	1259	1350	1459	1550	1550	...	1659	1750	1859	1950	...	2056	2110	2150
Bernburg d.	0456	0541	0620	0620	0711	0802	...	0816	0911	1002	1111	1202	1311	1402	1511	1602	1602	...	1711	1802	1911	2002	...	...	2122	2202
Köthen a.	0517	0603	0639	0639	0734	0825	...	0834	0934	1025	1134	1225	1334	1425	1534	1625	1625	...	1734	1825	1934	2023	...	...	2141	2223
Köthen d.	0522	0604	0640	0640	0735	0835	...	0835	0935	1035	1135	1235	1335	1435	1535	1635	1635	1651	1735	1827	1935	2035	...	...	2142	2224
Dessau Hbf a.	0546	0631	0703	0706	0757	0857	...	0857	0957	1057	1157	1257	1357	1457	1557	1657	1657	1719	1757	1846	1957	2057	...	...	2204	2246

g – On Ⓒ departs Aschersleben 1547, Güsten 1558.

j – 1716 on Ⓒ.

t – 0546 on Ⓐ.

862 MAGDEBURG - HALBERSTADT - THALE

HEX ◇

km			Ⓐ						C▲	Ⓐ	Ⓒ		Ⓒ	Ⓐ		Ⓒ	Ⓐ									L
	Berlin Ostbf **839** d.	...	...	...	...	...	...	...	0706	...	...	...	...	...	...	...	...	...	...	...	...	...	...	...	...	...
0	**Magdeburg** Hbf d.	...	0446	...	0555	0710	0810	0910	0910	0944	1010	1110	1144	1210	1310	1344	1410	1510	1610	1710	1810	1906	2017	2127	2217	2317
39	Oschersleben (Bode) d.	...	0520	...	0633	0741	0841	0941	0941	1024	1041	1141	1224	1241	1341	1424	1441	1541	1641	1741	1841	1942	2045	2204	2257	2355
59	**Halberstadt** a.	...	0540	...	0654	0756	0856	0956	0956	1045	1056	1156	1245	1256	1356	1445	1456	1556	1656	1756	1856	2000	2100	2224	2317	0016
59	**Halberstadt** d.	0500	...	0607	0706	0806	0906	1006	1006	1106	1106	1206	1306	1306	1406	1506	1506	1606	1706	1806	1906	2006	2106	2234	2318	...
77	Quedlinburg a.	0515	...	0623	0723	0823	0923	1023	1023	1123	1123	1223	1323	1323	1423	1523	1523	1623	1723	1823	1923	2023	2123	2249	2334	...
77	Quedlinburg d.	0519	...	0630	0730	0830	0930	1030	1030	1130	1130	1230	1330	1330	1430	1530	1530	1630	1730	1830	1930	2030	2130	2251	2335	...
87	**Thale** Hbf a.	0531	...	0642	0742	0842	0942	1042	1042	1142	1142	1242	1342	1342	1442	1542	1542	1642	1742	1842	1942	2042	2142	2303	2347	...

	Ⓐ			L			Ⓐ	Ⓒ				Ⓐ	Ⓒ						E▲							
Thale Hbf d.	...	...	0505	...	0616	0716	0816	0816	0916	1016	1116	1216	1216	1316	1416	1516	1616	1716	1716	1816	1916	2016	2116	2155	...	2319
Quedlinburg a.	...	...	0516	...	0628	0728	0828	0828	0928	1028	1128	1228	1228	1328	1428	1528	1628	1728	1728	1828	1928	2028	2128	2207	...	2331
Quedlinburg d.	...	...	0517	...	0633	0733	0833	0833	0933	1033	1133	1233	1233	1333	1433	1533	1633	1733	1733	1833	1933	2033	2133	2208	...	2336
Halberstadt a.	...	...	0537	...	0649	0749	0849	0849	0949	1049	1149	1249	1249	1349	1450	1549	1649	1749	1749	1849	1949	2049	2149	2224	...	2352
Halberstadt d.	0349	0450	0541	0613	0701	0801	0901	0912	1001	1112	1201	1301	1312	1401	1501	1601	1701	1801	1801	1912	2005	2105	2208	...	...	...
Oschersleben (Bode) d.	0405	0512	0602	0628	0716	0816	0916	0933	1016	1133	1216	1316	1333	1416	1516	1616	1716	1816	1816	1933	2020	2120	2229	...	...	...
Magdeburg Hbf a.	0440	0549	0645	0658	0742	0842	0942	1014	1042	1214	1242	1342	1414	1442	1544	1644	1742	1842	1842	2012	2052	2150	2306	...	...	...
Berlin Ostbf **839** a.	...	...	...	...	...	...	...	...	...	...	...	...	...	...	...	...	...	...	2048	...	...	...	...	...	...	...

C – ⑥⑦ only.

E – ⑤–⑦ only.

L – To / from Ilsenburg (Table **860**).

◇ – *Harz Elbe Express*. Operated by Veolia Verkehr Sachsen-Anhalt GmbH.

▲ – *HARZ-BERLIN-EXPRESS*. **DB tickets not valid for journeys from / to Berlin.** Conveys (2) Berlin - Halberstadt - Vienenburg and v.v. (Table **860**).

863 LÖHNE - HAMELN - HILDESHEIM - BRAUNSCHWEIG

DB (*RB* services); *eurobahn* ★

km		⚒	Ⓐ	⚒	⚒		Ⓐ							Ⓒ	Ⓐ					Ⓐ			Ⓐ			Ⓑ
	Bielefeld Hbf **810** d.	...	*0524*	...	*0624*	...	*0724*	...	*0824*	*0924*a	*1024*	*1124*a	*1224*	*1224*	...	*1324*a	*1424*	*1524*a	*1624*	*1724*	...	*1824*	*1924*	...	*2024*	*2024*
	Herford **810** d.	...	*0533*	...	*0633*	...	*0733*	...	*0833*	*0933*a	*1033*	*1133*a	*1233*	*1233*	...	*1333*a	*1433*	*1533*a	*1633*	*1733*	...	*1833*	*1933*	...	*2033*	*2033*
0	**Löhne** (Westf) d.	...	0545	...	0645	...	0745	...	0845	0945a	1045	1145a	1245	1245	...	1345a	1445	1545a	1645	1745	...	1845	1945	...	2048	2048
12	Vlotho d.	...	0559	...	0659	...	0759	...	0859	0959a	1059	1159a	1259	1259	...	1359a	1459	1559a	1659	1759	...	1859	1959	...	2059	2059
29	Rinteln d.	...	0610	...	0710	...	0810	...	0910	1010a	1110	1210a	1310	1310	...	1410a	1510	1610a	1710	1810	...	1910	2010	...	2110	2110
53	**Hameln** d.	0528	0628	0628	0728	0728	0828	0828	0928	1028	1128	1228	1327	1328	1335	1428	1528	1628	1728	1828	1828	1928	2028	2028	2127	2128
82	Elze a.	0553	0653	0653	0753	0753	0852	0852	0953	1052	1153	1252	...	1353	1402	1452	1553	1652	1753	1852	1852	1953	2052	2052	...	2153
82	Elze d.	0602	0702	0702	0802	0802	0907	0907	1002	1107	1202	1307	...	1402	1403	1507	1602	1707	1802	1907	1907	2002	2107	2107	...	2202
100	**Hildesheim** Hbf a.	0620	0720	0720	0820	0820	0925	0925	1020	1125	1220	1325	...	1420	1422	1525	1620	1725	1820	1925	1925	2020	2125	2125	...	2220

	Ⓐ	⚒	⚒	Ⓐ			Ⓐ			Ⓐ			Ⓐ			Ⓐ			Ⓐ			Ⓐ			Ⓑ
Hildesheim Hbf d.	...	0537	0634	0634	0737	0834	0834	0937	1034	1034	1137	1234	1234	1337	1434	1434	1537	1634	1634	1737	1834	1834	1937	2034	2137
Elze a.	...	0553	0650	0650	0753	0850	0850	0953	1050	1050	1153	1250	1250	1353	1450	1450	1553	1650	1650	1753	1850	1850	1953	2050	2153
Elze d.	...	0602	0702	0702	0802	0902	0902	1004	1102	1102	1202	1302	1302	1402	1502	1502	1602	1702	1702	1802	1902	1902	2002	2102	2205
Hameln d.	0529	0629	0727	0729	0829	0927	0929	1029	1127	1129	1229	1327	1329	1429	1527	1529	1629	1727	1729	1829	1927	1929	2029	2127	2230
Rinteln d.	0546	0646	...	0746	0846	...	0946	1046	...	1146	1246	...	1346	1446	...	1546	1646	...	1746	1846	...	1946	2046	...	...
Vlotho d.	0602	0702	...	0802	0902	...	1002	1102	...	1202	1302	...	1402	1502	...	1602	1702	...	1802	1902	...	2002	2102	...	...
Löhne (Westf) a.	0613	0713	...	0813	0913	...	1013	1113	...	1213	1313	...	1413	1513	...	1613	1713	...	1813	1913	...	2013	2113	...	...
Herford **810** a.	*0626*	*0725*	...	*0826*	*0925*	...	*1026*	*1125*	...	*1226*	*1325*	...	*1426*	*1525*	...	*1626*	*1725*	...	*1826*	*1925*	...	*2026*	*2125*	...	...
Bielefeld Hbf **810** a.	*0636*	*0736*	...	*0836*	*0936*	...	*1036*	*1136*	...	*1236*	*1336*	...	*1436*	*1536*	...	*1636*	*1736*	...	*1836*	*1936*	...	*2036*	*2136*	...	...

Hildesheim - Braunschweig

km		Ⓐ		◇⊙ ①–⑥	⚒		◇⊙	◇⊙		◇⊙	◇⊙		◇⊙	◇⊙		◇⊙	Ⓐ	◇⊙		◇⊙	◇⊙		◇⊙		◇	◇
0	**Hildesheim** Hbf d.	0559	0659	0734	0753	0859	0934	1034	1059	1134	1234	1259	1334	1434	1459	1534	1559	1634	1659	1734	1834	1859	1934	2059	2134	2234
43	**Braunschweig** Hbf a.	0645	0745	0758	0845	0945	0958	1058	1145	1158	1258	1345	1358	1458	1545	1558	1645	1658	1745	1758	1858	1945	1958	2145	2158	2258

	⚒	Ⓐ	◇		◇	◇		◇	◇		◇	◇		◇	Ⓐ	◇		◇	Ⓐ	◇	⚒	†	◇		◇Ⓑ	Ⓒ
Braunschweig Hbf d.	0615	0658	0758	0815	0858	0958	1015	1058	1158	1215	1258	1358	1415	1458	1515	1558	1615	1658	1715	1758	1815	1817	1958	2015	2058	2215
Hildesheim Hbf a.	0652	0730	0823	0856	0923	1023	1056	1123	1223	1256	1323	1423	1456	1523	1556	1623	1656	1723	1756	1823	1856	1856	2023	2056	2123	2256

a – Ⓐ only.

◇ – *ICE* train (see Table **900**).

⊙ – Until June 30 departs Hildesheim 3 minutes later, arrives Braunschweig 1 minute later.

★ – Löhne - Hildesheim operated by **eurobahn** Keolis Deutschland GmbH & Co. KG.

CANTUS Verkehrsgesellschaft (2nd class only) — GÖTTINGEN - KASSEL local services — 864

For fast trains Göttingen - Kassel Wilhelmshöhe and v.v. see Tables **900** (*ICE* services) and **902** (*IC* services).

km		Ⓐ	⑥k	⚒		⚒		⚒			Ⓒ	Ⓐ			Ⓐ	Ⓒ	Ⓑm	Ⓐ	Ⓒ	Ⓑm	⚒	Ⓑm	Ⓐ		Ⓒ	Ⓐ
0	**Göttingen** .... **908** d.	0455	0457	0614	0714	0814	0914	1018	1114	1218	1314	1332	1418	1514	1614	1618	1714	1814	1818	1914	2014	2118	2214	...	2335	2335
20	Eichenberg .... **908** a.	0509	0511	0628	0728	0828	0928	1032	1128	1232	1328	1346	1432	1528	1628	1632	1728	1828	1832	1928	2028	2132	2228	...	2350	2352
20	Eichenberg .... **865** d.	0513	0513	0633	0733	0833	0933	1033	1133	1233	1333	1349	1433	1533	1633	1633	1733	1833	1833	1933	2033	2133	2237	...	2354	...
43	Hann Münden .... **865** d.	0534	0534	0653	0753	0853	0953	1053	1153	1253	1353	1409	1453	1553	1653	1653	1753	1853	1853	1953	2053	2153	2258	...	0015	...
67	**Kassel** Hbf ⊡.... **865** a.	0554	0554	0713	0813	0913	1013	1113	1213	1313	1413	1430	1513	1613	1713	1713	1813	1913	1913	2013	2113	2213	2319	...	0036	...

	Ⓐ	⑥k	Ⓐ	Ⓐ	†	⑥k	⚒	†	⚒	⚒						Ⓑm	Ⓒ	Ⓐ		Ⓒ	Ⓐ	Ⓑm	⚒		Ⓐ	Ⓒ
Kassel Hbf ⊡......**865** d.	0426	0546	0546	0626	0646	0646	0746	0846	0846	0946	1046	1146	1246	1346	1446	1546	1646	1646	1746	1846	1846	1946	2046	2146	2302	2346
Hann Münden......**865** d.	0446	0606	0606	0646	0706	0706	0806	0906	0906	1006	1106	1206	1306	1406	1506	1606	1706	1706	1806	1906	1906	2006	2106	2206	2322	0006
Eichenberg ....**865** a.	0505	0626	0626	0706	0726	0726	0826	0926	0926	1026	1126	1226	1326	1426	1526	1626	1726	1726	1826	1926	1926	2026	2126	2226	2345	0026
Eichenberg ....**908** d.	0508	0627	0632	0707	0727	0732	0832	0927	0932	1032	1127	1232	1327	1432	1527	1632	1727	1732	1832	1927	1932	2032	2132	2227	2353	0027
Göttingen ....**908** a.	0522	0640	0645	0721	0740	0745	0845	0940	0945	1045	1140	1245	1340	1445	1540	1645	1740	1745	1845	1940	1945	2045	2145	2240	0007	0040

k – Not Oct. 3.

m – Also Oct. 3.

⊡ – See Tables **804**, **806** and **901** for connecting trains to / from Kassel Wilhelmshöhe.

DB (*RE* / *RB* services); EIB ◇ — ERFURT and HALLE - LEINEFELDE - KASSEL and GÖTTINGEN — 865

Timings Halle - Nordhausen and v.v. are subject to alteration to Aug. 1 (see note ▲) and from Oct. 19

km		⚒	◇Ⓐ	⚒		⚒	◇Ⓐ		◇	◇Ⓐ	◇Ⓒ	G			◇	◇	A		◇	◇	A		◇	◇
0	**Erfurt** Hbf.............. **849 850** d.	...	0400	...	0429y	...	...	...	*0559*	*0559*	0558	0710	...	...	...	0811	0910	...	...	1011	1110	...	...	1211
27	Gotha.................. **849 850** d.	...	|	...	0504	...	0539	...	0636	0636	|	0737	...	...	0839	|	0937	...	1039	|	1137	...	1239	|
48	Bad Langensalza ....d.	...	0452	...	0515	...	0602	...	0653	0654	0702	0749	...	...	0856	0902	0949	...	1056	1102	1149	...	1256	1302
67	Mühlhausen (Thür) ....d.	...	0509	...	0528	...	0617	...	▬	0714	0718	0802	...	...	▬	0918	1002	...	▬	1118	1202	...	▬	1318
	Halle (Saale) Hbf .... ◧ d.	...	|	...	|	...	|	*0412*	...	|	|	|	0535	0628	...	|	|	0835	...	|	|	1035	...	|
	Lutherstadt Eisleben...... ◧ d.	...	|	...	|	...	|	*0452*	...	|	|	|	0615	0711	...	|	|	0911	...	|	|	1111	...	|
	Sangerhausen .... ◧ d.	...	|	...	|	...	|	*0516*	...	|	|	|	0642	0738	...	|	|	0938	...	|	|	1138	...	|
	Nordhausen .... ◧ a.	...	|	...	|	...	|	*0556*	...	|	|	|	...	0813	...	|	|	1013	...	|	|	1213	...	|
	Nordhausen ....d.	...	|	0500	|	...	|	0621	0651	|	|	|	...	0821	0851	|	|	1021	1051	|	|	1221	1251	|
94	**Leinefelde**...........................a.	...	0535	0542	0546	←	0641	0655	0737	0741	0741	0818	...	0855	0937	0941	1018	1055	1136	1141	1218	1255	1336	1341
94	**Leinefelde**...........................d.	0431	0536	→	0548	0554	...	0656	...	0742	0742	0820	...	0856	...	0942	1020	1056	...	1142	1220	1256	...	1342
110	Heilbad Heiligenstadt ....d.	0446	0551	...	0559	0608	...	0706	...	0758	0758	0831	...	0906	...	0958	1031	1106	...	1158	1231	1306	...	1358
144	**Göttingen** ....a.	|	|	...	0625	|	...	|	...	|	|	0852	...	|	...	|	1052	|	...	|	1252	|	...	|
125	Eichenberg .... **864** d.	0500	0605	...	...	0622	...	0718	...	0812	0812	...	...	0918	...	1012	...	1118	...	1212	...	1318	...	1412
148	Hann Münden .... **864** a.	*0533*	0626	...	...	*0652*	...	0736	...	0831	0831	...	...	0936	...	1031q	...	1136	...	1231a	...	1336	...	1431b
172	**Kassel** Hbf .... **864** a.	*0554*	0650	...	...	*0713*	...	0753c	...	|	|	...	...	0953c	...	|	...	1153c	...	|	...	1353c	...	|
176	**Kassel** Wilhelmshöhe .... **864** a.	...	...	...	...	...	...	0754a	...	0850	0850	...	...	0954a	...	1050q	...	1154a	...	1250a	...	1355a	...	1450b

	A		◇	◇	A		◇	◇	A				◇	◇	A			◇	◇	A			◇	◇
Erfurt Hbf............... **849 850** d.	1310	...	...	1411	1510	...	...	1611	1710	...	...	...	...	1811	1910	...	...	...	2011	2110	...	...	...	2215
Gotha.................. **849 850** d.	1337	...	1439	|	1537	...	1639	|	1737	...	...	...	1839	|	1937	...	...	2039	|	2137	...	...	2245	|
Bad Langensalza ....d.	1349	...	1456	1502	1549	...	1656	1702	1749	...	...	...	1856	1902	1949	...	...	2056	2102	2150	...	...	2302	2312
Mühlhausen (Thür) ....d.	1402	...	▬	1518	1602	...	▬	1718	1802	...	...	...	▬	1918	2002	...	...	...	2118	2204	...	...	...	2330
Halle (Saale) Hbf............ ◧ d.	|	1235	...	|	|	1435	...	|	|	...	1604	1635	...	|	|	1835	1928	...	|	|	2103	2228	...	|
Lutherstadt Eisleben...... ◧ d.	|	1311	...	|	|	1511	...	|	|	...	1640	1711	...	|	|	1911	2011	...	|	|	2138	2311	...	|
Sangerhausen .... ◧ d.	|	1338	...	|	|	1538	...	|	|	...	1658	1738	...	|	|	1938	2035	...	|	|	2158	2335	...	|
Nordhausen .... ◧ a.	|	1413	...	|	|	1613	...	|	|	...	...	1816	...	|	|	2013	2112	...	|	|	2232	0012	...	|
Nordhausen ....d.	|	1421	1451	|	|	1621	1651	|	|	1751	...	1821	1851	|	|	2021	*2116*	...	|	|	2254	...	...	|
Leinefelde...........................a.	1418	1455	1536	1541	1618	1655	1736	1741	1819	1836	...	1855	1936	1941	2018	2055	*2158*	...	2141	2221	2338	...	...	2347
Leinefelde...........................d.	1420	1456	...	1542	1620	1656	...	1742	1820	1837	...	1856	...	1942	2020	2056	...	...	2203	▬	...	...	...	...
Heilbad Heiligenstadt ....d.	1431	1506	...	1558	1631	1706	...	1758	1831	1851	...	1906	...	1958	2031	2106	...	...	2217	...	...	...	...	...
Göttingen ....a.	1452	|	...	|	1652	|	...	|	1852	...	...	|	...	|	2052	|	...	...	|	Ⓐ	...	...	...	...
Eichenberg .... **864** d.	...	1518	...	1612	...	1718	...	1812	...	...	...	1918	...	2012	...	2118	...	...	2232	2237	...	...	...	...
Hann Münden................. **864** a.	...	1536	...	1631	...	1736	...	1831	...	...	...	1936	...	2031h	...	2136	...	...	...	2257	...	...	...	...
Kassel Hbf .... **864** a.	...	1553c	...	|	...	1753c	...	|	...	...	...	1953c	...	|	...	2153	...	...	...	2319	...	...	...	...
Kassel Wilhelmshöhe ..... **864** a.	...	1554a	...	1651	...	1754a	...	1851	...	...	...	1954a	...	2050h	...	...	...	...	...	...	...	...	...	...

km					Ⓐ		◇	◇	ⒶG	Ⓐ	Ⓒ	◇Ⓐ	A	◇			A	◇			A	◇		
0	**Kassel** Wilhelmshöhe .... **864** d.	...	...	...	...	...	...	...	...	...	...	...	...	...	...	0804a	...	0909	...	1004a	...	1109q	...	1204a
	Kassel Hbf .... **864** d.	...	...	*0426*a	...	...	...	...	...	0602	0605	...	...	0657a	...	0805c	...	|	...	1005c	...	|	...	1205c
23	Hann Münden................ **864** d.	...	...	*0446*a	...	...	...	...	...	0618	0621	...	...	0718a	...	0821	...	0927	...	1021	...	1127q	...	1221
46	Eichenberg .... **864** d.	...	...	0510r	...	...	...	...	...	0636	0640	...	...	0741a	...	0840	...	0949	...	1040	...	1149	...	1240
	Göttingen.........................d.	...	...	|	...	...	...	...	0603	|	|	...	0707	|	...	|	0907	|	...	|	1107	|	...	|
61	Heilbad Heiligenstadt ....d.	...	0446a	0523r	0559	...	...	...	0631	0649	0652	...	0730	0757a	...	0852	0930	1003	...	1052	1130	1203	...	1252
77	**Leinefelde**...........................a.	...	0502a	0538r	0613	...	...	...	0641	0659	0702	...	0741	0812a	...	0902	0941	1018	...	1102	1141	1218	...	1302
77	**Leinefelde**...........................d.	0433r	0503	0539	0614	...	0608a	...	0642	0700	0703	0708	0743	0821	0823	0903	0943	1021	1023	1103	1143	1221	1223	1303
119	**Nordhausen** ....a.	0515r	|	0620	0654	...	|	...	|	0733	0736	|	|	|	0905	0936	|	|	1106	1136	|	|	1305	1336
119	**Nordhausen** .... ◧ d.	0519	|	0624	...	0659	|	...	|	0738	0738	|	|	|	▬	0938	|	|	▬	1138	|	|	▬	1338
157	Sangerhausen .... ◧ d.	0602	|	0657	...	0742	|	...	|	0814	0814	|	|	|	...	1014	|	|	...	1214	|	|	...	1414
179	Lutherstadt Eisleben...... ◧ d.	0620	|	0716	...	0804	|	...	|	0833	0833	|	|	|	...	1033	|	|	...	1233	|	|	...	1433
217	**Halle** (Saale) Hbf .... ◧ d.	0654	|	0752	...	0849	|	...	|	0908	0908	|	|	|	...	1108	|	|	...	1308	|	|	...	1508
—	Mühlhausen (Thür) ....d.	...	0525	...	...	...	0636	...	0659	...	...	0731	0800	0844	◇	...	1000	1044	◇	...	1200	1244	◇	...
0	Bad Langensalza ....a.	...	0536	...	...	...	0652	0658	0708	...	...	0747	0810	0859	0902	...	1010	1059	1102	...	1210	1259	1302	...
	Gotha.................. **849 850** a.	...	0551	...	...	...	|	0716	0720	...	...	0810	0822	|	0920	...	1022	|	1120	...	1222	|	1320	...
38	**Erfurt** Hbf.............. **849 850** a.	...	0617	...	...	...	0747	...	0746	...	...	...	0847	0958	...	...	1047	1158	...	...	1247	1358	...	...

	A	Ⓐw	◇	Ⓒt	Ⓐw		A	◇			A	◇			G	◇			Ⓒ	Ⓑ	◇		◇	
Kassel Wilhelmshöhe ..... **864** d.	...	...	1309a	...	...	1404a	...	1509b	...	1604a	...	1709z	...	1804a	...	1909z	...	2004a	...	...	...	...	2109h	...
Kassel Hbf .... **864** d.	...	...	|	...	*1318*	1405c	...	|	...	1605c	...	|	...	1805c	...	|	...	2005c	...	...	...	...	|	...
Hann Münden................. **864** d.	...	...	1327a	...	*1340*	1421	...	1527b	...	1621	...	1727	...	1821	...	1927	...	2021	...	...	...	...	2127h	...
Eichenberg .... **864** d.	...	...	1349	...	1412	1440	...	1549	...	1640	...	1749	...	1840	...	1949	...	2040	...	...	...	...	2149	...
Göttingen..........................d.	1307	...	|	...	|	|	1507	|	...	|	1707	|	...	|	1907	|	...	|	...	...	...	2107	|	...
Heilbad Heiligenstadt ....d.	1330	...	1403	...	1426	1452	1530	1603	...	1652	1730	1803	...	1852	1930	2003	...	2052	...	...	...	2131	2203	...
Leinefelde...........................a.	1341	...	1418	...	1440	1502	1541	1618	...	1702	1741	1818	...	1902	1941	2018	...	2102	...	...	...	2142	2217	...
Leinefelde...........................d.	1343	1346	1421	1423	1442	1503	1543	1621	1623	1703	1743	1821	1823	1903	1943	2021	2023	2103	...	...	2108	2143	2227	2232
Nordhausen ....a.	|	1427	|	1505	1525	1536	|	|	1705	1736	|	|	1905	1936	|	|	2105	2136	...	...	|	|	|	2314
Nordhausen .... ◧ d.	|	...	|	▬	...	1538	|	|	▬	1738	|	|	▬	1938	|	|	▬	...	2159	2236	|	|	|	...
Sangerhausen .... ◧ d.	|	...	|	...	...	1614	|	|	...	1814	|	|	...	2014	|	|	...	...	2238	2319	|	|	|	...
Lutherstadt Eisleben....... ◧ d.	|	...	|	...	...	1633	|	|	...	1833	|	|	...	2033	|	|	...	...	2300	2341	|	|	|	...
Halle (Saale) Hbf............ ◧ d.	|	...	|	...	...	1708	|	|	...	1908	|	|	...	2108	|	|	...	...	2344	0024	|	|	|	...
Mühlhausen (Thür) ....d.	1400	...	1444	◇	...	...	1600	1644	◇	...	1800	1844	◇	...	2000	2044	◇	...	...	...	2134	2200	2250	...
Bad Langensalza ....a.	1410	...	1459	1502	...	...	1610	1659	1702	...	1810	1859	1902	...	2010	2059	2102	...	...	...	2149	2210	2305	...
Gotha.................... **849 850** a.	1422	...	|	1520	...	...	1622	|	1720	...	1822	|	1920	...	2022	|	2120	...	...	...	|	2222	2333	...
Erfurt Hbf................ **849 850** a.	1447	...	1558	...	...	...	1647	1758	...	...	1847	1958	...	...	2047	2154	...	...	...	...	2244	2250	0001	...

A – From / to Chemnitz and Zwickau (Table **858**).
G – From / to Gera (Table **858**).

a – Ⓐ only.
b – Ⓑ only.
c – Ⓒ only.
h – ⑤–⑦ only.
q – † only.
r – ⚒ only.
t – Ⓒ (daily June 25 - Aug. 5 and Oct. 10 – 25).
w – Not June 25 - Aug. 5, Oct. 12 – 23.
y – 0440 on Ⓒ.
z – 2 minutes earlier on ⑦.

◇ – Operated by Erfurter Bahn GmbH (2nd class only).
★ – No service from Nordhausen at 1447 (starts from Sangerhausen, d. 1529).
On ⑦ the 1647 from Nordhausen departs Lutherstadt Eisleben 1747, arrives Halle (Saale) Hbf 1830.
▲ – **Engineering work June 14 - Aug. 1**: All timings Halle - Nordhausen are subject to alteration during this period. Trains are replaced by 🚌 between Lutherstadt Eisleben and Sangerhausen with overall journey times extended by up to 35 minutes (earlier departures / later arrivals possible).
◧ – See panel below for additional services Halle - Nordhausen and v.v.

		▲	
Halle (Saale) Hbf......... d.	0743	and every	1743
Lutherstadt Eisleben ... d.	0823	**two** hours	1823
Sangerhausen .... d.	0845	until	1845
Nordhausen.............. d.	0924		1924

		★ ▲	
Nordhausen ....d.	1047	and every	2047
Sangerhausen ....d.	1129	**two** hours	2129
Lutherstadt Eisleben .....d.	1151	until	2151
Halle (Saale) Hbf..........a.	1234		2236

867 HARZER SCHMALSPURBAHNEN

2nd class only

Nordhausen - Wernigerode: *Die Harzquerbahn*; Eisfelder Talmühle - Stiege - Alexisbad - Quedlinburg: *Die Selketalbahn*; Drei Annen Hohne - Brocken: *Die Brockenbahn*

Summer service: Apr. 25 - Nov. 1, 2009

km			🚂	🚂	🚂🍷	🚂	🚂 B	🚂	🚂	🚂 B	🚂	
0	**Wernigerode** § d.	0725	0855	0940	1025	1155	...	1325	1455	...	1625	1625
15	Drei Annen Hohne a.	0802	0932	1017	1102	1232	...	1402	1532	...	1702	1702
15	Drei Annen Hohne ◇d.	0809	0945	1030	1115	1239	1245	1415	1551	1539	1716	1718
20	Schierke ◇d.	|	1005	1050	1135	|	1313	1440	1621	|	1748	|
34	**Brocken** ◇a.	|	1036	1121	1206	|	1344	1530	1652	|	1819	|
19	Elend d.	0821	▬	▬	...	1251	▬	▬	...	1551	...	1730
28	Sorge d.	0840	...	...	...	1310	...	...	...	1610	...	1749
31	Benneckenstein d.	0849	...	🚋	...	1319	...	...	...	1619	...	1758
44	Eisfelder Talmühle a.	0918	©	Ⓐ	...	1348	...	🚋	...	1648	...	1827
44	Eisfelder Talmühle d.	...	0920	*0920*	...	...	1357		...	1655	...	*1832*
50	Ilfeld d.	...	0941	0941	...	...	1412	1441	...	1711	...	*1846*
61	**Nordhausen** Nord § a.	...	1010*	1010*	...	...	1440c	1510*	...	1740	...	*1910**

		🚂 B	🚂	🚂		🚂	🚂🍷	🚂	🚂	🚂	
Nordhausen Nord § d.	*0829**	1014	...	...	1314	...	...	...	...	...	*1744**
Ilfeld d.	*0858*	1039	...	...	1339	...	...	...	...	...	*1809*
Eisfelder Talmühle a.	*0912*	1053	...	...	1353	...	...	...	...	...	*1823*
Eisfelder Talmühle d.	0937	1107	...	...	▬	1407	...	...	...	...	1837
Benneckenstein d.	1007	1137	...	...	...	1437	...	...	...	...	1907
Sorge d.	1015	1145	...	...	...	1445	...	...	...	...	1915
Elend d.	1035	1205	...	...	🚂 B	1505	...	...	...	...	1935
Brocken ◇d.	|	|	1136	1314	1451	|	1622	1707	1749	1831	|
Schierke ◇d.	|	|	1224	1355	1522	|	1703	1747	1830	1902	|
Drei Annen Hohne ◇a.	1046	1216	1236	1406	1533	1516	1714	1759	1841	1913	1946
Drei Annen Hohne d.	1108	...	1253	1423	...	1553	1723	1808	1853	1923	1953
Wernigerode § a.	1145	...	1333	1503	...	1633	1800	1845	1930	2000	2030

km		◐		🚂	◧			🚂	◧	◧		
0	**Quedlinburg** § ▲d.	0830	...	1030	1130	...	...	*1430*	1630	...	1730	2030
8	**Gernrode** ▲d.	0847	...	1047	1147	...	...	1447	1647	...	1747	2045
18	Mägdesprung d.	0918	...	1118	1219	...	...	1518	1718	...	1819	▬
	Harzgerode d.	|	0927	|	|	1326	1526	|	|	1826	|	...
23	Alexisbad a.	0932	0937	1132	1233	1336	1536	1532	1732	1836	1833	🚂
23	Alexisbad d.	▬	0941	*1140*	*1240*	1340	▬	1540	1740	▬	1840	1840
26	**Harzgerode** a.	...	|	*1149*	*1249*	|	...	|	1749	...	|	1849
26	Silberhütte d.	...	0953	...	...	1352	...	1552	▬	...	1852	...
30	Straßberg (Harz) d.	...	1004	...	...	1403	...	1603	...	...	1903	...
35	Güntersberge d.	...	1013	...	...	1412	...	1612	...	...	1912	...
	Hasselfelde d.	1006	|	...	...	|	1500	|	1748	...	|	...
44	Stiege a.	1027	1029	...	...	1428	1521	1628	1809	...	1928	...
44	Stiege d.	...	1030	...	...	1429	1531	1629	1810	...	1930	...
48	**Hasselfelde** a.	...	|	...	...	1450	|	1650	|	...	|	...
53	Eisfelder Talmühle d.	...	1055	...	...	...	1553	...	1832	1854	1958	...
59	Ilfeld d.	...	1111	...	...	...	1611	...	1846	1915	2013	...
70	**Nordhausen** Nord § a.	...	1140	...	...	...	1640	...	1910*	1940	2040*	...

					🚂	◧			🚂	⊙	🚂
Nordhausen Nord § d.	0629*	...	0829*	...	...	...	1114	1614	...	...	...
Ilfeld d.	0658	...	0858	...	...	...	1139	1639	...	...	...
Eisfelder Talmühle d.	0713	...	0920	...	...	...	1158	1658	...	...	...
Hasselfelde d.	|	0759	|	1006	...	...	|	|	1700	...	...
Stiege a.	0733	0820	0940	1027	...	...	1218	1718	1721	...	...
Stiege d.	0734	0821	0941	1037	...	...	1237	1723	1737	...	...
Hasselfelde a.	0755	|	1002	|	...	...	|	1744	|	...	...
Güntersberge d.	▬	0837	▬	1054	...	...	1253	▬	1753	...	...
Straßberg (Harz) d.	...	0847	...	1103	...	...	1302	...	1802	...	...
Silberhütte d.	...	0858	...	1115	...	...	1314	...	1814	...	...
Harzgerode d.	...	|	...	|	...	*1226*	|	1526	|	1826	1926
Alexisbad a.	...	0909	◧	1126	...	*1236*	1325	1536	1825	1836	1936
Alexisbad d.	...	0913	1001	1140	1201	1301	1340	1601	1840	1901	2001
Harzgerode a.	...	0923	|	1149	|	|	1349	|	1849	|	|
Mägdesprung d.	...	...	1015	...	1220	1315	...	1615	...	1915	2015
Gernrode ▲d.	0759	...	1059f	...	1259	1359f	...	1659f	...	1959f	2045
Quedlinburg § ▲a.	0815	...	1115	...	1315	1415	...	1715	...	2015	...

B – 🚃2 and 🍷 Brocken - Nordhausen and v.v.
c – © (also school holidays).
f – Arrives 14 minutes earlier.
🚂 – Steam train.
🚋 – Nordhausen Stadtbahn.
* – Nordhausen **Bahnhofsplatz**.
§ – Adjacent to DB station.

◧ – 🚂 on © (also May 22).
◐ – 🚂 (Gernrode - Alexisbad) on © (also May 22).
⊙ – 🚂 (Harzgerode - Gernrode) on © (also May 22).

▲ – Additional journeys Quedlinburg - Gernrode and v.v.
Quedlinburg d. 1330 🚂 → Gernrode a. 1345.
Gernrode d. 0959 🚂 → Quedlinburg a. 1015.
Gernrode d. 1559 ◧ → Quedlinburg a. 1615.

◇ – Additional journeys (🚂) Drei Annen Hohne - Brocken and v.v.:
From Drei Annen Hohne at 1200, 1339, 1506 and 1647.
From Brocken at 1051, 1221, 1359 and 1540.

Operator: Harzer Schmalspurbahnen GmbH.
Friedrichstraße 151, 38855 Wernigerode.
✆ + 49 (0) 3943 558 151. Fax + 49 (0) 3943 558 148.

868 ERFURT - NORDHAUSEN

RE / *RB* services

km		Ⓐ	⚒r															
0	**Erfurt** Hbf d.	...	0441	0604	0704	0804	0904	1004	1104	1204	1304	1404	1504	1604	1704	1804	1904	2004	2140
27	Straußfurt d.	...	0506	0626	0730	0826	0930	1026	1130	1226	1330	1426	1530	1626	1730	1826	1930	2026	2213
60	Sondershausen d.	0447	0552	0700	0810	0859	1010	1059	1210	1259	1410	1459	1610	1659	1810	1859	2010	2057	2245
80	**Nordhausen** a.	0510	0615	0720	0833	0919	1033	1119	1233	1319	1433	1519	1633	1719	1833	1919	2033	2118	2309

	Ⓐ	⚒r		Ⓐ	©													
Nordhausen d.	0417	0527	0637	0722	0728	0837	0928	1037	1128	1237	1328	1437	1528	1637	1728	1837	1928	2125
Sondershausen d.	0449	0553	0659	0753	0753	0859	0953	1059	1153	1259	1353	1459	1553	1659	1753	1859	1953	2145
Straußfurt d.	0527	0627	0731	0827	0827	0931	1027	1131	1227	1331	1427	1531	1627	1731	1827	1931	2027	2212
Erfurt Hbf a.	0552	0652	0752	0852	0852	0952	1052	1152	1252	1352	1452	1552	1652	1752	1852	1952	2052	2236

r – Not Oct. 31.

869 NORDHAUSEN - GÖTTINGEN

RB services

km		⚒																Ⓑt
0	**Nordhausen** d.	0538	0638	0738	0838	0938	1038	1138	1238	1338	1438	1538	1638	1738	1838	1938	2038	2142
20	Walkenried d.	0603	0703	0803	0903	1003	1103	1203	1303	1403	1503	1603	1703	1803	1903	2003	2103	2203
23	Bad Sachsa d.	0608	0708	0808	0908	1008	1108	1208	1308	1408	1508	1608	1708	1808	1908	2008	2108	2208
37	Bad Lauterberg ⊡ d.	0619	0719	0819	0919	1019	1119	1219	1319	1419	1519	1619	1719	1819	1919	2019	2119	2219
43	Herzberg (Harz) d.	0626	0726	0826	0926	1026	1126	1226	1329	1426	1526	1626	1726	1826	1926	2026	2126	2226
70	Northeim (Han) 904 a.	0650	0750	0850	0950	1050	1150	1250	1353	1450	1550	1650	1750	1850	1950	2050	2150	2250
90	**Göttingen** 904 a.	0715	0808	0915	1008	1115	1208	1315	1411	1515	1608	1715	1808	1920	2008	2120j	2208	2308

	⚒	⚒																©
Göttingen 904 d.	*0407*	0538	0638	0749	0838	0949	1038	1149	1238	1349	1438	1549	1638	1749	1838	1949	2038k	2149
Northeim (Han) 904 d.	0506	0606	0702f	0806	0906	1006	1106	1206	1306	1406	1506	1606	1706	1806	1906	2006	2106	2206
Herzberg (Harz) d.	0530	0630	0730	0830	0930	1030	1130	1230	1330	1430	1530	1630	1730	1830	1930	2030	2130	2230
Bad Lauterberg ⊡ d.	0536	0636	0736	0836	0936	1036	1136	1236	1336	1436	1536	1636	1736	1836	1936	2036	2136	2236
Bad Sachsa d.	0547	0647	0747	0847	0947	1047	1147	1247	1347	1447	1547	1647	1747	1847	1947	2047	2147	2247
Walkenried d.	0552	0652	0752	0852	0952	1052	1152	1252	1352	1452	1552	1652	1752	1852	1952	2052	2205	2252
Nordhausen a.	0615	0715	0815	0915	1015	1115	1215	1315	1415	1515	1615	1715	1815	1915	2015	2115	2227	2315

f – 0706 on ©.
j – 2108 on ①②③④⑥.
k – 2049 on ①②③④⑥.
t – Also Oct. 3.

⊡ – Bad Lauterberg im Harz Barbis

870 ERFURT - MEININGEN - SCHWEINFURT - WÜRZBURG

DB (*RE* services); *STB*; *EB*

km					▽ Ⓐ			▽		▽		▽		▽		▽		▽					▽		▽
0	**Erfurt** Hbf 872 d.	...	...	...	0414	0506	...	0645	0732	0845	0932	1045	1132	1245	1332	1445	1532	1645	1732	1830	1932	...	2045	2216	2345
23	Arnstadt Hbf 872 d.	...	...	...	0436	0523	...	0707	0750	0907	0950	1107	1150	1307	1350	1507	1550	1707	1750	1847	1950	...	2107	2233	0007
31	Plaue (Thür) d.	...	...	...	0444	0529	...	0718	0758	0918	0958	1118	1158	1318	1358	1518	1558	1718	1758	1854	1958	...	2118	2241	0016
37	Gräfenroda d.	...	...	...	0449	0534	...	0723	0803	0923	1003	1123	1203	1323	1403	1523	1603	1723	1803	1859	2003	...	2123	2246	0022
53	Oberhof (Thür) d.	...	...	...	0503	0546	...	0744	0814	0944	1014	1144	1214	1344	1414	1544	1614	1744	1814	1910	2014	...	2144	2259	0038
58	Zella-Mehlis d.	...	...	...	0509	0551	...	0751	0819	0951	1019	1151	1219	1351	1419	1551	1619	1751	1819	1915	2019	...	2151	2304	0044
64	Suhl d.	...	...	...	0515	0556	...	0758	0824	0958	1024	1158	1224	1358	1424	1558	1624	1758	1824	1920	2024	...	2158	2309	0050
84	Grimmenthal 873 a.	...	...	...	0536	0609	...	0814	0835	1014	1035	1214	1235	1414	1435	1614	1635	1814	1835	1938	2035	...	2214	2320	0106
92	**Meiningen** 873 a.	...	...	...	0544	*0633*a	...	0821	*0848*	1021	*1048*	1221	*1248*	1421	*1448*	1621	*1648*	1821	*1848*	1949	*2048*	...	2221	2327	0113
						|		▬	|	▬	|	▬	|	▬	|	▬	|	▬	|	▬	|				
		◇ Ⓐ	Ⓐ	◇		|	◇ Ⓐ	◇	|	◇	|	◇	|	◇	|	◇	|	◇	|	◇	|	◇ Ⓐ			...
	Meiningen 873 d.	0424	...	0530	...	*0549*a	0646	0741	*0822*	0945	*1022*	1145	*1222*	1345	*1422*	1545	*1622*	1745	*1822*	1945	*2022*	2051	...	...	...
84	Grimmenthal 873 d.	|	...	|	...	0610	|	|	0836	|	1036	|	1236	|	1436	|	1636	|	1836	|	2036	|	...	...	...
110	Mellrichstadt d.	0447	...	0553	...	0631	0712	0808	0848	1009	1048	1209	1248	1409	1448	1609	1648	1809	1848	2009	2048	2122	...	...	...
124	Bad Neustadt (Saale) d.	0456	...	0605	...	0639	0721	0818	0857	1018	1057	1218	1257	1418	1457	1618	1657	1818	1857	2018	2057	2141	...	...	...
134	Münnerstadt d.	0504	...	0613	...	0648	0729	0828	0903	1028	1103	1228	1303	1428	1503	1626	1703	1828	1903	2028	2103	2149	...	...	...
149	Ebenhausen (Unterfr) d.	0515	0518	0631	...	0701	0742	0841	0917	1041	1117	1241	1317	1441	1517	1641	1717	1842	1917	2040	2117	2201	...	...	...
163	**Schweinfurt** Hbf 876 a.	...	0532	0643	...	0716	0754	0852	0927	1052	1127	1252	1327	1452	1527	1652	1727	1852	1927	2052	2126	2213	...	...	...
206	**Würzburg** Hbf 876 a.	...	*0617*	*0719*	...	0747	*0823*	*0923*	0958	*1123*	1158	*1323*	1358	*1523*	1558	*1723*	1758	*1923*	1958	*2151*g	2158	*2253*	...	...	...

a – Ⓐ only.
g – *2123* on ©.

▽ – Operated by Süd Thüringen Bahn (STB; 2nd class only).
◇ – Operated by Erfurter Bahn (EB; 2nd class only).

DB (*RE* services); *STB*; *EB* — WÜRZBURG - SCHWEINFURT - MEININGEN - ERFURT — 870

							◇ Ⓐ	◇ Ⓐ	◇ ©		◇		◇		◇		◇		◇		◇			◇ Ⓐ	◇
Würzburg Hbf .. **876** ● d.	...	...	...	...	*0501*r	...	...	*0602*	*0602*	0801	*0836*	1001	*1036*	1201	*1236*	1401	*1436*	1601	*1636*	1801	*1836*	2001		*2036*	*2139*v
Schweinfurt Hbf **876** ● d.	...	...	...	...	0538	...	0619	0648	0705	0830	0906	1030	1106	1230	1306	1430	1506	1630	1706	1830	1906	2030	...	2106	2224
Ebenhausen (Unterf) ● d.	...	...	...	...	0549	...	0635	0701	0719	0840	0920	1040	1120	1240	1320	1440	1520	1640	1720	1840	1920	2040	...	2120	2243
Münnerstadt d.	...	...	...	...	0558	...	0648	0712	0732	0850	0932	1050	1132	1250	1332	1450	1532	1650	1732	1850	1932	2050	...	2131	2254
Bad Neustadt (Saale) d.	...	...	...	...	0605	...	0656	0722	0740	0857	0940	1057	1140	1257	1340	1457	1540	1657	1740	1857	1940	2057	...	2140	2303
Mellrichstadt d.	...	...	...	...	0614	...	0710	0731	0749	0905	0949	1105	1149	1305	1349	1505	1549	1705	1749	1905	1949	2105	...	2149	2312
Grimmenthal **873** a.	...	...	...	...	0629	...	|	|	|	0919	|	1119	|	1319	|	1519	|	1719	|	1919	|	2120	...	|	|
Meiningen **873** a.	...	...	...	...	|	...	0732	0756	0816	*0932*	1016	*1132*	1216	*1332*	1416	*1532*	1616	*1732*	1816	*1932*	2016	*2132*	...	2213	2335
	⚒t	▽ Ⓐ		▽	|		▽			|	▽	|	▽	|	▽	|	▽	|	▽	|	▽	|	▽		
Meiningen **873** d.	0342	0409	0510	0527	*0619*	0711	0733	...	...	*0907*	0933	*1107*	1133	*1307*	1333	*1507*	1533	*1707*	1733	*1907*	1933	*2107*	2133	...	...
Grimmenthal **873** d.	0348	0417	0516	0538	0630	0720	0740	...	...	0920	0940	1120	1140	1320	1340	1520	1540	1720	1740	1920	1940	2121	2140	...	...
Suhl d.	0400	0437	0531	0556	0641	0731	0758	...	...	0931	0958	1131	1158	1331	1358	1531	1558	1731	1758	1931	1958	2132	2158	...	...
Zella-Mehlis d.	0406	0449	0538	0602	0647	0737	0805	...	...	0937	1005	1137	1205	1337	1405	1537	1605	1737	1805	1937	2005	2138	2205	...	...
Oberhof (Thür) d.	0411	0455	0543	0608	0653	0742	0811	...	...	0942	1011	1142	1211	1342	1411	1542	1611	1742	1811	1942	2011	2143	2211	...	...
Gräfenroda d.	0422	0510	0556	0628	0703	0753	0828	...	...	0953	1028	1153	1228	1353	1428	1553	1628	1753	1828	1953	2028	2154	2228	...	...
Plaue (Thür) d.	0426	0516	0600	0639	0708	0758	0839	...	...	0958	1039	1158	1239	1358	1439	1558	1639	1758	1839	1958	2039	2159	2239	...	...
Arnstadt Hbf **872** d.	0434	0524	0609	0648	0715	0806	0848	...	...	1006	1048	1206	1248	1406	1448	1606	1648	1806	1848	2006	2048	2206	2248	...	...
Erfurt Hbf **872** a.	0450	0546	0624	0708	0729	0821	0908	...	...	1021	1108	1221	1308	1421	1508	1621	1708	1821	1908	2021	2108	2222	2308	...	...

r – ⚒ (not Aug. 15).
t – Not Oct. 31.
v – *2144* on ©.
▽ – Operated by Süd Thüringen Bahn (STB; 2nd class only).
◇ – Operated by Erfurter Bahn (EB; 2nd class only).
● – Trains between Würzburg, Schweinfurt and Ebenhausen are often combined with a service to Bad Kissingen. Passengers should take care to join the correct portion for their destination.

RE / *RB* services — LEIPZIG - GERA - HOF and SAALFELD — 871

km																											
		Ⓐ	⚒r					⑥H		R					R					R							
0	**Leipzig** Hbf d.	...	...	...	0455a	*0627*	0711	0827	*0827*	...	0911	*1027*	*1111*	1227	...	1311	1427	1511	1627	...	1711	1827	1920	2027	...	*2125*	2312
45	Zeitz d.	...	0445a	...	0545a	*0704*	0804	0904	*0904*	...	1004	*1104*	*1204*	1304	...	1404	1504	1604	1704	...	1804	1904	2004	2104	...	*2210*	2358
72	**Gera** Hbf a.	...	0515a	...	0617a	*0726*	0830	0926	*0926*	...	1030	*1126*	*1230*	1326	...	1430	1526	1630	1726	...	1830	1926	2030	2126	...	*2237*	0025
72	**Gera** Hbf d.	0437	0519	0609	0630	0744	0837	0928	0943	1009	1037	1145	1237	1345	1409	1437	1545	1637	1745	1809	1837	1945	2037	...	2200	2302	...
84	Weida d.	0456	0533	0623	0644	0759	0850	|	1003	1023	1050	1203	1253	1403	1423	1450	1603	1653	1803	1823	1850	2003	2050	...	2213	2321	...
156	**Hof** Hbf a.	|	|	0726	|	|	|	|	|	1126	|	|	|	|	1526	|	|	|	|	1926	|	|	|	...	...	|	...
99	Triptis d.	0509	0547	...	0657	0816	0910	|	1016	...	1110	1216	1310	1416	...	1510	1616	1710	1816	...	1910	2016	2110	...	...	2334	...
108	Neustadt (Orla) d.	0517	0555	...	0704	0824	0917	|	1024	...	1117	1224	1317	1424	...	1517	1624	1717	1824	...	1917	2024	2117	...	...	2342	...
139	**Saalfeld** (Saale) a.	0551	0627	...	0731	0854	0940	1018	1054	...	1140	1254	1340	1454	...	1540	1654	1740	1854	...	1940	2054	2140	...	...	0011	...

	⚒r	Ⓐ	⚒r					R					R				©	Ⓐ	R		⑥L						
Saalfeld (Saale) d.	...	...	0506	...	0622	0723	0819	...	0905	1019	1105	1219	...	1305	1419	1505	1619	1619	...	1705	1736	1819	1905	2019	...	2134	2229
Neustadt (Orla) d.	...	...	0537	...	0648	0752	0848	...	0941	1048	1141	1248	...	1341	1448	1541	1648	1648	...	1741	|	1848	1941	2048	...	2203	2258
Triptis d.	...	...	0549	...	0658	0801	0855	...	0949	1055	1149	1255	...	1349	1455	1549	1655	1655	...	1749	|	1855	1949	2055	...	2211	2306
Hof Hbf d.	...	...	|	...	|	|	|	0834	|	|	|	|	1234	|	|	|	|	|	1634	|	|	|	|	|	2034	|	|
Weida d.	...	*0453*	0602	...	0711	0815	0909	0938	1002	1109	1202	1309	1338	1402	1509	1602	1709	1715	1738	1802	|	1909	2002	2109	2138	2224	2319
Gera Hbf a.	...	*0507*	0614	...	0723	0827	0921	0948	1015	1121	1215	1321	1348	1415	1521	1615	1721	1729	1748	1815	1829	1921	2015	2121	2148	2236	2332
Gera Hbf ◐ d.	0452	0532	...	0630	...	0830	...	...	1030	...	1230	...	...	1430	...	1630	...	...	...	*1830*	1830	...	2030	...	...	2242	...
Zeitz ◐ d.	0524	0601	...	0654	...	0854	...	...	1054	...	1254	...	...	1454	...	1654	...	...	...	*1854*	1854	...	2054	...	...	2310	...
Leipzig Hbf ◐ a.	0614	0646	...	0729	...	0929	...	...	1129	...	1329	...	...	1529	...	1729	...	...	...	*1929*	1929	...	2131	...	...	2355	...

H – ⑥ until Oct. 31. To Rottenbach (1053), Obstfelderschmiede (1123), Katzhütte (1141).
L – ⑥ until Oct. 31. From Katzhütte (1617), Obstfelderschmiede (1635), Rottenbach (1703).
R – To / from Regensburg (Table **879**).
a – Ⓐ only.
r – Not Oct. 31.
◐ – Additional journeys Gera - Leipzig: From Gera Hbf 0712, 0912 and every **two** hours until 1912.

RE / *RB* services — ERFURT - SAALFELD and ROTTENBACH - KATZHÜTTE — 872

km		⚒r				C				
0	**Erfurt** Hbf **870** d.	0455	0638	*0732*	0840	then each	*1932*	2040	*2141*	2252
23	Arnstadt Hbf **870** d.	0518	0655	0802	0900	train runs	2002	2100	2212	2311
38	Stadtilm d.	0537	0708	0816	0913	every	2016	2113	2226	2326
54	Rottenbach d.	0554	0721	0835	0925	**two** hours	2035	2125	2245	2339
62	Bad Blankenburg d.	0601	0728	0842	0932	until	2042	2132	2252	2346
70	**Saalfeld** (Saale) a.	0609	0736	0850	0940		2050	2140	2300	2354

	⚒r								
Saalfeld (Saale) d.	0506	0612	0705	0819	0907	then each	2019	2107	2229
Bad Blankenburg d.	0513	0619	0712	0826	0914	train runs	2026	2114	2236
Rottenbach d.	0521	0626	0723	0833	0927	every	2033	2127	2243
Stadtilm d.	0536	0639	0737	0846	0941	**two** hours	2046	2141	2256
Arnstadt Hbf **870** a.	0550	0653	0751	0858	0955	until	2058	2155	2308
Erfurt Hbf **870** a.	0612	0712	*0814*	0916	*1021*		2116	2222	2326

km		Ⓐ			A			⑤⑦	
0	Rottenbach d.	0546	0641	0730	then each train	1841	1930	2041	...
15	Obstfelderschmiede ¶ a.	0610	0705	0754	runs every **two**	1905	1954	2105	...
25	Katzhütte a.	0628	0723	0812	hours until	1923	2012	2123	...

	Ⓐ				B			⑤⑦
Katzhütte d.	0540	...	0635	0746	then each train	1835	1946	2035
Obstfelderschmiede ¶ d.	0558	...	0653	0804	runs every **two**	1853	2004	2053
Rottenbach a.	0622	...	0717	0828	hours until	1917	2028	2117

A – On ⑥ until Oct. 31 the 1041 and 1641 from Rottenbach run 18 – 19 minutes later.
B – On ⑥ until Oct. 31 the 1035 and 1635 from Katzhütte run 18 – 19 minutes **earlier**.
C – On ⑥ until Oct. 31 Saalfeld a. 1054 (not 1050).
r – Not Oct. 31.
¶ – Station for the *Oberweißbacher Bergbahn* to Lichtenhain and Cursdorf.

Süd Thüringen Bahn (2nd class only) — EISENACH - MEININGEN - SONNEBERG — 873

km																									
		Ⓐ	Ⓐ	Ⓐ										©	Ⓐ		©	Ⓐ							
0	**Eisenach** d.	...	0400	0452	...	0608	0715	0815	0915	1015	1115	1215	1315	1415	1415	1515	1615	1615	1715	1815	1915	2015	2115	2220	2310
27	Bad Salzungen d.	...	0426	0521	...	0641	0741	0841	0941	1041	1141	1241	1341	1441	1441	1541	1641	1641	1741	1841	1941	2041	2141	2250	2333
41	Wernshausen d.	...	0441	0539	...	0657	0757	0857	0957	1057	1157	1257	1357	1457	1457	1557	1657	1657	1757	1857	1957	2057	2157	2304	...
61	**Meiningen** a.	...	0458	0600	...	0713	0813	0913	1013	1113	1213	1313	1413	1513	1513	1613	1713	1713	1813	1913	2013	2113	2213	2321	...
61	**Meiningen** **870** d.	0417	0549	0619	0619	0719	0822	0919	1022	1119	1222	1319	1422	1519	1519	1622	1719	1719	1822	1919	2022	2119	...	...	...
68	Grimmenthal **870** d.	0423	0556	0631	0631	0731	0831	0931	1031	1131	1231	1331	1431	1531	1541k	1631	1731	1741k	1831	1931	2031	2131	...	...	...
82	Themar d.	0440	0609	0644	0644	0744	0844	0944	1044	1144	1244	1344	1444	1544	1553	1644	1744	1753	1844	1944	2044	2144	...	...	...
94	Hildburghausen d.	0454	0621	0700	0700	0800	0900	1000	1100	1200	1300	1400	1500	1600	1606	1700	1800	1806	1900	2000	2100	2156	...	...	...
109	**Eisfeld** d.	0514	0643	0716	0716	0814	0916	1014	1116	1214	1316	1414	1516	1614	1621	1716	1814	1821	1916	2014	2114	2211	...	...	...
141	**Sonneberg** (Thür) Hbf a.	0558	0727	0800	0800	...	1000	...	1200	...	1400	...	1600	...	...	1800	...	...	2000	...	...	...	...	...	...

	Ⓐ	Ⓐ	Ⓐ	Ⓐ	Ⓐ		Ⓐ											©	Ⓐ		©	Ⓐ			
Sonneberg (Thür) Hbf d.	...	...	...	...	...	...	...	...	0600	...	0802	...	1002	...	1202	...	1402	...	...	1602	...	1630	1802	...	2002
Eisfeld d.	...	...	0412	...	...	...	0540	...	0645	0745	0845	0945	1045	1145	1245	1345	1445	1545	1545	1645	1745	1745f	1845	1945	2045
Hildburghausen d.	...	...	0427	...	...	...	0555	...	0659	0759	0859	0959	1059	1159	1259	1359	1459	1559	1606	1659	1759	1806	1859	1959	2059
Themar d.	...	...	0438	...	...	...	0611	...	0711	0811	0911	1011	1111	1211	1311	1411	1511	1611	1617	1711	1811	1817	1911	2011	2111
Grimmenthal **870** d.	...	...	0455	...	0537	...	0627	...	0726	0829	0926	1029	1126	1229	1326	1429	1526	1629	1629	1726	1829	1829	1926	2029	2126
Meiningen **870** a.	...	...	0501	...	0544	...	0633	...	0732	0835	0932	1035	1132	1235	1332	1435	1532	1635	1635	1732	1835	1835	1932	2035	2132
Meiningen d.	...	0423	...	0503	0549	0549	...	0639	0739	0839	0939	1039	1139	1239	1339	1439	1539	1639	1639	1739	1839	1839	1939	2039	2139
Wernshausen d.	...	0441	...	0520	0608	0608	...	0657	0757	0857	0957	1057	1157	1257	1357	1457	1557	1657	1657	1757	1857	1857	1957	2057	2157
Bad Salzungen d.	0410	0453	...	0533	0621	0621	...	0711	0811	0911	1011	1111	1211	1311	1411	1511	1611	1711	1711	1811	1911	1911	2011	2111	2211
Eisenach a.	0438	0519	...	0556	0646	0646	...	0739	0839	0939	1039	1139	1239	1339	1439	1539	1639	1739	1739	1839	1939	1939	2039	2139	2236

f – Arrives 1713.
k – Arrives 16 minutes earlier.

RE services — LEIPZIG - CHEMNITZ — 874

km			①–⑥							
0	**Leipzig** Hbf d.	0525	0630	...	0730		2130	...	2338	...
33	Bad Lausick d.	0549	0649	...	0749	and	2149	...	0002	...
44	Geithain d.	0557	0657	...	0757	hourly	2157	...	0010	...
66	Burgstädt d.	0611	0711	...	0811	until	2211	...	0024	...
81	**Chemnitz** Hbf a.	0624	0724	...	0824		2224	...	0037	...

			①–⑥					
Chemnitz Hbf d.	0423	...	0531	...	0631		2031	2244
Burgstädt d.	0435	...	0543	...	0643	and	2043	2256
Geithain d.	0449	...	0558	...	0658	hourly	2058	2310
Bad Lausick d.	0457	...	0606	...	0706	until	2106	2321
Leipzig Hbf a.	0519	...	0624	...	0724		2124	2352

875 NÜRNBERG - COBURG - SONNEBERG

RE / RB services except where shown

See Table **851** for faster *ICE* services Nürnberg - Erlangen - Bamberg - Lichtenfels and v.v.

Nürnberg - Bamberg subject to alteration Aug. 1 - Sept. 14. See note ⊠.

km		Ⓐ	Ⓐ		2				2				2					2				2			Ⓐ	
0	**Nürnberg** Hbf ‡ d.	...	0429	0553	...	0651	0745	0840	...	0846	0945	1040	...	1046	1145	1149	1240	...	1246	1345	1440	...	1446	1545	1614	1640
8	Fürth (Bay) Hbf ‡ d.	...	0438	0601	...	0659	0753	0848	...	0854	0953	1048	...	1054	1153	1158	1248	...	1254	1353	1448	...	1454	1553	1622	1648
24	Erlangen ‡ d.	...	0455	0613	...	0719	0806	0901	...	0913	1006	1101	...	1113	1206	1216	1301	...	1313	1406	1501	...	1513	1606	1634	1701
39	Forchheim (Oberfr) ‡ d.	...	0509	0621	...	0733	0816	0909	...	0929	1016	1109	...	1129	1216	1230	1309	...	1329	1416	1509	...	1529	1616	1645	1709
62	**Bamberg** ‡ a.	...	0532	0636	...	0752	0831	0924	...	0950	1031	1124	...	1150	1231	1250	1323	...	1350	1431	1524	...	1550	1631	1702	1724
62	**Bamberg** 876 d.	0449	0538	0638	0741	0754	0838	0926	0941	0954	1038	1126	1141	1154	1238	1252	1326	1340	1354	1438	1526	1541	1554	1638	1717	1726
	Würzburg Hbf 876 a.	|	|	|	|	|	|	1023	|	|	|	1223	|	|	|	|	1423	|	|	|	1623	|	|	|	|	1824
94	Lichtenfels 876 a.	0517	0610	0656	0800	0822	0856	...	1000	1023	1056	...	1200	1223	1256	1317	...	1400	1423	1456	...	1600	1623	1656	1746	...
94	Lichtenfels d.	0524	0622	0658	0810	0839	0906	...	1010	1039	1106	...	1210	1239	1306	1336e	...	1410	1439	1506	...	1610	1639	1706	1754	...
114	**Coburg** a.	0553	0642	0718	0833	0906	0930	...	1029	1106	1130	...	1229	1306	1330	1403e	...	1429	1506	1530	...	1629	1706	1730	1814	...
114	**Coburg** d.	0554	0701	0724	0835	...	0932	...	1035	...	1132	...	1235	...	1332	...	...	1435	...	1532	...	1635	1707q	1732	...	...
135	**Sonneberg** (Thür) Hbf a.	0621	0725	0745	0857	...	0954	...	1057	...	1154	...	1257	...	1354	...	...	1457	...	1554	...	1657	1739q	1754	...	...

	2				2						
Nürnberg Hbf ‡ d.	...	1646	1745	1840	...	1945	2040	...	2145	2253	0011
Fürth (Bay) Hbf ‡ d.	...	1654	1753	1848	...	1953	2048	...	2154	2307	0020
Erlangen ‡ d.	...	1713	1806	1901	...	2006	2101	...	2214	2325	0038
Forchheim (Oberfr) ‡ d.	...	1729	1816	1909	...	2016	2112	...	2228	2338	0053
Bamberg ‡ a.	...	1750	1831	1924	...	2031	2129	...	2248	2358	0115
Bamberg 876 d.	1741	1754	1838	1926	1941	2038	2138c	2141	2259	0021	...
Würzburg Hbf 876 a.	|	|	|	2023	|	|	2251c	|	|	|	...
Lichtenfels 876 a.	1800	1823	1856	...	2000	2056	...	2205	2324	0048	...
Lichtenfels d.	1810	1840	1909	...	2010	2109	...	2212	2325	...	...
Coburg a.	1829	1906	1930	...	2029	2126	...	2238	2345	...	...
Coburg d.	1835	...	1932	...	2035	...	...	2239	...	...	...
Sonneberg (Thür) Hbf a.	1857	...	1954	...	2057	...	...	2301	...	...	...

	Ⓐ	Ⓐ	Ⓒ	Ⓐ			Ⓐ	Ⓒ 2		
Sonneberg (Thür) Hbf d.	0433	...	...	0518	0612	...	0648	0656	...	0732e
Coburg a.	0456	...	...	0542	0634	...	0721	0721	...	0800e
Coburg d.	0457	0518	0518	0543	0636	0652e	0724	0732	...	0802e
Lichtenfels a.	0517	0539	0539	0604	0656	0717e	0749	0753	...	0823e
Lichtenfels 876 d.	0518	0542	0542	0605	0658	0736	0800	0800	...	0840
Würzburg Hbf 876 d.	|	|	|	|	|	|	|	|	0728h	|
Bamberg 876 a.	0547	0612	0612	0632	0722	0806	0819	0819	0834	0908
Bamberg ‡ d.	0549	0618	0628	0635	0727	0809	...	...	0836	0910
Forchheim (Oberfr) ‡ d.	0605	0632	0642	0650	0744	0831	...	...	0851	0932
Erlangen ‡ d.	0616	0645	0654	0714v	0756	0846	...	...	0900	0945
Fürth (Bay) Hbf ‡ d.	0628	0700	0708	0727	0808	0903	...	...	0912	1003
Nürnberg Hbf ‡ a.	0637	0708	0717	0734	0817	0912	...	...	0921	1011

			2				2				2				2				2				2			2
Sonneberg (Thür) Hbf d.	0807	...	0907	...	1007	...	1107	...	1207	...	1307	...	1407	...	1507	...	1607	...	1707	...	1807	...	1907	2007	...	2140
Coburg a.	0829	...	0929	...	1029	...	1129	...	1229	...	1329	...	1429	...	1529	...	1629	...	1729	...	1829	...	1929	2029	...	2203
Coburg d.	0835	0858	0932	...	1035	1058	1132	...	1235	1258	1332	...	1435	1458	1532	...	1635	1658	1732	...	1835	1858	1932	2035	2134	2204
Lichtenfels a.	0852	0920	0951	...	1052	1120	1151	...	1252	1320	1351	...	1452	1520	1551	...	1652	1720	1751	...	1852	1920	1951	2052	2154	2225
Lichtenfels 876 d.	0902	0936	1000	...	1102	1136	1200	...	1302	1337	1400	...	1502	1536	1600	...	1702	1736	1800	...	1902	1936	2000	2102	2200	2314
Würzburg Hbf 876 d.	|	|	|	0936	|	|	|	1136	|	|	|	1336	|	|	|	1536	|	|	|	1736	|	|	|	|	|	|
Bamberg 876 a.	0922	1006	1019	1034	1122	1206	1219	1234	1322	1406	1419	1434	1522	1606	1619	1634	1722	1806	1819	1834	1922	2006	2019	2127	2224	2342
Bamberg ‡ d.	0930	1009	...	1036	1130	1209	...	1236	1326	1409	...	1436	1530	1609	...	1636	1730	1809	...	1836	1930	2009	...	2130	...	2343
Forchheim (Oberfr) ‡ d.	0944	1030	...	1051	1144	1230	...	1251	1346	1430	...	1451	1544	1630	...	1651	1744	1830	...	1851	1944	2030	...	2144	...	0004
Erlangen ‡ d.	0956	1045	...	1101	1156	1245	...	1301	1356	1445	...	1501	1556	1645	...	1701	1756	1845	...	1901	1956	2052t	...	2156	...	0018
Fürth (Bay) Hbf ‡ d.	1008	1104	...	1113	1208	1304	...	1313	1408	1504	...	1513	1608	1704	...	1713	1808	1904	...	1913	2008	2113	...	2209	...	0037
Nürnberg Hbf ‡ a.	1017	1112	...	1121	1217	1312	...	1321	1417	1512	...	1521	1617	1712	...	1721	1817	1912	...	1921	2017	2120	...	2217	...	0045

c – Ⓒ only. On † departs Bamberg 2148, arrives Würzburg 2254.
e – Ⓐ only.
h – 0732 on Ⓒ.
q – ①–④ only.
t – Arrives 2044.
v – Arrives 0701.

‡ – Additional *RB* services Nürnberg - Bamberg and v.v.
From Nürnberg Hbf at 0106, 0618 ⚒, 0750, 0950, 1350, 1517 Ⓐ, 1550, 1715 Ⓐ, 1750, 1845, 1950 and 2047.
From Bamberg at 0353 Ⓐ, 0444 ⚒, 0505, 0542 Ⓒ, 0604 Ⓒ, 0706, 1110, 1310, 1510, 1654 Ⓐ, 1710, 1910 and 2210.
See Table **921** for other trains Nürnberg - Fürth and v.v.

⊠ – **Aug. 1 - Sept. 14** all services are replaced by 🚌 Forchheim - Bamberg and v.v. An amended train service operates Nürnberg - Fürth - Erlangen - Forchheim as follows:
From Nürnberg at 0538, 0619, 0737, 0832, 0940, 1029, 1141, 1233, 1341, 1432, 1541, 1629, 1741, 1829, 1941, 2032, 2145, 2254 and 2351.
From Forchheim at 0459, 0554, 0631, 0728, 0830, 0935, 1030, 1135, 1231, 1335, 1430, 1535, 1631, 1735, 1830, 1935, 2029, 2135, 2245 and 2348.
Please note that further amendments apply Sept. 11, 12, 13!
Trains Bamberg - Lichtenfels - Coburg - Sonneberg and v.v. run as per the normal schedule. However, be aware that overall journey times via the Forchheim - Bamberg 🚌 link are considerably extended during this period. Additional express (non-stop) 🚌 services operate Nürnberg - Bamberg and v.v.

876 WÜRZBURG - BAMBERG - HOF

RE / RB services

km		Ⓐ 2		⑥ k	Ⓐ						Ⓐ	Ⓒ	S	S					S	S	⊠		S	S	
0	**Würzburg** Hbf 870 d.	...	...	0501	0501	...	...	0602	...	...	0728	0732	...	...	0809	0836	0836	0936	...	...		1736	...	...	1809
43	Schweinfurt Hbf 870 d.	...	...	0538	0543	...	...	0636	...	...	0803	0803	...	...	0842	0903	0903	1003	...	...		1803	...	...	1842
68	Haßfurt d.	...	...	0556	0600	...	...	0653	...	...	0816	0816	...	...	0858	0918	0918	1017	...	...		1817	...	...	1858
100	**Bamberg** a.	...	...	0620	0625	...	...	0719	...	...	0834	0834	...	...	0923	0936	0936	1034	...	...	each train	1834	...	...	1923
100	**Bamberg** 851 875 d.	...	0449e	▬	...	0638	0638	...	0741	0741	0836*	0836*	0838	0838	...	0941	0941	1036*	1038	1038		1836*	1838	1838	...
	Nürnberg Hbf 875 a.	...	|	...	...	|	|	...	|	|	0921*	0921*	|	|	...	|	|	1121*	|	|	runs every	1921*	|	|	...
132	Lichtenfels 851 875 d.	0436	0550	...	...	0700	0700	...	0802	0802	...	...	0900	0900	...	1002	1002	...	1100	1100		...	1900	1900	...
162	Kulmbach d.	0505	0618	...	...	0718	0718	...	0821	0821	...	...	0918	0918	...	1021	1021	...	1118	1118	two hours	...	1918	1918	...
174	Neuenmarkt-Wirsberg a.	0519	0632	2	...	0727	0727	...	0833	0833	...	...	0927	0927	...	1033	1033	...	1127	1127		...	1927	1927	...
174	Neuenmarkt-Wirsberg d.	0520	0633	0637	...	0729	0733	...	0835	0837	...	...	0929	0933	...	1035	1037	...	1129	1133	until	...	1929	1933	...
196	**Bayreuth** Hbf a.	0548	|	0659	...	|	0755	...	0856	|	...	...	|	0955	...	1056	|	...	|	1155		...	|	1955	...
203	Münchberg 880 d.	...	0657	...	...	0754	...	...	...	0900	...	...	0954	...	...	...	1100	...	1154	...		...	1954	...	...
216	Schwarzenbach d.	...	0709	...	...	0804	...	...	...	0909	...	...	1004	...	...	...	1109	...	1204	...		...	2004	...	...
227	**Hof** Hbf 880 a.	...	0720	...	...	0816	...	...	...	0920	...	...	1014	...	...	...	1120	...	1214	...		...	2015	...	...

								Ⓒ	Ⓐ		
Würzburg Hbf 870 d.	1836	1836	1936	...	2009	2036	2036	2139	2139	...	2300
Schweinfurt Hbf 870 d.	1903	1903	2003	...	2042	2103	2103	2205	2212	...	2334
Haßfurt d.	1918	1918	2017	...	2058	2118	2118	2219	2229	...	2350
Bamberg a.	1936	1936	2034	...	2123	2136	2136	2237	2253	...	0016
Bamberg 851 875 d.	1941	1941	...	2038	...	2141	2141	...	...	2259	...
Nürnberg Hbf 875 a.	|	|	...	|	...	|	|	...	...	|	...
Lichtenfels 851 875 d.	2002	2002	...	2107	...	2206	2206	...	...	2329	...
Kulmbach d.	2021	2021	...	2134	...	2226	2226	...	...	2353	...
Neuenmarkt-Wirsberg a.	2033	2033	...	2148	...	2238	2238	...	...	0006	...
Neuenmarkt-Wirsberg d.	2035	2037	...	2148	...	2240	2242	...	...	0007	...
Bayreuth Hbf a.	2056	|	...	2207	...	2300	|	...	...	0029	...
Münchberg 880 d.	...	2100	...	...	...	...	2306	...	...	...	...
Schwarzenbach d.	...	2109	...	...	...	...	2315	...	...	...	...
Hof Hbf 880 a.	...	2120	...	...	...	...	2327	...	...	...	...

	Ⓒ	Ⓐ		Ⓐ 2	Ⓐ			⚒			
Hof Hbf 880 d.	...	...	...	...	...	0525	...	...	0638	...	...
Schwarzenbach d.	...	...	...	...	...	0533	...	...	0647	...	...
Münchberg 880 d.	...	...	...	...	...	0543	...	...	0656	...	...
Bayreuth Hbf d.	...	...	...	0452	...	|	0550	...	|	0703	...
Neuenmarkt-Wirsberg a.	...	...	...	0513	...	0606	0610	...	0721	0725	...
Neuenmarkt-Wirsberg d.	...	...	...	0520	...	0613	0613	...	0728	0728	...
Kulmbach d.	...	...	...	0532	...	0622	0622	...	0738	0738	...
Lichtenfels 851 875 d.	...	...	...	0601	...	0650f	0650f	...	0800	0800	...
Nürnberg Hbf 875 d.	...	...	...	|	...	|	|	...	|	|	...
Bamberg 851 875 a.	...	...	...	0632	...	0717e	0717e	...	0819	0819	...
Bamberg d.	0446	0455	0617	...	0643	...	...	0726	0824	0824	0838
Haßfurt d.	0508	0516	0634	...	0707	...	...	0742	0841	0841	0900
Schweinfurt Hbf 870 d.	0526	0543	0650	...	0725	...	...	0758	0856	0856	0918
Würzburg Hbf 870 a.	0600	0617	0719	...	0800	...	...	0823	0923	0923	0951

	S	S					♥				S	S						⑥ h	Ⓐ	†					
Hof Hbf 880 d.	...	0744	...	0841	...	...		1640	...	...	...	1744	...	1841	...	1940	...	...	...	...	2041	...	...	...	2237
Schwarzenbach d.	...	0752	...	0849	...	...		1648	...	...	...	1752	...	1849	...	1950	...	...	...	...	2049	...	...	...	2248
Münchberg 880 d.	...	0803	...	0858	...	...		1659	...	...	...	1803	...	1858	...	2002	...	...	...	...	2058	...	...	...	2301
Bayreuth Hbf d.	0801	|	...	|	0903	...	each train	|	1703	...	1801	|	...	|	1903	|	2003	...	...	...	|	2103	...	2211	|
Neuenmarkt-Wirsberg a.	0823	0828	...	0921	0925	...		1721	1725	...	1823	1828	...	1921	1925	2025	2029	...	...	...	2121	2125	...	2232	2331
Neuenmarkt-Wirsberg d.	0830	0830	...	0928	0928	...	runs every	1728	1728	...	1830	1830	...	1928	1928	▬	2030	...	...	...	2128	2128	...	2232	▬
Kulmbach d.	0838	0838	...	0938	0938	...		1738	1738	...	1838	1838	...	1938	1938	...	2038	...	...	...	2138	2138	...	2245	...
Lichtenfels 851 875 d.	0857	0857	...	1000	1000	...	two hours	1800	1800	...	1857	1857	...	2000	2000	...	2057	...	...	...	2200	2200	...	2305	...
Nürnberg Hbf 875 d.	|	|	0840*	|	|	...		|	|	...	|	|	1840*	|	|	...	|	2040*	...	2040*	|	|	...	|	...
Bamberg 851 875 a.	0922	0922	0924*	1019	1019	...	until	1819	1819	...	1922	1922	1924*	2019	2019	Ⓑ w	2127	2128*	...	2128*	2224	2224	...	2342	...
Bamberg d.	...	...	0926	1024	1024	1038		1824	1824	1838	...	...	1926	2024c	2024c	2038	...	2138	2145	2148	...	...	2259	...	0007
Haßfurt d.	...	...	0942	1041	1041	1100		1841	1841	1900	...	...	1942	2041c	2041c	2100	...	2159	2202	2205	...	...	2322	...	0030
Schweinfurt Hbf 870 d.	...	...	0958	1056	1056	1118		1856	1856	1918	...	...	1958	2056c	2056c	2118	...	2218	2219	2222	...	...	2342	...	0048
Würzburg Hbf 870 a.	...	...	1023	1123	1123	1151		1923	1923	1951	...	...	2023	2123c	2123c	2151	...	2251	2253	2254	...	...	0016	...	0122c

S – From / to Saalfeld (Table **851**).
c – ⑥⑦ only.
e – Ⓐ only.
f – Arrives 0642.
h – Not Oct. 3.
k – Not Aug. 15, Oct. 3.
w – Also Aug. 15, Oct. 3.
* – Not Aug. 1 - Sept. 14.
♥ – Hof Hbf d. 1141 / 1541 (not 1144 / 1544; also departs Schwarzenach 2 minutes earlier, Münchberg 1 minute earlier).
⊠ – The 1209 from Würzburg to Bamberg runs only on Ⓒ (daily Aug. 1 - Sept. 14 and Oct. 31 - Nov. 8).

LANDSHUT - MÜHLDORF - SALZBURG — 877

RB services

km		⑥k	Ⓐ								
0	**Landshut** (Bay) Hbf .... d.	...	...	0609r	0838	1038	1238	1438	1638	1838	2038
55	Mühldorf (Oberbay) ..... a.	...	...	0713r	0929	1129	1329	1530	1730	1929	2129
55	Mühldorf (Oberbay) ..... d.	0603	0609	0743	0942	1143	1343	1543	1743	1943	2146
120	Freilassing .... **890/1** a.	0702	0713	0841	1041	1241	1442	1641	1841	2041	2239
126	**Salzburg** Hbf.... **890/1** a.	*0716*	*0726*	0850	1050	*1316*	1450	1650	1849	*2116*	2247

	Ⓐ	⚒r								
Salzburg Hbf. **890/1** d.	*0510*	...	*0709*	0911	1110	*1314*	1510	1710	1911	...
Freilassing ..... **890/1** d.	0531	...	0720	0919	1118	1324	1520	1720	1920	*2114f*
Mühldorf (Oberbay)... a.	0624	...	0814	1013	1214	1416	1614	1814	2017	*2215f*
Mühldorf (Oberbay)... d.	...	0633	0830	1030	1231	1430	1630	1830	2030	2242
Landshut (Bay) Hbf.. a.	...	0723	0923	1123	1323	1523	1723	1923	2124	2328

f – ⑤ only. k – Not Aug. 15, Oct. 3. r – ⚒ (not Aug. 15).

MÜNCHEN - REGENSBURG — 878

DB (*RE* services); *ALX*

km		Ⓒ	Ⓐ	*ALX*	N	*ALX* P	N	*ALX*	N	*ALX*	N	*ALX*	N	Ⓐ	*ALX* P	*ALX* Ⓑ	N	Ⓐ	*ALX*	⑥k	N	*ALX*	*ALX* Ⓑ	⑥	*ALX*
0	**München** Hbf...... **944** d.	0536	0544	0644	0744	0844	0944	1044	1144	1244	1344	1444	1544	1623	1643	1643	1744	*1802*	1843	1904	1944	2043	2244	2244	2355
42	Freising .... **944** d.	0604	0609	0709	0808	0909	1008	1109	1208	1309	1408	1509	1608	1648	1708	1708	1808	*1831*	1908	1928	2008	2110	2311	2311	0019
76	Landshut (Bay) Hbf **944** d.	0628	0644	0732	0833	0932	1033	1132	1233	1332	1433	1532	1632	1713	1732	1732	1832	1900	1932	1954	2032	2132	2335	2335	0041
99	Neufahrn (Niederbay) .. d.	0644	0701	0748	0849	0948	1049	1148	1249	1348	1449	1547	1649	1730	1748	1748	1849	1916	1948	2011	2049	2148	2353	2353	0057
138	**Regensburg** Hbf........ a.	0713	0732	0811	0914	1011	1114	1211	1314	1411	1514	1611	1714	1757	1811	1811	1915	1949	2011	2038	2122	2211	0025	0025	0123
	Schwandorf **879 885** a.	...	...	0846	...	1048	...	1246	...	1446	...	1646	...	...	1847	1847	...	...	2046	...	...	2251	...	...	...
	Hof Hbf **879** .... a.	...	...	1018	...	...	...	1418	...	...	...	1818	...	...	...	2025	...	...	2220	...	...	...	...	...	...

	ALX ①–⑥	*ALX*	Ⓐ	⑥k	Ⓒ	Ⓐ	*ALX*	⑥k	N	*ALX*	N	*ALX*	N	*ALX* P	N	*ALX*	N	*ALX*	N	*ALX*	N	⑤–⑦ N		*ALX* P	N
Hof Hbf **879**............. d.	...	...	...	...	...	...	0536y	...	...	0740	...	0940	...	...	...	1340	...	...	...	1740	...	...	...	...	...
Schwandorf **879 885**. d.	...	0501y	...	...	...	...	0709	...	...	0908	...	1108	...	1311	...	1508	...	1708	...	1908	...	...	...	2121	...
Regensburg Hbf......... d.	0443	0547	0600	0603	0643	0701	0746	0831	0844	0946	1044	1146	1244	1346	1444	1546	1644	1746	1844	1947	2044	2044	...	2157	2244
Neufahrn (Niederbay) ... d.	0508	0611	0626	0636	0709	0727	0811	0857	0911	1010	1111	1210	1310	1410	1511	1610	1711	1810	1910	2010	2117	2117	...	2220	2315
Landshut (Bay) Hbf **944** d.	0526	0627	0646	0657	0729	0746	0826	0916	0929	1027	1129	1227	1329	1427	1529	1627	1729	1827	1929	2027	2134	2135	2144	2238	2334
Freising .... **944** d.	0547	0649	0709	0728	0751	0809	0847	0937	0952	1048	1153	1248	1351	1448	1549	1648	1749	1848	1951	2048	...	2156	2209	2259	2356
München Hbf....... **944** a.	0615	0716	0737	0757	0816	0836	0915	1002	1017	1115	1218	1315	1417	1515	1617	1715	1817	1915	2017	2115	...	2221	2236	2324	0021

N – To / from Nürnberg (Table **921**).
P – 🚂12 München - Schwandorf - Furth im Wald 🏛 - Praha and v.v. See also Tables **57** and **885**.
k – Not Aug. 15, Oct. 3.
y – ①–⑥ only.
ALX – *Arriva-Länderbahn-Express*. Operated by Regentalbahn AG - Die Länderbahn. Conveys 🍸.

REGENSBURG - HOF — 879

DB (*RE* services); *ALX*; Vogtlandbahn

km		2 Ⓐ	G	Ⓐ	2	*ALX*	2	G	2	*ALX*	⑤	2	*ALX*	G	2	*ALX*		2	*ALX*	*ALX* Ⓑ	2	2	*ALX*	2	*ALX*
	München Hbf **878**.... d.	...	...	...	...	0644	...	...	...	1044	...	...	1244	...	...	1444	...	...	1643	1643	...	...	1843	...	2043
0	**Regensburg** Hbf. **885** d.	...	0623	0729	0730z	0821	0931	1030	1130	1221	1321	1331	1419	1430	1528	1621	1737	1723	1819	1819	*1830*	1929	2021	2131	2221
42	Schwandorf .... **885** a.	...	0650	0756	0759z	0846	1000	1057	1159	1246	1348	1400	1446	1457	1557	1646	1758	1752	1847	1847	*1857*	1958	2046	2200	2251
42	Schwandorf .... d.	0502	0652	...	0801	0847	1001	1059	1201	1247	1349	1401	...	1459	1601	1647	1759	1802	...	1851	1902	2006	2047	2209	*2305*
86	Weiden (Oberpf).......... a.	0541	0719	...	0841	0913	1041	1122	1241	1313	1418	1441	...	1521	1641	1713	1823	1841	...	1918	1941	2046	2113	2249	*2344*
86	Weiden (Oberpf).......... d.	0551	0720	...	0851	0914	1051	1122	1251z	1314	1419	1451	...	1522	1651	1714	1824	1851	...	1919	1951e	2051	2114	2251	...
137	Marktredwitz .... **880** d.	0634	0755	...	0934	0950	1134	1155	1334z	1350	1455	1534	...	1555	1734	1750	1907g	1934	...	1956	2034e	2134	2152	2334	...
179	**Hof** Hbf .... **880** a.	0710	0819	...	1010	1018	1210	1219	1410z	1418	*1524*	1610	...	1619	1810	1818	1932	2011	...	2025	2110e	2210	2220	0010	...

	ALX ①–⑥	2 ¶	2 Ⓐ	*ALX* H		*ALX*	2	*ALX*	2	G	2	2 Ⓐ	*ALX*	2	G	*ALX*	2	*ALX*	2	⑦	G	2		2 Ⓐ	2
Hof Hbf .... **880** d.	...	...	...	0536	0642	0740	0748	0940	0948	1144	1148	...	1340	1348	1544	...	1548	1740	1748	*1837*	1944	1948	...	2048	2251
Marktredwitz .... **880** d.	...	...	...	0603	0713	0807	0824	1007	1024	1206	1224	...	1407	1424	1606	...	1624	1807	1824	1904	2007	2024	...	2124	2327
Weiden (Oberpf)........... a.	...	...	...	0641	0745	0840	0905	1041	1105	1237	1305	...	1441	1505	1637	...	1705	1841	1905	1940	2037	2105	...	2205	0008
Weiden (Oberpf)........... d.	*0414e*	0508	0541	0642	0746	0841	0914	1042	1114	1238	1314z	1322	1442	1514	1638	...	1714	1842	1914	1941	2038	2114z	...	2217	...
Schwandorf.................. a.	*0454e*	0548	0621	0708	0808	0907	0954	1107	1154	1300	1354z	1400	1507	1554	1700	...	1754	1907	1952	2008	2100	2154z	...	2255	...
Schwandorf........... **885** d.	0501	0552	0622	0709	0810	0908	1002	1108	1202	1301	1402z	1402	1508	1606	1702	1708	1804	1908	2006h	2009	2100	...	2206	*2303*	...
Regensburg Hbf .. **885** a.	0536	0621	0653	0736	0837	0937	1034	1136	1234	1330	1434z	1434	1536	1637	1730	1736	1836	1937	2037h	2037	2130	...	2237	*2332*	...
München Hbf **878**..... a.	0716	...	...	0915	...	1115	...	1315	...	...	...	...	1715	...	...	1915	...	2115	...	...	...	...	...	...	...

G – To / from Gera (Table **871**).
H – ①–⑥ (daily Schwandorf - München).
e – Ⓐ only.
g – Arrives 1857 (connects with 1901 departure to Dresden).
h – On ⑦ departs Schwandorf 1953, arrives Regensburg 2027.
z – Ⓒ only.
¶ – Change trains at Schwandorf on Ⓐ.
ALX – *Arriva-Länderbahn-Express*. Operated by Regentalbahn AG - Die Länderbahn. Conveys 🍸.

NÜRNBERG - HOF - DRESDEN — 880

IRE / *RE* / *RB* services

km			Ⓐ		L	Ⓐ			⚒N	⚒P	C									Ⓐ	E				
0	**Nürnberg** Hbf .... ● d.	0012	...	...	...	...	0548	0548	0642	0642	0648	0648	0748	0748	0842	0848	0848	0948	0948	1042	1048	1048	1148	1148	1242
28	Hersbruck (r Pegnitz)....... ● d.	0031	...	...	...	...	0606	0606	│	│	0706	0706	0806	0806	│	0906	0906	1006	1006	│	1106	1106	1206	1206	│
67	Pegnitz .... ● a.	0053	...	...	...	...	0627	0627	│	│	0727	0727	0827	0827	│	0927	0927	1027	1027	│	1127	1127	1227	1227	│
67	Pegnitz .... d.	0054	...	...	...	...	0629	0635	│	│	0729	0733	0829	0835	│	0929	0933	1029	1035	│	1129	1133	1229	1235	│
	Bayreuth Hbf .... **876** d.	0114	...	...	...	0519	│	0654	│	0732	│	0754	│	0854	0932	│	0954	│	1054	1132	│	1154	│	1254	1332
	Münchberg .... **876** d.	▬	...	...	...	0554	│	...	│	0805	│	...	│	...	1005	│	...	│	...	1205	│	...	│	...	1405
94	Kirchenlaibach .... d.	...	...	...	...	│	0643	...	│	│	0743	...	0843	...	│	0943	...	1043	...	│	1143	...	1243	...	│
125	Marktredwitz .... **879** d.	...	...	...	...	│	0701	...	0800t	│	0812	...	0901	...	│	1012	...	1101	...	│	1212	...	1301	...	│
167	**Hof** Hbf................. **876 879** a.	...	...	...	...	0618	0724	...	0823	0823	▬	...	0924	...	1023	...	...	1124	...	1223	▬	...	1324	...	1423
167	**Hof** Hbf......................... **881** d.	...	0428	0523	0602	0626	0728	...	0828	0828	...	...	0928	...	1028	...	...	1128	...	1228	...	...	1328	...	1428
215	Plauen (Vogtl) ob Bf ..... **881** d.	...	0455	0555	0632	0655	0755	...	0855	0855	...	...	0955	...	1055	...	...	1155	...	1255	...	...	1355	...	1455
240	Reichenbach (Vogtl) ob Bf **881** d.	...	0509	0609	0646	0709	0809	...	0909	0909	...	...	1009	...	1109	...	...	1209	...	1309	...	...	1409	...	1509
263	**Zwickau** (Sachs) Hbf........... d.	...	0526	0626	0703	0726	0826	...	0926	0926	0933	...	1026	...	1126	...	...	1226	...	1326	1333	...	1426	...	1526
279	Glauchau (Sachs)......... **858** d.	...	0535	0635	...	0735	0835	...	0935	0935	0949	...	1035	...	1135	...	...	1235	...	1335	1349	...	1435	...	1535
311	**Chemnitz** Hbf.............. **858** d.	0430	0600	0700	...	0800	0900	...	1000	1000	1030	...	1100	...	1200	...	...	1300	...	1400	1430	...	1500	...	1600
324	Flöha ....d.	0442	0615	0714	...	0815	0914	...	1015	1015	1042	...	1114	...	1215	...	...	1314	...	1415	1442	...	1514	...	1615
350	Freiberg (Sachs)................. d.	0507	0632	0731	...	0832	0931	...	1032	1032	1107	...	1131	...	1232	...	...	1331	...	1432	1507	...	1531	...	1632
390	**Dresden** Hbf..................... a.	0551	0702	0802	...	0902	1002	...	1102	1102	1151	...	1202	...	1302	...	...	1402	...	1502	1551	...	1602	...	1702

					Ⓐ						C					Ⓒ									⑥
Nürnberg Hbf.................. ● d.	1248	1248	1348	1348	1442	1448	1448	1548	1548	1642	1648	1648	1748	1748	1842	1842	1848	1848	1948	1948	2055	2148	2148	2250	2250
Hersbruck (r Pegnitz)........ ● d.	1306	1306	1406	1406	│	1506	1506	1606	1606	│	1706	1706	1806	1806	│	│	1906	1906	2006	2006	2114	2206	2206	2309	2309
Pegnitz .... ● a.	1327	1327	1427	1427	│	1527	1527	1627	1627	│	1727	1727	1827	1827	│	│	1927	1927	2027	2027	2136	2227	2227	2331	2331
Pegnitz .... d.	1329	1333	1429	1435	│	1529	1533	1629	1635	│	1729	1733	1829	1835	│	│	1929	1933	2029	2035	2137	2229	2233	2332	2332
Bayreuth Hbf............ **876** d.	│	1354	│	1454	1532	│	1554	│	1654	1732	│	1754	│	1854	1932	1932	│	1954	│	2054	2156	2250	│	2351	2357
Münchberg .... **876** d.	│	...	│	...	1605	│	...	│	...	1805	│	...	│	...	2005	2005	│	▬	│	▬	...	...	│	...	0047
Kirchenlaibach .... d.	1343	...	1443	...	│	1543	...	1643	...	│	1743	...	1843	...	│	│	1943	...	2043	...	...	...	2252	...	│
Marktredwitz .... **879** d.	1412	...	1501	...	│	1612	...	1701	...	│	1812	...	1901	...	│	│	2012	...	2101	...	...	...	2313	...	│
Hof Hbf ....**876 879** a.	...	...	1524	...	1623	▬	...	1724	...	1823	...	...	1924	...	2022	2022	▬	...	2124	◇2	...	...	2341	...	0112
Hof Hbf .... **881** d.	...	...	1528	...	1628	...	...	1728	...	1828	...	...	1928	...	2029	2029	...	...	▬	2224	...	...	...	...	...
Plauen (Vogtl) ob Bf...... **881** d.	...	...	1555	...	1655	...	...	1755	...	1855	...	...	1955	...	2056	2056	...	...	...	2313	...	...	...	...	...
Reichenbach (Vogtl) ob Bf. **881** d.	...	...	1609	...	1709	...	...	1809	...	1909	...	...	2009	...	2110	2110	...	...	...	2336	...	...	...	...	...
Zwickau (Sachs) Hbf .... d.	...	...	1626	...	1726	1733	...	1826	...	1926	...	...	2026	...	2126	2126	2133	2233	2333	...	...	...	...	...	...
Glauchau (Sachs).......... **858** d.	...	...	1635	...	1735	1749	...	1835	...	1935	...	...	2035	...	2135	2135	2149	2249	2349	...	...	...	...	...	...
Chemnitz Hbf.............. **858** d.	...	...	1700	...	1800	1830	...	1900	...	2000	...	...	2100	...	2159	2200	2230	2330	0023	...	...	...	...	...	...
Flöha .... d.	...	...	1714	...	1815	1842	...	1914	...	2015	...	...	2114	...	...	2215	2242	2342	...	...	...	...	...	...	...
Freiberg (Sachs).................... d.	...	...	1731	...	1832	1907	...	1931	...	2032	...	...	2131	...	...	2232	2307	0006	...	...	...	...	...	...	...
Dresden Hbf .... a.	...	...	1802	...	1902	1951	...	2002	...	2102	...	...	2202	...	...	2302	2351	...	...	...	...	...	...	...	...

C – To Cheb on ⑥⑦ (Table **1121**).
E – To Cheb (Table **1121**).
L – To Leipzig (Table **881**).
N – Until June 30.
P – From July 1.
t – Arrives 0749.
◇ – Operated by Vogtlandbahn GmbH.
● – Most trains between Nürnberg and Pegnitz convey portions for two separate destinations. Passengers should take care to join the correct portion for their destination.

880 DRESDEN - HOF - NÜRNBERG

IRE / RE services

km			Ⓐ	Ⓒ	Ⓒ	Ⓐ						⚒			C							Ⓐ			E
0	**Dresden** Hbf d.	...	...	...	...	...	...	...	...	...	...	0455g	0555	...	...	...	0655	0755	...	...	...	0855	0906	0955	...
40	Freiberg (Sachs) d.	...	...	...	...	...	...	...	...	...	0449	0526g	0627	...	...	...	0726	0827	...	...	...	0926	0949	1027	...
66	Flöha d.	...	...	...	...	...	...	...	...	...	0513	0545g	0643	...	...	...	0745	0843	...	...	...	0945	1013	1043	...
79	**Chemnitz** Hbf 858 d.	...	...	...	...	...	0415	...	...	...	0530	0559	0659	...	...	...	0759	0859	...	...	...	0959	1030	1059	...
111	Glauchau (Sachs) 858 d.	...	...	...	...	...	0449	...	...	...	0604	0621	0721	...	...	...	0821	0921	...	...	...	1021	1104	1121	...
127	**Zwickau** (Sachs) Hbf d.	...	...	...	...	...	0506	0521	...	...	0621	0634	0734	...	...	...	0834	0934	...	...	...	1034	1121	1134	...
150	Reichenbach (Vogtl) ob Bf 881 d.	...	...	...	...	...	—	0537	...	...	—	0650	0750	...	...	...	0850	0950	...	...	...	1050	—	1150	...
175	Plauen (Vogtl) ob Bf 881 d.	...	...	...	...	...	...	0552	...	...	...	0706	0806	...	...	...	0906	1006	...	...	...	1106	...	1206	...
223	**Hof** Hbf 881 a.	...	...	...	...	...	...	0626	...	...	...	0733	0833	...	...	...	0933	1033	...	...	...	1133	...	1233	...
223	**Hof** Hbf 876 879 d.	...	0420	0517	...	0517g	...	0628	...	...	...	0737	0837	...	...	...	0937	1037	...	...	...	1137	...	1237	...
	Marktredwitz 879 d.	...	0442	0539	...	0548	...	0656	...	0741	...	|	0859	...	0944	...	|	1059	...	1144	...	|	...	1300	1331t
	Kirchenlaibach d.	...	0506	0555	...	0605	...	0711	...	0812	...	|	0915	...	1012	...	|	1115	...	1212	...	|	...	1316	1412
247	Münchberg 876 d.	...	|	|	...	|	Ⓐ	|	...	|	...	0753	|	...	|	...	0953	|	...	|	...	1153	...	|	|
295	**Bayreuth** Hbf 876 d.	0503	|	|	0556	|	0605	|	0713	|	0812	0827	|	0912	|	1013	1027	|	1112	|	1213	1227	1305	|	|
322	Pegnitz a.	0524	0528	0613	0618	0623	0628	0731	0737	0831	0835	|	0931	0936	1029	1034	|	1131	1136	1229	1234	|	1326	1333	1429
322	Pegnitz d.	0530	0530	0620	0620	0630	0630	0739	0739	...	0836	|	0939	0939	1037	1037	|	1139	1139	1237	1237	|	1336	1336	1437
361	Hersbruck (r Pegnitz) d.	0552	0552	0642	0642	0653	0653	0801	0801	...	0858	|	1001	1001	1059	1059	|	1201	1201	1259	1259	|	1358	1358	1459
389	**Nürnberg** Hbf a.	0607	0607	0700	0700	0710	0710	0817	0817	...	0915	0919	1018	1018	1115	1115	1119	1218	1218	1315	1315	1319	1415	1415	1515

							Ⓐ								Ⓑ						Ⓒ		⑤		
Dresden Hbf d.	...	1055	1155	...	...	...	1255	1355	...	...	...	1455	1555	...	1655	1706	...	1755	...	1855	1855	1955	2055	2106	2306
Freiberg (Sachs) d.	...	1126	1227	...	...	...	1326	1427	...	...	...	1526	1627	...	1726	1749	...	1827	...	1926	1926	2027	2126	2149	2349
Flöha d.	...	1145	1243	...	...	...	1345	1443	...	...	...	1545	1643	...	1745	1813	...	1843	...	1945	1945	2043	2145	2213	0013
Chemnitz Hbf 858 d.	...	1159	1259	...	...	...	1359	1459	...	...	...	1559	1659	...	1759	1830	...	1859	...	1959	1959	2059	2159	2230	0025
Glauchau (Sachs) 858 d.	...	1221	1321	...	...	...	1421	1521	...	...	...	1621	1721	...	1821	1904	...	1921	...	2021	2021	2121	2221	2304	...
Zwickau (Sachs) Hbf d.	...	1234	1334	...	...	...	1434	1534	...	...	...	1634	1734	...	1834	1921	...	1934	...	2034	2034	2133	2234	2321	...
Reichenbach (Vogtl) ob Bf. 881 d.	...	1250	1350	...	...	...	1450	1550	...	...	...	1650	1750	...	1850	—	...	1950	...	2050	2050	*2209*	2250	*0007*	...
Plauen (Vogtl) ob Bf 881 d.	...	1306	1406	...	...	...	1506	1606	...	...	...	1706	1806	...	1906	...	...	2006	...	2106	2106	*2235*	2306	...	...
Hof Hbf 881 a.	...	1333	1432	...	...	...	1533	1633	...	...	...	1733	1833	...	1933	...	...	2033	...	2133	2133	...	2335	...	...
Hof Hbf 876 879 d.	...	1337	1437	...	...	...	1537	1637	...	...	...	1737	1837	...	1937	C	...	2037	...	—	2137	...	...	...	...
Marktredwitz 879 d.	...	|	1459	...	1544	...	|	1659	...	1744	...	|	1859	...	|	1944	...	2100	...	...	|	...	...	...	...
Kirchenlaibach d.	...	|	1515	...	1612	...	|	1715	...	1812	...	|	1915	...	|	2012	...	2116	...	...	|	...	...	...	...
Münchberg 876 d.	...	1353	|	...	|	...	1553	|	...	|	...	1753	|	...	1953	|	...	|	...	...	2153	...	...	...	...
Bayreuth Hbf 876 d.	1413	1427	|	1512	|	1613	1627	|	1712	|	1813	1827	|	1912	2027	|	2013	|	2116	2213	2233	...	...	...	...
Pegnitz a.	1434	|	1531	1536	1629	1634	|	1731	1736	1829	1834	|	1931	1936	|	2029	2034	2132	2137	2233	|	...	...	...	...
Pegnitz d.	1437	|	1539	1539	1637	1637	|	1739	1739	1837	1837	|	1939	1939	|	2037	2037	2140	2140	2234	|	...	...	...	...
Hersbruck (r Pegnitz) d.	1459	|	1601	1601	1659	1659	|	1801	1801	1859	1859	|	2001	2001	|	2108	2108	2202	2202	2256	|	...	...	...	...
Nürnberg Hbf a.	1515	1519	1618	1618	1715	1715	1719	1818	1818	1915	1915	1919	2018	2018	2119	2124	2124	2219	2219	2313	2325	...	...	...	...

C – From Cheb on ⑥⑦ (Table **1121**).
E – From Cheb (Table **1121**).
g – ① only.
t – 1344 on Ⓒ.

881 HOF and ZWICKAU - LEIPZIG

RE / RB services

km				①–⑥		①–⑤													Ⓐ	Ⓒ			
	Hof Hbf 880 d.	...	...	...	*0428*a	...	0602	*0626*a	...	*0828*r	...	...	*1028*	...	...	*1228*a	...	...	1428	1433	...	...	*1628*a
	Plauen (Vogtl) ob Bf 880 d.	...	...	...	*0455*a	*0507*e	0632	*0655*a	*0706*	0900	...	*0906*	*1055*	...	...	1300	...	*1306*	1455	1501	...	*1506*	*1642*g
	Reichenbach (Vogtl) ob Bf 880 d.	...	...	...	*0509*a	*0533*e	0646	*0709*a	*0731*	0915	...	*0931*	1114	...	...	1315	...	*1331*	1515	1515	...	*1531*	1714
0	**Zwickau** (Sachs) Hbf 858 880 d.	0341	...	0509	0541	0609	0712	0739	0809	|	0939	1009	|	1139	1209	|	1339	1409	|	|	1539	1609	|
9	Werdau 858 d.	0351	...	0519	0551	0618	0720	0749	0818	0925	0949	1018	1125	1149	1218	1325	1349	1418	1525	1525	1549	1618	1725
29	Gößnitz 858 d.	0409	...	0535	0609	0635	0736	0807	0835	0940	1007	1035	1140	1207	1235	1340	1407	1435	1540	1540	1607	1635	1740
45	Altenburg d.	0425	0525	0551	0625	0651	0751	0825	0851	0956	1025	1051	1156	1225	1251	1356	1425	1451	1556	1556	1625	1651	1756
89	**Leipzig** Hbf a.	0519	0619	0632	0719	0732	0833	0919	0932	1039	1119	1132	1239	1319	1332	1439	1519	1532	1639	1639	1719	1732	1841

						⊡		
Hof Hbf 880 d.	...	...	*1828*	...	...	*2029*	...	...
Plauen (Vogtl) ob Bf 880 d.	...	*1706*a	*1855*	...	*1906*	*2056*	...	...
Reichenbach (Vogtl) ob Bf 880 d.	...	*1731*a	1914	...	*1931*	*2110*	...	...
Zwickau (Sachs) Hbf 858 880 d.	1739	1809	|	1939	2009	2141	...	...
Werdau 858 d.	1749	1818	1925	1949	2018	2151	...	...
Gößnitz 858 d.	1807	1835	1940	2007	2035	2209	...	...
Altenburg d.	1825	1851	1956	2025	2051	2225	2225	2325
Leipzig Hbf a.	1919	1932	2039	2119	2133	2318	2318	0019

km				①–⑤	Ⓐe				
0	**Leipzig** Hbf d.	0016	...	0428	0434	0534	0623	0721	0734
44	Altenburg d.	0109	...	0508	0528	0627	0705	0802	0828
60	Gößnitz 858 d.	...	...	0521	0544	0643	0718	0815	0844
80	Werdau 858 d.	...	...	0537	0603	0703	0734	0831	0903
	Zwickau (Sachs) Hbf 858 880 a.	...	...	0546	0614	0716	0743	|	0915
97	Reichenbach (Vogtl) ob Bf 880 a.	...	...	...	*0649*	*0749*	*0822*	0844	*0949*
122	Plauen (Vogtl) ob Bf 880 a.	...	...	...	*0705*	*0805*	*0851*	*0905*	*1005*
170	**Hof** Hbf 880 a.	...	...	...	*0733*	*0833*	...	*0933*	*1033*

														Ⓑ									
Leipzig Hbf d.	0825	0921	0934	1024	1121	1134	1224	1321	1334	1424	1521	1534	1624	1725	1734	1825	1921	1934	2024	2121	2134	...	2225
Altenburg d.	0905	1002	1028	1105	1202	1228	1305	1402	1428	1505	1602	1628	1705	1805	1828	1905	2002	2028	2105	2202	2228	...	2305
Gößnitz 858 d.	0918	1015	1044	1118	1215	1244	1318	1415	1444	1518	1615	1644	1718	1818	1844	1918	2015	2044	2118	2215	2244	...	2318
Werdau 858 d.	0934	1031	1103	1134	1231	1303	1334	1431	1503	1534	1631	1703	1734	1834	1903	1934	2031	2103	2134	2231	2303	...	2334
Zwickau (Sachs) Hbf 858 880 a.	0943	|	1115	1143	|	1315	1343	|	1515	1543	|	1715	1743	1843	1915	1943	|	2115	2144	|	2312	...	2344
Reichenbach (Vogtl) ob Bf 880 a.	*1022*	1043	*1149*	...	1243	*1349*	*1422*a	1444	*1549*	*1622*	1644	*1749*	*1822*	*1932*	*1949*	*2022*	2043	...	*2208*j	2243	...	...	*0007*k
Plauen (Vogtl) ob Bf 880 a.	*1051*	1100	*1205*	...	1259	*1405*	*1450*a	*1505*t	*1605*	*1651*	*1705*	*1805*	*1851*	*2000*	*2005*	*2051*	2059	...	*2235*j	2300	...	...	...
Hof Hbf 880 a.	...	*1133*a	*1233*	...	1326	*1432*	...	*1533*a	*1633*	...	*1733*	*1833*	...	...	*2033*	...	2126	...	...	*2335*f	...	...	...

a – Ⓐ only.
e – Not Nov. 18.
f – ⑤ only.
g – *1655* on Ⓐ.
j – Change trains at Lichtentanne (a. 2140, d. *2152*).
k – Change trains at Lichtentanne (a. 2340, d. *2352*).
r – ⚒ only.
t – *1522* on Ⓒ.
⊡ – ①②③④⑦.

882 CHEMNITZ - VEJPRTY - CHOMUTOV

DB (RB services); ČD

km								①–⑤	⑥⑦		
0	**Chemnitz** Hbf 880 d.	0736	0836	0936	1136	1336	1436	1536	1636	1836	2036
13	Flöha 880 d.	0747	0847	0947	1147	1347	1447	1547	1647	1847	2047
31	Zschopau d.	0810	0908	1010	1210	1410	1510	1610	1710	1910	2110
57	Annaberg-Buchholz Unt. d.	0846	0940	1046	1246	1446	1546	1646	1746	1946	2146
64	Cranzahl ⊖ d.	0900	1000r	1100	1259	1459	1606	1705	1806	2006	2159
74	Bärenstein (Annab) d.	0913c	1013	1113	...	...	1620a	...	1820	...	...
75	Vejprty 🏛 a.	0915c	1015	1115	...	...	1621a	...	1821	...	...
75	Vejprty 🏛 d.	...	*1019*z	...	...	...	...	...	*1824*	...	...
133	Chomutov a.	...	*1141*z	...	...	...	...	...	*1951*	...	...

							⑥⑦	⑥⑦		
Chomutov d.	...	*0803*z	...	...	...	...	*1620*	...	...	...
Vejprty 🏛 a.	...	*0930*z	...	...	...	...	*1742*	...	...	...
Vejprty 🏛 d.	...	0940c	1140	...	...	1635a	1750	1840	...	...
Bärenstein (Annab) d.	...	0942c	1142	...	...	1637a	1752	1842	...	...
Cranzahl ⊖ d.	0756	0956	1156	1356	1550	1650	1806	1856	1949	2056
Annaberg Buchholz Unt. d.	0810	1010	1210	1410	1610	1710	1816	1910	2010	2110
Zschopau d.	0846	1046	1246	1446	1646	1746	1848	1946	2046	2146
Flöha 880 a.	0908	1108	1308	1508	1708	1808	1908	2008	2108	2208
Chemnitz Hbf 880 a.	0919	1119	1319	1519	1719	1819	1919	2019	2119	2219

⊖ – **Cranzahl - Kurort Oberwiesenthal** *Fichtelbergbahn* (17 km, narrow gauge steam). Journey: 60 minutes. Operator: SDG Sächsische Dampfeisenbahngesellschaft GmbH, Bahnhofstraße 7, 09484 Kurort Oberwiesenthal. ✆ + 49 (0) 37348 151 0.
From **Cranzahl** at 1010, 1110**k**, 1310, 1510**k**, 1710 and 1810**m**. From **Kurort Oberwiesenthal** at 0850, 0940**k**, 1140, 1340**k**, 1540 and 1640**m**.

a – ①–⑤ (not Nov. 18).
c – ⑥⑦ (also Nov. 18).
k – Not Nov. 2–20.
m – ⑥⑦ to June 21; daily June 27 - Aug. 30; ⑥⑦ from Sept. 5 (not Nov. 7–15).
r – Arrives 0950.
z – ⑥⑦ only.

883 CHEMNITZ - AUE

RB services

km											
0	**Chemnitz** Hbf d.	0610	0810	0910	1110	1310	1510	1710	1910	2110	2240
27	Thalheim d.	0658	0853	0958	1158	1358	1558	1758	1958	2158	2320
36	Zwönitz d.	0709	0904	1009	1209	1409	1609	1809	2009	2209	2331
47	Lößnitz unt Bf ⊗ d.	0720	0915	1020	1220	1420	1620	1820	2020	2220	2342
51	**Aue** (Sachs) a.	0725	0920	1025	1225	1425	1625	1825	2025	2225	2347

		Ⓐe									Ⓒz	
Aue (Sachs) d.	0403	0530	0629	0820	0929	1129	1329	1529	1729	1929	2031	2129
Lößnitz unt Bf ⊗ d.	0408	0536	0634	0825	0934	1134	1334	1534	1734	1934	2036	2134
Zwönitz d.	0420	0547	0646	0837	0946	1146	1346	1546	1746	1946	2048	2146
Thalheim d.	0436	0558	0658	0858	0958	1158	1358	1558	1758	1958	2059	2156
Chemnitz Hbf a.	0515	0640	0740	0940	1040	1240	1440	1640	1840	2040	2140	2234

e – Not Nov. 18.
z – Also Nov. 18.
⊗ – Trains stop on request only.

DB; ČD (2nd class only) ZWICKAU - JOHANNGEORGENSTADT - KARLOVY VARY 884

km		Ⓐe								
0	**Zwickau** (Sachs) Hbf ... d.	0505	0605	and	1905	2005	2105	2205	2305	...
27	Aue (Sachs) ... d.	0537	0637	hourly	1937	2037	2137	2237	2337	...
37	Schwarzenberg (Erzg) . d.	0556	0656	until	1956	2056	2156	2256	2350**z**	...
56	**Johanngeorgenstadt** . a.	0621	0721		2021	2121	2221	2321**z**	...	...

								Ⓒz
Johanngeorgenstadt ... d.	0430**e**	0530	0630	and	1930	2030	2130	2230
Schwarzenberg (Erzg) ... d.	0454	0554	0654	hourly	1954	2054	2154	2254
Aue (Sachs) ... d.	0507	0607	0707	until	2007	2107	2207	2307
Zwickau (Sachs) Hbf ... a.	0539	0639	0739		2039	2139	2239	2339

km	▶	Ⓐ					Ⓒ	Ⓐ			
0	**Johanngeorgenstadt** . d.	...	0725	1032	1245	...	1432	1432	1537**c**	1735	*2047*
1	Potůčky 🛃 ... d.	0608	0728	1039	1250	...	1437	1437	1541	1740	*2051*
28	Nejdek ... d.	0705	0818	1129	1342	1420	1525	1540	1635	1836	2225
44	**Karlovy Vary** ... a.	0734	0845	1155	1409**a**	1446	1551	1606	1701	1902	2250
47	**Karlovy Vary** dolní ... a.	0740	0854	1201	1415**a**	1458	1557	1613	1712	1908	2256

▶	Ⓒ				Ⓐ	Ⓒ			
Karlovy Vary dolní ... d.	0507	0541**a**	0745	0952	1214	1259	1448	1755	2103
Karlovy Vary ... d.	0513	0547**a**	0751	0958	1220	1306	1454	1801	2110
Nejdek ... d.	0539	0626	0819	1026	1308**f**	1337	1526	1830	2136
Potůčky 🛃 ... d.	...	0718	0908	1118	1358	1424	1618	1918	*2308*
Johanngeorgenstadt ... a.	...	0720	0910	1120	1400	1426	1620	1920	...

a – Ⓐ only.
c – Ⓒ only.
e – Ⓐ (not Nov. 18).
f – Arrives 1246.
z – Ⓒ (also Nov. 18).
▶ – Czech holiday dates apply (see page 2).

DB (*RE* / *RB* services); ČD REGENSBURG - SCHWANDORF - FURTH IM WALD - PLZEŇ 885

km		2	2 Ⓐ		351	2			2	2	355 ‡🍷	2	2 ⑥⑦	2 ⑥⑦	2	‡	353	2			2	2	357 ‡🍷	2	2	2
	München Hbf **878** .. d.	...	...	...	...	...	...	...	...	...	0844	...	...	...	...	1244	...	...	...	...	...	...	1643	...	...	...
0	**Regensburg** Hbf **879** d.	...	*0527*	0623	...	*0729*	0832	...	*0931*	...	1022	*1130*	*1230*	...	*1331*	1419	...	*1528*	1633	...	...	*1737*	1819	*1929*	*2031*	*2221*
	Nürnberg Hbf **886** .. d.	...	|	|	0540	|	|	0752	|	...	|	|	|	...	|	|	1339	|	|	1553	...	|	|	|	|	|
42	**Schwandorf** ...... **879** d.	...	0559	0650	0655	0803	0900	0905	1004	...	1056	1203	1305	...	1405	1446	1456	1602	1700	1705	...	1804	1856	2003	2107	2306
90	Cham (Oberpf) ... d.	...	0639	▬	0726	0839	▬	0940	1039	...	1124	1239	1339	...	1439	...	1524	1639	...	1740	...	1839	1924	2041	2142	2341
109	**Furth im Wald** 🛃 ..... a.	...	0656	2	0740	0856	2	0956	1056	...	1139	1256	1356	...	1456	...	1539	1657	...	1758	...	1856	1939	2058	2159	2358**f**
109	**Furth im Wald** 🛃 ..... d.	...	...	*0703*	0749	...	0906	...	...	1103	1149	...	...	1402	*1516*	...	1549	...	...	...	1806	...	1949	...	...	...
131	Domažlice ... d.	0606	...	0731	0810	...	0930	...	...	1127	1210	...	...	1426	*1540*	...	1610	...	...	...	1835	...	2010	...	...	...
190	**Plzeň** Hlavni ... a.	0731	...	0852	0857	...	*1055***v**	...	...	*1252*	1257	...	...	*1555*	...	...	1657	...	...	...	1955	...	2057	...	...	...
	Praha Hlavní **1120** . a.	...	...	...	1050	...	...	...	...	...	1450	...	...	...	...	...	1850	...	...	...	...	...	2250	...	...	...

	2 Ⓐ	2	Ⓐ	Ⓒ		2	350	2	2		2	2	354 ‡🍷	2 ⑥⑦	2 ⑥⑦	2	2	2	352	2	2	2	2	356 ‡🍷	2	2
Praha Hlavní **1120** .. d.	...	...	...	...	...	...	0511	...	...	...	...	...	0911	...	...	...	...	...	1311	...	...	...	...	1711	...	...
Plzeň Hlavni ... d.	...	...	...	...	...	...	0700	*0705*	...	...	*0808*	...	1100	*1105*	...	...	*1208*	...	1500	*1510***a**	...	...	...	1900	...	2252
Domažlice ... d.	...	0528	...	...	...	...	0746	0828	...	...	1028	...	1146	1228	...	...	1428	...	1546	1636	...	...	...	1946	...	0005
Furth im Wald 🛃 ...... a.	...	0552	...	...	...	...	0811	0852	...	...	1052	...	1211	1252	...	...	1452	...	1611	1700	...	...	...	2011	...	...
Furth im Wald 🛃 ...... d.	0448	...	0556	0600	...	0701**r**	0821	▬	0901	1002	▬	1102	1221	...	1301	1401	...	1502	1621	▬	1704	1800	*1902*	2021	2104	...
Cham (Oberpf) ... d.	0503	...	0612	0616	...	0726	0835	‡	0917	1017	...	1124	1235	...	1317	1417	...	1524	1635	‡	1718	1817	1928	2037	2120	...
Schwandorf ...... **879** a.	0539	...	0648	0648	0653	0759	0903	0908	0955	1055	1100	1157	1303	...	1357	1455	...	1600	1703	1708	1757	1855	2001	2105	2158	...
Nürnberg Hbf **886** ... a.	|	...	0806	0821	|	|	1009	|	|	1222	|	|	|	...	|	|	...	|	1809	|	|	|	|	|	|	...
Regensburg Hbf . **879** a.	*0621*	...	...	...	0722	*0834*	...	0937	*1034*	...	1129	*1234*	1337	...	*1434*	*1529*	...	*1637*	...	1736	*1836*	*1929*	*2037*	2148	*2237*	...
München Hbf **878** ... a.	...	...	...	...	...	...	...	1115	...	...	...	...	1515	...	...	...	...	...	...	1915	...	...	...	2324	...	...

a – Ⓐ only.
f – ⑤⑥ only.
r – ⚒ (not Aug. 15). Departs *0705* on ⑥ (change trains at Cham).
v – ①–⑥ (not July 6, Sept. 28).
‡ – *ALX* in Germany (operated by Arriva / Regentalbahn AG - Die Länderbahn).

RE services NÜRNBERG - SCHWANDORF and WEIDEN 886

Nürnberg - Schwandorf

km				Ⓐ	P								P			Ⓐ		Ⓐ								
0	**Nürnberg** Hbf .... ◧d.	0012	...	0434	0540	0648	0752	0848	0936	1048	1136	1248	1339	1353	1448	1536	1553	1636	1653	1736	1753	1848	1953	2055	2153	2250
28	Hersbruck (r Pegnitz) ◧d.	0029	...	0449	|	0712	0812	0912	0951	1112	1151	1312	|	1412	1512	1551	1612	1651	1712	1751	1812	1912	2012	2117	2212	2312
68	Amberg ... d.	0101	...	0532	0630	0743	0843	0943	1028	1143	1228	1341	1431	1443	1543	1629	1643	1731	1744	1828	1843	1943	2043	2147	2246	2347
94	**Schwandorf** ... a.	...	...	0551	0647	0757	0857	0957	1044	1157	1243	1357	1450	1457	1557	1644	1657	1746	1759	1843	1857	1957	2057	2203	2301	0001
	Furth im Wald **885** . a.	...	...	...	0740	...	0956	...	...	...	...	...	1539	...	...	...	1758	...	...	...	...	...	...	...	...	...

	Ⓐ	⚒	†	Ⓐ	⚒	†	Ⓐ	Ⓒ		P									P							
Furth im Wald **885** .. d.	...	...	...	...	...	...	0556	0600	...	0821	...	...	1002	...	...	...	...	...	1621	...	...	...	...	...	...	...
Schwandorf ... d.	0400	0513	0516	0544	0557	0609	0701	0709	0809	0904	0911	1009	1109	1209	1309	1409	1509	1609	1704	1711	1809	1907	2009	2113	2205	2309
Amberg ... d.	0416	0529	0532	0603	0615	0628	0718	0727	0824	0921	0929	1024	1124	1224	1326	1424	1524	1626	1721	1729	1824	1922	2024	2132	2222	2326
Hersbruck (r pegnitz) .. d.	0452**t**	0606	0606	0636**t**	0648	0707	0750	0806	0907	|	1007	1108	1207	1308	1406	1508	1607	1708	|	1807	1908	2007	2108	2207	2306	...
Nürnberg Hbf ... a.	0516	0621	0621	0656**z**	0706	0723	0806	0821	0923	1009	1022	1123	1222	1323	1421	1523	1622	1723	1809	1822	1923	2022	2124	2223	2321	...

Nürnberg - Weiden

km		Ⓐ								
0	**Nürnberg** Hbf .... ◧d.	0434	0535	0625	0737	0836	and	2036	...	2250
28	Hersbruck (r Pegnitz) ◧d.	0449	0551	0643	0752	0851	hourly	2051	...	2312
97	**Weiden** (Oberpf) .... a.	0541	0645	0745	0845	0945	until	2145	...	0007

	Ⓐ	⚒			❖				
Weiden (Oberpf) ... d.	0415	0505	0612	0710	and	1809	1910	2010	2213
Hersbruck (r Pegnitz) ... d.	0514**t**	0606	0707	0806	hourly	1908	2007	2108	2306
Nürnberg Hbf ... a.	0536	0621	0723	0821	until	1923	2022	2124	2321

P – To / from Praha (Table **885**).
t – Aug. 3 - Sept. 11 only.
z – 0701 Aug. 3 - Sept. 11.
❖ – Certain trains depart Weiden at 09 minutes past the hour.
◧ – Certain trains from Nürnberg and Hersbruck convey portions for two separate destinations. Passengers should take care to join the correct portion for their destination.

RB services BAYREUTH - WEIDEN 887

km		Ⓐ	Ⓐ			Ⓐ					Ⓐ			Ⓐ			Ⓐ		Ⓐ		Ⓐ		Ⓑw			
0	**Bayreuth** Hbf ... d.	0440	0543	0615	0716	0818	0818	0918	1018	1118	1218	1218	1318	1418	1418	1518	1618	1618	1644	1718	1818	1818	1918	1918	2018	2229
19	Kirchenlaibach .. a.	0457	0600	0632	0739	0839	0839	0939	1039	1139	1239	1239	1339	1439	1439	1539	1639	1639	1701	1739	1839	1839	1939	1939	2039	2246
19	Kirchenlaibach .. d.	*0532*	...	0655	0746	0846	...	0946	...	1146	1246	...	1346	1446	...	1546	1646	...	...	1746	1846	...	1946	...	...	...
59	**Weiden** ... a.	*0607*	...	0725	0817	0917	...	1017	...	1217	1317	...	1417	1517	...	1617	1717	...	...	1817	1917	...	2017	...	...	...

	Ⓐ	Ⓐ	⚒	Ⓐ	Ⓑw		Ⓐ					Ⓐ			Ⓐ			Ⓐ			Ⓐ				Ⓒ	
Weiden ... d.	0428	0524	...	0631	...	0731	0831	...	0931	...	1131	1231	...	1331	1431	...	1531	1631	...	1731	1831	...	1931	...	2131	...
Kirchenlaibach ... a.	0500	0557	...	0707	...	0808	0908	...	1008	...	1208	1308	...	1408	1508	...	1608	1708	...	1808	1908	...	2008	...	2203	...
Kirchenlaibach ... d.	0509	0608	0651	0717	0717	0819	0919	0919	1019	1119	1219	1319	1319	1419	1519	1519	1619	1719	1719	1819	1919	1919	2019	2119	...	2208
Bayreuth Hbf ... a.	0526	0629	0707	0734	0734	0836	0936	0936	1036	1136	1236	1336	1336	1436	1536	1536	1636	1736	1736	1836	1936	1936	2036	2136	...	2225

w – Also Oct. 3.

RB services; 2nd class only KEMPTEN - REUTTE IN TIROL - GARMISCH-PARTENKIRCHEN 888

km		B								
0	**Kempten** (Allgäu) Hbf ... d.	...	0717	0917	1017	1117	1317	1517	1717	1917
18	Oy-Mittelberg ... d.	...	0749	0948	1048	1148	1348	1549	1748	1948
24	Nesselwang ... d.	...	0800	0959	1059	1159	1359	1600	1759	1959
31	Pfronten-Ried ... d.	0631	0813	1013	1113	1213	1413	1613	1813	2013
33	**Pfronten-Steinach** 🛃 ... d.	0635	0818	1018	1128	1218	1418	1618	1818	2018
38	Vils 🛃 ... d.	0643	0826	1033	1137	1226	1426	1626	1841	2026
48	**Reutte in Tirol** ... a.	0658	0841	1048	1152	1241	1441	1641	1856	2041
	Change trains	**d**			|					
48	**Reutte in Tirol** ... d.	0700	0903	1103	1154**k**	1303	1500**h**	1703	1903	...
68	Lermoos ... d.	0726	0929	1129	1221**k**	1329	1527	1729	1929	...
71	Ehrwald Zugspitzbahn 🛃 ... d.	0731	0934	1134	1226**k**	1334	1533	1734	1934	...
93	**Garmisch**-Partenkirchen ... a.	0756	0959	1201	...	1359	1559	1759	1959	...

			⑥⑦c			⑥⑦c	A			
Garmisch-Partenkirchen .. d.	...	0804	0906	1004	1204	1404	1438	1604	1804	2006
Ehrwald Zugspitzbahn 🛃 . d.	...	0829	0935	1029	1229	1429	1503	1629	1829	2031
Lermoos ... d.	...	0833	0940	1033	1233	1433	1507	1633	1833	2035
Reutte in Tirol ... a.	...	0859	1005	1059	1259	1459	1536	1700	1859	2100
Change trains			⑥⑦c			**d**	▬			
Reutte in Tirol ... d.	0717	0917	1017	1103	1317	1517	...	1717	1917	2105
Vils 🛃 ... d.	0731	0931	1031	1117	1331	1531	...	1731	1931	2119
Pfronten-Steinach 🛃 ... d.	0741	0941	1041	1128	1341	1541	1639	1743	1943	2139
Pfronten-Ried ... d.	0747	0947	1047	1145	1347	1547	1645	1747	1947	2145
Nesselwang ... d.	0801	1001	1101	1201	1401	1601	1701	1801	2001	2206
Oy-Mittelberg ... d.	0812	1012	1112	1212	1412	1612	1712	1812	2012	2218
Kempten (Allgäu) Hbf ... a.	0843	1043	1143	1243	1443	1643	1743	1843	2043	2251

A – ①–⑤ (not Oct. 26, Dec. 8).
B – ①–⑥ (not Aug. 15, Oct. 26, Dec. 8).
c – Also Oct. 26, Dec. 8.
d – Runs daily from Reutte.
h – 1503 on ⑥⑦ (also Oct. 26, Dec. 8).
k – ①–⑤ (not July 13 - Sept. 11, Oct. 26, Dec. 8).

890 MÜNCHEN - SALZBURG

km		RB 30061 Ⓐ	RB 30063 Ⓐ		RB 30001 Ⓐ	RB 30003	EC* 61	RB 30007	EC 111	RE 30009	RJ 63	RB 30011	EC 317	RE 30013	RJ 65	RB 30015	EC 113	RB 30017	RJ 67	RB 30019	IC 2083	EC 115	RE 30021 30051	RJ 69
			2				✕		✕◆		B 🍷		✕◆		🍷		✕◆		B 🍷		🍷◆	✕◆		🍷
	Frankfurt Hbf **911** d.	...	...	...	...	...	...	...	...	...	...	...	...	...	...	...	0820	...	...	...	...	...	...	...
	Stuttgart Hbf **930** d.	...	...	...	...	...	...	...	...	...	...	...	0758	...	...	...	0958	...	...	...	...	1158	...	...
0	**München** Hbf **951** d.	...	...	...	0551	0638	0726	0741	0827	0847	0927	0941	1021	1047	1126	1141	1221	1241	1326	1341	...	1421	1446	1526
10	München Ost **951** d.	...	...	...	0600	0646	|	0750	|	0855	|	0949	1030	1055	|	1149	1230	1249	|	1349	1414	1430	1455	|
65	Rosenheim **951** d.	0542	...	...	0641	0731	|	0831	0904	0931	|	1030	1102	1131	|	1230	1302	1331	|	1430	1444	1502	1531	|
82	Bad Endorf d.	0554	...	...	0653	0742	|	0849	|	0942	|	1049	|	1142	|	1249	|	1342	|	1449	1457	|	1543	|
90	Prien am Chiemsee d.	0601	...	...	0701	0750	|	0856	0921	0950	|	1056	1119	1150	|	1256	1319	1350	|	1456	1504	1519	1550	|
118	Traunstein d.	0625	0656	...	0725	0814	|	0917	0940	1014	|	1117	1138	1214	|	1319	1338	1415	|	1519	1526	1538	1615	|
147	Freilassing **891** d.	0645	0718	...	0745	0834	|	0938	0959	1035	|	1138	1157	1235	|	1339	1357	1435	|	1540	1546	1557	1639	|
153	**Salzburg** Hbf 🏛 **891** a.	0652	0726	...	0752	0841	0854	0947	1006	1041	1054	1147	1204	1241	1254	1347	1404	1442	1454	1547	...	1604	1647	1654
	Wien Westbahnhof **950** a.	...	...	...	...	...	1140	...	...	...	1340	...	...	...	1540	...	...	...	1740	...	...	...	...	1940

	RB 30023	EC 319	RE 30025 Ⓐ	RE 30027	ICE 261	RB 30029 Ⓒ	RE 30031 Ⓐ	EC 117 Ⓑ	RE 30033	IC 2265 Ⓑ	RB 30035	EC 391	RE 30037	RB 27097	RB 30039		RE 30041	RB 5050		D 499	EN 463	RB 30043	RB 30043 ⑤⑥	RB 30067 Ⓐ
		✕◆			✕			✕◆		🍷◆		🍷◆						2		🍷◆	🍷◆			
Frankfurt Hbf **911** d.	...	1220	...	...	...	...	...	1420	...	...	...	1620	...	...	...	...	...	...	...	...	...	...	...	...
Stuttgart Hbf **930** d.	...	1358	...	...	...	...	...	1558	...	1653	...	1758	...	...	...	...	...	...	...	...	...	...	...	...
München Hbf **951** d.	1541	1622	1626	1647	1723	1739	1758	1820	1847	1921	1941	2024	2046	...	2148	...	2245	...	...	2340	2340	2350	2350	...
München Ost **951** d.	1549	1631	1636	1656	|	1748	1806	1830	1855	1930	1949	2034	2054	...	2156	...	2253	...	...	|	|	2358	2358	...
Rosenheim **951** d.	1630	1703	1709	1731	|	1838	1838	1902	1931	2002	2030	2105	2132	...	2237	...	2331	...	...	0020	0020	0038	0039	0042
Bad Endorf d.	1649	|	1721	1743	|	1850	1850	|	1942	2015	2049	2117	2143	...	2249	...	2342	...	...	|	|	...	0051	0055
Prien am Chiemsee d.	1656	1720	1728	1750	|	1857	1857	1919	1950	2023	2056	2125	2151	...	2256	...	2350	...	...	|	|	...	0058	0102
Traunstein d.	1719	1738	1753	1815	|	1921	1921	1938	2014	2041	2119	2144	2214	...	2319	...	0014	...	...	|	|	...	0121	0127
Freilassing **891** d.	1740	1757	1814	1838	|	1942	1942	1957	2035	2100	2140	2202	2235	2240	2340	...	0034	0039	...	|	|	...	0142	0148
Salzburg Hbf 🏛 **891** a.	1747	1804	...	1844	1853	1949	1949	2004	2042	2107	2147	2209	...	2247	2347	...	...	0047	...	0117	0117	...	0148	...
Wien Westbahnhof **950** a.	...	...	...	...	2140	...	...	...	...	...	...	...	...	...	...	...	...	...	...	...	0545h	...	...	...

	RB 30000 Ⓐ	EN 462	D 498		RB 30002 Ⓐ	RB 5051 Ⓐ	RE 30004	IC 2290 ①–⑥	RE 30006 Ⓐ	RB 30010 Ⓒ	RE 30008 Ⓐ	IC 2264 ⊡	IC 1916 ⑤	RB 30012 Ⓐ	RE 30014	EC 390 ①–⑥	RB 30016	ICE 260	RE 30018	IC 2082	EC 318	RB 30020	RJ 262	RB 30022
		🍷◆	🍷◆			2		🍷				🍷◆	🍷◆			🍷◆		✕		🍷◆	✕◆		🍷	
Wien Westbahnhof **950** d.	...	0009h	...	...	...	...	...	...	...	...	...	...	...	...	...	...	...	0614	...	...	...	...	0820	...
Salzburg Hbf 🏛 **891** d.	...	0428	0428	...	...	0510	...	0547	...	0607	*0611*r	0646	0646	...	0709	0753	0817	0902	0918	...	0957	1011	1103	1118
Freilassing **891** d.	0413	|	|	...	0452	0518	0522	0555	0607	0618	0622	0654	0654	0658	0725	0801	0824	|	0925	0942	1005	1019	|	1125
Traunstein d.	0433	|	|	...	0512	...	0543	0613	0628	0637	0650	0712	0712	0718	0745	0819	0845	|	0945	1000	1023	1039	|	1145
Prien am Chiemsee d.	0457	|	|	...	0535	...	0607	0631	0652	0708	0708	0730	0730	0741	0809	0837	0909	|	1009	1021	1041	1103	|	1209
Bad Endorf d.	0504	|	|	...	0542	...	0615	0639	0700	0715	0715	0738	0738	0748	0816	|	0916	|	1016	1029	|	1110	|	1216
Rosenheim **951** d.	0519	0528	0528	...	0557	...	0630	0653	0715	0730	0729	0753	0753	0803	0831	0856	0931	|	1031	1043	1100	1130	|	1231
München Ost **951** a.	0557	0602	0602	...	0635	...	0702	0721	0746	0807	0758	0821	0821	0840	0902	0924	1009	|	1102	1112	|	1208	|	1309
München Hbf **951** a.	0608	0615	0615	...	0645	...	0713	0733	0800	0817	0809	0833	0833	0853	0913	0935	1020	1031	1113	...	1137	1219	1231	1320
Stuttgart Hbf **930** a.	...	...	...	...	...	...	...	1000	...	...	...	1107	1107	...	...	1200	...	...	...	...	1400	...	...	...
Frankfurt Hbf **911** a.	...	...	...	...	...	...	...	1140	...	...	...	...	...	...	...	1340	...	...	...	...	1540	...	...	...

	EC 114	RB 30024	RJ 60	RE 30028	EC 112	RB 30030		RB 30032	EC 316	RB 30034	EC* 64	RE 30036		RB 30038	RJ 66	RE 30040	EC 110	RB 30042	RJ 68	RE 30044		RB 30070	RB 30062	
	✕◆		B 🍷		✕◆				✕◆		✕				B 🍷		✕◆		🍷					
Wien Westbahnhof **950** d.	...	...	1020	...	...	...	...	...	...	...	1420	...	...	...	1620	...	...	...	1820	...	...	...	...	...
Salzburg Hbf 🏛 **891** d.	1152	1211	1303	1314	1352	1411	...	1518	1552	1611	1702	1718	...	1812	1903	1918	1952	2013	2102	2118	...	2258	...	...
Freilassing **891** d.	1200	1219	|	1325	1400	1420	...	1525	1600	1619	|	1725	...	1819	|	1925	2000	2020	|	2125	...	2304	...	...
Traunstein d.	1218	1239	|	1345	1418	1440	...	1545	1618	1639	|	1745	...	1839	|	1945	2018	2040	|	2145	...	2326	...	...
Prien am Chiemsee d.	1236	1303	|	1409	1436	1503	...	1609	1636	1703	|	1809	...	1903	|	2009	2036	2110	|	2209	...	2351	0006	...
Bad Endorf d.	1244	1310	|	1416	|	1510	...	1616	|	1710	|	1816	...	1910	|	2016	|	2117	|	2216	...	...	0013	...
Rosenheim **951** d.	1258	1330	|	1431	1455	1530	...	1631	1655	1730	|	1831	...	1930	|	2031	2055	2131	|	2231	...	...	0025	...
München Ost **951** a.	|	1408	|	1502	1523	1607	...	1708	1723	1808	|	1902	...	2007	|	2102	2123	2208	|	2302	...	...	...	...
München Hbf **951** a.	1335	1418	1431	1513	1535	1617	...	1719	1735	1818	1833	1913	...	2018	2034	2113	2135	2219	2230	2313	...	...	...	...
Stuttgart Hbf **930** a.	1559	...	...	...	1800	...	...	...	2000	...	...	...	...	...	...	...	...	...	...	...	...	...	...	...
Frankfurt Hbf **911** a.	...	...	...	...	1940	...	...	...	...	...	...	...	...	...	...	...	...	...	...	...	...	...	...	...

◆ – **NOTES** (LISTED BY TRAIN NUMBER)

110/1 – ⟨12⟩ and ✕ Klagenfurt - Villach - München and v.v.; ⟨12⟩ Beograd (**210/1**) - Vinkovci - Zagreb - Dobova 🏛 - Ljubljana - Jesenice 🏛 - Villach - München and v.v.

112/3 – ⟨12⟩ and ✕ Klagenfurt - Villach - München - Frankfurt and v.v.; ⟨12⟩ Zagreb (**212/3**) - Dobova 🏛 - Ljubljana - Jesenice 🏛 - Villach - München - Frankfurt and v.v.

114 – WÖRTHERSEE – ⟨12⟩ and ✕ Klagenfurt - Villach - München - Mannheim - Mainz - Köln - Dortmund.

115 – WÖRTHERSEE – ⟨12⟩ and ✕ Münster - Köln - Mainz - Mannheim - München - Villach - Klagenfurt.

117 – ⟨12⟩ and ✕ Frankfurt - Stuttgart - München - Villach - Klagenfurt.

316/7 – ⟨12⟩ and ✕ Graz - Selzthal - Bischofshofen - Salzburg - Stuttgart - Mannheim - Saarbrücken and v.v.

318/9 – ⟨12⟩ and ✕ Graz - Selzthal - Bischofshofen - Salzburg - Stuttgart - Frankfurt and v.v.

390 – ⟨12⟩ and 🍷 Linz - Salzburg - Frankfurt.

391 – ⟨12⟩ and 🍷 Frankfurt - Salzburg (- Linz Ⓑ).

462/3 – KÁLMÁN IMRE – 🛏 1, 2 cl., ▬ 2 cl., ⟨2⟩ and 🍷 Budapest - Wien - München and v.v. 🛏 1, 2 cl. and ▬ 1, 2 cl. Bucureşti - Timişoara - Budapest - München and v.v.

498 – LISINSKI – 🛏 1, 2 cl., ▬ 2 cl. and ⟨2⟩ Zagreb - Dobova 🏛 - Ljubljana - Jesenice 🏛 - Villach - München; ⟨2⟩ Beograd (**418**) - Vinkovci (**748**) - Zagreb (**296**) - München. Until Sept. 18 (from Rijeka) conveys 🛏 1, 2 cl. and ▬ 2 cl. Rijeka (**480**) - Ljubljana (**296**) - München.

499 – LISINSKI – 🛏 1, 2 cl., ▬ 2 cl. and ⟨2⟩ München - Villach - Jesenice 🏛 - Ljubljana - Dobova 🏛 - Zagreb; ⟨2⟩ München - Zagreb (**741**) - Vinkovci (**419**) - Beograd. Until Sept. 19 conveys 🛏 1, 2 cl. and ▬ 2 cl. München - Ljubljana (**481**) - Rijeka.

1916 – ⟨12⟩ and 🍷 Salzburg - Köln - Dortmund - Berlin.

2082/3 – KÖNIGSEE – ⟨12⟩ Berchtesgaden - Augsburg - Hamburg and v.v. See Table **900** for timings to / from Hamburg.

2264/5 – ⟨12⟩ and 🍷 Salzburg - Karlsruhe and v.v.

B – ⟨12⟩ and 🍷 München - Wien - Hegyeshalom 🏛 - Györ - Budapest and v.v.

h – Wien **Hütteldorf**.

r – Not Oct. 26, Dec. 8.

***** – *RJ* from Sept. 6.

⊡ – ①②③④⑥.

891 (SCHWARZACH -) SALZBURG - BERCHTESGADEN

RB services (2nd class only)

km		L	Ⓐ		Ⓐ	Ⓒ					Ⓒ	Ⓐ	Ⓐ	Ⓒ			H								Ⓒ
	Schwarzach-St Veit ◐ d.	0453	...	...	0623	0623	0723	0823	0923	1023	1123	1123	1223	1223	1323	1423	...	1523	1623	...	1823	1923	...	2123	2223
	Bischofshofen ◐ d.	0509	...	...	0639	0639	0739	0839	0939	1039	1139	1139	1239	1239	1339	1439	...	1539	1639	1739	1839	1939	2039	2139	2239
0	**Salzburg** Hbf ◐ **890** d.	0611	...	*0709*	0742	0742	0842	0942	1042	1142	1242	1242	1342	1342	1442	1542	...	1642	1742	1845	1942	2042	2142	2242	2342
6	Freilassing **890** a.	0619	...	*0715*	0750	0750	0850	0950	1050	1150	1250	1250	1350	1350	1450	1550	...	1650	1750	1853	1950	2050	2150	2250	2350
6	Freilassing d.	...	0634	0720	0759	0759	0851	1001	1051	1159	1251	1252	1352	1359	1451	...	1600	1651	1800	1854	1959	2104	2203	2251	2352
21	Bad Reichenhall d.	...	0652	0741	0817	0817	0911	1019	1109	1217	1309	1314	1418	1418	1509	...	1619	1709	1818	1912	2017	2121	2220	2309	0008
39	**Berchtesgaden** Hbf a.	...	0727	0810	0855	0902	0945	1048	1138	1251	1339	1343	1447	1447	1539	...	1650	1744	1852	1941	2051	2150	2250	2338	...

	Ⓐ	⑥n	Ⓐ		Ⓐ		Ⓒ H	Ⓐ H						Ⓒ	Ⓐ						Ⓐ				
Berchtesgaden Hbf d.	*0505**	0620	0621	0709	0816	...	0827	0837	...	0910	1011	1102	1216	1302	1324	1411	1502	1613	1708	...	...	1817	1905	2016	2214
Bad Reichenhall d.	0546	0650	0656	0740	0847	0847	0910	0910	...	0940	1046	1135	1246	1336	1357	1445	1536	1647	1740	...	1817	1849	1939	2046	2247
Freilassing a.	0602	0706	0713	0756	0907	0907	0928	0928	...	0957	1106	1155	1307	1353	1414	1506	1556	1707	1759	...	1833	1912	1955	2103	2307
Freilassing **890** d.	0608	0708	*0718*	0808	0908	0908	...	...	0938	1008	1108	1208	1308	1408	1417	1508	1608	1708	...	1808	*1838*	1917	2008	2108	2308
Salzburg Hbf ◐ **890** a.	0616	0716	*0726*	0816	0916	0916	...	...	0947	1016	1116	1216	1316	1416	1425	1516	1616	1716	...	1816	*1844*	1924	2016	2116	2316
Bischofshofen ◐ a.	0720	0820	...	0920	1020	1020	...	...	...	1120	1220	1320	1420	1520	...	1620	1720	1820	...	1920	...	...	2120	2220	0023
Schwarzach-St Veit ◐ a.	0736	0836	...	0936	1036	1036	...	...	...	1136	1236	1336	1436	1536	...	1636	1736	1836	...	1936	...	...	2136	2236	...

H – *IC* **2082/3**: KÖNIGSSEE – ⟨12⟩ and 🍷 Berchtesgaden - Hamburg and v.v. Train category *RE* Berchtesgaden - Freilassing and v.v.

L – ①–⑥ (not Aug. 15, Oct. 26, Dec. 8).

n – Not Aug. 15, Oct. 3.

***** – By 🚌 to Bad Reichenhall.

◐ – For other services see Tables **960** / **970**.

FLUGHAFEN MÜNCHEN ✈ (S-Bahn services S1, S8) 892

2nd class only

km		S8	S8	S8	S8		S8	S1	S8	S1	S8	S1	S8		S1	S8	S1	S8	S1	S8	S8
0	**München** Pasing d.	0009	0049	0143	0309	and every	0449	...	0509	...	0529	...	0549	and at the	...	2249	...	2309	...	2329	2349
7	**München** Hbf (low level) d.	0018	0058	0152	0318	20 minutes	0458	0505	0518	0525	0538	0545	0558	same minutes	2245	2258	2305	2318	2325	2338	2358
11	**München** Ost d.	0027	0107	0201	0327	until	0507	|	0527	|	0547	|	0607	past each	|	2307	|	2327	|	2347	0007
44	**München Flughafen** Terminal ✈ a.	0057	0137	0231	0357		0537	0546	0557	0606	0617	0626	0637	hour until	2326	2337	2346	2357	0006	0017	0037

km*		S1	S8	S8	S8	S8		S8	S1	S8	S1	S8	S1	S8		S1	S8	S1	S8	S1	S8
0	**München Flughafen** Terminal ✈ d.	0011	0022	0042	0122	0402	and every	0542	0551	0602	0611	0622	0631	0642	and at the	2311	2322	2331	2342	2351	0002
	München Ost a.	|	0053	0113	0153	0433	20 minutes	0613	|	0633	|	0653	|	0713	same minutes	|	2353	|	0013	|	0033
41	**München** Hbf (low level) a.	0056	0103	0123	0203	0443	until	0623	0636	0643	0656	0703	0716	0723	past each	2356	0003	0016	0023	0036	0043
	München Pasing a.	...	0112	0133	0212	0452		0632	...	0652	...	0712	...	0732	hour until	...	0012	...	0032	...	0052

* – Via Neufahrn (b Freising).

☛ Many **S1** trains from München Hbf are combined with a Freising service - travel in the rear portion for the Airport.

MÜNCHEN - MÜHLDORF - SIMBACH 893

km				⚒r									Ⓐ	©	Ⓐ	©	Ⓐ		Ⓐ			Ⓐ				
0	**München** Hbf d.	...	...	*0602**	0707	0807**z**	0907	1009	1107	1207	1307	1407	1507	1507	*1526**	1607	1618	1707	1727	1748	1807	*1828**	1907	2028	2129	2228
10	**München** Ost d.	...	...	0616	0717	0817	0917	1018	1117	1217	1317	1417	1518	1518	1539	1617	1638	1717	1740	1758	1817	1840	1916	2038	2139	2238
85	**Mühldorf** (Oberbay) a.	...	...	0723	0816	0925	1016	1118	1216	1317	1417	1517	1620	1618	1646	1717	1732	1819	1828	1907	1918	1934	2021	2141	2238	2333
		H	⑦**w**										|	©	Ⓐ		**d**	©	|	|		|				
85	**Mühldorf** (Oberbay) d.	0637	0737	0737	0837	0937	1037	1136	1227	1337	1437	1536	1626	1637	1655	...	1737	1831	1831	1910	1936	1936	2030	2146	2246	...
98	Neuötting d.	0647	0747	0747	0853	0948	1047	1146	1237	1347	1447	1546	1638	1647	1711	...	1747	1841	1843	|	1946	1946	2041	2157	2257	...
124	**Simbach** (Inn) a.	0714	0813	0813	0924	1013	1116	1212	1258	1413	1513	1612	1700	1713	1731	...	1813	1908	1905	1935	2014	2014	2101	2217	2317	...
	Linz Hbf **962** a.	0850	0950	...	...	...	...	...	...	...	...	...	...	...	...	...	...	...	...	2109	...	...	...	...	...	...

		Ⓐ	⑥**k**	Ⓐ	Ⓐ			**G**											Ⓐ	©				©	▽	
Linz Hbf **962** d.	...	...	...	...	...	...	...	0653	...	...	...	...	...	...	...	...	...	...	...	...	...	...	...	1804	...	...
Simbach (Inn) d.	...	0507	0547	0554	0648	0648	0749	0826	0900	0949	1051	1148	1259	1349	1449	...	1548	...	1631	1649	...	1749	1844	1950	2106	2222
Neuötting d.	...	0528	0607	0616	0711	0711	0810	|	0921	1010	1112	1209	1320	1410	1510	...	1609	...	1658	1710	...	1810	1905	2011	2126	2242
Mühldorf (Oberbay) a.	...	0540	0619	0628	0724	0724	0822	0850	0932	1021	1125	1220	1332	1421	1521	...	1620	...	1709	1721	...	1821	1921	2022	2138	2257
	①–⑥	Ⓐ	©	|	|	©		|							Ⓐ	©	©	Ⓐ					©	|	
Mühldorf (Oberbay) d.	0522	0546	0623	0637	0730	0729	0830	0851	0937	1030	1137	1228	1339	1428	1539	1540	1628	1628	...	...	1737	1830	1939	2029	2146	...
München Ost a.	0625	0640	0724	0723	0823	0826	0927	0946	1045	1125	1245	1327	1445	1526	1646	1645	1725	1746	...	...	1846	1926	2044	2126	2247	...
München Hbf a.	0636	*0653**	0737	0737	0837	0837	0939	0956	1055	1141	1255	1338	1455	1539	1656	1656	1739	*1759**	...	...	1856	1938	2054	2139	2257	...

G – From Garsten (Table **977**).
H – ①–⑥ (not Aug. 15, Oct. 26, Dec. 8).
d – Daily from Mühldorf.
k – Not Aug. 15, Oct. 3.
r – Not Aug. 15.
w – Also Aug. 15, Oct. 26, Dec. 8.
z – © only.
* – München Hbf underground platforms (S-Bahn connection).
▽ – Change trains at Mühldorf on † (also Aug. 15).

MÜNCHEN - GARMISCH - INNSBRUCK 895

DB; ÖBB (2nd class only in Austria)

km											*ICE* **527** ⑥**W**				*ICE* **1707*** ⑥**K**		*ICE* **787** ⑥**H**									
			Ⓐ			⑦																				⑦
0	**München** Hbf d.	...	0537	0630	0732	0809	0832	0932	1032	1132	1209	1232	1332	1432	1443	1532	1557	1632	1732	1832	1932	2032	2132	2232	2333	2333
7	München Pasing d.	...	0544	0638	0739	0816	0839	0939	1039	1139	|	1239	1339	1439	|	1539	|	1639	1739	1839	1939	2039	2139	2240	2340	2340
40	Tutzing d.	...	0609	0701	0801	|	0901	1001	1101	1201	|	1301	1401	1501	|	1601	|	1701	1801	1901	2001	2101	2201	2301	0001	0001
54	Weilheim (Oberbay) d.	...	0631	0711	0813	0849	0911	1011	1111	1211	|	1311	1411	1511	|	1611	|	1711	1812	1911	2012	2111	2212	2312	0011	0011
75	Murnau d.	...	0650	0730	0832	0906	0930	1031	1130	1230	|	1331	1430	1530	|	1630	|	1730	1830	1930	2030	2130	2230	2330	0030	0030
101	**Garmisch**-Partenk. a.	...	0717	0759	0857	0933	0957	1057	1157	1256	1341	1357	1456	1557	1622	1658	1721	1757	1857	1957	2056	2157	2255	2356	0056	0056
101	**Garmisch**-Partenk. d.	0630	0727	0804	0900**e**	*0939*	1004	1100	1204	1300	...	1404	1500	1604	...	1700**t**	...	1804	1900	2004	2100	2200	2300	0000	...	0057
118	**Mittenwald** 🏛 d.	0654	0754	0826	0922**e**	*1007*	1026	1122	1226	1322	...	1426	1522	1626	...	1722**t**	...	1826	1922	2026	2122	2222	2322	0022	...	0118
125	Scharnitz ⊡ d.	0702	...	0834	...	...	1034	...	1234	...	...	1434	...	1634	...	...	...	1834	...	2034	...	...	...	...	...	...
135	Seefeld in Tirol ⊡ d.	0716	...	0846	...	...	1046	...	1246	...	...	1446	...	1646	...	...	...	1846	...	2046	...	...	...	...	...	...
160	**Innsbruck** Hbf ⊡ a.	0753	...	0922	...	...	1122	...	1322	...	...	1522	...	1722	...	...	...	1922	...	2122	...	...	...	...	...	...

									ICE **1708*** ⑥**K**		*ICE* **788** ⑥**H**							*ICE* **924** ⑥**W**								
	⚒r	Ⓐ	©	Ⓐ	Ⓐ	©										**A**										
Innsbruck Hbf ⊡ d.	...	...	...	...	...	...	0634	...	...	0838	...	...	1038	...	1238**c**	1304	...	...	1438	...	1638	...	1838	...	2038	...
Seefeld in Tirol ⊡ d.	...	...	...	...	...	...	0715	...	...	0915	...	...	1115	...	1315**c**	1345	...	...	1515	...	1715	...	1915	...	2115	...
Scharnitz ⊡ d.	...	...	...	...	...	...	0727	...	...	0927	...	...	1127	...	1327**c**	1357	...	...	1527	...	1727	...	1927	...	2127	...
Mittenwald 🏛 d.	...	...	0537	0553	0621	0633	0737	0837	...	0937	...	1037	1136	1237	1337	1406	1437**z**	...	1537	1637	1737	1837	1937	2037	2137	2237
Garmisch-Partenk. a.	...	...	0559	0615	0649	0700	0759	0859	...	0959	...	1059	1158	1259	1359	1433	1459**z**	...	1559	1659	1759	1859	1959	2059	2159	2259
Garmisch-Partenk. d.	0504	0557	0604	0623	0657	0704	0804	0904	0925	1004	1035	1104	1206	1308	1404	...	1504	1518	1604	1704	1804	1904	2004	2104	2204	2304
Murnau d.	0530	0624	0631	0651	0730	0730	0831	0931	|	1031	|	1131	1230	1333	1430	...	1530	|	1630	1731	1830	1930	2030	2130	2230	2330
Weilheim (Oberbay) d.	0548	0648	0649	0716	0749	0749	0849	0949	|	1049	|	1148	1249	1349	1449	...	1548	|	1649	1750	1850	1949	2049	2148	2249	2348
Tutzing d.	0559	0700	0700	0729	0800	0800	0900	1000	|	1100	|	1200	1300	1400	1500	...	1600	|	1700	1800	1900	2000	2100	2200	2300	0000
München Pasing a.	0621	0722	0722	0753	0819	0821	0919	1020	|	1119	|	1219	1319	1420	1520	...	1620	|	1720	1820	1919	2019	2119	2219	2319	0019
München Hbf a.	0629	0729	0729	0800	0827	0828	0927	1027	1059	1128	1211	1228	1327	1427	1527	...	1630	1645	1727	1827	1927	2027	2127	2226	2326	0027

München - Tutzing - Kochel

km			Ⓐ	Ⓐ	Ⓐ	Ⓐ	Ⓐ	Ⓐ	Ⓐ	Ⓐ	Ⓐ	Ⓐ	Ⓐ	Ⓐ	Ⓐ		Ⓐ	Ⓐ		©	©		©	©
0	**München** Hbf d.	Ⓐ	0640	0758	*0832*	*0932*	*1032*	*1132*	*1232*	*1332*	1446	1546	1646	1746	*1832*	and	*2232*	2333	©	*0630*	*0732*	and	*2232*	2333
7	München Pasing d.		0647	0805	*0839*	*0939*	*1039*	*1139*	*1239*	*1339*	1453	1553	1653	1754	*1839*	hourly	*2240*	2340		*0638*	*0739*	hourly	*2240*	2340
40	Tutzing d.		0715	0831	0905	1005	1105	1205	1310	1420	1519	1620	1720	1820	1905	until	2305	2400		0705	0805	until	2305	2400
75	**Kochel** a.		0748	0904	0936	1036	1136	1236	1348	1453	1553	1653	1753	1853	1936		2336	*0038*		0736	0836		2336	*0038*

		Ⓐ	Ⓐ	Ⓐ	Ⓐ	Ⓐ		Ⓐ	Ⓐ	Ⓐ	Ⓐ	Ⓐ	Ⓐ	Ⓐ	Ⓐ	Ⓐ	Ⓐ	Ⓐ		©	©		©	©
Kochel d.	Ⓐ	0517	0602	0638	0726	0813	and	1213	1300	1403	1503	1603	1703	1803	1913	2013	2113	2213	©	0618	0713	and	2213	2313
Tutzing a.		0550	0636	0710	0809	0852	hourly	1252	1333	1440	1540	1645	1745	1845	1952	2052	2152	2252		0652	0752	hourly	2252	2352
München Pasing a.		0614	0700	0741	0832	*0919*	until	*1319*	*1359*	1503	1604	1712	*1820*	*1919*	*2019*	*2119*	*2219*	*2319*		*0722*	*0821*	until	*2319*	*0019*
München Hbf a.		0621	0707	0749	0839	*0927*		*1327*	*1405*	1511	1612	1719	*1827*	*1927*	*2027*	*2127*	*2226*	*2326*		*0729*	*0828*		*2326*	*0027*

A – ①–⑤ (not Oct. 26, Dec. 8).
H – ⑥ until Oct. 24. WERDENFELSERLAND – [12] and ✕ Hamburg - Hannover - Nürnberg - Garmisch and v.v.
K – KARWENDEL – [12] and ✕ Berlin - Leipzig - Nürnberg - Garmisch and v.v.
W – WETTERSTEIN – [12] and 🍷 Dortmund - Köln - Frankfurt - Nürnberg - Garmisch and v.v.
c – ⑥⑦ (also Oct. 26, Dec. 8).
e – Ⓐ only.
r – Not Aug. 15.
t – 4 minutes later on ©.
z – © only.
* – Different train numbers Aug. 1 - Sept. 12: **1707** runs as **1697**; **1708** runs as **1666**.
⊡ – Additional ÖBB trains Scharnitz - Seefeld - Innsbruck and v.v.
From Scharnitz at 0634, 0734, 0934, 1303⚒, 1534, 1734, 1934Ⓐ and 2134.
From Innsbruck Hbf at 0738, 1208⚒, 1408, 1538, 1738Ⓐ and 1938.

A rack railway operates between Garmisch-Partenkirchen and the Zugspitz mountain: departures at 0815 and hourly to 1415, returning from Bf Zugspitzplatt at 0930 and hourly to 1630. All trains call at Eibsee (30 minutes from Garmisch, 49 minutes from Zugspitzplatt). Service may be suspended in bad weather conditions – please check locally before travelling. Cable cars run between Eibsee and Zugspitzgipfel (Eibsee-Seilbahn) and between Zugspitzplatt and Zugspitzgipfel summit (Gletscherbahn). **Operator**: Bayerische Zugspitzbahn AG ✆ + 49 (0) 88 21 7970.

MURNAU - OBERAMMERGAU 897

RB services ○

km		Ⓐ	Ⓐ						Ⓐ	©	Ⓐ	©									
0	**Murnau** d.	0602	0647	0742	0842	0942	1042	1142	1235	1242	1322	1342	1442	1542	1642	1742	1842	1942	2042	2142	2335
12	Bad Kohlgrub d.	0621	0707	0802	0902	1002	1102	1202	1254	1302	1341	1402	1502	1602	1702	1802	1902	2002	2102	2202	2353
20	Unterammergau d.	0635	0721	0816	0916	1016	1116	1216	1308	1316	1355	1416	1516	1616	1716	1816	1916	2016	2116	2216	0007
24	**Oberammergau** a.	0640	0726	0821	0921	1021	1121	1221	1313	1321	1400	1421	1521	1621	1721	1821	1921	2021	2121	2221	0012

	Ⓐ		Ⓐ					Ⓐ	©	Ⓐ	©									
Oberammergau d.	0559	0645	0740	0840	0940	1040	1140	1232	1240	1318	1340	1440	1540	1640	1740	1840	1940	2040	2140	2243
Unterammergau d.	0603	0649	0744	0844	0944	1044	1144	1236	1244	1322	1344	1444	1544	1644	1744	1844	1944	2044	2144	2247
Bad Kohlgrub d.	0620	0706	0801	0901	1001	1101	1201	1253	1301	1340	1401	1501	1601	1701	1801	1901	2001	2101	2201	2301
Murnau a.	0638	0725	0819	0919	1019	1119	1219	1312	1319	1359	1419	1519	1619	1719	1819	1919	2019	2119	2219	2319

900 NÜRNBERG and FRANKFURT - HAMBURG

See Table **901** for local services Frankfurt - Fulda - Kassel. See Table **902** for other *IC* services Frankfurt - Gießen - Kassel - Göttingen - Alfeld - Hannover - Hamburg.

km	See note ⊠	*IC* 2178	*CNL* 1288	*CNL* 1200	*IC* 2184	*EN* 490	*IC* 2176	*CNL* 478	*IC* 2280	*ICE* 988	*ICE* 876	*ICE* 876	*ICE* 672	*ICE* 1092	*ICE* 888	*ICE* 696	*ICE* 774	*ICE* 684	*ICE* 634	*ICE* 874	*ICE* 670	*ICE* 886	*ICE* 694	*ICE* 772
		①–⑤	[R]	[R]	①–⑤		①–⑤	[R]	①	①–⑥	①	①–⑥		①–⑤	①–⑤	①	①–⑥		A					
		🍷	✕♦	✕♦	🍷	♦	🍷	✕♦		✕	✕	✕	✕♦	D ⚡ ✕	✕	✕	✕	✕	✕	✕	✕	✕	✕	✕
	Zürich HB **510** d.	...	...	...	...	...	...	2042	...	...	...	...	...	...	...	...	...	...	...	...	...	...	...	...
	Basel SBB **912** 🏛 d.	...	...	...	...	...	...	2207	...	...	...	...	...	...	...	...	...	...	...	0412b	...	...	...	...
	Karlsruhe Hbf **912** d.	...	...	...	...	...	...	0011	...	...	...	...	...	...	...	...	...	...	...	0558	0651e	...	...	...
	Ulm Hbf **930** d.	...	...	...	...	...	...	|	...	...	...	...	...	...	...	...	...	...	...	|	|	...	...	...
	Stuttgart Hbf **930** d.	...	...	...	...	...	...	|	...	...	...	...	...	...	...	...	0509	...	...	|	|	...	0651	0727
	Mannheim Hbf **912** d.	...	...	...	...	...	...	|	...	...	...	...	...	...	...	...	0605	...	...	0631	0716e	...	0731	0806
	Frankfurt Flughafen ✈ § d.	...	...	...	...	...	...	|	...	...	...	...	0539	...	...	...	0642	...	...	|	|	...	|	0842
	Frankfurt (Main) Hbf **850** d.	...	...	...	...	...	...	|	...	0504	0510	...	0555	0614	...	...	0658	...	...	0713	0758	...	0813	0858
	Hanau Hbf **850** d.	...	...	...	...	...	...	|	...	0520	0526	...	0611	|	...	...	|	...	...	0729	|	...	0829	|
	München Hbf **904** d.	...	2252	2304	...	...	...	|	...	|	|	...	|	|	...	...	|	0517a	0517a	|	|	0620	|	|
	Augsburg Hbf **904** d.	...	2339	2345	...	...	...	|	...	|	|	...	|	|	...	...	|	|	|	|	|	|	|	|
0	**Nürnberg** Hbf **920 921** d.	...	|	|	...	0132	...	|	...	|	|	...	|	|	0534	...	|	0631	0631	|	|	0733	|	|
102	**Würzburg** Hbf **920 921** d.	...	|	|	...	0228	...	|	0503	|	|	...	|	|	0632	...	|	0730	0730	|	|	0832	|	|
195	Fulda **850** d.	...	|	|	...	|	...	|	0540	0604	0609	...	|	|	0707	...	|	0803	0803	0811	|	0904	0911	|
285	**Kassel** Wilhelmshöhe d.	...	|	|	...	|	...	|	0615	0636	0643	0643	0723	|	0739	0744	0823	0836	0836	0844*	0923	0936	0944*	1023
330	Göttingen d.	...	|	|	...	0508	0548	0611s	...	0656	0703*	0703*	0743	|	0759	0805*	0843	0856	0856	0903*	0943	0956	1003*	1043
	Hildesheim Hbf d.	...	|	|	...	|	|	|	...	|	0734*	0734*	|	|	|	0834*	|	|	|	0934*	|	|	1034*	|
	Braunschweig Hbf a.	...	|	|	...	|	|	|	...	|	0758	0758	|	|	|	0858	|	|	|	0958	|	|	1058	|
430	**Hannover** Hbf a.	...	0527s	|	...	0613	0656	0702s	...	0732	|	|	0817	|	0832	|	0917	0932	0932	|	1017	1032	|	1117
430	**Hannover** Hbf d.	0511	|	|	0555	0617	0659	|	...	0736	|	|	0820	|	0836	|	0920	0936	0945	|	1020	1036	|	1120
.	*Berlin Hbf* **810** a.	|	|	0741n	|	|	|	|	...	|	0925	0925	|	0952	|	1025	|	|	|	1125	|	|	1221	|
	Bremen Hbf **813** a.	|	0642j	...	|	|	|	|	...	|	...	...	|	...	|	...	|	|	1044	...	|	|	...	|
608	**Hamburg** Hbf a.	0644	0754	...	0728	0750	0826	0906z	...	0854	...	...	0934	...	0954	...	1034	1053	...	...	1134	1156	...	1234
615	**Hamburg** Altona a.	0658	0809	...	...	0804	0843	0936z	...	0909	...	...	0950	...	1008	...	1049	1107	...	...	1150	1210	...	1250

See note ⊠	*RE* 34604	*ICE* 682	*ICE* 632	*ICE* 872	*ICE* 78	*ICE* 882	*ICE* 692	*IC* 2170	*ICE* 770	*ICE* 680	*ICE* 630	*ICE* 278	*ICE* 76	*ICE* 880	*ICE* 690	*ICE* 578	*RE* 34612	*ICE* 588	*ICE* 538	*ICE* 276	*ICE* 74	*ICE* 788	*ICE* 598	*IC* 2082
			A					⑥⑦			A								B				‡	
		✕	✕	✕	✕	✕	✕	🍷♦	✕	✕	✕	R✕	K✕	✕	✕	✕		✕	✕	R✕	K✕	G✕	✕	🍷♦
Zürich HB **510** d.	...	...	...	...	0602	...	...	...	...	...	...	...	0802	...	...	...	...	...	...	...	1002	...	...	...
Basel SBB **912** 🏛 d.	...	...	...	0608	0704	...	...	...	...	...	...	0812	0904	...	...	...	...	...	...	1012	1104	...	...	...
Karlsruhe Hbf **912** d.	...	...	...	0800	0851	...	...	...	...	...	...	1000	1051	...	...	...	...	...	...	1200	1251	...	...	...
Ulm Hbf **930** d.	...	...	...	|	|	...	0751	...	...	...	...	|	|	...	0951	...	...	...	...	|	|	...	1151	...
Stuttgart Hbf **930** d.	...	...	...	|	|	...	0851	...	0927	...	...	|	|	...	1051	1127	...	...	...	|	|	...	1251	...
Mannheim Hbf **912** d.	...	...	...	0831	0916	...	0931	...	1006	...	...	1031	1116	...	1131	1206	...	...	...	1231	1316	...	1331	...
Frankfurt Flughafen ✈ § d.	...	...	...	|	|	...	|	...	1042	...	...	|	|	...	|	1242	...	...	...	|	|	...	|	...
Frankfurt (Main) Hbf **850** d.	...	...	...	0913	0958	...	1013	1017	1058	...	...	1113	1158	...	1213	1258	...	...	...	1313	1358	...	1413	...
Hanau Hbf **850** d.	...	...	...	0929	|	...	1029	1038	|	...	...	1129	|	...	1229	|	...	...	...	1329	|	...	1429	...
München Hbf **904** d.	...	0650	0650	|	|	0820	|	|	|	0915	0915	|	|	1020	|	|	...	1052	1052	|	|	1220	|	1114o
Augsburg Hbf **904** d.	...	0731	0731	|	|	|	|	|	|	|	|	|	|	|	|	|	...	1132	1132	|	|	|	|	1229
Nürnberg Hbf **920 921** d.	0804	|	|	|	|	0933	|	|	|	1032	1032	|	|	1133	|	|	1204	|	|	|	|	1333	|	|
Würzburg Hbf **920 921** d.	0919	0930	0930	|	|	1032	|	|	|	1130	1130	|	|	1232	|	|	1319	1330	1330	|	|	1432	|	1440
Fulda **850** d.	...	1003	1003	1011	|	1104	1111	1122	|	1203	1203	1211	|	1304	1311	|	...	1403	1403	1411	|	1504	1511	1518
Kassel Wilhelmshöhe d.	...	1036	1036	1044*	1123	1136	1144*	1159*	1223	1236	1236	1244*	1323	1336	1344*	1423	...	1436	1436	1444*	1523	1536	1544*	1554
Göttingen d.	...	1056	1056	1103*	1143	1156	1203*	1219*	1243	1256	1256	1303*	1343	1356	1403*	1443	...	1456	1456	1503*	1543	1556	1603*	1615
Hildesheim Hbf d.	...	|	|	1134*	|	|	1234*	|	|	|	|	1334*	|	|	1434*	|	...	|	|	1534*	|	|	1634*	|
Braunschweig Hbf a.	...	|	|	1158	|	|	1258	|	|	|	|	1358	|	|	1458	|	...	|	|	1558	|	|	1658	|
Hannover Hbf a.	...	1132	1132	|	1217	1232	|	1258	1317	1332	1332	|	1417	1432	|	1517	...	1532	1532	|	1617	1632	|	1654
Hannover Hbf d.	...	1136	1145	|	1220	1236	|	1301	1320	1336	1345	|	1420	1436	|	1520	...	1536	1545	|	1620	1636	|	1658
Berlin Hbf **810** a.	...	|	|	1325	|	|	1419	|	|	|	|	1525	|	|	1621	|	...	|	|	1725	|	|	1819	|
Bremen Hbf **813** a.	...	|	1244	...	|	|	...	|	|	|	1444	...	|	|	...	|	...	|	1645	...	|	|	...	|
Hamburg Hbf a.	...	1253	...	...	1334	1353	...	1429	1434	1454	...	...	1534	1555	...	1634	...	1654	...	...	1734	1754	...	1827
Hamburg Altona a.	...	1308	...	...	1350	1408	...	...	1450	1511	...	...	...	1609	...	1650	...	1709	...	...	...	1808	...	1842

See note ⊠	*IC* 1886	*IC* 1886	*ICE* 576	*RE* 34616	*ICE* 586	*ICE* 536	*ICE* 374	*ICE* 72	*ICE* 786	*ICE* 596	*IC* 1888	*ICE* 574	*ICE* 974	*ICE* 584	*ICE* 1084	*ICE* 370	*ICE* 776	*ICE* 70	*ICE* 784	*ICE* 1090	*ICE* 594	*IC* 1880	*IC* 1178	*IC* 1878
	⑥ C	⑥ A									⑦	⑥	Ⓑ	Ⓑ	⑥		Ⓑ			Ⓑ	⑥	⑦	⑤⑦	④
	🍷♦	🍷♦	✕		✕	✕	R✕	✕	✕	✕	F🍷	✕	K✕	L✕	✕	R✕	O✕	✕	✕	⚡✕	✕	T🍷	¶🍷	🍷
Zürich HB **510** d.	...	...	...	...	...	...	...	1202	...	...	...	...	...	...	...	...	...	...	...	...	...	...	...	...
Basel SBB **912** 🏛 d.	...	...	...	...	...	...	1212	1304	...	...	...	...	...	...	...	1412	...	1504	...	...	...	...	...	...
Karlsruhe Hbf **912** d.	...	...	...	...	...	...	1400	1451	...	...	...	...	...	...	...	1600	...	1651	...	...	...	...	...	...
Ulm Hbf **930** d.	...	...	...	...	...	...	|	|	...	1351	...	...	...	...	...	|	...	|	...	1551	1551	...	...	...
Stuttgart Hbf **930** d.	...	...	1327	...	...	...	|	|	...	1451	...	1527	1527	...	...	|	...	|	...	1651	1651	...	...	...
Mannheim Hbf **912** d.	...	...	1406	...	...	...	1431	1516	...	1531	...	1606	1606	...	...	1631	...	1716	...	1731	1731	...	...	...
Frankfurt Flughafen ✈ § d.	...	...	1442	...	...	...	|	|	...	|	...	1642	1642	...	...	|	...	|	...	|	|	...	...	...
Frankfurt (Main) Hbf **850** d.	...	...	1458	...	...	...	1513	1558	...	1613	...	1658	1658	...	...	1713	1716	1758	...	1813	1813	...	1822	1822
Hanau Hbf **850** d.	...	...	|	...	...	...	1529	|	...	1629	...	|	|	...	...	1729	1741	|	...	|	1829	...	1838	1838
München Hbf **904** d.	...	...	|	...	1251	1251	|	|	1420	|	1345	|	|	1515	1515	|	|	|	1616	|	|	1545	|	|
Augsburg Hbf **904** d.	...	...	|	...	1331	1331	|	|	|	|	1423	|	|	|	|	|	|	|	|	|	|	1623	|	|
Nürnberg Hbf **920 921** d.	1318	1318	|	1404	|	|	|	|	1533	|	|	|	|	1632	1632	|	|	|	1733	|	|	|	|	|
Würzburg Hbf **920 921** d.	1419	1419	|	1519-	1530	1530	|	|	1632	|	1635	|	|	1730	1730	|	|	|	1832	|	|	1835	|	|
Fulda **850** d.	1524	1524	|	...	1603	1603	1611	|	1704	1711	1717	|	|	1803	1803	1811	|	|	1907	|	1911	1913	1921	1930
Kassel Wilhelmshöhe d.	1601	1601	1623	...	1636	1636	1644*	1723	1736	1744*	1754	1823	1823	1836	1836	1844*	1851*	1923	1940	|	1944	1950	1959	2007
Göttingen d.	1622	1622	1643	...	1656	1656	1703*	1743	1756	1803*	1815	1843	1843	1856	1856	1903*	1912	1943	1959	|	2003	2012	2021	2028
Hildesheim Hbf d.	|	|	|	...	|	|	1734*	|	|	1834*	|	|	|	|	|	1934*	|	|	|	|	2034	|	|	|
Braunschweig Hbf a.	|	|	|	...	|	|	1758	|	|	1858	|	|	|	|	|	1958	|	|	|	|	2058	|	|	|
Hannover Hbf a.	1659	1659	1717	...	1732	1732	|	1817	1832	|	1855	1917	1917	1932	1932	|	1946	2017	2032	|	|	2051	2100	2110
Hannover Hbf d.	1706	1702	1720	...	1736	1745	|	1820	1836	|	1858	1920	1920	1936	1936	|	1949	2020	2036	|	|	2055	2105	2115
Berlin Hbf **810** a.	|	|	|	...	|	|	1925	|	|	2019	|	|	|	|	|	2128	|	|	|	2148	2226	|	2251	2300
Bremen Hbf **813** a.	|	1811	|	...	|	1845	...	|	|	...	|	|	|	|	|	...	2048	|	|	...	...	|	...	...
Hamburg Hbf a.	1831	1907	1834	...	1853	...	...	1934	1954	...	2029	2035	2037	2054	2054	...	...	2137	2154	...	...	2225	...	...
Hamburg Altona a.	1858	1921	1850	...	1912	...	...	1950	2008	...	...	2050	...	...	2108	...	...	2152	2208	...	...	2239	...	...

♦ – **NOTES** (LISTED BY TRAIN NUMBER)

478 – Daily until Nov. 1; ④–⑦ from Nov. 5. KOMET – 🛏 1, 2 cl., ▬ 2 cl., [2] (reclining) and ✕ Zürich - Hamburg.

490 – HANS ALBERS – 🛏 1, 2 cl., ▬ 2 cl., [2] and 🍷 Wien - Linz - Passau - Regensburg - Hamburg; conveys [2] (*D* **60490**) Nürnberg - Hamburg.

672 – [12] and ✕ Wiesbaden Hbf (d. 0500) - Mainz Hbf (d. 0511) - Frankfurt - Hamburg.

1200 – CAPELLA – 🛏 1 cl., ▬ 2 cl., [2] (reclining) and ✕ München - Berlin. For other stops see Table **851**. Train number **1210** Aug. 1 - Sept. 13.

1288 – PYXIS – 🛏 1 cl., ▬ 2 cl., [2] (reclining) and ✕ München - Hamburg. Also calls at München Pasing (d. 2301).

1886 – ROTTALER LAND – [12] and 🍷 Passau - Hamburg. Also calls at Gemünden (d. 1447).

2082 – KÖNIGSSEE – [12] and 🍷 Berchtesgaden - Hamburg; [12] Oberstdorf (**2084**) - Augsburg (**2082**) - Hamburg. Also calls at Treuchtlingen, Gunzenhausen, Ansbach and Steinach (Table **905a**).

2170 – WATTENMEER – [12] and 🍷 Frankfurt - Hannover - Hamburg - Westerland. See also Tables **902** / **821**.

A – From July 20.
B – ⑦ June 14 - July 12; daily from July 19.
C – Until July 18.
D – From Darmstadt Hbf (d. 0543).
F – To Flensburg (Table **823**). Also calls at Donauwörth (d. 1444), Treuchtlingen (d. 1507) and Ansbach (d. 1540).
G – From Garmisch-Partenkirchen on ⑥ until Oct. 24 (d. 1035).

K – To Kiel (Table **820**).
L – To Lübeck (Table **825**).
O – To Oldenburg on ①–⑤ from Sept. 28 (Table **813**).
R – From Interlaken via Bern (Table **560**).
T – Also calls at Donauwörth (d. 1644), Treuchtlingen (d. 1707) and Ansbach (d. 1740).

a – ①–⑤ only.
b – ① only. Basel **Badischer Bahnhof**.
e – ①–⑥ only.
j – From July 20.
n – 0959 Aug. 2 - Sept. 14.
o – München **Ost**.
s – Stops to set down only.
z – On ⑦ (also Oct. 3) arrives Hamburg Hbf 0845, Hamburg Altona 0900.

⊠ – **June 14 - July 19** all services Hannover - Hamburg are subject to alteration. Journey times extended by up to 25 minutes. Please confirm timings locally.
* – 3–8 minutes later until June 30.
‡ – Train number **998** on ⑦.
¶ – Train number **1878** on ⑤.
⚡ – *ICE SPRINTER*. [R] and supplement payable.
§ – Frankfurt Flughafen Fernbahnhof.

NÜRNBERG and FRANKFURT - HAMBURG 900

See Table **901** for local services Frankfurt - Fulda - Kassel and v.v. See Table **902** for other *IC* services Frankfurt - Gießen - Kassel - Göttingen - Alfeld - Hannover - Hamburg and v.v.

See note ⊠	*ICE*	*ICE*	*ICE*	*ICE*	*ICE*	*ICE*	*ICE*	*ICE*	*ICE*	*ICE*	*ICE*	*ICE*	*ICE*	*ICE*	*ICE*	*ICE*	*ICE*	*CNL*	*CNL*	*ICE*	*ICE*	*ICE*	*ICE*	*ICE*
	572	**582**	**870**	**376**	**782**	**732**	**592**	**782**	**732**	**570**	**524**	**580**	**580**	**980**	**272**	**272**	**372**	**482**	**482**	**780**	**590**	**992**	**698**	**990**
				⑤⑦		**B**			**B**	⑦		①–④	⑦	⑤	⑥	①–⑤	⑦	①–⑤	⑥⑦	⑦	⑥	⑦	⑤	⑦
	✕	✕	✕	R✕	✕	Q✕	✕	✕	Q✕	✕	🍷	✕	✕	✕	✕	✕	✕	✕♦	✕♦	✕	✕	✕	✕	
Zürich HB **510** d.	...	...	...	...	...	...	...	...	...	...	...	...	...	...	1702	1702	1702	...	...	...	...	...	...	...
Basel SBB **912** 🏛 d.	...	...	1612	1704	...	...	...	...	...	...	...	...	...	...	1812	1812	1812	...	...	...	...	...	...	...
Karlsruhe Hbf **912** d.	...	...	1801	1851	...	...	...	...	...	...	...	...	...	...	2000	2000	2000	...	...	...	...	...	...	...
Ulm Hbf **930** d.	...	...	|	|	...	...	1751	...	...	...	...	...	...	...	|	|	|	...	...	...	1951	1951	1951	2204
Stuttgart Hbf **930** d.	1727	...	|	|	...	...	1851	...	...	1927	...	...	...	...	|	|	|	...	...	...	2051	2051	2051	2305
Mannheim Hbf **912** d.	1806	...	1831	1916	...	...	1931	...	...	2006	...	...	...	...	2031	2031	2031	...	...	...	2131	2131	2131	2351
Frankfurt Flughafen ✈ § d.	1842	...	|	|	...	...	|	...	...	2042	...	...	...	...	|	|	|	...	...	...	|	|	|	0029
Frankfurt (Main) Hbf **850** d.	1858	...	1913	1958	...	...	2013	...	...	2058	...	...	...	...	2113	2113	2113	...	...	...	2222	2222	2222	0055
Hanau Hbf **850** d.	1914	...	1929	|	...	...	2029	...	...	|	...	...	...	...	2129	2129	2129	...	...	...	2238	2238	2238	0112
München Hbf **904** d.	|	1714	|	|	1820	1820	|	...	...	|	1855	1849	1849	1849	|	|	|	1900	1915	2020	|	|	|	|
Augsburg Hbf **904** d.	|	|	|	|	|	|	|	...	...	|	|	1932	1932	1932	|	|	|	|	|	|	|	|	|	|
Nürnberg Hbf **920 921** d.	|	1832	|	|	1933	1933	|	...	...	|	2000	|	|	|	|	|	|	2135	2135	2140	|	|	|	|
Würzburg Hbf **920 921** d.	|	1930	|	|	2032	2032	|	...	...	|	2054	2131	2131	2131	|	|	|	2233	2233	2237	|	|	|	|
Fulda **850** d.	|	2003	2011	|	2104	2104	|	...	...	|	...	2204	2204	2204	2211	2211	2211	2343j	2343j	2311	2323	2323	2323	0158
Kassel Wilhelmshöhe d.	2026	2036	2044	2123	2137	2137	2141	←	←	2223	...	...	2236	2236	2244	2244	2244	|	|	2342	2353	2356	0034	|
Göttingen d.	2045	2056	2103	2143	2155	2155	2201	2205	2205	2243	...	...	2256	2258	2305	2305	2303	|	|	...	...	0047	...	0325
Hildesheim Hbf d.	|	|	2134	|	→	→	2234	|	|	|	...	...	|	|	|	|	2334	|	|	...	...	|	...	|
Braunschweig Hbf a.	|	|	2158	|	...	...	2258	|	|	|	...	...	|	|	|	|	2358	|	|	...	...	|	...	|
Hannover Hbf a.	2118	2132	|	2217	...	...	|	2240	2240	2317	...	...	2332	2357	2341	0003	|	|	|	...	...	0146	...	0421
Hannover Hbf d.	2121	2136	|	2220	...	...	|	2243	2251	2320	...	...	2336	...	2345	0006	|	|	|	...	...	...	...	0424
Berlin Hbf **810** a.	|	|	2325	|	...	...	0027	|	|	|	...	...	|	...	|	|	0125	|	|	...	...	...	...	|
Bremen Hbf **813** a.	|	|	...	|	...	...	...	|	2349	|	...	...	|	...	|	|	...	|	|	...	...	...	...	|
Hamburg Hbf a.	2240	2254	...	2345	...	...	...	0003	...	0037	...	...	0103	...	0119	0134	...	0356	0356	...	...	...	...	0543
Hamburg Altona a.	2254	2309	...	2359	...	...	...	0018	...	0052	...	...	0117	...	0133	0148	...	...	...	...	...	...	...	...

km	See note ⊠	*ICE*	*CNL*	*CNL*	*ICE*	*ICE*	*ICE*	*ICE*	*ICE*	*ICE*	*ICE*	*ICE*	*ICE*	*ICE*	*ICE*	*ICE*	*ICE*	*ICE*	*ICE*	*ICE*	*ICE*	*ICE*	*ICE*	*RE*
		5	**483**	**483**	**591**	**591**	**999**	**781**	**781**	**373**	**531**	**581**	**571**	**1097**	**593**	**1091**	**783**	**783**	**71**	**375**	**533**	**583**	**1083**	**34613**
		①	②–⑦	①	①–⑤	①–⑥	⑦	①⑥	①–⑥	①–⑤	**D**		①–⑥	①–⑤	⑥⑦	①–⑤	⑥	①–⑥			①–⑥	①–⑥	⑦	
		R	✕♦	✕♦	✕	✕	✕	✕	✕	R✕	E✕	✕	✕	◧✕	✕	⚡✕	✕	✕	✕	R✕	N✕	L✕	✕	
	Hamburg Altona d.	...	...	...	0304	...	...	...	...	...	...	0444	0505	0552	...	...	0551	...	0604	...	...	...	0647	...
	Hamburg Hbf d.	0025	0031	0031	0318	...	...	...	...	...	...	0458	0519	0609	...	...	0605	...	0618	...	...	0701	0701	...
	Bremen Hbf **813** d.	|	|	|	|	...	...	...	...	...	0514	|	|	|	...	...	|	...	|	...	0714	|	|	...
	Berlin Hbf **810** d.	|	|	|	|	...	...	...	...	0432	|	|	|	|	0531	0608	|	...	|	0632	|	|	|	...
	Hannover Hbf a.	0147	|	|	0459	...	...	...	...	|	0614	0623	0638	0719	|	|	0721	...	0738	|	0814	0823	0821	...
	Hannover Hbf d.	0150	|	|	0518	0518	...	0526	...	|	0626	0626	0641	0722	|	|	0726	0726	0741	|	0826	0826	0826	...
0	**Braunschweig** Hbf d.	|	|	|	|	|	...	|	...	0558	|	|	|	|	0658	|	|	|	|	0758	|	|	|	...
43	Hildesheim Hbf d.	|	|	|	|	|	...	|	...	0625*	|	|	|	|	0725*	|	|	|	|	0825*	|	|	|	...
121	Göttingen d.	0247	|	|	0555	0555	...	0603	...	0655*	0703	0703	0717	|	0755*	|	0803	0803	0817	0855*	0903	0903	0903	...
166	**Kassel** Wilhelmshöhe d.	|	|	|	0615	0615	0615	0623	...	0715*	0723	0723	0737	|	0815*	|	0826	0826	0837	0915*	0923	0923	0923	...
256	Fulda **850** d.	0418	0456t	0513	0647	0647	0647	0656	0656	0747	0755r	0755r	|	|	0847	|	0858	0858	|	0947	0955	0955	0955	...
	Würzburg Hbf **920 921** d.	|	0536t	0551	|	|	|	0729	0729	|	0831	0831	|	|	|	|	0930	0930	|	|	1031	1031	1031	1040
	Nürnberg Hbf **920 921** a.	|	0645	|	|	|	|	0824	0824	|	0928	0928	|	|	|	|	1024	1024	|	|	|	|	|	1155
	Augsburg Hbf **904** a.	|	|	|	|	|	|	|	|	|	|	|	|	|	|	|	|	|	|	|	1223	1223	1223	...
	München Hbf **904** a.	|	0857	0857	|	|	|	0942	0942	|	1041	1041	|	|	|	|	1142	1142	|	|	1304	1304	1304	...
337	Hanau Hbf **850** d.	0506	...	...	0730	0730	0730	...	...	0829	...	...	|	|	0929	|	...	...	|	1029	...	...	...	...
360	**Frankfurt** (Main) Hbf **850** a.	0529	...	...	0744	0744	0744	...	...	0844	...	...	0900	0928	0944	0942	...	...	1000	1044	...	...	...	...
	Frankfurt Flughafen ✈ § a.	0550	...	...	|	|	|	...	...	|	...	...	0916	...	|	|	...	...	|	|	...	...	...	...
	Mannheim Hbf **912** a.	0625	...	...	0828	0828	0828	...	...	0928	...	...	0953	...	1028	1028	...	...	1042	1128	...	...	...	...
	Stuttgart Hbf **930** a.	|	...	...	0908	0908	0908	...	...	|	...	...	1033	...	1108	1108	...	...	|	|	...	...	...	...
	Ulm Hbf **930** a.	|	...	...	1006	1006	1006	...	...	|	...	...	...	...	1206	1206	...	...	|	|	...	...	...	...
	Karlsruhe Hbf **912** a.	0650	...	...	...	...	...	...	...	0958	...	...	...	...	...	...	...	...	1106	1158	...	...	...	...
	Basel SBB **912** a.	0847	...	...	...	...	...	...	...	1147	...	...	...	...	...	...	...	...	1255	1347	...	...	...	...
	Zürich HB **510** a.	...	...	...	...	...	...	...	...	...	...	...	...	...	...	...	...	...	...	...	...	...	...	...

See note ⊠	*ICE*	*ICE*	*IC*	*IC*	*IC*	*ICE*	*ICE*	*ICE*	*ICE*	*ICE*	*ICE*	*ICE*	*ICE*	*ICE*	*ICE*	*ICE*	*ICE*	*ICE*	*RE*	*ICE*	*ICE*	*ICE*	*ICE*	*ICE*
	973	**573**	**1887**	**1887**	**2083**	**595**	**785**	**73**	**871**	**535**	**585**	**575**	**597**	**787**	**75**	**277**	**537**	**587**	**34621**	**577**	**599**	**789**	**77**	**279**
	①–⑥	⑦	⑥**A**	⑥**C**						**A**							**A**							
	K✕	✕	🍷♦	🍷♦	🍷♦	✕	✕	K✕	✕	✕	✕	✕	✕	G✕	✕	R✕	✕	✕		✕	✕	✕	✕	R✕
Hamburg Altona d.	...	0709	0620	0704	0714	...	0747	...	...	...	0847	0909	...	0947	1009	...	...	1047	...	1109	...	1147	1209	...
Hamburg Hbf d.	0724	0724	0635	0718	0728	...	0803	0824	...	...	0901	0924	...	1001	1024	...	...	1101	...	1124	...	1201	1224	...
Bremen Hbf **813** d.	|	|	0737	|	|	...	|	|	...	0914	|	|	...	|	|	...	1114	|	...	|	...	|	|	...
Berlin Hbf **810** d.	|	|	|	|	|	0737	|	|	0832	|	|	|	0937	|	|	1031	|	|	...	|	1137	|	|	1232
Hannover Hbf a.	0838	0838	0846	0845	0858	|	0921	0938	|	1014	1023	1038	|	1121	1138	|	1214	1223	...	1238	|	1321	1338	|
Hannover Hbf d.	0841	0841	0849	0849	0901	|	0926	0941	|	1026	1026	1041	|	1126	1141	|	1226	1226	...	1241	|	1326	1341	|
Braunschweig Hbf d.	|	|	|	|	|	0858	|	|	0958	|	|	|	1058	|	|	1158	|	|	...	|	1258	|	|	1358
Hildesheim Hbf d.	|	|	|	|	|	0925*	|	|	1025*	|	|	|	1125*	|	|	1225*	|	|	...	|	1325*	|	|	1425*
Göttingen d.	0917	0917	0929	0929	0943	0955*	1003	1017	1055*	1103	1103	1117	1155*	1203	1217	1255*	1303	1303	...	1317	1355*	1403	1417	1455*
Kassel Wilhelmshöhe d.	0937	0937	0951	0951	1005	1015*	1023	1037	1115*	1123	1123	1137	1215*	1223	1237	1315*	1323	1323	...	1337	1415*	1423	1437	1515*
Fulda **850** d.	|	|	1028	1028	1043	1047	1055	|	1147	1155	1155	|	1247	1255	|	1347	1355	1355	...	|	1447	1455	|	1547
Würzburg Hbf **920 921** d.	|	|	1118	1118	1121	|	1129	|	|	1231	1231	|	|	1329	|	|	1431	1431	1440	|	|	1529	|	|
Nürnberg Hbf **920 921** a.	|	|	1232	1232	|	|	1224	|	|	1329	1329	|	|	1424	|	|	|	|	1555	|	|	1624	|	|
Augsburg Hbf **904** a.	|	|	...	...	1328	|	|	|	|	|	|	|	|	|	|	|	1626	1626	...	|	|	|	|	|
München Hbf **904** a.	|	|	...	...	1412o	|	1339	|	|	1443	1443	|	|	1543	|	|	1707	1707	...	|	|	1738	|	|
Hanau Hbf **850** d.	|	|	...	...	...	1129	...	|	1229	...	...	|	1329	...	|	1429	...	...	...	|	1529	...	|	1629
Frankfurt (Main) Hbf **850** a.	1100	1100	...	...	...	1144	...	1200	1244	...	...	1300	1344	...	1400	1444	...	...	...	1500	1544	...	1600	1644
Frankfurt Flughafen ✈ § a.	1116	1116	...	...	...	|	...	|	|	...	...	1316	|	...	|	|	...	...	...	1516	|	...	|	|
Mannheim Hbf **912** a.	1153	1153	...	...	...	1228	...	1242	1328	...	...	1353	1428	...	1442	1528	...	...	...	1553	1628	...	1642	1728
Stuttgart Hbf **930** a.	1233	1233	...	...	...	1308	...	|	|	...	...	1433	1508	...	|	|	...	...	...	1632	1708	...	|	|
Ulm Hbf **930** a.	...	...	...	...	...	1406	...	|	|	...	...	...	1606	...	|	|	...	...	...	...	1806	...	|	|
Karlsruhe Hbf **912** a.	...	...	...	...	...	...	...	1306	1358	...	...	...	...	...	1506	1558	...	...	...	...	...	...	1706	1758
Basel SBB **912** a.	...	...	...	...	...	...	...	1455	1547	...	...	...	...	...	1655	1747	...	...	...	...	...	...	1855	1947
Zürich HB **510** a.	...	...	...	...	...	...	...	1600	...	...	...	...	...	...	1800	...	...	...	...	...	...	...	2000	...

♦ – **NOTES** (LISTED BY TRAIN NUMBER)

482 – HANS CHRISTIAN ANDERSEN – 🛏 1, 2 cl., ▬ 2 cl. and (2.) München - Ingolstadt Hbf (d. 1947 ①–⑤ / 2013 ⑥⑦) - Flensburg - København (see also Tables **50**/**823**). Ⓡ for overnight journeys. For Warszawa and Moskva cars see Table **24**.

483 – HANS CHRISTIAN ANDERSEN – 🛏 1, 2 cl., ▬ 2 cl. and (2.) København - Flensburg - Ingolstadt Hbf (a. 0807) - München (see also Tables **50**/**823**). Ⓡ for overnight journeys. For Warszawa and Moskva cars see Table **24**.

1887 – ROTTALER LAND – (12.) and 🍷 Hamburg - Passau. Also calls at Gemünden (d. 1057).

2083 – KÖNIGSSEE – (12.) and 🍷 Hamburg - Berchtesgaden; (12.) Hamburg - Augsburg (**2085**) - Oberstdorf. Also calls at Steinach, Ansbach, Gunzenhausen and Treuchtlingen (Table **905a**). Until June 30 departs Göttingen 0942, Kassel 1004.

A – From July 20.
B – ⑦ June 14 - July 12; daily from July 19.
C – Until July 18.
D – ① June 15 - July 13; ①–⑤ from July 20
E – From Oldenburg on ① (d. 0447)
G – To Garmisch on ⑥ until Oct. 24 (a. 1721).
K – From Kiel (Table **820**).
L – From Lübeck (Table **825**).

N – From Sept. 28 starts from Oldenburg (d. 0642).
Q – To Oldenburg on ⑦ (Table **813**).
R – From / to Interlaken via Bern (Table **560**).

j – Arrives 2318.
o – München **Ost**.
r – 0758 until June 30.
t – On ⑦ Fulda d. 0513, Würzburg d. 0551.

⊠ – **June 14 - July 19** all services Hannover - Hamburg and v.v. are subject to alteration. Journey times extended by up to 25 minutes (earlier departures from Hamburg).
* – 3–5 minutes earlier until June 30.
⚡ – *ICE SPRINTER*. Ⓡ and supplement payable.
◧ – To Darmstadt Hbf (a. 0950). *ICE SPRINTER*. Ⓡ and supplement payable for journeys to Frankfurt and Darmstadt.
§ – Frankfurt Flughafen Fernbahnhof.

900 HAMBURG - FRANKFURT and NÜRNBERG

See Table **902** for other *IC* services Hamburg - Hannover - Alfeld - Göttingen - Kassel - Gießen - Frankfurt. See Table **901** for local services Kassel - Fulda - Frankfurt.

	ICE	*ICE*	*RE*	*ICE*	*IC*	*ICE*	*ICE*	*ICE*	*ICE*	*ICE*	*ICE*	*RE*	*ICE*	*IC*	*ICE*	*ICE*	*ICE*	*ICE*	*ICE*	*ICE*	*RE*	*ICE*	*IC*	*ICE*
See note ⊠	**539**	**589**	**34625**	**579**	**1881**	**691**	**881**	**79**	**873**	**631**	**681**	**34629**	**771**	**2171**	**693**	**883**	**671**	**875**	**633**	**683**	**34631**	**773**	**1897**	**695**
	A				⑤⑦					**A**				⑤–⑦					**D**				⑦	⑥
	✕	✕		✕	**E** 🍷	✕	✕	✕	✕	✕	✕		✕	🍷♦	✕	✕	✕	✕	✕	✕		✕	🍷	✕
Hamburg Altona ... d.	...	1247	...	1309	1314**v**	...	1347	1409	...	...	1447	...	1509	...	...	1547	1609	...	...	1647	...	1709	...	...
Hamburg Hbf ... d.	...	1301	...	1324	1328	...	1401	1424	...	...	1501	...	1524	1528	...	1603	1624	...	...	1701	...	1724	...	...
Bremen Hbf **813** ... d.	1314	|	...	|	|	...	|	|	...	1514	|	...	|	|	...	|	|	...	1714	|	...	|	...	...
Berlin Hbf **810** ... d.	|	|	...	|	|	1337	|	|	1432	|	|	...	|	|	1537	|	|	1633	|	|	...	|	1659	1735
Hannover Hbf ... a.	1414	1423	...	1438	1453	|	1521	1538	|	1614	1623	...	1638	1658	|	1723	1738	|	1814	1823	...	1838	1844	|
Hannover Hbf ... d.	1426	1426	...	1441	1456	|	1526	1541	|	1626	1626	...	1641	1702	|	1726	1741	|	1826	1826	...	1841	1901	|
Braunschweig Hbf ... d.	|	|	...	|	|	1458	|	|	1558	|	|	...	|	|	1658	|	|	1758	|	|	...	|	|	1858
Hildesheim Hbf ... d.	|	|	...	|	|	1525*	|	|	1625*	|	|	...	|	|	1725*	|	|	1825*	|	|	...	|	|	1925*
Göttingen ... d.	1503	1503	...	1517	1536	1555*	1603	1617	1655*	1703	1703	...	1717	1742	1755*	1803	1817	1855*	1903	1903	...	1917	1942	1955*
Kassel Wilhelmshöhe ... d.	1523	1523	...	1537	1559	1615*	1623	1637	1715*	1723	1723	...	1737	1803	1815*	1823	1837	1915*	1923	1923	...	1937	2004	2015
Fulda ... **850** d.	1555	1555	...	|	1635	1647	1655	|	1747	1755	1755	...	|	1840	1847	1855	|	1947	1955	1955	...	|	2046	2047
Würzburg Hbf ... **920 921** d.	1631	1631	1640	|	1716	|	1729	|	|	1831	1831	1840	|	|	|	1929	|	|	2031	2031	2040	|	|	|
Nürnberg Hbf ... **920 921** a.	|	|	1755	|	|	|	1824	|	|	|	|	1955	|	|	|	2024	|	|	|	|	2155	|	|	|
Augsburg Hbf **904** ... a.	1822	1822	...	|	1930	|	|	|	|	2022	2022	...	|	|	|	|	|	|	2222	2222	...	|	|	|
München Hbf **904** ... a.	1903	1903	...	|	2010	|	1938	|	|	2102	2102	...	|	|	|	2138	|	|	2302	2302	...	|	|	|
Hanau Hbf ... **850** d.	...	...	...	|	...	1729	...	|	1829	...	...	...	|	1925	1929	...	|	2029	...	...	...	|	2135	|
Frankfurt (Main) Hbf ... **850** a.	...	...	...	1700	...	1744	...	1800	1844	...	...	...	1900	1950	1944	...	2000	2044	...	...	...	2100	2152	2142
Frankfurt Flughafen ✈ § ... a.	...	...	...	1716	...	|	...	|	|	...	...	...	1916	...	|	...	|	|	...	...	...	2116	|	|
Mannheim Hbf **912** ... a.	...	...	...	1753	...	1828	...	1842	1928	...	...	...	1953	...	2028	...	2042	2127	...	...	...	2153	|	2228
Stuttgart Hbf **930** ... a.	...	...	...	1833	...	1908	...	|	|	...	...	...	2033	...	2108	...	|	|	...	...	...	2248	2339	2308
Ulm Hbf **930** ... a.	...	...	...	...	...	2006	...	|	|	...	...	...	...	...	2206	...	|	|	...	...	...	...	...	...
Karlsruhe Hbf **912** ... a.	...	...	...	...	...	...	...	1906	1958	...	...	...	...	...	...	...	2107	2158	...	...	...	...	...	...
Basel SBB **912** ... a.	...	...	...	...	...	...	...	2055	2147	...	...	...	...	...	...	...	2300**v**	2355	...	...	...	...	...	...
Zürich HB **510** ... a.	...	...	...	...	...	...	...	2200	...	...	...	...	...	...	...	...	...	...	...	...	...	...	...	...

	ICE	*ICE*	*ICE*	*ICE*	*ICE*	*ICE*	*ICE*	*ICE*	*IC*	*ICE*	*ICE*	*ICE*	*ICE*	*IC*	*ICE*	*ICE*	*ICE*	*CNL*	*EN*	*ICE*	*CNL*	*CNL*	*CNL*	*CNL*
See note ⊠	**1093**	**885**	**673**	**877**	**635**	**685**	**1517**	**775**	**1899**	**697**	**697**	**887**	**1087**	**2350**	**879**	**1687**	**879**	**479**	**491**	**889**	**1201**	**1211**	**1289**	**1289**
	Ⓑ				**C**		**1737**	⑦**H**	⑦	Ⓑ	⑤⑦	Ⓑ	⑥	⑦	⑦	⑦	⑦	🅁		Ⓑ**d**	**e** 🅁	**L** 🅁	**A** 🅁	**M** 🅁
	✕⚡	✕	✕♦	✕	✕	✕	✕	✕		✕	✕	✕♦	✕♦	♦	✕	✕	✕	✕♦	🍷♦	‡✕	**B**✕	**B**✕	✕♦	✕♦
Hamburg Altona ... d.	...	1745	...	...	...	1847	...	1909	...	...	...	1947	1947	...	...	2047	...	1903	2018	2113**z**	...	...	2146	2247**h**
Hamburg Hbf ... d.	...	1803	1824	...	...	1901	...	1924	...	...	...	2001	2001	...	...	2101	...	1918	2033	2127	...	...	2202	2306**h**
Bremen Hbf **813** ... d.	...	|	|	...	1914	|	...	|	...	...	...	|	|	...	...	|	...	|	|	|	...	...	2324	|
Berlin Hbf **810** ... d.	1805	|	|	1833	|	|	...	|	1909	1937	1937	|	|	1839	2032	|	...	|	|	|	2212	2212	|	|
Hannover Hbf ... a.	|	1922	1938	|	2014	2023	...	2038	2055	|	|	2121	2121	|	|	2218	...	|	2223	2256	|	|	|	|
Hannover Hbf ... d.	|	1926	1941	|	2026	2026	...	2041	2101	|	|	2126	2137	|	|	2221	...	2218**u**	2226	...	|	|	0046**u**	0046**u**
Braunschweig Hbf ... d.	|	|	|	1958	|	|	...	|	|	2058	2058	|	|	|	2158	|	...	|	|	...	|	|	|	|
Hildesheim Hbf ... d.	|	|	|	2025	|	|	...	|	|	2125	2125	|	|	|	2225	|	...	|	|	...	|	|	|	|
Göttingen ... d.	|	2003	2017	2055	2103	2103	...	2117	2142	2155	2155	2203	2214	|	2255	2302	...	2331**u**	2325	...	|	|	|	|
Kassel Wilhelmshöhe ... d.	|	2026	2037	2115	2123	2123	...	2137	2204	2213	2215	2223	2234	|	2315	2322	←	|	|	...	|	|	|	|
Fulda ... **850** d.	|	2059	|	2147	2155	2155	...	|	|	...	2247	2255	2304	2307	2346	2357	2358	|	|	...	|	|	|	|
Würzburg Hbf ... **920 921** d.	|	2134	|	|	2230	2230	...	|	|	...	|	|	|	2356	→	0032	|	|	0207	...	|	|	|	|
Nürnberg Hbf ... **920 921** a.	|	2228	|	|	2324	2324	2338	|	⊡	...	|	|	|	...	...	0126	|	|	0306	...	|	|	|	|
Augsburg Hbf **904** ... a.	|	|	|	|	|	|	|	|	|	...	|	|	|	...	...	...	|	|	...	...	0554**k**	0646	0622	0622
München Hbf **904** ... a.	|	2344	|	|	0038**j**	0038**j**	0049	|	|	...	|	|	|	...	...	...	|	|	...	...	0639	0731**o**	0705	0705
Hanau Hbf ... **850** d.	|	...	|	2229	...	...	...	|	|	...	2329	2340	0001	...	...	...	0041	|	...	...	...	...	...	...
Frankfurt (Main) Hbf ... **850** a.	2142	...	2200	2244	...	...	...	2300	0019	...	2344	2356	0017	...	...	...	0058	|	...	...	...	...	...	...
Frankfurt Flughafen ✈ § ... a.	|	...	|	|	...	...	...	|	...	...	...	0015	0038	...	...	...	0122	|	...	...	...	...	...	...
Mannheim Hbf **912** ... a.	2228	...	2242	2341	...	...	...	|	...	...	...	...	...	...	...	...	0200**r**	|	...	...	...	...	...	...
Stuttgart Hbf **930** ... a.	2308	...	|	|	...	...	...	0044	...	...	...	...	...	...	...	...	|	|	...	...	...	...	...	...
Ulm Hbf **930** ... a.	...	...	|	|	...	...	...	...	...	...	...	...	...	...	...	...	|	|	...	...	...	...	...	...
Karlsruhe Hbf **912** ... a.	...	...	2306	0013	...	...	...	...	...	...	...	...	...	...	...	...	0238	0437	...	...	...	...	...	...
Basel SBB **912** ... a.	...	...	0106	...	...	...	...	...	...	...	...	...	...	...	...	...	...	0654	...	...	...	...	...	...
Zürich HB **510** ... a.	...	...	...	...	...	...	...	...	...	...	...	...	...	...	...	...	...	0834**b**	...	...	...	...	...	...

♦ – **NOTES** (LISTED BY TRAIN NUMBER)

479 – Daily until Nov. 1; ④–⑦ from Nov. 5. KOMET – 🛏 1, 2 cl., ▬ 2 cl., [2] and ✕ Hamburg - Zürich.
491 – HANS ALBERS – 🛏 1, 2 cl., ▬ 2 cl., [2] and 🍷 Hamburg - Passau - Linz - Wien. Conveys [2] (*D* **60491**) Hamburg - Nürnberg. 🅁 for journeys beyond Nürnberg.
673 – [12] and ✕ Kiel - Hamburg - Karlsruhe (- Basel ⑥).
887 – [12] and ✕ Hamburg - Frankfurt - Mainz Hbf (a. 0044) - Wiesbaden Hbf (a. 0057).
1087 – [12] and ✕ Hamburg - Frankfurt - Mainz Hbf (a. 0059) - Wiesbaden Hbf (a. 0112).
1289 – PYXIS – 🛏 1 cl., ▬ 2 cl., [2] (reclining) and ✕ Hamburg - München.
2171 – WATTENMEER – [12] and 🍷 Westerland - Frankfurt.
2350 – [12] and 🍷 Stralsund - Berlin - Halle - Erfurt - Fulda - Gemünden (a. 2332) - Würzburg.

A – From July 20.
B – CAPELLA – Conveys 🛏 1 cl., ▬ 2 cl. and [2] (reclining). For other stops see Table **851**.
C – ⑥⑦ June 14 - July 12; daily from July 18.
D – ⑦ June 14 - July 12; daily from July 19.
E – Also calls at Ansbach (a. 1816), Treuchtlingen (a. 1845) and Donauwörth (a. 1907).

H – Also runs on ⑤ between Hannover and Frankfurt only.
L – Aug. 1 - Sept. 13 only.
M – Until July 19.

b – 0820 on ⑥⑦.
d – Not June 19, 26, July 3, 10, 17.
e – Not Aug. 1 - Sept. 13.
h – On ① Hamburg Altona d. 2217, Hamburg Hbf d. 2231.
j – Nürnberg - München on ⑦ only.
k – ①–⑥ only.
o – München **Ost**.
r – Not July 20, Aug. 3, 10.
u – Stops to pick up only.

v – ⑦ only.
z – ①–④ only.

⊠ – **June 14 - July 19** all services Hamburg - Hannover are subject to alteration. Journey times extended by up to 25 minutes (earlier departures from Hamburg).
* – 3–5 minutes earlier until June 30.
⊡ – Via Gießen (Table **806**).
‡ – Train number **1089** on ⑤⑦.
⚡ – *ICE* ***SPRINTER***. 🅁 and supplement payable.
§ – Frankfurt Flughafen Fernbahnhof.

901 Local services FRANKFURT - FULDA - KASSEL

RE / RB services

Other *ICE / IC* services: Table **850** for Bebra - Kassel Wilhelmshöhe and v.v., also Frankfurt - Fulda - Bad Hersfeld and v.v. Table **900** for Frankfurt - Fulda - Kassel Wilhelmshöhe and v.v.

Frankfurt - Fulda

km								
0	**Frankfurt** (Main) Hbf ... **921** d.	0526	and hourly until	2126	2226	2326	...	...
10	Offenbach (Main) Hbf ... **921** d.	0538		2138	2238	2338	...	...
23	Hanau Hbf ... **921** d.	0548		2148	2248	2348	...	...
104	**Fulda** ... a.	0649		2249	2350	0049	...	...

		ⒶB		ⒶB						
Fulda ... d.	0401	0438	0516	0600	0608	0708	0808	0908	and hourly until	2308
Hanau Hbf ... **921** d.	0500	0539	0616	0656	0709	0809	0909	1009		0009
Offenbach (Main) Hbf ... **921** d.	0509	0548	0625	|	0717	0817	0921	1017		0017
Frankfurt (Main) Hbf ... **921** a.	0520	0559	0636	0716	0728	0828	0932	1028		0028

Fulda - Kassel ♠

km		Ⓐ	Ⓐ	Ⓐ	†	⚒	Ⓐ																		Ⓐ
0	**Fulda** ... **908** d.	...	...	0548	0610	0616	...	0719	0819	*0900*	1019	*1100*	1219	*1300*	1419	*1500*	1619	*1700*	1819	*1900*	2019	*2118**	2221	2259	2357
42	Bad Hersfeld ... **908** d.	...	0521	0616	0639	0644	0715	0748	0848	0944	1048	1145	1248	1343	1448	1543	1648	1743	1848	1945	2048	2145	2250	2328	0028
56	Bebra ... **908** d.	0437	0535	0627	0650	0657	0727	0757	0857	0957	1057	1157	1257	1357	1457	1557	1657	1757	1857	1957	2059	2157	2301	2340	0038
62	Rotenburg (Fulda) ... d.	0443	0541	0634	0656	0704	0734	0804	0904	1004	1104	1204	1304	1404	1504	1604	1704	1804	1904	2004	2105	2204	...	...	...
84	Melsungen ... d.	0504	0600	0653	0715	0723	0753	0823	0923	1023	1123	1223	1323	1423	1523	1623	1723	1823	1923	2023	2124	2223	...	...	...
110	**Kassel** Wilhelmshöhe ... § a.	0531	0617	0713	0741	0742	0813	0842	0942	1042	1142	1242	1342	1442	1542	1642	1742	1842	1942	2042	2143	2243	...	...	...
114	**Kassel** Hbf ... § a.	0536	0623	0718	0747	0748	0818	0849	0949	1049	1149	1249	1349	1449	1549	1649	1749	1849	1949	2053	2153	2253	...	...	...

		ⒶB	Ⓐ	ⒶB	⚒	Ⓒ	Ⓐ		†	⚒														①–⑥	⑦
Kassel Hbf ... § d.	...	...	...	...	0506	0606	0629	0659	0806	0810	0910	1010	1110	1210	1310	1410	1510	1610	1710	1810	1910	2010	2105**r**	2309	2329
Kassel Wilhelmshöhe ... § d.	...	...	...	...	0510	0614	0633	0704	0814	0814	0914	1014	1114	1214	1314	1414	1514	1614	1714	1814	1914	2014	2114	2315	2335
Melsungen ... d.	...	...	...	...	0530	0634	0651	0731	0834	0834	0934	1034	1134	1234	1334	1434	1534	1634	1734	1834	1934	2034	2134	2343	2359
Rotenburg (Fulda) ... d.	...	...	...	...	0549	0652	0710	0751	0852	0852	0952	1052	1152	1252	1352	1452	1552	1652	1752	1852	1952	2052	2152	0001	0018
Bebra ... **908** d.	0315	0359	0425	0522	0558	0700	0717	0800	0900	0900	1000	1100	1200	1300	1400	1500	1600	1700	1801	1900	2000	2100	2200	0008	0024
Bad Hersfeld ... **908** d.	0325	0409	0437	0531	0608	0709	0726	0810	0909	0909	1010	1109	1211	1309	1411	1510	1610	1709	1811	1909	2010	2110	2210	...	...
Fulda ... **908** a.	0355	0436	0507	0558	0638	0738	0755	*0853*	0938	0938	*1053*	1138	*1253*	1338	*1453*	1538	*1653*	1738	*1853*	1938	*2053*	2139	2239	...	...

B – [12] Bebra - Fulda - Frankfurt.
r – 2110 on Ⓐ.
* – Connection by *ICE* train.
§ – See also Tables **804** and **806**.
♠ – Most services are operated by CANTUS Verkehrsgesellschaft. 2nd class only.

IC services ◇ KASSEL - HANNOVER - HAMBURG 902

See Table **900** for faster *ICE* trains Karlsruhe - Frankfurt - Kassel - Göttingen - Hannover - Hamburg and v.v. See Table **903** for other regional services operated by *metronom*.

km		*IC*	*IC*	*IC*	*IC*	*IC*	*IC*	*IC*	*IC*	*IC*	*IC*	*IC*	*IC*	*IC*	*IC*	*IC*	*EC*	*IC*	*IC*	*IC*	*IC*	*IC*	*IC*	*ICE*	*ICE*	*ICE*
	See note ⊠	**2178**	**2184**	**2176**	**2182**	**2182**	**2378**	**2376**	**2170**	**2170**	**2374**	**2174**	**2372**	**2082**	**2370**	**2270**	**340**	**1888**	**2276**	**2288**	**1880**	**2274**	**2274**	**580**	**272**	**272**
		①-⑤	①-⑤	①-⑤	①-⑤	①-⑥	①-⑥		⑥⑦		**P**	⑤			**H**	⑤⑦	⑧	⑦	①-⑥	⑦	⑦	⑤⑦	⑦	⑦	⑥	①-⑤
			O					**N**	**L**	**T**				**B**	**K**	**K**	**A**	**F**			**M**			**M**	**Z**	**Z**
		🍷	🍷	🍷			🍷	🍷	🍷	🍷	🍷	🍷	🍷	🍷	🍷	🍷		🍷	🍷	🍷	🍷			🍴	🍴	🍴
	Karlsruhe Hbf **911** d.	...	...	...	...	...	...	0647**e**	...	...	0854	0854	1054	...	1253	1253	...	...	1454	1454	...	1654	1654	...	2000	2000
	Frankfurt (M) Hbf ◐ d.	...	...	...	...	...	0623	0823	1017	...	1023	1023	1223	...	1423	1423	...	...	1623	1623	...	1823	1823	...	2113	2113
0	**Kassel** Wilhelmshöhe d.	...	...	...	0623	...	0828	1028	1159**h**	...	1228	1228	1428	1554	1628	1628	...	1754	1828	1828	1950	2029	2029	2236	2244	2244
45	**Göttingen** d.	...	...	0548	0645	...	0850	1050	1219**h**	...	1250	1250	1450	1615	1650	1650	...	1815	1850	1850	2012	2051	2051	2256	2305	2305
65	Northeim (Han) ▲ d.	...	...	0600	0658	...	0902	1102	|	...	1302	1302	1502	|	1702	1702	...	|	1902	1902	|	2103	2103	|	|	|
84	Kreiensen ▲ d.	...	...	0612	0711	...	0915	1115	|	...	1315	1315	1515	|	1715	1715	...	|	1915	1915	|	2115	2115	|	|	|
103	Alfeld (Leine) ▲ d.	...	...	0625	0724	...	0928	1128	|	...	1328	1328	1528	|	1728	1728	...	|	1928	1928	|	2128	2128	|	|	|
120	Elze (Han) ▲ d.	...	...	0637	0737	...	|	|	|	...	|	|	|	|	|	|	...	|	|	|	|	|	|	|	|	|
153	**Hannover** Hbf a.	...	...	0656	0756	...	0956	1156	1258	...	1356	1356	1556	1654	1756	1756	...	1855	1956	1956	2051	2156	2156	2332	2341	0003
153	**Hannover** Hbf d.	0511	0555	0659	0759	0759	0959	1159	1301	1301	1359	1359	1559	1658	1759	1759	...	1858	1959	1959	2055	...	2159	2336	2345	0006
194	Celle d.	0531	0620	0720	0820	0820	1020	1220	1321	1321	1420	1420	1620	1719	1820	1820	...	1918	2020	2020	2116	...	2220	2357	|	0027
246	Uelzen d.	0555	0643	0743	0843	0843	1043	1243	1344	1344	1442	1442	1643	1743	1843	1843	1937	1943	2043	2043	2143	...	2243	0019	0036	0051
259	Bad Bevensen d.	|	|	|	0850	0850	|	|	|	|	1450	1450	1651	|	|	|	|	|	|	|	|	...	|	|	|	|
282	Lüneburg d.	0614	0700	0800	0903	0903	1100	1300	1401	1401	1502	1502	1703	1759	1900	1900	1953	2000	2100	2100	2159	...	2300	0035	0052	0107
331	**Hamburg** Hbf a.	0644	0728	0826	0931	0931	1127	1328	1429	1429	1529	1529	1730	1827	1927	1927	2024	2029	2126	2126	2225	...	2327	0103	0119	0134
338	**Hamburg** Altona a.	0658	|	0843	|	|	1141	|	...	...	1546	|	|	1842	1955	|	2039	...	2141	|	2239	...	2342	0117	0133	0148
	Rostock Hbf **830** a.	...	0932	...	1132	1132	...	1532	...	...	...	1732	1932	...	...	2132	...	...	...	2341	...	...	...	...	...	...
	Stralsund **830** a.	...	1030	...	1230	1230**j**	...	1630	...	...	...	...	2032	...	...	2230	...	...	...	...	...	...	...	...	...	...

	ICE	*IC*	*IC*	*IC*	*EC*	*IC*	*IC*	*IC*	*IC*	*IC*	*IC*	*IC*	*IC*	*IC*	*IC*	*IC*	*IC*	*IC*	*IC*	*IC*	*IC*	*IC*	*ICE*	*ICE*	*IC*
See note ⊠	**591**	**2275**	**2179**	**2277**	**341**	**2083**	**2279**	**1879**	**2371**	**2348**	**2373**	**1881**	**2375**	**2171**	**2181**	**2377**	**2173**	**2379**	**2379**	**2379**	**2175**	**2183**	**889**	**1089**	**2185**
	①-⑤	①-⑤	①-⑤	①-⑥	①-⑥		①-⑥	⑤		⑤		⑤⑦		⑤-⑦	①-④		⑧		⑤⑦	⑤	**G**	⑦	①-④	⑤⑦	⑦
		S			**A**	**B**			**K**			**M**		**L**	**W**	**O**						**O**		**g**	
	🍴			🍷		🍷	🍷	🍷	🍷		🍷	🍷	🍷	🍷	🍷	🍷	🍷	🍷	🍷	🍷	🍷	🍴	🍴	🍴	
Stralsund **830** d.	...	...	...	...	...	...	0527	...	...	...	0927	...	...	...	...	1327	...	1527	1527	1527	...	1727	...	...	1927
Rostock Hbf **830** d.	...	...	...	...	...	...	0625	...	...	...	1025	...	...	...	...	1425	...	1625	1625	1625	...	1825	...	...	2025
Hamburg Altona d.	0304	...	0510	0609	0642	0714	|	0914	1014	1114	|	1314**v**	1414	...	...	|	1714	|	|	|	1914	|	2113	...	|
Hamburg Hbf d.	0318	...	0524	0628	0705	0728	0827	0928	1028	1128	1228	1328	1428	1528	1528	1628	1728	1828	1828	1828	1928	2028	2127	2127	2228
Lüneburg d.	0350	...	0553	0657	0734	0758	0857	0957	1057	|	1257	1357	1457	1557	1557	1657	1757	1857	1857	1857	1957	2057	2156	2156	2257
Bad Bevensen d.	|	...	0605	|	|	|	|	|	|	|	|	|	|	1609	1609	|	1809	|	|	|	|	|	|	|	|
Uelzen d.	0410	...	0614	0714	0754	0814	0914	1014	1114	1206	1314	1413	1514	1618	1618	1714	1818	1914	1914	1914	2016	2114	2212	2213	2314
Celle d.	0439	...	0636	0736	...	0838	0936	1037	1136	|	1336	|	1536	1639	1639	1736	1840	1936	1936	1936	2039	2136	2237	2236	2336
Hannover Hbf a.	0459	...	0656	0756	...	0858	0956	1056	1156	1246	1356	1453	1556	1658	1658	1756	1906	1956	1956	1956	2101	2156	2256	2256	2358
Hannover Hbf d.	0518	0600	...	0800	...	0901	1000	1059	1200	...	1400	1456	1600	1702	1702	1800	...	...	2000	2000	...	...	...	...	...
Elze (Han) ▲ d.	|	|	...	|	...	|	|	|	|	...	|	|	|	|	1722	|	...	...	|	|	...	...	...	...	...
Alfeld (Leine) ▲ d.	|	0628	...	0828	...	|	1028	|	1228	...	1428	|	1628	|	1732	1828	...	...	2028	2028	...	...	...	...	...
Kreiensen ▲ d.	|	0641	...	0841	...	|	1041	|	1241	...	1441	|	1641	|	1745	1841	...	...	2041	2041	...	...	...	...	...
Northeim (Han) ▲ d.	|	0655	...	0855	...	|	1055	|	1255	...	1455	|	1655	|	1758	1855	...	...	2055	2055	...	...	...	...	...
Göttingen d.	0555	0710	...	0910	...	0943**r**	1110	1140**r**	1310	...	1510	1536	1710	1742	1811	1910	...	...	2108	2110	...	...	...	...	...
Kassel Wilhelmshöhe a.	0613	0729	...	0929	...	1003	1129	1201**r**	1329	...	1529	1557	1729	1801	...	1929	...	...	...	2129	...	...	...	...	...
Frankfurt (Main) Hbf ◐ a.	0744	0933	...	1133	...	...	1333	1336	1533	...	1733	...	1933	1950	...	2133	...	...	...	2333	...	...	...	...	...
Karlsruhe Hbf **911** a.	...	...	...	1301	...	...	1501	...	1701	...	1901	...	2105**a**	...	...	2322**t**	...	...	...	...	...	...	...	...	...

A – WAWEL – [12] Kraków - Cottbus - Berlin - Stendal - Hamburg and v.v.
B – KÖNIGSSEE – [12] and 🍷 Berchtesgaden - München - Augsburg - Hamburg and v.v.; [12] Oberstdorf (**2084/5**) - Augsburg - Hamburg and v.v.
F – [12] and 🍷 München - Hamburg - Flensburg.
G – ①②③④⑦ only.
H – ①②③④⑥ only.
K – From / to Konstanz (Table **916**).
L – To / from Westerland (Table **821**).
M – From / to München (Table **900**).
N – To Ostseebad Binz on ⑥ (Table **844**).
O – To / from Ostseebad Binz (Table **844**).
P – Daily except ⑤.
S – To Stuttgart (Table **930**).
T – To Westerland (Table **821**) daily until Oct. 25, also ④-⑦ from Oct. 29. Train number **2180** on ①-③ from Oct. 26.
W – From Westerland (Table **821**) on ①-④ until Oct. 26, also ① from Nov. 2. Train number **2281** on ②-④ from Oct. 27.
Z – [12] and 🍴 Zürich - Basel - Hamburg.

a – ①-⑤ only.
e – ①-⑥ only.
g – Not June 19, 26, July 3, 10, 17.
h – Until June 28 departs Kassel 1204, Göttingen 1223.
j – 1249 on ⑥ until Oct. 24.
r – 1–5 minutes earlier until June 30.
t – ⑤⑦ only. Arrives 2304 on ⑦.
v – ⑦ only.

◇ – Also *ICE* trains making stops between Hannover and Hamburg.
▲ – On June 14, 15, 20, 21, 22 most *IC* trains do not call at Northeim, Kreiensen, Alfeld and Elze. On July 11, 12 most *IC* trains do not call at Kreiensen, Alfeld and Elze.
◐ – See Tables **806** (via Gießen) or **900** (via Fulda).
⊠ – **June 14 - July 19** all services are subject to alteration Hannover - Hamburg and v.v. Most *IC* trains in this table do not operate between Hannover and Hamburg during this period (see Table **900** for alternative services).

metronom Local services GÖTTINGEN - HANNOVER - UELZEN - HAMBURG 903

Services below are operated by ***metronom***. For *ICE* services see Table **900**. For *IC* services see Table **902**.

		⚒		⚒	†	⚒	◧			⊖	⊙		⊖◇							◇				◇	Ⓑr	⚒	†
Göttingen d.	...	...	...	0407	0502	*0502*	0607	0707	0812	0907	1012	1107	1212	1307	1412	1507	1612	1707	1812	1907	...	2012	...	2107	2207	2207
Northeim (Han) d.	...	...	...	0420	0515	*0515*	0620	0720	0825	0920	1025	1120	1225	1320	1425	1520	1625	1720	1825	1920	...	2025	...	2120	2220	2220
Kreiensen d.	...	...	...	0433	0533	*0533*	0633	0733	0838	0933	1038	1133	1238	1333	1438	1533	1638	1733	1838	1933	...	2038	...	2133	2233	2233
Alfeld (Leine) d.	...	...	...	0446	0546	*0546*	0646	0746	0851	0946	1051	1146	1251	1346	1451	1546	1651	1746	1851	1946	...	2051	...	2146	2246	2246
Elze (Han) d.	...	...	...	0458	0558	*0558*	0658	0758	0903	0958	1103	1158	1303	1358	1503	1558	1703	1758	1903	1958	...	2103	...	2158	2258	2258
Hannover Hbf a.	...	...	...	0521	0627	*0627*	0727	0828	0926	1028	1126	1227	1326	1428	1526	1628	1726	1828	1926	2028	...	2126	...	2228	2321	2321
Hannover Hbf d.	...	...	...	0540	0640	0640	0740	0840	0940	1040	1140	1240	1340	1440	1540	1640	1740	1840	1940	2040	...	...	2140	2248	2340	2351
Celle d.	...	0506	...	0606	0706	0706	0806	0906	1006	1106	1206	1306	1406	1506	1606	1706	1806	1906	2006	2106	...	...	2206	2316	0006	0019
Uelzen a.	...	0536	...	0637	0737	0737	0837	0937	1037	1137	1237	1337	1437	1537	1637	1737	1837	1937	2037	2137	...	...	2237	...	0039	0047
	⚒	⚒	⚒	d		|		⚒	|	|		|							|	†	⚒		|			
Uelzen d.	0501	0540	0628	0702	...	0800	0900	1001	1100	1200	1302	1400	1502	1600	1700	1800	1900	2000	2100	2200	2200	...	2300	...	...	...
Bad Bevensen d.	0510	0549	0636	0710	...	0809	0909	1009	1109	1209	1310	1409	1510	1609	1709	1809	1909	2009	2109	2209	2209	...	2309	...	...	...
Lüneburg d.	0524	0603	0651	0728	...	0828	0928	1028	1128	1228	1328	1428	1528	1628	1728	1828	1928	2028	2128	2228	2234	...	2323	...	...	...
Hamburg Hbf a.	0556	0635	0723	0802	...	0902	1004	1102	1202	1302	1402	1502	1602	1701	1802	1904	2001	2101	2203	2301	2319	...	2358	...	...	...

				Ⓐ	Ⓒ	⚒			⚒	⊖◇	⚒		⚒		⊙				◇						†	⚒
Hamburg Hbf d.	...	...	...	0544	0554	0652	...	0754	0857	0954	1057	1157	1257	1357	1457	1554	1657	1754	1857	1957	...	2057	2159	2255	2355	2355
Lüneburg d.	...	...	...	0617	0627	0722	...	0827	0933	1033	1133	1233	1333	1433	1533	1627	1733	1827	1933	2033	...	2133	2233	2328	0028	0041
Bad Bevensen d.	...	...	...	0632	0645	0741	...	0846	0949	1048	1149	1248	1349	1448	1549	1646	1749	1846	1949	2049	...	2147	2248	2343	0043	0055
Uelzen a.	...	...	...	0641	0653	0749	...	0854	0957	1056	1157	1256	1357	1456	1557	1654	1757	1854	1957	2057	...	2157	2256	2352	0052	0104
	⚒	⊖	◧	Ⓐ	Ⓒ	|	†		d	|	d		d		|				|	†	Ⓐ					
Uelzen d.	0413	0513	0609	0651	0709	0809	0809	0909	1009	1109	1209	1309	1409	1509	1609	1709	1809	1909	2009	2109	2128	2217	...	...	...	...
Celle d.	0447	0547	0647	0747**v**	0747	0847	0847	0947	1047	1147	1247	1347	1447	1547	1647	1747	1847	1947	2047	2149	2201	2251	...	...	...	...
Hannover Hbf a.	0514	0614	0714	0814	0814	0914	0914	1014	1114	1214	1314	1414	1514	1614	1714	1814	1914	2014	2114	2214	2226	2317	...	...	...	...
Hannover Hbf d.	0530	0633	0730**e**	0833	0833	*0933*	0933	1033	1130	1233	1330	1433	1530	1633	1730	1833	1930	2033	*2133*	2237	2237	2330	...	...	...	...
Elze (Han) d.	0558	0658	0758	0855	0855	*1001*	1001	1055	1158	1255	1358	1455	1558	1655	1758	1855	1958	2055	*2201*	2258	2258	2358	...	...	...	...
Alfeld (Leine) d.	0610	0710	0810	0906	0906	*1013*	1013	1106	1210	1306	1410	1506	1610	1706	1810	1906	2010	2106	*2213*	2310	2310	0010	...	...	...	...
Kreiensen d.	0623	0723	0823	0919	0919	*1026*	1026	1119	1223	1319	1423	1519	1623	1719	1823	1919	2023	2119	*2226*	2323	2323	0023	...	...	...	...
Northeim (Han) d.	0637	0737	0837	0934	0934	*1040*	1040	1134	1237	1334	1437	1534	1637	1734	1837	1934	2037	2134	*2240*	2337	2337	0037	...	...	...	...
Göttingen d.	0649	0749	0849	0946	0946	*1052*	1052	1146	1249	1346	1449	1546	1649	1746	1849	1946	2049	2146	*2252*	2349	2349	0049	...	...	...	...

d – Runs daily from Uelzen.
e – 0734 on Ⓐ.
r – Also Oct. 3.
v – Arrives 0728.
⊖ – Change trains at Hannover on ⚒.
◇ – Change trains at Uelzen on †.
◧ – Change trains at Hannover on Ⓐ.
⊙ – Change trains at Uelzen on ⚒.

904 MÜNCHEN - NÜRNBERG fast services

ICE and *IC* services

See Table **905** for regional services

	ICE	ICE	ICE	ICE	ICE	ICE	ICE	ICE	ICE	ICE	ICE	ICE	ICE	ICE	ICE	ICE	ICE	ICE	ICE	ICE	ICE	ICE	ICE	ICE	ICE
	1518	**1514**	**822**	**1714**	**684**	**1612**	**820**	**1126**	**886**	**728**	**682**	**1512**	**1610**	**726**	**882**	**724**	**680**	**108**	**1608**	**722**	**880**	**588**	**720**	**1508**	**628**
												1712											**1022**	**1708**	
	①	①–⑤	①	⑥	①–⑤	①–⑥	①–⑤	①						①–⑥											
See note ⊠	●	⊠	**E**	⊠	⊖	⊠	**E**				⊖	⊠	⊠	**D**			⊖	⊠**B**	⊠	**E**		⊖		⊠**G**	**E**
			🍷	✗	✗	✗	🍷	✗	✗	🍷	✗	✗	✗	🍷	✗	🍷	✗	✗	✗	🍷	✗	✗	🍷	✗	🍷
München Hbf ... **930** d.	0014	0431	0451	0516	0517	0530	0551	0614	0620	0651	0650	0720	0743	0755	0820	0855	0915	0921	0945	0955	1020	1052	1055	1120	1155
München Pasing ... **930** d.	0022	0439				0538					0658		0751						0953			1101			
Augsburg Hbf ... **930** d.	0054	0513				0615					0731		0822						1024			1132			
Donauwörth ... d.	0112	0532				0634					0752														
Treuchtlingen ... d.	0132	0553				0653																			
Ingolstadt Hbf ... d.			0529	0554	0557		0630		0659	0729		0759			0859			0959			1059			1159	
Nürnberg Hbf ... a.	0219	0626	0557	0626	0628	0727	0657	0726	0730	0757		0831	0926	0857	0930	0957	1023	1031	1127	1057	1130		1157	1231	1257
Würzburg Hbf **900 920** ... a.			0654		0727		0754	0825	0828	0854	0927			0954	1028	1054	1127			1154	1228	1327	1254		1354
Frankfurt (Main) Hbf **920** ... a.			0805				0905	0936		1005				1105		1205				1305			1405		1505
Köln Hbf **910** ... a.			0914**k**				1014**k**	1205		1140				1214**k**		1340				1414**k**			1540		1614**k**
Berlin Hbf **851** ... a.	0700	1100	...	1100		1205	...	...		...		1302	1405	...		...		1500	1605	...			...	1700	...
Hamburg Hbf **900** ... a.	...	...	...	...	1053	...	...	...	1156	...	1253	...	...	...	1353	...	1454	...	...	...	1555	1654	...	...	...

	ICE	ICE	ICE	ICE	ICE	ICE	ICE	ICE	ICE	ICE	ICE	IC	ICE	ICE	ICE	ICE	ICE	ICE	ICE	ICE	ICE	ICE	ICE	ICE	ICE
	788	**1606**	**586**	**626**	**1506**	**1604**	**624**	**786**	**622**	**584**	**1504**	**2206**	**928**	**620**	**926**	**784**	**1602**	**1700**	**528**	**582**	**1502**	**1600**	**526**	**782**	**980**
		1706			**1716**	**1704**				**1084**	**1724**	Ⓑ	⑦	①–⑤	⑥		Ⓑ	①–⑤	**924**		**1722**	Ⓑ	Ⓑ		⑤
See note ⊠	**Z**	⊠**R**	⊖		⊠	⊠	**D**		**D**	**S**	⊠		**D**		**D**		⊠**V**	¶	**T**		⊠	⊠	**D**	⊖	**H**
	✗	✗	✗	🍷	✗	✗	🍷	✗	🍷	✗	✗	🍷	🍷	🍷	🍷	✗	✗		🍷	✗	✗	✗	🍷	✗	✗
München Hbf ... **930** d.	1220	1225	1251	1255	1320	1341	1355	1420	1455	1515	1520	1529	1555	1555	1555	1616	1621	1638	1650	1714	1720	1745	1755	1820	1849
München Pasing ... **930** d.			1300									1537													1857
Augsburg Hbf ... **930** d.			1331			1419						1613						1714				1822			1932
Donauwörth ... d.												1632						1733				1842			1952
Treuchtlingen ... d.												1656						1755							2012
Ingolstadt Hbf ... d.	1259				1359			1459			1559					1659			1729		1759			1859	
Nürnberg Hbf ... a.	1330	1334		1357	1431	1523	1457	1530	1557	1623	1631	1733	1657	1657	1657	1730	1734	1829	1757	1823	1831	1928	1857	1930	
Würzburg Hbf **900 920** ... a.	1428		1527	1454			1554	1628	1654	1727		...	1754	1754	1754	1828	...	...	1854	1927			1954	2028	2129
Frankfurt (Main) Hbf **920** ... a.				1605			1705		1805			...	1905	1905	1905		...	...	2005				2105		...
Köln Hbf **910** ... a.				1732			1814**k**		1914**k**			...	2014**k**	2031	2040		...	...	2113**k**				2219**k**		...
Berlin Hbf **851** ... a.		1805		...	1900	2007	...		...		2100	...	...	...	...		...	...	...		2300	0014**p**	...		...
Hamburg Hbf **900** ... a.	1754	...	1853	...	...	...	...	1954	...	2054	...	...	...	...	...	2154	...	...	...	2254	...	...	...	0003	...

	ICE	ICE	ICE	ICE	ICE	ICE	ICE	ICE	ICE	ICE	ICE
	580	**524**	**1500**	**522**	**780**	**520**	**922**	**1120**	**920**	**920**	**1620**
	⊡				⑦	①–④	⑤–⑦	⑦	Ⓑ	⑦	⑥
See note ⊠	**Q**	**D**	⊠**L**		**A**						
	✗	🍷	✗	🍷	✗	🍷	✗	✗	🍷	🍷	✗
München Hbf ... **930** d.	1849	1855	1920	1951	2020	2055	2055	2154	2255	2255	2255
München Pasing ... **930** d.	1857										
Augsburg Hbf ... **930** d.	1932										
Donauwörth ... d.	1952										
Treuchtlingen ... d.	2012										
Ingolstadt Hbf ... d.			1959	2029	2059			2232	2333	2333	2333
Nürnberg Hbf ... a.		1957	2031	2057	2130	2157	2158	2304	0002	0002	0005
Würzburg Hbf **900 920** ... a.	2129	2054	...	2154	2235	2254	2255	0001	...	0100	...
Frankfurt (Main) Hbf **920** ... a.		2205	...	2300**f**	...	...	0013	0116	...	...	...
Köln Hbf **910** ... a.		2341**k**	...	...	...	...	...	...	...	...	...
Berlin Hbf **851** ... a.		...	...	...	...	...	...	...	...	...	...
Hamburg Hbf **900** ... a.	0103	...	...	...	...	...	...	...	...	...	...

	ICE	ICE	ICE	ICE	ICE	ICE	ICE	ICE	IC
	1701	**823**	**981**	**985**	**827**	**1601**	**1501**	**521**	**2201**
	①–⑤	①–⑤	①–⑤	①–⑤	①–⑤	①–⑤	①–⑥		①–⑥
See note ⊠							⊠**N**		
		🍷	✗	✗	🍷	✗	✗	🍷	
Hamburg Hbf **900** ... d.	...	...	...	...	...	...	...	...	...
Berlin Hbf **851** ... d.	...	...	...	...	...	...	...	...	...
Köln Hbf **910** ... d.	...	...	...	...	...	...	...	0420	...
Frankfurt (Main) Hbf **920** d.	...	...	...	...	...	...	...	0551	...
Würzburg Hbf **900 920** .. d.	...	...	...	...	0603	...	...	0705	...
Nürnberg Hbf ... d.	0412	0600	...	0627	0700	0618	0728	0802	0718
Ingolstadt Hbf ... d.		0629	...	0701	0729		0801		
Treuchtlingen ... d.	0445		...			0652			0752
Donauwörth ... d.	0506		0608			0712			0812
Augsburg Hbf ... **930** a.	0529		0627			0729			0832
München Pasing ... **930** a.	0559		0702			0800			0902
München Hbf ... **930** a.	0610	0706	0712	0738	0806	0810	0839	0904	0913

	ICE	ICE	ICE	ICE	ICE	ICE	ICE	ICE	ICE	ICE	ICE	ICE	ICE	ICE	ICE	ICE	ICE	ICE	ICE	ICE	ICE	ICE	ICE	ICE	ICE
	1603	**781**	**523**	**1123**	**581**	**1503**	**925**	**525**	**1605**	**783**	**527**	**1505**	**583**	**529**	**785**	**1607**	**621**	**1507**	**585**	**623**	**1609**	**787**	**625**	**1509**	**627**
	①–⑤	①–⑥	①–⑤	⑥		①–⑥	⑥⑦	①–⑤	①–⑥	①–⑥	①–⑥		**1083**			**1727**		**1707**			**1709**			**1719**	
See note ⊠	⊠**L**	**M**	**D**	**D**	⊖	⊠**J**	**D**	**D**	⊠**V**	**X**	**U**	⊠	**S**⊖	**D**		⊠	**D**	⊠**W**	⊖		⊠**R**	**Z**	**D**	⊠	
	✗	✗	🍷	🍷	✗	✗	🍷	🍷	✗	✗	🍷	✗	✗	🍷	✗	✗	🍷	✗	✗	🍷	✗	✗	🍷	✗	🍷
Hamburg Hbf **900** ... d.	...	...	...	...	0458	...	...	...	...	0605**r**	...	...	0701	...	0803	...	...	...	0901	...	...	1001	...	...	...
Berlin Hbf **851** ... d.	...	...	...	...		...	...	...	...		...	0652		...		0752	...	0858**e**		...	0952		...	1058	...
Köln Hbf **910** ... d.	...	...	0518**k**	0535**k**		...	0619**k**	0644**k**	...		0744**k**			0844**k**			0944**k**			1020			1144**k**		1220
Frankfurt (Main) Hbf **920** ... d.	...	...	0654	0654		...	0754	0754	...		0854			0954			1054			1154			1254		1354
Würzburg Hbf **900 920** ... d.	...	0729	0805	0805	0831	...	0905	0905	...	0930	1005		1031	1105	1129		1205		1231	1305		1329	1405		1505
Nürnberg Hbf ... d.	0823	0827	0902	0902	0931	0931	1002	1002	1023	1027	1102	1128		1202	1227	1229	1302	1328	1332	1402	1423	1427	1502	1528	1602
Ingolstadt Hbf ... d.		0901			1003					1101		1201			1301			1401				1501		1601	
Treuchtlingen ... d.																									
Donauwörth ... d.																									
Augsburg Hbf ... **930** a.						1032							1223			1332									
München Pasing ... **930** a.													1254												
München Hbf ... **930** a.	0938	0942	1004	1004	1041	1110	1104	1104	1137	1142	1204	1240	1304	1304	1339	1412	1404	1439	1443	1504	1539	1543	1604	1640	1704

	ICE	ICE	ICE	ICE	ICE	ICE	ICE	ICE	ICE	ICE	ICE	ICE	ICE	ICE	ICE	ICE	ICE	ICE	ICE	ICE	ICE	ICE	ICE	ICE	ICE
	587	**789**	**629**	**1711**	**109**	**589**	**721**	**881**	**1613**	**723**	**1513**	**681**	**725**	**883**	**727**	**1615**	**1515**	**683**	**729**	**1617**	**885**	**1025**	**821**	**685**	**1517**
			Ⓑ							Ⓑ					Ⓑ					⑦		★	⑤⑦	⑦	**1737**
See note ⊠	⊖		**D**	⊠**R**	⊠**B**	⊖	**D**		⊠	**E**	⊠	⊖	**D**		**E**	⊠	⊠	⊖	**E**	⊠				⊖	⊠
	✗	✗	🍷	✗	✗	✗	🍷	✗	✗	🍷	✗	✗	🍷	✗	🍷	✗	✗	✗	🍷	✗	✗	✗	🍷	✗	✗
Hamburg Hbf **900** ... d.	1101	1201	...	...	...	1301	...	1401	...	...	...	1501	...	1603	...	...	...	1701	...	...	1803	...	...	1901	...
Berlin Hbf **851** ... d.			...	1152	1258		...		1352	...	1458		...		...	1552	1658		...	1752		...	...		1858
Köln Hbf **910** ... d.			1344**k**				1428			1544**k**			1644**k**		1744**k**				1843**k**			1753	1928		
Frankfurt (Main) Hbf **920** ... d.			1454				1554			1654			1754		1854				1954			2018	2054		
Würzburg Hbf **900 920** ... d.	1431	1529	1605			1631	1705	1729		1805		1831	1905	1929	2005			2031	2105		2134	2130	2205	2230	
Nürnberg Hbf ... d.		1627	1702	1629	1728		1802	1827	1829	1902	1928		2003	2027	2102	2029	2129		2202	2224	2231	2235	2303	2328	2338
Ingolstadt Hbf ... d.		1701			1801			1901			2001			2101			2202		2231	2258	2304	2311		0001	0012
Treuchtlingen ... d.																									
Donauwörth ... d.	1608								1917							2117									
Augsburg Hbf ... **930** a.	1626			1731		1822			1934			2022				2134		2222							
München Pasing ... **930** a.	1656			1801		1853						2052				2205		2252							
München Hbf ... **930** a.	1707	1738	1804	1811	1838	1903	1904	1938	2012	2004	2040	2102	2105	2138	2204	2215	2240	2302	2307	2340	2344	2348	0005	0038	0049

A – To Kassel (Table **900**).
B – From / to Innsbruck (Table **951**).
D – To / from Dortmund (Table **800**).
E – To / from Essen (Table **800**).
G – From Garmisch on ⑥ (d. 0925).
H – To Hannover (Table **900**).
J – From Halle (Table **851**).
L – To / from Leipzig (Table **851**).
M – [12] and ✗ (Hannover ①⑥ -) Fulda - München.
N – From Lichtenfels on ①–⑤ (Table **851**).
Q – [12] and ✗ München - Fulda (- Hamburg ⑦).
R – To / from Warnemünde (via Rostock) on dates in Table **835**.
S – From / to Lübeck on dates in Table **825**.
T – [12] and 🍷 (Garmisch ⑥ -) München - Dortmund.
U – [12] and 🍷 Dortmund - München (- Garmisch ⑥).
V – [12] and ✗ München - Leipzig - Dresden and v.v.
W – [12] and ✗ (Berlin ①–⑥ -) Leipzig - München (- Garmisch ⑥).
X – [12] and ✗ (Hamburg ⑥ -) Hannover - München.
Z – To / from Garmisch on ⑥ until Oct. 24 (Table **895**).

f – Frankfurt (Main) **Süd**. Continues to Frankfurt Flughafen (a. 2315).
k – Köln **Messe/Deutz**.
p – Nürnberg - Berlin on ⑤⑦ only.
r – ⑥ only.

★ – Daily except ⑤.
⊡ – ①②③④⑦.
¶ – Train number *IC* **2200** on ⑤.
⊖ – Conveys [12] München - Hannover - Bremen and v.v. (Tables **900** / **813**).
● – Aug. 3 - Sept. 14 München Hbf d. 0128, Pasing d. 0136, Augsburg d. 0208, Donauwörth d. 0226, Treuchtlingen d. 0246, Nürnberg a. 0333, Berlin a. 0900 (train number **1576**).
⊠ – **Aug. 1 - Sept. 14** services to / from Berlin via Leipzig are subject to alteration. Trains on this route will run with different train numbers and altered timings north of Nürnberg (including later arrivals, earlier departures and altered destination/originating stations). Further details can be found in a special version of Table **851** on page 41. Timings between München and Nürnberg are unchanged during this period (unless shown otherwise).

RE / RB services — Regional services MÜNCHEN - NÜRNBERG — 905

See Table **904** for *ICE* and *IC* services

km		©	Ⓐ	⚒r				Ⓐ		⚒r		⚒r						⚒r					⚒r		
0	**München** Hbf ...... **930** d.	*0203*	...	...	...	0504	...	0526	0537	...	0625	...	0703	0729	0734	...	0829	*0834*	0905	0929	0934	1029	...	1105	1127
7	München Pasing .. **930** d.	*0209*	...	...	...	│	...	│	0543	**K**	│	...	│	│	0740	**L**	│	*0840*	│	│	0940	│	...	│	│
62	**Augsburg** Hbf ..... **930** d.	0327	...	0521	...	│	...	│	0628	0718	│	0721	│	│	0828	0918	│	0925	│	│	1028	│	1117	│	│
103	Donauwörth .... d.	0357	...	0559	...	│	...	│	0659	0739	│	0759	│	│	0859	0939	│	0959	│	│	1059	│	1159	│	│
	Pfaffenhofen (Ilm) .... d.	│	...	│	...	0529	...	0602	│	│	0701	│	0728	0805	│	│	0905	│	0930	1005	│	1105	│	1130	1205
	Ingolstadt Hbf .... a.	│	...	│	...	0548	...	0624	│	│	0723	│	0747	0827	│	│	0927	│	0949	1027	│	1127	│	1149	1227
	Ingolstadt Hbf .... d.	│	...	│	0529	0602	0627	0627	│	│	0726	│	0804	0830	│	│	0930	│	1004	1030	│	1130	│	1204	1230
	Kinding (Altmühltal) .. d.	│	...	│	│	0618	│	│	│	│	│	│	0820	│	│	│	│	│	1020	│	│	│	│	1220	│
	Allersberg (Rothsee) d.	│	...	│	│	0632	│	│	│	│	│	│	0834	│	│	│	│	│	1034	│	│	│	│	1234	│
	Eichstätt Bf ★ ...... d.	│	...	│	0556	│	0656	0656	│	│	0756	│	│	0856	│	│	0956	│	│	1056	│	1156	│	│	1256
137	**Treuchtlingen** .... a.	0417	...	0620	0620	│	0720	0720	0720	│	0820	0820	│	0920	0920	│	1020	1020	│	1120	1120	1220	1220	│	1320
137	**Treuchtlingen** .... d.	0418	0513	0625e	0626z	│	...	0726	0725z	│	0826z	0825e	│	0926e	0925z	│	1026z	1025e	│	1126e	1125z	1226z	1225e	│	1326e
146	Weißenburg (Bay) .... d.	0424	0519	0632e	0632z	│	...	0732	0732z	│	0832z	0832e	│	0932e	0932z	│	1032z	1032e	│	1132e	1132z	1232z	1232e	│	1332e
199	**Nürnberg** Hbf .... a.	0507	0604	0717e	0717z	0645	...	0817	0817z	0825	0917z	0917e	0849	1017e	1017z	1025	1117z	1117e	1047	1217e	1217z	1317z	1317e	1247	1417e

	△		⚒r						Ⓐ					Ⓐ	⑥⑦S						Ⓐ				†w
München Hbf .... **930** d.	1134	1229	...	1305	1329	1334	...	1429	*1434*	1505	1529	1536	1625	*1633*	1706	1705	1727	1734	...	1829	...	1905	1926	1933	...
München Pasing ... **930** d.	1140	│	...	│	│	1340	**L**	│	*1440*	│	│	1543	│	*1640*	│	│	│	1740	**L**	│	...	│	│	1940	**L**
Augsburg Hbf ...... **930** d.	1224	│	1318	│	│	1428	1518	│	1525	│	│	1628	│	1725	1743	│	│	1828	1918	│	1921	│	│	2028	2118
Donauwörth .... d.	1259	│	1359	│	│	1459	1539	│	1559	│	│	1659	│	1759	1805	│	│	1859	1939	│	1959	│	│	2059	2139
Pfaffenhofen (Ilm) ..... d.	│	1305	│	1330	1405	│	│	1505	│	1530	1605	│	1702	│	...	1730	1805	│	│	1905	│	1930	2002	│	│
Ingolstadt Hbf .... a.	│	1327	│	1349	1427	│	│	1527	│	1549	1627	│	1724	│	...	1749	1827	│	│	1927	│	1949	2025	│	│
Ingolstadt Hbf .... d.	│	1330	│	1404	1430	│	│	1530	│	1604	1630	│	1730	│	...	1804	1829	│	│	1930	│	2004	2031	│	│
Kinding (Altmühltal) ... d.	│	│	│	1420	│	│	│	│	│	1620	│	│	│	│	...	1820	│	│	│	│	│	2020	│	│	│
Allersberg (Rothsee) . d.	│	│	│	1434	│	│	│	│	│	1634	│	│	│	│	...	1834	│	│	│	│	│	2034	│	│	│
Eichstätt Bf ★ .... d.	│	1356	│	│	1456	│	│	1556	│	│	1656	│	1756	│	...	│	1856	│	│	1956	│	│	2056	│	│
Treuchtlingen .... a.	1320	1420	1420	│	1520	1520	│	1620	1620	│	1720	1720	1820	1820	...	│	1920	1920	│	2020	2020	│	2120	2120	│
Treuchtlingen .... d.	1325z	1426z	1425e	│	1526e	1525z	│	1626z	1625	│	1726e	1725z	1826z	1825	...	│	1926e	1925z	│	2026z	2025	│	2126e	2125z	│
Weißenburg (Bay) .... d.	1332z	1432z	1432e	│	1532e	1532z	│	1632z	1632	│	1732e	1732z	1832z	1832	...	│	1932e	1932z	│	2032z	2032	│	2132e	2132z	│
Nürnberg Hbf .... a.	1417z	1517z	1517e	1447	1617e	1617z	1625	1717z	1717	1648	1817e	1817z	1917z	1917	...	1847	2017e	2017z	2025	2117z	2117	2047	2217e	2217z	2225

		Ⓐ							
München Hbf .... **930** d.	2025	*2034*	2101	2109	2126	2203	2226	2301	2325
München Pasing ... **930** d.	│	*2040*	2107	│	│	2209	│	2307	│
Augsburg Hbf ...... **930** d.	│	2125	2154	│	│	2254	│	2354	│
Donauwörth .... d.	│	2159	2234	│	│	2332	│	0032	│
Pfaffenhofen (Ilm) ..... d.	2105	│	│	2134	2202	...	2302	...	0001
Ingolstadt Hbf .... a.	2128	│	│	2153	2224	...	2325	...	0024
Ingolstadt Hbf .... d.	2130	│	│	2158	2225	...	...	...	...
Kinding (Altmühltal) ... d.	│	│	│	2214	│	...	...	...	...
Allersberg (Rothsee) . d.	│	│	│	2228	│	...	...	...	...
Eichstätt Bf ★ .... d.	2156	│	│	│	2253	...	...	...	...
Treuctlingen .... a.	2220	2220	2255	│	2317	...	...	...	...
Treuchtlingen .... d.	2226z	2225	...	│	2322	...	...	...	...
Weißenburg (Bay) .... d.	2232z	2232	...	│	2328	...	...	...	...
Nürnberg Hbf .... a.	2317z	2317	...	2241	0011	...	...	...	...

km	km		©	Ⓐ			Ⓐ		Ⓐ	Ⓐ		©
0	0	**Nürnberg** Hbf .... d.	0046	...	0510	...	0437	0437z	0610	0526	0538z	...
	53	Weißenburg (Bay) .... d.	0128	...	│	...	0519	0519z	│	0608	0622z	...
	62	**Treuchtlingen** .... a.	0134	...	│	...	0526	0526z	│	0616	0630z	...
	62	**Treuchtlingen** .... d.	0135	0450	│	...	0527	0532	│	0631	0635	0635
	91	Eichstätt Bf ★ ...... d.	│	0514	│	...	│	0557	│	0655	│	0659
25		Allersberg (Rothsee) d.	│	│	0524	...	│	│	0623	│	│	│
59		Kinding (Altmühltal) .. d.	│	│	0539	...	│	│	0638	│	│	│
90	118	**Ingolstadt** Hbf .... a.	│	0532	0555	...	│	0623	0655	0723	│	0725
90	118	**Ingolstadt** Hbf .... d.	│	0533	0601	...	│	0633	0705	0732	│	0732
121	149	Pfaffenhofen (Ilm) .... d.	│	0555	0619	...	│	0656	0725	0756	│	0756
		Donauwörth .... d.	0158	│	│	0514	0603t	│	│	│	0658	│
		Augsburg Hbf ..... **930** a.	0222	│	│	0551	0641	│	│	│	0727	│
		München Pasing .. **930** a.	...	│	│	0645	...	│	│	│	0816	│
171	199	**München** Hbf ...... **930** a.	...	0633	0645	0652	...	0734	0752	0835	0824	0835

		⑥⑦S	⚒r				Ⓐ		⚒r		⑥h				⚒r		©				⚒r				
Nürnberg Hbf .... d.	0708	...	0629e	0633z	0738z	0738e	0835	0908	0839e	0839z	0935	0939z	0939e	1108	1038e	1038z	1134	1138z	1138e	1308	1238e	1238z	1338z	1338e	1508
Weißenburg (Bay) .... d.	│	...	0715e	0717z	0822z	0822e	│	│	0923e	0923z	│	1023z	1023e	│	1122e	1122z	│	1222z	1222e	│	1322e	1322z	1422z	1422e	│
Treuchtlingen .... a.	│	...	0723e	0725z	0830z	0830e	0905	│	0930e	0930z	│	1030z	1030e	│	1130e	1130z	│	1230z	1230e	│	1330e	1330z	1430z	1430e	│
Treuchtlingen .... d.	│	...	0735	0735	0835	0835	0906	│	0935	0936	│	1035	1035	│	1135	1135	│	1235	1240	│	1335	1336	1435	1435	│
Eichstätt Bf ★ .... d.	│	...	│	0759	│	0859	│	│	│	1000	│	│	1059	│	│	1159	│	│	1304	│	│	1400	│	1459	│
Allersberg (Rothsee) . d.	0721	...	│	│	│	│	│	0921	│	│	│	│	│	1121	│	│	│	│	│	1321	│	│	│	│	1521
Kinding (Altmühltal) ... d.	0736	...	│	│	│	│	│	0936	│	│	│	│	│	1136	│	│	│	│	│	1336	│	│	│	│	1536
Ingolstadt Hbf .... a.	0755	...	│	0825	│	0925	│	0955	│	1026	│	│	1125	1155	│	1225	│	│	1333	1355	│	1433	│	1525	1555
Ingolstadt Hbf .... d.	0805	...	│	0831	│	0931	│	1007	│	1031	│	│	1131	1205	│	1231	│	│	1334	1409	│	1434	│	1531	1605
Pfaffenhofen (Ilm) ..... d.	0825	...	│	0855	│	0955	│	1027	│	1055	│	│	1155	1225	│	1255	│	│	1356	1429	│	1456	│	1555	1625
Donauwörth .... d.	│	0752	0758	│	0858	│	0924	│	0958	│	1021	1058	│	│	1200	│	1221	1258	│	│	1358	│	1458	│	│
Augsburg Hbf ...... **930** a.	│	0819	0829	│	0929	│	0945	│	1030	│	1042	1129	│	│	1239	│	1242	1325	│	│	1430	│	1529	│	│
München Pasing ... **930** a.	│	│	*0914*	│	1014	│	...	│	*1114*	│	**L**	1214	│	│	...	│	**L**	1414	│	│	*1514*	│	1614	│	│
München Hbf .... **930** a.	0852	0859	*0922*	0934	1022	1035	...	1054	*1122*	1133	...	1222	1233	1252	...	1335	...	1422	1434	1453	*1522*	1535	1622	1633	1652

	Ⓐ		Ⓐ				Ⓐ						Ⓐ					Ⓐ		†w	Ⓐ	©			
Nürnberg Hbf .... d.	1438	1438z	1534	1538z	1538e	1708	1638	1638z	1734	1738z	1738e	1908	1838	1838z	1938z	1938e	2110	2038	2038z	2134	*2138*	2138	2138e	2233	2341
Weißenburg (Bay) .... d.	1522	1522z	│	1622z	1622e	│	1722	1722z	│	1822z	1822e	│	1922	1922z	2022z	2022e	│	2122	2122z	│	*2222*	2222	2222e	│	0023
Treuchtlingen .... a.	1530	1530z	│	1630z	1630e	│	1730	1730z	│	1830z	1830e	│	1930	1930z	2030z	2030e	│	2130	2130z	2204	*2230*	2230	2230e	2304	0031
Treuchtlingen .... d.	1535	1535	│	1635	1635	│	1735	1735	│	1835	1835	│	1935	1935	2035	2035	│	2138	2135	2205	2235	2235	2235	2305	...
Eichstätt Bf ★ .... d.	│	1559	│	│	1659	│	│	1759	│	│	1859	│	│	1959	│	2059	│	│	2159	│	│	│	2259	│	...
Allersberg (Rothsee) . d.	│	│	│	│	│	1721	│	│	│	│	│	1921	│	│	│	│	2123	│	│	│	│	│	│	│	...
Kinding (Altmühltal) ... d.	│	│	│	│	│	1736	│	│	│	│	│	1936	│	│	│	│	2138	│	│	│	│	│	│	│	...
Ingolstadt Hbf .... a.	│	1625	│	│	1725	1755	│	1825	│	│	1925	1955	│	2025	│	2125	2156	│	2225	│	│	│	2325	│	...
Ingolstadt Hbf .... d.	│	1631	│	│	1731	1805	│	1831	│	│	1931	2005	│	2031	│	2131	2206	│	2235	│	│	│	2332	│	...
Pfaffenhofen (Ilm) ..... d.	│	1655	│	│	1755	1825	│	1855	│	│	1955	2025	│	2055	│	2155	2226	│	2259	│	│	│	2356	│	...
Donauwörth .... d.	1558	│	1621	1658	│	│	1800	│	1821	1858	│	│	2000	│	2058	│	│	2200	│	2223	2256	2258	│	2327	...
Augsburg Hbf ...... **930** a.	1636	│	1642	1729	│	│	1839	│	1842	1926	│	│	2037	│	2129	│	│	2237	│	2244	...	2329	│	2348	...
München Pasing ... **930** a.	...	│	**L**	1814	│	│	...	│	**L**	2014	│	│	...	│	2219	│	│	...	│	**K**	...	*0019*	│	...	...
München Hbf .... **930** a.	...	1733	...	1822	1833	1852	...	1933	...	2022	2033	2052	...	2133	2226	2233	2253	...	2336	...	...	*0026*	0034	...	...

K – From / to Kempten (Table **935**).
L – From / to Lindau and Oberstdorf (Table **935**).
S – ⑥⑦ until July 26. [12] Aalen - München and v.v.
e – Ⓐ only.
h – Not Aug. 15, Oct. 3.
r – Not Aug. 15.
t – Arrives 0550.
w – Also Aug. 15.
z – © only.
△ – Change trains at Augsburg on ©.
★ – Eichstätt Bahnhof. Connecting trains operate to / from Eichstätt Stadt (*5km*, journey time: 9 minutes).

RB services (except train **A**) — TREUCHTLINGEN - WÜRZBURG — 905a

km		⚒2	©	Ⓐ	Ⓐ	©	Ⓐ	⑥k						Ⓐ	A 🍷										©	Ⓐ
0	**Treuchtlingen** .... d.	...	0506	0512	0612	0625	*0701*	0725	0825	0925	1025	1125	1225	1305	1308	1325z	1425	1525	1625	1725	1825	1925	2025	2125	2225	2225
24	Gunzenhausen .... d.	...	0519	0525	0626	0639	*0716*	0739	0839	0939	1039	1139	1239	1318	1324	1339z	1439	1539	1639	1739	1839	1939	2039	2139	2239	2239
51	Ansbach .... a.	...	0539	0545	0646	0659	*0739*	0759	0859	0959	1059	1159	1259	1339	1342	1359z	1500	1559	1659	1759	1859	1959	2059	2200	2259	2300
51	Ansbach .... d.	0443	0541	0607	0702	0710	0811	0811	0910	1010	1110	1210	1310	...	1344	1410	1510	1610	1710	1810	1910	2010	2110	2207e	2300	...
83	Steinach (b Rothenb) ◐ d.	0504	0602	0628	0723	0731	0832	0832	0931	1031	1131	1231	1331	...	1404	1431	1531	1631	1731	1831	1931	2031	2131	2229e	2321	...
140	**Würzburg** Hbf .... a.	0550	0647	0716	0809	0816	0917	0917	1016	1116	1216	1316	1416	...	1438	1519	1615	1715	1816	1916	2016	2116	2216	2313e	0006	...

	⚒	©	Ⓐ	Ⓐ	©	Ⓐ2					A 🍷	©	Ⓐ											①–⑥	⑦
Würzburg Hbf .... d.	0437	0531	0541	0632	0641	0710	0741	0841	0941	1041	1121	1141	1141	1241	1341	1441	1541	1641	1741	1841	1941	2041	2146	2241	2241
Steinach (b Rothenb) ◐ .... d.	0520	0615	0625	0716	0725	0755	0825	0925	1025	1125	1155	1225	1225	1327	1425	1525	1625	1725	1825	1925	2025	2125	2229	2325	2325
Ansbach .... a.	0542	0637	0646	0737	0746	0818	0846	0946	1046	1146	1214	1246	1246	1347	1446	1546	1646	1746	1846	1946	2046	2146	2251	2347	2347
Ansbach .... d.	0544	0654	0711	0754	0754	...	0854	0954	1054	1154	1216	1254	1315	1354	1454	1554	1654	1754	1854	1954	2054	2154	2254	2354	2358
Gunzenhausen .... d.	0603	0715	0732	0815	0815	...	0915	1015	1115	1215	1234	1315	1335	1415	1515	1615	1715	1815	1915	2015	2115	2215	2315	0015	0018
Treuchtlingen .... a.	0617	0730	0746	0830	0830	...	0930	1030	1130	1230	1250	1330	1349	1430	1530	1630	1730	1830	1930	2030	2130	2230	2330	0030	0033

◐ – Local trains **STEINACH** (b Rothenb) - **ROTHENBURG OB DER TAUBER** and v.v. 2nd class only *12 km* Journey time: 14 minutes.
From Steinach at 0524 ⚒, 0619 © **n**, 0627 ⑥⑦ **C**, 0631 Ⓐ, 0727 Ⓐ, 0735 ©, 0836, 0935, 1035, 1135, 1235 ©, 1245 Ⓐ, 1335, 1435, 1535, 1635 ©, 1645 Ⓐ, 1735, 1835, 1935, 2035 and 2233.
From Rothenburg ob der Tauber at 0437 ①–⑥ **C**, 0443 ⚒ **r**, 0543 ©, 0606 Ⓐ, 0657 Ⓐ, 0706 ©, 0806, 0906, 1006, 1106, 1206, 1309, 1406, 1506, 1606, 1706, 1806, 1906, 2006 and 2210.

A – *IC* **2082/3**. KÖNIGSSEE – [12] Berchtesgaden - Augsburg - Hamburg and v.v.; [12] Oberstdorf (**2084/5**) - Augsburg - Hamburg and v.v.
C – Oct. 5 - Nov. 20.
e – Ⓐ only.
k – Not Oct. 3.
n – Not Oct. 10 - Nov. 15.
r – Not Oct. 3 - Nov. 20.
z – © only.

906 GIESSEN - KOBLENZ; LIMBURG - FRANKFURT and WIESBADEN

DB (*RE* / *RB* services); VEC★

Gießen - Limburg - Koblenz △

km			Ⓐ		⚒	Ⓐ						†
0	**Gießen** .... **807** d.	...	0523	0618	0719	0723	0823	0919		1919	2023	2119
13	Wetzlar .... **807** d.	...	0533	0628	0729	0733	0833	0929		1929	2033	2129
36	Weilburg .... d.	...	0558	0655	0743	0758	0858	0943		1943	2058	2143
65	**Limburg** (Lahn).... a.	...	0635	0732	0808	0835	0935	1008	and	2008	2135	2208
			◧	◧	|	◧	◧	|	every	|	◧	|
		⚒	d			d		|	two	|	⚒	|
65	**Limburg** (Lahn).... d.	0545	0645	0745	0810	0845	0945	1010	hours	2010	2145	2210
68	Diez .... d.	0549	0649	0749	0814	0849	0949	1014	until	2014	2149	2214
91	Nassau (Lahn) ...... d.	0616	0716	0816	0832	0916	1016	1032		2032	2216	2232
99	Bad Ems .... d.	0625	0725	0825	0839	0925	1025	1039		2039	2225	2239
112	Niederlahnstein .. § d.	0645	0745	0845	0850	0945	1045	1050		2050	2245	2250
117	**Koblenz** Hbf .... § a.	0653	0753	0853	0858	0953	1053	1058		2058	2253	2259

	Ⓐ										
Koblenz Hbf .... § d.	0506	0656	0904		1704	1806	1904	1913	2006	2106	2317
Niederlahnstein § d.	0514	0703	0911		1711	1814	1911	1921	2014	2114	2323
Bad Ems .... d.	0532	0716	0921		1721	1832	1921	1936	2032	2132	2340
Nassau (Lahn) ... d.	0542	0727	0927	and	1727	1842	1927	1945	2042	2142	2349
Diez .... d.	0608	0745	0945	every	1745	1908	1945	2010	2108	2208	0013
Limburg (Lahn). a.	0613	0748	0948	two	1748	1913	1948	2014	2113	2213	0017
	◧	|	|	hours	|	◧	|	◧			
	⚒w	|	|	until	|	Ⓐ	|				
Limburg (Lahn). d.	0618	0749	0949		1749	1923	1949t	2023	...	...	...
Weilburg .... d.	0657	0815	1015		1815	1959	2015t	2059	...	...	...
Wetzlar .... **807** d.	0722	0833	1033		1833	2027	2033t	2127	...	...	...
Gießen .... **807** a.	0732	0843	1043		1843	2037	2043t	2137	...	...	...

Limburg - Niedernhausen - Frankfurt and Wiesbaden

km		⚒	Ⓐ	Ⓐ	⑥k	Ⓐ	Ⓐ	Ⓒ	Ⓐ	Ⓐ	Ⓐ	⚒	Ⓐ			Ⓐ			Ⓐ		Ⓐ	Ⓒ	Ⓐ		Ⓐ	Ⓒ
0	**Limburg** (Lahn) .... d.	0418	0448	0518	0518	0555	0608	0618	0623	0638	0655	0718	0755	0818	0918	0955	1018	1118	1155	1218	1318	1318	1355	1418	1518	1518
21	Bad Camberg .... d.	0442	0512	0542	0542	0614	0633	0642	0644	0703	0714	0742	0814	0842	0942	1014	1042	1142	1214	1242	1342	1342	1414	1442	1542	1542
30	Idstein .... d.	0451	0521	0551	0552	0621	0643	0651	0651	0713	0721	0751	0821	0851	0952	1021	1051	1152	1221	1251	1351	1352	1421	1451	1551	1552
38	Niedernhausen .... ‡ a.	0457	0527	0557	0559	0627	0651	0657	0657	0721	0727	0757	0827	0857	0959	1027	1057	1159	1227	1257	1357	1359	1427	1457	1557	1559
	Wiesbaden Hbf ..... a.	|	*0555*	*0625*	0625	*0655*	0714	*0725*k	|	0744	|	*0825*	*0857*	*0925*	1025	|	*1125*	1225	|	*1325*	*1425*	1425	|	*1525*	*1627*	1625
70	**Frankfurt** (Main) Hbf ‡ a.	0528	0558	0628	...	0658	...	0728	0728	...	0758	0828	0858	0928	...	1058	1128	...	1258	1328	1428	...	1458	1528	1631	...

	Ⓐ		Ⓐ	Ⓐ	Ⓒ	Ⓐ					
Limburg (Lahn) .... d.	1555	1618	1655	1718	1718	1755	1818	1918	2018	2118	2218
Bad Camberg .... d.	1614	1642	1714	1742	1742	1814	1842	1942	2042	2141	2241
Idstein .... d.	1621	1651	1721	1751	1752	1821	1851	1952	2052	2151	2251
Niedernhausen .... ‡ a.	1627	1657	1727	1757	1759	1827	1857	1959	2059	2157	2257
Wiesbaden Hbf ...... a.	|	*1727*	*1757*	*1827*	1825	*1857*	*1925*	2025b	...	...	...
Frankfurt (Main) Hbf ‡ a.	1658	1728	1758	1828	...	1858	1928	...	...	...	...

km			Ⓐ	Ⓒ	Ⓐ	Ⓐ	Ⓒ	Ⓐ		Ⓐ
	Frankfurt (Main) Hbf .... ‡ d.	...	0600	0630	0643	0730	...	...	0830	0857
0	**Wiesbaden** Hbf .... d.	0531h	*0601*	*0636*k	*0650*	*0720*	0736k	0801	*0836*r	|
20	Niedernhausen .... ‡ d.	0601	0631	0701	0718	0801	0801	0831	0901	0931
28	Idstein .... d.	0608	0638	0708	0725	0808	0808	0838	0908	0938
37	Bad Camberg .... d.	0617	0647	0717	0734	0817	0817	0847	0917	0945
58	**Limburg** (Lahn) .... a.	0640	0710	0740	0800	0840	0840	0910	0940	1003

			Ⓐ			Ⓐ	Ⓐ	Ⓒ		Ⓐ		Ⓐ	Ⓒ	Ⓐ	Ⓐ	Ⓐ	Ⓒ	Ⓐ		Ⓐ	Ⓐ	Ⓒ				
Frankfurt (Main) Hbf ‡ d.	...	1030	1100	...	1230	1300	1330	...	1430	1500	...	1600	1630	...	1700	1730	...	1800	1830	1900	1930	...	2030	...	...	...
Wiesbaden Hbf ..... d.	0936	*1036*	|	1136	*1236*	|	*1336*	1336	*1436*	*1501*	1536	*1606*	*1636*	1636	*1706*	*1736*	1736	*1806*	*1836*	|	*1936*	1936	*2036*e	...	...	...
Niedernhausen .... ‡ d.	1001	1101	1131	1201	1301	1331	1401	1401	1501	1531	1601	1631	1701	1701	1731	1801	1801	1831	1901	1931	2001	2001	2101	2201	2301	0001
Idstein .... d.	1008	1108	1138	1208	1308	1338	1408	1408	1508	1538	1608	1638	1708	1708	1738	1808	1808	1838	1908	1938	2008	2008	2108	2208	2308	0008
Bad Camberg .... d.	1017	1117	1145	1217	1317	1345	1417	1417	1517	1545	1617	1645	1717	1717	1745	1817	1817	1845	1917	1945	2017	2017	2117	2217	2317	0017
Limburg (Lahn) .... a.	1040	1140	1203	1240	1340	1403	1440	1440	1540	1603	1640	1703	1740	1740	1803	1840	1840	1903	1940	2003	2040	2040	2140	2240	2340	0040

b – Ⓑ (also Oct. 3).
d – Runs daily Limburg - Koblenz.
e – Ⓐ only.
h – ⚒ only. 0536 on ⑥.
k – ⑥ (not Oct. 3).
r – ⚒ only.

t – † only.
w – Runs 2 – 5 minutes later on ⑥.

◧ – Change trains at Limburg.
△ – Additional stopping trains operate.
§ – See also Table **914**.

★ – Vectus Verkehrsgesellschaft mbH.
‡ – **Additional S-Bahn** *S2* **services** Frankfurt - Niedernhausen and v.v. Journey time 35 minutes.
From Frankfurt (Main) Hbf (underground platforms): On ⚒ every 30 minutes 0522 – 2322; on † hourly 0522 – 1222, then every 30 minutes 1252 – 2322.
From Niedernhausen: On ⚒ every 30 minutes 0433 – 2303; on † hourly 0503 – 1203, then every 30 minutes 1233 – 2303.

907 GIESSEN - FULDA

RE / *RB* services

km		⚒c	⑥k	Ⓐ	⑥k	Ⓐ	Ⓒ	Ⓒ	Ⓐ	Ⓒ	⑥k	Ⓐ	Ⓐ	Ⓒ	Ⓒ	Ⓐ	Ⓐ	Ⓒ	⑥k	Ⓐ	Ⓒ	Ⓒ	Ⓐ	Ⓐ	Ⓒ	Ⓐ	Ⓒ
0	**Gießen** .... d.	...	*0619*	0621	0743	0843	0848	0943	1043	1048	1143	1143	1241	1248	1343	1343	1443	1448	1543	1643	1648	1743	1744	1843	1848	2043	2045
23	Grünberg .... d.	...	*0650*	0703	0806	0906	0920	1005	1108	1120	1205	1210	1308	1322	1406	1411	1508	1520	1606	1706	1720	1806	1808	1913	1922	2110	2117
60	Alsfeld............. d.	0555	0739	0741	0838	0937	1004	1037	1138	1204	1239	1257	1338	1405	1438	1453	1538	1604	1638	1740	1806	1839	1908j	1959	2003	2148	2155
79	Lauterbach...... d.	0613	0757	0801	0900	0951	1022	1059	1152	1223	1300	1316	1353	1424	1500	1516	1555	1623	1700	1803	1825	1854	1926	2018	2021	...	...
106	**Fulda**.............. a.	0641	0825	0826	0929	1016	1058f	1128	1217	1258	1329	1349	1417	1458h	1529	1554	1620	1658	1729	1833	1852	1924	1954	2049	2049	...	...

	Ⓐ	⑥k	Ⓐ	⑥k	⑥k	Ⓐ	Ⓒ	Ⓒ	Ⓐ	⑥k	Ⓒ	Ⓐ	Ⓒ	Ⓒ	Ⓐ	⑥k	Ⓒ	Ⓐ	Ⓐ	Ⓒ	Ⓒ	Ⓐ	Ⓐ	Ⓒ	Ⓐ	Ⓐ	†
Fulda ....d.	...	...	0457	0558	0710	0728	0832	0915	0936	1032	1115	1136	1232	1315	1321	1432	1515	1526	1605	1632	1715	1736	1819	1910	1938	2035	2125
Lauterbach ....d.	...	...	0530	0632	0738	0757	0857	0943	1005	1057	1143	1206	1257	1343	1354	1458	1543	1558	1638	1657	1743	1802	1847	1939	2019	2103	2153
Alsfeld ....d.	0503	0548	0603v	0653	0804	0813	0913	1005	1021	1113	1205	1221	1313	1406	1413	1514	1605	1617	1704	1713	1807	1819	1907	2004	2038	2122	2212
Grünberg ....d.	0541	0625	0636	0735	0847	0844	0944	1047	1050	1144	1247	1251	1346	1447	1451	1545	1647	1647	1747	1744	1849	1849	1945	2042	...	...	...
Gießen ....a.	0606	0651	0709	0805	0912	0914	1014	1112	1114	1212	1312	1314	1412	1512	1512	1612	1712	1714	1814	1812	1914	1914	2011	2109	...	...	...

c – Runs 17 – 18 minutes later on ⑥.
f – 1049 on †.
h – 1452 on †.
j – Arrives 1852.
k – Not Oct. 3.
v – Arrives 0549.

908 GÖTTINGEN - BEBRA - FULDA

CANTUS Verkehrsgesellschaft (2nd class only)

km		Ⓐ	⚒		⚒					Ⓐ	Ⓒ
0	**Göttingen** .... **864** d.	0455	0614	0714	0814	0914		1914	2014	2214	2214
20	Eichenberg .... **864** d.	0511	0630	0730	0830	0930	and	1930	2030	2230	2235
35	Bad Sooden-Allendorf .d.	0522	0639	0739	0839	0939	every	1939	2039	2239	2244
46	Eschwege West..........d.	0530	0647	0747	0847	0947	two	1947	2047	2247	2252
81	Bebra ....a.	0553	0712	0812	0912	1012	hours	2012	2111	2312	2317
81	Bebra .... **901** d.	*0558*	*0717*e	0814	*1000*	1014	until	2014	*2200*	...	...
95	**Bad Hersfeld** ...... **901** a.	*0608*	*0726*e	0824	*1010*	1024		2024	*2210*	...	...
137	**Fulda** .... **901** a.	*0638*	*0755*e	0853	...	1053		2053	*2239*	...	...

	Ⓐ	⚒		⚒					Ⓒ	Ⓐ
Fulda............... **901** d.	...	*0548*e	0700	*0719*	0900		1900	...	2221	2221
Bad Hersfeld ... **901** d.	*0521*	*0616*e	0729	*0748*	0929	and	1929	*1945*	2250	2250
Bebra............... **901** a.	*0532*	*0626*e	0741	*0756*	0941	every	1941	*1956*	2301	2301
Bebra.....................d.	0545	0645	0745	0845	0945	two	1945	2045	2302	2302
Eschwege West ....d.	0609	0709	0809	0909	1009	hours	2009	2109	2328	2328
Bad Sooden-Allendorf d.	0617	0717	0817	0917	1017	until	2017	2117	2335	2335
Eichenberg .... **865** d.	0632	0732	0832	0932	1032		2032	2132	2349	2353
Göttingen .... **865** a.	0645	0745	0845	0945	1045		2045	2145	0002	0007

e – Ⓐ only.

909 GEMÜNDEN - BAD KISSINGEN - SCHWEINFURT - WÜRZBURG

DB (*RB* services); EB ★

km			Ⓐ																Ⓐ				Ⓐ		
0	**Gemünden** (Main) ....d.	...	0621	0704	...	...	0904	...	...	1104	...	...	1304z	1313e	...	1504	...	...	1606	1706	...	...	1806	1906	2104
28	Hammelburg ....d.	...	0658	0736	...	...	0936	...	...	1136	...	...	1336z	1358e	...	1536	...	...	1636	1737	...	...	1837	1937	2136j
47	**Bad Kissingen** ....a.	...	0722	0800	...	...	1000	...	...	1200	...	...	1400z	1421e	...	1600	...	...	1659	1800	...	...	1900	2000	2200j
			|	|			|			|			|	|		|			Ⓐ	|			|	|	|
47	**Bad Kissingen** ....d.	0646	0728	0805	0825	0901	1005	1025	1101	1205	1225	1301	1405	1425	1501	1605	1626	1701	1729	1805	1825	1901	1929	2005	2230
56	Ebenhausen (Unterf)..... **870** d.	0701	0742	0817	0841	0917	1017	1041	1117	1217	1241	1317	1417	1441	1517	1617	1641	1717	1745	1817	1842	1917	1944	2017	2241
70	**Schweinfurt** Hbf... **870 876** a.	0716	0754	0829	0852	0927	1029	1052	1127	1229	1252	1327	1429	1452	1527	1629	1652	1727	1755	1829	1852	1927	1954	2029	2253
113	**Würzburg** Hbf ...... **870 876** a.	0747	*0823*	...	*0923*	0958	...	*1123*	1158	...	*1323*	1358	...	*1523*	1558	...	*1723*	1758	*1824*	...	*1923*	1958	*2023*	*2151*p	*0016*

									Ⓐ		Ⓒ	Ⓐ				Ⓐ							①–⑥	Ⓒ	
Würzburg Hbf.... ⊙ **870 876** d.	...	*0501*r	*0602*f	...	0801	*0836*	1001	*1036*	*1109*	1201	*1236*	*1236*	1401	*1436*	...	*1509*	1601	*1636*	...	1801	*1836*	2001	*2036*	*2109*q	*2139*v
Schweinfurt Hbf ⊙ **870 876** d.	0458	0538	0705	0730	0830	0931	1030	1131	1200	1230	1331	1331	1430	1506	1531	1600	1630	1706	1731	1830	1931	2030	2106	2149	2224
Ebenhausen (Unter) ...... **870** d.	0518	0551	0718	0744	0842	0945	1042	1145	1214	1242	1345	1345	1442	1518	1545	1616	1642	1718	1745	1842	1945	2042	2118	2202	2240
Bad Kissingen.................. a.	0528	0602	0727	0754	0853	0955	1053	1155	1223	1253	1355	1355	1453	1527	1555	1625	1653	1727	1755	1853	1955	2053	2127	2212	2250
		Ⓐ	|	|		|		|	|		|	|		|	|	Ⓐ		|	|	Ⓐ	|		|	|	
Bad Kissingen.................. d.	0545	0612	0732e	0801z	...	1001	...	1201	1257	...	1401	1434	...	1532e	1601z	1631	...	1732e	1801z	1904	2001	...	2132e	2219	...
Hammelburg .... d.	0612n	0658t	0823a	0823z	...	1023	...	1223	1322	...	1423	1458	...	1558e	1623z	1658	...	1758e	1823z	1925	2023	...	2153e	2240	...
Gemünden (Main) .... a.	0648n	0735	0854e	0854z	...	1054	...	1254	1354	...	1454	1534	...	1635e	1654z	1735	...	1835e	1854z	...	2054	...	...	2311	...

a – Ⓐ only. Arrives 0757.
e – Ⓐ only.
f – *0624* on Ⓐ.
j – On Ⓐ departs Hammelburg 2203, arrives Bad Kissingen 2225.
n – On Ⓒ departs Hammelburg 0609, arrives Gemünden 0639.

p – *2123* on Ⓒ.
q – † (also Aug. 15).
r – ⚒ (not Aug. 15).
t – Arrives 0640.
v – *2144* on Ⓒ.

z – Ⓒ only.
★ – Erfurter Bahn (2nd class only).
⊙ – Trains between Würzburg, Schweinfurt and Ebenhausen are often combined with a service to Meiningen or Erfurt. Passengers should take care to join the correct portion for their destination.

AACHEN - KÖLN - FRANKFURT via the high-speed line 910

See Tables **800**/**912** for services via Bonn and Koblenz.

km		ICE 521	ICE 523	ICE 1123	ICE 511	ICE 711	ICE 811	ICE 925	ICE 525	ICE 501	ICE 813	ICE 527	ICE 513	ICE 815	ICE 545		ICE 529	ICE 503	ICE 11	ICE 11	ICE 621	ICE 121	ICE 515
			①-⑤	⑥		①-⑤	①-⑤	⑥⑦	①-⑤		①-⑤	①-⑥		①-⑥	①-⑥				①-⑥	⑦		①-⑥	
		🍷	🍷	🍷	🍷		🍷	🍷	🍷	🍷	🍷	G 🍷	M 🍷	🍷	B ✕	◇	🍷	H 🍷	🍷	🍷	🍷	🍷	A 🍷
	Dortmund Hbf **800** d.	...	0401	0421	...	0502	...	0501	0523	0537	0559	0623	0638	0652	...	...	0723c	0737	...	...	0816c	...	0837
	Essen Hbf **800** d.	...	0423	0445	...	0524	...	0523	0553	│	0623	0650	0700	0715	...	...	0753x	│	...	...	0840	...	│
	Amsterdam Centraal **28** ⊡ d.	...	│	│	...	│	...	│	│	│	│	│	│	│	...	...	│	│	...	...	│	0704	│
	Düsseldorf Hbf **800** d.	...	0453	0513	...	0551	...	0553	0622	│	0653	0722	0727	0748	...	...	0822	│	...	...	0913	0923	│
	Brussels Midi/Zuid **21 400** d.	...	│	│	...	│	...	│	│	│	│	│	│	│	...	...	│	│	0718	0718	│	│	│
	Aachen Hbf **802 807** d.	...	│	│	...	│	...	│	│	│	│	│	│	│	0740	...	│	│	0839	0839	│	│	│
	Köln Hbf **802 807** a.	...	│	│	...	│	...	│	│	0646	0716	│	0749	│	0822	...	│	0846	0915	0915	│	│	0946
0	**Köln** Hbf **802 807** d.	0420	│	│	0554	│	0620	│	│	0654	0720	│	0754	│	...	0831	│	0854	0920	0920	│	│	0954
1	**Köln** Messe/Deutz **802** d.	│	0518	0535	│	0615	│	0619	0644	│	│	0744	│	0810	...	0833	0844	│	│	│	0944	0951	│
	Köln/Bonn Flughafen ✈ ⊖ **802** d.	│	0531	0547	│	│	│	0631	│	│	│	│	│	0821	...	...	│	│	│	│	│	│	│
25	Siegburg/Bonn 🚋 ⊖ **807** d.	0437	0543	│	0611	│	0636	0643	│	0711	0736	│	0811	0833	...	...	│	0911	│	│	│	│	1011
88	Montabaur d.	0458	0604	│	│	0646	0657	0704	│	│	0757	│	│	0857	...	...	│	│	│	0957	│	│	│
110	Limburg Süd d.	0510	0615	│	│	0657	0707	0715	│	│	0807	│	│	0907	...	...	│	│	│	1007	│	│	│
	Wiesbaden Hbf a.	│	│	│	│	0719	│	│	│	│	│	│	│	│	...	...	│	│	│	│	│	│	│
	Mainz Hbf a.	│	│	│	│	0744v	│	│	│	│	│	│	│	│	...	...	│	│	│	│	│	│	│
169	**Frankfurt** Flughafen Fernbf ✈ a.	0533	0634	0634	0651	│	0727	0734	0734	0751	0827	0834	0851	0926	...	...	0934	0951	1014	1026	1034	1043	1051
180	**Frankfurt** (Main) Hbf a.	0546	0648	0648	│	│	0741	0748	0748	│	0841	0848	│	0941	...	...	0948	│	1030	1040	1048	1102	│
	Nürnberg Hbf **920** a.	0759	0859	0859	│	│	...	0959	0959	│	...	1059	│	...	...	...	1159	│	...	...	1259	...	│
	Mannheim Hbf **912** a.	│	│	│	0724	0824	...	│	│	0824	...	│	0924	...	...	...	│	1024	...	...	│	...	1124
	Karlsruhe Hbf **912** a.	│	│	│	│	│	...	│	│	0858	...	│	│	...	...	...	│	1056	...	...	│	...	│
	Basel SBB **912** a.	│	│	│	│	│	...	│	│	1047	...	│	│	...	...	...	│	...	...	...	│	...	│
	Stuttgart Hbf **930** a.	│	│	│	0808	0923	...	│	│	...	...	│	1008	...	...	...	│	...	...	...	│	...	1208
	München Hbf **904 930** a.	0904	1004	1004	1031	...	...	1104	1104	...	...	1204	1230	...	...	...	1304	...	...	...	1404	...	1430

	ICE 623	THA 9407	ICE 105	ICE 505	ICE 625	ICE 517	ICE 627	THA 9415	ICE 507	ICE 507	ICE 123	ICE 629	ICE 519	ICE 15	ICE 721	ICE 721	ICE 509	ICE 125	THA 9427	RB 11860	ICE 723	ICE 611	ICE 817
									⑦			Ⓑ			⑥⑦						Ⓑ		
	🍷	Ⓡ P	🍷	🍷	🍷	🍷	🍷	Ⓡ P	🍷	🍷	🍷	🍷	🍷	🍷	🍷	🍷	🍷	🍷	Ⓡ P		🍷	🍷	🍷
Dortmund Hbf **800** d.	...	...	...	...	1023t	1038	...	...	1137	...	...	1223t	1238	...	1257	...	...	...	...	...	...	1438	...
Essen Hbf **800** d.	...	...	...	...	1053	1100	...	...	│	...	...	1253	1300	...	1324	...	...	...	...	...	1453	1500	...
Amsterdam Centraal **28** ⊡ d.	...	...	0804	...	│	│	...	...	│	...	1034	│	│	...	│	...	...	1234	...	...	│	│	...
Düsseldorf Hbf **800** d.	...	...	1022	...	1122	1127	...	...	│	...	1248	1322	1327	...	1353	...	...	1448	...	...	1522	1527	...
Brussels Midi/Zuid **21 400** d.	...	0755	│	...	│	│	...	0959	│	...	│	│	│	1218	│	...	...	│	1259	...	│	│	...
Aachen Hbf **802 807** d.	...	0939	│	...	│	│	...	1139	│	...	│	│	│	1339	│	...	...	│	1439	...	│	│	...
Köln Hbf **802 807** a.	...	1015	1045	...	│	1149	...	1215	1246	...	1312	│	1349	1415	1416	...	...	1512	1515	...	│	1549	...
Köln Hbf **802 807** d.	1020	...	1054	1054	│	1154	1220	...	1254	1254	1320	│	1354	1420	1428	1428	1454	1520	...	1524	│	1554	1620
Köln Messe/Deutz **802** d.	│	...	│	│	1144	│	│	...	│	│	│	1344	│	│	│	│	│	│	...	1526	1544	│	│
Köln/Bonn Flughafen ✈ ⊖ **802** d.	│	...	│	│	│	│	│	...	│	│	│	│	│	│	1441	1441	│	│	...	...	│	│	│
Siegburg/Bonn 🚋 ⊖ **807** d.	1037	...	1111	1111	│	1211	1237	...	1311	1311	│	│	1411	1436	│	│	1511	│	...	...	│	1611	1636
Montabaur d.	1058	...	│	│	│	│	1258	...	│	│	│	│	│	│	1509	1509	│	│	...	...	│	│	1657
Limburg Süd d.	1109	...	│	│	│	│	1309	...	│	│	│	│	│	1502	│	│	│	│	...	...	│	│	1707
Wiesbaden Hbf a.	│	...	│	│	│	│	│	...	│	│	│	│	│	│	│	│	│	│	...	...	│	│	│
Mainz Hbf a.	│	...	│	│	│	│	│	...	│	│	│	│	│	│	│	│	│	│	...	...	│	│	│
Frankfurt Flughafen Fernbf ✈ a.	1128	...	1151	1151	1234	1251	1328	...	1351	1351	1414	1434	1451	1522	1534	1534	1551	1614	...	...	1634	1651	1727
Frankfurt (Main) Hbf a.	1142	...	│	│	1248	│	1344	...	│	│	1430	1448	│	1540	1548	1548	│	1630	...	...	1648	│	1741
Nürnberg Hbf **920** a.	1359	...	│	│	1459	│	1559	...	│	│	...	1659	│	...	1759	1759	│	...	...	...	1859	│	...
Mannheim Hbf **912** a.	│	...	1224	1224	│	1324	│	...	1424	1424	...	│	1524	...	│	│	1624	...	...	...	│	1724	...
Karlsruhe Hbf **912** a.	│	...	1251	1251	│	│	│	...	1456	1456	...	│	│	...	│	│	1651	...	...	...	│	│	...
Basel SBB **912** a.	│	...	1447	1447	│	│	│	...	...	...	...	│	│	...	│	│	1847	...	...	...	│	│	...
Stuttgart Hbf **930** a.	│	...	...	...	│	1408	│	...	...	...	...	│	1608	...	│	│	...	...	...	...	│	1808	...
München Hbf **904 930** a.	1504	...	...	...	1604	1631	1704	...	...	...	...	1804	1830	...	1904	1904	...	...	...	...	2004	2030	...

	THA 9431	RB 11864	ICE 725	ICE 601	ICE 127	ICE 715	ICE 727	ICE 613	ICE 819	ICE 729	ICE 603	ICE 129	THA 9443	ICE 821	ICE 911	ICE 615	ICE 17	ICE 605	ICE 605	ICE 227	THA 9451	ICE 617	ICE 913
					S	①-⑤	Ⓑ		Ⓑ					⑤⑦	T				Ⓑ				
	Ⓡ P		🍷	🍷	🍷	🍷	🍷	🍷	🍷	🍷	🍷	🍷	Ⓡ P	🍷	🍷	🍷	🍷	🍷	🍷	🍷	Ⓡ P	🍷	🍷
Dortmund Hbf **800** d.	...	...	1522t	...	...	...	...	1638	...	...	...	...	...	...	...	1838	...	1923	1923	...	...	2038	...
Essen Hbf **800** d.	...	...	1553	...	...	...	1653	1700	...	1753	...	...	...	...	...	1900	...	1949	1949	...	...	2100	...
Amsterdam Centraal **28** ⊡ d.	...	...	│	...	1434	...	│	│	...	│	...	1634	...	...	...	│	...	│	│	1834	...	│	...
Düsseldorf Hbf **800** d.	...	...	1622	...	1648	...	1722	1727	...	1821	...	1848	...	...	...	1927	...	2022	2022	2048	...	2127	...
Brussels Midi/Zuid **21 400** d.	1359	...	│	...	│	...	│	│	...	│	...	│	1655	...	...	│	1818	│	│	│	1859	│	...
Aachen Hbf **802 807** d.	1539	...	│	...	│	...	│	│	...	│	...	│	1839	...	...	│	1939	│	│	│	2039	│	...
Köln Hbf **802 807** a.	1615	...	│	...	1712	...	│	1749	...	│	...	1912	1915	...	...	1949	2015	│	│	2112	2115	2149	...
Köln Hbf **802 807** d.	...	1624	│	1654	1720	1728	│	1754	1820	│	1854	1920	...	1928	1928	1958	2020	│	│	2120	...	2154	2254
Köln Messe/Deutz **802** d.	...	1626	1644	│	│	│	1744	│	│	1843	│	│	...	│	│	│	│	2044	2044	│	...	│	│
Köln/Bonn Flughafen ✈ ⊖ **802** d.	...	...	│	│	│	│	│	│	│	│	│	│	...	│	│	│	│	│	│	│	...	│	2307
Siegburg/Bonn 🚋 ⊖ **807** d.	...	...	│	1711	│	│	│	1811	1836	│	1911	│	...	1945	1945	2015	│	2100	2100	│	...	2211	│
Montabaur d.	...	...	│	│	│	1800	│	│	1857	│	│	│	...	2005	2005	│	│	2121	2121	│	...	│	2335
Limburg Süd d.	...	...	│	│	│	1811	│	│	1907	│	│	│	...	2015	2015	│	│	2132	2132	│	...	│	2345
Wiesbaden Hbf a.	...	...	│	│	│	1832	│	│	│	│	│	│	...	│	│	│	│	│	│	│	...	│	│
Mainz Hbf a.	...	...	│	│	│	1900	│	│	│	│	│	│	...	│	│	│	│	│	│	│	...	│	│
Frankfurt Flughafen Fernbf ✈ a.	...	...	1734	1751	1814	...	1834	1851	1927	1934	1951	2014	...	2035	2035	2055	2114	2151	2151	2218	...	2256	0010
Frankfurt (Main) Hbf a.	...	...	1748	│	1830	...	1848	│	1941	1948	│	2030	...	2048	2049	│	2130	│	│	2234	...	│	0023
Nürnberg Hbf **920** a.	...	...	1959	│	...	...	2059	│	...	2159	│	...	...	2259	...	│	...	│	│	...	...	│	...
Mannheim Hbf **912** a.	...	...	│	1824	...	...	│	1924	...	│	2024	...	...	│	...	2131	...	2224	2224	...	...	2337	...
Karlsruhe Hbf **912** a.	...	...	│	1851	...	...	│	│	...	│	2100	...	...	│	...	│	...	2300	2300	...	...	│	...
Basel SBB **912** a.	...	...	│	2047	...	...	│	│	...	│	2300z	...	...	│	...	│	...	...	0058b	...	...	│	...
Stuttgart Hbf **930** a.	...	...	│	...	...	...	│	2008	...	│	...	...	...	│	...	2208	...	...	...	...	...	0052k	...
München Hbf **904 930** a.	...	...	2105	...	...	...	2204	2232	...	2307	...	...	...	0005	...	0034	...	...	...	...	...	...	...

A – From Hamburg (Table **800**).
B – To Berlin (Tables **800**, **810**). Also calls at Düren (d. 0758).
G – [12] and 🍷 (Hannover ① -) Dortmund - München (- Garmisch ⑥).
H – From Hannover (Table **810**).
M – From Münster (d. 0601).
P – [12] and 🍷 Paris - Brussels - Liège - Köln.
S – Until Oct. 25.
T – ①②③④⑥.

b – Basel **Badischer Bahnhof**.
c – ⑥⑦ only.
k – 0040 on the mornings of ①⑦ (also July 11, 18, 25).
t – ⑦ only.
v – From Aug. 24.
x – ⑥⑦ until July 12; daily from July 18.
z – 2253 on ⑦.

◇ – *S-Bahn.*
⊡ – Amsterdam timings are subject to alteration on June 14, 27, 28, Aug. 9.
⊖ – For local connections Köln/Bonn Flughafen - Siegburg/Bonn see Tables **802** (Köln/Bonn Flughafen - Troisdorf) and **807** (Troisdorf - Siegburg/Bonn).

🚋 – Light-rail services operate Bonn Hbf - Siegburg/Bonn and v.v. Journey time: 25 minutes. Operator: Elektrische Bahnen der Stadt Bonn und des Rhein-Sieg-Kreises (SSB).

Departures from Bonn Hbf

On Ⓐ: 0016, 0046, 0133, 0418, 0438, 0458, 0518, 0528, 0543 and every 10 minutes until 1933, 1946, 2001, 2016, 2032, 2046 and every 15 minutes until 2246, 2316, 2346.

On ⑥: 0016, 0046, 0133, 0416 and every 30 minutes until 0746, 0801, 0816, 0831, 0846, 0856, 0906, 0916, 0925, 0932 and every 10 minutes until 1602, 1616 and every 15 minutes until 2246, 2316, 2346.

On †: 0016, 0046, 0133, 0511, 0541, 0616 and every 30 minutes until 1016, 1031 and every 15 minutes until 2246, 2316, 2346.

Departures from Siegburg/Bonn

On Ⓐ: 0022, 0052, 0122, 0202, 0454, 0514, 0534, 0554 and every 10 minutes until 1934, 1952, 2002, 2012, 2022 and every 15 minutes until 2222, 2232, 2252, 2302, 2322, 2352.

On ⑥: 0022, 0052, 0122, 0202, 0452 and every 30 minutes until 0752, 0814, 0834, 0854 and every 10 minutes until 1424, 1438, 1448, 1458, 1508, 1518, 1528, 1538, 1552, 1602, 1612, 1622, 1632, 1642, 1652 and every 15 minutes until 2222, 2232, 2252, 2302, 2322, 2352.

On †: 0022, 0052, 0122, 0202, 0552 and every 30 minutes until 1052, 1107 and every 15 minutes until 2222, 2232, 2252, 2302, 2322, 2352.

910 FRANKFURT - KÖLN - AACHEN via the high-speed line

See Tables 800/912 for services via Koblenz and Bonn.

km		ICE 828 ①–⑤ 🍷	ICE 826 🍷	◇	THA 9418 Ⓡ P	ICE 716 ①–⑤ 🍷	ICE 616 🍷	ICE 824 ①–⑤ D 🍷	ICE 16 🍷	ICE 226 🍷	ICE 604 🍷	ICE 822 ①–⑥ 🍷	ICE 818 ①–⑥ 🍷	ICE 1124 ⑦ 🍷	ICE 614 🍷	ICE 820 ①–⑤ 🍷	◇	THA 9430 Ⓡ P	ICE 128 🍷	ICE 602 🍷	ICE 728 🍷	ICE 612 🍷	ICE 726 ①–⑥ 🍷	◇
	München Hbf **904 930** d.	...	0032**g**	...	...	...	0317	...	...	...	...	0451**g**	...	...	0523	0551	...	...	...	...	0651	0723	0755	...
	Stuttgart Hbf **930** d.	...	0305	...	...	...	0551	...	...	...	...	|	...	...	0751	|	...	...	...	...	|	0951	|	...
	Basel SBB **912** d.	...	|	...	...	...	|	...	...	...	0516**b**	|	...	...	|	|	...	...	...	0712	|	|	|	...
	Karlsruhe Hbf **912** d.	...	|	...	...	...	|	...	...	...	0700	|	...	...	|	|	...	...	...	0907	|	|	|	...
	Mannheim Hbf **912** d.	...	0440	...	...	...	0635	...	...	...	0735	|	...	...	0835	|	...	...	...	0935	|	1035	|	...
	Nürnberg Hbf **920** d.	...	|	...	...	...	|	...	...	...	|	0600	...	...	|	0700	...	...	...	|	0800	|	0900	...
	Frankfurt (Main) Hbf d.	0510	0544	...	...	...	|	0702	0729	0729	|	0810	0816	0816	|	0910	...	...	0928	|	1010	|	1110	...
	Frankfurt Flughafen Fernbf ✈ d.	0524	0607	...	...	...	0709	0714	0743	0743	0809	0824	0831	0831	0909	0924	...	...	0943	1009	1024	1109	1124	...
0	**Mainz** Hbf d.	|	|	...	...	0609	|	|	|	|	|	|	|	|	|	|	...	...	|	|	|	|	|	...
10	**Wiesbaden** Hbf d.	|	|	...	...	0629	|	|	|	|	|	|	|	|	|	|	...	...	|	|	|	|	|	...
65	Limburg Süd d.	0544	0626	...	...	0650	|	0733	|	|	|	|	0850	0850	|	|	...	...	|	|	1044	|	|	...
87	Montabaur d.	0556	0637	...	...	0701	|	0744	|	|	|	|	0901	0901	|	|	...	...	|	|	1056	|	|	...
150	Siegburg/Bonn 🚋 ⊖ **807** d.	0618	0659	...	...	|	0749	0806	|	|	0849	|	0923	0923	0949	|	...	...	|	1049	1118	1149	|	...
166	Köln/Bonn Flughafen ✈ ⊖ **802** a.	0627	|	...	...	0726	|	|	|	|	|	|	|	|	|	|	...	...	|	|	1127	|	|	...
180	**Köln** Messe/Deutz **802** a.	|	0714	0727	...	|	|	0822	|	|	|	0914	|	0938	|	1014	1027	...	|	|	|	|	1214	1227
181	**Köln** Hbf **802 807** a.	0640	|	0729	...	0740	0805	|	0840	0840	0905	|	0940	|	1005	|	1029	...	1040	1105	1140	1205	|	1229
181	**Köln** Hbf **802 807** d.	0645	|	...	0744	...	0811	|	0844	0848	...	|	...	|	1011	|	...	1044	1048	...	...	1211	|	...
251	**Aachen** Hbf **802 807** a.	|	|	...	0820	...	|	|	0916	|	...	|	...	|	|	|	...	1120	|	...	...	|	|	...
	Brussels Midi/Zuid **21 400** a.	|	|	...	1001	...	|	|	1035	|	...	|	...	|	|	|	...	1301	|	...	...	|	|	...
	Düsseldorf Hbf **800** a.	0708	0737	...	...	...	0832	0844	...	0913	...	0937	...	1005	1032	1037	...	...	1111	...	...	1232	1237	...
	Amsterdam Centraal **28** ⊡ a.	|	|	...	...	...	|	|	...	1125	...	|	...	|	|	|	...	...	1325	...	...	|	|	...
	Essen Hbf **800** a.	0735**z**	0802**z**	...	...	...	0857	0917**z**	...	...	...	1002**z**	...	1039	1057	1102**z**	...	...	...	...	...	1257	1302**r**	...
	Dortmund Hbf **800** a.	...	0827**e**	...	...	...	0921	...	...	...	...	...	...	1102	1121	...	...	...	...	...	...	1321	1330**h**	...

	THA 9438 Ⓡ P	ICE 126 S 🍷	ICE 600 🍷	ICE 724 🍷	ICE 610 🍷	ICE 722 🍷	ICE 14 🍷	ICE 124 🍷	ICE 508 🍷	THA 9450 Ⓡ P	ICE 1128 ⑤ 🍷	ICE 720 T 🍷	ICE 1022 ⑤ 🍷	ICE 518 🍷	ICE 628 🍷	ICE 816 🍷	ICE 506 🍷	ICE 626 🍷	THA 9458 Ⓡ P	ICE 122 🍷	ICE 712 ①–⑤ 🍷	ICE 516 🍷	ICE 624 🍷	◇
München Hbf **904 930** d.	...	...	...	0855	0923	0955	...	...	...	...	1055	1055	1055	1123	1155	...	...	1255	...	...	...	1323	1355	...
Stuttgart Hbf **930** d.	...	...	...	|	1151	|	...	...	...	...	|	|	|	1351	|	...	...	|	...	...	1434	1551	|	...
Basel SBB **912** d.	...	...	...	|	|	|	...	...	1112	...	|	|	|	|	|	...	...	|	...	...	|	|	|	...
Karlsruhe Hbf **912** d.	...	...	1107	|	|	|	...	...	1307	...	|	|	|	|	|	...	1507	|	...	...	|	|	|	...
Mannheim Hbf **912** d.	...	...	1135	|	1235	|	...	...	1335	...	|	|	|	1435	|	...	1535	|	...	...	1533**k**	1635	|	...
Nürnberg Hbf **920** d.	...	...	|	1000	|	1100	...	...	|	...	1200	1200	1200	|	1300	...	|	1400	...	...	|	|	1500	...
Frankfurt (Main) Hbf d.	...	1128	|	1210	|	1310	1329	1329	|	...	1410	1410	1410	|	1510	1517	|	1610	...	1629	|	|	1710	...
Frankfurt Flughafen Fernbf ✈ d.	...	1143	1209	1224	1309	1324	1343	1343	1409	...	1424	1424	1431	1509	1524	1532	1609	1623	...	1643	|	1709	1724	...
Mainz Hbf d.	...	|	|	|	|	|	|	|	|	...	|	|	|	|	|	|	|	|	...	|	1623**v**	|	|	...
Wiesbaden Hbf d.	...	|	|	|	|	|	|	|	|	...	|	|	|	|	|	|	|	|	...	|	1645	|	|	...
Limburg Süd d.	...	|	|	1244	|	|	|	|	|	...	|	1444	1450	|	|	1551	|	1642	...	|	1706	|	|	...
Montabaur d.	...	|	|	1256	|	|	|	|	|	...	|	1456	1501	|	|	1601	|	1653	...	|	1717	|	|	...
Siegburg/Bonn 🚋 ⊖ **807** d.	...	|	1249	1318	1349	|	|	|	1449	...	|	1518	1523	1549	|	1623	1649	1714	...	|	1738	1749	|	...
Köln/Bonn Flughafen ✈ ⊖ **802** a.	...	|	|	1327	|	|	|	|	|	...	|	1527	|	|	|	|	|	|	...	|	1747	|	|	...
Köln Messe/Deutz **802** a.	...	|	|	|	|	1414	|	|	|	...	1514	|	|	|	1614	|	|	|	...	|	|	|	1814	1827
Köln Hbf **802 807** a.	...	1240	1305	1340	1405	|	1440	1440	1505	...	|	1540	1540	1605	|	1640	1705	1732	...	1740	1801	1805	|	1829
Köln Hbf **802 807** d.	1243	1248	1311**h**	...	1411	|	1444	1448	1511**h**	1544	|	...	...	1611	|	...	1711	...	1744	1748	...	1811	|	...
Aachen Hbf **802 807** a.	1320	|	|	...	|	|	1516	|	|	1620	|	...	...	|	|	...	|	...	1820	|	...	|	|	...
Brussels Midi/Zuid **21 400** a.	1501	|	|	...	|	|	1635	|	|	1801	|	...	...	|	|	...	|	...	2001	|	...	|	|	...
Düsseldorf Hbf **800** a.	...	1311	|	...	1432	1437	...	1511	|	...	1538	...	...	1632	1637	...	|	...	...	1811	...	|	1837	...
Amsterdam Centraal **28** ⊡ a.	...	1525	|	...	|	|	...	1725	|	...	|	...	...	|	|	...	|	...	...	2025	...	|	|	...
Essen Hbf **800** a.	...	...	|	...	1457	1502**z**	...	...	|	...	1603**z**	...	...	1657	1702**z**	...	|	...	...	...	...	|	1902	...
Dortmund Hbf **800** a.	...	...	1420**h**	...	1521	...	...	...	1620**h**	...	...	...	...	1721	...	...	1820	...	...	...	...	1920	1929	...

	THA 9462 Ⓡ P	ICE 814 ①–⑤ 🍷	ICE 914 ①–⑤ 🍷	ICE 104 ◧ 🍷	ICE 622 🍷	ICE 812 Ⓑ 🍷	ICE 10 🍷	ICE 812 Ⓑ 🍷	ICE 514 A 🍷	ICE 928 ⑦ H 🍷	ICE 620 ①–⑤ 🍷	ICE 926 ⑥ 🍷	ICE 120 Ⓑ 🍷	ICE 502 Ⓑ H 🍷	ICE 1002 ⑥ H 🍷	ICE 528 Ⓑ 🍷	ICE 924 ⑥ G 🍷	ICE 810 Ⓑ 🍷	ICE 512 M 🍷	ICE 526 Ⓑ 🍷	ICE 500 🍷	ICE 524 🍷	ICE 1110 ⑦ 🍷	ICE 1122 🍷
München Hbf **904 930** d.	...	...	...	...	1455	...	...	...	1523	1555	1555	1555	...	...	...	1650	1650	...	1723	1755	...	1855	1923	...
Stuttgart Hbf **930** d.	...	...	...	...	|	...	...	...	1751	|	|	|	...	...	...	|	|	...	1951	|	...	|	2151	...
Basel SBB **912** d.	...	...	...	1512	|	...	...	...	|	|	|	|	...	...	...	|	|	...	|	|	1912	|	|	...
Karlsruhe Hbf **912** d.	...	...	...	1707	|	...	...	...	|	|	|	|	...	1908	1908	|	|	...	|	|	2101	|	|	...
Mannheim Hbf **912** d.	...	...	...	1735	|	...	...	...	1835	|	|	|	...	1935	1935	|	|	...	2035	|	2135	|	2231	...
Nürnberg Hbf **920** d.	...	...	...	|	1600	...	...	...	|	1700	1700	1700	...	|	|	1800	1800	...	|	1900	|	2000	|	...
Frankfurt (Main) Hbf d.	...	1717	1717	|	1810	1816	1829	...	|	1910	1910	1910	1928	|	|	2010	2010	2016	|	2110	|	2210	|	2310
Frankfurt Flughafen Fernbf ✈ d.	...	1732	1732	1809	1824	1831	1843	...	1909	1924	1923	1923	1943	2009	2009	2024	2024	2031	2109	2124	2209	2224	2304	2324
Mainz Hbf d.	...	|	|	|	|	|	|	...	|	|	|	|	|	|	|	|	|	|	|	|	|	|	|	|
Wiesbaden Hbf d.	...	|	|	|	|	|	|	...	|	|	|	|	|	|	|	|	|	|	|	|	|	|	|	|
Limburg Süd d.	...	1751	1751	|	|	1850	|	←	|	|	1942	1942	|	|	|	|	|	2050	|	|	|	2243	|	2343
Montabaur d.	...	1801	1801	|	|	1859	|	1907	|	|	1953	1953	|	|	|	|	|	2101	|	|	|	2254	|	2354
Siegburg/Bonn 🚋 ⊖ **807** d.	...	1823	1836**c**	1849	|	→	1923	1929	1949	|	2014	2014	|	2049	2049	|	|	2128	2149	|	2254	2320	2349	0020
Köln/Bonn Flughafen ✈ ⊖ **802** a.	...	|	|	|	|	...	|	1937	|	|	|	2023	|	|	|	|	|	2137	|	|	|	2328	|	|
Köln Messe/Deutz **802** a.	...	|	1850	|	1914	...	|	|	|	2014	|	|	|	|	|	2113	2113	2150	|	2219	|	2341	|	|
Köln Hbf **802 807** a.	...	1840	|	1905	|	...	1940	1956	2005	|	2031	2040	2040	2105	2105	|	|	|	2205	|	2312	|	0005	0036
Köln Hbf **802 807** d.	1844	...	|	1917	|	...	1944	...	2011	|	...	2048	2048	2111	2111	|	|	|	2211	|	2317	|	...	0041
Aachen Hbf **802 807** a.	1920	...	|	|	|	...	2016	...	|	|	...	|	|	|	|	|	|	|	|	|	|	|	...	|
Brussels Midi/Zuid **21 400** a.	2101	...	|	|	|	...	2135	...	|	|	...	|	|	|	|	|	|	|	|	|	|	|	...	|
Düsseldorf Hbf **800** a.	...	...	1911	1938	1942	...	...	...	2032	2037	...	2111	2111	|	2132	2137	2137	2211	2232	2242	2338	0005	...	0103
Amsterdam Centraal **28** ⊡ a.	...	...	|	2155	|	...	...	...	|	|	...	|	2325	|	|	|	|	|	|	|	|	|	...	|
Essen Hbf **800** a.	...	...	1940	...	2008	...	...	...	2057	2102	...	2136	...	|	2158	2202	2202	2236	2257	2307	0007	0030	...	0131
Dortmund Hbf **800** a.	...	...	2003	...	2038	...	...	...	2121	2130	...	2159	...	2220	2221	2228	2228	2300	2321	2338	0030	0053	...	0154

A – To Hamburg (Table **800**).
D – From Darmstadt Hbf (d. 0637).
G – From Garmisch (d. 1518).
H – To Hannover (Table **810**).
M – To Münster (a. 2357).
P – 🅁 and 🍷 Köln - Liège - Brussels - Paris.
S – Until Oct. 25.
T – Daily except ⑤.

b – ①–⑥ only. Basel **Badischer Bahnhof**.
c – Arrives 1819.
e – ⑥⑦ from July 18.
g – ① only.

h – ⑥ only.
k – 1538 until Aug. 21.
r – ⑥ until July 11; ①–⑥ from July 18.
v – From Aug. 24.
z – From July 18.

◧ – Conveys 🅁 (*ICE* **504**) Basel - Köln.
⊡ – Amsterdam timings are subject to alteration on June 14, 27, 28, Aug. 9.
◇ – *S-Bahn*.
🚋 – Frequent light-rail services operate from/to Bonn Hbf. See page 419.
⊖ – For local connections Siegburg/Bonn - Köln/Bonn Flughafen see Tables **807** (Siegburg/Bonn - Troisdorf) and **802** (Troisdorf - Köln/Bonn Flughafen).

FRANKFURT - DARMSTADT - HEIDELBERG - KARLSRUHE 911

See Table **912** for *ICE* services via Mannheim. See Table **911a** for other local services.

km		*ICE* 181	*IC* 2395	*IC* 2273	*EC* 113	*ICE* 1097	*IC* 2275	*IC* 2293	*IC* 2277	*EC* 319	*IC* 2279	*IC* 2299	*EC* 117	*IC* 2371	*EC* 391	*IC* 2373	*IC* 2295	*IC* 2375	*IC* 1858	*IC* 2297	*IC* 2377	*IC* 2377	*IC* 2177	*IC* 1897	*ICE* 775
			①-⑤	①-⑥		①-⑤	①-⑤					⑥	Ⓑ				Ⓑ	Ⓑ	⑦	‡	⑦	⑤	①-④	⑦	⑦
		Z✕		🍷	F✕	✕⚡		🍷	🍷	G✕	🍷		K✕	N🍷	L🍷	🍷	🍷	🍷	R🍷		🍷	🍷		B🍷	✕
	Stralsund **830** d.	...	...	...	...	...	...	...	...	...	0527e	...	...	...	...	0927	...	...	...	...	1327	1327	...	...	...
	Hamburg Hbf **800 902** d.	...	...	...	...	0609	...	...	0628e	...	0827e	...	...	1028	...	1228	...	1428	...	...	1628	1628	...	...	1924
	Hannover Hbf **902** d.	...	...	...	...	0722	0600	...	0800e	...	1000e	...	...	1200	...	1400	...	1600	...	...	1800	1800	...	1901	2041
	Kassel Wilhelmshöhe **806** d.	...	...	0531	...	|	0731	...	0931	...	1131	...	...	1331	...	1531	...	1731	...	...	1931	1931	...	2004	2137
0	**Frankfurt** (Main) Hbf d.	0557	0642	0738	0820	0934	0938	1020	1138	1220	1338	1420	1420	1538	1620	1738	1820	1938	1955	2020	2138	2154	2154	2158	2310
28	Darmstadt Hbf d.	0615	0659	0755	0837	0950	0955	1037	1155	1237	1355	1437	1437	1555	1637	1755	1837	1955	2012	2037	2155	2211	2211	2216	2327
50	Bensheim d.	|	0714	0807	0849	...	1007	|	1207	1249	1407	1449	1449	1607	1649	1807	1849	2007	2025	2049	2207	2223	2223	|	|
64	Weinheim (Bergstr) d.	|	0727	0817	0900	...	1017	1056	1217	1300	1417	1500	1500	1617	1700	1817	1900	2017	2036	2100	2217	2233	2233	2236	|
87	**Heidelberg** Hbf d.	0657t	0742	0832	0914	...	1032	1110	1232	1314	1432	1514	1514	1632	1714	1832	1914	2032	2052	2114	2232	2249	2249	2251	0004
120	Bruchsal **931** d.	|	|	0848	|	...	|	|	1248	|	1448	|	|	1648	|	1848	|	2052h	|	|	2249	2306	2307	|	|
	Stuttgart Hbf **930** a.	0735	0833	|	0953	...	1123	1150	|	1353	|	1553	1553	|	1753	|	1953	|	2146	2154	|	|	|	2339	0044
	München Hbf **930** a.	...	...	|	1216	...	...	...	|	1616	|	...	1815	|	2016	|	2220	|	...	...	|	|	|	...	...
	Salzburg Hbf **890** a.	...	...	|	1404	...	...	...	|	1804	|	...	2004	|	2209	|	...	|	...	...	|	|	|	...	...
141	**Karlsruhe** Hbf **931** a.	...	...	0902	...	...	...	...	1301	...	1501	...	...	1701	...	1901	...	2105h	...	...	2304	2322	2322	...	...

	ICE 1092	*ICE* 824	*IC* 2278	*IC* 2296	*IC* 2376	*IC* 2294	*IC* 2374	*IC* 2290	*IC* 2290	*IC* 2372	*EC* 390	*IC* 2370	*IC* 2270	*EC* 318	*IC* 2276	*IC* 2288	*IC* 2292	*IC* 2274	*EC* 112	*IC* 2172	*IC* 2272	*IC* 1876	*IC* 1874		*ICE* 1580
	①-⑤	①-⑤	①-⑤	①-⑥	①-⑥	①-⑥	⊖	①-⑥	⑦			J	⑤⑦		①-⑥	⑦				⑦	①-⑤	⑦	⑦		
	B⚡	E🍷		✕	🍷	🍷	🍷	🍷		🍷	L🍷	N🍷	N🍷	G✕	🍷	S🍷	🍷	🍷	F✕	🍷	🍷				✕
Karlsruhe Hbf **931** d.	✕	...	0615	...	0647	...	0854	...	...	1054	...	1253	1253	...	1454	1454	...	1654	...	...	1854	...	...	...	...
Salzburg Hbf **890** d.	...	...	|	...	|	...	|	0547	...	|	0753e	|	|	0957	|	|	...	|	1352	...	|	...	...	...	...
München Hbf **930** d.	...	...	|	...	|	0516	|	0739	...	|	0940	|	|	1143	|	|	...	|	1541	...	|	...	...	...	...
Stuttgart Hbf **930** d.	...	...	|	0603	|	0805	|	1005	1005	|	1205	|	|	1405	|	|	1606	|	1805	1837	|	2009	...	...	2231
Bruchsal **931** d.	...	...	0633	|	0703	|	0906	|	|	1106	|	1306	1306	|	1506	1506	|	1706	|	|	1906	|	...	...	|
Heidelberg Hbf d.	...	...	0654	0658	0724	0847	0924	1047	1047	1124	1247	1324	1324	1447	1524	1524	1647	1724	1847	1924	1924	2050	2124	...	2317
Weinheim (Bergstr) d.	...	...	|	0714	0739	0900	0939	1100	1100	1139	1300	1339	1339	1500	1539	1539	1700	1739	1900	1939	1939	2104	2139	...	|
Bensheim d.	...	...	m	0729	0750	0910	0949	1110	1110	1149	1310	1349	1349	1510	1549	1549	1710	1749	1910	1949	1949	2115	2149	...	|
Darmstadt Hbf d.	0543	0637	|	0743	0802	0924	1002	1124	1124	1202	1324	1402	1402	1524	1602	1602	1724	1802	1924	2002	2002	2127	2202	...	0001
Frankfurt (Main) Hbf a.	0600	0656	0752	0800	0818	0940	1018	1140	1146	1218	1340	1418	1418	1540	1618	1618	1740	1818	1940	2018	2018	2144	2218	...	0019
Kassel Wilhelmshöhe **806** a.	...	...	...	...	1026	...	1226	...	...	1426	...	1626	1626	...	1826	1826	...	2027	...	2226	2226	...	0026	...	...
Hannover Hbf **902** a.	...	...	...	...	1156	...	1356	...	...	1556	...	1756	1756	...	1956	1956	...	2156f	...	...	...	...	...	...	...
Hamburg Hbf **902** a.	...	...	...	...	1328	...	1529	...	...	1730	...	1927	1927	...	2126	2126	...	2327v	...	...	...	...	...	...	...
Stralsund **930** a.	...	...	...	...	1630	...	...	...	...	2032	...	...	2230	...	...	...	...	...	...	...	...	...	...	...	...

B – To / from Berlin (Table **900**).
E – 🚃12 and 🍷 Darmstadt - Köln Messe/Deutz - Essen.
F – 🚃12 and ✕ Klagenfurt - Villach - Frankfurt and v.v.;
🚃12 Zagreb (**212/3**) - Ljubljana - Villach - Frankfurt and v.v.
G – 🚃12 and ✕ Graz - Salzburg - Frankfurt and v.v.
J – ①②③④⑥.
K – To Klagenfurt (Table **970**).
L – From / to Linz on dates in Table **950**.
N – From / to Konstanz (Table **916**).
R – From Leipzig (Table **850**).
S – To Rostock (Table **830**).
Z – To Zürich (Table **940**).

e – ①-⑥ only.
f – ⑤⑦ only.
h – Heidelberg - Karlsruhe on ①-⑤ only.
m – Via Mannheim (Table **912**).
t – Arrives 0649.
v – ⑦ only.

⊖ – Train number **2174** on ⑤.
‡ – Train number **2393** on ⑥. Conveys ✕ on Ⓑ, 🍷 on ⑥.
⚡ – *ICE SPRINTER*. 🅁 and supplement payable.

RE / RB services — Local services FRANKFURT and MAINZ - MANNHEIM - KARLSRUHE 911a

Frankfurt - Darmstadt - Heidelberg and Mannheim

	⚒	Ⓐ		Ⓐ			⚒					Ⓐ				Ⓐ	Ⓒ	Ⓐ						
Frankfurt (Main) Hbf **911/2** d.	0511	0506	0606	0630	0710	0706	0810	0806	0913	0906	this pattern runs every **two** hours until	1810	1806	1913	1906	2010	2006	2029	2113	2106	2206	2306	2318	0006
Darmstadt Hbf **911** d.	|	0530	0630	0653	|	0730	|	0830	|	0930		|	1830	|	1930	|	2030	2053	|	2130	2230	2330	|	0030
Bensheim **911** d.	◐	0552	0658	0709	◐	0752	◐	0858	◐	0952		◐	1858	◐	1952	◐	2058	2109	◐	2152	2254	2355	◐	0055
Weinheim (Bergstr) **911** d.	|	0608	0713	0722	|	0808	|	0913	|	1008		|	1913	|	2008	|	2113	2122	|	2208	2310	0010	|	0110
Mannheim Friedrichsfeld a.	|	0620	0726	0732	|	0817	|	0926	|	1017		|	1926	|	2018	|	2126	2131	|	2217	2323	0023	|	0123
Mannheim Hbf **912** a.	0621	*0644*	*0743*z	0743	0820	*0842*	0920	*0942*	1020	*1042*		1920	*1942*	2020	*2042*	2120	*2143*	*2143*	2220	*2242*	*2343*	|	0025	0138
Heidelberg Hbf **911** a.	...	0631	0738	...	...	0827	...	0939	...	1027		...	1939	...	2027	...	2139	2141	...	2227	2335	0035	...	...

	Ⓐ		Ⓐ		⚒				⚒					Ⓐ				Ⓐ				Ⓐ		
Heidelberg Hbf **911** d.	0424	0525	...	0625	...	0728	...	0821	...	0928	...	this pattern runs every **two** hours until	1821	...	1928	...	2021	...	2128	...	2221	...	2325	...
Mannheim Hbf **912** d.	|	*0516*r	0532	*0612*	0638	*0716*t	0738j	*0816*	0838j	*0916*	0938		*1816*	1838j	*1916*	1938	*2016*	2038j	*2116*	2138x	*2216*	2238	*2316*	0009
Mannheim Friedrichsfeld d.	0434	0534	|	0634	|	0737	|	0832	|	0938	|		1832	|	1938	|	2032	|	2138	|	2232	|	2335	|
Weinheim (Bergstr) **911** d.	0448	0549	◐	0648	◐	0749	◐	0845	◐	0949	◐		1845	◐	1949	◐	2045	◐	2149	◐	2245	◐	2349	◐
Bensheim **911** d.	0503	0603	|	0703	|	0803	|	0900	|	1003	|		1900	|	2003	|	2100	|	2203	|	2300	|	0004	|
Darmstadt Hbf **911** d.	0531	0630	|	0730	|	0830	|	0930	|	1030	|		1930	|	2030	|	2130	|	2230	|	2330	|	0029	|
Frankfurt (Main) Hbf **911/2** a.	0550	0648	0645	0748	0747	0848	0845	0948	0947	1048	1045		1948	1947	2048	2045	2148	2147	2248	2245	2348	2347	0048	0132

Mainz - Worms - Mannheim

km		Ⓐ	⚒	ⒶG		⚒		⚒		ⒶK				K			ⒶK			ⒶK			Ⓐ	ⒸK	Ⓐ	
0	**Mainz** Hbf **912** d.	0456	0515	0545	0552b	0621	0656	0722	0752	0813	0819e	0851	0952	1013	1051	1152	1213	1252	1351	1413	1451	1552	1613	1613	1628	1651
46	Worms Hbf a.	0540	0555	0614	0633b	0706	0740	0805	0835	0839	0903e	0935	1035	1039	1135	1235	1239	1335	1435	1439	1535	1635	1639	1639	1716	1735
46	Worms Hbf d.	0541	0556	0615	0635	0712	0746	0818	0848	0840	0916	0948	1048	1040	1148	1249	1240	1348	1448	1440	1548	1648	1640	1640	1717	1749
67	Ludwigshafen Hbf a.	0557	0615	0632	0652	0730	0804	0834	0908	0856	0936	1008	1108	1057	1208	1308	1256	1408	1508	1456	1608	1708	1654	1656	1736	1808
70	**Mannheim** Hbf **912** a.	0603	0623	...	0658	0737	0811	0841	0914	...	0942	1014	1114	...	1214	1314	...	1414	1514	...	1614	1714	1700	...	1742	1814

	ⒶG		K		Ⓐ		bK					
Mainz Hbf **912** d.	1719	1752	1813	1851	1922	1951	2013	2052	2152	...	2317	0022
Worms Hbf a.	1745	1835	1839	1935	2005	2035	2039	2135	2240	...	0000	0105
Worms Hbf d.	1746	1848	1840	1948	2018	2048	2040	2148	2241	...	0001	...
Ludwigshafen Hbf a.	1800	1908	1855	2008	2039	2108	2056	2208	2301	...	0017	...
Mannheim Hbf **912** a.	...	1914	...	2014	2046	2114	...	2214	2307	...	0024	...

	⚒	⚒	Ⓐ	⑥m	Ⓐ		⚒	ⒶG		ⒶG
Mannheim Hbf **912** d.	...	0427	0500	0527	0534	0550e	0618	...	0650	...
Ludwigshafen Hbf d.	...	0436	0505	0533	0543	0558e	0624	0655	0659	0750
Worms Hbf a.	...	0454	0523	0551	0601	0615e	0644	0712	0718	0804
Worms Hbf d.	0417	0455	0525	0553	0602	0620	0653	0713	0724	0805
Mainz Hbf **912** a.	0504	0538	0608	0637	0649	0706	0736	0747	0807	0835

	Ⓒ	Ⓐ		ⒶK	Ⓐ			K			ⒶK			ⒶK			K			K			ⒶK			
Mannheim Hbf **912** d.	0744	0748	0844	...	0916	0944	1044	...	1144	1244	...	1344	1444	...	1544	1644	...	1744	1844	...	1944	2044	...	2144	2248	0011
Ludwigshafen Hbf d.	0750	0755	0850	0904	0921	0950	1050	1104	1150	1250	1304	1350	1450	1504	1550	1650	1704	1750	1850	1904	1950	2050	2104	2150	2253	0017
Worms Hbf a.	0816	0816	0914	0919	0937	1014	1114	1119	1214	1311	1319	1414	1514	1519	1614	1714	1719	1814	1914	1919	2014	2114	2119	2214	2312	0039
Worms Hbf d.	0825	0825	0925	0920	0955	1025	1125	1120	1225	1324	1320	1425	1525	1520	1625	1725	1720	1825	1925	1920	2025	2125	2120	2223	2315	...
Mainz Hbf **912** a.	0908	0908	1008	0947	1038	1108	1208	1147	1308	1408	1347	1508	1608	1547	1708	1808	1747	1908	2008	1947	2108	2207	2147	2306	2359	...

Mannheim - Heidelberg - Karlsruhe

S-Bahn		Ⓒ	Ⓐ					❖			
Mannheim Hbf d.	0005	0535f	0544	0637v	0729h	0829	0929	and hourly until	2029	2137	2237
Heidelberg Hbf d.	0022	0558	0603	0707	0748	0848	0948		2048	2155	2255
Bruchsal d.	0048	0625	0630	0733	0817	0922	1018		2118	2221	2321
Karlsruhe Hbf a.	0106	0643	0648	0750	0832	0936	1032		2132	2235	2335

S-Bahn			Ⓒ	Ⓐ							
Karlsruhe Hbf d.	0333	0534	0615	0620	0728	and hourly until	1928	2030	2128	2228	2328
Bruchsal d.	0350	0558	0633	0638	0743		1943	2044	2143	2243	2343
Heidelberg Hbf d.	0418	0634	0700	0708	0814		2014	2114	2214	2314	0014
Mannheim Hbf a.	0434	0651	*0719*	0725	0829		2030	2132	2232	2332	0030

G – To / from Gemersheim (Table **918**).
K – To / from Karlsruhe via Germersheim (Table **918**).

b – Ⓑ (also Oct. 3).
e – Ⓐ only.

f – *0537* on ⑥ (not Oct. 3).
h – Change trains at Heidelberg on Ⓒ.
j – 4 minutes later until Aug 23.
m – Not Oct. 3.
r – ⚒ only.

t – *0720* on Ⓐ.
v – 0647 on Ⓐ.
x – 2142 on ⑦ until Aug. 23.
z – Ⓒ only.

◐ – Via Biblis.
❖ – Timings at Bruchsal and Karlsruhe may vary by up to 5 minutes on certain journeys.

912 (KÖLN -) KOBLENZ - FRANKFURT - MANNHEIM - KARLSRUHE - BASEL

km	km		IC 1591 ①–⑤	IC 997 ⑥ 🍷	IC 995 ⑦ 🍷	ICE 879 ⑦ 🍴	ICE 609 🍴K	CNL 40419 Ⓡ 🍷♦	CNL 479 Ⓡ 🍴♦	CNL 458 Ⓡ ◧ 🍷♦	CNL 1258 Ⓡ ◧ 🍴♦	IC 60458 ①–⑤ 2	IC 60458 ⑥⑦ 2	ICE 371 ①–⑤ Z🍴	ICE 672 ♦	ICE 991 ①–⑥ 🍴	ICE 5 ①–⑥ B🍴	ICE 5 B🍴	TGV 9578 ①–⑥ Ⓡ P 🍷	EN 468 Ⓡ 🍷♦	IC 2021 ⊖	ICE 511 🍷	ICE 271 Z🍴	CNL 473 Ⓡ 🍷♦	ICE 23 Q🍴
		Berlin Hbf **810** ▲ d.	...	...	...	2032	...	...	...	...	2222	...	...	...	...	...	...	...		...	...	...	...	...	...
		Hamburg Hbf **800 900** d.	...	...	...	|	1946	...	1918	...	|	...	...	...	...	...	0025g	...	...	...	2246	...	...	0031	...
		Dortmund Hbf **800** d.	...	...	...	|	2238	...	|	...	|	...	...	...	...	...	|	...	...	...	0203	...	...	|	0433
0		*Köln Hbf* **800 910** d.	...	...	...	|	2353	2346	|	...	|	...	...	...	...	...	|	...	...	...	0352	0554	...	|	0553
93		**Koblenz** Hbf **914** d.	...	...	...	|	0048	0044	|	...	|	...	...	...	...	...	|	...	...	...	0530	|	...	|	0648
154		Bingen (Rhein) Hbf **914** d.	...	...	...	|	0124¦	|	|	...	|	...	...	...	...	...	|	...	...	...	0609	|	...	|	|
		Wiesbaden Hbf d.	...	...	...	|	|	|	|	...	|	...	...	...	0500	0522	|	...	...	...	|	|	...	|	|
184		**Mainz** Hbf **914** a.	...	...	...	|	0141	|	|	...	|	...	...	...	0509	0536	|	...	...	...	0627	|	...	|	0738
184		**Mainz** Hbf **911a** d.	...	...	...	|	0143	|	|	...	|	...	...	...	0511	0540	|	...	...	...	0629	|	...	|	0740
	0	**Frankfurt** (Main) Hbf ◇ d.	0007	0018	0018	0109	|	|	|	...	|	0402x	0402x	...	|	|	0538	...	...	...	|	|	0650	|	|
210		**Frankfurt** Flughafen Fernbf ✈ a.	0023	0034	0034	0122	0202‡	|	|	...	|	|	|	...	0537	|	0550	...	...	...	0646	0651	|	|	0759
210		**Frankfurt** Flughafen Fernbf ✈ d.	0028	0039	0042	0127	0205‡	|	|	...	|	|	|	...	0539	|	0555	...	...	...	0648	0654	|	|	0802
221		**Frankfurt** (Main) Hbf a.	|	|	|	|	0217	|	|	...	|	|	|	...	0550	|	|	...	...	...	0702	|	|	|	0813
—	78	**Mannheim** Hbf **911a** a.	0104b	0110	0112c	0200b	0300r	|	|	0443s	0443s	0443	0443c	...	...	0622	0625p	...	...	...	...	0724	0728p	0750s	...
	78	**Mannheim** Hbf **911a** d.	0106b	0112	0114c	0202b	0302r	|	|	|	|	0445	0445c	...	...	0630	0627	...	...	...	...	0733	0736	|	...
		Heidelberg Hbf **911 911a** d.	0119	0125	0127	|	|	|	|	0458s	0458s	0500	0500	...	...	|	|	...	...	...	...	|	|	|	...
		Stuttgart Hbf **930** a.	0236	0249	0252	|	|	|	|	|	|	|	|	...	...	0708	|	...	...	...	...	0808	|	|	...
		München Hbf **930** a.	0519g	0521	0524	|	|	|	|	|	|	|	|	...	...	0930	|	...	...	...	...	1031	|	|	...
0	138	**Karlsruhe** Hbf **911 911a 916** d.	...	...	...	0238	0337	0437s	0437s	0540s	0540s	0542	0548	0552	...	...	0652q	0652q	0731	0754	...	...	0800	0818s	...
31	169	Baden-Baden **916** d.	...	...	...	...	0358	|	|	|	|	|	0609	0612	...	...	0714	0714	|	0819	...	...	|	|	...
	209	Offenburg ★ **916** d.	...	...	...	...	0416	0519s	0519s	0620s	0620s	0622	0629	0629	...	...	0730	0730	|	|	...	...	0829	0901s	...
84		**Strasbourg** ★ a.	...	...	...	...	|	|	|	|	|	|	|	|	...	...	|	|	0813	0859	...	...	|	|	...
	272	**Freiburg** (Brsg) Hbf ★ d.	...	...	...	...	0452	0556s	0556s	0653s	0653s	0655	0702	0702	...	...	0802	0802	...	...	...	...	0901	0939s	...
	333	**Basel** Bad. Bf ★ a.	...	...	...	...	0537	0644	0644	0746	0746	0746	0737	0737	...	...	0837	0837	...	...	...	...	0936	1027	...
	338	**Basel** SBB a.	...	...	...	...	0547	0654	0654	0755	0755	0755	0755	0747	...	...	0847	0847	...	...	...	...	0947	1037	...

	ICE 711 ①–⑤ Y	ICE 711 ①–⑤ t	ICE 591 ①–⑥ 🍴♦	ICE 999 ⑦ A🍴	ICE 501 🍷	TGV 9576 Ⓡ 🍷♦	IC 2319 ①–⑥ M	ICE 1597 ①–⑥ ⊙	ICE 1597 ⑦ D	ICE 513 M🍷	ICE 373 B🍴	ICE 571 ①–⑥ 🍴	IC 2102 N🍷	ICE 503 H🍷	ICE 593 ⑥⑦ 🍴	ICE 1091 ①–⑤ 🍴	ICE 25 Q🍴	ICE 71 🍴	EC 115 🍴♦	EC 7 🍴♦	ICE 1559 D🍴	ICE 515 🍷	ICE 375 B🍴	IC 119 🍷♦	ICE 973 🍴♦
Berlin Hbf **810** ▲ d.	...	...	...	...	...	...	...	...	...	...	0432a	...	...	...	0531	0608*	...	...	...	...	...	...	0632	...	...
Hamburg Hbf **800 900** d.	...	...	0318a	...	...	...	...	...	...	...	|	0519	...	...	|	|	...	0618	...	0442e	...	0537	|	...	0724
Dortmund Hbf **800** d.	0502	0502	|	...	0537	...	0538	...	...	0638	|	|	...	0737	|	|	0636	|	...	0738	...	0837	|	...	|
Köln Hbf **800 910** d.	0615d	0615d	|	...	0654	...	0653	...	...	0754	|	|	...	0854	|	|	0753	|	0818	0853	...	0954	|	0918	|
Koblenz Hbf **914** d.	|	|	|	...	|	...	0748	...	...	|	|	|	...	|	|	|	0848	|	0917	0948	...	|	|	1017	|
Bingen (Rhein) Hbf **914** d.	|	|	|	...	|	...	|	...	...	|	|	|	...	|	|	|	|	|	0951	|	...	|	|	1052	|
Wiesbaden Hbf d.	0724	0733	|	...	|	...	|	...	0824	|	|	|	...	|	|	|	|	|	|	|	1024k	|	|	|	|
Mainz Hbf **914** a.	|	0744	|	...	|	...	0837	...	0835	|	|	|	...	|	|	|	0938	|	1013y	1037	1035k	|	|	1111j	|
Mainz Hbf **911a** d.	|	0746	|	...	|	...	0838	0842	0842	|	|	|	...	|	|	|	0940	|	1015y	1038	1042	|	|	1113j	|
Frankfurt (Main) Hbf ◇ d.	|	|	0750	0750	|	...	|	|	|	|	0850	0905	...	|	0950	0950	|	1005	|	|	|	|	1050	|	1105
Frankfurt Flughafen Fernbf ✈ a.	|	|	|	|	0751	...	|	0859	0859	0851	|	0916	...	0951	|	|	0959	|	|	|	1100	1051	|	|	1116
Frankfurt Flughafen Fernbf ✈ d.	|	|	|	|	0754	...	|	0901	0901	0854	|	0920	...	0954	|	|	1002	|	|	|	1103	1054	|	|	1120
Frankfurt (Main) Hbf a.	|	|	|	|	|	...	|	0913	0913	|	|	|	...	|	|	|	1013	|	|	|	1114	|	|	|	|
Mannheim Hbf **911a** a.	0821	0824	0828	0828	0824p	...	0921	...	...	0924	0928p	0953	...	1024	1028	1028	...	1042	1101	1121	...	1124	1128p	1152	1153
Mannheim Hbf **911a** d.	0826	0826	0831	0831	0836	...	0923	...	...	0933	0936	0955	...	1026	1031	1031	...	1044	1103	1123	...	1133	1136	1154	1155
Heidelberg Hbf **911 911a** d.	0838	0838	|	|	|	...	0936	...	...	|	|	|	...	|	|	|	...	|	|	|	...	|	|	1206	|
Stuttgart Hbf **930** a.	0923	0923	0908	0908	|	...	1018	...	...	1008	|	1033	...	|	1108	1108	...	|	1153	|	...	1208	|	1246	1233
München Hbf **930** a.	...	...	1130	1130	|	...	...	...	...	1230	|	...	...	|	1330	1330	...	|	1416	|	...	1430	|	...	...
Karlsruhe Hbf **911 911a 916** d.	...	...	...	...	0900	0931	...	...	...	...	1000	...	1055	1056	...	...	...	1108	...	1149	...	...	1200	...	...
Baden-Baden **916** d.	...	...	...	...	0917	|	...	...	...	...	|	...	|	...	...	...	...	1126	...	1208	...	...	|	...	...
Offenburg ★ **916** d.	...	...	...	...	|	|	...	...	...	...	1029	...	1129	...	...	...	...	|	...	|	...	...	1229	...	...
Strasbourg ★ a.	...	...	...	...	|	1013	...	...	...	...	|	...	|	...	...	...	...	|	...	|	...	...	|	...	...
Freiburg (Brsg) Hbf ★ d.	...	...	...	...	1002	...	...	...	...	...	1101	...	1201	...	...	...	...	1211	...	1255	...	...	1301	...	...
Basel Bad. Bf ★ a.	...	...	...	...	1037	...	...	...	...	...	1136	...	1236	...	...	...	...	1247	...	1329	...	...	1336	...	...
Basel SBB a.	...	...	...	...	1047	...	...	...	...	...	1147	...	1247	...	...	...	...	1255	...	1337	...	...	1347	...	...

	ICE 105 🍷♦	ICE 595 🍴	ICE 27 Q🍴	ICE 73 🍴♦	TGV 9574 Ⓡ P🍷	IC 2005 ⑤⑥ 🍷♦	IC 2015 ①–④ 🍷♦	EC 101 🍴♦	ICE 1651 D🍴	ICE 517 🍷	ICE 871 🍴	IC 2013 🍷♦	ICE 575 🍴	IC 2100 N🍷	ICE 507 🍷	ICE 597 🍴	IC 2023 🍷	ICE 75 Z🍴	IC 2113 🍴	ICE 1653 t D🍴	ICE 519 🍷	ICE 277 B🍴	IC 1911 ⑤⑦ §	ICE 577 🍴	ICE 509 🍷
Berlin Hbf **810** ▲ d.	...	0737	...	...	...	...	...	...	...	...	0832	...	...	...	...	0937	...	...	...	...	...	1031	...	...	...
Hamburg Hbf **800 900** d.	...	|	...	0824	...	...	...	0646	...	...	|	...	0924	...	...	|	0746	1024	0846	...	...	|	...	1124	...
Dortmund Hbf **800** d.	...	|	0838	|	...	...	...	0938	...	1038	|	0952	|	...	1137h	|	1036	|	1138	...	1238	|	1152	|	...
Köln Hbf **800 910** d.	1054	|	0953	|	...	1018	1018	1053	...	1154	|	1118	|	...	1254	|	1153	|	1253	...	1354	|	1318	|	1454
Koblenz Hbf **914** d.	|	|	1048	|	...	1116	1116	1148	...	|	|	1217	|	...	|	|	1248	|	1348	...	|	|	1417	|	|
Bingen (Rhein) Hbf **914** d.	|	|	|	|	...	|	|	|	...	|	|	1252	|	...	|	|	|	|	|	...	|	|	1452	|	|
Wiesbaden Hbf d.	|	|	|	|	...	|	|	|	1224k	|	|	|	|	...	|	|	|	|	|	1424	|	|	|	|	|
Mainz Hbf **914** a.	|	|	1138	|	...	1212t	1212t	1237	1235k	|	|	1311j	|	...	|	|	1338	|	1437	1435	|	|	1511t	|	|
Mainz Hbf **911a** d.	|	|	1140	|	...	1217t	1217t	1238	1242	|	|	1313j	|	...	|	|	1340	|	1438	1442	|	|	1513t	|	|
Frankfurt (Main) Hbf ◇ d.	|	1150	|	1205	...	|	|	|	|	|	1250	|	1305	...	|	1350	|	1405	|	|	|	1450	|	1505	|
Frankfurt Flughafen Fernbf ✈ a.	1151	|	1159	|	...	|	|	|	1300	1251	|	|	1316	...	1351	|	1359	|	|	1500	1451	|	|	1516	1551
Frankfurt Flughafen Fernbf ✈ d.	1154	|	1202	|	...	|	|	|	1303	1254	|	|	1320	...	1354	|	1401	|	|	1503	1454	|	|	1520	1554
Frankfurt (Main) Hbf a.	|	|	1213	|	...	|	|	|	1314	|	|	|	|	...	|	|	1413	|	|	1515	|	|	|	|	|
Mannheim Hbf **911a** a.	1224	1228	...	1242	...	1307z	1307z	1321	...	1324	1328p	1352	1353	...	1424	1428	...	1442	1521	...	1524	1528p	1552	1553	1624
Mannheim Hbf **911a** d.	1226	1231	...	1244	...	1309	1312	1323	...	1333	1336	1354	1355	...	1426	1431	...	1444	1523	...	1533	1536	1554	1555	1626
Heidelberg Hbf **911 911a** d.	|	|	...	|	...	|	|	|	...	|	|	1406	|	...	|	|	...	|	1536	...	|	|	1606	|	|
Stuttgart Hbf **930** a.	|	1308	...	|	...	|	1358	|	...	1408	|	1446	1433	...	|	1508	...	|	1622	...	1608	|	1646	1632	|
München Hbf **930** a.	|	1530	...	|	...	|	...	|	...	1631	|	...	...	...	|	1730	...	|	...	...	1830	|	...	...	|
Karlsruhe Hbf **911 911a 916** d.	1254	...	...	1308	1331	1336	...	1349	...	...	1400	...	...	1455	1456	...	...	1508	...	...	...	1600	...	...	1654
Baden-Baden **916** d.	|	...	...	1326	|	1356	...	1408	...	...	|	...	...	|	...	...	...	1526	...	...	...	|	...	...	|
Offenburg ★ **916** d.	1329	...	...	|	|	1415	...	|	...	...	1429	...	...	1529	...	...	...	|	...	...	...	1629	...	...	1729
Strasbourg ★ a.	|	...	...	|	1415	...	...	|	...	...	|	...	...	|	...	...	...	|	...	...	...	|	...	...	|
Freiburg (Brsg) Hbf ★ d.	1401	...	...	1411	...	...	...	1455	...	...	1501	...	...	1601	...	...	...	1611	...	...	...	1701	...	...	1801
Basel Bad. Bf ★ a.	1436	...	...	1447	...	...	...	1529	...	...	1536	...	...	1636	...	...	...	1647	...	...	...	1736	...	...	1836
Basel SBB a.	1447	...	...	1455	...	...	...	1537	...	...	1547	...	...	1647	...	...	...	1655	...	...	...	1747	...	...	1847

♦ – **NOTES** (LISTED BY TRAIN NUMBER) for pages 422 and 423

7 – [12] and 🍴 (Hamburg ①–⑥ -) Dortmund - Basel - Zürich - Chur.

73 – [12] and 🍴 Kiel - Hamburg - Basel - Zürich.

101 – [12] and 🍴 Hamburg - Köln - Basel - Zürich - Chur.

105 – ICE INTERNATIONAL – [12] and 🍷 Amsterdam - Utrecht - Arnhem - Basel. Conveys [12] (*ICE* **505**) Köln - Basel

115 – WÖRTHERSEE – [12] and 🍴 Münster - Salzburg - Villach - Klagenfurt.

119 – [12] and 🍷 Münster - Stuttgart - Ulm - Lindau - Bregenz - Innsbruck.

360 – [12] and 🍷 München - Stuttgart - Strasbourg.

458 – CANOPUS – 🛏 1, 2 cl., ▬ 2 cl., [2] and 🍷 Praha - Dresden - Leipzig - Zürich.

468 – ORIENT EXPRESS – 🛏 1, 2 cl., ▬ 2 cl., [2] and 🍷 Wien - Salzburg - Strasbourg.

473 – AURORA – 🛏 1, 2 cl. and ▬ 2 cl. København - Basel; conveys 🛏 1, 2 cl. and ▬ 2 cl. Warszawa - Basel, also 🛏 1, 2 cl. Moskva - Basel.

479 – Daily until Nov. 1; ④–⑦ from Nov. 5. KOMET – 🛏 1, 2 cl., ▬ 2 cl., [2] (reclining) and 🍴 Hamburg - Zürich.

591 – [12] and 🍴 (Hamburg ①–⑤ -) Hannover - Frankfurt - München.

672 – [12] Wiesbaden - Frankfurt - Hamburg; 🍴 Frankfurt - Hamburg.

973 – [12] and 🍴 (Kiel ①–⑥ -) Hamburg - Stuttgart. Train number **573** on ⑦.

1125 – [12] and 🍴 Kiel - Köln - Nürnberg - Regensburg.

1258 – SIRIUS – 🛏 1, 2 cl., ▬ 2 cl., [2] (reclining) and 🍴 (Ostseebad Binz ● -) Berlin - Halle - Zürich.

1655 – [12] and 🍴 Wiesbaden - Frankfurt (- Leipzig - Berlin Ⓑ).

1657 – [12] and 🍴 Wiesbaden - Frankfurt (- Leipzig Ⓑ) (- Dresden ⑤⑦).

2005 – BODENSEE – [12] and 🍷 Emden - Münster - Konstanz.

2013 – ALLGÄU – [12] and 🍷 (Leipzig ① -) (Magdeburg ①–⑥ -) Hannover - Dortmund - Ulm - Oberstdorf.

2015 – [12] and 🍷 Emden - Münster - Stuttgart.

2027 – [12] and 🍴 Hamburg - Köln - Frankfurt - Nürnberg - Passau. On ①–⑥ until Oct. 3 (also July 19, 26, Aug. 2, 9, Oct. 4 and ⑤ from Oct. 9) starts from Puttgarden (Table **825**) and runs with train number **2327**.

2029 – [12] and 🍷 Hamburg - Köln - Frankfurt - Nürnberg.

2115 – [12] and 🍴 (Greifswald ①–⑤ -) Stralsund - Hamburg - Köln - Stuttgart.

2121 – [12] and 🍴 (Until Oct. 25: Puttgarden -) Hamburg - Köln - Frankfurt. Train number **2321** from Oct. 26.

2213 – RÜGEN – [12] and 🍴 Ostseebad Binz - Stralsund - Hamburg - Stuttgart.

9576 – [12] and 🍷 München - Stuttgart - Strasbourg - Paris.

40419 – Daily until Nov. 2; ①⑤⑥⑦ from Nov. 6. PEGASUS – 🛏 1, 2 cl., ▬ 2 cl., [2] (reclining) and 🍷 Amsterdam - Zürich.

NOTES CONTINUED ON NEXT PAGE →

(KÖLN -) KOBLENZ - FRANKFURT - MANNHEIM - KARLSRUHE - BASEL 912

	ICE 599	IC 2025	ICE 77	TGV 9572	IC 2115	ICE 1655	ICE 611	ICE 279	IC 1913	IC 1913	IC 1913	ICE 579	ICE 601	ICE 691	IC 2027	ICE 79	TGV 9570	IC 2311	ICE 1657	ICE 613	ICE 873	EC 360	IC 1915	ICE 771	ICE 693
				⑥⑦		t			Ⓑ¶	⑤	⑦						①–⑤						⑤⑦		
	✕		Z✕	[R]P	✕♦	✕♦	🍷	B✕		H🍷		✕	🍷	✕	✕♦	Z✕	[R]P	L✕	✕♦	🍷	✕	🍷♦	m	✕	✕
Berlin Hbf **810** ▲ d.	1137	...	...	🍷	...	...	...	1232	...	...	1010	...	...	1337	...	...	🍷	...	...	...	1432	...	1208	...	1537
Hamburg Hbf **800 900** ⊠ d.	|	0946	1224	...	1046	...	...	|	...	...	|	1324	...	|	1146	1424	...	1246	...	...	|	...	|	1524	|
Dortmund Hbf **800** d.	|	1236	|	...	1338	...	1438	|	...	1352	1352	|	...	|	1436	|	...	1538	...	1638	|	...	1552	|	|
Köln Hbf **800 910** d.	|	1353	|	...	1453	...	1554	|	1518	1518	1518	|	1654	|	1553	|	...	1653	...	1754	|	...	1718	|	|
Koblenz Hbf **914** d.	|	1448	|	...	1548	...	|	|	1617	1617	1617	|	|	|	1648	|	...	1748	...	|	|	...	1817	|	|
Bingen (Rhein) Hbf **914** d.	|	|	|	...	|	...	|	|	1652	1652	1652	|	|	|	|	|	...	|	...	|	|	...	1852	|	|
Wiesbaden Hbf d.	|	|	|	...	|	1624	|	|	|	|	|	|	|	|	|	|	...	|	1824t	|	|	...	|	|	|
Mainz Hbf **914** a.	|	1538	|	...	1637	1635	|	|	1711j	1711j	1711j	|	|	|	1738	|	...	1837	1835t	|	|	...	1911t	|	|
Mainz Hbf **911a** d.	|	1540	|	...	1638	1642	|	|	1713j	1713j	1713j	|	|	|	1740	|	...	1838	1842	|	|	...	1913t	|	|
Frankfurt (Main) Hbf ◇ d.	1550	|	1605	...	|	|	|	1650	|	|	|	1705	|	1750	|	1805	...	|	|	|	1850	...	|	1905	1950
Frankfurt Flughafen Fernbf ✈ a.	|	1559	|	...	|	1700	1651	|	|	|	|	1716	1751	|	1759	|	...	|	1900	1851	|	...	|	1916	|
Frankfurt Flughafen Fernbf ✈ d.	|	1602	|	...	|	1703	1654	|	|	|	|	1720	1754	|	1802	|	...	|	1903	1854	|	...	|	1920	|
Frankfurt (Main) Hbf a.	|	1613	|	...	|	1715	|	|	|	|	|	|	|	|	1813	|	...	|	1914	|	|	...	|	|	|
Mannheim Hbf **911a** a.	1628	...	1642	...	1721	...	1724	1728p	1752	1752	1752	1753	1824	1828	...	1842	...	1921	...	1924	1928p	...	1952t	1953	2028
Mannheim Hbf **911a** d.	1631	...	1644	...	1723	...	1733	1736	1754	1754	1754	1755	1826	1831	...	1844	...	1923	...	1933	1936	...	1954t	1955	2031
Heidelberg Hbf **911 911a** d.	|	...	|	...	1736	...	|	|	1806	1806	1806	|	|	|	...	|	...	1936	...	|	|	...	2006	|	|
Stuttgart Hbf **930** a.	1708	...	|	...	1825	...	1808	|	1846	1846	1846	1833	|	1908	...	|	...	2022	...	2008	|	...	2046	2033	2108
München Hbf **930** a.	1930	...	|	...	...	...	2030	|	...	2123	...	...	|	2133	...	|	...	...	...	2232	|	...	...	...	2330
Karlsruhe Hbf **911 911a 916** d.	...	...	1708	1731	...	...	...	1800	...	...	...	...	1855	...	...	1908	1931	...	...	...	2000	2006	...	...	...
Baden-Baden **916** d.	...	...	1726	|	...	...	...	|	...	...	...	...	|	...	...	1926	|	...	...	...	|	2024	...	...	...
Offenburg ★ **916** d.	...	...	|	|	...	...	...	1829	...	...	...	...	1929	...	...	|	|	...	...	...	2029	|	...	...	...
Strasbourg ★ a.	...	...	|	1815	...	...	...	|	...	...	...	...	|	...	...	|	2015	...	...	...	|	2101	...	...	...
Freiburg (Brsg) Hbf ★ d.	...	...	1811	...	...	...	...	1901	...	...	...	...	2001	...	...	2011	...	...	...	...	2101	...	...	...	...
Basel Bad. Bf 🏛 ★ a.	...	...	1847	...	...	...	...	1936	...	...	...	...	2036	...	...	2047	...	...	...	...	2136	...	...	...	...
Basel SBB a.	...	...	1855	...	...	...	...	1947	...	...	...	...	2047	...	...	2055	...	...	...	...	2147	...	...	...	...

	ICE 603	ICE 603	ICE 1025	ICE 1125	ICE 671	ICE 671	ICE 603	IC 2213	ICE 1659	ICE 615	ICE 875	ICE 773	IC 1917	ICE 605	ICE 695	ICE 1093	ICE 677	ICE 673	ICE 605	IC 2029	IC 2315	ICE 617	ICE 877	ICE 775	IC 2121
	①–⑥	⑦	♠	⑤		⑦	①–⑥			⊕			⑦		⑥	Ⓑ		⑥	Ⓑ					⑦	
	🍷	🍷	K✕	✕♦	✕	✕	🍷	✕♦	♥	🍷	✕	✕	🍷	🍷	✕	✕	K✕	K✕	🍷	🍷♦	R✕	🍷	✕	✕	✕♦
Berlin Hbf **810** ▲ d.	...	...	...	...	...	...	...	...	...	...	1633	...	1408	...	1735	1805*	...	...	...	...	...	...	1833	...	...
Hamburg Hbf **800 900** ⊠ d.	...	...	1346	1346	1624	1624	...	1446	...	...	|	1724	|	...	|	|	1824	1824	...	1546	1646	...	|	1924	1746
Dortmund Hbf **800** d.	...	...	1636	1636	|	|	...	1738	...	1838	|	|	1752	1923	|	|	|	|	...	1836	1938	2038	|	|	2036
Köln Hbf **800 910** d.	1854	1854	1753	1753	|	|	...	1853	...	1958	|	|	1918	2044d	|	|	|	|	...	1953	2053	2154	|	|	2153
Koblenz Hbf **914** d.	|	|	1848	1848	|	|	...	1948	...	|	|	|	2017	|	|	|	|	|	...	2048	2148	|	|	|	2248
Bingen (Rhein) Hbf **914** d.	|	|	|	|	|	|	...	|	...	|	|	|	2052	|	|	|	|	|	...	2123	|	|	|	|	|
Wiesbaden Hbf d.	|	|	|	|	|	|	...	|	2024	|	|	|	|	|	|	|	|	|	...	|	|	|	|	|	|
Mainz Hbf **914** a.	|	|	1938	1938	|	|	...	2037	2035	|	|	|	2111t	|	|	|	|	|	...	2140	2238	|	|	|	2338
Mainz Hbf **911a** d.	|	|	1940	1940	|	|	...	2038	2042	|	|	|	2113t	|	|	|	|	|	...	2142	2240	|	|	|	2340
Frankfurt (Main) Hbf ◇ d.	|	|	|	|	2005	2005	...	|	|	|	2050	2105	|	|	2150	2150	2205	2205	...	|	|	|	2300	2310	|
Frankfurt Flughafen Fernbf ✈ a.	1951	1951	1959	1959	|	|	...	|	2100	2055	|	2116	|	2151	|	|	|	|	...	2159	2258	2256	|	|	2359
Frankfurt Flughafen Fernbf ✈ d.	1954	1954	2002	2002	|	|	...	|	2103	2059	|	2120	|	2154	|	|	|	|	...	2202	2300	2306	|	|	0002
Frankfurt (Main) Hbf a.	|	|	2013	2013	|	|	...	|	2114	|	|	|	|	|	|	|	|	|	...	2213	2310	|	|	|	0013
Mannheim Hbf **911a** a.	2024p	2024	|	...	2042	2042	...	2121	...	2131	2127p	2153	2152p	2224	2228p	2228p	2242	2242	...	...	...	2337	2341p	|	...
Mannheim Hbf **911a** d.	2036	2036	|	...	2044	2044	...	2123	...	2133	2136	2157	2158	2236	2231	2231	2244	2244	...	...	...	2346	2349	|	...
Heidelberg Hbf **911 911a** d.	|	|	|	...	|	|	...	2136	...	|	|	2210	|	|	|	|	|	|	...	...	...	2359	|	0004	...
Stuttgart Hbf **930** a.	|	|	|	...	|	|	...	2222	...	2208	|	2248	|	|	2308	2308	|	|	...	...	...	0052f	|	0044	...
München Hbf **930** a.	|	|	2348	...	|	|	←	...	...	0034	|	...	|	|	...	...	|	|	←	...	...	...	|	...	...
Karlsruhe Hbf **911 911a 916** d.	2100	2102	...	...	2107	2111	2111	...	...	...	2200	...	2224	2300	...	...	2306	2311	2311	...	...	...	0013	...	...
Baden-Baden **916** d.	→	2119	...	...	...	2129	2129	...	...	...	2219	...	...	→	...	...	...	2330	2330	...	...	...	...	...	...
Offenburg ★ **916** d.	...	2135	...	...	...	2145	2145	...	...	...	2239	...	...	...	...	...	...	2350	2350	...	...	...	...	...	...
Strasbourg ★ a.	...	|	...	...	...	|	|	...	...	...	|	...	...	...	...	...	...	|	|	...	...	...	...	...	...
Freiburg (Brsg) Hbf ★ d.	...	2208	...	...	...	2217	2217	...	...	...	2311	...	...	...	...	...	...	0022	0022	...	...	...	...	...	...
Basel Bad. Bf 🏛 ★ a.	...	2243	...	...	...	2252	2252	...	...	...	2346	...	...	...	...	...	...	0058	0058	...	...	...	...	...	...
Basel SBB a.	...	2253	...	...	...	2300	2300	...	...	...	2355	...	...	...	...	...	...	0106	...	...	...	...	...	...	...

NOTES (CONTINUED FROM PREVIOUS PAGE)

A – From Kassel (Table **900**).
B – To Interlaken via Bern (Table **560**).
D – [12] and ✕ Wiesbaden - Leipzig - Dresden.
H – From Hannover (Table **810**).
K – From Kiel (Table **820**).
L – From Westerland (Table **821**).
M – From Münster (Table **800**).
N – [12] and 🍷 Nürnberg - Stuttgart - Basel.
P – [12] and 🍷 Stuttgart - Strasbourg - Paris.
Q – [12] and ✕ Dortmund - Nürnberg - Passau - Linz - Wien.
R – From Westerland until Oct. 25 (Table **821**). Train number **2215** from Oct. 26.
Y – Until Aug. 21.
Z – To Zürich (Table **510**).

a – ①–⑤ only.
b – Not July 20, Aug. 3, 10.
c – Not July 19, Aug. 2, 9.
d – Köln **Messe/Deutz**.
e – ①–⑥ only.
f – 0040 on the mornings of ①⑦ (also July 11, 18, 25).
g – ① only.
h – ⑦ only.
j – 4 minutes earlier until Aug. 23.
k – 5–7 minutes later until Aug. 23.
m – Conveys 🍷 on ⑦.
n – Not June 16, 17, 18, Oct. 20, 21, 22.
p – Connects with train in previous column.
q – 0656 from July 28.
r – Not July 19, 20, Aug. 1, 2, 8, 9.
s – Stops to set down only.
t – From Aug. 24.
v – Not June 15, 16, 17, Oct. 19, 20, 21.
w – Not Oct. 3.
x – Frankfurt (Main) **Süd**.
y – Not ①–⑤ July 13 - Aug. 21. On ⑥⑦ July 5 - Aug. 23 (also June 14, 21, 28) Mainz a. 1009, d. 1012.
z – 1251 until Aug. 22.

¦ – Not June 14, 15, 21, 22.
⊖ – Also calls at Boppard Hbf (d. 0543).
♠ – Daily except ⑤.
§ – Train number **1111** on ⑦.
¶ – Train number **1119** on ①③④. Conveys 🍷 on ①③⑤.
⊙ – Train number *IC* **2197** on ⑥.
⊕ – On June 20, July 4 terminates at Augsburg Hbf (a. 2352).
● – ⑥ July 4 - Aug. 22.
◧ – On the mornings of ⑥⑦ arrives Offenburg 0627, Freiburg 0700, Basel Bad. Bf 0737. On the mornings of July 19, Aug. 2, 9 does not call at Mannheim.
♥ – ①–⑥ (daily from Aug. 24). To Erfurt and Leipzig on dates in Table **851**.
* – [R] and supplement payable for journeys from Berlin.
‡ – Frankfurt Flughafen Regionalbahnhof.
◇ – See also Tables **911** (trains to Karlsruhe via Darmstadt and Heidelberg), **911a** (local services) and **919** (trains to Saarbrücken via Mannheim).
★ – See panel below for local services Offenburg - Strasbourg and Basel.
♣ – Jointly operated by DB and Ortenau-S-Bahn GmbH. 2nd class only. German holiday dates apply.
▲ – Berlin timings are subject to alteration June 20 - July 3. See Table **810**.
⊠ – Hamburg - Hannover timings are subject to alteration June 14 - July 19 (Hamburg departures may be up to 25 minutes **earlier**).

★ – Local services Offenburg - Strasbourg and Basel.

km	♣		Ⓐ		Ⓐ		Ⓐ	Ⓒ	Ⓐ	Ⓒ		Ⓐ	Ⓐ	Ⓒ		Ⓐ		Ⓐ		Ⓐ	Ⓐ		Ⓐ				
0	Offenburg d.	0632	0704	0734	0804	0834	0904	1004	1034	1206	1234	1304	1334	1403	1434	1504	1604	1634	1704	1734	1805	1834	1904	2004	2104	...	2325
21	Kehl 🏛 d.	0652	0722	0752	0822	0853	0922	1022	1052	1224	1252	1322	1356	1422	1452	1522	1622	1652	1722	1757	1822	1852	1922	2022	2122	...	2348
29	Strasbourg a.	0705	0734	0804	0834	0906	0935	1034	1104	1237	1305	1334	1407	1434	1505	1534	1634	1704	1734	1809	1834	1904	1934	2034	2134	...	2400v

♣				Ⓐ	Ⓒ	Ⓐ	Ⓐ	Ⓐ						Ⓐ		Ⓐ		Ⓐ		Ⓒ	Ⓐ	Ⓐ	Ⓐ			
Strasbourg d.	0005n	...	0622	0722	0749	0750	0822	0852	0922	1052	...	1252	1322	1422	1452	1522	1622	1652	1722	1750	1751	1822	1852	1922	2022	2152
Kehl 🏛 d.	0016	...	0634	0734	0804	0804	0834	0904	0934	1104	...	1304	1334	1434	1504	1534	1634	1704	1737	1804	1804	1834	1904	1934	2034	2204
Offenburg a.	0033	...	0652	0752	0822	0822	0852	0922	0952	1122	...	1322	1352	1452	1522	1552	1652	1722	1755	1822	1822	1852	1922	1952	2052	2222

	†		Ⓐ	Ⓐ	Ⓐ		①–⑥	Ⓐ	⚒																Ⓐ	
Offenburg d.	0049	...	0428	...	0525	...	0549	0634	0707	...	0807	0907	1007	1107	1204	1307	1404	1507	1607	1707	1807	1907	2007	2034	...	2243
Freiburg (Brsg) Hbf a.	0131	...	0528	...	0625	...	0649	0729	0756	...	0855	0955	1056	1156	1250	1355	1450	1555	1656	1755	1856	1955	2055	2133	...	2341
Freiburg (Brsg) Hbf d.	0132	...	0529	0609	0628	0628	0711	0734	0815	0815	0915	1015	1115	1215	1315	1415	1515	1615	1715	1815	1915	2015	...	2135	2235	2343
Basel Bad Bf a.	0220	...	0625	0703	0733	0733	0806	0813	0911	0911	1011	1111	1211	1311	1412	1511	1611	1711	1812	1911	2011	2111	...	2240	2340	0046

		Ⓐ	⚒	Ⓐ												Ⓐ		Ⓐ		Ⓒ						⑥w
Basel Bad Bf d.	0519	0549	...	0625	0634	0748	0848	0948	1048	1148	1248	1348	1448	1548	1648	1726	1748	1826	1848	1848	...	1948	...	2126	2258	2348
Freiburg (Brsg) Hbf a.	0615	0646	...	0718	0736	0847	0944	1044	1144	1244	1344	1444	1544	1644	1744	1823	1844	1923	1944	1944	...	2044	...	2219	0003	0050
Freiburg (Brsg) Hbf d.	0626	0656	0656	0720	0803	0903	1003	1103	1203	1307	1403	1507	1603	1703	1803	1825	1907	1925	...	2003	2026	...	2125	2225	0018	...
Offenburg a.	0719	0744	0744	0814	0851	0953	1053	1153	1253	1353	1450	1553	1650	1751	1850	1921	1953	2021	...	2050	2122	...	2221	2318	0113	...

See Table **910** for other Köln - Frankfurt ICE services via the high-speed line

912 BASEL - KARLSRUHE - MANNHEIM - FRANKFURT - KOBLENZ (- KÖLN)

km		ICE 826	ICE 826	IC 2120	ICE 774	IC 2310	ICE 874	ICE 616	IC 2278	ICE 670	ICE 604	ICE 694	IC 1114	IC 2028	IC 1114	ICE 678	ICE 676	ICE 772	IC 1118	IC 1112	EC 361	ICE 872	ICE 614	ICE 1656	IC 2116
		①			①–⑥	◐		◧	①–⑤	①–⑥			①–⑥		①–⑥	⑥	①–⑤		①–④	⑤				①–⑥	
		🍷♦	🍷♦	✕♦	✕	L✕	✕	🍷		✕	🍷	✕	t ⊡	🍷♦	E ⊡	S✕	✕	✕	¶	🍷	🍷♦	✕	🍷	✕♦	✕♦
	Basel SBB d.	...	...	...	...	...	...	...	...	...	...	...	...	...	...	...	...	...	...	...	...	0608	...	...	...
	Basel Bad. Bf ★ d.	...	...	...	...	...	0412g	...	...	...	0516e	...	...	...	...	0545	0545	...	...	...	...	0616	...	...	...
	Freiburg (Brsg) Hbf ★ d.	...	...	...	...	...	0447g	...	...	...	0552e	...	...	...	...	0623	0623	...	...	...	...	0652	...	...	...
	Strasbourg ★ d.	...	...	...	...	...	|	...	...	...	|	...	...	...	...	|	|	...	...	...	0653	|	...	...	...
	Offenburg ★ **916** d.	...	...	...	...	...	0520g	...	...	...	0626e	...	...	...	...	0657	0657	...	...	...	|	0725	...	...	...
	Baden-Baden **916** d.	...	...	...	...	...	0536g	...	...	...	0642e	...	...	...	...	0714	0714	...	...	...	0732	0742	...	...	...
	Karlsruhe Hbf **911 911a 916** d.	...	...	...	...	...	0558	...	0615	0651	0700	...	...	...	...	0732	0736	...	...	...	0752	0800	...	...	...
	München Hbf **930** d.	0032	...	...	...	...	|	0317	|	|	|	...	...	...	...	...	|	...	...	...	...	|	0523	...	...
	Stuttgart Hbf **930** d.	0305	0305	...	0509	...	|	0551	|	|	|	0651	0630	...	0630	...	|	0727	0714	0714	...	|	0751	...	0737
	Heidelberg Hbf **911 911a** d.	0428	0428	...	0547	...	|	|	0654	|	|	|	0720	...	0720	...	|	|	0755	0755	...	|	|	...	0825
	Mannheim Hbf **911a** a.	0438	0438c	...	0559	...	0622	0626p	0709	0714	0723	0728p	0731	...	0731	...	0800	0804	0806	0806	...	0822	0826p	...	0837
0	**Mannheim** Hbf **911a** d.	0440	0440c	...	0605	...	0631	0635	0711	0716	0735	0731	0733	...	0738	...	...	0806	0808	0808	...	0831	0835	...	0839
	Frankfurt (Main) Hbf d.	|	|	0542	|	0638	|	|	|	|	|	|	|	0742	|	...	...	|	|	|	...	|	|	0842	|
72	**Frankfurt** Flughafen Fernbf ✈ a.	0512	0512	0554	0638	0655	|	0706	|	|	0806	|	|	0754	|	...	...	0838	|	|	...	|	0906	0855	|
	Frankfurt Flughafen Fernbf ✈ d.	|	|	0557	0642	0657	|	0709	|	|	0809	|	|	0757	|	...	...	0842	|	|	...	|	0909	0858	|
	Frankfurt (Main) Hbf ◇ a.	0535	0535	|	0652	|	0708	|	0752	0752	|	0808	|	|	|	...	...	0853	|	|	...	0908	|	|	|
	Mainz Hbf **911a** a.	|	|	0616	|	0715	|	|	...	|	|	|	0815	0818	0831	...	...	|	0846t	0846t	...	|	|	0916	0918z
	Mainz Hbf **914** d.	|	|	0618	|	0717	|	|	...	|	|	|	...	0820	...	...	...	|	0848t	0848t	...	|	|	0922	0920z
	Wiesbaden Hbf a.	|	|	|	|	|	|	|	...	|	|	|	...	|	...	...	...	|	|	|	...	|	|	0933	|
	Bingen (Rhein) Hbf **914** d.	|	|	0635	|	|	|	|	...	|	|	|	...	|	...	...	...	|	0906t	|	...	|	|	...	|
	Koblenz Hbf **914** a.	|	|	0710	|	0810	|	|	...	|	|	|	...	0910	...	...	...	|	0941z	0941z	...	|	|	...	1010
	Köln Hbf **800 910** a.	0714d	0714d	0805	|	0905	|	0805	...	|	0905	|	...	1005	...	...	...	|	1042	1042	...	|	1005	...	1105
	Dortmund Hbf **800** a.	...	0827j	0920	|	1021	|	0921	...	|	...	|	...	1120	...	...	...	|	...	1208	...	|	1121	...	1221
	Hamburg Hbf **800 900** ⊠ a.	...	...	1212	1034	1312	|	...	...	1134	...	|	...	1412	...	...	...	1234	...	|	...	|	...	...	1511
	Berlin Hbf **810** ▲ a.	...	...	...	...	...	1125	...	...	...	...	1221	...	...	...	...	...	...	...	1551	...	1325	...	...	...

	ICE 1126	ICE 1026	ICE 78	ICE 602	ICE 692	ICE 770	ICE 278	ICE 612	ICE 1654	IC 2114	IC 2024	TGV 9571	ICE 76	ICE 690	IC 2101	ICE 600	IC 1920	IC 1920	IC 1916	ICE 578	ICE 276	ICE 610	ICE 1652	IC 2112	IC 2006
	①⑦	②–⑥							t			Ⓡ					⑦E	⑦T	⑤				t		⑥
	✕♦	✕♦	Z✕	🍷	✕	✕	B✕	🍷	✕♦	✕	✕♦	P🍷	✕♦	✕	N🍷	🍷			A🍷	✕	B✕	🍷	D✕	✕	🍷♦
Basel SBB d.	...	...	0704	0712	...	...	0812	...	...	...	...	...	0904	...	0912	...	...	...	...	...	1012	...	...	...	...
Basel Bad. Bf ★ d.	...	...	0713	0721	...	...	0822	...	...	...	...	...	0913	...	0922	...	...	...	...	...	1022	...	...	...	...
Freiburg (Brsg) Hbf ★ d.	...	...	0749	0756	...	...	0857	...	...	...	...	...	0949	...	0957	...	...	...	...	...	1057	...	...	...	...
Strasbourg ★ d.	...	...	|	|	...	...	|	...	...	...	...	0945	|	...	|	...	...	...	...	...	|	...	...	...	...
Offenburg ★ **916** d.	...	...	|	0828	...	...	0930	...	...	...	...	|	|	...	1030	...	...	...	...	...	1130	...	...	...	1139
Baden-Baden **916** d.	...	...	0833	0844	...	...	|	...	...	...	...	|	1033	...	|	...	...	...	...	...	|	...	...	...	1202
Karlsruhe Hbf **911 911a 916** d.	...	...	0851	0907	...	...	1000	...	...	...	...	1025	1051	...	1103	1107	...	...	...	...	1200	...	...	...	1221
München Hbf **930** d.	0614g	...	|	|	0628	...	|	0723	...	...	...	...	|	0824	...	|	...	...	0841	...	|	0923	...	...	|
Stuttgart Hbf **930** d.	|	...	|	|	0851	0927	|	0951	...	0937	...	...	|	1051	...	|	...	...	1114	1127	|	1151	...	1137	|
Heidelberg Hbf **911 911a** d.	|	...	|	|	|	|	|	|	...	1025	...	...	|	|	...	|	...	...	1155	|	|	|	...	1225	|
Mannheim Hbf **911a** a.	|	...	0914	0933	0928p	1004	1022	1026p	...	1037	...	...	1114	1128	...	1133	...	...	1206	1204	1222	1226p	...	1237	1250
Mannheim Hbf **911a** d.	|	...	0916	0935	0931	1006	1031	1035	...	1039	...	...	1116	1131	...	1135	...	...	1208	1206	1231	1235	...	1239	1252q
Frankfurt (Main) Hbf d.	0942	0942	|	|	|	|	|	|	1042	|	1144	...	|	|	...	|	1201	1215	|	|	|	|	1242	|	|
Frankfurt Flughafen Fernbf ✈ a.	0954	0954	|	1006	|	1038	|	1106	1055	|	1155	...	|	|	...	1206	1213	1226	|	1238	|	1306	1255	|	|
Frankfurt Flughafen Fernbf ✈ d.	0957	0957	|	1009	|	1042	|	1109	1058	|	1157	...	|	|	...	1209	1215	1228	|	1242	|	1309	1258	|	|
Frankfurt (Main) Hbf ◇ a.	|	|	0952	|	1008	1053	1108	|	|	|	|	...	1153	1208	...	|	|	|	|	1253	1308	|	|	|	|
Mainz Hbf **911a** a.	1017	1017	|	|	|	|	|	|	1116	1118z	1217	...	|	|	...	|	|	1246	1246t	|	|	|	1316	1318z	1340t
Mainz Hbf **914** d.	1020	1020	|	|	|	|	|	|	1122	1120z	1220	...	|	|	...	|	|	1248	1248t	|	|	|	1322	1320z	1342t
Wiesbaden Hbf a.	|	|	|	|	|	|	|	|	1133	|	|	...	|	|	...	|	|	|	|	|	|	|	1333	|	|
Bingen (Rhein) Hbf **914** d.	|	|	|	|	|	|	|	|	...	|	|	...	|	|	...	|	1306	1306	1306z	|	|	|	...	|	|
Koblenz Hbf **914** a.	1110	1110	|	|	|	|	|	|	...	1210	1310	...	|	|	...	|	1341	1341	1341z	|	|	|	...	1410	1441
Köln Hbf **800 910** a.	1205	1205	|	1105	|	|	|	1205	...	1305	1405	...	|	|	...	1305	1442	1442	1443	|	|	1405	...	1505	1542
Dortmund Hbf **800** a.	1320	1320	|	...	|	|	|	1321	...	1421	1520	...	|	|	...	1420h	1605	1605	1605	|	|	1521	...	1621	1703
Hamburg Hbf **800 900** ⊠ a.	1612	1612	1334	...	|	1434	|	...	...	1712	1812	...	1534	|	...	...	|	|	|	1634	|	...	...	1912	...
Berlin Hbf **810** ▲ a.	...	...	...	...	1419	...	1525	...	...	...	...	...	...	1621	...	...	1951	1951	1955	...	1725	...	...	...	...

	IC 2004	IC 2014	IC 2026	ICE 74	ICE 508	ICE 598	ICE 576	IC 2012	ICE 374	ICE 518	ICE 1650	EC 100	IC 2022	TGV 9573	ICE 72	ICE 596	IC 2103	ICE 506	ICE 712	ICE 712	ICE 574	ICE 974	IC 118	ICE 370	ICE 516
	⑦	①–⑤				‡								Ⓡ					①–⑤	①–⑤	⑥	⑧			
	🍷♦	🍷♦		✕♦	🍷	✕	✕	🍷♦	B✕	🍷	D✕	✕♦	🍷	P🍷	Z✕	✕	N🍷	🍷	t🍷	Y🍷	✕	K✕	🍷♦	B✕	🍷
Basel SBB d.	...	...	...	1104	1112	...	...	...	1212	...	...	1218	...	...	1304	...	1312	...	...	...	...	...	...	1412	...
Basel Bad. Bf ★ d.	...	...	...	1113	1122	...	...	...	1222	...	...	1227	...	...	1313	...	1322	...	...	...	...	...	...	1422	...
Freiburg (Brsg) Hbf ★ d.	...	...	...	1149	1157	...	...	...	1257	...	...	1304	...	...	1349	...	1357	...	...	...	...	...	...	1457	...
Strasbourg ★ d.	...	...	...	|	|	...	...	...	|	...	...	|	...	1345	|	...	|	...	...	...	...	...	...	|	...
Offenburg ★ **916** d.	1139	...	...	|	1230	...	...	...	1330	...	...	|	...	|	|	...	1430	...	...	...	...	...	...	1530	...
Baden-Baden **916** d.	1202	...	...	1233	|	...	...	...	|	...	...	1352	...	|	1433	...	|	...	...	...	...	...	...	|	...
Karlsruhe Hbf **911 911a 916** d.	1221	...	...	1251	1307	...	...	...	1400	...	...	1412	...	1425	1451	...	1503	1507	...	...	...	...	...	1600	...
München Hbf **930** d.	|	...	...	|	|	1023	...	...	|	1123	...	|	...	...	|	1223	...	|	...	...	...	...	...	|	1323
Stuttgart Hbf **930** d.	|	1209	...	|	|	1251	1327	1314	|	1351	...	|	...	...	|	1451	...	|	1434	1434	1527	1527	1512	|	1551
Heidelberg Hbf **911 911a** d.	|	|	...	|	|	|	|	1355	|	|	...	|	...	...	|	|	...	|	1520	1520	|	|	1555	|	|
Mannheim Hbf **911a** a.	1250	1250q	...	1314	1333	1328p	1404	1406	1422	1426p	...	1437	...	...	1514	1528	...	1532	1531	1531	1604	1604	1606	1622	1626p
Mannheim Hbf **911a** d.	1252q	1252q	...	1316	1335	1331	1406	1408	1431	1435	...	1439	...	...	1516	1531	...	1535	1533	1538	1606	1606	1608	1631	1635
Frankfurt (Main) Hbf d.	|	|	1344	|	|	|	|	|	|	|	1442	|	1542	...	|	|	...	|	|	|	|	|	|	|	|
Frankfurt Flughafen Fernbf ✈ a.	|	|	1355	|	1406	|	1438	|	|	1506	1455	|	1554	...	|	|	...	1606	|	|	1638	1638	|	|	1706
Frankfurt Flughafen Fernbf ✈ d.	|	|	1357	|	1409	|	1442	|	|	1509	1458	|	1557	...	|	|	...	1609	|	|	1642	1642	|	|	1709
Frankfurt (Main) Hbf ◇ a.	|	|	|	1353	|	1408	1453	|	1508	|	|	|	|	...	1553	1608	...	|	|	|	1653	1653	|	1708	|
Mainz Hbf **911a** a.	1340t	1340t	1417	|	|	|	|	1446z	|	|	1516	1518z	1617	...	|	|	...	|	1621	|	|	|	1646	|	|
Mainz Hbf **914** d.	1342t	1342t	1420	|	|	|	|	1448z	|	|	1522	1520z	1620	...	|	|	...	|	1623	|	|	|	1648	|	|
Wiesbaden Hbf a.	|	|	|	|	|	|	|	|	|	|	1533	|	|	...	|	|	...	|	1634	1632	|	|	|	|	|
Bingen (Rhein) Hbf **914** d.	|	|	|	|	|	|	|	1506	|	|	...	|	|	...	|	|	...	|	|	|	|	|	1706	|	|
Koblenz Hbf **914** a.	1441	1441	1510	|	|	|	|	1541	|	|	...	1610	1710	...	|	|	...	|	|	|	|	|	1741	|	|
Köln Hbf **800 910** a.	1542	1542	1605	|	1505	|	|	1642	|	1605	...	1705	1805	...	|	|	...	1705	1801	1801	|	|	1842	|	1805
Dortmund Hbf **800** a.	...	...	1720	|	1620h	|	|	1805	|	1721	...	1821	1921	...	|	|	...	1820	...	...	|	|	...	|	1920
Hamburg Hbf **800 900** ⊠ a.	...	...	2012	1734	...	|	1834	...	|	...	...	2112	2212	...	1934	|	...	...	...	...	2035	2037	...	|	...
Berlin Hbf **810** ▲ a.	...	...	...	...	...	1819	...	...	1925	...	...	...	...	...	...	2019	...	...	...	...	...	...	...	2128	...

♦ – **NOTES** (LISTED BY TRAIN NUMBER)

6 – [12] and ✕ Chur - Zürich - Basel - Dortmund (- Hamburg ⑧).
74/6 – [12] and ✕ Zürich - Basel - Hamburg - Kiel.
100 – [12] and ✕ Chur - Zürich - Dortmund - Hamburg (- Kiel ⑦). Train number **102** on ⑦.
104 – [12] and 🍷 Basel - Köln - Amsterdam; [12] (*ICE* **504**) Basel - Köln.
114 – WÖRTHERSEE – [12] and ✕ Klagenfurt - Villach - Salzburg - Dortmund.
118 – [12] and 🍷 Innsbruck - Bregenz - Lindau - Ulm - Münster. On ①–⑤ until Aug. 21 does not call at Mainz or Bingen and arrives Koblenz 1744. On ⑥⑦ until Aug. 23 Mannheim a. 1608, d. 1610, Mainz a. 1650, d. 1652, Bingen d. 1709.
361 – [12] and 🍷 Strasbourg - Stuttgart - München.
376 – [12] and ✕ Interlaken - Bern - Frankfurt (- Hamburg ⑤⑦).
459 – CANOPUS – 🛏 1, 2 cl., ▬ 2 cl., [2] (reclining) and 🍷 Zürich - Leipzig - Dresden - Praha.
469 – ORIENT EXPRESS – 🛏 1, 2 cl., ▬ 2 cl., [2] and 🍷 Strasbourg - Salzburg - Wien.
472 – AURORA – 🛏 1, 2 cl. and ▬ 2 cl. Basel - København. Conveys 🛏 1, 2 cl. and ▬ 2 cl. (*D* **50472**) Basel - Warszawa, also 🛏 1, 2 cl. (*D* **50472**) Basel - Moskva.
478 – Daily until Nov. 1; ④–⑦ from Nov. 5. KOMET – 🛏 1, 2 cl., ▬ 2 cl., [2] (reclining) and ✕ Zürich - Hannover - Hamburg.
826 – [12] (München ① -) Stuttgart - Duisburg (- Essen from July 18) (- Dortmund ⑥⑦ **j**).
1026 – [12] and ✕ Regensburg - Nürnberg - Frankfurt - Köln - Kiel.
1126 – [12] and ✕ (München - Nürnberg ① -) Frankfurt - Köln - Kiel.
1259 – SIRIUS – 🛏 1, 2 cl., ▬ 2 cl., [2] (reclining) and ✕ Zürich - Halle - Berlin (Zürich - Halle - Berlin - Ostseebad Binz on ⑤ July 3 - Aug. 21).
1654 – [12] and ✕ (Berlin ①–⑥ -) Leipzig - Erfurt - Frankfurt - Wiesbaden.
1656 – [12] and ✕ Leipzig - Erfurt - Frankfurt - Wiesbaden.
2004 – BODENSEE – [12] and 🍷 Konstanz - Karlsruhe - Münster - Emden.
2006 – BODENSEE – [12] and 🍷 Konstanz - Karlsruhe - Dortmund.
2012 – ALLGÄU – [12] and 🍷 Oberstdorf - Ulm - Stuttgart - Köln - Dortmund - Hannover (- Magdeburg ⑤⑦) (- Leipzig ⑦).
2014 – [12] and 🍷 Stuttgart - Münster - Emden.
2024 – [12] and ✕ Passau - Regensburg - Nürnberg - Frankfurt - Hamburg.
2028 – [12] and 🍷 Nürnberg - Frankfurt - Köln - Hamburg.
2116 – [12] and ✕ Stuttgart - Köln - Hamburg - Stralsund (- Greifswald ①–⑤).
2120 – [12] and ✕ Frankfurt - Köln - Hamburg (- Puttgarden until Oct. 25). Train number **2320** from Oct. 26.
2318 – [12] Stuttgart - Köln (- Dortmund ⑧) (- Münster ⑦).
9575 – [12] and 🍷 Paris - Strasbourg - Stuttgart - München.
40478 – Daily until Nov. 1; ④–⑦ from Nov. 5. PEGASUS – 🛏 1, 2 cl., ▬ 2 cl., [2] (reclining) and 🍷 Zürich - Amsterdam.

NOTES CONTINUED ON NEXT PAGE →

BASEL - KARLSRUHE - MANNHEIM - FRANKFURT - KOBLENZ (- KÖLN) 912

	ICE	EC	EC	ICE	ICE	ICE	ICE	IC	ICE	ICE	ICE	ICE	ICE	IC	TGV	ICE	ICE	ICE	IC	ICE	ICE	ICE	IC	ICE	ICE
	1558	6	114	70	104	1090	594	2316	26	572	1556	870	514	2318	9575	376	24	592	2105	502	1002	570	1910	1554	272
	t					⑧	⑥	⑧												⑧	⑥	⑦	⑦		①–⑥
	D✖	✖◆	✖◆	✖	🍷◆	✖	✖		Q✖	✖	D✖	✖	🍷	◆	Ⓡ◆	✖◆	Q✖	✖	❖🍷	H🍷	H🍷	✖		D✖	Z✖
Basel SBB d.	...	1418	...	1504	1512	...	...	...	...	...	...	1612	...	...	...	1704	...	...	1712	...	...	...	...	...	1812
Basel Bad. Bf 🏛 ★ d.	...	1427	...	1513	1522	...	...	...	...	...	...	1621	...	...	...	1713	...	...	1721	...	...	...	...	...	1822
Freiburg (Brsg) Hbf ★ d.	...	1504	...	1549	1557	...	...	...	...	...	...	1656	...	...	...	1749	...	...	1756	...	...	...	...	...	1857
Strasbourg ★ d.	...	|	...	|	|	...	...	...	...	...	...	|	...	...	1745	|	...	...	|	...	...	...	...	...	|
Offenburg ★ **916** d.	...	|	...	|	1630	...	...	...	...	...	...	1728	...	...	|	|	...	...	1828	...	...	...	...	...	1930
Baden-Baden **916** d.	...	1552	...	1633	|	...	...	...	...	...	...	1744	...	...	|	1833	...	...	1845	...	...	...	...	...	|
Karlsruhe Hbf **911 911a 916** d.	...	1612	...	1651	1707	...	...	...	...	...	...	1801	...	...	1825	1851	...	...	1902	1908	1908	...	...	...	2000
München Hbf **930** d.	...	|	1340	|	|	1423	1423	...	...	...	...	|	1523	...	...	|	...	1623	...	|	|	...	1612	...	|
Stuttgart Hbf **930** d.	...	|	1610**n**	|	|	1651	1651	1636	...	1727	...	|	1751	1741	...	|	...	1851	...	|	|	1927	1914	...	|
Heidelberg Hbf **911 911a** d.	...	|	|	|	|	|	|	1720	...	|	...	|	|	1825	...	|	...	|	...	|	|	|	1955	...	|
Mannheim Hbf **911a** a.	...	1637	1656**y**	1714	1733	1728**p**	1728**p**	1736	...	1804	...	1823	1826**p**	1837	...	1914	...	1928	...	1933	1933	2004	2006	...	2022
Mannheim Hbf **911a** d.	...	1639	1658**y**	1716	1735	1731	1731	1738	...	1806	...	1831	1835	1839	...	1916	...	1931	...	1935	1935	2006	2008	...	2031
Frankfurt (Main) Hbf d.	1642	|	|	|	|	|	|	|	1742	|	1842	|	|	|	...	|	1942	|	...	|	|	|	|	2042	|
Frankfurt Flughafen Fernbf ✈ a.	1655	|	|	|	1806	|	|	|	1754	1838	1855	|	1906	|	...	|	1954	|	...	2006	2006	2038	|	2055	|
Frankfurt Flughafen Fernbf ✈ d.	1658	|	|	|	1809	|	|	|	1757	1842	1858	|	1909	|	...	|	1957	|	...	2009	2009	2042	|	2058	|
Frankfurt (Main) Hbf ◇ a.	|	|	|	1753	|	1808	1808	|	|	1853	|	1908	|	|	...	1953	|	2008	...	|	|	2053	|	|	2108
Mainz Hbf **911a** a.	1716	1718**z**	1740**y**	|	|	|	|	1815**t**	1818	|	1916	|	|	1918**z**	...	|	2017	|	...	|	|	|	2046**z**	2116	|
Mainz Hbf **914** d.	1722	1720**z**	1742**y**	|	|	|	|	1822**t**	1820	|	1922	|	|	1920**z**	...	|	2020	|	...	|	|	|	2048**z**	2122	|
Wiesbaden Hbf a.	1733	|	|	|	|	|	|	1836	|	|	1933	|	|	|	...	|	|	|	...	|	|	|	|	2133	|
Bingen (Rhein) Hbf **914** d.	...	|	1806	|	|	|	|	...	|	|	...	|	|	|	...	|	|	|	...	|	|	|	|	...	|
Koblenz Hbf **914** a.	...	1810	1841	|	|	|	|	...	1910	|	...	|	|	2010	...	|	2110	|	...	|	|	|	2141	...	|
Köln Hbf **800 910** a.	...	1905	1942	|	1905	|	|	...	2005	|	...	|	2005	2105	...	|	2205	|	...	2105	2105	|	2242	...	|
Dortmund Hbf **800** a.	...	2021	2102	|	...	|	|	...	2120	|	...	|	2121	2221**b**	...	|	2320	|	...	2220	2221	|	2400	...	|
Hamburg Hbf **800 900** ⊠ a.	...	2314**b**	...	2137	...	|	|	...	...	2240	...	|	0020	...	...	2345**f**	...	|	...	...	...	0037	...	...	0134
Berlin Hbf **810** ▲ a.	...	...	...	...	...	2148*	2226	...	...	...	...	2325	...	...	...	...	...	0027	...	...	...	...	...	...	...

	ICE	ICE	IC	CNL	TGV	ICE	ICE	IC	ICE	IC	EN	ICE	ICE	ICE	IC	IC	ICE	ICE	ICE	ICE	CNL	CNL	CNL	CNL	ICE
	372	512	2110	472	9577	500	590	1196	22	1196	469	270	1110	510	2020	60459	990	990	887	1087	459	1259	478	40478	608
	⑦		⑧	Ⓡ	⑧		♠	⑦T		⑦E	Ⓡ		⑦	①–⑥				⑦	①–⑥	⑦	Ⓡ	Ⓡ	Ⓡ	Ⓡ	
	Z✖	M🍷	✖	🍷◆	ⓇP	🍷	✖		Q✖		🍷◆	Z✖	🍷	⊕	⊙	2	✖	✖	G	G	🍷◆	✖◆	✖◆	🍷◆	K🍷
Basel SBB d.	1812	...	...	1804	...	1912	...	...	...	...	...	2012	...	...	...	2107	...	...	...	...	2107	2107	2207	2207	2326
Basel Bad. Bf 🏛 ★ d.	1822	...	...	1817	...	1921	...	...	...	...	...	2022	...	...	...	2121	...	...	...	...	2121**u**	2121**u**	2219**u**	2219**u**	2334
Freiburg (Brsg) Hbf ★ d.	1857	...	...	1904**u**	...	1956	...	...	...	...	...	2057	...	...	...	2158	...	...	...	...	2158**u**	2158**u**	2257**u**	2257**u**	0014
Strasbourg ★ d.	|	...	...	|	1946	|	...	...	...	...	2037	|	...	...	...	|	...	...	...	...	|	|	|	|	|
Offenburg ★ **916** d.	1930	...	...	1937**u**	|	2028	...	...	...	...	|	2130	...	...	...	2230	...	...	...	...	2230**u**	2230**u**	2331**u**	2331**u**	0049
Baden-Baden **916** d.	|	...	...	|	|	2044	...	...	...	...	2118	|	...	...	...	|	...	...	...	...	|	|	|	|	0106
Karlsruhe Hbf **911 911a 916** d.	2000	...	...	2018**u**	2027	2101	...	...	...	...	2141	2200	...	...	...	2305	...	...	...	...	2305**u**	2305**u**	0011**u**	0011**u**	0129
München Hbf **930** d.	|	1723	...	|	...	|	1823	...	...	...	...	|	1923	1923	...	|	2040	2040	...	...	|	|	|	|	|
Stuttgart Hbf **930** d.	|	1951	1937	|	...	|	2051	2035	...	2035	...	|	2151	2151	...	|	2305	2305	...	...	|	|	|	|	|
Heidelberg Hbf **911 911a** d.	|	|	2025	|	...	|	|	2120	...	2120	...	|	|	|	...	2334	|	|	...	...	2334**u**	2334**u**	|	|	0210
Mannheim Hbf **911a** a.	2022	2026**p**	2037	|	...	2124	2128**p**	2133	...	2133	...	2222	2228**p**	2228**p**	...	2346	2342	2342	...	...	|	|	|	|	0222**x**
Mannheim Hbf **911a** d.	2031	2035	2039	2116**u**	...	2135	2131	2135	...	2138	...	2235	2231	2231	...	...	2351	2351	...	...	2359**u**	2359**u**	|	|	0224**x**
Frankfurt (Main) Hbf d.	|	|	|	|	...	|	|	|	2146	|	...	|	|	|	2314	...	|	|	0003	0022	...	|	|	|	0315
Frankfurt Flughafen Fernbf ✈ a.	|	2106	|	|	...	2206	|	|	2157	|	...	|	2302	2303	2326	...	0023	0023	0015	0038	...	|	|	|	0330**r**
Frankfurt Flughafen Fernbf ✈ d.	|	2109	|	|	...	2209	|	|	2159	|	...	|	2304	2313	2328	...	0029	0029	0027	0042	...	|	|	|	0346**r**
Frankfurt (Main) Hbf ◇ a.	2108	|	|	|	...	|	2208	|	|	|	...	2315	|	2325	|	...	0042	0042	|	|	...	|	|	|	|
Mainz Hbf **911a** a.	|	|	2118**z**	|	...	|	...	2215	2218	2231	...	...	|	...	2345	...	...	|	0044	0059	...	|	|	|	0406
Mainz Hbf **914** d.	|	|	2120**z**	|	...	|	...	2222	2220	2233	...	...	|	...	2347	...	...	|	0046	0101	...	|	|	|	0408
Wiesbaden Hbf a.	|	|	|	|	...	|	...	2233	|	2248	...	...	|	...	|	...	...	|	0057	0112	...	|	|	|	|
Bingen (Rhein) Hbf **914** d.	|	|	|	|	...	|	...	...	|	...	...	...	|	...	0006	...	...	|	...	...	...	|	|	|	0425¦
Koblenz Hbf **914** a.	|	|	2210	|	...	|	...	...	2310	...	...	...	|	...	0045	...	...	|	...	...	...	|	|	0445	0501
Köln Hbf **800 910** a.	|	2205	2305	|	...	2312	...	...	0005	...	...	...	0005	...	0148	...	...	|	...	...	...	|	|	0545	0605
Dortmund Hbf **800** a.	|	2321	...	|	...	0030	...	...	0122	...	...	...	...	...	0329	...	...	|	...	...	...	|	|	...	0721
Hamburg Hbf **800 900** ⊠ a.	|	...	...	0356	...	...	...	...	...	...	...	...	...	...	0651**k**	...	...	0543	...	...	...	|	0906**v**	...	1012
Berlin Hbf **810** ▲ a.	0125	...	...	...	...	...	...	...	...	...	...	...	...	...	...	...	...	...	...	...	...	0718	...	...	...

NOTES (CONTINUED FROM PREVIOUS PAGE)

- **A** – From Salzburg (Table **890**).
- **B** – From Interlaken via Bern (Table **560**).
- **D** – [12] and ✖ Dresden - Leipzig - Wiesbaden.
- **E** – Until Aug. 23.
- **G** – From Hamburg (Table **900**).
- **H** – To Hannover (Table **810**).
- **K** – To Kiel (Table **820**).
- **L** – To Westerland (Table **821**).
- **M** – To Münster (Table **800**).
- **N** – [12] and 🍷 Basel - Stuttgart - Nürnberg.
- **P** – [12] and 🍷 Paris - Strasbourg - Stuttgart.
- **Q** – [12] and ✖ Wien - Passau - Regensburg - Nürnberg - Dortmund.
- **S** – To Stuttgart (Table **930**).
- **T** – From Aug. 30.
- **Y** – Until Aug. 21.
- **Z** – From Zürich (Table **510**).

- **b** – ⑧ only.
- **c** – Not July 19, Aug. 2, 9.
- **d** – Köln **Messe/Deutz**.
- **e** – ①–⑥ only.
- **f** – ⑤⑦ only.
- **g** – ① only.
- **h** – ⑥ only.
- **j** – ⑥⑦ from July 18.
- **k** – 0756 on June 14, 21. 0743 on July 5, 12, 19.
- **n** – 1613 on © (also June 11).
- **q** – 6 minutes later from Aug. 24.
- **p** – Connects with train in previous column.
- **r** – Frankfurt Flughafen Regionalbahnhof.
- **t** – From Aug. 24.
- **u** – Stops to pick up only.
- **v** – 0845 on ⑦ (also Oct. 3).
- **x** – Not July 19, 20, Aug. 2, 3, 9, 10.
- **y** – On ⑥⑦ until Aug. 23 Mannheim d. 1701, Mainz a. 1744, d. 1746. On ①–⑤ July 13 - Aug. 21 Mannheim a. 1658, d. 1701 and does not call at Mainz.
- **z** – 3–8 minutes later until Aug. 23.

- ¦ – Not June 14, 21.
- ¶ – Train number **1918** on ③. Conveys 🍷 on ①. To Düsseldorf (Table **800**).
- ◧ – On June 21, July 5 starts from Augsburg Hbf (d. 0357).
- ‡ – Train number **998** on ⑦.
- ⊡ – Train number **2218** on ⑥.
- ⊕ – Train number **1010** on ⑤⑥. Conveys ✖ on ①–④, 🍷 on ⑤⑥.
- ♠ – Train number **698** on ⑤. Train number **992** on ⑦. To Kassel / Hannover on dates in Table **900**.
- ❖ – To Stuttgart, Nürnberg and Passau on dates in Tables **931**, **925** and **920**.
- ◐ – Also calls at Boppard Hbf (d. 0758).
- ⊙ – Also calls at Boppard Hbf (d. 0032).
- * – Ⓡ and supplement payable for journeys to Berlin.
- ◇ – See also Tables **911** (trains from Karlsruhe via Heidelberg and Darmstadt), **911a** (local services) and **919** (trains from Saarbrücken via Mannheim).
- ★ – See panel on page 423 for other local trains.
- ▲ – Berlin timings are subject to alteration June 20 - July 3. See Table **810**.
- ⊠ – Hannover - Hamburg timings are subject to alteration June 14 - July 19 (Hamburg arrivals may be up to 25 minutes later).

RE / RB services KÖLN - GEROLSTEIN - TRIER 913

km																										
		Ⓐ	⚒				†	⚒									©				⑤⑥	†	⚒	Ⓐ	
0	**Köln** Hbf d.	...	...	...	0611	0721	0811	0821	0921	1021	1121	1221	1321	1421	1521	1621	1721	1721	...	1821	1921	1921	2011	2027	2027	2211
40	Euskirchen d.	...	...	...	0659	0759	0859	0859	0959	1059	1159	1259	1359	1459	1559	1659	1759	1759	...	1859	1959	1959	2059	2110	2110	2259
55	Mechernich d.	...	...	...	0710	0810	0910	0909	1010	1109	1210	1309	1410	1509	1610	1709	1810	1810	...	1909	2010	2010	2110	2121	2121	2310
64	Kall d.	...	...	...	0720	0818	0920	0917	1018	1117	1218	1317	1418	1517	1618	1717	1818	1818	...	1917	2018	2018	2120	2131	2131	2320
80	Blankenheim d.	...	...	...	0736	0834	0936	0933	1034	1133	1234	1333	1434	1533	1634	1733	1834	1834	...	1933	2034	2034	2136	2147	2147	2336
93	Jünkerath d.	...	...	0654**e**	0750	0848	0950	0947	1048	1147	1248	1347	1448	1547	1648	1747	1848	1848	...	1947	2048	2048	2150	2201	2201	2350
112	**Gerolstein** a.	...	...	0711**e**	0807	0903	1007	1006	1103	1206	1303	1406	1503	1606	1703	1806	1903	1903	...	2006	2103	2103	2207	2223	2223	0007
112	**Gerolstein** d.	0449	0600	0712	0817	0904	1017	1017	1104	1217	1304	1417	1504	1617	1704	1817	...	1904	1912	2017	...	2104	2233**k**	...	2233	...
142	Bitburg-Erdorf d.	0522	0633	0745	0859	0933	1059	1059	1132	1259	1332	1459	1532	1659	1734	1859	...	1932	1945	2059	...	2134	2307**k**	...	2307	...
181	**Trier** Hbf a.	0607	0719	0839	0940	1009	1140	1140	1209	1340	1409	1540	1609	1740	1809	1940	...	2009	2039	2140	...	2210	2349**k**	...	2349	...

	⚒	⑥k	Ⓐ	⚒	⑥k	⚒	†	⚒		g									⑧m	⑥k		†	⚒		◧	⑤⑥
Trier Hbf d.	...	...	...	...	0528	...	0528	0556	0759	0816	0959	1016	1159	1216	1329**j**	1416	1559	1616	1759	1759	1816	1959	2028	2028	2216	2328
Bitburg-Erdorf d.	...	...	...	...	0606	...	0606	0657	0834	0859	1033	1058	1234	1258	1433	1458	1634	1658	1833	1833	1858	2034	2118	2118	2308	0013
Gerolstein a.	...	...	...	...	0643	...	0643	0732	0859	0932	1059	1132	1259	1332	1459	1532	1659	1732	1859	1859	1932	2059	2159	2159	2342	0048
Gerolstein d.	0445	0545	0555	0618	0644	0644	0644	0737**b**	0900	0945	1100	1145	1300	1345	1500	1545	1700	1745	1900	1900	1945	2100	2202	...	...	...
Jünkerath d.	0502	0602	0612	0635	0709	0709	0709	0810	0915	1010	1115	1210	1315	1410	1515	1610	1715	1810	1915	1915	2008	2115	2223	...	...	...
Blankenheim d.	0516	0616	0623	0649	0725	0725	0725	0824	0927	1024	1127	1224	1327	1424	1527	1624	1727	1824	1927	1927	2022	2127	2237	...	...	...
Kall d.	0533	0633	0639	0705	0742	0742	0742	0840	0942	1040	1142	1240	1342	1440	1542	1640	1742	1840	1942	1942	2039	2142	2254	...	...	...
Mechernich d.	0541	0641	0646	0714	0749	0749	0751	0847	0949	1047	1149	1247	1349	1447	1549	1647	1749	1847	1949	1949	2048	2149	2303	...	...	...
Euskirchen d.	0557	0659	0657	0729	0801	0801	0807	0901	1001	1101	1201	1300	1400	1501	1601	1701	1801	1901	2001	2007	2107	2207	2314	...	...	...
Köln Hbf a.	0639	0739	0739	0812	0839	0839	0851	0939	1039	1139	1239	1339	1439	1539	1639	1739	1839	1939	2039	2051	2151	2251	2354	...	...	...

- **b** – 0745 on ⑥.
- **e** – Ⓐ only.
- **g** – Change trains at Gerolstein on Ⓐ.
- **j** – 1359 on ©.
- **k** – Not Oct. 3.
- **m** – Also Oct. 3.
- ◧ – ①②③④⑦.

914 Local services KOBLENZ - WIESBADEN / MAINZ - FRANKFURT

RE / RB services

Koblenz - St Goarshausen - Wiesbaden - Frankfurt *(Rechte Rheinstrecke)*

km		Ⓐ	⚒	Ⓐ	Ⓐ		Ⓐ	Ⓒ						Ⓐ			Ⓐ			Ⓐ			Ⓐ			
0	**Koblenz** Hbf ...... 906 d.	...	...	0440	0510	0555	0652	0710	0755	0910	0955	1110	1155	1225	1310	1355	1410	1510	1555	1640	1710	1755	1810	1910	2010	2210
5	Niederlahnstein .. 906 d.	...	...	0446	0516	0601	0658	0716	0801	0916	1001	1116	1201	1231	1316	1401	1416	1516	1601	1646	1716	1801	1816	1916	2016	2216
11	Braubach .... d.	...	...	0453	0523	0608	0705	0723	0808	0923	1008	1123	1208	1238	1323	1408	1423	1523	1608	1653	1723	1808	1823	1923	2023	2223
23	Kamp-Bornhofen .... d.	...	...	0504	0534	0619	0716	0734	0819	0934	1019	1134	1219	1249	1334	1419	1434	1534	1619	1704	1734	1819	1834	1934	2034	2234
35	St Goarshausen .... d.	...	...	0514	0544	0630	0727	0744	0830	0944	1030	1144	1230	1259	1344	1430	1444	1544	1630	1714	1744	1830	1844	1944	2044	2244
46	Kaub .... d.	...	...	0523	0553	0640	0737	0753	0840	0953	1040	1153	1240	1308	1353	1440	1453	1553	1640	1723	1753	1840	1853	1953	2053	2253
52	Lorch (Rhein) .... d.	...	...	0529	0559	0645	0744	0759	0845	0959	1045	1159	1245	1314	1359	1445	1459	1559	1645	1729	1759	1845	1859	1959	2059	2259
64	Rüdesheim (Rhein) .... d.	0440	0510	0540	0610	0655	0755	0810	0855	1010	1055	1210	1255	1340	1410	1455	1510	1610	1655	1740	1810	1855	1910	2010	2110	2310
94	**Wiesbaden** Hbf .... a.	0514	0544	0614	0644	0724	0824	0844	0924	1044	1124	1244	1324	1414	1444	1524	1544	1644	1724	1814	1844	1924	1944	2044	2144	2344
94	**Wiesbaden** Hbf .... d.	0520	0550	0632	0700	0732	0832	0850	0932	1050	1132	1250	1332	1432	1450	1532	1550	1650	1732	1832	1850	1932	1950	2050	2150	2350
135	**Frankfurt** (Main) Hbf .. a.	0613*	0643*	0705	0735	0805	0905	0943*	1005	1143*	1205	1343*	1405	1505	1543*	1605	1643*	1743*	1805	1905	1943*	2005	2043*	2143*	2243*	0043*

	Ⓐ	⚒	⚒						Ⓐ	Ⓒ	Ⓐ				Ⓐ			Ⓐ	Ⓐ					†		
Frankfurt (Main) Hbf .. d.	...	...	0512*	0612*	0753	0812*	0953	1012*	1053	1153	1153	1212*	1353	1412*	1523	1553	1621e	1653	1723	1753	1823e	1953	2012*	2112*	2112*	2242*
Wiesbaden Hbf .... a.	...	...	0555	0655	0828	0855	1028	1055	1128	1228	1228	1255	1428	1455	1558	1628	1658e	1728	1758	1828	1858e	2028	2055	2155	2155	2325
Wiesbaden Hbf .... d.	...	0521e	0612	0712	0836	0912	1036	1112	1150	1236	1236	1312	1436	1512	1612	1636	1712	1742	1812	1836	1912	2036	2112	2212	2212	2342
Rüdesheim (Rhein) ...... d.	...	0554e	0644	0744	0902	0944	1102	1144	1224	1302	1302	1344	1502	1544	1644	1702	1744	1814	1844	1902	1944	2102	2144	2244	2244	0015
Lorch (Rhein) .... d.	...	0606e	0654	0754	0910	0954	1110	1154	1236	1310	1310	1354	1510	1554	1654	1710	1754	1824	1854	1910	1954	2110	2154	2254	...	...
Kaub .... d.	0515	0615	0701	0801	0916	1001	1116	1201	1245	1316	1318	1401	1516	1601	1701	1716	1801	1831	1901	1916	2001	2116	2201	2301	...	...
St Goarshausen .... d.	0524	0624	0710	0810	0925	1010	1125	1210	1254	1325	1327	1410	1525	1610	1710	1725	1810	1840	1910	1925	2010	2125	2210	2310	...	...
Kamp-Bornhofen .... d.	0535	0635	0721	0821	0935	1021	1135	1221	1305	1335	1337	1421	1535	1621	1721	1735	1821	1851	1921	1935	2021	2135	2221	2321	...	...
Braubach .... d.	0546	0646	0732	0832	0946	1032	1146	1232	1316	1346	|	1432	1546	1632	1732	1746	1832	1902	1932	1946	2032	2146	2232	2332	...	...
Niederlahnstein .... 906 d.	0553	0653	0739	0839	0953	1039	1153	1239	1323	1353	1353	1439	1553	1639	1739	1753	1839	1910	1939	1953	2039	2153	2239	2339	...	...
Koblenz Hbf .... 906 a.	0600	0701	0746	0846	1001	1046	1201	1246	1330	1401	1401	1446	1601	1646	1746	1801	1846	1918	1946	2001	2046	2201	2246	2346	...	...

Koblenz - Bingen - Mainz - Frankfurt *(Linke Rheinstrecke)* ⊠

km		Ⓐ◧	⚒◧	Ⓐ		Ⓐ			Ⓐ			Ⓐ			Ⓐ			Ⓐ			Ⓐ					
0	**Koblenz** Hbf .... d.	0450	0552	0607	0653	0707	0754	0853	0902	0954	1053	1102	1154	1253	1302	1354	1453	1502	1554	1653	1702	1754	1854	1954	2054	2154
19	Boppard Hbf .... d.	0505	0607	0621	0708	0721	0809	0908	0921	1009	1108	1121	1209	1308	1321	1409	1508	1521	1609	1708	1721	1809	1909	2009	2109	2209
24	Boppard-Bad Salzig .. d.	0509	0611	|	0712	|	0813	0912	|	1013	1112	|	1213	1312	|	1413	1512	|	1613	1712	|	1813	1913	2013	2113	2213
34	St Goar .... d.	0517	0619	|	0720	|	0821	0920	|	1021	1120	|	1221	1320	|	1421	1520	|	1621	1720	|	1821	1921	2021	2121	2221
41	Oberwesel .... d.	0523	0625	0635	0726	0735	0827	0926	0935	1027	1126	1135	1227	1326	1335	1427	1526	1535	1627	1726	1735	1827	1927	2027	2127	2227
47	Bacharach .... d.	0527	0629	|	0730	|	0831	0930	|	1031	1130	|	1231	1330	|	1431	1530	|	1631	1730	|	1831	1931	2031	2131	2231
61	Bingen (Rhein) Hbf ..... a.	0540	0642	0647	0743	0747	0844	0943	0947	1044	1143	1147	1244	1343	1347	1444	1543	1547	1644	1743	1747	1844	1943	2044	2144	2244
61	Bingen (Rhein) Hbf ..... d.	0548	0654	0648	0752	0748	0855	0955	0948	1055	1155	1148	1255	1352	1348	1455	1552	1548	1655	1752	1748	1855	1945	2056	2159	2250
62	Bingen (Rhein) Stadt .. d.	0551	0657	|	0755	|	0858	0958	|	1058	1158	|	1258	1355	|	1458	1555	|	1658	1755	|	1858	1947	2059	2202	2253
73	Ingelheim .... d.	0601	0707	0656	0805	0756	0908	1008	0956	1108	1208	1156	1308	1405	1356	1508	1605	1556	1708	1805	1756	1908	1957	2109	2213	2303
91	**Mainz** Hbf .... a.	0619	0725	0708	0822	0808	0926	1026	1008	1126	1226	1208	1326	1423	1408	1526	1623	1608	1726	1823	1808	1925	2017	2126	2231	2322
119	Frankfurt Flughafen ‡ a.	...	...	0735	...	0835	...	...	1035	...	...	1235	...	...	1435	...	...	1635	...	...	1835	...	...	...	...	...
130	**Frankfurt** (Main) Hbf .. a.	...	...	0751	...	0849	...	...	1049	...	...	1249	...	...	1449	...	...	1649	...	...	1849	...	...	...	...	...

	⚒		Ⓐ			Ⓐ			Ⓐ		▲	Ⓐ			Ⓐ		Ⓐ		Ⓐ	⊡	Ⓐ					⑤⑥¶
Frankfurt (Main) Hbf .. d.	...	...	0706	...	...	0908	...	...	1108	...	...	1308	...	...	1508	...	1608	...	1708	...	1808	...	...	...	...	...
Frankfurt Flughafen ‡ . d.	...	...	0719	...	...	0923	...	...	1123	...	...	1323	...	...	1523	...	1622	...	1723	...	1823	...	...	...	...	...
Mainz Hbf .... d.	0530e	0624	0751	0724	0830	0951	0935	1030	1151	1135	1230	1351	1330	1430	1551	1532	1650	1630	1751	1732z	1852k	1830	1933z	2030	2130	2350
Ingelheim .... d.	0549e	0644	0803	0743	0849	1003	0953	1049	1203	1153	1249	1403	1347	1449	1603	1550	|	1648	1803	1753z	1904	1848	1951z	2049	2148	0009
Bingen (Rhein) Stadt ...... d.	0559e	0657	|	0803	0907	|	1003	1100	|	1203	1302	|	1402	1507	|	1601	|	1659	|	1805z	|	1903	2003z	2107	2159	0019
Bingen (Rhein) Hbf .... a.	0602e	0700	0811	0806	0910	1011	1006	1104	1211	1206	1305	1411	1404	1510	1611	1604	1710	1702	1811	1807z	1912	1905	2006z	2109	2201	0021
Bingen (Rhein) Hbf .... d.	0607	0708	0811	0814	0914	1011	1015	1109	1211	1215	1309	1411	1415	1511	1611	1615	1711t	1716f	1811	1816	1913	1916	2011	2110	2208	0037
Bacharach .... d.	0619	0720	|	0827	0926	|	1027	1121	|	1227	1321	|	1427	1522	|	1627	|	1728f	|	1828	|	1928	2023	2122	2220	0048
Oberwesel .... d.	0624	0725	0823	0832	0931	1023	1032	1126	1223	1232	1326	1423	1432	1527	1623	1632	1722t	1733	1823	1833	1925	1933	2027	2127	2225	0053
St Goar .... d.	0630	0731	|	0838	0937	|	1038	1132	|	1238	1332	|	1438	1533	|	1638	|	1739	|	1839	|	1939	2033	2133	2231	0059
Boppard-Bad Salzig .... d.	0638	0739	|	0846	0945	|	1046	1140	|	1246	1340	|	1446	1541	|	1646	|	1747	|	1847	|	1947	2041	2141	2239	0107
Boppard Hbf .... d.	0642	0743	0838	0850	0949	1038	1050	1144	1238	1250	1344	1438	1450	1545	1638	1650	1738t	1751	1838	1851	1940	1951	2045	2145	2243	0111
Koblenz Hbf .... a.	0659	0800	0852	0907	1005	1052	1107	1201	1252	1307	1401	1452	1507	1601	1652	1707	1751t	1808	1852	1907	1954	2007	2101	2201	2300	0126

e – Ⓐ only.
f – On Ⓐ until Aug. 21 Bingen (Rhein) Hbf d. 1703, Bacharach d. 1715.
k – From Aug. 24.
t – 2–4 minutes later until Aug. 21.
z – Ⓒ only.

◧ – Runs daily Bingen (Rhein) Hbf - Mainz Hbf.
¶ – Runs daily Mainz Hbf - Bingen (Rhein) Hbf.
▲ – On ⑤⑦ Bingen Stadt d. 1259, Bingen Hbf a. 1302. On ⑥ until Aug. 21 Bingen Hbf d. 1303, Bacharach d. 1315.
⊡ – On ⑥⑦ until Aug. 23 Ingelheim d. 1749, Bingen Stadt d. 1759, Bingen Hbf a. 1802.

* – Underground platforms.
‡ – Frankfurt Flughafen Regionalbahnhof ✈.
⊠ – Stopping services Koblenz - Mainz and v.v. are operated by TransRegio Deutsche Regionalbahn GmbH. See Table **912** for long-distance *ICE / IC* services. See Table **917a** for other S-Bahn services Mainz - Frankfurt Flughafen ✈ - Frankfurt (Main) Hbf and v.v.

914a KÖLN - KOBLENZ - MAINZ

2009 service; KD (see shaded panel)

◐		A	A⛴	K	D	B	D	①E	A	G	L
750	**Köln** (Rheingarten) .... d.	A special service operates on "Rhein in Flammen" days Aug. 1, Sept. 12, 19						...	...	0930	0930
1600	**Bonn** .... d.							0730	...	1230	1230
1300	Bad Godesberg .... d.							0800	...	1300	1300
900	Königswinter Fähre ..... d.							0815	...	1330	1330
750	Bad Honnef (Rhein) .... d.	...	...	...	...	...	...	0835	...	1350	1350
400	Remagen .... d.	...	...	...	...	...	...	0910	...	1420	1420
750	Linz am Rhein .... d.	...	...	...	...	...	...	0930	...	1450	1450
1500	Bad Breisig .... d.	...	...	...	0800	...	...	1000	...	▬	1520
400	Bad Hönningen .... d.	...	...	...	0805	...	...	1005	...	...	1525
1200	Andernach .... d.	...	...	...	0850	...	...	1050	...	...	...
1500	Neuwied .... d.	...	...	...	0910	...	...	1110	...	...	...
2200	**Koblenz** ⊙ .... a.	...	...	...	1040	...	...	1300	...	G	...
2200	**Koblenz** ⊙ .... d.	...	0900	0945	1100	...	...	1305	1400	1810	...
600	Winningen (Mosel) ... a.	...	|	1055	|	...	...	1420	|	|	...
800	Cochem (Mosel) ...... a.	...	|	1500	|	...	...	...	|	|	...
750	Niederlahnstein .... d.	...	0930	▬	1130	...	...	...	1430	1835	...
150	Oberlahnstein .... d.	...	0940	...	1140	...	...	...	1440	1845	...
450	Braubach .... d.	...	1005	...	1205	...	...	...	1505	1910	...
400	**Boppard** .... d.	0900	1100	...	1300	...	1400	...	1600	2000	...
400	Kamp-Bornhofen .... d.	0910	1110	...	1310	...	1410	...	1610	...	...
300	Bad Salzig .... d.	0925	1125	...	1325	...	1425	...	1625	...	...
450	**St Goarshausen** ... ★ d.	1010	1210	...	1410	1410	1510	...	1710	...	...
250	**St Goar** .... ★ d.	1020	1220	...	1420	1420	1520	...	1720	...	...
450	Oberwesel .... d.	1050	1250	...	1450	1450	1550	...	1750	...	...
900	Kaub .... d.	1105	1305	...	1505	1505	1605	...	1805	...	...
600	Bacharach .... d.	1130	1330	...	1530	1530	1630	...	1830	...	...
900	Assmannshausen .... d.	1230	1430	...	1630	1630	1730	...	1930	...	...
400	**Bingen** (Rhein) .... d.	1300	1500	P	1700	1700	1800	...	2000	...	...
900	**Rüdesheim** (Rhein) .... d.	1315	1515	1530	1715	1715	1815	...	2015	...	...
1500	Wiesbaden-Biebrich .... d.	...	...	1730	1905	1905z	2005r	...	...	...	...
1600	**Mainz** .... a.	...	...	1800	1930	1930z	2030r	...	...	...	...

	A	D‡	①E	D	B	P	A	G	K	A⛴
Mainz .... d.	...	0845	...	0945r	0945z	1130	...	...	...	...
Wiesbaden-Biebrich . d.	...	0905	...	1005r	1005z	1150	...	...	...	...
Rüdesheim (Rhein) d.	0915	1015	...	1115	1115	1315	1415	1415	...	1615
Bingen (Rhein) .... d.	0930	1030	...	1130	1130	...	1430	1430	...	1630
Assmannshausen ..... d.	0945	1045	...	1145	1145	...	1445	1445	...	1645
Bacharach .... d.	1015	1115	...	1215	1215	...	1515	1515	...	1715
Kaub .... d.	1025	1125	...	1225	1225	...	1525	1525	...	1725
Oberwesel .... d.	1035	1135	...	1235	1235	...	1535	1535	...	1735
St Goar .... ★ d.	1055	1155	...	1255	1255	...	1555	1555	...	1755
St Goarshausen ★ d.	1105	1205	...	1305	1305	...	1605	1605	...	1805
Bad Salzig .... d.	1130	1230	...	1330	...	...	1630	1630	...	1830
Kamp-Bornhofen ...... d.	1140	1240	...	1340	...	...	1640	1640	...	1840
Boppard .... d.	1150	1250	...	1350	...	...	1650	1650	...	1850
Braubach .... d.	1220	1320	...	...	...	...	...	1720	...	1920
Oberlahnstein .... d.	1240	1340	...	...	...	...	...	1740	...	1940
Niederlahnstein .... d.	1250	1350	...	...	...	...	...	1750	...	1950
Cochem (Mosel) .... d.	|	|	...	...	...	...	...	|	1540	|
Winningen (Mosel) d.	|	|	1600	...	...	...	...	|	1845	|
Koblenz ⊙ .... a.	1310	1410	1700	...	...	...	...	1810	2000	2010
Koblenz ⊙ .... d.	▬	1430	1705	...	...	...	...	...	...	...
Neuwied .... d.	...	1520	1750	...	...	...	...	...	...	...
Andernach .... d.	...	1540	1805	...	...	...	...	...	...	...
Bad Hönningen .... d.	...	1615‡	1830	...	...	...	...	...	...	...
Bad Breisig .... d.	J	1620	1840	...	...					
Linz am Rhein .... d.	1450	1650	1905	...	...					
Remagen .... d.	1500	1700	1915	...	...					
Bad Honnef (Rhein) . d.	1525	1725	1940	...	...					
Königswinter Fähre .. d.	1540	1740	2000	...	...					
Bad Godesberg .... d.	1545	1745	2010	...	...					
Bonn .... d.	1615	1815	2030	...	...					
Köln (Rheingarten) .. a.	1800	2000	...	...	...					

Köln-Düsseldorfer Deutsche Rheinschiffahrt AG, Frankenwerft 35, D-50667 Köln.
✆ +49 (0) 221 20 88 319
Fax +49 (0) 221 20 88 345

A – Apr. 10 - Oct. 25.
B – Apr. 10–24 and Oct. 5–25.
D – Apr. 25 - Oct. 4.
E – ① May 25 - Sept. 28.
G – ①⑤⑥⑦ Apr. 10–20; daily Apr. 24 - Oct. 5; ①⑤⑥⑦ Oct. 9–25.
J – ①⑤⑥⑦ Apr. 10–20; ⑤⑥ Apr. 24 - Oct. 3; ①⑤⑥⑦ Oct. 5–25.

K – ①⑤⑥⑦ Apr. 25 - June 15; daily June 26 - Oct. 4.
L – ①②③④⑦ Apr. 26 - Oct. 4.
P – ①③⑥ May 4 - Oct. 17 (also Apr. 13, Oct. 21; not Aug. 8). Operated by Primus-Linie.
r – July and August only.
z – ①⑤⑥⑦ only.

⛴ – Operated by paddlesteamer *Goethe* Apr. 25 - Oct. 4.
⊙ – Koblenz (Konrad-Adenauer-Ufer).
‡ – Change ships at Bad Hönningen on ①②③④⑦.
◐ – Distance in metres from rail station to river landing stage.
★ – A passenger ferry links St Goar and St Goarshausen. Frequent trips 0600 (0800 on †) to 2100 (2300 May 1 - Sept. 30). Operator: Rheinschiffahrt Goar. ✆ +49 (0) 6771 26 20. Fax +49 (0) 6771 24 04.

RE / RB services except where shown — KOBLENZ - TRIER - LUXEMBOURG and SAARBRÜCKEN — 915

km		⑥ n	Ⓐ	Ⓐ	Ⓐ K	Ⓐ	N	K	Ⓐ	⚒	⚒			①–⑥	Ⓐ M	⚒				K	*IC* 338 ①–⑥ 🍷			K
	Norddeich Mole **812** d.	...	...	...	...	...	...	...	...	...	...	...	...	...	...	...	...	...	...	...	...	...	...	...	...
	Emden Hbf **812** d.	...	...	...	...	...	...	...	...	...	...	...	...	...	...	...	...	...	...	...	...	...	...	...	...
	Köln Hbf **800 802** d.	...	...	...	...	...	...	...	...	...	...	...	...	...	...	...	...	...	...	...	...	...	...	...	...
0	**Koblenz** Hbf d.	...	...	...	...	...	...	...	...	...	0559	...	...	0622j	...	0722	...	0731	0822	...	0924	...	0931	1022	1122
47	Cochem (Mosel) d.	...	...	...	...	...	...	...	0540	...	0635	...	...	0724	...	0758	...	0824	0858	...	0957	...	1024	1058	1158
59	Bullay d.	...	...	...	...	...	...	...	0554	...	0644	...	...	0735	...	0807	...	0835	0907	...	1007	...	1035	1107	1207
76	Wittlich Hbf d.	...	...	...	...	0515	...	...	0609	...	0657	...	...	0750	...	0820	...	0850	0920	...	1022	...	1050	1120	1220
112	**Trier** Hbf a.	...	...	...	...	0552	...	...	0647	...	0728	...	...	0830	...	0846	...	0930	0946	...	1049	...	1130	1146	1246
112	**Trier** Hbf ⊙ d.	0357	0413	0523	0529	...	0621	0636t	...	0701	0730	0730	0801r	...	0834	...	0901	...	0948	...	1055	1101	...	1148	1248
	Luxembourg ⊙ a.	|	|	|	|	...	|	|	...	|	|	|	|	...	|	...	|	...	|	...	1139	|	...	|	|
135	Saarburg d.	0422	0433	0541	0554	...	0641	0703t	...	0726	0748	0748	0826r	...	0852	...	0926	...	1006	...	...	1126	...	1206	1306
161	Merzig (Saar) d.	0449	0451	0559	0621	...	0700	0729	...	0751	0808	0808	0851	...	0910	...	0951	...	1023	1123	...	1151	...	1223	1326
173	Dillingen (Saar) d.	0500	0502	0609	0632	...	0709	0738	...	0802	0816	0816	0902	...	0918	...	1002	...	1031	1132	...	1202	...	1231	1336
177	Saarlouis Hbf d.	0504	0506	0613	0635	...	0713	0741	...	0805	0820	0820	0905	...	0922	...	1005	...	1035	1135	...	1205	...	1235	1340
190	Völklingen d.	0515	0517	0624	0645	...	0721	0750	...	0816	0831	0831	0916	...	0930	...	1016	...	1044	1144	...	1216	...	1244	1349
200	**Saarbrücken** Hbf a.	0529	0529	0634	0656	...	0731	0759	...	0827	0841	0841	0927	...	0939	...	1027	...	1054	1153	...	1227	...	1254	1358

		K	*IC* 336 🍷		Ⓒ	Ⓐ		*IC* 334 🍷	L			*IC* 332 Ⓑ 🍷	Ⓐ K				*IC* 330 🍷	Ⓐ K				*ICE* 856 B			⑤–⑦
Norddeich Mole **812** d.	...	...	...	...	...	...	...	0953x	...	...	...	1136y	...	...	...	...	1354p	...	...	...	...	...	...	...	...
Emden Hbf **812** d.	...	...	0834x	...	...	...	...	1033x	...	...	...	1233x	...	...	...	...	1433x	...	...	...	...	...	...	...	...
Köln Hbf **800 802** d.	...	...	1218	...	...	...	...	1418	...	...	...	1618	...	...	...	...	1818	...	...	...	...	2018	...	...	...
Koblenz Hbf d.	1222	...	1323	...	1331	1335	1422	1523	...	1531	1622	1723	...	...	1731	1822	1923	...	...	1931	2022	2123	...	2222	2318
Cochem (Mosel) d.	1258	...	1357	...	1424	1426	1458	1557	...	1624	1658	1757	...	...	1824	1858	1957	...	...	2024	2058	2158	...	2258	0009
Bullay d.	1307	...	1407	...	1435	1437	1507	1607	...	1635	1707	1807	...	...	1835	1907	2007	...	...	2035	2107	2208	...	2307	0022
Wittlich Hbf d.	1320	...	1422	...	1450	1452	1520	1622	...	1650	1720	1822	...	...	1850	1920	2022	...	...	2050	2120	2223	...	2320	0038
Trier Hbf a.	1346	...	1449	...	1530	1532	1546	1649	...	1730	1746	1849	...	...	1930	1946	2049	...	...	2130	2146	2251	...	2352	0116
Trier Hbf ⊙ d.	1348	...	1455	1501	...	...	1548	1655	1654	...	1748	1850	1854	1901	...	1948	2050	2055	2101	...	2148	...	2301	...	...
Luxembourg ⊙ a.	|	...	1539	|	...	...	|	1743v	|	...	|	1934	|	|	...	|	2134	|	|	...	|	...	|	...	...
Saarburg d.	1406	...	...	1526	...	...	1606	...	1712	...	1806	...	1912	1926	...	2006	...	2114	2126	...	2206	...	2326	...	...
Merzig (Saar) d.	1423	1523	...	1551	...	...	1623	...	1730	...	1823	...	1930	1951	...	2023	...	2131	2151	...	2223	...	2347	...	...
Dillingen (Saar) d.	1431	1532	...	1602	...	...	1631	...	1738	...	1832	...	1939	2002	...	2032	...	2138	2202	...	2232	...	2356	...	...
Saarlouis Hbf d.	1435	1535	...	1605	...	...	1635	...	1741	...	1835	...	1942	2005	...	2035	...	2142	2205	...	2235	...	0000	...	...
Völklingen d.	1444	1544	...	1616	...	...	1644	...	1749	...	1844	...	1950	2016	...	2044	...	2149	2216	...	2244	...	0008	...	...
Saarbrücken Hbf a.	1454	1553	...	1627	...	...	1654	...	1758	...	1854	...	1958	2027	...	2054	...	2200	2227	...	2254	...	0017	...	...

	Ⓐ		*ICE* 855 B	Ⓐ		Ⓐ	Ⓒ	Ⓐ	*IC* 331§ ①–⑥ 🍷		⚒			*IC* 333 🍷		K		K	*IC* 335 🍷			K		K	*IC* 337 🍷
Saarbrücken Hbf d.	...	...	...	0434	...	0522	0535	0550	...	...	0625	0703	0733	...	...	0817	0905	1001	...	...	1105	1201	1305	1401	...
Völklingen d.	...	...	...	0441	...	0532	0542	0557	...	...	0635	0710	0743	...	...	0825	0912	1008	...	...	1112	1209	1312	1408	...
Saarlouis Hbf d.	...	...	...	0450	...	0542	0551	0608	...	...	0646	0719	0753	...	...	0835	0921	1016	...	...	1121	1219	1321	1416	...
Dillingen (Saar) d.	...	...	...	0453	...	0545	0555	0612	...	...	0649	0722	0757	...	...	0838	0924	1019	...	...	1124	1223	1324	1419	...
Merzig (Saar) d.	...	...	...	0507	...	0556	0603	0621	...	...	0700	0731	0807	...	...	0846	0933	1027	...	...	1133	1233	1333	1427	...
Saarburg d.	...	...	...	0533	...	0621	0633	0642	...	...	0726	0750	0833	...	...	...	0952	1045	...	...	1152	1251	1352	1445	...
Luxembourg ⊙ d.	...	...	...	|	...	|	|	|	0620	...	|	|	|	0824	...	...	|	|	1024	...	|	|	|	|	1424
Trier Hbf ⊙ a.	...	...	...	0559	...	0648	0659	0702	0707	...	0757	0811	0859	0907	...	...	1011	1104	1107	...	1211	1311	1411	1504	1507
Trier Hbf d.	0355	...	0500	...	0613	...	...	...	0708	0721	...	0813	...	0908	0921	...	1013	...	1108	1121	1213	1313	1413	...	1508
Wittlich Hbf d.	0418	...	0525	...	0637	...	...	...	0733	0758	...	0837	...	0933	0958	...	1037	...	1133	1158	1237	1337	1437	...	1533
Bullay d.	0431	...	0540	...	0651	...	...	...	0748	0813	...	0851	...	0948	1013	...	1051	...	1148	1213	1251	1351	1451	...	1548
Cochem (Mosel) d.	0440	...	0551	...	0700	...	...	...	0758	0825	...	0900	...	0958	1025	...	1100	...	1158	1225	1300	1400	1500	...	1558
Koblenz Hbf a.	0520	...	0629	...	0738	...	...	...	0835	0920	...	0938	...	1035	1120	...	1138	...	1235	1320	1340	1438	1538	...	1635
Köln Hbf **800 802** a.	...	...	0742	...	...	...	...	...	0942	...	...	...	...	1142	...	...	...	...	1342	...	...	...	...	...	1742
Emden Hbf **812** a.	...	...	...	...	...	...	...	...	1325s	...	...	...	...	1525s	...	...	...	...	1725s	...	...	...	...	...	2125s
Norddeich Mole **812** a.	...	...	...	...	...	...	...	...	1404e	...	...	...	...	1604f	...	...	...	...	1804s	...	...	...	...	...	...

				Ⓐ K	*IC* 339 Ⓑ 🍷		Ⓒ K	Ⓐ M			K	Ⓑ q				K					⑤		⑥⑦		Ⓑ m
Saarbrücken Hbf d.	...	1505	1533	1601	...	...	1601	1623	1633	1705	1801	...	...	1905	1933	2003	...	2033	2115	...	...	2234	...	2319	2343
Völklingen d.	...	1512	1543	1608	...	...	1608	1632	1643	1712	1808	...	...	1912	1943	2010	...	2043	2123	...	...	2241	...	2329	2354
Saarlouis Hbf d.	...	1521	1553	1616	...	...	1617	1643	1653	1721	1816	...	...	1921	1953	2020	...	2053	2131	...	...	2251	...	2339	0006
Dillingen (Saar) d.	...	1524	1557	1619	...	...	1620	1647	1657	1724	1819	...	...	1924	1957	2024	...	2057	2135	...	...	2254	...	2343	0009
Merzig (Saar) d.	...	1533	1607	1627	...	...	1631	1657	1707	1733	1827	...	...	1933	2006	2033	...	2107	2144	...	...	2304	...	2352	0021
Saarburg d.	...	1552	1633	1645	...	...	...	1726	1733	1752	1846	...	...	1952	...	2054	...	2133	2205	...	...	2326	...	...	0041
Luxembourg ⊙ d.	...	|	|	|	1624	...	...	|	|	|	|	...	...	|	...	|	...	|	|	...	...	|	...	...	|
Trier Hbf ⊙ a.	...	1611	1659	1704	1707	...	...	1753	1759	1811	1906	...	...	2012	...	2116	...	2159	2227	...	...	2352	...	...	0101
Trier Hbf d.	1521	1613	...	...	1708	1721	...	...	...	1813	...	1913	1921	2013	...	...	2131	...	...	2242	2242	...	0001	...	...
Wittlich Hbf d.	1558	1637	...	...	1733	1758	...	...	...	1837	...	1937	1958	2037	...	...	2206	...	...	2319	2319	...	0038	...	...
Bullay d.	1613	1651	...	...	1748	1813	...	...	...	1851	...	1951	2013	2051	...	...	2218	...	...	2335	2335	...	0054	...	...
Cochem (Mosel) d.	1625	1700	...	...	1758	1825	...	...	...	1900	...	2000	2025	2100	...	...	2227	...	...	2347	2348	...	0107	...	...
Koblenz Hbf a.	1720	1738	...	...	1835	1920	...	...	...	1938	...	2038	2120	2138	...	...	2306	...	...	...	0042	...	...	...	...
Köln Hbf **800 802** a.	...	...	...	...	...	...	...	...	...	...	...	...	...	...	...	...	...	...	...	...	...	...	...	...	...
Emden Hbf **812** a.	...	...	...	...	...	...	...	...	...	...	...	...	...	...	...	...	...	...	...	...	...	...	...	...	...
Norddeich Mole **812** a.	...	...	...	...	...	...	...	...	...	...	...	...	...	...	...	...	...	...	...	...	...	...	...	...	...

Complete service Trier - Luxembourg and v.v.

km	🛃 at Igel	①–⑤ a	①–⑤ a	①–⑥ d	⑦ w	①–⑤ a				①–⑥ ‡				‡		‡	①–⑤ a		Ⓑ ‡	⑥		‡		①–⑤	
0	**Trier** Hbf d.	0534	0624	0641	0707z	0724	0752	0857	0952	1055	1152	1257	1352	1455	1552	1655	1726	1752	1850	1857	1952	2050	2152	2257	2357
51	**Luxembourg** a.	0633	0717	0745	0808	0817	0845	0941	1045	1139	1245	1345	1445	1539	1645	1743v	1814	1845	1934	1941	2041	2134	2241	2341	0041

🛃 at Wasserbillig	①–⑤ a	①–⑥ ‡	①–⑤		‡		‡				‡		Ⓑ ‡	⑥	①–⑤ a	⑥⑦ c	①–⑤ a	①–⑤ a	⑥⑦ c	①–⑤ a				①–⑤	
Luxembourg d.	0517	0620	0635	0717	0824	0917	1024	1117	1217	1317	1424	1517	1624	1624	1715	1717	1741	1815	1817	1841	1915	2017	2115	2152	2252
Trier Hbf a.	0606	0707	0734	0806	0907	1006	1107	1206	1306	1406	1507	1606	1707	1707	1804	1806	1832	1904	1904	1932	2006	2106	2206	2256	2356

B – [12] Trier - Hannover - Berlin and v.v.
K – To / from Kaiserslautern (Table **919**).
L – To Kaiserslautern on ⚒ (Table **919**).
M – To / from Mannheim (Table **919**).
N – To Mannheim on Ⓐ (Table **919**).

a – Not June 23.
c – Also June 23.
d – Not June 23, Aug. 15.
e – ①②③④⑥ from Oct. 26. Arrives 1445 Oct. 26 - Nov. 21.
f – 1618 on ⑦ Aug. 30 - Oct. 25; 1646 Oct. 26 - Nov. 22.
g – Sept. 5 - Oct. 4 Hagondange a. 2117, Metz a. 2129.
h – Sept. 5 - Oct. 4 Thionville d. 1806, Apach a. 1826.
j – 0631 on ⑥.
k – On ⑦ runs 3–7 minutes later Metz - Apach.
m – Also Aug. 15, Oct. 3.

n – Not Oct. 3.
p – 1309 Oct. 26 - Nov. 22.
q – Also Oct. 3.
r – ⚒ only.
s – 32–41 minutes later Oct. 26 - Nov. 22.
t – Ⓐ only.
v – 1739 on ⑥⑦ (also June 23).
w – Also June 23, Aug. 15.
x – 21–28 minutes earlier Oct. 26 - Nov. 22.
y – 1133 Oct. 26 - Nov. 22.
z – 0656 on June 23, Aug. 15.
* – By 🚌 Trier - Apach and v.v.
⊙ – See also panel below main table.
‡ – *IC* train (see main Table).
§ – Train **231** on ①②③④⑥ from Oct. 26.

BULLAY - TRABEN-TRARBACH — *13 km*

Journey time: 18–21 minutes.

From Bullay at 0704 ⚒, 0817, 0917 and hourly until 2117, then 2221.
From Traben-Trarbach at 0621 ⚒, 0745, 0845 and hourly until 2145.

TRIER - METZ — *Services on ⑥⑦ only*

Valid from July 5. No service on Aug. 15.

km		⑥⑦	⑥⑦		⑥⑦ k	⑥⑦
0	**Trier** Hbf d.	*0940**	*1940**	**Metz** d.	0745	1740
49	Apach d.	1046	2046	Hagondange d.	0757	1752
70	Thionville a.	1103	2102	Thionville d.	0807	1801**h**
82	Hagondange a.	1112	2112**g**	Apach a.	0825	1820**h**
100	**Metz** a.	1125	2125**g**	**Trier** Hbf a.	*0935**	*1935**

916 KARLSRUHE - OFFENBURG - KONSTANZ

IRE/RE services except where shown

km	See note ▲	⚒	Ⓐ	Ⓒ		Ⓐ	Ⓒ							IC 2005 ⑤⑥ N🍷				IC 2371 B🍷	IC 2364 ①–⑤ S		●		†	⚒ ●	⑤† ⊡
0	**Karlsruhe** Hbf ...... **912 943** d.	...	...	0501k	0604	*0638**	0704	0804	0904	1004	1104	1204	*1238**	1336	1404	1504	1604	1713	1733	1804	1904	2010	2116	2116	2227
23	Rastatt .... **943** d.	...	...	0515k	0616	0722	0719	0816	0916	1016	1116	1216	1323	|	1416	1516	1616	1728	1747	1816	1916	2023	2129	2129	2240
31	Baden-Baden .... **912** d.	...	...	0521k	0624	0729	0727	0824	0924	1024	1124	1224	1330	1356	1424	1524	1624	1735	1754	1824	1924	2030	2136	2136	2247
71	**Offenburg** .... **912 942** d.	...	0525	0554k	0658	0759	0759	0859	0959	1059	1159	1259	1359	1418	1459	1559	1659	1753	1818	1859	1959	2104	2207	2205	2323j
104	Hausach .... **942** d.	...	0550	0619k	0722	0818	0818	0921	1018	1121	1218	1321	1418	1439	1521	1618	1721	1813	...	1921	2018	2128	2231	2230	2348
114	Hornberg (Schwarzw) .... d.	...	0558	0627k	0730	0826	0826	0930	1026	1130	1226	1330	1426	1448	1530	1626	1730	1821	...	1930	2026	2136	2238	2237	2356
127	Triberg .... d.	...	0611	0640k	0744	0839	0839	0944	1039	1144	1239	1344	1439	1503	1544	1639	1744	1835	...	1944	2039	2149	2251	2250	0009
142	St Georgen (Schwarzw) .... d.	...	0627	0655k	0758	0854	0854	0958	1054	1158	1254	1358	1454	1520	1558	1654	1758	1850	...	1958	2054	2203	2305	2305	0023
157	Villingen (Schwarzw) ..... **938** d.	0553	0638	0705	0809	0904	0904	1009	1104	1209	1303	1409	1504	1531	1609	1703	1809	1901	...	2009	2104	2213	2314	2314	0032
171	Donaueschingen .... **938** d.	0603	0654j	0714	0818	0913	0913	1018	1113	1218	1313	1418	1513	1542	1618	1713	1818	1913	...	2018	2113	2222	2324	*2340*e	...
190	Immendingen .... **938** d.	0619	0706	0726	0829	|	|	1029	|	1229	|	1429	|	1554	1629	|	1829	|	...	2029	2124	2234	2336	*2353*e	...
206	Engen .... **940** d.	0633	0719	0738	0842	|	|	1042	|	1242	|	1442	|	|	1642	|	1842	|	...	2042	|	2247	2348	...	...
220	**Singen** .... **940** a.	0645	0733	0748	0850	0943	0943	1050	1143	1250	1343	1450	1543	1616	1650	1743	1850	1943	...	2050	2143	2300	2356	...	...
220	**Singen** .... **939** d.	0651	0735	0752	0853	0953	0953	1053	1153	1253	1353	1453	1553	1618	1653	1753	1853	1953	...	2053	2155b	2301	2357	...	...
230	Radolfzell .... **939** d.	0703	0746	0800	0900	1000	1000	1100	1200	1300	1400	1500	1600	1628	1700	1800	1900	2001	...	2100	2202b	2308	0004	...	...
250	**Konstanz** .... a.	0725	0810	0816	0916	1016	1016	1116	1216	1316	1416	1516	1616	1644	1716	1816	1916	2015	...	2116	2216b	2327	0020	...	...

See note ▲	IC 2365 ①–⑤ S🍴	⚒	⚒	Ⓐ	Ⓒ	●			IC 2006 ⑥ D🍷	IC 2004 ⑦ E🍷	IC 2370 A🍷								●		†			⑤	
Konstanz .... d.	...	...	0502e	0524	0551k	0638	0735	0838	0909	0909	0938	1038	1138	1238	1338	1438	1538	1638	1738	1838	1938	2038	2153	2153	2322
Radolfzell .... **939** d.	...	...	0516e	0545	0606k	0657	0758j	0855	0923	0923	0957j	1055	1158j	1255	1358j	1455	1558j	1655	1758j	1855	1958j	2055	2219	2219	2347
Singen .... **939** a.	...	...	0522e	0555	0612k	0704	0805	0902	0930	0930	1004	1102	1205	1302	1405	1502	1605	1702	1805	1902	2005	2102	2228	2228	2356
Singen .... **940** d.	...	...	0530	0558	0614	0706	0816	0905	0932	0932	1015	1105	1216	1305	1416	1505	1616	1705	1816	1905	2016	2105	2230	2230	0000
Engen .... **940** d.	...	...	0539	|	|	0716	|	0914	|	|	|	1114	|	1314	|	1514	|	1714	|	1914	|	2114	2244	2244	0013
Immendingen .... **938** d.	...	...	0552	0620	0634	0729	|	0928	0953	0953	|	1128	|	1328	|	1528	|	1728	|	1928	|	2127	2257	2257	▬
Donaueschingen .... **938** d.	...	*0503*e	0603	0630	0645	0741	0845	0939	1005	1005	1045	1139	1245	1339	1445	1539	1645	1739	1845	1939	2045	2140	2310	2310	...
Villingen (Schwarzw) ..... **938** d.	...	0535	0612	0641	0655	0751	0855	0949	1016	1016	1055	1149	1255	1349	1455	1549	1655	1749	1855	1949	2055	2150	2321	2322	...
St Georgen (Schwarzw) .... d.	...	0544	0620	0650	0703	0800	0903	0958	1026	1026	1104	1158	1303	1358	1503	1558	1703	1758	1903	1958	2103	2158	▬	2331	...
Triberg .... d.	...	0559	0635	0705	0718	0814	0918	1012	1042	1042	1120	1212	1318	1412	1518	1612	1718	1812	1918	2012	2118	2213	...	2345	*ICE*
Hornberg (Schwarzw) .... d.	...	0612	0648	0718	0731	0829	0928	1027	1057	1057	1134	1224	1328	1424	1528	1624	1728	1827	1928	2024	2131	2227	...	0000	**608**
Hausach .... **942** d.	...	0621	0657	0727	0739	0837	0939	1035	1105	1105	1143	1235	1339	1435	1539	1635	1739	1835	1939	2035	2139	2235	...	0008	🍷
Offenburg .... **912 942** a.	0558	0649	0718	0746	0758	0859	0958	1058	1125	1125	1202	1258	1358	1458	1558	1658	1758	1858	1958	2058	2158	2301	2323	0033	0049
Baden-Baden .... **912** a.	0615	0723	...	0822	0835	0935	1035	1135	1200	1200	1219	1335	1435	1535	1635	1735	1835	1935	2035	2135	2227	...	2346	...	0104
Rastatt .... **943** a.	0622	0730	...	0830	0841	0941	1041	1141	|	|	1227	1341	1441	1541	1641	1741	1841	1942	2041	2141	2233	...	2352	...	|
Karlsruhe Hbf .... **912 943** a.	0635	0744	...	0844	0854	0954	1054	1154	1219	1219	1245	1354	1454	1554	1654	1754	1854	1955	2054	2154	2248	...	0005	...	0127

A – SCHWARZWALD – (12) and 🍷 Konstanz - Frankfurt - Hamburg (- Stralsund ⑤⑦). Train number **2270** on ⑤⑦.
B – SCHWARZWALD – (12) and 🍷 Hamburg - Frankfurt - Konstanz.
D – BODENSEE – (12) and 🍷 Konstanz - Dortmund.
E – BODENSEE – (12) and 🍷 Konstanz - Köln - Münster - Emden.
N – BODENSEE – (12) and 🍷 Emden - Münster - Köln - Konstanz.
S – To/from Stuttgart (Table **931**).

b – Ⓑ (also Oct. 3). Connection available on ⑥ as follows: Singen d. 2212, Radolfzell d. 2222, Konstanz a. 2245.
e – Ⓐ only.
j – Arrives 7–10 minutes earlier.
k – ⑥ (not Oct. 3).

⊡ – ⑤† (runs daily Karlsruhe - Hausach).
* – Later departure possible by *ICE* train (see Table **912**).
● – Change trains at Offenburg on Ⓐ.
▲ – Services between Radolfzell and Konstanz are subject to alteration on June 20, 21.

917 FRANKFURT - MAINZ - IDAR OBERSTEIN - SAARBRÜCKEN

RB/RE services

km			Ⓐ	⚒	⚒												⑤			①–④				Ⓐ	
0	**Frankfurt** (Main) Hbf .... ‡ d.	...	...	...	...	...	...	0725	0825	...	1025	...	1225	...	1425	...	1531	1625	...	1734	1825	...	2025	2225	...
11	Frankfurt Flughafen ✈ § .... ‡ d.	...	...	...	...	...	...	0737	0838	...	1038	...	1238	...	1438	...	|	1638	...	|	1838	...	2038	2238	...
39	**Mainz** Hbf .... ‡ d.	...	...	0510e	b	0655	0730	|	0900	1000	1100	1155	1300	1355	1500v	1555	1606	1700	1755	1806	1900	1955	2100j	2300	2305
80	Bad Kreuznach .... d.	...	0501	0542e	0632e	0737	0812	0826	0926	1026	1126	1224	1326	1424	1526	1624	1643	1726	1824	1843	1926	2024	2126	2326	2344
102	Bad Sobernheim .... d.	...	0523	0603e	0654	0755	...	0844	0944	1044	1144	1244	1344	1444	1544	1644	1706	1744	1844	1906	1944	2044	2144	2344	0007
117	Kirn .... d.	...	0540	0619e	0712	0805	...	0854	0954	1054	1154	1254	1354	1454	1554	1654	1725	1754	1854	1925	1954	2054	2154	2354	0023
131	Idar-Oberstein .... d.	...	0558	0635	0729	0816	...	0905	1005	1105	1205	1305	1405	1505	1605	1705	1743	1805	1905	1943	2005	2105	2205	0005	0040
155	Türkismühle .... d.	0543	0628	0704	0759	0837	...	0926	1026	1126	1226	1326	1426	1526	1626	1726	...	1826	1926	...	2026	2126	2226	0026	...
170	St Wendel .... d.	0600	*0653*	0723	0818	0850	...	0938	1038	1138	1238	1338	1438	1538	1638	1738	...	1838	1938	...	2038	2138	2238	0038	...
179	Ottweiler (Saar) .... d.	0608	*0700*	0733	0826	0858	...	0945	1045	1145	1245	1345	1445	1545	1645	1745	...	1845	1945	...	2045	2145	2245	0045	...
184	Neunkirchen (Saar) .... d.	0615	*0707*	0740	0833	0905	...	0952	1052	1152	1252	1352	1452	1552	1652	1752	...	1852	1952	...	2052	2152	2252	0052	...
205	**Saarbrücken** Hbf .... a.	0642	*0725*	0800	0854	0924	...	1011	1111	1211	1311	1412	1511	1612	1711	1812	...	1911	2012	...	2111	2212	2311	0111	...

	Ⓐ	Ⓐ	⚒																		Ⓑ d	Ⓐ			
Saarbrücken Hbf .... d.	0348	...	0446	0546	0652	0750	0852	0950	1052	1150	1252	1350	1452	1550	1652	1750	1850	1935	...	2035	2105	...	2135	2235	2335
Neunkirchen (Saar) .... d.	0404	...	0504	0602	0708	0808	0908	1008	1108	1208	1308	1408	1508	1608	1708	1808	1908	2002	...	2108	2134	...	2214	2314	0004
Ottweiler (Saar) .... d.	0410	...	0510	0608	0713	0813	0913	1013	1113	1213	1313	1413	1513	1613	1713	1813	1913	2009	...	2115	2141	...	2221	2321	0011
St Wendel .... d.	0417	...	0517	0616	0721	0821	0921	1021	1121	1221	1321	1421	1521	1621	1721	1821	1921	2020	...	2125	2151	2202	2233	2331	0025
Türkismühle .... d.	0428	...	0528	0627	0732	0832	0932	1032	1132	1232	1332	1432	1532	1632	1732	1832	1932	2037	...	2141	...	2222	2253	2347	...
Idar-Oberstein .... d.	0449	...	0549	0649	0752	0852	0952	1052	1152	1252	1352	1452	1552	1652	1752	1852	1952	2103	...	...	...	2251	...	...	...
Kirn .... d.	0500	0505	0600	0700	0803	0903	1003	1103	1203	1303	1403	1503	1603	1703	1803	1903	2003	2117	...	...	...	...	...	...	...
Bad Sobernheim .... d.	0509	0523	0610	0710	0812	0912	1012	1112	1212	1312	1412	1512	1612	1712	1812	1912	2012	2131	...	...	...	...	...	...	...
Bad Kreuznach .... d.	0529	0602	0631	0731	0831	0933	1031	1133	1231	1333	1431	1533	1631	1733	1831	1933	2033	2153	2247	...	...	...	...	...	...
Mainz Hbf .... ‡ a.	0557	0639	0658	0756	0858	1004	1058	1204	1258	1404	1458	1604	1658	1804	1858	2004	2104	2220	2325	...	...	...	...	...	...
Frankfurt Flughafen ✈ § .... ‡ a.	0621	|	|	0821	0933t	...	1133t	...	1333t	...	1533h	...	1735	...	1933k	...	...	...	...	...	...	...	...	...	...
Frankfurt (Main) Hbf .... ‡ a.	0636	0724	0745	0836	0947t	...	1147t	...	1347t	...	1547h	...	1752f	...	1947k	...	...	...	...	...	...	...	...	...	...

b – From Bingen (Table **918**).
d – Also Aug. 15, Oct. 3.
e – Ⓐ only.
f – 1747 on ⑤–⑦.

h – On ⑤ (also June 14, 21, 28, July 5, 12, 19, 26, Aug. 2, 9, 16, 23) arrives Frankfurt Flughafen 1537, Frankfurt Hbf 1554.
j – Not June 14, 21, 28, July 5, 12, 19, 26, Aug. 2, 9, 16, 23.
k – On ⑤⑦ until Aug. 23 arrives Frankfurt Flughafen 1936, Frankfurt Hbf 1953.

t – 2–5 minutes later on †.
v – From Aug. 24.

‡ – See also Tables **912**, **914** and **917a**.
§ – Frankfurt Flughafen Regionalbahnhof ✈.

917a FRANKFURT - FRANKFURT FLUGHAFEN ✈ - MAINZ - WIESBADEN

S-Bahn 8/9

	⚒	†	⚒	⚒		⚒		⚒	†	⚒	⚒		†	⚒		†	⚒			†	⚒		†	⚒
Frankfurt (Main) Hbf ▽ d.	0417	0447	0447	0502	0517	0532	and at	1232	1247	1247	1302	1317	1331*	1332	1347	1401*	1402	1417	and at	2001*	2002	2017	2031*	2032
Frankfurt Flughafen ⊖ d.	0428	0458	0458	0513	0528	0543	the same	1243	1258	1258	1313	1328	1343	1343	1358	1412	1413	1428	the same	2012	2013	2028	2043	2043
Mainz Hbf .... d.	0456	|	0526	|	0556	|	minutes	|	|	1326	|	1356	|	|	1426	...	|	1456	minutes	...	|	2056	|	|
Mainz-Kastel .... d.	|	0524	|	0539	|	0609	past each	1309	1324	|	1339	|	1409	1409	|	...	1439	|	past each	...	2039	|	2109	2109
Wiesbaden Hbf .... a.	0507	0533	0537	0548	0607	0618	hour until	1318	1333	1339	1348	1407	1418	1418	1437	...	1448	1507	hour until	...	2048	2107	2118	2118

Frankfurt (Main) Hbf ▽ d.	2047	2117	2131*	2147	2217	2231*	2247	2317	2331*	0017
Frankfurt Flughafen ⊖ d.	2058	2128	2143	2158	2228	2243	2258	2328	2343	0028
Mainz Hbf .... d.	2126	2156	|	2226	2256	|	2326	2356	|	0056
Mainz-Kastel .... d.	|	|	2209	|	|	2309	|	|	0009	|
Wiesbaden Hbf .... a.	2139	2207	2218	2237	2307	2318	2337	0007	0018	0107

		⚒	†	⚒		⚒		⚒	†	⚒
Wiesbaden Hbf .... d.	0350	0420	0427	0442	0450	0512	and at	1120	1127	1142
Mainz-Kastel .... d.	|	|	0435	0450	|	0520	the same	|	1135	1150
Mainz Hbf .... d.	0402	0432	|	|	0502	|	minutes	1132	|	|
Frankfurt Flughafen ✈ .. ⊖ d.	0432	0502	0502	0517	0532	0547	past each	1202	1202	1217
Frankfurt (Main) Hbf .... a.	0444	0514	0514	0529	0544	0559	hour until	1214	1214	1229

		⚒				⚒			⚒														Ⓐ	Ⓒ	
Wiesbaden Hbf .... d.	1150	1212	1220	1242	1250	1312	...	and at	1912	...	1920	1942	1950	2020	2042	2050	2120	2142	2150	2220	2242	2250	2320	2327	2350
Mainz-Kastel .... d.	|	1220	|	1250	|	1320	...	the same	1920	...	|	1950	|	|	2050	|	|	2150	|	|	2250	|	|	2335	|
Mainz Hbf .... d.	1202	|	1232	|	1302	|	...	minutes	|	...	1932	|	2002	2032	|	2102	2132	|	2202	2232	|	2302	2332	|	0002
Frankfurt Flughafen ⊖ d.	1232	1247	1302	1317	1332	1347	1347	past each	1947	1947	2002	2017	2032	2102	2117	2132	2202	2217	2232	2302	2317	2332	0002	0002	0032
Frankfurt (Main) Hbf .. a.	1244	1259	1314	1329	1344	1359	1359	hour until	1959	1959	2014	2029	2044	2114	2129	2144	2214	2229	2244	2314	2329	2344	0014	0014	0044

▽ – From the underground platforms, except where shown by note *.
* – Departs from the main station (not underground platforms).

⊖ – Frankfurt Flughafen Regionalbahnhof ✈.

RB / S-Bahn services — RHEINLAND-PFALZ LOCAL SERVICES — 918

Pirmasens - Saarbrücken

km		Ⓐ	⚒	Ⓐ	⚒	†				
0	**Pirmasens** Hbf d.	0515	0552	0623	0732	0732	0832	and	1932	2032
7	Pirmasens Nord d.	0522	0602	0641	0743	0743	0843	hourly	1943	2043
31	Zweibrücken Hbf d.	0552	0640	0713	0813	0813	0913	until	2013	2113
67	**Saarbrücken** Hbf a.	0634	0721	0752	0851	0851	0951		2051	2151

	⚒	Ⓐ	⑥k			❖			
Saarbrücken Hbf d.	0602	0625	...	0704	0808	and	1908	2008	2108
Zweibrücken Hbf d.	0643	0713	...	0745	0845	hourly	1945	2045	2145
Pirmasens Nord a.	0715	0741	0747	0816	0916	until	2016	2116	2212
Pirmasens Hbf a.	0730e	0753	0755	0826	0926		2026	2126	2220

Pirmasens - Neustadt (Weinstr)

km		Ⓐ	⚒	Ⓐ																					
0	**Pirmasens** Hbf d.	0446	0544	0623	0701	0801	0901	1001	1101	1201	1301	1401	1501	1601	1701	1801	1901	2001	...	...	...	...	...	...	...
7	Pirmasens Nord d.	0457	0558	0639	0719	0819	0919	1019	1119	1219	1319	1419	1519	1619	1719	1819	1919	2019	...	...	...	...	...	...	...
55	**Landau** (Pfalz) Hbf a.	0550	0658	0737	0818	0918	1018	1118	1218	1318	1418	1518	1618	1718	1818	1918	2018	2118	...	...	...	...	...	...	...
73	**Neustadt** (Weinstr) Hbf a.	0618	0723	0758	0844	0944	1044	1144	1244	1344	1444	1544	1644	1744	1844	1944	2044	2156	...	...	...	...	...	...	...

	Ⓐ	Ⓐ	⚒	⑥k	Ⓐ	†	⑥k			†	⚒							Ⓒ	Ⓐ		Ⓒ	Ⓐ		
Neustadt (Weinstr) Hbf d.	0430	0554	0616	...	0659	0703	0717	...	0816	0916	0916	1016	1116	1216	1316	1416	1516	1616	1618	1716	1816	1818	1916	2016
Landau (Pfalz) Hbf d.	0533	0618	0635	0645	0711	0722	0737	0741	0841	0941	0941	1041	1141	1241	1341	1441	1541	1641	1641	1741	1841	1841	1941	2041
Pirmasens Nord a.	0636	0717	...	0740	...	...	...	0840	0940	1040	1040	1140	1240	1340	1440	1540	1640	1740	1740	1840	1940	1940	2040	2140
Pirmasens Hbf a.	0658	0730	...	0754	...	...	...	0858	0958	1058	1058	1158	1258	1358	1458	1558	1658	1758	1758	1858	1958	1958	2058	2158

Bingen - Kaiserslautern - Pirmasens

km		Ⓐ	⚒	⚒		Ⓐ																†		⚒	⑤⑥
0	**Bingen** (Rhein) Hbf d.	...	...	0548	...	0612	0646	...	0755	0855	0955	1055	1155	1255	1355	1455	1555	1655	1755	1855	1955	2102	...	2208	...
16	Bad Kreuznach d.	...	0509e	0609	...	0631	0710	...	0816	0916	1016	1116	1216	1316	1416	1516	1616	1716	1816	1916	2016	2130	...	2228	2247
43	Rockenhausen d.	...	0538e	0639	...	s	0740	...	0855	0955	1055	1155	1255	1355	1455	1555	1655	1755	1855	1955	2055	2159	...	...	2317
79	**Kaiserslautern** Hbf a.	...	0614e	0717	...	...	0819	...	0929	1026	1126	1226	1326	1426	1526	1626	1726	1826	1926	2026	2138	2237	...	...	2349
79	**Kaiserslautern** Hbf d.	0523	0630	...	0735	...	...	0835	0935	1035	1135	1235	1335	1435	1535	1635	1735	1835	1935	2035	...	...	2249	...	...
108	Pirmasens Nord a.	0555	0706	...	0806	...	...	0906	1006	1106	1206	1306	1406	1506	1606	1706	1806	1906	2006	2106	...	...	2320	...	...
115	**Pirmasens** Hbf a.	0609	0719	...	0818	...	...	0918	1018	1118	1218	1318	1418	1518	1618	1718	1818	1918	2018	2118	...	...	2330	...	...

	⚒	⚒	Ⓐ	⚒		⚒	†																⚒	†					⑤⑥
Pirmasens Hbf d.	...	...	0532	0614e	0641	0732	0741	...	0841	0941	1041	1141	1241	1341	1441	1541	1641	1741	...	...	1841	1941	2041	...	...
Pirmasens Nord d.	...	...	0540	0622e	0652	0750	0750	...	0850	0950	1050	1150	1250	1350	1450	1550	1650	1750	...	...	1850	1950	2050	...	...
Kaiserslautern Hbf a.	...	...	0615	0658e	0723	0826	0826	...	0926	1026	1126	1226	1326	1426	1526	1626	1726	1826	...	...	1926	2026	2126	...	...
Kaiserslautern Hbf d.	0522	0556	0640	0715	0737	...	...	0832	0932	1032	1132	1232	1332	1432	1532	1632	1732	...	1832	1836	1932	2032	...	2139	2306
Rockenhausen d.	0556	0636	0713	0750	0812	...	...	0901	1001	1101	1201	1301	1401	1501	1601	1701	1801	...	1901	1907	2001	2101	...	2209	2340
Bad Kreuznach d.	0642	0717	0743	0822	0842	...	...	0941	1041	1141	1241	1341	1441	1541	1641	1741	1841	...	1941	1941	2041	2133	...	2240	0011
Bingen (Rhein) Hbf a.	0701	0736	0802	...	0901	...	...	1000	1100	1200	1300	1400	1500	1600	1700	1800	1900	...	2000	2000	2100	2152	...	...	...

Neustadt (Weinstr) - Karlsruhe and Wissembourg

km		Ⓐ	Ⓐ	Ⓐ	Ⓐ	⚒	⚒	⚒	Ⓐ	Ⓒ							A	†B		A	†B			Ⓐ	Ⓒ
0	**Neustadt** (Weinstr) Hbf d.	0430	...	0511	...	0529	0616	...	0659	0703f	0736	0810	0836	0910	0936	1010	1036	1044	1110	1136	1145	1210	1236	1307	1310
18	Landau (Pfalz) Hbf d.	0448	...	0536	...	0554	0636	...	0712	0723	0758	0823	0858	0923	0958	1023	1058	1058	1123	1158	1159	1223	1258	1320	1323
31	Winden (Pfalz) d.	0502	0505	0551	0555	0601	0652	0658	0721	0731	0808	0831	0908	0931	1008	1031	1108	1108	1131	1208	1208	1231	1308	1331	1331
47	**Wissembourg** a.	|	0521	|	0615	|	|	0718	|	|	0828	|	0928	|	1028	|	1128	1128	|	1228	1228	|	1328	|	|
44	Wörth (Rhein) d.	0517	...	0605	...	0617	0708	...	0736	0744	...	0844	...	0944	...	1044	...	...	1144	...	...	1244	...	1344	1344
58	**Karlsruhe** Hbf a.	0530	...	...	...	0635	0726	...	0752	0754	...	0854	...	0954	...	1054	...	...	1154	...	...	1254	...	1354	1354

										⑥k
Neustadt (Weinstr) Hbf d.	1336	1410	and at	1910	1936	2010	2105	2138	2221	2321	2321
Landau (Pfalz) Hbf d.	1358	1423	the same	1923	1958	2023	2123	2158	2241	2341	2342
Winden (Pfalz) d.	1408	1431	minutes	1931	2008	2031	2131	2229	...	...	2357
Wissembourg a.	1428	|	past each	|	2029	|	|	|	...	...	|
Wörth (Rhein) d.	...	1444	hour until	1944	...	2044	2143	2243	...	...	0012
Karlsruhe Hbf a.	...	1454		1954	...	2054	2154	2256	...	...	...

	Ⓐ	Ⓐ	⚒	⚒	Ⓒ	Ⓐ	⑥k	Ⓐ
Karlsruhe Hbf d.	0431	...	0602	...	0707	0714	...	...
Wörth (Rhein) d.	0447	...	0618	...	0716	0735	...	...
Wissembourg d.	|	0527	|	0626e	|	|	0733	0733
Winden (Pfalz) d.	0502	0547	0630	0650	0727	0747	0753	0757
Landau (Pfalz) Hbf d.	0519	0609	0644	0702	0740	0757	0802	0806
Neustadt (Weinstr) Hbf a.	0542	0628	0705	0723	0758	0810	0824	0826

	Ⓐ	Ⓒ						Ⓐ	Ⓒ	†B	A		†B	A								⑥k		
Karlsruhe Hbf d.	0802	0806	...	0907	and at	1507	...	1603	1607	...	...	1705	...	...	1807	...	1907	...	2007	...	2106	...	2206	2315
Wörth (Rhein) d.	0817	0816	...	0917	the same	1517	...	1617	1617	...	...	1717	...	...	1817	...	1917	...	2017	...	2117	...	2217	2326
Wissembourg d.	|	|	0833	|	minutes	|	1533	|	|	1633	1633	|	1732	1732	|	1833	|	1932	|	2033	|	2203	|	|
Winden (Pfalz) d.	0829	0829	0853	0929	past each	1529	1553	1629	1629	1653	1653	1729	1753	1753	1829	1853	1929	1953	2029	2053	2128	2224	2228	2338
Landau (Pfalz) Hbf d.	0838	0839	0902	0938	hour until	1538	1602	1638	1638	1702	1702	1738	1802	1802	1838	1902c	1938	2002	2038	2102	2136	...	2236	2352
Neustadt (Weinstr) Hbf a.	0851	0852	0924	0951		1551	1624	1651	1651	1714	1724	1751	1816	1824	1851	1926	1951	2024	2051	2124	2156	...	2255	0011

Wörth and Karlsruhe - Speyer - Mannheim - Heidelberg

km	km			Ⓐ	Ⓐ	Ⓐ	⑥	Ⓐ	Ⓒ‡	Ⓐ	Ⓐ	Ⓒ		Ⓐ	Ⓒ	Ⓐ										Ⓐ
0		**Wörth** (Rhein) d.	...	...	0534	...	...	0622	...	...	0651	0718	...	0736	...	...	0818	...	0918	...	...	1018	...	1118	...	...
	0	**Karlsruhe** Hbf ⊠ d.	...	...	|	...	...	|	...	...	|	|	...	|	...	0808	|	...	|	...	1008	|	...	|	...	1208
27	38	Germersheim d.	0412e	0525	0605	0619	0622	0651	0703	0717	0725	0749	...	0810	0813	0838	0849	0913	0949	1013	1038	1049	1113	1149	1213	1238
41		Speyer Hbf d.	0426	0541	0621	0631	0635	0707	0716	0727	0738	0802	0802	0824	0826	0847	0902	0926	1002	1026	1047	1102	1126	1202	1226	1247
61		Ludwigshafen Hbf d.	0451	0607	0648	0651	0659	0732	0741	0748	0811	0820	0820	0847	0848	0903	0921	0948	1021	1048	1103	1121	1148	1221	1248	1303
64		**Mannheim** Hbf ⊡ a.	0456	0626	0658	m	0705	0747	0747	m	0817	0825	0825	0853	0853	m	0926	0953	1026	1053	m	1126	1153	1226	1253	m
81		**Heidelberg** Hbf ⊡ a.	0514	0646	0713	...	0723	0816	0816	...	...	0844	0844	0916	0916	...	0944	1016	1044	1116	...	1144	1216	1244	1316	...

					Ⓐ															Ⓐ					J		ⒸD
Wörth (Rhein) d.	1218	...	1318	...	...	1418	...	1518	...	...	1618	...	1718	...	...	1818	...	1918	...	2018	...	2119	2219	...	2330	...
Karlsruhe Hbf ⊠ d.	|	...	|	...	1408	|	...	|	...	1608	|	...	|	...	1808	|	...	|	2008	|	...	|	|	2225	|	...
Germersheim d.	1249	1313	1349	1413	1438	1449	1513	1549	1613	1638	1649	1713	1749	1813	1838	1849	1913	1949	2038	2049	2121	2202	2251	2322	2359	0020
Speyer Hbf d.	1302	1326	1402	1426	1447	1502	1526	1602	1626	1647	1702	1726	1802	1826	1847	1902	1926	2002	2047	2102	2137	2217	2303	2335	...	0033
Ludwigshafen Hbf d.	1321	1348	1421	1448	1503	1521	1548	1621	1648	1703	1721	1748	1821	1848	1903	1921	1948	2021	2103	2120	2200	2242	2328	2359	...	0102
Mannheim Hbf ⊡ a.	1326	1353	1426	1453	m	1526	1553	1626	1653	m	1726	1753	1826	1853	m	1926	1953	2026	m	2125	2205	2248	2333	0004	...	0108
Heidelberg Hbf ⊡ a.	1344	1416	1444	1516	...	1544	1616	1644	1716	...	1744	1816	1844	1916	...	1944	2016	2044	...	2153	...	2313	2353	0021	...	0134

	Ⓐ			Ⓐ	Ⓐ	Ⓒ	Ⓐ		①–⑥			Ⓐ										Ⓐ			Ⓒ	Ⓐ
Heidelberg Hbf ⊡ d.	0510	0534r	0603	...	...	0634	0644	...	0708	0744e	0814	...	0844	0914	0944	1014	...	1044	1114	1144	1214	...	1244	1314	1344	1347
Mannheim Hbf ⊡ d.	0530	0554	0622	m	0633	0656	0706	...	0730	0804	0831	m	0904	0931	1004	1031	m	1104	1131	1204	1231	m	1304	1331	1404	1404
Ludwigshafen Hbf d.	0536	0614	0627	0636	0638	0703	0714	...	0738	0810	0837	0858	0910	0937	1010	1037	1058	1110	1137	1210	1237	1258	1310	1337	1410	1410
Speyer Hbf d.	0558	0639	...	0655	0705	0726	0737	...	0804	0831	0856	0913	0931	0956	1031	1056	1113	1131	1156	1231	1256	1313	1331	1356	1431	1431
Germersheim a.	0612	0653	...	0709	0719	0740	0751	0812	0818	0844	0908	0921	0944	1008	1044	1108	1121	1144	1208	1244	1308	1321	1344	1408	1444	1444
Karlsruhe Hbf ⊠ a.	|	|	...	0754	|	...	...	|	...	...	|	0952	...	|	...	|	1152	...	|	...	|	1352	...	|	...	...
Wörth (Rhein) a.	0647	0724	...	...	0748	...	...	0840	...	...	0940	...	...	1040	...	1140	...	...	1240	...	1340	...	...	1440	...	...

		Ⓐ			Ⓒ	Ⓐ		Ⓒ	Ⓐ			Ⓐ	Ⓒ	Ⓐ							Ⓑh	Ⓒ	Ⓐ	¶	‡	H
Heidelberg Hbf ⊡ d.	1414	...	1444	1514	1544	1547	1614	...	...	1644	1714	...	1744	1747	1814	...	1844	1914	1944	2014	...	2105	2114	2144	2214	2314
Mannheim Hbf ⊡ d.	1431	m	1504	1531	1604	1604	1631	m	1644	1704	1731	m	1804	1804	1831	m	1904	1931	2004	2031	m	2136	2136	2214	2240	2336
Ludwigshafen Hbf d.	1437	1457	1510	1537	1610	1610	1637	1658	1700	1710	1737	1801	1810	1810	1837	1856	1910	1937	2010	2037	2057	2143	2143	2220	2246	2343
Speyer Hbf d.	1456	1513	1531	1556	1631	1631	1656	1713	1723	1733	1756	1818	1831	1831	1856	1915	1931	1956	2031	2056	2113	2205	2205	2243	2313	0008
Germersheim a.	1508	1521	1544	1608	1644	1644	1708	1721	1738	1745	1808	1830	1844	1844	1908	1923	1944	2008	2044	2108	2121	2218	2218	2256	2328	0021
Karlsruhe Hbf ⊠ a.	|	1552	...	|	...	...	|	1752	|	...	|	...	...	...	|	1952	...	|	...	|	2152	...	...	...	...	...
Wörth (Rhein) a.	1540	...	...	1640	...	...	1740	...	1814	...	1840	...	...	...	1940	...	...	2040	...	2140	...	...	...	...	...	...

A – ⚒ until Oct. 24; daily from Oct. 26.
B – † until Oct. 25.
D – Change trains at Schifferstadt (a. 0043, d. 0051).
H – On ①②③④⑦ (also Oct. 3) passengers travelling from Heidelberg to Speyer or Gemersheim should change trains at Schifferstadt (a. 2354, d. 2358).
J – Passengers travelling from Gemersheim or Speyer to Heidelberg should change trains at Schifferstadt (a. 2345, d. 2348).

c – 1907 on ⑥⑦.
e – Ⓐ only.
f – 0710 on ⑥ (not Oct. 3).
h – Also Oct. 3.
k – Not Oct. 3.
m – To/from Mainz (Table **911a**).
r – ⚒ only.

s – To Saarbrücken (Table **917**).
¶ – Change trains at Mannheim on Ⓐ.
‡ – Change trains at Mannheim on ⑥ (not Oct. 3).
⊡ – See also Tables **911a** and **923**.
❖ – Certain services depart Saarbrücken at 07 minutes past the hour.
⊠ – Additional connections available via Wörth (see Neustadt - Karlsruhe table above).

918a WIESBADEN - MAINZ - DARMSTADT - ASCHAFFENBURG

RB services

km																									
		⚒	Ⓐ	⚒		Ⓐ										Ⓐ		Ⓐ							
0	**Wiesbaden** Hbf ..... d.	...	...	0539	0639	0703	0739	0839	0939	1039	1139	1239	1339	1439	1539	1603	1639	1703	1739	1839	1939	2039	2139	2239	2339
10	**Mainz** Hbf ..... d.	...	...	0549	0649	|	0749	0849	0949	1049	1149	1249	1349	1449	1549	|	1649	|	1749	1849	1949	2049	2149	2249	2349
43	Darmstadt Hbf ..... a.	...	...	0623	0723	0743	0823	0923	1023	1123	1223	1323	1423	1523	1623	1643	1723	1751f	1823	1923	2023	2123	2223	2323	0023
43	Darmstadt Hbf ..... d.	0452	0549	0632	0732	0800	0832r	0932	1032r	1132	1232r	1332	1432r	1532	1632r	1700	1732	1800	1832e	1932	2032e	2132e	...	...	...
87	**Aschaffenburg** Hbf ..... a.	0535	0631	0713	0813	0841	0913r	1013	1113r	1213	1313r	1413	1513r	1613	1713r	1741	1813	1841	1913e	2013	2113e	2213e	...	...	...

	Ⓐ	Ⓐ	Ⓐ		Ⓐ		Ⓐ										Ⓐ		Ⓐ		Ⓐ				
Aschaffenburg Hbf ..... d.	...	...	0510	0542r	0606	0640r	0716	0746	0846r	0946	1046r	1146	1246r	1346	1446r	1546	1616	1646r	1716	1746	1816	1846e	1946	2046e	...
Darmstadt Hbf ..... a.	...	...	0552	0623r	0652	0727r	0759	0827	0927r	1027	1127r	1227	1327r	1427	1527r	1627	1659	1727r	1759	1827	1859	1927e	2027	2127e	...
Darmstadt Hbf ..... d.	0434	0530	0606	0634	0706	0734	0806	0834	0935	1035	1135	1235	1335	1435	1535	1634	1706	1735	1806	1834	1906	1934	2035	2135	2235
Mainz Hbf ..... d.	0513	0613t	|	0712	|	0812	|	0912	1012	1112	1212	1312	1412	1512	1612	1712	|	1812	|	1912	|	2012	2112	2212	2312
Wiesbaden Hbf ..... a.	0525	0625	0655	0725	0755	0825	0855	0925	1025	1125	1225	1325	1425	1525	1625	1725	1755	1825	1855	1925	1955	2025	2125	2225	2325

e – Ⓐ only. f – 1743 from Aug. 24. r – ⚒ only. t – Arrives 0604.

919 SAARBRÜCKEN - MANNHEIM (- FRANKFURT)

RE / S-Bahn services except where shown

km																									
				IC	*EC*		*IC*	*ICE*							*ICE*						*TGV*				
				2051	**317**		**2053**	**1557**							**9551**						**9553**				
				①–⑤			①–⑤	①–⑥			Ⓐ				①–⑥		Ⓐ						v		
					G✕	O	S🍷	D✕				O		O	R✕					O	R🍷		O	J	O
	Paris Est **390** ..... d.	...	...	...	...	...	...	...	...	...	...	...	...	...	0658	...	...	...	...	...	0909k	...	...	...	...
	Trier Hbf **915** ..... d.	...	...	...	...	...	...	...	...	0529a	0621	...	0636a	...	|	...	0834	...	...	...	|	...	...	...	...
0	**Saarbrücken** Hbf ..... d.	...	...	0440	0535	...	0621	0646	...	0658	0740	...	0802	...	0859	0903	0940	...	1002	...	1057	1103	...	1202	...
31	Homburg (Saar) Hbf ..... d.	...	...	0503	0558	0541r	0644	0707	...	0727	0804	0754c	0827	0854	|	0927	1004	...	1027	1054	|	1127	1154	1227	1254
67	**Kaiserslautern** Hbf ..... a.	...	...	0527	0622	0612r	0702	0727	...	0754	0825	0824c	0854	0924	0936	0954	1025	...	1054	1124	1135	1154	1224	1254	1324
		Ⓐ M	Ⓒ O	|	|	|	|	|	O	◧	|	|	◧	|	|	◧	|	O	◧	|	|	◧	|	◧	|
67	**Kaiserslautern** Hbf ..... d.	0456	0518	0529	0624	0614	0704	0729	0733	0758	0826	0832	0858	0930	0938	0958	1026	1032	1058	1130	1136	1158	1232	1258	1330
100	Neustadt (Weinstr) Hbf ..... d.	0527	0548	0553	0648	0651	0729	0752	0805	0830	0850	0905	0930	1005	|	1030	1050	1105	1130	1205	|	1230	1305	1330	1405
128	Ludwigshafen Hbf **911a 918** d.	0554	0613	0612	0705	0720	0746	|	0828	0857	|	0928	0957	1028	|	1057	|	1128	1157	1228	|	1257	1328	1357	1428
131	**Mannheim** Hbf ..... **911a 918** a.	0559	0619	0616	0709	0725	0751	0810	0834	0903	0910	0934	1003	1034	1016	1103	1110	1134	1203	1234	1214	1303	1334	1403	1434
131	**Mannheim** Hbf **911a 918** ▽ d.	0607	0637	0618	...	0729	0754	0812	0837	0907	*0929*	0937	1007	1037	1020	1107	*1129*	1137	1207	1237	1219	1307	1337	1407	1437
	Heidelberg Hbf **911a 918** a.	0624	0653	|	...	0744	0804	|	0853	0923	*0944*	0953	1023	1053	|	1123	*1144*	1153	1223	1253	|	1323	1353	1423	1453
191	Darmstadt Hbf ..... ▽ a.	...	...	0653	...	...	...	0845	...	...	...	...	...	...	|	...	...	...	...	...	|	...	...	...	...
219	**Frankfurt** (Main) Hbf ..... ▽ a.	...	...	0712	...	...	...	0903	...	...	...	...	...	...	1058	...	...	...	...	...	1258	...	...	...	...

	IC					*ICE*						*IC*	*IC*				*ICE*				*ICE*				
	2055					**9555**						**2057**	**2282**				**9557**				**9559**				
	Ⓑ											Ⓑ	⑥ L				Ⓑ								
	T🍷		O	K	O	R✕		O	J	O		🍷	🍷	O		O	R✕		O		R✕				
Paris Est **390** ..... d.	...	...	...	...	...	1309	...	...	...	...	...	...	...	...	...	...	1709	...	...	...	1905	...	...	...	...
Trier Hbf **915** ..... d.	...	...	...	1248	...	|	...	...	...	...	...	...	...	...	1654r	...	|	...	...	1854a	|	...	...	2055a	...
Saarbrücken Hbf ..... d.	1249	1302	...	1402	...	1459	1503	...	1602	...	1702	1741	1741	...	1802	...	1859	1903	...	2002	2059	...	2103	2202	2300
Homburg (Saar) Hbf ..... d.	1313	1327	1354	1427	1454	|	1527	1554	1627	1654	1727	1805	1805	1752	1827	1854	|	1927	1954	2027	|	...	2127	2227	2329
Kaiserslautern Hbf ..... a.	1336	1354	1424	1454	1524	1536	1554	1624	1654	1724	1754	1826	1826	1822	1854	1924	1936	1954	2024	2054	2136	...	2158	2258	0002
	|	◧	|	◧	|	|	◧	|	◧	|	◧	|	|	|	◧	|	|	◧	|	◧	|	M	◧ M	◧	◧
Kaiserslautern Hbf ..... d.	1338	1358	1432	1458	1530	1538	1558z	1632	1658	1730	1758	1828	1828	1832	1858	1930	1938	1958	2032	2058	2138	2141	2232*	2302	0006
Neustadt (Weinstr) Hbf ..... d.	1402	1430	1505	1530	1605	|	1630	1705	1730	1805	1830	1852	1852	1905	1930	2005	|	2030	2105	2130	|	2210	2300*	2330	0035
Ludwigshafen Hbf . **911a 918** d.	|	1457	1528	1557	1628	|	1657	1728	1759	1828	1857	|	|	1928	1957	2028	|	2057	2128	2200	|	2242	2328	2359	0102
Mannheim Hbf ..... **911a 918** a.	1420	1503	1534	1603	1634	1616	1703	1734	1804	1834	1903	1910	1910	1934	2003	2034	2016	2103	2134	2205	2216	2248	2333	0004	0108
Mannheim Hbf . **911a 918** ▽ d.	1424	1507	1537	1607	1637	1620	1707	1737	1807	1837	1907	1912	1912	1937	2007	2037	2020	2107	2137	2207	2220	2257	2337	0005	0117
Heidelberg Hbf . **911a 918** a.	1435	1523	1553	1623	1653	|	1723	1753	1823	1853	1923	|	|	1953	2023	2053	|	2123	2153	2223	|	2313	2353	0021	0134
Darmstadt Hbf ..... ▽ a.	...	...	...	...	...	|	...	...	...	...	...	1945	1945	...	...	...	|	...	...	...	|	...	...	...	...
Frankfurt (Main) Hbf ..... ▽ a.	...	...	...	...	...	1658	...	...	...	...	...	2004	2004	...	...	...	2058	...	...	...	2258	...	...	...	...

				ICE						*IC*		*ICE*										*ICE*			
				9558						**2058**		**9556**										**9554**			
		⚒		①–⑥	Ⓐ					①–⑤							v			Ⓐ					
	O		M	R✕	M		O	O	O	🍷	O	R✕	O		O		O		O			R✕	O		O
Frankfurt (Main) Hbf ..... ▽ d.	...	...	...	0600	...	...	...	...	...	0749	...	0901	...	...	...	...	...	...	...	...	...	1259g	...	...	...
Darmstadt Hbf ..... ▽ d.	...	...	...	|	...	...	...	...	...	0811	...	|	...	...	...	...	...	...	...	...	...	|	...	...	...
Heidelberg Hbf . **911a 918** d.	0014	...	0534r	|	0620	0634	0705	0735	0805	|	0835	|	0905	0935	1005	1035	1105	1135	1205	*1214*	1235	|	1305	1335	1405
Mannheim Hbf . **911a 918** ▽ a.	0030	...	0551r	0636	0635	0651	0719	0751	0821	0847	0851	0937	0921	0951	1021	1051	1121	1151	1221	*1229*	1251	1337	1321	1351	1421
Mannheim Hbf ..... **911a 918** d.	0031	0425	0554	0640	0643	0656	0721	0756	0826	0849	0856	0941	0926	0956	1026	1055	1126	1156	1226	1248	1256	1341	1326	1356	1426
Ludwigshafen Hbf . **911a 918** d.	0037	0432	0600	|	0650	0703	0727	0803	0832	|	0903	|	0932	1003	1032	1103	1132	1203	1232	|	1303	|	1332	1403	1432
Neustadt (Weinstr) Hbf ..... d.	0104	0506	0632	|	0715	0732	0802	0832	0858	0908	0932	|	1001	1032	1100	1132	1200	1232	1300	1309	1332	|	1401	1432	1500
Kaiserslautern Hbf ..... a.	0132	0534	0659	0720	0743	0759	0829	0859	0926	0930	0959	1020	1029	1059	1128	1159	1228	1259	1328	1331	1359	1420	1429	1459	1528
		◧	◧ J	|		◧	|	◧		|	◧	|	|	◧ K	|	◧	|	◧	|	|	◧	|	|	◧	|
Kaiserslautern Hbf ..... d.	...	0556	0703	0722	...	0803	0833	0903	...	0932	1003	1022	1033	1103	1133	1203	1233	1303	1333c	1332	1403	1422	1433	1503	1533c
Homburg (Saar) Hbf ..... d.	...	0624	0743	|	...	0831	0904	0931	...	0954	1031	|	1104	1131	1204	1231	1304	1331	1404c	1355	1431	|	1504	1531	1604c
Saarbrücken Hbf ..... a.	...	0657	0816	0758	...	0857	...	0957	...	1016	1055	1059	...	1157	...	1257	...	1400	...	1420	1455	1459	...	1557	...
Trier Hbf **915** ..... a.	...	...	...	|	...	...	...	1104	...	...	...	|	...	1311	...	...	...	1504	...	...	...	|	...	1704a	...
Paris Est **390** ..... a.	...	...	...	0950	...	...	...	...	...	...	...	1249h	...	...	...	...	...	...	...	...	...	1650	...	...	...

			IC		*IC*			*IC*		*TGV*				*IC*		*ICE*				*EC*		*ICE*		*IC*	
			2056		**2256**			**2054**		**9552**				**2052**		**9550**				**316**		**1594**		**2050**	
	Ⓐ		①–⑤		⑦			①–⑤						Ⓑ		Ⓑ						Ⓑ		⑦	
			V🍷	O	🍷		O	🍷		R🍷	O		O	S🍷		R✕	O		O	G✕		D✕	O	S	
Frankfurt (Main) Hbf ..... ▽ d.	...	...	...	...	1454	...	...	1554	...	1657	...	...	...	...	...	1901	...	...	...	...	...	2054	...	...	...
Darmstadt Hbf ..... ▽ d.	...	...	...	...	1512	...	...	1611	...	|	...	...	...	...	...	|	...	...	...	...	...	2111	...	...	...
Heidelberg Hbf . **911a 918** d.	*1414*	1435	...	1505	|	1535	1605	|	1635	|	1705	1735	1805	...	1835	|	1905	1935	2005	...	2035	|	2214	2255	2314
Mannheim Hbf . **911a 918** ▽ a.	*1429*	1451	...	1521	1547	1551	1621	1646	1651	1737	1721	1751	1821	...	1851	1937	1921	1951	2021	...	2051	2147	2232	2306	2332
Mannheim Hbf ..... **911a 918** d.	1448	1456	1539	1526	1549	1556	1626	1648	1656	1742	1726	1756	1826	1848	1856	1941	1926	1956	2026	2050	2056	2149	2240	2308	2336
Ludwigshafen Hbf . **911a 918** d.	|	1503	|	1532	|	1603	1632	1654	1703	|	1732	1803	1832	1854	1903	|	1932	2003	2032	|	2103	|	2246	|	2343
Neustadt (Weinstr) Hbf ..... d.	1509	1532	1558	1559	1608	1632	1700	1710	1732	|	1801	1832	1900	1910	1932	|	2001	2032	2100	2109	2132	2208	2316	2327	0016
Kaiserslautern Hbf ..... a.	1531	1559	1619	1629	1630	1659	1728	1731	1759	1822	1829	1859	1928	1931	1959	2020	2029	2059	2128	2131	2159	2228	2345	2349	0044
	|	◧	|	|	|	◧		|	◧	|	|	◧		|	◧	|	|	◧		|	◧	|	◧	|	|
Kaiserslautern Hbf ..... d.	1532	1603	1621	1633	1632	1703	...	1733	1803	1823	1833	1903	...	1933	2003	2022	2033	2103	...	2133	2203	2230	2355	2351	0045c
Homburg (Saar) Hbf ..... d.	1555	1631	1644	1707	1654	1731	...	1755	1831	|	1904	1931	...	1955	2031	|	2104	2131	...	2155	2231	2251	0026	0012	0116c
Saarbrücken Hbf ..... a.	1620	1657	1705	...	1716	1757	...	1816	1855	1901	...	1957	...	2019	2055	2059	...	2157	...	2218	2257	2310	0058	0033	...
Trier Hbf **915** ..... a.	1753	...	...	...	...	1906	...	...	...	|	...	2116	...	...	...	|	...	...	...	...	...	...	...	...	...
Paris Est **390** ..... a.	...	...	...	...	...	...	...	...	...	2053f	...	...	...	...	...	2253	...	...	...	...	...	...	...	...	...

D – [12] and ✕ Saarbrücken - Frankfurt - Erfurt - Leipzig - Dresden and v.v.
G – [12] and ✕ Graz - Salzburg - München - Stuttgart - Saarbrücken and v.v.
J – From / to Merzig (Table **915**).
K – From / to Koblenz (Table **915**).
L – To Kassel (Table **806**).
M – To / from Mosbach (Table **923**).
O – To / from Osterburken (Table **923**).
R – 🅁 for journeys to / from France.
S – To / from Stuttgart (Table **930**).

T – To Stuttgart on ⑤⑦ (Table **930**).
V – From Stuttgart Hbf (d. 1455) on ⑤.

a – Ⓐ only.
c – ⑥⑦ only.
f – 2104 on ⑥.
g – 1301 from Aug. 24.
h – 1253 on ⑦.
k – 0901 on ⑦.
r – ⚒ only.

v – Change trains at Kaiserslautern on ⑤.
z – On Ⓐ passengers travelling to Heidelberg should change trains at Neustadt.

* – On ⑥ passengers travelling to Heidelberg and beyond should change trains at Mannheim.
◧ – Change trains at Kaiserslautern.
▽ – Other services Mannheim - Frankfurt and v.v.: *ICE* trains see Table **912**. Local *RE / RB* trains see Table **911a**.

FRANKFURT - NÜRNBERG - PASSAU (- WIEN) 920

For other regional trains see Table 921 below.

km		ICE 827	ICE 521	ICE 21	ICE 523	ICE 1123	ICE 925	ICE 525	ICE 23	ICE 527	ICE 529	ICE 25	IC 1887	ICE 621	ICE 623	ICE 27	ICE 625	ICE 627	ICE 29	ICE 629	ICE 721	ICE 229	ICE 723	ICE 725	IC 2027
		①–⑤			①–⑤	⑥	⑥⑦	①–⑤		①–⑥			⑥							Ⓑ			Ⓑ		¶
		🍷	🍷	🍴	🍷	🍷	🍷	🍷	🍴	G 🍷	🍷	🍴	🍷	🍷	🍷	🍴	🍷	🍷	🍴	🍷	🍷	🍴	🍷	🍷	🍴
	Hamburg Hbf **800 900** ..... d.	...	...	...	...	...	...	...	...		...	...	0635v	...	...	...	...	...	...	...	...	...	...	...	1146
	Dortmund Hbf **800** ..... d.	...	...	...	0401	0421	0501	0523	0433	0623	0723c	0636	|	0816c	...	0838	1023h	...	...	1223h	1257c	...	...	1522h	1436
	Wuppertal Hbf **800** ..... d.	...	...	...	|	|	|	|	|	|	|	0714	|	|	...	|	|	...	...	|	|	...	...	|	1514
	Essen Hbf **800** ..... d.	...	...	...	0423	0445	0523	0553	0456	0650	0753t	|	|	0840	...	0900	1053	...	...	1253	1324c	...	1453	1553	|
	Düsseldorf Hbf **800** ..... d.	...	...	...	0453	0513	0553	0622	0523	0722	0822	|	|	0913	...	0927	1122	...	...	1322	1353c	...	1522	1622	|
	Köln Hbf **800 910** ..... d.	...	0420	...	|	|	|	|	0553	|	|	0753	|	|	1020	0953	|	1220	...	|	1428	...	|	|	1553
	Köln Messe/Deutz **910** ..... d.	...	|	...	0518	0535	0619	0644	|	0744	0844	|	|	0944	|	|	1144	|	...	1344	|	...	1544	1644	|
	Bonn Hbf **800** ..... d.	...	|	...	|	|	|	|	0614	|	|	0814	|	|	|	1014	|	|	...	|	|	...	|	|	1614
	Koblenz Hbf **912** ..... d.	...	|	...	|	|	|	|	0648	|	|	0848	|	|	|	1048	|	|	...	|	|	...	|	|	1648
	Mainz Hbf **912** ..... d.	...	|	...	|	|	|	|	0740	|	|	0940	|	|	|	1140	|	|	...	|	|	...	|	|	1740
0	**Frankfurt** Flughafen ✈ § ..... d.	...	0535	...	0637	0637	0737	0737	0802	0837	0937	1002	|	1037	1130	1202	1237	1330	...	1437	1537	...	1637	1737	1802
11	**Frankfurt** (Main) Hbf ..... d.	...	0551	0622	0654	0654	0754	0754	0818	0854	0954	1021	|	1054	1154	1221	1254	1354	1416	1454	1554	1621	1654	1754	1818
35	Hanau Hbf ..... d.	...	|	0638	|	|	|	|	0835	|	|	1038	|	|	|	1238	|	|	1439	|	|	1638	|	|	1835
57	Aschaffenburg Hbf ..... d.	...	0624	0652	0724	0724	0824	0824	|	0924	1024	|	|	1124	1224	|	1324	1424	|	1524	1624	|	1724	1824	1849
136	**Würzburg** Hbf ..... a.	...	0703	0731	0803	0803	0903	0903	0924	1003	1103	1131	1116	1203	1303	1331	1403	1503	1531	1603	1703	1731	1803	1903	1931
136	**Würzburg** Hbf ..... **900** d.	0603	0705	0734	0805	0805	0905	0905	0934	1005	1105	1134	1118	1205	1305	1334	1405	1505	1534	1605	1705	1734	1805	1905	1934
238	**Nürnberg** Hbf ..... **900** a.	0657	0759	0828	0859	0859	0959	0959	1028	1059	1159	1228	1232	1259	1359	1428	1459	1559	1628	1659	1759	1828	1859	1959	2028
238	**Nürnberg** Hbf ..... d.	0700	0802	0831	0902	0902	1002	1002	1031	1102	1202	1231	1235	1302	1402	1431	1502	1602	1631	1702	1802	1831	1902	2003	2031
	München Hbf **904** ..... a.	0806	0904	|	1004	1004	1104	1104	|	1204	1304	|	|	1404	1504	|	1604	1704	|	1804	1904	|	2004	2105	|
339	**Regensburg** Hbf ..... a.	...	...	0922	...	...	...	...	1122	...	...	1322	1335	...	...	1522	...	...	1722	...	...	1922	...	...	2131
339	**Regensburg** Hbf ..... d.	...	...	0924	...	...	...	...	1124	...	...	1324	1337	...	...	1524	...	...	1724	...	...	1924	...	...	2133
379	Straubing ..... d.	...	...	|	...	...	...	...	|	...	...	|	1400	...	...	|	...	...	|	...	...	|	...	...	2155
404	Plattling ..... **944** d.	...	...	0958	...	...	...	...	1158	...	...	1358	1414	...	...	1558	...	...	1758	...	...	1958	...	...	2210
456	**Passau** Hbf 🏨 ..... **944** a.	...	...	1026	...	...	...	...	1226	...	...	1426	1443	...	...	1626	...	...	1826	...	...	2026	...	...	2242
	Linz Hbf **950** ..... a.	...	...	1143	...	...	...	...	1343	...	...	1543	...	...	...	1743	...	...	1943	...	...	2143	...	...	...
	Wien Westbahnhof **950** ..... a.	...	...	1322	...	...	...	...	1522	...	...	1722	...	...	...	1922	...	...	2122	...	...	2322	...	...	...

	ICE 727	ICE 729	ICE 1025	ICE 1125	IC 2105	RB 32149	ICE 821	IC 2029		CNL 421	CNL 40401	EN 491
	Ⓑ		A	⑤	⑦	①–⑤	⑤⑦			①–④	⑤–⑦	L
	🍷	🍷	🍴	🍴	R 🍷	◇	🍷	🍷		N Ⓡ	P Ⓡ	Ⓡ
Hamburg Hbf **800 900** ..... d.	...	...	1346	1346	...	...	...	1546	...	...	...	2033
Dortmund Hbf **800** ..... d.	...	...	1636	1636	...	...	...	1836	...	1826	...	|
Wuppertal Hbf **800** ..... d.	...	...	1714	1714	...	...	...	1914	...	|	...	|
Essen Hbf **800** ..... d.	1653	1753	|	|	...	...	...	|	...	1904	...	|
Düsseldorf Hbf **800** ..... d.	1722	1821	|	|	...	...	...	|	...	1935	1935	|
Köln Hbf **800 910** ..... d.	|	|	1753	1753	...	...	1928	1953	...	2006	2006	|
Köln Messe/Deutz **910** ..... d.	1744	1843	|	|	...	...	|	|	...	|	|	|
Bonn Hbf **800** ..... d.	|	|	1814	1814	...	...	|	2014	...	2034	2034	|
Koblenz Hbf **912** ..... d.	|	|	1848	1848	...	...	|	2048	...	2115	2115	|
Mainz Hbf **912** ..... d.	|	|	1940	1940	...	...	|	2142	...	2212	2212	|
Frankfurt Flughafen ✈ § ..... d.	1837	1937	2002	2002	...	...	2037	2202	...	|	|	|
Frankfurt (Main) Hbf ..... d.	1854	1954	2018	2018	...	...	2054	2218	...	2305	2305	|
Hanau Hbf ..... d.	|	|	2035	2035	...	...	|	2235	...	|	|	|
Aschaffenburg Hbf ..... d.	1924	2024	2049	2049	...	...	2124	2249	...	2344	2344	|
Würzburg Hbf ..... a.	2003	2103	2128	2128	...	...	2203	2341	...	|	|	0205
Würzburg Hbf ..... **900** d.	2005	2105	2130	2130	...	...	2205	2343	...	|	|	0207
Nürnberg Hbf ..... **900** a.	2059	2159	2224	2224	...	...	2259	0038	...	|	|	0306
Nürnberg Hbf ..... d.	2102	2202	2235	2235	2240	2249	2303	...	...	|	|	0324
München Hbf **904** ..... a.	2204	2307	2348	|	|	|	0005	...	...	|	|	|
Regensburg Hbf ..... a.	...	...	...	2337	2342	0015	...	...	...	0427	0427	0427
Regensburg Hbf ..... d.	...	...	...	...	2344	0022	...	...	...	0430	0430	0430
Straubing ..... d.	...	...	...	...	0008	0053	...	...	...	|	|	|
Plattling ..... **944** d.	...	...	...	...	0022	0112	...	...	...	|	|	|
Passau Hbf 🏨 ..... **944** a.	...	...	...	...	0055	...	...	...	...	0532	0532	0532
Linz Hbf **950** ..... a.	...	...	...	...	...	...	...	...	...	0646	0646	0646
Wien Westbahnhof **950** ..... a.	...	...	...	...	...	...	...	...	...	0904	0904	0904

A – Daily except ⑤.
G – To Garmisch on ⑥ (a. 1341).
L – HANS ALBERS – 🛏 1, 2 cl., 🛌 2 cl., (2) and 🍷 Hamburg - Hannover - Wien.
N – ERIDANUS – 🛏 1, 2 cl., 🛌 2 cl., (2) and 🍷 Dortmund - Wien. Also calls at Gelsenkirchen Hbf (d. 1852).
P – ERIDANUS – 🛏 1, 2 cl., 🛌 2 cl., (2) and 🍷 Amsterdam - Wien.
R – (12) and 🍷 Basel - Karlsruhe - Stuttgart - Nürnberg - Passau.

c – ⑥⑦ only.
h – ⑦ only.
t – ⑥⑦ to July 12; daily from July 18.
v – 0718 until July 18.

¶ – Train number **2327** on ①–⑥ until Oct. 3 (also July 19, 26, Aug. 2, 9, Oct. 4) and ⑤ from Oct. 9.
◇ – Also calls at Neumarkt (Oberpf), d. 2325.
§ – Frankfurt Flughafen Fernbahnhof.

RE/ RB services — Local trains FRANKFURT - WÜRZBURG - NÜRNBERG - REGENSBURG - PASSAU 921

For faster *ICE/ IC* trains see Table **920** above.

km			Ⓒ	Ⓐ	†	⚒	Ⓐ	Ⓒ								Ⓒ	Ⓐ		Ⓒ	Ⓐ			†	⚒		⊠
0	**Frankfurt** (Main) Hbf .. d.	...	0442k	0442	0530	0634	0726	0730	0834	0930	1034	1130	1234	1330	1434	1530	1534	1634	1730	1734	1834	1930	2034	2034	2130	2236
4	**Frankfurt** (Main) Süd . d.	...	0448k	0448	0536	0640	0733	0736	0840	0936	1040	1136	1240	1336	1440	1536	1540	1640	1736	1740	1840	1936	2040	2040	2136	2242
10	Offenbach (Main) Hbf . d.	...	|	|	|	0645	0738	|	0845	|	1045	|	1245	|	1445	|	1545	1645	|	1745	1845	|	2045	2045	|	2248
24	Hanau Hbf ..... d.	...	0513k	0513	0614	0659	0759	0759	0859	0959	1059	1159	1259	1359	1459	1559	1559	1659	1759	1759	1859	1959	2059	2059	2159	2259
46	Aschaffenburg Hbf .... d.	0500	0602	0611	0710	0717	0817	0817	0917	1017	1117	1217	1317	1417	1517	1617	1617	1717	1817	1817	1917	2017	2117	2128v	2221	2322
84	Lohr Bahnhof ..... d.	0531	0633	0643	0741	0744	0844	0844	0944	1044	1144	1244	1344	1444	1544	1644	1644	1744	1844	1844	1944	2044	2144	2200	2253	2354
96	Gemünden (Main) ..... d.	0543	0645	0655	0752	0800	0900	0900	1000	1100	1200	1300	1400	1500	1556	1700	1656	1756	1900	1858	2000	2100	2156	2212	2304	0007
109	Karlstadt (Main) ..... d.	0554	0654	0703	0802	0808	0908	0908	1008	1108	1208	1308	1408	1508	1606	1708	1706	1806	1908	1908	2008	2108	2204	2220	2314	0016
136	**Würzburg** Hbf ..... a.	0617	0718	0718	0824	0824	0924	0924	1024	1124	1224	1324	1424	1524	1622	1724	1722	1822	1924	1924	2024	2124	2220	2236	2336	0040

km		2	2	Ⓐ								⑥♥									2	2			2	
0	**Würzburg** Hbf ..... d.	...	...	0510	0607	0638	...	0741	0840	0940	1040	1118	1140	1240	1340	1440	1540	1640	1740	1840	...	1946	2040	...	...	2255
23	Kitzingen ..... d.	...	...	0525	0623	0653	...	0800	0900	1000	1100	|	1200	1300	1400	1500	1600	1700	1800	1900	...	2006	2100	...	...	2314
61	Neustadt (Aisch) Bf .... d.	0456	0524	0551	0648	0719	...	0825	0925	1025	1125	1204v	1225	1325	1425	1525	1625	1725	1825	1925	2010	...	2125	...	2310	2338
94	Fürth (Bay) Hbf ..... d.	0528	0555	0618	0713	0741	...	0848	0948	1048	1148	|	1248	1348	1448	1548	1648	1748	1848	1948	2041	...	2148	...	2342	0008
102	**Nürnberg** Hbf ..... a.	0537	0605	0626	0721	0750	...	0855	0955	1055	1155	1232	1255	1355	1455	1555	1655	1755	1855	1955	2050	...	2155	...	2350	0017

	⚒r	△									◧			Ⓐ	Ⓒ			⊙								
Nürnberg Hbf ..... d.	...	0529e	0656	0736	...	...	0936	...	...	1136	...	...	1336	...	...	...	1536	...	1635e	1736	...	...	1936	...	...	2136
Neumarkt (Oberpf) ..... d.	0452	0554e	0719	0757	0801	0902e	0957	1001	1102e	1157	1201	1302e	1357	...	1401	1501e	1557	1601	1702e	1757	1801	1902e	1957	2001	...	2157
Regensburg Hbf ..... a.	0549	0649e	0758	0839	0857	0959e	1039	1057	1159e	1239	1257	1359e	1439	...	1457	1557e	1639	1657	1759e	1839	1857	1959e	2039	2057	...	2239
Regensburg Hbf ..... d.	0551	0651	0800	0844	0900	1001	1044	1059	1201	1244	1259	1401	1444	1457	1459	1559f	1644	1658	1800	1844	1859	2001	2044j	2059	2200	2244
München Hbf **878** ... a.	|	|	|	1017	|	|	1218	|	|	1417	|	|	1617	|	|	|	1817	|	|	2017	|	|	2221j	|	|	0021
Straubing ..... d.	0620	0721	0828		0928	1028	...	1128	1228	...	1328	1428	...	1528	1528	1628	...	1728	1828	...	1928	2028	...	2128	2229	...
Plattling ..... a.	0637	0739	0845	...	0945	1045	...	1145	1245	...	1345	1445	...	1546	1545	1645	...	1745	1846	...	1945	2045	...	2145	2246	...
Plattling ..... **944** d.	0644	0802	0900*	...	1004	1059	...	1204	1259	...	1404q	1459	...	1604	1604	1659	...	1804	1859	...	2004e	2101	...	2221	2305	...
Passau Hbf ..... **944** a.	0718	0837	0937*	...	1041	1136	...	1241	1336	...	1441q	1536	...	1641	1641	1736	...	1841	1936	...	2041e	2137	...	2258	2341	...

e – Ⓐ only.
f – 1601 on Ⓒ.
j – ⑤–⑦ only.
k – ⑥ (not Oct. 3).
q – 17 minutes later on ⑥.
r – Not Aug. 15.
v – Arrives 9–12 minutes earlier.

* – Through service on ⑥⑦ until Oct. 4 (Plattling d. 0847, Passau a. 0918).
⊠ – ⑤⑥ (runs daily Frankfurt - Gemünden).
△ – Change trains at Plattling on ⑥⑦.
◧ – Change trains at Plattling on ①–⑥.
⊙ – Change trains at Plattling on ①–⑤.
♥ – *IC* 1887: (12) and 🍷 Hamburg - Passau.

920 (WIEN -) PASSAU - NÜRNBERG - FRANKFURT

For other regional trains see Table **921** below.

	IC 2028	*ICE* 822	*ICE* 820	*IC* 2102	*ICE* 1026	*ICE* 1126	*ICE* 728	*ICE* 726	*IC* 2024	*ICE* 724	*ICE* 722	*ICE* 228	*ICE* 1128	*ICE* 720	*ICE* 628	*IC* 1886	*ICE* 28	*ICE* 626	*ICE* 624	*ICE* 26	*ICE* 622	*ICE* 620	*ICE* 928	*ICE* 926	*ICE* 24
		①–⑥	①–⑤	①	②–⑥	①		①–⑥					⑤	¶		⑥						①–⑤	⑦	⑥	
	🍷	🍷	🍷	K 🍷	🍴	🍴	🍷	🍷	🍴	🍷	🍷	🍴	🍷	🍷	🍷	🍷	🍴	🍷	🍷	🍴	🍷	🍷	H 🍷	🍷	🍴
Wien Westbahnhof **950** d.	...	...	...	...	...	...	...	...	...	...	...	0640	...	...	...	...	0840	...	...	1040	...	...	...	...	1240
Linz Hbf **950** d.	...	...	...	...	...	...	...	...	...	...	...	0816	...	...	...	...	1016	...	...	1216	...	...	...	...	1416
Passau Hbf 🚌 **944** d.	...	...	...	0512	...	...	...	...	0719	...	...	0930	...	...	...	1102	1130	...	...	1330	...	...	...	...	1530
Plattling **944** d.	...	...	...	0544	...	...	...	...	0752	...	...	0959	...	...	...	1133	1159	...	...	1400	...	...	...	...	1559
Straubing d.	...	...	...	0558	...	...	...	...	0806	...	...	|	...	...	...	1147	|	...	...	|	...	...	...	...	|
Regensburg Hbf a.	...	...	...	0619	...	...	...	...	0825	...	...	1031	...	...	...	1206	1230	...	...	1431	...	...	...	...	1631
Regensburg Hbf d.	...	...	...	0621	0622	...	...	...	0827	...	...	1033	...	...	...	1209	1232	...	...	1433	...	...	...	...	1633
München Hbf **904** d.	...	0451**g**	0551	|	|	0614	0651	0755	|	0855	0955	|	1055	1055	1155	|	|	1255	1355	|	1455	1555	1555	1555	|
Nürnberg Hbf a.	...	0557**g**	0657	0721	0721	0726	0757	0857	0925	0957	1057	1124	1157	1157	1257	1315	1325	1357	1457	1524	1557	1657	1657	1657	1724
Nürnberg Hbf **900** d.	0530	0600	0700	...	0729	0729	0800	0900	0928	1000	1100	1128	1200	1200	1300	1318	1328	1400	1500	1527	1600	1700	1700	1700	1727
Würzburg Hbf **900** a.	0624	0654	0754	...	0825	0825	0854	0954	1023	1054	1154	1225	1254	1254	1354	1417	1425	1454	1554	1625	1654	1754	1754	1754	1825
Würzburg Hbf d.	0626	0656	0756	...	0827	0827	0856	0956	1025	1056	1156	1227	1256	1256	1356	1419	1427	1456	1556	1627	1656	1756	1756	1756	1827
Aschaffenburg Hbf d.	0708	0736	0836	...	|	|	0936	1036	|	1136	1236	|	1336	1336	1436	|	|	1536	1636	|	1736	1836	1836	1836	|
Hanau Hbf d.	|	|	|	...	0920	0920	|	|	1120	|	|	|	|	|	|	|	1520	|	|	1720	|	|	|	|	1920
Frankfurt (Main) Hbf a.	0736	0805	0905	...	0936	0936	1005	1105	1136	1205	1305	1340	1405	1405	1505	|	1536	1605	1705	1736	1805	1905	1905	1905	1936
Frankfurt Flughafen ✈ § a.	0754	0821	0921	...	0954	0954	1021	1121	1155	1221	1321	...	1420	1421	1521	|	...	1621	1721	1754	1821	1921	1921	1921	1954
Mainz Hbf **912** a.	0818	|	|	...	1017	1017	|	|	1217	|	|	...	|	|	|	|	...	|	|	1818	|	|	|	|	2017
Koblenz Hbf **912** a.	0910	|	|	...	1110	1110	|	|	1310	|	|	...	|	|	|	|	...	|	|	1910	|	|	|	|	2110
Bonn Hbf **800** a.	0942	|	|	...	1142	1142	|	|	1342	|	|	...	|	|	|	|	...	|	|	1943	|	|	|	|	2142
Köln Messe/Deutz **910** a.	|	0914	1014	...	|	|	|	1214	|	|	1414	...	1514	|	1614	|	...	|	1814	|	1914	|	2014	|	|
Köln Hbf **800 910** a.	1005	|	|	...	1205	1205	1140	|	1405	1340	|	...	|	1540	|	|	...	1732	|	2005	|	2031	|	2040	2205
Düsseldorf Hbf **800** a.	|	0937	1037	...	|	|	...	1237	|	...	1437	...	1538	...	1637	|	...	...	1837	|	1942	...	2037	2111	|
Essen Hbf **800** a.	|	1002**t**	1102**t**	...	|	|	...	1302**j**	|	...	1502**t**	...	1603**t**	...	1702**t**	|	...	...	1902	|	2008	...	2102	2136	|
Wuppertal Hbf **800** a.	1041	...	...	...	1241	1241	...	|	1441	...	...	...	...	...	...	|	...	...	|	2041	|	...	|	|	2241
Dortmund Hbf **800** a.	1120	...	...	...	1320	1320	...	1330**k**	1520	...	...	...	...	...	...	|	...	...	1929	2120	2038	...	2130	2159	2320
Hamburg Hbf **800 900** a.	1412	...	...	...	1612	1612	...	...	1812	...	...	...	...	...	...	1907**v**	...	...	...	...	...	...	...	...	...

	ICE 528	*ICE* 924	*ICE* 526	*ICE* 22	*ICE* 524	*ICE* 522	*ICE* 20	*ICE* 520	*ICE* 922	*ICE* 1120	*ICE* 920	*EN* 490	*CNL* 40420	*CNL* 420
	Ⓑ	⑥	Ⓑ					①–④	⑤–⑦	⑦	⑦	L	P	N
	🍷	G 🍷	🍷	🍴	🍷	🍷	🍴	🍷	🍴	🍴	🍷	Ⓡ	Ⓡ	Ⓡ
Wien Westbahnhof **950** d.	...	...	...	1440	...	...	1640	...	...	...	...	1954	1954	1954
Linz Hbf **950** d.	...	...	...	1616	...	...	1816	...	...	...	...	2157	2157	2157
Passau Hbf 🚌 **944** d.	...	...	...	1730	...	...	1930	...	...	...	...	2306	2306	2306
Plattling **944** d.	...	...	...	1759	...	...	1959	...	...	...	...	|	|	|
Straubing d.	...	...	...	|	...	...	|	...	...	...	...	|	|	|
Regensburg Hbf a.	...	...	...	1831	...	...	2031	...	...	...	...	0012	0012	0012
Regensburg Hbf d.	...	...	...	1833	...	...	2033	...	...	...	...	0014	0014	0014
München Hbf **904** d.	1650	1650	1755	|	1855	1951	|	2055	2055	2154	2255	|	|	|
Nürnberg Hbf a.	1757	1757	1857	1924	1957	2057	2124	2157	2158	2304	0002	0113	|	|
Nürnberg Hbf **900** d.	1800	1800	1900	1927	2000	2100	2127	2200	2201	2307	0006	0132	|	|
Würzburg Hbf **900** a.	1854	1854	1954	2024	2054	2154	2227	2254	2255	0001	0100	0226	|	|
Würzburg Hbf d.	1856	1856	1956	2027	2056	2156	2229	...	2301	0003	...	0228	|	|
Aschaffenburg Hbf d.	1936	1936	2036	|	2136	2236	2310	...	2343	0045	...	|	|	|
Hanau Hbf d.	|	|	|	2120	|	|	2324	...	2356	0100	...	|	|	|
Frankfurt (Main) Hbf a.	2005	2005	2105	2136	2205	2300**z**	2339	...	0013	0116	...	|	0456	0456
Frankfurt Flughafen ✈ § a.	2020	2021	2121	2157	2221	2315	...	...	...	...	...	|	|	|
Mainz Hbf **912** a.	|	|	|	2218	|	...	...	...	...	...	...	|	0646	0646
Koblenz Hbf **912** a.	|	|	|	2310	|	...	...	...	...	...	...	|	0744	0744
Bonn Hbf **800** a.	|	|	|	2342	|	...	...	...	...	...	...	|	0817	0817
Köln Messe/Deutz **910** a.	2113	2113	2219	|	2341	...	...	...	...	...	...	|	|	|
Köln Hbf **800 910** a.	|	|	|	0005	|	...	...	...	...	...	...	|	0842	0842
Düsseldorf Hbf **800** a.	2137	2137	2242	0034	0005	...	...	...	...	...	...	|	0909	0909
Essen Hbf **800** a.	2202	2202	2307	0059	0030	...	...	...	...	...	...	|	...	0944
Wuppertal Hbf **800** a.	|	|	|	|	|	...	...	...	...	...	...	|	...	|
Dortmund Hbf **800** a.	2228	2228	2338	0122	0053	...	...	...	...	...	...	|	...	1006
Hamburg Hbf **800 900** a.	...	...	...	...	...	...	...	...	...	...	...	0750	...	...

G – From Garmisch (d. 1518).
H – To Hannover (Table **810**).
K – [12] and 🍷 Passau - Nürnberg - Stuttgart - Karlsruhe - Basel.
L – HANS ALBERS – 🛏 1, 2 cl., ▬ 2 cl., [2] and 🍷 Wien - Hannover - Hamburg.
N – ①②③⑦. ERIDANUS – 🛏 1, 2 cl., ▬ 2 cl., [2] and 🍷 Wien - Dortmund. Also calls at Duisburg (a. 0931).
P – ④⑤⑥. ERIDANUS – 🛏 1, 2 cl., ▬ 2 cl., [2] and 🍷 Wien - Amsterdam (Table **28**).

g – ① only.
j – ⑥ until July 11; ①–⑥ from July 18.
k – ⑥ only.
t – From July 18.
v – 1831 until July 18.
z – Frankfurt (Main) **Süd**. Change trains for Frankfurt (Main) Hbf (on ⚒ Süd d. 2310, Hbf a. 2316; on † Süd d. 2317, Hbf a. 2322).

§ – Frankfurt Flughafen Fernbahnhof.
¶ – Train number **1022** on ⑤.

921 Local trains PASSAU - REGENSBURG - NÜRNBERG - WÜRZBURG - FRANKFURT *RE / RB services*

For faster *ICE / IC* trains see Table **920** above.

	⚒r												⊙			⊙					Ⓒ	Ⓐ	⊙			
Passau Hbf **944** d.	*0438*	0549	*0604***g**	...	...	*0821*	*0912*	...	*1021*	1112	...	*1221*	1312	...	*1421*	1512	...	*1621*	1712	...	*1821**	*1821*	1912	...	*2023*	...
Plattling **944** a.	*0514*	0625	*0640***g**	...	...	*0856*	*0948*	...	*1056*	1148	...	*1256*	1348	...	*1456*	1548	...	*1656*	1748	...	*1856**	*1856*	1948	...	*2058*	...
Plattling d.	0521	0630	0704	0804**f**	...	0904	1004	...	1104	1204	...	1304	1404	...	1504	1604	...	1704	1804	...	1903	1904	2004	...	2104	2204
Straubing d.	0538	0646	0723	0823	...	0923	1023	...	1123	1223	...	1323	1423	...	1523	1623	...	1723	1823	...	1920	1923	2023	...	2123	2223
München Hbf **878** d.	|	|	|	|	0744	|	|	0944	|	|	1144	|	|	1344	|	|	1544	|	|	1744	|	|	|	1944	|	|
Regensburg Hbf a.	0609	0716	0752	0851	0914	0951	1051	1114	1151	1252	1314	1352	1451	1514	1551	1652	1714	1751	1851	1915	1948	1953	2053	2122	2152	2251
Regensburg Hbf d.	...	0720	0755**e**	0853	0919	0953**e**	1053	1120	1153**e**	1253**z**	1320	1353**e**	1453	1520	1553**e**	1654	1720	1753**e**	1853	1920	1950	*2021*	2053**z**	2125	...	2253
Neumarkt (Oberpf) d.	...	0802	0854**e**	0950	1002	1050**e**	1150	1202	1251**e**	1350**z**	1402	1450**e**	1550	1602	1650**e**	1752	1802	1850**e**	1950	2002	2031	*2124*	2150**z**	2209	...	2351
Nürnberg Hbf a.	...	0825	...	...	1027	...	...	1225	...	...	1425	...	...	1627	...	...	1827	...	...	2025	2053	...	...	2231	...	0026

	Ⓐ	⑥n	2												Ⓐ				2	2			2			
Nürnberg Hbf d.	0445	0446	0543	0604	0704	0804	0904	1004	1105	1204	1305	1404	1505	1604	1623	1705	1804	1905	...	2010	2108	...	2210	...	2335	...
Fürth (Bay) Hbf d.	0454	0455	0552	0613	0713	0813	0912	1013	1113	1213	1313	1413	1513	1613	1631	1713	1813	1913	...	2019	2117	...	2219	...	2345	...
Neustadt (Aisch) Bf d.	0524	0524	0621	0634	0734	0834	0934	1034	1134	1234	1334	1434	1534	1634	1703	1734	1834	1934	...	2049	2138	...	2249	...	0013	...
Kitzingen d.	0549	0549	...	0658	0758	0858	0958	1058	1158	1258	1358	1458	1558	1658	1729	1758	1858	1958	2056	...	2202	...	...	...	0036	...
Würzburg Hbf a.	0608	0608	...	0719	0819	0919	1019	1119	1219	1319	1419	1519	1619	1719	1750	1819	1919	2019	2116	...	2222	...	...	...	0056	...

	Ⓐ			Ⓒ	⑥n	Ⓐ								Ⓒ	Ⓐ							†	⚒		⑦	①–⑥
Würzburg Hbf d.	0424	0517	...	0611	0611	0635	0735	0835	0935	1035	1135	1235	1335	1435	1435	1535	1635	1735	1835	1935	2035	2136	2139	...	2305	2316
Karlstadt (Main) d.	0446	0541	...	0633	0633	0650	0750	0850	0950	1050	1150	1250	1350	1450	1450	1550	1650	1750	1850	1950	2050	2153	2201	...	2327	2338
Gemünden (Main) d.	0458	0553	...	0645	0645	0705	0805	0905	1005	1105	1205	1305	1405	1505	1505	1605	1705	1805	1905	2005	2105	2205	2212	...	2338	2349
Lohr Bahnhof d.	0508	0603	...	0655	0655	0715	0815	0915	1015	1115	1215	1315	1415	1515	1515	1615	1715	1815	1915	2015	2115	2215	2223	...	2348	2359
Aschaffenburg Hbf d.	0542	0640	0717	0726	0742	0744	0844	0944	1044	1144	1244	1344	1444	1544	1544	1644	1744	1844	1944	2044	2144	2244	2256	2313	0020	0031
Hanau Hbf d.	0604	0704**d**	0802**v**	...	0804	0804	0904	1003	1104	1203	1304	1403	1504	1603	1604	1704	1803	1904	2003	2104	2203	2303	...	0001**v**	...	...
Offenbach (Main) Hbf d.	0612	0712**d**	|	...	0812	0812	0912	|	1112	|	1312	|	1512	|	1612	1712	|	1912	|	2112	|	|	...	|	...	...
Frankfurt (Main) Süd a.	0616	0716**d**	0825	...	0816	0816	0916	1025	1116	1225	1316	1425	1516	1625	1616	1716	1825	1916	2025	2116	2225	2325	...	0025	...	...
Frankfurt (Main) Hbf a.	0624	0724**d**	0832	...	0826	0826	0924	1032	1124	1232	1324	1432	1524	1632	*1628*	1724	1832**p**	1924	2032	2124	2232	2332	...	0032	...	...

d – ⚒ only.
e – Ⓐ only.
f – 0730 on Ⓐ.
g – 11 minutes later on Ⓒ.
n – Not Oct. 3.
p – 1840 on ⑦.

r – Not Aug. 15.
v – Arrives 20 – 23 minutes earlier.
z – Ⓒ only.

* – Through service until Oct. 4 (Passau d. 1830, Plattling a. 1901).
⊙ – Change trains at Plattling on ①–⑤.

RE services WÜRZBURG - HEILBRONN - STUTTGART 922

km		Ⓐ	Ⓐ	Ⓐ		Ⓐ							†		Ⓑ		
0	**Würzburg** Hbf d.	...	...	...	0637	...	0837	0937	1037	1237	1437	1637	1736	1837	1936	2037	2137
43	Lauda d.	...	0532	...	0710	0719	0910	1008	1110	1310	1510	1710	1806	1910	2006	2110	2206
78	Osterburken d.	0502	0600	0609	0733	0802	0933	1032	1133	1333	1533	1733	1830	1933	2030	2133	2230
94	Möckmühl d.	0519	...	0626	0745	0819	0945	1044	1145	1345	1545	1745	1842	1945	2042	2145	2242
116	Bad Friedrichshall ⊖ d.	0544	...	0653	0801	0844	1001	1100	1201	1401	1601	1801	1858	2001	2058	2201	2258
127	**Heilbronn** Hbf **924** d.	0559	...	0712	0812	0856	1012	1110	1212	1412	1612	1812	1909	2012	2107	2210	2307
140	Lauffen (Neckar) **924** d.	0610	...	|	|	0904	|	|	|	|	|	|	|	|	2116	2218	2316
180	**Stuttgart** Hbf **924** a.	0651	...	0747	0853	0943	1053	1146	1253	1453	1653	1853	1949	2053	2155	2253	2353

	Ⓐ	†	Ⓐ	⑥k						†	Ⓐ		†	Ⓐ			⑥⑦h
Stuttgart Hbf **924** d.	0452	0456	0558	0559	0705	0907	1107	1307	1504	1605	1632	1704	1805	1809	1907	2031	2315
Lauffen (Neckar) **924** d.	0527	0532	|	0635	0739	|	|	|	|	|	|	|	|	|	|	2106	2352
Heilbronn Hbf **924** d.	0538	0544	0641	0647	0750	0947	1147	1347	1547	1647	1710	1747	1847	1844	1947	2117	0011
Bad Friedrichshall ⊖ d.	0549	0554	0649	0657	0800	0957	1157	1357	1557	1657	1722	1757	1857	1854	1957	2126	0024
Möckmühl d.	0605	0610	0713	0713	0816	1013	1213	1413	1613	1713	1755	1813	1913	1918	2013	2142	0048
Osterburken d.	0616	0622	0727	0727	0828	1027	1227	1427	1627	1727	1813	1827	1927	1930	2027	2154	0106
Lauda d.	0643	0650	0750	0750	0851	1050	1250	1450	1650	1750	...	1850	1954	1954	2050	2217	...
Würzburg Hbf a.	0722	0722	0822	0822	0922	1122	1322	1522	1722	1820	...	1922	2024	2024	2122	2247	...

h – Change trains at Heilbronn on ⑥.
k – Not Oct. 3.

⊖ – Bad Friedrichshall-Jagstfeld. See also Table **924**.

S-Bahn MANNHEIM - EBERBACH - OSTERBURKEN 923

km		Ⓐ	Ⓐ	Ⓐ	⑥k	Ⓐ						❖				⑥t	
	Kaiserslautern Hbf **919** d.	...	...	*0354*	0432	0456	0518z	0614	0733	0832	0930		1930	2032	2141	2141	2232*
0	**Mannheim** Hbf ¶ **924** d.	0422	...	*0457*	0537	0607	0637z	0729	0837	0937	1037		2037	2137	2257	2257	2337
17	**Heidelberg** Hbf ¶ **924** d.	0442	...	0555	0555	0630	0655	0755	0855	0955	1055	and	2055	2200	2315	2315	2355
28	Neckargemünd **924** d.	0456	...	0609	0609	0644	0709	0809	0909	1009	1109		2109	2214	2329	2329	0009
34	Neckarsteinach d.	0502	...	0615	0615	0650	0715	0815	0915	1015	1115	hourly	2115	2220	2335	2335	0015
41	Hirschhorn (Neckar) d.	0509	...	0622	0622	0657	0722	0822	0922	1022	1122		2122	2227	2342	2342	0022
50	Eberbach **924** d.	0516	...	0629	0629	0713f	0729	0829	0929	1029	1129	until	2129	2234	2349	2349	0029
69	Mosbach-Neckarelz **924** d.	0535	0623	0648	0648	0734	0748	0848	0948	1048	1148		2148	2258	0008	0008	0048
72	Mosbach (Baden) d.	0539	0627	0652	0652	0739	0752	0852	0952	1052	1152		2152	2302	0012	0012	0052
101	**Osterburken** a.	0612	0658	*0750*	0723	...	0823	0923	1023	1123	1223		2223	2333	...	0044	...

	⚒	Ⓐ	Ⓐ		Ⓐ		Ⓐ		Ⓐ	⚒				Ⓑm	⑥k	
Osterburken d.	...	...	0513	0536k	0606	0636z	0644	...	0706	...	0736		1836	1936	2036	2136	2236
Mosbach (Baden) d.	0435	0510	0543	0605	0635	0705	0718	...	0735	...	0805		1905	2005	2105	2205	2305
Mosbach-Neckarelz **924** d.	0440	0526f	0548	0610	0640	0710	0724	0729	0740	0740	0810	and	1910	2010	2110	2210	2310
Eberbach **924** d.	0459	0545	0607	0629	0659	0729	...	0743	0759	0759	0829		1929	2029	2129	2229	2329
Hirschhorn (Neckar) d.	0506	0552	0614	0636	0706	0736	...	|	0806	0806	0836	hourly	1936	2036	2136	2236	2336
Neckarsteinach d.	0512	0559	0620	0642	0712	0742	...	|	0812	0812	0842		1942	2042	2142	2242	2342
Neckargemünd **924** d.	0519	0605	0627	0649	0719	0749	...	|	0819	0819	0849	until	1949	2049	2149	2249	2349
Heidelberg Hbf ¶ **924** a.	0533	0619	0642	0703	0733	0803	...	0808	0833	0833	0903		2003	2103	2203	2303	0003
Mannheim Hbf ¶ **924** a.	0551	0635	0702	0719	0751	0821	...	0824	0851	0851	0921		2021	2132g	2232	2332	0030
Kaiserslautern Hbf **919** a.	0659	0743	0813	0829	0859	0926	...	...	0959	0959	1029		2128	...	2345	0044	0132

f – Arrives 10–12 minutes earlier.
g – 2121 on Ⓒ.
k – ⑥ (not Oct. 3).
m – Also Oct. 3.
t – Also Oct. 2.
z – Ⓒ only.

* – Change trains at Mannheim on ⑥ (not Oct. 3).
❖ – Passengers travelling from Kaiserslautern to stations beyond Eberbach may need to change trains at Neustadt (Weinstr) Hbf on certain trains / dates (Table **919**).
¶ – See also Tables **911a**, **918**, **919**.

RE / RB services MANNHEIM - HEILBRONN - STUTTGART 924

km		Ⓐ	Ⓒ	Ⓐ	Ⓐ		Ⓐ	Ⓐ	Ⓐ	Ⓒ		Ⓐ	Ⓐ												
0	**Mannheim** Hbf ¶ **923** d.	...	...	...	...	...	*0457*	...	0625	...	...	*0700*	0734	*0759*	0834	...	*0859*	0934	*0959*	1034	...	*1059*	1134	*1159*	1234
17	**Heidelberg** Hbf ¶ **923** d.	...	...	...	...	...	0541	...	0642	0641	...	0719	0749	0821	0849	...	0921	0949	1021	1049	...	1121	1149	1221	1249
29	Neckargemünd **923** d.	...	...	...	...	...	0553	...	|	0653	...	0733	|	0833	|	...	0933	|	1033	|	...	1133	|	1233	|
49	Sinsheim (Elsenz) d.	...	...	*0503*	...	...	0624	...	0713	0724	...	0759	|	0859	0919	...	0959	|	1059	1119	...	1159	|	1259	1319
52	Steinsfurt d.	...	...	*0508*	...	...	0629	...	0716	0729	...	0803	|	0903	|	...	1004	|	1103	|	...	1204	|	1303	|
72	Bad Wimpfen d.	...	...	*0535*	...	...	0657	...	0737	0751	...	*0834*	|	▬	0937	...	1034	|	▬	1137	...	1234	|	▬	1337
	Eberbach **923** d.	...	...	|	...	...	|	...	|	|	...	|	0814	...	|	...	|	1014	...	|	...	|	1214	...	|
	Mosbach-Neckarelz **923** d.	...	...	|	0552	0618r	|	0651	|	|	0752	|	0828	0852	|	0952	|	1028	1052	|	1152	|	1228	1252	|
75	Bad Friedrichshall-J. ⊖ **922** d.	...	...	0544	0612	0638r	0706	0711	0742	0756	0812	*0838*	0841	0912	0942	1012	1038	1042	1112	1142	1212	1238	1242	1312	1342
86	**Heilbronn** Hbf **922** a.	...	...	0557	0625	0651r	0720	0724	0752	...	0825	...	0851	0925	0952	1025	...	1051	1125	1152	1225	...	1251	1325	1352
86	**Heilbronn** Hbf **922** d.	0435	0554	0559	0627	0653	...	0725	*0756*	...	0826	...	*0856*	0926	*0956*e	1026	...	*1056*f	1126	*1156*e	1226	...	*1256*f	1326	*1356*e
99	Lauffen (Neckar) **922** d.	0445	0604	0610	0636	0704	...	0736	*0804*	...	0837	...	*0904*	0937	*1004*e	1037	...	*1104*f	1137	*1204*e	1237	...	*1304*f	1337	*1404*e
139	**Stuttgart** Hbf **922** a.	0525	0643	0651	0718	0743	...	0815	*0843*	...	0915	...	*0943*	1015	*1043*e	1115	...	*1143*f	1215	*1243*e	1315	...	*1343*f	1415	*1443*e

		◇										◇							Ⓑ						
Mannheim Hbf ¶ **923** d.	...	*1259*	1334	*1359*	1434	...	*1459*	1534	*1559*	1634	...	*1659*	1734	*1759*	1834	...	*1859*	1934	...	*1959*	2044	*2107*	2142	2242	...
Heidelberg Hbf ¶ **923** d.	...	1321	1349	1421	1449	...	1521	1549	1621	1649	...	1721	1749	1821	1849	...	1921	1949	...	2021	2059	2128	2157	2257	2305
Neckargemünd **923** d.	...	1333	|	1433	|	...	1533	|	1633	|	...	1733	|	1833	|	...	1933	|	...	2033	|	2145	|	|	2321
Sinsheim (Elsenz) d.	...	1359	|	1459	1519	...	1559	|	1659	1719	...	1759	|	1859	1919	...	1959	|	...	2058	2129	2212	|	|	2348z
Steinsfurt d.	...	1404t	|	1503	|	...	1604	|	1703	|	...	1804t	|	1903	|	...	2004	|	...	▬	2132	...	|	|	...
Bad Wimpfen d.	...	1434	|	▬	1537	...	1634	|	▬	1737	...	1834	|	▬	1937	...	2034	|	...	...	2149	...	|	|	...
Eberbach **923** d.	...	|	1414	...	|	...	|	1614	...	|	...	|	1814	...	|	...	|	2014	...	...	|	...	2223	2323	...
Mosbach-Neckarelz **923** d.	1352	|	1428	1452	|	1552	|	1628	1652	|	1752	|	1828	1852	|	1952	|	2028	...	2052	|	...	2237	2337	...
Bad Friedrichshall-J. ⊖ **922** d.	1412	1438	1442	1512	1542	1612	1638	1642	1712	1742	1812	1838	1842	1912	1942	2012	2038	2042	2058	2112	2154	...	2250	2350	...
Heilbronn Hbf **922** a.	1425	...	1451	1525	1552	1625	...	1651	1725	1752	1825	...	1851	1925	1952	2025	...	2051	2105	2125	2204	...	2300	2400	...
Heilbronn Hbf **922** d.	1426	...	*1456*f	1526	*1556*e	1626	...	*1656*f	1726	*1756*e	1826	...	*1856*e	1926	*2012*	2026	...	...	2107	2126	*2210*	...	*2307*	...	...
Lauffen (Neckar) **922** d.	1437	...	*1504*f	1537	*1604*e	1637	...	*1704*f	1737	*1804*e	1837	...	*1904*e	1937	|	2037	...	...	2116	2137	*2218*	...	*2316*	...	...
Stuttgart Hbf **922** a.	1515	...	*1543*f	1615	*1643*e	1715	...	*1745*f	1815	*1843*e	1915	...	*1943*e	2015	*2053*	2115	...	...	2155	2215	*2253*	...	*2353*	...	...

km		Ⓐ	Ⓐ	Ⓐ	⚒	Ⓐ		Ⓐ	Ⓐ	⑥k		Ⓐ													
0	**Stuttgart** Hbf **922** d.	...	...	...	...	*0452*	...	0545	0558	0559	...	...	*0705*	0745	*0809*v	...	0845	*0915*e	0945	*1009*v	...	1045	*1115*e	1145	*1209*v
40	Lauffen (Neckar) **922** d.	...	...	...	...	*0527*	...	0623	|	0635	0649e	...	*0739*	0822	*0844*v	...	0922	*0953*e	1022	*1044*v	...	1122	*1153*e	1223	*1244*v
53	**Heilbronn** Hbf **922** a.	...	...	...	...	*0538*	...	0633	0640	0646	0659e	...	*0748*	0832	*0854*v	...	0932	*1001*e	1032	*1054*v	...	1132	*1201*e	1233	*1254*v
53	**Heilbronn** Hbf **922** d.	...	0456	0500	0529	0542	0621	0634	0641	0647	0700	...	0805	0834	0905	...	0934	1005	1034	1105	...	1134	1205	1234	1305
64	Bad Friedrichshall-J. ⊖ **922** d.	...	0504	0515	0543	0554	0635	0646	0649	0657	0710	0718	0816	0847	0915	0918	0947	1016	1047	1115	1118	1147	1216	1247	1315
82	Mosbach-Neckarelz **923** d.	...	0518	|	0604	|	|	0702	...	...	0729	|	|	0906	0929	|	1006	|	1106	1129	|	1206	|	1306	1329
101	Eberbach **923** d.	...	0532	|	▬	|	|	...	...	...	0743	|	|	▬	0943	|	...	|	▬	1143	|	...	|	▬	1343
	Bad Wimpfen d.	...	|	0519	...	0558	0639	...	...	...	|	0721	0820	...	|	0921	...	1020	...	|	1121	...	1220	...	|
	Steinsfurt d.	...	|	0543	...	0616	0704	...	...	...	|	0751	|	0848	|	0951	...	|	1048	|	1151	...	|	1248	|
	Sinsheim (Elsenz) d.	0509	|	0549	0549	0620	0714	...	...	...	|	0759	0839	0859	|	0959	...	1039	1059	|	1159	...	1239	1259	|
123	Neckargemünd **923** d.	0534	|	0614	0614	|	0741	...	...	...	|	0824	|	0924	|	1024	...	|	1124	|	1224	...	|	1324	|
135	**Heidelberg** Hbf ¶ **923** a.	0548	0557	0629	0629	0648	0759	...	...	...	0808	0838	0908	0938	1008	1038	...	1108	1138	1208	1238	...	1308	1338	1408
152	**Mannheim** Hbf ¶ **923** a.	...	0614	*0651*	*0651*	0706	*0829*	...	...	...	0824	*0902*	0924	*1002*	1024	*1102*	...	1124	*1202*	1224	*1302*	...	1324	*1402*	1424

	◇					◇					◧										n		●		
Stuttgart Hbf **922** d.	...	1245	*1315*e	1345	*1409*v	...	1445	*1515*e	1545	*1609*v	...	1645	*1715*e	1745	*1813*	...	1845	*1915*e	...	*1945*	...	2115	2212	2315	0015
Lauffen (Neckar) **922** d.	...	1323	*1353*e	1422	*1444*v	...	1522	*1553*e	1622	*1644*v	...	1722	*1753*e	1823	*1850*	...	1922	*1953*e	...	*2022*	...	2153	2248	2352	0051
Heilbronn Hbf **922** a.	...	1333	*1401*e	1432	*1454*v	...	1532	*1601*e	1632	*1654*v	...	1732	*1801*e	1833	*1901*	...	1932	*2001*e	...	*2032*	...	2203	2300	0004	0102
Heilbronn Hbf **922** d.	...	1334	1405	1434	1505	...	1534	1605	1634	1705	...	1734	1805	1834	1905	...	1934	2005	...	2059	...	2221	...	...	...
Bad Friedrichshall-J. ⊖ **922** d.	1318	1347	1416	1447	1515	1518	1547	1616	1647	1715	1718	1747	1816	1847	1915	1918	1947	2016	...	2111	...	2235	...	...	...
Mosbach-Neckarelz **923** d.	|	1406	|	1506	1529	|	1606	|	1706	1729	|	1806	|	1906	1929	|	2006	|	...	2129	...	2254	...	...	...
Eberbach **923** d.	|	...	|	▬	1543	|	...	|	▬	1743	|	...	|	▬	1943	|	...	|	...	2143	...	...	...	...	...
Bad Wimpfen d.	1321	...	1420	...	|	1521	...	1620	...	|	1721	...	1820	...	|	1921	...	2020	...	|	...	...	...	...	...
Steinsfurt d.	1351	...	|	1448	|	1551	...	|	*1648*	|	1751	...	|	*1848*	|	1951	...	|	2053	|	...	...	...	...	...
Sinsheim (Elsenz) d.	1359	...	1439	1459	|	1559	...	1639	1659	|	1759	...	1839	1859	|	1959	...	2039	2059	|	2317	...	...	...	...
Neckargemünd **923** d.	1424	...	|	1524	|	1624	...	|	1724	|	1824	...	|	1924	|	2024	...	|	2124	|	2341	...	...	...	...
Heidelberg Hbf ¶ **923** a.	1438	...	1508	1538	1609	1638	...	1709	1738	1809	1838	...	1908	1938	2008	2038	...	2106	2138	2206	2358	...	...	...	...
Mannheim Hbf ¶ **923** a.	*1502*	...	1524	*1602*	1624	*1702*	...	1724	*1802*	1824	*1902*	...	1924	*2002*	2024	*2102*e	...	2124	*2202*	2224	*0030*	...	...	...	...

e – Ⓐ only.
f – 3–6 minutes later on Ⓒ.
k – Not Oct. 3.
n – Not Aug. 3 - Sept. 11.

r – ⚒ only.
t – 3 minutes later on Ⓐ.
v – 4–7 minutes later on Ⓐ.
w – Aug. 3 - Sept. 11 only.

z – Aug. 3 - Sept. 11 by 🚌 from Neckargemünd (arrives Sinsheim 0013).

● – ①②③④⑦.

⊖ – Bad Friedrichshall-Jagstfeld.
◇ – Change trains at Steinsfurt on Ⓐ.
◧ – Change trains at Sinsheim on Ⓐ.
¶ – See also Tables **911a**, **918**, **919**.

925 STUTTGART - BACKNANG / AALEN - NÜRNBERG

RE services except where shown

km	See note ⊠																							
		IC		*IC*		*IC*			*IC*			*IC*		*IC*		*IC*				*IC*		*IC*			
		2061		**2063**		**2065**			**2101**			**2069**		**2103**		**2163**				**2105**		**2167**			
		①–⑤					©	Ⓐ		©	Ⓐ					Ⓑ		Ⓐ	©	⑤⑦		⑦	Ⓐ	©	
				🍷		🍷			B🍷			🍷		B🍷		🍷				Q🍷					
	Karlsruhe Hbf **931** ... d.	...	...	0706e	...	0906	...	...	1106	...	...	1306	...	1506	...	1706	...	...	...	1906	...	2106	...	...	...
0	**Stuttgart** Hbf ... d.	0601	0640	0807	0840	1007	1040	1040	1207	1240	1240	1407	1440	1607	1642	1807	1840	1940	1940	2007	2058	2207	2258	2245u	2358
31	Backnang ... d.	0624	0706t	0829	0906	1029	1106	1106	1229	1306	1313	1429	1506	1629	1706	1829	1906	2006	2006	2029	2125	2229	2325	2328	0026
73	Schwäbisch H-H ⊡ ... a.	0652	0758	0857	0957	1057	1157	1157	1257	1357	1357	1457	1557	1657	1757	1857	1957	2048	2048	2057	2202	2257	0002	0004	0102
73	Schwäbisch H-H ⊡ ... d.	0701	0759	0901	0959	1101	1159	1159	1301	1359	1359	1501	1559	1701	1759	1901	1959	2051	2056k	2101	2203	2301	0003	0005	0103
100	Crailsheim ... d.	0726	0818	0926	1018	1125	1218	1218	1325	1418	1418	1525	1618	1725	1818	1925	2018	2109	2115k	2125	2221	2329	0021	0024	0121
146	Ansbach ... d.	0751	0851	0951	1051	1151	1251	1256	1351	1451	1456	1551	1651	1751	1851	1951	2051	...	...	2151	...	2355	...	...	...
190	**Nürnberg** Hbf ... a.	0818	0925	1018	1125	1216	1325	1342	1416	1525	1542	1616	1725	1816	1925	2016	2125	...	...	2216	...	0022	...	...	...

See note ⊠																								
					IC					*IC*		*IC*		*IC*			*IC*		*IC*		*IC*		*IC*		*IC*
					2164					**2102**		**2160**		**2100**			**2066**		**2064**		**2062**		**2060**		**1868**
	Ⓐ	Ⓐ	©	Ⓐ	①–⑤	©	Ⓐ	Ⓐ	©	①–⑥					Ⓐ	©							⑤⑦		⑦
					🍷					P🍷		🍷		B🍷			🍷		🍷		🍷		🍷		🍷
Nürnberg Hbf ... d.	...	...	...	...	0537	...	...	0614	0635	0741	0833	0941	1035	1141	1217	1235	1341	1435	1541	1635	1741	1835	1941	2035	2141
Ansbach ... d.	...	...	...	...	0604	...	...	0707v	0707	0807	0907	1007	1107	1207	1310v	1307	1407	1507	1607	1707	1807	1907	2007	2107	2207
Crailsheim ... d.	0452	0530	0540	0555	0632	0635	0638	0742	0742	0835	0942	1035	1142	1235	1343	1342	1435	1542	1635	1742	1835	1942	2035	2142	2235
Schwäbisch H-H ⊡ ... a.	0510	0548	0558	0613	0648	0653	0656	0800	0800	0852	1000	1052	1200	1252	1400	1400	1452	1601	1652	1801	1852	2000	2052	2200	2252
Schwäbisch H-H ⊡ ... d.	0511	0549	0559	0614	0653	0709	0708	0803	0803	0858	1003	1058	1203	1258	1403	1403	1458	1603	1658	1803	1858	2003	2058	2203	2258
Backnang ... d.	0551	0636	0651	0706	0722	0751	0751	0851	0851	0929	1051	1129	1251	1329	1451	1451	1529	1651	1729	1851	1929	2051	2129	2251	2329
Stuttgart Hbf ... a.	0618	0703	0718	0735	0753	0818	0818	0918	0918	0953	1118	1153	1318	1353	1518	1518	1553	1718	1753	1918	1953	2118	2153	2318	2355
Karlsruhe Hbf **931** ... a.	...	...	...	...	0853	...	...	...	...	1053	...	1253	...	1453	...	...	1653	...	1853	...	2053	...	2253	...	...

km	See note ▲																								
		Ⓐ		Ⓐ	Ⓐ		Ⓐ					Ⓐ		Ⓐ		Ⓐ				©			©		
0	**Stuttgart** Hbf ... d.	0424	0515	0549	0650	0719r	0746	0822		1422	1522	1549	1619r	1649	1719r	1755	1819r	1849	1922	1949	2022	2122	2149	...	2232
51	Schwäbisch Gmünd ... a.	0508	0603	0634	0734	0804	0834	0904		1504	1604	1631	1704	1734	1804	1839	1904	1933	2004	2034	2104	2204	2234	...	2316
51	Schwäbisch Gmünd ... d.	0513*	0608*	0640*	0740*	0810*	0840*	0910*	and	1510*	1610*	1637*	1710*	1740*	1810*	1843*	1910*	1940*	2010*	2040*	2110*	2210*	...	2240*	2322*
76	**Aalen** ... a.	0601*	0648*	0720*	0820*	0858*	0920*	0958*		1558*	1655*	1722*	1758*	1820*	1858*	1923*	1958*	2018*	2048*	2118*	2148*	2248*	...	2318*	2400*
									hourly																
		Ⓐ		d	d		d					d		d		d		Ⓑ		d					
76	**Aalen** ... d.	0641	...	0728	0828	...	0928	1028	until	1628	...	1728	...	1828	...	1928	...	2028	...	2133	...	...	...	2344	...
92	Ellwangen ... a.	0651	...	0745	0846	...	0945	1046		1645	...	1745	...	1845	...	1945	...	2046	...	2151	...	...	...	0003	...
92	Ellwangen ... d.	0657	...	0800	0900	...	1000	1100		1700	...	1800	...	1900	...	2000	...	2100f	...	2152	...	...	...	0004	...
113	**Crailsheim** ... a.	0712	...	0815	0915	...	1015	1115		1715	...	1815	...	1915	...	2015	...	2115f	...	2208	...	...	...	0020	...

See note ▲																									
			Ⓐ		Ⓐ																				
Crailsheim ... d.	...	...	0515	...	0607	...	0640	0745	0843		1243	1345	1443	1545	...	1643	...	1745	...	1843	...	1945	...	2043h	2146
Ellwangen ... a.	...	...	0531	...	0628	...	0656	0800	0859		1259	1400	1459	1600	...	1659	...	1800	...	1859	...	2000	...	2059h	2208
Ellwangen ... d.	...	...	0531	...	0629	...	0657	0800	0900	and	1300	1400	1500	1600	...	1700	...	1800	...	1900	...	2000	...	2100	2208
Aalen ... a.	...	...	0551	...	0650	...	0715	0819	0918		1318	1419	1518	1619	...	1718	...	1819	...	1918	...	2019	...	2118	2223
										hourly															
	Ⓐ		Ⓐ	©	Ⓐ	©														©		©		©	
Aalen ... d.	0402*	0509*	0559*	0559*	0656*	0656*	0800*	0900*	1000*	until	1400*	1500*	1600*	1630*	1700*	1730*	1800*	1830*	1900*	1930*	2010*	2040*	2110*	2140*	2240*
Schwäbisch Gmünd ... a.	0440*	0547*	0639*	0647*	0736*	0747*	0848*	0948*	1048*		1448*	1548*	1648*	1718*	1748*	1818*	1848*	1918*	1948*	2018*	2048*	2118*	2148*	2218*	2318*
Schwäbisch Gmünd ... d.	0445	0552	0645	0654	0746	0754	0854	0954	1054		1454	1554	1654	1726	1754	1824	1854	1924	1954	2024	2054	2124	2154	2224	2324
Stuttgart Hbf ... a.	0531	0642	0727	0738	0823	0838	0938	1038	1138		1538	1643j	1743j	1814	1843j	1913	1938	2010	2041	2110	2138	2210	2238	2310	0010

B – [12] Nurnberg - Basel and v.v.
P – [12] (Passau ① -) Nürnberg - Basel.
Q – [12] Basel - Nürnberg (- Passau ⑦).

d – Runs daily Aalen - Crailsheim.
e – ①–⑥ only.
f – ⑤⑦ only.

h – ⑤–⑦ only.
j – 5 minutes earlier on ©.
k – ⑥ only.
r – 3 minutes later on ©.
t – 0722 on Ⓐ.
u – From the S-Bahn (underground) platforms.
v – Arrives 7–9 minutes earlier.

* – By 🚌.
⊡ – Schwäbisch Hall-Hessental.
★ – See Table **920** for running dates from / to Passau.
⊠ – Service via Schwäbisch Hall-Hessental is valid **until Oct. 15**.

▲ – Service via Aalen is valid **until July 26**. Some additional train / 🚌 services operate on Ⓐ Stuttgart - Aalen and v.v. July 27 - Oct. 15 trains are replaced by 🚌 Schorndorf (*km 30*) - Schwäbisch Gmünd and v.v. Full details will be shown in the August and September editions.

926 HEILBRONN / ASCHAFFENBURG - CRAILSHEIM and AALEN - DONAUWÖRTH / ULM

RE / *RB* services

Aschaffenburg - Lauda - Crailsheim ⊠

km		Ⓐ								
0	**Aschaffenburg** Hbf ... d.	...	...	0652	0922	1122	1322	1522	1722	1922y
38	Miltenberg ... d.	...	...	0745j	0959	1159	1359	1559	1759	1959
69	Wertheim ... d.	...	0623a	0828j	1035	1235	1435	1635	1835	2035
93	Tauberbischofsheim ... d.	0559	0647a	0856	1056	1256	1456	1656	1856	2100
100	**Lauda** ... a.	0608	0659a	0906	1106	1306	1506	1706	1906	2106
100	**Lauda** ... d.	0613	0713	0913	1113	1313	1513	1713	1913	2113
110	Bad Mergentheim ... d.	0625	0725	0925	1125	1325	1525	1725	1925	2125
169	**Crailsheim** ... a.	0729	0831	1031	1231	1431	1631	1831	2031	...

	Ⓐ	©	Ⓐ							Ⓐ	©
Crailsheim ... d.	...	...	0520	0737	0930	1129	1328	1528	1728	1937	1937
Bad Mergentheim ... d.	0458	0606	0645	0834	1034	1234	1434	1634	1834	2053	2035
Lauda ... a.	0509	0617	0657	0844	1044	1244	1444	1644	1844	2104	2045
Lauda ... d.	0522	0622	0702	0853	1053	1253	1453	1653	1853	2114	2114
Tauberbischofsheim ... d.	0531	0630	0712	0859	1059	1259	1459	1659	1859	2120	2120
Wertheim ... d.	0559	0705	0738	0921	1121	1321	1521	1721	1921	2147	2147
Miltenberg ... d.	0643	0745	0845	0959	1159	1359	1559	1759	1959	2222	2222
Aschaffenburg Hbf ... a.	0730	0836	0930	1038	1238	1438	1638	1838	2038f	2305	2305

Heilbronn - Crailsheim ⊠

km	*Valid until Oct. 15*	Ⓐ	⑦	①–⑥						
0	**Heilbronn** Hbf ... d.	0550e	0803	0803r	1003r	1203r	1403r	1603r	1803r	2003r
54	Schwäbisch Hall ... d.	0642	0848	0848	1048	1248	1448	1648	1848	2048
61	Schwäbisch Hall-H ⊡ .. a.	0649	0855	0855	1055	1255	1455	1655	1855	2055
88	**Crailsheim** ... a.	◧	0914	◧	◧	1314	◧	◧	1916z	2128t

Valid until Oct. 15	©	Ⓐ	①–⑥	⑦						
Crailsheim ... d.	0635	0638	◧	0838	◧	1241	◧	◧	◧	2042
Schwäbisch Hall-H ⊡ ... d.	0658	0700	0901	0901	1101	1301	1501	1701	1901	2106
Schwäbisch Hall ... d.	0705	0706	0907	0907	1107	1307	1507	1707	1907	2113
Heilbronn Hbf ... a.	0751	0751	0952	0952	1152	1352	1552	1752	1952	2216d

Aalen - Donauwörth △

km		Ⓐ	©	Ⓐ	Ⓐ		⑥⑦§		❖			Ⓐ		Ⓐ		Ⓐ		Ⓐ		Ⓐ		Ⓐ			Ⓐ	©
0	**Aalen** ... d.	...	0531	...	0626	...	0653	...	0735	...	...	0835	0935	1035	1135	1235	1335	1435	1535	1635	1735	1835	1935	...	2035	2035
39	Nördlingen ... a.	...	0614	...	0706	...	0723	...	0814	...	...	0914	1014	1114	1219	1314	1414	1514	1614	1714	1814	1914	2014	...	2114	2114
39	Nördlingen ... d.	0525	0615	0619	0707	...	0724	...	0815	0815	...	0915	1015	1115	1220	1315	1415	1515	1615	1715	1815	1915	2015	...	2115	2115
68	**Donauwörth** ... a.	0552	0646	0652	0733	...	0749	...	0846	0846	...	0946	1046	1146	1247	1346	1446	1546	1646	1746	1846	1946	2046	...	2146	2146

	Ⓐ		Ⓐ				Ⓐ		Ⓐ		Ⓐ		Ⓐ		Ⓐ			⑥⑦§	Ⓐ				Ⓐ		
Donauwörth ... d.	...	...	0610	...	0708	...	0804	0904	1004	1104	1204	1304	1404	1504	1604	1704	...	1807	1804	...	1904	...	2004	...	2104
Nördlingen ... a.	...	...	0638	...	0740	...	0833	0933	1033	1133	1236	1333	1433	1533	1633	1733	...	1833	1833	...	1933	...	2033	...	2133
Nördlingen ... d.	0535	...	0641	...	0744	...	0844	0944	1044	1144	1244	1344	1444	1544	1644	1744	...	1836	1844	...	1944	...	2044	...	2134
Aalen ... a.	0619	...	0721	...	0826	...	0925	1025	1125	1225	1325	1425	1525	1625	1725	1825	...	1910	1925	...	2025	...	2125	...	2215

Aalen - Ulm ⊠

km		Ⓐ	⑥w	Ⓐ	Ⓐ	©	Ⓐ			Ⓐ			⊖							⊖			⊖			
0	**Aalen** ... d.	0501	0524	0554	0625	0633	0702	0733	0833	0908	0933	1033	1108	1133	1233	1333	1433	1533	1633	1708	1733	1833	1908	1936	2039	2133
23	Heidenheim ... d.	0524	0547	0617	0647	0659	0725	0756	0859	0924	0957	1059	1124	1157	1258	1357	1459	1557	1659	1724	1757	1859	1924	1958	2107	2157
73	**Ulm** Hbf ... a.	0621	0644	0709	0745	0744	0756	0844	0945	0956	1044	1145	1156	1245	1345	1445	1545	1644	1745	1756	1844	1945	1956	2041	2151	2254

	Ⓐ	Ⓐ	Ⓐ	©	Ⓐ	©	Ⓐ			⊖			⊖			⊖			⊖			⊖				
Ulm Hbf ... d.	0437	0548	0559	0614	0648	0712	0803	0812	0912	1003	1012	1112	1203	1212	1312	1403	1412	1512	1603	1612	1712	1803	1812	1912	2012	2218
Heidenheim ... d.	0527	0630	0657	0658	0759	0759	0835	0859	0959	1035	1059	1159	1235	1259	1359	1435	1459	1559	1635	1659	1759	1835	1859	1959	2058	2310
Aalen ... a.	0554	0651	0724	0721	0824	0824	0851	0924	1023	1051	1124	1223	1251	1324	1423	1451	1524	1623	1651	1724	1824	1851	1924	2024	2121	2333

a – Ⓐ only.
d – Change trains at Öhringen (a. 2136, d. *2138*).
e – Change trains at Öhringen (a. *0614*, d. 0618).
f – On Ⓐ arrive *2121* (change trains at Miltenberg).
j – On Ⓐ Miltenberg d. 0759, Wertheim d. 0835.
r – 2 minutes later on ①–⑤.

t – 2115 on ⑥.
y – 1928 on ⑥⑦.
z – ⑥ only. See Table **925** for connection on Ⓑ.
◧ – See Table **925** for *IC* connection.
❖ – ①–⑤ (daily from Oct. 16).
⊖ – ①–⑤ (daily from Oct. 12).

w – Not Oct. 3.

⊠ – 2nd class only.
§ – Until July 26. [12] Aalen - München and v.v. (see also Table **905**).
⊡ – Schwäbisch Hall-Hessental.
△ – Valid to July 26 and from Oct. 16. July 27 - Oct. 15 trains replaced by 🚌 Goldshöfe (7 km from Aalen) - Nördlingen and v.v. Full details will be shown in the August and September editions.

Deutsche Touring GmbH — ROMANTISCHE STRASSE (EUROPABUS 🚌 2009) — 927

Daily **May 2 - Oct. 19** Frankfurt → Füssen, **May 3 - Oct. 20** Füssen - Frankfurt. Reservation recommended. ✆ +49 (0)69 7903 261. Fax +49 (0)69 7003 156. www.touring.de

Frankfurt (Main) Hbf (Südseite) d. 0800 ⟶ Würzburg Hbf d. 0945 ⟶ Rothenburg ob der Tauber (Schrannenplatz) a. 1040, d. 1115 ⟶ Rothenburg ob der Tauber (Bahnhof) d. 1120 ⟶ Feuchtwangen (Marktplatz) d. 1145 ⟶ Dinkelsbühl (Schweinemarkt) a. 1205, d. 1240 ⟶ Nördlingen (Rathaus) a. 1320, d. 1335 ⟶ Augsburg Hbf d. 1435 ⟶ Augsburg (Rathaus) a. 1440, d. 1515 ⟶ **München** Hbf (Nord) d. 1625 ⟶ Oberammergau (Bahnhof) d. 1745 ⟶ Schwangau (Tourist-Info) d. 1835 ⟶ Hohenschwangau (Info Point) a. 1840 ⟶ **Füssen** (Bahnhof) a. 1900.

Füssen (Bahnhof) d. 0800 ⟶ Hohenschwangau (Info Point) d. 0820 ⟶ Schwangau (Tourist-Info) d. 0825 ⟶ Oberammergau (Bahnhof) d. 0940 ⟶ **München** Hbf (Nord) d. 1100 ⟶ Augsburg (Rathaus) a. 1205, d. 1235 ⟶ Augsburg Hbf d. 1240 ⟶ Nördlingen (Rathaus) a. 1345, d. 1400 ⟶ Dinkelsbühl (Schweinemarkt) a. 1440, d. 1510 ⟶ Feuchtwangen (Marktplatz) d. 1530 ⟶ Rothenburg ob der Tauber (Bahnhof) d. 1555 ⟶ Rothenburg ob der Tauber (Schrannenplatz) a. 1600, d. 1635 ⟶ Wüzburg Hbf a. 1730 ⟶ **Frankfurt** (Main) Hbf (Südseite) a. 1915.

20% discount available for holders of the Eurail and German Rail passes.

Operator: Deutsche Touring GmbH, Am Römerhof 17, 60486 Frankfurt (Main).

Bayerische Oberlandbahn GmbH — MÜNCHEN - BAYRISCHZELL, LENGGRIES and TEGERNSEE — 928

km																										
		Ⓐ	Ⓒ	Ⓐ				ⒸB																	⑤–⑦	
0	**München** Hbf...d.	0631	0642	0702	0742	...	0842	0902	0942	...	1042	1142	1242	...	1342	1442	1542	1642	1742	1842	1942	2042	2142	2242	2242	2342
37	Holzkirchen.......d.	0701	0709	0731	0809	...	0909	0929	1009	...	1109	1209	1309	...	1409	1509	1609	1709	1809	1909	2009	2109	2209	2309	2309	0009
61	Schliersee.........d.	0733	0737	0757	0837	...	0937	0955	1037	...	1137	1237	1337	...	1437	1537	1637	1737	1837	1937	2037	2137	2237	2333	2337	0037
78	**Bayrischzell**.....a.	0756	0800	...	0900	...	1000	...	1100	...	1200	1300	1400	...	1500	1600	1700	1800	1900	2000	2100	2200	2300	...	2400	0100

km																										
		Ⓐ	Ⓒ					ⒸB		ⒸB			Ⓒ	Ⓐ												
0	**München** Hbf...d.	0631	0642	...	0742	...	0842	0902	0942	1002	1042	1142	1242	1242	1342	1442	1542	1642	1742	1842	1942	2042	2142	2242	...	2342
37	Holzkirchen.......d.	0704	0711	...	0811	...	0911	0931	1011	1031	1111	1211	1311	1311	1411	1511	1611	1711	1811	1911	2011	2111	2211	2311	...	0011
47	Schaftlach.........d.	0719	0723	...	0823	...	0923	0948	1023	1048	1123	1223	1323	1327	1423	1523	1623	1723	1823	1923	2023	2123	2223	2323	...	0023
57	Bad Tölz...........d.	0733	0734	...	0834	...	0934	0959	1034	1059	1134	1234	1334	1338	1434	1534	1634	1734	1834	1934	2034	2134	2234	2334	...	0034
67	**Lenggries**........a.	0744	0745	...	0845	...	0945	1010	1045	1110	1145	1245	1345	1349	1445	1545	1645	1745	1845	1945	2045	2145	2245	2345	...	0045

km																										
		Ⓐ	Ⓒ							ⒸB			Ⓒ	Ⓐ												
0	**München** Hbf...d.	0631	0642	...	0742	...	0842	...	0942	1002	1042	1142	1242	1242	1342	1442	1542	1642	1742	1842	1942	2042	2142	2242	...	2342
37	Holzkirchen.......d.	0704	0711	...	0811	...	0911	...	1011	1031	1111	1211	1311	1311	1411	1511	1611	1711	1811	1911	2011	2111	2211	2311	...	0011
47	Schaftlach.........d.	0718	0724	...	0824	...	0924	...	1024	1048	1124	1224	1324	1326	1424	1524	1624	1724	1824	1924	2024	2124	2224	2324	...	0024
59	**Tegernsee**........a.	0738	0743	...	0843	...	0943	...	1043	1107	1143	1243	1343	1345	1443	1543	1643	1743	1843	1943	2043	2143	2243	2343	...	0043

	Ⓐ	Ⓐ			Ⓐ	Ⓐ	Ⓒ						Ⓐ							ⒸB				⑤–⑦		
Bayrischzell......d.	0455	...	0607	...	...	0703	0707	0807	0907	1007	1107	1207	...	1307	1407	1507	1607	...	1707	...	1807	1907	2007	2107	...	2207
Schliersee..........d.	0523	0555	0635	...	0705	0731	0735	0835	0935	1035	1135	1235	1312	1335	1435	1535	1635	...	1735	1811	1835	1935	2035	2135	2135	2235
Holzkirchen........d.	0550	0622	0702	...	0731	0802	0802	0902	1002	1102	1202	1302	1342	1402	1502	1602	1702	...	1802	1841	1902	2002	2102	2202	2202	2302
München Hbf....a.	0616	0649	0729	...	0800	0829	0829	0929	1029	1129	1229	1329	1412	1429	1529	1629	1729	...	1829	1909	1929	2029	2129	2229	2229	2329

	Ⓐ	Ⓐ	Ⓐ	Ⓒ	Ⓐ	Ⓐ	Ⓒ											ⒸB		ⒸB						
Lenggries.........d.	0511	0547	0622	0621	0653	0721	0721	0821	0921	1021	1121	1221	...	1321	1421	1521	1621	1700	1721	1800	1821	1921	2021	...	2121	2221
Bad Tölz............d.	0522	0558	0633	0634	0705	0735	0734	0834	0934	1034	1134	1234	...	1334c	1434	1534	1634	1711	1734	1811	1834	1934	2034	...	2134	2234
Schaftlach..........d.	0538	0610	0646	0650	0717	0748	0750	0850	0950	1050	1150	1250	...	1350	1450	1550	1650	1726	1750	1824	1850	1950	2050	...	2150	2250
Holzkirchen........d.	0550	0622	0702	0702	0731	0802	0802	0902	1002	1102	1202	1302	...	1402	1502	1602	1702	1741	1802	1841	1902	2002	2102	...	2202	2302
München Hbf....a.	0616	0649	0729	0729	0800	0829	0829	0929	1029	1129	1229	1329	...	1429	1529	1629	1729	1811	1829	1909	1929	2029	2129	...	2229	2329

	Ⓐ		Ⓐ	Ⓒ	Ⓐ	Ⓐ	Ⓒ						Ⓐ	Ⓒ				ⒸB								
Tegernsee........d.	0517	...	0621	0627	*0645**	0723	0727	0827	0927	1027	1127	1227	1307	1327	1427	1527	1627	1703	1727	...	1827	1927	2027	...	2127	2227
Schaftlach..........a.	0535	...	0640	0647	0717	0742	0747	0847	0947	1047	1147	1247	1325	1347	1447	1547	1647	1723	1747	...	1847	1947	2047	...	2147	2247
Holzkirchen........a.	0548	...	0656	0700	0727	0757	0800	0900	1000	1100	1200	1300	1339	1400	1500	1600	1700	1736	1800	...	1900	2000	2100	...	2200	2300
München Hbf....a.	0616	...	0729	0729	0800	0829	0829	0929	1029	1129	1229	1329	1412	1429	1529	1629	1729	1811	1829	...	1929	2029	2129	...	2229	2329

B – Until Nov. 1. **c** – 1337 on Ⓐ. * – By 🚌.

DB; ČD; 2nd class only — PLATTLING - BAYERISCH EISENSTEIN - PLZEŇ — 929

km					963						965							967						969
				Ⓐ	◇		Ⓐ	Ⓐ	⑥r		◇							◇						◇
0	**Plattling**..........d.	...	...	...	...	...	...	0520	0558	0659	...	0805	0905	...	...	1005	1105	...	1205	1305	1405	...	1505	...
9	Deggendorf Hbf.....d.	...	...	...	...	...	...	0532	0613	0709	...	0815	0915	...	...	1015	1115	...	1215	1315	1415	...	1515	...
33	Gotteszell.............d.	...	...	...	...	...	...	0554	0630	0732	...	0833	0933	...	...	1033	1133	...	1233	1333	1433	...	1533	...
48	Regen..................d.	...	...	...	...	...	...	0609	0645	0747	...	0848	0948	...	...	1048	1148	...	1248	1348	1448	...	1548	...
58	Zwiesel (Bay)........d.	...	...	...	...	...	...	0617	0658	0758	...	0858	0958	...	...	1058	1158	...	1258	1358	1458	...	1558	...
72	**Bayerisch Eisenstein** ☆ 🏛..a.	...	...	...	...	...	...	—	0711	0811	...	0911	1011	...	...	1111	1211	...	1311	1411	1511	...	1611	...
72	**Bayerisch Eisenstein** ☆ 🏛..d.	...	0410	...	...	...	0550	...	0713p	—	0842	0917	...	*1042*	...	1117j	1213h	1242	—	1413	—	1524	...	1642
76	Železná Ruda Město.....d.	...	0417	...	...	...	0557	...	0719p	...	0852	0923	...	*1052*	...	1123j	1219h	1252	...	1419	...	1533	...	1652
79	Špičák....................d.	...	0422	...	...	...	0602	...	0723p	...	0903	0927	...	*1103*	...	1127j	1223h	1303	...	1423	...	1543	...	1703
131	**Klatovy**................a.	...	0518	...	...	...	0710	...	...	...	0956	...	...	*1156*	...	...	...	1356	...	...	...	1639	...	1756
131	**Klatovy**................d.	0358	...	0527	0606	0635	...	0806	...	0846	1006	...	...	1206	1246	...	...	1406	1446	...	1606	1646	...	1806
141	Švihov u Klatov.........d.	0410	...	0538	0615	0648	...	0815	...	0858	1015	...	...	1215	1258	...	...	1415	1458	...	1615	1658	...	1815
170	**Plzeň** Hlavni..........a.	0459	...	0627	0656	0734	...	0856	...	0947	1056	...	...	1256	1347	...	...	1456	1547	...	1656	1747	...	1856
	Praha Hlavní **1120**......a.	...	...	...	0850	...	...	...	...	...	1250	...	...	...	...	...	...	1650	...	...	...	...	...	2050

Plattling..........d.	1605	1705	1805	...	1905	2005	2103	2223	2308
Deggendorf Hbf.....d.	1615	1715	1815	...	1915	2015	2113	2235	2318
Gotteszell.............d.	1633	1733	1833	...	1933	2033	2130	2253	2336
Regen..................d.	1648	1748	1848	...	1948	2048	2145	2308	2351
Zwiesel (Bay)........d.	1658	1758	1858	...	1958	2058	2153	2317	2359
Bayerisch Eisenstein ☆ 🏛...a.	1711	1811	1911	...	2011	2111	...	...	...
Bayerisch Eisenstein ☆ 🏛...d.	—	1813j	...	1930	—	...	...	...	...
Železná Ruda Město.....d.	...	1819j	...	1938	...	...	...	...	...
Špičák....................d.	...	1823j	...	1944	...	...	...	...	...
Klatovy................a.	◇	...	...	2041	...	...	...	...	...
Klatovy................d.	1846	...	...	...	2046	...	...	...	...
Švihov u Klatov.........d.	1858	...	...	...	2058	...	...	...	...
Plzeň Hlavni..........a.	1947	...	...	...	2147	...	...	...	...
Praha Hlavní **1120**......a.	...	...	...	...	...	...	...	...	...

	⚒r		Ⓐ	Ⓒ					k	
Praha Hlavní **1120**......d.	...	...	...	...	...	...	...	...	...	...
Plzeň Hlavni..........d.	...	...	...	...	...	...	0520	...	0702	...
Švihov u Klatov.........d.	...	...	...	...	...	...	0615	...	0743	...
Klatovy................a.	...	...	...	...	...	...	0627	...	0752	...
Klatovy................d.	...	...	...	...	0431	...	0651	...	0802	...
Špičák....................d.	...	...	...	...	0527	0730h	0748	...	0902	0932
Železná Ruda Město.....d.	...	...	...	...	0533	0734h	0753	...	0909	0936
Bayerisch Eisenstein ☆ 🏛.a.	...	...	...	...	0538	0740h	0800	...	0915	0942
Bayerisch Eisenstein ☆ 🏛.d.	...	...	...	...	...	0742	...	0842	...	0943
Zwiesel (Bay)........d.	0418	0529	0621	0655	...	0757	...	0857	...	0957
Regen..................d.	0427	0538	0630	0705	...	0806	...	0906	...	1006
Gotteszell.............d.	0442	0555	0645	0720	...	0820	...	0920	...	1020
Deggendorf Hbf.....d.	0500	0612	0710	0738	...	0844	...	0942	...	1042
Plattling..........a.	0510	0623	0720	0748	...	0854	...	0952	...	1052

			960						962							964							966	
			◇						◇		Ⓐ					◇							◇	
Praha Hlavní **1120**......d.	...	...	0711	...	...	...	...	...	1111	...	...	...	...	...	...	1511	...	...	...	...	...	...	1911	...
Plzeň Hlavni..........d.	0810	...	0902	...	...	*1102*	...	...	1302	...	*1410*	...	*1502*	...	...	1702	...	...	...	1810	*1910*	...	2102	2251
Švihov u Klatov.........d.	0859	...	0943	...	...	*1143*	...	...	1343	...	*1459*	...	*1546*	...	...	1743	...	...	...	1859	*1959*	...	2143	2339
Klatovy................a.	0911	...	0952	...	...	*1152*	...	...	1352	...	*1511*	...	*1555*	...	...	1752	...	...	...	1911	*2011*	...	2152	2351
Klatovy................d.	0919	...	1002	...	...	1202	...	...	1402	...	1515	...	1602	...	...	...	1802	...	...	...	2022	...	...	...
Špičák....................d.	1018	...	1102	1132j	1230h	1302	...	1430	1502	...	1610	...	1702	...	1830j	...	1902	...	...	...	2115	...	...	...
Železná Ruda Město.....d.	1025	...	1109	1136j	1234h	1309	...	1434	1509	...	1616	...	1709	...	1834j	...	1909	...	...	...	2120	...	...	...
Bayerisch Eisenstein ☆ 🏛...a.	1031	...	1115	1142j	1240h	1315	...	1440	1515	...	1622	...	1715	...	1840j	...	1915	...	...	...	2126	...	...	...
Bayerisch Eisenstein ☆ 🏛...d.	...	1042	...	1143	1242	...	1342	1442	...	1542	...	1642	...	1742	1842	...	...	1942	2042	...	...	2140	...	...
Zwiesel (Bay)........d.	...	1057	...	1157	1257	...	1357	1457	...	1557	...	1657	...	1757	1857	...	...	1957	2057	...	...	2154	...	...
Regen..................d.	...	1106	...	1206	1306	...	1406	1506	...	1606	...	1706	...	1806	1906	...	...	2006	2106	...	...	2203	...	...
Gotteszell.............d.	...	1120	...	1220	1320	...	1420	1520	...	1620	...	1720	...	1820	1920	...	...	2020	2132	...	...	2218	...	...
Deggendorf Hbf.....d.	...	1142	...	1242	1342	...	1442	1542	...	1642	...	1742	...	1842	1942	...	...	2042	2149	...	...	2235	...	...
Plattling..........a.	...	1152	...	1252	1352	...	1452	1552	...	1652	...	1752	...	1852	1952	...	...	2052	2159	...	...	2243	...	...

h – ⑥⑦ June 27 - Sept. 13.
j – June 22 - Sept. 13.
k – Change trains at Klatovy on Ⓐ.
p – ⑥ June 27 - Sept. 12 (not Aug. 15).
r – Not Aug. 15, Oct. 3.
☆ – Železná Ruda-Alžbětín in Czech.
◇ – Also conveys 🚃 Praha - Klatovy and v.v.

930 MANNHEIM - STUTTGART - MÜNCHEN

km		IC	IC	IC	IC	CNL	IC	IC	IC	RE	IC	IC	RE	ICE	ICE	IRE	IRE	ICE	ICE	EC	IRE	ICE	IC	IC	EC
		1591	**1591**	**997**	**995**	**419**	**60419**	**2095**	**2095**	**4161**	**2291**	**2291**	**37107**	**699**	**699**	**4219**	**4221**	**991**	**181**	**317**	**4223**	**511**	**2395**	**2053**	**361**
		②–⑤	①	⑥	⑦	[R]		①	①–⑤		①–⑤	①–⑥		⑦		①–⑤	⑥⑦	①–⑥					①–⑤	①–⑤	
				🍷	🍷	🍷♦					🍷	🍷		✕	✕	F	L	✕♦	✕♦	✕♦	L	🍷		A🍷	🍷♦
	Dortmund Hbf **800** d.	...	...	...	...	...	...	...	...	...	...	...	...	...	...	...	...	...	...	...	...	...	...	...	...
	Köln Hbf **800 910** d.	...	...	...	...	2346	...	...	...	...	...	...	...	...	...	...	...	...	...	...	...	0554	...	...	...
	Koblenz Hbf **912** d.	...	...	...	...	0044	...	...	...	...	...	...	...	...	...	...	...	...	...	...	...	|	...	...	...
	Frankfurt (Main) Hbf **911/2** d.	0007	0007	0018	0018	|	...	...	...	...	...	...	...	...	...	...	...	*0538*	0557	...	...	|	0642	...	...
	Frankfurt Flughafen ✈ **912** d.	0028	0028	0039	0042	|	...	...	...	...	...	...	...	...	...	...	...	*0555*	|	...	...	0654	|	...	...
0	**Mannheim** Hbf d.	0106	0106j	0112	0114j	|	...	...	...	...	...	...	...	...	...	...	...	0630	|	0712	...	0733	|	0754	...
	Heidelberg Hbf **931** d.	0119	0119	0125	0127	|	...	...	...	...	...	...	...	...	...	...	...	|	0657	|	...	|	0742	0806	...
	Karlsruhe Hbf **931** d.	|	|	|	|	|	...	...	...	...	0457	...	...	0607	...	...	...	|	|	|	...	|	|	|	0806
78	Vaihingen (Enz) **931** d.	0208	0208	0216	0219	|	...	...	...	...	0533	...	...	|	...	...	...	|	|	|	...	|	|	|	|
107	**Stuttgart** Hbf **931** a.	0236	0236	0249	0252	0419n	...	...	...	...	0549	...	...	0648	...	...	...	0708	0735	0754	...	0808	0833	0846	0849
107	**Stuttgart** Hbf **936** ★ d.	...	0241	0254	0257	|	0437n	0503	...	...	0553	0553	...	0656	0656	0659	0702	0712	...	0758	0802	0812	▬	...	0853
129	Plochingen **936** ★ d.	...	|	|	|	0451s	0453	0518	...	...	0609	0609	...	|	|	0713	0716	|	...	|	0816	|	*RE*	...	0909
149	Göppingen ★ d.	...	|	|	|	0504s	0506	0531	...	...	0621	0621	...	|	|	0725	0727	|	...	|	0827	|	**37109**	...	0921
168	Geislingen (Steige) ★ d.	...	|	|	|	0519s	0520	0544	...	...	|	|	...	|	|	0736	0738	|	...	|	0840	|		...	|
201	**Ulm** Hbf **945** ★ d.	...	0337	0351	0354	0542s	0544	0609	0609	0621	0655	0655	0724	0755	0755	0758	0759	0808	...	0855	0902	0908	0924	...	0955
225	Günzburg **945** d.	...	0355	0410	0413	0559s	0601	0627	0627	0642	0711	0711	0742	|	|	...	...	|	...	0910	...	|	0942	...	|
287	**Augsburg** Hbf **904 905** d.	...	0426	0441	0444	0633s	0636	0659	0659	0739	0741	0741	0839	0839	0839	...	...	0852	...	0941	...	0953	1039	...	1038
342	München Pasing **904 905** a.	...	0508	0512	0515	|	|	0728	0728	0816	0810	0810	0914	0908	0908	...	...	0920	...	|	...	1020	1114	...	1107
349	**München** Hbf **904 905** a.	...	0519	0521	0524	0716	0716	0738	0738	0824	0819	0819	0922	0917	0917	...	...	0930	...	1016	...	1031	1122	...	1116
	Salzburg Hbf **890** 🚌 a.	...	...	...	...	...	...	...	...	...	...	...	...	...	...	...	...	...	...	1204	...	...	...	...	...

	ICE	ICE	EC	IRE	ICE	IC	ICE	IC	ICE	IC	IC	EC	IRE	ICE	RE	ICE	IC	IC	ICE	EC	IRE	IC	ICE	RE	ICE
	591	**711**	**113**	**4225**	**513**	**2319**	**571**	**2093**	**1091**	**2275**	**2293**	**115**	**4227**	**515**	**37115**	**973**	**2261**	**119**	**595**	**319**	**4229**	**2015**	**517**	**37117**	**575**
		①–⑤				①–⑥	①–⑥	⑤	§	①–⑤												①–④			
	✕♦		✕♦	L	M🍷		H✕		B✕	♦	🍷	✕♦	L	G🍷		✕♦	🍷	🍷♦	B✕	✕♦	L	🍷♦	🍷		H✕
Dortmund Hbf **800** d.	...	0502	...	...	0638	0538	...	...	...	...	...	...	...	0837	...	...	...	...	...	...	...	...	1038	...	...
Köln Hbf **800 910** d.	...	0615d	...	...	0754	0653	...	...	...	...	...	0818	...	0954	...	...	...	0918	...	...	...	1018	1154	...	...
Koblenz Hbf **912** d.	...	|	...	...	|	0748	...	...	...	...	...	0917	...	|	...	...	...	1017	...	...	...	1117	|	...	...
Frankfurt (Main) Hbf **911/2** d.	0750	|	0820	...	|	|	0905	...	0950	0938	1020	|	...	|	...	1105	...	|	1150	1220	...	|	|	...	1305
Frankfurt Flughafen ✈ **912** d.	|	|	|	...	0854	|	0920	...	|	|	|	|	...	1054	...	1120	...	|	|	|	...	|	1254	...	1320
Mannheim Hbf d.	0831	0826	|	...	0933	0923	0955	...	1031	|	|	1103	...	1133	...	1155	...	1154	1231	|	...	1312	1333	...	1355
Heidelberg Hbf **931** d.	|	0838	0914	...	|	0936	|	...	|	1032	1110	|	...	|	...	|	...	1206	|	1314	...	|	|	...	|
Karlsruhe Hbf **931** d.	|	|	|	...	|	|	|	...	|	|	|	|	...	|	...	|	1206	|	|	|	...	|	|	...	|
Vaihingen (Enz) **931** d.	|	0905	|	...	|	|	|	...	|	1105	|	|	...	|	...	|	|	|	|	|	...	|	|	...	|
Stuttgart Hbf **931** a.	0908	0923	0953	...	1008	1018	1033	...	1108	1123	1150	1153	...	1208	...	1233	1249	1246	1308	1353	...	1358	1408	...	1433
Stuttgart Hbf **936** ★ d.	0912	...	0958	1002	1012	▬	...	1053	1112	...	...	1158	1202	1212	...	...	1253	1257	1312	1358	1402	...	1412	...	...
Plochingen **936** ★ d.	|	...	|	1016	|	*RE*	...	1109	|	...	...	|	1216	|	...	...	1309	|	|	|	1416	...	|	...	...
Göppingen ★ d.	|	...	|	1027	|	**37111**	...	1121	|	...	...	|	1227	|	...	...	1321	1327	|	|	1427	...	|	...	...
Geislingen (Steige) ★ d.	|	...	|	1040	|		...	|	|	...	...	|	1240	|	...	...	|	1340	|	|	1440	...	|	...	...
Ulm Hbf **945** ★ d.	1008	...	1055	1102	1108	1124	...	1155	1208	...	...	1255	1302	1308	1324	...	1355	1401	1408	1455	1502	...	1508	1524	...
Günzburg **945** d.	|	...	1110	...	|	1142	...	|	|	...	...	1310	...	|	1342	...	|	...	|	1510	...	...	|	1542	...
Augsburg Hbf **904 905** d.	1052	...	1141	...	1152	1239	...	1238	1252	...	...	1341	...	1352	1439	...	1438	...	1452	1541	...	...	1552	1639	...
München Pasing **904 905** a.	1120	...	|	...	1221	1314	...	1307	1320	...	...	|	...	1420	1514	...	1507	...	1520	|	...	...	1622	1714	...
München Hbf **904 905** a.	1130	...	1216	...	1230	1322	...	1316	1330	...	...	1416	...	1430	1522	...	1516	...	1530	1616	...	...	1631	1722	...
Salzburg Hbf **890** 🚌 a.	...	...	1404	...	...	...	...	...	...	...	...	1604	...	...	...	...	...	...	...	1804	...	...	...	...	...

	IC	ICE	IC	IC	EC	IRE	ICE	RE	IC	ICE	IC	IC	IRE	ICE	EC	IRE	ICE	IC	ICE	IC	IC	IC	IC	IC	ICE
	2013	**597**	**2055**	**2299**	**117**	**4231**	**519**	**37121**	**2113**	**577**	**1911**	**2265**	**4233**	**599**	**391**	**4235**	**611**	**2115**	**579**	**1119**	**1913**	**1913**	**2267**	**1913**	**691**
			⑤⑦	⑥	Ⓑ						⑤⑦		①–⑤							①–④	⑦	⑤		⑤	
	🍷♦	B✕	🍷A		✕♦	L	🍷		G✕	H✕	¶	🍷	L	B✕	Z🍷	L	🍷	✕♦	H✕	◐	B	R🍷	🍷	R🍷	B✕
Dortmund Hbf **800** d.	0952	...	...	...	...	...	1238	...	1138	...	1152	...	...	...	...	...	1438	1338	...	...	1352	1352	...	...	...
Köln Hbf **800 910** d.	1118	...	...	...	...	...	1354	...	1253	...	1318	...	...	...	...	...	1554	1453	...	1518	1518	1518	...	...	...
Koblenz Hbf **912** d.	1217	...	...	...	...	...	|	...	1348	...	1417	...	...	...	...	...	|	1548	...	1617	1617	1617	...	...	...
Frankfurt (Main) Hbf **911/2** d.	|	1350	...	1420	1420	...	|	...	|	1505	|	...	...	1550	1620	...	|	|	1705	|	|	|	...	...	1750
Frankfurt Flughafen ✈ **912** d.	|	|	...	|	|	...	1454	...	|	1520	|	...	...	|	|	...	1654	|	1720	|	|	|	...	...	|
Mannheim Hbf d.	1354	1431	1424	|	|	...	1533	...	1523	1555	1554	...	...	1631	|	...	1733	1723	1755	1754	1754	1754	...	...	1831
Heidelberg Hbf **931** d.	1406	|	1437	1514	1514	...	|	...	1536	|	1606	...	...	|	1714	...	|	1736	|	1806	1806	1806	...	...	|
Karlsruhe Hbf **931** d.	|	|	|	|	|	...	|	...	|	|	|	1606	...	|	|	...	|	|	|	|	|	|	1806	...	|
Vaihingen (Enz) **931** d.	|	|	1505	|	|	...	|	...	1605	|	|	|	...	|	|	...	|	1808	|	|	|	|	|	...	|
Stuttgart Hbf **931** a.	1446	1508	1523	1553	1553	...	1608	...	1622	1632	1646	1649	...	1708	1753	...	1808	1825	1833	1846	1846	1846	1849	←	1908
Stuttgart Hbf **936** ★ d.	1454	1512	...	...	1558	1602	1612	...	...	...	...	1653	1702	1712	1758	1802	1812	▬	...	...	...	→	1853	1858	1912
Plochingen **936** ★ d.	1509	|	...	...	|	1616	|	...	...	...	...	1709	1716	|	|	1816	|	*RE*	...	...	...	...	1909	1915	|
Göppingen ★ d.	1524	|	...	...	|	1627	|	...	...	...	...	1721	1727	|	|	1827	|	**37123**	...	...	...	...	1921	|	|
Geislingen (Steige) ★ d.	|	|	...	...	|	1640	|	...	...	...	...	|	1740	|	|	1840	|		...	...	...	...	|	1938	|
Ulm Hbf **945** ★ d.	1601	1608	...	...	1655	1702	1708	1724	...	...	...	1755	1802	1808	1855	1902	1908	1924	...	...	...	...	1955	2002	2008
Günzburg **945** d.	...	|	...	...	1710	...	|	1742	...	...	...	|	...	|	1910	...	|	1942	...	...	...	...	|	|	|
Augsburg Hbf **904 905** d.	...	1652	...	...	1741	...	1752	1839	...	...	...	1838	...	1852	1941	...	1952	2039	...	...	...	...	2038	2045	2052
München Pasing **904 905** a.	...	1720	...	...	|	...	1820	1914	...	...	...	1907	...	1920	|	...	2020	2118	...	...	...	...	2106	2112	2123
München Hbf **904 905** a.	...	1730	...	...	1815	...	1830	1922	...	...	...	1916	...	1930	2016	...	2030	2127	...	...	...	...	2116	2123	2133
Salzburg Hbf **890** 🚌 a.	...	...	...	...	2004	...	...	...	...	...	...	2107q	...	...	2209	...	...	...	...	...	...	...	...	...	...

	TGV	IC	IRE	ICE	IC	ICE	IC	IC	IC	ICE	RE	RB	IC	IC	ICE	IC	RB	ICE	EN	EN	ICE	RB	IC	ICE	ICE
	9575	**2295**	**4237**	**613**	**2311**	**771**	**1915**	**2269**	**2269**	**693**	**4185**	**19363**	**1858**	**2297**	**615**	**2213**	**19365**	**773**	**409**	**469**	**1093**	**19367**	**1897**	**617**	**775**
		Ⓑ					⑤⑦	♣	⑦				⑦		m				[R]	[R]	⊖		⑦		⑦
	🍷♦	🍷	F	🍷	✕♦	H✕	B		🍷	B✕			T🍷	⊙	🍷	✕♦		H✕	🍷♦	🍷♦	B✕		B🍷	🍷	✕H
Dortmund Hbf **800** d.	...	...	...	1638	1538	...	1552	...	...	...	...	...	...	...	1838	1738	...	...	...	...	...	...	...	2038	...
Köln Hbf **800 910** d.	...	...	...	1754	1653	...	1718	...	...	...	...	...	...	...	1958	1853	...	...	...	...	...	...	...	2154	...
Koblenz Hbf **912** d.	...	...	...	|	|	...	1817	...	...	...	...	...	...	...	|	1948	...	...	...	...	...	...	...	|	...
Frankfurt (Main) Hbf **911/2** d.	...	1820	...	|	|	1905	|	...	...	1950	...	...	1955	2020	|	|	...	2105	2000	...	2150	...	2158	|	2310
Frankfurt Flughafen ✈ **912** d.	...	|	...	1854	|	1920	|	...	...	|	...	...	|	|	2059	|	...	2120	|	...	|	...	|	2306	|
Mannheim Hbf d.	...	|	...	1933	1923	1955	1954r	...	...	2031	...	...	|	|	2133	2123	...	2157	2057	...	2231	...	|	2346	|
Heidelberg Hbf **931** d.	...	1914	...	|	1936	|	2006	...	...	|	...	...	2052	2114	|	2136	...	2210	|	...	|	...	2251	2359	0004
Karlsruhe Hbf **931** d.	1827	|	...	|	|	|	|	2006	2006	|	...	...	|	|	|	|	...	|	2156	2156	|	...	|	|	|
Vaihingen (Enz) **931** d.	|	|	...	|	2005	|	|	|	|	|	...	...	2128	|	|	2205	...	|	|	|	|	...	2323	|	|
Stuttgart Hbf **931** a.	1903	1953	...	2008	2022	2033	2046	2049	2049	2108	...	...	2146	2154	2208	2222	...	2248	2257	2257	2308	...	2339	0052k	0044
Stuttgart Hbf **936** ★ d.	1918	1958	2002	2012	▬	...	...	2053	2053	2112	...	2132	...	...	2212	...	2232	...	2307	2307	...	2332	...	...	...
Plochingen **936** ★ d.	|	|	2016	|	*RE*	...	...	2108	2108	|	...	2151	...	...	|	...	2253	...	|	|	...	2353	...	...	...
Göppingen ★ d.	|	|	2027	|	**37127**	...	...	2120	2120	|	...	2210	...	...	|	...	2313	...	|	|	...	0013	...	...	...
Geislingen (Steige) ★ d.	|	|	2040	|		...	...	2133	2133	|	...	2232	...	...	|	...	2339	...	|	|	...	0039	...	...	...
Ulm Hbf **945** ★ d.	2016	2055	2102	2108	2124	...	...	2154	2156	2208	2224	2302	...	...	2308	...	0005	...	0011	0011	...	0105	...	...	...
Günzburg **945** d.	|	2110	...	|	2142	...	...	...	2213	|	2242	...	...	...	|	...	...	...	|	|	...	...	...	...	...
Augsburg Hbf **904 905** d.	2101	2141	...	2152	2239	...	...	...	2243	2252	2339	...	...	...	2356	...	...	...	|	|	...	...	...	...	...
München Pasing **904 905** a.	|	2211	...	2223	2316	...	...	...	2310	2320	0019	...	...	...	0024	...	...	...	|	|	...	...	...	...	...
München Hbf **904 905** a.	2138	2220	...	2232	2325	...	...	...	2321	2330	0026	...	...	...	0034	...	...	...	|	|	...	...	...	...	...
Salzburg Hbf **890** 🚌 a.	...	...	...	...	...	...	...	...	...	...	...	...	...	...	...	...	...	...	0313	0313	...	...	...	...	...

♦ – **NOTES** (LISTED BY TRAIN NUMBER) for pages 436 and 437

112/3 – [12] and ✕ Klagenfurt - Villach - Salzburg - München - Frankfurt and v.v.; [12] Zagreb (**212/3**) - Ljubljana - Villach - Frankfurt and v.v.

114 – WÖRTHERSEE – [12] and ✕ Klagenfurt - Villach - Köln - Dortmund.

115 – WÖRTHERSEE – [12] and ✕ Münster - Köln - Villach - Klagenfurt.

117 – [12] and ✕ Frankfurt - München - Salzburg - Villach - Klagenfurt.

118/9 – [12] and 🍷 Innsbruck - Bregenz - Lindau - Ulm - Münster and v.v.

181 – [12] and ✕ Frankfurt - Stuttgart - Singen - Schaffhausen - Zürich.

316/7 – [12] and ✕ Graz - Bischofshofen - Salzburg - Saarbrücken and v.v.

318/9 – [12] and ✕ Graz - Bischofshofen - Salzburg - Frankfurt and v.v.

360/1 – [12] and 🍷 München - Strasbourg and v.v.

408 – 🛏 1, 2 cl., ▬ 2 cl., [2] and 🍷 Budapest (**460**) - Wien (**468**) - Karlsruhe (**408**) - Frankfurt.

409 – 🛏 1, 2 cl., ▬ 2 cl., [2] and 🍷 Frankfurt - Karlsruhe (**469**) - Wien (**461**) - Budapest.

418 – Daily until Nov. 1; ④–⑦ from Nov. 5. POLLUX – 🛏 1, 2 cl., ▬ 2 cl., [2] and 🍷 München - Amsterdam; conveys 🛏 1, 2 cl., ▬ 2 cl., [2] (*CNL* **40418** – CASSIOPEIA) München - Paris (Table **32**).

419 – Daily until Nov. 2; ①⑤⑥⑦ from Nov. 6. POLLUX – 🛏 1, 2 cl., ▬ 2 cl., [2] and 🍷 Amsterdam - München; conveys 🛏 1, 2 cl., ▬ 2 cl., [2] (*CNL* **40451** – CASSIOPEIA) Paris - München (Table **32**).

468/9 – ORIENT EXPRESS – 🛏 1, 2 cl., ▬ 2 cl., [2] and 🍷 Wien - Strasbourg and v.v.

MÜNCHEN - STUTTGART - MANNHEIM 930

km		ICE 826 ① E	ICE 826 X🍷	ICE 774 ①–⑥ H✕	RB 19300	ICE 616 🍷	IC 2296 ①–⑥ ✕	IC 1114 ①–⑥ J	RB 19304	EN 468 🄁 🍷♦	EN 408 🄁 🍷♦	ICE 694 B✕	IC 2268 ① 🍷
	Salzburg Hbf **890** 🚌 d.	...	...	...	...	...	...	...	...	0210	0210	...	...
	München Hbf **904 905** d.	0032	...	...	...	0317x	...	...	...	|	|	...	0425
	München Pasing **904 905** d.	0040	...	...	...	0325x	...	...	...	|	|	...	0433
	Augsburg Hbf **904 905** d.	0112	...	...	...	0357	...	...	...	|	|	...	0511
	Günzburg **945** d.	0144	...	...	...	|	...	...	...	|	|	...	0544
	Ulm Hbf **945** ★ d.	0202	...	...	0411	0440	...	...	0449	0519	0519	...	0602
	Geislingen (Steige) ★ d.	|	...	...	0436	|	...	...	0522	|	|	...	0625
	Göppingen ★ d.	|	...	...	0458	|	...	...	0547	|	|	...	0639
	Plochingen **936** ★ d.	|	...	...	0518	|	...	...	0607	|	|	...	0651
	Stuttgart Hbf **936** ★ a.	0300	...	...	0538	0537	...	...	0626	0630	0630	...	0707
0	**Stuttgart** Hbf **931** d.	0305	0305	0509	...	0551	0603	0630	...	0638	0638	0651	0711
29	Vaihingen (Enz) **931** d.	0336	0336	|	...	|	0620	0647	...	|	|	|	|
	Karlsruhe Hbf **931** a.	|	|	|	...	|	|	|	...	0749	0749	|	0753
92	**Heidelberg** Hbf **931** a.	0426	0426	0545	...	|	0647	0718	...	...	|	|	...
	Mannheim Hbf a.	0438	0438	0559	...	0626	|	0731	...	...	0848	0728	...
	Frankfurt Flughafen ✈ **912** a.	0512	0512	0638	...	0706	|	...	...	...	|	|	...
	Frankfurt (Main) Hbf **911/2** a.	0535	0535	0652	...	|	0800	...	...	...	0957	0808	...
	Koblenz Hbf **912** a.	|	|	...	...	|	...	...	...	...	...	...	...
	Köln Hbf **800 910** a.	0714d	0714d	...	...	0805	...	...	...	...	...	...	...
	Dortmund Hbf **800** a.	...	0827c	...	...	0921	...	...	...	...	...	...	...

	IC 2268 ①–⑤ 🍷	IC 1118 ①–④ △	IC 1112 ⑤ B🍷	ICE 772 H✕	IC 2116 ✕♦	ICE 614 🍷	IRE 4220 4222 F	IC 2294 ①–⑥ 🍷	RE 4160	TGV 9576 🍷♦	ICE 692 B✕	IC 2266 ①–⑥ 🍷
Salzburg Hbf **890** 🚌 d.	...	...	...	...	...	...	...	...	...	...	...	...
München Hbf **904 905** d.	...	...	...	...	...	0523	...	0516	0537	0620	0628	0641
München Pasing **904 905** d.	...	...	...	...	...	0531	...	0524	0543	|	0636	0649
Augsburg Hbf **904 905** d.	...	...	...	...	...	0604	...	0556	0625	0657	0708	0721
Günzburg **945** d.	...	...	...	...	...	|	...	0629	0716	|	|	|
Ulm Hbf **945** ★ d.	0602	...	...	...	...	0651	0654	0700	0735	0742	0751	0805
Geislingen (Steige) ★ d.	0625	...	...	...	...	|	0717	0722	...	|	|	|
Göppingen ★ d.	0639	...	...	...	...	|	0728	|	...	|	|	0839
Plochingen **936** ★ d.	0651	...	...	...	...	|	0739z	0746	...	|	|	0851
Stuttgart Hbf **936** ★ a.	0707	...	...	...	...	0747	0756	0800	...	0842	0847	0907
Stuttgart Hbf **931** d.	0711	0714	0714	0727	0737	0751	...	0805	...	0854	0851	0911
Vaihingen (Enz) **931** d.	|	|	|	|	0755	|	...	|	...	|	|	|
Karlsruhe Hbf **931** a.	0753	|	|	|	|	|	...	|	...	0929	|	0953
Heidelberg Hbf **931** a.	...	0753	0753	|	0823	|	...	0845	...	...	|	...
Mannheim Hbf a.	...	0806	0806	0804	0837	0826	...	|	...	...	0928	...
Frankfurt Flughafen ✈ **912** a.	...	|	|	0838	|	0906	...	|	...	...	|	...
Frankfurt (Main) Hbf **911/2** a.	...	|	|	0853	|	|	...	0940	...	...	1008	...
Koblenz Hbf **912** a.	...	0941b	0941b	...	1010	|	...	...	...	...	...	...
Köln Hbf **800 910** a.	...	1042	1042	...	1105	1005	...	...	...	...	...	...
Dortmund Hbf **800** a.	...	...	1208	...	1221	1121	...	...	...	...	...	...

	ICE 770 H✕	IC 2114 G✕	RE 37106	ICE 612 🍷	IRE 4224 L	IC 2290 ①–⑥ 🍷	IC 2290 ⑦	ICE 690 B✕	IC 2264 ♥ 🍷	IC 1916 ⑤ B🍷	ICE 578 H✕	IC 2112 G✕
Salzburg Hbf **890** 🚌 d.	...	...	...	...	...	0547	...	...	0646v	0646	...	...
München Hbf **904 905** d.	...	...	0636	0723	...	0739	...	0824	0841	0841	...	...
München Pasing **904 905** d.	...	...	0643	0731	...	|	...	0832	0850	0850	...	...
Augsburg Hbf **904 905** d.	...	...	0725	0803	...	0816	...	0903	0921	0921	...	...
Günzburg **945** d.	...	...	0822	|	...	0849	...	|	|	|	...	...
Ulm Hbf **945** ★ d.	...	...	0841	0851	0854	0905	...	0951	1005	1005	...	...
Geislingen (Steige) ★ d.	...	...	...	|	0917	|	...	|	|	|	...	...
Göppingen ★ d.	...	...	...	|	0928	|	...	|	1039	1039	...	...
Plochingen **936** ★ d.	...	...	...	|	0939	|	...	|	1051	1051	...	...
Stuttgart Hbf **936** ★ a.	...	...	...	0947	0956	1000	...	1047	1107	1107	...	...
Stuttgart Hbf **931** d.	0927	0937	...	0951	...	1005	1005	1051	1111	1114	1127	1137
Vaihingen (Enz) **931** d.	|	0955	...	|	...	|	|	|	|	|	|	1155
Karlsruhe Hbf **931** a.	|	|	...	|	...	|	|	|	1153	|	|	|
Heidelberg Hbf **931** a.	|	1023	...	|	...	1045	1045	|	...	1153	|	1223
Mannheim Hbf a.	1004	1037	...	1026	...	|	|	1128	...	1206	1204	1237
Frankfurt Flughafen ✈ **912** a.	1038	|	...	1106	...	|	|	|	...	|	1238	|
Frankfurt (Main) Hbf **911/2** a.	1053	|	...	|	...	1140	1146	1208	...	|	1253	|
Koblenz Hbf **912** a.	...	1210	...	|	...	...	...	...	...	1341b	...	1410
Köln Hbf **800 910** a.	...	1305	...	1205	...	...	...	...	...	1443	...	1505
Dortmund Hbf **800** a.	...	1421	...	1321	...	...	...	...	...	1605	...	1621

	RE 37110	ICE 610 🍷	IRE 4226 L	EC 390 Y🍷	IC 2014 ①–⑤ 🍷♦	ICE 598 ‡ B✕	IC 2012 🍷♦	ICE 576 H✕	RE 37112	ICE 518 🍷	IRE 4228 L	EC 318 ✕♦	ICE 712 ①–⑤ 🍷
Salzburg Hbf **890** 🚌 d.	...	...	...	0753e	...	...	...	...	...	...	...	0957	...
München Hbf **904 905** d.	0834	0923	...	0940	...	1023	...	...	1033	1123	...	1143	...
München Pasing **904 905** d.	0840	0931	...	|	...	1031	...	...	1040	1131	...	|	...
Augsburg Hbf **904 905** d.	0925	1003	...	1017	...	1103	...	...	1125	1203	...	1218	...
Günzburg **945** d.	1016	|	...	1049	...	|	...	...	1216	|	...	1249	...
Ulm Hbf **945** ★ d.	1035	1051	1054	1105	...	1151	1157	...	1235	1251	1254	1305	...
Geislingen (Steige) ★ d.	...	|	1117	|	...	|	|	...	...	|	1317	|	...
Göppingen ★ d.	...	|	1128	|	...	|	1235	...	...	|	1329	|	...
Plochingen **936** ★ d.	...	|	1139	|	...	|	1249	...	...	|	1339	|	...
Stuttgart Hbf **936** ★ a.	...	1147	1156	1200	...	1247	1305	...	...	1347	1356	1400	...
Stuttgart Hbf **931** d.	...	1151	...	1205	1209	1251	1314	1327	...	1351	...	1405	1434
Vaihingen (Enz) **931** d.	...	|	...	|	1226r	|	|	|	...	|	...	|	1453
Karlsruhe Hbf **931** a.	...	|	...	|	|	|	|	|	...	|	...	|	|
Heidelberg Hbf **931** a.	...	|	...	1245	|	|	1353	|	...	|	...	1445	1518
Mannheim Hbf a.	...	1226	...	|	1256t	1328	1406	1404	...	1426	...	|	1531
Frankfurt Flughafen ✈ **912** a.	...	1306	...	|	|	|	|	1438	...	1506	...	|	|
Frankfurt (Main) Hbf **911/2** a.	...	|	...	1340	|	1408	|	1453	...	|	...	1540	|
Koblenz Hbf **912** a.	...	|	...	...	1441	...	1541	...	...	|	...	...	|
Köln Hbf **800 910** a.	...	1405	...	...	1542	...	1642	...	...	1605	...	...	1801
Dortmund Hbf **800** a.	...	1521	...	...	...	...	1805	...	...	1721	...	...	...

	ICE 596 B✕	IC 118 🍷♦	IC 2260 🍷	ICE 974 ✕♦	RE 37114	ICE 516 🍷	IRE 4230 L	EC 114 ✕♦	IC 2292 🍷	IC 2316 Ⓑ W	ICE 1090 ◧ B✕	IRE 4232 ①–⑤ L
Salzburg Hbf **890** 🚌 d.	...	...	...	...	...	...	...	1152	...	...	...	...
München Hbf **904 905** d.	1223	...	1241	...	1234	1323	...	1340	...	...	1423	...
München Pasing **904 905** d.	1231	...	1249	...	1240	1331	...	|	...	...	1431	...
Augsburg Hbf **904 905** d.	1303	...	1321	...	1325	1403	...	1417	...	...	1503	...
Günzburg **945** d.	|	...	|	...	1416	|	...	1449	...	...	|	...
Ulm Hbf **945** ★ d.	1351	1356	1405	...	1435	1451	1454	1505	...	...	1551	1554
Geislingen (Steige) ★ d.	|	1420	|	...	...	|	1517	|	...	...	|	1618
Göppingen ★ d.	|	1433	|	...	...	|	1528	|	...	...	|	1630
Plochingen **936** ★ d.	|	|	1449	...	...	|	1539	|	...	...	|	1641
Stuttgart Hbf **936** ★ a.	1447	1458	1503	...	...	1547	1556	1559	...	...	1647	1656
Stuttgart Hbf **931** d.	1451	1512	1508	1527	...	1551	...	1610f	1606	1636	1651	...
Vaihingen (Enz) **931** d.	|	|	|	|	...	|	...	|	|	|	|	...
Karlsruhe Hbf **931** a.	|	|	1550	|	...	|	...	|	|	|	|	...
Heidelberg Hbf **931** a.	|	1553	...	|	...	|	...	|	1645	1718	|	...
Mannheim Hbf a.	1528	1606	...	1604	...	1626	...	1656	|	1736	1728	...
Frankfurt Flughafen ✈ **912** a.	|	|	...	1638	...	1706	...	|	|	...	|	...
Frankfurt (Main) Hbf **911/2** a.	1608	|	...	1653	...	|	...	|	1740	...	1808	...
Koblenz Hbf **912** a.	...	1741p	...	...	...	|	...	1841	...	...	...	...
Köln Hbf **800 910** a.	...	1842	...	...	...	1805	...	1942	...	...	...	...
Dortmund Hbf **800** a.	...	...	...	...	...	1920	...	2102	...	...	...	...

	IC 2362 ⑤ 🍷	ICE 572 H✕	IC 2318 N	RE 37118	ICE 514 G🍷	IC 2052 Ⓑ A🍷	IRE 4234 L	EC 112 ✕♦	IC 2172 ⑦ K🍷	ICE 592 B✕	IC 1910 ⑦	EC 360 🍷♦	ICE 570 ⑦ H✕
Salzburg Hbf **890** 🚌 d.	...	...	...	...	...	...	...	1352	...	...	...	...	...
München Hbf **904 905** d.	1441	...	...	1434	1523	...	...	1541	...	1623	1612	1643	...
München Pasing **904 905** d.	1449	...	...	1440	1531	...	...	|	...	1631	1620	1651	...
Augsburg Hbf **904 905** d.	1521	...	...	1525	1603	...	...	1617	...	1703	1653	1722	...
Günzburg **945** d.	|	...	...	1616	|	...	...	1649	...	|	1728	|	...
Ulm Hbf **945** ★ d.	1605	...	...	1635	1651	...	1654	1705	...	1751	1744	1805	...
Geislingen (Steige) ★ d.	|	...	...	...	|	...	1717	|	...	|	1816	|	...
Göppingen ★ d.	|	...	...	...	|	...	1728	|	...	|	1830	1839	...
Plochingen **936** ★ d.	1648	...	...	...	|	...	1739	|	...	|	|	1851	...
Stuttgart Hbf **936** ★ a.	1704	...	...	...	1747	...	1756	1800	...	1847	1858	1907	...
Stuttgart Hbf **931** d.	1708	1727	1741	...	1751	1757	...	1805	1837	1851	1914	1911	1927
Vaihingen (Enz) **931** d.	|	|	|	...	|	|	...	|	1855	|	|	|	|
Karlsruhe Hbf **931** a.	1753	|	|	...	|	|	...	|	|	|	|	1953	|
Heidelberg Hbf **931** a.	...	|	1823	...	|	|	...	1845	1922	|	1953	...	|
Mannheim Hbf a.	...	1804	1837	...	1826	1845	...	|	|	1928	2006	...	2004
Frankfurt Flughafen ✈ **912** a.	...	1838	|	...	1906	...	...	|	|	|	|	...	2038
Frankfurt (Main) Hbf **911/2** a.	...	1853	|	...	|	...	...	1940	2018	2008	|	...	2053
Koblenz Hbf **912** a.	...	...	2010	...	|	...	...	...	...	...	2141	...	...
Köln Hbf **800 910** a.	...	...	2105	...	2005	...	...	...	...	...	2242	...	...
Dortmund Hbf **800** a.	...	...	2221q	...	2121	...	...	...	...	...	2400	...	...

♦ – **NOTES** (LISTED BY TRAIN NUMBER) for pages 436 and 437

591 – [12] and ✕ (Hamburg ①–⑤ -) (Hannover ①–⑥ -) Kassel - Frankfurt - München. Train number **999** on ⑦.
973 – [12] and ✕ (Kiel ①–⑥ -) Hamburg - Stuttgart. Train number **573** on ⑦.
974 – [12] and ✕ Stuttgart - Hamburg (- Kiel Ⓑ). Train number **574** on ⑥.
991 – [12] and ✕ Wiesbaden - Mainz - München.
2012/3 – ALLGÄU – [12] and 🍷 Oberstdorf - Kempten - Ulm - Köln - Dortmund - Hannover (- Magdeburg - Leipzig ●) and v.v.
2014/5 – [12] and 🍷 Stuttgart - Köln - Münster - Emden and v.v.
2115/6 – [12] and ✕ (Greifswald ①–⑤ -) Stralsund - Hamburg - Köln - Stuttgart and v.v.
2213 – RÜGEN – [12] and ✕ Ostseebad Binz - Stralsund - Hamburg - Köln - Stuttgart.
2275 – [12] Hannover - Kassel - Gießen - Frankfurt - Stuttgart; conveys 🍷 on ⑤.
2311 – NORDFRIESLAND – [12] and ✕ Westerland - Hamburg - Köln - Stuttgart.
9575/6 – [12] and 🍷 Paris - Strasbourg - München and v.v. 🄁 for international journeys.

A – From / to Saarbrücken (Table **919**).
B – From / to Berlin (Tables **810**/**900**).
E – To Essen (Table **800**).
F – To / from Friedrichshafen (Table **933**).
G – From / to Hamburg (Table **800**).
H – From / to Hamburg (Table **900**).
J – To Mainz (Table **912**). Train number **2218** on ⑥.
K – To Kassel (Table **806**).
L – To / from Lindau (Table **933**).
M – From / to Münster (Table **800**).
N – To Münster on ⑦ (a. 2254).
R – From Hannover (Table **810**).
T – From Leipzig (Table **850**).
W – To Wiesbaden (Table **912**).
X – [12] and 🍷 Stuttgart - Düsseldorf - Duisburg (- Essen from July 18) (- Dortmund ⑥⑦ **c**).
Y – From Linz on ①–⑥ (Table **950**).
Z – To Linz on Ⓑ (Table **950**).

b – 5–6 minutes later until Aug. 21.
c – ⑥⑦ from July 18.
d – Köln **Messe/Deutz**.
e – ①–⑥ only.
f – 1613 on ⑥⑦.
g – ① only.
j – Not July 19, 20, Aug. 2, 3, 9, 10.
k – 0040 on the mornings of ①⑦ (also July 11, 18, 25).
m – On June 20, July 4 terminates at Augsburg Hbf.
n – Not July 10 - Oct. 5.
p – 1744 on ①–⑤ until Aug. 21.
q – Ⓑ only.
r – From Aug. 24.
s – Stops to set down only.
t – 1250 until Aug. 21.
u – Stops to pick up only.
v – ①②③④⑥.
x – Not June 21, July 5.
z – ⑥⑦ only.

♥ – ①②③④⑥⑦.
♣ – ①②③④⑦.
⊖ – Train number **695** on ⑥.
◧ – Train number **594** on ⑥.
⊙ – Train number **2393** on ⑥. Conveys ✕ on Ⓑ, 🍷 on ⑥.
⊕ – Train number **1010** on ⑤⑥. Conveys ✕ on ①–④, 🍷 on ⑤⑥.
⊡ – [12] and ✕ München - Frankfurt (- Kassel ⑤–⑦) (- Hannover ⑦). Train number **698** on ⑤. Train number **992** on ⑦.
§ – Train number **593** on ⑥⑦.
¶ – Train number **1111** on ⑦ (also Apr. 13, June 1).
‡ – Train number **998** on ⑦.
◐ – From Düsseldorf (Table **800**). Train number **1913** on ②. Conveys 🍷 on ①③.
△ – To Düsseldorf (Table **800**). Train number **1918** on ③. Conveys 🍷 on ①.
◇ – On ⑦ conveys [12] München - Frankfurt - Hamburg (Table **900**).
● – See Table **810** for days of running Hannover - Magdeburg - Leipzig and v.v.
★ – See panel on page 438 for additional *RE* services.

930 MÜNCHEN - STUTTGART - MANNHEIM

	IC 2110	RE 37120	ICE 512	IRE 4236	EC 316	IC 1876	IC 1196	ICE 590	IC 2092	RE 37124	ICE 510	ICE 1110	IRE 4238	IC 2050	ICE 1580	RB 19362	RB 19364	RE 4180	ICE 990	RE 19246	RB 37346	IC 2090	IC 60418	CNL 418	RB 37352
	⑧					⑦	⑦	⊡	⑧		①–⑥	⑦	⑥⑦	⑦		①–⑤	⑥⑦					⑦		🅁	
	✕		M🍷	L	✕◆		W	✕	🍷		⊕	🍷	L	A	✕				◇✕			🍷		🍷◆	
Salzburg Hbf **890** 🚌 d.	...	...	...	...	1552	...	...	...	...	...	...	...	...	...	...	...	...	...	...	...	...	...	...	...	...
München Hbf **904 905** d.	...	1633	1723	...	1740	...	...	1823	1844	1833	1923	1923	...	...	...	...	...	1933	2040	...	2101	2145	2244	2244	2301
München Pasing **904 905** d.	...	1640	1731	...	|	...	...	1831	|	1840	1932	1932	...	...	...	...	...	1940	|	...	2107	2153	|	|	2307
Augsburg Hbf **904 905** d.	...	1733	1803	...	1817	...	...	1903	1919	1925	2003	2003	...	...	...	...	...	2025	2117	...	2152	2224	2320	2320u	2352
Günzburg **945** d.	...	1822	|	...	1849	...	...	|	1949	2019	|	|	...	...	...	...	...	2121	|	...	2242	2254	2353	2353u	0042
Ulm Hbf **945** ★ d.	...	1840	1851	1854	1905	...	...	1951	2005	2038	2051	2051	2054	...	...	2103	2110	2139	2204	2242	2301	2310	0010	0010u	0101
Geislingen (Steige) ★ d.	...	...	|	1917	|	...	...	|	|	...	|	|	2117	...	...	2133	2138	...	|	2308	...	|	0034	0034u	...
Göppingen ★ d.	...	...	|	1928	|	...	...	|	2039	...	|	|	2128	...	...	2155	2158	...	|	2323	...	2343	0048	0048u	...
Plochingen **936** ★ d.	...	...	|	1939	|	...	...	|	2051	...	|	|	2139	...	...	2213	2215	...	|	2341	...	2356	0102	0102u	...
Stuttgart Hbf **936** ★ a.	...	...	1947	1956	2000	...	...	2047	2107	...	2147	2147	2156	...	...	2231	2232	...	2300	2400	...	0011	0116n	|	...
Stuttgart Hbf **931** d.	1937	...	1951	...	2005	2009	2035	2051	2111	...	2151	2151	...	2209	2231	...	...	...	2305	...	...	...	...	0126n	...
Vaihingen (Enz) **931** d.	1955	...	|	...	|	|	2052	|	|	...	|	|	...	2225	|	...	...	...	|	...	...	...	...	|	...
Karlsruhe Hbf **931** a.	|	...	|	...	|	|	|	|	2153	...	|	|	...	|	|	...	...	...	|	...	...	...	...	|	...
Heidelberg Hbf **931** a.	2023	...	|	...	|	2048	2118	|	...	...	|	|	...	2253	2314	...	...	...	|	...	...	...	...	|	...
Mannheim Hbf a.	2037	...	2026	...	2048	|	2133	2128	...	...	2228	2228	...	2306	|	...	...	...	2342	...	...	...	...	|	...
Frankfurt Flughafen ✈ **912** a.	|	...	2106	...	...	|	...	|	...	...	2303	2302	...	...	|	...	...	...	0023	...	...	...	...	|	...
Frankfurt (Main) Hbf **911/2** a.	|	...	|	...	...	2144	...	2208	...	...	2325	|	...	...	0019	...	...	...	0042	...	...	...	...	|	...
Koblenz Hbf **912** a.	2210	...	|	...	...	...	...	...	...	...	...	|	...	...	...	...	...	...	...	...	...	...	...	0445	...
Köln Hbf **800 910** a.	2305	...	2205	...	...	...	...	...	...	...	...	0005	...	...	...	...	...	...	...	...	...	...	...	0545	...
Dortmund Hbf **800** a.	...	...	2321	...	...	...	...	...	...	...	...	...	...	...	...	...	...	...	...	...	...	...	...	...	...

Additional *RE* trains Stuttgart - Ulm and v.v.

	①–⑤	⑥⑦	⑥⑦	①–⑤			⑥⑦	①–⑤	
Stuttgart Hbf d.	0622	0629	0717	0732	0832	each train	1917	1932	2032
Plochingen d.	0643	0647	0736	0749	0849	runs every	1936	1949	2049
Göppingen d.	0701	0705	0754	0807	0907	**two** hours	1955	2007	2107
Geislingen (Steige) d.	0719	0721	0815	0823	0923	until	2016	2023	2123
Ulm Hbf a.	0749	0747	0844	0848	0949		2044	2047	2148

	①–⑤	⑥⑦	①–⑤	⑥⑦		①–⑤	⑥⑦		①–⑤	⑥⑦	
Ulm Hbf d.	0523	0601	0706	0710	0810	0910	0910	each train	1910	1910	2010
Geislingen (Steige) d.	0555	0625	0732	0738	0833	0933	0938	runs every	1933	1938	2033
Göppingen d.	0609	0643	0751	0758	0850	0950	0958	**two** hours	1950	1958	2050
Plochingen d.	0623	0705	0805	0815	0908	1008	1015	until	2008	2015	2108
Stuttgart Hbf a.	0643	0724	0824	0832	0926	1026	1032		2026	2032	2126

← FOR NOTES SEE PAGES 437 AND 438

931 KARLSRUHE and HEIDELBERG - STUTTGART

See Table **930** for fast trains Heidelberg - Stuttgart and v.v.

km	km		IC 2291	IC 2363	ICE 699	IRE 4901	RE 19503	IC 2365	IC 2367	IC 2063	RE 19105	IC 2369	ICE 678	EC 361	IRE 4903	RE 19505	IC 2065	IRE 4905	TGV 9571	RE 19507	IC 2101	IC 2261	IRE 4907	RE 19509	IC 2069
			①–⑤	①–⑥	⑦	①–⑤	⑥⑦	①–⑤	①–⑤	①–⑥	⑥⑦	①–⑤	⑥												
					✕			O✕	✕	🍷		🍷	B✕	🍷			🍷		P🍷		B🍷	🍷			🍷
		Strasbourg **912** d.	...	...	...	...	...	...	...	...	...	...	...	0653	...	...	...	...	0945	...	...	...	...	...	...
0		**Karlsruhe** Hbf d.	0457	0559	0607	0601	...	0637	0659	0706	0719	0741	0741	0806	0805	...	0906	1005	1027	...	1106	1206	1205	...	1306
26		Pforzheim d.	|	|	|	0624	...	|	|	0727	0743	|	|	|	0826	...	0927	1026	|	...	1127	|	1226	...	1327
	0	**Heidelberg** Hbf **930** d.	|	|	|	|	0610	|	|	|	|	|	|	|	|	0810	|	|	|	1010	|	|	|	1210	|
	33	Bruchsal d.	0515	0617	0621	|	0632	0654	0719	|	|	0758	0758	0819	|	0833	|	|	|	1033	|	1219	|	1233	|
39	65	Mühlacker d.	|	|	|	0632	0655	|	|	0737	0755	|	|	|	0834	0859	0937	1034	|	1059	1137	|	1234	1259	1337
47	73	Vaihingen (Enz) **930** d.	0533	|	|	0639	0705	|	|	0746	0804	|	0815	|	0841	0907	0946	1041	|	1107	1146	|	1241	1307	1346
86	112	**Stuttgart** Hbf **930** a.	0549	0648	0648	0656	0738	0724	0750	0803	0837	0829	0831	0849	0858	0939	1003	1058	1103	1139	1203	1249	1258	1339	1403
		Nürnberg Hbf **925** a.	|	...	|	...	...	...	...	1018	...	...	...	|	...	...	1216	...	...	...	1416	|	...	...	1616
		München Hbf **930** a.	0819	...	0917	...	...	...	...	...	...	...	...	1116	...	...	...	...	...	...	...	1516	...	...	...

	IC 2263	IRE 4909	TGV 9573	RE 19511	IC 2103	IC 2265	IRE 4911	RE 19513	IC 2163	IC 2267	IRE 4913	TGV 9575	RE 19515	IC 2165	IC 2105	IC 2269	IRE 4915	TGV 9577	RE 19517	IC 2167	IC 2167	EN 469	IC 1867	RE 19133	RE 19135
	⑤								⑧					①–④	⑤–⑦	K		⑧		①–⑤	⑦	🅁	⑤		
	🍷		P🍷		B🍷	S🍷			🍷	🍷		P🍷		🍷	L🍷			P🍷		🍷		W	🍷	⊙	⊖
Strasbourg **912** d.	...	...	1345	...	...	...	...	...	...	...	...	1745	...	...	...	...	...	1946	...	...	...	2037	...	...	...
Karlsruhe Hbf d.	1406	1405	1427	...	1506	1606	1605	...	1706	1806	1805	1827	...	1906	1906	2006	2005	2029	...	2106	2106	2156	2208	2209	2318
Pforzheim d.	|	1426	|	...	1527	|	1626	...	1727	|	1826	|	...	1927	1927	|	2026	|	...	2127	2127	2219	|	2234	2340
Heidelberg Hbf **930** d.	|	|	|	1410	|	|	|	1610	|	|	|	|	1810	|	|	|	|	|	2010	|	|	|	|	|	|
Bruchsal d.	1419	|	|	1433	|	1619	|	1633	|	1819	|	|	1833	|	|	2019	|	|	2033	|	|	|	2226	|	|
Mühlacker d.	|	1434	|	1459	1537	|	1634	1659	1737	|	1834	|	1859	1937	1937	|	2034	|	2059	2137	2137	|	|	2245	2352
Vaihingen (Enz) **930** d.	|	1441	|	1507	1546	|	1641	1707	1746	|	1841	|	1907	1946	1946	|	2041	|	2107	2146	2146	|	2244	2254	0000
Stuttgart Hbf **930** a.	1449	1458	1503	1539	1603	1649	1658	1739	1803	1849	1858	1903	1939	2003	2003	2049	2058	2105	2139	2203	2203	2257	2301	2325	0036
Nürnberg Hbf **925** a.	...	...	...	...	1816	|	...	...	2016	|	...	|	...	...	2216r	|	...	...	...	...	0022	...	...	...	...
München Hbf **930** a.	...	...	...	...	...	1916	...	...	...	2116	...	2138	...	...	...	2321v	...	...	...	...	...	...	...	...	...

km ◧		RE 19138		IC 2368	RE 19500	EN 468	TGV 9578	RE 19104	IC 2268	RE 19106	RE 19108	IC 2164	RE 19502	TGV 9576	IRE 4902	IC 2266	IC 2102	RE 19504	IRE 4904	IC 2264	IC 2160	RE 19506	TGV 9574	IRE 4906	IC 2262
				①–⑤		🅁	①–⑥	①–⑤	①–⑤	⑥⑦	①–⑤	①–⑥				①–⑥	①–⑥								①–⑤
		⊕				W	P🍷		M🍷			🍷		P🍷		🍷	N🍷			S🍷	🍷		P🍷		🍷
	München Hbf **930** d.	...	...	...	...	...	...	...	0425g	...	...	...	...	0620	...	0641	...	...	...	0841h	...	...	...	...	...
	Nürnberg Hbf **925** d.	...	...	...	...	...	...	...	|	...	...	0537a	...	|	...	|	0741	...	...	|	0941	...	...	...	...
0	**Stuttgart** Hbf **930** d.	0019	...	0545	0614	0638	0654	0642	0711	0717	0719	0801	0819	0854	0900	0911	1001	1019	1059	1111	1201	1219	1254	1259	1311
29	Vaihingen (Enz) **930** d.	0052	...	0603	0644	|	|	0711	|	0750	0752	0816	0850	|	0916	|	1016	1050	1115	|	1216	1250	|	1315	|
	Mühlacker d.	0100	...	0611	0700	|	|	0717	|	0759	0800	0823	0859	|	0921	|	1023	1059	1121	|	1223	1259	|	1321	|
66	Bruchsal d.	|	...	|	0727	|	|	|	0740	|	|	|	0929	|	|	0940	|	1129	|	1139	|	1329	|	|	1340
	Heidelberg Hbf **930** a.	|	...	|	0747	|	|	|	|	|	|	|	0948	|	|	|	|	1148	|	|	|	1348	|	|	|
	Pforzheim d.	0113	...	0622	...	0722	|	0730	|	0813	0813	0834	...	|	0930	|	1034	...	1130	|	1234	...	|	1330	|
87	**Karlsruhe** Hbf a.	0136	...	0645	...	0749	0729	0753	0753	0838	0838	0853	...	0929	0953	0953	1053	...	1153	1153	1253	...	1329	1353	1353
	Strasbourg **912** a.	...	...	...	...	0859	0813	...	...	...	...	...	...	1013	...	...	...	...	...	...	...	...	1415	...	...

	IC 2100	RE 19508	IRE 4908	IC 2260	IC 2066	RE 19510	IC 2364	TGV 9572	IRE 4910	IC 2362	IC 2360	IC 2064	RE 19514	TGV 9570	IRE 4912	EC 360	RE 19130 19132	IC 2062	RE 19516	IRE 4914	IC 2092	IC 2060	RE 19134	RE 19136	IC 2366
							①–⑤	⑥⑦		⑧	①–⑤			①–⑤							⑧	⑧	⑥⑦	①–⑤	⑦
	B🍷			🍷	🍷		O	P🍷		🍷	🍷	🍷		P🍷		🍷		🍷			🍷	🍷	¶		🍷
München Hbf **930** d.	...	...	...	1241	...	...	...	...	...	1441f	...	...	...	...	...	1643	...	...	...	...	1844	...	...	...	...
Nürnberg Hbf **925** d.	1141	...	...	|	1341	...	...	...	...	|	...	1541	...	...	...	|	...	1741	...	...	|	1941r	...	...	...
Stuttgart Hbf **930** d.	1401	1419	1459	1508	1601	1617	1641	1654	1659	1708	1734	1801	1819	1854	1859	1911	1918	2001	2017	2059	2111	2201	2217	2218	2309
Vaihingen (Enz) **930** d.	1416	1450	1515	|	1616	1650	|	|	1715	|	|	1816	1850	|	1915	|	1950	2016	2050	2115	|	2216	2252	2252	|
Mühlacker d.	1423	1459	1521	|	1623	1659	|	|	1721	|	|	1823	1859	|	1921	|	1958	2023	2059	2121	|	2223	2300	2300	|
Bruchsal d.	|	1529	|	1537	|	1729	1714	|	|	1737	1804	|	1929	|	|	1939	|	|	2129	|	2140	|	|	|	2338
Heidelberg Hbf **930** a.	|	1548	|	|	|	1748	|	|	|	|	|	|	1948	|	|	|	|	|	2156	|	|	|	|	|	|
Pforzheim d.	1434	...	1530	|	1634	...	|	|	1730	|	|	1834	...	|	1930	|	2013	2034	...	2130	|	2234	2313	2313	|
Karlsruhe Hbf a.	1453	...	1553	1550	1653	...	1731	1729	1753	1753	1821	1853	...	1929	1953	1953	2038	2053	...	2153	2153	2253	2338	2338	2355
Strasbourg **912** a.	...	...	...	...	...	...	...	1815	...	...	...	...	...	2015	...	2101	...	...	...	...	...	...	...	...	...

B – From / to Basel (Table **912**).
K – ①②③④⑦. [12] Karlsruhe - Ulm (- München ⑦). Conveys 🍷 on ⑦.
L – [12] and 🍷 Basel - Stuttgart (- Nürnberg ⑤⑦) (- Passau ⑦).
M – [12] and 🍷 (München ① -) Ulm - Karlsruhe.
N – [12] and 🍷 (Passau ① -) Nürnberg - Basel.
O – From / to Offenburg (Table **916**).
P – From / to Paris (Table **390**). 🅁 for international journeys.
S – To / from Salzburg on dates in Table **890**.
W – ORIENT EXPRESS – 🛏 1, 2 cl., ▬ 2 cl., [2] and 🍷 Wien - Salzburg - Strasbourg and v.v.

a – ①–⑤ only.
f – ⑤ only.
g – ① only.
h – Daily except ⑤.
r – ⑤⑦ only.
v – ⑦ only.

¶ – Train number **4926** on ⑥⑦ Aug. 1 - Oct. 4.
⊙ – Train number **4927** on ⑥⑦ Aug. 1 - Oct. 4.
⊖ – Train number **4929** on ⑥⑦ Aug. 1 - Oct. 4.
⊕ – Train number **4928** on ①⑦ Aug. 2 - Oct. 5.
◧ – Via high-speed line.

S-Bahn 2/3 — FLUGHAFEN STUTTGART - ECHTERDINGEN ✈ — 932

Stuttgart Hbf (underground platforms) - **Stuttgart Flughafen** ✈ and v.v. *20 km.* Journey time: 27 minutes. On Oct. 3 services run as on ⑦.

From Stuttgart Hbf at 0455 Ⓐ, 0515 Ⓐ, 0525, 0545 Ⓑ, 0555 ⚒, 0615 Ⓐ, 0625, 0645 Ⓑ, 0655 ⚒, 0715 Ⓐ, 0725, 0745, 0755, 0815, 0825, 0845, 0855 and then at 15, 25, 45, and 55 minutes past each hour until 1815, 1825, 1845, 1855; then 1915 Ⓐ, 1925, 1945 Ⓐ, 1955, 2015 Ⓐ, 2025, 2045 Ⓐ, 2055, 2115 Ⓐ, 2125, 2155, 2225, 2255, 2325, 2355 and 0025.

From Stuttgart Flughafen ✈ at 0508, 0518 Ⓐ, 0538 ⚒, 0548 Ⓑ, 0608, 0618 Ⓐ, 0638 ⚒, 0648 Ⓑ, 0708, 0718 Ⓐ, 0738 ⚒, 0748 Ⓑ, 0808, 0818, 0838, 0848 and then at 08, 18, 38 and 48 minutes past each hour until 1808, 1818, 1838, 1848; then 1908, 1918, 1938, 1948 Ⓐ, 2008, 2018 Ⓐ, 2038, 2048 Ⓐ, 2108, 2118 Ⓐ, 2138, 2148 Ⓐ, 2208, 2238, 2308, 2338 and 0008.

IRE / RE services (except trains C and D) — ULM - LINDAU — 933

km			F	B	F		B			B			B	C 🍷		B			B						2
	Stuttgart Hbf 930 d.	...	...	...	0659k	0802	...	...	1002	...	...	1202	...	1257	1402	...	...	1602	...	1702e	1802	...	2002	...	...
0	**Ulm** Hbf d.	0550	0707h	0806	0812	0912	1006	1012	1112	1206	1212	1312	1406	1411	1512	1606	1612	1712	1806	1812	1912	2012	2112	2212	2320
37	Biberach (Riß) d.	0618	0734	0827	0835	0935	1027	1035	1135	1227	1235	1335	1426	1433	1535	1627	1635	1735	1827	1835	1936	2035	2139	2238	2352
62	Aulendorf d.	0637	0753	|	0854	0954	|	1053	1154	|	1253	1354	1442	1451	1553	1641	1654	1753	|	1854	1954	2054	2158	2258	0011
84	Ravensburg d.	0650	0806	0853	0907	1007	1053	1106	1207	1253	1306	1407	1456	1505	1606	1655	1707	1806	1853	1907	2007	2107	2211	2311	0025
95	Meckenbeuren d.	0658	0814	|	0915	1015	|	1114	1215	|	1313	1415	|	1513	1614	|	1714	1814	|	1915	2015	2115	2219	2319	0033
99	Friedrichshafen Flughafen ✈ d.	0703	|	0902	|	|	1102	1118	|	1302	1317	|	1505	|	|	1706	1718	|	1902	|	2019	|	2223	2323	|
103	Friedrichshafen Stadt ▲ a.	0714r	0823	0908	0924	1024	1108	1124	1224	1308	1324	1424	1511	1521	1624	1711	1724	1824	1908	1924	2026	2124	2231	2329	0041
103	Friedrichshafen Stadt ... 939 d.	*0727*	0829	...	0930	1032	...	1129	1230	...	1329	1429	...	1535	1634	...	1730	1834	...	1929	2034	2131	*2248*	*2339*	...
127	**Lindau** Hbf 939 a.	*0752*	0858	...	0951	1054	...	1154	1256	...	1351	1452	...	1554	1659	...	1751	1859	...	1951	2100	2154	*2320*	*0014*	...

	⑥⑦	①–⑤		F	F	B	F		B		D 🍷	B			B			B			B		B	2	2
Lindau Hbf 939 d.	...	*0513*	0558	0703k	0806	...	0906	1003	...	1101	1202	...	1305	1407	...	1503	1604h	...	1706	1807	...	1906	*2012*	*2102*	*2142*
Friedrichshafen Stadt 939 a.	...	*0544*	0622	0726	0827	...	0927	1024	...	1123	1219	...	1326	1426	...	1526	1626	...	1727	1827	...	1927	*2034*	*2123*	*2219*
Friedrichshafen Stadt ▲ d.	0521	0549	0628	0732	0832	0850	0932	1030	1050	1132	1233	1245h	1332	1432	1450	1532	1631	1650	1733	1832	1845	1933	2046	2128	2231
Friedrichshafen Flughafen ✈ d.	|	|	0632	|	0837	0855	|	1034	1055	|	|	1250h	|	1437	1456	|	1636z	1655	|	1836	1850	|	|	|	2236
Meckenbeuren d.	0529	|	0637	0739	0841	|	0940	1039	|	1139	1241	|	1339	1441	|	1539	1640	|	1740	1840	|	1940	2053	2135	2240
Ravensburg d.	0537	0601	0645	0747	0848	0904	0948	1047	1104	1148	1250	1259h	1347	1448	1505	1548	1648	1704	1748	1848	1901	1948	2100	2142	2249
Aulendorf d.	0552	|	0659	0803	0903	|	1003	1101	|	1203	1306	1314z	1403	1503	|	1603	1703	|	1803	1903	1915	2003	2113	2157	2304
Biberach (Riß) d.	0610	0627	0719	0820	0920	0930	1020	1120	1130	1220	1322	1330	1420	1520	1530	1620	1720	1730	1820	1920	1930	2021	2130	2212	2324
Ulm Hbf a.	0642	0650	0745	0845	0945	0953	1045	1145	1153	1245	1345	1353	1445	1545	1553	1645	1745	1753	1845	1945	1953	2045	2155	2237	2359
Stuttgart Hbf 930 a.	0756	0756	...	0956	...	...	1156	...	...	1356	1458	...	1556	1656e	...	1756	...	...	1956	...	...	2156z	...	...	...

B – To / from Basel Bad Bf (Table **939**).
C – *IC* **119**: 🚅 and 🍷 Münster - Köln - Stuttgart - Lindau - Bregenz - Innsbruck.
D – *IC* **118**: 🚅 and 🍷 Innsbruck - Bregenz - Lindau - Stuttgart - Köln - Münster.
F – Change trains at Friedrichshafen Stadt on ①–⑤.

e – ①–⑤ only.
h – 3–6 minutes later on ①–⑤.
k – 3 minutes later on ⑥⑦.
r – 0708 on ⑥⑦.

z – ⑥⑦ only.

▲ – Regular services operate to / from Friedrichshafen Hafen.

RE / RB services except where shown — MÜNCHEN, AUGSBURG and ULM - OBERSTDORF and LINDAU — 935

For services to / from Bad Wörishofen see pages 440 and 441

km	km			*ALX*													*ALX*			*EC* 196					
			⑥⑦	🍷		①–⑤			①–⑤	⑥⑦	⑥⑦	①–⑤	⑥⑦	①–⑤	⑥⑦			🍷			★✕			⑥⑦ L	●	
0		**München** Hbf ⊡ d.	...	0447r	...	...	...	...	...	...	0551	0551	...	0613	0613	...	...	0651	...	...	0712	...	...	0740	...	0751
7		München Pasing d.	...	0455r	...	...	...	...	...	...	0559	0559	...	0620	0620	...	...	0658	...	...	|	...	...	|	...	0759
42		Geltendorf d.	...	0515r	...	...	...	...	...	...	0622	0622	...	0644	0644	...	...	0720	...	...	|	...	...	0809	...	0822
56		Kaufering d.	...	0525r	...	...	...	...	...	...	0631	0631	...	0654	0654	...	...	0731	...	...	|	...	...	|	...	0832
	0	**Augsburg** Hbf d.	...	|	...	0503	...	...	0559	0603	|	|	...	|	|	...	0643	|	...	*0711*	|	...	...	|	0803	|
68	40	Buchloe ⊕ a.	...	0533r	...	0535	...	...	0630	0637	0640	0640	...	0702	0702	...	0712	0739	...	*0739*	0755	...	...	0824	0838	0841
68	40	Buchloe ⊕ d.	...	0535r	...	0536	...	...	▬	...	0641	0641	...	0703	0703	...	0715	0741	...	0744	0758	...	...	0825	...	0846
	48	Türkheim (Bay) d.	...	|	...	0542	...	...	...	...	0647	0700v	...	|	|	...	0725	|	...	0752	|	...	...	|	...	0852
88		Kaufbeuren d.	...	0550r	0617	|	...	...	...	...	|	|	...	0719	0719	0736	|	0755	0844	|	|	...	...	|	...	|
		Marktoberdorf d.	...	|	0642	|	...	...	...	...	|	|	...	|	|	0752h	|	|	0904	|	|	...	...	|	...	|
		Füssen a.	...	|	0724	|	...	...	...	...	|	|	...	|	|	0842	|	|	0946	|	|	...	...	|	...	|
	59	Mindelheim d.	...	|	▬	0554	...	...	①–⑤	...	0701t	0715	...	|	|	...	0732	|	▬	0800	|	...	...	|	...	0901
		Ulm Hbf d.	0509	|	...	|	0548e	...	0617	...	|	|	0659	|	|	...	|	|	...	|	|	0758	...	|	...	|
	86	Memmingen ⊕ a.	0555	|	...	0618	0649e	...	0710	...	0722	0735	0734	|	|	...	0757	|	...	0827	|	0825	...	0927	...	0922
	86	Memmingen ⊕ d.	0556	|	...	*0630*	0651e	...	0725	...	...	...	0735	|	|	...	...	|	...	...	|	0840	0833	0928	...	...
131		**Kempten** Hbf ⊕ a.	0622	0620r	...	|	0721e	...	0753	...	...	...	0759	0751	0751	...	...	0822	...	...	0841	0911	|	|	...	...
131		**Kempten** Hbf ⊕ d.	...	0629	*ALX*	|	0723	...	...	...	...	...	0800	0803	0808	...	...	0824	*ALX*	...	0843	0914	|	|	...	...
152		Immenstadt ⊕ a.	...	0644	◁ 🍷	|	0739	◁	...	...	...	...	0815	0819	0824	...	...	0839	◁	...	|	0930	|	|	...	...
152		Immenstadt ⊕ d.	...	0648	0653	|	0742	0748	...	...	...	...	0826	0826	0825	...	...	0842	0853	...	|	0943	|	|	...	...
		Sonthofen d.	...	|	0702	|	|	0758	...	...	...	...	0836	0836	|	...	...	|	0903	...	|	0954	|	|	...	...
		Oberstdorf a.	...	|	0725	|	|	0823	...	...	...	...	0853	0854	|	...	...	|	0922	...	|	1017	|	|	...	...
	118	Leutkirch d.	...	|	...	*0704*	|	...	...	...	...	...	...	...	|	...	...	|	...	...	|	...	0904	|	...	...
	129	Kißlegg **937** d.	...	|	...	*0717*	|	...	...	...	...	...	...	...	|	...	...	|	...	...	|	...	0920t	|	...	...
	142	Wangen (Allgäu) **937** d.	...	|	...	*0732*	|	...	...	...	...	...	...	...	|	...	...	|	...	...	|	...	0935	|	...	...
197	148	Hergatz **937** d.	...	0726	...	*0737*	0819	...	...	...	...	...	...	...	0901	...	...	0918	...	...	|	...	0940	|	...	...
220	171	**Lindau** Hbf a.	...	0744	...	*0755*	0835	...	...	...	...	...	...	...	0919	...	...	0934	...	...	0947	...	0956	1035	...	...

						ALX									*ALX*									*EC* 194		
						🍷					R				🍷				①–⑤	①–⑤	⑥⑦	N ⑥⑦		★✕		
München Hbf ⊡ d.	0819	...	...	0852	...	0919	...	...	0951	1019	...	...	1051	...	1119	...	...	1151	...	1219	1219	...	...	1234	1251	...
München Pasing d.	0827	...	...	0859	...	0927	...	...	0959	1027	...	...	1059	...	1127	...	...	1159	...	1227	1227	...	...	|	1259	...
Geltendorf d.	0849	...	...	0922	...	|	...	...	1022	1049	...	...	1122	...	|	...	...	1222	...	1250	1249	...	...	|	1322	...
Kaufering d.	0859	...	...	0931	...	0956	...	...	1032	1058	...	...	1131	...	1156	...	...	1232	...	1300	1258	...	...	|	1331	...
Augsburg Hbf d.	|	0844	...	|	0903	*0929*	...	1003	|	|	1045	...	|	1103	*1129*	...	1203	|	1233	|	|	1245	...	|	|	1303
Buchloe ⊕ a.	0907	0913	...	0940	0936	1003	...	1038	1041	1105	1112	...	1140	1136	1204	...	1238	1241	1306	1309	1306	1312	...	1316	1340	1336
Buchloe ⊕ d.	▬	0919	...	...	0944	1010	...	▬	1042	▬	1113	...	...	1144	1210	...	▬	1243	▬	1310	▬	1317	...	1318	...	1344
Türkheim (Bay) d.	...	|	...	...	0950	|	...	...	1049	...	|	...	...	1150	|	...	...	1250	...	|	...	|	...	|	...	1351
Kaufbeuren d.	...	0933	0940	...	|	1025	1044	...	|	...	1129	1140	...	|	1225	1244	...	|	...	1326	...	1331	1340	|	...	|
Marktoberdorf d.	...	|	1001	...	|	|	1104	...	|	...	|	1200	...	|	|	1302	...	|	...	|	...	|	1400	|	...	|
Füssen a.	...	|	1042	...	|	|	1146	...	|	...	|	1242	...	|	|	1346	...	|	...	|	...	|	1442	|	...	|
Mindelheim d.	...	|	▬	...	1001	|	▬	...	1101	...	|	▬	...	1201	|	▬	...	1301	...	|	...	|	▬	|	...	1401
Ulm Hbf d.	0859	|	...	...	|	|	...	0959	|	1059	|	...	...	|	|	...	1159	|	1259	|	...	|	...	|	...	|
Memmingen ⊕ a.	0938	|	...	...	1027	|	...	1027	1122	1135	|	...	...	1227	|	...	1227	1322	1337	|	...	|	...	1344	...	1421
Memmingen ⊕ d.	0939	|	...	...	1033	|	...	1042	...	1136	|	...	...	1233	|	...	1241	...	1338	|	...	|	...	1346	...	1445
Kempten Hbf ⊕ a.	0959	1002	...	...	|	1051	...	1113	...	1159	1157	...	...	|	1251	...	1312	...	1359	1356	...	1404	...	|	...	|
Kempten Hbf ⊕ d.	...	1004	...	...	|	1053	*ALX*	1115	...	...	1203	...	...	|	1253	*ALX*	1314	...	...	1403	①–⑤	1405	⑥⑦	|	...	|
Immenstadt ⊕ a.	...	1020	◁	...	|	1108	◁	1131	...	...	1219	◁	...	|	1308	◁	1330	...	...	1420	◁	1421	◁	|	...	|
Immenstadt ⊕ d.	...	1022	1027	...	|	1111	1116	1142	...	...	1222	1227	...	|	1311	1318	1342	...	...	1422	1427	1422	1427	|	...	|
Sonthofen d.	...	|	1038	...	|	|	1131	1152	...	...	|	1238	...	|	|	1332	1352	...	...	|	1438	|	1438	|	...	|
Oberstdorf a.	...	|	1056	...	|	|	1155	1214	...	...	|	1256	...	|	|	1355	1414	...	...	|	1456	|	1456	|	...	|
Leutkirch d.	...	|	...	...	1105	|	...	...	...	...	|	...	...	1305	|	...	...	...	...	|	...	|	...	|	...	1510
Kißlegg **937** d.	...	|	...	...	1120	|	...	...	...	...	|	...	...	1325v	|	...	...	...	...	|	...	|	...	|	...	1520
Wangen (Allgäu) **937** d.	...	|	...	...	1135	|	...	...	...	...	|	...	...	1336	|	...	...	...	...	|	...	|	...	|	...	1535
Hergatz **937** d.	...	1100	...	...	1140	1145	...	...	...	...	1300	...	...	1340	1345	...	...	...	...	1458	...	1459	...	|	...	1540
Lindau Hbf a.	...	1116	...	...	...	1203	...	...	...	...	1316	...	...	...	1403	...	...	...	...	*1531*	...	1516	...	1447	...	...

L – Until Oct. 4.
N – From Nürnberg (Table **905**).
R – From Nürnberg (Table **905**) on ⑥ (not Aug. 15, Oct. 3).

e – ①–⑤ only.
h – 0759 on ⑥⑦.

r – ①–⑥ (not Oct. 3, Aug. 15).
t – Arrives 6–7 minutes earlier.
v – Arrives 11–13 minutes earlier.

● – On ①–⑤ Augsburg d. 0812, Buchloe a. 0843.
★ – 🚅 and ✕ München - Bregenz - St Gallen - Zürich (Table **75**).

◁ – Detached from train in previous column at Immenstadt.
⊡ – Most trains in Table **935** use platforms 27–36 at München Hbf (minimum connecting time from other services is 10 minutes).
⊕ – Many services connect at Buchloe, Memmingen, Kempten and Immenstadt (connecting trains may be found in preceding columns). Minimum connectional time is 3 minutes.

ALX – *Arriva-Länderbahn-Express*. Operated by Arriva / Regentalbahn AG - Die Länderbahn.

935 MÜNCHEN, AUGSBURG and ULM - OBERSTDORF and LINDAU *RE / RB services except where shown*

For services to / from Bad Wörishofen see pages 440 and 441

	ALX 🍷		⑥⑦		IC 2085 H								ALX 🍷					⑥⑦	⑥⑦	N ①–⑤		EC 192 ★✕			ALX 🍷	
München Hbf ⊡ d.	1319	...	...	...	...	...	1351	...	1419	...	1451	...	1519	...	...	1551	1619	1619	...	...	...	1634	...	1651	1720	...
München Pasing d.	1327	...	...	...	...	...	1359	...	1427	...	1459	...	1527	...	...	1559	1627	1627	...	...	...	|	...	1659	1728	...
Geltendorf d.	|	...	...	...	...	...	1422	...	1449	...	1522	...	|	...	...	1622	1649	1649	...	...	...	|	...	1723	|	...
Kaufering d.	1356	...	...	...	...	...	1432	...	1458	...	1531	...	1556	...	...	1632	1658	1658	...	...	...	|	...	1732	1759	...
Augsburg Hbf d.	*1327*	...	...	...	1356	1403	|	...	|	...	|	1503	*1518*	...	1603	|	|	|	1644	1645	...	|	1703	|	*1729*	...
Buchloe ⊕ a.	1403	...	...	...	|	1438	1441	...	1506	...	1540	1538	1603	...	1638	1641	1706	1706	1710	1711	...	1715	1736f	1740	1808	...
Buchloe ⊕ d.	1410	...	...	...	|	...	1443	...	1512	...	...	1543	1610	...	▬	1643	▬	1712	▬	1712	...	1717	1737f	1754e	1811	...
Türkheim (Bay) d.	|	...	...	...	|	...	1455	...	|	...	...	1550	|	...	...	1650	...	|	...	|	...	|	1744f	|	|	...
Kaufbeuren d.	1425	1444	...	...	|	...	|	...	1529	1540	...	|	1625	1644	...	|	...	1729	...	1729	1740	|	|	1808e	1827	1844
Marktoberdorf d.	|	1502	...	...	|	...	|	...	|	1600	...	|	|	1703	...	|	...	|	...	|	1759	|	|	1821e	|	1904
Füssen a.	|	1546	...	...	|	...	|	...	|	1642	...	|	|	1746	...	|	...	|	...	|	1842	|	|	...	|	1946
Mindelheim d.	|	▬	...	...	|	...	1504	...	|	▬	...	1600	|	▬	A 🍷	1701	...	|	...	|	▬	|	1754f	...	|	▬
Ulm Hbf d.	|	...	1413	1413	|	...	|	1459	|	...	...	|	|	...	1607	|	1659	|	...	|	...	|	|	...	|	...
Memmingen ⊕ a.	|	...	1441	1441	|	...	1525	1530	|	...	...	1633	|	...	1636	1722	1729	|	...	|	...	1744	1816f	...	|	...
Memmingen ⊕ d.	|	...	1443	1443	|	...	...	1531	|	...	...	1645	|	...	1638	...	1730	|	...	|	...	1746	1845	...	|	...
Kempten Hbf ⊕ a.	1451	...	1512	1512	1524	...	...	1558	1603	...	...	|	1652	...	1701	...	1757	1803	...	1803	...	|	|	...	1855	...
Kempten Hbf ⊕ d.	1453	*ALX*	1517	1517	1531	...	...	...	1604	...	...	|	1653	*ALX*	1706	...	...	1804	⑥⑦	1804	①–⑤	|	|	...	1902	*ALX*
Immenstadt ⊕ a.	1508	◁	1533	1533	1547	...	...	...	1621	◁	...	|	1708	◁	1721	...	...	1820	◁	1820	◁	|	|	...	1916	◁
Immenstadt ⊕ d.	1511	1516	1536	1542	1602	...	...	...	1622	1628	...	|	1711	1717	1736	...	...	1822	1827	1822	1827	|	|	...	1919	1935
Sonthofen d.	|	1530	|	1552	1618	...	...	...	|	1638	...	|	|	1731	1745	...	...	|	1837	|	1837	|	|	...	|	1945
Oberstdorf a.	|	1550	|	1611	1639	...	...	...	|	1656	...	|	|	1749	1805	...	...	|	1856	|	1856	|	|	...	|	2001
Leutkirch d.	|	...	|	...	...	...	...	...	|	...	...	1710	|	...	...	...	...	|	...	|	...	|	1910	...	|	...
Kißlegg **937** d.	|	...	|	...	...	...	...	...	|	...	...	1720	|	...	...	...	...	|	...	|	...	|	1920	...	|	...
Wangen (Allgäu) **937** d.	|	...	|	...	...	...	...	...	|	...	...	1732	|	...	...	...	...	|	...	|	...	|	1935	...	|	...
Hergatz **937** d.	1547	...	1613	...	...	...	...	...	1700	...	...	1737	1746	...	...	...	...	1859	...	1859	...	|	1940	...	1955	...
Lindau Hbf 🚢 a.	1603	...	1630	...	...	...	...	...	1719	...	...	...	1803	...	...	...	...	1916	...	1916	...	1847	1957	...	2011	...

					N		EC 190 ★✕			ALX 🍷										ALX 🍷		❖	†		Q	
München Hbf ⊡ d.	...	1751	...	1819	...	...	1834	1851	...	1919	...	...	...	1951	...	...	2039	...	...	2141	...	...	...	2251	...	2353
München Pasing d.	...	1759	...	1827	...	...	|	1859	...	1927	...	...	...	1959	...	...	2046	...	...	2149	...	...	...	2259	...	0000
Geltendorf d.	...	1823	...	1849	...	...	|	1922	...	|	...	...	...	2022	...	...	2109	...	...	2210	...	...	...	2323	...	0023
Kaufering d.	...	1832	...	1858	...	...	|	1931	...	1956	...	...	...	2032	...	...	2119	...	...	2219	...	...	...	2333	...	0033
Augsburg Hbf d.	...	|	1803	|	1845	...	|	|	1903	*1940*	...	...	2003	|	...	2045	|	...	2147	|	...	←	...	|	2309	|
Buchloe ⊕ a.	...	1842	1838	1906	1912	...	1916	1940	1938	2003	...	...	2038	2041	...	2122	2128	...	2220	2228	...	2220	...	2342	2345	0042
Buchloe ⊕ d.	...	1844	1850	▬	1913	...	1918	...	1944	2011	...	...	▬	2044	...	2131	2130	...	2237	2233	...	2237	...	2348	2350	▬
Türkheim (Bay) d.	...	1851	|	...	|	...	|	...	1951	|	...	...	...	2051	...	2137	|	...	→	|	...	2243	...	2355	|	...
Kaufbeuren d.	...	|	1909	...	1928	1956	|	...	|	2026	2058	...	...	|	...	|	2144	2149	▬	2248	2253	|	...	|	0004	...
Marktoberdorf d.	...	|	1924	...	|	2011	|	...	|	|	2116	...	...	|	...	|	|	2205	...	|	2310	|	...	|	|	...
Füssen a.	...	|	...	...	|	2055	|	...	|	|	2157	...	...	|	...	|	|	2245	...	|	2349	|	...	|	|	...
Mindelheim d.	...	1901	...	...	|	▬	|	...	2001n	|	...	...	...	2059	...	2146	|	▬	...	|	▬	2251	...	0003	|	...
Ulm Hbf d.	1813	|	...	1859	|	...	|	...	|	|	...	2013	...	|	2059	|	|	...	2213	|	...	|	2314	|	|	2333
Memmingen ⊕ a.	1841	1923	...	1930	|	...	1944	...	2023n	|	...	2041	...	2119	2130	2207	|	...	2255	|	...	2312	2353	0029	|	0026
Memmingen ⊕ d.	1842	▬	...	1931	|	...	1946	...	...	|	...	2044	2046	...	2138	...	|	...	2256	|	...	2323	2355	...	|	...
Kempten Hbf ⊕ a.	1912	...	...	1958	2003	...	|	...	...	2052	...	2110	|	...	2204	...	2213	...	2322	2315	...	|	0021	...	0035	...
Kempten Hbf ⊕ d.	1917	...	...	...	2004	...	|	...	...	2102	...	2113	|	...	...	...	2216	...	...	2327	...	|	...	...	...	...
Immenstadt ⊕ a.	1933	◁	...	...	2020	◁	|	...	...	2117	...	2130	|	...	...	...	2233	...	...	2343	...	|	...	...	...	...
Immenstadt ⊕ d.	1938	1942	...	...	2024	2029	|	...	...	2124	...	2136	|	...	...	...	2234	2237	...	2344	2347	|	...	...	...	...
Sonthofen d.	|	1951	...	...	|	2039	|	...	...	|	...	2145	|	...	...	...	|	2246	...	|	2356	|	...	...	...	...
Oberstdorf a.	|	2011	...	...	|	2103	|	...	...	|	...	2204	|	...	...	...	|	2305	...	|	0015	|	...	...	...	...
Leutkirch d.	|	...	...	...	|	...	|	...	...	|	...	...	2113	...	...	...	|	...	...	|	...	2350	...	...	...	...
Kißlegg **937** d.	|	...	...	...	|	...	|	...	...	|	...	...	2124	...	...	...	|	...	...	|	...	0000	...	...	...	...
Wangen (Allgäu) **937** d.	|	...	...	...	|	...	|	...	...	|	...	...	2135	...	...	...	|	...	...	|	...	0011	...	...	...	...
Hergatz **937** d.	2015	...	...	...	2104	...	|	...	...	2200	...	...	2141	...	...	...	2312	...	...	0019	...	0016	...	...	...	...
Lindau Hbf 🚢 a.	2032	...	...	...	2120	...	2047	...	...	2217	...	...	2159	...	...	...	2329	...	...	0036	...	*0036*	...	...	...	...

km	*km*		ALX 🍷 ⚒r	①–⑤		①–⑤	①–⑤	N ①–⑤	①–⑤	①–⑤	①–⑤	⑥⑦	⑥⑦			ALX 🍷	⑥s	2 ①–⑤				N		①–⑤		
		Lindau Hbf 🚢 d.	...	...	...	...	...	...	...	...	...	...	...	...	0525	...	0602	*0601*	...	...	...	0638	0703k	...	...	...
		Hergatz **937** d.	...	...	...	...	...	...	...	...	...	...	...	...	0541	...	0619	0620	...	...	...	0657v	0723k	...	...	...
		Wangen (Allgäu) **937** d.	...	...	...	...	...	...	...	...	...	...	...	...	|	...	0624	0625	...	...	...	|	0728k	...	...	...
		Kißlegg **937** d.	...	...	...	*0516*	...	...	...	...	...	...	...	...	|	...	0634	0635	...	...	...	|	0739k	...	...	...
		Leutkirch d.	...	...	...	*0525*	...	...	...	...	...	...	...	...	|	...	0644	0644	...	...	...	|	0747k	...	...	...
	0	**Oberstdorf** d.	...	...	...	|	0503	...	...	...	...	...	...	0547	|	...	|	|	...	...	0705	|	|	...	...	...
	13	Sonthofen d.	...	...	...	|	0521	...	...	...	...	...	...	0605	|	...	|	|	...	...	0724	|	|	...	...	...
	21	Immenstadt ⊕ a.	...	...	...	|	0530	...	...	...	...	...	...	0616	0619	...	|	|	...	...	0734	0736	|	...	...	...
	21	Immenstadt ⊕ d.	...	...	...	|	0538	...	...	...	...	...	...	▷	0623	...	|	|	...	...	▶	0741	|	...	...	...
	46	**Kempten** Hbf ⊕ a.	...	...	...	|	0554	...	...	...	...	...	...	▬	0640	...	|	|	...	...	▬	0757	|	...	...	...
	46	**Kempten** Hbf ⊕ d.	0431	...	0542	|	0556	0603	...	...	0615	...	...	...	0643	0648	|	|	...	...	...	0758	|	...	0800	...
	81	Memmingen ⊕ a.	|	...	|	*0552*	0627	|	...	...	|	...	...	...	0712	|	0710	0710	...	...	...	|	0813	...	0826	...
	81	Memmingen ⊕ d.	|	0532	|	0600	0628	|	...	0622	|	0635	...	...	0714	|	...	▬	0738	...	...	|	0814	...	0828	0838
	133	**Ulm** Hbf a.	|	|	|	|	0725	|	...	|	|	|	...	...	0745	|	...	...	|	...	...	|	|	...	0858	|
		Mindelheim d.	|	0554	|	0621	▬	|	...	0644	|	0659	...	...	...	|	...	...	0800	...	⑥⑦	|	0831	...	...	0901
0		**Füssen** d.	|	|	|	|	...	|	...	|	|	|	...	0546	...	|	...	...	|	0703	0703	|	|	...	...	|
31		Marktoberdorf d.	|	|	|	|	...	|	...	|	|	|	...	0631	...	|	...	...	|	0751	0751	|	|	...	...	|
43		Kaufbeuren d.	0502	|	0615	|	...	0631	...	|	0647	|	...	0655	...	0720	...	...	|	0804	0816	0827v	|	0844	...	|
		Türkheim (Bay) d.	|	0602	|	0631	...	|	...	0653	|	0706	...	...	...	|	...	...	0809	...	|	|	|	|	...	0910
63		Buchloe ⊕ a.	0517	0609	0629	0637	⑥⑦	0646	...	0700	0702	0713	...	...	...	0734	...	①–⑤	0816	...	0830	0843v	0843	0900	...	0918
63		Buchloe ⊕ d.	0534	0610	0631	0640	0647	0649	0652	0713	0710	0714	0722	...	...	0735	...	0820	0820k	...	0831	0849	0851	0903	...	0920
103		**Augsburg** Hbf a.	*0607*q	|	|	0712	0716	0716	|	|	0743	|	0757	...	...	*0832*	...	|	0856	...	|	0916	|	|	...	|
		Kaufering d.	0542	0618	0640	...	...	...	0700	0721	...	0723	...	...	...	0743	...	0828	...	...	0840	...	0900	0912	...	0928
		Geltendorf d.	|	0628	0650	...	...	...	0710	0731	...	0732	...	...	...	|	...	0837	...	...	0849	...	0909	0923	...	0937
		München Pasing a.	0610	0652	0716	...	...	...	0734	0756	...	0753	...	...	...	0811	...	0858	...	...	0910	...	0933	0949	...	0958
		München Hbf ⊡ a.	0618	0700	0724	...	...	...	0745	0804	...	0801	...	...	...	0819	...	0908	...	...	0918	...	0941	0958	...	1007

A – ALLGÄU – (12) (*IC* **2013**) (Leipzig - Magdeburg on dates in Table **810** -) Hannover - Dortmund - Köln - Stuttgart - Ulm (*RE* **2013**) - Oberstdorf.
H – NEBELHORN – (12) Hamburg (**2083**) - Augsburg (**2085**) - Oberstdorf. See Table **900** for timings from Hamburg.
N – From / to Nürnberg (Table **905**).
Q – From Nürnberg (Table **905**) on † (also Aug. 15).

b – Change trains at Buchloe on ⑥⑦.
e – ①–⑤ only.
f – On ⑥⑦ Buchloe a. 1737, d. 1744, Türkheim d. 1751, Mindelheim d. 1801, Memmingen a. 1822.
k – 3–4 minutes later on ①–⑤.

n – On ①–⑤ Mindelheim d. 2006, Memmingen a. 2027.
q – *0557* on ⑥.
r – Not Aug. 15.
s – Not Oct. 3.
v – 3–5 minutes later on ⑥⑦.

• – Change trains at Buchloe and Türkheim.
★ – (12) and ✕ München - Bregenz - St Gallen - Zürich (Table **75**).
◁ – Detached from train in previous column at Immenstadt.
▷ – Attached to train in the next column at Immenstadt.
▶ – On ⑥⑦ attached to train in the next column at Immenstadt (change trains on ①–⑤).
♥ – On ⑥⑦ Türkheim d. 0714, Bad Wörishofen a. 0720.
❖ – Change trains at Memmingen on ①–⑤.
⊡ – Most trains in Table **935** use platforms 27 – 36 at München Hbf (minimum connecting time from / to other services is 10 minutes).
⊕ – Many services connect at Buchloe, Memmingen, Kempten and Immenstadt (connecting trains may be found in preceding columns). Minimum connectional time is 3 minutes.

ALX – Arriva-Länderbahn-Express. Operated by Arriva / Regentalbahn AG - Die Länderbahn.

km		♥	①–⑤	⑥⑦	①–⑤					①–⑤	⑥⑦											①–⑤	⑥⑦			
0	**Augsburg** Hbf d.	...	*0643*	0729	0733	0803**b**	0929	*1045*	1129	*1203*	*1245*	1327	*1444*	1518	1546	*1603*•	*1644*	1729	...	*1803*•	*1845*	1940	1940	*2045*	*2147*	*2309*•
40	Buchloe d.	*0641*	*0715*	0800	0820	0851	1000	1120	1200	1253	1323	1400	1522	1600	1620	*1643*	1723	1800	1837	*1844*	1923	2011	2020	*2131*	2237	*2348*
48	Türkheim (Bay) d.	0658	0727	0812	0831	0859	1012	1127	1212	1300	1330	1412	1529	1612	1631	1702	1730	1812	1844	1910	1930	2018	2031	2144	2246	2358
53	**Bad Wörishofen** a.	0704	0733	0818	0837	0906	1018	1133	1218	1306	1336	1418	1535	1618	1637	1708	1736	1818	1850	1916	1936	2024	2037	2151	2252	0004

RE / *RB* services except where shown **LINDAU and OBERSTDORF - ULM, AUGSBURG and MÜNCHEN** 935

For services to / from Bad Wörishofen see pages 440 and 441

			ALX	*ALX* 🍷			*EC* **191** ★✕					*IC* **2084** **H**	*IC* **2012** **A** 🍷	*ALX*	*ALX* 🍷			*EC* **193** ★✕						*ALX*	*ALX* 🍷	
Lindau Hbf 🏛 d.	...	0727	...	0747	...	0803	0912	...	0841	...	...	...	...	...	0959	...	1007	1112	...	1041	...	...	...	...	1159	...
Hergatz **937** d.	...	0744	...	0804	...	0823	|	...	0859	...	...	...	...	...	1016	...	1023	|	...	1059	...	...	...	...	1216	...
Wangen (Allgäu) **937** d.	...	|	...	|	...	0828	|	...	|	...	...	...	...	...	|	...	1028	|	...	|	...	...	...	...	|	...
Kißlegg **937** d.	...	|	...	|	...	0838	|	...	|	...	...	...	...	...	|	...	1039	|	...	|	...	...	...	...	|	...
Leutkirch d.	...	|	...	|	...	0847	|	...	|	...	...	...	...	...	|	...	1049	|	...	|	...	...	...	...	|	...
Oberstdorf d.	0750	|	0805	|	...	|	|	0900	|	...	...	0931	0945	1019	|	...	|	|	1101	|	...	...	1145	1219	|	...
Sonthofen d.	0808	|	0822	|	...	|	|	0922	|	...	...	0953	1007	1038	|	...	|	|	1120	|	...	...	1206	1238	|	...
Immenstadt ⊕ a.	0819	0822	0835	0839	...	|	|	0933	0939	...	...	1001	1015	1046	1051	...	|	|	1131	1139	...	...	1218	1246	1251	...
Immenstadt ⊕ d.	▷	0830	▷	0851	...	|	|	...	0940	...	...	1016	1033	▷	1058	...	|	|	▷	1140	...	...	1233	▷	1258	...
Kempten Hbf ⊕ a.	▬	0847	▬	0906	...	|	|	...	0956	...	...	1032	1049	▬	1112	...	|	|	...	1156	...	...	1249	▬	1312	...
Kempten Hbf ⊕ d.	...	0851	...	0907	...	|	|	...	0957	1004	...	1034	1052	...	1113	...	|	|	...	1158	1201	...	1252	...	1313	...
Memmingen ⊕ a.	...	0917	...	|	...	0914	1012	...	|	1027	...	|	1112	...	|	...	1115	1212	...	|	1227	...	1315	...	|	...
Memmingen ⊕ d.	...	0918	...	|	...	0934	1014	...	|	1028	1037	|	1124	...	|	...	1134	1214	...	|	1228	1240	1317	...	|	...
Ulm Hbf a.	...	0945	...	|	...	|	|	...	|	1058	|	|	1154	...	|	...	|	|	...	|	1258	|	1345	...	|	...
Mindelheim d.	...	...	...	|	...	1001	|	...	|	▬	1101	|	...	...	|	...	1201	|	...	|	▬	1301	▬	...	|	...
Füssen d.	...	...	0749	|	0854	|	|	...	|	...	|	|	...	1019	|	1055	|	|	...	|	...	|	...	1219	|	1253
Marktoberdorf d.	...	...	0835	|	0940	|	|	...	|	...	|	|	...	1105	|	1142	|	|	...	|	...	|	...	1304	|	1340
Kaufbeuren d.	...	...	0848	0933	0954	|	|	...	1027	...	|	|	...	1116	1139	1155	|	|	...	1228	...	|	...	1315	1339	1354
Türkheim (Bay) d.	...	...	...	|	|	1010	|	...	|	...	1110	|	...	...	|	|	1210	|	...	|	...	1310	...	...	|	|
Buchloe ⊕ a.	...	...	...	0947	1009	1017	1041	...	1043	...	1117	1135	...	...	1153	1209	1217	1241	...	1244	...	1316	...	...	1353	1409
Buchloe ⊕ d.	0922	...	...	0955	1020	1022	1043	...	1052	1048	1119	1136	...	...	1155	1220	1222	1243	...	1252	1248	1325	1322	...	1354	1420
Augsburg Hbf a.	0957	...	...	*1017*	|	1057	|	...	|	1119	|	1159	...	...	*1230*	|	1257	|	...	|	1317	|	1356	...	*1430*	|
Kaufering d.	...	...	...	1003	1028	...	|	...	1100	...	1128	...	...	...	1203	1228	...	|	...	1300	...	1337	...	...	1402	1428
Geltendorf d.	...	...	...	|	1037	...	|	...	1109	...	1137	...	...	...	|	1237	...	|	...	1310	...	1347	...	...	|	1437
München Pasing a.	...	...	...	1033	1058	...	|	...	1133	...	1158	...	...	...	1233	1258	...	|	...	1333	...	1410	...	...	1433	1458
München Hbf ⊡ a.	...	...	...	1041	1107	...	1128	...	1141	...	1207	...	...	...	1241	1307	...	1328	...	1341	...	1417	...	...	1441	1507

				N				*ALX*	*ALX* 🍷			*EC* **195** ★✕						⑥⑦	*ALX*	*ALX* 🍷		**G**	⊖	**N**	⑥⑦**L**	
Lindau Hbf 🏛 d.	...	...	...	1241	...	...	...	...	1359	...	...	1512	...	*1441*	...	...	...	1530	...	1559	1607**c**	...	...	1642	1703	...
Hergatz **937** d.	1222	...	...	1300	...	...	...	...	1416	...	1419	|	...	1504	...	...	...	1548	...	1616	1619**t**	...	...	1700	|	...
Wangen (Allgäu) **937** d.	1227	...	...	|	...	...	...	...	|	...	1428	|	...	|	...	...	...	|	...	|	1624**t**	...	...	|	|	...
Kißlegg **937** d.	1238	...	...	|	...	...	...	...	|	...	1440	|	...	|	...	...	...	|	...	|	1640	...	...	|	|	...
Leutkirch d.	1247	...	...	|	...	...	...	...	|	...	1450	|	...	|	...	...	...	|	...	|	1650	...	...	|	|	...
Oberstdorf d.	|	...	1301	|	...	...	1345	1419	|	...	|	|	1501	|	...	...	1539	|	1620	|	|	...	1659	|	|	1737
Sonthofen d.	|	...	1321	|	...	...	1406	1438	|	...	|	|	1521	|	...	...	1607	|	1639	|	|	...	1719	|	|	1807
Immenstadt ⊕ a.	|	...	1331	1336	...	...	1418	1446	1451	...	|	|	1531	1539	...	...	1618	1624	1646	1651	|	...	1728	1738	|	1818
Immenstadt ⊕ d.	|	...	▷	1339	...	...	1433	▷	1458	...	|	|	▷	1540	...	...	1638	1638	▷	1658	|	...	1734	1739	|	▷
Kempten Hbf ⊕ a.	|	...	...	1355	...	...	1449	▬	1512	...	|	|	...	1557	...	...	1654	1654	▬	1712	|	...	1750	1755	|	▬
Kempten Hbf ⊕ d.	|	1318	...	1404	...	...	1452	...	1513	...	|	|	...	1558	1600	...	1702	1702	...	1713	|	...	1758	1756	|	...
Memmingen ⊕ a.	1313	1356	...	|	...	...	1517	...	|	...	1524	1612	...	|	1623	...	1727	1727	...	|	1723	...	1819	|	1823	...
Memmingen ⊕ d.	1331	1358	...	|	...	1440	1531	...	|	...	1535	1614	...	|	1624	1635	1731	1731	...	|	1725**t**	...	1820	|	1824	1836
Ulm Hbf a.	|	1440	...	|	...	|	1559	...	|	...	|	|	...	|	1658	|	1758	1758	...	|	|	...	1858	|	|	|
Mindelheim d.	1401	...	...	|	...	1504	▬	...	|	...	1601	|	...	|	▬	1701	▬	...	...	|	1801	...	▬	|	|	1901
Füssen d.	|	...	...	|	...	|	...	1419	|	1454	|	|	...	|	...	|	...	...	1619	|	|	1655	...	|	|	|
Marktoberdorf d.	|	...	...	|	...	|	...	1505	|	1541	|	|	...	|	...	|	...	...	1705	|	|	1740	...	|	|	|
Kaufbeuren d.	|	...	...	1434	...	|	...	1516	1539	1554	|	|	...	1628	...	|	...	...	1716	1739	|	1756	...	1833	|	|
Türkheim (Bay) d.	1410	...	...	|	...	1511	...	...	|	|	1610	|	...	|	...	1710	...	...	...	|	1810	|	...	|	|	1910
Buchloe ⊕ a.	1417	...	...	1448	...	1518	...	...	1553	1608	1616	1641	...	1644	...	1717	...	...	...	1753	1816	1810	...	1848	1858	1917
Buchloe ⊕ d.	1423	...	...	1449	1452	1520	1522	...	1555	1619	1622	1643	...	1651	1648	1719	1723	...	...	1755	1820	1819	1850	1849	1909	1919
Augsburg Hbf a.	1457	...	...	1516	|	|	1557	...	*1630*	|	1657	|	...	|	1717	|	1757	...	...	*1830*	1856	|	|	1916	|	|
Kaufering d.	...	...	...	...	1500	1528	...	...	1603	1627	...	|	...	1700	...	1728	...	...	...	1803	...	1827	1859	...	|	1928
Geltendorf d.	...	...	...	...	1509	1537	...	...	|	1637	...	|	...	1710	...	1737	...	...	...	|	...	1837	1910	...	1925	1937
München Pasing a.	...	...	...	...	1533	1558	...	...	1633	1658	...	|	...	1734	...	1758	...	...	...	1833	...	1857	1933	...	|	1957
München Hbf ⊡ a.	...	...	...	...	1541	1607	...	...	1641	1707	...	1728	...	1742	...	1807	...	...	...	1841	...	1907	1941	...	1955	2007

		ALX	*ALX* 🍷		⑥⑦	①–⑤		**N** †**d**	⚒**e**	⑥⑦	①–⑤						⑥⑦	①–⑤	*EC* **197** ★✕	*ALX*	*ALX* 🍷			*ALX*		
Lindau Hbf 🏛 d.	1730	...	1758	...	...	...	...	1842	1842	...	...	...	...	...	1932	2009	...	...	2016	...	2030	...	...	2139	...	...
Hergatz **937** d.	1747	...	1816	...	1818	1818	...	1859	1859	...	...	...	...	...	1948	2029	...	...	|	...	2047	...	...	2156	...	...
Wangen (Allgäu) **937** d.	|	...	|	...	1828	1828	...	|	|	...	...	...	...	...	|	2034	...	...	|	...	|	...	...	|	...	...
Kißlegg **937** d.	|	...	|	...	1840	1840	...	|	|	...	...	...	...	...	|	2044	...	...	|	...	|	...	...	|	...	...
Leutkirch d.	|	...	|	...	1850	1850	...	|	|	...	...	...	...	...	|	2053	...	...	|	...	|	...	...	|	...	...
Oberstdorf d.	|	1816	|	...	|	|	1904	|	|	...	...	...	...	1949	|	|	...	...	|	2051	|	...	2151	|	...	...
Sonthofen d.	|	1839	|	...	|	|	1923	|	|	...	...	...	...	2011	|	|	...	...	|	2110	|	...	2214	|	...	...
Immenstadt ⊕ a.	1823	1846	1851	...	|	|	1934	1937	1939	...	...	...	...	2020	2025	|	...	...	|	2119	2123	...	2223	2231	...	...
Immenstadt ⊕ d.	1830	▷	1858	...	|	|	▶	1940	1940	...	...	...	...	▬	2026	|	...	...	|	▷	2132	...	▬	2233	...	...
Kempten Hbf ⊕ a.	1846	▬	1912	...	|	|	...	1956	1956	...	...	...	...	...	2043	|	...	...	2120	▬	2147	...	...	2249	...	...
Kempten Hbf ⊕ d.	1850	...	1913	...	|	|	...	1958	1959	1959	2014	...	...	2044	▬	|	2049	2113	2122	...	2151	2207	...	▬	2256	2259
Memmingen ⊕ a.	1915	...	|	...	1927	1927	...	|	|	2020	2039	...	...	|	...	2125	2116	2137	|	...	|	2233	...	...	2327	|
Memmingen ⊕ d.	1931	...	|	...	1929	1945	...	|	|	2021	2048	2046	...	|	...	...	2131	2138	|	2143	|	2234	2258	...	2328	|
Ulm Hbf a.	1959	...	|	...	|	|	...	|	|	2058	2149	|	...	|	...	...	2159	2222	|	|	|	2322	|	...	0001	|
Mindelheim d.	▬	...	|	...	2001	2006	...	|	|	▬	▬	2112		|	...	...	...	...	|	2211	|	...	2326	...	...	|
Füssen d.	...	1819	|	*1855*	|	|	...	|	|	...	...	|	2003	|	...	...	...	...	|	|	|	...	|	2222	...	|
Marktoberdorf d.	...	1905	|	1940	|	|	...	|	|	...	...	|	2049	|	...	...	...	...	|	|	|	...	|	2308	...	|
Kaufbeuren d.	...	1916	1939	1954	|	|	...	2027	2029	...	...	|	2102	2114	...	...	...	...	|	|	2219	...	|	2322	...	2331
Türkheim (Bay) d.	...	...	|	|	2011	2020	...	|	|	...	...	2119	...	|	←	...	...	...	|	2219	|	...	2334	...	...	|
Buchloe ⊕ a.	...	...	1953	2008	2017	2026	...	2043	2045	⚒**e**	†**d**	2125	...	2129	2125	...	...	...	2204	2226	2232	...	2341	...	...	2345
Buchloe ⊕ d.	1922	...	1955	2020**c**	2022	2027	...	2048	2051	2048	2051	2134	...	2141	2134	...	...	...	2206	2241	2234	...	2348	...	...	2346
Augsburg Hbf a.	1957	...	*2030*	|	2056	2103	...	2116	|	2116	|	→	...	2214	|	...	...	...	*2236*	2316	|	...	0021	...	...	|
Kaufering d.	...	...	2003	2028**c**	...	...	...	...	2059	...	2059	...	...	...	2143	...	...	...	|	...	2242	...	...	...	...	2356
Geltendorf d.	...	...	|	2037**c**	...	...	...	...	2109	...	2109	...	...	...	2152	...	...	...	|	...	2251	...	...	...	...	0006
München Pasing a.	...	...	2033	2058**c**	...	...	...	...	2129	...	2129	...	...	...	2214	...	...	...	|	...	2312	...	...	...	...	0029
München Hbf ⊡ a.	...	...	2041	2107**c**	...	...	...	...	2137	...	2137	...	...	...	2221	...	...	...	2245	...	2320	...	...	...	...	0039

A – ALLGÄU – (12) and 🍷 Oberstdorf - Ulm - Stuttgart - Köln - Dortmund - Hannover (- Leipzig on dates in Table **810**).
G – ⑥⑦ (runs daily Füssen - Kaufbeuren and Buchloe - München).
H – NEBELHORN – (12) Oberstdorf - Augsburg (**2082**) - Hamburg. See Table **900** for timings to Hamburg.
L – Until Oct. 4.
N – To Nürnberg (Table **905**).

c – ⑥⑦ only.
d – Also Aug. 15.
e – Not Aug. 15.
t – 5 minutes later on ⑥⑦.

• – Change trains at Türkheim and Buchloe.
⊖ – Change trains at Kempten on ①–⑤.
★ – (12) and ✕ Zürich - St Gallen - Bregenz - München (Table **75**).
▷ – Attached to train in the next column at Immenstadt.
▶ – On ⑧ attached to train in one of the next two columns at Immenstadt (change trains on ⑥).
⊡ – Most trains in Table **935** use platforms 27 – 36 at München Hbf (minimum connecting time to other services is 10 minutes).
⊕ – Many services connect at Buchloe, Memmingen, Kempten and Immenstadt (connecting trains may be found in preceding columns). Minimum connectional time is 3 minutes.

ALX – *Arriva-Länderbahn-Express*. Operated by Arriva / Regentalbahn AG - Die Länderbahn.

	①–⑤	①–⑤	①–⑤	⑥⑦	①–⑤	⑥⑦						①–⑤	⑥⑦									⑥⑦	①–⑤			
Bad Wörishofen d.	0544	0613	0643	0656	0711	0740	0823	0921	1023	1141	1223	1324	1341	1423	1540	1623	1651	1741	1823	1855	1941	2023	2029	2108	2208	2324
Türkheim (Bay) a.	0551	0620	0650	0703	0718	0746	0829	0928	1029	1147	1229	1330	1347	1430	1547	1629	1657	1748	1829	1902	1947	2029	2035	2115	2215	2331
Buchloe a.	*0609*	*0637*	*0700*	*0713*	*0730*	0757	0838	0935	1037	1158	1237	1337	1357	1437	1556	1637	*1717*	1758	1836	*1917*	1957	2037	2043	*2125*	*2226*	*2341*
Augsburg Hbf a.	*0647*•	*0712*	*0743*•	*0757*•	*0811*	0830	*0916*	1017	*1119*	1230	*1317*	1430	1430	*1516*	1630	*1717*	*1757*•	1830	*1916*	*1957*•	2030	*2116*	*2116*	*2214*•	*2316*	*0021*

936 STUTTGART - TÜBINGEN - HORB

IRE / RE services

km			Ⓐe	2	Ⓐ				
0	**Stuttgart** Hbf ..... 930 937 d.	0048	0520	0517g	0616	0722	0822	and hourly until	2322
22	Plochingen .... 930 d.	0107	0539	0557	0638	0742	0844		2344
35	Nürtingen .... d.	0119	0552	0609	0652	0755	0855		2355
57	Reutlingen Hbf .... 937 d.	0136	0609	0627	0709	0812	0912		0012
71	**Tübingen** Hbf .... 937 a.	0150	0620	0644	0721	0823	0923		0023

			Ⓒ	Ⓐ		Ⓒ	Ⓐ				
Tübingen Hbf .... 937 d.	0536	0628	0730	0737	0837	0932	0937	1037	and hourly until	2137	2236
Reutlingen Hbf .... 937 d.	0547	0638	0740	0748	0848	0943	0948	1048		2148	2250
Nürtingen .... d.	0603	0655	0757	0804	0904	0959	1004	1104		2204	2306
Plochingen .... 930 d.	0618	0705j	0818	0818	0918	1018	1018	1118		2218	2319
Stuttgart Hbf .. 930 937 a.	0638	0723j	0838	0838	0938	1038	1038	1138		2238	2338

TÜBINGEN Hbf - **HORB** *32 km.* 2nd class only. Journey time: 28 – 40 minutes.
From **Tübingen** at 0535 Ⓐ, 0558 Ⓐ, 0633 Ⓐ, 0641 Ⓒ, 0802, 0835 Ⓒ, 1004, 1035, 1204, 1235, 1303 Ⓐ, 1333 Ⓐ, 1404 Ⓒ, 1435, 1604, 1635, 1703 Ⓐ, 1804, 1835, 1933 Ⓐ, 2006, 2036, 2133 Ⓒ, 2236. From **Horb** at 0455 Ⓐ, 0619 Ⓐ, 0640 Ⓒ, 0648 Ⓐ, 0730 Ⓐ, 0750 Ⓒ, 0848, 0922, 1048, 1122, 1248, 1322, 1420 Ⓐ, 1448, 1522, 1648, 1722, 1817 Ⓐ, 1846, 1922, 2048, 2122, 2249 Ⓒ.

e – Not Aug. 3 - Sept. 11. **g** – *0532* on Ⓐ. **j** – On Ⓒ Plochingen d. 0709, Stuttgart a. 0728.

937 STUTTGART - TÜBINGEN - AULENDORF - HERGATZ

DB (IRE / RB services); HzL

km		⑥k	2Ⓐ	2Ⓐ	2Ⓐ	2Ⓒ	‡Ⓐ		‡Ⓒ	‡Ⓐ		‡	2	‡		‡		‡◧		‡◇		‡	2		†	‡
0	**Stuttgart** Hbf ..... 936 d.	...	...	...	...	...	...	...	...	0616	0816	0822	1016	1022	1216	1222	1416	1422	1616	1622	1816	1822	...	2016	...	2122
57	Reutlingen .... 936 d.	...	...	...	...	...	...	...	...	0709	0849	0912	1049	1112	1249	1312	1449	1512	1649	1712	1849	1912	...	2049	...	2212
71	**Tübingen** Hbf .... 936 d.	...	...	...	...	...	0546	0658	0725	0727	0900	0928	1100	1128	1300	1328	1500	1528	1700	1728	1900	1928	...	2100	...	2234
96	Hechingen .... d.	...	...	...	...	...	0616	0718	0749	0753	0919	0952	1119	1152	1320	1352	1519	1552	1719	1752	1918	1952	...	2119	...	2257
113	Balingen (Württ) .... d.	...	...	...	...	...	0638	0731	0808	0808	0932	1006	1132	1206	1335	1406	1535	1610	1732	1807	1930	2009	...	2133	...	2312
131	Albstadt-Ebingen .... d.	...	...	...	...	...	0659	0744	0829	0829	0947	1029	1145	1229	1347	1429	1547	1629	1745	1830	1945	2030	...	2150	...	2331
158	**Sigmaringen** .... a.	...	...	...	...	...	0723	0809	0853	0853	1010	1054	1209	1254	1411	1454	1611	1654	1811	1854	2009	2054	...	2211	...	2355v
158	**Sigmaringen** ...... 938 d.	...	...	0540	0645	0655	0727	0810	0901	0901	1011	1059	1210	1303	1412	1501	1611	1701	1811	1900	2011	...	2111	2213	2235	...
175	Herbertingen ...... 938 d.	...	...	0555	0708	0712	0743	0823	0917	0917	1024	1112	1225	1318	|	1518	1624	1717	1825	1917	2024	...	2130	2228	2249	...
184	Bad Saulgau .... d.	...	...	0609	0724	0725	...	0832	0927	0927	1033	1127	1234	1327	1432	1527	1633	1727	1834	1927	2033	...	2138	2237	2256	...
203	**Aulendorf** .... d.	...	...	0625	0741	0741	...	0848	0943	0943	1049	1143	1250	1343	1448	1543	1650	1742	1850	1942	2049	...	2153	2252	2309	...
	Change trains					2 d				2 d		2		2	2Ⓐ	2	2Ⓐ	2		2			2		2†	
203	**Aulendorf** .... d.	0556	0556	...	...	0808	...	...	...	1008	...	1208	...	1408	1515	1608	1715	1808	...	2013	...	...	2208	...	2314	...
213	Bad Waldsee .... d.	0604	0613	...	...	0816	...	...	...	1016	...	1216	...	1416	1524	1616	1724	1816	...	2021	...	...	2216	...	2322	...
233	Kißlegg .... 935 a.	0620	0632	...	...	0835	...	...	...	1035	...	1235	...	1435	1549	1635	1749	1835	...	2040	...	...	2235	...	2341	...
246	Wangen (Allgäu) . 935 a.	0647	0648	...	...	0850	...	...	...	1051	...	1250	...	1450	...	1651	...	1849	...	2056	...	...	2250	...	0010	...
252	**Hergatz** .... 935 a.	0653	0653	...	...	0855	...	...	...	1056	...	1255	...	1455	...	1656	...	1855	...	2101	...	...	2255	...	0016	...

	Ⓐ	2Ⓐ	‡Ⓒ	2Ⓐ	2	2			2		2		2		2	Ⓐ		2	2⑤		2			2		
Hergatz .... 935 d.	...	...	...	0533	...	0659	...	...	0902	...	1102	...	1302	...	1502	1619	...	1702	1818	...	1902	...	...	2106	...	...
Wangen (Allgäu) ... 935 d.	...	...	...	0538	...	0704	...	...	0907	...	1107	...	1307	...	1507	1624	...	1707	1828	...	1907	...	...	2111	...	...
Kißlegg .... 935 d.	...	0517	...	0554	0631k	0719	...	...	0922	...	1122	...	1324	...	1522	1637	...	1722	1841	...	1922	...	...	2126	...	...
Bad Waldsee .... d.	...	0535	...	0616	0647k	0737	...	...	0940	...	1140	...	1342	...	1540	1653	...	1740	1857	...	1940	...	...	2144	...	...
Aulendorf .... a.	...	0543	...	0624	0655k	0745	...	...	0948	...	1148	...	1350	...	1548	1701	...	1748	1905	...	1948	...	...	2151	...	...
Change trains		‡Ⓐ		Ⓐ	|	2	‡		‡		‡	2	‡		‡◧	|		‡			2	‡	2	2Ⓐ	2†	2
Aulendorf .... d.	...	0553	...	0633	0707	0812	...	0907	1012	1107	1212	1308	1412	1508	1612	1707	1707	1812	...	1908	2012	...	2118	2201	2201	2313
Bad Saulgau .... d.	...	0608	...	0650	0723	0833	...	0926	1033	1123	1234	1328	1433	1527	1633	1726	1726	1836	...	1927	2035	...	2139	2217	2217	2330
Herbertingen .... 938 d.	...	0616	...	0702	0732	0844	...	0935	1044	1132	1244	1338	1444	1538	1643	1736	1736	1844	...	1936	2046	...	2148	2229	2229	2339
Sigmaringen .... 938 a.	...	0630	...	0719	0747	0858	...	0947	1057	1146	1258	1349	1458	1549	1656	1749	1749	1858	...	1948	2102	...	2205	2244	2256	2355
Sigmaringen .... d.	0545	0634	0657	...	0748	...	0902	0949	1100	1149	1303	1350	1500	1550	1700	1750	1750	1910	...	1949	▬	2106	...	...	...	...
Albstadt-Ebingen .... d.	0608	0703	0722	...	0807	...	0926	1010	1124	1210	1327	1410	1528	1609	1724	1811	1811	1934	...	2008	...	2130	...	...	...	...
Balingen (Württ) .... d.	0620	0734	0746	...	0824	...	0950	1023	1149	1223	1350	1423	1553	1625	1749	1823	1823	1954	...	2025	...	2149	...	...	...	...
Hechingen .... d.	0634	0752	0804	...	0836	...	1007	1036	1207	1236	1407	1436	1607	1637	1807	1840	1840	2009	...	2038	...	2205	...	...	...	...
Tübingen Hbf ...... 936 a.	0653	0815	0828	...	0857	...	1030	1057	1230	1257	1430	1457	1630	1657	1830	1857	1857	2032	...	2059	2137	2229	...	...	...	...
Reutlingen .... 936 a.	0707	0847	0847	...	0908	...	1047	1108	1247	1308	1447	1508	1647	1708	1847	1908	1908	2047	...	2108f	2147	2249	...	...	...	...
Stuttgart Hbf .... 936 a.	0743	0938	0938	...	0943	...	1138	1143	1338	1343	1538	1543	1738	1743	1938	1943	1943	2138	...	2143f	2238	2338	...	...	...	...

d – Runs daily. **k** – ⑥ (not Oct. 3). ◇ – Change trains at Sigmaringen on ①–⑤. ‡ – Operated by Hohenzollerischen Landesbahnen (HzL)
f – ⑤–⑦ only. **v** – † only. ◧ – Change trains at Sigmaringen on ①–⑤ July 30 - Sept. 11 and Oct. 26 – 30. Tübingen - Sigmaringen and v.v. 2nd class only.

938 ULM and ROTTWEIL - NEUSTADT (Schwarzw) - FREIBURG

DB (RE / RB services); HzL

km		Ⓒ	Ⓐ	‡Ⓐ	2Ⓐ		Ⓐ	Ⓒ			⊖2	2		2		2		2		2		2		2	2†
0	**Ulm** Hbf .... d.	...	...	...	...	...	0554	0605	...	0810	0915	0915	1014	1115	1214	1315	1414	1515	1614	1715	1814	1916	2024	2112	2112
16	Blaubeuren .... d.	...	...	...	...	...	0609	0618	...	0822	0927	0927	1025	1127	1225	1327	1425	1527	1625	1727	1825	1928	2036	2131	2131
34	Ehingen (Donau) .... d.	...	...	...	...	...	0628	0634	...	0835	0943	0943	1038	1142	1238	1343	1438	1542	1638	1743	1838	1945	2053	2147	2147
76	Herbertingen .... 937 d.	...	...	...	...	...	0708	0701	...	0907	1012	1012	1112j	1214	1305	1411	1505	1611	1706	1811	1906	2013	2128	2216	2216
93	**Sigmaringen** .... 937 a.	...	...	...	...	...	0723	0716	...	0922	1028	1028	1125	1228	1322	1428	1521	1627	1721	1828	1921	2029	2142	2233	2233
93	**Sigmaringen** .... d.	...	...	...	...	...	0733	0717	...	0930	1030	▬	1130	▬	1330	▬	1530	▬	1730	▬	1930	▬	▬	▬	2239
135	Tuttlingen .... a.	...	...	...	...	...	0814	0750	...	1010	1108	...	1210	...	1410	...	1610	...	1810	...	2010	...	...	...	2313
135	Tuttlingen .... d.	...	...	...	...	...	0816	0816	...	1016	1111	...	1216	...	1416	...	1616	...	1816	...	2016	...	...	...	2314
145	Immendingen .... 916 d.	...	...	...	...	...	0824	0824	...	1024	1119	...	1224	...	1424	...	1624	...	1824	...	2024	‡	...	‡Ⓐ	2323
	Rottweil .... §d.	...	...	0558	0700	0705z	|	|	0911	|	|	1111	|	1311	|	1511	|	1711	|	1911	|	2119	...	2157	|
	Trossingen Bahnhof ▲ .. §d.	...	...	0608	0713	0716z	|	|	0920	|	|	1120	|	1320	|	1520	|	1720	|	1920	|	2129	...	2208	|
	Villingen (Schwarzw) 916 §d.	0605	0620	0629	0733	0738	|	|	0938	|	|	1138	|	1338	|	1538	|	1738	|	1938	|	2145	2213	2245f	|
164	Donaueschingen .... 916 §a.	0615	0640	0647	...	0749	0839	0839	0949	1039	1138	1149	1239	1349	1439	1549	1639	1749	1839	1949	2039	...	2221	2302	2336
164	Donaueschingen .... d.	0616	0642	...	...	0750	0848	0848	0950	1048	...	1150	1248	1350	1448	1550	1648	1750	1848	1950	2048	...	...	...	...
204	**Neustadt** (Schwarzw) .... a.	0656	0726	...	...	0826	0926	0926	1026	1126	...	1226	1326	1426	1526	1626	1726	1826	1926	2026	2126	...	...	...	...

km		2⑥k	‡⑥k	‡Ⓐ	Ⓐ	‡Ⓒ	Ⓒ	Ⓐ														⚒	2†	‡Ⓒ	
0	**Neustadt** (Schwarzw) .... d.	...	...	...	...	...	...	0627	0732	0832	0932	1032	1132	1232	1330	1432	1532	1632	1732	1832	1932	2032	2032	...	2202
40	Donaueschingen .... a.	...	...	...	...	...	...	0705	0809	0910	1009	1110	1209	1310	1409	1510	1609	1710	1809	1910	2009	2107	2109	...	2240
40	Donaueschingen .... 916 §d.	...	0458	0503	0518	0715	0720	0719	0810	0919	1010	1119	1210	1319	1410	1519	1610	1719	1810	1919	2010	2108	2119	2122	2241
54	Villingen (Schwarzw) 916 §d.	...	0518	0522	|	0736	|	|	0822	|	1022	|	1222	|	1422	|	1622	|	1822	|	2022	2118	|	2146j	2259
69	Trossingen Bahnhof ▲ .. §d.	...	0548h	0538	|	0752	|	|	0835	|	1035	|	1235	|	1435	|	1635	|	1835	|	2035	2143e	|	2201	...
81	**Rottweil** .... §a.	...	0559	0549	|	0802	|	|	0844	|	1044	|	1244	|	1444	|	1644	|	1844	|	2044	2153e	|	2211	...
	Immendingen .... 916 d.	...	▬	▬	0532	▬	0734	0740j	▬	0934	▬	1134	▬	1334	▬	1534	▬	1734	▬	1934	...	...	2134	...	...
	Tuttlingen .... a.	...	...	...	0539	...	0741	0748	...	0941	...	1141	...	1342	...	1541	...	1741	...	1941	...	...	2141	...	...
	Tuttlingen .... d.	...	...	...	0542	...	0751	0751	...	0947	...	1147	...	1347	...	1547	...	1747	...	1947	...	...	2156	...	...
	Sigmaringen .... a.	...	2Ⓐ	2Ⓒ	0622	2	0825	0825	2	1022	2	1222	2	1422	2	1622	2	1822	2	2022	...	...	2231	...	...
	Sigmaringen .... 937 d.	0520	0534	0611	0633	0727	0830	0830	0923	1030	1128	1230	1323	1430	1525	1629	1724	1830	1923	2032	...	...	2235	...	...
	Herbertingen .... 937 d.	0533	0548	0626	0646	0743	0845	0845	0937	1045	1143	1245	1339	1445	1538	1645	1737	1847	1939	2047	...	...	2248	...	...
	Ehingen (Donau) .... d.	0602	0617	0702	0715	0814	0917	0917	1011	1117	1211	1317	1411	1517	1611	1717	1810	1919	2014	2114	...	...	...	...	...
	Blaubeuren .... d.	0619	0633	0720	0732	0833	0930	0930	1026	1130	1226	1330	1426	1530	1626	1730	1829	1932	2026	2131	...	...	...	...	...
	Ulm Hbf .... a.	0637	0645	0740	0744	0845	0942	0942	1038	1142	1238	1342	1438	1542	1638	1742	1841	1943	2042	2142	...	...	...	...	...

km		Ⓐ🚌	Ⓐ	⚒	Ⓐ	Ⓐ🚌	Ⓐ	Ⓐ	Ⓒ	Ⓒ	Ⓐ	Ⓑm										🚌		
0	**Neustadt** (Schwarzw) d.	...	0531	0600	0610	...	0631	...	0701	0708	...	0731	0801	...	0831	...	and at the same	...	2031	...	...	2040	2131	2223
	Seebrugg .... d.	0503	|	|	|	0603	|	0641	|	|	0705	|	|	...	|	0839	minutes past	1939	|	...	2021	|	|	|
5	Titisee .... d.	0531	0538	0607	0616	0631	0638	0708	0708	0715	0731	0738	0808	...	0838	0908	each hour until	2008	2038	...	2048	2056	2138	2230
36	**Freiburg** (Brsg) Hbf .. a.	...	0617	0645	...	...	0719	0748	0748	...	...	0818	0848	...	0918	0948		2048	2118	...	...	2148	2218	2313

km		Ⓐ	Ⓐ	⑥k	Ⓐ	Ⓐ	Ⓒ	Ⓒ	Ⓐ	Ⓐ										🚌				
0	**Freiburg** (Brsg) Hbf ... d.	...	0540	🚌	...	0640	0640	...	0710	...	0742	...	0810	0840	and at the same	1910	1940	...	2010	...	...	2110	2225	2325
31	Titisee .... d.	0610	0617	0628	0630	0719	0722	0724	0749	0752	0819	...	0849	0919	minutes past	1949	2019	...	2049	2053	2058	2149	2301	0001
50	**Seebrugg** .... a.	0635	|	0659	0658	|	0748	|	|	0818	|	...	0915	|	each hour until	2015	|	...	|	2124	|	|	|	|
	Neustadt (Schwarzw) a.	...	0623	...	...	0725	...	0730	0755	...	0825	...	...	0925		...	2025	...	2055	...	2104	2155	2307	0007

e – Ⓐ only.
f – Arrives 2224.
h – Arrives 0533.
j – Arrives 7 – 8 minutes earlier.
k – Not Oct. 3.
m – Also Oct. 3.

z – Ⓒ only.
⊖ – ①–⑤ July 30 - Sept. 11.
‡ – Operated by Hohenzollerischen Landesbahnen (HzL). 2nd class only.
▲ – Regular services operate to / from Trossingen Stadt (operated by HzL). Journey time: 5 minutes.

§ – **Additional trains** (operated by HzL) Rottweil - Donaueschingen and v.v. Journey time: 48 – 54 minutes (64 – 66 minutes for trains marked *).
From Rottweil at 0646 Ⓐ, 0748 Ⓒ, 0754 Ⓐ, 0952, 1152, 1352, 1552, 1651 Ⓐ, 1754 and 1952, 2253 Ⓒ.
From Donaueschingen at 0546 Ⓐ, 0618 * Ⓐ, 0902 * Ⓒ, 0915 Ⓐ, 1115, 1315 Ⓒ, 1317 Ⓐ, 1515, 1618 Ⓐ, 1715 and 1915.

LINDAU - SCHAFFHAUSEN - BASEL

IRE / RB services — **939**

km																									
		Ⓐ			Ⓐ	Ⓒ	2Ⓐ	2Ⓒ	U	2	U	2	U	2	U	2	U	2	U	2	2	2†	2⚒	2†	2
0	**Lindau** Hbf 931 d.	...	...	...	0641	0647	0703	0706	0834	0906	1028	1101	1231	1305	1432	1503	1634	1706	1834	1906	2012	2012	2102	2102	2142
24	**Friedrichshafen** Stadt 931 d.	0436	...	...	0704	0713	0732	0732	0914	0938	1114	1138	1313	1338	1513	1538	1714	1740	1915	1933	2035	2035	2130	2130	2240
58	Überlingen d.	0514	...	...	0730	0733	0807	0807	0934	1012	1134	1212	1334	1412	1534	1612	1734	1814	1934	2010	2113	2113	2155	2155	2315
83	Radolfzell 916 d.	0540	...	0637	0752	0752	0843	0843	0953	1043	1153	1243	1353	1443	1553	1643	1753	1843	1953	2043	2140	2141	2213	2212	2341
93	**Singen** 916 a.	0547	...	0647	0759	0759	0856	0856	1000	1056	1200	1256	1400	1456	1600	1656	1800	1856	2000	2056	▬	2149	2222 ▬	2228	2350
				Ⓐ			Ⓐ			Ⓐ		Ⓐ		Ⓐ		Ⓐ		Ⓐ		2Ⓐ	2Ⓒ	2 d	2	2 d	
93	**Singen** 940 d.	0552	0552	0651	0802	0802	0902	...	1002	1102	1202	1302	1402	1502	1602	1702	1802	1902	2002	2106	...	2206	...	2306	...
112	**Schaffhausen** 940 d.	0611	0611	0710	0815	0815	0915	...	1015	1115	1215	1315	1415	1515	1615	1715	1815	1915	2015	2126	...	2225	2302	0002t	...
131	Erzingen (Baden) d.	0625	0625	0729	0829	0829	0929	...	1029	1129	1229	1329	1429	1529	1629	1729	1829	1929	2029	2142	...	...	2324	0024	...
151	Waldshut d.	0640	0640	0742	0842	0842	0942	...	1042	1142	1242	1344	1442	1542	1642	1742	1842	1942	2042	2157	2234	...	2342	...	...
174	Bad Säckingen d.	0654	0654	0755	0855	0855	0955	...	1055	1155	1255	1356	1455	1555	1655	1755	1855	1955	2055	2218	2256	...	...	...	...
191	Rheinfelden (Baden) d.	0704	0704	0805	0905	0905	1005	...	1105	1205	1305	1405	1505	1605	1705	1805	1905	2005	2105	2234	2311	...	...	...	...
206	**Basel** Bad Bf a.	0715	0715	0816	0916	0916	1016	...	1116	1216	1316	1416	1516	1616	1716	1816	1916	2016	2116	2250	2326	...	...	...	...

		2	2Ⓐ	2Ⓐ	2Ⓒ	U	Ⓐ	U	Ⓐ	U		Ⓐ	U	Ⓐ	U	Ⓐ	U	Ⓐ	U	Ⓐ	2		Ⓐ		2
Basel Bad Bf d.	...	...	...	0456	...	0638	0743	0843	0943	1043	...	1143	1243	1343	1443	1543	1643	1743	1843	1943	1947	...	2043	2143	2258
Rheinfelden (Baden) d.	...	...	...	0512	...	0647	0751	0851	0951	1051	...	1151	1251	1351	1451	1551	1651	1751	1851	1951	2001	...	2051	2151	2312
Bad Säckingen d.	...	...	...	0530	...	0657	0801	0901	1001	1101	...	1201	1301	1401	1501	1601	1701	1801	1901	2001	2017	...	2101	2201	2328
Waldshut d.	...	...	...	0556	0602	0712	0815	0915	1015	1115	...	1215	1315	1415	1515	1615	1715	1815	1915	2015	2039	...	2115	2215	2350
Erzingen (Baden) d.	...	...	0531	0625	0632	0729	0829	0929	1029	1129	...	1229	1329	1429	1529	1629	1729	1829	1929	2029	...	...	2128	2231	...
Schaffhausen 940 d.	...	0527	0556	0644	0659	0742	0842	0942	1042	1142	...	1242	1342	1442	1542	1642	1742	1842	1942	2042	...	...	2146	2244	...
Singen 940 a.	...	0547	0617	0702	0716	0756	0856	0956	1056	1156	...	1256	1356	1456	1556	1656	1756	1856	1956	2056	...	...	2202	2259	...
	2Ⓐ	2Ⓒ		d	d		d 2		d 2			d 2		d 2		d 2		d 2		d 2		2	d		
Singen 916 d.	0540	0610	0621	0709	0723	0758	0902	0958	1102	1158	...	1302	1358	1502	1558	1702	1758	1902	1958	2102	...	2202	2212	2305	...
Radolfzell 916 d.	0548	0618	0629	0718	0732	0806	0914	1006	1114	1206	...	1314	1406	1514	1606	1714	1806	1918	2006	2118	...	2223	2221	2316	...
Überlingen d.	0612	0642	0656	...	...	0824	0942	1024	1142	1224	...	1342	1424	1542	1624	1742	1824	1955	2025	2141	...	2246	...	2342	...
Friedrichshafen Stadt 931 a.	0649	0724	0743	...	...	0843	1022	1043	1222	1243	1329	1422	1443	1622	1643	1827	1843	2030	2044	2219	...	2324	...	0020	...
Lindau Hbf 931 a.	0738	0752	0817	...	...	0908	1054	1125	1256	1325c	1351	1452	1527	1659	1725	1859	1926	2100	2135	2244	...	0014	...	...	...

U – From / to Ulm (Table 933). c – Ⓒ only. d – Runs daily. t – Arrives 2327.

STUTTGART - SINGEN - SCHAFFHAUSEN - ZÜRICH

940

km																										
					‡ ①–⑤	⑥⑦		①–⑤	ICE 181 ✕ F		①–⑤	ICE 183 ✕		ICE 185 ✕ ❖		ICE 187 ✕		ICE 281 ✕		ICE 283 ✕			ICE 285 ✕ ⊖			
0	**Stuttgart** Hbf 942 d.	...	...	...	0518	0618	...	0618	0758	0818	0918	0955	1018	1153	1218	1355	1418	1553	1618	1755	1818	1918	1958	2018	2118	2225
26	Böblingen 942 d.	...	...	...	0538	0638	...	0638	|	0838	0938	|	1038	|	1238	|	1440	|	1638	|	1838	1938	|	2038	2138	2245
42	Herrenberg 942 d.	...	...	...	0547	0650	...	0650	|	0850	0947	|	1050	|	1250	|	1450	|	1650	|	1850	1948	|	2050	2147	2259
57	Eutingen im Gäu 942 d.	...	...	...	0600	0705	...	0705	|	0907	1004	|	1107	|	1307	|	1507	|	1707	|	1907	2004	|	2105	2203	2314
67	Horb d.	...	...	...	0608	0714	...	0717	0841	0917	1012	1040	1117	1240	1317	1440	1517	1640	1717	1840	1917	2012	2041	2114	2213	2322
110	Rottweil d.	...	...	...	0641	0744	...	0751	0910	0951	1047	1110	1151	1310	1351	1510	1551	1710	1751	1910	1951	2047	2110	2146	2249c	2353
138	Tuttlingen d.	...	...	...	0720	0805	...	0818j	0927	1014	...	1127	1214	1327	1414	1527	1614	1727	1814	1927	2014	...	2127	▬	▬	0014
157	Engen 916 d.	...	...	...	0736	0822	...	0835	|	1030	...	|	1230	|	1430	|	1630	|	1830	|	2030	...	|	...	...	0029
172	**Singen** 916 a.	...	...	...	0746	0833 ▬	...	0844	0949	1040 ▬	...	1149	1240 ▬	1349	1440 ▬	1549	1640 ▬	1749	1840 ▬	1949	2040 ▬	...	2149	...	...	0039
172	**Singen** 939 d.	0552	0631	0734	0751	...	0834e	0906	0954	1034	...	1154	1234	1354	1434	1554	1634	1754	1834	1954	2006	...	2156	2206	2306	0051c
191	**Schaffhausen** 939 a.	0604	0652	0753	0806	...	0853	0924	1007	1053	...	1207	1253	1407	1453	1607	1653	1807	1853	2007	2024	...	2209	2225	2327	0108c
191	**Schaffhausen** d.	0607	0707	0754	...	0809	0909	...	1009	1109	...	1209	1309	1409	1509	1609	1709	1809	1909	2009	2109	...	2211	2309	0009	...
219	Bülach d.	0630	0730	0826	...	0830	0930	...	1030	1130	...	1230	1330	1430	1530	1630	1730	1830	1930	2030	2130	...	2231v	2330	0038	...
239	**Zürich** HB a.	0648	0748	...	...	0848	0948	...	1048	1148	...	1248	1348	1448	1548	1648	1748	1848	1948	2048	2148	...	2248v	2348	0057	...

			2				ICE 284 ✕ ⊡			ICE 282 ✕		ICE 280 ✕		ICE 186 ✕		ICE 184 ✕ △			ICE 182 ✕		ICE 180 ✕					
Zürich HB d.	0017	...	...	...	0504	0610	0710	...	0810	0910	1010	1110	1210	1310	1410	1510	1610	1705	1710	1810	1910	...	2010	2110	2210	2310
Bülach d.	0040	...	...	...	0531	0631	0731	...	0831	0931	1031	1131	1231	1331	1431	1531	1631	1725	1731	1831	1931	...	2031	2131	2231	2331
Schaffhausen a.	0107	...	...	...	0610	0657	0750	...	0852	0950	1052	1150	1252	1350	1452	1550	1654	1749	1751	1854	1951	...	2052	2152	2252	2352
Schaffhausen 939 d.	0114c	...	0527	...	0629	0710	0752	...	0904	0952	1104	1152	1304	1352	1504	1552	1704	...	1752	1904	1953	...	2104	2204c	...	...
Singen 939 a.	0132c ▬	...	0547	...	0648	0729	0805	...	0924 ▬	1005	1124 ▬	1205	1324 ▬	1405	1524 ▬	1605	1724 ▬	...	1805	1924 ▬	2005	...	2126	2224c ▬	...	...
			①–⑤																				⑥⑦			
Singen 916 d.	...	...	0551	...	0714k	...	0809	...	0919	1009	1119	1209	1319	1409	1519	1609	1719	...	1809	1919	2009	...	2130	...	...	...
Engen 916 d.	...	...	0600	...	0724k	...	|	...	0928	|	1128	|	1328	|	1528	|	1728	...	|	1928	|	...	2139	...	...	...
Tuttlingen d.	①–⑤	...	0616	...	0739k	...	0832	...	0945	1032	1145	1232	1346	1432	1545	1632	1745	...	1832	1945	2032	...	2153	...	...	...
Rottweil d.	0507	0603	0641	0703	0810	...	0849	0908	1010	1049	1210	1249	1410	1449	1610	1649	1811	...	1849	2010	2049	...	2215	...	...	...
Horb d.	0541	0642	0711	0743	0846	...	0921	0943	1046	1121	1246	1321	1446	1521	1646	1721	1846	...	1921	2046	2121	2146	2246	①–⑤	...	...
Eutingen im Gäu 942 d.	0555	0655	|	0756	0857	...	|	0956	1057	|	1257	|	1457	|	1657	|	1857	...	|	2057	|	2159	2256	2256	...	...
Herrenberg 942 d.	0611	0711	0726	0811	0912	...	|	1011	1111	|	1311	|	1511	|	1711	|	1911	...	|	2111	|	2212	2310	2310	...	...
Böblingen 942 d.	0622	0722	0737	0822	0922	...	|	1022	1122	|	1322	|	1522	|	1722	|	1922	...	|	2122	|	2230	2322	2330	...	...
Stuttgart Hbf 942 a.	0642	0742	0757	0842	0942	...	1006	1042	1142	1202	1342	1406	1542	1602	1742	1806	1942	...	2007	2142	2206	2255	2342	2355	...	...

F – From Frankfurt (Table 911).

c – ⑥⑦ only.

e – 0838 on ⑥⑦.

j – Arrives 0811.

k – On ⑥⑦ departs Singen 0721, Engen 0731, Tuttlingen 0745.

v – Sept. 13–17 does not call at Bülach and arrives Zürich 2258.

‡ – Operated by Hohenzollerischen Landesbahnen Rottweil - Singen.

△ – Runs as *IC* **486** on ①–④.

❖ – Runs as *IC* **487** on ①–④.

⊖ – Runs as *IC* **489** on ①–③.

⊡ – Runs as *IC* **488** on ②–④.

PFORZHEIM - HORB and BAD WILDBAD

RB services (2nd class only) — **941**

km																										
		Ⓐ	Ⓒ	Ⓐ	Ⓐ	Ⓐ	Ⓒ					Ⓒ	Ⓐ		Ⓒ	Ⓐ		Ⓒ	Ⓐ		Ⓒ	Ⓐ				⑦
0	**Horb** d.	0453	0540	0548	0616	0649	0653	0751	0853	0953	1053	1131	1153	1253	1331	1353	1453	1531	1553	1653	1731	1753	1853	1934	2119	2251
15	Hochdorf (b. Horb) d.	0504	0551	0559	0627	0700	0704	0802	0904	1004	1104	1147	1204	1304	1347	1404	1504	1547	1604	1704	1747	1804	1904	1955v	2130	2305
25	Nagold d.	0518	0601	0609	0637	0710	0714	0813	0914	1014	1114	1214t	1214	1314	1414t	1414	1514	1614t	1614	1714	1814t	1814	1914	2014v	2141	2315
34	Wildberg (Württ) d.	0526	0609	0617	0645	0718	0722	0821	0922	1022	1122	1222	1222	1322	1422	1422	1522	1622	1622	1722	1822	1822	1922	2022	2149	2323
45	Calw d.	0537	0620	0628	0657	0731	0736	0832	0934	1033	1134	1235	1235	1333	1435	1433	1532	1635	1633	1732	1835	1833	1932	2033	2200	2334
52	Bad Liebenzell d.	0545	0629	0643v	0705	0744	0744	0843	0944	1043	1144	1243	1243	1344	1443	1444	1544	1643	1644	1744	1843	1844	1944	2041	2207	2342
71	**Pforzheim** Hbf a.	0607	0651	0706	0726	0808	0808	0907	1007	1107	1207	1307	1307	1407	1507	1507	1607	1707	1707	1807	1907	1907	2006	2107	2229	0006

	Ⓐ	Ⓐ		Ⓐ	Ⓒ		Ⓐ	Ⓒ		Ⓐ	Ⓒ		Ⓐ	Ⓒ		Ⓐ	Ⓒ	Ⓐ		Ⓐ					⑤–⑦
Pforzheim Hbf d.	0443	0638	0749	0849	0849	0949	1049	1049	1149	1249	1249	1349	1449	1449	1549	1649	1649	1719	1749	1819	1849	1949	2049	2142	2349
Bad Liebenzell d.	0505	0707v	0814	0915	0915	1014	1115	1115	1214	1315	1315	1414	1515	1515	1614	1715	1715	1745	1814	1845	1915	2014	2111	2209	0011
Calw d.	0512	0717	0822	0922	0922	1022	1122	1122	1222	1322	1322	1422	1522	1522	1622	1722	1722	1753	1822	1853	1922	2022	2118	2216	0018
Wildberg (Württ) d.	0527	0733	0835	0935	0935	1035	1135	1135	1235	1335	1335	1435	1535	1535	1635	1735	1735	1805	1835	1905	1935	2035	2130	2227	0030
Nagold d.	0538	0743	0843	0943	0950v	1043	1143	1159t	1243	1343	1358t	1443	1543	1558t	1643	1743	1758t	1815	1843	1915	1943	2043	2142	2235	0038
Hochdorf (b. Horb) d.	0548	0753	0853	0953	1012t	1053	1153	1212	1253	1353	1412	1453	1553	1612	1653	1753	1812	1824	1853	1924	1953	2053	2155	2252v	0048
Horb a.	0600	0805	0905	1005	1024	1105	1205	1224	1305	1405	1425	1505	1605	1625	1705	1805	1825	1835	1905	1935	2005	2105	2207	2304	0100

S-Bahn service **S6 Pforzheim** Hbf - **Bad Wildbad** Bf. *23 km*. Journey time: 26–34 minutes. Trains continue to / start from Bad Wildbad Kurpark (additional journey time: 3–4 minutes).

From Pforzheim Hbf at 0017, 0517 Ⓐ, 0612 Ⓐ, 0647 ⚒, 0705 Ⓐ, 0747, 0847, 0947, 1047, 1147, 1227 Ⓐ, 1247, 1317 Ⓐ, 1347, 1447, 1547, 1617 Ⓐ, 1647, 1717 Ⓐ, 1747, 1817 Ⓐ, 1847, 1917 Ⓐ, 1947, 2047, 2147, 2217 and 2317.

From Bad Wildbad Bf at 0509 Ⓐ, 0536 Ⓐ, 0605 Ⓐ, 0639 ⚒, 0701 Ⓐ, 0739, 0809 Ⓐ, 0839, 0909 Ⓐ, 0939, 1039, 1139, 1219 Ⓐ, 1239 Ⓒ, 1309 Ⓐ, 1339, 1439, 1539, 1609 Ⓐ, 1639, 1709 Ⓐ, 1739, 1809 Ⓐ, 1839, 1939, 2039, 2139, 2255 and 2355.

t – Arrives 13–18 minutes earlier. v – Arrives 7–11 minutes earlier.

942 STUTTGART - FREUDENSTADT - OFFENBURG

DB (RE/RB services); OSB★; 2nd class only

km																									
					Ⓐ		Ⓒ	Ⓐ															Ⓒ		Ⓒ
0	Stuttgart Hbf .... 940 d.	...	...	...	0518	0618	0718	0718	0818	0918	1018	1118	1218	1318	1418	1518	1618	1718	1818	1918	2018	2118	2225	2335u	...
26	Böblingen .... 940 d.	...	...	...	0538	0638	0738	0738	0838	0938	1038	1138	1238	1338	1440	1538	1638	1738	1838	1938	2038	2138	2245	2359	...
42	Herrenberg .... 940 d.	...	...	...	0547	0650	0747	0748	0850	0947	1050	1147	1250	1347	1450	1547	1650	1747	1850	1948	2050	2147	2259	0013	0017
57	Eutingen im Gäu .. 940 d.	...	...	...	0635	0709	0802	0809	0909	1004f	1109	1204f	1309	1404f	1509	1604f	1709	1804f	1909	2009	2109	2209	2319	...	0040
62	Hochdorf (b. Horb) ...... d.	...	...	...	0643	0714	0806	0814	0914	1010f	1114	1210f	1314	1410f	1514	1610f	1714	1810f	1914	2014	2114	2214	2324	...	0045
87	Freudenstadt Hbf ...... a.	...	...	...	0712	0740	0831	0840	0940	1040	1140	1240	1340	1440	1540	1640	1740	1840	1940	2040	2140	2240	2348	...	0109
	Change trains	Ⓐ	Ⓒ	Ⓐ		Ⓐ	Ⓒ	Ⓐ	Ⓐ		Ⓐ	Ⓒ									Ⓐ				
87	Freudenstadt Hbf .. ★ d.	0533	0633	0640	...	0743	0834	0843	0943	1043	1143	1243	1343	1443	1543	1643	1743	1843	1943	2043	2143	...	...	...	...
103	Alpirsbach .... ★ d.	0550	0650	0657	...	0800	0851	0900	1000	1100	1200	1300	1400	1500	1600	1700	1800	1900	2000	2100	2200	...	...	...	...
112	Schiltach .... ★ d.	0601	0701	0708	...	0811	0902	0911	1011	1111	1211	1311	1411	1511	1611	1711	1811	1911	2011	2111	2211	...	...	...	...
122	Wolfach .... ★ d.	0612	0712	0719	...	0822	0913	0922	1022	1122	1222	1322	1422	1522	1622	1722	1822	1922	2022	2122	2222	...	...	...	...
126	Hausach 916 .... ★ a.	0616	0716	0723	...	0826	0917	0926	1026	1126	1226	1326	1426	1526	1626	1726	1826	1926	2026	2126	2226	...	...	...	...
159	Offenburg 916 .... ★ a.	0649	0754	0746	...	0854	0954	0954	1054	1154	1254	1354	1454	1554	1654	1754	1854	1954	2054	2158q	2301	...	...	...	...

		Ⓐ		Ⓐ	Ⓒ	Ⓐ	Ⓐ		Ⓐ		Ⓐ	Ⓒ								Ⓐ				
Offenburg 916 .... ★ d.	...	0446	...	0558	0649	0702	0804	0904	1004	1104	1159	1204	1304	1404	1504	1604	1704	1804	1904	2004	...	...	...	2226
Hausach 916 .... ★ d.	...	0521	...	0627	0718	0730	0831	0931	1031	1131	1231	1231	1331	1431	1531	1631	1731	1831	1931	2031	...	...	...	2253
Wolfach .... ★ d.	...	0526	...	0632	0723	0735	0836	0936	1036	1136	1236	1236	1336	1436	1536	1636	1736	1836	1936	2036	...	...	...	2258
Schiltach .... ★ d.	...	0537	...	0643	0735	0747	0847	0947	1047	1147	1248	1248	1347	1447	1547	1647	1747	1847	1947	2047	...	...	...	2309
Alpirsbach .... ★ d.	...	0550	...	0700	0747	0800	0900	1000	1100	1200	1300	1300	1400	1500	1600	1700	1800	1900	2000	2100	...	...	...	2321
Freudenstadt Hbf .... ★ a.	...	0607	...	0717	0804	0817	0917	1017	1117	1217	1317	1317	1417	1517	1617	1717	1817	1917	2017	2117	...	...	...	2338
Change trains	Ⓐ	Ⓐ	Ⓒ	d ¶	Ⓒ	Ⓐ	d		d			d								d		Ⓒ	Ⓐ	
Freudenstadt Hbf ....d.	0518	0615	0619	0719	0808	0819	0919	1019	1119	1219	...	1319	1419	1519	1619	1719	1820	1919	2019	2119	...	2219	2219	...
Hochdorf (b. Horb) ....d.	0542	0641	0645	0744	0836	0845	0944	1044	1144	1244	...	1344	1444	1544	1644	1744	1845	1948	2044	2151	...	2247	2247	...
Eutingen im Gäu .... 940 a.	0546	0646	0649	0749	0840	0849	0949	1049	1150	1249	...	1350	1449	1550	1649	1750	1850	1953	2049	2155	...	2252	2252	...
Herrenberg .... 940 a.	0610	0710	0710	0810	0911	0911	1010	1110	1210	1310	...	1410	1510	1610	1710	1810	1910	2010	2110	2212	2217	2310	2310	...
Böblingen .... 940 a.	0621	0721	0721	0821	0921	0922	1021	1121	1221	1321	...	1421	1521	1621	1721	1821	1921	2021	2121	...	2230	2321	2330	...
Stuttgart Hbf .... 940 a.	0642	0742	0742	0842	0942	0942	1042	1142	1242	1342	...	1442	1542	1642	1742	1842	1942	2042	2142	...	2255	2342	2355	...

d – Runs daily.
f – 4–5 minutes later on Ⓐ.
q – † only.
u – Departs from the underground platforms.
¶ – Change trains at Eutingen on Ⓒ.
★ – Freudenstadt - Offenburg operated by Ortenau-S-Bahn GmbH.

943 KARLSRUHE - FREUDENSTADT

S-Bahn (2nd class only)

km																								
		Ⓐ	⑥k	Ⓐ	Ⓐ	Ⓒ	Ⓐ	Ⓒ	†			B	A	A										
0	Karlsruhe Hbf ... 916 d.	0514	0519	0547	0604	0618	0708	0718	0804	0818	0918	1004	1018	1118	Train A	1604	1622	1718	1804	1818	1918	2018	2118	2218	2318
24	Rastatt .... 916 d.	0533	0533	0609	0634	0638	0738	0738	0829	0838	0938	1029	1038	1138	runs	1629	1638	1738	1829	1838	1938	2038	2138	2238	2340
40	Gernsbach Bf.............. d.	0601	0600	0640	0701	0700	0800	0800	0844	0900	0959	1044	1100	1200	hourly	1644	1700	1800	1844	1900	2000	2100	2200	2300	0000
51	Forbach (Schwarzw) .. d.	0626	0618	0659	0718	0718	0818	0818	0900	0918	1018	1100	1118	1218	and	1700	1718	1818	1900	1918	2018	2118	2218	2318	0018
61	Schönmünzach .... d.	0638	0631	0711	0733	0731	0830	0830	0911	0931	1031	1111	1131	1231	train B	1711	1731	1831	1911	1931	2031	2131	2231	2331	0033
74	Baiersbronn Bf .... d.	0654	0649	0725	0752	0749	0848	0848	0922	0948	1049	1122	1149	1249	runs every	1722	1753	1849	1922	1949	2049	2145	2245	2345	0047
79	Freudenstadt Stadt .. a.	0701	0657	0733	0759	0757	0856	0856	0929	0956	1057	1129	1157	1256	two hours	1729	1801	1857	1929	1957	2057	2152	2253	2353	0054
82	Freudenstadt Hbf..... a.	0707	0707	0738	0809	0805	0906	0906	0937	1007	1107	1137	1208	1307	until	1737	1809	1907	1937	2008	2107	2158	2258	2358	0059

	Ⓐ	Ⓐ	Ⓒ	Ⓐ		Ⓐ	Ⓐ	Ⓒ	⚒	A	A	B						†		†				
Freudenstadt Hbf ..... d.	0448	0533	0602	0617	0653	0720	0745	0753	0823	0853	0953	1023	Train A	1453	1553	1623	1653	1723	1753	1823	1853	1953	2053	2202	2302
Freudenstadt Stadt... d.	0455	0540	0607	0633	0703	0733	0803	0803	0830	0903	1003	1030	runs	1503	1603	1630	1703	1730	1803	1830	1903	2003	2103	2208	2308
Baiersbronn Bf............ d.	0502	0547	0615	0641	0710	0740	0810	0810	0837	0910	1010	1037	hourly	1510	1610	1637	1710	1737	1810	1837	1910	2010	2110	2216	2316
Schönmünzach .... d.	0519	0605	0630	0658	0728	0751	0828	0828	0849	0928	1028	1049	and	1528	1628	1649	1728	1749	1828	1849	1928	2028	2128	2230	2330
Forbach (Schwarzw) ... d.	0530	0620	0640	0710	0740	0801	0840	0840	0901	0940	1040	1101	train B	1540	1640	1701	1740	1800	1840	1901	1940	2040	2140	2242	2342
Gernsbach Bf .... d.	0546	0640	0700	0729	0800	0816	0900	0900	0916	1000	1100	1116	runs every	1600	1700	1716	1800	1813	1900	1916	2000	2100	2200	2300	0000
Rastatt.................916 a.	0601	0704	0721	0751	0821	0830	0921	0921	0930	1021	1121	1130	two hours	1621	1721	1730	1821	1826	1921	1930	2021	2121	2221	2321	0021
Karlsruhe Hbf.....916 a.	0624	0726	0740	0820	0840	0920	0940	0940	0954	1040	1140	1154	until	1640	1740	1754	1840	1854	1940	1955	2040	2145	2240	2340	0040

A – Train runs hourly.
B – Train runs every **two** hours.
k – Not Oct. 3.

944 MÜNCHEN - PASSAU

RE / RB services

km																										
		①-⑥	†w	⑥k									⊡										Ⓐ		⑤	
0	München Hbf ..... 878 d.	...	0536	0621	0723	0805	...	0923	1005	...	1123	1205	...	1323	1344	1405f	...	1523	1603	...	1723	1802t	...	1923	2024	2123
42	Freising.............. 878 d.	...	0604	0648	0749	0833	...	0949	1033	...	1149	1233	...	1347	1408	1433	...	1549	1631	...	1749	1831t	...	1949	2052	2149
76	Landshut (Bay) Hbf 878 d.	0536	0655	0711	0814	0903	...	1014	1104	...	1214	1312	...	1414	1431	1504	...	1614	1704	...	1814	1902	...	2013	2126	2214
121	Landau (Isar) .... d.	0621	0730	0742	0845	0938	...	1045	1135	...	1245	1341	...	1445	...	1538	...	1645	1736	...	1845	1936	...	2045	2202	2244
139	Plattling.......... 920/1 d.	0636	0744	0756	0858	0952	1004	1057	1150	1204	1257	1354	1404	1457	...	1552	1604	1657	1750	1804	1857	1950	2004	2057	2215	2303
191	Passau Hbf 🚌 920/1 a.	0718	0837	0837	0937	1026*	1041	1136	1226*	1241	1336	1426*	1441	1536	...	1626*	1641	1736	1826*	1841	1936	2026*	2041	2137	2258	2341

	2⚒r	Ⓐ	Ⓒ	Ⓐ													Ⓒ	Ⓐ								
Passau Hbf 🚌..920/1 d.	0438	0604	0615	0644	0719*	0821	0912	0930*	1021	1112	1130*	1221	1312	1330*	1421	1512	1530*	1530*	1621	1712	1730*	1821	1912	1930*	2023	2208
Plattling ....920/1 d.	0516	0642	0653	0727	0801	0901	0948	1005	1058	1148	1205	1258	1348	1405	1458	1548	1605	1605	1658	1748	1805	1858	1948	2005	2100	2247
Landau (Isar).............. d.	0531	0655	0707	0742	0816	0913	...	1019	1109	...	1219	1309	...	1419	1509	...	1619	1619	1709	...	1819	1909	...	2019	2111	2258
Landshut (Bay) Hbf 878 d.	0605	0729	0747	0813	0900	0946	...	1057	1146	...	1257	1346	...	1457	1546	...	1657	1700	1746	...	1857	1946	...	2057	2144	2328
Freising ....878 a.	0628	0748	0808	0845	0927	1008	...	1126	1208	...	1326c	1408	...	1526	1608	...	1726	1728	1808	...	1926	2008	...	2126	2208	2355
München Hbf.........878 a.	0657	0816	0836	0915	0957	1036	...	1157	1236	...	1357c	1436	...	1556	1636	...	1757	1817	1836	...	1957	2036	...	2157	2236	0021

c – Ⓒ only.
f – ⑤-⑦ only.
k – Not Aug. 15, Oct. 3.
r – Not Aug. 15.
t – On Ⓒ departs München 1805, Freising 1833.
w – Also Aug. 15.
* – ICE or IC connection.
⊡ – 17 minutes later on ⑥.

945 REGENSBURG - DONAUWÖRTH - ULM

RB services (2nd class only)

km																										
		Ⓒ	Ⓐ	Ⓐ	Ⓐ	Ⓒ	Ⓐ	Ⓒ	Ⓐ	Ⓐ	Ⓒ	Ⓐ	Ⓐ	Ⓒ	Ⓐ	Ⓐ	Ⓒ	Ⓐ	Ⓐ	Ⓒ	Ⓐ	Ⓐ	Ⓒ	Ⓐ	Ⓐ	
0	Regensburg Hbf ...... d.	...	...	0511	0615	0644	0744	0845	0845	0944	1044	1044	1144	1244	1244	1344	1444	1444	1544	1644	1644	1744	1844	1844	1944	2044
46	Neustadt (Donau)...... d.	...	...	0556	0655	0731	0831	0931	0931	1031	1131	1131	1231	1331	1331	1431	1531	1531	1631	1731	1731	1831	1931	1931	2031	2131
74	Ingolstadt Hbf............ a.	...	...	0621	0718	0752	0852	0952	0952	1052	1152	1152	1252	1352	1352	1453	1552	1552	1652	1752	1752	1852	1952	1952	2052	2152
74	Ingolstadt Hbf........... d.	0606	0604	0702	0808	0807	0907	1007	1007	1107	1207	1207	1308	1407	1407	1507	1607	1607	1707	1807	1807	1907	2007	2007	2107	2207c
95	Neuburg (Donau) ...... d.	0621	0624	0719	0826	0826	0926	1026	1026	1126	1226	1226	1326	1426	1426	1526	1626	1626	1726	1826	1826	1926	2026	2026	2126	2226c
127	Donauwörth.............. a.	0648	0652	0753	0853	0853	0953	1053	1053	1153	1253	1253	1353	1453	1453	1553	1653	1653	1753	1853	1853	1954	2053	2053	2153	2253c
127	Donauwörth............... d.	0702	0705	0802	0902	0902	1002	1102	1102	1202	1302	1302	1402	1502	1502	1601	1702	1702	1802	1902	1902	2002	2102	2102	...	...
153	Dillingen (Donau) ...... d.	0725	0725	0824	0930	0926	1024	1126	1130	1225	1326	1330	1424	1526	1530	1622	1726	1730	1825	1925	1933	2025	2126	2133	...	...
176	Günzburg.............. 930 a.	0745	0742	0841	0947	0945	1041	1145	1147	1243	1345	1347	1441	1545	1547	1640	1745	1747	1843	1944	1953	2043	2145	2152	...	...
200	Ulm Hbf................ 930 a.	0809	0816	0939*	1017	1009	1139*	1209	1216	1316	1409	1416	1539*	1609	1616	1716	1809	1822	1939*	2009	2016	2139	2211	2246	...	...

	Ⓐ	Ⓒ	Ⓐ	Ⓒ	Ⓐ	Ⓐ	Ⓒ	Ⓐ	Ⓐ	Ⓒ	Ⓐ	Ⓐ	Ⓒ	Ⓐ	Ⓐ	Ⓒ	Ⓐ	Ⓐ	Ⓒ	Ⓐ	Ⓐ	Ⓒ	Ⓐ	Ⓐ	Ⓒ	Ⓐ
Ulm Hbf............930 ‡ d.	...	...	0446	0524*	0621	0744	0748	0819*	0944	0948	1019*	1144	1148	1244	1344	1348	1419*	1544	1548	1644	1744	1748	1836*	1944	1948	2024*
Günzburg.........930 ‡ d.	...	...	0510	0615	0653	0804	0804	0913	1004	1004	1113	1204	1204	1313	1404	1404	1513	1603	1604	1713	1804	1804	1913	2004	2004	2113
Dillingen.....................‡ d.	...	...	0529	0633	0710	0827	0822	0930	1027	1022	1130	1227	1222	1330	1427	1422	1530	1627	1622	1730	1827	1822	1930	2027	2024	2130
Donauwörth...............‡ a.	...	...	0553	0653	0737	0850	0847	0953	1050	1047	1153	1250	1247	1353	1450	1447	1553	1650	1647	1753	1850	1847	1954	2050	2048	2153
Donauwörth.................. d.	0500	0512	0601	0702	0803	0903	0903	1003	1103	1103	1203	1303	1303	1403	1503	1503	1603	1703	1703	1803	1903	1903	2003	2102	2102	...
Neuburg (Donau) .... d.	0531	0536	0635	0737	0837	0937	0937	1037	1137	1137	1237	1337	1337	1437	1537	1537	1637	1737	1737	1837	1937	1937	2037	2137	2128	...
Ingolstadt Hbf............ a.	0550	0555	0654	0755	0855	0955	0955	1055	1155	1155	1255	1355	1355	1455	1555	1555	1654	1755	1755	1855	1955	1955	2055	2154	2145	...
Ingolstadt Hbf........... d.	0600	0605	0705	0805	0905	1005	1005	1105	1205	1205	1306	1405	1405	1505	1605	1605	1705	1805	1805	1905	2005	2005	...	...	...	...
Neustadt (Donau) .... d.	0620	0627	0729	0831	0931	1031	1027	1131	1231	1227	1331	1431	1427	1531	1631	1627	1731	1831	1831	1931	2031	2027	...	...	...	...
Regensburg Hbf....... a.	0707	0712	0812	0912	1012	1112	1112	1212	1312	1312	1411	1512	1512	1612	1712	1712	1812	1912	1912	2012	2112	2112	...	...	...	...

c – Ⓒ only.
* – Earlier arrival / later departure possible by IC train (Table **930**).
‡ – **Additional trains.** On Ⓒ: Ulm Hbf d. 2200 → Günzburg d. 2219 → Dillingen d. 2236 → Donauwörth a. 2301. On Ⓐ: Ulm Hbf d. 2224 → Günzburg d. 2245 → Dillingen d. 2301 → Donauwörth a. 2322.

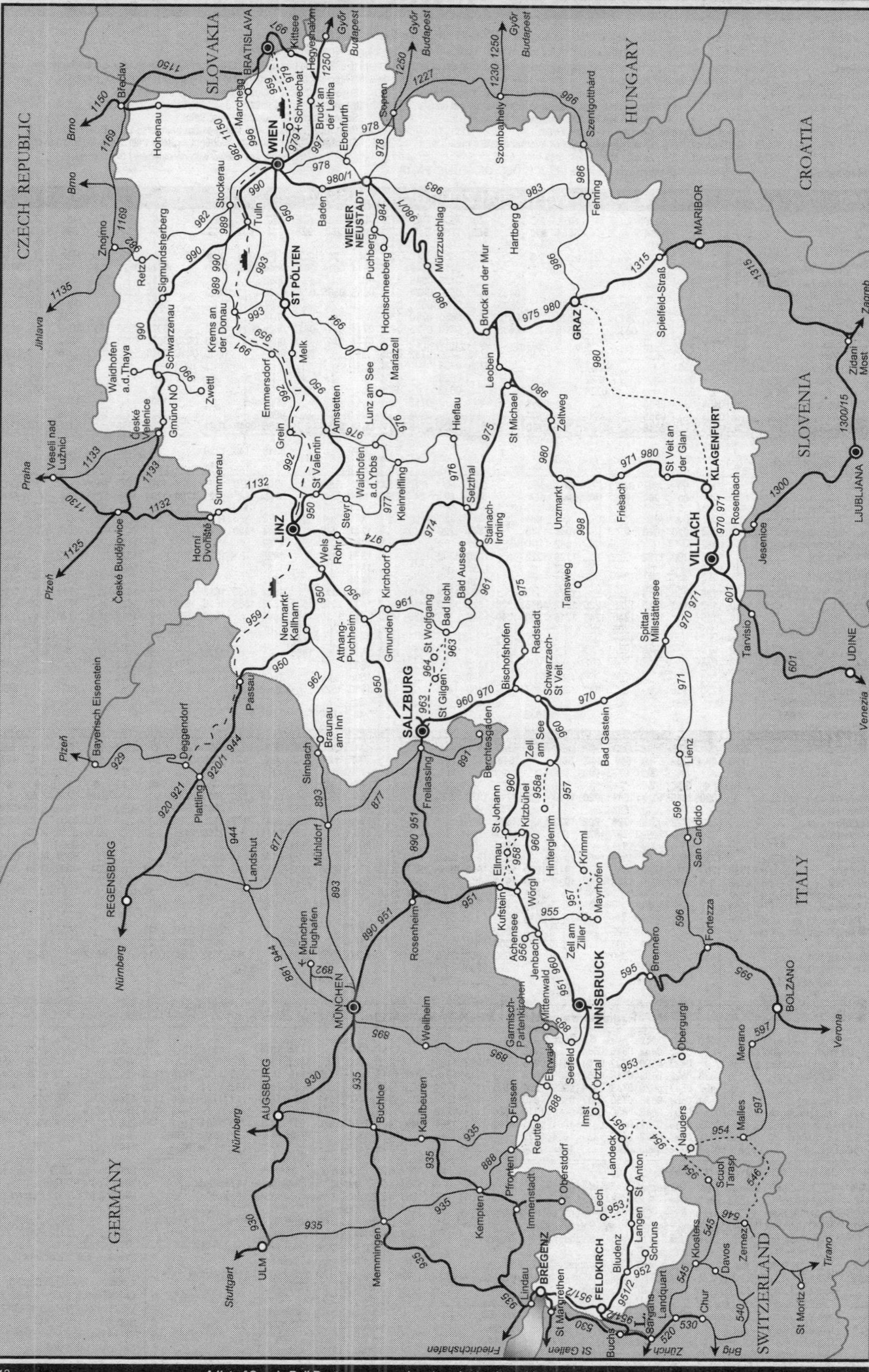
CZECH REPUBLIC
SLOVAKIA
HUNGARY
CROATIA
SLOVENIA
ITALY
SWITZERLAND
GERMANY
WIEN
BRATISLAVA
LINZ
ST PÖLTEN
SALZBURG
GRAZ
KLAGENFURT
VILLACH
INNSBRUCK
BREGENZ
FELDKIRCH
WIENER NEUSTADT
MÜNCHEN
AUGSBURG
ULM
REGENSBURG
MARIBOR
LJUBLJANA
BOLZANO
UDINE
Brno
Jihlava
Praha
Plzeň
Nürnberg
Stuttgart
Friedrichshafen
St Gallen
Zürich
Buchs
Sargans
Chur
Landquart
Klosters
Davos
Zernez
Scuol Tarasp
St Moritz
Tirano
Malles
Merano
Verona
Venezia
Zagreb
Zidani Most
Jesenice
Tarvisio
Győr
Budapest
Sopron
Szombathely
Szentgotthárd
Hegyeshalom
Břeclav
Znojmo
České Budějovice
České Velenice
Veselí nad Lužnicí
Horní Dvořiště
Summerau
Passau
Plattling
Deggendorf
Bayerisch Eisenstein
Landshut
Mühldorf
Simbach
Braunau am Inn
Freilassing
Berchtesgaden
Rosenheim
Kufstein
Wörgl
Jenbach
Achensee
Zell am Ziller
Mayrhofen
Kitzbühel
St Johann
Ellmau
Hinterglemm
Krimml
Zell am See
Schwarzach-St Veit
Bischofshofen
Radstadt
Bad Gastein
Spittal-Millstättersee
Lienz
San Candido
Fortezza
Brennero
Obergurgl
Ötztal
Imst
Landeck
St Anton
Langen
Lech
Bludenz
Schruns
Lindau
St Margrethen
Nauders
Seefeld
Mittenwald
Garmisch-Partenkirchen
Ehrwald
Reutte
Füssen
Pfronten
Immenstadt
Oberstdorf
Kempten
Memmingen
Buchloe
Kaufbeuren
Weilheim
München Flughafen
Gmunden
Attnang-Puchheim
Bad Ischl
St Wolfgang
St Gilgen
Bad Aussee
Stainach-Irdning
Selzthal
Kirchdorf
Wels
Neumarkt-Kallham
Steyr
Kleinreifling
Waidhofen a.d.Ybbs
Hieflau
Lunz am See
Amstetten
St Valentin
Grein
Emmersdorf
Melk
Mariazell
Krems an der Donau
Tulln
Stockerau
Hohenau
Marchegg
Schwechat
Kittsee
Bruck an der Leitha
Ebenfurth
Baden
Puchberg
Hochschneeberg
Mürzzuschlag
Bruck an der Mur
Leoben
St Michael
Zeltweg
Unzmarkt
Tamsweg
Friesach
St Veit an der Glan
Rosenbach
Spielfeld-Straß
Hartberg
Fehring
Gmünd NÖ
Zwettl
Waidhofen a.d.Thaya
Schwarzenau
Sigmundsherberg
Retz

AUSTRIA

Operator: Except where otherwise stated, rail services are operated by Österreichische Bundesbahnen (**ÖBB**).

Timings: Valid **June 14 - December 12, 2009** unless stated otherwise in individual tables. See page 2 for public holiday dates.

Services: Trains convey both first- and second-class seating unless footnotes show otherwise or there is a '2' in the train column. Overnight sleeping car (🛏) or couchette (▬) trains do not necessarily convey seating accommodation - refer to individual footnotes for details. Descriptions of sleeping and couchette cars appear on page 10.

Train categories:

RJ	**Railjet**	Austrian high-speed train. Conveys first and economy (2nd) class. *Premium class* also available to first class ticket holders (supplement payable).
ICE	**InterCity Express**	German high-speed train.
ÖEC	**ÖBB-EuroCity**	Quality international or internal express train.
ÖIC	**ÖBB-InterCity**	Quality internal express train.
EC	**EuroCity**	Quality international express train.
IC	**InterCity**	Internal or international express train.
D	**Schnellzug**	Ordinary fast train.
REX	**Regional Express**	Semi-fast regional train (also *EZ* – **Erlebniszug**).
EN	**EuroNight**	Quality overnight express train. Special fares payable.
		Local stopping trains are shown with no category / train number.

Reservations: Seats may be reserved on all express trains (*RJ, ICE, ÖEC, ÖIC, EC, IC, EN, D*).

950 WIEN - SALZBURG and PASSAU

km ♣		⚒ 2	⚒ 2	*REX* 1654 ⚒ 2	2	2	*REX* 6064 ⚒ 2	*EC* 390 ①–⑥ 🍷♦	⚒ 2	*D* 966	*REX* 1780 Ⓐ 2	*ÖIC* 540 🍷	*REX* 1782 Ⓒ 2	*ICE* 560 ✕	*ICE* 260 ✕	*ICE* 228 G✕	*ÖIC* 542 🍷	*ÖEC* 662 F✕	*ÖEC* 160 ✕♦	2	*ÖIC* 544 🍷	*RJ* 262 🍷	*ICE* 28 G✕	*ÖEC* 690 K✕	*EZ* 5918 W 2✕	*ÖEC* 162 ✕♦
0	**Wien** Westbahnhof ... d.	...	...	...	...	...	...	...	...	...	*0415*	0540	...	0614	0614	0640	0644	0657	0740	...	0744	0820	0840	0844	...	0940
6	**Wien** Hütteldorf ● .... d.	...	...	...	...	...	...	...	...	...	*0423*	0548	...	|	|	|	0652	|	|	...	0752	|	|	0852	0813	|
61	**St Pölten** Hbf .... d.	...	...	...	...	...	...	...	0433	...	*0529*	0624	...	0655	0655	0722	0728	|	0822	...	0828	0902	0922	0928	0909	1022
121	Amstetten .... d.	...	...	...	*0428*	...	0455	...	0535	...	0626	0653	0625	|	|	|	0757	|	|	...	0857	|	|	0957	1003	|
158	St Valentin .... **977** d.	0413	...	...	0513	...	0526	...	0613	...	0650	0710	0702	|	|	|	0814	|	|	...	0914	|	|	1014	1026	|
183	**Linz** Hbf .... **977** a.	0438	...	...	0538	...	0546	...	0638	...	0710	0725	0720	0744	0744	0813	0829	|	0913	...	0929	0950	1013	1029	1048	1113
183	**Linz** Hbf .... ‡ d.	▬	*0457*	0510	...	0547	...	0626	...	0653	0713	0728	0736	0747	0747	0816	0832	|	0916	0920	0932	0953	1016	1032	1052	1116
208	**Wels** Hbf .... ‡ d.	...	0523	0527	...	0616	...	0640	...	0713	0730	0742	0755	|	|	0830	0850	|	0930	0940	0946	|	1030	1046	1113	1130
	Neumarkt-Kallham. ‡ d.	...	0551	|	...	0647	...	|	...	0738	0758	|	0821	|	|	|	|	|	|	1008	|	|	|	|	1141	|
	Schärding .... d.	...	0624	|	...	0722	...	|	...	|	0828	|	0851	|	|	|	|	|	|	1042	|	|	|	|	1208	|
	Passau Hbf 🏛 ...... a.	2	0637	|	...	0736	...	|	...	|	0843	|	0906	|	|	0922	|	|	|	1055	|	|	1122	|	1220	|
238	Attnang-Puchheim..... d.	0459	...	0550	...	...	...	0658	...	⊙	...	0758	...	|	|	...	0907	|	|	...	1002	|	...	1102	...	|
243	Vöcklabruck .... d.	0503	...	0555	...	...	...	0704	...	|	...	0804	...	|	|	...	0913	|	|	...	1008	|	...	1108	...	|
308	**Salzburg** Hbf........... a.	0613	...	0648	...	...	...	0750	...	|	...	0848	...	0853	0853	...	0955	0948	1027	...	1050	1058	...	1150	...	1227
	München Hbf **890** .. a.	...	...	...	...	...	...	0935	...	0956	...	...	...	|	1031	...	|	|	|	...	...	1231	...	...	...	|
	Innsbruck Hbf **951**.. a.	...	...	...	...	...	...	...	...	...	...	...	...	1044	...	...	1348	1143	1230	...	...	...	...	...	...	1430
	Bregenz **951** .... a.	...	...	...	...	...	...	...	...	...	...	...	...	1312	...	...	...	...	...	...	...	...	...	...	...	...

	2	*ÖIC* 546 T🍷	*RJ* 60 🍷♦	*ICE* 26 H✕	*REX* 1788 2	*EC* 101 P✕	*ÖIC* 548 🍷	*ÖEC* 564 ✕	2	*ÖIC* 640 🍷	*RJ* 62 Z 🍷	*ICE* 24 H✕	*REX* 1790 Ⓐ 2	*ÖIC* 746 🍷	*ÖEC* 566 ✕	2	*ÖIC* 642 🍷	*ÖEC* 64 ◧ ✕	*ICE* 22 H✕	*REX* 1794 2	*REX* 1794 Ⓒ 2	*ÖIC* 692 K🍷	*REX* 1796 Ⓐ 2	*ÖEC* 568 ✕	2	*ÖIC* 644 🍷
Wien Westbahnhof .... d.	...	0944	1020	1040	...	...	1044	1140	...	1144	1220	1240	...	1244	1340	...	1344	1420	1440	...	...	1444	...	1540	...	1544
Wien Hütteldorf ● ..... d.	...	0952	|	|	...	...	1052	|	...	1152	|	|	...	1252	|	...	1352	|	|	...	...	1452	...	|	...	1552
St Pölten Hbf .... d.	...	1028	1102	1122	...	...	1128	1222	...	1228	1302	1322	...	1328	1422	...	1428	|	1522	...	...	1528	...	1622	...	1628
Amstetten .... d.	...	1057	|	|	...	...	1157	|	...	1257	|	|	...	1357	|	...	1457	|	|	...	...	1557	...	|	...	1657
St Valentin.......... **977** d.	...	1114	|	|	...	...	1214	|	...	1314	|	|	...	1414	|	...	1514	|	|	...	...	1614	...	|	...	1714
Linz Hbf .... **977** a.	...	1129	1150	1213	...	...	1229	1313	...	1329	1350	1413	...	1429	1513	...	1529	1550	1613	...	...	1629	...	1713	...	1729
Linz Hbf .... ‡ d.	1120	1132	1153	1216	1220	1226	1232	1316	1320	1332	1353	1416	1420	1432	1516	1520	1532	1553	1616	1620	1620	1632	1636	1716	1720	1732
Wels Hbf .... ‡ d.	1140	1146	|	1230	1240	1241	1246	1330	1340	1346	|	1430	1440	1446	1530	1540	1546	|	1630	1640	1640	1646	1654	1730	1740	1746
Neumarkt-Kallham ‡ d.	1208	|	|	|	1305	|	|	|	1408	|	|	|	1505	|	|	1608	|	|	|	1705	1705	|	1715	|	1808	|
Schärding.............. d.	1242	|	|	|	1337	|	|	|	1442	|	|	|	1537	|	|	1642	|	|	|	1738	1745	|	1745	|	1842	|
Passau Hbf 🏛 .... a.	1255	|	|	1322	1350	|	|	|	1455	|	|	1522	1550	|	|	1655	|	|	1722	...	1758	|	1758	|	1855	|
Attnang-Puchheim...... d.	...	1202	|	...	...	|	1302	|	...	1402	|	...	...	1502	|	...	1602	|	...	...	...	1702	...	|	...	1802
Vöcklabruck.............. d.	...	1208	|	...	...	|	1308	|	...	1408	|	...	...	1508	|	...	1608	|	...	...	...	1708	...	|	...	1808
Salzburg Hbf............ a.	...	1250	1258	...	...	1347	1352	1427	...	1450	1458	...	...	1550	1627	...	1650	1658	...	...	...	1750	...	1827	...	1850
München Hbf **890** .. a.	...	...	1431	...	...	...	...	|	...	...	...	...	...	...	|	...	...	1833	...	...	...	...	...	|	...	...
Innsbruck Hbf **951** .. a.	...	...	...	...	...	...	...	1633	...	...	...	...	...	...	1830	...	...	...	...	...	...	...	...	2031	...	...
Bregenz **951**.......... a.	...	...	...	...	...	...	...	1915	...	...	...	...	...	...	2105	...	...	...	...	...	...	...	...	2305	...	...

	REX 1798 Ⓐ 2	*RJ* 66 🍷♦	*ICE* 20 G✕	Ⓐ 2	*ÖIC* 646 🍷	*IC* 840 Ⓑ 🍷	*ÖEC* 660 ✕	2	*ÖIC* 648 🍷	*RJ* 68 🍷	*RJ* 762 Ⓑt 🍷	† 2	⚒ 2	*ÖIC* 740 🍷	*ÖEC* 764 ✕	*ÖIC* 742 🍷	*EN* 490 R ♦	*RJ* 42 Z 🍷	*IC* 744 🍷	*EN* 237 🅁 V	*D* 207 ♦	⚒ 2	*EN* 466 ♦	*EN* 246 △	*EN* 468 R ♦	*EN* 462 ♦
Wien Westbahnhof .... d.	...	1620	1640	...	1644	1720	1740	...	1744	1820	1820	...	...	1844	1920	1944	1954	2020	2040	2040	...	...	2125	2220	2240	...
Wien Hütteldorf ● ..... d.	...	|	|	...	1652	|	|	...	1752	|	|	...	...	1852	|	1952	2003	|	2048	2048	...	...	|	|	|	0009
St Pölten Hbf .... d.	...	|	1722	...	1728	1802	1822	...	1828	|	|	...	...	1928	|	2028	2041	2102	2125	2125	...	...	2209	2305	2325	0052
Amstetten .... d.	...	|	|	...	1757	1829	|	...	1857	|	|	...	...	1957	|	2057	2111	|	2155	2155	...	...	2239	2339	0000	|
St Valentin........... **977** d.	...	|	|	...	1814	|	|	...	1914	|	|	...	...	2014	|	2114	2130	|	2214	2214	...	...	|	0000	|	|
Linz Hbf .... **977** a.	...	1750	1813	...	1829	1856	1913	...	1929	1950	1950	...	...	2029	2050	2129	2145	2150	2229	2229	...	...	2311	0017	0035	0158
Linz Hbf .... ‡ d.	1736	1753	1816	1820	1832	...	1916	1920	1932	1953	1953	*1957*	2020	2032	2053	2132	2157	2153	2232	2232	2246	...	2314	0020	0038	0201
Wels Hbf .... ‡ d.	1756	|	1830	1840	1846	...	1930	1940	1946	|	|	2040	2040	2046	|	2146	2212	|	2246	2246	2303	2306	2329	0037	|	|
Neumarkt-Kallham ‡ d.	1822	|	|	1908	|	...	|	2008	|	|	|	2108	2108	|	|	|	|	|	|	|	|	2335	|	|	|	|
Schärding.............. d.	1853	|	|	1952	|	...	|	2042	|	|	|	2142	2142	|	|	|	2252	|	|	|	|	0009	|	|	|	|
Passau Hbf 🏛 .... a.	1906	|	1922	2005	|	...	|	2055	|	|	|	2155	2155	|	|	|	2304	|	|	|	|	...	|	|	|	|
Attnang-Puchheim...... d.	...	|	...	...	1902	...	|	...	2002	|	|	...	...	2102	|	2202	...	|	2305	2305	2323	...	|	0056	|	|
Vöcklabruck............... d.	...	|	...	...	1908	...	|	...	2008	|	|	...	...	2108	|	2208	...	|	2311	2311	2328	...	|	|	|	|
Salzburg Hbf............ a.	...	1858	...	...	1950	...	2027	...	2050	2058	2058	...	...	2150	2158	2250	...	2258	2352	2352	0014	...	0032	|	0155	0318
München Hbf **890**... a.	...	2034	...	...	...	...	|	...	...	2230	|	...	...	...	|	...	...	...	...	...	...	...	|	|	...	0615
Innsbruck Hbf **951** .. a.	...	...	...	...	...	...	2230	...	...	...	2300	...	...	...	2354	...	...	...	...	...	...	...	0237	0451	...	...
Bregenz **951**.......... a.	...	...	...	...	...	...	0056	...	...	...	...	...	...	...	...	...	...	...	...	...	...	...	...	0754	...	...

Regional trains WIEN - MELK - AMSTETTEN - LINZ (2nd class only)

km		⚒	Ⓐ L	⚒		S	W✕																			
0	**Wien** Westbahnhof ... d.	...	0415	*0452*	0610	0654	...	0918	...	1014	1118	...	1214*	1318	...	1414	1514	...	1614	1714	...	1814	1914	...	2129	2350
6	**Wien** Hütteldorf ● .... d.	...	0423	*0500*	0622	0701	0813	0926	...	1022	1126	...	1222*	1326	...	1422	1522	...	1622	1722	...	1822	1922	...	2136	2358
61	**St Pölten** Hbf .... d.	0433	0529	0602	0718	0752	0909	1015	1039	1115	1215	1239	1315	1415	1439	1515	1615	1639	1715	1815	1839	1915	2015	2129	2223	0047
85	Melk.......................... d.	0457	0547	0626	0743	0811	0929	1034	1103	1134	1234	1303	1334	1434	1503	1534	1634	1703	1734	1834	1903	1934	2034	2153	2241	0105
94	Pöchlarn .... d.	0504	0554	0633	0750	0817	0937	1040	1111	1140	1240	1311	1340	1440	1511	1540	1640	1711	1740	1840	1911	1940	2040	2200	2247	0112
107	Ybbs an der Donau ... d.	0517	0601	0646	0800	0826	0950	1049	1124	1149	1249	1324	1349	1449	1524	1549	1649	1724	1749	1849	1924	1949	2049	2213	2256	0121
124	Amstetten .... a.	0533	0616	0702	0813	0838	1001	1101	1140	1201	1301	1340	1401	1501	1540	1601	1701	1740	1801	1901	1940	2001	2101	2229	2308	0134
163	St Valentin .... **977** a.	0611	*0644*	0739	0840	...	1024	1139	...	1238r	1347	...	1439r	1538	...	1639r	1739	...	1839r	1939	...	2039r	*2141*	...	...	...
188	**Linz** Hbf .... **977** a.	0638	*0710*	*0808*	*0908*	...	1048	*1208*	...	*1308*r	...	...	*1508*r	*1608*	...	*1708*r	*1808*	...	*1908*a	*2008*	...	*2108*r	*2211*	...	...	...

♦ – **NOTES** (LISTED BY TRAIN NUMBER)

60/6 – [12] and ✕ Budapest - Györ - Hegyeshalom - Wien - München.

160 – VORARLBERG – [12] and ✕ Wien - Buchs 🏛 - Zürich.

162 – TRANSALPIN – [1] (panorama car), [12] and ✕ Wien - Buchs 🏛 - Zürich - Basel.

207 – MATTHIAS BRAUN – [12] Praha - Summerau 🏛 - Salzburg; 🛏 1, 2 cl. and ▬ 2 cl. Praha - Salzburg (**466**) - Zürich; 🛏 1, 2 cl. Praha - Salzburg (**499**) - Zagreb.

390 – [12] and 🍷 Linz - München - Stuttgart - Frankfurt.

462 – KÁLMÁN IMRE – 🛏 1, 2 cl., ▬ 2 cl. and [2] Budapest - München.

466 – WIENER WALZER – ▬ 2 cl. and [2] Budapest - Wien - Zürich; 🛏 1, 2 cl., ▬ 2 cl. and [2] Wien - Zürich. 🅁 for journeys to Switzerland.

468 – ORIENT-EXPRESS – 🛏 1, 2 cl., ▬ 2 cl. and [2] Wien - Strasbourg; 🛏 1, 2 cl., ▬ 2 cl. and [2] Budapest (**460**) - Wien (**468**) - Karlsruhe (**408**) - Frankfurt.

490 – HANS ALBERS – 🛏 1, 2 cl., ▬ 2 cl. and [2] Wien - Nürnberg - Hamburg. Conveys 🛏 1, 2 cl., ▬ 2 cl. and [2] (reclining) (*City Night Line* **420** / **40420** 🅁 Special fares – ERIDANUS) Wien - Nürnberg - Frankfurt - Köln - Dortmund / Amsterdam.

F – To Feldkirch (Table **951**).

G – [12] and ✕ Wien - Nürnberg - Frankfurt.

H – [12] and ✕ Wien - Nürnberg - Frankfurt - Köln - Dortmund.

K – To Klagenfurt (Table **970**).

L – To Kleinreifling (Table **976**).

P – JÓŽE PLEČNIK. From Praha (Table **1132**).

R – 🅁 for international journeys.

S – On Ⓒ continues to Schladming via Selzthal (Tables **975** and **977**).

T – Conveys [12] Wien - Attnang-Puchheim - Stainach-Irdning (Table **961**).

V – ALLEGRO DON GIOVANNI – 🛏 1, 2 cl., ▬ 2 cl. and [2] Wien - Villach - Tarvisio - Udine - Venezia (Table **88**).

W – Until Oct. 26. [2] and ✕ Wien Südbf (d. 0746) - Wien Meidling (d. 0753) - Passau.

Z – From Sept. 6.

a – Ⓐ only.

r – ⚒ only.

t – Not Oct. 25.

△ – Conveys 🛏 1, 2 cl., ▬ 2 cl. and [2].

* – 4 minutes later until Sept. 5.

◧ – Classification *RJ* from Sept. 6.

⊙ – Via Simbach (Tables **893**/**962**).

● – See note on page 447.

♣ – Via high-speed alignments.

‡ – See also Table **965**.

PASSAU and SALZBURG - WIEN 950

km		EN	EN	ÖIC		EN	REX	IC	EN	D		IC	EN	EN	REX		ÖEC		ÖIC	REX	REX	REX	RJ		ÖIC	ÖIC
		463	469	841		247	1783	843	467	206		745	236	491	1657		767		541	1785	1787	1663	43		543	765
			R		⚒		Ⓐ	①–⑥					🅁	R	⚒	⚒	◧			⚒	Ⓐ		①–⑥	⚒		
		♦	♦	🍷	2	△	2	🍷	♦	♦	2	🍷	V	♦	2	2	✕	2	🍷	2	2	2	z✕	2	🍷	🍷
	Bregenz **951** d.	...	...	...	...	2144	...	...	...	...	...	...	...	...	...	...	...	...	...	...	...	...	...	...	...	...
	Innsbruck Hbf **951** d.	...	...	...	...	0042	...	...	0227	...	...	...	...	...	...	...	...	...	...	...	...	...	0502	...	...	0605
	München Hbf **890** d.	2340	...	...	...	|	...	...	|	...	...	...	...	...	...	...	...	...	...	...	...	...	|	...	...	|
	Salzburg Hbf d.	0218	0316	...	...	|	...	...	0436	0441	...	0500	0500	...	0511	...	0600	...	0608	...	...	...	0703	...	0708	0808
	Vöcklabruck d.	|	|	...	...	|	...	...	|	|	...	0545	0545	...	0614	0631	|	...	0651	...	...	0704	|	...	0751	0851
	Attnang-Puchheim d.	0306	|	0420	...	0452	...	...	|	0528	...	0551	0551	...	0623	0635	0644	...	0657	...	...	0712	|	...	0757	0857
0	**Passau** Hbf 🏛 d.	|	|	|	...	|	0415	...	|	|	0430**c**	|	|	0535	|	...	|	0546	|	0604	0630	|	|	0645	|	|
14	Schärding d.	|	|	|	0401	|	0429	...	|	|	0444	|	|	0549	|	...	|	0600	|	0619	0643	|	|	0659	|	|
52	Neumarkt-Kallham ‡ d.	|	|	|	0435	|	0457	...	|	|	0520	|	|	|	|	...	|	0636	|	0647	0710	|	|	0735	|	|
81	**Wels** Hbf ‡ d.	0325	|	0438	0503	0512	0522	0529	0539	0547	0550	0613	0613	0631	0647	...	|	0706	0714	0717	0733	0737	|	0805	0814	0914
106	**Linz** Hbf ‡ a.	0340	0433	0452	0524	0528	0538	0542	0554	0602	0614	0627	0627	0646	0703	...	0707	0722	0727	0742	0751	0801	0807	0821	0827	0927
106	**Linz** Hbf **977** d.	0342	0436	0455	...	0531	...	0545	0557	...	...	0630	0630	0649	...	...	0710	...	0730	...	...	...	0810	...	0830	0930
131	St Valentin **977** d.	0402	|	0513	...	0550	...	0603	|	...	...	0648	0648	0711	...	...	|	...	0748	...	...	...	|	...	0848	0948
168	Amstetten d.	0425	0512	0532	...	0611	...	0620	0632	...	...	0707	0707	0739	...	...	|	...	0805	...	...	...	|	...	0905	1005
228	**St Pölten** Hbf d.	0500	0547	0605	...	0645	...	0650	0710	...	...	0739	0739	0819	...	...	|	...	0834	...	...	...	|	...	0934	1034
283	**Wien** Hütteldorf ● a.	0545	|	0647	...	0723	...	0728	0754	...	...	0818	0818	0855	...	...	|	...	0909	...	...	...	|	...	1009	1109
289	**Wien** Westbahnhof a.	...	0640	0657	...	0732	...	0737	0803	...	...	0827	0827	0904	...	...	0840	...	0918	...	...	...	0940	...	1018	1118

		ÖEC	ÖIC	ÖEC	ÖIC		ICE	RJ	ÖIC	ÖEC	ÖIC		ICE	RJ	ÖIC	REX	ÖEC	ÖIC	EC		ICE	RJ	ÖIC	REX	ÖEC	ÖEC
		61	547	561	693		21	63	549	563	747		23	65	641	1793	565	643	100		25	67	645	1795	163	691
		◧																						Ⓐ		
	2	✕	🍷	✕	K	2	G✕	🍷♦	🍷	✕	🍷	2	H✕	🍷	🍷	2	✕	🍷	P✕	2	H✕	🍷♦	🍷	2	✕♦	K✕
Bregenz **951** d.	...	...	...	0500	...	...	...	...	...	0650	...	...	...	...	...	...	0844	...	...	...	...	...	...	...	...	...
Innsbruck Hbf **951** d.	...	...	...	0730	...	...	...	...	...	0930	...	...	...	...	...	...	1130	...	...	...	...	...	...	...	1330	...
München Hbf **890** d.	...	0726	...	|	...	...	...	0927	...	|	...	...	...	1126	...	...	|	...	...	...	...	1326	...	...	|	...
Salzburg Hbf d.	...	0900	0908	0932	1008	...	...	1100	1108	1132	1208	...	...	1300	1308	...	1332	1408	1422	...	...	1500	1508	...	1532	1608
Vöcklabruck d.	...	|	0951	|	1051	...	...	|	1151	|	1251	...	...	|	1351	...	|	1451	|	...	...	|	1551	...	|	1651
Attnang-Puchheim d.	...	|	0957	|	1057	...	...	|	1157	|	1257	...	...	|	1357	...	|	1457	|	...	...	|	1557	...	|	1657
Passau Hbf 🏛 d.	0805	|	|	|	|	1005	1033	|	|	|	|	1205	1233	|	|	1311	|	|	|	1405	1433	|	|	1511	|	|
Schärding d.	0818	|	|	|	|	1018	|	|	|	|	|	1218	|	|	|	1325	|	|	|	1418	|	|	|	1525	|	|
Neumarkt-Kallham ‡ d.	0854	|	|	|	|	1054	|	|	|	|	|	1254	|	|	|	1357	|	|	|	1454	|	|	|	1557	|	|
Wels Hbf ‡ d.	0923	|	1014	1031	1114	1123	1131	|	1214	1231	1314	1323	1331	|	1414	1423	1431	1514	1520	1523	1531	|	1614	1623	1631	1714
Linz Hbf ‡ a.	0939	1004	1027	1043	1127	1139	1143	1204	1227	1243	1327	1339	1343	1404	1427	1439	1443	1527	1532	1539	1543	1604	1627	1639	1643	1727
Linz Hbf **977** d.	...	1007	1030	1046	1130	...	1146	1207	1230	1246	1330	...	1346	1407	1430	...	1446	1530	...	...	1546	1607	1630	...	1646	1730
St Valentin **977** d.	...	|	1048	|	1148	...	|	|	1248	|	1348	...	|	|	1448	...	|	1548	...	...	|	|	1648	...	|	1748
Amstetten d.	...	|	1105	|	1205	...	|	|	1305	|	1405	...	|	|	1505	...	|	1605	...	...	|	|	1705	...	|	1805
St Pölten Hbf d.	...	1059	1134	1139	1234	...	1239	1259	1334	1339	1434	...	1439	1459	1534	...	1539	1634	...	...	1639	1659	1734	...	1739	1834
Wien Hütteldorf ● a.	...	|	1209	1214	1309	...	|	|	1409	1414	1509	...	|	|	1609	...	1614	1709	...	...	|	|	1809	...	1814	1909
Wien Westbahnhof a.	...	1140	1218	1224	1318	...	1322	1340	1418	1424	1518	...	1522	1540	1618	...	1624	1718	...	...	1722	1740	1818	...	1824	1918

		ICE	RJ	ÖIC	ÖIC	IC	REX	ÖEC	EZ	ÖIC	ICE	ICE	ÖEC		ÖIC	ÖEC	D	ÖIC	ICE	REX			ICE		EC	
		27	69	15647	647	749	1797	569	5921	649	29	261	663		741	161	963	743	229	3435			661		391	
				⑦t	M	⑦t			W											Ⓒ					Ⓑ	
	2	H✕	🍷	T🍷	T🍷	🍷	2	✕	2✕	🍷	G✕	✕	F✕	2	🍷	✕♦		🍷	G✕	T 2	2	2	✕	2	🍷♦	2
Bregenz **951** d.	...	...	...	...	...	...	...	1246	...	...	...	...	...	...	...	...	...	...	...	...	...	...	1646	...	...	...
Innsbruck Hbf **951** d.	...	...	...	...	...	...	...	1530	...	1412	...	...	1702	...	...	1730	...	...	...	...	...	...	1930	...	...	...
München Hbf **890** d.	...	...	1526	...	...	...	...	|	...	|	...	1723	|	...	...	|	1748	...	...	...	...	...	|	...	2024	...
Salzburg Hbf d.	...	...	1700	1704	1704	...	...	1732	...	1808	...	1900	1904	...	1908	1932	|	2008	...	...	...	2108	2132	...	2215	2308
Vöcklabruck d.	...	...	|	1747	1747	...	...	|	...	1851	...	|	|	...	1951	|	|	2051	...	...	...	2224	|	...	2301	0019
Attnang-Puchheim d.	...	...	|	1753	1758	1758	...	|	...	1857	...	|	|	...	1957	|	⊙	2057	...	2200	...	2228	|	...	2307	0024
Passau Hbf 🏛 d.	1605	1633	|	|	|	|	1711	|	1717	|	1833	|	|	1846	|	|	|	|	2033	|	2107	...	|	...	|	...
Schärding d.	1618	|	|	|	|	|	1725	|	1732	|	|	|	|	1901	|	|	|	|	|	|	2120	...	|	...	|	...
Neumarkt-Kallham ‡ d.	1654	|	|	|	|	|	1757	|	1803	|	|	|	|	1935	|	|	2029	|	|	|	2156	...	|	...	|	...
Wels Hbf ‡ d.	1723	1731	|	1809	1814	1814	1823	1831	1834	1914	1931	|	|	2002	2014	2031	2053	2114	2131	2222	2223	...	2229	...	2325	...
Linz Hbf ‡ a.	1739	1743	1804	1822	1827	1827	1839	1843	1854	1927	1943	2004	|	...	2027	2043	2109	2127	2143	2237	...	...	2241	...	2342	...
Linz Hbf **977** d.	...	1746	1807	1825	1830	1830	...	1846	1902	1930	1946	2007	|	...	2030	2046	...	2130	2146	...	...	...	2243	2253	...	...
St Valentin **977** d.	...	|	|	1843	1848	1848	...	|	1930	1948	|	|	|	...	2048	|	...	2148	|	...	...	...	|	2318	...	...
Amstetten d.	...	|	|	1900	1905	1905	...	|	1957	2005	|	|	|	...	2105	|	...	2205	|	...	...	...	|	...	...	...
St Pölten Hbf d.	...	1839	1859	1929	1934	1934	...	1939	2053	2034	2039	2059	|	...	2134	2139	...	2234	2239	...	...	...	2335	...	...	...
Wien Hütteldorf ● a.	...	|	|	2004	2009	2009	...	2014	2131	2109	|	|	|	...	2209	2214	...	2309	|	...	...	...	|	...	...	...
Wien Westbahnhof a.	...	1922	1940	2013	2018	2018	...	2024	...	2118	2122	2140	2148	...	2218	2224	...	2318	2322	...	...	...	0015	...	...	...

Regional trains LINZ - AMSTETTEN - MELK - WIEN (2nd class only)

		⚒	⚒				L														ⒸS		W✕		
Linz Hbf **977** d.	...	*0441*	...	...	0700**r**	...	...	*0853***a**	...	*0953***a**	...	...	*1150***r**	*1253*	...	*1353***r**	*1450*	...	*1553***r**	*1653*	...	...	*1753*	1902	...	...
St Valentin **977** d.	...	0510	0525	0611	0721**r**	...	*0818***r**	0921**a**	...	1021**a**	1121**c**	...	1218**r**	1321	...	1421**r**	1518	...	1621**r**	1721	...	...	1821	1930	...	...
Amstetten d.	0415	0539	0614	0651	0758	0819	0858	0958	1019	1058	1158	1219	1255	1358	1419	1458	1555	1619	1658	1758	1819	1853	1915**j**	1957	2019	2215
Ybbs an der Donau d.	0428	0552	0627	0707	0810	0836	0910	1010	1036	1110	1210	1236	1307	1410	1436	1510	1607	1634	1710	1810	1836	1905	1927	2010	2036	2227
Pöchlarn d.	0435	0559	0636	0720	0819	0849	0919	1019	1049	1119	1219	1249	1316	1419	1449	1519	1616	1647	1719	1819	1849	1914	1936	2024	2049	2236
Melk d.	0442	0606	0643	0727	0825	0856	0925	1025	1056	1125	1225	1256	1322	1425	1456	1525	1622	1654	1725	1825	1856	1920	1942	2032	2056	2242
St Pölten Hbf d.	0505	0630	0706	0755	0846	0919	0946	1046	1119	1146	1246	1319	1344	1446	1519	1546	1644	1717	1746	1846	1919	1946	2002	2053	2119	2303
Wien Hütteldorf ● a.	0551	0718	0750	...	0932	...	1031	1132	...	1231	1332	...	1431	1532	...	1631	1732	...	1831	1932	...	2031	2047**q**	2131	...	2350
Wien Westbahnhof a.	0600	0728	0759	...	0944	...	1040	1144	...	1240	1344	...	1440	1544	...	1640	1744	...	1840	1944	...	2040	2056**q**	...	...	2359

♦ – **NOTES** (LISTED BY TRAIN NUMBER)

63/7 – [12] and 🍷 München - Wien - Hegyeshalom - Györ - Budapest.
161 – VORARLBERG – [12] and ✕ Zürich - Buchs 🏛 - Wien.
163 – TRANSALPIN – [1] (panorama car), [12] and ✕ Basel - Zürich - Buchs 🏛 - Wien.
206 – MATTHIAS BRAUN – [12] Salzburg - Linz - Summerau 🏛 - Praha; 🛏 1, 2 cl. and ▬ 2 cl. Zürich (**467**) - Salzburg (**206**) - Praha; 🛏 1, 2 cl. Zagreb (**498**) - Salzburg (**206**) - Praha.
391 – [12] and 🍷 Frankfurt - Stuttgart - München - Linz.
463 – KÁLMÁN IMRE – 🛏 1, 2 cl., ▬ 2 cl. and [2] München - Budapest.
467 – WIENER WALZER – ▬ 2 cl. and [2] Zürich - Wien - Budapest; 🛏 1, 2 cl., ▬ 2 cl. and [2] Zürich - Wien. 🅁 for journeys from Switzerland.
469 – ORIENT-EXPRESS – 🛏 1, 2 cl., ▬ 2 cl. and [2] Strasbourg - Karlsruhe - Wien; 🛏 1, 2 cl., ▬ 2 cl. and [2] Frankfurt (**409**) - Karlsruhe (**469**) - Wien (**461**) - Budapest.
491 – HANS ALBERS – 🛏 1, 2 cl., ▬ 2 cl. and [2] Hamburg - Hannover - Nürnberg - Wien. Conveys 🛏 1, 2 cl., ▬ 2 cl., [2] (reclining) and ✕ (*City Night Line* **40401** / **421** 🅁 Special fares – ERIDANUS) Amsterdam / Dortmund - Köln - Frankfurt - Nürnberg - Wien.

F – From Feldkirch (Table **951**).
G – [12] and ✕ Frankfurt - Nürnberg - Regensburg - Passau 🏛 - Wien.
H – [12] and ✕ Dortmund - Köln - Frankfurt - Nürnberg - Regensburg - Passau 🏛 - Wien.
K – From Klagenfurt (Table **970**).
L – From Kleinreifling (Table **976**).
M – ①–⑥ (also Oct. 25, Dec. 6; not Oct. 26, Dec. 8).
P – JÓŽE PLEČNIK. To Praha (Table **1132**).
R – 🅁 for international journeys.
S – From Schladming via Selzthal (Tables **975** and **977**).
T – Conveys [12] Stainach-Irdning - Attnang-Puchheim - Wien (Table **961**).
V – ALLEGRO DON GIOVANNI – 🛏 1, 2 cl., ▬ 2 cl. and [2] Venezia - Udine - Tarvisio - Villach - Salzburg - Wien (Table **88**).
W – Until Oct. 26. [2] and ✕ Passau - Wien Meidling (a. 2152) - Wien Südbahnhof (a. 2158).

a – Ⓐ only.
c – Ⓒ only.
j – Arrives 1856.
q – † only.
r – ⚒ only.
t – Also Oct. 26, Dec. 8; not Oct. 25, Dec. 6.
z – Not Oct. 26.

‡ – See also Table **965**.
△ – Conveys 🛏 1, 2 cl., ▬ 2 cl. and [2].
⊙ – Via Simbach (Tables **893/962**).
◧ – Classification *RJ* from Sept. 6.
● – S-Bahn trains operate every 10 – 15 minutes to / from Wien Heiligenstadt (journey time: 21 minutes). See panel below for Wien S-Bahn links to / from other Wien stations.

WIEN S-Bahn	Ⓐ		Ⓐ		Ⓐ					
Hütteldorf d.	0551	0622	0651	0722	0751	0822	0922		2322	2351
Meidling **981** a.	0602	0633	0702	0733	0802	0833	0933	and	2333	0002
Südbahnhof **981** a.	0609	0642	0709	0742	0809	0842	0942	hourly	2342	0009
Mitte **981** a.	0615	0648	0715	0748	0815	0848	0948	until	2348	0015
Praterstern **981** a.	0619	0652	0719	0752	0819	0852	0952		2352	0019

WIEN S-Bahn		Ⓐ		Ⓐ		Ⓐ				
Praterstern **981** d.	0510	0540	0610	0640	0710	0740	0810	0910		2310
Mitte **981** d.	0514	0544	0614	0644	0714	0744	0814	0914	and	2314
Südbahnhof **981** d.	0520	0550	0620	0650	0720	0750	0820	0920	hourly	2320
Meidling **981** d.	0528	0558	0628	0658	0728	0758	0828	0928	until	2328
Hütteldorf a.	0539	0609	0639	0711	0739	0814	0839	0939		2339

951 SALZBURG and MÜNCHEN - INNSBRUCK - BREGENZ - LINDAU

km		EN 466		D 15464	EN 464	EN 246		REX 1544	ÖEC 760	REX 5151			ÖEC 164	REX 1864	IC 118	EC 81			ICE 560	EC 85	REX 1504	ÖEC 662	REX 5179		ÖEC 160	EC 87
										⚒						R				R						R
		♦	2	Z	♦	△	2	S 2	✕	2	2	2	✕	2	🍷♦	✕♦	2	2	✕	✕♦	V 2	✕	2	2	✕	✕♦
	Wien Westbf **950** d.	2125	...	...	...	2220	...	...	...	...	...	...	...	...	...	...	...	...	0614	...	...	0657	...	...	0740	...
	Linz Hbf **950** d.	2314	...	...	...	0020	...	...	...	...	...	...	...	...	...	...	...	...	0747	...	...	|	...	...	0916	...
0	**Salzburg** Hbf d.	0044	...	...	...	|	...	...	...	...	...	...	0622	...	...	...	...	...	0856	...	...	0953	...	...	1031	...
	München Hbf. **890** d.	|	...	...	...	|	...	...	...	...	...	...	|	...	...	0730	...	*0741*	|	0931	...	|	...	*0941*	|	1130
	München Ost. **890** d.	|	...	...	...	|	...	...	...	...	...	...	|	...	...	0740	...	*0750*	|	0940	...	|	...	*0949*	|	1140
	Rosenheim **890** d.	|	...	...	...	|	...	...	...	...	...	0609**k**	|	...	...	0813	...	0835	|	1013	...	|	...	1035	|	1213
120	Kufstein 🏛 d.	|	...	...	...	|	...	*0514*	...	0554	...	0647	0738	...	...	0835	...	0906	|	1035	...	|	...	1109	1145	1235
134	Wörgl Hbf **960** d.	|	...	0255	...	|	...	0530	...	0610	...	0701	0749	...	...	0846	...	0920	|	1046	1103	|	...	1123	1156	1246
159	Jenbach **960** d.	|	...	|	...	0429	...	0549	...	0630	...	0723	0806	...	...	0900	...	0942	|	1100	1119	|	...	1145	1210	1300
193	**Innsbruck** Hbf **960** a.	0237	...	0337	...	0451	...	0616	...	0654	...	0757	0830	...	...	0921	...	1016	1044	1121	1140	1143	...	1218	1230	1321
193	**Innsbruck** Hbf d.	0241	...	0345	0402	0455	...	▬	0638	▬	0722	...	0839	...	0904	...	0952	...	1046	...	...	1146	1213	▬	1239	▬
239	Ötztal d.	|	...	|	|	0521	...	...	0705	...	0811	...	0903	...	0928	...	1044	...	1110	...	...	|	1251	...	1303	...
248	Imst-Pitztal d.	|	...	|	|	0532	...	*EN*	0714	...	0822	...	0912	...	0939	...	1059	...	|	...	...	|	1304	*REX*	1312	...
265	Landeck - Zams d.	|	...	0437	0456	0546	...	**246**	0727	...	0837	...	0926	...	0952	...	1113	...	1130	...	...	|	1318	**5570**	1326	...
293	St Anton am Arlberg d.	|	...	0503	0521	0612	...	△	0750	...	...	...	0950	...	1015	...	...	...	1152	...	...	|	▬		1350	*REX*
304	Langen am Arlberg d.	|	...	0513	0531	0623	...	←	0801	...	...	...	1001	...	1026	...	...	...	1203	...	...	|	...	2	1401	**1860**
329	Bludenz **952** d.	0427	...	0555	0615	0648	0659	0703	0828		...	...	1028	...	1057	...	...	...	1228	...	...	|		1330	1428	
350	**Feldkirch** **952** a.	0440	...	0609	0631	→	0712	0717	0840	2	...	...	1040	...	1109	...	...	...	1240	...	...	1332	2	1345	1440	2
350	**Feldkirch** **952** d.	0446	0458	0646	0646	...	0714	0721	0844	0846	...	...	1042	1046	1110	...	...	...	1244	...	...	...	1341	1346	1442	1446
369	**Buchs** 🏛 **952** a.	0502	|	0702	0702	...	0737	|	|	0909	...	...	1058	|	|	...	...	...	|	...	...	...	1358	|	1458	|
	Zürich HB **520** a.	0620	|	0820	0820	...	...	|	|	...	...	...	1220	|	|	...	...	...	|	...	...	...	...	|	1620	|
375	Dornbirn **952** d.	...	0527	...	...	...	...	0742	0903	...	...	...	...	1108	1132	...	...	...	1303	...	...	...	...	1408	...	1508
387	**Bregenz** 🏛 **952** a.	...	0542	...	...	...	...	0754	0912	...	...	...	...	1115	1140	...	...	...	1312	...	...	...	...	1415	...	1515
397	**Lindau** Hbf 🏛 **952** a.	...	0555	...	...	...	...	*0828*	*0928*	...	...	...	...	1128	1151	...	...	...	*1339*	...	...	...	...	1428	...	1528

	REX 5576		ÖEC 162	EC 89	ÖEC 668		ÖEC 564	EC 83		D 1281	ÖEC 566	REX 5195	EC 189			ICE 109	ÖEC 568			ÖEC 660	RB 5135	CNL 485	RJ 762	REX 5135		ÖEC 764
				R				R		⑥				⑥⑦	①–⑤	§						R	Ⓑt			
	2	2	✕♦	♦	✕♦	2	✕	♦	2	🍷♦	✕	2	✕	2	2	✕♦	✕	2	2	✕	2	✕♦	🍷	2	2	¶
Wien Westbf **950** d.	...	...	0940	...	...	...	1140	...	...	...	1340	...	...	...	...	...	1540	...	...	1740	...	...	1820	...	...	1920
Linz Hbf **950** d.	...	...	1116	...	...	...	1316	...	...	...	1516	...	...	...	...	...	1716	...	...	1916	...	...	1953	...	...	2053
Salzburg Hbf d.	...	...	1231	...	...	...	1431	...	...	...	1631	...	...	...	...	...	1831	...	...	2030	...	...	2106	...	...	2202
München Hbf **890** d.	...	*1141*	|	1330	...	*1341*	|	1530	*1541*	1600	|	...	1731	*1739*	*1752*	1841	|	*1847*	*1941*	|	*2046*	2103	|	...	...	|
München Ost **890** d.	...	*1149*	|	1340	...	*1349*	|	1540	*1549*	|	|	...	1741	*1748*	*1801*	|	|	*1855*	*1949*	|	*2054*	|	|	...	...	|
Rosenheim **890** d.	...	1234	|	1413	...	1436	|	1613	1634	1641	|	...	1813	1835	*1835*	|	|	1935	2035	|	2135	2143	|	←	...	|
Kufstein 🏛 d.	...	1306	1345	1435	...	1506	1545	1635	1706	1714	1745	...	1835	1909	1909	1940	1946	2006	2106	2145	2203	2209	2219	2223	...	|
Wörgl Hbf **960** d.	*1312*	1320	1356	1446	1459	1520	1556	1646	1720	1724	1756	...	1846	1920	1920	1951	1957	2020	2120	2156	→	2220	2228	2237	...	2322
Jenbach **960** d.	*1326*	1342	1410	1500	1513	1542	1610	1700	1742	...	1810	...	1900	1942	1942	2006	2011	2042	2142	2210	...	2236	|	2257	...	|
Innsbruck Hbf **960** a.	*1348*	1416	1430	1521	1535	1616	1633	1721	1816	...	1830	...	1921	2016	2016	2026	2031	2116	2216	2230	...	2256	2300	2323	...	2354
Innsbruck Hbf d.	1353	...	1439	▬	1539	▬	1639	▬	...	...	1839	1913	...	...	...	...	2039	...	...	2233	...	...	...	...	2330	...
Ötztal d.	1420	...	1503	...	1607	...	1703	...	...	...	1903	1951	...	...	...	...	2103	...	...	2300	...	...	...	...	0019	...
Imst-Pitztal d.	1429	...	1512	...	1620	...	1712	...	...	...	1912	2001	...	...	...	...	2112	...	...	2309	...	...	...	...	0029	...
Landeck - Zams d.	1442	...	1526	...	1634	...	1726		...	...	1926	2016	...	...	...	...	2126	...	...	2322	...	...	...	...	0044	...
St Anton am Arlberg d.	1504	...	1550	*REX*	1657	...	1750	...	...	...	1950	▬	...	...	...	...	2150	...	...	2345	...	...	...	...	...	...
Langen am Arlberg d.	1514	...	1601	**1862**	1708	...	1801	*D*	...	...	2001	...	...	...	...	...	2201	...	...	2356	...	...	...	...	...	...
Bludenz **952** d.	1600**f**	...	1628		1734	①–⑤	1828	**168**	...	...	2028		...	...	...	...	2228	...	...	0021	...	...	...	...	...	...
Feldkirch **952** a.	1615	...	1640	2	1746	2	1840		...	...	2040	2	...	...	...	...	2240	...	...	0032	...	...	...	...	...	...
Feldkirch **952** d.	1616	...	1642	1646	1750	1800	1844	1846	...	...	2042	2048	...	...	...	...	2242	...	...	0033	...	...	...	...	...	...
Buchs 🏛 **952** a.	|	...	1658	|	|	1822	|	1902	...	...	|	2111	...	...	...	...	|	...	...	|	...	...	...	...	...	...
Zürich HB **520** a.	|	...	1820	|	|	...	|	2020	...	...	|	...	...	...	...	...	|	...	...	|	...	...	...	...	...	...
Dornbirn **952** d.	1638	...	...	1708	1814	...	1903	...	...	...	2056	...	...	...	...	...	2256	...	...	0048	...	...	...	...	...	...
Bregenz 🏛 **952** a.	1645	...	...	1715	1822	...	1915	...	...	...	2105	...	...	...	...	...	2305	...	...	0056	...	...	...	...	...	...
Lindau Hbf 🏛 **952** a.	1658	...	...	1728	*1900*	...	*1929*	...	...	...	*2132*	...	...	...	...	...	*2325*	...	...	...	...	...	...	...	...	...

km		CNL 484	RJ 43	REX 5100	ÖIC 765	REX 5150		REX 5152	ÖEC 561	ICE 108		REX 5176		ÖEC 563	D 1280		REX 1879	EC 188	D 169	ÖEC 565		ÖEC 669	REX 1863	ÖEC 163		EC 82
		R	①–⑥	⚒				⚒		‡		⚒	①–⑤		⑥			R								
		✕♦	r 🍷	2	🍷	2	2	2	✕	✕♦	2	2	2	✕	🍷♦	2	2	♦		✕	2	✕♦	2	✕♦	2	✕♦
	Lindau Hbf 🏛 **952** d.	...	...	...	...	...	...	...	...	...	...	...	...	*0633*	...	...	0727	...	...	*0824*	...	*0924*	1030	...	...	...
	Bregenz 🏛 **952** d.	...	...	...	...	...	...	...	0500	...	...	...	...	0650	...	...	0740	...	...	0844	...	0942	1043	...	...	...
	Dornbirn **952** d.	...	...	...	...	...	...	...	0509	...	...	...	...	0700	...	...	0750	...	...	0855	...	0952	1052	...	...	...
	Zürich HB **520** d.	...	...	...	...	...	...	...	|	...	...	...	...	|	...	...	|	...	0740	|	...	|	|	0940	...	...
	Buchs 🏛 **952** d.	...	...	...	...	...	...	...	|	...	...	...	0602	|	...	0748	|	...	0856	|	...	|	|	1102	...	...
	Feldkirch **952** a.	...	...	...	...	...	...	...	0522	...	...	...	0624	0717	...	0812	0814	...	0912	0910	...	1007	1113	1118	...	...
	Feldkirch **952** d.	...	...	...	...	...	...	...	0524	...	...	...	▬	0720	...	▬	0815	...	...	0920	...	1017	▬	1120	...	...
	Bludenz **952** d.	...	...	...	...	...	...	...	0538	...	...	...	...	0735	...	...	0829	...	...	0935	...	1031	...	1135	...	...
	Langen am Arlberg d.	...	...	...	...	...	...	...	|	...	...	...	...	0800	...	...	0853	...	...	1000	...	1056	...	1202	...	...
	St Anton am Arlberg d.	...	...	...	...	...	...	...	0613	...	...	...	...	0812	...	...	0904	...	...	1012	...	1108	...	1213	...	...
	Landeck - Zams d.	...	...	0417	...	0515**a**	...	0557	0636	...	...	0723	...	0835	...	...	0926	...	...	1035	...	1131	*EC*	1240	...	...
	Imst-Pitztal d.	...	...	0432	...	0531**a**	...	0613	0650	...	...	0741	...	0848	...	...	0940	...	...	1048	...	1144	**88**	1253	...	...
	Ötztal d.	...	...	0443	...	0541**a**	...	0624	0700	...	...	0752		0858	...		0949	...	...	1058	...	1154	**R**	1303	...	...
	Innsbruck Hbf a.	...	...	0531	...	0620**a**	...	0654	0726	...	...	0825	2	0921	...	2	1020	...	...	1121	...	1217	♦	1326	...	...
0	**Innsbruck** Hbf **960** d.	0434	0502	0533	0605	0623	0642	0702	0730	0735	0742	...	0842	0930	...	0942	...	1036	...	1130	1142	1225	1236	1330	1343	1436
34	Jenbach **960** d.	0456	|	0559	|	0648	0717	0729	0750	0756	0817	...	0917	0950	...	1017	...	1057	...	1150	1217	1245	1257	1350	1417	1457
59	Wörgl Hbf **960** d.	0514	0534	0619	0637	0710	0739	0749	0805	0810	0839	...	0939	1005	1035	1039	...	1113	...	1205	1239	1259	1313	1405	1439	1513
73	Kufstein 🏛 d.	0530	0544	0634	|	0721	0754	0802	0816	0821	0856	...	0954	1016	1046	1054	...	1124	...	1216	1254	...	1324	1416	1454	1524
107	Rosenheim **890** a.	0551	|	0704**h**	|	...	0824	...	|	|	0924	...	1023	|	1113	1123	...	1143	...	|	1324	...	1343	|	1523	1543
162	**München** Ost. **890** a.	|	|	...	|	...	*0902*	...	|	|	*1009*	...	*1102*	|	|	*1208*	...	1214	...	|	*1408*	...	1414	|	*1607*	1614
172	**München** Hbf. **890** a.	0630	|	...	|	...	*0913*	...	|	0916	*1020*	...	*1113*	|	1153	*1219*	...	1225	...	|	*1418*	...	1427	|	*1617*	1626
	Salzburg Hbf a.	...	0656	...	0757	...	...	...	0929	...	...	...	...	1129	...	...	...	...	...	1329	...	...	...	1529	...	...
	Linz Hbf **950** a.	...	0807	...	0927	...	...	...	1043	...	...	...	...	1243	...	...	...	...	...	1443	...	...	...	1643	...	...
	Wien Westbf **950** a.	...	0940	...	1118	...	...	...	1224	...	...	...	...	1424	...	...	...	...	...	1624	...	...	...	1824	...	...

♦ – **NOTES** (LISTED BY TRAIN NUMBER)

81/2 – VAL GARDENA / GRÖDNERTAL – [12] and ✕ München - Bolzano/Bozen and v.v.

83 – GARDA – [12] München - Bolzano/Bozen - Verona.

85 – MICHELANGELO – [12] and ✕ München - Bolzano/Bozen - Verona - Bologna - Rimini.

87 – TIEPOLO – [12] and ✕ München - Bolzano/Bozen - Verona - Venezia.

88/9 – LEONARDO DA VINCI – [12] Milano - Verona - Bolzano/Bozen - München and v.v.

108/9 – [12] and ✕ Innsbruck - München - Nürnberg - Leipzig - Berlin and v.v.

118 – [12] and 🍷 Innsbruck - Lindau - Ulm - Stuttgart - Köln - Münster.

162/3 – TRANSALPIN – [1] (panorama car), [12] and ✕ Wien - Zürich - Basel and v.v.

188 – GARDA – [12] Verona - Bolzano/Bozen - München.

484/5 – LUPUS – 🛏 1, 2 cl., ▬ 2 cl., [2] and ✕ Roma - Verona - Brennero 🏛 - München and v.v.; 🛏 1, 2 cl., ▬ 2 cl. and [2] (**40484/5** – PICTOR) Venezia - Verona - München and v.v.

464 – ZÜRICHSEE – 🛏 1, 2 cl., ▬ 2 cl. and [2] Graz - Bruck a. d. Mur - Selzthal - Schwarzach - Zürich. Conveys from Schwarzach (except when train **Z** runs) 🛏 1, 2 cl.*, ▬ 2 cl.* and [2] Beograd (**414**) - Zagreb - Ljubljana - Villach - Schwarzach (**464**) - Zürich.

466 – WIENER WALZER – ▬ 2 cl. and [2] Budapest - Hegyeshalom 🏛 - Wien - Zürich; 🛏 1, 2 cl., ▬ 2 cl. and [2] Wien - Zürich; 🛏 1, 2 cl. and ▬ 2 cl. Praha (**207**) - Salzburg - Zürich and v.v. Ⓡ for journeys to Switzerland.

668/9 – [12] and ✕ Graz - Selzthal - Bischofshofen - Kitzbühel - Bregenz and v.v. Until Aug. 10 diverted between Selzthal and Wörgl (not running via Bischofshofen or Kitzbühel).

1280 – ⑥ June 27 - Aug. 29. GROSSGLOCKNER – [12] and 🍷 Zell am See - Wörgl - München.

1281 – ⑥ June 20 - Aug. 22. GROSSGLOCKNER – [12] and 🍷 München - Wörgl - Zell am See.

R – Ⓡ for journeys to / from Italy.

S – From Saalfelden (Table **960**).

V – From Schwarzach-St Veit (Table **960**).

Z – From Wörgl ①⑥⑦ to June 29, daily July 4 - Sept. 7, ①⑥⑦ Sept. 12 - Oct. 26 (also Nov. 1, 2). 🛏 1, 2 cl.*, ▬ 2 cl.* and [2] Beograd (**414**) - Zagreb - Ljubljana - Villach - Schwarzach (**15464**) - Feldkirch (**464**) - Zürich.

a – Ⓐ only.

f – Arrives 1549.

h – Not Oct. 3.

k – ①–⑥ (not Aug. 15, Oct. 3).

r – Not Oct. 26.

t – Not Oct. 25.

§ – Train number **309** Aug. 1 - Sept. 14.

‡ – Train number **308** Aug. 1 - Sept. 14.

¶ – Conveys ✕ Wien - Salzburg.

* – 🛏 1, 2 cl. and ▬ 2 cl. from / to Zagreb.

△ – Conveys 🛏 1, 2 cl., ▬ 2 cl. and [2].

LINDAU - BREGENZ - INNSBRUCK - MÜNCHEN and SALZBURG 951

		ÖEC		REX	ÖEC	REX	ÖEC		REX		IC	IC	ICE		EC	REX	ÖEC		ÖEC	REX	EN	REX	EN	D	REX	EN
		569		1861	663	5162	161		5190		119	15661	661		80	1869	165		761	1549	247	5587	465	15465	5589	467
						⑧						⑦w						①–⑤				Ⓐ		A		
	2	✕	2	2	✕	2	✕	2	2	2	🍷♦	2🍷	✕	2	✕	2	✕	2	✕	S 2	△	2	♦		2	♦
Lindau Hbf ▣ ..... **952** d.	...	*1229*	...	1415	...	...	...	...	...	...	1605	...	*1625*	...	...	1830	...	...	*2035*	...	*2127*	2227	...	...	2332	...
Bregenz ▣ .... **952** d.	...	1246	...	1428	...	...	...	...	...	...	1616	...	1646	...	...	1843	...	...	2055	...	2144	2240	...	...	2344	...
Dornbirn .... **952** d.	...	1257	...	1436	...	...	...	...	...	...	1625	...	1657	...	...	1853	...	...	2104	...	2153	2252	...	...	2356	...
Zürich HB **520** .... d.	...	|	...	|	...	...	1340	...	...	...	|	...	|	...	...	|	1740	...	|	...	|	|	2140	2140	|	2240
Buchs ▣ .... **952** d.	1254	|	...	|	...	...	1502	...	...	1602	|	...	|	...	...	|	1902	2055	|	...	|	|	2259	2259	|	0005
Feldkirch .... **952** a.	1316	1315	...	1457	...	...	1518	...	...	1624	1648	...	1715	...	...	1914	1918	2117	2118	...	2212	2313	2314	2314	0017	0020
Feldkirch .... **952** d.	...	1320	...	1506	1502	...	1520	...	...	*1633*	1650	...	1720	...	...	▬	1920	▬	2120	...	2220	2314	2332	2344	...	0022
Bludenz .... **952** d.	...	1335	...	1526	|	...	1535	...	...	*1653*	1704	...	1735	...	...	...	1935	...	2135	...	2240	2329	2348	0004	...	0039
Langen am Arlberg .... d.	...	1400	...	▬	|	...	1600	...	...	▬	1738	...	1800	...	...	...	2000	...	2200	...	2308	...	0020	0035	...	|
St Anton am Arlberg .. d.	...	1412	...	...	|	...	1612	...	...	...	1748	...	1812	...	...	...	2012	...	2212	...	2319	...	0031	0047	...	|
Landeck - Zams .... d.	...	1435	...	*EC*	|	...	1635	...	1721	*EC*	1811	1828	1835	...	...	...	2035	...	2235	...	2346	...	0055	0110	...	|
Imst-Pitztal .... d.	...	1448	...	**84**	|	...	1648	...	1740	**86**	1824	1842	1848	...	...	...	2048	...	2248	...	|	...	|	|	...	|
Ötztal .... d.	...	1458	...	**R**	|	...	1658	...	1751	**R**	1833	1852	1858	...	...	...	2058	...	2258	...	0009	...	|	|	...	|
Innsbruck Hbf .... a.	...	1521	...	✕♦	1650	...	1721	...	1826	✕♦	1857	1917	1921	...	...	2	2121	2	2325	...	0034	...	0140	0154	...	0224
Innsbruck Hbf ..... **960** d.	...	1530	1542	1636	1702	1708	1730	1742	...	1836	...	1920	1930	1942	2036	2042	2130	2242	...	2342	0042	...	0143	0158	...	0227
Jenbach .... **960** d.	...	1550	1617	1657	|	1736	1750	1817	...	1857	...	1940	1950	2017	2057	2117	2150	2317	...	0017	0105	...	|	|	...	|
Wörgl Hbf .... **960** d.	...	1605	1639	1713	|	1758	1805	1839	...	1913	...	1955	2005	2039	2113	2139	2205	2343	...	0038	0123	...	0216	0233	...	|
Kufstein ▣ .... d.	...	1616	1654	1724	|	1808	1816	1854	...	1924	...	2006	2016	2054	2124	2154	2216	2356	...	...	|	...	...	...	...	|
Rosenheim .... **890** a.	...	|	1723	1743	|	...	|	1924	...	1943	...	|	|	2123	2143	2223	|	...	...	...	|	...	...	...	...	|
München Ost ... **890** a.	...	|	*1808*	1814	|	...	|	*2007*	...	2014	...	|	|	*2208*	2214	*2302*	|	...	...	...	|	...	...	...	...	|
München Hbf ... **890** a.	...	|	*1818*	1827	|	...	|	*2018*	...	2027	...	|	|	*2219*	2226	*2313*	|	...	...	...	|	...	...	...	...	|
Salzburg Hbf .... a.	...	1729	...	...	1857	...	1929	...	...	...	...	2120	2129	...	...	...	2329	...	...	...	|	...	...	...	...	0424
Linz Hbf **950** .... a.	...	1843	...	...	|	...	2043	...	...	...	...	...	2241	...	...	...	...	...	...	...	0528	...	...	...	...	0554
Wien Westbf **950** .... a.	...	2024	...	...	2148	...	2224	...	...	...	...	...	0015	...	...	...	...	...	...	...	0732	...	...	...	...	0803

♦ – **NOTES** (LISTED BY TRAIN NUMBER)

84 – MICHELANGELO – (12) and ✕ Rimini - Bologna - Verona - Brennero ▣ - München.

86 – TIEPOLO – (12) and ✕ Venezia - Verona - Brennero ▣ - München.

119 – (12) and 🍷 Münster - Köln - Stuttgart - Ulm - Lindau - Innsbruck.

465 – ZÜRICHSEE – 🛏 1, 2 cl., ▬ 2 cl. and (2) Zürich - Schwarzach - Selzthal - Bruck a. d. Mur - Graz. Conveys Zürich - Schwarzach (except when train **A** runs) 🛏 1, 2 cl.*, ▬ 2 cl.* and (2) Zürich - Schwarzach (**415**) - Villach - Ljubljana - Zagreb - Beograd.

467 – WIENER WALZER – ▬ 2 cl. and (2) Zürich - Wien - Hegyeshalom ▣ - Budapest; 🛏 1, 2 cl., ▬ 2 cl. and (2) Zürich - Wien; 🛏 1, 2 cl. and ▬ 2 cl. Zürich - Salzburg (**206**) - Praha. Ⓡ for journeys to / from Switzerland.

A – ⑤–⑦ to June 28, daily July 3 - Sept. 6, ⑤–⑦ Sept. 11 - Oct. 25 (also Oct. 31, Nov. 1). 🛏 1, 2 cl.*, ▬ 2 cl.* and (2) Zürich (**465**) - Feldkirch (**15465**) - Schwarzach (**415**) - Villach - Ljubljana - Zagreb - Beograd.

R – Ⓡ for journeys from Italy.

S – To Saalfelden (Table **960**).

w – Also Oct. 26, Dec. 8; not Oct. 25.

△ – Conveys 🛏 1, 2 cl., ▬ 2 cl. and (2).

VORARLBERG LOCAL SERVICES 952

2nd class only (except where shown)

(Schruns ⊡ -) Bludenz - Bregenz - Lindau

		Ⓐv								⚒														Ⓐ			
Schruns .... ⊡ d.	...	...	...	0625a	0703r	...	...	...	...	...	...	...	1307	...	...	...	1505	...	...	1635	...	...	...	...	...	...	...
Bludenz ...... ⊡ d.	...	0506	0603	0650	0728	0807	0837	0937	...	1107	1137	1237	1330	...	1437	1507	1537	1600	...	1700	1800	1907	1937	2100	2137	2237	2337
Feldkirch ....d.	0458	0528	0618	0710	0746	0828	0858	0958	1046	1128	1158	1258	1346	1446	1458	1528	1558	1616	1646	1716	1816	1928	1958	2116	2158	2258	2358
Dornbirn ....d.	0527	0557	0639	0736	0808	0857	0927	1027	1108	1157	1231	1327	1408	1508	1527	1557	1627	1638	1708	1738	1838	1957	2027	2138	2227	2327	0027
Bregenz ▣ ....d.	0543	0613	0650	0749	0816	0916	0943	1043	1116	1213	1247	1343	1416	1516	1543	1615	1642	1646	1716	1746	1848	2013	2042	2148	2242	2342	0042
Lindau Hbf ▣ ..a.	0555	0625	0659	0800	0828	0928	0954	1055	1128	1225	1259	1355	1428	1528	1555	1627	...	1658	1728	1758	1900	2025	*2058*	2200	*2325*	...	...

	Ⓐ	⚒		⚒								⚒															
Lindau Hbf ▣ ..d.	...	...	...	*0650*	0727	0800	0903	1003	1030	*1100*	1200	*1229*	1330	1415	1501	1531	*1625*	1703	1729	1804	1830	1903	2001	*2056*	2203	...	...
Bregenz ▣ ....d.	0516	0546	0616	0711	0740	0813	0916	1016	1043	1116	1213	1246	1343	1428	1513	1546	1646	1716	1742	1816	1843	1916	2012	2116	2216	2316	0016
Dornbirn ....d.	0532	0602	0632	0722	0750	0822	0932	1032	1052	1132	1222	1302	1352	1436	1522	1602	1702	1732	1752	1832	1853	1932	2022	2132	2232	2332	0032
Feldkirch ....d.	0601	0632	0703	0745	0815	0844	1003	1103	1113	1203	1244	1333	1414	1506	1544	1633	1733	1803	1814	1903	1914	2003	2044	2203	2303	0003	0103
Bludenz ...... ⊡ a.	0621	0652	0723	0800	0828	0859	1023	1123	...	1223	1259	1353	1427	1526	1559	1653	1753	1823	1832	1923	...	2023	2059	2223	2323	0025	0123
Schruns .... ⊡ a.	0645	...	...	...	...	...	...	...	...	1256	...	...	1457	...	1623	...	...	...	...	...	...	...	...	...	...	...	...

St Margrethen - Bregenz - Lindau △

km						*EC* 191			*EC* 193							*EC* 195							*EC* 197			
			Ⓐ			Z			Z		⚒					Z				Ⓐ			Z			
0	St Margrethen ▣ ...... d.	0633	0652	0723	0819	0842	0919	...	1042	1154	...	...	...	1310	1354	1442	...	1554	1638	1710	1754	1854	1942	2033	...	2256
12	**Bregenz** ▣ .... a.	0645	0708	0739	0835	0853	0935	...	1053	1208	1213	1247	...	1326	1408	1453	...	1608	1701	1729	1808	1908	1953	2047	...	2312
22	**Lindau** Hbf ▣ .... a.	*0659*	*0732*	*0800*	*0855*	0905	*0954*	...	1105	...	1225	1259	...	1339	*1428*	1505	...	*1627*	*1728*	*1758*	*1828*	*1929*	2005	2058	...	2325

						EC 196								*EC* 194					*EC* 192					*EC* 190	
	Ⓐ						Z								Z			Ⓐ		Z		Ⓐ			Z	
Lindau Hbf ▣ .... d.	...	...	0650	*0727*	*0824*	...	0955	...	1100	...	1229	...	1400	1456	...	*1531*	1625	...	*1729*	1855	1903	1933	...	...	2056	2127
Bregenz ▣ .... d.	0542	0607	0703	0750	0850	...	1006	...	1111	1208	1242	...	1411	1507	...	1608	1638	1706	1808	1906	1915	1945	1950	...	2107	2147
St Margrethen ▣ .... a.	0558	0620	0719	0803	0903	...	1018	...	1124	1224	1258	...	1424	1519	...	1624	1654	1722	1824	1918	...	...	2003	...	2119	2203

Feldkirch - Buchs

km		①–⑤	①–⑤	B	①–⑥					①–⑤	
0	**Feldkirch** ....d.	0530	0633	0714	0747	0846	1341	1535	1730	1800	2048
16	Schaan-Vaduz ....d.	0549	0652	0734	0805	|	1355	1554	1749	1818	2108
19	**Buchs** ▣ ....a.	0552	0655	0737	0808	0909	1358	1557	1753	1822	2111

	①–⑤	①–⑤		①–⑥				①–⑤		①–⑤
Buchs ▣ ....d.	0602	0717	0748	1227	1254	1602	1702	1733	1803	2055
Schaan-Vaduz ....d.	0605	0721	0752	1230	1257	1605	1705	1737	1807	2058
Feldkirch ....a.	0624	0742	0812	1250	1316	1624	1724	1755	1825	2117

B – From Bludenz (Table **951**).

Z – (12) and ✕ Zürich - St Gallen - Lindau - München and v.v. See also Table **75**.

a – Ⓐ only.

r – ⚒ only.

v – Runs daily Bregenz - Lindau.

△ – Austrian holiday dates apply.

⊡ – Complete service **BLUDENZ - SCHRUNS** and v.v. (*12 km*, journey 20 minutes). Operated by Montafonerbahn AG ✆ +43 (0) 5556 9000.
From Bludenz at 0540 Ⓐ, 0625 ⚒, 0703, 0737, 0803, 0833, 0937, 1037, 1137, 1204 ⚒, 1235, 1307 ⚒, 1337, 1437, 1537, 1603, 1635, 1707, 1737, 1804, 1837, 1937, 2037, 2137, 2237.
From Schruns at 0512 Ⓐ, 0540 ⚒, 0625, 0703, 0737, 0803, 0903, 1003, 1105, 1137 ⚒, 1204, 1235 ⚒, 1307, 1337, 1505, 1537, 1603, 1635, 1707, 1737, 1804, 1903, 2003, 2103, 2203.

🚌 IMST - ÖTZTAL - OBERGURGL and ST ANTON - LECH 953

ÖBB-Postbus

km	🚌 Route **4194**		Ⓐ	Ⓒ								Ⓐ	Ⓒ	Ⓐ	Ⓒ				Ⓐ	Ⓒ			
0	**Imst** (Postamt) ....d.	0615	0640	0655	...	0755	0855	0955	1055	1155	...	1235	1255	1325	1355	...	1455	1555	1645	1655	...	1800	1900
13	**Ötztal** (Bahnhof) ....a.	0629	0654	0709	...	0809	0909	1009	1109	1209	...	1249	1309	1339	1409	...	1509	1609	1659	1709	...	1814	1914
13	**Ötztal** (Bahnhof) ....d.	0630	0700	0715	...	0815	0915	1015	1115	1215	...	1250	1315	1345	1415	...	1515	1615	1705	1715	...	1815	1915
21	Oetz (Posthotel Kassel) ....d.	0644	0714	0729	...	0829	0929	1029	1129	1229	...	1304	1329	1359	1429	...	1529	1629	1719	1729	...	1829	1929
54	Sölden (Postamt) ....d.	0732	0802	0817	...	0917	1017	1117	1217	1317	...	1352	1417	1447	1517	...	1617	1717	1807	1817	...	1917	2017
58	Zwieselstein (Gh Neue Post) ....d.	0740	0810	0825	...	0925	1025	1125	1225	1325	...	1400	1425	1455	1525	...	1625	1725	1815	1825	...	1925	2025
68	**Obergurgl** (Zentrum) ....a.	0755	0825	0840	...	0940	1040	1140	1240	1340	...	1415	1440	1510	1540	...	1640	1740	1830	1840	...	1940	2040

🚌 Route **4194**	Ⓐ	Ⓒ	Ⓐ								Ⓐ	Ⓒ	Ⓐ	Ⓒ	Ⓐ	Ⓒ	Ⓐ	Ⓒ					
Obergurgl (Zentrum) ....d.	...	...	...	...	0655	...	0815	0915	1015	1115	1205	1215	1255	1315	1355	1415	1455	1515	...	1615	1715	1815	1915
Zwieselstein (Gh Neue Post) ....d.	0520	0545	0555	...	0710	...	0830	0930	1030	1130	1220	1230	1310	1330	1410	1430	1510	1530	...	1630	1730	1830	1930
Sölden (Postamt) ....d.	0530	0555	0605	...	0720	...	0840	0940	1040	1140	1230	1240	1320	1340	1420	1440	1520	1540	...	1640	1740	1840	1940
Oetz (Posthotel Kassel) ....d.	0615	0640	0650	...	0810	...	0930	1030	1130	1230	1320	1330	1410	1430	1510	1530	1610	1630	...	1730	1830	1930	2030
Ötztal (Bahnhof) ....a.	0627	0652	0702	...	0822	...	0942	1042	1142	1242	1332	1342	1422	1442	1522	1542	1622	1642	...	1742	1842	1942	2042
Ötztal (Bahnhof) ....d.	...	0705	0705	...	0825	...	0945	1045	1145	1245	1335	1345	1425	1445	1525	1545	1625	1645	...	1745	1845	1945	2045
Imst (Postamt) ....a.	...	0720	0720	...	0840	...	1000	1100	1200	1300	1350	1400	1440	1500	1540	1600	1640	1700	...	1800	1900	2000	2100

🚌 Route **4248**: **ST ANTON AM ARLBERG - LECH** *20 km* Journey time: 30 – 36 minutes Summer service: **Valid June 6 - Sept. 27**.

From St Anton Bahnhof: 0828, 1028, 1228, 1508 and 1735. **From Lech** Postamt: 1158, 1438 and 1858.

☛ All services call at St Christoph a. Arlberg and Zürs (Postamt).

954 🚌 LANDECK - NAUDERS - SCUOL and MALLES

					⚒								©k	Ⓐe				
Landeck-Zams (Bahnhof) **951** d.	0650	0750	...	1000	1050	...	1150	...	1250	...	1350	...	1550	1605	1650	...	1750	1855
Ried im Oberinntal (Postamt) d.	0718	0818	...	1028	1118	...	1218	...	1318	...	1418	...	1618	1633	1718	...	1818	1923
Martina (posta) ⊞ d.	|	0900	0901	|	1200	1201	1300	1301	1400	1401	1500	1501	|	|	1800	1801	|	|
Scuol-Tarasp (staziun) **546** a.	|	|	0928	|	|	1228	|	1328	|	1428	|	1528	|	|	|	1828	|	|
Nauders (Postamt) a.	0758	0913	...	1108	1213	...	1313	...	1413	...	1513	...	1658	1713	1813	...	1858	2003

		⚒							⚒									
Nauders (Postamt) d.	0605	0650	...	0845	...	0945	...	1145	1259	...	1345	1500	...	1545	1705	...	...	1816
Scuol-Tarasp (staziun) **546** d.	|	|	0830	|	0930	|	1130	|	|	1330	|	|	1530	|	|	1730	...	|
Martina (posta) ⊞ d.	|	|	0858	0900	0958	1000	1158	1200	|	1358	1400	|	1558	1600	|	1758	*1800*n	|
Ried im Oberinntal (Postamt) d.	0648	0733	...	0942	...	1042	...	1242	1342	...	1442	1543	...	1642	1748	...	1857	1857
Landeck-Zams (Bahnhof) **951** a.	0715	0800	...	1009	...	1109	...	1309	1409	...	1509	1610	...	1709	1815	...	1924	1924

	⚒	⚒	⚒d		and hourly		⚒d
Nauders (Postamt) d.	...	0717	0817	0917	on ⚒d	1917	2017
Reschenpass/Passo di Resia ⊞ d.	0623	0723	0823	0923	(every **two**	1923	2023
Resia d.	0627	0727	0827	0927	hours on	1927	2027
Malles Stazione **597** a.	0658	0758	0858	0958	†v) until	1958	2058

	⚒	⚒d		⚒d	and hourly		⚒d	⚒
Malles Stazione **597** d.	0605	0705	0802	0902	on ⚒d	1802	1902	2002
Resia d.	0636	0736	0833	0933	(every **two**	1833	1933	2033
Passo di Resia/Reschenpass ⊞ d.	0640	0740	0837	0937	hours on	1837	1937	2037
Nauders (Postamt) a.	0646	0746	0843	0943	†v) until	1843	1943	...

d – Daily June 15 - Sept. 19.
e – Not July 13 - Sept. 11, Nov. 2.
k – Also Nov. 2; runs daily July 11 - Sept. 13.
n – Change at Nauders Mühlbach (a. *1811*, d. 1818).
v – † to June 14 and from Sept. 20.

Operators: Landeck – Scuol-Tarasp and v.v.: Bundesbus, Postautostelle, A-6500 Landeck: ✆ +43 (0) 5442 64 422.
Auto da posta, Agentura Scuol, CH-7550 Scuol: ✆ +41 (0) 81 86 41 683, Fax +41 (0) 81 86 49 148.
Malles – Nauders and v.v.: SAD – Servizi Autobus Dolomiti, Via Conciapelli 60, I-39100 Bolzano: ✆ +39 0471 97 12 59, Fax +39 0471 97 00 42.

955 JENBACH - MAYRHOFEN

2nd class only Narrow gauge Zillertalbahn *

km															
													🚂A	🚂B	
0	**Jenbach** Zillertalbahn § d.	0627	0652	...	0723	0753		1753	1823	...	1923	...	1035	1535	...
11	Fügen-Hart △ d.	0644	0709	...	0743	0813	and every	1813	1843	...	1943	...	1104	1604	...
13	Uderns d.	0648	0713	...	0748	0818		1818	1848	...	1948	also	1110	1610	...
17	Kaltenbach-Stumm d.	0655	0720	...	0755	0825	30 minutes	1825	1855	...	1955	...	1128	1628	...
21	Aschau im Zillertal △ d.	0702	0727	...	0803	0833		1833	1903	...	2003	...	1137	1637	...
25	**Zell am Ziller** d.	0711	0736	...	0812	0842	until	1842	1912	...	2012	...	1147	1647	...
32	**Mayrhofen** a.	0723	0748	...	0824	0854		1854	1924	...	2024	...	1205	1705	...

												🚂A	🚂B	
Mayrhofen d.	0547	0642	...	0735	0805		1805	1835	...	1935	...	1254	1724	...
Zell am Ziller d.	0559	0655	...	0748	0818	and every	1818	1848	...	1948	...	1311	1741	...
Aschau im Zillertal △ d.	0606	0702	...	0756	0826		1826	1856	...	1956	also	1320	1750	...
Kaltenbach-Stumm d.	0612	0708	...	0802	0832	30 minutes	1832	1902	...	2002	...	1337	1807	...
Uderns d.	0618	0714	...	0809	0839		1839	1909	...	2009	...	1347	1817	...
Fügen-Hart △ d.	0623	0719	...	0815	0845	until	1845	1915	...	2015	...	1355	1825	...
Jenbach Zillertalbahn § a.	0640	0736	...	0835	0905		1905	1935	...	2035	...	1420	1850	...

A – Daily May 1 - Oct. 18.
B – Daily May 30 - Sept. 6; ⑤⑥ Sept. 11 - Oct. 3.

🚂 – Steam train. Special fares apply.
§ – Adjacent to ÖBB station.

* – Zillertaler Vehrkehrsbetriebe, Austraße, A-6200 Jenbach. ✆ +43 (0) 5244 606 0.

956 JENBACH - ACHENSEE

Achenseebahn 2nd class only

Narrow gauge rack railway operated by steam locomotives. Special fares apply. **Service May 30 - October 4, 2009** *.

km									
0	**Jenbach** Achensee-Bahnhof § d.	0840	1015	1055	1215	1345	1500	1645	...
5	Maurach d.	0915	1050	1130	1250	1420	1535	1720	...
7	**Achensee** Seespitz-Bahnstation a.	0925	1100	1140	1300	1430	1545	1730	...

Achensee Seespitz-Bahnstation d.	0930	1110	1230	1400	1515	1600	...	1736
Maurach d.	0937	1117	1237	1407	1522	1607	...	1742
Jenbach Achensee-Bahnhof § a.	1010	1150	1310	1440	1555	1640	...	1815

§ – Adjacent to ÖBB station. **Operator**: Achenseebahn AG, A-6200 Jenbach: ✆ +43 (0) 5244 62243, Fax +43 (0) 5244 622435.

* – Service May 1–29 and October 5–25: **Jenbach** → **Achensee** at 1105, 1305 and 1505; **Achensee** → **Jenbach** at 1200, 1400 and 1600.

957 MAYRHOFEN - (🚌) - KRIMML - ZELL AM SEE

2nd class only

km	🚌 *Routes* **4094** *and* **670** *Valid June 6 - Oct. 4, 2009*									
			A		A ①–⑤	A ⑥⑦			A ◇	
0	**Mayrhofen** Bahnhof d.	0830	...	...	...	...	...	...	...	1830
8	Zell am Ziller Bahnhof d.	0852	...	1052	...	...	1322	1552	...	1847
28	**Gerlos** Gasthaus Oberwirt d.	0927	...	1127	...	...	1357	1627	...	1920
37	Königsleiten Sessellift d.	0934r	0944r	1140	1400	1400	1410	1636r	1644r	...
50	Krimml Wasserfälle a.	...	1004	...	1424	1424	...	...	1704	...
53	**Krimml** Bahnhof a.	...	*1014*	...	1434	*1436*	...	...	1714	...

🚌 *Routes* **670** *and* **4094** *Valid June 6 - Oct. 4, 2009*									
		A ⊖				A		A	
Krimml Bahnhof d.	...	0834	...	...	...	*1318*	...	*1538*	...
Krimml Wasserfälle d.	...	0841	...	...	...	1327	...	1547	...
Königsleiten Sessellift d.	...	0907	0950	...	1155	1353	1450	1613	1720
Gerlos Gasthaus Oberwirt d.	0700	...	1003	...	1208	...	1503	...	1733
Zell am Ziller Bf a.	0734	...	1036	...	1241	...	1536	...	1806
Mayrhofen Bahnhof a.	0748	...	...	...	...	...	...	...	1819

Train (narrow gauge) / 🚌 : KRIMML - ZELL AM SEE ⊡

km																									
		Ⓐ🚌	©D	⑥h	⚒	Ⓑ🚌	©D	Ⓐ🚌	©D	ⒶD	🚌	©D	ⒶD	⚒🚌		ⒶD	🚌	©D	B🚂	ⒶD	⚒🚌	C🍸	©D	ⒶD	
	Krimml Wasserfälle d.	0540	*0525**	*0553**	...	0633	*0730**	0808	*0830**	*0930**	1008	*1030**	*1130**	1208	*1230**	*1330**	1408	*1430**	*1440**	*1530**	1608	*1609**	*1630**	*1730**	*1830**
0	**Krimml** Bahnhof d.	0546	*0531**	*0559**	...	0639	*0736**	0814	*0836**	*0936**	1014	*1036**	*1136**	1214	*1236**	*1336**	1414	*1436**	*1450**	*1536**	1614	*1615**	*1636**	*1736**	*1836**
24	Mittersill Bahnhof d.	|	0611	0640	0640	|	0817	|	0917	1017	|	1117	1217	|	1317	1417	|	1517	1553	1617	|	1658	1717	1817	1917
53	**Zell am See** a.	0658	0703	0730	0730	0800	0910	0935	1010	1110	1135	1210	1310	1335	1410	1510	1535	1610	1659	1710	1735	1758	1810	1910	2010

		Ⓐ🚌	©D	🚌	ⒶD	Ⓐ🚌	©D	B🚂	⚒🚌	ⒶD	C🍸		🚌	ⒶD	©D	⚒🚌	ⒶD	©D	🚌	ⒶD	©D			Ⓑ🚌	⚒🚌
Zell am See d.	0627	0720	0752	0820	0852	0920	0952	1000	1020	1052	1100	1152	1220	1252	1352	1420	1452	1552	1620	1652	1752	1852	1952	2020	2050
Mittersill Bahnhof a.	0723	|	0843	|	0943	|	1043	1107	|	1143	1201	1243	|	1343	1443	|	1543	1643	|	1743	1843	1943	2043	|	|
Krimml Bahnhof a.	*0757**	0834	*0918**	0938	*1018**	1038	*1118**	*1207**	1138	*1218**	*1307**	*1318**	1338	*1418**	*1518**	1538	*1618**	*1718**	1738	*1818**	*1918**	*2018**	...	2125	2158
Krimml Wasserfälle a.	*0806**	0841	*0927**	0947	*1027**	1047	*1127**	*1215**	1147	*1227**	*1315**	*1327**	1347	*1427**	*1527**	1547	*1627**	*1727**	1747	*1827**	*1927**	*2027**	...	2134	2206

A – July 4 - Sept. 13.
B – ⑦ May 24 - Oct. 4 (also ④ July 2 - Sept. 3).
C – NATIONALPARKZUG. © May 23 - Oct. 4 (daily July 4 - Sept. 6). Loco-hauled diesel train.
D – Train Mittersill - Zell am See and v.v. runs daily.

h – Not Aug. 15.
r – Königsleiten Abzw Gerlospass.

* – By 🚌 to/from Mittersill.
🚂 – Steam train (and historic 🚌). Special fares payable.

◇ – Change at Krimml Wasserfälle on Ⓑ (also Aug. 15).
⊖ – Change at Krimml Wasserfälle on ①–⑤.
⊡ – Runs year round. All trains are currently replaced by 🚌 between Krimml and Mittersill.
Operator: Pinzgauer Lokalbahn.

958 🚌 WÖRGL - ELLMAU - KITZBÜHEL and ST JOHANN

ÖBB-Postbus routes **4006**, **4060**, **4902**

	Ⓐ	⑥h	⚒	⚒	⚒	⚒	⚒			⚒		Ⓐ	⚒	Ⓑ	⚒		⚒		†	⚒	Ⓐ	⚒	⚒	Ⓐ	Ⓑ
Wörgl Bahnhof d.	0550	...	...	0640	0740	...	0845	...	...	1120	...	1210	1210	...	...	...	1400	...	...	1615	...	1725	...	1825	...
Kufstein Bahnhof d.	*0545*	*0545*	...	|	*0735*	...	|	*0842*	1108	|	1208	|	|	...	...	1345	|	1520	...	*1620*	...	*1715*	1800	|	*1828*
Söll (Dorf) d.	0610	0612	...	0700	0802	...	0917	0917	1136	1140	1240	1240	1240	1240	...	1414	1430	1545	1545	1645	...	1755	1828	1855	1855
Scheffau ★ d.	0617	0619	...	...	0809	...	0927	0927	...	1147	...	1247	1247	1247	...	...	1439	...	1552	1653	...	1805	...	1903	1903
Ellmau (Dorf) d.	0626	0628	0630	...	0818	0900	0942	0942	...	1203	...	1303	1303	1303	1315	...	1456	...	1604	1706	1715	1820	...	1914	1914
Kitzbühel Bahnhof a.	|	|	0654t	...	|	0924t	|	|	...	|	...	|	...	|	1345	...	|	...	|	|	1745	|	...	|	|
St Johann in Tirol Bahnhof a.	0644	0646	...	...	0836	...	1002	1002	...	1225	...	1325	...	1325	...	...	1516	...	1627	1730	...	1840	...	1930	1930

	⚒	Ⓐ	⚒	†	⚒	⚒			⚒		⚒	Ⓐ	⑥h		⚒		⚒	Ⓐ	Ⓑ	Ⓐ	⚒	⚒	Ⓐ	Ⓐ	Ⓐ
St Johann in Tirol Bahnhof d.	0535	0535	0730	0750	...	0840	...	1055	1055	...	...	1230	...	1330	1330	...	1550	...	1700	1700	...	1740	1740	...	1850
Kitzbühel Bahnhof d.	|	|	|	|	0800	|	...	|	|	...	1215	|	...	|	|	...	|	1620	|	|	...	|	|	1815	|
Ellmau (Dorf) d.	0552	0552	0748	0812	0830	0902	...	1117	1117	...	1245	1257	1303	1352	1352	...	1612	1650	1722	1722	...	1759	1759	1843	1909
Scheffau ★ d.	0559	0559	0755	0818	...	0908	...	1123	1123	...	...	1303	1309	1358	1358	...	1618	...	1728	1728	...	1805	1805	...	1915
Söll (Dorf) d.	0612	0615	0805	0832	...	0925	0925	1137	1140	1240	...	1320	1323	1412	1415	1550	1635	...	1742	1745	1745	1817	1855	...	1925
Kufstein Bahnhof a.	*0640*	|	*0830*	...	...	|	0950	*1205*	|	1308	...	*1357*	|	*1447*	|	1622	*1710*	...	...	*1820*	|	*1853*	|	...	*1945*
Wörgl Bahnhof a.	...	0645	0835	...	...	0955	...	...	1210	...	...	1350	1350	...	1445	...	1705	...	...	1808	1808	...	1915	...	1945

h – Not Aug. 15.
t – 6–7 minutes later on ⑥.
★ – Scheffau Gh zum Wilder Kaiser.

ÖBB-Postbus Route 680 — ZELL AM SEE - HINTERGLEMM — 958a

km		⚒	E		E		E		A		A		A		E
0	**Zell am See** Bahnhof .... d.	0610p	0655	0820	0920	1020	1120	1220	1320	1420	1520	1620	1720	1820	1920
20	Saalbach Schattberg............. a.	0637	0725	0852	0952	1052	1152	1252	1352	1452	1552	1652	1752	1852	1952
23	**Hinterglemm** Ellmauweg...... a.	0643	0731	0858	0958	1058	1158	1258	1358	1458	1558	1658	1758	1858	1959

	⚒		E		E		E		A		A		A	E	
Hinterglemm Ellmauweg....... d.	0621	0657	0755	0920	1020	1120	1220	1320	1420	1520	1620	1720	1820	1913	...
Saalbach Schattberg.............. d.	0628	0703	0805	0930	1030	1130	1230	1330	1430	1530	1630	1730	1830	1918	...
Zell am See Bahnhof............ a.	0700	0735	0839	1004	1104	1204	1304	1404	1504	1604	1704	1804	1904	1944p	...

A – Daily June 14 - Oct. 2; Ⓐ Oct. 5 - Nov. 27; daily from Nov. 30.
E – Daily June 14 - Oct. 3; ⚒ Oct. 5 - Nov. 28; daily from Nov. 30.

p – Zell am See Postplatz (not Bahnhof).

Information: ✆ +43 (0) 6542 5444.

2009 service — Danube shipping: BUDAPEST - BRATISLAVA - WIEN - LINZ - PASSAU — 959

Hydrofoil services. 🍷.	V	W	B	R	V	V	P	Y	T
	🅁♠	🅁♠	🅁◇	⊙	🅁♠	🅁♠	⊙	⊙	🅁♠
Wien Reichsbrücke ▲.... d.	...	...	0900	0945	...	...	1700	1730	...
Wien Schwedenplatz ▲.. d.	0830	0900	|	|	1230	1630	|	|	1900
Bratislava...................... d.	0945	1015	1030u	1115	1345	1745	1830	1900	2015
Budapest §................... a.	...	...	1430	...	...	...	...	...	...

	Z	V	B	V	W	R	V		T
	⊙	🅁♠	🅁◇	🅁♠	🅁♠	⊙	🅁♠		🅁♠
Budapest §......................... d.	...	...	0900	...	...	...	...	...	...
Bratislava .... d.	0900	1030	1330s	1430	1700	1730	1830	...	2230
Wien Schwedenplatz............. a.	|	1200	|	1600	1830	|	2000	...	2400
Wien Reichsbrücke ▲........... a.	1045	...	1530	...	...	1915	...	...	...

All sailings convey ✕	④A	J	C	⑦N	D	⑦E	K	D	D
	⊖	⊡	◐	⊖	◐	🅁◐	⊡	◐	◐
Wien Reichsbrücke ▲.... d.	...	...	...	0730n	...	0830	...	...	...
Tulln .... d.	...	...	...	0950n	...	1120	...	...	...
Krems an der Donau ..... d.	0830	1010	1015	1220	1300	1355	1540	1545	...
Dürnstein .... d.	0900	1040	1050	1250	1330	1430	1610	1620	...
Spitz an der Donau .... d.	0955	1140	1145	1345	1420	...	1705	1715	1725
Melk............................ a.	1120	1300	1315	1510	1540	...	1820	...	1840
Grein .... d.	1430	...	...	1820	...	...	...	...	...
Linz Nibelungenbrücke ... a.	1830	...	...	2220	...	...	...	...	...

	K	D	C	J	⑥N	③A	⑦F	D	D
	⊡	◐	◐	⊡	⊖	⊖	🅁◐	◐	◐
Linz Nibelungenbrücke.......... d.	...	...	...	...	0900	0900	...	...	...
Grein.................................... d.	...	...	...	...	1200	1200	...	...	...
Melk.................................... d.	0825	1100	1350	1350	1440	1440	...	1615	...
Spitz an der Donau .... d.	0915	1150	1440	1445	1520	1520	...	1705	1720
Dürnstein .... d.	0940	1210	1510	1515	1600	1600	1640	...	1740
Krems an der Donau .... d.	1005	1240	1530	1535	1620	1620	1700	...	1800
Tulln.................................... d.	...	...	...	...	1820q	...	1855	...	...
Wien Reichsbrücke ▲........... a.	...	...	...	...	2030q	...	2100	...	...

All sailings convey ✕	G	M	L
	⊖	⊖	⊖
Linz Nibelungenbrücke ... d.	...	*0930*r	1420
Schlögen .... d.	...	1425	1755
Obernzell .... d.	1435	1615	1935
Passau Liegestelle 11 🚉 d.	1545	1715	2040
Deggendorf .... a.	2035	...	...

	L	M	G
	⊖	⊖	⊖
Deggendorf .... d.	...	...	0945
Passau Liegestelle 11 🚉 d.	0900	1200	1345
Obernzell .... d.	0945	1245	1435
Schlögen .... a.	1105	1410	...
Linz Nibelungenbrücke ... a.	1405	*1750*r	...

A – July 1 - Aug. 27.
B – Daily May 1 - Sept. 27.
C – Daily Apr. 5 - Oct. 26.
D – Daily Apr. 18 - Sept. 28.
E – ⑦ May 10 - Sept. 20 (also June 20; not June 7, 21, July 5, 19, Aug. 2, 9, Sept. 6).
F – ⑦ May 10 - Sept. 20 (not June 7, July 5, 19, Aug. 2, 9, Sept. 6).

G – ①②③④⑥⑦ Apr. 25 - Oct. 11.
J – Daily Apr. 11 - Oct. 26.
K – Daily May 1 - Oct. 4.
L – ②–⑦ Apr. 24 - Oct. 4 (also ⑥⑦ Oct. 10 – 25).
M – Apr. 25 - Oct. 11.
N – Apr. 25 - Oct. 4.
P – ⑤⑥ Sept. 4 – 26.
R – ③–⑦ Apr. 29 - Sept. 27.
T – ④–⑦ May 1 - Sept. 27.
V – Daily Apr. 4 - Nov. 1.
W – © Apr. 4 – 26; daily May 1 - Sept. 27; ⑥⑦ Oct. 3 - Nov. 1.
Y – ⑤⑥ May 1 – 23; ③–⑦ May 27 - Aug. 30.
Z – ⑤⑥ May 1 – 23; ③–⑦ May 27 - Aug. 30; ⑤⑥ Sept. 4 – 26.

n – Not June 21.
q – Not June 20.
r – ②–⑦ only. Change ships at Schlögen.
s – Calls to set down only.
u – Calls to pick up only.
§ – Nemzetközi hajóállomás (International shipping terminal).

▲ – DDSG operates Wien sightseeing cruises Schwedenplatz - Reichsbrücke and v.v. Daily Apr. 3 - Oct. 31.
From Schwedenplatz (duration 1 hr 55 m) at 1030 and 1400 (also 1130 and 1500 Apr. 25 - Sept. 27).
From Reichsbrücke (duration 1 hr 20 m) at 1230 and 1600 (also 1330 and 1700 Apr. 25 - Sept. 27).

Operators:
⊡ – Brandner Schiffahrt GmbH, Ufer 50, A-3313 Wallsee. ✆ +43 (0) 7433 25 90 21, Fax +43 (0) 7433 25 90 25.
◐ – DDSG Blue Danube Schiffahrt GmbH, Handelskai 265, A-1020 Wien. ✆ +43 (0)1 588 80, Fax +43 (0)1 588 80 440.
⊖ – Wurm und Köck, Höllgasse 26, D-94032 Passau. ✆ +49 (0) 851 929292, Fax +49 (0) 851 35518.
⊙ – SPaP - LOD – Slovenská Plavba a Prístavy - Lodná Osobná Doprava a.s., Fajnorovo nábrežie 2, 811 02 Bratislava. Reservation recommended. Check-in 15 minutes before departure. Bratislava: ✆ +421 2 529 32 226, Fax +421 2 529 32 231.
◇ – Operator: MAHART PassNave, H-1056 Budapest, Belgrád rakpart. Check-in 60 minutes before departure. Budapest: ✆ +36 1 4844 005, Fax +36 1 266 4201.
♠ – *Twin City Liner*. Central Danube GmbH, Handelskai 265, A-1020 Wien. Check-in 30 minutes before departure. ✆ +43 (0)1 588 80. Internet booking: www.twincityliner.com

SALZBURG - SCHWARZACH - INNSBRUCK — 960

km		*D* 15464 B		*EN* 464 M A	*EN* 464 Q A	*REX* 1544 2	⚒ 2	⚒ 2	*REX* 1518 † 2	*REX* 1500 ⚒ 2	*ÖEC* 590 ✕	*REX* 1502 2	*D* 1280 ⑥L 🍷	*REX* 1522 Ⓐ 2	*ÖEC* 592 ✕	*REX* 1504 2	2	Ⓐ 2	*REX* 1524 Ⓐ 2	*ÖIC* 542 🍷	2	*REX* 1526 Ⓐ 2	*ÖEC* 690 ✕	*ÖEC* 668 P Z✕	*ÖEC* 668 N Z✕
			2																						
	Wien Westbahnhof **950**.... d.	...	...	...	...	...	...	...	...	...	...	...	...	...	...	...	...	...	...	0644	...	...	0844	...	...
0	**Salzburg** Hbf...**951 970/5** ‡ d.	...	0018	...	...	...	...	...	...	...	0612	...	...	0710	0812	...	...	...	0910	1015	...	1110	1212	...	...
29	Golling-Abtenau .... **970** ‡ d.	...	0056	...	...	...	...	...	...	...	0633	...	...	0734	0833	...	...	...	0934	1040	...	1134	1233	...	...
	Graz Hbf **975**................. d.	...	|	1953	2138	...	...	...	...	...	|	...	...	|	|	...	...	...	|	|	...	|	|	0938	0938
53	**Bischofshofen** ...... **970/5** ‡ d.	...	0121	|	0108	...	...	...	0520	0527	0655	...	...	0756	0855	...	...	...	0956	1104	...	1156	1255	1249	|
61	St Johann im Pongau **970** ‡ d.	...	0131	|	|	...	...	...	0530	0537	0703	...	...	0805	0903	...	...	...	1005	1113	...	1205	1303	1258	|
67	**Schwarzach - St Veit 970** ‡ a.	...	0136	0118	0121	...	...	...	0535	0542	0709	...	...	0810	0909	...	...	...	1010	1119	...	1210	1309	1304	|
67	**Schwarzach - St Veit**.......... d.	0101	...	0145	0145	...	...	...	0536	0545	▬	0712	...	0812	▬	0912	...	...	1012	1121	...	1212	...	1312	|
99	**Zell am See**.................... d.	|	...	|	|	...	...	...	0612	0621	...	0746	0853	0846	...	0946	...	...	1046	1152	...	1246	...	1343	|
113	Saalfelden......................... d.	|	...	|	|	0415	0507	0601	0625	0636	...	0755	0902	0854	⚒	0955	...	...	1054	1201	1247a	1254	...	1353	◐
131	Hochfilzen.......................... d.	|	...	|	|	0429	0525	0619	0641	0653	2	0810	0918	...	2	1010	...	...	...	1217	1305	...	...	|	|
148	St Johann in Tirol................ d.	|	...	|	|	0444	0543	0637	0658	0710	0743	0825	0935	...	0943	1025	1043	1143	...	1233	1323	...	...	1421	|
157	**Kitzbühel** .... d.	|	...	|	|	0452	0552	0646	0706	0718	0752	0833	0944	...	0952	1033	1052	1152	...	1241	1332	...	...	1429	|
166	Kirchberg in Tirol................. d.	|	...	|	|	0502	0603	0657	0715	0727	0803	0841	0955	...	1003	1041	1103	1203	...	1249	1343	...	...	|	|
192	Wörgl Hbf .... **951** a.	0244	...	|	|	0528	0633	0727	0742	0754	0833	0902	1023	...	1033	1102	1133	1233	...	1311	1413	...	...	1458	1458
217	Jenbach .... **951** a.	|	...	|	|	0548	*0658*	0754a	*0805*	0811	*0859*	0918	...	...	*1059*	1118	*1209*	*1259*	...	1325	*1441*	...	...	1512	1512
251	**Innsbruck** Hbf............ **951** a.	0337	...	0358	0358	0616	*0728*	...	*0830*	0835	*0921*	0940	...	...	*1121*	1140	*1230*	*1321*	...	1348	*1516*	...	...	1535	1535

	REX 1540 2	⚒ 2	2	*REX* 1528 Ⓐ 2	*ÖEC* 113 F✕	*REX* 1510 2	*REX* 1530 Ⓐ 2	Ⓐ 2	Ⓒ 2	2	*EC* 115 D✕	*IC* 518 🍷	⚒ 2	*REX* 5165 Ⓐ 2	⚒ 2	*REX* 1532 2	*REX* 1552 Ⓐ 2	*ÖIC* 692 🍷	*REX* 1514 2	2	*REX* 1534 Ⓐ 2	*EC* 117 Ⓑ F✕	2	2	2
Wien Westbahnhof **950** .... d.	...	...	...	...	...	...	...	...	...	...	...	...	...	...	...	...	...	1444	...	...	...	...	...	...	...
Salzburg Hbf.... **951 970/5** ‡ d.	...	...	...	1310	1412	...	1510	...	...	1518	1612	...	...	...	1618	1712	1740	1812	...	...	1910	2012	...	2118	2218
Golling-Abtenau .... **970** ‡ d.	...	...	...	1334	1433	...	1534	...	...	1556	1633	...	...	...	1656	1733	1807	1833	...	...	1934	2033	...	2156	2256
Graz Hbf **975** .... d.	...	...	...	|	|	...	|	...	...	|	|	1338	...	...	|	|	|	|	...	...	|	|	...	|	|
Bischofshofen........**970/5** ‡ d.	...	...	...	1356	1455	...	1556	...	...	1621	1655	1649	...	...	1721	1755	1832	1855	...	...	1956	2055	...	2221	2321
St Johann im Pongau **970** ‡ d.	...	...	...	1405	1503	...	1605	...	...	1631	1703	1658	...	...	1731	1803	1840	1903	...	...	2005	2103	...	2231	2331
Schwarzach - St Veit. **970** ‡ a.	...	...	...	1410	1509	...	1610	...	...	1636	1709	1704	...	...	1736	1809	1846	1909	...	...	2010	2109	...	2236	2336
Schwarzach - St Veit........... d.	1318	...	...	1412	...	1512	1612	...	...	1638	...	1712	...	...	1738	1812	1847	▬	1912	...	2012	...	2112	2238	2338
Zell am See .... d.	1351	...	...	1446	...	1546	1646	...	...	1714	...	1743	...	...	1814	1846	1923	...	1946	...	2046	...	2148	2314	0014
Saalfelden .... d.	1401	...	...	1454	...	1555	1654	1707	...	1726	...	1753	1807	...	1826	1854	1935	...	1955	...	2054	...	2200	2326	0026
Hochfilzen............................ d.	1417	1425	1522	...	...	1610	...	1725	1742	...	...	|	1825	1906	...	...	...	2	2010	...	...	...	...	...	...
St Johann in Tirol .... d.	...	1443	1543	...	...	1625	...	1743	1800	...	...	1821	1843	1921	...	...	...	1943	2025	2043	...	...	...	...	...
Kitzbühel .... d.	...	1452	1552	...	...	1633	...	1752	1809	...	...	1829	1852	1929	...	...	...	1952	2033	2052	...	...	...	...	...
Kirchberg in Tirol .... d.	...	1503	1603	...	...	1641	...	1803	1820	...	...	|	1903	1937	...	...	...	2003	2041	2103	...	...	...	...	...
Wörgl Hbf .... **951** a.	...	1533	1633	...	...	1702	...	1833	1850	...	...	1858	1933	1958	...	...	...	2033	2102	2133	...	...	...	...	...
Jenbach.......................... **951** a.	...	*1609*	*1659*	...	...	1718	...	*1859*	...	...	...	1912	*2004*	*2041*	...	...	...	...	2118	*2209*	...	...	...	...	...
Innsbruck Hbf............... **951** a.	...	*1633*	*1721*	...	...	1740	...	*1921*	...	...	...	1935	*2026*	*2116*	...	...	...	...	2140	*2230*	...	...	...	...	...

A – ZÜRICHSEE – 🛏 1, 2 cl., ▬ 2 cl. and 🚃2 Graz - Feldkirch - Buchs 🚉 - Zürich. Conveys from Schwarzach (except when train **B** runs) 🛏 1, 2 cl.*, ▬ 2 cl.* and 🚃2 Beograd (**414**) - Zagreb - Ljubljana - Villach - Schwarzach (**464**) - Zürich.
B – From Schwarzach ①⑥⑦ to June 29, daily July 4 - Sept. 7, ①⑥⑦ Sept. 12 - Oct. 26 (also Nov. 1, 2). 🛏 1, 2 cl.*, ▬ 2 cl.* and 🚃2 Beograd (**414**) - Zagreb - Ljubljana - Villach - Schwarzach (**15464**) - Feldkirch (**464**) - Buchs 🚉 - Zürich.
D – WÖRTHERSEE – 🚃12 and ✕ Münster - Köln - Stuttgart - München - Klagenfurt.
F – 🚃12 and ✕ Frankfurt - Stuttgart - München - Klagenfurt.
L – ⑥ June 27 - Aug. 29. GROSSGLOCKNER. To München (Table **951**).

M – Until Aug. 9. Also calls at Bruck a. d. Mur (d. 2047) and Leoben (d. 2100).
N – Until Aug. 10.
P – From Aug. 11.
Q – From Aug. 10.
Z – To Bregenz (Table **951**).

a – Ⓐ only.

* – 🛏 1, 2 cl. and ▬ 2 cl. from Zagreb.
◐ – Diverted between Selzthal and Wörgl (via Kirchdorf and Salzburg).
‡ – See panel on page 452 for additional local stopping trains.

960 SALZBURG - SCHWARZACH - INNSBRUCK

	EN 465 P G	EN 465 N G¶	D 15465 F	REX 1551 2	REX 1521 ⚒ 2	2	REX 1523 Ⓐ 2	ÖIC 597 Ⓑ 🍷	2	2	REX 1505 2	ÖIC 693	⚒ 2	REX 1525 Ⓐ 2	⚒ 2⊙	IC 515 🍷	EC 114 D✕	2◇	REX 1527 Ⓐ 2	2	REX 1509 2	ÖEC 112 H✕	2	REX 1529 Ⓐ 2	⚒ 2
Innsbruck Hbf ... 951 d.	0143	0143	0158	...	...	...	0502	...	...	0533v	0605	...	0623	...	0735	0825	...	...	...	0930	1019	...	1036	...	1130
Jenbach ... 951 d.	|	|	|	...	...	...	|	...	...	0559v	|	...	0648	...	0756	0845	...	...	...	0950	1043	...	1057	...	1150
Wörgl Hbf ... 951 d.	0217	0217	0234	...	...	...	0548	...	0600v	0627	0658	...	0715	...	0814	0900	...	0911	...	1027	1058	...	1127	...	1227
Kirchberg in Tirol ... d.	|	|	|	...	...	...	0614	...	0631v	0658	0720	...	0746	...	0838	|	...	0942	...	1058	1120	...	1158	...	1258
Kitzbühel ... d.	|	|	|	...	...	...	0623	...	0642v	0709	0728	...	0757	...	0847	0930	...	0953	...	1109	1128	...	1209	...	1309
St Johann in Tirol ... d.	|	|	|	...	...	...	0631	...	0651v	0717	0736	...	0806	...	0854	0938	...	1001	...	1117	1136	...	1220	...	1318
Hochfilzen ... d.	|	|	|	...	...	...	0645	...	0708v	...	0750	...	0823	...	...	|	...	...	...	...	1150	...	1238	...	1335
Saalfelden ... d.	|	|	|	0459	0606	0634	0706	...	0734	...	0806	...	0841	0906	...	1008	...	...	1106	...	1206	...	1255a	1304	...
Zell am See ... d.	|	|	|	0508	0616	0646	0716	...	0746	...	0816	...	...	0916	...	1019	...	...	1116	...	1216	...	...	1313	...
Schwarzach - St Veit ... a.	0355	0355	0414	0541	0648	0721	0748	...	0821	...	0848	...	...	0948	...	1048	...	...	1148	...	1248	...	...	1345	...
Schwarzach - St Veit 970 ‡ d.	0400	0404	...	0542	0652	0723	...	0751	0823	...	...	0851	...	0952	...	1056	1051	...	1152	...	...	1251	...	1352	...
St Johann im Pongau 970 ‡ d.	|	|	...	0548	0658	0728	...	0757	0828	...	...	0857	...	0958	...	1102	1057	...	1158	...	...	1257	...	1358	...
Bischofshofen ... 970/5 ‡ d.	0413	|	...	0557	0708	0739	...	0808	0839	...	...	0908	...	1008	...	1113	1108	...	1208	...	...	1308	...	1408	...
Graz Hbf 975 ... a.	0737	0910	...	|	|	|	...	|	|	...	...	|	...	|	...	1422	|	...	|	...	...	|	...	|	...
Golling-Abtenau ... 970 ‡ d.	...	...	...	0619	0729	0802	...	0828	0902	...	...	0928	...	1029	...	...	1128	...	1229	...	...	1328	...	1429	...
Salzburg Hbf ... 951 970/5 ‡ a.	...	...	...	0645	0753	0840	...	0848	0940	...	...	0948	...	1053	...	...	1148	...	1253	...	...	1348	...	1453	...
Wien Westbahnhof 950 ... a.	...	...	...	...	...	...	...	...	...	...	...	1318	...	...	...	...	...	...	...	...	...	...	...	...	...

	ÖEC 669 P B✕	ÖEC 669 N B✕	ÖEC 691 ✕	2	REX 1531 Ⓐ 2	ÖIC 649 🍷	Ⓐ 2	REX 1533 Ⓐ 2	⚒ 2	⚒ 2	REX 1515 2	ÖEC 110 M✕	2	2	D 1281 ⑥E 🍷	REX 1535 Ⓐ 2	REX 5164 Ⓐ 2	2	REX 1517 2	ÖEC 593 ✕	2	REX 1519 2	2	REX 1547 2	REX 1549 2
Innsbruck Hbf ... 951 d.	1225	1225	...	1236	...	1412	1436	...	...	1530	1616	...	...	1636	...	...	1721	1730	1819	...	1836	1930	...	2130	2342
Jenbach ... 951 d.	1245	1245	...	1257	...	1433	1457	...	...	1550	1640	...	...	1657	...	...	1745	1750	1843	...	1857	1950	...	2150	0017
Wörgl Hbf ... 951 d.	1300	1300	...	1327	...	1449	1527	...	...	1627	1658	...	...	1727	1736	...	1801	1827	1858	...	1927	2011	...	2208	0039
Kirchberg in Tirol ... d.	|	|	...	1358	...	1511	1558	...	...	1658	1720	...	...	1758	1808	...	1827	1858	1920	...	1958	2037	...	2235	0104
Kitzbühel ... d.	1330	|	...	1409	...	1519	1609	...	...	1709	1728	...	...	1809	1819	...	1835	1909	1928	...	2009	2046	...	2244	0113
St Johann in Tirol ... d.	1338	|	...	1418	...	1527	1618	...	...	1718	1736	...	...	1818	1829	...	1843	1917	1936	...	2017	2054	...	2252	0121
Hochfilzen ... d.	|	|	...	1435	...	1543	1635	...	...	1735	1750	...	...	1835	1846	...	1856	▬	1950	...	...	2108	...	2307	0136
Saalfelden ... d.	1408	◐	...	1459	1506	1559	1653	1704	1734	1753	1806	...	1834	1853	1902	1906	...	...	2006	...	...	2127	...	2322	0151
Zell am See ... d.	1419	|	...	...	1516	1610	...	1713	1746	...	1816	...	1846	...	1911	1916	...	...	2016	...	...	2140	...	...	...
Schwarzach - St Veit ... a.	1448	|	...	...	1548	1639	...	1745	1821	...	1848	...	1921	...	...	1948	...	S 2	2048	...	...	2214	...	...	...
Schwarzach - St Veit 970 ‡ d.	1456	|	1451	...	1552	1641	...	1752	1823	...	...	1851	1923	...	...	1952	...	2023	2056	2051	...	...	2223	...	...
St Johann im Pongau 970 ‡ d.	1502	|	1457	...	1558	1647	...	1758	1828	...	...	1857	1928	...	...	1958	...	2028	2102	2057	...	...	2228	...	...
Bischofshofen ... 970/5 ‡ d.	1513	|	1508	...	1608	1657	...	1808	1839	...	...	1908	1939	...	...	2008	...	2037	2111	2108	...	...	2239	...	...
Graz Hbf 975 ... a.	1822	1822	|	...	|	|	...	|	|	...	...	|	|	...	...	|	...	...	...	|	...	...	|	...	...
Golling-Abtenau ... 970 ‡ d.	...	...	1528	...	1629	1719	...	1829	1902	...	...	1928	2002	...	...	2029	...	...	...	2128	...	...	2302	...	...
Salzburg Hbf ... 951 970/5 ‡ a.	...	...	1548	...	1653	1744	...	1853	1940	...	...	1948	2040	...	...	2053	...	...	...	2148	...	...	2340	...	...
Wien Westbahnhof 950 ... a.	...	...	1918	...	...	2118	...	...	...	...	...	...	...	...	...	...	...	...	...	...	...	...	...	...	...

B – From Bregenz (Table **951**).
D – WÖRTHERSEE – [12] and ✕ Klagenfurt - München - Stuttgart - Köln - Dortmund.
E – ⑥ June 20 - Aug. 22. GROSSGLOCKNER. From München (Table **951**).
F – From Zürich ⑤–⑦ to June 28, daily July 3 - Sept. 6, ⑤–⑦ Sept. 11 - Oct. 25 (also Oct. 31, Nov. 1). 🛏 1,2 cl.*, ▬ 2 cl.* and [2] Zürich (**465**) - Buchs ▣ - Feldkirch (**15465**) - Schwarzach (**415**) - Villach - Ljubljana - Zagreb - Beograd.
G – ZÜRICHSEE – 🛏 1,2 cl., ▬ 2 cl. and [2] Zürich - Buchs ▣ - Feldkirch - Graz. Conveys Zürich - Schwarzach (except when train **F** runs) 🛏 1,2 cl.*, ▬ 2 cl.* and [2] Zürich (**465**) - Schwarzach (**415**) - Villach - Ljubljana - Zagreb - Beograd.
H – [12] and ✕ Klagenfurt - München - Stuttgart - Frankfurt.
M – [12] and ✕ Klagenfurt - München.
N – Until Aug. 10.
P – From Aug. 11.
S – To Schladming (Table **975**).

a – Ⓐ only.
v – ⚒ only.
* – 🛏 1,2 cl. and ▬ 2 cl. to Zagreb.
◇ – Runs 16 minutes later on Ⓐ.
⊙ – On Ⓐ runs 4 minutes later Wörgl - St Johann.
¶ – Also calls at Leoben (a. 0759) and Bruck a. d. Mur (a. 0817)
‡ – See panel on right for additional local stopping trains.
◐ – Diverted between Wörgl and Selzthal (via Salzburg and Kirchdorf).
❖ – Change trains at Bischofshofen on the 1723 and 2023 from Schwarzach.

Salzburg Hbf ... d.	0618		2018
Golling-Abtenau ... d.	0656	and	2056
Bischofshofen ... d.	0721	hourly	2121
St Johann im Pongau ... d.	0731	until	2131
Schwarzach - St Veit ... a.	0736		2136
		❖	
Schwarzach - St Veit ... d.	0523		2123
St Johann im Pongau ... d.	0528	and	2128
Bischofshofen ... d.	0539	hourly	2139
Golling-Abtenau ... d.	0602	until	2202
Salzburg Hbf ... a.	0640		2240

961 ATTNANG-PUCHHEIM - STAINACH-IRDNING

2nd class only

km		⚒								A									
0	**Attnang-Puchheim** ... d.	...	...	0605	0713	0813	0913	1013	1113	1213	1313	1413	1513	1613	1713	1813	1913	2010	2113
12	**Gmunden** ... d.	...	...	0623	0734	0828	0934	1028	1134	1228	1334	1428	1534	1628	1734	1828	1934	2028	2134
17	Altmünster am Traunsee ... d.	...	...	0629	0740	0834	0940	1034	1140	1234	1340	1434	1540	1634	1740	1834	1940	2033	2140
22	Traunkirchen ... d.	...	...	0635	0746	0840	0946	1040	1146	1240	1346	1440	1546	1640	1746	1840	1946	2039	2146
27	Ebensee Landungsplatz ... d.	...	...	0643	0754	0846	0954	1046	1154	1246	1354	1446	1554	1646	1754	1846	1954	2046	2153
44	**Bad Ischl** ... d.	...	...	0706	0821	0905	1021	1105	1221	1305	1421	1505	1621	1705	1821	1905	2020	2105	2217
54	Bad Goisern ... d.	...	...	0721	0834	0916	1034	1116	1234	1316	1434	1516	1634	1716	1834	1916	2034	2117	...
64	Hallstatt ⊡ ... d.	...	...	0733	0849	0927	1049	1127	1249	1327	1449	1527	1649	1727	1849	|	|	|	...
67	Obertraun-Dachsteinhöhlen ... d.	...	...	0737	0852	0931	1052	1131	1252	1331	1452	1531	1652	1731	1852	1931	2052	2133	...
78	**Bad Aussee** ... d.	0440	0632	0750	...	0943	...	1143	...	1343	...	1543	...	1743	...	1943	2104	2145	...
93	Bad Mitterndorf ... d.	0457	0650	0805	...	1001	...	1200	...	1401	...	1600	...	1801	...	2001	...	...	...
108	**Stainach-Irdning** ... a.	0515	0707	0819	...	1017	...	1217	...	1417	...	1617	...	1817	...	2017	...	...	...

			⚒										B	△			©L	Ⓐ	
Stainach-Irdning ... d.	...	...	...	0611v	0714	...	0942	...	1142	...	1342	...	1542	...	1742	...	1942	1942	2050
Bad Mitterndorf ... d.	...	...	...	0628v	0731	...	1000	...	1200	...	1400	...	1600	...	1800	...	2000	2000	2107
Bad Aussee ... d.	...	0458	0601	0651	0810r	...	1017	...	1217	...	1417	...	1617	...	1817	...	2016	2018	2125
Obertraun-Dachsteinhöhlen ... d.	...	0510	0613	0704	0824	0907	1029	1107	1229	1307	1429	1507	1629	1707	1829	1907	2028	...	...
Hallstatt ⊡ ... d.	...	|	|	0708	0827	0911	1032	1111	1232	1311	1432	1511	1632	1711	1832	|	|	...	...
Bad Goisern ... d.	...	0525	0629	0722	0842	0925	1044	1125	1244	1325	1444	1525	1644	1725	1844	1925	2043	...	...
Bad Ischl ... d.	0439	0538	0643	0735	0853	0937	1054	1137	1254	1337	1454	1537	1654	1737	1854	1937	2054	...	...
Ebensee Landungsplatz ... d.	0502	0602	0709	0800	0915	1003	1115	1203	1315	1403	1515	1603	1715	1803	1915	2003	2115	...	...
Traunkirchen ... d.	0510	0610	0718	0808	0921	1011	1122	1211	1322	1411	1522	1611	1722	1811	1922	2011	2122	...	...
Altmünster am Traunsee ... d.	0516	0616	0724	0815	0927	1018	1128	1218	1328	1418	1528	1618	1728	1818	1928	2018	2128	...	...
Gmunden ... d.	0522	0622	0730	0828	0933	1028	1133	1228	1333	1428	1533	1628	1733	1828	1933	2028	2134	...	...
Attnang-Puchheim ... a.	0539	0639	0747	0846	0947	1045	1147	1245	1347	1445	1547	1645	1747	1845	1947	2045	2150	...	...

A – Conveys [12] Wien (**546**) - Attnang-Puchheim - Stainach.
B – Conveys [12] Stainach - Attnang-Puchheim (**647/15647**) - Wien.
L – To Linz (Table **950**).

r – Arrives 0749.
v – ⚒ only.

△ – Change trains at Bad Ischl on Ⓐ to July 9 and from Sept. 14.
⊡ – Connecting ⛴ services operate Hallstatt Bahnhof - Hallstatt Zentrum and v.v. **Operator**: Hallstättersee-Schifffahrt Hemetsberger KG ✆ +43 (0) 6134 8228.

962 LINZ - BRAUNAU - SIMBACH

2nd class only

km		⚒	Ⓐ	†	⚒	Ⓐ	G	Ⓐ	©		Ⓐ		©	⚒	Ⓐ		Ⓐ		©	Ⓐ	Ⓐ		B		
0	**Linz** Hbf ... 950 d.	0457	...	0547	0556	0556	0653	0713	0736	0920	1016	1120	1120	1220	1220	1320	1420	1520	1520	1620	1640	1720	1804	1920	2113
25	**Wels** Hbf ... 950 d.	0523	...	0621	0621	0621	0713	0730	0755	0940	1040	1140	1140	1240	1240	1340	1440	1540	1540	1640	1701	1740	1833	1940	2140
54	Neumarkt-Kallham. 950 d.	0550	0553	0651	0651	0651	0738	0810	0831	1010	1110	1210	1210	1310	1310	1410	1510	1610	1610	1707	1734	1810	1856	2010	2208
76	Ried im Innkreis ... d.	...	0614	0714	0714	0714	0754	0832	0854	1032	1132	1232	1232	1332	1332	1432	1532	1632	1632	1729	1754	1831	1913	2032	2228
113	**Braunau** am Inn ... a.	...	...	0740	0740	0740	0819	0910	0927	1110	1210	1310	1310	1410	1410	1510	1610	1710	1710	1806	1823	1904	1943	2108	...
115	**Simbach** (Inn) ▣ ... a.	...	...	...	...	0745	0823	0914	0932	1118	...	...	1314	...	1416	1516	...	...	1714	1811	...	...	1947	...	...

	⚒	Ⓐ	⚒	†		Ⓐ	⚒	†	⚒A		†A	Ⓐ			⚒	Ⓐ			Ⓐ	†	⑥n	Ⓐ		M	
Simbach (Inn) ▣ ... d.	...	...	...	...	...	...	...	...	0719	...	0815	...	0948	1148	...	1448	1523	...	...	1750	1750	1825	...	1938	...
Braunau am Inn ... d.	...	0510	0510	...	...	...	0629	0629	0725	0750	0820	0852	0952	1152	1252	1452	1526	1552	1715	1754	1754	1830	...	1944	1955
Ried im Innkreis ... d.	0455	0549	0549	0611	...	0619	0712	0712	0754	0831	0854	0931	1031	1231	1331	1531	...	1631	1807	1831	1831	1912	...	2011	2032
Neumarkt-Kallham 950 a.	0514	0612	0612	0630	0636	0638	0731	0731	0809	0850	0909	0950	1050	1250	1350	1550	...	1650	1828	1851	1851	1931	1935	2028	2051
Wels Hbf ... 950 a.	0548	0637	0637	...	0704	0715	0803	0803	0832	0921	0932	1021	1121	1321	1421	1621	...	1721	1859	1921	...	...	2002	2051	2121
Linz Hbf ... 950 a.	0614	0655	...	...	0722	0742	0821	0827	0850	0939	0950	1043	1139	1339	1439	1639	...	1739	1927	1943	...	...	2027	2109	2143

A – From Mühldorf (Table **893**).
B – [12] Linz - Mühldorf (- München ①–⑥ **z**). See also Table **893**.
G – *D* **966**. [12] Garsten - Linz - Simbach - München. See also Table **893**.
M – *D* **963**. [12] München - Simbach - Linz. See also Table **893**.
n – Not Aug. 15.
z – Not Aug. 15, Oct. 3.

Routes 150, 2560 — SALZBURG and ST WOLFGANG - STROBL - BAD ISCHL — 963

km	Route 150																								
		⚒	⚒		Ⓐ	⑥n		⚒		⑥n	Ⓐ	Ⓒ	Ⓐ	⚒		Ⓐ	Ⓒ	Ⓐ	Ⓐ		Ⓐ		Ⓐ	†	⚒
0	**Salzburg** Hbf △ d.	...	0555	...	*0625*	0645	0815	0915	1015	1115	1115	1215	1215	1315	1415	1515	1615	1625	1725	1815	1845	1915	2015	2115	2230
32	St Gilgen (Busbahnhof) d.	0600	0645	0645	0735	0735	0910	1010	1110	1210	1220	1310	1315	1410	1510	1610	1710	1710	1810	1910	1935	2005	2104	2205	2315
45	Strobl (Busbahnhof) d.	0618	0703	0703	0753	0753	0928	1028	1128	1228	1238	1328	1333	1428	1528	1628	1728	1728	1828	1928	...	2021	...	2221	2331
57	**Bad Ischl** Bahnhof a.	0640	0725	0725	0815	0815	0950	1050	1150	1250	1300	1350	1355	1450	1550	1650	1750	1750	1850	1950	...	2040	...	2240	2350

Route 150																								
	Ⓐ	⚒	Ⓐ	Ⓐ	⑥n		⚒					⑥n	Ⓐ	Ⓒ	Ⓐ	⑥n	Ⓐ		⚒		Ⓐ		Ⓐ	
Bad Ischl Bahnhof d.	...	0502	...	...	...	0611	0645	0745	...	0923	1023	1123	1123	1223	1223	1323	1333	1423	1523	1623	1723	1823	1923	2023
Strobl (Busbahnhof) d.	...	0518	0548	0615	...	0631	0707	0807	...	0945	1045	1145	1145	1245	1245	1345	1355	1445	1545	1645	1745	1845	1945	2045
St Gilgen (Busbahnhof) d.	0515	0535	0605	0630	0635	0646	0727	0827	...	1005	1105	1205	1220	1305	1315	1405	1415	1505	1605	1705	1805	1905	2005	2101
Salzburg Hbf △ a.	0553	0619	0649	0719	0719	0731	0819	0919	...	1057	1157	1257	1305	1357	1405	1457	1507	1557	1657	1757	1853	1953	2053	...

km	Route 2560																								
		Ⓐ	⚒	⚒	⑥n	†	Ⓐ	Ⓐ	Ⓐ				Ⓐ		Ⓐ			Ⓐ			Ⓐ				
0	**St Wolfgang** ⊡ ‡... ♥ d.	0500	0600	0648	0740	0740	0743	0753	0903	0928	1013	1028	1103	1210	1318	1410	1513	1513	1610	1713	1713	1813	1813	1913	2003
7	Strobl (Busbahnhof) ♥ d.	0513	0613	0700	0752	0753	|	0805	|	0942	|	1042	|	1225	1333	1425	1527	1528	1625	1727	1728	1827	|	1927	2017
19	**Bad Ischl** Bahnhof a.	0535	0642	...	...	0815	0815	...	0935	...	1045	...	1135	1252	1400	1452	...	1555	1652	...	1755	...	1845	...	...

Route 2560																								
	Ⓐ	⚒	⚒			Ⓐ	Ⓐ				⚒			Ⓐ			Ⓐ			Ⓐ				
Bad Ischl Bahnhof d.	0605	0645	...	0823	0913	...	1023	...	1113	...	1215	...	1333	1423	...	1518	1623	...	1713	1815	...	1913	...	...
Strobl (Busbahnhof) d.	0632	0708	0810	|	|	0930	1045	1045	|	1130	1245	1245	1355	1445	1445	1540	1645	1645	1735	1845	1845	|	1930	2045
St Wolfgang ⊡ ‡ a.	0645	0723	0825	0855	0945	0945	1100	1100	1145	1145	1300	1300	1410	1500	1500	1555	1700	1700	1750	1900	1900	1945	1945	2100

n – Not Aug. 15.

△ – All services also call at Mirabellplatz.

♥ – Additional services St Wolfgang - Strobl on Ⓒ: 1113 and 1313.

⊡ – St Wolfgang Schafbergbahnhof. All services also call at St Wolfgang Markt.

‡ – The **Schafbergbahn** narrow-gauge steam rack railway operates **St Wolfgang - Schafbergspitze** (*6 km*). Services operate subject to demand (minimum 20 passengers) and weather conditions **May 1 - Oct. 26**. 2nd class only. Special fares payable. **Journey time**: 45 minutes each way. ✆ +43 (0) 6138 2232 0.

Service June 11 - Sept. 6 — STROBL - ST GILGEN (WOLFGANGSEE) — 964

			⛴			⛴			⛴			⛴					
Strobl Schiffstation ⊡ d.	...	0845	...	0930	1030	...	1130	1230	...	1330	1430	...	1530	1630	1730	1820	1920
St Wolfgang Markt d.	...	0910	0935	1000	1100	1130	1200	1300	1330	1400	1500	1530	1600	1700	1800	1835	1933
St Wolfgang Schafbergbahnhof ‡ d.	0830	0920	0945	1008	1108	1140	1208	1308	1340	1408	1508	1540	1608	1708	1808	1845	1941
St Gilgen Schiffstation ● a.	0855	0955	1020	1045	1145	1220	1245	1345	1420	1445	1545	1620	1645	1745	1845	...	...

					⛴			⛴			⛴			⛴			
St Gilgen Schiffstation ● d.	...	...	0900	1000	1030	1100	1200	1230	1300	1400	1430	1500	1600	1630	1700	1800	1850
St Wolfgang Schafbergbahnhof ‡ d.	0825	0902	0937	1037	1110	1137	1237	1310	1337	1437	1510	1537	1637	1710	1737	1837	1935a
St Wolfgang Markt d.	|	0910	0950	1050	1120	1150	1250	1320	1350	1450	1520	1550	1650	1720	1750	1850	1925
Strobl Schiffstation ⊡ a.	0840	0925	1015	1115	...	1215	1315	...	1415	1515	...	1615	1715	...	1815	1915	...

a – Arrival time (calls after St Wolfgang Markt).

⛴ – From July 4 (subject to weather conditions). Operated by paddle-steamer *Kaiser Franz Josef I*. Supplement payable.

TAUERN TUNNEL CAR-CARRYING TRAINS — 969

BÖCKSTEIN - MALLNITZ-OBERVELLACH and v.v. *11 km*. Transit time: 11 minutes. Passengers without cars are also conveyed. ✆ 05-1717. E-mail: autoschleuse.tauernbahn@pv.oebb.at

From Böckstein at 0620, 0650 ⑥ **B**, 0720, 0750 ⑥ **B**, 0820, 0850 **C** and at 20 and 50 **C** minutes past each hour until 1620, 1650 **C**, then 1720, 1750 ⑦ **D**, 1820, 1850 ⑦ **D**, 1920, 2020, 2120, 2220.

From Mallnitz-Obervellach at 0550, 0650, 0720 ⑥ **B**, 0750, 0820 **C**, 0850 and at 20 **C** and 50 minutes past each hour until 1620 **C**, 1650, then 1720 ⑦ **D**, 1750, 1820 ⑦ **D**, 1850, 1950, 2050, 2150.

B – ⑥ until Sept. 12.

C – ⑥⑦ until Sept. 13.

D – ⑦ until Sept. 13 (also Aug. 15).

SALZBURG - VILLACH - KLAGENFURT — 970

km		*D* 499	*EN* 237	*EN* 234		*D* 415				*REX* 1563	*ÖEC* 590	*ÖEC* 592	*ÖEC* 111	*ÖEC* 690	*ÖEC* 113		*EC* 115	*ÖIC* 692	*EC* 117		*ÖIC* 596		
			Ⓡ						⚒							Ⓐ			Ⓑ		A		
		♦	♦	2		♦	2		2	2	✕	✕	✕♦	✕	✕♦	2	✕♦	🍷	✕♦		🍷	2	
	Wien Westbahnhof **950** d.	...	2040	...	...	...	...	...	...	...	...	...	...	0844	...	...	...	1444	...	...	...	...	...
	München Hbf **890** d.	2340	|	...	...	...	...	...	...	...	...	...	0827	|	1221	...	1421	|	1820	...	...	...	...
0	**Salzburg** Hbf **960 975** d.	0134	0134	...	...	...	...	...	...	...	0612	0812	1012	1212	1412	...	1612	1812	2012	...	2110	...	...
29	Golling-Abtenau **960** d.	|	|	...	...	...	...	...	...	...	0633	0833	1033	1233	1433	...	1633	1833	2033	...	2134	...	...
53	**Bischofshofen** **960 975** d.	|	|	...	...	...	...	...	...	...	0655	0855	1055	1255	1455	...	1655	1855	2055	...	2156	...	...
61	St Johann im Pongau **960** d.	|	|	...	...	...	...	...	...	...	0703	0903	1103	1303	1503	...	1703	1903	2103	...	2204	...	...
67	**Schwarzach - St Veit** **960** d.	0226	0226	...	...	0430	...	...	...	...	0711	0911	1111	1311	1511	...	1711	1911	2111	...	2211	...	...
86	Bad Hofgastein d.	|	|	...	...	0447	...	...	...	...	0729	0929	1129	1329	1529	...	1729	1929	2129	...	2229	...	...
97	Bad Gastein d.	|	|	...	...	0503	...	...	...	...	0741	0941	1141	1341	1541	...	1741	1941	2141	...	2241	...	...
113	Mallnitz-Obervellach d.	|	|	...	...	0518	...	...	0646	...	0755	0955	1155	1355	1555	1740	1755	1955	2155	...	2255	...	...
146	Spittal-Millstättersee **971** d.	|	|	...	...	0546	...	...	0717	0723	0821	1021	1221	1421	1621	1811	1821	2021	2221	...	2321	...	...
182	**Villach** Hbf **971** a.	0352	0352	...	...	0609	...	...	...	0748	0843	1043	1243	1443	1643	...	1843	2043	2245	...	2343	...	...
182	**Villach** Hbf **971** d.	...	...	0417	...	...	0620	...	...	0750	0846	1046	1246	1446	1646	...	1846	2046	2248	...	...	2350	...
198	Velden am Wörthersee **971** d.	...	...	|	...	...	0635	...	...	0801	0857	1057	1257	1457	1657	...	1857	2057	2259	...	...	0005	...
207	Pörtschach am Wörthersee **971** d.	...	...	|	...	...	0643	...	...	|	0903	1103	1303	1503	1703	...	1903	2103	2305	...	...	0013	...
220	**Klagenfurt** Hbf **971** a.	...	...	0438	...	...	0656	...	...	0816	0912	1112	1315	1512	1715	...	1915	2112	2317	...	...	0026	...

	D 498	*EN* 236				*REX* 1739	*ÖIC* 597	*ÖIC* 693	*EC* 114	*ÖEC* 112	*ÖEC* 691	*ÖEC* 591	*REX* 1747	*ÖEC* 110	*ÖEC* 593	*IC* 899		*REX* 1715	*D* 414				
		Ⓡ		⚒		⚒	Ⓑ						Ⓐ										
	♦	♦		2		2	🍷		✕♦	✕♦	✕	✕	2	✕♦	✕	✕*		2	♦				
Klagenfurt Hbf **971** d.	...	...	...	...	...	0530	0552	0646	0843	1033	1246	1446	1538	1631	1846	2046	...	2219	...	...	...	...	...
Pörtschach am Wörthersee **971** d.	...	...	...	...	...	0543	|	0655	0855	1045	1255	1455	1549	1643	1855	2055	...	2231	...	...	...	...	...
Velden am Wörthersee **971** d.	...	...	...	...	...	0550	|	0702	0902	1052	1302	1502	1555	1650	1902	2102	...	2237	...	...	...	...	...
Villach Hbf **971** a.	...	...	...	...	...	0606	0614	0713	0913	1103	1313	1513	1609	1703	1913	2113	...	2253	...	...	...	...	...
Villach Hbf **971** d.	0145	0145	...	0528	...	...	0616	0716	0916	1116	1316	1516	1610	1716	1916	2116	...	...	2300	...	...	...	...
Spittal-Millstättersee **971** d.	|	|	...	0603	...	...	0639	0739	0939	1139	1339	1539	1636	1739	1939	2139	...	...	2325	...	...	...	...
Mallnitz-Obervellach d.	|	|	...	0633	...	...	0707	0807	1007	1207	1407	1607	1707	1807	2007	2207	...	...	2359	...	...	...	...
Bad Gastein d.	|	|	...	...	...	...	0720	0820	1020	1220	1420	1620	...	1820	2020	2220	...	...	0015	...	...	...	...
Bad Hofgastein d.	|	|	...	...	...	...	0731	0831	1031	1231	1431	1631	...	1831	2031	2231	...	...	0026	...	...	...	...
Schwarzach - St Veit **960** d.	0320	0320	...	...	...	...	0751	0851	1051	1251	1451	1651	...	1851	2051	2251	...	...	0042	...	...	...	...
St Johann im Pongau **960** d.	|	|	...	...	...	...	0757	0857	1057	1257	1457	1657	...	1857	2057	2257	...	...	...	...	...	...	...
Bischofshofen **960 975** d.	|	|	...	...	...	...	0808	0908	1108	1308	1508	1708	...	1908	2108	2308	...	...	...	...	...	...	...
Golling-Abtenau **960** d.	|	|	...	...	...	...	0828	0928	1128	1328	1528	1728	...	1928	2128	2328	...	...	...	...	...	...	...
Salzburg Hbf **960 975** a.	0409	0409	...	...	...	...	0848	0948	1148	1348	1548	1748	...	1948	2148	2350	...	...	...	...	...	...	...
München Hbf **890** a.	0615	|	...	...	...	...	...	|	1335	1535	|	...	...	2135	...	...	...	...	...	...	...	...	...
Wien Westbahnhof **950** a.	...	0827	...	...	...	...	...	1318	...	...	1918	...	...	...	...	...	...	...	...	...	...	...	...

♦ – **NOTES** (LISTED BY TRAIN NUMBER)

110 – [12] and ✕ Klagenfurt - München; [12] Beograd (**210**) - Zagreb - Ljubljana - Villach (**110**) - München.

111 – [12] and ✕ München - Klagenfurt; [12] München - Villach (**211**) - Ljubljana - Zagreb - Beograd.

112 – [12] and ✕ Klagenfurt - München - Stuttgart - Frankfurt; [12] Zagreb (**212**) - Ljubljana - Villach (**112**) - München - Stuttgart - Frankfurt.

113 – [12] and ✕ Frankfurt - Stuttgart - München - Klagenfurt; [12] Frankfurt - Stuttgart - München - Villach (**213**) - Ljubljana - Zagreb.

114 – WÖRTHERSEE – [12] and ✕ Klagenfurt - München - Stuttgart - Köln - Dortmund.

115 – WÖRTHERSEE – [12] and ✕ Münster - Köln - Stuttgart - München - Klagenfurt.

117 – [12] and ✕ Frankfurt - Stuttgart - München - Klagenfurt.

236/7 – ALLEGRO DON GIOVANNI – [sleeper] 1, 2 cl., [couchette] 2 cl. and [2] Venezia - Udine - Tarvisio - Villach - Salzburg - Wien and v.v.

414 – [2] Beograd - Zagreb - Ljubljana - Villach - Schwarzach (**464/15464**) - Innsbruck - Feldkirch (**464**) - Zürich; [sleeper] 1, 2 cl. and [couchette] 2 cl. Zagreb - Ljubljana - Villach - Schwarzach (**464/15464**) - Innsbruck - Feldkirch (**464**) - Zürich.

415 – [2] Zürich (**465**) - Feldkirch (**465/15465**) - Innsbruck - Schwarzach (**415**) - Villach - Ljubljana - Zagreb - Beograd; [sleeper] 1, 2 cl. and [couchette] 2 cl. Zürich (**465**) - Feldkirch (**465/15465**) - Innsbruck - Schwarzach (**415**) - Villach - Ljubljana - Zagreb.

498 – LISINSKI – [sleeper] 1, 2 cl., [couchette] 2 cl. and [2] Zagreb - Ljubljana - Villach - Salzburg - München; [2] Beograd (**418**) - Vinkovci (**748**) - Zagreb (**296**) - München; [sleeper] 1, 2 cl. Zagreb - Salzburg (**206**) - Praha. Until Sept. 18 (from Rijeka) conveys [sleeper] 1, 2 cl. and [couchette] 2 cl. Rijeka (**480**) - Ljubljana (**296**) - München.

499 – LISINSKI – [sleeper] 1, 2 cl., [couchette] 2 cl. and [2] München - Ljubljana - Zagreb; [2] München - Zagreb (**741**) - Vinkovci (**419**) - Beograd; [sleeper] 1, 2 cl. Praha (**207**) - Salzburg (**499**) - Zagreb. Until Sept. 19 (from München) conveys [sleeper] 1, 2 cl. and [couchette] 2 cl. München - Ljubljana (**481**) - Rijeka.

A – Daily except ⑤.

* – Conveys ✕ on ⑧.

971 LIENZ - VILLACH - KLAGENFURT - FRIESACH (- WIEN)

		REX	ÖEC	REX	REX		REX	REX	REX	REX	IC	IC		REX	REX		ÖIC	REX			ÖIC	ÖIC			
		1740	532	1740	1700		1742	1742	1561	1565	534	534		1563	1744		536	1704			538	538			
	⚒	⚒	⚒	Ⓐ			Ⓐ	⚒	Ⓐ	Ⓒ	①–⑤				Ⓐ				Ⓐ		⑥				
	2	2	🍴	2	B2	2	2	2	2	2	🍷	🍷	B2	2	2	2	🍷	B2	2	2	🍷	🍷	B2	2	2
Lienz d.	...	...	...	...	...	...	...	...	0526	0526	0547	...	...	0623	...	0730	...	...	0830	0930	0950	...	...	...	1030e
Spittal-Millstättersee a.	...	...	...	...	...	...	...	...	0627	0627	0633	...	...	0722	...	0827	...	...	0927	1027	1038	...	...	...	1127
Spittal-Millstättersee 970 d.	...	0448	...	←	0535a	...	0601	0601	0630	0631j	0637	...	0641a	0723	...	0831	...	...	0931	1030	1044	...	...	...	1131
Villach Hbf 970 a.	...	0521	...	0521	0604a	...	0635	0635	0655	0705j	0701	...	0715a	0748	...	0905	...	...	1005	1104	1108	...	...	...	1205
		→		|	|		|	d 2	|		|		|	|					Ⓐ2	2	|				⚒2
Villach Hbf 970 d.	0500	...	0527	0530	0606	0620	0641	0645	0659	...	0716	0716	0720	0750	0820	...	0914	0920	1020	1050	1116	1116	1120	1150	1220
Velden am Wörthersee 970 d.	0515	...	|	0545	|	0635	0654	0700	0711	...	|	|	0735	0801	0833	...	0925	0935	1035	1105	|	|	1135	1205	1235
Pörtschach am W'see 970 d.	0523	...	|	0553	|	0643	0700	0708	|	...	|	|	0743	|	0839	...	|	0943	1043	1113	|	|	1143	1213	1243
Klagenfurt Hbf 970 a.	0536	...	0548	0606	0627	0656	0708	0721	0726	...	0737	0737	0756	0816	0849	...	0937	0956	1056	1126	1137	1137	1156	1226	1256
Klagenfurt Hbf 980 d.	...	...	0550	0608	0628	0704	...	...	...	...	0739	0739	0804	...	0851	...	0939	1004	1104	...	1139	1139	1204	...	1310
St Veit an der Glan 980 d.	...	...	0603	0628	0641	0724	...	...	...	...	0753	0753	0824	...	0903	...	0953	1024	1124	...	1153	1153	1224	...	1330
Friesach 980 a.	...	...	|	0700	0705	0756	...	...	...	...	|	|	0856	...	...	...	1015	1056	1156	...	|	|	1256	...	1402
Wien Südbahnhof 980 a.	...	...	0935	...	...	...	...	...	...	...	1135	1135	...	...	...	...	1335	...	...	...	1535	1535	...	...	...

		ÖEC	REX				ÖIC	REX				ÖEC	REX				ÖEC			IC				EC	
		732	1708				630	1710				530	1712				30			730				117	
	⚒					⚒			Ⓐ		⚒			†	⚒	⚒				⑦z		⚒		Ⓑ	
	2	🍴	B2	2	2	2	🍷	B2	2	2	2	🍴	B2	2	2	2	🍴	2	2	🍷	2	2	2	🍴	2
Lienz d.	1130	...	...	...	1230e	1330	...	...	...	1430e	1530	1550	...	1628	1630	1730	...	...	1830e	...	...	1930	2036	...	...
Spittal-Millstättersee a.	1227	...	...	...	1327	1427	...	...	...	1527	1627	1638	...	1727	1727	1827	...	...	1927	...	...	2027	2131	...	...
Spittal-Millstättersee 970 d.	1236	...	...	...	1331	1431	...	...	...	1531	1630	1644	...	1731	1731	1830	...	...	1931	...	...	2031	2132	2221	...
Villach Hbf 970 a.	1310	...	...	...	1405	1505	...	...	...	1605	1704	1708	...	1805	1805	1904	...	...	2005	...	...	2105	2205	2245	...
	2				⚒2	2				Ⓐ2	2	|		2	|	2			Ⓑ			d 2		|	
Villach Hbf 970 d.	1250	1316	1320	1350	1420	1450	1514	1520	1550	1630	1650	1714	1730	1750	1820	1850	1916	1920	1950	2020	2055	2150	...	2248	2350
Velden am Wörthersee 970 d.	1305	|	1335	1405	1435	1505	1525	1535	1605	1645	1705	|	1745	1805	1835	1905	|	1935	2005	|	2110	2205	...	2259	0005
Pörtschach am W'see 970 d.	1313	|	1343	1413	1443	1513	|	1543	1613	1653	1713	1729	1753	1813	1843	1913	|	1943	2013	|	2118	2213	...	2305	0013
Klagenfurt Hbf 970 a.	1326	1337	1356	1426	1456	1526	1537	1556	1626	1706	1726	1737	1806	1826	1856	1926	1937	1956	2026	2041	2131	2226	...	2317	0026
Klagenfurt Hbf 980 d.	...	1339	1404	...	1504	...	1539	1604	1628	1710	...	1739	1808	...	1904	...	1939	2004	...	2043	2133	2228	...	...	0028
St Veit an der Glan 980 d.	...	1353	1424	...	1524	...	1553	1624	1647	1730	...	1753	1833	...	1924	...	1953	2024	...	2057	2152	2248	...	...	0047
Friesach 980 a.	...	1415	1456	...	1556	...	|	1656	...	1802	...	1815	1905	...	1956	...	|	2056	...	|	...	2320	...	...	...
Wien Südbahnhof 980 a.	...	1735	...	...	...	...	1935	...	...	...	...	2135	...	...	...	...	2335	...	...	0035	...	...	...	...	...

km			REX				REX		REX		REX			REX	ÖEC		ÖEC		REX	ÖEC					REX
			1739				1741		1701		1721			1703	31		112		1705	531					1707
		⚒	⚒	⚒		Ⓐ	⚒		⚒	Ⓐ	Ⓐ					⚒					⚒		Ⓐ		
		2	2	2	2	2	2	2	B2	2	2	2	2	B2	🍴	2	🍴	2	A2	🍴	2	2	2	2	B2
	Wien Südbahnhof 980 d.	...	...	...	...	...	...	...	...	...	...	...	...	...	0623	...	...	...	...	0823	...	...	...	...	...
0	Friesach 980 d.	...	...	...	0522	0522	0545	0611r	0644	0706	...	...	0807	0907	|	...	...	...	1107	1145	...	...	1207	...	1307
33	St Veit an der Glan 980 d.	...	...	...	0556	0556	0616	0645	0720	0740	...	...	0840	0940	1009	...	...	...	1140	1209	...	...	1240	...	1340
53	**Klagenfurt** Hbf 980 a.	...	...	...	0615	0615	0631	0704	0740	0759	...	...	0859	0959	1021	...	...	...	1159	1221	...	...	1259	...	1359
53	**Klagenfurt** Hbf 970 d.	...	0530	0602	0622	0622	0633	0710	0742	0802	0817	0832	0902	1002	1023	...	1033	1132	1202	1223	...	1232	1302	1332	1402
66	Pörtschach am W'see 970 d.	...	0543	0616	0636	0636	0646	0721	0754	0816	|	0846	0916	1016	|	...	1045	1146	1216	1232	...	1246	1316	1346	1416
75	Velden am Wörthersee 970 d.	...	0550	0624	0644	0644	0653	0727	0801	0824	0832	0854	0924	1024	|	...	1052	1154	1224	|	...	1254	1324	1354	1424
91	**Villach** Hbf 970 a.	...	0606	0639	0659	0659	0709	0743	0817	0839	0846	0909	0939	1039	1044	...	1103	1209	1239	1246	...	1309	1339	1409	1439
			2	d 2		|		2			⚒2		2				|	2		|			d 2		
91	**Villach** Hbf 970 d.	0528	...	0656	...	0709	...	0756	...	...	0856	...	0956	...	...	1056	1116	1156	...	1253	1257	...	1356	...	...
127	Spittal-Millstättersee 970 a.	0601	...	0729	...	0734	...	0829	...	...	0929	...	1029	...	...	1129	1138	1229	...	1316	1330	...	1429	...	...
127	Spittal-Millstättersee d.	...	0626	...	...	0736	...	0831	...	...	0931	...	1031	...	...	1131	...	1231	...	1319	1331	...	1431	...	...
195	**Lienz** a.	...	0724	...	...	0825	...	0929	...	...	1029	...	1130	...	...	1229	...	1330	...	1409	1429	...	1530	...	...

	ÖIC					ÖEC		ÖEC		REX	REX	ÖIC	ÖIC					REX	ÖIC				REX	ÖEC	REX
	533					733		110		1749	1711	535	535					1713	537				1715	539	1715
		⚒		⚒			⚒		⚒	Ⓐ			Ⓑ	⚒		Ⓐ				⚒		⚒			
	🍷	2	2	2	B2	🍴	2	🍴	2	2	B2	🍷	🍷	2	2	2	2	B2	🍷	2	2	2	B2	🍴	B2
Wien Südbahnhof 980 d.	1023	...	...	...	...	1223	...	...	...	...	...	1423	1423	...	...	...	...	...	1623	...	...	...	...	1823	...
Friesach 980 d.	|	...	...	1407	1507	1545	...	...	1607	...	1707	|	|	...	...	1807	...	1907	1945	...	...	2007	2053	|	...
St Veit an der Glan 980 d.	1409	...	...	1440	1540	1609	...	...	1640	1724	1740	1809	1809	...	...	1840	...	1940	2009	...	...	2040	2126	2200	...
Klagenfurt Hbf 980 a.	1421	...	...	1459	1559	1621	...	...	1659	1736	1759	1821	1821	...	...	1859	...	1959	2021	...	...	2059	2145	2212	←
Klagenfurt Hbf 970 d.	1423	...	1432	1502	1602	1623	...	1631	1702	1738	1802	1823	1823	...	1832	1902	1932	2002	2023	...	2032	2102	→	2215	2219
Pörtschach am W'see 970 d.	|	...	1446	1516	1616	|	...	1643	1716	1749	1816	|	|	...	1846	1916	1946	2016	|	...	2046	2116		|	2231
Velden am Wörthersee 970 d.	1436	...	1454	1524	1624	|	...	1650	1724	1755	1824	|	|	...	1854	1924	1954	2024	2036	...	2054	2124	...	|	2237
Villach Hbf 970 a.	1446	...	1509	1539	1639	1644	...	1703	1739	1809	1839	1844	1844	...	1909	1939	2009	2039	2046	...	2109	2139	...	2236	2253
	2			d 2				|	d 2	|			|			d 2							Ⓑ2		
Villach Hbf 970 d.	1456	1456	...	1556	...	...	1656	1716	1756	1810	...	...	1853	1857	...	1957	...	...	...	2057	...	...	2145	...	...
Spittal-Millstättersee 970 a.	1529	1529	...	1629	...	...	1729	1738	1829	1835	...	...	1916	1930	...	2030	...	...	...	2130	...	...	2218	...	...
Spittal-Millstättersee d.	...	1531	...	1631	...	...	1731	...	1831	...	...	...	1919	1931	...	2031	...	...	...	2133	...	...	...	...	...
Lienz a.	...	1629	...	1730	...	...	1829	...	1930	...	...	...	2009	2029	...	2134	...	...	...	2230	...	...	...	...	...

A – From St Michael (Table **980**).
B – To / from Bruck a. d. Mur (Table **980**).
a – Ⓐ only.
d – Daily from Villach.
e – 2 minutes earlier on †.
j – On Oct. 26, Dec. 8 Spittal-Millstättersee d. *0630*, Villach a. *0655* (change trains at Spittal-Millstättersee).
r – ⚒ only.
z – Also Oct. 26, Dec. 8; not Oct. 25, Dec. 6.

974 LINZ - SELZTHAL

2nd class only (except *IC* trains)

km				IC				REX			REX		REX					REX		IC		REX				
				501				3903			3907		3915					3911		601		3913				
		⚒	Ⓐ													⚒	Ⓐ	Ⓒ		🍷	Ⓐ			Ⓐ	Ⓑ	
0	**Linz** Hbf d.	0506	0536	0610	0632	0736	0836	0858	1036	1136	1258	1336	1355	1436	1536	1636	1636	1658	1736	1810	...	1858	1936	2036	2136	2250
28	Rohr-Bad Hall d.	0540	0609	|	0709	0809	0909	0921	1109	1209	1321	1409	1421	1509	1609	1709	1709	1721	1809	|	...	1921	2009	2109	2209	2323
32	Kremsmünster d.	0545	0615	|	0715	0814	0914	0927	1114	1214	1325	1414	1426	1514	1614	1715	1715	1725	1814	|	...	1925	2014	2114	2214	2328
51	Kirchdorf a. d. Krems d.	0603	0633	0646	0740	0833	0933	0940	1140	1232	1340	1432	1447	1540	1632	1732	1740	1740	1833	1846	1857	1940	2034	2133	2232	2346
68	Hinterstoder d.	0625	...	|	0801	0853	...	1001	1201	...	1401	...	1508	1601	...	...	1802	1802	...	|	1918	2001	2058	...	...	...
82	Windischgarsten d.	0639	...	0715	0815	...	...	1015	1215	...	1415	...	1522	1615	...	...	1816	1816	...	1915	1932	2015	2112	...	...	...
87	Spital am Pyhrn d.	0646	...	|	0821	...	...	1021	1221	...	1421	...	1528	1621	...	...	1822	1822	...	|	1939	2021	2119	...	...	...
104	**Selzthal** 975 a.	0702	...	0735	0839	...	...	1038	1239	...	1439	...	...	1639	...	...	1840	1840	...	1935	1956	2039	2135	...	...	...
	Graz Hbf 975 a.	...	...	0905	|	...	...	...	|	...	|	...	...	|	...	...	...	...	...	2105	...	...	...	...	...	...
111	Liezen 975 a.	...	...	...	0856a	...	...	...	1256a	...	1456a	...	...	1656a	...	...	...	...	...	...	...	...	...	...	...	...

							REX			IC		REX				REX					REX				IC	
							3900			502		3904				3908					3912				602	
	⚒	Ⓐ	⚒	⚒	Ⓒ	Ⓐ	⚒			🍷									Ⓐ			⑥n			🍷	
Liezen 975 d.	...	...	...	...	...	...	...	...	...	...	...	0905a	...	...	...	1305a	...	1505a	...	...	1705a	...	...	...	...	...
Graz Hbf 975 d.	...	...	...	...	...	...	...	...	...	0655	...	|	...	...	...	|	...	|	...	...	|	...	...	...	1855	...
Selzthal 975 d.	...	0428	...	...	...	...	0547	0615	0721	0826	...	0921	...	1121	...	1321	...	1521	...	...	1717	...	...	1921	2026	...
Spital am Pyhrn d.	...	0445	...	...	...	...	0604	0631	0739	|	...	0939	...	1138	...	1338	...	1537	...	1643	1733	...	...	1938	|	...
Windischgarsten d.	...	0452	...	...	...	...	0610	0639	0745	0846	...	0945	...	1145	...	1345	...	1545	...	1650	1739	...	...	1946	2046	...
Hinterstoder d.	...	0505	...	...	...	...	0624	0654	0800	|	0902	1000	...	1200	...	1400	...	1600	...	1705	1753	...	...	2000	|	...
Kirchdorf a. d. Krems d.	0428	0526	0526	0556	0626	0626	0646	0726	0826	0915	0922	1021	1126	1226	1326	1421	1526	1626	1656	1726	1813	1826	1926	2021	2115	2126
Kremsmünster d.	0445	0546	0546	0615	0645	0645	0702	0744	0845	|	0945	1036	1145	1245	1346	1436	1545	1646	1715	1746	1832	1844	1946	2036	|	2145
Rohr-Bad Hall d.	0449	0550	0550	0619	0650	0650	0708	0749	0849	|	0949	1040	1149	1249	1350	1440	1549	1650	1721	1750	1837	1848	1950	2040	|	2149
Linz Hbf a.	0524	0624	0624	0654	0724	0728	0735	0824	0924	0948	1024	1104	1224	1324	1424	1504	1624	1724	1754	1824	1901	1924	2024	2104	2148	2224

a – Ⓐ only.
n – Not Aug. 15.

SALZBURG - BISCHOFSHOFEN - SELZTHAL - GRAZ 975

km	See note ⊠	REX 1991		EN 465	REX 1995	REX 1754	REX 4491	IC 501	REX 4471	IC 719	IC 534	REX 4473	IC 513	ÖIC 536	REX 4475	IC 515	ÖIC 538	REX 4477	EC 317	ÖEC 732	REX 4481	REX 3295	ÖEC 669	ÖEC 669	ÖIC 630
		⚒	Ⓐ	Y⊠	⚒	⚒	Ⓐ			⊠			⊠			⊠			⊠		Ⓑ	Ⓒ	Y	Z⊠	
		2	2	A	2	2	2		2	✕		⊗2	🍷		2	C🍷		2	S✕		2	T2	B✕	B✕	
0	**Salzburg** Hbf 960 970 d.	...	...	...	...	...	...	...	...	0615	...	...	0815	...	...	*1015*	...	...	1215	...	...	...	*1415*	1430	...
53	**Bischofshofen** 960 970 a.	...	...	...	...	...	...	...	...	0702	...	...	0902	...	...	*1102*	...	...	1302	...	...	...	*1502*	|	...
53	**Bischofshofen** d.	...	...	0413	...	...	...	...	...	0713	...	0740r	0913	...	...	1113	...	...	1313	...	...	...	1513	|	...
77	Radstadt d.	...	...	|	...	...	...	...	0610	0736	...	0809	0936	...	...	1136	...	1209	1336	...	1409	...	1536	|	...
94	Schladming d.	...	...	0451	0500	...	*0606*	...	0629	0752	...	0831	0952	...	1031	1152	...	1231	1352	...	1431	1511	1552	|	...
133	**Stainach-Irdning** d.	0427	...	0522	0541	...	*0647*	...	0710	0822	...	0912	1022	...	1112	1222	...	1312	1422	...	1512	1553	1622	|	...
145	Liezen d.	0438	...	|	0553	...	*0659*	...	0726	0833	...	0926	1033	...	1126	1233	...	1326	1433	...	1526	1605	1633	|	...
	Linz Hbf **974** d.	|	...	|	|	...	|	0610	|	|	...	|	|	...	|	|	...	|	|	...	|	|	|	|	...
152	**Selzthal** a.	0444	...	0539	0559	...	*0706*	0735	0732p	0840	...	0932	1040	...	1132	1240	...	1332	1440	...	1532	1612	1640	1640	...
152	**Selzthal** d.	0451	...	0548	0606	...	0714	0738	0742	0846	...	0939	1048	...	1139	1248	...	1339	1446	...	1539	...	1648	1648	...
158	Stadt Rottenmann d.	0458	...	|	0613	...	0720	0744	0748	0852	...	0945	|	...	1145	|	...	1345	1452	...	1545	...	|	|	...
169	Trieben d.	0506	...	|	0621	...	0728	|	0756	|	...	0953	|	...	1153	|	...	1353	|	...	1553	...	|	|	...
215	St Michael a.	0540	...	0625	0655	...	0802	|	0830	0921	...	1028	1121	...	1228	1321	...	1428	1521	...	1628	...	1721	1721	...
215	St Michael 980 d.	0541	0546	0626	0701	0707	0803	|	0843	0922	...	1033	1122	...	1233	1322	...	1433	1522	...	1633	...	1722	1722	...
225	Leoben Hbf 980 a.	0549	0553	0634	0708	0714	0810	0820	0850	0929	...	1040	1129	...	1240	1329	...	1440	1529	...	1640	...	1729	1729	...
225	Leoben Hbf 980 d.	0551	0554	0636	0709	0716	0811	0822	0851	0938	0934	1041	1138	1134	1241	1338	1334	1441	1538	1534	1641	...	1738	1738	1734
	Bruck a. d. Mur 980 a.	|	0608	0647	|	0729	0824	|	0903	|	0944	1053	|	1144	1253	|	1344	1453	|	1544	1653	...	|	|	1744
293	**Graz** Hbf 980 a.	0645	0711	0737	0801	...	...	0905	*0956*	1022	...	*1133*	1222	...	*1333*	1422	...	*1533*	1622	...	*1733*	...	1822	1822	...

See note ⊠	REX 4483	IC 611	ÖEC 530	IC 601	REX 4487	EC 319	ÖEC 30	REX 4489		
		⊠				⊠		Ⓑ		Ⓑ
	2	🍷		🍷	2	F✕		2	L 2	2
Salzburg Hbf 960 970 d.	...	1615	...	...	...	1815	...	...	*1918*	...
Bischofshofen 960 970 a.	...	1702	...	...	...	1902	...	...	*2020*	...
Bischofshofen d.	...	1713	...	...	*1738r*	1913	...	...	2038	...
Radstadt d.	1609	1736	...	...	1809	1936	...	...	2107	...
Schladming d.	1631	1752	...	...	1831	1952	...	2031	2125	2135
Stainach-Irdning d.	1712	1822	...	...	1912	2022	...	2112	...	2214
Liezen d.	1726	1833	...	...	1926	2033	...	2126	...	...
Linz Hbf **974** d.	|	|	...	1810	|	|	...	|	...	...
Selzthal a.	1732	1840	...	1935	1932p	2040	...	2132	...	...
Selzthal d.	1739	1848	...	1938	1942	2046	...	2142	...	...
Stadt Rottenmann d.	1745	|	...	1944	1948	2052	...	2148	...	...
Trieben d.	1753	|	...	|	1956	|	...	2156	...	...
St Michael a.	1828	1921	...	|	2030	2121	...	2230	...	...
St Michael 980 d.	1833	1922	...	|	*2035*	2122	...	2235	...	...
Leoben Hbf 980 a.	1840	1929	...	2020	*2042*	2129	...	2242	...	...
Leoben Hbf 980 d.	1841	1938	1934	2022	*2043*	2138	2134	2243	...	...
Bruck a. d. Mur 980 a.	1853	|	1944	|	*2055*	|	2144	2255	...	...
Graz Hbf 980 a.	*1933*	2022	...	2105	...	2222	...	*2333*	...	...

See note ⊠			REX 4470	EC 318		REX 1703	REX 4472	IC 502	ÖEC 31	IC 512
	⚒	⚒	Ⓐ	⊠	Ⓐ					⊠
	2	2	2	F✕	K2	2	2	🍷		🍷
Graz Hbf 980 d.	...	...	...	0545	...	*0613*	...	0655	...	0738
Bruck a. d. Mur 980 d.	...	...	*0530*	|	...	0708	...	|	0815	|
Leoben Hbf 980 a.	...	...	*0542*	0629	...	0720	...	0739	0825	0822
Leoben Hbf 980 d.	...	...	*0544*	0631	...	0721	...	0741	...	0831
St Michael 980 a.	...	...	*0552*	0637	...	0728	...	|	...	0837
St Michael d.	...	...	0600	0638	...	...	0730	|	...	0838
Trieben d.	...	...	0636	|	...	...	0805	|	...	|
Stadt Rottenmann d.	...	...	0644	0708	...	...	0812	0817	...	|
Selzthal a.	...	...	0650	0713	...	...	0818	0823	...	0911
Selzthal d.	...	0544	▬	0719	0740	...	0824	0826	...	0919
Linz Hbf **974** a.	...	|	...	|	|	...	|	0948	...	|
Liezen d.	...	0552	...	0726	0746	...	0832	...	...	0926
Stainach-Irdning d.	...	0604	2	0737	...	...	0845	...	...	0937
Schladming d.	0506	0648	0648	0810	...	...	0928	...	...	1010
Radstadt d.	0525	0707	0707	0826	...	...	...	...	...	1026
Bischofshofen a.	0554	0735	0735	0848	...	...	...	...	...	1048
Bischofshofen 960 970 d.	*0557*	*0739*	*0739*	0857	...	...	...	...	...	1057
Salzburg Hbf 960 970 a.	*0645*	*0840*	*0840*	0944	...	...	...	...	...	1144

See note ⊠	REX 4474	ÖEC 531	ÖEC 668	ÖEC 668	REX 3294	REX 4476	ÖIC 533	EC 316	REX 4478	ÖEC 733	IC 518	REX 4482	REX 1992	ÖIC 535	IC 610		REX 4486	REX 1994	ÖIC 537	IC 718	REX 4488	IC 602		REX 4490	EN 464
			Y	Z⊠	Ⓒ	Ⓑ⊗		⊠			⊠		⚒		⊠	⚒	Ⓑ	⚒		⊠			W		X⊠
	2		B✕	B✕	T2	△2		S✕	△2		C🍷	△2	2		🍷	2	△2	2		✕	△2	🍷	2	△2	A
Graz Hbf 980 d.	*0826*	...	0938	0938	...	*1026*	...	1138	*1226*	...	1338	*1426*	1500	...	1538	...	*1626*	*1700*	...	1738	*1826*	1855	...	*2026*	2138
Bruck a. d. Mur 980 d.	0908	1015	|	|	...	1108	1215	|	1308	1415	|	1508	|	1615	|	...	1708	|	1815	|	1908	|	...	2108	2227
Leoben Hbf 980 a.	0920	1025	1022	1022	...	1120	1225	1222	1320	1425	1422	1520	1554	1625	1622	...	1720	*1754*	1825	1822	1920	1939	...	2120	2238
Leoben Hbf 980 d.	0921	...	1031	1031	...	1121	...	1231	1321	...	1431	1521	1556	...	1631	...	1721	1801	...	1831	1921	1941	...	2121	2240
St Michael 980 a.	0928	...	1037	1037	...	1128	...	1237	1328	...	1437	1528	1605	...	1637	...	1728	1809	...	1837	1928	|	...	2128	2248
St Michael d.	0930	...	1038	1038	...	1130	...	1238	1330	...	1438	1530	1608	...	1638	...	1730	1810	...	1838	1930	|	...	2130	2250
Trieben d.	1005	...	|	|	...	1205	...	|	1405	...	|	1605	1644	...	|	...	1805	1846	...	|	2005	|	...	2205	|
Stadt Rottenmann d.	1012	...	|	|	...	1212	...	1308	1412	...	|	1612	1652	...	|	...	1812	1854	...	1908	2012	2017	...	2212	|
Selzthal a.	1018	...	1111	1111	...	1218	...	1313	1418	...	1511	1618	1658	...	1711	...	1818	1900	...	1913	2018	2023	...	2218	2327
Selzthal d.	1024	...	1119	1119	1135	1224	...	1319	1424	...	1519	1624	...	...	1719	1735	1824	...	...	1919	2024	2026	2058	2224	2339
Linz Hbf **974** a.	|	...	|	|	|	|	...	|	|	...	|	|	...	...	|	|	|	...	...	|	|	2148	|	|	|
Liezen d.	1032	...	1126	|	1144	1232	...	1326	1432	...	1526	1632	...	...	1726	1743	1832	...	...	1926	2032	...	2105	2231	|
Stainach-Irdning d.	1045	...	1137	|	1157	1245	...	1337	1445	...	1537	1645	...	...	1737	1755	1845	...	...	1937	2045	...	2117	2243	2356
Schladming d.	1129	...	1210	|	1248	1329	...	1410	1529	...	1610	1729	...	...	1810	1848	1928	...	...	2010	2128	...	2214	2330	0028
Radstadt d.	1152	...	1226	|	...	1352	...	1426	1552	...	1626	1752	...	...	1826	...	...	...	...	2026	...	...	...	2350	|
Bischofshofen a.	...	...	1248	|	...	...	...	1448	...	...	1648	...	...	...	1848	...	...	...	...	2048	...	...	...	...	0106
Bischofshofen 960 970 d.	...	...	*1257*	|	...	...	...	1457	...	...	*1657*	...	...	...	1857	...	...	...	...	2057	...	...	...	...	...
Salzburg Hbf 960 970 a.	...	...	*1344*	1356	...	...	...	1544	...	...	*1744*	...	...	...	1944	...	...	...	...	2144	...	...	...	...	...

A – ZÜRICHSEE – 1, 2 cl., 2 cl. and [2] Graz - Innsbruck - Buchs - Zürich and v.v.
B – [12] Graz - Schwarzach - Innsbruck - Bregenz and v.v.
C – [12] Innsbruck - Schwarzach - Graz and v.v.
F – [12] Graz - München - Stuttgart - Frankfurt and v.v.
K – From Kleinreifling (Table **976**).
L – From Schwarzach (Table **960**).
S – [12] Graz - München - Stuttgart - Saarbrücken and v.v.
T – [2] Wien - Amstetten - Selzthal - Schladming and v.v.

W – ①②③④⑦ (not Oct. 25).
X – From Aug. 10.
Y – From Aug. 11.
Z – Until Aug. 10.

p – Connects with train in previous column.
r – ⚒ only.

⊗ – Change trains at St Michael on †.
△ – Between Bruck a. d. Mur and St Michael combined with a service on the Klagenfurt route (Table **980**) – passengers should take care to join the correct portion for their destination.
⊠ – **June 11 - Aug. 10** *EC* and *IC* services are replaced by bus between Schladming and Stainach-Irdning (June 11 - July 7) or between Stainach-Irdning and Selzthal (July 8 - Aug. 10). Journey times extended by up to 15 minutes. During this period overnight trains **464/5** are diverted between Leoben and Schwarzach via Villach (see Table **960** for revised Graz, Bruck a. d. Mur and Leoben timings). *ÖEC* trains **668/9** are diverted between Selzthal and Wörgl (via Kirchdorf and Salzburg).

AMSTETTEN - KLEINREIFLING - SELZTHAL 976

2nd class only

km																										
		⚒	ⒶL	Ⓒ	w	Ⓐ	Ⓒ	Ⓐ	ⒸG	⚒	Ⓐ			Ⓐ	Ⓐ		Ⓐ		Ⓐ	Ⓐ	Ⓒ	Ⓐ		Ⓑm	ⒷB	
0	**Amstetten** d.	0449	...	...	0626	0718	0759	...	0840	0859	0959	1059	1159	...	1259	1359	1459	1559	...	1659	1759	1759	...	1859	...	1959
23	Waidhofen a. d. Ybbs. d.	0520	...	...	0708	0749	0829	...	0909	0928	1027	1129	1230	...	1329	1430	1530	1630	...	1730	1826	1830	...	1930	...	2027
41	Weyer d.	0545	...	...	0732	...	0849	...	0928	0946	...	1146	1249	...	1346	1449	1549	1649	...	1749	1845	1849	...	1951	...	...
47	**Kleinreifling** a.	0553	...	...	0740	...	0857	...	0937	0954	...	1154	1257	...	1354	1457	*1610*	1657	...	1757	1852	1857	...	1958	...	...
47	**Kleinreifling** d.	...	0616	0715	...	...	...	0915	0948	...	...	...	...	1324	...	*1524*	...	...	1724	...	...	...	1924	...	2002	...
82	Hieflau d.	...	0654	0755	...	...	...	1004	1031	...	...	...	...	1403	...	*1604*	...	...	1804	...	...	...	2004	...	2050	...
105	Admont d.	...	0719	0820	...	...	...	1029	1056	...	...	...	...	1430	...	*1629*	...	...	1829	...	...	...	2030	...	...	...
119	**Selzthal** a.	...	0733	0834	...	...	...	1043	1111	...	...	...	...	1443	...	*1643*	...	...	1843	...	...	...	2044	...	...	...

	⚒	Ⓐ		E		Ⓐ	w	Ⓐ	Ⓐ			⚒		Ⓐ			Ⓐ	Ⓐ	Ⓒ	Ⓐ	ⒸG	Ⓐ		†		Ⓐ
Selzthal d.	...	...	...	...	...	0549	...	...	0717	...	0918	...	...	...	...	1324	...	...	...	...	1626	...	1724	...	...	1924
Admont d.	...	...	...	...	...	0602	...	...	0733	...	0932	...	...	...	...	1338	...	...	...	...	1642	...	1738	...	...	1938
Hieflau d.	...	...	...	0536	...	0628	...	...	0758	...	0957	...	...	...	...	1403	...	...	...	...	1709	...	1803	...	...	2003
Kleinreifling a.	...	...	...	0614	...	0713	...	...	0838	...	1044t	...	...	...	...	1444	...	...	...	...	1749	...	1841	...	...	2041
Kleinreifling d.	...	0517	0603e	...	0635	0714	0801	...	...	0959	...	1102e	1159	1302	1359	...	1502	*1546*	1602	1701	1754	1801	...	1902	2003	...
Weyer d.	...	0525	0612e	...	0647	0722	0809	...	...	1011	...	1110e	1210	1310	1410	...	1510	1610	1610	1712	1804	1812	...	1910	2011	...
Waidhofen a. d. Ybbs. d.	0455	0548	0634	...	0708	...	0828	0931	...	1031	...	1131	1231	1331	1431	...	1531	1631	1631	1731	1825	1831	...	1931	2031	...
Amstetten a.	0524	0616	0701	...	0736	...	0856	0959	...	1059	...	1159	1259	1359	1459	...	1559	1659	1659	1759	1850	1859	...	1959	2059	...

Waidhofen a. d. Ybbs - Lunz am See

km	*Narrow gauge*	ⒸJ	Ⓐ¶	Ⓒ	Ⓐ	K	J	ⒶK	ⒶH	Ⓒ	
0	Waidhofen a. d. Ybbs. d.	0728	0752	0915	0932	1432	1432	1632	1632	1832	...
54	Lunz am See a.	0910	0919	1104	1118	1612	1618	1812	1820	2012	...

Narrow gauge	Ⓐv	ⒸJ	A	Ⓐ¶	ⒸK	ⒸJ		ⒶK	ⒶH	Ⓒ
Lunz am See d.	0541	0644	0744	0755	0829	0944	1240	1618	1628	1637
Waidhofen a. d. Ybbs a.	0725	0824	0925	0925	1012	1126	1428	1826	1827	1822

A – ①–⑤ July 13 - Sept. 4 (also Nov. 2).
B – Ⓑ (not Oct. 25). From Linz (Table **977**).
E – ①–⑥ (not Oct. 26). To Linz (Table **977**).
G – [2] Wien - Selzthal - Schladming and v.v.
H – Until Oct. 23.
J – Until Oct. 26.
K – From Oct. 27.
L – To Liezen (Table **975**).
e – ⑥ (not Aug. 15).
m – Also Aug. 15.
t – 1035 on Ⓐ.
v – Not July 13 - Sept. 4, Nov. 2.
w – From/to Wien (Table **950**).
¶ – Not July 13 - Sept. 11, Nov. 2.
By bus Großhollenstein (*25 km*) - Lunz and v.v.

977 LINZ - KLEINREIFLING

2nd class only

km																											
		⚒	⚒					⚒		Ⓐ	Ⓐ		Ⓐ			Ⓐ		Ⓐ		Ⓐ		Ⓐ	H				
0	**Linz Hbf** ... **950** d.	0441	0517	0618	0653	0750	*0830*	0853	0953	*1030*	*1130*	1150	1223	1253	1353	1423	1450	*1530*	1553	1623	1653	*1730*	1753	*1853*	1953	2153	2253
25	St Valentin **950** d.	0511	0544	0649	0722	0820	0852	0920	1020	1052	1152	1220	1252	1320	1420	1452	1520	1552	1620	1650	1720	1752	1820	1923	2020	2220	2320
45	Steyr .... d.	0535	0609	0715	0748	0848	0913	0946	1047	1113	1213	1247	1313	1347	1447	1518	1547	1613	1647	1712	1747	1813	1847	1948	2046	2245	2345
47	Garsten .... d.	0538	0612	0718	0752	0853	0917	0950	1051	1117	1215	1251	1317	1351	1451	1521	1550	1617	1651	1717	1751	1815	1851	1951	2050	2248	2347
91	**Kleinreifling** ... a.	0645	...	...	0849	0944c	1008a	...	1146c	1208	...	1348c	1408	1452a	1546c	1614	...	1710	1746c	1810	1844a	...	1947	...	2143	...	...

		Ⓐ	⚒	M	⚒	⚒	H			Ⓐ	Ⓒ	Ⓐ		⚒	Ⓐ			Ⓐ				Ⓐ		Ⓐ			
Kleinreifling ..... d.	...	0436	0511	...	...	...	0615	...	0750	...	...	0955	1014c	...	1155	1213c	...	1355	1413c	...	1615	...	1715a	...	1815	...	2024
Garsten .... d.	0437	0530	0600	0605	←	0637	0710	0809	0843	0909	0927	1043	1109	1208	1243	1309	1409	1443	1509	1609	1709	1743	1809	1843	1909	2009	2118
Steyr .... d.	0442	0535	0604	0610	0616	0641	0715	0814	0847	0914	0931	1047	1114	1213	1247	1314	1414	1447	1514	1614	1714	1747	1814	1847	1914	2014	2122
St Valentin . **950** a.	0505	0600	→	|	0639	0705	0741	0838	0906	0938	0954	1106	1140	1240	1306	1338	1440	1506	1540	1640	1740	1806	1840	1906	1940	2039	2144
Linz Hbf .... **950** a.	0538	0622	...	0643	0700	0738	0808	0908	*0929*	1008	1023	*1129*	1208	1308	*1329*	1408	1508	*1529*	1608	1708	1808	*1829*	1908a	*1929*	2008	2108	2211

H – To / from Hieflau on dates in Table **976**. M – To München via Simbach (Tables **962**/**893**). a – Ⓐ only. c – Ⓒ only.

978 WIEN and WIENER NEUSTADT - SOPRON

ÖBB / GySEV ● (2nd class only except where shown)

km																									
				Ⓐ		F	D ⁄		Ⓐ	B ⁄	Ⓐ		S		Ⓐ	S	Ⓐ			Ⓐ	Ⓐ	Ⓐ		V	
0	**Wien** Südbahnhof .... d.	...	*0538a*	*0623*	0628	0653	0726	...	0730	0753	*0823*	0836	...	*0923*	0936	...	*1023*	1036	*1123z*	1136	*1156*	*1223*	1236	...	*1323*
4	**Wien** Meidling .... d.	*0530a*	*0548a*	*0630*	0635	0700	0733	...	0737	0800	*0830*	0843	...	*0930*	0943	...	*1030*	1043	*1130z*	1143	*1203*	*1230*	1243	...	*1330*
	Wiener Neustadt Hbf ...... d.	0607	0632	0706	|	0732	0800	0807	|	0832	0907	|	0932	1007	|	1032	1107	|	1207	|	1237	1307	|	1332	1407
	Mattersburg .... d.	0631	0647	0731	|	0747	|	0831	|	0847	0931	|	0947	1031	|	1047	1131	|	1231	|	1259	1331	|	1347	1431
42	Ebenfurth .... d.	|	|	|	0714	|	|	|	0814	|	|	0914	|	|	1014	|	|	1114	|	1214	|	|	1314	|	|
74	**Sopron** 🏛 .... a.	0648	0658	0747	0750	0759	0826	0847	0850	0858	0947	0950	0958	1047	1050	1058	1147	1150	1247	1250	1315	1347	1350	1358	1447

	Ⓐ	Ⓐ	S		Ⓐ		Ⓐ	⚒	Ⓐ				Ⓐ		Ⓐ				Ⓐ	Ⓑq	Ⓐ		S		Ⓑ
Wien Südbahnhof .... d.	1336	...	*1423*	1436	*1456*	*1523*	1536	1553a	*1626*	1636	1653	*1723*	1736	1753a	*1826*	1836	*1853a*	*1926*	1936	...	*1956**	2036	...	*2147**	...
Wien Meidling .... d.	1343	...	*1430*	1443	*1503*	*1530*	1543	1600a	*1633*	1643	1700	*1730*	1743	1800a	*1833*	1843	*1900a*	*1933*	1943	...	*2006*	2043	...	*2200*	...
Wiener Neustadt Hbf .... d.	|	1432	1507	|	1537	1607	|	1632	1707	|	1732	1807	|	1832	1907	|	1932	2007	|	2032	2107	|	2132	2232	2235
Mattersburg .... d.	|	1446	1531	|	1559	1631	|	1646	1731	|	1747	1831	|	1846	1931	|	1947	2031	|	2046	2131	|	2147	2255	|
Ebenfurth .... d.	1414	|	|	1514	|	|	1614	|	|	1714	|	|	1814	|	|	1914	|	|	2014	|	|	2114	|	|	2248
Sopron 🏛 .... a.	1450	1458	1547	1550	1615	1647	1650	1658	1747	1750	1758	1847	1850	1858	1947	1950	2000	2047	2050	2058	2147	2150	2200	2311	2323

km																									
		Ⓐ	Ⓐ	Ⓐ	Ⓐ	Ⓐ	Ⓐ	S	Ⓐ					S	Ⓐ		F		Ⓐ	Ⓐ		S		Ⓐ	Ⓐ
0	**Sopron** 🏛 .... d.	0413	0416	0443	0502	0513	0543	0544	0602	0611	0633	0702	0711	0802	0811	0812	0902	0911	0915	1011	1015	1102	1111	1115	1211
	Ebenfurth .... d.	0456	|	0526	|	0556	0626	|	|	0653	|	|	0753	|	0853	|	|	0953	|	1053	|	|	1153	|	1253
17	Mattersburg .... d.	|	0431	|	0515	|	|	0601	0615	|	0701	0715	|	0814	|	0831	0914	|	0931	|	1031	1114	|	1131	|
33	**Wiener Neustadt** Hbf ...... a.	|	0453	|	0528	|	|	0623	0628	|	0724	0729	|	0827	|	0853	0927	|	0953	|	1053	1127	|	1153	|
77	**Wien** Meidling .... a.	0526	*0531*	0556	0600	0626	0656	...	0700	0724	...	0800	0824	*0858r*	0924	*0928r*	0955	1024	*1028*	1124	*1128*	*1158*	1224	*1228*	1324
81	**Wien** Südbahnhof .... a.	0532	*0538*	0602	0608	0632	0702	...	0708	0730	...	0808	0830	*0905r*	0930	*0935r*	1002	1030	*1035*	1130	*1135*	*1205*	1230	*1235*	1330

		V		Ⓐ	Ⓐ		S		Ⓐ	Ⓐ		V		Ⓐ	Ⓐ				Ⓐ			C ⁄	Ⓐ	A ⁄	
Sopron 🏛 .... d.	1215	1301	1311	1315	1411	1415	1502	1511	1515	1611	1615	1702	1711	1715	1811	1815	1900	1911	1915	2002	2015	2032	2115	2202	2240
Ebenfurth .... d.	|	|	1353	|	1453	|	|	1553	|	1653	|	|	1753	|	1853	|	|	1953	|	|	|	|	|	|	|
Mattersburg .... d.	1231	1313	|	1331	|	1431	1514	|	1531	|	1631	1714	|	1731	|	1831	1914	|	1931	2014	2031	|	2131	2214	2256
Wiener Neustadt Hbf .... a.	1253	1325	|	1353	|	1453	1527	|	1553	|	1653	1727	|	1753	|	1853	1927	|	1953	2027	2053	2058	2153	2227	2318
Wien Meidling .... a.	*1328*	*1358*	1424	*1428*	1524	*1528*	*1558*	1624	*1628*	1724	*1728*	*1758*	1824	*1828*	1924	*1928*	*1958*	2024	*2028*	*2058*	...	2126	...	2255	*2358*
Wien Südbahnhof .... a.	*1335*	*1405*	1430	*1435*	1530	*1535*	*1605*	1630	*1635*	1730	*1735*	*1805*	1830	*1835*	1930	*1935*	*2005*	2030	*2035*	*2105*	...	2132	...	2302	*0005*

A – Conveys 🚃12 Budapest (*IC* **918**) - Csorna (*IC* **938**) - Sopron (**9951**) - Wien. See also Table **1250**.
B – Conveys 🚃12 Wien - Sopron (*IC* **937**) - Csorna (*IC* **917**) - Budapest. See also Table **1250**.
C – *D* **284**: ZAGREB – 🚃12 Zagreb (*IC* **284**) - Gyékényes - Nagykanizsa - Szombathely - Sopron (*D* **284**) - Wien.
D – *D* **285**: ZAGREB – 🚃12 Wien - Sopron (*IC* **285**) - Szombathely - Nagykanizsa - Gyékényes - Zagreb.
F – To / from Fehring via Szombathely (Tables **1227** / **986**).
S – To / from Szombathely (Table **1227**).
V – 🚃2 Wiener Neustadt - Sopron - Szombathely - Szentgotthárd - Graz and v.v. (Tables **1227** / **986**).

a – Ⓐ only.
q – Not Oct. 25.
r – ⚒ only.
z – † only.
* – Suburban platforms 21 / 22.
● – GySEV / ROeEE: Győr-Sopron-Ebenfurti Vasút / Raab-Oedenburg-Ebenfurter Eisenbahn.
⁄ – Supplement payable in Hungary. Ⓡ for journeys from Hungary.

979 FLUGHAFEN WIEN ✈ Schwechat

CAT ★; S-Bahn (2nd class only)

km		★	★	★		★	★									⚒						
0	**Wien** Praterstern .... d.	CAT	...	...	and	...	...	...	S-Bahn	0428	0452	0504	0552	0613	0643	0652	0713	0743	and at	2213	2243	2343
2	**Wien** Mitte .... d.	→	0538	0608	every	2238	2308	...	→	0432	0456	0508	0556	0617	0647	0656	0717	0747	the same	2217	2247	2347
	Wien Südbahnhof ▲ d.		|	|	30	|	|	...		|	*0455*	|	*0549*	*0610*	*0643*	*0652*	*0710*	*0743*	minutes	*2210*	*2243*	*2343*
3	**Wien** Rennweg .... d.		|	|	minutes	|	|	...		0435	0459	0511	0559	0620	0650	0659	0720	0750	past each	2220	2250	2350
21	**Flughafen Wien** ✈ .... a.		0554	0624	until	2254	2324	...		0457	0521	0533	0621	0642	0712	0721	0744	0812	hour until	2244	2312	0012

km		★	★	★		★	★															
0	**Flughafen Wien** ✈ .... d.	CAT	0605	0635	and	2305	2335	...	S-Bahn	0539	0609	0639	0709	0739	0809	0845	0918	0941	and at	2241	2318	0018
18	**Wien** Rennweg .... a.	→	|	|	every	|	|	...	→	0600	0630	0700	0730	0800	0830	0906	0939	1006	the same	2306	2339	0039
20	**Wien** Südbahnhof ▲ a.		|	|	30	|	|	...		*0605*	*0641*	*0705*	*0735*	*0805*	*0835*	*0911*	*0950*	*1011*	minutes	*2311*	*2350*	*0056*
	Wien Mitte .... a.		0621	0651	minutes	2321	2351	...		0603	0633	0703	0733	0803	0833	0909	0942	1009	past each	2309	2342	0042
	Wien Praterstern .... a.		...	...	until	...	...	...		0607	0637	0707	0737	0807	0837	0913	0946	1013	hour until	2313	2346	0046

★ – *City Airport Train (CAT)*. Non-stop service with special fares.
▲ – Suburban platforms 21 / 22. Change trains at Rennweg (cross platform).

🚌 *Vienna Airport Lines*: Wien Westbahnhof – Wien Südbahnhof – Flughafen Wien ✈ and v.v.
🚌 From **Wien Westbahnhof**: 0500 and every 20 minutes until 1900, then every 30 minutes until 2300. Journey time: 35 minutes (from Westbahnhof), 20 minutes (from Südbahnhof).
🚌 From **Flughafen Wien** ✈: 0600 and every 20 minutes until 2000, then every 30 minutes until 2330, also 2359. Journey time: 20 minutes (to Südbahnhof), 40 minutes (to Westbahnhof).

🚌 ÖBB-Bahn Bus / SAD Bratislava: **Bratislava**, AS Mlynské nivy (bus station) – **Flughafen Wien** ✈ and v.v. Ⓡ (✆ +43 (0) 810 222 333-6). Journey time: 60 minutes.
Subject to alteration on Dec. 24, 25, 26, 31, Jan. 1.
🚌 From **Bratislava** AS Mlynské nivy at 0530, 0600, 0700 and hourly until 2000. 🚌 From **Flughafen Wien** ✈ at 0800, 0830, 0930, 1040, 1130, 1230 and hourly until 2330.

980 WIEN - GRAZ, KLAGENFURT and VILLACH

km		REX 1701				REX 1703	🚌 851	ÖEC 253	IC 512	ÖEC 31	🚌 853	ÖIC 553	REX 4474	REX 1705	ÖEC 151	ÖEC 668	ÖEC 531	ÖIC 555	REX 1707	🚌 855	ÖEC 255	EC 316	ÖIC 533	ÖIC 559	REX 1709
		⚒ 2	2	⚒ 2	⚒ 2	2	★	M✕	🍷	✕♦	★	🍷	2	2	‡ ✕♦	✕	L✕	§ 🍷	△2	★	M✕	✕	🍷	🍷	△2
0	**Wien** Südbahnhof .... **981** d.	...	...	...	...	...	...	0556	...	0623	...	0656	...	...	0756	...	0823	0856	...	...	0956	...	1023	1056	...
4	**Wien** Meidling ● .... **981** d.	...	...	...	...	...	...	0603	...	0630	...	0703	...	...	0803	...	0830	0903	...	...	1003	...	1030	1103	...
48	**Wiener Neustadt** Hbf .. **981** d.	...	...	...	...	...	...	0632	...	0657	...	0732	...	...	0832	...	0857	0932	...	...	1032	...	1057	1132	...
117	Mürzzuschlag .... **981** d.	...	0413r	...	0554	*0610*	...	0730	...	|	...	0830	...	...	0930	...	|	1030	...	...	1130	...	|	1230	...
	Graz Hbf .... **975** d.	*0345a*	|	*0423*	|	*0613*	0639	|	0738	|	0824	|	*0826*	...	|	0938	|	|	*1026*	1039	|	1138	|	|	*1226*
158	**Bruck** an der Mur .... **975** d.	0439	0457	0530	0639	0708	|	0758	|	0815	|	0858	0908	...	0958	|	1015	1058	1108	|	1158	|	1215	1258	1308
212	**Graz** Hbf .... a.	|	0544	|	0726	|	|	0833	|	|	|	0933	|	...	1033	|	|	1133	|	|	1233	|	|	1333	|
174	Leoben Hbf .... **975** d.	0453	...	0544	...	0721	|	...	0822	0827	|	...	0921	...	...	1022	1027	...	1121	|	...	1222	1227	...	1321
◧	St Michael .... **975** a.	0501	...	0552	...	0728	|	...	...	|	|	...	0928	...	...	...	|	...	1128	|	...	...	|	...	1328
◧	St Michael .... d.	0508	...	0601	...	0734	|	...	...	|	|	...	...	0934	...	...	|	...	1134	|	...	...	|	...	1334
205	Knittelfeld .... d.	0528	...	0619	...	0749	|	...	...	0846	|	...	...	0949	...	...	1046	...	1149	|	...	...	1246	...	1349
213	Zeltweg .... d.	0535	...	0627	...	0755	|	...	...	|	|	...	...	0955	...	...	|	...	1155	|	...	...	|	...	1355
220	Judenburg .... d.	0543	...	0635	...	0803	|	...	...	0900	|	...	...	1003	...	...	1100	...	1203	|	...	...	1300	...	1403
239	Unzmarkt .... d.	0558	...	0651	...	0818	|	...	...	0914	|	...	...	1018	...	...	1114	...	1218	|	...	...	1314	...	1418
276	Friesach .... **971** a.	0633	...	...	...	0852	|	...	...	|	|	...	...	1052	...	...	1144	...	1252	|	...	...	|	...	1452
309	St Veit an der Glan ...... **971** a.	0718	...	...	...	0939	|	...	...	1007	|	...	...	1139	...	...	1207	...	1339	|	...	...	1407	...	1539
329	**Klagenfurt** Hbf .... **970/1** a.	0740	...	...	...	0959	0839	...	...	1021	1024	...	...	1159	...	...	1221	...	1359	1239	...	...	1421	...	1559
367	**Villach** Hbf .... **970/1** a.	0817	...	...	...	1039	...	...	...	1044	...	...	...	1239	...	...	1246	...	1439	...	...	...	1446	...	1639

FOR NOTES SEE NEXT PAGE →

WIEN - GRAZ, KLAGENFURT and VILLACH 980

	🚌 857 ★	ÖIC 257 M🍷	IC 518 🍷	ÖEC 733 ✕	🚌 859 ★	ÖIC 653 🍷	REX 1711 △2	ÖIC 259 M🍷	IC 610 🍷	ÖIC 535 L🍷	ÖIC 657 🍷	REX 1713 △2	🚌 951 ★	REX 1763 ⚒ 2	EC 159 ✕♦	IC 718 ✕	ÖIC 537 🍷	ÖIC 659 🍷	REX 1715 △2	🚌 953 ★	REX 1765 Ⓐ 2	ÖEC 751 ✕	ÖEC 150 ✕	ÖEC 539 ✕	2
Wien Südbahnhof ... **981** d.	...	1156	...	1223	...	1256	...	1356	...	1423	1456	...	...	...	1556	...	1623	1656	...	...	...	1756	...	1823	...
Wien Meidling ● ... **981** d.	...	1203	...	1230	...	1303	...	1403	...	1430	1503	...	...	...	1603	...	1630	1703	...	...	...	1803	...	1830	...
Wiener Neustadt Hbf ... **981** d.	...	1232	...	1257	...	1332	...	1432	...	1457	1532	...	...	...	1632	...	1657	1732	...	...	...	1832	...	1857	...
Mürzzuschlag ... **981** d.	...	1330	...	|	...	1430	...	1530	...	|	1630	...	...	...	1730	...	|	1830	...	...	...	1930	...	|	...
Graz Hbf ... **975** d.	1239	|	1338	|	1424	|	*1426*	|	1538	|	|	*1626*	1639	1700	|	1738	|	|	*1826*	1839	1900	|	1926	|	...
Bruck an der Mur ... **975** d.	|	1358	|	1415	|	1458	1508	1558	|	1615	1658	1708	|	|	1758	|	1815	1858	1908	|	|	1958	2001	2015	...
Graz Hbf ... a.	|	1433	|	|	|	1533	|	1633	|	|	1733	|	|	|	1833	|	|	1933	|	|	|	2033	...	|	...
Leoben Hbf ... **975** d.	|	...	1422	1427	|	...	1521	...	1622	1627	...	1721	|	1757	...	1822	1827	...	1921	|	1955	...	...	2027	2033
St Michael ... **975** a.	|	...	...	|	|	...	1528	...	...	|	...	1728	|	|	...	...	|	...	1928	|	|	...	...	|	|
St Michael ... d.	|	...	...	|	|	...	1534	...	...	|	...	1734	|	|	...	...	|	...	1934	|	|	...	...	|	|
Knittelfeld ... d.	|	...	...	1446	|	...	1549	...	...	1646	...	1749	|	1817	...	...	1846	...	1949	|	2015	...	...	|	2056
Zeltweg ... d.	|	...	...	|	|	...	1555	...	...	|	...	1755	|	1825	...	...	|	...	1955	|	2023	...	...	|	2104
Judenburg ... d.	|	...	...	1500	|	...	1603	...	...	1700	...	1803	|	1833	...	...	1900	...	2003	|	2031	...	...	|	2112
Unzmarkt ... d.	|	...	...	1514	|	...	1618	...	...	1714	...	1818	|	1846	...	...	1914	...	2018	|	2044	...	...	|	2128
Friesach ... **971** a.	|	...	...	1544	|	...	1652	...	...	|	...	1852	|	...	...	...	1944	...	2052	|	...	...	...	|	...
St Veit an der Glan ... **971** a.	|	...	...	1607	|	...	1739	...	...	1807	...	1939	|	...	...	...	2007	...	2125	|	...	...	...	2159	...
Klagenfurt Hbf ... **970/1** a.	1439	...	...	1621	1624	...	1759	...	...	1821	...	1959	1839	...	...	...	2021	...	2145	2039	...	...	...	2212	...
Villach Hbf ... **970/1** a.	...	...	...	1644	...	...	1839	...	...	1844	...	2039	...	...	...	...	2046	...	2253	...	...	...	...	2236	...

	ÖIC 753 🍷	REX 1717 △2	EN 235 🍷♦	ÖIC 755 🍷	EN 1237 ⑤ 🅁♦	ÖIC 757 🍷	2	⑤–⑦ 2	D 1459 ⑤ ♦
Wien Südbahnhof ... **981** d.	1856	...	1923	1956	2023	2056	...	...	2156
Wien Meidling ● ... **981** d.	1903	...	1930	2003	2030	2103	...	...	2203
Wiener Neustadt Hbf ... **981** d.	1932	...	1958	2032	2057	2132	...	...	2232
Mürzzuschlag ... **981** d.	2030	...	|	2130	|	2230	...	...	2330
Graz Hbf ... **975** d.	|	*2026*	|	|	|	|	2204	...	|
Bruck an der Mur ... **975** d.	2058	2108	2125	2158	2222	2258	2250	2301	2358
Graz Hbf ... a.	2133	|	|	2233	|	2333	...	|	0033
Leoben Hbf ... **975** d.	...	2121	2140	...	2235	...	...	2313	...
St Michael ... **975** a.	...	2128	|	...	|	...	...	|	...
St Michael ... d.	...	2134	|	...	|	...	...	|	...
Knittelfeld ... d.	...	2149	2203	...	|	...	...	2336	...
Zeltweg ... d.	...	2155	|	...	|	...	...	2344	...
Judenburg ... d.	...	2203	|	...	|	...	...	2352	...
Unzmarkt ... d.	...	2218	|	...	|	...	...	0007	...
Friesach ... **971** a.	...	2252	2300	...	|	...	...	...	...
St Veit an der Glan ... **971** a.	...	...	|	...	|	...	...	...	...
Klagenfurt Hbf ... **970/1** a.	...	...	2336	...	0019	...	...	...	...
Villach Hbf ... **970/1** a.	...	...	0001	...	0043	...	...	...	...

	D 458 Ⓐ 2	D 1458 ♦	Ⓐ 2	ÖEC 550 ✕	EN 1236 🅁♦	EN 1238 🅁♦	REX 1750 ⚒ 2	EN 234 ♦	REX 1752 ⚒ 2	ÖIC 552 ⚒ 🍷	REX 1754 ⚒ 2
Villach Hbf ... **970/1** d.	...	...	...	...	0349	0349	...	0417	...	...	...
Klagenfurt Hbf ... **970/1** d.	...	...	...	...	0415	0415	...	0439	...	...	...
St Veit an der Glan ... **971** d.	...	...	...	...	|	|	...	|	...	...	0507
Friesach ... **971** d.	...	...	...	...	|	|	0459	|	...	...	0533
Unzmarkt ... d.	...	...	0441	...	|	|	0533	|	0557	...	0609
Judenburg ... d.	...	...	0458	...	|	|	0547	|	0614	...	0624
Zeltweg ... d.	...	...	0506	...	|	|	0555	|	0623	...	0632
Knittelfeld ... d.	...	...	0514	...	|	|	0602	|	0629	...	0639
St Michael ... a.	...	...	0534	...	|	|	|	|	|	...	0658
St Michael ... **975** d.	...	...	0546	...	|	|	|	|	|	...	0707
Leoben Hbf ... **975** d.	...	...	0554	...	0610	0610	0623	0628	0654	...	0716
Graz Hbf ... d.	...	0426	|	0540	|	|	|	|	|	0637	|
Bruck an der Mur ... **975** d.	...	0503	0608	0617	0625	0625	|	0641	0706	0714	0729
Graz Hbf ... **975** a.	...	|	*0700*	|	|	|	0715	|	...	|	*0815*
Mürzzuschlag ... **981** d.	0516	0530	...	0646	|	|	...	0708	...	|	...
Wiener Neustadt Hbf **981** a.	0615	0626	...	0745	0751	0751	...	0802	...	0831	...
Wien Meidling ● ... **981** a.	0646	0709	...	0816	0829	0850	...	0835	...	0858	...
Wien Südbahnhof ... **981** a.	0653	0717	...	0823	0838	0857	...	0842	...	0905	...

	ÖEC 532 ⚒ ✕	ÖEC 253 ✕	2	ÖIC 250 M🍷	🚌 852 ★	REX 1700 2	ÖIC 556 🍷	IC 534 L🍷	IC 719 ✕	ÖIC 252 M🍷	🚌 854 ★	2	ÖIC 650 🍷	ÖIC 536 🍷	IC 513 🍷	EC 158 ✕♦	🚌 856 ★	REX 1704 2	ÖIC 652 🍷	ÖIC 538 L🍷	IC 515 🍷	ÖEC 254 M✕	🚌 858 ★	REX 1706 2	ÖIC 656 🍷
Villach Hbf ... **970/1** d.	0527	...	...	...	...	0606	...	0716	...	...	...	0720	...	0914	...	...	...	0920	...	1116	...	...	...	1120	...
Klagenfurt Hbf ... **970/1** d.	0550	...	...	...	0720	0628	...	0739	...	...	0920	0804	...	0939	...	...	1120	1004	...	1139	...	...	1325	1204	...
St Veit an der Glan ... **971** d.	0603	...	...	...	|	0641	...	0753	...	...	|	0824	...	0953	...	...	|	1024	...	1153	...	...	|	1224	...
Friesach ... **971** d.	|	...	...	...	|	0706	...	|	...	...	|	0906	...	1016	...	...	|	1106	...	|	...	...	|	1306	...
Unzmarkt ... d.	|	...	0656	...	|	0741	...	0847	...	...	|	0941	...	1047	...	...	|	1141	...	1247	...	...	|	1341	...
Judenburg ... d.	|	...	0712	...	|	0756	...	0901	...	...	|	0956	...	1101	...	...	|	1156	...	1301	...	...	|	1356	...
Zeltweg ... d.	|	...	0720	...	|	0804	...	|	...	...	|	1004	...	|	...	...	|	1204	...	|	...	...	|	1404	...
Knittelfeld ... d.	|	...	0728	...	|	0811	...	0914	...	...	|	1011	...	1114	...	...	|	1211	...	1314	...	...	|	1411	...
St Michael ... a.	|	...	|	...	|	0826	...	|	...	...	|	1026	...	|	...	...	|	1226	...	|	...	...	|	1426	...
St Michael ... **975** d.	|	...	|	...	|	0833	...	|	...	...	|	1033	...	|	...	...	|	1233	...	|	...	...	|	1433	...
Leoben Hbf ... **975** d.	0734	...	0747	...	|	0841	...	0934	0938	...	|	1041	...	1134	1138	...	|	1241	...	1334	1338	...	|	1441	...
Graz Hbf ... d.	|	...	|	0726	|	|	0826	|	|	0926	|	|	1026	|	|	1126	|	|	1226	|	|	1326	|	|	1426
Bruck an der Mur ... **975** d.	0746	0758	0758	0803	|	0853	0903	0946	|	1003	|	1053	1103	1146	|	1203	|	1253	1303	1346	|	1403	|	1453	1503
Graz Hbf ... **975** a.	|	0833	*0856*r	|	0920	*0933*	|	|	1022	|	1120	*1133*	|	|	1222	|	1320	*1333*	|	|	1422	|	1525	*1533*	|
Mürzzuschlag ... **981** d.	|	...	...	0832	...	...	0932	|	...	1032	...	...	1132	|	...	1232	...	...	1332	|	...	1432	...	...	1532
Wiener Neustadt Hbf ... **981** a.	0902	...	...	0928	...	...	1028	1102	...	1128	...	...	1228	1302	...	1328	...	...	1428	1502	...	1528	...	...	1628
Wien Meidling ● ... **981** a.	0928	...	...	0958	...	...	1058	1128	...	1158	...	...	1258	1328	...	1358	...	...	1458	1528	...	1558	...	...	1658
Wien Südbahnhof ... **981** a.	0935	...	...	1005	...	...	1105	1135	...	1205	...	...	1305	1335	...	1405	...	...	1505	1535	...	1605	...	...	1705

	ÖEC 732 ✕	EC 317 ✕	ÖEC 256 ‡ M✕	🚌 950 ★	REX 1708 2	ÖIC 750 ¶ 🍷	ÖIC 630 🍷	ÖEC 669 ✕	ÖIC 258 M🍷	🚌 952 ★	REX 1710 2	ÖIC 752 🍷	ÖEC 530 L✕	IC 611 🍷	ÖEC 150 ✕♦	🚌 954 ★	REX 1712 2	ÖIC 754 ‡ 🍷	ÖEC 30 ✕♦	EC 319 ✕	IC 350 M🍷	⑦ 2	IC 730 ⑦z 🍷	⑤⑥ n2	⑦ 2
Villach Hbf ... **970/1** d.	1316	...	...	...	1320	...	1514	...	...	...	1520	...	1714	...	...	...	1730	...	1916	...	...	*1920*	2020	...	...
Klagenfurt Hbf ... **970/1** d.	1339	...	...	1520	1404	...	1539	...	...	1725	1604	...	1739	...	...	1920	1808	...	1939	...	...	*2004*	2043	...	...
St Veit an der Glan ... **971** d.	1353	...	...	|	1424	...	1553	...	...	|	1624	...	1753	...	...	|	1833	...	1953	...	...	*2024*	2057	...	...
Friesach ... **971** d.	1416	...	...	|	1506	...	|	...	...	|	1706	...	1816	...	...	|	1906	...	|	...	...	2102	|	...	...
Unzmarkt ... d.	1447	...	...	|	1541	...	1647	...	...	|	1741	...	1847	...	...	|	1941	...	2047	...	...	2137	|	2141	...
Judenburg ... d.	1501	...	...	|	1556	...	1701	...	...	|	1756	...	1901	...	...	|	1956	...	2101	...	...	2152	2201	2156	...
Zeltweg ... d.	|	...	...	|	1604	...	|	...	...	|	1804	...	|	...	...	|	2004	...	|	...	...	2200	|	2204	...
Knittelfeld ... d.	1514	...	...	|	1611	...	1714	...	...	|	1811	...	1914	...	...	|	2011	...	2114	...	...	2207	2214	2211	←
St Michael ... a.	|	...	...	|	1626	...	|	...	...	|	1826	...	|	...	...	|	2026	...	|	...	...	2222	|	2226	2222
St Michael ... **975** d.	|	...	...	|	1633	...	|	...	...	|	1833	...	|	...	...	|	2035	...	|	...	...	2235	|	2235	2235
Leoben Hbf ... **975** d.	1534	1538	...	|	1641	...	1734	1738	...	|	1841	...	1934	1938	...	|	2043	...	2134	2138	...	→	2234	2243	2243
Graz Hbf ... d.	|	|	1526	|	|	1626	|	|	1726	|	|	1826	|	|	1926	|	|	2026	|	|	2126j	...	|	|	|
Bruck an der Mur ... **975** d.	1546	|	1603	|	1653	1703	1746	|	1803	|	1853	1903	1946	|	2003	|	2055	2103	2146	|	2203	...	2246	2255	2255
Graz Hbf ... **975** a.	|	1622	|	1720	*1733*	|	|	1822	|	1925	*1933*	|	|	2022	|	2120	*2133*	|	|	2222	|	...	|	*2333*	*2333*
Mürzzuschlag ... **981** d.	|	...	1632	...	...	1732	|	...	1832	...	...	1932	|	...	2032	...	...	2132	|	...	2232	...	|	...	...
Wiener Neustadt Hbf ... **981** a.	1702	...	1728	...	...	1828	1902	...	1928	...	...	2028	2102	...	2128	...	...	2228	2302	...	2328	...	0002	...	...
Wien Meidling ● ... **981** a.	1728	...	1758	...	...	1858	1928	...	1958	...	...	2058	2128	...	2158	...	...	2258	2328	...	2358	...	0028	...	...
Wien Südbahnhof ... **981** a.	1735	...	1805	...	...	1905	1935	...	2005	...	...	2105	2135	...	2205	...	...	2305	2335	...	0005	...	0035	...	...

♦ – **NOTES** (CONTINUED FROM PREVIOUS PAGE)

30/1 – ALLEGRO JOHANN STRAUSS – 🚃12 and ✕ Venezia - Udine - Tarvisio 🏛 - Wien and v.v.

150/1 – EMONA – 🚃12 and ✕ Ljubljana - Maribor - Spielfeld-Straß 🏛 - Graz - Wien and v.v.; 🚃2 Rijeka (**482/3**) - Ljubljana - Wien and v.v.

158/9 – CROATIA – 🚃12 and ✕ Zagreb - Maribor - Spielfeld-Straß 🏛 - Graz - Wien and v.v. Conveys on dates in Table **91** 🛏 2 cl. Split - Wien and v.v.

234/5 – ALLEGRO TOSCA – 🛌 1, 2 cl., 🛏 2 cl. and 🚃2 Roma - Venezia - Wien and v.v.; 🛌 1, 2 cl. and 🛏 2 cl. Milano - Venezia - Wien and v.v. 🅁 for journeys from / to Italy.

1236 – Fom Villach on ⑦ until Sept. 27 (previous night from Roma). ALLEGRO ROSSINI – 🛌 1, 2 cl., 🛏 2 cl. and 🚃2 Roma - Firenze - Wien.

1237 – ⑤ until Sept. 25 (also Oct. 23, Dec. 4). ALLEGRO ROSSINI – 🛌 1, 2 cl., 🛏 2 cl. and 🚃2 Wien - Venezia - Firenze - Roma. Train number **1239** on Oct. 23, Dec. 4.

1238 – Oct. 26 and Dec. 8 only (from Villach, previous night from Roma). ALLEGRO ROSSINI – 🛌 1, 2 cl., 🛏 2 cl. and 🚃2 Roma - Firenze - Venezia - Wien.

1458 – ⑦ June 7 - Aug. 30 (previous night from Koper / Rijeka). ISTRIA – 🛏 2 cl. and 🚃2 Koper - Ljubljana - Wien; 🛏 2 cl. and 🚃2 Rijeka (**480**) - Ljubljana - Wien.

1459 – ⑤ June 5 - Aug. 28. ISTRIA – 🛏 2 cl. and 🚃2 Wien - Ljubljana - Koper; 🛏 2 cl. and 🚃2 Wien - Ljubljana (**481**) - Rijeka.

L – To / from Lienz (Table **971**).

M – To / from Maribor (Table **1315**).

a – Ⓐ only.

j – 2138 until Aug. 9.

n – Not Aug. 15.

r – ⚒ only.

z – Also Oct. 26, Dec. 8; not Oct. 25, Dec. 6.

¶ – On © runs with train number **15750** and also calls at Semmering (d. 1745).

§ – On © runs with train number **15555** and also calls at Semmering (d. 1015).

‡ – Also calls at Semmering (see Table **981**).

◧ – Leoben - St Michael is *10 km*. St Michael - Knittelfeld is *22 km*.

△ – Between Bruck a. d. Mur and St Michael combined with a service on the Selzthal route (Table **975**) – passengers should take care to join the correct portion for their destination.

● – See panel on page 447 for S-Bahn trains from / to Wien Hütteldorf. U-bahn line **U6** provides a direct link Wien Spittelau - Westbahnhof - Meidling.

★ – 🚌 **ÖBB** *IC Bus*. Rail tickets valid. 1st and 2nd class. 🍷 in first class. Number of seats limited so reservation is recommended.

981 Local trains WIEN - WIENER NEUSTADT - MÜRZZUSCHLAG — 2nd class only

WIEN - WIENER NEUSTADT

km				⚒	⚒						©B								M	P				
0	**Wien** Praterstern ... d.	0046	...	0446	0516	0546	0616	0646	0716	0746	...	...	0816	0846		2146	2216	...	2246	2346	...	...	...	...
2	**Wien** Mitte ... d.	0050	...	0450	0520	0550	0620	0650	0720	0750	...	...	0820	0850	and every	2150	2220	...	2250	2350	...	...	...	...
5	**Wien** Südbahnhof ▲. 980/3 d.	0056	...	0456	0526	0556	0626	0656	0726	0756	...	...	0826	0856	30 minutes	2156	2226	...	2256	2356	...	...	...	...
9	**Wien** Meidling ● ... 980/3 d.	0104	...	0506	0536	0606	0636	0706	0736	0806	0812	...	0836	0906	until	2206	2236	...	2304	0004	...	...	...	...
31	Baden ... d.	0120	...	0525	0555	0625	0655	0725	0755	0825	0835	...	0855	0925		2225	2255	...	2317	0017	...	...	...	...
53	**Wiener Neustadt** Hbf. 980/3 a.	0136	...	0545	0615	0645	0715	0745	0815	0845	0849	...	0915	0945		2245	2315	...	2329	0029	...	...	...	...

	ⒶM	⚒	Ⓐ		©M									©B									⚒	
Wiener Neustadt ... 980/3 d.	0502	0504	0534	0604	0617	0634	0704	0734	0810	0840		1710	1740	1804	1810	1840	1910	1940	2010	2040	2110	2140	2240	2342
Baden ... d.	|	0524	0554	0624	|	0654	0724	0754	0831	0901	and every	1731	1801	1821	1831	1901	1931	2001	2031	2101	2130	2201	2301	0008
Wien Meidling ● ... 980/3 a.	0531	0543	0613	0643	0646	0713	0743	0813	0852	0922	30 minutes	1752	1822	1842	1852	1922	1952	2022	2052	2122	2152	2222	2322	0049
Wien Südbahnhof ▲ .. 980/3 a.	0538	0551	0621	0651	0653	0721	0751	0821	0900	0930	until	1800	1830	...	1900	1930	2000	2030	2100	2130	2200	2230	2330	0057
Wien Mitte ... a.	...	0557	0627	0657	...	0727	0757	0827	0906	0936		1806	1836	...	1906	1936	2006	2036	2106	2136	2206	2236	2336	0103
Wien Praterstern ... a.	...	0601	0631	0701	...	0731	0801	0831	0910	0940		1810	1840	...	1910	1940	2010	2040	2110	2140	2210	2240	2340	0107

WIENER NEUSTADT - SEMMERING - MÜRZZUSCHLAG

km		Ⓐ	⚒	⚒		¶	©B	©¶				Ⓐ			Ⓐ			Ⓐ			Ⓐ			M	P
0	**Wiener Neustadt** Hbf .. 980 d.	...	*0605*	*0642*	*0805*	0832	0850	0932	*1005*	*1205*	1305	...	*1405*	1505	...	*1605*	1705	...	*1805*	1905	...	2005	2105	2331	0031
34	Payerbach-Reichenau ... a.	...	*0635*	*0712*	*0835*	|	0922	|	*1035*	*1235*	1335	...	*1435*	1535	...	*1635*	1735	...	*1835*	1935	...	2035	2138	0002	0102
34	Payerbach-Reichenau ... d.	0539	0639	0719	0839	|	0923	|	1039	1239	...	1339	1439	...	1539	1639	...	1739	1839	...	1939	...	2139	0002	...
55	Semmering ... d.	0607	0707	0744	0907	0915	0948	1015	1107	1307	...	1407	1507	...	1607	1707	...	1807	1907	...	2007	...	2207	0027	...
69	**Mürzzuschlag** ... 980 a.	0624	0724	0801	0924	0929	1007	1029	1124	1324	...	1424	1524	...	1624	1724	...	1824	1924	...	2024	...	2224	0041	...

	ⒶM	Ⓐ	©M	⚒		⚒					Ⓐ			Ⓐ			¶	Ⓐ	©B	©¶		Ⓐ			¶
Mürzzuschlag ... 980 d.	0349	0439	0511	0539	...	0629	...	0732	0935	1135	1235	...	1335	1435	...	1535	1632	1635	1645	1732	1735	1835	...	1935	2132
Semmering ... d.	0403	0456	0526	0556	...	0646	...	0754	0952	1152	1252	...	1352	1452	...	1552	1645	1652	1705	1745	1752	1852	...	1952	2145
Payerbach-Reichenau ... a.	0429	0525	0551	0625	...	0715	...	0821	1021	1221	1321	...	1421	1521	...	1621	|	1721	1730	|	1821	1921	...	2021	|
Payerbach-Reichenau ... d.	0430	*0529*	0552	...	0629	...	0729	*0824*	*1024*	*1224*	...	1324	*1424*	...	1524	*1624*	|	*1724*	1732	|	*1824*	...	1924	2022	|
Wiener Neustadt Hbf ... 980 a.	0500	*0559*	0615	...	0659	...	0759	*0854*	*1054*	*1254*	...	1354	*1454*	...	1554	*1654*	1728	*1754*	1800	1828	*1854*	...	1954	2054	2228

B – © from Nov. 28. (2) and ✕ Bratislava - Wiener Neustadt - Mürzzuschlag and v.v.
M – (2) Wien - Wiener Neustadt - Mürzzuschlag and v.v.
P – (2) Wien - Wiener Neustadt - Payerbach-Reichenau.

¶ – *EC* or *IC* train (see Table **980**).
▲ – Suburban platforms 21 / 22.
● – See panel on page 447 for S-Bahn trains from / to Wien Hütteldorf. U-bahn line **U6** provides a direct link Wien Spittelau - Westbahnhof - Meidling.

982 Local trains WIEN - BŘECLAV and ZNOJMO — 2nd class only

WIEN - BŘECLAV (see Table **1150** and **1161** for international express trains)

km		⚒	⚒						⚒		⚒	Ⓐ		Ⓐ	Ⓐ		Ⓐ	Ⓐ		Ⓑz				
0	**Wien** Meidling ... 981 d.	0500	0530	0600	...	0800	...	0954	1054	1154	1254	1324	1354	1454	1524	1554	1624	1654	1754	1854	1954	2054	...	2224
4	**Wien** Südbahnhof ▲ ... 981 d.	0507	0537	0607	...	0807	...	1001	1101	1201	1301	1331	1401	1501	1531	1601	1631	1701	1801	1901	2001	2101	...	2231
7	**Wien** Mitte ... 981 d.	0513	0543	0613	...	0813	...	1007	1107	1207	1307	1337	1407	1507	1537	1607	1637	1707	1807	1907	2007	2107	...	2237
9	**Wien** Praterstern ... 981 d.	0517	0547	0617	...	0817	...	1011	1111	1211	1311	1341	1411	1511	1541	1611	1641	1711	1811	1911	2011	2111	...	2241
40	Gänserndorf ... d.	0549	0629	0649	...	0849	...	1043	1143	1243	1343	1412	1443	1543	1612	1643	1712	1743	1843	1943	2043	2143	...	2313
74	Hohenau 🛃 ... a.	0621	0654	0721	...	0921	...	1115	1215	1315	1415	1443	1515	1615	1638	1715	1738	1815	1915	2015	2115	2215	...	2345
92	**Břeclav** 🛃 ... a.	0637	...	0737	...	0937	...	1131	...	1331	...	...	1531	...	...	1731	...	...	1931	...	2131	...	...	...

	Ⓐ	Ⓐ		⚒		⚒	⚒						⚒		⚒		Ⓐ		Ⓐ					
Břeclav 🛃 ... d.	...	...	0525	...	0625	...	0725	0825	...	1025	...	1225	...	1425	...	1625	...	1825	...	2025	...	2225	...	...
Hohenau 🛃 ... d.	0442	0518	0542	0612	0642	0712	0742	0842	...	1042	...	1242	1342	1442	1542	1642	1742	1842	1942	2042	...	2242	...	...
Gänserndorf ... d.	0514	0544	0614	0644	0714	0744	0814	0914	...	1114	...	1314	1414	1514	1614	1714	1814	1914	2014	2114	...	2314	...	...
Wien Praterstern ... 981 a.	0545	0615	0645	0715	0745	0815	0845	0945	...	1145	...	1345	1445	1545	1645	1745	1845	1945	2045	2145	...	2345	...	...
Wien Mitte ... 981 a.	0549	0619	0649	0719	0749	0819	0849	0949	...	1149	...	1349	1449	1549	1649	1749	1849	1949	2049	2149	...	2349	...	...
Wien Südbahnhof ▲ ... 981 a.	0556	0626	0656	0726	0756	0826	0856	0956	...	1156	...	1356	1456	1556	1656	1756	1856	1956	2056	2156	...	2356	...	...
Wien Meidling ... 981 a.	0603	0633	0703	0733	0803	0833	0903	1003	...	1203	...	1403	1503	1603	1703	1803	1903	2003	2103	2203	...	0003	...	...

WIEN - RETZ - ZNOJMO ★

km		⚒		D		⚒		⚒		⚒		Ⓐ		⚒		Ⓐ		
0	**Wien** Meidling ... 981/9 d.	0545	0645	0745	0845	0945	1045	1145	1245	1345	1445	1545	1645	1745	1845	1945	2045	2306
4	**Wien** Südbahnhof ▲ .. 981/9 d.	0552	0652	0752	0852	0952	1052	1152	1252	1352	1452	1552	1652	1752	1852	1952	2052	2313
7	**Wien** Mitte ... 981/9 d.	0558	0658	0758	0858	0958	1058	1158	1258	1358	1458	1558	1658	1758	1858	1958	2058	2319
9	**Wien** Praterstern ... 981/9 d.	0602	0702	0802	0902	1002	1102	1202	1302	1402	1502	1602	1702	1802	1902	2002	2102	2323
34	Stockerau ... 989 d.	0628	0728	0828	0928	1028	1128	1228	1328	1428	1528	1628	1728	1828	1928	2028	2127	2348
60	Hollabrunn ... d.	0645	0745	0845	0945	1045	1145	1245	1345	1445	1545	1645	1745	1845	1945	2045	2153	0009
90	**Retz** 🛃 ... d.	0715	0815	0912	1015	1112	1215	1312	1415	1512	1615	1712	1815	1912	2015	2112	2220	0036
96	Šatov 🛃 ... a.	0723	0823	...	1023	...	1223	...	1423	...	1623	...	1823	...	2023	...	...	...
		A																
96	Šatov ... 🚌★ d.	0725	0826	...	1026	...	1226	...	1426	...	1626	...	1826	...	2026	...	...	...
107	**Znojmo** ... 🚌★ a.	0742	0843	...	1043	...	1243	...	1443	...	1643	...	1843	...	2043	...	...	...

	Ⓐ	⚒		⚒		A			⚒		⚒		⚒		⚒		Ⓐ	
Znojmo ... 🚌★ d.	...	...	0522e	...	0642	0745	0848	...	1048	...	1248	...	1450	...	1649	...	1849	...
Šatov ... 🚌★ a.	...	...	0539e	...	0659	0802	0905	...	1105	...	1305	...	1506	...	1706	...	1906	...
						⚒												
Šatov 🛃 ... d.	...	...	0542e	...	0702	0804	0908	...	1108	...	1308	...	1508	...	1708	...	1908	...
Retz 🛃 ... d.	0418	0512	0552	0636	0715	0818	0918	1018	1118	1218	1318	1418	1518	1618	1718	1818	1918	2018
Hollabrunn ... d.	0445	0539	0621	0706	0746	0846	0946	1046	1146	1246	1346	1446	1546	1646	1746	1846	1946	2046
Stockerau ... 989 d.	0503	0557	0643	0729	0803	0903	1003	1103	1203	1303	1403	1503	1603	1703	1803	1903	2003	2103
Wien Praterstern ... 981/9 a.	0527	0627	0712	0757	0827	0927	1027	1127	1227	1327	1427	1527	1627	1727	1827	1927	2027	2127
Wien Mitte ... 981/9 a.	0531	0631	0716	0801	0831	0931	1031	1131	1231	1331	1431	1531	1631	1731	1831	1931	2031	2131
Wien Südbahnhof ▲ .. 981/9 a.	0538	0638	*0726*	0808	0838	0938	1038	1138	1238	1338	1438	1538	1638	1738	1838	1938	2038	2138
Wien Meidling ... 981/9 a.	0545	0645	*0733*	0815	0845	0945	1045	1145	1245	1345	1445	1545	1645	1745	1845	1945	2045	2145

A – ①-⑥ (not Dec. 8).
D – Daily until Oct. 31; ⚒ from Nov. 2.
e – ①-⑤ (not July 6, Sept. 28, Oct. 28, Nov. 17).
z – Not Oct. 25.

★ – All services between Šatov and Znojmo are operated by 🚌 until Nov. 30.
▲ – Suburban platforms 21 / 22 (allow 10 minutes to / from the main station).

983 (WIEN -) WIENER NEUSTADT - FEHRING — 2nd class only

km		Ⓐ	Ⓐ	◇	⚒			Ⓐ	⚒	†		†		Ⓐ		⚒	Ⓑz	
0	**Wien** Südbahnhof ... 980/1 d.	...	...	0656	0708*	...	0923	0923	*1056**	1123	1323	1323	1523	1626	1723	1826	1926	*2056*
4	**Wien** Meidling ... 980/1 d.	...	0530	0703	0718	...	0930	0930	*1106*	1130	1330	1330	1530	1633	1730	1833	1933	*2103*
48	**Wiener Neustadt** Hbf. 980/1 a.	...	0558	0728	0751	...	0955	0955	*1145*	1155	1355	1355	1555	1658	1755	1858	1958	*2128*
48	**Wiener Neustadt** Hbf ... d.	...	0600	...	...	0800	1000	1000	1200	1200	1400	1400	1600	1700	1800	1900	2000	2137
103	Friedberg ... d.	...	0702	...	...	0901	1058	1058	1301	1301	1502	1502	1701	1755	1902	1955	2100	2252
130	Hartberg ... d.	0613	0749	...	...	0947	1139	1145	1347	1347	1542	1547	1747	1846	1947	2047	2140	...
161	Fürstenfeld ... d.	0652	0826	...	...	1027	...	1223	1427	1427	...	1627	1827	...	2026	2132	...	...
181	**Fehring** ... a.	0722	0856	...	...	1056	...	1253	1456	1456	...	1656	1856	...	...	2201	...	...
	Graz Hbf **986** ... a.	0833	1021	...	...	1230	...	*1419*	*1603a*	*1603r*	...	1854	*2009a*	...	...	...	...	...

a – Ⓐ only.
r – Not Aug. 15.
z – Not Oct. 25.

* – Suburban platforms 21 / 22.
◇ – *ÖIC* **553**.

	Ⓐ	Ⓐ	⚒	⚒	Ⓐ		⚒	⚒					†			†	Ⓐ	
Graz Hbf **986** ... d.	...	...	...	...	...	...	...	...	...	...	...	*1144*	*1330*	...	*1519*	...	1743	...
Fehring ... d.	...	...	...	...	0451	...	...	0604	...	0902	...	1302	1502	...	1702	...	1902	...
Fürstenfeld ... d.	...	...	...	...	0520	...	...	0636	0734	0933	...	1333	1533	...	1733	...	1933	...
Hartberg ... d.	0409	0507	0507	...	0600	...	...	0714	0817	1015	1215	1415	1616	1616	1812	...	2012	...
Friedberg ... d.	0452	0549	0549	0608	0642	0642	0710	0805	0902	1102	1302	1502	1700	1700	1900	1942	2100	2100
Wiener Neustadt Hbf ... a.	0546	0645	0645	0659	0742	0742	0759	0859	0958	1156	1356	1556	1758	1758	1958	2028	2158	2158
Wiener Neustadt Hbf ... 980/1 d.	0547	0647	...	0702	*0747*	*0747*	0801	*0904*	1001	1201	1401	1601	1801	1801	2001	2030	*2230*	*2230*
Wien Meidling ... 980/1 a.	0616	0716	...	0731	*0816*	*0816*	0830	*0928*	1028	1228	1428	1628	1828	1828	2028	2055	*2255*	*2255*
Wien Südbahnhof ... 980/1 a.	0623	0723	...	0738	*0823*	*0823*	0838	*0935*	1035	1235	1435	1635	1835	1835	2035	2102	*2302*	*2302*

2nd class only — WIENER NEUSTADT - PUCHBERG am Schneeberg - HOCHSCHNEEBERG — 984

WIENER NEUSTADT - PUCHBERG am Schneeberg *28 km.* Journey time: 44–48 minutes.
From Wiener Neustadt at 0038 †, 0737, 0837 **A**, 0937, 1037 **E**, 1137, 1237 **E**, 1337, 1437 **E**, 1537, 1637, 1737, 1837 Ⓑ **w**, 1937, 2037 Ⓑ **w**, 2137.
From Puchberg at 0455 Ⓐ, 0525 Ⓐ, 0555 ⚒, 0624 Ⓐ, 0638 Ⓒ, 0647 Ⓐ, 0738, 0837, 0938 Ⓒ **G**, 1037, 1138 **E**, 1238, 1338 **E**, 1438, 1538 **E**, 1638, 1737, 1838, 1938 Ⓑ **w**, 2038 ⑤⑥ **r**.

PUCHBERG am Schneeberg - **HOCHSCHNEEBERG** *Schneebergbahn* (narrow-gauge rack railway). *9 km* Journey time: ± 50 minutes.
Services run **Apr. 25 - Oct. 26, 2009** subject to demand and weather conditions. **Operator**: NÖ Schneebergbahn GmbH, Bahnhofplatz 1, A-2734 Puchberg. ✆ +43 (0) 2636 3661 20.
From Puchberg at 0900, 1100, 1330 and 1530. **From Hochschneeberg** at 1000, 1200, 1430 and 1630. Additional trains operate when there is sufficient demand.

A – Daily until Oct. 30; Ⓐ from Nov. 2. **E** – Daily until Oct. 31; ⚒ from Nov. 2. **G** – Until Oct. 26. **r** – Also Oct. 25, Dec. 7. **w** – Not Oct. 25.

ÖBB, GySEV ●; 2nd class only — GRAZ - SZENTGOTTHÁRD - SZOMBATHELY — 986

km			S	A ⁄		S			S	⚒						V			⚒	Ⓐ		Ⓑ		Ⓐ		
0	**Graz** Hbf d.	...	...	0610	...	0807e	1007	...	1144	1236	...	1330	...	*1519*	1632	1743	1803	...	1841	1921	2011	2011	...	2115	2204	0004
30	Gleisdorf d.	...	...	0650	...	0845	1044	...	1220	1309	...	1405	...	*1551*	1705	1815	1843	...	1914	1959	2047	2047	...	2153	2239	0039
62	Fehring d.	...	0505	0726	...	0919	1123	...	1257	1350	...	1439	...	1623	1735	1846	1920	...	1942	2033	2122	2123	...	2226	2311	0111
82	Szentgotthárd 🛃 a.	...	0530	0744	...	0942	1144	...	1325	1412	...	1502	...	1645	1758	1907	1942	...	...	...	...	2146	...	*2252*	...	...
82	Szentgotthárd 🛃 d.	0408	0535	0754	0845	0955	1147	1225	1339	...	1428	...	1613	1703	1819	...	1943	2052	...	...	...	...	2220	...	...	...
110	Körmend a.	0444	0611	0827	0921	1032	1222	1303	1418	...	1506	...	1650	1739	1855	...	2020	2130	...	...	...	...	2257	...	...	...
146	**Szombathely** a.	0518	0645	0856	0955	1106	1255	1338	1454	...	1540	...	1724	1813	1931	...	2054	2205	...	...	...	...	2331	...	...	...

	Ⓐ	Z	⚒		⚒H		◇		S	W				⚒				S		Ⓐ			B ⁄			
Szombathely d.	...	0408	...	*0454*	...	*0620*	...	0716	0932	...	1020	...	1145	...	1315	...	1431	1551	1639	...	1818	...	1910	2029	2140	2245
Körmend d.	...	0445	...	*0531*	...	*0657*	...	0751	1008	...	1057	...	1223	...	1350	...	1505	1626	1714	...	1856	...	1941	2106	2218	2321
Szentgotthárd 🛃 a.	...	0520	...	*0606*	...	*0733*	...	0826	1042	...	1132	...	1258	...	1426	...	1540	1701	1750	...	1931	...	2012	2141	2252	2356
Szentgotthárd 🛃 d.	0404	...	0531	0620	...	0745	...	...	1059	...	...	*1148*b	...	1301	1437	1536	...	1711	*1817*	...	...	1944a	2040	2147	...	...
Fehring d.	0428	...	0557	0643	0730	0808	0920	...	1121	1124	...	1210	...	1323	1500	1600	...	1735	*1839*	1859	...	2009	2101	2211	...	...
Gleisdorf d.	0455	...	0626	0714	0759	0846	0953	...	...	1155	...	1244	...	1405	1529b	1639	...	1815	...	1935	...	2047	2129	...	...	...
Graz Hbf a.	0533	...	0702	0748	0833	0921	1021	...	...	1230	...	1321	...	1441	1603b	1721	...	1854	...	2009	...	2121	2203	...	...	...

A – 🚃2 Graz (*ER* **4760**) - Szentgotthárd (*IC* **917**) Györ - Budapest.
B – 🚃2 Budapest (*IC* **916**) - Györ - Szentgotthárd (*ER* **4761**) - Graz.
H – From Hartberg on Ⓐ (Table **983**).
S – To / from Wiener Neustadt via Sopron (Tables **1227** / **978**).
V – On Ⓐ conveys 🚃2 Graz - Fehring - Hartberg - Wiener Neustadt (Table **983**).
W – From Wiener Neustadt (Table **983**).
Z – ①–⑥ (not Aug. 20, 21, 22, Oct. 23, 24).
a – Ⓐ only.
b – Ⓑ only.
e – 0809 on †.
⁄ – Ⓡ and supplement payable in Hungary.
◇ – On Ⓐ from Wien Meidling via Hartberg (Table **983**).
● – GySEV: Györ-Sopron-Ebenfurti Vasút.

2nd class only — *Service until Sept. 27* — WIEN - STOCKERAU - KREMS an der Donau — 989

km		⚒	Ⓐ	⚒	ⒸE			⚒			Ⓐ					Ⓐ		Ⓐ		Ⓐ		Ⓐ			
0	**Wien** Meidling 981/2 d.	0515	0615	0715	...	0746	0846	0915	0946	1046	1115	1146	1246	1346	1446	1500	1546	1615	1646	1715	1746	1815	1846	1946	2118
4	**Wien** Südbahnhof ▲ 981/2 d.	0522	0622	0722	0723	0755	0855	0922	0955	1055	1122	1155	1255	1355	1455	1507	1555	1622	1655	1722	1755	1822	1855	1955	2125
7	**Wien** Mitte 981/2 d.	0528	0628	0728	│	0801	0901	0928	1001	1101	1128	1201	1301	1401	1501	1513	1601	1628	1701	1728	1801	1828	1901	2001	2131
9	**Wien** Praterstern 981/2 d.	0532	0632	0732	│	0805	0905	0932	1005	1105	1132	1205	1305	1405	1505	1517	1605	1632	1705	1732	1805	1832	1905	2005	2135
35	Stockerau 982 a.	0556	0656	0756	0815	0841	0941	0956	1041	1141	1156	1241	1341	1441	1541	1550	1641	1656	1741	1756	1841	1856	1941	2041	2211
		│	│	│	│			│			│					d		│		│		│			
35	Stockerau d.	0558	0658	0758	0817	0858	0958	0958	1058	1158	1158	1258	1358	1458	...	1558	1658	1658	1758	1758	1858	1858	1958	2058	2214
52	Absdorf-Hippersdorf 990 d.	0631t	0716	0816	0840	0916	1016	1016	1116	1216	1216	1316	1416	1516	...	1616	1715	1715	1816	1816	1916	1916	2016	2116	2231
84	**Krems** a. d. Donau 990 a.	0714	0748	0843	0906	0941	1041	1041	1141	1241	1241	1341	1441	1541	...	1641	1743	1743	1842	1842	1941	1941	2041	2148	2257

	⚒	⚒		Ⓐ	⑥n	Ⓐ	⚒					Ⓐ				Ⓐ		Ⓐ						ⒸE	
Krems a. d. Donau 990 d.	0439	0543	0613	0638	*0725*	0745	0850	0850	0950	1050	1148	1250	1250	1348	1450	1549	1549	1649	1649	1750	1850	...	1948	2019	2050
Absdorf-Hippersdorf 990 d.	0516	0615	0656	0718	0816	0816	0916	0916	1016	1116	1216	1316	1316	1416	1516	1616	1616	1716	1716	1816	1916	...	2016	2056	2116
Stockerau a.	0532	0632	0712	0734	0832	0832	0932	0932	1032	1132	1232	1332	1332	1432	1532	1632	1632	1732	1732	1832	1932	...	2032	2111	2132
	│	│		│		d	│					│				│		│						│	
Stockerau 982 d.	0533	0635	0719	0735	...	0849	0933	0949	1049	1149	1249	1333	1349	1449	1549	1633	1649	1733	1749	1849	1949	2003	2049	2112	2149
Wien Praterstern 981/2 a.	0557	0706	0754	0806	...	0924	0957	1024	1124	1224	1324	1357	1424	1524	1624	1657	1724	1757	1824	1924	2024	2027	2124	│	2224
Wien Mitte 981/2 a.	0601	0710	0758	0810	...	...	1001	...	...	...	1328	1401	1428	1528	1628	1701	1728	1801	1828	1928	...	2031	2128	│	2228
Wien Südbahnhof ▲ 981/2 a.	0608	0717	0805	0817	...	...	1008	...	...	...	1335	1408	1435	1535	1635	1708	1735	1808	1835	1935	...	2038	2135	2215	2235
Wien Meidling 981/2 a.	0615	0724	0816	0824	...	...	1015	...	...	...	1342	1415	1442	1542	1642	1715	1742	1815	1842	1942	...	2045	2142	...	2242

E – Ⓒ until Oct. 26. To / from Emmersdorf (Table **991**). **d** – Daily. **t** – Arrives 0614. **n** – Not Aug. 15. ▲ – Suburban platforms 21 / 22 (except train **E**).

2nd class only — WIEN - GMÜND — 990

SERVICE UNTIL SEPT. 27. All services Tulln - Absdorf-Hippersdorf and v.v. are operated by 🚌. See Table **989** for alternative rail services Wien - Absdorf-Hippersdorf and v.v.

km							Ⓐ			Ⓐ			Ⓐ		Ⓐ🚌				Ⓐ🚌						Ⓑk
	Wien Vienna Int. Centre d.	...	...	...	...	...	...	...	...	...	...	...	...	...	1535	...	...	...	1635	...	...	...	...	...	...
0	**Wien** Franz-Josefs-Bf ‡ d.	...	0534	0639	...	0810	0905	1005	...	1105	1205	...	1305	1405	│	1504	...	1552	│	1613	1730	...	1834	2005	2057
1	Wien Spittelau ● ‡ d.	...	0537	0642	...	0813	0908	1008	...	1108	1208	...	1308	1408	│	1507	...	1555	│	1616	1734	...	1837	2008	2100
3	Wien Heiligenstadt △ ‡ d.	...	0541	0646	...	0816	0911	1011	...	1111	1211	...	1311	1411	│	1510	...	1558	│	1619	1737	...	1840	2011	2103
33	Tulln ‡ a.	...	0601	0714	...	0843	0931	1031	...	1131	1231	...	1331	1431	│	1536	...	1618	│	1640	1803	...	1901	2031	2129
						▬	Ⓐ			Ⓐ			Ⓐ		│	🚌			│						
33	Tulln 🚌 d.	...	0607	0719	...	...	0937	1037	...	1137	1237	...	1337	1437	│	1541	...	1623	│	1645	1808	...	1907	2037	2133
44	Absdorf-Hippersdorf 🚌 a.	...	0639	0751	...	...	1009	1109	...	1209	1309	...	1409	1509	│	1613	...	1655	│	1717	1840	...	1939	2109	2205
				Ⓒ	Ⓐ		d			d			d		│	│	Ⓐ	A	│	D	⑥J	ⒶF			k🚌
44	Absdorf-Hippersdorf 989 d.	...	0700	0802	0820	...	1020	1120	...	1220	1320	...	1420	1520	│	1619	1629	1703	│	1732	1843	1844	1946	2124	2207
75	**Krems** a. d. Donau 989 a.	...	│	│	│	...	│	│	...	│	│	...	│	│	│	│	│	│	│	│	│	│	│	│	│
79	Eggenburg d.	Ⓐ	0727	0833	0850	...	1057	1150	...	1258	1350	...	1458	1550	│	1706	│	1734	1742	1756	1912	1912	2015	2152	2255
89	**Sigmundsherberg** d.	0614	0735	0842	0859	...	1106	1159	...	1307	1359	...	1507	1559	1650	1719	1700	1742	1755	1805	1920	1921	2023	2201	2308
121	Göpfritz d.	0640	0800	0906	0925	⚒	...	1224	Ⓐ	...	1424	Ⓐ	...	1624	...	...	1725	1812	...	1830	...	1945	2050	2226	...
138	Schwarzenau ⊡ d.	0656	0814	0921	0940	1151	...	1239	1318	...	1439	1536	...	1639	...	...	1741	1826	...	1845	...	2001	2104	2240	...
162	**Gmünd** NÖ a.	*0740**	0838	0943	1001	1213	...	1301	1342	...	1501	1559	...	1701	...	...	1803	1849	...	1906	...	2023	2125	2302	...

	Ⓐ	⚒G	ⒶH	Ⓐ🚌	Ⓐ		Ⓐ	Ⓐ🚌		⚒	Ⓐ🚌							⚒			Ⓐ		Ⓐ		
Gmünd NÖ d.	...	0346	0420	...	...	0513c	0531	...	0617	...	0741	0824	...	...	1129	...	...	1217	1329	...	1347	1511	1614	1718	1939
Schwarzenau ⊡ d.	...	0408	0442	...	0531	0535c	0552	...	0639	...	0810	0850	...	...	1151	...	...	1239	1351	...	1409	1534	1636	1740	2000
Göpfritz d.	...	0422	0457	...	0545	0550c	0605	...	0653	...	▬	0907	...	...	1205	...	...	▬	1405	...	▬	1548	▬	1753	2014
Sigmundsherberg d.	0411	0447	0522	0528	0609	0615	0629	0638	0717	0823	...	0932	1010	1121	1232	...	1321	...	1432	1521	...	1614	...	1821	2040
Eggenburg d.	0421	0456	│	│	...	0624	│	│	0726	0833	...	0940	1020	1131	1240	...	1331	...	1440	1531	...	1623	...	1829	2048
Krems a. d. Donau 989 d.	│	│	│	│	...	│	│	│	│	│	...	│	│	│	│	...	│	...	│	│	...	│	...	│	│
Absdorf-Hippersdorf 989 a.	0457	0525	0552	│	...	0652	0659	│	0754	0908	...	1008	1059	1208	1308	...	1408	...	1508	1608	...	1654	...	1900	2119
	Ⓐ	⚒	Ⓐ	│			Ⓐ	│		d															
Absdorf-Hippersdorf 🚌 d.	0505	0530	0557	│	...	0657	0705	│	0803	0921	...	1021	1121	1220	1313	1320	1420	...	1520	1620	...	1700	1820	1920	2125
Tulln 🚌 a.	0537	0602	0629	│	...	0729	0737	│	0835	0953	...	1053	1153	1252	1345	1352	1452	...	1552	1652	...	1732	1852	1952	2157
	Ⓐ	d	Ⓐ	│		⚒	d	│		⚒					Ⓐ		⚒			Ⓐ					
Tulln ‡ d.	0551	0618	0642	│	...	0739	0742	│	0850	1002	1019	1109	1218	1312	1349	1418	1502	1519	1602	1705	1708	1737	1909	2002	2202
Wien Heiligenstadt △ ‡ d.	0612	0642	0706	│	...	0800	0820	│	0911	1039	1043	1132	1244	1338	1418	1444	1539	1543	1639	1727	1745	1814	1931	2039f	2239f
Wien Spittelau ● ‡ d.	0615	0647	0710	│	...	0804	0823	│	0914	1043	1046	1136	1247	1342	1421	1447	1543	1546	1643	1730	1749	1818	1935	2043f	2243f
Wien Franz-Josefs-Bf ‡ a.	0618	0649	0713	│	...	0806	0825	│	0916	1045	1048	1138	1249	1344	1423	1449	1545	1548	1645	1732	1751	1820	1937	2045f	2245f
Wien Vienna Int. Centre a.	...	...	...	0644	...	...	...	0754	...	...	...	...	...	...	...	...	...	...	...	...	...	...	...	...	...

A – From Stockerau on Ⓐ (d. 1649).
D – From Stockerau on ⚒ (d. 1719).
F – From Stockerau (d. 1832).
G – To Stockerau (a. 0538).
H – To Stockerau (a. 0613).
J – ⑥ (not Aug. 15). From Stockerau (d. 1820).
c – Ⓒ only.
d – Daily.
f – 11–13 minutes earlier on Ⓒ.
k – Ⓑ (also Aug. 15).
n – Not Aug. 15.
* – By 🚌.
‡ – Additional trains operate Wien - Tulln and v.v.
△ – S-Bahn trains run every 15–20 minutes from / to Wien Hütteldorf (journey time: 21 minutes).
● – Direct U-bahn links: Line **U4** – Wien Mitte - Spittelau. Line **U6** – Wien Meidling - Westbahnhof - Spittelau.

⊡ – Local trains **Schwarzenau** to **Waidhofen** a. d. Thaya (*10 km*, journey 17–18 minutes) and **Zwettl** (*22 km*, journey 30–33 minutes).
Schwarzenau to **Waidhofen** at 0509 Ⓐ, 0555 ⚒, 0700, 0816, 0924 Ⓒ, 0943 Ⓐ, 1242, 1442, 1537, 1642, 1743, 1848, 2003 Ⓐ.
Waidhofen to **Schwarzenau** at 0531 Ⓐ, 0618 ⚒, 0754, 0900 Ⓒ, 0918 Ⓐ, 1129, 1329 Ⓒ, 1339 Ⓐ, 1512, 1615, 1718, 1805, 1938, 2042 Ⓐ.
Schwarzenau to **Zwettl** at 0520 ⑥ **n**, 0815 Ⓒ, 0923 Ⓒ, 0942 Ⓐ, 1241 Ⓒ, 1353 Ⓒ, 1359 Ⓐ, 1640, 1847. **Zwettl** to **Schwarzenau** at 0604 ⑥ **n**, 0850 Ⓒ, 1115, 1317 Ⓒ, 1459, 1809, 1924.

991 KREMS an der Donau - SPITZ an der Donau - EMMERSDORF an der Donau — 2nd class only

km		Ⓐ	⑥n	Ⓐ	⚒	E			©W						D		E	E		L	E	Ⓐ		
0	**Krems** an der Donau d.	0436	0456	0600	0643	0732	0801	0848	0920	...	1048	1148	...	1301	1343	1455	1548	1616	1648	1716	1748	1814	1848	1943
7	Dürnstein-Oberloiben d.	0449	0509	0614	0706	0745	0813	0901	0933	...	1101	1201	...	1316	1356	1509	1601	1631	1701	1732	1801	1827	1901	1956
13	Weißenkirchen d.	0459	0517	0623	0714	0753	0823	0918	0942	...	1118	1210	...	1324	1404	1522	1618	1639	1710	1741	1810	1835	1910	2004
18	**Spitz** an der Donau d.	0513	0526	0632	0722	0801	0831	0926	0950	...	1126	1218	...	1333	1417	1530	1626	1648	1718	1752	1818	1844	1918	2013
26	Aggsbach Markt d.	0539	0552	...	...	...	...	...	1018	...	...	...	...	...	1442	...	...	...	...	1822	...	...	...	...
34	**Emmersdorf** an der Donau a.	0550	0603	...	...	...	...	...	1030	...	...	...	...	...	...	...	...	...	...	1835	...	...	...	...

	Ⓐ	Ⓐ	⚒	Ⓐ	⑥n	⚒	⚒	E					L		D		D	E		E		©W		
Emmersdorf an der Donau d.	...	...	...	0600	0607	...	...	...	...	...	...	...	1146	...	...	...	...	...	...	...	...	1857	...	...
Aggsbach Markt d.	...	...	...	0612	0620	...	...	...	...	...	...	...	1158	...	...	...	1446	...	...	...	...	1909	...	...
Spitz an der Donau d.	0450	0525	0557	0639	0648	0648	0728	0814	0909	...	1109	1200	1226	1259	1355	1452	1513	1609	1700	1800	1900	1938	1938	2017
Weißenkirchen d.	0458	0533	0606	0647	0657	0657	0737	0822	0918	...	1123	1211	1235	1307	1405	1500	1521	1623	1723	1818	1914	1946	1946	2025
Dürnstein-Oberloiben d.	0507	0541	0614	0656	0705	0705	0745	0831	0932	...	1131	1219	1244	1315	1413	1509	1529	1631	1731	1831	1922	1956	1956	2033
Krems an der Donau a.	0520	0554	0627	0707	0718	0718	0758	0843	0945	...	1144	1232	1257	1328	1426	1520	1542	1644	1744	1844	1935	2009	2009	2046

D – Daily until Oct. 31; ⚒ from Nov. 2.
E – Daily until Oct. 30; Ⓐ from Nov. 2.
L – Daily until Oct. 26. From / to Linz (Table **992**).
W – © until Oct. 26. From / to Wien (Table **989**).
n – Not Aug. 15.

992 EMMERSDORF an der Donau - GREIN - ST VALENTIN and LINZ — 2nd class only

km		Ⓐ	Ⓐ	Ⓐ	⚒	Ⓐ	†			⚒		⚒		⚒		⚒		Ⓐ		Ⓐ			Ⓑ	K
0	**Emmersdorf** an der Donau d.	...	...	...	...	...	...	...	...	...	...	...	...	...	...	...	...	...	...	...	...	...	...	1837
37	St Nikola-Struden d.	...	...	0513	0524	...	0557	...	0629	...	0800	0900	...	...	...	...	...	...	...	...	...	1900a	1931	2026
43	Grein-Bad Kreuzen d.	0406	0442	0527	0538	0601	0611	0611	0643	0711	0814	0914	1014	1114	1214	1314	1414	1514	1614	1714	1814	1914	1946	2040
	St Valentin a.	0458	|	|	0634	|	0705	0705	|	0806	|	1008	|	1208	|	1408	|	1608	|	1808	|	|	2037	|
99	**Linz** Hbf a.	0538	0551	0632	0700	0705	0725	0725	0754	0829	0924	1029	1124	1229	1324	1429	1524	1629	1724	1829	1924	2024	2108	2200

km		Ⓐ	Ⓐ	⚒		L	K	⚒		⚒		⚒		Ⓐ	⚒	Ⓐ		Ⓐ	⚒	Ⓑ		ⒶL	ⒶN	
	Linz Hbf d.	...	0526	0618	0649	0837	0837	0930	1035	1130	1235	1330	1435	1450	1530	1602	1635	1702	1730	1753	1835	1935	1935	2035
0	**St Valentin** d.	0503	|	0648	0719	|	|	0951	|	1151	|	1351	|	1521	1551	|	|	|	1751	1823	|	|	|	|
38	Grein-Bad Kreuzen d.	0600	0642	0743	0814	0945	0949	1045	1145	1245	1345	1445	1545	1613	1645	1713	1745	1815	1845	1915	1946	2045	2101	2143
44	St Nikola-Struden a.	0612	...	0755	0826	...	1003	...	...	...	...	...	...	...	...	...	...	1827	...	1927	1958	2057	2114	...
81	**Emmersdorf** an der Donau a.	...	...	...	...	...	1145	...	...	...	...	...	...	...	...	...	...	...	...	...	...	...	...	...

K – Daily until Oct. 26. To / from Krems an der Donau (Table **991**).
L – From Oct. 27.
N – Until Oct. 23.
a – Ⓐ only.

993 ST PÖLTEN - KREMS and TULLN — 2nd class only

km		⚒	Ⓐ	Ⓐ	Ⓐ	⚒	⚒	⚒	⚒	†	⚒	†											Ⓐ		
0	**St Pölten** Hbf d.	0425	0450	0550	0556	0614	0633	0708	0731	0731	0731	0740	0811	0933	...	1036	1133	...	1236	1333	...	1436	1517	1534	...
11	Herzogenburg d.	0440	0506	0606	0611	0640	0647	0728	0752	0752	0754	0754	0821	0949	0952	1046	1149	1152	1246	1349	1352	1446	1526	1551	1552
	Tulln a.	0529	|	0659	|	0735	|	|	0836	0836	|	|	|	1035	|	|	1235	|	|	1435	|	|	|	1635	|
30	**Krems** an der Donau a.	...	0537	...	0639	...	0718	0756	...	...	0823	0823	0845	...	1024	1110	...	1224	1310	...	1424	1510	1555	...	1624

		Ⓐ				Ⓐ				
St Pölten Hbf d.	1636	1717	1733	...	1836	...	1935	...	2040	2141
Herzogenburg d.	1646	1726	1749	1752	1846	1848	1951	1954	2101	2153
Tulln a.	|	|	1835	|	|	1935	2035	|	|	|
Krems an der Donau a.	1710	1755	...	1824	1910	...	...	2027	2131	2220

km		Ⓐ	Ⓐ	Ⓐ	⚒	⚒	⚒		⚒	⚒	⚒
	Krems an der Donau d.	0433	0455	...	0539	...	0603	0616	...	0640	...
0	Tulln d.	|	|	0502	|	0542	|	|	0624	|	0704
38	Herzogenburg d.	0506	0527	0546	0611	0628	0632	0647	0709	0713	0743
49	**St Pölten** Hbf a.	0522	0541	0604	0627	...	0642	0703	0717	0723	0751

				⚒													Ⓐ				Ⓐ				Ⓑ
Krems an der Donau d.	0720	0836	...	...	0947	1034	...	1147	1234	...	1347	1434	...	1547	1634	...	...	1747	1834	...	...	1946	2020	...	2051
Tulln d.	|	|	0755	0907	|	|	1007	|	|	1207	|	|	1407	|	|	1607	1707	|	|	1807	1907	|	|	2007	|
Herzogenburg d.	0752	0907	0910	1010	1013	1105	1110	1213	1305	1310	1413	1505	1510	1613	1705	1710	1810	1813	1905	1910	1951	2015	2045	2101	2123
St Pölten Hbf a.	0808	...	0925	...	1022	...	1125	1222	...	1325	1422	...	1527	1622	...	1727	...	1822	...	1925	2006	2023	2055	2116	2132

994 ST PÖLTEN - MARIAZELL — Narrow gauge 2nd class only

km		▲	▲ ‡	P 🚂	▲ ⒶV	▲ ©	▲	▲	◇ Ⓐ	◇ ©	
0	**St Pölten** Hbf d.	0734	0834	0935	1034	1034	1334	1639	1954	2108	...
12	Ober Grafendorf d.	0757	0857	1010	1055	1056	1355	1700	2015	2129	...
31	Kirchberg a. d. Pielach d.	0832	0933	1046	1129	1129	1434	1736	2052	2203	...
43	Frankenfels d.	0852	0955	|	1149	1149	1455	1757	2113	2224	...
48	Laubenbachmühle d.	0902	1006	1130	1158	1159	1505	1808	2122	2233	...
57	Winterbach ● d.	0918	1023	|	1213	1214	1521	1824	...	...	...
67	Gösing d.	0937	1043	|	1230	1231	1537	1841	...	...	...
80	Mitterbach ● d.	1002	1108	|	1254	1255	1602	1905	...	...	...
84	**Mariazell** a.	1010	1115	1244	1300	1302	1608	1912	...	...	...

	◇	◇	z	R	▲ ⒶV	◇	P 🚂	◇ ©‡	◇ Ⓐ	◇ ©
Mariazell d.	...	0756	1153	1200	1304	1502	1627	1657	1659	1807
Mitterbach ● d.	...	0802	1159	1206	1310	1508	|	1703	1705	1813
Gösing d.	...	0827	1232	1239	1335	1538	|	1731	1731	1841
Winterbach ● d.	...	0842	1247	1254	1350	1553	|	1746	1746	1856
Laubenbachmühle d.	0650	0903	1304	1311	1406	1610	1736	1807	1807	1914
Frankenfels d.	0659	0912	1312	1320	1415	1618x	|	1815x	1816	1923
Kirchberg a. d. Pielach d.	0720	0934	1333	1341	1434	1639	1807	1836	1837	1944
Ober Grafendorf d.	0757	1009	1408	1416	1510	1714	1850	1909	1910	2019
St Pölten Hbf a.	0818	1029	1431	1443*	1531	1738	1916	1931	1930	2039

P – Runs on July 5 and Oct. 4 only. PANORAMIC 760. Conveys (12) and ✕. Steam train with special fares.
R – July 26 - Oct. 31.
V – Until Oct. 23.
x – Stops on request.
z – Not July 26 - Oct. 31.
‡ – Conveys ✕ on © until Oct. 26.
● – Trains stop on request.
* – On Ⓐ terminates at St Pölten Alpenbahnhof (a. 1435).
▲ – July 26 - Oct. 31 runs up to 19 minutes later.
◇ – July 26 - Oct. 31 runs up to 16 minutes **earlier**.

996 WIEN - BRATISLAVA via Marchegg — 2nd class only

km																					
0	**Wien** Südbahnhof d.	0528	0628	0728	0828	0928	1028	1128	1228	1328	1428	1528	1628	1728	1828	1928	2028	2128	2228	2324*	0024*
47	Marchegg 🏛 d.	0616	0704	0816	0904	1016	1104	1216	1304	1416	1504	1616	1704	1816	1904	2016	2104	2216	2304	0016	0116
53	Devínska Nová Ves 🏛 a.	0623	0711	0823	0911	1023	1111	1223	1311	1423	1511	1623	1711	1823	1911	2023	2111	2223	2311	0023	0123
66	**Bratislava** Hlavná a.	0637	0725	0837	0925	1037	1125	1237	1325	1437	1525	1637	1725	1837	1925	2037	2125	2237	2325	0037	0137

	①–⑤																				
Bratislava Hlavná d.	0450	0550	0700	0750	0900	0950	1100	1150	1300	1350	1500	1550	1700	1750	1900	1950	2100	2150	2300	2350	0050
Devínska Nová Ves 🏛 d.	0504	0604	0714	0804	0914	1004	1114	1204	1314	1404	1514	1604	1714	1804	1914	2004	2114	2204	2314	0004	0104
Marchegg 🏛 d.	0512	0614	0722	0814	0922	1014	1122	1214	1322	1414	1522	1614	1722	1814	1922	2014	2122	2214	2322	0014	0114
Wien Südbahnhof a.	0558	0658	0758	0858	0958	1058	1158	1258	1358	1458	1558	1658	1758	1858	1958	2058	2158	2258	2358	0103*	0203*

* – From / to suburban platforms 21/22.

997 WIEN - BRATISLAVA via Bruck an der Leitha

km		2		2	2	2	2	*IC* 405 K✕		2		2		*IC* 403 K✕	2	2	2	©M	2	2	2	*IC* 407 ✕	2
0	**Wien** Südbahnhof **1250** d.	0105	...	0510	0611	0705	0805	...	...	0905	and at	1505	...	...	1605	1705	1805	...	1912	2005	2105	...	2305
	Wien Westbahnhof **1250** d.	|	...	|	|	|	|	0800	...	|	the same	|	...	1536	|	|	|	...	|	|	|	2150	|
	Wien Meidling d.	|	...	|	|	|	|	0815	...	|	minutes	|	...	1550	|	|	|	1844	|	|	|	2205	|
41	Bruck an der Leitha **1250** d.	0132	...	0535	0639	0732	0832	|	...	0932	past each	1532	...	|	1632	1732	1832	1926	1939	2032	2132	|	2332
69	Kittsee 🏛 d.	0158	...	0553	0701	0758	0858	0908	...	0958	hour until	1558	...	1639	1658	1758	1858	1945	2005	2058	2158	2255	2358
74	**Bratislava** - Petržalka 🏛 a.	0203	...	0559	0707	0803	0903	0914	...	1003		1603	...	1645	1703	1803	1903	1952	2010	2103	2203	2302	0003
92	**Bratislava** Hlavná a.	...	...	...	...	...	...	0944	...	...		...	...	1715	...	...	...	...	...	...	...	2332	...

km		2Ⓐ	2©	*IC* 400 ✕	2	2Ⓐ	©M	2	2	2	2	*IC* 402 K✕		2		2		*IC* 404 K✕	2	2	2		2
0	**Bratislava** Hlavná d.	...	...	...	...	...	...	...	...	...	...	1052	...	...	and at	...	...	1841	...	...	...	...	...
18	**Bratislava** - Petržalka 🏛 d.	0429	0448	0547	0600	0638	0653	0733	0833	0933	1033	1122	...	1133	the same	1833	...	1911	1940	2033	2133	...	2333
23	Kittsee 🏛 d.	0434	0454	|	0606	0643	0700	0739	0839	0939	1039	1128	...	1139	minutes	1839	...	1917	1946	2039	2139	...	2339
51	Bruck an der Leitha **1250** d.	0500	0520	|	0631	0704	0732	0807	0907	1007	1107	|	...	1207	past each	1907	...	|	2014	2107	2207	...	0007
89	**Wien** Meidling a.	|	|	0646	|	|	0809	|	|	|	|	1219	...	|	hour until	|	...	2007	|	|	|	...	|
104	**Wien** Westbahnhof **1250** a.	|	|	0709	|	|	...	|	|	|	|	1232	...	|		|	...	2028	|	|	|	...	|
	Wien Südbahnhof **1250** a.	0533	0548	...	0700	0731	...	0834	0934	1034	1134	...	...	1234		1934	...	...	2041	2134	2234	...	0034

K – From / to Košice (Table **1180**).
M – © from Nov. 28. (2) and ✕ Bratislava - Mürzzuschlag and v.v. See also Table **981**.

UNZMARKT - TAMSWEG 998

2nd class only; Narrow gauge *Murtalbahn*

km		Ⓐe	Ⓐ		③B 🚂	Ⓐ	Ⓒ 🚌	②A 🚂		Ⓐ	Ⓒ 🚌	③B 🚂	Ⓒ	Ⓐ	Ⓐ	⑥k 🚌	† 🚌	†	Ⓐ 🚌
0	**Unzmarkt** d.	...	0715	0918	...	1118	1118	...	1318	1518	1518	...	1718	1718	1850	1850	1918	2049	2130
27	Murau-Stolzalpe d.	0632	0800	1000	1015	1200	1200	1250	1400	1600	1600	1655	1800	1812	1928	1930	2000	2125	2210
34	St Lorenzen d.	0644	0810	1010	1035	1210	1210	1310	1410	1610	1612	|	1810	1822	...	1938	2010s	2135	2218s
44	Stadl an der Mur d.	0702	0824	1024	1105	1224	1220	1343	1424	1624	1628	1745	1824	1836	...	1949	2020s	2149	2229s
65	**Tamsweg** a.	0735	0855	1055	1153	1255	1240	1431	1455	1655	1655	1830	1855	1907	...	2008	2040	2220	2250

	Ⓐ 🚌	Ⓐ			Ⓐe	Ⓐ	Ⓒ 🚌		Ⓐ	Ⓒ 🚌	③B 🚂		②A 🚂	Ⓒ 🚌	Ⓐ	Ⓐ 🚌	†	①–④ r 🚌	⑤⑥k 🚌
Tamsweg d.	...	...	...	0657	0752	0904	0905	1104	1304	1305	1335	1504	1615	1705	1704	1820	1900	...	2010
Stadl an der Mur d.	...	...	...	0728	0824	0935	0930	1135	1335	1330	1425	1535	1710	1730	1735x	1840	1931	1950	2030
St Lorenzen d.	...	...	...	0743	0838	0949	0945	1149	1349	1345	|	1549	1732	1745	1749	1853	1945	|	2043
Murau-Stolzalpe d.	0510	0615	...	0802	0850	1002	1000	1202	1402	1400	1500	1602	1745	1800	1810	1905	1958	2009	2053
Unzmarkt a.	0550	0653	...	0840	...	1040	1040	1240	1440	1440	...	1640	...	1840	1844	...	2036	2040	2130

A – ② June 23 - Sept. 8.
B – ③ June 24 - Sept. 9.

e – Not July 13 - Sept. 11, Nov. 2.
k – Not Aug. 15.
r – Not Oct. 26, Dec. 8.
s – Stops to set down only.
x – Stops on request.

🚂 – Steam train. Special fares payable.

Operator: Steiermärkische Landesbahnen. ✆ +43 (0) 3532 2233

POLAND

Operator: Polskie Koleje Państwowe (PKP).

Services: All trains convey first and second class seating, **except** where shown otherwise in footnotes or by '2' in the train column, or where the footnote shows sleeping and/or couchette cars only. Descriptions of sleeping (🛏) and couchette (▬) cars appear on page 10. As shown in the individual tables, Russian/Ukrainian sleeping car services cannot be used for journeys in or between Poland and Germany unless seating cars are also conveyed. Note that train numbers often change en route by one or two digits. In station names, Gł. is short for Główny or Główna, meaning main station.

Timings: Valid **December 14, 2008 - December 12, 2009**, incorporating ongoing amendments. Further changes are expected in June. Many trains, including long-distance and express services, do not run over the Christmas and Easter periods. A number of long-distance trains running only in high summer (particularly to coastal resorts) are not shown due to lack of space.

Tickets: A higher fare is payable for travel by all *EC*, *IC*, *Ex*, and *IR* trains. Special fares are payable on *TLK* (Tanie Linie Kolejowe / cheap railway lines) trains.

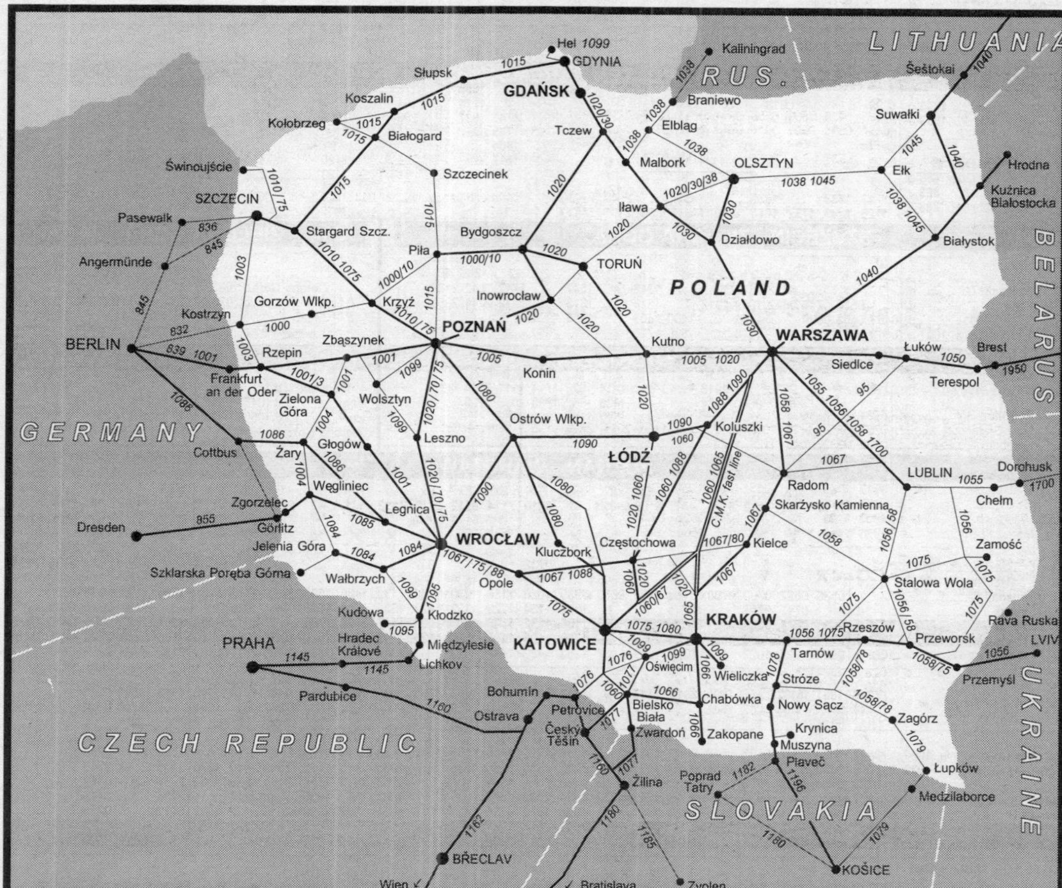

KOSTRZYN - KRZYŻ - PIŁA - BYDGOSZCZ 1000

km		82100 A	◇	◇	◇	◇	88100 81102	◇	◇	◇	◇ q	449 C
0	**Kostrzyn** d.	...	0535	0900	...	1100	1258	...	1630	1825	...	2244
43	Gorzów Wlkp. d.	0505	0616	0942	...	1144	1344	...	1714	1908	...	2331
103	Krzyż a.	0610	0709	1034	...	1236	1439	...	1806	1959	...	0028
103	Krzyż **1010** d.	0650	...	...	1040	...	1453	1630	...	...	2005	0128
161	**Piła 1010** a.	0753	...	...	1131	...	1557	1721	...	...	2056	0232
248	**Bydgoszcz 1010** a.	0919	...	...	...	...	1719	...	...	...	...	0413
	Warszawa ▲ a.	1310	...	...	...	...	2120	...	...	...	...	0810

	◇	◇ q	◇	18103 88101	◇	◇	◇	◇ q	◇	28101 A	◇	448 C
Warszawa ▲ d.	...	...	...	0647	...	...	...	...	...	1500	...	2130
Bydgoszcz 1010 d.	...	...	...	1052	...	...	...	...	...	1851	...	0134
Piła 1010 d.	...	0920	...	1225	...	1450	...	1720	...	2019	...	0256
Krzyż **1010** a.	...	1011	...	1323	...	1541	...	1811	...	2117	...	0352
Krzyż d.	0516	...	1114	1334	1445	...	1621	...	1815	2149	...	0449
Gorzów Wlkp. d.	0610	...	1210	1433	1540	...	1713	...	1910	2256	2310	0550
Kostrzyn a.	0650	...	1250	1517	1620	...	1752	...	1950	...	2350	0631

A – [12] Gorzów Wlkp. (**83106 / 38107**) - Krzyż (**82100**) - Warszawa - Lublin and v.v. [12] Gorzów Wlkp. - Krzyż - Poznań - Kraków - Rzeszów and v.v. Conveys [12] Szczecin - Krzyż - Lublin and v.v.

C – 🛏 1, 2 cl., ▬ 2 cl. and [2] (reclining) Berlin - Kostrzyn 🏛 - Warszawa and v.v. Conveys 🛏 1, 2 cl. Berlin - Kostrzyn 🏛 - Gdynia / Kaliningrad and v.v. Also conveys 🛏 1, 2 cl., ▬ 2 cl. and [2] (reclining) Berlin - Kostrzyn 🏛 - Poznań - Kraków and v.v.

q – To / from Chojnice.

◇ – Stopping train. 2nd class only.

▲ – Warszawa Centralna (Table **1020**).

1001 BERLIN - POZNAŃ and WROCŁAW

See Table **56** for train **441/440** Berlin - Moskva / St Petersburg and train **1248/440 441/1249** Berlin - Saratov (these are not available for journeys Germany - Poland or v.v.)

km		73100 73101 F	2 ◇	2 ◇ ①–⑤	2 ◇ ①–⑥	Ex 7111/0 [R]✕ Z	EN[R] 447 71008 J	67430 ◇ 2	EC 41 B	◇ 2	5881 ◇ 2	75103 75102 D	EC 341 [R]✕ M	◇ 2 b	EC 45 B	78243 ◇ 2 b	◇ 2 ①–⑤ q	5883 2 ◇	TLK 7116 ✕[R] Z	◇ 2 b	EC 47 B	5885 2 ◇	◇ 2	77200 81200 G	449 72002 A	449 83700 [R]🍷 U
	Berlin Hauptbahnhof .. **839** d.	...	...	...	...	...	0423	...	0629	...	...	...	0941	...	1229	...	...	...	...	...	1629	...	...	...	...	...
0	**Berlin** Ostbahnhof ...... **839** d.	...	...	...	...	...	0447	...	0640	...	...	...	0951	...	1240	...	...	...	...	...	1640	...	...	...	2104y	2104y
82	Frankfurt an der Oder. **839** a.	...	...	...	...	...	|	...	0730	...	...	...	|	...	1330	...	...	...	...	...	1730	...	...	...	|	|
82	Frankfurt an der Oder 🛃 ... d.	...	...	...	...	...	|	...	0733	...	0919	...	◐	...	1333	...	...	1519	...	...	1733	1846	...	...	◧	◧
93	Kunowice 🛃 .... d.	...	...	...	...	...	|	...	|	...	0932	...	|	...	|	...	...	1533	...	...	|	1859	...	...	|	|
105	Rzepin .... a.	...	...	...	...	...	|	...	0755	...	0943	...	|	...	1355	...	...	1544	...	...	1755	1910	...	...	|	|
105	Rzepin .... **1003** d.	...	0453	...	...	...	0602s	...	0805	0800	0956	...	|	1154	1405	...	*1448*	1558	...	1600	1805	1924	...	...	|	|
176	**Zielona Góra** .... **1003** d.	0546	0620	...	...	...	|	...	|	0928	|	...	|	1319	*1526*a	...	|	|	...	1727	|	2050	...	...	|	|
229	Glogów .... d.	0704	0745	...	...	...	|	0505	|	1045	|	...	|	1435	|	...	|	|	...	1845	|	...	...	...	|	|
**	**Zielona Góra** .... d.	|	|	...	...	0454	|	0640	|	|	|	1006	|	|	|	1400	|	|	1547	|	|	...	1845	2341	|	|
180	Zbąszynek .... **1099** d.	|	|	0359	0502	0604	|	0807	|	|	1053	1120	|	|	1443	1520	1604	1655	1714	|	|	...	1959	0054	|	|
186	Zbąszyń .... **1099** d.	|	|	0406	0509	|	|	0812	|	|	...	1127	|	|	|	1526	1610	1701	1722	|	|	...	2005	0101	|	|
261	**Poznań** Gł. .... a.	|	|	0515	0615	0655	0733	0915	0927	|	...	1218	|	|	1527	1635	1720	1805	1817	|	1927	...	2115	0150	|	0146
329*	**Wrocław** Gł. .... a.	0913	1003	...	...	|	|	...	|	1303	...	...	1537	1816	|	...	...	...	|	2103	|	...	...	|	|	0432
	Katowice **1075** .... a.	1225	...	...	...	|	|	...	|	...	...	...	1820	...	|	...	...	...	|	...	|	...	...	|	|	0725
	Kraków **1075** .... a.	1419	...	...	...	|	|	...	|	...	...	...	1956	...	|	...	...	...	|	...	|	...	...	|	|	0918
	Warszawa Centralna **1005**. a.	...	...	...	...	1000	1035	...	1220	...	...	...	...	...	1820	...	...	...	2210	...	2220	...	...	0605	0810	...
	Warszawa Wschodnia **1005**. a.	...	...	...	...	1022	1052	...	1232	...	...	...	...	...	1837	...	...	...	2222	...	2232	...	...	0617	0827	...

	5880 ◇ 2	77241 ◇ 2	TLK 1717 [R]✕ Z	◇ 2	EC 46 B	5882 77021 ◇ 2	EC 44 B	◇ 2 b	EC 340 [R]✕ M	77223 ◇ 2	57103 57102 D	5884 ◇ 2	◇ 2 b	77231 ◇ 2	◇ 2	7635 ◇ 2	EC 40 B	77231 ◇ 2	◇ 2	Ex 1711/0 [R]✕ Z	EN[R] 446 17009 J	37100 37101 F	448 27003 A	18201 77203 G	38704 448 [R]🍷 U	
Warszawa Wschodnia **1005** d.	...	...	0543	...	0723	...	1123	...	...	...	...	...	...	...	...	...	1623	...	...	1723	1742	...	2118	2232	...	...
Warszawa Centralna **1005** d.	...	...	0555	...	0735	...	1135	...	...	...	...	...	...	...	...	...	1635	...	...	1735	1755u	...	2130	2245	...	...
Kraków **1075** .... d.	...	...	|	...	|	...	|	...	0723	...	...	...	...	...	...	...	|	...	...	|	|	1347	|	|	1945	...
Katowice **1075** .... d.	...	...	|	...	|	...	|	...	0854	...	...	...	...	...	...	...	|	...	...	|	|	1534	|	|	2134	...
Wrocław Gł. .... d.	...	...	|	0550	|	...	|	0950	1132	...	...	...	1350	...	1550	...	|	...	1750	|	|	1836	|	|	0038	...
Poznań Gł. .... d.	...	0745	0923	|	1027	1045	1427	|	|	1445	1539	...	|	1645	|	1745	1927	1945	|	2034	2101u	|	|	0240	0305	...
Zbąszyń .... **1099** d.	...	0854	1016	|	|	1151	|	|	|	1553	1631	...	|	1753	|	1854	|	2052	|	|	|	|	|	0329	|	...
Zbąszynek .... **1099** d.	...	0901	1024	|	|	1158	1511	|	|	1600	1641	1645	|	1800	|	1901	|	2100	|	2127	|	|	|	0338	|	...
Zielona Góra .... a.	...	1012	1140	|	|	|	|	|	|	...	1757	|	|	...	|	2012	|	...	|	2239	|	|	|	0452	|	...
Glogów .... d.	...	...	...	0758	|	|	|	1158	|	...	...	|	1558	...	1759	2129	|	...	1958	...	|	2045	|	...	|	...
Zielona Góra .... **1003** d.	0620	...	...	0918	|	|	|	1314	|	...	...	|	1714	...	1911	...	|	...	2114	...	|	2159	|	...	|	...
Rzepin .... **1003** a.	0747	...	...	1054	1150	1257	1550	1437	|	...	...	1743	1837	...	2034	...	2050	...	2238	...	|	...	|	...	|	...
Rzepin .... d.	0802	...	...	...	1200	1315	1600	...	|	...	...	1753	...	...	...	...	2100	...	...	...	2242u	...	|	...	|	...
Kunowice 🛃 .... d.	0813	...	...	...	|	1328	|	...	|	...	...	1804	...	...	...	...	|	...	...	...	|	...	|	...	|	...
Frankfurt an der Oder 🛃 ... a.	0826	...	...	...	1222	1341	1622	...	◐	...	...	1817	...	...	...	...	2120	...	...	...	2308	...	◧	...	◧	...
Frankfurt an der Oder **839** d.	...	...	...	...	1227	...	1627	...	|	...	...	...	...	...	...	...	2123	...	...	...	2310	...	|	...	|	...
Berlin Ostbahnhof ...... **839** a.	...	...	...	...	1315	...	1715	...	1719	...	...	...	...	...	...	...	2215	...	...	...	0002	...	0806y	...	0806y	...
Berlin Hauptbahnhof ... **839** a.	...	...	...	...	1327	...	1727	...	1730	...	...	...	...	...	...	...	2227	...	...	...	0029	...	...	...	...	...

1003 SZCZECIN - ZIELONA GÓRA

km		◇ 2 h	◇ 2 h	◇ 2 h	◇ 2 p	◇ 2 h	◇ 2 p	◇ 2	◇ 2 h	◇ 2	◇ 2	◇ 2	◇ 2	◇ 2	84500 E	
0	**Szczecin** Gł. .... d.	...	...	...	0612	0812	1042	...	1242	1442	1542	...	1742	1942	2133	...
104	Kostrzyn .... d.	...	0510	0715	0842	1059	1312	...	1513	1712	1813	...	2012	2214	2355	...
136	Rzepin **1001** .... d.	0453	0553	0800	...	1154	...	1400	1600	...	1855	1924	...	...	|	...
207	**Zielona Góra** . **1001** a.	0619	0717	0926	...	1318	...	1526	1726	...	...	2050	...	...	0145	...

	◇ 2 p	48501 Q	◇ 2	◇ 2	◇ 2	◇ 2	◇ 2 h	◇ 2	◇ 2 p	◇ 2 h	◇ 2	◇ 2 h	◇ 2 h	◇ 2		
Zielona Góra .. **1001** d.	...	0215	...	...	0620	...	0918	...	...	1314	1525	1714	1911	2114	...	...
Rzepin **1001** .... d.	...	|	...	...	0747	0800	1054	...	...	1438	1652	1838	2055	2238	...	...
Kostrzyn .... d.	0322	0406	0422	0622	...	0842	...	1122	1322	1522	1735	1922	2137	...	...	...
Szczecin Gł. .... a.	0520	0553	0625	0820	...	1038	...	1320	1520	1721	1935	2120	...	...	...	...

1004 ZIELONA GÓRA - ŻAGAŃ

km		w 2 ◇	m 2 ◇	w 2 ◇	2 ◇	w 2 ◇	m 2 ◇	w 2 ◇
0	**Zielona Góra** d.	0622	...	1020	...	1530	...	1820
54	Żary .... d.	0732	0800	1133	1318	1640	1808	1930
67	Żagań .... a.	|	0814	|	1332	|	1822	*2027*
	Węgliniec .. a.	0825	...	1226	...	1733	...	2023

	2 ◇	2 ◇	w 2 ◇	m 2 ◇	w 2 ◇	m 2 ◇	w 2 ◇	w 2 ◇
Węgliniec ... d.	...	...	0742	...	1142	...	1602	2045
Żagań .... d.	0451	0811	|	1117	|	1539	|	|
Żary .... d.	0504	0826	0843	1129	1244	1552	1700	2140
Zielona Góra a.	0614	...	0953	...	1354	...	1809	...

1005 POZNAŃ - WARSZAWA

For other trains Warszawa - Wrocław and v.v. see Table 1090

km		IC 7100 [R] ✕ P	TLK 7118 [R] 🍷	Ex 7110 [R] ✕ Z	IC 6103 6102 [R]✕ ①–⑥	EN 447 71008 [R] J	IC 8102 [R] ✕ ①–⑥	IC 6105/4 [R] ✕ ①–⑤	EC 41 [R] ✕ B	TLK 8210 [R] 🍷 §	Ex 7114 [R] ✕ ②–⑥	Ex 6112 6113 [R] ✕	Ex 8110 81410 [R] ✕	Ex 7112 [R] ✕ V	TLK 71412 [R] ✕ ⑦ j	EC 45 [R] ✕ B	IC 6101 6100 [R]✕	IC 7102 [R] ✕ C	81102 81103	IC 8100 81400 [R]✕ ⑧	TLK 7116 [R] 🍷 Z	EC 47 [R] ✕ B	81200 77200 G	83700 81010 S
	Szczecin Gł. **1010** .... d.	...	...	...	...	...	0540	...	...	0732	...	...	1057	...	...	...	...	...	1307	1600	...	...	2315	2235
	Wrocław Gł. **1070** .... d.	...	...	...	0506	...	|	0606	...	|	...	1006	|	...	...	...	1406	...	|	|	...	...	|	|
0	**Poznań** Gł. .... d.	0630	0622	0700	0730	0733s	0800	0830	0930	1026	1130	1230	1330	1430	1430	1530	1630	1730	⊡	1830	1822	1930	0220	|
100	Konin .... d.	|	0743	0752	|	0827s	|	|	1020	1134	1222	1322	1421	1530	1534	1620	|	1829	|	|	1932	2020	0331	|
179	Kutno .... **1020** d.	|	0844	0838	|	0917s	0927	1006	1106	1232	1308	1406	1509	1617	1623	1706	|	|	1950	2007	2027	2106	0426	0639
306	**Warszawa** Centralna ... **1020** a.	0915	1010	1000	1020	1035s	1039	1120	1220	1405	1425	1520	1625	1735	1800	1820	1920	2035	2120	2125	2210	2220	0605	0810
311	**Warszawa** Wschodnia . **1020** a.	0927	1027	1022	1032	1052	1057	1137	1232	1422	1437	1542	1642	1747	1817	1837	1937	2047	2132	2137	2222	2232	0617	0827

	TLK 1716 1717 [R]✕ Z	IC 1801 18401 [R]✕ ①–⑥	18102 18103	EC 46 [R] ✕ B	IC 1600 1601 [R]✕	TLK 2811 [R] 🍷 §	Ex 1713 [R] ✕ V	EC 44 [R] ✕ B	Ex 1612 1613 [R] ✕	IC 1703 [R] ✕ C	Ex 1811 18411 [R] ✕	IC 1603 1602 [R]✕ ⑧	IC 1701 [R] ✕ L	EC 40 [R] ✕ B	IC 1803 [R] ✕ ⑧	Ex 1711 [R] ✕ Z	EN 446 17009 [R]✕ J	TLK 1719 [R] ✕	IC 1605 1604 [R]✕ ⑧	Ex 1715 [R] ✕ ⑧	18010 38705 [R] S	77203 18201 G		
Warszawa Wschodnia . **1020** d.	0543	0623	0647	0723	0818	0942	1018	1123	1218	1323	1418	1523	1618	1623	1643	1723	1742	1748	1824	1923	2118	2232	...	...
Warszawa Centralna ... **1020** d.	0555	0635	0700	0735	0835	0955	1035	1135	1235	1335	1435	1535	1630	1635	1655	1735	1755u	1800	1835	1935	2130	2245	...	...
Kutno .... **1020** d.	0720	0754	0829	0853	|	1122	1157	1253	1353	|	1554	|	|	1753	1813	1854	1919u	1929	1954	2054	2303	0019	...	...
Konin .... d.	0812	|	|	0932	|	1215	1243	1332	1434	1532	1637	|	|	1832	|	1936	2004u	2017	|	2136	|	0113	...	...
Poznań Gł. .... a.	0919	0929	⊡	1024	1124	1328	1352	1424	1526	1635	1731	1821	1916	1924	1937	2030	2101u	2132	2122	2231	|	0225	...	...
Wrocław Gł. **1070** .... a.	...	|	|	...	1353	|	...	...	1802	...	|	2051	...	...	|	...	...	...	2350	...	|	|	...	...
Szczecin Gł. **1010** .... a.	...	1159	1514	...	...	1611	...	...	...	...	2000	...	...	...	2159	...	...	...	...	...	0631	0529	...	...

NOTES FOR TABLES 1001 - 1005

A – 🛏 1, 2 cl., ▬ 2 cl. and [2] (reclining) Berlin - Warszawa and v.v. For other cars see Tables **51**, **56**.
B – BERLIN WARSZAWA EXPRESS – [12] and ✕ [R], Berlin - Warszawa and v.v. Special fares apply.
C – ⑧ Dec. 14 - June 19 and Sept. 1 - Dec. 12.
D – [12] Zielona Góra - Poznań - Bydgoszcz - Gdynia and v.v.
E – June 20 - Aug. 31: [12] Świnoujście - Szczecin - Katowice - Bielsko Biała.
F – [12] Zielona Góra - Wrocław - Przemyśl and v.v.
G – [12] Szczecin / Zielona Góra - Poznań - Warszawa - Terespol and v.v.
J – JAN KIEPURA – 🛏 1, 2 cl. Amsterdam / Basel / München - Warszawa - Moskva and v.v. (journey 2 nights). 🛏 1, 2 cl., ▬ 2 cl., [2] and 🍷 Amsterdam - Köln - Warszawa and v.v.; see Table **24**.
L – ⑧ Dec. 14 - June 26 and Aug. 30 - Dec. 12.
M – WAWEL – [12] and ✕ (Hamburg ♣) - Berlin - Wrocław - Katowice - Kraków and v.v.
P – ①–⑥ Dec. 14 - June 27 and Aug. 31 - Dec. 12.
Q – June 19 - Aug. 30: [12] Bielsko Biała - Katowice - Szczecin - Świnoujście.
S – 🛏 1, 2 cl. and ▬ 2 cl. Świnoujście - Szczecin - Warszawa and v.v.
U – 🛏 1, 2 cl., ▬ 2 cl. and [2] (reclining) Berlin - Kostrzyn 🛃 - Poznań - Kraków and v.v.
V – ①–⑤ Dec. 14 - June 19 and Sept. 1 - Dec. 12 (not Nov. 11).
Z – [12] and ✕ Zielona Góra - Poznań - Warszawa and v.v.

a – Arrival time.
b – From / to Szczecin.
h – To / from Wrocław Gł.
j – ⑦ Dec. 14 - June 14 and Sept. 6 - Dec. 12.
m – To / from Legnica.
p – Not Nov. 11.
q – Not Nov. 1, 11.
s – Stops to set down only.
u – Stops to pick up only.
w – To / from Jelenia Góra. (Table **1084**).
y – Berlin **Lichtenberg**.

◇ – Stopping train.
*** –** Via Zielona Góra.
§ – To / from Lublin.

♣ – For dates of running see Table **56**.
**** –** Zielona Góra - Zbąszynek: *58 km*.
◐ – 🛃 between Berlin and Wrocław is Forst / Zasieki; ticketing point is Forst.
◧ – 🛃 between Berlin and Poznań / Warszawa is Kostrzyn.
⊡ – Via Bydgoszcz.

SZCZECIN - POZNAŃ 1010

km																									
		2 ◇ ①–⑥	83106 83107	2 ◇	82100 82101	IC 8102 R ✕	83100 83101	84102 84103	TLK 8210 R ✕	2 ◇	83104 83105	Ex 8110 81410 R ✕	TLK 8310 83410 R ✕	81102 81103	81100 81101	2 ◇	IC 8100 81400	87102 87500	83500 83501	2 ◇	83510 83200	TLK 83704 83700	83700 81010	449 81010	81200 81201
		e	G		k	Q	P	m	h k	q	r				L		M		D		B	K	C	p	A
	Świnoujście d.	...	...	...	...	...	...	...	...	...	...	0918x	1011z	...	...	...	1422c	...	...	...	1755j	2043	2043	...	...
0	**Szczecin** Gł. **1015** d.	...	...	...	0505	0540	0550	0705	0732	...	0950	1057	1150	1307	1450	...	1600	1630	1655	1755	1955	2235	2235	...	2315
15	Szczecin Dąbie **1015** d.	...	...	...	0518	0553	0604	0719	0748	...	1005	1111	1204	1323	1504	...	1614	1645	1711	1813	2011	2215	2253	...	2330
40	Stargard Szczeciński **1015** d.	...	...	...	0536	0609	0623	0738	0806	...	1024	1128	1221	1341	1522	...	1632	1706	1734	1839	2035	2314	2314	...	2350
130	Krzyż **1000** d.	0515	0628	0625	0650	0659	0728	0842	0906	1040	1128	1224	1317	1453	1626	1630	1728	1814	1841	2004	2138	0049	0128	0128	0056
	Piła **1000** d.	0606	|	0716	0806	|	|	|	|	1131	|	|	|	1607	|	1721	|	|	|	*2056*	|	|	0302	0302	|
	Bydgoszcz **1000** a.	...	|	*0859*	0919	|	|	|	|	*1311*	|	|	|	1719	|	*1855*	|	|	|	|	|	|	0413	0413	|
213	**Poznań** Gł. a.	...	0730	...	|	0750	0830	0943	1010	...	1230	1318	1411	|	1725	...	1821	1915	1945	2120	2243	0146	|	|	0159
	Wrocław Gł. **1070** a.	...	1020	...	|	|	1120	...	|	...	1518	|	|	|	...	...	|	2220	...	...	0135	0432	|	|	|
	Warszawa Cent. **1005** a.	...	|	...	1310	1039	|	...	1405	...	|	1625	|	2120	...	...	2125	...	...	...	|	|	0810	0810	0605
	Kraków Gł **1075, 1080** a.	...	1519	...	...	...	1619	...	...	...	2018	...	2125	...	...	...	...	...	...	...	0657	0918	...	...	...

	2 ◇	38500 38501	65101 78101	2 ◇	IC 1801 18401	18100 18101	18102 18103	TLK 3811 38411 R ✕	TLK 2811 R ✕	38104 38105	2 ◇	48102 48103	78243 2 ◇	2 ◇	Ex 1811 18411 R ✕	38100 38101	IC 1803 R ✕ ⑧	38106 38107	28101 28100	448 18010	18010 38705	TLK 38704 38705	18200 18201	38201 38512	
		E			Q	L			h k	r		m	f			P	q	G	k	p	C	K	A	B	
Kraków Gł. **1075, 1080** d.	...	...	...	...	...	...	...	0535	..	0747	...	...	...	...	...	1147	...	1247	...	...	...	1945	...	2150	...
Warszawa Cent. **1005** d.	...	...	...	...	0635	...	0700	|	0955	|	...	...	...	...	1435	|	1655	|	1500	2130	2130	|	2245	|	...
Wrocław Gł. **1070** d.	...	...	0530	...	|	...	|	|	|	1235	...	...	...	...	|	1635	|	1735	|	|	|	0024	|	0312	...
Poznań Gł. d.	0640	0700	0838	...	0940	1103	|	1236	1338	1517	...	1630	1639	...	1741	1920	1946	2030	|	|	|	0305	0245	0600	...
Bydgoszcz **1000** d.	|	|	|	*0755*	|	|	1052	|	|	|	...	|	|	*1540*	|	|	|	|	1851	0134	0134	|	|	|	...
Piła **1000** d.	|	|	|	0920	|	|	1225	|	|	|	1550	|	|	1720	|	|	|	|	2013	0301	0301	|	|	|	...
Krzyż **1000** d.	0754	0815	0938	1011	1033	1204	1343	1330	1439	1619	1641	1732	1752	1811	1834	2022	2037	2129	2134	0357	0451	0451	0348	0703	...
Stargard Szczeciński **1015** d.	0915	0925	1038	...	1126	1307	1441	1428	1537	1721	...	1834	1915	...	1927	2123	2129	...	2234	...	0555	0555	0454	0807	...
Szczecin Dąbie **1015** a.	0937	0943	1055	...	1143	1324	1458	1445	1554	1738	...	1851	1937	...	1944	2140	2145	...	2251	...	0614	0614	0512	0825	...
Szczecin Gł. **1015** a.	0955	0959	1113	...	1159	1341	1514	1500	1611	1755	...	1908	1955	...	2000	2157	2159	...	2307	...	0631	0631	0529	0843	...
Świnoujście a.	...	...	...	...	1344b	...	...	1640t	...	...	...	...	...	...	2141v	...	...	...	...	...	0818	0818	...	1054j	...

km												
		◇ 2	◇ 2	◇ 2		◇ 2		◇ 2 S	◇ 2	◇ 2	◇ 2	
0	**Świnoujście** d.	0528	0640	0821	...	1150	...	1407	1528	1712	1940	...
101	Szczecin Dąbie a.	0708	0812	1000	...	1317	...	1548	1707	1846	2120	...
116	**Szczecin** Gł. a.	0727	1830	1017	...	1335	...	1606	1729	1904	2138	...

	◇ 2	◇ 2		◇ 2 q		◇ 2 S	◇ 2		◇ 2	◇ 2	
Szczecin Gł. d.	0512	0828	...	1143	...	1433	1543	...	1843	2043	...
Szczecin Dąbie d.	0527	0845	...	1159	...	1448	1601	...	1858	2059	...
Świnoujście a.	0710	1041	...	1329	...	1619	1743	...	2038	2229	...

A – Szczecin - Poznań - Warszawa - Terespol and v.v.
B – 1, 2 cl., 2 cl. and Szczecin - Poznań - Kraków - Przemyśl and v.v.; From Świnoujście to Przemyśl Apr. 9 - Sept. 27; from Przemyśl to Świnoujście Apr. 8 - Sept. 26.
C – 1, 2 cl., 2 cl. and Świnoujście - Szczecin - Warszawa and v.v.
D – June 19 - Aug. 30: 1, 2 cl., 2 cl. and Szczecin - Zakopane.
E – June 20 - Aug. 31: 1, 2 cl., 2 cl. and Zakopane - Szczecin.
G – Gorzów Wlkp - Krzyż - Poznań - Kraków - Rzeszów and v.v.
K – 1, 2 cl., 2 cl., and ✕ Świnoujście - Kraków and v.v.
L – Szczecin - Poznań - Ostrów Wlkp - Łódź and v.v.
M – ⑧ (not June 11).
P – Szczecin - Poznań - Kraków - Przemyśl and v.v.

Q – ①–⑥ (not June 12).
R – ①–⑥ (not June 12).
S – ①–⑤ (not Nov. 1, 11).
b – ⑥ June 20 - Aug. 29.
c – ⑦ June 21 - Aug. 30.
e – Not June 12, 13.
f – From Zielona Góra.
h – To / from Białystok.
j – Apr. 9 - Sept. 27.
k – To / from Lublin.

m – To / from Częstochowa.
p – To / from Berlin.
q – Not June 11.
r – To / from Rzeszow.
t – June 20 - Aug. 30.
v – June 19 - Aug. 31.
x – June 20 - Sept. 1.
z – June 21 - Aug. 31.
◇ – Stopping train.

SZCZECIN - KOSZALIN - GDYNIA - GDAŃSK 1015

km																								
		Ex 8114 R ✕	48201 48503	◇	TLK 8316 R ✕	85102 85103	2 ◇	Ex 83414 R ✕	◇ 2	81104 81113	85100 85101	48101 48100	2 ◇	2 ◇	38103 38102	2 ◇	2 ◇	85104 85105	TLK 83702 R ✕	82500 83202	2 ◇	38108 38109	2 ◇	81502 81503	
		O	C		p	G		J p		E	G	H		w	M			t	D	F		L		A	
0	**Szczecin** Gł. § d.	...	...	...	...	0555	...	...	0735	1005	1152	...	1235	...	...	1535	...	1703	...	...	...	...	1933	2010	...
15	Szczecin Dąbie § d.	...	...	...	...	0613	...	...	0755	1022	1209	...	1253	...	...	1553	...	1718	...	...	...	...	1953	2024	...
40	Stargard Szczeciński § d.	...	...	0455	...	0633	...	...	0821	1042	1227	...	1319	...	...	1619	...	1737	...	...	...	...	2019	2042	...
*231	**Poznań** Gł. d.	...	0121	|	...	|	0520	...	|	|	|	1125	|	1212	1322	|	1445	|	...	...	1645	1723	|	|	...
*135	Piła d.	...	0325	|	...	|	0730	...	|	|	|	1311	|	1418	1515	|	1647	|	...	...	1836	1916	|	|	...
*64	Szczecinek d.	...	0421	|	...	|	0839	...	|	|	|	1406	|	1534	1616	|	1756	|	...	...	1935	2016	|	|	...
151	Białogard a.	...	0512	0630	...	0804	0940	...	1002	1210	1356	1458	1457	1634	1708	1809	1859	1906	...	...	2034	2108	2157	2207	...
151	Białogard ▶ d.	...	0514	0646	...	0805	0941	...	1003	1213	1358	1500	1510	1636	1710	1811	1910	1909	...	...	2036	2110	2158c	2209	...
187	Kołobrzeg ▶ a.	...	0543	|	...	|	1017	...	|	|	|	|	|	1711	1740	|	1945	|	...	...	|	|	|	|	...
**43	Kołobrzeg d.	0258	...	|	0717	|	...	0925	|	|	|	|	|	...	...	|	...	|	1855	1940	|	|	|	|	...
175	**Koszalin** d.	0341	...	0708	0805	0825	...	1011	1027	1242	1417	1520	1535	...	...	1838	...	1927	1951	2034	2053	2131	2220c	2231	...
242	Słupsk d.	0428	...	...	0853	0918	...	1058	1120	1333	1505	1613	1640	...	...	1943	...	2017	2048	2132	...	2218	...	2322	...
294	Lębork d.	0503	...	...	0927	0954	...	1156	...	1407	1558	...	...	...	...	...	...	2052	2131	2218	...	...	...	2358	...
353	**Gdynia** Gł. ... **1020, 1030** a.	0546	...	...	1015	1042	...	1238	...	1455	1647	...	...	...	...	...	...	2140	2228	2305	...	...	...	0042	...
353	**Gdynia** Gł. ... **1020, 1030** d.	0600	...	...	1040	1054	...	1252	...	1518	1709	...	...	...	...	...	...	2143	2252	2325	...	...	...	0104	...
362	Sopot **1020** a.	0609	...	...	1049	1104	...	1302	...	1527	1718	...	...	...	...	...	...	2151	2303	2334	...	...	...	0113	...
374	**Gdańsk** Gł. ... **1020, 1030** a.	0626	...	...	1106	1121	...	1321	...	1545	1736	...	...	...	...	...	...	2208	2319	2352	...	...	...	0129	...
	Warszawa C. **1030** a.	1110	...	...	1600	...	...	1806	...	...	...	...	...	...	...	...	...	...	...	0455	...	...	...	...	...

	2 ◇	2 ◇	2 ◇	83109 83108	2 ◇	38203 28501	58105	TLK 38703 ✕	83102 83103	58101 58102	84101 84100	2 ◇	2 ◇	2 ◇	2 ◇	18105 18104	2 ◇	TLK 3816 R ✕	58103 58102	Ex 38415 R ✕	84200 84502	Ex 1815 R ✕	18503 18502		
				L	w	F	t	D	M	G	H					E		p	G	K p	C	P	B		
Warszawa C. **1030** d.	...	...	...	...	...	2220	...	...	...	...	...	...	...	...	...	...	...	1000	...	1300	...	1600	...	...	...
Gdańsk Gł. .. **1020, 1030** d.	...	...	...	...	...	0315	0602	0756	...	0916	...	...	...	...	...	1406	...	1455	1633	1745	...	2037	0219	...	...
Sopot **1020** d.	...	...	...	...	...	0332	0617	0812	...	0931	...	...	...	...	...	1421	...	1510	1648	1800	...	2052	0234	...	...
Gdynia Gł. ... **1020, 1030** a.	...	...	...	...	...	0342	0628	0823	...	0943	...	...	...	...	...	1431	...	1520	1659	1813	...	2104	0244	...	...
Gdynia Gł. ... **1020, 1030** d.	...	...	...	...	...	0403	0631	0852	...	1008	...	...	...	...	...	1450	...	1535	1713	1828	...	2117	0306	...	...
Lębork d.	...	...	...	...	...	0504	0723	0954	...	1057	...	...	...	...	...	1541	...	1633	1802	1915	...	2203	0400	...	...
Słupsk d.	...	...	0511	0528	...	0548	0758	1059	...	1133	1204	1227	...	1417f	...	1616	1737	1708	1837	1955	...	2238	0447	...	...
Koszalin d.	0434	...	0612	0626	...	0655	0855	1159	...	1220	1302	1329	...	1534	1643	1703	1837	1757	1928	2057	...	2327	0545	...	...
Kołobrzeg a.	|	...	|	|	...	0750	|	1247	...	|	|	|	...	|	|	|	|	1843	|	2144	...	0009	|	...	...
Kołobrzeg ▶ d.	|	...	|	|	0820	...	|	...	0950	|	|	|	1415	|	|	|	|	...	|	...	2230	...	|	...	...
Białogard ▶ a.	0452	...	0633	0643	0856	...	0911	...	1026	1236	1319	1352	1453	1557	1708	1719	1900	...	1944	...	2300	...	0608	...	...
Białogard d.	0453	0530	0636	0644	0857	...	0913	...	1028	1239	1325	1400	1503	1558	1712	1720	1908	...	1946	...	2304	...	0609	...	...
Szczecinek d.	|	0630	|	0736	1007	...	|	...	1124	|	1428	|	1617	|	1826	|	|	...	|	...	2359	...	|	...	...
Piła d.	|	0736	|	0832	1119	...	|	...	1222	|	1529	|	1727	|	1946	|	|	...	|	...	0056	...	|	...	...
Poznań Gł. a.	|	0936	|	1020	1326	...	|	...	1420	|	1718	|	1933	|	2144	|	|	...	|	...	0251	...	|	...	...
Stargard Szczeciński § d.	0640	...	0815	...	...	...	1050	...	...	1421	...	1545	...	1745	...	1853	2055	...	2119	...	...	...	0740	...	...
Szczecin Dąbie § a.	0703	...	0837	...	...	...	1109	...	...	1438	...	1607	...	1809	...	1910	2117	...	2137	...	...	...	0800	...	...
Szczecin Gł. § a.	0720	...	0855	...	...	...	1126	...	...	1454	...	1623	...	1827	...	1927	2135	...	2153	...	...	...	0817	...	...

A – June 20 - Aug. 31: 2 cl. and Szczecin - Białystok.
B – June 19 - Aug. 30: 2 cl. and Białystok - Szczecin.
C – Apr. 8 - Sept. 26 from Katowice; Apr. 9 - Sept. 27 from Kołobrzeg: 1, 2 cl., 2 cl. and Katowice - Kołobrzeg and v.v.
D – From Kołobrzeg June 20 - Aug. 30: Kołobrzeg - Warszawa - Katowice (arrive 0947) - Kraków (1148); from Kraków June 19 - Aug. 29: Kraków (depart 1914) - Katowice (depart 2117) - Warszawa - Kołobrzeg: 1, 2 cl., 2 cl., and ✕.
E – Szczecin - Gdańsk - Białystok and v.v.
F – From Sept. 1: 1, 2 cl., 2 cl. and Kołobrzeg - Kielce - Kraków and v.v.
G – Szczecin - Gdańsk - Olsztyn and v.v.
H – Katowice - Wrocław - Poznań - Słupsk and v.v.

J – June 21 - Aug. 31.
K – June 20 - Aug. 30.
L – Przemyśl - Poznań - Słupsk and v.v.
M – Kraków - Poznań - Kołobrzeg and v.v.
O – ①–⑥ (not June 12).
P – ⑧ (also Oct. 31; not June 11).

c – June 20 - Aug. 31 depart Białogard 2220, arrive Koszalin 2254.
f – ①–⑤ (not Nov. 1, 11).
j – Not Nov. 11.

p – To / from Kraków.
t – To / from Tczew.
w – From / to Wrocław.

* – Distance from Białogard.
** – Distance from Koszalin.
§ – See also Table **1010**.
◇ – Stopping train.

▶ – Other local trains: From Białogard to Kołobrzeg: 0550, 0640**j**, 0941, 1242, 1415, 1532, 1636, 2115. From Kołobrzeg to Białogard: 0550**j**, 0641**f**, 1200, 1531, 1625, 1830, 2024.

1020 GDYNIA - BYDGOSZCZ - ŁÓDŹ, POZNAŃ, KATOWICE and KRAKÓW

km		TLK 81010 449 D	52104 52105 Q	54110 54111 b	TLK 5112 Ⓡ✕ N	51108 51109 M h	56100 56101	56104 56105	82100 82101 B	54100 54101	54100 43103	57104 57105	53102 53103 E	57102 57103 G	52102 53103 Q ⑧	54102 54103	52100 52101 P	16112 16113 z	56102 56103	81102 81103 F	51502 51102 j	30500 57109 h	57100 57101 J	54502 54503 C	56510 56200 A	
0	**Gdynia** Gł. .... **1030** d.	...	...	...	...	...	0437	...	...	0732	0732	0844	...	1031	...	1134	...	...	1430	...	1530	...	1746	1851	2134	...
9	Sopot .... **1030** d.	...	...	...	...	...	0447	...	...	0742	0742	0854	...	1041	...	1144	...	...	1440	...	1540	...	1756	1901	2144	...
21	**Gdańsk** Gł. .... **1030** d.	...	...	...	...	...	0506	...	...	0800	0800	0912	...	1100	...	1201	...	...	1458	...	1559	...	1815	1921	2204	...
53	Tczew .... **1030** d.	...	...	...	...	...	0535	...	...	0828	0828	0939	...	1130	...	1227	...	...	1526	...	1627	...	1841	1949	2242	...
181	**Bydgoszcz** Gł. .... d.	0421	0512	0604	0630	0722	0720	...	0922	1025	1025	1125	1125	1319	1322	1425	1522	...	1713	1726	1825	...	2026	2152	0040	...
	Olsztyn .... d.	|	|	|	|	|	|	0624	|	|	|	|	|	|	|	|	|	1324	|	|	|	1707**x**	|	|	|	...
	Iława .... d.	|	|	|	|	|	|	0720	|	|	|	|	|	|	|	|	|	1422	|	|	|	1812**x**	|	|	|	...
232	**Toruń** Gł. .... d.	0520	0613	0706	0732	0828	|	0906	1023	1128	1128	|	1224	|	1421	1526	1621	1609	|	1831	1926	2010	|	2258	|	...
287	Włocławek .... d.	0602	0654	0747	0816	0910	|	|	1104	1207	1207	|	1304	|	1502	1606	1701	|	|	1912	2007	|	|	2342	|	...
227	Inowrocław .... d.	|	|	|	|	|	0802	0955	|	|	|	1209	|	1401	|	|	|	1653	1754	|	|	2056	2109	|	0125	...
342	Kutno .... d.	0639	0731	0825	0854	0946	|	|	1142	1246	1246	|	1342	|	1539	1645	1739	|	|	1950	2043	|	|	0021	|	...
410	**Łódź** Kaliska .... a.	|	|	1008	|	|	|	|	|	1414	1414	|	|	|	|	1815	|	|	|	|	2215	|	|	0200**e**	|	...
469	**Warszawa** Cent .... a.	0810	0900	|	1015	1115	|	|	1310	|	|	|	1510	|	1710	|	1910	|	|	2120	...	|	|	|	|	...
474	**Warszawa** Wsch .... a.	0827	0922	|	1037	1132	|	|	1322	|	|	|	1522	|	1722	|	1922	|	|	2132	...	|	|	|	|	...
283	Gniezno .... d.	...	...	|	...	...	0852	1044	...	|	|	1300	...	1450	...	|	...	1745	1845	...	...	2148	2201	|	0216	...
334	**Poznań** Gł. .... a.	...	...	|	...	...	0937	1133	...	|	|	1345	...	1534	...	|	...	1830	1930	...	...	2238	2247	|	0303	...
	Wrocław **1070** .... a.	...	...	|	...	...	1220	1420	...	|	|	...	...	...	...	|	...	2119	2220	...	...	...	...	|	0540	...
483	**Częstochowa Osobowa** ▲ d.	...	...	1226	...	...	...	...	...	1637	1647	...	...	...	...	2029	...	...	...	...	...	...	...	0407	...	...
526	Zawiercie .... ▲ d.	...	...	1301	...	...	...	...	...	1712	1721	...	...	...	...	2104	...	...	...	...	...	...	...	0448	...	...
561	Sosnowiec Gł. .... ▲ d.	...	...	1330	...	...	...	...	...	1740	|	...	...	...	...	2133	...	...	...	...	...	...	...	0524	...	...
569	**Katowice** .... ▲ a.	...	...	1341	...	...	...	...	...	1751	|	...	...	...	...	2144	...	...	...	...	...	...	...	0535	...	...
615	**Kraków** Gł. .... a.	...	...	...	...	...	...	...	...	...	1919	...	...	...	...	...	...	...	...	...	...	...	...	...	...	...

	75100 75101 K	75109 30501 h	15102 15502 j	18102 18103 F	65101 65100	25101 28511 P	45100 45101	61113 61112 z	75102 75103 G	25102 25103 Q ①–⑥	35102 35103 E	75104 75105	34102 45103	45102 45103	28100 28101 B	65105 65104	TLK 1513 1512 Ⓡ H	65102 65103	15108 15109 M h	45110 45111 b	25104 25105 Q	TLK 18011 448 D	65201 65200 A	45503 45502 C		
Kraków Gł. .... d.	...	...	...	...	...	...	...	...	...	...	...	...	0905	...	...	...	...	...	...	...	...	...	...	...	...	...
Katowice .... ▲ d.	...	...	...	...	...	...	0613	...	...	...	...	...	|	1010	...	...	...	...	...	1415	...	...	...	2245	...	...
Sosnowiec Gł. .... ▲ d.	...	...	...	...	...	...	0625	...	...	...	...	...	|	1022	...	...	...	...	...	1426	...	...	...	2257	...	...
Zawiercie .... ▲ d.	...	...	...	...	...	...	0656	...	...	...	...	...	1046	1052	...	...	...	...	...	1456	...	...	...	2328	...	...
Częstochowa Osobowa ▲ d.	...	...	...	...	...	...	0734	...	...	...	...	...	1140	1140	...	...	...	...	...	1534	...	...	...	0007	...	...
Wrocław **1070** .... d.	...	...	...	...	0535	...	|	0635	...	...	...	...	|	|	...	1335	...	1535	...	|	...	...	2335	|	...	...
Poznań Gł. .... d.	0523	0540	...	...	0823	...	|	0936	1223	...	...	1415	|	|	...	1618	...	1810	...	|	...	...	0228	|	...	...
Gniezno .... d.	0601	0642	...	...	0901	...	|	1017	1301	...	...	1450	|	|	...	1656	...	1849	...	|	...	...	0310	|	...	...
Warszawa Wsch .... d.	|	|	...	0647	|	0844	|	|	|	1047	1244	|	|	|	1437	|	1548	|	1653	|	1837	2118	|	|	...	...
Warszawa Cent .... d.	|	|	...	0700	|	0900	|	|	|	1100	1300	|	|	|	1500	|	1600	|	1705	|	1900	2130	|	|	...	...
Łódź Kaliska .... d.	|	|	0547	|	|	|	0953	|	|	|	|	|	1357	1357	|	|	|	|	|	1753	|	|	|	0203**e**	...	...
Kutno .... d.	|	|	0724	0829	|	1031	1125	|	|	1229	1429	|	1527	1527	1629	|	1730	|	1831	1924	2032	2303	|	0339	...	...
Inowrocław .... d.	0654	0735	|	|	0954	|	|	1109	1355	|	|	1541	|	|	|	1748	|	1943	|	|	|	|	0404	|	...	...
Włocławek .... d.	|	|	0801	0903	|	1107	1200	|	|	1306	1505	|	1601	1601	1706	|	1805	|	1906	1959	2108	2339	|	0415	...	...
Toruń Gł. .... d.	|	0825	0842	0946	|	1150	1241	1152	|	1350	1547	|	1644	1644	1751	1830	1848	|	1955	2041	2149	0021	|	0507	...	...
Iława .... d.	|	0941**x**	|	|	|	|	|	1317	|	|	|	|	|	|	|	1950	|	|	|	|	|	|	|	|	...	...
Olsztyn .... a.	|	1036**x**	|	|	|	|	|	1415	|	|	|	|	|	|	|	2049	|	|	|	|	|	|	|	|	...	...
Bydgoszcz Gł. .... d.	0753	...	0952	1043	1048	1247	1353	...	1454	1447	1644	1633	1757	1757	1848	...	1944	2040	2052	2139	2246	0116	0515	0627	...	...
Tczew .... **1030** d.	1026	...	1228	...	1321	...	1629	...	1726	...	...	1909	2034	2034	...	...	...	2316	...	...	...	...	0758	0903	...	...
Gdańsk Gł. .... **1030** a.	1052	...	1254	...	1347	...	1655	...	1751	...	...	1935	2102	2102	...	...	...	2342	...	...	...	...	0824	0929	...	...
Sopot .... **1030** a.	1108	...	1310	...	1404	...	1712	...	1808	...	...	1952	2119	2119	...	...	...	0001	...	...	...	...	0842	0948	...	...
Gdynia Gł. .... **1030** a.	1119	...	1322	...	1418	...	1724	...	1822	...	...	2006	2130	2130	...	...	...	0012	...	...	...	...	0855	0959	...	...

A – 🛏 1, 2 cl., ▬ 2 cl. and (12) Gdynia - Wrocław and v.v.
B – (12) Szczecin / Gorzów Wlkp. - Lublin and v.v.
C – ⑤⑦ (daily June 19 - Aug. 31) also Nov. 10, 11: 🛏 1, 2 cl., ▬ 2 cl. and (12) Gdynia - Katowice - Bielsko Biała and v.v.
D – 🛏 1, 2 cl., ▬ 2 cl. and (2) Świnoujście / Berlin - Warszawa and v.v.
E – (12) Bydgoszcz - Warszawa - Lublin - Przemyśl and v.v.
F – (12) Szczecin / Kostrzyn - Bydgoszcz - Warszawa and v.v.
G – (12) Gdynia - Poznań - Zielona Góra and v.v.

H – ⑧ (not June 11).
J – ⑧ (daily June 20 - Aug. 31).
K – ①–⑥ (daily June 20 - Aug. 31).
M – To / from Białystok (Table **1040**).
N – ①–⑥ (not June 12).
P – To / from Lublin.
Q – To / from Chełm.

b – To / Bielsko Biała.
e – Łódź **Widzew**.
h – Not Nov. 11.
j – From / to Hel June 20 - Aug. 31.
x – June 20 - Aug. 31.
z – From / to Ełk and Suwałki.

▲ – For additional trains see Table **1060**.

1030 GDYNIA - GDAŃSK - WARSZAWA

km		52106 52107 k ①–⑥	TLK 5210 Ⓡ U b	IC 5306 Ⓡ✕ ①–⑥	53100 53101	Ex Ⓡ 8114 51414 q	5302 53400 Ⓡ✕ z	54112 54113	7 55000 A	Ex 5310 Ⓡ✕ H	Ex 5410 Ⓡ✕ y	TLK 8316 Ⓡ✕ e	54104 54105 D g	Ex 5312 83414 Ⓡ t	IC 5300 Ⓡ ✕	51100 R	51530 2 G	IC 5100 Ⓡ ✕	Ex 51410 Ⓡ✕ D f	TLK 53702 Ⓡ C		83202 53502 B	
0	**Gdynia** Gł. .... **1038** ▲ d.	...	0345	0504	...	0600	0655	...	0807	0850	1000	1040	...	1252	1500	...	1623	1658	1812	1859	...	2325	...
9	Sopot .... **1038** ▲ d.	...	0355	0514	...	0610	0705	...	0816	0900	1010	1050	...	1303	1510	...	1632	1709	1823	1909	...	2335	...
21	**Gdańsk** Gł. .... **1038** ▲ d.	...	0415	0535	...	0630	0725	...	0834	0920	1030	1110	...	1325	1530	...	1649	1730	1840	1929	...	2355	...
53	Tczew .... **1038** d.	...	0442	|	...	0703	0755	...	0908	0951	1059	1136	...	1351	|	...	1721	1758	|	1956	...	0024	...
72	Malbork .... **1038** d.	...	0500	|	...	0721	0811	...	0925	1009	1117	1154	...	1409	1613	...	1740	1817	|	2015	...	0043	...
**	**Olsztyn** .... **1020 1038** d.	0515	|	|	0640	|	|	0837	...	|	|	|	1255	|	|	1705	|	|	|	|	...	|	...
141	Iława .... **1020 1038** d.	|	0550	|	|	0806	0857	0934	...	1054	1203	1246	|	1454	1659	|	1831	1902	2006	2106	...	0135	...
201	Działdowo .... d.	0641	0629	|	0819	0846	|	1016	...	1135	|	1329	1413	1537	|	1819	1915	1942	2047	2149	...	0220	...
251	Ciechanów .... d.	0716	0703	|	0851	|	|	1050	...	|	1310	1403	1448	|	|	1853	1952	|	|	2225	...	0301	...
345	**Warszawa** Wschodnia .... a.	0910	0845	0945	1040	1100	1145	1238	...	1344	1455	1547	1623	1745	1945	2039	2141	2155	2300	0009	...	0445	...
350	**Warszawa** Centralna .... a.	0922	...	1000	1050	1110	1201	1257	...	1400	1510	1600	1640	1806	2001	2050	2151	2205	2310	0025	...	0455	...
	Katowice **1060** .... a.	...	...	|	|	...	|	1654	...	|	1810	|	2054	|	|	...	...	...	...	0420	...	|	...
	Kraków Gł. **1065** .... a.	...	...	1310	1620	...	1510	...	...	1710	...	2128	...	2110	2302	...	...	...	...	0626	...	1034	...

	15101	IC 1501 Ⓡ ✕	Ex 15411 Ⓡ✕ D f	15531 2 G	IC 3500 3501 Ⓡ✕	TLK 3817 Ⓡ✕ e	45505 45105 J g	Ex 4511 Ⓡ y ①–⑥	Ex 3513 38415 Ⓡ p	Ex 3511 Ⓡ✕ H	45112 45113	Ex Ⓡ 1815 15415 q	IC 3507 Ⓡ✕ ⑧	8 55002 A	35100 35101	TLK 2511 Ⓡ U b	Ex 45411 Ⓡ✕ ⑦ y	3503 35401 Ⓡ✕ z	25106 25107 k ⑧	38203 35503 B		TLK 35702 Ⓡ C	
Kraków Gł. **1065** .... d.	...	...	...	...	0600	0450	...	...	1000	1200	...	...	1400	...	1210	...	...	1600	...	1710	...	2244	...
Katowice **1060** .... d.	...	...	...	...	|	|	0647	0900	|	|	1047	...	|	...	|	...	1500	|	...	|	...	0047	...
Warszawa Centralna .... d.	0640	0700	0800	0815	0900	1000	1105	1200	1300	1500	1522	1600	1700	...	1732	...	1800	1900	1938	2220	...	0445	...
Warszawa Wschodnia .... d.	0649	0709	0810	0823	0915	1010	1114	1215	1315	1515	1533	1610	1715	...	1748	1815	1815	1915	1947	2230	...	0500	...
Ciechanów .... d.	0832	|	|	1010	|	1156	1255	1358	|	|	1705	|	|	...	2014	1958	1958	|	2204	0015	...	0642	...
Działdowo .... d.	0910	|	1020	1047	|	1232	1331	|	1527	1724	1806	1823	|	...	2056	2034	2029	|	2239	0051	...	0719	...
Iława .... **1020 1038** d.	|	1001	|	1131	1201	1313	|	1512	1610	1807	1829	1904	|	...	|	2116	2113	2202	|	0137	...	0802	...
Olsztyn .... **1020 1038** a.	1022	|	|	|	|	|	1441	|	|	|	1942	|	|	...	2209	|	|	|	2349	|	...	|	...
Malbork .... **1038** d.	...	1048	1143	1223	1252	1405	...	1556	1656	1854	...	1949	|	2117	...	2207	2202	2249	...	0226	...	0851	...
Tczew .... **1038** d.	...	1106	|	1242	|	1424	...	1614	1715	1915	...	2008	|	2144	...	2226	2220	2309	...	0244	...	0910	...
Gdańsk Gł. .... **1038** ▲ a.	...	1133	1227	1307	1337	1452	...	1639	1742	1942	...	2034	2132	2210	...	2252	2246	2335	...	0310	...	0936	...
Sopot .... **1038** ▲ a.	...	1151	1240	1321	1355	1509	...	1656	1759	1959	...	2051	2149	2227	...	2310	2303	2352	...	0329	...	0954	...
Gdynia Gł. .... **1038** ▲ a.	...	1204	1252	1332	1409	1520	...	1709	1813	2012	...	2104	2203	2238	...	2322	2317	0006	...	0340	...	1006	...

A – (2) Gdynia - Malbork - Kaliningrad and v.v. Conveys Berlin - Kaliningrad cars and v.v.; see Tables **51 / 1038**.
B – Dec. 14 - June 18 and Aug. 31 - Dec. 12 to Kołobrzeg; June 19 - Aug. 30 to Hel. Dec. 14 - June 19 and Sept. 1 - Dec. 12 from Kołobrzeg; June 20 - Aug. 31 from Hel: 🛏 1, 2 cl., ▬ 2 cl., (12) and ✕ Kołobrzeg / Hel - Gdynia - Warszawa - Kielce - Kraków and v.v.
C – 🛏 1, 2 cl., ▬ 2 cl. and (2) Gdynia - Zakopane and v.v.
D – June 20 - Aug. 31.
G – June 6, 7, 11, 12, 13, 14, June 20 - Aug. 31.
H – To / from Przemyśl (Tables **1058 / 1075**).

J – June 19 - Dec. 12.
R – June 1 - Dec. 12.
U – ①–⑤ (not Nov. 11).

b – To / from Lublin.
e – From / To Kołobrzeg.
f – To / from Hel.
g – To / from Racibórz.
k – To / from Kielce.
p – June 20 - Aug. 30 to Kołobrzeg.

q – From / to Kołobrzeg on dates in Table **1015**.
t – June 21 - Aug. 31 from Kołobrzeg.
x – Not Apr. 12, May 2.
y – To / from Bielsko Biała.
z – To / from Zakopane on dates in Table **1066**.

** – Olsztyn - Działdowo: *84 km*.
▲ – Frequent local trains run between **Gdynia** and **Gdańsk**.

GDYNIA - GDAŃSK - OLSZTYN and KALININGRAD 1038

km		70140 70141 w	51104 51105	55000 7 A 2		85102 85103	70142 70143 2	81104 81105	85100 85101	81502 81503 C	
	Szczecin Gł. **1015** d.	...	...	...	...	0555	...	1010	1152	2010	...
0	**Gdynia** Gł. **1030** d.	0539	0724	0807	...	1054	1226	1518	1709	0104	...
9	Sopot **1030** d.	0548	0734	0816	...	1105	1235	1528	1719	0114	...
21	**Gdańsk** Gł. **1030** d.	0604	0753	0834	...	1124	1251	1547	1738	0132	...
53	Tczew **1030** d.	0634	0822	0908	...	1154	1324	1617	1812	0200	...
72	Malbork **1030** ▲ d.	0652	0842	0935	...	1215	1343	1640	1831	0221	...
101	Elbląg ▲ d.	|	0906	1000	...	1239	|	1706	1853	0246	...
156	Braniewo ▦ a.	|	|	1048	...	|	|	|	|	|	...
219	**Kaliningrad** § a.	|	|	1535	...	|	|	|	|	|	...
	Iława d.	0752	|	...	...	|	1441	|	|	|	...
200	**Olsztyn** a.	0846	1033	...	...	1406	1545	1833	2021	0408	...
471	*Białystok* **1045** a.	...	1508	...	...	...	...	2305	...	0840	...

	58101 58100	70120 70121	18105 18104		58103 58102	15105 15104	55002 8 B 2	70122 70123 m	18503 18502 D	
Białystok **1045** d.	...	...	0700	...	...	1240	...	...	1910	...
Olsztyn d.	0629	0820	1124	...	1340	1706	...	1953	2344	...
Iława d.	|	0928	|	...	|	|	...	2053	|	...
Kaliningrad § d.	|	|	|	...	|	|	1823	|	|	...
Braniewo ▦ d.	|	|	|	...	|	|	1950	|	|	...
Elbląg ▲ d.	0758	|	1253	...	1518	1839	2040	|	0108	...
Malbork **1030** ▲ d.	0826	1022	1318	...	1544	1905	2117	2146	0133	...
Tczew **1030** d.	0847	1043	1337	...	1605	1924	2144	2205	0152	...
Gdańsk Gł. **1030** a.	0913	1111	1403	...	1631	1950	2210	2233	0217	...
Sopot **1030** a.	0930	1125	1420	...	1647	2007	2227	2247	0233	...
Gdynia Gł. **1030** a.	0943	1135	1431	...	1659	2020	2238	2257	0244	...
Szczecin Gł. **1015** a.	1454	...	1927	...	2151	...	...	...	0817	...

A – Conveys 🛏 1, 2 cl. Berlin (**449**) (previous night) - Kostrzyn ▦ - Bydgoszcz (**65200**) - Gniezno (**65201**) - Tczew (**55001**) - Braniewo ▦ (**7**) - Kaliningrad (Table **51**).
B – Conveys 🛏 1, 2 cl. Kaliningrad (**8**) - Braniewo ▦ (**55002/3**) - Tczew (**56200**) - Gniezno (**56201**) - Bydgoszcz (**448**) - Kostrzyn ▦ - Berlin (Table **51**).
C – June 20 - Aug. 31: ▬ 2 cl. and [12] Szczecin - Białystok.
D – June 19 - Aug. 30: ▬ 2 cl. and [12] Białystok - Szczecin.

m – Not Aug. 15.
w – Not Aug. 16.

§ – Moskva time (2 hours ahead of Polish time, 1 hour ahead of Kaliningrad time).
▲ – Additional local trains run Malbork - Elbląg and v.v. Journey 30 minutes.

PKP, BCh, LG WARSZAWA - BIAŁYSTOK - VILNIUS and HRODNA 1040

km		79821 2 ①–⑤	77641 2	138 2	41500 41501 L	77621 2 ①–⑤	11201	77623 ⑥⑦ 2	91001 910	194 2	41103 ①–⑥ g	79825 2 ⑧	51109 51509 b	77625 2	134 2		61105 61104 S	77627 2	*TLK* 8210 T	31106 31107 N	77103 V	15107 W	79827 2	77645 2	41100 41101 P	140 19021 2	77119 2 ⑤⑦	🚌 99928 A Ⓡ
0	**Warszawa** Centralna d.	...	...	...	0405	...	0605	...	0725	...	0925	...	1125	...	...	...	1325	...	1415	1525	1625	1725	...	...	1925	...	2025	2300
5	**Warszawa** Wschodnia d.	...	...	...	0414	...	0625	...	0734	...	0940	...	1140	...	...	...	1334	...	1436	1534	1634	1734	...	...	1934	...	2034	|
184	**Białystok** a.	...	...	...	0645	...	0845	...	0955	...	1155	...	1356	...	...	...	1555	...	1651	1755	1855	1955	...	...	2155	...	2255	|
184	**Białystok** d.	0509	...	...	0700	0625	...	0900	1010	...	...	1205	1406c	1444	...	...	...	1655	...	1810	...	...	2005	...	...	2222	...	0200
225	Sokółka d.	0555	0627	...	0752	0711	...	0946	1056	...	...	1245	1449c	1531	...	...	...	1745	...	1855	...	...	2045	2050	...	2308	...	|
324	**Suwałki** d.	0727	|	...	0941	|	...	|	1244	...	...	1417	1634c	|	...	...	...	|	...	2035	...	...	2217	|	...	|	...	|
377	Šeštokai ▦ ◐ § a.	...	|	...	...	|	...	|	1448	1503	...	...	...	|	...	...	...	|	...	...	...	...	...	|	...	|	...	|
471	**Kaunas** **1810** § a.	...	|	...	...	|	...	|	...	*1709*x	...	...	...	|	...	...	...	|	...	...	...	...	...	|	...	|	...	0720
575	**Vilnius** § a.	...	|	...	...	|	...	|	...	1756	...	...	...	|	...	...	...	|	...	...	...	...	...	|	...	|	...	0900
241	Kuźnica Białostocka a.	...	0643	...	...	0728	...	1002	...	...	...	...	...	1548	...	...	...	1801	...	...	...	...	...	2106	...	2325	...	...
241	Kuźnica Białostocka ▦ d.	...	...	0715	...	...	...	...	...	...	...	...	...	...	1635	...	...	...	...	...	...	...	...	...	...	0025	...	...
268	Hrodna ▦ ‡ a.	...	...	0910	...	...	...	...	...	...	...	...	...	...	1830	...	...	...	...	...	...	...	...	...	...	0220	...	...

	77110 V	14100 14101 P	77622 2	*TLK* 2810 T	139 2	77640 2	79820 2	51106 W	77624 2	13106 13107 N	137 2	79822 2 ⑧	16104 16105 S	15508 15108 b	14103 ⑧g	77118 2 ⑤⑦		77628 2	77644 2	193 2	910 91002	79824 2	11200	133 19026 2	14500 14501 L		🚌 99927 B Ⓡ	
Hrodna ▦ ‡ d.	...	...	...	...	0535	...	...	...	...	...	1005	...	...	...	...	...	...	...	...	...	...	...	...	1950	...	...	...	...
Kuźnica Białostocka ▦ a.	...	...	...	...	0530	...	...	...	...	...	1000	...	...	...	...	...	...	...	...	...	...	...	...	1945	...	...	...	...
Kuźnica Białostocka d.	...	...	0520	...	...	0605	...	...	0733	...	...	...	...	...	...	...	...	1459	1643	...	...	...	...	2025	...	...	...	...
Vilnius § d.	...	...	|	...	...	|	...	...	|	...	...	...	...	...	...	...	...	|	|	1140	...	...	...	|	...	...	2200	...
Kaunas **1810** § d.	...	...	|	...	...	|	...	...	|	...	...	...	...	...	...	...	...	|	|	*1235*z	...	...	...	|	...	...	2330	...
Šeštokai ▦ ◐ § d.	...	...	|	...	...	|	...	...	|	...	...	...	...	...	...	...	...	|	|	1443	1508	...	...	|	...	...	|	...
Suwałki d.	...	...	|	...	...	|	0501	...	|	0730	...	0925	...	1058e	...	...	...	|	|	...	1525	1720	...	|	2048	...	|	...
Sokółka d.	...	...	0537	...	...	0621	0638	...	0749	0904	...	1058	...	1303e	...	...	...	1515	1659	...	1704	1857	...	2048	2227	...	|	...
Białystok a.	...	...	0620	...	...	...	0720	...	0832	0945	...	1136	...	1345e	...	...	...	1556	...	...	1745	1935	...	2132	2305	...	0220	...
Białystok d.	0500	0600	...	0700	...	...	...	0800	...	1000	...	...	1200	1400	1600	1655	...	...	...	...	1800	...	2000	...	2320	...	|	...
Warszawa Wschodnia a.	0720	0820	...	0919	...	...	...	1020	...	1220	...	...	1421	1620	1812	1920	...	...	...	...	2021	...	2217	...	0148	...	|	...
Warszawa Centralna a.	0734	0830	...	0950	...	...	...	1030	...	1230	...	...	1431	1700	1840	1945	...	...	...	...	2030	...	2235	...	0200	...	0500	...

A – ①③⑤ (daily June 13 - Sept. 12) 🚌 run by PKP InterCity. Ⓡ.
B – ②④⑥ (daily June 14 - Sept. 13) 🚌 run by PKP InterCity. Ⓡ.
L – From Bielsko Biała June 19 - Aug. 30; from Suwałki June 20 - Aug. 31: [12] Bielsko Biała - Warszawa - Suwałki and v.v.
N – [12] Kraków - Warszawa - Białystok - Suwałki and v.v.
P – [12] Bielsko Biała - Warszawa - Białystok and v.v.
S – [12] Wrocław - Częstochowa - Warszawa - Białystok and v.v.
T – [12] Szczecin - Poznań - Warszawa - Białystok and v.v.

V – ①–⑤ (not Nov. 1, 11).
W – To / from Ełk.
b – From / to Bydgoszcz (Table **1020**).
c – June 19 - Aug. 30.
e – June 20 - Aug. 31.
g – From / to Częstochowa.

x – Change at Marijampole (arrive 1539; depart 1558).
z – Change at Marijampole (arrive 1345; depart 1404).
§ – Lithuanian time (Polish time + 1 hour).
‡ – Belarus time (Polish time + 1 hour).
◧ – ▦ at Szypliszki (Poland) / Kalvarija (Lithuania).
◐ – ▦ at Trakiszki / Mockava; ticketing point is Mockava.

OLSZTYN - EŁK - BIAŁYSTOK 1045

km		◇ 2	51106 Y	81502 Z	◇ 2		◇ 2	◇ 2	51104 W	◇ 2 C	◇ 2	61113 A	◇ 2	81104 B	
0	**Olsztyn** d.	...	...	0411	...	...	0850	0943	1041	...	...	1425	1552	1845	...
120	Giżycko d.	...	...	0614	...	...	1116	|	1246	...	...	1637	|	2045	...
167	Ełk a.	...	...	0703	...	...	1205	1314	1332	...	...	1723	1920	2130	...
	Ełk d.	0541	0627	0715	0756	...	...	...	1344	1413	1620	1735	...	2144	...
	Suwałki a.	|	|	|	|	...	...	...	|	|	|	1930	...	|	...
271	**Białystok** a.	0721	0746	0840	0941	...	...	...	1508	1548	1755	...	...	2305	...

	◇ 2	◇ 2	18105 B	16112 A		15105 W	◇ 2	◇ 2	◇ 2 C	◇ 2	18503 Z	15107 Y		
Białystok d.	0526	...	0700	...	...	1240	1415	...	1700	1805	1910	2010	...	...
Suwałki d.	|	...	|	0820	...	|	|	...	|	|	|	|	...	...
Ełk a.	0706	...	0829	1013	...	1410	1601	...	1840	1942	2031	2128	...	...
Ełk d.	...	0747	0844	1028	...	1422	...	1625	...	...	2052	...	...	...
Giżycko d.	...	|	0934	1116	...	1509	...	1718	...	...	2149	...	...	...
Olsztyn a.	...	1110	1122	1316	...	1700	...	1926	...	...	2339	...	...	...

A – [12] Wrocław - Poznań - Olsztyn - Ełk - Suwałki and v.v.
B – [12] and ✕ Szczecin - Olsztyn - Ełk - Białystok and v.v.
C – ①–⑤ (also Nov. 1; not Nov. 11).

W – From / to Gdynia.
Y – To / from Warszawa.
Z – From / to Szczecin on dates in Table **1038**.

◇ – Stopping train.

WARSZAWA - BREST 1050

km		◇ 2 C	◇ 2		81201 B	◇ 2	◇ 2	◇ 2	◇ 2 C	209 A	◇ 2	31103 p	12 ⊠	◇ 2	◇ 2	◇ C 2		10 ⊠	10101 C	10105 q	◇ 2	◇	◇ 2	◇ 2	104 ⊠	◇ 2	◇ 2	441
0	**Warszawa** Centralna d.	...	...	...	0610	...	...	0804r	...	...	...	1115	...	...	1255r	...	...	1530	1630	1730	...	1750	...	1857r	2050	2057r	2257r	2315
5	**Warszawa** Wschodnia d.	...	...	...	0630	...	...	0813	...	...	...	1135	1250	...	1304	...	...	1540	1640	1739	...	1801	...	1906	2100	2106	2306	2342
93	Siedlce d.	...	...	...	0732	...	...	0948	...	...	...	1236	1347	...	1427	*1442*	...	1648	1740	1838	...	1937	...	2029	2208	2229	0029	⊠
121	Łuków d.	0530	0630	...	0752	0830	...	1019	1030	1100	1230	1257	|	1430	...	1530	...	1709	1800	1858	...	2008	2030	...	2230	...	...	|
173	Biała Podlaska d.	0622	0722	...	0837	0922	...	...	1122	1146	1322	1344	|	1522	...	1622	...	1756	1845	1945	...	...	2122	...	2317	...	...	|
210	Terespol ▦ a.	0709	0809	...	0925	1009	1123	...	1209	1237	1409	1430	1525	1609	...	1708	...	1842	1932	2035	2200	...	...	...	0003	...	...	0245
217	**Brest** ▦ ‡ a.	...	...	...	...	...	1244	...	...	1504	...	...	1741	...	...	...	...	2058	...	...	2318	...	...	...	0222	...	...	0516
	Moskva **1950** a.	...	...	...	...	...	...	...	...	0805	...	...	1059	...	...	...	...	1145	...	...	...	...	...	...	...	...	...	2035

	440	◇ 2	103 ⊠	◇ 2	◇ 2	10106 G	9 ⊠	◇ 2	◇ 2	◇ 2	◇ 2	10102 C	◇ 2	◇ 2 C	11 ⊠	13102 p	208 A	◇ 2	10502 ⑦	◇ 2	◇ 2	◇ 2	18200 B	◇ 2	◇ 2 C	◇ 2	◇ 2	
Moskva **1950** d.	0800	...	...	...	...	...	1650	...	...	...	...	...	...	...	2109	...	2344	...	...	...	...	...	...	...	...	...	...	...
Brest ▦ ‡ d.	2115	...	0240	...	...	...	0532	...	...	0750	...	...	...	...	1223	...	1440	...	...	...	...	...	...	1833	...	...	...	...
Terespol ▦ d.	2113	...	0238	...	...	0415	0530	0652	...	0708	0847	0915	...	1152	1248	1338	1438	1542	1620	1752	...	...	1905	1751	1952	...	...	...
Biała Podlaska d.	|	...	0327	...	...	0500	0613	0740	...	...	0932	1001	...	1240	|	1424	1518	1630	1704	1840	...	...	1953	...	2040	...	...	...
Łuków d.	⊠	...	0423	...	0457	0553	0705	0840	0858	...	1032	1054	...	1340	|	1519	1606	1730	1756	1940	1952	...	2048	...	2140	2200	...	...
Siedlce d.	|	0339	0445	0451	0530	0613	0725	...	0931	...	...	1113	1341	...	1436	1540	...	...	1819	...	2024	2045	2112	...	...	2232	2240	...
Warszawa Wschodnia a.	2351	0502	0549	0613	0641	0716	0830	...	1104	...	...	1210	1503	...	1529	1637	...	...	1926	...	...	2208	2212	...	...	...	0009	...
Warszawa Centralna a.	0107	0512r	0600	0623r	0650	0725	0840	...	1114r	...	...	1229	1513r	...	...	1700	...	...	1935	...	...	2218r	2240	...	...	...	0019r	...

A – VLTAVA – 🛏 1, 2 cl. Moskva - Praha and v.v. [2] Terespol - Łuków - Katowice and v.v. (for additional cars see Table **95**).
B – [12] Szczecin / Zielona Góra - Poznań - Warszawa - Terespol and v.v.
C – ①–⑥ (not Aug. 15, Nov. 11).
G – ①–⑤ (also Nov. 1; not Nov. 11).
p – [12] Kraków - Warszawa - Terespol. 🛏 1, 2 cl. Kraków - Moskva and v.v.

q – Not Aug. 15.
r – Warszawa **Śródmieście** (adjacent to Centralna).

◇ – Stopping train.

‡ – Belarus time (Polish time + 1 hour).
⊠ – Conveys only sleeping car passengers to / from Brest and points east thereof. For composition and days of running see **International** section (Tables **24 / 56 / 94**).

1055 WARSZAWA - LUBLIN - CHEŁM

For Warszawa - Lublin - Yahodyn - Kyïv sleeping car services, see Table **1700**

km		13108	*TLK*	52104	51108	82100	*TLK*	53103		52102		82511
		13109	5210/1	52105	12109	82101	8210/1	53102	12101	52103	12505	52101
			[R] ✕				[R] ✕		①–⑤	F		
		C	J	F	q	G	R	K	h	Ⓑ p	⑥	b
0	**Warszawa** Centralna d.	0715	...	0915	1125	1315	1415	1515	1615	1715	1715	1915
5	**Warszawa** Wschodnia d.	0724	0855	0924	1149	1324	1429	1524	1624	1724	1724	1924
125	Puławy Miasto d.	0906	1035	1109	1328	1508	1613	1706	1811	1918	1918	2109
175	**Lublin** a.	0945	1110	1145	1405	1545	1648	1743	1847	1954	1954	2145
175	**Lublin** d.	*1028*	...	1148	*1458*	*1558*	*1658*	*1758*f	*1858*	1956	*2028*	*2248*j
249	Chełm a.	*1141*	...	1256	*1611*	*1711*	*1811*	*1912*f	*2011*	2104	*2141*	*0001*j

		25100	*TLK*	25102	35102	28100	15109	*TLK*	25104	31108	
	21100	28510	2810/1	25103	35103	28101	21108	2510/1	25105	31109	
	①–⑤		[R] ✕	①–⑥				[R] ✕			
	h	b	R	F	K	G	q	J	F	C	
Chełm d.	...	*0400*j	*0550*f	0656	*0850*f	*1050*	*1220*j	*1350*	1459	*1650*f	...
Lublin a.	...	*0512*j	*0702*f	0812	*1002*f	*1202*	*1332*j	*1502*	1613	*1802*f	...
Lublin d.	0515	0615	0715	0815	1015	1215	1415	1530	1615	1815	...
Puławy Miasto d.	0550	0652	0750	0851	1050	1252	1450	1607	1650	1853	...
Warszawa Wschodnia a.	0736	0842	0928	1039	1242	1435	1638	1758	1835	2036	...
Warszawa Centralna a.	0745	0852	0950	1055	1252	1445	1700	...	1845	2045	...

FOR NOTES SEE TABLE 1058

1056 PRZEMYŚL - LVIV

km			13109	7310	7310	35
			52/107	51/107	52	⊗
			C	B ❖	D	T ❖
	Warszawa C. **1058** d.	...	0715	...	...	...
	Kraków Gł. **1075** d.	...	|	1340	1340	2115
0	**Przemyśl** d.	...	1924	1924	1924	0120
13	Medyka ⊞ d.	...	|	|	|	|
20	Mostiska II ⊞ ‡ d.	...	2222	2222	2222	0327
98	**Lviv** ‡ a.	...	2344	2344	2344	0447
	Chernivtsi **1720** a.	...	|	|	|	|
	Kyïv **1750** a.	...	|	|	1018	1428
	Odesa **1750** a.	...	1331	1331	...	...

	36	108/51	108/52	51	
	⊗	31108	3710	3710	
	U ❖	C	B ❖	D	
Odesa **1750** d.	...	1813	1813	...	...
Kyïv **1750** d.	2241	|	|	2042	...
Chernivtsi **1720** d.	|	|	|	|	...
Lviv ‡ d.	0835	0719	0719	0719	...
Mostiska II ⊞ ‡ d.	1028	0937	0937	0937	...
Medyka ⊞ d.	|	|	|	|	...
Przemyśl a.	1004	0926	0926	0926	...
Kraków Gł. **1075** a.	1410	|	1538	1538	...
Warszawa C. **1058** a.	...	2045	...	...	...

WARSZAWA - RAVA RUSKA - LVIV

	52105	52103
	22105	22103
	F	F Ⓑ
Warszawa Cent. d.	0915	1715
Warszawa Wsch. d.	0724	1724
Lublin a.	1145	1954
Lublin d.	1148	1956
Zawada d.	1407	2208
Zamość a.	1420	2220
Hrebenne ⊞ a.	...	...
Rava Ruska ‡ a.	...	...
Lviv ‡ a.	...	...

	22102	22104
	25102	25104
	F S	F
Lviv ‡ d.	...	...
Rava Ruska ‡ d.	...	...
Hrebenne ⊞ d.	...	...
Zamość d.	0522	1336
Zawada d.	0552	1404
Lublin a.	0812	1613
Lublin d.	0815	1615
Warszawa Wsch. a.	1039	1835
Warszawa Cent. a.	1055	1845

FOR NOTES SEE TABLE 1058

1058 WARSZAWA and LUBLIN - PRZEMYŚL

km		13109		*Ex*		53102		*Ex*	13511	
		13108		5311		53103		1309		
		C	...	[R] A		K		[R] P	c	
0	**Warszawa** Centralna d.	0715	...	...	...	1515	...	...	2245	...
5	**Warszawa** Wschodnia d.	0724	...	1352	...	1524	...	1703	2254	...
	Warszawa Centralna d.	|	...	1415	...	|	...	1715	|	...
175	**Lublin** d.	0956	...	|	...	1814	...	|	0133	...
278	Stalowa Wola Rozwadów d.	1156	...	k	...	2007	...	k	0337	...
	Rzeszów **1075** d.	|	...	1927	...	|	...	2235	|	...
353	Przeworsk **1075** d.	1334	...	2013	...	2139	...	2321	|	...
	Rzeszów **1075** a.	|	...	|	...	|	...	|	0555	...
	Zagórz **1078** a.	|	...	|	...	|	...	|	1030	...
368	Jarosław **1075** d.	1348	...	2027	...	2154	...	2335	...	...
403	**Przemyśl** **1075** a.	1420	...	2059	...	2226	...	0006	...	...

	Ex	35102		*Ex*		31108		31510	
	3108	35103		3510		31109			
	[R] P	K		[R] A		C		e	
Przemyśl **1075** d.	0401	0545	...	0814	...	1332	...	...	...
Jarosław **1075** d.	0430	0617	...	0842	...	1404	...	...	...
Zagórz **1078** d.	|	|	...	|	...	|	...	1735	...
Rzeszów **1075** d.	|	|	...	|	...	|	...	2151	...
Przeworsk **1075** d.	0443	0630	...	0854	...	1417	...	|	...
Rzeszów **1075** d.	0525	|	...	0935	...	|	...	|	...
Stalowa Wola Rozwadów d.	k	0816	...	k	...	1610	...	0027	...
Lublin d.	|	1015	...	|	...	1815	...	0248	...
Warszawa Centralna a.	1055	|	...	1455	...	|	...	|	...
Warszawa Wschodnia a.	1107	1242	...	1507	...	2036	...	0506	...
Warszawa Centralna a.	...	1252	...	...		2045	...	0515	...

A – [12] and ✕ Gdynia - Warszawa - Kraków - Przemyśl and v.v.
B – ❖ From Wrocław June 21 - Aug. 30; from Odesa June 22 - Aug. 31: ▬ 2 cl. Wrocław - Kraków - Odesa and v.v. ❖.
C – [12] Warszawa - Przemyśl and v.v. 🛏 2 cl. Warszawa - Odesa and v.v.
D – *TLK* 🛏 2 cl. Wrocław - Kraków - Przemyśl - Kyïv and v.v.
F – [12] Bydgoszcz - Lublin - Chełm / Zamość and v.v.
G – [12] Gorzów Wlkp / Szczecin - Warszawa - Lublin and v.v.
J – ①–⑤ (not Nov. 11): [12] and ✕ Gdynia - Warszawa - Lublin and v.v.
K – [12] Bydgoszcz - Warszawa - Przemyśl and v.v.
P – [12] and ✕ Warszawa - Kraków - Przemyśl and v.v.

R – From / to Szczecin.
S – ①–⑥.
T – ❖ ③⑤⑦ GEORGIJ KIRPA: 🛏 2 cl. Kraków - Kyïv.
U – ❖ ②④⑥ GEORGIJ KIRPA: 🛏 2 cl. Kyïv - Kraków.

b – From / to Bydgoszcz.
c – June 19 - Aug. 30.
e – June 20 - Aug. 31.

f – ①–⑤ (not Nov. 11).
h – Also Nov. 1; not Nov. 11.
j – ①–⑥ (not Aug. 15, Nov. 11).
k – Via Kraków (Tables **1065** and **1075**).
q – Not Nov. 11.

‡ – Ukrainian (East European) time.
❖ – Subject to confirmation.
⊗ – Only for sleeping car passengers to / from Lviv and beyond.

1060 WARSZAWA - KATOWICE - GLIWICE and BIELSKO BIAŁA

km		54502	*EC*103		13101	*Ex*	*Ex*	14100	*EC*114	54110	*Ex*	*EC*105	54112	*IC*	*Ex*	54100	54101	*IC*	54104	*IC*	*IC*	54102	203	*TLK*		
		54503	14001	13101	44101	1411	1405	14101	14005	54111	1615	14003	54113	1611	5410	54101	43103	1609	54506	1401	1403	54103	14011	53702		
			[R] ✕			[R]	14411		[R] ✕		[R] ✕	[R] ✕		[R] ✕	5411			[R]	q g	[R] ✕	[R] ✕			[R]		
		A	H	①–⑥	①–⑥	✕	[R] ✕	G	J	b	Ⓑ	E	q					✕		Ⓑ			C	B		
	Gdynia Gł. **1030** d.	1851	...	...	...	...	...	...	...	...	...	...	...	...	1000	0732	0732	...	...	...	...	1134	...	1859	...	...
0	**Warszawa** Wschodnia § d.	|	0613	...	...	0708	0808	0822	0913	...	1013	1113	1233	1413	1503	|	|	1613	1633	1713	1913	|	2047	0017	...	...
5	**Warszawa** Centralna. § d.	◐	0625	...	...	0725	0825	0850	0925	...	1025	1125	1250	1425	1525	◐	◐	1625	1650	1725	1925	◐	2100	0030	...	...
*194	**Łódź** Fabryczna d.	0204**e**	|	0615	0615	|	|	|	|	1013**r**	|	|	|	|	|	1417**r**	1417**r**	|	|	|	|	1819**r**	|	|	...	...
*167	Koluszki § d.	|	|	|	|	|	|	1006	|	|	|	|	1404	|	|	|	|	|	1801	|	|	|	|	|	...	...
*128	Piotrków Trybunalski § d.	0255	|	0710	0710	|	|	1036	|	1124	|	|	1435	|	|	1526	1526	|	1833	|	|	1926	|	|	...	...
*43	**Częstch Ob** ¶ **1020** § d.	0407	|	0826	0841	|	|	1139	|	1226	|	|	1539	|	|	1637	1647	|	1939	|	|	2029	|	0310	...	...
259	Zawiercie **1020** d.	0448	|	0900	0914	0931	1031	1214	|	1301	1231	|	1614	1631	1731	1712	1721	1831	2014	1931	2131	2104	2310	|	...	...
294	Sosnowiec Gł. **1020** a.	0524	0855	|	0942	0958	1058	1243	1155	1329	1258	1355	1643	1658	1758	1739	|	1858	2042	1958	2158	2132	2337	0408	...	...
302	**Katowice** **1020** a.	0535	0907	|	0952	1010	1110	1254	1207	1341	1310	1407	1654	1710	1810	1751	|	1910	2054	2010	2210	2144	2349	0420	...	...
	Kraków Gł. a.	|	...	1055	...	|	...	|	...	|	|	...	...	|	|	...	1919	|	...	|	|	...	...	0626	...	...
	Gliwice **1075** a.	|	...	...	...	|	...	|	...	|	1344	...	...	1744	|	...	...	1944	...	|	|	...	...	...	...	...
	Wrocław Gł. **1075** a.	|	...	...	...	|	...	|	...	|	1550	...	...	1947	|	...	...	2149	...	|	|	...	...	...	...	...
357	**Bielsko Biała** **1077** a.	0650	...	...	...	1118	...	1404	...	1451	...	...	...	...	1918	...	...	...	...	2118	2318	...	...	...	...	...

	202	*IC*	45100	45104	*IC*	*IC*	*Ex*	34102	45102	45112	*IC*		*EC*104	45110	41100	6114		*EC*115	*Ex*	*Ex*	*IC*		44100	*EC*102	45502	*TLK*
	41010	4102	45101	45105	6108	4100	4510	45102	45103	45113	6110		41002	45111	41101	6115	45410	41004	41410	4110	6106	31100	31100	41000	45503	35702
		[R] ✕		g q	[R]	[R]	[R] ✕				[R]		[R] ✕			[R] ✕	[R] ✕	[R] ✕	[R] 🍷	[R]	[R] ✕	🍷	🍷	[R] ✕		[R]
	C	①–⑥			✕	✕	①–⑥			q	✕		E	b	G	①–⑤	⑦	J	⑥⑦f	🍷	Ⓑ	Ⓑ	Ⓑ	H	A	B
Bielsko Biała **1077** d.	...	0455	...	...	...	0655	0755	...	...	...	...	...	...	1310	1340	...	1355	...	...	1655	...	...	...	...	2135	...
Wrocław Gł. **1075** d.	...	|	...	...	0425	|	|	...	...	...	0825	...	...	|	|	1225	|	...	...	|	1625	...	...	...	|	...
Gliwice **1075** d.	...	|	...	...	0624	|	|	...	...	...	1024	...	...	|	|	1424	|	...	...	|	1824	...	...	...	|	...
Kraków Gł. d.	...	|	...	...	|	|	|	0905	...	...	|	...	...	|	|	|	|	...	...	|	|	1715	...	...	|	2244
Katowice **1020** d.	0430	0600	0613	0647	0700	0800	0900	|	1010	1047	1100	...	1400	1415	1447	1500	1500	1600	1700	1800	1900	|	1810	2000	2245	0047
Sosnowiec Gł. **1020** d.	0442	0611	0625	0658	0711	0811	0911	|	1022	1058	1111	...	1411	1426	1458	1511	1511	1611	1711	1811	1911	|	1820	2011	2257	0059
Zawiercie **1020** d.	0509	0638	0656	0729	0738	0838	0938	1046	1052	1129	1138	...	|	1456	1529	1538	1538	|	1738	1838	1938	1856	1848	|	2328	|
Częstch Ob ¶ **1020** § d.	|	|	0734	0804	|	|	|	1140	1140	1204	|	...	|	1534	1604	|	|	|	|	|	|	1940	1940	|	0007	0158
Piotrków Trybunalski § d.	|	|	0849	0916	|	|	|	1252	1252	1314	|	...	|	1646	1715	|	|	|	|	|	|	2050	2050	|	0118	|
Koluszki § d.	|	|	|	0944	|	|	|	|	|	1344	|	...	|	|	1743	|	|	|	|	|	|	|	|	|	|	|
Łódź Fabryczna a.	|	|	0950**r**	|	|	|	|	1354**r**	1354**r**	|	|	...	|	1750**r**	|	|	|	|	|	|	|	2142	2142	|	0203**e**	|
Warszawa Centralna § a.	0720	0850	◐	1100	0950	1050	1150	◐	◐	1500	1350	...	1645	...	1900	1750	1750	1845	1950	2050	2150	...	...	2245	◐	0440
Warszawa Wschodnia § a.	0737	0902	|	1112	1002	1102	1207	|	|	1517	1402	...	1657	...	1932	1807	1807	1857	2002	2102	2202	...	...	2257	|	0452
Gdynia Gł. **1030** a.	...	...	1724	...	...	...	1709	2130	2130	...	...	...	...	...	...	...	0001	...	...	...	...	...	...	...	0959	1006

A – ⑤⑦ (daily June 19 - Aug. 31; also Nov. 10, 11): 🛏 1, 2 cl., ▬ 2 cl. and [12] Gdynia - Katowice - Bielsko Biała and v.v.
B – 🛏 1, 2 cl., ▬ 2 cl. and [2] Gdynia - Katowice - Kraków - Zakopane and v.v.
C – CHOPIN – 🛏 1, 2 cl., ▬ 2 cl. and [2] Warszawa - Bratislava / Budapest / Praha / Wien and v.v.
E – SOBIESKI – [12] and ✕ Warszawa - Zebrzydowice ⊞ - Wien and v.v.

G – [12] Białystok - Warszawa - Bielsko Biała and v.v.
H – POLONIA – [12] and ✕ Warszawa - Zebrzydowice ⊞ - Wien and v.v.
J – PRAHA – [12] and ✕ Warszawa - Zebrzydowice ⊞ - Praha and v.v.

b – To / from Bydgoszcz (Table **1020**).
e – Łódź **Widzew**.

f – Also Nov. 11.
g – To / from Racibórz.
q – From / to Olsztyn.
r – Łódź **Kaliska**.

* – Distance from Zawiercie.
◐ – Via Bydgoszcz (Table **1020**).
¶ – Full name is Częstochowa Osobowa.
§ – For Warszawa - Częstochowa see Table **1088**.

WARSZAWA - KRAKÓW 1065

Via CMK high-speed line ▲

*For trains via Kielce (including night trains) see Table **1067***

km	*For slow trains see **1067***	*Ex* 1311 13410 R ✕ K	*IC* 1301 R ✕	*Ex* 1313 13413 R ✕ Z	*IC* 1307 R ✕ ①–⑥	*IC* 5307 13407 R ✕	*IC* 1305 R ✕ F	*IC* 5303 53400 R ✕ z	*Ex* 5311 5310 R ✕ E	*Ex* 1315 13415 R ✕ G Z	*IC* 1303 R ✕	*Ex* 1309 R ✕ A	*Ex* 5313 83415 R ✕ q		*IC* 5301 5300 R ✕
	Gdynia Gł. **1030** ... d.	...	...	...	...	0504 j	...	0655	0850	...	...	...	1252	...	1500
0	**Warszawa** Wschodnia .. d.	0603	0658	0758	0903	0953	1058	1153	1352	1458	1603	1703	1758	...	1953
5	**Warszawa** Centralna ... d.	0615	0715	0815	0915	1015	1115	1215	1415	1515	1615	1715	1815	...	2015
297	**Kraków** Gł. ... a.	0910	1010	1110	1210	1310	1410	1510	1710	1810	1910	2010	2110	...	2302

	IC 3500 3501 R ✕	*IC* 3102 R ✕	*Ex* 3108 R ✕ A	*Ex* 3114 R ✕ ②–⑤	*Ex* 38414 R ✕ P q	*Ex* 3512 R ✕ Q q	*Ex* 3510 3511 R ✕ E	*IC* 3506 31406 R ✕	*Ex* 3104 31414 R ✕ J Z	*IC* 3502 35400 R ✕ z	*IC* 3100 R ✕	*IC* 3107 R ✕ ⑧	*Ex* 3112 31412 R ✕ Z	*Ex* 3110 31410 R ✕ K	
Kraków Gł. ... d.	0600	0700	0800	0900	1000	1025	1200	1400	1500	1600	1700	1800	1900	2000	...
Warszawa Centralna ... a.	0855	0955	1055	1155	1255	1340	1455	1655	1755	1855	1955	2055	2155	2255	...
Warszawa Wschodnia .. a.	0907	1012	1107	1212	1307	1347	1507	1707	1812	1907	2007	2107	2207	2307	...
Gdynia Gł. **1030** ... a.	1409	...	...	...	1813	1905	2012	2203t	...	0006	...	...	...	...	...

A – [12] Warszawa - Kraków - Przemyśl and v.v.
E – [12] and ✕ Gdynia - Kraków - Przemyśl and v.v.
F – Until June 19 and from Sept. 1: ①–⑤ (not Nov. 11).
G – ①–⑤.
J – ⑦ (⑧ until June 19 and from Sept. 1) not Nov. 11.
K – Conveys [12] Warszawa - Krynica and v.v. on dates in Table **1078**.
P – June 1 - Aug. 30.
Q – Aug. 31 - Dec. 12.
Z – Conveys [12] Warszawa - Kraków - Zakopane and v.v.; for dates of running see Table **1066**.

j – ①–⑥.
q – From / to Kołobrzeg on dates in Table **1015**.
t – Not ⑥.
z – To / from Zakopane on dates in Table **1066**.

▲ – Ticketing route is via Idzikowice.

KRAKÓW and KATOWICE - ZAKOPANE 1066

Ex trains convey ✕

km		13500 13501 L	◇ 2	83500 83501 C	◇ 2	*TLK* 53702 R F	🚂 A	◇ 2		*Ex*✕ 13413 R K	◇ 2	13105 13505 L	7311 33411 ⑥p	◇ 2	53401 R G	◇ 2	*Ex*✕ 13414 R R		◇ 2				
	Warszawa Cent **1065 1067** ... d.	2140	...	...	...	0030	...	...	...	0815	...	0655	...	...	1215	...	1515	...	...	...	...	...	...
	Katowice **1060** ... d.	|	...	0213	...	0435	...	...	...	|	...	|	1130	...	|	...	|	...	...	...	...	...	...
0	**Kraków** Gł. ... d.	0312	...	|	0528	0650	...	0725	...	1114	1131	1228	1329	1444	1515	1620	1814	...	2226	...	...	...	...
5	Kraków Płaszów ... d.	0332	...	|	0541	0718	...	0738	...	1133	1145	1251	1354	1457	1543	1643	1833	...	2239	...	...	...	...
68	Sucha Beskidzka ... d.	0449	0517	0615	0711	0840	...	0901	...	1246	1308	1414	1517	1622	1724	1816	2004	...	2359	...	...	...	...
103	Chabówka ... a.	0528	0558	0657	0752	0919	...	0940	...	1324	1349	1454	1556	1713	1806	...	2039	...	...	...	...	...	...
	Chabówka ... d.	0540	0615	0707	0806	0929	1009	0954	...	1334	1403	1507	1606	1727	1818	...	2049	...	...	...	...	...	...
126	Nowy Targ ... d.	0614	0647	0737	0836	1002	|	1028	...	1402	1432	1543	1654	1757	1852	...	2118	...	...	...	...	...	...
147	**Zakopane** ... a.	0636	0711	0804	0900	1028	1136	1052	...	1422	1459	1616	1713	1825	1913	...	2138	...	...	...	...	...	...

	◇ 2	◇ 2		◇ 2		*Ex*✕ 31414 R S	33410 3710 ⑦q	35400 R H	31504 31104 L	◇ 2	🚂 A	◇ 2	*Ex* 31412 R K		◇ 2	38500 38501 D		*TLK* 35702 R F		31500 31501 L		
Zakopane ... d.	...	...	...	0940	...	1117	1147	1201	1220	1238	1339	1432	1551	...	1746	1805	...	1845	...	2118	...	...
Nowy Targ ... d.	...	...	...	0959	...	1137	1207	1221	1244	1259	|	1455	1611	...	1807	1835	...	1915	...	2151	...	...
Chabówka ... a.	...	...	...	1029	...	1203	1233	1256	1310	1330	1505	1524	1637	...	1836	1909	...	1941	...	2217	...	...
Chabówka ... d.	...	...	...	1051	...	1216	1243	1306	1327	1351	...	1538	1647	...	1848	1920	...	1953	...	2227	...	...
Sucha Beskidzka ... d.	0451	0610	...	1134	...	1312	1356	1410	1423	1436	...	1625	1732	...	1933	2019	...	2052	...	2321	...	...
Kraków Płaszów ... a.	0607	0735	...	1305	...	1427	1507	1524	1532	1553	...	1741	1837	...	2048	|	...	2157	...	0030	...	...
Kraków Gł. ... a.	0620	0754	...	1318	...	1455	1538	1552	1556	1608	...	1754	1856	...	2101	|	...	2229	...	0053	...	...
Katowice **1060** ... a.	...	...	...	...	...	|	1729	|	|	...	...	...	|	...	...	0010	...	0025	...	|	...	...
Warszawa Cent **1065 1067** .. a.	...	...	...	...	...	1755	...	1855	2105	...	...	...	2155	...	...	...	...	0440	...	0556	...	...

A – June 21, 28, July 12, 19, Aug. 9, 16, 23, 30.
C – June 19 - Aug. 30: [sleeper] 1, 2 cl., [couchette] 2 cl. and [12] Szczecin - Zakopane (Tables **1010**, **1080**).
D – June 20 - Aug. 31: [sleeper] 1, 2 cl., [couchette] 2 cl. and [12] Zakopane - Szczecin (Tables **1010**, **1080**).
F – [sleeper] 1, 2 cl., [couchette] 2 cl. and [2] Gdynia - Warszawa - Katowice - Kraków - Zakopane and v.v.
G – ⑥: [12] Gdynia Gł. - Kraków - Zakopane.
H – ⑦: [12] Zakopane - Kraków - Gdynia Gł.
L – For dates of running see Table **1067**.
K – ⑥⑦ (daily June 6 - Oct. 4) also Nov. 11.

R – ⑤ (also June 10).
S – ⑦ (also June 12).

p – From Poznań, depart 0547.
q – To Poznań, arrive 2307.

🚂 – Normally hauled by steam locomotive (not guaranteed).
◇ – Stopping train.

WARSZAWA and LUBLIN - KIELCE - KRAKÓW 1067

km	*For fast trains to Kraków see Table* **1065**	◇ 2	◇ 2	83203 53503 A	23100 23101	23101 24103	13105 13505	52106 52107 ①–⑥ w	26100 26101	53100 53101 M	◇ 2	13106 13107 y		12110 12111 ①–⑥ p	*TLK* 8316 8317 E	23102 23103	23102 24105 h	◇ 2 ⑧	◇ 2	13102 13103 f	12112 12113	13500 13501 B	*TLK* 53702 R G		
0	**Warszawa** Wschodnia ... d.	...	...	0447	...	...	0637	0858	...	1043	...	1222	...	1442	1552	...	...	1628	...	1657	1842	2122	0017	...	...
5	**Warszawa** Centralna ... d.	...	...	0500	...	...	0655	0910	...	1055	...	1255	...	1455	1605	...	...	1640	...	1710	1855	2140	0030	...	...
	Lublin ... d.	...	...	|	0605	0605	|	|	1045	|	...	|	...	|	|	1645	1645	|	...	|	|	|	|	...	...
108	Radom ... d.	...	...	0657	0742	0742	0852	1108	1220	1248	...	1451	...	1700	1800	1825	1825	1840	...	1906	2057	2334	|	...	...
149	Skarżysko Kamienna ... d.	...	...	0747	0831	0831	0940	1156	1309	1336	...	1539	...	1750	1848	1913	1913	1936	1940	1955	2146	0023	|	...	...
193	Kielce ... d.	0535	0728	0831	0924	0935	1025	1237	1412	1422	1431	1625	...	1830	1930	2003	2014	...	2027	2038	2226	0106	|	...	...
	Katowice ... a.	0902	|	|	|	1150	|	...	|	|	1802	|	...	...	|	|	2233	...	...	|	...	|	0420	...	...
	Częstochowa Stradom ... d.	...	|	|	|	...	|	...	1622	|	...	|	...	...	|	|	...	...	...	|	...	|	|	...	...
	Wrocław Gł. ... a.	...	|	|	|	...	|	...	1926	|	...	|	...	...	|	|	...	...	...	|	...	|	|	...	...
325	**Kraków** Gł. ... a.	...	0942	1034	1121	...	1223	...	...	1620	...	1824	...	...	2128	2200	...	...	...	2238	...	0309	0626	...	...
330	Kraków Płaszów ... a.	...	...	1052	...	...	1236	...	...	1652	...	...	...	...	...	...	...	...	...	...	...	0320	0658	...	...
	Zakopane **1066** ... a.	...	...	...	...	...	1616x	...	...	...	...	...	...	...	...	...	...	...	...	...	...	0636	1035	...	...

	◇ 2	21112 21113	*TLK* 3816 3817 E	31102 31103 f	42104 32101 h	32100 32101	21110 21111 ①–⑥ p	◇ 2	31106 31107 y		35100 35101 M	◇ 2	62100 62101	25106 25105 ⑧ w	◇ 2	◇ 2	31504 31104	38202 35502 A	42100 32103	32102 32103	◇ 2	*TLK* 35702 R G	31500 31501 B		
Zakopane **1066** ... d.	...	...	...	...	...	...	...	...	...	...	...	...	...	...	...	...	1220x	...	...	...	...	1845	2118	...	...
Kraków Płaszów ... d.	...	...	...	...	...	...	...	...	...	...	1153	...	...	...	...	...	1548	1642	...	...	...	2221	0045	...	...
Kraków Gł. ... d.	...	...	0450	0610	...	0735	...	...	1010	...	1210	...	...	...	1437	...	1610	1710	...	1725	1910	2244	0056	...	...
Wrocław Gł. ... d.	...	...	|	|	...	|	...	...	|	...	|	...	1005	...	|	...	|	|	...	|	|	|	|	...	...
Częstochowa Stradom ... d.	...	...	|	|	...	|	...	...	|	...	|	...	1253	...	|	...	|	|	...	|	|	|	|	...	...
Katowice ... d.	...	...	|	|	0709	|	...	0748	|	...	|	1140	|	...	|	...	|	|	1705	|	|	0047	|	...	...
Kielce ... d.	...	0540	0637	0804	0945	0945	1002	1111	1203	...	1404	1454	1526	1610	1657	1712	1801	1906	1944	1944	2121	|	0252	...	...
Skarżysko Kamienna ... d.	0510	0622	0714	0843	1025	1025	1041	...	1241	...	1443	...	1607	1648	...	1756	1840	1947	2027	2027	...	|	0331	...	...
Radom ... d.	0545	0701	0753	0919	1102	1102	1116	...	1317	...	1519	...	1655	1724	...	...	1915	2031	2104	2104	...	|	0410	...	...
Lublin ... a.	|	|	|	|	1236	1236	|	...	|	...	|	...	1833	|	...	...	|	|	2240	2240	...	|	|	...	...
Warszawa Centralna ... a.	0735	0845	0945	1105	...	...	1305	...	1510	...	1705	...	...	1915	...	...	2105	2215	...	...	...	0440	0556	...	...
Warszawa Wschodnia ... a.	0757	0857	1007	1122	...	...	1317	...	1532	...	1717	...	...	1927	...	...	2122	2227	...	...	...	0452	0622	...	...

A – From Kołobrzeg until June 19 and from Sept. 1; From Hel June 20 - Aug. 31; To Kołobrzeg until June 18 and from Aug. 31; To Hel June 19 - Aug. 30: [sleeper] 1, 2 cl. and [12] Kołobrzeg / Hel - Warszawa - Kraków and v.v.
B – From Warszawa June 10, 11, June 19 - Aug. 30; from Zakopane June 13, 14, June 20 - Aug. 31: [12] Warszawa - Zakopane and v.v.
E – [12] Kołobrzeg - Warszawa - Kraków and v.v.
G – [sleeper] 1, 2 cl., [couchette] 2 cl. and [2] Gdynia - Warszawa - Katowice - Kraków - Zakopane and v.v.
M – [12] Olsztyn - Warszawa - Kraków and v.v.

f – From / to Terespol.
h – To / from Gliwice.
p – Not Aug. 15, Nov. 11.

x – June 20 - Aug. 31.
w – From / to Olsztyn.
y – From / to Suwałki.

◇ – Stopping train.

1070 POZNAŃ - WROCŁAW

FOR NOTES SEE TABLE 1075

km		449 83700	56200 56201		TLK 7310 ®✕	2 ◇	83106 83107	83100 83101	56100	2 ◇	83108 83109	IC 1601 1600	56104 56105	83104 83105	2 ◇	83102 83103	2 ◇	Ex 1612 1613	2 ◇	84100 84510	IC 1603 1602	16112 16113	56102 56103	IC 1605 1604	83201 83510
		D Y	E		Z	h w	A	m	n	h w	F	V	q	m p	j	B	h w	® V	g	G	® V	e	m n	® V	S
0	**Poznań** Gł. d.	0202	0307	...	0547	0645	0735	0835	0940	1000	1035	1127	1140	1235	1346	1435	1445	1535	1615	1735	1824	1835	1945	2125	2252
69	Leszno d.	0300	0408	...	0648	0747	0836	0939	1040	1118	1139	1222	1243	1339	1501	1538	1603	1630	1722	1837	1919	1937	2046	2220	2356
165	**Wrocław** Gł. a.	0432	0540	...	0820	0920	1020	1120	1220	1303	1320	1353	1420	1518	1650	1720	1738	1802	1903	2020	2051	2119	2220	2350	0135

	38200 38511	IC 6103 6102	65101 65100	IC 6105 6104	61113 61112	2 ◇	48100 48101	2 ◇	Ex 6113 6112	38102 38103	2 ◇	38104 38105	65105 65104	IC 6101 6100	38108 38109	65103	2 ◇	38100 38101	38106 38107		2 ◇	TLK 3711 ®✕	65201 65200	38704 448	
	S	M V	m n	X V	e	g	G	j	V	B	h w	m	q	V	F	n	h w	m	A		h w	Z	E	D Y	
Wrocław Gł. d.	0312	0506	0535	0606	0635	0735	0835	0854	1006	1035	1135	1235	1335	1406	1435	1535	1554	1635	1735	...	1935	2035	2340	0024	...
Leszno d.	0452	0630	0707	0731	0811	0913	1010	1039	1131	1212	1312	1411	1509	1531	1612	1707	1740	1813	1911	...	2107	2206	0112	0153	...
Poznań Gł. a.	0555	0727	0812	0827	0912	1032	1111	1155	1227	1312	1422	1512	1613	1627	1715	1807	1857	1915	2011	...	2211	2307	0214	0255	...

1075 WROCŁAW - KATOWICE - KRAKÓW - PRZEMYŚL

km		43100 43101	63100 63101	63100 32111	TLK 7310/1 ®✕	73100 73101	83106 83107	83106 32106	83100 83101	Ex 5311 ®✕	83108 83109	IR 63124 2	EC 341 73000 ®🍷	Ex 1309 ®✕	83104 83105	IR 63120 2	33011 35 ❖	83102 83103	TLK 8310 83411 ®✕	84100 84510	63200 63500	83200 83510	TLK 83700	449 83700
		H			Z	J	A			K	F	C	W	T		C	P	B		G	N	S	Y	D
	Świnoujście **1010** d.	...	...	...	...	...	...	...	...	...	...	...	...	...	...	...	...	...	1011v	...	...	1755c	2043	...
	Szczecin Gł. **1010** d.	...	...	...	...	...	...	...	0550	...	...	...	...	...	0950	...	...	...	1150	...	...	1955	2235	...
	Poznań Gł. **1070** d.	...	...	...	0547	...	0735	...	0835	...	1035	...	...	...	1235	...	...	1435	1414	1735	...	2252	0202	0202
0	**Wrocław** Gł. **1088** d.	...	0635	0635	0835	0935	1035	1035	1135	...	1335	1435	1540	...	1525	1635	...	1735	|	2035	2235	0142	0435	0435
42	Brzeg **1088** d.	...	0709	0709	0909	1009	1109	1109	1209	...	1409	1507	|	...	1557	1708	...	1809	|	2109	2310	0219	0506	0506
82	Opole Gł. **1088** d.	...	0740	0740	0940	1040	1140	1140	1240	...	1439	1540	1639	...	1630	1739	...	1840	◐	2140	2340	0256	0542	0542
162	Gliwice **1060** d.	...	0852	0852	1052	1152	1252	1252	1352	...	1552	1647	1748	...	1741	1847	...	1952	|	2252	0052	0415	0652	0652
190	**Katowice** **1060** a.	...	0925	0925	1125	1225	1325	1325	1425	...	1625	1719	1820	...	1815	1918	...	2025	1938	2325	0125	0449	0725	0725
	Katowice ▲ d.	0720	0930	0930	1130	1230	1330	1330	1430	...	1630	1722	1823	...	1828	1921	...	2030	1941	...	0130	0508	0730	0730
268	**Kraków** Gł. ▲ a.	0904	1119	1119	1319	1419	1519	1519	1619	...	1819	1904	1956	...	2018	2058	...	2219	2125	...	0318	0657	0918	0918
	Kraków Gł. **1078** d.	0928	1126	1126	1340	1422	1528	1528	1625	1720	1824	1911	...	2020	2025	...	2115	...	...	...	0321	0702	...	...
273	Kraków Płaszów **1078** d.	0937	1135	1135	1349	1431	1538	1538	1634	1729	1833	1919	...	2029	2035	...	|	...	...	...	0339	0726	...	...
346	Tarnów **1078** d.	1036	1234	1234	1447	1532	1641	1641	1732	1821	1932	2010	...	2130	2136	...	2213	...	...	...	0443	0827	...	...
379	Dębica d.	1102	1301	1301	1514	1600	1719	1733	1759	1846	1959	2035	...	2155	2202	...	2239	...	...	...	0512	0854	...	...
426	Rzeszów **1058** d.	1152	1354	1405	1556	1647	1800	|	1845	1927	2043	2115	...	2235	2244	...	2321	...	...	...	0558	0938	...	...
463	Przeworsk **1058** d.	1243	1446	1455	1647	1739	*1919*	|	1937	2013	2133	...	...	2321	...	...	|	...	...	...	0651	1030	...	...
478	Jarosław **1058** d.	1258	1501	1511	1702	1754	*1934*	|	1952	2027	2148	...	...	2335	...	...	|	...	...	...	0707	1045	...	...
* *	Zamość a.	|	|	1920	|	|	|	2230	|	|	|	...	...	|	...	...	|	...	...	...	|	|	...	...
513	**Przemyśl** **1058** a.	1332	1535	...	1734	1828	*2013*	...	2025	2059	2221	...	...	0006	...	...	0050	...	...	...	0741	1117	...	...

	48511 48101	TLK 3810 38410 ®✕	38102 38103	EC 340 37001 ®🍷	38104 38105	Ex 3108 ®✕	38108 38109	38100 38101	Ex 3510 ®✕	23107 38106	38106 38107	37100 37101	33012 36 ❖	IR 36121 2	TLK 3710/1 ®✕	23110 36100 36101	36100 36101	IR 36124 2	34100 34101	TLK 38704 ✕	38704 448	38200 38511	36501 36201	
	G		B	W		T	F		K		A	J	Q	C	Z			C	H	Y	D	S	N	
Przemyśl **1058** d.	...	...	...	...	...	0401	0550	0748	0814	...	...	0945	1034	...	1130	...	1229	...	1428	...	...	1728	2213	...
Zamość d.	...	...	...	...	...	|	|	|	|	0537	...	|	|	...	|	0825	|	...	|	...	...	|	|	...
Jarosław **1058** d.	...	...	...	...	...	0430	0622	0821	0842	|	...	1019	|	...	1202	1240	1302	...	1501	...	...	1759	2246	...
Przeworsk **1058** d.	...	...	...	...	...	0443	0636	0834	0854	|	...	1033	|	...	1216	1254	1316	...	1515	...	...	1813	2300	...
Rzeszów **1058** d.	...	...	...	...	0516	0525	0720	0918	0935	|	1009	1116	1153	...	1300	1418	1418	1603	1610	...	...	1857	2345	...
Dębica d.	...	...	...	...	0559	0605	0803	1002	1015	1102	1102	1159	1234	...	1342	1502	1502	1641	1654	...	...	1939	0029	...
Tarnów **1078** d.	...	...	...	...	0628	0643	0831	1031	1043	1131	1131	1229	1303	...	1412	1531	1531	1706	1723	...	...	2008	0100	...
Kraków Płaszów **1078** d.	...	...	...	...	0734	0742	0934	1134	1142	1234	1234	1334	|	...	1530	1634	1634	1759	1829	...	...	2128	0221	...
Kraków Gł. **1078** a.	...	...	...	...	0742	0750	0942	1142	1150	1242	1242	1342	1410	...	1538	1642	1642	1806	1837	...	...	2137	0230	...
Kraków Gł. ▲ d.	...	0535	0547	0723	0747	...	0947	1147	...	1247	1247	1347	...	1437	1547	1647	1647	1809	1847	1945	1945	2150	0247	...
Katowice ▲ a.	...	0712	0729	0852	0929	...	1129	1329	...	1429	1429	1529	...	1612	1729	1829	1829	1943	2029	2129	2129	2335	0429	...
Katowice **1060** d.	0534	0715	0734	0854	0934	...	1134	1334	...	1434	1434	1534	...	1615	1734	1834	1834	1948	...	2134	2134	2350	0434	...
Gliwice **1060** d.	0607	|	0807	0925	1007	...	1207	1407	...	1507	1507	1607	...	1645	1807	1907	1907	2019	...	2207	2207	0022	0507	...
Opole Gł. **1088** d.	0721	◐	0921	1034	1121	...	1321	1521	...	1621	1621	1721	...	1756	1921	2021	2021	2130	...	2321	2321	0147	0621	...
Brzeg **1088** d.	0749	|	0950	|	1149	...	1349	1549	...	1649	1649	1749	...	1824	1950	2049	2049	2159	...	2349	2349	0218	0648	...
Wrocław Gł. **1088** a.	0826	|	1026	1127	1226	...	1426	1626	...	1726	1726	1826	...	1858	2025	2126	2126	2233	...	0020	0020	0256	0726	...
Poznań Gł. **1070** a.	1111	1233	1312	...	1512	...	1715	1915	...	...	2011	...	...	...	2307	...	...	...	...	0255	0255	0555	...	...
Szczecin Gł. **1010** a.	...	1500	...	...	1755	...	...	2206	...	...	...	...	...	...	...	...	...	...	...	0631	...	0843	...	...
Świnoujście **1010** a.	...	1640o	...	...	...	...	...	...	...	...	...	...	...	...	...	...	...	...	...	0818	...	1053c	...	...

NOTES FOR TABLES 1070 and 1075

A – (12) Gorzów Wlkp - Krzyż - Poznań - Rzeszów and v.v.
B – (12) Kołobrzeg - Poznań - Kraków and v.v.
C – ⑤⑦ May 3 - June 21 and Sept. 4 - Dec. 12 (also Apr. 30).
D – Conveys 🛏 1, 2 cl., ▬ 2 cl. and (2) (reclining) Berlin - Kostrzyn 🏛 - Poznań - Kraków and v.v.
E – 🛏 1, 2 cl., ▬ 2 cl. and (12) Gdynia - Wrocław and v.v.
F – (12) Słupsk - Poznań - Wrocław - Przemyśl and v.v.
G – (12) Słupsk - Poznań - Wrocław - Katowice and v.v.
H – Also conveys (12) Katowice - Rzeszów - Zagórz and v.v.
J – (12) Zielona Góra - Wrocław - Przemyśl and v.v. Conveys (12) Zgorzelec - Wrocław - Przemyśl and v.v.
K – (12) and ✕ Gdynia - Warszawa - Kraków - Przemyśl and v.v. (Table **1030**).
M – ①–⑥.
N – (12) Wrocław - Przemyśl and v.v.
P – ❖ ③⑤⑦ GEORGIJ KIRPA: 🛏 2 cl. Kraków - Kyïv.
Q – ❖ ②④⑥ GEORGIJ KIRPA: 🛏 2 cl. Kyïv - Kraków.
S – (12) Szczecin - Poznań - Kraków - Przemyśl and v.v.
T – (12) and ✕ Warszawa - Kraków - Przemyśl and v.v.

V – (12) and ✕ ® Warszawa - Poznań - Wrocław and v.v.
W – WAWEL – (12) and ✕ Berlin - Wrocław - Kraków and v.v. For dates from/to Hamburg see Table **56**.
X – ①–⑤ (not June 12).
Y – 🛏 1, 2 cl., ▬ 2 cl., (2) and ✕ Świnoujście - Szczecin - Poznań - Wrocław - Katowice - Kraków and v.v.
Z – (12) Poznań - Wrocław - Przemyśl and v.v. Conveys 🛏 2 cl. Wrocław - Kraków - Przemyśl - Kyïv and v.v. and 🛏 1, 2 cl. Praha - Kraków - Kyïv and v.v. Conveys (12) Poznań - Kraków - Zakopane on dates in Table **1066**.

c – Apr. 9 - Sept. 27.
e – From/to Ełk and Suwałki.
g – From Wałbrzych Gł.
h – To/from Szklarska Poręba Górna. (Table **1084**).
j – From/to Kołobrzeg.
m – From/ to Szczecin.
n – From/to Bydgoszcz and Gdynia (Table **1020**).
o – June 20 - Aug. 30.

p – To / from Rzeszów.
q – To/from Toruń and Olsztyn (Table **1020**).
v – June 21 - Aug. 31.
w – To/from Kudowa Zdrój (Table **1095**).

❖ – Subject to confirmation.
◐ – Via Ostrow Wlkp (Table **1080**).
◇ – Stopping train.
* * – Dębica - Zamość: – *207 km.*
▲ – Additional trains run Katowice - Kraków and v.v. (Journey time: 80–106 minutes).

1076 KATOWICE and KRAKÓW - OSTRAVA

km		EC 118 ✕⚡ §	EC 118 EC 103 ✕ §	EC 103 ✕⚡ §	EC 114 ✕⚡ §	EC 105 ✕⚡ §	208	200 203	200	203	203 200
							V	K	W	C	S
	Warszawa Cent. **1060** d.	...	...	0625	0925	1125	...	...	...	2100	2100
0	**Katowice** d.	...	...	0909	1209	1409	2240	...	...	2353	2353
	Kraków Gł. **1099** d.	0653	0653	|	|	|	|	2215	2215	|	|
	Oświecim **1099** d.	0813	0813	|	|	|	|	2342	2342	|	|
74	Zebrzydowice 🏛 d.	0916	0916	1016	1316	1516	2357	0050	0050	0105	0105
94	Bohumín 🏛 **1160** a.	0935	0935	1035	1334	1534	0017	0109	0109	0126	0126
	Bohumín 🏛 **1160** d.	0950	1046	1046	1350	1546	0042	0215	0207	0215	0207
102	**Ostrava** Hlavní **1160** a.	0959	1054	1054	1359	1554	0051	0224	0216	0224	0216
	Praha Hlavní **1160** a.	1354	|	|	1754	|	0507	|	0654	|	0654
	Wien Südbf **995** a.	...	1402	1402	...	1902	...	0630z	...	0630z	...

	201 202	201	202	202 201	209	EC 104 ✕⚡ §	EC 115 ✕⚡ §	EC 102 ✕⚡ §	EC 102 EC 119 ✕ §	EC 119 ✕⚡ §
	S	W	C	K	V					
Wien Südbf **995** d.	...	...	2212z	2212z	...	0858	...	1458	1458	...
Praha Hlavní **1160** d.	2109	2109	|	|	2300	|	1009	|	|	1409
Ostrava Hlavní **1160** d.	0138	0138	0208	0208	0301	1206	1402	1806	1806	1800
Bohumín 🏛 **1160** a.	0147	0147	0217	0217	0310	1215	1410	1815	1815	1808
Bohumín 🏛 **1160** d.	0252	0307	0252	0307	0328	1229	1429	1829	1837	1837
Zebrzydowice 🏛 d.	0313	0329	0313	0329	0350	1250	1450	1850	1858	1858
Oświecim **1099** a.	|	0444	|	0444	|	|	|	|	2007	2007
Kraków Gł. **1099** a.	|	0633	|	0633	|	|	|	|	2146	2146
Katowice a.	0425	...	0425	...	0505	1357	1557	1957	...	...
Warszawa Cent. **1060** a.	0720	...	0720	...	...	1645	1845	2245	...	...

C – CHOPIN – 🛏 1, 2 cl., ▬ 2 cl. and (2) Warszawa - Wien and v.v. Conveys 🛏 1, 2 cl., ▬ 2 cl. and (2) Warszawa - Bratislava - Budapest and v.v. Conveys 🛏 1, 2 cl. Moskva - Wien / Budapest and v.v.
K – 🛏 1, 2 cl. (also ▬ 2 cl. Apr. 29 - Sept. 27 from Kraków; Apr. 30 - Sept. 28 from Wien) Kraków - Wien and v.v. 🛏 1, 2 cl. and ▬ 2 cl. Kraków - Bratislava - Budapest and v.v.
S – 🛏 1, 2 cl., ▬ 2 cl. and (2) Warszawa - Praha and v.v.
V – VLTAVA – 🛏 1, 2 cl. Moskva - Terespol - Katowice - Praha and v.v. For additional cars see Table **95**.
W – SILESIA – 🛏 1, 2 cl., ▬ 2 cl. and (12) Kraków - Praha and v.v.

z – Wien **Westbahnhof**.

⚡ – Supplement payable.
§ – ® in Poland.

TRAIN NAMES:
EC **104 / 105** SOBIESKI.
EC **114 / 115** PRAHA.
EC **102 / 103** POLONIA.
EC **118 / 119** COMENIUS.

KATOWICE and KRAKÓW - ŽILINA 1077

km		411	413	401	2221	415	335	417	3921	4411	419
		◇	◇	◇ 2	◇	◇ 2	34009	◇	◇	333	◇
		2	2	B		A		2	2		2
0	**Katowice** .... **1060** d.	0410**x**	0514	0621	0658	0711	...	1215	...	1524	1730
	Kraków Gł. .... **1099** d.	|	|	|	|	|	0705	|	...	|	|
	Oświecim .... **1099** d.	|	|	|	|	|	0834	|	...	|	|
	Bielsko Biała .... **1060** d.	0528	0631	0730	|	0829	0940	1331	...	1629	1852
	Zywiec .... d.	0609	0707	0804	|	0901	1006	1401	...	1656	1927
	Zwardoń .... d.	0734	0821	0912	|	1010	1128	1510	1542	1818	2036
	Cieszyn .... d.	...	...	...	0903	...	|	...	|	|	...
89	Český Těšín .... **1160** d.	...	...	...	0908	...	|	...	|	|	...
127	Čadca .... **1160** d.	...	...	...	...	...	1202	...	1635	1849	...
158	**Žilina** .... **1160** a.	...	...	...	...	...	1241	...	1717	1919	...

km		414	418	332	424	2224	3920	426	334	428	
		◇	◇	4412	◇	◇	◇	◇	43008	◇	
		2	2		2		2	2		2	
0	**Žilina** .... **1160** d.	...	...	0922	...	...	1346	...	1554	...	...
31	Čadca .... **1160** d.	...	...	0953	...	...	1430	...	1635	...	...
	Český Těšín .... **1160** d.	...	...	|	...	1610	|	...	|	...	...
	Cieszyn .... d.	...	...	|	...	1621	|	...	|	...	...
52	Zwardoń .... d.	0432	0628	1039	1434	|	1508	1557	1729	1928	...
89	Zywiec .... d.	0543	0743	1150	1550	|	...	1730	1848	2044	...
110	**Bielsko Biała** .... **1060** d.	0616	0816	1219	1623	|	...	1803	1917	2117	...
142	Oświecim .... **1099** a.	|	|	|	|	|	...	|	2020	|	...
207	**Kraków** Gł. .... **1099** a.	|	|	|	|	|	...	|	2211	|	...
	Katowice .... **1060** a.	0727	0927	1316	1726	1830	...	1915	...	2228	...

A – ①–⑤ (not Nov. 1, 11). **B** – ⑥⑦ (also Nov. 1, 11). **x** – ①–⑤ (not May 1, June 11). ◇ – Stopping train. TRAIN NAMES: **333/332** GORAL **335/334** SKALNICA

KRAKÓW - ZAGÓRZ and KRYNICA 1078

km			2					53513	53513		13501		623			2	Ex	43101							
			◇					53514	33513	621	33501	13511	2 ◇	33101		◇	13411	33511	66131	625				627	2
		2	①–⑤	2	2	2				2			①–⑤		2	①–⑤	R ✕		2	2		2	2	2	◇
		◇	j	◇	◇	◇	V	P	H	◇	F	A	j	◇	◇	j	G	V	◇	◇	V	◇	◇	◇	k
	Warszawa Cent. **1065** ..... d.	...	...	...	...	...	...	...	...	...	2140	2245	...	...	...	...	0615	...	...	...	...	...	...	...	...
	Katowice **1075** .... d.	...	...	...	...	...	...	...	...	...	|	|	...	...	...	...	|	0720	...	...	...	...	...	...	...
0	**Kraków** Gł. .... **1075** d.	...	...	...	...	...	...	0236	0236	...	0312	|	...	0622	...	...	0923	0928	1040	...	...	...	...	...	...
5	Kraków Płaszów .... **1075** d.	...	...	...	...	...	...	|	|	...	0348	|	...	0630	...	...	0932	0937	1048	...	...	...	...	...	...
78	Tarnów .... **1075** d.	...	...	...	...	...	...	0400	0400	0435	0447	|	0531	0747	...	...	1027	1036	1204	...	...	...	...	1442	...
136	Stróze .... d.	...	...	0433**y**	...	...	...	0534	0557	0551	0605	|	0648	0905	...	...	1130	|	1322	1443	...	...	...	1559	...
**	Rzeszów .... d.	...	...	|	0443	...	...	|	|	|	|	0607	|	|	...	...	|	1157	|	|	...	...	...	|	1531
182	Jasło .... d.	0441	0541	|	0630	0646	...	|	0740	|	|	0820	|	|	1255	1349	|	1407	|	|	...	1450	1548	|	1724
205	Krosno .... d.	0525	0631	|	...	0730	...	|	0831	|	|	0904	|	|	1340	1440	|	1500	|	|	...	1542	1638	|	...
244	Sanok .... d.	0641	0745	|	...	0841	...	|	0942	|	|	1015	|	|	1452	1603	|	1629	|	|	...	1703	1752	|	...
251	**Zagórz** .... a.	0653	0758	|	...	0854	...	|	0956	|	|	1030	|	|	1505	1617	|	1643	|	|	...	1716	1806	|	...
167	**Nowy Sącz** .... d.	...	...	0513	...	...	...	0617	...	0630	0658	...	0731	0947	...	...	1210	...	1403	1524	...	...	...	1639	...
	Krynica .... d.	...	...	|	...	...	0758	|	...	...	|	...	...	|	...	...	|	...	|	|	1721	...	...	...	...
217	Muszyna .... d.	...	...	0626	...	...	0815	0754**z**	...	...	0823**x**	...	...	1058	...	...	1323**x**	...	1512	1640	1738	...	...	...	...
228	**Krynica** .... a.	...	...	0643	...	...	|	0817	...	...	0841	...	...	1116	...	...	1340	...	1529	1657	|	...	...	...	...
231	**Plaveč** .... a.	...	...	...	...	...	0838	...	...	...	...	...	...	...	...	...	...	...	...	...	1801	...	...	...	...
	Košice **1196** .... a.	...	...	...	...	...	...	...	...	...	...	...	...	...	...	...	...	...	...	...	...	...	...	...	...

	73101	629	2221	66133	66135		Ex	33001		
							1309	1381		
		2		2	2		3309	🍷		
		◇		◇	◇		L R	C		
Warszawa Cent. **1065** ...... d.	...	...	...	...	...	...	1715	...	...	...
Katowice **1075** .... d.	1230	...	...	...	...	...	|	...	...	...
Kraków Gł. .... **1075** d.	1422	...	1630	1745	1938	...	2020	2245	...	...
Kraków Płaszów .... **1075** d.	1431	...	1639	1753	1946	...	2029	2254	...	...
Tarnów .... **1075** d.	1530	1552	1735	1910	2110	...	2139	2350	...	...
Stróze .... d.	...	1714	1847	2022	2222	...	2240	0055	...	...
Rzeszów .... d.	...	|	|	|	...	...	|	|	...	...
Jasło .... d.	...	|	|	|	...	...	|	|	...	...
Krosno .... d.	...	|	|	|	...	...	|	|	...	...
Sanok .... d.	...	|	|	|	...	...	|	|	...	...
Zagórz .... a.	...	|	|	|	...	...	|	|	...	...
Nowy Sącz .... d.	...	1755	1926	2102	...	...	2316	0136	...	...
Krynica .... d.	...	|	...	...	...	...	...	|	...	...
Muszyna .... d.	...	1913	...	...	...	...	...	0304	...	...
Krynica .... a.	...	1930	...	...	...	...	...	|	...	...
Plaveč .... a.	...	...	...	...	...	...	...	0325	...	...
Košice **1196** .... a.	...	...	...	...	...	...	...	0500	...	...

	6022		Ex	2222	66120	2	38108	6024		
			3308				38107			
	2	2	3108		2	◇		2	2	2
	◇	◇	M R		◇	k		◇	◇	◇
Košice **1196** .... d.	...	...	...	...	...	...	...	...	...	...
Plaveč .... d.	...	...	...	...	...	...	...	...	...	...
Krynica .... d.	...	...	...	...	0443	...	...	0608	...	...
Muszyna .... d.	...	...	...	...	0504	...	...	0630	...	...
Krynica .... a.	...	...	...	...	|	...	...	|	...	...
Nowy Sącz .... d.	0412	...	0451	0541	0616	...	...	0740	...	...
Zagórz .... d.	|	...	|	|	|	...	...	|	...	0353
Sanok .... d.	|	...	|	|	|	...	...	|	...	0406
Krosno .... d.	|	...	|	|	|	...	...	|	...	0527
Jasło .... d.	|	...	|	|	|	0442	...	|	...	0616
Rzeszów .... d.	|	0455	|	|	|	0640	0720	|	...	...
Stróze .... d.	0451	|	0526	0618	0657	...	|	0819	...	...
Tarnów .... **1075** d.	0609	0612	0643	0727	0807	...	0831	0930	0933	...
Kraków Płaszów ..... **1075** a.	...	0717	0741	0828	0919	...	0933	...	1046	...
Kraków Gł. .... **1075** a.	...	0731	0750	0837	0928	...	0942	...	1055	...
Katowice **1075** .... a.	...	...	|	...	...	...	1129	...	...	...
Warszawa Cent. **1065** .. a.	...	...	1055	...	...	...	...	...	...	...

	2						66122		33514		Ex				2						33516	35512	33506	33000	
	◇			6026			2 ◇	6030	34100	33102	31410				◇		6032		31510		35512	35513	31500	1380	
	①–⑤	2		2	2	2	①–⑤	2			R ✕	2	2	2	①–⑤	2	2	2						🍷	
	j	◇	V	◇	◇	◇	j	◇	W	◇	G	◇	◇	◇	j	◇	◇	◇	B	V	K	Q	J	D	
Košice **1196** .... d.	...	...	...	...	...	...	...	...	...	...	...	...	...	...	...	...	...	...	...	...	...	...	...	2304	...
Plaveč .... d.	...	...	0903	...	...	...	...	...	...	...	...	...	...	...	...	...	...	...	...	1811	...	...	...	0104	...
Krynica .... d.	...	...	|	1008	...	...	...	...	...	1454	1532	...	...	...	...	...	1745	...	...	|	...	1909	1956	|	...
Muszyna .... d.	...	...	0927	1030	...	...	...	...	...	1516	1558**x**	...	...	...	...	...	1807	...	...	1836	...	1940**x**	2022**x**	0135	...
Krynica .... a.	...	...	0944	|	...	...	...	...	...	|	|	...	...	...	...	...	|	...	...	1852	...	|	|	|	...
Nowy Sącz .... d.	...	...	...	1141	...	...	1425	1525	...	1627	1701	...	...	...	...	...	1915	...	...	...	...	2049	2130	0245	...
Zagórz .... d.	0443	0548	...	|	...	1033	|	|	1117	|	|	1259	...	...	1357	1510	|	...	1735	...	1755	|	|	|	...
Sanok .... d.	0456	0601	...	|	...	1045	|	|	1131	|	|	1312	...	...	1410	1523	|	...	1754	...	1815	|	|	|	...
Krosno .... d.	0629	0732	...	|	...	1158	|	|	1242	|	|	1436	...	...	1538	1641	|	...	1904	...	1925	|	|	|	...
Jasło .... d.	0719	0818	...	|	...	1241	|	|	1349	|	|	1525	1535	...	1624	1725	|	...	1955	...	2008	|	|	|	...
Rzeszów .... d.	...	...	...	|	...	...	|	|	1610	|	|	...	1728	1820	...	...	|	...	2151	...	|	|	|	|	...
Stróze .... d.	...	...	...	1218	...	...	1504	1604	|	1704	1737	...	...	|	...	...	1953	...	|	...	2139	2139	2208	0321	...
Tarnów .... **1075** d.	...	...	...	1330	1339	...	1621	1717	1723	1818	1843	...	...	1939	...	...	2104	2107	|	...	2311	2311	2320	0423	...
Kraków Płaszów .... **1075** a.	...	...	...	...	1452	...	1737	...	1828	1931	1941	...	...	2056	...	...	...	2224	|	...	|	|	0022	0521	...
Kraków Gł. .... **1075** a.	...	...	...	...	1500	...	1746	...	1837	1940	1950	...	...	2105	...	...	...	2233	|	...	0020	0020	0053	0529	...
Katowice **1075** .... a.	...	...	...	...	...	...	...	...	2029	...	|	...	...	...	...	...	...	...	|	...	...	...	|	...	...
Warszawa Cent. **1065** ...... a.	...	...	...	...	...	...	...	...	...	...	2255	...	...	...	...	...	...	...	0515	...	...	...	0556	...	...

A – June 19 - Aug. 30: [12] Warszawa - Zagórz.
B – June 20 - Aug. 31: [12] Zagórz - Warszawa.
C – CRACOVIA – June 18 - Aug. 30: [2] Kraków - Košice - Lökösháza; June 20 - Aug. 30: ▬ 2 cl. and [2] Kraków - Bucureşti. June 18 - Aug. 30: ▬ 2 cl. and [2] Kraków - Košice - Budapest - Keszthely. For additional cars to Varna and Burgas see Table **99**.
D – CRACOVIA – June 19 - Aug. 31: [2] Lökösháza - Košice - Kraków; June 19 - Aug. 29: ▬ 2 cl. and [2] Bucureşti - Kraków. June 19 - Aug. 31: ▬ 2 cl. and [2] Keszthely - Budapest - Košice - Kraków. For additional cars from Varna and Burgas see Table **99**.
F – June 10, 11, June 19 - Aug. 30: ▬ 2 cl. and [12] Warszawa - Kraków - Krynica.
G – ⑥⑦ (also Aug. 31, Nov. 11).
H – June 19 - Aug. 30 from Gdynia: [12] Gdynia (depart 1451) - Kraków - Zagórz.
J – June 13, 14, June 20 - Aug. 31: ▬ 2 cl. and [12] Krynica - Kraków - Warszawa.
K – June 20 - Aug. 31: [12] Zagórz - Kraków - Gdynia (arrive 1230).
L – ⑧ (also Oct. 31).
M – ①–⑥ (also Nov. 1).
P – June 19 - Aug. 30 from Gdynia: 🛏 1, 2 cl. and [12] Gdynia (depart 1451) - Krynica.
Q – June 20 - Aug. 31: 🛏 1, 2 cl. and [12] Krynica - Gdynia (arrive 1230).
V – June 20 - Aug. 30.
W – June 21 - Aug. 31.
j – Not Nov. 1, 11.
k – Not Aug. 15, 16, Nov. 11.
x – Arrive 10 minutes earlier.
y – ①–⑥.
z – Arrive 0732.
◇ – Stopping train.
** – Rzeszów - Jasło: *71 km*.

ZAGÓRZ - ŁUPKÓW - MEDZILABORCE - HUMENNÉ 1079

km			A	A			A	A		
		2 ◇	2 ◇	2 ◇	2 ◇	2 ◇	2 ◇	2 ◇	2 ◇	
	Jasło .... d.	0441	...	...	...	1255	...	...	...	...
0	**Zagórz** .... d.	0653	0657	...	...	1505	1509	...	...	...
48	Łupków .... d.	...	0838	0853	...	...	1650	1707	...	...
63	Medzilaborce Mesto **1194** d.	...	...	0902	0957	...	...	1726	1834	...
65	Medzilaborce .... **1194** d.	...	...	0905	1010	...	...	1729	1840	...
106	Humenné .... **1194** a.	...	...	...	1119	...	...	...	1943	...

		A	A				A	A	
	2 ◇	2 ◇	2 ◇	2 ◇		2 ◇	2 ◇	2 ◇	
Humenné .... **1194** d.	0626	...	...	...	...	1437	...	...	...
Medzilaborce .... **1194** d.	0734	0808	...	...	...	1558	1632	...	...
Medzilaborce Mesto **1194** d.	...	0812	...	...	...	1601	1636	...	...
Łupków .... d.	...	0832	0848	...	...	...	1656	1709	...
Zagórz .... a.	...	...	1029	1033	...	...	...	1850	...
Jasło .... a.	...	...	...	1241	...	...	...	...	...

A – ⑤⑥⑦ June 26 - Aug. 30. ◇ – Stopping train.

1080 POZNAŃ - OSTRÓW - KATOWICE - KRAKÓW

For other trains Poznań - Katowice - Kraków (via Wrocław) see Table **1075**

km		◇ 2	◇ 2	84102 m	◇ 2 f	◇ 2	◇ 2 P	TLK 8310	◇ 2	81100 81101 p	◇ 2	84200 84502 Q	83500 83501 A
	Szczecin Gł. **1010** .. d.	...	...	0705	...	...	...	1150	...	1450	...	...	1655
0	**Poznań** Gł. d.	...	0630	0946	1050	1250	...	1414	1520x	1735	1900	0254	1950
67	Jarocin d.	...	0740	1039	1156	1354	...	1504	1619x	1828	2003	0353	2054
114	Ostrów Wlkp ⊠ **1090** d.	...	0824	1117	1241	1437	1445	1539	1700	1905	2047	0432	2135
160	Kępno d.	...	0919	1153	1321	...	1528	1615	1747	...	2128	0510	2211
201	Kluczbork a.	...	1000	▬	1410	...	1615	|	1825	...	...	0545	2256
			◇ 2	◇ 2 j	◇ 2		◇ 2 j	|	◇ 2			|	|
	Kluczbork d.	...	1030	1230	1430	...	1640	|	1840	...	...	0547	2258
252	Lubliniec d.	0834	1131	1338	1532	...	1754	|	1949	...	...	0650	0000
302	Bytom d.	1009	1304	1512	1706	...	1925	1910	2125	...	...	0821	0133
320	**Katowice** a.	1037	1333	1541	1735	...	1954	1938	2154	...	...	0850	0201
398	**Kraków** Gł. a.	...	...	...	...	...	...	2125	...	...	...	...	...

	◇ 2	18101 18102 p	◇ 2	◇ 2	TLK 3811	◇ 2	◇ 2 j	◇ 2	◇ 2	◇ 2 j	48201 48503 P	38500 38501 B
Kraków Gł. d.	...	...	...	...	0535	...	...	...	...	...	...	...
Katowice d.	...	...	...	0543	0715	0750	0945	1145	1445	1751	1919	0022
Bytom d.	...	...	...	0612	0742	0819	1014	1214	1214	1820	1952	0051
Lubliniec d.	...	...	...	0738	|	0938	1138	1338	1338	1951	2114	0211
Kluczbork a.	...	...	...	0830x	|	1030	1230	1427	1427	2044	2206	0302
				▬	|	48103 m	◇ 2	◇ 2 f	▬		|	|
Kluczbork d.	...	...	0750	◇	|	...	1250	1450	◇ 2	...	2208	0304
Kępno d.	0524	...	0839	2	1014	1343	1337	1536	p	...	2252	0407
Ostrów Wlkp. ⊠**1090** d.	0620	0914	0921	0933	1049	1421	1441	1625	1630	...	2330	0459
Jarocin d.	0712	0954	...	1027	1134	1506	1535	...	1724	...	0010	0546
Poznań Gł. a.	0820	1058	...	1140	1233	1620	1705	...	1844	...	0118	0650
Szczecin Gł. **1010** .. a.	...	1341	...	...	1500	1908	...	...	...	...	...	0959

A – June 19 - Aug. 30: 🛏 1, 2 cl., ▬ 2 cl. and 🚃 Szczecin - Zakopane.
B – June 20 - Aug. 31: 🛏 1, 2 cl., ▬ 2 cl. and 🚃 Zakopane - Szczecin.
P – Apr. 8 - Sept. 26: 🛏 1, 2 cl., ▬ 2 cl. and 🚃 Katowice - Poznań - Kołobrzeg.
Q – Apr. 9 - Sept. 27: 🛏 1, 2 cl., ▬ 2 cl. and 🚃 Kołobrzeg - Poznań - Katowice.

f – Not Aug. 15.
j – Not Nov. 11.
m – To / from Częstochowa.
p – To / from Łódź.

x – ①–⑤ (not Nov. 11).
⊠ – Full name is Ostrów Wielkopolski.
◇ – Stopping train.

1084 WĘGLINIEC - JELENIA GÓRA - WAŁBRZYCH - WROCŁAW

km		◇ 2	◇ 2 p	◇ 2 j	◇ 2	◇ 2	◇ 2 p	60510 E	◇ 2	◇ 2 g	◇ 2 p	◇ 2	◇ 2 g	◇ 2 p	◇ 2 ⑦f	◇ 2	◇ 2	63500 Jq	◇ 2 ⑦	◇ 2 g	65502 C	61200 A	◇ 2 g	
0	Węgliniec d.	...	...	...	...	0544	...	...	...	0826	...	...	1227	...	...	1606	...	...	...	1734	...	...	2046	...
**	Szklarska Poręba Górna d.	...	...	...	...	|	0629	...	*0836*	|	1044	1244	|	1442	...	|	1642	...	...	|	...	1826z	|	...
74	**Jelenia Góra** d.	...	...	...	0548	0723	0749	0928	0949	0959	1149	1349	1359	1549	1654	1740	1749	1843	1902	1906	1931	1953	2219	...
121	Wałbrzych Gł. d.	...	0519	0619	0719	...	0919	1057	1119	...	1321	1519	...	1719	1824	...	1919	2009	2038	...	2058	2120	...	...
151	Jaworzyna Śląska d.	0511	0616	0716	0816	...	1016	1155	1216	...	1417	1616	...	1815	1923	...	2016	2107	2134	...	2156	2218	...	...
200	**Wrocław** Gł. a.	0623	0727	0827	0927	...	1127	1256	1327	...	1528	1727	...	1920	2027	...	2127	2214	2237	...	2305	2320	...	...

	◇ 2 g	◇ 2 R	56503 B	◇ 2	16201 A	◇ 2	◇ 2 g	36501 Jq	◇ 2	◇ 2 p	◇ 2 g	◇ 2	◇ 2	◇ 2 p	◇ 2 h	60501 F	◇ 2	◇ 2 j	◇ 2 p	◇ 2 R	◇ 2 p	◇ 2	◇ 2	
Wrocław Gł. d.	...	...	0439	0539	0555	0639	...	0749	...	0939	...	1139	...	1339	...	1428	1539	1639	1749	1839	1939	2039	2249	...
Jaworzyna Śląska d.	...	...	0540	0638	0657	0739	...	0856	...	1036	...	1239	...	1439	...	1525	1639	1739	1841	1938	2039	2139	2352	...
Wałbrzych Gł. d.	...	0539	0630	0724	0752	0827	...	0943	...	1123	...	1327	...	1528	...	1614	1727	1827	1927	2027	2128	2227	...	...
Jelenia Góra a.	0602	0715	0800	0855	0921	1001z	1006	1108	1153	1255	1406	1501	1606	1703	1913	1744	1901	...	2057	...	2301v	...	...	...
Szklarska Poręba Górna a.	|	...	...	1001	1042z	...	|	...	|	1409	|	1619	|	1820	|	...	...	...	2205	...	...	...	...	...
Węgliniec a.	0740	...	...	...	...	...	1140	...	1339	...	1540	...	1758	...	2044	...	...	...	...	...	...	...	...	...

A – 🛏 1, 2 cl., ▬ 2 cl. and 🚃 Jelenia Góra - Warszawa and v.v. June 19 - Sept. 26: ▬ 2 cl. and 🚃 Warszawa - Szklarska Poręba Górna; June 20 - Sept. 27 ▬ 2 cl. and 🚃 Szklarska Poręba Górna - Warszawa (Tables **1088** / **1090**).
B – June 19 - Aug. 30: ▬ 2 cl. and 🚃 Gdynia (depart 1943) - Wrocław - Jelenia Góra.
C – June 20 - Aug. 31: ▬ 2 cl. and 🚃 - Jelenia Góra - Wrocław - Gdynia (arrive 0923).
E – June 21 - Sept. 27: 🚃 Jelenia Góra - Wrocław - Warszawa.
F – June 20 - Sept. 26: 🚃 Warszawa - Wrocław - Jelenia Góra.
J – June 20 - Aug. 31.
R – ①–⑤ (not Nov. 11).

f – Also Nov. 11.
g – From / to Zielona Góra (Table **1004**).
h – To Zary (Table **1004**).
j – Not Nov. 11.
p – To / From Poznań (Table **1070**).
q – To / from Przemyśl.
v – ⑤⑥ (also Nov. 10).
x – ⑥⑦ (also Nov. 11).
z – June 20 - Sept. 27.

◇ – Stopping train.
** – Szklarska Poręba Górna - Jelenia Góra: *32 km.*

1085 GÖRLITZ - WROCŁAW

km		◇ 2	66100 P	17041 60002	◇ 2	61100 61101	◇ 2	17043 60004	◇ 2	17045 60006	
	Dresden Hbf. **855** ... d.	...	...	0727	...	...	...	1327	...	1727	...
0	**Görlitz** 🏛 d.	...	...	0845	...	...	...	1445	...	1845	...
2	Zgorzelec 🏛 d.	...	0646	0851	...	1028	...	1451	...	1851	...
30	Węgliniec d.	0550	0723	0912	0950	1107	1350	1512	...	1912	...
55	Bolesławiec d.	0610	0740	0928	1010	1125	1410	1528	...	1928	...
99	Legnica d.	0655	0810	0956	1055	1157	1455	1556	1755	1956	...
165	**Wrocław** Gł. a.	0816	0920	1100	1216	1317	1616	1700	1916	2100	...
	Warszawa C. **1090** ... a.	...	...	...	...	2000	...	...	...	...	...

	17040 60001	◇ 2	◇ 2	17042 60003	◇ 2	16100 16101	◇ 2	◇ 2	17044 60005	66101 P
Warszawa C. **1090** .... d.	...	...	...	...	...	0750	...	...	...	...
Wrocław Gł. d.	0705	0732	0832	1305	1332	1431	1532	1732	1805	1844
Legnica d.	0807	0855	0950	1407	1458	1538	1655	1855	1907	1953
Bolesławiec d.	0835	0934	...	1435	1537	1609	1735	1945	1935	2022
Węgliniec d.	0852	0955	...	1452	1558	1637	1757	2006	1952	2052
Zgorzelec 🏛 d.	0913	...	...	1513	...	1707	...	...	2013	2118
Görlitz 🏛 a.	0919	...	...	1519	...	...	...	...	2019	...
Dresden Hbf. **855** ..... a.	1032	...	...	1632	...	...	...	...	2132	...

P – 🚃 Zgorzelec - Wrocław - Przemyśl and v.v.

◇ – Stopping train.

1086 FORST - WROCŁAW

km		◇ 2	◇ 2	◇ 2	◇ 2	B	EC 341 A	◇ 2	◇ 2	◇ 2 C	◇ 2	B	◇ 2	◇ 2
	Berlin Hbf. **838** ... d.	...	...	...	...	...	0941	...	...	...	...	...	...	...
	Cottbus **854** ...... d.	...	0607	...	...	...	1121	...	...	...	...	...	1625	...
0	**Forst** 🏛 d.	...	0627	0632	...	...	1142	...	...	...	...	...	1655	1933
14	Tuplice d.	...	▬	0649	...	...	|	1256j	...	1607	...	...	1713	1949
35	Żary d.	0519	◇	0714	0800	...	1225	1318	1601	1631	1808	...	1738	2012
48	Żagań d.	0534	2	0731	0815	...	1245	1333	1616	...	1823	...	1755	2027
122	Legnica d.	0705	0737	...	0938	0956	1424	1519	1739	...	1944	1956	...	...
188	**Wrocław** Gł. a.	...	0856	...	...	1100	1537	...	*1916*	...	...	2100	...	...
	Katowice **1075** .... a.	...	...	...	...	...	1819	...	...	...	...	...	...	...
	Kraków Gł. **1075** . a.	...	...	...	...	...	1955	...	...	...	...	...	...	...

	◇ 2	◇ 2	◇ 2	◇ 2	◇ 2	◇ 2	EC 340 A	◇ 2	◇ 2	◇ 2	◇ 2	◇ 2
Kraków Gł. **1075** d.	...	...	...	...	...	...	0723	...	...	...	...	...
Katowice **1075** . d.	...	...	...	...	...	...	0854	...	...	...	...	...
Wrocław Gł. d.	...	...	...	...	0832	...	1132	*1232*	*1439*	...	...	...
Legnica d.	...	...	0544	...	0950	0955	1257	1415	1619	...	...	2000
Żagań d.	0513	...	0712	0811	...	1117	1424	1539	1749	...	...	2125
Żary d.	0528	...	0724	0826	...	1133	1442	1552	1802	1846	...	2138
Tuplice d.	0553	...	...	0851	...	1154j	|	...	...	1909	...	...
Forst 🏛 d.	0610	0633	...	0910	...	...	1528	...	...	1925	1933	...
Cottbus **854** ..... a.	...	0652	...	0932	...	...	1546	...	...	...	1952	...
Berlin Hbf. **838** . a.	...	...	...	...	...	...	1730	...	...	...	...	...

A – WAWEL – 🚃 and 🍷 Berlin - Wrocław - Kraków and v.v. 🅁 ✗. For dates from / to Hamburg see Table **56**.
B – 🚃 Dresden - Legnica - Wrocław.
C – ①–⑤ (not Nov. 11).
j – ⑥⑦ (also Nov. 11).
✗ – Supplement payable.
◇ – Stopping train.

1088 WARSZAWA - CZĘSTOCHOWA - WROCŁAW

§ – For other trains Warszawa - Wrocław (via Łódź) and additional trains Warszawa - Skierniewice - Koluszki see Table **1090**

km		*Ex* 🅁 16410 ⑥ f	16107 16106	14100 14101 T	54112 54113 p	16104 16105 B	54105 54506 p y	14102 14103 ⑧ b		16200 16201 A
0	**Warszawa** Wschodnia § d.	0548	0632	0822	1233	1423	1633	1832	...	2227
5	**Warszawa** Centralna § d.	0605	0650	0850	1250	1450	1650	1850	...	2250
71	Skierniewice § d.	|	0740	0940	1340	1540	1738	1940	...	2346
111	Koluszki **1060** § d.	|	0804	1006	1404	1604	1801	2004	...	0012
150	Piotrków Trybunalski **1060** d.	0734	0835	1036	1435	1636	1833	2035	...	0045
235	Częstochowa Osobowa **1060** d.	0836	0940	1137	1537	1742	1937	2137	...	0203
275	Lubliniec d.	|	1037	*1330*	*1652*	1843	...	...	...	0303
330	Opole Gł. **1075** d.	1026	1136	...	...	2005	...	...	...	0413
370	Brzeg **1075** d.	|	...	...	...	2036	...	...	...	0443
412	**Wrocław** Gł. **1075** a.	1120	...	...	...	2113	...	...	...	0521

	41102 ①–⑥ b	45105 45505 p y	61104 61105 B	45112 45113 p	41100 41101 T	61106 61107	*Ex* 61414 ⑥ 🅁	*Ex* 🅁 61411 ⑦ f	61200 61201 A
Wrocław Gł. **1075** d.	...	...	0715	...	...	...	1725	1725	2335
Brzeg **1075** d.	...	...	0749	...	...	...	|	|	0013
Opole Gł. **1075** d.	...	...	0823	...	...	1607	1820	1820	0057
Lubliniec d.	...	*0637*	0924	...	*1429*	1721	|	|	0205
Częstochowa Osobowa **1060** d.	0604	0804	1004	1204	1604	1802	1952	1952	0256
Piotrków Trybunalski **1060** d.	0716	0916	1113	1314	1715	1912	2100	2100	0408
Koluszki **1060** § d.	0746	0944	1142	1344	1743	1942	|	|	0439
Skierniewice § d.	0811	1007	1207	1408	1807	2006	|	|	0504
Warszawa Centralna § a.	0905	1100	1300	1500	1900	2100	2235	2235	0600
Warszawa Wschodnia § a.	0917	1112	1332	1517	1932	2117	2247	2247	0612

A – 🛏 1, 2 cl. and 🚃 Warszawa - Jelenia Góra and v.v. To / from Szklarska Poręba Górna on dates in Table **1084**.
B – 🚃 Białystok - Warszawa - Wrocław and v.v.
T – 🚃 Białystok - Warszawa - Częstochowa - Katowice - Bielsko Biała and v.v.

b – From / to Białystok.
f – To / from Jelenia Góra.
p – From / to Olsztyn.
y – To / from Racibórz.

WARSZAWA - ŁÓDŹ - WROCŁAW 1090

See Table **1005** for the through trains Warszawa - Wrocław via Poznań (also Łódź - Poznań via Kutno).

km		18101	18101	22500	22100	22102	16100	22502	22104	22504	22106	16103	22506	22108	22508	22110	16110	22510	2200	22512	16512	22514	22112	22516	22114
		18102	76101	22501	22101	22103	16101	22503	22105	22505	22107	16102	22507	22109	22509	22111	16111	22511	2201	22513	17112	22515	22113	22517	22115
			①–⑥	①–⑤			60501	①–⑤		①–⑤			①–⑤		①–⑤			①–⑤	①–⑤	⑥⑦	①–⑤	①–⑤		①–⑤	
		C	b	g			w	g		y			y		y			g	t	k		g		g	
0	**Warszawa** Wschodnia **1088** d.	...	...	0538	0608	0703	0732	0802	0908	1008	1108	1132	1208	1308	1408	1508	1537	1608	1648	1707	1738	1808	1908	2008	2107
5	**Warszawa** Centralna . **1088** d.	...	...	0550	0620	0720	0750	0820	0920	1020	1120	1150	1220	1320	1420	1520	1550	1620	1700	1720	1750	1820	1920	2020	2120
71	Skierniewice .... **1088** d.	...	...	0638	0710	0808	0840	0910	1010	1108	1208	1240	1308	1408	1508	1610	1640	1710	|	1810	1840	1908	2008	2108	2210
111	Koluszki .... **1088** d.	...	...	0700	0733	0830	0904	0934	1034	1130	1230	1304	1330	1430	1530	1634	1704	1734	|	1834	1904	1930	2030	2130	2234
132	Łódź Widzew ....d.	...	...	0713	0746	0843	0919	0949	1049	1143	1246	1321	1343	1443	1543	1649	1720	1749	1818	1849	1922	1943	2043	2146	2249
138	**Łódź** Fabryczna ....a.	...	...	0721	0754	0851	|	0957	1057	1151	1255	|	1351	1451	1551	1657	|	1757	1826	1857	|	1951	2051	2155	2257
147	**Łódź** Kaliska......................d.	0636	0636	...	...	...	0954	...	...	...	...	1358	...	...	...	...	1755	...	...	...	1959	...	...	...	...
260	Kalisz.................................d.	0828	0828	...	...	...	1147	...	...	...	...	1551	...	...	...	...	1953	...	...	...	2153	...	...	...	...
284	Ostrów Wielkopolski ... **1080** d.	0855	0911	...	...	...	1216	...	...	...	...	1620	...	...	...	...	2022	...	...	...	2219	...	...	...	...
390	**Wrocław** Gł. ....a.	...	1113	...	...	...	1410	...	...	...	...	1816	...	...	...	...	2214	...	...	...	0010**p**	...	...	...	...

	33501	33101	3301	33103	33503	61513	33105	33505	61111	33107	33507	33109	33509	61103	33111	33511	33113	33513	61100	33115	33117	67101	81100		
	33500	33100	3300	33102	33502	71113	33104	33504	61110	33106	33506	33108	33508	61102	33110	33510	33112	33512	61101	33114	33116	81100	81101		
	①–⑤		①–⑤		①–⑤	①–⑤		①–⑤			①–⑤		①–⑤			①–⑤		①–⑤	60510			⑧ f			
	g		t		g			y			y		y			g		g	w				C		
Wrocław Gł. ....d.	...	...	...	...	...	0342**z**	...	...	0530	...	...	...	...	0930	...	...	...	...	1330	...	...	1709	...	...	...
Ostrów Wielkopolski ... **1080** d.	...	...	...	...	...	0539	...	...	0737	...	...	...	...	1133	...	...	...	...	1536	...	...	1925	1925	...	...
Kalisz ....d.	...	...	...	...	...	0601	...	...	0759	...	...	...	...	1158	...	...	...	...	1559	...	...	1947	1947	...	...
Łódź Kaliska.....................d.	...	...	...	...	...	0803	...	...	1000	...	...	...	...	1401	...	...	...	...	1759	...	...	2134	2134	...	...
Łódź Fabryczna ....d.	0451	0551	0632	0651	0758	|	0858	0958	|	1058	1158	1258	1358	|	1458	1558	1651	1758	|	1856	2058	...	...	...	...
Łódź Widzew.......................d.	0459	0559	0639	0657	0805	0823	0905	1005	1022	1105	1205	1305	1405	1425	1505	1605	1659	1805	1824	1904	2105	...	...	...	...
Koluszki.................... **1088** d.	0515	0615	|	0715	0819	0847	0919	1019	1044	1119	1219	1319	1419	1444	1519	1619	1715	1819	1842	1919	2119	...	...	...	...
Skierniewice .... **1088** d.	0539	0639	|	0739	0841	0911	0941	1041	1108	1141	1241	1341	1441	1508	1541	1641	1739	1841	1906	1941	2141	...	...	...	...
Warszawa Centralna . **1088** a.	0629	0729	0800	0829	0929	1005	1029	1129	1200	1229	1329	1429	1529	1600	1629	1729	1829	1929	2000	2029	2229	...	...	...	...
Warszawa Wschodnia **1088** a.	0642	0742	0817	0842	0942	1017	1047	1141	1217	1241	1341	1442	1547	1617	1647	1742	1842	1942	2012	2042	2241	...	...	...	...

C – [12] Szczecin - Poznań - Ostrów Wlkp. - Łódź Kaliska and v.v.
b – Also Nov. 1; not Nov. 11.
f – Also Oct. 31; not Nov. 11.
g – Not Nov. 11.
k – Also Nov. 11.
p – ⑥ only.
t – ①–⑤ (also Nov. 1; not Nov. 11).
w – To / from Zgorzelec (Table **1085**). To / from Jelenia Góra on dates shown in Table **1084**.
y – Not June 22 - Aug. 28, Nov. 11.
z – ① only.

WROCŁAW - KŁODZKO - LICHKOV 1095

km		16201	250	2	2	2	2	2	252	2	2	2
		66511	66001	◇	◇	◇	◇	◇	66003	◇	◇	◇
		A	B		p			p	B		p	
	Warszawa C. **1090** ...d.	2250	...	...	...	...	...	...	...	...	...	...
0	**Wrocław** Gł. ....d.	0559	0625	0635	0935	1135	1135	1335	1425	1535	1745	1935
72	Kamieniec Ząbkowicki..d.	0727	0743	0805	1104	1303	1303	1504	1543	1706	1907	2105
94	Kłodzko Gł. ....a.	0749	0806	0829	1129	1331	1331	1529	1606	1731	1932	2130
	Kłodzko Gł. ....d.	...	0807	0855	1155	1347	1355**x**	1554	1607	1732	1958	2131
138	**Kudowa Zdrój** ....a.	...	|	1101	1425	|	1637	1847	|	|	2205	|
130	Międzylesie..................a.	...	0852	...	...	1432	...	...	1651	1824	...	2219
	Międzylesie 🏛 ....d.	...	0854	...	...	...	...	...	1654	...	...	...
139	**Lichkov** 🏛 ....a.	...	0903	...	...	...	...	...	1703	...	...	...
	Praha Hlavní **1145** ...a.	...	1247	...	...	...	...	...	2047	...	...	...

	2	2	2	251	2	2	2	2	2	253	66510
	◇	◇	◇	66000	◇	◇	◇	◇	◇	66002	61200
		p		B	p		p			B	A
Praha Hlavní **1145** d.	...	...	...	0711	...	...	...	...	...	1511	...
Lichkov 🏛 ....d.	...	...	...	1102	...	...	...	...	...	1902	...
Międzylesie 🏛 ....a.	...	...	...	1111	...	...	...	...	...	1911	...
Międzylesie ....d.	0630	...	...	1114	...	1436	...	1800	...	1914	...
Kudowa Zdrój ......d.	|	0657	0902	|	1111	|	1441	|	1650	|	...
Kłodzko Gł. ....a.	0717	0908	1122	1157	1317	1522	1659	1845	1856	1957	...
Kłodzko Gł. ....d.	0718	0923	1134	1158	1331	1523	1722	1908	1908	1958	2135
Kamieniec Ząbkowicki d.	0744	0948	1156	1222	1356	1549	1746	1934	1934	2022	2201
Wrocław Gł. ....a.	0911	1111	1321	1340	1523	1712	1914	2107	2107	2140	2319
Warszawa C. **1090**. a.	...	...	...	...	...	...	...	...	...	...	0600

A – From Warszawa June 19 - Sept. 26; from Kudowa Zdrój June 20 - Sept. 27: 🛏 2 cl. and [12] Warszawa - Wrocław - Kudowa Zdrój and v.v.
B – [12] Wrocław - Lichkov - Praha and v.v.
p – From / to Poznań (Table **1070**).
x – 1418 June 20 - Sept. 27.
◇ – Stopping train.

POLISH LOCAL RAILWAYS 1099

2nd class only

Certain trains Wolsztyn - Poznań and Wolsztyn - Leszno are hauled by steam locomotive - for details see www.parowozy.com.pl

km				🚂					🚂		
		①–⑥		W			⑧		J		
0	Zbąszynek .... d.	...	0640	...	0830	...	1234	1514	...	1900	...
6	Zbąszyń...................... d.	...	0646	...	0836	...	1241	1521	...	1906	...
28	Wolsztyn..................... d.	0507	0730	0800	0901	...	1313	1602	1750	1934	...
75	**Leszno**...................... a.	0603	0825	0853	0956	...	1407	1702	1855	2028	...

		🚂						🚂		
		H		F		⑧		X	⑧	
Leszno .... d.	0611	0958	1020	1215	1415	1540	1733	2030	2116	...
Wolsztyn .... d.	0714	1051	1116	1311	1518	1640	1828	2124	2212	...
Zbąszyń........................ a.	0739	...	1141	1336	1542	...	1852	...	...	...
Zbąszynek .... a.	0746	...	1203	1343	1549	...	1908	...	...	...

km			77325				77333				
		F	🚂				🚂				
0	**Wolsztyn** .... d.	0428	0505	0725	...	1145	1331	1601	...	1938	...
81	**Poznań** Gł. .... a.	0608	0701	0923	...	1323	1523	1743	...	2120	...

		77324					77332			
	F	🚂					🚂			
Poznań Gł. .... d.	0536	0635	0825	...	1336	1555	1712	1935	...	...
Wolsztyn.................... a.	0719	0831	1017	...	1515	1738	1908	2112	...	...

KRAKÓW - TRZEBINIA - OŚWIĘCIM (for Auschwitz) *65 km.* Journey time: 77–90 mins (from Kraków), 90–111 mins (from Oświęcim). Additional services by changing at Trzebinia.

From **Kraków Główny**: 0615, 0653 (*EC* **118**), 0705, 0845, 1105, 1445, 1539, 1841, 2142 ⑧, 2215 (*D* **200**).
From **Oświęcim**: 0356 ①–⑥, 0427, 0445 (*D* **201**), 0501, 0655, 0815, 1115, 1634 ⑦, 2008 (*EC* **119**), 2021.

KRAKÓW - SKAWINA - OŚWIĘCIM (for Auschwitz). *70 km.* Journey time: 106–110 mins (from Kraków), 111–118 mins (from Oświęcim).

From **Kraków Główny**: 0441, 0545 **F**, 1430, 1520, 1758.
From **Oświęcim**: 0350, 0535, 1318 **F**, 1536, 1738.

KATOWICE - OŚWIĘCIM. *33 km.* Journey time: 56–62 mins. From **Katowice**: 0540 **F**, 0650, 1435, 1534, 1855. From **Oświęcim**: 0517 **F**, 0632, 0818, 1550, 1830.

KRAKÓW - WIELICZKA (for Salt Mine). *15 km.* Journey time: 26 mins.

From **Kraków Główny**: 0503, 0554 **F**, 0630, 0736, 0835, 0935, 1135, 1335, 1435, 1535, 1635 **F**, 1736, 1835, 2038.
From **Wieliczka Rynek**: 0533, 0624 **F**, 0707, 0806, 0908, 1006, 1206, 1406, 1506, 1606, 1706 **F**, 1806, 1906, 2108.

WAŁBRZYCH - KŁODZKO. *51 km.*

From Wałbrzych Główny: 0614, 1154, 1554, 1934.
From Kłodzko Główne: 0441, 0941, 1341, 1741.

KRAKÓW - WADOWICE (Birth place of Pope John Paul II) *62 km.* Journey time 79–98 (minutes. Special fares payable. From **Kraków**: 0855 **n**, 1255 **m**, 1323, 1655 **m**. From **Wadowice**: 0744, 1030 **m**, 1500 **n**, 1830 **m**.

GDYNIA - HEL *77 km.* Local services only.

Dec. 14 - June 19 and Sept. 1 - Dec. 12. Journey time 96–109 mins.

From **Gdynia Gł.**: 0537, 0704, 1034, 1232, 1346, 1516, 1632, 1902, 2035.
From **Hel**: 0431, 0620, 0745, 0946, 1233, 1430, 1632, 1834.

June 20 - Aug. 31. Journey time 114–147 mins

From **Gdynia Gł.**: 0310, 0347, 0405 **h**, 0539, 0703, 0828, 0928, 0954, 1123, 1217, 1316, 1346, 1516, 1627, 1803 ⑧ **x**, 1943, 2149.
From **Hel**: 0402, 0627, 0834, 1048, 1130, 1300, 1425, 1507, 1607, 1642, 1732, 1852, 2011, 2058 **h**, 2126, 2214.

F – ①–⑤ (not Nov. 11).
H – HEFAJSTOS – May 2, Sept. 19: 🚂, [12] and ✕ Wrocław (depart 0806) - Lesno - Wolsztyn.
J – HEFAJSTOS – May 2, Sept. 19: 🚂, [12] and ✕ Wolsztyn - Lesno - Wrocław (arrive 2035).
W – THE WOLSZTYN EXPERIENCE – Feb. 14, Apr. 11, July 4, Aug. 28, Oct. 31 (dates subject to confirmation): 🚂, [12] and ✕ Wolsztyn - Lesno - Wrocław (arrive 1106).
X – THE WOLSZTYN EXPERIENCE – Feb. 14, Apr. 11, July 4, Aug. 28, Oct. 31 (dates subject to confirmation): 🚂, [12] and ✕ Wrocław (depart 1821) - Lesno - Wolsztyn.
h – From / to Warszawa and Kraków. Table **1030**.
m – May 1 - Sept. 30 (not June 15, 19, July 13, 24, Aug. 10, 28, Sept. 7, 25).
n – Not June 15, 19, July 13, 24, Aug. 10, 28, Sept. 7, 25, Oct. 5, 23, Nov. 2, 20, 30.
x – ⑧ (not Aug. 14).
🚂 – Normally hauled by steam locomotive (not guaranteed), except July / August.
⊠ – Operated on behalf of The Wolsztyn Experience. Special fares payable.

CZECH REPUBLIC

Services: Operator: České Dráhy (ČD). All daytime trains convey first and second classes of travel unless otherwise shown by '2' at the top of the column or by a note (which may be in the table heading). Overnight sleeping car (🛏) or couchette (▬) trains do not necessarily convey seating accommodation and individual footnotes should be checked carefully.

Timings: Valid **December 14, 2008 - December 12, 2009**, incorporating amendments from March 8. Further changes are due from June 14. A reduced service runs on the evening of Dec. 24, 31 and morning of Dec. 25, Jan. 1 (Christmas / New Year alterations are partially shown in the tables but cannot be shown in detail for space reasons, particularly local trains).

Reservations: It is possible to reserve seats on most Express trains.

Supplements: SuperCity (*SC*) trains are operated by tilting *Pendolino* units and have a compulsory reservation fee of 200 CZK or €7.00.

Station names: hlavní = main; západ = west; východ = east; horní = upper; dolní = lower; starý = old; město = town; předměstí = suburban; nádraží = station.

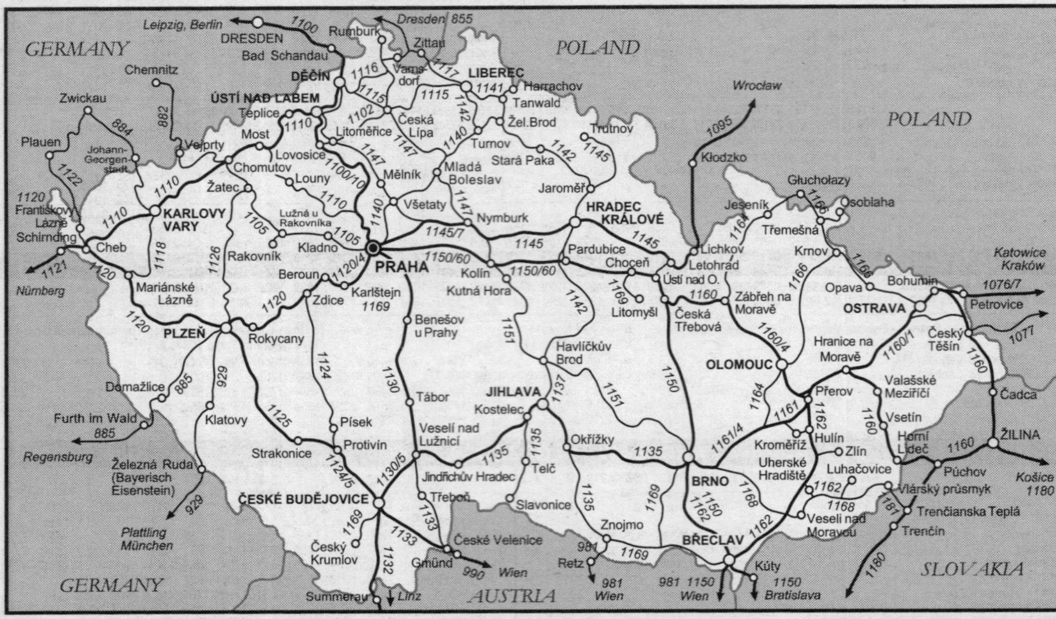

1100 PRAHA - ÚSTÍ NAD LABEM - DĚČÍN - DRESDEN

km	*Praha - Ústí : see also* **1110**	*EN* 476 ♦	440 ♦	◇	*EC* 178 ✕ ♦	770	*EC* 176 ✕ ♦	772	*EC* 378 ✕ ♦	774	*EC* 174 ✕ ♦	776	*EC* 172 ✕ ♦	778	976 Ⓐ	*EC* 170 ✕ ♦	780	782 Ⓐ	*EN* 456 ♦	*EN* 458 ♦	784	978 2 Ⓐ	786 ⊕	788 ⊗
0	**Praha** hlavní ▷ d.	...	0458	...	0629	...	...	...	...	...	...	...	...	...	...	...	...	...	1829	1829	...	...	...	...
0	**Praha** Masarykovo d.	...	|	...	|	0652	...	0852	...	1052	...	1252	...	1452	1552	...	1652	1752	|	|	1852	1952	2052	2322
3	**Praha** Holešovice ▷ d.	0340	0509	...	0640	|	0840	|	1040	|	1240	|	1440	|	|	1640	|	|	1840	1840	|	|	|	|
27	Kralupy nad Vltavou d.	|	0535	...	|	0717	|	0917	|	1117	|	1317	|	1517	1617	|	1717	1817	|	|	1917	2017	2117	2349
66	Roudnice nad Labem d.	|	0603	...	|	0743	|	0943	|	1143	|	1343	|	1543	1643	|	1743	1843	|	|	1943	2043	2143	0013
84	Lovosice d.	|	0620	...	|	0758	|	0958	|	1158	|	1358	|	1558	1658	|	1758	1858	|	|	1958	2058	2158	0026
106	**Ústí nad Labem** hlavní ▷ a.	0443	0639	...	0743	0815	0943	1015	1143	1215	1343	1415	1543	1615	1718	1743	1815	1915	1943	1943	2015	2115	2215	0042
106	**Ústí nad Labem** hlavní ▶ d.	0444	...	0700	0744	0817	0944	1017	1144	1217	1344	1417	1544	1617	*1727*	1744	1817	1917	1944	1944	2017	*2127*	2217	0044
129	**Děčín** ▶ a.	0500	...	0728	0800	0833	1000	1033	1200	1233	1400	1433	1600	1633	*1744*	1800	1833	1933	2000	2000	2033	*2144*	2233	0101
129	**Děčín** 🏛 ⊖ d.	0502	...	...	0802	...	1002	...	1202	...	1402	...	1602	...	...	1802	...	...	2002	2002	...	...	...	...
151	Bad Schandau 🏛 ⊖ **857** d.	|	...	...	0819	...	1019	...	1219	...	1419	...	1619	...	...	1819	...	...	2019	2019	...	...	...	...
191	**Dresden** Hbf **857** a.	0547	...	...	0846	...	1046	...	1246	...	1446	...	1646	...	...	1846	...	...	2047	2047	...	...	...	...

	771 ⊖	773	775 Ⓐ	777	*EN* 457 ♦	1156	979 2 Ⓐ	*EN* 459 ♦	779	*EC* 171 ✕ ♦	781	*EC* 173 ✕ ♦	783	*EC* 175 ✕ ♦	785	*EC* 177 ✕ ♦	787	*EC* 379 ✕ ♦	789 ⊗	*EC* 179 ✕ ♦	◇ ⊗	441 ♦	*EN* 477 ♦	
Dresden Hbf **857** d.	...	...	...	...	0710	...	...	0816	...	0910	...	1110	...	1310	...	1510	...	1710	...	1910	...	...	2210	...
Bad Schandau 🏛 ⊖ **857** d.	...	...	...	...	0738	...	...	0853	...	0938	...	1138	...	1338	...	1538	...	1738	...	1938	...	...	|	...
Děčín 🏛 ⊖ a.	...	...	...	...	0753	...	...	0912	...	0953	...	1153	...	1353	...	1553	...	1753	...	1953	...	...	2253	...
Děčín ▶ d.	0421	0521	0621	0721	0755	0818	...	0915	0921	0955	1121	1155	1321	1355	1521	1555	1721	1755	1921	1955	2028	...	2255	...
Ústí nad Labem hlavní ▶ a.	0438	0538	0638	0738	0812	0836	...	0932	0938	1012	1138	1212	1338	1412	1538	1612	1738	1812	1938	2012	2055	...	2312	...
Ústí nad Labem hlavní ▷ d.	0440	0540	0640	0740	0814	...	0840	0936	0940	1014	1140	1214	1340	1414	1540	1614	1740	1814	1940	2014	...	2114	2314	...
Lovosice d.	0458	0558	0658	0758	|	...	0858	|	0958	|	1158	|	1358	|	1558	|	1758	|	1958	|	...	2134	|	...
Roudnice nad Labem d.	0513	0613	0713	0813	|	...	0913	|	1013	|	1213	|	1413	|	1613	|	1813	|	2013	|	...	2148	|	...
Kralupy nad Vltavou d.	0539	0639	0739	0839	|	...	0939	|	1039	|	1239	|	1439	|	1639	|	1839	|	2039	|	...	2214	|	...
Praha Holešovice ▷ a.	|	|	|	|	0918	...	|	1040	|	1118	|	1318	|	1518	|	1718	|	1918	|	2118	...	2233	0018	...
Praha Masarykovo a.	0604	0704	0804	0904	|	...	1004	|	1104	...	1304	...	1504	...	1704	...	1904	...	2104	...	...	|	|	...
Praha hlavní ▷ a.	...	...	...	...	0956	...	...	1052	...	...	...	...	...	...	...	...	...	...	...	...	...	2245	0030	...

ADDITIONAL LOCAL TRAINS DĚČÍN - DRESDEN AND V.V. 2nd class

						E			
Děčín 🏛 ⊖ d.	0639	0858	1101	1301	1501	1608	1701	1901	...
Bad Schandau a.	0703	0933	1133	1333	1533	1625	1733	1933	...
Bad Schandau **857** d.	*0711*	*0941*	*1141*	*1341*	*1541*	1626	*1741*	*1941*	...
Dresden Hbf **857** a.	*0758*	*1029*	*1229*	*1429*	*1629*	1705	*1829*	*2028*	...

		E							
Dresden Hbf **857** d.	*0630*	0824	*0900*	*1100*	*1300*	*1500*	*1700*	*1900*	...
Bad Schandau **857** a.	*0716*	0858	*0946*	*1146*	*1346*	*1546*	*1746*	*1946*	...
Bad Schandau d.	0719	0859	0953	1153	1353	1553	1753	1953	...
Děčín 🏛 ⊖ a.	0750	0917	1024	1224	1424	1624	1824	2024	...

♦ – **NOTES** (LISTED BY TRAIN NUMBERS)

170/1 – HUNGARIA – [12] ✕ Budapest - Bratislava - Praha - Dresden - Berlin and v.v.
172/3 – VINDOBONA – [12] ✕ Wien - Praha - Dresden - Berlin - Hamburg ‡ and v.v.
174/5 – JAN JESENIUS – [12] ✕ Budapest - Bratislava - Praha - Dresden - Berlin - Hamburg ‡ and v.v.
176 – ALOIS NEGRELLI – [12] ✕ Brno - Praha - Dresden - Berlin - Hamburg ‡.
177 – JOHANNES BRAHMS – [12] ✕ Berlin - Dresden - Praha - Brno - Wien.
178 – JOHANNES BRAHMS – [12] ✕ Praha - Dresden - Berlin.
179 – ALOIS NEGRELLI – [12] ✕ Berlin - Dresden - Praha - Brno.
378 – CARL MARIA VON WEBER – [12] ✕ Wien - Praha - Dresden - Berlin - Stralsund - (Binz ◐).
379 – CARL MARIA VON WEBER – [12] ✕ (Binz ◐) - Stralsund - Berlin - Dresden - Praha - Brno.
440/1 – EXCELSIOR – 🛏 1, 2 cl., ▬ 2 cl., [12] Cheb - Karlovy Vary - Praha - Žilina - Košice and v.v.
456/7 – PHOENIX – [2] Praha - Dresden - Berlin and v.v.; 🛏 1, 2 cl., ▬ 2 cl., [2] (Ⓡ) Praha - Dresden - Berlin - Hannover - Amsterdam and v.v. Not June 6 from Praha or Berlin.
458/9 – CANOPUS – [2] Praha - Dresden - Leipzig - Erfurt and v.v.; 🛏 1, 2 cl., ▬ 2 cl., [2] (Ⓡ) Praha - Erfurt - Frankfurt Sud - Basel - Zürich and v.v. Not June 6 from Praha or Zürich.
476/7 – METROPOL – 🛏 1, 2 cl., ▬ 2 cl. and [2] Budapest - Bratislava - Brno - Praha - Dresden - Berlin and v.v.; 🛏 1, 2 cl., ▬ 2 cl. and [2] Wien Westbf - Brno - Praha - Dresden - Berlin and v.v.

E – ⑥⑦ Apr. 4 - Nov. 1.
◐ – Extended to / from Binz on dates in Table **844**.
▶ – Ústí nad Labem - Děčín: see also Table **1115** and foot of Table **1110**.
▷ – For other non-stop trains Praha - Ústí nad Labem and v.v. see Table **1110**.
⊖ – Routeing point for international tickets: Schöna.
‡ – Not Berlin - Hamburg or v.v. Mar. 1 - June 13.
◇ – Stopping train, 2nd class only.

⊕ – Not Dec. 24, 31.
⊗ – Not Dec. 24, 25, 31.
⊖ – Not Dec. 25, Jan. 1.

Other local services:

Praha Masarykovo - Lovosice: every 1-2 hours.

Lovosice - Ústí nad Labem: hourly.

LOVOSICE - LITOMĚŘICE - ČESKÁ LIPA 1102

Local trains, 2nd class

km										
0	**Lovosice 1100** d.	0601	0801	1001	1201	1401	1601	1801	2001	2213
8	Litoměřice horní d.	0616	0816	1016	1216	1416	1616	1816	2016	2226
50	**Česká Lípa** a.	0724	0924	1124	1324	1524	1724	1924	2124	...

		Ⓐ									
Česká Lípa d.	...	0440	0634	0834	1034	1234	1434	1634	1834	2034	...
Litoměřice horní d.	0010	0601	0740	0940	1140	1340	1540	1740	1940	2140	2213
Lovosice 1100 a.	0022	0616	0753	0953	1153	1353	1553	1753	1953	2153	2228

Also: Lovosice - Litoměřice horní: 0501, 0640 Ⓐ, 0701 Ⓐ, 0737, 0831, 0936, 1031, 1136, 1231, 1301 Ⓐ, 1336, 1436, 1501 Ⓐ, 1536, 1636, 1701 Ⓐ, 1736, 1836, 1901, 1936, 2031, 2136, 2301.
Litoměřice horní - Lovosice: 0441 Ⓐ, 0531, 0640 Ⓐ, 0701 Ⓐ, 0801, 0831 Ⓐ, 0910, 1001, 1110, 1201, 1301, 1401, 1440 Ⓐ, 1501, 1601, 1640 Ⓐ, 1701, 1800, 1840, 1900, 2000, 2110.

PRAHA - RAKOVNIK - CHOMUTOV - JIRKOV 1105

km			1284	1286	1288	1290	1292	1890	1294	1296	1298
		2						2Ⓐ			Ⓑh
0	**Praha** Masarykovo d.	*0515*	0702	0902	1102	1302	1502	1617	1702	1902	2102
31	Kladno d.	0621	0743	0943	1143	1343	1543	1709	1743	1943	2143
64	Lužná u Rakovnika a.	0702	0821	1021	1221	1421	1621	1751	1821	2021	2221
73	**Rakovník** a.	0720	0834	1034	1234	1434	1634	1804	1834	2034	2234

	1285	1883	1287	1289	1291	1293	1295	1297	1299	
	⚒n	2								2
Rakovník d.	0516	0620	0721	0921	1121	1321	1521	1721	1921	2207
Lužná u Rakovnika d.	0528	0635	0734	0934	1134	1334	1534	1734	1934	2222
Kladno d.	0608	0715	0815	1015	1215	1415	1615	1815	2015	2307
Praha Masarykovo a.	0646	0752	0852	1052	1252	1452	1652	1852	2052	2353

km	*2nd class*										
0	**Rakovnik** d.	0606	*0807*	*1007*	*1207*	*1408*	*1607*	...	*1807*	...	...
9	Lužná u Rakovnika d.	0624	0824	1024	1224	1424	1624	...	1824	...	...
50	Žatec **1126** d.	0710	0910	1110	1310	1510	1710	...	1910	...	...
75	**Chomutov** **1126** a.	0742	0942	1142	1342	1542	1742	...	1942	...	...
81	Jirkov a.	0756	0956	1156	1356	1556	1756	...	1956	...	...

Jirkov d.	...	0600	...	0800	1000	1200	1400	1600	1800	
Chomutov **1126** d.	...	0616	...	0812	1012	1212	1412	1612	1812	...
Žatec **1126** d.	...	0643	...	0843	1043	1243	1443	1643	1843	...
Lužná u Rakovnika a.	...	0727	...	0927	1127	1327	1527	1727	1927	...
Rakovník a.	...	0747	...	*0948*	*1148*	*1348*	*1548*	*1748*	*1948*	...

h – Not Dec. 24-26, 31, Apr. 12, July 5, Sept. 27.
n – Also Dec. 24, May 1, 8, Oct. 28, Nov. 17; not Dec. 27.

Change at Lužná u Rakovnika for connections to/from Chomutov (lower table).
Trains run hourly Praha - Kladno.

PRAHA - ÚSTI NAD LABEM - CHOMUTOV - KARLOVY VARY - CHEB 1110

km		1688	◇	1690	440	606	◇	608	◇	◇	610	1694	◇	612	◇	1696	614	◇	1698	616	◇	618	◇	◇
		2⊖		Ⓐ	E	c m	Ⓐ			Ⓐ		2Ⓐ	Ⓐ			2Ⓐ			Ⓐ		⊕	⊕	⊗	
0	**Praha** hlavní ▷ d.	...	...	...	0458	0729	...	0929	...	...	1129	...	...	1329	...	...	1529	...	...	1729	...	1929	...	...
3	**Praha** Holešovice ▷ d.	...	...	...	0509	0740	...	0940	...	...	1140	...	...	1340	...	...	1540	...	...	1740	...	1940	...	...
106	**Ústí nad Labem** hlavní ▷ a.	...	...	...	0639	0843	...	1043	...	...	1243	...	...	1443	...	...	1643	...	...	1843	...	2043	...	...
106	**Ústí nad Labem** hlavní d.	0048	...	0441	0649	0849	...	1049	...	...	1249	1347	...	1449	...	1547	1649	...	1747	1849	...	2049	...	*2224*
123	Teplice v Čechách d.	0109	...	0502	0706	0906	...	1106	...	...	1306	1407	...	1506	...	1607	1706	...	1807	1906	...	2106	...	*2244*
152	**Most** d.	0138	...	0531	0733	0933	...	1133	...	...	1333	1434	...	1533	*1612*	1634	1733	*1808*	1839	1933	...	2133	...	2320
177	**Chomutov** d.	0158	0529	0553	0755	0955	...	1155	...	...	1355	1454	...	1555	*1634*	1654	1755	*1834*	1859	1955	...	2153	2156	2340
196	Klášterec nad Ohří d.	▬	0544	▬	0810	1010	...	1210	1217	...	1410	▬	1534	1610	1657	...	1810	1857	...	2010	...	▬	2220	...
236	**Karlovy Vary** ⊙ a.	Ⓐ◇	0629	◇	0847	1047	...	1247	1302	...	1447	◇	1619	1647	1742	...	1847	1942	...	2047	...	◇	2305	...
236	**Karlovy Vary** ⊙ d.	0536	0631	0742	0849	1049	1200	1249	1316	1418	1449	1516	1622	1649	1744	...	1849	2000	...	2049	2115	2226	...	...
262	Sokolov d.	0604	0700	0816	0912	1112	1227	1312	1343	1446	1512	1544	1650	1712	1813	...	1912	2029	...	2112	2141	2251	...	...
291	**Cheb** a.	0639	0735	0851	0942	1142	1302	1342	1418	1521	1542	1619	1725	1742	1848	...	1942	2104	...	2142	2216	2325	...	...

	1689	605		609	1695	◇	611	◇	613	615	◇	617	◇	◇	619	◇	◇	607	◇	441	◇	◇	◇	◇
	2⊖	Ⓐ		⊖	2Ⓐ								Ⓐ	Ⓒ		Ⓐ		m		E b	Ⓐ	⊕	⊕	⊗
Cheb d.	...	...	0333	...	...	0540	0614	0708	0814	1014	1107	1214	1233	1256	1414	1430	1541	1614	1715	1814	...	...	2005	2233
Sokolov d.	...	...	0405	...	...	0618	0642	0750	0842	1042	1143	1242	1309	1333	1442	1506	1617	1642	1751	1842	...	...	2041	2308
Karlovy Vary ⊙ a.	...	...	0432	...	...	0644	0704	0817	0904	1104	1210	1304	1336	1400	1504	1533	1643	1704	1817	1904	...	...	2107	2332
Karlovy Vary ⊙ d.	...	...	0446	...	...	0649	0706	...	0906	1106	1221	1306	...	1421	1506	1537	1649	1706	*1821*	1906	2023	...	...	...
Klášterec nad Ohří d.	...	...	0533	...	...	0734	0743	...	0943	1143	1304	1343	...	1504	1543	1622	1734	1743	*1904*	1943	2106	2109	...	...
Chomutov d.	0323	0457	0550	0600	0700	...	0800	...	1000	1200	*1326*	1400	...	*1526*	1600	...	...	1800	...	2000	...	2132	...	...
Most d.	0344	0522	...	0622	0721	...	0822	...	1022	1222	*1349*	1422	...	*1549*	1622	...	...	1822	...	2022	...	2204	...	...
Teplice v Čechách d.	0413	0550	...	0650	0748	...	0850	...	1050	1250	...	1450	...	...	1650	...	...	1850	...	2050	...	2237	...	...
Ústí nad Labem hlavní a.	0435	0608	...	0708	0810	...	0908	...	1108	1308	...	1508	...	...	1708	...	...	1908	...	2108	...	2258	...	...
Ústí nad Labem hlavní ▷ d.	...	0614	...	0714	...	...	0914	...	1114	1314	...	1514	...	...	1714	...	...	1914	...	2114	...	...	...	...
Praha Holešovice ▷ a.	...	0718	...	0818	...	...	1018	...	1218	1418	...	1618	...	...	1818	...	...	2018	...	2233	...	...	...	...
Praha hlavní ▷ a.	...	0730	...	0830	...	...	1030	...	1230	1430	...	1630	...	...	1830	...	...	2030	...	2245	...	...	...	...

km	*via Louny (2 cl.)*	Ⓒn	Ⓑh
0	**Praha** Masarykovo d.	0657	1623
47	Slaný d.	0756	1730
90	Louny d.	0842	1818
115	**Most** a.	0910	...

via Louny (2 cl.)	⚒	Ⓒn
Most d.	...	1644
Louny d.	0534	1716
Slaný d.	0623	1801
Praha Masarykovo a.	0732	1854

Local trains (2 cl.)			
Děčín d.	0528	and	2028
Ústí nad Labem hlavní d.	0557	hourly	2057
Teplice v Čechách d.	0617	⊡	2117
Most a.	0650	until	2150

Local trains (2 cl.)			
Most d.	0504	and	2004
Teplice v Čechách d.	0537	hourly	2037
Ústí nad Labem hlavní d.	0600	⦵	2100
Děčín a.	0628	until	2128

E – EXCELSIOR – 🛏 1, 2 cl., ▬ 2 cl., [12] Cheb - Karlovy Vary - Praha - Žilina - Košice and v.v.
b – Conveys 🛏 1, 2 cl. Cheb - Karlovy Vary - Praha (**477**) - Bratislava (**811**) - Zvolen - Banská Bystrica.
c – Conveys 🛏 1, 2 cl. Banská Bystrica (**810**) - Zvolen - Bratislava (**476**) - Břeclav (**470**) - Praha (**606**) - Karlovy Vary - Cheb.
h – Not Dec. 24-26, 31, Apr. 12, May 1, 8, July 5.
m – Conveys 🛏 1, 2 cl. Cheb - Karlovy Vary - Praha (**209/8**) - Moskva and v.v.
n – Not Dec. 24.
▷ – For other non-stop trains see Table **1100**.
⊙ – Known locally as Karlovy Vary horní (upper).
◇ – Stopping train. 2nd class only.
⊕ – Not Dec. 24, 31.
⊗ – Not Dec. 24, 25, 31.
⊖ – Not Dec. 25, Jan. 1.
⊡ – Also Děčín - Ústí at 2128, 2228.
⦵ – Also Ústí - Děčín at 0450, 0522, 2230.

ÚSTÍ NAD LABEM - DĚČÍN - ČESKÁ LIPA - LIBEREC 1115

2nd class

km		1995	1155	◇	1157	1159	1161	1163	1165	1167	1169
		⊖		◧						⊗	Ⓑh
0	**Ústí nad Labem** hl. § d.	...	0727	...	0927	1127	1327	1527	1727	1927	2127
23	**Děčín** § a.	...	0744	...	0944	1144	1344	1544	1744	1944	2144
23	**Děčín** d.	0504	0745	0841	0945	1145	1345	1545	1745	1945	2145
54	Česká Lipa a.	0549	0821	0931	1021	1221	1421	1621	1821	2021	2221
54	Česká Lipa d.	0609	0826	*0939*	1026	1226	1426	1626	1826	2026	...
113	**Liberec** a.	0732	0944	*1111*	1142	1342	1542	1742	1942	2132	...

	1154	1156	1158	1160	◇	1162	1164	1166	1168	◇
	⚒				◐				⊗	⊕
Liberec d.	...	0627	0829	1027	1044	1227	1427	1627	1827	2038
Česká Lipa a.	...	0732	0937	1132	1221	1332	1532	1732	1932	2208
Česká Lipa d.	0610	0738	0938	1138	*1230*	1338	1538	1738	1938	2230
Děčín a.	0645	0814	1014	1214	*1316*	1414	1614	1814	2014	2316
Děčín § d.	0649	0818	1018	1218	...	1418	1618	1818	2018	...
Ústí nad Labem hl. § a.	0707	0836	1036	1236	...	1436	1636	1836	2036	...

h – Not Dec. 24-26, 31, Apr. 12, July 5, Sept. 27.
§ – See also Table **1100** and foot of Table **1110**.
◧ – Every 2 hours 0841 - 1841 (also 2041 to Č. Lipa).
◐ – Every 2 hours 1044 - 1844.
◇ – Stopping train. 2nd class.
⊕ – Not Dec. 24, 31.
⊗ – Not Dec. 24, 25, 31.
⊖ – Not Dec. 25, Jan. 1.

DĚČÍN - VARNSDORF / RUMBURK 1116

Local trains, 2nd class

km											
								Ⓐ			
0	**Děčín** d.	0615	0815	1015	1215	1415	1615	1703	1815	2015	2241
50	Rybniště a.	0725	0925	1125	1325	1525	1725	1838	1925	2125	2347
61	Varnsdorf a.	*0746*	*0946*	*1145*	*1345*	*1545*	*1745*	|	*1945*	*2145*	|
61	**Rumburk** a.	0739	0939	1139	1339	1539	1739	1853	1939	2139	2400

	Ⓐ								⑥	Ⓑ	
Rumburk d.	0416	0611	0815	1015	1215	1415	1615	1815	...	...	2015
Varnsdorf d.	|	*0602*	*0807*	*1004*	*1203*	*1407*	*1604*	*1803*	2000	2004	|
Rybniště d.	0430	0624	0828	1028	1228	1428	1628	1828	2017	2021	2028
Děčín a.	0536	0744	0944	1144	1344	1544	1744	1944	...	...	2144

VARNSDORF - ZITTAU - LIBEREC 1117

Local trains, 2nd class

km			d▽	⊖Ⓐ	Ⓒ		d		d▽			d	⑤⑥
0	**Varnsdorf** d.	0624	...	...	...	1053	...	1453	...	*1651*	1853	...	...
27	Zittau ⊞ ▷ d.	0644	0843	0914	0914	1115	1243	1514	1643	1715	1915	2043	2322
45	**Liberec** ▷ a.	0730	0918	0954	0954	1158	1318	1557	1718	1757	1955	2118	2356

		Ⓐ⊖	Ⓒ	d		d▽	⑥⑦		d		d▽
Liberec ▷ d.	0629	0700	0802	0838	0928	1238	1320	1458	1638	1827	2036
Zittau ⊞ ▷ a.	0709	0736	0837	0910	1002	1310	1357	1539	1710	1902	2110
Varnsdorf a.	0735	...	...	...	1024	...	1418	1601	...	1924	...

▷ – Additional trains: Zittau - Liberec 0432 Ⓐ, 0618 Ⓐ ⦵, 1223 Ⓐ ⦵, 1550 Ⓐ ⦵; Liberec - Zittau 0446 Ⓐ, 0736 Ⓐ ⦵, 1023 Ⓐ ⦵, 1320 Ⓐ ⦵, 1730 Ⓐ ⦵, 2245 ⑤⑥.
d – To/from Dresden (Table **855**).
⦵ – Operator: Railtrans / Sächsisch-Böhmische Eisenbahngesellschaft.
▽ – To/from Tanwald on Ⓒ (Table **1141**).

KARLOVY VARY - MARIÁNSKÉ LÁZNĚ 1118

Operator: Viamont. 2nd class

km										
0	**Karlovy Vary** dolní (lower) d.	0622	0900	1100	1300	1500	1700	1910	2100	...
33	Bečov nad Teplou d.	0652	0932	1134	1332	1532	1732	1941	2134	...
53	**Mariánské Lázně** a.	0739	1019	1221	1419	1619	1819	2028	2221	...

Mariánské Lázně d.	0602	0827	1045	1227	1427	1627	1850	2045	...
Bečov nad Teplou d.	0652	0917	1133	1315	1515	1715	1941	2133	...
Karlovy Vary dolní (lower) a.	0724	0949	1205	1349	1549	1749	2013	2205	...

1120 PRAHA - PLZEŇ - CHEB - FRANTIŠKOVY LÁZNĚ

km		970 2	750	350	752	960	754	354	756	962	758	352	760	964	762	356	764	966	766	968
		⚒n	G	N		z		M		z		N		k		M	△	k⊗	⊕	⊗
0	**Praha** hlavní .... **1124** d.	0011	0411	0511	0611	0711	0811	0911	1011	1111	1211	1311	1411	1511	1611	1711	1811	1911	2011	2211
4	Praha Smíchov .... **1124** d.	0019	0419	0519	0619	0719	0819	0919	1019	1119	1219	1319	1419	1519	1619	1719	1819	1919	2019	2219
43	Beroun .... **1124** d.	0048	0448	0548	0648	0748	0848	0948	1048	1148	1248	1348	1448	1548	1648	1748	1848	1948	2048	2248
52	Zdice .... **1124** d.	|	0500	|	0700	|	0900	|	1100	|	1300	|	1500	|	1700	|	1900	|	2100	|
91	Rokycany ....d.	0132	0532	0631	0732	0832	0932	1031	1132	1232	1332	1431	1532	1632	1732	1831	1932	2032	2132	2332
114	**Plzeň** hlavní ....a.	0151	0551	0650	0751	0851	0951	1050	1151	1251	1351	1450	1551	1651	1751	1850	1951	2051	2151	2351
114	**Plzeň** hlavní ....d.	...	0605	0700	0805	...	1005	1100	1205	...	1405	1500	1605	...	1805	1900	2005	...	2205	...
	Furth im Wald 🏛 **885** ....a.	...	|	0811	|	...	|	1211	|	...	|	1611	|	...	|	2011	|	...	|	...
147	Stříbro ....d.	...	0629	...	0829	...	1029	...	1229	...	1429	...	1629	...	1829	...	2029	...	2229	...
190	Mariánské Lázně ....d.	...	0721	...	0921	...	1121	...	1321	...	1521	...	1721	...	1921	...	2121	...	2321	...
220	**Cheb** ....a.	...	0757	...	0957	...	1157	...	1357	...	1557	...	1757	...	1957	...	2157	...	2357	...
220	**Cheb** .... ▶ d.	...	0801	...	1001	...	1201	...	1401	...	1601	...	1801	...	...	...	...	...	...	...
227	**Františkovy Lázně** .... ▶ a.	...	0808	...	1008	...	1208	...	1408	...	1608	...	1808	...	...	...	...	...	...	...

Engineering Work
March 19 - August 2
Service is by 🚌 between Stříbro and Mariánské Lázně in existing schedules

	971	961		751	963	753	351		755	965	757	355		759	967	761	353		763	969	765	357	767	
	⚒n	☆		⊖	k	▽	N			z		M			z		N			k⊗		M	G	
Františkovy Lázně.......... ▶ d.	...	...	...	...	...	...	...	...	...	...	0953	...	...	1153	...	1353	...	...	1553	...	1753	...	1953	...
Cheb .... ▶ a.	...	...	...	...	...	...	...	...	...	...	1000	...	...	1200	...	1400	...	...	1600	...	1800	...	2000	...
Cheb ....d.	...	...	...	0404	...	0604	...	...	0804	...	1004	...	...	1204	...	1404	...	...	1604	...	1804	...	2004	...
Mariánské Lázně ....d.	...	...	...	0436	...	0636	...	...	0836	...	1036	...	...	1236	...	1436	...	...	1636	...	1836	...	2036	...
Stříbro ....d.	...	...	...	0527	...	0727	...	...	0927	...	1127	...	...	1327	...	1527	...	...	1727	...	1927	...	2127	...
Furth im Wald 🏛 **885** ....d.	...	...	...	|	...	|	0749	...	|	...	|	1149	...	|	...	|	1549	...	|	...	|	1949	|	...
Plzeň hlavní ....a.	...	...	...	0551	...	0751	0857	...	0951	...	1151	1257	...	1351	...	1551	1657	...	1751	...	1951	2057	2151	...
Plzeň hlavní ....d.	0438	0508	...	0608	0708	0808	0908	...	1008	1108	1208	1308	...	1408	1508	1608	1708	...	1808	1908	2008	2108	2208	...
Rokycany................................d.	0457	0527	...	0627	0727	0827	0927	...	1027	1127	1227	1327	...	1427	1527	1627	1727	...	1827	1927	2027	2127	2227	...
Zdice .... **1124** d.	0530	0600	...	0700	|	0900	|	...	1100	|	1300	|	...	1500	|	1700	|	...	1900	|	2100	|	|	...
Beroun...................... **1124** d.	0543	0613	...	0713	0813	0913	1013	...	1113	1213	1313	1413	...	1513	1613	1713	1813	...	1913	2013	2113	2213	2313	...
Praha Smíchov............ **1124** a.	0612	0642	...	0742	0842	0942	1042	...	1142	1242	1342	1442	...	1542	1642	1742	1842	...	1942	2042	2142	2242	2342	...
Praha hlavní.............. **1124** a.	0620	0650	...	0750	0850	0950	1050	...	1150	1250	1350	1450	...	1550	1650	1750	1850	...	1950	2050	2150	2250	2350	...

G – [12] Františkovy Lázně - Plzeň - Praha and v.v.; [2] Františkovy Lázně - Plzeň - Praha (**440/1**) - Žilina - Košice and v.v.; 🛏 1,2 cl. and ▬ 2 cl. Plzeň - Praha (**440/1**) - Žilina - Košice and v.v.

M – [12] Praha - Furth im Wald - Regensburg - München and v.v. (Table **57**). Names: FRANZ KAFKA (**354/7**), ALBERT EINSTEIN (**355/6**).

N – [12] Praha - Schwandorf - Nürnberg and v.v. (Table **57**). Train names: KAREL ČAPEK (**350/3**), JAN HUS (**351/2**).

k – To/from Klatovy (Table **929**).
n – Also Dec. 24, May 1, 8, Oct. 28, Nov. 17; not Dec. 27.
z – To/from Klatovy, Železná Ruda (Table **929**).
⊕ – Not Dec. 24, 31.
⊗ – Not Dec. 24, 25, 31.
⊖ – Not Dec. 25, Jan. 1.
☆ – Not Dec. 25, 26, Jan. 1.

△ – Plzeň - Cheb: not Dec. 24, 31.
▽ – Cheb - Plzeň: not Dec. 25, Jan. 1.

▶ – Additional local trains (see also Table **1122**):
From Cheb: 0507 Ⓐ, 0556, 0647 Ⓐ, 0818, 1018, 1218, 1423, 1526 Ⓑ, 1626, 1818, 2018, 2235.
From Františkovy Lázně: 0517, 0631 Ⓐ, 0722, 0828 Ⓐ, 0936, 1136, 1336, 1536 Ⓑ, 1736, 1936, 2136.

1121 CHEB - MARKTREDWITZ - NÜRNBERG

27 km *	⊖	⊖	⊖		⊖	⊖		⊖	⊖	⊖		⊖
	C	A		C			d				C	
Cheb............... d.	0622	0651	0822	0915	1022	1222	1302	1422	1622	1822	1915	2022
Schirnding 🏛.... d.	0636	0705	0836	0929	1036	1240	1316	1436	1636	1836	1929	2036
Marktredwitz.... a.	0648	0717	0852	0942	1048	1252	1329	1448	1648	1852	1942	2048
Nürnberg **880** a.	*0817*	*0915*z	*1018*	1115	*1218*	*1415*	1515	*1618*	*1818*	*2018*	2124	*2219*

	⊖		⊖	⊖		⊖	⊖	⊖		⊖	⊖
		C							C		
Nürnberg **880** d.	*0548*	0648	*0748*	*0948*	1048	*1148*	*1348*	*1548*	1648	*1748*	*1948*
Marktredwitz... d.	0710r	0828	0910v	1110	1228	1310v	1510	1710	1828	1910v	2110
Schirnding 🏛... d.	0723r	0840	0923v	1123	1240	1326v	1523	1723	1840	1923v	2123
Cheb .... a.	0736r	0854	0936v	1136	1254	1339v	1536	1736	1854	1936v	2136

A – ①–⑤ (not Dec. 24-26, 31, Jan. 1, 6, Apr. 10-13, May 1, 21, June 1, 11).
C – ⑥⑦ (also Dec. 24-26, 31, Jan. 1, 6, Apr. 10-13, May 1, 21, June 1, 11).
d – Runs 13 minutes later to Marktredwitz on dates in note **C**.
r – On dates in note **A** runs 24-27 minutes later.
v – On dates in note **C** runs 3-9 minutes later.
z – Change at Marktredwitz and Pegnitz.
⊖ – Operator: Vogtlandbahn GmbH.
* – Cheb - Schirnding = 13 km; Cheb - Marktredwitz = 27 km.

1122 CHEB - FRANTIŠKOVY LÁZNĚ - PLAUEN - ZWICKAU

Local trains 1, 2 class

km										
0	**Cheb** .... ▶ d.	0609	0809	1009	1209	1409	1609	1809	2009	...
9	**Františkovy Lázně** .... ▶ d.	0617	0817	1017	1217	1417	1617	1817	2017	...
27	Bad Brambach 🏛 .... **881** d.	0638	0838	1038	1238	1438	1638	1838	2038	...
76	**Plauen** .... **880/1** d.	0802	1002	1202	1402	1602	1802	2002	2149	...
101	Reichenbach (Vogtl) ... **880/1** a.	0827	1027	1227	1427	1627	1827	2027	2214	...
124	**Zwickau** (Sachs) .... **880/1** a.	0851	1051	1251	1451	1651	1851	2051	2238	...

								c	
Zwickau (Sachs) .... **880/1** d.	...	0706	0906	1106	1306	1506	1706	1912	...
Reichenbach (Vogtl) **880/1** d.	0520	0728	0928	1128	1328	1528	1728	1933	...
Plauen .... **880/1** d.	0610	0811	1011	1211	1411	1611	1811	2010	...
Bad Brambach 🏛 .... **881** d.	0723	0923	1123	1323	1523	1723	1923	2123	...
Františkovy Lázně....... ▶ d.	0745	0945	1145	1345	1545	1745	1945	2145	...
Cheb 1110 .... ▶ a.	0752	0952	1152	1352	1552	1752	1952	2152	...

c – Change at Weischlitz (2022/2028).
▶ – See also Table **1120**.
Operator: Vogtlandbahn GmbH.

1124 PRAHA - BEROUN - PŘÍBRAM - PISEK - ČESKÉ BUDĚJOVICE

2nd class

km		1242	1242	1244	1246	1248	1250	1252	1254	1256
		Ⓐ	⊖							
0	**Praha** hlavní............... **1120** d.	0541	...	0741	0941	1141	1341	1541	1741	1941
4	Praha Smichov .... **1120** d.	0549	...	0749	0949	1149	1349	1549	1749	1949
43	Beroun .... **1120** d.	0618	...	0818	1018	1218	1418	1618	1818	2018
52	Zdice .... **1120** d.	0630	...	0830	1030	1230	1430	1630	1830	2030
82	Přibram.................................d.	0700	...	0900	1100	1300	1500	1700	1900	2100
100	Březnice ....d.	0717	0717	0917	1117	1317	1517	1717	1917	2117
142	Pisek ....d.	0759	0759	0959	1159	1359	1559	1759	1959	2159c
155	Protivín....................... **1125** d.	0815	0815	1015	1215	1415	1615	1815	2015	2215c
192	**České Budějovice** ...... **1125** a.	0845	0845	1045	1245	1445	1645	1845	2045	2245c

	1241	1243	1245	1247	1249	1251	1253	1255	1257
	Ⓐ								⑦c
České Budějovice ... **1125** d.	...	0508r	0708	0908	1108	1308	1508	1708	1908
Protivín .... **1125** d.	...	0543r	0743	0943	1143	1343	1543	1743	1943
Pisek ....d.	...	0558	0758	0958	1158	1358	1558	1758	1958
Březnice ....d.	0542	0642	0842	1042	1242	1442	1642	1842	2042
Přibram.................................d.	0600	0700	0900	1100	1300	1500	1700	1900	2100
Zdice .... **1120** d.	0630	0730	0930	1130	1330	1530	1730	1930	2130
Beroun........................ **1120** d.	0643	0743	0943	1143	1343	1543	1743	1943	2143
Praha Smichov .... **1120** a.	0712	0812	1012	1212	1412	1612	1812	2012	2212
Praha hlavní.............. **1120** a.	0720	0820	1020	1220	1420	1620	1820	2020	2220

c – ⑦ (also Apr. 13, July 6, Sept. 28, Nov. 17; not Apr. 12, July 5, Sept. 27, Nov. 15).
r – ⚒ only.
⊖ – Not Dec. 25, Jan. 1.

1125 PLZEŇ - ČESKÉ BUDĚJOVICE

km			667	669	665	663	661	925	923	921
		2Ⓐ	⊖				B	H		⊕
0	**Plzeň** hlavní ....d.	...	0603	0803	1003	1203	1403	1603	1803	2003
34	Nepomuk.....................................d.	...	0632	0832	1032	1232	1432	1632	1832	2032
59	Horaždovice předměstí ....d.	0541	0652	0852	1052	1252	1452	1652	1852	2052
76	Strakonice ....d.	0604	0707	0907	1107	1307	1507	1707	1907	2107
99	Protivín.......................... **1124** d.	0633	0726	0926	1126	1326	1526	1726	1926	2126
136	**České Budějovice** ...... **1124** a.	0722	0756	0956	1156	1356	1556	1756	1956	2156
	Jihlava **1135**...........................a.	...	1034	1234	1434	1634	1834	2033	...	...
	Brno **1135** ....a.	...	1237	1437	1637	1837	2045	...	...	...

	920	922	924	660	662	664	666	668	
	⊖		H	B				⊕	2
Brno **1135** ....d.	...	...	...	0718	0920	1120	1320	1520	...
Jihlava **1135**.........................d.	...	0524a	0724	0924	1124	1324	1524	1724	...
České Budějovice ... **1124** d.	0602	0802	1002	1202	1402	1602	1802	2002	2111
Protivín .... **1124** d.	0633	0833	1033	1233	1433	1633	1833	2033	2152
Strakonice....................................d.	0652	0852	1052	1252	1452	1652	1852	2052	2216
Horaždovice předměstí ......d.	0710	0910	1110	1310	1510	1710	1910	2110	...
Nepomuk ....d.	0730	0930	1130	1330	1530	1730	1930	2130	...
Plzeň hlavní.............................a.	0758	0958	1158	1358	1558	1758	1958	2158	...

B – [12] Plzeň - Brno - Ostrava - Bohumin and v.v.
H – [12] Plzeň - Brno - Jihlava - Havlíčkův Brod and v.v.
a – Ⓐ only.
⊖ – Not Dec. 25, Jan. 1.
⊕ – Not Dec. 24, 31.

1126 PLZEŇ - CHOMUTOV - MOST

2nd class

km		1190		1192		1194	1196		1990	1490	
							⊕		Ⓑh	⑦e	
0	**Plzeň** hlavní ....d.	0605	...	1005	...	1405	1605	...	1805	2005	...
59	Blatno u Jesenice ....d.	0710	...	1110	...	1510	1710	...	1910	2110	...
107	Žatec .... **1105** d.	0802	...	1202	...	1602	1802	...	|	2202	...
130	Chomutov .... **1110** a.	0827	...	1227	...	1627	1827	...	2022	2227	...
155	**Most**................... **1110** a.	0850	...	1250	...	1650	1850	...	2045	2250	...

	1991	1191		1193		1195		1197		1491
	⚒							⊕		⑦e
Most................... **1110** d.	0502	0705	...	0905	...	1305	...	1705	...	1905
Chomutov .... **1110** d.	0525	0728	...	0928	...	1328	...	1728	...	1928
Žatec .... **1105** d.	|	0753	...	0953	...	1353	...	1753	...	1953
Blatno u Jesenice.........d.	0646	0846	...	1046	...	1446	...	1846	...	2046
Plzeň hlavní.................a.	0755	0954	...	1154	...	1554	...	1954	...	2154

e – Also Apr. 13, July 6, Sept. 28, Nov. 17; not Apr. 12, July 5, Sept. 27, Nov. 15.
h – Not Dec. 24-26, 31, Apr. 12, July 5, Sept. 27.
⊕ – Not Dec. 24, 31.

PRAHA - TÁBOR - ČESKÉ BUDĚJOVICE — 1130

km		1831	631	942	*EC* 101	633	635	637	639	641	643	645	647	207	649	651	653	655
		Ⓒd	Ⓐ	⊖	J									M		⊕	⊕	⊗
0	**Praha** hlavní d.	0014	0514	0614	0714	0814	0914	1114	1214	1314	1414	1514	1614	1714	1814	1914	2014	2214
49	Benešov u Prahy d.	0107	0605	0705	0805	0905	1005	1205	1305	1405	1505	1605	1705	1805	1905	2005	2105	2305
103	**Tábor** d.	0155	0655	0755	0855	0955	1055	1255	1355	1455	1555	1655	1755	1855	1955	2055	2155	2355
130	Veselí nad Lužnicí △ d.	0219	0721	0821	0921	1021	1121	1321	1421	1521	1621	1721	1821	1921	2021	2121	2221	0021
169	**České Budějovice** △ a.	0250	0756	0856	0956	1056	1156	1356	1456	1556	1656	1756	1856	1956	2056	2154	2254	0054

	630	632	634	636	638	206	640	642	644	646	648	650	652	*EC* 100	940	654	1932	
	Ⓐ	⊖	⊖			M								J	⊗	⊕	⊗2	
České Budějovice △ d.	0401	0501	0601	0701	0801	0901	1001	1201	1301	1401	1501	1601	1701	1801	1901	2001	2110	...
Veselí nad Lužnicí △ d.	0433	0533	0633	0733	0833	0933	1033	1233	1333	1433	1533	1633	1733	1833	1933	2033	2153	...
Tábor d.	0459	0559	0659	0759	0859	0959	1059	1259	1359	1459	1559	1659	1759	1859	1959	2059	2223	...
Benešov u Prahy d.	0551	0651	0751	0851	0951	1051	1151	1351	1451	1551	1651	1751	1851	1951	2051	2151	2318	...
Praha hlavní a.	0641	0741	0841	0941	1041	1141	1241	1441	1541	1641	1741	1841	1941	2041	2141	2241	0005	...

J – JÓŽE PLEČNIK – (12) and ✕ Praha - Linz - Salzburg and v.v.
M – MATTHIAS BRAUN – (12) Praha - Linz - Salzburg and v.v.; 1, 2 cl., 2 cl. Praha - Linz - Innsbruck - Zürich and v.v.; 1, 2 cl. Praha - Linz - Salzburg - Ljubljana - Zagreb and v.v.
d – Daily to Tábor (not Dec. 25, 26, Jan. 1).
⊕ – Not Dec. 24, 31.
⊗ – Not Dec. 24, 25, 31.
⊖ – Not Dec. 25, Jan. 1.
△ – See also Table **1135**.

ČESKÉ BUDĚJOVICE - LINZ — 1132

2nd class (except trains **J** and **M**)

km				*EC* 101	1931				1933	207
				J			Ⓒ	Ⓐ		M
	Praha hlavní **1130** d.	...	...	0714	...	...	...	...	...	1714
0	**České Budějovice** d.	0533	...	1007	1212	1421	1631	1631	1815	2034
57	Horní Dvořiště 🏛 d.	0705	...	|	1316	1532	1755	1755	1917	|
64	Summerau 🏛 a.	0712	...	1112	1323	1539	1802	1802	1925	2142
64	Summerau d.	*0715*	0911	1113	1336	*1555*	*1804*	*1810*	1933	2147
73	Freistadt d.	*0724*	0920	1122	1345	*1604*	*1813*	*1819*	1941	2156
126	**Linz** Hbf a.	*0825*	1024	1218	1443	*1718*	*1919*	*1951*	2045	2244

	206	1938			1930	*EC* 100		1932	1934
	M					J	Ⓐ	Ⓒ	Ⓐ
Linz Hbf d.	0614	*0721*	1035	...	1308	1535	*1702*	1808	1830
Freistadt d.	0705	*0821*	1142	...	1405	1624	*1755*	1917	1924
Summerau a.	0714	*0830*	1151	...	1414	1633	*1804*	1926	1932
Summerau 🏛 d.	0715	0833	...	1226	1427	1644	1817	1935	1935
Horní Dvořiště 🏛 d.	|	0842	...	1234	1435	|	1834	1943	1943
České Budějovice a.	0820	0953	...	1348	1543	1748	1949	2053	2053
Praha hlavní **1130** a.	1141	...	...	...	...	2041	...	0005	0005

J – JÓŽE PLEČNIK – (12) and ✕ Praha - Linz - Salzburg and v.v.
M – MATTHIAS BRAUN – (12) Praha - Linz - Salzburg and v.v. For 1, 2 cl. / 2 cl. see Table **1130** note **M**.

ČESKÉ BUDĚJOVICE - ČESKÉ VELENICE - GMÜND — 1133

2nd class only

Gmünd - Wien is subject to alteration Mar. 22 - June 13 (see Tables **989**/**990** for altered timings)

km						1761																361				
		Ⓐ	Ⓐ	H			Ⓒ	F	G					Ⓐ	Ⓐ				H	Ⓐ	Ⓒ				Ⓐ	
0	**České Budějovice** d.	...	0503	0621	...	0712	...	...	...	1001	...	1145	...	1335	...	1504	...	1620	...	...	...	1819	1922	...	2104	...
*55	Veselí nad Lužnicí d.	0441	|	|	0550	|	0737	0845	0935	|	1131	|	1325	|	1438	|	1541	|	1624	1722	1740	|	|	1935	|	2234
*34	Třeboň d.	0505	|	|	0615	|	0805	0913	1001	|	1156	|	1348	|	1504	|	1605	|	1652	1745	1810	|	|	1956	|	2259
50	České Velenice a.	0552	0603	0719	0717	0809	0852	1000	1043	1104	1242	1253	1430	1435	1544	1605	1651	1723	1742	1827	1859	1911	2025	2036	2203	2339
50	České Velenice 🏛 d.	...	0605	0724	...	0811	...	...	...	1106	...	1255	...	1437	...	1607	...	...	...	...	...	1915	...	...	...	...
52	**Gmünd NÖ** 🏛 a.	...	0609	0728	...	0815	...	...	...	1110	...	1259	...	1441	...	1611	...	...	...	...	...	1919	...	...	...	...
	Wien FJB **990** a.	...	0832	...	...	1048	...	...	...	*1348*	...	*1548*	...	*1732*	...	...	...	...	...	...	...	2158	...	...	...	...

							360																1760			
		H	Ⓐ								Ⓐ			⑤f	H	Ⓐ			Ⓐ					⑥d		Ⓐ
Wien FJB **990** d.	...	...	...	...	...	...	0622	...	...	...	...	...	*1035*	*1035*	...	...	...	...	...	...	...	*1623*	1659	...	*1905*	...
Gmünd NÖ 🏛 d.	...	...	...	0629	0733**r**	...	0847	...	...	...	1219	...	1315	1315	...	1448	...	...	...	1645	...	1909	1928	...	2128	...
České Velenice 🏛 a.	...	...	...	0633	0737**r**	...	0851	...	...	...	1223	...	1319	1319	...	1452	...	...	...	1649	...	1913	1932	...	2132	...
České Velenice d.	0455	0609	0610	...	0742	0813	0855	0914	1034	1107	1225	1301	...	1324	1415	1453	1453	1502	1608	1654	1658	1915	1933	2042	2134	2218
Třeboň d.	|	|	0654	...	|	0852	|	1000	|	1157	|	1349	...	|	1503	|	|	1544	1651	|	1745	1956	|	2122	|	2259
Veselí nad Lužnicí a.	|	|	0718	...	|	0913	|	1026	|	1219	|	1415	...	|	1528	|	|	1608	1712	|	1811	2018	|	2144	|	2321
České Budějovice a.	0551	0711	...	...	0842	...	0946	...	1144	...	1321	...	...	1426	...	1555	1555	...	...	1753	...	...	2029	...	2232	...

F – Ⓒ June 14 - Sept. 12.
G – Ⓐ (daily Dec. 15 - June 13, Sept. 13 - Dec. 12).
H – Ⓐ to June 30/from Sept. 1.
d – Also Apr. 12, July 5, Sept. 27.
f – Also Apr. 30, May 7; not May 1, 8.
r – Ⓐ to June 30/from Sept. 1 only.
* – Distance from České Velenice.
Mar. 16 - May 23: trains from/to Veselí are replaced by 🚌 for last 6 km to České Velenice.

ČESKÉ BUDĚJOVICE - JIHLAVA - BRNO — 1135

km		1661	927	929	667	669	665	663	661		925
		⚒n	E						B⊕	2	k
	Plzeň **1125** d.	...	...	...	0603	0803	1003	1203	1403	...	1603
0	**České Budějovice** d.	...	0408	0608	0808	1008	1208	1408	1608	...	1808
39	Veselí nad Lužnicí ▷ d.	...	0445	0643	0843	1043	1243	1443	1643	...	1843
65	Jindřichův Hradec ▷ d.	...	0516	0716	0916	1116	1316	1516	1716	...	1916
117	Kostelec u Jihlavy d.	...	0616	0816	1016	1216	1416	1616	1816	...	2015
132	**Jihlava** a.	...	0634	0834	1034	1234	1434	1634	1834	...	2033
132	**Jihlava** d.	0531	0640	0840	1040	1240	1440	1640	1840	1930	...
161	Okříšky d.	0604	0710	0910	1110	1310	1510	1710	1910	2019	...
173	Trebíč d.	0620	0725	0927	1127	1327	1527	1727	1927	2039	...
236	**Brno** hlavní a.	0732	0837	1037	1237	1437	1637	1837	2045	2208	...

	922	924	660	662	664	666	668	926	928	
	Ⓐ	k	B					⊕	Ⓑh	
Brno hlavní d.	...	...	0718	0920	1120	1320	1520	1720	1920	...
Trebíč d.	...	...	0834	1032	1232	1432	1632	1832	2037	...
Okříšky d.	...	...	0848	1046	1246	1446	1646	1846	2052	...
Jihlava a.	...	...	0918	1118	1318	1518	1718	1918	2119	...
Jihlava d.	0524	0724	0924	1124	1324	1524	1724	1934	...	...
Kostelec u Jihlavy d.	0542	0742	0942	1142	1342	1542	1742	1952	...	...
Jindřichův Hradec ▷ d.	0645	0845	1045	1245	1445	1645	1845	2058	...	...
Veselí nad Lužnicí ▷ d.	0716	0916	1116	1316	1516	1716	1916	2129	...	...
České Budějovice a.	0748	0948	1148	1348	1548	1748	1948	2201	...	...
Plzeň **1125** a.	0958	1158	1358	1558	1758	1958	2158	...	...	...

CONNECTIONS OKŘÍŠKY - ZNOJMO

km		Ⓐ	⑥n			Ⓒ	Ⓐ	⑦e	Ⓐu		Ⓒ
0	Okříšky d.	0607	0715	0915	1120	1316	1415	1515	1615	1715	1920
32	Moravské Budějovice a.	0644	0753	0951	1155	1350	1449	1550	1656	1753	2000
70	Znojmo a.	0732	0844	1044	1244	1447	*1550*	*1646*	1752	1846	2040

	Ⓐu	⑥n	Ⓐ			⑦e	Ⓐ			z
Znojmo d.	0425	0512	*0532*	*0642*x	1103	1303	1401	1503	1703	1903
Moravské Budějovice d.	0524	0552	0625	0805	1158	1403	1456	1602	1804	1944
Okříšky a.	0558	0626	0704	0840	1238	1438	1536	1641	1838	2016

JIHLAVA - KOSTELEC U JIHLAVY - TELČ - SLAVONICE §

	Ⓐ		F	Ⓐ	Ⓒ	Ⓐ		Ⓐ	Ⓒ	Ⓐ		Ⓐ
Jihlava d.	*0535*	*0733*	*0937*	1055	*1152*	*1224*	*1350*	*1456*	*1553*	*1644*	*1837*	*2003*
Kostelec u J. a.	*0555*	*0759*	*1000*	1119	*1213*	*1248*	*1411*	*1518*	*1613*	*1709*	*1857*	*2032*
Kostelec u J. d.	0636	0819	1023	1124	1227	1309	1419	1527	1619	1713	1905	2037
Telč a.	0714	0858	1101	1200	1305	1352	1500	1602	1656	1751	1941	2113
Slavonice a.	...	0954**r**	1155**r**	1255	1358	1451	1604	...	1753	1855	2036	...

	Ⓐ	Ⓒ	Ⓐs	Ⓒ	Ⓐ		Ⓐ	Ⓒ	Ⓐ	Ⓒ	Ⓐ	Ⓒ
Slavonice d.	0703	0812	0842	*1006*	*1040*	1206**c**	...	1409	1502	1607	1712	1802
Telč d.	0805	0901	0935	1130	1204	1329	1439	1501	1609	1659	1814	1851
Kostelec u J. a.	0846	0937	1013	1210	1243	1406	1515	1539	1647	1739	1853	1935
Kostelec u J. d.	0851	*0942*	*1016*	*1216*	*1249*	*1416*	*1520*	*1542*	*1650*	*1816*	*1901*	*1952*
Jihlava a.	0912	*1006*	*1034*	*1234*	*1310*	*1434*	*1547*	*1602*	*1721*	*1834*	*1922*	*2013*

B – (12) Plzeň - Brno - Ostrava - Bohumin and v.v.; 1, 2 cl. (not Dec. 24, 31) České Budějovice - Brno - Přerov (**442/3**) - Košice and v.v.
E – Ⓐ from České Budějovice; ⚒**q** from Jihlava.
F – Ⓒ (daily July 1 - Aug. 30).
c – Ⓒ only.
e – Also Apr. 13, July 6, Sept. 28; not Apr. 12, July 5, Sept. 27, Nov. 15.
h – Not Dec. 24 - 26, 31, Apr. 12, July 5, Sept. 27.
k – To/from Havlíčkův Brod (Table **1137**).
n – Also Dec. 24, May 1, 8, Oct. 28, Nov. 17; not Dec. 27, May 2, 9.
q – Also Dec. 24, May 1, 8, Oct. 28, Nov. 17; not Dec. 27.
r – Ⓒ only.
s – Ⓐ July 1 - Aug. 28.
u – Not Dec. 29 - Jan. 2.
x – 0703 on Ⓒ (also July 1 - Aug. 28).
z – To Jihlava (arrive 2106).
▷ – Additional trains: from Veselí nad Lužnicí 0741, 0940, 1056 Ⓒ, 1210 Ⓐ, 1423, 1543, 1736, 1937, 2039, 2223; from Jindřichův Hradec 0738 Ⓒ, 0938, 1135, 1547, 1738, 1935, 2116. Journey 35 minutes.
⊕ – Not Dec. 24, 31.
§ – Kostelec - Telc *23 km*, Kostelec - Slavonice *53 km*.

HAVLÍČKŮV BROD - JIHLAVA — 1137

2nd class

km	*See note* ▲				924		1183										1181			913				
			Ⓐ		▽		△					Ⓐ			Ⓐ		△	Ⓐ		P				
0	Havlíčkův Brod d.	0449	0603	0645	0658	0805	0854	...	1005	1215	...	1311	1404	...	1511	1603	1651	1713	1805	1901	...	2004	2210	...
27	Jihlava a.	0518	0634	0718	0722	0835	0917	...	1035	1248	...	1345	1434	...	1545	1634	1718	1746	1836	1924	...	2034	2238	...

See note ▲	912					1180									1514		1182				925			
	P	Ⓐ		⚒		△				Ⓐn		Ⓐ		Ⓐ	†v		△				▽			
Jihlava d.	0532	0605	0653	0729	...	0843	0923	...	1122	1226	1321	1436	1522	1610	1622	...	1647	1723	1812	1925	2036	2242	...	...
Havlíčkův Brod a.	0555	0644	0734	0752	...	0912	0953	...	1152	1256	1352	1505	1553	1642	1646	...	1711	1753	1844	1953	2059	2310	...	...

P – (12) Praha - Havlíčkův Brod - Jihlava and v.v.
n – Not July 1 - Aug. 28.
v – Also Apr. 13, July 6, Sept. 28, Nov. 17; not Apr. 12, July 5, Sept. 27, Nov. 15. To Praha Mazarykovo (arrive 1901).
△ – To/from Pardubice (Table **1142**).
▽ – To/from České Budějovice (Table **1135**).
▲ – Service will be by 🚌 Mar. 17 - Apr. 27 in similar timings.

1140 PRAHA - MLADÁ BOLESLAV - TURNOV - LIBEREC / TANWALD

2nd class only

km			1138	1140	1142	1144	1146	1148	1840		
										⊕	Ⓑh
0	**Praha** hlavní d.	0547	0725	0925	1125	1325	1525	1725	1925	2105	2105
34	Neratovice d.	0632	0800	1000	1200	1400	1600	1800	2000	2149	2149
40	Všetaty d.	0640	0807	1007	1207	1407	1607	1807	2007	2157	2157
72	**Mladá Boleslav** a.	0718	0835	1035	1235	1435	1635	1835	2035	2232	2232
72	**Mladá Boleslav** d.	▬	0838	1038	1238	1438	1638	1838	2038	...	2240
88	Mnichovo Hradiště d.	...	0858	1058	1258	1458	1658	1858	2058	...	2259
102	**Turnov** a.	...	0912	1112	1312	1512	1712	1912	2115	...	2314
	Turnov **1142** d.	...	*0921*	*1121*	*1321*	*1521*	*1721*	*1921*	*2121*	...	*2318*
	Liberec **1142** a.	...	*0958*	*1158*	*1358*	*1558*	*1758*	*1958*	*2158*	...	*2356*
102	**Turnov** d.	...	0919	1119	1319	1519	1719	1919	...	...	...
116	Železný Brod a.	0701	0935	1135	1335	1535	1735	1935	...	...	...
133	**Tanwald** a.	0726	1004	1204	1404	1604	1804	2003	...	...	...

	1841	1137	1139	1141	1143	1145	1147	1149		
	Ⓐ									Ⓒ
Tanwald d.	...	0549	0752	...	1145	1345	1545	1745	2026	...
Železný Brod d.	...	0626	0820	...	1220	1420	1620	1820	2052	...
Turnov a.	...	0642	0836	...	1236	1436	1636	1836	▬	...
Liberec **1142** d.	*0400*	*0602*	*0802*	*1002*	*1202*	*1402*	*1602*	*1802*	...	*2031*
Turnov **1142** a.	*0438*	*0639*	*0839*	*1039*	*1239*	*1439*	*1639*	*1839*	...	*2112*
Turnov d.	0441	0644	0844	1044	1244	1444	1644	1844	...	2127
Mnichovo Hradiště d.	0459	0658	0858	1058	1258	1458	1658	1858	...	2144
Mladá Boleslav a.	0519	0715	0915	1115	1315	1515	1715	1915	...	2204
Mladá Boleslav d.	0521	0723	0924	1124	1324	1524	1724	1924	2037	2206
Všetaty d.	0551	0753	0953	1153	1353	1553	1753	1953	2121	2248
Neratovice d.	0600	0800	1000	1200	1400	1600	1800	2000	2130	2256
Praha hlavní a.	0638	0838	1038	1238	1438	1638	1838	2038	2211	2335

h – Not Dec. 24-26, 31, Apr. 12, July 5, Sept. 27. ⊕ – Not Dec. 24, 31.

1141 LIBEREC - TANWALD - HARRACHOV

km				Ⓐ	Ⓒd					Ⓐ	Ⓒd	⑤⑥
0	**Liberec** d.	0631	0837	0917	0920	0951	1117	1317	1517	1717	1720	1917
12	Jablonec △ d.	0656	0856	0936	0939	1016	1136	1336	1536	1736	1739	1936
27	Tanwald a.	0731	0931	1011	1011	1051	1211	1411	1611	1811	1811	2008
27	Tanwald d.	0732	0940**c**	*1021*	*1021*	1059**c**	1217	1418	1623	*1824*	*1824*	2017
39	**Harrachov** a.	0755	1006**c**	*1044*	*1044*	1130**c**	1240	1441	1646	*1847*	*1847*	2041

				Ⓒd						d	⑤⑥
Harrachov d.	0758	0900**z**	1026**c**	1113	...	1144**c**	1300	1458	1658	*1858*	2100
Tanwald d.	0821	0924**z**	1057**c**	1137	...	1208**c**	1323	1523	1723	*1923*	2123
Tanwald d.	0822	0942	1102	...	1140	1222	1340	1540	1740	1937	2137
Jablonec △ d.	0857	1017	1137	...	1217	1257	1417	1617	1817	2007	2207
Liberec a.	0916	1036	1206	...	1236	1316	1446	1636	1836	2027	2227

c – Ⓒ only.
d – To / from Dresden on Ⓒ (Table **1117** / **855**).
z – Ⓒ (daily Dec. 14 - Mar. 29, May 30 - Sept. 28).
△ – Jablonec nad Nisou.
Note: trains run every 40-90 mins Liberec - Tanwald and v.v.

1142 LIBEREC - TURNOV - HRADEC KRÁLOVÉ - PARDUBICE

2nd class

km		981	983	985	987	989	991	993	995	997
									⊗	⊗
0	**Liberec** d.	0400	0602	0802	1002	1202	1402	1602	1802	2002
38	Turnov d.	0439	0643	0842	1042	1242	1442	1642	1842	2042
52	Železný Brod d.	0456	0700	0900	1100	1300	1500	1700	1900	2100
76	Stará Paka d.	0525	0727	0927	1127	1327	1527	1727	1927	2127
107	Dvůr Králové nad Labem d.	0600	0800	1000	1200	1400	1600	1800	2000	2200
122	Jaroměř **1145** d.	0620	0821	1021	1221	1421	1621	1821	2021	2221
139	**Hradec Králové** **1145** a.	0634	0837	1037	1237	1437	1637	1837	2037	2237
139	**Hradec Králové** ▶ d.	0643	0840	1040	1240	1440	1640	1840	2040	2240
159	Pardubice-Rosice a.	0658	0858	1058	1258	1458	1658	1858	2058	2257
161	**Pardubice** ▶ a.	0702	0902	1102	1302	1502	1702	1902	2102	2301

	980	982	984	986	988	990	992	994	996
	☆								⊗
Pardubice ▶ d.	0455	0655	0855	1055	1255	1455	1655	1855	2055
Pardubice-Rosice d.	0500	0700	0900	1100	1300	1500	1700	1900	2100
Hradec Králové ▶ a.	0519	0719	0919	1119	1319	1519	1719	1919	2119
Hradec Králové **1145** d.	0523	0723	0923	1123	1323	1523	1723	1923	2123
Jaroměř **1145** d.	0542	0742	0942	1142	1342	1542	1742	1942	2142
Dvůr Králové nad Labem d.	0559	0759	0959	1159	1359	1559	1759	1959	2159
Stará Paka d.	0631	0831	1031	1231	1431	1631	1831	2031	2234
Železný Brod d.	0700	0900	1100	1300	1500	1700	1900	2100	2301
Turnov d.	0721	0921	1121	1321	1521	1721	1921	2121	2318
Liberec a.	0758	0958	1158	1358	1558	1758	1958	2158	2356

km		1183			1181	
0	**Pardubice** d.	0655	*0925*	*1125*	1455	*1725*
2	Pardubice-Rosice d.	0705	0930	1132	1503	1732
11	Chrudim d.	0725	0943	1150	1519	1745
92	**Havlíčkův Brod** a.	0853	1148	1353	1649	1920
	Jihlava **1137** a.	0917	...	...	1718	...

		1180			1182
Jihlava **1137** d.	...	0843	...	...	1647
Havlíčkův Brod d.	0648	0915	1214	1412	1715
Chrudim d.	0830	1041	1407	1637	1841
Pardubice-Rosice a.	0846	1054	1424	1654	1854
Pardubice a.	0851	1108	1442	1709	1908

▶ – Additional trains **Hradec Kralové - Pardubice** and v.v. Journey 20-30 minutes. *Subject to alteration Dec. 23 - Jan. 1.*
From Hradec Kralové: 0054, 0439 Ⓐ, 0505 and hourly to 2205 (also 0530 Ⓐ, 0731 Ⓒ, 0743 Ⓐ, 0930, 1130, 1330, 1530, 1730).
From Pardubice: 0127, 0424 Ⓐ, 0525 and hourly to 2125 (also 0608 Ⓐ, 0808, 1008, 1208, 1408, 1608, 1808, 2238).
⊗ – Not Dec. 24, 25, 31. ☆ – Not Dec. 25, 26, Jan. 1.

1145 PRAHA - HRADEC KRÁLOVÉ - TRUTNOV / WROCŁAW

km		791	849	251	851	793	853	795	855	797	857	253	859	799	953	955	957	959
		⊖	⊖									b§				⊕	✕	⊕
0	**Praha** hlavní d.	0511	0611	0711	0811	0911	1011	1111	1211	1311	1411	1511	1611	1711	1811	1911	2011	2211
35	Lysá nad Labem **1147** d.	0543	0643	0743	0843	0943	1043	1143	1243	1343	1443	1543	1643	1743	1843	1943	2043	2243
50	Nymburk **1147** d.	0556	0656	0756	0856	0956	1056	1156	1256	1356	1456	1556	1656	1756	1856	1956	2056	2256
57	Poděbrady **1147** d.	0602	0702	0802	0902	1002	1102	1202	1302	1402	1502	1602	1702	1802	1902	2002	2102	2302
116	**Hradec Králové** a.	0651	0751	0851	0951	1051	1151	1251	1351	1451	1551	1651	1751	1851	1951	2051	2151	2348
116	**Hradec Králové** **1142** d.	0705	0804	0905	1004	1105	1204	1305	1404	1505	1604	1705	1804	1905	*2002*	...	...	...
133	Jaroměř **1142** d.	│	0821	│	1021	│	1221	│	1421	│	1621	│	1821	│	*2021*	...	...	...
185	**Trutnov** a.	│	0921	│	1120	│	1321	│	1520	│	1720	│	1921	│	*2121*	...	...	...
137	Týniště nad Orlicí d.	0732	...	0932	...	1131	...	1331	...	1531	...	1732	...	1931	...	...	...	...
178	Letohrad d.	0830	...	1040	...	1230	...	1430	...	1630	...	1840	...	2027	...	...	...	...
199	**Lichkov** 🏛 a.	...	...	1101	...	...	...	...	...	...	...	1901	...	...	...	...	...	...
	Wrocław Gl **1095** a.	...	...	1340	...	...	...	...	...	...	...	2140	...	...	...	...	...	...

	950	952	790	846	792	848	250	850	794	852	796	854	798	856	252	858		
	⊖	⊖					c						⊕			⊕	2	2
Wrocław Gl **1095** d.	...	...	...	...	...	...	0625	...	...	...	...	...	...	...	1425	...	...	...
Lichkov 🏛 d.	...	...	...	...	...	...	0906	...	...	...	...	...	...	...	1704	...	...	...
Letohrad d.	...	...	0535	...	0737	...	0937	...	1137	...	1337	...	1537	...	1737	...	...	...
Týniště nad Orlicí d.	...	...	0630	...	0832	...	1032	...	1232	...	1432	...	1632	...	1832	...	...	...
Trutnov d.	...	...	│	0640	│	0841	│	1041	│	1241	│	1440	│	1640	│	1840	...	...
Jaroměř **1142** d.	...	...	│	0741	│	0941	│	1141	│	1341	│	1541	│	1741	│	1941	...	...
Hradec Králové **1142** a.	...	...	0653	0755	0854	0955	1054	1155	1254	1355	1454	1555	1654	1755	1854	1955	...	...
Hradec Králové d.	0508	0608	0708	0808	0908	1008	1108	1208	1308	1408	1508	1608	1708	1808	1908	2008	...	...
Poděbrady **1147** d.	0554	0654	0754	0854	0954	1054	1154	1254	1354	1454	1554	1654	1754	1854	1954	2054	2147	...
Nymburk **1147** d.	0602	0702	0802	0902	1002	1102	1202	1302	1402	1502	1602	1702	1802	1902	2002	2102	2206	2306
Lysá nad Labem **1147** d.	0616	0716	0816	0916	1016	1116	1216	1316	1416	1516	1616	1716	1816	1916	2016	2116	2225	2325
Praha hlavní a.	0647	0747	0847	0947	1047	1147	1247	1347	1447	1547	1647	1747	1847	1947	2047	2147	2302	0002

CONNECTIONS
Ústí nad Orlici - Letohrad ⊖

		⑥	n
Ústí nad Orlici d.	0839	0945	1745
Letohrad a.	0854	1005	1805
Lichkov a.	0921	...	...
Lichkov d.	1104	...	1804
Letohrad d.	1145	1745	1845
Ústí nad Orlici a.	1205	1808	1908

b – On Dec. 24, 31 runs only to Letohrad.
c – On Dec. 25, Jan. 1 starts from Letohrad.
n – Not Dec. 22 - Jan. 2.
⊕ – Not Dec. 24, 31.
⊖ – Not Dec. 25, Jan. 1.
⊖ – Local trains run 13-15 times daily. Only relevant connections (for Wroclaw trains) are shown.
§ – Conveys ✕ Praha - Hradec Králové.

1147 DĚČÍN - ÚSTÍ NAD LABEM - MĚLNÍK - KOLÍN

Dečín - Ústi: see Table **1100**

km		2Ⓐ	2	2		2	2	2	2	
0	**Děčín** hlavní d.	0425	0601	0801	...	1201	1401	1601	1801	...
28	**Ústí n. Labem** Střekov a.	0503	0641	0840	...	1240	1440	1640	1840	...

	2Ⓐ	2	2		2	2	2	2		
Ústí n. Labem Střekov d.	0517	0655	0913	...	1313	1513	1713	1913	...	...
Děčín hlavní a.	0555	0735	0956	...	1356	1556	1756	1956	...	...

km		711	713	715	717	719	721	723	725	
		⚒							⊕	2
0	**Ústí n. Labem** západ d.	0447	0641	0841	1041	1241	1441	1641	1841	2003
2	**Ústí n. Labem** Střekov d.	0452	0646	0846	1046	1246	1446	1646	1846	2008
27	Litoměřice město d.	0511	0705	0905	1105	1305	1505	1705	1905	2031
63	**Mělník** d.	0539	0734	0934	1134	1334	1534	1734	1934	2105
73	Všetaty d.	0547	0743	0943	1143	1343	1543	1743	1943	2114
85	Stará Boleslav d.	0557	0753	0953	1153	1353	1553	1753	1953	2126
111	Nymburk **1145** d.	0619	0817	1017	1217	1417	1617	1817	2017	...
118	Poděbrady **1145** d.	0626	0824	1024	1224	1424	1624	1824	2024	...
134	**Kolín** d.	0640	0838	1038	1238	1438	1638	1838	2038	...

			712	714	716	718	720	722	724	726
	2Ⓐ	2⊖							⊕	Ⓑh
Kolín d.	...	...	0715	0915	1115	1315	1515	1715	1915	2115
Poděbrady **1145** d.	...	...	0729	0929	1129	1329	1529	1729	1929	2129
Nymburk **1145** d.	...	...	0738	0938	1138	1338	1538	1738	1938	2138
Stará Boleslav d.	0428	0606	0759	0959	1159	1359	1559	1759	1959	2159
Všetaty d.	0441	0619	0809	1009	1209	1409	1609	1809	2009	2209
Mělník d.	0451	0629	0819	1019	1219	1419	1619	1819	2019	2219
Litoměřice město d.	0527	0704	0851	1051	1251	1451	1651	1851	2051	2251
Ústí n. Labem Střekov a.	0549	0726	0910	1110	1310	1510	1710	1910	2110	2310
Ústí n. Labem západ a.	0554	0731	0915	1115	1315	1515	1715	1915	2115	2315

km		2Ⓐ	2	2	2	2	2	2⊗	2Ⓒ	2Ⓐ
0	**Rumburk** d.	0457	...	0709	1109	1309	1509	1709	...	...
45	Česka Lipá d.	0625	0625	0824	1224	1424	1624	1824	2045	...
99	Mladá Boleslav d.	0722	0722	0922	1322	1522	1722	1922	2212	2241
129	Nymburk **1145** d.	0748	0748	0948	1348	1548	1748	1948	2301	2321
136	Poděbrady **1145** d.	0756	0756	0956	1356	1556	1756	1956	2310	2330
152	**Kolín** a.	0809	0809	1009	1409	1609	1809	2009	2329	2349

		2Ⓐ	2	2		2	2	2	2⊗	
Kolín d.	...	...	0747	0947	...	1347	1547	1747	1947	...
Poděbrady **1145** d.	...	...	0800	1000	...	1400	1600	1800	2000	...
Nymburk **1145** d.	...	...	0808	1008	...	1408	1608	1808	2008	...
Mladá Boleslav a.	...	...	0833	1033	...	1433	1633	1833	2033	...
Česka Lipá a.	...	0514	0934	1135	...	1535	1735	1935	2135	...
Rumburk a.	...	0609	1041	1241	...	1641	1841	2041	...	...

h – Not Dec. 24-26, 31, Apr. 12, July 5, Sept. 27. ⊕ – Not Dec. 24, 31. ⊗ – Not Dec. 24, 25, 31. ⊖ – Not Dec. 25, Jan. 1.

PRAHA - PARDUBICE - BRNO - BŘECLAV - WIEN / BRATISLAVA 1150

km			EC	EC•	EC	SC*	EC	EC		EC	EC	SC*	EC	EC	EC	EC•	EC	EC	EC	EC•	EC	SC*	EC	
		271	71	131	345	15	273	73	475	275	103	17	171	75	173	277	105	175	77	133	177	19	379	
			✕			🍷	✕	✕			✕	🍷	✕	✕	✕	🍷	✕	✕	✕		✕	🍷	✕	
				♦	♦	[R]			♦	E	♦	[R]	♦		♦		♦	♦		♦	♦	[R]§	♦	
	Praha Holešovice d.	...	...	...	...	...	0730	0830	...	0930	...	...	1130	1230	1330	1430	...	1530	1630	...	1730	...	1930	...
0	**Praha** hlavni ▷ d.	...	...	...	0528	0557	|	|	0918	|	...	1057	|	|	|	|	...	|	|	...	|	1823	|	...
62	Kolín ▷ d.	...	...	...	0613	|	0813	|	1013	1013	...	|	1213	|	1413	1513	...	1613	|	...	1813	|	2013	...
154	**Pardubice** ▷ d.	...	...	...	0636	0659	0836	0936	1036	1036	...	1159	1236	1336	1436	1536	...	1636	1736	...	1836	1925	2036	...
164	Česká Třebová ▷ d.	...	...	...	0711	|	0911	|	1111	1111	...	|	1311	|	1511	|	...	1711	|	...	1911	|	2111	...
255	**Brno** hlavní a.	...	...	...	0814	0825	1014	1114	1214	1214	...	1325	1414	1514	1614	1714	...	1814	1914	...	2014	2051	2214	...
255	**Brno** hlavní **1162** d.	...	0716	...	0816	0827	1016	1116	1216	1216	...	1327	1416	1516	1616	1716	...	1816	1916	...	2016	2053	...	...
314	**Břeclav** **1162** a.	...	0751	...	0851	0900	1051	1151	1251	1251	...	1400	1451	1551	1651	1751	...	1851	1951	...	2051	2126	...	...
314	**Břeclav** **991** d.	0553	0802	0755	0855	0902	1055	1202	1255	1255	1302	1402	1455	1602	1702	1755	1802	1855	2002	1955	2102	2130	...	...
	Wien Süd **991** a.	|	0902	|	|	1002	|	1302	|	|	1402	1502	|	1702	1802	|	1902	|	2102	|	2202	|	...	...
332	Kúty 🏛 d.	0610	...	0810	0910	...	1110	...	1310	1310	...	...	1510	...	...	1810	...	1910	...	2010	...	|	...	...
396	**Bratislava** Hlavná a.	0653	...	0853	0947	...	1147	...	1347	1347	...	...	1547	...	...	1850	...	1947	...	2050	...	2220	...	...
	Budapest Keleti **1170** a.	...	...	...	1232	...	1432	...	...	...	...	...	1832	...	...	...	...	2232	...	...	...	...	...	...

	IC	EC			471			EN	EN
	571	179		471	477	471		477	477
	Ⓑ	✕							
	h	♦		Y	X	W		♦b	V
Praha Holešovice d.	2030	2130	...	...	...	...	...	0020	0020
Praha hlavni ▷ d.	|	|	...	2140	2140	2140	...	0042	0042
Kolín ▷ d.	|	2213	...	2234	2234	2234	...	|	|
Pardubice ▷ d.	2136	2236	...	2308	2308	2308	...	|	|
Česká Třebová ▷ d.	2211	2312	...	2354	2354	2354	...	|	|
Brno hlavní a.	2314	0015	...	▽	▽	▽	...	0324	0324
Brno hlavní **1162** d.	...	...	...	▽	▽	▽	...	0327	0327
Břeclav **1162** a.	...	...	...	0223	0223	0223	...	0402	0402
Břeclav **991** d.	...	...	...	0335	0446	0459	...	0446	0459
Wien Süd **991** a.	...	...	...	|	|	0630**z**	...	|	0630**z**
Kúty 🏛 d.	...	...	...	0350	0501	...	...	0501	...
Bratislava Hlavná a.	...	...	...	0433	0540	...	...	0540	...
Budapest Keleti **1170** a.	...	...	...	0819	0832	...	...	0832	...

	IC	EC	SC*	EC		EC•	EC	EC	
	570	176	18	378		132	76	174	
	⚒	✕	🍷	✕			✕	✕	
	n	♦	[R]	♦		♦		♦	
Budapest Keleti **1170** d.	...	...	...	...	...	...	...	0528	...
Bratislava Hlavná d.	...	...	0539	...	...	0655	...	0801	...
Kúty 🏛 d.	...	...	|	...	...	0735	...	0841	...
Wien Süd **991** d.	...	...	|	0558	...	|	0658	|	...
Břeclav **991** a.	...	...	0629	0655	...	0748	0755	0854	...
Břeclav **1162** d.	...	...	0631	0704	...	...	0804	0904	...
Brno hlavní **1162** a.	...	...	0704	0739	...	...	0839	0939	...
Brno hlavní d.	0441	0541	0706	0741	...	...	0841	0941	...
Česká Třebová ▷ d.	0544	0644	|	0844	...	...	|	1044	...
Pardubice ▷ d.	0621	0720	0833	0920	...	...	1020	1120	...
Kolín ▷ d.	|	0743	|	0943	...	...	|	1143	...
Praha hlavni ▷ a.	|	|	0935	|	...	...	|	|	...
Praha Holešovice a.	0729	0829	...	1029	...	...	1129	1229	...

	EC	EC•	EC	SC*	EC	EC	EC			EC	SC*	EC	EC•	EC	EC	EC		EN	EN			476		
	104	276	172	14	170	74	274	474	270	102	16	272	130	72	344	70		476	476		470	470	470	
	✕		✕	🍷	✕	✕				✕	🍷	✕		✕		✕								
	♦		♦	[R]	♦		F	♦		♦	[R]		♦		♦			♦	V		W	Xc	Y	
Budapest Keleti **1170** d.	...	...	...	...	0928	...	...	...	...	...	...	1328	...	...	1528	...	...	1958	...	...	...	1958	1940	...
Bratislava Hlavná d.	...	0907	...	...	1201	...	1401	1401	1454	...	...	1601	1655	...	1801	...	...	2255	...	...	...	2255	2355	...
Kúty 🏛 d.	...	0948	...	...	1241	...	1441	1441	1539	...	...	1641	1735	...	1841	...	...	2335	...	...	...	2335	0041	...
Wien Süd **991** d.	0858	|	0958	1058	|	1258	|	|	|	1458	1558	|	|	1658	|	1858	...	|	2212**z**	...	2212**z**	|	|	...
Břeclav **991** a.	0955	1001	1055	1155	1254	1355	1454	1454	1554	1555	1655	1654	1748	1755	1854	1955	...	2348	2333	...	2333	2348	0054	...
Břeclav **1162** d.	...	1004	1104	1157	1304	1404	1504	1504	...	...	1657	1704	...	1804	1904	2004	...	0015	0015	...	0127	0127	0127	...
Brno hlavní **1162** a.	...	1039	1139	1230	1339	1439	1539	1539	...	...	1730	1739	...	1839	1939	2039	...	0050	0050	...	▽	▽	▽	...
Brno hlavní d.	...	1041	1141	1232	1341	1441	1541	1541	...	...	1732	1741	...	1841	1941	2041	...	0052	0052	...	▽	▽	▽	...
Česká Třebová ▷ d.	...	|	1244	|	1444	|	1644	1644	...	...	|	1844	...	|	2044	2144	...	|	|	...	0358	0358	0358	...
Pardubice ▷ d.	...	1220	1320	1359	1520	1620	1720	1720	...	...	1859	1920	...	2020	2120	2220	...	|	|	...	0448	0448	0448	...
Kolín ▷ d.	...	1243	1343	|	1543	|	1743	1743	...	...	|	1943	...	|	2143	|	...	|	|	...	0521	0521	0521	...
Praha hlavni ▷ a.	...	|	|	1501	|	|	|	1840	...	...	2001	2031	...	2131	2231	2331	...	|	|	...	0622	0622	0622	...
Praha Holešovice a.	...	1329	1429	...	1629	1729	1829	...	...	...	...	...	...	...	...	...	...	0329	0329	...	...	...	...	...

SLOWER TRAINS PRAHA - ČESKÁ TŘEBOVÁ - BRNO

km		1973	1975	865	867	869	871	1977	873	875	877	879
		⊙	Ⓐ					Ⓐ				⊗
0	**Praha** hlavní ▷ d.	...	...	0540	0740	0940	1140	*1240*	1340	1540	1740	1940
62	Kolín ▷ d.	...	...	0633	0833	1033	1233	*1333*	1433	1633	1833	2033
104	**Pardubice** ▷ d.	...	...	0706	0906	1106	1306	*1403*	1506	1706	1906	2106
139	Choceň ▷ d.	...	...	0730	0928	1128	1328	*1422*	1528	1728	1928	2128
154	Ústí nad Orlicí ▷ d.	...	...	0745	0943	1143	1343	*1437*	1543	1743	1943	2143
164	**Česká Třebová** ▷ a.	...	...	0754	0952	1152	1352	*1446*	1552	1752	1952	2152
164	**Česká Třebová** d.	0551	0651	0759	0957	1157	1357	1451	1559	1757	1959	...
181	Svitavy d.	0603	0703	0811	1010	1210	1410	1503	1611	1810	2011	...
208	Letovice d.	0630	0730	0830	1030	1230	1430	1530	1630	1830	2030	...
233	Blansko d.	0649	0749	0849	1049	1249	1449	1549	1649	1849	2049	...
255	**Brno** hlavní a.	0711	0811	0911	1111	1311	1511	1611	1711	1911	2111	...

	862	864	866	868	870	872	874	876	1974	878
	Ⓐ	⚒d					△	△	Ⓑh	⊗
Brno hlavní d.	...	0444	0644	0844	1044	1244	1444	1644	1744	1844
Blansko d.	...	0508	0708	0908	1108	1308	1508	1708	1808	1908
Letovice d.	...	0527	0727	0927	1127	1327	1527	1727	1827	1927
Svitavy d.	0456	0544	0744	0944	1144	1344	1544	1744	1851	1944
Česká Třebová a.	0507	0556	0756	0955	1156	1356	1556	1756	1902	1956
Česká Třebová ▷ d.	0509	0602	0805	1002	1202	1402	1602	1802	...	2002
Ústí nad Orlicí ▷ d.	0518	0612	0815	1012	1212	1412	1612	1812	...	2012
Choceň ▷ d.	0532	0628	0830	1027	1227	1427	1627	1827	...	2027
Pardubice ▷ d.	0555	0656	0856	1056	1256	1456	1656	1850	...	2056
Kolín ▷ d.	0625	0726	0926	1126	1326	1526	1726	1926	...	2126
Praha hlavní ▷ a.	0722	0822	1022	1222	1422	1622	1822	2022	...	2222

♦ – **NOTES** (LISTED BY TRAIN NUMBERS)

102/3 – POLONIA – [12] ✕ Warszawa - Ostrava - Břeclav - Wien and v.v.
104/5 – SOBIESKI – [12] ✕ Warszawa - Ostrava - Břeclav - Wien and v.v.
130/1 – MORAVIA – [12] Bohumin - Ostrava - Břeclav - Bratislava and v.v.
132/3 – DEVÍN – [12] Bohumin - Ostrava - Břeclav - Bratislava and v.v.
170/1 – HUNGARIA – [12] ✕ Berlin - Dresden - Praha - Budapest and v.v.
172/3 – VINDOBONA – [12] ✕ Hamburg - Berlin - Dresden - Praha - Wien and v.v.
174/5 – JÁN JESENIUS – [12] ✕ Hamburg - Berlin - Dresden - Praha - Budapest and v.v.
176 – ALOIS NEGRELLI – [12] ✕ Brno - Praha - Dresden - Berlin - Hamburg.
177 – JOHANNES BRAHMS – [12] ✕ Berlin - Dresden - Praha - Wien.
179 – ALOIS NEGRELLI – [12] ✕ Berlin - Dresden - Praha - Brno.
344/5 – AVALA – [12] ✕ Praha - Bratislava - Budapest - Beograd and v.v. Conveys ▬ 2 cl. Praha - Beograd - Thessaloniki on dates in Table **60** (summer only).
378 – CARL MARIA VON WEBER – [12] ✕ Wien - Praha - Berlin - Stralsund - Binz ◧.
379 – CARL MARIA VON WEBER – [12] ✕ Binz ◧ - Stralsund - Berlin - Praha - Brno.
474 – JADRAN – June 21 - Sept. 6 (previous day from Split). [12] Bratislava - Praha; 🛏 1, 2 cl., ▬ 2 cl. [2] Split - Zagreb - Bratislava - Praha (Table **92**).
475 – JADRAN – June 19 - Sept. 4. [12] Praha - Bratislava; 🛏 1, 2 cl., ▬ 2 cl. [2] Praha - Bratislava - Zagreb - Split (Table **92**).
476/7 – METROPOL – 🛏 1, 2 cl., ▬ 2 cl. and [2] Berlin - Dresden - Praha - Brno - Bratislava - Budapest and v.v. For other cars conveyed between Břeclav and Budapest see Tables **95** and **99**.

E – SLOVAN, not June 19 - Sept. 4.
F – SLOVAN, not June 21 - Sept. 6.
V – 🛏 1, 2 cl., ▬ 2 cl. and [2] Berlin - Dresden - Praha - Brno - Břeclav (**202/3**) - Wien Westbf and v.v.
W – AMICUS – 🛏 1, 2 cl. Praha - Olomouc - Břeclav - Wien and v.v.; [12] Praha - Přerov and v.v.
X – AMICUS – 🛏 1, 2 cl. and [2] Praha (**470/1**) - Břeclav (**476/7**) - Budapest and v.v.; conveys to Sept. 30 (to Sept. 29 from Bucuresti) 🛏 1, 2 cl. Praha (**470/1**) - Břeclav (**476/7**) - Budapest (**374/5**) - Bucureşti and v.v.
Y – AMICUS – May 28 - Sept. 28 from Praha, May 29 - Sept. 29 from Budapest. 🛏 1, 2 cl., ▬ 2 cl. and [12] Praha - Bratislava - Györ - Budapest and v.v. Conveys on dates in Table **60** (summer only) 🛏 1, 2 cl. and ▬ 2 cl. Praha - Burgas / Varna and v.v.
b – Conveys 🛏 1, 2 cl. Cheb (**441**) - Karlovy Vary - Praha (**477**) - Bratislava (**811**) - Zvolen - Banská Bystrica.
c – Conveys 🛏 1, 2 cl. Banská Bystrica (**810**) - Zvolen - Bratislava (**476**) - Břeclav (**470**) - Praha (**606**) - Karlovy Vary - Cheb.
d – Runs daily from Česká Třebová.
h – Not Dec. 24 - 26, 31, Apr. 12, July 5, Sept. 27.
n – Also Dec. 24, May 1, 8, Oct. 28, Nov. 17; not Dec. 27.
z – Wien **Westbf** (conveyed in train **202/3**).
◧ – Runs Stralsund - Binz and v.v. on dates in Table **844**.

△ – Other trains Brno - Česká Třebová: 1344 Ⓐ, 1544 Ⓑ.
▽ – Via Olomouc and Přerov (Table **1160**).
▷ – See also Table **1160**.
⊕ – Not Dec. 24, 31.
⊗ – Not Dec. 24, 25, 31.
⊖ – Not Dec. 25, Jan. 1.
⊙ – Not Dec. 25, 26, Jan. 1.
§ – [R] Praha - Břeclav.
• – *Ex* in Slovakia.
* – Pendolino tilting train. Classified *EC* in Austria.

OTHER TRAIN NAMES:
14/15 – SMETANA
16/17 – ANTONÍN DVOŘÁK
18/19 – SLOVENSKÁ STRELA
70/71 – GUSTAV MAHLER
72/73 – FRANZ SCHUBERT
74/75 – ZDENĚK FIBICH
76/77 – GUSTAV KLIMT
270/1 – RASTISLAV
272/3 – JAROSLAV HAŠEK
276/7 – FRANTIŠEK KŘIŽÍK

PRAHA - HAVLIČKŮV BROD - BRNO 1151

For faster trains Praha - Brno via Česká Třebová see Table **1150**

km		671	673	675	677	679	681	683	913	685	687	911
		⚒r	⊖						⊕		⊕	
0	**Praha** hlavni d.	...	0548	0756	0956	1156	1356	1556	1656	1756	1856	2056
62	Kolín d.	...	0650	0850	1050	1250	1450	1650	1750	1850	1950	2150
73	Kutná Hora d.	...	0700	0900	1100	1300	1500	1700	1800	1900	2000	2200
82	Čáslav d.	...	0709	0909	1109	1309	1509	1709	1809	1909	2009	2209
136	**Havlíčkův Brod** d.	0552	0802	1002	1202	1402	1602	1802	1901	2002	2102	2300
	Jihlava **1137** a.	|	|	|	|	|	|	|	1924	|	|	...
169	Ždár nad Sázavou d.	0620	0830	1030	1230	1430	1630	1830	...	2030	2130e	...
257	**Brno** hlavní a.	0724	0934	1134	1334	1534	1734	1934	...	2134	2234e	...

	910	912	670	672	674	676	678	680	682	684
	⊖	⊖	⊖							⊕
Brno hlavní d.	...	...	0524r	0624	0824	1024	1223	1423	1624	1824
Ždár nad Sázavou d.	...	...	0632r	0732	0932	1132	1332	1532	1732	1932
Jihlava **1137** d.	...	0532	|	|	|	|	|	|	|	|
Havlíčkův Brod d.	0458	0558	0658	0758	0958	1158	1358	1558	1758	1958
Čáslav d.	0550	0650	0750	0850	1050	1250	1450	1650	1850	2050
Kutná Hora d.	0559	0659	0759	0859	1059	1259	1459	1659	1859	2059
Kolín d.	0610	0710	0810	0910	1110	1310	1510	1710	1910	2110
Praha hlavni a.	0704	0804	0904	1004	1204	1404	1604	1805	2010	2204

e – ⑦ (also Apr. 13, July 6, Sept. 28, Nov. 17; not Apr. 12, July 5, Sept. 27, Nov. 15).
r – ⚒ (also Dec. 24, May 1, 8, Oct. 28, Nov. 17; not Dec. 27).
⊕, ⊖ – See Table above.

1160 PRAHA - OLOMOUC - OSTRAVA - ŽILINA

FASTEST TRAINS (calling only at points shown). See below for other services. *SC* (*SuperCity*) trains are named *SC PENDOLINO* and are operated by tilting trains.

km		*SC* 501	*SC* 503	*IC* 517	*SC* 505	*SC* 507	*SC* 509	*IC* 519	*SC* 511	
		Ⓡ🍷	Ⓡ🍷	✕	Ⓡ🍷	Ⓡ🍷	Ⓡ🍷	✕	Ⓡ🍷	
		Ⓐ					⊕	Ⓑh	⑦s	
0	**Praha** hlavní .... d.	0523	0923	1123	1323	1523	1723	1923	2023	...
104	Pardubice .... d.	0625	1025	1229	1425	1625	1825	2029	2125	...
252	**Olomouc** .... d.	0736	1136	1346	1536	1736	1936	2146	2236	...
353	Ostrava Svinov ♥ a.	0822	1222	1437	1622	1822	2022	2237	2322	...
358	**Ostrava** hlavní ♥ a.	0832	1232	1446	1632	1832	2032	2246	2332	...
366	Bohumín ♥ a.	...	...	1457	...	1842**y**	2042	2257	2342	...

	IC 518	*SC* 500	*SC* 502	*SC* 504	*SC* 506	*IC* 516	*SC* 508	*SC* 510	
	✕	Ⓡ🍷	Ⓡ🍷	Ⓡ🍷	Ⓡ🍷	✕	Ⓡ🍷	Ⓡ🍷	
	⚒n	⊖		Ⓐ				⑦s	
Bohumín ♥ d.	0400	0517	0717	...	...	1500	...	...	...
Ostrava hlavní ♥ d.	0411	0527	0727	0927	1327	1511	1727	1927	...
Ostrava Svinov ♥ d.	0419	0536	0736	0936	1336	1519	1736	1936	...
Olomouc .... d.	0513	0624	0824	1024	1424	1613	1824	2024	...
Pardubice .... d.	0629	0733	0933	1133	1533	1729	1933	2133	...
Praha hlavní .... a.	0735	0835	1035	1235	1635	1835	2035	2235	...

OTHER TRAINS. *SEE ABOVE FOR FASTEST TRAINS PRAHA - OSTRAVA*

km		441	2901	*Ex* 141	625	*Ex* 527	*IC* 583	705	*EC* 127	*EC* 143	627	*Ex* 529	*EC* 115	*EC* 235	707	*EC* 121	*EC* 147	629	*Ex* 525	331	*EC* 119	703	*EC* 129	*IC* 531	623
			2		✕		✕	✕	✕	✕	✕		✕	✕	✕	✕	✕	✕	✕	2	✕	✕		🍷	✕
		♦	Ⓐu			L		L	‡	‡		L	♦	♦‡	L				L		♦	V	‡		
0	**Praha** hlavní △ d.	0009	...	0408	...	0508	0609	0640	0709	0809	0840	0909	1009	1009	1040	1109	1209	1240	1309	...	1409	1440	1509	1609	1640
62	Kolín △ d.	0059	...	0459	...	0559	0659	0733	0759	0859	0933	0959	1059	1059	1133	1159	1259	1333	1359	...	1459	1533	1559	1659	1733
104	**Pardubice** △ d.	0123	...	0524	0600	0628	0724	0803	0828	0924	1003	1028	1124	1124	1205	1223	1324	1403	1428	...	1524	1603	1628	1724	1803
139	Choceň △ d.	0141	...	|	0619	|	|	0822	|	|	1022	|	|	|	1223	|	|	1422	|	...	|	1622	|	|	1822
154	Ústí nad Orlicí △ d.	0155	...	|	0634	|	|	0837	|	|	1037	|	|	|	1237	|	|	1437	|	...	|	1637	|	|	1837
164	Česká Třebová △ d.	0205	...	0602	0647	0706	0802	0848	0906	1002	1048	1106	1202	1202	1248	1306	1402	1448	1506	...	1602	1648	1706	1802	1848
206	Zábřeh na Moravé d.	|	...	0626	0718	|	0826	0918	|	1026	1118	|	1226	1226	1313	|	1426	1518	|	...	1626	1718	|	1826	1918
252	**Olomouc** a.	0251	...	0651	0748	0751	0851	0948	0951	1051	1148	1151	1251	1251	1341	1351	1451	1548	1551	...	1651	1748	1751	1851	1948
252	**Olomouc** d.	0254	...	0654	0757	0754	0854	0957	0954	1054	1157	1154	1254	1254	1357	1354	1454	1557	1554	...	1654	1757	1754	1854	1957
274	Přerov a.	0309	...	|	|	0809	|	1012	|	|	|	1209	|	|	1412	|	|	|	1609	...	|	1812	|	|	|
274	Přerov ▷ d.	0319	0424	|	|	...	|	*1027*	|	|	|	*1227*	|	|	*1427*	|	|	|	*1627*	...	|	*1827*	|	|	|
303	Hranice na Moravě ▷ d.	0338	0451	0725	0832	...	0924	*1045*	1026	1124	1232	*1245*	1324	1324	*1445*	1426	1524	1632	*1645*	...	1724	*1845*	1826	1924	2032
353	Ostrava Svinov ▷ d.	0416	0537	0752	|	...	0958	*1120*	|	1151	|	*1320*	1353	1407	*1520*	|	1551	|	*1720*	1736	1751	*1920*	|	1958	|
358	**Ostrava** hlavní ▷ d.	0426	0546	0801	|	...	1007	*1129*	|	1200	|	*1329*	1402	|	*1529*	|	1600	|	*1729*	1718*	1800	*1929*	|	2009	|
354	Ostrava Vitkovice d.	|	|	|	|	...	|	|	|	|	|	|	|	1414	|	|	|	|	|	1743	|	|	|	|	|
366	Bohumín ▷ a.	0435	0554	0809	|	...	1016	*1137*	|	1208	|	*1337*	1410	|	*1537*	|	1608	|	*1737*	|	1808	*1937*	|	|	|
366	Bohumín d.	0437	0556	0820	|	...	...	...	|	1220	|	...	1429	|	...	|	1620	|	...	1708*	...	...	|	|	|
	Katowice **1076** a.	|	|	|	|	...	...	...	|	|	|	...	1557	|	...	|	|	|	...	|	...	...	|	|	|
381	Karviná hlavní d.	0452	0610	0832	|	...	...	...	|	1232	|	...	...	|	...	|	1632	|	...	|	...	...	|	|	|
397	Český Těšín **1077** d.	0513	0629	0851	|	...	...	...	|	1251	|	...	...	1447	...	|	1651	|	...	1819	...	...	|	2050	|
435	Čadca 🏛 **1077** d.	0608	0727	0943	|	...	...	...	|	1343	|	...	...	1543	...	|	1743	|	...	1916	...	...	|	...	|
329	Valašské Meziříčí d.	|	|	|	0858	...	...	...	1052	|	1258	...	...	|	...	1452	|	1658	...	|	...	...	1852	...	2058
348	**Vsetín** d.	|	|	|	0914	...	...	...	1111	|	1314	...	...	|	...	1511	|	1716	...	|	...	...	1911	...	2114
366	Horní Lideč 🏛 d.	|	|	|	...	...	...	...	|	|	...	...	...	|	...	|	|	1733	...	|	...	...	|	...	...
394	Púchov **1180** d.	|	|	|	...	...	...	...	1151	|	...	...	...	|	...	1551	|	...	...	|	...	...	1951	...	...
Δ *439*	**Žilina** **1180** a.	0638	*0819*	1013	...	...	...	...	1228	1413	...	...	...	1613	...	1628	1813	...	...	1946	...	...	2028	...	...
	Košice **1180** a.	1007	...	...	...	...	...	...	...	...	...	...	...	...	...	1921	...	...	...	...	...	...	...	...	...

	Ex 523	*IC* 581	621	*Ex* 521	443	201	471	*EN* 425	447	209
		✕	✕					🛏		🛏
	Y⊕			⊗	♦	♦	♦	♦	♦	♦
Praha hlavní △ d.	1709	1809	1840	2009	2040	2109	2140	2204	2240	2300
Kolín △ d.	1759	1859	1933	2059	2133	2200	2234	2255	2333	2352
Pardubice △ d.	1828	1928	2003	2124	2158	2225	2308	2321	0004	0019
Choceň △ d.	|	|	2022	|	2219	|	2328	|	|	|
Ústí nad Orlicí △ d.	|	|	2037	|	2233	|	2342	|	|	|
Česká Třebová △ d.	1906	2005	2048	2202	2243	2305	2354	|	|	|
Zábřeh na Moravé d.	|	2029	2115	2226	|	2332	|	|	|	|
Olomouc a.	1951	2054	2150	2251	2329	2359	0041	0049	0123	0150
Olomouc d.	1954	2057	2153	2254	2332	0003	0044	0052	0126	0153
Přerov a.	2009	|	|	2309	|	0018	0059	|	|	|
Přerov ▷ d.	*2027*	|	|	...	|	0038	...	|	|	|
Hranice na Moravě ▷ d.	*2045*	2127	2228	...	0002	0058	...	|	|	|
Ostrava Svinov ▷ d.	*2120*	2201	|	...	0039	0129	...	|	0222	0252
Ostrava hlavní ▷ d.	*2129*	2210	|	...	0048	0138	...	|	0231	0301
Ostrava Vitkovice d.	|	|	|	...	|	|	...	|	|	|
Bohumín ▷ a.	*2137*	2219	|	...	0057	0147	...	|	0239	0310
Bohumín d.	...	2224	|	...	0120	0307	...	|	0240	0335
Katowice **1076** a.	...	|	|	...	|	0425	...	|	|	0505
Karviná hlavní d.	...	2235	|	...	0132	...	...	|	0252	...
Český Těšín **1077** d.	...	2252	|	...	0150	...	...	|	0311	...
Čadca 🏛 **1077** d.	...	...	|	...	0249	...	...	|	0407	...
Valašské Meziříčí d.	...	...	2254	...	|	...	...	|	|	...
Vsetín d.	...	...	2310	...	|	...	...	|	|	...
Horní Lideč 🏛 d.	...	...	...	...	|	...	...	|	|	...
Púchov **1180** d.	...	...	...	...	|	...	...	|	|	...
Žilina **1180** a.	...	...	...	...	0319	...	...	0329	0437	...
Košice **1180** a.	...	...	...	...	0707	...	...	0732	0813	...

	208	446	470	*EN* 424	200	*Ex* 520	442	*Ex* 522	620	*IC* 530
	🛏			🛏		🍷		✕	✕	✕
	♦	♦	♦	♦	♦	⊙	♦	Z⊖		
Košice **1180** d.	...	2005	...	2100	...	...	2202	...	...	...
Žilina **1180** d.	...	2339	...	0055	...	...	0142	...	...	...
Púchov **1180** d.	...	|	...	|	...	...	|	...	...	...
Horní Lideč 🏛 d.	...	|	...	|	...	...	|	...	...	...
Vsetín d.	...	|	...	|	...	...	|	...	0450	...
Valašské Meziříčí d.	...	|	...	|	...	...	|	...	0508	...
Čadca 🏛 **1077** d.	...	0012	...	|	...	...	0215	...	|	...
Český Těšín **1077** d.	...	0109	...	|	...	...	0312	...	|	0512
Karviná hlavní d.	...	0125	...	|	...	...	0328	...	|	|
Katowice **1076** d.	2240	|	...	|	2353	...	|	...	|	|
Bohumín a.	0017	0136	...	|	0126	...	0339	...	|	|
Bohumín ▷ d.	0042	0139	...	|	0207	...	0405	...	|	|
Ostrava Vitkovice d.	|	|	...	|	|	...	|	...	|	|
Ostrava hlavní ▷ d.	0053	0150	...	|	0218	...	0416	...	|	0555
Ostrava Svinov ▷ d.	0102	0159	...	|	0227	...	0425	...	|	0604
Hranice na Moravě ▷ d.	|	|	...	|	0256	...	0503	...	0533	0636
Přerov ▷ a.	|	|	...	|	0314	...	|	...	|	|
Přerov d.	|	|	0248	|	0339	0446	|	0548	|	|
Olomouc a.	0200	0252	0304	0351	0354	0501	0534	0602	0605	0705
Olomouc d.	0204	0255	0307	0354	0357	0504	0537	0608	0611	0708
Zábřeh na Moravé d.	|	|	|	|	0423	0529	0604	|	0646	0733
Česká Třebová △ d.	|	|	0358	|	0448	0558	0630	0653	0711	|
Ústí nad Orlicí △ d.	|	|	0409	|	0457	|	|	|	0721	|
Choceň △ d.	|	|	0424	|	0511	|	|	|	0735	|
Pardubice △ d.	0338	0434	0448	0520	0533	0636	0711	0736	0757	0838
Kolín △ d.	0411	0502	0521	0603	0559	0702	0738	0802	0826	0904
Praha hlavní △ a.	0507	0554	0622	0709	0654	0754	0830	0854	0922	0954

	Ex 524	622	*EC* 146	*EC* 128	702	340	*EC* 118	*Ex* 526	624	**1604** *EC*234	*EC* 234	*EC* 120	704	*EC* 114	*Ex* 528	626	*EC* 142	*EC* 126	706	*IC* 582	628	*Ex* 140	◇	2914	440
	✕	✕	🍷		✕	2	✕		✕	🍷	🍷	✕	✕	✕		✕	✕	✕	✕	✕	✕			2	
	V		‡	‡	L		♦	L			♦‡		L	♦	L		‡	‡	L						♦
Košice **1180** d.	...	...	...	...	...	...	...	...	...	...	...	0839	...	...	...	...	...	...	...	...	...	...	...	...	1802
Žilina **1180** d.	...	...	0542	0740	...	0742	...	...	...	...	0942	1140	...	...	...	...	1342	1540	...	...	...	1742	...	...	2137
Púchov **1180** d.	...	*0549*	|	0817	...	|	...	...	...	...	|	1217	...	...	...	...	|	1617	...	...	...	|	*2015*	...	|
Horní Lideč 🏛 d.	...	0627	|	|	...	|	...	...	...	...	|	|	...	...	...	...	|	|	...	...	1832	|	2102	...	|
Vsetín d.	...	0645	|	0854	...	|	...	...	1050	...	|	1254	...	...	...	1450	|	1654	...	...	1850	|	2144	...	|
Valašské Meziříčí d.	...	0704	|	0912	...	|	...	...	1108	...	|	1312	...	...	...	1508	|	1712	...	...	1908	|	2205	...	|
Čadca 🏛 **1077** d.	...	|	0615	|	...	0815	...	...	|	...	1015	|	...	...	...	|	1415	|	...	...	|	1815	|	2041	2210
Český Těšín **1077** d.	...	|	0706	|	...	0913	...	...	|	...	1108	|	...	...	...	|	1507	|	...	...	|	1907	|	2139	2306
Karviná hlavní d.	...	|	0722	|	...	0929	...	...	|	...	|	|	...	...	...	|	1523	|	...	...	|	1923	|	2159	2323
Katowice **1076** d.	...	|	|	|	...	|	...	...	|	...	|	|	...	1209	...	|	|	|	...	...	|	|	|	|	|
Bohumín a.	...	|	0733	|	...	0940	...	...	|	...	|	|	...	1334	...	|	1534	|	...	...	|	1934	|	2213	2334
Bohumín ▷ d.	*0623*	|	0745	|	*0823*	...	0950	*1023*	|	1132	|	|	*1223*	1350	*1423*	|	1550	|	*1623*	1745	|	1950	|	*2223*	2335
Ostrava Vitkovice d.	|	|	|	|	|	...	|	|	|	|	1140	|	|	|	|	|	|	|	|	|	|	|	|	|	|
Ostrava hlavní ▷ d.	*0633*	|	0755	|	*0833*	...	1001	*1033*	|	1142	|	|	*1233*	1401	*1433*	|	1601	|	*1633*	1756	|	2001	|	*2233*	2346
Ostrava Svinov ▷ d.	*0641*	|	0804	|	*0841*	...	1010	*1041*	|	1210**x**	1210**x**	|	*1241*	1410	*1441*	|	1610	|	*1641*	1804	|	2010	|	*2240*	2355
Hranice na Moravě ▷ d.	*0714*	0733	0836	0936	*0914*	...	1036	|	1133	1236	1236	1336	*1314*	1436	*1514*	1533	1636	1736	*1714*	1836	1933	2036	2247	...	0030
Přerov ▷ a.	*0731*	|	|	|	*0931*	...	|	*1131*	|	|	|	|	*1331*	|	*1531*	|	|	|	*1731*	|	|	|	2311	...	0048
Přerov d.	0746	|	|	|	0946	...	|	1146	|	|	|	|	1346	|	1546	|	|	|	1746	|	|	|	...	...	0057
Olomouc a.	0801	0805	0905	1005	1001	...	1105	1201	1205	1305	1305	1405	1401	1505	1601	1605	1705	1805	1801	1905	2005	2105	...	...	0112
Olomouc d.	0808	0811	0908	1008	1011	...	1108	1208	1211	1308	1308	1408	1411	1508	1608	1616	1708	1808	1811	1908	2011	2108	...	...	0115
Zábřeh na Moravé d.	|	0846	0934	|	1046	...	1134	|	1246	1334	1334	|	1446	1534	|	1646	1734	|	1846	1934	2046	2134	...	...	|
Česká Třebová △ d.	0853	0911	0958	1053	1111	...	1158	1253	1311	1358	1358	1453	1511	1558	1658	1711	1758	1853	1911	1958	2111	2158	...	...	0202
Ústí nad Orlicí △ d.	|	0921	|	|	1121	...	|	|	1321	|	|	|	1521	|	|	1721	|	|	1921	|	2121	|	...	...	|
Choceň △ d.	|	0935	|	|	1135	...	|	|	1335	|	|	|	1535	|	|	1735	|	|	1935	|	2135	|	...	...	|
Pardubice △ d.	0936	0957	1036	1136	1157	...	1236	1336	1402	1436	1436	1536	1557	1636	1736	1757	1836	1936	1957	2036	2157	2236	...	...	0240
Kolín △ d.	1002	1026	1102	1202	1226	...	1302	1402	1430	1502	1502	1602	1626	1702	1802	1826	1902	2002	2026	2102	2226	2302	...	...	0304
Praha hlavní △ a.	1054	1122	1154	1254	1322	...	1354	1454	1522	1554	1554	1654	1722	1754	1854	1922	1954	2054	2122	2154	2322	2354	...	...	0354

FOR NOTES SEE FOOT OF NEXT PAGE *Connections may be available at Olomouc with train in previous column* FOR FASTEST TRAINS SEE TOP OF PAGE

BRNO - PŘEROV - OSTRAVA - BOHUMÍN 1161

km	For notes see foot of page	202 ♦	731 ⊖	831 ⊖	733	EC 132 ♦‡	833	735	EC 104 ♦		737	835	739	837	741	EC 102 ♦	839	743	EC 130 ♦‡	841	745 ⊕	1539 ⑦e	661 R⊕
0	**Brno** hlavní **1164** d.	...	0502	0602	0702	...	0802	0902	...	...	1102	1202	1302	1402	1502	...	1602	1702	...	1802	1902	2002	2102
45	Vyškov na Moravě **1164** d.	...	0543	0643	0743	...	0843	0943	...	...	1143	1243	1343	1443	1543	...	1643	1743	...	1843	1943	2043	2141
	Wien Südbahnhof **1150** d.	2212z	|	|	|	...	|	|	0858	...	|	|	|	|	|	1458	|	|	...	|	|	|	|
	Bratislava Hlavná **1150** d.	|	|	|	|	0655	|	|	|	...	|	|	|	|	|	|	|	|	1655	|	|	|	|
	Břeclav **1162** d.	0018	|	|	|	0808	|	|	1008	...	|	|	|	|	|	1608	|	|	1808	|	|	|	|
88	**Přerov** a.	|	0624	0724	0824	0910	0924	1024	1110	...	1224	1324	1424	1524	1624	1710	1724	1824	1910	1924	2024	2124	2224
88	**Přerov** ▽ d.	|	0627	0727	0827	0912	0927	1027	1112	...	1227	1327	1427	1527	1627	1712	1727	1827	1912	1927	2027	2127	2227
117	Hranice na Moravě ▽ d.	|	0645	|	0845	0931	|	1045	|	...	1245	|	1445	|	1645	|	|	1845	1931	|	2045	|	2245
167	Ostrava Svinov ▽ a.	0157	0717	0810	0917	1000	1010	1117	1154	...	1317	1410	1517	1610	1717	1754	1810	1917	2000	2010	2117	2210	2317
172	**Ostrava** hlavní ▽ a.	0206	0727	0820	0927	1010	1020	1127	1204	...	1327	1420	1527	1620	1727	1804	1820	1927	2010	2020	2127	2220	2327
180	Bohumín ▽ a.	0217	0737	0830	0937	1021	1030	1137	1215	...	1337	1430	1537	1630	1737	1815	1830	1937	2021	2030	2137	2230	2337

	203 ♦		660 R⊖	830 ⊖	EC 131 ♦‡	730	832	732		734	EC 103 ♦	834	736	836	738	838	EC 105 ♦	740	840 ⊕	EC 133 ♦‡	742	1538 ⑦e	744 ⊕
Bohumín ▽ d.	0215	...	0423	0537	0541	0623	0737	0823	...	1023	1046	1137	1223	1337	1423	1537	1546	1623	1737	1741	1823	1937	2023
Ostrava hlavní ▽ d.	0226	...	0433	0547	0551	0633	0747	0833	...	1033	1056	1147	1233	1347	1433	1547	1556	1633	1747	1751	1833	1947	2033
Ostrava Svinov ▽ d.	0235	...	0441	0555	0559	0641	0755	0841	...	1041	1104	1155	1241	1355	1441	1555	1604	1642	1755	1759	1841	1955	2041
Hranice na Moravě ▽ d.	|	...	0514	|	0627	0714	|	0914	...	1114	|	|	1314	|	1514	|	|	1715	|	1827	1914	|	2114
Přerov ▽ a.	|	...	0531	0636	0644	0731	0836	0931	...	1131	1144	1236	1331	1436	1531	1636	1644	1732	1836	1844	1931	2036	2131
Přerov d.	|	...	0538	0639	0646	0739	0838	0938	...	1138	1146	1238	1338	1438	1538	1638	1646	1739	1838	1846	1938	2038	2138
Břeclav **1162** a.	0412	...	|	|	0746	|	|	|	...	|	1246	|	|	|	|	|	1746	|	|	1946	|	|	|
Bratislava Hlavná **1150** a.	|	...	|	|	0853	|	|	|	...	|	|	|	|	|	|	|	|	|	|	2050	|	|	|
Wien Südbahnhof **1150** a.	0630z	...	|	|	...	|	|	|	...	|	1402	|	|	|	|	|	1902	|	|	...	|	|	|
Vyškov na Moravě **1164** d.	...	...	0618	0718	...	0818	0918	1018	...	1218	...	1318	1418	1518	1618	1718	...	1818	1918	...	2018	2118	2218
Brno hlavní **1164** d.	...	...	0700	0757	...	0857	0957	1057	...	1257	...	1357	1457	1557	1657	1757	...	1857	1957	...	2057	2157	2257

OLOMOUC - UHERSKÉ HRADIŠTĚ - BŘECLAV - BRNO 1162

For direct services Olomouc - Brno see Table **1164**. Train **202/3** runs non-stop Ostrava - Břeclav and v.v. (see Table **1161**)

km	For notes see foot of page	800 ⊖	709 ✕	EC 131 ♦	802	◇	Ex 527 ✕	804	705 ✕	806	EC 103 ♦	Ex 529	808	707 ✕	810	Ex 525 ✕	EC 105 ♦	812	703 V✕	EC 133 ♦	814	Ex 523 Y⊕	816 ⊕	471 ♦
	Praha hlavní **1160** d.	...	...	...	...	...	0508	...	0640	...	...	0909	...	1040	...	1309	...	...	1440	...	...	1709	...	2140
0	**Olomouc** ▽ d.	...	0557	...	0706	...	0754	0906	0957	1106	...	1154	1306	1357	1506	1554	...	1706	1757	...	1906	1954	2106	0044
	Ostrava hlavní **1161** d.	...	|	0551	|	...	|	|	|	|	1056	|	|	|	|	|	1556	|	|	1751	|	|	|	|
22	Přerov ▽ d.	...	0614	0646	0723	0742	0811	0923	1014	1123	1146	1211	1323	1414	1523	1611	1646	1723	1814	1846	1923	2013	2123	0117
37	Hulín d.	...	0626	|	0735	0759	0824	0935	1027	1135	|	1224	1335	1427	1535	1624	|	1735	1827	|	1935	2025	2135	|
50	Otrokovice ★ d.	...	0636	0703	0745	0813	0834	0945	1037	1145	1203	1234	1345	1437	1545	1634	1703	1745	1837	1903	1945	2033	2145	0135
68	Staré Město u Uh. Hradiště d.	...	0658	0714	0756	0831	0858	0956	1058	1156	1214	1258	1356	1458	1556	1658	1714	1756	1858	1914	1956	...	2156	0146
73	Uherské Hradiště ⊖ d.	...	0705	|	|	|	0905	|	1105	|	|	1305	|	1505	|	1705	|	|	1904	|	|	...	|	|
90	Uherský Brod d.	...	0723	|	|	|	0923	|	1123	|	|	1323	|	1527	|	1723	|	|	...	|	|	...	|	|
104	**Luhačovice** a.	...	0741	|	|	|	0941	|	1141	|	|	1341	|	1547	|	1741	|	|	...	|	|	...	|	|
102	Hodonin d.	0617	...	0732	0817	0903	...	1017	...	1217	1232	...	1417	...	1617	...	1732	1817	...	1932	2017	...	2217	0207
122	**Břeclav** a.	0631	...	0746	0831	0924	...	1031	...	1231	1246	...	1431	...	1631	...	1746	1831	...	1946	2031	...	2231	0223
122	**Břeclav** **1150** d.	0638	...	...	0838	...	...	1038	...	1238	...	...	1438	...	1638	...	...	1838	...	...	2038	...	...	...
181	**Brno** hlavní **1150** a.	0724	...	...	0924	...	...	1124	...	1324	...	...	1524	...	1724	...	...	1924	...	...	2124	...	...	...

	470 ♦	Ex 520 🍷⊙	Ex 522 Z⊖	801 ⊖	Ex 524 V✕	803	EC 132 ♦	702 ✕	805	EC 104 ♦	Ex 526	807	704 ✕	809	Ex 528	811	EC 102 ♦	706 ✕	813	EC 130 ♦	708 ✕	815	◇	817 ⊕
Brno hlavní **1150** d.	...	...	...	...	...	0636	...	...	0836	...	...	1036	...	1236	...	1436	...	...	1636	...	...	1836	...	2036
Břeclav **1150** a.	...	...	...	...	...	0721	...	...	0921	...	...	1121	...	1321	...	1521	...	...	1721	...	...	1921	...	2121
Břeclav d.	0127	...	...	0528	...	0728	0808	...	0928	1008	...	1128	...	1328	...	1528	1608	...	1728	1808	...	1928	2039	2128
Hodonin d.	0143	...	...	0542	...	0742	0823	...	0942	1023	...	1142	...	1342	...	1542	1623	...	1742	1823	...	1942	2100	2142
Luhačovice d.	|	...	...	|	...	|	|	0812	|	|	1014	|	1214	|	1414	|	|	1614	|	|	1814	|	|	...
Uherský Brod d.	|	...	...	|	...	|	|	0833	|	|	1033	|	1233	|	1433	|	|	1633	|	|	1833	|	|	...
Uherské Hradiště ⊖ d.	|	...	...	|	0651	|	|	0851	|	|	1051	|	1251	|	1451	|	|	1651	|	|	1851	|	|	...
Staré Město u Uh. Hradiště d.	0203	0414	...	0603	0712	0803	0842	0912	1003	1042	1112	1203	1312	1403	1512	1603	1642	1712	1803	1842	1912	2003	2131	...
Otrokovice ★ d.	0217	0425	0527	0615	0724	0815	0853	0924	1015	1053	1124	1215	1324	1415	1524	1615	1653	1724	1815	1853	1924	2015	2156v	...
Hulín d.	|	0434	0536	0624	0734	0824	|	0933	1024	|	1133	1224	1333	1424	1533	1624	|	1733	1824	|	1933	2024	2207v	...
Přerov ▽ a.	0236	0445	0546	0635	0744	0835	0910	0944	1035	1110	1144	1235	1344	1435	1544	1635	1710	1744	1835	1910	1944	2035	2219v	...
Ostrava hlavní **1161** a.	|	|	|	|	|	|	1010	|	|	1204	|	|	|	|	|	|	1804	|	|	2010	|	|	...	...
Olomouc ▽ a.	0305	0501	0602	0652	0801	0852	...	1001	1052	...	1201	1252	1401	1452	1601	1652	...	1801	1852	...	2001	2052	...	...
Praha hlavní **1160** a.	0622	0754	0854	...	1054	...	...	1322	...	...	1454	...	1722	...	1854	...	...	2122	...	...	...	...	...	...

BRNO - PROSTĚJOV - OLOMOUC - JESENIK 1164

km		903	1701 ©	909	931	933	905	907	935	1707 ⊕	937 ⊕
0	**Brno** hlavní **1161** d.	0515	...	0718	0918	1118	1318	1518	1718	...	1918
45	Vyškov na Moravé **1161** d.	0600	...	0800	1000	1200	1400	1600	1800	...	2000
61	Nezamyslice d.	0619	...	0819	1019	1219	1419	1619	1819	...	2019
80	Prostějov d.	0635	...	0835	1035	1235	1435	1635	1835	...	2035
100	**Olomouc** a.	0651	...	0851	1051	1251	1451	1651	1851	...	2051
100	**Olomouc** **1160** d.	0658	0748	0858	...	*1258*	1458	1658	...	1858	...
146	Zábřeh na Moravé **1160** d.	0740	0830	0940	...	*1340*	1540	1740	...	1940	...
176	Hanušovice d.	0810	0901	1010	...	*1410*	1610	1812	...	2015	...
212	**Jesenik** a.	0915	1012	1124	...	*1516*	1715	1916	...	2120	...

	1646 ⚒	930	902	904	932	934	906	1704 ©	908	1436 ⑦e
Jesenik d.	...	...	0633	0838	...	*1241*	1438	1545	1638	*1859*
Hanušovice d.	...	...	0747	0947	...	*1345*	1547	1653	1747	*2001*
Zábřeh na Moravé **1160** d.	...	...	0832	1032	...	*1429*	1632	1730	1832	*2032*
Olomouc **1160** a.	...	...	0902	1102	...	*1502*	1702	1804	1902	*2102*
Olomouc d.	0600	0707	0907	1107	1307	1507	1707	...	1907	2107
Prostějov d.	0616	0725	0925	1125	1325	1525	1725	...	1925	2125
Nezamyslice d.	0637	0739	0939	1139	1339	1539	1739	...	1939	2139
Vyškov na Moravé **1161** d.	0659	0801	1001	1201	1401	1601	1801	...	2001	2159
Brno hlavní **1161** a.	0743	0838	1038	1238	1438	1638	1838	...	2038	2236

♦ – **NOTES FOR TABLES 1160/1161/1162/1164** (LISTED BY TRAIN NUMBER)

102/3 – POLONIA – [12] ✕ Wien Süd - Břeclav - Ostrava - Katowice - Warszawa and v.v.; [2] Wien Süd - Břeclav - Ostrava - Bohumín (**118/9**) - Kraków and v.v.

104/5 – SOBIESKI – [12] ✕ Wien Süd - Břeclav - Ostrava - Katowice - Warszawa and v.v.

114/5 – PRAHA – [12] ✕ Praha - Ostrava - Katowice - Warszawa and v.v.

118/9 – COMENIUS – [12] ✕ Praha - Ostrava - Kraków and v.v.

130/1 – MORAVIA – [12] Bratislava - Břeclav - Ostrava - Bohumin and v.v.

132/3 – DEVÍN – [12] Bratislava - Břeclav - Ostrava - Bohumin and v.v.

200/1 – SILESIA – 🛏 1, 2 cl., ▬ 2 cl. [12] Praha - Kraków and v.v.; 🛏 1, 2 cl., ▬ 2 cl. [2] Praha - Bohumín (**202/3**) - Warszawa and v.v.; [2] Praha - Ostrava - Bohumín and v.v.; 🛏 1, 2 cl. Praha - Kraków - Przemysl - Lviv - Kyïv and v.v. Conveys on days in Table **96** 🛏 1, 2 cl. Praha - Kraków - Lviv - Odesa and v.v.

202/3 – CHOPIN – 🛏 1, 2 cl., ▬ 2 cl., [2] Wien Westbf - Bohumín - Warszawa and v.v.; 🛏 1, 2 cl. Wien - Bohumín (**200/1**) - Kraków and v.v. (also ▬ 2 cl. on dates in Table **99**); 🛏 1, 2 cl. Wien - Bohumín (**208/9**) - Minsk - Moskva and v.v.; 🛏 1, 2 cl., ▬ 2 cl., [2] Budapest (**476/7**) - Bratislava - Břeclav (**202/3**) - Warszawa and v.v.; 🛏 1, 2 cl., ▬ 2 cl. Budapest (**476/7**) - Bratislava - Břeclav (**202/3**) - Bohumín (**200/1**) - Kraków and v.v.; 🛏 1, 2 cl. Budapest (**476/7**) - Bratislava - Břeclav (**202/3**) - Bohumín (**208/9**) - Moskva and v.v.

208/9 – VLTAVA – 🛏 1, 2 cl. Praha - Bohumín - Minsk - Moskva and v.v. (also Praha - Minsk on ②④⑦, Minsk - Praha on ①③⑥); 🛏 1, 2 cl. Cheb (**607/6**) - Karlovy Vary - Praha (**209/8**) - Moskva and v.v. Conveys on dates in Table **95**, 🛏 1, 2 cl. Praha - Brest - Orsha - St Peterburg and v.v.

234/5 – DETVAN – [12] Praha - Ostrava Svinov - Žilina - Zvolen and v.v.

424/5 – SLOVAKIA – 🛏 1, 2 cl., ▬ 2 cl. and [2] Praha - Poprad Tatry - Košice and v.v.

440/1 – EXCELSIOR – 🛏 1, 2 cl., ▬ 2 cl., [12] Cheb - Karlovy Vary - Praha - Žilina - Košice and v.v.; 🛏 1, 2 cl., ▬ 2 cl. Plzeň (**767/50**) - Praha (**440/1**) - Žilina - Košice and v.v.; [2] Fr. Lázně (**767/50**) - Plzeň - Praha (**440/1**) - Žilina - Košice and v.v.

442/3 – ŠIRAVA – 🛏 1, 2 cl., ▬ 2 cl., [12] Praha - Košice - Humenné and v.v.; 🛏 1, 2 cl. Praha - Žilina (**1846/7**) - Banská Bystrica - Zvolen and v.v.; ✕ Praha - Bohumín and v.v. Conveys (not Dec. 24, 31) 🛏 1, 2 cl. České Budějovice (**662/3**) - Brno - Bohumín (**442/3**) - Žilina - Košice and v.v.

446/7 – VIHORLAT – [12] Praha - Pardubice and v.v. On dates in Table **1180** conveys 🛏 1, 2 cl., ▬ 1, 2 cl., [2] Praha - Poprad Tatry - Prešov - Humenné and v.v. (train **860/1** on other dates).

470/1 – AMICUS – [12] Praha - Přerov and v.v. For portions to/from Wien, Budapest and Bucureşti see Table **1150**.

L – To/from Luhacovice (Table **1162**).

R – ROŽMBERK – [12] Bohumin - Ostrava - Přerov - Brno - Jihlava - České Budějovice - Plzeň and v.v.

V – [12] Praha - Přerov - Veseli nad Moravou and v.v. (Table **1162**). Arrive Veseli 1923/depart 0636.

Y – [12] Praha - Přerov - Zlín střed (arrive 2055).

Z – [12] Zlín střed (depart 0500) - Přerov - Praha.

e – Also Apr. 13, July 6, Sept. 28, Nov. 17; not Apr. 12, July 5, Sept. 27, Nov. 15.

h – Not Dec. 24-26, 31, Apr. 12, July 5, Sept. 27.

n – Also Dec. 24, May 1, 8, Oct. 28, Nov. 17; not Dec. 27.

s – Also Dec. 23, Apr. 10, 13, 30, May 7, June 30, July 6, Aug. 31, Sept. 28, Oct. 23, Nov. 13, 17; not Dec. 28, Apr. 12, July 5, Sept. 27, Nov. 15.

u – ⚒ **n** from Bohumín.

v – ⑤⑥⑦ only.

x – Arrive 1147.

y – ⚒ only.

z – Wien **Westbf**.

★ – Connection to **Zlín** by local train (1-2 per hour) or trolleybus (every 10 minutes), *11 km*.

♥ – *SC* trains do not carry passengers locally on the section Ostrava Svinov - Bohumín.

⊕ – Not Dec. 24, 31.

⊗ – Not Dec. 24, 25, 31.

⊖ – Not Dec. 25, Jan. 1.

⊙ – Not Dec. 25, 26, Jan. 1.

⊖ – Connecting trains run to/from Staré Město u Uherské Hradiště (journey 7 mins).

◇ – Local train, 2nd class.

△ – See also Table **1150**.

▷ – See also Table **1161**.

▽ – See also Table **1160**.

⊠ – International journeys only.

▵ – *466 km* via Ostrava.

‡ – Classified *Ex* in Slovakia.

* – Via Ostrava-Svinov.

1166 OLOMOUC / JESENIK - OPAVA - OSTRAVA

2nd class only

km		881 ⊖	819	1629	883	821	823	885	825	827	887	829 ⊕
0	**Olomouc** d.	...	0707	0904	...	1107	1307	...	1507	1707	...	1907
64	Bruntál d.	...	0832	1032	...	1232	1432	...	1632	1832	...	2032
• 58	**Jesenik** d.	0535	|	|	0935	|	|	1334	|	|	1734	|
• 17	Tremešná ve Slez. △ d.	0641	|	|	1041	|	|	1441	|	|	1841	|
87	Krnov d.	0706	0906	1057	1106	1306	1506	1506	1706	1906	1906	2057
116	Opava východ ▶ d.	0743	0943	...	1143	1343	1543	1543	1743	1936	1943	2137
144	**Ostrava** Svinov ▶ a.	0805	1004	...	1205	1403	1605	1605	1805	...	2005	...

	880	820	822	882	1628	824	884	826	828	886 ⊕
Ostrava Svinov ▶ d.	0606	...	0806	1006	...	1206	1406	...	1606	1806
Opava východ ▶ d.	0630	...	0830	1030	...	1230	1430	...	1630	1830
Krnov d.	0705	0709	0909	1105	1109	1309	1505	1509	1709	1905
Tremešná ve Slez. △ a.	0721	|	0930*	1121	|	|	1521	|	1731*	1921
Jesenik a.	0828	|	1054*	1228	|	|	1627	|	1852*	2038
Bruntál d.	...	0739	0937	...	1137	1337	...	1537	1737	...
Olomouc a.	...	0852	1052	...	1257	1452	...	1652	1852	...

⊕ – Not Dec. 24, 31.
⊖ – Not Dec. 25, Jan. 1.
• – Distance from Krnov.

△ – Station for narrow gauge line to Osoblaha (4 trains per day, *20 km*).
* – Local train, change at Krnov.

▶ – Fast trains **Opava** východ - **Ostrava** Svinov - **Ostrava** hlavní (journey 26 minutes): From Opava východ: every 2 hours 0614 - 1814. From Ostrava hlavní: every 2 hours 0651 - 1851. Local trains run approx hourly Opava východ - Ostrava Svinov and v.v.

1168 BRNO - UHERSKÉ HRADIŠTĚ - VLÁRSKÝ PRŮSMYK

2nd class only

km						b	b		b	
0	**Brno** hlavní d.	0733	0928	1128	1214	1328	1528	1728	1928	2128
67	Kyjov d.	0840	1032	1232	1338	1432	1632	1832	2032	2232
90	Veselí nad Moravou d.	0905	1101	1301	1412	1501	1711	1901	2106	2259
106	Kunovice a.	|	|	|	|	1518	1728	|	2124	...
108	Uherské Hradiště ▷ a.	0922	1120	1320	1436	1526	1739	1922	2128	...
113	**Staré Město u Uh. H.** ▷ a.	0930	1128	1328	1446a	1553c	1753	1930	2135	...

	Ⓐ	Ⓒ	⚒	b						⑦e	⚒
Staré Město u Uh. H ▷ d.	0503	...	0606	0806	1031	1231	1431	1606	1806	2006	2006
Uherské Hradiště ▷ d.	0531	...	0626	0827	1039	1239	1439	1620	1824	2032	2044
Kunovice d.	0540	...	0633	0834	|	|	|	1626	1832	2040	|
Veselí nad Moravou d.	0600	0600	0700	0900	1100	1300	1500	1700	1900	2105	2105
Kyjov d.	0628	0628	0728	0928	1128	1328	1528	1728	1928	2132	2132
Brno hlavní a.	0734	0734	0833	1033	1233	1433	1633	1833	2033	2235	2235

km						b	b		b	
0	**Staré Město u Uh. H.** ▷ d.	0737	0858	1058	1258	1458c	1722	1931	2055	...
5	Uherské Hradiště ▷ d.	0748	0925	1124	1324	1515	1729	1943	2117	...
7	Kunovice d.	0754	0932	1130	1330	1521	1734	1947	2124	...
22	Uherský Brod ▷ d.	0817	0953	1153	1353	1540	1753	2008	2150	...
35	Bojkovice a.	0837	1015	1215	1415	1559	1815	2031	2210	...
63	Bylnice a.	0917	1056	1256	1456	1641	1902	...	2248	...
68	**Vlárský průsmyk** 🏛. △ a.	0925	1107	1327	1504	...	1912	...	...	...

	b			Ⓒ	Ⓐ					⑦e	⚒
Vlárský průsmyk 🏛 △ d.	0703	...	1050	1250	1310	1410r	1550	...	1725v	1916	1916
Bylnice d.	0711	0852	1058	1258	1320	1418r	1603	...	1732v	1923	1923
Bojkovice d.	0753	0943	1143	1343	1359	1518	1643	1743	1843	2000	2000
Uherský Brod ▷ d.	0814	1004	1204	1404	1433	1540	1706	1812	1909	2020	2020
Kunovice a.	0833	1023	1223	1423	|	1601	1728	1831	1928	2037	2037
Uherské Hradiště ▷ a.	0840	1028	1228	1428	1449	1605	1739	1837	1933	2041	2041
Staré Město u Uh. H ▷ a.	0858c	1058	1258	1458	1458	1621	1753	1858c	1953	2048	2048

a – Ⓐ only.
b – Through train Brno to/from destinations in lower table.
c – Change at Kunovice and Uherské Hradiště.
e – Also Apr. 13, July 6, Sept. 28, Nov. 17; not Apr. 12, July 5, Sept. 27, Nov. 15.
r – Ⓑ (not Dec. 24-26, Jan. 1, Apr. 12, May 1, 8, July 5).
v – 10 minutes later on Ⓐ (through train).
▷ – See also Table **1162**.
△ – See Table **1181** for connections to Slovakia.

1169 OTHER LOCAL SERVICES

2nd class

BŘECLAV - ZNOJMO *69 km* Journey 90 minutes

From Břeclav: every 2 hours 0931 - 1931, also 0650**c**, 1231 Ⓐ **r**, 1431 Ⓐ **r**, 1631 Ⓐ **r**.
From Znojmo: every 2 hours 0900 - 1900, also 0557 Ⓐ **r**, 0658, 1200 Ⓐ **r**, 1400 Ⓐ **r**, 1600 Ⓐ **r**.

BRNO - ZNOJMO *89 km* Journey 2 hours Change at Hrušovany nad Jevišovkou

From Brno: 0646, 0846, 1046, 1246, 1446, 1646, 1946 Ⓑ **h**.
From Znojmo: 0658, 0900, 1100, 1300, 1500, 1700, 1900 Ⓒ.

ČESKÉ BUDĚJOVICE - ČESKÝ KRUMLOV *31 km* Journey 60 - 65 mins

To June 13 / from Sept. 13:
From České Budějovice: 0539, 0802, 1034, 1224, 1514, 1701, 1909, 2209 ⑦, 2246 Ⓐ.
From Český Krumlov: 0637, 0838, 1225, 1446, 1800, 2005.

June 14 - Sept. 12:
From České Budějovice: 0539, 0741, 0913*, 1034, 1220, 1454, 1716, 1909, 2209 ⑦, 2246 Ⓐ.
From Český Krumlov 0437, 0637, 0838, 1037, 1228, 1454, 1645, 1756*, 2004.

* – Praha (d. 0614) - Nové Údolí (a. 1150) and Nové Údolí (d. 1607) - Praha (a. 2141).

CHOCEŇ - LITOMYŠL *24 km* Journey 55 minutes ★

From Choceň: 0629 Ⓐ, 0637 Ⓒ, 0833 Ⓒ, 1030, 1230, 1430, 1542, 1630, 1830, 2142 Ⓐ.
From Litomyšl: 0641 Ⓐ, 0729 Ⓒ, 0834 Ⓐ, 1015 Ⓒ, 1210, 1405, 1521, 1635, 1815, 2012.

HULIN - KROMĚŘÍŽ *8 km* Journey 8 minutes

1 - 2 trains per hour, connecting with trains in Table **1162**.
Trains also run Kroměříž - Kojetin approx every 1 - 2 hours for connections to/from Brno.

PRAHA - KARLŠTEJN *33 km* Journey 42 minutes

From Praha hlavní: hourly 0716 - 2316 (every 30 mins 1216 - 1916). From Karlštejn: hourly 0501 - 2301 (every 30 mins 1301 - 2001). Trains continue to/from Beroun (9 mins to Beroun).

c – 0731 on Ⓒ (daily Dec. 29 - Jan. 2, July 1 - Aug. 28).
h – Not Dec. 24 - 26, 31, Apr. 12, May 1, 8, July 5, Sept. 27.
r – Not Dec. 29 - Jan. 2.
★ – Change at Vysoké Myto město on certain journeys.

SLOVAKIA

Operator: National railway company is Železničná spoločnosť Slovensko (ŽSSK) on the network of Železnice Slovenskej Republiky (ŽSR).

Services: All trains convey first and second class seating, **except** where shown otherwise in footnotes or by '2' in the train column, or where the footnote shows sleeping and/or couchette cars only. Descriptions of sleeping (🛏) and couchette (▬) cars appear on page 10.

Timings: Valid **December 14, 2008 - December 12, 2009**, incorporating amendments from March 8. Further amendments are due from June 14. Scheduled holiday variations are shown in the relevant tables. However, certain local trains may be cancelled during the period **Dec. 24 - Jan. 1** and these cancellations may not be shown in the tables.

Reservations: It is possible to reserve seats on most Express trains.

Supplements: A higher level of fares applies to travel by *EC* and *IC* trains.

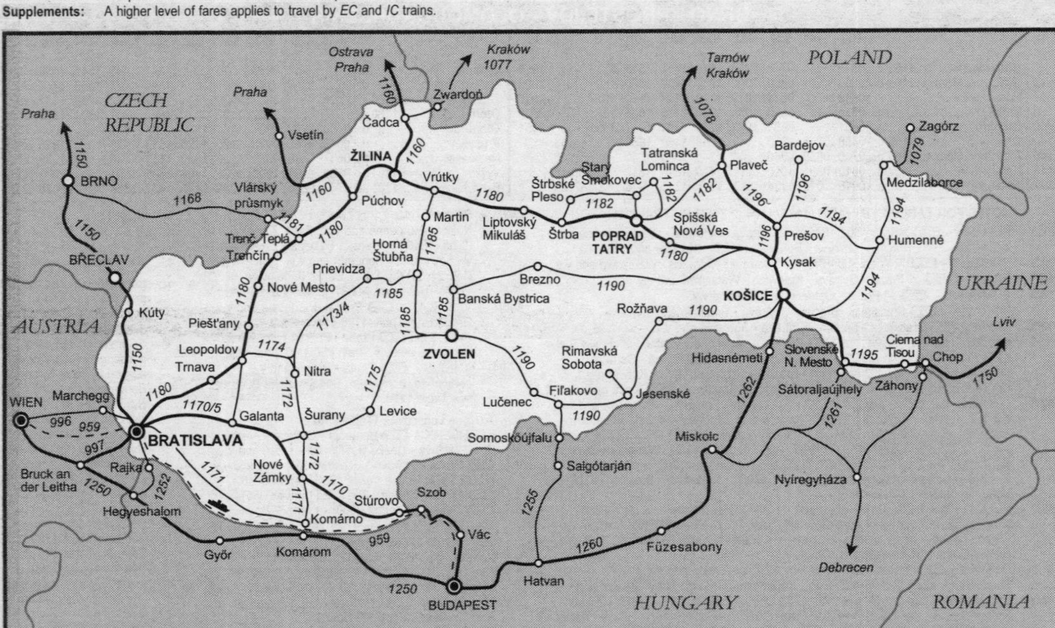

BRATISLAVA - ŠTÚROVO - BUDAPEST 1170

km			2137	471	471 477	EN* 477	◇	2135	◇	EC 345	◇	EC 273	1873	◇	◇	871	EC 171	◇	2111	873	875	EC 175	◇	◇
		★	2	Y	X	M		2		✕ A		✕	2 ⚒u	z		2 Ⓐk	✕ H	Ⓐ	2	2 d	2 Ⓐ	✕ J		
	Praha hlavní **1150** d.	...	...	2140	2140	0042	...	...	...	0528	...	0730h	...	...	...	...	1130h	...	...	...	...	1530h	...	...
	Brno hlavní **1150** d.	...	...	|	|	0327	...	...	...	0816	...	1016	...	...	...	...	1416	...	...	...	...	1816	...	...
	Břeclav **1150** 🚌 d.	...	...	0335	0446	0446	...	...	...	0855	...	1055	...	...	...	...	1455	...	...	...	...	1855	...	...
0	**Bratislava** hlavná **1175** d.	...	...	0456	0553	0553	0632n	...	0737	0950	1045	1150	1321	1346	1442	1521	1550	1628	...	1721	1921	1950	2056	2303
49	Galanta **1175** d.	...	...	|	|	|	0728	...	0835	|	1141	|	1356	1438	1535	1556	|	1710	...	1800	1956	|	2150	2356
91	Nové Zámky **1175** d.	...	*0533*	|	0649	0649	0813	*0829a*	0919	1043	1225	1243	1431	1535	1619	1624	1643	1747	*1752a*	1837	2026	2043	2249	0040
135	Štúrovo a.	...	*0616*	|	0715	0715	...	*0911a*	...	1108	...	1308	...	1615	...	...	1708	▬	*1835a*	1912	...	2108	2332	▬
135	Štúrovo 🚌 d.	...	0643	◐	0718	0718	...	0943	...	1112	...	1312	...	...	...	...	1712	★	1843	...	...	2112	...	★
150	Szob 🚌 ★ d.	0627	0657	|	|	|	...	0957	...	|	...	|	...	...	...	...	|	1757	1857	...	...	|	...	2204
163	Nagymaros-Visegrád ¶ ★ d.	0641	0711	|	|	|	...	1011	...	|	...	|	...	...	...	...	|	1811	1911	...	...	|	...	2218
180	Vác ★ d.	0658	0728	|	0750	0750	...	1028	...	1150	...	1350	...	...	...	...	1750	1828	1928	...	...	2150	...	2234
214	**Budapest** Nyugati ★ a.	0734	0754	|	|	|	...	1054	...	|	...	|	...	...	...	...	|	1854	1954	...	...	|	...	2316
214	**Budapest** Keleti a.	...	...	0819	0832	0832	...	...	...	1232	...	1432	...	...	...	...	1832	...	...	...	...	2232	...	...

	874	872	870	◇	◇	EC 174	1872		2112	◇	EC 170	◇	◇		EC 272	◇	EC 344	2136	1874	◇	EN* 476	476 470	470	
	2 Ⓐ	2 b	2 Ⓐk			✕ J	2 ⚒u	★	2		✕ H			★	✕		✕ A	2	2 ⑦W	k	M	X	Y	★
Budapest Keleti d.	...	...	...	...	...	0528	...	...	...	...	0928	...	...	...	1328	...	1528	...	...	...	1958	1958	1940	...
Budapest Nyugati ★ d.	...	...	...	...	0442	|	...	0707	0807	...	|	...	...	1207	|	...	|	1707	...	...	|	|	|	2107
Vác ★ d.	...	...	...	...	0527	0606	...	0734	0834	...	1006	...	...	1234	1406	...	1606	1734	...	...	2037	2037	|	2134
Nagymaros-Visegrád ¶ ★ d.	...	...	...	...	0542	|	...	0749	0849	...	|	...	...	1249	|	...	|	1749	...	...	|	|	|	2149
Szob 🚌 ★ d.	...	...	...	...	0557	|	...	0803	0904	...	|	...	...	1303	|	...	|	1804	...	...	|	|	|	2203
Štúrovo 🚌 a.	...	...	...	...	0610	0638	...	...	0917	...	1038	...	...	...	1438	...	1638	1817	...	...	2117	2117	◐	...
Štúrovo d.	...	0500	...	...	...	0641	*0741*	...	*0926a*	...	1041	...	1246	...	1441	...	1641	...	1818	*1840*	2120	2120	|	...
Nové Zámky **1175** d.	0415	0535	0635	0639	...	0707	0833	...	*1010a*	1016	1107	1139	1339	...	1507	1539	1707	...	1850	1939	2148	2148	|	...
Galanta **1175** d.	0447	0605	0705	0724	...	|	0909	...	...	1101	|	1225	1425	...	|	1625	|	...	1920	2025	|	|	|	...
Bratislava hlavná **1175** a.	0524	0640	0743	0824	...	0758	0944	...	...	1155n	1158	1319	1519	...	1558	1720	1758	...	1956	2119	2242	2242	2319	...
Břeclav **1150** 🚌 a.	...	...	...	...	...	0854	...	...	...	...	1254	...	...	...	1654	...	1854	...	...	...	2348	2348	0054	...
Brno hlavní **1150** a.	...	...	...	...	...	0939	...	...	...	...	1339	...	...	...	1739	...	1939	...	...	...	0050	...	...	...
Praha hlavní **1150** a.	...	...	...	...	...	1229h	...	...	...	...	1629h	...	...	...	2031	...	2231	...	...	...	0329h	0622	0622	...

A – AVALA – 🚃 ✕ Praha - Bratislava - Budapest - Beograd and v.v.
H – HUNGARIA – 🚃 ✕ Berlin - Dresden - Praha - Bratislava - Budapest and v.v.
J – JÁN JESENIUS – 🚃 ✕ Hamburg§ - Berlin - Dresden - Praha - Budapest and v.v.
M – METROPOL – 🛏 1, 2 cl., ▬ 2 cl. and 🚃 Berlin - Dresden - Praha - Bratislava - Budapest and v.v.; 🛏 1, 2 cl., ▬ 2 cl., 🚃 Warszawa (**202/3**) - Břeclav - Budapest and v.v.; ▬ 2 cl. Kraków (**200/1**) - Bohumín (**202/3**) - Břeclav - Budapest and v.v.; 🛏 1, 2 cl. Moskva - Katowice - Břeclav - Budapest and v.v. Conveys on days in Table **95** 🛏 1, 2 cl. St Peterburg - Katowice - Břeclav - Budapest - Zagreb and v.v.
W – ⑦ to June 28 / from Sept. 6 (also Jan. 6, Apr. 13; not Dec. 28, Jan. 4, Apr. 12).
X – AMICUS – 🛏 1, 2 cl. and 🚃 Praha (**470/1**) - Břeclav (**476/7**) - Budapest and v.v.; conveys to Sept. 30 (to Sept. 29 from Bucuresti) 🛏 1, 2 cl. Praha (**470/1**) - Břeclav (**476/7**) - Budapest (**374/5**) - Bucureşti and v.v.
Y – AMICUS – May 28 - Sept. 28 from Praha, May 29 - Sept. 29 from Budapest. 🛏 1, 2 cl., ▬ 2 cl. and 🚃 Praha - Budapest and v.v. Conveys on summer dates in Table **60** 🛏 1, 2 cl. and ▬ 2 cl. Praha - Burgas / Varna and v.v.

a – Ⓐ only.
b – Not Dec. 25, Jan. 1.
d – Not Dec. 24, 31.
h – Praha **Holešovice**.
k – To / from Komárno (Table **1172**).
n – Bratislava **Nové Mesto**.
u – Not Dec. 27, Apr. 11, Aug. 29.
z – Not Dec. 24 - Jan. 6.
◐ – Via Rajka 🚌 and Györ (Table **1250**).
◇ – Stopping train. 2nd class.
¶ – A ferry operates across the river to Visegrád.
§ – Will not run Berlin - Hamburg or v.v. Mar. 1 - June 13.

* – Classified *Ex* in Slovakia.

★ – **Budapest Nyugati - Vác - Szob** : From Budapest 0542, 0707 and hourly to 2107, also 2142, 2242, 2342. From Szob 0457, 0627, 0655, 0727, 0757, 0827 Ⓐ, 0857, 0927 Ⓐ, 0957 and hourly to 1857, also 2004, 2104, 2204, 2304.

OTHER TRAIN NAMES:
272/3 – JAROSLAV HAŠEK

2nd class BRATISLAVA - KOMÁRNO 1171

km		△		Ⓐb		Ⓐb	Ⓐ	Ⓒ	Ⓐb		
	Bratislava hl. **1170** d.	...	...	...	...	...	1521	...	...	...	...
0	Nové Zamky d.	0830	1130	1311	1442	1543	1632	1632	1750	1835	1946
29	Komárno a.	0857	1202	1343	1510	1611	1701	1701	1821	1902	2022

	Ⓐ		Ⓐb			Ⓐb		Ⓐb		▽	Ⓐb
Komárno d.	0602	0648	0734	1032	1302	1358	1453	1538	1633	1806	1907
Nové Zamky a.	0630	0720	0805	1100	1329	1425	1524	1613	1700	1832	1934
Bratislava hl. **1170** a.	0743	...	...	...	...	...	...	...	...	...	2119

km				b	Ⓐ	Ⓐ	Ⓒ	Ⓐ	Ⓐ		b
0	**Bratislava** hlavná d.	0605	1042	1303	1413	...	1531	1556	1633	...	2107
5	Bratislava Nové Mesto d.	0624	1053	1315	1422	1504	1540	1608	1648	1746	2117
42	Dunajská Streda d.	0731	1150	1420	1522	1544	1656	1656	1747	1853	2217
94	**Komárno** a.	0837	1257	1527	1630	...	1803	1803	1853	2003	2321

	Ⓐ	Ⓐ		b		Ⓐ	Ⓒ	Ⓐ	b	⑦a	
Komárno d.	0417	0502	0620	0900	...	1311	1456	1532	1704	1848	1905
Dunajská Streda d.	0531	0623	0730	1008	1214	1419	1619	1642	1826	1942	2018
Bratislava Nové Mesto a.	0615	0723	0829	1109	1312	1521	1720	...	1929	2027	2117
Bratislava hlavná a.	0633	0734	0838	1120	1321	1530	1730	...	1940	2036	2126

a – ⑦ to June 28 / from Sept. 6 (also Jan. 6, Apr. 13; not Dec. 28, Jan. 4, Apr. 12).
b – Not Dec. 24 - Jan. 6.
△ – Additional journeys: 0456, 0545 Ⓐ, 0652, 0736 Ⓐ b.
▽ – Additional journey: 2006.

2nd class NOVÉ ZAMKY - NITRA 1172

km		Ⓐ	Ⓒ		d							△
0	**Nové Zamky** d.	0638	0703	0745	0853	1110	1255	1452	*1540*	1638	1738	1836
10	Šurany d.	0650	0716	0757	0905	1128	1308	1504	1554	1653	1750	1847
36	**Nitra** a.	0731	0745	0830	0945	1201	1342	1538	1632	1735	1829	1928

				Ⓐd	⚒			Ⓐn		Ⓒ	Ⓐ§
Nitra d.	0639	0855	1206	1318	1423	1543	1643	1739	1836	1932	2035
Šurany a.	0713	0929	1241	1358	1455	1617	1715	1814	1911	2005	2109
Nové Zamky a.	0728	0941	1254	1411	1518	1629	1732	1825	1924	2019	2129

d – Not Dec. 24 - Jan. 6, July 1 - Aug. 31.
n – Not Jan. 2.
△ – Additional journeys: 2100 (not Dec. 24 - 28, Jan. 1, Apr. 12, 13), 2243 (not Dec. 24 - 26, Jan. 1, Apr. 12, 13).
§ – Additional journey: 2223 (not Dec. 24 - 26, Jan. 1, Apr. 12, 13).

2nd class NITRA - TOPOL'ČANY - PRIEVIDZA 1173

km			Ⓐ	Ⓒ	⚒	⑦	Ⓐ		Ⓐ		h	
0	Nitra d.	0642	0811	0946	1241	1346	1438	1539	1650	1838	1954	2225
33	Topoľčany a.	0737	0910	1035	1336	1443	1542	1636	1752	1938	2048	2318

		Ⓐ							Ⓑ	
Topoľčany d.	0523	0628	0744	...	1110	1422	1545	1656	1821	2025
Nitra a.	0621	0735	0835	...	1205	1516	1637	1801	1921	2123

km		Ⓐ	Ⓒ	Ⓐ	⑥	Ⓐd	Ⓐ		Ⓐ	Ⓒ	Ⓐ	△
0	Topoľčany ▷ d.	0642	0740	0921	1043	1203	1244	1342	1440	1448	1602	1702
44	Prievidza ▷ a.	0800	0845	1033	1155	1319	1411	1503	1549	1606	1725	1814

		Ⓐ			Ⓐd	Ⓐ	Ⓒ	Ⓐ		Ⓐd	⚒▽
Prievidza ▷ d.	0559	0654	0958	1216	1255	1343	1427	1439	1543	1700	1840
Topoľčany ▷ a.	0726	0803	1107	1318	1414	1511	1530	1600	1655	1818	2004

d – Not Dec. 24 - 31, July 1 - Aug. 31.
h – Not Dec. 24, 25, 31, Apr. 10 - 12.
△ – Additional journeys: 1943 Ⓐ, 2052 Ⓒ, 2222 Ⓐ.
▽ – Additional journeys: 1708 ⑦, 2011 ⑦, 2228 Ⓐ.
▷ – For fast trains see Table **1174**. Certain trains run through to / from Nitra (upper panel) or Nové Zamky (Table **1172**).

2nd class BRATISLAVA - NITRA and PRIEVIDZA 1174

km		1735 G	721 F	⚒		Ⓐ	725 G	1733 Ⓐn		723 Ⓑh		⚒
	Bratislava Petržalka d.	0633	0639	...	...	...	...	...	...	...	...	...
	Brat. Nové Mesto d.	0650	0656	...	...	...	...	...	...	...	...	...
0	**Bratislava** Hl. **1180** d.	|	|	*0831*	*1015*	...	1342	1540	*1610*	1645	*1815*	*1955*
46	Trnava **1180** d.	0737	0737	*0924*	*1108*	*1340*	1419	1619	*1642*	1725	*1907*	*2027*
63	Leopoldov **1180** a.	0751	0751	*0938*	*1122*	*1354*	1433	1633	*1654*	1738	*1923*	*2039*
63	Leopoldov d.	0759	0753	0945	1202	1403	1434	1635	1703	1740	1929	2059
87	Zbehy a.	|	0815	1025	1237	1437	1457	|	1736	1811	1959	2137
98	**Nitra** a.	0844	*0842*	1046	1307	1504	|	1717	1801c	*1834*	2019	2157
114	Topoľčany **1173** a.	...	0840	...	...	...	1523	...	...	1841	...	...
158	**Prievidza 1173** a.	...	0937	...	...	...	1622	...	...	1949	...	...

	1732 Ⓐn	722 ⚒u	F		Ⓐ	Ⓐ		720		1520 ⑦e	
Prievidza 1173 d.	...	0517	...	...	...	...	...	1638	...	1820	...
Topoľčany **1173** d.	...	0616	...	...	...	...	...	1733	...	1922	...
Nitra d.	0522	|	0756	0911	1139	1421	1527	*1737*	1810	|	2024
Zbehy d.	|	|	0819	0931	1201	1441	1547	1758	1832	|	2043
Leopoldov a.	0603	0707	0846	1004	1246	1522	1626	1821	1906	2010	2116
Leopoldov **1180** d.	0604	0708	...	1009	*1321*	*1557*	*1658r*	1823	*1921*	2011	*2121*
Trnava **1180** a.	0619	0724	...	1025	*1333*	*1612*	*1712r*	1836	*1933*	2027	*2133*
Bratislava Hl. **1180** a.	0702	0807	...	1120	*1408*	*1702*	*1802r*	|	*2008*	|	*2208*
Brat. Nové Mesto a.	...	...	...	...	...	...	...	1916	...	2108	...
Bratislava Petržalka a.	...	...	...	...	...	...	...	1930	...	2123	...

F – Ⓒ (daily Dec. 24 - Jan. 6, July 1 - Aug. 31).
G – Ⓐ (not Dec. 24 - Jan. 6, July 1 - Aug. 31).
c – Change at Lužianky.
e – ⑦ to to June 28 / from Sept. 6 (also Jan. 6, Apr. 13; not Dec. 28, Jan. 4, Apr. 12).
h – Also Oct. 31; not holidays or Apr. 12.
n – Not Jan. 2.
r – Ⓐ (not Dec. 24 - Jan. 6).
u – Also Nov. 1; not Apr. 11.

1175 BRATISLAVA - LEVICE - ZVOLEN

km		◇	811	831	833	833 933	835	835 935	Ex 531	837	801
		Ⓐ	H	b				Ⓑ	Ⓑ		Ⓑ
		v	△					d	x	u	P h
0	**Bratislava Hlavná 1170** d.	...	0621	1021	1221	1221	1421	1421	1621	1821	2342
49	Galanta **1170** d.	...	0656	1056	1256	1256	1456	1456	|	1856	0017
*10	Nové Zámky **1170** ▶ d.	0508	*0703*	*1110*a	*1255*	*1255*	*1452*	*1452*	*1638*	1937	0102
89	Šurany ▶ d.	0522	0728	1126	1327	1327	1526	1526	1717	1949	0113
131	Levice d.	0623	0815	1204	1409	1409	1608	1608	1755	2038	0152
198	Hronská Dúbrava **1185** d.	0809	0919	1305	1513	1513	1720	1720	|	2143	|
209	**Zvolen** osob. **1185** a.	0818	0929	1314	1523	1523	1730	1730	1900	2153	0304
	Banská Bystrica **1185** a.	...	0957	1342	1551	|	1804	|	1921	2221	|
	Košice **1190** a.	...	1359	...	...	1907	...	2223	...	...	0648
	Prešov **1183** a.	...	...	...	...	1958	...	...	...	...	0735

	820	Ex 530	830	930 830	832	932 832	834	1530 2	810	800
	Ⓐ	①–⑥					b	⑦	H	Ⓑ
	2	q						z	▽	P h
Prešov **1183** d.	...	...	...	...	...	0815	...	...	...	2231
Košice **1190** d.	...	...	...	0555r	...	0858	...	...	1448	2330
Banská Bystrica **1185** d.	...	0541	0847	|	1148	|	1501	1737	1853	|
Zvolen osob. **1185** d.	...	0602	0931	0931	1232	1232	1533	1806	1921	0323
Hronská Dúbrava **1185** d.	...	|	0942	0942	1243	1243	1544	1816	1932	|
Levice d.	0535	0706	1045	1045	1347	1347	1647	1919	2035	0440
Šurany ▶ d.	0616	0743	1129	1129	1434	1434	1734	2008	2115	0522
Nové Zámky **1170** ▶ a.	*0629*	*0824*	|	|	|	|	*1825*a	|	*2129*a	*0602*a
Galanta **1170** d.	0650	0810	1158	1158	1505	1505	1805	2038	2145	0553
Bratislava Hlavná 1170 a.	0725	0840	1233	1233	1540	1540	1840	2113	2220	0627

H – HOREHRONEC – [12] Bratislava - Banská Bystrica - Košice and v.v.
P – POL'ANA – 🛏 1, 2 cl. and [12]

a – Ⓐ only.
b – Not Dec. 24, 25.
d – Not Dec. 24, 25, 31, Apr. 10, 12.
h – Not Dec. 24 - 26, 31, Jan. 1, 2, Apr. 10, 12.
q – Not Dec. 25 - 27, Jan. 1.
r – ①–⑥ (not Dec. 25, 26, Jan. 1, Apr. 11, 13).
u – Not Dec. 24 - 26, 31, Jan. 1, 6, Apr. 10 - 13.
v – Daily Nové Zámky - Levice.
x – Not Dec. 24 - 26, 31.
z – Also Jan. 6, Apr. 13, Sept. 1; not Dec. 28, Jan. 4, Apr. 12, Aug. 30.

▶ – Local trains run 10 - 12 times per day.
◇ – Stopping train. 2nd class only.
△ – Conveys 🛏 1, 2 cl. Cheb (**441**) - Karlovy Vary - Praha (**477**) - Bratislava (**811**) - Banská Bystrica.
▽ – Conveys 🛏 1, 2 cl. Banská Bystrica - Bratislava (**476**) - Břeclav (**470**) - Praha (**606**) - Karlovy Vary - Cheb.
* – Distance from Šurany.

1180 BRATISLAVA - ŽILINA - KOŠICE

km		615	443	EN 425	447	701	441	IC 501		601	603	IC 405	605	607	IC 511	EC 121	609	1507	707	611	IC 403	703	1703	705	
								✕ Ⓡ	2	✕	✕	✕ Ⓡ	✕	✕	✕ Ⓡ	✕	✕			✕	✕ Ⓡ				2
		♦	♦ Y	♦	♦	R	♦	n					♦		Ⓑ h		⊖ △	⑤ g	Ⓐ			E	⑤ f	Y	
	Wien Westbf **997** d.	...	...	...	...	...	...	...	...	...	...	0800	...	...	...	...	...	...	...	...	1536	...	...	...	...
	Bratislava Petržalka d.	...	...	...	...	...	...	...	...	...	...	0924	...	...	...	...	...	...	...	...	1655	...	...	...	...
0	**Bratislava** hlavní **1174** d.	0010	...	...	...	...	...	0535	0430	0601	0810	0955	1010	1210	1335	...	1410	1455	1510	1610	1735	1810	1810	1955	2100
46	Trnava **1174** d.	0042	...	...	...	0438	...	0604	0526	0642	0842	1024	1042	1242	|	...	1442	1526	1542	1642	|	1842	1842	2027	2148
64	Leopoldov **1174** d.	0056	...	...	...	0452	...	|	0542	0656	0856	|	1056	1256	|	...	1456	|	1556	1656	|	1856	1856	2041	2202
81	Piešťany d.	0108	...	...	...	0504	...	|	0601	0708	0908	|	1108	1308	|	...	1508	|	1608	1708	|	1908	1908	2053	2216
99	Nové Mesto nad Váhom d.	0121	...	...	...	0517	...	|	0636	0721	0921	|	1121	1321	|	...	1521	|	1621	1721	|	1921	1921	2105	2229
123	**Trenčín** d.	0142	...	...	...	0538	...	0653	0706	0742	0942	1111	1142	1342	1447	...	1542	1615	1642	1742	|	1942	1942	2125	▬
131	Trenčianska Teplá d.	0151	...	...	...	0546	...	|	...	0751	0951	|	1151	1351	|	...	1551	|	1651	1751	|	1951	1951	2133	...
	Praha hlavní **1160** d.	|	2040	2204	2240	|	0009	|	...	|	|	|	|	|	|	1109	|	|	|	|	|	|	|	|	...
158	Púchov **1160** d.	0213	|	|	|	0610	|	|	...	0813	1013	|	1213	1413	|	1551	1613	1639	1713	1813	|	2013	2013	2156	...
203	**Žilina** **1160** a.	0250	0319	0329	0437	0649	0638	0751	...	0850	1050	1206	1250	1450	1541	1628	1650	1712	1750	1850	1952	2052	2052	2235	...
203	**Žilina** **1185** d.	0255	0355	0335	0455	...	0655	0754	...	0855	1055	1209	1255	1455	1544	1631	1705	1724	...	1855	1955	2055	2055	...	2
224	Vrútky **1185** d.	0314	0414	|	0514	...	0714	|	...	0914	1114	|	1314	1514	|	|	1724	|	...	1914	|	2112	2131	...	2116
242	Kraľovany d.	0329	0429	|	0529	...	0729	|	...	0929	1129	|	1329	1529	|	|	1739	|	...	1929	|	m	2145	...	2138
260	Ružomberok d.	0346	0446	0425	0546	...	0746	|	...	0946	1146	|	1346	1546	|	|	1756	1808	...	1946	|	▬	2202	...	2202
286	Liptovský Mikuláš d.	0405	0505	0449	0605	...	0805	0851	...	1005	1205	1306	1405	1605	1642	1728	1815	1828	...	2005	2052	...	2220	...	2228
325	Štrba d.	0434	0534	|	0637	...	0834	|	...	1034	1234	|	1434	1634	|	1756	1844	|	...	2034	|	2	|	...	2311r
344	**Poprad-Tatry** d.	0451	0551	0604c	0654	...	0851	0932	...	1051	1251	1347	1451	1651	1723	1811	1901	1911	...	2051	2132	2245	2302	...	2330r
370	Spišská Nová Ves d.	0511	0611	0628	0714	...	0911	|	...	1111	1311	|	1511	1711	1743	1831	1921	1932	...	2111	|	2315	2321	...	...
410	Margecany d.	0538	0638	|	0744	...	0938	|	...	1138	1338	|	1538	1738	|	|	1948	|	...	2138	|	2359	|	...	...
429	Kysak § **1183** a.	0553	0653	0716	0759	...	0953	1026	...	1153	1353	1441	1553	1753	1820	1908	2003	2010	...	2153	2226	...	|	...	...
445	**Košice** **1183** a.	0607	0707	0732	0813	...	1007	1038	...	1207	1407	1453	1607	1807	1832	1921	2017	2024	...	2207	2238	...	0009	...	...

	706	614	700	702	1510	600	IC 402	602	604	EC 120	606	704	608	IC 404	610	1506	1760	1508	612	IC 500	440	446	EN 424	442	
	⊖				①	✕	✕ Ⓡ	✕	✕	✕	✕		✕	✕ Ⓡ	✕		2	2	✕	✕ Ⓡ				⊖	
	Z	♦	Ⓐ	x	d	P			♦ ▽			Ⓑ k				⑦ e	Ⓐ	⑦ e		z	♦	♦	♦	♦ Z	
Košice **1183** d.	...	0002	...	...	...	0402	0535	0602	0802	0839	1002	...	1202	1325	1402	1500	1502	...	1602	1735	1802	2005	2100	2202	...
Kysak **1183** d.	...	0016	...	...	...	0416	0549	0616	0816	0853	1016	...	1216	1339	1416	1514	1516	...	1616	1749	1816	2019	2116	2216	...
Margecany d.	...	0033	...	...	...	0433	|	0633	0833	|	1033	...	1233	|	1433	|	1530	...	1633	|	1833	2036	|	2233	...
Spišska Nová Ves d.	...	0102	...	...	...	0502	|	0702	0902	0935	1102	...	1302	|	1502	1555	1605	...	1702	|	1902	2107	2207	2302	...
Poprad-Tatry d.	...	0125	...	...	...	0523	0645	0725	0925	0955	1125	...	1325	1436	1525	1615	1622	...	1725	1847	1925	2130	2249	2325	...
Štrba d.	...	0142	...	...	...	0539	|	0742	0942	1010	1142	...	1342	|	1542	|	...	...	1742	|	1942	2146	|	2342	...
Liptovský Mikuláš d.	...	0210	...	...	0500	0610	0726	0810	1010	1039	1210	...	1410	1518	1610	1657	...	...	1810	1929	2010	2216	2339	0010	...
Ružomberok d.	...	0231	...	...	0521	0631	|	0831	1031	|	1231	...	1431	|	1631	1718	...	...	1831	|	2031	2237	0003	0031	...
Kraľovany d.	...	0248	...	m	0538	0648	|	0848	1048	|	1248	...	1448	|	1648	|	...	...	1848	|	2048	2257	|	0048	...
Vrútky **1185** d.	...	0303	...	0456	0555	0703	|	0903	1103	|	1303	...	1503	|	1703	|	...	...	1903	|	2103	2312	|	0103	...
Žilina **1185** a.	...	0319	...	0519	0611	0719	0823	0919	1119	1137	1319	...	1519	1616	1719	1759	...	...	1919	2027	2119	2328	0050	0119	...
Žilina **1160** d.	0225	0325	0425	0525	0625	0725	0826	0925	1125	1140	1325	1425	1525	1619	1725	1811	...	1825	1925	2030	2137	2342	0055	0142	...
Púchov **1160** d.	0305	0405	0505	0605	0706	0805	|	1005	1205	1217	1405	1505	1605	|	1805	|	...	1905	2005	|	|	|	|	|	...
Praha hlavní **1160** a.	|	|	|	|	|	|	|	|	|	1654	|	|	|	|	|	|	...	|	|	|	0354	0554	0709	0830	...
Trenčianska Teplá d.	0327	0425	0526	0626	0730	0826	|	1025	1225	...	1425	1526	1625	|	1825	|	...	1930	2025	|	▬	...	...	...	...
Trenčín d.	0336	0434	0534	0635	0740	0835	|	1034	1234	...	1434	1534	1634	1713	1834	1911	...	1939	2034	2124	...	...	...	...	...
Nové Mesto nad Váhom d.	0357	0456	0556	0657	0806	0856	|	1056	1256	...	1456	1556	1656	|	1856	|	...	2004	2056	|	...	...	...	...	...
Piešťany d.	0409	0508	0608	0709	0818	0908	|	1108	1308	...	1508	1608	1708	|	1908	|	...	2016	2108	|	2	...	...	...	...
Leopoldov **1174** d.	0422	0521	0622	0722	0831	0921	|	1121	1321	...	1521	1621	1721	|	1921	|	...	2029	2121	|	2216	...	...	...	...
Trnava **1174** d.	0437	0535	0637	0737	0846	0935	|	1135	1335	...	1535	1635	1735	1800	1935	2001	...	2043	2135	2211*	2242	...	...	...	...
Bratislava hlavní **1174** a.	0508	0608	0709	0809	0923	1008	1035	1208	1408	...	1608	1708	1808	1829	2008	2034	...	2118	2208	2240	2330	...	...	...	...
Bratislava Petržalka a.	...	...	...	...	...	...	1112	...	...	...	...	...	...	1901	...	...	...	...	...	...	...	...	...	...	...
Wien Westbf **997** a.	...	...	...	...	...	...	1232	...	...	...	...	...	...	2028	...	...	...	...	...	...	...	...	...	...	...

♦ – **NOTES** (LISTED BY TRAIN NUMBERS)

424/5 – SLOVAKIA – 🛏 1, 2 cl., ▬ 2 cl., [2] Praha - Žilina - Košice and v.v.

440/1 – EXCELSIOR – 🛏 1, 2 cl., ▬ 2 cl., [12] Cheb - Karlovy Vary - Praha - Žilina - Košice and v.v.; 🛏 1, 2 cl., ▬ 2 cl. Plzeň (**767/50**) - Praha (**440/1**) - Žilina - Košice and v.v.; [2] Františkovy Lázně (**767/50**) - Plzeň - Praha (**440/1**) - Žilina - Košice and v.v.

442/3 – ŠÍRAVA – 🛏 1, 2 cl., ▬ 2 cl., [12] Praha - Žilina - Košice - Humenné and v.v.; 🛏 1, 2 cl. Praha - Žilina - Zvolen and v.v. Conveys (not Dec. 24, 31) 🛏 1, 2 cl. České Budějovice (**663/2**) - Brno - Žilina - Košice and v.v.

446 – VIHORLAT – ④⑤⑥⑦ June 25 - Sept. 6 (also Dec. 18, 19, 22, 23, Jan. 3, 4, Apr. 9, 10, 13, 14, 29, 30, May 9, 10, Oct. 27, 28, 31, Nov. 1). 🛏 1, 2 cl., ▬ 2 cl., [2] Košice - Žilina - Praha.

447 – VIHORLAT – ①⑤⑥⑦ June 26 - Sept. 7 (also Dec. 19, 20, 23, 24, Jan. 4, 5, Apr. 10, 11, 14, 15, 30, May 1, 10, 11, Oct. 28, 29, Nov. 1, 2). 🛏 1, 2 cl., ▬ 2 cl., [2] Praha - Žilina - Košice.

604/5 – DARGOV – [12] and ✕ Bratislava - Košice (**1902/3**) - Humenné and v.v.; [2] Bratislava - Košice - Čierna nad Tisou and v.v.

614/5 – ZEMPLÍN – 🛏 1, 2 cl., [12] Bratislava - Košice - Humenné and v.v. Not Dec. 24, 31 from Bratislava or Humenné.

E – Daily except ⑤ (will not run Dec. 18, Dec. 23 - 27, 31, Apr. 8, 9, 30, May 7).
P – ①–⑥ (not Dec. 24 - Jan. 1, Apr. 11).
R – ①–⑥ (not Dec. 25 - Jan. 6, Apr. 11, 13).
Y – Also conveys (not Dec. 24, 31) 🛏 1, 2 cl. Bratislava (**705**) - Žilina (**443**) - Košice.

Z – Conveys (not Dec. 24, 31) 🛏 1, 2 cl. Košice (**442**) - Žilina (**706**) - Bratislava. An additional 🛏 1, 2 cl. transfers at Žilina to train **700** (arrive Bratislava 0709), departing Košice on ①②③④⑦ (also Dec. 23 - Jan. 5, Apr. 9 - 12, Aug. 31, Sept. 14, Nov. 16).

c – Arrive 0537.
d – Also Jan. 7, Apr. 14, 15, Sept. 2, 16, Nov. 18; not Dec. 22, 29, Jan. 5, Apr. 13, June 29 - Aug. 31, Sept. 14, Nov. 16.
e – Also Jan. 6, Apr. 13, Sept. 1, 15, Nov. 17; not Apr. 12.
f – Also Dec. 18 - 23, Apr. 8, 9, 30, May 7; not Dec. 26, Jan. 2, Apr. 10, May 1, 8.
g – Also Dec. 23, Apr. 9, 30, May 7, Aug. 31; not Dec. 26, Apr. 10, May 1, 8.
h – Not Dec. 24 - Jan. 1, Apr. 12.
k – Not Dec. 24 - Jan. 5, Apr. 10, 12.
m – To / from Martin (Table **1185**).
n – Not Dec. 25 - Jan. 1, Apr. 11 - 13.
r – ⚒ only.
u – Also Jan. 7, Apr. 14, Sept. 1; not Dec. 28, Jan. 4, Apr. 12, July 5 - Aug. 30.
x – Not Dec. 25 - 28, Jan. 1.
z – Not Dec. 24 - 31, Apr. 10 - 12.
§ – Most trains call to set down only.
***** – Calls to set down only.

⊖ – Also conveys 🛏 1, 2 cl. Wien - Bratislava - Košice - Chop - Lviv and v.v. (extended to Kyïv on dates in Table **96**).
△ – Conveys on ①②④⑥ 🛏 1, 2 cl. Žilina - Košice - Chop - Moskva (journey 2 nights).
▽ – Conveys on ②④⑥⑦ (from Moskva) 🛏 1, 2 cl. Moskva - Chop - Košice - Žilina (journey 2 nights).

OTHER TRAIN NAMES:
120/1 – KOŠICAN
402/3 – ŠARIŠ
404/5 – TATRAN
500/1 – KRIVÁŇ

2nd class — TRENČIANSKA TEPLÁ - VLÁRSKÝ PRŮSMYK — 1181

km				S		⑦	①–⑤			
0	Trenčianska Teplá **1180** d.	0631	...	0955	...	1230	1340	...	1852	...
14	Vlárský průsmyk 🏛 **1168** a.	0648	...	1014	...	1248	1400	...	1910	...

				S		Ⓑ			
Vlárský průsmyk 🏛 **1168** d.	...	0658	...	1119	...	1506	...	1926	...
Trenčianska Teplá **1180** a.	...	0715	...	1136	...	1522	...	2020	...

S – July 1 - Aug. 31.

2nd class — LOCAL LINES IN POPRAD TATRY AREA — 1182

km		Ⓐ		Ⓐ				Ⓐ				
0	**Poprad Tatry** d.	0331	0501	0550	0711	0959	1136	1410	1457	1543	1902	2139
8	Studený Potok d.	0345	0513	0602	0730	1014	1148	1423	1509	1558	1915	2151
14	Kežmarok d.	0355	0524	0626	0740	1024	1158	1436	1519	1610	1925	2202
44	Stará Lubovňa d.	0441	0608	0709	0824	1106	1242	1532	1611	1713r	2009	2248
60	**Plaveč** a.	0459	0627	0728	0842c	1125	1301	...	1630	1731	2027	2306

		Ⓐ		Ⓐ	Ⓒ			Ⓐ		Ⓑ	
Plaveč d.	0419	0512	0732	0858	0901	1150	1438	...	1653	1916	2144
Stará Lubovňa d.	0438	0533	0751	0920	0920	1209	1457	1539	1712	1936	2212
Kežmarok d.	0523	0624	0838	1003	1003	1256	1546	1637	1755	2022	2259
Studený Potok d.	0533	0636	0847	1013	1013	1306	1556	1648	1806	2032	2308
Poprad Tatry a.	0546	0649	0901	1027	1027	1319	1609	1701	1819	2046	2321

km		Ⓒ	Ⓐ	Ⓐ			Ⓒ		Ⓐ			N	Ⓒ	Ⓐ	Ⓐ									
0	**Poprad Tatry** d.	0452	...	0550	...	0739	0950	0959	...	1105	1136	...	...	1410	...	1457	...	1543	...	1716	1753	2052	2139	...
8	Studený Potok d.	0502	0502	0602	0603	0751	1002	1010	1015	1117	1147	1158	1314	1422	1425	1509	1514	1554	1600	1728	1808	2103	2151	2156
17	**Tatranská Lomnica** a.	0516	0516	...	0616	0805	1016	...	1028	1131	...	1211	1327	...	1438	...	1527	...	1613	1742	1822	2117	...	2209

				Ⓐ	Ⓒ	Ⓐ		Ⓒ	Ⓒ	Ⓐ	N	Ⓒ		Ⓐ										
Tatranská Lomnica d.	0520	...	0619	...	0619	0831	...	0852	1020	1032	1135	1252	...	1336	1456	1543	...	1618	1750	...	1826	2138	2215	...
Studený Potok a.	0532	0533	0631	0636	0636	0843	0847	0906	1033	1045	1147	1304	1306	1348	1508	1555	1556	1631	1802	1806	1839	2150	2227	...
Poprad Tatry a.	...	0546	...	0649	0649	...	0901	0920	1046	1059	...	...	1319	...	...	...	1609	1645	...	1819	1852	...	2240	...

Poprad Tatry - Starý Smokovec (journey 25 minutes, *13* km, narrow gauge): 0353, 0514, 0614, 0654, 0742, 0830 **N**, 0908, 0952, 1055, 1155 **S**, 1253, 1337, 1427, 1526, 1616, 1726, 1815, 1907, 1957, 2052 **S**, 2147, 2246. Most journeys continue to Štrbské Pleso (see below).

Starý Smokovec - Štrbské Pleso (journey 40 - 45 minutes, *16* km, narrow gauge): 0539, 0639, 0732, 0811, 0859 **N**, 0937, 1026, 1125, 1221 **S**, 1321, 1412, 1458, 1551, 1641, 1753, 1841, 1932, 2028, 2124 **S**, 2218. Most journeys start from Poprad Tatry (see above).

Starý Smokovec - Tatranská Lomnica (14 mins, *6* km, nar. gauge): 0500, 0541, 0701, 0814, 0901 **N**, 0941, 1028, 1140, 1250, 1418 **N**, 1501, 1553, 1647, 1731 **a**, 1844, 2034, 2122.

Štrbské Pleso - Štrba (journey 17 - 18 minutes, *5* km, rack railway): 0513, 0617, 0721, 0812, 0919, 1010 **N**, 1119, 1310, 1412, 1458 **N**, 1539 **N**, 1635, 1721, 1833 **S**, 1921, 2011, 2235.

Starý Smokovec - Poprad Tatry (journey 25 minutes, *13* km, narrow gauge): 0422, 0538, 0702, 0733 Ⓐ, 0835 Ⓒ, 0900, 0940 **S**, 1001, 1121, 1244, 1345, 1415 **S**, 1457, 1551, 1643, 1731 **b**, 1842, 1933, 2022, 2120, 2213, 2310 **N**. Most start from Štrbské Pleso (see below).

Štrbské Pleso - Starý Smokovec (journey 40 - 45 minutes, *16* km, narrow gauge): 0500, 0622, 0647 Ⓐ, 0740 Ⓒ, 0819, 0852 **S**, 0921, 1034, 1206, 1305, 1331 **S**, 1417, 1505, 1559, 1649 **a**, 1801, 1849, 1940, 2036, 2132, 2226 **N**. Most journeys continue to Poprad Tatry (see above).

Tatranská Lomnica - Starý Smokovec (14 mins, *6* km, nar. gauge): 0521, 0620, 0718 **z**, 0837, 0919, 1004, 1104, 1228, 1328 **N**, 1440, 1530, 1619, 1710 **b**, 1824, 1913, 2100, 2151.

Štrba - Štrbské Pleso (journey 15 minutes, *5* km, rack railway): 0442, 0559, 0650, 0753, 0855, 0950 **N**, 1100, 1240, 1353, 1439 **N**, 1520, 1605 **N**, 1702, 1744 **S**, 1855, 1949, 2040.

N – Dec. 14 - Mar. 29, June 1 - Sept. 30.
S – June 1 - Sept. 30.
a – Štrbské Pleso - Tatranská Lomnica.
b – Tatranská Lomnica - Poprad Tatry.
c – Ⓒ (daily July 1 - Aug. 31).
r – Arrive 1659.
z – 0749 on ⑥† (daily July 1 - Aug. 31), also Dec. 22 - Jan. 7, Feb. 23 - 27, Apr. 9 - 14.

2nd class ✣ — ŽILINA - VRÚTKY - MARTIN - BANSKÁ BYSTRICA - ZVOLEN — 1185

km			1847 ①–⑥ P	Ⓐ	1849 ⑦ P	1855 ①–⑥ S	Ⓒ	Ⓒ	Ⓐ	Ⓒ	Ⓐ	Ⓐ c	1841		Ⓐ	Ⓐ		Ex 235 D	1843 n				1845 m	703 B	①–⑥ b
0	**Žilina 1180** d.	0445	0550	0620	0714	0726	0655	0855	0855	1055	1055	...	1324	1255	1408	1455	1524a	1626	1728	...	1757r	1855	1959	2055	2132
21	Vrútky **1180** a.	0508	0609	0646	0733	0743	0712	0912	0912	1112	1112	...	1340	1312	1424	1512	1548a	1642	1743	...	1819r	1912	2020	2112	2155
21	Vrútky d.	0510	0611	0649	0734	0744	0717	0924	0935	1119	1119	...	1341	1319	1429	1517	1554	1645	1745	...	1825	1925	2022	2113	2220
28	**Martin** d.	0519	0619	0658	0742	0751	0726	0934	0945	1128	1128	...	1348	1327	1439	1527	1604	1653	1752	...	1834	1935	2029	2120	2230
51	Diviaky d.	0548	|	0727	0759	|	0810	1002	1014	1156	1156	1205	1404	1417	1506	1600	1631	|	|	1835	1904	2003	|	...	2257
52	Turčianske Teplice d.	0551	0637	0731	0802	0809	0812	1005	1017	1159	1159	1208	1407	1420	1510	1604	1634	1710	1809	1838	1907	2006	2046	...	2300
61	Horná Štubňa a.	0602	|	0743	|	0817	0823	|	1029	1211	|	1218	|	1430	1522	|	1645	|	|	1849	|	2017	|	...	2312
99	**Prievidza** a.	0714	|	0847	|	|	0928	|	1138	1316	|	1316	|	1539	1634	|	1754	|	|	1944	|	2116	|	...	...
61	Horná Štubňa d.	0603	|	...	|	0818	...	|	...	1220	|	1220	|	...	...	|	1646	|	|	...	|	2018	|	...	...
80	Kremnica d.	0629	|	...	|	0841	...	|	...	1245	|	1245	|	...	...	|	1709	|	|	...	|	2045	|	...	...
106	Hronská Dúbrava § d.	0705	|	...	|	0911	...	|	...	1317	|	1317	|	...	...	|	1743	|	|	...	|	2118	|	...	...
97	**Banská Bystrica** a.	|	0727	...	0856	|	...	1049	...	|	1253	|	1453	...	...	1656	|	1751	1849	...	1959	|	2126	...	...
97	**Banská Bystrica** ▶ d.	|	0729	...	0900	|	...	...	...	|	1318	|	1501	...	...	1720	|	1753	1853	...	2014	|	2127	...	...
*118	**Zvolen** osob. ▶ a.	0715	0758	...	0924	0920	...	...	...	1327	1350	1327	1525	...	...	1752	1752	1814	1919	...	2047	2128	2152	...	...

	702 C		Ⓐ	1840 w	Ⓐ	Ⓒ	Ex 234 D		1854 S	Ⓐ	Ⓐ	Ⓐ	Ⓒ	Ⓐ	Ⓒ	1842 n	Ⓐ		1844				k		1846 P
Zvolen osob. ▶ d.	...	...	0416	0520	0617	0617	0728	...	0925	1021	...	1033	1055	...	...	1316	...	1424	1528	1530	...	1632	1819	1829	1928
Banská Bystrica ▶ a.	...	...	|	0551	|	|	0749	...	|	|	...	1104	|	...	...	1342	...	|	1551	|	...	1706	1851	|	1957
Banská Bystrica d.	...	...	|	0553	|	|	0751	...	|	|	...	1107	|	...	...	1354	...	|	1554	|	...	1722	1854	|	2000
Hronská Dúbrava § d.	...	...	0427	|	0627	0627	|	...	0934	1032	...	|	1105	...	...	|	...	1434	|	1541	...	|	|	1843	|
Kremnica d.	...	...	0512	|	0700	0719	|	...	1003	1110	...	|	1139	...	...	|	...	1510	|	1617	...	|	|	1921	|
Horná Štubňa a.	...	...	0549	|	0724	0745	|	...	1024	1135	...	|	1204	...	...	|	...	1535	|	1642	...	|	|	1947	|
Prievidza d.	...	...	0447	|	0611	0643	|	0857	|	|	1037	|	|	...	1211	|	1328	1436z	|	1508	1651	|	|	1839	|
Horná Štubňa d.	...	0506	0550	|	0725	0750	|	0953	1025	1135	1138	|	1205	1242	1330	|	1435	1536	|	1647	1750	|	|	1952	|
Turčianske Teplice d.	...	0517	0559	0633	0735	0759	0832	1003	1033	...	1148	1157	1215	1252	1339	1433	1445	1546	1633	1657	1759	1815	1953	2002	2045
Diviaky d.	...	0521	0602	|	0737	0802	|	1006	|	...	1150	1200	1219	1256	1342	|	1449	1549	|	1700	1801	1818	1955	2006	|
Martin d.	0446	0549	0628	0650	0803	0829	0849	1035	1052	...	...	1227	1246	1323	1409	1450	1518	1616	1649	1726	...	1845	...	2033	2102
Vrútky a.	0454	0558	0637	0656	0812	0838	0856	1043	1059	...	...	1236	1255	1332	1418	1456	1527	1625	1655	1735	...	1854	...	2043	2109
Vrútky **1180** d.	0456	0608	0644	0658	0817	...	0859	1054	1108	...	...	1303	1303	1337	1503	1507	1546	1703	1711	1736	...	1903	...	2103	2110
Žilina 1180 a.	0519	0628	0706	0714	0838	...	0914	1114	1126	...	...	1319	1319	1359	1519	1529	1607	1719	1730	1800	...	1919	...	2119	2131

▶ – *Full service:* ⊖	1840 w		Ⓐ		Ⓐ	Ex 234 D		811	Ⓐ		831 d	e		Ⓐ	833		Ⓐ	835	k	Ex 531 Ⓑ y	1846			837 v	b
Zvolen d.	0520	0600	0619	0646	0708	0728	0827	0933	1033	1155	1316	1333	1415	1506	1528	1632	1712	1735	1819	1903	1928	2010	2109	2155	2224
Banská Bystrica a.	0551	0631	0653	0720	0743	0749	0859	0957	1104	1228	1342	1402	1452	1538	1551	1706	1748	1804	1851	1921	1957	2039	2138	2221	2255

	Ex 530 R		Ⓐ		1847 ①–⑥		830	1849 ⑦	Ⓐ		Ⓐ	832		Ⓐ		834 d	Ⓐ		Ⓐ	e	Ex 235 D		810		1845 m
Banská Bystrica d.	0541	0605	0640	0656	0729	0816	0847	0900	0923	1038	1118	1148	1235	1318	1425	1501	1514	1552	1620	1720	1753	1826	1853	2014	2127
Zvolen a.	0600	0638	0705	0726	0758	0845	0913	0924	0952	1106	1150	1214	1305	1350	1456	1525	1545	1624	1651	1752	1814	1857	1919	2047	2152

B – (12) Bratislava - Žilina - Martin. Not Dec. 24 - 27, 31, Jan. 2, Apr. 10, May 1, 8. On ⑤ (also Dec. 18, 23, Apr. 8, 9, 30, May 7; not Dec. 26, Jan. 2, Apr. 10, May 1, 8) change at Vrutky; depart Vrutky 2118, arrive Martin 2125.
C – (12) Martin - Žilina - Bratislava. Not Dec. 25 - 28, Jan. 1.
D – DETVAN – (12) and ✕ Praha - Ostrava Svinov - Zvolen and v.v.
P – Conveys 🛏 1, 2 cl. Praha (**442/3**) - Žilina - Banská Bystrica - Zvolen and v.v.
R – ①–⑥ (not Dec. 25 - 27, Jan. 1).
S – July 1 - Aug. 31.
a – Ⓐ only.
b – Not Dec. 24 - 26, 31, Apr. 10 - 12.
c – Change at Horná Štubňa.
d – Not Dec. 24, 25.
e – Not Dec. 24 - 26, Apr. 10, 11.
f – Not Dec. 25 - 27, Jan. 1, Apr. 11 - 13.
g – Not Dec. 25, 26, Jan. 1, Apr. 11 - 13.
k – Not Dec. 24, 25, 31, Apr. 11, 12.
m – Not Dec. 24, 25, 31, Apr. 12.
n – Not Dec. 24, 25, Jan. 1.
r – ⚒ only.
v – Not Dec. 24 - 26, 31, Jan. 1, 6, Apr. 10 - 13.
w – Not Dec. 25, 26, Jan. 1, Apr. 13.
y – Not Dec. 24 - 26, 31.
z – Not ⑥.
▶ – For complete service see panel below main table.
✣ – 2nd class only, except trains with 3-digit train numbers.
⊖ – Also from Zvolen 0437 **g**; from Banská Bystrica 0446 **f**, 0525 **g**, 2140, 2232. Certain trains run to / from Bratislava (Table **1175**).
***** – *117* km via Kremnica.
§ – Junction for Banská Štiavnica (5 - 6 trains per day, journey 30 minutes). See also Table **1175**.

1190 ZVOLEN / BANSKÁ BYSTRICA - KOŠICE

km		931			1931			933		935	801
		2 Ⓐ	2	2	2 Ⓒ	2	2	2△	2	2▽ Ⓑv	Ⓑ h🛏
	Bratislava Hlavná 1175 d.	...	...	...	...	...	...	1221	...	1421	2342
0	**Zvolen** osob. d.	0557	0607	0821	0936	1000a	1331	1540	1821	1906	0316
54	Lučenec d.	0650	0718	0930	1023	1114	1438	1628	1933	1953	0407
70	Fil'akovo a.	0702	0737	0948	1035	1137	1456	1640	1952	2005	0420
70	Fil'akovo d.	0703	0819	...	1036	1147	1459	1642	...	2006	0421
98	Jesenské d.	0729	0902	...	1102	1227	1538	1709	...	2032	0449
109	Rimavská Sobota a.	0813	0921	...	1125r	1246	1602x	1727	...	2053	0516a
161	Rožňava d.	0824	...	...	1158	...	...	1807	...	2128	0547
233	**Košice** a.	0918	...	...	1257	...	...	1907	...	2223	0648
	Prešov 1196 a.	...	...	...	1348z	...	...	1958	...	...	0735

		930	932					934		800
	2 Ⓐ	2▷ P	2△	2	2 Ⓐ	2	2	2	2 Ⓐ	Ⓑ h🛏
Prešov 1196 d.	...	...	0815	...	...	...	...	1521z	...	2231
Košice d.	...	0555	0858	...	...	...	...	1556	...	2330
Rožňava d.	...	0655	1002	...	...	...	...	1649	...	0032
Rimavská Sobota d.	0543	0706	1007	1307	...	1436a	1515	1642	...	|
Jesenské d.	0606	0751	1058	1329	...	1456a	1542	1749	...	0129
Fil'akovo a.	0646	0816	1123	1407	...	1536a	1620	1814	...	0156
Fil'akovo d.	0650	0817	1124	...	1418	1557	...	1815	2024	0157
Lučenec d.	0717	0832	1138	...	1439	1615	...	1829	2041	0211
Zvolen osob. a.	0822	0929	1222	...	1551	1729	...	1916	2145	0307
Bratislava Hlavná 1175 a.	...	1233	1540	...	...	...	...	...	...	0627

km		2	2 c	811 H	2	2 Ⓐ	2 Ⓐ	2 E	2	2	2
0	**Zvolen** 1185 d.	0600	...	0933	1155	1415	...	...	1528	...	...
21	**Banská Bystrica** 1185 d.	0633	...	1010	1241	1458	...	...	1616	...	...
64	Brezno d.	0729	...	1057	1348	1559	1611	...	1727	1830	...
107	Červená Skala a.	0825	...	1145	...	...	1704	...	▬	1924	...
107	Červená Skala d.	...	0828	1146	...	...	...	1748	...	...	1926
135	Dedinky d.	...	0859*	1216	...	...	...	1818	...	...	1956*
192	Gelnica d.	...	1018	1315	...	...	...	1933	...	...	2109
200	Margecany a.	...	1030	1324	...	...	...	1945	...	...	2121
200	Margecany 1180 d.	...	1138	1332	...	...	...	...	1948	...	2138
219	Kysak 1180 a.	...	1153	1347	...	...	...	...	2003	...	2153
235	**Košice** 1180 a.	...	1207	1359	...	...	...	...	2017	...	2207

	2	2	2 d	2	2	810 H	2 F	2 Ⓑ	440	2
Košice 1180 d.	...	...	0822	...	...	1448	...	...	1802	...
Kysak 1180 d.	...	...	0839	...	...	1502	...	...	1816	...
Margecany 1180 a.	...	...	0902	...	...	1517	...	...	1831	...
Margecany d.	0519	...	0939	...	...	1525	1612	...	▬	1849
Gelnica d.	0531	...	0951	...	...	1534	1624	...	...	1902
Dedinky d.	0707	...	1110*	...	...	1638	1749	...	...	2101u
Červená Skala a.	0738	...	1141	...	...	1707	1820	...	...	...
Červená Skala d.	...	0836	...	1257	...	1708	...	1823	2	...
Brezno d.	...	0932	...	1352	1418	1754	...	1925	1945	...
Banská Bystrica 1185 a.	...	1036	...	...	1528	1840	...	...	2040	...
Zvolen 1185 a.	...	1106	...	...	1624	1919	...	...	2152	...

E – Ⓒ (daily July 1 - Aug. 31).
F – Ⓐ (not July 1 - Aug. 31).
H – HOREHRONEC – [12] Bratislava - Zvolen - Brezno - Košice and v.v.
P – ①-⑥ (not Dec. 25, 26, Jan. 1, Apr. 11, 13).
a – Ⓐ only.
c – Change at Nálepkovo (0929 / 0935).
d – Change at Nálepkovo (1035 / 1038).
h – Not Dec. 24 - 26, 31, Jan. 1, 2, Apr. 10, 12.
r – Not ⑥.
u – Ⓑ (not Dec. 24 - 26, 31, Apr. 10, 12, May 1, 8).
v – Not Dec. 24, 25, 31, Apr. 10, 12.
x – Change at Jesenské.
z – ⑦ (also Jan. 6, Apr. 13; not Dec. 28, Apr. 12).
🛏 – POL'ANA – 🛏 1, 2 cl. and [12].
△ – [2] Bratislava (833/2) - Zvolen (933/2) - Košice - Prešov and v.v.
▽ – [2] Bratislava (835) - Zvolen (935) - Košice.
▷ – [2] Košice - Zvolen (830) - Bratislava.
* – Request stop.

1194 KOŠICE / PREŠOV - HUMENNÉ - MEDZILABORCE

2nd class

km			615 Z	443 S	8907 n	8909	1901	1903 B	1905 u	1907 d	
	Bratislava 1180 d.	...	0010	...	...	...	...	...	...	...	...
0	**Košice** d.	...	0622	0732	1050	1420	1516	1638	1836	2242	...
68	Trebišov d.	...	0707	0817	1138	1508	1602	1725	1924	2327	...
88	Michalovce d.	...	0741	0851	1217	1543	1636	1756	1955	2358	...
112	**Humenné** a.	...	0809	0919	1249	1622	1708	1817	2020	0019	...

	1900 P	1902 B	8904 n	8906	8908	1904 u	1906 ⑦b	442 S	614 Z
Humenné d.	0338	0523	0620	0954	1144	1536	1829	1959	2151
Michalovce d.	0402	0546	0655	1023	1216	1557	1850	2023	2215
Trebišov d.	0434	0619	0730	1059	1255	1628	1925	2057	2250
Košice a.	0522	0707	0815	1145	1341	1714	2011	2141	2335
Bratislava 1180 a.	...	...	...	...	...	...	...	...	0608

km							Ⓐr			su	
0	Prešov d.	0333	0425	0546	0845	1128	1439	1511	1703	1852	2022
70	Humenné a.	0517	0615	0725	1018	1302	1555	1654	1838	2020	2215

Humenné d.	0408	0534	0735	1122	1455	1630	1755	2024	...
Prešov a.	0540	0714	0928	1257	1631	1819	1934	2205	...

km								m			
0	Humenné d.	0422	0626	0819	1021	1308	1437	1625	1823	2031	2227
41	Medzilaborce a.	0549	0734	0928	1139	1425	1555	1753	1932	2141	2334
43	Medzilaborce mesto a.	0554	0740a	0934			1601c	1759	1937	2146	

							m		
Medzilaborce mesto d.	0413	0600	0743a	0957	...	1419	1612	1834	2017
Medzilaborce d.	0418	0607	0804	1010	1158	1431	1619	1840	2023
Humenné a.	0520	0722	0916	1119	1305	1532	1727	1943	2125

B – Conveys [12] and ✕ Bratislava (604/5) - Žilina - Košice - Humenné and v.v.
P – ①-⑥ (not Dec. 24 - 27, Jan. 1, 6, Apr. 10, 11, 13).
S – ŠIRAVA – 🛏 1, 2 cl., ▬ 2 cl. and [12] Praha - Humenné and v.v.
Z – ZEMPLÍN – 🛏 1, 2 cl., ▬ 2 cl., [12] Bratislava - Košice - Humenné and v.v. Not Dec. 24, 31 from Bratislava or Humenné.
a – Ⓐ only.
b – ⑦ to June 28 / from Sept. 6 (also Jan. 6, Apr. 13; not Dec. 28, Jan. 4, Apr. 12).
c – Not on ⑤⑥⑦ June 26 - Aug. 30.
d – Not Dec. 24, 31.
m – Runs 15 - 20 minutes later on dates in note **b**.
n – Not Dec. 24 - 26, Apr. 10 - 12.
r – Ⓐ (not Dec. 22 - Jan. 7, Feb. 23 - 27, Apr. 9 - 14, July 1 - Aug. 31).
s – Change at Strážske (2007 / 2011).
u – Not Dec. 24 - 27, 31, Apr. 10 - 12.

1195 KOŠICE - ČIERNA NAD TISOU - CHOP

km		2	2	2 ①-⑥ d	2	2	2	605 b	2	2 ⊖△	2
0	**Košice** d.	0510	0740	1015	1220	1440	1540	1626	1840	2032	2251
62	Slovenské Nové Mesto d.	0617	0846	1121	1328	1545	1646	1717	1946	2138	0005
95	Čierna nad Tisou a.	0653	0923	1158	1406	1623	1723	1749	2023	2215	0042
95	Čierna nad Tisou d.	...	0929	...	...	1629	...	...	...	2235	...
105	**Chop** ⊕ a.	...	1115	...	...	1815	...	...	...	0021	...

	2	604 b △	2	2	2	2 ⑦ u	2 ①-⑥ h	2	2	2 ⊖
Chop ⊕ d.	...	0530	...	...	1215	...	...	...	...	1916
Čierna nad Tisou a.	...	0536	...	...	1221	...	...	...	...	1922
Čierna nad Tisou d.	0510	0615	0710	1000	...	1253	1340	1520	1821	1952
Slovenské Nové Mesto d.	0547	0644	0747	1037	...	1332	1417	1558	1858	2029
Košice a.	0654	0729	0850	1140	...	1437	1521	1703	2001	2130

b – From / to Bratislava (Table **1180**).
d – Not Dec. 24 - 26, Apr. 11.
h – Also Apr. 12; not Apr. 13, 14.
u – Also Apr. 13, 14; not Apr. 12.
⊕ – East European time (one hour ahead).
⊖ – Also conveys 🛏 1, 2 cl. Wien - Bratislava - Žilina - Košice - Lviv (- Kyïv on dates in Table **96**) and v.v.
△ – Conveys 🛏 1, 2 cl. Košice - Chop - Moskva and v.v. (Žilina - Košice - Moskva and v.v. on dates in Table **1180**).

1196 KOŠICE - PREŠOV - PLAVEČ

km		2 Ⓐ	2	2 ①-⑥ n	801 ①-⑥ Pn	2 ⑦ u	2 Ⓒ	2	2	2	1910 2	2 Ⓐ	1931 ⑦ 2q	2	2	2	2	2 Ⓑ h	2	2	2	933 ⊖	2	2	2	1380 C	2
0	**Košice** 1180 d.	0432	0554	0648	0703	0659	...	0749	...	1013	1153	1238	1305	1349	...	1453	1554	...	1651	1807	...	1929	2011	...	2213	2304	2310
16	Kysak 1180 d.	0450	0611	0707	0719	0719	...	0809	1006	1031	1209	1256	1325	1409	1445	1510	1610	...	1709	1825	1912	1942	2028	2156	2230	2318	2327
33	**Prešov** a.	0512	0633	0729	0735	0741	...	0836	1022	1053	1225	1324	1348	1435	1508	1531	1633	...	1736	1849	1935	1958	2050	2212	2252	2334	2353
33	**Prešov** d.	...	0635r	0746	...	0746	...	...	...	1055	1303r	▬	...	...	...	1539	1640	...	...	1850	...	...	...	...	2254	2336	...
65	Lipany a.	...	0715r	0824	...	0824	0827	...	...	1133	1341r	1402	...	...	...	1617	1719	1723	...	1929	...	...	...	...	2332	0004	...
88	**Plaveč** a.	...	...	...	...	...	0859	...	...	...	...	1436	...	...	...	1650	...	1757	...	2002	...	...	...	...	...	0035	...

	2	1381 C	2	2	2 Ⓐ	2	932 ⊖	2	2	2	2	2	2 Ⓑ h	934 ⑦ 2q	2 ⑦ e	2 ①-⑥ f	2	2 Ⓑ h	2	2	2 J	2 K	2	2	800 Ⓑ Pb	2 ⑦ d
Plaveč d.	...	0335	...	0428	...	0607	...	...	...	1130	...	...	...	...	...	...	...	1540	...	...	1827	1827	...	...	...	...
Lipany d.	...	0402	0433	0501	...	0645	...	0852r	1036r	1202	1221	...	...	...	1420	1453	...	1620	...	...	1859	1859	...	...	...	...
Prešov a.	...	0429	0511	0541	...	0727	...	0929r	1115r	...	1258	...	...	...	1502	1530	...	1700	...	...	1936	1936	...	...	...	...
Prešov d.	0346	0430	0513	0543	0642	0741	0815	0937	1118	...	1300	1341	1436	1521	1537	1537	1711	1711	1747	1824	1938	2001	2051	2141	2231	2354
Kysak 1180 a.	0409	0446	0536	0609	0705	0807	0831	1000	1141	...	1323	1404	1459	1537	1600	1600	1737	1737	1802	1851	2006	2024	2112	2211	|	0010
Košice 1180 a.	0426	0500	0551	0627	0723	0825	0844	1021	1159	...	1342	1425	1521	1552	1618	1618	1755	1755	...	1906	2026	2042	...	2228	2304	...

C – CRACOVIA – June 19 - Aug. 31. ▬ 1, 2 cl. and [2] Bucureşti - Miskolc - Košice - Kraków and v.v.; ▬ 2 cl. and [2] Keszthely - Budapest - Košice - Kraków and v.v.
J – Not dates in note **K**.
K – ⑤ to June 26 / from Sept. 4 (also Apr. 9, 30, May 7; not Dec. 26, Apr. 10, May 1, 8).
P – POL'ANA – 🛏 1, 2 cl. and [12] Bratislava - Košice - Prešov and v.v. (Table **1175**).
b – Not Dec. 24 - 26, 31, Jan. 1, 2, Apr. 10, 12.
d – Also Jan. 6, Apr. 13, Sept. 1, 15, Nov. 17; not Jan. 4, Apr. 12, Aug. 30, Sept. 13, Nov. 15.
e – Also Jan. 6, Apr. 13; not Jan. 4, Apr. 12.
f – Also Jan. 4, Apr. 12; not Jan. 6, Apr. 13.
h – Not Dec. 24 - 26, 31, Apr. 10, 12, May 1, 8.
n – Not Dec. 25 - 27, Jan. 1 - 3, Apr. 11, 13.
q – Also Jan. 6, Apr. 13; not Dec. 28, Apr. 12. To / from Zvolen (Table **1190**).
r – Ⓐ only.
u – Also Dec. 25 - 27, Jan. 1 - 3, Apr. 11, 13.
⊖ – To / from Bratislava via Zvolen (Table **1175**).

PREŠOV - BARDEJOV *45* km, 70 - 75 mins.
From Prešov: 0333, 0546, 0748, 1128, 1511, 1636, 1902, 2022, 2255 Ⓑ **h**.
From Bardejov: 0506, 0554 Ⓐ, 0710, 1144, 1405 ⑦ **e**, 1432 ①-⑥ **f**, 1642, 1824, 2033 Ⓑ **h**, 2217.

HUNGARY

Operator: MÁV-START, running on the network of MÁV, except the lines from Sopron to Györ and Szombathely which are operated by Györ - Sopron - Ebenfurthi Vasút (GySEV).

Services: All trains convey first and second class seating, **except** where shown otherwise in footnotes or by '2' in the train column, or where the footnote shows sleeping- and/or couchette cars only. Descriptions of sleeping- (🛏) and couchette (▬) cars appear on page 10. Certain international services, as indicated in the tables, cannot be used for internal journeys in Hungary, whilst others generally convey dedicated carriages for internal journeys, which may be made without reservation.

Timings: Valid **December 14, 2008** to **December 12, 2009**, with amendments from April 5. Summer alterations in the Balaton area will be shown in the July and August editions. Certain trains will not run at Christmas, notably on the evening of Dec. 24, 31 or on Dec. 25, Jan. 1, and these cancellations are **not** shown in the tables due to space constraints.

Reservations: Most **Domestic** InterCity (*IC*) and all InterPici (*IP*) trains have **compulsory** reservation, as shown by 🄁 in the tables. *IC* trains require a supplement of 520 HUF which includes the reservation fee. The price of the supplement may be reduced on certain journeys or on certain dates. Passengers having passes which include the supplement (e.g. Eurail) have to pay only the reservation fee of 130 HUF. For domestic journeys on **International** *EC*/*IC*/*EN* trains, the supplement is 390 HUF, but seat reservation is not possible. For international journeys on these trains the supplement does not apply (unless shown) but seat reservation is possible (and is **compulsory** on certain trains where shown).

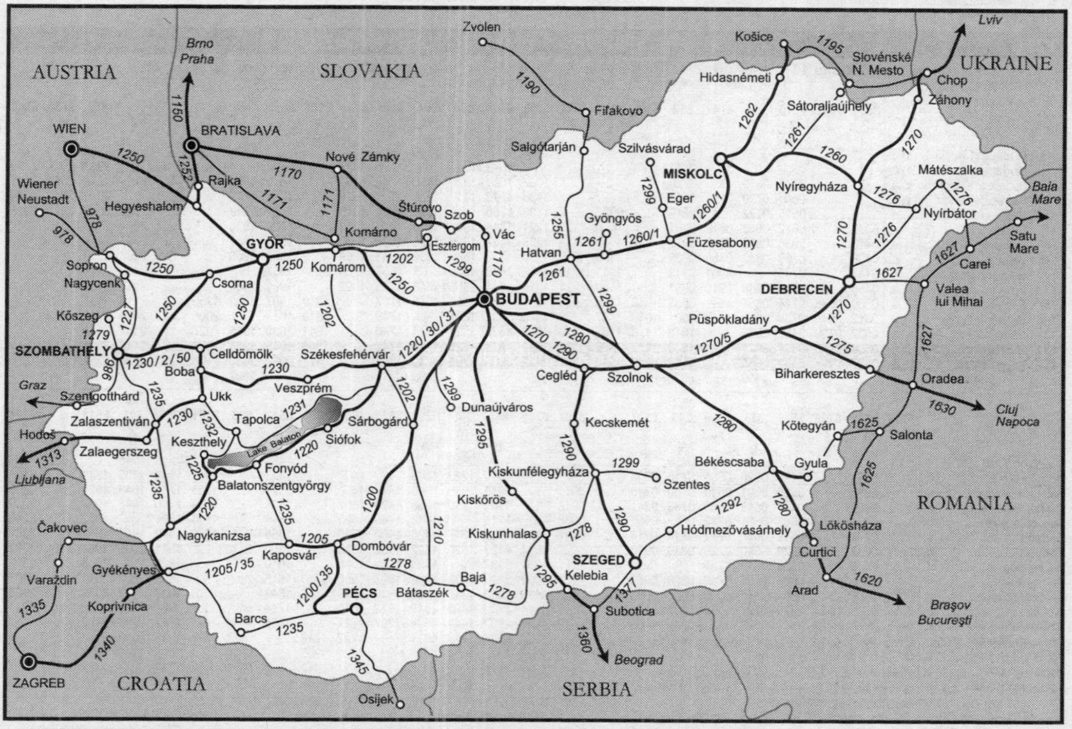

BUDAPEST - DOMBÓVÁR - PÉCS 1200

km		*IC* 800 🄁✕	*IC* 802 🄁✕		*IC* 259 🄁✕ S	*IC* 804 🄁✕	*IC* 814 🄁✕		*IC* 806 🄁✕	*IC* 828 🄁 n		*IC* 816 🄁✕	*IC* 808 🄁✕	
	Budapest Keleti .... § d.	0545	0745	...	0945	1145	1345	...	1545	...	...	1745	1945	...
0	**Budapest** Déli .... § d.	|	|	...	|	|	|	...	|	1653	...	|	|	...
4	Budapest Kelenföld .... § d.	0601	0801	...	1001	1201	1401	...	1601	1701	...	1801	2001	...
84	Sárbogárd .... § d.	0702	0902	...	1102	1302	1502	...	1702	1802	...	1902	2102	...
164	Dombóvár .... a.	0750	0950	...	1150	1350	1550	...	1750	1910	...	1950	2150	...
164	Dombóvár **1235** .... d.	0751	0951	...	1151	1351	1551	...	1751	...	...	1951	2151	...
209	Szentlörinc .... d.	0822	1022	...	1222	1422	1622	...	1822	...	...	2022	2223	...
228	**Pécs 1235** .... a.	0835	1035	...	1235	1435	1635	...	1835	...	...	2035	2235	...

	IC 809 🄁✕	*IC* 829 🄁 n	*IC* 807 🄁✕		*IC* 817 🄁✕	*IC* 805 🄁✕	*IC* 815 🄁✕		*IC* 258 🄁✕ S	*IC* 813 🄁✕		*IC* 801 🄁✕	2	
Pécs 1235 .... d.	0524	...	0724	...	0924	1124	1324	...	1524	1724	...	1924	2043	...
Szentlörinc .... d.	0538	...	0738	...	0938	1138	1338	...	1538	1738	...	1937	2102	...
Dombóvár **1235** .... a.	0611	...	0811	...	1011	1211	1411	...	1611	1811	...	2011	2155	...
Dombóvár .... d.	0613	0647	0813	...	1013	1213	1413	...	1613	1813	...	2013	...	...
Sárbogárd .... § d.	0702	0745	0902	...	1102	1302	1502	...	1702	1902	...	2102	...	...
Budapest Kelenföld ...... § a.	0758	0840	0958	...	1158	1358	1558	...	1758	1958	...	2158	...	...
Budapest Déli .... § a.	|	0847	|	...	|	|	|	...	|	|	...	|	...	...
Budapest Keleti .... § a.	0814	...	1014	...	1214	1414	1614	...	1814	2014	...	2214	...	...

S – To/from Sarajevo (Table **92a**). **n** – To/from Nagykanizsa (Table **1205**). § – See also **1210**.

2nd class LOCAL TRAINS 1202

90 km	⚒						
Györ **1250** .... d.	...	*0435*	...	*1133*	...	*1533*	*1833*
Komárom **1250** .. d.	0334	0546	...	1210	...	1644	1950
Almásfüzitö .... d.	0356	0559	0808	1221	1249	1657	2007
Esztergom .... a.	0509	0725	0922	...	1402	1807	2122

	⚒						
Esztergom .... d.	0517	0749	...	1333	1433	1833	2133
Almásfüzitö .... a.	0626	0904	0933	1446	1546	1945	2245
Komárom **1250** .. a.	*0646*	...	0946	1459	1600	2000	2258
Györ **1250** .... a.	*0725*	...	*1025*	...	...	*2112*	*2325*

82 km							
Komárom .... d.	0451	0806	...	1130	1603	2003	...
Székesfehérvár ... a.	0620	0934	...	1301	1731	2131	...

Székesfehérvár ... d.	0357	0550	...	1119	1509	1815	...
Komárom .... a.	0532	0723	...	1248	1642	1944	...

39 km							Ⓑ
Székesfehérvár ... d.	0548	0751	0945	1454	1748	1945	2254
Sárbogárd .... a.	0650	0853	1051	1556	1850	2051	2356

Sárbogárd .... d.	0504	0707	0907	1202	1622	1907	2105
Székesfehérvár ... a.	0610	0820	1009	1304	1729	2009	2207

DOMBÓVÁR - KAPOSVÁR - GYÉKÉNYES - NAGYKANIZSA 1205

For other services Budapest - Nagykanisza and v.v. (via Fonyód) see Table **1220**

km		7859 2 ⚒	7839 2	7829 2	7837 2	2	7827 2	7835 2	2	7825 2	*IC* 828 🄁	7833 2	7823 2 Ⓐ
	Budapest Déli **1200** . d.	...	...	...	...	...	...	...	...	...	1653	...	...
0	**Dombóvár** .... d.	0600	0800	1000	1200	1215	1400	1600	1615	1800	1912	2000	2200
2	Dombóvár alsó .... ◐ d.	|	|	|	|	1219	|	|	1619	|	|	|	|
31	**Kaposvár** .... ◐ a.	0640	0840	1040	1240	1312	1442	1640	1712	1840	1947	2040	2240
31	**Kaposvár** .... ◐ d.	0650	...	1050	...	1314	1450	...	1714	1850	1948	...	...
71	Somogyszob .... d.	0745	...	1145	...	1417	1545	...	1817	1945	2039	...	...
101	Gyékényes .... ◐ a.	0830	...	1230	...	1502	1630	...	1902	2030	2142	...	...
130	**Nagykanizsa** .... ◐ a.	*0910*	...	...	...	1539	*1710*	...	1945	*2110*	2211	...	...

	IC 829 🄁	7822 2	7834 2	2	7824 2	7836 2	7826 2	7838 2	2	7828 2 Ⓑ
Nagykanizsa ...... ◐ d.	0400	0454	*0640*	*0810*	...	*1040*	...	1445	*1610*	...
Gyékényes .... ◐ d.	0433	0529	0708	0905	...	1122	...	1523	1705	...
Somogyszob .... d.	0516	0616	0814	0952	...	1214	...	1614	1752	...
Kaposvár .... ◐ a.	0600	0716	0908	1046	...	1308	...	1708	1846	...
Kaposvár .... ◐ d.	0601	0731	0931	1048	1131	1331	1531	1731	1848	1922
Dombóvár alsó .. ◐ d.	|	|	|	1139	|	|	|	|	1939	|
Dombóvár .... a.	0644	0808	1008	1142	1208	1408	1608	1808	1942	2008
Budapest Déli **1200** . a.	0847	...	...	...	...	...	...	...	...	...

◐ – See also Table **1235**. *Many trains continue to Baja, Kiskunfélegyháza and Kecskemét (Table 1278).*

1210 BUDAPEST - SZEKSZÁRD - BAJA
2nd class

km		IP ® 830			IC 1834			IP ® 838	
		c			⑦n		c	c	c
0	**Budapest** Keleti .... **1200** d.	...	0745	...	...	1053**d**	1258**r**	1545	1745	1945
4	Budapest Kelenföld...... **1200** d.	...	0801	...	...	1100	1305	1601	1801	2001
84	Sárbogárd.................. **1200** a.	...	0858	...	...	1202	1430	1658	1858	2058
84	Sárbogárd..........................d.	0546	0905	0911	1151	1215	1440	1705	1905	2109
149	Szekszárd..........................a.	0707	1008	1041	1306	1340	1618	1835	2008	2230
168	Bátaszék .... **1278** a.	0743	1045	1120	1342	1436	1720	1937	2043	2309
188	**Baja** .... **1278** a.	0808	1104	...	1408	1452	1808	2008	2102	...

	IP ® 839						IP ® 833		
		c	c				c⊖		
Baja .... **1278** d.	...	0500	0543	0840**a**	1143	...	1500	1543	1743
Bátaszék................. **1278** d.	0425	0519	0625	0859	1223	1353	1519	1632	1815
Szekszárd.........................d.	0513	0555	0728	1011	1313	1441	1555	1711	1855
Sárbogárd.........................a.	0632	0656	0847	1124	1428	1554	1656	1826	2015
Sárbogárd................ **1200** d.	...	0702	0902	...	...	...	1702	...	...
Budapest Kelenföld... **1200** a.	...	0758	0958	...	...	...	1758	...	...
Budapest Keleti .... **1200** a.	...	0814	1014	...	...	...	1814	...	...

a – Ⓐ only.
c – Connection Budapest - Sárbogárd and v.v. is by *IC* train, ®.
d – Budpaest Déli.
n – ⑦ to June 14 / from Sept. 6.
r – Budapest Déli. Change at Pusztaszabolcs.
⊖ – On ⑦ to June 14 / from Sept. 6 runs 25 minutes later to Budapest Déli, arrive 1832 (train *IC* **1833**).

1220 BUDAPEST - SIÓFOK - FONYÓD - NAGYKANIZSA

Service to June 19 / from Aug. 24. *Service June 20 - Aug. 23 will be shown in the July edition (see also page 3)*

km		8530	8612	8510	IC 200	8742	852	8802	8512	8622	5209	8514	854	204	8524	8716	8806	8506	EN 240		908		858	8738	8748
		2	2	2	✕	2			2	2		2		M	2	2	2	2		2		2		2	
				u	K		b	P			A		b	⊖			Q		V					w	v
*	**Budapest** Keleti ..... ◧ d.	...	...	...	0605	...	...	...	...	...	1015	...	...	1405	...	...	...	...	1635	...	...	...	...	...	...
0	**Budapest** Déli .... ◧ d.	...	...	0338	|	...	0713	...	...	...	|	1043	1313	|	...	1443	...	1603	|	...	1803	...	1913	2043	2138
4	Budapest Kelenföld .. ◧ d.	...	...	0345	0620	...	0720	...	...	...	1032	1051	1320	1420	...	1451	...	1612	1650	...	1812	...	1920	2051	2145
67	**Székesfehérvár** ..... ◧ a.	...	...	0504	0720	...	0817	...	...	...	1136	1210	1417	1520	...	1610	...	1715	1747	...	1915	...	2018	2210	2304
67	**Székesfehérvár** ....d.	...	...	0515	0722	...	0819	...	0925	...	1138	1250	1419	1523	1500	1615	...	1721	1749	...	...	1920	2020	2220	2315
115	Siófok ....d.	0355	...	0612	0808	0812	0901	...	1020	1125	1221	1344	1505	1605	1610	1710	...	1809	1830	...	...	2014	2102	2313	0011
130	Balatonföldvár.............d.	0418	...	0635	0822	0832	0918	...	1043	1148	1239	1407	1520	1620	1634	1730	...	1830	1850	...	...	2037	2119	...	...
146	Balatonlelle.................d.	0438	...	0700	0843	0856	0938	...	1106	1210	1300	1428	1540	1636	1653	1749	...	1852	1908	...	...	2057	2139	...	...
149	Balatonboglár ....d.	0447	...	0705	|	0901	0943	...	1111	1215	1305	1435	1545	|	1657	1753	...	1857	|	...	...	2103	2144	...	...
157	**Fonyód** ....a.	0456	...	0714	0855	0910	0951	...	1120	1224	1316	1444	1553	1648	1705	1802	...	1905	1930	...	...	2112	2152	...	...
157	**Fonyód** ....d.	0500	0638	0724	0857	...	0953	1042	1126	1226	1317	1450	1557	1650	1707	...	1810	1907	1932	1955	...	2113	2154	...	...
165	Balatonfenyves ....d.	0512	0649	0734	|	...	1001	1052	1137	1236	1325	1502	1605	|	1719	...	1819	1917	|	2006	...	2126	2202	...	...
181	Balatonszentgyörgy.....a.	0532	0709	0752	0918	...	1018	1116	1157	1256	1342	1522	1621	1711	1740	...	1841	1939	1955	2027	...	2147	2219	...	...
181	Balatonszentgyörgy.....d.	0539	0710	0754	0921	...	1030	1122	1202	1258	1346	1524	1625	1715	1741	...	1846	1943	1956	2028	...	2148	2221	...	...
221	**Nagykanizsa**...............a.	0622	n	0841	0955	...	1106	n	1248	n	1423	1605	1705	1749	1821	...	n	2022	2030	2108	...	2229	2257	...	...
352	*Zagreb* **1340**............a.	...	...	...	1159	...	1333	...	...	...	...	...	...	2000	...	...	...	...	2307	...	...	...	...	...	...

	8719	8519	8729	8539	859	8529	EN 241	8507		8807	8715	855	205	5208	8615	1853		8513	903	8801	853	IC 201	8511		8531
		2	2	2		2		2	2	2	2		M		2	⑦	2	2				✕			2
	v		w		b		V			Q		b	⊖	A		b				P	b	K	u		
Zagreb **1340**............d.	...	...	...	...	...	...	0456	...	...	...	...	...	0958	...	...	...	...	...	...	...	...	1545	...	...	...
Nagykanizsa..............d.	...	0315	...	0455	0525	0605	0716	0800	...	n	...	1010	1222	1305	n	1407	...	1443	...	n	1653	1805	1841	...	2126
Balatonszentgyörgy......a.	...	0355	...	0535	0601	0649	0750	0840	...	0911	...	1049	1255	1345	1417	1450	...	1524	...	1708	1733	1843	1920	...	2208
Balatonszentgyörgy......d.	...	0402	...	0547	0613	0650	0752	0841	...	0918	...	1101	1256	1355	1420	1502	...	1526	...	1720	1745	1845	1922	...	2219
Balatonfenyves ....d.	...	0421	...	0608	0631	0712	|	0905	...	0938	...	1118	|	1413	1440	1523	...	1545	...	1746	1801	|	1942	...	2240
Fonyód.........................a.	...	0431	...	0619	0638	0722	0814	0914	...	0947	...	1126	1317	1420	1450	1530	...	1555	...	1755	1809	1907	1952	...	2251
Fonyód.........................d.	...	0432	...	0620	0640	0725	0816	0916	...	...	1044	1128	1320	1422	1452	1533	...	1600	...	...	1811	1909	1954	...	2252
Balatonboglár...............d.	...	0443	...	0629	0649	0735	|	0925	...	...	1054	1137	|	1433	1502	1545	...	1610	...	...	1820	|	2006	...	2302
Balatonlelle..................d.	...	0448	...	0634	0654	0740	0828	0929	...	...	1059	1142	1333	1438	1507	1550	...	1615	...	...	1825	1922	2011	...	2307
Balatonföldvár...............d.	...	0508	...	0657	0711	0800	0845	0955	...	...	1119	1202	1349	1458	1530	1610	...	1643	...	...	1844	1939	2031	...	2326
Siófok...........................d.	0350	0531	0625	0719	0727	0830	0901	1019	...	...	1144	1220	1403	1519	1612	1642	...	1714	...	...	1902	1954	2100	...	2347
Székesfehérvár...........a.	0443	0627	0723	...	0809	...	0940	1109	...	...	1240	1303	1441	1608	1707	1721	...	1808	...	...	1942	2036	2150	...	...
Székesfehérvár....... ◧ d.	0448	0643	0748	...	0811	...	0942	...	1148	...	1243	1306	1443	1611	...	1722	1748	...	1843	...	1943	2039	2153	...	...
Budapest Kelenföld.. ◧ a.	0605	0748	0905	...	0910	...	1041	...	1305	...	1340	1412	1554	1715	...	1820	1905	...	1940	...	2040	2140	2315	...	...
Budapest Déli .... ◧ a.	0612	0757	0912	...	0917	...	|	...	1312	...	1347	1419	|	|	...	1827	1912	...	1947	...	2047	|	2322	...	...
Budapest Keleti ...... ◧ a.	...	...	...	...	...	...	1059	...	...	...	...	...	1609	1734	...	...	...	...	...	...	...	2159	...	...	...

A – ⟨12⟩ Sátoraljaújhely - Miskolc - Budapest - Nagykanizsa / Keszthely and v.v.
K – KVARNER – ⟨12⟩ Budapest - Zagreb and v.v.
M – MAESTRAL – ⟨12⟩ Budapest - Murakeresztúr - Zagreb and v.v.
P – ⟨12⟩ Pécs - Fonyód - Tapolca - Celldömölk and v.v.
Q – ⟨2⟩ Kaposvár - Fonyód - Tapolca - Celldömölk - Szombathely and v.v.
V – VENEZIA – 🛏 1, 2 cl., ▬ 2 cl., ⟨2⟩ Venezia - Zagreb - Budapest and v.v.; 🛏 1, 2 cl. and ⟨2⟩ Venezia - Bucureşti and v.v. (also ▬ 1, 2 cl. June 1 - Sept. 21 from Venezia, May 30 - Sept. 19 from Bucureşti). For weekly 🛏 Venezia - Moskva see Table **97**. Special fares payable for international journeys.
W – ⑥⑦ to June 14 / from Aug. 29. ⟨2⟩ Keszthely - Szombathely (*IC* **981/2**) - Wien and v.v.
b – Conveys ⟨12⟩ Budapest - Keszthely and v.v. (Table **1225**).
c – To / from Celldömölk (Table **1232**).
f – From Fonyód (Table **1220**).
k – Budapest **Keleti**.
n – To / from Keszthely (Table **1225**).
s – From Siófok (Table **1220**).
t – To Székesfehérvár (Table **1220**).
u – Conveys ⟨2⟩ Budapest - Nagykanizsa and v.v.
v – Conveys ⟨12⟩ Budapest - Siófok and v.v.
w – Conveys ⟨2⟩ Budapest - Siófok and v.v.
* – Keleti - Kelenföld: *13 km.*
⊖ – Conveys on dates in Table **97**, 🛏 1, 2 cl. Moskva / Kyïv (**15 / 6**) - Budapest - Zagreb and v.v.
◧ – See also Tables **1230 / 31**.

1225 BALATONSZENTGYÖRGY - KESZTHELY - TAPOLCA

Service to June 19 / from Aug. 24. *Service June 20 - Aug. 23 will be shown in the July edition (see also page 3)*

km				8612			852 862		8802		8622		5209				854 866	19804			8806					
		2	2	2	2	2				2	2	2		2	2	2	2	2	2	2	2	2	2	2	2	
		⚒		f		c			P		s	c	A		c			W			Q		c			
	Budapest Déli **1220** .. d.	...	...	...	...	...	0713	...	...	...	...	...	1015**k**	...	...	...	1313	...	...	...	...	...	...	...	...	...
0	**Balatonszentgyörgy** ... d.	0359	0537	0710	0755	0920	1022	...	1122	1200	1258	...	1353	1419	...	1535	1633	...	1713	1745	1846	2000	...	2150	2222	...
10	Keszthely .... a.	0411	0549	0722	0808	0931	1033	...	1134	1213	1311	...	1405	1431	...	1546	1644	...	1724	1757	1857	2012	...	2202	2234	...
10	Keszthely .... d.	0412	0610	0732	...	0932	...	1042	1135	...	...	1337	...	...	1500	1549	...	1714	1730	...	1908	2025	2124	2237	...	...
35	**Tapolca** .... a.	0445	0639	0803	...	1002	...	1113	1203	...	...	1414	...	...	1531	1622	...	1738	1804	...	1939	2055	2154	2308	...	...

				869 859				8807		865 855		19807			9655 5208			1863 1853			8801	863 851				
	2	2	2		2	2	2	2	2			2	2	2		2	2	2⑦	2	2			2	2	2	2
			Ⓐc					Q				W		c	A	c	t		c		P			c		c
Tapolca.........................d.	...	0451	0516	...	...	0642	...	0824	1004	...	...	1140	1210	1245	...	1324	...	...	1425	1539	1625	...	1741	1833	1950	2105
Keszthely.........................a.	...	0523	0548	...	...	0716	...	0852	1038	...	...	1209	1240	1320	...	1359	...	...	1458	1609	1654	...	1816	1904	2023	2141
Keszthely.........................d.	0340	0524	...	0551	0615	0730	0822	0900	...	1040	1140	...	1241	...	1333	...	1406	1440	1505	1610	1657	1725	1825	1905	2042	2205
Balatonszentgyörgy.....a.	0352	0536	...	0602	0627	0742	0833	0911	...	1051	1153	...	1253	...	1344	...	1417	1451	1517	1622	1708	1735	1838	1918	2054	2217
Budapest Déli **1220**....a.	...	...	...	0917	...	...	...	...	...	1419	...	...	...	...	1734**k**	...	...	1827	...	...	...	2047	...	...	...	...

FOR NOTES SEE TABLE 1220 ABOVE

1227 SOPRON - SZOMBATHELY
Operated by GySEV

km				IC 285								
		2n	2	Z	2	2	2	2v	2	2	2	2
	Wien Süd **978** .....d.	...	0653	0726	...	...	...	...	...	...	...	...
	W. Neustadt **978** ..d.	...	0732	0800	0932	1032	...	1332	1507	...	...	2132
0	**Sopron**...................d.	0720	0811	0835	1015	1137	1318	1428	1600	1745	1911	2228
38	Bük...........................d.	0806	0855	0914	1103	1226	1401	1518	1649	1828	1956	2312
62	**Szombathely**..........a.	0828	0916	0933	1125	1248	1421	1542	1710	1850	2019	2334

										IC 284
	2	2	2	2v	2	2	2v	2	2n	Z
Szombathely.........d.	0618	0710	0934	1128	1308	1424	1516	1624	1852	1935
Bük.........................d.	0642	0733	0957	1150	1330	1446	1541	1649	1921	1954
Sopron...................a.	0729	0821	1042	1235	1415	1527	1629	1736	2006	2031
W. Neustadt **978** .a.	0827	0927	1127	1325	1527	...	1727	...	...	2058
Wien Süd **978**.....a.	...	1002	...	...	...	...	...	...	...	2132

Z – ZÁGRÁB – ⟨12⟩ and ✕ Wien - Zagreb and v.v. (Table **92**).
n – To / from Pécs (Table **1235**).
v – To / from Graz (Table **986**).

Additional trains: Sopron - Szombathely 0354, 0432, 0601; Szombathely - Sopron 0416, 0521, 2105, 2250.

BUDAPEST - SZÉKESFEHÉRVÁR - ZALAEGERSZEG and SZOMBATHELY 1230

km		900	900	902	902	246	246	904	906	906	908	908
			959		9525	9004				9511		951
					2		C	⚒				
0	**Budapest** Déli ....§d.	0603	0603	0905	0905	1203	1203	1403	1603	1603	1803	1803
4	B'pest Kelenföld ....§d.	0612	0612	0914	0914	1212	1212	1412	1612	1612	1812	1812
67	**Székesfehérvár** ...§a.	0715	0715	1016	1016	1315	1315	1515	1715	1715	1915	1915
67	**Székesfehérvár** .....d.	0717	0717	1018	1018	1317	1317	1517	1717	1717	1917	1917
90	Várpalota ....d.	0735	0735	1036	1036	1335	1335	1535	1735	1735	1935	1935
112	Veszprém.............d.	0800	0800	1100	1100	1400	1400	1600	1800	1800	2000	2000
148	Ajka ....d.	0829	0829	1129	1129	1429	1429	1629	1829	1829	2029	2029
181	Boba ....d.	0859	0910	1202	1206	1459	1505	1659	1859	1911	2059	2111
	Zalaegerszeg. ◐ a.	|	1009	|	1315	|	1605	|	|	2010	|	2209
191	Celldömölk ....d.	0909	...	1212	...	1509	...	1709	1909	...	2113	...
236	**Szombathely** ....a.	0943	...	1258	...	1543	...	1743	1943	...	2147	...

	909		905	9005	9514	9003	247	903	956	901	958
					9005	247			903		901
		2		Ⓑ	Ⓑ		C				
Szombathely ....d.	0605	0707	1005	1205	...	1400	...	1605	...	1805	...
Celldömölk ....d.	0641	0803	1041	1241	...	1441	...	1641	...	1841	...
Zalaegerszeg ◐ d.	0540**z**	|	0944**z**	|	1145	|	1351	|	1545	|	1744
Boba ....d.	0700	0815	1100	1300	1300	1500	1500	1700	1700	1900	1900
Ajka ....d.	0727	0857	1129	1327	1327	1527	1527	1727	1727	1927	1927
Veszprém.............d.	0802	0943	1202	1402	1402	1602	1602	1802	1802	2002	2002
Várpalota ....d.	0824	1010	1224	1424	1424	1624	1624	1824	1824	2024	2024
Székesfehérvár ...a.	0841	1037	1241	1441	1441	1641	1641	1841	1841	2041	2041
Székesfehérvár .§d.	0843	*1048*	1243	1443	1443	1643	1643	1843	1843	2045	2045
B'pest Kelenföld .§a.	0940	*1205*	1340	1540	1540	1740	1740	1940	1940	2145	2145
Budapest Déli ...§a.	0947	*1212*	1347	1547	1547	1747	1747	1947	1947	2152	2152

CELLDÖMÖLK - BOBA - ZALAEGERSZEG

km	See also △		959		9925		246			9511		951
		2	B	2	2B	2	C	2	2	B	2	B
0	**Celldömölk** .. **1232** d.	0756	0849	0953	1147	1356	...	1555	1800	*1841*	2002	...
10	Boba .... **1232** d.	0816	0910	1006	1206	1406	1505	1605	1810	1911	2012	2111
28	Ukk .... **1232** a.	0833	0925	1024	1224	1425	1521	1623	1828	1926	2037	2127
28	Ukk......................d.	0834	0927	1030	1229	1429	1526	1628	1829	1928	2038	2129
59	Zalaszentiván ....a.	0907	0956	1105	1304	1505	1554	1704	1905	1956	2112	2157
59	Zalaszentiván ....d.	0908	0959	1106	1305	1506	1556	1718	1906	2000	2113	2159
68	**Zalaegerszeg** ....a.	0918	1009	1115	1315	1515	1605	1727	1915	2010	2122	2209

	950		9512		9514		247	956		958	
	B	2	2B	2	ⒷB	2	C	B	2	B	2
Zalaegerszeg ......d.	0540	0840	0944	1040	1145	1240	1351	1545	1640	1744	1835
Zalaszentiván.........a.	0549	0848	0953	1048	1154	1248	1400	1553	1648	1753	1843
Zalaszentiván.........d.	0556	0849	1000	1049	1158	1249	1401	1556	1649	1758	1849
Ukk ....a.	0627	0925	1028	1123	1227	1324	1429	1625	1725	1827	1927
Ukk .... **1232** d.	0628	0927	1029	1126	1228	1326	1431	1627	1727	1829	1928
Boba .... **1232** a.	0645	0945	1046	1147	1243	1347	1448	1642	1746	1844	1946
Celldömölk 1232 a.	*0709*	0956	1109	1200	1311	1400	...	*1705*	1757	*1912*	2000

B – Conveys through portion Budapest - Boba - Zalaegerszeg and v.v. (see upper table).
C – CITADELLA – [12] Budapest - Hodoš - Ljubljana and v.v.
z – [12] Zalaegerszeg - Budapest.

◐ – See lower table.
△ – Additional journeys: 0555, 2156 Ⓑ from Celldömölk, 0640, 1437, 2043 from Zalaegerszeg.
§ – See also Tables **1220** and **1231**.

BUDAPEST - SZÉKESFEHÉRVÁR - BALATONFÜRED - TAPOLCA 1231

Service to June 19 / from Aug. 24. *Service June 20 - Aug. 23 will be shown in the July edition (see also page 3)*

km		9720	970	9712	9722	9714	974	9724	9716	9718	978	9738
		2		2	2	2		2	2	2		2Ⓑ
0	**Budapest** Déli ... § d.	*0338*	0618	*0713*	*0905*	*1043*	1213	*1313*	*1443*	*1603*	1813	*2043*
4	B'pest Kelenföld ... § d.	*0345*	0625	*0720*	*0914*	*1051*	1220	*1320*	*1451*	*1612*	1820	*2051*
67	**Székesfehérvár** .. § a.	*0504*	0726	*0817*	*1016*	*1210*	1322	*1417*	*1610*	*1715*	1922	*2210*
67	**Székesfehérvár** .....d.	0535	0740	0847	1047	1247	1340	1447	1647	1800	1940	2247
117	Balalatonalmádi......d.	0644	0839	0951	1151	1351	1439	1551	1752	1902	2039	2352
132	**Balatonfüred** ....d.	0706	0859	1015	1215	1415	1459	1615	1815	1926	2059	0012
157	Révfülöp ....d.	0745	0926	1101	1301	1501	1526	1701	1901	2009	2126	...
168	Badacsonytomaj.....d.	0759	0938	1116	1316	1516	1538	1716	1915	2023	2138	...
170	Badacsony ....d.	0802	0942	1119	1319	1519	1542	1719	1918	2026	2142	...
184	**Tapolca** ....a.	0821	0956	1138	1338	1538	1556	1738	1937	2045	2156	...

	9719	979	9717	9715	975	9725	9713	9723	971	9711	9721
			2	2		2	2	2		2	2
Tapolca ....d.	0429	0606	0823	1023	1206	1223	1423	1623	1806	1823	2110
Badacsony ....d.	0449	0621	0843	1043	1221	1243	1443	1643	1821	1843	2130
Badacsonytomaj...d.	0452	0625	0846	1046	1225	1246	1446	1646	1825	1846	2137
Révfülöp ....d.	0507	0636	0901	1101	1236	1301	1501	1701	1836	1901	2152
Balatonfüred ....d.	0550	0704	0945	1145	1304	1345	1545	1745	1904	1945	2231
Balalatonalmádi....d.	0611	0720	1009	1209	1320	1409	1609	1809	1920	2009	2252**r**
Székesfehérvár ...a.	0717	0814	1113	1313	1414	1512	1712	1912	2014	2112	2400**r**
Székesfehérvár .§d.	0730	0828	*1148*	*1348*	1428	*1548*	*1748*	*1943*	2028	*2153*	...
B'pest Kelenföld .§a.	0835	0935	*1305*	*1505*	1535	*1705*	*1905*	*2040*	2135	*2315*	...
Budapest Déli ...§a.	0842	0942	*1312*	*1512*	1542	*1712*	*1912*	*2047*	2142	*2322*	...

r – Ⓑ only.

§ – See also Tables **1220** and **1230**.

SZOMBATHELY - UKK - TAPOLCA 1232

km			8807	9627	19807	9615	9625	9635	9613	8801	9623	
		2	2k	2	W	2	2	2	2		2	2
	Wien Süd **978**.....d.	...	...	...	0726	...	...	...	...	...	...	...
	Sopron **1227**........d.	...	...	...	0835	...	...	...	...	...	...	...
0	**Szombathely**.........d.	...	0625	...	0946	*1005*	*1100*	*1205*r	...	*1427*a	*1625*a	...
45	Celldömölk ....a.	...	0706	...	1026	*1039*	*1142*	*1239*r	...	*1508*a	*1707*a	...
45	Celldömölk .... **1230** d.	*0555*	0716	*0849*	1035	1119	1214	1317	1420	1519	1717	1953
55	Boba............ **1230** d.	*0607*	0726	*0910*	|	1129	1224	1327	1430	1530	1728	2001
73	Ukk .... **1230** a.	*0625*	0746	*0925*	|	1151	1246	1346	1451	1546	1749	2027
73	Ukk.......................d.	0633	0747	0928	|	1152	1247	1347	1458	1547	1750	2028
81	Sümeg ....d.	0645	0756	0940	1112	1204	1259	1358	1511	1601	1804	2038
101	**Tapolca**.................a.	0710	0812	1003	1129	1232	1321	1421	1536	1621	1832	2100
	Keszthely **1225**...a.	...	0852	1038	1209	...	...	1458	1609	1654	1904	2141
	Fonyód **1220** ......a.	...	...	...	...	...	...	...	...	|	...	...
	Pécs **1235** ....a.	...	...	...	...	...	...	...	...	2139	...	...

	9652	9612	9622	8802	9614	9616	9626	19804	9636	8806	9628
	2	2	2		2	2	2c	W	2	2k	2⊡
Pécs **1235** ....d.	...	...	...	0731	...	...	...	...	...	...	...
Fonyód **1220** ....d.	...	...	...	|	...	...	...	...	...	...	...
Keszthely **1225**.d.	0610	0732	0931	1135	1337	1500	1549	1714	1730	1908	2124
Tapolca...............d.	0641	0834	1010	1204	1426	1540	1635	1740	1806	1940	2158
Sümeg ....d.	0706	0856	1032	1226	1448	1602	1656	1803	1828	1959	2219
Ukk.......................a.	0717	0907	1043	1237	1458	1613	1707	|	1839	2007	2227
Ukk............. **1230** d.	*0725*	*0927*	1044	1246	1459	1636	*1727*	|	1840	2008	2228r
Boba........... **1230** d.	*0746*	*0946*	1104	1306	1521	1654	*1747*	|	1903	2030	2247r
Celldömölk.. **1230** a.	*0758*	*0956*	1113	1318	1532	1705	*1757*	1836	1912	2039	2255r
Celldömölk ....d.	...	...	*1212*	*1348*	...	*1709*x	*1803*	1842	...	2049	...
Szombathely.......a.	...	...	*1258*	*1429*	...	*1743*x	*1846*	1920	...	2131	...
Sopron **1227**.....a.	...	...	...	...	...	...	...	2031	...	...	...
Wien Süd **978**...a.	...	...	...	...	...	...	...	2132	...	...	...

W – ⑥⑦ to June 14 / from Aug. 29. [2] Wien (*IC* **285/4**) - Szombathely - Keszthely and v.v.
a – Ⓐ only.
c – Change at Ukk and Celldömölk.
k – To / from Kaposvár (Table **1235**).
r – Ⓑ only.
x – ⚒ only.
⊡ – An additional journey operates Keszthely - Ukk at 2025.

SZOMBATHELY - NAGYKANIZSA - PÉCS 1235

km		8900	2	891	*IC* 285	2	2	2	2	8906	2	2
			⊡	s	Z						⊡	Ⓑ
	Wien Süd **978** ......d.	...	...	...	0726	...	...	...	...	...	...	...
	Györ **1250** ....d.	...	...	...	|	...	...	...	...	...	...	...
0	**Szombathely**.........d.	0510	0656	0913	0945	1057	1340	1453	1622	1713	1820	2153
49	Zalaszentiván.........a.	0551	0751	0954	1028	1151	1436	1552	1716	1754	1919	2249
49	Zalaszentiván .....d.	*0600*	|	*0959*	*1106*	|	1451	*1556*	*1718*	*1758*	|	*2305*
58	**Zalaegerszeg**.....a.	*0610*	|	*1009*	*1115*	|	1500	*1605*	*1727*	*1808*	|	*2315*
		|	|	|	|	|	2	|	|	|	|	|
	Zalaegerszeg.....d.	*0540*	|	*0944*	|	*1139*	1442	*1545*	*1640*	*1744*	*1835*	*2250*
	Zalaszentiván .....a.	*0549*	|	*0953*	|	*1148*	1451	*1553*	*1648*	*1753*	*1843*	*2258*
49	Zalaszentiván.........d.	0552	0801	0955	1029	1200	1500	1600	1717	1755	1920	2305
102	**Nagykanizsa** ....a.	0639	0903	1039	1114	1301	1608	1706	1820	1839	2029	0007
	Pécs ⊗ ....a.	0857	...	1257	...	...	...	...	...	2057	...	...

	2	8907	2	2	2	2	892	2	*IC* 284	2	8901
	⊙						s		Z	⊙	
Pécs ⊗ ....d.	...	0650	...	...	...	...	1450	...	...	...	1850
Nagykanizsa ....d.	0646	0911	1146	...	1445	1545	1711	...	1756	1900	2111
Zalaszentiván.......a.	0747	0955	1245	...	1546	1646	1755	...	1846	2002	2156
Zalaszentiván ...d.	|	*0959*	1250	...	*1556*	*1718*	*1758*	...	*1906*	*2012*	*2159*
Zalaegerszeg...a.	|	*1009*	1259	...	*1605*	*1727*	*1808*	...	*1915*	*2021*	*2209*
	|	|			|	|	|		|	|	|
Zalaegerszeg...d.	|	*0944*	1139	1432	*1545*	*1640*	*1744*	1739	*1835*	*1948*	|
Zalaszentiván ...a.	|	*0953*	1148	1441	*1553*	*1648*	*1753*	1748	*1843*	*1957*	|
Zalaszentiván.......d.	0755	1000	1200	1454	1605	1656	1800	1808	1847	2003	2159
Szombathely.......a.	0849	1042	1256	1550	1706	1759	1842	1906	1927	2059	2241
Györ **1250** ....a.	...	...	...	...	...	...	...	...	|	...	...
Wien Süd **978** ....a.	...	...	...	...	...	...	...	...	2132	...	...

km		8920	8900		8807	8912	891		8916	8801	8906	
		2		2	2	2	s	2	2	P		
	Szombathely ⊗ ...d.	...	0513	...	0625	...	0913	...	...	...	1713	...
0	**Nagykanizsa** ....d.	*0400*	0640	...	|	*0810*	1045	...	*1610*	...	1840	...
29	Gyékényes..............d.	0425	0704	...	n	0904	1109	...	1655	...	1904	...
84	Barcs ....d.	0534	0755	0835	|	1008	1159	1337	1757	...	1955	...
114	Szigetvár...............d.	0614	0823	0916	|	1053	1227	1421	1846	...	2023	...
	Fonyód .... ▶ d.	|	|	|	0957	|	|	|	|	1813	|	...
	Kaposvár .... ▶ d.	|	|	|	1121	|	|	|	|	2003	|	...
	Dombóvár alsó ...d.	|	|	|	...	|	|	|	|	2044	|	...
129	Szentlörinc.............d.	0635	0837	0940	...	1113	1241	1514	1912	2123	2037	...
148	**Pécs** ....a.	0703	0857	0959	...	1136	1257	1536	1934	2139	2057	...

	8919	8907	8802		8923	892	8806	8913	8901	8911	
	2		P	2	2	s	2	2		2Ⓑ	2
Pécs ....d.	0528	0650	0731	1009	1341	1450	...	1620	1850	1942	2156
Szentlörinc ....d.	0552	0707	0748	1033	1402	1507	...	1652	1907	2003	2225
Dombóvár alsó .d.	|	|	0837	|	|	|	...	|	|	|	|
Kaposvár ..... ▶ d.	|	|	0928	|	|	|	1650	|	|	|	|
Fonyód .... ▶ a.	|	|	1038	|	|	|	1808	|	|	|	|
Szigetvár.............d.	0617	0721	...	1053	1420	1522	|	1712	1921	2025	2244
Barcs ....d.	0657	0756	...	1134	1458	1556	|	1803	1956	2112	2325
Gyékényes ....a.	0810	0846	...	...	1602	1646	n	1903	2046	2215	...
Nagykanizsa ....a.	...	0910	...	...	...	1710	|	*1945*	2110	...	...
Szombathely ⊗ .a.	...	1042	...	...	...	1842	2131	...	2241	...	...

P – [12] Celldömölk - Tapolca - Fonyód - Pécs and v.v.
Z – ZÁGRÁB – [12] ✕ Wien Süd - Zagreb and v.v. (Table **92**).
n – Via Tapolca / Kesthely (Tables **1232/25**).
s – To / from Sopron (Table **1227**).
⊗ – See other section of the table.

⊡ – Additional journeys Szombathely - Zalaegerszeg: 0608, 1905, 2246.
⊙ – Additional journeys Nagykanizsa - Zalaegerszeg: 0525, 2007, 2231.

For JADRAN Praha - Bratislava - Zagreb - Split and v.v. (summer only) see Table 92.

▶ – Local trains **Fonyód - Kaposvár** and v.v. (2nd class, journey approx. 80 - 90 minutes):
From Fonyód 0325 Ⓐ, 0432, 0726, 1150, 1256 Ⓐ, 1506, 1625, 2000.
From Kaposvár 0240 Ⓐ, 0454, 0737, 1014 Ⓐ, 1321, 1434, 1829, 2246 Ⓑ.

1250 BUDAPEST - GYÖR - SOPRON / SZOMBATHELY / WIEN

See below main table for additional slower services. For other services Budapest - Szombathely see Table **1230**.

km		346	IC 910 / IC 930	IC 910	RJ 60	EC 962	IC 922 / IC 932	IC 922	EC 964		RJ 66	IC 924 / IC 934	IC 924	EC 968	IC 916 / IC 936	IC 916	EC 942	EN 466	EN 460	IC 918 / IC 938	IC 918	RJ 40	EN 462	
		✕	R	R ✕	✕	✕	R	R ✕	✕		✕	R	R ✕	✕	R	R ✕	✕	✕	✕	R	R ✕	✕		
		D			M						M					G		W	F	⊙			K	
0	**Budapest** Keleti d.	0555	0610	0610	0710	0910	1010	1010	1110	...	1310	1410	1410	1510	1610	1610	1710	1805	1905	1910	1910	2010	2105	...
13	Budapest Kelenföld d.	0610	0625	0625	0725	0925	1025	1025	1125	...	1325	1425	1425	1525	1625	1625	1725	1820	1920	1925	1925	2025	2120	...
75	Tatabánya d.	|	0659	0659	|	|	1059	1059	|	...	|	1459	1459	|	1659	1659	|	|	|	1959	1959	|	|	...
141	**Györ** a.	0723	0739	0739	0836	1036	1139	1139	1236	...	1436	1539	1539	1636	1739	1739	1836	1931	2031	2039	2039	2136	2231	...
141	**Györ** d.	0725	0741	0741	0838	1037	1141	1141	1237	...	1437	1541	1541	1637	1741	1741	1837	1933	2033	2041	2041	2137	2232	...
172	Csorna d.	|	0805	0812	|	|	1205	1212	|	...	|	1605	1612	|	1805	1812	|	|	|	2105	2112	|	|	...
226	**Sopron** 🏛 a.	|	0841	|	|	|	1241	|	|	...	|	1641	|	|	1841	|	|	|	|	2141	|	|	|	...
244	**Szombathely** a.	|	...	0902	|	|	...	1302	|	...	|	...	1702	|	...	1902	|	|	|	...	2202	|	|	...
	Graz **986** a.	|	...	...	|	|	...	...	|	...	|	...	...	|	...	2203	|	|	|	...	...	|	|	...
188	Hegyeshalom 🏛 d.	0758	...	...	0906	1106	...	...	1306	...	1506	...	...	1706	...	...	1906	2004	2106	...	...	2206	2301	...
219	Bruck an der Leitha **996** d.	0817	...	...	|	|	...	...	|	...	|	...	...	|	...	...	|	2024	2126	...	...	|	2321	...
261	Wien Meidling a.	|	...	...	0954	1154	...	...	1354	...	1554	...	...	1754	...	...	1954	|	2156	...	...	2254	2353	...
272	**Wien** Westbahnhof a.	0859	...	...	1008	1208	...	...	1408	...	1608	...	...	1808	...	...	2008	2105	2211	...	...	2308	...	...

	EN 463	IC 939 / IC 919	IC 919	RJ 41	EN 461	EN 467	IC 937 / IC 917	IC 917	EC 943		EC 961	IC 935 / IC 915	IC 915	RJ 63	IC 933 / IC 913	IC 913	EC 965		RJ 67	IC 931 / IC 911	IC 911	347 / 738	EC 969	
		R ✕	R ✕	✕	✕	✕	R	R	✕		✕	R	R ✕	✕	R	R ✕	✕		✕	R	R ✕	✕	✕	
	K				F	W	⊙	G						M					M			D		
Wien Westbahnhof d.	...	...	...	0650	0705	0825	...	...	0950	...	1150	...	...	1350	...	...	1550	...	1750	...	...	1850	1950	...
Wien Meidling d.	0600	...	...	0705	0722	|	...	...	1005	...	1205	...	...	1405	...	...	1605	...	1805	...	...	|	2005	...
Bruck an der Leitha **996** d.	0635	...	...	|	0758	0907	...	...	|	...	|	...	...	|	...	...	|	...	|	...	...	1933	|	...
Hegyeshalom 🏛 d.	0656	...	...	0757	0820	0930	...	...	1057	...	1257	...	...	1457	...	...	1657	...	1857	...	...	1957	2056	...
Graz **986** d.	|	...	...	|	|	|	...	0610	|	...	|	...	...	|	...	...	|	...	|	...	...	|	|	...
Szombathely d.	|	...	0606	|	|	|	...	0900	|	...	|	...	1300	|	...	1500	|	...	|	...	1900	|	|	...
Sopron 🏛 d.	|	0615	|	|	|	|	0910	|	|	...	|	1310	|	|	1510	|	|	...	|	1910	|	|	|	...
Csorna d.	|	0707	0707	|	|	|	1001	1001	|	...	|	1401	1401	|	1601	1601	|	...	|	2001	2001	|	|	...
Györ a.	0722	0726	0726	0819	0846	0957	1020	1020	1119	...	1319	1420	1420	1519	1620	1620	1719	...	1919	2020	2020	2030	2119	...
Györ d.	0724	0730	0730	0820	0847	0959	1022	1022	1120	...	1320	1422	1422	1520	1622	1622	1720	...	1920	2022	2022	2033	2120	...
Tatabánya d.	|	0808	0808	|	|	|	1100	1100	|	...	|	1500	1500	|	1700	1700	|	...	|	2100	2100	2126	|	...
Budapest Kelenföld a.	0839	0848	0848	0934	1003	1118	1137	1137	1234	...	1434	1537	1537	1634	1737	1737	1834	...	2034	2137	2137	2203	2234	...
Budapest Keleti a.	0854	0904	0904	0949	1019	1134	1154	1154	1249	...	1449	1554	1554	1649	1754	1754	1849	...	2049	2154	2154	2219	2249	...

SLOWER SERVICES BUDAPEST - GYÖR - SZOMBATHELY / SOPRON

See above for faster services

km					9200	990		9202		9204	992		9304			994	9206	9306		9208	9208	470	9408			☆
		2	2	2 ⚒			2		2			2 Ⓐ		2	2				2			A	B	2	2	2
0	**Budapest** Keleti d.	...	...	...	0640	...	...	0840	...	1040	...	...	1240	...	...	...	1440	1640	...	1840	1840	1940	1940	...	2123d	2323d
13	Budapest Kelenföld d.	...	...	...	0655	...	...	0855	...	1055	...	...	1255	...	...	...	1455	1655	...	1855	1855	1955	1955	...	2130	2330
75	Tatabánya ☆ d.	...	...	...	0731	...	...	0931	...	1131	...	...	1331	...	...	...	1531	1731	...	1931	1931	2031	2031	...	2215	0016
84	Tata ☆ d.	...	...	...	0739	...	...	0939	...	1139	...	...	1339	...	...	...	1539	1739	...	1939	1939	2039	2039	...	2226	0027
104	Komárom ☆ d.	...	...	...	0755	...	...	0955	...	1155	...	...	1355	...	...	...	1555	1755	...	1955	1955	2055	2055	...	2246	0046
141	**Györ** a.	...	...	...	0825	...	...	1025	...	1225	...	...	1425	...	...	...	1625	1825	...	2025	2025	2125	2125	...	2325	...
141	**Györ** d.	0555	0636	0657	0840	0835	0944	...	1050	1240	1235	1404	...	1445	1450	1604	1640	1840	1856	2040	2050	...	...	2240	...	...
213	Celldömölk a.	|	0802	|	1003	|	1114	...	|	1345	|	|	...	1643	|	|	1803	1945	|	2144	|	...	...	|	...	...
258	**Szombathely** ▷ a.	|	...	|	1046	|	...	...	|	...	|	|	...	...	|	|	1846	...	|	...	|	...	...	|	...	...
172	Csorna d.	0621	...	0731	...	0902	...	...	1121	...	1302	1434	...	...	1521	1633	...	...	1931	...	2118	...	...	2308	...	...
226	**Sopron** 🏛 a.	0717	...	0818	...	0945	...	...	1210	...	1345	1526	...	...	1611	1716	...	...	2027	...	2200	...	...	2355	...	...

		9406		471	9407	9209	999			995	9205			9305	993	9203		9303	991	9201	347		△		
	2		2 ⚒	A	B			2	2			2	2				2				D	2	2	2	2
Sopron 🏛 d.	0345	...	0458	...	...	...	0605	...	0740	1000	...	...	1140	...	1420	...	1552	...	1805	...	...	1945	...	...	2230
Csorna d.	0435	...	0553	...	...	...	0649	...	0834	1044	...	...	1234	...	1504	...	1647	...	1850	...	...	2037	...	...	2323
Szombathely ▷ d.	|	...	|	...	...	0519	|	...	|	|	0905	...	|	...	|	1305	|	1505	|	1705	...	|	...	...	|
Celldömölk d.	|	...	|	...	...	0605	|	0645	|	|	1006	1121	|	...	|	1406	|	1606	|	1806	...	|	...	2042	|
Györ a.	0505	...	0624	...	...	0716	0715	0813	0905	1108	1111	1255	1305	...	1528	1511	1714	1715	1914	1915	...	2107	...	2215	2348
Györ d.	...	0546	...	0633	0633	0733	0733	...	...	...	1133	...	...	1333	...	1533	...	1733	1933	1933	2033	...	2133	...	...
Komárom △ d.	...	0612	...	0702	0702	0802	0802	...	...	...	1202	...	...	1402	...	1602	...	1802	2002	2002	2102	...	2210	...	...
Tata △ d.	...	0626	...	0716	0716	0816	0816	...	...	...	1216	...	...	1416	...	1616	...	1816	2016	2016	2116	...	2229	...	...
Tatabánya △ d.	...	0636	...	0726	0726	0826	0826	...	...	...	1226	...	...	1426	...	1626	...	1826	2026	2026	2126	...	2242	...	...
Budapest Kelenföld a.	...	0713	...	0803	0803	0903	0903	...	...	...	1303	...	...	1503	...	1703	...	1903	2103	2103	2203	...	2329	...	...
Budapest Keleti a.	...	0729	...	0819	0819	0919	0919	...	...	...	1319	...	...	1519	...	1719	...	1919	2119	2119	2219	...	2337d	...	...

LOCAL TRAINS GYÖR - WIEN

2nd class

Györ d.	0445	0645	0745	0945	1145	1345	1545	1745	1945	2145
Mosonmagyaróvár d.	0510	0710	0810	1010	1210	1410	1610	1810	2010	2210
Hegyeshalom a.	0519	0719	0819	1019	1219	1419	1619	1819	2019	2219
Hegyeshalom 🏛 d.	0532	0722	0821	1021	1221	1421	1621	1821	2021	2221
Bruck an der Leitha d.	0558	0748	0847	1047	1247	1447	1647	1847	2047	2247
Wien Südbahnhof a.	0627	0819	0916	1116	1316	1516	1716	1916	2116	2316

Wien Südbahnhof d.	0540	0640	0840	1040	1240	1440	1640	1840	2040	2140
Bruck an der Leitha d.	0610	0710	0911	1110	1310	1510	1710	1910	2110	2210
Hegyeshalom 🏛 a.	0635	0735	0935	1135	1335	1535	1735	1935	2135	2235
Hegyeshalom d.	0641	0741	0941	1141	1341	1541	1741	1941	2141	2241
Mosonmagyaróvár d.	0649	0749	0949	1149	1349	1549	1749	1949	2149	2249
Györ a.	0713	0813	1013	1213	1413	1613	1813	2013	2213	2313

A – AMICUS – May 28 - Sept. 28 from Praha (next day from Bratislava), May 29 - Sept. 29 from Budapest. 🛏 1, 2 cl., ▬ 2 cl. and [12] Praha - Bratislava - Györ - Budapest and v.v. Conveys on dates in Table **60** (summer only) 🛏 1, 2 cl. and ▬ 2 cl. Praha - Burgas / Varna and v.v.

B – Runs when train **A** does not run (but not Dec. 20, 24 - 31, Jan. 1 - 3 from Budapest, not Dec. 14 - Jan. 4 from Rajka).

D – DACIA – 🛏 1, 2 cl., ▬ 2 cl., [2] and ✕ Wien - Budapest - Bucureşti and v.v.; [1] Wien - Budapest - Lököshaza and v.v.; 🛏 1, 2 cl. and ▬ 2 cl. Wien - Budapest - Beograd and v.v.; 🛏 1, 2 cl. Wien - Budapest - Beograd - Sofiya and v.v.

F – DANUBIUS – [12] and ✕ Wien - Budapest and v.v.; 🛏 1, 2 cl., ▬ 2 cl., [2] and ✕ Frankfurt (**408/9**) - Karlsruhe - Wien - Budapest and v.v.

G – HALÁSZBÁSTYA – [12] and ✕ Budapest - Szombathely - Graz and v.v.

H – JADRAN – June 19 - Sept. 4: 🛏 1, 2 cl., ▬ 2 cl., [2] Praha - Split (Table **92**).

J – JADRAN – June 20 - Sept. 5 (next day from Györ): 🛏 1, 2 cl., ▬ 2 cl., [2] Split - Praha (Table **92**).

K – KÁLMÁN IMRE – 🛏 1, 2 cl., ▬ 2 cl., [2] München - Wien - Budapest and v.v.; 🛏 1, 2 cl. and ▬ 1, 2 cl. München - Wien - Budapest - Arad - Bucureşti and v.v.

M – [12] and ✕ München - Wien - Budapest and v.v.

W – WIENER WALZER – [12] and ✕ Wien - Budapest and v.v.; ▬ 2 cl. and [2] Zürich - Wien - Budapest and v.v.

d – Budapest **Déli**.

▷ – For services via Székesfehérvár see Table **1230**.

⊙ – To / from Wien Süd (Table **978**).

☆ – Local trains run hourly 0423 - 2323 Budapest Déli - Komárom.

△ – Local trains run hourly 0710 - 2210 Komárom - Budapest Déli.

§ – See also Table **1250**.

• – *Railjet* service, supplement payable. Premium, first and economy class. Classified *RJ* in Austria.

OTHER TRAIN NAMES:

942 / 3 BARTÓK BÉLA

961 LISZT FERENC / FRANZ LISZT

962 SEMMELWEIS IGNAC / IGNAZ SEMMELWEIS

964 / 5 CSÁRDÁS

968 / 9 LÉHAR FERENC / LEHÁR

1252 GYÖR - BRATISLAVA

km				474						470	9408
		2	2	J	2	2	2	2	2	A	B
	Budapest Keleti **1250** d.	...	...	...	...	...	...	...	...	1940	1940
0	**Györ** § d.	0845	1045	...	1245	1445	1645	1845	2045	2127	2127
36	Mosonmagyaróvár § d.	0910	1110	...	1310	1510	1710	1910	2110	2149	2149
47	Hegyeshalom § d.	0922	1122	1239	1322	1522	1722	1922	2122	2207	2207
60	Rajka a.	0936	1136	1251	1336	1536	1736	1936	2136	2220	2220
60	Rajka 🏛 d.	...	...	1301	...	...	...	...	...	2235	...
79	Bratislava Petržalka a.	...	...	1320	...	...	...	...	...	2256	...
96	**Bratislava** hlavná a.	...	...	1341	...	...	...	...	...	2319	...

	9409	471	9407					475		
		A	B	2	2	2	2	H	2	2
Bratislava hlavná d.	...	0456	...	...	...	...	...	1447	...	...
Bratislava Petržalka d.	...	0518	...	...	...	...	...	1509	...	...
Rajka 🏛 a.	...	0537	...	...	...	...	...	1528	...	...
Rajka d.	0457	0550	0550	0826	1026	1226	1426	1539	1626	1826
Hegyeshalom § d.	0511	0602	0602	0841	1041	1241	1441	1553	1641	1841
Mosonmagyaróvár § d.	0519	0609	0609	0849	1049	1249	1449	...	1649	1849
Györ § a.	0543	0631	0631	0913	1113	1313	1513	...	1713	1913
Budapest Keleti **1250** a.	0729	0819	0819	...	...	...	...	...	...	...

FOR NOTES SEE TABLE 1250 ABOVE

BUDAPEST - SALGÓTARJÁN - FIL'AKOVO — 1255

2nd class

km								Ⓐ			
0	**Budapest Keleti** .... ◇ d.	...	*0703*	*0838*	*1103*	*1303*	*1503*	*1603*	*1703*	*1903*	*2038*
67	Hatvan .... ◇ d.	0410	0810	1010	1210	1410	1610	1710	1810	2010	2210
126	**Salgótarján** .... ▷ d.	0547	0947	1147	1347	1547	1747	1847	1947	2147	2340
132	Somoskőújfalu 🏛 .... a.	0557	0957	1157	1357	1557	1757	1857	1957	2157	2350
132	Somoskőújfalu .... d.	*0620*	*1005*	...	*1535z*	...	*1905*	*1905*	...	...	...
146	**Fil'akovo** .... a.	*0638*	*1024*	...	*1554z*	...	*1924*	*1924*	...	...	...

Fil'akovo .... d.	...	*0546*	...	*0936*	...	...	*1505z*	*1755*	...	...
Somoskőújfalu .... a.	...	*0605*	...	*0955*	...	...	*1524z*	*1814*	...	...
Somoskőújfalu 🏛 .... d.	0417	0610	0817	1017	1217	1417	1617	1817	2017	2217
Salgótarján .... ▷ d.	0428	0621	0828	1028	1228	1428	1628	1828	2028	2228
Hatvan .... ◇ a.	0550	0750	0950	1150	1350	1550	1750	1950	2150	2350
Budapest Keleti .... ◇ a.	*0712*	*0857*	*1122*	*1257*	*1457*	*1657*	*1857*	*2057*	*2322*	...

z – ⑦ (also Jan. 6, Apr. 13, Aug. 31; not Dec. 21, 28, Apr. 12, July 1 - Aug. 30).

▷ – On Ⓐ trains run Hatvan - Salgótarján hourly 0310 - 2210, returning 0228, 0328, 0428, 0528, 0621, 0721, 0828, 1028 and hourly to 2228.

◇ – See also Table **1261**.

BUDAPEST - MISKOLC - NYÍREGYHÁZA — 1260

Fast trains

For slower trains Budapest - Miskolc see Table **1261**. Most *IC* trains continue beyond Debrecen to/from Budapest Nyugati. For trains Budapest - Debrecen - Nyiregyháza see Table **1270**

km		*IC* 560	*IC* 659	*IC* 532		*IC* 657	*IC* 502		*IC* 564	*IC* 512		*IC* 655	*IC* 504		*IC* 566	*IC* 534		*IC* 653	*IC* 506		*IC* 568	*IC* 536		*IC* 508		
		[R] ✕ ⚒	[R] ✕	✕ R	2	[R] ✕	[R] ✕ Ⓐ	2	[R] ✕	[R] ✕ Ⓑ	2	[R] ✕	[R] ✕ Ⓑ	2	[R] ✕	✕ L	2	[R] ✕	[R] ✕ Ⓑ	2	[R] ✕	✕ H	2	[R] ✕ Ⓑ	2	2 Ⓑ
0	**Budapest** Keleti . ▶ d.	...	...	0633	...	0733	0833	...	0933	1033	...	1133	1233	...	1333	1433	...	1533	1633	...	1733	1833	...	1933	...	...
126	Füzesabony .... ▶ d.	...	...	0756	...	0856	0956	...	1056	1156	...	1256	1356	...	1456	1556	...	1656	1756	...	1856	1956	...	2056	...	...
183	**Miskolc** .... ▶ a.	...	...	0832	...	0932	1032	...	1132	1232	...	1332	1432	...	1532	1632	...	1732	1832	...	1932	2032	...	2132	...	...
183	**Miskolc** .... d.	0630	0734	...	*0837*	0934	...	*1037*	1134	...	*1237*	1334	...	*1437*	1534	...	*1637*	1734	...	*1837*	1934	...	*2037*	...	2137	2300
221	Szerencs .... d.	0655	0759	...	0915	0959	...	1115	1159	...	1315	1359	...	1515	1559	...	1715	1759	...	1915	1959	...	2115	...	2215	2336
239	Tokaj .... d.	0707	0811	...	0936	1011	...	1136	1211	...	1336	1411	...	1536	1611	...	1736	1811	...	1936	2011	...	2136	...	2236	2354
271	**Nyíregyháza** .... a.	0733	0834	...	1017	1034	...	1217	1234	...	1417	1434	...	1617	1634	...	1817	1834	...	2017	2034	...	2217	...	2317	0028
	Debrecen **1270** .... a.	0806	0906	...	...	1106	...	...	1306	...	...	1506	...	...	1706	...	...	1906	...	...	2106	...	...	...	...	...

	529	*IC* 519		*IC* 537	*IC* 569		*IC* 517	*IC* 650		*IC* 535	*IC* 567		*IC* 505	*IC* 652		*IC* 515	*IC* 565		*IC* 503	*IC* 654		*IC* 533	*IC* 563			
		[R] ✕	2	✕ H	[R] ✕	2	[R] ✕ ⚒	[R] ✕	2	[R] ✕ K	[R] ✕	2	[R] ✕ Ⓑ	[R] ✕	2	[R] ✕ Ⓑ	[R] ✕	2	[R] ✕ Ⓑ	[R] ✕	2	✕ R	[R] ✕	2	2	2
Debrecen **1270** .... d.	...	...	...	...	0654	...	...	0854	...	...	1054	...	...	1254	...	...	1454	...	...	1654	...	...	1854	...	...	...
Nyíregyháza .... d.	*0343*	0526	0543	...	0726	0743	...	0926	0943	...	1126	1143	...	1326	1343	...	1526	1543	...	1726	1743	...	1926	1943	2043	2243
Tokaj .... d.	*0418*	0550	0623	...	0750	0823	...	0950	1023	...	1150	1223	...	1350	1423	...	1550	1623	...	1750	1823	...	1950	2023	2123	2323
Szerencs .... d.	0445	0602	0640	...	0802	0840	...	1002	1040	...	1202	1240	...	1402	1440	...	1602	1640	...	1802	1840	...	2002	2040	2215	2342
Miskolc .... a.	0519	0626	*0719*	...	0826	*0919*	...	1026	*1119*	...	1226	*1319*	...	1426	*1519*	...	1626	*1719*	...	1826	*1919*	...	2026	*2121*	2249	...
Miskolc .... ▶ d.	0534	0628	...	0728	0828	...	0928	1028	...	1128	1228	...	1328	1428	...	1528	1628	...	1728	1828	...	1928	...	...	...	...
Füzesabony .... ▶ d.	0617	0703	...	0803	0903	...	1003	1103	...	1203	1303	...	1403	1503	...	1603	1703	...	1803	1903	...	2003	...	...	...	...
Budapest Keleti .. ▶ a.	0757	0827	...	0927	1027	...	1127	1227	...	1327	1427	...	1527	1627	...	1727	1827	...	1927	2027	...	2127	...	...	...	...

H – HERNÁD/HORNÁD – (12) Budapest - Miskolc - Košice and v.v.

K – (12) Košice (**7201**) – Hidasnémeti (*IC* **535**) - Budapest (Table **1262**).

L – (12) Budapest - Hidasnémeti (**7200**) - Košice (Table **1262**).

R – RÁKÓCZI – (12) Budapest - Miskolc - Košice and v.v.

▶ – For slower services see Table **1261**.

BUDAPEST - MISKOLC - SÁTORALJAÚJHELY — 1261

Slower trains

For fast trains Budapest - Miskolc - Szerencs see Table **1260**. For faster journeys use *IC* train (Table **1260**) and change at Füzesabony (for Eger) or Szerencs (for Sátoraljaújhely)

km		2	2	2	5500	5200	5510	520	5502	522	5512	524	5504	526	5506	528	5516	1528 ⑤E	5208 K	1380 C	5508	5008	5108	2
0	**Budapest** Keleti .... ▶ d.	...	...	...	0503	0603	0703	0803	...	1003	1103	1203	1303	1403	1503	1603	1703	1758	1803	...	1903	2003	2203	2238
67	Hatvan .... d.	...	...	*0505*	0558	0658	0758	0858	1015	1058	1158	1258	1358	1458	1558	1658	1758	|	1858	1912	1958	2058	2258	2353
87	Vámosgyörk ⊡ .... d.	...	...	*0521*	0613	0711	0813	0911	1036	1111	1213	1311	1413	1511	1613	1711	1813	|	1911	|	2013	2111	2311	0008
126	Füzesabony .... ▶ a.	...	...	*0557*	0649	0737	0849	0937	1111	1137	1249	1337	1449	1537	1649	1737	1849	1923	1937	1950	2049	2137	2337	0042
126	Füzesabony .... ▶ d.	...	...	0602	0706	0739	0906	0939	1112	1139	1306	1339	1506	1539	1706	1739	1906	1925	1939	2002	2106	2139	2339	...
143	**Eger** ⊙ .... a.	...	...	|	0724	|	0924	|	1130	|	1324	|	1524	|	1724	|	1924	|	|	|	2124	|	|	...
139	Mezőkövesd .... d.	...	...	0614	▬	0749	...	0949	▬	1149	▬	1349	▬	1549	▬	1749	▬	|	1949	2014	▬	2149	2349	...
183	**Miskolc** .... ▶ a.	...	...	0652	2	0820	...	1020	2	1220	2	1420	2	1620	2	1820	2	2003	2020	2052	2	2220	0020	...
183	**Miskolc** .... ▶ d.	*0537*	*0637*	...	*0737*	0837	...	1037	*1137*	1237	*1337*	1437	*1537*	1637	*1737*	1837	*1937*	2016	2037	...	*2137*	...	...	...
221	Szerencs .... ▶ d.	0613	0713	...	0813	0913	...	1113	1213	1313	1413	1513	1613	1713	1813	1913	2013	2045	2113	...	2224	...	...	...
257	Sárospatak .... a.	0700	0800	...	0900	1000	...	1200	1300	1400	1500	1600	1700	1800	1900	2000	2100	2131	2200	...	2305	...	...	...
267	**Sátoraljaújhely** 🏛 .... a.	0709	0809	...	0909	1009	...	1209	1309	1409	1509	1609	1709	1809	1909	2009	2109	2140	2209	...	2314	...	...	...
269	Slovenské Nové Mesto .... a.	...	...	...	...	...	...	...	...	...	...	...	...	...	...	...	...	...	...	...	...	...	...	...

	5009	5509	529	1381 D	5519	5209 K	1527 ⑥F	2	527		525	2	5205	2	523	2	521	2	5201	2	2	2	2	2
Slovenské Nové Mesto .... d.	...	...	...	...	...	...	...	...	...	...	...	...	...	...	...	...	...	...	...	...	...	...	...	...
Sátoraljaújhely 🏛 .... d.	...	...	0351	...	...	0547	0620	0647	0747	...	0947	1047	1147	1247	1347	1447	1547	1647	1747	1847	1947	...	2047	...
Sárospatak .... d.	...	...	0401	...	...	0601	0631	0701	0801	...	1001	1101	1201	1301	1401	1501	1601	1701	1801	1901	2001	...	2101	...
Szerencs .... ▶ d.	...	...	0445	...	...	0645	0712	0743	0845	...	1045	1143	1245	1343	1445	1543	1645	1743	1845	1943	2047	...	2143	*2215*
Miskolc .... ▶ a.	...	...	0519	...	...	0719	0738	*0819*	0919	...	1119	*1219*	1319	*1419*	1519	*1619*	1719	*1819*	1919	*2019*	2121	...	...	*2249*
Miskolc .... ▶ d.	0329	...	0534	0704	...	0734	0753	▬	0934	...	1134	▬	1334	▬	1534	▬	1734	▬	1934	...	...	2204	...	2304
Mezőkövesd .... d.	0407	...	0606	0742	...	0806	|	...	1006	...	1206	...	1406	...	1606	...	1806	...	2006	...	...	2242	...	2342
Eger ⊙ .... d.	|	0434	|	|	0634	|	|	0834	|	1034	|	1234	|	1434	|	1634	|	1834	|	...	...	|	...	|
Füzesabony .... ▶ a.	0418	0452	0615	0754	0652	0815	0831	0852	1015	1052	1215	1252	1415	1452	1615	1652	1815	1852	2015	...	...	2254	...	2354
Füzesabony .... ▶ d.	0419	0503	0617	0807	0709	0817	0832	0909	1017	1109	1217	1309	1417	1509	1617	1709	1817	1909	2017	...	...	...	...	...
Vámosgyörk ⊡ .... d.	0454	0539	0645	|	0745	0845	|	0945	1045	1145	1245	1345	1445	1545	1645	1745	1845	1945	2045	...	...	...	...	...
Hatvan .... d.	0511	0557	0700	0846	0802	0902	|	1001	1102	1202	1302	1402	1502	1602	1702	1802	1902	2002	2102	...	...	...	...	...
Budapest Keleti .... ▶ a.	0617	0712	0757	...	0857	0957	1002	...	1157	1257	1357	1457	1557	1657	1757	1857	1957	2057	2157	...	...	...	...	...

C – CRACOVIA – from Bucureşti June 19 - Aug. 31: 🛏 1, 2 cl. and (2) Bucureşti - Lőkösháza - Szolnok - Hatvan - Miskolc - Košice - Kraków.

D – CRACOVIA – from Kraków June 18 - Aug. 30: 🛏 1, 2 cl. and (2) Kraków - Košice - Miskolc - Szolnok - Lőkösháza - Bucureşti.

E – ⑤ Jan. 9 - June 12; ⑤ Sept. 4 - Dec. 11. *IC* train, [R].

F – ⑥ Jan. 17 - June 13, ⑥ Sept. 5 - Dec. 12 (also May 1, Oct. 23; not May 2, Oct. 24). *IC* train, [R].

K – (12) Sátoraljaújhely - Miskolc - Budapest - Nagykanizsa/Keszthely and v.v.

▶ – For faster trains see Table **1260**.

⊡ – Connecting trains **Vámosgyörk - Gyöngyös** and v.v. (journey 16 mins):
From Vámosgyörk : 0527, 0617 and hourly to 1917 (not 1017), also 2117.
From Gyöngyös : 0552 and hourly to 1952 (not 1052), also 2152.

⊙ – Full service **Füzesabony - Eger** and v.v. (journey 18 minutes):
From Füzesabony : 0420, 0506, 0606, 0634, 0706 and hourly to 2306.
From Eger : 0334 and hourly to 2234.

MISKOLC - KOŠICE — 1262

km		2	*IC* 532	2	5332 7202	2	*IC* 534 7200	2	*IC* 536	1380
			R		2		✕		✕ H	C
	Budapest Keleti **1260/1** .... d.	...	0633	...	...	...	1433	...	1833	...
	Füzesabony **1260/1** .... d.	0502	0756	0802	1002	1202	1556	1802	1956	2002
0	**Miskolc** .... d.	0606	0834	0906	1106	1306	1634	1906	2034	2106
61	Hidasnémeti .... a.	0713	0926	1013	1213	1413	1729	2013	2126	2213
61	Hidasnémeti 🏛 .... d.	...	0930	...	1222	...	1738	...	2130	2223
87	**Košice** .... a.	...	0950	...	1256	...	1814	...	2150	2243

	1381	*IC* 537		7201 *IC* 535		7203 5313		*IC* 533	
	D	✕ H	2	✕	2	2	2	R	2
Košice .... d.	0517	0613	...	0953	...	1457	...	1813	...
Hidasnémeti 🏛 .... a.	0537	0633	...	1026	...	1533	...	1833	...
Hidasnémeti .... d.	0547	0636	0947	1036	1347	1547	1647	1836	2147
Miskolc .... a.	0655	0726	1055	1126	1455	1655	1755	1926	2255
Füzesabony **1260/1** .... a.	0754	0802	...	1202	1554	1754	1854	2002	2354
Budapest Keleti **1260/1** .... a.	...	0927	...	1327	...	...	...	2127	...

C – CRACOVIA – from Bucureşti June 19 - Aug. 31: 🛏 1, 2 cl. and (2) Bucureşti - Lőkösháza - Szolnok - Hatvan - Miskolc - Košice - Kraków.

D – CRACOVIA – from Kraków June 18 - Aug. 30: 🛏 1, 2 cl. and (2) Kraków - Košice - Miskolc - Szolnok - Lőkösháza - Bucureşti.

H – HERNÁD/HORNÁD.

R – RÁKÓCZI.

Other local trains run Miskolc - Hidasnémeti.

1270 BUDAPEST - DEBRECEN - NYÍREGYHÁZA - ZÁHONY - CHOP

For trains to/from Romania see Table **1275**

km		IC 569 R✕ ◇	IC 650 R✕ ◇	IC 622 R✕ ⚒	IC 567 R✕ ◇	IC 612 R✕ ⚒	IC 652 R✕ ◇	IC 604 R✕ ⚒	IC 565 R✕ ◇	IC 614 R✕ ⑧	IC 654 R✕ ◇	IC 624 R✕	IC 563 R✕ ◇	IC 626 R✕ ⑧	IC 616 R✕	16 T	IC 608 R✕ ⑧
0	**Budapest** Nyugati ◧ d.	...	0623	0723	0823	0923	1023	1123	1223	1323	1423	1523	1623	1723	1823	1843k	1923
11	Kőbánya Kispest ◧ d.	...	0637	0737	0837	0937	1037	1137	1237	1337	1437	1537	1637	1737	1837	|	1937
18	Ferihegy ✈ ◧ d.	...	0643	0743	0843	0943	1043	1143	1243	1343	1443	1543	1643	1743	1843	|	1943
73	Cegléd ◧ d.	...	0719	0819	0919	1019	1119	1219	1319	1419	1519	1619	1719	1819	1919	|	2019
100	**Szolnok** ◧ d.	...	0739	0839	0939	1039	1139	1239	1339	1439	1539	1639	1739	1839	1939	2003	2039
177	Püspökladány d.	...	|	|	|	|	|	|	|	|	|	|	|	|	|	2056	|
201	Hajdúszoboszló d.	...	0839	0939	1039	1139	1239	1339	1439	1539	1639	1739	1839	1939	2039	2113	2139
221	**Debrecen** a.	...	0852	0952	1052	1152	1252	1352	1452	1552	1652	1752	1852	1952	2052	2126	2152
221	**Debrecen** d.	0654	0854	0954	1054	1154	1254	1354	1454	1554	1654	1757	1854	1954	2054	2129	2154
270	**Nyíregyháza** a.	0724	0924	1024	1124	1224	1324	1424	1524	1624	1724	1827	1924	2024	2124	2202	2224
270	**Nyíregyháza** d.	*0737*	...	1029	▬	...	...	...	...	...	...	1829	...	2026	...	2205	▬
313	Kisvárda d.	*0821*	...	1107	2	...	...	...	...	...	...	1900	...	2053	...	2237	2
335	Záhony ▦ ▶ a.	*0848*	...	1129	1159	...	...	...	...	...	...	1918	...	2111	...	2256	0452
341	**Chop** ▦ ⊙ ▶ a.	...	...	...	1316	...	...	...	...	...	...	...	...	...	...	0113	0609

SLOWER TRAINS — Debrecen - Záhony runs approx hourly *(connections available from IC at Nyíregyháza).*

Budapest Nyugati d.	...	0503	0628	E	1628	1828	2028	2228
Kőbánya Kispest d.	...	0517	0642	V	1642	1842	2042	2242
Ferihegy d.	...	0526	0648	E	1648	1848	2048	2248
Cegléd d.	...	0624	0724	R	1724	1924	2124	2324
Szolnok d.	...	0650	0750	Y	1750	1950	2150	2346
Püspökladány d.	0654	0754	0854		1854	2059	2254	0048
Hajdúszoboszló d.	0713	0813	0913	2	1913	2118	2313	▬
Debrecen a.	0728	0828	0928		1928	2133	2328	...
Debrecen d.	0737	0837	0937	H	1937	2137r	...	...
Nyíregyháza a.	0819	0919	1019	O	2019	2219r	...	2
Nyíregyháza d.	0837	0937	1037	U	2037	...	...	2252
Kisvárda d.	0921	1021	1121	R	2121	...	...	2336
Záhony a.	0948	1048	1148	S	2148	...	...	0003
Chop a.	...	...	...		...	...	...	...

	IC 609 R✕ ⚒	IC 627 R✕	IC 560 R✕ ⚒◇	15 T	IC 659 R✕ ◇	IC 607 R✕ ⚒	IC 657 R✕ ◇	IC 605 R✕	IC 564 R✕ ◇	IC 615 R✕ ⑧	IC 655 R✕ ◇	IC 623 R✕ ⑧	IC 566 R✕ ◇	IC 621 R✕ ⑧	IC 621 R✕ ⑦	IC 653 R✕ ◇	IC 568 R✕ ◇
Chop ▦ ⊙ ▶ d.	...	...	...	0500	...	...	...	...	...	...	...	*1435*	...	...	...	...	...
Záhony ▦ ▶ d.	...	0540	...	0652	...	...	...	...	...	...	...	1431	...	...	1631	...	...
Kisvárda d.	...	0559	...	0713	...	...	...	...	...	...	...	1450	...	...	1650	...	...
Nyíregyháza a.	...	0626	...	0747	...	...	...	...	...	...	...	1519	...	...	1719	...	...
Nyíregyháza d.	0536	0628	0736	0750	0836	0936	1036	1136	1236	1336	1436	1536	1636	1736	1736	1836	2036
Debrecen a.	0606	0658	0806	0825	0906	1006	1106	1206	1306	1406	1506	1606	1706	1806	1806	1906	2106
Debrecen d.	0608	0708	0808	0827	0908	1008	1108	1208	1308	1408	1508	1608	1708	1808	1808	1908	...
Hajdúszoboszló d.	0622	0722	0822	0841	0922	1022	1122	1222	1322	1422	1522	1622	1722	1822	1822	1922	...
Püspökladány d.	|	|	|	0858	|	|	|	|	|	|	|	|	|	|	|	|	...
Szolnok ◧ d.	0722	0822	0922	0957	1022	1122	1222	1322	1422	1522	1622	1722	1822	1922	1922	2022	...
Cegléd ◧ d.	0743	0843	0943	|	1043	1143	1243	1343	1443	1543	1643	1743	1843	1943	1943	2043	...
Ferihegy ✈ ◧ d.	0817	0917	1017	|	1117	1217	1317	1417	1517	1617	1717	1817	1917	2017	2017	2117	...
Kőbánya Kispest ◧ a.	0822	0922	1022	|	1122	1222	1322	1422	1522	1622	1722	1822	1922	2022	2022	2122	...
Budapest Nyugati ◧ a.	0837	0937	1037	1117k	1137	1237	1337	1437	1537	1637	1737	1837	1937	2037	2037	2137	...

SLOWER TRAINS — Záhony - Debrecen runs approx hourly *(connections available into IC at Nyíregyháza).*

Chop d.	0709	...	...	...		...	...	...
Záhony d.	0626	...	0602	0812	E	1612	1712	2012
Kisvárda d.	▬	...	0630	0840	V	1640	1740	2040
Nyíregyháza a.	...	...	0713	0923	E	1723	1823	2123
Nyíregyháza d.	...	0541	0741	0941	R	1741	1841	2141
Debrecen a.	...	0623	0823	1023	Y	1823	1923	2223
Debrecen d.	0422	0632	0832	1032		1832	1932	▬
Hajdúszoboszló d.	0439	0648	0848	1048	2	1848	1948	...
Püspökladány d.	0458	0708	0908	1108		1908	2008	2
Szolnok d.	0603	0815	1015	1215	H	2015	2124	2224
Cegléd d.	0628	0838	1038	1238	O	2038	2148	2248
Ferihegy d.	0717	0912	1112	1312	U	2112	2244	2344
Kőbánya Kispest a.	0722	0917	1117	1317	R	2117	2252	2352
Budapest Nyugati a.	0737	0932	1132	1332	S	2132	2307	0007

T – TISZA/TISSA – 🛏 2 cl. Budapest - Kyïv/Lviv/Moskva and v.v. 🛏 2 cl. Beograd - B'pest - Kyïv/Moskva and v.v.; [2] Záhony - Chop and v.v. See Table **97**.
k – Budapest **Keleti**.

r – June 20 - Aug. 23: Debrecen *2157*, N'háza *2239*.
◧ – Also **1290** Budapest - Cegléd; **1280** B'pest - Szolnok.
⊙ – Ukrainian (East European) time, one hour ahead.
◇ – To/from Miskolc (Table **1260**).

▶ – Other connections Záhony - Chop :

Záhony . d.	0806	1520	2000	Chop . ⊙ d.	1015	1735	2230
Chop ⊙ a.	0923	1637	2117	Záhony .. a.	0932	1652	2147

1275 BUDAPEST - BIHARKERESZTES - ORADEA

km		IC* 411 ⊖	IC* 409 H⊖	2	IC* 413 ⊖	2	IC* 365 A⊖	2	2	407 C⊖
0	**Budapest Keleti** ▷ d.	0543	0843	...	1143	...	1343	...	...	1743
100	Szolnok ▷ d.	0705	1005	...	1305	...	1505	...	...	1905
177	Püspökladány ▷ d.	0810	1110	1310	1410	1510	1610	1710	1810	2010
228	Biharkeresztes a.	0856	1156	1415	1456	1615	1656	1800	1903	2052
228	Biharkeresztes ▦ d.	0913	1213	...	1513	...	1713	...	...	2108
241	Episcopia Bihor ▦ ⊙ a.	1028	1328	...	1630	...	1828	...	...	2223
241	Episcopia Bihor ⊙ d.	1043	1348	...	1645	...	1843	...	...	2248
247	**Oradea** ⊙ a.	1051	1356	...	1653	...	1851	...	...	2256
	Cluj Napoca **1630** ⊙ a.	...	1640	...	...	...	2133	...	...	0138

	406 C⊖	2	IC* 364 A⊖	2	IC* 408 H⊖	2	IC* 412 ⊖	IC* 414 ⊖	2
Cluj Napoca **1630** ⊙ d.	0225	...	0623	...	1029	...	...	...	...
Oradea ⊙ d.	0503	...	0906	...	1310	...	1507	1807	...
Episcopia Bihor ⊙ a.	0513	...	0914	...	1318	...	1515	1815	...
Episcopia Bihor ▦ ⊙ d.	0533	...	0933	...	1333	...	1530	1830	...
Biharkeresztes ▦ a.	0448	...	0848	...	1248	...	1448	1748	...
Biharkeresztes d.	0504	0607	0904	1056	1304	1356	1504	1804	1905
Püspökladány ▷ a.	0550	0654	0950	1147	1350	1447	1550	1850	1952
Szolnok ▷ a.	0654	...	1054	...	1454	...	1654	1954	...
Budapest Keleti ▷ a.	0817	...	1217	...	1617	...	1817	2117	...

A – ADY ENDRE – [12] Budapest - Cluj Napoca and v.v.
C – CORONA – 🛏 1, 2 cl., ▬ 1, 2 cl. and [12] Budapest - Cluj Napoca - Deda - Braşov and v.v.; ▬ 2 cl. and [2] Budapest - Deda - Târgu Mureş and v.v.

H – HARGITA – [12] Budapest - Braşov and v.v.
⊙ – Romanian (East European) time.
⊖ – R for international journeys.

▷ – For connections Budapest **Nyugati** - Püspökladány see Table **1270**.
* – Classified *IC* only in Hungary.

1276 DEBRECEN and NYÍREGYHÁZA - MÁTÉSZALKA

2nd class

km									△			⑧
0	**Debrecen** d.	0510	0715	0915	1115	1315	1515	1715	1807	1920	2120	2245
58	Nyírbátor d.	0631	0836	1036	1236	1436	1636	1836	1910	2041	2241	0005
78	**Mátészalka** a.	0655	0900	1100	1300	1500	1700	1900	1928	2105	2306	0031

			▽								
Mátészalka d.	0410	0455	0530	0703	0903	1103	1303	1503	1703	1903	2109
Nyírbátor d.	0434	0519	0550	0727	0927	1127	1327	1527	1727	1933	2133
Debrecen a.	0556	0639	0652	0847	1045	1245	1445	1645	1850	2050	2250

km		⚒								⑧	⑧	
0	**Nyíregyháza** d.	0534	0829	1029	1229	1429	1629	1829	2042	2242	...	...
38	Nyírbátor d.	0703	1000	1200	1400	1553	1753	1953	2159	2358	0005	...
58	**Mátészalka** a.	0730	1022	1222	1423	1623	1816	2015	2228	...	0031	...

		▽						⑦	⚒		⑧
Mátészalka d.	0440	0530	...	0734	0935	1135	1334	1528	1535	1722	1950
Nyírbátor d.	0504	0549	0554	0759	0959	1159	1359	1559	1559	1759	2016
Nyíregyháza a.	0620	...	0710	0916	1116	1316	1516	1716	1716	1916	2132

△ – *IC* **624/638** from Budapest Nyugati, depart 1523, R.
▽ – *IC* **639/627** to Budapest Nyugati, arrive 0942, R.

Local trains Mátészalka - Tiborszállás ▦ - Carei : from Mátészalka 0535, 1235 (arrive 0751, 1446 Romanian time); from Carei 0924, 1639 (arrive Mátészalka 0950, 1652 Hungarian time).

1277 DEBRECEN - FÜZESABONY

2nd class

km										⑧	
0	**Debrecen** d.	0528	0726	0926	1126	1326	1526	1726	1929	2045	2240
42	Hortobágy d.	0618	0815	1015	1215	1415	1615	1815	2015	2136	2330
73	Tiszafüred d.	0659	0859	1059	1259	1459	1659	1859	2059	2211	0004
103	**Füzesabony** a.	0732	0932	1132	1332	1532	1732	1932	2132	2252	...

									⑧	
Füzesabony d.	0422	0622	0822	1022	1222	1422	1622	1822	2022	2200
Tiszafüred d.	0501	0701	0901	1101	1301	1501	1701	1901	2056	2235
Hortobágy d.	0536	0736	0936	1136	1336	1536	1736	1936	2139	...
Debrecen a.	0631	0831	1031	1231	1431	1631	1831	2028	2225	...

1278 DOMBÓVAR - BAJA - KISKUNFÉLEGYHÁZA - KECSKEMÉT

2nd class

km		7830	7840	7820	7822	7834	7824	7836	7826	7838	7828 ⑧
	Nagykanizsa **1205** d.	...	...	...	0454	...	...	...	...	1445	...
	Kaposvár **1205** d.	...	...	...	0731	0931	1131	1331	1531	1731	1922
0	**Dombóvár** d.	...	0418	0618	0818	1018	1218	1418	1618	1818	2018
60	Bátaszék **1210** d.	...	0546	0746	0946	1146	1346	1546	1746	1946	2140
80	**Baja 1210** d.	0409	0609	0809	1009	1209	1409	1609	1809	2009	...
156	Kiskunhalas a.	0520	0720	0920	1120	1320	1520	1720	1920	2120	...
156	Kiskunhalas d.	0532	0732	0932	1132	1332	1532	1732	*1932*	...	...
202	Kiskunfélegyháza **1290** a.	0614	0814	1014	1214	1414	1614	1814	*2014*	...	...
227	**Kecskemét** **1290** a.	0637	0837	1037	1237	1437	1637	1837	...	...	...

	7839	7829	7837	7827	7835	7825	7833	7823	7823 Ⓐ	7831
Kecskemét **1290** d.	...	...	0723	0923	1123	1323	1523	1723	1723	1923
Kiskunfélegyháza **1290** d.	...	...	0745	0945	1145	1345	1545	1745	1745	1945
Kiskunhalas a.	...	...	0825	1025	1225	1425	1625	1825	1825	2025
Kiskunhalas d.	0437	0637	0837	1037	1237	1437	1637	1837	1837	2037
Baja 1210 d.	0543	0743	0943	1143	1343	1543	1743	1943	1943	2142
Bátaszék **1210** a.	0608	0809	1009	1209	1409	1609	1809	2009	2009	...
Dombóvár a.	0745	0945	1145	1345	1545	1745	1945	2145	2145	...
Kaposvár **1205** a.	0840	1040	1240	1442	1640	1840	2040	...	2240	...
Nagykanizsa **1205** a.	...	...	...	...	...	...	...	...	...	...

1279 SZOMBATHELY - KOSZEG

2nd class

rom **Szombathely** : 0508 ⚒, 0605, 0708, 0805, 0908, 1005, 1108, 1205 Ⓐ, 1308, 1405 Ⓐ, 1508, 1605, 1708, 1805, 1908, 2108, 2247 ⑧.
rom **Köszeg** : 0430 ⚒, 0537, 0630, 0737, 0830, 0937, 1030, 1137 Ⓐ, 1230, 1337 Ⓐ, 1430, 1537, 1630, 1737, 1830, 2030, 2218.

18 km, journey time 25 - 30 minutes

BUDAPEST - BÉKÉSCSABA - LÖKÖSHÁZA - ARAD 1280

km			IC		IC	IC		IC	IC		IC		IC		EN		
			7400	75	1381	375	453	7302	355	355	7304	79	7306	455	7408	371	7308	347
		2		⊖		⊖	⊖		⊖	⊖		⊖		⊖		⊖		⊖
					B	P				N				u		W		D
0	**Budapest** Keleti **1270** d.	...	0613	0713	...	0913	1113	1213	1313	1313	1413	1513	1613	1713	1813	1913	2013	2313
100	Szolnok **1270** d.	...	0734	0834	0955	1034	1234	1334	1434	1434	1534	1634	1734	1834	1934	2034	2134	0037
141	Mezötúr d.	0527	0800	0900	1021	1100	1300	1400	1500	1500	1600	1700	1800	1900	2000	2100	2200	|
159	Gyoma d.	0546	0813	0913	1046	1113	1313	1413	1513	1513	1613	1713	1813	1913	2013	2113	2213	|
196	**Békéscsaba** a.	0618	0838	0938	1118	1138	1338	1438	1538	1538	1638	1738	1838	1938	2038	2138	2238	0140
196	**Békéscsaba** d.	0640	...	0943	1123	1143	1343	1443	1543	1543	1643	1743	1843	1943	...	2145	2243	0145
225	Lökösháza a.	0712	...	1010	1143	1205	1410	1507	1610	1610	1710	1810	1910	2005	...	2205	2305	0205
225	Lökösháza d.	...	...	1030	1230	1230	1430	...	1630	1630	...	1830	...	2030	...	2230	...	0230
236	Curtici ⊙ d.	...	...	1200	1357	1357	1557	...	1757	1757	...	2000	...	2157	...	2358	...	0357
253	**Arad** ⊙ a.	...	...	1217	1414	1414	1614	...	1814	1814	...	2017	...	2214	...	0015	...	0414
	Timişoara **1625** ⊙ a.	...	...	1305	|	|	|	...	|	|	...	2105	...	...	...	|	...	|
	Târgu Mureş **1630** ⊙ a.	...	...	...	|	|	|	...	2336	|	...	...	...	...	...	|	...	|
	Braşov **1620** ⊙ a.	...	...	...	2049	2049	2325	...	...	|	...	...	...	...	...	0702	...	1053
	Bucureşti Nord **1620** ⊙ a.	...	...	...	2355	2355	...	...	...	0619z	...	...	...	...	...	1028	...	1359

			EN		IC	IC	IC	IC		IC		IC			IC			
	346	7309	370	7307	78	454	354	354	7303	452	7403	374	1380	7301	74	7401		
	⊖		⊖		⊖	⊖	⊖	⊖		⊖		⊖	⊖		⊖		2	2
	D		W			v		N				P	C					
Bucureşti Nord **1620** ⊙ d.	1645	...	1950	...	...	...	...	2345z	...	...	...	0550	0550	...	...	...	...	...
Braşov **1620** ⊙ d.	1947	...	2248	...	...	...	...	|	...	0605	...	0904	0904	...	...	...	...	...
Târgu Mureş **1630** ⊙ d.	|	...	|	...	...	...	0605	|	...	|	...	|	|	...	...	...	...	...
Timişoara **1625** ⊙ d.	|	...	|	...	0700	...	|	|	...	|	...	|	|	...	1700	...	...	...
Arad ⊙ d.	0226	...	0545	...	0748	0948	1145	1145	...	1347	...	1552	1552	...	1748	...	...	...
Curtici ⊙ a.	0240	...	0559	...	0802	1002	1159	1159	...	1401	...	1606	1606	...	1802	...	...	...
Lökösháza a.	0210	...	0530	...	0730	0930	1130	1130	...	1330	...	1530	1530	...	1730	...	...	...
Lökösháza d.	0230	0458	0555	0652	0750	0950	1144	1144	1250	1350	...	1550	1610	1650	1750	1850	...	2050
Békéscsaba a.	0250	0520	0615	0716	0812	1012	1209	1209	1312	1412	...	1612	1636	1712	1812	1912	...	2112
Békéscsaba d.	0253	0525	0618	0718	0818	1018	1218	1218	1318	1418	1518	1618	1638	1718	1818	1918	2038	...
Gyoma d.	|	0559	0646	0746	0846	1046	1246	1246	1346	1446	1546	1646	1718	1746	1846	1946	2118	...
Mezötúr d.	|	0614	0659	0759	0859	1059	1259	1259	1359	1459	1559	1659	1734	1759	1859	1959	2133	...
Szolnok **1270** d.	0355	0649	0727	0827	0927	1127	1327	1327	1427	1527	1627	1727	1800	1827	1927	2027	...	...
Budapest Keleti **1270** a.	0517	0812	0847	0947	1047	1247	1447	1447	1547	1647	1747	1847	...	1947	2047	2147	...	...

BÉKÉSCSABA - GYULA

Journey 14 minutes

From **Békéscsaba**: 0525, 0601, 0642, 0744, 0844 **s**, 0944, 1044, 1144, 1244 Ⓑ, 1344, 1444, 1544, 1622 **s**, 1644, 1744, 1844 Ⓐ, 1944, 2044, 2244.

From **Gyula**: 0456, 0544, 0620 **s**, 0659, 0759, 0859, 0959, 1119 **s**, 1159, 1259, 1359, 1459 Ⓑ, 1559, 1659, 1720 **s**, 1759, 1859, 1959, 2059 Ⓐ.

NOTES (continued from below):

- **s** – To/from Szeged (Table **1292**).
- **u** – To Simeria, arrive 0018.
- **v** – From Simeria, depart 0734.
- **z** – Train **1822/1821** (in ⊏12⊐ change at Arad).
- ⊙ – Romanian (East European) time.
- ⊖ – Ⓡ for international journeys (and domestic journeys in Romania).

OTHER TRAIN NAMES:

- **74/75** – TRAIANUS
- **78/79** – KÖRÖS/CRIS
- **354/355** – MAROS/MURES
- **452/453** – TRANSILVANIA
- **454/455** – ZARÁND

B – CRACOVIA – from Kraków June 18 - Aug. 30: 1, 2 cl. and ⊏2⊐ Kraków - Košice - Miskolc - Szolnok - Lökösháza - Bucureşti.

C – CRACOVIA – from Bucureşti June 19 - Aug. 31: 1, 2 cl. and ⊏2⊐ Bucureşti - Lökösháza - Szolnok - Hatvan - Miskolc - Košice - Kraków.

D – DACIA – 1, 2 cl., 2 cl., ⊏2⊐ and ✕ Wien - Budapest - Bucureşti and v.v.; ⊏1⊐ Wien - Budapest - Lökösháza and v.v.

N – MAROS/MUREŞ – ⊏12⊐ Budapest - Arad - Târgu Mureş and v.v.; 1, 2 cl. and ⊏2⊐ Venezia (**241/0**) - Budapest - Arad - (**1822/1**) Bucureşti and v.v. (also 1, 2 cl. June 1 - Sept. 21 from Venezia, May 30 - Sept. 19 from Bucureşti).

P – PANNONIA – ⊏12⊐ and ✕ Budapest - Bucureşti and v.v.; 1, 2 cl., 1, 2 cl. München - Wien - Budapest - Bucureşti and v.v.; 1, 2 cl. Praha - Budapest - Bucureşti and v.v.

W – ISTER – 1, 2 cl., 1, 2 cl., ⊏2⊐ and ✕ Budapest - Bucureşti and v.v.; 1, 2 cl. Budapest - Bucureşti (**463/2**) - Sofija - Thessaloníki and v.v.

FOR OTHER NOTES SEE ABOVE

BUDAPEST - KECSKEMÉT - SZEGED 1290

km			IC	IC	IC		IC	IC		
			710	760	702		756	766	7008	7108
		2	Ⓡ✕	Ⓡ✕	Ⓡ✕		Ⓡ✕	Ⓡ✕		
0	**Budapest** Nyugati § d.	0403	0553	0653	0753		1753	1853	1953	2053
11	Köbánya Kispest § d.	0417	0607	0707	0807	and	1807	1907	2007	2107
18	Ferihegy ✈ § d.	0426	0613	0713	0813	hourly	1813	1913	2013	2113
73	Cegléd § d.	0530	0648	0748	0848	❖	1848	1948	2048	2203
106	**Kecskemét** d.	0604	0711	0811	0911	until	1911	2011	2111	2228
131	Kiskunfélegyháza d.	0631	0731	0831	0931		1931	2031	2131	2244
191	**Szeged** a.	0716	0816	0916	1016		2016	2116	2216	2328

		IC	IC	IC		IC	IC		
	7009	709	719	707		753	763	7001	17101
		Ⓡ✕	Ⓡ✕	Ⓡ✕		Ⓡ✕	Ⓡ✕		⑦
Szeged d.	0436	0546	0644	0744		1744	1844	1944	2044
Kiskunfélegyháza d.	0523	0631	0731	0831	and	1831	1931	2031	2131
Kecskemét d.	0539	0647	0747	0847	hourly	1847	1947	2047	2147
Cegléd § d.	0608	0713	0813	0913	❖	1913	2013	2117	2218
Ferihegy ✈ § d.	0657	0747	0847	0947	until	1947	2047	2152	2252
Köbánya Kispest § a.	0702	0752	0852	0952		1952	2052	2157	2257
Budapest Nyugati § a.	0717	0807	0907	1007		2007	2107	2212	2312

❖ – 1153 from Budapest and 1044 from Szeged run on ⑤–⑦ and holidays only.

§ – For additional trains see Table **1270**.

Note: on this line only, all *IC* trains have designated carriages for the use of passengers without seat reservations.

2nd class SZEGED - BÉKÉSCSABA 1292

km			z					z				
0	**Szeged** d.	0520	0620	0720	0920	1120	1320	1420	1520	1620	1720	1920
31	Hódmezövásárhely d.	0559	0703	0759	0959	1159	1359	1503	1559	1703	1759	1959
62	Orosháza d.	0629	0728	0829	1029	1229	1429	1528	1629	1728	1829	2029
97	**Békéscsaba** a.	0711	0807	0912	1109	1309	1509	1607	1709	1807	1909	2109

	z			z						
Békéscsaba d.	0645	0745	0945	1145	1345	1443	1545	1643	1745	1945
Orosháza d.	0730	0830	1030	1230	1430	1530	1630	1730	1830	2030
Hódmezövásárhely d.	0800	0900	1100	1300	1500	1600	1700	1800	1900	2100
Szeged a.	0833	0937	1137	1337	1537	1637	1737	1837	1937	2137

z – To/from Gyula (Table **1280**).

Additional trains: from Szeged 1820 ⑤⑦, from Békéscsaba 0545, 1845 ⑤⑦.

BUDAPEST - KISKUNHALAS - KELEBIA 1295

km							IC				
			790	1121	792	7902	345	7904	796	798	341
		2		S			A				B
0	**Budapest Keleti** d.	...	...	0705	...	...	1305	...	...	...	2300
0	Köbánya Kispest d.	...	0606	|	0806	1006	|	1406	1606	1806	|
61	Kunszentmiklós-Tass d.	0510	0709	0759	0909	1109	1359	1509	1709	1909	|
107	Kiskörös d.	0601	0801	0850	1001	1201	1450	1601	1801	2001	|
134	Kiskunhalas a.	0633	0833	0920	1033	1233	1520	1633	1833	2033	0102
163	**Kelebia** a.	0711	0911	0950	1111	1311	1550	1711	1911	2111	0130
	Beograd **1360** a.	...	...	1527	...	...	2030	...	...	...	0613

						IC				
	340	799	797	7907	795	344	7903	1120	791	7901
	B					A	T	S		
Beograd **1360** d.	2120	...	...	...	...	0730	...	1005	...	...
Kelebia d.	0220	0448	0648	0846	1046	1210	1446	1446	1646	1846
Kiskunhalas d.	0250	0524	0724	0924	1124	1241	1524	1524	1724	1924
Kiskörös d.	|	0600	0800	1000	1200	1311	1600	1600	1800	2000
Kunszentmiklós-Tass d.	|	0650	0850	1050	1250	1400	1650	1650	1850	2050
Köbánya Kispest a.	|	0750	0949	1149	1350	|	1749	|	1949	2149
Budapest Keleti a.	0504	...	...	...	...	1454	...	1749	...	...

A – AVALA – ⊏12⊐ and ✕ Praha - Budapest - Beograd and v.v. Conveys 2 cl. Moskva/Kyïv - Budapest - Beograd and v.v. (Table **97**).

B – BEOGRAD – for composition see Table **1360**.

S – IVO ANDRIC, June 11 - Sept. 23.

T – Not June 11 - Sept. 23.

Most trains 2nd class only OTHER LOCAL SERVICES 1299

BUDAPEST - DUNAÚJVÁROS *80* km, journey 85 minutes

From **Budapest** Déli: 0458, 0558, 0858, 1058, 1258, 1358, 1558, 1658, 1858, 1958, 2058, 2158.

From **Dunaújváros**: 0436, 0636, 0733, 0836, 1036, 1236, 1436, 1636, 1736, 1836, 2036, 2136, 2236.

BUDAPEST - ESZTERGOM *53 km*, journey 95 - 105 minutes

From **Budapest** Nyugati: 0610, 0721, 0820, 0852 Ⓐ, 0921 and hourly to 2321 (also on Ⓐ at 1352, 1452, 1552, 1652, 1752, 1852).

From **Esztergom**: 0333, 0413, 0457, 0532 Ⓐ, 0549 Ⓐ, 0605, 0638 Ⓐ, 0705, 0729 Ⓐ, 0809 and hourly to 2209 (also at 1233 Ⓐ).

BUDAPEST - VASÚTMÚZEUM (Railway Museum) *5 km*, journey time 8 minutes

Mar. 27 - Nov. 1, 2009 only. Trains continue to/from Esztergom.

From Budapest Nyugati: 1021, 1121, 1321. From Museum: 1030, 1330, 1630.

BUDAPEST - SZENTENDRE *21 km*, journey time 38 minutes

HÉV suburban trains from Budapest Batthyány tér, every 10 - 20 minutes (30 - 40 evenings).

EGER - SZILVÁSVÁRAD *34 km*, journey time 65 minutes

From **Eger**: 0446, 0746, 0946, 1346, 1446, 1746, 1946.

From **Szilvásvárad**: 0410, 0610, 0910, 1110, 1510, 1710, 1805 ⑦, 1910.

Via Szilvásvárad-Szalajkavölgy (for the forest railway), 6 minutes from Szilvásvárad.

HATVAN - SZOLNOK *68 km*, journey 71 - 73 minutes

From **Hatvan**: 0400, 0515 Ⓐ, 0615 and hourly (two-hourly on Ⓒ) until 2215.

From **Szolnok**: 0315, 0433, 0533 Ⓐ, 0633 and hourly (two-hourly on Ⓒ) until 2033, 2133.

KISKUNFÉLEGYHÁZA - CSONGRÁD - SZENTES *39 km*, journey time 55 minutes

From **Kiskunfélegyháza**: 0547 Ⓐ, 0632 Ⓒ, 0832, 1032, 1232, 1432, 1632, 1832, 2132.

From **Szentes**: 0610 Ⓐ, 0730 Ⓒ, 0930, 1130, 1330, 1530, 1730 (calls Csongrád 18 mins later).

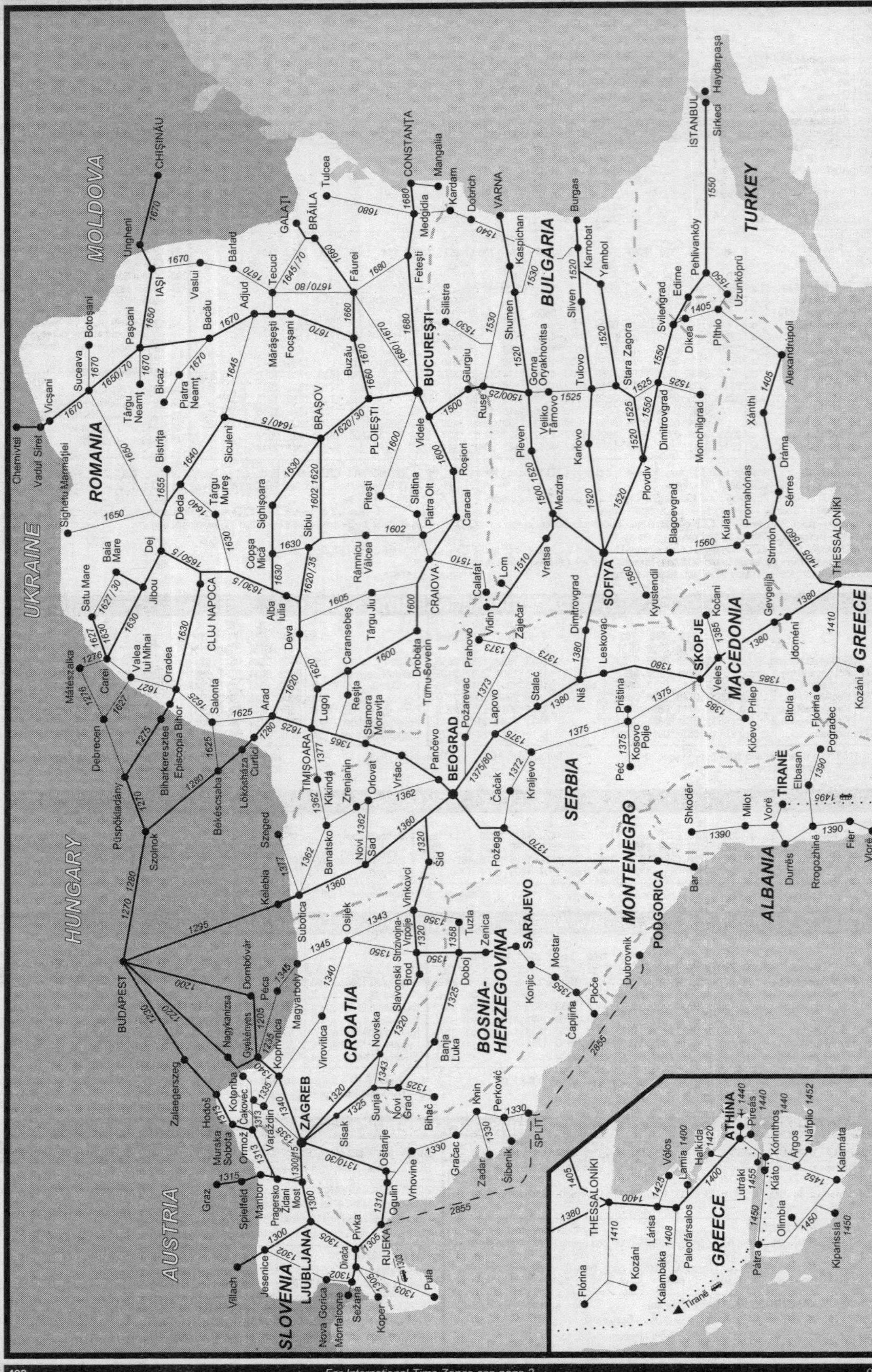
UKRAINE
MOLDOVA
ROMANIA
HUNGARY
AUSTRIA
SLOVENIA
CROATIA
BOSNIA-HERZEGOVINA
SERBIA
MONTENEGRO
ALBANIA
MACEDONIA
BULGARIA
GREECE
TURKEY
CHIŞINĂU
Ungheni
IAŞI
Paşcani
Suceava
Botoşani
Vicşani
Vadul Siret
Chernivtsi
Sighetu Marmaţiei
Satu Mare
Baia Mare
Jibou
Dej
Deda
Bistriţa
Târgu Mureş
Siculeni
Târgu Neamţ
Piatra Neamţ
Bicaz
Bacău
Vaslui
Bârlad
Adjud
Tecuci
Mărăşeşti
Focşani
GALAŢI
BRĂILA
Tulcea
Făurei
Buzău
CONSTANŢA
Mangalia
Medgidia
Feteşti
BUCUREŞTI
PLOIEŞTI
BRAŞOV
Sighişoara
Copşa Mică
Sibiu
CLUJ NAPOCA
Oradea
Valea lui Mihai
Carei
Mátészalka
Debrecen
Püspökladány
Szolnok
Biharkeresztes
Episcopia Bihor
Salonta
Békéscsaba
Lökösháza
Curtici
Arad
Alba Iulia
Deva
Râmnicu Vâlcea
Piteşti
Slatina
Piatra Olt
Caracal
Roşiori
Videle
Giurgiu
CRAIOVA
Calafat
Târgu Jiu
Drobeta Turnu Severin
Caransebeş
Lugoj
Reşiţa
Stamora Moraviţa
TIMIŞOARA
Kikinda
Zrenjanin
Orlovat
Vršac
Pančevo
BEOGRAD
Požarevac
Lapovo
Stalać
Niš
Leskovac
Prahovo
Zaječar
Dimitrovgrad
Kraljevo
Čačak
Požega
Priština
Kosovo Polje
Peć
Banatsko
Novi Sad
Subotica
Szeged
Kelebia
BUDAPEST
Dombóvár
Pécs
Magyarbóly
Nagykanizsa
Gyékényes
Zalaegerszeg
Hodoš
Kotoriba
Čakovec
Koprivnica
Murska Sobota
Ormož
Varaždin
ZAGREB
Graz
Spielfeld
Maribor
Pragersko
Zidani Most
LJUBLJANA
Jesenice
Villach
Nova Gorica
Monfalcone
Sežana
Divača
Pivka
Koper
RIJEKA
Pula
Ogulin
Oštarije
Vrhovine
Gračac
Zadar
Knin
Perković
Šibenik
SPLIT
Bihać
Novi Grad
Sunja
Sisak
Novska
Virovitica
Osijek
Vinkovci
Šid
Slavonski Brod
Strizivojna-Vrpolje
Banja Luka
Doboj
Tuzla
Zenica
SARAJEVO
Konjic
Mostar
Čapljina
Ploče
Dubrovnik
PODGORICA
Bar
Shkodër
Milot
Vorë
TIRANË
Durrës
Elbasan
Pogradec
Rrogozhinë
Fier
Vlorë
SKOPJE
Veles
Kičevo
Prilep
Bitola
Kočani
Gevgelija
Idoméni
Flórina
Kozáni
THESSALONÍKI
Strimón
Kulata
Promahónas
Sérres
Dráma
Xánthi
Alexandroúpoli
Píthio
Dikea
Svilengrad
Edirne
Pehlivanköy
Uzunköprü
İSTANBUL
Sirkeci
Haydarpaşa
SOFIYA
Kyustendil
Blagoevgrad
Vratsa
Mezdra
Lom
Vidin
Pleven
Ruse
Veliko Tarnovo
Gorna Oryakhovitsa
Shumen
Kaspichan
VARNA
Dobrich
Kardam
Silistra
Karlovo
Plovdiv
Dimitrovgrad
Momchilgrad
Stara Zagora
Tulovo
Sliven
Karnobat
Yambol
Burgas
THESSALONÍKI
Flórina
Kozáni
Lárisa
Kalambáka
Paleofársalos
Vólos
Lamía
Halkída
ATHÍNA
Pireás
Kórinthos
Lutráki
Kiáto
Pátra
Árgos
Náfplio
Olimbía
Kiparissía
Kalamáta
Tiranë

SLOVENIA, CROATIA and BOSNIA-HERZEGOVINA

Operators: Slovenske Železnice (SŽ); Hrvatske Željeznice (HŽ); Železnice Federacije Bosne i Hercegovine (ŽFBH) and Železnice Republike Srpske (ŽRS).

Services: All trains convey first and second class seating, **except** where shown otherwise in footnotes or by '2' in the train column, or where the footnote shows sleeping and / or couchette cars only. Descriptions of sleeping (🛏) and couchette (▬) cars appear on page 10. Travel on *ICS* trains in Slovenia requires compulsory reservation and payment of a special fare; second class, second plus and first class plus accommodation is conveyed.

Timings: Timings valid until **December 12, 2009** except where indicated otherwise. Readers should note, however, that some local trains are subject to alteration.

Tickets: A supplement is payable for travel by internal express trains. Reservation of seats is possible on most express trains.

SŽ, HŽ, ÖBB — VILLACH - JESENICE - LJUBLJANA - ZAGREB — 1300

km		EN 241 [R] ♦	2 Ⓐ	2	499 ♦	2	2		2 Ⓐ	2 Ⓐ	415 ♦	2 Ⓐ	2	2 Ⓐ	2	2 Ⓐ	2 Ⓐ	IC 313	2	2 Ⓐ	2 Ⓐ	EC 211 🍴 ♦	2 Ⓐ	631 2 Ⓑ	2	2	2 Ⓐ
	München Hbf **890** d.	...	...	...	2340	...	...	...	...	...	...	...	...	...	...	...	...	...	...	...	...	0826	...	...	...	...	...
	Salzburg Hbf **970** d.	...	...	...	0134	...	...	...	...	...	...	...	...	...	...	...	...	...	...	...	...	1012	...	...	...	...	...
0	**Villach** Hbf d.	...	...	...	0407	...	...	...	...	...	0626	...	...	...	...	...	...	1052	...	...	...	1254	...	...	...	...	...
38	**Jesenice** 🏛 a.	...	...	...	0444	...	...	...	...	...	0706	...	...	...	...	...	...	1130	...	...	...	1330	...	...	...	...	...
38	**Jesenice 1302** d.	...	...	...	0508	0532	...	...	0602	0623	0713	...	0751	...	...	...	1110	1135	...	...	1235	1336	...	...	1417	...	1526
51	Lesce-Bled d.	...	...	...	0521	0548	...	...	0617	0638	0727	...	0809	...	...	...	1124	1148	...	...	1249	1349	...	...	1433	...	1541
74	Kranj d.	...	...	...	0543	0612	...	...	0645	0706	0748	...	0835	...	...	...	1150	1211	...	...	1322	1409	...	...	1458	...	1612
102	**Ljubljana** a.	...	...	...	0605	0645	...	...	0722	0739	0810	...	0906	...	...	...	1220	1232	...	...	1353	1430	...	...	1530	...	1643
102	**Ljubljana 1315** d.	0200	0450	0550	0615	...	0655	...	...	...	0815	0845	...	0950	*1050*	1150	...	...	*1250*	1350	...	1435	1455	1530	...	1545	...
166	Zidani Most **1315** d.	0254	0555	0655	0712	...	0802	...	...	...	0909	0955	...	1055	1155	1255	...	...	1402	1455	...	1531	1600	1632	...	1655	...
182	Sevnica **1315** d.	0310	0615	0715	0728	...	0821	...	...	...	0925	1013	...	1113	1215	1314	...	...	1420	1514	...	1547	1619	1648	...	1714	...
215	Dobova **1315** 🏛 d.	0349	0642	0742	0805	...	0849	...	...	...	1005	1042	...	1142	1242	1342	...	...	1447	1542	...	1628	1647	1717	...	1742	...
245	**Zagreb 1315** a.	0418	...	...	0834	...	...	...	...	...	1034	...	...	...	...	...	...	...	...	...	...	1657	...	...	...	...	...
	Beograd **1320** a.	...	...	...	...	...	...	...	...	...	1718	...	...	...	...	...	...	...	...	...	...	2321	...	...	...	...	...

	IC 311	2 Ⓑ	2 Ⓐ	EC 213 ♦	2	2	2	315 ♦	2 N	
München Hbf **890** d.	...	...	...	1221	...	...	...	...	...	...
Salzburg Hbf **970** d.	...	...	...	1412	...	...	...	...	...	...
Villach Hbf d.	1452	...	...	1654	...	...	...	1927	...	...
Jesenice 🏛 a.	1530	...	...	1730	...	...	...	2005	...	...
Jesenice 1302 d.	1536	...	...	1735	...	1800	1908	2010	2020	...
Lesce-Bled d.	1549	...	...	1749	...	1816	1922	2023	2035	...
Kranj d.	1609	...	...	1808	...	1843	1949	2044	2100	...
Ljubljana a.	1629	...	...	1830	...	1914	2019	2108	2131	...
Ljubljana 1315 d.	1635	1655	1750	1835	1855	...	...	2115	...	...
Zidani Most **1315** d.	1731	1800	1855	1928	2000	...	...	2209	...	...
Sevnica **1315** d.	1746	1819	1914	1944	2019	...	...	2225	...	...
Dobova **1315** 🏛 d.	1827	1847	1942	2026	2047	...	...	2305	...	...
Zagreb 1315 a.	1856	...	...	2055	...	...	...	2334	...	...
Beograd **1320** a.	...	...	...	...	...	...	...	0621	...	...

	2 Ⓐ	2	2 Ⓐ	2	630 2 ①–⑥	2 Ⓒ N	632 2 Ⓐ	314 ♦	2	2 Ⓐ	2	EC 212 ♦	2
Beograd **1320** d.	...	...	...	...	...	...	...	2150	...	...	...	...	...
Zagreb 1315 d.	...	...	...	...	...	...	...	0500	...	...	...	0700	...
Dobova **1315** 🏛 d.	...	...	...	...	0452	...	0540	0545	0600	...	0705	0746	...
Sevnica **1315** d.	...	0413	...	0505	0526	...	0606	0611	0632	...	0735	0810	...
Zidani Most **1315** d.	...	0432	...	0524	0547	...	0621	0626	0700	...	0753	0825	...
Ljubljana 1315 a.	...	0535	...	0630	0646	...	0714	0722	0803	...	0857	0919	...
Ljubljana d.	0448	...	0610	...	...	0650	...	0726	...	0818	...	0927	0945
Kranj d.	0520	...	0645	...	...	0721	...	0748	...	0852	...	0949	1016
Lesce-Bled d.	0548	...	0707	...	...	0752	...	0809	...	0916	...	1010	1041
Jesenice 1302 a.	0601	...	0722	...	...	0809	...	0822	...	0930	...	1023	1055
Jesenice 🏛 d.	...	...	...	...	...	...	...	0829	...	...	...	1029	...
Villach Hbf a.	...	...	...	...	...	...	...	0906	...	...	...	1104	...
Salzburg Hbf **970** a.	...	...	...	...	...	...	...	...	...	...	...	1348	...
München Hbf **890** a.	...	...	...	...	...	...	...	...	...	...	...	1535	...

	IC 310	2 Ⓐ	2	2	2 Ⓐ	2 Ⓐ	2	2	EC 210 🍴 ♦	2	2 Ⓐ	2 Ⓐ	IC 312	2 Ⓐ	2	2	2	2 Ⓑ	2 Ⓐ	2	2 Ⓐ	414 ♦	2 Ⓑ	2 Ⓐ	498 ♦	2 Ⓑ	EN 240 [R] ♦
Beograd **1320** d.	...	...	...	...	...	...	...	...	0550	...	...	...	...	...	...	...	...	...	...	...	...	1035	...	...	...	...	...
Zagreb 1315 d.	0900	...	...	...	...	...	...	...	1300	...	...	...	...	...	...	...	...	...	...	...	...	1814	...	...	2110	...	2335
Dobova **1315** 🏛 d.	0946	1005	...	1105	...	1211	...	1305	1345	...	1405	...	...	...	1511	...	1611	...	1705	1805	...	1908	1911	2005	2154	2211	0040
Sevnica **1315** d.	1010	1035	...	1135	...	1240	...	1334	1408	...	1434	...	...	...	1540	...	1640	...	1734	1834	...	1930	1940	2034	2219	2239	0104
Zidani Most **1315** d.	1027	1053	...	1155	...	1300	...	1400	1423	...	1500	...	...	...	1600	...	1700	...	1800	1855	...	1945	2000	2100	2234	2300	0119
Ljubljana 1315 a.	1120	1157	...	1303	...	1403	...	1503	1518	...	1603	...	...	...	1703	...	1803	...	1903	1958	...	2040	2103	2203	2327	0003	0212
Ljubljana d.	1128	...	1250	...	1333	...	1441	...	1525	1533	...	1623	1652	1712	...	1750	...	1856	...	...	2025	2048	...	...	2350	...	...
Kranj d.	1150	...	1322	...	1409	...	1515	...	1548	1612	...	1658	1714	1746	...	1823	...	1929	...	...	2100	2116	...	...	0012	...	...
Lesce-Bled d.	1211	...	1349	...	1433	...	1549	...	1611	1636	...	1721	1735	1816	...	1846	...	1953	...	...	2124	2137	...	...	0033	...	...
Jesenice 1302 a.	1224	...	1403	...	1447	...	1602	...	1624	1651	...	1734	1753	1828	...	1859	...	2007	...	...	2137	2149	...	...	0044	...	...
Jesenice 🏛 d.	1229	...	...	...	...	...	...	...	1629	...	...	...	1757	...	...	...	...	...	...	...	...	2156	...	...	0054	...	...
Villach Hbf a.	1306	...	...	...	...	...	...	...	1704	...	...	...	1832	...	...	...	...	...	...	...	...	2232	...	...	0130	...	...
Salzburg Hbf **970** a.	...	...	...	...	...	...	...	...	1948	...	...	...	...	...	...	...	...	...	...	...	...	...	...	...	0409	...	...
München Hbf **890** a.	...	...	...	...	...	...	...	...	2135	...	...	...	...	...	...	...	...	...	...	...	...	...	...	...	0615	...	...

♦ – **NOTES** (LISTED BY TRAIN NUMBER)

210/1 – SAVA – [12] Beograd - Villach (**110/1**) - München and v.v.; 🍴 Beograd - Jesenice and v.v.

212/3 – MIMARA – [12] Zagreb - Villach (**112/3**) - Frankfurt and v.v.

240/1 – VENEZIA – For days of running and composition – see Table **1305**.

314/5 – 🛏 1, 2 cl., ▬ 2 cl. and [12] Beograd - Zagreb - Ljubljana - Villach and v.v.

414/5 – For days of running and composition – see Table **1320**.

498 – LISINSKI – 🛏 1, 2 cl., ▬ 2 cl. and [2] Zagreb - Salzburg (**462/3**) - München; [2] Beograd (**418**) - Vinkovci (**748**) - Zagreb - München; 🛏 1, 2 cl. Zagreb - Salzburg (**206**) - Praha. Conveys Mar. 27 - Sept. 18 (from Rijeka): ▬ 2 cl. (also 🛏 1, 2 cl. from Apr. 29) Rijeka (**480**) - Ljubljana - Salzburg - München.

499 – LISINSKI – 🛏 1, 2 cl., ▬ 2 cl. and [2] München (**463**) - Salzburg - Zagreb; [2] München - Zagreb (**741**) - Vinkovci (**419**) - Beograd; 🛏 1, 2 cl. Praha (**207**) - Salzburg - Zagreb. Conveys Mar. 28 - Sept. 19 (from München): ▬ 2 cl. (also 🛏 1, 2 cl. from Apr. 30) München - Salzburg - Ljubljana (**481**) - Rijeka.

N – Conveys on Ⓒ: [2] Nova Gorica - Jesenice - Ljubljana and v.v.

SŽ 2nd class only — JESENICE - NOVA GORICA - SEŽANA — 1302

km		Ⓐ	m	j	Ⓐ	N		Ⓐ	Ⓐ		Ⓑ		Ⓑ W
0	**Jesenice 1300** d.	...	0407	0407	0612	0818	1115	...	1435	1653	...	1901	2152
10	Bled Jezero d.	...	0423	0423	0628	0834	1130	...	1451	1708	...	1917	2204
28	Bohinjska Bistrica d.	...	0444	0444	0655	0902	1151	...	1513	1729	...	1939	2226
56	Most na Soči d.	...	0521	0521	0731	0939	1228	...	1605	1804	...	2014	2300
89	Nova Gorica a.	...	0608	0608	0816	1022	1309	...	1645	1843	...	2054	2335
89	Nova Gorica d.	0455	0612	...	0913	...	1410a	1530	...	...	1845	...	...
130	**Sežana 1305** a.	0557	0715	...	1013	...	1510a	1630	...	...	1944	...	...

	Ⓐ		Ⓐ			Ⓐ		Ⓐ	Ⓒ N	Ⓑ	h	Ⓑ
Sežana 1305 d.	...	...	0517	0638a	1018a	...	1430a	1632	...	...	2000	2045
Nova Gorica a.	...	...	0610	0730a	1110a	...	1522a	1724	...	...	2051	2137
Nova Gorica d.	0317	0528	...	0735	1115	1414	1524	...	1806	1933	2100	...
Most na Soči d.	0357	0609	...	0817	1158	1456	1603	...	1852	2016	2141	...
Bohinjska Bistrica d.	0446	0652	...	0900	1248	1540	1643	...	1939	2058	2225	...
Bled Jezero d.	0507	0713	...	0922	1310	1600	1711	...	1959	2119	2247	...
Jesenice 1300 a.	0524	0729	...	0939	1327	1616	1727	...	2014	2135	2303	...

N – Conveys on Ⓒ: [2] Ljubljana - Jesenice - Nova Gorica and v.v.
W – Runs 23–28 minutes later on Ⓐ.

a – Ⓐ only.
h – Ⓒ June 14 - Aug. 30.

j – ⑥ Apr. 4 - June 13, Sept. 5 - Dec. 12.
m – Ⓐ (also Ⓒ June 14 - Aug. 30).

HŽ, SŽ 2nd class only — DIVAČA - PULA — 1303

km			Ⓐ		1472 A		Ⓐ	Ⓐ	Ⓐ k		
	Ljubljana **1305** d.	...	...	...	0633	...	...	...	...	...	...
0	**Divača 1305** d.	...	...	...	0805	...	...	...	1505	...	...
12	Hrpelje-Kozina d.	...	...	...	0831	...	...	...	1519	...	...
48	Buzet 🏛 d.	...	0530j	0716	0922	1120	1310	...	1554	1600	1955r
61	Lupoglav ▲ d.	0455	0547	0734	0938	1138	1327	1507	...	1617	2012
135	**Pula** a.	0622	0728	0909	1051	1308	1458	1647	...	1752	2140

		Ⓐ		Ⓐ		Ⓐ k		Ⓐ	Ⓐ	r	1473 A	
Pula d.	0505	0655	0923	...	1318	...	1425	1530	1720	...	1810	1930
Lupoglav ▲ a.	0642	0830	1055	1240	1459t	...	1601	1710	1853	1855	1923	2106
Buzet 🏛 d.	0704	...	1113	1258	1528	1605	...	...	...	1913	1958	2128j
Hrpelje-Kozina d.	...	...	...	...	...	1644	...	...	...	...	2100	...
Divača 1305 a.	...	...	...	...	...	1658	...	...	...	...	2111	...
Ljubljana **1305** a.	...	...	...	...	...	...	...	...	...	...	2241	...

A – ISTRA – Apr. 25 - May 3, June 25 - Aug. 30: [2] Maribor (**1604/5**) - Hrpelje-Kozina - Pula and v.v.

j – Ⓐ Jan. 12 - June 12, Aug. 31 - Dec. 12.
k – Not Apr. 13, 27, May 1, June 25.
r – ⑦ Jan. 4 - June 7, Aug. 30 - Dec. 6 (also Apr. 13; not Apr. 12, 26, May 3, Nov. 1).
t – Depart 1510.

▲ – 🚌 service **Lupoglav - Rijeka and v.v.**: Journey 40 minutes.
From Lupoglav: 0645, 1100, 1610, 2110.
From Rijeka: 0600, 1015, 1425Ⓐ, 1520Ⓒ, 1920.

1305 LJUBLJANA (- RIJEKA, KOPER) - SEŽANA - MONFALCONE

SŽ, HŽ

km		*EN* 240	1459					481	1605	*ICS* 1011			*IC* 503							483		652			*IC* 509				
		♦⊖	♦[R]	2Ⓐ	2Ⓐp	2	2	♦	♦	♦[R]	2Ⓐ	2Ⓐ	♦	2	2Ⓐ	2Ⓐ	2	2Ⓐ	2Ⓐ	♦	2	Ⓑ	2Ⓐ	2Ⓑ		2	2Ⓐ	2m	2Ⓐ
	Maribor **1315** d.	...	0148	...	...	...	...	...	0350	0540	...	...	0650	...	...	...	...	...	...	...	...	...	...	...	...	...	...	...	...
0	**Ljubljana** d.	0230	0409	0430	...	0553	...	0620	0633	0740	0808	...	0932	...	1042	1210	1320	...	1433	1453	1540	1609	1653	...	1810	1850	1940	2040	2225
67	Postojna d.	0326	0504	0535	...	0658	...	0718	0730	0830	0914	0921	1028	...	1149	1316	1426	1454	1539	1554	1646	1707	1759	...	1911	1956	2047	2145	2331
80	Pivka d.	0338	0516	0548	...	0712	...	0731	0742	0841	0927	0934	1041	...	1202	1330	1439	1507	1552	1608	1659	1719	1812	1820	1923	2009	2100	2158	2342
	Ilirska Bistrica 🏛 d.	|	|	|	...	|	...	0758	|	|	|	0950	|	...	|	|	|	1523	|	1632	|	|	|	1845	|	|	|	|	...
	Šapjane 🏛 d.	|	|	|	...	|	...	0822	|	|	|	...	|	...	|	|	|	...	|	1656	|	|	|	1857	|	|	|	|	...
	Rijeka 1310 a.	|	|	|	...	|	...	0851	|	|	|	...	|	...	|	|	|	...	|	1725	|	|	|	*1945*	|	|	|	|	...
104	Divača **1303** d.	0401	0540	0613	0615	0736	0747	...	0804	0903	0951	...	1103	1108	1226	1355	1503	...	1616	...	1722	1741	1836	...	1947	2033	2125	2222	...
116	Hrpelje-Kozina ⊡ d.	|	0557	|	0630	|	0800	...	0822	0914	|	...	1116	|	|	|	|	...	|	...	1736	|	|	...	1959	|	|	|	...
153	**Koper** ⊡ a.	|	0632	|	0705	|	0836	...	0856	0945	|	...	1152	|	|	|	|	...	|	...	1810	|	|	...	2032	|	|	|	...
113	**Sežana** ▲ 🏛 a.	0410	...	0623	...	0746	...	...	...	...	1001	...	...	1118	1236	1404	1513	...	1626	...	...	1750	1847	...	...	2043	2135	2232	...
117	Villa Opicina ⊗ 🏛 a.	0428	...	...	...	...	...	...	...	...	...	...	...	...	...	...	...	...	...	...	...	...	...	...	...	...	...	...	...
150	**Monfalcone 605/6** a.	0542	...	...	...	...	...	...	...	...	...	...	...	...	...	...	...	...	...	...	...	...	...	...	...	...	...	...	...
	Venezia SL **605** a.	0716	...	...	...	...	...	...	...	...	...	...	...	...	...	...	...	...	...	...	...	...	...	...	...	...	...	...	...

km					*IC* 508						482					*IC* 502		*ICS* 1024		653					1604	480		1458	*EN* 241
		2Ⓐ	2m	2		2Ⓐ	2Ⓐ	2Ⓐ	2	2Ⓐ	♦	2Ⓐp	2Ⓐ	2Ⓐ	2	♦	2Ⓐ	♦[R]	2	2Ⓑ	2Ⓑ	2	2Ⓑ	2	♦	♦		♦[R]	♦⊖
	Venezia SL **605** d.	...	...	...	...	...	...	...	...	...	...	...	...	...	...	...	...	...	...	...	...	...	...	...	...	...	...	...	2120
	Monfalcone 605/6 d.	...	...	...	...	...	...	...	...	...	...	...	...	...	...	...	...	...	...	...	...	...	...	...	...	...	...	...	2259
	Villa Opicina ⊗ 🏛 d.	...	...	...	...	...	...	...	...	...	...	...	...	...	...	...	...	...	...	...	...	...	...	...	...	...	...	...	2348
	Sežana ▲ 🏛 d.	0440	0515	0600	...	...	0923	1042	...	1248	...	...	...	1425	1520	...	1652	...	1732	1833	1950	...	...	...	...	...	...	...	0005
	Koper ⊡ d.	|	|	|	0525	...	|	|	1003	|	...	1328	...	|	|	1445	|	1640	|	|	|	...	...	1912	2010	...	...	2215	|
	Hrpelje-Kozina ⊡ d.	|	|	|	0558	...	|	|	1036	|	...	1415	...	|	|	1518	|	1710	|	|	|	...	...	1947	2100	...	...	2250	|
	Divača **1303** d.	0451	0526	0609	0611	...	0934	1052	1058	1259	...	1428	...	1436	1530	1532	1703	1722	1743	1842	2000	...	...	2007	2112	...	...	2304	|
0	**Rijeka 1310** d.	|	|	...	|	...	|	...	|	|	1257	...	...	|	...	|	|	|	|	|	...	1815	...	|	|	2045	...	|	|
28	Šapjane 🏛 d.	|	|	...	|	...	|	...	|	|	1340	...	...	|	...	|	|	|	|	|	...	1851	1921	|	|	2128	...	|	|
40	Ilirska Bistrica 🏛 d.	|	|	...	|	0629	|	...	|	|	1401	...	1418	|	...	|	|	|	|	|	...	...	1942	|	|	2200	...	|	|
56	Pivka d.	0515	0550	...	0635	0648	0958	...	1125	1327	1417	...	1435	1500	...	1555	1727	1743	1807	1905	...	...	1958	2031	2134	2216	...	2328	0035
	Postojna d.	0528	0603	...	0648	0701	1011	...	1136	1340	1429	...	1446	1513	...	1610	1740	1754	1820	1917	...	...	...	2044	2146	2228	...	2342	0047
	Ljubljana a.	0633	0707	...	0747	0805	1114	...	1240	1444	1525	...	...	1616	...	1704	1843	1841	1924	2017	...	...	...	2147	2241	2322	...	0035	0141
	Maribor **1315** a.	...	...	...	...	...	...	...	...	...	...	...	...	...	...	1952	...	2043	...	...	...	...	...	...	0121	...	...	0300	...

♦ – NOTES (LISTED BY TRAIN NUMBER)

240/1 – VENEZIA – 🛏 1,2 cl., ▬ 2 cl., [2] and ✕ Budapest - Zagreb - Ljubljana - Venezia and v.v.; 🛏 1,2 cl. and [2] (also ▬ 1,2 cl. May 29 - Aug. 18 from Bucureşti, May 31 - Aug. 20 from Venezia) Bucureşti (**1821/2**) - Budapest - Venezia and v.v.; ▬ 2 cl. Beograd (**412/3**) - Zagreb - Venezia and v.v. Conveys on dates in Table **97**: 🛏 1,2 cl. Moskva / Kyïv (**15/6**) - Budapest - Venezia and v.v. Also conveys June 19 - Aug. 28 (from Budapest, June 21 - Aug. 30 from Rijeka): ▬ 2 cl. Budapest - Zagreb (**1901/84**) - Rijeka. Train **240** conveys ②⑤ June 19 - Aug. 28: 🛏 1,2 cl., ▬ 2 cl. and [12] Budapest - Zagreb (**1204**) - Split.

480/1 – OPATIJA – [12] Rijeka - Ljubljana and v.v. Conveys Mar. 27 - Sept. 18 (from Rijeka, one day later from München): ▬ 2 cl. (also 🛏 1,2 cl. Apr. 29 - Sept. 18 from Rijeka, one day later from München) Rijeka - Ljubljana (**498/9**) - Salzburg (**462/3**) - München and v.v. Conveys ⑥ June 6 - Aug. 29 (from Rijeka), ⑤ June 5 - Aug. 28 (from Wien): ▬ 2 cl. and [2] Rijeka - Ljubljana (**1458/9**) - Wien and v.v.

482/3 – LJUBLJANA – [12] Rijeka - Ljubljana and v.v.; [2] Rijeka - Ljubljana (**150/1**) - Wien and v.v.

502/3 – POHORJE – [12] and ✕ Koper - Maribor and v.v.; [12] Koper - Pragersko (**516/7**) - Hodoš and v.v.

1011/24 – Ⓒ June 14 - Aug. 30: [12] and 🍷 Maribor - Koper and v.v.

1458/9 – ⑥ June 6 - Aug. 29 (from Koper and Rijeka), ⑤ June 5 - Aug. 28 (from Wien): ▬ 2 cl. and [2] Koper - Wien and v.v.; ▬ 2 cl. and [2] Rijeka - Ljubljana (**480/1**) - Wien and v.v.

1604/5 – Apr. 25 - May 3, June 25 - Aug. 30: [2] and ✕ Maribor - Koper; [2] Maribor - Hrpelje-Kozina (**1472/3**) - Pula and v.v.

m – Ⓐ (daily June 20 - Aug. 31).

p – Not Feb. 16 - 20, Apr. 28 - 30, June 26 - Aug. 31, Oct. 26 - 30.

⊖ – [R] and special fares payable for journeys to / from Italy.

⊡ – 🚌 service (hourly 0630 – 1930) on ⚒ Koper - Trieste and v.v. An irregular 🚌 service also operates Trieste - Hrpelje-Kozina and v.v.

⊗ – 🚋 service (every 20 minutes, approximately 0700 – 2000) Villa Opicina (Stazione Trenovia) - Trieste (Piazza Oberdan) and v.v. Operator: Trieste Trasporti S.p.A. Villa Opicina tram terminus is ±20 minutes walk from railway station.

▲ – 🚌 service **Sežana - Trieste and v.v.**: Journey 28 minutes.
From **Sežana**: 0800◧, 0930◧, 1100◧, 1630♣, 1800♣, 1930♣.
From **Trieste** Autostazione: 0845◧, 1015◧, 1145◧, 1545♣, 1715♣, 1845♣.
Service subject to alteration. No service on ⑥⑦, Slovenian and Italian holidays.
Operators: ◧ – Avrigo D.D., Nova Gorica; ♣ – Trieste Trasporti S.p.A.

1310 RIJEKA - ZAGREB

2nd class only except where shown HŽ

km		1901		703				*IC* 501 [R]🍷		701	
		L		T	⚒			R			
0	**Rijeka 1305** d.	0020	...	0545	...	*0735*	...	1145	1340	1710	...
61	Delnice d.	0129	...	0654	...	*0851*	...	1246	1454	1818	...
90	Moravice d.	0211	0630	0738	0806	0948	1150	1315	1551	1906	1937
120	Ogulin **1330** d.	0248	0710	0811	0847	1024	1223	1345	1626	1936	2010
176	Karlovac **1330** d.	0345	0819	0900	0950	1135	1329	1428	1741	2026	2111
229	**Zagreb 1330** a.	0424	0911	0937	1043	1226	1418	1502	1829	2104	2203
	Osijek **1340** a.	1119	...	1428	...	...	...	...	...	...	...

	1984		*IC* 500 [R]🍷		700				702	
	M		R				Ⓐ		T	
Osijek **1340** d.	1932	...	...	...	...	...	...	...	1205	...
Zagreb 1330 d.	0110	0634	0650	0807	1235	1325	1422	1529	1650	1721
Karlovac **1330** d.	0151	0736	0725	0906	1316	1429	1532	1631	1728	1816
Ogulin **1330** d.	0245	0848	0810	1008	1408	1540	1640	1734	1816	1919
Moravice d.	0328	0918	0839	1053	1455	1610	1710	1804	1900	1955
Delnice d.	0357	...	0907	1125	1525	...	...	...	1931	...
Rijeka 1305 a.	0503	...	1005	1240	1628	...	...	...	2034	...

L – June 21 - Aug. 30: [2] Rijeka - Zagreb (**413**) - Vinkovci; [2] Rijeka - Zagreb (**783**) - Osijek; ▬ 2 cl. Rijeka - Zagreb (**241**) - Budapest.

M – June 19 - Aug. 28 (from Osijek, one day later from Zagreb): [2] Osijek - Zagreb - Rijeka; [2] Vinkovci (**412**) - Zagreb - Rijeka; ▬ 2 cl. Budapest (**240**) - Zagreb - Rijeka.

R – RIJEKA – [12] and 🍷 Zagreb - Rijeka and v.v.

T – [12] Osijek - Zagreb - Rijeka and v.v.

1313 MARIBOR - ČAKOVEC, MURSKA SOBOTA and ZALAEGERSZEG

2nd class only except where shown SŽ, MÁV

km											*IC* 247						506				1642	*IC* 518			*IC* 516		
		Ⓐ	Ⓐ	Ⓐ	Ⓐ	Ⓐ	Ⓐ	Ⓒ	Ⓐ	Ⓐ	C	Ⓐ	g	Ⓐ	Ⓐ	Ⓐ	H	Ⓐ			y	P		Ⓐ	M	Ⓐ	Ⓐ
	Ljubljana **1315** d.	...	...	...	...	...	...	...	...	...	0840	...	...	...	...	...	1245	...	...	...	1345	1515	...	...	1725	...	...
0	**Maribor 1315** d.	...	...	...	...	...	0700	0700	...	...	|	1034	1225	1225	1325	1425	|	...	1525	...	|	|	...	1832	|	...	2205
19	Pragersko **1315** d.	...	...	...	...	0617	|	0731	...	...	1057	1108	1257	1257	|	|	1510	...	|	...	1604	1722	...	|	1944	...	2236
37	Ptuj d.	...	...	...	...	0646	0747	0756	...	...	1111	1133	1320	1324	1407	1507	1525	...	1612	...	1634	1737	...	1920	1958	...	2302
59	Ormož d.	...	...	0449	0531	0709	0810	0819	0815	1055	1130	1157	1345	1349	1433	1529	1546j	1545	1636	1640	1704	1755	1800	1945	2020	2024	2326
	Središče 🏛 d.	...	...	0503	|	—	|	|	0826	|	|	—	|	|	1444	—	|	1556	|	1654	|	|	1811	...	|	2035	...
	Čakovec 1335 a.	...	...	0513	|	...	|	|	—	|	|	...	|	|	—	Ⓐ	|	...	|	1704	|	|	—	...	|	...	...
98	**Murska Sobota** d.	0310	0510	—	0624	...	0857	0906	...	1141	1210	...	1432	1435	...	1510	1630	...	1722	...	1753	1837	...	...	2115	...	...
127	Hodoš a.	0339	0545	...	...	...	...	...	...	...	1237	...	1459	...	...	1540	1657	...	...	...	...	1905	...	...	2149	...	...
127	Hodoš 🏛 d.	*0341*	*0610*	0810	...	1010	...	...	1152	...	1250	1407	...	...	1543	...	...	...	...	...	...	...	1912	...	...	...	...
174	**Zalaegerszeg** a.	*0458*	*0713*	0913	...	1119	...	...	1303	...	1334	1513	...	...	1645	...	...	...	...	...	...	...	2015	...	...	...	...
	Budapest D **1230** a.	...	...	...	...	...	...	...	...	...	1747	...	...	...	...	...	...	...	...	...	...	...	...	...	...	...	...

km			*IC* 519			*IC* 517															1641		*IC* 246				
			P	Ⓐ	Ⓐ	M	Ⓐ	Ⓐ		Ⓐ	Ⓐ		Ⓐ	Ⓐ	Ⓐ	g	Ⓐ	Ⓐ		Ⓐ	g		C				Ⓐ
	Budapest D **1230** d.	...	...	...	...	...	...	...	...	...	...	...	...	...	...	...	...	...	...	...	...	...	1203	...	...	...	...
	Zalaegerszeg d.	...	...	...	...	...	...	...	0530	...	...	1140	...	...	...	...	...	...	1350	...	...	...	1618	1730	...	2025	...
	Hodoš 🏛 a.	...	...	...	...	...	...	...	0628	...	...	1234	...	...	...	...	...	...	1457	...	...	...	1712	1828	...	2125	...
	Hodoš d.	...	0420	...	...	0505	0557	...	...	...	...	—	...	...	...	...	...	...	—	1553	1700	...	1740	...	...	...	2220
	Murska Sobota d.	...	0449	...	...	0540	0628	...	...	...	*0935*	...	1210	...	1457	1457	...	...	...	1624	1725	...	1803	...	1931	...	2248
0	**Čakovec 1335** d.	...	|	0525	...	|	|	...	...	...	|	...	|	...	|	|	...	...	1713	...	|	...	|	...	|	...	...
12	Središče 🏛 d.	0430	|	0538	...	|	|	...	...	1030	|	Ⓐ	|	1510	|	|	1604	...	1726	...	|	1827	|	...	|	...	...
22	Ormož d.	0442	0526	0550	0553	0627	0715	0718	...	1041	1045	1205	1258	1521	1544	1544	1615	1710	1738	...	1811	1838	1843	...	2017	...	...
	Ptuj d.	0507	0542	...	0618	0645	...	0746	...	...	1112	1229	1322	...	1614	1614	...	1736	...	...	1837	...	1903	...	2042	...	...
	Pragersko **1315** d.	0539	0609	...	0655	0719	...	0818	...	...	1144	1301	1359	...	1645	1645	...	1758	...	...	1909	...	1927	...	2112	...	...
	Maribor 1315 a.	0602	|	...	0717	|	...	0840	...	...	1207	1324	1422	...	1709	1709	...	...	...	...	|	...	|	...	2133	...	...
	Ljubljana **1315** a.	...	0813	...	...	0927	...	...	...	...	...	...	...	...	...	...	...	...	...	...	2114	...	2131	...	...	...	...

C – CITADELLA – [12] Budapest - Ljubljana and v.v.

H – [2] Ljubljana - Pragersko - Hodoš.

M – MURA – [12] Koper (**502/3**) - Pragersko - Hodoš and v.v.

P – PTUJ – Ⓐ: [2] Ljubljana - Hodoš and v.v.

g – ⑦ Dec. 14 - June 21, Sept. 6 - Dec. 6 (also Apr. 13; not Apr. 12, 26, Oct. 25).

j – Arrive 1541.

y – ⑤ Dec. 19 - June 19, Sept. 4 - Dec. 11 (not May 1).

SŽ, HŽ, ÖBB — LJUBLJANA and ZAGREB - MARIBOR - GRAZ — 1315

km		1458	IC 250	ICS 12	IC 252	ICS 14	EC 158	IC 247	IC 254		ICS 18	IC 256	IC 506		IC 258	1642	ICS 20	IC 518	EC 150	ICS 22	IC 502	IC 350	ICS 1124	ICS 1024	ICS 26		604	1604
		[R]	🍸	[R]	🍸	[R]	✕		✕	2	[R]	✕		2	🍸		[R]	2	✕	[R]		🍸	[R]	[R]	[R]	2		
		◆					◆	◆					◆			y		◆	◆	Ⓐ	◆		t	◆			w	◆
	Rijeka **1305** d.	2045	...	...	...	...	...	...	...	...	...	...	...	...	...	...	...	...	1257	...	...	...	...	...	...	...	...	...
0	**Ljubljana 1300** d.	0050	...	0545	...	0805	...	0840	...	1050	1213	...	1245	1250	...	1345	1450	1515	1600	1650	1725	...	1850	1850	1945	2050	2225	2250
*	**Zagreb 1300** d.	|	...	|	...	|	0725	|	...	|	|	...	|	|	...	|	|	|	|	|	|	...	|	|	|	|	|	|
	Dobova **1300** 🏛 d.	|	...	|	...	|	0813	|	...	|	|	...	|	|	...	|	|	|	|	|	|	...	|	|	|	|	|	|
	Sevnica **1300** d.	|	...	|	...	|	0839	|	...	|	|	...	|	|	...	|	|	|	|	|	|	...	|	|	|	|	|	|
64	Zidani Most **1300** d.	|	...	0630	...	0850	|	0938	...	1200	1259	...	1342	1400	...	1443	1535	1608	1654	1735	1824	...	1935	1935	2030	2200	2334	2352
89	Celje d.	0206	...	0650	...	0910	0918	1005	...	1225	1319	...	1409	1428	...	1510	1556	1635	1719	1756	1850	...	1956	1956	2050	2227	0001	0020
137	Pragersko **1313** d.	|	...	0722	...	0941	0958	1047	...	1311	1354	...	1449	1516	...	1551	1628	1719	1758	1830	1935	...	2030	2030	2124	2316	0045	0104
156	**Maribor 1313** a.	0300	...	0736	...	0953	1014	...	...	1331	1406	...	...	1541	...	...	1641	...	1814	1843	1952	...	2043	2043	2138	2341	0102	0121
156	**Maribor** d.	0305	0620	...	0822	...	1022	...	1222	...	...	1422	...	...	1622	...	...	...	1821	...	...	2022	...	...	...	...	...	...
172	Spielfeld-Straß 🏛 a.	0323	0637	...	0839	...	1039	...	1239	...	...	1439	...	...	1639	...	...	...	1839	...	...	2039	...	...	...	...	...	...
172	Spielfeld-Straß 🏛 d.	0351	0649	...	0851	...	1051	...	1251	...	...	1451	...	...	1651	...	...	...	1851	...	...	2051	...	...	...	...	...	...
219	**Graz Hbf** a.	0423	0723	...	0923	...	1123	...	1323	...	...	1523	...	...	1723	...	...	...	1923	...	...	2123	...	...	...	...	...	...
	Wien Südbf **980** a.	0717	1005	...	1205	...	1405	...	1605	...	...	1805	...	...	2005	...	...	...	2205	...	...	0005	...	...	...	...	...	...

	1459	605	1605		607	ICS 11	ICS 1011	IC 519	IC 503	IC 251	ICS 13	IC 253		EC 151	ICS 17	IC 255		IC 257	ICS 19	1611	IC 259	ICS 21	1615	1641	IC 246	ICS 23	EC 159	1613
	[R]			2	2	[R]	[R]	2			[R]	✕	2	✕	[R]	✕	2	🍸	[R]	2	🍸	[R]	2	2		[R]	✕	2
	◆	w	◆		Ⓐ	x	◆	◆	◆					◆						g		Ⓐ	g	g	◆		◆	g
Wien Südbf **980** d.	2156	...	...	...	...	...	...	...	...	...	...	0556	...	0756	...	0956	...	1156	...	...	1356	...	...	...	...	...	1556	...
Graz Hbf d.	0036	...	...	...	...	...	...	...	...	0634	...	0836	...	1036	...	1236	...	1436	...	...	1636	...	...	...	...	...	1836	...
Spielfeld-Straß 🏛 a.	0109	...	...	...	...	...	...	...	...	0709	...	0909	...	1109	...	1309	...	1509	...	...	1709	...	...	...	...	...	1909	...
Spielfeld-Straß 🏛 d.	0125	...	...	...	...	...	...	...	...	0721	...	0921	...	1121	...	1321	...	1521	...	...	1721	...	...	...	...	...	1921	...
Maribor a.	0142	...	...	...	...	...	...	...	...	0738	...	0938	...	1138	...	1338	...	1538	...	...	1738	...	...	...	...	...	1938	...
Maribor 1313 d.	0148	0350	0350	0515	0440	0540	0540	...	0650	...	0817	...	1015	1146	1245	...	1520	...	1545	1620	...	1650	1800	...	...	1945	1955	2005
Pragersko **1313** d.	|	0407	0407	0535	0457	0555	0555	0609	0719	...	0831	...	1035	1202	1259	...	1539	...	1559	1639	...	1703	1817	1909	1927	1959	2011	2021
Celje d.	0236	0451	0451	0621	0545	0633	0633	0652	0801	...	0906	...	1123	1241	1335	...	1623	...	1635	1724	...	1735	1859	1950	2007	2035	2049	2102
Zidani Most **1300** d.	|	0517	0517	0645	0610	0654	0654	0718	0828	...	0925	...	1147	1308	1354	...	1647	...	1654	1750	...	1754	1926	2015	2031	2054	|	2128
Sevnica **1300** d.	|	|	|	...	|	|	|	|	|	...	|	...	...	|	|	...	...	...	|	|	...	|	|	|	|	|	2127	|
Dobova **1300** 🏛 d.	|	|	|	...	|	|	|	|	|	...	|	...	...	|	|	...	...	...	|	|	...	|	|	|	|	|	2205	|
Zagreb 1300 a.	|	|	|	...	|	|	|	|	|	...	|	...	...	|	|	...	...	...	|	|	...	|	|	|	|	|	2234	|
Ljubljana 1300 a.	0351	0617	0617	...	0711	0738	0738	0813	0927	...	1009	...	...	1406	1438	...	...	...	1738	1844	...	1838	2025	2114	2131	2138	...	2221
Rijeka **1305** a.	0851	...	...	...	...	...	...	...	...	...	...	...	...	1725	...	...	...	...	...	...	...	...	...	...	...	...	...	...

ADDITIONAL SERVICES MARIBOR - ZIDANI MOST and v.v.: 2nd class only

	Ⓐ	Ⓐ	Ⓐ	Ⓐ	Ⓐ	Ⓐ		Ⓐ		Ⓐ	Ⓐ		Ⓑ	Ⓑ
Maribor d.	0615	0715	0755	1120	1215	1315	1415	1615	1715	1815	1920	2015	2100	2220
Pragersko d.	0635	0735	0814	1140	1235	1335	1435	1635	1735	1835	1938	2035	2119	2240
Celje d.	0723	0823	0910	1228	1323	1423	1523	1723	1823	1923	2023	2123	2207	2326
Zidani Most d.	0747	0847	0934	1252	1347	1447	1547	1747	1847	1947	2047	2147	2232	...

	Ⓐ		Ⓐ	Ⓐ	Ⓐ	Ⓐ	Ⓐ	Ⓐ			Ⓐ	Ⓑ		Ⓐ
Zidani Most d.	0556	0700	0800	0918	1000	1100	1304	1500	1600	1700	1800	1900	2000	2100
Celje d.	0622	0725	0825	0943	1025	1125	1329	1525	1625	1725	1825	1925	2025	2125
Pragersko d.	0711	0811	0912	1030	1112	1209	1415	1612	1712	1812	1912	2012	2112	2212
Maribor a.	0730	0831	0933	1050	1133	1228	1436	1633	1733	1833	1933	2033	2133	2233

◆ – **NOTES** (LISTED BY TRAIN NUMBER)

150/1 – EMONA – [12] and ✕ Ljubljana - Wien and v.v.; [2] Rijeka (**482/3**) - Ljubljana - Wien and v.v.
158/9 – CROATIA – [12] and ✕ Zagreb - Wien and v.v. Conveys ⑥ May 2 - Sept. 26 (from Split), ⑤ May 1 - Sept. 25 (from Wien): ▬ 2 cl. Split (**824/5**) - Zagreb - Wien and v.v.
246/7 – CITADELLA – [12] Budapest - Ljubljana and v.v.
502/3 – POHORJE – [12] and ✕ Koper - Maribor and v.v.; [12] Koper - Pragersko (**516/7**) - Hodoš and v.v.
506 – [12] Ljubljana - Pragersko - Hodoš.
518/9 – PTUJ – Ⓐ: [2] Ljubljana - Hodoš and v.v.
1011/24 – © June 14 - Aug. 30: [12] and 🍸 Maribor - Koper and v.v.
1458/9 – ⑥ June 6 - Aug. 29 (from Koper and Rijeka), ⑤ June 5 - Aug. 28 (from Wien): ▬ 2 cl. and [2] Koper - Wien and v.v.; ▬ 2 cl. and [2] Rijeka - Ljubljana (**480/1**) - Wien and v.v.
1604/5 – Apr. 25 - May 3, June 25 - Aug. 30: [2] and ✕ Maribor - Koper; [2] Maribor - Hrpelje-Kozina (**1472/3**) - Pula and v.v.

g – ⑦ Dec. 14 - June 21, Sept. 6 - Dec. 6 (also Apr. 13; not Apr. 12, 26, Oct. 25).
t – ⑦ Dec. 14 - June 7, Sept. 7 - Dec. 6 (also Apr. 13; not Apr. 12, 26).
w – Dec. 14 - Apr. 24, May 4 - June 24, Aug. 31 - Dec. 12.
x – Not © June 14 - Aug. 30.
y – ⑤ Dec. 19 - June 19, Sept. 4 - Dec. 11 (not May 1).
* – Zagreb - Celje: *104 km*.

SŽ, HŽ, ŽS — ZAGREB - VINKOVCI - BEOGRAD — 1320

km		413	741	419	415	743	745	EC 211	IC 551	747	315
		✕			✕	🍸		✕	[R] 🍸		
		◆	◆	◆	◆			◆			◆
	Ljubljana **1300** d.	...	...	...	0815	...	...	1435	...	...	2115
0	**Zagreb** d.	0603	0900	...	1100	1321	1514	1710	1820	2112	2355
105	Novska d.	0740	1033	...	1239	1458	1652	1847	|	2249	0128
191	Slavonski Brod d.	0836	1129	...	1333	1554	1748	1942	2036	2351	0225
224	Strizivojna-Vrpolje **1350** d.	0854	1146	...	1350	1611	1806	2000	2054	0012	0245
	Osijek **1350** a.	|	|	...	|	|	|	|	2140	|	|
256	**Vinkovci** d.	0929	1206	1230	1418	1631	1826	2030	...	0037	0321
288	Šid 🏛 d.	1042	...	1356	1533	...	...	2140	...	...	0436
407	**Beograd** a.	1225	...	1538	1718	...	...	2321	...	...	0621

	314	740	IC 550	742	744	EC 210	746	414	418	748	412
			[R] 🍸			✕		✕		🍸	✕
	◆					◆		◆	◆	◆	◆
Beograd d.	2150	...	...	...	...	0550	...	1035	1300	...	1535
Šid 🏛 d.	0054	...	...	...	...	0848	...	1332	1553	...	1828
Vinkovci d.	0147	0306	...	0605	0742	0949	1228	1449	1700	1725	1943
Osijek **1350** d.	|	|	0525	|	|	|	|	|	...	|	|
Strizivojna-Vrpolje **1350** d.	0207	0332	0611	0625	0802	1009	1248	1509	...	1750	2003
Slavonski Brod d.	0224	0354	0628	0644	0820	1027	1306	1526	...	1812	2021
Novska d.	0320	0458	|	0743	0915	1122	1402	1620	...	1912	2114
Zagreb a.	0453	0639	0846	0918	1053	1256	1545	1752	...	2050	2245
Ljubljana **1300** a.	0722	...	...	...	...	1518	...	2040	...	...	...

◆ – **NOTES** (LISTED BY TRAIN NUMBER)

210/1 – SAVA – [12] Beograd - Villach (**110/1**) - München and v.v.; ✕ Beograd - Jesenice and v.v.
314 – 🛏 1, 2 cl., ▬ 2 cl. and [12] Beograd - Zagreb - Ljubljana - Villach.
315 – 🛏 1, 2 cl., ▬ 2 cl. and [12] Villach - Ljubljana - Zagreb - Beograd; [2] (also [1] and 🍸 July 2 - Sept. 1) Banja Luka (**451**) - Vinkovci - Beograd.
412 – NIKOLA TESLA – [12] and ✕ Beograd - Zagreb; ▬ 2 cl. Beograd - Zagreb (**240**) - Venezia. Conveys June 19 - Aug. 28: [2] Vinkovci - Zagreb (**1984**) - Rijeka.
413 – NIKOLA TESLA – [12] and ✕ Zagreb - Beograd; ▬ 2 cl. Venezia (**241**) - Zagreb - Beograd. Conveys June 20 - Sept. 5 (from Split and Zadar, following day from Zagreb): [2] Split (**1822**) - Zagreb - Vinkovci; [2] Zadar (**1920**) - Knin (**1822**) - Zagreb - Vinkovci. Also conveys June 21 - Aug. 30 (from Rijeka and Zagreb): [2] Rijeka (**1901**) - Zagreb - Vinkovci.
414 – [2] Beograd - Schwarzach-St Veit (**464**) - Zürich; 🛏 1, 2 cl. and ▬ 2 cl. Zagreb - Schwarzach-St Veit - Zürich; [12] and ✕ Beograd - Ljubljana - Villach.
415 – [2] Zürich (**465**) - Schwarzach-St Veit - Beograd; 🛏 1, 2 cl. and ▬ 2 cl. Zürich (**465**) - Schwarzach-St Veit - Zagreb; [12] and ✕ Villach - Ljubljana - Beograd.
418 – [2] Beograd - Vinkovci; [2] (also [1] and 🍸 July 1 - Aug. 31) Beograd - Vinkovci (**450**) - Banja Luka; [2] Beograd - Vinkovci (**748**) - Zagreb (**498**) - Salzburg (**462**) - München.
419 – [2] Vinkovci - Beograd; [2] München (**463**) - Salzburg (**499**) - Zagreb (**741**) - Vinkovci - Beograd.
741 – [12] Zagreb - Vinkovci; [2] München (**463**) - Salzburg (**499**) - Zagreb - Vinkovci (**419**) - Beograd.
748 – [12] and 🍸 Vinkovci - Zagreb; [2] Beograd (**418**) - Vinkovci - Zagreb (**498**) - Salzburg (**462**) - München. Conveys June 19 - Sept. 4: [2] Vinkovci - Zagreb (**1823**) - Split; [2] Vinkovci - Zagreb (**1823**) - Knin (**1921**) - Zadar.

HŽ, ŽRS — 2nd class only except where shown — ZAGREB - BANJA LUKA - DOBOJ — 1325

km	km							397					451	399
					Ⓐ⊗			Z	⊗		⊗		L	S
0		**Zagreb 1343** d.	...	...	...	...	...	0855	...	...	...	...	...	2125
72		Sunja **1343** ⊡ d.	...	...	...	...	...	1016	...	...	...	...	...	2246
112	0	Novi Grad ⊡ d.	...	0512	...	...	...	1144	1155	1315	1715	1800	...	0011
	20	Blatna d.	...	0535	0540	...	...	|	1219	1338	1739	1823	...	|
	78	Bihać a.	...	...	0707	...	...	|	1346	▬	1906	▬	...	|
214		Banja Luka d.	0421	...	...	0730	0955	1315	...	1532	...	1930	2225	0143
324		**Doboj** a.	0637	...	...	0957	1218	1503	...	1810	...	2213	0009	0335
		Sarajevo **1350** a.	...	...	...	...	...	1805	...	...	...	...	|	0639
		Beograd **1320** a.	...	...	...	...	...	...	...	...	...	...	0621	...

								396			450	398
	Ⓐ⊗			⊗			⊗	Z			L	S
Beograd **1320** d.	...	...	...	...	...	...	...	...	...	...	1300	...
Sarajevo **1350** d.	...	...	...	...	...	...	...	1027	...	...	|	2120
Doboj d.	...	0659	0718	...	1107	...	...	1329	1525	1920	2021	0029
Banja Luka d.	...	0619	0935	...	1330	...	...	1529	1742	2137	2205	0221
Bihać d.	0356	▬	...	0944	...	...	1459	|	▬	...	...	|
Blatna d.	0523	0617	...	1112	...	1400	1627	|	1832	...	...	|
Novi Grad ⊡ d.	...	0640	...	1135	...	1423	1650	1657	1855	...	...	0348
Sunja **1343** ⊡ d.	...	...	...	...	...	...	...	1825	...	...	...	0522
Zagreb 1343 a.	...	...	...	...	...	...	...	1945	...	...	...	0642

L – [2] Banja Luka - Vinkovci (**315/418**) - Beograd and v.v. Also conveys [1] and 🍸 July 1 - Aug. 31 from Beograd, July 2 - Sept. 1 from Banja Luka.
S – [2] Zagreb - Sarajevo and v.v.
Z – [12] Zagreb - Sarajevo - Ploče and v.v.
⊗ – Not during 'heating' season (nominally until Apr. 15 or May 1).
⊡ – 🏛 at Volinja (Croatia) / Dobrljin (Bosnia-Herzegovina).

1330 ZAGREB - ZADAR and SPLIT — HŽ

km		ICN 521 🄡 🍷		ICN 1523 🄡 🍷		ICN 525 🄡 🍷		1823 1921	1823	825	825 5831	1204
			2	w	2		2	A	♦	♦	C	♦
0	**Zagreb 1310** d.	0650	...	1100	...	1522	...	2140	2140	2255	2255	2325
53	Karlovac **1310** d.	0723	...	1136	...	1600	...	2217	2217	2332	2332	|
109	**Ogulin 1310** d.	|	...	|	...	|	...	2312	2312	0028	0028	0105
225	Gospić d.	0930	...	1347	...	1805	...	0130	0130	0245	0245	|
269	Gračac d.	1003	...	|	...	1839	...	0206	0206	0328	0328	|
333	Knin a.	1052	...	1506	...	1928	...	0325	0325	0440	0440	0526
333	Knin § d.	1053	...	1507	1549	1929	1951	0342	0337	0441	0441	0528
	Zadar ⊡ § a.	|	...	|	|	|	|	0540	|	|	|	|
387	Perković § a.	1137	...	1549	1711	2012	2058	...	0439	0544	0544	0633
387	Perković § d.	1138	1144	1554	1713	2013	2103	...	0443	0555	0600	0650
	Šibenik ⊡ § a.	|	1212	|	1741	|	2131	...	|	|	0628	|
435	**Split** ⊡ § a.	1220	...	1642	...	2055	...	...	0548	0655	...	0759

		ICN 520 🄡 🍷		ICN 1522 🄡 🍷		ICN 524 🄡 🍷	1205	1920 1822	1822	5828 824	824
	2		2	w	2		♦	B	♦	D	♦
Split ⊡ § d.	...	0738	...	1054	...	1510	1600	...	2050	...	2210
Šibenik ⊡ § d.	0746	|	1027	|	1516	|	|	...	|	2245	|
Perković § a.	0817	0820	1058	1134	1547	1552	1708	...	2200	2315	2321
Perković § d.	...	0821	...	1139	...	1553	1720	...	2201	2332	2332
Zadar ⊡ § d.	...	|	...	|	...	|	|	2045	|	|	|
Knin § a.	...	0905	...	1221	...	1637	1821	2240	2305	0037	0037
Knin d.	...	0906	...	1222	...	1638	1827	2317	2317	0038	0038
Gračac d.	...	1004	...	|	...	1730	|	0048	0048	0210	0210
Gospić d.	...	1037	...	1346	...	1804	|	0126	0126	0249	0249
Ogulin 1310 d.	...	|	...	|	...	|	2315	0409	0409	0503	0503
Karlovac **1310** d.	...	1236	...	1545	...	2006	|	0458	0458	0554	0554
Zagreb 1310 a.	...	1310	...	1628	...	2041	0045	0535	0535	0631	0631

KNIN - ZADAR and v.v. :

km		A				Ⓐ	
0	Knin d.	0342	0417	0531	1102	1305	1645
57	Benkovac d.	0453	0537	0651	1222	1424	1805
95	Zadar a.	0540	0629	0741	1312	1523	1856

				Ⓐ	z	B	y
Zadar d.	0639	1003	1420	1545	1950	2045	2117
Benkovac d.	0736	1055	1514	1637	2042	2129	2209
Knin a.	0854	1217	1629	1801	2159	2240	2327

PERKOVIĆ - SPLIT and v.v. :

km				⚒			
0	Perković d.	0526	0824	1220	...	1720	2108
48	Split a.	0631	0929	1328	...	1825	2216

			⚒				
Split d.	0400	0706	1002	...	1529	1943	...
Perković a.	0505	0811	1107	...	1636	2055	...

KNIN - PERKOVIĆ - ŠIBENIK and v.v. (additional services) :

km			x	h				Ⓐv		x
0	Knin d.	0403	...	...	...	0708	...	...	1951	...
54	Perković d.	0509	0548	0600	0704	0822	1308	1442	2103	2325
76	Šibenik a.	...	0616	0628	0732	0850	1336	1506	2131	2349

		x					Ⓐv			
Šibenik d.	0432	0626	...	0746	1229	...	1405	...	2016	2245
Perković d.	0513q	0657	...	0833t	1300	...	1434	1638	2100r	2315
Knin a.	0624	...	...	0940	...	...	...	1745	2208	...

1335 ZAGREB - VARAŽDIN - NAGYKANIZSA — 2nd class only except where shown — HŽ, MÁV

km		7600	⚒		994			7602			Ⓐ	Ⓐ	992	790 ⚒			IC 590 🄡Z		7604	Ⓐ					⚒
0	**Zagreb** d.	...	0504	...	0705	...	0933	...	...	1121	...	1304	1413	1515	...	1526	1626	...	...	1623	...	1803	1904	2056	2223
38	Zabok d.	...	0555	...	0754	...	1033	...	...	1217	...	1410	1512	1602	...	1630	k	←	...	1725	...	1911	2009	2205	2316
104	**Varaždin** ▲ d.	0536	0744	...	0914	1023	1210	1309	...	1423f	1517	1556	1635	1716	...	1805	1817	1902	...	1918	1955	2040	2214p	2333	0043
115	Čakovec **1313** d.	0547	0758	...	0926	1034	...	1321	...	1439	1538	...	1647	1733	...	→	1827	1914	...	...	2008	2050	2225	2343	0053
145	Kotoriba 🏛 d.	0624	0832	...	1000	1107	...	1400	...	1519	1614	...	1725	1803	...	...	...	1954	2046	...	2043	...	2257	...	...
151	Murakeresztúr 🏛 d.	0631	...	...	...	...	...	1407	1525	...	...	...	...	...	...	...	...	...	2053	...	...	...	...	...	...
165	**Nagykanizsa** a.	*0741*	...	...	...	...	...	...	1539	...	...	...	...	...	...	...	...	...	*2110*	...	...	...	...	...	...

			⚒	991	IC 591 🄡Z		791 ⚒	7601	⚒		Ⓐ				Ⓐ		⚒	7603		995 K		997			
Nagykanizsa d.	...	...	...	...	...	...	...	*0640*	...	...	...	...	...	1119	...	...	...	...	...	...	...	...	2009	...	...
Murakeresztúr 🏛 d.	...	...	...	...	...	...	...	0729	...	...	...	...	...	1133	...	...	...	1442	...	...	...	...	2023	*2103*	...
Kotoriba 🏛 d.	...	...	...	0442	...	0553	0650	0742	...	...	1110	1158	1241	...	...	...	1403a	1450	...	1656	1808a	1924	...	2113	2210
Čakovec **1313** d.	...	0340	...	0520	0548	0634	0727	0822	1005	...	1151	1234	1322	...	1404	...	1437	1529	...	1735	1845	2010	...	2148	2249
Varaždin ▲ d.	0301	0351	0431	0535	0559	0647	0743	0832	1015	1038	1213	1244	1332	...	1414	1422	1447	1539	1542	1751	1904	2025	...	2158	2259
Zabok d.	0432	0521	0627	0657	k	0834	0907	...	...	1218	1348	...	...	...	...	1604	...	...	1727	1910	2041	2140	...	...	...
Zagreb a.	0526	0621	0729	0747	0748	0928	0953	...	...	1316	1443	...	...	...	...	1706	...	...	1823	2004	2134	2227	...	...	...

▲ – VARAŽDIN - KOPRIVNICA and v.v. 2nd class only except where shown:

km			Z				⚒			⑦Q		
0	Varaždin d.	0443	0559	0650	...	1033	1253	1417	1605	1702	1907	2217
42	Koprivnica a.	0532	0633	0733	...	1120	1342	1503	1651	1751	1953	2302

	⚒					Ⓐ			Z	⑦Q			
Koprivnica d.	0446	0550	0845	1150	1255	1414	1516	1705	1740	1815	1905	2014	2151
Varaždin a.	0533	0640	0931	1236	1341	1503	1602	1748	1815	1859	1952	2058	2243

1340 ZAGREB - KOPRIVNICA - NAGYKANIZSA and OSIJEK — HŽ, MÁV

km		1205	EN 241	1474	783	205	703	981	IC 201	IC 284	IC 590	IC 581	971	995
		♦	V	♦	♦	♦	🍷	2	♦	♦	🄡Z	🄡🍷	2	K
	Rijeka **1310** d.	...	...	...	0020d	...	0545	...	...	...	...	...	...	...
0	**Zagreb** d.	0055	0456	0640	0640	0958	0958	1300	1545	1545	1626	1705	1825	2015
57	Križevci d.	|	0537	0735	0735	1041	1041	1355	1625	1625	1703	1742	1919	2113
88	Koprivnica **1335** d.	0205	0611	0812	0821	1123	1125	1440	1656	1656	1732	1821	1959	2149
103	Gyékényes 🏛 d.	0240	0641	0851	|	1155	|	|	1722	1722	...	|	...	...
132	**Nagykanizsa** a.	0305	0714	0915	|	1220	|	|	1745	1745	...	|	...	...
	Budapest K **1220** a.	0659	1059	...	|	1609	|	|	2159	...	...	|	...	...
153	Virovitica d.	...	...	...	0925	...	1225	1600	...	...	...	1921	...	...
225	Našice d.	...	...	...	1037	...	1345	1737	...	...	...	2029	...	...
275	**Osijek 1345/50** a.	...	...	...	1119	...	1428	1829	...	...	...	2109	...	...

	980	IC 591	IC 580	IC 200	IC 285	702	204	782	1475	EN 240	1984
	2	🄡Z	🄡🍷	♦	♦	🍷	♦	♦	♦	V	♦
Osijek 1345/50 d.	0005	...	0532	...	...	1205	...	1622	...	...	1932
Našice d.	0053	...	0614	...	...	1249	...	1706	...	...	2032
Virovitica d.	0216	...	0724	...	...	1401	...	1820	...	...	2208
Budapest K **1220** d.	|	...	|	0605	...	|	1405	|	...	1635	|
Nagykanizsa d.	|	...	|	0957	1116	|	1751	|	1902	2032	|
Gyékényes 🏛 d.	|	...	|	1032	1203	|	1830	|	1943	2130	|
Koprivnica **1335** d.	0331	0641	0828	1049	1223	1508	1848	1944	2001	2150	2330
Križevci d.	0410	0711	0858	1119	1253	1538	1918	2014	2036	2222	0010
Zagreb a.	0505	0748	0936	1159	1333	1622	2000	2056	2126	2307	0051
Rijeka **1310** a.	...	...	...	...	...	2034	...	...	...	...	0503

♦ – **NOTES FOR TABLES 1330/35/40** (LISTED BY TRAIN NUMBER)

200 – KVARNER – [12] Budapest - Zagreb; ✕ Nagykanizsa - Zagreb.
201 – KVARNER – [12] and ✕ Zagreb - Budapest; [12] Zagreb - Nagykanizsa (**284**) - Wien.
204/5 – MAESTRAL – [12] Budapest - Gyékényes - Zagreb and v.v. Conveys on dates in Table **97**: 🛏 1, 2 cl. Moskva / Kyïv / St Peterburg - Budapest - Zagreb and v.v.
284 – ZAGREB – [12] and ✕ Zagreb (**201**) - Nagykanizsa - Wien.
285 – ZAGREB – [12] and ✕ Wien - Zagreb.
782 – [12] and 🍷 Osijek - Zagreb. Conveys June 19 - Sept. 4: [2] Osijek - Zagreb (**1823**) - Split.
783 – [12] and 🍷 Zagreb - Osijek. Conveys June 20 - Sept. 5 (from Split, one day later from Zagreb): [2] Split (**1822**) - Zagreb - Osijek; 🛏 1, 2 cl., ▬ 2 cl. and [2] Split (**1822**) - Zagreb - Koprivnica (**1474**) - Bratislava - Praha. Conveys June 21 - Aug. 30 (from Rijeka): [2] Rijeka (**1901**) - Zagreb - Osijek.
824 – 🛏 1, 2 cl. and [2] Split - Zagreb. Conveys ⑥ May 2 - Sept. 26: ▬ 2 cl. Split - Zagreb (**158**) - Wien.
825 – 🛏 1, 2 cl. and [2] Zagreb - Split. Conveys ⑤ May 1 - Sept. 25 (from Wien): ▬ 2 cl. Wien (**159**) - Zagreb - Split.
1204 – ADRIA – ②⑤ June 19 - Aug. 28 (from Zagreb): 🛏 1, 2 cl., ▬ 2 cl. and [12] Budapest (**240**) - Zagreb - Split.
1205 – ADRIA – ③⑥ June 20 - Aug. 29: 🛏 1, 2 cl., ▬ 2 cl. and [12] Split - Zagreb - Budapest.
1474 – JADRAN – June 20 - Sept. 5 (from Split, one day later from Zagreb): 🛏 1, 2 cl., ▬ 2 cl. and [2] Split (**1822**) - Zagreb (**783**) - Koprivnica - Bratislava - Praha.
1475 – JADRAN – June 19 - Sept. 4 (from Praha): 🛏 1, 2 cl., ▬ 2 cl. and [2] Praha - Bratislava - Zagreb (**1823**) - Split.
1822 – June 20 - Sept. 5: 🛏 1, 2 cl. and [2] Split - Zagreb; [2] Split - Zagreb (**413**) - Vinkovci; [2] Split - Zagreb (**783**) - Osijek; 🛏 1, 2 cl., ▬ 2 cl. and [2] Split - Zagreb (**783**) - Koprivnica (**1474**) - Bratislava - Praha.
1823 – June 19 - Sept. 4: 🛏 1, 2 cl. and [2] Zagreb - Split; [2] Vinkovci (**748**) - Zagreb - Split; [2] Osijek (**782**) - Zagreb - Split; 🛏 1, 2 cl., ▬ 2 cl. and [2] Praha (**1475**) - Bratislava - Zagreb - Split.
1984 – June 19 - Aug. 28: [2] Osijek - Zagreb - Rijeka; ▬ 2 cl. Budapest (**240**) - Zagreb - Rijeka.

A – June 19 - Sept. 4 (from Vinkovci and Zagreb, one day later from Knin): [2] Vinkovci (**748**) - Zagreb (**1823**) - Knin (**1921**) - Zadar.
B – June 20 - Sept. 5: [2] Zadar (**1920**) - Knin (**1822**) - Zagreb (**413**) - Vinkovci.
C – June 19 - Sept. 4: [2] Zagreb (**825**) - Perković (**5831**) - Šibenik.
D – June 20 - Sept. 5: [2] Šibenik (**5828**) - Perković (**824**) - Zagreb.
K – [2] Kotoriba - Zagreb - Koprivnica.
Q – Also Apr. 13; not Apr. 12.
V – VENEZIA – For days of running and composition – see Table **1305**.
Z – Ⓐ: [2] Čakovec - Zagreb and v.v. 🄡.

a – Ⓐ only.
d – June 21 - Aug. 30.
f – Arrive 1346.
h – June 6 - Sept. 5.
k – Via Koprivnica.
p – Arrive 2151.
q – Arrive 0503.
r – Arrive 2047.
t – Arrive 0817.
v – Not June 13 - Aug. 30.
w – June 12 - Sept. 13.
x – Not June 6 - Sept. 5.
y – Not June 20 - Sept. 5.
z – June 20 - Sept. 5.

§ – Additional local services operate – see separate panels.
⊡ – Frequent 🚌 services operate Zadar - Šibenik - Split and v.v.; some continue to Ploče and Dubrovnik. Bus station locations: Zadar, Split and Ploče are adjacent to rail station, Šibenik approximately 10 minutes walk.

1343 LOCAL SERVICES in Croatia — 2nd class only — HŽ

ZAGREB - SISAK CAPRAG and v.v.: Journey 60 – 75 minutes. All services call at Sisak (6 minutes from Sisak Caprag).
From Zagreb: 0543, 0648, 0748Ⓐ, 1048, 1146Ⓐ, 1349, 1448Ⓐ, 1548, 1647Ⓐ, 1748Ⓐ, 1842, 1948, 2046Ⓐ, 2249.
From Sisak Caprag: 0411⚒, 0513, 0617, 0718, 0818Ⓐ, 1018Ⓐ, 1217, 1418Ⓐ, 1518, 1618Ⓐ, 1718, 1818Ⓐ, 1919, 2116.

SISAK CAPRAG - SUNJA and v.v.: Journey 25 minutes.
From Sisak Caprag: 0342, 0722, 0803, 1218, 1456, 1659, 1920Ⓐ, 1957.
From Sunja: 0449, 0553, 0654, 1153, 1255, 1635, 1855, 2052, 2133Ⓐ.

SUNJA - NOVSKA and v.v.: Journey 70 minutes.
From Sunja: 0827, 1242Ⓐq, 1530, 2031.
From Novska: 0443, 0544, 1043, 1403Ⓐq, 1731.

VINKOVCI - OSIJEK and v.v.: Journey 44 minutes.
From Vinkovci: 0544, 0638, 1156, 1510, 1730.
From Osijek: 0827, 1415, 1628, 1940.

q – Not June 13 - Aug. 30.

PÉCS - OSIJEK 1345

HŽ, MÁV 2nd class only except where shown

km				8110				259			8114			
		Ⓐ					⚒	B						
	Budapest K **1200** d.	...	...	...	...	...	...	0945	...	...	...	...	...	...
0	**Pécs** d.	...	...	0652	...	...	...	1300	...	...	1652	...	...	...
43	Magyarbóly 🏛 d.	...	...	0811	...	...	...	1402	...	...	1810	...	...	...
54	Beli Manastir 🏛 d.	0545	0707	0824	0831	1055	1224	1430	1447	1607	1823	1843	2006	2210
82	**Osijek 1340/50** a.	0617	0739	...	0903	1127	1256	1457	1519	1640	...	1915	2039	2242

				8117			258				8111		
	Ⓐ					⚒	B						
Osijek 1340/50 d.	0503	0627	0743	...	0952	1144	1304	1350	1527	1801	...	1924	2120
Beli Manastir 🏛 d.	0535	0659	0815	0848	1024	1216	1347	1422	1559	1834	1900	1956	2152
Magyarbóly 🏛 d.	...	...	...	0916	...	...	1422	...	...	...	1932	...	...
Pécs a.	...	...	...	1016	...	...	1502	...	...	...	2039	...	...
Budapest K **1200** a.	...	...	...	...	...	...	1814	...	...	...	...	...	...

B – DRAVA – [12] Budapest - Pécs - Osijek - Sarajevo and v.v.

OSIJEK - DOBOJ - SARAJEVO 1350

HŽ, ŽFBH, ŽRS Most services 2nd class only

km								397			259		450	399
								Z			B		L	S
	Zagreb **1325** d.	...	...	...	...	...	...	0855	...	...	...	...	...	2125
	Beograd **1320** d.	...	...	...	...	...	...	|	...	...	...	...	1300	|
	Vinkovci **1320** d.	...	...	...	...	...	...	|	...	...	...	...	1740	|
0	**Osijek 1340/5** d.	...	...	...	...	...	...	|	...	...	1500	...	|	|
48	Strizivojna-Vrpolje d.	...	...	...	...	...	...	|	...	...	1547	...	1807	|
68	Slavonski Šamac 🏛 d.	...	...	...	...	...	...	b	...	...	1622	...	1839	b
72	Šamac 🏛 d.	...	0454	...	...	1016	...	|	...	...	1645	...	1900	|
144	**Doboj** d.	...	0625	...	...	1206	...	1503	...	...	1759	...	2021	0335
144	**Doboj** d.	0423	▬	0725	...	▬	1322	1512	1542	...	1814	1925	...	0345
167	Maglaj d.	0450	0500	0801	0940	...	1358	1539	1618	*1700*	1842	2001	...	0413
190	Zavidovici d.	▬	0528	▬	1008	...	▬	1600	▬	*1728*	1903	...	...	0434
239	Zenica d.	0452	0626	0750	1106	1129	1530	1647	...	1922	1951	...	...	0521
267	Kakanj d.	0525	...	0827	...	1207	1603	1713	1737	1955	2017	...	...	0547
285	Visoko d.	0546	...	0848	...	1228	1623	1730	1803	2016	2034	...	...	0604
292	Podlugovi d.	0554	...	0856	...	1236	...	1737	1811	2024	2041	...	...	0611
316	**Sarajevo 1355** a.	0628	...	0930	...	1310	...	1805	1845	2058	2109	...	...	0639

			258		396							451	398
			B		Z							L	S
Sarajevo 1355 d.	0436	...	0702	0721	1027	1142	...	1543	...	...	1906	...	2120
Podlugovi d.	0511	...	0731	0756	1056	1217	...	1618	...	...	1941	...	2149
Visoko d.	0519	...	0738	0804	1103	1230	...	1626	1736	...	1949	...	2156
Kakanj d.	0548	...	0755	0830	1120	1251	...	1646	1757	...	2019	...	2213
Zenica d.	0620	0725	0822	0902	1147	1323	1523	▬	1829	1925	2051	...	2240
Zavidovici d.	▬	0824	0908	▬	1233	▬	1622	...	...	2024	▬	...	2326
Maglaj d.	0554	0851	0929	1128	1254	1432	1649	1734	...	2051	2107	...	2347
Doboj a.	0630	▬	0955	1204	1320	1508	▬	1810	...	▬	2143	...	0013
Doboj d.	...	0732	1005	...	1329	...	1537	...	...	1950	...	0019	0029
Šamac 🏛 d.	...	0903	1131	...	|	...	1748	...	...	2127	...	0150	|
Slavonski Šamac 🏛 d.	...	...	1157	...	b	...	...	...	...	...	...	0223	b
Strizivojna-Vrpolje d.	...	...	1215	...	|	...	...	...	...	...	...	0238	|
Osijek 1340/5 a.	...	...	1302	...	|	...	...	...	...	...	...	|	|
Vinkovci **1320** a.	...	...	...	...	|	...	...	...	...	...	...	0258	|
Beograd **1320** a.	...	...	...	...	|	...	...	...	...	...	...	0621	|
Zagreb **1325** a.	...	...	...	...	1945	...	...	...	...	...	...	...	0642

B – DRAVA – [12] Budapest - Pécs - Osijek - Sarajevo and v.v.
L – [2] Banja Luka - Vinkovci (**315/418**) - Beograd and v.v. Also conveys [1] and 🍷 July 1 - Aug. 31 from Beograd, July 2 - Sept. 1 from Banja Luka.
S – [2] Zagreb - Sarajevo and v.v.
Z – [12] Zagreb - Sarajevo - Ploče and v.v.
b – Via Banja Luka (see Table **1325**).

SARAJEVO - PLOČE 1355

HŽ, ŽFBH Most services 2nd class only

km				391						397	
		⚒		P						Z	
	Zagreb **1325** d.	...	...	...	...	...	...	...	...	0855	...
0	**Sarajevo 1350** d.	...	...	0705	0715	...	1540	...	...	1818	1910
67	Konjic d.	...	...	0818	0841	...	1706	...	...	1931	2044
129	Mostar d.	...	...	0926	...	...	...	...	...	2043	...
149	Žitomislići d.	...	...	0946	...	...	...	...	...	2103	...
163	Čapljina 🏛 d.	...	...	1017	...	...	...	...	...	2134	...
173	Metković d.	0520	0715	1042	...	1325	...	1727	1855	2157	...
194	**Ploče** a.	0545	0740	1100	...	1350	...	1752	1920	2215	...

		396						390		
		Z						P		
Ploče d.	...	0600	0615	1247	...	1410	...	1700	...	1810
Metković d.	...	0633	0641	1313	...	1436	...	1733	...	1836
Čapljina 🏛 d.	...	0658	...	...	...	...	...	1802	...	...
Žitomislići d.	...	0715	...	...	...	...	...	1819	...	...
Mostar d.	...	0736	...	...	...	...	...	1840	...	...
Konjic d.	0514	0848	...	...	1124	...	1718	1947	...	...
Sarajevo 1352 a.	0640	1000	...	...	1250	...	1852	2059	...	...
Zagreb **1325** a.	...	1945	...	...	...	...	...	...	...	...

P – [12] (also 🍷 June 13 - Sept. 6) Ploče - Sarajevo and v.v.
Z – [12] Zagreb - Sarajevo - Ploče and v.v.

VINKOVCI - TUZLA and TUZLA - DOBOJ 1358

HŽ, ŽFBH, ŽRS 2nd class only

VINKOVCI - TUZLA and v.v.:

km				⊗		⊗	⚒
0	Vinkovci d.	0349	0920	...	1430	...	1930
46	Drenovci 🏛 d.	0444	1016	1050	1526	...	2025
55	Brčko d.	...	...	1120	...	1730	...
127	Tuzla a.	...	...	1325	...	1935	...

		⊗			⊗	⚒
Tuzla d.	...	0722	...	...	1514	...
Brčko d.	...	0941	...	...	1719	...
Drenovci 🏛 d.	0506	0954	1041	1621	...	2046
Vinkovci a.	0601	...	1136	1715	...	2141

Additional services on ⚒: Vinkovci d. 1212, Drenovci a. 1307; Drenovci d. 1326, Vinkovci a. 1420.

TUZLA - DOBOJ and v.v.:

km						
0	Tuzla d.	...	1036	...	1709	...
32	Petrovo Novo d.	0540	1120	1402	1753	2100
60	Doboj a.	0628	1208	1450	1841	2148

Doboj d.	0442	0728	1305	1528	1930
Petrovo Novo d.	0530	0817	1353	1617	2018
Tuzla a.	...	0900	...	1700	...

⊗ – Not during 'heating' season (nominally until Apr. 15 or May 1).

SERBIA, MONTENEGRO and MACEDONIA

MAP PAGE 492

Operators: **ŽS**: Železnice Srbije (Железнице Србије). **ŽCG**: Železnice Crne Gore (Железнице Црне Горе). **MŽ**: Makedonski Železnici (Македонски Железници). Services in Kosovo are overseen by the United Nations Interim Administration Mission in Kosovo (UNMIK), operating as **KŽ** Kosovske Železnice / **HK** Hekurudhat e Kosovës.

Services: All trains convey first- and second-class seating, except where shown otherwise in footnotes, by a '2' in the train column, or where the footnote shows that the train conveys sleeping- (🛏) and / or couchette (▬) cars only. Descriptions of sleeping- and couchette cars are given on page 10.

Timings: Valid until **December 12, 2009** except where indicated otherwise. Services may be amended or cancelled at short notice and passengers are strongly advised to check locally before travelling.

Tickets: A supplement is payable for travel by internal express trains. Reservation of seats is possible on most express trains.

Visas: Most nationals do not require a visa to enter Serbia and Montenegro, but must obtain an entry stamp in their passport, sight of which will be required by officials on leaving the country. These must be obtained at an authorised border point recognised by the government - this excludes Kosovo's external borders with Montenegro, Macedonia and Albania. Note also that the authorities in Serbia and Montenegro do not consider entry points from Kosovo to be official border crossing points. Visas are not required for entry into Macedonia for most nationals.

Currency: Visitors to Macedonia must declare all foreign currency on arrival. In Serbia and Montenegro this applies only to large amounts (currently €2000). A certificate issued by the customs officer must be presented on departure, otherwise any funds held may be confiscated.

Security: Following the declaration of independence by Kosovo (which has not been recognised by Serbia) caution should be exercised when travelling, particularly in southern Serbia and northern Kosovo. Caution is also advised in the northern and western border regions of Macedonia.

(BUDAPEST -) KELEBIA - SUBOTICA - BEOGRAD 1360

ŽS

km			541			1121	543		345	1139		437		341
		2	[R] 🍷	2	2		[R] 🍷	2	⚡	🍷	2	🍷	2	◐
						Q			A	G		P		B
	Budapest K **1295** d.	...	...	...	...	0705	...	...	1305	...	...	...	...	2300
0	**Kelebia** 🏛 d.	...	...	...	...	1020	...	...	1615	...	...	...	...	0155
10	**Subotica 1362** 🏛 a.	...	...	...	...	1033	...	...	1626	...	...	...	...	0206
10	**Subotica** ⊖ d.	0433	0545	0720	1029	1117	1422	...	1700	...	...	1840	...	0240
108	Novi Sad **1362** ⊖ a.	0654	0742	0930	1253	1354	1619	...	1859	...	...	2045	...	0437
108	Novi Sad d.	0728	0749	0945	1300	1357	1622	1810	1907	1940	1949	2109	2246	0450
181	Novi Beograd d.	0902	0909	1119	1428	1518	1736	1939	2021	2103	2130	2226	0014	0604
186	**Beograd** a.	0911	0918	1128	1437	1527	1745	1948	2030	...	2139	...	0023	0613

	436	1138	344		540	1120				542		340	
	🍷	🍷	⚡	2	[R] 🍷		2	2	2	[R] 🍷	2	◐	2
	P	G	A			Q						B	
Beograd d.	...	...	0730	0825	1005	1005	1105	1325	1636	1835	2035	2120	2255
Novi Beograd d.	0328	0605	|	0836	1016	1016	1116	1336	1646	1846	2046	|	2306
Novi Sad **1362** a.	0449	0727	0854	1007	1131	1131	1249	1510	1829	2011	2218	2245	0038
Novi Sad ⊖ d.	0509	...	0904	1010	1135	1135	1305	1525	...	2019	...	2252	...
Subotica 1362 ⊖ a.	0716	...	1100	1216	1332	1332	1517	1755	...	2218	...	0050	...
Subotica 🏛 d.	...	...	1136	...	...	1401	...	...	...	...	...	0125	...
Kelebia 🏛 a.	...	...	1210	...	...	1412	...	...	...	...	...	0136	...
Budapest K **1295** a.	...	...	1454	...	...	1749	...	...	...	...	...	0504	...

A – AVALA – [12] and ✕ Praha - Budapest - Beograd and v.v. Also conveys: June 12 - Sept. 20 (from Praha and Budapest) ▬ 2 cl. (Praha ②③⑤⑥ -) Budapest - Beograd (**335**) - Thessaloníki; June 13 - Sept. 21 (from Thessaloníki) ▬ 2 cl. Thessaloníki - Beograd (**334**) - Budapest (- Praha ③④⑥⑦); ① June 15 - Sept. 14 (from Bratislava, one day later from Thessaloníki) ▬ 2 cl. Bratislava - Thessaloníki and v.v.; June 10 - Sept. 18 (from Kyïv / Moskva) 🛏 2 cl. Kyïv ③ / Moskva ⑤ - Thessaloníki; June 12 - Sept. 21 (from Thessaloníki) 🛏 2 cl. Thessaloníki ① - Moskva, 🛏 2 cl. Thessaloníki ⑤ - Kyïv. Also conveys Kyïv / Moskva / Praha / Bratislava - Bar cars (see note **P**).
B – BEOGRAD – [2] Budapest - Beograd and v.v.; 🛏 1, 2 cl. and ▬ 2 cl. Wien - Budapest - Beograd and v.v.; 🛏 1, 2 cl. Wien - Beograd (**490/1**) - Sofija and v.v.
G – FRUŠKA GORA – June 19 - Aug. 31 (from Novi Sad, one day later from Bar): 🛏 1, 2 cl., ▬ 1, 2 cl., [2] and 🍷 Novi Sad - Bar and v.v.
P – PANONIJA – 🛏 1, 2 cl., ▬ 1, 2 cl., [2] and 🍷 Subotica - Novi Beograd - Bar and v.v. Also conveys: ②③⑥⑦ June 9 - Sept. 16 (from Praha), ①③④⑦ June 10 - Sept. 17 (from Bar) ▬ 2 cl. Praha - Budapest (**344/5**) - Subotica - Bar and v.v.; ⑤ June 12 - Sept. 18 (from Bratislava, one day later from Bar) ▬ 2 cl. Bratislava - Subotica - Bar and v.v.; June 14 - Sept. 20 (from Kyïv / Moskva) 🛏 2 cl. Kyïv ⑦ / Moskva ② - Bar; June 16 - Sept. 22 (from Bar) 🛏 2 cl. Bar ⑤ - Moskva, 🛏 2 cl. Bar ② - Kyïv.
Q – IVO ANDRIĆ – June 11 - Sept. 23: [2] Budapest - Beograd and v.v.

◐ – Supplement payable for travel in Serbia. ⚡ – Supplement payable for travel in Hungary and Serbia. ⊗ – Service reported to be suspended.

⊖ – Additional local services operate – see panel below.

SUBOTICA - NOVI SAD (additional services): 2nd class only

Subotica d.	1300	1548	1921	2222
Novi Sad a.	1518	1804	2128	0034

Novi Sad d.	0433	0738	1915	2220
Subotica a.	0642	0949	2126	0025

1362 SUBOTICA - KIKINDA, ZRENJANIN, NOVI SAD and PANČEVO
2nd class only ŽS

km											
	Subotica 1360 d.	0150	...	...	0725	...	1310	...	1544	...	2115
	Senta d.	0309	...	...	0842	...	1417	...	1659	...	2224
	Banatsko Miloševo d.	0401	...	...	0933	...	▬	...	1749	...	▬
0	**Kikinda 1377** d.	0418	0430	...	0950	1130	...	...	1806	1810	...
19	Banatsko Miloševo d.	▬	0450	...	...	1148	...	...	...	1828	...
71	**Zrenjanin** d.	0330	0640	1035	...	1331	1510	...	...	2011	2035
96	Orlovat stajalište d.	0426	0735	1134	...	...	1605	1653	...	...	2132
	Novi Sad **1360** a.	0633	|	1335	...	...	|	1852	...	...	|
145	**Pančevo** glavna **1365** a.	...	0845	...	...	...	1715	...	...	...	2242

Pančevo glavna **1365** d.	...	...	...	...	...	1155	...	1810	...	...	2300
Novi Sad **1360** d.	...	...	...	0710	...	|	1434	|	...	1920	|
Orlovat stajalište d.	0544	...	...	0915	...	1306	1634	1921	...	2134j	0010
Zrenjanin d.	0637	0700	...	1010	...	1410	▬	2016	2025	2229	0103
Banatsko Miloševo a.	▬	0844	...	...	...	1553	...	...	2209	▬	...
Kikinda 1377 a.	0430	0901	1000	...	...	1611	1830	...	2226	...	...
Banatsko Miloševo d.	0457	...	1024	...	...	...	1857	...	...	...	...
Senta d.	0549	...	1115	...	1427	...	1949	...	...	2236	...
Subotica 1360 a.	0656	...	1222	...	1534	...	2058	...	...	2345	...

j – Arrive 2122.

1365 BEOGRAD - VRŠAC - TIMIŞOARA
2nd class only except where shown ŽS, CFR

km								361 B				
0	**Beograd** d.	...	...	...	...	...	...	1555	...	...	...	...
	Beograd centar ▶ d.	0530	...	1030	...	1427	...	|	1850	...	2216	...
19	Pančevo glavna **1362** ▶ d.	0609	0636	1109	1130	1500	1520	1636	1925	1935	2252	2335
87	Vršac a.	...	0813	...	1301	...	1651	1753	...	2106	...	0106
87	Vršac d.	...	...	...	...	...	...	1818	...	...	...	...
107	Stamora Moraviţa § a.	...	...	...	...	...	...	1940	...	...	...	...
107	Stamora Moraviţa § d.	...	...	...	...	...	...	2002	...	...	...	...
163	**Timişoara** Nord § a.	...	...	...	...	...	...	2055	...	...	...	...
	Bucureşti N **1600** a.	...	...	...	...	...	...	0531	...	...	...	...

			360 B								
Bucureşti N **1600** d.	...	...	2121	...	...	...	...	...	...	...	...
Timişoara Nord § d.	...	...	0550	...	...	...	...	...	...	...	...
Stamora Moraviţa § a.	...	...	0643	...	...	...	...	...	...	...	...
Stamora Moraviţa § d.	...	...	0707	...	...	...	...	...	...	...	...
Vršac a.	...	...	0629	...	...	...	...	...	...	...	...
Vršac d.	0440	...	0654	0905	...	1330	...	1715	...	2145	...
Pančevo glavna **1362** ▷ d.	0604	0651	0817	1030	1051	1455	1537	1856	2006	2310	2329
Beograd centar ▷ a.	...	0724	|	...	1126	...	1617	...	2043	...	2359
Beograd a.	...	...	0854	...	...	...	...	...	...	...	...

B – BUCUREŞTI – 🛏 1, 2 cl., ━ 2 cl. and (12) Beograd - Timişoara - Bucureşti and v.v.
▶ – Beograd centar - Pančevo glavna: approximately hourly 0336 – 2216.
▷ – Pančevo glavna - Beograd centar: approximately hourly 0451 – 2329.
§ – Romanian (East European) time.

1370 BEOGRAD - PODGORICA - BAR
ŽCG, ŽS

km			1141							433	897				1131	515	781		513			1139	435	437	1343
		2		2	2	2	2	2	2	🍸		2	2		R ✕		⊗	2	2	2	2	🍸		🍸	
			♦							B	♦				y	z	K					G	L	P	A
0	**Beograd** d.	...	...	...	0315	...	0705	...	...	1010	...	...	1135	...	1310	1415	1515	1545	1725	...	1925	2105n	2210	2230n	2310
93	Valjevo d.	...	...	...	0523	...	0914	...	...	1141	...	...	1323	...	1438	1543	1644	1737	1900	...	2128	2229	2341	0006	|
	Kraljevo **1372/5** d.	...	0140	...	|	...	|	...	...	|	1125	...	|	...	|	|	1848p	|	|	...	|	|	|	|	|
159	Požega **1372** d.	...	|	...	0701	...	1030	...	...	1302	1302	...	1434	...	1545	1648	1751	1851	2000	...	2242	2326	0040	0112	0202
185	Užice d.	...	0350	...	0738	...	1110	...	...	1336	1336	...	1508	...	1615	1714	...	1932	2042	...	2310	2356	0123	0205	0239
288	Prijepolje d.	...	0535	...	0853	...	1301	...	...	1457	1457	...	1654	...	1741	...	...	2111	2155	...	...	0150	0254	0335	|
338	Bijelo Polje d.	0635	0722	...	0922	...	...	...	...	1633	1633	1745	...	...	1922	...	...	...	...	...	...	0337	0425	0515	0602
468	**Podgorica** d.	0914	1001	1013	...	1310	...	1443	1730	1901	1901	2030	...	...	2214	...	...	...	...	0530	...	0605	0654	0755	0830
524	**Bar** a.	1021	1101	1113	...	1414	...	1544	1826	2000	2000	2127	...	...	2313	...	...	...	...	0629	...	0705	0800	0849	0924

	512	780						432	896				1130	514					436	1140			1138	434	1342
	2	⊗	2	2	2	2	2	🍸		2		2	R ✕		2	2	2	2	🍸		2	2	🍸		
		K						B	♦				w	z					P	♦			G	L	A
Bar d.	...	...	...	...	0533	0647	...	1005	1005	...	...	1135	1200	...	1300	1450	1610	...	1800	1845	1920	...	2010	2100	2200
Podgorica d.	...	...	...	...	0640	0744	...	1110	1110	...	...	1231	1305	...	1356	1546	1713	...	1905	1952	2019	...	2119	2210	2305
Bijelo Polje d.	...	...	...	...	0915	...	...	1358	1358	...	...	...	1604	...	...	...	...	...	2153	2250	...	...	0016	0057	0151
Prijepolje d.	0330	...	0400	0736	...	...	1205	1513	1513	1530	...	...	1717	...	...	...	...	2007	2255	0005	...	...	0127	0205	|
Užice d.	0504	...	0602	0925	...	...	1400	1643	1643	1728	...	...	1850	1850	...	...	...	2156	0023	0138	...	0220	0304	0331	0438
Požega **1372** d.	0528	0550	0631	0955	...	...	1435	1730	1735	1758	...	...	1913	1913	...	...	...	...	0043	|	...	0250	0335	0400	0514
Kraljevo **1372/5** a.	|	0450p	|	|	...	...	|	|	1831	|	...	...	|	|	...	...	...	...	|	0314	...	|	|	|	|
Valjevo d.	0627	0649	0747	1115	...	...	1550	1830	...	1915	...	...	2018	2018	...	...	...	...	0151	...	...	0406	0433	0502	|
Beograd a.	0756	0816	0941	1319	...	...	1750	1959	...	2111	...	...	2147	2147	...	...	...	...	0328n	...	...	0601	0605n	0632	0741

A – AUTO-VOZ – May 29 - Sept. 12 (from Beograd, one day later from Bar): 🛏 1, 2 cl. and ━ 1, 2 cl. Beograd - Bar and v.v.
B – TARA – (12) and 🍸 Beograd - Bar and v.v.
G – FRUŠKA GORA – June 19 - Aug. 31 (from Novi Sad, one day later from Bar): 🛏 1, 2 cl., ━ 1, 2 cl., (2) and 🍸 Novi Sad - Bar and v.v.
K – (12) and 🍸 Beograd - Kraljevo and v.v.
L – LOVĆEN – 🛏 1, 2 cl., ━ 1, 2 cl. and (2) Beograd - Bar and v.v.
P – PANONIJA – 🛏 1, 2 cl., ━ 2 cl., (2) and 🍸 Subotica - Novi Beograd - Bar and v.v. Also conveys Kyïv / Moskva / Praha / Bratislava - Bar cars (see Table **1360**, note **P**).
n – **Novi Beograd**.
p – Via Požega.
w – May 28 - Sept. 26.
y – May 29 - Sept. 27.
z – Not May 28 - Sept. 27.
♦ – For days of running and composition – see Table **1380**.
⊗ – Service reported to be suspended.

1372 POŽEGA - KRALJEVO
2nd class only except where shown ŽS

tariff km		1140 ♦							896 ♦	781 ⊗K		
0	**Požega 1370** d.	...	...	0715	...	1255	1630	...	1735	1754	...	2135
45	Čačak d.	0245	...	0753	...	1332	1709	...	1804	1822	...	2213
83	**Kraljevo 1370/5** a.	0314	...	0837	...	1414	1753	...	1831	1848	...	2257
	Lapovo **1375/80** a.	0540	...	...	...	...	...	...	2053	...	...	...
	Niš **1373/80** a.	0807	...	...	...	...	...	...	2320	...	...	...

	780 ⊗K					897 ♦					1141 ♦
Niš **1373/80** d.	...	...	...	...	...	0645	...	...	...	...	2035
Lapovo **1375/80** d.	...	...	...	...	...	0900	...	...	...	...	2300
Kraljevo 1370/5 d.	0450	...	0530	...	1045	1125	...	1500	2000	...	0140
Čačak d.	0519	...	0615	...	1130	1158	...	1544	2045	...	0250
Požega 1370 a.	0546	...	0652	...	1207	1230	...	1620	2122	...	...

K – (12) and 🍸 Beograd - Požega - Kraljevo and v.v.
♦ – For days of running and composition – see Table **1380**.
⊗ – Service reported to be suspended.

1373 BEOGRAD - ZAJEČAR - NIŠ
2nd class only except where shown ŽS

tariff km													971 Z	
0	**Beograd** d.	...	...	...	...	...	0735	...	...	...	...	...	1620	1910
98	Požarevac d.	...	...	...	...	...	0944	...	...	...	...	...	1830	2112
199	Majdanpek d.	...	0405	...	...	0950	▬	...	...	1635	...	...	2120	...
★	Prahovo p d.	...	|	0420	0910	|	...	...	1730	|	...	2200	|	...
296	**Zaječar** d.	0340	0620	0625f	1059	1205	1210	1505	1930	1850	2010	2349	2314	...
343	Knjaževac d.	0441	...	0725	...	...	1322	1608	...	...	2112	...	...	...
420	**Niš 1372/80** a.	0619	...	0907	...	...	1502	1753	...	...	2249	...	...	...

		970 Z											
Niš 1372/80 d.	...	...	0255	...	...	0710	1100	...	...	1555	...	...	1928
Knjaževac d.	...	...	0446	...	...	0852	1241	...	...	1736	...	...	2117
Zaječar d.	...	0200	0548	0630	0645	0952	1341	1405	1515	1838	1905	1950	2219
Prahovo p a.	...	|	...	0817	|	...	▬	|	1702	...	|	2137	...
Majdanpek d.	...	0353	...	...	0858	...	...	1616	...	...	2116	...	...
Požarevac d.	0425	0700	...	...	...	...	1630	...	...	...	...	...	...
Beograd a.	0625	0837	...	...	...	...	1826	...	...	...	...	...	...

Z – (2) Beograd - Zaječar and v.v.
f – Arrive 0608.
★ – Prahovo - Zaječar: *81 km*.

1375 LAPOVO and PRIŠTINA - KOSOVO POLJE - SKOPJE
2nd class only except where shown ŽS, KŽ

km		881			891 ⊠	⊠	⊗ ⊠		761 ⊠		⊗ ⊠		
	Beograd **1380** d.	2250	...	...	...	...	...	...	...	...	...	...	...
0	**Lapovo 1380** d.	0127	0405	...	...	...	...	1135	...	...	...	1655	...
28	**Kragujevac** d.	0208	0505	...	...	...	...	1226	...	...	...	1746	...
82	Kraljevo **1370/2** d.	0403	0635	0710	...	...	...	1355	...	1445	...	1925	2330
163	Raška d.	0534	...	0845	...	...	...	▬	...	1622	...	▬	0104
180	Lešak d.	0610	...	0912	...	...	0955	...	...	1649	1650	...	...
210	Zvečan d.	0707	...	1015	...	...	1052	893	...	1750	1747	...	...
214	Kosovska Mitrovica d.	...	...	▬	...	...	1058	⊠	...	...	1753	...	...
	Priština d.	...	...	⊠	0624	0740	|	1250	1730	...	|	⊠	...
247	**Kosovo Polje** d.	...	...	0425	0636	0751	1159	1330	1740	...	1854	1900	...
*	Peć a.	...	...	|	|	0940	...	|	1906	...	...	|	...
276	Uroševac d.	...	...	0502	0709	...	...	1413	...	...	...	1946	...
304	Deneral Janković a.	...	...	0540	0747	...	...	1455	...	...	...	2027	...
331	**Skopje 1380/5** a.	...	...	...	0901	...	...	...	...	...	...	...	...

	760 ⊠	⊠	880	⊗ ⊠	890 ⊠		⊠	⊗ ⊠	892 ⊠		⊠
Skopje 1380/5 d.	...	...	...	...	...	...	...	...	1613	...	...
Deneral Janković d.	...	0557§	...	...	1058§	...	...	...	1730	...	2045§
Uroševac d.	...	0643	...	...	1146	...	...	...	1814	...	2129
Peć d.	0550	|	...	...	|	...	1120	...	|	...	|
Kosovo Polje d.	0722	0730	...	0735	1225	...	1321	1415	1857j	...	2209
Priština a.	0730	▬	...	|	1235§	...	1330	|	1908	...	...
Kosovska Mitrovica d.	▬	...	...	0837	...	...	▬	1517	▬	...	...
Zvečan d.	...	...	0805	0844	...	1045	...	1524	1810	...	...
Lešak d.	...	...	0915	0940	...	1148	...	1620	1914	...	...
Raška d.	0415	...	0943	...	...	1218	...	...	1943	...	...
Kraljevo **1370/2** d.	0600	0715	1135	...	...	1351	1425	...	2118	2200	...
Kragujevac d.	...	0851	1328	...	...	...	1557	...	...	2345	...
Lapovo 1380 a.	...	0943	1408	...	...	...	1640	...	...	0029	...
Beograd **1380** a.	...	...	1706	...	...	...	...	...	...	...	...

j – Arrive 1843.
⊗ – Currently suspended.
§ – Subject to confirmation.
⊠ – Service operated by KŽ (see country heading).
* – Kosovo Polje - Peć: *82 km*.

MINOR BORDER CROSSINGS — 1377
ŽS, MÁV, CFR

SUBOTICA - SZEGED and v.v. : (2nd class only)

km								
0	Subotica d.	0850	1028	*1435*	Szeged d.	0650	1230	1430
24	Horgoš ▣ d.	0952	1131	1533	Röszke ▣ d.	0719	1300	1500
31	Röszke ▣ d.	1022	1204	1604	Horgoš ▣ d.	0752	1333	1518
43	Szeged a.	1037	1219	1619	Subotica a.	0840	1420	*1737*

KIKINDA - TIMIŞOARA and v.v. : (2nd class only)

km															
0	Kikinda 1362 d.	...	...	...	0930	...	1630	...	Timişoara § d.	0703	0757	...	1324	1605	...	1929
19	Jimbolia ▣ § d.	0510	0610	0850	1049	1235	1749	1954	Jimbolia ▣ § d.	0751	0845	1135	1412	1653	1820	2033
58	Timişoara § a.	0559	0559	0939	...	1323	...	2054	Kikinda 1362 a.	...	...	1054	...	...	1739	...

§ – East European time, one hour ahead of Central European time.

BEOGRAD - NIŠ - SOFIYA, SKOPJE and THESSALONÍKI — 1380
ŽS, MŽ, BDŽ

km					1140	393			337	491						391			591		896			293	335
		2	2	2	N	S	2	2	Q	F	2	2	2	2	2	🍷	2	2	🍷		M	2	2	Z	H
0	Beograd 1375 d.	...	...	...	...	...	0340	0720	0750	0750	...	...	1025	...	...	1405	...	1530	1650	...	...	...	1935	2115	2200
110	Lapovo 1372/5 d.	0325	...	...	0605	...	0627	0948	0940	0940	...	...	1302	...	1532	1552	...	1757	1837	...	2118	...	2211	2306	2351
135	Jagodina d.	0349	...	...	0623	...	0657	1013	0958	0958	...	...	1326	...	1557	1610	...	1822	1855	...	2136	...	2240	2325	0010
155	Paraćin d.	0412	...	...	0643	...	0722	1035	1020	1020	...	...	...	...	1619	1630	...	1844	1917	...	2156	...	2302	2347	0034
176	Stalać 1372 d.	0435	...	...	0703	...	0747	1057	1040	1040	...	...	...	...	1642	1649	...	1906	1937	...	2216	...	2324	0007	0055
244	Niš 1372/3 a.	0606	...	...	0807	...	0913	1224	1137	1137	...	...	...	...	1810	1745	...	2040	2034	...	2320	...	0053	0110	0152
244	Niš d.	...	...	0720	0855	0855	...	...	1220	1240	...	1550	...	...	...	1800	1935	...	...	...	...	...	...	0215	0210
	Dimitrovgrad ▣ d.	...	...	|	|	|	...	...	|	1517	...	|	...	...	...	|	|	...	...	...	...	...	...	0452	|
	Dragoman ▣ § d.	...	...	|	|	|	...	...	|	1656	...	|	...	...	...	|	|	...	...	...	...	...	...	0626	|
	Sofiya § a.	...	...	|	|	|	...	...	|	1740	...	|	...	...	...	|	|	...	...	...	...	...	...	0715	|
288	Leskovac d.	...	...	0822	0936	0936	...	...	1300	...	...	1650	...	...	...	1841	2035	...	...	...	...	...	...	...	0250
392	Preševo ▣ d.	...	...	1102	1223	1223	...	...	1545	...	...	...	...	...	...	2128	2329	...	...	...	...	...	...	...	0535
401	Tabanovci ▣ d.	...	0723	...	1253	1253	...	...	1620	...	...	...	...	1955	...	2210	...	...	...	...	...	0505	...	...	0610
462	Skopje a.	...	0820	...	1349	1349	...	...	1700	...	...	...	...	2051	...	2250	...	...	...	...	...	0600	...	...	0650
462	Skopje 1375/85 d.	...	...	...	...	...	...	...	1715	...	1942	...	...	...	...	...	...	...	...	...	...	0609	...	...	0720
524	Veles 1385 d.	...	...	...	...	...	...	...	1757	...	2041	...	...	...	...	...	...	...	...	...	...	0705	...	...	0802
651	Gevgelija a.	...	...	...	...	...	...	...	1928	...	2224	...	...	...	...	...	...	...	...	...	...	0848	...	...	0929
651	Gevgelija ▣ d.	...	...	...	...	...	...	...	1955	...	...	...	...	...	...	...	...	...	...	...	...	...	...	...	1000
654	Idoméni ▣ a.	...	...	...	...	...	...	...	2100	...	...	...	...	...	...	...	...	...	...	...	...	...	...	...	1105
654	Idoméni d.	...	...	...	...	...	...	...	2145	...	...	...	...	...	...	...	...	...	...	...	...	...	...	...	1145
730	Thessaloníki 1400 § a.	...	...	...	...	...	...	...	2233	...	...	...	...	...	...	...	...	...	...	...	...	...	...	...	1231

km				590	897				390			490				336		1141		392			292		334
		2	2	🍷	M	2	2	2	T	2	2	F	2	2	2	P	2	N		2	2	2	Z		H
	Thessaloníki 1400 § d.	...	...	...	...	...	...	...	...	...	...	...	...	...	...	0945	...	...	...	...	...	...	...	...	1705
	Idoméni a.	...	...	...	...	...	...	...	...	...	...	...	...	...	...	1034	...	...	...	...	...	...	...	...	1753
	Idoméni ▣ d.	...	...	...	...	...	...	...	...	...	...	...	...	...	...	1107	...	...	...	...	...	...	...	...	1830
	Gevgelija ▣ a.	...	...	...	...	...	...	...	...	...	...	...	...	...	...	1012	...	...	...	...	...	...	...	...	1735
	Gevgelija d.	...	...	...	...	...	...	...	...	0459	...	...	...	...	...	1037	...	...	...	...	...	1552	...	...	1805
	Veles 1385 d.	...	...	...	...	...	...	...	...	0642	...	...	...	...	...	1205	...	...	...	...	...	1735	...	...	1933
	Skopje 1375/85 a.	...	...	...	...	...	...	...	...	0739	...	...	...	...	...	1245	...	...	...	...	...	1829	...	...	2014
	Skopje d.	...	...	...	...	0610	...	...	0741	...	...	...	...	...	...	1311	...	1311	...	1632	...	1840	...	...	2040
	Tabanovci ▣ a.	...	...	...	...	0707	...	...	0822	...	...	...	...	...	...	1351	...	1351	...	1729	...	1934	...	...	2120
	Preševo ▣ d.	...	0215	...	...	...	...	...	0915	...	...	...	...	1147	...	1502	...	1502	...	1808	...	...	...	...	2235
	Leskovac d.	...	0503	...	...	...	...	...	1141	...	...	...	...	1434	1710	1734	...	1734	...	2046	...	...	...	...	0045
0	Sofiya § d.	...	|	...	...	...	...	...	|	...	...	1155	...	|	|	|	...	|	...	|	...	...	2120	...	|
42	Dragoman ▣ § d.	...	|	...	...	...	...	...	|	...	...	1244	...	|	|	|	...	|	...	|	...	...	2213	...	|
63	Dimitrovgrad ▣ d.	...	|	...	...	...	...	...	|	...	...	1230	...	|	|	|	...	|	...	|	...	...	2200	...	|
161	Niš 1372/3 a.	...	0559	...	...	...	...	...	1219	...	...	1453	...	1529	1817	1820	...	1820	...	2124	...	...	0003	...	0133
	Niš d.	0326	...	0600	0645	...	0730	1020	1235	...	...	1520	1535	...	...	1835	1915	2035	...	...	2317	...	0050	...	0148
	Stalać 1372 d.	0454	...	0658	0743	...	0901	1151	1334	...	...	1619	1717	...	...	1934	2046	2134	...	...	0050	...	0149	...	0245
	Paraćin d.	0515	...	0718	0802	...	0922	1212	1353	...	...	1638	1738	...	...	1953	2107	2153	...	...	0111	...	0208	...	0304
	Jagodina d.	0539	...	0738	0822	...	0951	1236	1414	...	1449	1659	1802	...	...	2014	2131	2214	...	...	0135	...	0229	...	0324
	Lapovo 1372/5 d.	0620	...	0758	0840	...	1025	1301	1434	...	1524	1720	1838	...	...	2034	2206	2232	...	...	0200	...	0249	...	0344
	Beograd 1375 a.	0851	...	0957	...	...	1252	...	1633	...	1757	1918	2100	...	...	2223	0049	...	...	...	...	...	0448	...	0544

F – BALKAN – [12] Beograd - Sofiya and v.v.; 🛏 1, 2 cl. Beograd - Sofiya - İstanbul and v.v.; 🛏 1, 2 cl. Wien (**346/7**) - Budapest (**340/1**) - Beograd - Sofiya and v.v.

H – HELLAS EXPRESS – 🛏 1, 2 cl., ▬ 2 cl. and [12] Beograd - Skopje - Thessaloníki and v.v.; ▬ 2 cl. Skopje (**334/5**) - Niš - Sofiya and v.v. Also conveys: June 12 - Sept. 20 (from Praha and Budapest) ▬ 2 cl. (Praha ②③⑤⑥ -) Budapest (**345**) - Beograd - Thessaloníki; June 13 - Sept. 21 (from Thessaloníki) ▬ 2 cl. Thessaloníki - Beograd (**344**) - Budapest (- Praha ③④⑥⑦); ① June 15 - Sept. 14 (from Bratislava, one day later from Thessaloníki) ▬ 2 cl. Bratislava - Thessaloníki and v.v.; June 10 - Sept. 18 (from Kyïv / Moskva) 🛏 2 cl. Kyïv ③ / Moskva ⑤ - Thessaloníki; June 12 - Sept. 21 (from Thessaloníki) 🛏 2 cl. Thessaloníki ① - Moskva, 🛏 2 cl. Thessaloníki ⑤ - Kyïv.

M – Dec. 14 - June 11, Sept. 6 - Dec. 11 (from Niš, one day later from Bar): [2] Niš - Požega (**432/3**) - Bar and v.v.

N – NIŠAVA – June 12 - Sept. 5 (from Niš, one day later from Bar): 🛏 1, 2 cl., ▬ 2 cl. and [2] Niš - Bar and v.v.; 🛏 1, 2 cl. Skopje (**336/393**) - Niš - Bar and v.v.

P – OLYMPUS – [12] and 🍷 Thessaloníki - Beograd. Conveys June 27 - Aug. 29: 🛏 1, 2 cl. Skopje - Niš (**1141**) - Bar.

Q – OLYMPUS – [12] and 🍷 Beograd - Thessaloníki; ▬ 2 cl. Ljubljana (**315**) - Beograd - Skopje.

S – [2] Niš - Skopje. Conveys June 28 - Aug. 30 (from Bar): 🛏 1, 2 cl. Bar (**1140**) - Niš - Skopje.

T – KOČO RACIN – [12] and 🍷 Skopje - Beograd; ▬ 2 cl. Skopje - Beograd (**314**) - Ljubljana.

Z – 🛏 1, 2 cl., ▬ 2 cl. and [12] Beograd - Sofiya and v.v. Conveys June 27 - Sept. 4 (from Skopje), June 29 - Sept. 6 (from Sofiya): ▬ 2 cl. Skopje (**334/5**) - Niš - Sofiya and v.v.

* – Estimated time. § – East European time.

BRANCH LINES in Macedonia — 1385
MŽ

SKOPJE - KOČANI and BITOLA and v.v. : (2nd class only)

km												
0	Skopje 1380 d.	0222	0646	1430	1530	1815	Bitola d.	0333	...	1242	...	1843
62	Veles 1380 d.	0310	0739	1522	1621	1912	Prilep d.	0414	...	1332	...	1932
★	Kočani a.	0501	|	|	1811	|	Kočani d.	|	0521	|	1827	|
170	Prilep d.	...	0929	1707	...	2107	Veles 1380 d.	0555	0714	1523	2021	2116
228	Bitola a.	...	1017	1755	...	2145	Skopje 1380 a.	0644	0814	1620	2108	2205

SKOPJE - KIČEVO and v.v. : (2nd class only)

km								
0	Skopje d.	0250	0800	1630	Kičevo d.	0510	1215	1854
86	Tetovo d.	0347	0905	1735	Tetovo d.	0613	1319	1958
163	Kičevo a.	0445	1007	1837	Skopje a.	0715	1422	2059

★ – Veles - Kočani: *110 km*.

ALBANIA

SEE MAP PAGE 492

Operator: **HSH**: Hekurudha Shqiptarë.
Services: Trains convey one class of accommodation only. Tickets are not sold in advance, only for the next available departure.
Security: Most visits to Albania are now reported to be trouble free, but travellers are advised to avoid the north-east of the country.

Timings: Valid from **November 5, 2008**

ALBANIAN RAILWAYS — 1390
HSH One class only

Times for Milot, Vorë, Rrogozhinë, Lushnjë and Fier are subject to minor variation

km											
0	Shkodër a.	...	0555	...	...	...	...	...	...	...	...
47	Milot d.	...	0731*	...	...	...	...	...	...	...	...
	Tiranë d.	0555	|	0830	...	...	1410	1445	...	1615	2000
82	Vorë a.	0617*	0845	0852*	←	...	1432*	1507*	...	1637*	2022*
82	Vorë d.	0618	→	0854	0857	...	1438	1508	...	1641	2023
98	**Tiranë** a.	|	...	|	0921	...	|	|	...	|	|
102	**Durrës** a.	0653	...	0928	...	...	1507	1542	...	1712	2057
102	**Durrës** d.	0707	...	...	...	...	1525	1600	...	...	...
	Durrës Plazh a.	|	...	...	...	...	|	|	...	...	...
138	Rrogozhinë d.	0818*	...	...	...	...	1638*	1712*	...	...	...
179	Elbasan a.	0938	...	...	...	...	1755	|	...	...	...
255	Pogradec a.	1232	...	...	...	...	...	|	...	...	...
155	Lushnjë a.	...	...	...	...	...	...	1745*	...	...	...
187	Fier a.	...	...	...	...	...	...	1843*	...	...	...
221	Vlorë a.	...	...	...	...	...	...	1952	...	...	...

Vlorë d.	...	...	0540	...	...	...	...	...	...	...
Fier d.	...	...	0650*	...	...	...	...	...	...	...
Lushnjë d.	...	...	0748*	...	...	...	...	...	...	...
Pogradec d.	...	...	|	...	...	...	...	...	1250	...
Elbasan d.	...	0600	|	...	...	...	...	...	1555	...
Rrogozhinë d.	...	0713*	0822*	...	...	...	...	...	1712*	...
Durrës Plazh d.	...	|	|	...	...	...	...	...	|	...
Durrës a.	...	0828	0935	...	...	...	...	...	1820	...
Durrës d.	0610	0845	0950	...	1300	...	...	1730	1835	...
Tiranë d.	|	|	|	...	|	1315	...	|	|	...
Vorë a.	0645*	0921	1024	...	1335*	1340*	...	1805*	1909	...
Vorë d.	0647	0922	1025	...	1337	1345*	...	1807*	1911	...
Tiranë a.	0710	0946	1049	...	1401	|	...	1830	1935	...
Milot d.	...	...	...	...	...	1502*	...	...	...	...
Shkodër a.	...	...	...	...	...	1642	...	...	...	...

* – Estimated time.

GREECE

SEE MAP PAGE 492

Operator: Οργανισμος Σιδηροδρομων Ελλαδας - Organismós Sidiródromon Elládas / Hellenic Railways Organisation (ΟΣΕ - OSE). Some suburban services are operated by Proastiakos.

Services: All trains convey first and second class seating except where shown otherwise in footnotes or by '2' in the train column, or where the footnote shows sleeping and/or couchette cars only. Descriptions of sleeping (🛏) and couchette (▬) cars appear on page 10. Services that convey catering may vary from day to day.

Timings: Timings have been compiled from the latest information received. However, readers should be aware that a substantial amount of engineering work is taking place throughout the country and timetable amendments may come into effect at short notice.

Tickets: Reservation of seats is possible (and recommended) on most express trains. *IC* trains carry a supplement which varies depending upon distance travelled. Break of journey is only permitted when tickets are so endorsed before travel with the station quoted.

1400 ATHÍNA - LÁRISA - THESSALONÍKI

km		883 592	IC 70 ✕⚡	IC 50 ✕◇		884	500 🍷	IC 52 ✕⚡		1520 2	IC 54 ✕⚡	502 🍷		IC 40 🍷⚡	IC 48 🍷⚡	602 🍷 ♦⊗		1522 2	IC 56 ✕◇	IC 74 ✕⚡		504 [R] ♦	604 🍷 ♦	
0	**Athína** Lárisa **1420/40** d.	...	0650	0753	...	0821	0921	1051	...	1219	1321	1453	...	1553	1553	1651	...	1753	1928	2039	...	2255	2359	...
61	Inói **1420** d.	...	0734	|	...	0912	1010	1135	...	1317	1405	1542	...	1637	1637	1745	...	1846	|	2123	...	2350	0054	...
89	Thíva d.	...	0750	|	...	0929	1028	1151	...	1337	1422	1602	...	1654	1654	1803	...	1906	|	2140	...	0012	0115	...
129	Levadiá d.	...	0808	|	...	0950	1053	1209	...	1403	1440	1626	...	1714	1714	1828	...	1931	|	2159	...	|	0141	...
154	Tithoréa d.	...	|	|	...	1001x	1106	|	...	1421	1451x	1642	...	1725x	1725x	1847	...	1951	|	|	...	|	0156x	...
169	Amfíklia d.	...	|	|	...	1017	|	|	...	1433x	|	1654x	...	|	|	1859x	...	2003x	|	|	...	|	|	...
210	Lianokládi d.	...	0902	0948	...	1059	1157	1304	...	1515	1546	1739	...	1813	1813	1939	...	2055	2123	2256	...	0147	0303	...
	Lamia a.	...	|	|	...	|	|	|	...	1533	|	|	...	|	|	|	...	2114	|	|	...	|	|	...
291	Paleofársalos **1408** d.	...	1009	|	...	1216	1307	1407	...	...	1652	1854	...	1921	1923	2100	...	...	|	|	...	|	0434	...
	Kalambáka **1408** a.	0742	|	|	...	1303	|	|	...	...	|	|	...	|	2010	|	...	...	|	|	...	|	|	...
333	**Lárisa 1425** ▲ d.	0857	1030	1100	...	...	1342	1428	...	...	1713	1931	...	1941	...	2126	...	...	2235	0020	...	0358	0515	...
	Vólos **1425** a.	|	|	|	...	...	|	|	...	...	|	|	...	2025	...	|	...	...	|	|	...	|	|	...
417	Kateríni ▲ d.	0951	1113	|	...	...	1420	1506	...	...	1751	2009	...	...	...	2219	...	...	|	0058	...	0446	0609	...
465	Platí **1410** ▲ d.	1016	1134	|	...	...	1441	1530	...	...	1811	2030	...	...	...	2250	...	...	|	|	...	0511	0637	...
502	**Thessaloníki 1410** ▲ a.	1039	1154	1209	...	...	1502	1550	...	...	1831	2051	...	...	...	2313	...	...	2344	0138	...	0536	0700	...
	Alexandrúpoli Port **1405** a.	...	1716	...	...	...	...	...	...	...	...	...	...	...	...	0544	...	...	...	0653	...	...	1315	...

km		1521 2	IC 41 🍷⚡	IC 47 🍷⚡	IC 51 ✕◇		603 🍷 ♦⊗	IC 53 ✕⚡	IC 71 ✕⚡		501 🍷	IC 55 ✕⚡	1523 2		885	503 🍷	591 886	IC 57 ✕◇		605 🍷 ♦	505 [R] ♦		IC 75 ✕⚡	
	Alexandrúpoli Port **1405** a.	...	...	...	...	...	0051	...	0642	...	...	...	...	...	...	...	...	...	...	1522	...	...	2032	...
	Thessaloníki 1410 ▲ d.	...	...	...	0724	...	0735	1013	1140	...	1242	1454	...	...	...	1633	1759	1901	...	2259	2333	...	0151	...
	Platí **1410** ▲ d.	...	...	...	|	...	0758	1034	1201	...	1304	1515	...	...	...	1655	1824	|	...	2323	2359	...	|	...
	Kateríni ▲ d.	...	...	...	|	...	0829	1055	1222	...	1326	1536	...	...	...	1717	1849	|	...	2351	0025	...	0232	...
0	Vólos **1425** d.	...	0620	...	|	...	|	|	|	...	|	|	...	...	...	|	|	|	...	|	|	...	|	...
61	**Lárisa 1425** ▲ d.	...	0707	...	0834	...	0924	1136	1300	...	1418	1614	...	...	...	1809	1941	2011	...	0058	0126	...	0311	...
—	Kalambáka **1408** d.	...	|	0633	|	...	|	|	|	...	|	|	...	...	1736	|	2051	|	...	|	|	...	|	...
	Paleofársalos **1408** d.	...	0730	0730	|	...	0951	1157	1321	...	1439	1635	...	...	1824	1832	...	|	...	0125	|	...	|	...
0	Lamia d.	0615	|	|	|	...	|	|	|	...	|	|	1815	...	|	|	...	|	...	|	|	...	|	...
6	Lianokládi d.	0635	0838	0838	0947	...	1120	1305	1430	...	1551	1738	1835	...	1940	2009	...	2124	...	0250	0324	...	0434	...
—	Amfíklia d.	0717x	0924x	0924x	|	...	1202x	|	|	...	|	|	1922x	...	2019x	2053	...	|	...	|	|	...	|	...
	Tithoréa d.	0729	0936x	0936x	|	...	1214	1350x	|	...	1638	|	1934	...	2031x	2105x	...	|	...	0345x	|	...	0517x	...
	Levadiá d.	0748	0951	0951	|	...	1233	1402	1525	...	1651	1832	1954	...	2042	2118	...	|	...	0402	|	...	0528	...
	Thíva d.	0815	1011	1011	|	...	1258	1421	1543	...	1714	1850	2020	...	2102	2141	...	|	...	0430	0456	...	0546	...
	Inói **1420** d.	0835	1032	1032	|	...	1318	1437	1559	...	1730	1906	2042	...	2118	2158	...	|	...	0451	0518	...	0602	...
	Athína Lárisa **1420/40** a.	0932	1116	1116	1140	...	1410	1521	1643	...	1818	1950	2136	...	2208	2246	...	2317	...	0546	0612	...	0646	...

▲ – Local service Thessaloníki - Litóhoro - Lárisa and v.v.:

Thessaloníki d.	0508	0608	0808	0945	1215	1320	1410	1600	1734	1945	2105	2209
Platí d.	0534	0634	0834	1011	1241	1346	1436	1626	1800	2011	2131	2235
Kateríni d.	0557	0657	0857	1034	1304	1409	1459	1649	1823	2034	2154	2258
Litóhoro △ d.	0605	0705	0905	1042	1312	1417	1507	1657	1831	2042	2202	2306
Lárisa a.	0641	0741	0941	1118	1348	1453	1543	1733	1907	2118	2238	2342

Lárisa d.	0600	0650	0800	1002	1200	1400	1510	1553	1756	2000	2130	2250
Litóhoro △ d.	0637	0727	0837	1039	1237	1437	1547	1630	1833	2037	2207	2327
Kateríni d.	0645	0735	0845	1047	1245	1445	1555	1638	1841	2045	2215	2335
Platí d.	0708	0758	0908	1110	1308	1508	1618	1701	1904	2108	2238	2358
Thessaloníki a.	0733	0823	0933	1135	1333	1533	1643	1726	1929	2133	2303	0023

FOR NOTES SEE TABLE 1405

1405 THESSALONÍKI - ALEXANDRÚPOLI - SVILENGRAD

OSE, BDZh

km		1630 2	604 ♦🍷	1684 2	IC 70 ✕⚡	1632 2	614 🍷	1634 2⊗	IC 92 ✕⚡	444 ♦[R]	602 ♦⊗	IC 74 ✕⚡
	Athína **1400** d.	...	2359	...	...	...	...	...	...	...	1651	2039
0	**Thessaloníki** d.	0635	0718	...	1221	1302	1417	1636	1825	1937	2344	0201
42	Kilkís d.	0710	0752	...	1250	1340	1446	1710	1850	2002	0016	0227
97	Rodópoli d.	0754	0832	...	1322	1424	1524	1756	1323	|	0058	0259
130	Strimón d.	0825	0900	...	|	1455	1548	1826	|	|	0127	|
162	Sérres d.	0847	0926	...	1400	1517	1610	1848	2001	2117	0151	0337
232	Dráma d.	...	1021	...	1444	▬	1701	▬	2051	2205	0242	0421
327	Xánthi d.	...	1144	...	1557	...	1821	...	2212	2325	0406	0535
374	Komotiní d.	...	1217	...	1624	**1680**	1850	...	2239	2353	0441	0602
442	Alexandrúpoli a.	...	1310	...	1710	2	1941	...	2325	0039	0538	0647
443	**Alexandrúpoli** Port d.	...	1318	1507	1716	1756	2036	...	2331	|	0550	0658
556	Píthio d.	...	1459	1649	...	1941	2224	...	...	0252	0743	0835
*	*İstanbul Sirkeci* **1550** a.	...	*2131*	|	...	|	|	**1690**	...	0807	|	|
574	Néa Orestiáda d.	...	1604	1711	...	2003	2248	2	...	...	0807	0850
611	Díkea a.	...	1641	1745	...	2039	2324	0450	...	...	0850	0922
618	Orménio a.	...	1651	...	...	2048	...	0500	...	...	0900	...
627	Svilengrad 🏛 **1550** a.	...	...	...	...	...	...	...	...	...	0940	...

	445 ♦[R]	1681 2	IC 71 ✕⚡	613 🍷	1683 2	1691 2	605 ♦🍷	1635 2⊗	IC 91 ✕⚡	1693 2	IC 75 ✕⚡	1695 2	603 ♦⊗
Svilengrad 🏛 **1550** d.	...	...	...	...	...	1025	...	...	...	...	...	...	...
Orménio d.	...	...	...	0505	...	1050	...	...	1515	1700	...	2100	...
Díkea d.	...	0409	...	0516	0935	1100	1237	...	1530	1710	1801	2110	2211
Néa Orestiáda d.	...	0444	...	0551	1009	...	1313	...	1603	...	1834	...	2247
İstanbul Sirkeci **1550** d.	2100	|	...	|	|	...	|	...	*0830*	...	|	...	|
Píthio d.	0250	0459	...	0614	1033	...	1336	...	1618	...	1849	...	2304
Alexandrúpoli Port d.	|	0641	0642	0829	1218	...	1522	...	1755	...	2032	...	0051
Alexandrúpoli d.	0415	▬	0648	0835	▬	...	1528	...	1801	...	2038	...	0057
Komotiní d.	0503	...	0735	0929	...	...	1625	...	1849	...	2125	...	0151
Xánthi d.	0536	**1631**	0803	1001	**1633**	...	1701	...	1917	...	2153	...	0227
Dráma d.	0649	2	0913	1124	2	...	1828	...	2031	...	2308	...	0354
Sérres d.	0735	0900	0957	1213	1524	...	1919	2015	2116	...	2353	...	0458
Strimón d.	|	0929	|	1234	1549	...	1942	2038	|	...	|	...	0522
Rodópoli d.	|	1000	1033	1259	1622	...	2010	2114	2154	...	0029	...	0550
Kilkís d.	0854	1044	1105	1341	1711	...	2055	2159	2226	...	0107	...	0631
Thessaloníki a.	0920	1117	1130	1410	1743	...	2127	2233	2251	...	0132	...	0708
Athína **1400** a.	...	...	1643	...	...	...	0546	...	...	...	0646	...	1410

♦ – NOTES FOR TABLES 1400 / 1405 (LISTED BY TRAIN NUMBER)

444/5 – FILÍA - DOSTLUK EXPRESS – 🛏 1, 2 cl. Thessaloníki - İstanbul and v.v.
504/5 – 🛏 1, 2 cl. Athína - Thessaloníki and v.v.; 🛏 1, 2 cl. Athína - Thessaloníki (**360/3**) - Sofiya and v.v.
602 – (12) and 🍷 Athína - Thessaloníki - Díkea; ▬ 2 cl. Thessaloníki - Díkea; (2) Díkea - Svilengrad.
603 – (12) and 🍷 Díkea - Thessaloníki - Athína; ▬ 2 cl. Díkea - Thessaloníki.
604 – (12) and 🍷 Athína - Thessaloníki - Orménio; ▬ 2 cl. Athína - Thessaloníki.
605 – (12) and 🍷 Díkea - Thessaloníki - Athína; ▬ 2 cl. Thessaloníki - Athína.

x – Stops on request.
⚡ – [R] with supplement payable. *Icity* train.
◇ – [R] with supplement payable. *IcityE* train.
△ – Station for Mount Ólimbos.
⊗ – Service currently suspended.
* – Píthio - İstanbul: *268 km*.

1408 LÁRISA - PALEOFÁRSALOS - KALAMBÁKA

km		2	2	2	2	884	2⊖	2	2⊖	IC 48 🍷⚡	886
	Thessaloníki **1400** d.	...	...	...	...	...	...	...	...	...	1759
	Athína **1400** d.	...	...	...	...	0821	...	...	...	1553	|
	Lárisa 1400 d.	0500	0626	0725	...	|	...	...	...	|	1941
0	Paleofársalos **1400** d.	0522	0650	0756	1017	1213	1343	1444	1710	1923	2004
31	Kardítsa d.	0538x	0706	0815	1036	1229	1404	1500	1729	1939	2020
60	Tríkala a.	0554	0722	0833	1054	1245	1422	1516	1747	1955	2036
82	**Kalambáka 1400** ⊡ a.	0609	0737	0849	1110	1300	1438	1531	1808	2010	2051

	IC 47 🍷⚡	883	2	2		2	2⊖	885	2⊖	2
Kalambáka 1400 ⊡ d.	0633	0742	0853	1155	...	1331	1532	1736	1903	2100
Tríkala d.	0648	0757	0909	1211	...	1346	1548	1751	1919	2115
Kardítsa d.	0707	0816	0928	1233	...	1403	1607	1808	1940	2132
Paleofársalos **1400** a.	0722	0832	0946	1251	...	1418	1625	1823	1958	2147
Lárisa 1400 a.	|	0856	...	...	...	...	...	|	2030	2211
Athína **1400** a.	1116	|	...	...	...	...	...	2208	...	...
Thessaloníki **1400** a.	...	1039	...	...	...	...	...	...	...	...

x – Stops on request.
⊖ – Days and dates of running are subject to confirmation.
⚡ – [R] with supplement payable.
⊡ – An infrequent bus service operates Kalambáka - Igumenítsa and v.v. (approximately *250 km*).

THESSALONÍKI - ÉDESSA - KOZÁNI and FLÓRINA 1410

km		Ⓐ		k			Ⓐ	Ⓐk			k		Ⓐ				k		Ⓐ			k	Ⓐ		
0	**Thessaloníki 1400** d.	0428	0618	...	...	0657	0838	...	0954	1109	...	...	1231	1400	...	1511	...	...	1646	1751	1911	...	2013	2216	...
38	Platí **1400** d.	0452	0644	...	...	0728	0905	...	1025	1139	...	...	1259	1428	...	1537	...	...	1715	1818	1939	...	2040	2243	...
69	Véria d.	0517	0716	...	...	0803	0936	...	1054	1212	...	...	1330	1500	...	1610	...	...	1748	1850	2010	...	2118	2316	...
97	Skídra d.	0536	0738	...	...	0824	0957	...	1116	1234	...	...	1352	1523	...	1632	...	...	1809	1912	2031	...	2139	2337	...
112	**Édessa** d.	0548	0751	...	...	0836	1010	...	1128	1247	...	...	1404	1535	...	1645	...	...	1821	1924	2045	...	2151	2349	...
162	Amíndeo d.	...	0839	0838	...	...	1059	1058	...	1337	1336	...	...	...	...	1733	1734	...	...	...	2133	2134	...	...	...
	Kozáni a.	...	|	0920	...	...	|	1141	...	|	1419	...	...	...	...	|	1817	...	...	...	|	2217	...	...	...
196	**Flórina** a.	...	0904	...	...	...	1124	...	...	1402	...	...	...	...	...	1758	...	...	...	...	2158	...	...	...	...

km			Ⓐ								Ⓐ	Ⓐ		Ⓐ					Ⓐ						Ⓐ
	Flórina d.	...	...	...	0608	...	...	...	0941	...	...	1219	...	...	...	1501	...	...	...	...	...	...	1926	...	...
0	Kozáni d.	...	...	0548	|	...	...	0926	|	...	1155	|	...	...	1438	|	...	...	...	...	...	1903	|	...	...
60	Amíndeo d.	...	...	0631	0638	...	...	1007	1011	...	1238	1249	...	...	1521	1531	...	...	...	...	...	1946	1956	...	...
	Édessa d.	0440	0640	...	0725	0917	...	...	1100	1152	...	1337	...	1444	...	1617	...	1712	1830	1951	...	...	2044	...	2156
	Skídra d.	0453	0653	...	0739	0930	...	...	1114	1205	...	1351	...	1457	...	1631	...	1725	1843	2004	...	...	2057	...	2209
	Véria d.	0515	0715	...	0802	0953	...	...	1133	1228	...	1412	...	1518	...	1650	...	1747	1906	2027	...	...	2118	...	2230
	Platí **1400** d.	0546	0746	...	0833	1026	...	...	1202	1307	...	1445	...	1555	...	1714	...	1820	1938	2059	...	...	2149	...	2300
	Thessaloníki 1400 a.	0615	0815	...	0901	1058	...	...	1228	1333	...	1515	...	1621	...	1740	...	1846	2004	2125	...	...	2215	...	2326

k – Connection from train in previous column.

ATHÍNA - INÓI - HALKÍDA 1420

Local rail service. 2nd class. *83 km.* Journey: 70–90 minutes.
All trains call at Inói (± 60 minutes from Athína).

From **Athína** Lárisa: 0506Ⓐ, 0545Ⓐ, 0623, 0723, 0841, 1024, 1144, 1337, 1415Ⓐ, 1524, 1629, 1723Ⓐ, 1831, 2014, 2214, 2325.
From **Inói**: 0533Ⓐ, 0614, 0652Ⓐ, 0735, 0914, 0948, 1136, 1343, 1448, 1520Ⓐ, 1646, 1748, 1940, 2135, 2326.

Service currently suspended Inói - Halkída and v.v. owing to engineering work; a replacement 🚌 service will operate (approximately hourly 0600 - 2200).

LÁRISA - VÓLOS 1425

Local rail service. Journey: ± 60 minutes.
See Table **1400** for *IC* services from / to Athína.

From **Lárisa**: 0526, 0555, 0706, 0803, 0930, 1106, 1207, 1352, 1438, 1602, 1722, 1841, 2025, 2140, 2247.
From **Vólos**: 0540, 0703, 0822, 0928, 1039, 1227, 1312, 1457, 1557, 1707, 1901, 1951, 2128, 2244, 2347.

PIREÁS, ATHÍNA and ATHÍNA AIRPORT ✈ - KÓRINTHOS - KIÁTO 1440

2nd class

km																										
0	Pireás ▲ d.	0436	...	...	0544	...	...	...	...	...	...	0644	and	...	...	...	...	...	...	2244	...	...	...	...	...	...
10	**Athína** Lárisa **1400** ▲ d.	0457	...	...	0606	...	...	...	...	...	...	0706	at the	...	...	...	...	...	...	2306	...	...	...	...	...	...
	Athína Airport ✈ ▲ d.	|	0539	...	|	0554	0609	...	0623	0639	...	|	same	2154	2209	...	2223	2239	...	|	2254	2309	...	2323	2339	...
	Neratziótissa ▲ d.	|	0600	0606	|	0615	0630	0635	0644	0700	0706	|	minutes	2215	2230	2235	2244	2300	2306	|	2315	2330	2335	2344	0000	0006
20	Ano Liosia ▲ d.	0510	...	0615	0619	...	...	0644	...	...	0715	0719	past each	...	...	2244	...	...	2315	2319	...	...	2344	...	...	0020
90	**Kórinthos** (new station) d.	...	...	...	0713	...	...	...	...	...	...	0813	hour	...	...	...	...	...	...	0013	...	...	...	...	...	...
111	**Kiáto 1450** a.	...	...	...	0727	...	...	...	...	...	...	0827	until	...	...	...	...	...	...	0027	...	...	...	...	...	...

km																										
	Kiáto 1450 d.	...	...	...	...	...	...	0536	...	...	...	...	...	...	and	2136	...	...	...	...	...	...	2236	...	...	...
	Kórinthos (new station) d.	...	...	...	...	...	...	0551	...	...	...	...	...	...	at the	2151	...	...	...	...	...	...	2251	...	...	...
0	Ano Liosia ▲ d.	0545	...	...	0622	...	...	0647	0650	...	...	0722	...	...	same	2247	2250	...	...	2322	...	...	2347	2350	...	...
9	Neratziótissa ▲ d.	0554	0605	0620	0631	0635	0649	|	0659	0705	0720	0731	0735	0749	minutes	|	2259	2305	2320	2331	2335	2349	|	2359	0005	...
34	Athína Airport ✈ ▲ a.	...	0627	0642	...	0657	0711	|	...	0727	0742	...	0757	0811	past each	|	...	2327	2342	...	2357	0011	|	...	0027	...
	Athína Lárisa **1400** ▲ d.	...	...	...	...	...	...	0704	...	...	...	...	...	...	hour	2304	...	...	...	...	...	...	0004	...	...	...
	Pireás ▲ a.	...	...	...	...	...	...	0722	...	...	...	...	...	...	until	2322	...	...	...	...	...	...	0022	...	...	...

▲ – Frequent Metro services operate as follows:
Line 1: Pireás - Monastiraki - Omónia - Attiki - Neratziótissa (journey time: ± 45 minutes).
Line 2: Syntagma - Omónia - Athína Lárisa (for **Athína** mainline station) - Attiki (journey time: ± 7 minutes).
Line 3: Monastiraki - Syntagma - Athína Airport ✈ (journey time: ± 37 minutes). *Currently subject to partial 🚌 replacement.*
Operators: ISAP Line 1; Attiko Metro Lines 2 and 3.

Allow sufficient time for connecting shipping services at Pireás as the port is very large.

KIÁTO - PÁTRA - KALAMÁTA 1450

Narrow gauge. 2nd class only (except *IC* trains)

km		308		*IC* 20	300		*IC* 22		302	304	*IC* 24	306	*IC* 12
				⚡			⚡				⚡		⚡
0	**Kiáto 1440** d.	0052	...	0747	0955	...	1247	...	1353	1453	1647	1951	2147
13	Xilókastro d.	0106	...	0759	1009	...	1259	...	1410	1507	1659	2008	2159
56	Diakoftó d.	0152	...	0837	1055	...	1337	...	1456	1555	1737	2057	2237
109	**Pátra** a.	0249	...	0927	1154	...	1427	...	1555	1652	1830	2154	2327
		|	**1350**	|	**1352**	**1354**	|	**350**	|	**1356**	|	**1358**	
109	**Pátra** d.	0301	0617	0930	1200	...	1433	...	1558	1706	1834	...	...
175	Kavásila d.	0416x	0733x	1037	1316x	...	1539	...	1713x	1821x	1942	...	...
209	**Pírgos** d.	0457	0814	1108	1401	1422	1608	1610	1758	1903	2013	...	...
266	Kaloneró d.	0601	0920	1203	...	1528	...	1705	1904	...	2107	...	...
272	Kiparissía ◧ a.	0608	*0929*	*1212*	...	*1537*	...	*1714*	*1915*	...	*2116*	2154	...
339	**Kalamáta 1452** a.	0752	1042	1319	...	1657	...	1821	2023	...	2227	2330	...

	1351	1353	*IC* 21	1357	1355	351	*IC* 23	305		*IC* 25	1359	309
			⚡				⚡			⚡		
Kalamáta 1452 d.	0559	...	0643	...	0928	1044	...	1234	...	1546	1736	2212
Kiparissía ◧ d.	0736	...	*0750*	0952	1103	*1151*	...	*1349*	...	1653	*1852*	2353
Kaloneró d.	...	...	0800	1000	...	1202	...	1359	...	1704	1906	0001
Pírgos d.	...	0611	0855	1110	...	1255	1257	1504	...	1759	2012	0106
Kavásila d.	...	0651x	0925	1150x	...	...	1327	1546x	...	1829	2052x	0146x
Pátra d.	...	0806	1031	1305	...	...	1432	1702	...	1934	2206	0300
	IC 11 ⚡	**301**	|		**303**		|	|	**307**	|		|
Pátra d.	0530	0710	1034	...	1210	...	1435	1707	1806	1937	...	0312
Diakoftó d.	0621	0808	1125	...	1308	...	1526	1807	1907	2028	...	0410
Xilókastro d.	0659	0857	1203	...	1357	...	1604	1854	1954	2106	...	0457
Kiáto 1440 a.	0710	0910	1214	...	1413	...	1615	1907	2010	2117	...	0510

x – Stops on request. ⚡ – Ⓡ with supplement payable, 🍷. ◧ – Kiparissía passengers are required to change train at Kaloneró where times are shown in *italics*.

KÓRINTHOS - ÁRGOS - KALAMÁTA 1452

Service by 🚌 during reconstruction of the narrow gauge line. Árgos - Náfplio is currently suspended. For connections Athína - Kórinthos see Table **1440**

			🚌			🚌			
Kórinthos (new) 1440 d.	...	...	0930	...	...	1540	...	...	...
Árgos d.	...	...	|	...	...	|	...	...	...
Náfplio a.	...	...	|	...	...	|	...	...	...
Trípoli d.	...	...	1031	...	...	1630	...	...	...
Kalamáta 1450 a.	...	...	1230	...	...	...	...	...	...

			🚌			🚌			
Kalamáta 1450 d.	...	...	...	...	...	1233	...	...	...
Trípoli d.	...	...	0825	...	...	1433	...	...	...
Náfplio d.	...	...	|	...	...	|	...	...	...
Árgos d.	...	...	|	...	...	|	...	...	...
Kórinthos (new) 1440 a.	...	...	0925	...	...	1533	...	...	...

PELOPÓNNISOS narrow-gauge branches 1455

Athína – Lutráki *Service currently suspended* 2nd class only

km		⑥⑦	
0	**Athína** Ágii Anárgiri ◇ d.	0710	1600
79	Isthmós d.	0840	1730
85	**Lutráki** a.	0851	1741

	⑥⑦	
Lutráki d.	0909	1809
Isthmós d.	0921	1821
Athína Ágii Anárgiri ◇ a.	1050	1950

Diakoftó – Kalávrita *Service currently suspended* 2nd class only, rack railway

km				S		S
0	**Diakoftó** d.	0653	0900	1058	1302	1458
23	**Kalávrita** a.	0800	1009	1207	1411	1607

			S		S
Kalávrita d.	0926	1124	1328	1524	1730
Diakoftó a.	1035	1233	1437	1633	1837

Diakoftó - Kalávrita service expected to recommence from June 1 - schedules not yet available.

Katákolo – Pírgos – Olimbía 2nd class only

km				⊖			⊖		⊖			
0	Katákolo d.	...	0836	0931	1013	1106	1200	1252	1353	1451	1547	1652
12	Pírgos a.	0655	0856	0951	1031	1126	1220	1312	1413	1511	1605	1710
33	Olimbía a.	0724	0917	1012	...	1152	1241	1341	1434	1538	...	...

						⊖		⊖		⊖	
Olimbía d.	0730	...	0922	...	...	1103	1127	1249	1346	1448	1542
Pírgos d.	0801	0858	0950	...	1043	1127	1221	1313	1414	1512	1612
Katákolo a.	0819	0916	1008	...	1101	1145	1239	1331	1432	1530	1630

S – Operates only when sufficient demand.
⊖ – Days and dates of running are subject to confirmation.
◇ – Ágii Anárgiri is situated 5 km north of Athína Lárisa station.

BULGARIA and TURKEY IN EUROPE

SEE MAP PAGE 492

Operator: Български Държавни Железници – Bâlgarski Dârzhavni Zheleznitsi (БДЖ - BDZh); Türkiye Cumhuryeti Devlet Demiryolları (TCDD).

Services: All trains convey first and second class seating, except where shown otherwise in footnotes or by '2' in the train column, or where the footnote shows sleeping and/or couchette cars only. Descriptions of sleeping (🛏) and couchette (▬) cars appear on page 10. Reservation of seats is possible on most express trains. Services covering Turkey in Asia and beyond are given in the **Thomas Cook Overseas Timetable**.

Timings: BDŽ schedules are valid **December 14, 2008 - December 12, 2009**. Timetable amendments are possible at short notice so please confirm timings locally before travelling. TCDD schedules are the latest available. Please refer to Tables **60**, **98** and **99** for international through cars to / from Burgas and Varna (summer only).

1500 BUCUREŞTI - RUSE - SOFIYA

km		4611		463 465 [R] T	463 [R] R		383 [R] B			
0	**Bucureşti** Nord d.	...	...	1216	1216	...	2004	...	...	...
114	Giurgiu Nord a.	...	...	1405	1405	...	2150	...	...	...
114	Giurgiu Nord 🏛 d.	...	...	1420	1420	...	2205	...	...	...
131	**Ruse** 🏛 a.	...	...	1445	1445	...	2230	...	...	...
131	**Ruse 1525** d.	0600	...	1520	1520	...	2330	...	...	...
242	Gorna Oryakhovitsa **1520/25** d.	0814	...	1719	1725	...	0139	...	...	...
342	Pleven **1520** d.	0934	...	...	1845	...	0300	...	...	...
448	Mezdra **1520** d.	1050	...	...	1956	...	0415	...	...	...
536	**Sofiya 1520** a.	1230	...	...	2133	...	0600	...	...	...

	464 462 [R] T	462 [R] R		4612		382 [R] B		4627 2	
Sofiya 1520 d.	...	0745	...	1530	...	1930	...	2300	...
Mezdra **1520** d.	...	0923	...	1703	...	2108	...	0100	...
Pleven **1520** d.	...	1036	...	1821	...	2232	...	0217	...
Gorna Orykahovitsa **1520/25** d.	1205	1205	...	1947	...	2359	...	0342	...
Ruse 1525 a.	1405	1405	...	2148	...	0205	...	0541	...
Ruse 🏛 d.	1448	1448	...	...	...	0315	...	...	...
Giurgiu Nord 🏛 a.	1513	1513	...	...	...	0340	...	...	...
Giurgiu Nord d.	1528	1528	...	...	...	0355	...	...	...
Bucureşti Nord a.	1719	1719	...	...	...	0544	...	...	...

B – BULGARIA EXPRESS – 🛏 1, 2 cl. and (12) Bucureşti - Sofiya and v.v.; 🛏 1, 2 cl.* Moskva - Kyïv - Sofiya and v.v. Conveys on dates in Table **98**: 🛏 2 cl.* Minsk - Kyïv - Sofiya and v.v., 🛏 2 cl.* Lviv - Sofiya and v.v.

R – ROMANIA – (2) Sofiya - Bucureşti and v.v.; 🛏 1, 2 cl. and ▬ 1, 2 cl. Thessaloníki - Sofiya - Bucureşti and v.v.; 🛏 1, 2 cl. Sofiya - Bucureşti (**370/1**) - Budapest and v.v.;

T – BOSPHOR – 🛏 1, 2 cl. and ▬ 2 cl. Bucureşti - Svilengrad 🏛 - Kapıkule 🏛 - İstanbul and v.v.; (2) Bucureşti - Dimitrovgrad and v.v.

* – Only available for journeys from / to Russia, Belarus or Ukraine.

1510 SOFIYA - VIDIN - CALAFAT - CRAIOVA

km		70102 2	7620	1602 P [R]	7622	7624	7630	70241 2
0	**Sofiya 1520** d.	...	0712	0923	1225	1625	1900	...
88	Mezdra **1520** d.	0541	|	|	1413	|	2049	...
106	Vratsa d.	0602	0905	1102	1431	1808	2107	...
182	Brusartsi ⊖ d.	0745	1029	...	1558	1919	2232	2237
204	Lom ⊖ a.	|	|	...	|	|	2300	|
269	**Vidin** 🏛 ★ a.	0938	1208	...	1741	2051	...	0020

	7631	7621	1601 P [R]	7623	70103 2	7625
Vidin 🏛 ★ d.	...	0612	...	1245	1355	1608
Lom ⊖ d.	0540	|	...	|	|	|
Brusartsi ⊖ d.	0610	0744	...	1426	1554	1801
Vratsa d.	0746	0856	1335	1551	1726	1929
Mezdra **1520** a.	0801	|	|	1606	1745	|
Sofiya 1520 a.	1000	1042	1522	1803	2021	2120

km					▲			Ⓑ
0	**Calafat** 🏛 ★ d.	0335	0558	...	1138	1300	1515	1928
107	**Craiova 1600** a.	0652	0915	...	1515	1542	1840	2241

	⚒					
Craiova 1600 d.	0508	0801	0945	1406	1650	1942
Calafat 🏛 ★ a.	0828	1120	1230	1747	2018	2257

P – (1) Vratsa - Plovdiv and v.v. Higher fares payable.

⊖ – Additional journeys Brusartsi - Lom and v.v. Journey time: 27 – 33 minutes.
From Brusartsi at 0627, 0750, 1040, 1430, 1615, 1800, 1925 and 1955. **From Lom** at 0708, 0830, 0945, 1340, 1515, 1710, 1845 and 2125.

▲ – During engineering work: Calafat 1324, Craiova 1635.

★ – An infrequent vehicle / passenger ⛴ service operates Vidin - Calafat and v.v. (the ferry terminal at Vidin is approx. 5 km north of the railway station). Only operates with a full load of vehicles so a long wait may be possible. Journey time: 20 minutes.

1520 SOFIYA - PLOVDIV - BURGAS and VARNA

km	km		2655	⊙	⊙	⊙	8605 ϟ[R] 🍷	8601 ϟ[R]	2601 ϟ[R]	⊙	3621	2611 🍷	8611	8611 8661	2613	8615	4612 R	4640 A	3601 ϟ[R]	8603 ϟ[R] 🍷	2607 ϟ[R]	2637 B	8637 △	3637 △	8627 △	2627 ▲
0	0	**Sofiya 1500 1510** ⊡ d.	...	...	...	...	...	0630	0705	...	0710	0955	1040	1040	1325	1345	1530	...	1600	1630	1730	2110	...	2220	2240	2335
	119	Pazardzhik ⊡ d.	...	...	...	...	...	0806	|	...	|	|	1237	1237	|	1538	|	...	|	1807	|	|	...	|	0040	|
	156	**Plovdiv** ⊡ a.	...	...	...	...	...	0827	|	...	|	|	1304	1304	|	1605	|	...	|	1829	|	|	...	|	0110	|
	156	**Plovdiv** d.	...	...	...	...	0658	0830	|	...	|	|	1310	1310	|	1610	|	...	|	1834	|	|	2255	|	0120	|
		Karlovo d.	...	...	...	...	|	|	|	0600	0947	|	|	|	|	|	|	...	1826	|	|	|	|	0051	|	|
		Tulovo d.	...	...	...	...	|	|	|	0758t	1115v	|	|	|	|	|	|	...	1938	|	|	|	|	0215v	|	|
		Sliven d.	...	0545	...	...	|	|	|	0926	1223	|	|	|	|	|	|	...	2044	|	|	|	|	0326	|	|
	262	Stara Zagora d.	...	|	...	...	0841	1005	|	▬	|	|	1455	1455	|	1805	|	...	|	2028	|	|	0052v	|	0323t	|
	340	Yambol d.	...	|	0652	0845	0944	1107	|	...	|	|	1600	1600	|	1919	|	...	|	2128	|	|	0201	|	0428	|
	389	Karnobat **1530** d.	...	0645	0744	0936	1031	1144	|	...	1310	|	1648	1710	|	2003	|	...	2128	...	|	|	0252	0417	0513	|
	450	**Burgas 1530** a.	...	0804	0901	1051	◇	1227	|	...	1400	|	|	1800	|	2052	|	...	2214	...	|	|	|	|	0602	|
88		Mezdra **1500 1510** d.	...	...	...	...	|	...	0835	...	...	1132	|	...	1507	...	1703	...	...	...	1900	2252	|	|	...	0115
194		Pleven **1500** d.	0650	...	...	...	|	...	0948	...	...	1300	|	...	1628	...	1821	...	...	...	2014	0015	|	|	...	0233
294		Gorna Oryakhovitsa **1500** a.	0804	...	...	...	|	...	1055	...	...	1417	|	...	1743	...	1935	...	...	...	2125	0128	|	|	...	0350
294		Gorna Oryakhovitsa d.	0809	...	...	...	|	...	1100	⊙	...	1427	|	...	1752	...	...	1953	...	...	...	0135	|	|	...	0400
435		Shumen **1530** d.	1002	...	...	...	|	...	1244	1310	...	1621	|	...	1946	...	...	2158	...	...	...	0328	|	|	...	0607
459		Kaspichan **1530** d.	1022	...	...	...	|	...	|	1337	...	1641	|	...	2006	...	...	...	...	...	...	0347	|	|	...	0627
518		Povelyanovo **1530** d.	1111	...	...	...	|	...	|	1447	...	1729	1849	...	2052	...	...	...	...	...	...	...	0459	0617	...	0720
543	546	**Varna 1530** a.	1136	...	...	...	1246	...	1404	1522	...	1755	1912	...	2118	...	...	...	...	...	...	...	0525	0643	...	0745

km		2608 ϟ[R]	8604 ϟ[R] 🍷	3602 ϟ[R]	4641 A	4611 R	8610	⊙	⊙	2602 ϟ[R]	8660 8614	8614	2610 🍷	2612	3622	8602 ϟ[R]	⊙	8606 ϟ[R] 🍷	2654	⊙	⊙	8626 △	3636 △	2626 ▲	8636 △	2636 C
	Varna 1530 d.	...	...	...	...	...	...	...	0630	0755	...	0920	1055	1240	...	...	1410	1510	1720	...	1935	...	2140	2230	2305	...
	Povelyanovo **1530** d.	...	...	...	...	...	...	...	0704	|	...	0944	|	1304	...	...	1443	1531	|	...	2013	...	2204	2254	2329	...
	Kaspichan **1530** d.	...	...	...	...	...	...	...	0812	|	...	|	1205	1353	...	...	1550	|	1828	...	2117	...	|	2341	|	0035
	Shumen **1530** d.	...	...	...	0555	...	...	...	0840	0911	...	|	1225	1414	...	...	1615	|	1849	...	2142	...	|	0002	|	0055
	Gorna Oryakhovitsa a.	...	...	...	0802	...	...	...	▬	1055	...	|	1417	1605	...	...	▬	|	2041	...	▬	...	|	0154	|	0245
	Gorna Oryakhovitsa **1500** d.	0500	...	...	...	0814	...	...	...	1100	...	|	1427	1615	...	...	...	|	2048	...	...	...	|	0202	|	0252
	Pleven **1500** d.	0616	...	...	...	0934	...	...	...	1213	...	|	1549	1735	...	...	...	|	2202	...	...	...	|	0324	|	0411
	Mezdra **1500 1510** d.	0731	...	...	...	1050	...	...	...	1323	...	|	1714	1856	...	...	...	|	...	...	⊙	...	|	0445	|	0537
0	**Burgas 1530** d.	|	...	0530	...	|	0655	0712	...	|	1040	|	|	|	1420	1540	...	|	...	1748	1945	2215	|	|	|	|
61	Karnobat **1530** d.	|	...	0618	...	|	0746	0830	...	|	1150	1150v	|	|	1508	1625	...	1723	...	1915v	2107	2307	0008	|	0127	|
	Yambol d.	|	0515	|	...	|	0831	|	...	|	1236	1236	|	|	|	1704	...	1803	...	|	2157	2350	|	|	0219	|
	Stara Zagora d.	|	0620	|	...	|	0947	|	⊙	|	1346	1346	|	|	|	1807	⊙	1906	...	|	...	0100	|	|	0344t	|
119	Sliven d.	|	|	0702	...	|	|	0925	*0940*	|	|	|	|	|	1555	|	1739	|	...	2014	...	|	0058	|	|	|
195	Tulovo d.	|	|	0807	...	|	|	...	1125	|	|	|	|	|	1720v	|	1947z	|	...	...	...	|	0208	|	|	|
269	Karlovo d.	|	|	0917	...	|	|	...	1257	|	|	|	|	|	1848	|	2116	|	...	...	...	|	0323	|	|	|
	Plovdiv a.	|	0756	|	...	|	1135	...	...	|	1536	1536	|	|	|	1935	...	2040	...	...	...	0245	|	|	0526	|
	Plovdiv ⊡ d.	|	0800	|	...	|	1145	...	...	|	1540	1540	|	|	|	1940	...	...	...	...	...	0252	|	|	...	|
	Pazardzhik ⊡ d.	|	0829	|	...	|	1217	...	...	|	1612	1612	|	|	|	2007	...	...	...	...	...	0323	|	|	...	|
418	**Sofiya 1500 1510** ⊡ a.	0908	1020	1140	...	1230	1420	...	...	1458	1817	1817	1854	2036	2115	2155	...	...	...	...	...	0535	0600	0630	...	0725

	8601 ϟ[R]	⊙	1621	8611	8615	⊙	1601 ϟF	8603 ϟ[R]	1623	1651 D	8627
Sofiya d.	0630	0638	0830	1040	1345	1415	1530	1630	1730	1835	2240
Pazardzhik d.	0806	0904	1022	1237	1538	1639	1707	1807	1924	2025	0040
Plovdiv a.	0827	0940	1048	1304	1605	1715	1729	1829	1952	2050	0110

	8626	1650 D	1602 ϟF	8604 ϟ[R]	8610	⊙	1620	⊙	8614	⊙	1622	8602 ϟ[R]
Plovdiv d.	0252	0600	0700	0800	1145	1200	1300	1410	1540	1725	1810	1940
Pazardzhik d.	0323	0633	0728	0829	1217	1241	1331	1454	1612	1804	1845	2007
Sofiya a.	0535	0837	0918	1020	1420	1507	1534	1730	1817	2030	2046	2155

A – (12) Plovdiv - Veliko Târnovo - Shumen and v.v. (Table **1525**).

B – ▬ 2 cl. and (12) Sofiya - Dobrich - Kardam (Table **1540**). Conveys ▬ 2 cl. and (2) Sofiya - Kaspichan (**9636**) - Samuil - Silistra (Table **1530**).

C – ▬ 2 cl. and (12) Kardam - Dobrich - Sofiya (Table **1540**). Conveys ▬ 2 cl. and (2) Silistra (**9637**) - Samuil - Kaspichan (**2636**) - Sofiya (Table **1530**).

D – To / from Dimitrovgrad (Table **1550**).

F – (1) Vratsa - Sofiya - Plovdiv and v.v. [R].

R – To / from Ruse (Table **1500**).

t – Arrives 19 – 21 minutes earlier.

v – Arrives 12 – 15 minutes earlier.

z – Arrives 1911.

⊙ – Local stopping train. 2nd class only.

◇ – June 19 - Sept. 13 conveys (12) Plovdiv - Karnobat (**8681**) - Burgas (a. 1127)

▲ – Conveys 🛏 1, 2 cl., ▬ 2 cl. and (12).

△ – Conveys 🛏 1, 2 cl. and (12).

ϟ – Express Train. Higher fares payable.

⊡ – See panel below main table for complete service Sofia - Plovdiv and v.v.

RUSE - STARA ZAGORA - PLOVDIV — 1525

km					4641				463 465	4647	8636
		⊙	⊙	⊙	S	⊙	⊙	⊙	[R] B		
0	**Ruse 1500** d.	...	...	...	*0600*	0802	1115	1310	1520	2155	...
111	Gorna Oryakhovitsa **1500** a.	...	...	...	*0804*	1036	1356	1550	1719	2354	...
111	Gorna Oryakhovitsa d.	...	...	0505	0816	*1120*	1430	1625	1748	0001	...
125	Veliko Târnovo d.	...	...	0527	0834	*1145*	1451	1651	1806	0020	...
226	Tulovo d.	...	...	0819	1114t	...	1715	1942	2016	0236	...
253	Stara Zagora a.	...	...	0900	1150	...	1753	2022	2052	0312	...
253	Stara Zagora **1520** d.	0455	...	...	1200	...	...	...	2057	0333	0344
310	Dimitrovgrad **1550** a.	0625	0740	...	|	...	...	...	2210	0454	|
411	Momchilgrad **1550** a.	...	1030	...	|	...	...	...	...	*0812*	|
359	**Plovdiv 1520** a.	...	...	...	1342	...	...	...	...	...	0526

			464 462		4640			8637	4646
	⊙	⊙	[R] B	⊙	S	⊙	⊙		
Plovdiv 1520 d.	...	...	...	...	1415	...	...	2255	...
Momchilgrad **1550** d.	...	...	...	...	|	...	*1650*	|	*1930*
Dimitrovgrad **1550** d.	...	...	0650	...	|	...	2004	|	2310
Stara Zagora **1520** a.	...	...	0806	...	1604	...	2128	0040	0026
Stara Zagora d.	...	0705	0816	1024	1610	1840	...	...	0104
Tulovo d.	...	0748	0915	1105	1702t	1929	...	...	0159t
Veliko Târnovo d.	0635	1027	1123	1349	1923	2226	...	...	0428
Gorna Oryakhovitsa a.	0657	1049	1140	1407	1941	2246	...	...	0444
Gorna Oryakhovitsa **1500** d.	0709	1115	1205	1446	*1947*	...	...	...	0451
Ruse 1500 a.	0940	1338	1405	1716	*2148*	...	...	...	0711

B – BOSPHOR – 1, 2 cl. and 2 cl. Bucureşti - Ruse - İstanbul and v.v.; (2) Bucureşti - Dimitrovgrad and v.v.

S – To / from Shumen (Table **1520**).

t – Arrives 16 – 19 minutes earlier.

⊙ – Local stopping train. 2nd class only.

RUSE - SILISTRA, VARNA and BURGAS — 1530

km		9636	9621	3660*			8661	9623			9637
		K	🍷	2	⊙	⊙			⊙	⊙	L
0	**Ruse** d.	...	0608	0608	0730	...	...	1620	1730	...	...
71	Razgrad d.	...	0737	0737	0911	...	...	1740	1919	...	...
93	Samuil d.	0503	0800	0800	0934	0936	...	1801	1940	2025	2320
206	**Silistra** a.	0720	|	|	|	1202	...	|	...	2306	|
142	Kaspichan a.	...	0900	0900	1041	▬	...	1905	...	...	0021
142	Kaspichan **1520** d.	...	0907	0924	*1050*	⊙	...	1906	...	...	...
166	Shumen **1520** d.	...	|	0944	*1113*	*1345*	...	|	...	...	...
216	Komunari d.	...	|	1054	...	1523	...	|	...	...	...
299	Karnobat **1520** a.	...	|	1212	...	1657	1710	|	...	...	...
360	**Burgas 1520** a.	...	|	1315	...	...	1800	|	...	...	...
201	Povelyanovo **1520** d.	...	|	...	...	...	...	1955	...	...	...
226	**Varna 1520** a.	...	1020	...	...	...	...	2020	...	...	...

	9636				9620	8605				9622	3661	9637
	K	⊙	⊙	⊙		⚡	⊙	⊙	⊙	🍷	2	L
Varna 1520 d.	...	...	...	...	0850	...	...	...	...	1730	...	...
Povelyanovo **1520** d.	...	...	...	...	0915	...	...	...	...	1755	...	...
Burgas 1520 d.	...	...	...	...	|	*0850*	...	...	...	|	1500	...
Karnobat **1520** d.	...	...	...	...	|	1031	...	...	...	|	1600	...
Komunari d.	...	...	...	...	|	1140	1211	...	...	|	1720	...
Shumen **1520** d.	...	...	...	*0607*	|	...	1330	...	*1621*	|	1832	...
Kaspichan **1520** a.	...	...	...	*0626*	1003	...	▬	...	*1640*	1851	1850	...
Kaspichan d.	0355	...	...	0708	1005	...	...	...	1650	1907	1907	...
Silistra d.	|	...	0505	|	|	...	⊙	1505	|	|	|	2055
Samuil d.	0453	0552	0741	0823	1101	...	1555	1733	1802	2010	2010	2310
Razgrad d.	...	0614	...	0845	1122	...	1617	...	1825	2029	2029	...
Ruse a.	...	0757	...	1014	1238	...	1802	...	2000	2149	2149	...

K – 2 cl. and (2) Sofiya (**2637**) - Kaspichan (**9636**) - Samuil - Silistra.

L – 2 cl. and (2) Silistra - Samuil - Kaspichan (**2636**) - Sofiya.

* – Train **9621** Ruse - Kaspichan.

⊙ – Local stopping train. 2nd class only.

⚡ – Express Train. Higher fare payable. [R].

VARNA and SOFIYA - DOBRICH - KARDAM — 1540

km		2637	2627				1132		2613	
		△	▲	2	2	2	★✕			2
0	**Varna 1520 1530** d.	...	...	0700	1105	1430	1530	...	...	2025
	Sofiya 1520 d.	2110	2335	|	|	|	|	...	1325	|
25	Povelyanovo **1520 1530** a.	|	0719	0732	1138	1502	|	...	2051	2058
25	Povelyanovo d.	|	...	0733	1139	1503	|	...	...	2059
93	**Dobrich** a.	0620	...	0910	1306	1624	1709	...	...	2231
131	Kardam a.	0737	...	1020	...	1730	1820	...	...	...

		8614			2612	1131				2636
	2			2		★✕	2		2	△
Kardam d.	...	...	...	1028	...	1202	...	...	1742	2040
Dobrich d.	0638	...	...	1135	...	1309	1355	...	1848	2206
Povelyanovo a.	0804	...	...	1258	...	|	1525	...	2008	|
Povelyanovo **1520 1530** d.	0805	0944	...	1306	1304	|	1533	...	2009	|
Sofiya 1520 a.	|	1817	...	|	2036	|	|	...	|	0725
Varna 1520 1530 a.	0840	...	...	1340	...	1445	1607	...	2041	...

★ – June 15 - Sept. 6. (12) Bucureşti - Negru Vodă - Varna and v.v.

△ – Conveys 2 cl. and (12).

▲ – Conveys 1, 2 cl., 2 cl. and (12).

BDŽ; TCDD — PLOVDIV - İSTANBUL — 1550

km	Bulgarian/Greek train number					1641	1651	444	491	463/5
	Turkish train number			81721				81021	81031	81031
		2	2		2	2		[R] T	[R] R	[R] B
	Bucureşti **1500** d.	...	...	...	...	...	...	...	...	1216
	Beograd **1380** d.	...	...	...	...	...	...	...	0750	|
0	*Sofiya* **1540** d.	...	...	...	...	*1630*	1835	...	1910	|
156	**Plovdiv** d.	0537	1423	...	1800	1855	2101	...	2132	|
234	Dimitrovgrad **1525** d.	0738	1615	...	2001	2029	2246	...	2322	2322
	Momchilgrad **1525** a.	|	|	...	|	2250	▬	...	|	|
299	Svilengrad a.	0855	1740	...	2127	▬	...	...	0033	0033
299	Svilengrad 🛃 d.	▬	▬	...	▬	**81731**	...	...	0105	0105
318	Kapıkule 🛃 a.	...	...	...	...		...	...	0130	0130
318	Kapıkule d.	...	...	0700	**82901**	1535	...	...	0330	0330
338	Edirne d.	...	...	0733	2	1603	...	...	0355	0355
	Thessaloníki **1405** d.	...	**82861**	|	*0718*	|	**81741**	1937	|	|
	Píthio 🛃 d.	...	2	|	1530	|		0251	|	|
	Uzunköprü 🛃 d.	...	0750	|	1601	|	1640	0400	|	|
385	Pehlivanköy d.	**81601**	0815	0828	...	1658	1702	0421	|	|
406	Alpullu d.		0837	0852	...	1717	1732	0448	0502	0502
506	Çerkezköy d.	0700	...	1036	...	...	1919	0606	0621	0621
593	Halkalı d.	0837	...	1221	...	...	2103	0727	0743	0743
621	**İstanbul** Sirkeci a.	0919	...	1304	...	...	2133	0807	0825	0825

km	Turkish train number	81742	81732	82902	81722	82864	81602	81022	81032	81032
	Bulgarian/Greek train number							445	490	464/2
				2		2		[R] T	[R] R	[R] B
0	**İstanbul** Sirkeci d.	0830	...	...	1550	...	1800	2100	2200	2200
28	Halkalı d.	0916	...	...	1635	...	1839	2136	2238	2238
115	Çerkezköy d.	1101	...	...	1819	...	2018	2259	0002	0002
215	Alpullu d.	1258k	1250	...	2005	2015	▬	0026	0124	0124
237	Pehlivanköy d.	1319	1311	...	2026	2038	...	0045	|	|
258	Uzunköprü 🛃 d.	1339	|	1410	|	2059	...	0140	|	|
268	Píthio 🛃 a.	▬	|	1438	|	...	...	0208	|	|
	Thessaloníki **1405** a.	...	|	*2251*	|	...	...	0920	|	|
	Edirne d.	...	1405	▬	2118	...	...	▬	0230	0230
	Kapıkule a.	...	1432	...	2145	...	...	...	0252	0252
	Kapıkule 🛃 d.	...	▬	...	▬	...	...	...	0405	0405
	Svilengrad 🛃 a.	2	2	2	2	...	...	**1640**	0430	0430
	Svilengrad d.	0540	1040	1524	1827	...	**1650**	2	0505	0505
	Momchilgrad **1525** d.	|	|	|	|	...		0345	|	|
	Dimitrovgrad **1525** d.	0705	1214	1710f	1956	...	0410	0607	0636	0650
	Plovdiv a.	0909	1358	1858	2153	...	0550	0741	0815	|
	Sofiya **1540** a.	...	...	...	...	...	0837	*1020*	1050	|
	Beograd **1380** a.	...	...	...	...	...	...	...	1918	|
	Bucureşti **1500** a.	...	...	...	...	...	...	...	...	1719

B – BOSPHOR – 1, 2 cl. and 2 cl. Bucureşti - İstanbul and v.v.

R – BALKAN EXPRESS – 1, 2 cl. Sofia - İstanbul and v.v. Conveys June 1 - Oct. 30 (from Sofia), June 2 - Oct. 31 (from İstanbul) 2 cl. Sofia - İstanbul and v.v. Conveys June 8 - Dec. 12 (from Beograd) / June 7 - Dec. 12 (from İstanbul) 1, 2 cl. Beograd - İstanbul and v.v.

T – FILIA - DOSTLUK EXPRESS – 1, 2 cl. Thessaloníki - İstanbul and v.v.

f – Arrives 1650.

k – Arrives 1243.

IDO — BOSPHORUS FERRIES — 1555

service **İstanbul Karaköy - Haydarpaşa** (for Asian rail services) and v.v. *2 km*

Journey time: 20 - 35 minutes

Operator: IDO – İstanbul Deniz Otobüsleri.

From İstanbul Karaköy: On ⚒ at 0630, 0700, 0730, 0750 and every 20 minutes until 1930, then 2000, 2030, 2100, 2130, 2200, 2230, 2300. On † at 0630 and every 30 minutes until 2300.

From Haydarpaşa: On ⚒ at 0635, 0705, 0725, 0750, 0810 and every 20 minutes until 1950, then 2005, 2035, 2105, 2135, 2205, 2235, 2305. On † at 0635, 0705, 0735, 0850, 0920 and every 30 minutes until 2320.

BDŽ, OSE — SOFIYA - KULATA - THESSALONÍKI — 1560

km		361	5621	6621	5611	6623	5623	363	363	6625	5625	463
			2	2	2	2	2		V [R]	2		T [R]
0	**Sofiya** d.	0701	0733	0812	1200	1414	1532	1705	1705	1725	1935	2253
33	Pernik d.	|	0828	0910	1256	1509	1632	|	|	1814	2033	2337
48	Radomir d.	|	0854	0932	1319	1531	1655	|	|	1834	2057	|
102	**Kyustendil** a.	|	|	1055	|	1655	|	|	|	1957	|	|
91	Dupnitsa d.	|	0952	...	1403	...	1749	|	|	...	2158	0041
123	**Blagoevgrad** d.	0903	1037	...	1435	...	1822	1907	1907	...	2231	0110
186	Sandanski d.	1008	1143	...	1542	...	1929	2007	2007	...	...	0211
210	Kulata a.	1025	1215	...	1613	...	2000	2025	2025	...	...	0230
210	Kulata 🛃 d.	1045	...	...	...	...	...	2045	2045	...	...	0300
211	Promahónas 🛃 a.	1050	...	...	...	...	...	2050	2050	...	...	0305
211	Promahónas d.	1111	...	...	...	...	...	2110	2110	...	...	0350
225	Strimón **1405** d.	1134	...	...	...	...	...	2134	2134	...	...	0415
354	**Thessaloníki 1405** a.	1254	...	...	...	...	...	2252	2252	...	...	0540
	Athína **1400** a.	...	...	...	...	...	...	...	0612	...	...	...

	462	5620	6620	5622	360	360	6622	5624	6624	5610	362
	T [R]		2	2	Z [R]		2	2	2	2	
Athína **1400** d.	...	...	...	...	2255	...	...	...	...	...	...
Thessaloníki 1405 d.	2349	...	...	...	0640	0640	...	...	...	...	1734
Strimón **1405** d.	0127	...	...	...	0811	0811	...	...	...	...	1903
Promahónas a.	0140	...	...	...	0823	0823	...	...	...	...	1915
Promahónas 🛃 d.	0205	...	...	...	0843	0843	...	...	...	...	1935
Kulata 🛃 a.	0210	...	...	...	0848	0848	...	...	...	...	1940
Kulata d.	0240	...	...	0605	0914	0914	...	1410	...	1715	2004
Sandanski d.	0301	...	...	0643	0933	0933	...	1445	...	1751	2028
Blagoevgrad d.	0405	0620	...	0759	1034	1034	...	1601	...	1909	2129
Dupnitsa d.	0434	0700	...	0837	|	|	...	1635	...	1945	|
Kyustendil d.	|	|	0718	|	|	|	1115	|	1810	|	|
Radomir d.	|	0751	0841	0923	|	|	1237	1718	1938	2029	|
Pernik d.	0536	0813	0900	0943	|	|	1258	1741	2000	2053	|
Sofiya a.	0635	0912	0952	1032	1232	1232	1351	1831	2048	2152	2325

T – ROMANIA – 1, 2 cl. and 1, 2 cl. Bucureşti - Sofiya - Thessaloníki and v.v.; 1, 2 cl. and (2) Sofiya - Thessaloniki and v.v.

V – 1, 2 cl. Sofiya - Thessaloníki (**505**) - Athína.

Z – 1, 2 cl. Athína (**504**) - Thessaloníki - Sofiya.

ROMANIA

SEE MAP PAGE 492

Operator: CFR – Compania Naţională de Căi Ferate (www.cfr.ro).

Services: Trains convey 1st- and 2nd-class seating accommodation unless otherwise indicated. Sleeping- (🛏) and couchette (▬) cars are described on page **10**. Russian-type sleeping-cars, as used in trains to and from destinations in Belarus, Moldova, Russia and Ukraine, are described on page **512**; these cars are not accessible to passengers making journeys wholly within Romania or between Romania and Bulgaria.

Timings: Valid until **December 12, 2009** unless stated otherwise.

Tickets: Reservation is obligatory for travel by all services for which a train number is shown in the tables, and passengers boarding without a prior reservation are surcharged. Supplements are payable for travel by **Intercity** (*IC*) and most other fast trains. Trains shown without numbers are slow stopping-services calling at all, or most, stations.

1600 BUCUREŞTI - CRAIOVA - TIMIŞOARA

km		991	1762		791	591	797	821		593		1693	693	823	1725		595	795	1823	825	1691		360		695	1821
						IC				*IC*							*IC*									
		M	2E	2		✕	⑤©	R		✕					T		✕		T	R			B		V	A
0	**Bucureşti** Nord ▼ d.	0005n	...	...	0545	0645	0845	0945	...	1045	...	...	1245	1345	1445	...	1545	1645	1745	1845	1945	...	2121	...	2245	2345
51	Videle d.	|	...	...	0629	|	0929	1033	...	1129	...	...	|	1428	1530	...	1626	1730	1830	1929	2030	...	2204	...	2327	0030
100	Roşiori Nord d.	0134	...	...	0713	0805	1011	1113	...	1214	...	...	1416	1507	1612	...	1707	1814	1915	2008	2114	...	2247	...	0006	0112
155	Caracal d.	0218	...	...	0757	|	1056	1158	...	1300	...	...	1500	1550	1700	...	|	1857	2005	2055	2203	...	2332	...	|	0201
209	**Craiova** ▼ a.	0258	...	...	0836	0926	1141	▬	...	1339	...	...	1539	...	1740	...	1826	1936	2045	...	2242	...	0011	...	0125	0240
209	**Craiova** 1605 d.	0310	...	0345	0839	0833	...	...	1232	1345	...	1430	1547	...	1745	...	1832	...	2050	...	2253	2235	0021	...	0135	0252
245	Filiaşi 1605 d.	0338	...	0430	0906	|	...	...	1326	1412	...	1506	1614	...	1810	...	|	...	2115	...	2321	2329	0047	...	|	0319
	Deva 1605 a.	|	...	|	|	|	...	...	|	|	...	|	|	...	...	...	|	...	...	...	|	|	|	...	|	0748
323	Drobeta Turnu Severin d.	0455	...	0636	1042	1114	...	...	1520	1532	...	1632	1735	...	...	1820	2013	...	...	...	0047	0132	0203	...	0313	|
347	Orşova d.	0525	...	0715	...	|	...	1513	...	1600	...	1702	1806	...	...	1855	|	...	...	...	0116	0205	0232	←	|	|
364	Băile Herculane d.	0546	...	...	...	1159	...	1537	...	1620	←	1721	1831	...	...	1917	2056	...	...	...	0140	0228	0252	0228	0400	|
435	Caransebeş d.	0716	0636	...	...	1320	...	1812	...	1748	1812	1901	1952	...	...	2132	2217	...	...	...	0302	→	0412	0448	0530	|
474	Lugoj 1620 d.	0759	0715	...	...	1352	...	→	...	1820	1900	1943	2025	...	...	2218	2249	...	...	...	0334	...	0443	0540	0604	|
533	**Timişoara** Nord 1620 a.	0843	0803	...	...	1433	...	...	...	1900	2018	2041	2106	...	...	2312	2330	...	...	...	0415	...	0524	0647	0655	|
	Arad 1625 a.	...	...	...	...	...	...	...	...	...	...	...	...	...	...	...	...	...	...	...	...	...	|	...	...	0957
	Budapest Keleti 1280 a.	...	...	...	...	...	...	...	...	...	...	...	...	...	...	...	...	...	...	...	...	...	|	...	...	1447
	Beograd 1365 a.	...	...	...	...	...	...	...	...	...	...	...	...	...	...	...	...	...	...	...	...	...	0854	...	...	...

	794	820	1724	592	594		798	822	792	1824		694		824		596		1761	992	1692	361		1822	696	1694	
				IC	*IC*											*IC*										
		R	T	✕	✕		⑤©	R		T	2		2	R		✕		2E	M		B		A	V		
Beograd 1365 d.	...	...	...	...	...	...	...	...	...	...	...	...	...	...	...	...	...	...	...	...	1555	...	...	...	...	...
Budapest Keleti 1280 d.	...	...	...	...	...	...	...	...	...	...	...	...	...	...	...	...	...	...	...	...	|	...	1313	...	...	...
Arad 1625 d.	...	...	...	...	...	...	...	...	...	...	...	...	...	...	...	...	...	...	...	...	|	...	2012	...	...	...
Timişoara Nord 1620 d.	...	...	...	0600	0700	...	...	...	...	...	...	1350	...	...	1403	1600	...	1632	1901	2005	2120	...	|	2245	2335	...
Lugoj 1620 d.	...	...	...	0642	0742	...	...	...	...	...	...	1441	...	...	1512	1642	...	1715	1944	2058	2203	...	|	2338	0032	...
Caransebeş d.	...	...	...	0714	0814	...	...	...	...	...	...	1513	...	...	1558	1715	...	1743	2031	2130	2237	...	|	0020	0112	...
Băile Herculane d.	...	...	...	0829	0929	...	...	...	...	...	...	1636	...	...	1752	1830	...	...	2156	2252	2352	...	|	0139	0251	...
Orşova d.	...	...	...	|	0956	...	...	...	...	...	1610	1703	←	...	1825	|	←	...	2224	2320	0019	...	|	|	0319	...
Drobeta Turnu Severin d.	...	...	...	0921	1024	...	...	...	1420	...	1700	1732	1700	...	1925	1922	1925	...	2302	2350	0048	...	|	0249	0353	...
Deva 1605 d.	...	...	...	|	|	...	...	...	|	...	→	|	|	...	→	|	|	...	|	|	|	...	2214	|	|	...
Filiaşi 1605 d.	...	...	0638	|	1142	...	...	...	1540	1728	...	1849	1912	...	...	|	2126	...	0043	0110	0202	...	0246	|	0526	...
Craiova 1605 a.	...	...	0705	1058	1209	...	...	...	1607	1755	...	1916	2010	...	...	2057	2200	...	0110	0137	0229	...	0315	0440	0600	...
Craiova ▲ d.	0500	...	0710	1104	1215	...	1320	...	1612	1800	...	1926	...	...	...	2103	...	...	0125	0147	0238	...	0325	0450	...	...
Caracal d.	0542	0725	0752	|	1258	...	1402	1618	1654	1841	...	2007	...	2030	...	|	...	...	0207	0228	0319	...	0405	|	...	...
Roşiori Nord d.	0629	0813	0844	1234	1344	...	1448	1706	1740	1932	...	2053	...	2120	...	2225	...	...	0253	0319	0405	...	0453	0612	...	...
Videle d.	0710	0852	0928	1313	1424	...	1528	1745	1821	2014	...	|	...	2159	...	|	...	...	|	0401	0445	...	0534	0653	...	...
Bucureşti Nord ▲ a.	0756	0935	1015	1405	1510	...	1616	1828	1907	2100	...	2215	...	2244	...	2345	...	...	0424n	0447	0531	...	0619	0738	...	...

km	▼	1891	1789	1791	1893	1793	1795	1895	1797	1799	
0	**Bucureşti** Nord d.	0520	0720	0920	1120	1320	1520	1720	1920	2120	...
108	Piteşti d.	0714	0900	1100	1307	1500	1707	1914	2100	2300	...
189	Slatina d.	0827	...	...	1420	...	1820	2034	...	...	...
206	Piatra Olt 1602 d.	0846	...	...	1439	...	1838	2053	...	...	...
250	**Craiova** 1602 a.	0928	...	...	1530	...	...	2135	...	...	...

▲	1788	1892	1790	1792	1794	1894	1796	1896	1798	
Craiova 1602 d.	...	0445	...	...	...	1245	...	1645	...	...
Piatra Olt 1602 d.	...	0529	...	...	...	1328	...	1728	1932	...
Slatina d.	...	0550	...	...	...	1348	...	1748	1952	...
Piteşti d.	0515	0715	0915	1115	1315	1515	1715	1915	2115	...
Bucureşti Nord a.	0711	0905	1112	1316	1505	1705	1906	2106	2305	...

A – [12] Constanţa - Bucureşti - Târgu Jiu - Arad and v.v.; 🛏 1, 2 cl., ▬ 2 cl. and [12] Bucureşti - Arad and v.v. Conveys 🛏 1, 2 cl. and [2] (also ▬ 1, 2 cl. May 29 - Aug. 18 from Bucureşti, May 31 - Aug. 20 from Venezia) Bucureşti - Budapest (**240/1**) - Venezia and v.v.
B – BUCUREŞTI – 🛏 1, 2 cl., ▬ 2 cl. and [12] Bucureşti - Beograd and v.v.
D – 🛏 1, 2 cl. and [12] Bucureşti - Caransebeş - Reşiţa and v.v. Ⓡ.
E – [2] Reşiţa - Caransebeş - Timişoara and v.v. Ⓡ.

M – June 19 - Sept. 12 (from Timişoara / Reşiţa, one day later from Mangalia): [12] Timişoara / Reşiţa - Mangalia and v.v. Ⓡ.
R – To / from Râmnicu Vâlcea (Table **1602**).
T – To / from Târgu Jiu (Table **1605**).
V – VALAHIA – 🛏 1, 2 cl., ▬ 2 cl. and [12] Bucureşti - Timişoara and v.v.; 🛏 1, 2 cl. and [12] Bucureşti - Caransebeş - Reşiţa and v.v.

n – Bucureşti Băneasa.

REŞIŢA - CARANSEBEŞ: Journey: ± 65 minutes
From Reşiţa Sud: 0435, 0538 **E**, 0624, 1247, 1520, 1731, 1914 **M**, 2055, 2308 **D**.
From Caransebeş: 0448, 0538 **D**, 0735 **M**, 0818, 1330, 1602, 1751 **E**, 1910, 2220.
Local trains also operate 4–5 times daily **Reşiţa** Sud - **Timişoara** Nord and v.v.; journey ± 2 hrs 55 mins.

1602 SIBIU - RÂMNICU VÂLCEA - CRAIOVA

km		1828	820		802		822		828	824		884	804
			B				B	2		B		804*	
0	**Sibiu** 1620 d.	0255	...	0305	0730	0759	...	1215	1454	...	1546	1827	...
	Braşov 1620 d.	|	...	|	|	|	...	|	|	...	|	|	1649
22	Podu Olt 1620 d.	0321	...	0344	|	0838	...	1253	1520	...	1625	1905	1905
83	Călimăneşti d.	0437	...	0543	|	1042	...	1444	|	...	1836	|	|
99	**Râmnicu Vâlcea** d.	0500	0540	0614	0926	1110	1416	1515	1653	1842	1915	2050	2050
186	Piatra Olt 1600 ◧ d.	0614	0652	0829	1033	...	1547	1751	...	2000	2126	2154	2158
	Caracal ◧ a.	0640	0722	|	|	...	1615	1835	...	2026	|	|	|
230	**Craiova** 1600 a.	...	...	0955	1115	...	...	...	...	...	2231	2238	2240

	829			801	801		821		803	823	1827	825
		2			881*		B	2		B		B
Craiova 1600 d.	...	...	0505	0715	0715	...	...	1212	1500	...	...	...
Caracal ◧ d.	...	...	|	|	|	...	1200	|	|	1554	1725	2100
Piatra Olt 1600 ◧ d.	...	0400	0618	0800	0800	...	1229	1320	1546	1635	1752	2132
Râmnicu Vâlcea d.	0525	0640	0846	0912	0912	...	1342	1542	1700	1748	1920	2252
Călimăneşti d.	|	0706	0933	|	|	...	1359	1610	|	...	1942	...
Podu Olt 1620 a.	0715	0920	1159	1046	1052	...	...	1802	|	...	2125	...
Braşov 1620 a.	|	|	|	1300	|	...	...	|	|	...	|	...
Sibiu a.	0740	1002	1241	...	1115	...	...	1845	1853	...	2150	...

km	◧												
0	Piatra Olt d.	0355	...	0530	...	0835	...	1330	...	1559	...	1925	...
32	Caracal a.	0435	...	0620	...	0915	...	1415	...	1646	...	2016	...

◧												
Caracal d.	0530	0740	...	1225	1418	...	1620	1740	...	2028	...	2110
Piatra Olt a.	0611	0825	...	1308	1500	...	1721	1832	...	2113	...	2156

B – [12] Râmnicu Vâlcea - Bucureşti and v.v.

* – Number from Podu Olt.

1605 CRAIOVA - TÂRGU JIU - DEVA

km		839	1821	995	631			1695				1725	1823	
			A ⊖	M		2			2		2			2
	Bucureşti N 1600 d.	...	2345	0005n	...	...	...	...	...	...	...	1445	1745	...
0	**Craiova** 1600 d.	...	0252	0310	0505	0800	...	0844	1400	...	1555	1745	2050	1950
36	Filiaşi 1600 d.	...	0319	0658	0531	0918	...	0912	1507	...	1649	1812	2117	2043
107	**Târgu Jiu** d.	0210	0429	0530	0640	1102	...	1020	1652	...	1835	1937	2230	2218
157	Petroşani d.	0323	0540	0645	0753	...	1112	...	1828	1844	2005	...	...	*0017*
237	Simeria ▲ 1620 d.	0515	0740	0847	|	...	1402	...	...	2122	...	...	...	*0219*
246	**Deva** 1620 a.	0523	0748	0857	|	...	1412	...	...	2131	...	...	...	...
	Cluj Napoca 1620 a.	0854	|	...	1251	...	...	...	...	...	...	...	...	...
	Arad 1620 a.	...	0957	...	...	...	...	...	...	...	...	...	...	...

	1724				1696	1824				632	838	996	1822
				2				2				M	A ⊖
Arad 1620 d.	...	...	...	...	...	...	...	...	1502	...	...	...	2012
Cluj Napoca 1620 d.	...	...	...	...	...	...	...	...	|	1448	1555	...	|
Deva 1620 d.	...	...	...	...	...	...	1541	...	1707	|	1925	1935	2214
Simeria ▲ 1620 d.	...	...	0739	...	...	...	1611	...	1721	|	1858j	1948	2228
Petroşani d.	...	0750	1015	1132	...	...	1842	1905	1928	1950	2121	2140	0020
Târgu Jiu d.	0510	0929	...	1318	1342	1617	...	2052	2120	2105	2233	2257	0135
Filiaşi 1600 a.	0636	1109	...	1502	1448	1726	...	2250	...	2213	...	0020	0244
Craiova 1600 a.	0705	1203	...	1600	1516	1755	...	2345	...	2242	...	0110	0315
Bucureşti N 1600 a.	1015	...	...	...	...	2100	...	...	...	...	...	0424n	0619

A – [12] Constanţa - Bucureşti - Târgu Jiu - Arad and v.v.; 🛏 1, 2 cl., ▬ 2 cl. and [12] Bucureşti - Arad and v.v.
M – June 19 - Sept. 12 (from Deva, one day later from Mangalia): [12] Deva - Mangalia and v.v.

j – Via Deva.
n – Bucureşti Băneasa.
⊖ – Subject to alteration.

▲ – Service **Simeria** - **Hunedoara** and v.v.: Journey time: ± 30 minutes
From Simeria: 0500, 0710 ①–⑤, 1234, 1409, 1620, 1920, 2232.
From Hunedoara: 0548, 0800 ①–⑤, 1330, 1530, 1721, 2014, 2320.

BUCUREŞTI - BRAŞOV - SIBIU - ARAD 1620

km		811	IC 454	1821 354 A	1837 Q	354 T		IC 452		374 P		1621		838 R			813	IC 525 V	804 883*	827	346 D	1752 X	1924 S	EN 370 J	1765 N	1635 Z	1821 Y
0	**Bucureşti** Nord **1630** d.	...	...	2345	...	...	...	...	...	0550	...	0942	...	...	...	...	...	1300	...	1530	1645	...	...	1950	...	2033	2345
59	Ploieşti Vest **1630** d.	...	...	|	...	...	...	...	...	0633	...	1025	...	...	...	...	...	1342	...	1613	1727	...	...	2031	...	2116	|
121	Sinaia **1630** d.	...	...	|	...	...	...	...	...	0744	...	1143	...	...	...	...	...	1447	...	1723	1838	...	...	2137	...	2229	|
140	Predeal **1630** d.	...	...	|	...	...	...	...	...	0822	...	1219	...	...	...	...	...	1518	...	1756	1909	...	...	2208	...	2304	|
166	**Braşov 1630** a.	...	...	|	...	...	...	...	...	0852	...	1249	...	...	...	...	...	1548	...	1826	1939	...	...	2238	...	2334	|
166	**Braşov 1630** d.	...	...	|	...	...	...	0605	0617	0904	...	1301	1426	...	...	...	...	1600	1649	1838	1947	2026	...	2248	...	2358	|
	Sighişoara **1630** d.	...	...	|	...	...	...	|	|	1109	...	|	|	...	...	...	...	1758	|	|	2145	|	...	0046	...	|	|
231	Făgăraş d.	...	...	▽	...	...	...	0716	0755	|	...	1412	1603	...	...	...	...	|	1803	1944	|	2146	...	|	...	0108	▽
293	Podu Olt **1602** d.	...	...	|	...	...	...	|	0916	|	...	|	1729	...	...	...	...	|	1905	|	|	|	...	|	...	|	|
315	**Sibiu 1602 1635** a.	...	...	|	...	...	...	0832	0949	|	...	1530	1808	...	...	...	...	|	1933	2057	|	2313	...	|	...	0222	|
315	**Sibiu 1635** d.	0420	...	|	...	...	...	0840	▬	|	...	1540	...	...	...	...	1728	|	...	...	|	...	...	|	...	...	|
389	Sebeş Alba **1635** d.	0546	...	|	...	...	...	1013	...	|	...	1715	...	...	...	...	1855	|	...	...	|	...	...	|	...	...	|
397	Vinţu de Jos **1635** a.	0554	...	|	...	...	...	1023	...	|	...	1724	...	...	...	...	1903	|	...	...	|	...	...	|	...	...	|
	Cluj Napoca **1635** d.	|	...	|	0512	...	...	|	...	|	...	|	...	1555	...	|	|	...	...	...	|	...	2201	|	2349	...	|
	Alba Iulia 1630 1635 d.	|	...	|	0727	0820	...	|	...	1250	...	|	...	1802	...	|	2009	...	...	...	2325	...	0015	0252	0202	...	|
397	Vinţu de Jos **1635** d.	0559	...	|	0738	0831	...	1036	...	|	...	1726	...	1813	...	1915	2019	...	...	...	|	...	0026	|	0212	...	|
441	Simeria **1605** d.	0640	0734	0740	0835	0922	...	1120	1200	1346	1535	1814	...	1858	...	2001	2101	...	...	...	0019	...	0115	|	0302	...	0740
450	Deva **1605** d.	0650	0743	0750	0846	0932	...	1130	1212	1356	1548	1825	...	1906	...	2011	2111	...	...	...	0028	...	0125	0348	0313	...	0750
474	Ilia d.	0714	0806	0815	0910	|	...	|	1244	|	1620	1848	...	...	...	|	|	...	...	...	|	...	0149	|	0339	...	0815
564	Radna d.	|	0912	0925	|	|	...	|	1441	|	1807	|	...	...	...	|	|	...	...	...	|	...	0259	|	0448	...	0925
599	**Arad 1625** a.	|	0944	0957	|	1126	...	1344	1527	1551	1852	|	...	...	...	|	2307	...	...	...	0224	...	0331	0543	0531n	...	0957
557	Lugoj **1600** d.	0842	|	|	1100	|	...	|	...	|	...	2035	...	...	...	2159	...	...	...	...	|	...	|	|	|	...	...
616	**Timişoara** Nord **1600/25** a.	0951	|	|	1214	|	...	|	...	|	...	2149	...	...	...	2308	...	...	...	...	|	...	0437	|	0629	...	...
	Budapest Keleti **1280** a.	...	1247	1447	...	1447	...	1647	...	1847	...	...	...	...	...	...	...	...	...	...	0517	...	...	0847	...	...	...

	1636 Z	826	839 R	834	347 D	882 801*	812				1622	IC 526 V	375 P		H	1766 N	1751 X	IC 453	814		355 T	1838 Q	355 1822 B	1822 Y	IC 455	EN 371 J
Budapest Keleti **1280** d.	...	...	...	...	2313	...	...	...	...	...	...	...	0913	...	...	...	...	1113	...	...	1313	...	1313	...	1713	1913
Timişoara Nord **1600 1625** d.	...	...	...	...	|	...	0519	...	...	...	0815	...	|	...	1335	1515	...	|	1550	...	|	1747	|	...	|	|
Lugoj **1600** d.	...	...	...	...	|	...	0633	...	...	...	0946	...	|	...	|	|	...	|	1702	...	|	1903	|	...	|	|
Arad 1625 d.	...	...	...	...	0416	...	|	0630	...	...	|	1220	1416	...	1502	1558n	...	1616	|	...	1837	|	2012	2012	2216	0017
Radna d.	...	...	...	...	|	...	|	0707	...	...	|	|	|	...	1530	1644	...	|	|	...	|	|	2040	2040	2243	|
Ilia d.	...	...	...	...	|	...	0812	0912	...	...	1125	|	|	...	1647	1758	...	|	|	...	|	2100	2153	2153	2350	|
Deva **1605** d.	...	...	0543	...	0604	...	0833	0945	...	...	1147	1410	1605	...	1707	1818	...	1804	1847	...	2025	2123	2214	2214	0009	|
Simeria **1605** d.	...	...	0555	...	0624	...	0843	0959	...	...	1158	1421	1622	...	1717	1831	...	1815	1857	...	2037	2152	2228	2228	0018	|
Vinţu de Jos **1635** a.	...	...	0634	...	|	...	0919	...	...	...	1241	1458	|	...	...	1914	...	1853	1934	...	2117	2235	|	|	...	|
Alba Iulia 1630 1635 d.	...	...	0650	...	0709	...	|	...	...	...	|	1509	1707	...	...	1926	...	|	|	...	2128	2245	|	|	...	0256
Cluj Napoca **1635** a.	...	...	0854	...	|	...	|	...	...	...	|	|	|	...	...	2129	...	|	|	...	...	0051	|	|	...	|
Vinţu de Jos **1635** d.	...	...	...	0648	|	...	0936	...	...	...	1242	|	|	...	...	...	...	1906	1939	...	...	...	|	|	...	|
Sebeş Alba **1635** d.	...	...	...	0658	|	...	0945	...	...	...	1253	|	|	...	...	...	...	1917	1951	...	...	...	|	|	...	|
Sibiu 1635 a.	...	...	...	0823	|	...	1118	...	...	...	1427	|	|	...	...	...	...	2048	2126	...	...	...	|	|	...	|
Sibiu 1602 1635 d.	0234	0618	...	...	|	1016	...	...	...	1208	1437	|	|	1722	...	...	2012	2058	...	...	...	...	|	|	...	|
Podu Olt **1602** d.	|	|	...	...	|	1058	...	...	...	1245	|	|	|	1750	...	...	|	|	...	...	...	...	▽	▽	...	|
Făgăraş d.	0353	0745	...	...	|	1153	...	...	...	1411	1604	|	|	1911	...	...	2137	2216	...	...	...	...	|	|	...	|
Sighişoara **1630** d.	|	|	...	...	0901	|	...	...	...	|	|	1733	1859	|	...	...	|	|	...	...	...	...	|	|	...	0512
Braşov 1630 a.	0500	0851	...	...	1053	1300	...	...	...	1538	1713	1923	2049	2052	...	...	2247	2325	...	...	...	...	|	|	...	0702
Braşov 1630 d.	0527	0905	...	...	1102	...	...	...	...	...	1725	1937	2100	...	...	...	...	...	...	...	...	...	|	|	...	0714
Predeal **1630** d.	0606	0938	...	...	1134	...	...	...	...	...	1800	2016	2138	...	...	...	...	...	...	...	...	...	|	|	...	0753
Sinaia **1630** d.	0639	1005	...	...	1207	...	...	...	...	...	1837	2046	2210	...	...	...	...	...	...	...	...	...	|	|	...	0820
Ploieşti Vest **1630** d.	0754	1125	...	...	1319	...	...	...	...	...	2002	2200	2314	...	...	...	...	...	...	...	...	...	|	|	...	0941
Bucureşti Nord **1630** a.	0837	1215	...	...	1359	...	...	...	...	...	2045	2241	2355	...	...	...	...	...	...	...	...	...	0619	0619	...	1028

A – MUREŞ – (12) Bucureşti - Arad; 🛏 1,2 cl. and (2) (also ▬ 1,2 cl. May 29 - Aug. 18) Bucureşti - Budapest (**240**) - Venezia.
B – MUREŞ – (12) Arad - Bucureşti; 🛏 1,2 cl. and (2) (also ▬ 1,2 cl. May 31 - Aug. 20 from Venezia) Venezia (**241**) - Budapest - Bucureşti.
D – DACIA – (12) Bucureşti - Curtici and v.v.; 🛏 1,2 cl., ▬ 2 cl. (2) and ✕ Bucureşti - Budapest - Wien and v.v.
H – (12) Timişoara - Arad - Târgu Jiu.
J – ISTER – 🛏 1,2 cl., ▬ 2 cl., (2) and ✕ Bucureşti - Budapest and v.v.; 🛏 1,2 cl. Thessaloníki - Bucureşti - Budapest and v.v. Supplement payable.
N – (12) Iaşi - Timişoara and v.v.
P – PANNONIA – (12) and ✕ Bucureşti - Budapest and v.v.; 🛏 1,2 cl., ▬ 1,2 cl. Bucureşti - Budapest - Wien - München and v.v.; conveys to Sept. 29 (to Sept. 30 from Praha) 🛏 1,2 cl. Bucureşti - Budapest - Praha and v.v.
Q – ▬ 2 cl. and (12) Iaşi - Timişoara and v.v.
R – (12) Cluj - Deva - Târgu Jiu and v.v. (Table **1605**).
S – (12) Sighetu - Timişoara and v.v.
T – MUREŞ – (12) Târgu Mures - Lökosháza - Budapest and v.v.
V – AUREL VLAICU – (12) and ✕ Bucureşti - Teius (**525/6**) - Arad and v.v.
X – (12) Suceava - Braşov - Sibiu - Copşa Mică and Sibiu - Suceava.
Y – (12) Constanţa - Bucureşti - Târgu Jiu - Arad and v.v.; 🛏 1,2 cl., ▬ 2 cl. and (12) Bucureşti - Arad and v.v.
Z – (12) Constanţa - Bucureşti - Sibiu and v.v.
n – Aradu Nou.
▽ – Via Craiova (Table **1600**).
* – Number from Podu Olt.
☛ For Bucureşti - Timişoara and v.v. via Craiova, see Table **1600**.

TIMIŞOARA - ARAD - ORADEA 1625

km		IC 232 2	1834 J	78 C	1945	1947	2	1743 M	74 T	IC 234 2	1923 A
0	**Timişoara** Nord **1620** ▲ d.	0557	0642	0700	0747	1250	1255	1610	1700	1733	2310
33	Vinga d.	|	|	|	|	|	1330	|	|	|	|
57	**Arad 1620** ▲ a.	0643	0740	0746	0839	1346	1406	1659	1746	1819	2359
57	**Arad** d.	0650	0752	...	0845	1351	1419	1701	...	1822	0011
139	Salonta d.	0816	0924	...	1015	1516	1629	1829	...	1941	|
178	**Oradea** a.	0842	0953	...	1042	1541	1711	1854	...	2016	|
	Cluj Napoca **1630** a.	1109	1239	...	...	...	...	...	...	2242	0532

	1944 A	1744 M	1946	IC 234 2	75 T	1948		1836 J	79 C	IC 233 2
Cluj Napoca **1630** d.	2201	...	...	0710	...	...	...	1453	...	1728
Oradea d.	|	0445	0618	0937	...	1527	1543	1739	...	2004
Salonta d.	|	0517	0647	1014	...	1602	1628	1809	...	2032
Arad a.	0331	0641	0817	1131	...	1722	1833	1948	...	2147
Arad 1620 ▲ d.	0348	0644	0821	1136	1219	1728	1906	2000	2019	2150
Vinga d.	|	|	|	|	|	|	1932	|	|	|
Timişoara Nord **1620** ▲ a.	0437	0737	0910	1222	1305	1826	2012	2049	2105	2236

km		2	2	2
0	Békéscsaba **1280** d.	0642	1044	1644
16	Gyula **1280** d.	0659	1059	1659
36	Kötegyán 🏛 HU a.	0723	1123	1723
50	Salonta 🏛 RO a.	0853	1253	1853
89	Oradea a.	...	...	...

	2	2	2
Oradea d.	...	...	...
Salonta 🏛 RO d.	0901	1301	1901
Kötegyán 🏛 HU d.	0831	1231	1831
Gyula **1280** d.	0859	1259	1859
Békéscsaba **1280** a.	0913	1315	1913

▲ – Additional trains:
Timişoara Nord - **Arad**: 0428, 0542, 0750, 1335, 1557Ⓑ, 1724, 1821, 1944, 2345Ⓐ.
Arad - **Timişoara** Nord: 0440, 0549, 0752, 1310, 1425, 1618, 1747Ⓑ, 2338Ⓐ.

HU – Hungary (Central European Time).
RO – Romania (East European Time).

A – (12) Timişoara - Sighetu and v.v. Via Alba Iulia (Tables **1620** and **1635**).
C – CRIŞ – (12) Timişoara - Budapest and v.v.
J – (12) Timişoara - Iaşi and v.v.
M – (12) Timişoara - Baia Mare and v.v.
T – TRAIANUS – (12) Timişoara - Budapest and v.v.

DEBRECEN and ORADEA - SATU MARE - BAIA MARE 1627

km			1741 B		2	367		Ⓐ		369	1743 T	
0	**Debrecen** d.	...	...	...	0712	1112	...	...	...	1512	...	...
30	Nyirábrány 🏛 HU a.	...	...	...	0751	1151	...	...	...	1551	...	...
**	**Oradea** d.	0312	0627	0756	|	|	...	1431	1550	|	1858	1945
39	Valea lui Mihai 🏛 RO d.	0452	0731	0915	0927	1347	1215	1550	1707	1757	1955	2102
	Oradea a.	|	|	...	...	1511	|	...	|	|	|	|
70	Carei **1630** d.	0529	0800	...	...	...	1253	...	1758	1827	2022	2139
106	**Satu Mare 1630** ▲ a.	0610	0829	...	...	...	1335	...	1839	1856	2050	2220
165	Baia Mare **1630** ▲ a.	...	...	...	...	...	...	...	...	2112	2226	...

	1744 T		Ⓐ	368		2			1742 B	366	
Baia Mare **1630** ▲ d.	0130	...	...	0422	...	...	...	...	...	...	...
Satu Mare 1630 ▲ d.	0249	0336	...	0641	0742	...	1440	1535	1656	...	2007
Carei **1630** d.	0319	0415	...	0730	0837	...	1518	1617	1726	...	2059
Oradea d.	|	|	...	|	|	...	...	|	|	1647	|
Valea lui Mihai 🏛 RO d.	0342	0448	0534	0837	0920	1037	...	1716	1753	1837	2147
Oradea a.	0440	0614	0706	|	1056	|	...	1838	1856	|	2309
Nyirábrány 🏛 HU d.	...	...	...	0809	...	1009	...	...	...	1809	...
Debrecen a.	...	...	...	0848	...	1048	...	...	...	1848	...

B – 🛏 1,2 cl., ▬ 2 cl. and (12) Bucureşti - Satu Mare and v.v.
T – (12) Timişoara - Baia Mare and v.v.

** – Oradea - Valea lui Mihai: *66 km*.

HU – Hungary (Central European Time).
RO – Romania (East European Time).

▲ – Additional local services **Satu Mare - Baia Mare and v.v.**:
Journey time: ±1 h. 45 m.
From **Satu Mare**: 0410, 0813, 1118⚒, 1615.
From **Baia Mare**: 0738, 1224⚒, 1550, 1941.

1630 BUCUREŞTI - BRAŞOV - SIGHIŞOARA - CLUJ - ORADEA and SATU MARE

km		408 ✕	1537	1633	935 Z	374 P	1833 U	1745	1533	831	846	1937	IC 531 ✕	1637 ✕	1735	406 C	346 D	1643 S	1741 N	741 M	370 J	1631	1641 N	844	364 E	IC 231 K
0	**Bucureşti** Nord **1620** d.	...	0500	...	...	0550	...	0730	0736	0830	...	...	1300	...	1620	...	1645	1733	1830	1950	1950	2033	2133	...	...	...
59	Ploieşti Vest **1620** d.	...	0547	...	0442	0633	...	0813	0827	0912	...	...	1342	...	1708	...	1727	1818	1916	2031	2031	2116	2219	...	...	...
121	Sinaia **1620** d.	...	...	...	0617	0744	...	0927	...	1027	...	...	1447	...	...	...	1838	1930	2042	2137	2137	2229	2340	...	...	...
140	Predeal **1620** d.	...	...	...	0648	0822	...	1007	...	1101	...	...	1518	...	...	...	1909	2005	2115	2208	2208	2304	0011	...	...	...
166	**Braşov 1620** a.	...	...	...	0718	0852	...	1037	...	1138	...	...	1548	...	...	...	1939	2035	2145	2238	2238	2334	0041	...	...	...
166	**Braşov 1620** d.	0314	...	0430	0732	0904	...	1054	...	▬	...	...	1600	1846	...	1910	1947	▬	2157	2248	2248	2342	0053	...	...	...
294	Sighişoara **1620** d.	|	...	0628	0936	1109	...	1302	...	...	...	...	1758	2043	...	|	2145	...	2357	0046	0046	0140	|	...	...	...
333	Mediaş d.	|	...	0659	1010	1139	...	1335	...	...	...	...	1828	2113	...	|	2215	...	0030	|	|	0210	|	...	...	...
344	Copşa Mică ¶ d.	|	...	0712	1025	|	...	1348	...	...	...	...	|	2126	...	|	|	...	0043	|	|	|	|	...	...	...
374	Blaj d.	|	...	0739	1053	1217	...	1414	...	...	...	...	1907	2153	...	|	2252	...	0109	|	|	0248	|	...	...	...
407	**Alba Iulia 1620** a.	|	...	|	|	1250	...	|	...	...	...	...	|	|	...	|	2325	...	|	|	0252v	|	|	...	...	...
395	Teiuş **1635** d.	◐	...	0758	1115	▬	...	1433	...	...	...	...	1933	2212	...	◐	...	...	0128	0212	0228	0307	◐	...	...	...
408	Aiud **1635** d.	|	...	0810	1128	...	...	1444	...	...	...	...	1945	2223	...	|	...	...	0140	|	▬	0319	|	...	...	...
429	Războieni **1635** ▼ d.	|	...	0832	1158	...	...	1505	...	...	...	...	2007	2244	...	|	...	...	0201	|	...	0340	|	...	...	...
	Târgu Mureş ▼ a.	|	...	|	|	...	...	|	...	*IC*	...	...	|	|	...	|	...	...	|	|	...	|	|	...	...	...
446	Câmpia Turzii **1635** d.	|	...	0848	1213	**1935**	...	1522	...	**233**	...	...	2023	2301	...	|	...	...	0218	|	...	0357	|	...	...	...
497	**Cluj Napoca 1635** a.	1017	...	0941	1309		...	1615	...	**K**	...	...	2116	2354	...	0210	...	...	0311	|	...	0451	|	...	...	...
497	**Cluj Napoca** d.	1029	...	...	...	1405	1453	1627	...	1728	1814	1941	2133	...	...	0225	...	...	0331	|	...	0509	|	0607	0623	0710
547	Huedin d.	1124	...	...	...	1500	1552	|	...	1820	|	2037	2228	...	...	0320	...	...	0430	|	...	0602	|	|	0716	0803
650	**Oradea** a.	1307	...	...	...	1646	1735	|	...	1959	|	2240	0004	...	...	0457	...	...	0616	|	**941**	0751	|	|	0901	0932
	Budapest K **1275** a.	1617	...	...	...	...	▬	|	...	...	|	...	...	...	...	0817	...	...	|	|	**Q**	...	|	|	1217	...
556	Dej Călători d.	...	...	...	...	...	...	1729	...	...	1912	...	...	...	...	...	...	...	|	0423	0610	...	0742	0701	...	...
632	Jibou **1627** d.	...	...	...	...	...	1906	1840	...	...	2018	...	...	...	...	...	...	0329	⊡	0539	0743	...	0909	0819	...	...
655	Zalău Nord **1627** d.	...	...	...	...	...	1945	|	...	...	|	...	...	...	...	...	...	0408	|	|	|	...	|	|	...	...
743	Carei **1627** a.	...	...	...	...	...	2131	|	...	...	|	...	...	...	...	...	...	0556	0758	|	|	...	|	|	...	...
690	**Baia Mare 1627** a.	...	...	...	...	...	|	1929	...	...	2107	...	...	...	...	...	...	|	|	0627	0844	...	1012	0909	...	...
749	**Satu Mare 1627** a.	...	...	...	...	...	2239	2112	...	...	2242	...	...	...	...	...	...	0700	0829	0754	1106	...	...	1034	...	...

	1638 ✕		347 D	1936	1746	IC 232 K	843	1834 U	IC 532 ✕	375 P	409	1634		942 Q	1642 N		1938	365 E	1742 N	845	IC 234 K	1632	1534	742 M	371 J	407 C
Satu Mare 1627 d.	...	0318	...	...	0515	...	0736	...	...	...	...	...	...	1410	...	1440	...	...	1656	1738	...	...	...	2140	...	...
Baia Mare 1627 d.	...	|	...	...	0645	...	0910	...	...	...	...	...	...	1546	1635	|	...	...	|	1855	...	...	...	2307	...	...
Carei **1627** d.	...	0405	...	...	|	...	|	...	...	...	...	...	...	|	|	1533	...	...	1726	|	...	...	...	|	...	...
Zalău Nord **1627** d.	...	0620	...	...	|	...	|	...	...	...	...	...	...	|	|	1722	...	...	|	|	...	...	...	|	...	...
Jibou **1627** d.	...	0658	...	...	0742	...	0959	...	...	...	...	...	...	1641	1748	1803	...	...	⊡	1956	...	...	...	2357	...	...
Dej Călători d.	...	▬	...	...	0854	...	1105	...	...	...	...	...	...	1758	1923	▬	...	...	|	2107	...	...	...	0114	...	...
Budapest K **1275** d.	...	...	...	...	|	...	|	...	...	...	0843	...	...	...	|	...	...	1343	|	|	...	...	...	|	...	1743
Oradea d.	...	...	...	0600	|	0845	|	1001	1101	...	1402	...	1536	...	|	...	1733	1853	1911	|	2019	2046	...	|	...	2301
Huedin d.	...	...	...	0741	|	1019	|	1145	1242	...	1549	...	1822	...	|	**936**	1930	2040	2056	|	2152	2226	...	|	...	0047
Cluj Napoca a.	...	...	...	0835	0958	1109	1154	1239	1335	...	1640	...	1940	...	|	**Z**	2024	2133	2152	2200	2242	2316	...	|	...	0138
Cluj Napoca 1635 d.	0500	...	...	▬	1010	...	...	...	1347	...	1654	1712	...	...	|	2025	...	...	2212	▬	...	2331	...	|	...	0150
Câmpia Turzii **1635** d.	0557	...	...	...	1107	...	...	...	1445	...	|	1810	...	...	|	2123	...	...	2309	...	...	0028	...	|	...	|
Târgu Mureş ▲ d.	|	...	...	...	|	...	...	...	|	...	|	|	...	...	|	|	...	...	|	...	...	|	...	|	...	|
Războieni **1635** ▲ d.	0615	...	...	...	1125	...	...	...	1503	...	|	1827	...	...	|	2159	...	...	2326	...	...	0047	...	|	...	|
Aiud **1635** d.	0633	...	...	...	1144	...	...	...	1522	...	|	1845	...	...	|	2218	...	...	2344	...	...	|	...	|	...	|
Teiuş **1635** d.	0649	...	...	...	1201	...	...	...	1551	...	◐	1902	...	...	◐	2235	...	...	0000	...	...	0126	...	0339	0339	◐
Alba Iulia 1620 d.	|	...	0709	...	|	...	...	...	|	1707	|	|	...	...	|	|	...	...	|	...	...	|	...	|	0256v	|
Blaj d.	0711	...	0744	...	1229	...	...	...	1614	1741	|	1925	...	...	|	2258	...	...	0022	...	...	0149	...	|	|	|
Copşa Mică ¶ d.	0740	...	|	...	1259	...	...	...	|	|	|	1954	...	...	|	2328	...	...	0051	...	...	|	...	|	|	|
Mediaş d.	0752	...	0821	...	1312	...	...	...	1653	1819	|	2006	...	...	|	2341	...	...	0102	...	...	0227	...	|	|	|
Sighişoara **1620** d.	0832	...	0901	**832**	1354	...	...	...	1733	1859	|	2046	...	...	|	0021	...	...	0144	**1644**	...	0307	...	0512	0512	|
Braşov 1620 a.	1030	...	1053		1549	...	...	...	1923	2049	0009	2237	...	...	0213	0216	...	...	0336	**S**	...	0457	...	0702	0702	0908
Braşov 1620 d.	...	...	1102	1404	1603	...	...	...	1937	2100	...	...	...	...	0225	0234	...	...	0348	0413	...	0527	...	0714	0714	...
Predeal **1620** d.	...	**1736**	1134	1436	1635	...	...	...	2016	2138	...	...	...	...	0305	0316	...	...	0426	0452	...	0606	...	0753	0753	...
Sinaia **1620** d.	...		1207	1510	1704	...	...	...	2046	2210	...	...	...	...	0331	0344	...	...	0454	0523	...	0639	...	0820	0820	...
Ploieşti Vest **1620** d.	...	1248	1319	1617	1819	...	...	...	2200	2314	...	...	...	...	0444	0451	...	...	0611	0642	...	0754	0838	0941	0941	...
Bucureşti Nord **1620** a.	...	1336	1359	1659	1901	...	...	...	2241	2355	...	...	...	...	0526	...	...	...	0653	0725	...	0837	0934	1028	1028	...

km	▼				856		948 Z	2Ⓐ		1540		355 A
0	Războieni d.	0330	0424	0718	1048	1129	1213	1513	1718	1925	2010	2234
19	Luduş d.	0359	0503	0752	1109	1158	1234	1543	1746	1944	2115	2255
59	**Târgu Mureş** a.	0514	0623	0904	1149	1311	1318	1704	1849	2027	2218	2336

▲		1549	354 A		2Ⓐ			855		949 Z	
Târgu Mureş d.	0339	0523	0605	0728	1249	1435	1548	1638	1930	2030	2240
Luduş d.	0454	0603	0645	0831	1359	1546	1650	1717	2038	2114	2349
Războieni a.	0521	0624	0706	0858	1429	1616	1716	1747	2107	2135	0018

A – MUREŞ – [12] Târgu Mureş - Arad - Budapest and v.v. See Table **1620**.

C – CORONA – 🛏 1,2 cl., ▬ 1,2 cl. and [12] Budapest - Cluj Napoca - Deda - Braşov and v.v.; ▬ 2 cl. and [2] Budapest - Deda - Târgu Mureş and v.v.

D – DACIA – [12] Bucureşti - Curtici and v.v.; 🛏 1,2 cl., ▬ 2 cl., [2] and ✕ Bucureşti - Budapest - Wien and v.v.

E – ADY ENDRE – [12] Cluj - Budapest and v.v.

J – ISTER – 🛏 1,2 cl., ▬ 2 cl., [2] and ✕ Bucureşti - Budapest and v.v.; 🛏 1,2 cl. Thessaloníki - Bucureşti - Budapest and v.v. Supplement payable.

K – [2] Cluj - Oradea - Timişoara and v.v. (Table **1625**).

M – MARAMUREŞ – 🛏 1,2 cl., ▬ 2 cl. and [2] Bucureşti - Satu Mare and v.v.

N – Conveys 🛏 1,2 cl., ▬ 2 cl. and [12].

P – PANNONIA – [12] and ✕ Bucureşti - Budapest and v.v.; 🛏 1,2 cl., ▬ 1,2 cl. Bucureşti - Budapest - Wien - München and v.v.; 🛏 1,2 cl. Bucureşti - Budapest - Praha and v.v.

Q – June 19 - Sept. 12 (from Satu Mare / Sighetu Marmaţiei, one day later from Mangalia): [12] Satu Mare / Sighetu Marmaţiei - Mangalia and v.v.

S – 🛏 1,2 cl., ▬ 2 cl. and [12] Bucureşti - Sighetu Marmaţiei and v.v.

U – [12] Iaşi - Timişoara and v.v.

Z – June 19 - Sept. 12 (from Cluj / Târgu Mureş, one day later from Mangalia): [12] Cluj Napoca / Târgu Mureş - Mangalia and v.v.

v – Via Teiuş.

◐ – Via Miercurea Ciuc (Table **1640**).

⊡ – Via Valea lui Vihai (Table **1627**).

¶ – **COPŞA MICĂ - SIBIU and v.v.**: Journey time: ± 75 minutes.
From **Copşa Mică**: 0435, 0754, 1303, 1621, 1754, 2137.
From **Sibiu**: 0438, 0720, 1226, 1547, 1918, 2325.

1635 SIBIU - ALBA IULIA - CLUJ

km		1923 S	811	839 J	856	631 D			1766	355 T	1838 C
0	**Sibiu 1620** d.	...	0420	...	...	...	...	1556	...	...	...
74	Sebeş Alba **1620** d.	...	0546	...	...	...	...	1756	...	...	...
	Timişoara Nord **1620** d.	2310	|	...	...	...	...	|	1515	...	1747
82	Vinţu de Jos **1620** d.	0314	0554	0640	0941	1026	1545	1832	1916	2118	2236
92	**Alba Iulia 1620** d.	0325	...	0650	0951	1036	1555	1841	1926	2128	2245
111	Teiuş **1630** d.	0348	...	0712	1013	1103	1625	1917	1947	2150	2307
124	Aiud **1630** d.	0400	...	0724	1025	1115	1638	1930	1959	2201	2319
145	Războieni **1630** d.	0421	...	0744	1048	1143	1703	2030	2020	2234	2341
	Târgu Mureş **1630** a.	|	...	|	1149	|	|	2218	|	2336	|
162	Câmpia Turzii **1630** d.	0439	...	0801	...	1159	1722	...	2036	...	2358
213	**Cluj Napoca 1630** a.	0532	...	0854	...	1251	1838	...	2129	...	0051
	Iaşi **1650** a.	...	...	...	...	...	...	...	0619	...	0938

	1837 C		838 J	814			1924 S	1765	855	354 T	632 D
Iaşi **1650** d.	2042	...	...	...	...	...	...	1500	...	...	...
Cluj Napoca 1630 d.	0512	1216	1555	...	...	1950	2201	2349	...	...	1448
Câmpia Turzii **1630** d.	0610	1328	1651	...	...	2103	2258	0047	...	...	1546
Târgu Mureş **1630** d.	|	|	|	...	1548	|	|	|	1638	0605	|
Războieni **1630** d.	0628	1349	1708	...	1719	2124	2316	0104	1747	0721	1604
Aiud **1630** d.	0647	1411	1724	...	1746	2147	2335	0122	|	0740	1622
Teiuş **1630** d.	0704	1434	1739	...	1803	2201	2352	0139	1823	0757	1644
Alba Iulia 1620 d.	0727	1503	1802	...	1836	...	0015	0202	1843	0820	1706
Vinţu de Jos **1620** d.	0736	1513	1812	1939	1929	...	0024	0211	1855	0830	1715
Timişoara Nord **1620** a.	1214	...	...	|	|	...	0437	0629	...	...	...
Sebeş Alba **1620** d.	...	...	...	1951	1956	...	...	...	...	...	...
Sibiu 1620 a.	...	...	...	2126	2155	...	...	...	...	...	...

C – ▬ 2 cl. and [12] Timişoara - Iaşi and v.v.

D – From / to Craiova (Table **1605**).

J – From / to Târgu Jiu.

S – [12] Timişoara - Cluj - Sighetu Marmaţiei and v.v.

T – [12] Târgu Mures - Lökosháza - Budapest and v.v.

BRAŞOV - DEDA - DEJ - CLUJ 1640

km		941	1641	408		1973			IC549		406	406	1643
		Q	Y	✕							D	C	S
	Bucureşti Nord **1630** d.	...	2133	...	...	...	...	...	...	...	...	...	1733
0	**Braşov 1645** d.	...	0053	0314	0405	...	1126	...	1558	1605	...	1910	2047
32	Sfântu Gheorghe **1645** d.	...	0123	0344	0448	...	1216	...	1628	1649	...	1941	2118
	Galaţi **1645** d.	...	|	|	|	0540	|	...	|	|	...	|	|
95	**Miercurea Ciuc 1645** d.	...	0232	0452	0627	|	1353	1530	1751	1832	...	2049	2231
103	Siculeni **1645** d.	0059	0244	0503	0638	1208	1405	1541	1803	1857	...	2059	2244
150	Gheorghieni d.	0158	0336	0547	0749	1257	1513	1650	1849	2014	...	2143	2343
184	Topliţa d.	0231	0414	0634	0832	1333	1614	1733	1926	2106	...	2218	0023
	Târgu Mureş d.	|	|	|	|	|	|	|	|	|	2209	|	|
228	Deda a.	0343	0536	0746	1003	1445	1747	1857	2041	2242	2327	2330	0136
228	Deda ▼ d.	0347	0544	0748	...	1457	1759	1937	2102	2303	2345	2345	0139
	Târgu Mureş ▼ a.	|	|	|	...	1617	1940	2113	2227	0048	|	|	|
275	Sărăţel ‡ d.	0454	0648	0839	...	...	...	...	...	...	0036	0036	0228
300	Beclean pe Someş ‡ d.	2530	0710	0901	...	...	...	...	...	...	0058	0058	0247
324	Dej Călători ‡ d.	0551	0742	0924	...	...	...	...	...	...	0120	0120	...
	Baia Mare **1630** a.	...	1012	|	...	...	...	...	...	...	|	|	...
383	**Cluj Napoca** ‡ a.	...	...	1017	...	...	...	...	...	...	0213	0213	...
	Budapest K **1275** a.	...	...	1617	...	...	...	...	...	...	0817	0817	...

		1974	IC540			409	942	1642	1644		407	407
						✕	Q	Y	S		C	D
Budapest K **1275** d.	...	...	...	...	...	0843	...	...	...	...	1743	1743
Cluj Napoca ‡ d.	...	...	...	...	...	1654	...	...	...	...	0150	0150
Baia Mare **1630** d.	...	...	...	...	...	|	...	1635	...	...	|	|
Dej Călători ‡ d.	...	...	...	...	...	1751	1811	1923	...	...	0245	0245
Beclean pe Someş ‡ d.	...	...	...	...	...	1815	1852	1944	2150	...	0306	0306
Sărăţel ‡ d.	...	...	...	...	...	1839	1913	2020	2212	...	0328	0328
Târgu Mureş ▲ d.	1013	1158	1300	1430	1555	|	|	|	|	...	|	|
Deda ▲ a.	1148	1322	1417	1612	1744	1930	2005	2109	2259	...	0419	0419
Deda d.	1201	1336	1429	1624	1819	1932	2008	2128	2302	0227	0429	0452
Târgu Mureş a.	|	|	|	|	|	|	|	|	|	|	|	0613
Topliţa d.	1334	1456	1556	1802	1956	2050	2138	2249	0022	0412	0542	...
Gheorghieni d.	1420	1531	1632	1850	2056	2124	2226	2325	0056	0458	0618	...
Siculeni **1645** d.	1544	1659	1721	2006	2207	2219	2326	0018	0148	0617	0707	...
Miercurea Ciuc 1645 d.	1554	|	1732	2016	2216	2230	...	0030	0159	0628	0720	...
Galaţi **1645** a.	|	2310	|	|	...	|	...	|	|	|	|	...
Sfântu Gheorghe **1645** d.	1745	...	1841	2205	...	2340	...	0145	0321	0811	0840	...
Braşov 1645 a.	1833	...	1909	2244	...	0009	...	0213	0400	0855	0908	...
Bucureşti Nord **1630** a.	...	...	...	...	...	...	...	0526	0725	...	...	...

km	▼		641		1843			1973				549	
		2			b	⑧	①–⑤	G	2			d	
0	**Deda** d.	0400	0452	0516	0557	1020	1205	1457	1619	1759	1937	2102	2303
22	Reghin d.	0448	0524	0556	0629	1109	1245	1527	1659	1837	2016	2133	2351
54	**Târgu Mureş** a.	0545	0613	0652	0716	1216	1344	1617	1756	1940	2113	2227	0048

▲				1974		540				1844	642	
		2		G		d				b		
Târgu Mureş d.	0250	0723	1013	1158	...	1300	1430	1555	...	1921	2209	2235
Reghin d.	0342	0815	1105	1247	...	1343	1528	1700	...	2017	2253	2352
Deda a.	0425	0858	1148	1322	...	1417	1612	1744	...	2100	2327	0035

C – CORONA – 1, 2 cl., 1, 2 cl. and (12) Budapest - Cluj Napoca - Deda - Braşov and v.v.; 2 cl. and (2) Budapest - Deda - Târgu Mureş and v.v.
D – 2 cl. and (2) Târgu Mureş - Deda - Budapest and v.v.
G – From / to Galaţi.
Q – June 19 - Sept. 12 (from Satu Mare / Sighetu Marmaţiei, one day later from Mangalia): (12) Satu Mare / Sighetu Marmaţiei - Mangalia and v.v.
S – 1, 2 cl., 2 cl. and (12) Bucureşti - Sighetu and v.v.
Y – 1, 2 cl., 2 cl. and (12) Bucureşti - Baia Mare and v.v. Conveys (12) Bucureşti - Deda (**1843/4**) - Târgu Mureş and v.v., (12) Bucureşti - Sărăţel - Bistriţa and v.v.
b – From / to Bucureşti.
d – From / to Braşov (see table above).
‡ – See also Tables **1630 / 50 / 55**.

BRAŞOV- MIERCUREA CIUC - ADJUD - GALAŢI 1645

km		1751		IC550							1974		942
		S		B							G		Q
0	**Braşov 1640** d.	2303	...	...	...	0405	...	...	...	...	...	...	...
32	Sfântu Gheorghe **1640** d.	2339	...	...	...	0448	...	...	...	...	...	...	...
	Târgu Mureş **1640** d.	|	...	...	...	|	...	...	...	...	1158	...	...
	Siculeni d.	|	...	...	...	|	...	...	...	...	|	...	...
95	**Miercurea Ciuc 1640** d.	0057	...	...	...	0627	0717	...	...	...	|	1931	...
103	Siculeni **1640** d.	0109	...	...	0430	0635	0727	...	...	...	1659	1942	2343
144	Ghimeş d.	0208	...	...	0547	▬	0849	...	...	1345	1815	2053	0054
179	Comăneşti d.	0248	...	0410	0637	...	0949	1300	...	1433	1855	2139	0139
216	Oneşti d.	0338	...	0457	0741	...	...	1357	...	1540	1944	2331	0235
254	**Adjud 1670** d.	0440	...	0538	0843	⑧	...	1500	...	1640	2032	0046	0324
279	Mărăşeşti **1670** d.	0506	0627	...	0917	1043	...	1532	1542	...	2057	0118	0349
	Iaşi **1670** a.	0836	|	...	...	|	...	...	|	...	|	...	...
298	Tecuci **1670** a.	...	0657	...	...	1112	...	...	1616	...	2132	...	...
383	**Galaţi 1670** a.	...	0913	...	...	1330	...	...	1837	...	2310	...	...

		1973			1752				IC559			941
		G			S				B	Ⓐ		Q
Galaţi 1670 d.	...	0540	0750	...	...	...	...	...	...	1525	...	...
Tecuci **1670** d.	...	0727	1013	...	...	...	...	...	...	1745	...	...
Iaşi **1670** d.	...	|	|	...	1037	...	...	...	...	|	...	...
Mărăşeşti **1670** d.	0420	0752	1040	1225	1359	1444	...	1714	...	1811	1910	2026
Adjud 1670 d.	0509	0828	...	1302	1508	1522	...	1807	1910	...	1946	2056
Oneşti d.	0600	0903	...	1358	1546	1611	...	1855	1947	...	2038	2138
Comăneşti d.	0658	0955	...	1454	1640	1704	...	1957	2034	...	2141	2247
Ghimeş d.	0752	1035	...	1539	1721	1747	...	2054	...	...	2229	2343
Siculeni **1640** d.	0903	1208	...	...	1820	1856	2006	2202	...	...	...	0041
Miercurea Ciuc 1640 d.	0914	|	...	...	1831	1906	2016	...	...	...	...	...
Siculeni a.	...	|	...	...	|	...	|	...	...	...	...	...
Târgu Mureş **1640** a.	...	1617	...	...	|	...	|	...	...	...	...	...
Sfântu Gheorghe **1640** d.	...	...	...	...	1942	...	2205	...	...	...	...	...
Braşov 1640 a.	...	...	...	...	2010	...	2244	...	...	...	...	...

B – (12) Comăneşti - Bucureşti and v.v.
G – (12) Galaţi - Târgu Mureş - Timişoara and v.v.
Q – June 19 - Sept. 12 (from Satu Mare / Sighetu Marmaţiei, one day later from Mangalia): (12) Satu Mare / Sighetu Marmaţiei - Mangalia and v.v.
S – (12) Iaşi (**1664/5**) - Adjud - Sibiu and v.v.; (12) Suceava - Adjud - Sibiu and v.v.

IAŞI - SUCEAVA - DEJ - CLUJ 1650

km		1653	1942	1833	1859	943	1931	1924	853	1644	1765	1837
		B				Q				A		J
0	**Iaşi** d.	...	...	0626	0800	...	1032	...	...	...	1500	2042
76	Paşcani **1670** d.	0308	...	0736	0907	...	1143	...	...	...	1611	2152
122	Vereşti **1670** d.	0351	...	0809	|	...	1216	...	...	...	1644	2224
137	**Suceava 1670** d.	0415	...	0829	0953	...	1238	...	...	...	1657	2245
140	Suceava Nord **1670** a.	|	...	|	|	...	|	...	...	...	1705	|
140	Suceava Nord d.	|	...	|	|	...	|	...	...	...	1725	|
187	Gura Humorului Oraş d.	0504	...	0917	1039	...	1326	...	...	...	1813	2335
219	Câmpulung Moldovenesc d.	0548	...	1000	1118	...	1411	...	...	...	1859	0021
257	Vatra Dornei Băi d.	0659	...	1104	1217	...	1516	...	1820	...	1959	0128
351	Năsăud d.	...	...	1254	...	...	1714	...	2008	...	2150	0311
	Sighetu Marmaţiei d.	...	0125	|	...	1300	|	1620	|	1721	|	|
	Vişeu de Jos d.	...	0327	|	...	1447	|	1815	|	1916	|	|
357	Salva d.	...	0539	1303	...	1656	1724	2007	2017	2111	2200	0323
379	Beclean pe Someş **1640** d.	...	0559	1325	...	1718	1750	2031	2039	2134	2224	0345
402	Dej Călători **1640** ▲ d.	...	0644	1347	...	...	1813	2055	2101	...	2246	0406
460	**Cluj Napoca 1640** ▲ a.	...	0739	1439	...	...	1903	2146	2153	...	2337	0457
	Oradea **1630** a.	...	...	1735	...	...	...	|	...	...	|	|
	Timişoara N **1620 / 35** a.	...	...	2049	...	...	...	0437	...	...	0629	1214

	1838	1646	944	1923	854	1932	1858	1834	1654	1943	1766
	J	A	Q						B		
Timişoara N **1620 / 35** d.	1747	...	...	2310	...	...	...	0642	...	...	1515
Oradea **1630** d.	|	...	...	|	...	...	...	1001	...	...	|
Cluj Napoca 1640 ▲ d.	0109	...	...	0552	0600	0905	...	1257	...	1538	2149
Dej Călători **1640** ▲ d.	0206	...	...	0649	0656	1001	...	1355	...	1701	2244
Beclean pe Someş **1640** d.	0233	0300	0608	0715	0721	1024	...	1415	...	1722	2305
Salva d.	0255	0337	0631	0751	0743	1046	...	1437	...	1800	2327
Vişeu de Jos d.	|	0522	0820	0940	|	|	...	|	...	2035	|
Sighetu Marmaţiei a.	|	0714	1030	1131	|	|	...	|	...	2235	|
Năsăud d.	0312	...	...	...	0752	1055	...	1446	...	...	2334
Vatra Dornei Băi d.	0458	...	...	...	0941	1249	1608	1639	2142	...	0117
Câmpulung Moldovenesc d.	0602	...	...	...	...	1352	1702	1747	2245	...	0223
Gura Humorului Oraş d.	0643	...	...	...	...	1436	1739	1834	2336	...	0307
Suceava Nord a.	|	...	...	...	...	|	|	|	|	...	0358
Suceava Nord **1670** d.	|	...	...	...	...	|	|	|	|	...	0415
Suceava 1670 d.	0741	...	...	...	...	1536	1834	1934	0037	...	0422
Vereşti **1670** d.	0753	...	...	...	...	1548	|	1946	0103	...	0434
Paşcani **1670** d.	0833	...	...	...	...	1628	1921	2028	0140	...	0514
Iaşi a.	0938	...	...	...	...	1733	2023	2133	...	...	0619

A – 1, 2 cl., 2 cl. and (12) Sighetu - Bucureşti and v.v.
B – 1, 2 cl., 2 cl. and (12) Bucureşti - Vatra Dornei Băi and v.v.
J – 2 cl. and (12) Iaşi - Timişoara and v.v.
Q – June 19 - Sept. 12 (from Satu Mare / Sighetu Marmaţiei, one day later from Mangalia): (12) Satu Mare / Sighetu Marmaţiei - Mangalia and v.v.
▲ – See also Tables **1630** and **1655**.

BISTRIŢA - DEJ - CLUJ 1655

km			1949									1845
			Ⓐ				Ⓐ					A
0	**Bistriţa** Nord d.	0418	0528	0725	0732	1215	1451	1523	1535	1917	1930	1943
11	Sărăţel ‡ d.	0435	0540	0741	0806	1232	1508	1554	1552	1948	1946	1955
58	Deda **1640** a.	|	|	|	0920	...	|	1702	|	2056	|	...
36	Beclean pe Someş ‡ d.	0509	0605	0827	...	...	1545	...	1628	...	2018	...
60	Dej Călători ‡ d.	0546	0644	0929	...	...	1618	...	1703	...	2046	...
119	**Cluj Napoca** ‡ a.	0712	0739	1053	...	...	...	...	1830	...	...	...

			1846					1940			
			B	Ⓐ				Ⓐ			
Cluj Napoca ‡ d.	...	...	...	...	...	...	1206	1538	...	...	1957
Dej Călători ‡ d.	...	0508	...	0559	...	...	1324	1645	1720	...	2127
Beclean pe Someş ‡ d.	...	0546	...	0630	...	...	1358	1713	1756	...	2204
Deda **1640** d.	0445	|	...	|	...	1238	|	|	|	1718	|
Sărăţel ‡ d.	0611	0621	0652	0706	0910	1403	1430	1736	1829	1841	2238
Bistriţa Nord a.	0629	0639	0704	0724	0936	1421	1447	1747	1846	1859	2256

A – (12) Bistriţa - Sărăţel (**1642**) - Bucureşti.
B – (12) Bucureşti (**1641**) - Sărăţel - Bistriţa.
‡ – See also Tables **1630 / 40 / 50**.

BUCUREŞTI - GALAŢI 1660

km			IC571		875	1671	1675	1673		IC575	1871	1731	871
			✕	F ⊖									
0	**Bucureşti** Nord **1670** d.	...	0535	...	0701	0930	1235	1341	...	1540	...	...	1910
	Ploieşti Sud **1670** d.	...	|	...	0745	|	1318	|	...	1625	...	...	|
**	Buzău **1670** d.	0430	|	...	0850	|	1429	|	1515	1728	...	2000	|
	Constanţa **1680** d.	|	|	...	|	|	|	|	|	|	1714	|	|
138	Făurei d.	0538	0746	0830	0947	1140	1525	1551	1627	1824	|	2056	2122
	Constanţa **1680** a.	|	|	|	|	|	|	|	2011	|	|	|	|
198	Brăila d.	0638	0825	0936	1026	1225	1607	1635	...	1902	2115	2137	2200
229	**Galaţi** a.	0725	0858	1020	1100	1301	1643	1713	...	1935	2151	2213	2233

	IC572	1872	1732	876	1672		1676	1674	IC576		872	
	✕									F ⊖		
Galaţi d.	0500	0550	0640	0655	0940	...	1130	1350	1515	1648	1750	1940
Brăila d.	0534	0629	0717	0730	1018	...	1209	1429	1550	1739	1825	2028
Constanţa **1680** d.	|	|	|	|	|	0723	|	|	|	|	|	|
Făurei d.	0614	|	0800	0812	1103	1133	1255	1514	1631	1842	1905	2131
Constanţa **1680** a.	|	1002	|	|	|	|	|	|	|	...	|	|
Buzău **1670** d.	|	...	0858	0910	|	1244	1355	|	1728	...	|	2243
Ploieşti Sud **1670** d.	|	...	1001	1021	|	...	1507	|	1829	...	|	...
Bucureşti Nord **1670** a.	0817	...	...	1102	1314	...	1551	1729	1914	...	2111	...

F – (12) Feteşti - Galaţi and v.v. (Table **1680**).
⊖ – Subject to alteration.
** – Buzău - Făurei: *40 km*.

1670 BUCUREŞTI - BUZĂU - BACĂU - IAŞI and SUCEAVA

km		1751	1956	1665	1851	1964	IC 551	IC 564	382	IC 555	1866	751	661	651	1966	1861	IC 557	1661	1552	IC 553	IC 561	402	1653	1677	663	753
		V			H⊖		✕	✕	A	✕				F		C⊖	T			✕	2	D	N	⑦	de	d
0	**Bucureşti** Nord **1660** d.	...	...	...	...	...	0602	0602	0626	0900	...	1103	1200	1400	...	...	1500	1600	...	1701	1750	1957	2100	2230	2300	2350
59	Ploieşti Sud **1660** d.	...	...	...	...	...	0644	0644	0717	1002	...	1149	1247	1445	...	...	1545	1645	...	1743	1834	2049	2146	2316	2345	0035
128	**Buzău 1660** d.	...	...	...	0405	...	0747	0747	0822	1118	...	1254	1356	1550	...	...	1649	1753	...	1847	1937	2201	2257	0024	0050	0142
161	Râmnicu Sărat d.	...	...	...	0442	...	|	|	|	1157	...	1330	1432	1625	...	...	|	1829	...	|	|	|	2334	0101	0126	|
199	Focşani d.	...	...	...	0524	...	0855	0855	0934	1233	...	1409	1511	1704	...	...	1758	1909	...	1955	2043	2313	0014	0141	0206	0257
219	Mărăşeşti **1645** d.	...	...	...	0556	...	|	|	|	1302	...	1440	|	|	...	...	1827	|	...	|	|	|	0046	0211	|	0329
244	Adjud **1645** d.	0450	...	0440	0623	...	0945	0945	|	1326	...	1505	|	1759	...	...	1851	|	2038	2045	|	|	0113	▬	|	0355
303	**Bacău** ◧ d.	0539	0547	|	0706	...	1027	1027	1115	1407	...	1548	|	1852	...	...	1933	|	2134	2127	|	0054	0156	...	|	0439
346	Roman d.	0611	0620	|	0738	...	1059	1059	|	▬	...	1620	|	1924	...	...	...	|	2206	2159	|	0130	0228	...	|	0512
	Galaţi 1645 d.	|	|	|	|	0600	|	|	|	...	1150	|	|	|	1615	...	...	|	|	|	|	|	|	...	|	|
	Tecuci **1645** d.	|	|	0531n	|	0733	|	|	|	...	1331	|	1612	|	1805	1905	...	2012	|	|	2131n	|	|	...	0308	|
	Bârlad d.	|	|	0619	|	0820	|	|	|	...	1406	|	1656	|	1841	1949	...	2055	|	|	2205	|	|	...	0352	|
	Vaslui d.	|	|	0725	|	0916	|	|	|	...	1502	|	1753	|	1937	2054	...	2155	|	|	2259	|	|	...	0452	|
	Iaşi a.	|	0809	0836	|	1016	|	1247	|	2	1607	|	1901	|	2037	2210	...	2308	2339	|	2358	0307	|	2	0600	|
	Iaşi 1650 ‡ RO d.	|	...	...	|	...	|	...	|	1300	...	|	...	|	...	...	...	...	...	|	...	0310	|	0450	...	|
	Ungheni **1730** .. 🏛 MD a.	|	...	...	|	...	|	...	|	1450	...	|	...	|	...	...	...	...	...	|	...	0524	|	0638	...	|
	Chişinău 1730 a.	|	...	...	|	...	|	...	|	...	...	|	...	|	...	...	...	...	...	|	...	0852	|	...	...	|
387	Paşcani **1650** ▼ d.	0642	...	...	0810	...	1134	...	1231	...	...	1700	...	1957	...	...	...	...	...	2234	...	...	0308	...	...	0552
432	Vereşti **1650** ★ a.	0713	...	...	0852	...	|	...	|	...	...	1749	...	2030	...	...	...	...	...	|	...	...	0351	...	...	0647
476	Botoşani ★ a.	|	...	...	|	...	|	...	|	...	...	1855	...	|	...	...	...	...	...	|	...	...	|	...	...	0746
448	**Suceava** a.	0726	...	...	0902	...	1211	...	1315	...	...	1757p	...	2041	...	...	...	...	...	2311	...	...	0404	...	...	0647p
450	**Suceava** Nord **1650** . § RO a.	0735	...	...	0911	...	1220	...	|	...	...	1806p	...	2050	...	...	...	...	...	2320	...	...	...	...	...	0655p
539	Chernivtsi § UA a.	...	...	...	...	...	...	...	1816	...	...	...	...	...	...	...	...	...	...	...	...	...	...	...	...	...

km*		1654		IC 552	1551	IC 562	1662	1963	652	1865	1664	1752	383	IC 556	754		662	IC 554	IC 563	1955	1965	1852	1862	752	664	401
		N	2	✕		2			G			V	B			2		✕	✕			H⊖	C⊖	d	de	E
	Chernivtsi § UA d.	...	...	...	...	...	...	...	...	...	...	...	0704	...	...	...	...	...	...	...	...	...	...	...	...	...
	Suceava Nord **1650** . § RO d.	...	...	0505	...	...	...	...	0741	...	...	1147	|	...	1310q	...	...	1635	...	...	...	2129	...	2259q	...	...
	Suceava d.	0037	...	0512	...	...	...	...	0748	...	...	1154	1234	...	1317q	...	...	1642	...	...	...	2136	...	2306q	...	...
	Botoşani ★ d.	|	...	|	...	...	...	...	|	...	...	|	|	...	1227	...	...	|	...	...	...	|	...	2215	...	...
	Vereşti **1650** ★ d.	0103	...	|	...	...	...	...	0759	...	...	1206	|	...	1345	...	...	|	...	...	...	2149	...	2334	...	...
	Paşcani **1650** ▼ d.	0149	...	0558	...	...	...	...	0840	...	...	1246	1333	...	1433	...	...	1741	...	...	...	2231	...	0021	...	...
0	**Chişinău 1730** d.	|	...	|	...	...	...	...	|	...	...	|	|	...	|	...	...	|	...	...	...	|	...	|	...	1710
107	Ungheni **1730** .. 🏛 MD d.	|	0755	|	...	...	...	...	|	...	...	|	|	...	|	1740	...	|	...	...	...	|	...	|	...	2110
128	**Iaşi 1650** ‡ RO a.	|	0921	|	...	...	...	...	|	...	...	|	|	...	|	1907	...	|	...	...	...	|	...	|	...	2326
128	**Iaşi** d.	|	▬	|	0500	0530	0606	0717	|	1025	1037	|	|	...	|	▬	1456	|	1615	1808	1810	|	2254	|	2330	2331
196	Vaslui d.	|	...	|	|	0630	0724	0817	|	1127	1153	|	|	...	|	...	1610	|	|	|	1910	|	0020	|	0042	|
248	Bârlad d.	|	...	|	|	0717	0819	0906	|	1217	1252	|	|	...	|	...	1701	|	|	|	2001	|	0117	|	0135	|
297	Tecuci **1645** d.	|	*IC*	|	|	0754n	0913	0940	|	1259	1331n	|	|	...	|	...	1755	|	|	|	2043	|	0200	|	0228	|
382	**Galaţi 1645** a.	|	**558**	|	|	|	|	1115	|	1442	|	|	|	...	|	...	|	|	|	|	2223	|	...	|	|	|
	Roman d.	0219	**T**	0625	0635	|	|	...	0908	...	|	1314	|	...	1503	...	|	1807	1807	1958	...	2301	...	0051	|	0110
	Bacău ◧ d.	0255	0459	0702	0717	|	|	...	0957	...	|	1353	1439	1503	1539	**1678**	|	1843	1843	2032	...	2338	...	0127	|	0149
	Adjud **1645** d.	0341	0557	0746	0759	|	|	...	1056	...	1425	1435	|	1549	1625	⑦	|	1928	1928	...	...	0025	...	0214	|	|
	Mărăşeşti **1645** d.	0407	0621	|	...	|	|	...	|	...	...	...	|	1613	1650	1720	|	|	|	...	...	0051	...	0239	|	|
	Focşani d.	0437	0650	0833	...	0842	0959	...	1156	...	...	...	1619	1641	1720	1750	1844	2016	2016	...	...	0121	...	0309	0319	0329
	Râmnicu Sărat d.	0519	|	|	...	|	1038	...	1242	...	...	...	|	1720	1800	1832	1926	|	|	...	...	0203	...	0350	0401	|
	Buzău 1660 d.	0559	0803	0946	...	0954	1116	...	1324	...	...	...	1736	1757	1838	1910	2004	2131	2131	...	...	0237	...	0430	0439	0453
	Ploieşti Sud **1660** d.	0706	0911	1048	...	1058	1228	...	1429	...	...	...	1840	1902	1940	2017	2106	2233	2233	...	...	...	...	0534	0544	0556
	Bucureşti Nord **1660** a.	0750	0959	1137	...	1151	1311	...	1512	...	...	...	1931	1948	2023	2101	2148	2314	2314	...	...	...	...	0618	0627	0647

km	◧		①–⑤						J	IC 557	
0	**Bacău** d.	0420	0602	0933	1147	...	1413	1659	1907	1938	2138
60	Piatra Neamţ a.	0557	0740	1103	1318	...	1543	1847	2014	2044	2316
86	**Bicaz** a.	0643	...	...	...	...	1629	1933	...	2115	...

◧	IC 558			K			①–⑤			
Bicaz d.	0320	...	0710	...	...	...	...	...	1650	1958
Piatra Neamţ d.	0351	0507	0750	0826	...	1125	1425	1613	1730	2052
Bacău a.	0457	0643	0916	0932	...	1301	1601	1740	1856	2219

A – BULGARIA EXPRES – 🛏 1, 2 cl. Sofiya (**9647**) - Ruse (**382**) - Vadul Siret (**60**) - Kyïv - Moskva; 🛏 2 cl. Sofiya - Kyïv. ◇
B – BULGARIA EXPRES – 🛏 1, 2 cl. Moskva (**59**) - Kyïv - Vadul Siret (**383**) - Ruse (**9646**) - Sofiya; 🛏 2 cl. Kyïv - Sofiya. ◇
C – [12] Iaşi - Constanţa (- Mangalia, summer only) and v.v.
D – PRIETENIA – 🛏 2 cl. Bucureşti - Ungheni (**106**) - Chişinău. *May run alternate days only.*
E – PRIETENIA – 🛏 2 cl. Chişinău (**105**) - Ungheni - Bucureşti. *May run alternate days only.*
F – Conveys [12] Bucureşti - Bacău (**657**) - Piatra Neamţ.
G – Conveys [12] Piatra Neamţ (**658**) - Bacău - Bucureşti.
H – [12] Suceava - Constanţa (- Mangalia, summer only) and v.v.
J – [12] Bucureşti (**651**) - Bacău (**657**) - Piatra Neamţ.
K – [12] Piatra Neamţ (**658**) - Bacău (**652**) - Bucureşti.

N – 🛏 1, 2 cl., ━ 2 cl. and [12] Bucureşti - Vatra Dornei Băi and v.v.
T – [12] Bucureşti - Bicaz / Comăneşti and v.v.
V – [12] Sibiu - Suceava and v.v.
d – Also conveys 🛏 1, 2 cl.
e – Also conveys ━ 2 cl.
n – Tecuci Nord.
p – Portion detached from main train at Vereşti.
q – Portion attached to main train at Vereşti.
y – Not June 16 - Sept. 15.
z – June 16 - Sept. 14.

⊖ – Subject to alteration. ◇ – See also Table **98**.
MD – Moldova. RO – Romania. UA – Ukraine.

▼ – **PAŞCANI - TÂRGU NEAMT and v.v.**: Journey: ± 45 minutes.
From **Paşcani**: 0315, 0705**y**, 0820**z**, 1631, 2029.
From **Târgu Neamt**: 0505, 0957, 1742, 2136.

★ – **VEREŞTI - BOTOŞANI and v.v.**: Journey: ± 65 minutes.
From **Vereşti**: 0358 Ⓡ, 0446 Ⓡ, 0815, 1238, 1631, 2003.
From **Botoşani**: 0544, 1009, 1413, 1520 Ⓡ, 1807, 2340 Ⓡ.

‡ – 🏛: Nicolina (RO).
§ – 🏛: Vicşani (RO) / Vadul Siret (UA).
* – Other distances: Tecuci Nord - Focşani: *35 km*; Iaşi - Roman: *114 km*.

1680 BUCUREŞTI - CONSTANŢA - MANGALIA

Valid from June 14

Engineering work may affect services between Bucureşti and Constanţa

km		10917		1852	1862			992	942	1872	1131	985	936		1822		987	1636			681						685
		x	v2	Q	J	2	2	Tx	Mx	G	V	w	Cx		A		y✕	S	v2	2	✕	2		v2	2	F	
0	**Bucureşti** Nord d.	0146	...	...	...	...	...	0439n	...	...	0625	...	...	...	0717	...	0839	0929	...	...	1400	...	...	...	...	...	1854
	Buzău d.	|	...	0307	...	...	...	|	0551q	...	|	...	0608	...	|	0705	|	|	...	...	|	...	1515	...	...	...	|
	Făurei d.	|	...	0404	0421	...	...	|	0647	...	|	...	0715	...	|	0824	|	|	...	...	|	...	1627	...	...	1911	|
146	Feteşti d.	0422	...	0526	0551	...	0656	0726	0809	0822	|	...	0845	...	0958	1002	1109	1205	...	...	1632	1657	1805	...	...	2050	2203
190	Medgidia d.	0517	...	0610	0636	0658	0749	|	|	0919	0931	0940	0955	...	1042	...	1152	1250	...	1551	1716	1805	1908	...	2014	...	2246
334	**Tulcea** Oraş a.	|	...	|	|	1000	|	|	|	|	...	|	|	...	|	...	|	|	...	1853	|	|	|	...	2242	...	|
225	**Constanţa** a.	0609	...	0637	0706	...	0840	0848	0931	0946	...	1007	1040	...	1109	...	1218	1317	...	...	1743	1854	2003	...	...	...	2313
225	**Constanţa** d.	...	0615	0657x	0728x	...	...	0904	0943	...	...	1022	1052	...	1136x	...	1232	...	1545	...	1805z	...	...	2052	...	...	...
239	Eforie Nord d.	...	0639	0720x	0756x	...	...	0933	1005	...	...	1045	1115	...	1200x	...	1300	...	1609	...	1828z	...	...	2113	...	...	...
268	**Mangalia** a.	...	0739	0817x	0850x	...	...	1027	1055	...	...	1139	1222	...	1320x	...	1401	...	1710	...	1930z	...	...	2220	...	...	...

km			680				684				1861		941		1635	1871	988			1821	986	10918	1132	991		935	1851
		F		2v	2		✕	2	2v		J		Mx		S	G	y✕	2		A	w	z	V	Tx	2v	Cx	Q
0	**Mangalia** d.	...	...	0525	...	...	0602y	...	0829	...	1201x	...	1300	...	...	...	1606	...	...	1725x	1750	...	...	1825	1909	2109	2200x
29	Eforie Nord d.	...	...	0615	...	...	0700y	...	0930	...	1259x	...	1353	...	...	...	1702	...	...	1830x	1851	...	...	1929	2010	2208	2258x
43	**Constanţa** a.	...	...	0641	...	...	0720y	...	0954	...	1321x	...	1414	...	...	...	1724	...	...	1852x	1912	...	...	1950	2034	2229	2320x
43	**Constanţa** d.	...	0549	...	...	0723	0742	...	...	1148	1339	...	1429	...	1544	1727	1745	...	1808	1918	1938	1944	...	2029	...	2252	2335
	Tulcea Oraş d.	...	|	...	0515	|	|	0701	...	|	|	...	|	...	|	|	|	1555	|	|	|	|	...	|	...	|	|
78	Medgidia d.	...	0618	...	0754	0828	0815	1005	...	1243	1408	...	|	...	1614	1758	1815	1852	1900	1948	2006	2035	2048	|	...	2339	0007
122	Feteşti d.	0559	0700	...	...	0928	0912	...	...	1343	1449	...	1531	1700	1706	1844	1903	...	1954	2031	...	2202	|	2136	...	0032	0050
211	Făurei d.	0805	|	...	...	1133	|	...	...	|	1649	...	1723	1909	|	...	|	...	...	|	...	|	|	|	...	0221	0240
251	Buzău a.	...	|	...	...	1244	|	...	...	|	...	...	...	2021	|	...	|	...	...	|	...	|	|	|	...	0322	0335
268	**Bucureşti** Nord a.	...	0947	...	...	...	1204	...	...	1718o	...	...	...	...	1941	...	2137	...	...	2316	...	0050	2359	0001n	...	...	...

A – From / to Arad.
C – From / to Cluj Napoca / Târgu Mureş.
F – [12] Galaţi - Feteşti and v.v. (Table **1660**).
G – ①⑤⑥⑦ (daily June 23 - Sept. 11): [12] Galaţi - Constanţa and v.v.
J – Fom / to Iaşi.
M – From / to Satu Mare / Sighetu Marmaţiei.
Q – From / to Suceava / Botoşani.
S – From / to Sibiu / Oradea.
T – From / to Timişoara / Reşiţa / Deva.
V – June 15 - Sept. 6: [12] and ✕ Bucureşti - Negru Vodă - Varna and v.v. See Table **1540**.
n – Bucureşti Băneasa.
o – Bucureşti Obor.
q – Buzău Sud.
v – June 9 - Sept. 18.
w – June 15 - Sept. 6.
x – June 20 - Sept. 13.
y – June 19 - Sept. 13.
z – June 19 - Sept. 12.

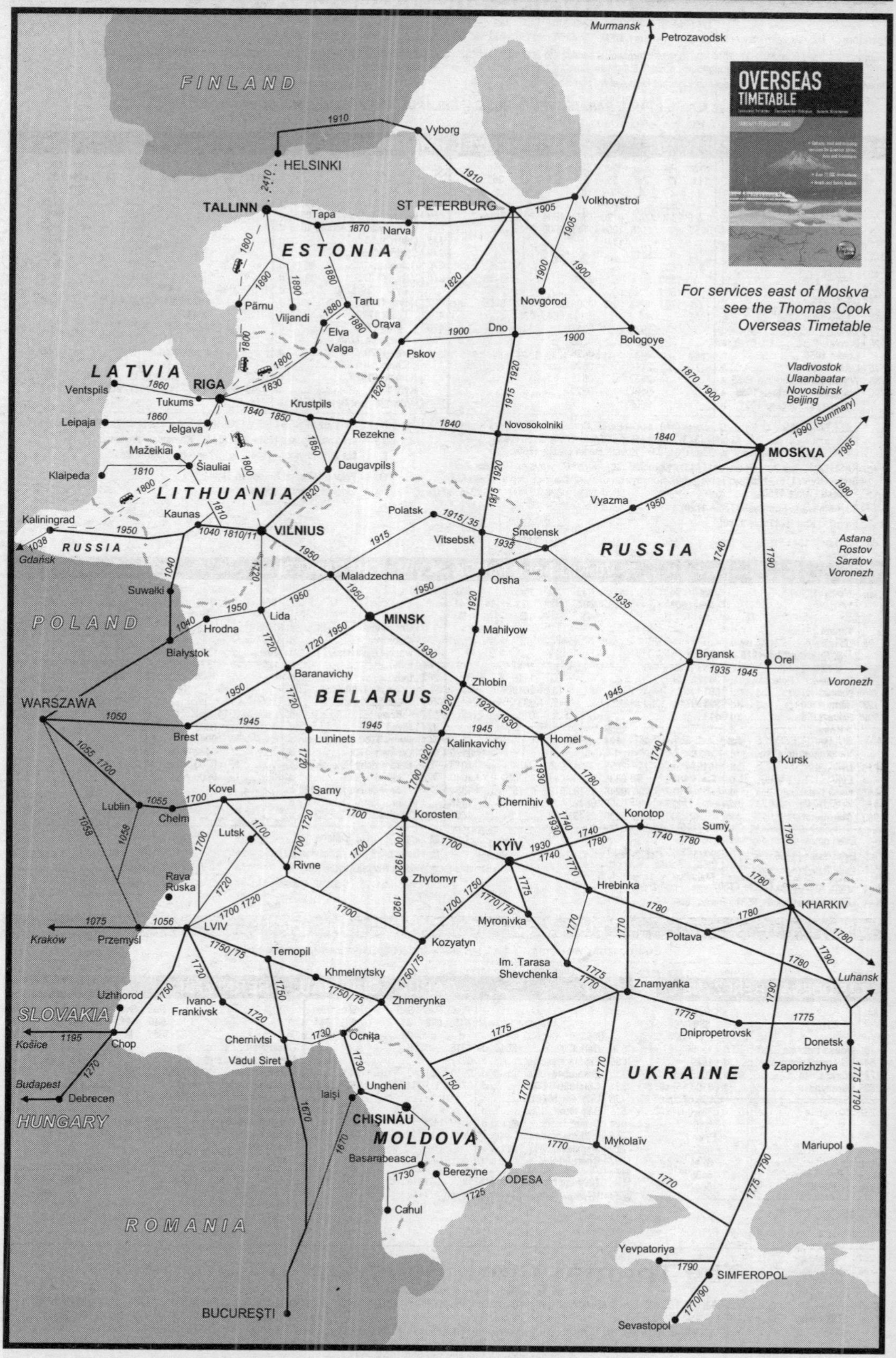
FINLAND
ESTONIA
LATVIA
LITHUANIA
RUSSIA
POLAND
BELARUS
RUSSIA
UKRAINE
MOLDOVA
ROMANIA
SLOVAKIA
HUNGARY
OVERSEAS
TIMETABLE
For services east of Moskva
see the Thomas Cook
Overseas Timetable
Murmansk
Petrozavodsk
HELSINKI
Vyborg
TALLINN
Tapa
Narva
ST PETERBURG
Volkhovstroi
Novgorod
Pärnu
Viljandi
Tartu
Elva
Orava
Valga
Pskov
Dno
Bologoye
RIGA
Ventspils
Tukums
Leipaja
Jelgava
Krustpils
Rezekne
Novosokolniki
Vladivostok
Ulaanbaatar
Novosibirsk
Beijing
MOSKVA
Mažeikiai
Šiauliai
Klaipeda
Daugavpils
Kaliningrad
Gdańsk
Kaunas
VILNIUS
Polatsk
Vitsebsk
Smolensk
Vyazma
Astana
Rostov
Saratov
Voronezh
Maladzechna
Orsha
Suwałki
Lida
Hrodna
MINSK
Mahilyow
Białystok
Baranavichy
Bryansk
Orel
Voronezh
Zhlobin
WARSZAWA
Brest
Luninets
Kalinkavichy
Homel
Kursk
Lublin
Chełm
Kovel
Sarny
Korosten
Chernihiv
Konotop
Sumy
Lutsk
Rivne
KYÏV
Zhytomyr
Hrebinka
Rava Ruska
Mryonivka
KHARKIV
Kraków
Przemyśl
LVIV
Kozyatyn
Poltava
Ternopil
Khmelnytsky
Im. Tarasa Shevchenka
Luhansk
Uzhhorod
Ivano-Frankivsk
Zhmerynka
Znamyanka
Košice
Chop
Chernivtsi
Ocniţa
Dnipropetrovsk
Donetsk
Vadul Siret
Budapest
Debrecen
Iaşi
Ungheni
Zaporizhzhya
CHIŞINĂU
Mykolaïv
Mariupol
Basarabeasca
Berezyne
ODESA
Cahul
Yevpatoriya
SIMFEROPOL
BUCUREŞTI
Sevastopol

UKRAINE and MOLDOVA

SEE MAP PAGE 509

Operators : **UZ**: Ukrzaliznytsya (УЗ : Укрзалізниця). **CFM**: Calea Ferată din Moldova. Other operators as indicated in the table headings and notes.

Timings : Valid from **May 31, 2009**. Timings of international services to and from non-CIS countries should be verified from the international tables at the front of this book. Local time is used throughout : i.e. East European Time for Ukraine and Moldova – for other countries, see the time comparison chart on page **2**.

Tickets : Prior reservation is necessary except for travel by purely local trains.

SEE ALSO THE PANEL ***RAIL TRAVEL IN RUSSIA, BELARUS, UKRAINE, and MOLDOVA*** ON PAGE 515

1700 KYÏV - KOVEL - WARSZAWA — UZ, PKP

km		*Sko* 111 H	*Fir* 77	*Sko* 29 A	*Sko* 55 Y	*Sko* 67 K	*Pas* 659	*Fir* 43 F	*Fir* 363	
	Moskva Kiyevskaya **1740** d.	...	1638	...	1908	...	...	...	...	...
0	**Kyïv 1750** d.	0421	0546	0924	0720	1533	1604	1916	2115	...
156	Korosten **1920** d.	0650	|	1148	1004	1743	1900	2133	|	...
241	Zhytomyr **1920** a.	|	|	|	1140	|	|	|	|	...
311	Sarny **1720** d.	|	|	1412	...	|	2315	|	|	...
159	Kozyatyn **1750** d.	|	0832	|	...	|	|	|	2352	...
383	Rivne **1720** d.	|	1330	|	...	2130	|	|	0458	...
469	Lutsk **1720** d.	|	1509	|	...	|	|	|	0647	...
453	**Kovel 1720** d.	|	1701	1638	...	0008	0217	|	0858	...
652	**Lviv 1720 1750** a.	1445	...	|	...	|	0643	0352	...	...
512	Yahodyn 🏛 UA d.	...	...	1932	...	0317	...	...	...	...
520	Dorohusk 🏛 PL a.	...	...	1850	...	0238	...	...	...	...
541	Chełm **1055** a.	...	...	2022	...	0426	...	...	...	...
615	Lublin **1055** a.	...	...	2114	...	0526	...	...	...	...
785	Warszawa Wschodnia **1055** a.	...	...	2339	...	0811	...	...	...	...
790	**Warszawa** Centralna **1055** a.	...	...	0107	...	0820	...	...	...	...
	Berlin Lichtenberg **1001** a.	...	...	0900	...	...	...	...	...	...

km		*Sko* 112 H	*Fir* 44 F	*Fir* 364	*Pas* 660	*Sko* 68 K	*Fir* 78	*Pas* 344 Z	*Sko* 30 B	
	Berlin Lichtenberg **1001** d.	...	...	...	...	...	...	...	2139	...
0	**Warszawa** Centralna **1055** d.	...	...	...	...	1645	...	...	0445	...
5	Warszawa Wschodnia **1055** d.	...	...	...	...	1654	...	...	0459	...
175	Lublin **1055** d.	...	...	...	...	1941	...	...	0728	...
249	Chełm **1055** d.	...	...	...	...	2031	...	...	0819	...
270	Dorohusk 🏛 PL d.	...	...	...	...	2143	...	...	0930	...
278	Yahodyn 🏛 UA d.	...	...	...	...	0110	...	...	1248	...
	Lviv 1720 1750 d.	1705	2130	...	1927	|	...	...	|	...
337	**Kovel 1720** d.	|	|	1820	0049	0222	0928	...	1400	...
421	Lutsk **1720** d.	|	|	2041	|	|	1145	...	|	...
473	Rivne **1720** d.	|	|	2227	|	0425	1311	...	|	...
705	Kozyatyn **1750** d.	|	|	|	|	|	1806	...	|	...
	Sarny **1720** d.	|	|	|	0351	|	|	...	1606	...
	Zhytomyr **1920** d.	|	|	|	|	|	|	1714	|	...
	Korosten **1920** d.	0037	0353	|	0758	0812	|	1932	1905	...
	Kyïv 1750 a.	0248	0620	0607	1034	1027	2017	2145	2112	...
	Moskva Kiyevskaya **1740** a.	...	...	...	...	...	1130	1432	...	...

A – KASHTAN – 🛏 2 cl. Kyïv - Dorohusk (**440** / **444**) - Berlin. Conveys on ②⑤ from Kharkiv (③⑥ from Kyïv) 🛏 2 cl. Kharkiv (**343**) - Kyïv - Berlin (Table **1780**). Conveys on ①②③⑥ (②③④⑦ from Kovel) 🛏 2 cl. Odesa (**84** / **83**) - Kovel - Berlin (Table **1750**).

B – KASHTAN – 🛏 2 cl. Berlin (**441** / **445**) - Dorohusk (**30**) - Kyïv. Conveys on ④⑦ 🛏 2 cl. Berlin - Kyïv (**118**) - Kharkiv (Table **1780**). Conveys on ①③④⑤ 🛏 2 cl. Berlin - Kyïv (**123**) - Odesa (Table **1750**).

F – To / from Ivano-Frankivsk (Table **1720**).

H – From / to Kharkiv (Table **1780**).

K – KYÏV EKSPRES / KIEV EXPRESS – 🛏 1, 2 cl. Kyïv - Warszawa and v.v.

Y – 🛏 2 cl. Moskva (**55**) - Kyïv (**343**) - Korosten - Zhytomyr.

Z – 🛏 2 cl. Zhytomyr (**344**) - Korosten - Kyïv (**56**) - Moskva.

PL – Poland (Central European Time).

UA – Ukraine (East European Time).

1720 VILNIUS and MINSK - LVIV - CHERNIVTSI — LDZ, LG, BCh, UZ

km		*Pas* 47 J	*Pas* 608		*Pas* 668	*Pas* 604 ◇	*Fir* 43	*Pas* 371 E		*Sko* 141 M
0	**Vilnius** § LT d.	...	...	...	...	...	...	...	...	...
95	Lida § BY d.	...	...	...	...	...	...	...	...	...
	St Peterburg Vit. **1920** d.	1245	...	...	...	...	...	...	...	...
	Minsk d.	0153	...	...	...	...	...	1547	...	...
200	Baranavichy Polesskiye d.	0412	...	...	...	...	...	1819	...	...
316	Luninets **1700** ‡ BY d.	0616	...	...	...	...	...	2019	...	...
422	Sarny **1700** ‡ UA d.	0947	...	...	...	...	...	2331	...	...
509	Rivne **1700** d.	1131	...	...	...	...	...	0114	...	...
	Kovel d.	|	...	...	1559	...	...	|	...	...
	Lutsk d.	|	...	...	1821	...	...	|	...	...
	Kyïv **1700 1750** d.	|	...	...	|	...	1916	|	...	0120
716	**Lviv** a.	1519	...	...	2255	...	0352	0454	...	1013
	Lviv d.	...	1645	...	2335	2130	0417	0520*	...	1040
857	Ivano-Frankivsk d.	...	2012	...	0240	0518	0702	1115*	...	1334
912	Kolomyya d.	...	2125	...	0358	0642	...	...	...	1446
983	**Chernivtsi** a.	...	2300	...	0530	0843	...	...	...	1607

km		*Sko* 608		*Pas* 372 N	*Fir* 44	*Sko* 48 K	*Pas* 668	*Pas* 604 ◇	*Sko* 142 M	
0	**Chernivtsi** d.	0735	...	...	...	...	1517	2016	2212	...
71	Kolomyya d.	0907	...	...	...	...	1713	2240	2341	...
126	Ivano-Frankivsk d.	1025	...	1304*	1815	...	1850	0035	0114	...
267	**Lviv** a.	1259	...	1837*	2105	...	2159	0804	0400	...
267	**Lviv** d.	...	...	1900	2130	2312	2230	...	0420	...
	Kyïv **1700 1750** a.	...	...	|	0620	|	|	...	1322	...
443	Lutsk a.	...	...	|	...	|	0256	...	...	...
527	**Kovel** a.	...	...	|	...	|	0520	...	...	...
474	Rivne **1700** d.	...	...	2303	...	0305	...	...	...	...
561	Sarny **1700** ‡ UA d.	...	...	0048	...	0445	...	...	...	...
667	Luninets **1700** ‡ BY d.	...	...	0422	...	0815	...	...	...	...
783	Baranavichy Polesskiye d.	...	...	0703	...	1032	...	...	...	...
923	**Minsk** a.	...	...	0900	...	1222	...	...	...	...
	St Peterburg Vit. **1920** a.	...	...	...	...	0525	...	...	...	...
	Lida § BY d.	...	...	...	...	...	...	...	...	...
	Vilnius § LT a.	...	...	...	...	...	...	...	...	...

E – Even dates.

J – Even dates [... *30, 1, 4* ...] (daily May 25 - Oct. 2; not Oct. 1).

K – Even dates (daily May 24 - Sept. 28).

M – From / to Moskva (Table **1750**).

N – Uneven dates [... *31, 3* ...].

◇ – Runs via Stry (*105 km* from Lviv, *108 km* from Ivano-Frankivsk).

▮ – 🏛 : Joniškis (LT) / Meitene (LV).

§ – 🏛 : Benyakoni (BY) / Stasylos (LT).

‡ – 🏛 : Horyn (BY) / Udrytsk (UA).

* – Summer (May 26 - Sept. 6) only.

BY – Belarus.

LT – Lithuania.

LV – Latvia.

UA – Ukraine.

1725 ODESA - BEREZYNE — UZ

km		*Pas* 686 y	
0	**Odesa** Holovna d.	1545	...
84	Bilhorod-Dnistrovsky d.	1820	...
174	Artsyz d.	2035	...
209	**Berezyne** a.	2303	...

		Pas 686 y	
Berezyne d.	...	2323	...
Artsyz d.	...	0244	...
Bilhorod-Dnistrovsky d.	...	0438	...
Odesa Holovna a.	...	0642	...

y – May 25 - Oct. 10.

1730 CAHUL - CHIŞINĂU - CHERNIVTSI — UZ, CFM

km		*Pas* 645 d	*Pas* 609 d	*Sko* 47 M		*Sko* 61 S	*Sko* 341 M
0	**Cahul** d.	1616	...	...	...	...	...
136	Basarabeasca a.	0227	...	...	...	...	...
136	Basarabeasca d.	0313	...	...	...	...	...
331	**Chişinău 1670** d.	0715	...	1150	...	1928	2000
438	Ungheni **1670** d.	...	...	|	...	2211	2308
516	Bălţi Oraş d.	...	...	1513	...	2352	0050
614	Ocniţa 🏛 MD d.	...	1425	1719	...	0253	0401
768	**Zhmerynka** ‡ UA a.	...	|	2202	...	0745	0919
729	Mamalyha 🏛 UA a.	...	1804	...	...	...	...
787	**Chernivtsi** a.	...	1942	...	...	...	...

	Pas 646 d	*Sko* 341 M	*Pas* 610 d	*Sko* 47 M		*Sko* 61 S
Chernivtsi d.	...	...	0848	...	...	...
Mamalyha 🏛 UA d.	...	...	1030	...	...	...
Zhmerynka ‡ UA d.	...	0646	|	1247	...	1903
Ocniţa 🏛 MD d.	...	1209	1400	1736	...	0031
Bălţi Oraş d.	...	1446	...	1926	...	0300
Ungheni **1670** d.	...	1659	...	|	...	0515
Chişinău 1670 d.	1905	2015	...	2248	...	0727
Basarabeasca a.	0331	...	...	...	...	...
Basarabeasca d.	0516	...	...	...	...	...
Cahul a.	1139	...	...	...	...	...

M – To / from Moskva (Table **1750**).

S – To / from St Peterburg (Table **1750**).

d – (4) only.

‡ – 🏛 : Mohyliv-Podilski (UA).

MD – Moldova.

UA – Ukraine.

RZhD, UZ — MOSKVA - BRYANSK - SUMY, CHERNIHIV and KYÏV — 1740

km		Sko 59 Ad		Sko 33 U		Sko 141	Sko 341	Sko 89 Z		Sko 73	Sko 41	Sko 41 V⊗	Fir 77 K		Sko 55 LX	Sko 117	Sko 47	Fir 5	Fir 23	Sko 15 S	Fir 1 F	Fir 3	Fir 3 Ac	Sko 21 g
0	**Moskva** Kiyevskaya d.	0025	...	1048	...	1235	1243	1343	...	1546	1646	1646	1638	...	1908	1801	1937	2023	2120	2213	2323	2129	2129	2250
387	Bryansk Orlovski d.	0642	...	1705	...	1900	1919	1948	...	2200	2349	2349	2326	...	0114	0025	0216	0252	0323	0426	|	0357	0357	0454
504	Suzemka 🏛 RU d.	|	...	|	...	|	|	2146	...	|	|	|	0125	...	|	0240	|	|	|	|	0457	0556	0556	|
519	Zernove 🏛 UA d.	|	...	|	...	2016	|	|	...	|	|	|	|	...	|	0228	|	|	|	|	|	|	|	0610
651	Konotop **1780** d.	0943	...	1958	...	2221	2233	2300	...	0118	0217	0217	0258	...	0340	0440	0530	0523	0555	0757	|	0725	0725	0802
780	**Sumy 1780** d.	|	...	|	...	|	|	|	...	|	|	|	|	...	|	0732	|	|	|	|	|	|	|	|
829	**Chernihiv** a.	|	...	|	...	|	|	|	...	|	|	0556	|	...	|	...	|	|	|	|	|	|	|	|
872	**Kyïv** a.	1308	...	|	...	0104	0140	0122	...	0353	0510	...	0529	...	0624	...	0820	0750	0834	1042	0800	0958	0958	1108
	Odesa Holovna **1750 1770** a.	|	...	1156	...	|	|	...	...	|	...	...	...	...	...	...	|	...	1909	|	...	...	|	...
	Chişinău **1750** a.	|	...	...	...	|	2015	...	...	|	...	...	...	...	...	...	2248	...	...	|	...	...	|	...
	Lviv **1750** a.	|	...	...	...	1013	...	...	...	1357	...	...	...	...	...	...	...	...	...	2052	...	...	|	...
	Chernivtsi **1750** a.	0620	...	...	...	1607	...	...	...	...	...	...	...	...	...	...	...	...	...	...	...	...	0620	...

	Sko 56 LY	Fir 24	Sko 47		Sko 34 G		Sko 60 Ba		Sko 142	Sko 341	Sko 658 W⊗	Sko 42	Sko 42 Bb		Sko 22 h		Fir 2 F	Fir 6	Sko 74	Sko 117	Sko 90 Z	Sko 16 T	Fir 78 K	Fir 4
Chernivtsi **1750** d.	...	...	...	...	...	...	1856	...	2212	...	...	...	1856	...	...	...	...	...	...	...	...	...	...	...
Lviv **17507** d.	...	...	...	...	...	...	|	...	0420	...	...	...	|	...	...	...	...	...	0837	...	...	1057	...	...
Chişinău **1750** d.	...	...	1150	...	...	...	|	...	|	2000	...	...	|	...	...	...	...	...	|	...	...	|	...	...
Odesa Holovna **1750 1770** d.	...	1504	|	...	1800	...	|	...	|	|	...	...	|	...	...	...	...	...	|	...	...	|	...	...
Kyïv d.	0023	0121	0218	...	|	...	2117	...	1342	1348	...	1435	1435	...	1704	...	2009	1905	1847	...	2015	2036	2042	2117
Chernihiv d.	|	|	|	...	|	...	|	...	|	|	1447	|	|	...	|	...	|	|	|	...	|	|	|	|
Sumy 1780 d.	|	|	|	...	|	...	|	...	|	|	|	|	|	...	|	...	|	|	|	1913	|	|	|	|
Konotop **1780** d.	0308	0357	0506	...	0953	...	0008	...	1644	1654	1821	1821	1821	...	2002	...	|	2149	2121	2238	2304	2330	2339	0008
Zernove 🏛 UA d.	|	|	|	...	|	...	|	...	1919	|	|	|	|	...	|	...	|	|	|	0105	|	|	0154	|
Suzemka 🏛 RU d.	0628	0720	|	...	|	...	1617	...	2103	|	|	|	|	...	|	...	0135	|	|	|	0242	|	0338	|
Bryansk Orlovski d.	0815	0910	1044	...	1507	...	1735‡	...	2245	2304	2335	2335	2335	...	0050	...	|	0233	0256	0408	|	0427	0523	0445
Moskva Kiyevskaya a.	1432	1516	1623	...	2118	...	2236	...	0452	0518	0533	0533	0533	...	0619	...	0639	0902	0910	1004	0931	0959	1130	1058

FOR NOTES, SEE TABLE **1750** BELOW.

UZ, CFM — KYÏV - ODESA, CHERNIVTSI and LVIV / ODESA - CHERNIVTSI and LVIV — 1750

km		Sko 141	Sko 89	Sko 341	Sko 73	Sko 111	Sko 55	Sko 47	Fir 23	Sko 15	Sko 15 D	Sko 15 S	Sko 59 A	Sko 61	Sko 115	Fir 43 N	Sko 13	Fir 108 R	Sko 51 P	Fir 26	Fir 123 M	Fir 91	Sko 9 y	Sko 19 H	Sko 7 E
	Moskva Kiyevskaya **1740** d.	1235	1343	1243	1546	...	1908	1937	2120	2213	2213	2213	2129e	...	...	...	...	...	...	...	...	...	...	...	...
	Kharkiv **1780** d.	|	|	|	|	1911	|	|	|	|	|	|	|	...	0712	...	1101	...	...	...	...	...	...	...	...
0	**Kyïv 1700** d.	0120	0152	0204	0408	0421	0646	0837	0902	1110	1110	1110	1540k	...	1659	1916	2012	...	2042	...	1821	2215	2259	...	2358
	St Peterburg Vitebski **1920** d.	|	|	|	|	|	|	|	|	|	|	|	|	1620r	|	|	|	...	|	...	|	|	|	2355q	|
159	Kozyatyn **1700** d.	|	0423	0433	0629	|	0856	1047	1112	1329	1329	1329	1804	1700	1921	|	|	...	2311	...	2035	|	0113	0159	0221
221	Vinnytsya d.	|	0519	0534	0726	|	0951	1141	1208	1424	1424	1424	1900	1754	2019	|	|	...	0006	...	2140	|	0211	0255	0322
	Odesa Holovna d.	|	|	|	|	|	|	|	|	|	|	|	|	|	|	|	|	1813	|	1900	|	|	|	|	|
268	Zhmerynka **1775** d.	|	0610	0646	|	|	|	1247	1317	|	|	|	|	1903	2129	|	|	0015	0113	0122	2255	|	0319	0410	|
654	**Odesa** Holovna a.	|	...	|	|	◧	|	|	1909	|	|	|	|	|	|	◧	|	|	|	|	0541	|	0850	1018	|
	Chişinău **1730** a.	|	...	2015	|	|	|	2248	...	|	|	|	|	0727	|	|	|	|	|	|	...	|	...	...	|
367	Khmelnytsky **1775** d.	|	...	...	0939	|	1147	...	...	1624	1624	1624	2107	...	2315	|	|	0142	0242	0251	...	|	...	...	0545
486	Ternopil **1775** d.	|	...	...	1139	|	...	...	...	1837	1837	1837	2335	...	0117	|	|	0342	0437	0450	...	|	...	...	0744
594	**Chernivtsi** a.	1607j	...	...	|	|	...	...	...	|	|	|	0623	...	|	|	|	|	|	|	...	|	...	...	|
	Bucureşti Nord **1670** a.	|	...	...	|	|	...	...	...	|	|	|	1913	...	|	|	|	|	|	|	...	|	...	...	|
	Sofiya **1500** a.	|	...	...	|	|	...	...	...	|	|	|	0605	...	|	|	|	|	|	|	...	|	...	...	|
627	**Lviv 1775** a.	1013	...	...	1357	1445	...	...	...	2052	2052	2052	...	...	0331	0352	0537	0557	0651	0710	...	0633	...	...	0959
627	**Lviv** d.	...	...	...	...	...	...	...	...	2120	2120	2120	...	...	...	...	0604	0623	...	...	...	...	...	...	1026
852	Mukacheve d.	...	...	...	...	...	...	...	...	0155	0155	0155	...	...	...	...	1039	1110	...	...	...	...	...	...	1459
893	**Chop** a.	...	...	...	...	...	...	...	...	0245	0245	0245	...	...	...	...	1132	1214	...	...	...	...	...	...	1547
	Košice **1195** a.	...	...	...	...	...	...	...	...	|	0729	|	...	...	...	...	|	|	...	...	...	...	...	...	2130
	Budapest Keleti **1270** a.	...	...	...	...	...	...	...	...	|	...	1117	...	...	...	...	|	|	...	...	...	...	...	...	...
915	**Uzhhorod** a.	...	...	...	...	...	...	...	...	0403	...	...	...	...	...	...	1235	1316	...	...	...	...	...	...	...

	Sko 52 Q	Fir 107 R	Sko 8	Sko 61	Sko 142	Sko 341		Sko 74	Sko 14	Sko 90	Sko 16 DE	Sko 16 T	Sko 16	Sko 116	Sko 56	Fir 24	Sko 47	Sko 112	Sko 20 J	Fir 26	Fir 44 N	Fir 92	Fir 84 C	Sko 10 w	Sko 60 B
Uzhhorod d.	...	1805	...	...	...	...	...	...	2145	...	...	...	0135	...	...	...	...	...	...	...	...	...	...	...	...
Budapest Keleti **1270** d.	...	|	...	...	...	...	...	...	|	...	...	1843	|	...	...	...	...	...	...	...	...	...	...	...	...
Košice **1195** d.	...	|	...	...	...	...	...	...	|	...	2032	|	|	...	...	...	...	...	...	...	...	...	...	...	...
Chop d.	...	1855	2026	...	...	...	...	...	2243	...	0434	0434	0434	...	...	...	...	...	...	...	...	...	...	...	...
Mukacheve d.	...	2003	2138	...	...	...	...	...	2357	...	0538	0538	0538	...	...	...	...	...	...	...	...	...	...	...	...
Lviv a.	...	0057	0223	...	...	...	...	...	0450	...	1031	1031	1031	...	...	...	...	...	...	...	...	...	...	...	...
Lviv 1775 d.	0011	0140	0246	...	0420	...	...	0837	0516	...	1057	1057	1057	1240	...	...	...	1705	...	1943	2130	2247	...	...	...
Sofiya **1500** d.	|	|	|	...	|	...	...	|	|	...	|	|	|	|	...	...	...	|	...	|	|	|	...	...	1930
Bucureşti Nord **1670** d.	|	|	|	...	|	...	...	|	|	...	|	|	|	|	...	...	...	|	...	|	|	|	...	...	0638
Chernivtsi d.	|	|	|	...	2212j	...	...	|	|	...	|	|	|	|	...	...	...	|	...	|	|	|	...	...	1856
Ternopil **1775** d.	0228	0355	0503	...	|	...	...	1059	|	...	1307	1307	1307	1504	...	...	...	|	...	2203	|	|	...	...	0155
Khmelnytsky **1775** d.	0437	0601	0712	...	|	...	...	1315	|	...	1511	1511	1511	1745	1904	...	...	|	...	0009	|	|	...	...	0359
Chişinău **1730** d.	|	|	|	1928	|	2000	...	|	|	...	|	|	|	|	|	...	1150	|	...	|	|	|	...	...	|
Odesa Holovna d.	|	|	|	|	|	|	...	|	|	...	|	|	|	|	|	1504	|	◧	1832	|	◧	|	2300	2319	|
Zhmerynka **1775** d.	0626	0745	|	0810	|	0938	...	|	|	1526	|	|	|	1942	|	2119	2224	|	0050	0156	|	|	|	0438	|
Odesa Holovna a.	|	1331	|	|	|	|	...	|	|	|	|	|	|	|	|	|	|	|	|	0750	|	|	|	|	|
Vinnytsya d.	0713	...	0913	0901	|	1025	...	1516	|	1621	1706	1706	1706	2034	2104	2204	2308	|	0138	...	|	|	|	0526	0613
Kozyatyn **1700** d.	0807	...	1012	1020	|	1121	...	1616	|	1735	1759	1759	1759	2150	2200	2258	0001	|	0252	...	|	|	0526	0621	0712
St Peterburg Vitebski **1920** a.	|	...	|	1243z	|	|	...	|	|	|	|	|	|	|	|	|	|	|	0615z	...	|	|	...	|	|
Kyïv 1700 a.	1018	...	1222	...	1322	1330	...	1827	1433	1946	2001	2001	2001	0010	0003	0101	0208	0248	...	...	0620	0726	...	0832	0926
Kharkiv **1780** a.	...	...	...	...	|	|	...	|	2253	|	|	|	|	1020	|	|	|	1145	...	...	...	...	...	...	|
Moskva Kiyevskaya **1740** a.	...	...	...	...	0452	0518	...	0910	...	0931	0956	0956	0956	...	1432	1516	1623	...	...	...	...	...	...	...	0533f

A – BOLGARIYA EKSPRESS – 🛏 1, 2 cl. Moskva (**3** ▽) - Kyïv - Vadul Siret (**383**) - Sofiya. Conveys on ⑥ (also ② June 16 - Sept. 1) 🛏 2 cl. Minsk (**86**) - Kyïv - Sofiya. Conveys, on dates shown in Table **98**, 🛏 2 cl. Moskva - Ruse - Varna and 🛏 2 cl. Moskva - Ruse - Burgas.
B – BOLGARIYA EKSPRES – 🛏 1, 2 cl. Sofiya (**382**) - Vadul Siret (**60**) - Kyïv (**42** △) - Moskva. Conveys on ② (also ⑤ June 14 - Sept. 2) 🛏 2 cl. Sofiya - Kyïv - Minsk. Conveys, on dates shown in Table **98**, 🛏 2 cl. Varna - Ruse - Moskva and 🛏 2 cl. Burgas - Ruse - Moskva.
C – Conveys on ①②③⑥ 🛏 2 cl. Odesa - Kozyatyn - Berlin.
D – 🛏 1, 2 cl. Moskva - Chop - Košice and v.v. (extended to / from Žilina on dates shown in Table **1180**).
E – Conveys on dates shown in Table **96** 🛏 1, 2 cl. Kyïv / Lviv - Chop - Bratislava - Wien and v.v.
F – Uneven dates in Aug., Nov., Dec. Even dates in June, July, Sept., Oct.
G – Even dates (daily May 26 - Sept. 14, Dec. 26 - 31).
H – From St Peterburg ①③⑤ (daily May 25 - Oct. 1).
J – ③⑤⑦ (daily May 24 - Oct. 3).
K – To / from Kovel (Table **1700**).
L – To / from Khmelnytsky (Table **1750**).
M – Conveys on ①③④⑤: 🛏 2 cl. Berlin - Kyïv - Odesa.
N – To / from Ivano-Frankivsk (Table **1720**).
P – To Przemyśl (Table **1056**). Conveys 🛏 1, 2 cl. Kyïv - Praha; 🛏 2 cl. Kyïv - Wrocław (Table **96**).
Q – From Przemyśl (Table **1056**). Conveys 🛏 1, 2 cl. Praha - Kyïv; 🛏 2 cl. Wrocław - Kyïv (Table **96**).
R – Conveys 🛏 2 cl. Odesa - Lviv - Przemyśl - Warszawa and v.v. Table **1056**. Conveys on dates shown in Table **96** 🛏 1, 2 cl. Odesa - Praha and v.v.
S – TISSA – 🛏 2 cl. Moskva - Kyïv - Záhony (**629**) - Budapest (**794**) - Kelebia (**345**) - Beograd. Conveys on dates shown in Table **97** 🛏 1, 2 cl. Moskva - Budapest - Zagreb / Venezia; 🛏 2 cl. Kyïv - Budapest - Zagreb.
T – TISSA – 🛏 2 cl. Beograd (**344**) - Kelebia (**793**) - Budapest (**628**) - Záhony - Kyïv - Moskva. Conveys on dates shown in Table **97** 🛏 1, 2 cl. Venezia / Zagreb (**205**) - Budapest - Moskva; 🛏 2 cl. Zagreb - Budapest - Kyïv.
U – Uneven dates (daily May 25 - Sept. 13, Dec. 25 - 30).
V – Moskva - Nizhyn (**58**) - Chernihiv.
W – Chernihiv - Nizhyn (**42**) - Moskva.
X – Conveys 🛏 2 cl. Moskva - Kyïv (**29**) - Korosten (**642**) - Zhytomyr. See Table **1700**.
Y – Conveys 🛏 2 cl. Zhytomyr (**642**) - Korosten (**30**) - Kyïv - Moskva. See Table **1700**.
Z – To / from Zhmerynka (Table **1750**).

a – June 14 - Sept. 4 (previous day from Chernivtsi).
b – Until June 13 and from Sept. 5 (previous day from Chernivtsi).
c – Until June 12 and from Sept. 4.
d – June 14 - Sept. 4.
e – 0025 June 14 - Sept. 4.
f – 2236 June 14 - Sept. 4.
g – May 29 - Oct. 2, Dec. 24 - 30.
h – May 30 - Oct. 3, Dec. 25 - 31.
j – Via Lviv.
k – 1404 June 14 - Sept. 4.
q – Two days earlier.
r – Previous day.
w – Sept. 2 - Dec. 31.
y – Sept. 1 - Dec. 31.
z – Next day.

▽ – Train **59** June 14 - Sept. 4.
△ – Train **60** June 14 - Sept. 4.
RU – Russia (Moskva Time).
UA – Ukraine (East European Time).
◧ – Via Korosten (Table **1700**).
‡ – Bryansk Lgovski.
⊗ – Subject to confirmation.

1770 KYÏV and ODESA - SEVASTOPOL *UZ*

km		Fir 23 Z	Fir 40	Sko 250 E	Fir 12 S	Fir 28	Fir 650 B	Fir 121	Pas 382 Q	Sko 33 C
	Moskva Kiyevskaya **1740** d.	2120	...	...	...	...	...	...	...	1048
0	Konotop d.	0555	...	...	...	...	...	...	...	1958
414	Znamyanka d.	|	...	...	...	...	...	...	...	0505
	Kyïv 1775 d.	0902	1252	...	1751	2021	...	1904	...	|
	Myronivka **1775** d.	|	1424	...	|	|	...	2202	...	|
	Minsk **1930** d.	|	|	...	|	|	...	|	0948	|
	Chernihiv d.	|	|	1205	|	|	...	|	1856	|
	Hrebinka d.	|	|	1605	|	|	...	|	2340	|
	Cherkasy d.	|	|	1742	|	|	...	|	0115	|
	Im. T. Shevchenka **1775** d.	|	1606	1859	2055	2317	...	0001	0219	|
826	**Odesa** Holovna a.	1909	|	|	|	|	2329	|	|	1156
	Mykolaïv d.	...	d	0043	d	0448	0425	0553	d	...
	Kherson d.	...	|	0220	|	0600	0527	...	|	...
	Simferopol **1775 1790** a.	...	0415	0736	0850	1106	1155	...	1546	...
	Sevastopol 1775 1790 a.	...	0616	...	...	1306	...	...	...	...

km		Sko 250 F	Fir 122	Fir 12 S	Fir 40	Fir 28	Fir 650 A	Fir 24 Z	Pas 382 P	Sko 34 D
0	**Sevastopol 1775 1790** d.	...	...	...	1324	1452	...	...	...	...
78	Simferopol **1775 1790** d.	1014	...	1626	1537	1710	1925	...	2154	...
360	Kherson d.	1536	...	|	|	2212	0202	...	|	...
415	Mykolaïv d.	1637	1923	d	d	2334	0338	...	d	...
	Odesa Holovna d.	|	|	|	|	|	0810	1504	|	1800
726	Im. T. Shevchenka **1775** d.	2227	0120	0443	0433	0526	...	|	1301	|
756	Cherkasy d.	2308	|	|	|	|	...	|	1357	|
848	Hrebinka d.	0129	|	|	|	|	...	|	1552	|
1054	**Chernihiv** a.	0534	|	|	|	|	...	|	1950	|
	Minsk **1930** a.	...	|	|	|	|	...	|	0529	|
835	Myronivka **1775** d.	...	0301	|	|	|	...	|	...	|
942	**Kyïv 1775** a.	...	0530	0742	0708	0845	...	0101	...	|
	Znamyanka d.	...	...	...	...	...	...	|	...	0040
	Konotop a.	...	...	...	...	...	...	0337	...	0919
	Moskva Kiyevskaya **1740** a.	...	...	...	...	...	...	1516	...	2118

A – Uneven dates in Jan., Apr., May; even dates in Feb., Mar.; daily May 26 - Aug. 31; uneven dates in Sept., Oct.; even dates in Nov., Dec.
B – Uneven dates in Jan., Apr., May; even dates in Feb., Mar.; daily May 27 - Aug. 31; uneven dates in Sept., Oct.; even dates in Nov., Dec.
C – Uneven dates [... *29, 1* ...] (daily May 25 - Sept. 13, Dec. 25–30).
D – Even dates (daily May 26 - Sept. 14, Dec. 26–31).
E – Even dates June 20 - Aug. 30.
F – Uneven dates June 21 - Aug. 31.
P – Even dates.
Q – Even dates [... *30, 1, 4* ...].
S – SLAVUTICH.
Z – Via Zhmerynka (Table **1750**).
d – Via Dnipropetrovsk (Table **1775**).

1775 LVIV and KYÏV - MARIUPOL and SEVASTOPOL *UZ*

km		Fir 40	Fir 84 Y	Fir 84 Z	Fir 12 S h	Sko 86	Fir 38 D	Fir 72	Fir 80 N p	Sko 22 T	Sko 70 E
0	**Lviv 1750** d.	...	...	...	...	0944	...	...	...	1623	1747
141	Ternopil **1750** d.	...	...	...	...	1202	...	...	...	1844	2010
260	Khmelnytsky **1750** d.	...	...	...	...	1400	...	...	...	2100	2220
359	Zhmerynka **1750** d.	...	...	...	...	1545	...	...	...	2247	0005
468	Kozyatyn **1750** d.	...	...	...	...	1742	...	...	...	|	0204
	Kyïv 1770 d.	1252	1505	1636	1751	|	1923	2027	2312	|	|
663	Myronivka **1770** d.	1424	1633	1808	|	2019	|	2150	0028	|	0449
772	Im. T. Shevchenka **1770** d.	1606	1821	2018	2055	2154	2218	2336	0200	|	0640
864	Znamyanka d.	1727	1947	2150	2210	2314	2334	0051	0317	0800	0800
973	Pyatykhatky d.	|	2141	2341	|	0107	|	0246	0510	0959	0959
1052	Dniprodzerzhynsk d.	|	2247	0043	|	0208	|	0352	0613	1114	1114
1088	**Dnipropetrovsk** Holovny d.	2114	0015	0136	0146	0259	0306	0445	0657	1214	1214
1357	Donetsk a.	|	0504	0615	|	|	0710	|	...	1650	1650
1489	**Mariupol** a.	|	0807	0847	|	|	...	|	...	...	2000
1214	Zaporizhzhya **I 1790** d.	2312	...	...	0350	0453	...	0642	...	...	...
1326	Melitopol **1790** d.	0103	...	...	0532	0637	...	...	...	...	...
1570	Simferopol **1770 1790** a.	0415	...	...	0850	0950	...	...	...	...	...
1648	**Sevastopol 1770 1790** a.	0616	...	...	...	...	...	...	...	...	...

	Sko 70 U	Sko 21 E	Sko 86	Fir 12 S	Fir 72	Fir 79 N q	Fir 37 D	Fir 40 k	Fir 84	
Sevastopol 1770 1790 d.	...	...	...	...	...	...	...	1324	...	...
Simferopol **1770 1790** d.	...	...	1312	1626	...	...	...	1537	...	...
Melitopol **1790** d.	...	...	1645	1954	...	...	...	1858	...	...
Zaporizhzhya **I 1790** d.	...	...	1814	2133	1925	...	...	2030	...	...
Mariupol d.	1007	...	|	|	|	...	...	|	1649	...
Donetsk d.	1349	1349	|	|	|	...	1920	|	2003	...
Dnipropetrovsk Holovny d.	1830	1830	2025	2357	2157	2245	2322	2330	0030	...
Dniprodzerzhynsk d.	1906	1906	2101	|	2235	2323	|	|	0115	...
Pyatykhatky d.	2018	2018	2210	|	2348	0038	|	|	0232	...
Znamyanka d.	2215	2232	0008	0319	0141	0240	0256	0309	0434	...
Im. T. Shevchenka **1770** d.	2347	|	0137	0443	0304	0408	0416	0433	0643	...
Myronivka **1770** d.	0129	|	0312	|	0437	0536	|	|	0825	...
Kyïv 1770 a.	|	|	|	0742	0556	0654	0701	0708	1004	...
Kozyatyn **1750** d.	0441	|	0619	...	...	...	...	...	...	...
Zhmerynka **1750** d.	0654	0835	0826	...	...	...	...	...	...	...
Khmelnytsky **1750** d.	0828	1012	0955	...	...	...	...	...	...	...
Ternopil **1750** d.	1040	1217	1150	...	...	...	...	...	...	...
Lviv 1750 a.	1307	1433	1409	...	...	...	...	...	...	...

D – DONBAS.
E – Even dates.
N – DNIPRO.
S – SLAVUTICH.
T – Uneven dates [... *31, 3* ...].
U – Uneven dates [... *29, 1* ...].
Y – Daily May 26 - Sept. 30.
Z – Daily Oct. 1 - Jan. 31, 2010.
h – On ②⑤ from Berlin (③⑥ from Kyïv) conveys 2 cl. Berlin - Kyïv - Simferpol.
k – On ④⑦ from Simferopol conveys 2 cl. Simferpol - Kyïv - Berlin.
p – Daily May 25 - June 30; even dates July; uneven dates Aug.; daily Sept. 1 - Dec. 31.
q – Daily May 25 - June 29; uneven dates July; even dates Aug.; daily Aug. 31 - Dec. 31.

1780 KYÏV and HOMEL - KHARKIV and LUHANSK *BCh, UZ*

km **		Sko 112	Fir 164 S	Pas 312 E	Fir 20	Pas 606	Sko 14	Sko 100 R	Sko 118 J	Fir 64	Pas 116
	Uzhhorod **1750** d.	...	...	...	...	...	2145	...	...	...	...
	Lviv **1750** d.	1705	...	...	...	...	0516	...	...	...	1240
0	**Kyïv** d.	0313	0633	...	1840	...	1453	...	1948	2225	0042
148	Hrebinka d.	0527	|	...	2035	...	1654	...	2200	0030	|
333	**Poltava** Kyïvska d.	0905	1035	...	2328	...	2017	...	0139	0344	|
	Kaliningrad **1950** d.	|	|	1403	|	...	|	...	|	|	|
	Minsk **1930** d.	|	|	0057	|	...	|	0825	|	|	|
	Homel § BY d.	|	|	0635	|	...	|	1404	|	|	|
	Konotop **1740** § UA d.	|	|	1236	|	...	|	1932	|	|	0349
	Sumy **1740** d.	|	|	1530	|	1650	|	2206	|	|	0623
491	**Kharkiv** a.	1145	1228	1921	|	2120	2253	0121	0417	0621	1020
	Simferopol **1790** a.	...	...	...	|	|	...	1055	...	...	...
814	**Luhansk** a.	...	...	...	0947	1022	...	...	...	...	...

	Fir 20	Pas 311 U	Pas 606	Sko 115	Sko 13	Fir 163 S	Sko 111	Pas 343 K	Fir 63	Sko 100 Q
Luhansk d.	1649	...	1803	...	...	...	...	...	...	...
Simferopol **1790** d.	|	...	|	...	...	...	...	...	...	1335
Kharkiv d.	|	0050	0636	0712	1101	1627	1911	1835	2255	2314
Sumy **1740** d.	|	0442	1200	1109	|	|	|	2320	|	0238
Konotop **1740** § UA d.	|	0733	...	1353	|	|	|	0247	|	0510
Homel § BY a.	|	1339	...	|	|	|	|	|	|	1038
Minsk **1930** a.	|	1917	...	|	|	|	|	|	|	1612
Kaliningrad **1950** a.	|	0856	...	|	|	|	|	|	|	...
Poltava Kyïvska d.	0327	...	...	|	1415	1840	2233	|	0148	...
Hrebinka d.	0620	...	...	|	1758	|	0158	|	0455	...
Kyïv a.	0806	...	...	1639	1952	2217	0401	0613	0715	...
Lviv **1750** a.	...	...	...	0331	0537	...	1445	...	...	...
Uzhhorod **1750** a.	...	...	...	...	1235	...	...	...	...	...

E – Even dates.
J – On ④⑦ from Berlin (②⑥ from Kyïv) conveys 2 cl. Berlin (**441 / 445**) - Kyïv - Kharkiv.
K – On ②⑤ conveys 2 cl. Kharkiv - Kyïv (**440 / 444**) - Berlin.
Q – Even dates (daily June 2 - Oct. 2).
R – Uneven dates [... *29, 1* ...] (daily June 1 - Oct. 1).
S – STOLICHNY EKSPRES.
U – Uneven dates [... *29, 1* ...].
§ – : Terekowka (BY) / Khorobychi (UA).
** – Homel - Konotop: *222 km.* Sumy - Kharkiv: *195 km.* Kharkiv - Luhansk: *439 km.*
BY – Belarus.
UA – Ukraine.

1790 MOSKVA - KHARKIV - MARIUPOL and SEVASTOPOL *RZhD, UZ*

km		Sko 7 S p	Sko 25 y	Fir 29 z	Sko 17	Sko 100 R	Sko 9	Fir 15	Sko 67 K x	Sko 77
0	**Moskva** Kurskaya d.	0403	0824	0944	1032	...	1440	1449	1611	1629
194	Tula **I** d.	0645	1130	1226	1319	...	1726	1734	1951	2007
383	Orel d.	0932	1420	1506	1555	...	2007	2015	2227	2259
537	Kursk d.	1159	1635	1717	1825	...	2230	2243	0030	0100
697	Belgorod § RU d.	1551	2008	2039	2148	...	0140	0156	0341	0413
	Kyïv **1780** d.	|	|	|	|	...	|	|	|	|
	Minsk **1780** d.	|	|	|	|	0825	|	|	|	|
781	**Kharkiv** § UA a.	1655	2036	2149	2245	0121	0205	0246	0402	0510
781	**Kharkiv** d.	1728	2116	2209	2310	0139	0244	0313	0445	0530
1098	Donetsk a.	|	|	|	|	|	0833	|	|	1230
1230	**Mariupol** a.	|	|	|	|	|	...	|	|	1505
1081	Dnipropetrovsk Holovny a.	|	|	|	|	|	...	0741	|	...
1108	Zaporizhzhya **I 1775** d.	2225	0134	0220	0332	0600	...	...	0926	...
1220	Melitopol **1775** d.	0007	0314	0351	0517	0733	...	...	1135	...
1464	Simferopol **1770 1775** a.	0310	|	0648	0840	1055	...	...	1440	...
1543	Yevpatoriya a.	|	0716	...	|	...	...	...	...	...
1542	**Sevastopol 1770 1775** a.	0505	...	...	1045	...	...	...	...	...

	Fir 16	Sko 10	Sko 78	Sko 68 K z	Sko 100 Q	Fir 30 w	Sko 18	Sko 26 v	Sko 8 S q
Sevastopol 1770 1775 d.	...	...	...	...	...	...	1705	...	2215
Yevpatoriya d.	...	...	...	...	...	...	|	1929	|
Simferopol **1770 1775** d.	...	...	...	1212	1335	1445	1936	|	0050
Melitopol **1775** d.	...	...	...	1526	1652	1743	2255	2341	0407
Zaporizhzhya **I 1775** d.	...	...	...	1704	1836	1911	0024	0108	0550
Dnipropetrovsk Holovny d.	1415	...	...	|	|	|	|	|	|
Mariupol d.	|	...	1050	|	|	|	|	|	|
Donetsk d.	|	1444	1332	|	|	|	|	|	|
Kharkiv a.	1848	2043	2049	2130	2254	2355	0454	0547	1026
Kharkiv § UA d.	1928	2115	2109	2203	2314	0034	0514	0601	1056
Minsk **1780** a.	|	|	|	|	1612	|	|	|	|
Kyïv **1780** a.	|	|	|	|	...	|	|	|	|
Belgorod § RU d.	2223	0011	0037	0100	...	0330	0847	0928	1352
Kursk d.	0116	0250	0333	0343	...	0653	1142	1225	1720
Orel d.	0317	0500	0537	0547	...	0852	1350	1430	1957
Tula **I** d.	0535	0743	0815	0823	...	1134	1629	1656	2228
Moskva Kurskaya a.	0906	1036	1109	1115	...	1444	1934	2014	0110

K – KRYM.
Q – Even dates (daily June 2 - Oct. 2).
R – Uneven dates [... *29, 1* ...] (daily June 1 - Oct. 1).
S – From / to St Peterburg (Table **1900**).
p – Even dates (from St Peterburg) [... *30, 1, 4* ...] (daily May 1 - Nov. 5, Dec. 24 – 31).
q – Even dates [... *30, 1, 3, 6* ...] (daily May 1 - Nov. 5, Dec. 24 – 31).
v – May 25 - Oct. 1.
w – May 26 - Oct. 3.
x – May 25 - Oct. 3.
y – May 27 - Oct. 3.
z – May 24 - Oct. 1.
RU – Russia (Moskva Time).
UA – Ukraine (East European Time).
§ – : Krasny Khutor (RU) / Kozacha Lopan (UA).
For services Moskva - Kharkiv - Rostov and beyond, see the *Thomas Cook Overseas Timetable*.

LITHUANIA, LATVIA and ESTONIA

SEE MAP PAGE 509

Operators: Lithuania: **LG** (Lietuvos Geležinkeliai). Latvia: **LDz** (Latvijas Dzelzceļš). Estonia: **Edelaraudtee** (except for international trains, which are operated by **GoRail**).

Services: Trains convey first- and second-class seating unless indicated otherwise. International trains to and from CIS countries (Belarus, Russia, Ukraine) are composed of Russian-style sleeping-cars (for details of train types and classes of travel in the CIS, see the panel on page **515**).

Timings: Valid from **May 31, 2009**. Timings are expressed in local time at the station concerned (time comparison chart: page **2**).

Reservations: Reservation is compulsory for travel by long-distance and international services – *i.e.* all those for which a train number is shown.

KALININGRAD and VILNIUS - RIGA - TARTU and TALLINN — 1800

Operators:	A	E	E	E	E	E	T	E	E	E	E
Kaliningrad d.	2100	...	...	...	...	...	...	...	...	...	...
Vilnius d.	|	...	...	0700	...	...	1330	...	...	...	2100
Riga d.	0600	0700	0830	1130	1230	1530	1800	1830	1845	2340	0125
Valga d.	...	|	|	...	|	|	...	|	2120	|	|
Tartu a.	...	|	|	...	|	|	...	|	2245	|	|
Pärnu d.	...	0935	1120	...	|	1800	...	2105	...	0215	0420
Tallinn harbour *term. A* a.	...	|	|	...	|	|	...	|	...	0400	0620
Tallinn harbour *term. D* a.	...	|	|	...	|	|	...	|	...	0400	0620
Tallinn bus station a.	...	1125	1300	...	1655	2000	...	2255	...	0410	0630

Operators:	E	E	E	E	E	T	E	A	E	E	E
Tallinn bus station d.	...	0700	...	1000	1230	...	1700	...	1830	2100	0030
Tallinn harbour *term. D* d.	...	|	...	1010	|	...	|	...	|	|	|
Tallinn harbour *term. A* d.	...	|	...	1010	|	...	|	...	|	|	|
Pärnu d.	...	0850	...	1205	|	...	1855	...	2020	2300	0220
Tartu d.	0645	|	...	|	|	...	|	...	|	|	|
Valga d.	0805	|	...	|	|	...	|	...	|	|	|
Riga a.	1050	1125	1230	1435	1655	1800	2135	2210	2255	0150	0515
Vilnius a.	...	...	1700	...	...	2205	...	|	...	0620	...
Kaliningrad a.	...	...	...	...	...	...	...	0710	...	...	...

A – Also on ①④⑥ Kaliningrad dep. 0920, arrive Riga 1820; on ②⑤⑦ depart Riga 1000, arrive Kaliningrad 1900.

E – Mootor Reisi (www.eurolines.ee).

T – Toks or BAL (www.eurolines.lt).

☛ Also: Vilnius - Riga at 1000 (**E**), 1300 (**T**), 1600 (**T**), 1830 (**E**); Riga - Vilnius at 0800 (**E**), 1000 (**T**), 1530 (**E**), 1845 (**E**).

LG — VILNIUS - KLAIPEDA — 1810

km			17		19			21		
		c		2		2	c		2	
0	**Vilnius 1040, 1811** d.	...	0630	...	0900	...	...	1730	...	...
‡	Kaunas I **1040, 1811** d.	...	|	...	|	...	...	|	...	...
192	Radviliškis d.	0607	0844	...	1122	1430	1503	1946	...	...
212	Šiauliai d.	0630	0906	0920	1142	1504	1536	2008	2030	...
***	Mažeikiai a.	|	|	1036	|	1620	|	|	2146	...
376	**Klaipeda** a.	0918	1103	...	1351	...	1826	2203	...	...

		18			20			22	
	2		c	2		c	2		
Klaipeda d.	...	0625	0812	...	1139	1504	...	1700	...
Mažeikiai d.	0649	|	|	1149	|	|	1714	|	...
Šiauliai d.	0804	0833	1101	1306	1341	1751	1829	1905	...
Radviliškis d.	...	0851	1133	1338	1359	1826	...	1923	...
Kaunas I **1040, 1811** d.	...	|	...	...	|	...	...	|	...
Vilnius 1040, 1811 a.	...	1108	...	...	1614	...	...	2140	...

c – 3rd class only. ‡ – Kaunas - Radviliškis *138 km*. *** *78 km* Šiauliai - Mažeikiai. Kaunas I (Kaunas -1) is a temporary station during the closure of Kaunas tunnel.

LG 3rd class — VILNIUS - KAUNAS — 1811

km		①–⑤	①–⑤											
0	Vilnius **1040** d.	0520	0528	0640	0730	0836	1020	1155	1400	1435	1630	1725	1827	1920
104	Kaunas I **1040** a.	0618	0705	0745	0845	1013	1126	1305	1507	1612	1728	1824	2004	2028

	①–⑤		①–⑤										
Kaunas I **1040** d.	0500	0540	0645	0825	0910	1100	1200	1340	1540	1753	1851	1940	2055
Vilnius **1040** a.	0633	0722	0744	0934	1052	1242	1309	1521	1649	1902	2033	2049	2206

Kaunas I (Kaunas -1) is a temporary station during the closure of Kaunas tunnel.

LG, LDz, RZhD — VILNIUS - ST PETERBURG — 1820

km						*Pas*		*Fir*
		c	c	c	c	92	c	38
								B
0	**Vilnius** d.	0505	0750	1200	1455	1820	1849	...
147	Turmantas ▦ LT a.	0751	1032	1442	1737	|	2136	...
173	Daugavpils ▦ LV a.	...	...	...	...	2027	...	...
173	Daugavpils d.	...	...	...	...	2047	...	...
	Riga **1840** d.	...	...	...	...	|	...	1930
260	Rezekne I d.	...	...	...	...	2202	...	2250r
304	Karsava ▦ LV d.	...	...	...	...	2325	...	0018
337	Pytalovo ▦ RU d.	...	...	...	...	0148	...	0243
431	Pskov d.	...	...	...	...	0347	...	0428
715	**St Peterburg** Vitebski a.	...	...	...	...	0821	...	0908

		Pas		*Fir*			
	c	91	c	37	c	c	c
				B			
St Peterburg Vitebski d.	...	2030	...	2208	...	...	...
Pskov d.	...	0110	...	0246	...	...	...
Pytalovo ▦ RU d.	...	0334	...	0507	...	...	...
Karsava ▦ LV d.	...	0352	...	0525	...	...	...
Rezekne I d.	...	0436	...	0635r	...	...	...
Riga **1840** a.	...	|	...	0935	...	...	...
Daugavpils a.	...	0547	...	...	...	...	...
Daugavpils ▦ LV d.	...	0607	...	...	...	...	...
Turmantas ▦ LT d.	0438	|	0810	...	1126	1515	1803
Vilnius a.	0710	0815	1052	...	1407	1756	2055

B – BALTIYA – 🛏 1, 2 cl., ▬ 3 cl. and ④.

c – 3rd class only.

r – Rezekne II.

LT – Lithuania.

LV – Latvia (East European Time).

RU – Russia (Moskva Time).

LDz — RIGA - CESIS - VALGA — 1830

km												①–⑤		
0	**Riga** d.	0558	0635	0752	0907	1042	1151	1354	1540	1724	1805	1900	2100	...
53	Sigulda d.	0712	0740	0906	1021	1150	1305	1502	1654	1838	1858	2014	2212	...
93	Cesis d.	...	0822	...	...	1237	...	1545	...	...	1941	...	2254	...
121	Valmiera d.	...	0854	...	...	1308	...	1617	...	...	2013	...	2325	...
164	Lugaži ▦ LV a.	...	0941	...	...	...	...	1705	...	...	2101	...	...	...
168	**Valga** ▦ EE a.	...	0948	...	...	...	...	1711	...	...	2107	...	...	...

	①–⑤											⑧	
Valga ▦ EE d.	...	...	0525	...	...	...	1027	...	...	...	...	1729	
Lugaži ▦ LV d.	...	...	0533	...	...	...	1035	...	...	...	...	1737	
Valmiera d.	...	0523	0618	...	...	...	1120	...	1426	...	...	1822	...
Cesis d.	...	0550	0649	...	...	...	1153	...	1459	...	...	1854	...
Sigulda d.	0556	0629	0731	0817	0957	1114	1232	1350	1541	1707	1852	1937	2131
Riga a.	0704	0740	0840	0931	1110	1227	1339	1503	1652	1820	2005	2039	2244

EE – Estonia. LV – Latvia.

LDz, RZhD — RIGA - REZEKNE - MOSKVA — 1840

km			*Pas*			*Fir*		*Fir*	*Fir*
			662			2		4	38
			N			L		J	B
0	**Riga 1850** d.	1028	...	1127	...	1620	1645	1810	1930
129	Krustpils (Jekabpils) **1850** d.	1233	...	1317	...	1812	1901	2008	2113
224	**Rezekne** II d.	1412	...	1429	...	1937	2039	2129	2250
	St Peterburg Vitebski **1820** a.	|	...	...	...	|	|	|	0908
279	Zilupe ▦ LV d.	1514	...	...	...	2113	2141	2304	...
305	Sebezh ▦ RU d.	...	1537	...	...	2336	...	0127	...
416	Novosokolniki d.	...	1820	...	...	|	...	0305	...
445	**Velikiye Luki** a.	...	1913	...	...	0135	...	0338	...
445	**Velikiye Luki** d.	...	2045	...	...	0200	...	0400	...
686	Rzhev d.	...	0213	...	...	0536	...	0747	...
921	**Moskva** Rizhskaya a.	...	0642	...	...	0941	...	1216	...

		Fir	*Fir*	*Fir*	*Pas*			
		37	1	3	661			
		B	L	J	N			
Moskva Rizhskaya d.	...	...	1910	2102	2008	...	...	...
Rzhev d.	...	...	2301	0100	0039	...	...	...
Velikiye Luki a.	...	...	0224	0424	0650	...	...	...
Velikiye Luki d.	...	...	0250	0445	0850	...	...	...
Novosokolniki d.	...	...	|	0519	1006	...	...	...
Sebezh ▦ RU d.	...	...	0558	0755	1225	...	...	...
Zilupe ▦ LV d.	0335	...	0610	0807	...	...	1550	...
St Peterburg Vitebski **1820** d.	|	2208	|	|	...	...	|	...
Rezekne II d.	0439	0635	0705	0902	...	1500	1655	...
Krustpils (Jekabpils) **1850** d.	0617	0752	0822	1019	...	1616	1840	...
Riga 1850 a.	0830	0935	1010	1205	...	1800	2040	...

B – BALTIJA – 🛏 1, 2 cl. and ▬ 3 cl.

J – JURMALA – 🛏 1, 2 cl.

L – LATVIJAS EKSPRESIS – 🛏 1, 2 cl.

N – 🛏 2 cl. and ▬ 3 cl.

LV – Latvia (East European Time).

RU – Russia (Moskva Time).

LDz, BCh — RIGA - DAUGAVPILS - POLATSK — 1850

km			❖				D		
0	**Riga 1840** d.	0710	0845	1028	1300	1525	1610	1725	2052
129	Krustpils (Jekabpils) **1840** d.	0931	1113	1233	1503	1750	1759	1937	2315
218	Daugavpils § LV d.	1053	...	...	1635	...	1903	2103	...
379	**Polatsk** § BY a.	...	...	...	...	...	...	...	...

			D		❖			
Polatsk § BY d.	...	...	...	...	...	...	...	...
Daugavpils § LV d.	...	...	0614	0724	...	1315	...	1800
Krustpils (Jekabpils) **1840** d.	0500	0617	0722	0851	1154	1440	1811	1940
Riga 1840 a.	0729	0830	0906	1058	1420	1650	2031	2152

D – DINABURGA express service: special fares payable. BY – Belarus. LV – Latvia. ❖ – Subject to confirmation. § – ▦: Indra (LV) / Bihosava (BY).

LDz — RIGA AREA local trains — 1860

RIGA - JELGAVA and v.v. *43 km*
1–2 trains per hour. Journey ± 49 minutes.

RIGA - VENTSPILS and v.v. Daily. *176 km*.
Riga depart 1815, Ventspils arrive 2058.
Ventspils depart 0620, Riga arrive 0905.

RIGA - LIELVARDE and v.v. *51 km*
1–2 trains per hour. Journey ± 60 minutes. Certain of these trains continue to / start from **Aizkraukle** *82 km* ± 86 minutes.

RIGA - SAULKRASTI and v.v. *48 km*
1–2 trains per hour. Journey ± 60 minutes. Certain of these trains continue to / start from **Skulte** *56 km* ± 70 minutes.

RIGA - SLOKA (JURMALA) and v.v. *35 km*
1–2 trains per hour. Journey ± 52 minutes. Certain of these trains continue to / start from **Tukums** *65 km* ± 84 minutes.

RIGA - LIEPAJA and v.v. daily. *223 km*. Riga dep. 1100 and 1830, Liepaja arr. 1407 and 2135; Liepaja dep. 0600 and 1435, Riga arr. 0910 and 1748.

1870 TALLINN - ST PETERBURG and MOSKVA
Edelaraudtee, GoRail, RZhD

km		🚌 ①–⑤	🚌	🚌	🚌	🚌	222 B	34 A	224 B	🚌	🚌
0	**Tallinn 1880** d.	0600	0700	1015	1100	1430	1605	1710	1820	2300	2359
77	Tapa **1880** d.	|	|	|	|	|	1738	1826	1955	|	|
104	Rakvere d.	|	|	1145	1230	|	1802	1854	2018	|	0130
163	Jõhvi d.	|	0920	1305	1350	1650	1900	1941	...	|	0240
209	Narva EE d.	0830	1020	1400	1455	1750	1946	2103	...	0200	0335
380	**St Peterburg** Baltiski RU a.	1300	1530	1845	2015	2250	...	|	...	0705	0830
633	Bologoye **1900** RU a.	...	...	...	...	...	...	0548	...	...	...
797	Tver **1900** a.	...	...	...	...	...	...	0734	...	...	...
964	**Moskva** Oktyabrskaya **1900** a.	...	...	...	...	...	...	0920	...	...	...

	221 B	34 A	223 B	🚌	🚌	🚌 ⑧	🚌 ⑧	🚌	🚌	🚌
Moskva Oktyabrskaya **1900** d.	...	1805	...	...	...	...	...	...	...	...
Tver 1900 d.	...	2034	...	...	...	...	...	...	...	...
Bologoye 1900 RU d.	...	2232	...	...	...	...	...	...	...	...
St Peterburg Baltiski RU d.	...	|	...	0715	1115	1400	1645	1800	2300	2345
Narva EE d.	...	0505	0627	1025	1425	1710	1955	|	0150	0255
Jõhvi d.	...	0556	0714	1120	1525	1805	2050	|	0315	0355
Rakvere d.	0543	0656	0812	|	1645	|	|	|	0435	0515
Tapa 1880 d.	0607	0720	0836	|	|	|	|	|	|	|
Tallinn 1880 a.	0735	0827	1002	1335	1810	2020	2305	2320	0600	0640

A – *Firmenny.* 🛏 1, 2 cl. Ⓡ.
B – 🚃 (*tavaklassi*; general class).
EE – Estonia (East European Time).
RU – Russia (Moskva Time).
🚌 – Operated by Eurolines Estonia. Timings apply to bus, not rail, stations except for St Peterburg Baltiski rail station.

1880 TALLINN - TARTU - ORAVA and VALGA
Edelaraudtee

km		❖		❖	A	①–⑤ ◇	❖	⑤⑦ ◇		⑧	❖	◇	⑤⑦ ◇
0	**Tallinn 1870** d.	...	0640	...	...	0746	...	1355	1442	...	...	1645	1959
77	Tapa **1870** d.	...	0814	...	...	0900	...	1509	1612	...	...	1759	2113
142	Jõgeva d.	...	0910	...	...	0944	...	1553	1714	...	...	1848	2157
190	**Tartu** a.	...	0950	...	...	1015	...	1624	1756	...	...	1919	2228
190	**Tartu** d.	0457	...	1019	1024	...	1130	...	...	1814	1910	...	...
233	Põlva d.	|	...	|	1119	...	|	...	...	1909	|	...	...
262	**Orava** a.	|	...	|	1148	...	|	...	...	1938	|	...	...
215	Elva d.	0546	...	1103	...	...	1219	...	...	...	2000	...	...
273	**Valga** a.	...	...	...	...	...	...	...	...	...	...	...	...

	①–⑥ ◇	❖	①–⑥		❖	⑤⑦ ◇	A	⑧ ◇	❖		❖	⑤⑦ ◇
Valga d.	...	...	...	...	...	...	...	...	...	...	...	...
Elva d.	...	0632	...	...	1229	...	...	...	1718	...	1811	...
Orava d.	...	|	0553	...	|	...	1548	...	|	...	|	...
Põlva d.	...	|	0625	...	|	...	1620	...	|	...	|	...
Tartu a.	...	0720	0720	...	1317	...	1715	...	1803	...	1859	...
Tartu d.	0639	...	...	0734	...	1405	...	1723	...	1804	...	1954
Jõgeva d.	0711	...	...	0813	...	1437	...	1755	...	1847	...	2026
Tapa **1870** d.	0756	...	...	0918	...	1526	...	1841	...	1946	...	2112
Tallinn 1870 a.	0859	...	...	1047	...	1629	...	1944	...	2115	...	2215

A – May 31 - Sept. 30.
❖ – Subject to confirmation.
◇ – Conveys 🚃 12 (and 🍷 in 1st class). All other trains convey 🚃 (*tavaklass*; general class).
☛ Express 🚌 services operate Tallinn - Tartu and v.v. 20+ times daily (journey: 2½ hrs).

1890 TALLINN - PÄRNU and VILJANDI
Edelaraudtee

km						⑤⑥⑦						
0	**Tallinn** d.	0658	0750	0837	1035	1334	1422	1635	1725	1825	1920	2125
54	Rapla d.	0812	0846	0951	1146	1429	1535	1728	1835	1940	2033	2235
72	Lelle d.	0832	0901	...	...	1445	1550	1743	1852	...	2049	2250
136	**Pärnu** a.	0943	|	...	...	|	...	|	2001	...	|	|
98	Türi d.	...	0924	...	...	1506	...	1806	...	...	2113	2314
151	**Viljandi** a.	...	1018	...	...	1603	...	1902	...	...	...	...

	①–⑤				⑥⑦			⑤⑥⑦				
Viljandi d.	...	...	0639	...	...	...	...	1324	...	1622	...	...
Türi d.	0526	0620	0735	...	0930	...	...	1420	...	1718	...	...
Pärnu d.	|	|	|	0717	|	...	...	|	...	|	1709	...
Lelle d.	0550	0645	0757	0829	0954	...	...	1443	1615	1741	1819	...
Rapla d.	0606	0700	0811	0845	1009	1040	1222	1457	1632	1755	1835	1949
Tallinn a.	0715	0807	0908	0954	1105	1148	1330	1552	1742	1848	1948	2103

☛ All trains convey 🚃 (*tavaklass*; general class).

RUSSIA and BELARUS

SEE MAP PAGE 509

Operators: **RZhD**: Rossiskiye Zheleznye Dorogi (РЖД: Российские Железные Дороги). **BCh**: Belaruskaya Chyhunka (БЧ: Беларуская Чыгунка).

Timings: Valid from **May 31, 2009**. Moskva Time is used for all Russian stations (including Kaliningrad, where local time is one hour behind Moskva Time). The timings of international services to and from non-CIS countries should be verified from the international tables at the front of this book.

Tickets: Except for travel by purely local trains, prior reservation is necessary and passports and visas must be presented when purchasing tickets.

SEE ALSO THE PANEL ***RAIL TRAVEL IN RUSSIA, BELARUS, UKRAINE, and MOLDOVA*** ON THE FACING PAGE

1900 MOSKVA - ST PETERBURG
RZhD

km		*Fir* 38	*Sko* 16	*Sko* 30 B	*Sko* 8 C	*Sko* 802 ❖		*Fir* 24 △		*Sko* 814	*Fir* 160 △	*Sko* 18	*Fir* 10	*Sko* 56	*Fir* 28 D	*Sko* 66 F	*Sko* 42	*Fir* 32	*Fir* 26	*Fir* 6 B❖	*Sko* 54 ⊠	*Fir* 2	*Fir* 4
	Sevastopol **1790** d.	...	...	...	2215	...	...	...	...	...	...	...	...	...	...	...	...	...	...	...	...	...	...
0	**Moskva** Oktyabrskaya § **1870** d.	0030	0050	0105	0125**k**	...	...	1230	...	1530	1630	1825	1923	2020	2130	2130	2150	2250	2300	2330	2340	2355	2359
167	Tver **1870** d.	0226	0240	0301	0334	...	...	1416	...	1722	1754	2045	2155	2305	2352	2352	0021	0054	0117	|	|	|	|
331	Bologoye **1870** d.	0410	0436	0510	0527	...	...	1611	...	1925	1921	2232	0030	0124	0150	0150	0219	|	|	|	|	|	|
588	Dno d.	|	|	|	|	...	...	|	...	|	|	|	0543	|	|	|	|	|	|	|	|	|	|
687	**Pskov** a.	|	|	|	|	...	...	|	...	|	|	|	0730	|	|	|	|	|	|	|	|	|	|
606	Novgorod na Volkhove d.	|	|	|	|	0805	...	|	...	|	|	|	...	|	|	|	0610	|	|	|	|	|	|
650	**St Peterburg** Glavny ‡ a.	0848	0838**c**	0946	1008	1121	...	1952	...	2309	2200	|	...	0500	0528	0528	...	0602**c**	0645	0740	0835	0755	0800
	Helsinki **1910** a.	...	|	...	...	...	...	...	...	...	...	|	...	...	...	...	...	1206	...	...	...	...	...
	Petrozavodsk **1905** a.	...	1628	...	...	...	...	...	...	...	...	0850	...	...	...	...	...	...	...	...	...	...	...
	Murmansk **1905** a.	...	1157	...	...	...	...	...	...	...	...	...	...	...	...	...	...	...	...	...	...	...	...

km		*Fir* 31	*Sko* 17	*Sko* 55	*Fir* 23 △		*Fir* 159 △	*Sko* 813	*Sko* 801 ❖	*Fir* 165	*Sko* 7 C	*Sko* 42	*Sko* 29 B	*Fir* 37	*Fir* 27 E	*Sko* 65 D	*Fir* 10	*Sko* 15	*Fir* 25	*Fir* 5 B❖	*Sko* 53 ⊠	*Fir* 1	*Fir* 3
	Murmansk **1905** d.	...	...	...	...	...	...	...	...	...	...	...	...	...	...	...	...	1941	...	...	...	...	...
	Petrozavodsk **1905** d.	...	1900	...	...	...	...	...	...	...	...	...	...	...	...	...	...	1517	...	...	...	...	...
	Helsinki **1910** d.	1752	|	...	...	...	...	...	...	...	...	...	...	...	...	...	...	|	...	...	...	...	...
0	**St Peterburg** Glavny ‡ d.	0149**c**	|	0040	1305	...	1600	1505	1718	1830	2000	...	2201	2220	2237	2237	...	2251**c**	2300	2330	2340	2355	2359
192	Novgorod na Volkhove d.	|	|	|	|	...	|	|	2024	|	|	2120	|	|	|	|	...	|	|	|	|	|	|
	Pskov d.	|	|	|	|	...	|	|	...	|	|	|	|	|	|	|	1800	|	|	|	|	|	|
	Dno d.	|	|	|	|	...	|	|	...	|	|	|	|	|	|	|	2017	|	|	|	|	|	|
319	Bologoye **1870** d.	|	0447	0510	1706	...	1842	1849	...	|	0007	0112	0155	0207	0219	0219	0213	0247	|	|	|	|	|
483	Tver **1870** d.	0628	0651	0719	1855	...	1959	2031	...	|	015	0330	0337	0351	0407	0407	0358	0443	0450	|	|	|	|
650	**Moskva** Oktyabrskaya § **1870** a.	0825	0857	0953	2055	...	2130	2213	...	2300	0348**k**	0532	0550	0602	0556	0556	0625	0654	0700	0710	0835	0755	0800
	Sevastopol **1790** a.	...	...	...	...	...	...	...	...	...	0505	...	...	...	...	...	...	...	...	...	...	...	...

B – ⑧ (daily May 1 - Aug. 29).
C – Even dates (daily May 1 - Nov. 5; Dec. 24 – 31).
D – Uneven dates [... *31, 3* ...].
E – Even dates.
F – Even dates [... *30, 1, 4* ...].
c – St Peterburg Ladozhski.

k – Moskva Kurskaya.
❖ – Subject to confirmation.
△ – Conveys 🚃 Sd seating.
§ – Also known as *Leningradski vokzal.*
‡ – Also known as *Moskovski vokzal.*
⊠ – *Grand Express* 🛏 1, cl. with ensuite, shower, sofa, air conditioning, TV, DVD and wi-fi.

Named trains:

1/2	KRASNAYA STRELA	25/26	SMENA
3/4	EKSPRESS	31/32	LEV TOLSTOI
5/6	NIKOLAYEVSKI EKSPRESS	37/38	AFANASI NIKITIN
7/8	NEVA	42	ILMEN
17/18	KARELIYA	159/160	AVRORA

1905 (MOSKVA and) ST PETERBURG - PETROZAVODSK - MURMANSK
RZhD

km		*Sko* 18 K	*Sko* 382	*Sko* 16	*Sko* 12 C	*Sko* 212 A		*Sko* 22	*Pas* 658
	Moskva Oktyabrskaya **1900** d.	1825	2045	0050	...	0117	...	...	...
0	**St Peterburg** Ladozhski d.	|	|	0856	0934	1102	...	1720	2202
* 114	Volkhovstroi I d.	0350	|	1115	1145	1321	...	1939	0033
394	**Petrozavodsk** d.	0850	1145	1645	1703	1832	...	0057	0650
773	Belomorsk d.	...	2110	2340	0015	0219	...	0758	...
1161	Kandalaksha d.	...	0451	0640	0731	0910	...	1502	...
1438	**Murmansk** a.	...	1108	1157	1308	1444	...	2019	...

	Sko 11 D	*Sko* 21		*Sko* 211 B	*Sko* 15	*Sko* 17 K	*Sko* 381	*Pas* 657
Murmansk d.	0154	0905	...	1741	1941	...	1844	...
Kandalaksha d.	0713	1429	...	2303	0107	...	0152	...
Belomorsk d.	1419	2130	...	0559	0755	...	0937	...
Petrozavodsk d.	2200	0446	...	1309	1517	1900	1957	2300
Volkhovstroi I d.	0256	1006	...	1816	2025	0039	0101	0505
St Peterburg Ladozhski a.	0500	1211	...	2030	2231	|	|	0707
Moskva Oktyabrskaya **1900** a.	...	...	...	0418	0654	0857	1115	...

A – May 31 - Sept. 6.
B – June 1 - Sept. 7.
C – July 18 - Sept. 6.
D – July 19 - Sept. 5.
K – KARELIYA.
* – Moskva - Vokhovstroi: *641 km.*

ST PETERBURG - HELSINKI 1910

RZhD, VR

km		Fir 790 TA	Fir 32 TB	Fir 34 RC	Sko 36 SC
	Moskva Okt. **1900** . d.	1745	2250	...	...
***	**St Peterburg** Lad. ◧ d.	0216	0607	...	...
0	**St Peterburg** Finl. § a.	|	|	0717	1630
129	Vyborg .... a.	0415	0759	0857	1820
	Vyborg .... RU d.	0455	0834	0927	1850
159	Vainikkala ...... FI a.	0500	0845	0932	1854
	Vainikkala .... d.	0600	0905	0952	1914
250	**Kouvola 797** .... a.	0700	1004	1047	2006
312	Lahti **797** .... a.	0742	1053	1138	2053
400	Tikkurila **797** .... a.	0947	1148	1232	2142
413	Pasila **797** .... a.	0958	1159	1242	2152
416	**Helsinki 797** .... a.	1006	1206	1248	2158

	Sko 35 SC	Fir 33 RC	Fir 31 T
Helsinki 797 .... d.	0700	1500	1752
Pasila **797** .... d.	0706	1506	1758
Tikkurila **797** .... d.	0716	1517	1809
Lahti **797** .... d.	0812	1622	1911
Kouvola 797 .... d.	0857	1710	2009
Vainikkala .... a.	0948	1806	2109
Vainikkala ...... FI d.	1011	1826	2134
Vyborg .... RU a.	1155	2023	2318
Vyborg .... d.	1225	2053	2353
St Peterburg Finl. § a.	1415	2251	|
St Peterburg Lad. ◧ a.	...	...	0144
Moskva Okt. **1900**. a.	...	...	0825

A – ① June 1 - Aug. 24.
B – ②–⑦ May 31 - Aug. 30; daily Aug. 31 - Dec. 12.
C – ①③④⑤⑥⑦ May 31 - Aug. 30; daily Aug. 31 - Dec. 12.
R – REPIN – 1 cl., 2 and ✕ Ⓡ St Peterburg - Helsinki and v.v.
S – SIBELIUS – 12 and ✕ Ⓡ. St Peterburg - Helsinki and v.v.
T – LEV TOLSTOI – 1, 2 cl. and ✕.
§ – Finlyandski vokzal.
◧ – Ladozhski vokzal.
FI – Finland (East European Time).
RU – Russia (Moskva Time).
*** *143 km* St Peterburg Ladozhski - Vyborg.

ST PETERBURG - MALADZECHNA 1915

RZhD, BCh

km		Sko 79 E
0	**St Peterburg** Vit. **1920** .... d.	1815
245	Dno **1920** .... d.	2222
421	Novosokolniki **1920** ..... ‡ RU d.	0147
568	Vitsebsk **1920** .... d.	0354
670	Polatsk .... ‡ BY d.	0552
868	**Maladzechna** .... a.	0858
	Vilnius **1950** .... a.	1242
	Kaliningrad **1950** .... a.	2029

	Sko 80 C
Kaliningrad **1950** .... d.	0950
Vilnius **1950** .... d.	1548
Maladzechna .... d.	1913
Polatsk .... ‡ BY d.	2253
Vitsebsk **1920** .... d.	0043
Novosokolniki **1920** .. ‡ RU d.	0447
Dno **1920** .... d.	0731
St Peterburg Vit. **1920** ...a.	1110

C – Uneven dates [... *29, 1* ...] (daily June 5 - Sept. 5).
E – Even dates (daily June 6 - Sept. 6).
‡ – : Yezyaryshcha (BY) / Zaverezhye (RU).
BY – Belarus (East European Time).
RU – Russia (Moskva Time).

ST PETERBURG - HOMEL and KOZYATYN 1920

RZhD, BCh, UZ

km		Sko 47 D	Sko 49 A	Sko 53	Sko 61	Fir 55	Sko 83 K	Fir 51	Sko 19 BR
0	**St Peterburg** Vitebski **1915** ......d.	1245	1500	1558	1620	...	1747	1908	2355
245	Dno **1915** .... d.	1630	1903	1955	2008	...	2136	2306	0357
421	Novosokolniki **1915** .... § RU d.	1934	2200	2300	2340	...	0044	0222	0725
568	Vitsebsk .... § BY d.	2116	2351	0038	0119	...	0306	0408	0921
	Moskva Belorusskaya **1950** ....d.	|	|	|	|	2119	|	|	|
652	**Orsha** Tsentralnaya .... a.	2238	0107	0200	0239	0325	0425	0540	1047
652	**Orsha** Tsentralnaya .... d.	2259	0127	0217	0259	0344	0441	0600	1111
	Minsk Passazhirski **1950** .... a.	0140	0355	|	|	|	|	0851	|
	Lviv **1720** .... a.	1519	|	|	|	|	|	...	|
	Brest Tsentralny **1950** .... a.	...	0824	|	|	|	|	...	|
726	Mahilyow I .... d.	...	...	0356	0437	0548	0626	...	1257
853	Zhlobin **1930** .... d.	...	...	0621	0709	0805	0857	...	1608
	Homel 1930 .... a.	...	...	0740	|	0932	1027	...	|
	Kyïv Passazhirski **1930** .... a.	...	...	1440	|	...	...	...	|
954	Kalinkavichy **1700** .... ‡ BY d.	...	...	...	0850	...	...	...	1811
1109	Korosten **1700** .... ‡ UA d.	...	...	...	1308	...	...	...	2218
1191	Zhytomyr **1700** .... d.	...	...	...	1501	...	...	...	2358
1267	**Kozyatyn** .... a.	...	...	...	1640	...	...	...	0136
	Odesa Holovna **1750** .... a.	...	...	...	|	...	...	...	1018
	Chişinău **1750** .... a.	...	...	...	0727	...	...	...	...

	Sko 48 E	Sko 20 BS	Fir 52	Sko 50	Sko 54	Sko 83 L	Sko 61 A	Fir 55
Chişinău **1750** .... d.	...	...	...	...	...	...	1928	...
Odesa Holovna **1750** .... d.	...	1832	...	...	...	...	|	...
Kozyatyn .... d.	...	0252	...	...	...	...	1020	...
Zhytomyr **1700** .... d.	...	0432	...	...	...	...	1207	...
Korosten **1700** .... ‡ UA d.	...	0626	...	...	...	...	1355	...
Kalinkavichy **1700** .... ‡ BY d.	...	1028	...	...	...	...	1745	...
Kyïv Passazhirski **1930** .... d.	...	|	...	...	1030	...	|	...
Homel 1930 .... d.	...	|	...	...	1655	1818	|	1936
Zhlobin **1930** .... d.	...	1215	...	...	1817	1945	1935	2104
Mahilyow I .... d.	...	1454	...	...	2048	2204	2255	2347
Brest Tsentralny **1950** .... d.	...	|	...	1405	|	|	|	|
Lviv **1720** .... d.	2312	|	...	|	|	|	|	|
Minsk Passazhirski **1950** .... d.	1240	|	1740	1848	|	|	|	|
Orsha Tsentralnaya .... a.	1536	1611	2013	2119	2210	2327	0041	0112
Orsha Tsentralnaya .... d.	1556	1637	2030	2135	2233	2345	0103	0134
Moskva Belorusskaya **1950** ....a.	|	|	|	|	|	|	|	0955
Vitsebsk .... § BY d.	1751	1831	2214	2315	0006	0140	0234	...
Novosokolniki **1915** .... § RU d.	2158	2254	0206	0316	0402	0524	0621	...
Dno **1915** .... d.	0125	0220	0512	0601	0702	0835	0905	...
St Peterburg Vitebski **1915** .....a.	0525	0615	0853	0940	1044	1204	1243	...

A – Conveys (on dates shown in Table **95**) 1, 2 cl. St Peterburg - Orsha - Brest - Praha and v.v.
B – Conveys (on dates shown in Table **56**) 1, 2 cl. St Peterburg - Orsha - Berlin and v.v.
D – Even dates [... *30, 1, 4* ...] (daily May 25 - Oct. 2; not Oct. 1).
E – Even dates (daily May 24 - Sept. 28).
K – Uneven dates [... *31, 3* ...].
L – Even dates.
R – ①③⑤ (daily May 25 - Oct. 1).
S – ③⑤⑦ (daily May 24 - Sept. 30).
§ – : Yezyaryshcha (BY) / Zaverezhye (RU).
‡ – : Slovechno (BY) / Berezhest (UA).
BY – Belarus (East European Time).
RU – Russia (Moskva Time).
UA – Ukraine.

Named trains:
51/52 ZVYAZDA
53/54 LYBID
55/56 SOZH

MINSK - HOMEL - KYÏV 1930

BCh, UZ

km		Pas 312 E	Pas 134 B	Sko 53 L	Sko 100 H	Pas 382 D	Sko 94 F		Sko 86 A
	Kaliningrad **1950** .... d.	1403	2011	...	...	...	...	...	...
	Vilnius **1950** .... d.	2000	0204	...	...	...	...	...	...
0	**Minsk** Passazhirski .... d.	0057	0648	...	0825	0948	1131	...	2050
	St Peterburg Vitebski **1920** ....d.	|	|	1558	|	|	|	...	|
214	Zhlobin **1920** .... d.	0430	1021	0621	1217	1327	1513	...	0036
304	**Homel 1920** .... a.	0600	1149	0740	1344	1447	1636	...	0156
304	**Homel** .... ‡ BY d.	0635	...	0803	1404	1512	1701	...	0221
	Kharkiv Passazhirski **1780** .....a.	1921	...	|	0121	|	|	...	|
415	Chernihiv .... ‡ UA d.	...	...	1141	|	1856	2052	...	0604
	Simferopol **1775 1790** .... a.	...	...	|	1055	1546	|	...	|
624	**Kyïv** Passazhirski **1700 1720** ....a.	...	...	1440	...	...	0003	...	0851
	Odesa **1750** .... a.	...	...	...	...	...	1027	...	...

	Sko 94 G	Sko 100 J	Pas 311 C	Sko 54 L	Pas 133 E		Pas 382 E	Sko 86 A
Odesa **1750** .... d.	1430	...	...	...	...	...	...	...
Kyïv Passazhirski **1700 1720** ....d.	0052	...	...	1030	...	...	...	1822
Simferopol **1775 1790** .... d.	|	1335	...	|	...	...	2154	|
Chernihiv .... ‡ UA d.	0415	|	...	1324	...	...	2010	2133
Kharkiv Passazhirski **1780** .....d.	|	2314	0050	|	...	...	|	|
Homel .... ‡ BY a.	0734	1038	1339	1625	...	...	2337	0051
Homel 1920 .... d.	0813	1111	1402	1655	1705	...	2358	0115
Zhlobin **1920** .... d.	0933	1238	1543	1817	1833	...	0145	0239
St Peterburg Vitebski **1920** ....a.	|	|	|	1044	|	...	|	|
Minsk Passazhirski .... a.	1256	1612	1917	...	2206	...	0529	0558
Vilnius **1950** .... a.	...	...	0055	...	0255	...	...	...
Kaliningrad **1950** .... a.	...	...	0856	...	1032	...	...	...

A – Conveys (on dates shown in Table **98**) 2 cl. Minsk - Kyïv - Sofiya and v.v.
B – Uneven dates [... *31, 3* ...].
C – Uneven dates [... *29, 1* ...].
D – Even dates [... *30, 1, 4* ...].
E – Even dates.
F – ①⑤ (daily June 13 - Sept. 30).
G – ②⑥ (daily June 14 - Oct. 1).
H – Uneven dates [... *29, 1* ...] (daily June 1 - Oct. 1).
J – Even dates (daily June 2 - Oct. 2).
L – LYBID.
‡ – : Teryukha (BY) / Homostayivka (UA).
BY – Belarus.
UA – Ukraine.

RAIL TRAVEL IN RUSSIA, BELARUS, UKRAINE, and MOLDOVA

CARRIAGE TYPES

As trains generally operate over very long distances, most accommodation is designed for overnight as well as day use. Carriage types (with their Russian names) are:

Spálny vagón СВ (1 cl. in the tables) – 2-berth compartments (9 per carriage)

Kupéiny К (2 cl. in the tables) – 4-berth compartments (9 per carriage)

Platskártny ПЛ (3 cl. in the tables) – Dormitory-style carriage with 54 bunks

Óbshchi О (4 in the tables) – 4th-class hard seating (81 places per carriage) ★
★ Not recommended for long-distance travel and not normally indicated in the tables.

A few day trains convey more comfortable *Sidyáchi* (seating) accommodation with 54–62 places per carriage (shown as Sd in the tables).

TRAIN TYPES

Ordinary long-distance trains are classified *Passazhirsky* (shown as *Pas* in the tables): they normally convey at least 3 cl. and 2 cl.

Faster long-distance trains are classified *Skóry* (shown as *Sko* in the tables): they normally convey at least 3 cl. and 2 cl. and often also 1 cl.

The top grade of fast long-distance trains are classified *Firménny* (shown as *Fir* in the tables). They are composed of higher-quality carriages dedicated to a particular, and usually named, service. They normally convey 2 cl. and 1 cl. carriages.

International services to, from and via Poland, Slovakia, Hungary and Romania convey through sleeping cars of the normal European ('RIC') types, with single and double compartments in first class, and 3- or 4-berth compartments in second class. The railways of the former Soviet Union being of broad gauge (1520mm), the bogies (trucks) of these through cars are changed at the frontier with these countries.

DAYS OF RUNNING

Many trains run on alternate days only: even dates or uneven dates. The examples below illustrate the system used to indicate exceptions to the pattern of even or uneven dates at the end of a month with 31 days and at the beginning of the month following:

e.g. "Uneven dates [... *29, 1* ...]" means that the train does not run on the 31st of a month with 31 days.

e.g. "Even dates [... *30, 1, 4* ...]" means that the train, **following a month with 31 days**, runs exceptionally on the 1st, but not the 2nd, of the month.

1935 VORONEZH - POLATSK

RZhD, BCh

km		Pas 468 A	Fir 39 D
0	**Voronezh** d.	0250	...
246	Kursk d.	1110	...
324	Lgov d.	1300	...
541	Bryansk Orlovski a.	1824	...
541	Bryansk Orlovski d.	1854	...
	Moskva Beloruss. **1950** d.	|	2144
796	Smolensk a.	0145	0329
796	Smolensk d.	...	0356
937	Vitsebsk § RU d.	...	0555
1039	**Polatsk** § BY a.	...	0738

	Pas 467 B	Fir 39 D
Polatsk § BY d.	...	1758
Vitsebsk § RU d.	...	2007
Smolensk a.	...	2325
Smolensk d.	0702	2355
Moskva Beloruss. **1950** a.	|	0549
Bryansk Orlovski a.	1306	...
Bryansk Orlovski d.	1336	...
Lgov a.	1755	...
Kursk a.	1945	...
Voronezh a.	0200	...

1945 VORONEZH - HOMEL - BREST

RZhD, BCh

km		Sko 75	Pas 376 Y	Pas 663
0	**Voronezh** d.	...	1800	...
**	Moskva Beloruss. d.	1553	|	...
548	Bryansk Orlovski d.	0045	0738	...
776	Zlynka RU d.	0503	1226	...
802	Dobrush BY d.	0436	1151	...
827	**Homel** a.	0502	1218	...
827	**Homel** d.	0522	...	2055
956	Kalinkavichy **1700** d.	0753	...	2340
1133	Luninets **1700** d.	1118	...	0325
1361	**Brest** Tsentr. **1700** a.	1548	...	0743

	Pas 376 Z	Sko 76	Pas 664
Brest Tsentr. **1700** d.	...	1014	1934
Luninets **1700** d.	...	1429	0008
Kalinkavichy **1700** d.	...	1740	0351
Homel a.	...	1941	0625
Homel d.	1739	2010	...
Dobrush BY d.	1810	2044	...
Zlynka RU d.	1936	2211	...
Bryansk Orlovski a.	0010	0240	...
Moskva Beloruss. a.	|	1140	...
Voronezh a.	1145	...	...

NOTES FOR TABLES **1935** and **1945**:

A – Uneven dates [... *31, 2, 5* ...]. June 25 - Sept. 25.
B – Uneven dates [... *29, 1* ...]. June 23 - Sept. 25.
D – DVINA.
Y – Uneven dates [... *31, 2, 5* ...].
Z – Uneven dates [... *31, 3* ...].
** – Moskva - Bryansk: *485 km.*
§ – : Zavolsha (BY) / Rudnya (RU).
BY – Belarus (East European Time).
RU – Russia (Moskva Time).

1950 MOSKVA - MINSK, VILNIUS, KALININGRAD and BREST

RZhD, BCh, LG

km		Fir 105	Sko 69 S	Sko 19 B	Sko 19 U	Sko 13 M	Pas 301 N	Pas 311 K	Sko 25	Sko 103		Pas 133 GY	Fir 29		Sko 27	Sko 47 H	Sko 9 P	Fir 77	Sko 5	Sko 49 J	Sko 147 F	Sko 11 A	Pas 395	Fir 55 X
0	**Moskva** Belorusskaya d.	...	...	...	...	0800	...	...	1027	...	...	...	1357	...	1543	...	1650	1700	1855	...	1855	2109	1937	2119
243	Vyazma d.	...	0745	...	...	1036	...	...	1402	...	...	...	1740	...	1915	...	1945	2051	2223	...	2250	0035	2344	0046
419	Smolensk § RU d.	...	1117	...	...	1220	...	...	1620	...	...	...	2000	...	2139	...	2132	2307	0016	...	0116	0231	0238	0300
	St Peterburg Vitebski ▲ d.	...	|	2355	2345	|	...	...	|	...	...	...	|	...	|	1245	|	|	|	1500	|	|	|	|
538	Orsha Tsentralnaya § BY a.	...	1157	1047	1047	1235	...	...	1653	...	...	...	2029	...	2208	2238	2143	2331	0034	0107	0145	0257	0309	0325
538	Orsha Tsentralnaya d.	...	1213	1250	1250	1250	...	...	1707	...	...	...	2044	...	2221	2259	2153	2344	0047	0127	0200	0311	0322	...
750	**Minsk** a.	...	1445	1504	1504	1504	...	...	2006	...	...	...	2321	...	0053	0140	0009	0210	0311	0355	0456	0549	0635	...
750	**Minsk** d.	1333	1503	1529	1529	1529	1813	1945	2040	2040	...	2226	2346	...	0110	0153	0019	0232	0333	0408	0515	0619	0649	...
828	Maladzechna ‡ BY d.	|	|	|	|	|	1924	2119	|	|	...	2345	0103	...	|	|	|	0344	0444	|	0644	|	|	...
956	Lida d.	|	|	|	|	|	|	|	|	|	...	|	|	...	|	|	|	0624	|	|	|	|	|	...
1088	Hrodna a.	|	|	|	|	|	|	|	|	|	...	|	|	...	|	|	|	0839	|	|	|	|	|	...
944	**Vilnius** ‡ LT a.	|	|	|	|	|	2205	0055	|	|	...	0255	0421	...	|	|	|	...	0800	|	1014	|	|	...
944	**Vilnius** ¶ LT d.	|	|	|	|	|	...	0115	|	|	...	0315	0441	...	|	|	|	...	...	|	1034	|	|	...
1286	**Kaliningrad** ¶ Ka a.	|	|	|	|	|	...	0856	|	|	...	1032	1157	...	|	|	|	...	...	|	1807	|	|	...
892	Baranavichy Tsentralnye d.	1522	1653	|	|	|	...	...	2224	2224	...	...	...	...	0300	0412p	|	...	...	0556	...	0804	0918p	...
	Lviv **1720** a.	|	|	|	|	|	...	...	|	|	...	...	...	...	|	1519	|	...	...	|	...	|	|	...
1094	**Brest** Tsentralny a.	1756	1856	1855	1855x	1855	...	...	0029x	0029x	...	...	...	...	0535	...	0342	...	...	0824	...	1011	1218	...
	Warszawa Wschodnia **1050** a.	...	2351	2351	0549	2351	...	...	0549	0549	...	...	...	...	...	...	0830	...	...	...	...	1529	...	...

	Fir 39 D	Fir 3 Y	Fir 7 R	Pas 305	Fir 1	Sko 131	Sko 21 V	Sko 79 L	Fir 51
Moskva Belorusskaya d.	2144	2334	2334	...	2225	2334	2344	...	...
Vyazma d.	0124	0204	0204	...	0207	0253	0309	...	...
Smolensk § RU d.	0329	|	|	...	0420	0455	0505	...	...
St Peterburg Vitebski ▲ d.	...	|	|	...	|	|	|	1815	1908
Orsha Tsentralnaya § BY a.	...	0342	0342	...	0443	0520	0528	|	0540
Orsha Tsentralnaya d.	...	0352	0352	...	0456	0533	0542	|	0600
Minsk a.	...	0606	0606	...	0729	0824	0807	|	0851
Minsk d.	...	...	...	0630	...	0838	0825	|	...
Maladzechna ‡ BY d.	...	...	...	0754	...	|	|	0915	...
Lida d.	...	...	...	|	...	|	|	|	...
Hrodna a.	...	...	...	|	...	|	|	|	...
Vilnius ‡ LT a.	...	...	...	1108	...	|	|	1242	...
Vilnius ¶ LT d.	...	...	...	...	...	|	|	1300	...
Kaliningrad ¶ Ka a.	...	...	...	...	...	|	|	2029	...
Baranavichy Tsentralnye d.	...	...	...	...	...	1027	1014	...	...
Lviv **1720** a.	...	...	...	...	...	|	|	...	...
Brest Tsentralny a.	...	...	...	...	...	1242	1226	...	...
Warszawa Wschodnia **1050** a.	...	...	...	...	...	...	...	...	...

	Sko 104	Sko 104 132	Fir 106	Pas 302 N	Sko 14 W	Sko 14 M	Sko 14 Q	Sko 70 T	Sko 48 E
Warszawa Wschodnia **1050** d.	2100	2100	...	...	2100	2342	2342	2342	...
Brest Tsentralny d.	0410z	0430z	0620	...	0720z	0720	0720	0720	...
Lviv **1720** d.	|	|	|	...	|	|	|	|	2312
Baranavichy Tsentralnye d.	0618	0657	0855	...	|	|	|	0928	1032p
Kaliningrad ¶ Ka d.	|	|	|	...	|	|	|	|	|
Vilnius 1850 ¶ LT a.	|	|	|	...	|	|	|	|	|
Vilnius ‡ LT d.	|	|	|	0640	|	|	|	|	|
Hrodna d.	|	|	|	|	|	|	|	|	|
Lida d.	|	|	|	|	|	|	|	|	|
Maladzechna ‡ BY d.	|	|	|	0920	|	|	|	|	|
Minsk a.	0804	0837	1037	1040	1046	1046	1046	1114	1222
Minsk d.	...	0852	...	...	1111	1111	1111	1127	1240
Orsha Tsentralnaya a.	...	1136	...	...	1332	1332	1332	1408	1536
Orsha Tsentralnaya § BY d.	...	1150	...	...	1637	1348	1637	1426	1556
St Peterburg Vitebski ▲ a.	...	|	...	...	0615	|	0615	|	0534
Smolensk § RU d.	...	1413	...	...	...	1604	...	1655	...
Vyazma d.	...	1639	...	...	...	1805	...	1937	...
Moskva Belorusskaya a.	...	1954	...	...	...	2035	...	...	...

	Fir 52	Fir 39 D	Sko 50	Sko 26	Pas 306	Sko 80 C	Sko 22 V	Sko 22 Jd	Fir 4 R	Fir 8 Y	Fir 2	Sko 6	Sko 28	Fir 30	Fir 56 X	Fir 78	Sko 12 A	Pas 312 K		Sko 10 P	Sko 148 L	Pas 396		Pas 134 GZ
Warszawa Wschodnia **1050** d.	...	...	...	...	...	...	...	...	...	...	...	...	...	...	...	...	1250	...	...	1540	...	...	...	...
Brest Tsentralny d.	...	...	1405	...	...	...	1707	1707	...	...	...	...	1740	...	...	...	1942	...	...	2230	...	2144	...	...
Lviv **1720** d.	...	...	|	...	...	...	|	|	...	...	...	...	|	...	...	...	|	...	...	|	...	|	...	...
Baranavichy Tsentralnye d.	...	...	1646	...	...	...	1921	1921	...	...	...	...	2014	...	...	...	2155	...	...	|	...	0117p	...	...
Kaliningrad ¶ Ka d.	...	...	|	...	...	0950	|	|	...	...	...	...	|	1202	...	...	|	1403	...	|	1627	|	...	2011
Vilnius 1850 ¶ LT a.	...	...	|	...	...	1531	|	|	...	...	...	...	|	1731	...	...	|	1940	...	|	2222	|	...	0144
Vilnius ‡ LT d.	...	...	|	...	1416	1548	|	|	...	...	...	1700	|	1748	...	...	|	2000	...	|	2239	|	...	0204
Hrodna d.	...	...	|	...	|	|	|	|	...	...	...	|	|	|	...	1722	|	|	...	|	|	|	...	|
Lida d.	...	...	|	...	|	|	|	|	...	...	...	|	|	|	...	1935	|	|	...	|	|	|	...	|
Maladzechna ‡ BY d.	...	...	|	...	1728	1913	|	|	...	...	...	2010	|	2057	...	2157	|	2313	...	|	0145	|	...	0515
Minsk a.	...	...	1828	...	1846	|	2102	2102	...	...	...	2140	2203	2216	...	2312	2336	0030	...	0158	0258	0316	...	0629
Minsk d.	1740	...	1848	1826	...	|	2118	2118	2147	2147	2155	2203	2218	2237	...	2332	0002	...	...	0211	0324	0340	...	...
Orsha Tsentralnaya a.	2013	...	2119	2131	...	|	2344	2344	0002	0002	0018	0032	0050	0103	...	0206	0227	...	...	0424	0605	0632	...	...
Orsha Tsentralnaya § BY d.	2030	...	2135	2145	...	|	2359	0103	0014	0014	0031	0051	0103	0119	0134	0221	0240	...	...	0434	0623	0646	...	...
St Peterburg Vitebski ▲ a.	0853	...	0940	|	...	1110	|	1243	|	|	|	|	|	|	|	|	|	...	...	|	|	|	...	...
Smolensk § RU d.	...	2355	...	0012	...	...	0229	...	|	|	0300	0313	0334	0342	0355	0446	0501	...	...	0648	0856	0935	...	...
Vyazma d.	...	0235	...	0244	...	...	0443	...	0412	0412	0522	0530	0555	0603	0620	0714	0723	...	...	0852	1151	1232	...	...
Moskva Belorusskaya a.	...	0549	...	0556	...	...	0805	...	0625	0625	0846	0858	0920	0927	0955	1026	1059	...	...	1145	1548	1623	...	...

A – VOSTOK-ZAPAD EKSPRESS – 1, 2 cl. Moskva - Warszawa - Amsterdam, Basel and München and v.v. See Table **24**. Conveys 1, 2 cl. Kraków - Moskva and v.v.
B – 2 cl. St Peterburg - Orsha (**13**) - Berlin. For days of running, see Table **56**.
C – Uneven dates [... *29, 1* ...] (daily June 5 - Sept. 5).
D – DVINA – to / from Polatsk (Table **1935**).
E – Even dates (daily May 24 - Sept. 28).
F – Uneven dates [... *31, 3* ...] (daily June 7 - Sept. 7).
G – 2 cl. and 3 cl. Homel - Kaliningrad and v.v.
H – Even dates [... *30, 1, 4* ...] daily May 25 - Sept. 30.
J – Conveys (on dates shown in Table **95**) 2 cl. St Peterburg - Praha and v.v.
K – Uneven dates [... *29, 1* ...] from Kharkiv; even dates from Kaliningrad. 2 cl., 3 cl. Kharkiv - Kaliningrad and v.v.
L – Even dates (daily June 6 - Sept. 6).
M – MOSKVA EKSPRESS – 1, 2 cl. Moskva (**13**) - Terespol (**442**) - Warszawa (**440**) - Berlin, and Berlin (**441**) - Warszawa (**443**) - Brest (**14**) - Moskva. For days of running, see Table **56**. Conveys 1, 2 cl. Moskva - Paris and v.v. For days of running, Table **24**.
N – 2 cl. and 2 Minsk - Vilnius and v.v.
P – POLONEZ – 1, 2 cl., 1, 2 cl. (Lux) and Warszawa - Moskva and v.v. ✕ Brest - Moskva and v.v.
Q – 2 cl. Berlin (**441**) - Orsha (**20**) - St Peterburg. For days of running, see Table **56**.
R – Uneven dates [... *29, 1* ...].
S – ④ (④⑥ June 4 - Oct. 10) from Saratov (⑤ (⑤⑦ June 5 - Oct. 11) from Vyazma). 1, 2 cl. Saratov - Vyazma - Berlin; 2 cl. Novosibirsk (**113**) - Brest - Berlin. For other through coaches, see Tables **1980** and **1985**.
T – ⑥ (①⑥ June 6 - Oct. 12): from Berlin and Warszawa, 1, 2 cl. Berlin - Vyazma - Saratov; 2 cl. Berlin - Minsk (**64**) - Novosibirsk. For other through coaches, see Tables **1980** and **1985**.
V – VLTAVA – 1, 2 cl. Moskva - Cheb, Budapest, Praha and Wien and v.v. ✕ Moskva - Brest. See Table **95**.
U – ①③⑤ Dec. 14 - May 29; ①②③⑤⑦ May 31 - Oct. 16; ①③⑤ Oct. 19 - Dec. 12: 2 cl. St Peterburg (**19**) - Orsha (**13**) - Brest (**103**) - Warszawa (journey 2 nights).
W – ③⑤⑦ Dec. 14 - May 31; ②③④⑤⑦ June 2 - Oct. 19; ①③⑤ Oct. 21 - Dec. 12: 2 cl. Warszawa (**104**) - Brest (**14**) - Orsha (**20**) - St Peterburg (journey 2 nights).
X – SOZH – to / from Homel (Table **1920**).
Y – Even dates.
Z – Uneven dates [... *31, 3* ...].

d – Train **61** from Orsha.
p – Baranavichy Polesskiye.
x – Depart 0240.
z – Arrive 0222.
§ – : Osinovka (BY) / Krasnoye (RU).
‡ – : Hudahai (BY) / Kena (LT).
¶ – : Kybartai (LT) / Nesterov (Ka).
BY – Belarus (East European Time).
Ka – Kaliningrad region of Russia (Moskva Time).
LT – Lithuania (East European Time).
RU – Russia (Moskva Time).
▲ – See Tables **1915** and **1920**.

Other named trains:

1/2 BELORUSSIYA / BELARUS
3/4 MINSK
7/8 SLAVYANSKI EKSPRESS
29/30 YANTAR
77/78 NEMAN / NYOMAN
103/104 SUZORYE
105/106 BUH

RZhD, KTZh — VYAZMA - ADLER and ASTANA — 1980

km		Sko 70 A	Sko 70 C
	Berlin Hbf **56** d.	1515 ⑥	1515 ⑥
	Warszawa W. **1050** d.	2342 :	2342 :
	Brest Tsentr. **1950** d.	0720 ⑦	0720 ⑦
	Minsk **1950** d.	1127 :	1127 :
0	**Vyazma** d.	2000 :	2000 :
470	Ryazan d.	0337 ①	0337 ①
680	Michurinsk a.	0623 :	0623 :
680	Michurinsk d.	0703 :	0724 :
1058	Rossosh a.	| :	1347 :
1498	**Rostov na Donu** a.	| :	2237 :
2032	**Adler** a.	| :	1012 ②
753	Tambov d.	0824 :	...
1133	**Saratov** a.	1516 :	...
1133	**Saratov** d.	2325 :	...
3315	**Astana** ‡ a.	2038 ③	...

	Sko 104 D	Sko 107 B
Astana ‡ d.	...	1142 ②
Saratov a.	...	1036 ④
Saratov d.	...	1129 :
Tambov d.	...	1807 :
Adler d.	1713 ③	| :
Rostov na Donu d.	0251 ④	| :
Rossosh d.	0925 :	| :
Michurinsk a.	1443 :	1932 :
Michurinsk d.	2004 :	2004 :
Ryazan d.	2332 :	2332 :
Vyazma a.	0722 ⑤	0722 ⑤
Minsk **1950** a.	1445 :	1445 :
Brest Tsentr. **1950** a.	1856 :	1856 :
Warszawa W. **1050** a.	2351 ⑥	2351 ⑥
Berlin Hbf **56** a.	0900 :	0900 :

BCh, RZhD — MINSK - NOVOSIBIRSK — 1985

km		Sko 70 N
	Berlin Hbf **56** d.	1515 ⑥
	Warszawa W. **1050** d.	2342 :
	Brest Tsentr. **1950** d.	0720 ⑦
0	**Minsk 1950** d.	1136 :
212	Orsha **1950** § BY d.	1925 :
331	Smolensk **1950** § RU d.	2148 :
507	Vyazma **1950** d.	0056 ①
1346	Sergach a.	1643 :
1615	**Kazan** a.	2047 :
1919	Agryz a.	0131 ②
2265	Krasnoufimsk a.	0726 :
2490	**Yekaterinburg** (Sverdlovsk) a.	1131 :
2816	Tyumen a.	1729 :
3388	Omsk a.	0208 ③
4015	**Novosibirsk** a.	1052 :

	Sko 113 P
Novosibirsk d.	1858 ②
Omsk d.	0401 ③
Tyumen d.	1205 :
Yekaterinburg (Sverdlovsk) d.	1757 :
Krasnoufimsk d.	2138 :
Agryz d.	0317 ④
Kazan d.	0845 :
Sergach d.	1332 :
Vyazma **1950** a.	0454 ⑤
Smolensk **1950** § RU a.	0752 :
Orsha **1950** § BY a.	0824 :
Minsk 1950 a.	1201 :
Brest Tsentr. **1950** a.	1732 :
Warszawa W. **1050** a.	2351 ⑥
Berlin Hbf **56** a.	0900 :

NOTES FOR TABLES **1980** and **1985**:

A – 2 cl. Berlin - Saratov. 2 cl. Warszawa - Saratov (**108**) - Astana.
B – 2 cl. Astana - Saratov (**69**) - Warszawa. 2 cl. Saratov (**69**) - Berlin.
C – 1, 2 cl. Berlin - Michurinsk (**87**) - Adler.
D – 1, 2 cl. Adler - Michurinsk (**69**) - Berlin.

N – 2 cl. Berlin - Orsha (**64**) - Novosibirsk.
P – 2 cl. Novosibirsk - Brest (**69**) - Berlin.
‡ – Kazak Eastern Time (= Moskva Time + 3 hrs).

§ – : Osinovka (BY) / Krasnoye (RU).
BY – Belarus (East European Time).
RU – Russia (Moskva Time).

RZhD, MTZ, CR — TRANS-SIBERIAN RAILWAY (Summary Table) — 1990

For full details of this and other services east of Moskva, see the Thomas Cook Overseas Timetable in the blue cover

km	*All timings in Russia are in Moskva Time*	Sko 4 ②		Fir 2 Ra		Sko 20 ⑤	
0	**Moskva** Yaroslavskaya d.	2135	*1st day*	2125	*1st day*	2355	*1st day*
461	Nizhni-Novgorod (Gorki) d.	0349	*2nd day*	0339	*2nd day*	0623	*2nd day*
917	Vyatka (Kirov) d.	1008	*2nd day*	0958	*2nd day*	1241	*2nd day*
1397	Perm d.	1752	*2nd day*	1742	*2nd day*	2037	*2nd day*
1778	**Yekaterinburg** (Sverdlovsk) d.	2353	*2nd day*	2343	*2nd day*	0224	*3rd day*
2676	Omsk d.	1142	*3rd day*	1132	*3rd day*	1526	*3rd day*
3303	**Novosibirsk** d.	1918	*3rd day*	1933	*3rd day*	2312	*3rd day*
4065	Krasnoyarsk d.	0709	*4th day*	0745	*4th day*	1102	*4th day*
5153	**Irkutsk** d.	0013	*5th day*	0133	*5th day*	0432	*5th day*
5609	Ulan-Ude d.	0830	*5th day*	0910	*5th day*	1135	*5th day*
6266	Ulaanbaatar ‡ a.	0730	*6th day*	|	|	|	|
6166	Chita d.	|	|	1839	*5th day*	2112	*5th day*
7573	**Harbin** § a.	|	|	|	|	1250	*7th day*
8120	Shenyang § a.	|	|	|	|	1918	*7th day*
****	**Beijing** § a.	1404	*7th day*	|	|	0531	*8th day*
8493	Khabarovsk a.	...	...	1100	*7th day*	...	...
9259	**Vladivostok** a.	...	...	2348	*7th day*	...	...

All timings in Russia are in Moskva Time	Sko 3 ③		Fir 1 Rb		Sko 19 ⑥	
Vladivostok d.	...	...	1500	*1st day*	...	...
Khabarovsk d.	...	...	0345	*2nd day*	...	...
Beijing § d.	0745	*1st day*	|	|	2256	*1st day*
Shenyang § d.	|	|	|	|	0850	*2nd day*
Harbin § d.	|	|	|	|	1510	*2nd day*
Chita d.	|	|	2006	*3rd day*	2102	*3rd day*
Ulaanbaatar ‡ d.	1350	*2nd day*	|	|	|	|
Ulan-Ude d.	0340	*3rd day*	0531	*4th day*	0634	*4th day*
Irkutsk d.	1105	*3rd day*	1249	*4th day*	1345	*4th day*
Krasnoyarsk d.	0407	*4th day*	0652	*5th day*	0713	*5th day*
Novosibirsk d.	1617	*4th day*	1906	*5th day*	2005	*5th day*
Omsk d.	2356	*4th day*	0316	*6th day*	0307	*6th day*
Yekaterinburg (Sverdlovsk) d.	1208	*5th day*	1551	*6th day*	1608	*6th day*
Perm d.	1745	*5th day*	2129	*6th day*	2145	*6th day*
Vyatka (Kirov) d.	0101	*6th day*	0447	*7th day*	0501	*7th day*
Nizhni-Novgorod (Gorki) d.	0650	*6th day*	1046	*7th day*	1058	*7th day*
Moskva Yaroslavskaya a.	1428	*6th day*	1758	*7th day*	1813	*7th day*

R – ROSSIYA – 1, 2 cl. and 3 cl. Moskva - Vladivostok and v.v.
a – From Moskva on uneven dates [... *29, 1* ...].
b – From Vladivostok on even dates (also on the 1st, 3rd and 5th – not the 2nd, 4th or 6th – of Jan., Feb., Apr., June, Aug., Sept., Nov.).

**** *7622 km* via Ulaanbaatar (Trans-Mongolian Railway). *8961 km* via Harbin (Trans-Manchurian Railway).

‡ – Mongolian Time.
§ – Chinese Time.

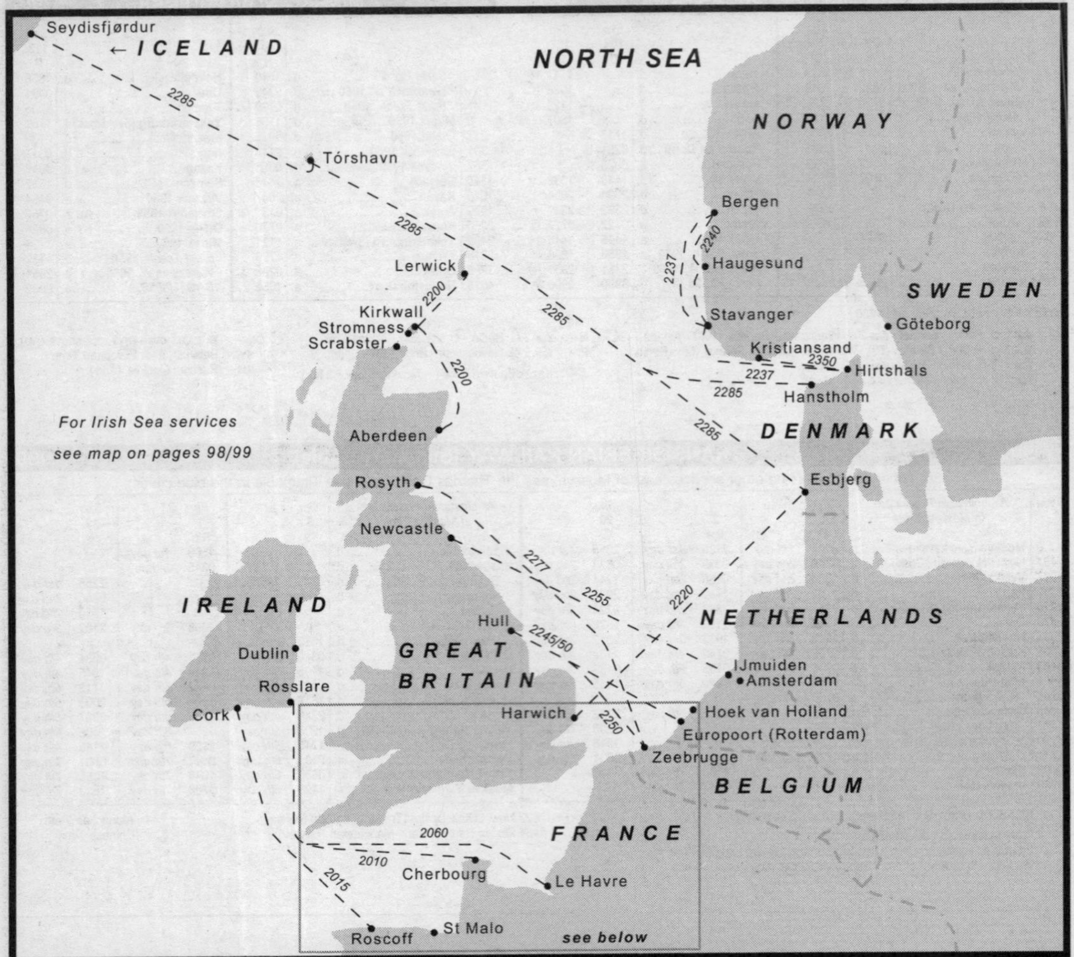
Seydisfjørdur
← ICELAND
NORTH SEA
NORWAY
2285
Tórshavn
2285
Bergen
2240
2237
Haugesund
Lerwick
2200
Kirkwall
Stromness
Scrabster
2285
Stavanger
SWEDEN
Göteborg
Kristiansand
2350
Hirtshals
2237
2285
Hanstholm
2200
For Irish Sea services
see map on pages 98/99
Aberdeen
2285
DENMARK
Rosyth
Esbjerg
Newcastle
2277
2255
2220
IRELAND
NETHERLANDS
Hull
2245/50
GREAT
BRITAIN
Dublin
IJmuiden
Amsterdam
Rosslare
Cork
Harwich
Hoek van Holland
2250
Europoort (Rotterdam)
Zeebrugge
BELGIUM
FRANCE
2060
2010
Cherbourg
2015
Le Havre
St Malo
Roscoff
see below

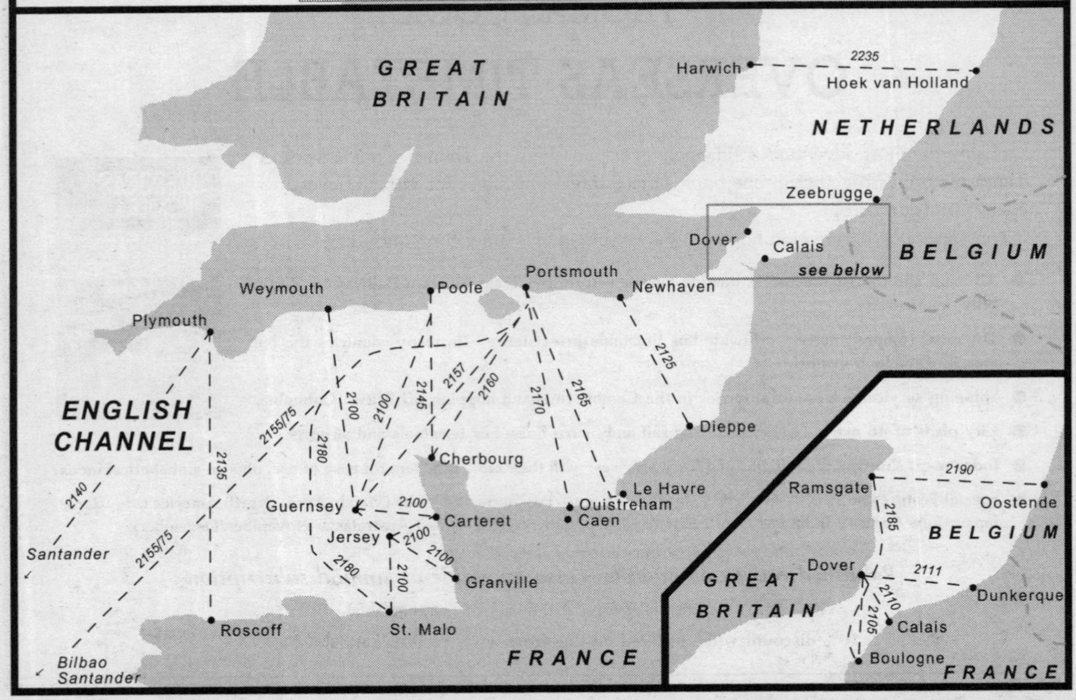
GREAT
BRITAIN
Harwich
2235
Hoek van Holland
NETHERLANDS
Zeebrugge
Dover
Calais
see below
BELGIUM
Weymouth
Poole
Portsmouth
Newhaven
Plymouth
2125
ENGLISH
CHANNEL
2100
2100
2145
2157
2160
2170
2165
Dieppe
2155/75
2180
2135
Cherbourg
2140
Guernsey
2100
Carteret
Le Havre
Ouistreham
Caen
Jersey
2100
2100
Santander
2155/75
2180
2100
Granville
Roscoff
St. Malo
Bilbao
Santander
FRANCE
Ramsgate
2190
Oostende
2185
BELGIUM
Dover
2111
GREAT
BRITAIN
2110
Dunkerque
2105
Calais
Boulogne
FRANCE

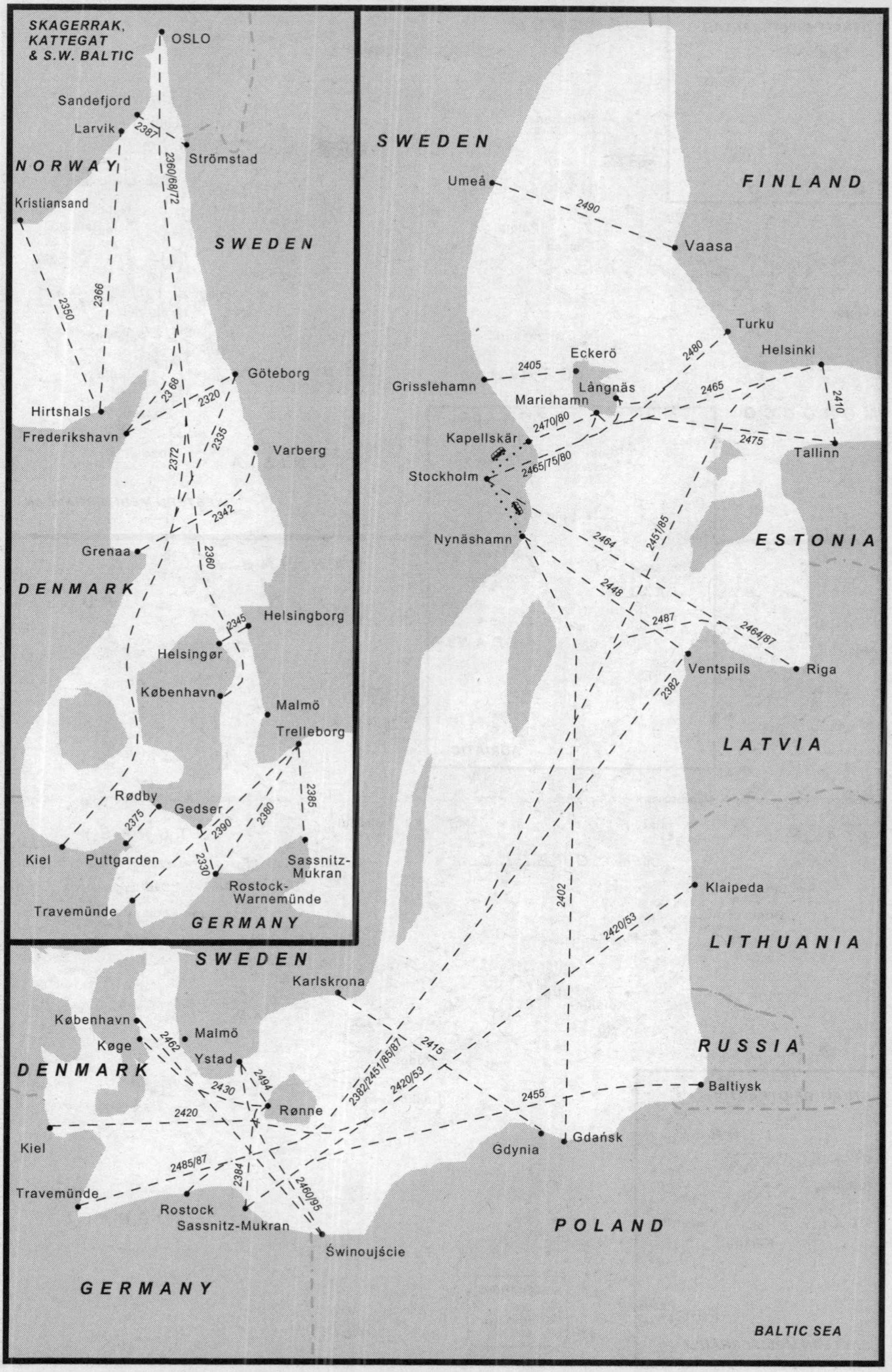
SKAGERRAK, KATTEGAT & S.W. BALTIC
OSLO
Sandefjord
Larvik
2387
Strömstad
NORWAY
2360/68/72
Kristiansand
SWEDEN
2350
2366
Göteborg
Hirtshals
2368
2320
Frederikshavn
2335
Varberg
2372
2342
Grenaa
2360
DENMARK
2345
Helsingborg
Helsingør
København
Malmö
Trelleborg
Rødby
Gedser
2385
2375
2390
2380
Kiel
Puttgarden
2330
Sassnitz-Mukran
Rostock-Warnemünde
Travemünde
GERMANY
SWEDEN
Umeå
2490
FINLAND
Vaasa
Turku
2480
Helsinki
Eckerö
2405
Grisslehamn
Långnäs
2465
Mariehamn
2410
2470/80
Kapellskär
2475
Tallinn
Stockholm
2465/75/80
Nynäshamn
2464
2451/85
ESTONIA
2448
2487
2464/87
Ventspils
Riga
2382
LATVIA
2402
Klaipeda
2420/53
LITHUANIA
SWEDEN
Karlskrona
København
Malmö
2462
Køge
Ystad
2415
RUSSIA
DENMARK
2494
2430
2382/2451/85/87
2420/53
Baltiysk
Rønne
2455
2420
Kiel
Gdynia
Gdańsk
2485/87
2384
2460/95
Travemünde
Rostock
Sassnitz-Mukran
POLAND
Świnoujście
GERMANY
BALTIC SEA

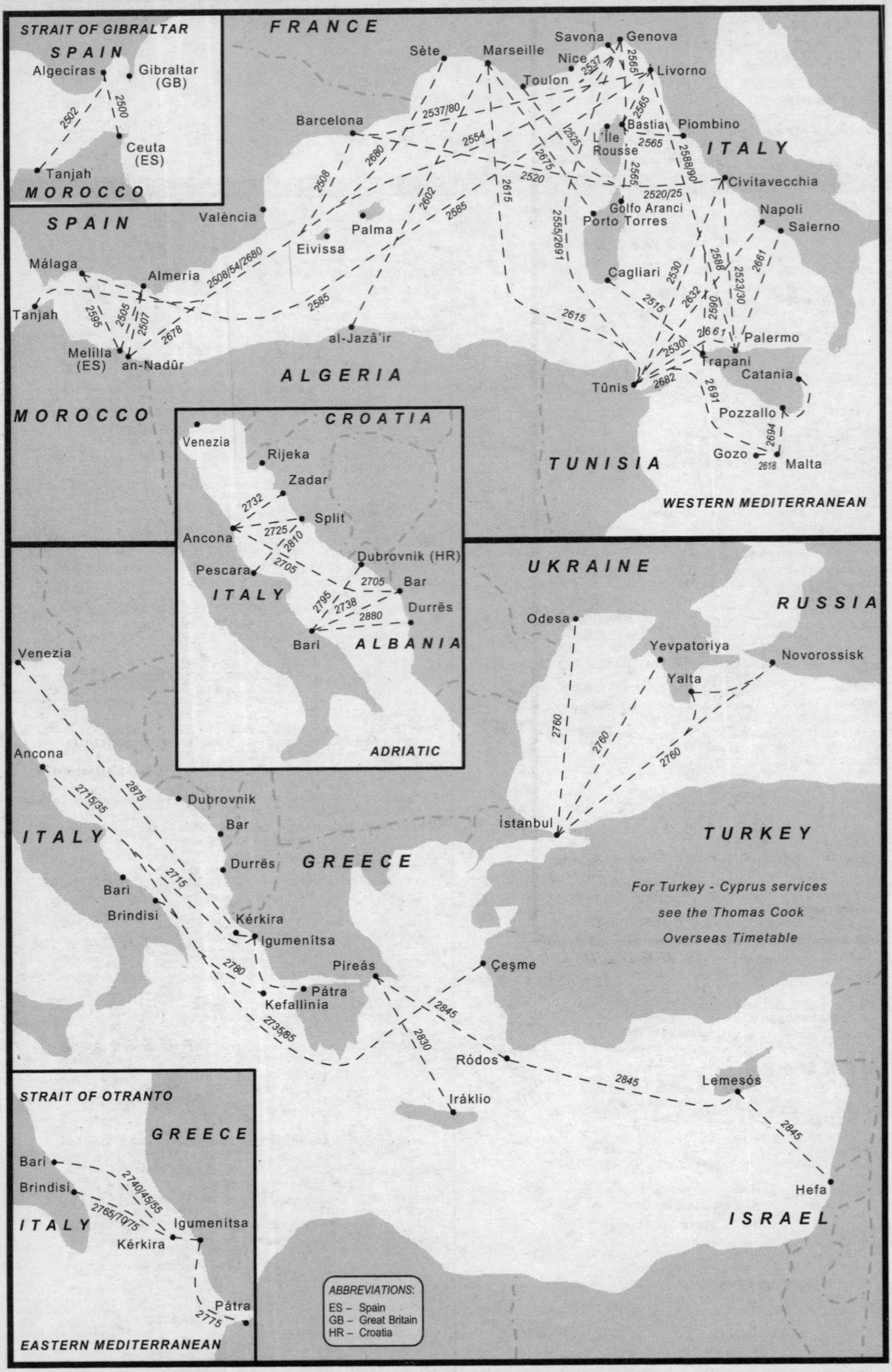

For domestic shipping routes please see relevant country maps

SHIPPING CONTENTS

SHIPPING OPERATORS

A G EMS: Postfach 11 54, 26691 Emden-Außenhafen.
✆ +49 (0)1805 180 182, fax +49 21 / 89 07 405.

ALILAURO: Via Caracciolo 11, 80122 Napoli.
✆ +39 081 76 14 909, fax +39 081 76 14 250.

ALSTRAFIKKEN: ✆ +45 70 23 15 15.

ANEK LINES: 32 Akti Possidonos, 185 31 Pireás.
✆ +30 210 4118611, fax +30 210 4115465.
UK agent: Viamare, Suite 3, 447 Kenton Road, Harrow, HA3 0XY. ✆ 020 8206 3420, fax 020 8206 1332.

ARKADIA LINES: Kifissias Ave 215, 15124 Maroussi, Greece.
✆ +30 210 6123402, fax +30 210 6126206.
UK agent: Viamare (see Anek Lines) ✆ 020 8206 3420, fax 020 8206 1332.

AZZURRA LINE: Old Bakery Street, Valletta, Malta.
Italy agent: Pier Paola Santelia, Stazione marittima, Bari ✆ +39 080 52 31 824, fax +39 080 52 30 287.
Croatia agent: Elite Shipping Agency, Gruska obala 1, 20000 Dubrovnik, Croatia.
✆ +385 (20) 31 31 78, fax +385 (20) 31 31 80.

BALEÀRIA (EUROLÍNIES MARÍTIMES): Estació Marítima, 03700 Dénia.
✆ +34 902 160 180, fax +34 (96) 578 76 06.

BLUE LINE: Postboks 36, Englandsvej 370, DK 2770 Kastrup, Denmark.
Italy agent: ✆ +39 071 20 40 41, fax +39 071 20 26 18.
Croatia agent: ✆ +385 21 352 533, fax +385 21 352 482.
UK agent: Viamare (see Anek Lines) ✆ 020 8206 3420, fax 020 8206 1332.

BLUE STAR FERRIES: 26, Akti Posidonos, 185 31 Pireás.
✆ +30 210 422 5000, fax +30 210 422 5265.
UK agent: Viamare (see Anek Lines) ✆ 020 8206 3420, fax 020 8206 1332.

BORNHOLMSTRAFIKKEN: Havnen, 3700 Rønne.
✆ +45 56 95 18 66, fax +45 56 91 07 66.

BRITTANY FERRIES: Millbay, Plymouth, PL1 3EW. ✆ 08709 076 103.
Wharf Road, Portsmouth, PO2 8RU. ✆ 0990 360 360, fax 023 9289 2204.
42 Grand Parade, Cork. ✆ +353 (0)21 277801, fax +353 (0)21 277262.
Gare Maritime, Port du Bloscon, 29688 Roscoff. ✆ +33 825 828 828.
Estación Maritima, 39002 Santander. ✆ +34 942 36 06 11.

BUMERANG SHIPPING COMPANY TOURISM TRAVEL & TRADE S.A.: Rihtim Cad. Veli Alemdar Han Kat. 6, 80030 Karaköy - Istanbul.
✆ +90 (0)212 251 7373, fax +90 (0)212 251 1472.

CAREMAR: Campania Regionale Marittima S.p.A., Molo Beverello, 80133 Napoli.
✆ +39 081 58 05 111, fax +39 081 55 14 551.

COLOR LINE: Postboks 1422 Vika, 0115 Oslo.
✆ +47 810 00 811, fax +47 22 83 07 76.

COMARIT: 7 Rue du Mexique, Tanjah (Tangiers), Morocco.
✆ + 212 (0)9 32 00 32, fax + 212 (0)9 32 59 00.

COMPAGNIE MAROCAINE DE NAVIGATION (COMANAV):
7 Boulevard de la Résistance, Casablanca 05.
✆ +212 (0)2 30 30 12, fax +212 (0)2 30 84 55.
U.K. Agent: Southern Ferries, 30 Churton Street, Victoria, London SW1V 2LP.
✆ 0844 815 7785, fax 0844 815 7795.

COMPAGNIE TUNISIENNE DE NAVIGATION: Dag Hammarskjoeld Avenue 5, Tûnis.
✆ +216 (1) 341777, fax +216 (1) 335714.
UK agent: Southern Ferries (see Comanav). ✆ 0844 815 7785, fax 0844 815 7795.
France agent: SNCM, Marseille. ✆ +33 (0)4 91 56 30 10, fax +33 (0)4 91 56 31 00.

CONDOR FERRIES LTD.: New Harbour Rd. South, Hamworthy, Poole, BH15 4AJ.
✆ 01202 207 216.
The Quay, Weymouth, Dorset DT4 8DX. ✆ 01305 761 551, fax 01305 760 776.
Jersey: ✆ 01534 872 240. Guernsey 12023 (local calls only).
Reservations: ✆ 0870 243 5140.

CORSICA FERRIES: (including SARDINIA FERRIES), 5 bis, Rue Chanoine Leschi, 20296 Bastia. ✆ +33 (0)4 95 32 95 95, fax +33 (0)4 95 32 14 71.

DESTINATION GOTLAND: PO Box 1234, 621 23 Visby, Gotland, Sweden.
✆ +46 (0)498 20 10 20, fax +46 (0)498 20 18 90.

DFDS LISCO: Ostuferhafen 15, 24149, Kiel.
✆ +49 (0)431 20976 420, fax +49 (0)431 20976 102.
Reservations: ✆ +370 46 393616.

DFDS SEAWAYS: Scandinavia House, Parkeston Quay, Harwich CO12 4QG.
✆ 0871 522 9955; Reservations: ✆ 08702 520 524.
International Ferry Terminal, Royal Quays, North Shields, NE29 6EE.
Axelborg Vesterbrogade 4A, 1620 København V. ✆ +45 33 156341, fax +45 33 936330.
Skandiahamnen, P.O. Box 8895, 402 72 Göteborg. ✆ +46 (0)31 65 06 00, fax +46 (0)31 54 3925.
Van-den-Smissen Strasse 4, 2000 Hamburg 50. ✆ +49 (0)40 389 0371, fax +49 (0)40 389 03120.
P.O. Box 548, 1970 BA, IJmuiden. ✆ +31 (0)255 534 546, fax +31 (0)255 535 349.

ECKERÖ LINJEN: Keskuskatu 1, 00100 Helsinki.
✆ +358 (0)9 22 88 544, fax (0)9 22 88 5222.
Torggatan 2, Box 158, 22101 Mariehamn.
✆ +358 (0)18 28 000, fax +358 (0)18 28 380.
Grisslehamn: ✆ +46 (0)175 30 920, fax +46 (0)175 30 820.
Eckerö: ✆ +358 (0)18 28 300, fax +358 (0)18 38 230.

EIMSKIP: Iceland Steamship Company Ltd, P.O. Box 220, 121 Reykjavik.
✆ +354 525 7000, fax +354 525 7179.

ENDEAVOR LINES: Posidonos Av 35, 183 44 Moschato.
✆ +30 210 9405222, fax +30 210 9405066.
Reservations: Nautilus Shipping Agencies, 72 Othonos Amalias Av, 26221 Patras.
✆ +30 2610 620061 / 622676, fax +30 2610 620031.
Brindisi: +39 0831 548116, fax +39 0831 548118.

E N T M V: Enterprise Nationale de Transport Maritime de Voyageurs, Gare Maritime, Quai d'Ajaccio, al-Jazâ'ir. ✆ +213 (021) 42 30 48.
Alacant: ✆ +34 965 14 90 10, fax +34 965 20 82 90.

EUROFERRIES: www.euroferries.co.uk

FANØTRAFIKKEN: ✆ +45 70 23 15 15.

FERRIMAROC: Muelle de Ribera s/n, 04002 Almería.
✆ +34 (50) 27 48 00, fax +34 (50) 27 63 66.
UK agent: Wasteels London. ✆ 020 7834 7066, fax 020 7630 7628.

FERRYS RAPIDOS DEL SUR (FRS): C/ Alcade Juan Núñez 10, Edificio Santa Catalina, Bloque 2, Bajo A, 11380 Tarifa - Cádiz. ✆ +34 956 68 18 30, fax +34 956 62 71 80.

FINNLINES DEUTSCHLAND AG: Finnlines Passagierdienst, Einsiedelstrasse 45, 23554 Lübeck. ✆ +49 (0)451 1507 443, fax +49 (0)451 1507 444.
Finland agent: Nordic Ferry Center, Itämerenkatu 21, 5th floor, 00180 Helsinki.
✆ +358 (0)9 2510 200, fax +358 (0)9 2510 2022.
Finnlines UK Ltd., 8 Heron Quay, London. ✆ (0)207 519 7300, fax (0)207 536 0255.

FJORD LINE: Rosenkrantzgt 3, Postboks 4008 Dreggen, 5023 Bergen.
✆ +47 55 323 770, fax +47 55 323 815.

FLAGGRUTEN: Partrederiet Flagruten ANS, Postboks 2005 Nordnes, 5024 Bergen.
✆ +47 55 23 87 00, +47 55 23 87 01.

FÖRDE REEDEREI SEETOURISTIK: Norderhofenden 19 - 20, D 24937 Flensburg.
✆ +49 (0)461 864 0, fax +49 (0)461 864 30.

GOZO CHANNEL: Hay Wharf, Sa Maison, Malta.
✆ +356 21 243964.

GRANDI NAVI VELOCI: Via Fieschi 17, 16121 Genova.
✆ +39 010 58 93 31, fax +39 010 55 09 225.
UK agent: Viamare (see Anek Lines) ✆ 020 8206 3420, fax 020 8206 1332.

GRIMALDI FERRIES: Via M. Campodisola 13, Napoli.
✆ +39 081 496 444, fax +39 081 551 7716.
UK agent: Viamare (see Anek Lines) ✆ 020 8206 3420, fax 020 8206 1332.

HURTIGRUTEN (NORWEGIAN COASTAL VOYAGE):
Havnegata 2, N - 8501 Narvik. ✆ +47 76 96 76 00.
Booking ✆ +47 810 30000, +47 76 11 82 45.
Kirkegata 1, N - 9291 Tromsø.

INTERNATIONAL MARITIME TRANSPORT CORPORATION (I M T C): 122 Bd Anfa, Casablanca. ✆ +212 (0)2 299 209, fax +212 (0)2 299 202.
Spain agent: Vapores Suardiaz Andalucia S.A. (VS), Avda. Del Puerto 1 - 6, 11006 Cádiz. ✆ +34 956 282 111, fax +34 956 282 846.

IRISH FERRIES: 2 - 4 Merrion Row, Dublin 2. ✆ +353 (0)1 890 31 31 31.
Corn Exchange Building, Ground Floor, Brunswick Street, Liverpool L2 7TP.
✆ 08705 17 17 17, fax 0151 236 0562.

ISLE OF MAN STEAM PACKET CO.: Imperial Buildings, Douglas, Isle of Man IM1 2BY.
✆ 08705 523 523, fax 01624 645697.

ISLES OF SCILLY STEAMSHIP CO.: The Weighbridge, Quay Street, Penzance, Cornwall, TR18 4BZ. ✆ 0845 710 5555, fax 01736 51223.

ITALIAN RAILWAYS: Piazza della Croce Rossa, 00161 Roma.
✆ +39 06 884 0724, fax +39 06 883 1108.

JADROLINIJA: Riva 16, 51000 Rijeka, Croatia.
✆ +385 (51) 66 61 11, fax +385 (51) 21 31 16.
UK agent: Viamare (see Anek Lines) ✆ 020 8206 3420, fax 020 8206 1332.

KYSTLINK: Kongshavn 8, 3970 Langesund, Norway.
✆ +47 35 96 68 00, fax +47 35 96 68 01.
Denmark: ✆ +45 96 56 00 68, fax +45 96 56 00 69.
Sweden: ✆ +46 526 14 000, fax +46 526 14 125.

L D LINES: Continental Ferry Port, Wharf Road, Portsmouth, PO2 8QW.
✆ 0870 428 4335, fax 01235 84 56 08.
Terminal de la Citadelle, BP 90746, F-76060 Le Havre. +33 2 35 19 78 78, fax +33 (0)2 35 19 78 82..

LINDA LINE OY: Makasiiniterminaali, 00140 Helsinki.
✆ +358 (0)9 668 9700, fax +358 (0)9 668 97070.
Tallinn: ✆ +372 -6 412 412.

LINEAS FRED. OLSEN: Polígono Industrial de Añaza, 38109 Santa Cruz de Tenerife.
✆ +34 (902) 10 01 07, fax +34 (922) 62 82 32.

MANCHE ÎLES EXPRESS: Albert Quay, St Helier, Jersey.
✆ 01534 880 756, fax 01534 880 314.
Terminal Building, New Jetty, White Rock, St Peter Port, Guernsey
✆ 01481 701 316, fax 01481 701 319.

MARMARA LINES:
Germany agent: RECA Handels GmbH, Neckarstrasse 37, 71065 Sindelfingen.
✆ +49 (0)7031 86 60 10, fax +49 (0)7031 87 65 68.

MED LINK LINES: 49 Corso Garibaldi Str., 72100 Brindisi.
✆ +39 0831 52 76 67, fax +39 0831 56 40 70.

MEDMAR LINEE LAURO: Piazza Municipo 88, 80133 Napoli. ✆ +39 081 551 33 52, fax +39 081 552 43 29.
UK agent: Viamare (see Anek Lines) ✆ 020 8206 3420, fax 020 8206 1332.

MINOAN LINES: 2 Vassileos Konstantinou Ave. (Stadion), 116 35 Athína.
✆ +30 210 7512356, fax +30 210 7520540.
UK agent: Magnum Travel, 747 Green Lanes, Winchmore Hill, London N21 3SA.
✆ 020 8360 5353, fax 020 8360 1056.

MOBY LINES: Via Ninci 1, 57037 Portoferraio, Italy.
✆ +39 0565 91 81 01, fax +39 0565 91 67 58.
UK agent: SMS, London. ✆ 020 7244 8422, fax 020 7244 9829.

MOLS-LINIEN: Færgehavnen, 8400 Ebeltoft.
✆ +45 89 52 52 52, fax +45 89 52 52 92.

MONTENEGRO LINES: Barska Plovidba, Obala 13 jula bb, 85000 Bar.
✆ +381 85 312-366/312-809/311-465, fax +381 85 311-652.

NAUTAS FERRY:
✆ +34 902 161 181, fax +34 (96) 578 76 06.

NAVIERA ARMAS: Juan Rejón 32-5y6, 35008 Las Palmas de Gran Canaria, España.
✆ +34 (928) 22 72 82, fax +34 (928) 46 99 91.

NAVIGAZIONE LIBERA del GOLFO: Molo Beverello, 80133 Napoli.
✆ +39 081 55 20 763, fax +39 081 55 25 589.

NORDIC JET LINE: Kanavaterminaali, 00161 Helsinki.
✆ +358 (0)9 681 770, fax +358 (0)9 681 77 111.

NORDIC FERRY SERVICES: www.nordic-ferry.com

NORDLANDSEKSPRESSEN: OVDS, Bodø.
✆ +47 75 52 10 20, fax +47 75 52 08 35.

NORFOLK LINE: Reservations: ✆ 0870 870 1020.

NORFOLK LINE IRISH SEA FERRIES: 12 Quays Terminal, Tower Road, Birkenhead, CH41 1FE. ✆ 0151 906 2700, fax 0151 906 2718.
Victoria Business Park, 9 West Bank Road, Belfast, BT3 9JL. ✆ 028 9077 9090.
Reservations: UK ✆ 0870 600 4321, Republic of Ireland ✆ +353 (0)1 819 2999.

NORTHLINK FERRIES: Kiln Corner, Ayre Road, Kirkwall, Orkney KW15 1QX.
✆ 01856 851 144, fax 01856 851 155.
Reservations: ✆ 0845 6000 449.

P & O FERRIES:
United Kingdom: Channel House, Channel View Road, Dover, CT17 9TJ.
King George Dock, Hedon Road, Hull HU9 5QA.
Peninsular House, Wharf Road, Portsmouth PO2 8TA.
✆ 08705 980 333.
Belgium: Leopold II Dam 13, Kaaien 106-108, 8380, Zeebrugge.
✆ +32 070 70 77 71.
France: 41 Place d'Armes, BP 888, 62225, Calais.
Gare Maritime Transmanche, BP 46, 50652, Cherbourg.
Terminal de la Citadelle, BP 439, 76057, Le Havre.
✆ +33 0825 12 01 56.
Netherlands: Europoort Beneluxhaven, Havennummer 5805, Rotterdam/Europoort, Postbus 1123, 3180 AC, Rozenburg.
✆ +31 020 200 8333.
Spain: Cosme Echevarrieta 1, 48009, Bilbao.
✆ +34 902 02 04 61.

P & O IRISH SEA: Larne Harbour, Larne BT40 1AQ.
✆ 0870 24 24 777.

POLFERRIES: Polish Baltic Shipping Co., ul. Portowa 41, 78 100 Kolobrzeg.
✆ +48 (0)965 252 11, fax +48 (0)965 266 12.

POSEIDON LINES: 32 Alkyonidon Avenue, 166 73 Voula, Athína.
✆ +30 210 965 8300, fax +30 210 965 8310.
UK agent: Viamare (see Anek Lines) ✆ 020 8206 3420, fax 020 8206 1332.

REEDEREI CASSEN EILS: Bei der Alten Liebe 12, 27472 Cuxhaven.
✆ +49 (0)4721 35082, fax +49 (0)4721 31161.

RG LINE: Satamaterminaali, Vaskiluoto, 65170 Vaasa.
Bookings: ✆ 0207 716 810, fax 0207 716 820.

SALAMIS LINES: 28th October Avenue, P.O. Box 531, Limassol, Cyprus.
✆ +357 (0)5 35 55 55, fax +357 (0)5 36 44 10.
Greece agent: Salamis Lines (Hellas), 9 Filellinon Str., 18536 Pireás.
✆ +30 210 429 4325, fax +30 210 429 4557.
Salamis Cruise Lines: ✆ +357 2586 0000, fax +357 2537 4437.

SAMSØTRAFIKKEN: Strandbakkevej 2, Kolby Kås, DK-8305 Samsø, Denmark.
✆ +45 70 10 17 44.

SARDINIA FERRIES: see Corsica Ferries.

SCANDLINES: DSB Kunde, Vester Farimagsgade 3, København.
✆ +45 33 151515, fax +45 33 151020.
Gedser: ✆ +45 54 160 055, fax +45 54 160 0533.
Helsingborg: ✆ +46 (0)42 186 100, fax +46 (0)42 187 410.
Helsingør: ✆ +45 49 258 892, fax +45 49 258 895.
Rødby: ✆ +45 54 605 166, fax +45 54 605 834.
Rønne: ✆ +45 56 951 069, fax +45 56 958 910.
Trelleborg: ✆ +46 410 65000, fax +46 410 13386.

SCANDLINES DEUTSCHLAND GmbH: Am Warnowkai 8, 18147 Rostock Seehafen.
✆ +49 (0)381 673 12 92, fax +49 (0)381 673 12 99.
Puttgarden: ✆ +49 (0)4371 86 51 61, fax +49 (0)4371 86 51 62.
Sassnitz: ✆ +49 (0)38392 644 20, fax +49 (0)38392 644 29.
Klaipeda: ✆ +370 6 314 376, fax +370 6 311 121.

SCANDLINES EUROSEABRIDGE: Uberseehafen, 18147 Rostock.
✆ +49 (0)381 458 4448, fax +49 (0)381 458 4442.

SEA CONTAINERS FINLAND: Makasiiniterminaali M4, Eteläsatama, 00140 Helsinki.
✆ +358 9 180 4678, fax ✆ +358 9 180 4699.
Reservations: ✆ +372 610 0000, fax +372 610 0011.

SEAFRANCE: Eastern Docks, Dover, Kent CT16 1JA. ✆ 0871 663 2546.

SILJA LINE: Mannerheimintie 2, 00100 Helsinki.
✆ +358 (0)9 180 4422, fax +358 (0)9 180 4279.
Reservations: ✆ +358 600 174 552.

SIREMAR: Sicilia Regionale Marittima, Via Principe di Belmonte 1/c, 90139 Palermo.
✆ +39 091 58 26 88, fax +39 091 58 22 67.

SMYRIL LINE: Jonas Broncksgøta 37, Postboks 370, 110 Tórshavn.
✆ +298 315 900, fax +298 315 707.

SNAV FERRIES: Via Giordano Bruno 84, 80122 Napoli.
✆ +39 081 428 5555, fax +39 081 428 5259.
UK agent: Viamare (see Anek Lines) ✆ 020 8206 3420, fax 020 8206 1332.

S N C M: Société Nationale Maritime Corse Mediterranée, 61, Boulevard des Dames, 13002 Marseille. ✆ +33 (0)4 91 56 30 10, fax +33 (0)4 91 56 31 00.
UK agent: Southern Ferries (see Comanav). ✆ 0844 815 7785, fax 0844 815 7795.

SPLIT TOURS: ✆ +385 (0)21 352 533.

STENA LINE: Stena House, Station Approach, Holyhead, LL65 1DQ. ✆ 08705 70 70 70.
Prince's Dock, 14 Clarendon Road, Belfast, BT1 3GB. ✆ 08705 204 204.
The Ferry Terminal, Dun Laoghaire, Co. Dublin. ✆ 01 204 7777.
Masthuggskajen, 405 19 Göteborg. ✆ +46 (0)31 704 00 00, fax +46 (0)31 85 85 95.
Trafikhavn, 9900 Frederikshavn. ✆ +45 98 424366, fax +45 98 422750.
Box 94, 432 22, Varberg. ✆ +46 (0)340 690 900, fax +46 (0)340 851 25.
Box 150 8500, Grenaa. ✆ +45 87 58 75 00, fax +45 86 32 01 18.
Box 104 371 22, Karlskrona. ✆ +46 (0)455 665 50, fax +46 (0)455 220 99.

SUPERFAST FERRIES: 157 C. Karamanli Av., 166 73 Voula, Athína.
✆ +30 210 969 1100, fax +30 210 969 1190.
Reservations: ✆ +30 210 89 19 130, fax +30 210 89 19 139.
United Kingdom: The Terminal Building, Port of Rosyth, Fife, KY11 2XP.
✆ 0870 234 0870, fax 0138 360 8020.
UK agent: Viamare (see Anek Lines) ✆ 020 8206 3420, fax 020 8206 1332.
Germany: ✆ +49 451 88 00 61 66, fax +49 451 88 00 61 29.

SWANSEA CORK FERRIES: 52 South Mall, Cork, Ireland.
✆ +353 (0)21 271166, fax +353 (0)21 275061.
Swansea: ✆ 01792 456116, fax 01792 644356.

TALLINK: Erottajankatu 19, 00130 Helsinki.
✆ +358 (0)9 2282 1211, fax +358 (0)9 635311.

TIRRENIA: Rione Sirignano 2, Casella Postale 438, 80121 Napoli.
✆ +39 081 720 11 11, fax +39 081 720 14 41.
UK agent: S.M.S. Travel & Tourism, 40/42 Kenway Road, London SW5 0RA.
✆ 020 7373 6548, fax 020 7244 9829.

TOREMAR: Via Calafati 6, Casella Postale 482, 57123 Livorno.
✆ +39 0586 22 45 11, fax +39 0586 22 46 24.

TRANSEUROPA FERRIES: Slijkensesteenweg 2, B-8400 Oostende.
✆ +32 (0)59 340 260, fax +32 (0)59 340 261.
Ferry Terminal, New Port, Ramsgate CT11 9FT. ✆ 01843 595522.

TRANSMANCHE FERRIES: Harbour, Newhaven, BN9 0BG. ✆ 0800 917 12 01.
Quai Gaston Lalitte, 76200 Dieppe. ✆ +33 (0)800 650 100, fax +33 (0)2 32 14 52 00.

TRASMEDITERRANEA: Obenque 4, Alameda de Osuna, 28042 Madrid.
✆ +34 (91) 322 91 00, fax +34 (91) 322 91 10.
UK agent: Southern Ferries (see Comanav). ✆ 0844 815 7785, fax 0844 815 7795.

TT-LINE: Mattentwiete 8, 20457 Hamburg.
✆ +49 (0)40 3601 442 446, fax +49 (0)40 3601 407.

UKRFERRY SHIPPING COMPANY: 4a Sabanskiy lane, Odesa, 65014, Ukraine.
✆ +380 (482) 344 059, fax +380 (482) 348 297, 348 108.

UNITY LINE: Plac Rodła 8, 70419, Szczecin, Poland.
✆ +48 (0)91 35 95 592, fax +48 (0)91 35 95 673.
Sweden agent: Pol-Line AB, Färjeterminalen, 27139 Ystad.
✆ +46 (0)411 55 69 00, fax +46 (0)411 55 69 53.

USTICA LINES: Via A. Staita 23, 91100 Trapani, Sicily.
✆ +39 092 322 200, fax + 39 092 323 289.
Reservations: ✆ +39 0923 873 813, fax +39 0923 593 200.

VENTOURIS FERRIES: 91 Pireos Avenue, 185 41 Pireás.
✆ +30 210 4825815, fax +30 210 4832919.

VIKING LINE: P.O. Box 35, 22101 Mariehamn.
✆ +358 (0)18 26011, fax +358 (0)18 15811.
UK agent: Emagine UK Ltd, Leigh, WN7 1AZ. ✆ 01942 262662, fax 01942 606500.

VIRTU FERRIES LTD: Sea Passenger Terminal, Pinto Road, Valletta, Malta.
Reservations: ✆ +356 21 228777, fax +356 21 235435.

CAIRNRYAN - LARNE 2005

P & O Irish Sea **by ship** Journey 1 hour 45 minutes **2009 service**

January 1 - March 12 and October 6 - December 31

Depart Cairnryan: 0415①②③④⑤⑥, 0730, 1030①②③④⑤⑥, 1300⑦, 1330①②③④⑤⑥, 1630, 2000, 2300⑦, 2359①②③④⑤.

Depart Larne: 0415①②③④⑤⑥, 0730, 1030①②③④⑤⑥, 1300⑦, 1330①②③④⑤⑥, 1630, 2000, 2300⑦, 2359①②③④⑤.

March 13 - October 5

Depart Cairnryan: 0415①②③④⑤⑥, 0730, 1030, 1300⑦, 1330①②③④⑤⑥, 1630, 2000, 2300⑦, 2359①②③④⑤.

Depart Larne: 0415①②③④⑤⑥, 0730, 1030①②③④⑤⑥, 1300⑦, 1330①②③④⑤⑥, 1630, 2000, 2300⑦, 2359①②③④⑤.

Subject to alteration during Xmas/New Year period.

P & O Irish Sea **by fast ferry** **March 13 - October 5, 2009 (No winter service)**

Cairnryan		Larne	Larne		Cairnryan
1500	→	1600	1255	→	1355

CHERBOURG - ROSSLARE 2010

Irish Ferries **Service to December 21, 2009**

Cherbourg		Rosslare	
1800	→	1130	June 1, 3, 9, 15, 17, 23, 29, July 1, 7, 13, 15, 19, 21, 27, 29, Aug. 2, 4, 8, 10, 12, 16, 18, 20, 24, 26, 30, Sept. 1, 3, 7, 9, 13, 15, 21, 23, 27, 29.
2000	→	1400	② Oct. 6 - Dec. 15 (also Dec. 21).
2130	→	1430	⑥ Oct. 3 - Dec. 19.
2130	→	1530	④ Oct. 1 - Dec. 17.
Rosslare		**Cherbourg**	
1530	→	1100	May 17, 19, 25, 31, June 2, 8, 14, 16, 22, 28, 30, July 6, 12, 14, 18, 20, 26, 28, Aug. 1, 3, 7, 9, 11, 15, 17, 19, 23, 25, 29, 31, Sept. 2, 6, 8, 12, 14, 20, 22, 26, 28, 30.
1800	→	1400	⑦ Feb. 1 - May 10, Oct. 4 - Dec. 20.
2300	→	1830	③⑤ Feb. 4 - May 13, Oct. 2 - Dec. 18.

CORK - ROSCOFF 2015

Brittany Ferries **Service to October 31, 2009 (No winter service)**

Sailings from Cork (Ringaskiddy) and Roscoff.

Cork		Roscoff		Roscoff		Cork	
1600	→	0700	⑥ Apr. 4 - Oct. 31.	2130	→	1030	⑤ Apr. 3 - Oct. 30.

Departure times may vary owing to tidal conditions.

DOUGLAS - BELFAST 2020

Isle Of Man Steam Packet Co. **by SEACAT catamaran** **2009 service (No winter service)**

Sailings from Belfast Donegall Quay.

Douglas		Belfast		Belfast		Douglas	
0600	→	0855	Aug. 23, 30 only.	1045	→	1340	See note E.
0700§	→	0955	See note E.	1100	→	1355	Aug. 23, 30 only.
1000	→	1255	See note H.	1400	→	1655	See note H.
1200	→	1455	Sept. 13, 27 only.	1600	→	1855	Sept. 13, 27 only.
1345	→	1640	See note F.	1815	→	2110	See note J.
				1900	→	2155	May 27, 29 only.

E – Apr. 5, 8, 12, 16, 19, 30, May 5, 14, 17, 21, July 12, 17, Sept. 6, 10, 24.
F – May 27, 29, July 5, 20, 26, Aug. 2, 9, 16.
H – July 2, 8, 23, 30, Aug. 6, 13, 20, 25, Sept. 3.
J – July 5, 20, 26, Aug. 2, 9, 16.
§ – July 17 depart 0630.

A special service will operate during the TT Race period (May 30 - June 28)

DOUGLAS - DUBLIN 2025

Isle Of Man Steam Packet Co. **by SEACAT catamaran** **2009 service (No winter service)**

Sailings from Dublin North Wall.

Douglas		Dublin		Dublin		Douglas	
0700	→	0955	Apr. 13 only.	1045	→	1340	Apr. 13 only.
1000	→	1255	See note A.	1400	→	1655	See note E.
1345	→	1640	See note B.	1815	→	2110	See note C.
1530	→	1825	Apr. 10 only.	1915	→	2210	See note D.
1800	→	2055	Sept. 4 only.	2130	→	0025	Sept. 4 only.

A – May 24, July 3, 6, 10, 16, 19, 24, 31, Aug. 7, 14, 21, 24, 27, 31, Sept. 7.
B – May 28, July 13, 27, Aug. 3, 10, 17.
C – July 6, 13, 19, 27, Aug. 3, 10, 17, 31.
D – Apr. 10, May 28.
E – July 3, 10, 16, 24, 31, Aug. 7, 14, 21, 24, 27, Sept. 7.

A special service will operate during the TT Race period (May 30 - June 28)

FISHGUARD - ROSSLARE 2030

Stena Line **by ship** **2009 service (No service Dec. 25, 26)**

Fishguard		Rosslare		Rosslare		Fishguard	
0245	→	0615		0900	→	1230	
1430	→	1800	Not Dec. 24.	2115	→	0030	Not Dec. 24.

Stena Line **by *LYNX* catamaran** **May 14 - September 12, 2009 (No winter service)**

Fishguard		Rosslare	Rosslare		Fishguard
1130	→	1330	0800	→	1000
1830	→	2030	1500	→	1700

FLEETWOOD - LARNE 2032

Stena Line **by ship** Journey 8 hours **2009 service**

Conveys passengers with vehicles only

Departure times vary – contact operator for details

HEYSHAM - DOUGLAS 2035

Isle Of Man Steam Packet Co. **by ship** **Service to January 5, 2010 (No service Dec. 25)**

Heysham		Douglas	
0215	→	0545	Daily June 17 - Dec. 19, Dec. 21 - 24, 27, Dec. 29 - 31, Jan. 2 - 5 (not June 4 - 6, 21, July 5, Aug. 16, Sept. 13, Oct. 4, Nov. 1, Dec. 6).
0300	→	0630	June 4 - 6 only.
1415	→	1745	Daily June 17 - Nov. 6; ①②③④⑤ Nov. 9 - Jan. 5.
Douglas		**Heysham**	
0815	→	1145	Aug. 20 - 22, 28, 29 only.
0845	→	1215	Daily June 17 - Nov. 6; ①②③④⑤ Nov. 9 - Jan. 5 (not Aug. 20 - 22, 28, 29).
1945	→	2315	①②③④⑤⑦ June 17 - Jan. 5 (not Dec. 24, 27, 31).
2000	→	2330	⑥ June 27 - Jan. 2 (not July 4, Aug. 15, Sept. 12, Oct. 3, Dec. 5, 19).

A special service will operate during the TT Race period (May 30 - June 16)

HOLYHEAD - DUBLIN 2040

Irish Ferries **by ship** **2009 service (No service Dec. 25, 26)**

Sailings from Holyhead and Dublin Ferryport.

Holyhead		Dublin	Dublin		Holyhead
0240	→	0555	0805	→	1130
1410	→	1725	2055	→	0020

Sailing times may vary owing to tidal conditions.

Bus: Dublin Ferryport - Dublin Busaras (Central Bus Station).

Irish Ferries **by fast ferry** Journey 1 hour 55 minutes **2009 service (No service Dec. 25, 26)**

Sailings from Holyhead and Dublin Ferryport.

Depart Holyhead: 1200**A**, 1715. Depart Dublin: 0845**A**, 1430.

Bus: Dublin Ferryport - Dublin Busaras (Central Bus Station).

A – Daily Apr. 3 - 19; ⑤⑥⑦ Apr. 20 - May 14; daily May 15 - Oct. 4; ⑤⑥⑦ Oct. 5 - Nov. 1.

Stena Line **2009 service (No service Dec. 25, 26)**

Sailings from Holyhead and Dublin Ferryport.

Holyhead		Dublin		Dublin		Holyhead	
0230	→	0545		0820	→	1135	
1350	→	1705		1600	→	1915	See note A.
2130	→	0045	See note A.	2115	→	0030	

A – ①②③④⑤⑥ Jan. 6 - Mar. 1, Mar. 15 - Dec. 31.

Subject to alteration during Xmas/New Year period

HOLYHEAD - DUN LAOGHAIRE 2045

Stena Line **by *HSS* fast ferry** **2009 service (No service Dec. 25, 26)**

Sailings from Holyhead and Dun Laoghaire.

Holyhead		Dun Laoghaire	Dun Laoghaire		Holyhead
1025	→	1225	1330	→	1530

Bus: Dun Laoghaire - Dublin Busaras (Central Bus Station).

BIRKENHEAD (LIVERPOOL) - DUBLIN 2049

Norfolk Line Irish Sea Ferries **2009 service**

Sailings from Birkenhead Twelve Quays Terminal and Dublin Port Passenger Terminal.

Birkenhead		Dublin		Dublin		Birkenhead	
1000	→	1700	②③④⑤⑥	1000	→	1700	②③④⑤⑥
2200	→	0500		2200	→	0500	

BIRKENHEAD (LIVERPOOL) - BELFAST 2050

Norfolk Line Irish Sea Ferries **2009 service**

Sailings from Birkenhead Twelve Quays Terminal and Belfast.

Birkenhead		Belfast		Belfast		Birkenhead	
1030	→	1830	②③④⑤⑥⑦	1030	→	1830	②③④⑤⑥⑦
2200	→	0600	①	2200	→	0600	①
2230	→	0630	②③④⑤⑥⑦	2230	→	0630	②③④⑤⑥⑦

LIVERPOOL - DUBLIN 2052

P & O Irish Sea **2009 service**

Conveys passengers with vehicles only

Liverpool		Dublin		Dublin		Liverpool	
1000	→	1800	②③④⑤⑥	1000	→	1800	②③④⑤⑥
2200	→	0600		2200	→	0600	

Subject to alteration during holiday periods

LIVERPOOL - DOUGLAS 2053

Isle Of Man Steam Packet Co. **by *SeaCat*** **Service to January 5, 2010**

Liverpool		Douglas	
1130	→	1400	Daily June 17 - Sept. 5; ①⑤⑥ Sept. 7 - Oct. 3.
1600	→	1830	Aug. 29, Sept. 5, 6 only.
1930	→	2200	Daily June 17 - Aug. 26, Sept. 8 - Oct. 18, Oct. 21 - 26, Oct. 29 - Nov. 1 (not Aug. 23).
2030	→	2300	Daily Aug. 27 - Sept. 7 (also Aug. 23).
Douglas		**Liverpool**	
0600	→	0830	Aug. 28, 29 only.
0730	→	1000	Daily June 17 - Sept. 5; ①⑤⑥ Sept. 7 - Oct. 3 (not Aug. 28, 29).
1000	→	1230	⑥ Oct. 10 - 31.
1100	→	1330	Aug. 29, Sept. 5, 6 only.
1530	→	1800	Daily June 17 - Aug. 31, Sept. 8 - Oct. 9, Oct. 11 - 16; ①④⑤⑦ Oct. 18 - Nov. 1 (also May 31).
1630	→	1900	Daily Sept. 1 - 7.

Additional sailings by ferry ⑥⑦ Nov. 7 - Jan. 3: Liverpool depart 1400; Douglas depart 0800.

A special service will operate during the TT Race period (May 30 - June 16)

PEMBROKE - ROSSLARE 2055

Irish Ferries **2009 service (No service Dec. 25, 26)**

Pembroke		Rosslare	Rosslare		Pembroke
0245	→	0630	0845	→	1230
1430	→	1815	2100	→	0045

Sailing times may vary owing to tidal conditions

For shipping operator details – see pages 521/522

IRISH SEA continued

2060 ROSSLARE - LE HAVRE

L D Lines by ship — 2009 service

Rosslare		Le Havre		Le Havre		Rosslare	
1745	→	1645	See note P.	2000	→	1430	See note R.
0100	→	2200	See note Q.	2359	→	2130	See note S.

P – ⑥ (not May 23, June 6, 20, July 4, 18, Aug. 1, 15, 29, Sept. 12, 26).
Q – May 24, June 7, 21, July 5, 19, Aug. 2, 16, 30, Sept. 13, 27.
R – ⑤ (not May 22, June 5, 19, July 3, 17, 31, Aug. 14, 28, Sept. 11, 25).
S – May 22, June 5, 19, July 3, 17, 31, Aug. 14, 28, Sept. 11, 25.

2065 ROSSLARE - ROSCOFF

Irish Ferries — 2009 service (No winter service)

Rosslare		Roscoff	
1600	→	1030	May 21, 23, 27, 29, June 4, 6, 10, 12, 18, 20, 24, 26, July 2, 4, 8, 10, 16, 22, 24, 30, Aug. 5, 13, 21, 27, Sept. 4, 10, 16, 18, 24.
1730	→	1100	May 15 only.
Roscoff		**Rosslare**	
1800	→	1100	May 16, 22, 24, 28, 30, June 5, 7, 11, 13, 19, 21, 25, 27, July 3, 5, 9, 11, 17, 23, 25, 31, Aug. 6, 14, 22, 28, Sept. 5, 11, 17, 19, 25.

2070 STRANRAER - BELFAST

Stena Line by *HSS* fast ferry — Service to January 5, 2010 (No service Dec. 25, 26)

Sailings from Stranraer and Belfast.

Stranraer		Belfast	Belfast		Stranraer
0440	→	0700	0725	→	0925
0950	→	1150	1215	→	1415
1440	→	1640	1705	→	1925
1950	→	2200	2235	→	0055

Subject to alteration during Xmas / New Year period

Stena Line by ship — Service to January 5, 2010 (No service Dec. 25, 26)

Sailings from Stranraer and Belfast.

Stranraer		Belfast		Belfast		Stranraer	
0710§	→	1010§	②③④⑤⑥	0320§	→	0610§	②③④⑤⑥
1515§	→	1815§	⑤ May 1 - Sept. 30.	1100§	→	1350§	See note S.
1550§	→	1850§	See note T.	1920§	→	2210§	①②③④⑤
2320§	→	0220§	①②③④⑤	2000	→	2250	⑥⑦
2359	→	0300	⑥⑦				

S – ⑤⑦ May 1 - Sept. 30 (also ⑥ July 1 - Aug. 31).
T – ⑦ May 1 - June 30; ⑥⑦ July 1 - Aug. 31; ⑦ Sept. 1 - 30.
§ – No foot passengers conveyed.

Subject to alteration during Xmas / New Year period

2080 TROON - LARNE

P & O Irish Sea by fast ferry — March 13 - October 5, 2009 (No winter service)

Troon		Larne	Larne		Troon
1005	→	1155	0715	→	0905
2020	→	2210	1730	→	1920

ENGLISH CHANNEL

2100 CHANNEL ISLAND SERVICES

POOLE and WEYMOUTH - GUERNSEY - JERSEY by fast ferry

Condor Ferries — Service to September 30, 2009

Sailings from St Helier Elizabeth Terminal and St Peter Port.

Weymouth - Guernsey - Jersey: 1–3 sailings per week Jan. - Mar.; 5–6 sailings per week Apr. - Sept., (daily July 15 - Sept. 7). Journey time 2 hours 10 minutes (Guernsey), 3 hours 25 minutes (Jersey).

Poole - Guernsey: 2–5 sailings per week Apr. 3 - Sept. 26 (daily July 18 - Sept. 1). Journey time 2 hours 30 minutes.

Poole - Jersey (most services via Guernsey): 2–5 sailings per week Apr. 3 - Sept. 26 (daily July 30 - Sept. 2). Journey time 3 hours.

Departure times vary owing to tidal conditions.

POOLE and WEYMOUTH - GUERNSEY - JERSEY - ST MALO by fast ferry

Condor Ferries — Service to September 30, 2009

Sailings by catamaran from St Helier Elizabeth Terminal or Albert Quay, St Malo Gare Maritime de la Bourse and St Peter Port.

Weymouth - St Malo: 1–2 sailings per week (5–7 sailings Apr. 2 - Sept. 30). Journey 5 hours 15 minutes. A change of vessel may be necessary in either Guernsey or Jersey in summer (extended journey time).

Poole - St Malo (via Guernsey or Jersey): up to 6 sailings per week May 6 - Sept. 26; journey 4 hours 35 minutes.

OTHER SERVICES:

Manche îles Express operate catamaran services in summer from Jersey to Carteret, Granville, Sark and Guernsey, and from Alderney to Diélette and Guernsey.

2105 DOVER - BOULOGNE

L D Lines by fast ferry — Service from June 1, 2009

Dover		Boulogne		Boulogne		Dover	
0415§	→	0615§	①②③④⑤	0700	→	0700	①②③④⑤
0745	→	0945		1045§	→	1100§	
1230§	→	1430§		1700	→	1700	
1900	→	2100		2230§	→	2245§	

§ – No foot passengers conveyed on this service.

L D Lines by ship — Service from June 1, 2009

Dover		Boulogne		Boulogne		Dover	
1045	→	1330	⑥⑦	0430	→	0515	①②③④⑤
1645	→	1930	①②③④⑤	0900	→	0945	⑥⑦
2215	→	0100		2030	→	2115	

2110 DOVER - CALAIS

P & O Ferries Journey 75-90 minutes — 2009 service (No service Dec. 25)

Sailings from Dover Eastern Docks and Calais Maritime.
Conveys passengers with vehicles only on night services.

Depart Dover: 0115, 0320, 0425, 0530, 0640, 0830, 0925, 1020, 1110, 1300, 1355, 1450, 1540, 1730, 1825, 1920, 2015, 2215, 2315, 2355.

Depart Calais: 0130, 0235, 0340, 0440, 0645, 0750, 0855, 0950, 1140, 1235, 1330, 1420, 1610, 1705, 1800, 1850, 2040, 2135, 2235, 2335.

Minor schedule changes are possible.
A reduced service will operate on Dec. 24, 26 (no service Dec. 25)

🚌 connections:
Dover Eastern Docks - Dover Priory station: from Dover Eastern Docks 0700–2100 on arrival of ship; from Dover Priory station 0715–1930.
Calais Port - Calais (Place d'Armes) - Calais Ville station - Calais Port 1000–1915.

SeaFrance Journey 70 - 100 minutes — 2009 service

Sailings from Dover Eastern Docks and Calais Maritime.

Depart Dover: 0045§, 0230§, 0500§, 0645§, 0800, 0930, 1105§, 1220, 1350, 1525§, 1625, 1750, 1950§, 2100§, 2230§.

Depart Calais: 0015§, 0245§, 0515§, 0645§, 0815, 1000§, 1105, 1235, 1410§, 1515, 1645, 1830§, 1930, 2100§, 2245§.

§ – Conveys passengers with vehicles only.

🚌 connections: Dover Eastern Docks - Dover Priory station.
Calais Port - Calais (Place d'Armes) - Calais Ville station - Calais Port 1000–1915.

2111 DOVER - DUNKERQUE

Norfolk Line by ship *Conveys passengers with vehicles only* — 2009 service

Sailings from Dover Eastern Docks and Dunkerque. Journey 1 hour 45 minutes

Depart Dover: 0200①②③④⑤⑥, 0400①②③④⑤⑥, 0600②③④⑤⑥, 0800, 1000, 1200, 1400, 1600, 1800, 2000①②③④⑤⑦, 2200, 2359①②③④⑤⑦.

Depart Dunkerque: 0200①②③④⑤⑥, 0400②③④⑤⑥, 0600, 0800, 1000, 1200, 1400, 1600, 1800①②③④⑤⑦, 2000, 2200①②③④⑤⑦, 2359①②③④⑤⑦.

2115 DOVER - DIEPPE

L D Lines by ship — Service from June 1, 2009

Dover		Dieppe		Dieppe		Dover	
0615	→	1130	①②③④⑤	1230	→	1545	①②③④⑤

2125 NEWHAVEN - DIEPPE

Transmanche Ferries by ship — Service to September 30, 2009 (No service Dec. 25)

Sailings from Newhaven and Dieppe.

Newhaven		Dieppe		Dieppe		Newhaven	
0800	→	1300	⑦	0500	→	0800	①②③④⑤⑥
0930	→	1430	①②③④⑤⑥	1800	→	2100	①②③④⑤⑦
2230	→	0330	①②③④⑤⑦	2000	→	2300	⑥

Departure times may vary owing to tidal conditions.

2130 PENZANCE - ST. MARY'S

Isles Of Scilly Steamship Co. — 2009 service ▲ (No winter service)

Sailings from Penzance Lighthouse Pier and St Mary's.

Penzance		St Mary's		St Mary's		Penzance	
0630	→	0910	⑥ May 18 - 30.	0945	→	1225	⑥ May 18 - 30.
0915	→	1155	See note A.	1500	→	1740	⑥ July 20 - Aug. 29.
1030	→	1310	⑥ July 20 - Aug. 29.	1630♣	→	1910♣	See note A.
1345	→	1625	⑥ May 18 - 30.	1700	→	1940	⑥ May 18 - 30.

A – ①③⑤⑥ Mar. 30 - Apr. 11; ①②③④⑤⑥ Apr. 13 - May 16; ①②③④⑤ May 18 - 30; ①②③④⑤⑥ June 1 - July 18; ①②③④⑤ July 20 - Aug. 29; ①②③④⑤⑥ Aug. 31 - Oct. 3; ①③⑤⑥ Oct. 5 - 31.
♣ – June 3 depart 1415 (Penzance a. 1655).
▲ – Subject to alteration Apr. 30 - May 4.

Departure times may vary owing to tidal conditions.

PLYMOUTH - ROSCOFF 2135

Brittany Ferries — Service to November 18, 2009

Sailings from Plymouth Millbay, Roscoff and St Malo Terminal Ferry du Naye.

April 1 - 19, May 21 - 31 and July 16 - September 6

Plymouth		Roscoff		Roscoff		Plymouth	
0800	→	1500	②③⑤⑦	0830	→	1230	⑤
1430	→	2030	⑤	0830	→	1330	①④⑥
1500	→	2200	①④⑥	0915	→	1330	⑦
2200	→	0630	④	1630	→	2130	③⑤⑦
2300	→	0700	③⑤⑦	2330	→	0630	①②④⑥

April 20 - May 20, June 1 - July 15 and September 7 - November 1

Plymouth		Roscoff		Roscoff		Plymouth	
1230	→	1900	⑤	0915	→	1330	⑦
2200	→	0800	①②③④⑤	1500	→	2000	①②③④⑤⑥
2200	→	1000	⑥	1630	→	2130	⑦
2300	→	0800	⑦				

November 2 - 18

Plymouth		Roscoff		Roscoff		Plymouth	
2200	→	0800		1500	→	2030	①②③④⑦
				2200	→	0800	⑤⑥

PLYMOUTH - SANTANDER 2140

Brittany Ferries — Service to November 1, 2009 (No service Jan., Feb.)

Sailings from Plymouth Millbay and Santander.

Plymouth		Santander	
1200⑦	→	1200①	Mar. 18-29, Nov. 2-18.
1600⑦	→	1230①	Mar. 30 - Nov. 1.

Santander		Plymouth	
1500④	→	0930⑤	Apr. 20 - May 17, June 1 - July 12, Sept. 7 - Nov. 1.
1600④	→	1500⑤	Mar. 18-29, Nov. 2-18.
2100③	→	1800④	Mar. 30 - Apr. 19, May 18-31, July 13 - Sept. 6.

POOLE - CHERBOURG 2145

Brittany Ferries by ship — March 24 - November 18, 2009

Poole		Cherbourg		Cherbourg		Poole	
0900	→	1445	③⑤⑦	0900	→	1245	②④⑥
1415	→	1930	②④⑥	1830	→	2145	①③⑤⑦
2315	→	0700	①③⑤⑦	2300	→	0630	②④⑥

🚌 Cherbourg Port - Cherbourg station (operated by Zéphir).

Brittany Ferries by fast ferry — May 18 - September 27, 2009 (No winter service)

Poole		Cherbourg	Cherbourg		Poole
0730	→	1045	1130	→	1245

PORTSMOUTH - BILBAO 2155

P & O Ferries — 2009 service

Sailings from Portsmouth Continental Ferry Port and Bilbao (Santurtzi).
Santurtzi is located approximately 13 km to the north west of Bilbao city centre.

Portsmouth		Bilbao		Bilbao		Portsmouth	
2000	→	0800§	See note M.	1230	→	1715¶	See note R.
2115	→	0800§	See note P.	1315	→	1715¶	See note S.

M – Feb. 4, 7, 11, 14, 18, 21, 25, 28, Mar. 4, 7, 11, 14, 18, 21, 25, 28, Apr. 1, 4, 8, 11, 15, 18, 22, 25, 29, May 2, 6, 9, 13, 16, 20, 23, Sept. 26, 30, Oct. 3, 7, 10, 14, 17, 21, 24, 28, 31, Nov. 4, 7, 11, 14, 18, 21, 25, 28, Dec. 2, 5, 9, 12, 16.

P – May 26, 29, June 1, 4, 7, 10, 13, 16, 19, 22, 25, 28, June 1, 4, 7, 10, 13, 16, 19, 22, 25, 28, July 1, 4, 7, 10, 13, 16, 19, 22, 25, 28, 31, Aug. 3, 6, 9, 12, 15, 18, 21, 24, 27, 30, Sept. 2, 5, 8, 11, 14, 17, 20, 23.

R – Feb. 6, 9, 13, 16, 20, 23, 27, Mar. 2, 6, 9, 13, 16, 20, 23, 27, 30, Apr. 3, 6, 10, 13, 17, 20, 24, 27, May 1, 4, 8, 11, 15, 18, 22, 25, Sept. 25, 28, Oct. 2, 5, 9, 12, 16, 19, 23, 26, 30, Nov. 2, 6, 9, 13, 16, 20, 23, 27, 30, Dec. 4, 7, 11, 14, 18.

§ – Approximate time (two days later). ¶ – Approximate time (following day).

PORTSMOUTH - CHANNEL ISLANDS 2157

Condor Ferries — 2009 service (No service Dec. 24-26, 31, Jan. 1)

Sailings from Portsmouth Continental Ferry Port, St Helier and St Peter Port.

Portsmouth		St Peter Port		St Peter Port		St Helier		St Helier		Portsmouth
0900 **A**	→	1600 **A**	→	1730 **A**	→	1930 **A**	→	2100 **A**	→	0630 **B**

A – ①②③④⑤⑥. B – ②③④⑤⑥⑦.

Departure times may vary owing to tidal conditions.

PORTSMOUTH - CHERBOURG 2160

Brittany Ferries by fast ferry — Service to November 2, 2009 (No winter service)

Sailings from Portsmouth Continental Ferry Port and Cherbourg.

Portsmouth		Cherbourg		Cherbourg		Portsmouth	
0800	→	1200	See note **P**.	1730	→	1930	See note **P**.
1545	→	1945	See note **Q**.	2030	→	2230	See note **Q**.

P – ①②③④ Apr. 1 - Sept. 27; daily Sept. 28 - Nov. 2.
Q – ⑤⑥⑦ Apr. 1 - Sept. 27.

🚌 Cherbourg Port - Cherbourg station (operated by Zéphir).

Condor Ferries by ship — 2009 service (No winter service)

Sailings from Portsmouth Continental Ferry Port and Cherbourg.

Portsmouth		Cherbourg		Cherbourg		Portsmouth	
0930	→	1430	⑦ May 24 - Sept. 6.	1700	→	2200	⑦ May 24 - Sept. 6.

PORTSMOUTH - LE HAVRE 2165

L D Lines — 2009 service

Sailings from Portsmouth Continental Ferry Port and Le Havre Quai de Southampton.

Portsmouth		Le Havre		Le Havre		Portsmouth	
1015	→	1645	See note **D**.	1600	→	2045	See note **E**.
1200	→	1830	See note **C**.	1700	→	2130	See note **F**.
2300	→	0800		2300	→	0715	See note **G**.
				2359	→	0715	May 24 - Sept. 14.

C – ②③④ (also ① May 25 - Sept. 14; May 22, June 5, 19, July 3, 17, 31, Aug. 14, 28, Sept. 11, 25).
D – ⑤ (not May 22, June 5, 19, July 3, 17, 31, Aug. 14, 28, Sept. 11, 25).
E – ⑤⑦ (not May 22, 24, June 5, 7, 19, 21, July 3, 5, 17, 19, 31, Aug. 2, 14, 16, 28, 30, Sept. 11, 13, 25).
F – ①②③④⑥ (also May 22, 24, June 5, 7, 19, 21, July 3, 5, 17, 19, 31, Aug. 2, 14, 16, 28, 30, Sept. 11, 13, 25).
G – ①②③④ (also May 31, June 14, 28, July 12, 26, Aug. 9, 23, Sept. 6).

PORTSMOUTH - OUISTREHAM (CAEN) 2170

Brittany Ferries by ship — Service to November 18, 2009 (No service Dec. 25)

Sailings from Portsmouth Continental Ferry Port and Ouistreham.

March 1 - 31 and November 1 - 18

Portsmouth		Ouistreham		Ouistreham		Portsmouth	
0730	→	1430	④⑥⑦	0800	→	1300	①②③④⑥⑦
0830	→	1530	①②③	1600	→	2100	④⑤⑥⑦
1230	→	1930	⑤	1700	→	2130	③
1430	→	2130	①②③④⑥⑦	1700	→	2200	①②
2230	→	0630	⑤⑥⑦	2300	→	0600	③⑤⑥
2230	→	0800	④	2300	→	0700	①②④⑦
2330	→	0630	①②③				

April 1 - September 27

Portsmouth		Ouistreham		Ouistreham		Portsmouth	
0800	→	1500	④⑤⑥⑦	0800	→	1300	①②④⑤⑥⑦
0830	→	1530	①②	1630	→	2130	③④⑤⑥⑦
1230	→	1930	③	1700	→	2200	①②
1430	→	2130	①②④⑤⑥⑦	2300	→	0630	③④⑤⑥
2230	→	0630	③	2300	→	0700	①②⑦
2300	→	0630	④⑤⑥⑦				
2330	→	0630	①②				

September 28 - October 31

Portsmouth		Ouistreham		Ouistreham		Portsmouth	
0730	→	1430	④⑤⑥⑦	0800	→	1300	①②④⑤⑥⑦
0830	→	1530	①②	1600	→	2100	③④⑤⑥⑦
1230	→	1930	③	1700	→	2200	①②
1430	→	2130	①②④⑤⑥⑦	2300	→	0600	③④⑤⑥
2230	→	0630	③④⑤⑥⑦	2300	→	0700	①②⑦
2330	→	0630	①②				

🚌 Ouistreham - Caen station (journey 45 minutes) to connect with most sailings.

Brittany Ferries by fast ferry — April 1 - September 27, 2009 (No winter service)

Sailings from Portsmouth Continental Ferry Port and Ouistreham.

Portsmouth		Ouistreham		Ouistreham		Portsmouth	
0700	→	1145	⑤⑥⑦	1230	→	1500	⑤⑥⑦

PORTSMOUTH - SANTANDER 2175

Brittany Ferries — Service to November 18, 2009

Sailings from Portsmouth Continental Ferry Port and Santander.

Portsmouth		Santander	
1100③	→	1200④	Mar. 18-29, Apr. 20 - May 17, June 1 - July 12, Sept. 7 - Nov. 18.
1700②	→	1800③	Mar. 30 - Apr. 19, May 18-31, July 13 - Sept. 6.

Santander		Portsmouth	
1500①	→	1400②	Mar. 30 - Apr. 19, May 18-31, July 13 - Sept. 6.
1600①	→	1700②	Mar. 18-29, Apr. 20 - May 17, June 1 - July 12, Sept. 7 - Nov. 18.

PORTSMOUTH - ST MALO 2180

Brittany Ferries — Service to November 18, 2009

Sailings from Portsmouth Continental Ferry Port and St. Malo Terminal Ferry du Naye.

Portsmouth		St. Malo		St. Malo		Portsmouth	
2030	→	0815	See note **A**.	1030	→	1815	See note **B**.
				2200	→	0800	⑥ until Mar. 14.

A – ①②③④⑤⑦ until Mar. 17; daily Mar. 18 - Nov. 18.
B – ①②③④⑤ until Mar. 17; daily Mar. 18 - Nov. 18.

Departure times may vary owing to tidal conditions.

RAMSGATE - BOULOGNE 2185

Euroferries — 2009 service

Ramsgate Boulogne — Boulogne Ramsgate

SERVICE TO COMMENCE 2009 – contact operator for details

RAMSGATE - OOSTENDE 2190

Transeuropa Ferries — 2009 service

Conveys passengers with vehicles only

Ramsgate		Oostende		Oostende		Ramsgate	
0700	→	1200	⑥⑦	0800	→	1100	
0800	→	1300	①②③④⑤	1330	→	1630	
1200	→	1700	⑥⑦	1800	→	2100	⑥
1330	→	1830	①②③④⑤	2100	→	2359	①②③④⑤
1830	→	2330		2130	→	0030	⑦

2200 ABERDEEN - KIRKWALL - LERWICK

NorthLink Ferries **2009 service**

Aberdeen		Kirkwall		Kirkwall		Lerwick
January 1 - March 31 and November 1 - December 31						
1700④⑥⑦	→	2300④⑥⑦	→	2345④⑥⑦	→	0730⑤⑦①
1900①②③⑤	→	→	→	→	→	0730②③④⑥
April 1 - October 31						
1700②④⑥⑦	→	2300②④⑥⑦	→	2345②④⑥⑦	→	0730③⑤⑦①
1900①③⑤	→	→	→	→	→	0730②④⑥

Lerwick		Kirkwall		Kirkwall		Aberdeen
January 1 - March 31 and November 1 - December 31						
1730③⑤	→	2300③⑤	→	2345③⑤	→	0700④⑥
1900①②④⑥⑦	→	→	→	→	→	0700②③⑤⑦①
April 1 - October 31						
1730①③⑤	→	2300①③⑤	→	2345①③⑤	→	0700②④⑥
1900②④⑥⑦	→	→	→	→	→	0700③⑤⑦①

Subject to alteration February - April during ship maintenance

A 🚌 transfer service is available Kirkwall - Stromness and v.v. in conjunction with evening sailings.

2220 HARWICH - ESBJERG

DFDS Seaways **2009 service**

Sailings from Harwich International Port and Esbjerg Englandskajen.

Harwich		Esbjerg	
1745	→	1300	③⑤⑦ until May 17; uneven dates May 19 - 31; even dates June 2 - July 30; uneven dates Aug. 1 - 31; even dates Sept. 2 - 20; ③⑤⑦ Sept. 23 - Dec. 20 (also Dec. 22, 28, 30).

Esbjerg		Harwich	
1845	→	1200	②④⑥ until May 16; even dates May 18 - 30; uneven dates June 1 - July 31; even dates Aug. 2 - 30; uneven dates Sept. 1 - 19; ②④⑥ Sept. 22 - Dec. 19 (also Dec. 21, 27, 29).

For rail services from / to London – see Table **204**

2235 HARWICH - HOEK VAN HOLLAND

Stena Line **by ship** **Service to December 23, 2009 (No service Dec. 24, 25)**

Sailings from Harwich International Port and Hoek van Holland.

Harwich		Hoek	
0900	→	1630	See note **H**.
1100	→	1815	Jan. 1 only.
2345	→	0745	See note **J**.

Hoek		Harwich	
1430	→	2000	See note **K**.
2200	→	0630	Not Dec. 31, Mar. 7.

H – Not Dec. 26, Jan. 1, Mar. 8.
J – Not Dec. 31, Mar. 21 - 24.
K – Not Dec. 26, Mar. 21 - 24.

See Table **15a** for connecting rail services London - Harwich and v.v. and Hoek van Holland - Amsterdam and v.v.

Subject to alteration during Xmas / New Year period

2237 HIRTSHALS - STAVANGER - BERGEN

Fjord Line **Service to December 20, 2009**

Hirtshals		Stavanger		Bergen	Bergen	Stavanger	Hirtshals
0800⑥	→	1930⑥		...	1000⑤	1800⑤	0600⑥
1230④⑦	→	0015⑤①	→	0800⑤①	1230①③	2030①③	0800②④
1430②	→	0200③	→	1000③	...	2100⑥	0830⑦

Subject to alteration during Xmas / New Year period

2240 NORWEGIAN COASTAL SERVICES

Flaggruten **2009 service**

BERGEN - HAUGESUND - KOPERVIK - STAVANGER

Sailings from Bergen Strandkaiterminalen, Haugesund Hurtigbåtterminalen, Kopervik and Stavanger Hurtigbåtterminalen.

Bergen		Haugesund		Kopervik		Stavanger	
...		0640	→	0700	→	0800	①②③④⑤
0950	→	1300	→	1320	→	1420	①②③④⑤
1010	→	1325	→	1350	→	1445	⑥
...		1500	→	1520	→	1620	①②③④⑤
1240	→	1535	→	1600	→	1655	⑦
1615	→	1920	→	1940	→	2040	①②③④⑤
1630	→	1920	→	1945	→	2040	⑦

Stavanger		Kopervik		Haugesund		Bergen	
0720	→	0815	→	0835		...	①②③④⑤
0930	→	1025	→	1050	→	1350	①②③④⑤
0950	→	1045	→	1110	→	1410	⑥
1200	→	1255	→	1320	→	1605	⑦
1645	→	1740	→	1805	→	2110	①②③④⑤
1715	→	1810	→	1835	→	2120	⑦
2045	→	2140	→	2210		...	①②③④⑤

Hurtigruten **2009 service**

BERGEN - TRONDHEIM - TROMSØ - KIRKENES

WINTER SERVICE – **January 1 - April 14 and September 15 - December 31**

NORTHBOUND	*arrive*	*depart*	*day*	SOUTHBOUND	*arrive*	*depart*	*day*
Bergen ♣	...	2230	A	Kirkenes	...	1245	A
Florø		0445	B	Vadsø		|	A
Måløy		0730	B	Vardø	1600	1700	A
Ålesund	1200	1500	B	Honningsvåg		0615	B
Molde		1830	B	Hammerfest	1115	1245	B
Kristiansund		2300	B	Tromsø	2345	0130	B/C
Trondheim	0600	1200	C	Finnsnes		0445	C
Rørvik		2115	C	Harstad	0800	0830	C
Brønnøysund		0100	D	Stokmarknes		1515	C
Sandnessjøen		0415	D	Svolvaer	1830	2000	C
Bodø	1230	1500	D	Stamsund		2200	C
Stamsund		1930	D	Bodø	0200	0400	D
Svolvaer	2100	2200	D	Sandnessjøen		1330	D
Stokmarknes		0100	E	Brønnøysund		1700	D
Harstad	0645	0800	E	Rørvik		2130	D
Finnsnes		1145	E	Trondheim	0630	1000	E
Tromsø	1430	1830	E	Kristiansund		1700	E
Hammerfest	0515	0645	F	Molde		2130	E
Honningsvåg	1145	1515	F	Ålesund	2359	0045	E/F
Vardø	0400	0415	G	Måløy		0545	F
Vadsø		0800	G	Florø		0815	F
Kirkenes	0945	...	G	Bergen ♣	1430	...	F

SUMMER SERVICE – **April 15 - September 14**

NORTHBOUND	*arrive*	*depart*	*day*	SOUTHBOUND	*arrive*	*depart*	*day*
Bergen ♣	...	2000	A	Kirkenes	...	1245	A
Florø		0215	B	Vadsø		|	A
Måløy		0430	B	Vardø	1600	1700	A
Ålesund	0845	0930	B	Honningsvåg		0615	B
Geiranger ▲		1330	B	Hammerfest	1115	1245	B
Ålesund		1845	B	Tromsø	2345	0130	B/C
Molde		2200	B	Finnsnes		0445	C
Kristiansund		0145	C	Harstad	0800	0830	C
Trondheim	0815	1200	C	Stokmarknes		1515	C
Rørvik		2115	C	Svolvaer	1830	2000	C
Brønnøysund		0100	D	Stamsund		2200	C
Sandnessjøen		0415	D	Bodø	0200	0400	D
Bodø	1230	1500	D	Sandnessjøen		1330	D
Stamsund		1930	D	Brønnøysund		1700	D
Svolvaer	2100	2200	D	Rørvik		2130	D
Stokmarknes		0100	E	Trondheim	0630	1000	E
Harstad	0645	0800	E	Kristiansund		1700	E
Finnsnes		1145	E	Molde		2130	E
Tromsø	1430	1830	E	Ålesund		|	E
Hammerfest	0515	0645	F	Geiranger		|	E
Honningsvåg	1145	1515	F	Ålesund	2359	0045	E/F
Vardø	0400	0415	G	Måløy		0545	F
Vadsø		0800	G	Florø		0815	F
Kirkenes	0945	...	G	Bergen ♣	1430	...	F

A – 1st day .... **G** – 7th day.
♣ – Sailings from Bergen Frilenesset.
▲ – Embarkation and disembarkation take place by tender - passengers are required to be at the quay 30 minutes before departure.

Other ports served: Torvik, Nesna, Ørnes, Sortland, Risøyhamn, Skjervøy, Øksfjord, Havøysund, Kjøllefjord, Mehamn, Berlevåg, Båtsfjord.

Nordlandsekspressen **Service to April 5, 2010**

BODØ - SVOLVÆR

Bodø		Svolvær	
1715	→	2050	①②③④⑥
1800	→	2135	⑤
2030	→	2330	⑦

Svolvær		Bodø	
0630	→	1000	①②③④⑤⑥
1600	→	1930	⑦

HELGOLAND (Germany) services — 2242

The following services operate:

Route:		Operator:
BÜSUM - HELGOLAND	Summer only	**Reederei Cassen Eils**
CUXHAVEN - HELGOLAND	Summer service	**Förde Reederei Seetouristik**
	Winter service	**Reederei Cassen Eils**
HAMBURG - HELGOLAND	Summer service	**Förde Reederei Seetouristik**
WILHELMSHAVEN - HELGOLAND	Summer only	**A G Ems**

HULL - ROTTERDAM — 2245

P & O Ferries — **2009 service**

(No service Jan. 1, Dec. 25, 26, Dec. 31)

Sailings from Hull King George Dock and Rotterdam Europoort.

Hull		Rotterdam	Rotterdam		Hull
2100	→	0815	2100	→	0800

connections (reservation recommended):
Hull railway station (depart 1715) - King George Dock and v.v.
Rotterdam Centraal Station (depart 1700) - Europoort and v.v.
Amsterdam Centraal Station (depart 1700) - Europoort and v.v.

HULL - ZEEBRUGGE — 2250

P & O Ferries — **2009 service**

(No service Dec. 25, 26, 31)

Sailings from Hull King George Dock and Zeebrugge Leopold II Dam.

Hull		Zeebrugge		Zeebrugge		Hull	
1800	→	0845§	See note **L**.	1800	→	0815◇	See note **N**.
1900	→	0845§	See note **M**.	1900	→	0815◇	See note **P**.

L – Jan. 23, 25, 26, 28, 30, Feb. 1, 3, 5, 7, 9.
M – Not Jan. 22, 24, 27, 29, 31, Feb. 2, 4, 6, 8, 10.
N – Jan. 22, 24, 25, 27, 29, 31, Feb. 2, 4, 6, 8.
P – Not Jan. 21, 23, 26, 28, 30, Feb. 1, 3, 5, 7, 9.
§ – On ⑥⑦ arrive 0930. ◇ – On ⑥⑦ arrive 0900.

connections (reservation recommended):
Hull railway station (depart 1715) - King George Dock and v.v.
Brugge Station (depart 1730) - Zeebrugge and v.v.

NEWCASTLE - IJMUIDEN (AMSTERDAM) — 2255

DFDS Seaways — **2009 service**

Sailings from Newcastle International Ferry Terminal, Royal Quays and IJmuiden Felison Terminal.

Newcastle		IJmuiden		IJmuiden		Newcastle	
1700	→	0930	Not Dec. 24, 25, 31.	1730	→	0900	Not Dec. 24, 25, 30.

connections:
Newcastle rail station - International Ferry Terminal (North Shields) and v.v.
(depart Newcastle station 2½ and 1¼ hours before sailing; depart Ferry Terminal following arrival of ship).
Victoria Hotel Amsterdam (near Centraal station) - IJmuiden and v.v.
(depart hotel every 10 minutes 1530 - 1630; depart Ferry Terminal following arrival of ship).

ROSYTH - ZEEBRUGGE — 2277

Norfolk Line — **2009 service**

Rosyth		Zeebrugge	Zeebrugge		Rosyth
1700②④⑥	→	1400③④⑦	1800①③⑤	→	1300②④⑥

SCRABSTER - STROMNESS — 2280

NorthLink Ferries — **2009 service**

Scrabster		Stromness		Stromness		Scrabster	
0845	→	1015	See note **A**.	0630	→	0800	See note **A**.
1200	→	1330	⑥⑦	0900	→	1030	⑥⑦
1315	→	1445	See note **A**.	1100	→	1230	See note **A**.
1900	→	2030	Daily.	1645	→	1815	Daily.

A – ①②③④⑤ (also ⑥ June 13 - Aug. 15).

ICELAND and the FAEROE ISLANDS — 2285

Smyril Line — **2009 service**

	arrive	*depart*	
	February 1 - April 3		
Esbjerg	0900⑥	1500⑥	First sailing Feb. 5, 2100 Tórshavn - Esbjerg.
Tórshavn	0500①	2100④	
	April 4 - June 12		
Esbjerg	0900⑥	1500⑥	
Tórshavn	0500①	1400①	
Seydisfjördur	0900②	2000③	
Tórshavn	1500④	2100④	
	June 13 - August 28		
Hanstholm	1400⑥	1800⑥	
Tórshavn	2330⑦	0200①	
Hanstholm	0800②	1100②	
Tórshavn	1630③	1800③	
Seydisfjördur	1000④	1300④	
Tórshavn	0430⑤	0730⑤	

SKAGERRAK, KATTEGAT & SOUTH WEST BALTIC

ÅRHUS - KALUNDBORG — 2300

Mols-Linien **by ship** Journey 2 hours 40 minutes — **2009 service**

April 14 - June 26 and August 31 - October 10

Depart Århus: 0300①②③④⑤, 0700②③④⑤, 0900⑥, 1000⑦, 1100①②③④⑤, 1230 (June 20, Oct. 10 only), 1400⑦, 1500①②③④⑤, 1900①②③④⑤⑦, 2300①②③④⑤⑦.

Depart Kalundborg: 0300②③④⑤, 0700①②③④⑤, 0900 (June 20, Oct. 10 only), 1000⑦, 1100①②③④⑤, 1230⑥, 1400⑦, 1500①②③④⑤, 1900①②③④⑤⑦, 2300①②③④⑤⑦.

June 27 - August 9

Depart Århus: 0300①②③④⑤, 0700②③④⑤, 0800⑥, 1000⑦, 1100①②③④⑤⑥, 1400⑦, 1430⑥, 1500①②③④⑤, 1730⑥, 1900①②③④⑤⑦, 2300①②③④⑤⑦.

Depart Kalundborg: 0300②③④⑤, 0700①②③④⑤, 0800⑥, 1000⑦, 1100①②③④⑤⑥, 1400⑦, 1430⑥, 1500①②③④⑤, 1730⑥, 1900①②③④⑤⑦, 2300①②③④⑤⑦.

August 10 - 30

Depart Århus: 0300①②③④⑤, 0700②③④⑤, 0900⑥, 1000⑦, 1100①②③④⑤, 1230⑥, 1400⑦, 1500①②③④⑤, 1900①②③④⑤⑦, 2300①②③④⑤⑦.

Depart Kalundborg: 0300②③④⑤, 0700①②③④⑤, 0900⑥, 1000⑦, 1100①②③④⑤, 1230⑥, 1400⑦, 1500①②③④⑤, 1900①②③④⑤⑦, 2300①②③④⑤⑦.

Subject to alteration during holiday periods

BØJDEN - FYNSHAV — 2304

Alstrafikken (Nordic Ferry Services) Journey 50 minutes — **2009 service**

Depart Bøjden: 0500 **A**, 0700, 0900, 1000 **S**, 1100, 1200 **S**, 1300, 1400 **S**, 1500, 1600 **S**, 1700, 1900, 2100 **B**.

Depart Fynshav: 0600 **A**, 0800, 1000, 1100 **S**, 1200, 1300 **S**, 1400, 1500 **S**, 1600, 1700 **S**, 1800, 2000, 2200 **B**.

A – ①②③④⑤⑥.
B – ⑦ (daily June 1 - Aug. 31).
S – June 1 - Aug. 31.

Subject to alteration on and around holidays

EBELTOFT - SJÆLLANDS ODDE — 2310

Mols-Linien **by catamaran** Journey 65 minutes — **2009 service**

Ebeltoft - Sjællands Odde and v.v.: 6 - 13 sailings daily in summer; 5 - 9 in winter.

Subject to alteration during holiday periods

ESBJERG - FANØ — 2312

Fanøtrafikken (Nordic Ferry Services) Journey 12 minutes — **2009 service**

Departures every 40 minutes (0630 - 1950 from Esbjerg, 0650 - 2010 from Fanø).

Subject to alteration on and around holidays

FREDERIKSHAVN - GÖTEBORG — 2320

Stena Line **by ship** — **2009 service**

Sailings from Frederikshavn Trafikhavn and Göteborg.

Frederikshavn		Göteborg		Göteborg		Frederikshavn	
			March 31 - May 13				
0345	→	0715	②	0800	→	1115	See note **H**.
0830	→	1145	① (not Apr. 6).	0930	→	1255	See note **L**.
1150	→	1515	See note **H**.	1100	→	1400	Apr. 9 only.
1330	→	1655	Apr. 9, 13 only.	1600	→	1915	
1430	→	1745	Apr. 13 only.	1845	→	2200	See note **K**.
1430	→	1755	See note **J**.				
2000	→	2315					
2245	→	0215	See note **K**.				
			May 14 - June 28				
0345	→	0715	June 26 - 28 only.	0800	→	1115	See note **P**.
0900	→	1215	May 16 only.	0930	→	1255	See note **Q**.
1150	→	1515	②③④⑤⑥⑦	1100	→	1400	May 21 only.
1330	→	1645	May 24, 24 only.	1600	→	1915	Not May 16.
1430	→	1745	May 24 only.	1845	→	2200	See note **R**.
1430	→	1755	See note **M**.	2355	→	0315	June 25 - 28 only.
2000	→	2315	Not May 16.				
2245	→	0215	See note **N**.				

G – ①②③④⑤⑥ (not Feb. 23).
H – ②③④⑤⑥⑦ (also Apr. 13, 20).
J – ①③④⑤⑥⑦ (not Apr. 9, 13, 20, 22).
K – ①②③④⑤⑦ (not Apr. 20, 21).
L – ①③④⑤⑥⑦ (not Apr. 20, 22).
M – ①③④⑤⑥⑦ (not May 16, 21, 24).
N – ①②③④⑤⑦ (also May 16, June 27; not May 15, June 24).
P – ⑥⑦ (also May 21, 22, June 26).
Q – ①③④⑤⑥⑦ (not May 16, June 25).
R – ①②③④⑤⑦ (also May 16, June 27).

Stena Line **by *HSS* fast ferry** Journey 2 hours — **2009 service**

Sailings from Frederikshavn Trafikhavn and Göteborg. — **(no winter service)**

May 14 - June 28

Depart Frederikshavn: 1000 **K**, 1530 **L**, 1730 **M**, 2030 **L**.
Depart Göteborg: 0730 **K**, 1245 **L**, 1500 **M**, 1800 **L**.

June 29 - August 9

Depart Frederikshavn: 0945, 1515 **N**, 1730 **P**, 2030 **N**.
Depart Göteborg: 0700, 1230 **N**, 1500 **P**, 1800 **N**.

K – ①②③④⑤⑥ (also May 24, June 28).
L – May 20, 23, 24 only.
M – ⑤⑥⑦ (also May 21; not May 23, 24).
N – ④⑤⑥⑦ (also July 20 - 22, 27 - 29).
P – June 29 - July 1, July 6 - 8, 13 - 15, Aug. 3 - 5.

2330 GEDSER - ROSTOCK

Scandlines Deutschland — **2009 service**

Sailings from Rostock Überseehafen and Gedser.
Journey 1 hour 45 minutes

Depart Gedser: 0200 **D**, 0230 **D**, 0345 **D**, 0700, 0900, 1100, 1300, 1500, 1700, 1900, 2100, 2315 **D**, 2345 **D**.

Depart Rostock: 0130 **D**, 0215 **D**, 0400 **D**, 0430 **D**, 0600, 0900, 1100, 1300, 1500, 1700, 1900, 2100, 2345 **D**.

D – Not daily – contact operator for details.

Subject to alteration on and around holidays

2335 GÖTEBORG - KIEL

Stena Line — **2009 service**

Sailings from Kiel Schwedenkai and Göteborg. **(No service Dec. 24, 25)**

Göteborg		Kiel	Kiel		Göteborg
1900	→	0900	1900	→	0900

2342 GRENAA - VARBERG

Stena Line Journey 4 - 5½ hours — **2009 service**

Grenaa		Varberg		Varberg		Grenaa	
Until May 17 and September 21 - December 23							
0100	→	0615	①②③④⑤	0900	→	1315	See note **E**.
1425	→	1840	①②③④⑤⑦	1945	→	2400	See note **F**.
May 18 - June 25							
0100	→	0615	Not May 24, 31.	0900	→	1315	
1425	→	1840		1945	→	2400	Not May 23, 30.
June 26 - August 9							
0100	→	0615	June 26 only.	0800	→	1215	
1315	→	1730		1830	→	2245	
2345	→	0415					
August 10 - September 20							
0100	→	0615	See note **G**.	0900	→	1315	Not Sept. 13, 20.
1425	→	1840		1945	→	2400	

E – ①②③④⑤ (also Apr. 12).
F – ①②③④⑤⑦ (not Apr. 10, Dec. 23).
G – Not Aug. 10, Sept. 13, 20.

2345 HELSINGØR - HELSINGBORG

Scandlines Journey 20 minutes — **2009 service**

From Helsingør and Helsingborg: Sailings every 20 minutes 0640 - 2140 (every 30 minutes at other times).

Subject to alteration on and around holidays

2350 HIRTSHALS - KRISTIANSAND

Color Line by ship — **2009 service**

Hirtshals		Kristiansand		Kristiansand		Hirtshals	
March 1 - April 13, April 22 - June 25 and August 10 - December 23							
1215	→	1530	See note **H**.	0800	→	1115	See note **H**.
2045	→	2400		1630	→	1945	
April 14 - 21							
2115	→	0030		0800	→	1115	
June 26 - August 9							
0445	→	0800	⑥	0045	→	0400	⑥
0530	→	0845	⑦	0130	→	0445	⑦
0630	→	0945	①	0230	→	0545	①
1215	→	1530	②③④⑤	0800	→	1115	②③④⑤
1315	→	1630	⑥	0900	→	1215	⑥
1415	→	1730	⑦	1000	→	1315	⑦
1445	→	1800	①	1030	→	1345	①
2045	→	2400	②③④⑤ (not July 8).	1630	→	1945	②③④⑤ (not July 8).
2130	→	0045	⑥	1730	→	2045	⑥
2230	→	0145	⑦	1830	→	2145	⑦
2315	→	0230	①	1900	→	2230	①

H – Not Mar. 2, 30, Apr. 27, May 11, 25, June 8, 22, Aug. 17, 31, Sept. 14, 28, Oct. 12, 26, Nov. 9, 23, Dec. 7, 21.

2355 KALUNDBORG - SAMSØ

Samsøtrafikken (Nordic Ferry Services) — **Service to September 27, 2009**

Journey 1 hour 50 minutes

May 4 - June 25

Depart Kalundborg: 0855⑦**S**, 0955①②③④⑤⑥**T**, 1325⑦**S**, 1430⑤⑥**V**, 1800①②③④⑦**W**, 1900⑤⑥**V**, 2225⑦**S**.

Depart Kolby Kås (Samsø): 0640⑦**S**, 0740①②③④⑤⑥**T**, 1110⑦**S**, 1215⑤⑥**V**, 1540①②③④⑦**W**, 1645⑤⑥**V**, 2015⑦**S**.

June 26 - August 16

Depart Kalundborg: 0855⑤⑥⑦, 0955①②③④, 1325⑤⑥⑦, 1800, 2225.

Depart Kolby Kås (Samsø): 0640⑤⑥⑦, 0740①②③④, 1110⑤⑥⑦, 1540, 2015.

August 17 - September 27

Depart Kalundborg: 0855⑦, 0955①②③④⑤⑥, 1325⑦, 1430①②③④⑤⑥, 1800⑦, 1900①②③④⑤⑥, 2225⑦.

Depart Kolby Kås (Samsø): 0640⑦, 0740①②③④⑤⑥, 1110⑦, 1215①②③④⑤⑥, 1540⑦, 1645①②③④⑤⑥, 2015⑦.

S – Also May 7, 20, 29, June 1; not May 31.
T – Also May 31; not May 7, 20, 29, June 1.
V – Also May 21, 31; not May 9, 23, 29.
W – Also May 9, 23, 29; not May 21, 31.

Subject to alteration during holiday periods

2360 KØBENHAVN - OSLO

DFDS Seaways — **2009 service**

Sailings from København Dampfærgevej and Oslo Vippetangen (Utstikker 2).

København		Oslo	Oslo		København
1700	→	0930	1700	→	0930

2366 LARVIK - HIRTSHALS

Color Line — **2009 service** **(no service Sept. 7 - 10)**

Larvik		Hirtshals		Hirtshals		Larvik	
March 1 - 29							
0800		1145	②③④⑤	0200		0600	⑤
1245		1630	⑥⑦	0800		1145	⑥⑦
1730		2115	①②③④	1245		1630	①②③④⑤
1900	→	2245	⑤	1730	→	2115	⑥⑦
2215		0200	⑥⑦	2215		0200	①②③
March 30 - April 13 and April 22 - December 23							
0800	→	1145	See note **L**.	1245	→	1630	See note **L**.
1730	→	2115	Not July 1.	2215	→	0200	Not July 1.
April 14 - 21							
1645	→	2030		1215	→	1600	

L – ②③④⑤⑥⑦ (also ① June 22 - Aug. 3; Apr. 13, June 1).

2368 OSLO - FREDERIKSHAVN

Stena Line — **2009 service**

Sailings from Oslo Vippetangen and Frederikshavn.

Oslo		Frederikshavn		Frederikshavn		Oslo	
1930	→	0730	See note **F**.	0930	→	1830	See note **J**.
				1000	→	1830	See note **G**.
				1830	→	0730	See note **H**.

F – ②③④⑤⑥⑦ (daily June 19 - Aug. 23).
G – ③④⑤⑥⑦ Jan. 1 - June 18; daily June 19 - Aug. 23.
H – ① Jan. 1 - June 19, Aug. 24 - Dec. 31.
J – ③④⑤⑥⑦ Aug. 24 - Dec. 31.

Subject to alteration during Xmas/New Year period

2372 OSLO - KIEL

Color Line — **2009 service**

Sailings from Oslo Color Line Terminalen, Hjortnes and Kiel Oslo-Kai.

Oslo		Kiel		Kiel		Oslo	
1400	→	1000	See note **K**.	1400	→	1000	See note **L**.

K – Not Apr. 13, 15, 17, 19, 21, May 10, 12.
L – Not Apr. 14, 16, 18, 20, 22, May 11, 13.

Oslo Color Line Terminal - Oslo Sentral rail station.
Kiel Oslo-Kai - Hamburg ZOB (Central Bus Station).

2375 PUTTGARDEN - RØDBY

Scandlines Deutschland Journey 45 minutes — **2009 service**

Departures every 30 minutes (40 minutes 2215 ⑥⑦ - 0615 ⑦①).

Subject to alteration on and around holidays

2380 ROSTOCK - TRELLEBORG

Scandlines Deutschland — **2009 service**

Sailings from Rostock Überseehafen and Trelleborg.
Journey 5 hours 45 minutes (§ – 7½ hours)

Depart Rostock: 0745②③④⑥⑦, 1500, 2245§.
Depart Trelleborg: 0730②③④⑥⑦, 1500, 2245§.

Subject to alteration on and around holidays

TT Line by ship — **2009 service**

Sailings from Rostock Überseehafen and Trelleborg.

Rostock		Trelleborg		Trelleborg		Rostock	
0800	→	1345		0800	→	1345	②③④⑤⑥⑦
1530	→	2100	②③④⑤⑥⑦	1530	→	2100	①②③④⑤⑥
2130	→	0530	⑦	1530	→	2200	⑦
2300	→	0600	①②③④⑤⑥	2300	→	0630	
2330	→	0630	⑦				

Subject to alteration during holiday periods

ROSTOCK - VENTSPILS 2382

Scandlines Deutschland — Service to December 21, 2009

Sailings from Rostock Überseehafen and Ventspils.
Journey 26 hours

Depart Rostock: 1730②③⑤⑥. Depart Ventspils: 0400②④⑤⑦.

Subject to alteration on and around holidays

SASSNITZ-MUKRAN - RØNNE 2384

Bornholmstrafikken (Nordic Ferry Services) — 2009 service

Up to 3 sailings per week (daily in summer), journey 3 hours 30 minutes.

SASSNITZ-MUKRAN - TRELLEBORG 2385

Scandlines Deutschland Journey 4 hours — 2009 service

Sailings from Trelleborg and Fährhafen Sassnitz-Mukran.

Depart Sassnitz-Mukran: 0215, 0745, 1245, 1745, 2230**A**.
Depart Trelleborg: 0300**B**, 0745, 1245, 1745, 2230②③④⑤⑥⑦.

A – ⑦ (also ⑤⑥ June 1 - Sept. 6). B – ① (also ⑥⑦ June 1 - Sept. 6).

Subject to alteration on and around holidays

STRÖMSTAD - SANDEFJORD 2387

Color Line Journey 2½ hours — 2009 service

January 23 - June 18 and August 17 - December 23

Depart Strømstad: 1000**S**, 1300, 1630**S**, 1930, 2230②③④⑤⑥⑦**S**.
Depart Sandefjord: 0700**S**, 1000, 1300**S**, 1630, 1930②③④⑤⑥⑦**S**.

June 19 - August 16

Depart Strømstad: 1000, 1330, 1700, 2000, 2300 (not July 6).
Depart Sandefjord: 0700, 1000, 1330, 1700, 2000 (not July 6).

December 24 - 31

Depart Strømstad: 1000**T**, 1300**V**, 1630**W**, 1930**W**, 2230**X**.
Depart Sandefjord: 0700**T**, 1000**V**, 1300**W**, 1630**W**, 1930**X**.

S – Not Mar. 30, 31, Apr. 14.
T – Not Dec. 25, 31.
V – Not Dec. 24, 25.
W – Not Dec. 24, 31.
X – Not Dec. 24, 25, 28, 31.

TRAVEMÜNDE - TRELLEBORG 2390

TT Line — 2009 service

Sailings from Travemünde Skandinavienkai and Trelleborg.

Travemünde		Trelleborg		Trelleborg		Travemünde	
0300	→	1045	②③④⑤⑥	0230	→	1045	②③④⑤
0330	→	1100	①	0630	→	1500	①
1000	→	1715		1000	→	1830	①②③
1430	→	2200	⑤	1000	→	1830§	④⑤⑥⑦
1645	→	0015	①②③④	1345	→	2100	⑥
2200	→	0730		1715	→	0015	①②③
2300	→	0630	⑥	1715	→	0045	④⑤⑦
				2200	→	0730	

§ – Arrive 1715 June 13 - Aug. 30.

Subject to alteration during holiday periods

🚌 connection available Trelleborg - Malmö railway station and v.v. for certain sailings.

BALTIC SEA

GDAŃSK - NYNÄSHAMN 2402

Polferries — Service to January 10, 2010

Gdańsk		Nynäshamn		Nynäshamn		Gdańsk	
1800	→	1200	See note **A**.	1800	→	1200	See note **C**.
1800	→	1300	See note **B**.	1800	→	1300	See note **D**.

A – ①③⑤ Mar. 2 - 13; ①③⑤ Mar. 30 - June 12; uneven dates June 15 - July 31; even dates Aug. 2 - 28; ①③⑤ Aug. 31 - Dec. 11; uneven dates Dec. 13 - 29; even dates Jan. 2 - 10 (not Apr. 10, 13, Dec. 23, 25).
B – ②④⑦ Mar. 1 - June 18; even dates June 20 - July 30; uneven dates Aug. 1 - 27; ②④⑦ Aug. 30 - Dec. 3; even dates Dec. 6 - 20; uneven dates Jan. 5 - 11 (not Apr. 12).
C – ②④⑦ Mar. 1 - 15; ②④⑦ Mar. 31 - June 14; even dates June 16 - July 30; uneven dates Aug. 1 - 27; ②④⑦ Aug. 30 - Dec. 3; even dates Dec. 6 - 30; uneven dates Dec. 3 - 11 (not Apr. 12, 14, Dec. 24, 26).
D – ①③⑤ Mar. 2 - June 19; uneven dates June 21 - July 31; even dates Aug. 2 - 28; ①③⑤ Aug. 31 - Dec. 4; uneven dates Dec. 7 - 21; even dates Jan. 6 - 10 (not Apr. 13).

GRISSLEHAMN - ECKERÖ 2405

Eckerö Linjen Journey 2 hours — Service to January 10, 2010 (No service Dec. 24, 25)

May 1 - August 30

Depart Grisslehamn: 1000, 1500, 2000.
Depart Eckerö: 0830, 1330, 1830.

August 31 - January 10

Depart Grisslehamn: 1000 (not Jan. 1), 1500, 2000④⑤⑥⑦ (not Dec. 31).
Depart Eckerö: 0830①⑤⑥⑦ (not Jan. 1), 1330, 1830.

🚌 connections: Stockholm Cityterminalen (near Central station) - Grisslehamn and v.v. (departing 2 hours before ship departure).
Eckerö - Mariehamn and v.v. (departing 1 hour before ship departure).

HELSINKI - TALLINN 2410

Eckerö Line by ship — 2009 service (No service Dec. 24, 25, 31)

Sailings from Helsinki Länsiterminaali and Tallinn A-terminal.

Helsinki		Tallinn		Tallinn		Helsinki	
0800	→	1100	①②③④⑤	1600	→	1930	⑦
0800	→	1130	⑥	1700	→	2030	①②③④⑤⑥
1030	→	1330	⑦				

Linda Line Oy by hydrofoil — April 2 - September 27, 2009

Linda Line Express Journey 1 hour 30 minutes
Sailings from Helsinki Makasiiniterminaali and Tallinn Linnahalli.

April 2 - June 24 and August 17 - September 27

Depart Helsinki: 0800①②③④⑤⑥, 1000, 1200, 1500⑤⑦, 1700, 1900, 2100⑤⑦.
Depart Tallinn: 0800①②③④⑤⑥, 1000①②③④⑤⑥, 1200⑤⑥⑦, 1500①②③④⑤⑦, 1700, 1900, 2100⑤⑥⑦.

June 25 - August 16

Depart Helsinki: 0800①②③④⑤⑥, 1000, 1200, 1400①②③④⑤⑥, 1500⑦, 1700, 1900, 2100.
Depart Tallinn: 0800①②③④⑤⑥, 1000, 1200①②③④⑤⑥, 1300⑦, 1500, 1700, 1900, 2100.

Services operate during the ice-free period only (generally from mid-April to November/ December)

continued

Tallink by ship — Service to December 23, 2009

Sailings from Helsinki Länsiterminaali and Tallinn D-terminal.

Helsinki		Tallinn	Notes	Tallinn		Helsinki	Notes
0730	→	0930	①②③④⑤	0730	→	0930	See note **V**.
0830	→	1030	⑥	1100	→	1300	①②③④⑤⑦
1030	→	1230		1130	→	1330	⑥
1430	→	1630	Not Aug. 4.	1300	→	1630	See note **T**.
1730	→	1930	Not Aug. 4.	1400	→	1600	
1830	→	2200	See note **W**.	1730	→	1930	
2200	→	2400		2100	→	2300	Not Aug. 4.

T – Not June 7, 8, July 25, 26, Aug. 4, 5. V – ①②③④⑤⑥ (not Aug. 5).
W – Not June 6, 7, July 24 - 26, Aug. 4.

Subject to alteration during Xmas/New Year period

Viking Line by ship Journey 2½ hours — 2009 service

Sailings from Helsinki Katajanokka terminal and Tallinn A-terminal.

Depart Helsinki: 1130, 2000⑦, 2130①②③④⑤⑥.
Depart Tallinn: 0800, 1630⑦, 1800①②③④⑤⑥.

Variations: last departure before Xmas 1800 from Tallinn Dec. 23; first departure after Xmas 1130 from Helsinki Dec. 26.

KARLSKRONA - GDYNIA 2415

Stena Line — 2009 service

Karlskrona		Gdynia		Gdynia		Karlskrona	
Until June 21 and August 31 - December 13							
0900	→	1930	②③④⑥⑦	0900	→	1930	②③④⑥⑦
1930	→	0730	⑤	1930	→	0730	①
2030	→	0730	⑥	2000	→	0730	⑤
2030	→	0830	⑦	2100	→	0730	②③⑥⑦
2100	→	0730	①②③④	2100	→	0900	④
June 22 - August 30							
0900	→	1930		0900	→	1930	
2100	→	0730		2100	→	0730	

Subject to alteration Apr. 6 - 13

KIEL - KLAIPEDA 2420

DFDS Lisco — Service to December 21, 2009

Sailings from Kiel Ostuferhafen and Klaipeda International Ferry Port.

Kiel		Klaipeda	Klaipeda		Kiel
1400①	→	1200②	1500①	→	1100②
1600②	→	1400③	1700②	→	1300③
1800③	→	1600④	1900③	→	1500④
2000④	→	1800⑤	2100④	→	1700⑤
2200⑤	→	2000⑥	2300⑤	→	1900⑥
2300⑥	→	2100⑦	0100⑦	→	2100⑦

Subject to alteration during Xmas/New Year period

2430 KØGE - RØNNE

Bornholmstrafikken (Nordic Ferry Services) **Service to January 4, 2010**

Køge	Rønne		Rønne	Køge	
0800	1345	See note **K**.	1430	2030	See note **K**.
2330	0600		2330	0600	

K – ① June 15 - 22; ①⑥⑦ June 27 - Aug. 16; ① Aug. 17 - Sept. 7 (also Apr. 2, 8, 16, 23, 30, May 7, 14, 20, 28; not June 27, 28, Aug. 15, 16).

2445 NYNÄSHAMN - VISBY

Destination Gotland **2009 service**

Nynäshamn	Visby		Visby	Nynäshamn	
		May 4 - June 14			
0900	1220	① (not May 4).	0705	1025	See note **S**.
1105	1425	See note **S**.	0805	1120	See note **T**.
1200	1515	See note **T**.	1255	1555	⑤ (not May 22).
1630	1930	⑤ (not May 22).	1600	1915	See note **V**.
2005	2320	See note **V**.	1645	2000	See note **W**.
2105	0020	See note **W**.	1920	2235	See note **X**.
		June 15 - 21			
0700	1015	④⑤	0705	1005	④⑤
1040	1340	④⑤	0705	1025	①②③⑦
1105	1425	①②③⑦	0835	1135	①③④
1210	1510	①③④	0835	1150	⑦
1230	1545	⑦	0940	1240	⑦
1315	1615	⑦	1045	1400	④⑥
1445	1800	④⑥	1255	1555	②⑥⑦
1630	1930	②⑥⑦	1510	1825	⑦
1920	2220	③④⑦	1545	1845	③④
2025	2325	⑦	1645	2000	①②③
2105	0020	①②③	1650	1950	⑦
2320	0235	④	1900	2215	④
		June 22 - July 2			
0950	1250	①⑥⑦ (not June 22).	0705	1025	
1105	1425		0835	1135	
1210	1510		1545	1845	Not June 24.
1920	2220	Not June 24.	1645	2000	
2105	0020		1835	2135	⑤⑥⑦
		July 3 - August 10			
0450	0805	①⑥⑦ (not July 4).	0050	0405	①⑥⑦ (not July 4).
0730	1045	①⑤⑥⑦ (not July 3).	0330	0645	①⑤⑥⑦ (not July 3).
0950	1250	③④	0705	1005	①⑤⑥⑦
1040	1340	①⑤⑥⑦	0705	1025	②③④
1105	1425	②③④	0835	1135	②③④
1210	1510	②③④	0850	1205	①⑤⑥⑦
1250	1605	①⑤⑥⑦	1415	1715	①⑤⑥⑦
1750	2050	①⑤⑥⑦	1545	1845	②③④
1920	2220	②③④	1645	2000	②③④
2105	0020	②③④	1755	2055	① (not July 6).
2130	0030	① (not July 6).	1835	2135	②③
2330	0245	①⑤⑥⑦	1910	2225	①⑤⑥⑦

S – ①②③④⑤⑥ (also May 24, June 14). **T** – ⑦ (not May 24, June 14).
V – ⑤⑥⑦ (not June 12 - 14). **W** – ①②③④ (also June 12 - 14).
X – ⑦ (not May 24, June 14).

Subject to alteration during Easter and Xmas / New Year periods

🚐 service Stockholm Cityterminalen - Nynäshamn connects with most sailings.

2448 NYNÄSHAMN - VENTSPILS

Scandlines **Service to December 21, 2009**

Journey 11 hours

Depart Nynäshamn: 0830⑦, 1030①, 1900②, 2200⑤, 2230③.
Depart Ventspils: 0030②, 0930③, 1800⑥, 2030④, 2330⑦.

2450 OSKARSHAMN - VISBY

Destination Gotland **2009 service**

Oskarshamn	Visby		Visby	Oskarshamn	
		May 4 - June 11			
1100	1400	③ (not May 20).	0720	1020	③⑥ (not May 20).
1540	1835	⑦	1200	1455	⑦ (not May 24).
1910	2210	⑥	1230	1510	May 24.
2110	2350	⑦	1705	2000	See note **B**.
2110	0005	①②④⑤	1735	2015	⑦ (not May 24).
2115	0010	③			
		June 12 - July 2			
1100	1400	Not June 13, 20, 21.	0720	1020	Not June 20, 21.
2110§	0005§	See note **B**.	1705	2000	Not June 13, 19.
2115	0010	③			
		July 3 - August 10			
1035	1315	⑤⑥⑦	0720	1000	⑤⑥⑦
1100	1400	②③④ (not July 7).	0720	1020	②③④ (not July 7).
1510	1805	①⑤⑥⑦	1130	1425	①⑤⑥⑦
2110	0005	①②④⑤⑥⑦	1705	2000	
2115	0010	③			

B – ①②④⑤⑥⑦ (not June 19). § – 2 hours earlier June 13.

Subject to alteration during Easter and Xmas / New Year periods

2451 ROSTOCK - HELSINKI

Tallink Journey 23 - 24 hours **2009 service**

Sailings from Rostock Überseehafen and Helsinki Vuosaari▲.

Rostock	Helsinki	Helsinki	Rostock
0500③④⑥⑦	0800④⑤⑦①	2100①②④⑤	2300②③⑤⑥

▲ – 🚐 connection (number 90 B) from Tallink terminal to Helsinki Vuosaari metro station for onward journeys to Helsinki centre (Rautatientori metro station).

2453 SASSNITZ-MUKRAN - KLAIPEDA

DFDS Lisco **Service to December 20, 2009**

Sailings from Sassnitz Fahrhafen and Klaipeda International Ferry Port.

Sassnitz-Mukran	Klaipeda	Klaipeda	Sassnitz-Mukran
1600⑥	1100⑦	1600⑦	1000①

2455 SASSNITZ-MUKRAN - BALTISK

DFDS Lisco **Service to April 30, 2009**

Sailings from Sassnitz Fahrhafen and Baltisk Ferry Terminal.

Sassnitz-Mukran	Baltisk	Baltisk	Sassnitz-Mukran
1700③	1000④	1800④	1000⑤

2460 ŚWINOUJŚCIE - RØNNE

Polferries **July 4 - August 29, 2009 (No winter service)**

Świnoujście	Rønne	Rønne	Świnoujście
1000⑥	1515⑥	1730⑥	2245⑥

2462 ŚWINOUJŚCIE - KØBENHAVN

Polferries **Service to January 11, 2010**

Świnoujście	København	København	Świnoujście
	March 1 - June 24 and August 20 - January 11		
2000②④⑥§	0800③⑤⑦	1000⑦	1900⑦
2100⑦	0800①	2000①③⑤	0800②④⑥
	June 25 - August 19		
1000④⑤	1900④⑤	1000⑦	1900⑦
2000②	0800③	2000①③	0800②④
2100⑦	0800①	2100④⑤	0800⑤⑥
2330⑥	0830⑦		

§ – Depart 2330 Aug. 22, 29.

No departure from Świnoujście Apr. 11, Dec. 24, 26, 31; from København Apr. 12, Dec. 25, 27, Jan. 1

2464 STOCKHOLM - RIGA

Tallink **2009 service**

Sailings from Stockholm Frihamnterminalen and Riga passenger port.

Stockholm	Riga	Riga	Stockholm
1700	1100	1730	0930

2465 STOCKHOLM - MARIEHAMN - HELSINKI

Silja Line **2009 service**

Sailings from Stockholm Värtahamnen and Helsinki Olympiaterminaali.

Stockholm	Mariehamn	Helsinki		Helsinki	Mariehamn	Stockholm	
1600	2355	1400	Dec. 24.	1600	0425	1200	Dec. 24.
1700	2355	0955	Note **B**.	1700	0400	0900	May 29.
1700	2355	1100	Dec. 25.	1700	0425	0930	Note **A**.
2100	0355	1330	May 30.				

A – Not Not Dec. 24, May 29.
B – Not Dec. 24, 25, May 30.

🚐 Stockholm Värtahamnen - Ropsten metro station (for Stockholm Centralen).

Viking Line **2009 service (No service Dec. 24, 25)**

Sailings from Stockholm Stadsgården and Helsinki Katajanokka.

Stockholm	Mariehamn	Helsinki		Helsinki	Mariehamn	Stockholm	
1645	2345	0945	Note **A**.	1730	0435	0940	Note **B**.

A – Not Sept. 7, 9, 11, 13, 15, 17. **B** – Not Sept. 6, 8, 10, 12, 14, 16.

Connections:

🚐 Stockholm Cityterminalen (near Central station) - Slussen metro station - Viking Line terminal. Tram no. 4T runs daily from Helsinki city centre to the Viking Line Terminal.

2470 (STOCKHOLM -) KAPELLSKÄR - MARIEHAMN

Viking Line Sailings from Kapellskär and Mariehamn. **2009 service (No service Dec. 24 - 26)**

Stockholm (*by* 🚐)	Kapellskär	Mariehamn		Mariehamn	Kapellskär	Stockholm (*by* 🚐)	
			June 1 - August 30				
0710♦	0900	1200	Note **K**.	0730	0830	*1000*♦	Note **K**.
1310♦	1500	1800		1245	1400	*1530*♦	
1810♦	2000	2300	Note **L**.	1830	1930	*2100*♦	Note **L**.
			August 31 - December 31				
0710♦	0900	1200	⑤⑥	0730	0830	*1000*♦	⑤⑥
1010♦	1200	1530	①②③④	0800	0915	*1045*♦	①②③④
1210♦	1400	1730	⑦	1200	1315	*1445*♦	⑦
1310♦	1500	1800	⑤⑥	1245	1400	*1530*♦	⑤⑥
1710♦	1900	2200	①②③④	1600	1730	*1900*♦	①②③④
1810♦	2000	2300	⑤⑥⑦	1830	1930	*2100*♦	⑤⑥⑦

K – Not June 20. **L** – Not June 19.

Variations: no service Dec. 24, 25, 26. Last sailing before Xmas 1900 on Dec. 23.

♦ – Connecting 🚐 service from / to Stockholm Cityterminalen (near Central station).

2475 STOCKHOLM - TALLINN

Tallink **2009 service**

Sailings from Stockholm Värtahamnen and Tallinn D-terminal.

Stockholm	Mariehamn	Tallinn	Tallinn	Mariehamn	Stockholm
1745	0100	1000	1800	0500	1000

For international shipping maps – see pages 518 - 520

STOCKHOLM - TURKU via Mariehamn / Långnäs — 2480

Silja Line — **2009 service**

Sailings from Stockholm Värtahamnen and Turku.

Stockholm		Mariehamn ⊡		Långnäs §		Turku	
0710	→	1345	→	→	→	1915	See note A.
1930	→	→	→	0255	→	0700	See note B.

Turku		Långnäs §		Mariehamn		Stockholm	
0815	→	→	→	1345	→	1815	See note C.
2015	→	0045	→	→	→	0610	See note D.

A – Not May 26, 27, Sept. 21 - 27.
B – Not May 12, 13, 29 - 31.
C – Not May 12, 13, May 29 - June 1.
D – Not May 25, 26, 29, Sept. 20 - 26.
§ – Långnäs is 28km from Mariehamn.
⊡ – No sailings May 28 - June 5.

Nearest metro station to Stockholm Värtahamnen is Gärdet (for Stockholm Centralen).

Viking Line — **2009 service**

Sailings from Stockholm Stadsgården and Turku Linnansatama. **(No service Dec. 24, 25)**

Stockholm		Mariehamn		Långnäs §		Turku	
0745	→	1425	→	→	→	1950	Not Sept. 22 - 24.
2010	→	→	→	0330	→	0735	Not Sept. 22 - 24.

Turku		Långnäs §		Mariehamn		Stockholm	
0845	→	→	→	1425	→	1855	Not Sept. 22 - 24.
2100	→	0110	→	→	→	0630	Not Sept. 21 - 23.

§ – Långnäs is 28km from Mariehamn.

🚌 connections: Stockholm Cityterminalen (near Central station) - Slussen metro station - Viking Line terminal; Turku city centre - harbour (bus no. 1).

TRAVEMÜNDE - HELSINKI — 2485

Finnlines Deutschland — **2009 service**

Sailings from Travemünde Skandinavienkai and Helsinki Hansaterminaali.

Travemünde		Helsinki	Helsinki		Travemünde
0300②③④⑤⑦	→	0645③④⑤⑥①	1500⑦	→	0700②
0300⑥	→	0700⑦	1800①②③④⑤⑥	→	2000②③④⑤⑥⑦
1500⑦	→	0645②	2200②⑤	→	0700④⑦
1900③	→	0645⑤			
1900⑤	→	0700⑦			

TRAVEMÜNDE - RIGA — 2487

DFDS Lisco — **2009 service**

Sailings from Travemünde Skandinavienkai and Riga Vecmilgravis.

Travemünde		Riga	Riga		Travemünde
2100③	→	0800⑤	0200②	→	1100③
1000⑦	→	2100①	2100⑤	→	0600⑦

VAASA - UMEÅ (HOLMSUND) — 2490

R G Line — **Service to August 31, 2009** **(No service May 1)**

Vaasa		Umeå		Umeå		Vaasa	
May 2 - June 28							
0800	→	1130	⑦ (also June 27).	0800	→	1330	③
0900	→	1230	④⑤	0900	→	1430	①②
1500	→	1830	③	1300	→	1830	⑦ (also June 27).
2000	→	2330	①②⑦	1800	→	2330	④⑤
				2000	→	0130	③
June 29 - August 4							
0730	→	1030	Aug. 2 only.				
0800	→	1100	②④⑥⑦ (not Aug. 2).	0800	→	1300	①③⑤ (not Aug. 3).
1430	→	1730	①③⑤	1130	→	1630	Aug. 2 only.
1730	→	2030	Aug. 2 only.	1230	→	1730	②④⑦
1900	→	2200	②④⑦ (not Aug. 2).	1300	→	1800	⑥
				1900	→	2359	①③⑤
				2130	→	0230	Aug. 2 only.
August 5 - 31							
0800	→	1130	⑦ (also Aug. 8).	0800	→	1330	③
0900	→	1230	④⑤	0900	→	1430	①②
1500	→	1830	③	1300	→	1830	⑦ (also Aug. 8).
2000	→	2330	①②⑦	1800	→	2330	④⑤
				2000	→	0130	③

Subject to alteration during Xmas / New Year and Easter periods

YSTAD - RØNNE — 2494

Bornholmstrafikken (Nordic Ferry Services) by fast ferry — **2009 service**

Up to 5 sailings daily, journey 75 minutes.

See Table **727** for rail connections Ystad - København and v.v.

Bornholmstrafikken (Nordic Ferry Services) by ship — **2009 service**

Up to 3 sailings daily, journey 2 hours 30 minutes.

See Table **727** for rail connections Ystad - København and v.v.

YSTAD - ŚWINOUJŚCIE — 2495

Polferries — **Service to January 11, 2010** **(No service Dec. 24, 25, 31, Jan. 1)**

Ystad		Świnoujście		Świnoujście		Ystad	
1400	→	2030	Not Apr. 11, 12, Dec. 26, Jan. 2.	2330	→	0630	Not Apr. 10, 11, Dec. 23, 30.

Unity Line — **2009 service** **(No service Dec. 24, 25, 31)**

Ystad		Świnoujście	Świnoujście		Ystad
1330	→	2000	1300	→	1945
2200	→	0700	2300	→	0700

A connecting 🚌 service operates Świnoujście terminal - Szczecin Hotel Radisson SAS and v.v.: Świnoujście depart 0730, Szczecin arrive 0900. Return journey Szczecin depart 1000, Świnoujście arrive 1130.

WESTERN MEDITERRANEAN

ALGECIRAS - CEUTA — 2500

Baleària (Eurolínies Marítimes) by fast ferry — **Service to November 2, 2009**

Journey 30 minutes

Depart Algeciras: 0700, 1000, 1300, 1600, 1900, 2200.
Depart Ceuta: 0830, 1130, 1430, 1730, 2030, 2330.

Trasmediterranea by fast ferry Journey 45 mins. — **2009 service**

Subject to alteration at Easter and Christmas

Depart Algeciras: 0600, 0800, 0900, 1100, 1200, 1400, 1500, 1700, 1800, 2000, 2100.
Depart Ceuta: 0730, 0930, 1030, 1230, 1330, 1530, 1630, 1830, 1930, 2130, 2230.

ALGECIRAS - TANJAH (TANGIERS) — 2502

Nautas Ferry Journey 90 minutes — **Service to June 15, 2009**

From Algeciras: 0900, 1330, 1730. From Tanjah: 0930, 1330, 1730.

Trasmediterranea (& associated operators) Journey 2½ hours — **2009 service**

From Algeciras and Tanjah: Up to 4 departures daily in winter (additional services in summer). Also 2 – 4 sailings by hydrofoil.

ALMERÍA - MELILLA — 2505

Trasmediterranea Journey 6 - 8 hours — **Service to June 14, 2009**

Depart Almería: 1630①, 2359②③④⑤⑥⑦.
Depart Melilla: 0900①, 1200②③④⑥⑦, 1430 **M**.

M – ②③④⑤⑥⑦ until Apr. 29; ⑤ from May 1.
P – ②③④⑥⑦ from Apr. 30.

Subject to alteration during Easter and Xmas / New Year periods

ALMERÍA - AN-NADÛR (NADOR) — 2507

Ferrimaroc / Trasmediterranea Journey 5 - 10 hours — **2009 service**

From Almería and an-Nadûr: 1 – 3 sailings daily, departure times vary.

BARCELONA - TANJAH (TANGIERS) — 2508

Grandi Navi Veloci — **2009 service**

Barcelona		Tanjah	Tanjah		Barcelona
1400⑦	→	1430①	2355①	→	0830③

BALEARIC ISLANDS (see map page 320) — 2510

Trasmediterranea — **Service to May 31, 2009**

BARCELONA - EIVISSA (IBIZA) by catamaran Journey 4½ - 7 hours
Depart Barcelona: *no sailings.*
Depart Eivissa: *no sailings.*

BARCELONA - EIVISSA (IBIZA) by ship Journey 9 - 14 hours
Depart Barcelona: **Apr. 1 - May 31**: 2300②④⑤⑥.
Depart San Antoni: **Apr. 1 - May 31**: 1030③⑤, 1900⑥, 2200⑦.

BARCELONA - MAÓ (MAHÓN) by ship Journey 8 - 9 hours
Depart Barcelona: **Apr. 14 - May 31**: 2300①③⑤.
Depart Maó: **Apr. 14 - May 31**: 1130②④⑥.

BARCELONA - PALMA by ship Journey 6½ - 8½ hours
Depart Barcelona: **Apr. 14 - May 31**: 1300①②③④⑤, 2300.
Depart Palma: **Apr. 14 - May 31**: 1230①②③④⑤, 2330.

BARCELONA - PALMA by catamaran Journey 3½ - 4 hours
Depart Barcelona: *no sailings.*
Depart Palma: *no sailings.*

PALMA - EIVISSA (IBIZA) by ship Journey 4 - 5 hours
Depart Palma: **Apr. 14 - May 31**: 0900⑥, 1045⑥.
Depart Eivissa: **Apr. 14 - May 31**: 1900⑥.

PALMA - EIVISSA (IBIZA) by catamaran Journey 2 - 2½ hours
Depart Palma: *no sailings.*
Depart Eivissa: *no sailings.*

PALMA - MAÓ (MAHÓN) by ship Journey 5½ hours
Depart Palma: **Apr. 5 - May 31**: 0800⑦.
Depart Maó: **Apr. 5 - May 31**: 1730⑦.

VALÈNCIA - EIVISSA (IBIZA) by catamaran Journey 3 - 3½ hours
Depart València: *no sailings.*
Depart Eivissa: *no sailings.*

VALÈNCIA - MAÓ (MAHÓN) via Palma by ship Journey 15 hours
Depart València: **Apr. 4 - May 31**: 2300⑥.
Depart Maó: **Apr. 4 - May 31**: 1730⑦.

VALÈNCIA - PALMA by ship Journey 7 - 9½ hours
Depart València: **Apr. 1 - May 31**: 2300①②③④⑤⑥.
Depart Palma: **Apr. 1 - May 31**: 1045⑥, 1145②③④⑤, 2359⑦.

VALÈNCIA - PALMA by catamaran Journey 4 - 6½ hours
Depart Valencia: *no sailings*
Depart Palma: *no sailings.*

continued

Baleària (Eurolínies Marítimes) — Service to October 31, 2009

DÉNIA - EIVISSA (IBIZA) - PALMA by fast ferry

Dénia		Eivissa		Palma		Palma		Eivissa		Dénia	
1700	→	1900/2000	→	2200	Note A.	0800	→	1000/1100	→	1300	Note A.
2030	→	0045/0130	→	0630		0930	→	1345/1430	→	1845	

A – ①④⑤⑥⑦ until May 14; daily from May 15 (also Apr. 7, 8, 14).

OTHER SERVICES:

Dénia - Sant Antoni and v.v.: 1–2 sailings daily, journey 4 hours.
València - Palma and v.v.: 1 sailing daily except ②, journey 6½ hours by fast ferry (some services via Eivissa).

2512 CANARY ISLANDS

Lineas Fred. Olsen — 2009 services

CORRALEJO (FUERTEVENTURA) - PLAYA BLANCA (LANZAROTE) Journey 30 mins.
Depart Corralejo: 0745①②③④⑤, 0900, 1100, 1330①②③④⑤, 1500, 1700, 1900.
Depart Playa Blanca: 0710①②③④⑤, 0830, 1000, 1230①②③④⑤, 1400, 1600, 1800.

LOS CRISTIANOS (TENERIFE) - SANTA CRUZ (PALMA) Journey 5 hours
Depart Los Cristianos: 1930①②③④⑤⑦. Depart Santa Cruz: 0600①②③④⑤⑥.

LOS CRISTIANOS (TENERIFE) - VALVERDE (EL HIERRO)
Depart Los Cristianos: 1200②⑤⑦. Depart Valverde: 1500②⑤⑦.

SAN SEBASTIÁN (GOMERA) - LOS CRISTIANOS (TENERIFE) Journey 30 mins.
Depart San Sebastián: 0730, 0800, 1030②⑤⑥⑦, 1130, 1230①③④, 1650, 1700.
Depart Los Cristianos: 0830, 0900, 1200②⑤⑦, 1330①③④⑥, 1400, 1830, 1930.

SANTA CRUZ (TENERIFE) - AGAETE (GRAN CANARIA) Journey 60 minutes
Departures from Santa Cruz and Agaete: 0700①②③④⑤, 0900, 1300①②③④⑤, 1600, 1800, 1930.

Naviera Armas — 2009 services

Corralejo (Fuerteventura) - Playa Blanca (Lanzarote) and v.v.	5-7 sailings daily.
Las Palmas (Gran Canaria) - Arrecife (Lanzarote) and v.v.	5 sailings per week.
Las Palmas (Gran Canaria) - Morro Jable (Fuerteventura) and v.v.	1 sailing daily.
Las Palmas (G. Canaria) - Puerto del Rosario (Fuerteventura) and v.v.	3 sailings per week.
Las Palmas (Gran Canaria) - Santa Cruz (La Palma) and v.v.	2 sailings per week.
Las Palmas (Gran Canaria) - Santa Cruz (Tenerife) and v.v.	1-3 sailings daily.
Los Cristianos - San Sebastián Gomera and v.v.	1-3 sailings daily.
Santa Cruz (La Palma) - Arrecife (Lanzarote) and v.v.	1 sailing per week.
Santa Cruz (Tenerife) - Arrecife (Lanzarote) and v.v.	5 sailings per week.
Santa Cruz (Tenerife) - Santa Cruz (La Palma) and v.v.	3 sailings per week.
Santa Cruz (Tenerife) - Valverde and v.v.	3 sailings per week.

Other inter-Island services operate

Trasmediterranea — Service to May 31, 2009

CÁDIZ - GRAN CANARIA - TENERIFE - PALMA - LANZAROTE - CÁDIZ

	arrive	*depart*
Cádiz	1000①	1700②
Lanzarote (Arrecife)	2300③	0130④
Gran Canaria (Las Palmas)	0800④	1400④
Tenerife (Santa Cruz)	1800④	2330④
Palma (Santa Cruz)	0800⑤	1800⑤
Tenerife (Santa Cruz)	2330⑤	1100⑥
Gran Canaria (Las Palmas)	1430⑥	1630⑥
Lanzarote (Arrecife)	2300⑥	0005⑦

OTHER SUMMER SERVICES:

Las Palmas - Morro Jable and v.v.	2-7 sailings per week by hydrofoil.
Santa Cruz Tenerife - Morro Jable and v.v.	2-7 sailings per week by hydrofoil.
San Sebastián Gomera - Los Cristianos and v.v.	3-4 sailings daily by hydrofoil, 1-2 sailings daily by ferry.
Valverde - Los Cristianos and v.v.	1-6 sailings per week.
Santa Cruz Tenerife - Las Palmas and v.v.	up to 3 sailings daily.
Santa Cruz Tenerife - Santa Cruz Palma and v.v.	1 sailing per week.

2520 CIVITAVECCHIA - BARCELONA

Grimaldi Lines — 2009 service

Civitavecchia		Barcelona		Barcelona		Civitavecchia	
2215	→	1715	See note X.	2215	→	1715	See note X.

X – ①②③④⑤⑥ (daily July 20 - Sept. 5).

2523 CIVITAVECCHIA - PALERMO

SNAV — May 27 - September 12, 2009 (No winter service)

Civitavecchia		Palermo	Palermo		Civitavecchia
1900	→	0900	1900	→	0800

2525 CIVITAVECCHIA - TOULON

Grimaldi Lines — 2009 service

Civitavecchia		Toulon		Toulon		Civitavecchia	
2100	→	1230	①③⑤	1800	→	0930	⑥
				2100	→	1230	②④

2530 CIVITAVECCHIA - PALERMO - TÛNIS

Grandi Navi Veloci — 2009 service

Civitavecchia		Palermo		Tûnis		Palermo		Civitavecchia
2000①③	→	0800②④		...		2000②④	→	0800③⑤
2000⑤	→	0800/1100⑥	→	2000/2300⑥	→	1000/2000⑦	→	0800①

Grimaldi Ferries — 2009 service

Civitavecchia		Tûnis	Tûnis		Civitavecchia
2359③	→	1500④	2130②	→	1600③

2537 GENOVA - BARCELONA

Grandi Navi Veloci — 2009 service

Genova		Barcelona		Barcelona		Genova	
1800	→	1200	⑥	1500	→	0900	③
2000	→	1400	See note G.	2000	→	1400	See note J.
2115	→	1515	See note H.	2115	→	1515	②④ (not Dec. 24).
				2355	→	1755	⑥ (not May 23).

G – ④ Apr. 30 - May 14, Nov. 5 - Dec. 17.
H – ①③⑤ (not May 22, Dec. 25).
J – ⑤ Apr. 24 - May 15, Nov. 6 - Dec. 18.

2547 GENOVA - PALERMO

Grandi Navi Veloci — 2009 service (No service Dec. 24, 25)

Genova		Palermo		Palermo		Genova	
2100	→	1700	See note P.	2100	→	1700	See note P.
2200	→	1800	See note Q.	2200	→	1800	See note Q.

P – June 15 - Sept. 12; ①②③④⑤⑥ Sept. 14 - Oct. 3 (not June 21, Aug. 16).
Q – ①②③④⑤⑥ Apr. 27 - June 13, Oct. 5 - Dec. 30.

2554 GENOVA - TANJAH (TANGIERS)

Cie. Marocaine de Navigation (Comanav) — 2008 service

Depart 1300 from Genova and Tanjah. Sailings arrive 2 days later.

Departures from Genova: ⑥ Apr. 5 - June 14; June 19, 25, July 1, 7, 13, 19, 25, 31, Aug. 6, 12, 18, 24, 30, Sept. 5, 11, 17, 23, 29, Oct. 5; ⑥ Oct. 11 - Nov. 8; Nov. 14, 20, 26, Dec. 2, 8, 14, 20, 26.

Departures from Tanjah: ② Apr. 1 - June 17; June 22, 28, July 6, 10, 16, 22, 28, Aug. 3, 9, 15, 21, 27, Sept. 2, 8, 14, 20, 26, Oct. 2, 8; ② Oct. 14 - Nov. 11; Nov. 17, 23, 29, Dec. 5, 11, 17, 23, 29.

Grandi Navi Veloci — 2009 service

Genova		Tanjah	Tanjah		Genova
1800⑥	→	1430①	2355①	→	0830④

All sailings via Barcelona (see Table **2508**)

2555 GENOVA - TÛNIS

Compagnie Tunisienne de Navigation / S N C M — 2009 service

Departure times vary. Journey 20-24 hours

From Genova: Apr. 4, 11, 18, 25, May 2, 9, 16, 23, 30, June 6, 13, 18, 20, 22, 23, 25, 27, 30, July 2, 3, 4, 8, 11, 12, 15, 16, 18, 20, 21, 25, 27, 30, 31, Aug. 1, 3, 6, 8, 11, 14, 15, 16, 19, 22, 26, 29, 30, Sept. 2, 4, 5, 7, 10, 12, 13, 16, 19, 26, 28, Oct. 3, 10, 17, 24, 31, Nov. 7, 14, 21, 24, 28, Dec. 5, 12, 19, 21, 26, 28.

From Tûnis: Apr. 3, 10, 17, 24, May 1, 8, 15, 22, 29, June 5, 12, 17, 19, 20, 22, 24, 26, 29, July 1, 3, 7, 10, 11, 14, 16, 17, 20, 24, 26, 29, 31, Aug. 2, 7, 10, 12, 14, 15, 18, 21, 24, 25, 28, 29, Sept. 1, 3, 4, 6, 9, 11, 12, 15, 18, 25, 27, Oct. 2, 9, 16, 23, 30, Nov. 6, 13, 20, 23, 27, Dec. 4, 11, 17, 18, 20, 25, 27.

Grandi Navi Veloci — 2009 service

Departure times vary. Journey 24 hours

From Genova: ③⑥ Apr. 29 - June 24; ①③⑤⑥ June 26 - Aug. 8; ②⑤⑦ Aug. 11 - Sept. 20; ③⑥ Sept. 23 - Dec. 26.

From Tûnis: ④⑦ Apr. 30 - June 25; ②④⑦ June 28 - Aug. 9; ①③⑥⑦ Aug. 12 - Sept. 21; ④⑦ Sept. 24 - Dec. 27.

2560 GULF OF NAPOLI (including Gulf of Salerno and Ponziane Islands)

Alilauro — 2009 services (subject to confirmation)

Napoli Mergellina or Beverello - Capri: 5-11 sailings daily.
Napoli Mergellina - Forio: 5 sailings daily (summer only).
Napoli Beverello - Ischia: 2-6 sailings daily by ship, 4-8 sailings daily by catamaran.
Napoli Mergellina - Ischia: 4-7 sailings daily.
Napoli Mergellina or Beverello - Sorrento: 5-9 sailings daily.
Napoli - Sorrento - Positano - Amalfi: summer only, infrequent sailings.
Pozzuoli - Ischia: frequent service by ship.
Sorrento - Capri: 7-16 sailings daily by catamaran, also 1-6 sailings by ship.
Salerno - Amalfi - Positano - Capri: summer only, infrequent sailings by catamaran.

Additional infrequent services to Capri operate (summer only) from Ischia, Castellammare di Stábia, Torre Annunziata, Positano and Amalfi.

Caremar — 2009 services

Napoli - Capri: 6 sailings daily by catamaran, 3 sailings by ship.
Napoli - Ischia: 9 sailings daily by catamaran, 5 sailings by ship.
Napoli - Procida: 8 sailings daily by catamaran, 5 sailings by ship.
Pozzuoli - Procida - Ischia: 2 sailings daily by catamaran, 2 sailings by ship.
Sorrento - Capri: 4 sailings daily by catamaran.

Additional infrequent services operate between Procida and Ischia, Formia and Ventotene, Formia and Ponza, Anzio and Ponza.

Navigazione Libera del Golfo by *Linea Jet* — 2009 services

Napoli (Molo Beverello) - Capri: 4 sailings daily (9-10 in summer). Journey 40 minutes.
Sorrento - Capri: 6-8 sailings daily (19-20 in summer). Journey 25 minutes.

Additional services operate (summer only) between Castellammare di Stábia and Capri.

SNAV Journey 40 minutes — 2009 service

Napoli (Beverello) - Capri: 0710⚒, 0930, 1135, 1440, 1735.
Capri - Napoli (Beverello): 0815⚒, 1035, 1335, 1630, 1835.

For international shipping maps – see pages 518 - 520

CORSICA 2565

Sailings from mainland FRANCE

MARSEILLE - AJACCIO 2009 service

S N C M Journey 9 - 12 hours

From Marseille and Ajaccio: Feb. - Oct.: up to 2 sailings daily (most sailings overnight). Departure times vary.

MARSEILLE - BASTIA 2009 service

S N C M Journey 10 - 13 hours

From Marseille and Bastia: Feb. - Oct.: up to 2 sailings daily (most sailings overnight). Departure times vary.

MARSEILLE - L'ÎLE ROUSSE 2009 service

S N C M Journey 8 - 11½ hours

From Marseille and L'Île Rousse: Apr. - Oct.: 13–17 sailings per month (all sailings overnight). Departure times vary.

MARSEILLE - PORTO VECCHIO 2009 service

S N C M Journey 14 hours

From Marseille and Porto Vecchio: Apr. - Oct.: 13–18 sailings per month (all sailings overnight). Departure times vary.

MARSEILLE - PROPRIANO 2009 service

S N C M Journey 9½ - 12½ hours.

From Marseille and Propriano: Mar. - Oct.: 13–18 sailings per month (most sailings overnight). Departure times vary.

NICE - AJACCIO 2009 service

Corsica Ferries Departure times vary. Journey 4½ - 10 hours

From Nice:
day sailings: Apr. 4, 9, 11, 13, 18, 20, 25; May 1, 3, 8, 10, 14, 16, 21, 23, 28, 30.
night sailings: no sailings.
From Ajaccio:
day sailings: Apr. 4, 9, 11, 13, 18, 20, 25; May 1, 3, 8, 10, 14, 16, 21, 23, 28, 30.
night sailings: no sailings.

NICE - BASTIA 2009 service

Corsica Ferries Departure times vary. Journey 5 - 10 hours

From Nice:
day sailings: Apr. 4, 5, 9 - 14, 16 - 21, 23 - 30, May 1 - 4, 7 - 10, 15 - 17, 20 - 24, 29 - 31.
night sailings: no sailings.
From Bastia:
day sailings: Apr. 4, 5, 9 - 14, 16 - 21, 23 - 30, May 1 - 4, 7 - 10, 15 - 17, 20 - 24, 29 - 31.
night sailings: no sailings.

S N C M Journey 5 hours

From Nice and Bastia: Apr. - Sept.: up to 11 sailings per month (all day sailings). Departure times vary.

NICE - CALVI 2009 service

Corsica Ferries Departure times vary. Journey 3 - 6 hours (night = 10 hours)

From Nice:
day sailings: Apr. 9, 13, 20, May 1, 8, 14, 23, 28.
night sailings: no sailings.
From Calvi:
day sailings: Apr. 9, 13, 20, May 1, 8, 14, 23, 28.
night sailings: no sailings.

S N C M Departure times vary (all day sailings). Journey 3 - 4 hours

From Nice and Calvi: Apr. - Sept.: up to 20 sailings per month (all day sailings). Departure times vary.

NICE - L'ÎLE ROUSSE 2009 service

Corsica Ferries Departure times vary (all day sailings). Journey 4 - 5½ hours

From Nice: no sailings.
From L'Île Rousse: no sailings.

S N C M Journey 3 - 6½ hours (night = 12 hours)

From Nice and L'Île Rousse: Mar. - Oct.: 1 sailing per week (up to 20 sailings per month in peak summer). Departure times vary.

TOULON - AJACCIO 2009 service

Corsica Ferries Departure times vary. Journey 6 - 10 hours

From Toulon:
day sailings: Apr. 8, 10 - 12, 14, 17 - 19, 21, 24 - 26, May 1, 2, 4, 8, 9, 15 - 17, 21 - 24, 29 - 31.
night sailings: Apr. 1, 3, 5, 6, 8, 10, 12, 14, 15, 17, 19, 21, 22, 24, 26, 27, 29, 30, May 2, 4, 6, 7, 9, 11, 13, 15, 17, 18, 20, 22, 24, 25, 27, 29, 31.
From Ajaccio:
day sailings: Apr. 6, 8, 10 - 12, 14, 15, 17 - 19, 21, 22, 24 - 27, 30, May 1, 2, 4, 7 - 9, 15 - 18, 21 - 25, 29 - 31.
night sailings: Apr. 2, 4, 7, 9, 11, 13, 16, 18, 20, 23, 25, 28, May 1, 3, 5, 8, 10, 12, 14, 16, 19, 21, 23, 26, 28, 30.

TOULON - BASTIA 2009 service

Corsica Ferries Departure times vary (all sailings overnight). Journey 8½ - 10 hours

From Toulon: daily Apr. 1 - May 31.
From Bastia: daily Apr. 1 - May 31.

TOULON - L'ÎLE ROUSSE 2009 service

Corsica Ferries Departure times vary (all day sailings). Journey 6 hours

From Toulon: May 3, 10, 24.
From L'Île Rousse: May 3, 10, 24.

Sailings from ITALY

GENOVA - BASTIA 2009 service (no winter service)

Moby Lines

Genova		Bastia	Bastia		Genova	
0900	→	1345	1445	→	1930	Daily May 28 - Sept. 13; ⑥⑦ Sept. 19 - 27.

LIVORNO - BASTIA 2009 service

Corsica Ferries Departure times vary. Journey 3 - 4 hours (night = 7 hours)

From Livorno:
day sailings: Mar. 1, 3, 5 - 8, 10, 12 - 15, 17 - 20, 22, 24 - 27, 29, 31, Apr. 1 - 5, 7 - 12, 14 - 19, 21, 23 - 30; daily May 1 - Nov. 3 (not Oct. 11).
night sailings: no sailings.
From Bastia:
day sailings: Mar. 1, 3 - 8, 10 - 15, 17 - 20, 22, 24 - 27, 29, 31, Apr. 1 - 5, 7 - 12, 14 - 19, 21, 23 - 30; daily May 1 - Nov. 3 (not Oct. 11).
night sailings: ⑤⑥ May 9 - July 26; July 27, 31, Aug. 1 - 4, 7 - 11, 14 - 17, 21 - 25, 28 - 31, Sept. 1, 5; ⑥ Sept. 6 - Oct. 4.

Moby Lines

Livorno		Bastia		Bastia		Livorno	
0900	→	1300	See note **R**.	0130	→	0630	See note **T**.
2030	→	0030	See note **S**.	1500	→	1900	See note **R**.

R – Daily Apr. 9 - 14, 17 - 20, 23 - 30, May 1 - 5, 8 - 11, 15 - 18, May 22 - Sept. 13.
S – ⑤⑥⑦ Aug. 1 - 30.
T – ①⑥⑦ Aug. 1 - 31 (also July 31).

PIOMBINO - BASTIA 2009 service

Corsica Ferries Departure times vary (all day sailings). Journey 2 hours

From Piombino and Bastia: Apr. - May: no sailings.

SAVONA - BASTIA 2009 service

Corsica Ferries Departure times vary. Journey 4½ - 10 hours

From Savona:
day sailings: May 3, 10, 19, 22 - 24, 29 - 31.
night sailings: Apr. 7, 8, 10, 12, 14, 15, 17, 19, 21, 22, 24, 26, 28, 30, May 1, 4, 5, 7, 8, 11, 13, 15, 17, 20, 22, 25, 27, 29 - 31.
From Bastia:
day sailings: Apr. 8, 12, 15, 19, 22, 26, May 1, 3, 5, 8, 10, 17, 22, 23, 29 - 31.
night sailings: Apr. 9, 13, 16, 20, 23, 27, 29, May 3, 6, 10, 12, 14, 18, 19, 21, 23, 24, 26, 28, 30, 31.

CORSICA - SARDINIA

BASTIA - GOLFO ARANCI 2009 service

Corsica Ferries Departure times vary (all day sailings). Journey 3½ hours

From Bastia and Golfo Aranci: Apr. - May: no sailings.

BONIFACIO - SANTA TERESA DI GALLURA 2009 services

Moby Lines Journey 50 minutes **Apr. 9 - Sept. 20 only**

From Bonifacio: 0830, 1300, 1700, 2030.
From Santa Teresa di Gallura: 0700, 1000, 1510, 1900.

Saremar

Up to 3 sailings per day, journey 1 hour.

2570 ITALIAN COASTAL SERVICES (including Egadi and Eolian Islands)

Alilauro — **2009 services**

Napoli Mergellina - Stromboli - Panarea - Salina - Vulcano - Lipari and v.v.: 3 sailings per week (daily late July – late Aug.).

Siremar — **2009 services**

NAPOLI - MILAZZO via Stromboli, Ginostra, Panarea, Lipari and Vulcano. Also serves Rinella and S.M. Salina on certain days. Journey 16 - 20 hours.

Sailings from Napoli: 2000②⑤. Sailings from Milazzo: 1500①④.

See Table 2621 for faster sailings Napoli - Milazzo and v.v. (summer only).

OTHER SERVICES by ship:

Milazzo - Vulcano - Lipari: 2 – 3 sailings per day; journey 2 hours.
Milazzo - Vulcano - Lipari - Panarea - Ginostra - Stromboli: 1 – 3 sailings per week; journey 6 hours.
Milazzo - Vulcano - Lipari - S. M. Salina - Filicudi - Alicudi: 4 – 5 sailings per week; journey 6 hours.
Trapani - Favignana - Levanzo - Marettimo: 6 – 7 sailings per week; journey 3 hours.
Palermo - Ustica: 5 – 7 sailings per week; journey 2½ hours.
Trapani - Pantelleria: 6 – 7 sailings per week; journey 4½ - 5½ hours.
Porto Empedocle (Agrigento) - Linosa - Lampedusa: 6 – 7 sailings per week; journey 8 hours.

OTHER SERVICES by hydrofoil 2 – 6 sailings per day:

Lipari - Panarea - Ginostra - Stromboli.
Lipari - S. M. Salina - Rinella.
Milazzo - Vulcano - Lipari.
Milazzo - Vulcano - Lipari - Rinella - Filicudi - Alicudi.
Milazzo - Vulcano - Lipari - S. M. Salina.
Palermo - Ustica.
Trapani - Levanzo - Favignana - Marettimo.

Ustica Lines by hydrofoil — **2009 services** (subject to alteration)

EGADI & EOLIAN ISLANDS

The Sicilian ports of Cefalù, Messina, Milazzo, Palermo and Trapani are linked by island-hopping services serving Alicudi, Favignana, Filicudi, Levanzo, Lipari, Marettimo, Panarea, Salina Rinella, Salina S. M., Stromboli and Vulcano.

Services operate to differing frequencies (additional sailings in summer).

LAMPEDUSA - LINOSA by hydrofoil Journey 1 hour

Depart Lampedusa: 0730①③④⑤⑥⑦**D**▲, 0900**B**, 0930**F**, 1315③⑥**A**▲, 1635**B**, 1715**F**.
Depart Linosa: 1015**C**, 1045**F**, 1115③⑥**A**▲, 1735①③④⑤⑥⑦**E**▲, 1740**C**, 1815①③④⑤⑥⑦**F**▲, 1830**F**.

A – Jan. 1 - Apr. 30, Nov. 1 - Dec. 31.
B – Apr. 1 - 30, Sept. 16 - Oct. 31.
C – Apr. 1 - 30, Sept. 16 - Nov. 4.
D – May 1 - Oct. 31.
E – Sept. 16 - Oct. 31.
F – May 1 - Sept. 15.
▲ – From / to Porto Empedocle (for Agrigento); additional journey time 3 – 3¼ hours.

MILAZZO - VULCANO by hydrofoil Journey 45 minutes

Jan. 1 - May 31, Sept. 17 - Dec. 31: 6 – 7 departures daily; June 1 - Sept. 16: 8 daily.

PALERMO - MILAZZO - CEFALÙ - PALERMO by hydrofoil

Palermo		Cefalù		Milazzo		Cefalù		Palermo	
...		...		0620	→	→	→	1135	June 1 - Sept. 16.
...		...		0630	→	1110	→	1220	①⑤⑦ until May 31 and from Sept. 17.
...		...		1510		2010	→	2105	June 1 - Sept. 16.
0655	→	0805	→	1245		...		...	June 1 - Sept. 16.
1400	→	→	→	1920		...		...	June 1 - Sept. 16.
1400	→	1510	→	2000		...		...	①⑤⑦ until May 31 and from Sept. 17.

TRAPANI - PANTELLERIA by hydrofoil June 10 - Oct. 10 only Journey 2½ hours

Depart Trapani: 1800. Depart Pantelleria: 0830.

2580 LIVORNO - BARCELONA

Grimaldi Lines — **2009 service**

Livorno		Barcelona	Barcelona		Livorno
2330①③⑤	→	2200②④⑥	2359②④⑥	→	1930③⑤⑦

2585 LIVORNO - MÁLAGA

Ustica Lines — **Service from March 20, 2009**

Livorno		Málaga	Málaga		Livorno
1900①	→	0700④	1700⑤	→	0700①

2588 LIVORNO - PALERMO

Grandi Navi Veloci — **2009 service**

Livorno		Palermo	Palermo		Livorno
2359①③⑤	→	1900②④⑥	2359②④⑥	→	1900③⑤⑦

2590 LIVORNO - TRAPANI

Ustica Lines — **2009 service**

Livorno		Trapani	Trapani		Livorno
0200③⑦	→	0700④①	1930①⑤	→	2100②⑥

2595 MÁLAGA - MELILLA

Trasmediterranea Journey 7 - 8 hours — **Service to June 14, 2009**

Depart Málaga and Melilla: 1 – 2 sailings daily. Also daily sailings by fast ferry in summer (journey 4 hours)

Subject to alteration during Easter and Xmas / New Year periods

2602 MARSEILLE - AL-JAZÂ'IR (ALGIERS)

SNCM / ENTMV Journey 20 hours — **Service to June 15, 2009**

Departures from Marseille: Apr. 1, 4, 6, 7, 11, 14, 15, 18, 20, 21, 25, 28, 29, May 2, 4, 5, 9, 12, 13, 16, 18, 19, 23, 25, 26, 27, 30, June 1, 6, 8, 9, 10, 13.

Departures from al-Jazâ'ir: Apr. 1, 2, 6, 8, 9, 11, 13, 15, 16, 20, 22, 25, 27, 29, 30, May 4, 6, 9, 11, 13, 14, 18, 20, 23, 25, 27, 28, 30, June 1, 3, 8, 10, 11, 13, 15.

Departure times vary

Other services operate from Marseille to Annâbah, Bijâyah, Sakîkdah, Wâhran (Oran) and v.v.

2615 MARSEILLE - TÛNIS

Compagnie Tunisienne de Navigation / S N C M — **2009 service**

Departure times vary. Journey 20 - 24 hours

Departures from Marseille: Apr. 2, 4, 9, 11, 16, 18, 20, 23, 25, 30, May 2, 4, 7, 9, 14, 16, 21, 23, 28, 30, June 4, 6, 11, 13, 18, 20 - 23, 25, 27 - 30, July 2, 3, 5 - 7, July 9 - Aug. 14, Aug. 16 - 19, 21 - 25, 27, 28, 30, 31, Sept. 2 - 4, 6, 7, 9, 10, 12 - 14, 16, 17, 19, 24, 26, Oct. 1, 3, 8, 10, 15, 17, 22, 24, 29, 31, Nov. 5, 7, 12, 14, 19, 21, 26, 28, Dec. 3, 5, 10, 12, 17, 19, 22, 24, 26, 29, 30.

Departures from Tûnis: Apr. 1, 5, 8, 12, 15, 19, 22, 26, 29, May 3, 5, 10, 13, 17, 20, 24, 27, 31, June 3, 7, 10, 14, 17, 19, 21, 23 - 26, 28, 29, July 1, 4 - 8, 10, 11, 13 - 23, 25, 27, 29, 31, Aug. 1 - 5, 7 - 12, 14 - 23, 25, 26, 29 - 31, Sept. 1 - 9, 11, 13, 15, 16, 20, 23, 27, 30, Oct. 4, 7, 11, 14, 18, 21, 25, 28, Nov. 1, 4, 8, 11, 15, 18, 22, 25, 29, Dec. 2, 6, 9, 13, 16, 20, 21, 23, 27 - 29.

2618 MGARR (Gozo) - CIRKEWWA (Malta)

Gozo Channel Co. Journey 25 minutes — **2009 service**

Departures from Mgarr and Cirkewwa: every 30 - 45 minutes 0600 - 1930 (less frequent at other times).

2621 NAPOLI - MILAZZO

Ustica Lines by hydrofoil — **June 29 - September 16, 2008** **(No winter service)**

Napoli		Milazzo	Milazzo		Napoli
0800	→	1450	1200	→	2100

See Table 2570 for alternative sailings Napoli - Milazzo and v.v. (all year).

2625 NAPOLI - PALERMO

Tirrenia — **2009 service**

Napoli		Palermo		Napoli	
2015	→	0630 / 2015	→	0630	Apr. 1 - July 31.

SNAV — **2009 service**

Napoli		Palermo		Palermo		Napoli	
0900	→	1900	Aug. 1 - 30.	0900	→	1900	Aug. 1 - 30.
2000	→	0630		2000	→	0630	
2100	→	0730	Aug. 1 - 30.	2100	→	0730	Aug. 1 - 30.

2630 NAPOLI - TRAPANI

Ustica Lines by hydrofoil — **June 1 - September 30, 2008** **(No winter service)**

①④⑥ ▲: Napoli 1500 → Ustica 1915 → Favignana 2130 → Trapani 2205.
①④⑥ ▲: Trapani 0630 → Favignana 0655 → Ustica 0915 → Napoli 1315.

▲ – Also ⑤ July 1 - Aug. 31.

2632 NAPOLI - TÛNIS

Medmar — **2009 service**

SERVICE SUSPENDED

2660 REGGIO DI CALABRIA - MESSINA

Ustica Lines by hydrofoil Journey 15 minutes — **2009 service**

From Reggio di Calabria and Messina: 3 sailings in summer, 2 in winter.

2661 SALERNO - PALERMO - TÛNIS

Grimaldi Ferries — **2009 service**

Salerno		Palermo		Tûnis		Palermo		Salerno
1900①	→	0600② / 1000②	→	2030② / 2330④	→	0930⑤ / 1200⑤	→	2100⑤
0500⑥	→	1600⑥ / 2000⑥	→	0830⑦ / 1100⑦	→	2200⑦ / 0100①	→	1000①

SARDINIA 2675

Sailings from FRANCE

MARSEILLE - PORTO TORRES — 2009 service

S N C M — Journey 16-19 hours

From Marseille and Porto Torres: Mar. - Oct.: 7–16 sailings per month (most sailings overnight). Departure times vary.

Sailings from mainland ITALY

CIVITAVECCHIA - ARBATAX — 2009 service

Tirrenia

Civitavecchia		Arbatax	
1830	→	0500	③⑤ Apr. 1 - June 26; ⑤⑦ July 3 - Sept. 13; ③⑤ Sept. 16-30.
Arbatax		**Civitavecchia**	
2359	→	1030	③⑦ Apr. 1 - June 28; ⑤⑦ July 3 - Sept. 13; ③⑦ Sept. 16-30.

CIVITAVECCHIA - CAGLIARI — 2009 service

Tirrenia

Civitavecchia		Cagliari	
1830	→	0900	Daily **except** when service below sails.
1830	→	1115	③⑤ Apr. 1 - June 26; ⑤⑦ July 3 - Sept. 13; ③⑤ Sept. 16-30 (via Arbatax).
Cagliari		**Civitavecchia**	
1800	→	0830	Daily **except** when service below sails.
1800	→	1030	③⑦ Apr. 1 - June 28; ⑤⑦ July 3 - Sept. 13; ③⑦ Sept. 16-30 (via Arbatax).

CIVITAVECCHIA - GOLFO ARANCI — 2009 service

Sardinia Ferries — Journey 5-11 hours.

From Civitavecchia and Golfo Aranci: up to 3 sailings daily. Departure times vary.

CIVITAVECCHIA - OLBIA — 2009 service

Moby Lines

Civitavecchia		Olbia		Olbia		Civitavecchia	
1500	→	1945	See note **C**.	0900	→	1345	See note **C**.
2200	→	0800	May 28-31.	1200	→	1900	May 29-31.

C – Apr. 2-5, 9-11, 13, 14, 17-19, 24-30, May 1-4, 8-10, 15-17, 21-31.

Tirrenia

Civitavecchia		Olbia	
2230	→	0530	Apr. 1 - July 30, Sept. 1-30.
2359	→	0630	July 31 - Aug. 31.
Olbia		**Civitavecchia**	
2230	→	0530	Apr. 1 - July 30, Sept. 1-30.
2359	→	0630	July 31 - Aug. 31.

Additional sailings available June - mid-Sept.

GENOVA - ARBATAX — 2009 service

Tirrenia

Genova		Arbatax	
1800	→	1200	①⑤ Apr. 3 - June 12; ②⑤ June 16 - July 17.
1930	→	1200	②⑤ Sept. 1-29 (also July 21, 24).
2130	→	1200	①③ July 27 - Aug. 12; ①④ Aug. 17-27.
Arbatax		**Genova**	
1400	→	0715	③⑥ Sept. 2-30 (also July 22, 25).
1400	→	1000	②⑥ Apr. 4 - June 13; ③⑥ June 17 - July 18.
1500	→	0715	②④ July 28 - Aug. 13; ②⑤ Aug. 18-28.

GENOVA - OLBIA — 2009 service

Grandi Navi Veloci

Genova		Olbia		Olbia		Genova	
1000	→	1900	See note **D**.	1000	→	1900	See note **F**.
2130§	→	0730§	See note **E**.	2130	→	0730	See note **G**.

D – Aug. 17 - Oct. 10 (June 2).
E – May 22, 23, 29-31, June 3-6, June 8 - Aug. 15.
F – May 23, 30, 31, June 4-6, June 9 - Aug. 15.
G – Aug. 16 - Oct. 10 (also May 24, June 1, 2, 7).
§ – May 22 depart 2030.

Moby Lines

Genova		Olbia		Olbia		Genova	
2200	→	0730	May 22 - Oct. 10.	2200	→	0730	May 21 - Oct. 10.

Tirrenia

Genova		Olbia	
1800	→	0715	①③⑤ Apr. 1 - June 12; ②⑤⑦ June 14 - July 17.
Olbia		**Genova**	
2030	→	1000	②④⑥ Apr. 2 - June 13; ①③⑥ June 15 - July 18.

GENOVA - PORTO TORRES — 2009 service

Grandi Navi Veloci Journey 11 hours Departure times vary.

From Genova: ①③⑤⑦ Apr. 6 - May 13; daily May 15 - Aug. 15; ①②③④⑤⑦ Aug. 17 - Sept. 25; ①③④⑤ Sept. 28 - Oct. 30; ①③⑤ Nov. 2 - Dec. 30 (also Apr. 30).

From Porto Torres: ②④⑥⑦ Apr. 7 - May 14; daily May 16 - Sept. 26; ②④⑤⑥ Sept. 29 - Oct. 31; ②④⑥ Nov. 3 - Dec. 29 (also May 1).

Moby Lines

Genova		Porto Torres		Porto Torres		Genova	
1000	→	2000	See note **P**.	1000	→	2000	See note **S**.
2200	→	0800	See note **R**.	2200	→	0800	See note **T**.

P – ①④⑤⑥⑦ Aug. 17 - Sept. 27.
R – ①③④⑤⑥⑦ May 28 - Aug. 15; ② Aug. 18 - Sept. 22.
S – ①④⑤⑥⑦ May 29 - Aug. 15.
T – ② June 2 - Aug. 11; ①③④⑤⑥⑦ Aug. 16 - Sept. 27.

Tirrenia

Genova		Porto Torres	Porto Torres		Genova	
2030	→	0630	2030	→	0630	Apr. 1 - July 31.

LIVORNO - GOLFO ARANCI — 2009 service

Sardinia Ferries — Journey 6½-10 hours.

From Livorno and Golfo Aranci: up to 3 sailings daily. Departure times vary.

LIVORNO - OLBIA — 2009 service

Moby Lines

Sailings from Livorno Marittima, Varco Galvani and Olbia.

Jan. - Mar.: 1 sailing per day; Apr. - May: 1-2 sailings per day; June - Sept.: 2-3 sailings per day; Oct. - Dec. 1 sailing per day. Departure times vary.

NAPOLI - CAGLIARI — 2009 service

Tirrenia

Napoli		Cagliari	
1915	→	1130	④ Apr. 2 - July 30; ②④ Aug. 4 - Sept. 3; ④ Sept. 17-24.
Cagliari		**Napoli**	
1830	→	1045	③ Apr. 1 - July 29; ①③ Aug. 3 - Sept. 2; ③ Sewpt. 16-30.

PIOMBINO - OLBIA — 2009 service

Moby Lines

Piombino		Olbia		Olbia		Piombino	
0800	→	1230	May 30, 31 only.	1430	→	1900	May 23, 30, 31 only.
1000	→	1630	See note **Q**.	2200	→	0430	See note **Q**.

P – ①②③④⑤⑥ Oct. 1 - Dec. 23; daily Dec. 27, 28, Jan. 2, 4; ①②③④⑤⑥ Jan. 5-31.
Q – ①②③④⑤ Apr. 1 - May 20 (not May 1).

Sailings from SICILY

PALERMO - CAGLIARI — 2009 service

Tirrenia

Palermo		Cagliari		Cagliari		Palermo	
1700⑥	→	0630⑦	Apr. 4 - Sept. 26.	1900⑤	→	0930⑥	Apr. 3 - Sept. 25.

TRAPANI - CAGLIARI — 2009 service

Tirrenia

Cagliari		Trapani	
1000	→	2000	⑦ Apr. 5 - Sept. 27.
Trapani		**Cagliari**	
2359	→	1000	⑦ Apr. 5 - Sept. 27.

SÈTE - AN-NADÛR (NADOR) 2678

Cie. Marocaine de Navigation (Comanav) — **2009 service** (subject to alteration)

Depart 1900 from Sète, 1800 from an-Nadûr. Sailings arrive 2 days later.
Departures from Sète: June - Oct.: up to 6–8 sailings per month.
Departures from an-Nadûr: June - Oct.: up to 6–8 sailings per month.

SÈTE - TANJAH (TANGIERS) 2680

Cie. Marocaine de Navigation (Comanav) — **2009 service** (subject to alteration)

Depart 1900 from Sète, 1800 from Tanjah. Sailings arrive 2 days later.
Departures from Sète: June - Oct.: up to 6–8 sailings per month.
Departures from Tanjah: June - Oct.: up to 6–8 sailings per month.

TRAPANI - TÛNIS 2682

Ustica Lines — 2008 service

Trapani		Tûnis	Tûnis		Trapani
1030①③	→	2000①③	2230①③	→	0800②④

VALLETTA - CATANIA 2690

Virtu Ferries by catamaran — 2009 service

Valletta		Catania	
0500	→	0800	⑥ Apr. 4-25; ②⑥ May 2 - Sept. 29; ⑥ Oct. 3 - Dec. 26.
Catania		**Valletta**	
1930	→	2230	⑥ Apr. 4-25.
2000	→	2300	②⑥ May 2 - Sept. 29; ⑥ Oct. 3 - Dec. 26.

VALLETTA - GENOVA 2691

Grandi Navi Veloci — 2009 service

Valletta		Genova	Genova		Valletta
1500①	→	2030②	1800⑥	→	0830①

Departure times may vary

VALLETTA - POZZALLO 2694

Virtu Ferries by catamaran Journey 1½ hours — 2009 service

1–2 sailings daily on ①③④⑤⑦ only; departure times vary.

2695 VILLA S. GIOVANNI - MESSINA

Italian Railways Journey 35 minutes **Service to June 13, 2009**

From Villa S.G.: 0055, 0140, 0215, 0335, 0420, 0500, 0625, 0705, 0735, 0900, 0935, 1005, 1140, 1215, 1250, 1425, 1510, 1530, 1655, 1750, 1825, 1935, 2030, 2105, 2215, 2300, 2340.

From Messina: 0020, 0055, 0215, 0300, 0335, 0455, 0540, 0615, 0740, 0820, 0850, 1020, 1055, 1130, 1300, 1350, 1410, 1540, 1630, 1650, 1815, 1910, 1945, 2055, 2145, 2225, 2335.

2699 OTHER SERVICES

Moby Lines **2009 services**

Piombino - Portoferraio (Elba): 7 sailings daily in winter, 13 - 16 sailings in summer, journey 1 hour (no service on Dec. 25).

Toremar **2009 services**

Services operate from Piombino to Cavo, Pianosa, Portoferraio and Rio Marina; from Livorno to Capraia and Gorgona; and from Porto Santo Stefano to Isola del Giglio.

ADRIATIC / EASTERN MEDITERRANEAN / BLACK SEA

2705 ANCONA - BAR

Montenegro Lines **2009 service (No winter service)**

Ancona		Bar	
1600	→	0700	④⑥ July 4 - Sept. 5 (also Aug. 24, 31).
Bar		**Ancona**	
1600§	→	0700§	③⑤ July 3 - Sept. 4 (also Aug. 23, 30).

§ – Sails 4 hours later on ③ Aug. 19, 26, Sept. 2.

2715 ANCONA - PÁTRA via Igumenítsa

Anek Lines **Service to January 10, 2010**

February 17 - March 29 and November 3 - January 10
(from Pátra, following day from Ancona)

Ancona		Igumenítsa		Pátra
1600①③④⑤⑥⑦	→	0830②④⑤⑥⑦①	→	1400②④⑤⑥⑦①
Pátra		**Igumenítsa**		**Ancona**
1700②③④⑤⑥⑦	→	2230②③④⑤⑥⑦	→	1300③④⑤⑥⑦①

March 31 - November 1 ▲
(from Pátra, following day from Ancona)

Ancona		Igumenítsa		Pátra	Pátra		Igumenítsa		Ancona
1600	→	0800	→	1330	1700	→	2230	→	1230

▲ – No sailings from Pátra (following day from Ancona): Apr. 13, 27, May 11, June 1, 8, 22, July 27, Sept. 14, 28, Oct. 12, 26.

🚌 connection Pátra - Pireás - Athína and v.v. operates most days in summer.

Minoan Lines **Service to October 31, 2009**

Ancona		Igumenítsa		Pátra	Pátra		Igumenítsa		Ancona
1700	→	0900	→	1500	1800	→	2330	→	1400

No sailings from Pátra: Mar. 4, 11, 18, 25, Apr. 1, 8, 15, 22, 29, May 6, 13, 20, 27, June 3, 10, 17, July 15, Aug. 12, Sept. 9, 16, 23, 30, Oct. 7, 14, 21, 28 (one day later from Ancona).

Superfast Ferries **2009 service**

Ancona		Igumenítsa		Pátra		Pátra		Igumenítsa		Ancona	
1330	→	0530	→	1130		1430	→	2000	→	1030	
1800	→	1000	→	1600	②④⑥	1900	→	2359	→	1500	①③⑤

Subject to alteration during ship maintenance periods

🚌 connection Pátra - Pireás - Athína and v.v.

Tickets available on-board ship and from 30 Amalías av., Síndagma, Athína.

2725 ANCONA - SPLIT

Blue Line Journey 9 hours **2009 service**

March 29 - July 23 and September 6 - October 31
Depart Ancona: 2030①②③④⑤⑥. Depart Split: 2030①②③④⑤⑦.

July 24 - August 27
Depart Ancona: 1030 **A**, 2030. Depart Split: 1030 **A**, 2030.

August 28 - September 5
Depart Ancona: 2030. Depart Split: 2030 (not Sept. 5).

November 1 - December 20
Depart Ancona: 2030①③⑤. Depart Split: 2030②④⑦.

A – ⑤⑥⑦ July 31 - Aug. 9; ①⑥⑦ Aug. 10 - 27.

Jadrolinija **2009 service**

Ancona		Split		Split		Ancona	
			February 1 - July 9 and September 4 - 30				
2100	→	0700	①③⑤	2100	→	0700	②④⑦
			July 10 - September 3				
1130	→	1915	⑦	2200	→	0700	②④
2100	→	0600	①③⑤	2200	→	0900	⑥⑦ (via Hvar).

SNAV by catamaran *Croazia Jet* **June 13 - September 6, 2009 (No winter service)**
Journey 4½ hours

Ancona		Split	Split		Ancona
1100	→	1530	1700	→	2130

2732 ANCONA - ZADAR

Jadrolinija **2009 service**

Ancona		Zadar		Zadar		Ancona	
			February 1 - May 31				
2200	→	0700	②④⑥	2200	→	0700	①③⑤
			June 1 - July 16 and September 2 - 30				
2200	→	0700	②④⑤⑥	1200	→	1800	⑤⑥
				2200	→	0700	①③
			July 17 - September 1				
1230	→	1830	⑦	0800	→	1400	⑥
1600	→	2200	⑥	1200	→	1800	②③④⑤
2200	→	0530	⑤	2200	→	0700	⑦
2200	→	0600	①②③④	2345	→	0700	⑥

2735 ANCONA - ÇEŞME

Marmara Lines **2009 service (No winter service)**

Ancona		Çeşme	
2230⑥	→	0630②	May 2 - June 27, Aug. 15 - Oct. 24.
2230⑥	→	2330①	July 4 - Aug. 8.
Çeşme		**Ancona**	
1100④	→	1800⑥	Apr. 30 - July 30, Sept. 17 - Oct. 22.
1430④	→	1800⑥	Aug. 6 - Sept. 10.

2738 BARI - BAR

Azzurra Line Journey 8½ – 10 hours **2009 service (No winter service)**

Departure times vary.

From Bari: Apr. 21, 28, May 5, 6, 12, 19, 26, June 9, 13, 16, 20, 27, July 2, 9, 16, 23, Aug. 3, 6, 13, 20, 27, Sept. 5, 12.

From Bar: Apr. 22, 29, May 13, 20, 27, June 10, 14, 17, 21, 28, July 3, 10, 17, 24, Aug. 4, 7, 14, 21, 28, Sept. 6, 13.

Montenegro Lines **2009 service**

Bari		Bar		Bar		Bari	
1000	→	1900	③ Aug. 19 - Sept. 2.	1200	→	2100	See note **C**.
1200	→	2100	See note **B**.	2200	→	0800	See note **D**.
2200	→	0800	See note **A**.				

A – ①③⑤ Jan. 1 - June 30; ①③⑤⑥ July 1 - 11; ①③⑤⑥⑦ July 13 - 26; daily July 27 - Aug. 12; ② Aug. 18 - Sept. 1; ①③⑤ Sept. 7 - Dec. 19 (also June 27, Aug. 16, 17, Dec. 19, 21, 22, 23, 28, 30).

B – Aug. 14, 15, 20 - 24, 27 - 31, Sept. 3 - 6, 13.

C – ⑥ July 4 - 11; ⑥⑦ July 18 - 26; ④⑤⑥⑦ July 30 - Aug. 9 (also June 27, Dec. 19, 22, 23).

D – ②④⑦ Jan. 1 - July 26; ①②⑦ July 27 - Aug. 11; daily Aug. 13 - Sept. 6; ②④⑦ Sept. 8 - Dec. 19 (also Sept. 12, Dec. 20, 27, 29).

2740 BARI - KÉRKIRA (CORFU)

Ventouris Ferries **Service to September 30, 2009**

From Bari and Kérkira: 1 - 2 per week (6 - 7 per week in summer). Departure times vary.

2745 BARI - IGUMENÍTSA

Ventouris Ferries Journey 12½ hours **Service to September 30, 2009**

From Bari and Igumenítsa: Up to 6 sailings per week (1 - 2 per day in summer). Departure times vary.

2755 BARI - PÁTRA via Kérkira and Igumenítsa

Blue Star Ferries / Superfast Ferries **2009 service**

Bari		Kérkira		Igumenítsa		Pátra
1200⑦	→	2100⑦	→	2230⑦	→	0600①
2000①–⑥	→	0500②–⑦§	→	0630②–⑦	→	1230②–⑦
Pátra		**Igumenítsa**		**Kérkira**		**Bari**
1800	→	2359	→	0130⊡	→	0830

§ – Kérkira sailings operate ⑤⑥ July 24 - Aug. 29 only.

⊡ – Kérkira sailings operate ⑥⑦ Aug. 1 - Sept. 6 only.

Subject to alteration during ship maintenance periods

🚌 connection Pátra - Pireás - Athína and v.v.

Tickets available on-board ship and from 30 Amalías av., Síndagma, Athína.

 For international shipping maps – see pages 518 - 520

BLACK SEA services 2760

Bumerang Shipping Company Tourism Travel & Trade S.A.

İSTANBUL - YALTA - NOVOROSSISK Irregular sailings, journey 30 hours

İSTANBUL - YEVPATORIYA Journey 24 hours

Ukrferry **2009 service**

İSTANBUL - ODESA

İstanbul		Odesa	Odesa		İstanbul
2359④	→	1300⑥	2100①	→	0800③

Schedules subject to change at short notice

BRINDISI - IGUMENÍTSA 2765

Endeavor Lines **2009 service**

From Brindisi: Daily May 1 - Sept. 30 (not Aug. 14). Additional sailing June 3.
From Igumenitsa: Daily May 1 - Sept. 29 (not May 4, June 4, 8, 10, 16, 18, 22, 24, 30, July 2, Sept. 16, 18, 22, 24, 28). Additional sailing May 3, June 2, 3, 5-7, 9, 11, 13-15, 17, 19-21, 23, 25, 27-29, July 1, 3-31, Aug. 1-14, 16-31, Sept. 1-15, 17, 19, 21, 23, 25-27, 29).

Departure times vary

BRINDISI - KÉRKIRA (CORFU) 2770

Endeavor Lines **2009 service**

Brindisi		Kérkira		Kérkira		Brindisi	
1800	→	0845	See note **A**.	0915	→	1445	See note **B**.

A – May 28, 29, June 4, 5, 10, 12, 13, 18, 19, 24, 26, 27, July 2-8, 10-15, 17-29, 31, Aug. 1-5, 7-12, 15-19, 21-26, 28-31, Sept. 1, 2, 4, 5, 11-13.
B – May 4, June 3, 5, 6, 11, 13, 14, 19, 20, 25, 27, 28, July 3-9, 11-16, 18-30, Aug. 1-6, 8-13, 16-20, 22-27, 29-31, Sept. 1-3, 5, 6, 12-14.

Departure times may vary

BRINDISI - PÁTRA 2775

Endeavor Lines **2009 service**

Brindisi		Pátra		Pátra		Brindisi	
1830	→	1030	May 1 - Sept. 30.	1730	→	0830	May 1 - Sept. 30.

Departure times may vary

BRINDISI - SÁMI (Kefallinía) 2780

Endeavor Lines **2009 service**

Brindisi		Sámi		Sámi		Brindisi	
1830	→	0645	See note **K**.	2045	→	0830	See note **L**.

K – June 5, 6, 10, 12-14, 19, 20, 24, 26-28; daily July 2 - Sept. 6.
L – June 7, 10, 12-14, 19-21, 24, 26-28, 30; daily July 3 - Sept. 13 (also Sept. 19, 20).

Sailings also operate from Brindisi to Zákinthos (Zante); June 1 - Sept. 30.

BRINDISI - ÇEŞME 2785

Marmara Lines **2008 service (No winter service)**

Brindisi		Çeşme		Çeşme		Brindisi	
1130③	→	2435④	July 2 - Sept. 10.	0715⑤	→	1830⑥	July 4 - Sept. 5.
2230⑥	→	1245①	July 5 - Sept. 6.	1930①	→	0700③	June 30 - Sept. 8.

DUBROVNIK - BARI 2795

Azzurra Line Journey 9–10 hours **2009 service (No winter service)**

Departure times vary.
From Dubrovnik: Apr. 11, 14, May 1, 3, 30, June 2, 13, 20, 24, 27, July 4, 11, 18, 25, 28, 31, Aug. 1, 8, 11, 12, 15, 18, 19, 22, 25, 26, 29, Sept. 1, 8.
From Bari: Apr. 10, 14, 30 May 3, 29, June 2, 12, 19, 23, 26, July 3, 10, 17, 24, 27, 30, 31, Aug. 7, 10, 11, 14, 17, 18, 21, 24, 25, 28, 31, Sept. 7.

Jadrolinija **Service to September 30, 2009**

Dubrovnik		Bari	
1130	→	1930	⑤ June 5 - Sept. 25.
1230	→	2000	⑦ June 7 - Sept. 27.
1530	→	2130	⑥ Apr. 11 - May 30.
1600	→	2200	⑥ June 5 - Sept. 25.
2300	→	0800	② Feb. 3 - May 26; ①②③ June 1 - Sept. 28.
Bari		**Dubrovnik**	
2200	→	0700	③ Feb. 4 - May 27; ②③④⑤⑦ June 2 - Sept. 30.
2230	→	0700	⑦ Apr. 11 - May 30.
2359	→	0700	⑥ June 6 - Sept. 26.

GREEK ISLANDS 2800

Summary table of regular ⛴ services to the Greek Islands.

Each route is operated by various shipping companies to differing schedules.
Further details are given in the **Thomas Cook Guide to Greek Island Hopping**.
Additional inter-island routes are operated at less regular intervals.

Pireás to Égina, Póros, Ídra, Spétses, Kíthira, Andikíthira.
Pireás to Sérifos, Sífnos, Mílos, Folégandros.
Pireás to Páros, Íos, Thíra (Santorini), Iráklio.
Pireás to Náxos, Amorgós, Astipálea.
Pireás to Pátmos, Léros, Kálimnos, Kos, Nísiros, Tílos, Sími, Ródos, Kárpathos, Kásos.
Pireás to Ikaria, Sámos, Híos, Lésvos.
Pireás and **Rafína** to Síros, Dílos, Míkonos, Tínos, Ándros.
Pátra to Zákinthos (Zante), Kefallinía, Itháki, Kérkira (Corfu), Igumenítsa.
Vólos, Ágios Konstantínos and **Kími** to Skíathos, Skópelos, Alónissos, Skíros.
Kavála to Thásos, Samothráki, Límnos.

PESCARA - SPLIT 2810

Jadrolinija **2009 service (No winter service)**

Pescara	Split	Split	Pescara

NO SERVICE SUMMER 2009

SNAV by catamaran *Croazia Jet* **June 13 - September 6, 2009 (No winter service)**

Pescara		Split	Split		Pescara
1030	→	1615	1700	→	2330

PIREÁS - IRÁKLIO 2830

Superfast Ferries **2009 service**

Pireás		Iráklio	Iráklio		Pireás
1530	→	2200	2345	→	0615

2845 PIREÁS - LEMESÓS (LIMASSOL) - HEFA

Salamis Lines — **2009 service**

Salamis Cruise Lines operate 2/3 day cruises Apr. - Oct. – contact operator for details.

2855 RIJEKA - SPLIT - DUBROVNIK

Jadrolinija — **2009 service**

February 1 - May 31

Rijeka	Split	Stari Grad	Korčula	Dubrovnik	
1900① →	0700② →	0900② →	1300② →	1615②	Until Mar. 30.
2000① →	0700② →	0900② →	1300② →	1615②	From Apr. 6.
1900⑤ →	0700⑥ →	0900⑥ →	1300⑥ →	1615⑥	Until Apr. 3.
2000⑤ →	0630⑥ →	0815⑥ →	1130⑥ →	1430⑥	From Apr. 10.

Dubrovnik	Korčula	Stari Grad	Split	Rijeka	
0900④ →	1235④ →	1630④ →	1930④ →	0700⑤	
0900⑦ →	1235⑦ →	1630⑦ →	1930⑦ →	0700①	Not May 31.

June 1 - September 30

Rijeka	Split	Stari Grad	Korčula	Dubrovnik	
...	...	...	1800① →	2150①	
2000① →	0700② →	0900② →	1300② →	1615②	
...	...	...	1800③ →	2150③	Not Sept. 30.
2000⑤ →	0630⑥ →	0815⑥ →	1130⑥ →	1430⑥	
...	1800⑥ →	→	→ 2200⑥	...	June 27 - Sept. 5.
...	...	...	0700⑦ →	1050⑦	

Dubrovnik	Korčula	Stari Grad	Split	Rijeka	
0830① →	1240①	...	...	...	
0830③ →	1240③	...	...	...	
1000④ →	1330④ →	1700④ →	2000④ →	0700⑤	
0830⑥ →	1240⑥	...	...	...	
...	1330⑥ →	→	→ 1730⑥	...	June 27 - Sept. 5.
1000⑦ →	1330⑦ →	1700⑦ →	2000⑦ →	0700①	

2875 VENEZIA - PÁTRA via Igumenítsa and Kérkira (Corfu)

Anek Lines — **Service to January 8, 2010**

January 8 - April 6 and October 8 - January 8

(from Pátra, 2 days later from Venezia)

Venezia	Igumenítsa	Kérkira	Pátra	Pátra	Kérkira	Igumenítsa	Venezia
1900② →	2100③ →	2300③ →	0600④	2359① →	→	0800② →	0730③
1900③ →	2100④ →	→	0600⑤	2359④ →	→	0800⑤ →	0730⑥
1200⑥ →	1400⑦ →	→	2100⑦	2359⑤ →	0615⑥ →	0800⑥ →	0730⑦
1200⑦ →	1400① →	→	2100①	2359⑦ →	→	0800① →	0730②

April 9 - October 5

(from Pátra, 2 days later from Venezia)

Venezia	Igumenítsa	Kérkira	Pátra	Pátra	Kérkira	Igumenítsa	Venezia
1900② →	2030③ →	2230③ →	0600④	2359① →	0630② →	0830② →	0730③
1900③ →	2030④ →	2230④ →	0600⑤	2359④ →	0630⑤ →	0830⑤ →	0730⑥
1200⑥ →	1300⑦ →	1430⑦ →	2100⑦	2359⑤ →	0630⑥ →	0830⑥ →	0730⑦
1200⑦ →	1300① →	1430① →	2100①	2359⑦ →	0630① →	0830① →	0730②

Minoan Lines — **2009 service**

January 26 - March 31

(from Pátra, 2 days later from Venezia)

Venezia	Kérkira	Igumenítsa	Pátra	Pátra	Kérkira	Igumenítsa	Venezia
1700① →	→	→ 2015② →	0500③	2359① →	0700② →	0900② →	0800③
1400③ →	1115④ →	1230④ →	1930④	2359③ →	→	→ 0900④ →	0800⑤
1400⑤ →	→	→ 1300⑥ →	1930⑥	2359④ →	0700⑤ →	0900⑤ →	0800⑥
1700⑥ →	1900⑦ →	2015⑦ →	0500①	2359⑥ →	→	→ 0900⑦ →	0800①

April 1 - October 31

(from Pátra, 2 days later from Venezia)

Venezia	Igumenítsa	Kérkira	Pátra	Pátra	Kérkira	Igumenítsa	Venezia
1700① →	2000② →	2130② →	0500③	2359① →	0700② →	0900② →	0800③
1400③ →	1200④ →	1330④ →	2000④	2359③ →	0700④ →	0900④ →	0800⑤
1400⑤ →	1200⑥ →	1330⑥ →	2000⑥	2359④ →	0700⑤ →	0900⑤ →	0800⑥
1700⑥ →	2000⑦ →	2130⑦ →	0500①	2359⑥ →	0700⑦ →	0900⑦ →	0800①

Subject to alteration during Xmas/New Year period

2880 BARI - DURRËS

Tirrenia — **Service to September 30, 2009**

Bari	Durrës		Durrës	Bari
2300 →	0800		2300 →	0800

Ventouris Ferries Journey 10 hours — **2009 service**

March 1 - May 31

From Bari and Durrës: 4–5 sailings per week (most departures overnight).

June 1 - September 30

From Bari and Durrës: 1–3 sailings per day (most departures overnight).

2899 OTHER SERVICES

Jadrolinija — **2009 services**

Many local services operate to the Islands along the Croatian coast.

Split Tours — **2009 services**

Many local Island services operated from Split.

Venezia Lines — **2009 services**

Summer services from Venezia to Mali Lošinj, Piran, Poreč, Pula, Rabac and Rovinj.

TGV Atlantique

PARIS - LE MANS - RENNES and NANTES 280 (Summer)

Service July 5 - Aug. 30. *For service to July 4 and from Aug. 31 see page 184*

Many trains continue to destinations in Tables **284**, **285** and **288**. For other trains Massy - Nantes via St Pierre des Corps see Table **335**.

km	*July 5 - Aug. 30*				TGV 8903	TGV 8003	TGV 8905		TGV 8009*	TGV 8909	TGV 8613*	TGV 5486	TGV 8813	TGV 8715	TGV 8713			TGV 8923	TGV 8619	TGV 5214	TGV 5213	TGV 5350	TGV 5360	TGV 5365
		Ⓐ	⑥	Ⓐ	Ⓐ	①–⑥	①–⑥	Ⓐ							⑥	⑦						Ⓑ	⑥	⑥
			t			n	n					☆				e						♠	♣	♣
	Lille Europe **11** d.	...	...	...	...	...	...	...	...	...	...	...	...	...	...	...	...	...	...	0846	0846	...	...	...
	Charles de Gaulle ✈ d.	...	...	...	...	...	...	...	...	...	...	...	...	...	...	...	...	...	...	1027	1027	...	...	...
	Marne la Vallée - Chessy § d.	...	...	...	...	...	...	...	...	...	...	0900	...	...	...	...	...	...	...	1042	1042	...	...	...
0	**Paris Montparnasse** d.	...	...	...	0700	0705	0730	...	0805	0900	0905	|	1000	1005	1025	...	...	1100	1105	|	|	...	...	...
14	Massy TGV d.	...	...	...	|	0716	0741	...	|	|	|	0933	|	|	|	...	...	|	|	1117	1117	1131	1131	1131
202	**Le Mans** d.	0620	0637	0650	|	0808	0832	0840	0902	|	|	1023	1057	|	|	1104	1104	|	1202	1209	1213	1222	1222	1225
292	Laval d.	0725	0729	|	|	0851	|	|	0943	|	|	|	|	|	|	1150	|	|	1244	|	|	|	|	|
327	Vitré d.	0749	0754	|	|	|	|	|	|	|	|	|	|	|	|	1214	|	|	|	|	|	|	|	|
365	**Rennes** a.	0819	0815	|	|	0926	|	|	1020	|	1108	|	|	1208	1229	1245	|	|	1321	1327	|	1340	1333	|
251	Sablé d.	...	...	0713	|	...	0854	0859	...	|	...	|	|	...	...	...	1124	|	...	...	|	...	...	|
299	Angers St Laud **289** d.	...	...	0738	|	...	0916	0922	...	1033	...	1102	1137	...	...	...	1145	|	...	...	1253	...	...	1305
387	**Nantes 289** a.	...	...	0818	0901	...	0952	1002	...	1108	...	1140	1213	...	...	...	1231	1304	...	...	1333	...	...	1342

July 5 - Aug. 30		TGV 8823	TGV 5470	TGV 8719*	TGV 8929	TGV 8621	TGV 8933*	TGV 5224	TGV 5227	TGV 8051	TGV 8625	TGV 8835		TGV 8651			TGV 8837*	TGV 8729*		TGV 5375	TGV 5371	TGV 8843	TGV 8033*	TGV 8031	
	⚒				⑤	⑤				⑤	⑦	⑤	⑤	L	⑤				Ⓐ	⑦	⑦	⑤	Ⓑ	⑥	
			☆								e									♠e	♠e				H
Lille Europe **11** d.	...	...	...	...	...	...	...	1210	1210	...	...	...	...	...	...	...	...	...	...	...	...	...	...	...	...
Charles de Gaulle ✈ d.	...	...	...	...	...	...	...	1316	1316	...	...	...	...	...	...	...	...	...	...	...	...	...	...	...	...
Marne la Vallée - Chessy § d.	...	...	1122	...	...	...	...	1329	1329	...	...	...	...	...	...	...	...	...	...	...	...	...	...	...	...
Paris Montparnasse d.	...	1200	|	1205	1300	1305	1400	|	|	1405	1405	1430	...	1435	...	...	1500	1505	...	...	...	1600	1605	1605	...
Massy TGV d.	...	|	1200	|	|	|	|	1401	1401	|	|	|	...	|	...	...	|	|	...	1532	1532	|	|	|	...
Le Mans d.	1228	|	1253	1302	|	1402	1457	1453	1502	|	|	1524	1535	|	1539	...	|	|	1629	1622	1626	|	|	1702	1706
Laval d.	1325	|	1335	|	|	|	|	|	|	1539	1539	...	|	1609	1627	...	|	|	1723	|	1709	|	|	1743	|
Vitré d.	...	|	|	|	|	|	|	|	|	1558	1558	...	|	1628	1644	...	|	|	...	|	|	|	|	|	|
Rennes a.	...	|	1410	1413	|	1515	|	1607	|	1619	1619	...	|	1649	1703	...	|	1708	...	|	1743	|	1808	1820	|
Sablé d.	...	|	...	...	|	...	|	...	|	...	...	...	1555	...	...	...	|	...	...	|	...	|	...	...	1726
Angers St Laud **289** d.	...	1339	...	...	1435	...	1538	...	1542	...	...	...	1618	...	...	...	1632	...	...	1702	...	1733	...	...	1749
Nantes 289 a.	...	1414	...	...	1511	...	1612	...	1617	...	...	...	1657	...	...	...	1707	...	...	1736	...	1808	...	...	1830

July 5 - Aug. 30	TGV 5232	TGV 5216	TGV 8737*			TGV 8849		TGV 8747*	TGV 8745		TGV 8953*	TGV 8649*		TGV 8955	TGV 8957	TGV 8861	TGV 8657	TGV 8659	TGV 8653		TGV 8093*	TGV 8965	TGV 8873	TGV 8869	TGV 8871
	①–⑥	⑦	Ⓐ	Ⓐ	†	Ⓐ	Ⓐ	①–⑥	⑦		①–⑥	⑤	Ⓐ	Ⓐ	Ⓒ	⑤	Ⓐ	⑦	⑥	Ⓒ	Ⓐ	①–⑥	A	⑤	⑤
	n	e						n	e		n							e				n			
Lille Europe **11** d.	1447	1447	...	...	...	...	...	...	...	...	...	...	...	...	...	...	...	...	...	...	...	...	...	...	...
Charles de Gaulle ✈ d.	1542	1542	...	...	...	...	...	...	...	...	...	...	...	...	...	...	...	...	...	...	...	...	...	...	...
Marne la Vallée - Chessy § d.	1557	1557	...	...	...	...	...	...	...	...	...	...	...	...	...	...	...	...	...	...	...	...	...	...	...
Paris Montparnasse d.	|	|	1635	...	...	1700	...	1705	1705	...	1730	1735	...	1750	1750	1800	1805	1805	1805	...	1835	1830	1845	1845	1900
Massy TGV d.	1631	1631	|	...	...	|	...	|	|	...	|	|	...	|	|	|	|	|	|	...	|	|	|	|	|
Le Mans d.	1722	|	1732	1738	1745	1757	1800	|	1801	...	|	1832	1835	1847	1847	|	|	1902	1902	1910	|	|	1942	1942	|
Laval d.	|	|	1813	1823	|	|	|	|	1843	...	|	1913	1926	|	|	|	|	|	1943	2010	2012	|	|	|	|
Vitré d.	|	◐	|	1842	|	|	|	|	|	...	|	|	...	|	|	|	|	|	2003	...	2031	|	|	|	|
Rennes a.	1836	|	1855	1904	|	|	|	1908	1920	...	|	1950	...	|	|	|	2008	2015	2024	...	2049	|	|	|	|
Sablé d.	...	|	...	...	1805	|	1820	...	...	...	|	...	...	|	|	|	...	...	...	...	...	|	2002	2002	|
Angers St Laud **289** d.	...	1815	...	...	1828	1836	1843	...	...	...	|	...	...	1931	1927	|	...	...	...	...	...	|	2025	2031	|
Nantes 289 a.	...	1854	...	...	1908	1912	1923	...	...	...	1930	...	...	2008	2003	2002	...	...	...	...	...	2033	2102	2112	2102

July 5 - Aug. 30	TGV 5373	TGV 5363	TGV 8665	TGV 8669	TGV 5236*		TGV 5231	TGV 8763*	TGV 8879*	TGV 8071	TGV 5387	TGV 8775	TGV 8887*	TGV 5488	TGV 8077	TGV 8679	TGV 8069	TGV 5234	TGV 5390	TGV 5210	TGV 5247	TGV 8895	TGV 8073	TGV 8075	
	①–⑥	①–⑥	①–⑥	⑦		Ⓑ			Ⓑ		①–④	⑤		☆	G	⑤	⑦	①–④	⑤⑦	⑤⑦	⑦	⑤⑦	⑤	⑦	
	♠n	♠n	n	e							♣n						e	n	♣e	e	e	e▽		e	
Lille Europe **11** d.	...	...	...	...	1729	...	1729	...	...	...	...	...	...	...	...	...	...	1939	...	2014	2014	...	...	...	...
Charles de Gaulle ✈ d.	...	...	...	...	1824	...	1824	...	...	...	...	...	...	...	...	...	...	2034	...	2109	2109	...	...	...	...
Marne la Vallée - Chessy § d.	...	...	...	...	1840	...	1840	...	...	...	...	...	...	2024	...	...	...	2050	...	2125	2125	...	...	...	...
Paris Montparnasse d.	...	...	1905	1905	|	...	|	1935	2000	2005	...	2035	2100	|	2105	2105	2105	|	...	|	|	2200	2205	2205	...
Massy TGV d.	1901	1901	|	|	1917	...	1921	|	|	|	2032	|	|	2101	|	|	|	2131	2137	2201	2201	|	|	|	...
Le Mans d.	1952	1957	2002	|	2008	2020	|	|	|	2102	2122	|	|	2157	|	2202	2202	2222	2227	2253	2258	2257	|	|	...
Laval d.	2034	|	|	2039	2048	|	|	|	|	2143	|	|	|	|	|	|	2244	|	|	|	|	|	2340	2343	...
Vitré d.	|	|	|	2058	|	|	◐	|	|	|	|	|	|	|	|	2258	2304	|	|	|	|	|	|	|	...
Rennes a.	2110	|	2115	2119	2125	|	|	2138	|	2220	2234	2238	|	|	2308	2317	2323	|	2339	|	0010	|	0016	0019	...
Sablé d.	...	|	...	...	...	2040	|	...	|	...	...	...	|	|	...	...	...	|	...	|	...	|	...	...	...
Angers St Laud **289** d.	...	2038	...	...	...	2103	2108	...	2133	...	...	...	2231	2239	...	...	...	2304	...	2331	...	2337	...	...	...
Nantes 289 a.	...	2116	...	...	...	2143	2147	...	2208	...	...	...	2308	2314	...	...	...	2338	...	0007	...	0016	...	...	...

July 5 - Aug. 30	TGV 8800	TGV 8802	TGV 8004		TGV 5252	TGV 5254	TGV 8902		TGV 8808	TGV 8906	TGV 8806		TGV 8908	TGV 8008*		TGV 8812	TGV 5312			TGV 8716*	TGV 8014	TGV 8816	TGV 5478	TGV 8618*	
	①	Ⓐ	Ⓐ		①–⑥	①–⑥	①		①	②–⑤	⑥	Ⓐ	①	①–⑥	Ⓐ				Ⓐ	Ⓐ	Ⓒ	Ⓐ			
	g				n	n	g		g	n			g	n			♠						☆		
Nantes 289 d.	0500	0530	...	...	0604	...	0630	...	...	0630	0634	0634	0700	...	...	0730	0735	...	0739	...	...	0830	0834	...	...
Angers St Laud **289** d.	0542	0608	...	...	0643	...	|	...	0715	0715	0715	0719	|	...	...	0809	0813	...	0820	...	...	0907	0913	...	...
Sablé d.	|	0630	...	...	|	...	|	...	|	|	|	0744	|	...	...	|	|	...	0841	...	...	|	|	...	...
Rennes d.	|	|	0558	...	|	0610	|	...	|	|	|	|	|	0705	0710	|	|	...	|	0805	0805	|	|	0905	...
Vitré d.	|	|	0620	...	|	|	|	...	|	|	|	|	|	|	0728	|	|	...	|	|	|	|	|	|	...
Laval d.	|	|	0639	...	|	|	|	...	|	|	|	|	|	|	0748	|	|	...	|	0841	0841	|	|	|	...
Le Mans d.	0623	0652	0724	...	0731	0731	|	...	0759	0759	0759	0805	|	0819	0835	0849	0854	...	0903	0929	0929	|	0956	|	...
Massy TGV a.	|	|	|	...	0818	0818	|	...	|	|	|	...	|	|	...	|	0943	...	...	|	|	|	1047	|	...
Paris Montparnasse a.	0720	0750	0820	...	|	|	0835	...	0855	0855	0855	...	0905	0915	...	0945	...	...	...	1025	1025	1040	|	1110	...
Marne la Vallée - Chessy § a.	...	...	...	...	0900	0900	...	...	...	...	...	...	...	...	...	...	...	...	...	...	...	...	1123	...	...
Charles de Gaulle ✈ a.	...	...	...	...	0914	0914	...	...	...	...	...	...	...	...	...	...	...	...	...	...	...	...	...	...	...
Lille Europe **11** a.	...	...	...	...	1008	1008	...	...	...	...	...	...	...	...	...	...	...	...	...	...	...	...	...	...	...

July 5 - Aug. 30	TGV 8818	TGV 5318	TGV 5272	TGV 5270	TGV 8922	TGV 8620*	TGV 8726*			TGV 8936	TGV 8022	TGV 8926		TGV 5324	TGV 5322	TGV 8932	TGV 8930	TGV 8084	TGV 8732*	TGV 8836	TGV 5326		TGV 5278	TGV 5280	TGV 8942
										Ⓑ	Ⓐ	⑥	⚒	F		Ⓒ	Ⓐ				⑤⑥				
		♠												♣	♠						♠				
Nantes 289 d.	0900	...	...	0910	1100	...	...	...	1144	1200	...	1200	...	...	1252	1300	1300	...	...	1400	...	...	1435	...	1500
Angers St Laud **289** d.	0937	...	...	0948	1138	...	...	...	1227	1239	...	1238	...	...	1337	|	|	...	...	1438	...	...	1513	...	1537
Sablé d.	|	...	...	|	|	...	...	...	1248	|	...	|	...	...	|	|	|	...	...	|	...	...	|	...	|
Rennes d.	|	0910	0915	|	|	1105	1125	...	|	|	1205	|	...	1230	|	|	|	1305	1405	|	1414	...	|	1435	|
Vitré d.	|	|	|	|	|	|	|	...	|	|	|	|	...	|	◐	|	|	|	|	|	|	...	|	|	|
Laval d.	|	0946	0952	|	|	1142	|	...	|	|	|	|	1240	|	|	|	|	1340	|	|	|	...	|	|	|
Le Mans d.	1019	1029	1041	1041	|	1228	|	...	1309	|	1319	1319	1338	1351	|	|	1414	|	|	1519	1529	...	1557	1557	|
Massy TGV a.	|	1118	1133	1133	|	|	|	...	...	|	|	|	...	1438	1518	|	|	|	|	|	1618	...	1647	1647	|
Paris Montparnasse a.	1115	...	|	|	1310	1325	1330	...	...	1410	1415	1415	...	...	...	1505	1510	1515	1610	1615	...	...	|	|	1710
Marne la Vallée - Chessy § a.	...	...	1223	1223	...	...	...	...	...	...	...	...	...	...	...	...	...	...	...	...	...	...	1728	1728	...
Charles de Gaulle ✈ a.	...	...	1237	1237	...	...	...	...	...	...	...	...	...	...	...	...	...	...	...	...	...	...	1741	1741	...
Lille Europe **11** a.	...	...	1341	1341	...	...	...	...	...	...	...	...	...	...	...	...	...	...	...	...	...	...	1838z	1838z	...

A – Daily except ⑤.
F – ①②③④⑦ only.
G – ①②③④⑥ (not July 14).
H – ①②③④⑥ (not July 14, Aug. 15).
L – ①②③④⑥ only.

e – Also July 14.
g – Also July 15; not July 13.
n – Not July 14.
t – Not Aug. 15.
z – Lille **Flandres**.

TGV –🅁, supplement payable, 🍷.

NOTES CONTINUED ON NEXT PAGE →

280 (Summer) NANTES and RENNES - LE MANS - PARIS

Service July 5 - Aug. 30. *For service to July 4 and from Aug. 31 see page 185*

July 5 - Aug. 30	TGV 8844	TGV 8040*	TGV 5346	TGV 5480			TGV 8646	TGV 8752	TGV 8852	TGV 5334	TGV 5460		TGV 8958		TGV 8088	TGV 8662	TGV 8862	TGV 8862	TGV 8860	TGV 8864*	TGV 5338	TGV 8762	TGV 8864	TGV 5290
	⑤		①–④		Ⓑ	⑥				⑦		†		Ⓐ			①–④	⑤	Ⓒ	Ⓐ	⑦		⑦	
			♠n	☆						♣e	☆		△				n				♣e		e	
Nantes 289 d.	...	...	...	1520	1527	1527	...	...	1700	1708	...	1712	1730	1734	...	...	1800	1800	1800	1830	...	...	1830	...
Angers St Laud **289** d.	...	...	...	1600	1609	1610	...	...	1737	1744	...	1753	|	1816	...	...	1838	1838	1838	|	...	...	|	...
Sablé d.	...	...	...	|	1631	1633	...	...	|	|	...	1814	|	1838	...	...	1901	1901	1858	|	...	...	|	...
Rennes d.	...	1505	1514	|	|	|	1605	1705	|	|	1710	|	|	|	1735	1805	|	|	|	|	1827	1835	|	1840
Vitré d.	...	|	|	|	|	|	|	|	|	|	|	|	|	|	1757	|	|	|	|	|	|	|	|	|
Laval d.	...	|	|	|	|	|	1641	|	|	|	1746	|	|	|	1819	|	|	|	|	|	|	|	|	|
Le Mans d.	1609	|	1630	1640	1652	1703	1725	|	1819	1825	1835	1836	|	1859	1904	|	|	|	|	|	1952	|	1948	2000
Massy TGV a.	|	|	1717	1727	...	...	|	|	|	1912	1922	...	|	...	|	|	|	|	|	|	2042	|	|	2048
Paris Montparnasse a.	1705	1715	...	|	...	...	1820	1910	1915	...	|	...	1935	...	2000	2010	2015	2020	2020	2035	...	2040	2045	|
Marne la Vallée - Chessy § a.	...	...	...	1803	...	...	...	...	...	...	2003	...	...	...	...	...	...	...	...	...	...	...	...	2129
Charles de Gaulle ✈ a.	...	...	...	...	...	...	...	...	...	...	...	...	...	...	...	...	...	...	...	...	...	...	...	2146
Lille Europe **11** a.	...	...	...	...	...	...	...	...	...	...	...	...	...	...	...	...	...	...	...	...	...	...	...	2318

July 5 - Aug. 30	TGV 5288	TGV 8672	TGV 8670	TGV 8866	TGV 8966	TGV 5344	TGV 5342	TGV 8986	TGV 8774*	TGV 8980*	TGV 8780	TGV 8782	TGV 8096	TGV 5294	TGV 8688	TGV 8692*	TGV 8890	TGV 8896	TGV 8076	TGV 8098	TGV 8996	TGV 8686	TGV 8898	TGV 8078
		Ⓐ	Ⓒ	①–⑥	⑦	⑤	⑤	⑦	⑦		G	⑤	⑦	⑦	⑦		⑤	⑦	⑤	⑦	⑦	⑦	⑦	⑦
				n	e	♣	♣	e	e				e	e	e			e		e	e	e	e	e
Nantes 289 d.	1835	...	...	1900	1900	...	1904	1930	...	2000	...	...	...	...	...	...	2100	2100	...	...	2200	...	2230	...
Angers St Laud **289** d.	1912	...	...	1939	1941	...	1944	|	...	2039	...	...	...	...	...	...	2139	2143	...	...	|	...	2308	...
Sablé d.	|	...	...	|	|	...	|	|	...	|	...	...	...	...	...	...	|	|	...	...	|	...	|	...
Rennes d.	|	1904	1905	|	|	1909	|	|	1935	|	2005	2005	2005	2020	2035	2105	|	|	2130	2135	|	2205	|	2245
Vitré d.	|	|	|	|	|	|	|	|	|	|	|	|	2027	|	|	|	|	|	|	|	|	|	|	|
Laval d.	|	|	|	|	|	|	|	|	|	|	2041	2044	2047	|	|	|	|	|	2204	|	|	|	|	2319
Le Mans d.	2000	|	|	2019	2019	2030	2030	|	|	|	|	2129	2132	2138	|	|	2219	2225	|	|	|	|	|	|
Massy TGV a.	2048	|	|	|	|	2118	2118	|	|	|	|	|	|	2227	|	|	|	|	|	|	|	|	|	|
Paris Montparnasse a.	|	2110	2110	2115	2115	...	...	2135	2140	2210	2215	2225	2230	|	2240	2310	2315	2325	2340	2340	0005	0010	0040	0055
Marne la Vallée - Chessy § a.	2129	...	...	...	...	...	...	...	...	...	...	...	...	2301	...	...	...	...	...	...	...	...	...	...
Charles de Gaulle ✈ a.	2146	...	...	...	...	...	...	...	...	...	...	...	...	2316	...	...	...	...	...	...	...	...	...	...
Lille Europe **11** a.	2318	...	...	...	...	...	...	...	...	...	...	...	...	0010	...	...	...	...	...	...	...	...	...	...

NOTES - CONTINUED FROM PREVIOUS PAGE

§ – Station for Disneyland Paris.
♣ – From/to Lyon (Table **335**).
♠ – From/to Lyon and Marseille (Table **335**).
◐ – Via St Pierre des Corps (Table **335**).
☆ – From/to Strasbourg (Table **391**).
△ – On July 4 Nantes d. 1710, Paris a. 1915.
▽ – Runs 10 minutes earlier on Aug. 21, 28.

* – **The train number shown is altered as below:**
5236 runs as 5238 on ⑤.
8008 runs as 8702 on ①.
8009 runs as 8097 on Ⓒ.
8033 runs as 8633 on ⑤⑦.
8040 runs as 8744 on ⑥⑦.
8089 runs as 8087 on ⑤.
8093 runs as 8095 on ⑤.
8613 also runs as 8693.
8618 runs as 8016 on ⑦.
8620 runs as 8622 on Ⓒ, 8624 on ①.
8649 also runs as 8695.
8692 runs as 8696/8794 on ⑦ (also as 8790 on ①⑤⑥).
8716 runs as 8714 on ①.
8719 runs as 8717 on ⑦.
8726 runs as 8728 on ⑦.
8729 runs as 8087 on ⑤.
8732 runs as 8730 on ⑥, 8734 on ⑦, also runs as 8638 on ①–⑥, 8634 on ⑦.
8737 runs as 8739 on ⑤.
8747 runs as 8741 on ⑥.
8763 runs as 8761 on ⑦.
8774 also runs as 8676.
8837 runs as 8937 on ⑥.
8864 runs as 8964 on ⑤.
8879 runs as 8979 on ⑤.
8887 runs as 8987 on ⑤.
8933 runs as 8833 on ⑤⑥.
8953 runs as 8951 on ⑤.
8980 runs as 8880 on ⑤.

281 (Summer) RENNES - ST MALO

Service July 5 - Aug. 30. *For service to July 4 and from Aug. 31 see page 185*

km	*TGV trains*, Ⓡ	TGV 8097	TGV 8083	TGV 8085	TGV 5224	TGV 8089*	TGV 8093	TGV 8095	TGV 8099	
		Ⓒ	Ⓒ	Ⓐ	⑤⑦		①–④	⑤	⑦	
					e		n		e	
	Paris Montparnasse **280** d.	0805	1005	1005	...	1505	1835	1835	1905	...
	Lille Europe **11** d.	|	|	|	1210	|	|	|	|	...
0	**Rennes 272** d.	1023	1215	1215	1610	1715	2058	2058	2126	...
58	Dol **272** d.	1056	|	1249	|	|	|	2132	|	...
81	**St Malo** a.	1109	1258	1303	1656	1801	2144	2147	2210	...

TGV trains, Ⓡ	TGV 8084	TGV 8088	TGV 5290	TGV 8096	TGV 8094	TGV 8092	TGV 5294	TGV 8098	
			⑤	⑦	⑤	G	⑦	⑦	
				e			e	e	
St Malo d.	1214	1640	1745	1908	1911	1914	1930	2044	...
Dol **272** d.	|	1657	|	1925	|	|	|	|	...
Rennes 272 a.	1300	1730	1830	2000	1956	1956	2015	2130	...
Lille Europe **11** a.	|	|	2318	|	|	|	0010	|	...
Paris Montparnasse **280** a.	1515	2000	...	2230	2225	2215	...	2340	...

July 5 - Aug. 30	Ⓐ	Ⓐ	⑥	†	⚒	Ⓐ	⑥	†	†		⚒	†	⚒	⑤	Ⓐ	Ⓐ	⑥	Ⓐ		Ⓐ	†	⑥	⚒	⑤	
			t				t										t					t			
Rennes 272 d.	0630	0730	0730	0930	0941	1030	1100	1100	1130	...	1340	1350	1430	1530	1645	1730	1730	1800	1830	1930	1930	1930	2150	2253	...
Dol **272** d.	0711	0809	0814	1006	1017	1104	1133	1149	1204	...	1420	1426	1506	1604	1726	1806	1810	1844	1906	2006	2008	2018	2228	2327	...
St Malo a.	0730	0825	0833	1020	1031	1118	1148	1208	1218	...	1439	1440	1520	1618	1742	1820	1828	1903	1920	2020	2022	2032	2241	2341	...

July 5 - Aug. 30	⚒	Ⓐ	⑥	Ⓐ	Ⓒ	Ⓐ		⚒	†	†	⚒		H	Ⓑ	⑤	†	Ⓐ	⑥	†	Ⓐ	†		⑤	G	
			t															t							
St Malo d.	0550	0620	0630	0650	0750	0750	...	0950	0950	1250	1250	...	1450	1550	1650	1720	1720	1720	1750	1820	1830	1950	2030	2050	...
Dol **272** d.	0604	0639	0650	0706	0805	0805	...	1004	1005	1304	1309	...	1505	1604	1704	1734	1738	1740	1811	1838	1844	2003	2044	2104	...
Rennes 272 a.	0641	0720	0740	0744	0840	0845	...	1039	1043	1341	1350	...	1537	1636	1736	1808	1819	1823	1905	1919	1916	2038	2116	2136	...

G – ①②③④⑥ (not July 14). H – ①②③④⑥ (not July 14, Aug. 15). e – Also July 14. n – Not July 14. t – Not Aug. 15.

282 (Summer) DOL - DINAN

2nd class

Service July 5 - Aug. 30. *For service to July 4 and from Aug. 31 see page 185*

July 5 - Aug. 30	Ⓐ	⑥		Ⓐ		⚒		†	⑥		†	Ⓐ		⑥	†	Ⓐ		①–④	†	⑤		⑤⑥		
		t		⊙					t					t				m				t		
Dol d.	0702	0818	...	1025	...	1301	...	1433	1511	...	1702	1730	...	1814	1815	1848	...	2011	2015	2137	...	2235	...	...
Dinan a.	0725	0841	...	1048	...	1323	...	1456	1542	...	1732	1801	...	1842	1838	1918	...	2034	2038	2200	...	2258	...	...

July 5 - Aug. 30	Ⓐ	⚒	Ⓒ		①–④	⑤		†	Ⓐ	⑦	⚒	
					m					e		
Dinan d.	0630	0732	0927	1227	1437	1536	1624	1740	1810	1852	1936	...
Dol a.	0657	0800	0957	1255	1500	1559	1647	1803	1833	1915	1959	...

e – Also July 14.
m – Not July 14, Aug. 15.
t – Not Aug. 15.
⊙ – To/from St Brieuc (Table **299**).

283 (Summer) MORLAIX - ROSCOFF

2nd class

Service July 5 - Aug. 30. *For service to July 4 and from Aug. 31 see page 185*

km	*July 5 - Aug. 30*	🚌 Ⓐ	🚌 ⚒	⑥	⑦	Ⓐ	🚌 †				🚌 ①–④	🚌 ⑤	🚌 †	🚌 ①–④	🚌 ⑥	🚌 †	🚌 ①–④
					e			z			n			n	t		n
0	**Morlaix 284** d.	0803	0929	1021	1037	1041	1150	1247	1519	...	1630	1705	1806	1840	1840	2010	2057
28	**Roscoff** a.	0833	1004	1050	1106	1110	1220	1316	1548	...	1700	1735	1841	1910	1910	2040	2132

July 5 - Aug. 30	🚌	🚌 Ⓒ					🚌 Ⓐ	Ⓐ		Ⓒ	🚌 ①–④		🚌 Ⓐ	🚌 †		🚌 ⑤	
	△										n						
Roscoff d.	0643	0830	...	1133	1339	...	1530	1634	...	1710	1730	...	1839	1925	...	2030	...
Morlaix 284 a.	0713	0905	...	1201	1409	...	1605	1702	...	1745	1800	...	1914	2000	...	2105	...

e – Also July 14.
n – Not July 14.
t – Not Aug. 15.
z – Runs 10 minutes later on ⑤.
△ – Subject to confirmation.

All services call at St Pol de Léon (*21 km*/15 mins from Morlaix). 🚌 call at Roscoff port on days of sailings.

RENNES - ST BRIEUC - MORLAIX - BREST 284 (Summer)

Service July 5 - Aug. 30. *For service to July 4/from Aug. 31 see page 186*

km	*TGV* trains convey 🍷	Ⓐ	Ⓐ	Ⓐ	⑥	Ⓐ u	Ⓐ	⑥	55803 Ⓐ	Ⓐ	⑥ t	55811 ①-⑥ n	①-⑥ n	⑦ e	⑦ e	*TGV* 8609 ①-⑥ n	*TGV* 8613	⚒	*TGV* 8693				*TGV* 8619	
	Paris Montparnasse **280** d.	...	...	...	...	...	...	...	...	...	...	...	...	...	...	0835	0905	...	0905	...	...	...	1105	...
0	**Rennes** d.	...	...	0605	...	...	0620	0640	0700	0720	0830	0936	...	1006	...	|	1111	...	1119	...	1220	...	1324	...
80	Lamballe **299** d.	...	...	0647	...	0704	0724	0745	|	0809	0909	1012	...	1043	...	|	|	...	1159	...	1256	...	|	...
101	**St Brieuc 299** d.	...	...	0701	0708	0723	0737	0759	0748	0823	0922	1024	...	1055	...	1126	|	...	1212	...	1308	...	1413	...
132	Guingamp d.	...	...	0719	0724	0746	...	...	|	...	0940	1042	1050	1113	...	1143	|	...	1230	...	1325	...	1430	...
158	Plouaret-Trégor d.	...	...	0734	0738	0802	...	...	|	...	0954	|	1106	1127	1134	|	|	...	1246	...	1343	1345	1446	1450
175	Lannion a.	...	...	|	|	0818	...	...	|	...	|	|	1123	|	1151	|	|	...	1302	...	|	1401	|	1507
189	Morlaix d.	0616	0637	0759	0800	...	...	...	0831	...	1012	1112	...	1145	...	1211	1235	1245	...	...	1400	...	1505	...
215	Landivisiau d.	0632	0700	0814	0815	...	...	...	|	...	1027	|	...	1159	...	|	|	1308	...	...	1415	...	|	...
230	Landerneau **286** d.	0643	0715	0830	0828	...	...	...	|	...	1036	|	...	1209	...	|	|	1321	...	...	1425	...	1530	...
248	**Brest 286** a.	0657	0732	0842	0840	...	...	...	0902	...	1048	1143	...	1220	...	1245	1308	1338	...	...	1437	...	1542	...

July 5 - Aug. 30		*TGV* 8627 ①-④ n	⑤	⑥⑦ e	*TGV* 8621 ⑤	⑤	①-④ n	⑤	*TGV* 8625 ⑦ e	⑦ e	⑦ e	⑤	⑤	*TGV* 8651 L	L	L		⚒	⑦ d	Ⓐ	Ⓐ		*TGV* 8633 ⑤⑦ e	⑦ e
Paris Montparnasse **280** d.	...	1205	...	...	1305	...	...	...	1405	...	...	...	...	1435	...	...	...	...	...	...	...	...	1605	...
Rennes d.	1333	1420	1426	1426	1518	...	...	...	1622	...	...	1636	...	1652	...	...	...	1700	1723	1746	...	...	1812	...
Lamballe **299** d.	1435	|	1504	1502	1559	...	...	...	1703	...	...	1716	...	1733	...	...	...	1801	1759	1821	...	...	|	...
St Brieuc 299 d.	1450	1511	1516	1514	1612	...	...	...	1716	...	...	1730	1738	1747	...	1755	...	1815	1812	1834	...	...	1900	...
Guingamp d.	...	1530	1534	1532	1629	...	...	...	1734	...	1742	1749	1803	1805	...	1820	...	...	1830	1852	...	...	1918	1926
Plouaret-Trégor d.	...	|	|	1546	|	...	...	1707	|	...	1758	1805	1820	|	...	1838	...	...	1844	1907	1931	...	|	1942
Lannion a.	...	|	|	|	|	...	...	1724	|	...	1815	|	1836	|	...	1854	...	...	|	|	1948	...	|	1959
Morlaix d.	...	1600	1604	1604	1658	1714	1722	...	1803	1809	...	1824	...	1834	1844	...	...	...	1902	1924	...	...	1946	...
Landivisiau d.	...	|	|	1619	|	1738	1745	...	|	1828	...	1843	...	|	1903	...	...	...	1917	1939	...	...	|	...
Landerneau **286** d.	...	|	|	1628	|	1752	1758	...	|	1838	...	1855	...	|	1913	...	...	...	1926	1949	...	...	2011	...
Brest 286 a.	...	1630	1635	1640	1732	1810	1815	...	1838	1853	...	1907	...	1907	1928	...	...	...	1938	2000	...	...	2023	...

July 5 - Aug. 30	⑥	⑥	Ⓑ	*TGV* 8647 ⑤	①-④ n	⑤	⑤	①-④ n	⑦ d	*TGV* 8649 ⑤	*TGV* 8695 ⑤	*TGV* 8657 Ⓐ	*TGV* 8659 ⑦ e	*TGV* 8653 ⑥		*TGV* 8665 ①-⑥ n	①-⑥ n	*TGV* 8669 ⑦ e	⑦ e	*TGV* 5238 ⑤ ♥	⑦ e		*TGV* 8679 ⑤	*TGV* 8689 ⑦ q
Paris Montparnasse **280** d.	...	...	...	1710	...	...	...	...	...	1735	1735	1805	1805	1805	...	1905	...	1905	...	...	...	...	2105	2355
Rennes d.	1846	...	1838	|	1908	1919	...	1925	1935	1953	2001	2011	2018	2027	...	2120	...	2122	...	2130	2235	...	2320	|
Lamballe **299** d.	1921	...	1936	|	1947	1957	...	2017	2010	|	2041	|	|	|	...	2202	...	2204	...	2212	2311	...	|	|
St Brieuc 299 d.	1934	...	1949	1959	2000	2010	...	2028	2023	|	2054	2103	2108	2118	...	2215	...	2217	...	2226	2323	...	0013	0423
Guingamp d.	1951	...	...	|	2017	2028	...	...	2040	|	2111	2123	2126	2134	...	2232	...	2234	...	2245	2342	...	0031	0440
Plouaret-Trégor d.	2006	2011	...	|	|	2043	2052	...	|	|	2128	|	|	|	...	2247	2252	2249	2254	|	2356	...	|	|
Lannion a.	|	2028	...	|	|	|	2109	...	|	|	2145	|	|	|	...	|	2309	|	2311	|	|	...	|	|
Morlaix d.	2023	...	...	|	2046	2100	...	...	2110	2119	...	2151	2154	2202	...	2305	...	2307	...	2316	0014	...	0101	0512
Landivisiau d.	2038	...	...	|	|	|	...	...	|	|	...	|	|	|	...	|	...	|	...	|	0029	...	|	|
Landerneau **286** d.	2048	...	...	|	|	2122	...	...	|	|	...	|	|	|	...	2330	...	|	...	|	0038	...	|	0537
Brest 286 a.	2059	...	...	2109	2117	2133	...	...	2141	2153	...	2222	2229	2236	...	2343	...	2341	...	2348	0050	...	0132	0552

July 5 - Aug. 30	① g	*TGV* 8604 ① g	②-⑤ c	⚒	① g	Ⓐ	Ⓐ	†	⚒	*TGV* 8618 ①-⑥ n	Ⓐ	†	⚒	① g	*TGV* 8624 ① g	*TGV* 8626 ① g	②-⑤ w§	*TGV* 8620 ②-⑤ w	Ⓒ	*TGV* 8622 Ⓒ		⑦ e	⑥ t	
Brest 286 d.	...	0448	...	...	...	0536	...	...	...	0648	0800	...	...	...	0843	0852	...	0848	...	0844	...	0956	1042	1112
Landerneau **286** d.	...	|	...	...	...	0548	...	...	...	0701	0818	...	...	...	|	|	...	|	...	|	...	1008	1054	1129
Landivisiau d.	...	|	...	...	...	0557	...	...	...	|	0830	...	...	...	|	|	...	|	...	|	...	1017	|	1141
Morlaix d.	...	0520	...	...	...	0613	...	...	...	0723	0853	...	...	...	|	0926	...	0921	...	0916	...	1032	1116	1206
Lannion d.	0505	|	...	...	0603	|	...	...	0656	|	...	...	...	0900	|	|	0908	|	0910	|	...	|	|	...
Plouaret-Trégor d.	0520	|	...	...	0620	0630	...	...	0711	|	...	...	...	0917	|	|	0924	|	0927	0935	...	1049	|	...
Guingamp d.	0537	0550	0548	...	...	0645	0707	0720	0731	0752	...	...	...	0931	0942	|	0940	0951	...	0951	...	1103	1145	...
St Brieuc 299 d.	...	0609	0605	0633	...	0705	0730	0738	0751	0811	...	0935	0935	...	1011	1011	...	1011	...	1011	...	1120	1202	...
Lamballe **299** d.	...	0621	0616	0645	...	0717	0744	0751	...	|	...	0946	0947	...	|	|	...	|	...	|	...	1131	1213	...
Rennes a.	...	0700	0653	0748	...	0755	0840	0850	...	0900	...	1040	1045	...	1056	1056	...	1056	...	1056	...	1209	1250	...
Paris Montparnasse **280** a.	...	0915	...	...	...	...	...	...	...	1110	...	...	...	...	1325	1325	...	1325	...	1325	...	...	...	...

July 5 - Aug. 30		*TGV* 8638 ①-⑥ n	*TGV* 8634 ⑦ e	⑤		*TGV* 8646		A	⑤	⑤	*TGV* 8658	*TGV* 8662	①-④ n	⑤	⑦ e	⑦ e	⑤	⑤	*TGV* 5290 ⑦ ♠e	⑦ e	①-④ n	*TGV* 8670 Ⓒ	*TGV* 8672 Ⓐ	⑥
Brest 286 d.	...	1144	1148	1214	...	1345	...	1437	...	1454	...	1546	...	...	...	1556	...	1608	1621	...	...	1644	1650	...
Landerneau **286** d.	...	|	|	1226	...	|	...	1449	...	1506	...	|	...	...	...	1608	...	1620	|	...	...	|	|	...
Landivisiau d.	...	|	|	|	...	|	...	1459	...	1516	...	|	...	...	...	1618	...	1630	|	...	...	|	|	...
Morlaix d.	...	1216	1220	1248	...	1418	...	1514	...	1532	...	1618	...	...	...	1635	...	1646	1654	...	...	1716	1723	...
Lannion d.	1208	|	|	|	1406	|	...	|	1523	|	1603	|	...	...	1625	|	1633	|	|	1704	1712	|	|	...
Plouaret-Trégor d.	1225	1234	1238	|	1422	|	...	1531	1539	|	1621	|	...	...	1641	|	1650	1703	|	1720	1728	|	|	...
Guingamp d.	...	1249	1253	1317	1437	1448	...	1546	1553	1607	1636	|	...	...	1655	1708	...	1717	1725	1736	1743	1746	1753	...
St Brieuc 299 d.	...	1308	1312	1334	...	1509	...	1603	...	1625	1705	1705	1713	1714	...	1726	...	1735	1744	...	1801	1807	1812	1825
Lamballe **299** d.	...	1320	|	1345	...	1521	...	1614	...	1636	1718	1718	1728	1728	...	1737	...	1746	1757	...	1812	1820	|	1839
Rennes a.	...	1400	1400	1422	...	1600	...	1655	...	1716	1800	1800	1829	1815	...	1817	...	1825	1834	...	1850	1900	1859	1943
Paris Montparnasse **280** a.	...	1610	1610	...	...	1820	...	...	...	...	2010	2010	...	...	...	...	...	...	...	...	...	2110	2110	...

July 5 - Aug. 30	①-④ n	⑤	Ⓐ	*TGV* 8676 ⑦ e	Ⓐ	⑦ e	⑥ t	⑥	Ⓐ	⑦ e	⑦ e	*TGV* 8688 ⑦ e	⑥	⑥	Ⓐ	Ⓐ	*TGV* 8696 ⑦ e	*TGV* 8692 ①-⑥ n		⑦ e	①-④ n	⑤	*TGV* 8686 ⑦ e	⑤
Brest 286 d.	...	...	1705	1718	...	1723	...	1728	1740	...	...	1811	...	1817	1821	...	...	1851	...	1902	1920	1935	1950	...
Landerneau **286** d.	...	...	1721	|	...	1736	...	1740	1752	...	...	|	...	1832	1839	...	...	|	...	1914	1938	1952	2002	...
Landivisiau d.	...	...	1732	|	...	1746	...	1750	|	...	...	|	...	1843	1851	...	...	|	...	1923	1950	2005	|	...
Morlaix d.	...	...	1749	1751	...	1804	...	1807	1816	...	...	1842	...	1901	1914	...	...	1924	...	1939	2005	2020	2025	...
Lannion d.	1735	1753	|	|	...	|	1802	|	|	...	1820	|	1900	|	...	1911	1921	|	...	|	...	...	|	2020
Plouaret-Trégor d.	1752	1810	1815	|	...	1823	|	1825	|	...	1838	|	1917	1926	...	1927	|	|	...	1956	...	...	|	2037
Guingamp d.	1807	1825	...	1821	...	1839	1830	1846	1847	...	1854	1917	...	1943	...	1944	1950	1954	...	2010	...	...	|	...
St Brieuc 299 d.	1827	...	...	1839	1832	1858	...	1903	1904	1910	...	1940	...	...	...	...	2009	2013	...	2027	...	...	2108	...
Lamballe **299** d.	...	...	...	|	1848	1911	...	1914	1915	1924	...	|	...	...	...	...	2022	|	...	2038	...	...	|	...
Rennes a.	...	...	...	1926	1945	1952	...	1952	1952	2019	...	2030	...	...	...	...	2100	2100	...	2115	...	...	2156	...
Paris Montparnasse **280** a.	...	...	...	2140	...	...	...	...	...	...	...	2240	...	...	...	...	2310	2310	...	...	...	...	0010	...

A – Daily except ⑤.
L – ①②③④⑥ (not July 14).

c – Also July 13; not July 15.
d – Also July 14, Aug. 15.
e – Also July 14.
g – Also July 15; not July 13.
n – Not July 14.
q – Also July 14; not July 12.

t – Not Aug. 15.
u – From/to Dinan, Table **299**.
w – Also July 13; not July 14, 15.

TGV – Ⓡ, supplement payable, 🍷.

♥ – From Lille Europe, depart 1729 (Table **11**).
♠ – To Lille Europe, arrive 2318 (Table **11**).
§ – Subject to alteration on ⑤ Aug. 7 - Sept. 25 and ②③④ Sept. 1 - 24.

285 (Summer) RENNES and NANTES - QUIMPER

TGV trains convey 🍸

Service July 5 - Aug. 30. *For service to July 4 / from Aug. 31 see page 187*

km	*TGV trains convey* 🍸	Ⓐ	Ⓐ	⑥ t	Ⓐ	⑥ t	4546 4547 Ⓡ Y	Ⓐ	Ⓐ	Ⓒ	⚒	⚒	† ◇	TGV 8701	†	†		Ⓐ	⑥ t	⑥ t	TGV 8715	TGV 8713 ⑥	⑤	⑥ t	TGV 8721 ①–④ n
0	*Paris* ⊡ **280** d.	...	...	...	...	...	...	...	...	...	...	...	...	0830	...	...	...	...	...	...	1005	1025	...	...	1105
365	**Rennes 287** d.	...	...	...	...	0625	...	0711	...	0830	0936	...	0939	|	...	1040	...	...	...	1149	1211	1232	1302	...	1328
	Nantes ◧ d.	...	...	...	...	|	0641	|	0650	|	|	0920	|	|	1003	|	...	1140	1140	|	|	|	|	1312	|
	Savenay ◧ d.	...	...	...	...	|	|	|	0714	|	|	0942	|	|	1026	|	...	1203	1202	|	|	|	|	1336	|
437	Redon **287** ◧ d.	...	...	...	0710	0711	0726	0752	0752	0908	1019	1019	1022	|	1053	1115	...	1229	1234	1234	1249	|	1338	1403	|
492	Vannes d.	...	0700	0706	0742	...	0754	0822	0822	...	1049	1049	1057	1133	...	1141	...	1257	1304	1304	1316	1333	1407	...	1428
511	Auray d.	...	0714	0721	0754	...	0811	0835	0835	...	1101	1101	1110	1146	...	1154	...	1310	1317	1317	1329	1347	1420	...	1441
545	Lorient d.	0645	0746	0748	0812	...	0831	0856	0856	...	1122	1122	...	1206	...	1214	...	1329	1335	1335	1350	1408	1438	...	1459
565	Quimperlé d.	0657	0801	...	...	...	0845	0908	0908	...	1134	1134	...	|	...	1227	...	1341	1347	1347	1403	|	1450	...	...
612	**Quimper** a.	0728	0828	...	...	...	0915	0934	0934	...	1200	1200	...	1241	...	1253	...	1408	1414	1414	1431	1442	1517	...	...

July 5 - Aug. 30	Ⓒ	①–④ n	TGV 8717 ⑦	TGV 8719 ①–⑥ n	Ⓒ	Ⓐ	Ⓒ	13895	TGV 8723 ⑤	①–④ n	⑤	⑤	①–④ n	①–④ n	⑥ t	⑥ t	†	†	⑤	TGV 8729 A	①–④ n	⚒	⑦ e	†	Ⓐ
Paris ⊡ **280** d.	...	...	1205	1205	...	...	...	...	1345	...	...	...	...	...	...	...	...	...	...	1505	...	...	...	...	...
Rennes 287 d.	1340	1353	1416	1416	...	1426	1430	...	|	...	1610	...	1639	...	1637	...	...	1646	1700	1711	1644	...	...	1735	...
Nantes ◧ d.	|	|	|	|	...	|	|	1450	|	...	|	1622	|	1622	|	1622	1622	|	|	|	|	...	1723	|	1728u
Savenay ◧ d.	|	|	|	|	...	|	|	|	|	...	|	1645	|	1643	|	1643	1644	|	|	|	|	...	1748	|	1749
Redon **287** ◧ d.	1418	1428	|	|	...	1503	1515	1535	|	...	1649	1716	1721	1721	1723	1723	1712	1724	1741	|	1740	1755	1813	1828	1821
Vannes d.	1448	1458	1517	1517	...	...	...	1605	1647	1700	1719	...	1747	1747	1753	1753	...	1754	1811	1812	...	1831	...	1900	...
Auray d.	1501	1511	1530	1530	...	...	...	1618	1700	1714	1732	...	1759	1759	1805	1805	...	1807	1823	1826	...	1845	...	1915	...
Lorient d.	1523	1528	1551	1551	1600	...	...	1640	1720	1746	1753	...	1822	1822	1826	1826	...	1829	1845	1847	...	1911	...	1940	...
Quimperlé d.	1535	...	|	1604	1614	...	...	1652	|	1801	1804	...	1834	1834	1838	1838	...	1841	1857	|	...	...	...	...	...
Quimper a.	1602	...	1626	1632	1645	...	...	1719	1754	1832	1832	...	1901	1901	1904	1904	...	1908	1923	1924	...	...	...	...	...

July 5 - Aug. 30	Ⓐ	⑤	⑥ t	†	3854 3855 ♠	TGV 5232 ①–⑥ ♥n	TGV 8737 ①–④ n	TGV 8739 ⑤	TGV 8747 Ⓐ	TGV 8741 ⑥	TGV 8745 ⑦ e	TGV 8757 ⑤	Ⓐ	①–④ n	⑦	⑥ t	⑦ e	TGV 5236 ⑦ ♥e	3856 ⑤⑦ ♠e	L	TGV 8763 ①–⑥ n	TGV 8761 ⑦ e	TGV 8775 ⑤		TGV 8799 ⑦ q
Paris ⊡ **280** d.	...	...	...	...	...	...	1635	1635	1705	1705	1705	1810	...	...	...	...	...	...	...	...	1935	1935	2035	...	2355
Rennes 287 d.	1745	...	1815	1824	...	1844	1858	1855	1911	1911	1923	|	...	2025	2025	2034	...	2129	...	...	2141	2141	2241	...	|
Nantes ◧ d.	|	1809	|	|	1818	|	|	|	|	|	|	|	1944	|	|	|	2043	|	2116	2126	|	|	|	...	|
Savenay ◧ d.	|	|	|	|	1841	|	|	|	|	|	|	|	2015	|	|	|	2104	|	2141	2147	|	|	|	...	|
Redon **287** ◧ d.	1828	1853	1855	1904	1910	1928	1937	1937	|	1949	2000	|	2044	2103	2103	2111	2135	2206	2207	2212	2219	2219	2318	...	|
Vannes d.	1857	1922	...	...	1942	1955	2002	2004	2016	2015	2027	2115	...	2133	2133	...	...	2233	...	...	2246	2246	2345	...	0449
Auray d.	1910	1935	...	...	1957	2009	...	2017	2029	2028	2040	2128	...	2146	2146	...	...	2246	...	...	2258	2258	2358	...	0505
Lorient d.	1931	1957	...	...	2018	2028	...	2036	2049	2048	2100	2148	...	2208	2208	...	...	2305	...	...	2318	2318	0018	...	0525
Quimperlé d.	1943	2008	...	...	|	2040	...	|	2102	2102	2113	|	...	2220	2220	...	...	2319	...	...	|	2332	0031	...	|
Quimper a.	2009	2035	...	...	2056	2107	...	2116	2128	2130	2141	2222	...	2247	2247	...	...	2346	...	...	2355	2359	0059	...	0600

July 5 - Aug. 30	TGV 8702 ① g	Ⓐ	TGV 8714 ① g	TGV 8716 ②–⑤ j	†	⑥ t	Ⓐ	Ⓐ	Ⓐ	TGV 5272 ♣	⑥ t	Ⓐ b	Ⓐ	3832 3833 ♠	⚒	TGV 8728 ⑦ e	TGV 8726 ①–⑥ n		13894	TGV 8732 Ⓐ	TGV 8730 ⑥	TGV 8734 ⑦ e	⑥ t	①–④ n	①–④ n
Quimper d.	0442	...	0537	0542	...	...	0601	0601	...	0646	0705	0707	0725	0739	...	0853	0858	1024	1112	1137	1144	1147	...	1234	1234
Quimperlé d.	|	...	0606	|	...	...	0628	0628	...	0715	0734	0737	0752	|	...	0922	0927	1051	1139	1205	|	|	...	1301	1301
Lorient d.	0517	...	0620	0620	...	...	0640	0640	0700	0729	0748	0751	0805	0819	...	0941	0946	1104	1153	1219	1219	1222	1300	1314	1314
Auray d.	0536	...	0640	0640	...	...	0701	0701	0728	0749	...	...	0826	0841	...	1000	1005	1128	1218	1239	1239	1242	1328	1333	1333
Vannes d.	0549	...	0653	0653	...	...	0713	0713	0741	0803	...	...	0838	0856	...	1014	1018	1141	1233	1254	1254	1255	1342	1347	1347
Redon **287** d.	0618	0646	0724	0724	0736	0734	0747	0750	0811	0829	...	...	0909	0928	1022	1044	|	1211	1303	1321	1321	|	...	1420	1423
Savenay ◧ d.	|	0734	|	|	|	|	|	0817	...	|	...	...	|	|	|	|	|	|	1327	|	|	|	...	|	1446
Nantes ◧ d.	|	0810	|	|	|	|	|	0840	...	|	...	...	|	1012	|	|	|	|	1350	|	|	|	...	|	1507
Rennes 287 ◧ a.	0656	...	0800	0800	0814	0820	0829	...	...	0904	...	...	0945	...	1101	1120	1120	1248	...	1357	1357	1357	...	1455	...
Paris ⊡ **280** a.	0915	...	1025	1025	...	...	...	...	...	...	...	...	...	...	...	1330	1330	...	...	1610	1610	1610	...	...	...

July 5 - Aug. 30	⑤	TGV 8744 Ⓒ	⑤	⑤	⑥ t	⑥ t	†	Ⓐ	⑥ t	†	TGV 8752		Ⓐ	⑦ e	⑤	†	Ⓒ	①–④ n	⑤	†	TGV 8762	Ⓐ	Ⓐ	Ⓐ	①–④ n
Quimper d.	1240	1237	1321	1321	1333	1333	...	...	...	...	1437	...	1512	...	...	1531	...	...	1547	1603	1613	...	...	...	1706
Quimperlé d.	1308	1306	1348	1348	1400	1400	...	...	...	...	1505	...	1539	...	...	1558	...	...	1614	1630	|	...	...	...	1734
Lorient d.	1321	1324	1400	1400	1412	1412	...	...	...	...	1523	...	1552	...	...	1611	...	...	1632	1642	1654	...	1714	...	1746
Auray d.	1341	1346	1417	1417	1434	1434	...	...	...	...	1542	...	1614	...	...	1634	...	...	1654	1704	1715	...	1739	...	1805
Vannes d.	1354	1359	1430	1430	1446	1446	...	...	...	...	1556	...	1627	...	...	1647	...	...	1707	1716	1730	...	1750	...	1817
Redon **287** d.	1420	1426	1503	1507	1520	1526	1526	1538	1548	1540	1626	...	1658	1658	1705	1719	1729	1729	1737	1748	|	1809	...	1832	1846
Savenay ◧ d.	|	|	|	1530	|	1549	1549	|	|	|	|	...	1722	1730	|	|	|	|	|	1816	|	|	...	1904	|
Nantes ◧ d.	|	|	|	1550	|	1610	1610	|	|	|	|	...	1745	1750	|	|	|	|	|	1836	|	|	...	1932	|
Rennes 287 ◧ a.	1455	1500	1540	...	1555	...	...	1616	1626	1617	1700	...	...	...	1804	1755	1823	1822	1811	...	1829	1906	...	...	1920
Paris ⊡ **280** a.	...	1715	...	...	...	...	...	...	...	...	1910	...	...	...	...	...	...	...	...	...	2040	...	...	...	...

July 5 - Aug. 30	⑥ t	TGV 8774 ⑦ e	⑥	Ⓐ	4446 4447 Ⓡ Z	⑥	Ⓐ	⑤	TGV 8776 ⑦ e	TGV 8780 ①–④ n	TGV 8780 ⑥	TGV 8782 ⑤	⑤⑥ t	⑦ e	†	Ⓐ	⑤	TGV 8794 ⑦ e	TGV 8790 ① g	TGV 8790 ⑤⑥	②–④ w	TGV 8798 ⑦ e	† ◇	†	
Quimper d.	...	1717	...	...	1715	1732	...	1735	1746	1748	1748	1750	...	1753	...	1757	...	1836	1846	1846	1846	1950	...	2025	...
Quimperlé d.	...	|	...	...	1747	1759	...	1803	|	|	|	|	...	1821	...	1827	...	1905	|	|	|	|	...	2053	...
Lorient d.	1740	1753	...	1754	1803	1812	...	1815	1822	1827	1827	1827	...	1834	...	1843	...	1919	1922	1922	1921	2026	...	2107	...
Auray d.	1807	1811	...	1820	1856	1835	...	1833	1842	1847	1847	1847	...	1854	...	1912	...	1939	1941	1941	1942	2046	2053	2127	...
Vannes d.	1819	1824	...	1835	1911	1848	...	1845	1857	1901	1901	1901	...	1907	...	1923	...	1953	1955	1955	1955	2059	2106	2140	...
Redon **287** d.	1847	1854	1901	1909	1940	1919	1921	1918	|	|	|	|	1936	1938	1947	...	2026	2020	|	|	|	|	2141	2207	...
Savenay ◧ d.	...	|	1928	...	|	|	1949	|	|	|	|	|	|	|	2016	...	2054	|	|	|	|	|	|	|	...
Nantes ◧ d.	...	|	1950	...	2025	|	2012	|	|	|	|	|	|	|	2036	...	2116	|	|	|	|	|	|	|	...
Rennes 287 ◧ a.	...	1930	...	...	...	1952	...	1950	|	2000	2000	2000	2015	2010	...	...	...	2056	2056	2056	2053	2200	2223	2240	...
Paris ⊡ **280** a.	...	2140	...	...	...	...	...	...	2200	2215	2215	2225	...	...	...	...	...	2310	2310	2310	...	0010	...	...	...

Auray - Quiberon *June 27 - Aug. 30*

28 km	S	T	T	S §	⑦E	T	S	S	T	S	S
Rennes (above) d.	...	...	...	...	0939	...	...	...	...	...	...
Auray d.	0800	0858	1009	1112	1112	1201	1352	1604	1735	1841	2045
Quiberon a.	0844	0948	1058	1203	1203	1244	1436	1654	1825	1930	2129

	S	T	T	S	S	T	S	T	S	⑦F	S
Quiberon d.	0854	1005	1108	1255	1449	1600	1731	1837	1949	1949	2140
Auray a.	0937	1049	1151	1337	1534	1643	1816	1920	2032	2032	2223
Rennes (above) a.	...	...	...	...	...	...	...	...	...	2223	...

A – Daily except ⑤.
E – ⑦ July 5 - Aug. 30 (also July 14, Aug. 15).
F – ⑦ June 28 - Aug. 30 (also July 14, Aug. 15).
L – ①②③④⑥ (not July 14, Aug. 15).
S – June 27 - Aug. 30.
T – July 4 - Aug. 30.
Y – 🛏 1, 2 cl. and 2 (reclining) Genève - Lyon - Nantes - Quimper (see Table **290** Night Trains panel).
Z – 🛏 1, 2 cl. and 2 (reclining) Quimper - Nantes - Lyon - Genève. On ⑦ (also July 14) depart Quimper 1656 and runs up to 19 minutes earlier. See Table **290** Night Trains panel.

b – From Brest (Table **286**).
e – Also July 14.
g – Also July 15; not July 13.
j – Also July 13; not July 15.
n – Not July 14.
q – Not July 12.
t – Not Aug. 15.
u – Depart 1725 on ⑤.
w – Also July 13; not July 14, 15.

TGV –Ⓡ, supplement payable, 🍸.

⊡ – Paris Montparnasse.
◇ – To / from Quiberon (see below main table).
◧ – See also **287** Nantes - Redon, **287/8** Nantes - Savenay.
♥ – From Lille Europe (**5232** departs 1447, **5236** departs 1729, Table **11**).
♣ – To Lille Europe (arrive 1341, Table **11**).
♠ – To / from Bordeaux (Table **292**).
§ – On June 27, 29, 30, July 1 - 3 d. 1108, a. 1152.

PUBLICATIONS LIST AND ORDER FORM

To view our full range of titles visit our website: www.thomascookpublishing.com

To order publications please tick the boxes for the titles required, note the prices in the shaded columns and fill in the reverse of this form. Please add postage and packing overleaf.

TIMETABLES AND RAIL MAPS

£

☐ **EUROPEAN RAIL TIMETABLE** ● Published monthly, this timetable has guided generations of travellers throughout Europe. Ideal as a planning aid and for easy en route reference. *Edition required* . . . .

Price: £13.99 *excluding postage and packing*

☐ **Independent Travellers Edition** ● Available through bookshops, this special edition of the European Rail Timetable contains an additional section of country by country travel information. Editions: Summer (June) and Winter (December).

Price: £15.99 *excluding postage and packing*

EUROPEAN RAIL TIMETABLE SUBSCRIPTION
Annual subscription (12 issues) including post and packing to:
☐ UK £150 ☐ Europe £174 ☐ Rest of World £192
Starting issue . . . .

☐ **OVERSEAS TIMETABLE** ● For world (and armchair) travellers, the only rail and public transport timetable to cover the whole world outside Europe. Published every two months at the beginning of January, March, May, July, September and November. *Edition required* . . . .

Price: £13.99 *excluding postage and packing*

☐ **Independent Travellers Edition** ● Published twice a year in May (Summer) and November (Winter), this special edition of the Overseas Timetable contains a host of additional travel tips and essential country by country information. Also available from bookshops.

Price: £15.99 *excluding postage and packing*

OVERSEAS TIMETABLE SUBSCRIPTION
Annual subscription (6 issues) including post and packing to:
☐ UK £75 ☐ Europe £87 ☐ Rest of World £96
Starting issue . . . .

☐ **RAIL MAP OF EUROPE** ● 17th edition. Covers all of Europe, with central Europe enlarged on the reverse. Scenic routes are highlighted.

Price: £8.99 *excluding postage and packing*

☐ **RAIL MAP OF BRITAIN & IRELAND** ● 6th edition. Lines colour-coded to show operating companies. Includes tourist information guide.

Price: £8.99 *excluding postage and packing*

PHRASEGUIDES

PhraseGuides are designed to make the languages of major holiday destinations accessible to all travellers. Each guide includes a two-way dictionary and sections on greetings, eating out, shopping, getting around and accommodation.

☐ Arabic ☐ Bulgarian ☐ Croatian ☐ French
☐ German ☐ Greek ☐ Italian ☐ Japanese
☐ Latin American Spanish ☐ Mandarin Chinese
☐ Polish ☐ Portuguese ☐ Russian ☐ Spanish
☐ Turkish

Price: £3.99 *excluding postage and packing*

PHRASEBOOKS

☐ **EUROPEAN 12-Language Phrasebook** ● French, German, Italian, Spanish, Portuguese, Polish, Czech, Hungarian, Romanian, Bulgarian, Greek and Turkish.

Price: £4.99 *excluding postage and packing*

☐ **EASTERN EUROPEAN 12-Language Phrasebook** ● Bulgarian, Croatian, Czech, Estonian, Hungarian, Latvian, Lithuanian, Polish, Romanian, Russian, Slovenian, Ukrainian.

Price: £4.99 *excluding postage and packing*

☐ **SOUTH-EAST ASIAN 9 Language Phrasebook** ● Contains Burmese, Indonesian, Malaysian, Chinese (Mandarin), Filipino, Cambodian, Laotian, Thai and Vietnamese.

Price: £5.99 *excluding postage and packing*

INDEPENDENT TRAVELLERS

£

☐ **EUROPE BY RAIL** ● Features over 300 cities, towns and villages. Detailed city and journey maps. Cross- referenced to the European Rail Timetable table numbers.

☐ **GREEK ISLAND HOPPING 2009** ● The only guide to include details of all the island ferry services as well as advice on exploring this fascinating region, finding accommodation, and sightseeing.

Price: £14.99 *per title, excluding postage and packing*

TRAVELLERS

A range of popular, compact guidebooks perfect for planning all sorts of holidays - whether long-haul, short-haul, regional tours or city breaks. Full of useful information on walks and tours, eating out, shopping options and top travel tips. All you need for your holiday right at your fingertips.

☐ Algarve and Southern Portugal		☐ Amsterdam
☐ Andalucia inc Seville	☐ Argentina	☐ Australia (East Coast)
☐ Australia (South East inc. Tasmania)		☐ Austria
☐ Bali & Lombok	☐ Baltic Cruising	☐ Barcelona
☐ Bavaria inc Munich	☐ Belgium	☐ Berlin
☐ Bosnia, Serbia & Montenegro		☐ Boston
☐ Brazil	☐ Brittany	☐ Budapest
☐ Bulgaria	☐ Calabria	☐ California
☐ Cambodia	☐ Cape Town	☐ Cape Verde
☐ Caribbean Cruising inc Miami		☐ Catalonia
☐ Chile	☐ China - Beijing	☐ China - Shanghai
☐ Costa Rica	☐ Crete	☐ Croatia
☐ Cuba		☐ Cyprus
☐ Delhi, Agra & Rajasthan		☐ Denmark
☐ Devon and Cornwall		☐ Dominican Republic
☐ Dubai		☐ Dublin
☐ Ecuador and the Galapagos Islands		☐ Egypt
☐ Estonia	☐ Finland	☐ Florence & Tuscany
☐ Florida	☐ Gambia	☐ Goa
☐ Gran Canaria & Tenerife		☐ Greek Islands
☐ Hawaii	☐ Ibiza	☐ Iceland
☐ Ireland	☐ Italian Lakes	☐ Jamaica
☐ Japan	☐ Jordan	☐ Kenya
☐ Kerala & Southern India		☐ Krakow
☐ Lake District	☐ Lanzarote & Fuerteventura	
☐ Las Vegas	☐ Latvia	☐ Lithuania
☐ London	☐ Madeira	☐ Madrid
☐ Maldives	☐ Mallorca	☐ Malta & Gozo
☐ Mauritius	☐ Mediterranean Cruising	
☐ Menorca	☐ Mexico	☐ Morocco
☐ Moscow & St. Petersburg		☐ Namibia
☐ Naples & the Amalfi Coast		☐ New York
☐ New Zealand	☐ Normandy	☐ Northern Italy
☐ Norway	☐ Oman	☐ Ontario & Quebec
☐ Paris	☐ Peru	☐ Poland
☐ Prague	☐ Provence	☐ Puglia
☐ Romania	☐ Rome	☐ San Francisco
☐ Sardinia	☐ Scottish Highlands	☐ Seychelles
☐ Sicily	☐ Singapore & Malaysia*	☐ South Africa
☐ Sri Lanka	☐ Sweden	☐ Switzerland
☐ Syria	☐ Tanzania	☐ Thailand
☐ Tunisia		☐ Turkey
☐ Vancouver & British Columbia		☐ Venice
☐ Vietnam		☐ Warsaw

Titles marked with an asterisk are £8.99 each.

Price: £9.99 *per title, excluding postage and packing*

To view the entire range of Thomas Cook Publishing titles go to:

www.thomascookpublishing.com

PUBLICATIONS LIST AND ORDER FORM

To view our full range of titles visit our website: www.thomascookpublishing.com

To order publications please tick the boxes for the titles required, note the prices in the shaded columns and fill in the reverse of this form. Please add postage and packing below.

HOTSPOTS

Pocket guides covering main resorts and excursion destinations. Includes maps, eating out, shopping, sightseeing, useful phrases and menu decoders.

☐ Algarve ☐ Bali ☐ Brazil
☐ Bulgaria - Black Sea Resorts ☐ Corfu
☐ Corsica ☐ Costa Blanca
☐ Costa del Sol & Almeria ☐ Costa Brava & Costa Dorada
☐ Cote d'Azur ☐ Crete ☐ Croatia - Dalmatian Coast
☐ Cuba ☐ Cyprus ☐ Dominican Republic
☐ Egypt Red Sea Resorts ☐ Fuerteventura
☐ Gibraltar ☐ Goa ☐ Gran Canaria
☐ Greek Islands ☐ Guernsey ☐ Halkidiki
☐ Hawaii ☐ Ibiza ☐ Ionian Islands
☐ Kenya - Indian Ocean Resorts ☐ Lanzarote
☐ Jamaica ☐ Jersey ☐ Madeira
☐ Maldives ☐ Mallorca ☐ Malta
☐ Menorca ☐ Mexico ☐ Morocco
☐ Neopolitan Riviera ☐ Orlando ☐ Rhodes & Kos
☐ Santorini ☐ Sardinia ☐ Seychelles
☐ Sicily ☐ Skiathos ☐ Sri Lanka
☐ Tenerife ☐ Thailand ☐ Tunisia
☐ Turkey - Aegean Coast ☐ Turkey - Lycian Coast
☐ Turkey - Mediterranean Coast

Price: £4.99 *per title excluding postage and packing*

DRIVE AROUND

These unique guidebooks for driving holidays include road safety information, full colour detailed maps, descriptive introductions to routes, and a glossary of road signs appropriate to the destination.

☐ Andalucia & the Costa del Sol ☐ Australia
☐ Bavaria & the Austrian Tyrol ☐ Brittany & Normandy
☐ Burgundy & the Rhône Valley ☐ California
☐ Canadian Rockies ☐ Catalonia & Spanish Pyrenees
☐ Dordogne & Western France ☐ England & Wales
☐ Florida ☐ Ireland
☐ Italian Lakes & Mountains ☐ Languedoc & Southwest France
☐ Loire Valley ☐ New England
☐ Portugal ☐ Provence & the Côte d'Azur
☐ New Zealand ☐ Scotland
☐ Tuscany & Umbria ☐ Vancouver & British Columbia
☐ Washington D.C.

Price: £15.99 *per title excluding postage and packing*

£

CITYSPOTS

New from Thomas Cook Publishing. Perfect for pleasure-seeking city breakers wanting to quickly pinpoint the city's most entertaining highlights and decide what to see and do in a limited time with essential advice on shopping, sightseeing, eating and drinking, plus great entertainment ideas too.

New and revised editions:

☐ Aarhus ☐ Antwerp ☐ Belfast ☐ Belgrade
☐ Biarritz ☐ Bologna ☐ Bordeaux ☐ Brussels
☐ Budapest ☐ Cairo ☐ Cape Town ☐ Cork
☐ Dubai ☐ Dubrovnik ☐ Fez ☐ Gdansk
☐ Geneva ☐ Hamburg ☐ Hannover ☐ Helsinki
☐ Hong Kong ☐ Istanbul ☐ Kiev ☐ Krakow
☐ Leipzig ☐ Lisbon ☐ Ljubljana ☐ Marrakech
☐ Marseille ☐ Moscow ☐ Nice ☐ Palma
☐ Palermo ☐ Piza ☐ Reims ☐ Riga
☐ Rome ☐ Rotterdam ☐ Sarajevo ☐ Seville
☐ Sofia ☐ St. Petersburg ☐ Tirana ☐ Toulouse
☐ Tallinn ☐ Valencia ☐ Verona ☐ Vilnius
☐ Warsaw ☐ Zagreb

Price: £6.99 *per title excluding postage and packing*

☐ Amsterdam ☐ Athens ☐ Bangkok ☐ Barcelona
☐ Berlin ☐ Bilbao ☐ Bratislava ☐ Bruges
☐ Bucharest ☐ Cardiff ☐ Cologne ☐ Copenhagen
☐ Dublin ☐ Dusseldorf ☐ Edinburgh ☐ Florence
☐ Frankfurt ☐ Genoa ☐ Glasgow ☐ Gothenburg
☐ Granada ☐ Kuala Lumpur ☐ Lille ☐ London
☐ Los Angeles ☐ Lyon ☐ Madrid ☐ Milan
☐ Monte Carlo ☐ Munich ☐ Naples ☐ New York
☐ Oslo ☐ Paris ☐ Porto ☐ Prague
☐ Reykjavik ☐ Salzburg ☐ Singapore ☐ Stockholm
☐ Strasbourg ☐ Tokyo ☐ Turin ☐ Venice
☐ Vienna ☐ Warsaw ☐ Zagreb ☐ Zurich

Price: £5.99 *per title excluding postage and packing*

BED & BREAKFAST FRANCE

☐ **BED AND BREAKFAST FRANCE 2009** • Describes over 650 selected quality properties in all regions of France, with details of rates, rooms, facilities and locations. Also features maps showing where you can enjoy the best in local cuisine, and where to buy local specialities.

Price: £14.99 *excluding postage and packing*

£

WAYS TO PAY

- £ Sterling cheque drawn on UK bank.
- Bank transfer to HSBC Bank plc., City of London Corporate Office, PO Box 125, 27-32 Poultry, LONDON, EC2P 2BX, UK. Account name Thomas Cook Tour Operations Ltd., Account no. 31212508, sort code 40-02-50. IBAN no: GB09MIDL4002503121508
- Credit card: Mastercard, Visa or American Express.
- Switch / Maestro / Delta / Solo.
- *Any bank or similar charges incurred to be paid by remitter.*

VAT Registration No. GB 239 3841 42

* If you order more than three items you only pay postage for three

VAT / TVA / IVA
If you are registered for VAT or equivalent please enter your registration number:

SUB TOTAL FROM ALL COLUMNS £

ADD POSTAGE AND PACKING:

TO UK - £1.50 per item * £

TO EUROPE - £3.50 per item * £

REST OF WORLD - £5.00 per item * £

TOTAL ENCLOSED £

Please complete the following and send form to Thomas Cook Publishing, Unit 9, Coningsby Road, Peterborough PE3 8SB, United Kingdom.
✆ +44 (0)1733 416477 fax +44 (0)1733 416688
publishing-sales@thomascook.com

FOR CREDIT CARD PAYMENTS – please complete:

☐ Mastercard ☐ Visa ☐ American Express ☐ Switch / Delta

Cardholders name ____________________

Signature ____________________

Card number |_|_|_|_|_|_|_|_|_|_|_|_|_|_|_|_|

Card expiry date __________ Card issue number __________

Card security number (Last 3 digits) __________

Address ____________________

Postcode ____________________

Daytime Telephone No. ____________________

Delivery details (if different from above):

Name ____________________

Address ____________________

____________________ Postcode __________